1 MONTH OF
FREE
READING

at
www.ForgottenBooks.com

By purchasing this book you are eligible for one month membership to ForgottenBooks.com, giving you unlimited access to our entire collection of over 1,000,000 titles via our web site and mobile apps.

To claim your free month visit:
www.forgottenbooks.com/free1273815

ISBN 978-0-364-79268-1
PIBN 11273815

𝔓𝔲𝔟𝔩𝔦𝔠𝔞𝔱𝔦𝔬𝔫𝔰 𝔬𝔣 𝔱𝔥𝔢 𝔄𝔯𝔫𝔬𝔩𝔡 𝔄𝔯𝔟𝔬𝔯𝔢𝔱𝔲𝔪. 𝔑𝔬. 3

THE BRADLEY BIBLIOGRAPHY

A GUIDE TO THE LITERATURE OF THE WOODY PLANTS OF THE WORLD
PUBLISHED BEFORE THE BEGINNING OF
THE TWENTIETH CENTURY

COMPILED AT THE ARNOLD ARBORETUM OF HARVARD UNIVERSITY
UNDER THE DIRECTION OF CHARLES SPRAGUE SARGENT

BY

ALFRED REHDER

VOLUME V

INDEX OF AUTHORS AND TITLES
SUBJECT INDEX

CAMBRIDGE
𝔓𝔯𝔦𝔫𝔱𝔢𝔡 𝔞𝔱 𝔗𝔥𝔢 ℜ𝔦𝔳𝔢𝔯𝔰𝔦𝔡𝔢 𝔓𝔯𝔢𝔰𝔰
MCMXVIII
1918

INTRODUCTION TO VOLUME V

VOLUME V. of the Bradley Bibliography contains the index of authors and titles enumerated in the preceding volumes and in the additions and corrections which appear in this volume; it also contains the subject index to all the volumes.

To confine the index to one volume it has been found necessary to shorten the titles as much as possible; this has been done, however, without loss of clearness. The first words of every title are always given in full and the omission of any words within the title as so given is indicated by dots. Articles in serials, like the *Botanical Magazine*, the *Botanical Register, Hooker's Icones* and the *Flore des Serres*, which are devoted entirely to the illustration and description of single species, have been omitted, as they are not strictly independent articles; these may be found under the name of the genus by consulting the subject index for its place in the systematic arrangement. Likewise names of plants excerpted from books or articles and appearing in the systematic arrangement as separate entries in brackets have been omitted.

Anonymous publications are arranged alphabetically under the first word of the title which is not an article or preposition, but anonymous articles in serials or periodicals published with only a botanical name as the title have been omitted, as they may be found under the name of the genus by consulting the subject index for their place in the systematic arrangement. Anonymous articles published without title in serials or periodicals and enumerated in the systematic arrangement with a supplied title are also omitted, unless they have also been issued as separate publications.

Serial publications of societies and corporate bodies will be found under the title of the publishing body, and government publications of a serial nature under the name of the country. Other publications, however, not of a serial nature, issued occasionally by societies, corporate bodies or governments are arranged alphabetically under the title of the publication to insure uniform treatment, as in many such publications taken from other bibliographies or sent by contributors to the Bradley Bibliography the name of the publishing body was not correctly given or was omitted.

This volume completes this work, the first volume of which was published in 1911. In it will be found more than one hundred thousand entries of the titles of books and articles relating to trees and other woody plants, their botanical characters, uses and cultivation. The enumeration is certainly not complete, for a bibliography of a subject so great can never be made complete, but it is believed that in the Bradley Bibliography will be found the best key to the literature of trees which has been made.

The Bradley Bibliography was begun and has been finished by Mr. Alfred Rehder of the Arboretum staff, who has devoted sixteen years of intelligent, enthusiastic and uninterrupted labor to this work.

C. S. SARGENT.

JANUARY, 1918.

1918

TABLE OF CONTENTS

ADDITIONS AND CORRECTIONS
TO VOLUMES I–IV

The figures at the beginning of each entry indicate the page where the additional entry is to be inserted according to its chronological sequence, or where the entry to be corrected will be found.

VOLUME I

I. AUXILIARY AND MISCELLANEOUS PUBLICATIONS

A. BIBLIOGRAPHY

1. GENERAL

1. **Cobres**, J. P. [von]. Deliciae Cobresianae . . . **1782.** *Lines 2–3 read:* 2 pts. ([4]+28+956+[1] pp.) O. [Augsburg, **1782.**] — *After line 3 add as a note:*
Pflanzenreich (pp. 471–674).

2. **Zuchold**, E. A. Additamenta ad Georgii Augusti Pritzelii Thesaurum literaturae botanicae. **1853.** — *Line 5 add:* — *Reprinted:* 16 pp. O. Lipsiae, 1866.

2. **Chatin**, Ad[olphe]. Notice sur les travaux scientifiques de M. Ad. Chatin. 11+102 pp. Q. Versailles, **1866.**

2. **Bureau**, É[douard]. Notice sur les travaux scientifiques. 37+[1] pp. sq. Q. Paris, **1874.** — [Another ed.] 68+[3] pp. sq. Q. Paris, 1894.

2. **Ekama**, C. Fondation Teyler. Catalogue de la bibliothèque. V . I.–II. Q. Harlem, **1885–89→**

3. **Baillon**, [E.]. Notice sur les titres scientifiques de M. H. Baillon. ⌐ pp. sq. Q. Tours, **1894.**

2. NORTH AMERICA

3. **Kellerman**, W. A. Bibliography of Ohio botany. **1893.** — *Line 3 add:* — Additions to the bibliography . . . pp. 5–18. O. n.-t-p. [Columbus, 1896.] — *From: "Ohio state academy of science. Annual report,* IV. 1896."

B. PERIODICALS AND SERIALS

1. NORTH AMERICA
b. United States

5. **Botanical** gazette. Hanover (Ind.) & Chicago, 1875–1900→ — *Transfer the note after the entry "* Boston society of natural history. Anniversary memoirs *" to line 4 of the* BOTANICAL gazette, *and take out note.*
"Consists of separates and reprints."

4. EUROPE
c. Denmark

9. **Kön. Dänische Gesellschaft der Wissenschaften.** Schriften der physikalischen Klasse; aus dem Dänischen. Vol. I.–III. O. Kopenhagen, 1801–05.
Is a translation of Kongelige Danske Videnskaber(ne)s Selskab. Skrifter.

e. German Empire

10. **Annalen** der Physik und Chemie. Halle & Leipzig, 1799–1900→ — *Transfer the note after the entry "* Annalen der Pharmacie *" to line 4 of* Annalen der Physik . . .

13. **Naturhistorischer Verein in Augsburg.** Bericht. Vol. I.–XXXIV. Q. & O. Augsburg, 1848–81. — *Continued: as* Naturwissenschaftlicher Verein für Schwaben und Neuburg. Bericht. Vol. XXXV.–LIV. O. Augsburg, 1882–1900→

g. Belgium

16. **Académie royale des sciences, des lettres et des beaux-arts de Belgique.** Mémoires sur les questions proposées. — *Lines 6–7 read:* sq. Q. Bruxelles, 1844–1900→ — Collection in 8° . . .

i. France

21. **Bulletin** de pharmacie . . . 1809–14→ — *Line 5 add:* Table analytique du Bulletin et du Journal de pharmacie [ser. 1, vol. I.– ser. 2, vol. XVI. (1809–30)], suivie de celle des auteurs et de celle des ouvrages annoncés ou analysés dans ces journaux. Par A. E. Baudrimont. [2]+424 pp. O. Paris, 1831. — Table alphabétique des auteurs cités [et table méthodique des matières] dans les volumes XVII.–XXVII. [ser. 2], (1831–42). 66 pp. O. [Paris, 1842?] —Table générale des auteurs et des mémoires cités dans les tomes I.–XLVI. (1842–64), de la 3e série. 412 pp. O. Paris, 1872. Table générale des auteurs et des mémoires cités dans les tomes I.-XXX. (1865–80), de la 4e série. 312 pp. O. Paris, 1880.

21. **Introduction** aux observations sur la physique, sur l'histoire naturelle et sur les arts. Par l'abbé Rozier. 18 vol. D. Paris, 1771–72. — Ed. 2. 2 vol. Q. Paris, 1777. — *Continued as:* Observations et mémoires sur la physique, sur l'histoire naturelle et sur les arts et métiers. Par l'abbé Rozier. Vol. I. Q. Paris, 1773. — *Continued as:* Observations sur la physique, sur l'histoire naturelle et sur les arts. Par l'abbé Rozier [from 1778] et J. A. Mongez [from 1785] et de la Méthérie. Vol. II.–XLIII. Q. Paris, 1773–93. — *Continued as:* Journal de physique, de chimie, d'histoire naturelle et des arts. Par Jean Claude Laméthérie [from 1817] et H. M. Ducrotay de Blainville; [from vol. LXXXV. by de Blainville alone]. Vol. XLIV.–XCVI. Q. Paris, 1794–1823. ‖ — Suppléments. 2 vol. Q. Paris, 1778–82.
Ed. 2, vol. II. has also the title: Tableau du travail annuel de toutes les académies de l'Europe: ou, Observations sur la physique, sur l'histoire naturelle et sur les arts et métiers. — Vol. X., XXIX. & LVI. contain indices. — No volumes published from 1795 to 1797.

22. **Musée d'histoire naturelle.** Annales. — *Line 2 add:* Vol. XXI. Contenant table des auteurs . . . suivi d'une table générale et analytique des matières. Q. Paris, 1827. —

k. Italy

25. **(Reale) istituto lombardo di scienze e lettere.** Giornale . . . e biblioteca italiana. — *After line 3 add as a note:*
Is a continuation of Biblioteca italiana.

26. **Zoologische Station zu Neapel.** Mittheilungen. Vol. I.–XIII. il. pl. O. Leipzig, 1879–99→

m. Austria-Hungary

28. **Naturhistorisches Ladnes-Museum** von Kärnten. — *Line 1 read:* **Naturhistorisches Landes-Museum** . . .

C. MISCELLANEOUS PUBLICATIONS OF GENERAL CHARACTER

30. **Aristoteles.** Problemata quæ ad stirpium genus & oleracea pertinent. (*In* BRASAVOLA, A. M. Examen omnium simplicium medicamentorum . . . pp. 530–542. **1539.**)

30. **Bayle**, [François]. Dissertationes physicæ in quibus principia proprietatum in mistis, oeconomia corporum in plantis & animalibus . . . demonstrantur . . . [14]+208+[3] pp. 1 pl. D. Hagæ-Comitis, **1678.†**

31. **Linné**, Carl von. Opera varia . . . **1758.** — *Lines 2–3 read:* ; Systema naturae in quo proponuntur naturae regna tria secundum classes, ordines, genera & species. 376 pp. 1 pl. D. Lucae, **1758.**

33. **Voigt**, F. S. Almanach der Natur. 1 pl. O. Jena, **1832.†**
Contains: Tafel verschiedener Temperaturen zum Gedeihen von Pflanzen (pp. 72–73). Einfluss der Kälte auf die Gewächse (pp. 74–75). Alter und Höhen verschiedener Bäume (pp. 81–84). Alter und Dicke merkwürdiger Bäume (pp. 85–88). Allmähliges Wachsthum einiger Bäume (pp. 87–88). Hitzkraft verschiedener Hölzer (p. 92).

34. **Lindley**, John & **Moore**, Thomas. The treasury of botany . . . 1866. — *Lines 3–4 read:* 2 vol. (20+1254 pp.) il. 20 pl. S. London, 1866. — New ed. 2 vol. (20+1254 pp.) Il. 20 pl. O. London, 1870. — The treasury . . . with supplement. New ed. 2 vol. (20+1352 pp.) il. 20 pl. O. London, 1876. — [Reissue.] 2 vol. (20+1352 pp.) il. 20 pl. O. London, etc., 1899.

34. **Ito**, Tokutaro. A memorial work, chiefly on botany and zoology in commemoration of the ninetieth anniversary of Keisuke Ito. 2 vol. il. 1 por. O. Nagoya, 1893.

Text in Japanese.

D. COLLECTIONS, ARBORETUMS, BOTANIC GARDENS, MUSEUMS ETC.

1. TECHNIQUE OF COLLECTING

35. **Lauremberg**, Wilhelm. Botanotheca hoc est modus conficiendi herbarium vivum . . . 1626. — *Lines 5–10 read:* pp. 731–799. 1653). — Botanotheca Laurembergiana, hoc est methodus conficiendi herbarium vivum ad usum Societatis medicae in Universitate altdorffina Norimbergensium accommodata a Mauritio Hoffmanno. [26] pp. sq. O. Altdorffi, 1662. — [Another ed.] 28 pp. O. Altdorffi, 1693.

36. **Bailey**, W. W. The botanical collector's handbook. 14+139 pp. D. Salem, Mass., & London, 1881. (Naturalist's handy series, III.)

36. *Conservazione degli erbari.* (*Nuov. Riv. Forest.* VI. 203. 1883.)

2. LABORATORY TECHNIQUE, MICROTECHNIQUE

36. **Reinicke**, Friedrich. Beiträge zur neueren Mikroskopie. 1858.† — *Lines 1–2 read:* [4]+57 pp. 7 pl. O. Dresden, 1858.

36. **Naegeli**, Karl & **Schwendener**, Simon. Das Mikroskop. 1865–67. — *Line 3 read:* Ed. 2. 12+679 pp. O. Leipzig, 1877.

36. **Behrens**, W. J. Hilfsbuch zur Ausführung mikroskopischer Untersuchungen im botanischen Laboratorium. 12+398 pp. il. O. Braunschweig, 1883.

For English translation see BEHRENS, J. W. The microscope in botany. 1885. Vol. I. 521.

37. **Schaffner**, J. H. General methods in botanical microtechnique. [7] pp. O. Columbus, 1899. (Ohio state university bulletins. Botanical series, II.) — *From:* " Journal of applied microscopy, II."

4. WOOD COLLECTIONS

b. Description of special collections

37. **Hildt**, J. A. [Beschreibung in- und ausländischen Holzarten . . .] [1797–98?] — *For corrected entry see under* TECHNOLOGY OF WOOD, vol. IV. p. 407.

37. **Burkart.** Sammlung der wichtigsten europäischen Nutzhölzer . . . 1880. — *Line 2 read:*, ausgeführt von F. M. Podany. 75+[1] pp. 40 pl. O. Brünn, 1880. — [Another ed.] 71+[1] pp. O. Brünn, 1881.

5. BOTANIC GARDENS, ARBORETUMS, MUSEUMS ETC.

b. North America

I. CANADA

38. **Brunet**, [L.] O. Notice sur le Musée botanique de l'Université Laval . . . 14 pp. O. Québec, 1867.

II. UNITED STATES

38. [**Delacoste**.] Catalogue of the natural productions and curiosities, which compose the collections of the Cabinet of natural history . . . 87 pp. O. New York, 1804.

Botanical objects (pp. 62–77).

38. **Prince**, William. Catalogue of fruit and ornamental trees and plants . . . 1822. — *Line 5 add:* Annual catalogue of fruit and ornamental trees and plants cultivated at the Linnæan botanic garden and nurseries. William Prince & Sons, proprietors. Ed. 26. 91 pp. D. New York, [1831].

38. **Carr**, Robert. Periodical catalogue of American trees, shrubs, plants and seeds, cultivated and for sale at the Bartram botanic garden, near Philadelphia. pp. 63–84. D. Philadelphia, 1831.

From a larger work.

d. South America

40. **Rodrigues**, J. B. Relatorio sobre trabalhos do Jardim botanico . . . 28 pp. O. Rio de Janeiro, 1893.

e. Europe

II. RUSSIA

42. **Lindberg**, S. O. Plantae nonnullae Horti botanici helsingforsiensis. [1871.] — *Line 3 add:* — *Separate:* sq. Q. Helsingforsiae, 1871.

III. GERMAN EMPIRE

43. **Vater**, Abraham. Catalogus plantarum imprimis exoticarum Horti academici wittenbergensis . . . 1721. — *Line 4 add:* — [Another ed.] [20]+28 pp. 1 pl. sq. O. Wittenbergae, 1722. — *Lines 6–7 read:* hucusque auctus est. [10]+20 pp. 1 pl. sq. O. Wittenbergæ, 1724.

47. **Goeppert**, H. R. Ueber botanische Museen, insbesondere ueber das an der Universitaet Breslau. 8+68 pp. O. Goerlitz, 1856.

48. **Cohn**, Ferdinand & **Engler**, A[dolf]. Das botanische Museum der Universität Breslau. Reden, gehalten zur Einweihung desselben am 29. April 1888. 48 pp. D. Breslau, 1888.

48. **Kraus**, Gregor. Der botanische Garten der Universität Halle. 2 pts. il. por. pl. maps. O. Leipzig, 1888–94.

49. **Potonié**, H[enry]. Die pflanzengeographische Anlage im Kgl. botanischen Garten zu Berlin. 48 pp. 2 pl. O. Berlin, 1890. (Allgemeinverständliche naturwissenschaftliche Abhandlungen, XIII.) — *From:* Naturw. Wochenschr.

49. **Haupt**, [A.] (*Dr.*). Vermehrung des Kgl. Naturalienkabinets in Bamberg seit 50 Jahren. 15+120 pp. O. t-p-c. Bamberg, 1893.

Botanik (pp. 99–102).

49. **Hickel**, R. Les jardins botaniques . . . 1899–1900. — *Line 3 add:* — [Extract.] (*Rev. Eaux For.* XXXIX. 155–156. 1900.)

IV. BELGIUM

50. **Houtte**, Louis van. Hortus Vanhoutteanus . . . 1845.— *Line 7 read:* 50 pp. 7 pl. O.

VI. BRITISH ISLANDS

51. An **English** catalogue of the trees and plants in the physicke garden of the university of Oxford . . . 1648. — *Lines 1–5 read:* [Bobart, Jakob.] An English catalogue of the trees and plants in the Physicke garden of the universitie of Oxford, with the Latine names added thereunto. 51 pp. T. Oxford, 1648. (*Appended to his* Catalogus plantarum Horti medici oxoniensis . . . [pt. 2.] 1648.)

Is a translation of his Catalogus plantarum Horti medici oxoniensis . . . pt. 2.

51. [**Bobart**, Jakob.] Catalogus plantarum Horti medici oxoniensis . . . 1648. — *Line 2 read:* ensis Sc. latino-anglicus & anglico-latinus. Eas alphabetico ordine accuratè exhibens. 2 pts. ([2]+54+51 pp.) T. [Oxonii], 1648. — *Line 6 on p. 53 read:* [Browne] A. M. adhibitis.

55. **Göppert**, [H. R.] Der botanische Garten zu Kew bei London. (*Schles. Forstver. Verh.* [1863], pp. 245–249.)

VII. FRANCE

56. **Le Lectier.** Catalogue . . . 1628. — *Line 2 read:* Orleans, 1628.

IX. ITALY

60. [**Cortuso**, J. A.] L'Horto dei simplici di Padova . . . 1591. — *Line 1 read:* [Porro, Girolamo.] L' Horto dei semplici . . . — *Line 3 read:* & indi — *Lines 4–5 read:* [142] pp. 1 por. 3 pl. S. Venetia, 1591.

60. **Ambrosini**, Giacinto. Hortus studiosorum . . . 1657. — *Lines 1–6 read:* Hortus studiosorum; sive, Catalogus arborum, fruticum, suffruticum, stirpium, & plantarum omnium, quæ hoc anno 1657 in studiosorum Horto publico bonon. coluntur. 103 pp. il. O. [colophon:] Bononiæ, 1657.

61. [**Viviani**, Domenico.] Elenchus plantarum hor. botanici J. Car. Diuegro . . . 1802. — *Line 2 read:* Car. Dinegro . . .

63. **Bertoloni**, Antonio. Continuatio historiae horti botanici . . . [1837.] — *Line 5 read:* 18 pp. 2 pl. Q. Bononiae, 1827 [1837].

64. **Bargellini**, Demetrio. Arboretum istrianum. 1882–87. — *Line 6 add:* — *Reprinted under the title:* L' arboreto istriano; ossia, Descrizione degli alberi coltivati nel giardino della principessa Elena Koltzoff-Massalsky (Dora d' Istria); dei loro usi economici, industriali e medicinali nonchè delle proprietà generali delle loro famiglie secondo le quali furon classati. [2]+110 pp. O. Firenze, 1887.

64. **Flückiger**, F. A. La Mortola . . . 1886. — *Line 2 read:* Strasburg, 1886. — La Mortola; a short description of the garden of Thomas Hanbury, Esq. Translated from the German by Helen P. Sharpe. 20 pp. 3 pl. O. [Edinburgh], 1885.

64. **Penzig**, O[tto]. L' Istituto botanico Hanbury della R. università di Genova. 14 pp. 7 pl. O. t-p-c. Genova, [1892]. — *From:* Congr. Bot. Intern. Genova 1892 Atti, 1893,

64. Il **centenario** dell' Orto botanico di Palermo. (*Eco Campi Boschi*, I. 354. **1894**.)

XI. AUSTRIA-HUNGARY

66. **Schubert**, Karl. Der Park von Abbatia, seine Bäume & Gesträuche. Mit einer Schilderung der Vegetation der Umgebung von Abbatia von Günther Ritt. v. Beck. 12+113 pp. 17 pl. Wien, **1894**.

f. Asia and Malay Archipelago

IV. JAVA

68. **Clautriau**, G[eorges]. Les installations botaniques et l'organisation agricole de Java et de Ceylan. 56+[2] pp. 5 pl. O. Ciney, **1899**. — *From: Ingén. Agric. Gembloux*, 1899.

h. Australasia

69. **Brisbane** botanic **garden**. Report for 1874, '79, '80. F. [Brisbane, **1874**–80.]

69. **South Australia — Botanic garden & government** plantations. Report on the progress . . . *1879*–90. — *Lines 3–6 read:* and government plantations, 1869, 1873, 1877–83, 1885–89. pl. F. Adelaide, [**1870**]–90.

In 1869 title reads: Report of director of Adelaide botanic garden. In 1886–89 title reads: Report on the progress and condition of the Botanic garden.

69. **Condition** and management of the Brisbane botanic gardens. Return to an order made by the Honourable the Legislative assembly of Queensland . . . Copies of all reports, correspondence, or regulations bearing upon the condition and management of the Brisbane botanic gardens from the date of the retirement of the late curator to the 30th of June last. 11 pp. F. [Brisbane, **1882**.] (Queensland. Legislative assembly, 1882.)

E. GLOSSARIES, DICTIONARIES, NOMENCLATORS ETC.

1. TERMINOLOGY

69. **Linné**, Carl von (p*i* sees). Termini botanici. [1762.] — *Line 2 add:* [Ano* ed.] 28+8 pp. O. Edinburgi, 1764.

70. **Eberle**, John. Botanical terminology or pocket companion for students of botany. 73 pp. S. Philadelphia, 1818.

70. **Dierbach**, J. H. Die botanische Terminologie älterer Zeiten. 32 pp. D. n. p., [**1824**]. — *From: "Magazin für die Pharmacie (Geiger)*, 1824."

70. **Eaton**, Amos. Botanical grammar and dictionary. **1836**. — *Lines 1–2 read:* Grammar of botany [and vocabulary]. (*In his* A manual of botany . . . Ed. 4, pp. 11–93. 1824.) — Botanical grammar and dictionary. Ed. 3. 53+71 pp. D. Albany, 1828. — (*Also appended to his* Manual of botany . . . Ed. 5, pp. 13–63+[71] pp. 1829.) — Botanical grammar modernized down to 1836. Ed. 4. 125 pp. D. Albany, 1836. — (*Also appended to his* Manual of botany . . . Ed. 7. 1836.) — Botanical dictionary, modernized for 1840. Ed. 5. (*In his* North American botany . . . Ed. 8, pp. 567–625. 1840.)

For earlier editions see his A botanical dictionary . . . 1816, vol. I. 70.

70. **Henslow**, J. S. [A dictionary of English-Latin terms used in botanical descriptions. London, 1837–51?]

Issued in portions with the botanic garden and the botanist. — For later editions see his A dictionary of botanical terms . . . [1850].

71. **Müller**, J. B. Botanisch-prosodisches Wörterbuch, nebst einer Charakteristik der wichtigsten natürlichen Pflanzenfamilien . . . 6+504 pp. Q. Brilon & Paderborn, 1840 [–41].

71. **Lindley**, John. A glossary of technical terms used in botany. **1848**. — *Line 2 read:* 100 pp. 433 il. O. London, 1848.

71. **Metzner**, R[einhold]. Botanisch-gärtnerisches Taschenwörterbuch . . . **1836**. — *Line 6 read:* 12+286 pp. S. Berlin, 1836.

71. **Moll**, J. W. Handboek der plantbeschrijving. 8+143 pp. 3 il. D. Groningen, 1900.

2. DICTIONARIES AND LISTS OF VERNACULAR NAMES

a. General

71. **De** latinis et graecis nominibus arborum, fruticum . . . **1544**. — *Line 1 read:* [Estienne, Charles.] De latinis . . . — *Lines 6–7 read:* Ed. 2 enl. 123 pp. S. Lutetiae, 1545.

72. **Mentzel**, Christian. Πίναξ βοτανώνυμος πολύγλωττος καθολικός. **1682**. — *Line 18 add:* Lexicon plantarum polyglotton universale, ex diversis europaeorum, asiaticorum, africanorum & americanorum, antiquis & modernis linguis, earumque dialectis variis, quotquot ex probatis autoribus excerpi potuerunt . . . accessit pugillus plantarum rariorum . . . item corollarium quarundam satis rariorum plantarum Africae & orientalis Indiae . . . [12]+331+[24] pp. 13 pl. F. Berolini, 1715.

72. **Monti**, Giuseppe. Plantarum varii indices ad usum demonstrationum . . . **1724**. — *Lines 3–11 read:* quotannis habentur. Iis praefixa est dissertatio ibidem habita anno 1723 ad easdem demonstrationes auspicandas. [Cum Exoticorum simplicium medicamentorum varii indices ad usum exercitationum . . .] 20+78+[2]+39+[1] pp. 1 pl. O. Bononiae, 1724.

d. Europe

III. GERMAN EMPIRE

73. **Salomon**, Carl. Wörterbuch der deutschen Pflanzen-Namen, besonders der im Volksmunde gebräuchlichen Benennungen wichtiger heimischer wie fremder Gewächse, mit Beifügung der botanischen Namen. 4+183 pp. T. Stuttgart, **1881**.

IV. HOLLAND, BELGIUM, LUXEMBURG · ¹

73. **K**[erchove de Denterghem, Oswald], *comte* de. À propos d'Ypréaux. (*Rev. Hort. Belge*, XXI. 238–240. **1895**. — *Soc. Centr. For. Belg. Bull.* II. 817–819. 1895.)

VI. FRANCE

74. **Le Hé**richer, Édouard. Essai sur la flore populaire de Normandie . . . **1857**. — *Line 2 read:* 103 pp. O. Avranches & Paris, **1857**. — Additions . . . 14 pp. O. n. t-p. [Avranches, 1857?]

74. **D.** Ypréaux. (*Rev. Hort. Belge*, XXI. 144. **1895**. — *Soc. Centr. For. Belg. Bull.* II. 556–557. 1895.)

e. Asia and Malay Archipelago

I. CHINA AND JAPAN

75. **Faber**, Ernst. Chinese names of plants identified in Japan, classified under their natural orders and arranged alphabetically. (*In* BRETSCHNEIDER, Emil. Botanicon sinicum, II. 411–434. **1892**. — *As. Soc. N. China Branch Jour.* new ser. XXV. 411–434. 1892.)

3. ETYMOLOGY OF BOTANICAL NAMES

76. **Obermüller**, Wilhelm. Kleines practisches Gärtner-Lexicon . . . **1880**. — *Line 7 add:* Kleines praktisches Blumen-Lexicon . . . Ed. 2 enl. 8+119 pp. S. Frankfurt a. M., 1859. — Ed. 3. 123 pp. S. Frankfurt a. M., 1883. — Ed. 4. 141 pp. O. Basel, 1886.

4. BOTANICAL NOMENCLATORS

a. General nomenclators and indices

77. **Henckel von Donnersmarck**, L. F. V. Nomenclator botanicus . . . **1803**. — *Lines 1–5 read:* Nomenclator botanicus, sistens plantas omnes in Caroli a Linné Speciebus plantarum ab . . . Carolo Ludovico Willdenow enumeratas. 4 pp.+ 677 col. O. Halae Magdeb., 1803–[07]. — Index generum ad Caroli a Linné Species plantarum a Carolo Ludovico Willdenow editarum in tom. I. II. III. et IV. pars I. [et II.] curante Jo. Chr. Hendel. 58 pp. O. Halae, 1806–[07].

77. **Hendel**, J. C. Index generum ad Caroli a Linné Species plantarum . . . **1806**. — Delete the entry.

77. **Lichtenstein**, A. G. G. Index alphabeticus generum botanicorum . . . **1814**. — *Line 2 read:* quotquot a Willdenovio in Speciebus plantarum et a Persoonio in Synopsi plantarum recensentur, continuatus. 8+88 pp. O. Helmstadii, 1814.

II. INTRODUCTORY PUBLICATIONS

A. PHILOSOPHY, ENCOMIUMS

79. **Ray**, John. The wisdom of God manifested in the works of the creation. In two parts, viz. The heavenly bodies, elements, meteors, fossils, vegetables . . . O. London, 1691.† — Ed. 2. O. London, 1692.† — Ed. 3. O. London, 1701.† — Ed. 4 rev. & enl. [14] + 464 pp. 1 por. D. London, 1704. — Ed. 8. [24]+405 pp. O. London, 1722.† — Ed. 9 rev. [6]+405 pp. O. London, 1727. — Ed. 12. 405 pp. O. London, 1759. — New ed. by Wernerian club. Pt. 1–4. O. London, 1845–47.

B. HISTORY

1. GENERAL

79. **Bischoff**, G. W. Die Botanik in ihren Grundrissen mit Rücksicht auf ihre historische Entwicklung. [1]+138+[1] pp. O. Stuttgart, **1848**. — *From:* " Neue Encyklopädie der Wissenschaften und Künste . . . III."

79. **Martens**, Édouard. Les plantes alimentaires des anciens. 42 pp. O. Bruges, **1858**. — *From: " Revue de l'instruction publique en Belgique,* new ser. I."
79. **Sachs**, Julius. Geschichte der Botanik . . . **1875**. — *Line 5 add:* —— Histoire de la botanique du XVIᵉ siècle à 1860. Traduction française par Henri de Varigny. O. Paris, 1895.
80. **Pammel**, L. H. Botanists and botanical discoveries of the last decade. (*Iowa State Hort. Soc. Rep.* XXX. (1895), pp. 140–145. **1896**.)

2. NORTH AMERICA

80. **Goode**, G. B. The beginnings of natural history in America. An address delivered at the 6th anniversary meeting of the Biological society in Washington. (*Biol. Soc. Wash. Proc.* III. 35–105. **1884–86**.) — *Separate:* t-p. Washington, 1886. — (*Smithson. Inst. Ann. Rep.* 1897, U. S. National Museum, pt. II. 355–406. 1898.)
80. **Goode**, G. B. The beginnings of American science. The third century. An address delivered at the 8th anniversary meeting of the Biological society at Washington. (*Biol. Soc. Washington Proc.* IV. 9–94. **1886–88**.) — *Separate:* t-p. Washington, 1888. — (*Smithson. Inst. Ann. Rep.* 1897, U. S. National Museum, pt. II. 407–466. 1898.)

3. CENTRAL AND SOUTH AMERICA

80. **Wittmack**, [Ludwig]. Die Nutzpflanzen der alten Peruaner. 24 pp. O. [Berlin, **1888**.] — *From: Congr. Intern. Amer. Compt. Rend.* 7ᵉ session, 1888.

4. EUROPE

c. German Empire

80. **Fischer-Benzon**, R[udolf] von. Zur Geschichte unseres Beerenobstes. **1895**. — *Line 3 add:* — *Reprinted:* O. Kassel, 1895.†

5. ASIA

81. **Faber**, Ernst. General remarks [on Dr. Bretschneider's Botanicon sinicum]. (*In* BRETSCHNEIDER, Emil. Botanicon sinicum, II. 402–410. **1892**. — *As. Soc. N. China Branch Jour.* new ser. XXV. 402–410. 1892.)

6. AFRICA

81. **Braun**, A[lexander]. Die Pflanzenreste des ägyptischen Museums in Berlin; aus dem Nachlasse des Verfassers herausgegeben von P. Ascherson und P. Magnus. 24 pp. Q. Berlin, **1877**.
Read at the meeting of the Berliner Anthrop. Gesellschaft, April 15, 1871.

C. TEXTBOOKS AND WORKS INTRODUCTORY TO GENERAL BOTANY

1. RELATING TO WOODY PLANTS ONLY

82. **Schacht**, H[ermann]. Der Baum . . . **1853**. — *Line 10 add:* — Ed. 3 enl. [2]+11+[1]+456 pp. 212 il. [14] pl. Q. Paris & Bruxelles, 1865.

2. GENERAL

82. **Gorter**, David de. Elementa botanica methodo cl. Linnaei accommodata . . . **1749**. — *Lines 2–3 read:* [8]+88+ [2] pp. 11 pl. O. Harderovici, 1749.
83. **Brotero**, Felix de Avellar. Compendio de botanica . . . **1788**. — *Lines 6–7 read:* [Ed. 2.] 2 vol. 37 pl. O. Lisboa, 1837–39.
84. **Koch**, J. F. W. Botanisches Handbuch . . . **1797–98**. — *Lines 1–2 read:* Botanisches Handbuch für deutsche Liebhaber der Pflanzenkunde und für Gartenfreunde, Apotheker und Oekonomen. 3 vol. S. Magdeburg, 1797–98.
85. **Richard**, Achille. Nouveaux élémens de botanique . . . **1819**. — *Lines 17–18 read:* Neuer Grundriss der Botanik und der Pflanzenphysiologie, nach der vierten mit den Characteren der natürlichen Familien des Gewächsreiches vermehrten und verbesserten Originalausgabe übersetzt, und mit Zusätzen, Anmerkungen, einem Sach- und Wort-Register versehen von Mart. Balduin Kittel. Ed. 2 rev. & enl. 32+804 pp. 8 pl. O. Nürnberg,1831. (Buchner, J. A. Vollständiger Inbegriff der Pharmacie . . . Div. 4, II.)
85. **Sagra**, Ramon de la. Principios fundamentales para servir de introducción a la Escuela botanica-agricola de la Habana. [6]+151 pp. O. Habana, 1824.
85. **Oken**, Lorenz. Lehrbuch der Naturgeschichte. Theil II. Botanik. 2 vol. 6 tab. D. Jena, **1825–26**.
Theil I. is Mineralogie, Theil III. Zoologie.

86. **[Phelps]**, *Mrs.* A. H. (Lincoln). Familiar lectures on botany . . . **1829**. — *Line 23 add:* New ed. rev. & enl. 246+ 220 pp. 158 il. 8 pl. O. New York, 1846. —
89. **Czerwiakowski**, I. R. Opisanie roślin skrytopłciowych lékarskich i przemysłowych. Botaniki szczególnéj. [Description of cryptogamous plants, medical and economical. Special botany.] 6 vol. (8+3545 pp.) O. Kraków, **1849–63**. (Biblioteka naukowa wydawana staraniem C. K. Towarzystwa naukowego krakowskiego.)
Vol. II. has the title: Opisanie roślin jednolistniowych [monocotyledonous] lékarskich . . . Vol. III.–VI. have the title: Opisanie roślin dwulistniowych [dicotyledonous] lékarskich . . .
89. **Bill**, J. G. Grundriss der Botanik für Schulen. O. Wien, **1854**.† — Ed. 2. O. Wien, 1857.† — Ed. 3. O. Wien, 1860.† — Ed. 4. 8+264 pp. il. O. Wien, 1866.
90. **Provancher**, L[éon]. Traité élémentaire de botanique à l'usage des maisons d'éducation et des amateurs qui voudraient se livrer à l'étude de cette science sans le secours d'un maître. 7+118 pp. 87 il. D. Quebec, **1858**.
91. **Masters**, M. T. Botany for beginners; an introduction to the study of plants. 13+185 pp. il. O. London, [1872.]
91. **Brown**, Robert. A manual of botany, anatomical and physiological . . . 18+614 pp. il. O. Edinburgh & London, **1874**.
91. **Thomé**, O. W. Lehrbuch der Botanik . . . **1874**. — *Lines 1–2 read:* Lehrbuch der Botanik für Realschulen, Gymnasien, forst- und landwirtschaftliche Lehranstalten, pharmaceutische Institute etc. sowie zum Selbstunterrichte. Ed. 3 rev. & enl. 8+389 pp. 633 il. map. O. Braunschweig, 1874.
91. **Wood**, Alphonso. Leaves and flowers; or, Object lessons in botany with a flora, prepared for beginners in academies and public schools. 346 pp. 665 il. 1 pl. D. New York & Chicago, 1877 [°1860].
91. **Lürssen**, Christian. Grundzüge der Botanik, Repetitorium für Studirende der Naturwissenschaften und Medicin und Lehrbuch für polytechnische, land- und forstwirthschaftliche Lehranstalten. 11+405 pp. il. O. Leipzig, **1877**. — Ed. 2. 4+483 pp. il. O. Leipzig, 1879. — Ed. 3 rev. 11+490 pp. il. O. Leipzig, 1881. — Ed. 4 rev. & enl. 8+578 pp. il. O. Leipzig, 1885. — Ed. 5 rev. 12+586 pp. 366 il. O. Leipzig, 1893.
91. **Baenitz**, C. Leitfaden für den Unterricht in der Botanik. Ed. 2. 4+164 pp. 754 il. O. Berlin, **1879**.
91. **Baenitz**, C. Handbuch der Botanik in populärer Darstellung. Ed. 2 rev. & enl. 4+516 pp. 1700 il. O. Berlin, **1880**.
91. **Oudemans**, C. A. J. A. & **Vries**, Hugo de. Leerboek der plantenkunde . . . Vol. I.–III. Amsterdam, etc., **1880–84→**
Is a much enlarged and revised edition of OUDEMANS, C. A. J. A. Leerboek der plantenkunde, 1866–70.
92. **Waeber**, R[obert]. Lehrbuch für den Unterricht in der Botanik, mit besonderer Berücksichtigung der Kulturpflanzen. 242 pp. il. 8 pl. O. Breslau, **1885**. — Ed. 5 rev. 315 pp. 240 il. 24 pl. O. Leipzig, 1896.
92. **Frank**, A. B. Lehrbuch der Botanik nach dem gegenwärtigen Stand der Wissenschaft. 2 vol. (6+669 pp.) 227 il. O. Leipzig, **1892–93**.
92. **Giesenhagen**, K[arl]. Lehrbuch der Botanik. 7+[1]+ 335 pp. 310 il. O. München & Leipzig, **1894**.

3. POPULAR

93. **Wood**, W. Zoography; or, The beauties of nature displayed in select descriptions from the animal and vegetable, with additions from the mineral kingdom systematically arranged; illustrated with plates, designed and engraved by William Daniell. 3 vol. 4 il. pl. Q. London, **1807**.
Plants (III. 1–331).
94. **Taylor**, Joseph. The wonders of trees, plants and shrubs, recorded in anecdotes . . . 192+[8] pp. 6 pl. D. London, [1823].
96. **Vries**, Hugo de. Het leven der bloem. 147+[2] pp. 64 il. O. Haarlem, **1877**. — Ed. 2 rev. [2]+165 pp. 63 il. D. Haarlem, 1900.
96. **Meetkerke**, C. E. The guests of flowers, a botanical sketch for children. 61 pp. D. London, **1881**.
96. **Schubert**, A. Pflanzenkunde. Theil I. 164 pp. O. Berlin, **1888**.
96. **Wurm**, W. Waldgeheimnisse. Ed. 2 rev. & enl. 16+ 232 pp. il. 1 pl. O. Stuttgart, **1895**.

III. MORPHOLOGY AND ANATOMY

A. GENERAL

1. MISCELLANEOUS PUBLICATIONS

98. Kieser, D. J. Mémoire sur l'organisation des plantes. **1814.** — *Lines 1–2 read:* ; ou, Réponse à la question physique proposée par la Société Teylérienne. Par la quelle on demande: Que l'on cherche à décider au moyen d'observations nouvelles, autant que par la comparaison de celles, qui ont été faites déja, ce qu'il y a d'incontestable dans ce que l'on a avancé sur l'organisation des plantes . . . [2]+21+345 pp. 22 pl. Harlem, **[1814].** (*Teyler's Tweed. Genoot. Verh.* XVIII. 1814.)

B. VEGETATIVE PARTS

1. ROOT

103. Grew, Nehemiah. An idea of a phytological history propounded . . . **1673.** — *Lines 3–4 read:* , and an account of the vegetation of roots grounded chiefly thereupon. [20]+ 144+[32] pp. 7 pl. D. London, **1673.**

C. REPRODUCTIVE PARTS

11. SEEDLINGS

123. Lubbock, *Sir* John. A contribution to our knowledge of seedlings. **1892.** — *Line 2 add:* — [Another ed.] 2 vol. il. O. London, 1892. — Popular edition. 6+288 pp. il. O. London, 1896. (International scientific series, LXXIX.)

D. HISTOLOGY

2. STRUCTURE OF WOOD

a. General

124. [Houttuyn, Martin.] Houtkunde . . . [1773]–91. — *For corrected entry see* vol. IV. 17 *under* [SEELIGMANN, (*publisher*).] Abbildung inn- und ausländischer Hœlzer . . . **1773–78,** *and* SEPP, J. C. (*publisher*). Houtkunde . . . **[1773]–91.**

126. Blits, G. A. De anatomische bouw der Oostindische Ijzerhoutsoorten en van het Djatihout, benevens een overzicht van alle thans bekende Ijzerhoutplanten. 53 pp. il. 6 pl. (*Kol. Mus. Haarlem Bull.* XIX. **1898.**) — [Abstract by A. H. Berkhout.] (*Ind. Mercuur*, XXI. 621. 1898.)

4. TEGUMENTARY TISSUES

b. Bark

130. Müller, Rudolf. Die Rinde unserer Laubhölzer. (Diss.) [2]+35+[1] pp. O. Breslau, **[1875].**

131. Lamonette, [B.]. Recherches sur l'origine morphologique . . . **1890.** — *Line 3 add: Separate:* Paris, 1891. (Thèses présentées à la Faculté des sciences de Paris . . . sér. A, no. 149.)

8. SECRETORY TISSUES

a. General

135. Tschirch, A[lexander]. Ueber Secrete und Secretbildung. (*Bot. Centr.* LX. 289–293. **1894.**)

135. Sieck, Willy. Die schizolysigenen Secretbehälter. **1895.** — *Line 3 add:* — *Reprinted:* (Thèse.) [2]+46 pp. 4 pl. O. Berlin, 1895.

135. Biermann, Rudolf. Ueber Bau und Entwicklungsgeschichte der Oelzellen und die Oelbildung in ihnen. **1898.** *Line 3 add:* — [Abstract.] (*Arch. Pharm.* CCXXXVI. 74–80. 1898.)

E. CYTOLOGY

3. CRYSTALS

138. Unger, F[ranz]. Über Krystallbildungen in den Pflanzenzellen. [1838?] — *Line 2 add:* — *Separate:* (*In* BENTHAM, George & others. Phytologische Abhandlungen . . . 1841.).

F. TERATOLOGY

2. STEM

144. Boehmer, G. R. De Melocacto . . . **1757.** — *Line 2 read:* sq. O. [Wittenbergae, **1757.**]

5. DOUBLE FLOWERS

145. Majer, Gustavus. Observationes de antherarum excisione ad efficiendos flores plenos. Observationes de efficacia natri muriatici in plantis . . . (Diss.) 27 pp. O. Tübingen, 1830.

IV. PHYSIOLOGY

A. MISCELLANEOUS AND GENERAL PUBLICATIONS

147. Malbranche, A[lexandre]. Physiologie végétale. L'ori-

gine des espèces en botanique et de l'apparition des plantes sur le globe. 20 pp. O. Rouen, 1853.

C. PHYSICS OF PLANT BODY

2. TURGIDITY AND TENSION

149. Effect of hot water in reviving flowers. (*Edinb. Philos. Jour.* II. 395. **1820.**)

D. PHYSIOLOGICAL CHEMISTRY AND NUTRITION

2. TEXTBOOKS

152. Schlossberger, J. E. Lehrbuch der organischen Chemie, mit besonderer Rücksicht auf Physiologie und Pathologie, auf Pharmacie, Technik und Landwirthschaft. Ed. 2 rev. & enl. 16+546+[1] pp. O. Stuttgart, **1852.** — Ed. 3 rev. & enl. 10+722 pp. O. Stuttgart, 1854. — Ed. 4 rev. & enl. 12+884 pp. O. Leipzig & Heidelberg, 1857. — Ed. 5 rev. & enl. 8+1047+[1] pp. O. Leipzig & Heidelberg, 1860.

3. PLANT CONSTITUENTS AND COMPOSITION

a. General

153. Garreau, Lazare. Recherches expérimentales . . . **1859.** — *Line 8 read:* Nouvelles recherches sur la distribution des matières minérales fixes . . .

154. Planta, A. von. Ueber die Zusammensetzung einiger Nektararten. pp. 227–247. O. [Strassburg, **1886.**] — *From: Zeitschrift für physiologische Chemie*, X. — Sur la composition de quelques espèces de nectars. (*Jour. Pharm. Chim. Paris*, ser. 5, XIV. 275–277. **1886.**)

b. Wood and woody plants

155. [Emmons, Ebenezer.] The fruit and forest trees; of the composition of the ash of fruit and forest trees, with remarks on the distribution of the elements in the parts and organs composing them. pp. 305–343. pl. 8–14. sq. Q. [Albany, **1849.**] — *From his* Agriculture of New York, II. 1849.

4. NUTRITION IN GENERAL

160. Ebermayer, [Ernst]. Untersuchungen und Studien über die Ansprüche der Waldbäume . . . **1893.** — *Line 5 add:* (*Ann. Sci. Agron. Franç. Étrang.* ser. 2, ann. 1 (1894–95), I. 234–259. 1895.) — *Reprinted.*

6. CONDUCTION OF FLUIDS AND GASES

163. Féburier, [C. R.]. Essai sur les phénomènes de la végétation expliqués par les mouvemens des sèves ascendante et descendante . . . 4+188 pp. O. Paris & Versailles, 1812.

164. Göppert, [H. R.]. Ueber die Existenz eines absteigenden Saftes in unseren einheimischen Bäumen. 6 pp. 1 ll. D. Breslau, 1852. — *From: Schles. Forstver. Verh.* 1852, p. 355.

164. Sorauer, [Paul]. [Ringelungsversuch an Kirschen.] (*Bot. Zeit.* XXX. 748–749. **1872.**) — *From: "Gesellschaft deutscher Naturforscher und Aerzte. Tageblatt der Versammlung*, 45."

166. Hartig, Robert. Ueber den Ort der Saftleitung im Holze. **1889.** — *Line 2 read:* — [Extract.] (*Oesterr. Forst-Zeit.* VII. 106. 1889.)

12. METABOLIC PROCESSES AND PRODUCTS

a. General

175. Lassaigne, J. L. Sur le mode de transporte des phosphate et carbonate de chaux . . . 1849. — *Line 6 read:* Mémoire sur le mode de transporte des phosphate et carbonate de chaux dans les organes des plantes. (*Jour. Pharm. Chim. Paris*, ser. 3, XV. 258–264. 1849.)

c. Storage and transfer of reserve material

179. Russow, E. [A. F.]. Über das Schwinden und Wiederauftreten von Stärke . . . **1884.** — *Line 3 add:* — Hamburg. Gart. Blumenzeit. XLI. 59–60. 1885.) — *From: Humboldt*, 1884.

e. Gums and resins

181. Rehmann, Anton. O utworach żywicznych roślin szyszkowych j wydzielinach roślinnych w ogólności. [On resin formation in conifers and in different plants in general.] 53 pp. 3 pl. O. Kraków, **1869.** — *From: "Rocznika Tow. nauk. krak.* XXXIX."

g. Oils and fats

182. Mesnard, Eugène. Recherches sur la formation des huiles grasses . . . **1893.** — *Line 3 add:* — *separate:* (Thèse.) O. Paris, 1894.

13. COLOR

a. General

185. **Rupe**, Hans. Die Chemie der natürlichen Farbstoffe. 12+332 pp. O. Braunschweig, **1900**. (Bolley, P. A. Handbuch der chemischen Technologie, V. pt. 4.)

b. Leaves, particularly their autumnal coloration

185. **Kny**, L[eopold]. Ueber Laubfärbungen. 28 pp. 7 il. O. Berlin, **1889**. — *From: Naturw. Wochenschr.*

14. GENERATION OF HEAT

186. **Bohm**, Josef & **Breitenlohner**, Jakob. Die Baumtemperatur in ihrer Abhängigkeit von äusseren Einflüssen. **1877**. — *Line 1 read:* **Böhm** . . . — *Line 4 add:* —— La temperatura dell' albero in relazione cogli agenti esterni, [trad. de A. Lunardoni.] (*Nuov. Riv. Forest.* IV. 49–67. 1881,)

E. GROWTH

4. INCREASE OF WOOD AND BARK

190. **Wieler**, A[rwed]. Ueber Beziehungen zwischen dem sekundären Dickenwachsthum und den Ernährungsverhältnissen der Bäume. (*Tharand. Forstw. Jahrb.* XLII. 72–225, 2 pl. **1892**.) — *Reprinted:* 155 pp. 2 pl. O. [Dresden, 1892.]

6. PERIODICITY AND ARREST OF GROWTH

a. General

191. **Baranetzki**, J. Die tägliche Periodicität im Längenwachsthum der Stengel. 91 pp. 5 il. 5 pl. St.-Pétersbourg, **1879**. (*Acad. Sci. St. Pétersb. Mém.* ser. 7, XXVII. no. 2. 1880.)

b. Leaf fall

192. **Tison**, A[drien]. Recherches sur la chute des feuilles chez les dicotylédones. **1899**–1900. — *Line 3 add:* — *Reprinted:* (Thèse.) 207 pp. 5 pl. sq. Q. Caen, 1900.

c. Casting off of branches

192. **Höhnel**, Franz, *Ritter von.* Ueber den Ablösungsvorgang der Zweige einiger Holzgewächse und seine anatomischen Ursachen. (*Mittheil. Forstl. Versuch. Oesterr.* I. pt. 3, pp. 255–268. **1878**.) — Weitere Untersuchungen über den Ablösungsvorgang von verholzten Zweigen. [1879.] (*Mittheil. Forstl. Versuch. Oesterr.* II. pt. 2, pp. 247–256, pl. 6. 1881.)

7. VITALITY

a. General

192. **Ehrenstein**, von (*Forst-Inspektor, Rauden*). [Mittheilung über langjährige Keimfähigkeit von Kiefersaamen.] (*Schles. Forstver. Verh.* [1846], pp. 124–126.)

G. REPRODUCTION

2. FECUNDATION

a. General

201. **Pammel**, L. H. Pollination of flowers. (*Iowa State Hort. Soc. Rep.* XXVI. (1891), pp. 130–177, il. 1–45. **1892**.) With a bibliography.

V. PATHOLOGY

C. WOUNDS AND MUTILATIONS

1. GENERAL

207. **Sorauer**, [Paul]. [Ringelungsversuch an Kirschen.] (*Bot. Zeit.* XXX. 748–749. **1872**.) — *From: "Gesellschaft Deutscher Naturforscher und Aerzte. Tageblatt der 45ten Versamm. Bot. Sect.*

6. ENCLOSURES AND INSCRIPTIONS IN TREES

210. **Goeppert**, [H. R.]. Über das Saftsteigen und über Inschriften und Zeichen an Bäumen. **1880**. — *Line 5 add:* — *Schles. Forstver. Jahrb.* 1879, pp. 335–339. 1880.

VI. ECOLOGY

A. ECOLOGY IN GENERAL AND ECOLOGICAL PHYTOGEOGRAPHY

1. GENERAL

217. **Humboldt**, F. H. A. von. Ansichten der Natur. **1808**. — *Lines 1–3 read:* Ed. 2 rev. & enl. 2 vol. T. Stuttgart & Tübingen, 1826. — Ed. 2. 2 vol. D. Stuttgart, 1827.† — Ansichten der Natur mit wissenschaftlichen Erläuterungen. Ed. 3 rev. & enl. 2 vol. D. Stuttgart & Tübingen, 1849. —

Line 10 add: — Views of nature; or contemplations on the sublime phenomena of creation with scientific illustration. Translated from the German by E. C. Otté and H. G. Bohm. 30+452 pp. 2 pl. London, 1869.

B. PHENOLOGY

1. GENERAL

221. **Günther**, Siegmund. Die Phänologie, ein Grenzgebiet zwischen Biologie und Klimakunde. 51 pp. O. Münster, **1895**. — *From: "Natur und Offenbarung,* XLI."

4. EUROPE

a. General

222. **Ihne**, E[gon]. Ueber den Einfluss der geographischen Länge auf die Aufblühzeit von Holzpflanzen in Mitteleuropa. [Abstract by Müttrich.] (*Zeitschr. Forst. Jagdwes.* XXVI. 633–635. **1894**.) — *From: "Gesellschaft deutscher Naturforscher und Aerzte. Verhandlungen."*

d. German Empire

225. **Goeppert**, [H. R.]. Über das Verhältniss der Pflanzenwelt zur gegenwärtigen Witterung. **1873**. — *Line 3 add:* — *Schles. Forstver. Jahrb.* 1872, pp. 378–382. 1873.) — Ueber die Pflanzenwelt in dem vergangenen Winter. (*Schles. Forstver. Jahrb.* 1872, pp. 383–391. 1873.) — *From: "Bresl. und Schles. Zeit.* December 18, 1872."

k. Austria-Hungary

227. **Fritsch**, Karl. Phänologische Beobachtungen aus dem Pflanzen- und Thierreiche. Vol. VIII. 4+180 pp. 2 maps. F. Wien, **1869**.

C. VEGETATIVE INTERRELATIONS AND NUTRITIVE ADAPTATIONS

6. ATMOSPHERIC INFLUENCES

233. **Mémoire** sur l'influence des astres et en particulier de la lune sur les végétaux. (*Soc. Sci. Phys. Lausanne Mém.* II. (1784–86), [4]+4 pp.+pp. 17–18, [4]+4+80+[2]+4+344+[2] pp.+pp. 89–119. **1789**.)

7. PARASITISM

233. **Unger**, F[ranz]. Beiträge zur Kenntniss der parasitischen Pflanzen . . . **1840**. — *Line 4 read:* Separate. — (*Also in* BENTHAM, George & others. Phytologische Abhandlungen . . . 1841.)

G. MIGRATION

1. GENERAL

241. **Kraus**, Gregor. Ueber die Bevölkerung Europas mit fremden Pflanzen. (*Gartenfl.* XLII. 142–147, 168–174. **1893**.) — *From: "Gesellschaft Deutscher Naturforscher und Aerzte. Verhandlungen."*

2. INTRODUCTION BY MAN

242. **Goeze**, E[dmund]. Das Vaterland der in Europa angebauten Früchte. (*Hamburg. Gart. Blumenzeit.* XL. 434–449. **1884**.) — *From: Humboldt, 1884.*

VIII. PHYTOGRAPHY

A. CLASSIFICATION

251. **Bernhardi**, J. J. Ueber den Begriff der Pflanzenart und seine Anwendung. 8+68 pp. O. Erfurt, **1834**.

B. NOMENCLATURE

253. **Candolle**, Alphonse de. Réponse à diverses questions et critiques faites sur le recueil des Lois de la nomenclature botanique, tel que le Congrès international de 1867 l'a publié. (*Soc. Bot. France Bull.* XVI. 64–81. **1869**.)

254. **Saint-Lager**, [Jean]. Quel est l'inventeur de la nomenclature binaire . . . **1883**. — *Line 2 read:* (*Soc. Linn. Lyon Ann.* XXIX. 367–382. 1883.) — *Reprinted:* 16 pp. O. Paris, 1883.

254. **Saint-Lager**, [Jean]. Remarques historiques sur les mots plantes mâles et plantes femelles. (*Soc. Bot. Lyon Ann.* XI. (1883), pp. 1–48, 1 pl. **1884**.) — *Reprinted under the title: Recherches historiques sur les mots " plante mâle et plante femelle."* 48 pp. 1 pl. Q. t-p-c. Paris, 1884.

254. **Harms**, H[ermann]. Die Nomenclaturbewegung der letzten Jahre, im Auftrage der Nomenclaturcommission besprochen. 32 pp. (*Bot. Jahrb.* XXIII. Beibl. 56. **1897**.) — *Separate:* t-p-c. Leipzig, 1897.

D. MISCELLANEOUS AND GENERAL TAXONOMY

1. TEXTBOOKS

254. **Gouan**, Antoine. Explication du système botanique du Chevalier von Linné . . . **1787**. — *Line 3 add:* —— Explicacion del sistéma botánico del caballero Cárlos Linneo, para que sirva de introducción al estudio de la botánica . . . Traducida del frances al castellano por Don Antonio Paláu y Verdéra. 178 pp. 1 por. (*Appended to* LINNÉ, Carl von. Parte práctica de botánica . . . VIII. 1788.)

255. **Liebe**, Theodor. Grundriss der speciellen Botanik. **1866**. — *Line 2 add:* Ed. 2. 4+144 pp. 1 pl. O. Berlin, 1879.

256. **Kanitz**, Ágost. A növényrendszer áttekintése. Systematis vegetabilium janua, in usum auditorum R. Universitatis claudiopolitanae. Ed. 2 rev. [4]+96 pp. O. Kolozsvárt, **1887**.

2. GENERAL TAXONOMY

257. **Sistema** der natuurlyke historie, in IV. ryken, dieren, planten, mineralen, en wateren. Quadrupedia. Pt. 1. Regnum vegetabile. Pt. 1. 2 pts. (20+40 pp.) 24 pl. F. Hagæ-Comitum, **1765**.

In Dutch, French and English. — Has also titles: Sistème d'histoire naturelle, en IV. règnes, l'animal, le végétal . . . des eaux. System of natural history, in IV. reigns, animals, vegetables . . . Half t-p. reads: Sistema historiæ naturalia, in IV. regna diviaum, animals, vegetablie . . . — Sometimes wrongly attributed to Linnæus.

258. **Linné**, Carl von. Systema vegetabilium secundum classes . . . **1774**. — *Lines 52–53 read:* Système sexuel des végétaux, suivant les classes, les ordres, les genres et les espèces, avec les caractères et les différences. Première interprétation française, calquée sur les editions de Murray, de Person, de Wildenow; augmentée et enrichie de notions élémentaires, de notes diverses, d'une concordance avec la méthode de Tournefort, et les familles naturelles de Jussieu, etc., etc. par N. Jolyclerc. Ed. 2 rev. & enl. 2 vol. O. Paris, 1810.

258. **Linné**, Carl von. Systema plantarum . . . **1779**. — *After line 4 add:* —— Parte práctica de botánica del caballero Cárlos Linneo, que comprehende las clases, órdenes, géneros, especies y variedades de las plantas, con sus caracteres genéricos y específicos, sinónimos mas selectos, nombres triviales, lugares donde nacen, y propiedades. Traducida del latin en castellano é ilustrada por Don Antonio Paláu y Verdéra . . . 8 vol. 1 pl. O. Madrid, 1784–88. — Sistema de los vegetables; o, Resumen de la Parte práctica de botánica del caballero Cárlos Linneo, que comprehende las clases, órdenes, generos y especies de las plantas, con algunas de sus variedades; por Don Antonio Paláu y Verdéra. 12+713 pp. O. Madrid, 1788.

258. **Boehmer**, G. R. Tabularum synopticarum . . . 1790. — *Lines 1–2 read:* Genera plantarum in tabulis synopticis disponenda commendat. 2 pts. (11+16 pp.) sq. O. [Vitebergae, 1790.]

Title of Pt. II. reads: Tabularum synopticarum, quibus genera plantarum disponuntur, exempla proponente pergit.

260. **Fuhlrott**, Karl. Jussieu's und De Candolle's natürliche Pflanzensysteme . . . 1829. — *Lines 4–5 read:* Mit einer Vorrede von . . . C. G. Nees von Esenbeck. 6+242 pp. 2 maps. O. Bonn, 1829.

3. MISCELLANEOUS TAXONOMIC PUBLICATIONS

261. **S.**, H. W. Vegetabilium omnium generum icones. 2 vol. 640 [652] pl. F. [Wien], **1736–37**.

Most of the plates are "nature printed," many are hand-colored and a few are drawn in water-colors. Apparently a manuscript.

261. **Brückmann**, F. E. Centuriae tertiae epistola itineraria LVI. sistens fragmentorum collegii botanici a H. B. Ruppio . . . incepti. pp. 744–775. sq. O. [Wolffenbuttelæ, 1752.] — *From his* Centuria epistolarum itinerariarum. Centuria 3, 1750–53?

261. **Brückmann**, F. E. Centuriae tertiae epistola itineraria LVIII. offerens notas et animadversiones in H. B. Ruppii . . . Floram jenensem edit. primae. pp. 781–789. sq. O. [Wolffenbuttelæ, 1752.] — *From his* Centuria epistolarum itinerariarum. Centuria 3, 1750–53?

261. **Gmelin**, P. F. Otia botanica . . . 1760. — *Line 5 read:* [6]+200+[15] pp. O. Tubingae, 1760.

262. **Lipp**, F. J. Έγχειρίδιον βοτανικόν. Specimen inaugurale. 74+[15] pp. 11 pl. O. Vindobonæ, **1765**. — Ed. 2. O. Vindobonae, 1779.†

Has also the title: Enchiridium botanicum, sistens delineationem plantæ Carl v. Linné, definitam, exemplis et figuris illustratam.

263. **L'Héritier** de Brutelle, C. L. Stirpes novae . . . **1784-85**. — *Line 3 read:* 1784[-91].

Published in 6 parts. — See Jour. Bot. XLIII. 268 for dates of publication.

263. **Martyn**, Thomas. Thirty-eight plates with explanations . . . **1788**. — *Line 6 add:* — New ed. 6+72 pp. 38 pl. O. London, 1817.

266. **Trattinick**, Leop[old]. Botanisches Album; oder, Sammlung ausgewählter, naturgetreuer Abbildungen, der merkwürdigsten Pflanzen, Blumen, Früchte, Bäume, Sträucher u. s. w., nebst deren Benennung. Zusammengetragen aus Leop. Trattinick's sämmtlichen botanischen Werken. 150 pl. O. Wien, [182 .7].

266. **Salm-Reifferscheid-Dyck**, Joseph, *Fürst und Altgraf.*] Observationes botanicae in Horto Dickensi notatae, anno 1822. 47 pp. S. Coloniae, [1822].

267. **Rafinesque**, C. S. The school of flora. 1827, pp. 31–33, 73–75, 113–115, 153–155, 193–195, 231–234, 268–270, 316–318, 355–357, 438–440, 481–482, 42 il.; 1828, pp. 42–43, 90–91, 138–139, 184–185, 236–237, 272, 332, 379–380, 428, 475, 523, 568, 24 il.; 1830, pp. 86–87, 138, 188–189, 232–233, 284–285, 328–329, 376, 425–426, 474, 521–522, 568, il.; 1831, pp. 43–44, 89–90, 134–135, 187, 235–236, 283, 332, 379, 423–424, 476–477, 513, 573, il.; 1832, pp. 3, 42–43, 91, 139, 185, 236, 282, 331, 424–427, il. O. [Philadelphia, 1827–32.] — *From: "The Casket,* 1827–32."

268. **Presl**, K. B. Symbolae botanicae . . . 1832 [1830–52]. — *Line 3 read:* 1832 [1830–58].

268. **Bentham**, George *& others.* Phytologische Abbandlungen aus den Annalen des Wiener Museums der Naturgeschichte, I. und II. Bandes, von G. Bentham, St. Endlicher, E. Fenzl und F. Unger. various pag. [15] pl. sq. Q. Wien, **1841**.

Consists of a collection of reprints.

269. **Seemann**, B[erthold]. —— Endlicher's Paradisus vindobonensis. **1844–60**. — *Lines 1–6 read:* Hartinger, Anton. Endlicher's Paradisus vindobonensis. Abbildungen seltener und schönblühender Pflanzen der Wiener und anderer Gärten und Museen, von A. Hartinger . . . erläutert von . . . B. Seemann . . . (Illustrations of rare and ornamental plants . . .) 2 vol. 84 [81] pl. F. Wien, 1844–60.

Published in 21 pts. The title of pt. 1 reads: Auswahl der seltensten und ausgezeichnetesten Blumen in naturgetreuen Abbildungen. Later the title reads: Paradisus vindobonensis, Auswahl von seltenen und schönblühenden Pflanzen der Wiener Gärten . . . — The preparation of the text was confided to S. Endlicher, who prepared the manuscript for sixty of the plates, and on his death to E. Fenzl, who contributed nothing. In 1858 B. Seemann carried on the work. — Text in Latin, German and English.

270. **Witte**, H[einrich]. Schetsen uit het plantenrijk. [**1870**.] — *Line 2 read:* 156 il. 42 pl. O. Haarlem, 1870.

271. **Fünfstück**, M[oritz]. Naturgeschichte des Pflanzenreichs; grosser Pflanzenatlas mit Text für Schule und Haus. 172 pp. il. 80 pl. F. Stuttgart, [1885?].

271. **Suringar**, W. F. R. Het plantenrijk. (Regnum vegetabile.) Phylogenetische schets. 16 pp. 1 pl. D. Leeuwarden, 1895.

5. PRE-LINNEAN BOTANY

a. Classic and early botanical writers

271. **Theophrastos Eresios**. (371–**286** B. C.) Theophrasti de historia et de causis plantarum . . . 1483. — *Line 1 read:* Theophrasti de historia plantarum lib. IX. et decimi principium duntaxat eiusdem de causis plantarum lib. V. [VI.] [Theodoro Gaza interprete]. [15]+284 ff. S. n. p., [148 .7] — *Lines 4–6 read:* Theophrasti de historia et causis plantarū, libri quindecim, Theodoro Gaza interprete. Ejusdē, tabulas duas capita librorū complectentes, quarū unam libris de historia, alteram de causis plantarū, unacū vocabulis quibusdam graecorū & latinorum nominum, praefixas invenies lector. Theodoro Gaza interprete. [32]+343+[43]+354+ [23] pp. S. Parisiis, 1529. — *Lines 14–15 of p. 872 read:* [3]+72 [68] ff. S. Vinegia, 1549. — La storia delle piante. Volgarizzata e annotata da Mons. Filippo Ferri Mancini. 40+580+[3] pp. O. Roma, 1900.

272. **Nikandros Kolophonios.** (About 200–**135** B. C.) Alexipharmaca et theriaca. 1499. — *Line 3 read:* Νικάνδρου Θηριακά. Τοῦ αὐτῦ Ἀλεξιφάρμακα. 'Ερμήνεια τῦ αἰωνύμου συγγραφέωs εἰs Θηριακά. Σχόλια διαφόρων συγγραφέων εἰs Ἀλεξιφάρμακα. Ἐξήγησιs σαφῶν, μέτρων, σημείων, καὶ χαρακτήρων. Theriaca eiusdem alexipharmaca. Interpretatio innominati authoris in Theriaca. Commentarii diversorum authorū in Alexipharmaca. Expositio ponderū, mensurarum, signorum, & characterum. 92 [90] ff. O. [colophon:] Venetiis, 1522–23. — *Line 8 read:* 70+[1] ff. S. Parisiis, 1549.

272. **Scribonius Largus.** (About '40.) De compositionibus medicamentorum . . . 1529. — *Lines 8–9 read:* [18]+144+ 465+[40] pp. il. O. Patavii, 1655.

272. **Dioscorides**, Pedakios, Anazarbeus. (About 77.) Πεδακίου Διοσκορίδου Ἀναζαρβέως περὶ ὕλης ἰατρικῆς λόγοι ὄξ. 1499. — *Line 3 read:* Πεδακίου Διοσκορίδου περὶ ὕλης ἰατρικῆς λόγοι ὄξ. Pedacii Dioscoridis de materia medica libri six. — *Line 4 read:* [11]+235[244] ff. O. — *Lines 7–15 read:* Πεδακίου Διοσκορίδου Ἀναζαρβέως περὶ ὕλης ἰατρικῆς βιβλία ἔ . . . Pedacii Dioscoridae Anazarbei de medica materia libri V. de letalibus venenis eorumque precautione & curatione . . . lib. unus. Interprete⁀ Marcello Vergilio. Ejusdem Marcelli Vergilii in hosce Dioscoridis libros comm̄etarii doctissimi, in quibus præter omnigenam variā̃q̃ eruditionē, collatis aliorum interpretum versionibus, suæ tralationis ex utriusq̃ linguæ autoribus certissima adferuntur documenta . . . [With Hermolai Barbari, In Dioscoridem corollariorū libri quinque.] [26]+753+[1] pp.+ 78 ff. F. Coloniæ, 1529. — *Line 20 of p. 273 add:* Pharmacorum simplicium, reiq̃ medicæ libri VIII. [IX.], Jo. Ruellio interprete. Una cum Herm. Barbari corollarijs, & Marc. Vergilij in singula capita obscuris, sive annotationibus . . . [3]+ 361+[13] pp. F. Argentorato, 1529. — *Lines 34–37 of p. 273 read:* Oū ejusdē annotationibus, nuperq̃ diligētissime excusi. Addito indice eorų, q̃ digna notatu visa sunt. [5]+352+[6] ff. F. [*colophon:*] Florentiæ, 1518. — *Line 44 add:* Simplicium medicamentorū, reiq̃ medicæ libri VI. interprete Marcello Vergilio. Quibus accessit, præter pharmacorum simplicium catalogum, novus omnium ferè medelarum sive curationum index. [30]+684+[130] pp. S. Basileæ, 1532. — *Line 50 of p. 273 read:* Pedanii . . . nunc primum studio cuiusdam viri doctissimi ad græcum exemplar recogniti, ac eadem opera in juniorum gratiam vulgatis officinarum nominib. passim aspersis. Una cum duplici indice, quorum primus quidem stirpium nom̄eclaturas Dioscoridi; alter seplasiariorum & herbariis usitatas continebit. [30]+617+ [49] pp. T. Lugduni, 1543. — Pedanii . . . His accessit, præter pharmacorum simplicium catalogum, copiosus omniū fermē medelarum sive curationum index. [28]+543+[139] pp. Tt. Lugduni, 1546. — *Line 52 of p. 273 read:* Pedanii Dioscoridis Anazarbei de medica materia . . . His accessit, præter pharmacorum simplicium catalogum, copiosus omnium fermē medelarū sive curationum index. 274+[90] ff. Tt. Venetiis, 1550. — *Line 82 of p. 273 read:* 128+[8] pp. sq. O. Vinegia, 1548, — *Lines 34–35 of p. 273, col. 2 read:* [26]+616+[27] pp. il. 1 por. Q. Salamanca, 1570.

273. **Plinius Secundus**, Cajus. (23–79.) Historiae naturalis libri XXXVII. 1469. — *Lines 14–15 read:* cum commentariis & adnotationibus Hermolai Barbari, Pintiani, Rhenani, Gelenii, Dalechampii, Scaligeri, Salmasii, G. Vossii, & variorum. Accedunt praeterea variae lectiones ex MS. S. . . . Item J. F. Gronovii notarum liber singularis ad illustrem virum Johannem Capelanum. 3 vol, O. Lugd. Batav. & Roterodami, 1668–69. — *Line 15 add:* Naturalis historiae libri XXXVII. Interpretatione et notis illustravit Joannes Harduinus. 5 vol. sq. Q. Parisiis, 1685. — *Line 1 of p. 274 add:* The historie of the world; commonly called, The naturall historie. Translated into English by Philemon Holland. [Ed. 2.] 2 vol. F. London, 1634–35. — *Line 10 of p. 274 add:* — Index in C. Plinii Nat. hist. libros locupletior, & castigatior quàm qui hactenus impressi sunt . . . [250] ff. S. Venetiis, 1538.

274. **Macer Floridus** (*pseud.* for Odo). De viribus herbarum. 1487. — *Line 3 add:* — De viribus herba ̃2J Famosissimus medicus et medico ̃2J Speculum. [51] ff. il. D. n. p., n. d.

274. **Albertus de Bollstaedt** (Albertus Magnus). (1193–1280.) Tabula tractatuum parvorum naturalium . . . 1517. — *Lines 2–3 of p. 274 — line 2 of p. 275 read:* Tabula tractatuum parvorum naturalium. De sensu ̃7 sensato, de memoria ̃7 reminiscentia . . . de vegetabilibus ̃7 plantis . . . [5]+233 ff. F. [*colophon:*] Venetiis, 1517. — *Line 10 of p. 275 read:* De vegetabilibus ̃7 plantis (1517 ed. ff. 122–179).

275. **Bartholomaeus Anglicus** (Bartholomaeus de Glanvilla). (About 1300.) Liber de proprietatibus rerum. 1481. — *Line 2 add:* [Liber de proprietatibus rerum.] [*Folium 1, sign. a. 2:*] Incipit prohemium de proprietatib' rerum fratris Bartholomei Anglici de ordine fratrum mino ̃2J. [320] ff. F. n. p., [1480]. — *Line 7 add:* Liber de proprietatib' rerū. [256] ff. Q. [*colophon:*] Argentine, 1491.

275. **Matthaeus Sylvaticus**. (?–1342.) Liber pandectarum medicine omnia medicine simplicia continē . . . n. d. — *Line 5 read:* [307] ff. F. [Argentorati, 14 . ?] — [Another ed.] 356 ff. — *Line 6 add:* — Liber pandectarum medicine: omnia medicine simplicia cōtinēs: quæ ex oībus antiquo ̃2J

libris aggregauit eximius artiū ̃7 medicine doctor . . . [235] ff. F. [*colophon:*] Venetijs, 1480. — *Line 8 add:* Opus pādectarū medicine nuper impressus cū quottatiōb ̃9 oīus auctorī in locis ppriis et cū Simone Janūesi additis ē tnonullis captis simpliciū medicinarū in aliis nō repertis . . . 212+ [3] ff. Q. [*colophon:*] n. p., 1512.

b. Works of authors after 1400

275. **Ortus sanitatis** . . . [148 . ?] — *Cancel lines 1–2 of col. 1 and lines 1–2 of col. 2 up to — and read:* [Gart der Gesundheit.] [*Fol. 1a, sign. aij:*] Offt und vil . . . [Mencz, 1485.] *See col. 2 line 5 and the following German editions. After these insert:* Ortus sanitatis. [453] ff. il. pl. F. [*colophon:*] Moguntiae, 1491. — Ortus sanitatis: de herbis ̃7 plantis, de animalibus ̃7 reptilibus, de auibus ̃7 volatilibus, de piscibus ̃7 natatilibus . . . [*Fol. 2a, sign. aij:*] OMnipotētis eterniq̃ dei: totius nature creatoris opera mirabilia admirandaq̃ mecū vicibus iteratis crebrius p̃cogitādo reuolui . . . [360] ff. il. F. n. p. [149 . ?] — *Line 2 of col. 2 add:* — Ortus sanitatis: De herbis et plantis, de animalibus ̃7 reptilibus, de auibus et volatilibus . . . [*Fol. 2a, sign. aij:*] oMnipotētis eterniq̃ dei: toti ̃9 nature creatoris opa. [360] ff. il. F. n. p., [1497?].

275. **Herbarius**. [Aggregator practicus de simplicibus.] 1484. — *Line 4 of p. 276 read:* [Herbolarium.] Incipit tractatus de virtutibus herbarum. [3]+150+[17] ff. il. O. [*colophon:*] Venetiis, 1509. — *Line 3 of p. 276 read:* Herbolario volgare, nelquale se dimostra a conoscer le herbe, & le sue virtu, & il modo di operarle, cō molti altri simplici, di novo venute in luce, & il latino in volgare tradutte, con gli suoi repertorii da ritrovar le herbe, & li remedii alle infirmita. New ed. [397] pp. il. S. [Vinegia], 1536.

276. **Arbolayre** contenant la qualitey . . . [1485.] — *Line 12 read:* Le grant herbier en francoys, contenant les qualitez, vertus & proprietes des herbes, arbres, gommes & semences. Extraict de plusieurs traictes de medecine cōme de Avincēne, de Rasis de Constantin, de Isaac & de Plataire. Selon le commun usage. 108+[12] ff. il. Q. n. p. n. d.

276. **Leoniceno**, Nicolo. De Plinii et aliorum medicorum erroribus. 1492. — *Lines 2–3 read:* De Plinii, & plurium aliorū medicorum in medicina erroribus . . . [3]+95+[3] ff. O. [*colophon:*] Ferrariæ, 1509.

276. **Ardoynis**, Santes de. Incipit liber de venenis quem magister santes de Ardoynis . . . 1492. — *Lines 6–7 read:* In quo naturalis primum historia venenatorū omnium, sive natura sive arte constent, fidelissime proponitur . . . Adiunximus ejusdem generis commentarium . . . Ferdinandi Ponzetti . . . [14]+573 [569]+[14] pp. F. Basiliæ, [1562].

276. **Barbarus**, Ermolao (Barbarus, Hermolaus). Castigationes Plinianae. 1492–93. — *Line 2 read:* nii [et Secundae castigationes.] 2 pts. [316] pp. ? F. [Romae, 1492–93.]

276. **Brunfels**, Otto. Herbarum vivae cicones . . . 1530. — *Line 12 add:* — [Another ed.] 313+[5] pp. il. F. Argent., 1536.

276. **Champier**, Simphorien. Campus Elysius Galliae . . . 1533. — *Lines 4–6 read:* [6]+135 pp. S. Lugduni, 1533.

276. **Champier**, Simphorien. Hortus gallicus . . . 1533. — *Line 3 read:* [10]+83 pp.

276. **Petri**, Cornelis. Annotatiunculae . . . 1533. — *Lines 1–3 read:* Annotatiunculae aliquot in quatuor libros Dioscoridis Anazarbei. Experimenta & antidota contra varios morbos. De rebus occultis in natura mirandis, & alia quaedam lectu digna. [97] pp. 1 pl. S. [*colophon:*] Antwerpiae, 1533.

276. **Estienne**, Charles.] Arbustum, fonticulus, spinetum. 1533. — *Line 2 add:* [Another ed.] 37+[3] pp. T. Parisiis, 1538. —

277. **Estienne**, Charles.] De re hortensi libellus. . . 1533. — *Lines 2–3 read:* ac fruticum, qui in hortis conseri solent nomina latinis vocibus efferre docens ex probatis authoribus . . . 99+[13] pp. S. Parisiis, 1535. — *Line 3 add:* [Another ed.] 99+[13] pp. T. Parisiis, 1536. — *Line 4 add:* [Another ed.] 140 pp. S. Parisiis, 1539.

277. **Brasavola**, A. M. Examen omnium simplicium medicamentorum . . . 1536. — *Line 7 add:* — Examen omnium simplicium quorum usus in publicis est officinis . . . [Ed. 5.] 862+[27] pp. O. Lugduni, 1546.† — Examen omnium simplicium, quorum usus in publicis est officinis; opus perinsigne, & medicinam facientibus perutile; ab ipso authore recognitum & auctum. 862+[64] pp. T. Lugduni, 1556.

277. **Ruel**, Jean (Joannes Ruellius). De natura stirpium libri tres. 1536. — *Line 6 read:* [90]+666 pp. F. Basileae, 1543.

277. Bock, Hieronymus. New Kreutter-Buch . . . **1539.** — *Line 6 add:* Kreütter Büch, darin Underscheid, Würckung und Namen der Kreütter so in deutschen Landen wachsen, auch der selbigen eigentlicher und wolgegründter gebrauch inn der Artznet fleissig dargeben . . . Von newem fleissig übersehen, gebessert und gemehret . . . darüber findestu drei volkomene nutzliche Register . . . [18]+353 ff. il. F. [Strassburg], 1546. — *Line 28 read:* [Another ed.] [17]+413+ [6] ff. il. 1 por. Q. Strassburg, 1560. — *Lines 59–60 read:* [64]+1200+[62] pp. il. 1 por. O. [colophon:] Argentorati, 1552.

278. Fuchs, Leonhard. De historia stirpium commentarii insignes . . . **1542.** — *Line 9 read:* [11]+362+[6] ff. D. Parisiis, 1543. — [Another ed.] — *Lines 12–13 read:* De historia stirpium commentarii insignes, adjectis earundem vivis, & ad naturæ imitationem artificiose expressis imaginibus . . . accessit iis succincta admodum vocum quarundam subobscurarum in hoc opere passim occurrentium explanatio . . . [28]+352+[12] pp. il. D. Lugduni, 1551. — *Line 49 read:* [30]+607 pp. il. Q. Lion, 1558.

278. Fuchs, Leonhard. Primi de stirpium historia commentariorum tomi vivae imagines . . . **1545.** — *Lines 4–5 read:* [13]+516 pp. 516 il. S. Basileae, 1549. — *Line 9 read:* [20]+516 pp. 516 il. 1 por. T. Lugduni, 1552.

278. Cardano, Geronimo. De subtilitate libri XXI. **1550.** — *Line 3 add:* De subtilitate . . . Addita insuper Apologia adversus calumniatorem, qua vis horum librorum aperitur. [86]+1426+[4] pp. il. 1 por. D. Basileae, [1560]. — *Line 4 add:* —— Les livres intitules de la subtilité & subtiles inventions, ensemble les causes occultes & raisons d'icelles. Traduits de latin en françois par Richard le Blanc. Nouvellement reveus, corrigez & augmentez sur le dernier exemplaire latin . . . [32]+478 ff. il. S. Paris, 1584. — *Line 5 add:* —

De plantis (Ed. 1560, pp. 515–624).

279. Belon, Pierre. Les observations de plusieurs singularitez et choses memorables, trouvées en Grèce . . . **1553.** — *Lines 4–6 read:* [Rev. ed.] [11]+211+[1] ff. il. 1 por. 1 pl. O. Paris, 1554. — Les observations . . . Reveuz de rechef, & augmentes de figures, avec une nouvelle table de toutes les matières traictées en iceux. [7]+375+[33] ff. il. 1 por. 1 pl. S. Anvers, 1555.

279. Mattioli, Pierandrea. Commentarii in libros sex Pedacii Dioscoridis Anazarbei De medica materia . . . **1554.** — *Line 10 read:* [20]+776+46 pp. il. F. Venetiis, 1560. — *Line 21 add:* —— I discorsi nei sei libri di Pedacio Dioscoride Anazarbeo Della materia medicinale . . . [118]+802 pp. il. F. Venetia, 1559. — *Line 31 add:* —— Dei discorsi . . . Dal proprio autore, innanzi la sua morte ricorretta, ampliata, & all' ultima perfettione ridotta . . . 2 vol. ([164]+1527+ [11] pp.) il. por. F. Venetia, 1604. — *Line 38 add:* —— Commentaires de M. P. André Matthiolus . . . sur les six livres de Pedacius Dioscoride Anazarbéen De la matière medicinale; traduits de latin en français par M. Antoine du Pinet, & de nouveau accreus d'un bon nombre de figures, & reveus & augmentes en plus de mille lieux sur la dernière edition de l'autheur . . . [138]+605+[32] pp. il. 1 por. F. Lyon, 1573. — *Line 44 add:* Les commentaires sur les six livres de Pedacius Dioscoride Anazarbéen De la matière médecinale . . . [126]+605+[32] pp. il. 1 por. F. Lyon, 1642. — *Lines 51 52 read:* latino & françoise. [4] | 95+[14]+636+[33] pp. il. 1 por. F. Lyon, 1680.

280. Cardano, Girolamo. De rerum varietate libri XVII. [10]+707+[32] pp. il. F. Basileæ, **1557.**

280. Lonitzer, Adam. Kreuterbuch . . . **1557.** — *Lines 53–64 read:* Vollständiges Kräuter-Buch; oder, Das Buch über alle drey Reiche der Natur. Erstens die Destillirkunst, sodann von Bäumen, Stauden, Hecken, Kräutern, Getraiden . . . und Benennungen in deutscher, griechischer, lateinischer, französischer, italiänischer und spanischer Sprache. Zweytens von allen Gattungen der Thiere der Erde, Vögeln der Luft . . . Alles in deutlichen Abbildungen, mit Beschreibung ihrer Eigenschaften, Wirkungen, und nützlichen Gebrauch . . . von Peter Uffenbach . . . übersehen; und mit drey vollständigen Registern bereichert, nachmals mit einer Zugabe von den neuest entdeckten Beobachtungen vermehrt von Balthasar Ehrhart, nun aber aufs neue verbessert, und nach der heutigen Mundart eingerichtet. [6]+750+[30]+ 136 pp. il. nar. F. Augsburg, 1783.

280. Anguillara, Luigi. Semplici . . . **1561.** — *Line 2 read:* nobili huomini scritti appaiono, et nuovamente . . . — *Line 3 read:* S. Vinegia, **1561.**

280. Du Pinet, Antoine. Historia plantarum . . . **1561.** — *Line 10 read:* Paris, 1584. — *Line 11 add:* —— Ed. 2 rev. & enl. 720+240+[56] pp. il. Tt. Paris, [1619–]22.

281. Sansovino, Francesco. Della materia medicinale libri IV. . . **1561.** — *Line 5 add:* Della materia medicinale libri quattro. Nel primo & secondo de quali si contengono i semplici medicamenti . . . Nel terzo s' insegna il modo di preparare & comporre i medicamenti . . . Nel quarto . . . son poste le malattie che vengono al corpo humano . . . [19]+ 332+[1] ff. il. O. Venetia, 1562 [colophon:] 1561.

281. Cordus, Valerius. Stirpium descriptionis liber quintus . . . **1563.** — *Line 8 read:* Iosiam Rihelium, anno 1560. 13 ff. F. Argentorati, **1563.**

281. Mattioli, Pierandrea. Opusculum de simplicium . . . **1569.** — *Line 2 read:* locos & genera. Accesserunt quoque præfationes quædam huic opusculo ad modum necessariæ, quarum enarrationem epistola ad lectorem indicabit. 328+ [2] ff. il. nar. T. Venetiis, 1569.

282. Langham, William. The garden of health . . . **1579.** — *Line 5 read:* Ed. 2 rev. & enl. [6]+702+[66] pp. O. London, 1633.

282. Durante, Castore. Herbario nuovo . . . **1585.** — *Line 14 add:* [Another ed.] [6]+480+[27] pp. il. F. Venetia, 1718. —

283. Tabernaemontanus, J. T. Neuw Kreuterbuch . . . **1588.** — *Lines 39–40 read:* 3 vol. ([10]+1529+[96] pp.) il. Fᵉ. Basel, 1731.

284. Sweert, Emanuel. Florilegium . . . **1612.** — *Lines 4–5 cancel:* [Another ed.] F. Amstelodami, 1620.† — *Line 10 read:* 2 pts. ([34] pp.) 110 pl. Fᵉ. Amstelodami & Francofurti, [1614]–20. — [Another ed.] — *Line 13 read:* 2 vol. 1 por. 110 pl. Fᵉ. Amstelodami, 1654–55.

284. Colonna, Fabio. Minus cognitarum rariorumque nostro coelo orientium stirpium . . . **1616.** — *Lines 1–5 read:* Minus cognitarum stirpium aliquot, ac etiam rariorum nostro coelo orientium ἔκφρασις, qua non paucae ab antiquioribus, Theophrasto, Dioscoride, Plinio, Galeno, aliisque memoratae declarantur, officinarum usui perquam utiles. Item, de aquatilibus aliisq; animalibus quibusdam paucis libellus . . . Opus nunc primm in lucem editum. [8]+340+ 73+[7] pp. il. O. Romæ, **1606.** — Minus cognitarum plantarum prima, & secunda pars. Purpura; & aliorum aquatilium observationes. Omnia fermé nunc primum edita. 3 pts. ([4]+340+73+[7]+[10]+99+[4]+42 pp.) il. 1 por. O. [Romæ, 1616.]

The 1616 edition comprises three parts. The first part under the title: Minus cognitarum rariorumque nostro celo orientium stirpium . . . is a reissue of Minus cognitarum stirpium aliquot . . . of 1606, except the preliminary sheets, comprising the title-page and preface, which have been reset. The second part is Minus cognitarum stirpium pars altera; the third part is Purpura. Each part is paged separately and has its respective title-page.

285. Alpino, Prospero. De plantis exoticis libri duo . . . **1627.** — *Line 4 add:* — [Another ed.] [14]+344 pp. il. O. Venetiis, 1699.

285. Jacobs, Heymann. Den cleynen herbarius . . . **1627.** — *Line 1 read:* J[acobs], H[eymann]. Den cleynen herbarius; ofte, Kruydt-boecxken, inhoudende de kracht' ende operatie van alle de ghemeene kruyderen ende bekende vruchten die men dogelicx gebruyckt waer deur men met Gods hulpe een yder zijne ghesontheydt can onder houden ende veelder hande sieckten te genesen. Van nieus oversien en op veel plaetsen verbetert ende vermeerdert . . . 192 pp. T. Amsterdam, 1606. —

285. Cornut, J. [P.]. Canadensium plantarum . . . **1635.** — *Line 4 add:* — Ed. 2. [14]+238+[2] pp. il. O. Parisiis, 1651. — Ed. 2. [14]+238+[2] pp. il. sq. O. Parisiis, 1662.

285. Nieremberg, J. E. Historia naturae maxime peregrinae libris XVI. distincta . . . **1635.** — *Line 1 read:* Curiosa filosofia y tesoro de marauillas de la naturaleza . . . [2] vol. S. Madrid & Barcelona, [1633]–44. — *Line 6 read:* Antverpiac, 1635. — *Line 9 add as a note:* Vol. [II.] has the title: Oculta filosofia . . .

285. Pauli, Simon. Quadripartitum botanicum . . . **1639.** — *Lines 5–6 read:* — [Ed. 3.] [18]+811+[108] pp. sq. O. Francofurti ad Moenum, 1708.

285. Curtus, Franciscus. Ad vivium [sic] exprimebat. 32 pl. F. [Bologna, 1640?]

A collection of etchings of flowers; almost identical with those in Robert, Nicolas. Variae ac multiformes florum . . . 1665.

286. Ambrosini, Giacinto. Novarum plantarum hactenus non sculptarum historia. (In his Hortus studiosorum . . . pp. 69–103. 1657.)

286. [**Kentmann**, Theophilus.] Tabula locum et tempus, quibus uberius plantæ potissimum spontaneæ vigent ac proveniunt, exprimens. [8] pp. sq. O. Lipsiæ, **1659.**

286. **Robert**, N[icolas]. Variæ ac multiformes florum species expressæ ad vivum et æneis tabulis incisæ. 30 pl. F'. Romæ, **1665.**

The plates are almost identical with those in CURTUS, Franciscus. Ad vivium [*sic*] exprimebat. [1640?]

286. **Charas**, Moyse. Histoire naturelle des, animaux des plantes . . . **1668.** — *Lines 3–4 read:* [24]+310+[9] pp. S. Paris, **1668.** — *Line 6 read:* New ed. 5+305+[8]+12 pp. D. Paris, 1685. — *New ed. rev. & enl.* — *After line 10 add as a note:*

The 1668 ed. has also the title: Thériaque d'Andromachus.

287. **Nylandt**, Petrus. De Nederlandtse herbarius . . . **1670.** — *Lines 11–12 read:* [Another ed.] [6]+342+[24] pp. il. sq. O. Amsterdam, 1682.

287. **Zanoni**, Giacomo. Istoria botanica . . . **1675.** — *Line 6 add:* —— Rariorum stirpium historia ex parte olim edita, nunc centum plus tabulis ex commentariis auctoris ab ejusdem nepotibus ampliata opus universum digessit, latine reddidit, supplevitque Cajetanus Montius. [38]+247 pp. 186 pl. por. F'. Bononiae, 1742.

288. **Redi**, Francesco. Esperienze intorno a diverse cose naturali e particolarmente a quelle, che ci son portate dall' Indie . . . [2]+122 pp. 6 pl. O. Firenze, 1686.

288. **Saumaise**, Claudius. Exercitationes de homonymis hyles iatricæ nunquam antehac editæ, ut et de manna et saccharo. [10]+27+259+20 pp. F'. Trajecti ad Rhenum, **1689.** (*Appended to his* Plinianæ exercitationes . . . 1689.)

288. **Saumaise**, Claudius (Salmasius). Plinianæ exercitationes in Caji Julii Solini Polyhistora . . . **1689.** — *Lines 5–6 read:* 2 vol. ([46]+63+943+16+157+[1]+[10]+27+259+20 pp.) il. F'. Trajecti ad Rhenum, 1689.

Contains scattered references to plants.

289. **Salmon**, William. Botanologia . . . **1710–11.** — *Line 7 add:* [Another ed.] [4]+24+1296+[43] pp. il. F'. London, 1760.

289. **Valentini**, M. B. Historia simplicium reformata . . . **1716.** — *Lines 6–7 read:* [26]+664+[28] pp. il. 1 tab. nar. F'.

290. **Blair**, Patrick. Pharmaco-botanologia . . . **1723.** — *Line 4 read:* London, 1723–[28].

291. **Morandi**, J. B. Historia botanica practica . . . **1744.** — *Line 7 read:* [10]+32+164 pp.

292. **Gmelin**, P. F. & **Böhmer**, G. R. Thesaurus rei herbariae . . . **1788–89.** — *Line 6 read:* 2 vol. pl. F. Nuremberg, 1770–72.† — New ed. rev. 2 vol. 403 pl. F'. Nürnberg, 1788–89.

E. DENDROGRAPHY

1. GENERAL

293. **Loudon**, J. C. An encyclopædia of trees and shrubs . . . **1841.** — *Line 4 read:* 71+[1]+1162 pp. il. O. London, **1842.** — [Another ed.] 71+[1]+1162 pp. il. O. London, **1853.** — [Another ed.] 71+[1]+1162 pp. il. O. London, **1869.** — *Line 6 read:* 71+[1]+1162 pp. il. O. London, **1875.** — [Another ed.] 71+[1]+1162 pp. il. O. London, 1883.

293. **Hartig**, Theodor. Vollständige Naturgeschichte der forstlichen Culturpflanzen Deutschlands. **1851.** — *Lines 2–3 read:* [4]+17+580+[18]+8+[4] pp. 120 pl. sq. O. Berlin, [1840–]51. (Lehrbuch der Pflanzenkunde in ihrer Anwendung auf Forstwirthschaft . . . Erste Abtheilung.)

294. **Турскій**, М. & **Яшновъ**, Л. Опредѣленіе древесины . . . **1885.** — *Line 1–2 read:* **Турскій**, М. & **Яшновъ**, Л., [Turski, M. & Yashnof, L.] Опредѣленіе древесины и вѣтвей главнѣйшихъ. . . . — *Line 5 read:* [1]+124 pp. 40 il. 1 pl. O. Москва,

3. INDIVIDUAL NOTEWORTHY TREES

b. North America

295. **Sahut**, Félix. La culture fruitière aux États-Unis. **1893.** — *Line 3 add:* —.*Reprinted:* 77 pp. il. O. Montpellier, 1894.

d. Europe

V. BRITISH ISLANDS

296. **Walker**, John. A catalogue of some of the most considerable trees in Scotland. (*In his* Essays on natural history and rural economy, pp. 1–90. **1812.**)

F. GEOGRAPHICAL DISTRIBUTION

1. GENERAL

a. Miscellaneous

298. **Barton**, John. A lecture on the geography of plants. **1827.** — *Lines 3–4 read:* ouvrage traduit de l'anglais et augmenté de notes pour l'amélioration de l'industrie nationale des Pays-Bas par J. Marchal. 84 pp. 4 maps. O. Bruxelles, 1829.

301. **Hansen**, Adolf. Pflanzengeographische Tafeln. No. 1–5. 5 pl. 75×100 cm. Berlin-Steglitz, 1899 →

301. **Thevenot**, Melchisedec. Relation de divers voayges [*sic*] curieux qui n'out point esté publiées, ou qui sont esté traduites d'Hacluyt, de Purchas, et d'autres voyageurs anglois, hollandois, portugais, allemands, espagnols . . . 4 vol. pl. maps. F. Paris, 1683.†

The secondary titles bear earlier dates.

302. **Kotzebue**, Otto von. Entdeckungs-Reise in die Süd-See . . . **1821.** — *Line 4 add:* —A voyage of discovery into the South Sea and Beering's Straits for the purpose of exploring a north-east passage, undertaken in the years 1815–1818 at the expense of His Highness the chancellor of the empire, Count Romanzoff, in the ship Rurick . . . 3 vol. por. pl. maps. O. London, 1821.

303. **Moseley**, H. N. Notes by a naturalist on the "Challenger" . . . **1879.** — *Line 5 add:* — New ed. rev. 24+540 pp. il. por. map. O. London, 1892.

303. **North**, Marianne. Recollections of a happy life . . . **1892.** — *Line 3 add:* — Some further recollections of a happy life selected from the journals of Marianne North chiefly between the years 1859 and 1869 edited by her sister Mrs. J. A. Symonds. 8+316 pp. 2 por. O. London, 1893.

2. NORTH AMERICA

a. General

Dendrography

304. **Michaux**, F. A. Histoire des arbres forestiers . . . **1810–13.** — *Line 18 add:* — [Another ed.] 3 vol. 156 pl. Q. Philadelphia, 1855.

304. **Nuttall**, Thomas. The North American sylva . . . **1842–49.** — *Line 9 add:* — [Another ed.] 3 vol. 121 pl. Q. Philadelphia, 1855. — *Line 11 read:* Called also vol. IV.–VI. of Michaux, F. A. The North American sylva . . .

304. **Browne**, D. J. Trees of America . . . **1846.** — *Line 1 read:* The trees of America, native and foreign . . . scientifically and popularly described, being considered principally with reference to their geography and history, soil and situation, propagation and culture, accidents and diseases, properties and uses . . . — *Line 2 add:* — [Another ed.] 12+520 pp. il. O. New York, 1851.

General Phytography

305. **Michaux**, A[ndré]. Flora boreali-americana . . . **1803.** — *Lines 3–4 read:* New ed. 2 vol. 51 pl. O. Parisiis, 1820.

305. **Lounsberry**, Alice. A guide to the trees; with . . . plates and . . . diagrams by Mrs. Ellis Rowan. With an introduction by Dr. N. L. Britton. 20+313 pp. il. pl. D. New York, [°1900].

306. [**Rich**, O. O.] A synopsis of the genera of American plants . . . **1814.** — *Line 1 read:* [Rich, Obadiah.]

306. [**Eaton**, Amos.] A manual of botany for the northern states . . . **1817.** — *Line 3 add:* Ed. 7 enl. 672+125 pp. D. Albany, 1836.

307. **Wood**, Alphonso. A class-book of botany . . . **1845.** — *Line 6 add:* Ed. 2 rev. & enl. 645 pp. il. D. Claremont (N. H.), 1847. — *Line 13 add:* Ed. 41 rev. & enl. 645+[1]+4 pp. il. O. Claremont, (N. H.), & Boston, 1855 [°1846]. — *Line 21 add:* — [Another ed.] 20+832+3 pp. il. 5 pl. O. New York, 1870.

307. **Gray**, Asa. The genera of the plants of the United States . . . **1848.** — *Line 3 read:* Boston (vol. I.) & New York (vol. II.), 1848–49. — [Another ed.] 2 vol. 186 pl. O. New York, 1849.

307. [**Pech**, F.] Catalogue of the United States plants in the Department of agriculture. 27 pp. O. t-p-c. [Washington, 1867?].

c. Canada east and Newfoundland

General Phytography

310. **Barnston**, James. Catalogue of Canadian plants in the Holmes' herbarium in the cabinet of the University of McGill college. (*Canad. Naturalist*, IV. 101–116. **1859.**) — *Reprinted:* 20 pp. O. Montreal, 1859.

310. **Lawson**, George. Some account of plants collected in the counties of Leeds . . . 1863. — *Line 3 add: — Edinb. New Philos. Jour.* new ser. XVII. 197–208. 1863.)

310. **Moyen**, J. Cours élémentaire de botanique et flore du Canada, à l'usage des maisons d'éducation. 334 pp. 46 pl. D. Montreal, **1871**.

f. Northeastern United States

312. **Flagg**, Wilson. A year among the trees . . . **1881.** — *Lines 1–2 read:* The woods and by-ways of New England. 18+442 pp. 22 pl. O. Boston, 1872. — A year among the trees; or, The woods and by-ways of New England. 18+ 335 pp. D. Boston, 1881. — [Another ed.] [10]+308 pp. 2 il. D. Boston, 1890.

312. **Russell**, L. W. Native trees . . . **1891.** — *Line 3 add:* Ed. 5 rev. & enl. 6+103 pp. il. 4 pl. D. Boston, 1894. —

312. **Miller**, John. Wooded areas. [Providence, **1894.**] — *From: "Providence Sunday journal,* April 29, 1894."

This article gives an excellent account of the trees of Rhode Island with their distribution. It is based on an interview with James L. Bennett, author of "Plants of Rhode Island."

313. **Green**, Jacob. Catalogue of plants indigenous to the state of New York. pp. 91–136. [Albany, **1814.**] — *From: Soc. Trans. Usef. Arts Albany Trans.* III.

314. **Olney**, S. T. Catalogue of plants collected by the botanical department of the Providence Franklin Society, principally in Rhode Island, in 1844. 8 pp. O. t-p-c. Providence, **1845.** — Rhode Island plants, or additions and emendations to the Catalogue of plants published by the Providence Franklin society in March 1845. 24 pp. O. [Providence, 1846.] — *From: "Providence Franklin society. Proceedings,* I. no. 1, 1846." — Rhode Island plants, 1846, or additions to the published lists of the Providence Franklin society. pp. 25–42. O. [Providence, 1847.] — *From: "Providence Franklin society. Proceedings,* I. no. 2, 1847."

314. **Hale**, T. J. Additions to the flora of Wisconsin; [supplement to Lapham's Plants of Wisconsin, 1852]. 8 pp. O. [Madison, **1860**.] — *From: Wisconsin Agric. Soc. Trans.* V. 417–424. — Additions . . . for 1860 and 1861. 4 pp. O. [Madison, 1861?]

314. **Clinton**, G. W. Preliminary list of plants of Buffalo and its vicinity. 12 pp. O. Buffalo, **1864.**

314. **Perkins**, G. H. Catalogue of the flowering plants of Vermont. pp. 161–166, 181–190, 215–218, 231–234, 252–253. O. [Newport, Vt., **1872–74**.] — *From: " Orleans county society of natural sciences. Archives of science,* I."

315. **Phinney**, A. J. Catalogue of the flora of central-eastern Indiana, (Alpine or elevated district of the state). pp. 194–236. O. [Indianapolis, **1883**.] — *From: Indiana Dept. Geol. Ann. Rep.* XII.

315. **Meyncke**, O. M. The flora of Franklin county, [Indiana]. pp. 13–38, 45–49. O. n. . [**1885–86**.] — *From: " Brookville society of natural history.* Bulletin, I.–II."

315. **Bradner**, E. A partial catalogue of the flora of Steuben county, [Indiana]. (*Indiana Dept. Geol. Ann. Rep.* XVII. (1891), pp. 135–159. **1892**.)

316. **Pieters**, A. J. The plants of Lake St. Clair. 10+[2] pp. map. O. Lansing, **1894.** (*Michigan fish commission.* Bulletin, II.)

316. **Coulter**, Stanley. A report upon certain collections of phanerogams presented to the State biological survey. pp. 169–182. O. t-p-c. Indianapolis, [**1896**]. — *From: Indiana Acad. Sci. Proc.* 1895, no. 5.

316. **Coulter**, Stanley. Noteworthy Indiana phanerogams. pp. 183–198. O. t-p-c. Indianapolis, [**1896**]. — *From: Indiana Acad. Sci. Proc.* 1895, no. 5.

316. **Harvey**, F. Le R. Notes upon Maine plants. (*Torr. Bot. Club Bull.* XXIII. 275–276; XXIV. 50–51; XXV. 210–211. **1896–98**.) — *Separate*.

316. **Bailey**, W. W. New England wild flowers and their seasons. 4+150 pp. D. Providence, **1897.**

Includes lists of Alpine and coast plants.

316. **Coulter**, Stanley. Contributions to the flora of Indiana. No. IV.–V. 2 pts. (13 pp.+pp. 158–165.) O. t-p-c. Indianapolis, [**1897–98**]. — *From: Indiana Acad. Sci. Proc.* 1896–97.

g. Southeastern United States

Dendrography

317. **Cooper**, J. G. On the forests and trees of Florida and the Mexican boundary. (*Smithson. Inst. Ann. Rep.* XV. (1860), pp. 439–442. **1861**.)

General Phytography

317. **Catesby**, Mark. The natural history of Carolina . . . 1731–43. — *Lines 5–6 read:* (Histoire naturelle de la Caroline, de la Floride, & les Isles Bahama . . .) 2 vol. 220 pl. map. F°. London, 1731–43. — *Lines 7–8 read:* revis'd by Mr. Edwards. 2 vol. 220 pl. map. F°. London, 1754.

318. **Darby**, John. A manual of botany . . . **1841.** — *Line 4 add:* — [Another ed.] 156+20+344 pp. 145 il. D. Savannah, 1847.

318. **Riddell**, J. L. New and hitherto unpublished plants of the South West, mostly indigenous in Louisiana, and preferred to by name in the " Catalogus floræ ludovicianæ," published in the New Orleans medical and surgical journal, vol. VIII., pages 743 to 764, May no., 1852, and embraced in the MS. " Plants of Louisiana," illustrated by specimens and drawings, deposited in the Smithsonian institution in 1851. (*New Orleans Med. Surg. Jour.* IX. 609–618. **1853**.)

Contains Quercus Carpenterii (p. 613), Q. Peckiana, Q. Andromeda, Q. rhombifolia, and Q. bumeliaefolia (p. 614).

319. **Lesquereux**, Leo. Botanical and palæontological report on the Geological state survey of Arkansas. pp. [295]–399. 6 pl. O. [Philadelphia, **1860**.] — *From: " Arkansas geological survey. Annual report,* 1860."

A catalogue of the plants of Arkansas (pp. 346–399).

319. **Ward**, L. F. List of plants added to the flora of Washington from April 1, 1882, to April 1, 1884. (*Biol. Soc. Washington Proc.* II. (1882–84), pp. 84–87. **1885**.)

Supplementary to his Guide to the flora of Washington, 1881.

319. **Knowlton**, F. H. Additions to the flora of Washington and vicinity, from April 1, 1884, to April 1, 1886. (*Biol. Soc. Washington Proc.* III. (1884–86), pp. 106–132. **1886**.)

Supplementary to WARD, L. F. Guide to the flora of Washington, 1881.

319. **Holm**, Theo. Third [and fourth] list of additions to the flora of Washington, D. C. (*Biol. Soc. Washington Proc.* VII. 105–132; X. 29–43. **1892**–96.)

Supplementary to WARD, L. F. Guide to the flora of Washington, 1881.

319. **Mell**, P. H. The flora of Alabama. Pt. V. [Leguminosæ and Rosaceæ]. pp. 276–296. O. Montgomery, Ala., **1896.** (*Alabama Agric. Exper. Stat. Bull.* LXX.)

320. **Hyams**, C. W. The flora of North Carolina from Ranunculaceae to Salviniaceae. pp. [289]–365. O. Raleigh, [**1899**]. (*North Carolina Agric. Exper. Stat. Bull.* CLXIV.)

h. Western United States

Dendrography

320. **Call**, R. E. Notes on the native forest trees of eastern Arkansas. **1890.** — *Transfer from vol. I.* 317: PHYTOGRAPHY. SOUTHEASTERN UNITED STATES.

320. **Bush**, B. F. The trees, shrubs and vines of Missouri. **1895.** — *Transfer from vol. I.* 317: PHYTOGRAPHY. SOUTH- EASTERN UNITED STATES.

321. **Pammel**, L. H. Some observations on trees and shrubs in the Rocky Mountains. (*Iowa State Hort. Soc. Rep.* XXXI. (1896), pp. 350–352. **1897.**)

General Phytography

321. [**Nuttall**, Thomas.] A catalogue of new and interesting plants, collected in upper Louisiana . . . **1813.** — *Transfer from vol. I.* 318: PHYTOGRAPHY. SOUTHEASTERN UNITED STATES.

321. **Nuttall**, Thomas. A journal of travels into the Arkansas Territory during the year 1819 . . . **1821.** — *Transfer from vol. I.* 318: PHYTOGRAPHY. SOUTHEASTERN UNITED STATES.

321. **Nuttall**, Thomas. Collections towards a flora of the territory of Arkansas. **1837.** — *See* vol. I. 318: PHYTOGRAPHY. SOUTHEASTERN UNITED STATES.

322. **Abert**, J. W. Notes [of a journey from Fort Leavenworth to Bent's Fort]. **1848.** — *Transfer from vol. I.* 318: PHY- TOGRAPHY. SOUTHEASTERN UNITED STATES.

322. **Torrey**, John. Plantae Frémontianae . . . **1854.** — *Line 3 read:* 1854.) — *Separate:* t-p. Washington City, **1853.**

324. **Arthur**, J. C. Contributions to the flora of Iowa; a catalogue of the phænogamous plants. 43 pp. O. Charles City, **1876.**

324. **Bush**, Frank. Flora of Jackson county, [Missouri]. **1882.** — *Transfer from* vol. I. 318: PHYTOGRAPHY. SOUTHEAST- ERN UNITED STATES.

325. **Upham**, Warren. Catalogue of the flora of Minnesota, including its phænogamous and vascular cryptogamous plants, indigenous, naturalized and adventive. 193 pp. O. Minneapolis, **1884.** (*Minnesota Geol. Nat. Hist. Surv. Rep.* XII. pt. 6. 1884.) — Supplement to the flora of Minnesota. (*Minnesota Geol. Nat. Hist. Surv. Bull.* III. 46–54. 1887.)

325. **Havard**, V[alery]. Report on the flora of western and southern Texas. [**1885.**] (*United States Nat. Mus. Proc.* VIII. 449–533. 1886.)

325. **Tracy**, S. M. Catalogue of the phænogamous and vascular cryptogamous plants of Missouri. **1886.** — *Transfer from vol.* I. 319: PHYTOGRAPHY. SOUTHEASTERN UNITED STATES.

325. **Chapin**, F. H. Mountaineering in Colorado; the peaks about Estes Park. 168 pp. il. pl. D. Boston, 1889.
A partial list of plants growing in Estes Park, Colorado (pp. 163–168).

326. **Smyth**, B. B. Check list of the plants of Kansas . . . 1892. — *Line 4 read:* Ed. 2. 34 pp. O. Topeka, (Kansas), 1892. — Check list . . . [with Supplement, March 15, 1893]. Ed. 2. 36 pp. O. Topeka, (Kansas), 1892–[93].

326. **Bush**, B. F. Notes on the mound flora of Atchison county, Missouri. (*Missouri Bot. Gard. Rep.* VI. 121–134. 1895.) — *Separate.*

326. **Eastwood**, Alice. Description of some new species of Californian plants. (*California Acad. Sci. Proc.* ser. 2, VI. (1896), pp. 422–430. **1897.**) — *Reprinted:* 9 pp. 7 pl. [San Francisco, 1897.]

327. **Heller**, A. A. Corrections and additions to the flora of Minnesota. [**1898.**] (*Minnesota Bot. Stud.* II. 30–32. 1898–1900→)

327. **Bogue**, E. E. An annotated catalog of the ferns and flowering plants of Oklahoma. 48 pp. O. Stillwater, (Okl.), [1900]. (Oklahoma agricultural experiment station. Bulletin, XLV.)

3. CENTRAL AND SOUTH AMERICA

b. Mexico

331. **Rio de la Loza**, L. & **Craveri**, E. Opusculo sobre los pozos artesianos y las aguas naturales de mas uso en la ciudad de Mexico; con algunas noticias relativas al corte geológico del valle, y una lista de las plantas que vegetan en las inmediaciones del desierto viejo. 39 pp. 2 pl. 1 tab. D. Mexico, 1854.
Contains lists of plants (pp. 24–29).

332. [**Conzatti**, Cassiano.] Clave analitica para la determinacion de las familias de las plantas fanerogamas que nacen silvestres y cultivadas en Mexico. 58 pp. O. Jalapa, 1889.
T-p-c. has the date 1890.

332. **Heilprin**, Angelo. Observations on the flora of northern Yucatan. (*Amer. Philos. Soc. Proc.* XXIX. 137–144. **1891.**)

d. West Indian Islands

337. **Provancher**, L[éon]. Une excursion aux climats tropicaux; voyage aux Îles-du-Vent, St-Kitts, Névis, Antigue, Montserrat, La Dominique, La Guadeloupe, Ste-Lucie, La Barbade, Trinidad. 359+[1] pp. il. O. Québec, 1890.
Table alphabétique des noms de genres et d'espèces mentionnés (pp. 357–359). — Contains a few notes on plants.

f. Guiana

338. **Barrère**, Pierre. Essai sur l'histoire naturelle de la France équinoxiale . . . 1741. — *Lines 2–6 read:* des animaux & des minéraux, qui se trouvent dans l'isle de Cayenne, les isles de Remire, sur les côtes de la mer, & dans le continent de la Guyane . . . 24+215+[7] pp. S. Paris, 1741. — [Another ed.] 24+315+[215]+[7] pp. S. Paris, 1749.

338. Barrère, Pierre. Nouvelle relation de la France équinoxiale . . . 1743. — *Lines 2–5 read:* dans la Guiane; de l'isle de Cayenne . . . 4+250+[1] pp. 16 pl. 3 maps. S. Paris, 1743.

g. Colombia and Ecuador

340. **Linden**, J[ean] & **Planchon**, J. É. Troisième voyage de J. Linden dans les parties intertropicales de l'Amérique, au Venezuela, dans la Nouvelle-Grenade, à la Jamaïque et dans l'île de Cuba . . . pendant . . . 1841 à 1845. Pt. I. Botanique. Plantae Columbianae. Vol. I. (88+64 pp.) O. Bruxelles, 1863.

j. Brasil

343. **Warming**, Eugen. Une excursion aux montagnes du Brésil. [**1883.**] — *Line 2 add:* — *Reprinted:* 29 pp. O. Liège, 1883. — *Line 3 read:* French extract from: *Natur Halle*, 1881, pp. 156, 170, 194, 203.

343. **Abreu Lacerda**, Augusto de. A bacia do Rio das Mortes por Augusto de Abreu Lacerda. Nota sobre calcareos e traços geraes da bacia do Rio das Mortes por Alvaro A. da Silveira. 124 pp. il. pl. map. O. Rio de Janeiro, 1895. (Commissão geographica e geologica do estado de Minas Geraes. Boletim, III.)
Traços geraes da vegetação da bacia do Rio das Mortes (pp. 115–124).

k. Argentina with Patagonia, Uruguay and Paraguay

344. **Leybold**, Federico. Escursion a las pampas arjentinas . . . 1873. — *Line 2 add:* —— Ein Ausflug nach den Argentinischen Pampas; Tagebuchblätter; aus dem Spanischen übersetzt von Dr. R. G. Lorentz. pp. 97–100, 113–116. [Buenos Aires, 1875.] — *From:* "*La Plata Monatsschrift,* 1875."

344. **Lorentz**, P. G. Reiseskizzen aus Argentinien. 4+43 pp. D. n. s Aires, 1875. — *From:* "*La Plata Monatsschrift,* III. 'Bue 0"
Consists of: 1. LORENTZ, P. G. & STUELENER, A. Ein Winterausflug nach dem Norden der Sierra von Córdoba.

344. **Lorentz**, P. G. Reiseskizzen aus Argentinien, III. pp. 100–103, 116–119, 145–151, 161–164; IV. 1–5, 25–28, 110–111, 117–120, 129–133; VI. 1–3, 5–? [Buenos Aires, 1875]–77. — *From:* "*La Plata Monatsschrift,* III.–VI."

344. **Lorentz**, P. G. Ferienreise eines argentinischen Gymnasial-Schullehrers mit seinen Schülern. pp. 43–45, 49–54, 81–87. F. t-p-c. Buenos Ayres, 1876. — *From:* "*La Plata Monatsschrift,* IV. 1876."

344. **Lorentz**, P. G. Reiseskizzen aus Argentinien; aus dem Gran Chaco. 31 pp. F. t-p-c. Buenos Ayres, 1877. — *From:* "*La Plata Monatsschrift,* 1877."

344. [**Niederlein**, Gustav.] Herbario "Bettfreund;" enumeración sistemática de las plantas recogidas en Buenos Aires y sus alrededores. Ed. 2 rev. & enl. 48+[1] pp. O. Buenos Aires, 1898. — *From:* *Mus. Prod. Argent. Bol.* no. 29, 1890.

l. Chile

346. **Gray**, Asa. List of the dried plants brought from Chile by the U. S. N. astronomical expedition. (*In* GILLISS, J. M. The U. S. Naval astronomical expedition to the southern hemisphere . . . II. 265–269. **1855.**)

4. EUROPE

a. General

348. **Smith**, [Sir] J. E. A sketch of a tour on the continent, in the years 1786 and 1787. 3 vol. O. London, 1793.
Interspersed with many notes on plants.

349. **Graumüller**, J. C. F. Diagnose der bekanntesten, besonders europäischen Pflanzengattungen. **1811.** — *Lines 2–3 read:* nach dem verbesserten Linnéischen Systeme zum analytischen Gebrauche für seine Vorlesungen so wie auch zum Selbstunterricht entworfen . . . Nebst einer Vorrede vom Herrn Geheimen Hofrath Gruner. 8+435 pp. O. Eisenberg, 1811.
Cancel the correction in vol. I on p. 531.

350. **Masclef**, A[médée]. Les plantes d'Europe. Préface de M. Gaston Bonnier. 6+79+[4] pp. 72 pl. obl. T. Paris, [189.?].

b. Scandinavia

352. **Acerbi**, Giuseppe. Travels through Sweden . . . **1802.** — *Lines 3–4 read:* 1 por. 15 pl. map. sq. Q. London, 1802.
Of Lapland botany (II. 257–263).

356. **Schübeler**, F. C. Die Culturpflanzen Norwegens . . . **1862.** — *Line 4 add:* — Uebersicht der vegetabilischen Produkte Norwegens. [Abstract.] (*Hamburg. Gart. Blumenzeit.* XVIII. 510–516, 544–552. 1862.) — *Line 8 add:* —— Synopsis of the vegetable products of Norway. Translated from the MS. by M. R. Barnard. 31 pp. 1 pl. map. Q. Christiania, 1862. —— L'horticulture en Norwège; observations sur l'acclimatation des plantes. [Abstract.] (*Belg. Hort.* XIII. 145–150. 1863.)

356. **Falck**, Alfred. Bidrag till kännedomen om den sydsvenska vegetationens ursprung och vägen för dess invandring. (Diss.) [2]+57 pp. O. Lund, 1868.

356. **Brotherus**, V. F. Anteckningar till Norra Tavastlands flora. [**1872.**] (*Sällsk. Fauna Fl. Fenn. Notis.* XIII. 185–217. 1874.)

357. **Lange**, Joh[an]. Bemærkninger ved det tredie (sidste) Supplementhæfte til Flora danica. 1874. — *Line 3 read:* n. t-p. [Kjøbenhavn, 1874.]

357. **Thomsen**, C. Roskilde-Egnens Flora . . . **1874.** — *Line 2 read:* [4]+92 pp. D. Roskilde, 1874. (Indbydelsesskrift til Afgangsprøven og Aarsprøverne i Roskilde Kathedralskole, 1874.)

357. **Larsson**, L. M. Öfversigt af Sveriges vigtigare fanerogama växtslägten ordnade efter det friesiska systemet. 80 pp. O. Karlstad, [1877].

357. Olsson, P[eter]. Jemtlands fanerogamer och ormbunkar, upptecknade med angifvande af växtlokaler. (*Svensk. Vetensk. Akad. Öfvers.* XLI. (1884), no. 9, pp. 41–155. **1885**.)

357. Reichardt, H. W. Flora der Insel Jan Mayen, gesammelt von Dr. F. Fischer, bearbeitet unter Mitwirkung von Theodor Fries in Upsala, Eduard Hackel in St. Pölten und Ferdinand Hauck in Triest. 16 pp. sq. Q. Wien, **1886**. — *From:* "Die INTERNATIONALE Polarforschung, 1882–83. Die österreichische Polarstation Jan Mayen, III."

358. Jørgensen, E[ugen]. Om floraen i Nord-Reisen og tilstødende dele af Lyngen. 104 pp. O. Christiania, **1894**. — *From: Vidensk. Selsk. Christiania Forh.* 1894, no. 8.

358. Dahl, Ove. Plantegeografiske undersøgelser i ydre Søndmøre, 1894. 44 pp. O. Christiania, **1895**. — *Reprinted from: Vidensk. Selsk. Christiania Forh.* 1894, no. 11.

358. Dahl, Ove. Kystvegetationen i Romsdal, Nord- og Søndfjord. 76 pp. O. Christiania, **1896**. — *Reprinted from: Vidensk. Selsk. Christiania Forh.* 1896, no. 3.

358. Dahl, Ove. Botaniske undersøgelser i Søndfjords og Nordfjords fjorddistrikter i 1896–97. 71 pp. O. Christiania, **1898**. — *Reprinted from: Vidensk. Selsk. Christiania Forh.* 1898, no. 3.

c. Russia

I. GENERAL

366. Stenroos (afterwards Kiwirikko), K. E. Nurmijärven pitäjän siemen- ja saniais-kasvisto. [Vegetation of the Nurmi lake region.] 52 pp. Helsingissä, **1894**. (*Soc. Faun. Flor. Fenn. Act.* IX. no. 11. 1893–94.)

d. German Empire

Dendrography

370. Oelhafen von Schöllenbach, C. C. Abbildung der wilden Bäume, Stauden und Buschgewächse . . . **1773** [1767–1804]. — *Line 9 read:* Nürnberg, 1767–[1804]. — *Lines 15–16 read:* contenant des descriptions exactes de tout ce qui concerne leur nature et leur culture . . . Traduit de l'allemand par Godefroi Bepistant. Première partie, contenant les arbres à feuilles étroites et longues, et qui conservent toujours leur verdure. 80 pp. 34 pl. Q. Nuremberg, 1775. — *After line 16 add a note:*
Some copies contain a separate t-p. for vol. I.: Carl Christoph Oelhafens von Schöllenbach, Abbildung der wilden Bäume . . . Erster Theil, welcher die Tangel- oder immergrünen Bäume enthält. 1773. — *After vol. I. continued by Johann Wolf.*

371. Plüss, B. Unsere Bäume und Sträucher . . . **1884**. — *Line 1 read:* Plüss, B[enjamin]. — *Line 7 add:* Ed. 2. 6+[2]+120 pp. 80 il. 1 pl. S. Freiburg im Breisgau, 1888. — *Line 10 add:* — Ed. 5. 6+[2]+146 pp. 112 il. 2 pl. S. Freiburg im Breisgau, 1899.

General Phytography

372. Menzel, Christian. Plantarum circa nobile Gedanum sponte nascentes adjecta appendicis loco ad elenchum plantarum gedanensium . . . Nicolai Oelhafii . . . excursu quinque mensium . . . facto collecta et edita. Dantisci, 1650.† — (*Also in* REYGER, Gottfried. Tentamen florae gedanensis . . . II. 201–224. 1766.)

375. Borkhausen, M. B. Flora der obern Grafschaft Catzenelnbogen . . . 1795–96. — *Line 1 read:* Flora der oberen Grafschaft Catzenelnbogen nach dem System vom Staude, der Verbindung und dem Verhältniss der Staubfäden. (*Obercattische Flora.*] (*Rhein. Mag. Erweit. Naturk.* I. 393–607. 1793.) — Flora . . . . — *Line 4 read:* Halle, 1795–96.

375. Frenzel, J. S. T. Verzeichniss wild wachsender Pflanzen und ihres Standortes in der Nähe um Wittenberg für Kräutersammler. 32 pp. nar. D. Wittenberg, 1799.

375. Dietrich, F. G. Die Weimarsche Flora; oder, Verzeichniss der im Herzoglichen Park in Weimar befindlichen Bäume, Sträucher und Stauden. 16+224 pp. O. Eisenach, 1800. — Ed. 2. O. Eisenach, 1808. — Ed. 3. 6+364 pp. · 1 pl. O. Eisenach, 1811.†

375. La Vigne, G. F. de. Flore germanique . . . 1801–02. — *Line 1 read:* Delavigne, G. F. — *Line 3 read:* Enrichie des figures coloriées de la Flore germanique de J. Sturm. 4 pts. (22+[2]+128 pp.) 64 pl. T. Erlang, 1801–02.

375. Rebentisch, J. F. Prodromus florae Neomarchicae . . . 1804. — *Line 1 read:* Prodromus florae neomarchicae . . .

376. Jungk, C. L. Observationes botanicae in Floram halensem. 1807. — *Line 2 read:* D. Halis Saxonum, [1807]. — *Add as a note:*
Acer Pseudoplatanus (p. 8): Salix aquatica (p. 12).

377. Pappe, K. W. L. Enumerationis plantarum phaenogamarum lipsiensium specimen. 1827. — *Line 2 read:* (Diss.) 20+42 pp. O. Lipsiae, [1827].

378. Reichenbach, [H. G.] L. Index in herbarium floras germanicae. Editum a Societate botanicorum ultra saxaginta. 18 pp. Q. n. t-p. n. p., [183.?].

379. Prahl, J. F. Index plantarum, quae circa Gustroviam sponte nascentur . . . 1837. — *Line 2 read:* nascuntur phanerogamarum. 4+66 pp. O. Gustroviae, 1837.

379. Koch, W. D. J. Synopsis florae germanicae et helveticae . . . 1837. — *Lines 26–27 read:* 3 vol. (68+1210 pp.) O. Leipzig, 1846–47.

381. Meyer, G. F. W. Flora des Königreichs Hannover . . . 1842–54. — *Lines 5–6 read:* 3 vol. F°. Göttingen, 1842–54. — *Line 10 add as a note:*
Published in parts with separate t-p. Vol. I.–II. ([4]+12+240+32 pp.) is "begründender Theil"; vol. III. (six parts, unpaged) "beschreibender Theil."

383. Bischoff, G. W. Beiträge zur Flora Deutschlands und der Schweiz. 20+341+[1] pp. O. Heidelberg, 1851.

383. [Emmert, Friedrich & Segnitz, Gottfried von.] Das Florengebiet der Stadt Schweinfurt. (*In* Zur GESCHICHTE der Säcularfeier der Kaiserlichen Leopoldinisch-carolinischen Akademie der Naturforscher am 21. September 1852. 1. Einladungs- und Eröffnungs-Programm. [2]+42 pp. sq. Q. [Breslau and Bonn, 1852.] *See* pp. 23–42. — *Leop.-Carol. Akad. Naturf. Verh.* XXIV. Vorwort. Besondere Ausgabe, pp. 23–42. 1853. — *Leop.-Carol. Akad. Naturf. Verh.* XXIV. pt. I. xxxi–L. 1854.)

383. Postel, Emil. Der Führer in die Pflanzenwelt; Hülfsbuch zur Auffindung und Bestimmung der in Deutschland wild wachsenden Pflanzen . . . 752 pp. il. O. Langensalza, 1856. — Ed. 2. 752 pp. il. 5 pl. O. Langensalza, 1858. — Ed. 3. 752 pp. il. 5 pl. O. Langensalza, 1861. — Ed. 4. 791 pp. il. 1 pl. O. Langensalza, 1866. — Ed. 5. 850 pp. 14 pl. O. Langensalza, 1871.† — Ed. 6. 866 pp. il. 4 pl. O. Langensalza, 1875. — Ed. 7. 866 pp. 744 il. O. Langensalza, 1876.

384. Wilde, O. Die Pflanzen und Raupen Deutschlands . . . 1860–61. — *Lines 2–3 read:* 2 vol. 10 pl. O. Berlin, 1860–61.

385. Schildknecht, J. Nachtrag zu Spenners Flora friburgensis. 6+62 pp. O. Freiburg i. B., [1862]. (Beilage zum Programm der höhern Bürgerschule Freiburg. Schuljahr 1861/62.)

385. Deutschlands Flora oder Abbildung und Beschreibung der daselbst wildwachsenden Pflanzen. Ed. 7 rev. & enl. 36 pp. pl. Q. Leipzig, [1864–68]. — Ed. 8 rev. & enl. 36 pp. 500 pl. Leipzig, [1868–?]. — Deutschlands Flora; oder, Abbildung und Beschreibung der wildwachsenden Pflanzen in der mitteleuropäischen Flora. Text von Dr. Ernst Hallier. Ed. 9 rev. 224+21 pp. Q. Leipzig, [1873–75]. — Atlas. 4 vol. 500 pl. Q. Leipzig, [1873–75].
Ed. 7–8 are anonymous. — May be a new edition of STURM, Jakob. Deutschlands Flora . . . 1798–1861. The plates are almost identical, but the text is different.

385. Hoffmann, H[ermann]. Untersuchungen zur Klima- und Bodenkunde mit Rücksicht auf die Vegetation. 1865. — *Line 3 add:* — [Abstract.] (*Allg. Forst. Jagd-Zeit. Suppl.* VI. 52–78. 1867.)

386. Frank, A. B. Pflanzen-Tabellen . . . 1869. — *Line 3 add:* — Ed. 6. 36+238 pp. il. D. Leipzig, 1892. — Ed. 7 rev. & enl. Leipzig, 1897.

386. Wünsche, Otto. Excursionsflora für das Königreich Sachsen und die angrenzenden Gegenden; nach der analytischen Methode. 48+319 pp. D. Leipzig, 1869. — Ed. 2. 55+422 pp. D. Leipzig, 1875. — Ed. 3. 64+420 pp. D. Leipzig, 1878. — Ed. 4. 64+422 pp. O. Leipzig, 1883. — Ed. 5. 424 pp. Leipzig, 1887. — Ed. 6 rev. 28+468 pp. D. Leipzig, 1891. — Ed. 7. 475 pp. Leipzig, 1895.† — Die Excursionsflora des Königreichs Sachsen . . . Ed. 8. 24+447 pp. D. Leipzig, 1899.

387. Kramer, F. C. Phanerogamen-Flora von Chemnitz. 1875. — *Lines 1–2 read:* Kramer, F. A. Phanerogamen-Flora von Chemnitz und Umgegend. 4+38 pp. map. Q. Chemnitz, 1875. (Königl. Gymnasium zu Chemnitz. Programm.)

388. Huth, Ernst. Flora von Frankfurt a. d. Oder und Umgebung . . . 1880. — *Line 2 read:* bung. 48+4 pp. sq. Q. Frankfurt a. O., 1880. (Oberschule (Realschule erster Ordnung) zu Frankfurt an der Oder. Jahresbericht, 1880. Progr. nr. 89.)

388. Troost, J. Genaue Beschreibung von 250 häufig vorkommenden, wild wachsenden Pflanzen. 16+265 pp. 203 il. O. Wiesbaden, 1884.

388. **Rehder**, Alfred. Beiträge zur Flora des Muldenthals. (*Ver. Naturk. Zwickau Jahresber.* 1885, pp. 29–33. **1886.**) — *Reprinted:* 5 pp. O. [Zwickau, 1886.]

388. **Knuth**, Paul. Flora der Provinz Schleswig-Holstein, des Fürstentums Lübeck, sowie des Gebietes der freien Städte Hamburg und Lübeck.   12+902+25 pp. D. Leipzig, **1887.**

Verzeichnis der Litteratur und Beobachter der schleswig-holsteinischen Flora . . . (pp. 55–64).

389. **Knuth**, P[aul]. Einige Bemerkungen meine Flora von Schleswig-Holstein betreffend. 28 pp. D. Leipzig, **1888.**

389. **Knuth**, Paul. Schulflora der Provinz Schleswig-Holstein, des Fürstentums Lübeck, sowie des Gebietes der freien Städte Hamburg und Lübeck. 4+406 pp. D. Leipzig, **1888.**

389. **Lutze**, G[ünther]. Flora von Nord-Thüringen, mit Bestimmungstabellen zum Gebrauche auf Exkursionen, in Schulen und beim Selbstunterrichte. 12+398 pp. D. Sondershausen, **1892.**

389. **Beckhaus**, K[onrad]. Flora von Westfalen. Die in der Provinz Westfalen wildwachsenden Gefässpflanzen. Nach des Verfassers Tode herausgegeben von L. A. W. Hasse. 22+1096 pp. O. Münster, **1893.**†

389. **Buchenau**, Franz. Flora der nordwestdeutschen Tiefebene. 14+[4]+550 pp. 1 il. D. Leipzig, **1894.**

Bibliography (pp. 526–533).

389. **Graebner**, P[aul]. Studien über die norddeutsche Heide. **1895.** — *Line 2 add:* — *Reprinted:* 155 pp. 2 pl. O. Leipzig, 1895.

390. **Gräbner**, P[aul]. Ueber die Bildung natürlicher Vegetationsformationen im norddeutschen Flachlande. pp. 133–161. O. [**1898.**] — *From:* "*Brandenburgia Archiv,* IV."

e. Holland

390. **Gorter**, David de. Flora gelro-zutphanica. **1745.** — *Lines 1–2 read:* Flora gelro-zutphanica, exhibens plantas per ducatum Gelriæ et comitatum Zutphaniæ crescentes. [8]+204+[2] pp. O. Harderovici, **1745.**

390. **Schuurmans Stekhoven**, H. Kruidkundig handboek . . . **1815.** — *Line 4 read:* Vol. I. Plantæ phanerogamicæ. 16+465+[2] pp. S. Amsterdam, **1815.**

390. **Hall**, H. C. van. Flora Belgii septentrionalis . . . **1825**–32. — *Lines 3–4 read:* Vol. I. 20+9+[1]+861+[2] pp. O. Amsterdam, **1825**[–36]. — *Line 8 add:* —

Vol. II. deals with cryptogams.

391. **Gevers Deynoot**, P. M. E. & **Abeleven**, T. H. A. J. Flora noviomagensis . . . **1848.** — *Lines 2–3 read:* noviomagensis; sive, Enumeratio plantarum circa Noviomagum sponte crescentium. (Plant. phanerog. et cryptog. contin.) Flora van Nijmegen; of, Naamlijst en opgave van groeiplaatsen der in het wild voorkomende planten, in en rondom Nijmegen . . . [4]+2+169+9 pp. O. Nijmegen, **1848.**

391. **Hoven**, F. J. J. [Slingsby] van. Flora van 's Hertogenbosch. **1848.** — *Lines 1–2 read:* Flora van 's Hertogenbosch; of, Naamlijst van de planten welke in de stad 's Hertogenbosch en omstreken in het wild gevonden worden, met aanwijzing van derzelver groeiplaatsen. 4+[2]+36 pp. Q. Heusden, **1848.**

391. **Prodromus** Florae batavae . . . **1851.** — *Line 1 read:* inprimis — *Lines 3–4 read:* 2 vol. O. [Leyden], **1850**–66.

391. **Oudemans**, C. A. J. A. De flora van Nederland ten behoeve van het algemeen beschreven. **1859**–62. — *Lines 6–7 read:* Ed. 2 enl. 3 vol. il. O. Amsterdam, 1872–74. — *After line 8 add as a note:*

T-p-c. of vol. I.–III. of ed. 2 has the date 1872.

f. Belgium and Luxemburg

391. **Necker**, N. J. Deliciae gallo-belgicae silvestres . . . **1768.** — *Line 1 read:* Necker, N. J. de. — *Line 6 read:* 2 vol. (24+568+[42] pp.) 3 pl. S.

392. **Hocquart**, Léopold. Flore du département de Jemmape . . . **1814.** — *Line 1 read:* Jemmape. — *Lines 2–3 read:* faites d'après le système de Linnée, à l'usage des élèves en botanique. 8+303+[1] pp. S. Mons, **1814.**

392. **Thielens**, Arm[and]. Nouvelles additions à la flore de la partie septentrionale du Brabant. (*Soc. Bot. Belg. Bull.* III. 141–149. **1864.**) — *Reprinted:* 11 pp. O. .Bruxelles, [1864].

392. **Dumoulin**, L. J. G. Guide du botaniste dans les environs de Maestricht . . . **1868.** — *Line 8 read:* ; ou, Indication des phanérogames et des cryptogames vasculaires croissant spontanément dans ces environs. 176 pp. D. Maestricht, **1868.**

393. **Bamps**, Constant. Les plantes rares des environs de Hasselt. (*Soc. Bot. Belg. Bull.* XII. 3–25. **1873.**) — *Reprinted:* 25 pp. O. Gand, 1873.

g. British Islands

Dendrography

393. **Coleman**, W. S. Our woodlands . . . [**1859.**] — *Line 3 read:* 8+146+[1] pp. il. 8 pl. S. London, 1859. — [Another ed.] — *Line 4 read:* [pref. 1859]. — [Another ed.] 8+146+[1] pp. il. 8 pl. S. London, 1865. — [Another ed.] 8+198+[1] pp. il. 8 pl. S. London, 1866. — Ed. 13. 8+198+[1] pp. il. 8 pl. S. London, 1892.

393. **Lees**, Edwin. The forest and chace of Malvern . . . **1870.** — *Line 2 add:* — *Reprinted:* 62+[1] pp. 11 pl. O. Worcester, 1877.

General Phytography

394. **Cajus**, John. De rariorum animalium et stirpium historia liber I. **1570.** — *Lines 6–7 read:* 15+[1]+249+[7] pp. D. Londini, 1729. *See* pp. 37–122.)

394. **Plot**, Robert. The natural history of Oxfordshire. **1677.** — *Lines 1–2 read:* P[lot], R[obert]. The natural history of Oxfordshire, being an essay toward the natural history of England. [8]+358+[12] pp. 16 pl. map. F. Oxford, **1677.** — *Line 3 read:*

Of plants (Ed. 1677, pp. 143–174).

394. **Leigh**, Charles. The natural history of Lancashire . . . **1700.** — *Lines 2–3 read:* with an account of the British, Phoenician, Armenian, Gr. and Rom. antiquities in those parts. [20]+4+196+[2]+97+112 [120]+[35] pp. 24 pl. map. F. Oxford, **1700.**

394. **Blackstone**, John. Fasciculus plantarum circa Harefield (Middlesex) sponte nascentium . . . **1737.** — *Lines 1–3 read:* Blackstone, John.] Fasciculus plantarum circa Harefield sponte nascentium; cum appendice ad loci historiam spectante. 8+118 pp. S. Londini, 1737.

394. **Wilson**, John. Synopsis of British plants . . . **1744.** — *Lines 4–5 read:* [4]+17+272+[8] pp. il. 2 pl. O. Newcastle upon Tyne, 1744.

396. **Garnett**, T[homas]. Observations on a tour through the Highlands and part of the western isles of Scotland, particularly Staffa and Icolmkill . . . 2 vol. il. 52 pl. 2 maps. sq. Q. London, 1800.

Contains a few notes on the occurrence of rarer plants.

396. **Evans**, J[ohn]. A tour through part of North Wales in . . . 1798, and at other times, principally undertaken with a view to botanical researches . . . 8+416+[1] pp. O. London, 1800. — Ed. 2. O. London, 1802.†

396. **Hunter**, R. E. A catalogue of plants growing wild in Thanet. (In his A short description of the isle of Thanet, being chiefly intended as a directory for the company resorting to Margate, Ramsgate, and Broadstairs . . . and a Thanet flora. [6]+129+[2] pp. map. S. London, 1802. *See* pp. 97–107.)

396. **Walker**, John. Essays on natural history and rural economy. 2+629 pp. O. London & Edinburgh, 1812.

397. **Jones**, J. P. & **Kingston**, J. F. Flora devoniensis . . . **1829.** — *Line 3 read:* Devon; arranged both according to the Linnæan and natural systems, with an account of their geographical distribution, &c. 47+[1]+162+67+[1]+217+[1] pp. O. London, 1829.

397. **Patrik**, William. A popular description of the indigenous plants of Lanarkshire . . . **1831.** — *Line 1 read:* Patrick, William. — *Line 2 read:* ; with an introduction to botany, and a glossary of botanical terms. 34+399 pp. S. Edinburgh, 1831. — Ed. 2. 34+399 pp. S. Edinburgh, etc., 1832.

398. **Winch**, N. J. Flora of Northumberland and Durham. **1831.** — *Lines 1–2 read:* [1832.] (*Nat. Hist. Soc. Northumberland Trans.* II. 1–149. 1838.)

399. **Ralfs**, John. The British phænogamous plants . . . **1839.** — *Lines 1–2 read:* The British phænogamous plants & ferns; arranged on the Linnæan system, and analyzed after the method of Lamarck, with a short comparative analysis of the natural families. 16+208 pp. D. London, 1839.

399. [**Russell**, Anna.] Catalogue of plants . . . **1839.** — *Line 1 read:* [Russell, Mrs. A. W.] Catalogue of plants found in the neighbourhood of Newbury. 31 pp. O. t-p-c. [Speenhamland], 1839.

399. **Munford**, George. A list of flowering plants found growing wild in western Norfolk. (*Ann. Mag. Nat. Hist.* VIII. 171–191. 1842.) — *Reprinted:* 23 pp. O. London, 1841.

399. **Lubbock**, Richard. Observations on the fauna of Norfolk, and more particularly on the district of the Broads. 8+156 pp. map. O. Norwich, 1845. — Observations ... with additions from unpublished manuscripts of the author, and notes by Thomas Southwell; also a memoir by Henry Stevenson ... and botany of the county. New ed. 36+239 pp. pl. map. O. Norwich, 1879.

Botany (1879 ed. pp. 215–219).

400. **Cumming**, J. G. The Isle of Man; its history, physical, ecclesiastical, civil, and legendary. 36+376 pp. 10 pl. 8 maps. O. London, 1848.

On the flora of the Isle of Man by E. Forbes (pp. 360–364).

400. **Duck**, J. N. The natural history of Portshead; comprising a guide to the locality, with an appendix containing an ornithological, entomological, and botanical catalogue for the neighbourhood. 65 pp. 3 pl. map. D. Bristol, 1852.

Botanical list (pp. 63–65).

400. **Salmon**, J. D. On the division of the county of Surrey into botanical districts ... 1852. — *Line 3 add:* — *Reprinted with additions, under the title:* A flora of Surrey; being a catalogue of indigenous plants found wild in the county, with the localities of the rarer species. 17 pp. map. O. London, 1852.

401. **Hobkirk**, C. C. P. Huddersfield ... 1859. — *Line 2 read:* A descriptive, historical, geological, botanical, and zoological sketch of the town and neighbourhood. 6+[2]+164 pp. 2 pl. D. London, 1859. — *Add as a note:*

Botanical (pp. 105–132).

401. **Henslow**, J. S. & **Skepper**, Edmund. Flora of Suffolk. [1860.] — *Line 1 read:* Flora of Suffolk; a catalogue of the plants (indigenous or naturalized) found in a wild state in the county of Suffolk. 10+[2]+140 pp. D. London, [pref. 1860].

401. **Ravenshaw**, T. F. A new list of the flowering plants ... of Devon ... 1860. — *Line 2 read:* 8+92+[1]+7 pp. — *Line 3 add:* — Re-issue, with supplement. 8+110+[1]+7 pp. D. London, 1872.

401. **Lawson**, George. Some account of plants collected in the counties of Leeds ... Upper Canada ... 1863. — *Cancel this entry.*

402. **Purchas**, W. H. Flora of Herefordshire. 1867. — *Lines 1–2 read:* A flora of Herefordshire. Pt. 1. [2]+24+25 pp. map. O. Hereford, 1867. — *From:* " *Woolhope naturalists' field club. Transactions, 1866.*"

402. **Flora wellingtonensis.** First list. 8 pp. O. [London, 1868.] — Botanical list. pp. 51–59, 38–40, 29–41. O. [London, 1869–74.] — *From:* " *Wellington college natural history society. Annual report, I.–II., IV.*"

402. **Botanical notices.** pp. 28–36. map. O. [Cheltenham, 1871] — *From:* "*Cheltenham college natural history society. Report, 1870.*"

402. **Britten**, James. Contributions to a flora of Berkshire. pp. 33–59. map. O. [Newbury, 1871.] — *From:* "*Newbury district field club. Transactions, I.*"

402. **Brown**, Robert. The botanical history of Angus. (*Jour. Bot.* IX. 321–327. 1871.) — *Reprinted:* 8 pp. O. [London, 1871.] —— Histoire botanique du comté d'Angus. (*Soc. Bot. France Bull.* XIX. 214–222. 1872.)

Read before the Edinburgh natural history society, January 26, 1792.

402. **Warren**, J. [B.] L. [*3d baron* De Tabley]. The flora of Hyde Park and Kensington Gardens. (*Jour. Bot.* IX. 227–238. 1871.) — *Reprinted:* 14 pp. O. London, 1871.

402. **List** of flowering plants, ferns, &c. found within seven miles from Winchester. pp. 37–52. O. [Winchester, 1872.] — *From:* " *Winchester and Hampshire scientific and literary society. Report of proceedings, 1870–71.*"

402. **Alcock**, R. H. List of plants noticed by the Bury natural history society within fifteen miles of Bury. pp. 14–23. O. [Bury, 1872.] — *From:* " *Bury natural history society. Report, 1872.*"

402. **The flora** of Liverpool; a list of the indigenous flowering plants and ferns growing within fifteen miles of the Liverpool exchange and two miles of Southport; published by the Liverpool naturalists' field club . . . 6+178+[4] pp. O. Liverpool, 1872. — Appendix. [Notes of additions ...] 14 pp. O. [Liverpool], 1873. — Second appendix. 24 pp. O. [Liverpool], 1875.

402. **Warren**, J. [B.] L. [*3d baron* De Tabley]. Notes on a projected Cheshire flora. 16 pp. O. [London, 1873.]

402. **Hodgson**, E. North or Lake Lancashire; a sketch of its botany, geology, and physical geography. (*Jour. Bot.* XII. 268–277, 296–305, map. 1874.) — *Reprinted:* 21 pp. map. O. [London, 1874.]

402. **Cotter.** The flora of the county Cork. (*In* Cusack, M. F. A history of the city and county of Cork. 22+[2]+586+2 pp. pl. map. 1 tab. O. Dublin & Cork, 1875. *See* pp. 467–479.)

402. **Pryor**, R. A. Notes on a proposed re-issue of the Flora of Hertfordshire. 14 pp. O. Hertford, 1875. — Notes ... with supplementary remarks on the botany of the Watford district. [1875.] (*Watford Nat. Hist. Soc. Hertfordshire Field Club Trans.* I. 17–32. 1878.) — *Reprinted:* 16 pp. map. O. [Watford, 1875.]

402. **Geldart**, H. D. Fauna and flora of Norfolk. Pt. VI. Flowering plants and ferns. [1875–84.] (*Norfolk Norwich Nat. Soc. Trans.* II. 71–110, 229–242; III. 719–729. 1879–84.) — *Reprinted in part:* 54 pp. O. [Norwich, 1875.]

403. **Pryor**, R. A. On the botanical work of the past season. 13 pp. O. [Watford, 1876.] — *From:* "*Watford Nat. Hist. Soc. Hertfordshire Field Club Trans.* March, 1876.

403. **A Snowdrop**, (*pseud.*). The berries and heaths of Rannoch. 24 pp. [13] pl. Q. London, 1881.

Contains Ericaceæ, Empetrum and Rubus Chamæmorus.

403. **Allin**, Thomas. The flowering plants and ferns of the county Cork. [2]+13+113 pp. map. O. Weston-super-Mare, 1883.

403. **Webster**, A. D. The forest flora of Carnarvonshire, more particularly the Penrhyn estate. (*Jour. For.* X. 207–210, 258–267, 354–361, 447–450. [1885.])

404. **Bunbury**, *Sir* C. J. F. Notes on wild plants found in the parish of Great Barton. Mildenhall, 1889. (*In his* Botanical notes at Barton . . . pp. 199–235. 1889.)

404. **B[unbury]**, *Sir* C. J. F. List of flowering plants and ferns found in the parish of Mildenhall, Suffolk. Mildenhall, 1889. (*In his* Botanical notes at Barton . . . pp. 237–285. 1889.)

404. **Lee**, J. R. Plants of the Kenmuir district of the Clyde. [1896.] (*Anderson. Nat. Soc. Ann.* II. 8–15. 1900.)

404. **Murray**, R. P. The flora of Somerset. 1896. — *Line 2 add:* (Somersetshire archaeological and natural history society. Proceedings. XXXIX.–XLII. [Supplement.])

h. France

I. GENERAL

Dendrography

404. **Martins**, C. [F.]. Sur l'origine paléontologique des arbres . . . [1876.] — *Line 7 add:* — Origine paléontologique de quelques arbres du midi de la France. (*Rev. Eaux For.* XVI. 157–159. 1877.)

General Phytography

405. **Barbeu-Dubourg**, Jacques. Le botaniste français . . . 1767 — *Lines 1–4 read:* Barbeu Dubourg [Jacques]. Le botaniste françois, comprenant toutes les plantes communes & usuelles, disposées suivant une nouvelle méthode & décrites en langue vulgaire. 2 vol. S. Paris, 1767. — *Add as a note:*

Title of vol. II. reads: Le botaniste françois; ou, Manuel d'herborisation.

407. **Plée**, Auguste & François. Herborisations artificielles aux environs de Paris . . . 1811. — *Line 6 read:* 12 pp. 99 pl. O. Paris, 1811.

408. **Guépin**, [J. P.]. Flore de Maine et Loire. 1830. — *Lines 5–6 read:* Supplément à la troisième édition de la Flore de Maine et Loire. [4]+51 pp. D. Angers, 1850. — *Add as a note:*

For a second supplement see his Notice sur une flore angevine manuscrite . . . 1853.

408. **Mutel**, A[uguste]. Flore française destinée aux herborisations . . . 1834–37. — *Lines 6–7 read:* Flore française . . . Table générale et supplément final. [2]+189+[1] pp. S. Paris & Strasbourg, 1838.

410. **Le Jolis**, Auguste. Observations sur quelques plantes rares découvertes aux environs de Cherbourg. (*Ann. Sci. Nat. Bot.* ser. 3, VII. 214–231, pl. 13. 1847.) — *Reprinted with additions:* 32 pp. 1 pl. O. [Paris, 1847.]

411. **Lloyd**, James. Flore de l'ouest de la France . . . 1854. — *Lines 5–6 read:* Ed. 2. 215+[1]+644 pp. T. Nantes, 1868. — *Line 10 read:* 71+[1]+454+[1] pp. D. Nantes & Paris, 1886. — *Line 12 read:* Ed. 5. — *Line 13 read:* 1897. — Ed. 5. 124+[1]+458+[2] pp. O. Nantes, [1898]. — *Add as a note:*

Part of the 1897 ed. has date 1898.

412. **Companyo**, Louis. Histoire naturelle du département des Pyrénées orientales. **1861**-64. — *Line 3 read:*
(II. 939+[1] pp.)

412. **Gillet**, [C. G.] & **Magne**, J. H. Nouvelle flore française . . . **1863**. — *Line 1 read:* **Gillet**, [C. C.] & **Magne**, J. H. — *Line 6 add:* 26+[2]+618+[2] pp. il. D. Paris, 1862. — [Another ed.] — *Line 7 read:* 1863. — *Line 10 add:* Ed. 5 rev. 24+775+[1] pp. il. D. Paris, 1883. —

413. **Baillet**, [C.], Jeanbernat, [Ernest] & **Timbal-Lagrave**, E[douard]. Une excursion botanique sur le massif de Cagire, et dans la haute vallée du Ger (Haute-Garonne). (*Acad. Sci. Toulouse Mém.* ser. 6, II. 383-409. **1864.**) — *Reprinted:* 27 pp. O. [Toulouse, 1864.]

413. **Blanche**, [H.] & **Malbranche**, [Alexandre]. Catalogue des plantes cellulaires et vasculaires de la Seine-Inférieure. **1864**. — *Line 1 read:* **Blanche**, [Emmanuel] & **Malbranche**, [Alexandre]. — *Line 3 read:* Rouen, 1864. — *From:* Acad. Sci. Rouen Précis, 1863-64.

413. **Crouan**, P. L. & H. M. Florule du Finistère, contenant les descriptions de 360 espèces nouvelles de sporogames, de nombreuses observations et une synonymie des plantes cellulaires et vasculaires qui croissent spontanément dans ce département . . . 10+262 pp. 31 [33] pl. O. Paris & Brest, **1867.**

415. **Héribaud-Joseph**, (*frère*). Quelques plantes de la flore d'Auvergne non comprises dans la Clef analytique du frère Gustave. (*In his* Plantes nuisibles aux diverses productions culturales de l'Auvergne, pp. 65-75. **1878.**)

416. **Debeaux**, [J.] O. Des plantes caractéristiques de la flore méditerranéenne dans le Roussillon. 12 pp. O. Paris, **1882**. — *From:* Soc. Sci. Pyrén. Or. Bull. XXV.

416. **Aubouy**, A[ntonin]. Florule de Palavas (Hérault); ou, Catalogue des plantes vasculaires observées aux environs de cette localité. (*Rev. Bot.* III. 171-206. **1884**-85.) — *Reprinted:* 36 pp. O. t-p-c. Auch, **1884.**

416. **Gentil**, Amb[roise]. Petite flore mancelle, contenant l'analyse et la description sommaire des plantes phanérogames de la Sarthe. 220 pp. D. Le Mans, **1884.**
Documents relatifs à la flore de la Sarthe (pp. 5-6).

417. **Masclef**, A[médée]. Catalogue raisonné des plantes vasculaires du département du Pas-de-Calais. 52+214+[1] pp. O. Arras & Paris, **1886.**

417. **Magnin**, [Antoine]. B. Vaivolet et les premiers explorateurs de la flore du Beaujolais. (*Soc. Bot. Lyon. Ann.* XIV. 37-160. **1887.**)

417. [Huet, Edm.] Catalogue des plantes de Provence; résultat des herborisations faites pendant plus de dix années dans les départements des Bouches-du-Rhône, du Var et des Alpes-maritimes par MM. R. Shuttleworth, A. Huet et Jacquin, Hanry . . . 165 pp. O. Pamiers, **1889.**

417. **Baichère**, Éd[ouard]. Contributions à la flore du bassin de l'Aude et des Corbières. Fasc. I. 46 pp. O. t-p-c. Carcassonne, [1891]. — *From: " Société d'études scientifiques de l'Aude, Bulletin.* II." — Contributions à la flore des Corbières et du bassin de l'Aude. Fasc. II. pp. 49-90. Q. [Carcassonne, 1893.] — *From: " Société des arts et sciences de Carcassonne. Mémoires,* VI. pt. 2."

418. **Huteau**, H. & **Sommier**, F. Catalogue des plantes du département de l'Ain. 212 pp. O. Bourg, **1894**. — *From: "Société d'émulation, agriculture, sciences, lettres et arts de l'Ain. Annales."*

418. **Maire**, R[ené]. Flore grayloise; ou, Catalogue des plantes de l'arrondissement de Gray. 102 pp. O. Gray, **1894.**

418. **Pontarlier** & **Marichal**. Catalogue des plantes vasculaires et spontanées du département de la Vendée . . . **1894**-95. — *Line 4 add:* — *Reprinted:* 99 pp. O. Paris, 1895.

418. **Briquet**, John. Notes sur la flore du Massif de Platé. 53 pp. O. Genève, **1895**. (Contributions à l'histoire phytogéographique des Alpes occidentales.) — *From: " Le Globe, journal géographique,* XXXIV."

418. **Marcailhou d'Ayméric**, H[ippoly]te & Alex[andre]. Catalogue raisonné des plantes phanérogames & cryptogames indigènes du bassin de la haute Ariège. 2 pts. (*Soc. Hist. Nat. Autun Bull.* XI. 248-376; XIII. 1-125, map. **1898**-1900→)

i. Iberian peninsula

I. GENERAL

419. **Secall**, José. Catálogo metódico . . . **1888**. — *Line 3 read:* (*Rev. Mont.* XII. 377-382, 401-405. **1888**.) — *Reprinted:* 15+[1] pp. O. Madrid, 1888.

423. **Marcailhou d'Ayméric**, H[ippoly]te. Contribution à la flore de l'Andorre. Ascensions au puig de Coma Pedrosa (2946ᵐ) et au puig dels Pessons (2865ᵐ). pp. 28-58. O. Toulouse, **1898**.] — *From: " Société Ramond. Bulletin,* ser. 2, II."

j. Italy

I. GENERAL

424. **Pontedera**, Julius. Compendium tabularum botanicarum . . . [1718.] — *Line 5 add:* — [Another ed.] [6]+18+[4]+ 168+24+[2] pp. sq. Q. Patavii, 1718.

424. **Santi**, Giorgio. Viaggio al Montamiata. **1795**. — *Line 2 add:* — Viaggio secondo per le due provincie Senesi che forma il seguito del Viaggio al Montamiata. 451 pp. 9 pl. map. O. Pisa, 1798. — *Line 11 add as a note:*
The 1795 ed. has half t-p.: Viaggio primo per la Toscana; 1798 ed.: Viaggio secondo per la Toscana. —

426. **Thomas**, Emanuel. Catalogue des plantes de Sardaigne qui se vendent à Bex, canton de Vaud en Suisse . . . 1837. 4 pp. O. n. t-p. [Lausanne, 1837.] — [Another ed.] O. [Lausanne, 1841.]†

429. **Terracciano**, Nicola. Osservazioni sulla vegetazione . . . **1881**. — *Line 5 add:* — *From: " Stazione agraria de Caserta Ann.* VIII. 49-64, 97-112. 1879-80." — — Die Wirkungen der Kälte im Winter 1879-80 auf gewisse Pflanzen der warmen Zone, welche zu Caserta unter freiem Himmel kultivirt werden. [Translated by C. Bolle.] (*Deutsch. Gart.* 1881, pp. 159-164, 1 il.)

429. **Marco**, Gennaro de. Flora di Montecassino; ossia, Guida alla determinazione delle piante spontanee di detto luogo. 2 pts. (32+268+47 pp.) 15 pl. O. Montecassino, **1886**-87.
T-p-c. has the date 1887.

429. **Marchesetti**, Carlo. La flora di Parenzo. **1890**.— *Transfer to* PHYTOGRAPHY. AUSTRIA-HUNGARY, p. 443.

II. SICILY

431. **Lojacono**, M[ichele]. Le isole Eolie . . . **1878**. — *Line 1 read:* **Lojacono[-Pojero}**, M[ichele].

432. **Lojacono**, M[ichele]. Sulla influenza dell' esposizione considerata sulla vegetazione . . . **1879**. — *Line 1 read:* **Lojacono[-Pojero}**, M[ichele].

432. **Pojero**, M. L. Flora sicula . . . **1888**-91. — *Line 1 read:* **Lojacono-Pojero**, M[ichele].

432. **Pojero**, Lojacono. Schizzo orografico della Sicilia . . . **1890**. — *Line 1 read:* **Lojacono-Pojero**, [Michele].

k. Switzerland

General Phytography

432. **Bauhin**, Kaspar. Catalogus plantarum circa Basileam sponte nascentium . . . **1622**. — *Line 2 read:* synonymiis & locis — *Line 4 read:* +[15] pp. S. Basileae, [1622].

433. **Haller**, Albert von. Iter helveticum anni 1739. **1740**. — *Lines 1-2 read:* [4]+120 pp. 2 pl. sq. O. Gottingae, 1740.

433. **Hugi**, F. S. Naturhistorische Alpenreise. 10+378 pp. . 1 il. 2 maps. 16 pl. 9 tab. D. Leipzig, 1830.

434. **Gaudin**, J. F. G. P. Synopsis florae helveticae . . . **1836**. — *Line 1 read:* **Gaudin**, J. [F. G. P.]. — *Lines 2-3 read:* editum a I. P. Monnard. 16+824+[3] pp. S. Turici, 1836.

434. **Moritzi**, Alexander. Die Pflanzen Graubündens; ein Verzeichniss der bisher in Graubünden gefundenen Pflanzen, mit besonderer Berücksichtigung ihres Vorkommens. Die Gefässpflanzen. 158 pp. 6 pl. O. (*Allg. Schweiz. Ges. Naturwiss. Neu. Denkschr.* III. [pt. 4]. **1839**.) — *Reprinted:* 158 pp. 6 pl. sq. Q. Neuchâtel, 1839.
Phytogeographical notes and list with localities.

435. **Fischer**, L[udwig]. Taschenbuch der Flora von Bern . . . **1855**. — *Line 10 read:* Flora von Bern . . . Ed. 6 rev. 36+309 pp. map. D. Bern, 1897.

435. **Weber**, J. K. Die Alpen-Pflanzen Deutschlands und der Schweiz in colorirten Abbildungen nach der Natur und in natürlicher Grösse mit einem erläuternden Text von C. A. Kranz. 4 vol. 400 pl. T. München, **1856**. — Ed. 2. 4 vol. 400 pl. T. München, 1872.† — Ed. 3. 4 vol. T. München, 1879.

l. Austria-Hungary

I. GENERAL

438. **Hacquet**, [Balthasar]. Mineralogisch-botanische Lustreise . . . **1780**. — *Line 4 add:* Mineralogisch-botanische Lustreise . . . im Jahre 1779 und 1781. Ed. 2 rev. & enl. 149 pp. 4 pl. D. Wien, 1783.

.439. **Sartori,** ·Franz. Specimen nomenclatoris plantarum phaenogamarum in Styria sponte crescentium . . . **1808.** — *Line 3 read:* D. [Viennae], **1808.**

441. **Kolenati,** [F. A.]. Die Höhenflora des Altvaters (Hohen Gesenkes der Sudeten) von 3700 bis 4708 Fuss Meereshöhe. (*Forstwirthe Mähr. Schles. Verh.* XLI. 20–84. 1860.)

·441. **Zwanziger,** G. A. Botanische Reise im Juli 1862 von Salzburg nach dem Radstädter Tauern bis Mauterndorf im Lungau, dann dem Grossarler Thale im Pongau . . . (*Zool.-Bot. Ges. Wien Verh.* XIII. 965–1002. 1863.)

443. **Pospichal,** Eduard. Flora des Flussgebietes der Cidlina und Mrdlina . . . 103 pp. Q. Prag, **1881.** — *From:* " *Archiv der naturwissenschaftlichen Landesdurchforschungen von Böhmen,* IV. no. 5."

443. **Marchesetti,** Carlo de. La flora di Parenzo. 98 pp. O. · Trieste, **1890.** — *Reprinted from:* " *Museo civile di storia naturale di Trieste,* 1890, pp. 25–122."

443. **Beck von Mannagetta,** Günther, *Ritter.* Flora von Niederösterreich; Handbuch zur Bestimmung sämmtlicher in diesem Kronlande und den angrenzenden Gebieten wildwachsenden, häufig gebauten und verwildert vorkommenden Samenpflanzen, und Führer zu weiteren botanischen Forschungen; für Botaniker, Pflanzenfreunde und Anfänger. 2 vol. (10+1396 pp.) il. Q. t-p-c. Wien, **1890–93.**

443. **Schönach,** Hugo. Beiträge zur Flora von Tirol und Vorarlberg. pp. 3–22. O. [Feldkirch, **1892.**] — *From:* " *K. k. Real- und Obergymnasium in Feldkirch. Jahresbericht,* XXXVII. 1892.**"

II. Hungary

445. **Lang,** A. F. Enumeratio plantarum in Hungaria sponte · nascentium, quas in usum botanicorum legit. **1822.** — *Line 2 read:* (*Flora,* 1823, II. Beil. 1, pp. 19–32.) — *Reprinted:*

·446. **Porcius,** Florian. Diagnosele plantelorŭ fanerogame şi · criptogame vasculare carī crescŭ spontaneĭ în Transilvania · şi nu sunt descrise in opulă luī Koch: " Synopsis floræ germanicæ et helveticæ." pp. 11–360. Q. [Bucuresci, **1893.**] — *From:* " *Academieĭ romane. Analele,* ser. 2, XIV. Memorĭile secţiuneĭ sciinţifice.*"*

III. Austrian Littoral, Bosnia and Herzegovina

448. **Beck [von Mannagetta],** Günther, *Ritter* von. [Die Vegetation der Umgebung von Abbazia.] (*In* Schubert, Karl. Der Park von Abbazia . . . **1894.**)

m. Balkan peninsula

448. **Sonnini de Manoncour,** C. S. Voyage en Grèce et en · Turquie. **1801.** — *Lines 3–4 read:* London, 1801. — Atlas. 6 pl. 4 maps. sq. Q. in. t-p. [London, 1801.]

449. **Dingler,** H[ermann]. Das Rhodopegebirge in der europäischen Türkei und seine Vegetation. 29 pp. O. [München, **1877.**] — *From:* " *Deutscher und österreichischer Alpen-Verein. Zeitschrift,* VIII, 195–223."

451. **Heldreich,** Th[eodor] von. Flore de l'île d'Égine. 1898. — *Line 1 read:* 60 pp. (*Herb.* — *Line 2 add:* — *Separate:* t-p-c. Genève, 1898.

451. [**Grecescu,** Demetrius.] Plantele indigene din Românīea alese din herbariile elevilor în farmacie spre a fi intercalate în colecţia laboratoriuluī în anul 1898, octombre. 5 [4]+15 pp. O. Bucureşti, **1899.** (Laboratoriul de botanică medicală din Bucureşti) — Plantele indigene din Românīea culese în excursiile făcute cu studenţiī în medicină şi cu ceī în farmacie în vara anuluī 1899 cum şi cele ce aŭ fost alese din herbariile elevilor în farmacie spre a fi intercalate în colecţiea · botanică a laboratoriuluī în ₎anuľ 1899 octobre. 47 pp. O. Bucureşti, **1900.** (Facultatea de medicină din Bucureşti. Laboratoriul de botanică.)

n. Mediterranean region in general and islands

451. **État des graines d'arbres, arbrisseaux, plantes, oignons à** fleurs, qu'il seroit n₂cessaire de faire venir du Levant, pour les jardins botaniques, & d'agrémens, de Sa Majesté. 8+40 pp. O. Paris, 1779.

5. Asia and Malay Archipelago

a. General

454. **Sommier,** Stéphen. Un' estate in Siberia fra Ostiacchi, Samoiedi, Siriéni, Tatári, Kirghisi e Baskíri. 8+634 pp. il. 3 maps. Q. Firenze, Torino & Roma, **1885.**
Contains notes on the vegetation.

c. East Siberia

455. **Middendorff,** A. T. von. Reise in den äussersten Norden . . . **1847.** — *Lines 2–3 read:* 4 vol. il. pl. F. St. Petersburg, **1847–75.**

455. **Trautvetter,** E. R. von. Phaenogame Pflanzen aus dem Hochnorden. **1856.** — *Lines 3–4 read:* I., Theil 2, Abtheil. 1, 9 pp.+pp. 1–190, pl. 1–8. 1856.) — *Reprinted in advance:* 9+190 pp. 8 pl. F. St. Petersburg, **1847.**

455. **Trautvetter,** E. R. von & Meyer, C. A. Florula ochotensis phaenogama. **1856.** — *Line 2 read:* [**1855.**] — *Line 4 read:* Theil 2, Abtheil. 2, pp. 1–133, 146–148, pl. 19–31. 1856.)

455. **Trautvetter,** E. R. von & others. Einleitung, Klimatologie . . . **1856.** — *Line 2 read:* 9+435+148 pp. — *Line 5 read:* I., Theil 2. 1856.)

e. China

I. General

Dendrography

·457. **Bois,** D[esiré]. Nouvelles espèces d'arbres . . . **1900.** — *Line 4 read:* Nuovi alberi.

General Phytography

457. **Boym,** Michael. Flora sinensis . . . **1656.** — *Line 3 add:* —— Flora sinensis; ou, Traite des fleurs, des fruits, des plantes, et des animaux particuliers à la Chine. (*In* Thevenot, Melchisedec. Relations de divers voyages curieux . . . vol. II. Briefve Relation de la Chine . . . pp. 15–30, 5 pl. 1696.)

458. **Wu K 'i-sün.** Chi wu ming shi t'u k'ao. 10 vol. il, O. T'ai-yüan-fu (Shansi), **1848.**
For bibliographical notes see: Bretschneider, Emil. Botanicon sinicum . . . (*As. Soc. N. China Branch Jour.* new ser. XVI. (1881), pt. I, pp. 72–73. 1882.)

f. Japan

I. General

Dendrography

461. **Dai-Nihon ju-moku shi-ryaku.** [Japanese trees figured and explained. Published by the Geographical bureau of the Department of the interior.] unp. 100 pl. Q. [Tokyo, 1878.]
In Japanese.

General Phytography

461. **Siebold,** G. F. von. Flora japonica . . . **1826–70.** — *Line 4 and note read:* **1835–70.**
Vol. I. fasc. 1–20 and vol. II. fasc. 1–5 edited by J. G. Zuccarini and published 1835–44; vol. II. fasc. 6–10 edited by F. A. W. Miquel and published in 1870. — There is another t-p. referring to the erection of a monument to Kaempfer and Thunberg in 1826.

462. **Siebold,** P. F. von & Zuccarini, J. G. Florae japonicae familiae naturales . . . **1843–46.** — *Line 2 read:* 1845–46.†

462. **Gray,** Asa. Remarks on the botany of Japan . . . **1860.** — *Line 1 read:* Diagnostic characters of new species of phænogamous plants, collected in Japan by Charles Wright, botanist of the U. S. North Pacific exploring expedition . . . With observations upon the relations of the Japanese flora to that of North America and of other parts of the northern temperate zone. [1859.] (*Amer. Acad. Mem.* new ser. VI. 077–453. 1857.) Extract from the concluding part of a Memoir on the botany of Japan in its relations to that of North America. (*Amer. Jour. Sci.* ser. 2, XXVIII. 187–200. 1859.) — Remarks on the botany of Japan in its relations — *Line 4 cancel* — *From:* " American journal . . ." *and insert:* —— Observations sur les rapports qui existent entre la flore du Japon, celle du nord de l'Amérique et d'autres parties de la zone tempérée boreale. (*Bibl. Univ. Genève Arch. Sci. Phys.* new per. IX. 32–43. 1800.)

h. Malay peninsula and archipelago

IV. Java

469. [**Warburg,** Otto.] Ein Besuch der Kina-Districte und Waldzone Preangers in Java. 22 pp. O. Hamburg, **1887.**

469. **Massart,** Jean. Notes javanaises. 44 pp. O. Bruxelles, **1896.** — *In part from:* " *Revue de l'Université de Bruxelles,* I. 53–69, 181–196."
Popular treatment.

V. Borneo

469. **Hallier,** H[ans]. Die botanische Erforschung Mittelborneos. pp. 75–81, 85–93, 95–101, 109–114. [Berlin, 1896.] — *From:* " *Naturw. Wochenschr.* XI."

j. British India

I. General

471. [**Wallich,** Nathanael.] [A numerical list of dried specimens . . . **1828.** — *Line 5 add as a note:*
For dates of publication see Kew Bull. Misc. Inform. 1913, p. 255.

I. Ceylon

476. **Haeckel,** Ernst. A visit to Ceylon. Translated by Clara Bell. 8+337 pp. O. London, **1883.**

k. Pérsia, Afghanistan, Baluchistan and Pamir

477. **Stapf**, Otto. Der Landschaftscharakter der persischen Steppen und Wüsten. pp. 227–251, 348–366; V. 51–62, 155–165. [Wien, **1888**.] — *From:* "*Oesterreichisch-Ungarische Revue, IV.–V.*"

1. Asiatic Turkey and Arabia

I. GENERAL

479. **Fellows**, *Sir* Charles. Travels and researches in Asia Minor, more particularly in the province of Lycia. 16+510 pp. il. pl. maps. O. London, **1852**.
.Contains a few notes on plants.

II. SYRIA AND PALESTINE

479. **Hasselquist**, Fredric. Iter palaestinum . . . **1757**. — *Line 7 read:*, in the years 1749, 50, 51, 52; containing observations in natural history, physick, agriculture and commerce, particularly on the Holy Land and the natural history of the Scriptures . . . [4]+8+456 [384] pp. map. O. London, 1766. — *Line 8 read:* Voyages dans| le Levant, dans les années 1749, 50, 51 & 52; contenant des observations sur l'histoire naturelle, la médecine, l'agriculture & le commerce, & particulièrement sur l'histoire naturelle de la Terre Sainte. 2 vol. S. Paris, 1769. — *Line 9 read:*
pp. 240–267 of the English and II. 67–94 of the French ed.

480. **Tristram**, H. B. The survey of western Palestine. The fauna and flora of Palestine. **1888**. — *Line 3 read:* **1884**. — [Another issue.] 22+455 pp: 201 pl. sq. Q. London, 1888.

6. AFRICA AND MADAGASCAR

a. General

482. **Dapper**, [Olfert]. Naukeurige beschrijvinge der Afrikaensche gewesten van Egypten . . . **1668**. — *Lines 4–5 read:* drachten . . . 2 pts. [6]+728 [762]+[18]+120 [128]+ [4] pp.) il. 31 pl. 13 maps. Fº. Amsterdam, **1668**.
482. **Dapper**, [Olfert]. Naukeurige beschrijvinge der Afrikaensche eylanden . . . **1668**. — *Line 5 read:* zeeden . . . *Lines 6–8 read:* 120 [128]+[4] pp. il. 5 pl. 4 maps. Fº. Amsterdam, **1668**. (*Appended to his* Naukeurige beschrijvinge der Afrikaensche gewesten . . . 1668.)

b. Mediterranean States

484. **Debeaux**, O[don]. Une excursion botanique dans la haute Kabylie. **1858**. — *Line 2 add:* — *Reprinted:* 11 pp. O. [Bordeaux, 1858.]

c. Northeast Africa

488. **Schweinfurth**, Georg. The heart of Africa; three years' travels and adventures in the unexplored regions of Central Africa from 1868 to 1871. Translated by E. E. Frewer. With an introduction by Winwood Reade. 2 vol. il. pl. maps. O. New York, **1874**.
Contains a few notes on plants.

e. Congo State and Angola

491. **Johnston**, *Sir* H. H. The river Congo, from its mouth to Bólóbó; with a general description of the natural history and anthropology of its western basin. 17+470 pp. 11 pl. il. 2 maps. O. London, **1884**. —— Der Kongo; Reise von seiner Mündung bis Bolobo, nebst einer Schilderung der klimatischen, naturgeschichtlichen und ethnographischen Verhältnisse des westlichen Kongogebietes. Autorisirte deutsche Ausgabe. Aus dem Englischen von W. von Freeden. 21+ 437 pp. il. pl. maps. O. Leipzig, 1884.
Botanik (pp. 292–298).

f. East Africa

493. **Engler**, A[dolf], (*ed.*). Die Pflanzenwelt Ost-Afrikas und der Nachbargebiete. Theil A–C. 3 vol. il. pl. map. Q. Berlin, **1895**. (Deutsch-Ost-Afrika . . . V.)
CONTENTS: Theil A. Grundzüge der Pflanzenverbreitung in Deutsch-Ost-Afrika und den Nachbargebieten. Theil B. Die Nutzpflanzen Ost-Afrikas. Theil C. Verzeichniss der bis jetzt aus Ost-Afrika bekannt gewordenen Pflanzen.

g. South Africa

493. **Kolbe**, Peter. Beschreibung des Vorgebirgs der Guten Hoffnung oder der Hottentotten. **1719**. — *Line 4 read:* behelzende een zeer omstandig verhaal — *Lines 5–7 read:* toestant van dat vermaarde gewest . . . haven, sterkte, regerings-vorm . . . nevens een geleerde beschri[ving van het klimaat en art van dat landschap, van deszelfs dieren, visschen, vogelen, planten, kruiden . . . 2 vol. 1 por. 47 pl. 6 maps. Fº. Amsterdam, 1727. — *Line 13 add:*
Van de bomen, bloemen, wortelen en andere gewassen (Ed. 1727, I. 283– 325).

493. **Sparrman**, Anders. Resa till Goda-Hopps Udden . . . **1783**. — *Lines 13–14 read:* Voyage au Cap de Bonne-Espérance et autour du monde avec le capitaine Cook, et principalement dans le pays des Hottentots et des Caffres. Traduit par M. Le Tourneur. 3 vol. 16 pl. map. D. Paris, 1787.
494. **Le Vaillant**, François. Voyage dans l'intérieur de l'Afrique par le Cap de Bonne-Espérance dans|les années 1780– 1785. **1790**. — *Line 8 add:* — Second voyage dans l'intérieur de l'Afrique par le Cap de Bonne-Espérance dans les années 1783, 84 et 85. 3 vol. 22 pl. O. Bruxelles & Amsterdam, 1797.
494. **Latrobe**, C. I. Journal of a visit to South Africa in 1815 and 1816, with some account of the missionary settlements of the United Brethren, near the Cape of Good Hope. 7+ 395 pp. O. New York, **1818**.
List of trees, shrubs and plants (pp. 385–386). — Only the most common plants listed.

i. Azores, Madeira, Canary and Cape Verde Islands

498. **Taylor**, E. M. Madeira; its scenery and how to see it . . . and lists of the trees, flowers, ferns and seaweeds. 16+ 261 pp. 1 pl. 2 maps. D. London, **1882**.
Trees, fruits, flowers (pp. 164–175).

7. AUSTRALASIA

d. Australia

500. **Tuckey**, J. H. An account of a voyage to establish a colony at Port Philip in Bass's Strait, on the south coast of New South Wales in His Majesty's ship Calcutta, in the years 1802–3–4. 15+239 pp. O. London, **1805**.
List of plants (pp. 218–219). — No botanical names given.

500. **Hügel**, Carl, *Freiherr* von. Botanisches Archiv . . . **1837**. — *Line 6 read:* 11 ff.
500. **Endlicher**, Stephan. Stirpium australasicarum herbarii Hügeliani decades tres. **1838**. — *Line 3 add:* — Separate. (*In* BENTHAM, George & others. Phytologische Abhandlungen . . . 1841.)
501. **Mueller**, F[erdinand, *Baron* von]. First [and second] general report . . . **1854**–55. — *Lines 2–3 read:* [of Victoria, Australia]. (*Bot. Gard. Melbourne Gen. Rep.* 1853, pp. 1–7; 1854, pp. 1–7. 1853–54.) — (*Hooker's Jour.* . . . — *Line 4 read:* 1854–55.)
501. **Mueller**, Ferdinand, [*Baron* von]. Enumeration of plants, collected by A. C. Gregory, Esq., along and near Cooper's river and its tributaries in sub-central Australia. (*In* DR. LEICHHARDT; papers relative to expedition in search of. 10 pp. nar. F. n. t-p. [Sydney, **1859**.] *See* pp. 4– 10.) (Legislative assembly, New South Wales, 1858–9.)
505. **Helms**, Richard. La flore et la faune de l'Australie occidentale. (*In* L'AUSTRALIE occidentale; publiée par la Commission royale de l'Australie occidentale . . . Traduction de l'édition anglaise autorisée par le gouvernement de l'Australie occidentale. 8+197 pp. por. pl. O. Paris, **1900**. (Exposition universelle de Paris, 1900.) *See* pp. 32–46.)
La flore (pp. 32–38).

8. PACIFIC ISLANDS

a. General

509. **Endlicher**, Stephan. Bemerkungen über die Flora der Südseeinseln. **1836**. — *Line 3 add:* — (*Also in* BENTHAM, George & others. Phytologische Abhandlungen . . . 1841.)

d. Fiji, Friendly, Samoan, Phoenix and Ellice Islands

510. **Cooper**, H. S. Coral lands. 2 vol. il. O. London, **1880**.
Appendix: [Extracts from Dr. Seeman's Report on the Fijian calendar, woods, birds, fishes, and flora] (I. 301–339).

IX. ETHNOBOTANY

A. GENERAL AND VARIOUS

511. **Howell**, James. Δενδρολογία, Dodona's grove . . . **1650**. — *Line 1 insert:* Dendrologia; or, Dodonna's grove. pl. O. London, 1640.† — *Line 2 read:* London, 1650. —— Dendrologie; ou, La forest de Dodonne. pl. O. Paris, 1641.†
511. **Austen**, Ralph. The spirituall use of an orchard; or, Garden of fruit trees, held forth in diverse similitudes between naturall and spirituall fruit-trees, in their natures, and ordering, according to scripture and experience. [10]+41 pp. sq. D. [Oxford, **1653**.] (*Appended to his* A treatise of fruit-trees . . . 1653.) — Ed. 2 enl. [18]+208 pp. sq. D. Oxford, 1657. (*Appended to his* A treatise of fruit trees . . . 1657.)

511. [**Hey**, *Mrs.*] The moral of flowers, illustrated by coloured engravings . . . Ed. 2. 14+[2]+227 pp. 24 pl. O. London, **1835**.

511. **Unger**, Franz. Botanische Streifzüge auf dem Gebiete der Culturgeschichte. Pt. 1–6. (*Akad. Wiss. Wien Sitzber.* XXIII. 159–254, map; XXIV. 383–454; XXIII. (1858), pp. 303–356, 3 il.; XXXVIII. (1859), pp. 69–140, il., pl. 1–9; XLV. pt. 2, pp. 75–88, 1 pl.; L. (1864), pt. 1, pp. 211–223. **1857–65**.) — *Separate:* Pt. 4, 6. — *Reprinted:* Pt. 1–3. il. map. O. Wien, 1857–59.

512. **Deas**, Lizzie. Flower favourites, their legends, symbolism and significance. 8+229 pp. D. London, **1898**.

B. BIBLE PLANTS

512. **Lemnius**, Levinus. Herbarum atque arborum quae in Bibliis . . . **1566**. — *Lines 11–12 read:* [6]+134+[2] ff. S. Antverpiæ, 1568.

512. **Brown**, Thomas. Observations upon several plants mention'd in Scripture. (*In his* Certain miscellany tracts. [6]+ 215+[6] pp. D. London, **1684**. *See* pp. 1–88.)

513. Botanique biblique; ou, Courtes notices sur les végétaux mentionnés dans les Saintes Écritures. 6+195 pp. 18 pl. D. Genève, **1862**.

513. **Hamilton**, Frédéric. La botanique de la Bible; étude scientifique, historique, littéraire et exégétique des plantes mentionnées dans la Sainte-Écriture. 19+196 pp. 25 pl. O. Nice, **1871**.

C. PLANTS IN ANCIENT LITERATURE

514. **Annecy**, Tôchon d'. Dissertation sur l'inscription grecque ΙΑΞΟΝΟΣ ΔΤΚΙΟΝ (Jasonis lycium) et sur les pierres antiques qui servaient de cachets aux médecins oculistes. (*Jour. Pharm. Paris*, V. 93–95. **1819**.)

514. **Euchholz**, J. B. Flora Homerica. **1848**. — *Lines 1–2 read:* Euchholz, [J. B.]. Flora Homerica. 30 pp. sq. O. Culm, [1848]. (Königliches katholisches Gymnasium zu Culm. Jahresbericht, 1847–48.)

514. **Visiani**, Roberto de. Sopra l'Acanto degli scrittori greci e latini; studii critici. (*Istit. Veneto Sci. Mem.* VII. 45–51. **1857**.) — *Separate.*

The name has been used for several species of Acacia and for other plants.

514. **Bubani**, Pietro. Flora Virgiliana . . . [1870.] — *Lines 3–4 read:* 135 pp. O. [Bologna, 1869.] — Illustrazioni ulteriori . . . pp. 137–144. O. n. t-p. [Bologna, 1870.] — Ultime note . . . 7+[1] pp. O. n. t-p. [Bologna, 1876.]

E. EMBLEMATIC BOTANY

515. **Rinaldi**, Giovanni de'. Il mostruosissimo mostro . . . **1584**. — *Line 6 add:* — [Another ed.] 78+[1] ff. T. Venetia, 1626.

515. **Camerarius**, Joachim. Symbolorum et emblematum ex re herbaria desumtorum centuria una collecta. **1590**. — *Line 8 add:* Symbolorū & emblematum . . . centuria una [et altera] collecta. 2 pts. (102+103 ff.) il. 1 por. D. Francofurti, 1654.

515. [**Hohberg**, W. H. *Freiherr* von.] Die mit teutschen Saiten überzogene heilige Kron-Harffe; oder, Verfassung des gantzen Psalter Davids in teutsche Reim-Gebände; vermittelst sonderbarer darzu mit dem Basso continuo, neuverfertigter Kunst-Melodeyen abzusingen unter lieblichen Sinn-Blumen und Bildungs-Gewächsen, als wie in einem Geisterfreudiger Lust- und Artzney-Garten . . . [14]+526 [516]+[1] pp. 150 pl. S. Nürnberg, **1680**.

With figures of plants.

F. ESTHETIC BOTANY

516. **Harding**, J. D. The park and the forest. 25 pl. F°. [London], **1841**.

516. **Berge**, Hermann. Pflanzenphysiognomie; Besprechung der landschaftlich wichtigen Gewächse. 12+288 pp. 328 il. O. Berlin, **1880**.

G. PLANT LORE

2. PLANT LORE IN GENERAL

517. **Reivas** dell Tbis. Miti e simboli delle piante presso i Greci e Romani. **1857**. — *Lines 1–2 read:* I miti e i simboli delle piante presso i Greci ed i Romani. 58 pp. Q. Verona & Milano, 1857. — *From:* "*Gazz. uff. di Verona*, III."

518. **Strantz**, M. von. Die Blumen in Sage und Geschichte. 6+471 pp. O. Berlin, **1875**.

518. **Bergen**, F. D. Animal and plant lore. 180 pp. O. Boston, **1899**. — *From:* "*American folk lore society. Memoirs*, VII."

VOLUME II

I. GYMNOSPERMAE

4. PINACEAE

12. **Beinling**, Theodor. Ueber die geographische Verbreitung der Coniferen. **1858**. — *Line 3 add:* — Die Nadelhölzer, Koniferen, und deren geographische Verbreitung. [Abstract.] (*Schles, Forstver. Verh.* [1858], pp. 159–169.)

13. [**Kent**, A. H.] A manual of the Coniferae . . . **1881**. — *Line 9 add:* —— Manuale dei Coniferi, comprendente una rivista generale della famiglia, una sinossi delle specie rustiche coltivate nella Gran Bretagna; loro posto ed uso nell' orticoltura, ecc., ecc. 351 pp. il. pl. O. Milano, 1882.

13. **Goeze**, E[dmund]. Die Palmen und Nadelhölzer; eine pflanzengeographische Skizze. (*Hamburg. Gart. Blumenzeit.* XL. 108 211, 244 260. **1884**.) *From:* Humboldt, 1883, pt. 7, 8 & 10.

13. [**Ravenscroft**, Edward.] The pinetum britannicum . . . **1884**. — *Line 4 read:* Edinburgh & London, [1863]–84. — *After line 4 add as-a note.*

The work is sometimes known as Lawson's Pinetum britannicum, and was so styled on the plates to the first thirty-three parts, which were issued from the private press of Peter and Charles Lawson. — For further bibliographical information see Gard. Chron. ser. 3, XXXVI. 36–37. 1904.

15. **Murray**, Andrew. Monographic sketch of the Conifers of Japan . . . **1862**. — *Line 3 read:* Reprinted under the title: Pines and Firs of Japan.

17. **Russow**, E[dmund]. Zur Kenntniss des Holzes, insonderheit des Coniferenholzes. **1883**. — *Line 3 add:* Reprinted: 50 pp. 2 il. 5 pl. O. t-p-c. Kassel, 1883.

17. **Pfiırtscheller**, Paul. Beiträge zur Anatomie der Coniferenhölzer. **1885**. — *Line 3 add:* — Zur Anatomie der Coniferenhölzer. [Extract.] (*Oester. Forst-Zeit.* III. 309. 1885.)

19. **Hejberg**, P. Betragtninger over den af Prof. Ørsted fremsatte Tydning af Gymnospermernes Blomster. (*Bot. Tidsskr.* II. 89–146, 8 il. **1867**.)

PINUS

Morphology

40. **Gordon**, James. Male flowers of Pines. An argument for their leaf origin. (*Jour. For.* III. 388–389. **1879**.)

SEQUOIA

3. Wellingtonia:

51. — **Labhrt-Luatz** . . . **1869**. — *Line 1 read:* Labhart-Luatz.

51. — **Williams**, J. O. Mammoth trees of California, illustrated by a comparison with other noted trees, ancient and modern, with a hand-book in brief . . . 54+[1] pp. il. O. Boston, 1871.

TAXODIUM

T. mucronatum:

52. — **Reyes**, M. O. El gigante de la flora mexicana . . . **1884**. — *Line 3 add:* — Ein Riesenbaum. (*Oesterr. Forst-Zeit.* I. 363. **1883**.)

TSUGA

53. **T. japonica:** Shirasawa, Homi. Eine neue Coniferenart in Japan. (*Bot. Mag. Tokyo*, IX. 86–84, pl. 3. **1895**.) — *Reprinted:* 3+[3] pp. 1 pl. O. t-p-c. [Tokyo, 1895.]

II. ANGIOSPERMAE

A. MONOCOTYLEDONEAE

8. PALMAE

61. **Goeze**, E[dmund]. Die Palmen und Nadelhölzer; eine pflanzengeographische Skizze. (*Hamburg. Gart. Blumenzeit.* XL. 198–214, 244–259. **1884**.) — *From:* Humboldt, 1883, pt. 7, 8 & 10.

Morphology

62. **Mohl**, Hugo von. De Palmarum structura. [1823.] — *Line 3 read:* 1831.]) — *Reprinted:* 52 pp. F°. Monachii, 1831. — Atlas. 16 pl. F°. n. t-p. [Monachii, 1831.]

64. **ARCHONTOPHOENIX** — *Add:* (Ptychosperma spec., Seaforthia spec.)

ARECA (Cocos spec.)

64. **A. Normanbyi**: Hill, Walter. [Cocos Normanbyi.] (*In* Brisbane botanic garden. Report, 1874, p. 6.)

KENTIA (Areca spec.)

69. **K. minor**: Hill, Walter. [Areca minor.] (*In* Brisbane botanic garden. Report, 1874, p. 6.)

12. LILIACEAE

ALOË

78. **A. grandidentata**: [Salm-Reifferscheid-Dyck, Joseph, *Fürst und Allgraf.*] (*In his* Observationes botanicae in Horto Dickensi notatae . . . pp. 3–4. [1822.])

79. **A. spinulosa**: [Salm-Reifferscheid-Dyck, Joseph, *Fürst und Allgraf.*] (*In his* Observationes botanicae in Horto Dickensi notatae . . . p. 4. [1822.])

DRACAENA

D. **Draco**: Noteworthy individuals

82 — Humboldt, F. H. A. von. (*In his* Ansichten der Natur . . . Ed. 2, II. 83–85. **1826.** — Ed. 3, II. 104–108. 1849.)

B. I. DICOTYLEDONEAE. Subcl. ARCHI-CHLAMYDEAE

18. PIPERACEAE

PIPER

93. Heister, Lorenz. De Pipere. **1740.** — *Lines 1–2 read:* Heister, Lorenz (*praeses*). De Pipere. (Diss.) (G. K. Pfeffer.) 48+[1] pp. 1 pl. sq. D. Helmaestadii, **1740.**

21. SALICACEAE

SALIX

Taxonomy

Germany

101. **Schwaiger**, L[udwig]. Bestimmung der bairischen Weidenarten . . . **1877.** — *Line 3 add:* — Separate under the title: Bestimmung der Weiden-Arten nach den Blättern.

105. **S. babylonica**: Brückmann, F. E. Epistola itineraria LXXI. sistens Chamaecerasum hungaricum et Salicem orientalem Davidis ad . . . Georgium Clifford . . . 12 pp. 1 pl. sq. O. Wolffenb., 1738.

26. JUGLANDACEAE

JUGLANS

J. **regia**: Physiology

114. — Cardan, M. Observations on the vegetation . . . 1849. — *Line 1 read:* Observations sur la végétation du Noyer commun (Juglans regia). [Extract.] (*Acad. Sci. Paris Compt. Rend.* XXVII. 650–653. **1848.**) — *Line 2 read:* 1849.

29. BETULACEAE

Taxonomy

115. **Hartig**, Theodor. Monographie der Betulaceen. 113 pp. Q. Berlin, 1849.

From his Vollständige Naturgeschichte der forstlichen Culturpflanzen Deutschlands, pp. 259–373. [1840–]51.

30. FAGACEAE

QUERCUS

Q. **Robur**: Taxonomy

136. — Thümen, F[elix] von. Eine neue und schöne Eichen-varietät. (*Oester. Forst. Jagd.-Zeit.* 1886, p. 284.) — Una nuova varietà di Querce. (*Nuov. Riv. Forest.* X. 25–27. 1887.)

34. PROTEACEAE

EMBOTHRIUM (Oreocallis)

160. **E. Wickhamii**: Hill, Walter. [Oreocallis Wickhami.] (*In* Brisbane botanic garden. Report, 1874, pp. 6–7.)

41. LORANTHACEAE

Physiology

174. **Scott**, John. Loranthaceae . . . 1871. — *Line 1 read:* Loranthaceae.

48. AIZOACEAE

MESEMBRYANTHEMUM

193. [Salm-Reifferscheid-Dyck, Joseph, *Fürst und Allgraf.*] (*In his* Observationes botanicae in Horto Dickensi notatae . . . pp. 10–47. [1822.])

53. RANUNCULACEAE

CLEMATIS

C. **Vitalba**:

200. — Boerlage, J. G. [Clematis Vitalba var. biternata.] (*In his* Catalogus plantarum phanerogamarum quae in horto botanico bogoriensi coluntur herbaceis exceptis, pt. 1, pp. 1–2. 1899.)

82. ROSACEAE

PRUNUS

Taxonomy

270. **Tenore**, M[ichele]. Intorno all' Amygdalus pumila . . . 1847. — *Line 3 add:* — Istit. Incor. Sci. Nat. Napoli Atti. VIII. 135–149. 1855.) — *Reprinted:* 15 pp. sq. Q. n. t-p. [Napoli, 1847.]

P. **fruticosa**:

274. **Brückmann**, F. E. Epistola itineraria LXXI. sistens Chamaecerasum hungaricum et Salicem orientalem Davidis ad . . . Georgium Clifford . . . 12 pp. 1 pl. sq. O. Wolffenb., 1738.

RUBUS

Taxonomy

German Empire

302. **Krause**, E. H. L. Die elsässischen Brombeerarten. pp. 17–34. pl. 2–3. O. [Strassburg, 1897.] — *From:* "Philomathische Gesellschaft in Elsass-Lothringen. Mittheilungen, V. pt. 2."

France

303. [Boulay, J. N.] [Ronces vosgiennes; description des espèces.] [2]+152+12 pp. D. t-p. w. [Rambervillers, 1864–69.]

SORBUS

312. **S. cuspidata**: Bertoloni, Antonio : . . 1864. — *Line 1 read:* **S. granulosa**: Bertoloni . . . and insert after S. GRACILIS.

84. LEGUMINOSAE

ACACIA

Physiology

323. **Emery**, Carlos. Hormigas de Costa Rica que viven en las Acacias. (*Mus. Nac. Costa Rica Anal.* I. 65–67. 1888–89.) — Die in Akaziendornen lebenden Ameisen in Costa Rica. — Zur Biologie der Ameisen, I. (*Biol. Centralbl.* XI. 165–168. 1891.)

CASSIA

C. **moschata**:

344. **Hamburg**, Daniel. Note . . . 1863. — *Line 1 read:* Hanbury, Daniel.

ERYTHROPHLEUM

358. **E. couminga**: Baillon . . . 1871–73. — *Line 1 read:* **E. couminga**.

PROSOPIS

379. — **P. Vidaliana**: Náves, Andrés. Descripción de la especie botánica Prosopis Vidaliana de la flora de Filipinas. 17 pp. 2 pl. O. Manila, 1877.

PUERARIA

P. **Thunbergiana**:

380. — Wittmack, Ludwig. Pueraria Thunbergiana . . . 1896. — *Line 3 read:* Schlingpflanze.

93. SIMARUBACEAE

AILANTHUS

A. **glandulosa**: Taxonomy

413. — Ellis, Walter. [Rhus glandulosa.] . . . **1758.** — *Line 1 read:* [Rhus sinense foliis alatis . . .]

102. EUPHORBIACEAE

CUNURIA

440. **Wawra** [von Fernsee], H[einrich], Ritter. [Cunaria [sic] pruceana.] . . . **1883.** — *Line 2 read:* Spruceana.]

116. ACERACEAE
ACER
Taxonomy
Europe
476. .Borbás, Vince[nz] von.   Magyarország és a Balkánfél-
sziget Juharfáiról . . . 1891. — *Line 3 add:* — *Separate.*

122. VITACEAE
Morphology
501. Velten, Wilhelm. Vitis vinifera L. u. Ampelopsis bede-
racea Michaux; eine morphologische Studie.   pp. 149–165.
pl. 8–9. [Heidelberg, 1873?] — *From: Ann. Oenol. III.*

126. TILIACEAE
TILIA
T. Braunii:
517. — T[hümen], F[elix] von.   Eine neue Lindenart. (*Oesterr.
Forst. Jagd-Zeit.* 1887, pp. 2–3.) —— Una nuova specie di
Tiglio. (*Nuov. Riv. Forest.* X. 147–148.   1887.)

128. BOMBACACEAE
ADANSONIA
A. digitata: Noteworthy individuals
529. — Humboldt, F. H. A. von.   (*In his* Ansichten der Natur . . . Ed. 2, II. 105–107.   1826. — Ed. 3, II. 108–112.
1849.)

129. STERCULIACEAE
BRACHYCHITON
532. **B. discolor:** Hooker, *Sir* J. D. Sterculia (Brachychiton) discolor. (*Bot. Mag.* CVIII. pl. 6608.   1882.)
STERCULIA
538. **S. discolor:** *Transfer to* BRACHYCHITON *as* **B. discolor,** p. 532.

139. DIPTEROCARPACEAE
DRYOBALANOPS
D. aromatica:
560. — [Jones, *Sir* William.] On the Dryobalanops Camphora
. . . 1816. — *Line 1 read:* — [Colebrooke, H. T.]

159. CACTACEAE
Taxonomy
584. [Salm-Reifferscheid-Dyck, Joseph, *Fürst und Altgraf.*]
(*In his* Observationes botanicae in Horto Dickensi notatae
. . . pp. 4–10. [1822.])
586. Brinkmaier.   Die Cactuspflanzen in ihrer Heimat.
(*Wien. Ill. Garten-Zeit.* XVIII. 18–21. 1893.) — *From his*
"Naturbilder."
CEPHALOCEREUS
591. L[emaire], Ch[arles].   Pilocereus chrysomallus Ch. L.
.(*Flore Sert.* III. 242. c1847.)
PILOCEREUS
598. **P. chrysomallus** *transfer to* CEPHALOCEREUS, p. 591.

173. MYRTACEAE
634. **UGNI** (EUGENIA) *read* **UGNI** (EUGENIA *spec.*)

**B. II. DICOTYLEDONEAE. Subcl. META-
CHLAMYDEAE**

182. ERICACEAE
VACCINIUM
V. Myrtillus:
686. — Ascherson, P[aul] & Magnus, P[aul].   Die weisse Hei-
delbeere . . . 1889. — *Line 6 read:* — [Extract.] (*Oesterr.
Forst-Zeit.* VIII. 76.   1890.)

192. STYRACACEAE
STYRAX
704. — Torrey, John. On the Darlingtonia californica, a new
pitcher-plant from northern California.   7+[1] pp. pl. 12.
[*Smithson. Contr. Knowl.* VI. art. 4. 1854.) — *Separate:* t-p.
[Washington, D. C., 1853.]
Contains Styrax californicum and S. platinifolium (p. 4).
S. officinalis:
705. — Κρίνος, Σ. Δ. . . . 1862. — *Line 1 read:* Κρῖνος, Σ. Δ.

202. VERBENACEAE
TECTONA
T. grandis:
761. — Koórders, S. H. De kiemontwikkeling van Tectona
grandis . . . 1890. — *Line 3 read:* 1892.

207. BIGNONIACEAE
PANDOREA
789. **P. jasminoides:** *Insert here the three entries under*
TECOMA JASMINOIDES, p. 791.
TECOMA
791. **T. jasminoides:** *Transfer to* PANDOREA *as* **P. jasminoides,** p. 789.

215. RUBIACEAE
CINCHONA
Taxonomy
812. Weddell, H. A. Notes sur les Quinquinas.   1869. —
Line 4 add: —— Übersicht der Cinchonen. Deutsch bear-
beitet von Dr. F. A. Flückiger. 43 pp. O. Schaffhausen
& Berlin, 1871.

216. CAPRIFOLIACEAE
LONICERA
838. **L. hispida:** Lindley, John . . . 1836. — *Transfer to*
L. hispidula, p. 838.
L. hispidula:
838. Lindley, John.   Caprifolium hispidulum. (*Bot. Reg.*
XXI. 1761, pl. 1836.)
838. **L. iberia:** Marschall von Bieberstein, F. A. . . .
1810–[43].) — *Line 1 read:* **L. iberica.**

SUBJECT INDEX
911. Lasiandra, 641 read: Lasiandra, 641.

VOLUME III

**I. AUXILIARY AND INTRODUCTORY
PUBLICATIONS**

B. PERIODICALS AND SERIALS
4. EUROPE
b. Scandinavia
10. Kongl. Svenska landtbruks-academiens.   Annaler. —
Line 1 read: Kong. Svenska landtbruks-academien. —
Annaler.
g. France
18. Annales de flore et de pomone. — *Cancel this entry, and
see under* JOURNAL et flore des jardins, p. 20.
l. Balkan peninsula
26. Ύπουργεῖον ἐσωτερικῶν τρῆμα γεωργίας. — *Line 1 read:*
Ύπουργεῖον ἐσωτηρικῶν τρῆμα γεωργίας.

C. COLLECTIONS, GARDENS, ARBORETUMS
1. NORTH AMERICA
27. [Franceschi, Francesco.]   Southern California acclimatizing association . . . general catalogue and garden guide
for the South, comprising summary description, degree of
hardiness, hints to culture of 2,000 sorts of plants. [2]+112
pp. 1 il. D. t-p-c. [Santa Barbara, 1900.]

D. ENCYCLOPEDIAS AND DICTIONARIES
1. TERMINOLOGY, GLOSSARIES, DICTIONARIES
30. Metzner, R[einhold]. Botanisch-gärtnerisches Taschenwörterbuch . . . 1896. — *Line 6 read:* 12+286 pp. S.
Berlin, 1896.

II. PRINCIPLES AND FUNDAMENTAL SCIENCES

F. DESCRIPTIVE BOTANY

1. GENERAL

b. Medicinal

55. **Scannagatta**, Josue. Appendix specierum plantarum officinalium Linneana methodo distributarum. 123 pp. O. Bononiæ, **1805**. (*Appended to* LINNÉ, Carl von. Systema vegetabilium . . . 1805.)

4. EUROPE

a. General

66. **Botanique practique** . . . **1878**. — *Line 3 add:* — Botanique pratique Suisse et Savoie. Choix de 319 plantes alpines. 2 ser. New ed. Genève, 1885.†

d. German Empire

70. **Jesemann**, (*Obergärtner. Ungar. Altenburg*) . . . **1885**. — *Line 1 read:* Iisemann.

h. FRANCE

85. **Congrès** pour l'étude des fruits à cidre. Supplément aux procès-verbaux des sessions. 37 pp. O. t-p-c. Rouen, 1873.

85. **Liste** générale des fruits adoptés par le Congrès pomologique de 1900 et " La géographie pomologique du territoire français." 32 pp. O. Lyon, 1900.

88. **Sauviago**, Émile . . . **1899**. — *Line 1 read:* **Sauvaigo,** Émile.

III. ARBORICULTURE

B. MISCELLANEOUS PUBLICATIONS INCLUDING REPORTS AND STATISTICS

7. AUSTRALASIA

a. Australia

132. **Bernays**, L. A.] Economic tropical horticulture in Northern Queensland; report . . . 5 pp. F. [Brisbane, **1880**.] (Queensland. Legislative assembly, 1880.)

C. PUBLICATIONS RELATING TO THE CULTIVATION OF PARTICULAR GROUPS

1. FRUIT TREES

c. Europe

VII. France

143. **Butret**, C[harles, *baron* de]. Taille raisonnée des arbres fruitiers . . . **1795**. — *Line 9 add:* New ed. 16+95+[4] pp. 4 pl. D. Lyon, 1832.

VII. ECONOMIC PRODUCTS AND THEIR USES

D. SPECIAL PRODUCTS

6. FIBRES

234. **Höhnel**, Franz, *Ritter* von. Die Mikroskopie der technisch verwendeten Faserstoffe. Ein Lehr- und Handbuch der mikroskopischen Untersuchung der Faserstoffe, Gewebe und Papiere. 8+163 pp. 69 il. O. Wien, Pest & Leipzig, **1887**.

E. MATERIA MEDICA

3. MEDICINAL PRODUCTS, DRUGS

239. **Brunschwig**, Hieronymus. The vertuose boke 'of distyllacyon . . . **1527**. — *Line 1 read:* Hie anfahen ist das Büch genannt liber de arte distillandi, von der Künst der Distillierung, zusammen colligiert und gesetzt von Hieronymo Brunsthwygk . . . 212 ff. il. F. Strassburg, **1500**.† — Das neuwe distilier-buoch. F. Strassburg, 1531.† —— *Line 4 read:* London, 1527.

239. **Apollinaris**, Quintus. Kurtz Handtbüchlin und Experiment vieler Artzneyen . . . Sampt lebendiger Abcontrafactur eticher gemeiner Kreuter, und daraus mancherley gebrauten und distillirten Gewässer. Jetzundt von nuwem gemehrt und gebessert an vielen Orten. 152 ff. pref. ind. il. O. Franckfurt am Mayn, **1550**.† — [Another ed.] O. Strassburg, 1571.† — Kurtzs Handtbüchlin uund Experiment viler Artzneyen, durch den gantzen Cörper dess Menschens . . . Sampt . . . Abcontrafactur eticher . . . Kreuter . . . Jetzund . . . gemehret und gebessert. Sampt dem Experiment-Büchlin von XX Pestilents wurtzlen dess . . . T. Oeyori. 213 pp.+[25] ff. O. Strassburg, 1589. — [Another ed.] O. Strassburg, 1599.† — [Another ed.] 212 ff. ind. il. O. Strassburg, 1633.† — [Another ed.] [4]+212 pp.+[34] ff.

O. Strassburg, 1651. —— [Latin translation.] Opera Rudolphi Goclenii. il. O. Francofurti, 1610.†

240. **[Yûhannâ ibn Masawaih.**] Opera de medicamentorum purgantium delectu, castigatione & usu, libri duo, quorum priorem Canones universales, posteriorem de simplicibus vocant. Grabadin, hoc est compendii secretorum medicamentorum, libri duo, quorum prior Antidotarium; posterior de appropriatis vulgò inscribitur . . . His accessere plantarum in libro simplicium descriptarum . . . reliqua verò, quæ cum Mesuæ operibus exire solent, in aliud volumen conjecimus, quod nomine supplementi in Mesuen inscriptum est . . . [5]+252+[5]+278+[11] ff. il. F. Venetiis, **1623**. *See* De simplicibus (I. 24–82).

240. **[Yûhannâ ibn Masawaih.**] Supplementum in secundum librum, compendii secretorum medicinæ Jo. Mesues . . . Petri Apponi . . . Francisci de Pedemontium . . . [5]+278+[11] ff. F. Venetiis, **1623**. (*Appended to his* Opera de medicamentorum purgantium delectu . . . 1623.)

240. **Bayle**, F[rançois]. Dissertationes medicæ in quibus receptæ communiter circa subjectam materiam, veterum ac recentiorum opiniones erroneæ refelluntur, & veræ morborum ac symptomatum causæ assignantur & demonstrantur. Ed. 3 enl. 2 vol. 1 pl. T. Tolosæ, **1681**. De forma plantarum (II. 35–60). — Vol. II. has the title: Dissertationes physicæ in quibus principia proprietatum in mistis, oeconomia corporum in plantis & animalibus . . . demonstrantur . . .

240. **Tryon**, Thomas. The way to health, long life and happiness; or, A discourse of temperance and the particular nature of all things requisite for the life of man . . . to which is added a treatise of most sorts of English herbs . . . Ed. 2 rev. [12]+500+18 pp. D. London, **1691**.

5. PHARMACOGNOSY AND PHARMACOLOGY

b. Relation of properties to affinity and habit

259. **Lefebvre**, Léopold. Essai sur les analogies botaniques et les différences médicales des plantes. (Thèse.) 47 pp. sq. Q. Paris, 1860. (École supérieure de pharmacie de Paris.)

F. ECONOMIC PRODUCTS PLACED ACCORDING TO COUNTRIES

1. NORTH AMERICA

d. United States

IV. WESTERN UNITED STATES

264. **Coville**, F. V. The Panamint Indians of California. (*Amer. Anthropol.* V. 351–361, pl. 4. **1892**.) — *Separate:* t-p-c. Washington, 1892.

5. AFRICA

e. Congo state and Angola

281. **Bateman**, C. S. L. The first ascent of the Kasaï, being some records of service under the Lone star. 20+192 pp. il. pl. 2 maps. O. London, 1889.

VIII. TAXONOMIC ARRANGEMENT

A. GYMNOSPERMAE

4. PINACEAE

JUNIPERUS

J. communis: Economic

303. — Baier, J. J. (*praeses*). De Junipero. **1719**. — *Lines 1–2 read:* Klein, J. C. De Junipero. (Diss.) 24 pp. sq. D. [Altdorf], 1719.

B. ANGIOSPERMAE

B. II. DICOTYLEDONEAE

27. MORACEAE

MORUS

Descriptive and cultural

373. **Manni**, D. M. Della piantagione e coltivazione de' Gelsi in Toscana, cagione di ricchezza ragionamento. 20 pp. O. Firenze, 1767.

375. **Kamm**, J. M. Das Gemeinnützigste und Nothwendigste über die Maulbeerbaum- und Seidenraupen-Zucht, oder theoretisch praktische Anleitung hiezu. Für die Jugend der deutschen Volksschulen sowie für den Bürger und Landmann. 8+37+[2] pp. D. Marktbreit a. M., **1839**.

376. **[Zollinger**, C. von.] Praktisches Handbuch über die Fortpflanzung und Kultur des Maulbeerbaumes . . . [2]+16+208 pp. 5 pl. O. Innsbruck, **1843**.

377. **Schulz**, C. F. Gründliche Anleitung für Maulbeerbaumzucht und Seidenbau. 6+58+[1] pp. 6 pl. O. Berlin, **1854**.

63. ROSACEAE

MALUS

429. **M. spectabilis**: M[oore], T[homas]. Pyrus . . . (*Flor.* Pomol. 1852, p. 25, pl.) — *Line 2 read:* 1872.

PYRUS

446. **P. communis**: Galloway, B. T. Pear leaf blight; its cause and treatment. (*Amer. Assoc. Nurserym. Proc.* XV. 88–89, 1 il. 1890.)

ROSA

Descriptive and general

449. [Achenbach, (*Oberconsistorial-Secretair*), **Noack**, R. & **Gernet**, (*Hofgärtner, Jugenheim*).] Ueber Geschichte, Vaterland und Verbreitung der Rose. Die verschiedenen Arten der Rose. Ueber Kultur der Rose. Drei Vorträge, den Besuchern der Allgemeinen Rosen-Ausstellung zu Darmstadt am 25., 26. und 27. Juni 1870 gewidmet. 47 pp. O. Darmstadt, 1870.

449. **Noack**, R. Die verschiedenen Arten der Rose. (*In* ACHENBACH, NOACK, R. & GERNET. Ueber Geschichte, Vaterland . . . der Rose . . . pp. 14–28. 1870.)

450. **Theunen**, Auguste. Guide à l'usage des amateurs de Roses. 1893. — *Line 1 read:* **Theunen**, August. Handleiding voor rozenliefhebbers. 118+[1] pp. D. Antwerpen, 1891. —— Guide . . . *Line 2 read:* Anvers, 1893.

451. [**Graveraux**, Jules.] Roseraie de l'Haÿ (Seine). Collection botanique du genre Rosa. 18+[1] pp. O. [Paris, 1899.]

· Cultural

451. **Vollständige** Anweisung schöne Rosen . . . 1820. — *Line 4 read:* 55 pp. nar. D. Ulm, 1820.

452. **Gernet**, (*Hofgärtner, Jugenheim*). Ueber Kultur der Rosen. (*In* ACHENBACH, NOACK, R. & GERNET. Ueber Geschichte, Vaterland . . . der Rose . . . pp. 29–47. 1870.)

65. LEGUMINOSAE

CAESALPINIA

468. **CAESALPINIA** (BALSAMOCARPON ; POINCIANIA spec.). — *Read:* POINCIANA.

72. RUTACEAE

SKIMMIA

505. **Carrière**, E. A. Des Skimmias. (*Rev. Hort.* 1880, 55–58, il. 10–13.)

96. VITACEAE

VITIS

General

545. **Kohn**, Ch. Histoire ancienne de la Vigne. (*Rev. Sci. Bourbonnais*, XI. 33–37. 1898.) — *From:* "*Fauna, Verein luxemburger Naturfreunde*, VII."

Pathological

582. Ξανθόπουλος, Σ. [Xanthopoulos, S.] 1900. — *Line 1 read:* Ξανθόπουλος, Σ.

108. THEACEAE

THEA

T. japonica: Cultural

599. —— Soulange-Bodin, [Étienne]. Notice sur les soins à donner aux Camellias. 1827. — *Lines 3–4 read:* frei bearbeitet und vermehrt von F. A. Lehmann. 15 pp. S. Dresden, 1828.

T. sinensis: Economic

606. —— The history of the Tea plant . . . [1819]. — *Lines 5–6 read:* 60 pp. 1 [13] pl. O. London, [1820].

141. ERICACEAE

ERICA

651. **E. ventricosa**: **Carrière**, E. A. Erica ventricosa coccinea minor. (*Rev. Hort.* 1880, 50, pl.)

169. RUBIACEAE

COFFEA

Economic

739. [**Lindley**, John, **Hooker**, *Sir* J. D. & others.] [On Coffee, its substitutes and adulteration.] 8+13+[1]+37+33 pp. 11 pl. F. n. t-p. [London, 1852–53.]

Lithographed. — Contains also communications by Tho[mas] Graham, John Stenhouse, Dugald Campbell, W. B. Carpenter & A. S. Taylor.

VOLUME IV

I. AUXILIARY AND INTRODUCTORY PUBLICATIONS

B. PERIODICALS AND SERIALS

3. EUROPE

h². Portugal

13. **Portugal** — Direcção geral da agricultura. Annuario dos serviços florestaes. Vol. 1.–? Lisboa, 18 . . ?–1900→

m. Balkan Peninsula

15. Привредни Гласник. [The agricultural messenger; journal of the Serbian agricultural society.] O. Belgrad, 1899–1900→
Contains silvicultural articles.

15. Тежак. [The farmer.] F. Belgrad, 1869–1900→
Contains silvicultural articles.

C. COLLECTIONS, FOREST GARDENS

3. EXHIBITIONS

d. Europe

III. HOLLAND AND BELGIUM

19. **Wesmael**, A[lfred]. Tentoonstelling te Namen, voor producten van boschkultur. (*Tijdschr. Boomteelk.* 1869, pp. 218–222.)

V. FRANCE

20. **Siemoni**, [G.] C. & Devincenzi . . . 1866. — *Line 1 read:* **Siemoni**, [G.] C. & Devincenzi.

20. **Hooker**, [*Sir*] J. D. On seeds and saplings of forest trees. (*Canad. Naturalist*, ser. 2, III. 453–457. 1868. — *Reprinted under the title:* Report on seeds and saplings of forest trees. 4 pp. O. n. t-p. [Montreal, 1868.]
From a report on the Paris exhibition of 1867; chiefly on French forestry exhibits.

e. Asia

III. BRITISH INDIA

21. **Catalogue** of the collections of forest products exhibited by the Northern circle, Madras forest department, at the Edinburgh international forestry exhibition 1884, with a short account of the forests. 28 pp. O. Madras, 1884.

21. **Alexander**, J[ohn]. Descriptive catalogue of the exhibits sent from the island of Ceylon to the Edinburgh international forestry exhibition. 26 pp. D. [Edinburgh], 1884.

F. EDUCATION

2. FOREST SCHOOLS AND PUBLICATIONS ON EDUCATION

b. Europe

XIII. AUSTRIA-HUNGARY

36. **Hohenbruck**, Arthur, *Freiherr* von & Zimmerauer, Friedrich . . . 1890. — *Line 1 read:* **Hohenbruck**, Arthur, *Freiherr* von & Zimmerauer, Friedrich.

5. ARBOR DAY

a. North America

UNITED STATES

42. **Northrop**, B. G. Arbor day in schools. 1892. — *Line 2 add:* — *Reprinted:* 22 pp. O. Boston, 1892.

G. FOREST INFLUENCES

1. FOREST INFLUENCES IN GENERAL AND EFFECTS OF DEFORESTATION

43. **Maistre**, J[ules]. Influence des forêts sur le climat et sur le régime des sources. [1867.] — *Line 2 add:* — De l'influence des forêts et des cultures sur le climat et sur le régime des sources. 46 pp. O. Montpellier, 1881. — Ed. 3. 94 pp. O. Montpellier, 1883. — Ed. 4. 89 pp. O. Clermont-L'Hérault, 1889.

d. Europe

VI. FRANCE

47. Guénot. Des effets du déboisement dans les Pyrénées; communication faite au Congrès national des sociétés françaises de géographie, le 5 Août 1895. 25 pp. O. Bordeaux, **1896.**

4. SANITARY INFLUENCES

55. Destruction of mangrove forests (despatches respecting the injurious effect on climate by the). 3 pp. F. [Brisbane, **1884.**]

II. PRINCIPLES OF FORESTRY AND FUNDAMENTAL SCIENCES

H. BOTANY

7. DENDROGRAPHY

d. Europe

III. RUSSIA

80. Медвѣдевъ, Я. С. [Medvyedef, J. S.] Деревья и кустарники Кавказа. 1882. — *Line 2 read:* 300 pp.

III. GENERAL FORESTRY

A. TEXTBOOKS AND MANUALS

2. EUROPE

d. German Empire

94. Fleming, H. F. von. Der vollkommene teutsche Jäger, darinnen die Erde, Geburge, Kräuter und Bäume, Wälder, Eigenschaft der wilden Thiere und Vögel, so wohl historice, als physice und anatomice . . . [20]+400+111+[33] . pp. 1 por. 62 pl. F. Leipzig, 1719.

The 1st part (pp. 1–78) deals with silviculture and forestry.

g. France

98. Bridel, J. B. Manuel pratique du forestier; ouvrage dans lequel on traite de l'estimation, exploitation, conservation, aménagement, repeuplement, des semis & plantations des forêts; avec les moyens de prévenir la disette des bois de construction & de chauffage, &c. On y a joint des moyens simples & faciles de toiser les bois tant en grume qu'équarris. 215+[1] pp. D. Paris, an VI. [1798].

IV. SILVICULTURE

A. TEXTBOOKS AND MANUALS

2. EUROPE

e. German Empire

106. König, G[ottlob]. Die Waldpflege aus der Natur und Erfahrung neu aufgefasst . . . 1849. — *Line 3 add:* —Die Waldpflege . . . Zweite vermehrte Auflage von Dr. Carl Grebe. 16+354 pp. il. O. Gotha, 1859.

h. British Islands

107. Cook, M[oses]. The manner of raising, ordering and improving forrest-trees . . . 1676. — *Line 6 read:* —The manner of raising, ordering and improving forest and fruit-trees, also how to plant, make and keep woods, walks, avenues, lawns, hedges, &c. with several figures in copper-plates, proper for the same . . . [14]+204+[3] pp. 4 pl. sq. Q. London, 1679.

i. France

108. Poedeste, de. Manuel de l'arboriste . . . 1774. — *Line 1 read:* **Poederlé,** E. J. C. H. d'Obnen, *baron.* For correct entry see: III. 106.[1]

B. MISCELLANEOUS PUBLICATIONS ON SILVICULTURE

2. NORTH AMERICA

a. Dominion of Canada

111. Chapais, J. C. The Canadian forester's illustrated guide. 1885. — *Line 1 read:* Guide illustré du sylviculteur canadien. 193 pp. 126 il. 1 tab. O. Montréal, 1883. ——-*Line 3 read:* 1885.

b. United States

111. Warder, J. A. An essay on timber planting in Ohio. 9 pp. O. Columbus, 1880.†

4. EUROPE

i. British Islands

120. Standish, A. New directions of experience . . . 1613. — *Line 1 read:* **Standish,** Arthur. — *Line 8 add:* — New directions of experience authorized by the Kings most excellent Maiesty, as may appeare, for the increasing of timber and fire-wood, with the least waste and losse of ground, with a neare estimation, what millions of acres the kingdome doth containe, what acres is waste ground, whereon little profit for this purpose will arise . . . and how a great store of fire-wood may be raised, forth of hedges, as may plentifully mainetaind the kingdome for all purposes, without losse of ground, so as within thirty yeares all spring-woods may be converted to l g and pasture. [18]+28 pp. sq. D. [London?], 16[85] a e

7. AUSTRALASIA

a. Australia

124. Cultivation of forest trees. Return in connection with the cultivation of forest trees, showing the description of trees and cost of cultivation. [1] p. F. [Brisbane, **1882.**] (Queensland. Legislative assembly, 1882.)

E. COMPOSITION OF FORESTS AND TREATMENT OF PURE AND MIXED FORESTS

1. GENERAL

137. Brandis, *Sir* Dietrich. Pure forests and unmixed forests 1899. — *Line 1 read:* Pure forests and mixed forests.

H. AFFORESTATION

4. EUROPE

j. France

162. [Suzzoni & others.] Rapport sur le reboisement · des forêts de la Corse. [Par une commission, M M. Suzzoni, Benedetti, Casale et Arrighi.] 31 pp. O. Bastia, 1860. (Société d'agriculture, sciences et arts de Bastia.)

162. Germain, Félix. Rapport sur le reboisement présenté au Conseil général de la Drôme, séance du 28 août, 1873. 100 pp. O. Paris & Valence, 1873.

163. Levavasseur, T., *jr.* Traité pratique du boisement . . . 1878. — *Line 8 read:* St. Petersburg, 1877.

V. FOREST PROTECTION

B. PUBLICATIONS RELATING TO CERTAIN COUNTRIES

4. EUROPE

i. Italy

181. Sartorelli, G. B. Mezzi di conservare i boschi. Milano, **1826.** — *Lines 1–2 read:* Osservazioni sopra i mezzi di conservare i boschi mediante la regolarità dei tagli. 117+[1] pp. O. Milano, **1826.**

6. AUSTRALASIA

a. Australia

181. Reserves for timber and state forests. Return to an order made by the Honourable the Legislative Assembly of Queensland . . . showing number and area of all·reserves for timber and state forests in the colony; the district where each is situated; number of nurseries or plantations for growing seedlings for distribution, and where located . . . 4 pp. F. [Brisbane, **1885.**] (Queensland. Legislative assembly, 1885.)

C. FOREST FIRES AND·PROTECTIONS THEREFROM

5. AFRICA

Algeria

184. [Thibault, R.] Des incendies de forêts en Algérie, de leurs causes et des moyens préventifs et défensifs à·leur opposer. [2]+73 pp. O. Constantine & Paris, 1866.

F. INJURIES CAUSED BY METEORIC AND CLIMATIC INFLUENCES

3. INJURIES CAUSED BY FROST

191. Bodde, B. Ideen über die Anwendung der Frühlings-Nachtfröste . . . 1807. — *Line 1 read:* Ideen über die Abwendung.

7. Diseases and injuries caused by insects
e. Various insects of Europe
III. German Empire
206. **Brestchneider**, C. B. . . . . **1798.** — *Line 1 read:*
Bretschneider, C. B.

VII. FOREST MANAGEMENT

A. MANUALS AND HANDBOOKS OF FOREST MANAGEMENT

239. **Däzel**, G. A. Praktische Anleitung zur Forstwirthschaft, besonders zur Vermessung, Taxirung und Eintheilung der Wälder. Ein Handbuch für junge Förster. [8]+474+[6] pp. 4 pl. S. München, **1788.**

B. VARIOUS PUBLICATIONS

3. Europe
a. Scandinavia
247. — Driftsplan . . . **1896.** — *Line 1 read:* Oppermann, A. Driftsplan . . .

d. Belgium
248. **Houba**, J[ulien]. Projet d'amenagement des bois de Rochefort. 84 PP. O. Liège, **1881.**

j. Austria-Hungary
250. **Houba**, J[ulien]. Projet . . . **1881.** — *Transfer to* Belgium, p. 248.

F. VARIOUS PUBLICATIONS ON FOREST VALUATION

256. **Jäger**, [Hermann]. . . . **1873.** — *Line 1 read:* Jäger, (*Forstdirektor*).

VIII. FOREST ENGINEERING

A. GEODESY

263. **Wilke**, C. H. Abhandlung über die fürstl. Jablonowskische Preisaufgabe aus der Erdmesskunst " einen unzugänglichen und undurchsichtigen Wald oder Morast " auf die beste Weise auszumessen, u. s. w." . . . 32 pp. 1 pl. sq. Q. Danzig, 1770.

IX. FOREST POLICY AND ECONOMICS

B. PUBLICATIONS RELATING TO CERTAIN COUNTRIES

1. North America
b. United States
271. **[Wright**, Elizur.] The voice of a tree from the Middlesex Fells. 28 pp. Tt. Boston, **1883.**

6. Australasia
a. Australia
280. **Forest** conservancy. Return to an address of the Honorable the Legislative Assembly . . . Copies of all correspondence . . . within or without the colony . . . upon the subject of forest conservancy; copies of all proclamations, regulations and instructions . . . having for their object the reservation and protection of timber tracts, the preservation of particular species of timber trees, or the prevention of the felling of trees in an immature state. 13 pp. F. [Brisbane, **1876.**] (Queensland. Legislative assembly, 1875.)
280. **Report** from the Select committee on forest conservancy together with the proceedings of the committee and the minutes of evidence. 8+55 pp. F. Brisbane, **1875.** (Queensland. Legislative assembly, 1875.)

XI. FOREST LAWS

A. PRINCIPLES OF FOREST LAWS

313. **Ruginelli**, J. C. Resolutiones de arboribus controversis. **1688.** — *Line 2 add:* — De arboribus controversis resolutionum; id est, Baum-Recht, liber singularis, ex quibus omnes ferè de hac re disceptationes quovis modo obvenientes, facilè dirimi possunt . . . [2]+272+[34] pp. 1 .pl. sq. D. Norimbergae, 1719.

XII. FOREST DESCRIPTIONS, FOREST STATISTICS AND REPORTS ON FOREST CONDITIONS

D. EUROPE

4. German Empire
i. Prussia
352. **Middledorpf**, (*Oberförster, Stoberau*). [Massen-Angaben einiger Weissbuchen und Kiefern im königlichen Forstrevier Stoberau; desgleichen von Eichenblöcken daselbst.] (*Schles. Forstver. Verh.* [1854], pp. 259–260.)

6. Belgium
357. **Crahay**, N. I. & Blondeau, A. Excursion forestière de septembre 1898. La forêt de Mormal. (*Soc. Centr. For. Belge Bull.* VI. 1–16, 61–71. **1899.**)

8. British Islands
b. England
357. **Forresta** de Windsor . . . **1646.** — *Line 4 read:* by inquisition . . . intituled an act for the certainty of forrests . . . 14 pp. D. London, **1646.**

9. France
362. **Crahay**, N. I. & Blondeau, A. Excursion forestière . . . **1899.** — *Transfer to* Belgium, p. 357.

E. ASIA

8. British India
377. **Brandis**, *Sir* Dietrich. On the geographical distribution of forests in India. (*Jour. Bot.* X. 283–285. **1872.** — *Brit. Assoc. Adv. Sci.* XLII. (1872), Note & Abstr., pp. 205–207. 1873.) — On the distribution of forests in India. (*Ocean Highways*, IV. 200–206, map. 1872. — *Scott, Arb. Soc. Trans.* VII. 88–113, map. 1875. — *Ind. For.* IX. 173–183, 221–233, map. 1883.) —— Forstliche Verhältnisse aus den britischindischen Waldungen. (*Burckhardt Aus dem Walde*, VIII. 36–65. 1877.)

XIII. FOREST UTILIZATION

B. VARIOUS ARTICLES ON FOREST EXPLOITATION IN GENERAL

382. **[König**, F. W.] Beyträge zur practischen Forst- und Holzhandels-Wissenschaft. **1790.** — *Line 1 read:* Beyträge zur practischen Forst- und Flozhandels-Wissenschaft.

C. LUMBERING

4. Further conversion of timber
d. Potash
395. **Dossie**, Robert. [The production of pot-ash in our American colonies.] (*In his* Memoirs of agriculture . . . Ed. 2, I. 202–211. 1769.)

D. FOREST PRODUCTS

2. North America
b. Canada
397. **Drummond**, A. T. Canadian timber trees; their destruction . . . 1879. — *Line 1 read:* Canadian timber trees; their distribution.

c. United States
397. Of the **different** uses to which the woods of the American forests are applied in the various parts of the United States. From the French of Mons. Michaux. By the corresponding secretary. (*Mass. Agric. Repos. Jour.* V. 180–188. 1819.)

3. Central and South America
e. Argentina
398. **Niederlein**, Gustav. La riqueza florestal de la Republica Argentina en la Exposicion universal de Paris de 1889. 101 pp. il. Q. n. t-p. [Buenos Aires, **1889.**]

7. Australasia
a. Australia
401. **[Hill**, Walter & Bailey, F. M.] Colonial timber (despatch respecting). 11 pp. F. [Brisbane, **1875.**]
401. **[Hill**, Walter.] Timber, &c. on Frazer's Island; (report of curator of Botanic gardens). 3 pp. F. [Brisbane, **1879.**] (Queensland. Legislative assembly, 1879.)

G. USES OF TIMBER IN CONSTRUCTION

2. RAILWAY CONSTRUCTION, CHIEFLY TIES

424. **Coüard.** Note sur la durée des traverses en bois. XIV. pt. 2, pp. 239–246, pl. 26; XV. pt. 2, pp. 3–13, pl. 1–2; XVI. pt. 1, pp. 235–254, pl. 27–29. [1891–93.] — *From: " Revue générale des chemins de fer, 1891–93."*

4. SHIP- AND BOAT-BUILDING

424. **Instruction** sur les bois de marine; contenant des détails relatifs à la physique & à l'analyse du Chêne, & en ce qui concerne l'économie & l'amélioration du bois en général. 24+230+[4] pp. pl. D. Paris, 1780.

I. FOREST PRODUCTS OTHER THAN WOOD, INCLUDING REFUSE WOOD

6. FOREST SEEDS

438. **Weinzierl,** Theodor von. Die Production und Klengung der Nadelholzsamen in Tirol. (*Oesterr. Vierteljahrsschr. Forstw.* XXXVIII. 42–44. 1888.)

XIV. TAXONOMIC ARRANGEMENT

A. GYMNOSPERMAE

3. PINACEAE

AGATHIS

447. **A. robusta:** [McDowall, A.] Cultivation of Kaurie pine on Fraser island (papers in connection with the). 2 pp. F. [Brisbane, 1882.] (Queensland. Legislative assembly, 1882.)

447. — [McDowall, A. & Hooper, E. D. M.] Kauri pine plantation, Fraser Island (report of district surveyor, Maryborough). 4 pp. 3 maps. F. [Brisbane, 1885.] (Queensland. Legislative assembly, 1885.)

PICEA

P. Abies:

454. — **Tutein Nolthenius,** G. E. H. De invloed . . . 1889. — *Transfer to* PINUS SYLVESTRIS, p. 473.

PINUS

Silviculture

461. **Decrept,** Alfred. L'arbre vert en Picardie, poix et ses coteaux, utilité des résineux dans les sols calcaires. New ed. 24 pp. O. Amiens, 1885.

P. halepensis:

464. **Montvalon,** *comte* de. De la reproduction, de l'éducation et de l'aménagement des bois de Pins. (*Acad. Sci. Aix Mém.* IV. 249–260. 1840.)

P. Pinaster: Forest management

468. — **Burnet,** Raymond. Le Pin maritime . . . [187 . ?] — *Line 1 read:* Brunet, Raymond.

P. sylvestris: Silviculture

473. — **Tutein Nolthenius,** G. E. H. De invloed van den zaaittijd op te ontwikkeling van eenjarige Grove Dennen. (*Nederl. Heidemaat. Tijdschr.* I. 20–22. 1889.)

474. — **Smets,** G[érard]. La culture du Pin sylvestre en Campine. 41+[4] pp. O. Hasselt, Bruxelles & Gand, 1892.

B. ANGIOSPERMAE

B. II. DICOTYLEDONEAE

FAGUS

F. sylvatica: Silviculture

495. **Géne.** Ueber Bodenbearbeitung . . . 1873. — *Line 1 read:* Gené.

27. LEGUMINOSAE

ROBINIA

R. Pseudacacia: Forest management

524. — **Profits** of growing Locust timber. (*United States Commis. Patents Rep. Agric.* 1845, pp. 981–982. 1846.)

BRADLEY BIBLIOGRAPHY

INDEX OF AUTHORS AND TITLES

Page numbers printed in italics denote duplicate or incomplete entries; if several page numbers in arabic figures are given, the entries differ or supplement each other.

a. Der Aschen- und Phosphorgehalt von Holz. 1888. IV. 64.[1]

A. Bark and bark stripping. 1891. IV. 434.[2]

A. Cantua dependens. 1873. III. 694.[3]

A. Cereus triangularis. 1900. III. 622.[1]

A. Conifers in the Edinburgh bot. gardens. 1868. III. 292.

A. Cuatro palabras sobre las instrucciones para el servicio de las ordenaciones. 1891. IV. 550.[1]

A. Dracaena Dennisoni. .1873. III. 335.[1]

A. Euphorbia jacquiniaeflora. 1873. II. 442.[2]

A. Le Ficus elastica. 1845. III. 370.[3]

A. The flow of the sap. 1877. I. 165.

A. El Liparis monacha. 1890. IV. 548.[2]

A. El ministro de agricultura en Austria. 1884. IV. 279.[1]

A. Los montes enajenables en hacienda. 1883. IV. 276.[3]

A. De quelques arbres à introduire dans l'Afrique française. 1854. III. 130.[1]

A. Real decreto sobre ordenación de los montes públicos. 1890. IV. 550.[1]

A. Rimboschimento nel comune di Sirolo. 1864. IV. 165.

A. Russelia juncea as a basket plant. 1873. III. 704.[1]

A. The Stag's-horn Sumach. 1886. III. 528.[1]

A. Verwendung des Rhus typhinia. 1886. III. 528.[3]

A. Voyage à la recherche des Cactus monstres. 1845. III. 622.[1]

A. Der Wald und die Ueberschwemmungen in Venetien. . 1884. IV. 48.[1]

A., A. Repoblacion de los montes. 1889. IV. 546.[1]

A., B. Rimboschimenti. 1889. IV. 166.[1]

A., C. Iets over het oppotten. · 1899. IV. 374.[2]

A., C. S. F. The twelve best autumn-flowering ·Clematises. 1899. III. 391.[1]

A., D. A. Nueva· mira para trabajos topográficos. 1886. IV. 265.

A., E. A. Några rön och försök, angående honungs dagg. 1745. I. 213.[1]

A., F. Exploitabilité relative au taux de placement. 1886. IV. 257.

A., H. B. Dimensions of Minnesota Pine. 1894. IV. 470.[2]

A., H. B. Divi-divi. 1886. .III. 468.[3]

A., H. B. Theekistenhout. 1886. IV. 427.[1]

A., I. De Ficubus e trunco arboris enatis. 1741. II. 149.[2]

A., L. E. La nouvelle maison de campagne. 1854. III. 113.

A., M. Wald . . . in Bosnien. 1889. IV. 374.[2]

A., M. Woods and rainfall. 1884. IV. 51.

A., R. I boschi dell' Umbria. 1881. IV. 364.

A., S. Niektóre wiadomości o gospodarstwie w dobraeh Młyńcu. 1846. IV. 345.

A., S. See A., C. (Russian alphabet.)

A., T. Report on the cultivation of the quiniferous Cinchonae. 1863. III. 713.[3]

A., V. J. Essais de culture en Ardennes . . . de Conifères. 1896. IV. 126.[2]

A., V. J. Revision cadastrale des propriétés boisées. 1898. IV. 266.[1]

A., W. P. Sea-coast gardening. 1873. III. 41.[3]

A.-Z. Freymüthige Gedanken über Holzmangel. 1802. IV. 280.[3]

A friend to improvement, (pseud.). White Thorn. 1842. III. 422.[2]

A noble man's flower gardener, (pseud.). The Magnolia. 1857. III. 399.[1]

A planter from the South, (pseud.). The native Pine of Scotland. 1881. II. 46.[3]

A Rambler, (pseud.). Brussels. 1900. III. 370,[2] 743.[1]

A Sussex naturalist, (pseud.). The Butcher's Broom. 1900. II. 84.[2]

— Some Sussex fruits. 1899. III. 79.

A Tea dealer, (pseud.). Tsiology. 1826. III. 606.

Aa, Christian Pieter E., ROBIDÉ VAN DER. See ROBIDÉ VAN DER AA, C. P. E.

Aa, P. van der. Icones arborum fructicum et herbarum exoti-carum. See ICONES . . . 1720. I. 290.

Aagsaard, K. Veiledning ved en Gaards Drift i Hedeegne. 1811. III. 165.

Aaken, J. M. (or N.) van. Cacao-kultuur. 1880. III. 592.[2]

Over het aankweeken van den Lariks. See OVER het aank-weeken . . . 1822. IV. 448.[3]

Het aankweeken van den Witten Moerbeiboom. 1868. III. 377.

Over den **aanlag** en de bewerking van woeste gronden voor houtcultuur in de provincie Drenthe. · See OVER den aan-lag . . . 1842. IV. 159.[2]

Aanprijzing van boomen en planten ter bevordering van den groei met zeepwater . . . te bevochtigen. 1822. III. 38.[1]

Aanteekeningen betreffende de Kakaokultuur. 1859. III. 592.[1]

Aanteekeningen om te strekken tot handleiding bij de Kaneelkultuur. 1837. III. 405.[2]

Aargau. Abschätzung von Wildschaden. 1894. IV. 197.[1]

Aargauische landwirtschaftliche Mittheilungen. See MIT-THEILUNGEN über Haus-, Land- und Forstwirthschaft . . . III. 24.[1]

Aargauische Weinbaugesellschaft. Jahrheft. III. 24.[1]

Aasen, Ivar. Norske plantenavne. 1860. I. 73.[1]

Aasheim, Arnold Niklas. Descriptiones rariorum plantarum . . . e terra surinamensi fragmentum. See ROTTBÖLL, C. F. 1776. I. 338.[2]

Abacher, N. J. Der vollkommene Blumengärtner. 1819. III. 104.

Abad, José Ramon. La república dominicana. 1888. I. 336.

Abänderung des ¶13 der Dienst-Instruction für die Staats-förster. 1835. IV. 306.

Abazadze, A. See AБАЗАДЗЕ.

Abbad y Lasierra, Iñgo, Fray. Historia geográfica, . . . de la isla de San Juan Bautista de Puerto-Rico. 1788. I. 334.[2]

Abbadie, Antoine Thomson d'. Sur l'usage du café. 1850. III. 739.

Abbado, Michele. Divisione della nervatura . . . in alcune foglie di Buxus. 1895. II. 453.[1]

— L'ibridiamo nei vegetali. 1898. I. 246.[1]

— Mostruosità in fiori di Paeonia Moutan. 1896. II. 200.[2]

Abbans, de JOUFFROY D'. See JOUFFROY D'ABBANS, de.

Abbay, Rev. Richard: New Caledonia. 1077. II. 96.[1]

— Observations on Hemileia vastatrix. 1880. III. 735.

— A visit to the Big trees. 1877. II. 51,[1] 624.[1]

Abbe, Cleveland. Smoke from forest fires. 1895. IV. 193.[1]

— Wirkung der Waldbrände. 1895. IV. 193.[1]

Abbene, Angelo. Essai physiologico-chimique sur . . . mag-nésie. 1838. I. 157.

— Saggio fisiologico-chimico . . . magnesia. 1838. I. 157.

Abbes Gabema, S. Friesche lust-gaärde. 1687. I. 283.

Abbeville — Société d'émulation. See SOCIÉTÉ . . . I. 23.

Abbey, George. On the destruction of an Elm-tree. 1898. III. 365.[1]

Abbey grounds. Tresco, Scilly. 1898. III. 334.[2]

Abbildung der Bäume und Sträuche . . . in Deutschland. 1788. III. 68,[2] IV. 81.[2]

Abbildung in- und ausländischer Höltzer. See HOUTTUYN, Martin. 1773. I. 124.

Abbildung inn- und ausländischer Hoelzer. See SEELIGMANN. 1773. IV. 17.

Abbildung und Beschreibung der gefährlichsten . . . Gift-gewächse. 1842. III. 73.

Abbildung von 51 Pfirsich Gattungen. See ANTOINE, Franz. 1821. III. 439.[3]

Abbildungen . . . empfehlenswerther Haselnüsse. 1885. ·III. 357.[1]

Abbildungen von Arzeneygewächsen. See ZORN, Johannes. 1779. III. 55.

Abbildungen von mehr als 30,000 Pflanzenarten. See DIET-RICH, D. N. F. 1846. I. 269.

Abbot, Charles. Flora bedfordiensis. 1798. I. 396.
Abbot, H. B. Changes in our streams. 1895. IV. 51.
— Changes in the volume of streams. 1894. IV. 51.
Abbott, Charles Conrad. Acorns and Oaks. 1889. II. 132.[1]
— Last year's leaves. 1888. III. 205.[2]
Abbott, Francis. Catalogue of plants . . . Royal society's gardens, Queen's Park, Hobart Town. 1865. I. 69.[1]
— Tasmania. 1888. III. 283.[1]
Abbott, Helen Cecilia De Silver. The chemical basis of plant forms. 1887. I. 154.
— A chemical study of Yucca angustifolia. 1886. ·II· 87.[2]
— On haematoxylin in the bark of Saraca. 1887. II. 383.[2]
— Plant analysis as an applied science. 1887. IV. 64.[1]
— Preliminary analysis of the bark of Fouquieria. 1885. III. 612.[2]
— Yucca angustifolia; a chemical study. 1886. II. 87.[2]
Abbott, Rosa G. Electrical attraction of trees. 1897. IV. 412.[2]
Abbott, Thomas W. The original Ribston Pippin Apple tree. 1857. II. 267.[2]
Abbott, W. E. Forest destruction in New South Wales. 1889. IV. 49.[1]
— Ringbarking and its effects. 1880. ·IV· 385.[1] ·
— Report on certain Indian fibres. 1896. III. 762.[2] 763.[1]
— Silk-cotton (floss) of Calotropis procera. 1897. III. 692.[1]
Abel, Friedrich. Die Familie der Cycadeen und ihre Arten. 1886. III. 284.[1]
— Die Gattung Citrus. 1898. III. 497.[2]
— Rhododendron diversifolium Vesely. 1899. II. 679.[1]
— Ueber die Yucca und ihre Arten. 1886. III. 339.[2]
Abel, G. F. See REITER, J. D. & ABEL, G. F.
Abel, Heinrich Kaspar. Neu angelegtes medizinisches Kräuter-Paradies-Bärtlein. 1719. I. 290.
Abel, Lothar. Altes und Neues über Anpflanzungen. 1885. IV. 24.[1]
— Die Bäume. 1894. I. 516.
— Die Baumpflanzungen. 1882. III. 202.[1]
— Remarks about planting both old and new. 1885. IV. 24.[1]
Abel, W. Ueber Fuchsien-Kultur. 1845. . III. 639.[2]
— Ueber Thee-Kultur. 1845. III. 600.[1]
Abela y Sainz de Andino, Eduardo. El Naranjo. 1879. II. 401.[1] III. 494.[2]
Abeleven, Th. H. A. J. · Grondbeginselen der plantenkunde. 1868. I. 91.
— See also GEVERS DEYNOOT, P. M. E. & ABELEVEN, T. H. A. J.
The Abelias. 1885. III. 748.[1]
Abelien. 1897. III. 748.[1]
Abell, A. S. Co. Maryland, its resources. 1893. III. 264.[1]
Abels, A. P. G. Koffie-kultuur. 1871. III. 726.[2]
— Het kunstmatig droogen van koffij. 1866. III. 592,[1] 786.[2]
— De kwaliteitsachteruitgang der Java koffij. 1867. III. 729.[2]
Aben Mohamed Ben Ahmed Ebn el Awam. See YAḤYÁ IBN MUḤAMMAD IBN AḤMAD IBN AL 'AWAMM (abū Zakariyā) al Abišālī.
Abendroth, Wilhelm Friedrich. De Coffea. 1825. III. 738.
Abercrombie, John. The British fruit-gardener. 1779. III. 141.
— The complete forcing-gardener. 1781. III. 176.[1]
— The complete wall-tree pruner. · 1783. III. 171.
— The garden vademecum. 1789. III. 81.
— The gardener's pocket dictionary. 1786. III. 30.
— A general system of trees and shrubs. 178.? III. 78.[1]
— The propagation and botanical arrangements of plants. 1784. III. 81.
— Der Treibhausgärtner. 1781. III. 176.[1]
— The universal gardener's kalendar. 1789. III. 109.
— Vollständige Anleitung zur Erziehung . . . aller . . . Obst- und Fruchtbäume. 1779. III. 141.
— See also MAWE, Thomas & ABERCROMBIE, John.
Abert, James W. Notes [of a journey from Fort Leavenworth to Bent's Fort]. 1848. I. 318, V. xvii.[1]

— On Palm trees. 1884. II. 64.[1]
— Report . . . of his examination of New Mexico. 1848. I. 322.
L' Abete d' Obersold. 1863. IV. 447.[1]
Abhängigkeit der Blitzschläge von der Bodenbeschaffenheit. 1882. IV. 194.
Abhängigkeit der Quellen. 1830. IV. 49.[2]
Abhandlung über den ökonomischen Nutzen des wilden Kastanien-Baums. 1806. III. 537.[2]
Abhandlung vom Caffe. See LA ROQUE, Jean de. 1717. III. 738.
Abhandlung vom Pottaschsieden. See WILDENHAYN. 1771. IV. 395.
Abhandlung vom wilden Kastanienbaume. 1772. III. 537.[1]
Abhandlung von den Maulbeerbäumen. See POMIER. 1754. III. 372.[2]
Abhandlung von der Regalität derer Jagten in Teutschland. See BURI, F. C. von. 1744. IV. 316.
Abhandlungen aus dem Forst- und Jagdwesen. IV. 13.[2]
Abhandlungen aus dem Gebiete der Naturwissenschaften. See NATURWISSENSCHAFTLICHER VEREIN IN HAMBURG. I. 14.
Abhandlungen über wichtige Gegenstände des Forstwesens. 1806. IV. 213, 394.
Abhandlungen und Vorträge aus dem Gesammtgebiete der / Naturwissenschaften. See SAMMLUNG naturwissenschaftlicher Vorträge. I. 14.
Abich, Hermann. Ueber Natronseen auf der Araxes-Ebene. 1847. II. 187.[2]
Abl. On the use of Coca leaves. 1865. III. 492.[1]
Ablaing van Gressenberg, d' & others. Het snoeijen der . boomen. 1854. III. 170.
Ablett, William H. Arboriculture for amateurs. 188.? III. 106.[1]
— The culture of Osiers. 1880. III. 348.
— English trees and tree-planting. 1880. III. 106.[2]
Abnormal growth in Hyophorbe indica. 1900. II. 69.[1]
Abnormal pears. 1881. II. 280.[1]
Abo, R. E. N. d'. De landbouw in de bergstreken. 1872. III. 128.
Aboville, R. d'. Rapport sur les effets de l'hiver 1890-91. 1891. III. 49.[1]
Abramowski, (Landrath des ·Elbinger Kreises). Über die Anlage der Obstbaumschulgärten. 1834. III. 137.
Abrégé des élémens de botanique. See TOURNEFORT, J. P. de. 1749. I. 254.[2]
Abrégé des instructions sur le jardinage. See ARDÈNE, J. P. R. d'. · 1767. III. 112.
Abreu Lacerda, Augusto de. A bacia do Rio das Mortes. 1895. V. xviii.[1]
Abric, A. Sur l'emploi du bitume de Judée. 1882. III. 560.
Abrine. 1892. III. 462.[2]
L'Abrine. 1892. III. 462.[2]
Abriss von der Forstbewirthschaftung in den königlich Preussischen Staaten. 1792. IV. 25.
Abromeit, Johannes. Über die Anatomie des Eichenholzes. 1884. II. 131.[2]
— Berichtigung des Sanio'schen Aufsatzes. 1885. I. 388.
— Botanische Ergebnisse der . . . Grönlandsexpedition. 1899. I. 309.[2]
— Flora von Ost- und Westpreussen. 1898. I. 390.
— Ueber Lycium-Arten. 1892. II. 772.[2]
— Über neue Pflanzen in Ostpreussen. 1893. II. 277.[2]
— Über die in Preussen bis jetzt beobachteten wilden Rosen. 1893. II. 284.[2]
— Zwei für Nordostdeutschland neu entdeckte Pflanzen. 1899. II. 107.[2]
Abrus precatorius Willd. and its therapeutic use. 1884. II. 462.[2]
Abschätzungs- und Einrichtungs-Operat des Gemeinde-waldes von Ebringen. See SCHERER & WASMER. 1846. IV. 247.[2]
Abschieds-Rede des Zirbel-Baumes zu Hammel. 1762. II. 41.[1]
Abschrift eines Erkenntnisses des königl. Gerichtshofes zur Entscheidung der Kompetenz-Konflikte. 1859. IV. 320.
Absorption of ammonia by . . . plants. 1879. I. 161.[1]
Absorption of water by . . . plants. 1879. I. 161.[1]
Ueber die Abstammung . . . des Kautschuks. 1874. III. 231.
Das Absterben der Pflänzchen in Nadelholz-Saaten. 1856. IV. 209.[2]
An abstract of several sorts of trees. See LAWSON. 1733. III. 261.[1]

Abstract of the general results which form the basis of Galesio's "Theory of the reproduction." 1820. I. 205.
Abt, Johann. Gründliche Anweisung zur Ausmessung und Berechnung des Bau- und Nutz-Holzes. 1783. IV. 220.
Die Abtheilung derer Gehölze in jährliche Gehaue. 1760. IV. 250.
Abū 'Ali. See IBN SĪNĀ.
Abu Zacaria Iáhia Aben Mohamed Ben Ahmed Ebn el Awam. See YAḤYĀ IBN MUḤAMMAD IBN AḤMAD IBN AL 'AWĀMM (abū Zakariyā) al Abishīli.
Les abus du déboisement. 1897. IV. 551.
Acacia, (pseud.). Wattle cultivation as an industry. 1884. IV. 520.
L'Acacia commun. See Ueber den GEMEINEN . . . 1858. IV. 523.
L'Acacia convient-il en Ardenne (schistes rouges)? 1900. IV. 523.
Acacia de Sainte-Hélène. 1832. III. 466.
Academia caes.-leopoldina naturae curiosorum. Ephemerides. See ACADEMIA NATURAE CURIOSORUM. I. 10.
Academia cæssarea leopoldino-carolina germanica naturæ curiosorum. See ACADEMIA NATURAE CURIOSORUM. I. 10.
Academia caesarea leopoldino-carolina naturae curiosorum. Acta. See ACADEMIA NATURAE CURIOSORUM. I. 10.
Academia das sciencias de Lisboa. See ACADEMIA REAL . . . I. 24.
Academia de ciencias exactas . . . de Madrid. See REAL ACADEMIA . . . I. 24.
Academia de ciencias médicas, físicas y naturales de la Habana. See REAL ACADEMIA . . . I. 7.
Academia electoralis scientiarum et elegantiorum literarum Theodoro-palatina. Historia. I. 10.
Academia medica de Madrid. See REAL ACADEMIA . . . I. 24.
Academia nacional de ciencias en Córdoba. Boletin. I. 7.
Academia naturae curiosorum. Miscellanea. I. 10.
Academia real das sciencias de Lisboa. Jornal. Memorias. I. 24.
Academia real das sciencias de Lisboa. Memorias. III. 23.
Academia Rheno-Traiectina. Annales. I. 15.
Academia scientiarum imperialis petropolitana. Acta. Commentarii. I. 9, 519.
Academia scientiarum instituti bononiensis. Novi commentarii. See BONONIENSIS SCIENTIARUM . . . I. 24.
Academia Theodoro-palatina. Acta. See ACADEMIA ELECTORALIS SCIENTIARUM ET ELEGANTIORUM LITERARUM THEODORO-PALATINA. I. 10.
Académie d'horticulture de Gand. Journal. See SOCIÉTÉ D'HORTICULTURE . . . III. 15.
Académie d'horticulture (de Paris). Journal. III. 18.
Académie de Marseille. Mémoires. I. 20.
Académie de médicine. See ACADÉMIE ROYALE . . . I. 20.
Académie de Metz. See SOCIÉTÉ DES LETTRES, SCIENCES, ARTS . . . DE METZ. I. 15.
Académie de Reims. See ACADÉMIE NATIONALE . . . I. 20.
Académie de Stanislas. Mémoires. See SOCIÉTÉ ROYALE DES SCIENCES ET BELLES-LETTRES DE NANCY. I. 24.
Académie des inscriptions et belles-lettres de l'Institut impérial de France. See ACADÉMIE ROYALE DES SCIENCES. I. 20.
Académie des sciences . . . See also ACADÉMIE ROYALE DES SCIENCES . . .
Académie des sciences, agriculture, arts et belles-lettres d'Aix. Bulletin. Mémoires. See SOCIÉTÉ DES AMIS DES SCIENCES . . . I. 520.
Académie des sciences, arts et belles-lettres de Dijon. Mémoires. I. 20.
Académie des sciences, belles-lettres et arts de Clermont-Ferrand. Annales. Mémoires. I. 20.
Académie des sciences, belles-lettres et arts de Rouen. Précis. I. 20.
Académie des sciences de Cracovie. Bulletin. I. 27.
Académie des sciences [de Paris]. Comptes rendus. See ACADÉMIE ROYALE DES SCIENCES. I. 20.
Académie des sciences, des lettres et des beaux-arts de Belgique. See ACADÉMIE ROYALE DES SCIENCES . . . I. 16.
Académie des sciences et belles-lettres d'Angers. Mémoires. See SOCIÉTÉ ACADÉMIQUE DE MAINE-ET-LOIRE. I. 22.
Académie des sciences et belles-lettres de Bruxelles. See ACADÉMIE ROYALE DES SCIENCES . . . DE BELGIQUE. I. 16.
Académie des sciences et lettres de Montpellier. Mémoires. I. 20.
Académie (imperiale) de Metz. Mémoires. See SOCIÉTÉ DES LETTRES, SCIENCES, ARTS . . . DE METZ. I. 15.

Académie impériale des sciences . . . See also ACADÉMIE ROYALE DES SCIENCES . . .
Académie impériale des sciences de St.-Pétersbourg. Bulletin. Mélanges biologiques. Mémoires. Recueil. See ACADEMIA SCIENTIARUM IMPERIALIS PETROPOLITANA. I. 9, 519.
Académie impériale et royale des sciences et belles-lettres de Bruxelles. See ACADÉMIE ROYALE DES SCIENCES . . . DE BELGIQUE. I. 16.
Académie internationale de géographie botanique. Bulletin. See LE MONDE des plantes. I. 22.
Académie nationale de Reims. Travaux. I. 20.
Académie nationale des sciences . . . See ACADÉMIE ROYALE DES SCIENCES . . .
Académie royale de Belgique. Bulletin. See ACADÉMIE ROYALE DES SCIENCES . . . DE BELGIQUE. I. 16.
Académie royale de médicine (Paris). Bulletin. Mémoires. I. 20.
Académie (royale) des inscriptions et belles-lettres de l'Institut impérial de France. Mémoires. See ACADÉMIE ROYALE DES SCIENCES. I. 20.
Académie royale des sciences . . . See also ACADÉMIE DES SCIENCES . . .
Académie royale des sciences, arts et belles-lettres de Caen. Mémoires. I. 20.
Académie royale des sciences, belles-lettres et arts de Besançon. Séances. I. 20.
Académie royale des sciences, belles-lettres et arts de Bordeaux. Actes. Recueil. I. 20.
Académie royale des sciences, belles-lettres et arts de Lyon. Mémoires. I. 20.
Académie royale des sciences de Turin. Mémoires. See MISCELLANEA philosophico-mathematica . . . I. 25.
Académie royale des sciences, des lettres et des beaux-arts de Belgique. Bulletins. Mémoires. I. 16, V. VII.
Académie royale des sciences et belles-lettres de Bruxelles. Mémoires. Nouveaux mémoires. See ACADÉMIE ROYALE DES SCIENCES . . . DE BELGIQUE. I. 16.
Académie royale des sciences et des lettres de Berlin. Histoire. Mémoires. I. 10.
Académie royale des sciences, inscriptions et belles-lettres de Toulouse. Bulletin. Histoire. Mémoires. I. 20.
Académie royale des sciences (Paris). Histoire. Mémoires. I. 20.
Academy of natural sciences of Philadelphia. Journal. Proceedings. I. 4.
Academy of science of St. Louis. Transactions. I. 4.
L'Acajou au Congo. 1896. IV. 407.
L'Acajou-cedra. 1894. IV. 525.
Acajou-olie. 1883. III. 524.
Accademia d' agricoltura, arti . . . dello stato veneto. Raccolta . . . I. 24.
Accademia d' agricoltura . . . di Verona. Memorie. I. 24.
Accademia de' fisiocritici. See REALE ACCADEMIA DELLE SCIENZE DETTA DE' FISIOCRITICI. I. 25.
Accademia de' georgofili. See REALE ACCADEMIA ECONOMICO-AGRARIA DEI GEORGOFILI. III. 23.
Accademia degli aspiranti naturalisti. Annali. Bullettino. I. 24.
Accademia dei lincei. See REALE ACCADEMIA . . .
Accademia delle scienze . . . See also REALE ACCADEMIA DELLE SCIENZE . . .
Accademia delle scienze dell' istituto di Bologna. Memorie. See BONONIENSIS SCIENTIARUM . . . I. 24.
Accademia delle scienze di Torino. See MISCELLANEA philosophico-mathematica . . . I. 25.
Accademia delle scienze fisiche . . . di Napoli. Atti. Rendiconti. I. 24.
Accademia di scienze . . . See REALE ACCADEMIA . . . I. 25.
Accademia di scienze . . . di Padova. See CESAREO-REGIA ACCADEMIA . . . I. 24.
Accademia di scienze e lettere . . . di Palermo. Atti. See ACCADEMIA PALERMITANA. . I. 24.
Accademia economico-agraria dei georgofili di Firenze. See REALE ACCADEMIA . . . III. 23.
Accademia Gioenia di scienze naturali in Catania. Atti. I. 24.
Accademia lucchese di scienze. See REALE ACCADEMIA . . . I. 25.
Accademia napolitana delle scienze. See REALE ACCADEMIA DELLE SCIENZE, SEZIONE DELLA SOCIETÀ REALE BORBONICA. I. 25.
Accademia palermitana. Saggi . . . I. 24.
Accademia pontaniana. Atti. I. 24.
Accademia pontificia de' nuovi lincei. Atti. I. 24.

Accademia valdarnese del Poggio. Memorie. I. 24.¹
Acción de la luz sobre las plantas. *See* AZIONE delle luce . . . 1890. IV. 543.²
A acclimação de Coniferas estrangeiras. 1894. IV. 125.¹
Acclimatation en Europe du Rhus vernicifera. 1892. III. 528.²
Acclimatisation of exotic trees in Scotland. 1873. III. 488.²
Acclimatisation society of Victoria. Report. III. 27.¹
Acclimatization experiments with medicinal plants. 1878. III. 482.²
Acclimatization in Queensland. 1877. III. 50.¹
Acclimazione del Bagolaro in Francia. 1863. IV. 126.²
Acclimazione del Bambu'. 1863. IV. 485.¹
Acclimazione del Mogano. 1865. IV. 127.¹
Acclimazione di alberi del Canadà. 1864. IV. 127.¹
Acclimazione di Palme dell' Australia. 1863. IV. 127.¹
Acclimazione in Francia dell' Albero a pane. 1863. IV. 519.¹
An account of a sort of sugar made of the juice of the Maple in Canada. 1686. IV. 526.²
Account of brucine. 1820. III. 507.¹
An account of East Florida. *See* STORK, William. 1767. I. 317.¹
Account of Mr. Saul's fruit-gatherer. 1822. III. 173.²
An account of the Cinnamon tree in Ceylon. 1731. II. 224.¹
An account of the Larch plantations. 1832. IV. 449.
An account of the Oak at Cowthorp. *See* MAUDE, Thomas. 1774. II. 137.¹
An account of the petrological, botanical and zoölogical collections made in Kerguelen's Land. 1879. I. 303.
Account of the qualities and uses of coal-tar. 1785. IV. 436.¹
Account of the Rasamala. 1806. III. 416.²
An account of the Sugar Maple-tree. 1797. III. 536.¹
An account of the vertues of faba S.ti Ignatii. 1700. III. 682.¹
Accum, Friedrich. Physische und chemische Beschaffenheit der Baumaterialien. . 1826. IV. 408.
An accurate description of the Cacao-tree. 1673. III. 592.¹
Acebal, Ricardo. Los trabajos de repoblación . . . de Covadonga. 1884. IV. 165.
— Los trabajos de repoblación en la montaña de Covadonga. 1888. IV. 546.²
Aceite de madera. 1886. IV. 433.¹
Los aceites de madera de Cochinchina. 1887. IV. 528.²
Acer californicum Koch. 1898. IV. 526.²
Acer platanoides, anomalie. 1886. IV. 526.²
Acerbi, Giuseppe. Travels through Sweden. 1802· I. 352, V. XVIII.²
— Delle Viti italiane. 1825. III. 546.
Achard, E. L. La culture des plantes à caoutchouc en Cochinchine. 1899. III. 149.
— Les écorces tannantes de l'Inde. 1900. IV. 435.
— Les maladies de l'Aréquier. 1900. III. 320.¹
— Rapport sur les champs d'essais de la Cochinchine. 1900. III. 129.¹
— Rapport sur un essai de plantation . . . d'Isonandra gutta. 1900. III. 149.
Achard, Franz Karl. Verzeichniss einer Sammlung Treib-, Gewächs-, u. Orangeriehauspflanzen. 1796. I. 44.
Acharius, Erik. Rosa senticosa, ny svensk Törnbuske. 1813. II. 298.²
Achenbach, (*Oberconsistorial-Secretair*), Noack, & Gernet. Ueber Geschichte . . . der Rose. 1870. V. XXIX.¹
Achenbach, H. *See* АХЕНБАХЪ, Г.
Achilles, K. Eucalyptus globulus. 1864. III. 634.²
Achintre, Joseph. *See* FONVERT, Amédée de & ACHINTRE, Joseph.
Acht, Kazimierz. Katalog szczegółowy dla zbiorowej wystawy. 1894. III. 127.¹
— Nasze gospodarstwo lasowe. 1898. IV. 369.
Acide gymnémique. 1894. III. 693.¹
Acide gynocardique; l'huile de Chaulmoogra. 1893. III. 614.²
Acker, E. von. Kleine Mittheilungen. 1883. III. 524,² 648.¹
Acker und Wald. 1867. IV. 274.¹
Ackerbauministerium in Wien. *See* K. K. ACKERBAUMINIS-TERIUM . . . III. 25.
Ackerman, Rich. Arr. Landtmanna genväg til fruktträn. *See* TROZELIUS, C. B. 1780. III. 134.¹
Ackermann. Nachricht und Beschreibung einer . . . Obst-Sorten. *See* HEINECKEN, K. H. von. 1803. III. 70.¹
Ackermann. Der Waldbau in ökonomischer und technischer Beziehung. 1824. IV. 117.
Ackermann, Eugène. Au pays du caoutchouc. 1900. III. 230.
Ackermann, Jakob Fidelis. Ueber die Natur der Gewächse. 1812. I. 33.
Ackermann, M. W. Th. Het enten van ·Koffie. 1896. III. 733.¹
Acloque, Alexandre. Sur un cas de foliation anormale chez Syringa. 1894. II. 716.¹
— L'inflorescense de Chèvrefeuille Périclymène. 1893. II. 839.¹
Acoluthus, Johannes Carolus. Ex abusu baccarum Juniperi diabetes. 1754. III. 303.²
Acorambonus, Felix. Explanatio sententiarum difficilium in Theophrasti libris de plantis. 1590. I. 283.
"Acorn," (*pseud.*). English timber. 19 . . ? IV. 398.²
Acosta, F. de P. Estudios sobre las materias colorantes de Venezuela. 1868. III. 236, 613.¹
Acosta, José d'. *See* ACOSTA, Joseph de.
Acosta, Joseph de. Histoire naturelle et moralle des Indes. 1590. III. 217.
— Historia natural y moral de las Indias. 1590. III. 217.
— Historia naturale e morale delle Indie. 1590. III. 217.
— Historie naturael ende morael van de westersche Indien. 1590. III. 217.
— Naturalis et moralis Indiae Occidentalis historia. 1590. III. 217.
— The naturall and morall historie of the East and West Indies. 1590. III. 217.
Acosta, TELLÈS D'. *See* TELLÈS D'ACOSTA.
Acqua, Camillo. Alcune osservazioni sul luogo di origine dell' ossalato calcico. 1889. I. 139.
— Contribuzione alla conoscenza della cellula vegetale. 1891. I. 137.
— Contribuzione allo studio dei cristalli. 1888. I. 139.
— Sulla distribuzione dei fasci fibrovascolari. 1887. I. 134.¹
— Sulla formazione dei granuli d' amido. 1897. I. 140.²
— Sulla formazione dei granuli d' amido nel Pelargonium. 1893. II. 391.²
— Sulla formazione dell' ossalato calcico. 1889. I. 139.
— La formazione della parete cellulare nei peli aerei della Lavatera cretica. 1894. II. 525.¹
— Nuova contribuzione allo studio dei cristalli di ossalato di calcio. 1889. I. 139.
Le acque e le foreste in Italia. 1861. IV. 48.¹
Acquisition de forêts ou de terrains à boiser. 1899. IV. 274.²
Acrel, Johan. Bästa sättet at för röta, sprickor och mask länge förvara Ek-virke. 1776. IV. 416.²
Acrel, Johan Gustaf. De usu Linnaeae medico. 1788. III. 749.²
Acrelius, Israel. A history of New Sweden. 1874. III. 263.¹
An act for the protection of the forests, fish and game of the state. 1900. IV. 314.²
An act to codify and amend the laws relative to the preservation of trees. 1899. IV. 314.²
An act to encourage the planting of timber-trees. 1733. IV. 40.²
An act to establish a forest commission. 1885. IV. 314.²
An act to preserve the forests from destruction by fire. 1878. IV. 314.¹
An act to preserve the forests from destruction by fire. 1896. IV. 181.²
An act to remove doubts regarding the Madras forest act. 1882. IV. 332.¹
Acta eruditorum. I. 10.
Acta helvetica . . . *See* SOCIETAS PHYSICO-MEDICA BASILIEN-SIS. I. 27.
Acta literaria et scientiarum Sueciae. *See* ACTA literaria Sueciae. I. 8.¹
Acta literaria Sueciae. I. 8.¹
Actenmässige Nachricht von denen Wald-Nuzungs-Etats. 1790. IV. 247.²
Actes de la Conférence phylloxérique internationale. 1878. III. 571.
Actes du congrès de vignerons . . . en France. 1843. III. 554.²

Actes du congrès de vignerons et de pomologistes. 1847. III. 124.[1]

Action du gaz sulfureux. 1895. I. 211.

Action nuisible de l'acide sulfureux. 1881. I. 211.

The **action** of light . . . upon cuttings. 1844. III. 157.[2]

The **action** of the New Jersey state federation of women's clubs . . . 1896. IV. 39.[1]

Sur l'**action** physiologique du kola. 1897. III. 590.[2]

Acton, E. Hamilton. *See* DARWIN, Francis & ACTON, E. H.

Acuña, Cristoval d'. A new discovery of the great river of the Amazons. 1641. III. 268.[2]

— Nuevo . . . s . . . m, n, del gran rio de las Amazonas. 1641. III. 268.[de cubri ie to]

Adair, D. L. Fruit bud grafting. 1861. III. 164.[1]

— Improvement and domestication of the Wild Cherry. 1860. III. 442.[2]

— Improvement of the native Plum. 1869. III. 432.[2]

— Inarching. An improvement. 1861. III. 161.

— The Persimmon. 1860. III. 670.[1]

Adair, John. On the acclimation of plants. 1870. III. 43.

— Hints on the culture of ornamental plants. 1878. III. 110.[1]

Adam. Anacardium occidentale. 1854. III. 523.[2]

Adam. Culture . . . des Poinsettia pulcherrima. 1880. III. 518.[1]

Adam. Taschenbuch zur richtigen Berechnung des Holzes. 1801. IV. 221.

Adam, Georg & **Keyser**, G. A. Ueber die Veredlung des Obstes. 1800. III. 50.[1]

— *See also* KEYSER, G. A. & ADAM, Georg.

Adam, James. Reports on collecting . . . the seeds of forest trees. 1832. IV. 147.[1]

Adam, Johann Michael Friedrich. Decades quinque novarum specierum plantarum Caucasi et Iberiae. 1805. I. 368.[2]

Adam, V. E. La Vigne; traité pratique. 1886. III. 561.

Adam, William. The gem of the Peak. 1838. I. 398, 533.

Adams, W. R. HORA. *See* HORA ADAMS, W. R.

Adamek, Karel. Lesni hospodářstvi Francie. 1879. IV. 360.

Adami, Ernst Daniel. Freye Gedanken über das Seltne . . . an einem zu Landeshut 1755 gefällten Buchenbaum . . . 1756. I. 210.[1]

Adami, J. A. De oleo cajeput. 1783. III. 636.

Adamović, Lujo. Beiträge zur Flora von Südostserbien. 1892. II. 350.[1]

— Die mediterranen Elemente der serbischen Flora. 1899. I. 451.

— Die Vegetationsformationen Ostserbiens. 1898. I. 451.

— *See also* Адамовић, Лујо.

Adams, Andrew Leith. Letter . . . relative to poisoning with Euphorbia. 1862. III. 512,[2] 513.[1]

Adams, Arthur. On the variation of colour. 1840. I. 184, 244.[1]

— **Baikie**, W. B. & **Barron**, Charles. A manual of natural history for the use of travellers. 1854. I. 35.

Adams, C. K. The needs of education in forestry. 1892. IV. 30.[1]

Adams, D. W. A common-sense view of pruning. 1868. III. 170.

— Evergreens — A great necessity for Iowa. 1868. III. 117.[2]

— Fruits in northern Iowa. 1870. III. 133.

— List of Apples for Iowa. 1869. III. 425.[7]

Adams, F. N. New Zealand botany. 1885. I. 507.

Adams, George. Essays on the microscope. 1787. I. 36.[1]

— Micrographia illustrata. 1746. I. 36.[1]

Adams, J. S. Florida; its climate, soil. 1869. III. 264.[1]

Adams, James. On the botany of Hikurangi Mountain. 1898. I. 508.[1]

— On the botany of Te Aroha Mountain. 1885. I. 507.

— On the botany of Te Moehau Mountain. 1889. I. 508.[1]

— On the botany of the Thames goldfields. 1884. I. 503.

Adams, James Foster Alleyne. Sanitary forest-culture. 1884. IV. 55.[1]

Adams, Michael F. Descriptio novae speciei Azaleae. 1810. II. 679.[2]

— Descriptiones plantarum minus cognitarum Sibiriae. 1817. I. 453.[1]

Adams, T. W. The Ash. 1896. III. 72.[1]

— The Elm. 1896. III. 364.[1]

— Forest tree planting. 1891. IV. 124.[2]

— Forest trees. Effect of long drought. 1886. IV. 192.[1]

— Growth of trees in New Zealand. 1896. III.132.[1]

— List of trees growing at Greendale. 1897. IV. 18.[1]

— Notes on tree planting. 1896. III. 132.[2]

— Planting trees for shelter. 1897. III. 215.[2]

— Trees and shrubs growing at Greendale. 1898. IV. 18.[2]

Adams, W. Bridges. Yerva de Paraguay. 1856. III. 530.[2]

Adamski, Max Joseph Adalbert Andreas Anton. Dissertatio sistens Prodromum historiae rei herbariae in Polonia. 1825. I. 80.[1]

Adamski, Wojciech. Materjały do flory W. Ks. Poznańskiego Zebral. 1896. I. 389.

Adamson, James. Botanic institution [of Cape Town]. 1848. I. 69.[1]

Adámszky, József. A Clematis. 1898. III. 389.[2]

Adanson, Aglaé. Catalogue des arbres, arbrisseaux, arbustes et plantes . . . à Baleine. 1825. I. 57.

— Extrait d'une lettre au sujet des Hortensias bleus. 1841. III. 412.[1]

— Lettre au sujet du Cytise Adam. 1840. II. 368.[2]

— La maison de campagne. 1825. III. 113.

Adanson, G. de ROCQUIGNY-. *See* ROCQUIGNY-ADANSON, G. de.

Adanson, Michel. Description d'un arbre . . . appelé Baobab. 1763. II. 528.[2]

— Deuxième mémoire sur le Gommier blanc. 1781. III. 463.[1]

— Examen de la question si les espèces changent. 1772. I. 243.[2]

— Familles des plantes. 1763. I. 257, 530.[1]

— Familles naturelles des plantes. 1763. I. 530.[1]

— Histoire de la botanique. 1763. I. 257,

— Histoire naturelle du Sénégal. 1757. I. 490.

— Premier mémoire sur l'Acacia des anciens. 1777. III. 463.[1]

— A voyage to Senegal. 1757. I. 490.

Adanson, Paul Napoléon, DOÛMET-. *See* DOÛMET-ADANSON, P. N.

Adansonia. I. 20.

Adcock, George Henry. Census of plants of the Cape Otway forest. 1895. I. 504.

— Census of plants of the Geelong district. 189. ? I. 504.

— On the flora of Australia. 1898. I. 505.

Addenet, R. F. De la destruction des forêts dans ses rapports physiques. 1839. IV. 43.

Additions to the Hortus Kewensis. *See* HOOKER, W. J. 1846. I. 54.

Additions to Warner's Plantae woodfordienses. *See* FORSTER, Edward. 1784. I. 395.

Address to the Botanical society of Edinburgh. *See* DICKSON, Alexander. 1866. II. 1.

The **addresses** of the president and treasurer at the . . . meeting of the subscribers to the Hull botanical garden. 1812. I. 522.[1]

Adee, Alvey A. Fruit culture in foreign countries. 1890. III. 132.[2]

Adelaide — Philosophical society. *See* PHILOSOPHICAL . . . I. 29.[1]

Adelante. 1892. IV. 551.[2]

Adelkofer, Marquart. Gründliche Gartenschule. 1778. III. 103.

Adelmann, Heinrich. Kurze praktische Anleitung zum Obstbau. 1881. III. 138.

Adema, W. R. Beschouwingen over de plantwijzen van de Djagoeng- en Koffie-kultuur. 1886. III. 730.

— Handleiding voor de . . . kennis van de plantwijzen. 1899. III. 100.

— Nadere beschouwingen betreffende de plantwijze . . . ten behoeve van de Koffiecultuur. 1886. III. 730.

Aden barilla. 1891. III. 387.[2]

Aden senna. 1892. III. 471.[1]

Adena, H. Ter zake van de groene luis. 1899. III. 737.

Ader, Frédérique. Iets over Djeroeks. 1900. III. 497.[2]

Ader, Rudolf. Die Fusicladien unserer Obstbäume. 1896. III. 195,[1] 444.[2]

— Glasige Äpfel. 1895. III. 428.[1]

— Milchglanz des Steinobstes. 1895. III. 431.[1]

— Zur Monilia-Epidemie. 1897. III. 436.[2]

— Mycosphaerella cerasella. 1900. III. 432.[2]

— Notizen über einige . . . Pflanzenkrankheiten. 1895. III. 435,[1] 431.[1]

— Ueber die . . . Schäden und Krankheiten unserer Obstbäume. 1899. III. 191.

— Studien über . . . Krankheit der Aprikosenbäume. 1893. III. 435.[1]

— Unserer Obstbäume Hausarst. 1900. III. 180.[1]

Adhesion between two Beeches. 1882. I. 209,[1] III. 360.[1]

Adie, Alexander J. On Taxus baccata variegata seedlings. 1868. III. 288.[1]

The **Adirondack** forests in danger. 1888. IV. 178.¹
Adirondack league club. Constitution. 1893. IV. *3*,¹ 39.¹
Adjudicataire responsable. 1900. IV. 327.
Adlam, R. W. Forestry in the Transvaal. 1899. IV. 169.¹
— A visit to the Durban botanic gardens. 1888. I. 69.¹
Adler, Arthur. Untersuchungen über die Längenausdehnung der Gefässraume. 1892. I. 134.¹
Adler, Hermann. Alternating generations. 1881. IV. 510.
— Über den Generationswechsel der Eichengallen. 1881. IV. 510.
Adler, Wilhelm. Flora des Ziegenrücker Kreises. 1819. I. 376.
Adlerheim, Pehr. Berättelse om et gjordt försök, til frost-fjärilars hindrande. 1770. III. 188.²
— *See also* CRONSTEDT, C. J. & ADLERHEIM, Pehr.
Adlerskron, Bekhagel von. *See* BEKHAGEL VON ADLERSKRON.
Adlerstam, Johann Patricius von. *See* LEDEBOUR, K. F. & ADLERSTAM, J. P.
Adlerz, Ernst. Bidrag till knoppfjällens anatomi. 1880. I. 108.¹
Adlum, John. A memoir on the cultivation of the Vine. 1823. III. 549.²
Administration des eaux et forêts. Recrutement. 1894. IV. 540.¹
Administration des eaux et forêts — Recrutement . . . Programme. 1894. IV. 540.¹
Administration des forêts. Annuaire. ₁ IV. 12.²
Administration des forêts. Circulaire. 1822. IV. 303.²
L'**administration** des forêts au concours régional de Troyes. 1875. IV. 20.¹
Administration forestière. Recrutement. 1895. IV. 552.²
Administration forestière. — Recrutement. 1897. IV. 540.¹
Admiraal, K. De kankerziekte der boomen. 1889. III. 194.
Adolph. Eine deutsche Musterforstwirtschaft in Rumätlien. 1892. IV. 375.¹
Adolphi, A. W. Sur le goudron de Tremble. 1894. IV. 487.¹
— Zur Kenntniss des Espen-Theers. 1894. IV. 487.¹
Adoption du système métrique aux États-Unis. 1893. IV. 214.¹
Ador, DEMOLE-. *See* FATIO, Victor & DEMOLE-ADOR.
Ador, Émile. Note sur l'apparition du phylloxera. 1874. III. 567.¹
— Observations relatives au Phylloxera. 1874. III. 566.¹
Adriaans, Adriaan. De kaneelkultuur in Krawang. 1855. III. 406.¹
Adrian, Louis Alphonse. Arbutine. 1894. III. 648.²
— De l'influence du climat . . . sur la quantité d'acide cyan-hydrique . . . de Laurier-cerise. 1862. III. 438.¹
— Juglandine. 1894. III. 354.²
— Note on Sandal wood. 1891. III. 384.²
— Note sur le Santal. 1891. III. 384.²
— Note sur les principaux Quinquinas. 1891. III. 718.
— Note sur les tannins. 1892. III. 237.²
— Note sur les térébenthines. 1891. IV. 443.²
— & **Trillat**, A. Sur un nouveau principe cristallisé retiré de la grande absinthe. 1898. III. 754.²
Adriani, Arius. On guttapercha, catechu. 1851. III. 230.
— Over gutta-percha en caoutchouc. 1850. III. 228.²
— Specimen chemicum inaugurale, de Gutta Percha. 1850. III. 230.
— Verhandeling over gutta percha. 1850. III. 230.
Adumbratio novæ Pharmacopoeæ austriacæ. *See* PHARMACOPŒA austriaca. 1818. III. 256.¹
Adventitious buds on the roots of the Elm. 1873. II. 144.²
Adventitious leaves in Rhus. 1880. II. 459.¹
Æbletræernes Bladlus. 1850. III. 427.¹
Aehrenthal, Johann Lexa, *Freiherr* von. Anleitung unter den . . . bekanntesten Kernobstsorten . . . Wahl selbst treffen zu können. 1845. III. 71.
— Deutschlands Kernobstsorten. 1833. III. 71.
— Systematische Uebersicht aller . . . Kernobstsorten. 1833. III. 71.
— Verzeichniss derjenigen Obstsorten . . . in den Freiherrl. ₇v. Aehrenthal'schen Gärten. 1840. III. 90.¹
Ahrling, Ewald. Carl von Linnés ungdomsskrifter. 1888. I. 520.²
Aejmelaeus, Christen. Arbor toxicaria macassariensis. *See* THUNBERG, C. P. 1788. II. 145.¹
Aelbroeck, J. L. van. Werkdadige landbouw-konst der Vlamingen. 1823. III. 122.¹
Der **älteste** Baum der Erde. 1888. IV. 519.¹
Der **älteste** Baum der Welt. 1899. II. 52.¹
Aemilianus, PALLADIUS RUTILIUS TAURUS. *See* PALLADIUS RUTILIUS TAURUS AEMILIANUS.

Ændringer og Tilføielser til Instruxen af 29/9 1870 angaaende "Udførelsen af den 10aarige Revision." 1887. IV. 296.²
Aengelen, Petrus van. Herbarius kruyt en bloemhof. 1663. I. 286, *III. 76*.
— Der verständige Gärtner. 1663. III. 104.²
— Verstandige gardenier. 1663. III. 104.²
— De verstandige hovenier. 1663. III. 104.²
Ærbødigst Taksigelse . . . i Anledning af Brænde-Auctionens Udsættelse. 1797. IV. 281.²
Ueber das **ätherische** Oel von Pinus Abies. 1843. IV. 459.²
Aetherische olien. 1884. III. 611.²
Aetherisches Oel von Pinus silvestris. 1844. IV. 482.²
Afanasef, P. A. *See* АФАНАСЬЕВЪ, П. А.
Afbeelding van in- en uitlandsche houten. *See* HOUTTUYN, Martin. 1773. I. 124.
Afbeeldingen der Artseny-gewaassen. *See* OSKAMP, D. L. 1796. III. 55.
Affaitat, Casimir. Il semplice ortolano. 1734. III. 115.¹
Affleck, Thomas. Hedging and hedging plantations. 1869. III. 213.
Afforestation in China. 1889. IV. 168.¹
Afouage; partage en argent. 1899. IV. 334,² *555.*¹
Aux **affouagistes**. 1897. IV. 555.¹
Affourtit, R. C. Overzicht van de geschiedenis . . . der Roos. 1848. III. 448.
— Tuinboekje voor iedereen. 1861. III. 106.¹
Afhandling om Kultilvirkning. 1799. IV. 394.
L'**afide** lanigero. 1866. III. 189.
African Oil Palm. 1891. III. 325.¹
African rubber and Indian. 1892. III. 229.
De **Afrikaansche** rubber-boomen. 1885. III. 229.
Afrikanische Gesellschaft in Deutschland. Mittheilungen. I. 10.
Het **afvallen** der bladeren. 1872. I. 191.²
Afzel, Adam. *See* AFZELIUS, Adam.
Afzelius, Adam. Anmärkningar vid svenska vaxternas kännedom. 1787. II. 106.²
— De origine myrrhae controversa. 1818. II. 418.¹
— Remedia guineensia. 1813. III. 93,¹ 475.²
— De Rosis suecanis. 1804. II. 283.²
— Stirpium in Guinea medicinalium species cognitae. *See* FLYGARE, Axel & ALNER, A. 1817. III. 93.¹
— Stirpium in Guinea medicinalium species novae. 1818. III. 93.¹
— & **Elgenstierna**, N. W. Genera plantarum guineensium. 1804. I. 490.
Afzelius, J. A. Spartium scoparium funnen inom Stockholmsflorans område. 1853. II. 351.²
Afzelius, Peter Conrad. Novitiae florae gotlandicae. 1844. I. 354.
Agallochum praestantissimum. *See* CELSIUS, Olof. 1737. I. 513.
Agardh, Carl Adolf. Aphorismi botanici. 1817. I. 98, *259.*
— Über die Eintheilung der Pflanzen nach den Kotyledonen. 1826. I. 123.¹
— Enumeratio plantarum in regione landscronensi. *See* DUBEN, M. W. VON. 1835. I. 353.
— Essai de réduire la physiologie végétale à des principes fondamentaux. 1828. I. 146.
— Essai sur le développement intérieur des plantes. 1829. I. 123.²
— Ett nytt växtställe för Salix daphnoides. 1849. II. 106.²
— Om inskrifter i lefvande träd. 1829. I. 210.¹
— Lärobok i botanik. 1829. I. 86.
— Lehrbuch der Botanik. 1829. I. 86.
— Novitiae florae suecicae. *See* FRIES, E. M. 1814. I. 352.
— Öfver en ny art Vinbär. 1823. II. 243.²
— Observationer på blomdelarnes plana ställning såväl inbördes. 1850. II. 320.¹
— Om Sveriges skogsväsen. 1857. IV. 344.¹
Agardh, Jacob Georg. Om äggets läge inom ovariet. 1860. I. 117.²
— Om byggnaden . . . af monocotyledonernas stam. 1854. I. 105.
— Exempel på bark förekommande i den inre vedmassan. 1861. I. 127.¹
— Öfver den sammanvuxna calyx hos några Lonicera-arter. 1846. II. 836.¹
— Om den Stadsbergska drif-vedens ursprung. 1869. I. 242.²
— Theoria systematis plantarum. 1858. I. 261.
— Tre slags blommor hos Hippophaë rhamnoides. 1851. II. 608.¹
— Om växternas stipler. 1849. I. 111.

L'agaric miellé. 1895. IV.-550.[1]
Agassiz, Louis. Lake Superior. 1850. I. 304.
— Tableau synoptique des principales familles naturelles des plantes . . . en Suisse. 1833. I. 434.
Age and leafing of trees. 1877. I. 221.
Age and size of trees. 1838, 1839. I. 193.[1]
The age and size of trees. 1879. I. 297.[1]
The age of English trees. 1863. I. 297.[1]
Age of the giant Gum trees. 1880. II. 623.[1]
On the age of trees. 1850. I. 193.[1]
The age of trees. 1878, 1896. I. 193.[2]
Agema, J. Samenvatting van hetgeen over het vergiftig Steranijs is bekend gemaakt. 1881. III. 398.[1]
Agenda du forestier. IV. 12.[3]
Gli agenti forestali. 1866. IV. 293.[2]
Ages of trees. 1886. I. 193.[2]
Aggeenko, Vladimir (Naumovitch). See Агтеенко, B. H.
Agitation. See .'. Agitation. 1885. IV. 34.[2]
Aglcmerados de corcho. 1885. IV. 518.[1]
Agnethler, Michael Gottlieb. De Lauro. 1751. III. 406.[2]
Agnew, William. Reports on Tea cultivation . . . in Assam. 1863. III. 603.
Agosti, Giuseppe. De re botanica tractatus. 1770. I. 424.
Agostinetti, Giacomo. Cento e dieci ricordi, che formano il buon fattor di villa. 1679. III. 115.[1]
Agrandissement du domaine forestier de l'état. 1898. IV. 274.[3]
Agrémens de la campagne. 1750. III. 139.
Les agrémens de la campagne. See DE LA COURT, Pieter. 1738. III. 105.
Agri-horticultural society, Bombay. Transactions. III. 26.[1]
Agricola, (pseud.). Iets over het proefstation voor Koffiecultuur. 1900. III. 732.[1]
— Miscellaneous observations on planting . . . timber-trees. See ANDERSON, James. 1777. IV. 120.
— De waarde van landbouwonderwijs voor de Koffiecultuur. 1900. III. 732.[1]
Agricola, Georg Andreas. L'agriculture parfaite. 1716. III. 152.
— The experimental husbandman and gardener. 1716. III. 152.
— Kurtzer Bericht von dem Ursprunge der neu- und höchstnutzbaren Universal-Vermehrung. 1715. III. 152.
— Neu-und nie-erhörter . . . Versuch der Universal-Vermehrung. 1716. III. 152.
— Nieuwe en ongehoorde . . . queekkonst van boomen, heesters. 1715. III. 152.
— A philosophical treatise of husbandry. 1715. III. 152
— Versuch einer allgemeinen Vermehrung aller Bäume. 1715. III. 152.
Agricola, Johann. Medicinae herbariae libri duo. 1539. I. 277.
L' agriculture chinoise. III. 24.[1]
L' Agriculteur praticien. III. 18.
O agricultor brasileiro. III. 757.[1]
Agricultural and horticultural society of India. Journal. Transactions. III. 26.[1]
Agricultural bulletin of the Malay peninsula. III. 26.[1]
Agricultural department, Assam. Bulletin. III. 26.[1]
Agricultural experiment stations (United States). See under respective states.
Agricultural gazette of New South Wales. III. 27.[1]
Agricultural journal, Cape Colony. III. 26.[3]
The agricultural ledger. III. 26.[1]
Agricultural ledger: special forest series. IV. 16.[1]
Agricultural resources of Zanzibar. 1892. III. 281.[2]
Agricultural review. See AMERICAN AGRICULTURAL ASSOCIATION. III. 2.
Agricultural science. III. 2.
Agriculture forestière, législation. 18 . . ? IV. 275.
Agriculture française. 1843. III. 124.[1]
L'Agriculture nouvelle. III. 18.
Agriculture of Pennsylvania. See PENNSYLVANIA BOARD OF AGRICULTURE. III. 7.
Les agronomes latins. See SCRIPTORES rei rusticae. 1470. III. 97.
Agronomika. See 'АГРОНОМИКА.
Agronomische Zeitung. III. 11.
Agronoom, (pseud.). Hybriden van Liberia en Java-Koffie. 1893. III. 742.[1]
— Monosoeko-tuinen. 1887. III. 730.
— Een paar vijanden van den Dadapboom. 1894. III. 476.[1] III. 114.[1]
Aguado, Ramon Romualdo. Tratado del arbolista. 1864.

Agucchi. Proclama. 5 dicembre 1810. . 1810. IV. 276.[2]
Agüera, Mariano de la Paz GRAELLS Y DE LA. See GRAELLS Y DE LA AGÜERA, Mariano de la Paz.
Aguillon, Camille Calendrier horticultural toulonnais. 1832. III. 113.
— Sur les greffes d'arbres à fruits et à fleurs. 1839. III. 164.[2]
— Quelques mots sur la maladie de la Vigne. 1853. III. 575.[2]
Aguirre Miramon, Severo de. Enfermedades del Manzana. 1880. III. 427.[1]
— Instituciones agrarias y forestales en Guipúzcoa. 1884. IV. 135.[2]
Ahl, Jonas Nicolaus. De Benzoë. See THUNBERG, C. P. 1793. III. 671.[1]
Ahlberg, C. G. Plantarum brasiliensium. See THUNBERG, C. P. 1817. I. 341.
Ahlburg, Hermann. Beiträge zur Cultur der Hortensie. 1875. III. 411.[3]
— Mitteilungen über japanischen Obstbau. 1878. III. 273.[2]
— Ein neues japanisches Pflanzengenus. 1878. II. 819.[1]
— Reiseberichte aus Japan. 1877. I. 462.
Ahlén, Gustaf. Des Landmann's Obstbau. 1883. III. 139.
Ahlfrengren, Fredrik Elias. Bidrag till kännedomen om Composité-stammens anatomiska byggnad. 1896. II. 850.[2]
— Om induktionselektricitets inverkan på fröns gronings energi. 1898. I. 204.
Ahlich, J. Den svenske lust-örte och trä-gården. 1722. III. 100.[2]
Ahlin, Erik. Om Pilplanteringar. See FRIES, Elias. 1836. II. 100,[1] III. 350.[2]
Ahlisch, Louis. Die Beschreibung . . . der Codiaeum-(Croton)-Arten. 1887. III. 516.[1]
— Hexenbesen. See HEXENBESEN . . . 1886. I. 528.[2]
Ahlquist, Abraham. Anmärkningar om Ölands fysiska beskaffenhet. 1821. I. 353.
— Flora runsteniensis. 1815. I. 352.
Ahlquist, Petrus. Novitiae florae suecicae. See FRIES, E. M. 1814. I. 352.
Ahnfelt, C. N. Stirpes agri femsionensis. See FRIES, E. M. 1825. I. 353.
Ahrendts, L. Blüthenkalender der Bäume und Sträucher. 1884. I. 225.
Ahrens, (Oberförster, Schoningen). Das Bedecken der Eichenkampsaat. 1872. IV. 506.
Ahrens, August. Ueber die Natur und Bildung der Blumen. 1813. I. 114.[1]
Ahrens, Cd. MEYER-. See MEYER-AHRENS, Cd.
Ai camphor. 1895. III. 754.[2]
Aichenhayn, Joseph, AICHINGER VON. See AICHINGER VON AICHENHAYN, Joseph.
Aichholzer, Josef. Anbauversuche mit Eucalyptus globulus. 1878. IV. 532.[2]
— Bericht über die Aufastungs-Versuche. 187 . ? IV. 171.
— Einiges über die Pinie. 1879. IV. 468.[2]
— Eis als forstliche Nebennutzung. 1878. IV. 434.
— Der Fichtennadelrost. 1875. IV. 456.
— Das Schiffbauholz. 1875. IV. 425.[1]
Aichinger von Aichenhayn, Joseph. Botanischer Führer in und um Wien. 1847. I. 440.
Aide mémoire à l'usage des jardiniers . . . des plantations d'agrément. 1879. III. 200.
Aignan, A. Determination de l'huile de résine. 1897. II. 45,[1] IV. 468.[3]
Aignan, François. Le prestre médecin. 1696. III. 605, 741.[2]
Aigner, Hans von. Tabellen für den Kubik-Inhalt runder Stammhölzer. 1863. IV. 225.
Aigubelle, Charles d'. Homographie. 1828. III. 217.
Aikin, Arthur. On timber. 1836. I. 126.
Aikin, John. The woodland companion. 1802. I. 393.[1]
Aikin, William E. A. Catalogue of phænogamous plants . . . of Baltimore. 1837. I. 318.
The Ailanthus. 1888. III. 507.[1]
Aims and methods of the College of forestry. 1898. IV. 30.[1]
Ain — Société d'horticulture pratique. See CHRONIQUE HORTICOLE. III. 19.
Ainslie, Sir Whitelaw. Materia indica. 1813 III. 277.
— Materia medica of Hindoostan. 1813. I. 75,[2] III. 277.
Ainsworth, William. Researches in Assyria, Babylonia. 1838. I. 478.
Ainsworth, William Francis. The river Karûn. 1890. III. 279.[2]
Ainu names of Hokkaido plants. See MIYABE, Kingo. 1895. I. 75.[2]

Aire d'habitation du Sapin de Douglas. 1899. IV. 483.²
Airlie, *earl of.* Report on the planting of lands on the Airlie estates. 1831. IV. 358.²
Airoles, Jules de LIRON D'. *See* LIRON D'AIROLES, Jules de.
Airy, Hubert. On leaf-arrangement. 1873. I. 102.
Aitchison, James Edward Tierney. The botany of the Afghan delimitation commission. 1888. I. 477.³
— A catalogue of the plants of the Punjab. 1869. I. 474.
— Ueber einige Pflanzen Afghanistans. 1887. III. 93.¹
— On the flora of Kuram Valley, etc., Afghanistan. 1880. I. 477.²
— Flora of the Hushiarpur district. 1871. I. 474.
— Flora of the Jhelum district of the Punjab. 1865. I. 474.
— Hand-book of the trade products of Leh. 1874. III. 278.
— Notes to assist in a further knowledge of the products of western Afghanistan. 1890. III. 279.²
— Remarks on the vegetation of the islands of the Indus River. 1865. I. 474.
— Some plants of Afghanistan. 1887. *I.* 477,² III. 93.¹
— On the vegetation of the Jhelum district. 1865. I. 474.
— The vegetation of the Kuram and Hariab valleys. 1880. I. 477.²
— Hortus kewensis. 1789. I. 53.
Aitken, Andrew P. Leaf-mould. 1898. III. 41.²
— The nitrogenous food of plants. 1900. I. 160.
Aitken, John M. On the Hylobius abietis. 1879. IV. 445.
Aiton, William Townsend. Delineations of exotick plants cultivated in the Royal garden at Kew. *See* BAUER, Franz. 1796. II. 664.¹
— An epitome of the second edition of Hortus kewensis. 1814. I. 53.
— Hortus kewensis. 1789. I. 53.
Aix — Académie des sciences, agriculture . . . *See* SOCIÉTÉ DES AMIS DES SCIENCES . . . I. 520.¹
Aix — Société des amis des sciences, des lettres . . . *See* SOCIÉTÉ . . . I. 520.¹
Ajmere forest regulation. 1874. IV. 307.²
Ajmere-Merwara. *See* INDIA — AJMERE-MERWARA.
Ajtay, Sándor. Korai és késői Bükk. 1888. II. 126.²
Akacya. 1861. IV. 523.¹
Akácz-fatermési táblák. 1887. IV. 524.¹
Akademie der Wissenschaften in Krakau. Anzeiger. *See* ACADÉMIE DES SCIENCES DE CRACOVIE. I. 27.
Akademie der Wissenschaften, [Wien]. *See* KAISERLICHE AKADEMIE . . . I. 27.
Akademie der Wissenschaften zu Berlin. *See* KÖNIGLICHE AKADEMIE . . . I. 13.
Akademie der Wissenschaften zu München. *See* KÖNIG-LICHE BAYERISCHE AKADEMIE . . . I. 13.
Akademie van wetenschappen. *See* KONINKLIJKE AKADEMIE . . . I. 16.
Akademija umiejetności w Krakowie. Pamiętnik. Roz-prawy. Sprawozdanie. I. 27.
Die Akazie. 1894. IV. 523.²
The Akee. 1892. III. 539.¹
Aken, Franz Joachim von. Svenska medicinal och apothekar växterna. 1764. III. 66.²
Akerly, Samuel. Remarks on the cultivation of the Locust tree. 1817. III. 486.²
Akhmatof, M. & Kosyanenko, V. *See* АХМАТОВЪ, М. и Кос-янянко, В.
Akinfiyef, I. Ja. *See* АКИНФІЕВЪ, И. Я.
Akisato, Ritō. To rinsen meishō zukai. n. d. I. 298.
Die Akklimatisation fremder Nadelhölzer. 1874. IV.·124.²
Zur Akklimatisirung des Bambus. 1872. III. 314.¹
Aktsioner. *See* АКЦІОНЕРЪ.
Aktsionernoye obshtchestvò. *See* АКЦІОНЕРНОЕ ОБЩЕСТВО.
Al dyeing and cloth printing. 1896. III. 746.¹
Al Fresco, (*pseud.*). Florida and her resources. 1874. III. 264.¹
— Orange culture in Florida. 1868. III. 499.²
Alabama — Agricultural and mechanical college — Agricul-tural experiment station. Annual report. Bulletin. III. 2.
Alabama agricultural experiment station. *See* ALABAMA — AGRICULTURAL AND MECHANICAL COLLEGE. III. 2.
Aladin, P. *See* АЛАДЬИНЪ, П.
Alamanni, Luigi. La coltivatione. 1539. III. 114.¹
— La coltivazione. 1539. III. 114.¹
Alas, A. V. Análisis de una planta indígena. 1882. III. 629.²
Albanese, V. G. Sulle legislazioni italiane forestali. 1864. IV. 328.
Albany institute. Transactions. I. 519.¹
The Albany lumber trade, its history and extent. 1872. IV. 403.²

Albareda, José Luis. Instrucciones de servicio para el cuerpo de ingenieros de montes. 1881. IV. 304.¹
Albarella, Salvatore. Memoria sulla radice de' vegetali. 1867. I. 161.
Albéniz, Enrique. Aspiraciones. 1897. IV. 553.²
Alberda van Ekenstein. Sur la caroubinose. 1897. III. 472.¹
Degli alberi ed arbusti. *See* BOZOLI, G. M. 1851. III. 88.¹
Gli alberi in Algeria. 1861. IV. 49.¹
Albero a succhero scoperto in Spagna. 1812. III. 647.²
L' albero dai quaranta scudi. 1863. IV. 440.¹
L' albero del burro. 1889. IV. 534.²
L' albero della Chinchina. 1864. IV. 538.²
L' albero della morte. 1882. IV. 440.¹
L' albero della pioggia. 1882. IV. 522.¹
L' albero ed il verme della cera. 1864. III. 226.¹
Albero giganteseo. 1865. IV. 520.²
Albert, Abel. Botanique du Var. 1884. I. 416.
— Clematis hybrida Albert. 1889. II. 198.¹
Albert, Federico. Las dunas del centro de Chile. 1900. I. 347.
Albert, Georg. Beiträge zur Lehre von der Ueberführung des Mittelwaldes in Hochwald. 1859. IV. 128.
Albert, H. Beiträge zur Frage der Rebendüngung. 1895. III. 549.¹
Albert, Joseph. Die Arbeitstheilung in der Forstverwaltung. 1876. IV. 287.
— Die Errichtung forststatistischer Bureaux. 1871. IV. 336.¹
— Zur forstlichen Reinertragstheorie. 1876. IV. 256.
— Eine gemeinsame Grundlage für Forststatistik. 1876. IV. 336.¹
— Lehrbuch der forstlichen Betriebsregulirung. 1861. IV. 240.
— Lehrbuch der Forstservituten-Ablösung. 1868. IV. 333.
— Lehrbuch der Forstverwaltung. 1883. IV. 287.
— Lehrbuch der gerichtlichen Forstwissenschaft. 1864. IV. 313.
— Lehrbuch der Staatsforstwissenschaft. 1875. IV. 269.
— Lehrbuch der Waldwerthberechnung. 1862. IV. 253.
— Die schwedische Forstverwaltung im Jahre 1877. 1881. IV. 288.²
— Die Waldbodenrente. 1872. IV. 255.
Albert, Paul. Beiträge zur Entwickelungsgeschichte der Knospen. 1894. I. 108.²
Albert, W. Die Ablösung der Weideservituten. 1845. IV. 333.
Alberti, Antonio. Flora medica. 1817. III. 56.
Alberti, Jacopo. Dell' epidemica mortalità de Gelsi. 1773. III. 378.
Alberti, Michael. De camphorae circumspecto usu medico. 1722. III. 404.²
— De coffee potus usu noxio. 1730. III. 741.¹
— De Roremarino. 1718. III. 698.¹
— De Succino. *See* BAUMER, Johannes. 1750. III. 227.¹
Albertinus, Aegidius. Der Welt Tummel- und Schauplatz. 1612. I. 284.
Albertis, Luigi Maria d'. New Guinea. 1880. *See* BECCARI, Odoardo. 1880. I. 499.
Albertoni, Pietro. Action physiologique et thérapeutique de la cotoïne. 1884. III. 407.²
Alberts, G. *See* THOORN, N. A. M. von der & ALBERTS, G.
Alberts, J. Caoutchouc-cultuur, [in Guatemala]. 1899. III. 149.
— Tentoonstelling van Aucuba's te Boskoop. 1879. III. 645.¹
Alberts, L. G. Demerara Groenhart. 1893. IV. 520.¹
— Greenheart geen Geelhart. 1894. IV. 520.¹
— *See also* THOORN, N. A. M. von der & ALBERTS, G.
Albertus de Bollstaedt. Alberti Magni . . . de vegetabili-bus libri VII. 1280. I. 275.²
— Beati Alberti Magni . . . opera. . . . Parva natur-alia. 1280. I. 275.¹
— Liber aggregationis. *See* LIBER aggregationis. 1481. I. 275.²
— Tabula tractatum parvorum naturalium. 1280. I. 274, V. XIV.¹
Albertus Magnus. *See* ALBERTUS DE BOLISTAEDT.
Albini, Frid. Bernhard. De Thee. 1817. III. 605.
Albini, Giuseppe. Ueber den Nahrungswerth der echten Cas-tanien. 1854. III. 360.¹
— Ricerche chimiche sul frutto del Castagno. 1854. III. 360.¹
— & Fienga, A. Ricerche chimiche sulle Castagne comuni. 1867. II. 124.¹
Albizzia lophantha as a 'reboisement' plant. 1894. IV. 521.¹

Albochâri, A. A. A. IBN SÎNÂ. *See* IBN SÎNÂ ALBOCHÂRI, A, A. A.
Alboff, Nicolas. Contributions à la flore de la Terre de Feu. 1896. · I. 347.[2]
— Contributions á la flore de la Transcaucasie. 1893. I. 369.
— La flore alpine des calcaires de la Transcaucasie. 1895. I. 370.
— Les forêts de la Transcaucasie. 1896. I. 368,[1] *IV. 81.*
— La naturaleza en la Tierra de Fuego. 1896. I. 347.[3]
— Rapport préliminaire sur une excursion botanique dans la Sierra Ventana. 1895. I. 345.
— The western Caucasus and its flora. 1892. I. 369.
— *See also* АЛЬБОВЪ, Н. М.
Albonico, Johann Heinrich. Nützliche Bemerkungen für Garten- und Blumenfreunde. 1795. III. 121.[1]
Albrecht, Hermann. Note sur le Carica Papaya. 1882. III. 617.[2]
Albrecht, Johann Peter. Klar entdeckte Unschuld der Thee- und Kaffee-getränke. 1696. III. 222.
Albrecht, Johannes Sebastian. De ligno . . . in tenebris lucente. 1740. I. 154.
— De Salicum rosis fictis. 1748. I. 517,[1] *II. 104.*[2] — 1752. III. 350.[1]
Albrecht; Joseph. Woody plants of Louisiana. 1885. I. 317,[1] *IV. 77.*[2]
Albrecht fóherczeg O Fensége bellyei uradalmának leirása. 1883. IV. 373.
Albret, d'. Cours . . . de la taille des arbres fruitiers. 1840. III. 172.
— Het enten. 1851. III. 160.
— Grafting. 1851. III. 160. ·
Album der natuur. I. 15.
Albungh, N. H. Budding. 1885. IV. 149.[1]
Alby, Ed. *See* MÜNTZ, Achille & ALBY, Ed.
Alcenius, Otto. Finlands kärlvexter. 1863. I. 362.
Alciati, Napoleone. Cenni sul morbo delle Viti. 1857. III. 559.[3]
— Note sur un liquide employé contre la maladie de la Vigne. 1859. III. 577.
Alcinet, José. Nuevas utilidades de la China. 1763. III. 272.[2]
Alcocer, Pascual. Estudio de algunos principios astringentes vegetales. 1887. III. 260.[1]
Alcock, Alfred William. Report on the natural history results of the Pamir boundary commission. *See* DUTHIE, J. F. 1898. I. 477.[2]
Alcock, Randal Hilbert. Botanical names for English readers. 1876. I. 76.[2]
— List of plants noticed by the Bury natural history society. 1872. V. xxi.[1]
Alcock, *Sir* Rutherford. Capital of the Tycoon. *See* VEITCH, J. G. 1863. I. 462.
Los alcornocales de Túuez, 1893. IV. 559.[2]
El Alcornoque. 1894. IV. 517.[2]
Alcott, William Alexander. Tea and coffee. 1839. III. 222.
Sopra alcune malattie e danni che soffrono alcune piante forestali. *See* SOPRA alcune . . . 1881. IV. 196.[1]
Di alcuni mezzi speciali d' insegnamento nello Istituto forestale di Vallombrosa. 1878. IV. 35.[1]
Sopra alcuni strumenti topografici. *See* SOPRA alcuni . . . 1889. IV. 265. ·
Aldéguier, Thérèse Joseph Hippolyte d'. Opinion sur la cession des bois dits de l'état. 1817. IV. 325.
Aldenbrück. Zur Holzmesskunst. Die richtige Construktion der Kluppe. 1864. IV. 231.[3]
Of the Alder. 1733. III. 356.[2]
Alderman. Garden Ivies, their uses and cultivation. 1876. III. 642.[2]
The Alders. 1899. III. 356.[3]
Alderson, John. Versuch über das Rhus Toxicodendron. 1799. III. 528.[1]
Alderton, George E. Treatise . . . of Orange-culture in Auckland. 1884. III. 500.[1]
Aldinus, Tobias. Exactissima descriptio . . . plantarum . . . in Horto farnesiano. 1625. I. 60.[3]
Aldrovandi, Ulisse. Δενδρολογία; sive, Arboretum libris II. 1667. I. 292.[2] ·
— Dendrologiae naturalis . . . libri duo. 1667. I. 292.[2]
— Pomarium curiosum. 1667. I. 292.[3]
Alechamps, J. de. *See* DALECHAMPS, Jacques.
Alefeld, F. riedrich· Beiträge zur Malvaceenkunde. 1863. II. 519.[1]
— Die Bienenflora Deutschlands. 1856. III. 73, 224.[1]
— Ueber einige Kulturpflanzen. 1865. II. 402.[3]

— Ueber die Familie der Pyrolaceen. 1856. II. 657.[2]
— Ueber Filamentenverlängerung einiger Papilionaceen. 1861. II. 359.[1]
— Ueber die Formen mehrerer Kulturpflanzen. 1867. II. 340,[1] 847.[2]
— Gynatrix. 1862. II. 527.[1]
— Ueber Hibiscus Lampas Cav. 1861. II. 523.[1]
— Ueber Jughans L. 1861. II. 112.[2]
— Ueber die Malveen. 1862. II. 519.[1]
— Ueber Parochetus, Reinwardtia und Napaea. 1867. II. 393,[1] 526.[3]
— Ueber die Stellung der Gattung Gossypium. 1861. II. 522.[1]
— Ein Wacholderbaum. 1860. II. 31.[1]
Alegre, Paulo PORTO-. *See* PORTO-ALEGRE, Paulo,
Aleksandrovitch, Gh. *See* АЛЕКСАНДРОВИЧЪ, Г.
Aleksandrowicz, Benedykt. O drzewie i jego użytkach. 1855. IV. 269.
— IV. kongres leśny, jego obrady. 1879. IV. 40.[1]
— Las jak chodować. 1860. IV. 94.
Aleksandrowicz, Benedykt. O trzebieży i znaczeniu jej w gospodarstwie leśnem. 1774 (*error for* 1874?). IV. 385.[1]
— Wyrachowanie miąższości drzewa. 1874. IV. 227.
Aleksandrowicz, Bron. Obecny stan lasów i sadów owocowych w Królestwie.Polskiem. 1880. IV. 346.
Aleksandrowicz, Jerzy. Kurs organografii roślin. 1865. · I. 100.[3]
— Szkoła ogrodnicza prywatna w Warszawie. 1882. III. 32.[1]
— Urządzenie szkoły ogrodniczej prywatnej w Warszawie pod kierunkiem. 1880. III. 32.[1]
Alemann, Friedrich Adolph von. Ueber Forst-Culturwesen. 1851. IV. 118.
— Ueber das Vorkommen schädlicher Forstinsekten. 1861. IV. 207.
Alers, Georg. Das v. Alemann'sche Forstculturverfahren. 1852. IV. 152.
— Altes und Neues über die Aufastung. 1891. IV. 172.[1]
— Ueber das Aufästen der Nadelhölzer. 1868. IV. 171.
— Über das Aufästen der Waldbäume. 1868. IV. 171.
— Ueber Aufastung der Waldbäume. 1876. IV. 171.
— Ueber das Auftreten der Schütte. 1882. IV. 477.
— Beleuchtung der Homburg'schen Nutzholzwirthschaft. 1879. IV. 129.
— Ueber Eichenheisterpflanzungen. 1887. IV. 507.
— Der Einfluss des Waldes auf die Bodenfeuchtigkeit. 1883. IV. 51.
— Es wird fortgeästet! 1879. IV. 171.
— Der Frost in seiner Einwirkung auf die Waldbäume. 1884. IV. 66.[2]
— Noch ein Wort über das Schütten junger Kiefern. 1853. IV. 475.
— Russische Beobachtungen über die Schütte. 1883. IV. 477.
— Schutz den jungen Kiefern . . . gegen Frühfrost. 1878. IV. 477.
— Ueber den Ueberwaltungsprocess. 1879. IV. 171.
— Wald- und Bodenfeuchtigkeit. 1890. IV. 51.
Alessandro, Arnaud. A proposito del vincolo forestale. 1887. IV. 328.
Alexander, Catherine. Observations on the glands . . . of Myoporum laetum. 1887. II. 806.[3]
Alexander, *Sir* James Edward. Experiments with the Osage Orange. 1856. III. 372.[1]
— Notice regarding the Little Andaman Island. 1827. I. 481.[1]
Alexander, John. On the best modes of starting . . . Coniferae. 1873. III. 294.[1]
— Descriptive catalogue of the exhibits . . . of Ceylon. 1884. III. 279,[1] V. xxix.[2]
— Notes on the ravages of tree . . . destroying insects. 1885. IV. 550.[1]
— Notes on the various methods of producing and harvesting Cinchona bark. 1885. III. 712.[3]
— Propagation of the newer Coniferae. 1873. III. 294.[1]
— Tonga. 1881. III. 697.[1]
Alexander, N. Cultivation of Indigo. 1838. III. 479.[1]
Alexander, R. C. Botanical excursion in lower Styria. 1846 I. 440.
— Notes on the botany of Jamaica. 1850. I. 335.
Alexander, S. A remarkable forest [tree] in Michigan. 1900. · II. 135.[2]
Alexanderson, Adolph. Novitiae florae suecicae. *See* FRIES, E. M. 1814. I. 352.
Alexandre, Nicolas. Dictionnaire botanique et pharmaceutique. 1716. III. 241.
— Sur une nouvelle sorte de cire. 1724. III. 352.[1]

Alexandrinus, Georgius. Enarrationes vocum priscarum in libris de re rustica. 1549. III. 29.[1]

Aleyboom, C. Remarks on a disease affecting the Tea plant called " roest " (rust). 1878. III. 604.[2]

Alfaro, Agustin. *See* COLLANTES, A. E. & ALFARO, Agustin.

Alfaro, Anastasio. Lista de las plantas . . . in Costa Rica. 1888. I. 334.

Alfast, O. Figentræets Dyrkning paa Friland. 1896. III. 369.[2]

Alföld, Károly, FLATT VON. *See* FLATT, Károly ALFÖLDI.

Alfonso, Ferdinando. Monografia sul Nocciuolo. 1886. III. 357.[2]

— Trattato sulla coltivazione degli Agrumi. 1875. III. 500.[1]

Alfroy, (*jr.*). Notice sur divers Chênes. 1829. III. 357,[1] 361.[1]

— Notice sur les avantages que présente la culture du Thuya de la Chine. 1832. III. 311.[2]

Alfroy, Charles Thomas. Catalogue des arbres et arbrisseaux. 1790. I. 56.

— Catalogue des arbres fruitiers. 1821. I. 57.

Altthan, O. Lonicera coerulea fråu södra Karelen. 1871. II. 836.[2]

Algan, H. Le calepin dendromètre. 1896. IV. 216.

— Cubage mental des Chênes. 1900. IV. 513.

— Cubage mental des Sapins. 1900. IV. 446,[2] 550.[1]

— Une emphytéose forestière. 1893. IV. 309.[1]

— Estimation des Sapins sur pied. 1890. IV. 237.

— Une formule fille du Sapin. 1896. IV. 444.[1]

— Tarifs de cubage. 1894. IV. 219.

Algemeen verslag wegens den staat van den landbouw. 1852. III. 122.[1]

Algemeene konst en letterbode. I. 15.

Algemeene landhuishoudelijke courant. III. 14.

Alger, W. S. Peaches. 1893. III. 441.[1]

Algeria — Bulletin agricole . . . *See* BULLETIN . . . III. 27.[1]

Algeria — Gouvernement général — Service botanique . . . Bulletin. III. 27.[1]

Algeria — Ligue du reboisement. *See* LIGUE . . . IV. 16.[1]

Algeria — Société d'horticulture d'Alger. *See* REVUE horticole de l'Algérie. III. 27.[1]

Algeria — Société de climatolcgie, sciences physiques & naturelles. *See* SOCIÉTÉ . . . I. 29.[2]

Algeria — Société des sciences physiques . . . *See* SOCIÉTÉ DE CLIMATOLOGIE, SCIENCES PHYSIQUES . . . I. 29.[2]

Algérie; horticulture générale. *See* RIVIÈRE, Charles. 1889. III. 130.[2]

Algérie; plantes médicinales. *See* BATTANDIER, J. A. & TRABUT, Louis. 1889. III. 93.[1]

L'Algérie agricole. III. 26.[2]

El Algodonero en Filipinas. 1886. IV. 399.[2]

Alheilig, M. Recette, conservation et travail des bois outils. n. d. IV. 427.[2]

La Aliaga. 1893. III. 490.[1]

Alibert, J. L. Considérations physiologiques sur le fruit du Coignassier. 1798. II. 263.[2]

— Nouveaux élémens de therapeutique. 1804. III. 242.

Aliceholt and Woolmer forest. 1878. IV. 358.[1]

L'aliénation des forêts de l'état. 1865. IV. 275.

L'aliénation des forêts de l'état devant l'opinion publique. *See* ROTHSCHILD, Jules. 1865. IV. 275.

De **l'aliénation** projetée des forêts de l'état. *See* SAINT-ANGE, Legros. 1848. IV. 275.

Alienazione dei beni demaniali. 1863. IV. 277.

Alienazione dei boschi demaniali. 1864. IV. 277.

Alifio, B. Giner. The disease affecting the Elm trees. 1899. III. 365.[1]

Aliquis, (*pseud.*). On preserving timber, &c. from . . . white ant. 1840. IV. 417.

Alix. Catalogue des arbres, arbustes. 1819. I. 57.

Alkemade, J. van Rijn van. *See* RIJN VAN ALKEMADE, J. van.

All the year round. III. 16.

Allais, Alphonse. Les arbres qui ont peur des moutons. 1895. I. 517.[1]

Allamanda fruiting. 1894. III. 686.[1]

Allan, Alex. McD. Some lessons we have learned. 1883. IV. 271.[2]

Allan, James T. American Bird Cherry. 1881. IV. 112.

— Conifers on the prairies. 1881. IV. 441.

— Essay on forest growing. 1873. IV. 111.[2]

— Sketch of the distribution of forest-trees in Nebraska. 1861. I. 320, *IV. 77.*[2]

Allard, Gaston. Effets du froid pendant l'hiver 1894–95. 1896. III. 49.[1]

Allard, J. Remarques sur la résistance au froid de certains arbres. 1891. III. 49.[1]

— La rusticité en Anjou des plantes sarmenteuses. 1891. III. 49.[1]

Allard, Marie. Étude pratique du phylloxéra. 1889. III. 762.

Allardyce, James. Remarks on the vegetation of the Neilgherries. 1836. I. 472.

Une **allée** de Palmiers. 1900. III. 322.[2]

Allegazione de' possessori di boschi. 179 . ? IV. 276.[2]

Allegretti, A. Gli esami nell' amministrazione forestale. 1899. IV. 294.[1]

Allemagne; une nouvelle société forestière. 1900. IV. 541.

Allemandi-Ehinger. Die Maulbeerbäume. 1837. III. 375.

Allemão, Francisco Freire. Apocynea. 1846. II. 726.[2]

— Apontamentos que poderão servir para a historia das arvores florestaes do Brasil. 1851. I. 340,[2] *IV. 78.*[2]

— Artocarpea. Soaresia nitida. 1854. II. 148.[1]

— Combretacea. Vicentia acuminata. 1844· II. 617.[2]

— Considerações sobre a estructura e usos de alguns pellos. 1851. I. 112.[2]

— Descripção da arvore . . . Bainha de Espada. 1857. II. 155.[2]

— Drypetes sessiliflora. 1844. II. 441.[1]

— Euphorbiacea. Hyeronima ·alchorneoides. 1848. II. 445.[2]

— Euphorbiacea. Ophthalmoblapton. 1849. II. 448.[1]

— Laurinea. 1848. II. 226.[2]

— Leguminosa. 1847. II. 374.[1]

— Leguminosa. 1848. II. 374.[1]

— Leguminosa. 1851. II. 374.[2]

— Leguminosa. Ferreirea. 1851. II. 358.[1]

— Leguminosa. Machaerium heteropterum. 1850. II. 387.[1]

— Noticia de algumas plantas. 1851. II. 148.[1]

— Nyctagenea. 1845. II. 190.[1]

— Ophthalmoblapton. 1850. II. 448.[2]

— Origem . . . dos vasos nos embryões da Jatropha Curcas. 1852. II. 436,[1] 446.[1]

— Plantas novas do Brasil. 1844. I. 342.

— Secção botanica. 1861. I. 342.

— Vicentia acuminata. 1844. II. 617.[2]

— & others. Breve noticia sobre a collecção das madeiras do Brasil. 1867. IV. 19.[1]

Allemão, Manoel Freire. Considerações sobre as plantas medicinaes da flora cearense. 1862. III. 65.[1]

Allen, Charles Linnaeus. A few good climbers and creepers. 1890. III. 205.[1]

— The scientific education of gardeners. 1891. III. 31.[2]

Allen, Charles P. Wooden stave pipe for high water pressure. 1887. IV. 426.[1]

Allen, Edwin West. Untersuchungen über Holzgummi. 1890. I. 181.[1]

Allen, George Young. *See* PERKIN, A. G. & ALLEN, G. Y.

Allen, Grant. The colours of flowers. 1882. I. 115,[1] 336.[2]

— Ghost worship and tree worship. 1893. I. 517.[2]

— Hazel and Filbert. 1889. II. 121.[1]

— The story of the plants. 1895. I. 96.

— Under the Willows. 1897. II. 104.[2]

Allen, H. Viburnum prunifolium. 1880. III. 753.[2]

— Sur le Viburnum prunifolium. 1880. III. 753.[2]

Allen, James. *See* MACDONALD, George & ALLEN, James.

Allen, Joel Asaph. Alpine flora of the province of Quebec. 1883. I. 310.

— Notes on the natural history of portions of Dakota. 1874. I. 323.

Allen, John Fisk. The culture of the Grape. 1847. III. 549.[1]

— A practical treatise on the culture . . . of the Grape. 1847. III. 549.[2]

— Remarks on the Grape disease of Europe. 1855. III. 576.

Allen, Lewis F. Ornamental trees — The Cotton-wood. 1856. III. 345.[1]

— Ornamental trees. — The Lombardy Poplar.· 1856. III. 346.[1]

Allen, Martin. Tree-planting on the plains. 1833. IV. 112.

Allen, Timothy Field. A critical examination of the materia medica. 1881. III. 243.

Allen, W. J. Fumigating trees for pests. 1900. III. 198.[2]

— Fumigation table. 1900. III. 198.[2]

— Olive culture. 1900. III. 677.[1]

— The Orange. 1900. III. 500.[2]

— The Passion fruit. 1898. III. 615.[2]

— Pruning, grafting, and budding. 1898. III. 147.[2]

— Red scale. 1899. III. 193.[1]
— Some experiments in spraying and fumigating. 1900. III. 198.[2]
—, Blunno, M., **Froggatt**, W. W. & **Guthrie**, F. B. Insect and fungus diseases of fruit-trees. 1899. III. 180.[1]
Allen, William. Experiments upon a substance called da-pêche. 1807. III. 230.
Allent, B. Les végétaux curieux. 1824. I. 94.
Alleon du Lac, J. L. Mélanges d'histoire naturelle. 1763. I. 261.
— Mémoires pour servir à l'histoire naturelle des provinces de Lyonnois. 1765. I. 405.
Allerhöchst bestätigte Verordnung den Schuts der Privat-wälder in Ehstland betreffend. 1875. IV. 286.[1]
Allerhöchst bestätigte Verordnung den Schuts der Privat-wälder in Kurland betreffend. 1874. IV. 286.[1]
Allerhöchst bestätigte Verordnung den Schuts der Privat-wälder in Livland. 1877. IV. 180.[1]
Allescher, Andreas. Zur Blattfleckenkrankheit des Epheu's. 1895. III. 643.[1]
— Zwei gefährliche Parasiten der Gattung Codiaeum. 1895. III. 516.[1]
L,'**allevamento** dei bachi da seta in Ungheria. 1895. III. 148.[2]
Per **allevare** Castagni in breve tempo. 1865. IV. 492.[2]
Alleyne, James. Ars præscribendi. 1731. III. 252.
— A new English dispensator in four parts. 1733. III. 252.
Allgemeine Anordnung betreffs Vorsorge gegen den Frass der Nonnenraupe. 1890. IV. 300.[2]
Allgemeine Bedingungen für Holzhauerlohns-Accorde in den k. württembergischen Staatswaldungen. 1871. IV. 303.[2]
Allgemeine Bestimmungen über Ausbildung und Prüfung für den k. Forstverwaltungsdienst. 1864. IV. 302.
Allgemeine botanische Bibliothek des 19. Jahrhunderts. See BOTANISCHE Zeitung, welche Recensionen . . . I. 11.
Allgemeine botanische Zeitschrift. I. 10.
Allgemeine deutsche Garten- und Blumenzeitung. See NEUE allgemeine . . . III. 13.
Allgemeine deutsche Garten-Zeitung. III. 11.
Allgemeine Disciplinar- und Dienst-Vorschriften für die Forstschutz-Beamten. 1851. IV. 301.
Allgemeine Forst- und Jagd-Zeitung. IV. 6.
Allgemeine Forstbeschreibung der . . . Domaine-Kammer Teschen. See STRZEMCHA, Karl. 1873. IV. 369.
Allgemeine Gärtner-Zeitung. III. 24.[2]
Allgemeine Gartenzeitung. III. 11.
Allgemeine Grundsätze und Regeln für den . . . Culturbe-trieb in Württemberg. 1865. IV. 118.—186 .? IV. 248.[1]
Allgemeine Historie der Reisen zu Wasser und Lande. See MOORE, Francis. 1738. III. 281.[1]
Allgemeine Holz-Industrie-Zeitung. See ALLGEMEINE Holz-Zeitung. IV. 6.
Allgemeine Holz- u. Jagd-Verordnung, für die Städte . . . in den Herzogthümern Schleswig u. Holstein. 1781. IV. 006.[1]
Allgemeine Holz-Zeitung. IV. 6.
Allgemeine Jahrbücher der Forst- und Jagdkunde. See NEUE Jahrbücher . . . IV. 10, and ZEITSCHRIFT für das Forst- und Jagdwesen . . . IV. 11.
Allgemeine land- und forstwirtschaftliche Zeitung. IV. 13.[2]
Allgemeine Landesverordnung . . . gegen die Verheerung durch Insektenschaden. 1798. IV. 205.[2]
Allgemeine neue Forst- u. Jagd Verordnung für die Aemter . . . in den Herzogthümern Schleswig u. Holstein. 1784. IV. 296.[1]
Allgemeine österreichische Zeitschrift für den Landwirth, Forstmann und Gärtner. III. 24,[1] IV. 13.[2]
Allgemeine österreichische Zeitung für Forstcultur. IV. 14.
Allgemeine praktische Forstnaturgeschichte Deutschlands. See MOSER, Heinrich Christoph. IV. 1.
Allgemeine Regeln für die Anpflanzung von Bäumen in Städten. 1900. III. 210.
Allgemeine Sätze über die Pflanzenwelt. See M. 1800. I. 146.
Allgemeine schweizerische Gesellschaft für die gesammten Naturwissenschaften. Denkschriften. Eröffnungsrede. Naturwissenschaftlicher Anzeiger. Verhandlungen. I. 26.[1]
Allgemeine thüringische Gartenzeitung. III. 11.
Allgemeine waldwirtschaftliche Verhältnisse der Herrschaft Mähr.-Kromau. 1892. IV. 369.
Die **allgemeinen** Holzbestandsvorraths-Tabellen von B. Borggreve und A. König. 1892. IV. 231.[1]
Allgemeiner Anzeiger für den Forstprodukten-Verkehr. IV. 6.
Allgemeiner Arbeitsplan für Durchforstungsversuche. 1884. IV. 173.

Allgemeiner Holz- und Forst-Anzeiger. See ALLGEMEINE Holz-Zeitung. IV. 6.
Allgemeiner Holzverkaufs-Anzeiger. IV. 6.
Allgemeiner Kameral-, Oekonomie-, Forst- und Technologie-Korrespondent . . . IV. 6.
Allgemeiner österreichischer Apotheker-Verein. Zeit-schrift. III. 24.[2]
Allgemeiner österreichischer Gartenkalender. See FROMME's Österreichisch-ungarischer Gartenkalender. III. 24.[1]
Allgemeiner Plan der königlichen sächsischen Forstaka-demie zu Tharandt. See KÖNIGLICH sächsische Akademie . . . zu Tharandt. 1830. IV. 31.[1]
Allgemeiner Verein deutscher Gerber. See VEREIN . . . III. 14'
Allgemeines Forst- und Jagd-Archiv. See FORST- UND JAGD-ARCHIV. IV. 7.
Allgemeines Forst- und Jagd-Journal. IV. 14.
Allgemeines Literatur-Repertorium der Technologie, Forst-wissenschaft. 1842. IV. 1.
Allgemeines öconomisches Forst-Magazin. IV. 6.
Allgemeines Repertorium der forstwissenschaftlichen Litera-tur. See GAETTNER, C. W. J. 1796. IV. 1.
Allgemeines teutsches Garten-Magazin. III. 11.
Allgulin, Johan Magnus. De plantis cibariis romanorum. See RETZIUS, A. J. 1808. III. 88.[1]
Alliaume: Solanum betaceum. 1880. III. 699.[2]
Allibert. Résultats obtenus par le traitement des Vignes phyl-loxérées. 1876. III. 569.[1]
Allies, F. Application directe du sulfure de carbone: 1876. III. 568.
— Lettre à M. Dumas sur l'emploi du sulfure de carbone. 1876. III. 568.
— Nouvelle note concernant les résultats obtenus par le traite-ment des Vignes phylloxérées. 1876. III. 569.[2]
— Le phylloxéra. 1876. III. 760.
— Sur un procédé d'application directe du sulfure de carbone. 1876. III. 568.
— Résultats obtenus dans le traitement, par le sulfure de car-bone. 1876. III. 569.[1]
— Résultats obtenus par l'application du sulfure de carbone. 1877. III. 570.[2]
Allin, Thomas. The flowering plants . . . of the county Cork. 1883. V. XXI.[2]
Allioni, Carlo. Flora pedemontana. 1785. I. 424.
— Stirpium praecipuarum littoris agro nicaeensis enumeratio. 1757. I. 405.
— Synopsis methodica stirpium Horti taurinensis. 1760. I. 61.
Allman, William. Analysis per differentias constantes . . . generum plantarum. 1828. I. 349.
Allmann, Georg J. The past winter near Bournemouth. 1887. III. 123.[2]
Allnutt, Henry. The Cactus and other tropical succulents. 1877. II. 586.[2]
De l'allongement de la révolution dans les taillis. 1090. IV. 252.
De l'allongement de la révolution des taillis sous futaie. 1896. IV. 252.
Allport, M. Action of teredo on Blue Gum. 1875. IV. 531.[1]
Alluaud, François, (sr.). Mémoire sur le reboisement. 1845. IV. 121, 161.[1]
Allut. See MALAPERT & ALLUIT.
Allut, Louis César CAZALIS-. See CAZALIS-ALLUT, L.C.
Alm, Jacob. Plantae surinamenses. See LINNÉ, Carl von. 1775. I. 338.[2]
Almanach de Carlsbad. See ORTMANN, Anton. 1831. I. 439.
Almanach der kruidkunde. 1800. I. 33.
Almanach du jardinier. III. 18.
Almedingen, A. See АЛЬМЕДИНГЕНЪ, A.
Almeida, Avelino Nunes d'. Breves palavras sobre a cul-tura das Oliveiras. 1899. III. 676.[2]
Almeida, L. FURQUIM D'. See FURQUIM D' ALMEIDA, L.
Almeida, Verissimo d' & Motta Prego, João da. Les maladies de la Vigne en Portugal. 1895. III. 581.
Almeida Pinto, José de. Diccionario de botanica bra-sileira. See ARRUDA DA CAMARA, Manoel. 1873. I. 343.
Almindelig dansk Gartnerforening. See GARTNER-TIDENDE. III. 10.[2]
Almindelige Bestemmelser for Besigtelse og Klassifikation af Ege- og Fyrre-Materiale ved Orlogsværftet. 1895. IV. 425.[2]
Det. 6. **almindelige** Møde af danske Skovbrugere i Kjøbenhavn. 1891. IV. 39.[2]

Almond, T. R. The lofty Bhotan Pine. 1898. III. 307.[1]
The **Almond** trees of Tunis. 1898. III. 434.[2]
Almquist, Johan Magnus. Om utländske träd, buskar och blomstervixter. *See* THUNBERG, C. P. 1820. I. 266.
— *See* also HAMMARIN, J. I., ALMQUIST, J. M. & HUMBLE, A. H.
Almquist, Sigfrid Oskar Immanuel. Om den floristiska behandlingen af polymorfa slägten. 1880. I. 252.
— Om gruppindelning inom fam. Rosaceæ. 1887. II. 256.[1]
— Om Hippophaë rhamnoides' förekomst i Bohuslän. 1891. II. 608.[1]
Alner, Federicus Ad. *See* FLYGARE, Axel & ALNER, F. A.
Aloes in Natal. 1887. II. 78.[1]
Aloi, Alberto. Sulla necessità di ricorrere ancora a' metodi . . . nella lotta contro la fillossera. 1898. III. 762.
Aloi, Antonio. Caratteri botanici degli Agrumi. 1899. II. 401.[2]
— Dell' influenza dell' elettricità. 1895. I. 231.[2]
— L' Olivo e l' olio. 1898. III. 676.[2]
— Relazioni esistenti tra la traspirazione . . . ed il movimento delle cellule stomatiche. 1891. I. 168.[1]
— Una rivendicazione di priorità. 1884. III. 578.
Alonso de Beraza, J. M. Los derechos de exportación; el corcho. 1898. IV. 559.[2]
Alopäus, S. Nachricht von der Bereitung . . . des Wacholderbaums. 1791. III. 303.[2]
Alp, A. von LILIENFELD. *See* LILIENFELD-ALP, A. von.
Die **Alpenerle** in Tirol. 1862. II. 117.[1]
Alpers, Ferdinand. Verzeichnis der Gefässpflanzen der Landdrostei Stade. 1875. I. 387.
Alpes-Maritimes–Société centrale d'agriculture, d'horticulture . . . *See* SOCIÉTÉ CENTRALE D'AGRICULTURE . . . DE NICE . . . III. 20.
Alpha, (*pseud.*). The Black Austrian Pine. 1881. III. 308.[1]
— Boronia serrulata. 1853. III. 496.[1]
— The Colletias. 1882. III. 541.[2]
— Die Colletias. 1882. III. 541.[2]
— The different kinds of Laurels. 1882. III. 437.[2]
— The Forsythias. 1881. III. 671.[2]
— Greenhouse Rhododendron. 1884. III. 655,
— The Himalayan Spruce. 1881. III. 306.[1]
— Kalmia latifolia. 1882. III. 652.[2]
— Leptospermum grandiflorum. 1854. III. 636.
— More wall plants. 1883. III. 205.[1]
— Propagating Coniferae. 1880. III. 294.[1]
— The Retinosporas. 1880. III. 300.[2]
— Select Thorns. 1882. III. 421.[2]
— Select varieties of Pyrus. 1882. III. 459.[1]
— Shrubby Spiraeas. 1883. III. 460.[1]
— The Swiss Pine. 1881. III. 307.[1]
— Variableness of Conifers. 1882. II. 18.
— Varieties of Pernettya mucronata. 1883. III. 653.[2]
— Varieties of Portugal Laurel. 1882. III. 438.[1]
— The White Alders. 1881. III. 646.[2]
— Zenobia speciosa. 1882. III. 664.[2]
Alphand, Jean Charles Adolphe. Arboretum et fleuriste de la ville. 1875. (*By error entered under* ALPHAND, Alphonse.) II[1]. 8[1].
Alpherts, G. A. De cortice Rhamni Frangulae. 1854. III. 543.[1]
Alpherts, W. I. Flora culenbergensis. 1863. I. 391.[1]
Alphonse, Jean. *See* CARTIER, Jacques, ROBERVAL & ALPHONSE, Jean.
Alpina. I. 26.[1]
The **Alpine** Forest Heath. 1898. III. 651.[1]
Alpine forestry. 1888. IV. 36.[2]
The **alpine** forests of Europe. 1873. I. 531,[1] *IV. 79.*[1]
Alpino, Prospero. *See* ALPINUS, Prosper.
Alpinus, Prosper. De balsamo dialogus. 1591. III. 510.[1]
— Historia du baulme. 1591. III. 510.[1]
— Historiae Aegypti naturalis. 1735. III. 280.[1]
— Liber de balsamo. 1591. III. 510.[1]
— Medicina Aegyptiorum. 1718. III. 280.[1]
— De plantis Aegypti liber. 1592. III. 280.[1]
— De plantis exoticis libri duo. 1627. I. 285,[1] V. xv.[2]
Alschinger, Andreas. Das Brennholz in Zara. 1860. IV. 399.[1]
— Flora jadrensis. 1832. I. 447.
— Unser Brennholz in Zara. 1858. IV. 431.[1]
Alston, Charles. A dissertation on botany. 1753. I. 83.
— Index plantarum praecipue officinalium . . . in Horto medico edinburgensi. 1740. I. 52.
— Lectures on the materia medica. 1770. III. 241.
— Tirocinium botanicum edinburgense. 1753. I. 83, 523.

Alston, E. R. & others. Notes on the fauna and flora of the west of Scotland. *See* RAMSAY, James. 1876. I. 403.
Alstorphius Grevelink, P. W. De houtteelt in de kolonien. 1840. IV. 356.[1]
— Statistiek van de provincie Drenthe. 1840. III. 122.[1]
Alströmer, Clas. Beskrifning på svenska Slok-granen. 1777. II. 34.[1]
Alt, Otto. Tägliche Durchmesserschwankungen der Zweige. 1898. I. 150.[1]
Altamirano, Federico. El Zoapatle. 1873. III. 755.[1]
Altamirano, Fernando. El árbol del Mamey. 1876. III. 667.[2]
— Informe . . . á la Secretaria de fomento . . . O. *See* RAMIREZ, José. 1895. I. 332.
— Leguminosas indígenas medicinales. 1879. III. 462.[2]
— Necesidad de la repoblación de los bosques. 1897. IV. 155.[2]
— & **Ramírez**, José. Lista de nombres vulgares y botánicos de árboles. 1894. I. 331, *IV. 78,*[2] *113.*[1]
Alte Akasien. 1900. II. 383.[2]
Alte Eibenbäume. 1891. IV. 440.[2]
Alte Waldbäume. 1886. I. 297.[2]
Alte Waldbäume im Hochgebirge. 1888. I. 298.[1]
Alten, H. & **Jännicke**, Wilhelm. Krankheitserscheinungen an Camellia. 1891. III. 600.[1]
— — Eine Schädigung von Rosenblättern durch Asphaltdämpfe. 1891. III. 185.[2]
Alten, Johann Wilhelm von. Augsburgische Blumenlese. 1822. I. 376.
Alten, P. von. Eichen-Fassholz. 1884. IV. 514.[1]
— Die Einbürgerung fremder Baumarten. 1898. IV. 126.[1]
— Ergebniss der Holzsamen-Ernte. *See* ERGEBNISS der Holzsamen-Ernte. 1875. IV. 438.[1]
— Die Federegge von Ingermann. 1886. IV. 143.[1]
— Frost-Schäden im Weiden-Heeger. 1885. III. 350.[1]
— Neue Keimapparate. 1886. III. 157.
— Die Pflanharke. 1891. IV. 150.
— Schaden durch Treibeis. 1884. IV. 185.[1]
— Senkerbildung der Weymouthskiefer. 1882. II. 46.[1]
— Unsere Nadelholz-Keimlinge. 1885. II. 18.
— Versuche . . . mit Rothbuchen-Nutzholz. 1895. IV. 499.
— Weymouthskiefern-Holz. 1882. IV. 470.[2]
— Wie wirkt die Saatzeit auf die Erziehung von Kiefern-Jährlinge? 1887. IV. 473.
Alter Wachholderbaum. 1887. II. 31.[1]
Altération du bois de Chêne. 1898. IV. 514.[1]
Altern die Pflanzensorten? *See* DEGENERACY of races. 1857. I. 205, *248.*[1]
Alternation of generations. 1897. I. 101,[1] *205.*
Altheer, J. J. Chemisch-physiologisch onderzoek naar . . . Cocculus crispus. 1860. II. 208.[2]
— Examen chimico-physiologique du . . . Cocculus crispus. 1860. II. 208.[2]
— Scheikundig onderzoek . . . van Cerbera odollam. 1863. III. 687.[1]
— Scheikundig onderzoek van den bast van Nauclea. 1858. III. 746.[2]
— Scheikundig onderzoek . . . van den wortel der Cicca disticha. 1858. III. 521.[2]
Alting Siberg, J. Beschrijving van het eiland Bawean. 1846. I. 465.
Altmann, L. Die nützlichen und schädlichen Forstinsekten. 1844. IV. 92.
— Die nützlichen und schädlichen Forstkäfer. 1844. IV. 92.
Altmayer, Nicolas. Mémoire sur cette question: Quels sont les avantages . . . du défrichement des forêts? 1842. IV. 282.[2]
— Quels sont les avantages et les inconvénients généraux ou spéciaux du défrichement des forêts? 1842. IV. 43.
Altomari, Donati Antonio. De mannae differentijs. 1562. III. 220.[2]
— De vinacceorum facultate, ac usu. 1563. III. 218.[2]
Altomètre Philippe. 1894. IV. 550.[1]
Alton, St. Eloy d'. Notes on the plants indigenous to . . . Victoria. 1898. I. 505.
Altona — **Garten- und Blumen-Verein**. *See* GARTEN-. . . III. 12.
Altra causa che rende le piene ognor più gravi. 1880. IV. 50.
Altra causa che tende ad aumentare le piene. 1880. IV. 50.
Altum, Bernhard. Zur Abwehr einer Kiefernspannergefahr. 1895. IV. 479.
— Agrotis tritici, Getreideeule. 1878. IV. 477.

— Der Ahornbockkäfer. 1875. III. 534.[1]
— Der Alpenbockkäfer. 1879. IV. 497.
— Antheeren der Nadelholztriebe gegen Wildverbiss. 1879. IV. 196.[2]
— Das Antinonnin im Dienste des Forstschutzes. 1893. IV. 201.
— Aradus cinnamomeus Pz. 1879. IV. 477.
— Das Auftreten der Gespinnstblattwespen. 1882. IV. 207.
— Das Auftreten der Kiefernnadelscheiden-Gallmücke. 1892. IV. 478.
— Ueber Baumbeschädigungen durch Spechte. 1896. IV. 199.[1]
— Behandlung des mausefrässigen Buchenaufschlages. 1880. IV. 497.
— Die Bekämpfung der Nonne. 1892. IV. 201.
— Bekämpfung der waldschädlichen Mäuse. 1893. IV. 198.[2]
— Beschädigungen an Eichen durch Eichhörnchen. 1873. IV. 198.[1]
— Beschädigungen . . . durch Eichhörnchen. 1873. I. 207,[2] IV. 198.[1]
— Buprestis (Chrysobothris) affinis. 1880. IV. 510.
— Cerambyx fascicularis, Bostrichus bidens. 1875. IV. 477.
— Drei Eichenblattzerstörer. 1896. IV. 511.
— Der Eichenerdfloh. 1878. IV. 510.
— Einfluss des Raupenleims auf die . . . Bäume. 1894. IV. 200.
— Zur Entwicklungsgeschichte und Vertilgung des grossen braunen Rüsselkäfers. 1884. IV. 207.
— Ueber den Erfolg der künstlichen Verbreitung der Flacheriebazillen. 1893. IV. 201.
— Ueber den Erfolg der Versuche zur Vertilgung der Engerlinge mittels Fangknüppel. 1885. IV. 203.
— Erreichung einer einheitlichen Nomenclatur. 1890. IV. 57.
— Feinde des Buchenaufschlags. 1888. IV. 497.
— Zur Förderung des Fichtensamen-Anfluges. 1889. IV. 456.
— Die Folgen der letzten Massenvermehrung der Nonne. 1880. IV. 477.
— Die forstliche Verwendbarkeit neuer Mittel zur Vertilgung der Mäuse. 1895. IV. 198.[2]
— Die forstlichen Beschädigungen des Siebenschläfers. 1878. IV. 198.[1]
— Die forstschädlichen Elateren. 1879. IV. 207.
— Forstzoologie. 1872. IV. 90.[1]
— Ueber den Frass des Kiefernspanners. 1890. IV. 478.
— Der gebänderte Kiefernspanner. 1889. IV. 478.
— Genaueres über die Lebensweise des grossen braunen Rüsselkäfers. 1879. IV. 442.
— Der grosse schwarze Eschenbastkäfer. 1879. IV. 535.[1]
— Kahlfrass von Birken durch Cimbex lucorum. 1879. IV. 490.[3]
— Kieferninsecten auf einer Brandfläche. 1880. IV. 477.
— Die Kiefernnadelmotte. 1887. IV. 479.
— Die Kiefernsaat-Eule. 1875. IV. 207.
— Der Kiefernstangen-Rüsselkäfer. 1879. IV. 477.
— Der Krahe'sche Käfer-Fangapparat für Weidenheger. 1899. III. 350.[3]
— Kukuk und Prozessionsraupe. 1870. IV. 199.[1]
— Lachnus exsicator. 1878. IV. 497.
— Die langschnäbelige Baumlaus. 1879. IV. 207.
— Lebensweise der Chrysomela vitellinae. 1880. III. 350.[1]
— Zur Lebensweise . . . des Kieferprozessionsspinners. 1895. IV. 479.
— Lebensweise und Bekämpfung der Lyda pratensis. 1899. IV. 479.
— Der Linden-Prachtkäfer. 1880. III. 585.[1]
— Das massenhafte Auftreten der Kiefern-Buschhornblattwespe. 1898. IV. 479.
— Mittheilungen aus dem Walde über Vertilgungsmittel forstschädlicher Insecten. 1878. IV. 199.[1]
— Mittheilungen . . . über den Kiefernspinner und die Nonne. 1879.[1] IV. 477.
— Die Nadelholzprocessionsspinner. 1878. IV. 442.
— Neue Erfahrungen über schädliche Weideninsecten. 1882. III. 350.[1]
— Neuere Beobachtungen über den Kiefernprozessionsspinner. 1896. IV. 479.
— Die Nonne (Liparis monacha) in Kiefern. 1878. IV. 477.
— Ornias araneiformis Schrk. 1892. III. 350,[3] IV. 511.
— Pissodes validirostris Schoenh. 1886. IV. 478.
— Primäre und secundäre Insectenfrass. 1879. IV. 207.
— Das "Rabenfederchen." 1894. IV. 489.[1]
— Der Raupenleim. 1892. IV. 199.[3]

— Resultate von neuen Versuchen zur Vernichtung unserer Borkenkäfer. 1885. IV. 204.
— Rüsselkäfergefahr für Eichenkulturen. 1887. IV. 511.
— Zum Schutze gegen die verderblichen Eichenrüsselkäfer. 1879. IV. 510.
— Sehr starker Raupenfrass in Buchen. 1898. IV. 497.
— Die Spechtringelbäume. 1873. I. 207,[2] IV. 198.[2]
— Das Streurechen zur Vertilgung forstschädlicher Insecten. 1886. IV. 199.[1]
— Die durch Thiere erzeugten Baumringelungen. 1877. IV. 196.[1]
— Tortrix chlorana. 1873. III. 352.[2]
— Tortrix (Grapholitha) Zebeana Ratz. 1886. IV. 451.
— Unsere Mäuse in ihrer forstlichen Bedeutung. 1880. IV. 198.[1]
— Unsere Spechte und ihre forstliche Bedeutung. 1878. IV. 90.[1]
— Untersuchungen über die Boden-Temperatur, bei welcher das Aufbäumen der Raupen des Kiefernspinners erfolgt. 1872. IV. 476.
— Aus Veranlassung des . . . auftretenden Massenfrasses der Nonne. 1890. IV. 456.
— Zur Vertilgung der Borken- und Rüsselkäfer. 1883. IV. 199.[3]
— Vertilgung der Engerlinge. 1888. IV. 203.
— Zur Vertilgung der Maikäferlarven. 1887. IV. 203.
— Zur Vertilgung der Rothschwanzraupe. 1889. IV. 207.
— Zur Vertilgung der wurzelbrütenden Hylesinen. 1887. IV. 199.[2]
— Zur Vertilgung des Kiefernspanners. 1885. IV. 478.
— Zur Vertilgung des Kiefernspinners. 1876. IV. 199.[1]
— Vertilgung verschiedener . . . Insectenspecies. 1881. IV. 199.[2]
— Waldbeschädigungen durch Thiere. 1889. IV. 196.[1]
— Die den Weidenhegern schädlichen Insecten. 1879. III. 350.[1]
— Ueber Weideninsecten. 1888. III. 350.[1]
— Ueber den Werth der Brutknüppel. 1888. IV. 207.
— Durch wilde Kaninchen angerichtete Schäden. 1900. IV. 198.[2]
— Wipfeldürre der Kiefernuberständer. 1884. IV. 477.
— Ueber Woll- und Schildläuse. 1885. IV. 207.
— Zerhacken junger Bäume durch den grossen Buntspecht. 1875. IV. 198.[1]
— Zerstörung der Eichenknospen durch Rüsselkäfer. 1896. IV. 511.
— Zerstörung junger Fichtenpflanzen durch Strophosomus coryli. 1885. IV. 456.
— Zerstörung von Baum . . . knospen durch Vögel. 1897. IV. 199.[1]
— Zerstörung von Eichen- und Kiefernsaaten. 1899. IV. 479, 511.
— Zerstörung zweijähriger Fichtenbüschelpflanzen. 1894. IV. 457.
— Zwei Eichheister-Prachtkäfer. 1879. IV. 510.
— Der zweibindige Prachtkäfer. 1879. IV. 510.
— Der zweipunktirte Eichenprachtkäfer. 1879. IV. 510.
— See also Альтум, Бернард.

Alvarez, Francisco. Noticia del establecimiento y poblacion de las colonias inglesas en la America septentrionale. 1778. III. 261.[2]

Alvares Alvistur, Luis. Los frutos de la tierra. 1878. III. 218.[1]

Alvarez de Quindos y Baena, Juan Antonio. Descripción historica del real bosque y casa de Aranjuez. 1804. I. 60.[1]

Alvarez Perez, José. Apuntes sobre el Argan. 1877. III. 666.[2]

Alvarez Sereix, Rafael. De algunas escuelas de montes. 1880. IV. 30.[1]
— Causa de la ascensión de la savia. 1884. I. 165.
— Escuela de montes de Vallombrosa. 1880. IV. 35.[2]
— Estudios botánico-forestales. 1884. I. 271,[1] IV. 85.[2]
— Estudios botánico-forestales. 1886. IV. 86.[1]
— Influencia de los montes en el clima. 1884. IV. 44.
— Los montes de América. 1881. IV. 271.[2]
— Los montes públicos en Francia. 1884. IV. 361.
— Neustadt-Eberswalde. 1880. III. 38.[1]
— Una polemica sobre montes. 1886. IV. 276.[3]
— La venta de los montes. 1886. IV. 276.[3]
— Voz de alarma. 1881. IV. 547.[2]

Alves, G. M. Catalpa posts. 1880. IV. 538.[2]
Alves Pereira da Fonseca, A. A. M. V. See PEREIRA DA FONSECA, A. A. M. V. ALVES.

Alvistur, Luis ALVAREZ. See ALVAREZ ALVISTUR, Luis.

Alvord, William. The consumption of wood in the Comstock mines. 1895. IV. 425.²
— The forests of California. 1892. IV. 340.³
Et par **alvorlige** Ord i Tide til S. T. Magistraten, angaaende Brændets ubilige Priis. 1797. IV. 281.³
Alwood, William B. & Phillips, J. L. Growing forest tree seedlings. 1898. IV. 543.³
Alyon, Pierre Philippe. Cours de botanique. 1787. III. 51.
Alzate y Ramirez, José Antonio de. Memoria acerca del ambar amarillo. 1884. III. 227.
— Memoria en que se trata del insecto grana ó cochinilla. 1795. III. 624.¹
Amacher, Chr. Bauern und Förster. 1895. IV. 278.³
Amadeo, Antonio José. The botany of the island of Porto Rico. 1888. I. 336.
Amado, Hilarion RUIZ. *See* RUIZ AMADO, Hilarion.
Amandelolie. 1883. III. 434.³
Amann, Nicolaus N. Flora alpina. *See* LINNÉ, Carl von. 1756. I. 219.³
Amateur gardening for the lovers . . . of flowers. III. 2.
Amati, Michael. De opobalsami specie. 1722. III. 510.²
Amatore, Un, (*pseud.*). La Nyssa villosa. 1888. III. 632.¹
Amatus Lusitanus, (*pseud.*). In Dioscoridis Anazarbei De materia medica libros enarrationes. 1553. I. 279, 530.²
— Index Dioscoridis. 1536. I. 277.
Amblard, Désiré. Culture des arbres à branches renversées. 1892. III. 174.¹
— Note sur les variétés de Vignes. 1885. III. 556.
Amblard, Francisque. Recherches pour servir à l'étude . . . du Dividivi. 1870. II. 339.³
Ambodik, Nestor Maksimovich. Novum dictionarium botanicum rosso-latino-germanicum. 1808. I. 72.¹
— Plantae medicinales. 1783. III. 55.
Ambronn, Hermann. Einige Bemerkungen zu den Abhandlungen des Herrn Wortmann. 1886. I. 196.³
— Über die Entwickelungsgeschichte . . . des Collenchyms. 1879. I. 134.³
— Ueber heliotropische und geotropische Torsionen. 1884. I. 194.
— Zur Mechanik des Windens. 1884. I. 196.³
— Ueber das optische Verhalten der Cuticula. 1888. I. 129.³
— Das optische Verhalten . . . des Kirschgummis. 1889. I. 181.¹
— Über Poren in den Aussenwänden von Epidermiszellen. 1884. I. 129.³
— *See also* WESTERMAIER, Max & AMBRONN, Hermann.
Ambrosi, Francesco. Flora del Tirolo meridionale. 1854. I. 441.
Ambrosini, Bartolomeo. De Capsicorum varietate . . . brevis historia. 1630. II. 769.³
— Panacea ex herbis quæ a sanctis denominantur. 1630. III. 238.¹
Ambrosini, Giacinto. Hortus studiosorum (Bononiae). 1657. I. 60,³ V. VIII.²
— Novarum plantarum . . . historia. 1657. V. XV.³
— Phytologiae . . . tomus primus. 1666. I. 72,¹ (*by error* 1656), 286.
Ambrosini, Hyacintho. *See* AMBROSINI, Giacinto.
Amé, Georges. Le Jardin d'essai du Hamma à Mustapha près d'Alger. 1884. I. 69.¹
The **Amelanchier**. 1878. II. 258.¹
Amélioration et aménagement du domaine forestier communal. 1898. IV. 248.¹
Améliorations à apporter dans un domaine. 1900. IV. 129.
Les **améliorations** agricoles et forestières. 1899. IV. 135.¹
Aménagement de la forêt de Haguenau. 1860. IV. 248.³
L'**aménagement** de nos forêts. 1899. IV. 248.³
De l'**aménagement** en taillis. *See* Zum LAUBHOLZ-Niederwald-Betrieb. 1858. IV. 132.¹
Amendement zu dem Berichte der verstärkten Agrar-Kommission . . . betreffend die Bildung von Waldgenossenschaften. *See* BERICHT der verstärkten Kommission. 1869. IV. 308.³
Ament. De cultuur . . . der West-Indische Koffie. 1836. III. 729.¹
La **America** cientifica e industrial. *See* AMERICAN agriculturist. III. 2.
An **American**. *See* AMERICAN husbandry. 1775. III. 261.¹
American; a national weekly journal of politics. III. 2.
American academy of arts and sciences. Memoirs. Proceedings. I. 4.²
American agricultural association. Journal. III. 2.
American agriculturist. III. 2.
American almanac. III. 2.

American and British Larch. 1875. IV. 448.²
American anthropologist. III. 2.
American antiquarian society. Transactions. I. 4.²
American Arbor vitae. 1874. II. 52.²
American architect. IV. 3.
American association for the advancement of science. Proceedings. I. 4.²
American association of nurserymen. Proceedings. Report. III. 2.
The **American Beech**. 1891. III. 360.¹
American botanist. I. 4.²
The **American Buckeyes**. 1891. II. 481.¹
American builder. Cleveland. IV. 3.
American builder. New York. IV. 3.
American builders' journal. *See* ARCHITECTURAL review. IV. 3.
American chemical journal. I. 4.²
American cultivator. III. 2.
American druggist and pharmaceutical record. I. 4.²
American druggists' circular. I. 4.²
American economic association. Publications. III. 2.
The **American Elm**. 1890. II. 143,³ 144.¹
American field. *See* CHICAGO field. IV. 3.
American florist. III. 2.
American forest; or, Uncle Philip's conversations. 1834. I. 304.
The **American forest-fires**. 1894. IV. 182.¹
American forest trees in spring. 1895. III. 203.
American forestry. 1880. IV. 155.¹
American forestry association. *See* AMERICAN FORESTRY CONGRESS. IV. 3.
The **American** forestry congress — Cincinnati meeting. 1882. IV. 39.¹
The **American** forestry congress — Montreal meeting. 1882. IV. 39.¹
American forestry congress. Proceedings. IV. 3.
The **American forests**. 1881. IV. 337.¹
American forests and forestry. 1883. IV. 337.¹
American furniture gazette. IV. 3.
American garden. III. 2.
American gardener's magazine. *See* MAGAZINE of horticulture. III. 5.
American gardening. *See* AMERICAN garden. III. 2.
The **American Hawthorns**. 1892. III. 421.³
American historical record. *See* POTTER'S American monthly. III. 7.
American horticultural annual. III. 2.
American horticultural society. Transactions. *See* MISSISSIPPI VALLEY HORTICULTURAL SOCIETY. III. 6.
American horticulturist. III. 2.
American husbandry. 1775. III. 261.¹
American institute. Journal. III. 2.
American institute of mining engineers. Transactions. IV. 3.
American institute of the city of New York. Annual report. III. 2.
American journal of forestry. IV. 3.
American journal of horticulture. III. 2.
American journal of pharmacy. I. 4.²
American journal of science and arts. I. 4.²
American journal of the medical sciences. I. 4.²
The **American Larch** (Larix microcarpa). 1885. III. 304.²
The **American Locust tree**. *See* The LOCUST tree. 1890. II. 383.¹
American lumber in foreign markets. 1894. IV. 403.²
American lumberman. IV. 3.
American medical association. Journal. Transactions. I. 5.
American monthly magazine and critical review. I. 5.
American monthly review of reviews. *See* REVIEW of reviews. New York. III. 8.
American naturalist. I. 5.
American Oaks. 1876. III. 128.³
American paper and pulp association. Report. IV. 3.
American paper trade and wood pulp news. IV. 3.
American pharmaceutical association. Proceedings. I. 5.
American philosophical society held at Philadelphia. Proceedings. Transactions. I. 5.
American Pitch Pine. 1858. IV. 462.³
The **American Pitch Pine**. 1887. III. 308.²
American pomological society. Proceedings. III. 2.
American Poplars. 1892. II. 96.¹
American public health association. Public health reports. IV. 3.
The **American Rose culturist**. *See* SAXTON, C. M. 1852. III. 448.

An **American** school of forestry. 1888. IV. 30.[1]
American silk and fruit culturist. III. 2.
American society of civil engineers. Transactions. III. 2.
American statistical association. Publications. IV. 3.
The **American** timber supply. 1880. IV. 403.[2]
American wood preserving company. See THILMANY, Walde-
mar. 1875. IV. 419.
American wood-worker. IV. 3.
Die **amerikanische** Möbelpolsterung mit Holzspänen. 1868.
IV. 429.
Der **amerikanische** Urwald. 1890. I. 308.
Amerikansk Dvergkirsebaer. 1895. III. 442.[2]
Amérique contre Europe. 1895. IV. 557.[1]
Amerling, Karl. Ueber Asynapta lugubris auf Pflaumen-
bäumen. 1859. III. 433.[2]
— Einige neu entdeckte Feinde der Birkenwaldungen. 1860.
IV. 490.[2]
— Einige physiokratische Beobachtungen an den Obstbäumen.
1858. III. 178.
— Die Heteroemphyteuse. 1867. III. 165.
— Ueber Hibernakel-Ringe. 1858. I. 108.[1]
— Uiber [sic] Naturcomplexe einiger Nutzpflanzen. 1868.
II. 508.[1]
— Ueber naturökonomische und physiokratische Tabellen.
1858. III. 189.
— Die Siechperiode der Birken. 1857. II. 118.[1]
— Über die wissenschaftlichen Grundlagen der Pomologie.
1864. III. 90.[1]
Amersfoordt, J. P. Esschen schildluis. 1863. IV. 535.[1]
— Losmaken van den grond voor bosschen. 1860. IV. 143.[1]
— Wilgen pooten. 1860. III. 347.
Amery, C. F. Notes on forestry. 1875. IV. 124.[2]
— Report on the forests of India. 1878. IV. 377.[2]
— The special survey branch. 1876. IV. 295.[1]
Ames, Oakes. Concerning Acalypha hispida. 1898. III.
514.[2]
Amherst, _Hon._ Alicia Margaret Tyssen. A history of garden-
ing in England. 1895. III. 33.[2]
Amici, Giovanni Battista. Beiträge zur Pflanzen-Anatomie
und Physiologie. 1823. I. 98.
— On the disease of the Vine. 1853. III. 576.
— De druivenziekte. 1853. III. 576.
— Microscopical observations. 1823. I. 123.[2]
— Note sur le mode d'action du pollen sur le stigmate. 1830.
I. 200.
— Observations microscopiques sur diverses espèces de plantes.
1823. I. 98.
— Osservazioni microscopiche sopra varie piante. 1823. I.
98, 123.[2]
L'**Amico** dei campi. III. 24.[2]
Amm, Anton. Untersuchungen über die intramolekulare
Athmung. 1893. I. 171.
Ammann, Johann. De Betula pumila. 1744. II. 119.[2]
— De Lapatho orientali. 1751. II. 184.[1] \.
— Quinque nova plantarum genera. 1741. I. 291.
— Stirpium rariorum in imperio rutheno. 1739. I. 359.
Ammann, August. Die Pflanzenkrankheiten. 1867. III. 179.
Ammann, Johann. See AMMAN, Johann.
Ammann, Paul. Character plantarum naturalis. 1676. I.
287.
— Curae secundae quibus character plantarum naturalis
. . . redditus. 1676. I. 287.
— Hortus Bosianus. 1686. I. 43.
— Supellex botanica. 1675. I. 43.
Ammersin, Wendelin. Brevis relatio de electricitate propria
lignorum. 1754. IV. 412.[3]
L'**amministrazione** dei boschi demaniali inalienabili. 1887.
IV. 293.[2]
Dell' **amministrazione** dei boschi in Piemonte. 1861. IV.
293.[1]
Amministrazione forestale. 1865. IV. 293.[2]
Amministrazione forestale del Portogallo. 1866. IV. 293.[1]
Per l' **amministrazione** forestale del regno d' Italia. 1869. IV.
328.
Amney, J. C. Empleurum serrulatum. 1895. III. 504.[1]
Amo y **Mora**, Mariano del. Flora fanerogámica de la penin-
sula iberica. 1871. I. 421.
— Memoria sobre la distribucion geografica de . . . Cruci-
feras, Leguminosas. 1861. I. 421.
— See also CUTANDA, Vicente & AMO, Y MORA, Mariano del.
El **amoniaco** en la vegetación. 1889. IV. 543.[1]
El **amoniaco** y las tierras de cultivo. 1890. IV. 543.[2]
Amor, Fernando. Recuerdos de un viage á Marruecos.
1859. I. 421.

Amoretti, Carlo. Elettrometria de' vegetali. 1816. I. 231.[1]
— Viaggio da Milano ai tre laghi Maggiore. 1824. I. 426.
Amoreux, Pierre Joseph. Dissertation philologique sur les
plantes religieuses. 1817. I. 513.
— Dissertation . . . sur l'origine du cachou. 1812. III.
463.[1]
— Dissertation sur les Pommes d'or des Hespérides. 1809.
III. 499.[1]
— État de la végétation sous le climat de Montpellier. 1809.
I. 226.[de]
— Mémoire sur les haies. 1787. III. 212.[2]
— Traité de l'Olivier. 1784. III. 674.[2]
— Traité des haies vives. 1787. III. 212.[2]
Gli **amori** delle piante. See DARWIN, Erasmus. 1789. I. 93.
Amorim Castro, Joaquim de. Memoria sobre a cochonilha do
Brasil. 1790. III. 624.[1]
— Memoria sobre o Malvaisco . . . da Cachoeira. 1791.
III. 589.[1]
Les **amours** des plantes. See DARWIN, Erasmus. 1789. I.
93.
Les **amours** des plantes. See MELLEVILLE. 1835. I. 199.
Ampelografia italiana. 1878. III. 547.
Ampelopsis an Ulmus americana. 1900. III. 545.[1]
Amrhyn, X., _Freiherr_. Etwelche Bemerkungen über das
Forstgesetz des Kantons Luzern. 1858. IV. 330.
— Uebersicht über das Forstwesen im Kanton Luzern. 1843.
IV. 365.
Amsig, Edm. L'arbre Pécher en Belgique. 1856. III.
440.[2]
Amsterdam — **Congrès international de botanique et d'hor-
ticulture.** See CONGRÈS . . . I, 15.
Amsterdam — **Congrès international de botanistes, d'horti-
culteurs** . . . See CONGRÈS . . . I, 15.
Amsterdam — **Genootschap ter bevordering van natuur-
genees- en heelkunde.** See GENOOTSCHAP . . . I. 15.
Amsterdam — **Koninklijk nederlandsch instituut van weten-
schappen, letterkunde** . . . See KONINKLIJK . . . I, 15.
Amsterdam — **Maatschappij ter bevordering van den land-
bouw.** See MAATSCHAPPIJ . . . III. 14.
Amtliche Mittheilungen aus der Abteilung für Forsten des K.
preuss. Ministeriums. See AMTLICHE Mittheilungen be-
treffend die Wirthschaftsergebnisse. 1892. IV. 354.
Amuat, Xavier. Ueber die Aufästung der Waldbäume.
1861. IV. 170.
— Des défauts dans le traitement des forêts communales.
1868. IV. 309,[1] 366.
— Sur l'ébranchage des arbres forestiers. 1861. IV. 170.
— Holz-Tabellen; Berechnung des kantigen und runden
Holzes in Kubikmass. 1858. IV. 224.
— Quelle est le meilleur procédé à suivre dans le traitement des
pâturages boisés. 1863. IV. 135.[2]
— Quelles sont les mesures à prendre pour favoriser la réussite
des plantations sur les sols argileux. 1868. IV. 68.
— Tarif pour le cubage des bois ronds. n. d. IV. 224.
— Welches ist das zweckmässigste Verfahren in Behandlung
. . . von Waldungen auf Wytweiden. 1863. IV. 123,[1] 135.[3]
An English resident, (_pseud._). Forest economy in Sweden.
1880. IV. 344.[2]
— Les forêts en Suède. 1880. IV. 344.[2]
Anales de ciencias naturales. See ANALES de historia natural.
I. 24.[1]
Anales de historia natural. I. 24.[1]
Analisi vegetabili. See TOMMASELLI, Giuseppe. 1794.
I. 254.[xlei]
Analogy between alpine and arctic vegetation. 1850. I. 219.
Sur l'**analyse** des feuilles de Séné. 1874. III. 470.[2]
Analyse des plantes vasculaires du Lyonnais. 1838. I. 409.
Analyse du sol. Renseignements à en tirer relativement au
choix des essences. 1900. IV. 70.
Analyse von upas antiar. 1838. III. 366.[2]
Analysis mali Citrei compendiosa. See GRUBE, Hermann.
1668. III. 498.[2]
Analysis of returns in reply to queries relating to colonial tim-
ber. 1878. IV. 396,[2] 405.[1]
Analytical key to the chief arboreous Conifers of the Punjab
Himalaya. 1874. II. 15.[1]
Anatomia vegetale. 1861. IV. 62.[1]
Anbau der Edelkastanie. 1878. IV. 493.[3]
Anbau der Kiefer. 1833. IV. 471.
Vom **Anbau** der vorzüglichsten inn- und ausländischen Holz-
arten. 1789. IV. 116.
Der **Anbau** der weissen Akazie. 1837. IV. 523.[1]
Der **Anbau** des Weissen Maulbeerbaums. See Het AANK-
WEEKEN . . . 1868. III. 377.

Anbau exotischer Holzarten. 1887. IV. 127.[2]
Anbau-, Forst- und Erntestatistik. *See* MAYET, P. 1894. IV. 349.[2]
Anbau und Erziehung der Buche durch Pflanzung. 1842. IV. 494.
Anbau von Vaccinium macrocarpum Hort. 1876. III. 663.[2]
Die **Anbauversuche** ausländischer Nadelholzarten in Grossbritannien. *See* CULTURE des arbres conifères exotiques. 1852. IV. 126.[2]
Anbauversuche mit fremden Holzarten in Preussen. 1885. IV. 125.[2]
Anbauversuche mit fremdländischen Holzarten. 1891. IV. 127.[2]
Anceau. Le Bambou comestible de la Chine. 1861. III. 814.[1]
Ancelon. De la nature de la maladie de la Vigne. 1864. III. 577.
Anchald, Henry d'. La foudre et les arbres. 1900. IV. 195.[1]
Anciennes lois forestières anglaises. *See* ANCIENT English forest laws. 1878. IV. 323.[1]
Ancient English forest laws. 1878. IV. 323.[1]
Ancient Pinus Cambra. 1858. II. 41.[1]
Ancient Yew. 1845. II. 10.[2]
Anckeveen, G. de WAAL VAN. *See* WAAL VAN ANCKEVEEN, G. de.
Ancona, Cesare d'. Bignonia magnifica. 1887. III. 705.
— La Brahea Roezlii. 1883. III. 321.[1]
— Camoënsia maxima. 1886. III. 469.[2]
— Epacris onosmaeflora flore-pleno nivalis. 1884. III. 665.[1]
— Erica Cavendishiana. 1885. III. 651.[1]
— Le foglie in autunno. 1877. III. 207.[1]
— La Kentia Belmoreana Wendl. 1884. III. 325.[2]
— Luculia gratissima Sweet. 1889. III. 745.[2]
— Nannorhops Ritchieana. 1887. III. 327.[2]
— Pithecoctenium buccinatorium. 1888. III. 707.[1]
— Rhododendron × Countess of Haddington. . 1885. III. 658.[2]
Ancona, Giovachino F."M. de. Succinto trattato che porta per titolo: La seconda ricchezza del Moro. 1844. III. 379.[2]
Ancora della malsania del Nocciolo. 1898. IV. 492.[1]
Ancora gl' insetti! 1866. IV. 209.[2]
Ancora la legge forestale 20 Giugno 1877. -1895. IV. 329.
Ancora sulla riforma della legge forestale. 1896. IV. 329.
Ancora sulla ruggine dell' Ulivo. 1897. III. 678.[1]
Andalorius, Andreas. Il Caffée descritto ed esaminato. 1703. III. 738.
Andaman Islands. *See* INDIA-ANDAMAN ISLANDS.
Andeer, Peter Justus. Der Albula. 1858. I. 435.
— & others. Flora Galliae & Germaniae exsiccata. 1864. I. 413.
Een en ander betreffende kweek . . . van Liberiakoffie. 1895. III. 743.[1]
Een en ander over Thee. 1884. III. 602.[1]
Anderegg, Felix. Die Obstbaumpflanzungen an Strassen im Kanton Bern. 1887. III. 211.[1]
— & Ernst. Agriculture. 1895. III. 1.
— Landwirthschaft; die Literatur von ihren Anfängen. 1895. III. 1.
Anderes. Mittheilungen über die Zucht des Ailanthusspinners. 1865. III. 507.[2]
Anderlind, Leo. Die Dorneckereiche. 1892. II. 140.[2]
— Ueber die Einwirkung des Salzgehaltes der Luft auf den Baumwuchs. 1894. III. 42.[1]
— Der kalifornische Giftstrauch. 1891. III. 527.[1]
— A note on the Californian Poison Oak. 1891. III. 527.[1]
— Die Waldbewässerung als Mittel zur Vertilgung 'forstschädlicher Thiere. 1896. IV. 200.
— Die Waldbewässerung als Mittel zur Vertilgung hauptsächlich der . . . Kerfe. 1896. IV. 200.
Andersen, F. J. Bemærkninger om langenske Plantager paa öte Kronborg Skovdistrikt. 1872. IV. 343.[1]
Andersen, M. P. Virkningerne af Kryds- og Selvbefrugtning. 1879. I. 245.
Anderson. *See also* ANDERSSON.
Anderson, (*Dr.*). Analysis of the ash of Larch seed. 1851. II. 33.[1]
Anderson, Alexander. Observations on the Clove plant. 1802. II. 627.[2]
— State of some of the most valuable plants in . . . botanical gardens in the island of St. Vincent. 1798. III. 64.[1]
Anderson, Alexander Pierce. Ueber abnorme Bildung von Harzbehältern. 1896. I. 207,[1] *IV. 66,[1] 442.*
— Comparative anatomy of . . . Abies balsamea. 1897. II. 22.[2]

— Comparative anatomy of . . . Abies balsamea. 1898. IV. 444.[1]
— On the formation . . . of abnormal resin-ducts. 1896. II. 16.[2]
— Stomata on the bud-scales of Abies. 1897. II. 23.[2]
Anderson, Charles Lewis. A catalogue of Nevada flora. 1870. I. 323.
— A few Californian Willows. 1879. II. 99.[2]
— A few of our native Willows. 1879. II. 99.[2]
— A monoecious Willow. 1890. II. 107.[2-]
Anderson, George. Description of a new British Rubus. 1815. II. 309.[1]
— A monograph of the genus Paeonia. 1818. II. 200.[1]
— & Peter. Guide to the highlands . . . of Scotland. 1834. I. 398.
Anderson, Graham. Jottings on Coffee . . . in Mysore. 1879. III. 732.[2]
Anderson, Hjalmar & Källström, Ernst. Folia Uvae ursi. 1896. III. 648.[2]
Anderson, Isaac. Sikkim Rhododendrons. 1858. III. 654.[1]
Anderson, James. The conclusion of the letters on the culture of silk. 1792. ' III. 373.
— The continuation of letters on the progress . . . of the culture of silk. 1792. III. 373.
— Correspondence for the introduction of cochineal insects from America. 1791. III. 129.[2]
— A letter . . . shewing that a great proportion of the timber used in shipping is decayed. 1834. IV. 413.[2]
— Letters for the culture of bastard Cedar trees. 1794. III. 129.[2]
— Letters . . . on the subject of cochineal insects. 1788. III. 235.[2]
— Miscellaneous observations on planting . . . timber-trees. 1777. IV. 120.
— Some additional letters principally regarding the culture of raw silk. 1792. III. 373.
Anderson, James F. Lodoicea Seychellarum. 1883. II. 70.[2]
Anderson, Johann. Beschryving van Island, Groenland. 1746. I. 351.
— Histoire naturelle de l'Islande. 1746. I. 351.
— Nachrichten von Island, Grönland. 1746. I. 351.
Anderson, John. The strength of materials. 1872. IV. 410.
— The strength of timber. 1872. IV. 410.
Anderson, Peter. *See* ANDERSON, George & Peter.
Anderson, Thomas. Catalogue of plants cultivated in the Royal botanical gardens, Calcutta. 1865. I. 67.[1]
— Catalogue of plants indigenous in the neighborhood of Calcutta. 1862. I. 473.
— On the colouring matter of the Morinda citrifolia. 1848. III. 746.[1]
— On the colouring matter of the Rottlera. 1855. III. 520.[1]
— Composition of the Locust or Carob bean. 1859. III. 472.[1]
— On the cultivation of the quiniferous Cinchonas. 1864. III. 714.
— Effects of the cyclone of the 5th Oct. 1864. 1867. III. 184.[1]
— An enumeration of the Indian species of Acanthaceae. 1867. II. 796.[1]
— An enumeration of the Palms of Sikkim. 1871. II. 62.[1]
— An enumeration of the species of Acanthaceae. 1864. II. 796.[1]
— Ueber den Farbstoffe der Morinda citrifolia. 1848. III. 746.[1]
— On the flora of Behar. 1863. I. 473.
— Florula adenensis. 1860. I. 480.
— On the identification of the Acanthaceae of the Linnean herbarium. 1864. II. 796.[1]
— List of Acanthaceae cultivated. 1869. II. 796.[1]
— On Lycium mediterraneum. 1857. II. 773.[2]
— Sur la matière colorante du Morinda citrifolia. 1848. III. 746.[1]
— A new species of manna from New South Wales. 1849. IV. 533.[2]
— Note on the use of subacetate of lead. 1858. I. 156.[2]
— Notes on the flora of Lucknow. 1859. I. 473.
— Notes on the Indian species of Lycium. 1857. II. 772.[2]
— Notice of the flower garden attached to the Cinchona nursery at Rungyroong. 1869. I. 67.[1]
— Sur une nouvelle espèce de manne. 1849. IV. 533.[2]
— On a presumed case of parthenogenesis in . . . Aberia. 1864. II. 570.[2]
— Remarks on the yield of quinine. 1863. III. 718.
— Report of the cultivation of Cinchonae at Darjeeling. 1866. III. 714.

— Report on the cultivation of Cinchona in Bengal. 1869. III. 714.
— On Sphaeroooma. 1861. II. 194.[2]
— On two species of Guttiferae. 1867. II. 555,[1] 558.[1]
— & Cleghorn, James. Report on the cultivation . . . of the Mahogany tree. 1867. III. 513.[1]
Anderson, William. Bemerkungen über den Ursprung der Thränenbäume. 1829. III. 204.[1]
— On the origin of weeping trees. 1829. III. 204.[1]
Anderson-Henry, Isaac. See HENRY, Isaac, ANDERSON-.
Andersonian naturalists' society. Annals. III. 16.
Andersson, Gunnar. Die Geschichte der Vegetation Schwedens. 1896. I. 358.
— Studier öfver svenska växtarters utbredning. 1893. II. 115.[2]
— Svenska växtvärldens historia. 1896. I. 358.
Andersson, Nils Johan. Angående slägtet Betula. 1849. II. 117.[2]
— Anteckningar under en resa i Umeå. 1846. I. 354.
— Aperçu de la végétation . . . de la Suède. 1867. I. 356, III. 120,[1] IV. 79.[2]
— Arbres et arbrisseaux d'origine étrangère . . . en Suède. 1867. I. 293, III. 66,[1] IV. 79.[2]
— Atlas öfver den skandinaviska florans naturliga familjer. 1849. I. 355.
— Bidrag till kännedomen om de i Nordamerika förekommande Pilarter. 1858. II. 99.[2]
— Botaniske maanedsbilleder. 1888. I. 96.
— Bref fråu resande naturforskare. 1853. I. 303.
— Conspectus vegetationis lapponicae. 1846. I. 354.
— On East Indian Salices. 1851. II. 103.[1]
— Excursioner i det sydliga Schlesien. 1850. II. 101.[2]
— Femhundra afbildningar af . . . svenska växter. 1870. I. 356.
— Om Galapagos-öarnes vegetation. 1853. I. 510.[1]
— Inledning till botaniken. 1859. I. 90.
— Lärobok i botanik. 1859. I. 90.
— Lärobok i botaniken. 1851. I. 89.
— Monographia Salicum. 1867. II. 99.[1]
— Några ord om form-begreppet hos Pilslägtet. 1846. II. 100.[2]
— Norges Salices. 1874. II. 100.[2]
— Notes on the Rev. J. E. Leefe's Salictum britannicum. 1851. II. 102.[1]
— Ost-Indiens hittills kända Pilarter. 1851. II. 103.[1]
— Plantae vasculares circa Quickjock. 1844. I. 354.
— Resebref fråu N. Andersson om vegetationen i Kina. 1853. I. 303.
— Salices boreali-americanae. 1858. II. 99.[2]
— Salices Lapponiae. 1845. II. 100.[2]
— Salicineae. 1868. II. 95.[2]
— Salix. 1867. II. 99.[1]
— Samtidiga (fenologiska) observationer. 1849. I. 223.[1]
— Schweden und seine Pflanzen. 1867. I. 356.
— Skånska växter. 1849. II. 100.[1]
— Om slägtet Salix. 1866. II. 100.[1]
— Söderhafsöarnas vegetation. 1853. I. 303.
— Om tvenne Pilarter. 1858. II. 100.[1]
— Underrättelser fråu resande naturforskare. 1852. I. 329.
— Ueber die Vegetation der Galapagos-Inseln. 1853. I. 510.[1]
— The Willows of the East Indies hitherto known. 1851. II. 103.[1]
— & Thedenius, K. F. Svensk skol-botanik. 1853. I. 89.
Anderweite [speyersche] Verordnung in Brennholtz-Sachen. 1733. IV. 299.
Andés, Louis Edgar. Das Conserviren des Holzes. 1895. IV. 421.
Andeutung über die Ursachen der Entstehung der Wald-bräude. 1858. IV. 151.[2]
Andeutungen über die notwendige Beachtung des Klimas bei dem Holzanbau. 1829. IV. 72.
Andino, Eduardo, ABELA Y SAINZ DE. See ABELA Y SAINZ DE ANDINO, Eduardo.
Andino, Julian, DIEZ DE. See DIEZ DE ANDINO, Julian.
Andouard, Ambroise. Le cuivre dans les vins provenant de Vignes. 1887. III. 561.
Andrada e Silva, José Bonifacio de. Memoria sobre a necessidade . . . do plantio de novos bosques em Portugal. 1815. IV. 164.[1]
Andrade Corvo, João de. Memoria sobre a " mangra " ou doença das Vinhas. 1855. III. 576.
Andrade Corvo, Luiz de. Sur le rôle des bacilles. 1885. III. 561.

Andrae, Carl Justus. Beiträge zur Kenntniss der Flora des südlichen Banates. 1853. I. 445.
— A new European Oak. 1856. II. 139.[2]
André, A. Th. Bijdrage tot de kennis van . . . Koffieblad-ziekte. 1890. III. 736.
— Cultuur en bereiding van indigo. 1891. III. 479.[1]
André, Édouard. Abelia rupestris grandiflora. 1886. III. 748.[2]
— Abies Menziezii (sic) Parryana. 1876. III. 306.[1]
— Abies pectinata Massonii. 1870. III. 296.[2]
— Abutilon Thompsoni flore pleno. 1885. III. 587.[1]
— L'Acacia gommifère de Tunisie. 1875. III. 466.[1]
— Acacia linifolia. 1882. III. 465.[2]
— Acalypha Chantrieri. 1899. II. 435.[1]
— Acalypha hispida. 1898. II. 435.[2]
— Actinidia Kolomikta. 1898. II. 541.[1]
— Aesculus × plantierensis. 1894. II. 481.[2]
— Aesculus intermedia. 1867. III. 537.[1]
— Aesculus turbinata. 1888. III. 539.[1]
— Allamanda nobilis. 1897. III. 686.[1]
— Alloplectus vittatus. 1870. III. 708.[1]
— Les Aloe Dyckiana, roseo-cincta. 1886. III. 333.[1]
— Les Amaraboya. 1871. III. 638.[1]
— Die amerikanischen Araliaceen mit grosser Belaubung. 1884. II. 646.[2]
— Amorpha canescens. 1896. II. 332.[1]
— Anemopaegma clematideum. 1890. II. 785.[1]
— Les Araliacées américaines. 1884. II. 646.[2]
— Les Aralias filiformes. 1877. III. 642.[1]
— Les Aralias japonais. 1893. II. 646.[2]
— Araucaria Balansae. 1875. II. 26.[1]
— Araucaria Rulei F. Mueller. 1875. II. 26.[2]
— L'arboretum de la Maulevrie. 1896. I. 59.
— L'arboriculture en Russie. 1869. III. 120.[1]
— L'Arbousier de Menzies. 1893. II. 660.[1]
— L'arbre de Judée à fleurs pendantes. 1899. III. 472.[2]
— L'Arbre du voyageur. 1890. II. 91.[3]
— Arbres fruitiers et arbres utiles. 1870. III. 492.[2]
— Les arbres pleureurs. 1874. III. 204.[1]
— Les arbustes à tige. 1889. III. 204.[1]
— Arbustes d'ornement en espalier. 1878. III. 205.[1]
— Aristolochia arborea. 1895. II. 181.[2]
— Aristolochia elegans. 1898. II. 182.[1]
— L'art des jardins. 1879. III. 201.
— Die Arten der Gattungen Kalmia und Andromeda. 1865. III. 647.[1]
— Autumnal foliage tints in eastern Europe. 1891. III. 207.[1]
— De l'Avocatier sur le littoral Méditerranéen. 1900. III. 407.[2]
— Azalées. 1865. III. 654.[1]
— Les Azalées dites de l'Inde. 1865. III. 654.[2]
— Les Azaléodendrons. 1893. III. 655.
— L' Azzeruolo sprone di gallo. 1886. III. 422.[1]
— Baccharis trimera. 1896. II. 852.[2]
— Les Baculls de l'Amazone. 1079. II. 65.[1]
— Bamboo poisoning. 1872. III. 316.[1]
— Les Bambous de Péradénia. 1889. II. 60.[1]
— Bauhinia grandiflora. 1897. II. 335.[1]
— Bauhinia purpurea. 1885. III. 467.[2]
— Begonia Duchartrei. 1892. III. 618.[1]
— Begonia Lubbersii. 1888. III. 618.[1]
— Bentinckia nicobarica. 1886. III. 320.[2]
— Berberis Thunbergii. 1883. III. 395.[1]
— Berberis Thunbergii. 1894. II. 205.[1]
— Bignonia argyrea. 1885. III. 705.
— Bignonia buccinatoria. 1898. III. 790.[1]
— Bleuissement des Hortensias. 1871. III. 412.[2]
— Blue-flowered Hydrangeas. 1871. III. 412.[2]
— Un bois de Wellingtonias en Alsace. 1879. III. 310.[1]
— Le Bonduc du Canada. 1897. II. 363.[1]
— De boomteelt in Rusland. 1869. III. 120.[1]
— Boronia heterophylla. 1889. III. 495.[2]
— Le Bouleau à feuilles pourpres. 1872. III. 357.[1]
— Bouturage des Oreopanax. 1874. III. 643.[2]
— Brahea nitida. 1887. II. 65.[3]
— Le Brahea Roezlii. 1883. II. 65.[3]
— Brownlea. 1880. II. 337.[2]
— Buddleia Colvilei. 1893. III. 717.[1]
— Buddleia variabilis. 1899. III. 681.[2]
— Burchellia capensis. 1890. III. 711.[1]
— Bursaria spinosa. 1883. III. 415.[1]
— Les Cactées rustiques. 1877. III. 619.
— Les Cactées rustiques. 1894. III. 620.[1]

André, Édouard (*continued*).
— Caesalpina japonica. 1899. II. 339.[1]
— The Canary Island Date Palm. 1888. III. 328.[1]
— Carpinus japonica. 1895. II. 121.[1]
— Caryopteris Mastacanthus. 1892. II. 754.[1]
— Catalpa speciosa. 1895. II. 787.[1]
— Cedrela sinensis. 1891. II. 420.[1]
— Le centenaire des Fuchsias. 1888. III. 640.[1]
— The centenary of the Fuchsia. 1888. III. 640.[1]
— Les Cephalanthus cultivés. 1889. II. 811.[1]
— Le Cératozamier du Mexique. 1861. III. 284.[2]
— Cerises jumelles. 1873. II. 273.[2]
— Chaenomeles japonica serotina. 1894. III. 420.[2]
— Chaenomeles japonica Simonii. 1883. III. 420.[1]
— Chariot-traineau à transplantation. 1884. III. 168.[1]
— Le Châtaignier de Drouilly-les-Hayes. 1894. II. 125.[1]
— Le Chêne-Bouleau des Loges. 1870. II. 118.[2]
— Le Chêne lacinié de Doumet. 1894. III. 363.[1]
— Le Chêne unilatéral de la côte californienne. 1889. III. 184.[2]
— La chlorose des arbres. 1887. III. 181.[1]
— Le Cierge géant du Méxique. 1872. III. 621.[1]
— Circulation de la sève. 1888. I. 166.
— Citrus triptera. 1885. III. 503.[1]
— Classification des Roses. 1885. II. 282.[2]
— Clematis coccinea et ses variétés. 1888. III. 390.[1]
— Clematis rhodochlora. 1887. II. 199.[1]
— Clématite François Morel. 1884. III. 391.[2]
— Clématite hybride de Pitcheri et coccinea. 1893. III. 390.[1]
— Les Clématites hybrides. 1893. III. 390.[1]
— Clématites ornementales. 1899. III. 389.[1]
— Clerodendron hastatum. 1893. II. 755.[2]
— Le Coca. 1884. II. 394.[1]
— Le Cocotier des Seychelles. 1891. II. 70.[2]
— Les Cocotiers sur le littoral méditerranéen. 1900. III. 322.[1]
— Coffea liberica. 1890. III. 742.[1]
— Collection d'Agaves de M. de Jonge-Van Ellemeet. 1872. III. 340.[1]
— Les Columnea. 1883. III. 708.[1]
— Les Conifères du parc des Côtes. 1892. III. 291.
— Cornus florida flore rubro. 1889. III. 646.[1]
— Cornus florida rubra. 1894. III. 646.[1]
— Les Cornus sericea et stolonifera. 1888. III. 645.[2]
— Les Cotoneaster frigida et nepalensis. 1875. III. 420.[2]
— Cotoneaster horizontalis. 1885. III. 421.[1]
— Cotoneaster horizontalis. 1889. II. 259.[2]
— Cotoneaster reflexa. 1892. II. 260.[1]
— Les Cotonéasters à rameaux pendants. 1893. III. 421.[1]
— Couverture des Palmiers rustiques. 1871. III. 317.
— Le Cranberry. 1885. III. 663.[1]
— Crataego-mespilus Dardari. 1900. II. 260.[1]
— Crataegus Oxyacantha semperflorens. 1883. III. 422.[1]
— Crataegus pauciflora. 1898. III. 443.[2]
— Crossandra infundibuliformis. 1891. III. 709.[1]
— Croton musaicus. 1882. III. 516.[1]
— Croton Veitchianum. 1867. III. 515.[1]
— Culture de la Coca. 1893. III. 492.[1]
— Culture des Allamandas. 1882. III. 686.[1]
— Culture des Dipladenia. *See* Die KULTUR der Dipladenia. 1882. III. 687.[2]
— La culture du Caféier à Nice. 1900. III. 729.[1]
— Cupressus Goveniana compacta. 1896. III. 302.[2]
— Cydonia sinensis. 1889. III. 420.[1]
— Cytisus schipkaensis. 1900. II. 350.[1]
— Le Dattier des Canaries. 1888. III. 328.[1]
— Debregeasia velutina. 1896. II. 157.[1]
— De la dégénérescence. 1875. I. 248.[2]
— Deutzia corymbosa. 1897. III. 410.[2]
— Deutzia parviflora. 1892. II. 239.[1]
— Deux beaux Eucalyptus. 1893. III. 634.[1]
— Dichogamie protérandre chez le Kentia Belmoreana. 1896. II. 69.[1]
— Les Diospyros. 1884. III. 669.[1]
— Diospyros Kaki var. costata Carrière. 1871. II. 701.[1]
— Disjonction dans le Retinospora plumosa. 1872. II. 28.[2]
— Dombeya Cayeuxii. 1897. II. 533.[2]
— Les Échinocactes aux États-Unis. 1873. III. 622.[2]
— Effets des inondations sur les plantes. 1883. III. 185.[1]
— L'élagage des arbres d'alignement. 1887. III. 211.[2]
— Contre l'élagage des Conifères. 1865. III. 295.[1]
— Emploi de l'Ailante en corbeilles. 1890. III. 507.[1]
— Emploi ornemental du Sumac Fustet. 1891. III. 524.[1]
— Empoisonnement . . . par le Laurier-Amande. 1870. III. 438.[1]

— Empoisonnement par les Bambous. 1872. III. 316.[1]
— Les Epiphyllum. 1886. III. 623.[1]
— L'Érable à sucre. 1886. III. 534.[1]
— Étude sur les Phyllocactus. 1898. III. 625.[2]
— Eucalyptus calophylla. 1888. III. 634.[1]
— Eucalyptus calophylla. 1890. II. 624.[1]
— Eucalyptus globulus. 1863. III. 634.[2]
— Eucalyptus gomphocephala. 1893. II. 624.[2]
— Eugenia Guabiju. 1897. II. 626.[2]
— Eugenia Michelii. 1889. III. 635.[1]
— Eupatorium serrulatum. 1894. III. 755.[1]
— Evonymus europaeus foliis argenteo-variegatis. 1885. III. 532.[1]
— Une excursion dans quelques jardins du Midi. 1867. I. 58.
— Expériences sur les arbres . . . dé vorés ou respectés par les lapins. 1882. III. 186.[1]
— Fagus tricolor. 1885. III. 360.[2]
— Fendlera rupicola. 1891. II. 240.[1]
— Fendlera rupicola. 1899. III. 411.[1]
— Le Ferdinanda eminens. 1862. III. 755.[2]
— Les feuillages de l'automne en Orient. 1891. III. 207.[1]
— Ficus barbata. 1897. III. 371.[2]
— Ficus stipulata. 1891. III. 371.[2]
— Les fleurs . . . du Phillyrea Vilmoriniana. 1895. II. 714.[1]
— Fleurs et fruits de l'Howea . . . Belmoreana. 1897. II. 69.[1]
— Floraison anormale du Deutzia gracilis. 1891. III. 410.[1]
— Sur la floraison de l'Astrapaea Wallichii. 1865. III. 591.[1]
— Floraison de l'Hamamelis japonica. 1889. III. 417.[1]
— Floraison du Chaenomeles sur racines. 1872. II. 258.[2]
— Floraison et fructification du Washingtonia filifera. 1895. II. 75.[2]
— Flowers on the roots of Pyrus japonica. 1872. II. 258.[2]
— Fourcroya Bedinghausii. 1895. II. 89.[2]
— Fourcroya Roeslii. 1887. III. 341.[2]
— Fructification . . . de l'Aloe roseo-cincta. 1896. II. 79.[1]
— Fructification de l'Avocatier en plein air. 1890. III. 407.[2]
— Fructification de la Passiflore quadrangulaire. 1898. II. 580.[1]
— Fructification des Aucuba. 1866. III. 644.[2]
— Fructification des Phoenix sur le littoral français. 1893. II. 72.[1]
— Fructification du Brahea nitida. 1887. II. 65.[2]
— Fructification du Cycas revoluta. 1896. II. 5.[1]
— Fructification du Prunus triloba. 1883. III. 443.[2]
— Fructification du Prunus triloba. 1884. III. 436,[1] *443.*[2]
— Fructification du Xanthoceras. 1873. III. 540.[2]
— Le fruit de l'Encephalartos villosus. 1897. II. 6.[1]
— Le fruit du Feijoa Sellowiana. 1899. II. 632.[1]
— Les fruits de l'Erythea edulis. 1899. II. 68.[2]
— Le Fruticetum des Barres. 1900. I. 60.[1]
— Gardenia Stanleyana. 1894. II. 829.[2]
— Ueber die Gattung Azalea. 1845. III. 654.[2]
— Die Gattung Rhododendron und deren Verbreitung. 1870. II. 675.[2]
— Genista tinctoria flore pleno. 1899. III. 477.[2]
— Le genre Aesculus. 1891. II. 481.[1]
— Genre Kalmia et genre Andromeda. 1865. III. 647.[1]
— The giant Vine of Montecito. 1877. II. 509.[1]
— Les Glycines. 1862. II. 490.[1]
— Les Gogants de Saint-Cergues. 1891. II. 24.[2]
— Goldfussia isophylla. 1892. II. 804.[1]
— La gomme des arbres fruitiers. 1884. I. 528.[1]
— Le Goyavier de Passé. 1890. II. 632.[2]
— Les graines de l'Exochorda. 1889. III. 424.[1]
— Greffage des Poiriers sur Cotoneaster. 1875. III. 445.[2]
— Le greffage du Poirier sur le Pirus salicifolia. 1891. III. 445.[2]
— La greffe des Camellias en plein air. 1874. III. 599.[2]
— Grevillea longifolia. 1882. III. 383.[1]
— Grevillea Thelemanniana splendens. 1882. III. 383.[2]
— Greyia Sutherlandi. 1894. II. 491.[2]
— Les gros arbres des Landes. 1895. II. 125.[1]
— Le gros Chêne de Razat. 1894. II. 139.[1]
— Les gros Figuiers du jardin de Péradénia. 1890. II. 150.[1]
— Guevina Avellana. 1884. II. 160.[2]
— Les guirlandes de Clematis montana. 1891. III. 391.[1]
— Les haies d'Aserolier ergot-de-coq. 1886. III. 422.[1]
— Les haies de Roses dans le Midi. 1874. III. 452.
— Hamamelis japonica. 1891. II. 253.[1]
— Hardenbergia Makoyana. 1882. III. 480.[1]
— Hedera Helix aurantiaca. 1884. III. 642.[2]

— Un Héliotrope géant. 1899. II. 751.[1]
— Hibiscus cisplatinus. 1898. II. 522.[2]
— Hibiscus subviolaceus. 1884. III. 588.[1]
— Histoire et usages du Mutisia viciaefolia. 1891. III. 755.[2]
— Holboellia latifolia. 1890. II. 201.[1]
— Hoya imperialis. 1900. II. 739.[2]
— Das hundertjahrige Jubiläum der Fuchsien. 1888. III. 640.[1]
— Hybrides d'Azalea mollis. 1886. III. 660.[2]
— Hypericum densiflorum. 1899. II. 556.[1]
— Hypericum Moserianum. 1889. III. 610.[1]
— Iochroma flavum. 1898. II. 772.[1]
— Jacaranda mimosaefolia. 1897. II. 789.[1]
— Le Jacquier à feuilles entières. 1891. III. 367.[1]
— Les Kakis dans le midi de la France. 1893. III. 669.[2]
— Kalmia latifolia Favarti. 1888. III. 652.[1]
— Kalmia myrtifolia. 1883. III. 652.[1]
— Kentia (Kentiopsis?) Balmoreana Ch. Moore. 1874. II. 69.[1]
— Kentiopsis macrocarpa. 1884. III. 326.[1]
— Les Keteleeria. 1900. II. 32.[1]
— La Ketmie hérissée. 1862. III. 587.[1]
— Une larve inédite nuisible aux Rosiers. 1882. III. 453.[2]
— Le Laurier du Parana. 1898. II. 227.[1]
— Lettre sur le Brownea Ariza. 1881. II. 337.[2]
— Le Lierre à fruits rouges. 1882. II. 642.[2]
— Ligustrum japonicum Alivoni. 1886. III. 673.[2]
— Ligustrum japonicum elegans. 1898. III. 673.[2]
— Le Lilas en arbre du Japon. 1894. II. 715.[1]
— Longévité des arbres. 1873. I. 193.[1]
— Lucuma Sellowii. 1900. III. 668.[1]
— La lutte pour l'existence chez les végétaux. 1887. II. 46.[1]
— Macaranga Porteana. 1888. III. 520.[1]
— Maclura aurantiaca inermis. 1896. III. 372.[1]
— Les magasins de vivres des pic-verts d'Amérique. 1871. I. 234.[2]
— Le Marronnier bifère. 1889. III. 537.[1]
— Le Marronnier géant de Fontenay-le-Comte. 1898. II. 482.[2]
— De Marseille à Gênes. 1875. . III. 125.
— Melaleuca fulgens. 1895. II. 629.[2]
— Melianthus major. 1867. III. 541.[1]
— Monnina obtusifolia. 1883. III. 513.[2]
— Les mouches des poires. 1890. III. 446.[2]
— Le mouvement horticole. 1866. III. 33.[1]
— Multiplication des Araucarias. 1891. III. 297.[2]
— Mutisia viciaefolia. 1891. II. 861.[1]
— Myrmecodia Beccarii. 1887. III. 746.[1]
— Neillia thyrsiflora. 1888. II. 268.[2]
— A new fruit, Diospyros Kaki. 1871. II. 701.[2]
— A new fruiting tree, Feijoa. 1898. II. 632.[1]
— New varieties of Oleander. · 1873. III. 689.[2]
— Le Noisetier d'Australie. 1891. II. 164.[1]
— Note sur le Streptosolen Jamesoni. 1882. III. 702.[1]
— Notes sur l'horticulture à La Plata. 1890. III. 119.[1]
— Un nouveau mode de greffage de la Vigne. 1894. III. 543.[1]
— Un nouveau Phoenix hybride. 1888. III. 329.[1]
— Nouveaux détails sur l'Eucalyptus globulus. 1868. III. 624.[2]
— Nouveaux Kakis. 1887. III. 669.[2]
— Les nouveaux Nérions de M. Sabut. 1873. III. 689.[2]
— Les nouveaux Yuccas de M. Deleuil. 1883. III. 339.[2]
— Un nouvel arbre fruitier, Feijoa. 1898. II. 632.[1]
— Nouvelle multiplication des Orangers. 1874. II. 403.[1]
— Une nouvelle Passiflore. 1885. II. 581.[1]
— Nouvelles forêts de Wellingtonias. 1870. II. 51.[1]
— Nouvelles Pivoines en arbre. 1898. III. 392.[2]
— N   s plantes à feuillage ornemental. 1863, · III. 701.Jouvelle
— Nouvelles variétés de Clématites. 1899. III. 392.[1]
— Les Olives de Tunisie. 1898. III. 676.[1]
— Les Opuntia. 1873. III. 625.[1]
— L'Opuntia à chapelets. 1885. II. 597.[1]
— Les Opuntia nord-américains. 1873. II. 596.[1]
— Oranger de Jaffa. 1899. III. 500.[2]
— Les Orangers économiques. 1886. III. 443.[2]
— Oranges monstrueuses. 1900. II. 403.[1]
— Oreopanax Andreanum. 1882. III. 651.[1]
— Oreopanax Epremesnilianum. 1882. III. 643.[2]
— L'Orme de la Vieille-Verrerie. 1899. II. 144.[2]
— L'Orme géant de Grignon. 1892. II. 144.[2]
— Les Ormes de la Malle. 1897. II. 144.[2]

— Les ovaires vivipares des Opuntia. 1870. II. 596.[1]
— Ozothamnus thyrsoideus. 1900. II. 858.[2]
— Les Palmarès de Ceroxylon. 1878. III. 321.[2]
— Les Palmes du dimanche des rameaux. 1871. III. 319.[1]
— Le Palmier nain d'Afrique. 1892. II. 66.[2]
— Les Palmiers cultivés. See WATSON, William. 1884. III. 318.[1]
— Les Palmiers dans la Floride centrale. 1888. III. 318.[1]
— Les Palmiers dans la région méditerranéenne. 1879. III. 317.
— Les Palmiers hybrides en Provence. 1892. III. 328.[1]
— Les Palmiers nouveau à l'Exposition quinquennale. 1898. III. 318.[1]
— Les Pandanus. 1862. III. 313.[1]
— Passiflora atomaria. 1883. III. 615.[2]
— Passiflora atomaria. 1884. III. 615.[2]
— Passiflora violacea. 1885. II. 581.[1]
— Passiflora Weberiana. 1887. II. 581.[1]
— Passiflores hybrides. 1883. III. 615.[2]
— Les Pernettyas. 1884. III. 653.[2]
— Le Phillyrea Vilmoriniana. 1889. III. 680.[1]
— Phyllanthus Chantrieri. 1883. III. 521.[1]
— Phyllanthus salviaefolius. 1883. III. 521.[2]
— Phyllocalyx edulis. 1884. II. 627.[1]
— Pinus peuce. 1883. III. 308.[1]
— Pircunia dioica. 1895. II. 193.[1]
— Plantation des arbustes grimpants. 1897. III. 205.[1]
— Plantation et tuteurage des arbres. 1888. III. 199.
— Les plantations dans le Midi. 1878. III. 124.[1]
— Les plantations en ligne à Paris. 1873. III. 209.
— Une plante nouvelle . . . Acalypha Sanderi. 1898. II. 435.[1]
— Les plantes à feuillage ornemental. 1866. III. 205.[2]
— Plantes de terre de Bruyères. 1865. III. 87.
— Plantes nouvelles. 1897. III. 514,[1] 516.[2]
— Les plantes nouvelles . . . à l'Exposition quinquennale. 1898. III. 78.[1]
— Plantes nouvelles et inédites. 1873. III. 386.[1]
— Plantes nouvelles ou rares. 1872. III. 87.
— Les Plaqueminiers. 1874. III. 669.[1]
— Platycarya strobilacea. 1888. III. 356.[2]
— Poinciana Gilliesii. 1893. II. 339.[1]
— Pritchardia Vuylstekeana. 1883. III. 330.[2]
— Procédés pour mesurer la hauteur des arbres. 1889. IV. 216.
— Prolongation axile des fleurs . . . de Cryptomérias. 1887. II. 29.[1]
— La Prune Kelsey. 1887. III. 443.[1]
— Prunes Mariana et Masu. 1894. III. 438.[2]
— Prunier Mirobolan à feuilles panachées. 1894. III. 436.[1]
— Les Prunopsis. 1890. II. 270.[2]
— Prunus Botan. 1895. III. 443.[1]
— Prunus cerasifera contorta. 1895. III. 436.[1]
— Pseudophoenix Sargenti. 1897. II. 74.[1]
— Pseudophoenix Sargenti. 1888. II. 74.[1]
— Sur le Pseudotsuga glaucescens. 1895. II. 49.[1]
— Quelques mots sur les Berberis cultivés. 1899. III. 394.[1]
— Quelques plantes des jardins Dognin. 1883. I. 59.
— Quelques plantes rares. 1873. III. 509.[1]
— Rameaux aoûtés sur un Pin maritime. 1896. II. 44.[2]
— Raphiolepis × Delacourii. 1900. II. 281.[1]
— Remijia pedunculata. 1897. II. 600.[1]
— Les Rémijias. 1887. II. 830.[1]
— Rhododendron × Halopeanum. 1896. II. 680.[1]
— Rhododendron argenteum. 1888. III. 659.[1]
— Rhododendron Cavroni. 1885. III. 658.[1]
— Rhododendron ciliicalyx. 1899. II. 678.[2]
— Les Rhododendrons de serre froide. 1873. III. 655.
— Ribes speciosum. 1900. II. 246.[2]
— Les Ricins. 1872. II. 450.[2]
— Der Riesen-Weinstock von Montécito. 1877. II. 509.[1]
— Robinia Decaisneana rubra. 1890. III. 487.[1]
— Robinia neo-mexicana. 1895. II. 382.[1]
— Rondeletia speciosa. 1891. III. 747.[2]
— Rosa Regeliana. 1871. II. 298.[1]
— Rosa rugosa calocarpa. 1891. III. 456.[2]
— Les Rosa rugosa et Regeliana. 1872. III. 456.[3]
— Rosa sinica. 1889. III. 455.[1]
— Rose hedges in the south of France. 1874. III. 452.
— Rosier Cramoisi sarmenteux de Turner. 1894. III. 456.[1]
— Rubus nubigenus H. B. K. var. macrocarpus. 1878. II. 309.[1]
— Rubus rosaefolius. 1898. II. 310.[1]
— Rudgea nivosa. 1866. III. 747.[2]

André, Édouard (continued).
— Ruellia Makoyana. 1896. II. 803.[1]
— Rusticité de quelques plantes à Paris. 1873. III. 48.
— Salix Humboldtiana fastigiata. 1896. II. 107.[2]
— Sambucus racemosa plumosa. 1889. · III. 752.[2]
— Les Saules de l'Amérique du Nord. 1878. III. 348.
— Le Schinus Molle dans l'Écuador. 1889. II. 460.[2]
— Securinega ramiflora. 1882. III. 522.[2]
— Solanum albidum Poortmani. 1886. II. 775.[1]
— Solanum muricatum. 1892. II. 777.[1]
— Solanum Seaforthianum. 1897. II. 777.[2]
— Le Sophora japonica de Villennes. 1887. II. 384.[2]
— Spiraea Foxii. 1900. III. 461.[1]
— Staphylea × Coulombieri. 1887. II. 473.[2]
— Stephanotis floribunda. 1887. III. 694.[1]
— Streptosolen Jamesoni. 1883. III. 702.[1]
— Syringa vulgaris Chamaethyrsus. 1894. II. 716.[1]
— La taille des arbres en une leçon. ·1866. III. 170.
— De la taille des arbustes à fleurs. 1872. III. 172.
— Telopea speciosissima. 1883. III. 384.[1]
— Thunbergia coccinea. 1890. III. 710.[1]
— Tournefortia cordifolia. 1887. III. 695.[2]
— De la transplantation des Conifères. 1872. III. 294.[2]
— La transplantation des gros arbres. 1863. III. 167.
— De la transplantation des gros arbres. 1872. III. 167.
— Transplantation des gros arbres. 1888. III. 168.[1]
— Transplantation des gros arbres sans chariot. 1899. ·III. 168.[1]
— Transplanting Pines and evergreen shrubs. 1872. III. 294.[2]
— Urostigma subtriplinervium. 1900. II. 153.[1]
— L'utilisation du bois d'Eucalyptus. 1887. IV. 531.[1]
— Variegated Ash-leaved Maple. 1861. III. 535.[1]
— Une variété de l'Érable à feuilles de Frêne. 1861. III. 535.[1]
— Les variétés de l'Evonymus japonicus. 1883. III. 532.[2]
— Les variétés de l'If commun. 1886. III. 288.[1]
— Variétés du Cupressus Lawsoniana. 1870. III. 301.[1]
— Variétés du Cytisus purpureus. 1872. III. 474.[2]
— The varieties of the Common Yew. 1886. III. 288.[1]
— La végétation dans l'Uruguay. 1891. I. 345.
— Veitchia Joannis. 1883. III. 331.[1]
— Veitchia Joannis. 1884. III. 332.[1]
— Vigne épineuse Madame Victor Caplat. 1897. III. 584.[1]
— La Vigne géante de Montécito. 1877. II. 509.[1]
— Visnea Mocanera. 1882. III. 608.[1]
— Vitis capensis. 1887. III. 545.[1]
— Washingtonia robusta. 1885. II. 75,[2] III. 532.[1]
— Washingtonia robusta. 1900. II. 75.[2]
— Wellingtonia gigantea pendula. 1875. III. 310.[1]
— Les Wigandias et leur culture. 1861. III. 695.[1]
— Xanthorraea et Dasylirion. 1887. III. 337.[2]
— Yucca Carrierei. 1895. II. 87.[2]
— Yucca Whipplei. 1886. III. 340.[2]
— Yucca Whipplei violacea. 1884. III. 340.[2]
— Les Yuccas baccata et Treculeana. 1887. III. 339.[2]
— See also Carrière, E. A. & André, Édouard; Micheli, Marc & André, Édouard; Pynaert, Édouard & André, Édouard.
André, Emil. Einfachste den höchsten Ertrag . . . sicher stellende Forstwirthschafts-Methode. 1832. IV. 240.
— Kubik-Tabellen für alle runden Hölzer. 1844. IV. 223.
— Versuch einer zeitgemässen Forstorganisation. 1823. IV. 239.
— Die vorzüglichsten Mittel, den Wäldern einen höhern Ertrag abzugewinnen. 1826. IV. 242.
André, Gustave. Étude de quelques transformations . . . chez les plantes étiolées. 1900. III. 40.
— Remarques sur les transformations de la matière organique pendant la germination. 1900. I. 204.
— Sur les transformations chimiques qui se passent pendant la décolouration du bourgeon. 1900. I. 178.
— See also Berthelot, M. P. E. & André, G.
André, Karl. Die Forst- und Jagdliteratur der letzten zwanzig Jahre. 1860. IV. 1.
André, L. Gekyaniseerd hout. 1883. IV. 420.
André, M. F. d'. Bambous et cours d'eau. 1892. III. 314.[2]
Andreä. Baumverpflanzung in der Blüthezeit. 1844. III. 168.[1]
Andreae, D. J. Verslag over den landbouw in Nederland. 1886. III. 122.[2]
Andreae, Ernst. Ueber abnorme Wurzelanschwellungen bei Ailanthus. 1893. II. 413.[2]
Andreae, Jakob Heinrich. Karakteristik innländischer Forstbäume. 1790. IV. 1, 81.

Andrée, Adolf. Salzabscheidungen durch die Blätter. 1885. I. 169.[1]
Andrés, Erwin. A practical treatise of the fabrication of volatile and fat varnishes. 1882. III. 232.[2]
Andrés y Tubilla, Tomás. See Lázaro é Ibiza, Blas & Andrés y Tubilla, Tomás.
Andresen, C. Ist für das Herzogthum Schleswig ein Holz- u. Torfmangel zu befürchten? 1818. IV. 282.[2]
Andresen, C. C. Om Klitformationen. 1861. IV. 145.
Andrew, George L. On the sanitary value of forests. 1879. IV. 55.[1]
Andrews. See Giannazi, Bugalini & Andrews.
Andrews, Alexander. Descriptive catalogue of the collection . . . by the colony of Western Australia. · 1862. IV. 21.[2]
Andrews, Charles William. A monograph of Christmas Island (Indian Ocean). See Baker, E. G. & others. 1900. I. 481.[2]
Andrews, Christopher Columbus. The Minnesota park. 1900. IV. 179.[2]
— Report on forestry in Sweden. 1872. IV. 344.[2]
— Report to the Department of state on the forests and forest-culture of Sweden. 1872. IV. 344.[2]
Andrews, D. M. Hardy Cacti. 1897. III. 620.[1]
Andrews, Edward R. The Hayford process. 1878. IV. 420.
Andrews, Henry. Botanist's repository. See Botanist's . . . I. 17.
Andrews, Henry C. Coloured engravings of Heaths. 1802. II. 664.[1]
— Geraniums. 1805. II. 389.[2]
— The Heathery; or, A monograph of the genus Erica. 1804. II. 664.[1]
— Roses. 1805. II. 281.[2]
Andrews, John. Notes on the genus Rhus. 1886. IV. 526.[1]
— Sobre los Zumaques. 1886. IV. 526.[1]
Andrews, Luman. List of the flowering plants . . . of Meriden Mountain. 1900. I. 317.[1]
Andrews, William. On certain woods . . . of New Zealand. 1870. IV. 402.[1]
Andreyevski, G. See Андреевскій, Г.
Andrieux. Catalogue raisonné des plantes. 1771. I. 56.
Andrieux, François Guillaume Jean Stanislas. L'Olivier, le Figuier. 1793. I. 513.
Andrieux, Vilmorin-, & Cie. See Vilmorin-Andrieux & Cie. ·
Andry de Boisregard, Nicolas.· Le Thé de l'Europe. 1712. III. 605.
Andryaska, Stanis. Ogrodnictwo dla wszystkich. 1886. III. 99.
Andrzejowski, Anton Lukianowicz. Dictionarium glossologiae botanicae. 1825. I. 70.
— Flora Ukrainy. 1869. I. 363.
— Nauka wyrazów botanicznych. 1825. I. 70.
— Objazd w przedmiotach historyi naturalnej. 1823. I. 94.
— Rys botaniczny krain swiedzonych w podróżach pomiędzy Bohem i Dniestrem. 1823. I. 360.
— Rys botaniczny krain swiedzonych w podróżach pomiędzy Bohem i Dniestrem. 1830. I. 360.
— & Besser, W. S. J. G. von. Naswiska róslin Grekom starożytnym znanych. 1828. I. 73.[1]
Andy, S. Pulney. On branched Palms in southern India. 1869. II. 65,[1] 67.[1]
Andsheïkovitch, A. See Анджейкович, A.
Die Anerziehung und .Schonung des Waldmantels. 1869. IV. 177.[1]
Anez. Traitement par submersion des Vignes. 1872. III. 564.[2]
Anez, Hippolyte. Mortalité des Vignes. 1874. III. 759.
Anfragen der Durchforstungen. 1831. IV. 172.[2]
Ange, Legros, Saint-. See Saint-Ange, Legros.
Die Angehörigen der Land- und forstwirthschaftlichen Akademie Hohenheim. 1868. IV. 32.
Angelbeek, C. van. Korte schets van het eiland Lingga. 1826. · III. 275.[1]
Angeliny, Augustin Rose. Lettres sur l'éducation des vers-à-soie. 1806. III. 373.
Angelita, G. F. I pomi d'oro. 1607. II. 149.[2]
Angerer, J. Die Waldwirthschaft in Tirol. 1883. IV. 28.[1]
Angers — Académie des sciences et belles-lettres. See Société académique de Maine-et-Loire. I. 22.
Angers — Société d'agriculture, sciences et arts. See Société . . . III. 21.
Angers — Société d'études scientifiques. See Société . . . I. 23.
Angers — Société d'horticulture. See Société d'horticulture de Maine-et-Loire. III. 21.

Angers — Société industrielle. *See* Société . ; . III. 22.
Anglicus, Bartholomaeus. *See* Bartholomaeus Anglicus.
An Anglo-Canadian forest school. 1886. IV. 30.[1]
Angot, Alfred. Influence de l'altitude. 1883. I. 218.
— Influence de l'altitude sur la végétation. 1885. I. 218.
Angran de Rueneuve. Observations sur l'agriculture et le jardinage. 1712. III. 125.
Angrand. Bouturage dans l'eau. 1877. III. 158.
Angreville, J. E. d'. La flore vallaisanne. 1862. I. 435, 535.[2]
Anguillara, Luigi. Semplici. 1561. I. 280, V. xv.[1]
Anguisola, Antonius. Compendium simplicium et compositorum medicamentorum. 1587. III. 240.
Angyal, Dezső. A Pirus és Malus diszfajai. 1895. III. 444.[1]
— Terméketlen Diófa. 1887. II. 114.[1]
Anheisser, Roland. Ueber die aruncoide Blattspreite. 1900. I. 219.[1]
Anjubault, P. A. Le Gui du Chêne. 1866. II. 179.[1]
— Recherches sur les principales causes qui ont nui à la production des Pommiers à cidre. 1858. III. 427.[1]
Ankarcrona, Theodor. Beskrifning om Berberis trän eller buskar. 1749. III. 394.[2]
Ankel, Otto. Grundzüge der Landesnatur des Westjordanlandes. 1887. I. 480.
Ankündigung einer Gesellschaft forstwissenschaftlicher Freunde. *See* Liebhaber, E. A. W. von. 1822. IV. 40.[1]
Ankündigung, eines Privat-Forst-Lehrunterrichts zu Aarau. 1815. IV. 36.[1]
Om Anlæg af Pileplantninger. 1878. III. 348.
Die Anlage und Behandlung der . . . Pflanzkämpe. 1878. IV. 150.
Ueber die Anlage von Erlensaatkämpen. 1886. IV. 488.[2]
I Anledning af de jydske Heeders Bebyggelse. *See* Rothe, T. 1760. IV. 155.[3]
Anleitung für die Landleute in Absicht auf das Ausstocken und die Pflanzung der Wälder. 1765. IV. 110.[1]
Anleitung für Landleute über die Anlegung . . . der Obstbäume. 1786. III. 145.[2]
Anleitung über das Verfahren beim Schneideln der Eiche. 1860. IV. 505.
Anleitung über das Verfahren beim Schneideln der Eiche. 1865. IV. 505.
Anleitung über den Vollzug der Distrikts-Bezeichnung . . . kgl. Regierung zu Trier. 1861. IV. 302.
Anleitung unter den . . . bekanntesten Kernobstsorten . . . Wahl selbst treffen zu können. *See* Aehrenthal, J. L. Freiherr von. 1845. III. 71.
Anleitung zu den Witterungs-Beobachtungen. 1827. IV. 59.[1]
Anleitung zu der neuen . . . Forstschätzung. *See* Wiesenhaven, L. H. J. 1794. IV. 250,[2] *253*.
Anleitung zu der Pflanzenkenntniss. *See* Schinz, Salomon. 1774. III. 55.
Anleitung zu einer zu errichtenden Holz-Sammlung. 1823. I. 37,[2] *IV. 17*.
Anleitung zu zweckmässiger Behandlung der Wälder. 1824. IV. 99.[1]
Anleitung zum Forstbau, zum Gebrauche des Landvolkes in der Schweiz. 1768. IV. 110.[1]
Anleitung zur Anfertigung der Fällungs-Nachweisung. 1831. IV. 299.
Anleitung zur Anlage . . . der Laub- und Nadelholz-Saatbeete. 1862. III. 154,[1] *IV. 150*.
Anleitung zur Aufnahme und Berechnung von Probeflächen in Hochwaldungen. 1840. IV. 216.
Anleitung zur Ausführung der Taxations-Revisionen. 1852. IV. 301.
Anleitung zur Ausführung des v. Buttlar'schen Forst-Kultur-Verfahrens. 1866. IV. 152.
Anleitung zur Behandlung der Streuwerksabgaben. 1839. IV. 300.[1]
Anleitung zur Behandlung der Waldgrunderwerbungen. 1863. IV. 300.[1]
Anleitung zur Erziehung . . . des Maulbeerbaums. 1854. III. 377.
Anleitung zur Führung des Flächenregisters. 1857. IV. 251.[1]
Anleitung zur Führung des Taxations-Notizenbuchs. 1870. IV. 248.[1]
Anleitung zur Geschäftsbehandlung der Gemeinde- und Stiftungs-Waldungen der Pfalz. 1858. IV. 300.[1]
Anleitung zur Gewinnung der Eichen-Spiegelborke. 1842. IV. 512.

Anleitung zur Kultur . . . des Rujastrauches. 1813. III. 524.[1]
Anleitung zur Untersuchung der Kieferspinner-Raupen. 1877. IV. 477.
Anleitung zur Verbesserung der bündnerischen Waldwesens. *See* Bohl, J. 1838. IV. 110.[1]
Anleitung zur Vornahme von Untersuchungen . . . des jährlichen Waldstreuanfalles. 1866. IV. 71.
Anleitung zur Vornahme von Untersuchungen über die Wirkungen der Durchforstungen. 1870. IV. 173.
Anleitung zur Waldwerthberechnung. 1866. IV. 255, 302.
Anleitung zur Werthsberechnung bei Waldankäufen. 1844. IV. 300.[1]
Anleitung zur Zuckererzeugung aus dem Safte inländischer Ahornbäume. 1812. III. 534.[2]
Anmärkningar om natural-historiens lärande. *See* Trafvenfelt, E. C. 1818. I. 78.[2]
Anmärkningar om Tall- eller Furu-skogen. 1769. IV. 480.
Anmerkungen über das bairische Mandat, welches in Betreff der Wildschützen . . . *See* Schollenberg und Reutha, J. T., Freiherr zu. 1778. IV. 318.
Anmuthigkeiten des Landlebens. *See* De la Court, Pieter. 1738. III. 105.
Annaberg-Buchholzer Verein für Naturkunde. Jahresbericht. I. 10.
Annalen der Blumisterei. III. 11.
Annalen der Botanick. I. 26.[1]
Annalen der Chemie und Pharmacie. *See* Annalen der Pharmacie. I. 10.
Annalen der deutschen Landwirthschaft. *See* Land- und Forstwirthschaftliche Zeitschrift . . . IV. 10.
Annalen der Erd-, Völker- und Staatenkunde. *See* Hertha, Zeitschrift . . . I. 12.
Annalen der Forst- und Jagd-Wissenschaft. IV. 7.
Annalen der Gärtnerey. III. 11.
Annalen der Gewächskunde. *See* Literaturblätter . . . 1828. I. 1.
Annalen der Oenologie. III. 11.
Annalen der Pharmacie. I. 10.
Annalen der Physik und Chemie. I. 10, V. vii.[1]
Annalen der Societät der Forst- und Jagdkunde. *See* Annalen der Forst- und Jagd-Wissenschaft. IV. 7.
Annales administratives et scientifiques de l'agriculture. *See* Annales de l'agriculture. III. 18.
Annales agronomiques. III. 18.
Annales belgiques des sciences. III. 15.[1]
Annales d'horticulture et de botanique. III. 14.
Annales d'hygiène publique. III. 18.
Annales de chimie. I. 20.
Annales de flore et de pomone. *III. 18, V. xxvii*. *See* Journal et flore des jardins. III. 20.
Annales de géographie. I. 20.
Annales de l'agriculture française. III. 18.
Annales de l'Extrême Orient. I. 20.
Annales de l'horticulture en Belgique. III. 15.[1]
Annales de la science agronomique française. III. 18.
Annales de médecine vétérinaire. I. 16.
Annales de pharmacie. I. 16.
Annales de pomologie belge. III. 15.[1]
Annales des arts et manufactures. III. 18.
Annales des jardiniers amateurs. *See* Société d'agronomie pratique. IV. 21.
Annales des mines. *See* Journal des mines. IV. 12.[2]
Annales des ponts et chaussées. IV. 12.[1]
Annales des sciences naturelles. I. 21.
Annales des sciences physiques et naturelles d'agriculture . . . *See* Société royale d'agriculture, histoire naturelle . . . de Lyon. I. 24.[1]
Annales encyclopédiques. *See* Magasin encyclopédique. I. 22.
Annales européennes. IV. 12.[2]
Annales forestières. IV. 12.[2]
Annales forestières. Bulletin administratif. IV. 12.[2]
Annales forestières, faisant suite au Mémorials forestier. IV. 12.[2]
Annales forestières; revue des eaux . . . *See* Revue des eaux et forêts. IV. 12.[2]
Annales françaises et étrangères d'anatomie. I. 21.
Annales générales des sciences physiques. I. 16.
Annales maritimes et coloniales. III. 18.
Annales scientifiques, litteraires . : . de l'Auvergne. *See* Académie des sciences, belles-lettres et arts de Clermont-Ferrand. I. 20.
Annales télégraphiques. III. 19.

Annali civili del regno delle due Sicilie. I. 24.[2]
Annali dell' agricoltura del regno d' Italia. III. 23.[1]
Annali delle scienze del regno Lombardo-Veneto. I. 24.[2]
Annali di agricoltura. III. 23.[1]
Annali di botanica. I. 24.[2]
Annali di storia naturale. I. 24.[2]
Annali di viticoltura ed enologia italiana. III. 23.[1]
Annals and magazine of natural history. I. 17.
Annals of botany. Balfour. I. 17.
Annals of botany. Konig & Sims. I. 17.
Annals of horticulture. III. 16.
Annals of horticulture in North America. III. 2.
Annals of natural history. See ANNALS and magazine of natural history. I. 17.
Annals of philosophy. I. 17.
Annals of Scottish natural history. I. 17.
Annand, John Fowler. The formation of plantations. 1893. IV. 142.
Le annate di siccità e la vegetazione forestale. 1895. IV. 73.[1]
Annatto. 1887. III. 613.[1]
Annatto. 1888. III. 613.[1]
Annecy, Tôchon d'. Dissertation sur l'inscription grecque. 1819. V. xxv.[1]
Annecy — Association florimontane. See ASSOCIATION . . . I. 21.
Année champêtre. See ARDÈNE, J. P. R. d'. 1769. III. 112.
Annel, PANNELIER d'. See PANNELIER D'ANNEL.
Annenkof, Nikolai Ivanovitch. Observations sur la floraison de quelques plantes. See ANNENKOW, N. 1849. I. 223.[3]
— Observations sur les plantes indigènes des environs de Moscou. See ANNENKOW, N. 1851. I. 223.[2]
— See also АВНЕНКОВЪ, Н. И.
Annenkof, S. See АВНЕНКОВЪ, С.
Annenkow, Nicolaus. See ANNENKOF, N. I.
Annesley, Lord. See ANNESLEY, Hugh, 5th earl.
Annesley, Hugh, 5th earl. A list of plants hardy in the garden at Castlewellan, Co. Down. 1890. I. 55.
Anniversaria in memoriam reipublicae sacrae. See HORNE-MANN, J. W. 1819. I. 490.
Anniversary leaflet . . . for . . . Arbor day. 1897. IV. 42.[2]
Annotazioni sopra la Coltivazione di Luigi Alamanni. See BENINI, Vincenzo. 1745. III. 115.[2]
Annuaire de l'herboriste. 1802. I. 33.
Annuaire de l'horticulteur. See ALMANACH du jardinier. III. 18.
Annuaire des eaux et forêts. IV. 12.[1]
Annuaire forestier. 1860. IV. 292.
Annuaire général du commerce des bois. IV. 12.[2]
Annual report on the Sind forests. See DALZELL, N. A. 1859. IV. 377.[1]
Annuario forestale. IV. 13.[1]
Annuario scientifico-forestale. IV. 13.[1]
Anomoeus, Clemens. Sacrarum arborum . . . Decas. 1609. I. 512.
Anonymus, Philomusus. See CARRICHTER, Bartholomaeus.
Anordning om Besigtelsesmaaden af Ege-Tømmer. 1825. IV. 425.[1]
Another Bougainvillea. 1861. III. 388.[1]
Another mysterious tree. 1878. I. 213.[2]
Another new fruit. 1898. III. 637.[1]
Anouilh de Salies, d'. Des moyens d'arriver . . . à la destruction complète du puceron lanigère. 1866. III. 427.[1]
Ueber die Anpflanzung . . . der verschiedenen Weidenarten. 1834. III. 347.
Anpflanzung des Götterbaumes. 1878. IV. 525.
Die Anpflanzung von Fremdhölzern. 1883. IV. 127.[2]
Ueber die Anpflanzung von Kastanien-Wäldern. 1837. IV. 492.[1]
Ansberque, Edme. See CUSIN, Louis & ANSBERQUE, Edme.
Das Anschlemmen der Pflanzen-Wurzeln. 1855. IV. 152.
Ansiaux, Léon. Les déchets de laine. 1898. IV. 144.[2]
— Le Lupin. 1898. IV. 145.
Ansichten über den Anbau der Fichte. 1868. IV. 453.
Ansichten über die Beibehaltung des Mittel und Niederwald-Betriebes. 1856. IV. 128.
Ansichten über Forst-Taxationen und Betriebs-Regulierungen in der Schweiz. 1856. IV. 249.[3]
Anslijn, Nicolaas. Afbeelding der artsenij-gewassen. 1832. III. 57.
— Handleiding in de leer der botanie. 1831. I. 86.
— Handleiding tot de kennis der artzenijgewassen. 1837. III. 57.

Ansoryamar, Ch. Hauteur, grosseur et âge de certains arbres. 1899. I. 193.[2]
Antananarivo annual. I. 29.[2]
Anteeren als Mittel gegen Wildverbiss. 1900. IV. 197.[1]
Anthoine, d'. Cynipédologie du Chêne Roure. 1794. IV. 509.
Anthologia Meriana. 1776. I. 262.
Anthophilus, Isidor. Wohlbewährtes Garten-Buch. 1758. III. 103.
Anthropological society of Bombay. Journal. I. 28.[3]
Antill, Edward. An essay on the cultivation of the Vine. 1771. III. 549.[3]
The Antiquary. I. 17.
Antoine. Forest renovation in Dalmatia. 1872. IV. 167.[1]
Antoine, (frère). Manuel théorique et pratique d'horticulture. 1883. III. 113.
Antoine, A. Les beautés de la nature. 1814. I. 94.
Antoine, Franz. Abbildung von 51 Pfirsich Gattungen. 1821. III. 439.[2]
— Die Coniferen nach Lambert, Loudon. 1840. II. 12.[3]
— Die Cupressineen-Gattungen. 1857. II. 30.[1]
— Ueber Eucalypti-Anpflanzungen. 1874. IV. 529.[2]
— Japanische Coniferen mit blossgelegten Wurzeln. 1881. III. 175.[2]
— Myrmecodia echinata Gaud. 1882. II. 824.[2]
— Das Pflanzenreich auf der Wiener Weltausstellung. 1875. III. 29.[1]
— Pinus leucodermis Ant. 1864. II. 42.[3]
— Ueber das Wachsthum der Pinus leucodermis. 1879. II. 42.[2]
— & Kotschy, Theodor. Arceuthos. 1854. II. 31.[2]
— — Coniferen des Cilicischen Taurus. 1855. II. 15.[1]
— — Eine neue Tanne vom Taurus-Gebirge. 1853. II. 22.[3]
Antommarchi, C. Francesco. Les derniers momens de Napoléon. 1825. I. 498.
— Esquisse de la flore de Saint-Hélène. 1825. I. 498.
— Mémoires. 1825. I. 498.
Anton, C. Die Giftgewächse Deutschlands. 1879. III. 73.
Anton Ramirez, Bráulio. Diccionario de bibliografía agronómica. 1865. III. 1.
Antonacci, Pietro. Nozioni elementari di botanica. 1852. III. 58.
Antonesco, Constantin S. Du salicylate de quinine. 1877. III. 721.
Antonescu, Petre S. See ANTONESCU-REMUS, Petre S.
Antonescu-Remus, Petre S. Cercetarea causelor şi remediului innecurilor si depunerilor din basinul superior al Prahovei. 1887. IV. 188.[1]
— Comparaţie între pădurile ţărei nóstre şi cele din Ungaria. 1887. IV. 375.[1]
— Notiţe economice asupra taerii pădurilor din ţérra. 1880. IV. 383.[1]
— Pădurile din Salzkammergut. 1896. IV. 369.
— Studiu asupra corecţiunei torentului Zauchbach. 1894. IV. 188.[1]
— Studiu asupra economiei forestiere în Austria. 1896. IV. 279.[1]
— Studiu asupra regulelor de esploatarea pădurilor. 1885. IV. 382.[1]
— Studiu privitor la domeniul agricol Brăneşti-Cernica-Paserea. 189.? IV. 375.[1]
— Studiu torenţilor din diferitele state ale Europei. 1900. IV. 188.[1]
— Tratamentul grădinărit şi aplicaţiunea sa în România. 1892. IV. 131.
Antoni, Joseph Friedrich. Ueber die Benutzung einiger Sumacharten. 1820. III. 237.[1]
Antonielli, Giuseppe. See GIRELLI, Giuseppe & ANTONIELLI, Giuseppe.
Antonnici. Bignonia Catalpa. 1835. III. 706.[1]
Antonof, A. A. See АНТОНОВЪ, А. А.
Antony. Propriété des feuilles de Pêchers. 1837. III. 442.[3]
Antony, A. Sulla struttura e sulla funzione degli stomi. 1898. I. 132.[1]
Antrag, from der Erlass eines Waldschutzgesetzes für Sachsen betreffend. 1877. IV. 180.[3]
Auts, Karl Casar & Clemen, R. E. Flora von Düsseldorf. 1846. I. 381.
Anuario forestal de España. IV. 13.[1]
Anvers — Congrès international de botanique et d'horticulture d'Anvers . . . 1885. See CONGRÈS . . . I. 16.
Anvers — Société de pharmacie. See JOURNAL de pharmacie. I. 16.
Anvers — Société phytologique. See SOCIÉTÉ . . . I. 17.

Anvers — Société royale de géographie. See Société ... III. 15.

Anviisning for Bouden i den skovløse Egn til vilde Træers Opelskning. See SARAUW, G. 1829. III. 119.[2]

Anviisning for Gaardmændene . . . til at opelske Shov paa deres Lodder. See HOLSTEIN, F. A. von. 1811. IV. 113.[1]

Anviisning til Behandling . . . af private Skove. See BAASTRUP, F. v. 1863. IV. 113.[2]

Anvisning att bruka räkne skalan till upplösande af åtskilliga arithmetiska frågor. 1824. IV. 213.

Anvisningar och formulärer vid skogstjenste-förvaltningen. 1860. IV. 243.

Anweisung den Gebrauch der Waldarbeiter-Nummerhämmer . . . in den sächs. Staatsforstrevieren betreffend. 1897. IV. 303.[1]

Die Anweisung, Fällung . . . der Dürrständer, Schneebrüche . . betreffend. 1847. IV. 299.

Anweisung für das Holzaufbereitungsgeschäft im Forstbezirk Grillenburg. 1883. IV. 303.[1]

Anweisung nach welcher in Zukunft das Oberjägermeisterey- und Oberqueichische Forst-Amt . . . achten sollen. 1770. IV. 317.[2]

Anweisung über das bei den Forsttaxations-Nachträgen zu beobachtende Verfahren. See BESTIMMUNGEN und Erläuterungen . . . 1887. IV. 303.[1]

Anweisung über Visitation der National-Waldungen. 1801. IV. 306.

Anweisung vom 7. Mai 1868 für das Verfahren bei den Vermessungsarbeiten. 1868. IV. 264.

Anweisung zu Anlegung und Wartung guter Hecken. 1786. III. 212.[2]

Anweisung zu dem Gebrauche der Waldarbeiter-Nummerhämmer. 1889. IV. 303.[1]

Anweisung zu einer einträglichen Akazienpflanzung. See NEEB, J. 1829. IV. 522.[2]

Anweisung zum Anpflanzen lebendiger Hecker. 1791. III. 212.[2]

Anweisung zum Fertigen der von der k. sächsischen Forsteinrichtungs-Anstalt zu liefernden Forstkarten. 1878. IV. 303.[1]

Anweisung zum zweckmässigen Gebrauch der Schneidelstreu. 1833. IV. 437.[2]

Anweisung zur Akazien-Saat. 1797. IV. 522.[1]

Anweisung zur Anfertigung der Anschläge über die vorzunehmenden Forstverbesserungen. 1835. IV. 302.

Anweisung zur Anlegung und Führung des Controlbuchs. 1864. IV. 302.

Anweisung zur Anlegung und Führung des Controlbuchs. 1870. IV. 302.

Anweisung zur Anlegung und Führung des Controlbuchs. 1875. IV. 248.[1]

Anweisung zur Anlegung und Führung des Controlbuchs. 1895. IV. 302.

Anweisung zur Aufnahme und Erhaltung der ständigen Versuchsflächen in den Domänenwaldungen. 1861. IV. 248.[1]

Anweisung zur Fertigung der Forstkarten. 1898. IV. 266.[1]

Anweisung zur richtigen Kenntnis der Krankheiten der Wald- und Gartenbäume. 1795. IV. 195.[1]

Anweisung zur sichern Holzersparnis. See SANDHOF, K. A. 1792. IV. 280.[1]

Anweisung zur Veranschlagung . . . der Ausführung der Forstverbesserungen. 1000. IV. 303.[1]

Anwendung des Dampfpfluges zur Forstkultur. 1859. IV. 143.[1]

Zur Anwendung des Gesetzes vom 13. Juni 1873. 1873. IV. 334.[1]

Anwendung des Holzes und der Rinde des ächten Kastanien-Baums. 1834. IV. 493.[1]

Anzi, Martino. Auctarium ad floram novo-comensem. 1881. I. 429.

Ueber die Anzucht der Eiche im Hochwald. 1853. IV. 504.

Anzucht der Palmen aus Samen. 1885. III. 318.[1]

Ueber die Anzucht der Weiden. 1858. IV. 487.[1]

d'Aoust, Pierre Théodore VIRLET. See VIRLET D'AOUST, P. T.

Apáthi, Vilmos. A fák vezérhajtásáról. 1895. I. 107.[1]

Apchier de Pruns, marquis d'. Les Abiétinées. 1895. III. 293.

— Cultures de Conifères. 1894. III. 293.

— Pertes occasionnées par l'hiver 1879–1880. 1880. III. 48.

Aperçu général sur l'industrie des thés dans . . . Fo-Kieng. 1839. III. 601.[2]

Aperçu succinct sur les vignobles en Russie. 1897. III. 575.[1]

Apéry, Pierre. Des Myrobalans. 1888. III. 632.[2]

Apgar, Austin Craig. Extraordinary vitality in a girdled limb. 1889. I. 207.[3]

— Pocket key of trees . . . of the northern United States. 1891. I. 312, IV. 77.[1]

— Trees of the northern United States. 1892. I. 312, IV. 77.[1]

L'Apiculture. See BULLETIN d'insectologie agricole. III. 19.

Aplicaciones de la pasta de papel. 1886. IV. 430.

Aplin, T. H. Memorandum on Teak sowings. 1887. IV. 536.[1]

Apocynea. See ALLEMÃO, F. F. 1846. II. 726.[2]

Apoiger, F. See WITTSTEIN, G. C. & APOIGER, F.

Apollinaris, Quintus. Kurtz Handtbüchlin. 1550. V. XXVIII.[2]

Apologie der Bäume. Der patriotischen Gesellschaft zugeeignet von einer alten abgängigen Ulme. 1792. II. 143.[2]

Apologie du thé. See ÉLOY, N. F. J. 1751. III. 605.

Apotheker-Zeitung. I. 10.

Appalachia. I. 5.

Appalachian mountain club. Journal. See APPALACHIA. I. 5.

Appareil de mesurage des arbres. 1898. IV. 232.

Appel, Otto. Beiträge zur Flora von Baden. 1889. II. 177.[2]

— Kritische . . . Pflanzen aus der Flora von Coburg. 1891. II. 177.[2]

— Ueber Zoo- und Phyto-Morphosen. 1898. I. 214.[2]

Un appello ai paesi minacciati dal Po. 1881. IV. 186.[2]

Appenzell a. Rhodes. 1878. II. 11.[1]

Appenzell a. Rh. Schätzung der Gemeindewaldungen. 1896. IV. 262.

Appenzell I.-Rh. Ueberwachung der Privatforstwirtschaft. 1896. IV. 286.[2]

Applegarth, John. On manna and honey-dew. 1875. I. 213.[1]

Appleton, Francis H. The embellishment of grounds with trees. 1881. III. 202.[1]

Appleton's journal of literature, science and art. III. 2.

Applications du Quassia amara. 1881. III. 508.[2]

Appun, Karl Ferdinand. Ueber die Behandlung von Sämerein . . . des tropischen Süd-Amerika. 1858. III. 64,[2] 150.[1]

— Beiträge zur Pflanzenphysiognomie Venezuela's. 1856. I. 338.[1]

— Roraima. 1893. I. 339.[2]

— Unter den Tropen. 1871. I. 330.

— Volksnamen einiger . . . Pflanzen Venezuela's. 1856. I. 72.[3]

Aprikosen- und Pfirsichbaumzucht. 1821. III. 430.[1]

Aprovechamiento de la Retama. 1887. IV. 521.[2]

Aprovechamiento de los montes de California. 1892. IV. 403.[3]

Apuleius Barbarus. Herbarium Apuleji Platonici. See APULEIUS PLATONICUS. 400. I. 274.

— De herbarum virtutibus. See APULEIUS PLATONICUS. 400. I. 274.

— De medicaminibus herbarum. See APULEIUS PLATONICUS. 400. I. 274.

— De viribus herbarum. See APULEIUS PLATONICUS. 400. I. 274.

Apuleius Platonicus. See APULEIUS BARBARUS.

Apuntes acerca de la rectificación del catálogo de los montes públicos. 1888. IV. 363.[2] See also CATALOGO razonado. . . . 1888. III. 271.[3]

Apuntes sobre la vegetacion ecuatoriana. 1874. I. 340.[1]

The Arabian drug waras or wars. 1898. III. 477.[1]

Arago, Dominique François Jean. Rapport sur les travaux exécutés en Abyssinie. 1844. I. 487.

— On thunder and lightning. 1838. IV. 193.[2]

— Sur le tonnerre. 1838. IV. 193.[2]

Araliacées japonaises en culture à Leide. 1858. II. 648,[2] 649.[1]

Die Aralien. 1883. III. 641.[1]

Arango, Posada-. See POSADA-ARANGO.

Arata, Pedro N. Sobre el ácido quebrachitánico. 1879. II. 460.[1]

— Sur l'alcaloïde du Mio-Mio. 1879. III. 754.[2]

— The alkaloid of Mio-Mio. 1879. III. 754.[2]

— Análisis de la madera del Calafate. 1879. II. 203.[1]

— Apuntes sobre la cera . . . de la Yerba-mate. 1877. III. 531.[1]

— Contribución al estudio del tanino contenido en la Yerba-mate. 1877. III. 531.[1]

— Estudio de la corteza de Winterverdadera. 1888. III. 397.[2]

— Estudio de la Persea Lingue. 1880. II. 227.[3]

Arata, Pedro N. (*continued*).
— Sobre la goma del Quebracho Colorado. 1878. II. 460.[1]
— Eine neue Untersuchung der echten Winterrinde. 1888. III. 397.[2]
— Nota sobre la pretentida identidad de la Paitina con la Aspidospermina. 1881. III. 686.[2]
— Nota sobre la Thevetia Yccotli. 1880. III. 691.[2]
Arató, Gyula Julius. Erdészetünk az 1896. 1898. IV. 374.[1]
— A magyar erdőgazdaság az ezredéves országos kiállításkor. 1896. IV. 374.[1]
Die **Araucaria-Arten.** 1881. III. 297.[2]
The **Araucaria** of New Guinea. 1888. II. 26.[1]
Die **Araucarienwälder** in Chile und Argentinien. 1899. IV. 447.[2]
Arbaumont, Jules d'. Sur l'anatomie et la morphologie des Ampélidées. 1881. II. 501.[2]
— Contribution à l'histoire des racines adventives. 1878. II. 504.[1]
— Sur la disposition des faisceaux dans la tige . . . des Ampélidées. 1881. II. 501.[2]
— Effets produits sur certains végétaux par les gelées de l'hiver dernier 1879–1880. 1881. III. 48.
— Famille des Ampélidées. 1881. II. 501.[2]
— Sur le mode de formation de quelques nodosités phyllox-ériques. 1878. III. 571.
— Note sur le péricycle. 1886. I. 128.[2]
— Observations sur les stomates . . . du Cissus. 1877. II. 504.[1]
— Quelques observations sur le Myrsine africana. 1900. II. 694.[2]
— Sur les ramifications de la tige des Ampélidées. 1882. II. 501.[2]
— La tige des Ampélidées. 1880. II. 501.[2]
— Sur une Vigne à inflorescence monstrueuse. 1896. II. 507.[2]
— *See also* VIALLANES, Alfred & ARBAUMONT, Jules d'.
Zu den Arbeiten der K. k. forstlichen Versuchsanstalt. 1895. IV. 28.[2]
Arbeitsplan für die Anbauversuche mit ausländischen Holzarten. 188.? IV. 125.[2]
Arbeltier de la Boullaye. Les forêts de l'Aube. 1899. IV. 362.
— Rapport sur "L'art de greffer." 1889. IV. 163.[1]
— Rapport sur le mémoire de M. Labourasse. 1896. IV. 462.[1]
— Rapport sur le reboisement des terrains en pente . . . Chaumont. 1878. IV. 163.
Arbey, L. Tecnologia forestale. 1888. IV. 427.[1]
Arbois de Jubainville, A. d'. Bois de Pin, comme bois de râperie. 1893. IV. 430.
— Cœur rouge du Hêtre. 1883. IV. 497.
— Culture du Cerisier. 1888. III. 432.[1]
— Dunes de la Vendée. 1877. IV. 162.
— Émondage des branches gourmandes du Chêne. 1895. IV. 508.
— Extension à donner à la culture du Sapin pectiné. 1894. IV. 446.[2]
— Faculté asséchante du Pin sylvestre. 1877. IV. 481.
— Hydnum diversidens Fr. 1884. IV. 211.[2]
— Hylésine piniperde. 1885. IV. 461.[2]
— La maladie du rond. 1877. IV. 467.[2]
— Manuel du défrichement des forêts. 1865. IV. 381.
— Merulius lacrymans. 1886. IV. 415.[1]
— Mode de combattre l'invasion des pineraies. 1894. IV. 209.[1]
— Mortalité parmi les souches des taillis de Chêne. 1893. IV. 511.
— Mycologie forestière. 1890. IV. 212.
— Mycologie forestière. 1892. IV. 212.
— Le mytilaspis du Hêtre. 1893. IV. 497.
— Le Nectria ditissima. 1885. IV. 211.[2]
— Nocuité de l'entaille circulaire au pied des Chênes à écorcer. 1892. IV. 513.
— Un nouveau dendromètre. 1870. IV. 215.
— Observations sur la vente des forêts de l'état. 1865. IV. 275.
— Le Peridermium pini. 1886. IV. 478.
— Peuplier du Canada et Peuplier blanc. 1877. IV. 485.[1]
— Pineraies de la Champagne. 1894. IV. 478.
— Polyporus borealis Fr. 1885. IV. 456.
— Polyporus dryadeus. 1883. IV. 510.
— Polyporus fulvus Scop. 1881. IV. 211.[2]
— Polyporus igniarius Fr. 1882. IV. 211.[2]
— Polyporus vaporarius Fr. 1884. IV. 211.[2]

— Pruning epicormic branches of Oak. 1895. IV. 508.
— Recépage des taillis incendiés. 1890. IV. 181.[2]
— Recherches sur les tailles sous futaie. 1860. IV. 130.
— Stereum hirsutum Fr. 1882. IV. 211.[2]
— Le Stereum purpureum Fr. 1890. IV. 415.[1]
— Utilité des assolements forestiers. 1864. IV. 68.
— & Vesque, Julien. Les maladies des plantes cultivées. 1878. III. 179.
Arbol colosal, la Sounina. 1865. I. 296.[1]
Arbolado, 1871. IV. 47.[2]
Arbolado; ó, Influencia de los árboles. 1887. IV. 541.
Arbolayre contenant la qualitey . . . des herbes. 1485. I. 276, V. XIV.[2]
Los **árboles** enanos japoneses. 1892. III. 176.[1]
Arbor, (*pseud.*). Cladrastis lutea. 1874. III. 472.[2]
— The planting of roadside trees. 1885. III. 210.
Arbor day. 1888. IV. 41.[2]
Arbor day. 1895. IV. 42.[1]
Arber-day. 1897. IV. 42.[1]
Arbor day, 1889–1900. 1889. IV. 42.[1]
Arbor day, May, 1892–96, 1898. 1892. IV. 42.[1]
Arbor day, 1894–95. 1894. IV. 42.[2]
Arbor-day for Italy. 1899. IV. 42.[1]
Arbor day in Japan. 1896. IV. 42.[2]
Arbor day in the United States. 1888. IV. 41.[2]
Arbor day tree planting. 1889. IV. 42.[1]
An **arboreal** junk. 1894. III. 202.[2]
Arboreal physiology and an important experiment. 1884. I. 159.
L'**Arboretum** de Grafrath. 1896. IV. 18.[2]
Arboretum floridum. 1689. I. 530.[2]
Arboricultural notes. — Notices on trees. 1855. I. 295.[2]
Arboriculture. 1886. III. 32.[1]
Arboriculture; culture du Pêcher. 1831. III. 440.[2]
L'arboriculture fruitière aux États-Unis. 1899. III. 134.[1]
Arboriculture in its relation to climate. 1876. IV. 55.[1]
Arboriculture on hill sides. 1884. IV. 72.
Un arbre à caoutchouc du Brésil. 1899. III. 688.[2]
L'arbre à chandelles. 1870. III. 706.[1]
Arbre à cire. 1882. III. 324.[2]
Arbre à lait de l'Amérique du Sud. 1849. III. 367.[2]
L'**Arbre** à laque. 1879. III. 528.[2]
Arbre à pluie. 1877. I. 213.[1]
L'**Arbre** à pluie. 1892. I. 213.[2]
L'**Arbre** à sucre et à alcool. 1887. III. 667.[2]
Sur l'arbre à suif. 1848. III. 522.[1]
Un arbre curieux. 1894. IV. 491.[2]
Sur l'arbre de quercitrin. 1824. IV. 518.[2]
L'arbre électrique de la Nouvelle-Guinée. *See* The ELECTRIC tree . . . 1885. I. 517.[1]
Un arbre incombustible. 1878. I. 508.[2]
Arbre remarquable, Sapin recourbé. 1845. II. 37.[1]
Pour les arbres. 1897. IV. 541.
Les arbres curieux. 1895. II. 139,[1] IV. 493.[2]
Nos arbres curieux. 1897. IV. 558.[2]
Les arbres de Wilhelmine. 1898. III. 34.
Les arbres des promenades de Paris. 1898. III. 42.[2]
Les arbres des quais. *See* AYNARD, Théodore. 1887. III. 211.[2]
Les arbres en cas d'orage. 1896. IV. 195.[1]
Arbres et plantes d'ornement. *See* POMMIER, A. 188.? III. 87.
Les arbres exotiques en Angleterre. 1896. IV. 126.[2]
Les arbres fruitiers le long des routes. 1896. III. 211.[1]
Les arbres les plus hauts du monde. 1896. IV. 75.[2]
Sur les arbres morts par la gelée de 1709. 1712. III. 181.[2]
Arbres-piège pour les dermestes. *See* BORKENKÄFER-FANG-BÄUME. 1858. IV. 204.
Arbres remarquables, Cèdre de Montigny. 1852. II. 28.[1]
Arbres remarquables par leurs dimensions. 1877. I. 296.[2]
Sur un arbrisseau d'Amérique qui porte de la cire. 1727. III. 352.[2]
Arbustum, fonticulus, spinetum. *See* ESTIENNE, Charles. 1533. I. 276, V. XIV.[2]
The **Arbutes.** 1878. III. 647.[2]
The **Arbutus,** Croome's variety. 1875. III. 647.[2]
Arbutus Unedo at Balcarres. 1893. III. 647.[2]
Arcangeli, Giovanni. Sopra alcune mostruosità. 1897. II. 40.[1]
— Alcune osservazioni sull' Araujá albens. 1899. II. 736.[1]
— Sopra alcune piante della Repubblica Argentina. 1894. II. 395.[2]
— Sopra alcune piante di Araucaria brasiliensis. 1900. II. 26.[1]

— Sopra alcune piante di Araucaria coltivate. 1899. III. 298.[1]
— Sopra alcuni Cocos. 1878. II. 67.[1]
— Sopra alcuni esemplari di Araucaria Bidwillii. 1899. III. 298.[1]
— Altre osservazioni sull' Araucaria. 1900. II. 26.[2]
— Ancora sull' Araucaria imbricata. 1899. II. 26.[2]
— Appunti sulle Cicadacee. 1876. III. 284.[1]
— Sull' Araucaria imbricata . . . di Pisa. 1862. III. 299.[1]
— Sulla caprificazione. 1881. II. 152.[2]
— Sopra al Castagno d'India . . . dell' Orto pisano. 1892. II. 482.[2]
— Comparsa di un tetranychus sulle Viti. 1891. III. 564.[1]
— Compendio della flora italiana. 1882. I. 429.
— Compendio di botanica. 1889. I. 92.
— La comunicazione preliminare sopra la cellula del canale nella Cycas. See IKENO, Seiitsiro. 1896. II. 5.[1]
— Sugli effetti del freddo nell' Orto botanico di Torino. 1880. III. 49.[2]
— Sopra un esemplar di Cycas media. 1876. III. 285.[1]
— Sopra l' esperimento di Kraus. 1889. I. 185.[1]
— La festa degli alberi. 1900. IV. 42.[3]
— Sul germogliamento dei grani pollinici. 1897. I. 201.[2]
— Germogliamento dei semi del Podocarpus chinensis. 1876. II. 9.[3]
— Sull' influenza della luce nell' accrescimento. 1888. I. 191.[1]
— Sulla Larrea cuneifolia e sulle piante bussola. 1893. II. 395.[2]
— Sopra la malattia dell' Olivo. 1886. III. 677.[2]
— Sopra una malattia della Vite. 1877. III. 577.
— Sull' ossalato calcico criptocristallino. 1891. I. 139.
— Osservazioni sopra alcune Vite. 1886. III. 579.
— Le piante arboree dell' Orto botanico di Pisa. 1872. I. 64.
— Sulla polvere cristallina . . . d' ossalato calcico. 1891. I. 139.
— Ricerche sul contegno del polline nel Gingko biloba. See HIRASE, Sakugoro. 1894. II. 7.[2]
— Sul rossore della Vite. 1896. III. 562.[1]
— Gli spermatozoi della Cycas revoluta. See IKENO, Seiitsiro. 1897. II. 5.[1]
— Sur la structure de la fleur femelle des Conifères. 1880. II. 19.
— Sulla struttura del frutto della Cyphomandra. 1890. II. 771.[1]
— Sulla struttura e sulla funzioni degli stomi. See CHESTER, G. D. 1897. I. 132.[1]
— Gli studi dello Czapek. 1899. I. 37.[1]
— Sopra i tubercoli radicali delle Leguminose. 1891. III. 321.[1]

Archbald, A. B. Flora dell' alto Serchio e del Lima. 1874. I. 428.
Archenegg, Adolf Noé von. Uber atavistische Blattformen des Tulpenbaumes. 1894. II. 211.[1]
Archer, John. A compendious herbal. 1673. III. 54.
Archer, Thomas Croxen. First steps in economic botany. 1853. III. 217.
— The Guarana of Brazil. 1863. III. 539.[2]
— Popular economic botany. 1853. III. 217.
— Profitable plants. 1853. III. 217.
— Some account of Paullinia sorbilis. 1863. II. 488.[1]
— Some account of Paullinia sorbilis. 1864. III. 539.[2]
— On two fibres from Brazil. 1855. III. 319.[1] 631.[1]
— The vegetable products of the world. 1862. III. 319.[1]
— The useful products of . . . Palmaceae. 1856. III. 319.[1]
Archer, William. Note on Microcachrys. 1850. II. 9.[1]
— Notes on the vegetable products of Tasmania. 1863. III. 282.[1]
— On the value of hairs as a character in . . . Eurybia. 1861. II. 861.[2]
Archer, William Henry & others. Die Colonie Victoria in Australien. See MUELLER, Ferdinand, Baron von. 1861. I. 502.
Archibald, Joseph. The botanist's and nurseryman's companion. 1791. III. 81.
Archief voor de Kina-cultuur. III. 26.[2]
Archief voor den landbouw der bergstreken. III. 26.[2]
Architect. London. IV. 12.[1]
Architect and builder. Kansas City. IV. 3.
Architect and builder. Milwaukee. IV. 3.
Architect, builder and woodworker. See AMERICAN builder. New York. IV. 3.
Architects' and builders' magazine. See BUILDING. IV. 3.

Architectural and building monthly. IV. 3.
Architectural era. See AMERICAN builder. New York. IV. 3.
Architectural review. IV. 3.
Architecture and building. See BUILDING. IV. 3.
Archiv der Pharmacie des Apotheker-Vereins. See ARCHIV des Apothekervereins. I. 10.
Archiv des Apothekervereins. I. 10.
Archiv for Haugevæsen. III. 10.[2]
Archiv for Mathematik og Naturvidenskab. I. 8.[1]
Archiv for Pharmacie. I. 8.[2]
Archiv für Anatomie und Entwickelungsgeschichte. See ARCHIV für die Physiologie. I. 10.
Archiv für Anatomie und Physiologie. See ARCHIV für die Physiologie. I. 10.
Archiv für die Botanik. I. 10.
Archiv für die gesammte Naturlehre. I. 520.[1]
Archiv für die Naturkunde Liv-, Ehst- und Kurlands. See DORPATER NATURFORSCHER-GESELLSCHAFT. I. 9.[3]
Archiv für die naturwissenschaftliche Landesdurchforschung von Böhmen. I. 27.
Archiv für die Physiologie. I. 10.
Archiv für die systematische Naturgeschichte. I. 10.
Archiv für experimentelle Pathologie und Pharmakologie. I. 10.
Archiv für Natur. See ARCHIV von Merkwürdigkeiten . . . III. 11.
Archiv für Naturgeschichte. I. 10.
Archiv scandinavischer Beiträge zur Naturgeschichte. I. 10.
Archiv von Merkwürdigkeiten aus dem Reiche der Natur. III. 11.
Archiv zemědělský. I. 27.
Archives botanique du nord de la France. I. 21.
Archives cosmologiques. I. 16.
Archives de botanique. I. 21.
Archives de flore. I. 10.
Archives de l'agriculture du nord de la France. III. 19.
Archives de la flore d'Europe. See ARCHIVES de flore. I. 10.
Archives de la flore jurassienne. I. 21.
Archives de médecine et de pharmacie militaires. See JOURNAL de médecine, de chirurgie . . . I. 21.
Archives de pharmacodynamie. I. 16.
Archives de physiologie normale. See JOURNAL de la physiologie . . . I. 21.
Archives des sciences physiques et naturelles. See BIBLIOTHÈQUE universelle des sciences. I. 26.[1]
Archives internationales de pharmacodynamie. See ARCHIVES de pharmacodynamie. I. 16.
Archives italiennes de biologie. I. 24.[2]
Archives néerlandaises des sciences exactes et naturelles. I. 15.
Archivo rural. III. 23.[1]
Archon, (pseud.). How to measure timber. 1854. IV. 216.
Arcozzi-Masino & Panizzardi. Descrizione . . . intorno ad esperimenti di coltivazione di alcuni banchi di sabbia. 1864. IV. 165.
Arcueil-Société. See SOCIÉTÉ . . . I. 23.
Arcularius, Rudolf. Ein Fall von Wurzelkropf bei Abies pichta. 1897. III. 297.[1]
Ardant, P. Études théoriques et expérimentales sur l'établissement des charpentes. 1840. IV. 408.
Ardène, Jean Paul Rome d'. Abrégé des instructions sur le jardinage. 1767. III. 112.
— Année champêtre. 1769. III. 112.
Arderne, H. M. The Norfolk Pine at Cape Town. 1891. III. 298.[2]
Ardoino, Honoré. Catalogue des plantes vasculaires . . . de Menton et de Monaco. 1862. I. 412.
— Flore analytique du département des Alpes-Maritimes. 1867. I. 413.
Ardoynis, Santes de. Incipit liber de venenis. 1492. I. 276, V. XIV.[2]
— Opus de venenis. 1492. I. 276, III. 260.[1]
Arduino, Giovanni. Memoria sopra la coltura dei boschi di Roveri. 1790. IV. 504.
Arduino, Pietro. Animadversionum botanicarum specimen. 1759. I. 424.
— Catalogo primo delle piante . . . nel Real orto di agricoltura di Padova. 1807. I. 61.
— Memoire di osservazioni . . . sopra la coltura e gli usi di varie piante. 1766. III. 51.
Arechavaleta, José. Contribución al conocimiento de la flora Uruguayá. 1896. I. 345.
— Flora uruguaya. 1898. I. 345.
— Las Gramíneas Uruguayas. 1894. II. 58.[1]

Arena. III. 2.

Arena, Filippo. La natura e coltura·de fiori. 1767. III. 126.²

Arenas, Bernardino, NUÑEZ DE. *See* NUÑEZ DE ARENAS, Bernardino.

Arenas, Domingo A. Repoblacion del monte Auseba. 1877. IV. 164.³

Arenberg, *prince* de. Fixation des terrains siliceux. 1899. IV. 146,¹ 545.³

— Plantaciones protectoras en el Istmo de Suez. 1899. IV. 545.²

Arends, Georg. Fuchsia triphylla hybrida. 1894. III. 640.³

Arendt, J. J. F. Scholia osnabrugensia in Chloridem hannoveranam. 1837. I. 379.

— Tabellarische Uebersicht der Flora . . . Deutschlands. 1831. I. 378.

Arendts, H. Atlas historyi naturalnej. 1900. I. 93.

Arenstorff, C. F. Comparatio nominum plantarum officinalium. 1762. III. 72.

Areschoug, Fredrik Wilhelm Christian. Abstract of researches on the anatomy of bud-scales. 1871. I. 108.¹

— Om bastcellers ombildning i kristalförande parenchym. 1861. II. 497.³

— Beiträge zur Biologie der Holzgewächse. 1875. I. 217.

— Om de i " Beiträge zur Biologie der Holzgewächse " använda benämningar. 1879. I. 105.

— Betrachtungen über die Organisation . . . der nordischen Bäume. 1888. I. 218.

— Bidrag till den Skandinaviska Vegetationens Historia. 1866. I. 356.

— Der Einfluss des Klimas auf . . . Pflanzen. 1882. I. 218.

— Om . den europeiska vegetationens ursprung. 1869.— I. 349.

— Exsicatverk öfver nordiska Rubi. 1886. II. 301.¹

— Förberedande redogörelse för några undersökningar öfver bladets anatomi. 1874. I. 110.

— Ueber gegitterte Parenchymzellen in der Rinde. 1870. II. 264.¹

— Om de mekaniska cellväfnaderna i. bladen 1877. I. 134.¹

— Monografi öfver Skånes Rubus-arten. 1855. II. 301.¹

— Norges Rubi. 1876. II. 301.¹

— Ueber ein Paar Weihe'scher Rubi. 1876. II. 301.²

— Über die physiologischen Leistungen . . . des Grundgewebes des Blattes. 1897. I. 111.

— Plantae . . . circa Guayaquil collectae. 1858. I. 340.¹

— Rubus. 1876. II. 301.¹

— Ueber Rubus affinis Whe. 1888. II. 306.¹

— Om Rubus affinis Whe. och R. relatus. 1888. II. 301.¹

— Om Rubus Idaeus L., dess affiniteter. 1872. II. 308.¹

— On Rubus Idaeus L.; its affinities and origin. 1872. II. 308.¹

— Ueber Rubus obovatus. 1889. II. 301.²

— Om de s. k. bladspårens förhållande. 1873. I. 105. ·

— Om de skandinaviska Rubusformerna. 1871. II. 301.¹

— Skånes flora. 1866. I. 356. .

— Some observations on the genus Rubus. 1885. II. 301.¹

— Om stambygnaden hos Leycesteria. 1879. II. 835.¹

— Växtanatomiska undersökningar. 1867. I. 110.

— Ytterligare om Rubus Idaeus. 1875. II. 308.¹

Areschoug, Johan Erhard. Bidrag och anmärkningar till Götheborgs flora. 1840. I. 354.

— Botanikens elementer lärobok. 1863. I. 90.

— Lärobok i botanik. 1860. I. 90.

— Plantae cotyledoneae florae gothoburgensis. 1836. I. 53.

— Stirpes in regione cimbritshamnensi. 1831. I. 353.

Aretin, Georg, *Freiherr* von. Aktenmässige Donaumoos-Kulturs-Geschichte. 1795. IV. 143.²

Aretius, Benedictus. Stoechornii et Nessi . . . stirpium brevis descriptio. 1561. I. 432.²

Arévalo, Ricardo. Estudio sobre la corteza de Copalchi. 1887. III. 517.¹

The 'Argan' tree of Marocco. 1879. III. 666.²

L'Arganier du Maroc en Algérie. 1895. III. 667.¹

Argel leaves. 1891. III. 694.¹

Argence, Louis. La géographie des Palmiers. 1890. II. 61.¹

Argenta, Vicente, MARTIN DE. *See* MARTIN DE ARGENTA, Vicente.

Argenteuil — Société d'horticulture, d'arboriculture et de viticulture du canton . . . *See* SOCIÉTÉ . . . III. 21.

Argentine palm kernels. 1897. III. 319.¹

Argentine Republic — **Museo de productos argentinos.** *See* MUSEO . . . I. 7.²

Argosy. III. 16.

Arici, Cesare. La coltivazione degli Olivi. 1808. III. 675.¹

On the **aridity** of Spain. *See* BROWN, J. C. 1884. IV. 47.²

Aristolochia-covered verandah. 1885. III. 386.¹

Aristolochia gigas Sturtevantii at Washington. 1896. III. 386.¹

Aristoteles. Aristoteles graece ex recognitione Immanuelis Bekkeri. 321. I. 271.³

— Aristoteles latine interpretibus variis. 321. I. 271.³

— Aristotelis opera. 321. I. 271.³

— Aristotelis qui ferebantur librorum fragmenta. 321. I. 271.³

— Fragmente Aristotelischer Phytologie. 321. I. 271.³

— Phytologiae Aristotelicae fragmenta. 321. I. 271.³

— Problemata quæ ad stirpium genus. 1539. V. VII.³

— Scholia in Aristotelem, collegit C. A. Brandis. 321. I. 271.³

Arizmendi, Antonio de. Prontuario ó tarifa por sucesiva progresion de dimensiones de las piezas de madera. 1789. IV. 220.

Arizona — **Agricultural experiment station.** · Annual report. Bulletin. III. 2.

Arizona — **University of** — **Arizona agricultural experiment station.** *See* ARIZONA — *See* AGRICULTURAL EXPERIMENT STATION.

An Arizona Agave. 1895. II. 89.¹

Arizona shellac. 1880. III. 465,¹ 494.³

Arkansas — Bureau of mines, manufactures and agriculture. Biennial report. III. 2.

Arkansas agricultural experiment station. *See* ARKANSAS INDUSTRIAL UNIVERSITY. III. 2.

Arkansas industrial university — **Arkansas agricultural experiment station.** Annual report. Bulletin. III. 2.

Arkhipof, S. N. *See* АРХИПОВЪ, С. Н.

Arlidge, John Thomas. On the monstrosity of a Rose. 1853. III. 289.²

Arloing, Saturnin. Sur un nouveau mode d'administration de l'éther . . . à la Sensitive. 1879. II. 373.¹

— Recherches . . . sur le bouturage des Cactées. 1876. II. 588,¹ III. 619.

Arlt, Carl. Eine abnorme Fichte. 1884. II. 36.¹

Arma, Joannes Franciscus. Opus de venenis in dialogos. 1557. III. 260.¹

Armailhacq, A. d'. La culture des Vignes. 1855. III. 555.

Armano, Filippo. Catalogus plantarum Horti r. b. braydensis. 1812. I. 62.

Armendaris, Eduardo. Necesidad de la conservacion de los bosques. 1895. IV. 179.³

— *See also* VILLADA, M. M. & ARMENDARIS, Eduardo.

Armenteras, A. Aclaración. 1899. IV. 554.

— El criterio desamortizador. 1896. IV. 552.¹

— La escala cerrada. 1900. IV. 554.

— Miscelánea forestal. 1900. IV. 544.³

— El personal de montes. 1900. IV. 554.

— La zona forestal de la provincia de Madrid. 1897. IV. 556.²

Armesto, Rodrigo. Noticia sobre el Árbol del azucar. 1811. III. 647.³

Armit, William E. Notes on certain plants of north-western Queensland. 1884. I. 503.

Armitage, Edward. A lecture on the botany of Natal. 1854. I. 494.

— *See also* SANDERSSON, John & ARMITAGE, Edward.

Armitage, H. P. C. A few notes on some statistics for working plans in the north of Ceylon. 1900. IV. 250.³

Armstrong, C. Spearman. Tea cultivation in Ceylon. 1884. III. 603.

Armstrong, Clive. Durability of Yellowbox timber. 1897. IV. 533.³

Armstrong, Henry Edward. Indian turpentines. 1896. III. 386.³

— Preliminary report on two Burmese turpentines. 1899. IV. 463.¹

Armstrong, J. B. Descriptions of new and rare New Zealand plants. 1881. I. 507.

— On the genus Corallospartium. 1881. II. 347.³

— The New Zealand Cordylines. 1881. II. 79.³ ·

— Planting in towns. 1880. III. 42.¹

— A short sketch of the flora . . . of Canterbury. 1880. I. 507.

— The southern Alps of New Zealand. 1883. I. 507.

— A synopsis of the New Zealand species of Veronica. 1881. II. 782.²

Armstrong, John. Histoire naturelle et civile de l'Isle de Minorque. 1752. III. 126.[1]
— The history of the island of Minorca. 1752. III. 126.[1]
Armstrong, John F. New Zealand Veronicas. 1883. II. 783.[1]
— On some new species of New Zealand plants. 1872. II. 783.[1]
— On the vegetation . . . of Christchurch. 1870. I. 506.[2]
The army and the forests. 1890. IV. 178.[2]
Arnaud, Albert Léon. Sur la composition élémentaire de la strophantine. 1888. III. 690.[2]
— Dosage de la carotine. 1887. I. 176.
— Sur les écorces des Quinquinas Cuprea. 1882. III. 723.
— Sur la matière cristallisée active des flèches empoisonnées des Comalis. 1888. III. 685.[3]
— Sur la matière cristallisée active, extraite des semences du Strophantus. 1888. III. 690.[1]
— Sur un nouvel alcaloïde des quinquinas. 1881. III. 723.
— Sur les produits de dédoublement de l'ouabaïne. 1898. III. 685.[2]
— Recherches sur l'ouabaïne. 1898. III. 685.[2]
— Recherches sur la carotine. 1889. I. 177.
— Recherches sur la cinchonamine. 1883. III. 747.[2]
— Recherches sur la composition de la carotine. 1886. I. 185.[1]
— Recherches sur la digitaline et sur la tanghinine. 1889. III. 691.[1]
— Recherches sur les matières colorantes des feuilles. 1885. I. 185.[2]
— Sur la tanghinine cristallisée. 1889. III. 691.[1]
— See also GRIMAUX, Édouard & ARNAUD, A. L.; ROCHE-BRUNNE, A. T. & ARNAUD, A. L.
— & Padé, Léon. Recherche chimique de l'acide nitrique. 1884. I. 180,[2] III. 747.[2]
— & Verneuil, Auguste Victor Louis. Sur un nouveau procédé d'extraction du caoutchouc. 1900. III. 232,[1] 688.[2]
Arnaud, Alessandro. Brighe, traverse e serbatoi artificiali. 1884. IV. 186.[2]
Arnaud, J. A. M. Flore du département de la Haute-Loire. 1825. I. 407.
Arnaud, J. B. Calendrier républicain, botanique. 1799. I. 33.
Arnaud, Marius Henri. Le Laurier-cerise est-il une Amygdalée? 1900. II. 270.[2]
Arnaudon, Giovanni. On the Amaranth wood. 1863. IV. 63.[2]
— Études sur quelques produits naturels applicables à la teinture. 1858. III. 238.
— Faits pour servir à l'histoire du bois d'Andromène. 1858. IV. 401.[2]
— On a means of rendering ostensible the specific gravity of woods . . . 1864. IV. 411.[1]
Su di un mezzo per rendere ostensibile il peso specifico dei legni. 1864. IV. 411.[1]
— The Owala or Opochala. 1863. III. 483.[1]
— Recherches sur la coloration des bois. 1858. I. 155.
— Recherches sur les bois d'amarante. 1858. III. 236.
— Recherches sur un nouvel acide extrait du bois de Taigu du Paraguay. 1858. III. 232.[2]
— The seed of Owala or Opochala. 1863. III. 483.[1]
— On the tanning materials and dyestuffs. 1862. III. 236.
Arnaudon, J. J. De l'Algarobille. 1894. III. 469.[1]
Arnault de la Noblevile, Louis Daniel. Description abrégée des plantes usuelles. 1767. III. 54.
Arnd. Das Unstatthafte der einfachen Zinsrechnung bei Werthschätzung der Wälder. 1824. IV. 253.
Arndt, (Oberförster, Ullersdorf). Zur Durchforstungsfrage. 1888. IV. 174.
— Geht unsere Waldwirthschaft zurück? 1895. IV. 119.[1]
— Die gesetzliche Versicherung der Privatforstbeamten. 1890. IV. 301.[1]
— Hat die ostpreussische Fichtenwirthschaft eine Zukunft? 1894. IV. 454.
— Kann der National-Wohlstand durch . . . Scheidung der drei Culturarten . . . gefördert werden? 1889. IV. 270.
— Mängel der Privatforstwirtschaft. 1900. IV. 308.[1]
— Die Nachzucht von Fichte und Tanne. 1887. IV. 138,[1] 444,[2] 454.
— Aus der Praxis der Eichenverjüngung. 1899. IV. 509.
— Schirmverjüngung von Fichte. 1890. IV. 444,[3] 454.
— Die zweckmässige Verwerthung des Holzeinschlages. 1887. IV. 388.[1]
Arndt, C. Eiche durch den Blitz entzündet. 1878. IV. 194.

— Ilex Aquifolium var. senescens. 1875. II. 463.[2]
Arndt, E. M. Ein Wort über die Pflegung und Erhaltung der Forsten. 1820. IV. 268.
Arndt, Ernst. Die Privatforstwirthschaft in Preussen. 1889. IV. 98,[2] 286.[2]
Arndt, F. Der Rückgang der Kirschenerträge des Dresdener Elbthals. 1892. III. 435.[1]
Arndts. Ueber das Gewicht der Laubstreu. 1873. IV. 71.
Arnell, Hampus Wilhelm. Anmärkningar angående Sorbus Aucuparia L. f. minor. 1884. II. 312.[1]
— En egendomlig, ny form af Rönn. 1883. II. 312.[1]
— Naturens misshushållning. 1879. II. 104.[1]
— Tvenne i norra Småland funna reliktformer. 1891. II. 100.[2]
Arnold. Reise nach Mariazell in Steyermark. 1785. II. 43.
Arnold. Forstwirthschaftliche Benützung des Bodens. See Die LANDWIRTHSCHAFT im Regierungsbezirk Oberbáyern. 1885. IV. 351.[1]
Arnold, (colonel). See АРНОЛЬДЪ, (ПОЛКОВНИКЪ).
Arnold, (Lehrer, Bitburg). See DAU, BECKER, ESSER & ARNOLD.
Arnold, (Professor, Moscow). Eine neue russische Taxations-Instruction. 1885. IV. 247.[1]
Arnold, Bruno. De graecis florum et arborum amantissimis. 1885. I. 514.[2]
Arnold, Edwin Lester. Coffee; its cultivation. 1886. III. 727.
Arnold, Frederick Henry. Flora of Sussex. 1887. I. 403.
Arnold, Friedrich von. Russlands Wald. See АРНОЛЬДЪ, Ѳ. К. 1890. IV. 346.
— See also АРНОЛЬДЪ, Ѳ. К.
Arnold, G. C. De monumentis historiae naturalis Poloniae literariis. 1882. I. 39.
Arnold Arboretum. Report of the director. See SARGENT, C. S. 1874. I. 39.
Arnoldi, W. Beiträge zur Morphologie der Gymnospermen. 1900. II. 8,[2] 20.[1]
— Beiträge zur Morphologie einiger Gymnospermen. 1900. II. 50.[1]
— Ueber die Knospenlage der Blätter. 1900. I. 109.[1]
Arnold's London chronicle. 1503. III. 106.[3]
Arnoldus de Villa Nova. De virtutibus herbarum. See HERBARIUS.
Arnott, George Arnott Walker-. Botany. 1842. I. 268.
— Characters of three genera of Indian plants. 1834. I. 470.[1]
— Descriptions of some new or rare Indian plants. 1839. I. 472.
— Sur le genre Torreya. 1838. II. 12.[1]
— On the genus Torreya. 1838. II. 12.[1]
— Historical notice of some celebrated trees. See ARNOTT, WALKER-. 1835. I. 295.
— Names of orders, sub-orders and tribes. 184.? I. 399.
— New genera of plants. 1834. II. 738.[1]
— Note on Hypericum anglicum. 1860. II. 556.[1]
— Note on Samara laeta Linn. 1851. II. 693.[2]
— Note relative to . . . Hya-hya. 1830. III. 691.[1]
— Note sur la plante qui produit la Coque du Levant. 1834. IV. 206.[2]
— Notes on some South African plants. 1841. I. 494.
— Observations on some new . . . plants. 1838. I. 268.
— Observations sur quelques plantes . . . de Sénégambie. 1834. I. 490.
— Professori D. F. L. de Schlechtendal haec pauca de Grabowskia scribit. 1837. II. 772.[1]
— Fugilus plantarum Indiae orientalis. 1836. I. 472.
— On the Rhizophoreae. 1838. II. 612.[2]
— Swan River plants. 1840. I. 500.
— Tour to the south of France. 1826. I. 408.
— See also HOOKER, Sir W. J. & ARNOTT, G. A. WALKER-WIGHT, Robert & ARNOTT, G. A. WALKER-.
Arnott, Samuel. Cytisus purpureus. 1899. III. 474.[2]
— Spiraea bullata. 1900. III. 461.[1]
— Veronica Lindsayi. 1899. III. 704.[2]
Arnould, Auguste. Les forêts et l'impôt. 1895. IV. 285.
— La réforme de l'impôt foncier. 1896. IV. 285.[1]
— Le revenu cadastral des forêts. 1896. IV. 259,[2] 285.[1]
Arnould, J. E. Mode de production de l'alcool au moyen des fibres végétales. 1854. IV. 432.[1]
Arnoult, Georges. Rapport présenté à l'Association bretonne sur l'établissement d'un jardin fruitier. 1875. I. 59.
Arnoux, F. De l'Anagyrie fétide. 1870. III. 467.[1]

Arnsperger, C. Die Forsttaxation behufs der Servitutablö-
sung. 1841. IV. 254.
— Die Forstwirthschaft in der Umgegend von Carlsruhe.
1840. IV. 117.
— Das Verfahren bei der Taxation . . . im Grossherzogthum
Baden. 1846. IV. 247.²
Arnsperger, C. F. Erneuertes Lagerbuch über die schiffer-
schaftlichen Waldungen im Murg-Thal. 1818. IV. 350.¹
Arnstein, Adolf, *Freiherr* von PEREIRA-. *See* PEREIRA-ARN-
STEIN, Adolf, *Freiherr* von.
Arntzenius, G. Cultuur en volk. beschouwingen over de gou-
vernementskoffiecultuur op Java. 1891. III. 730.
The Arolla or Swiss Stone Pine. 1887. III. 307.¹
Aromatari, Giuseppe degli. Epistola . . . de generatione
plantarum. 1625. I. 202.¹
Aromatum et simplicium . . . historia. *See* HUERTO, Garcia
del. 1563. III. 240.
Aron, Ede. Gyakorlati utmutatás az Eperfa és selyem-hernyó
tenyésztésre. 1870. III. 377.
Around the world. III. 3.
Arppe, Adolph Eduard. Om gutta percha. 1849. III.
230.
Arquimbau, Ramon MASFERRER Y. *See* MASFERRER Y
ARQUIMBAU, Ramon.
Arquistade, A. de FAYMOREAU D'. *See* FAYMOREAU D'AR-
QUISTADE, A. de.
Arrest des juges en dernier ressort des eaux et forêts de France.
1778. IV. 325.
Arrest du Conseil d'estat du roy, qui ordonne que des baux
. . . distraction en sera faite des . . . amendes des eaux &
forests. 1715. IV. 324.
Arrest du Conseil d'état du roi, qui fait défenses . . . de re-
lever ailleurs qu'au siége de la table de marbre les appels des
sentences rendues. 1780. IV. 325.
Arrest du Conseil d'état du roi, qui ordonne que dans les forêts
& bois les plus voisins des ports . . . il sera fait délivrance.
1785. IV. 325.
Arrest du parlement, qui pourvoit au commerce, & à la
police du bois de chauffage. 1715. IV. 324.
Arrêt du Conseil d'état du roi, concernant les matériaux à
prendre dans tous les endroits non clos. 1786. IV. 325.
Arrêt du Conseil d'état du roi, qui maintient les marchands
& négociants dans l'exemption des droits pour les bois. 1786.
IV. 325.
Arrêté du directoire du département de la Haute-Marne.
1792. IV. 275.
Arrêté du 3 juillet 1897 portant réglementation du droit
d'exploitation des produits des forêts à Madagascar. 1897.
IV. 295.²
Arrêté fédéral concernant la création d'une station centrale
d'essais forestiers. 1885. V. 38.³
Arrêté fédéral modifiant l'article 25, alinéa 2, de la loi fédérale
concernant la haute surveillance. 1881. IV. 331.¹
Arrhenius, Axel. Beriktigande angående Rubus nemoralis.
1900. II. 309.¹
— En för Finland ny Rosaart. 1891. II. 293.²
— Ueber die für die Flora Finnlands neue Rosa coriifolia.
1891. II. 293.¹
— Linnaea borealis med hvita blommor. 1896. II. 835.²
— Några anmärkningsvärda Salix-hybrider. 1895. II. 101.¹
— Salixhybrider från Finland. 1882. II. 105.¹
— Salixhybrider från Finland. 1883. II. 101.¹
— Sorbus Aucuparia. 1879. II. 312.¹
— Sorbus Aucuparia × S. fennica. 1900. II. 312.¹
— Trenne Salix-hybrider från Åland. 1883. II. 101.¹
— Tvänne för Finlands flora nya Rubus-hybrider. 1900. II.
306.²
— Tvänne kollektioner kärlväxter. 1900. II. 312,¹ 686.²
— Tvenne Salixhybrider från Finland. 1882. II. 105.¹
— Vaccinium intermedium från Pommern. 1898. II. 686.¹
— Vaccinium Myrtillus var. leucocarpum. 1893. II. 686.²
— Växter från Åland. 1881. II. 312.¹
Arrhenius, J. G. Stirpes agri femsionensis. *See* FRIES,
E. M. 1825. I. 353.
Arrhenius, Johan Pehr. Botanikens första grunder. 1859.
I. 90.
— Elementarkurs i botaniken. 1845. I. 88.
— Om de karakterer . . . vid bestämmandet af Rubus-
arterne. 1840. II. 301.¹
— Monographia Ruborum Sueciae. 1839. II. 301.¹
— Ruborum Sueciae disposito. 1839. II. 301.¹
— För Sverige och Danmark nya Rubus-arter. 1844. II.
301.¹
— Udkast till växt-rikets terminologie. 1842. I. 71.

Arrian, Alexander. The voyage of Nearchus from the Indus
to the Euphrates. 1807. III. 277.
Arrillaga, Francisco de P. La producción forestal. 1875.
IV. 21.¹
Arrondeau, E. F. Sur quelques monstruosités végétales.
1874. II. 307.¹
— Transformation d'étamines en pétales. 1874. II. 307.¹
Arrondeau, E. Théodore. Catalogue des plantes . . . [Morbi-
han]. 1867. I. 413.
— Études sur la flore de Toulouse. 1849. II. 285.²
— Flore toulousaine. 1854. I. 411.
Arosto, Francesco. Monografia degli Agrumi. 1835. III.
497.¹
Arruda da Camara, Manoel. Diccionario de botanica bra-
sileira. 1873. I. 343.
— Dissertação sobre as plantas do Brazil. 1810. III. 233.¹
— A dissertation upon the plants of Brazil. 1810. III. 233.¹
— An essay on the utility of establishing gardens in . . .
Brazil. 1816. III. 65.¹
Ars medendi; sive, Doses et vires medicamentorum. 1760.
III. 241.
Arsenef, S. *See* АРСЕНЬЕВЪ, С.
Arsonval, Arsène d' & Couty, Louis. De l'action du maté sur
les gas du sang. 1881. III. 531.¹
L'art d'économiser les bois de chauffage. 1828. IV. 280.³
L'art de conserver et d'employer les fruits. 1823. III. 174.¹
L'art de cultiver les Mûriers-Blancs. *See* PÓMIER. 1754.
III. 372.²
L'art de tailler les arbres fruitiers. *See* VENETTE, Nicolas.
1683. III. 171.²
Art-journal. III. 16.
The art of pruning fruit-trees. *See* VENETTE, Nicolas. 1683.
III. 171.²
L'art ou la manière de tailler les arbres fruiters. 1699. III.
171.²
Art-union. *See* ART-JOURNAL. III. 16.
Artaria, Ferdinando Augusto. Contribuzione alla flora della
provincia di Como. 1893. I. 430.¹
— Seconda contribuzione alla flora della provincia di Como.
1893. I. 430.¹
Dell' arte dei giardini inglesi. *See* SILVA, Ercole, *conte.*
1801. III. 201.
Artélls, Antonio, FENECH Y. *See* FENECH Y ARTÉLLS, An-
tonio.
Artemare, C. GONOD D'. *See* GONOD D'ARTEMARE, C.
Sur l'artemisine. 1895. III. 754.²
Die Arten des Geschlechtes Laburnum. 1884. III. 430.¹
Arthur, Charles. Pharmacopoeia of the Royal infirmary,
Edinburgh. 1892. III. 255.¹
Arthur, Joseph Charles. Contributions to the flora of Iowa.
1876. V. XVII.²
— Development of vegetable physiology. 1896. I. 148.
— History and biology of Pear blight. 1887. III. 446.²
— The mildew on growing plants. 1884. III. 193.²
— Native shrubs for cultivation. 1881. III. 60.
— New station for the dwarf Mistletoe. 1900. II. 174.²
— Pear blight and its cause. 1885. III. 446.¹
— Prolonged vitality of seeds. 1882. II. 267.²
— Proof that bacteria are the direct cause of . . . Pear blight.
1885. III. 446.¹
— Report on botanical work in Minnesota. 1887. I. 325.
— On some characteristics of the vegetation of Iowa. 1879.
I. 324.
— The special senses of plants. 1894. I. 194.
— & MacDougal, D. T. Living plants and their properties.
1898. I. 219.¹
— Bailey, L. H. & Holway, E. W. D. Plants collected be-
tween Lake Superior and the international boundary. 1887.
I. 325.
El art. 8°. de la ley sobre modificación de impuestos. 1896.
IV. 552.²
Artigas, Gustavo R. Estudio sobre la Flor de Noche Buena.
1877. III. 443.²
Artigas, Primitivo. *See* ARTIGAS Y TEIXIDOR, Primitivo.
Artigas y Teixidor, Primitivo. Alcornocales é industria
corchera. 1895. IV. 518.¹
— Alcornocales, industria taponera. 1885. IV. 518.¹
— El Alcornoque. 1884. IV. 518.¹
— Alcornoque y la industria taponera. 1875. IV. 517.²
— Bosquejo forestal de los alrededores de Bagur. 1880. IV.
363.²
— Breve reseña crítica . . . "Notas sobre los alcornocales."
1884. IV. 517.²
— Breves apuntes sobre repoblacion. 1878. IV. 164.²

— Breves consideraciones con motivo de las tempestades . . . de Agosto. 1880. IV. 189.[1]
— Los catálogos de montes públicos. 1899. IV. 552.[1]
— Le Chêne-Liège. 1893. IV. 517.[1]
— El cólera y los montes. 1886. IV. 542.[2]
— El corcho en el Senado. 1892. IV. 518.[1]
— The Cork tree. 1875. IV. 517.[2]
— Los derechos de exportación del corcho. 1898. IV. 559.[2]
— Dunas. 1885. IV. 165.
— Las dunas del golfo de Rosas. 1896. IV. 556.[2]
— Dunas procedentes del golfo de Rosas. 1889. IV. 546.[2]
— La enseñanza forestal en Francia. 1882. IV. 34.[2]
— Escuela práctica de agricultura . . . en Saint-Pau. 1891. IV. 540.[2]
— Exceso de previsión y no falta de orientación. 1900. IV. 552.[1]
— Forestales españoles. 1898. IV. 539.[1]
— La industria corchotaponera. 1892. IV. 518.[1]
— Ingenieros, montes de aprovechamiento. 1893. IV. 552.[1]
— Las inundaciones y los montes. 1898. IV. 542.[1]
— La lagarta en los encinares y alcornocales. 1894. IV. 501.[1]
— Memoria relativa á la excursión . . . á los montes públicos . . . de Gerona. 1885. IV. 363.[2]
— Memoria relativa á las observaciones . . . de la Escuela especial de ingenieros de montes. 1893. IV. 542.[2]
— Modificación del arancel de exportación del corcho. 1877. IV. 517.[2]
— Montes de utilidad pública. 1896. IV. 552.[1]
— Noticia sobre el Alcornoque. 1888. IV. 517,[2] 518.[1]
— Partes de servicio de los distritos forestales. 1898. IV. 554.
— Reorganización de la Administración central de montes. 1900. IV. 554.
— Reseña crítica . . . Le Chêne-Liège en Algérie par M. A. Lamey. 1881. IV. 517.[2]
— Selvicultura. 1890. IV. 109.[2]
— Los torrentes de Barcelonnette. 1881. IV. 186.[2]
— & Castel y Clemente, Cárlos. Más sobre la Escuela especial de ingenieros de montes. 1887. IV. 540.[2]
The artistic aspect of trees. 1888. I. 516.
Artocarpus exsculpta Hort. Bull. 1878. II. 146.[1]
Artus, Wilhelm Friedrich Wilibald. Atlas aller in den neuesten Pharmacopoen Deutschlands aufgenommenen officinellen Gewächse. 1864. III. 58.
— Hand-Atlas sämmtlicher medicinisch-pharmaceutischer Gewächse. 1876. III. 59.[1]
— De strychnino. 1835. III. 682.[2]
Artzt, F. F. A. Vorarbeiten zur Phanerogamen-Flora des sächsischen Vogtlandes. 1876. I. 387.
Arvet-Touvet, Casimir. Essai sur les plantes du Dauphiné. 1871. I. 414.
Arsneibuch für das Deutsche Reich. See Pharmacopoea Germaniae. 1865. III. 249.
Arsneiliches und Giftiges unserer Holzgewächse. 1878. IV. 63.[2]
Arrruní, Andréas. Ueber das Safrol. 1876. III. 408.[1]
Asa Gray bulletin. I. 5.
Asal, Karl. Das badische Forstrecht. 1898. IV. 318.
Asbjørnsen, Peter Christen. Einige Notizen über das Vorkommen der Lärche. 1859. II. 871.[1]
— Om skovene og et ordnet skovbrug i Norge. 1855. IV. 79,[1] 113.[2]
— Om skovtørk og mark* at. 1861. IV. 195.[2]
Ascárate y Fernández, Casildo. Insectos y criptógamas que invaden los cultivos en España. 1893. III. 179.
Ascensión de la sève. 1884. IV. 63.[2]
The ascent of sap. 1874. I. 165. — 1896. I. 166.
On the ascent of sap. 1896. I. 166.
The ascent of water in plants. 1884. I. 165.
Ascertained effects of the winter of 1853-54. 1854. III. 46.[1]
Aschan, Johannes Laurentius. De Acere. See Thunberg, C. P. 1793. II. 476.[1]
Der Aschen- und Phosphorgehalt von Holz. 1891. IV. 64.[1]
Ascherson, Ferdinand Moritz. Pharmaceutische Botanik. 1831. III. 56.
Ascherson, Paul Friedrich August: Afrikanische von H. Soyaux . . . gesammelte Pflanzen. 1876. II. 6.[1]
— Ueber den afrikanischen Ursprung aegyptischer Kulturpflanzen. See Schweinfurth, Georg.
— Alphabetisches Verzeichniss der in diesem Werk vorkommenden einheimischen Pflanzennamen. 1888. I. 522.[2]
— Eine zur Anfertigung von Schirmstöcken verwendete Luftwurzel von Eugeissona. 1877. III. 325.[1]

— Anfrage das Vorkommen der Mistel. 1871. II. 179.[1]
— Ueber einen Ast einer Carpinus Betulus var. incisa. 1876. II. 120.[1]
— Beitrag zur Flora Aegyptens. 1879. I. 489.
— Beitrag zur Flora des nordwestlichen Kleinasiens. 1883. I. 479.
— Eine bemerkenswerte Spielart der Populus tremula. 1896. II. 98.[1]
— Beobachtungen über die Flora des Fürstenthums Waldeck. 1858. I. 384.
— Blühende Exemplare von Daphne Mezereum. 1883. II. 602.[1]
— Botanisch-ethnographische Notizen aus Guinea. 1879. III. 281.[1]
— Eine botanische Excursion unter dem 39° N. Br. 1863. I. 427.
— Ueber den botanischen Nachlass des . . . .Eug. de Pruyssenaere. 1877. III. 131.[1]
— Braungefärbte Dattelpalmen-Blattrippen. 1881. III. 329.[1]
— Ueber Carpinus Betulus forma quercifolia. 1880. II. 120.[1]
— Eine aus Ceylon stammende, nach Veilchen riechende Droge. 1888. III. 610.[2]
— Ueber eine chinesische . . . Drogue. 1877. III. 488.[1]
— Zur Chronik der märkischen Flora. 1900. II. 11,[2]313.[2]
— Cissus rotundifolius (Forsk.) Vahl. 1884. III. 544.[2]
— Doppelfrüchte der . . . Hyphaene. 1878. II. 69.[1]
— Erscheinungen in der Entwicklung der Vegetation. 1877. I. 225.
— Eine Excursion unter dem 39° N. Br. 1863. I. 427.
— Farbenabänderung der Blattrippe von Phoenix dactylifera. 1874. II. 72.[2]
— Der Farbenwechsel des Saftmals in den Blüten der Rosskastanie. 1888. II. 482.[2]
— Flora der Provinz Brandenburg. 1864. I. 385.
— Flora der Provinz Brandenburg. 1866. I. 385.
— Florula der Oasengruppe Kufra. 1882. I. 485.
— Formenwechsel der Blätter bei Populus euphratica. 1872. II. 97.[2]
— Die Gärten von Esneh in Aegypten. 1876. III. 131.[1]
— Keimlinge von Boscia senegalensis. 1878. II. 230.[1]
— Keimpflanze in Innern eines Borsdorfer Apfels. 1875. II. 267.[2]
— Ueber die Kultur der Coffea liberica. 1879. III. 742.[2]
— Ligustrum vulgare L. 1882. II. 711.[2]
— Loranthus europaeus Jacq. 1883. II. 175.[2]
— Aus dem mittleren Nordafrika stammende, dort zum Gerben benutzte Pflanzen-Rohstoffe. 1882. III. 237.[2]
— Noch einige Bemerkungen über . . . Meleguetta-Pfeffer. 1876. III. 402.[1]
— Note sur l'hétérophyllie du Populus euphratica. 1872. II. 97.[2]
— Pflanzenreste aus den . . . Sarkophagen. 1882. II. 110.[1]
— Plagianthus discolor. 1861. III. 526.[2]
— Plantarum Africae septentrionalis . . . conspectus. 1881. I. 485.
— Sambucus nigra mit schmutzighell-olivengrünen Früchten. 1900. II. 841.[1]
— Schmalblättrige Populus balsamifera. 1883. II. 97.[1]
— Die springenden Tamarisken-Früchte. 1891. III. 612.[1] IV. 501.[1]
— Studiorum phytographicorum de Marchia brandenburgensi specimen. 1853. I. 383.
— Subflorale Axen als Flugapparate. 1881. I. 240.[2]
— Taxus baccata L. in der Prignitz? 1893. II. 11.[1]
— Ueber die Veränderungen, welche die Blüthenhüllen bei . . . Homalium . . . erleiden. 1880. II. 571.[1]
— Die verwilderten Pflanzen in der Mark Brandenburg. 1854. I. 383.
— Vorläufiger Bericht über die botanischen Ergebnisse der Rohlfs'schen Expedition. 1874. I. 488.
— Ueber die Wirkung der Frucht von Sideroxylon dulcificum. 1879. III. 690.[1]
— Zwei Früchte von Adansonia digitata. 1876. II, 529.[1]
— See also Braun, Alexander & Ascherson, P. F. A.; Schweinfurth, G. A. & Ascherson, P. F. A.
— & Graebner, Paul. Flora des norddeutschen Flachlandes. 1898. I. 390.
— Synopsis der mitteleuropäischen Flora. 1896. I. 350.[1]
— & Janka, August. Catalogus cormophytorum . . . Serbiae, Bosniae. 1877. I. 447.
— & Magnus, Paul. Die Verbreitung der hellfrüchtigen Spielarten der europäischen Vaccinien. 1891. II. 685.[1]

Ascherson, Paul Friedrich August & **Magnus,** Paul. (continued.)
— Die weisse Heidelbeere. 1889. II. 686,[2] V. xxvii.[2]
— & **Schweinfurth,** Georg August. Illustration de la flore d'Égypte. 1887. I. 489.
— & others. Botanik [von Ost-Afrika]. 1869. I. 492.[2]
Aschoff, Carl. Ueber die Bedeutung des Chlors. 1890. I. 159.
— De l'importance du chlore dans la plante. 1890. I. 159.
Aschoff, O. Beobachtungen über die Wurzelfäule an Kiefern. 1892. IV.478.
— Ein Gang durch die Heiden von Schleswig-Holstein. 1892. IV. 354.
Ascholin, Carl. De Evonymo. See **Hellenius,** C. N. 1786. II. 467.[2]
Sur l'**Asedarach.** 1814. III. 512.[2]
Ash, Henry W. Street trees. 1890. III. 208.[2]
— Trees of the forest. 1892. IV. 112.
Ash, Thomas. Carolina. 1682. III. 263.[2]
The **Ash.** 1842. IV. 534.[2]
The **Ash.** 1886. II. 707.[1]
Asham, Anton. A little herbal of the properties of herbes. 1550. I. 278.
Ashburner, John. Remarks on an East-Indian medicine. 1831. III. 693.[1]
Ashe, William Willard. The American system of gathering turpentine. 1897. IV. 437.[1]
— Contribution from my herbarium. 1897. II. 382.[1]
— Contributions from my herbarium. 1899. I. 305, II. 260.[3]
— Contributions from my herbarium. 1900. II. 260.[2]
— Forest fires. 1895. IV. 182.[1]
— The forests . . . of eastern North Carolina. 1894. IV. 340.
— The Long Leaf Pine and its struggle for existence. 1894. II. 44.[1]
— New East American species of Crataegus. 1899. II. 260.[2]
— A new Hickory — Hicoria pallida. 1897. II. 112.[2]
— New North American plants. 1900. II. 260.[2]
— Notes on Darbya and Buckleya. 1897. II. 168.[1]
— Notes on the forest resources of North Carolina. 1893. IV. 340.
— Notes on the Hickories of the United States. 1896. II. 112.[1]
— Notes on the Sumacs — Rhus caroliniana. 1895. II. 458.[2]
— Notes on the woody plants of the south Atlantic states. 1897. I. 317,[2] IV. 77.[2]
— The possibilities of a maple sugar industry in western North Carolina. 1897. IV. 527.[2]
— Robinia Boyntonii. 1897. II. 382.[1]
— Woodland pasture and cattle value. 1898. IV. 197.[2]
— See also **Pinchot,** Gifford & **Ashe,** W. W.
Ashik, V. A. See **Ammk,** B. A.
Ashmead, Samuel. See **Durand,** Elias, **James,** T. P. & **Ashmead,** Samuel.
Ashworth, H. P. C. The dispersal of Mistletoe. 1896. II. 175.[2]
Asiatic quarterly review. I. 17.
Asiatic society . . . See also **Royal Asiatic Society.**
Asiatic society of **Bengal.** Asiatick researches. Journal. Proceedings. I. 28.[2]
Asiatic society of **Great Britain and Ireland.** See **Royal Asiatic** . . . I. 19.
Asiatic society of **Japan.** Transactions. I. 28.[2]
Asiatick researches. See **Asiatic society of Bengal.** I. 28.[2]
Asis Vera, Francisco de. La polilla de mar en Cádiz. 1893. IV. 557.[2]
Askenasy, Eugen. Beiträge zur Kenntniss der flachen Stämme. 1872. I. 105.
— Botanisch-morphologische Studien. 1872. I. 105.
— Ueber explodirende Staubgefässe. 1880. I. 238.
— Ueber die jährliche Periode der Knospen. 1877. I. 108.[1]
— Ueber das Saftsteigen. 1896. I. 166.
Asō, Kejiro. A physiological function of oxydase in Kakifruit. 1900. II. 701.[2]
Asociación de defunciones. 1893. IV. 554.
Asociación de ingenieros de montes. 1889, 1890, 1892, 1893. IV. 541.
Aspden, N. Hartley. Through Sherwood forest. 1883. IV. 358.[1]
Aspect of the Oak in landscape. 1886. III. 363.[1]
The **aspect** of trees in winter. 1892. III. 208.[1]
Aspegren, Gustaf Carsten. Försök till en Blekingsk flora. 1823. I. 353.

— Växt-rikets familje-träd. 1828. I. 259.
Aspelin, E. F. & **Thurén,** A. Bidrag till Tavastehus-regionens flora. 1867. I. 356.
Aspelin, Elias. Flora oeconomica. See **Linné,** Carl von. 1748. III. 66.[2]
— Hushållsnyttan af de . . . wildt wäxande örter. See **Linné,** Carl von. 1748. III. 66.[2]
L'**assainissement** des fanges. 1898. IV. 144,[1] 161.[1]
L'**assainissement** des fanges du Luxembourg. 1898. IV. 160.[2]
Assainissement et culture forestière. See **Chambrelent,** Jules. 1855. IV. 162.
Assainissement et culture forestière des Landes de la Gironde. 1855. IV. 359.[2]
Assam, (pseud.). Beneficial results of the Sau tree. 1885. III. 466.[2]
Assam. See also **India** — **Assam.**
Assam — Agricultural department. See **Agricultural** . . . III. 26.[1]
Assam; sketch of its history, soil. 1839. III. 602.[2]
The **Assam** forest regulation, 1891. 1892. IV. 307.[2]
Assam rubber for West Africa. 1891. III. 370.[2]
Asseler, Thomas. Viridarium adriaticum. 1686. I. 424.
Assfahl, E. Ueber die Ernährung grüner Pflanzenzellen mit Glycerin. 1892. I. 160.
— De la nutrition des plantes vertes par la glycerine. 1892. I. 160.
Assmann, Richard Adolph. Auftreten des Curculio pini. 1875. IV. 207.
— Der Duft- und Schnee-Anhang auf dem Brocken. 1885. IV. 190.
— Das Pflanz-Lineal. 1875. IV. 152.
Assmus, (Revierförster, Biedenkopf). Ueber den Obstbau an und in Waldgebirgen. 1852. IV. 134.[2]
Assmuss, Eduard Philibert. Die trockene Destillation des Holzes. 1867. IV. 432.[2]
— See also **Ассмусъ,** 9.
Asso, Ignacio Jordan de. See **Asso y del Rio,** Ignacio Jordan de.
Asso y del Rio, Ignacio Jordan de. Enumeratio stirpium in Arragonia. 1784. I. 419.[2]
— Introductio in oryctographiam et zoologiam Aragoniae. 1784. I. 419.[2]
— Mantissa stirpium indigenarum Aragoniae. 1779. I. 419.[2]
— Synopsis stirpium indigenarum Aragoniae. 1779. I. 419.[2]
Association des anciens élèves de l'École nationale d'horticulture de Versailles; Bulletin. III. 19.
Association des anciens élèves de l'Institut agricole de l'état à **Gembloux.** Journal. III. 15.
Association florimontane d'**Annecy.** Bulletin. Revue. I. 21.
Association française de botanique. I. 21.
Association française pour l'avancement des sciences. Comptes-rendus. I. 21.
Association Haut-Marnaise d'horticulture. III. 19.
Association of engineering societies. Journal. III. 3.
Association philomatique vogéso-rhénane. Annales. I. 10.
Association pomologique de l'Ouest. Bulletin. III. 19.
Association pour la protection des plantes . . . Bulletin. I. 26.[1]
Associazione dei naturalisti e medici per la mutua istruzione. Bulletino. III.23.[1]
Astafel, R. F. See **Астафьевъ,** Р. Ѳ.
Astaix, J. B. Essai sur la théorie des stipules. 1841. I. 111.
Astaurof, A. See **Астауровъ,** А.
Astheimer, Romanus. Phytologia generalis. 1773. I. 32.
Asti, Felice. Lettera intorno alla nuova China-china. 1791. III. 720.
Astié, F. Le Bouleau pleureur élégant. 1869. III. 357.[1]
— Introduction et propagation des Bambous. 1871. III. 314.[1]
Astier. Sur les fonctions physiologiques des épines. 1826. I. 236.[2]
Astley, Francis Dukinfield. Hints to planters. 1807. III. 122.[2]
Astronomical observatory of Harvard College. Annals. III. 3.
Astruc. See L'**Hoste** & **Astruc.**
Astruc, Jean. Conjecture sur le redressement des plantes inclinées à l'horizon. 1709. I. 195.[1]
— Mémoires pour l'histoire naturelle . . . de Languedoc. 1737. I. 405.
Ateneo di Brescia. Commentari. I. 24.[2]

Athenaeum. I. 17.
Athenaeum français. I. 21.
Athenstaedt, Wilhelm. Aschenanalyse von Ledum. 1885. III. 653.[1]
Atienza y Sirvent, Melitón. Breves consideraciones acerca del establecimiento de un jardin de aclimatacion. 1879. I. 60.[1]
— Memoria acerca del plan de una obra de arquitectura de jardines. 1855. III. 126.[1]
— " Proyecto de establecimiento de un jardin de aclimatacion." 1879. I. 60.[1]
Atkinson, Edwin Thomas. Economic products of the North-Western Provinces. 1876. III. 278.
— The Himálayan districts of the North-Western Provinces of India. 1882. I. 474.
Atkinson, George Clayton. First[-second] instalment of a catalogue of the more remarkable trees of Northumberland. 1877. I. 297.[1]
Atkinson, George Francis. Elementary botany. 1898. I. 92.
— Leaf curl and Plum pockets. 1894. III. 431.[1]
— Nectria on Currant canes. 1897. III. 415.[1]
— Some tendencies . . . in the evolution of species among parasitic fungii. 1896. III. 195.[1]
Atkinson, Robert Witlam. Yatsu-ga-take, Haku-san, and Tate-yama. 1880. I. 462.
Atkinson, Thomas William. Travels in the regions of the upper and lower Amoor. 1860. I. 455.
Atkinson, W. G. American shade trees. 1880. III. 208.[2]
Atkinson, William. Observations on the quality of the Oak timber. 1835. IV. 514.[1]
Atlantic journal. I. 5.
Atlantic monthly. III. 3.
Atlantis. I. 17.
Atlas, (pseud.). Araucaria seed. 1843. III. 298.[3]
Una atrevida empresa. 1889. IV. 390.[2]
Attar of Roses. 1890. III. 454.[1]
Attems, Heinrich, Graf von. Oesterreich's Obstbau auf der Triester Export-Ausstellung. 1883. III. 146.[2]
— Österreichs Obstbau auf der Weltausstellung. 1900. III. 147.[1]
Atterberg, Albert. Om Dvergtallens eteriska olja. 1881. IV. 465.[1]
— Sur les térébènes . . . du Pinus sylvestris de Suède. 1877. II. 48.[1]
— Die Terpene . . . aus Pinus sylvestris. 1877. II. 48.[1]
Attfield, John. On the food-value of the kolanut. 1865. III. 590.[1]
— A note on sap. 1883. I. 169.[1]
Atti amministrativi. 1864. IV. 305.
Atti del governo. 1861. IV. 304.[2]
Atti del governo. 1864. IV. 305.
Atti del governo. 1865. IV. 305.
Atti del governo concernente l' amministrazione forestale italiana. 1863. IV. 304.[2]
Atti del governo concernente le foreste. 1863. IV. 304.[2]
Atti del secondo Congresso degli orticoltori italiani. 1883. III. 126.[2]
Atti ufficiali. 1862. IV. 304.[2]
L' attività dell' Associazione forestale elvetica. 1882. IV. 41.[2]
Les attributions de l'administration forestière française. 1898. IV. 293.[1]
Attwell, C. B. Abnormal Roses. 1889. II. 290.[1]
Atwater, Wilbur Olin. On fertilisers. 1878. III. 151.
Atwood, George A. White variety of American Wistaria. 1887. III. 490.[1]
Atwood, George G. See ROBERTS, I. P. & ATWOOD, G. G.
Atzendorf, Salomon, FISCHER VON. See FISCHER VON ATZENDORF, Salomon.
Aubaret, G. Histoire et description de la basse Cochinchine. See IRANG-HOÏ-DUC. 1863. III. 276.[2]
Aube — Société académique d'agriculture, des sciences, arts, . . . See SOCIÉTÉ D'AGRICULTURE, SCIENCES ET ARTS . . . DE L'AUBE. I. 22.
Aube — Société d'agriculture, sciences et arts . . . See SOCIÉTÉ . . . I. 22.
Aube — Société d'horticulture de l'. See SOCIÉTÉ . . . III. 21.
Aube — Société horticole, vigneronne et forestière. See SOCIÉTÉ . . . III. 22.
Aubenton, C. MILLET D'. See MILLET D'AUBENTON, C.
Aubergier. Sur l'état des Vignes de Mézel. 1877. III. 560.

— Résultats obtenus, au moyen du sulfocarbonate de potassium. 1875 III. 568.
— Résultats obtenus par l'emploi des sulfocarbonates. 1876. III. 569.[2]
Aubert, Auguste. Considérations sur les moyens d'utiliser les plantations de Mûriers multicaules. 1837. III. 380.[2]
— Note rectificative au sujet du Maclura mâle. 1839. III. 372.[1]
— Observations sur le Mûrier multicaule. 1837. III. 380.[2]
Aubert, Bellamy. Lettre sur la culture de la Vigne. 1825. III. 558.[1]
Aubert, Ephrem. Recherches physiologiques sur les plantes grasses. 1892. I. 147.
— Recherches sur la respiration. 1892. I. 171, 174.
— Recherches sur la turgescence. 1892. I. 168, II. 235,[1] 588.[2]
— Sur la répartition des acides organiques. 1890. I. 180.[2]
— Respiration comparée des plantes grasses. 1892. I. 171.
Aubert, Eugène. Production du copahu en Amazonie. 1885. III. 473.[1]
Aubert, Pierre Léonce. Organogénie de la fleur dans le genre Salix. 1873. II. 103,[2] 104,[2] III. 550.[2]
Aubert, Samuel. La flore de la vallée de Joux. 1900. I. 438.
— Les Pommiers de la vallée de Joux. 1896. III. 89,[1] 426.[3]
Aubert du Petit-Thouars, Louis Marie Aubert. See DU PETIT-THOUARS, L. M. A.
Aubin, L. C. P. Élémens succincts de la langue et des principes de botanique. 1803. I. 93.
Aublet, Jean Baptiste Christophe Fusée. Histoire des plantes de la Guiane françoise. 1775. I. 338.[2]
— Observations sur la culture du Café. 1786. III. 726.[1]
Aubles, Ant. Sur un passage de Strabon relatif à un traitement de la Vigne. 1892. III. 561.
Anbouy, Fulcran Antonin Édouard. Catalogue des plantes . . . de Lodève. See AUBOUY, Q. 1874. I. 414.
— Deux herborisations dans le département de l'Hérault. 1875. I. 414.
— Florule de Palavas. 1884. V. XXII.[1]
— Des plantes interessantes . . . de Lodève. 1870. I. 414.
Aubriot, L. & Daguin, Arthur. Flore de la Hte.-Marne 1885. I. 417.
Aubry de la Mottraie. Exercices d'histoire naturelle à l'école . . . du Morbihan. 1801. I. 406.
Aubry-Lecomte, C. Culture et production du cacao. 1866. III. 592.[1]
— Culture et production du Café. 1865. III. 726.[2]
— Exploitation des matières textiles dans les colonies françaises. 1866. III. 234.
Auch einige Bemerkungen über Holzmangel und die Mittel demselben abzuhelfen. See EINIGE . . . 1844. IV. 280.[2]
Auch etwas über den Mittelwaldbetrieb. 1844. IV. 130.
Aucher-Éloy, P. M. R. Relations de voyages en Orient. 1843. I. 478.
Auckland, Lord. Note on the progress . . . in the cultivation of the Tea plant. 1842. III. 602.[2]
The auctarium of the Botanic garden. See MAUND, Benjamin. 1825. III. 123.[2]
Les Aucubas. See The MALE Aucuba. 1869. III. 644.[2]
Aude — Société d'agriculture. See SOCIÉTÉ . . . III. 21.
Audibert. Fécondation du Chamaerops humilis. 1854. III. 322.[1]
Audibert, (aîné). Catalogue des végétaux. 1817. I. 57.
— Catalogue(s) des principaux arbres, arbustes et autres plantes. 1810. I. 57.
Audibert. frères. Catalogue des arbres, arbrisseaux, arbustes. 1831. I. 57.
Audibert & Audibert, E. Quelques variétés de Figuiers. 1854. III. 369.[2]
Audiffred. Exposé visant la transformation, par le reboisement . . . de la Loire. 1900. IV. 164.[2]
— Les reboisements de la Loire. 1900. IV. 164.[2]
Audin, Marius. La chlorose de la Vigne. 1900. III. 562.[1]
Audot, Cereus militaris. 1845. III. 620.[3]
— Extraction et raffinage de sucre de Palmiers. 1844. III. 319.[1]
— Sur les fleurs bleues de l'Hortensia. 1847. III. 412.[1]
— Sur l'Hortensia bleu. 1839. III. 412.[1]
— Notes sur les jardins du sud de l'Italie. 1840. III. 126.[1]
— Observations sur les Hortensias bleus. 1847. III. 412.[1]
— Première floraison en France . . . Aristolochia gigas. 1845. III. 386.[1]

Audouin, Jean Victor. Communication verbale sur une éducation faite à Paris d'un ver à soie de la Louisiane. 1841. III. 148.[1]
— Considérations nouvelles sur les dégâts occasionnés par la pyrale de la Vigne. 1837. III. 562.[2]
— Histoire des insectes nuisibles à la Vigne. 1842. III. 562.[2]
— Notice sur les ravages causés . . . par la pyrale de la Vigne. 1837. III. 562.[2]
— Observations sur certains insectes qui attaquent les bois. 1840. IV. 414.[1]
— Quelques considérations nouvelles sur l'insecte qui attaque les Vignes d'Argenteuil. 1837. III. 562.[2]
Audouit, Edmond. L'herbier des demoiselles. 1865. I. 95.
— Les plantes curieuses. 1850. I. 95.
Audoynaud. Discussion des expériences exécutées sur les Vignes phylloxérées à Las-Sorrès. 1877. III. 570.[1]
— Discussion des expériences faites au Mas de Las-Sorres. 1875. III. 567.[2]
— Falsifications de l'huile d'olive comestible. 1885. III. 679.[1]
Audoynaud, Alfred. De l'influence qu'exercent sur la Vigne les engrais potassiques. 1877. II. 508.[1]
— L'Olivier dans les Alpes-Maritimes. 1876. III. 675.[2]
— Sur la résistance des Vignes dans les terres sableuses. 1884. III. 556.
Audubon, John James! The birds of America. 1827. I. 306.
Aué. Remède contre la maladie de la Vigne. 1854. III. 576.
Auer, Andreas. Abhandlung über die geometrische Aufgabe einen unzugänglichen . . . Wald . . . auszumessen. 1767. IV. 263.
— Disquisitio problematis mathematici mensurare . . . sylvam . . . inaccessibilem. 1767. IV. 263.
Auerbach, Michael Levin. Nonnulla de salicinio novo medicamine. 1831. III. 350.[2]
Auerhahn, Joh. R. Die sibirische Tanne. 1852. IV. 447.[1]
Auersperg, Johann, *Graf* von. Abhandlung über die Krankheiten der Pflanzen. 1779.‘ I. 206.[1]
Auerswald, Bernard. Botanische Unterhaltungen. 1856. I. 384.
— & **Rossmässler**, E. A. ·Botanische Unterhaltungen. 1856. I. 384.
— — : *See also* Россмесслеръ, Э. А. & Ауэрсвальдъ.
Das **Aufästen** der Waldbäume. 1886. IV. 172.[1]
Aufastungen in jungen Beständen. 1856. IV. 170.
Der **auffallende** Wuchs einer Kiefer. 1859. II. 871.[2]
Auff'm Ordt, P. Die Lupinen-Kiefern-Kultur. 1885. IV. 473.
Aufforderung an alle edel denkende Deutsche. *See* AUFFORDERUNG an meine Landsleute . . . 1798. IV. 522.[2]
Aufforderung an meine Landsleute in Bayern. 1798. IV. 522.[2]
Aufforstung der Sanddünen in Preussen. 1893. IV. 159.
Ueber die **Aufforstung** einer Ackerfläche. 1888. IV. 142.
Die **Aufforstungsbestrebungen** in Dänemark. 1882. IV. 156.[1]
Die **Aufforstungsbestrebungen** in der Schweiz. 1882. IV. 166.[1]
Die **Aufforstungsbestrebungen** in Frankreich. 1882. IV. 163.
Die **Aufforstungsbestrebungen** in Italien. 1882. IV. 166.[1]
Aus den **Aufforstungsgebieten** Westpreussens. 1893. IV. 159.
Die **Aufgaben** der forstlich-meteorologischen . . . Stationen in Preussen. *See* — ? —. Die Aufgaben . . . 1895. IV. 60.[1]
Der **aufmerksame** Forstmann. IV. 7.
Aufmkolk, Friedrich Wilhelm. De cortice caribaeo. 1793. III. 244.
Aufmunterung zur Anpflanzung von Hickoryholz. 1877. III. 353.[2]
Aufrecht. Gonorol. 1899. III. 384.[2]
Von der **Aufrechthaltung** der Betriebsregulierungen. 1841. IV. 242.
Der **aufrichtige** Baumgärtner. 1797. III. 101.[2]
Aufruf eines praktischen Forstmannes. *See* GRIESHEIM, L. W. von. 1801. IV. 100.[2]
Aufschlaeger, J. F. Description historique . . . des deux départemens du Rhin. *See* KIRSCHLEGER, Friedrich. 1826. I. 377.
Die **Aufschliessung** der Schwarzmeer-Forsten für den Handel. 1898. IV. 404.[2]
Auftreten der Arven-Miniermotte. 1895. IV. 464.[1]

Das **Auftreten** der Nonne in Böhmen. 1892. IV. 201.
Das **Auftreten** der Nonne in Oesterreich. 1890. IV. 200.
Aufzählung der in der Umgebung von Linz wildwachsenden . . . Gefäss-Pflanzen. 1871. I. 442.
Augé. Notices: 1. Sur les deux dernières éducations du ver Trivoltini. 1841. III. 381.[1]
Auger, L. SEBILLE. *See* SEBILLE-AUGER, L.
Augier, Augustin. Essai d'une nouvelle classification des végétaux. 1801. I. 251.
Augmentation de la durée du bois de Hêtre. *See* ERHÖHUNG der Dauer . . . 1865. IV. 499.[1]
Augustin, F. L. Pharmacopoea extemporanea. 1809. III. 248.
Augustin, Samuel. Prolegomena in systema sexuale. 1777. I. 258.
Aulagnier, A. F. Dictionnaire des substances alimentaires. 1830. III. 219.[1]
Auld, William. *See* BALDWIN, D. D. & AULD, William.
Auleitner, Antoni. Gospodarstwo leśne. 1845. IV. 94.
— Łatwy sposób zaprowadzenia plantacyj Drzew Morwowych. 1853. III. 376.
— O potrzebach intensywnego gospodarstwa leśnego. 1879. IV. 102.
— Przewodnik leśny. 1850. IV. 94.
— Rzut oka na gospodarstwo obecne w lasach ziemiańskich w Polsce. 1844. IV. 273.[1]
— Środki praktyczne zagospodarowania lasów prywatnych. 1852. IV. 307.[2]
— O szkodliwych skutkach zaniedbania dozoru leśnego. 1849. IV. 269.
L'Aulne. 1898. II. 116.[2]
Aumann. Beitrag zur Durchforstungsfrage. 1887. IV. 174.
— Fichtenwirthschaft in Höhenlagen. 1893. IV. 454.
— Frostempfindlichkeit ausländischer : . . Holzarten. 1887. IV. 191.[2]
— Weidenheegerbetrieb in Flussniederungen. 1894. III. 349.
Aumento dell' organico dell' amministrazione forestale. 1864. IV. 293.[2]
L'Aune à feuilles en cœur. 1883. IV. 489.[1]
L'aune blanc. 1895. IV. 489.[2]
Aurange, Léon. Culture des Ericas dans le midi. 1872. III. 650.[1]
— La floraison rapide de l'Acacia dealbata. 1891. III. 464.[2]
— Les Nériums. 1872. III. 689.[1]
— Pritchardia filifera. 1878. III. 332.[1]
— Le Yucca superbe. 1890. III. 340.[2]
Aurell, August. Afhandling om de wäxter som i Bibelen omtalas. *See* THUNBERG, C. P. 1828. I. 513.
Aurich, von, (*Oberforstmeister, Pless*). Aeusserung oder Betrachtung zu der Abhandlung des . . . Oberförsters Hrn. Thiem. 1853. IV. 453.
— Anfrage über Eichenschälwald-Anlagen. 1850. IV. 504.
— Anmerkungen betreffend das Schütten der jungen Kiefern. 1853. IV. 475.
— Eine Anregung,‾ betreffend die Forst-Lehrlinge. 1864. IV. 32.
— Beantwortung aufgrgebenen [*sic*] Thema's,‘ betreffend die Vermehrung . . . der Bodengüte beim Forsthaushalte. 1851. IV. 68.
— Beitrag zu der Lehre über Pflanzungsform. 1860. IV. 154.[1]
— Bemerkungen·über den Aufsatz; Die Boden-Konservation betreffend. 1853. IV. 68.
— Ueber das Biermannssche Kulturverfahren. 1855. IV. 141.
— Ueber den Einfluss des Gesteins auf die Vegetation. . 1862. IV. 68.
— Etwas über die Hiebsregeln. 1866. IV. 132.[1]
— Rigol-Streifen zur Kiefer-Pflanzung. 1863. IV. 472.
— Thema betreffend die Bonitirung des Waldbestandes. 1850. IV. 242.
— Thema betreffend die Verbesserung . . . des Waldbodens. 1850. IV. 142.
— Weiden-Kultur. 1853. IV. 487.[1]
Aus allen Welttheilen. I.‘ 11.
Aus dem Walde; Mittheilungen. IV. 7.
Aus dem Walde; Wochenblatt. IV. 7.
Aus unseren heimischen Wäldern. IV. 14.
Aus Wald und Haide. IV. 14.
Das **Auslästen** und Schneideln der Waldbäume. 1858. IV. 170.
Die **Auslästung** der Eichenlohstangen. 1878. IV. 507.

Die Ausbildung des Forstpersonals in Baden. 1876. IV. 32.

Ausbildung für das Forstfach, Versuchs-Vereinswesen und Statistik. 1889. IV. 33.[1]

Ueber Ausbildung und Anstellung der Privatforstbeamten. 1889. IV. 33.[2]

Ausdehnung des Holzes durch Wasseraufnahme. 1889. IV. 412.[1]

Ausius, Henrik. Disputatio physica de plantis. 1640. I. 30.

— De plantis in genere. 1640. I. 30.

Ausländische Holzarten. 1899. IV. 126.[1]

Ausländische Waldbäume, insbes. der Gingko. 1842. III. 286.[2]

Ausland. I. 11.

Die Ausrottung der Wälder in Russland. 1893. IV. 282.[1]

Das Ausschneiden der Aeste. 1891. III. 171.

Aussereuropäische Forstculturstationen. 1892. IV. 37.[2]

Die Ausstellung der österreichischen Actien-Gesellschaft für Forst-Industrie. 1873. IV. 21.[1]

Austen, Ralph. A dialogue . . . betweene the husbandman and fruit-trees. 1676. III. 141.

— Observations upon some part of Sr. Francis Bacon's naturall history. 1658. III. 141.

— The spirituall use of an orchard. 1653. III. 140,[1] V. xxiv.[3]

— A treatise of fruit-trees. 1653. III. 140.[3]

Die austernförmige Schildlaus, Aspidiotus. 1898. III. 191.

Australasia — Royal geographical society. See ROYAL . . . I. 30.

Australasian association for the advancement of science. Reports. I. 29.[2]

Australasian medical gazette. I. 29.[2]

Australian big timber. 1885. II. 624.[1]

Australian Cycads. 1874. II. 2.[2]

The Australian handbook. 1884. III. 282.[2]

Australian horticultural and agricultural society. Proceedings. See SYDNEY, magazine of science . . . III. 27.[1]

Australian horticultural magazine. III. 27.[1]

Australian species of Macrozamia. 1877. III. 285.[2]

Australian timber. 1899. IV. 401.[3]

Australian timber supplies. 1885. IV. 401.[2]

Australian wild flowers. 1896. I. 505.

L'Australie occidentale. See HELMS, Richard. 1900. V. xxiv.[2]

Der australische Weihnachtstrauch. 1887. III. 416.[1]

Austria — Forst-Verein. See FORST-VEREIN FÜR ÖSTERREICH . . . IV. 14.

Austria — Forst-Verein für Oberösterreich und Salzburg. See FORST-VEREIN FÜR ÖSTERREICH . . . IV. 14.

Austria — K. k. Ackerbauministerium. See K. K. ACKER-BAUMINISTERIUM. IV. 14.

Austria — Mittheilungen aus dem forstlichen Versuchswesen See MITTHEILUNGEN . . . IV. 15.

The Austrian Briars. 1893. III. 455.[2]

Austrian Pine at home. 1880. II. 43.[2]

Der auswärtige Holzhandel mit Bezug auf Oesterreich. 1867. IV. 406.[2]

Eine Auswahl von fünfzig der besten Eriken. 1849. III. 650.[1]

Auswahl von Pflanzen und Gesträuchen. See CLAIRVILLE, J. P. de. 1796. I. 284.

Auszüge aus alten Forstgesetzen. 1861. IV. 330.

Auszüge aus alten Forstgesetzen. Vorsorge wider den Holz-Mangel. 1862. IV. 330.

Auszug aus dem Gutachten des Ausschusses für die Baum-zucht über . . . Gleditschien. 1829. III. 477.[2]

Auszug aus den Abhandlungen . . . Welchen Einfluss äussern die Erd- und Düngerarten. 1832. III. 151.

Auszug aus der Dienst-Instruction für den Forst-Taxations-Inspector. See INSTRUCTION für die Forstbetriebs - Einrich-tungs-Commissionen des Kurstaates. 1864. IV. 302.

Auszug aus der Forst-Statistik des Kantons Bern. 1867. IV. 366.

Auszug aus der generellen Beschreibung des k. Forstamts Sailauf. n. d. IV. 350.[2]

Auszug der Abhandlung über das Verpflanzen der capischen Eriken. 1835. III. 649.[2]

Auszug der vornehmsten Gründe welche den . . . in der Zill-bacher Holz-Abgabe- und Verkaufs-Sache . . . ergriffenen Recurs rechtfertigen. 1782. IV. 25.

Autenrieth, Hermann Friedrich. Ueber die ächte Angustura-Rinde. 1841. III. 503.[2]

— De discrimine sexuali jam in seminibus. 1821. I. 120, 99.[2]

Autenrieth, Johann Heinrich Ferdinand von. De Diosma crenata. 1830. III. 495.[2]

— Gründliche Anleitung zur Brodzubereitung aus Holz. 1834. III. 219.[2]

Autran, Eugène. See POST, G. E. & AUTRAN, E.; SCHINZ, Hans & AUTRAN, Eugène.

— & Durand, Théophile. Hortus Boissierianus. 1896. I. 65.[1]

— — Liste des Conifères cultivés dans le parc de la Pierreière, à Chambésy. 1896. I. 65.[1]

Autumn-planted evergreens. 1884. III. 169.[1]

Autun — Société d'histoire naturelle. See SOCIÉTÉ . . . I. 23.

Auvergne, Jules d'. Planchette-dendromètre à fenêtre. 1858. IV. 231.[1]

Auvergne — Société d'horticulture de l'. See SOCIÉTÉ . . . III. 21.

Auzende, Joseph. Nouvelles observations sur la plantation de gros arbres. 1863. III. 167.

Ava, or Kava-kava. 1876. III. 343.[1]

Sur l'Ava ou Kava-Kava. See AVA, or Kava-kava. 1876. III. 343.[1]

Avannes, d'. Des droits d'usage dans les bois de l'État. 1837. IV. 334.[1]

Sur les avantages obtenus par des plantations d'arbres dans l'Île de l'Ascension. 1875. IV. 44.

Avanzini, Gius. Lezione accademica in lode della ciocco-lata. 1728. III. 594.

Avé-Lallemant, Julius Leopold Eduard. De plantis quibus-dam Italiae borealis. 1829. I. 349.

Avé Lallemant, Robert Christian Bernhard. See LALLEMANT, R. C. B. A.

Avebury, Sir John LUBBOCK, 1st baron. See LUBBOCK, Sir John.

Aveleyra, Ramón N. Sustituciones de algunas drogas in-dígenas. 1887. III. 264.[3]

Aveling, Edward. An introduction to the study of botany. 1891. I. 92.

Avellar Brotero, Felix de. See BROTERO, Felix de AVELLAR.

Avellino, Giulio. Sulla necessità di creare nelle provincie al di qua del faro nuove industrie agrarie. 1842. III. 527.[1]

— See also PASQUALE, G. A. & AVELLINO, Giulio.

Avenarius, R. Die Konservirungs-Methoden des Holzes. 1882. IV. 420.

Avennes, Prisse d'. Culture du Caféier à Ceylan. 1853. III. 732.[1]

Avenue of Dracaenas in a garden in the Scilly Isles. 1876. III. 334.[2]

An avenue of Elms. 1893. III. 365.[1]

An avenue of Live Oaks. 1893. III. 363.[1]

An avenue of Palms. 1887. III. 328.[1]

Avenues of tapering trees. 1873. III. 204.[1]

Avequin, J. B. De la culture de la Vigne. 1857. III. 550, 456,[3] III. 525.[1]

— Essais analytiques sur la graine de mangue. 1861. II. 456,[3] III. 525.[1]

— Maple sugar of the United States. 1857. IV. 527.[1]

— Du sucre d'Érable aux États-Unis. 1857. IV. 527.[1]

Averill, Charles K. The distribution of certain trees . . . in western Connecticut. 1900. I. 313, IV. 77.[1]

Avetta, Carlo. Contribuzione all' anatomia . . . dell' An-tigonon leptopus. 1888. II. 184.[1]

— Contribuzione alla flora dello Scioa. 1889. I. 489.

— Contribuzione allo studio delle anomalie di struttura nelle radici. 1887. I. 104.

— Materiali per la flora dello Scioa. 1897. I. 489.

— Ricerche anatomiche . . . sugli organi vegetativi della "Pueraria." 1885. II. 380.[2]

— Ricerche . . . sul fusto . . . dell' Atraphaxis. 1888. II. 184.[2]

Avice, Louis Claude Théod. Note sur un bois d'Arbousiers. 1896. III. 660.[2]

— Note sur une variété maritime du Solanum Dulcamara L. 1896. III. 776.[1]

Avicenna. See IBN-SÎNÂ.

Avignon. Sur l'emploi du goudron. 1881. III. 573.

— See also LAGUNA Y VILLANUEVA, Maximo & ÁVILA, Pedro de.

Ávila, Pedro de. Zoologia descriptiva. 1888. IV. 544.[1]

Avis aux cultivateurs touchant l'économie des bois. 1779. IV. 123.[1]

Avis pour le transport par mer des arbres. See DU HAMEL DU MONCEAU, H. L. 1753. III. 154.[2]

Avis sur les mesures à prendre pour s'opposer à l'extension des ravages du phylloxéra. 1877. III. 760.

Avoine, P. J. d' & **Morren**, Charles F. A.   Concordance des espèces végétales décrites . . . par Rembert Dodoens. 1850.   -I. 78.[1]
Sur les **avortements** des parties des fleurs.   *See* VIREY, J. J. 1838.   I. 114.[2]
Avrainville, A. d'.   Manière de conserver les graines de certains Palmiers.   1875.   III. 317.
d'**Avrigni**, A. E. C.   LOEUILLART-.   *See* LOEUILLART-D' AVRIGNI, A. E. C.
Avril, Didion, & Mary.   Rapport sur les résultats des essais faits par M. Boucherie.   1850.   IV. 417.
— — — Report of the results of experiments made by M. le docteur Boucherie.   1850.   IV. 417.
L' **avvenire** del Canadà.   1897.   IV. 337.[2]
Degli **avvisi** d' asta per provvista di legnami.   1865.   IV. 305.
Aweng, Eugen.   Contribution à l'étude . . . de l'écorce de Bourdaine.   1897.   III. 543.[1]
The **axe** in its relation to ornamental trees.   1890.   III. 202.[2]
Axel.   Les arbres des routes.   1899.   III. 210.
Axell, Johan Severin.   Om det färgade hyllets betydelse för växten.   1868.   I. 237.
Axenborg, Pehr.   Afhandling om de wäxter som i Bibelen omtalas.   *See* THUNBERG, C. P.   1828.   I. 513.
Axmann, August.   Ueber Schirmverjüngung.   1895.   IV. 140.
— Vorbeugungsmittel gegen die Beschädigungen durch Lasius. 1895.   IV. 208.[1]
Axtius, Johann Konrad.   Tractatus de arboribus coniferis. 1679.   IV. 436,[1] *443.*[1]
Ayasse, Étienne.   Sur un Saule nouveau, 1879.   II. 109.[1]
Aygalliers, P. d'.   L'état actuel . . . de la culture de l'Olivier. 1898.   III. 676.[2]
— L'Olivier et l'huile d'olive.   1900.   III. 679.[2]
Ayméric, MARCAILHOU D'.   *See* MARCAILHOU D'AYMÉRIC.
Aynard, Théodore.   Les arbres des quais . . . de Lyon. 1887.   III. 211.[2]
Ayrer, G. A.   De iure sibi habendi arbores in fundum villaticis turbine deiectas.   1755.   IV. 313.
Ayres, Horace Beemer.   The Flathead forest reserve. 1900.   IV. 341.[2]
— Forest fires.   1893.   IV. 182.[1]
— Forest fires.   1895.   IV. 182.[1]
— Hemlock in Minnesota.   1893.   II. 53.[1]
— Lewis and Clarke forest reserve.   1900.   IV. 341.[2]
— The Muskeag Spruce.   1894.   II. 38.[1]
— Native evergreens.   1896.   I. 312.
— Notes on the Norway Pine.   1888.   IV. 468.[2]
— Suggestions from the White Pine forests of Minnesota. 1893.   IV. 469.
— Timber conditions of the Pine region of Minnesota.   1900. IV. 341.[2]
— The value of Lodgepole Pine.   1900.   IV. 465.[1]
— Washington forest reserve.   1899.   IV. 341.[1]
— A word for the Jack Pine.   1889.   IV. 463.[1]
— *See also* GREEN, S. B. & AYRES, H. B.
Ayres, Richard.   On the management of . . . Citrus.   1822. III. 496.[1]
Ayres, William O.   A huge Californian tree.   1856.   II. 50.[2]
Ayres, William P.   The Coral tree as an open air plant.   1843. III. 476.[1]
— Cupressus Lamberti or macrocarpa.   1854.   III. 302.[1]
— Sur les Cupressus Lambertiana ou C. macrocarpa.   1854. III. 302.[2]
— Dillwynia scabra.   1852.   III. 475.[2]
— Gastrolobium pyramidale.   1852.   II. 359.[1]
— New hybrid Heaths.   1852.   III. 650.[1]
Ayudantes de montes.   1891.   IV. 553.[2]
Azais, G.   Catalogue botanique.   1871.   I. 74.[1]
Azalus, Pompilius Placentinus.   De omnibus rebus naturalibus.   1544.   I. 278.
Azam, Eugène.   Le phylloxera dans . . . la Gironde.   1876. III. 570.[2]
Azara, Félix de.   Descripción é historia del Paraguay.   1809. III. 65.[2]
— Voyages dans l'Amérique méridionale.   1809.   III. 65.[2]
Azcarate, Gumersindo de.   La propiedad colectiva del suelo. 1886.   IV. 270.
Azémar.   Notice sur la taille de l'Olivier.   1854.   III. 675.[2]
— & Guiraud de Saint-Marsal.   Mémoire sur l'état présent de la culture du Chêne-Liége.   1851.   IV. 516.[2]
Azione della luce sulle piante.   1890.   IV. 67,[2] 543.[2]
El **ázoe** de las plantas.   1890.   IV. 543.[2]
Azuni, Domenico Alberto.   Histoire géographique . . . de la Sardaigne.   1798.   I. 424.

B.   Over het aankweeken der planten door zaad.   1846.   I 247.
B.   Acacia lineata.   1886.   III. 465.[2]
B.   Acacias.   1885.   III. 463.[1]
B.   Ueber die Administration der Köhlerei.   1827.   IV. 394.
B.   Die Aufforstung in Tunesien.   1893.   IV. 168.[2]
B.   Autumn Blue Berry.   1879.   III. 415.[2]
B.   Beaufortia splendens.   1883.   III. 633.[1]
B.   Beplantingen aan onze wegen.   1881.   III. 209.
B.   Bericht über eine . . . Erlen-Verwüstung.   1843.   IV. 489.[1]
B.   De bevruchting der Koffie-bloemen.   1886.   III. 727.
B.   Bignonia Chamberlayni.   1885.   III. 705.
B.   Bignonia purpurea.   1886.   III. 706.[2]
B.   Bignonias.   1884.   III. 705.
B.   Bignonias.   1891.   III. 705.
B.   Der Blessing'sche Schraubenkeil.   1895.   IV. 384.[1]
B.   Bottle grafting.   1876.   III. 162.
B.   Das Buchenholzproblem.   1885.   IV. 499.
B.   Burtonias and Johnsonias.   1886.   III. 468.[1]
B.   The Californian Elder.   1877.   III. 751.[2]
B.   Callicoma serratifolia Andrew.   1898.   III. 416.[1]
B.   Campsidium filicifolium.   1874.   III. 705.
B.   The Carapa tree.   1874.   III. 511.[2]
B.   Carmine-tinted Thibaudia.   1876.   III. 647.[1]
B.   The Cashew nut.   1877.   III. 524.[1]
B.   Chinese mode of propagating Aralias.   1877.   III. 159.[1]
B.   Cissus porphyrophylla.   1877.   III. 343.[2]
B.   The Coca plant.   1876.   II. 394.[1]
B.   Commerce du bois.   1897.   IV. 557.[1]
B.   The Crossandras.   1883.   III. 709.[1]
B.   Croton Youngii.   1873.   III. 515.[2]
B.   The Cycads.   1882.   III. 284.[1]
B.   Cycas revoluta.   1874.   III. 285.[1]
B.   Desfontainea spinosa in Ireland.   1879.   III. 682.[1]
B.   An early spring-flowering shrub.   1876.   III. 429.[2]
B.   The edible Passion-flower.   1874.   III. 616.[1]
B.   Ueber Eichenrinde.   1888.   IV. 507.
B.   Einiges über Schonungsgatter.   1888.   IV. 146.[2]
B.   Elaeocarpus cyaneus.   1883.   III. 584.[2]
B.   Epigynium leucobotrys.   1874.   III. 664.[2]
B.   Ertrag von Platanen.   1894.   IV. 520.[2]
B.   Ein Feind der Tanne.   1877.   IV. 445.
B.   The forests of Bavaria.   1875.   IV. 351.[1]
B.   The forests of Switzerland.   1875.   IV. 367.
B.   Formzahlen und Massentafeln.   1891.   IV. 231.[1]
B.   Zum Forstwesen Australiens.   1894.   IV. 401.[2]
B.   Fuchsia as climbers.   1891.   III. 640.[1]
B.   The Fuchsia-flowered Ribes.   1876.   III. 415.[2]
B.   Garden Yuccas.   1885.   III. 339.[2]
B.   Garrya elliptica in fruit.   1876.   III. 352.[2]
B.   Giftige Holzgewächse . . . der Papilionaceen.   1880. IV. 524.[2]
B.   Hakea laurina and other species.   1884.   III. 383.[2]
B.   The hardy Dracaena.   1873.   III. 335.
B.   Die Holzarten des Harzes.   1892.   IV. 354.
B.   Holzwirthschaftliche Glossen.   1886.   IV. 237.
B.   Voor houttelers.   1865.   IV. 402.[2]
B.   Hoya Cumingiana.   1885.   III. 693.[1]
B.   Hybrid Epacrises.   1884.   III. 665.[1]
B.   Hypocalymna robustum.   1882.   III. 635.[1]
B.   Influenza privativa delle foreste.   1881.   IV. 53.
B.   Zur Konservirung des Buchenholzes.   1870.   IV. 499.
B.   Ueber die Krebskrankheit der Lärche.   1895.   IV. 451.
B.   The Kumquat.   1874.   III. 502.[1]
B.   Ueber die Lage des Mittelstammes.   1877.   IV. 245.
B.   Lagerstroemia indica.   1873.   III. 629.[2]
B.   The large-flowered Jasmine.   1876.   III. 673.[1]
B.   La législation forestière en Suisse.   1899.   IV. 331.[1]
B.   Leiden die Wälder in der Nähe grosser Städte durch Steinkohlenrauch?   1897.   IV. 193.[1]
B.   The Lemon-scented Gardenia.   1874.   III. 747.[1]
B.   Leschenaultia biloba major.   1884.   III. 754.[1]
B.   Lichtungs-Zuwachs bei Rothbuchen.   1876.   IV. 498.
B.   Long-tailed Croton.   1877.   III. 515.[2]
B.   Mächtige Bäume.   1894.   IV. 486.[1]
B.   Making hedges.   1900.   III. 214.[1]
B.   Mountain Aralias.   1886.   III. 643.[2]
B.   De natuurlijke eigenschappen van het hout.   1868.   IV. 408.
B.   The Necklace-flowered Chamaedorea.   1876.   III. 322.[1]
B.   'A new berry-bearing shrub.   1877.   III. 614.[1]
B.   New double white Epacris.   1876.   III. 665.[1]
B.   New Spiral-leaved Croton.   1877.   III. 515.[2]

B. The North American Custard Apple. 1876. III. 401.[2]
B. Notes on Hoyas. 1883. III. 693.[1]
B. Die österreichische Cameraltaxe rehabilitiert, 1893. IV. 250.[1]
B. Olio solubile d' Abete insetticida. 1882. IV. 209.[2]
B. Ornamental Cycads. 1874. III. 285.[2]
B. Ornamental hedges. 1873. III. 214.[2]
B. Pavonia Wiotii. 1883. III. 588.[2]
B. The Pepper tree. 1884. III. 529.[1]
B. Philesia buxifolia. 1883. III. 337.[2]
B. Phyllanthus roseus pictus. 1876. III. 521.[2]
B. Le Pin de Corse au domaine de Clabecq. 1898. IV. 465.[2]
B. Posoqueria formosa. 1885. III. 746.[2]
B. Aus der Praxis der Holzmassenaufnahme. 1878. IV. 217.
B. Ptychosperma singaporensis. 1884. III. 330.[2]
B. Die rankenden Clematis. 1882. III. 389.[1]
B. Zum Reinertragswaldbau. 1890. IV. 258.
B. Ueber die Relationen zwischen den Bodenwerthen isolierter . . , Waldgrundparcellen. 1889. IV. 257.
B. Rhus Vernix. 1877. III. 528.[2]
B. Riesenbäume in Australien. 1895. IV. 532.[1]
B. A royal Palm. 1876. III. 321.[1]
B. Sambas. 1896. III. 276.[1]
B. The Scarlet Scutellaria. 1876. III. 698.[2]
B. Select dwarf Cereus. 1885. III. 621.[1]
B. A showy white-flowered Bramble. 1876. III. 458.[1]
B. A shrubby Composite (Barnardesia [sic] rosea). 1880. III. 754.[2]
B. A stately Fan Palm. 1876. III. 332.[1]
B. La sylviculture à l'Exposition de Barcelone. 1888. IV. 20.[2]
B. Systematik der Blumendüfte. 1900. I. 182.[2]
B. The Tasmanian Tea tree. 1879. III. 636.[1]
B. Tecoma (Bignonia) radicans. 1882. III. 705.
B. Thunbergia laurifolia. 1877. III. 710.[2]
B. Thunbergias. 1886. III. 710.[1]
B. Tinnaea aethiopica. 1884. III. 698.[2]
B. The Turquoise-berried Vine. 1876. III. 544.[1]
B. Vegetable Ivory. 1883. III. 330.[1]
B. Ueber die Verbindung des Obstbaues mit der Wildbolzzucht. 1861. IV. 134.[2]
B. Die Verwendung buchener Eisenbahnschwellen. 1897. IV. 499.
B. Vorschläge zur Verbesserung der Kiefernholzsaat, 1785. III. 309,[1] IV. 471.
B. Die Wälder der Erde. 1894. IV. 336.[2]
B. Weeping Broom. Genista prostrata. 1877. III. 474.[2]
B. Wo empfiehlt sich im allgemeinen die natürliche Verjüng ng. 1886. IV. 140.
B.,u. The Wood Sorrels. 1882. III. 492.[1]
B. Zebra-striped Dragon tree. 1876. III. 336.[2]
B. & J. Aristolochia Duchartréi Ed. André, 1880. III. 356.[1]
B., v. Ueber die Frostbeschädigungen . . , in Elsass-Lothringen. 1881. IV. 194.[1]
B., van. Dennenwol en dennen-olie. 1855. IV. 443.[2]
B., A. Conservation des bois. 1832. IV. 416.[2]
B., A. Die Flora Homer's. 1897. I. 514.[2]
B., A. Frühtreiberei algemeiner Aetherisirung. 1900. III. 177.
B., A. Large Yew trees. 1878. II. 11.[1]
B., A. The Madroña. 188/. III. 647.[2]
B., A. El presupuesto de los montes públicos. 1887. IV. 553.[1]
B., A. A winter-flowering Honeysuckle. 1874. III. 750.[1]
B., A. C. Taxodium distichum var. pendula. 1899. III. 311.[1]
B., A. F. Street planting. 1881. III. 211.[1]
B., A. H. Notices regarding the flowering of Bamboos. 1882. II. 58.[2]
B., A. H. The tree Rose. 1845. III. 452.
B., A. P. F. Abentheur von allerhand Mineralien, Wurtzeln . . . See PLEYER. 1656. III. 272.[2]
B., C. Apparition en Belgique de la rouille courbeuse du Pin sylvestre. 1899. IV. 479.
B., C. Les arbres du Parc de Bruxelles. 1899. IV. 84.[2]
B., C. Les arbres géants. 1896. IV. 484.[2]
B., C. Culture des champs et culture des bois. 1892. IV. 270.
B., C. La détermination des bois. 1898. IV. 62,[2] 409.
B., C. Les maladies infectieuses des arbres. 1896. IV. 212.
B., C. L'origine de notre flore forestière. 1896. IV. 75.[1]
B., C. Un pays soustrait à la tyrannie du régime forestier. 1892. IV. 276.[1]

B., C. Production de la forêt domaniale de La Fuvelle. 1892. IV. 237.
B., C. Recettes utiles. 1892. IV. 153.[1]
B., C. Recettes utiles: Élagage. 1892. IV. 172.[1]
B., C. C. Un nouveau puceron. 1878. IV. 444.[1]
B., Sir C. J. F. List of flowering plants. See BUNBURY, Sir C. J. F. 1889. V. xxi.[2]
B., C. W. De scheikunde in hare toepassing op den landbouw. 1856. III. 37.[1]
B., D. Les Chamaecyparis. 1899. III. 300.[2]
B., D. Henschels Theorie omtrent het plantenrijk. 1821. I. 251.
B., D. Le Pêcher à fruit plat. 1887. III. 440.[1]
B., D. Wederlegging van Henschels theorie. 1821. I. 251.
B., D. J. Cultivation of the Cranberry. 1858. III. 663.[2]
B., D. J. Planting and management of quickset hedges. 1855. III. 213.
B., D. J. R. Verjonging van Eikenstobben. 1889. IV. 508.
B., E. Appauvrissement des forêts communales. 1889. IV. 276.[1]
B., E. Aufforstungen in Algier. 1886. IV. 168.[2]
B., E. Die Aufforstungen . . . in den französischen Alpen. 1885. IV. 163.
B., E. Die Bäume der Stadt Paris. 1885. III. 124.[1]
B., E. Die·Bewaldung der Sologne. 1885. IV. 361.
B., E. Forêts en Sibérie. 1886. IV. 376.[1]
B., E. Die forstlichen Verhältnisse Rumäniens. 1886. IV. 375.[1]
B., E. Pariser Promenaden. 1886. III. 210.
B., E. Die Waldungen Sibiriens. 1886. IV. 376.[1]
B., E. v. Z. Kaspische Zandwilg. 1877. III. 351.[1]
B., E. B. Ameisen-Pflanzen. 1900. II. 824.[2]
B., E. B. Myrmecophilous plants. 1898. III. 746.[1]
B., E. C. Terrassen in Koffietuinen. 1875. III. 726.[2]
B., E. G. Plurality of embryos in Quercus alba. 1886. II. 132.[2]
B., Mrs. E. V. Ros Rosarum ex horto poetarum. See BOYLE, Mrs. E. V. 1896. II. 290.[2]
B., Em. Cradine, nouveau ferment peptique. 1891. III. 370.[1]
B., F. Beobachtungen über Stummelpflanzen. 1888. IV. 154.[1]
B., F. Ueber die Durchforstung. 1883. IV. 175.[2]
B., F. Ein Urteil über die Ertragsfähigkeit der ungarischen Eichenwaldungen. 1888. IV. 508.
B., F. von. Cryptomeria Lobbiana. 1853. III. 302.[1]
B., F. W. Anthocercis viscosa. 1879. III. 698.[2]
B., F. W. Araujia albens entrapping insects. 1899. II. 736.[1]
B., F. W. The birth of the Chilian Pine. 1883. II. 26.[2]
B., F. W. A chapter on Agaves. 1876. III. 340.[2]
B., F. W. Colletia bictoniensis (cruciata). 1899. III. 541.[2]
B., F. W. The Creeping Fuchsia. 1880. III. 640.[2]
B., F. W. Daemonorops accidens. 1872. III. 321.[1]
B., F. W. Dwarf Palms. 1872. III. 327.[1]
B., F. W. Dwarf Palms; Geonomas. 1872. III. 325.[2]
B., F. W. A few hints on propagating Conifers. 1876. III. 294.[1]
B., F. W. Ficus diversifolia. 1881. - III. 370.[1]
B., F. W. The gardens at Battle Abbey. 1875. III. 393.[2]
B., F. W. Glossy-flowered Tutsan. 1880. III. 610.[1]
B., F. W. The Great-leaved Vine of Japan. 1896. III. 584.[1]
B., F. W. The Indian or Sikkim Yulan. 1895. III. 399.[2]
B., F. W. Jasminum pubescens. 1881. III. 673.[1]
B., F. W. The Nepaulese Tutsan. 1880. III. 610.[1]
B., F. W. The Rain tree. 1880. II. 377.[2]
B., F. W. Shrubby St. John's worts. 1883. III. 610.[1]
B., F. W. Some of the rarer climbing and trailing plants. 1900. III. 205.[1]
B., F. W. Tropical Rhododendrons. 1884. III. 658.[2]
B., F. W. Yucca gloriosa. 1873. III. 340.[1]
B., Félix. De la greffe par application. 1852. III. 161.
B., G. L'Orme et ses ennemis. 1886. III. 364.[2]
B., G. Planting trees on mounds. 1877. III. 166.
B., G. Podocarpus. 1877. III. 287.[2]
B., G. The Pyrenean Pine. 1877. III. 308.[1]
B., G. Shrubs . . . which· thrive under the drip of trees. 1872. III. 42.[1]
B., G. E. The Amherstia nobilis in India. 1876. II. 331.[2]
B., H. Quelques réflexions sur le jardinage. 1887. IV. 131.
B., H. See also USINX, G. W. & B., H.
B., H. C. Carya alba Nutt. 1880. II. 112.[2]
B., J. Bemerkungen über Mäusefrass. 1862. IV. 197.[2]

B., J. De Berk en de bliksem. 1900. IV. 195.¹
B., J. Le Bouleau et la foudre. 1900. IV. 195.¹
B., J. El ensanche de Las Majadas. 1891. IV. 551.²
B., J. A nurseryman's paradise. 1897. I. 64.
B., J. Las reformas en el servicio forestal. 1899. IV. 554.
B., J. Refutación al folleto publicado por un vecino de Las Majadas. 1892. IV. 552.¹
B., J. Sikkim and Bhotan Rhododendra. 1862. III. 654.²
B., J. Trees in towns. 1877. III. 42.²
B., J. Winter bedding and other plants. 1886. III. 208.¹
B., J. See also BEALE, John; BLAGRAVE, Joseph.
B., J. C. Magnolia grandiflora. 1879. III. 400.¹
B., J. C. & others. Propagating Rhododendrons. 1883. III. 656.
B., J. H. Botany. 1878. I. 270.
B., J. H. Historical trees of Rhode Island. 1884. I. 295.²
B., J. W. Diospyros virginiana, the Persimmon. 1892. III. 670.¹
B., J. W. The forests of Switzerland. 1883. IV. 367.
B., J. W. The Persimmon. 1894. III. 670.¹
B., L. La carte dendrologique de la Belgique. 1899. IV. 119.²
B., L. Chêne à tanin (Quercus densiflora), en Amérique. 1895. IV. 503.¹
B., L. Création de taillis de Chênes rouges. 1894. IV. 516.¹
B., L. Downings Ever-bearing Mulberry. 1858. II. 154.²
B., L. L'excursion forestière de septembre 1898. 1898. IV. 362.
B., L. Die Forstwirthschaft in Russland. 1883. IV. 114.
B., L. Le gaz de bois. 1899. IV. 433.²
B., L. La glandée de 1898. 1898. IV. 509.
B., L. Les plantations routières aux Chambres législatives. 1900. III. 210.
B., L. Promesses de quelques arbres exotiques en Campine. 1894. IV. 545.¹
B., L. Revision cadastrale des propriétés non bâties. 1899. IV. 285.¹
B., L. Trois heures à la forêt de Soignes. 1897. IV. 556.¹
B., L. See also BILLECARD, L.; BIVORT, Alexandre & B., L.
B., M. Le monopole du camphre au Japon. 1900. III. 405.¹
B., M. Rsecz o Modrzewiach. 1851. IV. 452.¹
B., M. J. Deformed Walnuts. 1883. II. 113.²
B., M. J. Gardenia Rothmanni. 1855. II. 818.²
B., M. J. Lilac fungus. 1881. III. 680.²
B., M. J. Monstrous flowers. 1852. II. 274.¹
B., M. J. Witches' brooms on Silver Firs. 1856. IV. 445.
B., M. V. Robinier and Sophora. 1898. IV. 523,² 524.²
B., N. Déductions d'économie forestière . . . du Chêne des partisans. 1850. II. 138.¹
B., N. Eucalyptus als Zwergbaum. 1877. III. 634.²
B., N. Ueber den neuen amerikanischen blüthenlosen Apfel. 1890. II. 267.¹
B., N. Opuntien. 1877. III. 624.¹
B., N. Wellingtonia gigantea var. pendula. 1877. III. 310.¹
B., N. Winterharte Cactus. 1877. III. 622.¹
B., N. Wisteria Nutt. 1878. III. 490.¹
B., N. Zijdeteelt in Indie. 1900. III. 148.³
B., N. L. Branched catkins of Salix. 1879. II. 107.¹
B., N. L. A large Grape vine. 1881. II. 506.²
B., R. Le camphre en extrême-orient. 1900. III. 405.¹
B., R. Ein eindringliches Mahnwort an alle Forstwirte. 1895. IV. 129.
B., R. Estudio acerca de " el Ahuacate." 1887. II. 227.²
B., R. Die forstlichen Verhältnisse im Kanton Baselland. 1898. IV. 278.²
B., R. Ein Mittel gegen Engerlinge. 1896. IV. 203.
B., R. Natürliche und künstliche Mischungen. 1899. IV. 137.²
B., R. In a north-western American forest. 1874. I. 311.¹
B., R. Note accompanying figure of a bifurcated Bamboo. 1890. II. 59.¹
B., R. La producción de madera de construcción. 1900. IV. 544.²
B., R. La production . . . du thé en extrême-orient. 1900. III. 608.¹
B., R. Reisebrief an das Feuilleton der Schweiz. Zeitschrift für Forstwesen. 1898. IV. 374.²
B., R. H. Lindenia rivalis. 1899. III. 745.¹
B., R. H. Portlandia grandiflora. 1898. III. 746.²
B., S. Pyrus Aucuparia. 1858. III. 460.¹
B., S. v. Skov-Culturen. See S. v. B. 1847. IV. 113.¹

B., S. L. Notes about the Acacia. 1862. III. 486.²
B., T. The Alder. 1885. IV. 489.²
B., T. Autumn and winter Heaths. 1883. III. 650.²
B., T. Crotons. 1883. III. 516.¹
B., T. Cutting and felling garden hedges. 1879. III. 213.
B., T. Eriostemons. 1891. III. 504.¹
B., T. Evergreen shrubs. 1886. III. 206.¹
B., T. Iledaroma (Darwinia) tulipifera. 1891. III. 633.²
B., T. Osiers. 1884. III. 348.
B., T. Osiers on sewage farms. 1885. III. 349.
B., T. Pimeleas. 1891. III. 628.¹
B., T. Rhododendrons in dry soils. 1885. III. 656.
B., T. A. Brugmansia suaveolens. 1834. III. 700.¹
B., T. A. Végétation extraordinaire du Brugmansia suaveolens. 1834. III. 700.¹
B., T. F. Seeding of Bamboos. 1887. II. 60.¹
B., T. W. Forests in Alsace-Lorraine. 1883. IV. 349.²
B., W. Befaria glauca. 1891. III. 648.²
B., W. E. Propagation of the Mango by inarching or grafting by approach. 1894. III. 525.¹
B., W. G. A large Horse Chestnut tree. 1877. II. 482.²
B., W. J. Prunus Jacquemonti. 1896. II. 274.²
B., W. J. See also BEAN, W. J.
B., W. W. Androgynous Alder. 1879. II. 115.²
B., Z. Cultivated Hibbertias. 1880. III. 596.¹
B., Z. Cyoas undulata. 1881. III. 285.¹
B., Z. The Eranthemums. 1880. III. 709.¹
B., Z. The Hoyas or Honey plants. 1880. III. 693.¹
B., Z. Noble Melastomads. 1881. III. 638.¹
B . . . . r. Zur. Lebensweise des grossen Eichenbockkäfers. 1889. IV. 511.
B——. Ueber die Schwarze Wallnuss. 1875. IV. 488.¹
B——a, N. F. See B——a, H. Φ.
B.** Benagen der Rinde an Lärchen. 1842. IV. 450.
B.***, Mme. Botanique à l'usage de la jeunesse. 1845. I. 94.
B***, M. Traité ou abrégé curieux et très utile touchant les jardinages. 1706. III. 143.
Ba. Nochmals Tipula crocata. 1878. IV. 445.
Baalen, Petrus van. De cortice peruviano ejusque . . . usu. 1735. III. 719.
Baarschers. Dennen zaaien. 1870. III. 294.¹
Baarzahlung, oder Zahlungsfristen beim Holzverkauf? 1879. IV. 388.¹
Baastrup, F. v. Anviisning til Behandling . . . af private Skove. 1863. IV. 113.²
Baath, (Stadt- und Zoll-Richter). Über die Abwendung . . . schädlicher Thiere. 1831. III. 186.¹
Bab, Arthur. Die Bewaldung der Pampa. 1899. III. 346,¹ 552.²
Babcock, Henry Homes. First annual report of the Chicago botanical garden. 1876. I. 39.
Baber, Edward Colborne. On the Chinese Tea-trade with Tibet. 1886. III. 601.²
— Travels and researches in western China. 1882. III. 607.
Baber, J. The medicinal properties of some New Zealand plants. 1887. III. 283.²
— On the rate of growth of native trees. 1873. III. 38.²
Baber Muhammad. Denkwürdigkeiten des Zehir-Eddin Muhammed Baber. 1826. III. 496.²
— Memoirs of Zehir-Ed-Din Muhammed Baber. 1826. III. 496.²
Babey, Claude· Marie Philibert. Flore jurassienne. 1845. I. 410.
Babington, Charles Cardale. On the· arrangement of the British Salices. 1863. II. 102.¹
— The British Rubi. 1869. II. 303.¹
— Cork-tree at Summertown. 1863. II. 140.¹
— Descriptions of Rubi. 1852. II. 303.¹
— Effects of the bad summer and winter of 1860. 1861. III. 46.³
— Flora bathoniensis. 1834. I. 398, 533.
— Flora of Cambridgeshire. 1860. I. 401.
— On Hedera Canariensis as an Irish plant. 1865. II. 649.¹
— Hints towards a Cybele hibernica. 1859. I. 401.
— On Hypericum anglicum. 1855. II. 556.¹
— List of plants gathered during a short visit to Iceland. 1847. I. 355.
— Localities of several species of British plants. 1836. II. 660.¹
— Manual of British botany. 1843. I. 399.
— Nativity of the Box-tree. 1853. II. 452.¹
— Note on Dr. Planchon's paper on Ulex Gallii. 1849. II. 387.¹

— Notes on British Rubi. 1886. II. 303.[1]
— Notes on Rubi. 1878. II. 303.[1]
— Primitiæ floræ sarnicæ. 1839. I. 398.
— Professor Babington on Rubus in 1891. 1896. II. 303.[1]
— Propagation of Rubi. 1867. II. 306.[1]
— On the Pyrus Aria of England. 1851. II. 312.[1]
— Remarks upon British plants. 1853. II. 556.[1]
— A revision of the flora of Iceland. 1871. I. 356.
— Rubus dumnoniensis. 1890. II. 307.[1]
— On the Rubus nitidus. 1849. II. 309.[1]
— Rubus Reuteri Merc. 1873. II. 309.[1]
— Supplement to Notes on Rubi. 1886. II. 303.[1]
— A syllabus of lectures on botany. 1868. I. 34.
— A synopsis of the British Rubi. 1846. II. 302.[2]
— On Ulex. 1840. II. 387.[1]
— Ulex strictus. 1861. II. 388.[1]
— On the varieties of Dryas octopetala. 1842. II. 263.[2]
— See also BALFOUR, J. H. & BABINGTON, C. C.
Babo, von. Akkerbouw-scheikunde. 1849. III. 36.[2]
Babo, A. von. Schnitt der Maulbeer-Hochstämme. 1855. III. 377.
Babo, August, Freiherr von & Mach, E. Handbuch des Weinbaues. 1881. III. 553.[1]
— & Rümpler, Theodor. Kultur . . . der amerikanischen Weintrauben. 1885. III. 553.[1]
Babo, Lambert, Freiherr von. Der Weinbau. 1842. III. 552.
— Über den Weinbau der Bergstrasse. 1860. III. 553.[1]
— Der Weinstock und seine Varietäten. 1844. III. 546.
— & Metzger, Johann. Die Wein- und Tafeltrauben. 1836. III. 546.
Babu Daulat Ram. See DAULAT RAM (Babu).
Babu Upendranath Kanjilal. See UPENDRANATH KANJILAL, (Babu).
Babuty Desgodetz & Le Camus de Mézieres, [Nicolas]. Dissertation de la compagnie des architectes. 1763. IV. 382.[1]
— — Essai sur les bois de charpente. 1763. IV. 422.[2]
Babylonian and oriental record. I. 17. -
Baccanelli, Giovanni. Liber de consensu medicorum. 1554. III. 237.[2]
Baccarini, Pasquale. Appunti intorno ad alcuni sferocristalli. 1888. I. 139.
— Contributo alla conoscenza dell' apparecchio albuminoso tannico della Leguminose. 1892. II. 321.[1]
— Contribuzione allo studio dei colori. 1886. I. 185.[1]
— Sui cristalloidi borali di alcune Leguminose. 1895. II. 321.[1]
— Sopra un curioso cecidio della Capparis. 1893. III. 408.[2]
— Intorno agli elementi speciali della Glycine. 1889. II. 388.[2]
— Sulla Genista aetnensis e le Genista junciformi. 1897. II. 359.[1]
— Sul mal nero delle Viti. 1894. III. 581.
— Sul mal nero delle Viti in Sicilia. 1892. III. 580.
— Intorno ad una malattia dei grappoli dell' Uva. 1888. III. 579.
— Intorno ad una malattia della Palma da datteri. 1895. III. 329.[1]
— Osservazioni anatomiche sopra alcuni ricettacoli florali. 1885. I. 115.[1]
— Intorno ad una particolarità dei vasi cribrosi. 1892. II. 891.[1]
— La Peronospora viticola nel settentrione d' Italia. 1895. III. 579.
— Intorno ad una probabile funzione meccanica dei cristalli di ossalato calcico. 1885. I. 139.
— Sul sistema secretore delle Papilionacee. 1890. II. 321.[2]
— Studio comparativo sulla flora vesuviana e sulla Etnea. 1881. I. 429.
— & Scalia, Giuseppe. Appunti per la conoscenza di due acarocecidii. 1896. I. 215,[2] III. 897,[1] 700.[2]
Baccelli, G. Passeggiata scolastica . . . per celebrare la festa degli alberi. 1899. IV. 42.[1]
Bacci, Andrea. De naturali vinorum historia. - 1596. III. 582.
Bach, Alexis. Contribution à l'étude des phénomènes chimiques de l'assimilation. 1893. I. 174.
— Sur le dédoublement de l'acide carbonique. 1893. I. 174.
— Sur le mécanisme chimique de la réduction des azotates. 1896. I. 178.
Bach, C. See NERLINGER, Th. & BACH, C.
Bach, Ernest. Floraison des Cereus cinerascens et Bomplandi. 1864. III. 621.[1]
— Floraison du Cereus rostratus. 1865. III. 621.[2]
— Floraison du Cereus strigosus. 1865. III. 622.[1]

Bach, M. Taschenbuch der rheinpreussischen Flora. 1873. I. 387.
Bach, O. Recherche de l'Aloès. 1875. III. 333.[2]
Bachabiolos, I. See BAXABIÓAOΣ, 'I.
Bache, Franklin. See WOOD, G. B. & BACHE, Franklin.
Bachelot de la Pylaie, Auguste Jean Marie. Flore de l'île de Terre-Neuve. 1829. I. 310.
La bachicoltura nelle Puglie. 1898. III. 148.[1]
Bachlechner, Gregor. Verzeichniss der phanerogamen Pflanzen . . . von Brixen. 1859. I. 441.
Bachman, John. Catalogue of phænogamous plants . . . of Charleston. 1834. I. 318.
Bachmann. Gegenfeuer bei der Lösphung von Waldbränden. 1894. IV. 182.[2]
Bachmann, Ewald Theodor. Beschaffenheit . . . des Arillus einiger Leguminosen. 1885. II. 352.[1]
— Darstellung der Entwickelungsgeschichte . . . der Samenschalen der Scrophularineen. 1880. II. 779.[1]
— Die Entwickelungsgeschichte . . . der Samenschalen der Scrophularineen. 1880. II. 779.[1]
— Über Korkwucherungen auf Blättern. 1879. I. 130.
Bachmann, Friedrich. Die landeskundliche Literatur über die Grossherzogtümer Mecklenburg. 1889. I. 3.[2]
Bachmann, Otto. Untersuchungen über die . . . Schildhaare. 1886. I. 113.[1]
Bachs, M. Flora der Rheinprovins. 1899. I. 390.
Bachy, Charles. Question de physiologie végétale. 1868. I. 164.
Il bacino del Po. 1880. IV. 186.[2]
Back, Sir George. Narrative of the Arctic land expedition. 1836. I. 310.
— Reise durch Nord-Amerika bis zur Mündung des grossen Fischflusses. 1836. I. 310.
Backer, Gerard. De radicum plantarum physiologia. 1829. I. 160.
Backer Overbeek, A. A. Bericht omtrent zaden en olie. See OVERBEEK, Backer. 1874. III. 615.[1]
— De Granaatboom. 1875. III. 630.[2]
Backhouse, James. On the esculent plants of Van Diemensland. 1833. III. 283.[1]
— Index plantarum . . . Van Diemen's Land. 1834. I. 505.
— The names Abies and Picea. 1886. II. 21.[2]
— A narrative of a visit to the Australian colonies. 1842. III. 283.[1]
— Native country of Tecomaria. 1864. II. 792.[1]
— Observations on the purple Laburnum. 1865. II. 368.[1]
— Remarks on the . . . productions of Tasmania. 1842. III. 283.[1]
— On the roots . . . of Van Diemens Land. 1833. III. 283.[1]
Backhouse, Thomas & James. A catalogue of fruit and forest-trees, evergreen and deciduous shrubs. 1816. I. 53.
Dacon, C. A. The Kumquat Orange in Florida. 1893. III. 502.[1]
Bacon, Francis, Viscount St. Albans. Histoire naturelle. 1627. I. 30.
— Sylva sylvarum. 1627. I. 30.
Bacon, Louis. Notice d'une analyse du Thé de James. 1823. III. 652.[2]
Baczewski, Max. Chemische Untersuchung der Samen von Nephelium. 1893. II. 407.[1]
Badcock, Richard. A letter concerning the farina fœcundans of the Yew tree. 1748. II. 10.[2]
— A letter to Mr. Henry Baker, containing some microscopical observations on the farina fœcundans. 1748. I. 116.[1]
Baden — Botanischer Verein. See BOTANISCHER VEREIN FÜR DEN KREIS FREIBURG . . I. 11.
Baden — Domänendirection. Dienstanweisung über Forsteinrichtung. 1869. IV. 299.[1]
Baden — Forstliche Mittheilungen. See FORSTLICHE . . . IV. 8.
Baden-Powell, Baden Henry. The " Chôs " of Hoshiárpur. 1880. IV. 377.[2]
— Commutation of rights. 1896. IV. 335.
— Concessions. 1900. IV. 335.
— Forest conservancy in its popular aspect. 1877. IV. 181.[2]
— Forest law. 1893. IV. 314.[1]
— Forest laws. 1893. IV. 332.[2]
— Forest settlements in India. 1892. IV. 134.[1]
— The forest system of British Burma. 1874. IV. 294.[2]
— The forests of New Zealand. See WALKER, J. CAMPBELL-. 1876. IV. 380.[2]

Baden-Powell, Baden Henry (*continued*).
— Hand-book of the economic products of the Punjab. *See* POWELL, B. H. BADEN-. 1868. III. 278.
— The influence of forests on rainfall. *See* BRANDIS, Dietrich. 1887. IV. 49.[1]
— Kashmir products. *See* POWELL, B. H. BADEN-. 1892. III. 279.[1]
— A manual of jurisprudence for forest officers. 1882. IV. 332.[1]
— On methods of cutting . . . Pine forests. *See* REGIMBEAU. 1878. IV. 461.[1]
— Mochras. 1882. III. 589.[2]
— The natural reproduction treatment of Deodar forests. 1878. IV. 447.[2]
— The nature . . . of the servitude . . . in forest estates. *See* DANCKELMANN, Bernhard. 1884. IV. 333.[1]
— Note on the Dehra Doon. 1876. IV. 377.[2]
— Note on the demarcation of the forest area. 1876. IV. 287.
— Note on the demarcation of the forest area. 1877. IV. 295.[1]
— Papers relating to the establishment of a forest terminology in English. 1874. IV. 23.[1]
— The political value of forest conservancy. 1877. IV. 279.[1]
— A study on the reboisement of denuded slopes. 1877. IV. 155.[1]
— *See also* BAILEY, Frederick & BADEN-POWELL, B. H.; BRANDIS, *Sir* Dietrich, BADEN-POWELL, B. H. & STENHOUSE, W.
— & Gamble, J. S. Report of the proceedings of the forest conference . . . at Lahore, 1874. *See* FOREST CONFERENCE. IV. 16.[1]
— & Macdonell, J. C. Report of the proceedings of the forest conference . . . at Lahore. 1872. *See* FOREST CONFERENCE. IV. 16.[1]
Badens Kernobst-Sorten auf der Landes-Obstausstellung. 1881. III. 71.
Badetty, R. Le Teck au Siam. 1900. IV. 537.[1]
Badger, *Mrs.* C. M. Wild flowers. 1859. I. 307.
Badier, de. Abhandlung über die Chinchina-Piton. 1789. II. 816.[1]
— Mémoire sur le Quinquinapiton. 1789. II. 816.[2]
Das badische Forstgesetz in seiner jetzigen Fassung. 1855. IV. 317.[2]
Badische Pharmakopöe. *See* PHARMACOPOEA badensis. 1841. III. 249.[1]
Die badische Verordnung über das Verfahren in Forststrafsachen. 1882. IV. 317.[1]
Badischer botanischer Verein. Mitteilungen. *See* BOTANISCHER VEREIN FÜR DEN KREIS FREIBURG . . . I. 11.
Badischer Forst-Verein. Statuten. 1863. IV. 40.[2]
Badischer Forst-Verein. Verhandlungen. *See* FORSTLICHER VEREIN . : . IV. 8.
Bado, Sebastiano. *See* BALDI, Sebastiano.
Badoux, Henri. Accroissement en longueur d'un rameau de Glycine. 1897. II. 389.[1]
— L'Épicéa à verrues du "Moos." 1899. II. 37.[1]
— L'Épicéa de l'Himalaya. 1899. IV. 460.[2]
— Ueber grosse Bäume in Zürich. 1898. I. 298.
— L'hylésine du Frêne. 1898. III. 354.[2]
— Längenwachstum eines Glycinezweiges. 1897. II. 389.[1]
— Lichtversuche mit Deckgittern. 1898. IV. 151.[2]
— Un nouveau rôle protecteur de la forêt. 1898. IV. 168.[1]
— Les plus beaux arbres de Zurich. 1898. I. 298.
— Quelques notes sur l'accroissement . . . du Sapin & de l'Épicéa. 1898. IV. 446.[2] 459.[1]
— Représentation graphique de l'accroissement. 1896. IV. 234.
— Über Rhytisma acerinum. 1899. III. 534.[1]
— Untersuchungen über das Wachstum auf verschiedenen Bodenarten. 1895. IV. 70.
— Untersuchungen über Körnerzahl. 1895. IV. 147.[1]
— Untersuchungen über die Sickerwassermengen. 1898. IV. 73.[2]
— Versuche über Einfluss der Saatzeit. 1899. III. 157.
Badstübner. Der nordschwedische Wald und seine Feinde. 1887. IV. 344.[2]
— Untersuchungen über die Wuchsverhältnisse der nordschwedischen Kiefer. 1888. IV. 481.
— Ueber Verwaltung . . . der schwedischen Staatsforsten. 1888. IV. 289.[1]
Bächtold, M. Der Staatswald und das Bergwerk am Gonsen. 1890. IV. 367.
Bäck, Abraham. Tilläggning om Faua Pichurim ifrån Brasilien. 1759. III. 403.[2]
— Tilläggning til föregäende rön. 1765. III. 475.[1]

Bädeker, Franz Gotthilf Heinrich Jakob. Kurzer und fasslicher Unterricht in der einfachen Obstbaumzucht. 1796. III. 135.
Bägenholm, Jakob. Examen classis monoeciae. *See* THUNBERG, C. P. 1825. I. 251.
Bähr, O. Der hessische Wald. 1879. IV. 26, 321.
The Bael fruit and its properties. 1866. III. 495.[1]
Baelz, Erwin. *See* FROMMULLER, C. & BAELZ, Erwin.
Baena, J. A., ALVAREZ DE QUINDOS Y. *See* ALVAREZ DE QUINDOS Y BAENA, J. A.
Bänitz, Carl Gabriel. Beiträge zur Flora des Königreichs Polen. 1865. I. 385.
— Beiträge zur Flora des Königreichs Polen. 1871. I. 363.
— Flora der östlichen Niederlausitz. 1861. I. 384.
— Handbuch der Botanik. 1880. V. x.[2]
— Leitfaden für den Unterricht in der Botanik. 1879. V. x.[2]
— Ribes rubrum L. var. pseudo-petraeum. 1892. II. 246.[1]
— Ueber seltene und neue Rubi. 1898. II. 300.[1]
— Ueber seltene und neue schlesische Rubi. 1896. II. 302.[2]
— Ueber Vaccinium uliginosum L. var. globosum. 1891. II. 687.[1]
Baer, F. L. Chemische Untersuchung der Seidelbast-Rinde. *See* GMELIN, C. G. 1822. III. 627.[1]
Baer, Karl Ernst von. Dattel-Palmen an den Ufern des Kaspischen Meeres. 1859. II. 72.[2]
— Ergänzende Nachrichten über Dattelpalmen am Kaspischen Meere. 1860. II. 72.[2]
— Die uralte Waldlosigkeit der südrussischen Steppe. 1856. I. 362.
Bärsch, G. & Weber, C. O. Briefliche Mittheilung über den Anbau von Sorbus. 1857. III. 660.[1]
Die bäuerliche Waldgenossenschaft in Oesterreich. 1881. IV. 309.[2]
Bäume und Sträucher mit Zierfrüchten. 1891. III. 208.[1]
Baeumler, G. Ph. A. Quaedam animadversiones de Piperis Cubebae efficacitate. 1826. III. 342.[2]
Bäumler, Konrad. Azaleen-Befruchtung. 1877. III. 656.
— Die Waldstreu. 1894. IV. 72.
Baffico, C. G. Modo pratico di coltivare l' Ulivo. 1857. III. 675.[2]
Baginsky, Adolf. Présence de la xanthine . . . dans le thé. 1884. III. 607.
Baglietto, Francesco. Florula della valle del Lagaccio in Genova. 1886. I. 429.
Bagnall, James Eustace. The distribution of the genus Rosa in Warwickshire. 1886. II. 285.[1]
— The flora of Warwickshire. 1891. I. 404.[1]
— A new Bramble. 1892. II. 308.[2]
— Notes on Sutton Park. 1876. I. 403.
— Notes on the Rubi of Warwickshire. 1882. II. 303.[1]
Bagnall, L. J. Notes on the occurrence of Kauri-gum. 1897. II. 25.[2]
Bagneris, Gustave. Elements of sylviculture. - 1873. IV. 109.[2]
— Manual of sylviculture. 1873. IV. 109.[2]
— Manuel de sylviculture. 1873. IV. 109.[2]
— & Broillard, Charles. Étude sur la production du Chêne. 1870. IV. 512.
Bagnol, Eugène. Acclimatation en Tunisie. 1894. III. 130.[2]
— Exploitation du Pistachier Lentisque. 1896. III. 525.[2]
— Le Jujubier Lotus. 1897. II. 500.[1]
Bagot, William, *Lord.* An account of the cultivation of the Mespilus japonica. 1820. III. 422.[2]
Bagshawe, C. Memorandum on the forests of the Kuram assigned district. 1881. IV. 378.
— Memorandum on the system of management of the . . . forest divisions of the Central circle. 1888. IV. 250.[2]
Baguenault de Viéville, G. Le Chêne. 1875. IV. 512.
— Observations pratiques sur la culture . . . des Pins maritimes et sylvestres. 1875. IV. 461.[1]
Baguer, Jaime R. de. La repoblación de los montes del Carso. 1900. IV. 547.[1]
Bahama Islands. 1888. III. 267.[1]
Bahia Piassava. 1889. III. 320.[2]
Bahnschwellen-Imprägnazion. 1880. IV. 423.[2]
Bahrdt, Heinrich August. De pilis plantarum. 1849. I. 112.[2]
Baichère, Édouard. Contributions à la flore des Corbières et du bassin de l'Aude. 1891. V. XXII.[1]
— Contributions à la flore du bassin de l'Aude. 1891. V. XXII.[1]

Baier. Beobachtungen über den Fichtenrüsselkäfer. 1840. IV. 206.
Baier. *See also* BAJER.
Baier, Anton. Die .Heimat des gemeinen Flieders. 1883. II. 715.[2]
Baier, Johann Jakob. De Aristolochia. 1719. III. 386.[1]
— Horti medici Academiae altdorfiensis historia. 1727. I. 43.
— De hortis Germaniae botanico-medicis. 1726. I. 43.
— De Junipero. 1719. III. 303.[2]
— De malo Punica. 1712. II. 611.[1]
— De sanguine Draconis. 1712. III. 336.[2]
— De Senna. 1733. III. 470.[1]
— De Visco. 1706. II. 177.[2]
Baierische botanische Gesellschaft in Regensburg. *See* KÖNIGLICH BAIERISCHE . . . I. 13.
Baikie, William Balfour. African Palms. 1862. II. 62.[1]
— African Palms. 1863. III. 319.[1]
— *See also* ADAMS, Arthur, BAIKIE, W. B. & BARRON, Charles.
Bail, Demetrius. *See* БАЙКОВЪ, Дм.
Bail, Theodor. Ueber androgyne Blüthenstände. 1869. I. 145.[1]
— Botanische Notizen. 1886. II. 275.[2]
— Ein Eibenwald in Westpreussen. 1873. II. 11.[1]
— Pilz-Epidemie an der Forleule. 1869. IV. 476.
— Ueber Pilzepizootien. 1869. IV. 199.[1]
— Viscum album auf Rosa canina. 1869. II. 179.[1]
Baildon, Samuel. Tea in Assam. 1877. III. 603.
— The Tea industry in India. 1882. III. 603.
Bailey & Co. Forest culture. 1875. IV. 111.[2]
Bailey, Charles. On the natural ropes used for packing. 1870. III. 234.
Bailey, Frederick. The Bo'ness pit-wood trade. 1899. IV. 425.[2]
— Damage to woods and agricultural crops. 1900. IV.183.[1]
— Export works of the Mandi forest company. 1889. IV. 389.
— Forest schools and model forests in Scotland. 1899. IV. 34.[2]
— A forest tour among the dunes of Gascony. 1887. IV. 361.
— A forest tour in Provence and the Cevennes. 1886. IV. 361.
— Forestry in France. 1886. IV. 361.
— Forestry in Hungary. 1888. IV. 374.[1]
— Grazing in the French forests. 1885. IV. 135.[1]
— The Indian forest school. 1885. IV. 37.[1]
— The Indian forest survey. 1885. IV. 295.[1]
— Introduction to course of forestry lectures. 1893. IV. 177.[2]
— Memorandum on the timber export works in the Bashahr division. 1889. IV. 389.
— Note on modern works on forestry in the English language. 1897. IV. 2.
— Plan or scheme of management of the woods of the Novar estate. 1899. IV. 243.[2]
— Sales and export of timber in France. 1886. IV. 405.[1]
— State model forest for Scotland. 1899. IV. 243.[2]
— Timber export works in Bashahr. 1889. IV. 389.
— A visit to Dr. Schlich's forests. 1900. IV. 357.[1]
See also BRANDIS, Sir Dietrich & BAILEY, Frederick.
— & Baden-Powell, B. H. Compounding forest offences. 1882. IV. 332.[1]
— & Macdonald, G. U. Raith estate; plan or management scheme. 1898. IV. 248.[2]
— — Working plan for the pit-wood working circle, Raith. 1898. IV. 248.[2]
Bailey, Frederick Manson. An abnormal growth in a Papaw fruit. 1900. II. 582.[2]
— Botanic notes. 1895. I. 504.
— Botanical note. 1889. II. 326.[2]
— Botany abridged . . . for the Queensland student. 1894. I. 504.
— Catalogue of plants in the two metropolitan gardens, the Brisbane botanic garden and Bowen park. 1885. I. 69.[1]
— Catalogue of the . . . plants of Queensland. 1890. I. 504.
— A classified index of the . . . plants of Queensland. 1883. I. 503.
— A companion for the Queensland student of plant life. 1893. I. 71.
— Contributions to the flora of New Guinea. 1898. I. 499.[2]
— Contributions to the flora of Queensland. 1897. I. 505.
— Contributions to the Queensland flora. 1885. I. 503.
— Contributions to the Queensland flora. 1891. I. 504.
— Description of a new Eucalypt. 1894. II. 624.[2]
— Description of the Queensland form of Nipa. 1889. II. 71.[2]
— Edible fruits indigenous to Queensland. 1898. III. 94.[3]
— Fasciation in Bouvardia triphylla. 1887. II. 810.[2]
— A few remarks on the distribution . . . of Queensland plants. 1879. I. 502.
— A few words about the flora of the islands of Torres Straits. 1898. I. 505.
— On the flora of Stradbroke Island. 1882. I. 503.
— Indigenous rubber plant, Excœcaria Dallachyana. 1898. III. 518.[2]
— The Kei apple, Aberia caffra. 1899. III. 614.[1]
— Medicinal plants of Queensland. 1881. III. 94.[1]
— Notes on the vegetation of New Guinea. 1899. I. 499.[2]
— Notes upon some plant specimens. 1892. III. 94.[1]
— Occasional papers on the Queensland flora. 1886. I. 503.
— Official guide to the Museum of economic botany. 1891. I. 69.[2]
— Peculiarities of the phanerogamic flora of Queensland. 1895. I. 504.
— Peculiarities of the Queensland flora. 1895. I. 504.
— Plants reputed poisonous to stock. 1897. III. 94.[2]
— The Queensland flora. 1899. I. 505.
— Queensland woods. 1888. I. 499,[2] IV. 89.[2]
— Queensland woods. Catalogue. 1886. IV. 22.[1]
— Rubber-bearing Fig of Rigo. 1897. II. 153.[1]
— A sketch of the economic plants of Queensland. 1888. III. 94.[1]
— On some of the introduced plants of Queensland. 1880. I. 502.
— A synopsis of the Queensland flora. 1883. I. 503.
— Useful tables for the height of trees. 1882. IV. 215.
— *See also* HILL, Walter & BAILEY, F. M.
— & Gordon, P. R. Plants reputed poisonous and injurious to stock. 1887. III. 94.[1]
— & Keys, James. A contribution towards a flora of Mount Perry. 1885. I. 503.
— & Woods, J. E. TENISON-. A census of the flora of Brisbane. 1880. I. 502.
Bailey, Henry. Management of forest trees. 1849. IV. 120.
— Theory and practice of pruning. 1851. III. 170.
Bailey, John Frederick. Coca, Erythroxylon Coca. Lam. 1897. III. 493.[2]
— Jaborandi, Pilocarpus Jaborandi. 1898. III. 505.[1]
— Lignum vitae, Guaiacum officinale. 1898. III. 494.[2]
— Ngai or Ai Camphor. 1898. III. 755.[1]
— The Papaw, Carica Papaya Linn. 1897. III. 618.[1]
— Plants of the rabbit-infested country, Bulloo River. 1898. I. 505.
— Poisonous weeds in the Springsure district. 1900. III. 94.[2]
— Report on the timber trees of . . . Queensland. 1899. IV. 89.[3] 401.[2]
Bailey, Katherine. The Irish flora. 1833. I. 398.
Bailey, Liberty Hyde. Acclimatization; does it occur? 1887. III. 44.[1]
— Ackermann's Phyllocactus. 1890. III. 625.[2]
— American Grape training. 1893. III. 551.[1]
— American Thorns as ornamental plants. 1906. III. 421.[2]
— An analysis of grafting. 1890. III. 163.[1]
— Annals of horticulture in North America. *See* ANNALS . . . III. 2.
— Apricot growing in western New York. 1894. III. 434.[2]
— The Black Maple. 1888. II. 479.[1]
— Blackberries. 1895. III. 457.[2]
— The bloomless Apple. 1889. III. 425.[2]
— Botany; an elementary text for schools. 1900. I. 93.
— Bud on a Pear stem. 1887. II. 280.[1]
— Cape Cod Cranberries. 1890. III. 663.[2]
— Chippeway plant names. 1887. I. 72.[2]
— Climbers and their uses. 1886. III. 205.[1]
— Cross-breeding and hybridizing. 1892. III. 51.
— The cultivated Chestnuts. 1891. II. 123.[2]
— The cultivated native Plums and Cherries. 1892. III. 430.[2]
— The cultivated Poplars. 1894. III. 344.[2]
— Cyclopedia of American horticulture. 1900. III. 31.
— The Dewberries. 1890. II. 300.[2]
— The Dewberries. 1891. III. 457.[2]
— Electricity and plant-growing. 1894. I. 231.[1]
— Evaporated Raspberries. 1895. III. 458.[1]

Bailey, Liberty Hyde (*continued*).
— Experimental evolution amongst plants. ·1896· I. 248.[1]
— False Shag-bark Hickory. 1890. II. 112.[2]
— Field notes on Apple culture. 1886. III. 426.[2]
— Four new types of fruits. 1893. III. 61.[2]
— The Frost or River-bank Grape. 1893. II. 509.[1]
— The Goumi, Elaeagnus longipes. 1896. III. 629.[1]
— The horticulturist's rule-book. 1889. III. 99.
— Hybridisation in the United States. 1900. III. 51.
— Impressions of the Peach industry. 1894. III. 441.[1]
— The improvement of our native fruits. 1897. I. 248.[1]
— Is grafting a devitalizing process? 1892. I. 208.[2]
— The Japanese Plums in North America. 1894. III. 443.[1]
— The Japanese Walnut. 1890. III. 356.[2]
— Lessons with plants. 1898. I. 92.
— A list of ornamental plants which are hardy in Michigan. 1887. III. 63.[1]
— The long-spurred Thorn. 1890. II. 262.[1]
— Michigan lake shore plants. 1880. II. 97.[1]
— Mulberries. 1892. III. 378.
— The native dwarf Cherries. 1894. III. 432.[1]
— The new American Mulberry. 1890. III. 378.
— The Norway Spruce in Michigan. 1888. III. 305.[1]
— Notes from a garden herbarium. 1890. II. 300.[3]
— Notes from a garden herbarium. 1891. II. 123,[2] 266,[1] III. 432.[1]
— Notions about the spraying of trees. 1895. III. 198.[1]
— The nursery-book. 1891. III. 153.
— Old Cherry trees. 1893. II. 273.[1]
— Our Blackberries and Raspberries. 1890. III. 300.[2]
— Our Elms. 1885. II. 142.[2]
— Peach yellows. 1894. III. 442.[1]
— Peaches and yellows. 1891. III. 442.[1]
— The philosophy of the crossing of plants. 1892. III. 51.
— Piece-roots vs. whole-roots. 1891. III. 164.[1]
— Pines, Hemlocks and Spruces. 1891. III. 291.
— Plant-breeding. 1895. I. 248.[1]
— Plants collected or observed on Hunters' Island. 1887. I. 310.
— Plants collected or observed on the Bluff at Duluth. 1887. I. 325.
— The principles of fruit growing. 1897. III. 134.[1]
— Les Pruniers japonais. 1894. III. 443.[1]
— Prunus hortulana. 1892. II. 274.[1]
— Pyrus ioensis. 1892. II. 268.[1]
— Pyrus nigra Sargent. 1890. III. 419.[2]
— The recent Apple failures of western New York. 1895. III. 428.[1]
— Root-grafting and budding. 1890. III. 163.[1]
— Rules for planting wind-breaks. 1888. III. 215.[1]
— Say's Rose. 1890. III. 298.[2]
— Sketch of the evolution of our native fruits. 1898. I. 248,[1] *III. 68.*[1]
— Sketch of the flora of Vermilion Lake. 1887. I. 325.
— Sketch of the relationship between American and eastern Asian fruits. 1895. III. 61.[1]
— The Soulard Crab and its kin. 1891. II. 266.[1]
— Species of Japanese flowering Cherries. 1891. III. 432.[1]
— A study of the native Plum as now under cultivation. 1892. II. 270.[2]
— A study of windbreaks. 1889. III. 215.[2]
— Suggestions for the planting of shrubbery. 1896. III. 202.[1]
— On the supposed correlations of quality in fruits. 1892. I. 243.[2]
— The survival of the unlike. 1896. I. 248.[1]
— Top-grafting old trees. 1890. III. 163.[1]
— The tree Tomato. 1890. III. 699.[2]
— What a Lilac bush did. 1884. I. 150,[1] *187.*
— *See also* ARTHUR, J. C., BAILEY, L. H. & HOLWAY, E. W. D.; BEACH, S. A. & BAILEY, L. H.; WILLARD, S. D. & BAILEY, L. H.
— & **Powell**, G. H. Cherries. 1895. III. 432.[1]
— & others. Spraying notes. 1900. III. 198.[1]
Bailey, Loring Woart. Epigaea with abnormal flowers. 1868. II. 663.[2]
— The woods of New Brunswick. 1887. IV. 397.[1]
— & **Jack**, Edward. The woods and minerals of New Brunswick. 1876. IV. 76.[2]
Bailey, Nathan. Dictionarium rusticum & urbanicum. 1704. III. 30.
— Dictionarium rusticum urbanicum & botanicum. 1704. III. 30.
Bailey, W. H. Bouvardia Humboldtii corymbiflora. 1876. III. 711.[1]

Bailey, William L. Trees, plants and flowers. 1870. I. 95.
Bailey, William O. Report on the Michigan forest fires. 1882. IV. 182.[1]
Bailey, William Whitman. Aestivation of Mahernia verti- cillata. 1879. II. 536.[1]
— The botanical collector's handbook. 1881. V. VIII,[1]
— Botanizing. 1899. I. 36.[1]
— Crow's Nest Mountain. 1884. I. 315.
— Dimorphism. 1876. II. 810.[1]
— A double Epigaea repens. 1881. II. 663.[2]
— Fission of leaves in the Peach. 1879. II. ·276.[2]
— Ilex with yellow berries. 1882. II. 465.[1]
— New England wild flowers. 1897. ·V. XVII.[1]
— Note on Abutilon striatum. 1887. II. 521.[1]
— Notes on Mahernia. 1884. II. 536.[1] ·
— Notes on the plants found in the Franconia Valley. 1883. I. 315. ·
— Recollections of the West Humboldt Mountains. 1885. I. 325. ·
— A remarkable Orange tree. 1891. I. 207,[2] *III. 498.*[2]
— Among Rhode Island wild flowers. 1895. I. 316.
— Rondeletia (Rogiera) cordata. 1881. II. 830.[3]
— Synspermy in the Horsechestnut. 1884. II. 482.[1]
— Vernation of Carya. 1897. II. 112.[1]
Bailhache, G. *See* RIVIÈRE, Gustave & BAILHACHE, G.
Baillet, C., **Jeanbernat**, Ernest & **Timbal-Lagrave**, Édouard. Une excursion botanique. 1864. V. XXII.[1]
Bailleul, L. L'arboriculture moderne. 1888. III. 144.
Baillie, D. C. A new method of.tree-planting. 1896. III. 166.
Baillie, Edmund James. The city flora. 1878. I. 403.
— The decorative character of Conifers. 1892. III. 291.
— Forest trees for commercial purposes. 1895. IV. 121.
Baillie, William. Report on an instrument for measuring the heights of trees. 1869. IV. 215.
Baillon, Emmanuel. Memoire . . . sur les causes du dé- périssement des bois. 1794.· IV. 282.[2]
— Quelles sont les causes du dépérissement des bois? 1801. IV. 282.[2]
Baillon, Henri Ernest. Sur les affinités des Erythrospermum. 1868. II. 570.[2]
— Sur les affinités des Helwingia. 1877. II. 656.[2]
— Les affinités des Verbénacées. 1890· II.·752.[2]
— Sur les affinités du genre Trisciadia. 1879. II. 814.[1]
— Sur les ailes séminales de certaines Rubiacées. 1876. II. 808,[1] *815,*[2] *851.*[2]
— Sur l'Akania. 1879. II. 484.[1]
— Sur l'Aloès. 1867. III. 333.[1]
— Sur un Amandier à ovules anormaux. 1868. II. 272.[1]
— Anatomie et physiologie végétales. 1882. I. 91.
— Sur l'androcée des Rhizophoracées. 1875. II. 613.[1]
— Anonaceae Mexicanae Liebmannianae. ·1867. II. 215.[1]
— Une Anonacée nouvelle de Madagascar. 1885. II. 219.[1]
— Sur les Anones de l'Afrique. 1887. II. 215.[1]
— Sur les anthères de quelques Apocynacées. 1889. II. 722.[1]
— Anthostemidearum . . . descriptionem . . . tentat. 1858. ·II. 433.[2]
— Sur les Apama. 1886. II. 181.[1]
— Sur l'Apetahi de raiatea. 1882. II. 845.[1]
— Les appendices stipulaires des Leycesteria. 1887. II. 835.[1]
— Sur les Aquilariées des herbiers de la Hollande. 1873. II. 800.[1]
— Sur une Asclépiadacée comestible du Laos. 1889. II. 743.[1]
— Sur les Asimina. 1887. II. 215.[2]
— De Asteropeiae structura et positione. 1886. II. 548.[1]
— Un Ateleia brésilien. 1882. II. 334.[1]
— Balanops. 1871. II. 111.[2]
— Sur les Baobabs de Madagascar. 1890. II. 528.[2]
— Sur le baume de Guatémala. 1880. III. 482.[2]
— Sur une Bixacée à ovaire uniloculaire. 1887. II. 574.[1]
— Le Bonamia de Dupetit-Thouars. 1890. II. 744.[1]
— Sur le Bosqueia. 1862. II. 146.[2]
— Botanical origin of the balsams of Tolu and Péru. 1874. II. 374.[2]
— Broussonetia papyrifera. 1866.· II. 147.[1]
— Sur une Bruyère à gynécée monstrueux. 1860. II. 658.[2]
— Sur une Canellacée de l'ancien continent. 1866. II. 566.[2]
— Sur le Canthopsis. 1879. II. 829.[1]
— Sur les caractères du genre Negria. 1879. II. 795.[1]
— Les caractères . . . du genre Ruscus. 1894. II. 84.[2]
— Sur les caractères généraux des Araliacées. 1878. II. 647.[1]

— Sur les caractères spécifiques des Toluifera. 1874. II. 374.²
— Sur un cas apparent de parthénogenèse. 1864. II. 574.¹
— Sur le Cephaelis ixoraefolia des jardins. 1879. II. 811.¹
— Sur certaines fleurs hermaphrodites du Corylus. 1868. II. 121.¹
— Sur un Chimonanthus à feuilles alternes. 1868. II. 214.²
— Sur des Clématites à préfloraison imbriquée. 1882. II. 196.¹
— Sur le Coffea microcarpa DC. 1879. II. 816.¹
— Constitution du genre Dombeya. 1885. II. 533.¹
— Sur la constitution du genre Paropsia. 1881. II. 572.²
— Sur le Craspidospermum. 1889. II. 725.¹
— Sur le Cremixora. 1880. II. 820.²
— Crescentia nigripes. 1882. III. 704.²
— Sur la culture et la floraison du Dillenia speciosa. 1866. II. 541.²
— Cyrillées. 1860. II. 461.²
— Description d'un nóuveau genre de Tiliacées. 1871. II. 512.¹
— Description d'un nouveau genre . . . des Humiriacées. 1861. II. 393.²
— Description du genre Longetia. 1865. II. 446.²
— Description du nouveau genre Brandzeia. 1868. II. 337.¹
— Description du nouveau genre Grisollea. 1863. II. 474.²
— Sur deux Artocarpées anormales. 1880. II. 572.¹
— Sur deux cas de monstruosités. 1880. II. 710.¹
— Sur deux Euphorbiacées brésiliennes. 1865. II. 434.¹
— Sur deux genres de Moniniacées. 1871. II. 221.¹
— Sur deux genres . . . des Ménispermées. 1867. II. 206.¹
— Sur les deux genres Potameia et Dilobeia. 1868. II. 227.²
— Sur deux nouveaux genres apétales. 1871. II. 111,² 614.²
— Deux nouveaux types de Loranthacées. 1892. II. 170,¹ 177.²
— Développement de la fleur des Sterculiées. 1871. II. 531.⁶
— Développement de la fleur femelle du Sarcobatus. 1887. II. 188.²
— Sur le développement des feuilles des Carapa. 1874. II. 420.¹
— Sur le développement des ovules des Pyrus. 1876. II. 278.²
— Sur le développement et les affinités des Olinia. 1876. II. 599.²
— Développement et structure des feuilles du Copaifera. 1882. II. 347.²
— Dichapetaleae. 1886. II. 432.²
— Dictionnaire de botanique. 1876. I. 34.
— Sur le Didierea. 1880. II. 485.¹
— Les Didierea de Madagascar. 1895. II. 485.²
— Didierea madagascariensis. 1880. II. 485.²
— Sur une différence fondamentale entre . . . Bauhiniées et . . . Amherstiées. 1869. II. 220.²
— Le Dilobeia femelle. 1883. II. 160.¹
— Divisions du genre Amphitecna. 1883. II. 785.¹
— Sur l'écorce dite de Josse. 1879. II. 823.¹
— Emendanda. 1881. I. 271.¹
— Sur l'émission des tubes polliniques des Helianthemum. 1861. II. 565.¹
— Énumération des Euphorbiacées cultivées dans les jardins botaniques de Paris. 1800. II. 400.⁹
— Épacridées. 1860. II. 688.¹
— Errorum Decaisneanorum . . . centuria. 1879. I. 270.
— Essai sur les lois de l'entraînement dans les végétaux. 1876. II. 560.
— Étude botanique de l'Hazigne. 1884. II. 558.¹
— Étude des Prestonia. 1889. II. 731.¹
— Étude générale du groupe des Euphorbiacées. 1858. II. 433,² 434.²
— Étude sur les Actephila australiens. 1865. II. 435.²
— Étude sur les Connaracées de l'Afrique tropicale. 1867. II. 316.²
— Étude sur le Copaifera. 1877. II. 347.²
— Étudesorganogéniques . . . de Byttnériacées. 1861. II. 531.²
— Études sur l'herbier du Gabon. 1864. I. 490.
— Études sur la structure . . . des Philésiacées. 1860. II. 77.²
— Examen des genres . . . des Antidesmées. 1857. II. 433.²
— Expériences physiologiques sur l'enroulement des vrilles d'une Ampélidée. 1887. II. 503.¹
— De la famille des Aurantiacées. 1855. II. 397.¹

— Les feuilles anormales des Codiaeum. 1888. II. 438.²
— Sur la fleur femelle du Muscadier. 1864. II. 220.²
— Les fleurs de l'Anisacanthus virgularis. 1890. II. 797.¹
— Les fleurs du Saccllium [sic] lanceolatum. 1890. II. 751.²
— Sur les fleurs et les fruits des Napoleona. 1875. II. 612.²
— Les fleurs mâles du Podoon. 1889. II. 456.¹
— Sur des fleurs monstrueuses de Sassafras. 1868. II. 228.¹
— Sur la floraison d'un Livistona australis. 1864. II. 70.¹
— Sur le fruit d'une nouvelle Chlaenacée. 1871. II. 511.¹
— Le fruit des Osteospermum. 1881. II. 862.²
— Le fruit du Durian. 1883. II. 530.¹
— Le fruit du Santalina. 1890. II. 831.¹
— Sur les Gaertnera. 1879. II. 817.¹
— Sur un Gaertnera de l'Afrique tropicale occidentale. 1880. II. 817.¹
— La gamopétalie et les fleurs doubles. 1881. I. 145.²
— Le Garcinia Balansae. 1890. II. 555.¹
— Genera Euphorbiacea tria nova. 1860. II. 422,² 445,¹ 451.¹
— De genere novo Ficrella. 1871. II. 415.¹
— Generum novorum quatuor descriptio. 1860. II. 433.²
— Le genre Amblyocalyx. 1883. II. 724.¹
— Sur le genre Arthroclianthus. 1868. II. 333.¹
— Sur le genre Bruea. 1866. II. 147.¹
— Sur un genre de Magnoliacées. 1866. II. 214.¹
— Sur le genre de Passifloracées Tetrastylis. 1885. II. 580.¹
— Sur le genre Dobera. 1871. II. 473.¹
— Le genre Humblotia. 1886. II. 445.²
— Sur le genre Kaleniczenkia. 1868. II. 337.¹
— Sur le genre Makokoa. 1886. II. 604.²
— Du genre Nettoa. 1865. II. 514.²
— Le genre Newtonia. 1888. II. 374.²
— Sur le genre Pierardia. 1863. II. 437.²
— Le genre Ramisia. 1887. II. 192.¹
— Sur le genre Thelyra. 1867. II. 269.¹
— Sur le genre Tribeles. 1885. II. 247.¹
— Sur les genres australiens . . . des Rubiacées. 1879. II. 808.¹
— Sur les genres Chasmanthera et Jateorhiza. 1868. II. 206,² 807.²
— Les genres de Cassini Glycideras et Henricia. 1880. II. 858.¹
— Sur les genres Eulobus, Cienkowskia. 1877. II. 456,¹ 748.¹
— The genus Copaifera. 1877. II. 347.¹
— Sur une gousse chinoise de Shangai. 1875. II. 363.¹
— Sur les gousses chinoises de Shang-Hai. 1875. II. 363.¹
— Sur les graines des Diervilla. 1879. II. 834.²
— Sur les graines du Bouchardatia. 1868. II. 400.²
— Sur le groupe des Tacazzées. 1889. II. 743.¹
— Guide de l'étudiant au . . . jardin botanique de la Faculté de médecine de Paris. 1865. I. 58.
— Sur gynéocées monstrueux d'un Kalmia latifolia. 1880. II. 672.²
— Les herborisations parisiennes. 1890. I. 417.
— De l'hermaphroditisme accidentel chez les Euphorbiacées. 1857. II. 434.²
— L'hermaphroditisme apparent de certains Kadsura. 1882. II. 210.²
— Histoire des plantes. 1867. I. 261.
— Sur l'histologie des Dilléniacées. 1867. II. 540.²
— Sur l'Hoûna-hoûna de Madagascar. 1881. II. 571.²
— Homea madagascariensis. 1882. II. 571.²
— Humiriacées. 1861. II. 393.²
— Iconographie de la flore française. 1885. I. 417.
— Sur l'Imantina. 1879. II. 823.²
— Les inflorescences localisées. 1888. I. 113.²
— Sur les Jaborandi. 1875. II. 409,² III. 504.²
— Le jardin botanique de la Faculté de médecine de Paris. 1884. I. 59.
— Sur le Lepipogon. 1884. II. 522.¹
— Sur les limites du genre Amaioua. 1879. II. 809.¹
— Sur les limites du genre Barbacenia. 1894. II. 90.¹
— Sur les limites du genre Cephaloeroton. 1864. II. 438.¹
— Sur les limites du genre Genista. 1882. II. 359.¹
— Sur les limites du genre Guettarda. 1876. II. 819.¹
— Sur les limites du genre Ixora. 1876. II. 820.¹
— Liste des plantes de Madagascar. 1882. I. 496.
— Sur un Lysinema monstrueux. 1890. II. 690.¹
— Mémoire sur la famille des Anonacées. 1867. II. 215.¹
— Mémoire sur la famille des Magnoliacées. 1866. II. 208.²
— Mémoire sur le développement du fruit des Morées. 1860. II. 145.²
— Mémoire sur les genres Canthium et Hypobathrum. 1876. II. 820,² 827.¹

Baillon, Henri Ernest *(continued).*
— Mémoire sur les Loranthacées. 1861. II. 172.[1]
— Mémoire sur les ovules des Protéacées. 1868. II. 158.[1]
— Mémoire sur les Uragoga. 1876. II. 828.[1]
— Sur une Ménispermacée à carpelles nombreux. 1868. II. 206,[1] *205.*[2]
— Sur le Microsplenium. 1879. II. 833.[2]
— Modifications de la caractéristique des Muscadiers. 1884. II. 220.[2]
— Monographie des Buxacées. 1859. II. 452.[2]
— Monographie des Phyllanthus. 1860. II. 449.[1]
— Monographie des Rosacées. 1867. II. 255.[2]
— Sur le Monotheca. 1891. II. 700.[1]
— Des mouvements dans les organes sexuels des végétaux. 1856. I. 197,[2] *199.*
— Sur les mouvements des anthères des Pyrolées. 1877. II. 657.[1]
— The natural history of plants. 1867. I. 261.
— Sur la nature axile des ovaires infères. 1895. I. 118.[1]
— Sur le Neolindenia. 1890. II. 801.[2]
— Note sur l'Atamisquea. 1871. II. 229.[2]
— Note sur l'organisation florale du Greyia Sutherlandi. 1891. II. 491.[2]
— Note sur le Berberidopsis corallina. 1879. III. 614.[1]
— Note sur le Burasaia Dup.-Th. 1861. II. 206.[2]
— Note sur le Canotia. 1871. II. 465.[2]
— Note sur le Pancovia (W.). 1868. II. 486.[1]
— Note sur le Rigiostachys. 1871. II. 415.[1]
— Note sur le Rosa microphylla. 1871. II. 296.[1]
— Note sur le Spiraeopsis. 1871. II. 250.[2]
— Note sur les fleurs des Schizandrées. 1862. II. 208.[2]
— Note sur les fruits . . . de l'Anona Cherimolia. 1869. II. 216.[1]
— Note sur les ovules des Ternstroemiacées. 1871. II. 547.[2]
— Note sur les Storckiella. 1868. II. 385.[2]
— Note sur quelques Xylopia africains. 1863. II. 219.[2]
— Note sur une nouvelle espèce du genre Sorocea. 1860. II. 155.[2]
— Note sur une production anomale chez les Podocarpus. 1859. II. 9.[2]
— Notes sur les Bixacées. 1871. II. 565.[2]
— Notes sur les Crescentiées. 1887. II. 784.[1]
— Notes sur les Plombaginées. 1891. II. 696.[1]
— Notes sur les Tiliacées. 1871. II. 512.[1]
— Notice sur les titres scientifiques. 1894. V. vii.[1]
— Sur un nouveau Baillonia. 1890. II. 753.[1]
— Sur un nouveau Bosqueia. 1867. II. 146.[2]
— Sur un nouveau Brongniartia. 1868. II. 337.[2]
— Un nouveau Cinnamodendron. 1882. II. 566.[2]
— Sur un nouveau Didierea. 1895. II. 485.[2]
— Le nouveau genre Anisocycla. 1893. II. 206.[2]
— Sur le nouveau genre Bernieria. 1884. II. 223.[2]
— Sur le nouveau genre Bouchardatia. 1866. II. 400.[2]
— Du nouveau genre Ctenodon. 1868. II. 330.[1]
— Sur un nouveau genre d'Anonacées. 1868. II. 219.[1]
— Sur un nouveau genre de la famille des Myrtacées. 1861. II. 633.[2]
— Sur un nouveau genre de Saxifragacées. 1879. II. 238.[2]
— Le nouveau genre Grevellina. 1894. II. 422.[2]
— Sur le nouveau genre Lanessania. 1875. II. 153.[2]
— Sur le nouveau genre Leioclusia. 1880. II. 557.[2]
— Sur le nouveau genre Maxwellia. 1871. II. 530.[1]
— Sur le nouveau genre Oncotheca. 1891. II. 869.[2]
— Sur un nouveau genre Payera. 1878. II. 826.[1]
— Le nouveau genre Periestes. 1890. II. 802.[1]
— Sur le nouveau genre Poissonia. 1868. II. 378.[2]
— Sur un nouveau genre polyandre de Ménispermacées. 1871. II. 208.[1]
— Le nouveau genre Siphocolea. 1887. II. 790.[2]
— Sur le nouveau genre Solenixora. 1880. II. 831.[2]
— Sur le nouveau genre Sphenostemon. 1875. II. 465.[1]
— Sur le nouveau genre Thiersia. 1876. II. 832.[1]
— Un nouveau mode de monoecie du Papayer. 1887. II. 582.[2]
— Sur un nouveau Plocosperma. 1880. II. 719.[2]
— Sur un nouveau Strychnos. 1880. II. 720.[1]
— Sur un nouveau Thenardia du Mexique. 1890. II. 730.[1]
— Un nouveau type aberrant, de Madagascar. 1884. II. 240.[1]
— Un nouveau type apérianthé. 1887. II. 456.[1]
— Un nouveau type de Caesalpiniées monopétales. 1884. II. 332.[2]
— Sur un nouveau type de Rubiacées. 1879. II. 832.[1]
— Sur un nouveau type de Saxifragacées. 1879. II. 238.[2]

— Un nouveau type réduit de Portulacées. 1886. II. 194.[1]
— Sur les nouveaux arbres à Caoutchouc. 1885. II. 444.[1]
— Les nouveaux Caféiers des Comores. 1885. II. 814.[1]
— Sur un nouvel exemple de monoecie du Coelebogyne. 1874. II. 436.[2]
— Sur un nouvel Eysenhardtia. 1868. II. 358.[1]
— Sur un nouvel usage du Redoul. 1880. III. 523.[2]
— Sur une nouvelle Mappiée. 1879. II. 476.[1]
— Sur une nouvelle Mappiée du Congo. 1892. II. 474.[1]
— Nouvelles notes sur les Hamamélidées. 1871. II. 252.
— Nouvelles observations sur les Aquilariées. 1873. II. 600.[1]
— Nouvelles observations sur les Chlénacées. 1886. II. 511.[2]
— Nouvelles observations sur les Euphorbiacées. 1873. II. 433.[2]
— Nouvelles observations sur les Olinia. 1878. II. 599.[2]
— Nouvelles observations sur les plantes du curare. 1876. II. 719.[2]
— Nouvelles recherches sur la fleur femelle des Conifères. 1864. II. 19.
— Observations relatives aux crêtes de glace. 1870. I. 212;
— Observations sur l'anatomie des Dilléniacées. 1868. II. 540.[2]
— Observations sur l'Antholma. 1861. II. 509.[2]
— Observations sur l'Euphorbia paucifolia. 1860. II. 438.[1]
— Observations sur le genre Canotia. 1878. II. 463.[2]
— Observations sur le Myosurandra. 1868. II. 251.[1]
— Observations sur le Tapiscia. 1895. II. 473.[2]
— Observations sur les affinités du genre Barbeuia. 1862. II. 192.[2]
— Observations sur les affinités du Macarisia. 1862. II. 613,[1] *613.*[2]
— Observations sur les Gesnériacées. 1888. II. 792.[2]
— Observations sur les Légumineuses-Papilionacées. 1868. II. 352,[2] 364.[2]
— Observations sur les limites . . . des Célastracées. 1873. II. 465.[2]
— Observations sur les Monimiacées. 1868. II. 221.[2]
— Observations sur les Nauclées. 1876. II. 807.[1]
— Observations sur les Rutacées. 1871. II. 397.[1]
— Observations sur les Sapotacées de la Nouvelle-Calédonie. 1890. II. 696.[2]
— Sur un Ochrocarpus anormal de Madagascar. 1876. II. 558.[1]
— Olacineae Phytocreneae. 1873. II. 170.[2]
— Sur les organes sexuels d'un Chrysopia. 1882. II. 558.[1]
— Sur l'organisation de l'Olostyla. 1885. II. 814.[1]
— Sur l'organisation des Humbertia. 1889. II. 745.[1]
— Sur l'organisation du fruit de l'Arbre à pain. 1863. II. 146.[1]
— Sur l'organisation . . . du genre Morinda. 1879. II. 823.[2]
— Sur l'organisation . . . du genre Pterostemon. 1868. II. 243.[1]
— Sur l'organisation et les affinités des Axinandra. 1877. II. 636.[1]
— Sur l'organisation et les affinités du Jackia. 1878. II. 821.[2]
— Sur l'organisation florale d'un Wormia. 1866. II. 543.[2]
— Sur l'organisation florale du Condalia. 1868. II. 494.[1]
— Organogenic researches on the female flower of the Coniferae. 1860. II. 19.
— Organogénie florale d'un Cedrela. 1895. II. 420.[2]
— Organogénie florale des Amentacées. 1872. II. 121.[1]
— Organogénie florale des Cordiacées. 1892. II. 747.[2]
— Sur l'organogénie florale . . . des Garrya. 1877. II. 110.[2]
— Organogénie florale des Garrya. 1878. II. 110.[2]
— Organogénie florale des Illicium. 1865. II. 210.[1]
— Sur l'organogénie florale des Jussieua. 1858. II. 645.[2]
— Organogénie florale des Moringa. 1869. II. 234.[2]
— Organogénie florale des Papayées. 1879. II. 582.[1]
— Sur l'organogénie florale des Podocarpus. 1874. II. 9.[1]
— Organogénie florale du Pleurandra. 1862. II. 541.[2]
— Sur l'organogénie florale du Triphasia trifoliata. 1858. II. 411.[2]
— L'orientation de la fleur des Passiflores. 1885. II. 577.[1]
— Organogénie florale des Badianes. 1867. II. 209.[2]
— Sur l'origine de la pulpe . . . du fruit des Courbarils. 1876. II. 364.[2]
— Sur l'origine des baumes de Tolu. 1874. III. 482.[1]
— Sur l'origine du macis de la Muscade. 1874. II. 220.[2]
— L'ovule des Acokanthera. 1888. II. 722.[2]

— Les ovules des Corylopsis. 1894. II. 252.²
— Sur les ovules des Cyrillées. 1878. II. 461.²
— Sur les ovules des Gardneria. 1878. II. 718.²
— Les ovules des Oléacées. 1882. II. 705.²
— Les ovules des Peupliers. 1887. II. 96.²
— Les Palmiers malgaches à petites fleurs. 1894. II. 62.¹
— Sur le Paragenipa. 1879. II. 825.²
— Sur le Patagus. 1871. II. 165.¹
— Le Pentanura du Yunnan. 1889. II. 741,¹ 742.²
— Les Phelline de la Nouvelle-Calédonie. 1891. II. 465.¹
— Sur le Picraenia excelsa. 1875. III. 508.¹
— Sur un pied fleuri de Picraena excelsa. 1875. II. 415.¹
— Sur les Pilocarpus dits Jaborandi. 1878. II. 409.²
— Sur les Pittosporum à ovules définis. 1880. II. 248.¹
— La place des Connaracées dans la classification. 1894. II. 316.²
— La place du Minquartia d'Aublet. 1886. II. 171.¹
— Sur les Platycarpum. 1879. II. 826.¹
— Sur le Plectaneia. 1888. II. 730.¹
— Sur le Pleurocoffea. 1880. II. 827.¹
— La plus longue fleur de la famille des Légumineuses. 1883. II. 335.¹
— Sur plusieurs Acanthacées à fleurs involucrées. 1890. II. 796.¹
— Sur le Podophania. 1880. II. 863.²
— Sur une poire monstrueuse. 1879. . II. 280.¹
— Sur le poison de Cay-Chui. 1878. III. 366.²
— Sur un Polycardia nouveau. 1881. II. 471.¹
— Sur la position des Chloranthacées. 1871. II. 95.¹
— Sur la position des Geissoloma. 1874. II. 599.¹
— Sur la préfloraison de la corolle dans les Rubiacées. 1878. II. 808.²
— Sur la préfloraison des étamines. 1855. I. 116.¹
— Première [et deuxième] étude sur les Mappiées. 1862. II. 474.¹
— La prétendue adhérence du nucelle des Conifères. 1892. II. 19.
— Les primefeuilles des Noyers. 1886. II. 113.¹
— Sur une Protéacée et une Laurinée polycarpellées. 1861. II. 163,² 222.¹
— Sur le Psiloxylon. 1871. II. 573.¹
— Sur le Quapoya scandens Aubl. 1876. II. 558.²
— Sur les Quararibea. 1871. II. 531.¹
— Sur quelques affinités des Erythropalum. 1892. II. 171,¹ 704.²
— Sur quelques Euphorbiacées ornementales. 1865. II. 433.²
— Sur quelques genres de Rubiacées. 1879. II. 807.¹
— Sur quelques Gynopogon néo-calédoniens. 1889. II. 723.²
— Sur quelques Loganiacées néo-calédoniennes. 1880. II. 719.¹
— Sur quelques Melodinus néo-calédoniens. 1889. II. 728.²
— Sur quelques Geniostoma. 1880. II. 719.¹
— Quelques nouveaux types de la flore du Congo. 1890. I. 492.¹
— Sur quelques Ourouparia. 1879. II. 832.²
— Sur quelques plantes à curare. 1880. II. 719.²
— Sur quelques types anomaux d'Acanthacées. 1890. II. 796.¹
— Une question de nomenclature à propos des Bignonia. 1888. II. 785.²
— Sur les rapports des Hamiltonia. 1879. II. 819.²
— Les rapports du Podocon et du Dobinea. 1890. II. 456.¹
— Recherches histologiques sur la moelle . . . 'des Magnoliacées. 1867. II. 209.¹
— Recherches nouvelles sur les Araliées. 1876. II. 646,¹ 652.¹
— Recherches organogéniques sur la fleur . . . de l'Arceuthobium. 1877. II. 174.²
— Recherches organogéniques sur la fleur femelle des Conifères. 1860. II. 19.
— Recherches organogéniques sur les Amentacées. 1876. I. 524.¹
— Recherches organogéniques sur les Eupomatia. 1868. II. 217.²
— Recherches sur l'Aucuba. 1864. II. 654.¹
— Recherches sur l'organisation . . . des Caprifoliacées. 1860. II. 833.²
— Recherches sur l'organisation . . . des Éricoidées. 1860. II. 658.²
— Recherches sur l'organisation des Euphorbiacées. 1858. II. 434.¹
— Recherches sur l'organisation . . . des Salvadorées. 1868. II. 472.²

— Recherches sur l'organogénie florale des Corylées. 1873. II. 115.¹
— Recherches sur l'organogénie florale des Noisetiers. 1873. II. 121.²
— Recherches sur le développement de la Châtaigne. 1876. II. 124.²
— Recherches sur le développement du fruit des Morées. 1850. II. 145.²
— Recherches sur le groupe des Chaillétiées. 1874. II. 432.
— Recherches sur le Ravensara. 1868. II. 227.²
— Recherches sur les ovules des Evonymus. 1858. II. 467.
— Reconstitution de la famille des Boraginacées. 1890. II. 747.²
— Sur le Reiné-ala et ses usages. 1885. II. 529.¹
— Remarques générales sur les Phyllanthées. 1861. II. 449.¹
— Remarques sur l'organisation des Berbéridées. 1861. II. 201.²
— Remarques sur l'organisation florale de . . . Bruniacées. 1862. II. 170,¹ 251.²
— Remarques sur le genre Thenardia. 1888. II. 733.¹
— Remarques sur les Dilléniacées. 1865. II. 540.¹
— Remarques sur les Ternstroemiacées. 1887. II. 547.²
— Remarques sur quelques Mostuea. 1880. II. 719.¹
— Remarques sur une nouvelle . . . Menarda. 1861. II. 449.¹
— Sur le retour à l'état complet des étamines dans les fleurs anormales de Berberis. 1879. II. 202.¹
— Révision des Acacia médicinaux. 1863. II. 322,¹ III. 463.²
— Révision des Aristoloches médicinaux. 1867. II. 181.¹
— Les Ropalocarpées. 1883. II. 573.¹
— Sur une Rose de l'Anjou. 1881. II. 291.²
— Le Santal de Madagascar. 1890. II. 831.¹
— Sur un Saule à placentas uniovulés. 1884. II. 107.²
— Les Scépacées doivent-elles constituer un ordre. 1857. II. 433.²
— Sur la section Torquearia du genre Genipa. 1882. II. 813.²
— Sur la signification des diverses parites de l'ovule. 1877. I. 122.
— Species Euphorbiacearum; Euphorbiacée Neo-Caledonicae. 1861. II. 434.¹
— Species Euphorbiacearum; Euphorbiacées africaines. 1860. II. 434.¹
— Species Euphorbiacearum; Euphorbiacées américaines. 1863. II. 434.¹
— Species Euphorbiacearum; Euphorbiacées australiennes. 1865. II. 434.¹
— Species Euphorbiacearum; recherches complémentaires. 1866. II. 434.²
— Sur les stipules des Fuchsia à feuilles alternes. 1880. II. 643.¹
— Sur les stipules des Onagrariées. 1880. II. 642.²
— Stirpes exoticae novae. 1867. I. 270.
— Stirpes exoticae novae. 1873. II. 412.²
— Sur le Strophanthus hispidus. 1890. II. 732.¹
— Sur un Strychnos anormal de Delagoa. 1880. II. 720.²
— Le support des fleurs femelles des Cycadacées. 1885. II. 3.¹
— Sur la symétrie florale des Trigoniées. 1873. II. 428.¹
— Sur le Taluha au hombé de Madagascar. 1891. II. 967.¹
— Sur le Tanghin de Ménabé. 1890. II. 741.¹
— Termes usuels appliqués aux arbres. 1877. I. 74.¹
— Sur le Tetracera de l'Afrique orientale. 1866. II. 543.¹
— Sur les Toluifera. 1874. II. 374.²
— Traité de botanique médicale. 1884. II. 59.¹
— Traité du développement de la fleur et du fruit. 1868. I. 100.¹
— Traité du développement de la fleur et du fruit — Hydrocharidées — Garryacées — Loranthées. 1876. II. 110.³
— Sur la tribu des Labordiées. 1880. II. 719.¹
— Le Tripinna de Loureiro. 1888. II. 761.¹
— Sur trois Stephanotis néo-calédoniens. 1889. II. 742.²
— Types nouveaux d'Apocynacées. 1888. II. 721.²
— Types nouveaux de la flore malgache. 1890. II. 869.²
— Sur l'Uragoga lycioides. 1879. II. 828.¹
— Sur le Vacacoua de Madagascar. 1880. II. 720.²
— Sur la valeur de genre Herminiera. 1883. II. 330.¹
— De la valeur . . . des étamines pour la classification des Anonacées. 1883. II. 215.³
— Sur la valeur du genre Rhyssocarpus. 1883. II. 823.¹.
— Sur le véritable organisation du Buis. 1856. II. 452.²
— Sur le véritable Piptocoma. 1880. II. 863.³

Baillon, Henri Ernèst (continued).
— Sur la Vigne d'Alfissach. 1890. II. 507.[1]
— Sur le Vouacapou de la Guyane. 1868. II. 332.[2]
— Sur le Vouacapou de la Guyane. 1870. II. 332.[2]
— Sur un Wunderlichia du Brésil. 1881. II. 868.[2]
— Du Xanthocercis. 1868. II. 389.[1]
— Les Xylolaena et la valeur . . . des Chlénacées. 1884. II. 512.[1]
— Sur les Zuccagnia de la flore du Chili. 1868. II. 389.[1]
— See also WITTMACK, Ludwig & BAILLON, Henri.
Baillon, J. See KRALIK, Louis & BAILLON, J.
— & Drake de Castillo, Emmanuel. Histoire naturelle des plantes [de Madagascar]. 1886. I. 496.
Baillon, J. F. Emmanuel. Quelles sont les causes du dépérissement des bois? 1791. IV. 121.
Bailly. Le Wigandia de Caracas. 1859. III. 695.[1]
Bailly, Charles François. De l'incision annulaire. 1825. III. 174.[2]
— Manuel complet . . . du jardinier. 1824. III. 113.
Bailly, Edmond Constant Marie. Contribution à l'étude du Strophantus. 1888. III. 690.[2]
Bailly, Ém. L'Abies cephalonica robusta. 1889. III. 296.[1]
— Sur l'Abies insignis. 1893. II. 22.[2]
— Abies insignis et Abies Nordmanniana. 1890. III. 295.[3]
— Le Biota meldensis. 1889. III. 311.[3]
— Bouture en écusson. 1860. III. 158.
— Calycanthe précoce à fleurs jaunes. 1861. III. 401.[1]
— Les Cèdres du Liban . . . près Gien. 1891. II. 28.[2]
— Culture des Conifères. 1894. III. 293.
— Sur la culture des Mûriers. 1850. III. 376.
— Effets produits par l'hiver 1890–91. 1891. III. 49,[1] 293.
— Essais de greffe sur vieux arbres. 1857. III. 161.
— Les forêts des Vosges à travers les âges. 1893. IV. 27.[2]
— Hybride d'Abies Pinsapo et d'Abies cephalonica. 1889. III. 296.[1]
— Pseudotsuga glaucescens. 1895. II. 49.[1]
— Du rôle protecteur du feuillage chez les Conifères. 1894. II. 21.[1]
— Le Thuiopsis Standishii. 1896. II. 52.[2]
— Trois Conifères nouvelles remarquables. 1889. III. 291.
— Sur une variété . . . du Sapin de Céphalonie. 1888. III. 296.[1]
— Vermehrung durch Knospen in der Rinde. 1860. III. 158.
Bailly de Merlieux, C., Bixio, Alexandre & Malepeyre. Maison rustique du 19. siècle. See MALEPEYRE, (sr.). 1837. IV. 98.[2]
Bain. Du Mûrier et du ver à soie en Touraine. 1838. III. 375.
Bain, A. A Cocoanut analysis. 1900. II. 67.[2]
Bain, John. Ueber ein erfolgreiches Experiment mit einem Drachenbaum. 1849. III. 336.[1]
— On a successful experiment with the Dragoon tree. 1849. III. 336.[1]
Bain, Samuel M. Some experiments with fungicides. 1895. III. 198.[1]
Bainbridge, George. On an instance of fructification in a staminiferous plant, Carica Papaya. 1886. II. 582.[2]
Baines, Henry. The flora of Yorkshire. 1840. I. 399.
Baines, Thomas. Autumn tints. 1874. III. 207.[1]
— Bignonia venusta. 1882. III. 707.[1]
— Clematiseae. 1881. III. 389.[1]
— Clerodendron squamatum. 1881. III. 696.[3]
— The Clerodendrons. 1877. III. 696.[1]
— Clerodendrons. 1883. III. 696.[1]
— Les Clérodendrons. 1883. III. 696.[1]
— Cutting down Arbutus unedo. 1879. III. 647.[2]
— Decorative trees. 1882. III. 203.
— Dipladenia profusa. 1881. III. 688.[1]
— The Dipladenias. 1875. III. 687.[1]
— Double variety of Jasminum Sambac. 1881. III. 673.[1]
— Dracaenas. 1884. III. 334.[2]
— Eastnor Castle, Ledbury. 1878. II. 28,[1] III. 308.[3]
— Erica obbata. 1878. III. 651.[1]
— Eurya japonica variegata. 1875. II. 548.[2]
— A few good wall shrubs. 1886. III. 205.[1]
— Franciseeas and their culture. 1877. III. 698.[2]
— Franciseeas and their culture. 1883. III. 698.[1]
— Les Franciséas et leur culture. 1883. III. 698.[2]
— Die Franciseeen und ihre Cultur. 1883. III. 698.[3]
— Handcross Park. 1880. III. 336.[1]
— Hedges. 1880. III. 214.[1]
— Hexacentris mysorensis. 1883. III. 710.[2]
— Horizontal extension of tree-roots. 1879. I. 188.

— Ixoras. 1878. III. 745.[1]
— Kentia Canterburyana. 1877. III. 326.[1]
— Levens Hall, Westmoreland. 1874. III. 202.[2]
— Lopping deciduous trees. 1879. III. 173.[1]
— Mussaenda frondosa. 1878. III. 746.[1]
— Planting for autumnal effects. 1874. III. 207.[1]
— Pritchardia grandis. 1877. III. 326.[1]
— Quality of Wellingtonia timber. 1879. IV. 484.[1]
— Renovating coniferous trees. 1885. III. 292.
— Rondeletia speciosa major. 1883. III. 747.[1]
— The Scarlet Mitre-flower. 1877. III. 708.[1]
— Stephanotis floribunda. 1880. III. 694.[1]
— Stove Palms. 1883. III. 317.
— Street trees. 1876. III. 209.
— Theophrastas. 1872. III. 665.[2]
— Tortworth Court. 1880. II. 125.[1]
— Toxicophlæa Thunbergi. 1883. III. 686.[1]
— Transplanting evergreens. 1883. III. 169.[1]
— Trees that thrive in indifferent soil. 1878. III. 41.[1]
— The variegated Javanese Screw Pine. 1873. III. 314.[1]
— Varieties of Epiphyllum truncatum. 1878. III. 623.[1]
— What and when to plant. 1884. III. 294.[3]
Baird, Spencer Fullerton. Contributions towards a catalogue of the trees . . . of Cumberland county. 1844. I. 312.
La baisse du revenu des forêts. 1897. IV. 259.[2]
Bajer. Handbuch der badischen Forstverwaltung. 1842. IV. 289.[2]
— Handbuch des badischen Forst- und Jagdrechts. 1838. IV. 317.[1]
Bake, H. W. A. van den WALL. See WALL BAKE, H. W. A. van den.
Bake, W. A. Over het bewaren van het hout door middel van bijtend kwik. 1837. IV. 417.
Baker, Edmund Gilbert. Catalogue of plants collected [in British East Africa]. 1896. I. 493.
— On a new form of Rosa tomentosa Woods. 1892. II. 299.[3]
— New Somaliland polypetalae. 1898. I. 490.
— A new tree Senecio from tropical Africa. 1894. II. 865.[2]
— Notes on Guttiferae. 1894. II. 552.[2]
— Notes on Malvaviscus. 1899. II. 525.[2]
— Notes on Thespesia. 1897. II. 528.[1]
— An officinal Aloe from central Madagascar. 1882. III. 333.[2]
— Rhodesian Polypetalae. 1899. I. 495.
— Synopsis of genera and species of Malveae. 1890. II. 519.[1]
— Tilia cordata Mill. 1898. II. 517.[1]
— Two old American types. 1898. II. 514.[2]
— See also BRITTEN, James & BAKER, E. G.; ROSE, J. N. & BAKER, E. G.; SCHÖNLAND, Selmar & BAKER, E. G.
— & Rendle, A. B. New African plants. 1896. I. 489.
— & others. Botany. 1900. I. 481.[2]
Baker, Edward. Facts . . . illustrative of the tanghen. 1833. III. 691.[1]
Baker, Floyd P. & Furnas, R. W. Preliminary report on the forestry of the Mississippi valley. 1883. IV. 340.
Baker, H. C. Experiments on the strength and elasticity of Indian woods. 1833. IV. 409.
— List of specimens of wood from India. 1836. IV: 17.
Baker, Henry. Het mikroskop. 1778. I. 36.[1]
— Nuttig gebruik van het mikroskop. 1770. I. 36.[1]
Baker, John Gilbert. Agave paucifolia Baker. 1878. II. 89.[2]
— Agaves and arborescent Liliaceae. 1892. III. 333.[1]
— Aloe aurantiaca, n. sp. 1892. II. 78.[1]
— Aloe (Eualoe) penduliflora. 1888. II. 78.[1]
— Aloe heteracantha. 1894. II. 78.[2]
— Aloe Lynchii × Baker. 1881. II. 78.[1]
— Aloe (Pachidendron) chloroleuca. 1877. II. 78.[1]
— Aloe (Pachidendron) drepanophylla. 1875. II. 78.[2]
— Aloe (Pachidendron) platylepis. 1877. II. 79.[1]
— Barbacenia squamata. 1890. II. 90.[1]
— On the botanical origin of Roses. 1875. III. 454.[1]
— British Roses. 1871. II. 285.[1]
— A classification of garden Roses. 1885. II. 282.[2]
— Classified list of . . . Apicra and Haworthia. 1879. II. 79,[1] 83.[2]
— Compositae. 1873. II. 849.[1]
— Connaraceæ et Ampelideæ. 1871. II. 316,[2] 501.[2]
— A contribution to the flora of North China. 1884. I. 459.
— Contributions to the flora of central Madagascar. 1882. I. 496.
— Contributions to the flora of Madagascar. 1884. I. 496.

— On Dasylirion and Beaucarnea. 1872. II. *81,*[1] 84.[1]
— Descriptions of three new Brasilian Vernoniaceae. 1875. II. 849.[1]
— On Dracaena and Cordyline. 1872 (1873). II. 79,[3] *81.*[2]
— Dracaena Godseffiana. 1894. II. 82.[2]
— Elementary lessons in botanical geography. 1875. I. 300.
— Essai d'une classification des Rosiers. 1885. II. 282.[2]
— False Sisal of Florida. 1892. II. 89.[1]
— A few remarks on the genus Rosa. 1889. II. 283.[1]
— Flora of Aldabra Islands. 1894. I. 482.
— On the flora of Madagascar. 1881. I. 496.
— Flora of Mauritius and the Seychelles. 1877. I. 482.
— A flora of the English lake district. 1885. I. 403.
— The flowering plants and ferns of Great Britain. 1855. I. 400.
— On the fruit of Yuccas. 1871. II. 86.[2]
— Die Gattung Beaucarnea und deren Arten. 1872. II. 84.[1]
— Genera of Malagasy plants. 1883. I. 496.
— The genus Agave. 1877. II. 88.[2]
— On Gorcebxia. 1882. II. 858.[1]
— Handbook of the Amaryllideae. 1888. II. 88.[2]
— Hermaphrodite florets in Salix Caprea. 1853. II. 106.[1]
— On Kew gardens. 1886. I. 55.
— The known forms of Yucca. 1870. II. 86.[2]
— A monograph of the British Roses. 1871. II. 285.[1]
— Monographie des Beaucarnea. 1872. II. 84.[1]
— On the natural history of Madagascar. 1881. I. 496.
— A new Dracaena from Singapore. 1881. II. 81.[8]
— On new Dracaenas from tropical Africa. 1874. II. 81.[3]
— New genera of Malagasy plants. 1881. I. 496.
— New petaloid monocotyledons from Cape Colony. 1889. II. 78.[1]
— New plants from the Zambesi country. 1884. II. 78.[2]
— A new Strongylodon from Madagascar. 1891. II. 385.[1]
— North Yorkshire. 1863. I. 401.
— Notes on a collection of flowering plants made . . . in Madagascar. 1881. I. 496.
— Notice sur les Rubus des environs de Spa. 1886. II. 302.[2]
— Olearia macrodonta n. sp. 1884. II. 862.[1]
— Periodic phenomena of vegetation. 1855. I. 226.[1]
— Physical history of the Vale of Mowbray. 1858. I. 400.
— On the present state of our knowledge of the geography of British plants. 1883. I. 403.
— Recent additions to our knowledge of the flora of Fiji. 1884. I. 510.[1]
— On the relation of the British forms of Rubi. 1886. II. 303.[1]
— Report on the Liliaceae, Iridaceae . . . of Welwitsch's Angolan herbarium. 1878. I. 491.
— Review of the British Roses. 1864. II. 285.[1]
— Revision of . . . Asparagaceae. 1875. II. 77.[1]
— Rivista delle Agave. 1877. II. 89.[1]
— On Rosa apennina. 1873. II. 291.[1]
— On Rosa collina Iaeq as a British plant. 1865. II. 293.[1]
— On Rosa sepium Thuill. 1870. II. 285.[1]
— Rubus latifolius Bab. 1853. II. 308.[1]
— On Salix acutifolia Willd. 1856. II. 104.[2]
— On Salix Grahami Borrer. 1867. II. 109.[2]
— The species of Fourcroya. 1879. II. 89.[2]
— A synopsis of Aloineae and Yuccoideae. 1881. II. 77.[1]
— A synopsis of . . . Museae. 1893. II. 91.[1]
— 0 of the African species of Xerophyta 1875 II 90. ynopsis
— Synopsis of the East Indian species of Dracaena and Cordyline. 1873. II. 79,[3] 81.[3]
— Vier neue Bromelien aus British Guiana. 1883. II. 76.[2]
— Yucca Whipplei Torr. 1876. II. 88.[1]
— See also SCHUMANN, Karl, BAKER, J. G., ROLFE, R. A. & COGNIAUX, Alfred.
— & MOORE, S. Le M. Descriptive notes on a few of Hildebrandt's East African plants. 1877. I 492.[2]
— & NOWELL, John. A supplement to Baines' Flora of Yorkshire. 1854. I. 400.
— & TATE, G. R. A new flora of Northumberland. 1868. I. 402, 534.[1]
— & others. Botany of the Hadramaut expedition. 1894. I. 481.[1]
Baker, R. C. The Golynos Oak. 1873. II. 138.[2]
Baker, Richard Thomas. On an apocynaceous plant yielding . . . tubers. 1900. II. 730.[1]
— On the botany of Rylstone. 1896. I. 505.
— On the Cinnamomums of New South Wales. 1898. II. 224.[1]
— Contributions to a knowledge of the flora of Australia. 1898. I. 505.

— Description of a new Isopogon. 1895. II. 163.[2]
— Descriptions of two new species of Acacia. 1898. II. 323.[1]
— Descriptions of two new species of Pultenaea. 1898. II. 381.[1]
— Explanation of the vernacular name " Cut-tail." 1900. II. 624.[2]
— On a new species of Angophora. 1900. II. 620.[1]
— Note on a new variety of Acacia decurrens. 1896. II. 324.[2]
— Some New South Wales plants. 1892. I. 504.
— On some new species of Eucalyptus. 1900. II. 623.[2]
— On a supposed new genus of the N. O. Myrtaceae. 1898 II. 633.[1]
— On three new species of Eucalyptus. 1900. II. 623.[1]
— On two new species of Casuarina. 1900. II. 92.[2]
— On two new species of Eucalyptus. 1898. II. 623.[1]
— On two well-known . . . species of Eucalyptus. 1898 II. 623.[1]
— See also MAIDEN, J. H. & BAKER, R. T.
— & Smith, H. G. On the Darwinias of Port Jackson. 1899. III. 633.[3]
— — On the essential oil . . . in the " Sydney Peppermint." 1897. II. 625.[1]
— — On " Grey Gum." 1897. IV. 534.[1]
— — On the " Stringybark " trees of N. S. Wales. 1898. IV. 532.[1]
Baker, Walter & Co. The Chocolate-plant. 1891. III. 595.[1]
— Cocoa and chocolate. 1886. III. 595.[1]
Baker, Y. G. Agaves and arborescent Liliaceae on the Riviera. 1892. III. 340.[3]
Bakker, H. P. A. De Tengkawang. 1884. III. 611.[1]
— Tengkawang fat or vegetable tallow. 1885. III. 611.[2]
Bąkowski, Jan Nep. Jaksa. Holz-Vermehrung. 1838. IV. 141.
— Przyczynienie drzewa przez użycie miejsc zaciemnionych w lesie. 1838. IV. 141.
— Reproduction des forêts. 1838. IV. 141.
Balaguer y Primo, Francisco. Cria del gusano del Mora 1878. III. 380.[1]
— Industria corchera. 1879. IV. 518.[1]
— Materias tintóreas. 1878. III. 236.
Balan. Neue Abhandlung von dem Baume Acacia. 1762. IV. 522.[1]
— Nouveau traité sur l'arbre nommé Acacia. 1762. IV. 522.[1]
Balansa, Benjamin. Ascension du Mont Humboldt. 1872 I. 509.[1]
— Catalogue des Graminées de l'Indochine. 1890. II. 58.
— Sur le mode de végétation de l'Arceuthobium. 1856. II. 174.[2]
Balard. Rapport sur plusieurs mémoires . . . sur les charbons de bois. 1854. IV. 431.[2]
Balás, Árpád. Az élődi fagyöngy vagy Gyimbor. 1863. II. 178.[2]
— Magyarországi fontosabb vadon termő és miveleti fák és cserjék rendszeres leirása. 1870. I. 444.
De balata-industrie. 1885. III. 668.[1]
De balata-industrie in Surinamen. 1892. III. 668.[1]
Balázs, István. A pöllenröl. 1896. I. 117.[1]
Balbes, Alexandros. See BAABHΣ, 'Αλέξανδρος.
Balbi, Marco, I. Rapporto sulla materia boschiva. 1858. IV. 364.
Balbiani, Édouard Gérard. Sur l'éclosion de l'œuf d'hiver du phylloxera. 1876. III. 568.
— Sur l'éclosion prochaine des œufs d'hiver du phylloxera. 1876. III. 568.
— Sur les œufs des badigeonnages goudronneux. 1884. III 573.
— Die Eichen-Phylloxera? 1875. IV. 510.
— Sur l'existence d'une génération sexuée hypogée chez le Phylloxera. 1874. III. 567.[1]
— Lettre sur la nécessité de détruire l'œuf d'hiver. 1882. III. 573.
— Mémoire sur la reproduction du phylloxera du Chêne. 1874. IV. 510.
— Mémoires sur le phylloxera présentés à l'Académie. 1876. III. 569.[3]
— Nouvelles observations sur le phylloxera du Chêne. 1876. III. 569,[1] *IV. 510.*
— Observations, à propos d'une communication récente de M. Lichtenstein. 1874. III. 566.[2]
— Observations relatives à une note récente de M. Rommier. 1874. III. 567.[1]

Balbiani, Édouard Gérard (*continued*).
— Observations sur la reproduction du phylloxera de la Vigne. 1874. III. 567.[2]
— Sur la parthénogénèse du phylloxera. 1876. III. 560, 760.
— Sur le phylloxera ailé. 1874. III. 566.[2]
— Le phylloxera du Chêne. 188 .? IV. 510.
— Le phylloxera du Chêne. 1884. III. 573.
— Les phylloxeras sexués et l'œuf d'hiver. 1875. III. 568.
— Sur la première génération annuelle du phylloxera du Chêne. 1874. IV. 510.
— Sur la prétendue migration des phylloxeras. 1874. III. 566,[2] *IV. 503*.[1]
— Recherches sur l'action du coaltar. 1874. III. 567.[1]
— Recherches sur la structure . . . des œufs du phylloxera. 1876. III. 569.[2]
— Recherches sur la vitalité des œufs du phylloxera. 1876. III. 569.[2]
— Remarques au sujet d'une note de M. Derbès sur les Pemphigus. 1873. IV. 510.
— Remarques au sujet d'une note récente de M. Lichtenstein. 1876. III. 569.[1]
— Remarques au sujet des notes récentes de MM. Signoret et Lichtenstein. 1874. III. 567,[1] *IV. 510*.
— Remarques relatives à une communication de M. **Boiteau**. 1879. III. 571.
— Remarques . . . sur les pucerons. 1882. IV. 510.
— Réponse à la note précédente de M. Targioni-Tozzetti. 1883. III. 573.
— Sur la reproduction du phylloxera du Chêne. 1873. IV. 509.
— Sur le traitement des Vignes phylloxérées. 1882. III. 573.
— Sur l'utilité de la destruction de l'œuf d'hiver. 1885. III. 573.
— & others. Mémoires sur le phylloxera. 1876. III. 569.[2]
Balbis, Giovanni Battista. Catalogus plantarum Horti botanici taurinensis. 1807. I. 61.
— Catalogus stirpium Horti acad. taurinensis. 1811. I. 61.
— Elenco delle piante . . . di Torino. 1801. I. 424.
— Enumeratio plantarum officinalium Horti botanici taurinensis. 1805. I. 61.
— Flora taurinensis. 1806. I. 425.
— Flore lyonnaise. 1827. I. 408.
— Horti acad. taurinensis stirpium . . . icones et descriptiones. 1810. I. 61.
— Miscellanea botanica. 1804. I. 425.
— Synopsis plantarum Horti taurinensis. 1801. I. 61.
— *See also* NOCCA, Domenico & BALBIS, G. B.
Balch, D. M. On native Grapes. 1866. III. 583.[1]
Baldacci, Antonio. Affinità delle Aristolochiacee. 1894. II. 180.[2]
— Ἐκ τοῦ ἀνὰ τὴν Ἀλβανίαν ὁδοιπορικοῦ μου. 1899. I. 451.
— Altre notizie intorno alla flora del Montenegro. 1892. I. 450.
— Considerazioni preliminari sulla fitogeografia dell' Albania. 1898. I. 451.
— Contributo alla conoscenza della flora dalmata. 1894. I. 450.
— Contributo alla conoscenza della flora del confine Montenegrino-Albanese. 1900. .I. 451.
— Una corsa botanica nell' Isola di Santa Maura. 1896. II. 498.[1]
— Crnagora; memorie di un botanico. 1897. I. 451.
— Fiora del piano del Cetinje. 1886. I. 449.
— I Giardini sperimentali di colture tropicali nell' Eritrea. 1900. I. 69.[1]
— Itinerari albanesi. 1896. I. 451.
— Itinerari albanesi. 1900. I. 451.
— Nel Montenegro; cenni . . . intorno alla flora. 1890. I. 450.
— Die pflanzengeographische Karte von Mittel-Albanien und Epirus. 1897. I. 451.
— Del posto che occupa . . . la flora del Bolognese. 1897. I. 430.
— Ricerche sulla stuttura [*sic*] . . . della Forsythia europaea. 1899. II. 706.[2]
— Ricordi di un viaggio botanico fra Prevesa e Janina. 1893. I. 450.
— Risultati botanici del viaggio compiuto in Creta. 1895. I. 452.
— Rivista critica della collezione botanica . . . in Albania. 1894. I. 450.
— Rivista della collezione botanica . . . in Albania. 1896. I. 451.
— Rivista della collezione botanica . . . in Albania. 1897. I. 451.
— La stazione delle "doline." 1893. I. 450.
— Die westliche akrokeraunische Gebirgskette. 1896. I. 479.
— & **Filippucci**, F. Contribuzioni allo studio delle gemme. 1894. I. 108.[2]
Baldamus, August Carl Eduard. Schützet die Vögel? 1868. IV. 90.[2]
Baldamus, Eduard. Die deutsche Literatur der Forst- und Jagdwissenschaft. 1866. IV. 1.
— Die Erscheinungen der deutschen Literatur auf dem Gebiete der Forst- und Jagdwissenschaft. 1866. IV. 1.
— Die Erscheinungen der deutschen Literatur auf dem Gebiete der Land-, Forst- und Hauswirthschaft. 1866. IV. 1.
— Die literarischen Erscheinungen der letzten 5 Jahre. 1866. IV. 1.
— Die literarischen Erscheinungen der letzten 10 Jahre. 1866. IV. 1.
Balde, D. Eerste bijdragen tot de nasporingen of de plantgewassen warmtestof in zich onthouden. 1812. I. 186.
Balden, James. Accounts of insects injurious to forest trees. 1843. IV. 208.[2]
— On converting into use the small twigs . . . of Oak copse. 1843. IV. 512.
— On the disease of the Silver Fir. 1839. IV. 445.
Balderama, Jenaro. Ensayo descriptivo de las Palmas de San Martin Casanare. 1871. II. 61.[2]
Baldi, Baldo. Due lettere sopra il balsamo. 1640. III. 510.[2]
— Opobalsami orientalis in conficienda theriaca. 1640. II. 417,[2] *III. 510*.[2]
— Del vero opobalsamo orientale discorso. 1646. III. 510.[2]
Baldi, Sebastiano. Anastasis cortiosi Peruviæ. 1613. III. 719.
— Cortex Peruviae redivivus profligator febrium. 1656. III. 719.
Baldinger, Ernst Gottfried. Index plantarum Horti et agri jenensis. 1773. I. 44.
— Ueber Litterar-Geschichte der . . . Botanik. 1794. I.1.
— Ueber das Studium der Botanik. 1770. I. 78.[1]
Baldini, T. Arturo. Di alcune particolari escrescenze del . . . Laurus. 1886. III. 406.[2]
— Sopra alcune produzioni radicali del genere Podocarpus. 1887. II. 9.[1]
— Le gemme della Pircunia dioica. 1888. II. 193.[1]
Baldrati, Isaia. Appunti di oecidiologia. 1900. I. 216.[1]
— Contributo alla ricerca della eziologia della antracnosi. 1897. III. 581.
— Istruzioni popolare contro la Diaspis. 1900. III. 379.[2]
— Il nero della Pesca. 1900. III. 442.[1]
— Rossore, perforazione e antracnosi. 1900. III. 582.
Baldwin, A. S. The age of trees. 1884. I. 128.[1]
Baldwin, David Dwight & **Auld**, William. List of indigenous Hawaiian woods. 1890. III. 94.[2]
Baldwin, Ebenezer. Catalogue of the phenogamous plants and the ferns . . . within five miles of Yale college, Ct. 1831. I. 313.
Baldwin, Elmer. History of La Salle county, Illinois. *See* WILLIAMS, R. 1877. I. 314.
Baldwin, William. Reliquiæ Baldwinianae. 1843. I. 307.
Bale, M. Powis. Saw mills. 1883. IV. 393.
Baleful Mistletoe. 1882. II. 180.[1]
Balester, Octave. Le sagou et l'exploitation des Sagoutiers. 1899. III. 276.[2]
Balestreri, Demetrio. Sopra la coltura dei boschi. 1871. IV. 277.
— Esperimenti di riboscamento delle crete sanesi. 1865. IV. 165.
— Sulle pinete di Ravenna. 1866. IV. 364.
— Principii generali pel governo e pella coltura. 1866. IV. 248.[2]
— Trattato della scienza forestale. 1864. IV. 57.
Balfe, Ambrose. Petraea volubilis. 1877. III. 697.[1]
Balfour, Edward Green. Cyclopaedia of India. 1857. III. 278.
— Influence exercised by trees on the climate. 1878. IV. 49.[1]
— Notes on the influence exercised by trees on climate. 1849. IV. 52.
— The timber trees, timber . . . of India. 1858. III. 272.[2]
Balfour, Isaac Bayley. Aspects of the . . . vegetation of Rodriguez. 1878. I. 481.[2]
— Botany [of Rodriguez]. 1879. I. 481.[2]

— Coco-nut, not Cocoa-nut. 1887. II. 67.²
— Description of a new species of Pandanus. 1884. II. 57.¹
— Diagnoses plantarum . . . socotrensium. 1882. I. 489.
— The Dragon's Blood tree of Socotra. 1883. II. 82.¹
— The flora of Socotra. 1883. I. 489.
— Forestry. 1894. IV. 357.²
— Forestry in Britain. 1894. IV. 357.²
— Latania Verschaffeltii. 1879. II. 70.¹
— On a new genus of Turneraceae. 1877. II. 574.²
— Observations on the genus Pandanus. 1880. II. 56.²
— & others. Botany of Socotra. 1888. I. 489.
Balfour, James Melville. Results of a series of experiments on the strength of New Zealand . . . woods. 1875. IV. 410.
Balfour, John Hutton. Account of a botanical excursion to Switzerland. 1859. I. 435.
— Account of a botanical trip to Ben Ledi. 1861. I. 401.
— Botanical intelligence on the vitality of seeds. 1859. I. 193.¹
— The botanist's companion. 1860. I. 35.
— Botany and religion. 1851. I. 95.
— Botany of the Bass. 1848. I. 533.
— Class book of botany. 1852. I. 89.
— Description of a new species of Clerodendron. 1862. II. 756.²
— Description of the fruit . . . of Clerodendron Thomsonae. 1863. II. 756.²
— Description of the plant which produces the ordeal bean. 1859. II. 376.²
— The elements of botany. 1869. I. 91.
— Encyclopaedia metropolitana . . . Botany. 1849. I. 89.
— On the flora of the Bass Rock. 1847. I. 399.
— Guide to the Royal botanic garden, Edinburgh. 1873. I. 55.
— List of medicinal and poisonous plants . . . of Edinburgh. 1859. I. 55.
— A manual of botany. 1849. I. 89.
— Notes of a trip to the north of Italy. 1862. I. 349.
— Notes of an excursion to Connemara. 1876. I. 403.
— Notes on a botanical excursion . . . to the mountains of Braemar. 1848. I. 400.
— Notice of a diseased condition of Beeches. 1862. IV. 496.
— Notice of a species of Trichoscypha. 1868. II. 461,² 831.¹
— Notice of Pandanus odoratissimus. 1863. II. 57.¹
— Notice of plants at Dr. Shapter's garden. 1879. III. 334.²
— Notice of plants which have flowered recently in the Royal botanic garden. 1848. III. 82.
— Notice of some plants which have flowered recently in the Edinburgh botanic garden. 1848. III. 82.
— Notice of some plants which have flowered recently in the Royal botanic garden. 1849. II. 224,² 415.¹
— Observations on temperature in connection with vegetation. 1901. III. 16.¹
— Outlines of botany. 1854. I. 89.
— Phyto-theology. 1851. I. 95.
— The plants of the Bible. 1857. I. 513.
— Remarks on plants furnishing varieties of Ipecacuan. 1873. II. 828.²
— Remarks on the Ipecacuan plant. 1872. II. 828.²
— Remarks on the state of the forests in Pegu. 1856. IV. 377.¹
— Short notice of a botanical trip to the highlands of Scotland. 1842. I. 399.
— On the structure of the bark of Araucaria imbricata. 1862. II. 26.²
— & Babington, C. C. An account of the vegetation of the Outer Hebrides. 1841. I. 399.
— & Sadler, John. Flora of Edinburgh. 1863. I. 401.
Balfour, Thomas Alexander Goldie. Note on the effect of soot on some Coniferae. 1879. III. 292.
Balicka-Iwanowska (Mrs.) G. See CHODAT, Robert & BALICKA-IWANOWSKA, (Mrs.) G.
Balissat, L. Note concernant la destruction du phylloxera. 1872. III. 565.¹
Baliveau, (pseud.f). Culture du Pin sylvestre. 1898. IV. 474.
— Les recherches et les expériences en matière forestière. 1895. IV. 541.
— Le taillis sous futaie. 1896. IV. 131.
Ball, Carleton Roy. The genus Salix in Iowa. 1900. II. 99.³
— Notes on some western Willows. 1899. II. 99.²
Ball, Charles James. Note on the wood called urkarha. 1889. II. 452.²

Ball, John. A new compendious dispensatory. 1769. III. 253.
— Pharmacopoeia domestica nova. 1760. III. 252.
Ball, John (1818–1889). Botanical notes of an excursion through Portugal and Spain. 1851. I. 421.
— Considérations sur l'origine de la flore alpine européenne. 1879. I. 349.
— Contributions to the flora of North Patagonia. 1884. I. 345.
— Contributions to the flora of the Peruvian Andes. 1885. I. 340.²
— Descriptions of some new species . . . in Marocco. 1873. I. 485.
— The distribution of plants on the south side of the Alps. 1896. I. 438.
— Notes of a naturalist in South America. 1887. I. 330.
— Notes on the botany of western South America. 1887. I. 330.
— On the origin of the flora of the European Alps. 1879. I. 349.
— Spicilegium florae maroccanae. 1878. I. 485.
— See also HOOKER, Sir J. D. & BALL, John.
Ball, Samuel. An account of the cultivation . . . of Tea in China. 1848. III. 601.³
Ball, Valentine. A commentary on the colloquies of Garcia de Orta. 1889. III. 279.¹
— On the identification of . . . plants of India . . . known to early Greek authors. 1879. I. 514.¹
— On the jungle products. 1868. III. 278.
— Notes on the flora of Manbhúm. 1869. I. 474.
— Remarks on a kind of farina from . . . Pandanus. 1871. III. 313.¹
— Sticks used in producing fire by friction. 1882. IV. 431.²
Balland, Joseph Antoine Félix. Sur la composition et la valeur alimentaire. 1899. III. 220.²
— Expériences relatives à l'alcool . . . de la Figue de Barbarie. 1876. III. 624.²
— Marrons et châtaignes. 1897. III. 360,¹ 533.²
— Note sur la présence de l'acide cyanhydrique dans . . . Néflier du Japon. 1876. II. 264.¹
— Sur le Phytolaque dioïque. 1881. II. 193,¹ III. 388.¹
— Sur le vin de Palmier récolté à Laghouat. 1879. III. 319.²
Ballard, Edward & Garrod, A. B. Elements of materia medica. 1845. III. 243.
Ballard, G. On the culture of Indigo in Bengal. 1838. III. 479.¹
— Method of treating the Grape vine at Bombay. 1838. III. 559.¹
Ballard, Stephen. A treatise on the nature of trees and the pruning. 1833. III. 169.²
Ballé, Emile. Sur deux productions gallaires . . . sur divers Rubus. 1890. III. 457.²
— Sur les hémiptérocécidies de l'Épicéa. 1890. IV. 457.
— Du rôle du bois secondaire. 1898. I. 126.
Ballet, Jules. La Guadeloupe. 1890. I. 337.
Ballou, William Hosea. Natural and industrial history of the White Pine in Michigan. 1881. IV. 470.²
— The White Pine of Michigan. 1881. IV. 470.²
Ballus, Paul von. Über die Anzucht des Weinstockes. 1837. III. 548.¹
— Beschreibung der, den Obstbäumen . . . schädlichsten Raupenarten. 1830. III. 188.²
Bally, V. Notice sur les avantages de la culture du Mûrier. 1851. III. 376.
Balmanno, Robert. On reverse budding. 1848. III. 164.²
Balmaseda, Francisco Javier. Tesoro del agricultor cubano. 1885. III. 100.¹
Balme, L. Expériences sur un mode de traitement des Vignes phylloxérées. 1874. III. 567.¹
Balmer, J. A. Forest tree plantation. 1894. IV. 112.
Balog, Joseph D. M. Specimen inaugurale sistens praecipuas plantas, in M. Transsilvaniae. 1779. I. 444.
The Balsam Fir. 1881. III. 295.¹
Balsam of Copaiba. 1877. III. 473.¹
Balsam of Peru. 1861. III. 482.¹
Balsamo, Francesco. Ricerche sulla penetrazione delle radiazioni. 1892. I. 230.
Il balsamo del Perú. 1863. III. 245, 482.¹
Balsiger, R. Ueber die neuern Verfahren der forstlichen Wirthschafts-Einrichtung. 1875. IV. 244.
Baltet, Charles. De l'action du froid sur les végétaux pendant l'hiver 1879–80.. 1881. III. 48.
— L'arbre fruitier est le premier arbre d'ornement. 1877. III. 203.

Baltet, Charles (*continued*).
— Des arbres et arbrisseaux d'ornement. 1898. III. 173.[1]
— Les arbustes de pleine terre. 1886. III. 84.[1]
— L'art de greffer les arbres. 1869. III. 161.
— The art of grafting. 1869. III. 162.
— The art of grafting and budding. 1869. III. 162.
— Berberis dulcis. 1857. III. 394.[2]
— Les bonnes poires. 1859. III. 445.[1]
— Les bonnes poires d'hiver. 186.? III. 444.[2]
— Causerie sur la Rose en Champagne. 1894. III. 450.
— Le congrès de l'Association pomologique de l'Ouest. 1892. III. 85.
— Congrès pomologique de Lyon. 1857. III. 85.
— El corrimiento de las Uvas. 1890. III. 561.
— La coulure des raisins. 1887. III. 579.
— Culture des arbres fruitiers. 1870. III. 144.
— Culture du Poirier. 1859. III. 445.[1]
— Die Doppelveredelung der Gewächse. 1888. III. 162.
— Effets de la greffe sur les Rhododendrons javanais. 1893. III. 656.
— Un ennemi du Peuplier. 1889. III. 344.[2]
— Étude comparative des différents sujets propres au greffage des Rosiers. 1897. III. 453.[1]
— Étude sur les meilleurs arbustes de pleine terre. 1886. III. 84.[1]
— Fruit culture in France. 1895. III. 145.[1]
— Les fruits populaires. 1889. III. 144.
— Grafting the Walnut. 1868. III. 354.[1]
— Le greffage de la Vigne. 1882. III. 548.[2]
— Le greffage du Sorbier des oiseleurs. 1879. III. 459.[1]
— Greffage sur racine de l'Exochorda. 1884. III. 424.[1]
— Greffe du Noyer à fruit comestible. 1868. III. 354.[1]
— Greffe du Noyer d'Europe. 1868. III. 354.[1]
— Griffeling van den gewonen Notelaar. 1868. III. 354.[1]
— L'horticulture dans les cinq parties du monde. 1895. III. 116.[2]
— L'horticulture en Belgique. 1865. III. 122.[1]
— L'horticulture française. 1892. III. 33.[2]
— Influence du sujet sur le greffon. 1897. III. 40.
— Le Marronnier du vingt mars. 1886. II. 482.[2]
— Les meilleurs Pommes à cultiver. 1879. III. 425.[2]
— Moyens de combattre le phylloxera. 1871. III. 564.[2]
— The Myrobalan and Mirabelle Plums. 1896. III. 436.[1]
— Praktische Anleitung zur Baumzucht. 1865. III. 101.[2]
— À propos d'un nouveau mode de greffage. 1897. III. 163.[1]
— À propos du Marronnier du vingt mars. 1886. II. 482.[2]
— Le Prunus triloba. 1872. III. 420,[1] 448.[2]
— Prunus triloba Lindl. 1865. III. 443.[1]
— Ptelea trifoliata L. als plaatsvervanger der hop. 1880. III. 505.[2]
— Quelques greffes peu connues. 1889. III. 165.
— Quelques greffes rajeunies. 1880. III. 162.
— Quelques mots à propos de la dégénérescence. 1866. .I. 248.[2]
— Quelques observations sur le greffage. 1878. III. 165.
— Rapport sur le Cèdre du Liban des Fallets. 1862. II. 27,[1] 96.[2]
— Reconstitution des arbres gelés. 1882. III. 183.[1]
— Regreffage des arbres. 1879. III. 162.
— Le Rosier dans le département de l'Aube. 1892. III. 453.[1]
— Les routes fruitières. 187.? II. 211.[1]
— Le surgreffage des végétaux. 1888. III. 162.
— Taille de la Spirée. 1898. III. 460.[2]
— Traité de la culture fruitière. 1884. III. 144.
— La Vallée suisse. 1872. III. 87.
— Visite à la villa Tourasse à Pau. 1881. I. 59.
— Les Yucca. 1887. III. 339.[2]
— *See also* CHARGUERAUD, A. & BALTET.
Baltet, Ernest. Sur l'écorce et l'aubier des Chênes. 1895. IV. 508.
— Historique du phylloxera dans l'Aube. 1899. III. 575.[1]
— Les maladies de la Vigne. 1874. III. 560.
— Des semis d'arbres fruitiers pour la recherche des nouvelles variétés. 1882. I. 247.
— Het zaaien van vruchtboomen tot het winnen van nieuwe varieteiten. 1882. I. 247.
Baltet-Petit. Essai sur la plantation . . . des arbres verts. 1836. III. 291.
Balthasar. Ueber Mäusefrass in Buchenschonungen. 1869. IV. 198.[1]
— Ueber das Verhalten der Eiche als Waldrechter. 1869. IV. 506.
Baltimore Cactus journal. III. 3.

Baltischer Forstverein. Verhandlungen. IV. 6.
Baltz. Zur Akazienpflanzung. 1900. IV. 523.[2]
— Anbau ausländischer Holzarten. 1897. IV. 126.[1]
— Die Bedeutung der Bodenbearbeitung. 1896. IV. 143.[2]
— Bestandespflege in gemischten Eichen- und Buchenbeständen. 1898. IV. 138.[1]
— Die Bewirtschaftung der Gemeindeforsten in der Rheinprovinz. 1898. IV. 309.[1]
— Die Lärche (Larix europaea) im deutschen Walde. 1897. IV. 450.
— Lichtstand und Unterbau. 1898. IV. 129.
— Rauchschaden am Walde. 1900. IV. 193.[1]
— Verhalten von Kiefer und Fichte. 1897. IV. 138.[1]
— Wachstum des Epheus. 1898. IV. 534.[1]
— Welchen Ursachen ist die sogenannte Wipfeldürre der Eichen zuzuschreiben? 1899. IV. 511.
— In welcher Richtung der Spirale wachsen unsere Laubbölzer. 1898. IV. 62.[1]
— Die Zopftrocknis . . . der Eiche! 1897. IV. 511.
— *See also* FEEGER, BALTZ & MÜCKE, Fritz.
Baltzer, Leonhard Volkmar. Das Kyffhäuser-Gebirge. 1880. I. 388.
Baluchistan. *See* INDIA-BALUCHISTAN.
The Baluchistan agency forest law. 1890. IV. 332.[1]
Balzer, A. Ueber das Sandarachars. 1896. III. 299.[2]
Bamber, M. Kelway. First report on . . . the inquiry relating to Tea soils. 1891. III. 604.[1]
— Report on Ceylon Tea soils. 1900. III. 604.[1]
Bamberger, Max. Zur Analyse der Harze und Balsame. 1891. I. 181.[1]
— Zur Kenntniss der Überwallungsharze. 1891. III. 228.[1]
— Zur Kenntniss der Xanthorrhoeaharze. 1893. III. 339.[1]
The Bamboo. 1874. III. 314.[1]
Bamboo and Arundo. 1893. III. 315,[1] 316.[2]
The Bamboo as a paper material. 1866. III. 315.[1]
Bamboo brooms. 1898. III. 315.[1]
Bamboo for paper-making. 1879. III. 315.[1]
Bamboo paper. 1881. III. 315.[1]
Bamboos. 1889. III. 58.[1]
Bamboos at Shrubland Park. 1890. III. 314.[2]
Il Bambù commestibile. 1881. III. 315.[1]
Die Bambusen. 1889. III. 314.[1]
Bamford, *Mrs.* C. E. Silk culture. 1886. III. 378.
Bamps, Constant. Les plantes rares . . .'de Hasselt. 1873. V. xx.[2]
— Recherches sur les insectes parasites des Conifères. 1890. IV. 549.[2]
Banal, Antoine. Catalogue des plantes usuelles. 1755. III. 51.
Bancroft, Edw. Nath. An account of the tree which produces the Hog-gum. 1842. II. 557.[2]
Bancroft, Edward. An essay on the natural history of Guiana. 1769. III. 267.[2]
— Naturgeschichte von Guiana. 1769. III. 267.[2]
Bancroft, Joseph. Duboisia Pituri. 1882. II. 771.[2]
— Further remarks on the Pituri group. 1877. III. 700.[1]
— Pituri and Duboisia. 1877. III. 700.[1]
— Pituri and tobacco.' 1879. III. 700.[1]
— Respiration in the roots of shore-plants. 1889. I. 171.
Bancroft, Thomas Lane. On the discovery of saponin in Acacia delibrata. 1888. II. 324.[2]
— Distillation of native essential oils. 1891. IV. 532.[1]
— Note on bacterial diseases of the roots of the Leguminosae. 1894. III. 462.[1]
— On the physiological action of Cryptocarya. 1888. III. 406.[1]
— On the physiological action of Daphnandra. 1888. III. 403.[1]
— Preliminary notes on some new poisohous plants. 1887. III. 94.[1]
— Preliminary notes on some new poisonous plants. 1892. III. 94.[1]
— Preliminary notes on the pharmacology of Carissa. 1894. III. 687.[1]
— Preliminary notes on the pharmacology of some new poisonous plants. 1890. III. 94.[1]
Bandelow, Adolphus Davides. Foliorum Ilicis Aquifolii analysin . . . submittit. 1898. III. 530.[1]
Bandi, V. L' anarchia in pratica nel regime forestale. 1896. IV. 293.[1]
— I boschi degli enti morali. 1897. IV. 329.
— Nel bosco e fuori. 1895. IV. 70.
— Concorso per le promozioni di merito nell' amministrazione forestale. 1898. IV. 293.[2]

— Per la conservazione dei boschi. 1895. IV. 277.
— Il crescente disordine dei fiumi. 1895. IV. 48.[1]
— La critica di una critica. 1896. IV. 487.[1]
— Elenchi di vincolo ed altro. 1896. IV. 329.
— La flora delle sabbie mobili. 1899. IV. 146.[1]
— La forza del destino . . . forestale. 1897. IV. 293.[2]
— Sulla frugalità delle piante legnose. 1895. IV. 70.
— Il giro di servizio. 1897. IV. 293.[2]
— L' imposta sulle terre incolte. 1895. IV. 41.[1]
— Sull' insegnamento scientifico nell' Istituto forestale di Vallombrosa. 1895. IV. 35.[2]
— Istruzione forestale. 1896. IV. 35.[2]
— Istruzione forestale. 1899. IV. 36.[1]
— La legge forestale del 20 Giugno 1877. 1895. IV. 329.
— Nodi al pettine. 1898. IV. 35.[2]
— Per la nuova legge forestale. 1898. IV. 329.
— L' ovo di Colombo. 1898. IV. 277.
— Piene e disastri. 1896. IV. 45.
— Le prescrizioni di massima. 1897. IV. 329.
— Quali sarebbero le terre incolte? 1895. IV. 166.[1]
— Una questione nuova. 1896. IV. 329.
— Per la revisione della legge forestale. 1896. IV. 329.
— Per la riforma della legge forestale. 1896. IV. 329.
— Per la riforma della legge forestale. 1897. IV. 329.
— Per le riforme forestali. 1897. IV. 277.
— Rimboschimento o conservazione. 1895. IV. 166.[1]
— Sepultus est. 1898. IV. 329.
— Gli studi forestali dell' avvocato Mantovani. 1897. IV. 277.
— Terre incolte e colonizzazione interna. 1898. IV. 277.
Bando, (Forstmeister, Katholisch-Hammer). Ueber das Ablegen der Eier von Microgaster. 1870. IV. 199.[2]
— Ueber das Auftreten . . . der Forleule. 1851. IV. 475.
— Auszug aus dem vom . . . Bando gelieferten Aufsatz über Eichenschälwald-Erziehung. 1850. IV. 504.
— Über den Erfolg des Köpp'schen Fertilisationsmittels. 1849. IV. 146.[2]
— Ueber Holzpflasterung. 1880. IV. 426.[1]
— Der japanische Lackbaum. 1881. III. 528.[2]
— Saatlinte und Säehorn. 1869. IV. 149.[1]
— Die Veränderungen in den wirthschaftlichen Verhältnissen des königl. Forstlehr-Reviers Liege. 1880. IV. 354.
— & Hagen, von. Ueber die Anlage . . . von Eichenschäl-waldungen. 1854. IV. 504.
Banerjei, N. N. Monograph on dyes . . . in Bengal. 1896. III. 237.[1]
Banesius Faustus Naironus. See NAIRONI, Antonio Fausto.
Bang, Axel Olof. De Junipero. 1708. III. 303.[2]
Bang, Christian Friedrich. De plantis quibusdam saerae botanicae. 1767. I. 513.
Bang, F. De rosenske Saamskiner. 1867. IV. 149.[1]
— & Jensen-Tusch. Ahlgennembrydninger i Hannover. 1870. IV. 143.[1]
Bang, Jens. Iagttagelse ved et Bøgetræ. 1798. II. 127.[1]
— Kortfattet Veiledning til at opelske Træer. 1828. IV. 156.[1]
Bang, Jens Pul Fredrik. Om de nord- og vestjydske Klitters Beplantning. 1889. IV. 156.[2]
Bang, Niels E. HOFMAN-. See HOFMAN-BANG, N. E.
Bânge, C. O. Remedia guineensia. See AFZELIUS, Adam. 1813. III. 93.[1]
Banger, George S. History of the Susquehanna Boom Co. 1876. IV. 403.[2]
Banger, Karl. Anleitung zur Forstwirthschaft. 1792. IV. 95, 239.
— Systematischer Forst-Katechismus. 1790. IV. 95.
Banister, Thomas. Wellingtonia gigantea. 1856. II. 50.[2]
Bank, F. J. J. Die preussischen Gesetze zum Schutze der Forsten und Forstbeamten. 1867. IV. 320.
Bank. Der Schnücke'sche Zahnkeil. 1896. IV. 384.[1]
Banks, George. An introduction to the study of English botany. 1823. I. 397.
— The Plymouth and Devonport flora. 1830. I. 397.
Banks, Sir Joseph. Aanteekeningen aangaande de eerste ontdekking van de Aphis lanigera. 1817. III. 427.[1]
— An account of the method of cultivating the American Cranberry. 1812. III. 663.[1]
— Catalogus bibliothecae historico-naturalis. See DRYANDER, Jonas. 1796. I. 1.
— On the horticultural management of the . . . Chestnut tree. 1812. III. 358.[2]
— Icones selectae plantarum quas in Japonia collegit. See KAEMPFER, Engelbert. 1791. I. 461.

— Journal of . . . Sir Joseph Banks, bart. . . . during Capt. Cook's first voyage. 1896. I. 304.
— Notes relative to the first appearance of Aphis lanigera. 1817. III. 427.[1]
— Plants of the coast of Coromandel. See ROXBURGH, William. 1795. I. 471.
— & Solander, Daniel. Illustrations of the botany of Captain Cook's voyage. 1900. I. 505.
Banknoten-oile. 1884. III. 514.[2]
Die Bannbriefe über Waldbannungen. 1896. IV. 181.[1]
Banning. Die Brombeeren der Gegend von Minden. 1874. II. 301.[2]
Bannister, Richard. Sugar, coffee, tea and cocoa. 1890. III. 223.[1]
Bannwarten-Unterricht. 1858. IV. 36.[1]
Banti, Adolfo. La cocciniglia dell' Evonimo. 1893. III. 532.[2]
— Descrizione e figure dello Aspidiotus Ceratoniae. 1893. III. 471.[2]
Bantschev, Stojan. Eine Locusta-Art. 1891. IV. 210.[1]
The Banyan. 1873. II. 152.[1]
Le Banyan de Calcutta. See The BANYAN tree. 1889. II. 152.[1]
The Banyan tree. 1888. II. 152.[1]
The Banyan tree. 1889. II. 152.[1]
Banyer, Henry. Pharmacopœia pauperum. 1721. III. 252.
The Baobab tree. 1888. II. 529.[1]
The Baobab tree. 1896. III. 589.[2]
Bapst von Rochlitz, Michaëlis. Juniperetum oder Wacholder-Garten. 1605. III. 303[2]
Baptista, Manoel Dias. Ensaio de huma descripçaõ . . . de Coimbra. 1789. I. 535.
Baraban, Léopold. Catalogue de l'exposition forestière . . . à Niort. 1882. IV. 361.
— Les dunes de Belgique. 1890. IV. 160.[2]
— Recherches des causes de dépérissement des Pins maritimes. 1881. IV. 467.[2]
— A travers la Tunisie. 1887. I. 485, IV. 379.[1]
— En Tunisie. 1886. IV. 146.[1]
Baranda, José, SAINZ DE. See SAINZ DE BARANDA, José.
Baranetzki, Iosif Vasilevich. Sur le développement des points végétatifs. 1897. I. 132.[2]
— Ueber den Einfluss einiger Bedingungen auf die Transpiration. 1872. I. 167.
— Épaississement des parois. 1886. I. 138.[1]
— Die kreisförmige Nutation. 1883. I. 196.[2]
— Recherches sur les faisceaux bicollatéraux. 1900. I. 134.[2]
— Die tägliche Periodicität im Längenwachsthum. 1879. V. XII.[1]
Baranetzki, O. V. See Баранецкiй, О. В..
Baranetzki, P. V. See Баранецкiй, П. В.
Baraudière, Jacques BOYCEAU DE LA. See BOYCEAU DE LA BARAUDIÈRE, Jacques.
Barbadoes. 1888. III. 267.[1]
Barbadoes Aloes in Saint Helena. 1884. III. 334.[1]
Barbados — Botanical station. See BOTANICAL . . . 1891. I. 39.
Barbaro, Ermolao. Castigationes Plinianae. 1492. I. 276, V. XIV.[2]
— Corollarii in Dioscoridem libri quinque. 1516. I. 276.
— In Dioscoridem Corollariorum libri quinque. 1516. I. 276.
Barbarus, APULEIUS. See APULEIUS BARBARUS.
Barbarus, Hermolaus. See BARBARO, Ermolao.
Barbazita, Francesco. Saggio della flora lucona. 1840. I. 426.
Barbe, Arn. Essai sur la culture des Érica du Cap. 1829. III. 649.[3]
Barbe, Paul. L'Oranger, son histoire. 1880. III. 501.[1]
Barbe, Pierre Joseph. Étude sur l'Olivier. 1875. III. 675.[2]
Barber, Charles Alfred. The botanic station, Montserrat. 1892. III. 27.[2]
— The botanical station, Antigua. 1892. III. 27.[2]
— On the nature . . . of the corky excrescences. 1892. I. 107,[2] II. 411.[2]
— Reports on Furcraea fibre plantations. 1893. III. 341.[2]
Barber, Emil. Die Flora der Görlitzer Heide. 1893. I. 389.
Barber, George. The pharmaceutical . . . map of the world. 1869. III. 59.[1]
— The student's pocket companion to the British and London pharmacopœias. 1872. III. 255.[1]
Barber, Mrs. M. E. The Aloe, its habits and culture. 1870. II. 77.[2]
— On the fertilization . . . of Duvernoia adhatodoides. 1871. II. 799.[1]

Barberry as a tree. 1880. III. 394.[1]
Barbeu-Dubourg, Jacques. Le botaniste françois. 1767. I. 405, V. xxi.[2]
— Manuel de botanique. 1768. I. 405.
— Usage des plantes. 1767. III. 217.
Barbey, Auguste. Une invasion de la Fidonie du Pin. 1895. IV. 479.
— Quelques ennemis de nos forêts. 1896. IV. 209.[2]
Barbey, C. & William. Herborisations au Levant, Égypte. 1882. I. 479.
Barbey, William. Florae sardoae compendium. 1884. I. 429.
— Le Linnaea borealis L. appartient-il à la flore française? 1881. II. 835.[2]
— Lydie, Lycie, Carie. 1890. I. 479.
— See also BARBEY, C. & William; BURNAT, Émile & BARBEY, William; MAJOR, C. I. FORSYTH-, & BARBEY, William; STEF-ANI, Carlo de, MAJOR, C. I. FORSYTH- & BARBEY, William.
Barbié du Bocage, Victor Amédée. Boisement des terrains agricoles improductifs. 1881. IV. 163.
— Le commerce des bois. 1883. IV. 405.[1]
— État du commerce des bois. 1883. IV. 405.[1]
— Réponse à la première question . . . Traiter des influences météorologiques sur la végétation forestière. 1878. IV. 67.[1]
Barbier, Achille. Des moyens de grossir les graines. 1861. I. 247.
Barbier, J. Le Coprosma Stocki hort. 1877. III. 743.[2]
— Le Tacsonia insignis Mast. 1877. III. 616.[2]
Barbier, Jean Baptiste Grégoire. Elementos de materia médica. 1819. III. 242.
— Traité élémentaire de matière médicale. 1819. III. 242.
Barbier, Philippe. Dérivés et constitution du rhodinol. 1893. III. 454.[2]
— Sur l'essence de licari kanali. 1892. III. 404.[1]
— See also MONNET, P. & BARBIER, Philippe.
— & Bouveault, L. Sur le citronnellal. 1896. IV. 533.[2]
— — Sur la constitution du rhodinol. 1894. III. 491.[2]
— — Constitution du rhodinol. 1896. III. 491.[2]
— — Sur l'essence de Linaloë. 1895. III. 510.[1]
— — Sur l'essence de Pelargonium. 1894. III. 491.[2]
— — Extraction du rhodinol. 1896. III. 491.[2]
— & Hilt, J. Recherches sur l'australène. 1889. IV. 467.[1]
Barbieri, J. See SCHULZE, E. & BARBIERI, J.
Barbieri, Paolo. Osservazioni microscopiche. 1828. I. 98.
— Proseguimento di esperienze . . . intorno la semplice circolazione della linfa. 1831. I. 98.
Barbosa, Antonio Maria. Recherches sur l'action de la fève de Calabar. 1874. III. 484.[1]
Barbosa, Antonio Soares. Memoria sobre a causa da doença. 1791. III. 677.[1]
Barbosa, Joaquim Casimiro. O jardim; manual do jardineiro-amador. 1892. III. 114.[2]
Barbosa Rodrigues, João. See RODRIGUES, João BARBOSA.
Barceló y Combis, Francisco. Apuntes para una flora de las islas Baleares. 1867. I. 423.
— Flora de las islas Baleares. 1879. I. 423.
Bárcena, Mariano. Aclimatación de plantas en la república. 1873. II. 44.[1]
— El árbol de Manitas. 1876. II. 533.[1]
— El bosque de Chapultepec. 1897. III. 184.[1]
— Calendario botánico del valle de Mexico. 1882. I. 222.[1]
— Descripcion de . . . Gaudichaudia Enrico-Martinesii. 1878. II. 425.[2]
— Ensayo práctico de repoblacion de bosques. 1897. IV. 55.[1]
— Fenómenos periódicos de la vegetacion. 1881. I. 222.[1]
— La Hauya elegans. 1876. II. 645.[2]
— El Jardin botánico . . . de Guadalajara. 1891. I. 39.
— El Marañon. 1870. III. 523.[2]
— Noticia científica de una parte del estado de Hidalgo. 1877. I. 332.
— Observaciones de plantas características de climas. 1873. II. 792.[1]
— Selvicultura. 1892. IV. 113.[1]
— & others. Dictámen sobre la repoblacion vegetal. 1884. IV. 155.[2]
Barcia, Andres Gonzalez. Historiadores primitivos de las Indias Occidentales. 1749. III. 266.
Barcianu, D. P. Ueber die Blüthenentwicklung der Cupheen. 1875. II. 608.[2]
Barck, Harald. On the foliation of trees. See LINNÉ, Carl von. 1753. I. 222.[1]
— Vernatio arborum. See LINNÉ, Carl von. 1753. I. 222.[1]
Barckhausen, Gottlieb. Specimen botanicum . . . plantarum ex Flora comitatus lippiaci. 1775. I. 374.

Barclay, Arthur. Commoner rusts and mildews of Indian crops. 1895. III. 195.[2]
— A descriptivo list of the Uredineae . . . of Simla. 1888. III. 195.[2]
— Leaf-fungus on Ehretia serrata. 1892. III. 695.[1]
— On a new species of uredine parasitic on Cedrus Deodara. 1886. IV. 447.[2]
— Rhododendron Uredineae. 1891. III. 657.[1]
— On a second species of uredine affecting Abies Smithiana. 1886. III. 306.[2]
— On a uredine affecting the Himalayan Spruce-Fir. 1886. III. 306.[2]
Bardenwerper, Paul. Veredlung der Picea pungens glauca. 1898. III. 306.[1]
— & others. Veredlung der Coniferen. 1896. III. 294.[2]
— — Vermehrung der Coniferen durch Stecklinge. 1893. III. 294.[2]
Bardet, George. L'Arbre à la vache. 1879. III. 367.[2]
— Saules remarquables pour l'ornementation. 1885. III. 349.
Bardili, Karl Wilhelm Adolf. De Diosma crenata. See AUTENRIETH, J. H. F. von. 1830. III. 495.[2]
Bardy, Charles & Bordet, L. Sur la préparation de l'éther méthylformique. 1879. IV. 432.[2]
Barème forestier. See TARIF de cubage. 18 . . ? IV. 229.
Barentin, Friedrich Wilhelm. Die Vegetation in der Mark Brandenburg. 1840. I. 380.
Barfrost oder Auswintern. 1860. IV. 191.[1]
Barfuss, Josef. Der Beerenbau. 1892. III. 147.[2]
— Himbeere und Brombeere. 1899. III. 457.[1]
Bargagli, Piero, marchese. Di alcuni insetti nocivi ai rami di Querce. 1878. IV. 501.[1]
— Notizie sopra alcuni entomocecidi. 1895. IV. 511.
— Nuova stazione del Pinus sylvestris. 1891. II. 47.[1]
— I rimedi contro la Phylloxera. 1879. III. 760.
Bargagli-Petrucci, Gino. Ricerche anatomiche sopra la Chamaerops. 1900. II. 63.[2]
Bargellini, Demetrio. L'arboreto istriano. 1882. V. VIII.[2]
— Arboretum istrianum. 1882. I. 64, V. VIII.[2]
— I latte delle piante. 1893. III. 219.[1]
— Sulla provenienza e sugli usi della Terebintina. 1881. III. 526.[1]
Bargellini, G. Come renderebbe l' imboscamento. 1896. IV. 166.[1]
— Concimazione degli orti forestali. 1897. IV. 151.[2]
— Foreste ed energia meccanica. 1897. IV. 52.
— Le frane dell' argilla scagliosa. 1898. IV. 146.[1]
— Frane e boschi nell' alta montagna. 1898. IV. 48.[1]
— Piante esotiche dell' orto dendrologico dei sigg. Rovelli in Pallanza. 1896. IV. 18.[2]
— La scomparsa del Faggio. 1898. IV. 500.[2]
— Sempre sul Faggio. 1899. IV. 500.[2]
— Il solfuro di carbonio per uccidere le . . . melolonte. 1895. IV. 203.
— I terreni incolti e paludosi d' Italia. 1898. IV. 166.[2]
Barger, Ständiger Waldweidebetrieb. 1896. IV. 136.[1]
Barger, Vinzenz. Forst-Beschreibung der fürstlich Collalto'-schen Domäne Pirnitz. 1850. IV. 368.
Bargmann, Bernhard Alexander. Die Erhaltung des Wassers. 1898. IV. 73.[2]
— Der Wald in seiner Beziehung zur Hochwassergefahr. 1900. IV. 52.
Barham, Henry. An essay upon the silk-worm. 1719. III. 372.[2]
— Hortus americanus. 1794. III. 63.[2]
Bari — Reale istituto tecnico. See REALE . . . III. 23.[2]
Barillé, Auguste Éloi. Coloration artificielle d'oranges. 1892. III. 583.[2]
Barillet, F. Le Livistona australis du Jardin botanique de Munich. 1870. II. 70.[1]
— Quelques arbres remarquables. 1873. I. 295.[1]
Barillot. See VIGNON, Léo & BARILLOT.
Barillot, Ernest. La distillation des bois. 189 . ? IV. 433.[1]
— La distillation du bois. 1896. IV. 433.[1]
— Sur les produits de la distillation du bois. 1896. IV. 433.[1]
— Sur le rendement des diverses essences de bois en charbon. 1896. IV. 433.[2]
Baring, Walter. A tour in the neighbourhood of Cettinje. 1888. III. 583,[1] IV. 374.[2]
Barisch, Bernhard Johann. Observationes phytotomicae. 18 . .? I. 97.
Barisic, Paul. Los montes de Esclavonia. 1886. IV. 373.
Bark, L. See Баркъ, Л.
Bark-cloth of Uganda. 1892. III. 468.[1]
Bark peeling. 1884. IV. 515.[1]

Barker, A. & others. Evils of grafting. 1889. I. 208.[2]
Barker, George M. A Tea-planter's life in Assam. 1884. III. 603.
Barker, John G. Ornamental climbing plants. 1887. III. 205.[1]
— Shade trees. 1875. III. 208.[2]
Barker, Thomas. Abstract of a register of the barometer. 1788. III. 38.[1]
Barkhausen. Heinrich Burckhardt's Durchforstungs-Grundsätze. 1888. IV. 174.
— Zwanglose Beiträge zur Kenntnis der forstlichen Verhältnisse . . . Lüneburg. 1888. IV. 354.
Barkly, Sir Henry. Notes on the fauna and flora of Round Island. 1870. I. 482.
Barlet, G. Note sur l'Higginsia regalis. 1862. III. 744.[2]
— Note sur la Rose pimprenelle à fleur double. 1862. III. 457.[1t]
— Note sur le Phyllagathis rotundifolia. 1862. III. 639.[1]
— Le Physostigma venenosum. 1864. III. 483.[2]
— Notice sur le Plumbago rosea. 1863. III. 666.[2]
Barlow, Peter. An essay on the strength and stress of timber. 1817. IV. 409.
— Experiments on the strength of different kinds of wood. 1832. IV. 409.
— On the strength of the Fir of the Forest of Mar. 1841. IV. 482.[1]
— On the strength of timber. 1867. IV. 410.
— A treatise on the strength of timber. 1817. IV. 409.
Barnades, Miguel. Principios de botanica. 1767. I. 83.
Barnard, Charles. Talks about our useful plants. 1894. III. 117.[2]
Barnard, George. Barnard's trees. 1868. I. 295.[1]
Barnard, John. See REDWOOD, Theophilus, BENTLEY, Robert & BARNARD, John.
Barnéoud, F. Marius. Mémoire sur le développement de l'ovule . . . dans les Renonculacées. 1845. II. 195,[1] 667.[1]
— Monographie générale . . . des Plantaginées. 1845. II. 807.[1]
— Note sur l'organogénie des corolles irrégulières. 1846. I. 115.[2]
— Observations sur l'organogénie de l'ovaire. 1847. I. 117.[2]
— Recherches sur le développement . . . des Plantaginées. 1844. II. 695.[2]
— Second mémoire sur l'organogénie des corolles irrégulières. 1847. I. 114.[2]
Barner. Universalkluppe von A. Treffurth. 1888. IV. 231.[2]
Barnes. Barnes's Behandling af Ericaer. 1851. III. 650.[1]
Barnes, Charles Reid. Catalogue of . . . plants . . . in Jefferson county. 1878. I. 314.
— The occurrence of cork . . . in the stem of Catalpa speciosa. 1884. II. 787.[1]
— Plant life. 1898. I. 92.
— The progress and problems of plant physiology. 1898. I. 48.
— The so-called "sap" of trees. 1893. I. 166.
Barnes, Henry J. Irrigation with fresh sewage. 1892. III. 151.
Barnes, James. Araucaria imbricata. 1867. III. 298.[2]
— Araucaria imbricata. 1871. III. 298.[3]
— Coning of Wellingtonia. 1872. III. 292.
— The Deodar. 1869. III. 300.[1]
— On the effects of the winter in Devonshire. 1850. III. 46.[2]
— The hardy Bamboos. 1872. III. 314.[1]
— Magnolia brandy. 1873. III. 400.[1]
— Magnolia grandiflora. 1873. III. 400.[1]
— The Monterey Cypress. 1872. III. 302.[2]
— Pinus insignis as a sea-coast tree. 1873. III. 308.[2]
— Pinus Lindleyana. 1868. III. 307.[2]
— Pinus patula. 1868. III. 308.[1]
— Pinus Russelliana. 1868. III. 307.[2]
— The propagation of fruit-trees. 1847. III. 158.
— Quercus glabra. 1868. III. 362.[1]
— Sea-side trees and shrubs. 1872. III. 41.[2]
— On the seeding of Conifers. 1866. II. 20.[2]
— Ueber die Vermehrung von Frucht- und anderen Bäumen. 1847. III. 158.
Barnes, Thomas. A new method of propagating fruit-trees. 1759. III. 152.
Barnet Lyon, G. H. See SCHLUCH, P. G., BARNET LYON, G. H. & GONGRYP, J. R. C.
Barnett, J. The story of Hawaii's departed forests. 1894. IV. 49.[2]

Barnett, William N. Grape culture in gardens. 1876. III. 550.
Barneveld, Willem van. Over de ijzer-roest-kleurige vlekken op de bladeren der Pereboomen. 1813. III. 445.[2]
— Proeve van onderzoek, omtrent de herstelling van bedorven lucht door den groei. 1784. III. 34.[1]
— Proeven van onderzoek omtrent de hoeveelheid van bederf. 1781. III. 34.[1]
— & Müller, J. F. Verhandeling over het planten van boomen binnen en rondom de steden. 1793. III. 34.[1]
— — Wat heeft men te denken aangaande het planten van boomen. 1785. III. 34.[1]
Barnéwitz, A. Kopfweidenüberpflanzen. 1898. I. 234.[2]
Barney, E. E. Additional facts . . . in relation to the Catalpa tree. 1877. II. 786,[2] IV. 538.[2]
— Le Catalpa. 1877. IV. 538.[2]
— The Catalpa and its uses. 1878. III. 705.
— Facts . . . in relation to the Catalpa tree. 1877. II. 786,[2] IV. 538.[1]
— On the new variety of Catalpa. 1879. III. 706.[1]
— The varieties of Catalpa. 1878. III. 705.
Barnhart, John Hendley. Family nomenclature. 1895. I. 254.[1]
— Nomenclatural notes. 1899. II. 837.[1]
Barnier. Observations relatives au Phylloxera. 1874. III. 566.[2]
Barnier, (Dr.). Les Kakis du Japon. 1882. III. 669.[2]
Barnston, George. On a collection of plants from British Columbia. 1878. I. 311.[2]
Barnston, James. Catalogue of Canadian plants. 1859. V. XVI.[2]
Baroch, Josef. Der Borkenkäfer. 1878. IV. 204.
Baron, P. Alexis. Flore des départemens méridionaux de la France. 1823. I. 407.
Baron, Philibert. Note sur la greffe en coulée. 1861. III. 161.
— Nouveaux principes de taille des arbres fruitiers. 1858. III. 172.
Baron, Richard. Economic plants of Madagascar. 1890. III. 93.[2]
— The flora of Madagascar. 1890. I. 496.
— Genera of Madagascar plants. 1881. I. 496.
— Jottings on some of the plants of Imerina. 1873. I. 496.
— A Malagasy forest. 1890. I. 496.
— La phyllotaxie. 1881. I. 102.
Baroni, Eugenio. Sopra una fioritura anormale nella Deutzia. 1899. II. 239.[1]
— Sulle gemme di Corylus tubulosa. 1895. III. 358.[1]
— Ricerche anatomiche sul frutto . . . di Eugenia myrtillifolia. 1892. II. 627.[1]
— Sulla struttura del seme dell' Evonymus. 1891. II. 468.[2]
— Sulla struttura delle glandole fiorali di Fachira. 1893. II. 530.[2]
— Supplemento generale al Prodromo della flora toscana. 1897. I. 430.
— See also GUERCIO, Giacomo del & BARONI, Eugenio.
Baroni, Gaetano. Del Pistacchio. 1841. III. 526.[1]
— Dell' utilità della Myrica cerifera. 1844. III. 352.[2]
Baroni, Paolo. Alberi più notevoli esistenti nell' Orto bot. de' semplici. 1877. I. 64.
— Fruttificazione e sementa della Medinilla magnifica. 1876. III. 638.[2]
— La Rosa Banksiae R. Br. di fiore scempio. 1877. III. 454.[2]
Baronnet, Michel. Naturalisation de végétaux en Tunisie. 1894. III. 130.[2]
Barot, Alexandre. Notions élémentaires d'agriculture et d'horticulture. 1885. III. 113.
Barotte, Edmond. Le Poirier greffé sur l'Aubépine. 1893. III. 445.[2]
Barral, Étienne Victor. Sur une Badiane toxique. 1890. III. 398.[1]
Barral, Jean Augustine. Clématite hybride splendide. 1865. III. 391.[1]
— Conférence sur le phylloxera. 1882. III. 573.
— Dictionnaire d'agriculture. 1886. III. 31.
— Influence de l'humidité souterraine . . . sur la végétation des Vignes. 1883. III. 556.
— De l'influence exercée par l'atmosphère. 1860. I. 233.[1]
— & Sagnier, Henry. Notions d'agriculture et d'horticulture. 1883. III. 113.
Barrande, Note sur un nouveau dendromètre. 1845. IV. 215.
Barrandon, Auguste. See LORET, Henri & BARRANDON, Auguste.

Barras, Paul. Les barrages d'avalanches . . . Oberruckwald. 1895. IV. 188.²
— Des coupes rases dans les hautes régions. 1900. IV. 130.
— Note sur le Bois de Boulogne. 1900. IV. 362.
— Noticias acerca de la familia de las Palmas en Andalucia. 1891. III. 318.¹
— Un ravageur des semis d'Arole. 1896. IV. 464.¹
Barratt, Joseph. Salices americanae. 1840. II. 99.²
Barratte, Gustave. *See* BONNET, Edmond & BARRATTE, Gustave.
Barrau de Muratel, Maurice? de. Emploi de la [*sic*] tannée pour les semis de Chênes. 1880. III. 361.²
— Semis de Chêne et de Châtaignier. 1881. IV. 198.¹
Barraud, (*sr. & jr.*). Catalogue des Rosiers. 1822. III. 448, 491.¹
Barré. . Sur une source nouvelle des premiers termes des acides de la série grasse. 1869. IV. 432.²
Barré, Henri & Roussel, Lucien. Manuel d'arpentage et de lever des plans. 1873. IV. 264.
— Notice sur les procédés de lever des plans. 1878. IV. 265.
Barreira, Frey Isidoro de. Tractado das significaçoens das plantas . . . na Sagrada Escriptura. 1622. I. 512. .
Barrel, Edmund. Observations of a difference of sex in Misleto. 1729. II. 178.¹
Barrel and box. IV. 3.
Barrelier, Jacques. Plantae per Galliam, Hispaniam et Italiam observatae. 1714. I. 348.²
Barrenstein, (*in Rovno*). Beitrag zur Kultur der Allamanda Schottii. 1853. III. 686.¹
— Liriodendron tulipifera. 1853. III. 399.¹
— Ueber das Trocknen . . . von überseeischem Samen. 1852. III. 154.²
Barrère, Pierre. Essai sur l'histoire naturelle de la France équinoxiale. 1741. I. 328, 338,² V. XVIII.¹
— Nouvelle relation de la France équinoxiale. 1743. I. 338,² V. XVIII.¹
Barret, J. On the cultivation of the Gooseberry. 1848. III. 414.²
Barreto, Adolfo PARADA Y. *See* PARADA Y BARRETO, Adolfo.
Barrett, J. M. *See* HUSTON, H. A. & BARRETT, J. M.
Barrett, Joseph Osgood. The forest tree planter's manual. 1891. IV. 103.¹
— Forestry in our schools. 1895. IV. 30.¹
— How to manage seeds, seedlings. 1894. III. 153.
Barrie, James. Old and remarkable trees on the Rolle estate. 1890. I 297.¹
Barrière, J. de. Verschaffeltia splendida Herm. 1896. III. 332.¹
Barrière à relèvement. 1883. IV. 146.²
Barrio, Matias & Mier.· Proposición de ley [acerca de los montes.] 1891. IV. 327.
Barrit, J. J. MORTENSEN-. *See* MORTENSEN-BARRIT, J. J.
Barron, Archibald F. Abutilon-Arten und Varietäten. 1879. III. 586.²
— Abutilons grown for trial. 1879. · III. 586.²
— British Apples. 1884. III. 425.²
— La culture de la Vigne. 1893. III. 553.²
— Experiments on grafting various sorts of fruit on different kinds of stocks. 1872. III. 39.
— Malus floribunda. 1870. III. 429.¹
— Report on Abutilons grown for trial. 1879. III. 586.²
— Vines and Vine-culture. 1873. III. 554.¹
— Die Weinrebe und ihre Kultur. 1893. III. 553.² ·
Barron, Charles. *See* ADAMS, Arthur, BAIKIE, W. B. & BARRON, Charles.
Barron, H. P. T. On the Alto-Douro wine district of Portugal. 1862. III. 558.¹
Barron, James. On the causes of dry rot. 1828. IV. 414.²
Barron, John. Abies Engelmanni. 1877. III. 305.²
Barron, William. The British winter garden. 1852. ·III. 291.
— The Buckland Yew. 1880. II. 11,¹ *III. 163.*¹
— Coniferous nomenclature. 1871. .III. 305.¹
— Coniferous nomenclature. 1881. II. 22.²
— The Dovaston Yew. 1876. III. 294.¹
— On grafting the Cedrus Deodara. 1838. III. 299.²
— Home grown Fir-seeds. 1865. III. 294.¹
— Picea nobilis. 1859. III. 296.²
— Picea Parsonsiana. 1876. II. 22.¹
— Transplanting Pines and evergreen shrubs.· 1874. III. 294.²
— Ueber das Veredeln der Cedrus Deodara. 1838. III. 299.²

— & others. Evidence as to the best time for transplanting evergreens. 1874. III. 169.¹
Barron's transplanting machine. 1879. III. 167.
Barros Gomes, Bernardino. *See* GOMES, Bernardino BARROS.
Barros da Silva, Francisco Manuel. Memoria sobre a verdadeira origem . . . do catto. 1814. III. 464.¹
Barroso, Agustin. Apuntes sobre la vegetacion del Istmo de Tehuantepec. 1880. I. 332.
Barrot, F. Observations sur la . . . l'Eucalyptus globulus en Algerie. 1872. IV. 532.² ˎ
Barrow, *Sir* John. An account of travels into the interior of southern Africa. 1801. I. 494.
— Travels in China. 1804. I. 458.
— A voyage to Cochinchina. 1806. I. 469.²
Barrows, David Prescott. The ethno-botany of the Coahuilla Indians. 1900. I. 518.
Barruel-Beauvert, *vicomte*. Note sur le Mûrier-lou. 1843. III. 380.¹
— Nouvelle espèce de Mûrier. 1843. III. 380.¹
Barry, B. The Maples. 1872. III. 533.²
Barry, *Sir* Edward. Observations historical . . . on the wines of the ancients. 1775. III. 582.
Barry, J. B. Hints for the formation of Tea gardens. 1863. III. 603.
Barry, J. S. Old trees. 1874. I. 295.¹
Barry, John W. French forestry at the Paris exhibition. 1879. IV. 20,¹ 379.¹
— The lumberman's actuary. 1893. IV. 228.
— On the measurements of trees. 1884. IV. 218.
— Some observations on the mode of measuring timber. 1878. IV. 228.
— A substitution for pitting in planting. 1880. IV. 152.
— Woods of Greece. 1879. IV. 375.²
— The woods . . . of Scotland. 1879. ·IV. 358.¹
Barry, P. The Big tree of California. 1855. II. 50.¹
— Drooping trees. 1850. III. 204.¹
— The fruit garden. 1851. III. 133.
— Pinus ponderosa and P. Benthamiana. 1869. III. 306.²
Barry, William Crawford. New coniferous trees. 1884. III. 290.
— Weeping Birches. 1881. III. 357.¹
— Weeping trees. 1880. III. 204.¹
Barsanti, Adelmo. Pro arboribus. — Cattedre ambulanti. 1896. IV. 35.²
— Bandinelle per gli orti forestali. 1896. IV. 151.²
— I boschi . . . nel circondario di Lagonegro. 1889. IV. 364.
— Il Castagno nel Basso Piemonte. 1897. IV. 493.¹
— Cattedre di selvicoltura. 1898. IV. 35.²
— Ciuccieide . . . forestale. 1897. IV. 277.
— Contribuzione alla tecnologia forestale. 1895. IV. 514.¹
— Contribuzione alla tecnologia forestale. 1897. IV. 382.²
— Sulla difficoltà di rimboscare i terreni denudati. 1897. IV. 142.
— Gli effetti del disboscamento in Basilicata. 1888. IV. 48.¹
— Elenchi di vincolo forestale. 1898. IV. 277.
— Farnia o Rovere? 1896. IV. 501.¹
— Fiori di lingua e . . . d' altro. 1899. IV. 36.¹
— Giurisprudenza forestale. 1898. IV. 329.
— Sulla importanza dei boschi dal lato economico. 1896. IV. 270.
— Sull' insegnamento dell' Istituto di Vallombrosa. 1895. IV. 35.²
— Insetti dannosi ai boschi. 1889. IV. 209.²
— Macchie, bestie e comitati. 1899· IV. 135.²
— Le matricine migliori. 1895. IV. 140.
— Pei nostri forestali. 1897. IV. 293.²
— Le note alsometriche del Sotto-Ispettore. 1898. IV. 219.
— Nuova giurisprudenza forestale italiana. 1897. IV. 329.
— Per la nuova legge forestale. 1898. IV. 277.
— Per la nuova legge forestale. — I boschi del Teramano. 1896. IV. 329.
— Per la nuova legge forestale. — Rimboschimenti. 1898. IV. 166.¹
— Panelli e farina di cocco. 1895. III. 324,¹ *IV. 485.*²
— Quistione di giustizia e di cuore. 1899. IV. 311.²
— La quotizzazione dei boschi. 1898. IV. 123.¹
— Rari Nantes. 1899. IV. 283.¹
— Rassegna forestale del 1897. 1898. IV. 35.²
— Rimboscamenti volontari. 1888. IV. 166.²
— Il rimboscamento in Italia. 1896. IV. 166.¹
— Il rovescio della medaglia. 1899. IV. 277.
— Sic itur ad imum. 1899. IV. 42.¹
— La silvicoltura all' Esposizione di Bologna. 1888. IV. 20.²

— Per la sistemazione dei torrenti. 1897. IV. 186.²
— Sognando. 1899. IV. 123.¹
— Tutela dei boschi. Il coniglio. 1888. IV. 198.¹
Barstad, H. S. Beretning om stipendiereise til Jylland. 1889. III. 119.²
Barstow, Thomas. On planting Oak. 1845. III. 361.²
Barsukof, A. F. See Барсуковъ, A. Ө.
Bartalini, Biagio. Catalogo delle piante . . . di Siena. 1776. I. 424.
Bartel, Alfred. Ueber die Vertheilung des Gerbstoffes in der Rinde. 1891. IV. 515.²
Bartelink, E. J. Bijvoegsel tot de beschrijving van de kultuur . . . der kakao. 1881. III. 592.²
— The Cacao planters' manual. 1885. III. 592.²
— Handboek voor Kakao-planters. 1885. III. 592.²
— Handleiding voor de Cacao-cultuur. 1885. III. 592.²
— Handleiding voor Kakao-planters. 1885. III. 592.¹
— & Schimmelpenninck van der Oye, A. J. Kultuur . . . van de kakao. 1880. III. 592.²
Bartels. Wie das Manna in Calabrien gewonnen wird. 1790. IV. 536.¹
Bartels, Max Karl August. Der Eucalyptus in Italien. 1883. IV. 530.
— Über luftgeschorene . . . Wälder. 1893. I. 233.²
Bartels, Murray. Die Kultur der Ardisia crenulata. 1892. III. 666.¹
Bartels, Wilhelm. Studien über die Cangoura. 1894. III. 462.¹
Barter. Shea butter. 1859. III. 667.¹
Bartet. Météorologie comparée, agricole et forestière. 1890. IV. 60.¹
Bartet, E. On certain experiments made in the forest nursery at Bellefontaine. 1892. IV. 151.¹
— Deuxième mémoire sur l'influence· des éclaircies. 1888. IV. 174.
— Época de la corta en monte bajo. 1890. IV. 545.²
— Étude sur la place de production no. 2. 1889. IV. 38,² 245.
— De l'influence exercée par l'époque de l'abatage sur la production . . . des rejets de souches. 1890. IV. 140, 545.²
— Note sur les travaux exécutés . . . relativement à l'influence des éclaircies. 1888. IV. 174.
— Observations phénologiques sur les Chênes. 1892. II. 137.²
— Première étude sur les peuplement réguliers de Sapin. 1889. IV. 444.²
— Sur quelques expériences effectuées à la pépinière forestière de Bellefontaine. 1892. IV. 151.¹
— Recherches sur la production ligneuse. 1888. IV. 237, 245.
— Recherches sur le couvert des arbres de taillis sous futaie. 1892. IV. 131.
— Recherches sur le mode d'accroissement des Chênes. 1891. IV. 234, 513.
— Station d'expériences à Nancy 1891 IV. 38 ¹
— La station d'expériences institué à . . . Nancy. 1889. IV. 34, 38.²
— See also Reuss, Eduard & Bartet, E.
— & Vuillemin, Paul. Recherches sur le rouge des feuilles du Pin sylvestre. 1888. IV. 478.
— — Le rouge des feuilles du Pin sylvestre. 1888. IV. 478.
Barth. Om en særegen foryngelsesmaade af Birkeskoven. 1902. II. 110.¹
Barth, A. M. De corticis peruviani usu. · See Triller, D. W. 1758. III. 719.
Barth, Anton. Barth's Pflanzschnabel. 1891. IV. 153.¹
Barth, Ernst Adolph. Beobachtungen über die Verwandlung von Antheren in Carpelle. See Mohl, Hugo von. 1836. I. 145.¹
Barth, Fernand. Anatomie comparée . . . des Trigoniacées. 1896. II. 483,¹ 492.²
Barth, Heinrich. Reisen und Entdeckungen in Nord- und Central-Afrika. 1857. I. 483.¹
— Voyages et découvertes dans l'Afrique septentrionale. 1857. I. 483.¹
Barth, Hermann. Studien über den mikrochemischen Nachweis von Alkaloiden. 1898. I. 157.
Barth, Jacob Böchmann. Om almindingsskovene. 1857. IV. 343.²
— Om grantorken og barkbillen. 1880. IV. 199.¹
— Knudsbø eller fjeldfloraen. 1880. I. 357.
— Lidt af naturens egen skovhusholdning. 1882. II. 36.¹
— Nogle ord om Norges afskovning. 1881. IV. 282.¹
— Om skovene i deres forhold til nationaloeconomien. 1857. IV. 273.¹

— Om skovforbholdene i Finmarken. 1858. IV. 343.²
— Om skovforbholdene i Gulbrandsdalen. 1859. IV. 343.²
— Veiledning i det vigtigste af den norske skovhuusholdning. 1864. IV. 103.²
Barth, Ludwig, Ritter von. Die Geschichte der Flösserei im Flussgebiet der oberen Kinzig. 1895. IV. 390.²
— & Goldschmiedt, Guido. Sur l'acide ellagique. 1878. II. 339.¹
— — Ueber die Reduction der Ellagsäure. 1878. II. 338.²
— — Studien über die Ellagsäure. 1879. II. 339.¹
Barth, M. Die Blattfallkrankheit der Reben. 1892. III. 561.
Barth, Theodor. , Die Erhöhung der Holzzölle. 1883. IV. 284.¹
Barthe, Firmin & Boutineau, F. E. Analyse de l'huile de noix du Noyer d'Amérique. 1897. III. 354.²
Barthe-Labastide, Louis Jacques Guillaume. Opinion sur la dotation de la caisse d'amortissement [bois de l'état]. 1817. IV. 325.
Barthelat, Gilbert Joseph. Les laticifères de l'Eucommia. 1900. ·II. 254.¹
Barthélemy. Barème de cubage des bois en grume. 1878. IV. 228.
Barthélemy, Aimé. De l'absorption des bicarbonates. 1876. I. 161.
— De l'action de la chaleur. 1884. I. 232.²
— De l'évaporation des plantes. 1873. I. 167.
— De l'exhalation aqueuse des plantes. 1873. I. 167.
— Expérience sur la sève descendante. 1877. I. 165.
— De l'influence de la tension hydrostatique. 1880. I. 149.²
— Du mouvement des plantes dans Lamarck. 1883. I. 194.
— Note concernant un procédé pour combattre les ravages du Phylloxera. 1871. III. 564.²
— Note sur la floraison d'un Dasylirium. 1893. II. 81.¹
— Note sur la floraison intempestive d'un Cerisier. 1859. II. 273.¹
— Note sur les éducations automnales de vers à soie. 1857. III. 370.²
— Du passage des gaz à travers des membranes. 1873. I. 150.¹
— De la respiration et de la circulation des gaz. 1874. I. 170.
— Du rôle des stomates. 1877. I. 170.
— Du rôle que joue la cuticule dans la respiration. 1868. I. 170.
— Théorie de la respiration des plantes. 1868. I. 170·
Barthélemy-Lapommeraie, Christophe Jerôme. De la mouche de l'Olivier. 1844. III. 677.¹
Barthes, M. Glossaire botanique languedocien. 1873. I. 74.¹
Bartholinus, Thomas. Epistola de simplicibus medicamentis inquilinis. 1669. IV. 240.
Bartholomaeus Anglicus. Batman upon Bartholome, his book de proprietatibus rerum. 1300. I. 275.¹
— Boeck van den proprietevten der dinghen. 1300. I. 275.¹
— Liber de proprietatibus rerum. 1300. I. 275,¹ V. xiv.¹
Bartholomaeus de Glanvilla. See Bartholomaeus Anglicus.
Bartholow, Roberts. A practical treatise on materia medica. 1876. III. 243.
Bártik, A. Die künstliche Füllung. 1884. ·I. 248.¹
Bartl, Josef. Die Bewegung der Hölzer auf den Holzriesen. 1889. IV. 390.¹
Bartlett, John Russell. Personal narrative of explorations . . . in Texas. 1856. I. 494.
Bartling, Fridericus Theophilus. See Bartling, Friedrich Gottlieb.
Bartling, Friedrich Gottlieb. Beiträge zur Flora der oesterreichschen Küstenländer. 1825. I. 447.
— Der Botanische Garten zu Göttingen. 1837. I. 47.
— Diosmeas Diosmearum capensium. ·1843. II. 396.²
— Diosmeae A. Juss. 1844. II. 397.¹
— De Galphimiis mexicanis annotationes. 1839. ·II. 425.²
— Labiatae Juss. 1844. II. 762.¹
— De littoralibus ex insulis maris liburnici. 1820. I. 451.
— Myoporineae. 1844. II. 805.²
— Ordines naturales plantarum. 1830. I. 260.
— Plantae Eckionianae: Laurineae. 1837. I. 494.
— & Wendland, H. L. Beiträge zur Botanik. 1824. I. 267.
— — Diosmeae descriptae et illustratae. 1824. II. 396.²
Bartolotti, Pierre. L'essence de Myrte. 1892. III. 637.¹
— Kamala et rottlérine. 1894. III. 520.¹
Barton, Benjamin H. & Castle, Thomas. The British flora medica. 1837. IV. 80.
Barton, Benjamin Smith. Collections pour un essai sur la matière médicale des États-Unis. 1798. III. 262.¹

Barton, Benjamin Smith (*continued*).
— Collections . . , toward a materia medica of the United States. 1798. III. 262.[1]
— Elements of botany. 1803. I. 84, 523.
— An epitome of Mr. Forsyth's Treatise on the culture . . . of fruit-trees. *See* FORSYTH, William. 1802. III. 141.
— Fragments of the natural history of Pennsylvania. 1799. I. 313.
— Specimen of a geographical view of the trees and shrubs. 1809. I. 306.
Barton, John. A lecture on the geography of plants. 1827. I. 298, V. XVI.[2]
— Lecture sur la géographie des plantes. 1827. I. 298.
Barton, William Paul Crillon. Compendium Florae philadelphicae. 1818. I. 313.
— Engravings of fifty medicinal plants. 1832. III. 62.
— A flora of North America. 1821. I. 306.
— Florae philadelphicae prodromus. 1815. I. 313.
— Vegetable materia medica of the United States. 1817. III. 62.
Bartosságh, Joseph von. Beobachtungen . . . über den Götterbaum. 1841. III. 506.[2]
Bartram, Frank M. Nuts and nut culture. 1899. III. 134.[1]
Bartram, Isaac. A memoir on the distillation of Persimons. 1771. III. 670.[1]
Bartram, William. Reisen durch Nord- und Südkarolina. 1791. I. 318.
— Reizen door Noord- en Zuid Carolina. 1791. I. 318.
— Travels through North and South Carolina. 1791. I. 317.[2]
— Voyage dans les parties sud de l'Amérique septentrionale. 1791. I. 318.
Baruffi, G. B. Carbon fossile. 1866. IV. 55.[1]
Baruffi, G. F. Baco della Querce. 1866. IV. 502.[1]
Barvic, K. Vernichtung des Borkenkäfers. 1875. IV. 204.
Barville de Livet, Léon, *marquis* de. La Tunisie. 1880. IV. 379.[1]
Barvitius, Carlo. Catalogo delle piante che coltivansi nel D. Giardino di Colorno. 1825. III. 29.[1]
Bary, de. Bush-tea vom Cap der Guten Hoffnung. 1870. III. 473.[2]
Bary, Anton de. *See* BARY, H. A. de.
Bary, Erwin de. Le dernier rapport d'un Européen sur Ghât. 1898. I. 486.
Bary, Heinrich Anton de. Beiträge zur Morphologie . . . der Pilze. 1864. III. 433.[2]
— Comparative anatomy of the vegetative organs. 1877. I. 100.[1]
— Corypha- und Phoenix-Krankheiten. 1884. III. 318.[2]
— Disease of Palms. 1884. III. 318.[2]
— Die Erscheinung der Symbiose. 1879. I. 233.[2]
— Morphologie und Physiologie der Pilze. *See* HOFMEISTER, Wilhelm. I. 90.
— Über einen neuen . . . der Kiefer verderblichen Pilz. 1864. IV. 476.
— Notizen über die Blüthen einiger Cycadeen. 1870. II. 3.[1]
— De plantarum generatione sexuali. 1853. I. 199.
— Der schwarze Brenner. 1878. III. 577.
— Ueber den sogenannten Brenner. 1874. III. 577.
— "Verbänderung" an Tanacetum. 1868. II. 602.[1]
— Vergleichende Anatomie der Vegetationsorgane. 1877. I. 100,[1] 524.[1] *See also* HOFMEISTER, Wilhelm. 1865. I. 90.
— Ueber die Wachsüberzüge der Epidermis. 1871. I. 129.[2]
— *See also* MIDDELDORPF, (*Oberförster*) & BARY, Anton de; Де-Бари, А.
Bas, F. P. de. Opgave van eenige proeven, ten bewijze dat veele van Hollands duinen . . . kunnen gebezigd worden. 1775. IV. 159.
Bas-Rhin — Société des sciences, agriculture et arts. *See* SOCIÉTÉ DES SCIENCES . . . DE LA BASSE-ALSACE. I. 15.
Basarow. *See also* BAZAROF.
Basarow, Aleksandr Ivanovich. Le Genévrier en Crimée. 1886. III. 303.[1]
Basel, W. H., SENN VAN BASEL, W. H.
Basel — Naturforschende Gesellschaft. *See* NATURFORSCHENDE . . . I, 26.[1]
Basel — Societas physico-medica basiliensis. *See* SOCIETAS . . . I. 27.
Baselice, Luigi. Flora biccarese. 1842. I. 426.
Basile, Gioacchino. Sullo adattamento delle Viti americane in Sicilia. 1890. III. 558.[1]
Basiner, Theodor Friedrich Julius. Ein Beitrag zur vergleichenden Klimatologie. 1860. III. 217.
— Ueber die Biegsamkeit der Pflanzen gegen klimatische Einflüsse. 1857. III. 43.

— Enumeratio monographicé specierum generis Hedysari. 1845. II. 363.[2]
— Gedrängte Darstellung der Herbstvegetation am Aral-See. 1844. I. 456.
— Naturwissenschaftliche Reise durch die Kirgisensteppe. 1848. I. 456.
— Schädlicher Einfluss des Schnee's auf Bäume. 1861. III. 184,[2] IV. 190.
Baskerville, Thomas. Affinities of plants. 1839. I. 251.
Bassagaña, Pedro. Flora médico-farmacéutica abreviada. 1859. III. 58.
Basse-Alsace — Société des.sciences, agriculture et arts. *See* SOCIÉTÉ . . . I. 15.
Bassermann, Fried. Ueber Nanary. 1834. III. 693.[1]
Basses-Pyrénées — Société d'horticulture et de viticulture. *See* SOCIÉTÉ . . . III. 22.
Basset, (*Oberförster, Ullersdorf*). Beitrag zur Beantwortung der . . . Frage: " Welche Regeln sind bei Gewinnung des nachhaltigen Natural-Ertrages . . . zu befolgen?" 1847. IV. 130.
— Welche Massregeln werden . . . angewendet, um den Verheerungen durch Stürme . . . vorzubeugen? 1854. IV. 189.[1]
— & others. Konferenzverhandlung über . . . Behandlung des Plänterwaldes. 1849. IV. 130.
Bassett, William F. Kalmia poisonous to sheep. 1882. III. 652.[2]
— Trees with showy autumn foliage. 1887. III. 207.[1]
Bassi, Agostino. Tre nuove memorie . . . la prima versa sulla coltura del Gelsi. 1844. III. 376.
Bassières, E. Notice sur la Guyane. 1900. III. 268.[1]
Bassus, Ferdinandus. Novae plantarum species. 1783. II. 737.[2]
Bastard, Toussaint. Essai sur la flore du département de Maine et Loire. 1809. I. 407.
— Notice sur les végétaux . . . du Jardin des plantes d'Angers. 1810. I. 75.
Über Bastard-Erzeugung. *See* On THE PREDOMINATION- . . . 1855. I. 248.[1]
Bastelaer, Desiré Alexandre van. Promenades d'un botaniste. 1865. I. 392.
Bastelica, A. M. COSTA DE. *See* COSTA DE BASTELICA, A. M.
Baster, Job. Natuurkundige uitspanningen. 1762. I. 261.
— Verhandeling over de voortteeling. 1765. I. 205.
— Welke boomen, graanen . . . zonde men met vrucht in ons land kunnen invoeren? 1779. III. 270.[2]
Bastian, Fr. Destruction du phylloxéra. 18 . . ? III. 758.[1]
Bastian, Henry Charlton. Flora of Falmouth. 1850. I. 400.
Bastick, William. Analysis of ashes of the bark of the Beech tree. 1844. IV. 500.[1]
Bastien, Jean François. Année du jardinage. 1800. III. 125.
— Calendrier du jardinier. 1807. III. 113.
— Dictionnaire botanique et pharmaceutique. 1802. I. 33.
— La flore jardinière. 1809. III. 86.
— Nouveau manuel du jardinier. 1807. III. 113.
Bastin, Edson Sewell. Elements of botany. 1887. I. 92.
— Laboratory exercises in botany. 1895. I. 37.[1]
— & Trimble, Henry. A contribution to the knowledge of some North American Coniferae. 1896. II. 14.[1]
Bastoulh, de. Observations sur la culture du Châtaignier. 1845. III. 359.[1]
Basu, B. C. Note on the cultivation of Black Pepper in Assam. 1898. III. 343.[2]
— Note on the lac industry of Assam. 1900. III. 232.[2]
Bataafsch genootschap der proefondervindelijke wijsbegeerte te Rotterdam. Nieuwe verhandelingen. I. 15.
Bataafsche maatschappij der wetenschappen te Haarlem. Natuurkundige verhandelingen. *See* HOLLANDSCHE MAATSCHAPPIJ DER WETENSCHAPPEN. I. 15.
Batalin, Alexander. Aperçu des travaux russes sur la géographie des plantes. 1870. II. 716.[1]
— Beobachtungen über die Bestäubung einiger Pflanzen. 1870. II. 716.[1]
— Einführung der parasitischen Pflanzen. 1880. III. 385.[1]
— Neue asiatische Bäume und Gesträuche. 1894. I. 457.
— Neue asiatische Gehölze. 1893. I. 457.
— Notae de plantis asiaticis. 1891. I. 459.
— Über die Wirkung des Lichtes. 1871. I. 230.
— *See also* БАТАЛИН, А. Ө.
Bâtard. *See* BASTARD, Toussaint.
Batavia — Gesellschaft der Künste und Wissenschaften. *See* GESELLSCHAFT . . . I. 12.

Batavia, de hoofdstad van Neerlands O. Indien. 1782. I. 467.

Bataviaasch genootschap van kunsten en wetenschappen. Catalogus van de Bibliotheek. *See* BLEEKER, Pieter. 1853. I. 2.

Bataviaasch genootschap van kunsten en wetenschappen. Verhandelingen. I. 29.[1]

Batavian society of arts and sciences. Transactions. *See* BATAVIAASCH GENOOTSCHAP VAN KUNSTEN EN WETENSCHAPPEN. I. 29.[1]

Batchelor, John & Miyabe, Kingo. Ainu economic plants. 1893. III. 91.[3]

Bate, George. Pharmacopoea Bateana, na qual se contem. 1688. III. 251.

—Pharmacopoea Batheana. Osteapotheek. 1688. III. 251.

— Pharmacopoeia Bateana. 1688. III: 251.

— Pharmacopoeia Bateana; or, Bate's dispensatory. 1688. III. 251.

Bateham, M. B. Osage Orange hedges. 1849. III. 372.[1]

— Our centennial Magnolia tree. 1876. II. 211.[3]

Batelli, Andrea. · Contribuzione (prima-terza) sulla flora umbra. 1885. I. 429.

Bateman, C. S. L. The first ascent of the Kasai. 1889. V. XXVIII.[2]

Bateman, James. Particulars respecting . . . cultivation &c. of the Averrhoa. 1842. III. 491.[3]

— Quelques particularités . . . de culture, etc., de l'Averrhoa. 1842. III. 491.[3]

Bates, Henry Walter. The naturalist on the river Amazons. 1863. I. 342.

— *See also* БЕТСЪ, В. Г.

Bateson, Anna. On the change of shape exhibited by turgescent pith in water. 1889. I. 129.[1]

Bateson, William. Problems of heredity. 1900. I. 248.[3]

Bath — Society instituted at Bath for the encouragement of agriculture. *See* SOCIETY . . . III. 18.

Bath and West of England society for the encouragement of agriculture. Letters. *See* SOCIETY INSTITUTED AT BATH . . . III. 18.

Bath natural history and antiquarian field club. Proceedings. I. 17.

Bathgate, G. Einiges über Weissdorn-Hecken. 1868. III. 422.[2]

Bathgate, A. Araucaria and Eucalypti. 1900. III. 298,[1] 634.[1]

Batise, Jules. Essai sur les plantes grimpantes. 1883. III. 204.[3]

— De l'incision annulaire. 1886. III. 175.[1]

Batka, Johann B. Ueber die Abstammung der Sennes-Blätter. 1849. II. 342.[3]

— Analyse des follicules de séné. 1836. III. 470.[3]

— Artemisia glomerata Sieber. 1827. II. 852.[1]

— Om China rubra og China Savanilla, 1851, III 721.

— Ueber China rubra und Savanilla. 1851. III. 721.

— Über die Entstehung der Harze. 1850. I. 180.[3]

— Om folia Sennae og de planter, der levere dem. 1849. II. 342.[3]

— Mémoire sur divers objets de la matière médicale. 1830. III. 244.

— Monographie der Cassien Gruppe Senna. 1866. II. 342.[2] On the plants from which Senna leaves are obtained. 1849 (1850). II. 342,[2] III. 470.[3]

— Ueber Senna. 1849. II. 342.[3]

— Ueber Senna. 1854. II. 342.[3]

— Senna Hookeriana. 1863. II. 343.[1]

— On Vateria indica. 1832. II. 561.[1]

— Sur le Vateria indica. 1832. II. 561.[1]

— On Vateria indica and some other plants. 1832. II. 225.[3]

— Sur le Vateria indica et quelques autres plantes. 1832. II. 225.[3]

— Ueber den Weihrauch. 1872. III. 509.[3]

Batka, Wenceslaus. Lauri Malabathri Lamarckii adumbratio. 1835. II. 224.[3]

Bátky, Károly. Futóhomok megfogása és használása módjáról. 1842. IV. 145.

Batlle, José. Contestación al artículo "Aspiraciones." 1897. IV. 553.[3]

Batsch, August Johann Georg Karl. Analyses florum. 1790. I. 97.

— Ausartung einer Blume von Yucca gloriosa. 1791. II. 88.[1]

— Bau der Cypressenblätter. 1791. II. 29.[1]

— Beiträge und Entwürfe zur pragmatischen Geschichte der drei Naturreiche. 1801. I. 264.

— Beweglichkeit des Cactus mammillaris. 1791. II. 595.[1]

— Blätterdrüsen von Nyctanthes Sambac. 1791. II. 711.[1]

— Blume von Cotyledon orbiculata. 1791. II. 235.[3]

— Blume von Nyctanthes Sambac. 1791. II. 711.[1]

— Blumenfüllung von Nerium Oleander. 1791. II. 729.[1]

— Blumenzergliederungen. 1790. I. 97.

— Botanik for Fruentimmer. 1795. I. 93.

— Botanik für Frauenzimmer. 1795. I. 93.

— Botanique pour les femmes. 1795. I. 93.

— Botanische Bemerkungen. 1791. I. 264.

— Botanische Unterhaltungen für Naturfreunde. 1793. I. 93.

— Catalogus plantarum Horti botanici ducalis, Jenae. 1797. I. 44.

— Cistus ladaniferus. 1791. II. 564.[3]

— Conspectus Horti botanici ducalis jenensis. . 1795. I. 44.

— Dispositio generum plantarum Europae. 1794. I. 348.[3]

— Dispositio generum plantarum jenensium. 1786. I. 374.

— Drehung von Baumstämmen. 1791. I. 107.[1]

— Entstehung der Dornen. 1791. II. 289.[1]

— Frucht der grossen Cocosnuss. 1791. II. 67.[3]

— Frucht von Cocos lapidea. 1791. II. 67.[1]

— Fruchtartiger Stengelknoten. 1791. II. 837.[1]

— Der geöffnete Blumengarten. 1798. I. 93.

— Geschlechtstheile von Decumaria barbara. 1791. II. 238.[3]

— Geschlechtstheile von Philadelphus coronarius. 1791. II. 242.[1]

— Geschlechtstheile von Plumbago zeylanica. 1791. II. 696.[1]

— Grundzüge der Naturgeschichte des Gewächsreichs.. 1801. I. 84.

— Narben der vorigen Blume [Crassula coccinea]. 1791. II. 237.[1]

— Staubgefässe der Cassien. 1791. II. 343.[1]

— Staubgefässe von Crassula coccinea. 1791. II. 237.[1]

— Synopsis . . . generum plantarum. 1794. I. 259.

— Tabula affinitatum regni vegetabilis. 1802. I. 259.

— Ueberzug des gemeinen Oehlbaumes. 1791. II. 713.[1]

— Ueberzug von Elaeagnus angustifolia. 1791. II. 607.[1]

— Versuch einer Anleitung zur Kenntnis und Geschichte der Pflanzen. 1787. I. 83.

Battandier, Jules Aimé. Considérations sur les plantes . . . de la flore algérienne. 1895. I. 486.

— Contribution à l'étude des caractères taxonomiques tirés de la chimie végétale. 1897. II. 322.[1]

— Sur l'histoire des alcaloïdes des Fumariacées. 1895. III. 408.[3]

— Note sur quelques plantes d'Algérie. 1880. I. 485.

— Plantes médicinales. 1900. III. 93.[1]

— & Malosse, Th. Sur un nouvel alcaloïde. 1897. II.361.[1]

— & Trabut, Louis. L'Algérie. 1898. I. 486.

— — Algérie; plantes médicinales. 1889. III. 93.[1]

— — Contributions à la florule . . . d'Alger. 1879. I. 405.

— — Extraits d'un rapport sur quelques voyages botaniques en Algérie. 1891. I. 486.

— — Flore d'Alger. 1884. I. 485.

— — Flore de l'Algérie. 1888. I. 486.

Batten, Edmund Chisholm. The forest trees of Somerset. 1890. IV. 358.[2]

Batten, G. H. M. Boehmeria njveą. 1878. III. 382.[1]

Batten, John Hallet. Notes and recollections on Tea . . . in Kumaon. 1878. III. 603.

Un battesimo commemorativo. 1880. III. 34.[1]

Batteux, Charles. Mémoires concernant l'histoire . . . des Chinois. 1777. I. 458.

— Le Mou-tan ou Pivoine. 1778. II. 200.[1]

Battle, K. P. *See* PHILLIPS, James & BATTLE, K. P. & R. H.

Battuš, Carolus. Het secret boek — van boomen. 1694. I. 288.

Baty, William. The management of plantations in Cumberland. 1884. IV. 120.

Bau-Instruktion für die Organe der k. k. Staats- und Forst- und Domänenverwaltung. 1887. IV. 307.[1]

Baubigny, Henry. Recherches sur le camphre. 1869. III. 233.[1]

Bauby. Restauration et conservation des terrains en montagne. 1900. IV. 164,[3] 186.[1]

Bauchery, A. · Les arbres & arbustes à feuilles panachées. 1895. III. 206.[3]

Baud, H. W. L. De cultuur van Liberiakoffie. 1894. III. 742.[2]

Baudet. L'emploi de naphtaline pour combattre le phylloxera. 1871. III. 564.[2]

Baudet, P. J. H. Over de bereiding van het hout tegen be-
derf. 1868. IV. 419.
Baudet-Lafarge, J. A. Agriculture du département du Puy-
de-Dôme. 1860. III. 125.
Baudin, Émile. Utilisation du gaz de bois. 1900. IV. 433.[2]
— Valeur calorifique du bois de Sapin. 1900. IV. 413.[1]
Baudisch, Friedrich. Absterben von Lärchentriebspitzen.
1881. IV. 451.
— Zur Anzucht der Lärche. 1900. IV. 450.
— Ein Beitrag zur Schädlichkeit der Fichtenquirl-Schildlaus.
1885. IV. 456.
— Beschädigungen durch den Hallimasch. 1879. IV. 211.[2]
— Eine Betrachtung zu Gunsten der Tanne. 1885. IV. 444.[2]
— Bildet die obligatorische Kranken- und Unfallversicherung
der forstwirthschaftlichen Arbeiter ein Gebot der Nothwen-
digkeit? 1898. IV. 311.[1]
— Die Bildung der Hiebszüge. 1887. IV. 245.
— Callidium luridum L. 1896. IV. 457.
— Einfluss des Nonnenraupenfrasses auf den Zuwachs. 1895.
IV. 202.
— Einige Worte über Durchforstungen. 1884. IV. 173.
— Einiges über den Mittelwaldbetrieb. 1896. IV. 131.
— Die Elater-Larve als Tannenschädling. 1884. IV. 445.
— Die Frage des Umtriebes für die reinen Tannen . . .
bestände. 1889. IV. 446.[2]
— Fragmentarisches zur Forsteinrichtungsfrage. 1886. IV.
245.
— Genügt der Schutz der jungen Kiefern gegen Frühfrost.
1881. IV. 477.
— Ist die Nachzucht der Rothbuche . . . empfehlenswerth?
1898. IV. 499.[1]
— Ueber die Lärche in Mähren. 1895. IV. 450.
— Eine Lanze für die Tanne. 1897. IV. 444.[2]
— Ueber den Lichtungsbetrieb. 1889. IV. 131.
— Ueber den Lösbieb und die Hiebsfolge. 1883. IV. 244.[2]
— Ueber Nectria ditissima. 1895. IV. 212.
— Ueber die Nonne. 1891. IV. 200.
— Die Pflanzlanze. 1879. IV. 152.
— Ueber " Phytophthora omnivora." 1888. IV. 497.
— Der Plänterbetrieb und der Kleinwaldbesitz. 1885. IV.
131.
— Reflexionen über die Verbandweite. 1883. IV. 154.[1]
— Ueber Schneedruck-Schaden. 1884. IV. 190.
— Eine Studie über die Umwandlung herabgekommener Nie-
derwälder. 1883. IV. 132.[1]
— Die Tannenrindenlaus. 1882. IV. 445.
— Ueber den Tulpenbaum. 1886. III. 398.[2]
— Ueber die Umwandlung von Niederwald in Nadelholz-
hochwald. 1899. IV. 129.
— Untersuchung von Probebäumen auf . . . Nonne. 1892.
IV. 201.
— Ueber das Vorkommen des krummzähnigen Tannen-
Borkenkäfers auf der Weymouthskiefer. 1893. IV. 470.[1]
— Wind und Wald. 1884. IV. 189.[2]
— Ein Wort über die Kernschäle. 1882. IV. 445.
— Ein Wort über die Rothbuche. 1881. IV. 495.
Baudrillart, Jacques Joseph. Code forestier. 1827. IV. 324.
— Dictionnaire général raisonné et historique des eaux et
forêts. 1823. IV. 22.[2]
— Economie forestière. Amélioration. 1812. IV. 242.
— Extraits des ouvrages . . . de Hartig et de Burgsdorff, sur
les moyens de lever les sables. 1806. IV. 145.
— Forst-Gesetzbuch. 1827. IV. 324.
— Mémoire sur l'aménagement des forêts. 1812. IV. 242.
— Mémoire sur la pesanteur spécifique des bois. 1815. IV.
411.[1]
— Mémoire sur le déboisement des montagnes. 1831. IV.
42.[1]
— Mémoire sur les incendies dans les forêts. 1810 .? IV. 183.[1]
— Mémoire sur les moyens de favoriser l'éducation des bois
courbes. 1812. IV. 425.[1]
— Notes sur les caractères du dépérissement des arbres. 1822.
I. 193.[1]
— Recueil chronologique des réglemens forestiers. 1821.
IV. 323.[2]
— Signs of increase, maturity and decay in trees. 1828.
I. 192.[1]
— Traité général des eaux et forêts. 1821. IV. 101.
— See also Bosc, L. A. G. & Baudrillart, J. J.
— & Rast-Maupas. Plantations des routes et des avenues.
1809. III. 209.
Baudrimont, Alexandre Édouard. Sur la cire des fruits.
1843. I. 182.[1]
— Études relatives au phylloxera. 1874. III. 567.[1]

— Expériences faites avec des agents vénéneux sur des Vignes
saines. 1874. III. 560.
— Expériences faites sur des rameaux de Vigne. 1874. III.
560.
— Leçon sur le phylloxéra. 1874. III. 759.
— Observations relatives aux expériences communiquées ré-
cemment par M. A. Poëy. 1872. I. 230.
— Observations sur l'existence de la matière minérale dans les
plantes. 1872. I. 153.
Baudrimont, Ernest. Sur les bourgeons de Sapin des phar-
macies. 1873. IV. 443.[3]
— Explication des phénomènes que présente l'iodure bleu
d'amidon. 1860. I. 140.[1]
Bauer. See also **Baur.**
Bauer, (*Hauptmann*). Kurze Anleitung zur zweckmässigen
Kultur der Wildgründe. 1850. IV. 155.[1]
Bauer, F. E. & **Hilger,** Albert. Beiträge zur chemischen
Kenntnis der Pfefferfrucht. 1896. III. 343.[1]
Bauer, Ferdinand Lucas. Icones plantarum norfolkicarum.
182 .? I. 508.[2]
— Illustrationes florae Novae Hollandiae. 1813. I. 500.
Bauer, Franz Andreas. Delineations of exotick plants. 1796.
II. 664.[1]
— Tabulae ineditae plantarum in prima Cookiana expeditione
. . . collectarum. 177 .? I. 499.[3]
Bauer, Johann Adam. De Cydoniis. See **Heister,** Lorenz.
1744. III. 423.[3]
Bauer, Johann Lorenz. Herkunft der schädlichen Wald-
raupen. 1797. IV. 205.[2]
— Versuch eines Unterrichts für den Forstmann zur Ver-
hütung der Waldverheerung durch Insecten. 1800 .• IV. 206.
Bauer, Josef. Das Invaliditäts- und Altersversicherungs-
Gesetz. 1890. IV. 310.[1]
Bauer, Karl. Die Bedeutung des normalen Holzvorrathes.
1894. IV. 246.
— Zur Frage der Wälderbesteuerung. 1870. IV. 285.[1]
— Untersuchungen über gerbstoffführende Pflanzen. 1890.
I. 183.
Bauer, S. Landwirthschaftliche und technische Naturge-
schichte. 1839. IV. 61.[1]
Bauernschmitt, Josef Erhardt Franz Lothar. Die Pflanzen-
welt. 1846. I. 515.
Bauhin, Johann. De plantis a divis sanctisve nomen haben-
tibus. 1591. I. 72.[1]
— De plantis Absynthii nomen habentibus. 1593. II. 851,[1]
III. 754.[1]
— & **Cherler,** J. H. Historia plantarum universalis. 1619.
I. 284.
— — Historiae plantarum generalis. 1619. I. 284.
Bauhin, Johann Kaspar. Positionum botanico-anatomicarum
centuria. See **Eglinger,** Nicolas. 1685. I. 97.
Bauhin, Kaspar. Animadversions in Historiam generalem
plantarum. 1601. I. 283.
— Catalogus plantarum circa Basileam. 1622. I. 432,[1]
V. xxii.[2]
— Φυτοπίναξ. 1596. I. 283.
— Πίναξ theatri botanici. 1623. I. 284.
— Πρόδρομος theatri botanici. 1620. I. 284.
— Theatri botanici. 1658. I. 286.
Bauholz-Verkauf. 1860. IV. 358.[1]
Bauke. Wie verfährt man bei der Aufnahme eines Schlages.
1886. IV. 387.[2]
Baum, H. Die Standorte der Tumboa Bainesii. 1900. II.
55.[2]
Baum, O. M. See Баумъ, О. М.
Baum, Otto Ernst. Abhandlung über die ungeschlechtliche
Vermehrung. 1850. III. 153.
— Die ungeschlechtliche Vermehrung. 1850. I. 205.
Baum-Album der Schweis. 1896. I. 298.
Baumann, (*Gebrüder*). Unterweisung über das Verfahren . . .
beim Empfange von Gewächsen. 1837. III. 155.
Baumann, Aegid. Kurzer Unterricht zur Erziehung der Obst-
bäume. 1809. III. 136.
Baumann, Charles A. von Napoléon. Bollweilerer Camellien-
sammlung. 1828. II. 550.[1]
Baumann, Christian. Der Seidenbau in Deutschland. 1784.
III. 373.
Baumann, F. J. Catalogue des arbres fruitiers. 1788. III.
70.
Ein baumartiger Wachholder, Juniperus communis in Nor-
wegen. 1886. II. 31.[1]
Baumbach, von, (*Oberforstmeister, Meiningen*). Ueber das
forstliche Verhalten der bunten Mergel. 1868. IV. 68.
— Die Weymuthskiefer betreffend. 1868. IV. 469.

Baumbach, von, (*Landforstmeister, Berlin*). Ueber die Verwendung der transportablen Eisenbahnen. 1885. IV. 391.

Baumbach, Christian Friedrich. Tabellarische Ausrechnungen des Holz-, Stamm- und Pflanz-Geldes. 1825. IV. 254.

Baumé, Antoine. Mémoire sur les Marrons d'Inde. 1797. *II. 481*,[2] III. 537.[2]

Baume de gurgum. 1870. III. 611.[1]

Baumer, Heinrich. Allgemeine Uebersicht der Forste des Allodialgutes Lissitz. 1895. IV. 369.

— Die Betriebseinrichtung in den fürstl. Liechtenstein'schen Forsten. 1889. IV. 230.[1]

— Die Schwarznuss . . . als Waldbaum. 1886. IV. 488.[1]

Baumer, Johannes. De Succino. 1750. III. 227.[1]

Baumer, Wilhelm von. Betrachtungen über die Abnahme der Wälder. 1846. IV. 43.

Baumes. *See* VINCENS, J. C. & BAUMES.

Über den Baumfrevel. 1790. IV. 196.[2]

Baumgaertner, Johann Christian. Gartenlust in Geheimnissen. 1732. III. 103.

— Vollständige, liebliche und annehmliche Gartenlust. 1730. III. 103.

Baumgardt, E. Ueber die Flora der Insel Rügen. 1845. I. 381.

— Flora der Mittelmark. 1856. I. 383.

Baumgarten, F. L. Agriculture in Malacca. 1849. III. 320.[1]

— Uses of the Borassus gomutus. 1849. III. 320.[1]

Baumgarten, Johann Christian Gottlob. De corticis Ulmi campestris natura. 1791. III. 365,[1] *365*.[2]

— Enumeratio stirpium . . . Transsilvaniae. 1816. I. 445.

— Flora lipsiensis. 1790. I. 374.

— Sertum lipsicum. 1790. I. 44.

Baumgarten-Crusius, Arthur. Das Forststrafgesetz für das Königreich Sachsen. 1848. IV. 322.[1]

Baumgartner, Julius. Ueber den Begriff "Wald." 1891. IV. 56.

— Zur Durchforstungsfrage. 1890. IV. 174.

— Ueber ein in Frankreich übliches Taxationsverfahren. 1891. IV. 249.[1]

— Aus den Kinderjahren der Forsteinrichtung in Oesterreich. 1886. IV. 368.

— Ueber die Verjüngung von Mittelgebirgsforsten. 1898. IV. 140.

Baumhauer, Édouard Henri von. Sur la composition de la gutta percha. 1860. III. 231.

— Over de middelen om het . . . hout tegen de vernieling door den paalworm te vrijwaren. 1866. IV. 419.

— Over de middelen om het hout tegen de vernieling van den paalworm te beschutten. 1868. IV. 419.

— Ueber die Mittel das . . . Holz gegen die Zerstörung des Holzwurms zu bewahren. 1868. IV. 419.

— Sur les moyens de préserver le bois des attaques du taret. 1868. IV. 419.

— Ontleding van de zaden van den Phytelephas. 1843. III. 330.[1]

— Scheikundige onderzoekingen . . . van de harde bekleedsels der vruchten. 1845. I. 152.[2]

— Over eene stof, voorkomende in de perispermia der zaden. 1846. I. 152.[2]

— Sur le taret et les moyens de préserver le bois. 1866. IV. 419.

— Untersuchung der Samen von Phytelephas. 1843. III. 330.[1]

Der Baumhöhenmesser von T. Christen. 1892. IV. 216.

Baumpflanzungen mit Kanonen. 1886. III. 166.

Baumriesen. 1890. II. 51.[1]

Ueber Baumroden und Stocksprengung. 1863. IV. 386.

Die Baumschulen von André Leroy. *See* KOCH, Karl. 1864. I. 58.

Baumsetzlingssucht in Töpfen. 1863. III. 161.

Baumstark, Edward. Ueber staats- und landwirthschaftliche Academien. 1839. IV. 29.

Baumstümpfe zerstören. 1883. IV. 387.[1]

Baup, André. Mémoire sur la culture des Vignes. 1819. III. 554.[1]

Baup, Samuel. Harz von Arbol-a-brea und Elemiharz. 1851. III. 510.[1]

— Sur les résines de l'Arbol-abrea. 1851. III. 245, *510*.[1]

Baur. *See also* BAUER.

Baur, Alfred. Ueber das Burseraceen-Opoponax. 1894, 1895. III. 509,[2] *511*.[1]

Baur, Carl. Die Araucarien und ihre Kultur. 1891. III. 297.[2]

Baur, František. Vyšetřování ohledně klíčivosti semen jednotlivých dřevin. 1880. I. 527, *IV. 65*.[2]

Baur, Franz Adolph Gregor. Anleitung zur Aufnahme der Bäume und Bestände. 1861. IV. 214.

— Ueber die Aufstellung von Holzertragstafeln. 1878. IV. 236.

— Bemerkungen . . . über Prof. Pressler's neue Baum- und Bestandesschätzungs-methode. 1859. IV. 213.

— Ueber die Berechnung der zu leistenden Entschädigungen für die Abtretung von Wald. 1868. IV. 255..

— Die Bildung der Ackererde. 1883. IV. 69.

— Der Blitz als Waldverderber. 1873. IV. 194.

— Nach dreissigjährigem Kriege. 1889. IV. 258.

— Ueber Durchforstungen. 187.? IV. 173.

— Zur Ehrenrettung des Waldes. 1872. IV. 101.

— Ein einfaches Bonitirungsverfahren. 1877. IV. 244.

— Einige Resultate von Durchforstungsversuchen. 1894. IV. 174.

— Etwas über Ocularschätzung. 1866. IV. 217.

— Expériences sur les écorces de Chêne. 1876. IV. 515.[1]

— Fichte. 1898. IV. 459.[1]

— Die Fichte in Bezug auf Ertrag. 1876. IV. 458.

— Form und Wesen der österreichischen Cameraltaxe. 1882. IV. 250.[1]

— Formzahlen und Massentafeln für die Fichte. 1890. IV. 458.

— Forstakademie oder allgemeine Hochschule? 1875. IV. 29.

— Ueber forstliche Versuchsstationen. 1868. IV. 38.[1]

— Zur forstlichen Unterrichtsfrage. 1875. IV. 29.

— Zur Frage des Zinsfusses, insbesondere bei Servituten-Ablösungen. 1878. IV. 256.

— Die Frosterscheinungen des Jahres 1869. 1870. IV. 191.[1]

— Der gegenwärtige Stand der Durchforstungsfrage. 1892. IV. 174.

— Zur Geschichte der Durchforstungen. 1882. IV. 24,[1] *173*.

— Ueber Durchforstungen . . . des Holzes. 1892. IV. 461.[1]

— Grundsätze und Ergebnisse der Waldbesteuerung im Grossherzogthum Hessen. 1874. IV. 284.[1]

— Handbuch der Waldwertberechnung. 1886. IV. 253.

— Die Holzmesskunde. 1861. IV. 214.

— Die Holzmesskunst. 1861. IV. 214.

— An den kgl. preuss. Forstmeister Herrn W. Weise in Eberswalde in Sachen der Ertragstafeln. 1883. IV. 237.

— Die Kgl. württemb. forstliche Versuchsanstalt in Hohenheim. 1874. IV. 38.[1]

— Lehrbuch der niederen Geodäsie. 1858. IV. 264.

— Zur Lehre von der mittleren Bestandeshöhe. 1882. IV. 215.

— Neue Formzahlen für die Gemeine Kiefer. 1881. IV. 481.

— Ein neuer Baumhöhen- und Stärkenmesser. 1883. IV. 215.

— Ein neuer Zuwachsstab. 1883. IV. 233.

— Die neuesten Kundgebungen über meine . . . Waldwerthberechnung betreffenden Veröffentlichungen. 1886. IV. 257.

— Die ökonomische und socialpolitische Seite des Waldes. 1885. IV. 270.

— Die Rothbuche in Bezug auf Ertrag. 1881. IV. 498.

— Ueber die Sonderstellung des Waldes. 1895. IV. 45.

— Ueber die Sonderstellung des Waldes. 1895. IV. 270.

— Taxation af Træmassen i Skoven. 1869. IV. 217.

— Ueber Theorie und Praxis der heutigen Waldwerthberechnung. 1885. IV. 257.

— Ueber unmotivirte Kahlschlagwirthschaft. 1871. IV. 129.

— Untersuchung über den Einfluss der Grösse der Eicheln. 1880. II. 137.[2]

— Untersuchungen über den Festgehalt und das Gewicht der Hölzer. 1874. IV. 415.[2]

— Untersuchungen über den Festgehalt und das Gewicht des Schichtholzes und der Rinde. 1879. IV. 217.

— Untersuchungen über die Brusthöhenformzahlen der Fichte. 1876. IV. 458.

— Untersuchungen über die Keimkraft. 1880. III. 156.[2]

— Untersuchungen über die Normalformzahlen der Fichte. 1876. IV. 458.

— Untersuchungen über die Tiefe der Bedeckung . . . bei Saaten. 1880. IV. 149.[1]

— Untersuchungen über Eichengerbrinden. 1875. IV. 512.

— Die verdächtigte Bruttoschule. 1887. IV. 257.

Baur, Franz Adolph Gregor (*continued*).
— Vergleichende Untersuchungen über die Gewinnung des Stockholzes. 1874. IV. 386.
— Ueber die Verwendung von Wasserapparaten zu Derbgehaltsversuchen. 1876. IV. 214.
— Der Wald und seine Bodendecke. 1869. IV. 43.
— Zwei einfache forstliche Vermessungsinstrumente. 1871. IV. 215, 264.
— *See also* Баурь, Ф.
Baur, Karl Friedrich. Forststatistik der deutschen Bundesstaaten. 1842. IV. 348.[2]
Bauschinger, Johann. Beschlüsse . . . über einheitliche Untersuchungs-Methoden bei Prüfung von Bau- und Constructions-Materialien. 1893. IV. 415.[1]
— Einige Resultate über die Festigkeit von Bauhölzern. 1879. IV. 410.
— Untersuchungen über die Elasticität . . . verschiedener Nadelhölzer. 1887. IV. 410.
— Untersuchungen über die Elasticität . . . von Fichten- und Kiefern-Bauhölzern. 1883. IV. 410.
— Ueber die Veränderung der Festigkeit des Nadelholzes. 1887. IV. 410, 413.[2]
— & others. Beschlüsse . . . über einheitliche Untersuchungs-Methoden bei der Prüfung von Bau- und Constructions materialien. 1887. IV. 415.[2]
Bauše, Bohumil. Japonská hortikultura. 1890. III. 127.[2]
— Lesy v Cechách. 1897. IV. 372.
Bausteine zum forstlichen Kulturbetrieb. 1866. IV. 141.
Bauthor. Manière et façon d'enter . . . Meuriers blancs. 1604. III. 372.[2]
Bautier, Alexandre. Flores partielles de la France comparées. 1868. I. 413.
— Tableau analytique de la flore parisienne. 1827. I. 408.
Bauve, Adam de. Extrait d'une lettre . . . sur un nouveau fébrifuge. 1836. III. 268.[1]
Bavaria. *See also* **Bayern.**
Bavaria. Landes- und Volkskunde des Königreichs Bayern. 1860. I. 384.
Bavaria — Forstliche Mittheilungen. *See* **Forstliche . . .** IV. 3.
Bavaria; " Ministerial-Forsteinrichtungs-Bureau." *See* **Anleitung** zur Aufnahme und Berechnung von Probeflächen in Hochwaldungen. 1840. IV. 216.
Bavarskiya massoviya tablitsy. *See* **Баварскія массовыя таблицы.**
Bavay, L. de. Du Mûrier. 1854. III. 381.[1]
— Du Néflier. 1856. III. 429.[1]
— Traité . . . de la taille des arbres fruitiers. 1850. III. 172.
Bavink, F. G. Entrup. *See* **Entrup Bavink, F. G.**
Bavoux, Vital. Notice sur quelques plantes . . . du Doubs. 1855. II. 602.[1]
Baxter, H. F. Does magnetism influence vegetation? 1857. I. 231.[1]
— An experimental inquiry, undertaken with the view of ascertaining whether any signs of current electricity are manifested in plants. 1858. I. 231.[1]
Baxter, Robert. On the best kinds of wood for charcoal. 1878. IV. 395.
— Carbon. 1879. IV. 395.
— Charcoal. 1879. IV. 395, 432.[1]
— Underwood. 1881. IV. 132.[2]
Baxter, Sylvester. Climbing plants on Boston buildings. 1894. III. 205.[1]
— The forestry work of the tenth census. 1881. IV. 337.[2]
— The Lynn public forest. 1889. IV. 339.
Baxter, Thomas. A key to the natural orders of British wild flowering plants. 1871. I. 402.
Baxter, William. An account of the Fig tree which was planted in 1648. 1820. II. 151.[1]
— British phænogamous botany. 1834. I. 398.
Baxter, William Hart. Ailantus. 1870. IV. 413.[2]
Bay, Jens Christian. Material for a monograph on the tannoids. 1893. I. 183.
— Tillæg til " Den danske botaniske Literatur." 1890. I. 3.[1]
Bay rum. 1891. III. 637.[1]
Bay State monthly. III. 3.
Bayer, Edvin. Abnormální větev borová. 1896. II. 47.[2]
— Palmy z rodu Raphia. 1890. III. 330.[2]
— Žlutokap nizký. 1888. III. 339.[1]
Bayer, G. C. Anweisung zum Obstbau. 1836. III. 137.
Bayer, Johann N. Botanisches Excursionsbuch für das Erzherzogthum Oesterreich. 1869. I. 442.

— Linden mit kappenförmigen Blättern. 1860. II. 516.[1]
— Monographia Tiliae generis. 1862. II. 515.[1]
— Notizen über Rubus. 1859. II. 504.[1]
— Pinus-Formen. 1854. II. 43.[2]
— Praterflora. 1869. I. 442.
Bayer, Robert Kaufmann-. *See* **Kaufmann-Bayer,** Robert.
Bayerische Akademie der Wissenschaften zu München. *See* **Königliche Akademie der Wissenschaften . . .** I. 13.
Bayerische botanische Gesellschaft zur Erforschung der heimischen Flora. Berichte. I. 11.
Ueber die bayerische Forstverwaltung. 1849. IV. 289.[2]
Bayerische Gartenbau-Gesellschaft in München. Jahresberichte. III. 11.
Bayerische Pharmacopoe auf königlichen Befehl herausgegeben. *See* **Pharmacopœa** bavarica jussu regio edita. 1822. III. 248.
Bayern. *See also* **Bavaria.**
Bayern; Churfürstl. General-Landes-Commissariat. *See* Die **Bedingnisse** heym Verkauf der Staatswaldungen betreffend. 1805. IV. 299.[2]
— **K. Finanz-Ministerium.** *See* **Anleitung** zur Werthsberechnung bei Waldankäufen. 1844. IV. 300.[1]
— **K. Ministerial-Forstbureau.** *See* Die **Forstverwaltung** Bayerns beschrieben . . . 1861. IV. 289.[2]
— **K. Regierung der Pfalz.** *See* **Anleitung** zur Behandlung der Streuwerksabgaben. 1839. IV. 300.[1]
— **K. Staatsministerium der Finanzen.** *See* **Anleitung** zur Anfertigung . . . 1831. IV. 299; **Anleitung** zur Anlage . . . 1862. IV. 150; **Programm** und Satzungen . . . 1888. IV. 33.[1]
— **Ministerial-Forstabtheilung.** *See* **Allgemeine** Anordnung betreffs Vorsorge . . . 1890. IV. 300.[1]
Ueber die bayern vorkommende fremdländische Holzarten. 1883. IV. 125.[3]
Bayersche Pharmakopöe. *See* **Pharmacopœa** bavarica jussu regio edita. 1822. III. 248.
Bayle, François. Dissertationes medicæ. 1681. V. xxviii.[2]
— Dissertationes physicæ. 1678. V. vii.[2]
— Dissertationes physicæ. 1681. V. xxviii.[2]
Bayles, William Eduard. La nomenclature des produits commerciaux. 1883. III. 30.
— Les produits commerciaux et industriels. 1881. III. 218.[1]
Baylies, A. The Buttonwood disease. 1851. III. 418.[2]
Bayne, Lewis. The different ages at which various timber trees may be . . . felled. 1875. IV. 383.[2]
— On the distances at which forest trees should be planted. 1878. IV. 154.[1]
— On the drainage of plantations. 1875. III. 150.[2]
— On the general management of plantations. 1875. IV. 20.
— On planting in exposed and maritime situations. 1876. III. 41.[2]
— On the rearing . . . of hardwood plantations. *See* **Baine,** Lewis. 1881. IV. 137.[2]
— On transplanting trees and shrubs. 1873. III. 166.
Baynon, T. Caparrapi balsam. 1893. III. 407.[1]
Bayonne — Société d'horticulture de l'arrondissement . . . *See* **Société . . .** III. 21.
Bayrische Vorstordnung. 1568. IV. 299.
Bayrische Vordnung. 1598. IV. 39.
Bažant, (Dr.) & others. Ueber den Holzhandel. 1882. IV. 403.[1]
Bazarof. *See also* **Basarow.**
Bazarof, A. *See* **Базаровъ, А.** и **Монтеверде, Н.**
Bazelaire, Hippolyte de. Manuel du planteur du reboisement. 1846. IV. 109.[1]
— Traité du reboisement. 1846. IV. 109.
Bazillac, Louis de. Sur l'hybridation des végétaux par le croisement des séves. 1865. III. 759.
Bazille, J. F. Gaston. Études sur le phylloxéra. 1872. III. 759.
— Nouvelles observations sur les migrations dù phylloxera. 1874. III. 566.[1]
— Résultats d'expériences faites . . . sur la destruction du phylloxera. 1873. III. 565.[1]
— **Planchon, J. E.** & **Sahut, Félix.** Sur une maladie de la Vigne. 1868. III. 560.
Bazin. Note sur une modification apportée à la greffe en fente. 1868. III. 161.
Bazin. Horticulture, arboriculture, floriculture. 1854. III. 113.
Bazin, Armand. Notes sur les maladies de plusieurs de nos plantes usuelles. 1854. III. 563.
— Observations sur la maladie du Noyer. 1854. III. 356.[1]

Bazin, Ch. Sur deux espèces de chenilles. 1870. IV. 209.[1]
Bazin, Gilles Augustin. Observations sur les plantes. 1741. I. 31.
Baring. Waldvernachlässigung und Waldverwüstung in Tirol. 1872. IV. 283.[2]
Bazire, Alphonse. Notice sur plusieurs substances apportées de Guatemala. 1834. III. 265.[1]
Bazot, Louis. Plantes vasculaires . . . de Vitry-le-François. 1893. I. 417.
Beach, Spencer Ambroise. Currants. 1895. III. 414.[1]
— Fumigation of nursery stock. 1900. III. 198.[2]
— Notes on self-pollination of the Grape. 1892. II. 506.[1]
— The self-pollination of the Grape. 1892. II. 506.[1]
— & Bailey, L. H. Spraying in bloom. 1900. III. 198.[2]
Beach, Wooster. Medical and botanical dictionary. 1847. III. 243.
The Beach or Sand Plum. 1872. III. 438.[2]
Beadle, Chauncey Delos. Bamboo. 1900. III. 314.[3]
— Notes on the botany of the southeastern states. 1898. I. 319.
— Studies in Crataegus. 1899. II.. 260.[2]
Beadle, Clayton. See CROSS, C. F., BEVAN, E. J. & BEADLE, Clayton.
Beadon, C. & others. Correspondence regarding the intro-·duction of the quiniferous Cinchonas. 1859. III. 713.[2]
Beal, Foster Ellenborough Lascelles. Preliminary report on the food of woodpeckers. 1895. IV. 90.[2]
Beal, John. Some hints for the horticulture of Scotland. 1675. III. 123.[1]
Beal, John. See also BEALE, John.
Beal, William James. Acorns planted at different depths. 1890. I. 204, III. 154,[2] 361,[2] IV. 65,[2] 148.
— Agency of insects in fertilizing plants. 1868. I. 237.
— Branches of Sugar Maple and Beech. 1898. II. 125, 480.[2]
— Comparison of the flora of . . . Michigan. 1888. I. 315.
— Dispersion of some tree seeds. 1886. I. 240.[2]
— The forest. 1876. IV. 397.
— The forests of Michigan. 1876. I. 295.[3]
— The growth and structure of a tree. 1883. I. 82.[2]
— Hairs and glandular hairs of plants. 1878. I. 112.[2]
— Hints for Arbor day. 1888. IV. 41.[3]
— Inequilateral leaves. 1872. I. 110.
— The leaves of the Red Astrachan Apple. 1898. III. 428.[2]
— Lumbering in Michigan. 1890. IV. 382.[2]
— Methods of reforesting Pine stump lands. 1898. IV. 155.[2]
— Movements of fluids in plants. 1892. I. 166.
— Observations on the succession of forests. 1888. IV. 74.[2]
— Among the Pines of northern Michigan. 1899. IV. 339.
— Planting the Locust. 1894. IV. 523.[2]
— A remarkable increase in size of leaves of Kalmia angusti-folia. 1898. III. 652.[2]
— Seed dispersal. 1898. I. 241.[1]
— The structure and growth of a tree. 1883. I. 82.[2]
— The Sugar Maples of central Michigan. 1894. II. 480.[2]
— Tree planting on the Jack Pine plains. 1888. IV. 112.
— The venation of a few odd leaves. 1876. II. 7.[2]
— Why not plant a grove? 1889. IV. 112.
— & Wheeler, C. F. Michigan flora. 1892. I. 316.
Beale, F. & Tonge, Ezerel. Some communications relating to the queries about vegetation. 1669. I. 162.
Beale, John. Herefordshire orchards. 1657. III. 141.
— New improvements of planting and gardening. 1657. III. 141.
Beale, John. See also BEAL, John.
Bean, William Jackson. Akebias. 1897. III. 393.[1]
— The Almond and its varieties. 1898. III. 434.[1]
— Amelanchiers. 1897. III. 419.[3]
— Andromeda and its allies. 1896. III. 647.[1]
— Aplopappus ericoides. 1898. III. 754.[1]
— Arbutus Menziesii. 1898. III. 647.[3]
— Bamboos and the past winter. 1895. III. 314.[2]
— The Beech and its varieties. 1900. III. 360.[1]
— The Beeches. 1899. III. 360.[1]
— Berberis stenophylla. 1894. III. 395.[1]
— Berberis stenophylla. 1897. III. 395.[1]
— Betula Maximowicziana. 1896. III. 357.[1]
— Betula nigra. 1899. III. 357.[1]
— Buddleia variabilis. 1899. III. 681.[f]
— Calycanthus. 1898. III. 401.[1]
— Caraganas. 1899. III. 469.[2]
— Catalpas. 1896. III. 705.
— Catalpas. 1900. III. 705.
— Ceanothuses. 1899. III. 541.[1]

— Chimonanthus fragrans. 1899. III. 401.[1]
— The Cistuses. 1898. III. 612.[3]
— Clerodendron trichotomum. 1895. III. 696.[2]
— The Cock's spur Thorn. 1900. III. 422.[1]
— Cockspur Thorn. 1900. III. 422.[1]
— Cotoneaster rotundifolia. 1899. III. 421.[1]
— Cotoneasters. 1899. III. 420.[3]
— Crataegus. 1897. III. 421.[2]
— Crataegus mollis. 1896. II. 262.[1]
— Crataegus punctata. 1896. III. 423.[1]
— Cytisus Ardoini. 1896. III. 474.[1]
— Cytisus kewensis. 1896. III. 351.[1]
— Cytisus praecox. 1899. III. 474.[3]
— Cytisus praecox ×. 1897. III. 474.[2]
— Les Daphniphyllum. 1895. III. 517.[3]
— Daphniphyllums. 1895. III. 517.[3]
— Disanthus cercidifolia Maximowicz. 1897. III. 416.[2]
— A double-flowered Hydrangea. 1900. III. 412.[1]
— Early flowering shrubs. 1895. III. 207.[3]
— Elaeagnus macrophylla. 1897. III. 628.[2]
— Elaeagnus macrophylla. 1900. III. 628.[2]
— The Elders. 1898. III. 751.[2]
— Erica lusitanica. 1898. III. 651.[2]
— Erinacea pungens. 1896. III. 475.[2]
— Escallonia Philippiana. 1893. III. 411.[1]
— Eucryphia pinnatifolia. 1893. III. 596.[1]
— The flowering Cherries. 1900. III. 431.[1]
— Francisceas. 1891. III. 699.[1]
— The genus Prunus. 1896. III. 430.[2]
— Gleditschia japonica. 1900. III. 477.[3]
— Hardy Bamboos. 1894. III. 314.[3]
— The hardy Heaths. 1898. III. 650.[2]
— Hardy shrubby Araliads. 1896. III. 641.[1]
— The hardy species of Clematis. 1897. III. 389.[2]
— The hardy Sumachs. 1898. III. 526.[2]
— The Hazels. 1898. III. 357.[2]
— Hedysarum multijugum. 1898. III. 478.[2]
— Hibiscus syriacus. 1897. III. 588.[2]
— Himalayan Rhododendrons. 1895. III. 655.
— †Himalayan Rhododendrons hardy near London. 1898. III. 655.
— The Horse-Chestnut and its allies. 1897. III. 536.[2]
— Hydrangea Hortensia var. Mariesi. 1898· III. 412.[1]
— Hydrangeas. 1896. III. 411.[1]
— Hypericum galioides. 1898. III. 610.[1]
— Hypericum Hookerianum. 1900. III. 610.[1]
— Ilex Sieboldi. 1900. III. 531.[3]
— The Irish Heath. 1897. III. 649.[1]
— Itea virginica. 1897. III. 413.[1]
— Juglans Sieboldi. 1895. III. 356.[2]
— Kalmias. 1897. III. 652.[2]
— Kew notes. 1895. III. 83.[2]
— Laburnums. 1897. III. 480.[1]
— Larix occidentalis. 1900. III. 304.[2]
— Ledum glandulosum Nutt. 1897. III. 652.[4]
— Lespedeza Sieboldi. 1896. II. 369.[2]
— The Lilacs. 1898. III. 680.[2]
— The Limes. 1895. III. 585.[1]
— Magnolia glauca. 1895. III. 399.[2]
— Magnolia parviflora. 1898. III. 400.[1]
— Magnolias. 1894. III. 399.[1]—1900. III. 399.[1]
— Mock Oranges. 1900. III. 477.[1]
— The Mount Etna Broom. 1900. III. 477.[1]
— A new Witch-hazel. 1898. III. 417.[1]
— Notes on shrubs in flower. 1899. III. 417.[1]
— Nuttallia cerasiformis. 1898. III. 429.[2]
— Osmanthuses. 1896. III. 679.[2]
— Paulownia imperialis. 1898 . III. 703.[2]
— Picea Omorica. 1897. III. 305.[2]
— Pieris formosa. 1898. III. 654.[1]
— Pinus flexilis. 1897. III. 307.[1]
— The Privets. 1897. III. 673.[2]
— Prunus Amygdalus var. persicoides. 1898. III. 434.[1]
— Prunus Davidiana. 1897. III. 436.[2]
— Prunus humilis. 1896. III. 437.[1]
— Prunus Jacquemontiana. 1897. III. 437.[1]
— Prunus Mume. 1897. III. 438.[2]
— Prunus Padus. 1896. III. 439.[1]
— Prunus Pseudo-Cerasus fl.-pl. . 1899. III. 443.[1]
— Prunus Pseudo-Cerasus (single var.). 1899. III. 443.[1]
— Prunus Simoni. 1898. III. 443.[1]
— Pterocaryas. 1898. III. 356.[2]
— Pyrus floribunda. 1897. III. 429.[1]
— Pyrus salicifolia. 1898. III. 447.[1]

Bean, William Jackson (*continued*).
— Pyrus thianschanica. 1899. III. 460.[1]
— Rhododendron Aucklandi. 1900. III. 659.[1]
— Rhododendron (Azalea) rhombicum. 1896. III. 662.[1]
— Rhododendron campylocarpum. 1900. II. 678.[1]
— Rhododendron decorum. 1899. III. 658.[2]
— Rhododendron fulgens. 1896. III. 659.[1]
— Rhododendron kewense ×. 1898. III. 660.[2]
— Rhododendron kewense vars. 1897. III. 660.[2]
— Rhododendron Mrs. Thiselton-Dyer. 1897. III. 659.[1]
— Rhododendron niveum. 1896. III. 661.[2]
— Rhododendron rhombicum. 1896. III. 662.[1]
— Rhodothamnus Chamaecistus. 1898. III. 663.[1]
— Rhus cotinoides. 1896. II. 455.[2]
— Ribes. 1897. III. 414.[1]
— Robinias. 1897. III. 486.[1]
— Rosa hispida. 1896. III. 457.[1]
— Rosa hispida. 1899. III. 457.[1]
— Rosa setigera. 1895. III. 457.[1]
— Rosa spinosissima var. altaica. 1895. II. 299.[1]
— Rosa Wichuraiana. 1895. III. 457.[1]
— Rubus australis. 1895. III. 458.[1]
— Rubus deliciosus. 1894. III. 458.[1]
— Rubus lasiostylus. 1895. III. 458.[2]
— St. Dabeoc's Heath. 1898. III. 649.[1]
— The Scarlet Oak. 1900. III. 362.[1]
— The Sea Buckthorn. 1898. III. 629.[1]
— The shrubby St. John's worts. 1898. III. 610.[1]
— Snowdrop trees, Halesias. 1900. III. 670.[2]
— Some new Rhododendrons. 1899. III. 656.
— The species of Azalea. 1898. III. 655.
— The species of Camellia. 1898. III. 599.[1]
— The Spindle tree. 1900. II. 468.[1]
— Spiraea arguta × Zabel. 1897. III. 460.[2]
— Spiraea Millefolium. 1897. III. 459.[1]
— Stachyurus praecox. 1897. III. 615.[1]
— Stephanandras. 1898. III. 462.[1]
— Tamarisks. 1899. III. 612.[1]
— Tecoma Smithi. 1895. III. 707.[2]
— Trees & shrubs in winter. 1900. III. 208.[2]
— The Tupelo, or Sour Gum. 1898. III. 632.[1]
— Two American Birches. 1899. III. 357.[1]
— Two new Rhododendrons from Yunnan. 1898. III. 655.
— Viburnums. 1899. III. 753.[1]
— Viburnums. 1900. III. 753.[1]
— The Vines. 1895. III. 545.[2]
— Vines in autumn. 1898. III. 545.[1]
— Vitis heterophylla. 1898. III. 544.[1]
— The weeping Willows. 1898. III. 349.
— The white-stemmed Brambles. 1898. III. 457.[2]
— The wild Roses. 1899. III. 451.[1]
— Wild Roses. 1900. III. 451.[1]
— Wistarias. 1895. III. 490.[1]
— Wistarias. 1898. III. 490.[1]
— The Yellow-berried Holly. 1899. III. 530.[1]
— Yuccas. 1900. III. 339.[1]
Beardslee, Henry Curtis. Catalogue of the plants of Ohio. 1874. I. 314.
— Poisoning by Rhus. 1876. III. 526.[2]
A **bearing** Cocoanut tree. 1889. III. 323.[1]
Beaton, D. On the cultivation . . . of the Cactus tribe. 1842. III. 618.[2]
— Fuchsias, climbers &c. 1852. III. 204.[2]
— On grafting Ipomoeas. 1839. III. 694.[1]
— De la greffe des Ipomaea. 1839. III. 694.[2]
— Den hensigtsmæssigste Behandlingsmaade for haardføre Slyngplanter. 1852. III. 204.[2]
— New Ribes. 1842. III. 414.[1]
— On root-grafting. 1841. III. 164.[1]
— On the transmission of cuttings to India. 1843. III. 155.
Beatson, Alexander. Notes on planting trees. 1864. III. 132.[1]
— Tracts relative to the island of St. Helena. 1816. I. 498.
Beaucantin, A. J. Ch. Notice sur une plantation d'arbres verts. 1837. III. 291.
Beaufays. Flore verviétoise. 1857. I. 532.[2]
— Flore verviétoise. 1872. I. 392.
Beaulieu, Camille LE HARDY DE. *See* LE HARDY DE BEAULIEU, Camille.
Beaulieux, PHILIPPE-. *See* PHELIPPE-BEAULIEUX.
Beaume, G. Emploi des eaux d'épuration du gaz d'éclairage. 1874. III. 566.[2]
Beaumetz, DUJARDIN-. *See* DUJARDIN-BEAUMETZ.
Beaumont. Note sur les plantations de Balnen-Bouzareh. 1878. III. 130.[2]

Beaumont, J. B. P. de. Traité du cassis. 1757. III. 415.[1]
Beaumont, Jean Baptiste Armand Louis Léonce ÉLIE DE. *See* ÉLIE DE BEAUMONT, J. B. A. L. L.
Beaumont de Miras Peralta, Ricardo. Manual del forestal. 1877. IV. 99.[1]
— Observaciones atmosféricas. 1872. IV. 47.[2]
— Protesta justificada. 1898. IV. 554.
Beaune — Société vigneronne . . . *See* SOCIÉTÉ . . . III. 22.
Beaunier, Stanislas. Le guide des propriétaires et des jardiniers. 1821. III. 110.[1]
— Précis sur les greffes. 1821. III. 160.
Beaupré, Charles GAUDICHAUD-. *See* GAUDICHAUD-BEAU-PRÉ, Charles.
Beauregard, (*Forstdirector*). Die Bedeutung der Akazie für die ungarische Tiefebene. 1887. IV. 523.[3]
— Pasture in relation to forests. 1885. IV. 135.[1]
— Válass Illés Nándor urnak "Egy érdekes Akáczsállabról" szóló czikkére. 1877. IV. 523.[1]
— Die Weide in ihren Beziehungen zu den Forsten. 1885. IV. 135.[1]
Beauregard, Henri. Recherches pour servir à l'histoire des Daphne. 1876. II. 601.[1]
— Remarques sur la structure des écorces . . . du Grenadier. 1880. II. 611.[1]
— Structure . . . du fruit des Daphne. 1877. II. 602.[1]
— & **Galippe,** L. M. V. Guide . . . pour les travaux pratiques de micrographie. 1880. I. 36.[2]
Beaurepaire-Rohan, Henrique, *visconde* de. Diccionario de vocabulos brazileiros. 1889. I. 73.[1]
Beautés méridionales de la flore de Montpellier. *See* BELLE-VAL, Charles de. 1826. I. 407.
Beauties and wonders of vegetable life. 185 . ? I. 95.
A **beautiful** shrub (Rhodotypus kerrioides). 1874. III. 447.[2]
A **beautiful** variety of the Bird Cherry. 1879. III. 439.[1]
The **beauty** of evergreens in snow. 1892. III. 208.[1]
The **beauty** of our trees in spring. 1892. III. 203.
Beauvais, Joseph. Lippia mexicana. 1887. III. 697.[1]
Beauvais, VINCENT DE. *See* VINCENT DE BEAUVAIS.
Beauvais Raseau, de. L'art de l'indigotier. 1770. III. 478.[2]
Beauvais — Société d'horticulture et · de botanique. *See* SOCIÉTÉ . . . III. 22.
Beauvert, *vicomte* BARRUEL-. *See* BARRUEL-BEAUVERT, *vicomte*.
Beauvisage, Georges Eugène Charles. Cercueils pharaoniques en bois d'If. 1895. III. 288.[2]
— Contribution à l'étude des origines botaniques de la gutta percha. 1881. III. 229.
— Deuxième note sur l'herbier du R. P. Montrouzier. 1897. II. 771.[2]
— Fleurs de Gleditschia à deux carpelles. 1894. II. 362.[1]
— Observations sur deux Roses prolifères. 1888. II. 290.[1]
— Observations sur les canaux à résine du Pinus silvestris. 1885. II. 47.[1]
— Recherches sur quelques bois pharaoniques. 1896. I. 82.[1]
— Revision de quelques . . . plantes néo-calédoniennes. 1894. I. 509.[1]
— Toxicité des graines de Ricin. 1894. III. 522.[1] ·
Beauvoir, Ludovic, *comte* de. Pékin, Yeddo, San Francisco. 1872. II. 51.[1]
Beauvoir, Josse-. *See* JOSSE-BEAUVOIR.
Beauvois, A. M. F. J., PALISOT DE. *See* PALISOT DE BEAUVOIS, A. M. F. J.
Bebb, Michael Schuck. Note on Salix sitchensis and its affinities. 1882. II. 110.[1]
— Notes on North American Willows. 1888. II. 99.[1]
— Notes on some arborescent Willows of North America. 1895. II. 99.[2]
— Salix alba × lucida, S. nigra × alba. 1895. II. 104.[2]
— Salix balsamifera Barratt. 1879. II. 105.[3]
— Salix Barclayi Anders. 1878. II. 105.[2]
— Salix flavescens Nutt. var. Scouleriana. 1882. II. 105.[3]
— Salix macrocarpa Nutt. not of Anderson. 1885. II. 108.[1]
— White Mountain Willows. 1888. II. 99.[1]
— Willows of California. 1879. II. 99.[2]
Du Bébéeru. 1851. IV. 407.[3]
Bec, P. de. De la plantation des Vignes. 1844. III. 555.
Becalli, Angelo. Di alcune vecchi arbusti. 1892. III. 206.[1]
— Gli effetti del freddo nell' inverno 1890-91. 1891. III. 49.[2]
— Degli Eucalyptus e specialmente dell' E. Amygdalina. 1884. III. 633.[3]
— Gli Hibiscus rosa sinensis di fior doppio. 1887. III. 588.[1]
— Idesia polycarpa. 1888. III. 614.[3]
Beccari, Odoardo. Le Bombaceae Malesi. 1886. II. 528.[3]

— Cenni sopra la flora di Assab. 1881. I. 489.
— Descrizione di una nuova . . . Myrmecodia. 1874. II. 824.²
— Della disseminazione delle Palme. 1877. II. 63.²
— Illustrazione di nuove specie di piante bornensi. 1869. I. 469.²
— Malesia. 1877. I. 466.
— Metroxylon Rumphii. 1877. III. 327.²
— Note sopra alcune Palme bornensi. 1871. II. 62.¹
— Notes on the plants collected . . . in New Guinea. 1880. I. 499.
— Nuove Palme asiatiche. 1886. II. 62.²
— Nuove specie di Palme . . . Nuova Guinea. 1888. II. 62.²
— Nuovi studi sulle Palme asiatiche. 1886. II. 62.²
— Su di un nuovo genere . . . delle Olacineae. 1877. II. 171.¹
— Sul nuovo genere Scorodocarpus. 1877. II. 170 ² 172.¹
— Della organogenia dei fiori feminei del Gnetum Gnemon. 1877. II. 55.¹
— Osservazioni sulla Ximenia americana. 1877. II. 172.¹
— Le Palme del genere Pritohardia. 1886. II. 74.¹
— Le Palme incluse nel genere Cocos. 1887. II. 61,¹ 67.¹
— Le Fennec e Monetti contro Vitali. 1886. II. 136.¹
— Piante nuove o rare dell' Arcipelago malese. 1877. I. 466.
— Piante ospitatrici . . . della Malesia. 1884. I. 235,¹ 466.
— Sulle piante raccolte alla Nuova Guinea. 1877. II. 474.¹
— Pinanga malaiana. 1884. III. 330.²
— Plantes à fourmis de l'Archipel indo-malais. 1884. I. 235.¹
— Reliquiae Schefferianae. 1885. II. 62.¹
— Revista monografica . . . del genere Phoenix. 1886. II. 72.¹
— Il Sagu della Nuova Guinea. 1877. III. 327.¹
— Le specie di Palme raccolte alla Nuova Guinea. 1877. II. 62.²
— Studio monografico sopra . . . Icacineae. 1877. II. 206,¹ 474.¹
— Turgescenza dei petali di Magnolia Yulan. 1887. II. 213.¹

Bech, A. W. Om Skovdyrkningens Fremme. 1866. IV. 156.¹
Béchamp, Antoine. Sur le blessissement des Sorbes. 1874. II. 312.²
— Sur le dosage du glucose dans le vin. 1875. III. 560.
— Sur l'existence de plusieurs acides . . . dans le fruit du Gingko. 1863. II. 8.¹
— Faits pour servir à l'histoire de l'origine des bactéries. 1869. I. 212.
— Faits pour servir à l'histoire de la fécule. 1860. I. 151,¹ 175.
— Ueber die in den Früchten von Gingko biloba enthaltenen Säuren. 1863. II. 8.¹
— Sur l'innocuité des vapeurs de créosote. 1866. IV. 433.²
— Sur les microzymas de l'orge germée. 1876. I. 175.
— Sur les microzymas de l'orge germée. 1877. II. 272.²
— Nouvelles études sur l'amidou. 1854. I. 140.¹
— *See also* ROUX, J. A. PAOÈS, Hippolyte & BÉCHAMP, Antoine.
Béchamp, Marie Joseph & **Dujardin**, A. De la zymase du Jéquirity. 1885. III. 462.³
Becher, Johann Joachim. Parnassus medicinalis illustratus. 1662. III. 53.
Becheraz, Achille. Ueber die Sekretbildung in den schizogenen Gängen. 1893. I. 135.
— Ueber die Sekretbildung in den schizogenen Gängen. 1894. I. 135.
Bechstädt, J. C. Vollständiges niedersächsisches Land- und Gartenbuch. 1772. III. 103.
Bechstein, (*Oberlehrer Dr.*). Merkwürdige Bäume in Elsass-Lothringen. 1898. I. 296.¹
Bechstein, Johann Matthäus. Der Bastardvogelbeerbaum. 1797. II. 313.¹
— Die Forst- und Jagdwissenschaft. 1818. IV. 96.
— Forstbotanik. 1810. I. 370, IV. 82.
— Forstinsectologie. 1818. IV. 91.¹
— Gemeinnützige Naturgeschichte Deutschlands. 1789. IV. 56.
— Kurze aber gründliche Musterung aller . . . als schädlich geachteten Thiere. 1792. IV. 196.¹
— Kurzgefasste gemeinnützige Naturgeschichte der Gewächse. 1796. I. 264.
— Naturgeschichte der schädlichen Waldinsecten. 1797. IV. 91.¹
— Die Oxelbirne oder Oxel-Azerole. 1816. II. 313.¹

— Der spitzblättrige Hagedorn. 1797. II. 262.¹
— Taschenblätter der Forstbotanik. 1798. I. 370, IV. 81.
— Die Waldbenutzung. 1821. IV. 381.
— Die Waldbeschützungs-Lehre. 1818. IV. 177.¹
— Die wohlriechende Birke, Betula odorata. 1797. II. 118.²
— & Scharfenberg, G. L. Vollständige Naturgeschichte der schädlichen Forstinsekten. 1804. IV. 91.¹
Bechstein, Ludwig. Dr. Johann Matthäus Bechstein und die Forstacademie Dreissigacker. 1855. IV. 32.
Bechtel, F. Die Anwendung ein- und zweijähriger Kiefernpflanzen. 1846. IV. 472.
— Bemerkungen zu der Uebersicht über die Forstculturen bei Bisenz. 1850. IV. 370.
— Ueber die Benutzung der jungen Buchenpflanzen. 1850. IV. 494.
Bechtel, S. F. Eine Delicatesse des Waldes. 1891. IV. 439.
Bechtner. Ueber das Decken der Hügelpflanzen. 1865. IV. 153.²
Beck, Carl Felix. Wie schützt sich der Landwirt am sichersten vor Frostschäden? 1895. III. 183.²
Beck, Friedrich Joseph. Untersuchungen über die mittlere Zeit der Blüthenentwicklung. *See* SCHÜBLER, Gustav. 1831. I. 224.³
Beck, Günther. *See* BECK VON MANNAGETTA, Günther, *Ritter*.
Beck, Johann Jodocus. Tractatus de jurisdictione forestali. 1733. IV. 316.
Beck, John. Lectures on materia medica. 1851. III. 243.
Beck, Lewis Caleb. Adulterations of various substances used in medicines. 1846. III. 258.
— Botany of the northern and middle states. 1833. I. 313.
— Botany of the United States north of Virginia. 1833. I. 313.
Beck, Michael. Uva magna Cananaea. 1679. II. 509.¹
Beck, Otto. Der Gesetzentwurf, betreffend die Erhaltung . . . von Waldschutzwaldungen. 1875. IV. 180.²
— Instruktion über das Pflanzen und die Pflege der Alleebäume. 1873. III. 209.
— Land und volkswirthschaftliche Tagesfragen. 1873. IV. 314.¹
— Die Waldschutzfrage in Preussen. 1860. IV. 180,¹ 286.¹
— Die Wurzellaus des Rebstocks. 1873. III. 759.
Beck, Richard. Katalog der Bibliothek der K. sächs. Forstakademie Tharandt. 1900. IV. 2.
— Ueber eine Pilzkrankheit der Weisstanne. 1900. IV. 446.¹
— Die Verbreitung der Hauptholzarten im Königreiche Sachsen. 1899. I. 372, IV. 84.¹
Beck von Mannagetta, Günther, *Ritter*. Allamanda Hendersoni. 1894. II. 723,¹ 805.¹
— Die alpine Vegetation der südbosnisch-hercegovinischen Hochgebirge. 1888. I. 448.¹
— Ueber die Baumgrenze in den . . . Alpen. 1891. I. 438, IV. 87.¹
— Bericht über die botanischen Ergebnisse der Expedition. 1888. I. 489.
— Botanischer Ausflug auf den Troglav. 1897. I. 448.²
— Coniferen-Hybriden. 1890. II. 39.³
— Ueber die Entwicklung . . . der Schwimmorgane von Neptunia. 1889. II. 374.²
— Das Erfrieren von Pflanzen. 1897. I. 212.
— Ueber die Familie der Cycadeen. 1893. III. 284.¹
— Flora des Gebietes [von Hernstein]. 1886. I. 443.
— Flora des Stewart-Atolls im Stillen Ocean. 1888. I. 508.¹
— Flora von Nieder-Österreich. 1890. I. 443, V. XXIII.¹
— Flora von Südbosnien. 1886. I. 448.¹
— Gärtnerische Reflexionen über Dalmatien. 1894. III. 127.¹
— Interessante Nadelhölzer im Occupationsgebiete. 1889. II. 42.²
— Itinera principium S. Coburgi. *See* WAWRA VON FERNSEE, Heinrich, *Ritter*. 1883. I. 303.
— Zur Kenntniss der Torf bewohnenden Föhren Niederösterreichs. 1888. II. 41.²
— Die Königsblume (Daphne Blagayana). 1893. II. 601.¹
— Ueber Mischfrüchte (Xenien). 1895. I. 201.²
— Mittheilungen aus der Flora von Niederösterreich. 1888. I. 443.
— Die Nadelhölzer Niederösterreichs. 1890. II. 15,¹ IV. 144.¹
— Notizen zur Flora von Niederösterreich. 1895. I. 443.
— Die periodische Entwickelung der Pflanzen. 1897. I. 222.¹
— Physiognomische Betrachtungen. 1890. I. 218.

Beck von Mannagetta, Günther, *Ritter (continued)*.
— Pinus leucodermis Antoine. 1889. III. 307.[2]
— Ruscus Hypoglossum für Niederösterreich neu. 1885. II. 84.[3]
— Ueber die Schädlichkeit der Flechten. 1896. III. 193.[1]
— Die Spermatozoiden der Gymnospermen. 1897. II. 1.
— Die in den Torfmooren Niederösterreichs vorkommenden Föhren. 1887. II. 39.[3]
— Uebersicht der hybriden Pinus-Arten. 1890. II. 39.[3]
— Die Vegetation der Umgebung von Abbazia. 1894. V. XXIII.[1]
— Ueber die Verbreitung der Schwarzföhre. 1895. II. 43.[3]
— Versuch einer neuen Classification der Früchte. 1891. I. 119.
— Was ist Pinus Wettsteinii Fritsch? 1892. II. 49.[1]
— Die Wechselwirkung zwischen Edelreis und Unterlage. 1895. III. 40.
— Ziele . . . der Acclimatisation der Pflanzen. 1894. III. 44.[1]
— & **Szyszylowicz**, Ignaz von. Plantae a Dre I. Szyszylowicz . . . lectae. 1889. I. 450.
Beckensteiner. Du phylloxera et des moyens de le combattre. 1875. III. 567.[1]
Becker. Alte und seltene Waldbäume. 1893. II. 139.[1]
Becker. See DAU, BECKER, ESSER & ARNOLD.
Becker, Alexander. Beiträge zu meinen Verzeichnissen der um Sarepta und am Bogdo vorkommenden Pflanzen. 1880. I. 364.
— Mittheilungen einer botanischen . . . Reise. 1865. I. 369.
— Reise in die Kirgisensteppe. 1866. I. 369.
— Reise nach Baku, Lenkoran. 1873. I. 369.
— Reise nach dem Kaukasus. 1868. I. 369.
— Reise nach dem Magi Dagh. 1875. I. 477.[3]
— Reise nach dem südlichen Daghestan. 1882. I. 369.
— Reise nach den Salzseen Baskuntschatskoje und Elton. 1873. I. 369.
— Reise nach Derbent. 1869. I. 369.
— Reise nach Krasnowodsk und Daghestan. 1878. I. 369.
— Verzeichniss der um Sarepta wildwachsenden Pflanzen. 1858. I. 362.
Becker, B. Die Coniferen zu Miechowitz. 1877. III. 290.
Becker, C. Die Feinde der Obstbäume. 1878. III. 190.
Becker, Cuno. Citrus medica var. Cedrata. 1900. III. 502.[1]
— Pritchardia filifera Lind. 1900. III. 332.[1]
Becker, Daniel. Kleine Hausapothek. 1650. III. 303.[3]
— De Pipere et opio. 1624. III. 343.[3]
Becker, E. D. H. Ueber Kiefern-Culturen. 1873. IV. 480.
Becker, G. Vinterblomstrende Rhododendron. 1892. III. 655.
Becker, Hermann Friedrich. Beschreibung der Bäume und Sträucher . . . in Mecklenburg. 1791. I. 370.
— Ueber Cultur, künstliche Bildung und Fällung des Schiffsbauholzes. 1804. IV. 424.[3]
— Om Skibsbygningstømmers Kultur. 1804. IV. 424.[3]
Becker, Johann Friedrich Adolf. Experimenta circa mutationem colorum. 1779. I. 184.
Becker, Johann Philipp. Chemische Untersuchung der Pflanzen. 1786. I. 152.[1]
Becker, Johannes. Flora der Gegend um Frankfurt a. M. 1828. I. 377.
Becker, K. Eriobotrya japonica. 1898. III. 424.[1]
Becker, Karl Joseph Theodor. De acidi hydro-cyanici vi perniciosa in plantas. 1823. I. 210.[3]
Becker, Moritz Alois von. Hernstein in Niederösterreich. See BECK VON MANNAGETTA, Günther, Ritter. 1886. I. 443.
Becker, Wilhelm. Floristische und systematische Beiträge zur Flora Nord-Thüringens. 1899. II. 106.[1]
Becker, Wilhelm Gottlieb. Miscellen für Gartenfreunde, Botaniker und Gärtner. 1802. III. 121.[1]
— Der plauische Grund bei Dresden. See PURSH, F. T. 1799. I. 375.
Beckers, Georges. Procédé graphique pour l'évaluation des bois. 1894. IV. 551.[1]
Beckerstedt, Karl Jacob. En örtebook. 1758. I. 291.
Beckhaus, Konrad. Flora von Westfalen. 1893. V. XX.[1]
Becking, B. E. J. H. Bericht over eenige proefnemingen ter bepaling van . . . kina-alkaloïd. 1875. III. 721.
Beckmann, J. A. Acacias. 1854. III. 463.[1]
Beckmann. Merkwürdige Folgen eines Blitzschlages. 1900. IV. 195.[1]
— Das Reifrauchen als Schutz gegen Frostgefahr. 1900. III. 183.[2]

Beckmann, Johann. Anfangsgründe der Naturhistorie. 1767. I. 93.
— Beiträge zur Geschichte der Erfindungen. 1780. III. 238.[3]
— Grundsätze der deutschen Landwirthschaft. 1769. IV. 116.
— History of inventions and discoveries. 1780. III. 238.[3]
— Lexicon botanicum. 1801. I. 70, 76.[1]
— Physikalisch-ökonomische Bibliothek. 1770. I. 1.
Beckmann, Johann Christoph. Catalogus plantarum in tractu francofurtano. 1676. I. 372.
— Historische Beschreibung der Kur und Mark Brandenburg. 1751. I. 373.
Beckmann, Johann Gottlieb. Anweisung zu einer pfleglichen Forstwirthschaft. 1759. IV. 104.[2]
— Beyträge zur Verbesserung der Forstwissenschaft. 1763. IV. 94.
— Forst-Calender. 1764. IV. 116.
— Forst-Calender. 1765. IV. 94.
— Gegründete Versuche und Erfahrungen von der . . . Holzsaat. 1756. IV. 104.[3]
— Versuche und Erfahrungen von der Holzsaat. 1785. IV. 105.
— *See also* БЕКМАНЪ, I. Г.
Becks, F. Ueber einige Wachsthums-Erscheinungen. 1839. I. 189.
Beckström, W. & **Hagen**, L. Merkwürdige Bäume. 1889. IV. 66.[3]
Beckurts, Heinrich August. Über den Alkaloïdgehalt . . . von Strychnos. 1892. III. 683.[3]
— Beiträge zur chemischen Kenntnis der Kakaobohnen. 1893. III. 595.[1]
— Sur le dosage des alcaloïdes. 1890. I. 177.
— Zur Kenntniss der Angustura alkaloïde. 1895. III. 504.[1]
— Sur les principes immédiats de l'écorce d'Angustura-Cusparine. 1895. III. 504.[1]
— *See also* BRÜCHE, W. & BECKURTS, H.
— & **Hartwich**, Carl. Beiträge zur . . . Kenntnis der Kakaobohnen. 1892. III. 595.[1]
— & **Nehring**, Paul. Ueber die Bestandtheile der Angusturarinde. 1891. III. 504.[1]
— — Sur les principes immédiats de l'écorce d'Angustura. 1891. III. 504.[1]
— & **Troeger**, J. Sur la composition de l'huile . . . d'Angustura. 1898. III. 504.[1]
Beckwith, Florence, **Macauley**, M. E. & **Fuller**, J. B. Plants of Monroe county. 1896. I. 316.
Beckwith, Milton H. The Ridgely Chestnut. 1894. III. 360.[1]
Beckwith, N. W. Our Canadian forests. 1872. IV. 337.[1]
Becmann, Karl Hilmar. De chocolata analepticorum principe. See CARTHEUSER, J. F. 1763. III. 594.
Becœur. Maladie des Vignes attribuée aux piqûres. 1853. III. 563.
Bécourt, Henri. Débit et emploi des bois de bateau. 1898. IV. 425.[2]
Becquerel, Antoine César. De l'action de l'électricité sur les tissus colorés. 1871. I. 184.
— De l'action du sel sur la végétation. 1847. I. 158.
— Des climats et de l'influence qu'exercent les sols boisés et non boisés. 1853. IV. 52.
— Concerning the experiments on the temperature of plants. 1859. I. 186.
— Sur la culture de la Vigne. 1872. III. 555.
— Sur la culture des Orangers. 1858. III. 499.[3]
— Deuxième mémoire sur la décoloration des fleurs. 1871. I. 184.[3]
— Des effets du déboisement sur les sources. 1854. IV. 49.[3]
— Forests and their climatic influence. 1865. IV. 53.
— Des forêts et de leur influence sur les climats. 1865. IV. 53.
— On the influence of forests on climate. 1865. IV. 53.
— Mémoire sur l'intervention des forces physico-chimiques. 1876. I. 159.
— Mémoire sur la décoloration des fleurs. 1871. I. 184.[3]
— Mémoire sur la propriété forestière dans l'intérieur de la France. 1853. IV. 359.[3]
— Mémoire sur la situation de la propriété forestière dans l'intérieur de la France. 1853. IV. 359.[3]
— Mémoire sur la température de l'air, au nord, observée avec le thermomètre ordinaire. 1860. IV. 53.
— Mémoire sur la température de l'air au nord prés du sol. 1860. IV. 53.
— Mémoire sur les effets électriques. 1850. I. 231.[1]

— Mémoire sur les forêts et leur influence. 1865. IV. 53.
— Nogle Bemærkninger om den Indflydelse, som Skovens Borthugning har paa Kilder. 1871. IV. 50.
— Note sur la decoloration de certains feuilles. 1872. III. 40.
— Note sur la température de l'air hors du bois et sous bois. 1869. IV. 53.
— Observations sur les moyens à employer pour évaluer la température des végétaux 1839. I. 186.
— Sur la proportion plus considérable de salin fournie par les cendres de bois vert. 1832. I. 154.
— Quatrième mémoire sur la physique des végétaux. 1860. I. 186.
— Recherches sur la température de l'air au-dessus des arbres. 1860. IV. 53.
—Recherches sur là température de l'air au nord. 1864. V. 53.
— Recherches sur la température des végétaux et de l'air. 1864. I. 186.
— Recherches sur les causes du dégagement de l'électricité. 1850. I. 231.[1]
— Second mémoire sur la température moyenne de l'air. 1862. IV. 53.
— De la température des végétaux et du sol. 1860. I. 186.
— Du thermomètre électrique. 1858. I. 186.
—Troisième mémoire sur la décoloration des fleurs par l'électricité. 1871. I. 184.[2]
— Troisième mémoire sur la température des végétaux. 1859. I. 186.
— & A. E. Mémoire sur la température de l'air sous bois. 1866. IV. 53.
— — Mémoire sur la témperature de l'air sous bois et hors des bois. 1869. IV. 53.
— — Mémoire sur les quantités d'eau tombées près et loin des bois. 1869. IV. 50.
— Des pluies dans les lieux boisés et non boisés. 1866. IV. 50.
— Des quantités d'eau tombées prés et loin des bois. 1869. IV. 50.
Becquet, Charles. Mémoire sur la conversion des taillis sous futaie. 1866. IV. 128.
Bedall, C. Ueber das Koussin. 1862. III. 424.[2]
— Sur la Koussine. 1862. III. 424.[2]
— Sur la Koussine. 1874. III. 424.[2]
— Neue chemische Untersuchung der Brayera. 1859. III. 424.[1]
Ueber den Bedarf an Eisenbahnschwellen. 1888. IV. 424.[1]
Beddome, Richard Henry. Acrocarpus fraxinifolius. 1877. IV. 521.[1]
— Contributions to the botany of southern India. 1861. I. 473.
— Extract from Report on the vegetable products of the Pulney Hills. 1858. I. 473.
— Flora . . . of the Nilagiri district. 1880. I. 474.
— The flora sylvatica for southern India. 1869. I. 470,[1] IV. 88.[2]
— Forest flora of the Nilgiris. 1876. I. 474.
— The forests and flora of the Nilgíris. 1876. I. 474.
— The forests and flora of the Tinnevelly district. 1878. I. 474.
— Icones plantarum Indiae orientalis. 1874. I. 474.
— The Jeypore forests. 1878. IV. 377.[2]
— A list of the exogenous plants found in the Anamallay Mountains. 1865. I. 474.
— On a new genus of Ternstroemiaceae. 1865. II. 558.[1]
— Oorea and botanical list of the trees in the Gomsúr forests. 1864. I. 75,[2] IV. 88.[2]
— Report upon the Nelambur Teak plantations. 1878. IV. 536.[2]
— The trees of the Madras presidency. 1863. I. 470,[1] IV. 88.[1]
— & others. L'Eucalyptus dans l'Inde. 1885. IV. 530.
— — On Eucalyptus plantations in India. 1885. IV. 530.
Bédel. Le ballvage dans les taillis composés. 1886. IV. 513.
— Le Chêne vert. 1866. IV. 503.[1]
— Des conversions. 1885. IV. 128.
— Un mot sur le traitement des sapinières, 1885. IV. 446.[1]
Bedel, Léon. Chute des feuilles. 1900. IV. 543.[1]
Bedemar, Vargas de. See VARGAS DE BEDEMAR.
Bedford, duke of & Pickering, S. U. First report on . . . the Woburn experimental fruit farm. 1897. III. 142.
Bedinghaus, Émile. L'Acacia alata R. Br. 1899. III. 463.[2]
— Acacia longifolia Wild. [sic] var. 1899. III. 465.[2]

— Acacia rupicola. 1900. III. 466.[1]
— Anopterus glandulosus. 1899. III. 409.[2]
— Aotus gracillima Meisn. 1900. III. 467.[2]
— Beaufortia purpurea. 1899. III. 633.[1]
— Cytisus albus pendulus. 1900. III. 474.[1]
— Cytisus canariensis. 1900. III. 474.[1]
— Escallonia macrantha Hook. et Arnott. 1896. II. 239.[2]
— Hardenbergia monophylla Benth. 1896. II. 367.[1]
— Le Pimelea spectabilis Líndl. 1900. III. 628.[1]
— Polygala Dalmaisiana. 1899. III. 514.[1]
— Le Russelia sarmentosa. 1899. III. 704.[1]
— Thibaudia macrantha Hook. 1900. III. 647.[2]
— Tremandra ericoides. 1899. III. 513.[1]
— Tremandra verticillata. 1897. III. 513.[2]
Die Bedingnisse beym Verkauf der Stattswaldungen. 1805. IV. 299.
Bedingungen zum Verkaufe von Holz aus den Kronsforsten des Baltischen Gouvernements. 1881. IV. 298.[1]
Bedő, Albert. A Bálványgesztről. 1864. IV. 525.
— Carte synoptique de toutes les forêts de l'état hongrois. 1885. IV. 373.
— Description économique et commercial des forêts de l'état de Hongrie. 1878. IV. 373.
— Description économique et commerciale des forêts de l'état hongrois. 1885. IV. 373.
— A Douglas-fenyő, Abies Douglasii. 1878. IV. 483.[2]
— A Dugasztölgy és ipara. 1868. IV. 517.[2]
— Az erdészet. 1873. IV. 373.
— Erdészet. 1896. IV. 374.[1]
— Erdészetünk leirása. 1873. IV. 373.
— Erdőőr. 1874. IV. 99.[2]
— Forstliche Mittheilungen über Ungarn. 1885. IV. 373.
— Das Forstwesen als Gegenstand der internationalen Statistik. 1874. IV. 336.[1]
— A magyar állam erdőségeinek gazdasági és kereskedelmi leirása. 1885. IV. 373.
— A magyar állam összes erdőségeinek átnezeti térképe. 1885. IV. 373.
— A magyar kir. államerdők gazdasági és kereskedelmi leirása 1878. IV. 373.
— Übersichtskarte sämmtlicher Wälder des ungarischen Staates. 1885. IV. 373.
— A Vörösfenyőről. 1867. IV. 449.
— Die Wälder Ungarns. 1885. IV. 373.
— Die wirthschaftliche und commercielle Beschreibung der königl.-ungarischen Staatsforste. 1878. IV. 373.
— Die wirthschaftliche und commercielle Beschreibung der Wälder des ungarischen Staates. 1885. IV. 373.
Bédos, S. Rapport sur la maladie de la Vigne. 1858. III. 577.
Beebee, W. W. Fruit and fruit-trees. 1868. III. 44.[1]
The Beech. 1896. III. 360.[2]
Without the Beech. 1882. IV. 498.
Of the Beech-tree. 1733. III. 360.[1]
The Beech-tree, a nonconductor of lightning. 1827. IV. 193.[2]
Beecher. Transplanting evergreens. 1879. III. 169.[1]
Beecher, H. W. Birches and Aspens. 1874. III. 346,[2] 357.[1]
— The music of trees. 1874. I. 516.
Beechey, Frederick William. The botany of Captain Beechey's voyage. See HOOKER, Sir W. J. & ARNOTT, G. A. W. 1830. I. 302.
— Note of the Cloth tree. 1851. III. 368.[1]
Beeck, F. George MUELLER-. See MUELLER-BEECK, F. G.
Beek, Albert van. Température propre des plantes. 1840. I. 186.
— & Bergsma, C. A. Expériences sur la température des végétaux. 1839. I. 186.
Beeldsnijder. Catalogue des plantes . . . Rupelmonde. 1823. I. 51.[1]
Been, Johannes Nicolai. Dissertatio evincere contendens, quod spinae et tribuli ante lapsum creati exstiterint. 1702. I. 107.[1]
Béer, C. de. Rapport sur le service forestier du département des Basses-Alpes. 1857. IV. 292.
Beer, Joseph Georg. Ueber Befaria Lin. 1848. II. 661.[1]
— Grundzüge der Obstbaukunde. 1872. III. 146.[2]
— Neue Methode, die . . . Heiden . . . zu ziehen. 1846. III. 650.[1]
Beermann, F. H. A. Anviisning til Skov- og Hegnsplantning. 1852. IV. 103.[1]
— De Buttlarske og Biermanske Cultur-methoder. 1849. IV. 152.

Beermann, F. H. A. (*continued*).
— Forslag til Forsøg navnlig med Gjennemhugninger. 1848. IV. 173.
— Die Holzzucht im dänischen Forstreviere Odsherred. 1880. IV. 113.[2]
Beesley, Alfred. The history of Banbury. *See* BEESLEY, Thomas. 1841. I. 399.
Beesley, Thomas. Botany of the neighbourhood of Banbury. 1841. I. 399.
Beets, M. N. Woordenboek van droogerijen. 1825. III. 242.
Beggiato, Francesco Secondo. Per le faustissime nozze Mainardi-Valvasori. 1838. II. 154.[2]
Beginnings of professional forestry in the Adirondacks. 1900. IV. 339.
Begonia Ingramii. 1850. III. 618.[1]
Begrootingen over 100 en 300 bouws woeste gronden bestend om met Koffie te worden beplant. *See* C., J. V. H. n. d. III. 729.[1]
Beguillet, Edme B. Oenologie. 1770. III. 554.[1]
Beguinot, Augusto. Notizie preliminari sulla flora dell' Arcipelago ponziano. 1900. I. 430.
— Prodromo ad una flora dei bacini Pontino. 1897. I. 430.
Béhague, Amédée, *comte* de. Sur la culture des Pins. 1874. IV. 461.[1]
— Note sur quelques travaux agricoles . . . de Dampierre. 1841. III. 125.
Béhal, Auguste. Sur les campholènes. 1894. III. 233.[1]
— & **Choay,** E. Composition qualitative des créosotes officinales. 1894. I. 156,[1] IV. 500,[2] 515.[2]
— Composition quantitative des créosotes de bois. 1894. IV. 433.[1]
— — Recherche qualitative des phénols. 1894. IV. 433.[2]
Behandeling, kweeking en opgave van . . . Camellia's. 1853. III. 599.[2]
Om **Behandlingen** af de danske Statsskove. *See* HEMPEL, S. 1868. IV. 288.[2]
Die **Behandlung** der Arve im Oberengadin. 1850. IV. 463.[1]
Ueber die **Behandlung** der Weidflächen. 1859. IV. 135.[1]
Ueber die **Behandlung** des Nutzholzes zum Zwecke besserer Conservirung. 1863. IV. 418.
Behauptete Vorrechte deren alten königlichen Bann-Forste. *See* BURI, F. C. von. 1742. IV. 319.[2]
Béheré, Jean Baptiste Joseph. Tableau méthodique du système corolliste de Tournefort. 1802. I. 259.
Beherzigenswerthe Rathschläge . . . um die heutige Nonnen-Calamität endgiltig aus der Welt zu schaffen. 1892. IV. 201.
Behlen, Stephan. Anleitung zur Kenntniss der königlich bayerischen Forstverwaltung. 1826. IV. 289.[3]
— Archiv der Forst- und Jagdgesetzgebung der deutschen Bundesstaaten. 1835. IV. 316.
— Die Bearbeitung der deutschen Forstmannssprache. 1845. IV. 23.[1]
— Beiträge zur Lehre von den Taxen der Forstprodukte. 1828. IV. 402.[3]
— Botanisches Handbuch. 1824. I. 370, IV. 88.
— Catechismus der forstlichen Zoologie. 1838. IV. 91.[2]
— Catechismus der Forstwissenschaft. 1838. IV. 97.
— Catechismus vom dem Anbau der Hoch-, Nieder- und gemischten Waldungen. 1838. IV. 139.[1]
— Clima, Lage und Boden in ihrer Wechselwirkung. 1823. IV. 52.
— Die Forstkunstsprache. 1831. IV. 23.[1]
— Forstliche Baukunde. 1845. IV. 266.[1]
— Grundsätze des Geschäftsstyls. 1826. IV. 311.[3]
— Lehrbuch der beschreibenden Forstbotanik. 1823. IV. 82.
— Lehrbuch der deutschen Forst- und Jagd-Geschichte. 1831. IV. 25.
— Lehrbuch der Forst- und Jagdthiergeschichte. 1826. IV. 89.[3]
— Lehrbuch der Forstnaturgeschichte. 1831. IV. 56.
— Lehrbuch der Gebirgs- und Bodenkunde. 1826. IV. 60.[2]
— Real- und Verbal-Lexikon der Forst- und Jagdkunde. 1840. IV. 22.[3]
— Sammlung der königlich bayerischen Forst- und Jagdgesetze. 1846. IV. 318.
— Der Spessart. 1823. IV. 350.[2]
— & **Desberger,** F. A. Forstbotanik. 1833. IV. 82.
— Naturgeschichte und Beschreibung der deutschen Forst-Kryptogamen. 1835. IV. 82.
— & **Laurop,** C. P. Dienst-Instructionen für das königlich baierische Forst-Personal des äusseren Dienstes. 1832. IV. 300.[1]

— Systematische Sammlung der Forst- und Jagdgesetze der deutschen Bundesstaaten. 1827. IV. 316.
— & **Merkel,** J. Geschichte und Beschreibung von Aschaffenburg. 1843. IV. 350.[2]
— & **Reber,** Peter. Handbuch der Forstwissenschaft. 1827. IV. 97.
Behm, E. Grubenholz-Kubiktabelle. 1897. IV. 229.
Behm, Florian. Från botaniska excursioner i Jemtland. 1887. II. 100.[2]
Behm, H. Hülfstafeln für forstliche Taxwerth- und Preis-Berechnungen. 1875. IV. 256.
— Kubik-Tabelle zur Bestimmung des Inhalts von Rundhölzern. 1870. IV. 226.
— Massen-Tafeln zur Bestimmung des Gehaltes stehender Bäume. 1872. IV. 230.
Behm, Moritz. Beiträge zur anatomischen Charakteristik der Santalaceen. 1895. II. 168.[1]
Behne, H. Ueber Datura oder Brugmansia. 1878. III. 699.[2]
Behnick, Erich B. Randia Stanleyana. 1897. III. 747.[1]
Behr, von. Anleimen oder Anteeren. 1900. IV. 197.[1]
Behr, Hans Hermann. *See* BEHR, Hermann H.
Behr, Hermann. Ueber die Verhältnisse der südaustralischen Flor. 1847. I. 501.
Behr, Hermann H. Changes in the fauna and flora of California. 1896. I. 326.
— Changes in fauna and flora of California. 1889. I. 325.
— Synopsis of the genera of vascular plants . . . of San Francisco. 1884. I. 324.
— *See also* KELLOGG, Albert & BEHR, H. H.
Behrend, Recherches sur le principe actif de l'Uva ursi. 1883. III. 648.[1]
Behrend, P. Beiträge zur Chemie des Obstweines. 1892. I. 154.
Behrens, H. Ueber den Anbau der Schwarzkiefer. 1855. IV. 465.[1]
Behrens, Johannes. Über die anatomischen Beziehungen zwischen Blatt und Rinde der Coniferen. 1886. II. 18.
— Ein bemerkenswertes Vorkommen von Nectria. 1895. III. 295.[2]
— Botrytis Douglasii Tub. 1895. IV. 483.[2]
— Ueber einige ätherisches Oel secernirende Hautdrüsen. 1886. III. 390.[1]
— Nutzpflanzen. 1900. III. 53.
— Phytopathologischen Notizen, I. 1895. IV. 483.[3]
Behrens, Wilhelm Julius. Anatomisch-physiologische Untersuchungen der Blüthen-Nectarien. 1878. I. 118.[2]
— Beiträge zur Geschichte der Bestäubungs-theorie. 1878. I. 237.
— Der Bestäubungsmechanismus bei . . . Cobaea. 1880. II. 746.[2]
— Hülfsbuch zur Ausführung mikroskopischer Untersuchungen. 1883. V. VIII.[1]
— The microscope in botany. 1885. I. 521.[1]
— Die Nectarien der Blüthen. 1878. I. 118.[2]
Behringer, Martin. Ueber den Einfluss wirthschaftlicher Massregeln auf Zuwachsverhältnisse. 1891. IV. 234.
— Schätzung stehender Fichtenholzes. 1900. IV. 459.[1]
Beiche, W. Eduard. Der kleine Botaniker. 1867. I. 386.
— Die schädlichen und nützlichen Vögel Deutschlands. 1868. IV. 198.[2]
— Taschenbuch der Pflanzenkunde. 1869. III. 73.
— Vollständiger Blüthenkalender der deutschen Phanerogamen-Flora. 1872. I. 387.
Beijerinck, Martinus Willem. Beobachtungen über . . . Cynipidengallen. 1882. I. 214.[1]
— Beobachtungen . . . über Wurzelknospen und Nebenwurzeln. 1886. I. 104.
— Bijdrage tot de morphologie der plantegallen. 1877. I. 214.[1]
— De la cecidie produite par le Namatus Capreae. 1887. III. 351.[2]
— La cécidiogénèse . . . chez le Cynips callicis. 1897. IV. 511.
— Over het cecidium van Nematus Capreae. 1887. III. 50.[1]
— Ueber Gallbildung. 1896. I. 214,[2] IV. 511.
— The Gardenia-root disease. 1897. III. 744.[1]
— De gomziekte der vruchtboomen is besmettelijk. 1882. I. 528.[1]
— L. Beissner's Untersuchungen bezüglich der Retinisporafrage. 1890. II. 18.
— Over een middel tegen de " zonnebarsten." 1889. III. 184.[1]

— Over normale Wortelknoppen. 1884. I. 104.
— Onderzoekingen over de besmettelijkheid der gomziekte. 1883. I. 528.[1]
— Over het ontstaan van knoppen . . . uit bladen. 1882. I. 108.[2]
— Recherches sur la contagiosité de la maladie de gomme. 1884. I. 213,[1] 528.[1]
— Schade door insecten in de Dennen. 1878. IV. 442.
— Verslag omtrent de schade veroorzaakt door insecten. 1878. IV. 549.[2]
Bell, Anton. Beschreibung einer sehr einfachen Säemaschine. 1845. IV. 148.
— Die Feldholzzucht in Belgien. 1842. IV. 134.[2]
— Forstwirthschaftliche Kulturwerkzeuge. 1846. IV. 176.[2]
— Frankfurt's Stadtwaldung. 1840. IV. 352.
— Massregeln gegen die Maikäfer. 1865. IV. 202.
Beilagen zur Instruktion über die Aufstellung von Wirthschafts-Plänen. 1841. IV. 300.[1]
Beille, Lucien. Sur les altérations produites par l'Heterodera. 1899. III. 617.[1]
— De la limite altitudinale du Châtaigner. 1888. II. 124.[1]
— Note sur l'organogénie florale des " Pedilanthus." 1900. II. 448.[2]
— Note sur le développement de la fleur mâle du " Ricinus." 1899. II. 451.[1]
— Note sur le développement des Disciflores. 1900. I. 115.[2]
— Note sur le développement des fleurs mâles du Cluytia. 1900. II. 438.[2]
— Note sur le développement floral des Vitis. 1900. II. 506.[1]
Beilschmied, Karl Traugott. Characteres distinctivi. 1833. I. 255.
— Ueber einige bei pflanzengeographischen Vergleichungen zu berücksichtigende Punkte. 1829. I. 378.
Beinert, Karl Christian. Ueber die Nutzanwendung von Juniperus communis. 1864. IV. 448.[2]
Beinling, Theodor Rudolf Berthold. Ueber die geographische Verbreitung der Coniferen. 1858. II. 12,[1] V. xxv.[1]
— Die Nadelhölzer. 1858. V. xxv.[1]
— De Smilacearum structura. 1850. II. 77,[1] 85.[1]
Beins, C. A. G. Practische handleiding ter bevordering der . . . snoeiwijze. 1876. III. 170.
Beirão, C. M. F. da S. See Gomes, B. A. & Beirão, C. M. F. da S.
Beisly, Sidney. Shakspere's garden. 1864. I. 514.[2]
Ein Beispiel der Wiederherstellung eines abgewirthschafteten Forstkomplexes. 1893. IV. 248.[2]
Beissner, Ludwig. Abies nobilis Lindl. 1899. III. 296.[2]
— Abies Nordmanniana. 1891. III. 296.[2]
— Abies numidica de Lannoy. 1891. III. 296.[3]
— Aralia papyrifera . . . als Staude. 1882. III. 644.[1]
— Araucaria imbricata. 1891. III. 296.[1]
— Eine Aufzählung von Pflanzen . . . an der Mittelmeerküste. 1876. III. 119.[1]
— Die Baumschulkulturen in Angers. 1878. I. 59.
— Bemerkungen über verschiedene Ziergehölze. 1878. III. 46.
— Beobachtungen über ächte und falsche Chamaecyparis. 1879. II. 28.[2]
— Biota orientalis aurea hort. 1891. III. 311.[2]
— Chionanthus virginica. 1883. III. 671.[2]
— Conifere della China. 1897. II. 16.[1]
— Coniferenfrage . . . 1900. II. 18.
— Zur Coniferenfrage. 1887. III. 300.[2]
— Conifères de Chine. 1897. II. 16.[1]
— Cryptomeria japonica. 1891. III. 302.[1]
— Cryptomeria japonica . . . var. elegans. 1884. II. 29.[1]
— Deutzia Lemoinei. 1898. III. 410.[1]
— Eigenthümliche Verwachsung zweier Sämlinge. 1881. II. 52.[2]
— Einheitliche Coniferen-Benennung. 1887. II. 13.[2]
— Einheitliche Coniferen-Benennung. 1893. II. 13.[2]
— Einige alte Gärten Deutschlands. 1893. I. 48.
— Einige Bemerkungen über die Nomenclatur der Coniferen. 1886. II. 13.[1]
— Einige besonders dekorative Coniferen. 1877. III. 290.
— Empfehlenswerte ausländische Coniferen. 1899. IV. 126.[1]
— Ueber Formveränderung der Coniferen. 1881. III. 290.
— Ueber Formveränderung von Coniferen-Sämlingen. 1879. II. 17.[2]
— Die Freiland-Coniferen. 1897. III. 291.
— Die Hänge- oder Trauerbäume. 1898. III. 204.[2]
— Die Hängefichte im Park zu Reinhardsbrunn. 1899. III. 305.[2]

— Handbuch der Coniferen-Benennung. 1887. II. 13.[2]
— Handbuch der Nadelholzkunde. 1891. II. 13.[2]
— Ueber Jugendformen von Pflanzen. 1888. II. 18.
— Juniperus virginiana reptans. 1896. III. 304.[1]
— Knospenvariation. 1895. I. 244.[2]
— Durch Knospenvariation entstandene Pflanzenformen. 1898. I. 245.
— Zur Koniferen-Frage. 1887. III. 290.
— Lespedeza bicolor Turcz. und Lespedeza Sieboldi. 1885. II. 369.[2]
— Monographie der Abietineen . . . von Dr. Heinrich Mayr. 1892. II. 16.[1]
— Neues auf dem Gebiete der Nadelholzkunde. 1893. III. 91.
— Noch ein Wort über die Retinispören. 1881. II. 28.[1]
— Pflanzenphysiologische Betrachtungen. 1900. I. 219.[1]
— Philadelphus Lemoinei Lem. 1898. III. 413.[2]
— Picea alba Lk. compacta gracilis. 1893. III. 305.[2]
— Picea excelsa Lk. var. virgata. 1894. III. 305.[2]
— Picea pungens. 1891. III. 306.[1]
— Pinus Cembra L. var. columnaris. 1898. III. 307.[1]
— Pinus Cembra und ihre Formen. 1891. III. 307.[1]
— Pinus excelsa. 1889. III. 308.[1]
— Die pyramidenförmigen Taxus. 1891. III. 288.[1]
— Reife Frucht von Stephanotis. 1890. III. 694.[1]
— Reiseerinnerungen. 1897. I. 49.
— Die Schlangenfichte in Bückeburg. 1889. III. 305.[1]
— Die schönsten Nadelhölzer, IV–VII, IX–XIV, XVI. 1891. III. 306,[1] 302,[1] 307,[1] 288,[1] 311,[1] 296,[2] 310,[2] 312,[1] 302,[1] 299.[1]
— Die schönsten Nadelhölzer, XVII. 1893. III. 305.[2]
— Sequoia gigantea und ihre Formen. 1891. III. 310.[2]
— Sorbus Aucuparia L. var. dulcis lacinata. 1899. III. 459.[2]
— Stangenholz im Park und Garten. 1882. III. 202.[2]
— Der Strassen-Gärtner. 1887. III. 210.
— Thuya gigantea und ihre Formen. III. 312.[1]
— Thuya occidentalis L. var. umbraculifera. 1891. III. 311.[1]
— Vaccinium Myrtillus L. β baccis albis. 1889. II. 686.[2]
— Vegetationsverhältnisse . . . von Hyères. 1869. I. 58.
— Vermeidung einer Doppelbenennung. 1895. III. 311.[1]
— Das Verpflanzen einer grossen Palme. 1876. III. 167, 317.
— Ueber verschiedene Entwickelungsstadien. 1897. I. 101.[1]
— Verzeichniss derjenigen Holzgewächse . . . in den Gärten am Starnberger See. 1881. III. 69.
— Zusammenstellung von Ziergehölzen, welche . . . Kontraste hervorbringen. 1876. III. 203.
— Zwei zu selten kultivirte Pflanzen. 1883. III. 400,[2] 533.[1]
— Die Zypressen. 1891. III. 302.[1]
See also Förster, F. C. & Beissner, Ludwig; Jäger, Hermann & Beissner, Ludwig.
Beithar, Ibn. See Ibn Beithar.
Beiträge zum Buchenhochwaldbetrieb. 1857. IV. 494.
Beiträge zur Biologie der Pflanzen. I. i.
Beiträge zur Forststatistik des Deutschen Reichs. 1884. IV. 349.[1]
Beiträge zur Forst-Statistik von Böhmen. 1885. IV. 371.
Beiträge zur Forststatistik von Elsass-Lothringen. IV. 7.
Beiträge zur Forstwissenschaft. IV. 7.
Beiträge zur gesammten Forstwissenschaft. IV. 7.
Beiträge zur gesammten Natur- und Heilwissenschaft. I. 27.
Beiträge zur Geschichte der Kieferraupe. 1800. IV. 4/5.
Beiträge zur Kenntniss der amerikanischen Holzverarbeitung. 1894. IV. 382.[1]
Beiträge zur Kenntniss der forstwirthschaftlichen Verhältnisse der Provinz Hannover. 1881. IV. 354.
Beiträge zur Kenntniss der Land- und Forstwirthschaft im Grossherzogthum Baden. See Dengler, Leopold. 1860. IV. 350.[1]
Beiträge zur Kenntniss der land- und forstwirthschaftlichen Verhältnisse im Königreich Hannover. See Burckhard, Heinrich. 1852. IV. 352.[2]
Beiträge zur Kenntniss des Forstwesens in Deutschland. IV. 7.
Beiträge zur Kenntniss des Russischen Reiches. I. 9.[2]
Beiträge zur künstlichen Kultur der . . . deutschen Holzarten. 1817. IV. 117.
Beiträge zur Pflanzenkunde. I. 11.
Beiträge zur Pflanzenkunde des russischen Reiches. I. 9.[2]
Beiträge zur praktischen Forst- und Jagdwissenschaft. IV. 7.
Beiträge zur rheinischen Naturgeschichte. See Gesellschaft für Beförderung der Naturwissenschaften in Freiburg i. B. I. 12.

Beiträge zur St. Gallischen Volksbotanik. 1861. I. 517.[2]
Beiträge zur Statistik der inneren Verwaltung des Grossherzogthums Baden. IV. 7.
Beiträge zur Statistik des Grossherzogthums Hessen. IV. 7.
Beiträge zur wissenschaftlichen Botanik. I. 11.
Beiträge zur Würdigung und Ausbildung des Fehmelwaldbetriebs. 1857. IV. 130.
Beiträge . . . See also BEYTRÄGE . . .
Beitrag zu den allgemeinen Grundsätzen der Forstökonomie. 1798. IV. 242. See also BRANDENSTEIN, von. 1798. IV. 117.
Beitrag zu den Erfahrungen über die Benutzung der Eichenrinde. 1865. IV. 512.
Beitrag zur Durchforstungsfrage. 1899. IV. 175.[2]
Beitrag zur Forst-Statistik des Kantons Bern. 1855. IV. 365.
Ein Beitrag zur Frage über die Pflicht der Entschädigung wegen Waldbränden. 1860. IV. 182.[3]
Ein Beitrag zur Frage über die vortheilhafteste Benutzung schadhafter alter Eichen. 1859. IV. 505.
Beitrag zur Kenntniss der Feinde des Kiefernspinners. 1861. IV. 207.
Beitrag zur schweiz. Forstgesetzgebung. 1852. IV. 330.
Beitrag . . . See also BEYTRAG . . .
Baitter, Albert. Pharmacognotisch-chemische Untersuchung der Catha. 1900. III. 551.[3]
— Réactions digitaliques. 1897. III. 724.[1]
Beivinkler, Karl. Anleitung zur Waldwerthberechnung. 1855. IV. 253.
— Ueber die Bindung des Flugsandes. 1861. IV. 145.
— Erdőgazda. 1853. IV. 99.[3]
— Utmutatás az erdőérték kiszámitására. 1855. IV. 253.
Beiwinkler, Károly. See BEIVINKLER, Karl.
Bejthe, Stephan. Stirpium nomenclator pannonicus. 1584. I. 444.
Ueber die Bekämpfung der Kiefernschütte. 1900. IV. 559.[2]
Die Bekämpfung der Reblaus. 1878. III. 761.
Bekarevitch, N. See Бекаревичъ, Н.
Beke, Charles Tilstone. Discoveries of Sinai in Arabia. 1878. I. 481.[1]
— Remarks on Mr. Carter's paper on the Gopherwood. 1834. I. 513.
Bekény, Aladár. Máramaros erdőmivelési viszonyai. 1897. IV. 374.[1]
Békétoff, Andreas. Cours de botanique. 1864. I. 90.
— De l'influence du climat sur la croissance de quelques arbres résineux. 1869. II. 20.[3]
— Mémoire sur la stabilité et la régularité des proportions relatives des parties foliaires. 1858. I. 109.[3]
— Notice sur la germination. 1859. I. 203.
— Sur une station . . . du Sapin de Sibérie. 1866. II. 25.[1]
— Sur la structure de l'écorce du Bouleau. 1866. II. 119.[1]
— See also Бекетовъ, А. Н.
Bekhagel von Adlerskron. See Вехагель-фонъ Адлерскронъ.
Bekow, Daniel. Die Beheerwurm der Wälder des Kreises Kuba. 1900. IV. 46.[3]
Bekuhrs. Ein vom Blitz getroffener Eichen-Drehling. 1888. IV. 194.
Bel, Jules. Monographie des Rosiers du Tarn. 1890. II. 286.[1]
— Les plantes médicinales du midi de la France. 1897. III. 86.
— La Rose; histoire et culture. 1892. III. 450.
Un bel exemplaire d'Araucaria. 1894. III. 299.[1]
Belajeff, W. C. Zur Lehre von dem Pollenschlauche der Gymnospermen. 1891. II. 1.
Bélanger, Charles. Voyage aux Indes-orientales. 1846. I. 303.
Belchilgen, count & Cope, J. A. An essay on the properties . . . of Ginseng tea. 1786. III. 605.
Belda, Vincente LAJARA. See LAJARA BELDA, Vincente.
Belehrung über die zweckmässigste Art der Anpflanzung von Alleen. 1836. III. 209.
Beleuchtung der Ansprache des Klosters Pfäffers. 1831. IV. 329.
Beleuchtung eines Leitartikels. 1857. I. 205, 248.[2]
Belfort — Société forestière de Franche - Comté & Belfort. See SOCIÉTÉ . . . IV. 13.[1]
Belfort de la Roque, L. de. La destruction du phylloxéra. 1884. III. 761.
— Guide pratique de la fabrication du chocolat. 189.? III. 595.[1]
Belgique: création de la direction générale des eaux et forêts. 1900. IV. 553.[1]

Belgique horticole. III. 15.
Belgium — Académie royale de Belgique. See. ACADÉMIE ROYALE DES SCIENCES . . . DE BELGIQUE. I. 16.
Belgium — Académie royale des sciences des lettres . . . See ACADÉMIE . . . I. 16.
Belgium — Cercle professoral pour le progres de l'arboriculture. See CERCLE . . . III. 15.
Belgium — Fédération des sociétés d'horticulture. See FÉDÉRATION . . . III. 15.
Belgium — Leeraarskring tot volmaaktere boomteeltkunde. See LEERAARSKRING . . . III. 15.
Belgium — Ministère de l'agriculture. See MINISTÈRE . . . III. 15.
Belgium — Société centrale d'agriculture. See SOCIÉTÉ . . . III. 15.
Belgium — Société centrale d'arboriculture. See ANNALES de l'horticulture . . . III. 15.
Belgium — Société malacologique. See SOCIÉTÉ . . . I. 17.
Belgium — Société royale de botanique. See SOCIÉTÉ . . . I. 17.
Belgrand, Eugène. De l'influence des forêts. 1854. IV. 49.[3]
Belgrove, William. A treatise upon husbandry and planting. 1755. III. 99.
Belházy, Emil BÖLCSHÁZAI-. See BÖLCSHÁZAI-BELHÁZY, Emil.
Belházy, Jenő. Az Erdei-fenyő csemeték túhullatásáról. 1885. IV. 477.
Belhomme. Sur le choix des Chênes destinés à la nourriture du Bombyx yama-maï. 1865. IV. 501.[2]
— Note sur un nouveau Salix. 1856. II. 106.[2]
— Recherches sur la persistance du pouvoir fécondant dans le pollen. 1864. I. 201.[1]
Beling, Theodor. Zur Ablösung von Forstservituten. 1880. IV. 334.[1]
— Ueber Absprünge bei Fichten. 1872. IV. 456.
— Auffällige Baumtrocknis und Blitzschläge. 1884. IV. 194.
— Ein ausgeheilter Schneedruck-Schaden im jungen Buchen-Hochwalde. 1876. IV. 497.
— Beitrag zur Naturgeschichte des Bostrychus. 1873. IV. 204.
— Bemerkenswerthe Blitzschläge in Wald und Flur. 1886. IV. 194.
— Ueber die Berechnung der Pflanzenzahl. 1881. IV. 154.[1]
— Beschädigung junger Fichten durch Eichhörnchen. 1881. IV. 456.
— Beschädigungen des Waldes durch Mäuse. 1880. IV. 198.[1]
— Ueber Blitzschläge an Bäumen. 1873. IV. 194.
— Entomologische Mittheilungen. 1883. IV. 207.
— Das forstliche Verhalten der Lärche. 1886. IV. 449.
— Ein Frass der Buchenspinner- oder Rothschwanz-Raupe am Harze. 1871. IV. 456.
— Der grosse, schwarze Fichten-Rüsselkäfer. 1887. IV. 207.
— Der Heerwurm. 1883. IV. 207.
— Die Lärchenkrankheit am Harze. 1882. IV. 451.
— Noch, etwas über die sogenannten Fichten-Absprünge. 1872. IV. 456.
— Rasenasche und Kohlenstübbe. 1858. IV. 144.[3]
— Reproductionsfähigkeit der Lärche. 1874. II. 33.[1]
— Rindenringelungen an Waldbäumen. 1878. IV. 207.
— Ueber Rindenrisse an Bäumen. 1888. I. 207,[3] IV. 66.[3]
— Ueber Samenjahre bei der Eiche. 1877. I. 200, IV. 66.[3]
— Ueber Schnellkäfer-Larven. 1879. IV. 207.
— Die sogenannte Ringelkrankheit der Waldbäume. 1878. IV. 207.
— Die Standgewächse der Mistel. 1873. IV. 179.[1]
— Ueber Standortgewächse der Mistel. 1884. II. 872.[1]
— Der Stangenholzbetrieb. 1874. IV. 2.[1]
— Der Stockausschlag der Rothbuche. 1878. IV. 495.
— Waldbeschädigungen durch die Röthelmaus. 1886. IV. 198.[1]
— & Pannewitz, Julius von. Blitzschläge an Buchen und an Nadelhölzern. 1867. IV. 194.
Belke, Gustave. Notice sur l'histoire naturelle du district de Radomysl. 1866. I. 362.
Bell. Sur le papier de Calabar. 1865. III. 483.[2]
Bell. Report on the fruits and fruit trade of Madeira. 1896. III. 147.[1]
Bell, Jacob. On the adulteration of Senna. 1843. III. 470.[1]
— On the Ægle Marmelos. 1851. III. 495.[1]
— Babul bark. 1851. III. 464.[1]
— Bush tea of the Cape of Good Hope. 1854. III. 473.[2]
— Clove bark. 1845. III. 405,[1] 406.[1]

— On Hemidesmus indicus. 1844. III. 693.[1]
— Mitcham. 1851. III. 454.[1]
— Sago. 1852. III. 327.[3]
— On the varieties of the Almond. 1847. II. 272.[2]
— Zabucajo, a new esculent nut. 1851. III. 631.[2]
Bell, James. The analysis and adulteration of foods. 1881. III. 222.
Bell, John. The plants of the west coast of Newfoundland. 1869. I. 310.
— A practical dictionary of materia medica. 1841. III. 242.
Bell, Martin RODON Y. See·RODON Y BELL, Martin.
Bell, Robert. Forest fires in northern Canada. 1889. IV. 181.[2]
— The forests of Canada. 1885. IV. 337.[2]
— The forests of Canada. 1886. IV. 337.[1]
— The geographical distribution of forest trees in Canada. 1897. I. 309,[1] IV. 76.[2]
— The northern limits of . . . forest trees of Canada. 1882. I. 309,[2] IV. 76.[2]
Bell, William. On the effects of woods on climate. 1841. IV. 52.[2]
— Notes on the varieties of Tea cultivated in India. 1870. II. 552.[1]
— Remarks on tea manufacture in the North-West Provinces of India. 1873. III. 607.
— On the Whin as a fence. 1837. III. 489.[2]
— See also SADLER, John & BELL, William.
Bell, William Abraham. New tracks in North America. See PARRY, C. C. 1869. I. 323.
Un bell' esempio da imitare. 1881. IV. 166.[1]
Bella, Joaõ Antonio dalla. Memoria sobre a cultura das Oliveiras em Portugal. 1786. III. 674.[2]
— Memorias e observações sobre . . . azeite de Oliveira. 1784. III. 678.[2]
Bellair, C. Le placage du Lierre pour bordures sous bois. 1894. III. 643.[1]
Bellair, G. Ad. L'Abricotier, le Cerisier, et le Prunier. 189.? III. 144.
— Les arbres fruitiers. 1891. III. 145.[1]
— Engrais applicables à l'horticulture. 189.? III. 151.
— Le Figuier, le Framboisier. 189.? III. 147.[2]
— Le Pêcher, sa culture. 189.? III. 441.[1]
— Le Poirier, sa culture. 189.? III. 445.[2]
— Le Pommier, le Cognassier et le Néflier. 189.? III. 144.
Bellair, Georges. L'arboriculture d'ornement à l'Exposition universelle. 1900. III. 202.[1]
— De·la brûlure des jeunes pousses du Poirier. 1887. III. 446.[2]
— Les cépées de Paulownia. 1890. III. 703.[2]
— Hybrides anormaux. 1899. II. 260.[1]
— Les insectes utiles. 1885. III. 95.
— Le Marron d'Inde. 1894. III. 538.[2]
— Le parfum du Magnolia glauca. 1894. III. 399.[2]
— Procédés de bouturage . . . des Rosiers. 1890. III. 453.[1]
— Les Ruscus. 1894. III. 338.[1]
— Sciadophyllum pulchrum. 1894. III. 644.[1]
— Stabilité des arbres d'alignement. 1891. III. 210.
— Tecoma capensis et Tecoma jasminoides. 1895. III. 707.[1] 707.[3]
— Traité d'horticulture pratique. 1892. III. 113.
— & Saint-Léger, L. Les plantes de serre. 1900. III. 88.[1]
Bellairs, Nona. Wayside flora. 1866. I. 427.
Bellamy, Félix. See LECHARTIER, G. & BELLAMY, Félix.
Bellamy, John Cremer. The natural history of South Devon. 1839. I. 398.
Bellani, Angelo. Delle funzioni delle radici. 1843. I. 161.
— Della indefinibile durabilità della vita. 1836. I. 192.[2]
— Memoria sui boschi. 184.? IV. 165.
Bellardi, Carlo Antonio Lodovico. Appendix ad Floram pedemontanam. 1792. I. 424.
— De Mimosa sentiente. 1764. II. 372.[2]
— Osservazione botaniche . . . Flora pedemontana. 1788. I. 424.
Bellardi, Luigi. Quadri iconografici di botanica. 1863. I. 90.
Bellati, Giambattista. I ricordi di Nane Castaldo. 1884. III. 558.[1]
Belle, C. E. Étude sur le système forestier en France. 1876. IV. 292.
Belle, Louis. Maladie des Citronniers. 1899. III. 502.[2]
— Le " ver du Citronnier." 1899. III. 498.[2]
Bellecourt, DUCHESNE DE. See DUCHESNE DE BELLECOURT.
Bellecroix, Ernest. Guide pratique du garde-chasse. See LA RUE, Adolphe de. 1886. IV. 382.[1]

Bellenghi, Albertino. Articoli sulla coltivazione dei boschi. 1816. IV. 122.[2]
Bellenghi, Filippo. Processo sulle tinte. 1811. III. 236.
Bellerie, LE SEURRE DE LA. See LE SEURRE DE LA BELLERIE.
Bellerive, de. Dissémination des plantes par l'intermédiaire. 1892. I. 240.[2]
— L'écorce du " Tanner's Cassia." 1894. III. 470.[2]
— Le foin de fagots. 1892. III. 223.[2]
Bellermann, Franz. Landschafts- und Vegetations-Bilder aus den Tropen Süd-Amerikas. 1894. I. 330.
Bellermann, Johann Bartholomaeus. Abbildungen zum Kabinet der vorzüglichsten . . . Holzarten. 1788. I. 37,[2] III. 68,[3] IV. 17.
Belleroche, John. Nouvelles observations sur le Physianthus albens. 1869. II. 736.[1]
— Observations sur les cellules fibreuses de l'anthère. 1864. I. 116.[1]
Bellerue, de. De l'exploitabilité commerciale. 1886. IV. 259.[2]
Belleval, Charles de. Beautés méridionales de la flore de Montpellier. 1826. I. 407.
— Nomenclateur botanique languedocien. 1840. I. 74.[1]
— Questions et observations particulièrement philologiques sur quelques plantes. 1830. I. 511.
Belleval, Pierre Richer de. Dessein touchant la recherche des pays de Languedoc. 1605. I. 404.[2]
— Onomatologia. See BELLEVAL, Richier de. 1598. I. 32, 56.
— Opuscules. 1785. I. 32.
Belleville, Gabriel. Der Stalldünger und die Waldstreu. 1878. IV. 438.[1]
Bellevoye, Adolphe. Communication sur le Phylloxera vastatrix. 1874. III. 567.[2]
— Les insectes nuisibles au Tilleul. 1876. III. 585.[2]
— & Laurent, Jules. Les plantations de Pins dans la Marne. 1897. IV. 461.[1]
Belli, Saverio. Rosa Jundzilli Besser. 1896. II. 295.[1]
Bellier, A. Du Caféier. 1864. III. 726.[2]
Bellini, Raffaello. See CERIO, Ignazio & BELLINI, Raffaello.
Belloy Espinosa, Domingo. Apuntes para la flora de Puerto-Rico. 1881. I. 336.
Belloc. Préparation de la fécule de marrons d'Inde. 1849. III. 538.[1]
Bellonius, Petrus. See BELON, Pierre.
Bellot des Minières & Sabatier, J. Gelées et fumées dans les vignobles. 1899. III. 549.[3]
Bellovacensis, VINCENTIUS. See VINCENTIUS BELLOVACENSIS.
Bellucci, Giuseppe. Sulla pretesa emissione dell' ozono dalle piante. 1872. I. 170.
Bellucci, J. Sur le prétendu dégagement de l'ozone des plantes. 1874. I. 170.
Bellucci, Toma. Plantarum index Horti pisani. 1662. I. 60.[2]
Bellus, Honorius. Aliquot epistolae, de varioribus quibusdam plantis. 1601. I. 451, 486.
— Nonnullae ejusdem stirpes insignes in Creta. 1601. I. 451, 486.
Bellynck, Auguste Alexis Adolphe Alexandre. Catalogue des plantes soit spontanées . . . en Belgique. 1876. I. 393.[1]
— Flore de Namur. 1855. I. 411.
Belmont, Abel. Dictionnaire historique et artistique de la Rose. 1896. II. 290,[1] III. 481.[1]
Belohoubek, August. Über Ebenholz und dessen Farbstoff. 1884. III. 701.[2]
— Untersuchungen von Ebenholz. 1884. III. 701.[2]
Belon, Pierre. De arboribus coniferis, resiniferis. 1553. I. 292.
— De neglecta plantarum cultura. 1558. III. 110.[2]
— De neglecta stirpium cultura. 1558. III. 110.[1]
— Les observations de plusieurs singularites. 1553. I. 279, V. xv.[1]
— Plurimarum singularium .& memorabilium rerum in Graecia . . . observationes. 1553. I. 279.
— Les remonstrances sur le default du labour et culture des plantes. 1558. III. 110.[3]
— Traicté nouveau de l'agriculture & manière de planter. See TRAICTÉ nouveau . . . 1551. III. 110.[1]
Below, Jakob Fredrik. De vegetabilibus in genere. 1700. I. 30.
Belt, Thomas. The naturalist in Nicaragua. 1874. I. 333.
Belzung, Ernest. Anatomie et physiologie végétales. 1900. I. 93.
— Sur divers principes issus de la germination. 1892. I. 177, 204.

Belzung, Ernest (*continued*).
— Nature des sphérocristaux des Euphorbes. 1893. II. 442.[1]
— Note additionnelle sur les sulfates et nitrates. 1893. I. 204.
— Note sur le développement de l'amidon. 1885. I. 204.
— Recherches morphologiques . . . sur l'amidou. 1887. I. 140,[2] *142*.
— Remarques sur le verdissement. 1881. I. 142.
Bemærkninger om Maaden at drive afskaarne Grene af Siirtræer i Vand. 1838. III. 176.[1]
Bemærkninger over de Fordele, som Skibs . . . *See* WOLFF, J. 1832. IV. 416.[2]
Bement, C. N. American evergreen trees. 1862. III. 206.[1]
— American shade trees. 1861. III. 208.[2]
Bemerkenswerte Eibe. *See* APPENZELL a. Rh. . . . 1878. II. 11.[1]
Bemerkenswerthe Bäume. 1887. I. 297.[3]
Bemerkungen auf einer Reise nach Harbke. *See* HENNERT, C. W. 1792. IV. 352.
Bemerkungen betreffend das Vorwaldsystem. 1846. IV. 128.
Bermerkungen des Abgeordneten Bening . . . die Bildung von Waldgenossenschaften betreffend. *See* BERICHT der verstärkten Kommission. 1869. IV. 308.[1]
Bemerkungen des Ausschusses für die Obstbaumzucht. 1839. III. 433.[2]
Bemerkungen eines badischen Forstmannes über die Forstschule zu Karlsruhe. 1832. IV. 31.
Bemerkungen über das Pfropfen. 1851. III. 163.[3]
Bemerkungen über die Buchen-Nachzucht. 1885. IV. 495.
Bemerkungen über die Cultur . . . der Ceder vom Libanon. 1825. III. 300.[1]
Bemerkungen über die Erfolge des Biermanns'schen Kulturverfahrens. 1860. IV. 141.
Bemerkungen über die sächsische Forstwirthschaft. 1797. IV. 355.[1]
Bemerkungen über die Weymouthskiefer. 1838. IV. 469.
Einige Bemerkungen über die Würkung welche die Kälte . . . auf die Waldbäume gehabt. 1790. IV. 191.[1]
Bemerkungen über die Zuwachsberechnung. 1839. IV. 232.
Bemerkungen über die Zuwachsprocente. 1850. IV. 232.
Bemerkungen über ein . . . Schutzmittel gegen den Raupenfrass. 1833. III. 196.
Bemerkungen und Erfahrungen in Rücksicht der Mittel zur Verminderung der Baumraupen. 1791. III. 188.[3]
Bemerkungen zu den von der General-Kommission in Schlesien. *See* PFEIL, Wilhelm. 1846. IV. 333.
Bemesting van Koffietuinen. 1897. II. 734.[1]
Bemmelen, J. A. van. Algemeen verslag wegens den staat van den landbouw. 1847. III. 122.[1]
— Algemeen verslag wegens den staat van den landbouw. 1849. III. 122.[1]
— Iets over de Radix Sarsaparillae. '1830· III. 338.[1]
Bemmelen, J. F. van. Dwars door Midden-Sumatra. 1896. I. 467.
Benade, (*Rektor, Hoyerswerda*). · Über das Pfropfen hinter die Rinde. 1824. III. 160.
Bénard, Jules. La guerre aux hannetons. 1899. IV. 203.
— Les plantations sur les routes. 1896. III. 210.
— Les routes fruitières. 1900. III. 211.[1]
Bénardeau, Fabien. La restauration des montagnes. 1887. IV. 185.[2]
— *See also* LABBÉ, Henry & BÉNARDEAU, Fabien.
— & Labbé, Henry. Essences forestières principales. 1889. IV. 85.[2]
— — La science forestière illustrée. 1889. IV. 122.[1]
Benbow, John. Fàtsia japonica (Aralia Sieboldi). 1894. II. 648.[2]
Bencze, Gergely. A különféle fafajok hőhatásának megitélésére szolgáló analytikai adatok. 1900. IV. 413.[1]
Bender, Carl. Das Gas der Hülsen von Colutea. 1875. II. 347.[1]
Bender, E. & Vermorel, V. Le vigneron moderne. 1893. III. 557.[1]
Bending tests of wood. 1899. IV. 411.[1]
Bendixen, Chr. Den første Behandling af nysindplantede Roser. 1889. III. 452.
Benecke, (*Prediger, Schönerlinde bei Berlin*). Die Vertilgung der Raupen. 1842. III. 196.
Benecke, Franz. Beiträge zur Kenntniss der Begoniaceen. 1882. II. 583.[3]
— Beitrag zur Kenntniss der Ursachen des Wachsthums. 1884. I. 187.

Benecke, Wilhelm. Ein Beitrag zur mineralischen Nahrung der Pflanzen. 1894. I. 160.
— Die Nebenzellen der Spaltöffnungen. 1892. I. 131.[2]
Beneckendorff, von. Theoretisch-praktische Anleitung zur neueren Forstwissenschaft. 1783. IV. 95.
Benedikt, Rudolf. Analyse der Fette und Wachsarten. 1886. III. 225.
Benefizi provenienti dall' arboratura. 1865. IV. 43.
Bénéguet. *See* REBOUL & BÉNÉGUET.
Benekendorff, Karl Friedrich. Abhandlung von Anlegung eines Obstgartens. 1792. III. 135.
— Abhandlung von Baumschulen. 1776. III. 153.
Benemann, Johann Christian. Die Rose. 1742. II. 290.[3]
Benes, János. Coniferák, Toboztermők. 1887. III. 290.
Benese, *Sir* Richard de. The boke of measuryng. 156.[?] III. 200.[1]
Bénévent, B. Déboisement et reboisement dans les Basses-Pyrénées. 1894. IV. 362.
Benevides, Antonio Albino FONSECA. *See* FONSECA BENEVIDES, A. A.
Bengal. *See also* INDIA—BENGAL.
Bengal — Asiatic society. *See* ASIATIC . . . I. 28.[2]
Bengal — Government Cinchona plantation and factory . . . Annual report. 1894. III. 715.
Bengal — Selections from the records . . . *See* SELECTIONS . . . III. 26.[1]
The Bengal forests. 1882. IV. 377.[2]
The Bengal pharmacopœia. 1844. III. 257.[1]
Benge, J. M. De Thee. *See* ALBINI, F. B. 1684. III. 605.
Bengein. Indian arts and manufactures, II. 1832. III. 323.[3]
— The Palm or Toddy tree. 1832. III. 323.[2]
Bengy-Puyvallée, C. A. de. Mémoire de la culture du Pécher. 1831. III. 440.[2]
I beni incolti comunali da imboschire. 1894. IV. 328.
Béninga, Bojung Scato Georg LANTZIUS-. *See* LANTZIUS-BÉNINGA, B. S. G.
Benini, Vincenzo. Annotazioni sopra la Coltivazione di Luigi Alamanni. 1745. III. 115.[2]
Benjamin, C. I. 108.[1]
Benjamin, Ludwig. Über intrapetiolare Knospenbildung. 1852. I. 482.[1]
— Morphologische Entwickelungsgeschichte des Blattes von Aesculus. 1849. II. 482.[1]
Benjamin, S. G. W. The trees of Persia. 1890. I. 477.[2]
Bennet, Henry. Araucaria excelsa. 1888. III. 298.[2]
— The Date Palm. 1882. III. 328.[3]
— The history of a Passiflora on the Genoese Riviera. 1884. III. 615.[3]
— Is Ivy parasitic? 1888. II. 650.[1]
— The Olive. 1874. II. 713.[2]
— The Palm forest at Elche. 1883. III. 328.[2]
— Der Palmenwald zu Elche. 1883. III. 328.[3]
— Pinus canariensis. 1888. III. 307.[1]
Bennett, Alfred William. Acclimatization of foreign trees. 1870. III. 46.[2]
— Conspectus Polygalarum europaearum. 1878. II. 430.[2]
— The flora of the Alps. 1891. I. 437, 535.
— Foreign trees and plants in English gardens. 1870. III. 46.[3]
— Insects and flowers. 1875. I. 237.
— On the medicinal products of . . . Simarubeae. 1875. III. 506,[2] *509*.[2]
— Notes on Indian Burseraceae. 1876. II. 416.[1]
— Notes on Indian Simarubae. 1873. II. 413.[1]
— Polygalae americanae novae. 1879. II. 430.[2]
— Polygaleae. 1874. II. 429.[2]
Bennett, Arthur. Ledum palustre L. in Scotland. 1894. II. 673.[1]
— Notes on the flora of Surrey. 1880. I. 403.
Bennett, E. C. Evergreens for the farm. 1892. III. 118.[1]
Bennett, Edward. The Orange or Golden-berried Mountain Ash. 1895. III. 459.[2]
— Transplanting and removing evergreens. 1874. III. 169.[1]
Bennett, Frederick Debell. Narrative of a whaling voyage. 1840. I. 303.
Bennett, George. An account of the medicinal properties &c. of the Kava shrub. 1832. III. 384.[1]
— An account of the Sandal wood tree. 1832. III. 384.[2]
— Bemerkung über einige Arzneipflanzen. 1833. III. 366.[1]
— Bougainvillea spectabilis in New South Wales. 1866. III. 388.[2]
— Capparis Mitchellii, der australische Granatapfel. 1877. II. 231.[2]
— A case of poisoning by . . . Macrozamia spiralis. 1872. III. 286.[1]

— The Chinese Date Plum. 1863. III. 669.[1]
— The Cocoa-nut tree. 1834. III. 323.[2]
— Curious Epiphytes from Cape York. 1868. II. 820,[1] *824*.[2]
— Flowers and folk-lore. 1882. I. 536.[2]
— Gatherings in Australia. 1869. I. 502.
— Gatherings of a naturalist in Australasia. 1860. I. 499.[1]
— On the introduction . . . of the Orange. 1867. III. 499.[1]
— Mittheilungen aus [seinen] Reisenotizen. 1863. III. 282.[2]
— Nachrichten von neusellándischen Pflanzen. 1833. I. 506.[1]
— The native Pomegranate of 'Australia. 1877. II. 231.[2]
— Notes on a visit to the Bottle tree of Queensland. 1876. II. 538.[2]
—₇ Notes on two species of the genus Alstonia. 1867. II. '23.[1]
— Observations on the coniferous trees of New Zealand. 1832. II. 16.[1]
— Observations on the introduction . . . of the Orange-tree in New South Wales. 1867. III. 499.[1]
— Observations on the Rice-paper tree. 1864. III. 644.[1]
— The Orange-tree in Australia. 1860. III. 499.[2]
— The Paper bark trees of New South Wales. 1868. II. 619.[2]
— A remarkable Eucalyptus. 1872. II. 625.[2]
— On the Tanghinia veneniflua. 1868. II. 733.[2]
— Ueber Telopea speciosissima. 1865. II. 167.[2]
— On variation of colour in the flowers of the Warratah. 1868. II. 167.[2]
—Wanderings in New South Wales, Batavia. 1834. I. 302.
— The Waratah. 1865. II. 167.[2]
Bennett, J. L. Plants of Rhode Island. 1888. I. 315.
Bennett, John Joseph. Description of the Bungo. 1855. II. 319.[2]
— Description of the Kobo-tree. 1857. II. 347.[1]
— Note on the species of Croton described . . . under . . . Clutia. 1860. II. 439.[1]
— Plantae javanieae rariores. 1838. I. 468.
— Révision des genres Turraea et Munronia. 1841. II. 421,[2] *422*.[2]
Bennett, John Whitchurch. Ceylon and its capabilities. 1843. III. 279.[1]
— A selection of rare & curious fruits . . . Ceylon. 1850. III. 279.[1]
Bennett, K. H. Notes on the method of obtaining water from Eucalyptus roots. 1884. IV. 531.[2]
— Remarks on the decay of certain . . . Eucalypti. 1886. II. 623.[2]
Bennetts, W. J. Additions to the flora of Milwaukee county. 1900. I. 317.[1]
Benoist, (député, Maine-et-Loire). Opinion sur le titre XI. du projet de budget. 1817. IV. 326.
Benoist, Constant, baron de. De l'amélioration de la culture du Pommier 1887 III. 426.[2]
Benoit, Madame. Herbier élémentaire. 1811. III. 85.
Benoit, A. Das Buchsbaumwäldchen in Pieterlen. 1898. IV. 525.[2]
Benoit, T. T. W. Botanist's pocket companion. 1838. I. 94.
Benoni, J. Pěstování Palem v pokoji. 1893. III. 318.[1]
— Přezimování Růží. 1889. III. 452.
Denouard, Alfred, (jr.). Cultivo y descortezamiento del Ramié. 1890. III. 381.[1]
Benque, W. Die Einwirkung des Continentalklimas. 1871. I. 217.
Benseler, Friedrich. Ueber den Einfluss der Insecten . . . auf die Entstehung von Varietäten. 1880. I. 244.[2]
— Leichtlin's botanischer Privatgarten in Baden-Baden. 1883. I. 48.
— Ueber die Wichtigkeit der Acclimatisationgärten. 1876. I. 38,[1] *III. 43*.
Bensen, C. A. Over Tjendana-Djengkeh. 1862. IV. 399.[2]
Benson, Albert H. Apple culture. 1894. III. 426.[2]
— Fruit culture in Queensland. 1900. III. 497.[2]
— General hints on the pruning of deciduous fruit-trees. 1892. III. 172.
— Orange culture. 1893. III. 500.[1]
— Pruning. 1893. III. 172.
— Spraying. 1897. III. 198.[1]
— & Tryon, Henry. Experiments in cyaniding Oranges. 1899. III. 501.[1]
Benson, Carlos. Contribution to the study of Cangoura. 1892. III. 265.[1]
Benson, Margaret. Contributions to the embryology of the Amentiferae. 1894. I. 524.[2]

Bent, C. D. How to secure hardy Peach trees. 1898. III. 441.[1]
— Twenty years experience with the Peach. 1896. III. 441.[1]
Bent, Thomas. The way of making pitch. 1699. IV. 436.[1]
Bentham, George. Account of Indian Labiatae. 1833. II. 762.[2]
— Account of two new genera allied to Olacineae. 1841. II. 170.[1]
— On African Anonaceae. 1862. II. 215.[2]
— Bemerkungen über Loganiaceen. 1856. II. 716.[2]
— The botany of the voyage of H. M. S. Sulphur. 1844. I. 303.
— Catalogue des plantes . . . des Pyrénées. 1826. I. 408.
— Centralamerikas Rubiaceer. See ØRSTED, A. S. 1852. II. 807.[2]
— Chaunochiton loranthoides Benth. 1867. II. 170.[2]
— Commentationes de Leguminosarum generibus. 1837. II. 318.[1]
— Contributions to the flora of Guiana. 1848. II. 423.[2]
— Contributions toward a flora of South America. 1840. I. 339.[1]
— Description of a new species of Bolivaria. 1846. II. 712.[1]
— Description of some . . . tropical Leguminosae. 1865. II. 319.[2]
— Description of two American species of Gnetum. 1856. II. 54.[2]
— Discours sur la géographie des êtres vivants. 1816. I. 300.
— Enumeration of Leguminosae. 1843. II. 318.[1]
— Enumeration of the plants collected by Mr. Schomburgk, British Guiana. 1839. I. 338.[2]
— Ericeae. 1839. II. 657.[2]
— On Fissicalyx, a new genus of Dalbergieae. 1861. II. 358.[2]
— On Fissicalyx and Prioria. 1861. II. 358,[2] *379*.[1]
— Flora australiensis. 1863. I. 502.
— Flora hongkongensis. 1861. II. 460.[2]
— On the genera Sweetia Sprengel. 1865. II. 386.[1]
— On the genus Henriquezia of Spruce. 1859. II. 819.[2]
— On the geographical distribution . . . of species. 1868. I. 300.
— Handbook of the British flora. 1858. I. 400.
— On Henriquezia verticillata Spruce. 1854. II. 819.[2]
— Kennedya Marryattiana. 1838. II. 367.[2]
— Labiatae. 1831. II. 762.[1]
— Labiatae. 1848. II. 762.[1]
— Labiatarum genera et species. 1832. II. 762.[1]
— Leguminosae. 1859. II. 318.[2]
— Leguminosae inter plantas nilgherrenses. 1851. II. 358.[2]
— De Leguminosarum generibus commentationes. 1837. II. 318.[1]
— On Leopoldinia Piassaba Wallace. 1860. II. 70.[1]
— New Guinea region. 1844. I. 499.[1]
— On the North Brazilian Euphorbiaceae. 1854. II. 434.[1]
— Note on Leonia cymosa. 1853. II. 567.[2]
— Note on the genera Darwinia. 1867. II. 381,[1] *622*.[2]
— Notes on Anonaceae. 1861. II. 215.[1]
— Notes on Bixaceae and Samydaceae. 1861. II. 565,[2] *568*.[2]
— Notes on Euphorbiaceae. 1880. II. 433.[2]
— Notes on Homalium. 1860. II. 571.[1]
— Notes on Humiriaceae. 1853. II. 393.[2]
— Notes on Loganiaceae. 1856. II. 716.[2]
— Notes on Malvaceae and Sterculiaceae. 1862. II. 519,[1] *551*.[1]
— Notes on Menispermaceae. 1861. II. 206.[1]
— Notes on Mimoseae. 1842. II. 318.[1]
— Notes on Myrtaceae. 1869. II. 619.[1]
— Notes on Ternstroemiaceae. 1861. II. 547.[2]
— Notes on the American species of Myristica. 1853. II. 220.[1]
— Notes on the classification . . . of Compositae. 1873. II. 848.[1]
— Notes on the gamopetalous orders. 1877. II. 705.[2]
— Notes on the styles of Australian Proteaceae. 1873. II. 158.[2]
— Notes on Tiliaceae. . 1861. 'II. 512.[1]
— Notes on two little-known genera. 1853. II. 265,[1] *433*.[1]
— Notice of the rediscovery of the genus Asteranthos. 1859. II. 611.[1]
— Observations on some genera of plants . . . of Guiana. 1841. I. 339.[1]
— Observations on some new . . . Scrophulariaceae. 1836. II. 778.[2]

Bentham, George (*continued*).
— Observations on the distinctive characters of the Papilionaceae and Caesalpinieae. 1841. II. 318.[1]
— Plantae Hartwegianae. 1839. I. 331.
— Plantae Muellerianae. Mimoseae. 1853. II. 323.[1]
— Plantae Regnellianae. 1849. I. 342.
— Polemoniaceae. 1845. II. 746.[2]
— On Professor Nees von Esenbeck's genera of Acanthaceae. 1857. II. 796.[1]
— Report on some of the more remarkable . . . plants raised in the Horticultural society's garden. 1834. II. 243.[2]
— Report on the dried plants collected . . . in North Brazil. 1850. I. 342.
— Revision of the genera of Scrophulariaceae. 1836. II. 778.[2]
— Revision of the genus Cassia. 1871. II. 342.[2]
— Revision of the suborder Mimoseae. 1875. II. 318.[1]
— Scrophulariaceae. 1846. II. 778.[2]
— Scrophularineae indicae. 1835. II. 778.[1]
— Some new Anonaceae. 1853. II. 215.[1]
— On some new . . . Brazilian Rubiaceae. 1853. II. 807.[2]
— On the species and genera of plants. 1861. I. 244.[1]
— The species of Ventilago. 1861. II. 499.[3]
— Synopsis of Legnotideae. 1859. II. 612.[2]
— Synopsis of the Dalbergieae. 1860. II. 318.[1]
— Synopsis of the genus Clitoria. 1858. II. 347.[1]
— On three new genera connected with the Indian flora. 1853. II. 489.[3]
— On the tree supplying the Sabicù wood of Cuba. 1854. II. 370.[2]
— *See also* CHAMPION, J. G. & BENTHAM, George; HINDS, R. B. & BENTHAM, George; HOOKER, *Sir* J. D. & BENTHAM, George.
— & Hooker, J. D. Genera plantarum. 1862. I. 261.
— — Note on the embryo of Ancistrocladus. 1864. II. 584.[3]
— & Ørsted, A. S. Labiatae centroamericanae. 1853. II. 762.[2]
— — Leguminosae centroamericanae. 1853. II. 318.[3]
— — Scrophularineae centroamericanae. 1853. II. 778.[3]
— & others. Phytologische Abhandlungen. 1841. V. XIII.[2]
Bentheim, Otto von. Was uns Noth thut! Wildschadenersatz. 1888. IV. 136.[2]
— Wie sind reine Buchenhochwaldungen zu bewirthschaften? 1890. IV. 495.
Benthem van den Bergh, J. F. van. Eene proef tot bestrijding van de groene schildluis. 1899. III. 737.
Bentley, Robert. Cerasus (Prunus) virginiana. 1864. III. 443.[2]
— The characters, properties . . . of Eucalyptus globulus. 1874. IV. 533.[1]
— Eucalyptus globulus. 1878. IV. 533.[1]
— A manual of botany. 1861. I. 90.
— Monstrosity in the flower of the Rose. 1857. II. 289.[2]
— New American remedies. 1863. II. 412.[1]
— Physiological botany. 1886. I. 92.
— Ptelea trifolia Linn. 1863. III. 505.[2]
— Sur la Salsepareille de Guatémala. 1853. III. 339.[1]
— Xanthorrhiza apiifolia. 1863. III. 393.[1]
— Xanthoxylon fraxineum Willd. 1863. II. 412,[1] *III. 506.*[1]
— *See also* REDWOOD, Theophilus, BENTLEY, Robert & BARNARD, John.
— & Trimen, Henry. Medicinal plants. 1880. III. 59.[1]
Bentsch, Daniel. Untersuchungen über die fetten Oele. 1828. III. 224.[1]
Bentzen, Edv. Nye Krydsningsvarieteter af Rosa Wichuraiana. 1899. III. 457.[1]
Bentzien, Julius August. Abies Douglasii, Menziesii og Engelmannii. 1878. III. 290.
— Abutilon. 1882. III. 586.[2]
— Acclimatisering af exotiske Naale- og Løvtræer. 1858. III. 43.
— Acrophyllum venosum. 1859. II. 250.[1]
— Ælmetræet. 1856. III. 363.[2]
— Til Anbefaling for Koglebærende Træer. 1865. III. 289.
— Om " Arbeidet med Øxen." 1857. III. 173.[2]
— Arbutus Unedo eller Jordbærtræet. 1864. III. 647.[2]
— Aucuba japonica og de nyere Varieteter. 1872. III. 645.[1]
— Om Behandling af større Træplantninger. 1851. IV. 12.[1]
— Bemærkninger om . . . af Slægten Lonicera. 1875. III. 749.[2]
— Bemærkninger om de rankende Arter af Slægten Clematis. 1881. III. 389.[1]
— Bemærkninger om forskjellige Arter af Ligustrum. 1872. III. 481,[1] *673.*[1]

— Bemærkninger om forskjellige Sorter Buske. 1875. III. 66.[1]
— Bemærkninger om forskjellige Træer og Buske. 1867. III. 66.[1]
— Bemærkninger om Kjernefrugternes indre Egenskaber. 1876. III. 66.[3]
— Bemærkninger om nogle Arter . . . af Berberis. 1872. III. 393.[2]
— Bemærkninger om nogle Arter Aralia. 1880. III. 641.[1]
— Bemærkninger om nogle ikke rankende Arter af Slægten Lonicera. 1875. III. 749.[2]
— Bemærkninger om nogle tildels nyere Sirtræer. 1873. III. 66.[2]
— Bemærkninger om Plantning af Træer og Buske. 1853. III. 166.
— Bemærkninger om Slægten Deutzia. 1874. III. 410.[1]
— Bemærkninger om Træfrugtens Foranderlighed. 1873. I. 244.[1]
— Om Beskæring af Buxbom. 1870. III. 522.[2]
— Beskæring af Camellier. 1871. III. 599.[2]
— Beskæring af Pyramidetræer. 1858. III. 170.
— Beskæring af Skovtræer. 1856. IV. 170.
— Beskrivelse og Tegning af 31 . . . Pære- og Æblesorter. 1864. III. 66.[2]
— Birketræet óg dcts Arter. 1863. III. 357.
— Bocconia frutescens. 1864. III. 408.[2]
— Bør vi beskære de Træer, vi plante? 1855. III. 170.
— Om Brugen og Kulturen af Berberissen. 1863. III. 395.[2]
— Caryverse eller de nordamerikanske Hickory-træer. 1878. III. 353.[2]
— Om Charakteren af Træbeplantninger. 1856. I. 516.
— Citrus japonica. 1859. III. 501.[2]
— Coniferæ eller de koglebærende Planters Familie. 1856. III. 289.
— Drivning af forskjellige træagtige Planter. 1877. III. 176.[3]
— Om Drivning af nogle træagtige Frilandsplanter. 1858. III. 176.[2]
— Om Dyrkning af Clerodendron. 1870. III. 696.[1]
— Om dyrkning af Epacris. 1853. III. 665.[1]
— Dyrkning af Epacris. 1881. III. 665.[1]
— Dyrkning af Erica. 1874. III. 650.[1]
— Om Dyrkning af Granattræet. 1857. III. 630.[1]
— Om Dyrkning af Ilex. 1863. III. 529.[2]
— Om Dyrkning af Lyngplanter. 1854. III. 650.[1]
— Om Dyrkning af Magnolia. 1859. III. 399.[1]
— Dyrkning af Rhododendron. 1854. III. 656.
— Om Dyrkning af Rhododendron. 1861. III. 656.
— Om Dyrkning af Rhododendron. 1875. III. 656.
— Om Dyrkning af Slægten Acacia. 1853. III. 463.[1]
— Om Dyrkning af Slægten Chorizema. 1853. III. 472.[2]
— Om Dyrkning af Slægten Citrus. 1854. III. 497.[1]
— Om Dyrkning af Slægten Correa. 1853. III. 503.[1]
— Om Dyrkning af Tecoma. 1856. III. 705.
— Om Dyrkning af træagtige Calceolarier. 1867. III. 702.[2]
— Dyrkning af Vaccinium macrocarpum. 1877. III. 663.[2]
— Om Dyrkning af Wellingtonia gigantea. 1857. III. 310.[1]
— Om Dyrkning og Anvendelse af Gran-, Fyr- og andre Naaletræer. 1862. IV. 441.
— Ege med brogede Blade. 1875. III. 361.[1]
— Eugenia Ugni og Myrtus filiformis. 1864. III. 633.[1]
— Figenslægten i gartnerisk Henseende. 1878. III. 368.[2]
— Den forløbne Vinters.Indflydelse paa forskjellige træagtige Planter. 1867. III. 44.[3]
— Om de formeentlig skadelige Virkninger af Podning. 1859. I. 208.[1]
— Formering af Buske ved urteagtige Skud. 1877. III. 158.
— Formering af- de indiske Azaleer. 1850. III. 660.[1]
— Om Formering af Kirsebærtræer ved Stiklinger. 1855. III. 435.[1]
— Om Formering af koglebærende Træer. 1874. III. 294.[1]
— Formering af koglebærende Træer. 1881. III. 294.[1]
— Om Formering af . . . Naaletræer. 1859. III. 294.[1]
— Om Formering af Roser. 1872. III. 452.
— Om Formering af Roser. 1872. III. 452.
— De forskjellige Arter af Lycium. 1876. III. 700.[2]
— Forskjellige smukke og anvendelige Buske. See ØRSTED, A. S. (*by mistake*). 1867. III. 66,[1] 757.[2]
— Forskjellige Træer og Buske. 1877. III. 67.[1]
— Forskjellige Træer, som ere anvendelige til økonomisk Brug. 1865. III. 67.[1]
— Forskjellige Træsorters . . . Anvendelighed til Vei- og Alleebeplantning. 1857. III. 209.
— Forsøg med Dyrkning af uyere Sorter Naaletræer. 1860. III. 292.

— Til Forsvar for Hyldebærbusken. 1870. III. 751.[2]
— Frøets Modning. 1845. I. 223,[1] III. 156.[1]
— Frostens Virkning paa Frugttræernes Blomster. 1870. III. 182.
— Fuldstændig Haandbog for Havedyrkere. 1865. III. 100.[2]
— Fuldstændig Haugekalender for Hvermand. 1853. III. 120.[1]
— Grundstammens Indflydelse paa Æbletræets Frugtbarhed. 1864. III. 426.[1]
— Haandbog for Frugttrædyrkere. 1861. III. 134.[2]
— Haugedyrknings-Catechismus. 1853. III. 120.[1]
— Hestekastaniens Nytte. 1860. III. 538.[1]
— En historisk Bemærkning om Hvidtornen. 1863. III. 422.[1]
— Den Hooibrinkske Befrugtningsmaade. 1864. III. 175.[1]
— Hovedprinciperne for Vinterbeskæring af Træer. 1860. III. 170.
— Hvad er Pomologiens Hovedopgave. 1855. III. 66.[2]
— "Hvilke lave træagtige Planter egne sig bedst til Plantning paa Stenhøie?" 1873. III. 205.[1]
— Hvilke Sorter Ege ere de mest anvendelige til Plantning. 1872. III. 361.[1]
— "Hvilke Sorter Naaletræer egne sig bedst til Plantning for at give Læ?" 1868. III. 215.[1]
— "Hvilke Sorter Tjørn ere de smukkeste." 1867. III. 421.[2]
— Hvorledes beskytte vi bedst vore Planter imod Frostens skadelige Indvirkninger? 1845. III. 153.[1]
— Hvorledes forskjellige Træer og Buske forholde sig i Hensende til Lys og Skygge. 1867. I. 230.
— Hvorledes Man kan erstatte det afbrudte Topskud paa Naaletræer. 1858. III. 295.[1]
— Hyldebusken (Sambucus nigra). 1855. III. 751.[2]
— Iagttagelser over Løvets Farver. 1856. III. 205.[2]
— Juglans regia laciniata. 1859. III. 355.
— Knækning af Grene. 1863. III. 174.[2]
— Om Knopper eller Øine paa Planter og Okulation. 1861. III. 161.
— Om Kræft og Brand hos Frugttræer. 1860. III. 193.[2]
— Lærketræet. 1855. III. 304.[2]
— Leptadactylon californicum. 1860. III. 695.[1]
— Lidt om Tjørnevarieteterne med fyldte Blomster. 1858. III. 422.[1]
— Et lille Udvalg af Naaletræer. 1874. III. 290.
— Om Lindetræer. 1868. III. 585.[1]
— Løvfarverne i dette Efteraar. 1861. III. 207.[1]
— En meget sandsynlig Formodning om Anledning til Kræft hos Frugttræer. 1859. III. 193.[2]
— Midler, hvorved Træer kunne bringes til at ansætte Frugt. 1856. III. 174.[2]
— Morbærtræet, Morus. 1855. III. 377.
— Morbærtræets Historie. 1877. III. 378.
— Om Nedbøjningen af Grene. 1849. III. 174.[1]
— Nogle af de bedste Arter af Spiræa. 1858. III. 460.[1]
— Nogle af de Midler at Skuddene paa vore Frugt- og Zirtræer modnes for Vinteren. 1870. III. 174.[2]
— Nogle af de smukkeste Sorter Weigelia. 1882. III. 748.[2]
— Nogle Arter af Enebærslægten Juniperus. 1861. III. 303.[1]
— Nogle Arter af Liguster. 1873. III. 673.[1]
— Nogle Arter af Slægten Kennedya. 1872. III. 480.[1]
— Nogle Arter Vitis, som egne sig til almindelig Brug hos os. 1870. III. 545.[1]
— Nogle Bemærkninger om Anvendelse . . . af Naaletræer. 1861. III. 292.
— Nogle Bemærkninger om Aucuba. 1874. III. 645.[1]
— Nogle Bemærkninger om Caprifolier. 1865. III. 749.[2]
— Nogle Bemærkninger om de forskjellige Sorter Hasselrødder. 1867. III. 357.[1]
— Nogle Bemærkninger om Dyrkning af Nerier. 1859. III. 689.[1]
— Nogle Bemærkninger om forskjellige Arter . . . af Krisebærslægten. 1865. III. 435.[1]
— Nogle Bemærkninger om Indsamling af Frø. 1864. III. 156.[1]
— Nogle Bemærkninger om Kjernefrugternes ydre Egenskaber. 1876. III. 66.[2]
— Nogle Bemærkninger om Pæretræers Livsvarighed. 1864. II. 280.[1]
— Nogle Bemærkninger om . . . Pandanus. 1875. III. 313.[1]
— Nogle Bemærkninger om Slægten Berberis. 1866. III. 393.[2]
— Nogle Bemærkninger om Slægten Clematis. 1873. III. 389.[1]

— Nogle Bemærkninger om Slægten Cotoneaster. 1869. III. 420.[2]
— Nogle Bemærkninger om Slyngplanter. 1864. III. 204.[2]
— Nogle Bemærkninger om Søileroser. 1865. III. 449.
— Nogle Buske. 1869. III. 66.[1]
— Nogle Buske, som særlig egne sig til at drives i Blomst. 1867. III. 176.[2]
— Nogle Buske . . . vist sig aldeles haardføre. 1877. III. 66.[2]
— Nogle Egesorter. 1867. III. 361.[1]
— Nogle hos os lidet kjendte Sirtræer og Buske. 1876. III. 66.[2]
— Nogle meget smukke Ornamenttræer. 1868. III. 66.[1]
— Nogle nye stedsegrønne Træer. 1852. III. 289.
— Nogle uyere smukke Zirtræer. See ØRSTED, A. S. (by error). 1865. III. 66,[1] 757.[2]
— Nogle uyere smukke Zirtræer. 1867. III. 66.[1]
— Nogle uyere Sorter af Acacia. 1855. III. 463.[1]
— Nogle uyere Sorter Naaletræer. 1868. III. 289.
— Nogle uyere . . . Sorter Naaletræer. 1873. III. 290.
— Nogle særdeles smukke, haardføre Buske. 1870. III. 66.[2]
— Nogle sildigt blomstrende Buske og Træer. 1876. III. 207.[2]
— Nogle smukke Arter af Slægten Viburnum. 1871. III. 53.[1]
— Nogle smukke Sirtræer. 1874. III. 444.[1]
— Nogle smukke Sorter Juniperus. 1866. III. 303.[1]
— Nogle smukke Træer og Buske. 1882. III. 66.[2]
— Nogle smukke Zirtræer. 1868. III. 419.[1]
— Nogle smuktblomstrende Arter af Blommeslægten. 1868. III. 430.[2]
— Nogle Sorter Ahorn. 1877. III. 533.[2]
— Nogle Sorter Ask. 1870. III. 672.[1]
— Nogle Sorter Cornus. 1876. III. 645.[1]
— Nogle Sorter Skovranke, Clematis. 1868. III. 389.[1]
— Nogle Sygdomme og Insekter. 1856. III. 427.[1]
— Nogle Træers Forhold til forskjellige Jordboniteter. 1868. III. 41.[1]
— De nordamerikanske Hickorytræer. 1866. III. 353.[2]
— Nye Planter. 1848. III. 67.[1]
— Nyere Planter. 1853. III. 67.[1]
— Oculering paa det sovende Øje. 1849. III. 164.[1]
— Omplantning af større Træer. 1855. III. 167.
— Oversigt over Arter og Afarter af Ahornslægten. 1858. III. 533.[2]
— Oversigt over de vigtigste Arter af Træer og Buske. 1852. III. 66.[1]
— Paradisæblet. 1870. III. 425.[2]
— Pimpinellerosen, Rosa spinosissima. 1861. III. 457.[1]
— Pinus sylvestris Bujotii. 1863. III. 289.
— Plantning af Hækker. 1852. III. 213.
— Plantning af Hvidtornshækker. 1856. III. 422.[2]
— Om Plantning af Naaletræer. 1857. III. 291.
— Om Plantning af Naaletræer. 1869. III. 292.
— Om Plantning . . . af Træer og Buske. 1859. III. 110.[2]
— De til Plantning i Haver mest anvendelige Sorter Rønnebærtræer. 1866. III. 758.[2]
— Om Plataner. 1875. III. 418.[1]
— Poppelers Uundværlighed · til Læplantning. 1868. III. 344.[1]
— Rhamnus immeretina. 1871. III. 543.[2]
— Rhododendrerne frå Sikkim. 1881. III. 655.
— Rhyncospermum jasminoides. 1867. III. 691.[1]
— Roser med hængende Grene. 1854. III. 448.
— Schinus molle. 1860. III. 529.[1]
— De sikkimske Rhododendrer. 1858. III. 654.[2]
— Skal man beskære Rødderne paa Træer. 1867. III. 173.[1]
— Slægten Abelia. 1853. III. 748.[1]
— Slægten Adenocarpus. 1876. III. 466.[1]
— Slægten Andromeda. 1862. III. 647.[1]
— Slægten Aralia. 1863. III. 641.[1]
— Slægten Araucaria. 1858. III. 297.[2]
— Slægten Boronia. 1857. III. 495.[2]
— Slægten Boronia. 1867. III. 495.[2]
— Slægten Calycanthus. 1867. III. 401.[1]
— Slægten Ceanothus. 1877. III. 541.[1]
— Slægten Clerodendron. 1873. III. 696.[1]
— Slægten Deutzia. 1876. III. 410.[1]
— Slægten Evonymus eller Benved. 1873. III. 532.
— Slægten Forsythia. 1877. III. 671.[2]
— Slægten Gleditschia. 1877. III. 477.[2]
— Slægten Glycine eller Wistaria. 1874. III. 490.
— Slægten Hibiscus. 1861. III. 587.[1]
— Om Slægten Jasminum. 1855. III. 672.[2]

Bentzien, Julius August (*continued*).
— Slægten Mahonia. 1852. III..395.[2]
— Slægten Tamarix. 1874. III. 612.[1]
— Slægten Thuja. 1858. III. 311.[1]
— Slægten Weigelia. 1864. III. 748.[2]
— Slægterne Brugmansia og Datura. 1858. III. 699.[2]
— Smukke mindre hyppigt forekommende Zirtræer. 1869. III. 66.[1]
— De smukkeste Arter Rhus. 1879. III. 526.[1]
— Søileroser. 1854. III. 448.
— Om stedsegrønne Træer. 1854. III. 205.[2]
— Systematisk Inddeling af Æbler. 1874. III. 425.[2]
— Taxodium distichum Rich. 1861. III. 310.[2]
— Tilia alba spectabilis. 1877. III. 586.[1]
— Tiltrækning af nye Frugtsorter. 1854. III. 50.[2]
— Tjørneslægten. 1852. III. 421.[1]
— De træagtige Pioners Historie og Kultur. 1858. III. 392.[2]
— Træagtige Planter, som egne sig til Drivning om Vinteren. 1856. III. 176.[2]
— Træer og Buske med smukke Frugter. 1854. III. 207.[2]
— Træers og Buskes Udtæring og Hensygnen i ny Anlæg. 1869. III. 42.[1]
— Træers Plantning. 1845. III. 166.
— Træers Plantning. 1848. III. 166.
— Om Udplantning af Træer og Buske. 1853. III. 166.
— Udtyndning og Fornyelse af Beplantningerne. 1855. III. 173.[1]
— Udvalg af de fortrinligste . . . nyere Siirvæxter. 1848. III. 67.[1]
— Et Udvalg . . . af Guldregn. 1870. III. 480.[1]
— Udvalg af nyere og ældre Sir-Træer. 1848. III. 66.[1]
— Et Udvalg af Palmer. 1872. III. 317.
— Valdnøddetræet. 1858. III. 355.
— Ved hvilke Midler kunne vi bedst bidrage til at nylig plantede Træer hurtig fæste Rod i Jorden. 1865. III. 166.
— Veddets Modenhed. 1849. III. 174.[2]
— Vedets Modning. 1881. III. 170.
— Om Vedligeholdelse af Buskadser. 1863. III. 119.[2]
— Vedligeholdelse af Livskraften hos Stikkelsbærbuske. 1860. III. 414.[1]
— Veiledende Bemærkninger om Plantning af enkelte Træer. 1858. III. 201.
— Vinterhaver i det Frie. 1845. III. 208.[1]
Die Benutzung der Acacie. 1840. IV. 524.[1]
Ueber die Benutzung der amerikanischen weissen Fichte. 1835. III. 305.[2]
Ueber die Benutzung der gemeinen Hülse. 1828. III. 530.[1]
Von Benutzung der Mast in Wirtemberg. 1794. IV. 438.[1]
Die Benutzung der Stachelbeeren. 1846. III. 414.[1]
Benutzung des Lindenholzes zur Bastbereitung. 1853. IV. 528.[1]
Benzenberg, Johann Friedrich. Vollständiges Handbuch der angewandten Geometrie. 1814. IV. 263.
Benzon, Alfr. Om Kilderne til et Par Pharmaca i Pharmacopoea norvegica. 1861. III. 247.[2]
Benzon, Rudolph von FISCHER. *See* FISCHER-BENZON, Rudolph von.
Benzoni, Girolamo & Léry, Jean de. Historia Indiae Occidentalis. 1586. III. 266.
Benzoni, V. Alcune ricerche fisico-chimiche sulla terra . . . di Vallombrosa. 1881. IV. 69.
— Il Larice delle Alpi. 1879. IV. 449.
— I terricolo dell' Abetaia di Vallombrosa. 1879. IV. 69.
Beobachter, (*pseud.*). Tree-pruning. 1844. IV. 170.
Beobachtungen an den forstlich-meteorologischen Stationen Adlisberg und Haidenhaus. 1892. IV. 60.[1]
Beobachtungen in Fichtenpflanzbeständen. 1888. IV. 454.
Beobachtungen über Abänderung der Farben der Blumen. 1832. I. 245.
Beplanten van woeste duingronden met Dennen. 1864. IV. 160.[1]
Beplanting der duinen. 1869. IV. 160.[1]
Een te beproeven middel tegen de Theeluis. 1876. III. 604.[2]
Berail, H. Over meststoffen. 1858. III. 151.
Béral, M. Les pignadas des Landes. 1896. IV. 122.[1]
Béranger-Féraud & Dujardin-Beaumetz. Du traitement du ténia par la pilletiérene. 1886. III. 631.[1]
Berar. *See* INDIA—HYDERABAD ASSIGNED DISTRICTS.
Berar forest law amendment. Law 1892. 1892. IV. 332.[1]
Bérard. Taschenbuch für Theetrinker. 1836. III. 606.
Bérard, (*sr.*) (*du Mans*). Mémoire en réponse aux questions sur les semis. 1833. III. 39.
Bérard, E. Paul. Note sur le salant. 1871. I. 228.[2]

Bérard, Jacques Étienne. Mémoire sur la maturation des fruits. 1821. I. 178.
Bérard, René Charles, (*sr.*). Mémoires sur l'origine des arbres . . . acclimatés en France. *See* BÉRARD, [A.], (sr.) 1823. I. 241.[2]
Béraud. Mémoire sur la culture du Câprier. 1787. III. 408.[2]
Béraud, Érasme. De l'alternance des essences. 1858. IV. 74.[1]
— De l'ancienne . . . culture des forêts de Chêne en futaie. 1861. IV. 505.
— Le Chêne rouvre et le Chêne pédonculé. 1864. IV. 505.
— Du département de la Sarthe. 1861. IV. 360.
— Études sur le Chêne et sur ses auxiliaires. 1863. IV. 512.
— De la propriété forestière. 1871. IV. 27.[2]
— Régeneração dos Carvalhos nos talhadios. 1877. IV. 507.
— De la régénération du Chêne dans les taillis. 1877. IV. 507.
— Dell' utilità di talune piante basse nelle foreste di Quercia ad alto fusto. 1865. IV. 505.
— De l'utilité de certaines basses plantes dans les forêts de Chêne en futaie. 1865. IV. 505.
— De la végétation spontanée des plantes naturelles forestières. 1867. I. 413.
Béraud, Jean Jacques. Mémoire sur la manière de resserrer le bit des torrens. 1791. IV. 185.[1]
Beraud, Toussaint Charles. Recherches sur les causes accidentelles de la mortalité des arbres des promenades. 1857. III. 212.[1]
— Rosa Boraeana (Beraud). 1846. II. 291.[2]
Bérauld, B. La Vigne et le vin devant la Bible. 1885. II. 509.[1]
Beraza, J. M. ALONSO DE. *See* ALONSO DE BERAZA, J. M.
Berberich, Herman. Jamaica Dogwood. 1898. II. 377.[1]
— Proximate analysis of the bark of Piscidia. 1898. II. 377.[1]
Berberids. 1887. 1887. III. 394,[1] 396.[1]
Berchem, Berthout van, (*jr.*). Description et histoire naturelle du bouquetin. 1789. IV. 197.[2]
Berchem, Berthout van, (*sr.*). Conditions de croissance d'un arbre. 1789. III. 169.[1]
— Observations sur les dégâts faits par la larve du hanneton. 1789. IV. 202.
Berchoire, Pierre. Reductorii moralis libri XIV. 1477. I. 275.[1]
Berchtold, Bedřich, *hrabě*. *See* BERCHTOLD, Friedrich, *Graf* von.
Berchtold, Friedrich, *Graf* von. Ueber die hohe Esche. 1838. IV. 535.[2]
— Das Todte Meer. 1851. I. 513.
— & Presl, J. S. O přirozenosti rostlin aneb rostlinář obsahujcej popsání a vyobrazení rostlin. 1823. I. 439.
— Seidl, W. B. & Opitz, P. M. Oekonomisch-technische Flora Böhmens. 1836. III. 90.[2]
Berck, F. H. van. Over de olifants torretjes. 1807. III. 427.[1]
— Verhandeling ten bewijze, dat niet de zwarte vliegen . . . de bedervers zijn van de bloesems der vruchtboomen. 1807. III. 427.[1]
Berck, L. van den. Le Lupin comme engrais vert. 1898. IV. 145.
— Oseraies. Rajeunissement. 1897. III. 349.
Berckmans, P. J. Les Araucarias en Californie. 1895. III. 298.[1]
— De Araucarias in Californië. 1895. III. 298.[1]
— Fruiting of a male tree of Cephalotaxus Fortunii. 1882. II. 8.[1]
— Sequoia gigantea and sempervirens. 1895. III. 310.[1]
— Sequoia gigantea et Sequoia sempervirens. 1895. III. 310.[1]
Bercy, L. de. Le Mussaenda borbonica. 1888. III. 744.[1]
Berdau, Feliks. Botanika leśna. 1890. IV. 80.
— Flora cracoviensis. 1859. I. 441.
— Flora Tatr, Pienin i Beskidu Zachodniego. 1890. I. 446.
— O rosie miodowej jako chorobie drzew naszych. 1887. I. 213.[2]
— O roślinach Korei. 1887. I. 461.
— Spostrzeżenia nad przyswojeniem się sosny amerykańskiej i akacyi swycząjnej. 1887. III. 45.
— Wycieczka botaniczna w Tatry odbyta w r. 1855. I. 445.
Bereau, B. Sur la coloration des Hortensias. 1847. III. 412.[1]
De bereiding van kamfer in Japan. 1883. III. 404.[2]
Bereitung von Birkentheer in den Blue Mountains. 1883. IV. 491.[2]

Berendes, Johannes. *See* SCHMIDT, Ernst & BERENDES, Johannes.

Berendes, Julius. Die Pharmacie bei den alten Culturvölkern. 1891. III. 239.
— Pharmacie bei den alten Kulturvölkern. 1889. III. 239.

Bérenger, Adolfo di.` Ueber die alte und neue Nomenclatur der europäischen Eichenarten. 1865. *II. 129,*[2] IV. 502.[1]
— Dell' antica storia . . . forestale in Italia. 1859. IV. 28,[1] *527.*
— Dell' arte e della scienza forestale. 1865. IV. 56.
— Beiträge zur Geschichte der Forstwissenschaft. 1865. IV. 24,[1] *502.*[1]
— Dizionario enciclopedico forestale trilingue. 1853. IV: 23.[1]
— Elenco delle principali opere. *See* ELENCO . . . 1895.
— Entlaubung eines Eichenforstes durch Tinea. 1855. IV. 509.
— Sulla fondazione . . . del R. istituto forestale di Vallombrosa. 1871. IV. 35.[1]
— Guida per il coltivatore di vivai boschivi. 1880. IV. 109.[1]
— Idea di legge forestale. 1863. IV. 327.
— Idea di legge forestale. 1864. IV. 313.
— Eine neue Waldtaxationsmethode. 1875. IV. 244.
— Nuovo metodo di tassare i boschi. 1871. IV. 243.
— Della Picchiola odierna malattia delle Viti. 1852. III. 559.[2]
— Principii di amminastrazione e direzione boschive. 1883. IV. 287.
— Dei provvedimenti idraulici degli antichi. 1880. IV. 50.
— Rudimenti di matematica applicata. 1865. IV. 58.
— Saggio storico della legislazione veneta forestale. 1863. IV. 327.
— Selvicoltura. 1887. IV. 110.[1]
— Tariffa per la vendita dei legnami di Quercia. 1865. IV. 405.[2]
— L' utilizzazione della corteccia. 1844. IV. 434, *512.*

Bérenger, G. M. Adolfo di. *See* BÉRENGER, Adolfo di.

Bérenger-Feraud, Laurent Jean Baptiste. Note sur trois Sabliers. 1876. III. 519.[2]

Berens, Reinhold. De Dracone arbore Clusii. 1770. II. 81.[1]

Beretning om Bistrup Godses Skove. 1871. IV. 343.[1]

Beretning om de Arbeider, der ere udførte af det danske Hedeselskab. 1872. IV. 156.[2]

Beretning om det i Odense . . . om Oldenborresagen afholdte Delegeretmøde. 1891. IV. 549.[1]

Beretning om Lolland-Falsters Forstmandsforenings Udflugt til Rostocker Heide. *See* BUCH. 1889. IV. 354.

Berg, *Freiherr* von. Forststatistisches aus Elsass-Lothringen. 1880. IV. 349.[1]
— Mittheilungen über die forstlichen Verhältnisse in Elsass-Lothringen. 1883. IV. 349.[2]

Berg, Albert. Physiognomy of tropical vegetation in South America. 1854. I. 342.

Berg, Alexander. Anleitung zur Erkennung der in der Arzneikunde gebräuchlichen . , . Gewächse. 1832. III. 57.
— Beschreibung einiger neuen Cacteen. 1840. II. 585.[2]
— Sur la culture des Cactées. 1839. III. 618.[2]
— Ueber die Kultur der Cacteen. 1839. III. 618.[2]
— Temperatur-Verhältnisse der Cacteen. 1838. II. 588.[2]

Berg, C. *Samling af Træsorter fra de dansk-vest-indiske Øer.* 1888. IV. 398.[1]

Berg, Carlos. Sobre la Carpocapsa saltitans. 1891. II. 439.[1]
— Enumeración de las plantas Européas . . . en la provincia de Buenos Aires. 1877. I. 344.
— Sobre plantas Europeas . . . en las repúblicas Argentina y Oriental. 1877. I. 344.
— La reina de las flores. 1880. IV. 282.[2]

Berg, Edmund, *Freiherr* von. *See* BERG, Karl Heinrich Edmund, *Freiherr* von.

Berg, Ernst von. Additamenta ad Thesaurum literaturae botanicae. 1858. I. 2.
— Catalogue alphabétique et méthodique des dessins de plantes. 1857. I. 2, 77.
— Catalogus systematicus bibliothecae Horti imperialis botanici petropolitani. *See* CATALOGUS . . . 1852. I. 2.
— Vollständiger Bericht über . . . Rudolstädter Ausartungen. 1843. I. 143.

Berg, Friedrich, *Graf.*` Einige Spielarten der Fichte. 1887.` II. 35.[1]

Berg, John. Untersuchungen über Obst- und Weintrauben-Arten Würtembergs. 1827. III. 552. *See also* SCHÜBLER, Gustav. 1827. III. 546.

Berg, Julius. De Angusturae cortice spurio. 1844. III. 503.[2]

Berg, Karl Heinrich Edmund, *Freiherr* von. Akademische Nachrichten. 1850. IV. 32.
— Der alte Taxus bei Somsdorf. 1851. II. 10.[2]
— Anleitung zum Verkohlen des Holzes. 1830. IV. 394.
— Ueber die Anwendung der Büschel- oder Einzelnpflanzungen bei der Fichte. 1853. IV. 453.
— Anzucht, Saat und Pflanzung. — Beiträge zur forstlichen Kenntniss der Eiche. 1848. IV. 504.
— Das Auftreten des Kieferntrieb-Wicklers. 1857. IV. 475.
— Ueber die Ausführung der forstlichen Kartirungen. 1857. IV. 251.[1]
— Der Bakony Wald. 1875. IV. 373.
— Die Baum- und Strauchvegetation auf den schwedischen Schären. 1875. I. 350.[2]
— Beantwortung der Frage: Wie ist die Nachzucht der Rothbuche . . . zu erzielen? 1851. IV. 494.
— Beiträge zur Beantwortung der Frage: Wie ist dem Schaden des . . . Kiefern-Rüsselkäfers zu begegnen? 1854. IV. 206.
— Beiträge zur Lehre von der Mittelwaldswirthschaft. 1850. IV. 130.
— Beitrag über die Holzerträge in Reihenpflanzungen. 1848. IV. 480.
— Bemerkungen über die Erle. 1835. IV. 489.[1]
— Bemerkungen über die Holzverkohlung. 1855. IV. 394.
— Beschreibung einer Varietät der Fichte. 1833. II. 34.[1]
— Betrachtungen über den Einfluss der kleineren deutschen Staaten auf die Entwickelung . . . des Forstwesens. 1867. IV. 25, *274.*[1]
— Betrachtungen über Eichen-Pflanzungen. 1867. IV. 506.
— Bruchstück aus meinem Reise-Tagebuche. Die östreichische Schwarzkiefer. 1852. IV. 465.[1]
— Ueber die Buchen-Hochwaldwirthschaft. 1848. IV. 494.
— Zur Buchen- und Eichen-Nachzucht. 1851. IV. 137.[2]
— Über die Büschelpflanzung bei der Fichte. 1833. IV. 452.[2]
— Über das v. Buttlar'sche Kulturverfahren. 1847. IV. 141.
— Die Durchforstung. 1851. IV. 173.
— Ueber die Durchforstungen der Fichte und Buche. 1846. IV. 173.
— Dynamit als Sprengmittel beim Holze. 1872. IV. 386.
— Ueber den Einfluss der nachtheiligen Naturereignisse auf . . . Fichte. 1833. IV. 455.
— Ueber die Fabrikation der Spankörbe. 1853. IV. 429.
— Fichtenerträge am grossen Brandholze. 1851. IV. 458.
— Ueber Fichten-Pflanzung in Gebirgsforsten. 1826. IV. 452.[2]
— Fichtensamen-Oel. 1831. IV. 459.[2]
— Die forstliche Organisation in Finland. 1858. IV. 289.[1]
— Die forstlichen Verhältnisse der Schweiz. 1868. IV. 366.
— Die forstlichen Verhältnisse Skandinaviens. 1858. IV. 342.[5]
— Gegenwärtiger Stand des Forstculturwesens. 1847. IV. 141.
— Geschichte der deutschen Wälder. 1871. IV. 26.
— Zur Geschichte des Forsteinrichtungswesens in Sachsen. 1854. IV. 248.[1]
— Kertomus Suomen metsistä. 1859. IV. 289.[1]
— Ueber die Kultur-Methoden bei der Fichte. 1826. IV. 452.[2]
— Mancherlei aus dem Gebiete des Waldbaues. 1850. IV. 118.
— Notizen über den Weihmuthskiefern-Bestand. 1851. IV. 470.[1]
— Die obeern Baumgrenzen. 1873. I. 220.[1] .
— Organisation der Forstlehranstalten in Schweden und Finland. 1863. IV. 30.[2]
— Ueber die Pflanzweite bei der Fichte. 1860. IV. 154.[1]
— Pürschgang im Dickicht der . . . Forstgeschichte. 1869. IV. 24.[1]
— Soll der Forstmann forsttechnische Gewerbe leiten? 1861. IV. 392.
— Die Staatsforstwirthschaftslehre. 1850. IV. 269.
— Starke Weisstannen. 1848. II. 64.[1]
— Ueber die Vegetations-Verhältnisse in Skandinavien. 1855. I. 531.[2]
— Veränderung des Wässerstandes der Flüsse. 1867. IV. 50.
— Die Verbreitung der Kiefer im Norden. 1868. II. 46.[2]
— Das Verdrängen der Laubwälder im nördlichen Deutschlande durch die Fichte und die Kiefer. 1844. I. 370, *IV. 82, 348.*[2]

Berg, Karl Heinrich Edmund, *Freiherr* von (*continued*).
— Ueber die Verkohlung in stehenden Meilern. 1854. IV.
394.
— Das Vorkommen des Aprikosenspinners. 1857. IV. 455.
— Vortrag . . . die Forstreform betreffend. 1849. IV. 291.¹
— Die Wälder im Banate. 1861. IV. 123.²
— Die Wälder in Polen. 1866. IV. 345.
— Der Wald und das Wild. 1865. IV. 196.²
— Wald-Entwässerungen. 1851. IV. 143.²
— Zum Waldfeldbaue. 1851. IV. 133.
— Welche Bedeutung·hat die Lerche. 1854. IV. 449.
— Die Wirkungen der Luftbewegungen auf die Baumsamen.
1872. I. 240.¹ *IV. 74.*¹
— Ein Zeitbild von der Erziehung, Bildung und dem Unter-
richte der Forstleute. 1862. IV. 29.
— Die Zuchtversuche mit der japanesischen Seidenraupe.
1870. IV. 502.¹
Berg, N. P. van den.   Historical-statistical notes on . . .
Coffee. 1879. III. 739.
— Historisch-statistische aanteekeningen over . . . Koffie.
1879. III. 739.
Berg, Otto Karl. Das Anacahuite-Holz. 1860. II. 748.²
— Anatomischer Atlas zur pharmazeutischen Waarenkunde.
1865. I. 99, *III. 58.*
— Die Balsamodendron-Arten der Berliner Herbarien. 1862.
II. 417.²
— Bemerkungen, die chilenischen Myrtaceen . . . betreffend.
1857. II. 619.¹
— Beschreibung einiger neuen Droguen vom Cap. 1860.
III. 281.²
— Ueber die bis jetzt bekannten Arten der Gattung Kra-
meria. 1856. II. 367.²
— Botanik. 1845. III. 58.
— Charakteristik der für die Arzneikunde . . . wichtigsten
Pflanzen-Gattungen. 1845. III. 57.
— Die Chinarinden der pharmakognostischen Sammlung zu
Berlin. 1865. II. 813.¹
— Cortex Quillajae. 1861. II. 281.¹
— Florae brasiliensis Myrtographia. 1858. II. 619.¹
— Handbuch der pharmaceutischen Botanik. 1845. III.
58.
— Mantissa 1–3 ad revisionem Myrtacearum Americae.
1858. II. 619.¹
— Mexikanische Sarsaparille. 1861. II. 85,¹ *III. 338.²*
— Myrtaceae. 1857. II. 619.¹
— Myrtaceae centroamericanae. See ØRSTED, A. S. 1856.
II. 619.¹
— Ueber die officinellen Buckoblätter. 1853. II. 399,¹ *405.²*
— Pharmaceutische Waarenkunde. 1857. III. 258.
— Pharmazeutische Botanik. 1845. III. 58.
— Revisio Myrtacearum Americae. 1854. II. 619.¹
— Die Zimmtwurzel aus Japan. 1861. III. 404.¹
— & **Schmidt**, C. F. Atlas der officinellen Pflanzen. 1858.
III. 58.
— — Darstellung . . . in der Pharmacopoea borussica aufge-
führten officinellen Gewächse. 1858. III. 58.
Berg, Petrus Ulricus. De medicina Africanorum. See
THUNBERG, C. P. 1785. III. 281.²
Berg, Walter Gilman. Berg's complete timber test record.
1899. IV. 416.¹
Berg, Wilhelm, *Freiherr* von. Die Eisenbahnschwelle und
der Wald. 1877. IV. 423.²
— Erfahrungen über das Futterlaub. 1864. IV. 438.²
— Zur Nachweisung der wirklichen Erträge beim Buchen-
Hochwalde. 1843. IV. 497.
— Notiz über einige Durchforstungs-Versuche. 1841. IV.
73.
— Reiseeindrücke aus Bosnien und Herzegowina. 1895. IV.
374.²
— Eine Rollbahn. 1875. IV. 391.
— Stammholzflösserei und Klosholztrift. 1874. IV. 390.¹
— & K. H. E. von. Denkschriften über das Forstwesen im
Königreiche Polen. 1864. IV. 345.
Bergamaschi, Giuseppe. Sopra i danni sommi che derivano dal
diboscamento. 1814. IV. 42.²
— Gita botanica agli Appennini. 1823. I. 425.
— Lettera seconda sopre varie piante degli Apennini. 1823.
I. 425.
— Peregrinazione statistico-fitologica fatte nelle Valli Camo-
nica. 1853. I. 427.
Bergamo, · Gennaro. Teoria delle spostazioni fillotassiche.
1900. I. 103.
Berge, Fr. & **Riecke**, V. A. Giftpflanzenbuch. 1845. III.
59.²

Berge, Hermann. Beiträge zur Entwicklungsgeschichte von
Bryophyllum. 1877. II. 235.¹
— Pflanzenphysiognomie. 1880. V. xxv.²
Bergellini, G. Legge e forestali. 1897. IV. 329.
Bergemann, Joh. G. Der chinisische Thee. 1810. III. 606.
Bergen, de. Quinquinas. 1830. III. 721.
Bergen, *Mrs.* Fanny Dickerson. Animal and plant lore.
1899. V. xxv.²
— Popular American plant-names. 1892. I. 72.²
Bergen, Heinrich von. Versuch einer Monographie der China.
1826. II. 812.
Bergen, J. Y., (*jr.*). Elements of botany. 1896. I. 92.
Bergen, Karl August von. De Aloide. 1753. III. 333.¹
— Catalogus stirpium . . . quas hortus medicus Academiae
viadrinae complectitur. 1744. I. 43.
— Flora francofurtana. 1750. I. 373.
— De Laburno. 1759. II. 368.¹
— Propempticon inaugurale . . . utri systematum an Tourne-
fortiano an Linneano potiores partes deferendae sint? 1742.
I. 250.
Bergendal, David. Några ord med anledning utaf " Bidrag
till knoppfjällens anatomi." 1882. I. 108.²
Bergenhold, Johann Ferdinand SCHMIDT VON. See SCHMIDT
VON BERGENHOLD, J. F.
Bergens museum. Aarbog. I. 8.²
Berger. Der Forst- und Jagdschutz in Deutschland. 1889.
IV. 317.¹
— Wildschaden. 1890. IV. 197.¹
Berger, (*Dr.*). Wald und Witterung. 1865. IV. 53.
Berger, Alexander Mal. Calendarium florae. See LINNÉ,
Carl von. 1756. I. 222.²
— *See also* STILLINGFLEET, Benjamin & BERGER, A. M.
Berger, Alwin. Agaven. 1898. III. 341.¹
— Aloe plüridens Haw. 1900. III. 334.¹
— Aloe Schweinfurthi. 1898. III. 334.¹
— Cantua dependens. 1898. III. 694.²
— Melianthus major and M. pectinatus. 1899. III. 541.¹
— Melianthus major und pectinatus. 1899. III. 541.¹
— Rosa gigantea. 1898. III. 455.²
— Tacsonia manicata Juss. 1899. III. 581.²
— Tecoma Ricasoliana hort. Mort. 1898. II. 789.²
Berger, C. & Severin, G. Projet de règlement sur les insectes
nuisibles. 1899. IV. 303.²
Berger, Christian Gottlieb. Taschenbuch für Blumenfreunde.
1802. III. 74.
Berger, Ernest. Cestrum nocturnum. 1890. III. 699.²
— Chamaerops excelsa. 1890. III. 331.²
— *See also* NARTS, A. & BERGER, E.
Berger, Ernst Friedrich. Die Bestimmung der Gartenpflan-
zen auf systematischem Wege. 1855. I. 269.
— Catalogus herbarii. 1841. I. 380.
Berger, Franz. Beiträge zur Anatomie der Coniferen. 1889.
II. 16.²
Berger, Friedrich Christian. Handbuch der Pflanzenkennt-
niss für Oekonomen. 1801. III. 51.
Berger, J. L. Abhandlung vom gegenwärtigen Forsthaus-
halte. 1794. IV. 116.
Berger, Johann Gottfried. De Cinchona ab iniquis judiciis
vindicata. 1711. III. 719.
Berger, L. De l'âge auquel il faut abattre les arbres. 1896.
IV. 252.
— Allongement des révolutions dans les taillis. 1896. IV. 252.
— Un bois selon les idées nouvelles. 1894. IV. 555.²
— La culture du Robinier. 1896. IV. 523.²
— De la sendroculture en Flandre. 1894. IV. 544.²
— Une expérience intéressante en sylviculture. 1896. I. 51.²
— La flore forestière des environs de Turnhout. 1897. IV.
556.¹
— La flore forestière maritime de la Belgique. 1896. IV. 84.²
— De l'indemnisation des dommages causés par les planta-
tions routières. 1898. III. 200.²
— Note sur les dommages causés par les plantations routières.
1894. III. 84.²
— Le Noyer noir en Belgique. 1895. IV. 488.¹
— Les pépiniéristes à l'Exposition de Tervueren. 1897. III.
122.²
— Les plantations routières à la Chambre des représentants.
1895. III. 210.
— Les plantations routières . . . du Brabant. 1895. III. 210.
— Un programme d'études sylvicoles pour la Campine. 1894.
IV. 544.²
— Une visite aux arbres exotiques . . . de la Campine.
1895. IV. 545.¹
— & **Lecart**, A. Du soutrage. 1895. IV. 438,¹ *543.*²

Berger, Louis J. Notice sur les essences d'arbres à choisir en Belgique pour les plantations des routes. 1892. III. 210.
Bergeret, Jean. Flore des Basses-Pyrénées. 1803. I. 406.
Bergeret, Jean Pierre. Phytonomatotechnie universelle. 1783. I. 263.
Bergerie, J. B., *baron* ROUGIER DE LA. *See* ROUGIER DE LA BERGERIE, J. B., *baron*.
Berggrén, Gustaf. De plantis cibariis romanorum. *See* RETZIUS, A. J. 1808. III. 88.[1]
Berggren, Jonas. Examen classis polygamiae. *See* THUNBERG, C. P. 1825. I. 251.
— Resor . . . Europa och Österländerne. *See* WAHLENBERG, G. G. 1826. I. 353.
Berggren, Sven. Bidrag till kännedomen om fanerogamfloran vid Disko-bugten. 1871. I. 309.[1]
— En botanisk exkursion på Nya Zeeland. 1875. I. 507.
— Contributions to the botany of New Zealand. 1885. I. 536.[2]
— Om förkrympta Barrträd vÃ¤xande i en myr i södra Småland. 1873. IV. 480.
— New New-Zealand plants. 1880. I. 507.
— Resebref från Nya Zeeland. 1874. I. 507.
— Om rotbildniagen hos australa Coniferer. 1887. II. 18.
— Ueber die Wurzelbildung bei australen Coniferen. 1887. II. 18.
Bergh, J. F. van BENTHEM VAN DEN. *See* BENTHEM VAN DEN BERGH, J. F. van.
Berghaus, Heinrich Karl Wilhelm. Allgemeiner pflanzengeographischer Atlas. 1851. I. 299.
— On the epochs of vegetation. 1841. I. 220.[2]
Berghe, Maximilien van den. *See* VANDEN-BERGHE, Maximilien.
Berghes, C. de. Abbildung sämmtlicher Holzpflanzen . . . des mittleren Europa. 1825. IV. 78.[2]
Bergholz. Ueberbrückung eines beschädigten Theiles der Rinde bei einem Rebenstock. 1866. I. 207,[2] *III. 560.*
Berghuis, S. De Nederlandsche boomgaard. 1864. III. 76.
— Niederländischer Obstgarten. 1864. III. 76.
Bergius, Bengt. Ueber die Lechereyen. 1785. III. 219.[1]
— Tal om läckerheter. 1785. III. 219.[1]
Bergius, P. F. Om de sibiriske Cedrer. 1796. II. 41.[1]
Bergius, Peter Jonas. Anmärkningar om Libidibibönan. 1774. III. 468.[2]
— Beskrifning och ritning på . . . Perdicium. 1772. II. 867.[1]
— Beskrifning på Hudsonia ericoides. 1778. II. 565.[2]
— Croton spicatum. 1769. II. 440.[1]
— Croton spicatum, das sehrentragende Croton. 1769. II. 440.[1]
— A description of a . . . plant of the Brownaeae kind. 1773. II. 337.[2]
— Descriptiones plantarum ex Capite Bonae Spei. 1767. I. 493.
— Echites semidigyna. 1773. II. 726.[2]
— Försök till fullständigare uppställning af Leucadendri genus. 1766. II. 164.[1]
— Grubbia. 1767. II. 170.[1]
— Ledum buxifolium. 1778. II. 673.[1]
— Materia medica e regno vegetabili. *See* BERG, P. J. 1778. III. 241.
— Nyctanthes elongata. 1772. II. 709.[1]
— Von Obstgärten . . . in Schweden. 1780. III. 134.[1]
— Örten Aristolochia trilobata. 1764. III. 380.[1]
— Pterocarpus Ecastaphyllum, en americanisk växt. 1769. II. 352.[2]
— Spermacoce capitata descripta -et delineata. 1770. II. 831.[2]
— Svenska bränvins-ämnen, utom spannmål. 1776. III. 222.
— Tal om frukt trägårder. 1780. III. 134.[1]
Bergman. Over het aanwezen van Blauwzuur . . . in de basten. 1813. III. 439.[1]
Bergman, Ernest. Notes horticoles sur le Portugal. 1890. III. 126.[1]
Bergman, Torbern Olof. Et sällsamt galläple. 1762. IV. 509.
— Uplysning om de skadelige Tallmaskarne. 1769. IV. 474.
Bergmann, Emil. Recherches sur la présence des acides formique et acétique dans lés plantes. 1882. I. 180.[2]
— Untersuchungen über das Vorkommen der Ameisensäure. 1882. I. 180.[1]
Bergrath & Medikus, L. W. Beytrag' zur forstbotanischen Beschreibung der Arve. 1802. IV. 464.[1]
Bergroth, J. Ossian. Anteckningar om vegetationen i gränstrakterna mellan Åland. 1894. I. 366.
Bergsma. Over het gebruik van inlandsch hout voor meubelen. 1848. IV. 426.[2]

Bergsma, A. P. Over de ontdekking van Tiemann en Haarmann. 1875. II. 20.[2]
Bergsma, Arnold Jacob. Over de parthenogenesis. 1857. I. 202.[1]
— Over de zoogenaamde ademhaling der planten. 1859. I. 170.
Bergsma, Cornelis Adriaan. Aanmoediging . . . tot het aanweeken van de Witte Moerbezieboomen. 1832. III. 374.
— Eenige aanmerkingen betrekkelijk het werk van Dr, J. Liebig. 1841. III. 36.[3]
— Handboek voor de vaderlandsche landhuishoudkunde. 1841. III. 105.
— Lijst van werken, waarin onze inlandsche planten . . . beschreven zijn. 1834. I. 3.[2]
— Over de literatuur der inlandsche flora. 1834. I. 3.[2]
— De Thea. 1825. III. 606.
— De Vlaamsche landbouw. 1845. III. 122.[1]
— *See also* BEEK, Albert van & BERGSMA, C. A.
Bergsøe, Adolf Frederik. Den danske Forst- og Jagt-Lovgivning system fremstillet. 1842. IV. 315.[1]
Bergsøe, V. Oldenborrens Naturhistorie. 1862. IV. 548.[2]
— Oldenborrens Udryddelse. 1891. IV. 549.[1]
— On Oldenborrens Udryddelse ved Masse-Indsamling. 1883. IV. 548.[2]
— Resultaterne af Oldenborreindsamlingen. 1895. IV. 549.[1]
Bergstrand, Carl Erik. Naturalhistoriska anteckningar om Öland. 1851. I. 355.
Berber, Eugène. Catalogue des plantes . . . des Vosges. 1876. I. 415.
Bericht an den Bundesrath über das Forstwesen in der Schweiz. 1856. IV. 365.
Bericht der Commission für die Flora von Deutschland. 1899. I. 390.
Bericht der Deputation des forstlichen Ausschusses . . . [Diejenigen wesentlichen Aenderungen . . . anzugeben, welche . . . in der Forstverwaltung als . . . wünschenswert anzusehen sind.] 1849. IV. 291.[1]
Bericht der ständeräthlichen Commission . . . betreffend eidgenössische Oberaufsicht über die Forstpolizei . . . *See* WEBER, J. 1875. IV. 330.
Bericht der verstärkten Kommission für die Agrar-Verhältnisse über . . . Bildung von Waldgenossenschaften. 1869. IV. 308.[1]
Bericht des eidgenössischen Handels- und Landwirthschafts-departements . . . Forstwesen. 1885. IV. 367.
Bericht einer Reise durch die süderdithmarsischen Hölzungen. 1861. IV. 353.
Bericht over de beste wijze om ledige plekken in houtlanden aantevullen. 1794. IV. 169.[2]
Bericht over Liberia-Koffie. 1879. III. 742.[2]
Bericht über das Auftreten der Phylloxera. 1874. III. 759.
Bericht über das eidgenössische Forstwesen. IV. 13.[1]
Bericht über den Stand der Verbreitung der Reblaus. 1883, III. 573.
Bericht über die Holzsamen-Ernte der Provinz Schlesien. 1876. IV. 438.[1]
Bericht über die in der Engepromenade bei Bern befindliche Sammlung von Bäumen. *See* BRUNNER, Samuel. 1828. I. 65.[1]
Bericht über die Leistungen . . . im Waldbau. *See* JAHRES-BERICHT . . . in der Forstwirthschaft. IV 9
Bericht über die Trocknung der Eichenlohrinde. 1891. IV. 513.
Bericht über die Verbreitung der Reblaus. 1883. III. 761.
Bericht über Mittel und Wege zu Hebung des bündnerischen Forstwesens. 1846. IV. 41.[2]
Bericht über neue und wichtigere Beobachtungen aus dem Jahre 1884–91. 1885. I. 388.
Bericht über österreichische Literatur der Zoologie, Botanik. 1855. I. 4.[1]
Bericht und Antrag des Direktors der Domänen und Forsten an den Grossen Rath über das Forstwesen. 1857. IV. 365.
Bericht wegens het teelen en planten van mast of Dennen bosschen. 1794. IV. 452.[2]
Berichten uit Suriname. 1895. III. 118.[2]
Berigt over de inrichting van een plantentuin in Buitenzorg. 1819. I. 67.[2]
Berigten wegens reeds gedane ontginningen en verbeteringen van woeste gronden. 1808. IV. 159.
Beriktigande of Dr. Beilschmieds uppfattning. *See* LINDBLOM, A. E. 1845. II. 143.[1]
Beringer, Johann Bartholomaeus Adam & Dercum, L. A. Plantarum quarundam exoticarum . . . in Horto medico herbipolensi. 1722. I. 43.

Beringer, Martin. *See* Берингеръ, Мартинъ.
Berkeley, Miles Joseph. Hairs from seed of Adenium obesum. 1877. II. 722.[2]
— Note on a diseased state . . . of Pleroma vimineum. 1849. III. 639.[2]
— A notice of a mould attacking the Coffee plantations. 1849. III. 734.[2]
— On the ravages of ants. 1865. IV. 414.[1]
— On two species of Rudgea. 1866. II. 830.[2]
— Variegated plants of the seventeenth century. 1866. III. 206.[2]
Berkeley, T. B. H. The Leeward Islands. 1880. I. 336.
Berkenhout, John. Clavis anglica linguae botanicae. 1764. I. 69.[2]
— Outlines of the natural history of Great Britain and Ireland. 1769. I. 395.
— Pharmacopoeia medici. 1766. III. 253.
— Synopsis of the natural history of Great Britain and Ireland. 1769. I. 395.
Berkenkamp, W. A. Catalogus plantarum Horti botanici coloniensis. 1816. I. 45.
Berkhey, Jan Le Francq van. Expositio characteristica structurae florum qui dicuntur compositi. 1760. II. 850.[1]
— Welke boomen, heesters en planten . . . dewelke op de zandduinen . . . kunnen geplant worden? 1779. IV. 159.
— Welke zijn de beste middelen, om onze landen . . . ten meesten voordeele aan te leggen. 1765. III. 122.[1]
Berkhout, A. H. Aanplanting van nuttige boomsoorten in Nederlandsch Indië. 1884. III. 128.
— De anatomische bouw der Oostindische Ijzerhoutsoorten. 1898. II. 225,[3] 761,[1] IV. 400.[1]
— Boheemsche boschtoestanden. 1900. IV. 373.
— Boschbouw op Java. 1895. IV. 124.[1]
— Boschbouwkundige beschrijving van het eiland Banka. 1895. IV. 377.[1]
— Het boschwezen in Nederlandsch-Indië. 1894. IV. 376.[1]
— Caoutchouc-cultuur. 1898. III. 149.
— Caoutchouc en getah-pertja. 1895. III. 231.
— De Coca, Cuca. 1885. III. 442.[1]
— Djaticultuur op Java. 1885. IV. 536.[1]
— De exploitatie der Australische Eucalyptusbosschen. 1898. IV. 532.[1]
— F. W. van Eedens catalogus van Ned. Indische houtsoorten. 1886. IV. 124.[1]
— Gemengde boschaanplantingen. 1894. IV. 124.[1]
— Getah-pertja. 1899. III. 230.
— Gunstige invloed van den Albizzia stipulata op . . . Theeheester. 1886. III. 602.[1]
— De heer Cordes over het boschwezen in Indië. 1895. IV. 377.[1]
— Hout sprokkelingen. 1886. IV. 396.[3]
— Kickxia africana. 1898. III. 688.[2]
— De Kinakultuur op Java. 1894. III. 717.[1]
— De Koffiecultuur op Java. 1893. III. 730.
— De mexikaansche Gomelastiek-boom. 1897. III. 368.[1]
— Het nieuwe boschreglement. 1897. IV. 307.[1]
— Nogmaals het boschwezen der Djatibosschen op Java. 1896. IV. 536.[2]
— The oldest India-rubber plantation in the world. 1898. III. 370.[2]
— Ons papier. 1892. III. 235.[2]
— De Oost-indische houtsoorten. 1894. IV. 400.[1]
— Opbrengst van Indische Caoutchouc boomen. 1885. III. 149.
— De rentabiliteit der caoutchouc en getah-pertja-cultuur. 1899. III. 149.
— De rentabiliteit der caoutchouc en getah-pertja-cultuur. 1900. III. 149.
— De rentabiliteit van eene Kina onderneming. 1887. III. 16.
— Reorganisatie van het Indische boschwezen. 1896. IV. 294.[2]
— Het rooien van stronken en boomen. 1899. IV. 387.[1]
— Terrassenaanleg. 1892. IV. 124.[1]
— Over de toekomst der caoutchouc-cultuur. 1885. III. 149.
— De toekomst der Djatibosschen in gevaar? 1899. IV. 37.[1]
— De toekomst der Kinacultuur op Java. 1889. III. 716.
— Verbetering der Kinaprijzen. 1892. III. 718.
— Voordracht over de rentabiliteit der caoutchouc- en getah-pertja-cultuur. 1899. III. 149.
— Zagen bij de boschexploitatie. 1894. IV. 384.[1]
Berlandier, Jean Louis. Grossularieae. 1828. II. 243.[1]
— Mémoire sur la famille des Grossulariées. 1826. II. 243.[1]

Berlepsch, von. Entwurf eines Unterrichts von den nöthigsten Stücken bey der Forstwissenschaft. 1788. IV. 116.
Berlepsch, von, (*Oberland forstmeister, Dresden*). Ueber die Entbehrlichkeit der Waldstreu. 1859. IV. 71.
Berlepsch, von, (*Forstinspector*). Flächen-oder Massen-Etat? 1873. IV. 236.
Berlepsch, Hermann Alexander von. Schweizerkunde, Land und Volk. 1858. I. 435.
Berlese, Amedeo. Rapporti fra la Vite ed i saccaromiceti. 1897. III. 582.
Berlese, Antonio. Acari dannosi alle piante coltivate. 1886. III. 190.
— Di alcuni insetticidi. 1893. III. 197.
— Sulla azione delle soluzioni di rubina sopra insetti. 1892. III. 197.
— Della azione di alcuni liquidi insetticidi. 1892. III. 564.[1]
— Intorno alle cocciniglie degli Agrumi. 1892. III. 498.[2]
— Le cocciniglie degli Agrumi. 1896. III. 498.[2]
— Le cocciniglie italiane viventi sugli Agrumi. 1893. III. 498.[2]
— Estratto di una memoria sulla Mytilaspis fulva. 1893. III. 498.[2]
— Insetticidi ed insettifughi. 1894. III. 197.
— Nuove proposte contro la Cochylis ambiguella. 1895. III. 564.[1]
— Contro l'Oeneria dispar L. 1892. III. 197,
— Osservazioni circa proposte per allontanare i parassiti. 1899. III. 197.
— I parassiti vegetali. 1894. III. 193.[1]
— & **Bocchicchio**, Nicola. Sugli effetti di alcuni insetticidi. 1892. III. 197.
— & **Leonardi**, Gustavo. Notizie intorno all' effetto degli insettifughi. 1896. III. 564.[1]
— — Notizie intorno alle cocciniglie americane. 1898. III. 192.[1]
Berlese, Augusto Napoleone. Alcune idee sulla flora micologica del Gelso. 1887. III. 379.[1]
— Alcune idee sulla predisposizione delle piante all' infezione parassitaria. 1893. I. 206.[2]
— Una alterazione parassitaria della corteccia del Castagno. 1893. III. 359.[3]
— Sopra due parassiti della Vite . . . trovati in Italia. 1888. III. 561.
— La fitoptosi del Pero. 1892. III. 446.[2]
— Fungi moricolae. 1889. III. 379.[1]
— Le malattie del Gelso. 1885. III. 379.[1]
— Le malattie del Gelso. 1897. III. 379.[2]
— Una nuova malattia del Fico. 1893. III. 270.[1]
— Sopra una nuova malattia fungina del Leccio. 1892. IV. 503.[1]
— Osservazioni critiche sulla Cercospora Vitis. 1892. III. 580.
— Parassiti del Gelso a nuovo rovi. 1894. III. 379.[2]
— La Peronospora del Faggio. 1895. IV. 497.
— Rapporti tra Dematophora e Rosellinia. 1892. III. 580.
— Relazione sull' infezione della peronospora. 1893. III. 581.
— Saccharomyces e dematium. 1897. III. 581.
— Il seccume del Castagno. 1893. III. 359.[2]
— Sulla struttura e sviluppo della Pileolaria. 1897. III. 525.[1]
— Studi anatomici sul Gelso. 1887. II. 154.[2]
— Studi la forma, struttura . . . nelle Ampelidee. 1892. II. 501.su 1
— & **Sostegni**, L. Ricerche sul comportamento di alcuni sali di rame in rapporto al terreno ed alla Vite. 1894. III. 561.
Berlèse, L. M. Conservation extraordinaire d'un Jasmin blanc. 1833. III. 175.[2]
Berlèse, Laurent, (*abbé*). Sur l'Acacia subcaerulea. 1835. III. 466.[1]
— Beschreibung und Cultur der Camellia. 1838. III. 763.[2]
— Camellia de Bonnard. 1842. III. 598.[1]
— Ueber Camellien. 1837. III. 598.[1]
— Sur la chlorose des plantes. 1852. III. 181.[1]
— Crassula obliqua odorata. 1835. III. 466.[2]
— Cultur . . . der schönsten . . . Camellien. 1838. III. 598.[1]
— Description de variétés nouvelles de Camellia. 1849. III. 598.[2]
— Deux nouveaux Camellia. 1835. III. 597.[2]
— Excursion horticole en Belgique. 1835. III. 122.[1]
— Iconographie du genre Camellia. 1841. III. 598.[1]
— Mémoire sur un Prunier fébrifuge. 1830. III. 436.[3]
— Monographie du genre Camellia. 1837. III. 598.[1]

— Monography of the genus Camellia. 1837. III. 598.[1]
— Note sur la fécondation artificielle du Camellia. 1838. III. 599.[2]
— Note sur le Brugmansia sanguinea. 1837. III. 700.[1]
— Note sur un nouveau Camellia. 1847. III. 598.[2]
— Notice sur l'Erythrina crista galli. 1831. III. 476.[1]
— Notice sur la matière colorante . . . dans le Sophora. 1829. III. 488.[1]
— Notice sur la transplantation de plantes. 1828. III. 168.[2]
— Nouvelle méthode de classification du Camellia. 1844. III. 598.[1]
— Nouvelles observations sur le Morus multicaulis. 1832. III. 380.[1]
— Sur la panachure des fleurs du Camellia. 1847. III. 600.[1]
— Du Pistachier. 1847. III. 526.[1]
— Sur les progrès de la culture du Camellia. 1844. III. 598.[1]
— & Payen, Anselme. Rapport sur des cordes faites avec les fibres de la Mauve en arbre. 1835. III. 588.[3]
Berlese, Lorenzo. See BERLÈSE, Laurent, (abbé).
Berlet. Erfahrungen über den strengen Winter 1890–91. 1892. III. 46.[1]
Berlin, August. Kärlväxter, insamlade . . . Grönland 1883. 1884. I. 309.[1]
Berlin, Nils Johan. Commentarius medico-practicus in Pharmacopoeæ suecicæ editionem septimam. 1858. III. 247.[2]
— Om några blommers luktämnen. 1861. I. 182.[2]
— In Pharmacopoeam suecicam et militarem commentarius. 1858. III. 247.[1]
— Den svenska farmakopeen. 1851. III. 247.[1]
Berlin — Académie royale des sciences et des lettres. See ACADÉMIE . . . I. 10.
Berlin — Deutsche chemische Gesellschaft. See DEUTSCHE . . . I. 11.
Berlin — Gesellschaft für Erdkunde. See GESELLSCHAFT . . . I. 12.
Berlin — Kaiserliches Gesundheitsamt. See KAISERLICHES . . . I. 13, IV. 9.
Berlin — Königliche Akademie der Wissenschaften. See KÖNIGLICHE . . . I. 13.
Berlin — Königliche landwirthschaftliche Hochschule. Führer durch die vegetabilische Abtheilung. See WITTMACK, Ludwig. 1886. III. 28.[1]
Berlin — Königliche technische Versuchsanstalten. See KÖNIGLICHE . . . IV. 9.
Berlin — Königlicher botanischer Garten und botanisches Museum. See KÖNIGLICHER . . . I. 13.
Berlin — Königlicher botanischer Garten und Museum. See KÖNIGLICHER . . . 1895. I. 49.
Berlin — Königliches landwirthschaftliches Museum. Allgemeiner Katalog. See WITTMACK, Ludwig. 1869. III. 28.[1]
Berliner allgemeine Gartenzeitung. See ALLGEMEINE Gartenzeitung. III. 11.
Berliner Gesellschaft für Anthropologie. See ZEITSCHRIFT für Ethnologie. I. 15.
Berliner Gesellschaft für Anthropologie . . . Verhandlungen. 1889. IV. 210.[1]
Berlinische Gesellschaft naturforschender Freunde. Beschäftigungen. I. 11.
Berlioz, Antoine. See CORNIL, A. V. & BERLIOZ, Antoine.
Berlu, J. Jacob. The treasury of drugs unlock'd. 1690. III. 240bhn
Bermuda. 1888. III. 267.[1]
The Bermuda Juniper. 1891. II. 30.[2]
The Bermuda Palmetto. 1891. II. 75.[1]
Bern. Aufforstung am Brienzerberg. 1894. IV. 166.[2]
— Borkenkäferschaden im Lauterbrunnenthal. 1897. IV. 204.
— Entschädigung an Minderung des Bodenwertes durch Aufforstung. 1895. IV. 166.[2]
— Ueber Mass und Gewicht im Handel mit Brennmaterialien. 1896. IV. 406.[2]
— Ein Nussbaum mit . . . spätem Laubausbruch. 1898. II. 114.[1]
Bern — Naturforschende Gesellschaft. See NATURFORSCHENDE . . . I. 16.[2]
Bernál, Francisco LOSCOS Y. See LOSCOS Y BERNÁL, Francisco.
Bernard. Mémoire pour servir à l'histoire naturelle de l'Olivier. 1782. III. 678.[1]
— Mémoire sur l'histoire naturelle du Figuier. 1787. III. 369.[1]
— Mémoire sur l'Olivier. 1782. III. 678.[1]
— Mémoires pour servir à l'histoire naturelle de la Provence. 1782. III. 678.[1]
— Mémoires pour servir à l'histoire naturelle de la Provence. 1787. III. 85.
— Premier mémoire sur l'Amandier. 177 . ? III. 434.[1]
— Réponse aux observations sur le traité de l'Olivier. 1786. III. 675.[1]
Bernard, Alfred Karl Isaak. Vergleichung der Floren des Westindischen und Ostindischen Archipels. 1877. I. 336, 466.
Bernard, Augustin. L'archipel de la Nouvelle-Calédonie. 1895. I. 509.[1]
Bernard, Bayle (Mrs.). Our common fruits. 1866. III. 79.
Bernard, Claude. Action du curare. 1872. III. 683.[1]
— Analyse physiologique . . . au moyen du curare. 1856. III. 682.[1]
— Note sur les effets physiologiques de la curarine. 1865. III. 683.[1]
— See also PELOUZE, J. & BERNARD, Claude.
Bernard, E. Le Caryopteris Mastacanthus. 1893. III. 695.[2]
Bernard, François Marie Claude Charles. Restauration et conservation des terrains en montagne; correction des ruines de Pellafol. 1900. IV. 186.[1]
— Restauration et conservation des terrains en montagne; les terrains et les paysages torrentiels. 1900. IV. 186.[1]
Bernard, Johann. Vollständige Forst- und Jagdlehre. 1811. IV. 99.[2]
Bernard, Pierre & others. Le Jardin des plantes. 1842. I. 58.
Bernard, Pierre Frédéric B. Tableau de la flore du Jura. 1823. I. 407.
Bernardi, A. B. Stirpium rariorum . . . in Sicilia. 1813. I. 431.
Bernardi, Antonio BIVONA-. See BIVONA-BERNARDI, Antonio.
Bernardin, Jean de Waele. L'Afrique centrale. 1877, IV. 280,[2] 281.[1]
— Classification de 100 caoutchoucs. 1872. III. 229.
— Classification de 160 huiles et graisses végétales. 1871. III. 224.[2]
— Classification de 250 fécules. 1876. III. 220.[3]
— Classification de 250 matières tannantes. 1872. III. 237.[2]
— Classification de 40 savons végétaux. 1875. III. 226.[1]
— Classification de 350 matières tannantes. 1872. III. 237.[2]
— Classification des huiles et des graisses végétales. 1871. III. 224.[2]
— Nomenclature usuelle de 550 fibres textiles. 1872. III. 234.
— Les produits végétaux exotiques. 1886. I. 72,[2] III. 30.
— Les richesses naturelles du globe. 1885. III. 218.[1]
— Visite à l'Exposition de Vienne. 1874. III. 218.[1]
— Woods of the Philippine Islands. 1885. IV. 399.[2]
Bernardin de Saint-Pierre, Jacques Henri. See SAINT-PIERRE, J. H. B. de.
Bernaroli, U & Delpino, Federico. Pseudanzia di Camellis e di Geum. 1891. II. 550.[2]
Bernas, W. · Der Kiefernspannerfrass . . . Waldsteinruh. 1889. IV. 210.[1]
Bernat, Josef. Výnos lesů. 1885. IV. 371.
Bernatz, (Oberbaurath). Ueber Triftbauten. 1863. IV. 390.[1]
Bernatz, Wilhelm. Der Engerling und der Maulwurf. 1869. III. 180.
Bernatzik, W. Commentar zur oesterreichischen Militär-Pharmacopöe. 1872. III. 256.[2]
Bernatzki, A. See Бернацкий, A.
Bernays, Herbert L. Poisoning by Virginia Creeper. 1876. III. 545.[1]
Bernays, Lewis Adolphus. Cultural industries for Queensland. 1883. III. 147.[2]
— Description of exotic fruits new to Queensland. 1885. III. 147.[3]
— Dillenia speciosa Thunb. 1899. III. 595.[2]
— Economic tropical horticulture in Northern Queensland. 1880. V. XXVIII.[1]
— Notes on the Palm Caryota urens. 1887. III. 321.[3]
— The Olive and its products. 1872. III. 675.[3]
— The Palm Raphia (Sagus) ruffia. 1886. III. 330.[2]
Berne, A. Manuel d'arboriculture fruitière. 1898. III. 145.[1]
Berneaud, Arsenne THIÉBAUT DE. See THIÉBAUT-DE-BERNEAUD, Arsenne.
Bernegau, L. Die Bedeutung der Kola-Nuss. 1897. III. 591.[1]
— Étude sur la Kola. 1900. III. 591.[1]

Bernegau, L. (*continued*).
— Kola in Kamerun. 1900. III. 590.[1]
— Die Kola-Nuss als Arznei- und Genussmittel. 1897. III. 591.[1]
— Studien über die Kola. 1900. III. 591.[1]
Bernelot-Moens, Johann Carel. *See* MOENS, J. C. BERNELOT.
Berner, H. E. Indkjöb af skov for kommunerne. 1896. IV. 273.[1]
Bernerus, Gottlieb Ephraim. Germinatio vegetabilium in vegetabili. 1747. I. 234.[1]
Bernfus, Heinrich. Die Auwaldwirthschaft. 1895. IV. 131.
— Die Donauregulirung und die Wälder. 1892. IV. 124.[1]
— Die Eiche. 1895. IV. 502.[2]
— Zur Ermittlung der Bodenerwartungswerthe. 1898. IV. 259.[1]
— Die Ertragstafeln für die Weichhölzer der Auwälder. 1892. IV. 237.
— Die Martineit'schs Formel für den Bestandeswert. 1898. IV. 259.[1]
— Niederwaldculturen mit Fruchtzwischenbau. 1890. IV. 134.[1]
— Der Waldrentirungswerth. 1897. IV. 259.[1]
Bernhard. Die Umwandlung der sog. Reutberge in Eichenschälwaldungen betreffend. 1862. IV. 133.
Bernhard, Martin. Catalogus plantarum . . . in hortis regiis Warsaviae. 1652. I. 41.
Bernhardi, Johann Jakob. Anleitung zur Kenntniss der Pflanzen. 1804. I. 84.
— Ueber den Begriff der Pflanzenart. 1834. V. XII.[2]
— Bemerkungen über cultivirte Hollunderarten. 1846. III. 751.[1]
— Bemerkungen über die Gattung Monsonia. 1839. II. 389.[2]
— Beobachtungen über Pflanzengefässe. 1805. I. 133.
— Catalogus plantarum Horti erfurtensis. 1799. I. 45.
— Einige Bemerkungen über Cistaceen. 1838. II. 563.[2]
— Sur la formation de graines. 1839. I. 202.[1]
— Ueber die Gattung Laurophyllus. 1838. II. 456.[2]
— Ueber die Gattungen Methyscophyllum. 1846. II. 466.[1]
— Ueber die Kennzeichen der Hedysareae. 1842. II. 318.[1]
— Ueber die Metamorphose der Pflanzen. 1843. I. 101.[2]
— Recherches sur la metamorphose des plantes. 1843. I. 101.[2]
— Revue du genre Monsonia. 1839. II. 389.[2]
— Ricerche sulla metamorfosi delle piante. 1843. I. 101.[2]
— Systematisches Verzeichniss der Pflanzen . . . um Erfurt. 1800. I. 375.
Bernhardt, August. Ueber die Benutzung des praktischen Bienniums. 1873. IV. 32.
— Die Dampf-Entrindung. 1870. IV. 434.
— Die Drewitz'sche Kiefern-Säemaschine. 1875. IV. 149.[1]
— Eichen-Schälwald-Katechismus. 1877. IV. 506.
— Zur Etymologie des Wortes " Forst." 1871. IV. 56.
— Die forstlichen Verhältnisse des europäischen Russland. 1875. IV. 345.
— Die forstlichen Verhältnisse von Deutsch-Lothringen. 1871. IV. 349.[2]
— Forststatistik Deutschlands. 1872. IV. 349.[1]
— Forstwirthschaftliche Probleme. 1873. IV. 139.[2]
— Gedanken über das Forstunterrichtswesen in Preussen. 1872. IV. 32.
— Zur Geschichte der Staatsforstwirthschaftslehre. 1873. IV. 24.[1]
— Geschichte des Waldeigenthums. 1872. IV. 26.
— Gesetz-Entwurf, betreffend die Erhaltung . . . von Schutzwaldungen. 1874. IV. 180.[2]
— Die Gesetzgebung zum Schutz der Wälder. 1877. IV. 180.[2]
— Die Haubergswirthschaft im Kreise Siegen. 1877. IV. 133.
— Die Haubergswirthschaft im Kreise Siegen. 1868. IV. 133.
— Ueber die historische Entwicklung der Waldwirthschaft und Forstwissenschaft in Deutschland. 1871. IV. 26.
— Nordamerikanische Waldzustände. 1878. IV. 337.[2]
— Der sächsische Kammerirschlägel. 1874. IV. 387.[2]
— Schneebruchschaden in . . . Alt-Krakow und Stolp. 1876. IV. 190.
— Die Umwandlung der preussischen Staats-Domänen in Staats-Forsten. 1878. IV. 274.[1]
— Die Umwandlung der sog. Reutberge in Eichenschälwaldungen. 1862. IV. 505.
— Die Verbreitung der Lärchen-Krankheit. 1874. IV. 450.

— Die Verheerungen der preussischen Staatsforsten durch den Kiefernspinner. 1875. IV. 207.
— Die Waldbeschädigungen durch Sturm-und Schneebruch. 1880. IV. 189.[1] 195.[2]
— Waldbeschädigungen durch Windbruch. 1877. IV. 190.
— Die Waldflächen Europas. 1872. IV. 342.[1]
— Ueber Waldgenossenschaften. 1870. IV. 307.[2]
— Die Waldwirthschaft und der Waldschutz. 1869. IV. 180.[2]
— Der Weise'sche Höhenmesser. 1874. IV. 215.
— *See also* ERGEBNISS der Holzsamen-Ernte. 1875. IV. 438.[1]
— *See also* OEHLSCHLÄGER, O. & BERNHARDT, August.
Bernhardt, R. Kiefernmisbildung. 1877. II. 47.[2]
Der Bernhardzeller Wald ist kein Eigenthum der Ortsgemeinde Bernhardzell. 1843. IV. 330.
Bernieau, 'Léon. Traité des espèces . . . du genre Ilex. 1874. .III. 529.[2]
Bernigau, Christian Ferdinand. Specimen . . . sistens observationes quasdam de corticis Ulmi . . . usu medico. 1790. III. 365.[1]
Bernisches statistisches Bureau. Mittheilungen. IV. 13.[1]
Bernock, Heinrich. Ueber Eichen-Veredlungen im Freien. 1895. III. 361.[3]
Bernou, E. Estudio de la corteza del Zapote Chico. 1884. II. 697.[2]
— Étude de l'écorce de Sapotillier. 1883. II. 697.[1]
Bernoulli, Daniel. Positiones anatomico-botanicae. 1721. I. 97.
Bernoulli, Karl Gustav. Beiträge zur Pflanzen-Teratologie. 1869. II. 577,[1] 814.[2]
— Durchwachsene Frucht von Passiflora. 1869. II. 577.[1]
— Zur Kenntniss dimorpher Blüthen. 1869. II. 567,[2] 814.[2]
— Ueber scheinbar terminale Blätter. 1869. II. 814.[2]
— Uebersicht der . . . Arten von Theobroma. 1869. II. 539.[1]
Bernstein, J. G. Anti-Typographus. 1793. IV. 203.
— Etwas über den Borkenkäfer. 1786. IV. 455.
Bernuth, von, (*Oberförster*). Ueber Ackerculturen. 1874. IV. 133.
— Ueber ausländische Holzgewächse. 1881. IV. 125.[2]
— Ueber die Erziehung gemischter Holzbestände. 1872. IV. 138.[1]
— Forstinsectologisches. 1885. IV. 207.
— Ueber den Kieferspinner. 1870. IV. 476.
— Ueber den Rückgang der Erlen- und Birken-Niederwälder im Ertrage. 1885. IV. 132.[1]
— Ueber die Schütte der Kiefern. 1866. IV. 476.
— Zur Ueberbürdung der Oberförster mit Arbeit. 1885. IV. 290.[2]
— Ueber Waldfeldbau in Pommern. 1886. IV. 134.[1]
Beroaldus, Philippus. Enarrationes in XIII. Columellæ libros. 1549. III. 98.
Beroth, Berosch. ברוש יער 2 Sam. VI. 5. . . . 1736. I. 513.
Berregaard, F. V. Bøgeskovens Foryngelse. 1872. IV. 495.
Berriz, P. Bernardo Villareal de. *See* VILLAREAL DE BERRIZ, P. B.
Berro, Mariano B. La vegetación Uruguaya. 1899. III. 269.[2]
Berry, Edward Wilber. Abnormal flowers of Dogwood. 1900. II. 655.[1]
Berry, George. The Abele or White Poplar. 1877. III. 345.[1]
— The Abele Poplar and its uses. 1879. III. 345.[1]
— Autumn tints in trees and shrubs. 1879. III. 207.[1]
— The Californian Buckeye. 1877. III. 536.[2]
— Game coverts. 1872. III. 215.[1]
— Golden Conifers. 1878. III. 290.
— The Huon Pine. 1877. III. 287.[1]
— Improvement of park scenery. 1877. III. 201.
— The Lombardy Poplar. 1877. III. 346.[1]
— The Major Oak at Thoresby Park. 1876. II. 138.[2]
— Picea Nordmanniana in Wiltshire. 1877. III. 296.[2]
— The Plane trees. 1881. III. 418.[2]
— The Redwood in England. 1877. III. 310.[2]
— Remarkable Silver Fir. 1881. IV. 447.[1]
— Sabine's Pine. 1877. III. 308.[2]
— The Silver Fir. 1877. III. 296.[2]
— Two useful forest-trees. 1882. IV. 488,[2] 520.[2]
Berry-Reynal, (*ancien forestier*). Mémoire sur un nouvel aménagement des bois. 1858. IV. 242.
Berryhill, James G. Commercial growing of the Cherry in Iowa. 1897. III. 432.[1]

— The Plum. 1898. III. 433.[1]
— Sensible legislation on the forestry question. 1895. IV. 272.
Bersch, Josef. Die Verwerthung des Holzes auf chemischem Wege. 1883. IV. 433.[1]
Bersezio, V. I boschi e la metallurgia in Italia. 1861. IV. 277.
Bert. Les forêts de la Cochinchine. ' 1880. IV. 377.[1]
Bert, Joseph. Étude sur les plantations. 1886. IV. 124.[2]
— Note sur les dunes de Gascogne. 1900. IV. 122.[2]
Bert, Paul. Sur la cause intime des mouvements périodiques. 1878. I. 197.[2]
— Influence de la lumière verte sur la Sensitive. 1870. II. 373.[1]
— Influence des diverses couleurs. 1871. I. 230.
— Recherches expérimentales sur l'influence que les changements dans la pression barométrique exercent. 1873. I. 233.[2]
— Recherches sur les mouvements de la Sensitive. 1866. II. 373.[1]
— Sur la température comparée . . . de la Sensitive. 1869. II. 373.[1]
Berta, Tommaso Luigi. Iconografia del sistema vascolare delle foglie. 1830. I. 109.[1]
— Iconografia di scheletri di diverse foglie. 1828. I. 109.[1]
— Memoria sull' anatomia delle foglie. 1829. I. 109.[1]
Bertagnini, Cesare. Ueber das Phillyrin. 1854. III. 680.[1]
— & Luca, S. de. Ueber die chemische Constitution des Phillyrins. 1860. III. 680.[1]
— — Recherches sur la constitution chimique de la phyllyrine. 1860. III. 680.[1]
Bertani, Pellegrino. Nuovo dizionario di botanica. 1817. I. 70.
Bertaud. Mémoire sur la culture du Mûrier. 1835. III. 374.
Bertauf, René. See DETHAN, Georges & BERTAUT, René.
Bertero, Carlo Giuseppe. List of the plants of Chile. 1831. III. 65.[2]
— Specimen medicum . . . stirpes continens exoticis succedaneas. 1811. III. 88.[1]
Bertero, M. D. Continuacion del catalogo de plantas. 1829. I. 346.
Berthault. Quelques notes sur la végétation à Buenos Ayres. 1874. III. 119.[1]
Berthelot, Léon. Influence de l'intensité lumineuse. 1883. I. 230.
Berthelot, Marcellin Pierre Eugène. Sur l'absorption de l'azote libre. 1876. I. 159.
— Sur l'absorption des matières salines. 1888. I. 161.
— Chimie végétale et agricole. 1899. I. 152.[1]
— Sur les combinaisons des matières azotées avec les acides. 1886. I. 190.[1]
— Détermination du matériel, de l'accroissement. 1886. IV. 237.
— Sur les diverses sortes d'essence de térébenthine. 1853. IV. 443.[2]
— Sur le dosage du phosphore . . . dans les végétaux. 1899. I. 526.[1]
— Sur la force de la poudre. 1870. IV. 432.[1]
— Un the manna of Sinai. 1861. III. 221.[1]
— Sur la manne du Sinaï. 1861. III. 221.[1]
— Sur la présence et le dosage du chlore. 1899. I. 154.
— Sur la présence universelle des azotates. 1884. I. 154.
— Sur quelques matières sucrées. 1855. II. 42,[1] IV. 531.[1]
— Remarques concernant l'influence de l'électricité. 1887. I. 231.[1]
— Remarques sur la formation de l'alcool. 1899. I. 171.
— Remarques sur la formation des azotates. 1890. I. 159.
— Synthèse de l'esprit-de-bois. 1857. I. 155.
— & André, G. Sur l'acide oxalique dans la végétation. 1885. I. 156.[1]
— — Sur l'état de la potasse dans les plantes. 1887. I. 154.
— — Sur l'état du soufre et du phosphore dans les plantes. 1887. I. 154.
— — Études sur la formation de l'acide carbonique. 1894. I. 171.[1]
— — L'existence .·. de principes-dédoublables. 1894. I. 177.[1]
— — Sur la formation de l'acide oxalique. 1884. I. 180.[2]
— — Sur la formation du salpêtre. 1884. I. 176.
— — Sur le phosphore . . . dans la végétation. 1888. I. 154.
— — Sur la présence de l'alumine. 1895. I. 154.

— — Recherches sur la végétation. 1884. I. 156,[2] 159.
— — Sur la silice dans les végétaux. 1892. I. 154.
— & Buignet, Henri. Recherches sur la maturation des fruits. 1860. I. 179.[1]
Berthelot, Pierre Eugène Marcellin. See BERTHELOT, M. P. E.
Berthelot, Sabin. De l'acclimatation en Algérie des principales essences forestières des Iles Canaries. 1860. IV. 127.[2]
— Arboles y bosques. 1880. I. 496,[2] IV. 89.[1]
— Considérations sur l'acclimatement. 1844. III. 43.
— Coup d'œil sur les forêts canariennes. 1836. I. 496,[2] IV. 89.[1]
— Sur les essences forestières des Canaries. 1862. IV. 380.[1]
— De l'industrie de la cochenille aux Iles Canaries. 1851. III. 624.[1]
— Observations sur l'accroissement. 1832. I. 193.[1]
— Observations sur le Boehmeria arborea. 1829. II. 157.[1]
— Observations sur le Dracaena Draco. 1827. II. 82.[1]
— Observations sur le Dracaena Draco. 1328. II. 82.[1]
— See also WEBB, P. B. & BERTHELOT, Sabin.
Berthemot, J. B. Examen chimique du produit blanchâtre qui recouvre les fruits. 1846. I. 182.[1]
— & Dechastelus, de. Nouvel examen chimique du Guarana. 1840. III. 539.[2]
Bertherand, Émile Louis. La Cassie au point de vue de la culture. 1885. III. 465.[1]
— Le Celastrus edulis. 1889. III. 531.[2]
— Emploi thérapeutique du Schinus Molle. 1888. III. 529.[1]
— L'Eucalyptus au point de vue de l'hygiène en Algérie. 1876. IV. 531.[2]
— Hygiène publique. 1882. IV. 49.[1]
— Influence des plantations d'Eucalyptus. 1886. IV. 531.[1]
— Matière médicale arabe. 1888. III. 279.[1]
— Le noyau des dattes. 1882. III. 329.[2]
Berthereau de la Giraudière, A. L. Mémoire sur les semis et plantations d'arbres verts. 1829. IV. 441.
Berthier, Charles. Étude physiologique de l'If. 1896. III. 288.[2]
Berthier, Pierre. Recherche des substances organiques dans les sarments de Vigne. 1852. III. 582.
Berthold, Franz Josef. Die Loretto- und Sebastiani-Allee zu Rosenheim. 1890. III. 344.[2]
— Pflanzenphänologie im Dienste der Klimatologie. 1888. I. 221.
Berthold, G. Ueber das Vorkommen von Protoplasma in Intercellularräumen. 1884. I. 137.
Berthold, Johann Christoph Friedrich. De granorum kermes. 1743. III. 362.[1]
Berthold, Karl. Beitrag zur vergleichenden Anatomie der Coniferen-blätter. 1875. II. 17.[3]
— Darstellungen aus der Natur. 1869. I. 386.
— Uebersichten der forêts de montagne. 1870. IV. 264.
— Extrait du rapport annuel de l'inspecteur des forêts du canton des Grisons. 1866. IV. 366.
— Extrait du rapport sur l'administration des forêts domaniales du canton de Zurich. 1865. IV. 366.
— Les forêts et les pâturages de la Marche. 1865. IV. 135.[2]
— L'homme en guerre avec la forêt. 1878. IV. 196.[2]
— Note sur les effets de l'hiver 1879–80. 1880. III. 49.[3]
— Notes sur l'action du vent sur la position de blocs de rocher. 1880. III. 184.[2]
— Notice sur les forêts du Jura vaudois. 1887. IV. 367.
— Notices sur la forêt cantonale du Risoud. 1882. IV. 367.
— Quelques arbres de nos forêts. 1871. IV. 86.[2]
— Quelques arbres de nos forêts. 1876, (1877.) IV. 271,[3] IV. 86.[1]
— See also GREYERZ, Walo von & BERTHOLET, Charles; KOPP, J. & BERTHOLET, Charles; LANDOLT, Elias & BERTHOLET, Charles; MEISTER, Charles; SCHLUP & BERTHOLET, Charles; WEBER & BERTHOLET, Charles.
— & Meister, Ulrich. Die l'économie des forêts domaniales en Suisse. 1872. IV. 278.[1]
Berthollet, Paul. Le bois rouge de l'Épicéa. 1896. II. 36,[1] IV. 558.[1]
— Causerie. 1894. II. 126.[1]
— De la germination du Sapin blanc au Jorat. 1897. II. 24,[1] IV. 558.[1]
— La madera roja de Abeto. 1896. IV. 558.[2]
— Un nouveau bois d'œuvre. 1896. IV. 447.[1]
— Le Pitch pine au pont des Greniers. 1896. IV. 462.[2]
— À la recherche de la meilleure scie passepartout. 1896. IV. 393.

Bertholon de St. Lazare, Pierre. De l'eau la plus propre à la végétation des plantes. 1789. IV. 73.[1]
— Ueber die Eleċtricität in Beziehung auf die Pflanzen. 1783. I. 230.
— De l'électricité des végétaux. 1783. I. 230.
— De la taille de la Vigne. 1790. III. 548.[3]
Berthoule, Amédée. Acclimatation du Cufé au Brésil. 1891. III. 728.[3]
— L'Elaeagnus longipes. 1889. III. 628.[3]
— L'Érable à sucre. 1888. IV. 527.[1]
— Les forêts en Tunisie. 1888. IV. 379.[1]
Berthoumieu, G. Victor. La miellée des Tilleuls. 1900. II. 516.[3]
— Sur les tuberculoïdes des Légumineuses. 1898. II. 322.[1]
Berti, C. Coronedi. *See* Coronedi Berti, C.
Berti, P. & **Cavazza**, D. Saggio di frutticultura. 1883. III. 145.[3]
— & **Magliani**. Disegno di legge . . . disposizioni intese e promuovere i rimboscamenti. 1882. IV. 166.[1]
Bertin. Lettre au sujet de la multiplication des Pivoines. 1841. III. 393.[1]
Bertin, Exuperius Joseph. An potus ex foliis Thé ad sanorem diaetam . . . pertineat ? 1739. III. 605.
Bertin, Jules. Étude sur la réorganisation de l'administration des forêts. 1878. IV. 292.
— Études forestières. 1879. IV. 102.
— & **Vallée**, George. Étude sur les forestiers . . . de Flandre. 1876. IV. 27.[1]
Bertin, Victor. Danaida racemosa. 1882. III. 336.[1]
— Une Glycine gigantesque. 1878. II. 389.[1]
— *See also* Renault, Bertin & Boschi.
Bertog, (*sr.*). Der Obstbau . . . für Mittel- und Nord-deutschland. 1885. III. 139.
Bertog, Hermann. Ueber die Genauigkeit der Ermittelung der Stammgrundfläche. 1899. IV. 219.
— Mittheilungen über Schneebruchschäden. 1899. IV. 191.[1]
— Untersuchungen über den Wuchs . . . der Weisstanne und Fichte. 1895. II. 23,[2] *36*.[1]
— Verhalten der Eiche . . . in Buchenbeständen. 1900. IV. 138,[1] *496*.
Bertola, V. F. Appendix ad floram taurinensem. 185. ? II. 262.[3]
Bertoloni, Antonio. Amoenitates italicae. 1819. I. 425.
— De anatome monocotyledonearum. 1853. I. 133.
— Cactus pseudococchinillifer. 1823. II. 597.[1]
— De cedria et de cedrio. 1861. II. 28.[1]
— Il Cinnamomo. 1862. II. 224.[1]
— De Citro. 1854. II. 402.[1]
— Commentarius de itinere neapolitano. 1837. I. 426.
— Continuatio historiae horti botanici et scholae bot. Archigymnasii bononiensis. 1837. I. 63, V. viii.[3]
— Descriptiones plantarum . . . in expeditione Chesneyana per Euphratem. 1842. I. 477.[1]
— Descrizione di una nuova specie di Sida. 1843. II. 520.[1]
— Dissertatio de quibusdam novis plantarum speciebus. 1835. II. 364.[3]
— De Ebeno. 1849. I. 79.[3]
— Elenchus plantarum vivarum quas . . . exhibet hortus botanicus Archigymnasii bononiensis. 1820. I. 62.
— Excerpta de re herbaria. 1823. I. 266.
— Flora italica. 1833. I. 426.
— Florula guatimalensis. 1840. I. 333.
— Horti botanici bononiensis plantae. 1826. I. 62.
— Horti botanici bononiensis plantae novae. 1838. I. 63.
— De iconibus Panphytonis siculi. 1823. I. 431.
— Institutiones rei herbariae. 1807. I. 84.
— Iter per Apenninum della Futa. 1850. I. 427.
— Itinera ad Alpes apuanas. 1851. I. 427.
— Lucubrationes de re herbaria. 1822, (1823). *I. 266, 530*,[1] II. 358.[3]
— De Malogranato. 1857. II. 611.[1]
— Manipolo primo [e secondo] di piante dello Liguria. 1847. I. 427.
— Mantissa plantarum florae alpium apuanarum. 1832. I. 426.
— Memoria sopra l'Agallocum. 1865. II. 600.[1]
— Memoria sopra l'erbario . . . del Cesalpino. 1819. I. 8.[1]
— La mirra. 1862. III. 227.
— Miscellanea botanica. 1842. I. 268.
— De Monte Caprione. 1849. I. 427.
— Observationes botanicae. 1817. I. 266.
— Piante asiatiche. 1863. I. 473.

— Piante del Brasile. 1819. I. 341.
— Piante nuove asiatiche. 1864. I. 473.
— On the plant which furnishes the . . . ebony. 1848. II. 371.[3]
— De planta dicta Ethob in Sacris Literis. 1859. II. 764.[1]
— Plantae albamenses. 1844. I. 318.
— Plantae genuenses. 1804. I. 425.
— Praelectiones rei herbariae. 1827. I. 86.
— De quibusdam novis plantarum. 1835. II. 364.[3]—1836., II. 522.[1]
— Rapporto sulla collezione di piante fatta in Egitto. 1830. I. 487.
— Rariorum Italiae plantarum. Decas II.–III. 1803. I. 425.
— Rariorum Italiae plantarum descriptio. 1818. I. 425.
— Rariorum Liguriae plantarum. Decas I. 1803. I. 425.
— Viridarii bononiensis vegetabilia. 1824. I. 62.
Bertoloni, Antonio, (*jr.*). Nuovo Oïdium del Lauroceraso. 1879. III. 437.[3]
— Torna più giovevole il seminare o l'innestare? 1881. III. 153.
Bertoloni, Giuseppe. Alcune considerazioni sulla teoria degli innesti. 1875. I. 208.[1]
— Azione venefica dei Rhus. 1877. III. 528.[1]
— Del Castagno e della sua coltivazione. 1857. III. 359.[1]
— Come si comporta il midollo. 1861. I. 129.[1]
— Dei danni che ha incontrato il Pioppo della Virginia. 1866. III. 345.[3]
— De duobus insectis Ulmo . . . infensis. 1844. III. *364*,[1] *365*,[2] 427.[1]
— Florole delle due isolette più piccole del Golfo della Specia. 1866. I. 427.
— Illustrazione di piante mozambicesi. 1850. I. 492.[1]
— Iter in Apenninum bononiensem. 1841. I. 426.
— Delle malattie . . . del Pero. 1859. III. 446.[1]
— Modo facile di distruggere l'insetto . . . dell' Olmo. 1838. III. 364.[1]
— Nota posteriore. 187. ? III. 164.
— Notizie intorno a cose naturali osservate nei monti italiani. 1863. I. 427.
— Notizie intorno alle piante spontanee dei Monti porrettani. 1864. I. 427.
— Di una nuova galla dell' Eschia. 1873. IV. 510.
— Osservazioni posteriori intorno alla malattia del falchetto del Gelso. 1878. III. 379.[1]
— Di quattro diverse specie d'insetti nocivi ai Pini. 1878. IV. 442.
— Raccolta straordinaria di un gas entro il tronco di una Quercia. 1838. I. 208,[1] *IV. 509*.
— Intorno a tre galle del bolognese. 1872. IV. 501.[1]
— Ulteriori osservazioni intorno alla mortalità degli alberi. 187. ? III. 194.
— Vegetazione dei monti di Porretta. 1867. I. 428.
— Vegetazione . . . di lido marittimo italiano. 1869. I. 428.
Berton. Sur l'emploi de l'huile d'asphalte. 1879. III. 571.
Bertoni, Moïse. Le Noisetier. 1883. III. 358.[1]
— Sur quelques végétaux de la République Argentine. 1887. III. 65.[1]
Bertot. Procédé pour prendre l'empreinte des plantes. 1876. I. 37.[1]
Bertram, Julius. *See* Walbaum, Heinrich & Bertram, Julius.
— & **Gildemeister**, E. Betelöl. 1889. III. 342.[3]
— — Sur l'essence de Bétel. 1889. III. 342.[1]
Bertram, Werner. Flora von Braunschweig. 1876. I. 387.
— Nachtrag zu der Flora von Braunschweig. 1883. I. 388.
Bertrand, (*sr.*). Note sur l'Ortie blanche. 1860. III. 381.[1]
Bertrand, A. Notice sur les reboisements du Puy-de-Dôme. 1885. IV. 163.
— Les reboisements dans le Puy-de-Dôme. 1886. IV. 163.
Bertrand, Charles Eugène. Sur les Abietinées. 1872. IV. 13.[1]
— Anatomie comparée des . . . Gnétacées et les Conifères. 1874. II. 17,[1] *53*.[2]
— Anatomie comparée des . . . Gnétacées et les Conifères. 1875. II. 1.
— Anatomie comparée des téguments de la graine. 1878. I. 120.
— Définitions des membres des plantes. 1881. I. 100.[1]
— Étude sur les téguments séminaux des . . . gymno-spermes. 1878. II. 1.
— Sur le genre Abies. 1870. II. 21.[1]
— Loi des surfaces libres. 1884. I. 130.
— Note sur le genre Abies. 1871. II. 22.[1]
— Traité de botanique. 1881. I. 91.

— Traitement et aménagement des bois taillis. 1892. IV. 246.
— Le Welwitschia mirabilis D. Hook. 1877. II. 55.²
— & Renault, Bernard. Remarques sur les faisceaux foliaires des Cycadées. 1882. II. 3.¹
Bertrand, C. F. Le parfumeur impérial. 1809. III. 226.²
Bertrand, Émile. Les bois des fagnes de l'Entre Sambre et Meuse. 1894. IV. 555.²
Bertrand, Gabriel. Action de la bacterie du sorbose sur le sucre de bois. 1898. I. 178.
—L'Arbre à chilté et le chilté. 1899. III. 519.²
—Sur la composition chimique de l'essence de Niaouli. 1893. I I. 636.
— Sur la composition chimique du Kôsam. 1900. III. 508.¹
— Sur la diffusion de la pectase. 1895. I. 177.
— Sur l'existence de diastases oxydantes. 1896. I. 178.
— Sur le latex de l'Arbre à laque. 1894. III. 526.¹
— Mannocellulose in gymnosperms. 1899. II. 2.
— Nouvelles recherches sur les ferments oxydants. 1897. I. 178.
— Sur la presence de la mannocellulose. 1899. II. 2.
— Sur la recherche et la présence de la laccase. 1895. I. 177.
— Recherches sur la composition immédiate des tissus. 1892. I. 154.
— See also DYBOWSKI, Jean, BERTRAND, Gabriel & PHISALIX, C.
— & Mallèvre, A. Sur la diffusion de la pectase. 1896. I. 178.
— — — & Poirault, G. Sur la matière colorante du pollen. 1892. I. 201.²
Bertrand, J. La viticulture algérienne. 1889. III. 559.¹
— La viticulture et la vinification en Algérie. 1900. III. 559.²
Bertrand, Julien. D'une nouvelle espèce de vers à soie. 1844. IV. 501.²
Bertrand-Geslin, baron. La forêt de Paimpont. 1887. IV. 334.¹
Bertuch, Friedrich. See GUENTHER, Johann & BERTUCH, Friedrich.
Berwald, Johann Gottfried. Abhandlung vom Geschlecht der Pflanzen. 1778. I. 200.
Berwick, Thomas. The formation . . . of forest-tree nurseries. 1885. IV. 151.¹
Berzelius, Benedictus. Nomenclator botanicus. See LINNÉ, Carl von. 1759. I. 72.¹
Berzelius, Jöns Jacob. Sur la couleur jaune des feuilles en automne. 1836. I. 185.¹
— Lettre de M. Berzelius à M. Felouze. 1838. I. 140.²
— Några undersökningar af den färg. 1836. I. 185.¹
— Undersökning af bladgrönt . . . 1837. I. 140.²
Berzhinski, V. O. See БЕРЖИНСКІЙ, В. О.
Besançon — Académie royale des sciences, belles-lettres et arts. See ACADÉMIE . . . I. 20.
Besançon — Société d'horticulture et d'arboriculture du Doubs. See SOCIÉTÉ . . . III. 22.
Besanez, Eugen Franz Cajetán, Freiherr von GORUP-. See GORUP-BESANEZ, E. F. C., Freiherr von.
Beschädigung der Holzgewächse . . . durch Eichhörnchen. 1863. IV. 197.²
Beschluss der Verwaltungs-Kammer des Kantons Luzern betreffend . . . Frevel an den Wäldern. 1800. IV. 306.
Beschluss des eidg. Bundesrathes in Bezug der Gebirgs-Waldungen. 1858. IV. 283.¹
Die Beschornerien. 1859. III. 341.²
Die Beschränkung der Privatwaldwirthschaft. 1883. IV. 180.¹
Beschreibung der am 4. August 1873 in die Forste der . . . Herrschaft Drhowle unternommenen Exkursion. 1873. IV. 371.
Beschreibung der Domäne Janowitz. 1896. IV. 369.
Beschreibung der Domainenwaldungen in den Forstbezirken Baden, Gernsbach und Herrenwies. 1857. IV. 350.¹
Beschreibung der Excursionstour des Böhm. Forstvereines in den Forsten der Herrschaften Rožmital. 1891. IV. 372.
Beschreibung der Excursionstour des Böhm. Forstvereins in obgenannte Forste. See WAGNER, Theodor. 1894. IV. 372.
Beschreibung der Excursionstour . . . in die Forste der . . . Fideikom.-Domäne Reichenau. 1883. IV. 371.
Beschreibung der Exkursion des Böhmischen Forstvereines . . . in die Wälder der kgl. Stadt Pilsen. 1885. IV. 371.
Beschreibung der Exkursion in die Waldungen des Hrabiner Berges bei Troppau. 1851. IV. 368.

Beschreibung der Exkursion veranstaltet vom Böhm. Forstvereine . . . in die Forste der Herrschaft Worlik. 1890. IV. 372.
Beschreibung der Exkursionstour des Böhm. Forstvereines in den Forsten der Domäne Hofowitz. 1892. IV. 372.
Beschreibung der fürstlich Fürstenbergischen Waldsamen-Darre. 1836. IV. 147.²
Beschreibung der fürstlich Schwarzenberg'schen Domäne Wittingau. 1873. IV. 371.
Beschreibung der Gangloff'schen Stockholzrodemaschine. 1856. IV. 385.²
Beschreibung der italienischen Kohlungs-Methode. See HERBURGER, G. von. 1812. IV. 394.
Beschreibung der Land- und forstwirthschaftlichen Akademie Hohenheim. 1863. IV. 32.
Beschreibung der Obstsorten in der Central-Obst-Baumschule zu Grätz. 1827. III. 90.¹
Beschreibung der Reichsdomäne Brandeis. See URBAN, Josef. 1856. IV. 370.
Beschreibung der Reviere Kimratshofen und Kirnach. 1856. V. 351.¹
Beschreibung der verschiedenen besonders nützlichen . . . Holzgattungen. See WALBERG, T. W. von. 1787. IV. 86.²
Beschreibung der von Böhmischen Forstvereine . . . in die Forste der Herrschaft Nachod unternommenen Exkursion. 1878. IV. 371.
Beschreibung der Waldungen auf dem bunten Sandsteingebirge der Pfalz. See FORSTLICH-CHARAKTERISTISCHE. Skizze . . . 1845. IV. 350.²
Beschreibung des Neuburgerwaldes. 1851. IV. 350.²
Beschreibung des Reichswaldes bei Nürnberg. 1853. IV. 350.²
Beschreibung des Wermsdorfer Waldes. 1856. IV. 355.²
Beschreibung des zur Fürst Johann von und zu Liechtenstein'-schen Herrschaft Landskron gehörigen Revieres Lichwe. 1900. IV. 373.
Beschreibung einer Methode, aus inländischen . . . Pflanzen . . . Wolle zu bereiten. 1812. III. 272.¹
Beschreibung einer neuerfundenen Hebmaschine. 1780. IV. 385.²
Beschreibung eines sibirischen Forstreviers. 1898. IV. 376.¹
Beschreibung mehrerer Wälder der Korporation von Luzern. 1855. IV. 365.
Beschreibung schweizerischer Obstsorten. 1870. III. 89.¹
Beschreibung und Gebrauchs-Anleitung der Gangloff'schen Stockrode-Maschine. 1855. IV. 385.²
Beschreibung und Wirthschaftsplan über die Stadt-Waldungen von Luzern. 1870. IV. 366.
Beschreibung von Encephalartos Lehmanni. 1836. II. 6.¹
Beschrijving der vruchtsoorten. 1842. III. 76.
Beschrijving van de Koffij-en Suiker-cultuur. See HENNY, G. T. H. 1858. III. 729.¹
Beschrijving van de Wongindo. 1790. III. 507.²
Beschrijving van het eiland Soemba. 1855. III. 274.¹
Bese, A. Die freie Benutzung und Bewirthschaftung der Privatholzgrundstücke. 1854. IV. 308.¹
Om Beskæring af Rødderne paa Pæretræer. 1848. III. 445.¹
Beskrifning om askebränning i skogar. 1753. IV. 398.
Beskrifning om tilverknings sätten af harts. 1774. IV. 436.¹
Besler, Basilius. Fasciculus rariorum . . . varii generis. 1010. I. 204.
— Hortus eystettensis. 1613. I. 42.
— & M. R. Rariora musei Besleriani. 1716. I. 43.
Besler, Michael Rupert. Gazophylacium rerum naturalium. 1642. II. 271.²
Besnard, Anton Franz. Bayern's Flora. 1866. I. 365.
Besnier, Pierre Charles Louis. Le jardinier botaniste. 1705. III. 112.
Besnou, Léon. Catalogue raisonné des plantes composant l'école botanique au Jardin d'Avranches. 1881. I. 416.
— La flore de la Manche. 1881. I. 416.
— Note sur l'acclimatation . . . de l'Araucaria imbricata. 1868. III. 298.²
— Observations relatives au désévage des bois. 1867. IV. 419.
— & Lachênée, Bertrand. Catalogue raisonné des plantes . . . de Cherbourg. 1862. I. 412.
Eine besonders grosse Eiche. 1828. II. 137.² .
Der besorgte Forstmann. IV. 7.
Besquet, Jules. Méthode de torréfaction du bois. 1863. IV. 431.¹
Bessa, Pancrace. Des fleurs jardiniers. 1836. III. 86.
De Bessengaarde. 1855. III. 415.¹
Besser, Otto Ludwig von. De salicinio. 1831. III. 350.²

Besser, Wilibald Swibert Josef Gottlieb von. Aperçu de la géographie physique de Volhynie. 182 . ? I. 439.
— De Artemisia virente Moenchii. 1841. II. 851.²
— Catalogue des plantes du Jardin botanique de Krzemieniec en Volhynie. 1810. I. 41.
— Catalogus plantarum in Horto botanico gymnasii volbyniensis Cremeneci. 1810. I. 41.
— Dracunculi. 1835. II. 851.¹
— Enumeratio Artemisiarum illarum. 1835. II. 851.¹
— Enumeratio plantarum hucusque in Volhynia, Podolia . . . collectarum. 1822. I. 360.
— Monographiae Artemisiarum sectio 1, Dracunculi. 1843. II. 851.²
— Primitiae florae Galiciae. 1809. I. 439.
— Revisio Artemisiarum. 1841. II. 851.¹
— Ueber russische Artemisien. 1841. II. 851.²
— Rzut oka na jeografią fizyczną Wołynia i Podolia. 1828. I. 360.
— De Seriphidiis. 1834. II. 851.¹
— Supplementum ad synopsin Absynthiorum. 1836. II. 851.¹
— Tentamen de Abrotanis. 1832. II. 851.¹
— See also ANDRZEJOWSKI, A. L. & BESSER, S. W.
Besserer, C. Mexico and its coniferous plants. 1857. II. 14.²
Bessey, Charles Edwin. Are the trees receding from the Nebraska plains? 1897. I. 321, IV. 78.²
— Botany for high schools and colleges. 1880. I. 91.
— The botany of the Grape. 1895. III. 547.
— The botany of the Grape and . . . Prunus. 1895. III. 430,² 547.
— Botany of the Plums and Cherries. 1895. III. 430.²
— The Box-Elder on the plains. 1896. III. 535.¹
— The diseases of plants. 1882. III. 178.
— Evolution and classification. 1894. I. 253.¹
— The forests and forest trees of Nebraska. 1900. IV. 341.¹
— The functions of the leaf. 1884. III. 37.²
— A large Grape-vine. 1882. II. 506.²
— The natural spreading of timber areas. 1900. I. 219.¹ IV. 74.²
— Notes on the distribution of the Yellow Pine in Nebraska. 1895. II. 45.¹
— Phylogeny and taxonomy of the angiosperms. 1897. I. 249.²
— Preliminary report on the native trees . . . of Nebraska. 1891. I. 320, IV. 78.¹
— Sargent's studies of the forests of Japan. 1895. I. 461, IV. 87.¹
— Some observations on the action of frost. 1883. I. 212.
— Synopsis of a lecture upon the leaf. 1880. III. 37.²
— & Webber, H. J. Report of the botanist on the grasses . . . and the catalogue of plants. See WEBBER, H. J. 1890. I. 325.
— & Woods, A. F. The botany of the Apple tree. 1894. III. 425.¹
— Transpiration. 1892. I. 168.
Bessey, Ernst Athearn. See WEBBER, H. J. & BESSEY, E. A.
Besson, Émile. Leçons d'anatomie et de physiologie végétales. 1891. I. 92.
Best, George Newton. Examination of Pine-seed wings. 1886. II. 42.²
— North American Roses. 1889. II. 283.¹
— Pinus pungens in New Jersey. 1886. II. 45.²
— Remarks on the group Carolinae of . . . Rosa. 1887. II. 295.¹
— Remarks on the group Cinnamomeae. 1890. II. 283.¹
— Rosa humilis Marsh. var. plena. 1889. II. 295.¹
The best autumn-flowering shrub. 1884. III. 412.²
The best hedge plants. 1847. III. 213.
The best season for coppice fellings in Bombay. 1900. IV. 132,² 385.¹
The best time for cutting timber, etc. 1850. IV. 384.²
Beständig, Clemens. Tabellen, worin der kubische Gehalt eines jeden Stammes . . . berechnet zu finden. 1832. IV. 222.
Ueber Bestandespflege . . . in Buchengehegen. 1887. IV. 495.
Ueber die Bestandsgründung in den Theilwaldungen des K. Forstreviers Jachenau. 1883. IV. 118.
Die Bestimmung der Güteklasse des Bodens. 1852. IV. 68.
Bestimmung der Samenmenge nach dem Boden. 1850. IV. 148.
Bestimmung des Werths der für Zwecke der K. bayrischen Eisenbahnen abzutretenden Staats-Waldtheile. 1857. IV. 254.

Bestimmungen in Betreff der Forstdienstprüfungen. 1885. IV. 33.¹
Bestimmungen über Ausbildung und Prüfung für den königlichen Forstverwaltungsdienst. 1883. IV. 33.¹
Bestimmungen und Erläuterungen über das bei den Forsttaxationsnachträgen zu beobachtende Verfahren. 1850. IV. 302.
Bestimmungen und Erläuterungen über das bei den Forsttaxations-Nachträgen zu beobachtende Verfahren. 1887. IV. 303.¹
Bestimmungen und Erläuterungen über das bei den k. sächs. Forstvermessungsarbeiten zu beobachtende Verfahren. 1841. IV. 302.
Bestimmungen und Erläuterungen über das bei den Taxations-Nachträgen zu beobachtende Verfahren. 1873. IV. 303.¹
Bestrebungen zur Hebung der Forstwirtschaft in den Privatwaldungen. 1898. IV. 309.¹
Ein Besuch der Kina-Districte. See WARBURG, Otto. 1887. V. XXIII.²
Beta. Mittheilungen über das Verpflanzen grosser Bäume. 1878. III. 167.
Betænkning, afgiven af den . . . Commission betræffende Skyldsætningen af Kongerigets Skove. 1858. IV. 260.¹
Betænkning fra det af Dansk Skovforening og Garverforeningen . . . angaaende Barkhandelen. 1895. IV. 435.
Betancourt, A. Milchsaft von Hippomana Manzanillo. 1889. III. 519.²
Betche, Ernst. Vegetations-Charakter der Samoa-Inseln. 1881. I. 510.¹
— Vegetationsskizze der Marshalls-Inseln. 1884. I. 510.¹
— See also MAIDEN, J. H. & BETCHE, Ernst.
Betcke, Ernst Friedrich. Monographische Beschreibung der Brombeersträucher Meklenburgs. 1850. II. 301.²
Die Betheiligung der Frauen an der Lösung der Waldfrage in Nordamerika. 1896. IV. 272.
Betel nut chewing. 1873. III. 320.¹
Betham, G. K. Some notes on the connection existing between forestry and agriculture in India. 1889. IV. 134.¹
Betham, J. A. Uses of the Screw Palm. 1889. III. 313.¹
Bethe, (Geheimer Ober-Regierungs-Rath), & Lenné, P. J. Über Trift- und Feld-Pflanzungen. 1826. III. 214.²
Bethune, Charles James Stuart. Some recent work in economic entomology. 1900. III. 197.
Betrachtungen über die Zusammenlegung und den Austausch kleiner Waldparzellen. 1855. IV. 309.¹
Betrachtungen über verschiedene Gegenstände . . . einer pfleglichen Forstwissenschaft im Nordgau . . . nachtheilig. 1797. IV. 289.³
Die Betriebs-Einrichtung der [österreichischen] Staatsforste. 18 . . ? IV. 249.¹
Die Betriebseinrichtung des ärarischen Waldes von Haye. 1883. IV. 249.¹
Die Betriebseinrichtung für den Kobernauser Wald. 1873. IV. 250.¹
Betriebseinrichtung und Wirtschaftsführung. 1900. IV. 247.¹
Betriebs-Regulierungen. 1857. IV. 242.
Betten, Robert. Die Rose, ihre Ansucht. 1897. III. 451.¹
Bettfreund, Carl. Flora Argentina. 1898. I. 345.
Die Bettlertanne von Villmergen. 1890. II. 24.²
Bettoni, Giovanni. Di notizie relative alla materia zuccherina. 1812. III. 220.¹
Betts, Charles. The Bur-Oak. 1860. III. 362.²
Betz, Karoly. Rhus Cotinus. 1896. III. 524.¹
— Die Ueberwinterung des Granatbaumes. 1900. III. 630.¹
Beucker, J. J. de. Boomteeltkunde. 1871. III. 121.²
— Het schildgriffelen. 1868. III. 164.¹
— Voorsorgen by het enten van vruchtboomen. 1866. III. 161.
— Welke is de beste wijze om boomgaarden te leggen. 1868. III. 154.¹
— De wortelenting. 1868. III. 164.¹
— See also HEURCK, Henri van & BEUCKER, J. I. de.
Beuermann & others. Über Streulaubnutzung. 1866. IV. 71.
Beughem, Cornelius van. Bibliographia medica. 1681. III. 1.
Beugin. Valeur nutritive pour chevaux et vaches du diss. 1893. IV. 401.¹
Beugon, Meschiny & Noirot. Rapport . . . l'état et le succès de diverses plantations nouvellement faites. 1808. IV. 121.

— — — "Rapport sur la coupe des bois entre deux terres." 1808. IV. 121.
Beunie, J. B. de. Antwoord op de vraege, welk zyn de profytelykste planten van dit land. 1772. III. 270.²
Beurling, Pehr Johan. Bidrag till Portobellos flora. 1854. I. 333.
— Plantae vasculares . . . Scandinaviae. 1859. I. 355.
Beurmann, (Forstmeister, Saupark). Einfriedigung mit transportabeln Hürden. 1865. IV. 146.²
Beurre de cay-cay de la Cochinchine. 1886. III. 508.¹
Beust. Schlüssel zum Bestimmen aller in der Schweiz wildwachsenden Blütenpflanzen. 1881. I. 436.
Beust, Fritz. Untersuchung über fossile Hölzer aus Grönland. 1884. I. 308.
Bevan, E. J. See Cross, C. F. & Bevan, E. J.; Cross, C. F., Bevan, E. J. & Beadle, C.
The beverages we infuse. 1854. III. 222.
Beveridge, James. L'industrie de la cellulose de bois en Scandinavie. 1897. I. 48.
— L'industrie de la cellulose en Scandinavie. 1899. IV. 430, 558.¹
Beverly, Robert. Histoire de la Virginie. 1705. III. 263.²
— The history and present state of Virginia. 1705. III. 263.¹
— The history of Virginia. 1705. III. 263.²
Bevérwyck, J. van. Inleijdingh tot de hollandtsche geneesmiddelen. 1656. III. 76.
Bewährte Garten-Geheimnüsse. 1735. III. 121.¹
Die Bewaldung des Bodens in ihrem Einflusse. 1882. IV. 50.
Die Bewaldungsverhältnisse der Erde. 1892. IV. 75.²
Die Bewaldungsverhältnisse der deutschen Reiches. 1885. IV. 349.¹
Bewaldungsversuche in der Umgegend von Tiflis. 1873. III. 184,¹ IV. 157.
Bewick, J. W. Hedges and their management. 1895. III. 214.¹
Bewick, Thomas. The different kinds of fences. 1898. IV. 146.²
— On the woods . . . of Streatlam. 1890. IV. 358.²
Bexell, Johann Jacob. Hallands Historia och Beskrifning. 1817. I. 352.
Bey, de, Foerster, A. & Monheim, V. Botanischer Garten der Stadt Aachen. 1879. I. 48.
Bey, A. B., Clot-. See Clot-Bey, A. B.
Beyer, A. Ein Beitrag zur Kenntniss über die Stoffmetamorphose der Früchte. 1865. I. 179.¹
— Sur la maturation des fruits. 1865. I. 179.¹
Beyer, A. de. Opmerkingen omtrent den wasdom van eenige . . . houtsoorten. 1834. III. 363.¹
Beyer, Friedrich. Quercus pedunculata umbraculifera Ligini. 1893. III. 363.¹
Beyer, Hermann. Die spontanen Bewegungen der Staubgefässe. 1888. I. 197.²
Beyer, J. Quaestiones de plantis. 1623. I. 30.
Beyer, Johan Markus. Forst- und Jagd-Wörterbuch. 1801. IV. 22.²
Beyer, Konrad. Wilhelm von Braumüller und Heinrich von Cotta. 1881. IV. 2.
— Zillbach . . . dessen Bedeutung als Forstlehranstalt. 1878. IV. 32.
Beyer, Michael. Spalding's Feldeisenbahn. 1884. IV. 391.
Beyer, P. Ergebnisse der bisherigen Arbeiten bezüglich der Ueberpflanzen. 1896. I. 234.²
— Weitere Beobachtungen von Ueberpflanzen. 1894. I. 234.²
Beyer, Robert Alexander. Die sächsischen Forststraf- und Jagdgesetze. 1864. IV. 322.¹
Beyerinck, Martinus Willem. See Beijerinck, M. W.
Beyreuther, (Forstconducteur). Einige Beobachtungen über . . . Streunutzung in Kiefernwaldungen. 1868. IV. 476.
Beyrich, Carl. Bemerkungen über die Eigenschaften . . . der Brotfrucht. 1824. III. 367.¹
— Nachricht von Herrn Beyrich aus Nordamerika. 1834. III. 60.
— Eine Schilderung des Gartenbaues in den südlichen atlantischen Staaten von Nordamerika. 1835. III. 117.²
Beythe, András. Fives könüv fiveknek és faknac névökröl, termeszetökröl és hasznokrul. 1595. I. 283.
Beyträge zur Beförderung der Naturkunde. I. 11.
Beyträge zur Forstwissenschaft aus der praktischen Geometrie. See Hennert, C. W. 1783. IV. 213.¹
Beyträge zur practischen Forst- und Holzhandels-Wissenschaft. See König, F. W. 1790. IV. 382,¹ V. xxxi.¹
Beytrag zur Geschichte der Schädlichkeit . . . der frischen Acajoukerne. 1784. III. 523.²

Het bezaaijen . . . van een deel der duinen. 1867. IV. 160.¹
Beze, Claude de. Descriptions de quelques arbres . . . de Malaque. 1731. I. 464.¹
Bezeth, S. Gutta-percha. 1848. III. 230.
— Gutta-Percha, haar oorsprong. 1848. III. 228.²
Über die Beziehungen zwischen Landwirthschaft und Forstwirthschaft. 1885. IV. 134,¹ 550.²
Béziers — Société d'étude des sciences naturelles. See Société . . . I. 23.
Bgtr., J. Die Schneebruchfestigkeit der Weymouthskiefer. 1894. IV. 469.
Bhai Sadhu Singh. Report on the better conservancy of forests on hills surrounding Mount Abu. 1888. IV. 378.
The Bhotan Pine. 1887. III. 307.¹
Biancardi, Gian Antonio. Flora dei dintorni d' Avola. 1844. I. 431.
— Monografia del Mandorlo comune. 1872. III. 434.¹
Biancardi, Dionigi. Formula algebraica generale. 1877. IV. 256.
— Teoria per la valutazione. 1856. IV. 254.
Bianchedi, C. L' Olivo sulle colline parmensi. 1880. III. 675.²
Bianchi, Casimir. Vademecum botanico. 1763. I. 257.
Bianciardi, E. D. R. Under the Olives. 1883. III. 679.¹
Bianconi, Gian Antonio. Alcune ricerche intorno alla estensione della superficie respirante dei vegetabili. 1868. I. 170.
Bianconi, Giovanni Giuseppe. Di alcuni movimenti . . . per la diffusione de' semi. 1841. I. 240.¹
— Sul sistema vascalore delle foglie. 1838. I. 109.¹
Biasoletto, Bartolomeo. Escursioni botaniche sullo Schneeberg. 1846. I. 447.
— Relazione del viaggio . . . nell' Istria, Dalmazia e Montenegro. 1841. I. 447.
Bibb, A. B. Notes on some European systems of forest administration. 1900. IV. 288.¹
Bibb, Richard. The Eucalyptus globulus. 1876. IV. 533.¹
Bibliografia agronomica. 1844. III. 1.
Bibliographie des œuvres d'Auguste Mathieu. 1892. IV. 2.
Bibliographie nationale suisse. Forêts. See Forêts . . . 1894. IV. 2.
Bibliography of forestry. 1886. IV. 2.
Bibliography of Indiana; botany. 1894. I. 3.¹
Biblioteca italiana. I. 24.²
Biblioteka i zbiory Towarzystwa ogrodniczego w Krakowie. 1900. III. 2.
Bibliotheca botanica. I. 11.
Bibliotheca guanabarense. See Sociedade vellosiana. I. 519.²
Bibliotheca historico-naturalis. 1851. I. 2.
Die Bibliothek der Ökonomischen Gesellschaft im Königreiche Sachsen. 1876. III. 1.
Bibliothek für Physik, Medecin og Oeconomie. See Physikalox-oekonomiske . . . Bibliothek for Danmark . . . I. 9.¹
Bibliothek für Lustgärtner und Blumenfreunde. 1808. III. 1.
Bibliothèque britannique. See Bibliothèque universelle des sciences. I. 26.¹
Bibliothèque britannique. Agriculture anglaise. III. 24.¹
Bibliothèque des propriétaires ruraux. III. 19.
Bibliothèque universelle. See Bibliothèque universelle des sciences. I. 26.¹
Bibliothèque universelle. Agriculture. See Bibliothèque britannique. III. 24.¹
Bibliothèque universelle de Genève. See Bibliothèque universelle des sciences. I. 26.¹
Bibliothèque universelle des dames. Botanique. 1786. I. 93.
Bibliothèque universelle des sciences. I. 26.¹
Bibra, Ernst, Baron von. Der Kaffee und seine Surrogate. 1858. III. 740.²
— Die narkotischen Genussmittel. 1855. III. 222.
Bicchi, Cesare. Aggiunta alla flora lucchese de B. Puccinelli. 1860. I. 427.
— Alcuni alberi notevoli dell' Orto botanico di Lucca. 1877. I. 297.²
— La flora lucchese. 1877. I. 428.
— Le Uve della provincia di Lucca. 1874. III. 547.
Biche, B. Catalogue des plantes cultivées au Jardin botanique du Collège de Pézenas. 1875. I. 59.
— Flore des environs de Roque-haute. 1881. I. 618.
Bicheno, James Ebenezer. On systems and methods in natural history. 1827. I. 251.
Bicheyre, A. Traité d'agriculture théorique et pratique. 1884. III. 113.

Bickmore, Albert Smith. Reizen in den Oost Indsche Archipel. 1868. I. 466.
— Travels in the East Indian Archipelago. 1868. I. 466.
Bicknell, Clarence. Flora of Bordighera and San Remo. 1896. I. 430.
— Flowering plants . . . of the Riviera. 1885. I. 429.
Bicknell, Eugene Pintard. Salix. 1880. II. 103.[2]
— Stamens within the ovary of Salix. 1881. II. 103.[1]
Bidard. Structure de la fleur des Graminées. 1869. II. 58.[2]
— See also GIRARDIN & BIDARD.
Bidauld, P. Sur un moyen d'empêcher le développement du phylloxera. 1881. III. 573.
Bidaut, Eugène. Culture du Sapin. 1857. IV. 444.[1]
Biddle, John B. Materia medica. 1853. III. 243.
— Review of materia medica. 1853. III. 243.
Biddulph, *Sir* Robert. The Cedar forest of Cyprus. 1884. II. 28.[1]
Bidell, Hermann. Effects of lightning. 1890. IV. 194.
Biden, H. B. Abnormal inflorescence in Cereus speciosissimus. 1883. II. 591.[2]
Bidet, Nicolas. Abhandlung von Anbau . . . des Weinstocks. 1752. III. 554.[1]
— L' agricoltore sperimentato. 1752. III. 554.[1]
— Traité sur la nature . . . de la Vigne. 1752. III. 554.[1]
— Trattato sopra la coltivazione delle Viti. 1752. III. 554.[1]
— See also DU HAMEL DU MONCEAU, H. L. & BIDET, Nicolas.
Bidie, George. Catalogue of specimens of Cinchona. 1883. II. 813.[1]
— Catalogue of the raw products of southern India. 1878. III. 278.
— Cinchona cultivation in India. 1882. III. 714.
— Cinchona culture in British India. 1879. III. 714.
— Climate and flora of Ootacamund. 1867. I. 474.
— Coca, its source, culture. 1885. III. 493.[1]
— Indian timbers for fishing rods. 1896. IV. 428.[2]
— List of the Madras drugs. 1884. III. 278.
— Notes on the woods used for fishing rods. 1896. IV. 428.[2]
— Report on Neilgherry loranthaceous parasitical plants. 1874. II. 173,[1] III. 195.[1]
— Report on the ravages of the borer in Coffee estates. 1869. III. 735.
— The Seegoor Ghaut, Neilgherries. 1867. I. 474.
— The timber trees of India. 1862. IV. 400.[3]
— The useful plants of the Nilagiris. 1880. III. 92.[2]
Bidlake, W. H. Dry-rot in timber. 1888. IV. 415.[1]
Bidloo, Lambert. Dissertatio de re herbaria. 1683. I. 30.
Bidwill, H. On a new species of Araucaria. 1842. II. 25,[3] 177.[1]
Bidwill, J. S. Another coniferous tree detected in Australia. 1849. II. 25.[1]
Bie, H. C. J. de. De Arenpalm.in de Preanger. 1891. III. 320.[1]
— De Klapper (Cocos nucifera). 1895. III. 323.[1]
Bieber, D. Die Weymouthskiefer. 1859. IV. 470.[1]
Bieberstein, Friedrich August, *Freiherr* von MARSCHALL VON. *See* MARSCHALL VON BIEBERSTEIN; F. A., *Freiherr* von.
Biedenfeld, Ferdinand, *Freiherr* von. Das Buch der Rosen. 1840. III. 448.
— Handbuch aller bekannten Obstsorten. 1854. III. 71.
— Aus meiner Pilgertasche; der Schlossgarten zu Karlsruhe. 1860. I. 48.
— Von der natürlichen und künstlichen Befruchtung der Pflanzen. *See* LECOQ, Henri. 1845. III. 50.[2]
— Wörterbuch der Synonymen sämmtlicher Pflanzen. 1848. I. 77.
Biedermann, Detlev, *Freiherr* von. Die Blattformen der Palmen. 1879. II. 63.[1]
— Die Nutzungen der Palmen. 1876. III. 319.[1]
Biedermann, E. Beiträge zu den Jahresberichten . . . der forstlich-meteorologischen Stationen. 1885. IV. 72.
— Ueber Durchwinterung von Eicheln. 1890. IV. 508.
— Ueber das Verfahren bei der Verwerthung der Holzernte. 1883. IV. 388.[1]
Biedermann's Centralblatt für Agrikulturchemie. *See* CENTRALBLATT . . . III. 11.
Biedersfeld, N. B. von. Die Waldbrände Slavoniens. 1875. IV. 184.[1]
Biehler. Ueber Raumgehalt und Gewicht von aufgespaltenen Prügelholzklaftern. 1871. IV. 387.[2]
— Der Schälwaldbetrieb. 1875. IV. 506.
Biehler, Johann Friedrich Theodor. Plantarum novarum ex herbario Sprengelii centuriam. 1807. I. 265.
Biel, J. Zur Prollius'schen Untersuchungsmethode für Chinarinden. 1882. III. 725.[1]

Biel, Johann Christian. Exercitatio de lignis ex Libano . . . petitis. 1740. IV. 443.[1]
Bielawski, B. H. Note sur le genre Chimonanthus. 1867. III. 401.[1]
Bielefeld, Rudolf. Beitrag zur Flora Ostfrieslands. 1896. I. 389.
Bieler, Ambrosius Karl. Phytanthoza iconographia. *See* WEINMANN, J. W. 1735. I. 290.
Bielitz, Julius. De manna. *See* HEISTER, Lorentz. 1725. IV. 536.[1]
Bielke, Sten Carl. Beskrifning om det sibiriska Ärte-trädet. 1750. II. 341.[1]
Bielkin, W. W. Beiträge zur Kenntniss der Quillaja-Rinde. 1888. III. 447.[2]
— **Kobert & Pachorukoff.** Sur les principes actifs de l'écorce de Panama. 1889. III. 447.[1]
Bielozerski, O. M. *See* БѢЛОЗЕРСКІЙ, O. M.
Bielski, Wladysl. *See* SKÓRKOWSKI, Kazimierz & BIELSKI, Wladysl.
Biels, Eduard Albert. Die in Siebenbürgen wildwachsenden Arten der Syringa. 1886. II. 714.[2]
— Das Vorkommen . . . des Sade-Wachholders . . . in Siebenbürgen. 1886. II. 32.[1]
Biemüller, Julius. Die Absprünge der Fichte. 1897. IV. 457.
— Clematis graveolens. 1899. III. 391.[2]
— Hochstämmige Fuchsien. 1900. III. 640.[1]
Bieneck, R. Promemoria über die Art der Feststellung der Waldstreu-Massen. 1846. IV. 437.[3]
— Referat über das v. Buttlarsche . . . Kultur-Verfahren. 1851. IV. 152.
— Referat über die bei . . Biermanns . . . vorgefundenen Resultate seiner Kulturmethode. 1851. IV. 141.
Biener, Christian Gottlob. De suprema principis in silvas inspectione. 1796. IV. 313.
Bienert, Theophil. Baltische Flora. 1872. I. 363.
— Riga; Vegetations-Periode. 1857. I. 223.[2]
Bierau, (*Oberförster, Rothau*). Zur Erziehung der Lärche. 1892. IV. 450.
Bierbach, Oskar. Fagus sylvatica L. var. Zlatia. 1898. II. 126.[1]
— Prunus Laurocerasus L. var. serbica. 1898. III. 437.[3]
Bierdimpfel. Ueber die Bewirthschaftung der Staatswaldungen des kgl. bayr. Forstamtes Freising. 1881. IV. 118.
Bierdimpfel, Eduard. Culturversuch mit landwirthschaftlicher Zwischennutzung. 1858. IV. 133.
Bierer, Hermann & **Frisch**, Friedrich. Das Forststrafgesetz. 1880. IV. 322.[3]
Bierkander, Clas. *See* BJERKANDER, Clas.
Bierl, E. Wem gehört der Stechtenknubelwald? 1885. IV. 331.[1]
Biermann, Max. Beiträge zur Kenntnis der Entwickelungsgeschichte der Früchte von Citrus. 1896. II. 402.[1]
Biermann, Rudolf. Ueber Bau . . . der Oelzellen. 1898. I. 135, V. xi.[1]
Biermanns, (*Oberförster*). Die Anwendung der Streifen-Schläge. 1852. IV. 128.
— Die Anwendung der Streifenschläge betreffend. 1853. IV. 128.
— Ueber die Eichenholz-Zucht. 1850. IV. 504.
— Vorschläge zu . . . Bewirthschaftungsart der Nieder- und Mittelwaldungen. 1852. IV. 128.
Biern, Sewer. *See* BJÖRN, Sören.
Biernacki, J. F. Dokładny praktyczny ogrodnik. 1855. III. 101.[1]
Biersack, (*Geheimrath, Dr.*). Die Grundsätze der Waldwerthberechnung. 1860. IV. 255.
Biese, Franz. Die Philosophie des Aristoteles. 1835. I. 292.
Bietrix, Antoine. Le Thé: botanique et culture. 1892. III. 608.[1]
Bietti. Sur l'aribine, nouvel alcaloïde. 1862. III. 467.[1]
Biffen, R. H. The coagulation of latex. 1898. I. 181.[3]
— Coagulation of rubber-milk. 1898. III. 232.[1]
— The functions of latex. 1897. I. 181.[2]
— Methods of preparing rubber. 1899. III. 232.[1]
A big Deodar log. 1899. II. 2.
The **Big** trees and the Yosemite. 1880. II. 51.[1]
Big trees in California. The Three Sisters. 1873. II. 51.[1]
The **Big** trees of California. 1859. II. 50.[1]
Bigazzi, Pietro. Catalogo della biblioteca della R. accademia dei georgofili. 1863. I. 2.
Bigelow, Cassie M. Study of glands in the Hop-tree. 1895. II. 410.[1]
Bigelow, Jacob. American medical botany. 1817. III. 62.

— Facts serving to show the comparative forwardness of the spring season. 1818. I. 222.[1]
— Florula bostoniensis. 1814. I. 313.
— Nature in disease. 1854. III. 607, 742.[1]
— A treatise on the materia medica. 1822. III. 242, 245.
— See also ENGELMANN, George & BIGELOW, J. M.
Bigelow, John Milton. Description of forest trees . . . 1856. I. 320, IV. 77.[2]
— General description of the botanical character of the country . . . explored by Lieut. A. W. Whipple. 1856. I. 323.
Bigelow, Robert Payne. New York state college of forestry. 1898. IV. 30.[1]
Bigge, H. On the destruction of Orange trees. 1838. III. 500.[2]
The biggest tree in Berar. 1899. II. 529.[1]
Bignonia grandiflora. 1833. III. 705.[2]
Bignonias. 1878. III. 705.[1]
Bijblad van de landbouw courant. See ALGEMEENE . . . courant. III. 14.
Bijdrage tot de kennis der insekten . . . den Kakao-boom nadeelig. 1859. III. 593.[2]
Eene bijdrage tot verbetering van de Koffij-cultuur. 1892. III. 727.
Bijdragen tot de bevordering van de kennis van de Nederlandsche West-Indische kolonien. See WEST INDIË. Bijdragen . . . III. 10.[1]
Bijdragen tot de kennis van . . . voortbrengselen van Nederlandsch Indie. 1860. III. 274.[2]
Bijdragen tot de natuurkundige wetenschappen. I. 15.
Bijlert, A. van. Onderzoek van eenige grondsoorten in Deli. 1897. III. 41.[2]
The Bijou Lemon. 1876. III. 502.[1]
Bijzondere aanmerkingen over het aanleggen van landhuizen. See DE LA COURT, Pieter. 1738. III. 105.
Bijzonderheden over caoutchouc en gedrah-pertja. 1894. III. 229.
Bijzonderheden wegens het cultiveren van duingronden. 1806. IV. 159.
Bilancio delle rendite e delle spese dell' Amministrazione forestale in Francia. 1862. IV. 261.[2]
Bilberg, Immanuel. Plantarum brasiliensium. See THUNBERG, C. P. 1817. I. 341.
Bildiche und beschreibende Darstellung der . . . Natur und Kunstgärten in Europa. See DESCRIPTION des principaux parcs . . . 1812. III. 27.[2]
Die Bildung der Forstschutzbeamten. 1840. IV. 31.
Ueber Bildung und Bedeutung der Altersklassen. 1859. IV. 243.
Bilek, Fr. Die Bepflanzung der Baumschulen. 1877. III. 154.[1]
— Einfluss der Lage auf die Widerstandsfähigkeit zarterer Nutz- und Zierhölzer. 1881. III. 40.
Bílek, Johann Georg. Grundriss der Botanik für Schulen. 1854. V. x.[2]
A bill to make better provision for the planting, conservation and protection of forests. 1882. IV. 332.[2]
Billaudel. Mémoire sur les proportions relatives des espèces . . . de la flore bordelaise. 1830. I. 408.
Billberg, Gustav Johan. Botanicon Scandinaviae. 1822. I. 353.
Billebaut. Note relative à l'emploi du goudron de gaz. 1871. III. 564.[1]
Billecard, L. Notice sur le dixième arrondissement forestier, Hautes Alpes. 1889. IV. 361.
Billerbeck, Julius Heinrich Ludwig. Flora classica. 1824. I. 514.[1]
Billet, Henri. Causerie et conseils . . . sur la taille des arbres. 1879. . III. 172.
Billiard, L. C. Baccharis halimifolia. 1870. III. 754.[2]
— Les Chamaecerisiers. 1861. III. 749.[2]
— Hibiscus syriacus monstrosa plena. 1868. III. 588.[2]
— Liste d'espèces et variétés de Spiraea. 1861. III. 460.[2]
— Liste de quelques espèces de Spirées. 1866. III. 460.[2]
— Liste de Spiraea. 1864. III. 460.[2]
— Les Spiraea. 1862. III. 460.[2]
— De la taille des Spirea. 1864. III. 460.[2]
Der Billich in Krain. 1874. IV. 198.[1]
Billiet, P. Un grand Araucaria imbricata en Auvergne. 1896. III. 299.[1]
Billige Sämaschine für Wald und Feld. 1862. IV. 12.[1]
Billington, William. Acacia or Locust tree. 1842. III. 486.[1]
— Reclaiming umbrella-headed trees. 1855. III. 170.

— A series of facts . . . on . . . raising young plantations of Oaks. 1825. IV. 120.
Billot, Paul Constant. Annotations à la flore de France et d'Allemagne. 1855. I. 349.
— Quelques observations sur les centuries. 1855. I. 349.
Billotia. I. 21.
Billotte, Henri. Le phylloxéra en Lorraine. 1900. III. 575.[1]
Bills, F. D. How Roses are propagated and grown. 1895. III. 453.[1]
Billson, H. G. Notes on the tour of the forest school students in the Western Dün. 1894. IV. 378.
Billwiller, R. & Bühler, Anton. Die forstlich-meteorologischen Stationen. 1891. IV. 60.[1]
Bimbhat, DAULAT RAM. See DAULAT RAM BIMBHAT.
Binazzi, A. Il bosco e le frane profonde. 1897. IV. 70.
— Danni economici derivanti dalla distruzione dei boschi comunali. 1896. IV. 48.[1]
— Sulla delimitazione dei terreni vincolati. 1896. IV. 329.
— Il progetto che modifica la legge forestale. 1898. IV. 329.
Binder, Josef. Instruction für die Anfertigung der forstwirthschaftlichen Betriebspläne. 1881. IV. 250.[1]
Binder von Kriegelstein, Carl, Freiherr. Beyträge zur Würdigung der verschiedenen Brennstoffe. 1844. IV. 281.[1]
— Die Kiefer im Urgebirge. 1852. II. 46.[1]
— Materialien zur Bildung forstwissenschaftlicher Grundbegriffe. 184. ? IV. 101.
— Sind unsere Waldungen im Stande den Bedarf des Landes zu decken? 1843. IV. 278.[2]
— Ueber Sinn und Wesen der periodischen Durchforstungen. 1834. IV. 173.
— Über die Verbindung des Wald- und Feldbaues. 1836. IV. 133.
— Vorträge: 1. Über die Verbindung des Wald- und Feldbaues. 1836. IV. 471.
Bindseil, E. Einfache und zusammengesetzte Bestandesformen. 1887. IV. 128.
— Einiges über Beseitigung bezw. Pflege der . . . Vorwüchse. 1887. IV. 169.[1]
— Empfiehlt es sich . . . die Erziehung von Starkholz im gruppenweisen Stande anzustreben? 1887. IV. 128.
— Empfiehlt sich der Anbau der Weymouthskiefer? 1887. IV. 469.
— Gehört die Aspe zu den Forstunkräutern? 1887. IV. 486.[2]
— Pritchardia grandis. 1884. III. 326.[2]
— Wo empfiehlt sich im allgemeinen die Saat? 1887. IV. 142.
Binet, Paul. See PREVOST, J. L & BINET, Paul.
Bingham, C. T. Note on the sea-borne export trade in timber from Tenasserim. 1893. IV. 407.[2]
Bingham, J. Evidence on the Peach and Nectarine mystery. 1850. II. 276.[1]
Bingham, Mrs R. F. The Eucalyptus and the honey bee. 1890. II. 623.[2]
— Medicinal plants growing wild in Santa Barbara. 1890. III. 63.[1]
Bingley, William. Practical introduction to botany. 1817. I. 85.
— Useful knowledge. 1808. III. 217.
Binnendijk, Simon. Sur quelques arbres d'ornement . . . de Duitenzorg. 1076. I. 68.[1]
— See also TEYSMANN, J. E. & BINNENDIJK, Simon.
— & Teysmann, J. E. Nieuwe plantensoorten in 's Lands plantentuin. 1852. I. 469.[1]
Binns, John A. A treatise on practical farming. 1803. III. 132.[1]
Binswanger, Max. Analysis of barks of Rhamnus. 1850. III. 542.[1]
— Pharmakologische Studien über Rhamnus. 1850. III. 542.[1]
— Rinde von Rhamnus Frangula. 1850. III. 543.[1]
Binz, Carl. Das Chinin. 1875. III. 721.
— Lectures on pharmacology. 1884. III. 259.[1]
— Vorlesungen über Pharmakologie. 1884. III. 259.[1]
Binz, F. C. Antiseptisk Behandling ved Stikning. 1886. III. 166.
— Das mehrmalige Blühen von Obstgehölzen. 1887. I. 221.
Binzer, C. A. L. von. Die Bewaldungsverhältnisse . . . in Schleswig-Holstein. 1871. IV. 354.
— Die Communal-Forstwirthschaft im Regierungsbezirke Arnsberg. 1875. IV. 308.[2]
— Holzpflanzen-Kalender. 1874. I. 225, IV. 73.[1]
— Hülfs-Tafeln zum Gebrauch für praktische Forstbeamte. 1871. I. 225, IV. 72, 230.

Binzer, C. A. L. von (*continued*).
— Insekten-Kalender. 1878. IV. 207.
— Die Oberaufsicht des Staates über die Waldungen. 1876. IV. 285.[2]
— Sammlung der wichtigsten Instruktionen . . . für kgl. preuss. Forstschutsbeamte. 1871. IV. 320.
— Schädliche und nützliche Forstinsekten. 1880. IV. 92.
Biörlingsson, Karl Julius. De elementis physiologiae plantarum. 1828. I. 146.
Biörn, Sören. Über die Erlen und deren Behandlung. 1817. IV. 488.[2]
— Raut oka na pożytki z przyzwoitego traktowania Wierzb pruskich wynikajace. 1804. III. 347.
— Uebersicht der . . . Benutzung der preussischen Weidenarten. 1804. III. 347.
— Ueber die vortheilhafteste Behandlungs-Methode bei Besamung . . . der Kiefern. 1807. IV. 145, *471*.
Biographical memoir of Father Rasles. 1826. III. 262.[1]
Bioletti, Frederic T. Californian flowering shrubs. 1894. I. 320.
— The causes of frogging and bloating of Prunes. 1896. III. 433.[2]
— The Olive knot. 1898. III. 678.[1]
— & Colby, G. E. Olives. 1899. III. 676.[2]
Biolley, H. E. Atmosphère et accroissement. 1897. IV. 543.[1]
— Le cantonnement de la forêt dans les pâturages boisés. 1900. IV. 136.[1]
— À propos de la classification uniforme des produits forestiers. 1896. IV. 396.[2]
— Une question de méthode. 1893. IV, 252.
— *See also* BLONAY, H. de, BIOLLEY, H. & JOREZ, H.
Biological society of Washington. Proceedings. I. 5.
Biologische Abtheilung für Land- und Forstwirthschaft, Kaiserliches Gesundheitsamt Berlin. *See* KAISERLICHES GESUNDHEITSAMT BERLIN . . . I. 13.
Biologisches Centralblatt. I. 11.
Biot, Jean Baptiste. Sur un caractère optique. 1833. I. 156.[1]
— Expériences sur l'essence liquide . . . remise par M. Felouze. 1841. III. 611.[1]
— Sur le mouvement et la nature de la sève. 1833. I. 163.
— Nouveaux faits pour servir à l'histoire de la végétation. 1833. I. 172.
— Observations sur la difference physique qui existe entre l'amidou et la dextrine. 1837. I. 139.
— Rapport sur un mémoire de M. Pallas, relatif à l'influence de la fructification. 1842. I. 157.
— Remarques scientifiques, à l'occasion de la lettre de M. Boucherie. 1841. I. 163, *IV. 417*.
— & Pasteur, Louis. Observations optiques sur la populine. 1852. II. 96.[2]
Birbal. The manufacture of turpentine . . . Dehra Dûn. 1900. IV. 437.[1]
— & Upendranath Kanjilal. Rearing India-rubber plants in Dehra Dun. 1900. IV. 519.[1]
Birch, Deburgh. Topographical report on the Neilgherries. 1838. I. 472.
The Birch. 1842. IV. 491.[1]
Birdwood, *Sir* George Christopher Molesworth. Catalogue of the economic products . . . of Bombay. 1862. III. 278.
— Catalogue of the vegetable productions . . . of Bombay. 1862. III. 278.
— Frankincense or olibanum. 1871. III. 509.[2]
— On the genus Boswellia. 1870. II. 416.[2]
— Indian forestry. - 1884. IV. 378.
— Sweet Chestnuts. 1892. III. 360.[1]
— & others. Reports on the cultivation of the Spanish Chestnut. 1892. III. 359.[1]
Birdwood, Herbert Mills. A catalogue of the flora of Matheran. 1886. I. 475.[1]
— The hill forests of western India. 1898. IV. 378.
Biré, de FONTAINES. *See* FONTAINES BIRÉ, de.
Birkbeck, George. Extracts from a lecture on the preservation of timber. 1835. IV. 417.
— A lecture on the preservation of timber. · 1835. IV. 417.
Birkbeck, Robert. Eucalyptus in this country. 1899. III. 634.[1]
Die Birke saugt den Boden aus. 1853. IV. 490.[1]
Die Birke und ihr Werth als Forstholz. 1857. IV. 490.[1]
Birkett, Herbert. New plan of watering street trees. 1878. III. 211.[2]
Birkholz, Adam Michael, (*praeses*). De corticis peruviani virtute. 1785. III. 720.

Birkinger, X. Die Rose. 1891. III. 450.
Birmingham, William. On the Larch grown on Killerton. 1864. IV. 452.[1]
The Birmingham botanic garden. III. 16.
Birmingham natural history and philosophical society. Proceedings. *See* BIRMINGHAM PHILOSOPHICAL SOCIETY. I. 17.
Birmingham philosophical society. Proceedings. I. 17.
Birnbaum, Karl. Zur Waldschutzfrage. 1870. IV. 50.
Birnie, D. Bestrijding van de rupsenplaag in Koffietuinen. 1896. III. 736.
Birno, Franz. Vollständige Anweisung zur Holzfärberei. 1804. IV. 422.[2]
Biroli, Giovanni. Catalogus plantarum Horti bot. novariensis. 1810. I. 61.
— Catalogus plantarum Regii horti botanici taurinensis. 1813. I. 62.
— Catalogus stirpium . . . taurinensis. 1813. I. 62.
— Flora aconiensis. 1808. I. 425.
— Flora economica . . . dell' Agogna. 1805. III. 88.[1]
Biron, Claude. Curiositez de la nature et de l'art. 1703. III. 266.
Bisceglia, Vito. Sulla flora della provincia di Bari. 1809. III. 271.[2]
Bischof, Karl Gustav Christoph. *See* NEES VON ESENBECK, C. G., BISCHOF, C. G. & ROTHE, H. A.
Bischof, Karl Wilhelm. De alcalibus in plantis. 1848. I. 175.
Bischoff, Gottlieb Wilhelm. Beiträge zur Flora Deutschlands. 1851. V. XIX.[2]
— On the botanical origin of Senna leaves. · 1850. II. 342.[2]
— Die Botanik in ihren Grundrissen. 1848. V. IX.[2]
— Die botanische Kunstsprache. 1822. · I. 70.
— Ueber die Cassia-Arten, welche . . . Sennesblätter liefern. 1850. II. 342.[2]
— Ueber Cassia Ehrenbergii. 1844. II. 343.[1]
— Grundriss der medicinischen Botanik. 1831. III. 57.
— Handbuch der botanischen Terminologie. 1829. I. 70.
— Lehrbuch der Botanik. 1834. I. 87.
— Medicinisch-pharmaceutische Botanik. 1843. III. 57.
— Plantae medicinales secundum methodum Candollei. 1829. III. 56.
— Plantarum species novae in catalogo seminum Horti bot. heidelbergensis. 1848. I. 47.
— Wörterbuch der beschreibenden Botanik. 1839. I. 70.
Bischoff, Theodor Ludwig Wilhelm von. De vera vasorum plantarum spiralium structura. 1829. I. 33.
Biscoe, W. F. Lebdieropsis [*sic*] orbicularis. 1896. III. 520.[1]
Biscup, C. Anbau des Götterbaumes. 1877. IV. 525.
Biseau d'Hauteville, (de. Note sur le froid anormal de la nuit du 17 au 18 mai dernier. 1871. III. 48.
Bisexual Hazel. 1895. II. 121.[2]
Über den bisherigen Verlauf und Erfolg . . . Anbauversuche mit ausländischen Holzarten. 1884. IV. 125.[2]
Bishop, A. C. The ancient forests of Hants. 1881. IV. 358.[1]
— The New forest. 1881. IV. 358.[1]
Bishop, David. Casual botany. 1829. I. 244.[1]
Bishop, J. B. Peril to forest reserves. 1898. IV. 179.[1]
Bishop, James Nathaniel. A catalogue of all phænogamous plants . . . in the state of Connecticut. 1885, I. 315.
Bishop, Thomas. Report on the introduction of . . . forest trees. 1837. III. 306.[1]
Bisschop-Grevelinck, Arnold Hermann. *See* GREVELINCK, A. H. BISSCHOP-.
Bisschop van Tuinen, K. Diersoorten nuttig voor landbouw of houtteelt. 1896. III. 95.
— Nederlandsche planten.. 1874. III. 77.
Bisset, G. F. Nouvelles expériences relatives à la désinfection antiphylloxérique. 1888. III. 574.
Bisset, William. Unusual blooming of the Hawthorn. 1879. II. 262.[2]
Bissmarck, Fredrik August. Botanico-oeconomisk afhandling om Berberis-buskens nytta och skada. *See* RETZIUS, A. J. 1807. IV. 202,[2] *III. 394.*[1]
Bitely, N. H. More about the yellows. 1882. III. 441.[1]
Bitler, F. L. The present forest area of Pennsylvania. 1894. I. 312, *IV. 77.*[1]
Bitter, Georg. Ergebnisse einer Reise nach dem Pacific. 1900. I. 510.[1]
— Die phanerogamische Pflanzenwelt der Insel Laysan. 1900. I. 510.[1]
Bittersweet, (*pseud.*). The Climbing Staff. 1890. III. 532.[1]
Bittinger. Forests of Canada. 1899. IV. 337.[2]

Bittner. Ungarns Forstwirthschaft auf der Millenniumsaus-stellung in Budapest. 1896. IV. 21.[2]
Bittner, (*Kratzkau*). Lässt sich die Obstbaumzucht mit der Waldwirtschaft verbinden? 1881. IV. 134.[2]
— Ueber die Verbindung der Obstbaumzucht mit der Wald-wirthschaft. 1880. IV..134.[2]
Biuso, S. Monografia sul Fico d'India in Sicilia. 1879. II. 596.[1]
Bivona, Andrea. Sull' importanza de' boschi. 1844. IV. 43.
Bivona-Bernardi, Antonio. Sicularum plantarum centuria. 1806. I. 431.
— Stirpium rariorum . . . in Sicilia . . . descriptiones. 1813. II. 359.[2]
Bivort, Alexandre. Les fruits du jardin Van Mons. 1868. III. 77.
— & B., L. Album de pomologie. 1847. III. 77.
Bixio, Alexander. Der Landwirth des neunzehnten Jahr-hunderts. 1846. III. 104.
— *See also* BAILLY DE MERLIEUX, C., BIXIO, Alexandre & MALEPEYRE.
Bizarrerie sur un Oranger portugais. 1831. II. 402.[2]
Bizio, Bartholomeo. Analyse du liquide . . . dans le fruit du Coco. 1833. II. 67.[2]
— Sulla condizione dell' azoto nella gomma arabica. 1844. II. 323.[2]
— Memoria sopra una lacca verde ottenuta dal Caffé. 1819. III. 740.[1]
Bizot de Fonteny. Cubage des bois sans tarif. 1897. IV. 219.
— Rapport fait . . . relativement à la protection des oiseaux. 1893. IV. 326.
Bjalobrzeski, M. Chemische Untersuchung der Folia Bucco. 1896. III. 495.[2]
Bjaur, Jacob. Incrementa botanices proxime praeterlapsi semisaeculi. *See* LINNÉ, Carl von. 1753. I. 79.[1]
Bjerkander, Clas. Anmärkning om socker på Gran. 1784. II. 36.[2]
— Anmärkningar, huru tidigt trän . . . blommade. 1794. I. 223.[1]
— Anmärkningar öfver några träd och örter. 1778. III. 44.[1]
— Anmärkningar öfver träds och örters växande på Kinne-kulle. 1776. I. 352.
— Anmärkningar vid hvilken tid trän och örter fingo mogen frugt och frön innevarande år. 1794. I. 223.[1]
— Anmärkningar vid örternas utdunstning. 1773. I. 169.[1]
— Beskrifning på en härtilg okänd hallonmask. 1781. III. 458.[2]
— Beskrifning på hallon-mask. 1783. III. 458.[2]
— Beskrifning på tvenne maskar. 1785. III. 188.[2]
— Biens flora. 1774. III. 224.[1]
— Blomster-almanach i Vester-Göthland. 1786. I. 222.[2]
— Blomster-almanach i Wester-Göthland. 1780. I. 222.[2]
— Försök til et thermometrum florae. 1770. I. 222.[2]
— Förtekning på de örter, som blommade i November. 1789. I. 223.[1]
— Ytterligare försök med svenska thermometern insatt i lefvande träd. 1792. I. 181.
Bjerregaard, H. Endnu et Opraab til Træplantning. 1840. IV. 39.[2]
— En kort Anviisning til Træavl. 1828. III. 100.[1]
Björkmann, C. A. T. Handbok i skogs-skötsel. 1868. IV. 103.[1]
Björnlund, Benedictus. *See* BJÖRNLUND, Bengt.
Björnlund, Bengt. Fundamentum differentiae specificae plantarum. 1771. I. 250.
— Händelser, rörande Ledi . . . bruk. 1782. III. 653.[1]
— Rön, om värkan af häggbarks decoct. 1784. III. 439.[1]
Bjørnsen, S. M. Bœgebesaaninger paa større Sletter og fri Mark. 1857. IV. 494.
Björnström, Fredrik Johan. Bidrag til kännedomen om Stockholms skärgårds-flora. 1853. II. 30.[2]
Bjurzon, J. Skandinaviens wäxtfamiljer i sammandrag. 1846. I. 354.
Blachère, E. Le reboisement dans l'Ardèche. 1877. IV. 162.
Black. Report on the Teak trade in Siam. 1895. IV. 538.[1]
— De teakhandel in Siam. 1895. IV. 538.[1]
Black, Allan A. Catalogue of Japan plants. 1861. I. 462.
— Mexico vergeleken met Ceylon als een Koffie produceerend land. 1895. III. 740.[1]
— Systematisches Verzeichniss aller seit Thunberg in Japan gesammelten Pflanzen. 1861. I. 462.
Black, John J. The cultivation of the Peach and the Pear. 1886. III. 133.
Black Birch, Sweet Birch, Cherry Birch. 1898. II. 119.[2]

The black-knot of the Plum and Cherry. 1892. III. 431.[1]
Black resinous varnish used at Silbet in Bengal. 1821. III. 524,[2] 589.[1]
The Black Walnut. 1879. II. 113.[2]
The Black Walnut. 1885. II. 113,[2] III. 354.[2]
The Black Walnut tree. 1880. IV. 488.[1]
Blackie, George S. Contributions to the medical flora of Nashville. 1860. III. 264.[1]
— On the Cornus florida of the United States. 1861. II. 655.[1]
Blacklaw, A. Scott. *See* CRÜWELL, G. A. & BLACKLAW, A. S.
Blackman, F. Frost. Experimental researches on vegetable assimilation. 1895. I. 171.
— Recherches sur l'assimilation et la respiration. 1895. I. 171.
Blackman, Vernon H. On the cytological features of fertiliza-tion . . . in Pinus silvestris. 1898. II. 48.[2]
Blacknall, O. W. New and enlarged manual on berry fruit culture. 1900. III. 148.[1]
Blackstone, John. Fasciculus plantarum circa Harefield. 1737. I. 394, V. xx.[2]
— Specimen botanicum. 1746. I. 394.
Blackwell, Elizabeth. A curious herbal. 1737. I. 291.
— Herbarium Blackwellianum. 1737. I. 291.
— Vermehrtes und verbessertes Blackwellisches Kräuter-Buch. 1737. I. 291.
Blackwood's Edinburgh magazine. I. 17.
Bladon, James. Monstrosities in the flowers of a Fuchsia. 1843. II. 643.[1]
Bladziekte bij de Koffieboomen. 1879. III. 735.
Bläscke, W. *See* BLÄSKE, W.
Blaese, G. H. Die natürlichen Familien der wildwachsenden Phanerogamen der baltischen Provinzen. 1868. I. 363.
Bläske, W. Die Königs-Fichte im Forst-Reviere Nessel-grund. 1842. IV. 460.[1]
— Die Sumpfkiefer. 1842. IV. 464.[2]
Blagrave, Joseph. The epitome of the art of husbandry. 1675. III. 107.
— New additions to the art of husbandry. 1675. III. 107.
— Supplement or enlargement to Nich. Culpepper's English physician. 1666. III. 79.
Blaikie, Francis. The farmer's instructor for the planting . . . of forest trees. 1810. IV. 108.[1]
— A treatise on the management of hedges. 1821. III. 214.[2]
Blaikie, James. Observations on the uses to which Alder, Birch, Hazel . . . may be applied. 1829. IV. 433.[2]
Blain, Frédéric. De l'acclimatation en France du Bombyx Cynthia. 1861. III. 507.[1]
— Notice pratique pour servir à l'éducation du ver à soie du Chène. 1866. IV. 502.[1]
— Rapport sur une éducation en Anjou du ver du Chène. 1865. IV. 501.[1]
Blair, Patrick. Botanick essays. 1720. I. 31.
— Miscellaneous observations in the practise of physick. 1718. III. 238.[1]
— Observations upon the generation of plants. 1723. I. 198.
— Pharmaco-botanologia. 1723. I. 290, V. xvi.[1]
Blair, William N. The building materials of Otago. 1877. IV. 402.[1]
— The building materials of Otago. 1879. IV. 402.[1]
Blake, James. On paralysis. 1878. III. 569.[2]
— Remedy for the phylloxera. 1877. III. 570.[1]
Blake, Joseph. *See* GOODALE, G. L. & BLAKE, Joseph.
Blake, Stephen. The compleat gardiners practice. 1664. III. 107.
Blake, William Phipps. On the great trees of Mariposa. 1863. II. 50.[2]
— Note upon a peculiarity of the " Redwood." 1856. II. 49.[2]
— Notes upon the grove of " Mammoth trees." 1856. II. 50.[2]
— Notice of a peculiar astringent gum . . . of the Sequoia gigantea. 1863. II. 50.[2]
— Origin of the submerged forests in the Columbia River. 1863. I. 320.
Blanc. Établissement . . . d'une plantation de Café dans l'ouest de la Cochinchine. 1900. III. 732.[1]
Blanc, (*abbé*). Essai de botanique pratique. 1784. III. 51.
Blanc, A. A wonderland of Cactuses; novelties, curiosities. 1890. III. 619.
— & Co. Catalogue and hints on Cacti. 1886. III. 619.
— Hints on Cacti. 1886. III. 619.
Blanc, Édouard. L'arbre à prières de Goumboum. 1895. I. 298.

Blanc, Édouard (continued).
— L'Arbre des Lotophages. 1889. II. 500.[2]
— Étude sur le résinage. 1885. IV. 436.[2]
— La forêt de Gommiers du Bled-Tahla. 1887. II. 328.[2]
— La forêt de Gommiers du Bled Thalah. 1889. IV. 379.[1]
— Les Landes, leur passé et leur avenir. 1883. IV. 361.
— Note sur l'arbre à prières du monastère de Goumboum. 1896. I. 298, II. 715.[2]
— Notes botaniques recueillis. 1889. I. 486.
— Notes recueillies . . . dans le sud de la Tunisie. 1889. I. 486.
— Recherches sur le Lotus d'Afrique. 1889. III. 544.[1]
— Le sud de la Tunisie. 1889. III. 130.[2]
Blanc, Léon. Déformations produites sur les tiges , . . de Saule. 1892. II. 104.[1]
— Fasciation de Sambucus nigra. 1898. II. 841.[2]
Blancard, Stephanus. See BLANKAART, Stephen.
Blanchan, Neltje. Nature's garden. 1900. I. 239,[1] 308.[2]
Blanchard, Charles Émile. Sur une cicadelle. 1880. III. 563.
— La connaissance des flores et des faunes. 1885. I. 300.
— De la dissemination des espèces végétales et animales. 1885. I. 300.
— Sur une expérience devant être exécutée en vue de la destruction du phylloxera. 1876. III. 569.[1]
— Notas sueltas. Variabilidad de las especies. 1891. IV. 543.[1]
— Note sur Coûi-dean. 1869. III. 516.[2]
— À propos de Reiset, Jules. Mémoire sur les dommages causés . . . par le hanneton. 1867. IV. 202.
— Rapport sur un mémoire de M. le Dr. Aug. Vinson. 1863. III. 469.[1]
— Remarques à la suite des observations verbales de M. Pasteur. 1880. III. 563.
— See also CONDAMINE & BLANCHARD, C. E.
Blanchard, Edme. Traité de la coupe des bois. 1729. IV. 392.
Blanchard, Fréd. Des arbres à flèche. 1859. III. 292.
Blanchard, J. H. Acacia dealbata. 1883. III. 464.[2]
— Aperçu sur la végétation de l'ancienne Armorique. 1882. I. 416.
— Araucaria imbricata. 1892. III. 299.[1]
— Aristolochia labiosa Ker. 1888. III. 386.[1]
— Le Bambusa gracilis des horticulteurs. 1886. III. 316.[1]
— Bignonia unguis. 1884. III. 705.
— Camellia Donkelaari [sic]. 1893. III. 599.[1]
— Le Chamaerops excelsa dans l'ouest. 1887. III. 331.[2]
— Curieuse germination de l'Araucaria Bidwillii. 1892. II. 26.[1]
— Le Dracaena indivisa. 1888. III. 335.
— Effets produits . . . par les froids de 1890–91. 1891. III. 49.[1]
— Encore l'Araucaria imbricata. 1880. III. 299.
— Les Eucalyptus dans l'ouest. 1890. IV. 530.
— Les Eucalyptus dans l'ouest de la France. 1888. III. 634.[1]
— Le Figuier de Roscoff. 1879. II. 151.[1]
— Floraison du Macrozamia spiralis. 1895. II. 6.[1]
— Le Néflier à fruits sans noyaux. 1893. III. 429.[2]
— Observations relatives à l'action des derniers hivers. 1872. III. 48.
— Olearia Forsteri. 1888. III. 756.[1]
— Une particularité de l'Araucaria imbricata. 1884. II. 26.[2]
— Phénomène morphologique observé sur un If. 1891. II. 10.[2]
— Pinus insignis Dougl. 1890. III. 308.[2]
— Pittosporum tenuifolium. 1888. III. 416.[1]
— Quelques plantes remarquables du Jardin des plantes de Tours. 1895. I. 59.
— Quelques vieux Chênes bretons. 1894. II. 139.[1]
— La rusticité des végétaux exotiques en Bretagne. 1891. III. 49.[1]
— Rusticité du Livistona chinensis. 1885. III. 327.[1]
— Une visite au domaine de Catros. 1887. I. 59.
— Un Yucca gloriosa gigantesque. 1866. III. 340.[1]
— See also PAUGAM, L. & BLANCHARD, J.
Blanchard, Théophile. Liste de noms patois de plantes. 1900. I. 74.[2]
Blanche, Emmanuel. Jardin des plantes, Rouen. 1869. I. 58.
— & Malbranche, A. F. Catalogue des plantes . . . de la Seine-Inférieure. 1864. I. 413, V. XXII.[1]
Blanchet, Charles. Des arbres sur lesquels on rencontre le Gui. 1864. II. 179.[1]

— Catalogue des plantes vasculaires du sudouest de la France. 1891. I. 417.
Blanchet, Rodolphe. Catalogue des plantes . . . dans le canton de Vaud. 1836. I. 434.
— Essai sur l'art de tailler la Vigne. 1844. III. 172, 548.[2]
— Mémoire sur . . . production de l'écorce de Chêne en Suisse. 1858. IV. 505.
— Notice sur les différents plants de Vigne. 1852. III. 546.
Blanchis, Moïse Bertoni de. Influence des basses températures. 1886. I. 212, IV. 531.[1]
Blanck, Siegfried. Ueber die Wirkungskraft einiger Strychninsalze. 1895. III. 684.[1]
Blanckmeister, von. Forstliche Mittheilungen aus Russland. 1875. IV. 31.
Blanco, F. M. Flora de Filipinas. 1837. I. 464.[1]
Blanco, José GARCÍA. See GARCÍA BLANCO, José.
Blanco y Fernandez, Antonio. Arboricultura. 1864. III. 114.[1]
— Ensayo de zoología agrícola y forestal. 1859. IV. 90.[1]
— Introduccion al estudio de las plantas. 1845. I. 88.[1]
— Tratado elemental de botánica. 1834. I. 87.
Bland, Thomas. On the relations of the flora and fauna of Santa Cruz. 1880. I. 336.
Blandeau. Étrennes littéraires aux grands hommes. 1824. II. 738.
Blandford, Walter Fielding Holloway. Insects injurious to Coniferae. 1892. III. 295.[2]
Blanford von. On the influence of Indian forests. 1887. IV. 49.[1]
Blankaart, Stephen. Haustus polychresti. See BONTEKOE, Cornelis & BLANKAART, Stephen. 1686. III. 221.[2]
— See also BONTEKOE, Cornelis & BLANKAART, Stephen.
Blankenburg, (Oberförster). Ueber das Aufästen der Eichen. 1872. IV. 506.
— Beantwortung der Frage . . . Weidenstecklingspflanzungen im Frühjahre oder im Herbste. 1853. IV. 487.[1]
— Bericht über den Frass der Arvicola glareola. 1858. IV. 197.[2]
— Bericht über die . . . forstliche Reise in Deutschland. 1858. IV. 348.[2]
— Durchforstungs-Erträge von Eichenschonungen. 1864. IV. 512.
— Ueber die Folgen der vorjährigen Oderüberschwemmung. 1855. IV. 185.[1]
— Zur Frage. Wie klein kann ein Forstgrundstück sein? 1851. IV. 242.
— Monographie der Strehlener Berge. 1850. IV. 352.
— See also WAGNER, BLANKENBURG & ROSENBERG, Baron von.
— & Lüttwitz, Baron von (Oberförster, Nimkau). Gutachten über die Baden'sche Baum-Säge. 1863. IV. 170.
— & Pannewitz, von, (Oberförster, Panten). Bericht über die . . . in die Trachenberger Fürstenthumsforsten vorgenommenen Exkursionen. 1857. IV. 353.
Blankenhorn, Adolph. An alle diejenigen, die sich mit dem Studium der Phylloxera-Frage befassen. 1878. III. 760.
— Aufruf zur Einsendung von Objecten für die . . . ampelographische Versuchsstation. 1876. III. 760.
— Beiträge zur Frage der natürlichen Feinde der Phylloxera. 1877. III. 760.
— Catalogue des préparations du phylloxéra. 1880. III. 61.
— Les ennemis naturels du phylloxéra. 1877. III. 570.[2]
— Ueber eine zu errichtende internationale Phylloxeracommission. 1877. III. 760.
— List of preparations of phylloxera. 1880. III. 761.
— Ueber die Phylloxera vastatrix. 1876. III. 569.[2]
— Ueber die Phylloxera vastatrix. 1878. III. 570.[2]
— A tutti coloro che fanno studii e ricerche sulla phylloxera. 1878. III. 760.
— Verzeichniss der Präparate der Phylloxera. 1880. III. 61.
— & Moritz, J. Die Wurzellaus des Weinstockes. 1875. III. 567.[1]
Blanquart de Sept-Fontaines, Louis Marie. See SEPT-FONTAINES, Louis Marie BLANQUART DE.
Blanqueo de la pasta de papel por el ozono. 1890. IV. 430.
Blanqueo instantáneo de la pasta de papel. 1886. IV. 430.
Blanqui, Jérôme Adolphe. Du déboisement des montagnes. 1846. IV. 282.[2]
— Voyage en Bulgarie pendant l'année 1841. 1843. II. 15.[2]
Blas. Sur la thévétine. 1869. III. 691.[2]

Blaschke, Eduard. Index plantarum . . . a cel. Karelin et Kirilow in regionibus altaicis . . . collectarum. 1842. I. 453.[2]
— Topographia medica Portus novi-archangelscensis. 1842. I. 531.[1]
Blasdale, Walter C. The California Nut Pine. 1895. II. 42.[1]
Blase, S. W. Amtliche Vorschrift über die Berechnung des Waldwerthes. 1865. IV. 255.
— Aufhilfe des Buchenaufschlags in Nadelholzbeständen. 1848. IV. 494.
— Ueber ein einfaches Baum-Mess-Instrument. 1865. IV. 215.
— Nachrichten über die Kiefernschütte. 1853. IV. 475.
Blasio, Abele de. Influenza dell' uretano sulla Mimosa pudica. 1889. II. 373.[1]
Blasius, I. H. Reise im europäischen Russland. 1844. I. 361.
Blasius, Wilhelm. Herbstblüthen von Aesculus Hippocastanum. 1897. II. 482.[2]
Blass, J. Untersuchungen über die physiologische Bedeutung des Siebtheils. 1890. I. 134.[1]
Blasting tree stumps. 1900. IV. 387.[1]
Blasy, E. Pinus Cembra in der Tatra. 1869. II. 41.[1]
Blatchley, Willis Stanley. Notes on some phanerogams new . . . to the state. 1897. I. 316.
Blath, (Prof. Dr.)." Die Blutlaus, ihr Auftreten. 1899. III. 192.[1]
Blau, A. Zur gegenwärtigen Lage des Obstbaues in den baltischen Gouvernements. 1885. III. 120.[1]
Blau, Ernst Otto Friedrich Hermann. Reisen in Bosnien und der Herzegowina. 1877. I. 447.
Blauel, J. C. A. Ueber den den Mangel des Holzes . . . ersetzenden Lerchenbaum. 1830. IV. 449.
Blauw, R. J. Sterfte in Populieren. 1879. III. 344.[2]
Das Blauwerden des Kiefernholzes. 1898. IV. 482.[2]
Blavet, J. L. See NOLIN & BLAVET, J. L.
Blażek, Józef & Pawlikowski, Gwalbert. Spis roślin w pomarańczarni i szklarni ogrodu Medyckiego. 1834. I. 66.[1]
Blażka, František. O Tisu vyhynujicím stromu lesním v západním Prusku. 1894. II. 11.[1]
— Zřůdnost Jablka. 1899. II. 267.[1]
Blechynden, A. H. Note on Cacao. 1886. III. 592.[1]
— Note on the cultivation of the Tea plant in the Andamans. 1890. III. 604.[1]
— Note on the Muddar or Ak. 1886. III. 692.[2]
Blechynden, Richard, (jr.). Divi-divi, or American Sumach. 1890. III. 468.[2]
— Final report on the . . . cultivation of certain fibre-yielding plants. 1890. III. 235.[1]
— Some suggestions in favor of the hybridization . . . of the Tea-plant. 1891. III. 604.[1]
Bleeker, Pieter. Bijdrage tot de kennis der genees- en artsenijmengkunde onder de Chinezen. 1844. III. 273.[1]
— Bijdrage tot de medische topographie van Batavia. 1843. III. 275.[1]
— Bijdragen tot de geneeskundige topographie van Batavia. 1844. III. 275.[2]
— Catalogus van de Bibliotheek van het Bataviaasch genootschap van kunsten en wetenschappen. 1853. I. 2.
— Enumeratio specierum plantarum . . . in insula Nusa Kambangan. 1850. I. 465.
— Fragmenten eener reis over Java. 1849. I. 468.
— De invoering der volkszijdeteelt in Nederlandsch Indie. 1863. III. 148.[1]
— On Nutmeg culture in the Banda Islands. 1861. III. 402.[2]
— Reis door de Minahassa. 1856. I. 465.
Bleeker, S. Geschiedkundig overzigt der theorien over de bevruchting. 1871. I. 201.[1]
— Handboek over bloemisterij. 1897. III. 106.[1]
— See also IDE, A. & BLEEKER, S.
— & Greef, H. de. Appel en Peer. 1900. III. 140.[1]
Bleekrode, S. Getah-lahoe, eene nieuwe soort plantenwas. 1854. III. 371.[2]
— Grondstoffen voor papierbereiding. 1857. III. 235.[1]
— De Klapper (Kokos) olie. 1857. III. 323.[2]
— Nog iets over . . . Inkoe en weifa. 1856. III. 488,[1] 542.[1]
— Note sur la getah-laboe. 1854. III. 371.[2]
— Notice sur la gutta-percha de Surinam. 1857. II. 699,[1] III. 231.

— De Surinaamsche getah-pertja. 1857. III. 668.[1]
— Verdere bijzonderheden over het Chineesche groen. 1857. III. 542.[1]
Bleekrode, S. A., (jr.). Onderzoek naar het vetgehalte der zaden van Penaga. 1868. III. 224.[2]
— Onderzoek van eenige Damar-soorten. 1863. II. 25.[2]
— & Gon Netscher, van der. De Koffiebereiding. 1861. III. 739.
Blegny, Nicolas de. Le bon usage du thé. 1687. III. 244.
— Le remède anglois pour la guérison des fièvres. 1682. III. 719.
Bleibinhaus, J. See WEISS, J. E., KRAUSE, M. & BLEIBINHAUS, J.
Bleicher, Marie Gustave. Nouveaux aperçus sur la théorie des rapports botanico-chimiques. 1862. I. 151.[1]
Bleisch, Eduard. De Amygdalino. 1838. II. 272.[2]
Blengini, Domenico. Expériences sur la quantité de potasse. 1839. III. 582.
Blenk, Paul. Die durchsichtigen Punkte der Blätter. 1884. I. 110.
— Ueber die durchsichtigen Punkte in den Blättern. 1884. I. 110.
Blenkarn, John. British timber trees. 1859. IV. 108.[2]
Blériot & others. Note sur une Vigne très remarquable. 1846. II. 509.[1]
Blessner, G. Flora sacra. 1864. I. 513.
Bleuel, Georg. Ueber den Einfluss des Streuentzugs. 1891. IV. 72, 495.
Bley, Franz. Die Flora des Brockens. 1896. I. 532.[2]
Blézy. Traitement de la maladie de la Vigne. 1854. III. 576.
Ein Blick in die Gemeindewaldwirtschaft im Kanton Zürich. 1854. IV. 365.
Bligh, W. G. Metal versus wooden sleepers. 1888. IV. 424.[1]
Blight, Robert. Mistletoe. 1898. II. 174.[1]
Blijdenstein, A. J. Iets over de cultuur van buitenlandsche Dennensoorten. 1889. IV. 126.[2]
— Wat er uit een heideveld door ontginning worden kann. 1890. IV. 160.[1]
— & Brants, I. R. De boschbeplanting op de nederlandsche zeeduinen. 1892. IV. 160.[2]
— Onderzoek omtrent de boschbeplantingen op de zeeduinen. 1890. IV. 160.[2]
— & Lovink, H. J. Verslag over den toestand der ontginning en houtteelt in ons land. 1893. IV. 356.[1]
Een blik op de vooruitzichten der Kinacultuur. 1883. III. 716.
Blik op het bestuur van Nederlandsch-Indië. 1835. III. 127.[2]
Blin, A. J. Cordyline a Dracaeny pestrolisté. 1881. III. 334.[2]
Blin, Henri. Culture de l'Olivier en Tunisie. 1896. III. 676.[2]
— Soins culturaux à donner à la Vigne. 1896. III. 557.[1]
Blin, L. See BLUM FAILLET & BLIN, L.
Blink, H. Iets over de geschiedenis der bosschen in Nederland. 1897. IV. 27.[1]
— Overzicht van de uitgestrektheid der bosschen. 1891. IV. 356.[2]
Bliss, G. The fruit grower's instructor. 1825. III. 142.
Blisson. Observations sur la grosseur extraordinaire d'un Orme. 1843. II. 143.[2]
Blüth, Walter. The English improver. 1649. III. 107.
Blitz, A. De anatomische bouw der Oost-indische Ijzerhoutsoorten. 1898. II. 761,[1] IV. 400,[2] V. XI.[1]
— Houtsoorten uit de familie der Samydaceae. 1898. II. 873.[2]
— Kurkhouten. 1899. IV. 400.[2]
Der Blitz schlägt auch in die Buchen. 1788. IV. 193.[2]
Ueber Blitzschläge in Waldungen. 1875. IV. 194.
Bloch, Georg Castaneus. Tentamen phoinicologie saerae. 1767. II. 63.[2]
Bloch, Johannes Erasmus. Horticultura danica. 1647. III
Blochwitz, Martin. Anatomia Sambuci. 1631. III. 752.[1]
— Beschreibung des Hollunders. 1631. III. 752.[1]
Block. Moyens d'activer la croissance des jeunes arbres. 1847. III. 124.[1]
Block, (Forstassistent, Braunschweig). Die . Smaliansche Formel zur Berechnung des mittleren Bestandsalters. 1888. IV. 235.[1]
Block, Hermann. Über die Bestandteile der Epheupflanze. 1888. III. 650.[1]
— Die Bestandtheile der Epheupflanze. 1888. III. 643.[1]
— Sur les principes . . . dans le Lierre. 1888. III. 643.[1]

Block, Maurice. Du rendement en graines . . . de Pin. 1856. III. 306.[2]
Blocken, Felix von. Kubik-Tafeln zur Bestimmung des Inhaltes der runden Hölzer. 1871. IV. 226.
Błocki, Bronisław. Ein Beitrag zur Flora von Ost-Galizien. 1892. II. 274.[2]
— Ér yczynek do flory Galicyi. 1881. I. 443.
— Rosa ciliato-sepala nov. spec. 1890. II. 292.[2]
— Rosa gypsicola nova spec. 1889. II. 294.[2]
— Rosa Hedevigae n. spec. 1887. II. 294.[2]
— Rosa Herbichiana n. sp. 1887. II. 294.[2]
— Rosa Knappii nova spec. 1889. II. 295.[2]
— Rosa Liechtensteinii. 1888. II. 295.[2]
— Rosa thyraica nova spec. 1889. II. 299.[2]
— Roślinność letnia i jesienna okolic Bilcza. 1880. I. 442.
— Zwei neue Cytisus-Arten. 1895. II. 349.[2]
Blöcke oder Betriebsklassen? 1855. IV. 251.[1]
Over de bloemen der Vijgen. See OVER de bloemen . . . 1772. II. 149.[2]
Bloemen Waanders, H. L. van. Nota omtrent eenige uit Banka'sche vruchten getrokken olien. 1860. III. 224.[2]
— Note sur quelques espèces d'huiles extraites de fruits. 1860. III. 224.[2]
Bloemen Waanders, P. L. van. Bijdragen tot de kenenis van het eiland Bali. 1868. III. 276.[1]
Bloemkundig woordenboek. 1821. III. 76.
Bloemkundig woordenboek. 1866. I. 71.
Blohm, Ernst. Untersuchungen über die Dicke des assimilirenden Gewebes. 1895. I. 174.
Blohmer, (Oberforstmeister). Das Verhalten gemischter Nadelholzbestände. 1870. IV. 189.[1]
Blom, Anthony. Verhandeling over den landbouw in de colonie Suriname. 1786. III. 118.[1]
Blom, Carolus Magnus. Betula hybrida, Ornäs-Björkén. 1786. II. 120.[1]
— Lignum Quassiae. See LINNÉ, Carl von. 1763. III. 508.[2]
— Het Quassie-hout uit Suriname. 1764. III. 508.[2]
Blom, G. DUFFER. See DUFFER BLOM, G.
Blomefield, Leonard. The Bournemouth Firs. 1889. II. 48.[2]
— Case of abnormal development of wood in the root of a Spanish Chestnut. 1882. II. 124.[2]
Blomqvist, Anton Gabriel. Kulovalkeista. 1888. IV. 181.[2]
— Kuusi. 187.? IV. 453.
— Mänty. 187.? IV. 472.
— Några iakttagelser rörande fröbildningens periodicitet. 1876. II. 20.[2]
— Några ord till belysning af den närvarande skogsfrågen i Finland. 1874. IV. 273.[2]
— Eine neue Methode den Holzwuchs . . . bildlich darzustellen. 1879. I. 218, IV. 217.
— Puiden karsimisesta ja hirsipuiden kasvattamisesta. 1879. IV. 171.
— Studien über den Welthandel mit Holz. 1883. IV. 273.[2]
— Suomen puulajit metsänhoidolliselta kannalta. I. 187.? IV. 472.
— Suomen puulajit metsänhoidolliselta kannalta, II. 187.? IV. 453.
— Tabeller framställande utvecklingen af jemnåriga och slutna skogsbestånd. 1872. IV. 233, 347.
— Undersökningar af tjocklekstillväxten hos timmerträd af Tall och Gran. 1897. IV. 348, 443.[1]
Blomspråk; eller, Blommornas betydelse efter Finska Runor. 1831. I. 515.
Blomsterspråket; eller, Blommornas betydelse. 1827. I. 515.
Blomstrand, Christian Wilhelm. Om barken af Rhamnus catharcica. 1861. III. 124.
Blomstrende Rhododendron ved Juletid. See GREENHOUSE Rhododendrons at Christmas. 1891. III. 655.
Blonay, Henri de. Équation de la courbe d'accroissement. 1892. IV. 234.
— Méthode destinée à déterminer l'état dans lequel la forêt donne le maximum de produits. 1898. IV. 550.[2]
— Sur la méthode du contrôle. 1897. IV. 246.
— Méthode nouvelle d'exploitation forestière. 1897. IV. 238.
— Note sur une nouvelle méthode forestière. 1890. IV. 237.
— Biolley, H. & Jobez, H. Barême du tarif conventionnel unique. 189.? IV. 218.
Blonay, Henri William de. See BOREL, William & BLONAY, H. W. de
Blondain, K. M. Der Wald als Objekt für Hypothekar. Darlehen. 1876. IV. 256.

Blondeau, (jr.). Rapport sur une thèse de M. Desnoix. 1854. III. 682.[2]
Blondeau, A. See CRAHAY, N. I. & BLONDEAU, A.
Blondeau, Ch. Action exercée par le courant d'induction. 1867. I. 231.[1]
— Sur l'irritabilité des végétaux. 1867. I. 194, II. 373.[1]
— On the irritability of plants. 1867. I. 194.
Blondeau, Lucien. Excursion forestière de juin 1899. 1899. IV. 357.[1]
— Excursion forestière en 1894. 1895. IV. 555.[2]
— Une visite aux papeteries de Virginal. 1900. IV. 430.
Blondein, K. M. Zur Borkenkäfer-Frage. 1874. IV. 92.
— Einige Bemerkungen über die Femel-Schlagswirthschaft. 1878. IV. 131.
— Die gemeine Kiefer auf theilweise nassen . . . Böden. 1875. IV. 472.
Blondein, Karl. Die gewerbliche Aufgabe der Staats-Forstwirthschaften. 1853. IV. 269.
— Die lichte Erziehung der Waldbestände. 1854. IV. 129.
Blondel, Raoul. Sur l'écorce et les graines de l'Holarrhena. 1887. III. 688.[1]
— L'industrie de la Badiane au Tonkin. 1889. III. 398.[1]
— Sur le parfum et son mode de production chez les Roses. 1889. III. 454.[1]
— Les produits odorants des Rosiers. 1889. III. 454.[1]
— Les Strophantus du commerce. 1888. III. 690.[1]
Blondus, Michael Angelus. De ancipiti ligni indici propriétate. 1542. III. 235.[2]
Błoński, Franciszek. Kilka uwag o nowych dla królestwa roślinach. 1897. I. 367.
— Przyczynek do sprawy jedno-lub wielogatunkowości Jemioly. 1900. II. 177.[2]
Bloomer, H. G. On the scientific name of the " Big trees." 1863. II. 52.[1]
Blosse, R. C. Lynch. The Wistarias. 1897. III. 491.[1]
Blot, Frédéric. Mémoire sur le puceron lanigère. 1830. III. 427.[1]
Blot, Natalis Sebastian. Quaestio botanico-medica. 1747. III. 259.[1]
Blottière, René. Étude anatomique . . . des Menispermées. 1886. II. 206.[1]
— See also HÉRAIL, J. J. M. & BLOTTIÈRE, René.
Blotz, J. F. Die Gartenkunst. 1795. III. 103.
Bloudeau, Henri. La culture selon la science. 1883. III. 113.
Blount, Sir Thomas Pope. A natural history. 1693. III. 217.
Bloxam, Andrew. Note on the British Rubi. 1848. II. 302.[2]
— On Rubus Briggsii Blox. 1869. II. 306.[2]
— Rubus obliquus Wirtg. 1870. II. 309.[1]
Bloys van Treslong Prins, A. H. J. Het enten van Kinaboomen. 1879. III. 716.
Eine blühende Araucaria excelsa. 1871. II. 26.[2]
Blühende Cunninghamia lanceolata. 1834. III. 302.[1]
Blümml, Emil K. Rhodologische Miscellaneen. 1899. II. 288.[2]
Blümml, Emil R. Die Blattgallen des Weinstockes. 1899. III. 564.[1]
Blüthe- und Reifezeiten mehrerer . . . Pflanzen . . . als Massstäbe. 1844. I. 224.[2]
Bluff, Mathias Joseph & Fingerhuth, K. A. Compendium florae Germaniae. 1825. I. 377.
Bluhm, Erich. Das Rechnungswerk eines mit einer Privatforstverwaltung verbundenen Kassenwesens. 1895. IV. 312.
Blum, J. Die Pyramideneiche bei Harreshausen. 1895. II. 136.[2]
— Die zweizeilige Sumpfcypresse. 1898. II. 51.[2]
— & Jännicke, W. Botanischer Führer durch die städtischen Anlagen in Frankfurt a / M. 1892. III. 28.[1]
Blum, O. F. Anleitung zum Studium der Botanik. 1849. I. 89.
Blum-Paillet & Blin, L. Statisque botanique de l'arrondissement St. Quentin. 1863. I. 412.
Blume. Die amerikanische Esche in den anhaltischen Elbforsten. 1885. IV. 535.[1]
Blume, Karl Ludwig, Ritter von. De alia Antiaris specie minus noxia. 1835. II. 145.[2]
— De aliis quibusdam Coryphinis Indiae orientalis. 1836. II. 61.[2]
— De aliis quibusdam Palmarum generibus . . . Arecinearum. 1836. II. 61.[2]
— Anonaceae. 1828. II. 215.[1]
— Antwoord aan den Heer W. H. de Vriese. 1850. II. 8,[2] 42.

— Balsamifluae. 1828. II. 252.¹
— Beschrijving van Calamus Draco. 1832. II. 65.²
— Beschrijving van eenige gewassen, waargenomen op cenen togt naar den Salak. 1823. I. 468.
— Bijdrage tot de kennis onzer Javaansche Eiken. 1823. II. 131.¹
— Bijdragen tot de flora ván Nederlandsch Indië. 1825. I. 468.
— Catalogus van eenige der merkwaardigste . . . gewassen . . . in 's Lands plantentuin te Buitenzorg. 1823. I· 67.²
— De Ceratolobo et Korthalsia. 1836. II. 66,¹ 70.¹
— Chloranthcae. 1828. II. 95.¹
— Collectanea ad cognitionem Myristicearum Indiae. 1835. II. 220.¹
— De Coniferis quibusdam. 1847. .II. 15.²
— Cupuliferae. 1828. II. 123.¹
— De Cycade circinali. 1848. II. 4.²
— Descriptio Laurinearum indicarum. 1835. II. 224.¹
— Dipterocarpeae. 1828. .II. 559.¹
— Over eenige Oost-indische houtsoorten. 1859. IV. 399.²
— Over eenige Oost-Indische . . . Melastomaceae. 1831. II. 635.¹
— Over eenige Oost-indische planten. 1843. III. 233.²
— Eenige waarnemingen omtrent den Culilawanboom. 1834. II. 224.¹
— Einige Bemerkungen über den Culilawan-Baum. 1834. II. 224.¹
— Ueber einige ostindische . . . Melastomaceen. 1831. II. 635.¹
— Enumeratio plantarum Javae. 1827. I. 468.
— Flora Javae. 1828. I. 468.
— De genere Calamo. 1847. II. 62.¹
— De genere Cardiopteris. 1847. II. 474.²
— De genere Caryota. 1836. II. 65.²
— De genere Sago. 1836. II. 71.¹
— De genere Saguero. 1836. II. 64.²
— De genere Zalacca. 1836. II. 75.¹
— Over de gesteldheid van het gebergte Gede. 1825. I. 468.
— De Gnetaceis. 1848. II. 54.¹
— De houtteelt verbonden met den akkerbouw. 1860. IV. 133.
— De Ipo; sive, Arbore toxicaria. 1835. II. 146.¹
— Juglandeae. 1828. II. 112.²
— De Licuala. 1836. II. 61.¹
— Lorantheae. 1828. II. 173.¹
— Magnoliaceae. 1828. II. 208.²
— Monographie der Oost-indische Pepersoorten. 1826. II. 94.¹
— Museum botanicum lugduno-batavum. 1849. I. 269.
— Myriceae. 1828. II. 111.¹
— Naamlijst van Oost-indische en bepaaldelijk Javaansche gewassen. 1844. III. 122.¹
— Naschrift op den brief van Junghuhn. 1827. I. 465.
— Neesia, genus plantarum javanicum. 1835. II. 530.¹
— De Nipa. 1847. II. 71.²
— De nominibus . . . quibusdam Palmarum generibus inditis. 1836. II. 62.¹
— Notice sur quelques Barringtoniées. 1851. II. 611.¹
— De novis quibusdam plantarum familiis expositio. 1833. I. 468.
— De novis quibusdam plantarum familiis expositio. 1864. I. 268.
— De novo quodam genere e familia Laurinearum. 1835. II. 225.¹
— Over het nut der invoering van vreemde gewassen. 1844. III. 122.¹
— Observationes de genere Helicia Lour. 1834. II. 163.¹
— Observationes sur la structure des Poivres. 1827. I. 93.¹
— Opheldering over de inlichtingen van den heer Fr. Junghuhn. 1850. I. 465.
— De Pangieis. 1848. II. 568.²
— De quibusdam Apocyneis, Asclepiadeis . . . Indiae orientali propriis. 1848. I. 465.
— De quibusdam generibus e tribu Arecinearum. 1836. II. 61.²
— De quibusdam Palmis domesticis. 1847. II. 67,¹ III. 319.¹
— De quibusdam Passifloreis Indiae. 1855. II. 575.²
— De quibusdam plantis . . . e familia Pandanearum. 1835. II. 56.¹
— De quibusdam Sapindaceis. 1847. II. 483.²
— Revue des Palmiers de l'archipel des Indes. 1838. II. 62.¹
— Rudera Padjajarana prope Bogor. 1836. I. 468.
— Rumphia. 1835. I. 472.
— Rumphii de quibusdam Melastomaceis. 1835. II. 635.¹
— Schizandreae. 1828. ·II. 208.²
— Ueber ein Surrogat des chinesischen Thees. 1845. III. 739.
— De Upas Radja. 1835. II. 720.¹

Blume, W. Kubic-Tabelle für runde Hölzer. 1869. IV. 226.

Blumen, von, (Forstmeister, Görlitz). Bericht über die . . . in die k. Forsten des Zobtenberges stattgefundene Exkursion. 1860. IV. 353.

Blumen und Insektenbuch. 17..? I. 288.

Blumenau, H. Aufbewahrung und Versendung von Kernen. 1881. III. 156.²
— Deux nouveaux Cocotiers. 1881. II. 67.¹
— Der Mangababaum. 1900. III. 688.²
— Notizen über Palmen. 1881. II. 64,² 67.¹·
— Waldverwüstung, Aufforstung. 1900. IV. 111.¹

Blumenberg, Carl Fr. De cortice Angusturae. See THUNBERG, C. P. 1793. III. 503.²

Blumenduft und Insecten. 1900. I. 239.¹

Die Blumenesche und das Manna. 1873. III. 221,³ IV. 536.¹

Blumenthal, Johann. Handbuch für Förster. 1830. IV. 103.²

Blumenthal, Julius. See БЛЮМЕНТАЛЬ, Ю.

Blumenwitz, Julius. Eicheln als Handelsartikel. 1875. IV. 515.¹

Blumen-Zeitung. 1811. 11.

Blumer-Heer, J. J. See HEER, Oswald & BLUMER-HEER, J. J.

Blunno, M. See ALLEN, W. J., BLUNNO, M., FROGGATT, W. W. & GUTHRIE, F. B.
— & Froggatt, W. W. Phylloxera of the Grapevine. 1900. III. 575.¹

Bly, C. H. de. De Koffiecultuur in Palembang. 1900. III. 732.¹

Blydenstein, & others. Rapport over de ontginning van heidegronden. 1887. IV. 119.²

Blytt, Axel. Bidrag til kundskaben om vegetationen i . . . Norge. 1872. I. 356.
— Bidrag til kundskaben om vegetationen paa Nowaja Semlja. 1873. I. 363.
— Botanisk reise i Valders. 1864. I. 356.
— Christiania omegns phanerogamer. 1870. I. 356.
— Essay on the immigration of the Norwegian flora. 1876. I. 357.
— Forsøg til en theori om indvandringen af Norges flora. 1876. I. 357.
— Zur Geschichte der nordeuropäischen . . . Flora. 1893. I. 350.¹
— En ny Rubus fra Norge. 1875. II. 306.¹
— Theori om indvandringen af Norges flora. 1881. I. 357.
— On the vegetation of the Sogne Fjord. 1866. I. 356.
— Om vegetations-forholdene ved Sognefjorden. 1869. I. 356.

Blytt, Mathias Numsen. Enumeratio plantarum vascularium . . . circa Christianiam. 1844. I. 354.
— Fortegnelse over de i . . . Norge vildvaxende Traearter. 1837. I. 350,¹ IV. 79.¹
— Norsk Flora. 1847. I. 355.
— & A. G. Norges flora. 1861. I. 356.

Boardman, Samuel L. The Hemlock in Maine 1883 IV. 484.²
— United States census forestry report. 1885. IV. 338.¹

Boas, Johan Erik Vesti. Cossus ligniperda i Eg. 1890. IV. 511.
— Dansk Forstzoologi. 1896. IV. 90.¹
— Det store Bladhvepseangreb paa Lærkene. 1897. IV. 451.¹
— Erfaringer vedrørende Strykninhvedens Anvendelse. 1896. IV. 198.²
— Om et Angreb af Snudebillen. 1889. III. 350.¹
— Et Besøg paa de af Nonnen angrebne svenske Skovdistrikter. 1899. IV. 202.
— Om et nyt Middel imod Markmusene. 1892. IV. 198.²
— Et Skadedyr paa unge Æbletræer. 1899. III. 428.²
— Forsøg med den Lœffler'ske Musetyfus-Bacil. 1892. IV. 198.²
— Forsøg med Musetyfusbacillen. 1894. IV. 198.²
— Fortsatte Forsøg med Musetyfus-Bacillen. 1893. IV. 198.²
— Granbarkvikleren, Tortrix pactolana. 1889. IV. 456.
— Iagtagelser . . . ved rørende Oldenborrene. 1892. IV.549.¹
— Kortfattet Udsigt over forstskadelige Dyrs Optræden. 1888. IV. 205.¹

Boas, Johan Erik Vesti (*continued*).
— Musene i vore Skove. 1891. IV. 198.[1]
— Nogle Bemærkninger om Spætternes forstlige Betydning. 1889. IV. 90.[2]
— Nonnen. 1899. IV. 202.
— Om en Rodlus . . . paa Ædelgran. 1890. IV. 445.
— Rødmusegnav paa Weymouthsfyr. 1896. IV. 198.[3]
— Træbukken Tetropium luridum i Lærk. 1890. IV. 451.
Boate, Gerard. Irelands naturall history. 1652. IV. 359.[1]
Bobart, Jakob. Catalogus plantarum Horti medici oxoniensis. 1648. I. 51,[2] V. VIII.[1]
— An English catalogue of the trees and plants in the physicke garden. *See* An ENGLISH catalogue . . . (*By error*). 1648. I. 51,[3] V. VIII.[2]
Bobbink, L. C. Multiplication des Vitex. 1892. III. 697.[2]
Boberski, Wład. Choroby roślinne. 1881. III. 179.
Bobet, Réné. Le caoutchouc et la gutta-percha. 1889. III. 231.
Boblaye, POUILLON-. *See* POUILLON-BOBLAYE.
Bobrinsky, *Graf* von. Über das Blühen der Gewächse. 1851. I. 220.[2]
— Über die Wurzeln und ihren Einfluss. 1853. III. 173.[1]
Bocage, Victor Amédée BARBIÉ DU. *See* BARBIÉ DU BOCAGE, V. A.
Bocarmé, VISART DE. *See* VISART DE BOCARMÉ.
Boccone, Paolo. Elegantissimarum plantarum . . . semina. 1668. I. 60.[2]
— Icones & descriptiones rariorum plantarum. 1674. I. 287.
— Iconum Musei rariorum plantarum index. 1697. I. 288.
— Manifestum botanicum de plantis siculis. 1668. I. 430.
— Museo di piante rare della Sicilia. 1697. I. 288.
— Naspeuringen van den groeij der planten. 1745. I. 187.
— Osservazioni naturali. 1684. I. 184.
— Recherches et observations naturelles. 1671. I. 430. *
Bochdanecký, Josef. Die Umtriebsseiten. 1880. IV. 252.
Bochefontaine, Louis Théodore. Pouvoir toxique de la quinine. 1883. III. 722.
— *See also* SÉE, Germain & BOCHEFONTAINE, L. T.
— & **Freitas**, Cypriano de. Note sur l'action physiologique du Pao Pereira. 1877. III. 688.[1]
— & **Rey**, Ph. Sur quelques expériences relatives à . . . l'Erythrina corallodendron. 1881. III. 476.[1]
— **Féris**, Bazile & **Marcus**. Propriétés physiologiques de l'écorce du Doundaké. *See* BOCHEFONTAINE, F. B. & MARCUS. (*By error.*) 1883. III. 747.[2]
Bochicchio, Nicola. *See* BERLÈSE, Antonio & BOCHICCHIO, Nicola.
Bochmann, Friedrich Ferdinand Eduard. Ueber die Benutzung der Rosskastanien. 1848. III. 537,[2] *IV. 514.[2]*
Bock, C. Reis in Oost en Zuid Borneo. 1887. I. 469.[2]
Bock, Hieronymus. Herbarum aliquot dissertationes et censurae. 1531. I. 276.
— Kräutterbuch. 1539. I. 277.
— Kreüter Büch, darin Underscheid. 1539. V. XV.[1]
— Kreutterbüch. 1539. I. 277.
— New Kreutter-Buch. 1539. I. 277, V. XV.[1]
— De stirpium . . . usitatis nomenclaturis. 1539. I. 277.
— Verae atque ad vivum expressae imagines omnium herbarum. 1553. I. 279.
Bock, Joseph. Plantarum secundum Pharmacopeam austriacam . . . descriptio. 1832. III. 90.[3]
Bock, Karl. Die Anzucht der Eiche im Mischbestande. 1888. IV. 508.
Bockström, H. Montrösa blommor af Fuchsia. 1878. II. 643.[1]
Bocquillon, Henri T. Description d'un genre nouveau . . . des Verbénacées. 1861. II. 753.[2]
— Mémoirs sur le groupe des Tiliacées. 1866. II. 512.[1]
— Observations sur le genre Oftia Adans. 1861. II. 806.[2]
— Observations sur les genres Oxera. 1861. II. 759.[2]
— Organogénic du Lantana camara. 1861. II. 758.[1]
— Organogénie florale de l'Holmskioldia. 1861. II. 758.[1]
— Organogénie florale du Callicarpa. 1861. II. 754.[1]
— Organogénie florale du Citharexylum. 1861. II. 755.[1]
— Organogénie florale du Clerodendron. 1861. II. 755.[1]
— Organogénie florale du Petrea. 1861. II. 760.[1]
— Organogénie florale du Vitex incisa. 1861. II. 761.[2]
— Revue du groupe des Verbénacées. 1861. II. 752.[2]
— La vie des plantes. 1868. I. 95.
Bocquillon-Limousin, Henri. Étude du Condurango de l'équateur. 1898. III. 693.[2]
— Note sur le Gonolobus Condurango. 1891. II. 738.[2]
— Les plantes alexitères de l'Amerique. 1891. III. 63.[1]
— Les plantes utiles de la Tunisie. 1894. III. 93.[1]

— Rendement en extrait de plantes . . . dans la thérapeutique. 1895. III. 245.
— Les Thés du commerce. 1883. III. 607.
Bodach, Carl Fr. Novitiae florae suecicae. *See* FRIES, E. M. 1814. I. 352.
Bodard, Pierre Henri Hippolyte. Analyse du cours de botanique médicale-comparée. 1809. III. 85.
— Cours de botanique médicale comparée. 1810. III. 55.
— Tableau des plantes médicinales exotiques. 1815. III. 56.
Bodde, Bernard. Ideen über die Abwendung der Frühlings-Nachtfröste. 1807. IV. 191,[1] V. XXX.[2]
Bode, Adolph Friedrich. Beitrag zur Würdigung der Forstwirthschaft in Russland. 1851. IV. 80, 289.[1]
— Handbuch zur Bewirthschaftung der Forsten. 1840. IV. 94.
— Notizen gesammelt auf einer Forstreise durch einen Theil des europäischen Russlands. 1854. IV. 345.
— Verbreitungs-Gränsen der . . . Holzgewächse . . . Russlands. 1851. I. 358,[2] *IV. 80.*
— Waldberichte aus Kurland 1838. 1840. IV. 347.
— *See also* БОДЕ, A. K.
Bode, Alexander. Gärtnerische Mitteilungen aus Singapore. 1889. III. 129.[1]
— Winterschutz der Araucaria imbricata. 1891. III. 299.[1]
Boden. Die Aufbewahrung von Eicheln. 1900. IV. 509.
— Ueber Erziehung von Pflanzen . . . von Pinus rigida und Pinus Banksiana. 1898. IV. 461.[1]
— Zum Insertionswesen bei Holzverkäufen. 1892. IV. 388.[2]
— Vergleichende Untersuchungen über Mittel gegen Wild-Verbiss. 1894. IV. 197.[1]
Boden, Franz. Betrachtungen über die Schicksale eines Reichswaldes. 1879. IV. 26.
— Die Lärche. 1899. IV. 450.
— Zur Ringelbaumfrage. 1876. I. 207,[3] *IV. 199.[1]*
Boden, W. Die Kultur der Eiche. 1892. IV. 508.
— Ueber Umzäunungen im Walde. 1890. IV. 146.[2]
Die **Bodencultur** Oesterreichs. *See* WESSELY, Josef. 1873. IV. 368.
Die **Bodenkultur** des deutschen Reichs. 1881. IV. 349.[1]
Bodenmüller, F. J. Die Malkäfer und Engerlinge. 1866. IV. 548.[2]
Bodenstein, J. V. Die selbstregistrirende "Typkluppe." 1892. IV. 231.[3]
Bodin, Étienne SOULANGE-. *See* SOULANGE-BODIN, Étienne.
Bodin, J. Herbier agricole. 1856. III. 86.
Bodor, Gyula. A havasi Fenyő, törpe Fenyő és Tiszafa tenyészete az Unö-Omuluj hegységben. 1895. II. 15.[1]
Bodry, János. Himalayai Rhododendronok. 1899. III. 655.
Bodungen, F. von. Die Aufforstung der öden Ebenen. 1881. IV. 153.
— Die Verwandlungen der öden Gründe. 1876. IV. 158.
— Die vormalige Grafschaft Lützelstein. 1879. IV. 349.[2]
— Die Waldrechte in Elsass-Lothringen. 1878. IV. 334.[1]
Böck, J. B. Naturgetreue Abbildungen der . . . wilden Holzarten. 1844. I. 371, *IV. 82.*
Böck, R. Kubik-Preisrechner für beschlagene und runde Hölzer. 1877. IV. 227.
Böckel, Godwin. Culture des plantes naines. 1855. III. 175.[1]
— Etymologisch-botanische Nachlese. 1854. I. 76.[3]
— Ueber Formen der Myrica Gale. 1854. II. 111.[1]
— How to grow lilliputian plants. 1855. III. 175.[1]
— Ueber die Zucht der Liliputpflanzen. 1855. III. 175.[2]
— Ueber zwei neue Prunus-Arten. 1853. II. 271.[1]
Böcker, F. W. Action du sucre, du café. 1849. III. 741.[2]
Böckh, Georg Andreas. Nützliche Haus- und Feldschule. 1666. IV. 115.
Boecklin. Vermischte freye Gedanken eines Forstliebhabers bey den Klagen über Holzmangel. 1776. IV. 280.[1]
Boeoler, Johann. Cynosura materiæ medicæ continuata. 1729. III. 241.
— Cynosura materie medicæ continuatæ continuata. 1729. III. 241.
Boedecker, C. *See* ECKARD, G. E., BOEDECKER, C. & LUTTER-KORTH, H.
Boedo y Cardois, Manuel. Elementos de agricultura. 1836. III. 114.[3]
Bøgh, G. J. Frugttrædyrkning i Jylland. 1865. III. 134.[3]
Bøgh, V. Nogle Undersøgelser over Egebarkens Garvestofindhold. 1890. IV. 515.[3]
— Nogle Undersøgelser over forskjellige indenlandske Barksorters Garvestofindhold. 1892. IV. 435.

Böhm, August. Ein Beitrag zum Capitel "Darrscheit." 1884. IV. 387.²
— Einiges über die Waldstreunuzung. 1871. IV. 71.
— Zur Reinertrags-Theorie. 1873. IV. 256.
— Welche Bahnen wären einzuschlagen . . . um unsere geringen Walderträge zu erhöhen. 1883. IV. 41,² 279.¹
Böhm, Bernard. Ueber das Absterben von Thuja Menziesii. 1894. III. 312,¹ IV. 483.²
— Anleitung zur Buch- und Rechnungsführung für Privatforstreviere. 1897. IV. 312.
— Fichten-Varietäten. 1893. II. 35.¹
— Untersuchungen über das Holz der wichtigsten . . . nordamerikanischen Holzarten. 1896. IV. 397.
Böhm, Ferdinand. Vom Erfrieren der Pflanzen. 1865. IV. 66.²
— Die mechanischen Wirkungen der Luft. 1862. IV. 189.¹
— Das Wasser und die Vegetation. 1862. IV. 73.¹
— Die Wirkungen des Sturmes auf die . . . Blätter. 1860. IV. 189.¹
Boehm, Georg. Cause dell' ascensione della linfa. 1880. IV. 63.¹
Böhm, Josef Anton. Ueber Aufforstung von Torf- und Moorböden. 1888. IV. 167.²
— Beiträge zur Kenntniss des Chlorophylls. 1867. I. 141.
— Beiträge zur näheren Kenntniss der Genesis und Function von Pflanzen-Farbstoffen. 1862. I. 184.
— Beiträge zur näheren Kenntniss des Pflanzengrüns. 1863. I. 141.
— Über die Bildung von Sauerstoff. 1872. I. 173.
— Capillarität und Saftsteigen. 1893. I. 166.
— Sur la cause de l'ascension de la sève. 1889. I. 166.
— De la cause du mouvement de l'eau. 1881. I. 167.
— Les causes de l'ascension de la sève. 1878. I. 165.
— Ueber Druckkräfte in Stammorganen. 1880. I. 168.
— Ueber einen eigenthümlichen Stammdruck. 1892. I. 169.¹
— Über Einfluss der Kohlensäure auf das Ergrünen. 1873. I. 173.
— Über den Einfluss der Sonnenstrahlen auf die Chlorophyllbildung. 1859. I. 172.
— Über den Einfluss des Leuchtgases. 1873. III. 185.²
— Über die Entwickelung von Gasen. 1866. I. 151.¹
— Ueber die Entwickelung von Sauerstoff aus grünen Zweigen. 1877. I. 170.
— Über Function und Genesis der Zellen in den Gefässen des Holzes. 1866. I. 125.
— Über das Keimen von Samen in reinem Sauerstoffgase. 1874. I. 203.
— Ueber Krankheiten, Alter . . . der Pflanzen. 1888. I. 92.²
— Die Nährstoffe der Pflanzen. 1886. I. 159.
— De la nature des gaz . . . dans les tissus. 1883. I. 151.²
— Die Pflanze und die Atmosphäre. 1883. I. 173.
— Physiologische Bedingungen der Bildung von Nebenwurzeln. 1867. I. 208,² III. 352.¹
— Physiologische Untersuchungen über blaue Passifiorabeeren. 1857. II. 577.¹
— Über die physiologischen Bedingungen der Chlorophyllbildung. 1865. I. 141.
— De la respiration des plantes terrestres. 1877. I. 170.
— Über die Respiration von Landpflanzen. 1873. I. 170.
— Über die Schmarotzernatur der Mistel. 1865. II. 179.¹
— Ein Schulversuch über die Wasserversorgung transpirirender Blätter. 1892. I. 170.
— Sind die Bastfasern Zellen oder Zellfusionen? 1866. I. 130,¹ 136.²
— Ueber Stärkebildung in verdunkelten Blatttheilen. 1877. I. 525.
— Transpiration gebrühter Sprosse. 1892. I. 168.
— Umkehrung des aufsteigenden Saftstromes. 1890. I. 166.
— Ueber die Ursache der Wasserbewegung. 1881. I. 167.
— Ursache der Wasserbewegung in transpirirenden Pflanzen. 1890. I. 168.
— Ueber die Ursache des Absterbens der Götterbäume. 1881. III. 507.¹
— Über die Ursache des Saftsteigens. 1863. I. 164.
— Ursache des Saftsteigens. 1880. I. 166.
— Ueber die Verfärbung grüner Blätter. 1877. I. 141, 230.
— Ueber das Verhalten von vegetabilischen Geweben . . . zu Gasen. 1883. I. 151.²
— Warum steight der Saft in den Bäumen? 1878. I. 165.
— Ueber die Wasserbewegung. 1877. I. 167.
— Wird das Saftsteigen . . . durch Diffusion . . . bewirkt? 1865. I. 164.

— Zwei neue Versuche über die Wasserversorgung. 1890. I. 168.
— & Breitenlohner, Jakob. Die Baumtemperatur. 1877. I. 186, V. xii.¹
— — La temperatura dell' albero. 1877. V. xii.¹
Boehm, Rudolph Albert Martin. Ueber Curare und Curarealkaloide. 1897. III. 684.¹
— Das südamerikanische Pfeilgift Curare. 1895. III. 684.¹
Boehm, W. M. Tabelaryczny przegląd nadzwyczaj starych oraz rzadkich drzew w lasach zachodniej Galicyi. 1866. I. 298.
Böhme, (Dr.). Resultate der Untersuchungen mit imprägnirten und nicht imprägnirten Holzproben. 1886. IV. 420.
Böhme, (Forstmeister). Anwendung des Plenterschlages. 1890. IV. 74.²
— Ein Beitrag zur Frage über die Pflanzung von jungen Kiefern mit entblösster Wurzel. 1886. IV. 473.
— Ein Beitrag zur Lehre vom Waldwertzunahme-Prozent. 1887. IV. 257.
— Zur Ehrenrettung der Lärche. 1891. IV. 450.
— Ueber Holzanbau auf öden Kalkflächen. 1892. IV. 159
— Rentabilität eines 34jährigen Eichen-Schälwald-Bestandes. 1885. IV. 513.
— Ueber die Ueberführung des Mittelwaldes in Hochwald 1885. IV. 128.
Böhme, Paul. Datura sanguinea. 1899. III. 700.¹
— Fuchsia fulgens als Hockstamm. 1896. III. 640.¹
— Hamamelis virginica. 1890. III. 417.¹
— Nochmals Styrax japonicus und Pterostyrax. 1890. III. 670,² 671.¹
— Polygonum vaccinifolium. 1896. III. 387.¹
— Sciadopitys verticillata S. et Z. 1890. III. 309.²
— & others. Winterschutz der Magnolia Soulangeana 1889. III. 400.¹
Böhmen. See Bohemia.
Boehmer, Georg Rudolf. Bibliotheca scriptorum historiae naturalis. 1785. I. 1.
— De coeruleo colore. 1786. I. 184.
— Commentatio-physico-botanica de plantarum semine. 1777. I. 120.
— Dissertationes de nectariis florum additamenta. 1762. I. 118.¹
— In essentiae coffeae . . . virtutem inquirit. 1782. III. 41.³
— Flora Lipsiae indigena. 1750. I. 373.
— De foliis arborum deciduis. 1797. I. 191.¹
— Genera plantarum in tabulis synopticis. 1790. V. xiii.¹
— Handbuch der Naturgeschichte, Oeconomic. 1785. I. 1.
— Lexicon rei herbariae tripartitum. 1802. I. 33, 70, 76.¹
— De nectariis florum. 1758. I. 118.¹
— Novum contra frigus hybernum arbores defendendi adminiculum describit. 1773. III. 182.
— Ordinis medici in Academia wittebergensi . . . commoda, quae arbores a cortice accipiunt. 1773. I. 157.
— De ornamentis, quae praeter nectaria in floribus reperiuntur. 1758. I. 114.¹
— De plantarum superficie exercitatio. 1770. I. 97.
— Plantas fabulosas . . . recenset. 1800. I. 517.³
— De plantis fasciatis. 1752. I. 144.²
— De plantis in cultorum memoriam nominatis. 1770. I. 76,¹ 511.
— De plantis monadelphis. 1797. I. 264.
— De Sambuco in totum medicinali. 1771. III. 752.¹
— De serendis vegetabilium seminibus monita. 1761. III. 156.¹
— Spermatologia vegetabilis. 1777. I. 120.
— Tubularum synopticarum . . . exempla. 1790. I. 258, V. xiii.¹
— De Taxo baccato. 1796. III. 288.¹
— Technische Geschichte der Pflanzen. 1794. III. 51.
— De Toxicodendro. 1800. III. 528.¹
— De vario coffeae potum parandi modo. 1782. III. 738.
— De vegetabilium celluloso contextu. 1753. I. 123.³
— De vegetatione plantarum inversa. 1794. I. 146.
— De viribus radicis Sassaprifolae antisyphiliticis. 1803. III. 388.¹
— See also Gmelin, P. F. & Böhmer, G. R.
Boehmer, M. Louis. General observations of the flora of Hokkaido. 1876. I. 462.
Boehmer, Philipp Adolph. De cortice Cascarillae. See Hoffmann, Friedrich. 1738. III. 719.
— De cortice peruviano. See Neigebind, T. G. 1775. III. 720.

Böhmerle, Emil. Die Goldenhöher Schlangenfichte. 1881. II. 34.[2]
— Der Hainburger Herrenwald. 1889. IV. 369.
— Tafeln zur Berechnung der Cubikinhalte stehender Kohl-meiler. 1877. IV. 227, *335*.
— Das waldtrockene Holz. 1879. IV. 411.[1]
Böhmerle, Karl. Ueber das Alter der deutschen Waldbäume. 1886. I. 527, *IV. 65*.[1]
— Die Aluminiumkluppe. 1897. IV. 232.
— Die Astmasse der Schwarzföhre. 1884. IV. 466.[1]
— Bisherige Erfahrungen aus einigen Durchforstungs- und Lichtungsversuchsflächen. 1900. IV. 175.[2]
— Ueber charakteristische Jahresringe. 1882. I. 525.
— Durchforstungsstudien. 1896. IV. 175.[1]
— Einfluss verschiedener Wachsthumsgebiete auf . . . Schwarzföhre. 1888. IV. 466.[1]
— Études sur le sujet d'éclaircies. 1896. IV. 175.[1]
— Formzahlen und Massentafeln für die Schwarzföhre. 1893. IV. 466.[2]
— Der Huber'sche Mittelstamm. 1893. IV. 246.
— Kluppen aus Aluminium. 1898. IV. 232.
— Die Pfister'sche Zuwachsuhr. 1883. IV. 233.
— Ueber Schneeschäden. 1898. III. 185.[1]
— Ueber vergleichende Zuwachsuntersuchungen. 1895. IV. 234.
— Ueber den Verpachtungsmodus bei der Harznutzung der Schwarzföhre. 1883. IV. 466.[2]
— Versuche über Bestandesmassenaufnahmen. 1898. IV. 219.
— Zuwachs an geharzten Schwarzföhren. 1881. IV. 466.[1]
— Zuwachs an geharzten Schwarzföhren. 1885. IV. 466.[1]
— **Kunze**, Max F. & **Schuberg**, Karl. Entwurf einer über-einstimmenden Formelschreibung. 1895. IV. 215.
Böhmische Forstschule zu Weisswasser. Jahresheft. IV. 14.
Böhmische Gesellschaft der Wissenschaften. See KÖNIG-LICHE BÖHMISCHE . . . I. 27.
Böhmischer Forstverein. Bericht. IV. 14.
Böhmischer Forstverein. Vereinsschrift für Forst . . . und Naturkunde. See VEREINSSCHRIFT . . . IV. 15.
Böhn, H. G. Roses planted at North End House. 1852. III. 448.[1]
Böhnke-Reich, Heinrich. Der Kaffee in seinen Beziehungen zum Leben. 1875. III. 739.
Böhringer, Chr. & **Koerner**, G. Sur les alcaloïdes . . . d'Angusture. 1885. III. 503.[2]
Boeken, Hubert J. Der Sisalhanf. 1900. II. 89.[2]
Boekhold, F. van. Relaas van een reisje na en op den berg Marbaboe. 1792. I. 468.
— Relaas van 2 togten na den brandenden berg. 1792. I. 468.
Bökmann, A. Beschreibung eines . . . Höhenmessers. 1815. IV. 215.
Bölcsházai-Belházy, Emil. Az erdőrendezéstan kézikönyve. 1895. IV. 241. *See also* BELHÁZY, Emil. 1895. IV. 111.[1]
Boele, R. De gouvernements' Koffiecultuur ter Sumatra's westkust. 1897. III. 731.
— Nogmaals de gouvernements Koffiecultuur. 1898. III. 731.
— De zegen der gouvernements Koffiecultuur. 1898. III. 731.
Bölling, G. Beiträge zur Kenntniss einiger alkaloidhaltiger Pflanzen. 1900. I. 178.
Böning, Reinhold Johan. Rön och Anmärkningar om ut-ländska wäxter. See GADD, P. A. 1777. III. 120.[1]
Boening, Robert. Anatomie des Stammes der Berberitze. 1885. II. 202.[2]
Boeninger, Theodor Konrad. De plantis venenatis. 1790. III. 72.
Boenneken, Joann Wolfg. Frider. De cortice Simarubae. 1759. III. 501.[1]
Bönninghausen, Clemens Maria Friedrich, *Freiherr* von. Kurze und fassliche Anleitung zur Anlegung von Lohschlagen, 1825. IV. 504.
— Nomenclator botanicus sistens plantas . . . in circulo Coesfeldiae-Westphalorum. 1821. I. 377.
— Prodromus florae monasteriensis Westphalorum. 1824. I. 377.
Boer, G. Cytisus Adami. 1876. III. 480.[2]
Boer, Petrus de. Coniferae Junghuhnianae posteriores. 1867. II. 9.[1]
— Specimen botanicum inaugurale de Coniferis Archipelagi indici. 1866. II. 15.[2]
— De verklaring van het karakter der vegetatie. 1883. I. 218.

— De waarde van het vergelijkend onderzoek voor de béoef-ening der plantenkunde. 1871. I. 79.[2]
Boer, R. W. Aanwijzingen bij het snoeijen van boomen. 1880. III. 170.
— Aanwijzingen voor de behandeling der beplantingen. 1850. III. 209.
— Het anatomisch zamenstel van het hout. 1858. I. 124.
— Bijdragen tot de kennis der houtteelt. 1854. IV. 119.[1]
— Bijdragen tot de kennis der houtteelt. 1875. IV. 107.[1]
— Dennencultuur in de duinen. 1879. IV. 160.[1]
— Eenige waarnemingen omtrent den groei van boomen. 1869. III. 38.[1]
— Gronden, naar welke de houtteler de boschinsekten te beoordeelen heeft. 1857. IV. 208.[1]
— Haagsche bosch. 1877. IV. 356.[2]
— In hoeverre is een zekere wisselbouw ook van toepassing voor de houtteelt? 1870. IV. 74.[2]
— Iets over duinbeplantingen. 1883. IV. 160.[1]
— Het omplaggen en spitten der akkermaalsbosschen. 1865. IV. 505.
— De ontginning van heidegronden. 1867. IV. 160.[1]
— Opmerkingen over houtsoorten. 1858. IV. 398.[1]
— Practische handleiding voor de houtteelt. 1862. IV. 107.[1]
— Ulex europaeus. 1878. III. 489.[2]
— Waarde, die aan verschillende middelen tegen de bosch-insecten aanbevolen, moet toegekend worden. 1857. IV. 208.[2]
— Waarom is het in den winter gevelde hout zoo veel voor-treffelijker. 1858. IV. 384.[2]
— Wat behoeft de Nederlandsche houtteler in een handboek over houtteelt? 1857. IV. 119.[2]
— Wat staat den mensch tegenover de plantenziekten te doen? 1869. III. 196.
Børgesen, Frederik C. E. Sur l'anatomie des feuilles des plantes arctiques. 1895. I. 220.[1]
— Beretning om et Par Exkursioner i Sydspanien. 1897. I. 423.
— Bidrag til Kundskaben om arktiske Planters Bladbygning. 1895. I. 220.[1]
— Nogle Ericineae-Haars Udviklingshistorie. 1890. II. 658.[2]
— *See also* ULDALL, F. P. & BØRGESEN, F. C. E.
— & **Ostenfeld**, C. E. H. Planter samlede paa Færøerne. 1896. I. 358.
— & **Paulsen**, Ove. La végétation des Antilles danoises. 1898. I. 337.
— Om Vegetationen paa de dansk-vestindiske øer. 1898. I. 337.
Boerhaave, Hermann. Historia plantarum quae in Horto academico Lugduni-Batavorum crescunt. 1727. I. 290.
— Index alter plantarum . . . in Horto academico lugduno-batavo. 1720. I. 50.
— Index plantarum . . . in Horto acad. lugduno-batavo. 1710. I. 289, *521*.[3]
— Libellus de materie medica. 1727. III. 241.
Boerlage, Jacob Gijsbert. Aanteekeningen omtrent de kennis der flora van Nederlandsch Indië. 1888. I. 466.
— Bijdrage tot de kennis der houtanatomie. 1875. I. 125, *II. 145*.[2]
— Catalogus plantarum phanerogamarum . . . in Horto botanico bogoriensi. 1899. I. 68.[3]
— Chondrostylis Bancana Boerl. 1897. II. 438.[1]
— Enumération des végétaux producteurs de caoutchouc. 1900. III. 230.
— Het geslacht Achyranthes. 1889. II. 189.[2]
— Handleiding tot de kennis der flora van Nederlandsch Indië. 1890. I. 466.
— Sur l'Indovethia. 1894. II. 544.[2]
— Inlandsche . . . Synonymen der Rhizophoren. 1895. II. 614.[1]
— De Koffiebladziekte. 1885. III. 735.
— Sur la manière de flotter . . . des fruits du Heritiera. 1898. II. 535.[1]
— Notes sur les Anonacées. 1899. II. 215.[1]
— Révision de quelques genres des Araliacées. 1887. II. 646.[2]
— Sur Roucheria Griffithiana Planch. 1894. II. 393.[2]
— Over de soorten van het geslacht Erythrina. 1892. II. 356.[2]
— Systematische lijst der verzamelte planten. 1884. I. 467.
— Uitheemsche planten om Buitenzorg verwilderd. 1889. I. 469.[1]
— De verspreidingsmiddelen der planten. 1875. I. 240.[1]

— Voorloopige mededeelingen omtrent eenige Indische Araliaceën. 1886. II. 646.²
— Welken botanischen naam moet men geven aan de soort van Erythrina . . . onder den naam van Dadap. 1894. II. 357.²
— *See also* HASSELT, A. L. van & BOERLAGE, J. G.
— & **Koorders**, S. H. Erythroxylon latifolium Burck var. longipetiolatum. 1897. II. 394.³
— — De Mangirboom van Java. 1896. III. 539.¹
— — Een nieuw Javaansch Woudboomen-geslacht. 1893. II. 704.¹
— — Een nieuwe Javaansche boomsoort. 1896.· II. 708.²
Börner. *See* UFFELMANN & BÖRNER.
Boerner, Friedrich. De Aemilio Macro. 1754. I. 291.
Börner, Gottlob. Alphabetisches Verzeichniss grösstentheils nordamerikanischer . . . Bäume. 1786. I. 44.
— Catalogue alphabétique d'arbres, d'arbrisseaux. 1786. I. 44.
Börner, R. Die Schütte-Krankheit an Kiefern. 1862. IV. 476.
Börsch, Otto. Anleitung zur Berechnung der rechtwinkligen sphärischen Coordinaten. 1868. IV. 58.
Boëry, Pascal. Les plantes oléagineuses. 1888. III. 225.
Böse, Christian. Generale Haushalts-Principia von Berg-. . . und Forstwesen. 1753. IV. 115, 352.
Boese, E. Die echten Nadelhölzer . . . des Freilandes. 1868. III. 289.
— Die Eibengehölze oder Taxineen. 1868. III. 287.¹
— Die Koniferen . . . des freien Landes. 1868. III. 292.
— Die unechten Nadelhölzer . . . des Freilandes. 1868. III. 289.
Bösemann, Fr. Aug. Deutschlands Gehölze im Winterkleide. 1884. I. 294,³ *IV.* 84.¹
Bösen, Jobst. Verbesserte . . . Hebmaschine. 1771. IV. 385.¹
Boesen, N. Graapilen. 1900. III. 351.²
Boethius, Jacob. Försökt medet, af afhälla myror. 1763. III. 188.²
Boetius de Boot, Anselm. *See* BOOT, A. B. de.
Böttcher, Emil. Die Vermehrung durch Ableger. 1857. III. 159.¹
Böttcher, Friedrich Wilhelm. Abhandlung über Holz-Ersparungen. 1815. IV. 280.²
Boettger, Christoph Heinrich. Beschreibung des botanischen Gartens zu Kassel. 1777. I. 44.
— Verzeichniss der Bäume und Stauden im Park zu Weissenstein. 1777. I. 44.
Bötger, Ludwig. Beyträge zur Erläuterung des Forstrechts. 1802. IV. 313.
Boetticher, Karl. Der Baumkultus der Hellenen. 1856. I. 517.¹
Böttinger, G. Sur l'acide tannique du bois de Chêne. 1888. IV. 515.¹
Böttinger, Heinrich. Analysen der Aschen einiger Hölzer. 1844. I. 155.
Böttner, Johannes C. Lehre der Obstkultur und Obstverwertung. 1885. III. 139.
— Unsere besten Obstsorten. 1896. III. 72.
Bötz, (*Dodenau*). Die Krankheit der Lärche. 1866. IV. 450.¹
Bötz, (*Oberförster, Ermenrod*). Das Entasten. 1856. IV. 170.
Bötzel, (*Forstmeister*). Ein Waldpflug. 1892. IV. 143.²
Bötzel, A. Ueber den Pflanzenwechsel in den Kämpen. 1885. IV. 151.¹
Bogaardt, A. *See* HARST, C. van der & BOGAARDT, A.
Bogenhard, Carl. Taschenbuch der Flora von Jena. 1850. I. 382.
Bogner, Pietro. Breve guida per la tassazione delle foreste. 1864. IV. 243.
— Krótka wskazówka szacowania lasów. 1867. IV. 255.
— Kurze Anleitung zur Forst-Taxation. 1864. IV. 217.
— Tafeln zur Bestimmung des Kubikinhaltes von bezimmerten Hölzern. 1864. IV. 225.
Bogoslovski. *See* БОГОСЛОВСКІЙ.
Bogsch, Johann. Anleitung nützliche Obstbäume . . . zu ziehen. 1793. III. 146.¹
— Kurze . . . Anleitung, nützliche –Obstbäume . . . zu erziehen. 1793. III. 146.¹
Bogucki, Adolf. Jedwabnictwo nasze i obce. 1890. III. 378.
— Prawidłowy sposób zasiewu i hodowli Morwy. 1891. III. 378.
Bogue, Ernest Everett. An annotated catalog of . . . plants of Oklahoma. 1900. V. XVIII.¹

Boguslof, I. *See* БОГУСЛОВЪ, I.
Bohadsch, Johann Tauffer. Dienst- und nutzbarer patriotischer Vorschlag. 1758. IV. 524.¹
Bohdanecký, Josef. Bericht über die . . . 1879 in Fiume stattgefundene gemeinschaftliche Karstversammlung. 1880. IV. 167.²
— Beschreibung der Exkursionstour . . . in den Forsten der . . . Herrschaft Worlik. 1893. IV. 372.
— Der Durchforstungs- und Lichtungszuwachsbetrieb. 1895. IV. 176.¹
— Führer zur Excursion . . . in die . . . Forste der Herrschaft Worlik. 1899. IV. 373.
— Naturgetreue Abbildungen des Holzzuwachses. 1889. IV. 234.
— Popis vychásky . . . do lesů panství Vorlického. 1893. IV. 372.
— Průvodce k vycházce . . . do lesů . . . na panství Vorlickém. 1899. IV. 373.
— Statisticko-topografický a lesnický popis knížecích Schwarzenbergských lesů panství Vorlíka. 1890. IV. 372.
— Statistisch-topografische und forstliche Beschreibung der . . . Güter Tochowic und Altsattel-Hrádek. 1891. IV. 372.
— Statistisch-topographische und forstliche Beschreibung der . . . Herrschaft Worlik. 1890. IV. 372.
Bohemia — Archiv für die naturwissenschaftliche Landesdurchforschung. *See* ARCHIV . . . I. 27.
Bohemia — Gesellschaft des Vaterländischen Museums. *See* GESELLSCHAFT . . . III. 24.¹
Bohemia — Verein deutscher Forstleute. *See* VEREIN . . . IV. 15.
Bohl, J. Anleitung zur Verbesserung des bündnerischen Waldwesens. 1838. IV. 110.¹
— Entruidament tra l' ameglioraziun della Economia d' usuls Grischuns. 1838. IV. 110.¹
— Eine Stimme aus dem Walde über die Verrichtungen des St. Gallischen Forstpersonals. 1844. IV. 294.¹
Bohlin, Knut Harald. Ett exempel på ömsesidig vikariering mellan en fjäll- och en kustform. 1900. I. 219.¹
Bohman, Johan. Omberg (in Ostrogothia) och dess omgifningar. 1829. I. 353.
— Wettern och dess küster. 1840. I. 354.
Bohn, Johann Conrad. Anleitung zu Vermessungen in Feld und Wald. 1876. IV. 264.
Bohnenberger, Christoph Heinrich. Chemische Untersuchung der ächten Angustura Rinde. *See* GMELIN, C. G. 1830. III. 503.²
Das **Bohne'sche** Universalinstrument. 1881. IV. 265.
Bohnhof, Ernst. Die forstliche Statistik Belgiens. 1887. IV. 357.¹
Bohnhorst, J. *See* RELING, H. & BOHNHORST, J.
Bohnsach, Berendt Joch. Öm Ek-ållons säning. 1749. IV. 503.²
Bohnstedt, Reinhold. Flora luccaviensis. 1882. I. 532.¹
Bohutinsky, Hugo. Statisticko-topografický popis velkostatku Zelče. 1887. IV. 372.
— Statistisch-topographische Beschreibung der . . . Domäne Zelč. 1887. IV. 372.
Bohutinsky, Joseph. Ueber Ursache und Entstehung der Baumkrankatas. n. d. IV. 454.
Boiret, H. Emploi des feuilles d'arbres comme nourriture du bétail. 1894. III. 223.²
Boirivant, Auguste. Recherches sur les organes de remplacement. 1897. I. 100,² 208.¹
— Sur le remplacement de la racine principale par une radicelle. 1897. I. 104.
— Sur le remplacement de la tige principale par une de ses ramifications. 1898. ·I. 107.¹
— Sur tissu assimilateur des tiges privées de feuilles. 1897. I. 174.
Bois, Désiré. Aperçu historique sur la Société nationale d'horticulture de France. 1900. III. 33.³
— Les Araucaria imbricata de Penandreff. 1893. III. 299.¹
— Atlas des plantes de jardins. 1896. III. 87.
— L'Avocatier. 1900. III. 407.¹
— Las Cactaceas útiles. 1888. III. 620.²
— Les Cactées utiles. 1888. III. 620.¹
— Le Cereus giganteus Engelm. 1888. ·II. 590.¹
— Une Clématite à fleurs odorantes. 1900. III. 391.²
— Ehretia serrata Roxb. 1888. III. 695.¹
— Fructification du Persica Davidiana. 1893. II. 274.¹
— Le Gustavia augusta L. 1892. III. 631.¹

Bois, Désiré (*continued*).
— Herbolisations dans le département de la Manche. 1887. I. 417.
— Jacquinia aurantiaca. 1892. III. 665.²
— Kopsia fruticosa. 1893. II. 727.¹
— Le Mollé Poivrier du Pérou. 1890. III. 529.¹
— Un nouvel arbrisseau . . . le Decaisnea. 1900. II. 201.¹
— Nouvelles espèces d'arbres et d'arbrisseaux du Yunnan. 1900. I. 457, V. xxiii.²
— Nuovi alberi e nuovi arbusti della China. 1900. I. 457.
— Le Palmier nain. 1888. III. 322.¹
— Les plantes d'appartement et les plantes de fenêtres. 1891. III. 87.
— Les plantes nouvelles. 1893. III. 28.²
— Les plantes nouvelles et les plantes d'Australie. 1898. III. 78.¹
— Les plantes utiles des colonies à l'Exposition universelle. 1900. III. 29.¹
— Rhododendron ciliicalyx. 1895. III. 658.¹
— Solandra grandiflora. 1891. III. 701.¹
— Solanum betaceum Cavanilles. 1890. III. 699.²
— Solanum Seaforthianum. 1893. II. 777.²
— Le thé et ses succédanés. 1889. III. 222.
— *See also* Paillieux, Auguste & Bois, Désiré.
— & **Gibault,** Georges. L'arboriculture et la culture maraichère en Tunisie. 1897. III. 130.²
— — L'horticulture dans la Nouvelle-Galles. 1897. III. 132.¹
— — La végétation . . . des Iles Canaries. 1895. III. 282.¹
— & **Maury,** Paul. Les fruits des tropiques. 1888. III. 85, 220.¹
— & others. Dictionnaire d'horticulture, illustré. 1893. III. 31.
Bois. IV. 12.¹
Le **Bois.** Liège. IV. 539.¹
Le **Bois.** Paris. IV. 539.¹
Les bois à Odessa. 1900. IV. 404.²
Bois contre fer. 1898. IV. 409.
Bois d'Érable. 1899. IV. 526.²
Les bois de la République Argentine. 1898. IV. 342.¹
Les bois de Norwège. 1894. IV. 557.¹
Du bois de Pin et de Peuplier. 1853. IV. 413.¹
Le bois de Teck. 1899. IV. 537.¹
Bois de Teck. Consommation en Europe. 1898. IV. 538.¹
Bois de Teck du Haut-Laos. 1899. IV. 538.¹
Les bois du Congo. 1896. IV. 379.²
Les bois en Italie. 1879. IV. 364.
Le bois métallisé. 1899. IV. 557.²
Un bois productif. 1894. IV. 486.¹
Bois soumis au régime forestier. 1899. IV. 388.¹
Le bois-pierre. 1894. IV. 558.¹
Boisard, J. Diplothemium caudescens Martius. 1872. III. 325.¹
Boisbaudran, François Lecoq de. *See* Lecoq de Boisbaudran, François.
Boisclaireau, *comte de, (député, Sarthe).* Opinion sur la dotation de la caisse d'amortissement. 1817. IV. 326.
Boisdhyver, Marrier de. *See* Marrier de Boisdhyver.
Boisduval. Coup d'œil sur l'histoire naturelle de la Savoie. 1866. I. 413.
Boisduval. Essai sur l'entomologie horticole. 1867. III. 189.
— Insects infesting fruit trees. 1855. III. 445.²
— Note relative à un insecte qui vit sur les branches du Poirier. 1855. III. 445.²
— Note sur divers insectes nuisibles aux plantes. 1864. III. 189.
— Note sur la teigne du Pêcher. 1864. III. 441.²
— Note sur le kermès des Limons. 1867. III. 498.¹
Boisduval, Jean Baptiste Alphonse Déchauffour de. Flore française. 1828. I. 408.
Boisement. Sol calcaire, sec, gazonné. 1898. IV. 153.¹
Boisement d'un mauvais terrain sablonneux. 1898. IV. 161.¹
Boisement d'un sol sablonneux. 1900. IV. 143.²
Boisement d'un terrain marneux. 1899. IV. 70.
Boisement d'une butte sablonneuse. 1898. IV. 161.¹
Boisement dans la région du Condroz. 1900. IV. 161.¹
Boisement de feuillus. 1899. IV. 138.¹
Boisement de pâtures-sarts dans la Famenne. 1900. IV. 161.¹
Boisement de terrains incultes (Famenne). 1900. IV. 161.¹
Boisement de terrains sablonneux et humides. 1899. IV. 142.
Boisement des dunes. 1894. IV. 546.²
Boisement des pays les plus importants. 1895. IV. 336.²
Boisement en Aune et Bouleau. 1899. IV. 142.

Boismont, Alexandre Jacques François Brierre de. *See* Brierre de Boismont, A. J. F.
Boissaye, Pierre. Le Pitchpin. 1896. IV. 467.¹
Boisse, *baron de* Mortemart de. *See* Mortemart de Boisse, *baron de.*
Boisselot, A. Le Chêne de la Tranchée. 1861. II. 138.¹
— Influence du greffon sur le sujet. 1881. III. 39.
— Poinciana Gilliesii. 1870. III. 469.¹
Boissier, Edmond. Abies Pinsapo Boiss. 1861. II. 24.²
— Description d'une nouvelle espèce de Sapin. 1838. II. 24.²
— Diagnoses plantarum orientalium. 1842. I. 452.
— Elenchus plantarum . . . quas in itinere hispanico legit. 1838. I. 420.
— Flora orientalis. 1867. I. 449, *452.*
— Icones Euphorbiarum. 1866. II. 441.²
— Note on some new facts in botanical geography. 1866. I. 300.
— Note sur quelques nouveaux faits de géographie botanique. 1866. I. 300
— Notice sur l'Abies Pinsapo. 1838. II. 24.²
— Plantae Aucherianae orientales. 1841. I. 478.
— Plantarum orientalium novarum decas I. 1875. II. 674.¹
— Plantes nouvelles recueillies par M. P. de Tchihatcheff. 1854. II. 297.²
— Plumbaginaceae. 1848. II. 696.¹
— Voyage botanique dans le midi de l'Espagne. 1839. I. 420.
— & **Buhse,** Fedor. Aufzaehlung der auf einer Reise durch Transkaukasien und Persien gesammelten Pflanzen. 1860. I. 477.²
— & **Reuter,** G. F. Diagnoses plantarum novarum hispanicarum. 1842. I. 420.
— — Pugillus plantarum novarum Africae. 1852. I. 452.
Boissier de la Croix de Sauvages, F. Methodus foliorum. 1751. I. 405.
— Observations sur quelques plantes venimeuses. *See* Sauvages de la Croix. 1741. III. 523.¹
Boissier de la Croix de Sauvages, Pierre Augustin. Mémoires sur l'éducation des vers à soie. 1763. III. 373.
Boissier de Sauvages, Pierre Augustin. *See* Boissier de la Croix de Sauvages, P. A.
Boissier—L'Herbier. *See* L'Herbier Boissier. I. 26.²
Boissieu, C. V. de. Flore d'Europe. 1805. I. 348.²
Boissieu, Henri de. Les Ericacées du Japon. 1897. II. 658.²
— Espèces . . . nouvelles pour la flore du Japon. 1897. II. 246.²
— Les Légumineuses du Japon. 1898. II. 319.¹
— Les Renonculacées du Japon. 1899. II. 196.¹
Boitard, M. *See* Bréant, Victor & Boitard, M.
Boitard, Pierre. La botanique des dames. 1821. I. 94.
— Botanique des demoiselles. 1835. I. 94.
— Flore de la botanique des dames. 1821. I. 94.
— Manuel complet de botanique. 1826. I. 86.
— Manuel complet de l'amateur de Roses. 1836. III. 448.
— Manuel d'histoire naturelle. 1827. I. 255.
— Manuel de physiologie végétale. 1829. I. 148.
— Manuel du cultivateur-forestier. 1834. IV. 85,¹ *109.*¹
— Traité de la culture du Mûrier. 1828. III. 374.
— *See also* Noisette, Louis & Boitard, Pierre.
Boiteau, Pierre. Sur le degré d'efficacité du sulfure de carbone. 1877. III. 570.²
— Eclosion de l'œuf d'hiver du phylloxera. 1876. III. 568.
— Effets du sulfure de carbone sur . . . la Vigne. 1879. III. 560.
— Sur l'emploi du sulfure de carbone. 1880. III. 572.
— Études sur la reproduction du phylloxera. 1885. III. 573.
— Sur les générations parthénogénésiques du phylloxera. 1883. III. 573.
— Sur les générations parthénogénésiques du phylloxera. 1883. III. 573.
— Lettre à M. Dumas. 1876. III. 569.²
— Sur les mœurs du phylloxera. 1887. III. 574.
— Observations diverses sur le phylloxera. 1877. III. 570.²
— Observations faites en 1881 sur le phylloxera. 1881. III. 573.
— Observations faites pendant la campagne viticole. 1882. III. 573.
— Observations pour servir à l'étude du phylloxera. 1882. III. 573.
— Observations relatives à l'influence exercée par la saison dernière sur le . . . phylloxera. 1880. III. 572.
— Observations sur le développement et les migrations du phylloxera. 1876. III. 569.¹

— Sur l'œuf d'hiver du phylloxera. 1876. III. 568.
— Sur le phylloxera aérien. 1876. III. 569.[1]
— Le phylloxéra ailé. 1876. III. 760.
— Sur le phylloxera issu de l'œuf d'hiver. 1876. III. 568.
— Sur la préparation et l'emploi du liquide destiné à badigeonner les Vignes. 1877. III. 570.[1]
— Sur la présence . . . d'œufs d'hiver du phylloxera. 1879. III. 571.
— Procédés pratiques pour la destruction du phylloxera. 1877. III. 570.[1]
— Sur quelques-uns des résultats obtenus dans le traitement des Vignes phylloxérées. 1878. III. 570.[2]
— Recherches sur les causes de réinvasion des vignobles phylloxérées. 1879. III. 571.
— Réponse à M. Balbiani. 1879. III. 571.
— Réponse à quelques-uns des critiques . . . sur la reproduction du phylloxera. 1885. III. 573.
— Résultat des traitements effectués sur les Vignes atteintes par le phylloxera. 1880. III. 572.
— Suite des résultats obtenus par l'élevage, en tubes, du phylloxera. 1886. III. 574.
— Sur le traitement des Vignes par le sulfure de carbone. 1881. III. 572.
— Traitement des Vignes phylloxérées. 1876. III. 569.[2]
Boitel, A. Culture du Cédratier en Corse. 1875. III. 502.[1]
Boitel, Amédée. Mise en valeur des terres pauvres par le Pin maritime. 1848. IV. 467.[2]
— Du Pin maritime. 1848. IV. 467.[1]
Boive, (Dr.). Code des loix des trois mandemens de la plaine du gouvernement d'Aigle. 1772. IV. 329.
Boixo, P. de. Les forêts et le reboisement dans les Pyrénées-Orientales. 1894. IV. 362.
— Les inondations de 1888 à 1891. 1892. IV. 47.[1]
— Inondations des 8 et 9 novembre 1892. 1892. IV. 185.[2]
— Notice sur les forêts . . . dans les Pyrénées-Orientales. 1893. IV. 361.
— Notice sur les inondations de 1888. 1892. IV. 47.[1]
— La sylviculture dans la Haute-Garonne. 1898. IV. 122.[1]
— Vente au printemps des coupes à écorcer. 1896. IV. 388.[2]
Bojer, Wenzel. Botanical description of the Tanghin. 1833. II. 733.[2]
— Sur la culture du Thé à l'Ile Maurice. 1845. III. 604.[1]
— Description du genre Labourdonnaisia. 1841. II. 698.[2]
— Descriptiones et icones plantarum . . . in insulis Africae. 1835. I. 483.[1]
— Descriptiones plantarum . . . in insulis Africae. 1843. I. 483.[1]
— Descriptions d'espèces nouvelles. 1836. I. 483.[1]
— Descriptions de diverses plantes . . . de Madagascar. 1842. I. 482.
— Hortus mauritianus. 1837. I. 482.
— Planches relatives au genre Gaertnera. 1847. II. 817.[1]
Bokof, V, E. See Бокофъ, B. E.
Bokorny, Thomas. Ueber Aggregation. 1889. I. 147.
— Die durchsichtigen Punkte der Blätter. 1882. I. 110.
— Ueber die durchsichtigen Punkte in den Blättern. 1882. I. 110.
— Einiges über die Proteinstoffe der Samen. 1900. I. 204.
— Die Keimung der Samen. 1888. I. 204.
— Ueber den Nachweis des Transpirationsstromes. 1891. I. 168.
— Ueber den Ort der Wasserleitung in den Pflanzen. 1890. I. 166.
— Die Wege des Transpirationsstromes. 1890. I. 168.
Bolander, Henry N. Caractères généraux de la végétation californienne. 1868. I. 323.
— Enumeration of shrubs and trees . . . of San Francisco Bay. 1863. I. 320.
— On Menzies' Spruce. 1875. II. 38.[2]
— Names of California plants. 1867. I. 323.
— Remarks on California trees. 1863. I. 320.
Boldi, Lodovico. Le foreste e la loro influenza. 1899. IV. 45.
Le Boldo. Peumus boldus. 1872. II. 222.[1]
Boldt, Johan Georg Robert. Ek i Kuopio. 1898. II. 136.[2]
Boleg. See Болегъ.
Bolet, Louis Madelaine. Essais sur la culture du Mûrier blanc. 1766. III. 373.
Boletim de agricultura, mineria é industrias. III. 9.
Boletin de agricultura tropical. 1898. II. 10.[1]
Boletin de fomento de la industria nacional corcho-taponera. 1893. IV. 541.
Bolfbar, Jerónimo. El corcho laminado como calorífugo. 1890. IV. 559.[2]
Bolingbroke, Henry. A voyage to the Demerary. 1809. III. 267.[2]

Bolivian Cinchona forests. 1884. II. 813.[1]
Boll, Ernst. Flora von Mecklenburg. 1860. I. 384.
— Flora von Mecklenburg-Strelitz. 1849. I. 382.
— Merkwürdige Bäume in Meklenburg. 1857. I. 296.[1]
Boll, Jacob. Verzeichniss der Phanerogamen- & Kryptogamen-Flora von Bremgarten. 1869. I. 435.
Bollaert, William. Products of New Granada. 1861. III. 268.[1]
Bolle, Giovanni. See Bolle, Johann.
Bolle, Johann. L' infezione fillosserica in Istria. 1886. III. 762.
— I rimedi contro la fillossera. 1882. III. 761.
— Der Seidenbau in Japan. 1898. III. 378.
— La sommersione delle Vigne affette dalla Phylloxera. 188 . ? III. 761.
Bolle, Karl August. Addenda ad floram Atlantidis. 1859. I. 497.
— Die Aktinidien-Schlinge. 1881. III. 595.[2]
— Ampelopsis Graebneri. 1899. III. 545.[1]
— Andeutungen über die freiwillige Baum- und Strauchvegetation der Provinz Brandenburg. 1886. I. 371.
— The arboretum of Dr. Dieck at Zoeschen. 1890. I. 49.
— Argyranthemum crithmifolium. 1861. II. 854.[2]
— Die Arten und Formen der Platanen. 1875. III. 418.[1]
— Ein Baumgärtchen unter der Erde. 1892. I. 49, III. 183.[2]
— A bit of forgotten history. 1890. II. 46.[1]
— Botanische Rückblicke auf die Inseln Lanzarote. 1893. I. 498.
— Der Capollin fruchttragend. 1898. III. 435.[2]
— Ueber Catalpa. 1879. III. 706.[1]
— Drei Gehölzporträts. 1881. III. 69.
— Die Eichenfrucht als menschliches Nahrungsmittel. 1891. IV. 515.[3]
— Etwas über Ahorne. 1894. II. 476.[2]
— Die Eukalyptusweide. 1890. III. 351.[1]
— Die Fichte von Hasselwerder. 1878. II. 48.[1]
— Florula insularum olim Purpurariarum. 1892. I. 498.
— Grafting Oaks. 1890. III. 361.[2]
— Die in Italien einheimischen Koniferen. 1869. II. 15.[1]
— Ein Kapitel über die Eichen in . . . Brandenburg. 1888. II. 130.[2]
— Ueber Lärchenbäume. 1873. III. 304.[2]
— Unter den Linden des Werbellin. 1890. III. 517.[2]
— The Lindens for city-planting. 1889. III. 585.[1]
— A mysterious Conifer. 1890. III. 25.[1]
— Nachtrag zur Florula der Kopfweiden. 1892. I. 234.[2]
— The naturalization of exotic forest-trees in Prussia. 1891. IV. 126.[1]
— Eine neue Pyramideneiche. 1894. III. 363.[1]
— Noch ein Wort über Gattungsnamen der Nadelhölzer. 1886. II. 13.[1]
— Die Omorika-Fichte. 1877. II. 38.[1]
— Ein paar Worte über Pinus mitis. 1879. III. 307.[1]
— Die Palmen auf den Canarischen Inseln. 1854. I. 496, II. 62.[1]
— Zum Rätsel der Eichlerstaone. 1890. III. 297.[1]
— Die Rosskastanie. 1880. II. 481.[2]
— Salix daphnoides X argenteo-repens. 1863. II. 101.[2]
— Siebold's Wallnussbaum. 1881. II. 114.[2]
— Die Sternmagnolie. 1881. III. 400.[2]
— Ulmus effusa. 1888. II. 144.[2]
— Zur Variabilität der Eiche in der Mark. 1891. II. 130.[2]
— De vegetatione alpina in Germania. 1846. I. 381.
— Wann erscheint die Weymouthskiefer zuerst in Europa? 1890. II. 46.[1]
— Der Weinstock. 1860. II. 507.[1]
— Wiederauffindung der Eibe, als wild in der Mark Brandenburg. 1898. II. 13.[1]
— Ein Wort zu Gunsten des dendrologischen Gartens. 1877. I. 53,[1] 48.
Boller, Wilhelm. Untersuchungen über die Bodentemperaturen. 1894. IV. 70.
Bolles, Frank. Sap-sucking woodpeckers. 1891. IV. 199.[1]
Bollettino ufficiale per l' amministrazione forestale italiana. IV. 13.[1]
Bolley, Henry Luke & Waldron, L. R. The occurrence of calcium oxalate . . . during the differentiation of the buds of Prunus. 1898. II. 272.[1]
— A preliminary list of . . . plants of North Dakota. 1900. I. 327.
Bolley, P. A. Ueber den Farbstoff des Sandelholzes. 1847. III. 384.[1]

Bolley, P. A. (continued).
— Ueber den gelben Farbstoffe der Quercitronrinde. 1841. II. 140.[2]
— Sur la matière colorante du bois de Santal. 1847. III. 384.[1]
— De mest, scheikundige samenstelling. 1851. III. 151.
Bollmann, Carl. See ZIPPEL, Hermann & BOLLMANN, Carl.
Bollstaedt, ALBERTUS DE. See ALBERTUS DE BOLLSTAEDT.
Bologna — Academia scientiarum instituti bononiensis. See BONONIENSIS SCIENTIARUM . . . I. 24.[2]
Bologna — Accademia delle scienze dell' istituto. See BONONIENSIS SCIENTIARUM . . . I. 24.[2]
Bologna — Bononiensis scientiarum . . . institutum atque academia. See BONONIENSIS . . . I. 24.[2]
Bologna — Società agraria della provincia . . . See SOCIETÀ . . . III. 23.[2]
Bolotow, A. Wie man Wälder auf die vortheilhafteste Art fällen . . . könne. 1774. IV. 113.[2]
Bolt, W. N. Het bevestigen van Heide-duinen. 1855. IV. 472.
— Dennen zonder kluiten. 1862. IV. 152.
Bolton, James. A catalogue of plants . . . of Halifax. 1775. I. 395.
Bolton, Robert. The history of the several towns, manors . . . of the county of Westchester. See WILLIS, O. R. 1881. I. 315.
Boltshauser, Heinrich. Blattflecken des Wallnussbaums. 1898. III. 356.[1]
— Krankheiten unserer Kirschbäume. 1898. III. 435.[2]
Bolus, Harry. Contributions to South-African botany. 1888. I. 495.
— Contributions to the flora of South Africa. 1894. I. 495.
— Grundzüge der Flora von Südafrika. 1886. I. 495.
— Sketch of the flora of South Africa. 1886. I. 495.
— See also MACOWAN, Peter & BOLUS, Harry.
Bomare, Jacques Christophe VALMONT-. See VALMONT-BOMARE, J. C.
Bomasch, Gustav. Der Holzhandel in Ost- und Westpreussen. 1893. IV. 404.[2]
Bombast von Hohenheim, Aureolus Philippus Theophrastus. Das Holtzbüchlein . . . gebrauch des Franzosenholzes. 1564. III. 494.[1]
Bombay — Agri-horticultural society. See AGRI-HORTICULTURAL . . . III. 26.[1]
Bombay — Anthropological society. See ANTHROPOLOGICAL . . . I. 28.[2]
Bombay — Medical and physical society. See MEDICAL . . . I. 29.[1]
Bombay Aloe fibre. 1890. III. 341.[1]
Bombay Aloe fibre. 1892. III. 341.[1]
Bombay branch of the Royal Asiatic society. See ROYAL ASIATIC SOCIETY . . . I. 29.[1]
Bombay geographical society. Journal. Proceedings. Transactions. I. 28.[2]
Bombay natural history society. Journal. I. 29.[1]
Bombay Presidency. See INDIA — BOMBAY PRESIDENCY.
Bomberger, W. M. Blackberry culture. 1889. III. 457.[2]
— Grape pruning. 1889. III. 549.[1]
— Grape pruning. 1891. III. 549.[2]
— Recent experiences in top-grafting. 1895. III. 163.[1]
— In the vineyard. 1893. III. 551.[1]
Bombicci, Luigi. Il diboscamento sulle montagne. 1874. IV. 48.[1]
Bombien, Otto HILLER-. See HILLER-BOMBIEN, Otto.
Bomboletti, Annesio. I vini del Reno. 1880. III. 583.[1]
Le Bombyce moine en Campine. 1898. IV. 202.
Bombyx Cynthia or Ailanthus silkworm. 1862. III. 507.[1]
Bomme, Leendert. Naturkundige waarneming van een bevruchten Oranje-Appel. 1780. II. 402.[2]
Bommer, Charles. Musée forestier. Rapport. 1898. IV. 18.[2]
— La pourriture rouge de l'Épicéa. 1899. IV. 457.
— Sequoia gigantea Torr. 1896. III. 310.[2]
— See also CRAHAY, N. I. & BOMMER, C.
Bommer, Jean Édouard. Considérations sur la panachure. 1867. I. 141.
— De la fécondation artificielle des Palmiers. 1867. III. 317.
— Des matières colorantes des feuilles. 1866. I. 185.[1]
— Notice sur le Jardin botanique de Bruxelles. 1871. I. 50.
— Les Platanes et leur culture. 1869. II. 254.[2]
Bompard, J. P. Abrégé sur la culture de l'Olivier. 1842. III. 675.[2]
Bomplan. Sur la récolte de quinquina au Pérou. 1809. III. 720.

Bon. Moyens de rendre utiles les Marons d'Inde. 1722. III. 537.[2]
Le Bon cultivateur. III. 19.
Le Bon jardinier. III. 19.
Bona, Giovanni dalla. Dell' uso e dell' abuso del Caffè. 1751. III. 741.[1]
— L' uso e l' abuso del caffè. 1751. III. 741.[1]
Bona y Garcia de Tejada, Casimiro de. Memoria sobre la explotación de los Robles por la marina. 1881. IV. 514.[1]
Bonadei, Carlo. Intorno all' accrescimento in grossezza. 1864. I. 187.
Bonafous, Matthieu. Analyse de la feuille du Mûrier. 1823. II. 154.[2]
— Aperçu de la culture du Mûrier. 1830. III. 374.
— Ueber die Cultur des Maulbeerbaums. 1822. III. 374.
— De la culture des Mûriers. 1822. III. 373.
— De la culture des Mûriers. 1825. III. 374.
— Culture du Mûrier en prairie. 1832. III. 374.
— Expériences comparative sur l'emploi des feuilles du Mûrier. 1829. III. 379.[2]
— Expériences comparatives sur l'emploi des feuilles du Mûrier. 1832. III. 374.
— Des feuilles du Maclura. 1835. III. 372.[1]
— Sul Gelso delle Filippine. 1833. III. 380.[1]
— De la greffe du Mûrier. 1836. III. 375.
— De la greffe du Mûrier blanc. 1836. III. 375.
— Mémoire sur la culture du Mûrier. 1831. II. 154,[1] III. 374.
— Mémoire sur le Mûrier à papier. 1829. III. 367.[2]
— Mûrier remarquable. 1842. II. 154.[2]
— Recherches sur les moyens de remplacer la feuille du Mûrier. 1826. III. 168.[1]
— Saggio sui gelseti. 1831. III. 374.
— Traité de l'éducation des vers à soie. 1824. III. 374.
Bonafous, Norbert. Notice sur le Dacus Oleae. 1860. III. 677.[2]
Bonald, de, (député, Aveyron). Opinion sur l'article 1er du titre XI. du projet de loi de finances. 1817. IV. 325.
Bonami, François. Florae nannetensis prodromus. 1782. I 406.
Bonamicus, Franciscus. De alimento libri V. 1602. III. 219.[1]
Bonamy, François. Lettre à Bernard de Jussieu. 1895. II. 212.[1]
— Le plus ancien Magnolia de France. 1895. II. 212.[1]
Bonamy's Weeping Birch. 1895. III. 357.[1]
Bonanno, Alfio. Dell' uso del Pepe nero. 1831. III. 343.[2]
Bonard, Ernest. Code forestier. 1827. IV. 275.
— Des forêts de la France. 1826. IV. 275.
— Plantes nouvelles. 1869. III. 87.
— Plantes nouvelles pour 1864. 1864. III. 711,[2] 749.[1]
— Rusticité du Poinciana Gilliesii. 1866. III. 469.[1]
Bonastre, J. F. Analyse du baume de copalme d'Amérique. 1831. III. 417.[2]
— Analyse du piment de la Jamaïque. 1825. III. 637.[1]
— Chemische Untersuchung der Früchte von Myristica sebifera. 1833. III. 403.[2]
— Considerations sur la résine alouchi. 1824. III. 397.[2]
— A dissertation on some ancient plants of Egypt. 1834. I. 81.[2]
— Essai comparatif entre la manne dite de Briançon. 1833. IV. 534.[2]
— Sur l'essence licari kanali. 1882. III. 404.[1]
— Examen analytique de la fève de Péchurim. 1825. III. 404.[1]
— Examen analytique du baume de la Mecque. 1832. III. 510.[2]
— Examen chimique d'une nouvelle résine. 1829. IV. 452.[1]
— Examen chimique de l'écorce Mossoy. 1829. III. 407.[1]
— Examen des baies du Laurier. 1824. III. 406.[2]
— Examen des dattes. 1832. III. 329.[1]
— Examen des fruits du Myristica sebifera. 1833. III. 403.[1]
— Examen du baume de Sucrier de montagne. 1826. III. 511.[2]
— Expériences sur le produit résineux du Palmier à cire. 1828. III. 321.[2]
— Fruit du Hura. 1824. III. 519.[2]
— Sur l'huile essentielle du Thuya. 1825. III. 311.[1].
— De l'huile volatile de Cèdre de Virginie. 1837. III. 304.[1]
— Note sur les fleurs du Mimosa odorata. 1831. III. 465.[1]
— Notice sur quelques végétaux représentés sur les anciens monumens de l'Égypte. 1830. I. 523.

— Sur une nouvelle espèce de Myrrhe. 1829. III. 510.²
— Observations sur du baume de la Mecque. 1832. III. 510.²
— Sur la présence de la fécule dans la noix muscade. 1823. III. 402.²
— Sur quelques végétaux qui ont acquis en 1834 un volume extraordinaire. 1835. I. 187.
— Recherches chimiques sur quelques substances végétales trouvées dans l'intérieur des cercueils. 1828. I. 523.
— Recherches sur le Cinnamomum des anciens. 1828. III. 402.² 405.²
— Du styrax ou storax de Bogota. 1830. III. 244.
— Untersuchung der Datteln. 1832. III. 329.²
— See also MORINGLANE, DUPONCHEL & BONASTRE, J. F.
Bonato, J. A. Catalogus plantarum Horti bot. patavini. 1811. I. 61.
Bonavia, Emanuel. Antiquity of the Citron-tree in Egypt. 1894. II. 402.²
— The Arabian Date-tree in India. 1899. III. 329.¹
— Befruchtung ohne Pollen. 1890. I. 202.¹
— The Carawnda bush. 1885. III. 687.¹
— Citrus décoction as a fever remedy. 1886. III. 499.¹
— The cone-fruit of the Assyrian monuments. 1887. II. 402.¹
— The cultivated Oranges and Lemons. 1890. II. 401,⁷ III. 497.²
— The Date Palm. 1885. III. 328.²
— The Date Palm in India. 1898. III. 329.¹
— Did the Assyrians know the sexes of the Date-palms? 1889. II. 73.¹
— Erythrina suberosa. 1885. III. 476.²
— Eucalyptus globulus. 1899. IV. 533.²
— Eucalyptus rostrata at Lucknow. 1878. III. 634.²
— Fertilisation without pollen. 1890. I. 202.¹
— A few notes on the oranges . . . of the London market. 1890. III. 499.¹
— The flora of the Assyrian monuments. 1894. I. 81,² 516.
— The future of the Date Palm in India. 1885. III. 328.²
— The gardener's note book. 1867. III. 497.¹
— Indian notes. 1885. III. 129.²
— Note on an Orange having a distinct streak of lemon colour on the rind. 1899. II. 402.²
— Oil from the Lawsonia inermis. 1865. III. 630.¹
— On the probable wild source of . . . true Limes. 1887. II. 401.¹
— Propagation . . . of the Malta Orange. 1867. III. 497.¹
— Ruscus hypophyllum var. latifolius. 1885. III. 338.¹
— The sacred trees of the Assyrian monuments. 1888. I. 514.²
— Some account of the orange . . . in India. 1890. III. 499.¹
Bonavia, G. The fruits of India. 1888. III. 279.¹
Boncenne, F. Les arbres fruitiers à fleurs doubles. 1862. III. 207.¹
— Chorosema Henchmanni. 1861. III. 472.²
— Sur la Clématite à calice. 1859. III. 390.¹
— Étymologie du genre Chorosema. 1861. II. 345.²
— Euphorbia jacquiniaeflora. 1870. III. 518.¹
— Gomphocarpus fruticosus. 1863. III. 692.²
— Leucopogon verticillatus. 1861. III. 665.¹
— Passiflore Belotii. 1859. III. 615.²
— Le Solanum crispum. 1860. III. 701.²
Boncerf. Mémoire sur les moyens de mettre en culture les terres incultes. 1790. IV. 101.²
Bondam, R. Flora kampensis. 1845. I. 391.¹
— & Top, W. G. Flora kampensis. See BONDAM, R. 1845. I. 391.¹
Bondaroy, Auguste Denis FOUGEROUX DE. See FOUGEROUX DE BONDAROY, A. D.
Bondault, P. C. See GLÉNARD, Alexandre & BONDAULT, P. C.
Bondonneau, Lucien. De l'amylogène ou amidon soluble. 1875. I. 140.¹
— De l'iodure d'amidon. 1877. I. 140.¹
— De la saccharification des matières amylacées. 1875. I. 175.
— & Foret. De la saccharification directe. 1887. I. 177.
Bondt, Nikolaus. De cortice Geoffreae surinamensis. 1788. III. 467.¹
Bondurant, C. S. L'hydrangine de l'Hydrangea arborescens. 1887. III. 411.¹
Bonelli, Georgio. Hortus romanus. 1772. I. 292.
— Memoria intorno al olio di Ricino. 1782. III. 522.¹
Bonelli, Luigi Giorgio. Pei nostri forestali? 1897. IV. 293.²
— Pei nostri monti. 1897. IV. 166.¹
Bonfiglioli, Giuseppe. Index plantarum Aetnae. 1636. I. 430.
Bongard, Heinrich Gustav. Bauhiniae et Pauletiae, species brasilienses novae. 1836. II. 334.²

— Compositae brasilienses novae. 1839. II. 860.²
— Descriptiones plantarum novarum. 1839. I. 342.
— Esquisse historique des travaux sur la botanique entrepris en Russie. 1834. I. 80.¹
— Mémoire sur la végétation des îles de Bonin-Sima. 1837. I. 462.
— Observations sur la végétation de l'île de Siteha. 1831. I. 311.²
— Plantae quatuor brasilienses novae. 1836. I. 341.
— Quatuor plantae brasilienses. 1836. I. 341.
— & Meyer, C. A. Verzeichniss der . . . am Saisang-Nor und am Irtysch gesammelten Pflanzen. 1841. I. 453.¹
Boni, Ferdinand. Des contraventions forestières. 1877. IV. 326.
Bonificamento delle regioni di malaria lungo le ferrovie d'Italia. 1882. IV. 55.¹
Bonjean, Edmond. Sur la présence naturelle de grandes proportions de chlorure de potassium. 1898. III. 583.²
Bonjour, Samuel. See MARCHAND, Ernest & BONJOUR, Samuel.
Bonn — Niederrheinische Gesellschaft für Natur- und Heilkunde. See NIEDERRHEINISCHE . . . I. 14.
Bonnafont. Les racines assainissantes de l'Eucalyptus. 1882. IV. 533.²
Bonné, Philippe. Le Caroubier ou l'Arbre des Lotophages. 1867. III. 471.²
Bonnechose, A. de. Recherches historiques sur les progrès de l'horticulture. 1844. III. 33.²
Bonnefond, A. Du Pin Mugho. 1880. II. 43.¹
Bonnefons, Nicolas de. The French gardiner. 1651. III. 111.
— Le jardinier françois. 1651. III. 111.
Bonnegens, de. Rapport . . . sur l'échange de la forêt de Brix. 1791. IV. 281.²
Bonnel. Clematis Vitalba. 1882. III. 392.¹
— Phoenix cycadaefolia. 1881. III. 328.¹
Bonnel, Benoit. Maladies de la Vigne. 1855. III. 576.
Bonnelle, F. C. Le jardinier d'Artois. 1763. III. 112.
Bonnemère, Lionel. Greffe du Châtaignier sur le Chêne. 1896. III. 359.¹
Bonner, W. G. The Redwoods of California. 1884. II. 49,² IV. 484.¹
Bonnêt. Fruit monstrueux; poire prolifère. 1827. II. 279.²
Bonnet, (Inspecteur adj. des forêts). Souvenirs d'une mission forestière en Nouvelle-Calédonie. 1887. IV. 380.²
Bonnet, A. See RAVAZ, Louis & BONNET, A.
Bonnet, Charles, (1720–1793). Betrachtung über die Natur. 1764. I. 31.
— Betrachtungen über die organisirten Körper. 1762. I. 31.
— Considérations sur les corps organisés. 1762. I. 31.
— Contemplation de la nature. 1764. I. 31.
— Onderzoek over het gebruik der bladen in de plantgewassen. 1754. I. 172.
— Recherches sur l'usage des feuilles. 1754. I. 172.
— Untersuchungen über den Nutzen der Blätter. 1754. I. 172.
Bonnet, Charles. Notes sur la rusticité de quelques plantes. 1873. III. 48.
Bonnet, Charles Henri. Traité de l'agriculture des bois. 1814. IV. 109.¹
Bonnet, Edmond. Aperçu historique sur les plantes de Tunisie. 1894. I. 82.¹
— De la disjonction des sexes dans l'Evonymus. 1878. II. 468.¹
— Énumération des plantes recueillies . . . dans le Sahara. 1883. I. 485.
— Essai d'une monographie des Canellées. 1876. II. 566.²
— Florule des îles Saint-Pierre et Miquélon. 1895. I. 310.
— Géographie botanique de la Tunisie. 1895. I. 486.
— Histoire du Gui. 1879. II. 179.¹
— Ministère de l'instruction publique et des beaux-arts. 1890. I. 523.
— Une mission française en Afrique. 1891. I. 523.
— Note sur les Ephedra. 1877. II. 54.¹
— Nouveaux documents relatifs à l'ambassade d'Éthiopie. 1890. I. 523.
— Petite flore parisienne. 1883. I. 416.
— Le piante egiziane del Museo reale di Firenze. 1895. I. 82.¹
— Plantes représentées sur les vases de Boscoreale. 1900. I. 81.¹
— Recherches sur la nomenclature . . . de genre Erica. 1882. II. 664.²
— Remarques sur quelques plantes indiquées en Tunisie. 1897. I. 486.

Bonnet, Edmond (*continued*).
— Revue des plantes nouvelles pour la flore française. 1879. I. 416.
— & **Barratte**, Gustave.   Catalogue raisonné des plantes . . . de la Tunisie.   1896.   I. 486.
—— Illustrations de la partie botanique.   1896.   I. 486.
— & **Maury**, Paul.   D'Aïn-Sefra à Djenien-Bou-Resq.   1888. I. 485.
— & **Maury**, Pierre.   Étude sur le Warionia Saharae.   1890. II. 868.²
— & **Richter**, J. A.   Notes sur quelques plantes de la Côte-d'Or.   1882.   II. 312.¹
Bonnet, G.   Jardin botanique de Lyon.   1859.   I. 58.
— & **Faivre**, E.   Jardin . . . de Lyon.   1862.   I. 58.
Bonnet, L.   Transformation des vrilles de la Vigne.   1894. II. 507.²
Bonnet, L. NOIROT-.   See NOIROT-BONNET, L.
Bonnet, Marcellin.   Facies plantarum.   1810.   I. 33.
Bonnet, Maurice.   See FOURNIER, Eugène & BONNET, Maurice.
Bonnet, Michel.   Une invasion de chenilles à Valdoniello. 1897.   IV. 209.¹
Bonnet, Valère.   See HÉRAIL, Joseph & BONNET, Valère.
Bonnewyn, H.   Considérations sur le Thé.   1856.   III. 607.
Bonnier, Gaston Eugène Marie.   Anatomie de la Rose à prolifération centrale.   1881.   II. 289.¹
— Sur l'assimilation des plantes parasites à. chlorophylle. 1891.   I. 174.
— L'assimilation du Gui comparée à celle du Pommier.   1889. II. 179.³
— Cultures expérimentales sur l'adaptation des plantes. 1899.   I. 219.¹
— Sur la différence de transmissibilité des pressions.   1892. I. 149.²
— Sur la différenciation des tissus vasculaires de la feuille et de la tige.   1900.   I. 111, *134*.³
— Étude anatomique et physiologique des nectaires.   1879. I. 118.²
— Étude sur l'anatomie et la physiologie des nectaires.   1878. I. 115,¹ *800*.
— Les études sur l'origine de la flore arctique.   1880.   I. 220.¹
— Études sur la végétation de la vallée d'Aure.   1890.   I. 422.
— Études sur la végétation de la vallée de Chamonix.   1889. I. 437.
— La flore des Pyrénées comparée à celle des Alpes françaises. 1893.   I. 417.
— De la greffe-bouture.   1886.   III. 548.²
— Influence de la lumière électrique continue et discontinue. 1892.   I. 230.
— Influence de la lumière électrique continue sur la forme. 1895.   I. 230.
— Influence des hautes altitudes.   1891.   IV. 73.¹
— Sur la miellée des feuilles.   1896.   I. 213.³
— Mouvements de la Sensitive développée dans l'eau.   1898. II. 373.¹
— Les nectaires.   1879.   I. 118.¹
— Note sur la pression transmise à travers les tiges.   1892.   I. 150.¹
— Observations sur les Berbéridées.   1890.   II. 205.¹
— Observations sur les Renonculacées.   1889.   II. 196.¹
— Sur l'ordre de formation des éléments du cylindre central dans la racine et la tige.   1900.   I. 106.¹
— Les plantes arctiques comparées.   1894.   II. 109.²
— Sur les qualités de chaleur dégagées et absorbées par les végétaux.   1886.   I. 186.
— Quel   observations sur la flore alpine d'Europe.   1880. I. 349.ques
— Recherches expérimentales sur l'adaptation des plantes au climat alpin.   1895.   I. 220.¹
— Recherches expérimentales sur les variations de pression dans la Sensitive.   1892.   II. 373.¹
— Recherches sur la chaleur végétale.   1893.   I. 186.
— Recherches sur la transmission de la pression.   1893. I. 150.¹
— Sur le rôle attribué aux parties colorées des organes floraux. 1878.   I. 237.
— Sur la structure des plantes de Spitzberg.   1894.   I. 220.¹
— De la variation avec l'altitude.   1880.   I. 236.²
— Les variations de la structure chez une même espèce.   1892. II. 30.²
— & **Flahault**, Charles.   Observations sur les modifications des végétaux.   1878.   I. 217.
— & **Layens**, Georges de.   Flore complète de la France. 1894.   I. 418.

—— Nouvelle flore des environs de Paris.   1887.   I. 417.
—— Nouvelle flore pour la détermination facile des plantes sans mots techniques.   1887.   I. 417.
—— Tableaux synoptiques des plantes vasculaires de la flore de la France.   1894.   I. 418.
— & **Mangin**, Louis.   L'action chlorophyllienne.   1885.   I. 142, *171*.
—— L'action chlorophyllienne dans l'obscurité ultraviolette. 1886.   I. 173, 142.¹
—— Sur les échanges gazeux entre les plantes vertes et l'atmosphère.   1885.   I. 173.
—— La fonction respiratoire chez les végétaux.   1885.   I. 171.
—— Influence de la lumière sur la respiration.   1884.   I. 171.
—— Note sur l'action chlorophyllienne.   1885.   I. 173.
—— Recherches sur la respiration des feuilles à. l'obscurité. 1884.   I. 171.
—— Recherches sur les variations de la respiration.   1885. I. 171.
—— Sur la respiration . . . aux différentes saisons.   1885. I. 171.
—— Sur la respiration des végétaux.   1885.   I. 171.
Bonnieu, Pierre.   Note sur la rusticité de quelques Pins du Méxique.   1871.   III. 292.
Bononiensis scientiarum . . . institutum atque academia. Commentarii.   I. 24.²
Bonpland, Aimé de.   Berigt wegens het inzamelen van den Kinabast in Peru.   1810. `III. 717.³
— Communication faite par M. François Delessert.   1854.   I. 329.
— Description des plantes rares cultivées à Malmaison et à Navarre.   1813.   I. 57. .
— Ilex paraguayensis.   1854.   III. 530.²
— Mémoire sur le Ceroxylon. ,1804.   II. 66.¹
— See also HUMBOLDT, F. H. A. von & BONPLAND, Aimé.
Bonplandia.   I. 11.
Bonsall, Spencer.   Tea: its culture and manufacture.   1861. III. 600.²
Bonse, (*Forstassessor*).   Versuche mit dem Schnücke'schen Zahnkeil.   1886.   IV. 384.¹
Bontekoe, Cornelis.   Een kort tractaat . . . van de chocolate. 1679.   III. 594.
— Een kort tractaat van de kragten . . . van de coffi.   1679. III. 741.¹
— Tractaat van het excellenste kruyd thee.   1679.   III. 221,³ *605*.
— & **Blankaart**, Stephen.   Gebruik en misbruik van de thee. 1686.   III. 221.³
— Haustus polychresti.   1686.   III. 221.³
Bontius, Jacob.   Historiae naturalis & medicae Indiae orientalis libri VI.   1642.   III. 277.   *See also* PISO, Willem. 1658.   III. 266.
— De medicina Indorum libri IV.   1642.   III. 277.
— Notae in Garciam ab Horto.   1642.   III. 268.²
Bonvalet.   Culture des Eucalyptus en Orient.   1893.   IV. 530.
Bonvalot.   Note. sur l'odeur de la Crassula lactea. · 1835. II. 236.²
Bonvalot, Gabriel.   De Paris au Tonkin.   1892.   I. 460.²
Bonvier, L.   Mont Cenis . . . sa végétation.   1863.   I. 412.
Bonynge, Frank.   Tea, cultivation, Assam, India.   1851. III. 602.²
Bonzom, E. & others.   Du Caroubier et de la caroube.   1878. III. 471.²
Boodle, Leonard A.   See CALVERT, Agnes & BOODLE, L. A.
— & **Worsdell**, W. C.   On the comparative anatomy of the Casuarineae.   1894.   II. 92.¹
Boodt, Anselm Boethius de.   See BOOT, A. B. de.
Boogh, J.   Nederduitsch woordenboek, of alphabeth van alle kruiden.   1794.   I. 73.²
A book of fruits & flowers.   1656.   III. 51.
The book of trees.   1837.   I. 293,¹ *IV. 75*.¹
A booke of beast, birds, flowers, fruits.   1630.   I. 285.¹
Boole, *Miss* Lucy Everest.   See DUNSTAN, W. R. & BOOLE, *Miss* L. E.
De boomen en bosschen in den omtrek van Constantinopel. 1853.   I. 448.²
Boon Mesch, Anton Hendrik van der.   Over het kaoutschouh of elastieke gom.   1833.   III. 230.
— Over de noodzakelijkheid van de beoefening der natuurkundige wetenschap voor den landbouw in Nederland.   1846. III. 36.¹
—Scheikundig onderzoek . . . van het Kamhout of Camwood.   1833.   II. 334.¹

Boon Mesch, Hendrik Carel van der. Commentatio de vi lucis. 1819. I. 229.
— De ratione quae est inter structuram et formam externam plantarum. 1818. I. 98.
— Responsio ad quaestionem botanicam . . . quaeritur de ratione quae est inter structuram et formam externam plantarum. 1818. I. 98.
Boone, A. J. M. Les Conifères exotiques en Campine. 1897. IV. 545.[1]
Boone, Alphonse. *See* CRAHAY, N. I. & BOONE, Alphonse.
Boorsma, Willem Gerbrand. Eerste resultaten van het onderzoek naar de plantenstoffen. 1894. I. 154, III. 275.[1]
— Iets over de saponine-achtige bestanddeelen . . . der Assamthee. 1891. III. 608.[1]
— Over kola-noten. 1894. III. 590.[2]
— Nadere resultaten van het onderzoek naar de plantenstoffen. 1894. I. 154.
— Ueber philippinische Pfeilgifte. 1900. III. 274.[1]
— Plantaardige enzymen. 1893. I. 177.
— Sur les substances analogues à la saponine. 1891. III. 608.[1]
Boos, Josef & **Fritsch,** Karl. Ueber die Blüthezeit der Linden. 1862. II. 516.[1]
— — Phänologische Notizen, I. 1862. II. 516.[1]
Boos, Joseph. Schönbrunn's Flora. 1816. I. 65.[2]
Boot, Anselm Boetius de. Florum, herbarum, ac fructuum selectiorum icones. 1640. I. 285.[2]
Booth, George. Sieg der Rose " Königin von Dännemark." 1834. III. 448.
Booth, John. Abies oder Picea? 1887. II. 21.[2]
— Antwort auf den in . . . Artikel über die Douglasfichte. 1892. IV. 483.[2]
— Apropos de l'arboretum. 1898. IV. 18.[2]
— Ausländische Holzarten in der deutschen forstlichen Literatur. 1894. IV. 126.[1]
— Die ausländischen Holzarten in Bayern. 1893. IV. 126.[1]
— Beskrivelse af nogle haardføre Arter af Slægten Magnolia. 1839. III. 398.[1]
— Die Douglas-Fichte. 1877. IV. 441, *483.*[1]
— Einfluss des Samens auf die Pflanzenerziehung. 1881. I. 247, *IV. 74.*[1]
— Einige allgemeine Betrachtungen über die Wirkungen des Winters 1879/1880. 1881. IV. 191.[2]
— Feststellung der Anbauwürdigkeit ausländischer Waldbäume. 1880. IV. 125.[2]
— Forestry in North America. 1880. IV. 336.[1]
— Forêts de l'Amérique du Nord. 1892. IV. 337.[1]
— Ein letztes Wort an den Besitzer des sog. National-Arboretums, Herrn Dr. Dieck. 1890. IV. 483.[2]
— Die nadellosen Douglas-Fichten des Herrn Köhler. 1891. IV. 483.[2]
— Die Naturalisation ausländischer Waldbäume. 1882. IV. 125.[2]
— Die Naturalisation der Douglasfichte. 1890. IV. 483.[2]
— Ein neues Mittel zum Schutz von Nadelholzsaaten. 1878. IV. 199.[1]
— Die nordamerikanischen Holzarten und ihre Gegner. 1896. IV. 126.[1]
— Notizen über einige exotische Waldbäume. 1843. III. 120.[2]
— Le Pinus rigida. 1894. IV. 469.
— Pinus sylvestris von Riga. 1881. IV. 473.
— Quercus tinctoria. Quercitron-Egen. 1843. IV. 518.[2]
— Verzeichniss der Kiefern- und Tannen-Arten. 1841. IV. 441.
— Die Waldfrage in Nordamerika. 1880. IV. 271.[2]
— Die weitere Behandlung der Versuche mit ausländischen Holzarten. 1893. IV. 126.[1]
— Welche fremden Holzarten empfehlen sich für den Anbau als Waldgehölze. 1878. IV. 125.[2]
Booth, Thomas J. Neue Rhododendron von Assam und Bootan. 1854. III. 654.[2]
— The new Rhododendrons of Assam & Bootan. 1854. III. 654.[2]
Booth, William Beattie. Aucuba japonica. 1843. III. 644.[2]
— Cereus latifrons. 1849. III. 626.[1]
— Curious notices of the formation of roots. 1853. I. 188.
— History and description of the species of Camellia. 1830. II. 550.[2]
— *See also* CHANDLER, Alfred & Booth, W. B.
Booth, W. S. Mexican fibre or Istle. 1890. III. 341.[1]
Die Booth'sche Gärtnerei in Flottbeck bei Hamburg. 1858. I. 48.
Boott, Francis. Two introductory lectures on [vegetable] materia medica. 1827. III. 242.

Bopp, Alexander Andreas Stephanus. De acido quercitanico. 1855. IV. 514.[2]
Boppe, Lucien. L'aménagement et la propagation du gibier. 1900. IV. 136.[1]
— Création de peuplements artificiels. 1882. IV. 142.
— Le dendromètre Christen. 1892. IV. 216.
— English and Scotch forests. 1882. IV. 357.[2] -
— Exposé des faits généraux relatifs à la production forestière. 1882. IV. 63.[2]
— Les forêts de la Grande-Bretagne. 1882. IV. 357.[2]
— Les forêts du bassin inférieur de la Loire. 1898. IV. 362.
— Galerie Daubrée à l'École forestière . . . de Nancy. 1897. IV. 18.[2]
— Notice sur le contrôle. 1878. IV. 244.
— Les produits forestiers à l'Exposition . . . de Budapest. 1886. IV. 21.[1]
— Rapports de MM. Mallot & Le Grix père, datant de 1819 à 1825 et concernant . . . bois propres aux constructions navales. 1898. IV. 425.[2]
— Report on a visit to the English and Scotch forests. 1882. IV. 357.[2]
— Les tournées de l'École forestière en 1898. 1898. IV. 362.
— Traité de sylviculture. 1889. IV. 109.[2]
— Trois heures à la forêt de Soignes. 1897. IV. 357.[1]
— *See also* BROILLARD, Charles & BOPPE, Lucien.
— & Reuss, Eduard. L'enseignement forestier en Autriche et en Bavière. 1886. IV. 36.[2]
— — La enseñanza forestal en el extranjero. 1890. IV. 540.[1]
— — La forêt du Spessart. 1886. IV. 351.[1] ·
— Missions forestières à l'étranger. 1886. IV. 342.[2]
Borbás, Vincenz von. Abauj-Torna vármegye flórája. 187 . ? I. 446.
— Abies sive Picea eblipsonis. 1900. II. 37.[2]
— Abweichende Blätter bei Sorbus domestica. 1884. II. 312.[2]
— Adatok Arbe és Veglia szigetek nyári flórája közelebbi ismeretéhez. 1876. I. 447.
— Az Alnus barbata C. A. Mey. 1885. II. 116.[1]
— Ueber Arten der Gattung Tilia. 1889. II. 515.[2]
— Balanographiai magyarázatok. 1887. II. 130.[1]
— Balanographische Kleinigkeiten. 1884. II. 130.[1]
— Balanographische Mittheilung. 1887. II. 130.[1]
— A Balaton tavának és partmellékének növényföldrajza és edényes növényzete. 1900. I. 447.
— Békésvármegye flórája. 1881. I. 446.
— Biologiai fajta Tölgyek. 1887. II. 132.[1]
— A bolgár flóra vonatkozása hazánkra. 1893. I. 446.
— Budapest flórájának Disstфлátái. 1899. II. 99.[1]
— Budapestnek és környékének növényzete. 1879. I. 446.
— Clusius Szedre (Rubus Clusii). 1885. II. 306.[2]
— Coronilla emeroides Boiss. et Sprunn. 1886. II. 348.[1]
— A Coronilla Emerus és emeroides cserjék hazánkban. 1886. II. 347.[2]
— Daphne arbuscula. 1891. II. 601.[1]
— Dendrologiai apróságok. 1894. II. 100.[1]
— Dioszeg und Fazekas. 1897. II. 130.[1]
— A fák ikergyümölcseiről. 1884. I. 525.
— A fás növényzet, mint a klima képviselője Vas megyében. 1884. I. 444.
— A fehér-vagy hegyi Juhar egy eltérő alakja. 1885. II. 479.[2]
— A fenyvesek és a fenyvek magyar nevei Vasmegyében. 1883. I. 75, *II. 15.*[1]
— Zur Flora von Deutschland. 1886. II. 130.[1]·
— Floristische Mittheilungen. 1885. II. 116.[1]
— Die Gallen der ungarischen Eiche. 1887. II. 133.[1]
— Görbe fenyőt helyettesítő Fűz. 1885. II. 107.[1]
— A gyalogfenyő boróka fajtái. 1886. II. 31.[1]
— A havasi rózsák (Rhododendronok). 1886. II. 601.[1]
— Havasvölgyi bokor a magyar haza legalacsonyabb pontján. 1886. II. 562.[1]
— A hazai fenyvek magyar nevei. 1888. I. 75.[1]
— A hazai Orgonafa-fajokról. 1887. II. 714.[1]
— Hazánk Füzféinak fajvegyülékei. 1883. II. 102.[2]
— Hazánknak egy új Lonicerája. 1882. II. 837.[1]
— A homoki Szömörcze. 1886. II. 455.[2]
— Husszonöt bogyós bokor Alföldünk homokpusztáin. 1885. I. 444.
— Die Hybriden der pentapetalen Linden. 1889. II. 515.[2]
— A kaszárbokor. 1885. II. 54.[1]
— A Keoskerágó mássdvirágzasa. 1896. II. 468.[1]
— Késsötölgy. 1887. II. 130.[1]
— Die Knospengallen einiger Eichen. 1887. IV. 501.[1]
— Közlemények Békés és Bihar vármegyék flórájából. 1891. II. 130.[2]

Borbás, Vincenz von (*continued*).
— Kurze Bemerkungen zu Halácsy & Braun's Nachträge. 1883. II. 287.[2]
— Linden-Hybriden und anderes. 1887. II. 515.[2]
— A lisztes Berkenye gyümölcse. 1879. III. 459.[2]
— A magyar birodalom vadon termő Rózsái monographiájának kísérlete. 1880. II. 287.[2]
— A magyar Nagy-Alföld Tölgyei. 1887. II. 130.[2]
— A magyar nemzeti muzeum növénytani kézirataiból, 1889. II. 715.[1]
— Magyarország és a Balkánfélsziget Juharfáiról. 1891. II. 476,[2] V. XXVII.[1]
— A Mocsárfa s nevezetesebb Tölgyeink magyar nevei. 1886. II. 130.[1]
— Die Nadelholzwälder des Eisenburger Comitates. 1884. I. 444.
— Natürlichere Beweise für die Achsengebilde der Hagebutte. 1884. II. 289.[1]
— Néhány Füzbokor másodszori virágzásáról. 1887. II. 104.[1]
— A németországi Tölgyek pelyhessége. 1886. II. 130.[1]
— Az örökzöld és kitelelő lomb. 1890. I. 192.[1]
— Pflanzen mit ausnahmsweise quirlständigen Blättern. 1881. II. 715.[2]
— Pirostobzú kárpáti Fenyő. 1900. II. 35.[2]
— Polygala Chamaebuxus in Ungarn. 1885. II. 431.[1]
— Quercus Budenziana. 1890. II. 130.[2]
— A Quercus conferta Kit. 1886. II. 130.[1]
— Quercus coriacea Bechst. 1886. II. 140.[1]
— A Quercus Csatói. 1887. II. 133.[2]
— Ueber Quercus Csatói Borb. 1887. II. 133.[2]
— A Quercus Fekete! Simk. tetőrügyének a makkcsészével való összeforradása. 1887. II. 133.[2]
— Quercus hiemalis Stev. hazánkban. 1886. II. 136,[2] *IV. 511.*
— A Quercus hungarica Hubeny legelő forrása. 1886. II. 133.[1]
— Quercus hybrida és Qu. decipiens Bechstein. 1886. II. 130.[1]
— Quercus malacophylla Schur. 1886. II. 136.[2]
— Quercus Széchenyianá. 1887. II. 140.[2]
— Rákosi Füz. 1887. II. 109.[1]
— Régi nevü uj Cytisus bokor. 1887. II. 351.[2]
— A rezgő Nyárfának másodízbeli virágzása. 1887. II. 98.[2]
— Rhamni Hungariae. 1887. II. 497.[1]
— Rhamnusaink áttekintése. 1885. II. 497.[1]
— Rhodo- und bathographische Kleinigkeiten. 1883. II. 282.[2]
— Rhodologische Bemerkungen. 1880. II. 283.[2]
— Ribiszkéink és Egreseink áttekintése. 1885. II. 243.[2]
— Ueber Rosa belgradensis Panč. 1880. II. 291.[2]
— Ueber Rosa cuspidatoides Crép. 1881. II. 293.[1]
— Rosa Pokornyana Kmet. 1883. II. 297.[2]
— Rosa Szabói Borbás. 1882. II. 299.[2]
— Rubus ulmifolius Franciaországban. 1885. II. 310.[2]
— Rubus ulmifolius Schott fil. Galliae civis. 1885. II. 310.[2]
— Samenreifende Doppelrosen. 1884. II. 290.[1]
— A slavoniai Quercus conferta. 1886. II. 133.[1]
— Sorbusainkról. 1883. II. 311.[2]
— Species Acerum Hungariae atque peninsulae Balcanae. 1891. II. 476.[2]
— Spiraea-csérjéink összeállítása. 1889. II. 314.[1]
— Syringa dichroa kétszenü Orgonafa. 1895. II. 715.[1]
— A Syringa Josikaea Jacqu. fil., magyarföldi . . . Orgona fá sorsa. 1887. II. 715.[1]
— A Syringa Josikaea leírásának kelte. 1884. II. 715.[2]
— Syringa prunifolia Kit. 1885. II. 715.[1]
— Szederjeink csoportjainak áttekintése. 1885. II. 304.[2]
— A szelid Gesztenye csirázásához. 1879. II. 124.[1]
— A szelid Gesztenye hazai termőhelyéről és termeléséről. 1885. II. 124.[1]
— A szelid Gesztenye hazánkban. 1879. II. 124.[1]
— Szúrós bokrok havasáinkon. 1885. I. 236.[2]
— Taraczkoló Tölgy. 1887. II. 140.[2]
— Zur Teratologie der Wallnuss. 1887. II. 113.[2]
— Tilia Richteri Borb. n. sp. hybr. 1889. II. 515.[2]
— Tilia semicuneata Rupr.? in Galizien. 1889. II. 518.[1]
— A tissafa egylakisága. 1886. II. 10.[1]
— A Tölgyek makkcsészéjének morphologiai értéke. 1887. II. 131.[2]
— Uj Boróka-bokor hazánkban. 1887. II. 31.[2]
— Ueber die Umwandlung der Blattdrüsen der Weide in Blätter. 1894. II. 107.[1]

— Ueber ungarische Sorbusarten. 1883. II. 311.
— Vasvármegye növényföldrajza és flórája. 1887. I. 446.
— A vénhedő Tiszafa. 1895. II. 11.[2]
— Vierzig beerentragende Sträucher in den ungarischen Sandpuszten. 1885. I. 444.
— Die Weidenhybride Ungarns. 1883. II. 102.[2]
— Weitere Beiträge zur Kenntniss der verwachsenen Blätter. 1879. I. 144.[2]
— A Zanótbokor virágszine kapcsolatban az évszakkal. 1898. II. 350.[1]
— Zwei neue Rosenformen aus Istrien. 1880. II. 287.[2]
— & Csató, Johann von. Alsó-Fehérmegye Tölgyei. 1886. II. 130.[1]
Borch, A. P. R. C. van der. *See* BORCH VAN VERWOLDE, A. P. R. C. van der.
Borch, B. van der. Aanleg van het landgoed Valkenberg. 1804. IV. 159.
— Over het enten van vruchtboomen. 1805. III. 139, *159.*[2]
— Over het zaaijen en planten van Dennen. 1804. IV. 452,[2] *471.*
Borch, L. W. P. van der. Berigt van het insekt Phalaena Bombyx Pityocampa. 1807. IV. 441.
— Berigt wegens de Phalaena Bombyx pityocampa. 1806. IV. 471.
Borch, Ole. Kurzer Begriff von Gebrauch der einländischen Kräuter. 1690. III. 270.[1]
— De usu plantarum indigenarum. 1690. III. 270.[1]
Borch, Wilhelm Friedrich, *Freiherr* von der. Die Ceder Libanons. 1830. IV. 448.[1]
— Johann Adolph Irrwalds Lehrjahre. 1828. IV. 101.
Borch tot Verwolden, P. A. van der. Plan van ontginning van heidegronden. 1868. IV. 160.[1]
Borch van Verwolden, A. P. R. C. van der. Proeven wegens het aanleggen van onbebouwde gronden tot Dennen. 1802. IV. 159.
— Verhandeling over de nederlandsche woudboomen. 1820. IV. 84.[2]
— Verhandeling over de Schotsche Spar. 1806. IV. 471.
— Verslag . . wegens de aanplanting van den Mastpijn. 1814. IV. 471.
Borchardt, (*Revierförster*). Der Holzdiebstahl. 1842. IV. 196.[2]
— Die landwirthschaftliche Holzzucht. 1843. IV. 106, *117.*
Borchers, Carl. Anleitung zur Vervollkommnung des Obstbaues. 1863. III. 138.
Borchert, (*Oberförster*). Beleuchtung des Werthes des Pressler'schen Zeitmessknechtes. 1857. IV. 264.
— Beschreibung und Holzmassen-Aufnahme einiger Lärchenhorste. 1855. IV. 452.[1]
Borchmeyer, Wilh. Ant. Auch Nadelhölzer lassen sich durch Stecklinge fortpflanzen. 1826. IV. 149.[2]
— Deutschlands Baumzucht. 1823. III. 69.
— Erziehung der Kirsch-Pflaume. 1827. III. 435.[2]
— Über Fortpflanzung der Nadelhölzer durch Stecklinge. 1827. III. 293.
— Über die Kultur einiger Holzgewächse. 1830. III. 120.[2]
— Oekonomische Musterung der . . . ausländischen Holzarten. 1829. IV. 125.[1]
— Die Weimouths-Kiefer. 1829. IV. 469.
Borckhausen, Moritz Balthasar. *See* BORKHAUSEN, M. B.
Bordage, Edmond. Notice sur les parasites du Caféier à l'Ile de la Réunion. 1899. III. 737.
— *See also* DEWÈVRE, Alfred & BORDAGE, Edmond.
Bordas, Léonard. Contribution à l'histoire naturelle de quelques Gryllidae. 1900. III. 737.
Borde de Tempest, Ernest. Phylloxéra, sa destruction certaine. 1873. III. 759.
Bordeaux, E. Note sur la multiplication dans l'eau de la Vigne. 1877. III. 158.
Bordeaux — Académie royale des sciences, belles-lettres et arts. *See* ACADÉMIE . . . I. 58.
Bordeaux — Jardin-des-plantes. *See* JARDIN-DES-PLANTES. 1864. I. 58.
— **Société** de géographie commerciale. *See* SOCIÉTÉ . . . II. 22.
Bordeaux — Société des sciences physiques et naturelles. *See* SOCIÉTÉ . . . I. 23.
Bordeaux — Société Linnéenne. *See* SOCIÉTÉ . . . I. 23.
Bordes. Sur une maladie nouvelle du vin en Algérie. 1888. III. 561.
Bordes, De. Bederfwerende bereiding van hout. 1854. IV. 417.
Bordet, L. *See* BARDY, Ch. & BORDET, L.
Bordiga, Benedetto. Storia delle piante forastiere le più importanti. 1791. III. 51.

Bordley, John Beale. Essays and notes on husbandry. 1799. III. 117.²

Bordone, (Dr.). Considérations générales sur la maladie du Mûrier. 1865. III. 379.

Bordot, Anatole. Les fleurs qui parlent. 1860. I. 515.

Boreau, Alexandre. Catalogue raisonné des plantes . . . de Maine-et-Loire. 1859. I. 412.

— Flore du centre de la France. 1840. I. 409.ʳ

— Notes sur quelques espèces de plantes françaises. 1844. I. 410.

— Notice historique sur le Jardin des plantes d'Angers. 1851. I. 411.

— Notice sur les plantes recueillies en Corse. 1857. I. 419.¹

— Observations sur les enveloppes.florales. 1826. I. 115.²

— Précis des principales herborisations faite en Maine-et-Loire. , 1862. I. 412.

— Programme de la flore du centre de la France. 1835. I. 408.

— Voyage aux montagnes du Morvan. 1832. I. 408.

Borecki, Józef. Podręcznik botaniczny kieszonkowy dla ogrodników polskich. 1882. III. 30.

— Wskazówka sadzenia drzewek owocowych. 1887. III. 135.

Borel, Pierre. Les antiquitez, raretez, plantes . . . de Castres. 1649. I. 404.²

— Hortus seu armamentarium simplicum. 1669. I. 286.

Borel, William. Un compas forestier enrigistreur. 1892. IV. 265.

— Étude sur l'aménagement des bois de Chêne. 1898. IV. 513.

— Observations sur quelques méthodes pour calculer la possibilité. 1892. IV. 246.

— Rapport sur les bois du canton de Genève. 1899. IV. 367.

— & Blónay, H. W. de. Dosages de tanin dans des écorces de Chêne. 1898. IV. 515.³

Borellus, Johann. De plantis verno tempore efflorescentibus. See NEBEL, Daniel. 1706. III. 72.

Borenius. Die Kiefer in Finland. 1886. IV. 481.

Borenius, A. Pajuistutuksesta. 1890. IV. 487.²

Borg, John. Orange culture and diseases. 1900. III. 501.¹

Borg, Väinö. Anmärkningsvärda fanerogamer från södra Tavastland. 1896. II. 109.²

— Dvärgform af Granen. 1895. II. 35.²

— Fysiilis-maantieteellisiä tutkimuksia Kalvolan pitäjässä. 1898. I. 367.

Borgata, J. Catalogus omnium vegetabilium . . . in Viridario saponariensi. 1868. I. 64.

Borges, Joaquim FERREIRA. See FERREIRA BORGES, Joaquim.

Borggreve, Bernhard. Abermaliger Frass von Elateriden-Larven. 1878. IV. 477.

— Abnorme Buchenkapseln. 1889. II. 126.²

— Anderthalb Dutzend Thesen über Mäuseschaden. 1891. IV. 198.¹

— Zur Aufforstungs-Frage in Preussen. 1880. IV. 158.

— Die ausgedehntere Anwendung der Buchen-Dielung. 1884. IV. 500.¹

— Zur Baumhöhenschätzung. 1888. IV. 216.

— Ueber die Bedingungen der Blüthenproduktion. 1880. I. 529, IV. 65.³

— Ueber die Beziehungen zwischen Wald, Sumpf und Quellen. 1890. IV. 51.

— Doppeltes Ergrünen der Lärche. 1877. II. 33.¹

— Ueber Düngungs-Versuche. 1884. IV. 144.²

— Eine eigenthümliche Art von Dichogamie von Abies excelsa. 1875. II. 36.²

— Der Einfluss des Waldes auf die Strom-Ueberschwemmungen. 1884. IV. 51.

— Einige Bemerkungen über die deutschen Rüstern-Arten. 1883. II. 143.¹

— Ueber die Einwirkung des Sturmes. 1872. III. 184.¹

— Ueber Erblichkeit und Zuchtwahl bei Waldbäumen. 1889. I. 529, IV. 75.¹

— Experimentelle Proben auf die Plenterdurchforstung. 1892. IV. 174.

— Die Forstabschätzung. 1888. IV. 233.

— Die Forstreinertragslehre. 1878. IV. 256.

— Fruchtträger des Agaricus melleus. 1887. IV. 211.²

— Führer zur Besichtigung der mündener Lehrforstreviere. 1890. IV. 354.

— Gedanken . . . über die Beschneidung der Holzpflänzlinge. 1878. IV. 154.¹

— Zur Generation der forstschädlichen Rüsselkäfer. 1881. IV. 207.

— Georg Ludwig Hartig's Lehrbuch für Förster. 1871. IV. 98.¹

— Die gesetzliche Regelung der Feld- und Forst-Polizei. 1880. IV. 314.¹

— Getreide- und Sauerdorn-Rost. 1884. III. 395.¹

— Ueber die Haide. 1872. I. 387.

— Haide und Wald. 1872. I. 387.

— Die Holzzucht. 1885. IV. 107.¹

— Imprägnirung des — echten — Buchenkernholzes. 1889. IV. 499.

— Die Kehrseite der Buchenschwellen-Verwerthung. 1888. IV. 500.¹

— Ueber die Lärchenkrankheit. 1889. IV. 451.

— Der Lichtungshieb mit Unterbau. 1883. IV. 131.

— Ueber Lichtungszuwachs. 1899. IV. 235.¹

— Lichtungszuwachs an Kiefern-Waldrechtern? 1887. IV. 481.

— Das mittlere Zuwachs-Procent. 1889. IV. 234.

— Ueber das nachträgliche Aufwärtsbiegen horizontaler Stammtheile. 1877. I. 194.

— Eine neue (?) Art von Frostschaden an Eichen. 1870. IV. 509.

— Die neue Buchenkrankheit. 1879. IV. 497.

— Die neuen Ertragstafeln der deutschen forstlichen Versuchsanstalten. 1883. IV. 237.

— Neues über Hüttenrauch-Schaden. 1880. IV. 192.²

— Zum Nonn enfrass in Süddeutschland. 1890. IV. 200.

— Über die öfter im Innern des Holzes . . . gefundenen fremdartigen Körper. 1879. I. 210.¹

— Zur Plänterdurchforstung. 1887. IV. 174.

— Zur Plenterdurchforstung. 1892. IV. 131.

— Für die Rentabilität einer Kiefernaufforstung. 1886. IV. 481.

— Ueber das Robert Hartig'sche Kennzeichen der Rauchbeschädigung an Fichten. 1897. IV. 193.¹

— Die sogenannte Lärchenkrankheit. 1875. IV. 450.

— Das sogenannte " Lieben " der Pflanzen. 1892. I. 229.

— Der sogenännte " Wurzeldruck." 1892. I. 169.ʳ

— Studien über den Lichtungszuwachs. 1877. IV. 233.

— Untersuchungs-Ergebnisse betreffend die forstliche Bedeutung zweier Coniferen-Rostpilze. 1877. IV. 211.²

— Die " Verbesserung der Bestandsordnung." 1882. IV. 244.

— Die Verbreitung . . . der wichtigeren Waldbaumarten. 1888. I. 371, IV. 84.¹

— Verminderung der Blattgrösse. 1889. I. 529, IV. 65.²

— Waldschäden im oberschlesischen Industriebezirk. 1895. IV. 193.¹

— Ueber Waldschäden in der Umgebung industrieller Anlagen. 1877. IV. 192.²

— Ueber die " weisse " bez. grünfruchtige Heidelbeere. 1891. II. 686.²

— Weitere Proben auf die Plenterdurchforstung 1894. IV. 174.

— Die Wirthschaftsregeln zur Erziehung gemischter Hochwaldungen. 1886. IV. 138.²

— See also MÄRKER, C. & BORGGREVE, Bernhard; MICHAELIS, C. & BORGGREVE, Bernhard.

— & König, A. Die allgemeinen Holzbestandsvorraths-Tabellen. 1892. IV. 237.

Borggreve, F. Ein Beitrag zu dem Kapitel über Wald und Fluth. 1884. IV. 51.

Borghers. Considérations sur une variété exotique de la Vigne. 1827. III. 546.

Borghesi, Giovanni. Lettera . . . racconto del viaggio . . . alle coste dell' Indie Orientali. 1705. III. 277.

Borghstyn, J. De Mimosa. 1880. III. 237.²

Borgmann, Hugo. Beschädigung des Buchenaufschlags. 1889. IV. 497.

— Horst- und gruppenweise Lichtwuchsdurchforstung. 1893. IV. 174.

— Neue Beobachtungen und Untersuchungen über Lärchenfeinde. 1892. IV. 451.

— Neuere Beobachtungen über die Eschenzwieselmotte. 1893. IV. 535.³

— Die Zwieselbildung der Esche. 1887. IV. 535.²

Borgmann, Wilhelm. Betriebseinrichtung . . . im Kiefernplenterwald. 1890. IV. 482.¹

— Kronenfreiheib . . . der Fichte. 1897. IV. 459.¹

Borgström, Ferd. Ludvig. Anteckningar öfver temperaturen. 1841. I. 223.¹

— En excursion i Villands härad. 1844. I. 354.

— Några bidrag till Vermlands flora. 1842. I. 354.

Borie, Victor. Araujo albens Don. 1857. III. 692.¹ .

Borie, Victor (*continued*).
— Clematis florida Thbg. 1856. III. 390.[2]
— Clematis montana Wall. 1856. III. 391.[1]
— Lonicera flava. 1856. III. 750.[1]
— Siphocampylus betulaefolius. 1857. III. 754.[1]
Bories, A. Caractères botaniques . . . du Thé. 1863. III. 607.
Bories, P. Acclimatation et culture des Quinquinas. 1865. III. 712.[1]
— Catalogue des végétaux qui se trouvent à la Réunion. 1864. I. 482.
Der Borkenkäfer. 1844. IV. 204.
Borkenkäfer-Fangbäume. 1858. IV. 204.
Borkhausen, Moritz Balthasar. Beyträge zur deutschen Flora. 1794. II. 310.[2]
— Botanisches Wörterbuch. 1797. I. 70.
— Flora der oberen Grafschaft Catzenelnbogen. 1795. I. 375, V. xix.[1]
— Ueber die Linnéische Gattung Viburnum. 1797. II. 842.[1]
— Ueber die Linneischen Gattung Crataegus. 1798. II. 255.[2]
— Ueber Linné's Prunus und Amygdalus-Gattungen. 1797. II. 270.[2]
— Tentamen dispositionis plantarum Germaniae. 1792. I. 375.
— Theoretisch-praktisches Handbuch der Forstbotanik. 1800. I. 370, *IV: 88.*.
— Versuch einer forstbotanischen Beschreibung . . . im Freien wachsenden Holzarten. 1790. I. 293, *IV. 81.*
— *See also* GUENDERRODE, F. J., *Freiherr* von & BORKHAUSEN, M. B.
Bormann, (*Forstmeister, Hermsdorf*). Mittheilung über den Ertrag eines . . . Eichen-Schälwaldes. 1856. IV. 512.
Born, Joseph, *Freiherr* von. Freymüthige Briefe über den Holzmangel. 1791. IV. 283.[1]
Borne, von dem. Bebosching van woeste gronden door den staat in Pruisen. 1896. IV. 546.[1]
— Boisement par l'état des terrains incultes en Prusse. 1896. IV. 546.[1]
— Denkschrift, betreffend die Waldverhältnisse der Provinzen Ost- und Westpreussen. 1900. IV. 119.[1]
— Ueber den Fortgang der Oedlandserwerbungen. 1896. IV. 159, 546.[1]
— Die Oedlands-Ankäufe. 1892. IV. 736.[1]
Bornemann, C. E. Versuch einer systematischen Abbandlung von Kohlen. 1775. IV. 394.
Bornemann, Georg. Die flüchtigen Oele des Pflanzenreiches. 1891. III. 225.
Bornemann, J. G. Uprawa Wina około budynków, murów, chłodników i drzew. 1842. III. 558.[2]
Bornemissza, Zoltán. Az Almafa. 1896. III. 426.
— A Cseresznyefa. 1896. III. 432.[1]
— A Diófa. 1896. III. 354.[1]
— A Kajszinbarackfa. 1897. III. 434.[2]
Bornet, Edouard. Sur un projet de note, relative à une Rose prolifère. 1896. II. 290.[1]
Bornitz, Fridericus Augustus. De corticis Angusturae patria. 1804. III. 503.[2]
Bornmüller, Joseph. Beiträge zur Kenntniss der Flora des bulgarischen Küstenlandes. 1888. I. 450.
— Ein Beitrag zur Eichenflora des südöstlichen Europa. 1889. II. 130.[2]
— Ein Beitrag zur Kenntniss der Flora von Syrien. 1898. I. 480.
— Ein Beitrag zur Kenntniss der Küstenflora des Persischen Golfes. 1894. I. 477.[1]
— Conservirung von Abietineen. 1887. I: 36.[1]
— Crataegus tanacetifolia. 1894. II. 263.[2]
— Zur Flora von Oberbaiern. 1895. II. 102.[1]
— Hypericum pumilio, Cerasus hippophaoides. 1899. II. 271.[2]
— Nachtrag zu Florula insulae Thasos. 1894. I. 450.
— Noch Einiges über Populus Steiniana. 1888. II. 96.[1]
— Populus Steiniana Brnmllr. 1888. II. 98.[1]
— Reisebriefe aus Persien. 1893. I. 477.[2]
— Rhamnus orbiculata Bornm. 1897. II. 498.[2]
— Rhamnus orbiculata Brnmllr. n. sp. 1887. II. 498.[2]
— Salix Caprea pendula, die zhängende Salweide. 1888. III. 351.[2]
Bornstedt, von. Ueber die Ansetzung der Kulturkosten bei Waldwerthberechnungen. 1880. IV. 256.
— Die Regelung des Plenterwald-Betriebes. 1896. IV. 131.
— Sind "Kopfdurchforstungen" . . . Hauptnutzungshiebe? 1899. IV. 175,[2] 247.[1]

Borodin, Ivan P. *See* BORODIN, Johann.
Borodin, Johann. Sur les conditions qui déterminent l'intensité de la respiration des plantes. 1880. I. 170.
— Recherches physiologiques sur la respiration des rameaux feuillus. 1878. I. 170.
— Recherches sur la respiration des végétaux. 1881. I. 171.
— Sur la répartition des cristaux d'oxalate de chaux. 1885. I. 139.
— Untersuchungen über die Pflanzenathmung. 1881. I. 171.
— Über die Wirkung des Lichtes auf . . . Chlorophyllkörner. 1869. I. 141.
— *See also* FAMINTZIN, André & BORODIN, Johann; Бородинъ, И. П.
Boronia heterophylla als Kronenbäumchen. 1893. III. 495.[2]
Borovski, I. *See* Боровскій, I.
Borowski, Georg Heinrich. Ueber die Anpflanzung ausländischer Holzarten. 1787. IV. 125.[1]
Borregaard, P. Chr. F. Foraarsblomstrende Træer og Buske. 1892. III. 207.[2]
— Morbærtræet. 1893. III. 378.
— Pyrus angustifolia fl. pl. 1894. III. 425.[1]
Borrich, Ole. *See* BORCH, Ole.
Borrichius, Olaus. *See* BORCH, Ole.
Borries, Herman. Beretning angaaende . . . Forekomst af Bladhvepsen. 1890. III. 191.
— De danske Lophyrus-Arter. 1892. IV. 549.[1]
— Uddrag . . . af en entomologisk Undersøgelsesrejse. 1889. III. 190.
Borruat. Du reboisement des pâturages communaux. 1871. IV. 166.[2]
Borščow, Elias. *See* BORSHTCHOF, I. G.
Borszczow, Elias. *See* BORSHTCHOF, I. G.
Borshchov, Il'ya Ghrighor'evīch. *See* BORSHTCHOF, I. G.
Borshtchof, Ilya Grigorevitch. Action du protoxyde d'azote sur les plantes. 1868. I. 211.
— Die Aralo-Caspischen Calligoneen. 1860. II. 184.[2]
— Beiträge zur Histochemie der Pflanzen. 1874. I. 151.[2]
— Compte rendu général sur les résultats botaniques obtenus . . . dans les régions Aralo-Caspiennes. 1859. I. 456.
— Einige vorläufige Versuche über das Verhalten der Pflanzen im Stickoxydulgase. 1868. I. 211.
— Über gegitterte Parenchymzellen . . . von Ceropegia . . . aphylla. 1869. II. 736.[2]
Borszczow. *See* BORSHTCHOF.
Bort, Leon TEISSERENC DE. *See* TEISSERENC DE BORT, Leon.
Borthwick, A. W. On the development of quadrifoliar spurs in Pinus Laricio. 1900. II. 44.[1]
— On interfoliar buds in Pines. 1900. II. 40.[1]
— Notes on the witches' broom of Pinus sylvestris. 1900. IV. 480.
Borthwick, John. On a simple means of safely guiding the fall of trees. 1845. IV. 383.[2]
Bortier, P. Beplanting der zeekusten en duinen. 1873. IV. 160.[1]
— Boisement du littoral et des dunes de la Flandre. 1874. IV. 160.[1]
— El empleo de la madera en la fabricación del papel. 1877. IV. 429.
— Met hout beplanting des kustgronds. 1873. IV. 160.[1]
— Papier d'aubier de Tremble. 1877. IV. 429.
Bory de Saint Vincent, Jean Baptiste George Marcellin. Sur les Cèdres de l'Atlas. 1844. IV. 447.[2]
— Sur une espèce de Chêne. 1843. II. 135.[2]
— Essais sur les isles Fortunées. 1803. I. 497.
— Sur une excursion aux extrémités . . . de l'Algérie. 1844. I. 484.
— Sur la flore d'Algérie. 1843. I. 484.
— Florule de la Sierra-Nevada. 1820. I. 420.
— Sur les Grenadilles ou Passionaires. 1819. II. 576.[2]
— Sur la Mocanère Visnea Mocanera. 1819. II. 552.[1]
— Note sur une excursion à Miliana. 1841. I. 484.
— Notice sur les travaux de la Commission scientifique de l'Algérie. 1841. I. 484.
— Voyage dans les . . . iles des mers d'Afrique. 1804. I. 482.
— *See also* CHAUBARD, L. A. & BORT DE SAINT-VINCENT, J. B. G. M.; FAUCHÉ, BRONGNIART, Adolphe, CHAUBARD, L. A. & BORY DE SAINT-VINCENT, J. B. G. M.
— & others. Dictionnaire classique d'histoire naturelle. 1822. I. 33.
Borzì, Antonino. L' acqua in rapporto alla vegetazione. 1893. I. 233.[1]
— Di alcune lenticelle fogliari. 1887. I. 132.[2]

— Ancora della Quercus macedonica. 1888. II. 135.[1]
— Bauerella, novum Rutacearum genus. 1897. II. 399.[2]
— Cenni sulla biologia del Phloeosinus Aubei. 1883. IV. 204.
— Compendio della flora forestale italiana. 1885. I. 423, IV. 86.[1]
— Contribuzioni alla biologia dei pericarpi. 1893. I. 171.
— Contribuzioni alla biologia del frutto. 1894. I. 171.
— Contribuzioni alla biologia vegetale. See CONTRIBUZIONI . . . I. 24.[1]
— Diagnosi di specie nuove o critiche. 1897. I. 271.[1]
— Esperienze di acclimatamento. 1897. I. 64.
— Flora forestale italiana. 1879. I. 423, IV. 86.[1]
— Formazione delle radici laterali. 1887. I. 104.
— Germinazione dei semi delle Salicinee. 1897. II. 96.[1]
— Ibridi di Salix pedicellata Desf. 1887. II. 108.[2]
— L'Ilixi-Suergiu. 1881. II. 135.[2]
— Inzengaea, nuovo fungo parassita delle Olive. 1885. III. 677.[2]
— Note alla biologia delle xerofile. 1894. I. 219.[2]
— Phoenix dactylifera × canariensis. 1897. II. 72.[2]
— Quercus Fragnus Longo. 1888. II. 135.[1]
— La Quercus macedonica Alph. DC. in Italia. 1888. II. 135.[1]
— Reliquiae Tineanae. 1897. II. 459.[1]
— Saggio di ricerche sull' incremento in grossezza. 1878. IV. 233.
— I silofagi della fauna forestale. 1878. IV. 209.[2]
— Le specie di Ficus . . . nel R. ortò botanico di Palermo. 1897. III. 369.[1]
— Thunbergia elegans Borzi. 1897. II. 804.[2]
— Un tipo anemofilo delle Eparcidacee. 1897. II. 688.[1]
Bos, H. P. M. van den. See HORN VAN DEN BOS, H. P. M. van der.
Bos, Hemmo. Beknopt leerboek der plantkunde. 1898. I. 92.
— Beschadiging van Seringen. 1899. III. 680.[2]
— Leerboek der plantkunde. 1892. I. 92.
— Nut of schade. 1898. III. 191.
— Oorwormen. 1898. III. 191.
— De rusttijd der planten. 1898. I. 191.[1]
— De verhouding der mieren tot de plantenwereld. 1890. I. 235.[1]
— Verwondingen. 1900. I. 208.[1]
Bos, J. RITZEMA. See RITZEMA Bos, J. & LOVINK, H. J.
Bos, R. Flora. Uitstapjes in het plantenrijk. 1893. I. 96.
Bosc, J. J. Tableau de quelques végétaux indigènes. 1893. I. 74.[2]
Bosc, Joseph Antoine. Traité de physique végétale appliquée à l'agriculture. 1839. I. 148.
— Traité élémentaire de physique végétale. 1824. I. 148.
Bosc, Louis Augustin Guillaume. Collection de mémoires . . . aux effets sur les Oliviers de la gelée. 1822. III. 675.[1]
— De la culture des pépinières. 18.. ? III. 153.
— Decumaria sarmentosa. 1792. II. 238.[2]
— Exposition . . . du plan . . . pour étudier . . . Vignes cultivées. 1808. III. 546.
— Mémoire sur l'utilité des clôtures. 1807. III. 212.[3]
— Mémoire sur les différentes espèces de Chênes. 1807. II. 128.[1]
— Note sur les moyens de remédier à la gelée des Oliviers. 1803. III. 675.[1]
— Notice agronomique sur . . . Frênes. 1809. II. 707.[1]
— Notice sur un emploi économique des baies du Vaccinium Myrtillus. 1795. III. 664.[1]
— Rapport sur les moyens à substituer à l'élagage. 1811. III. 211.[3]
— Rapport sur un mémoire de M. Devèze de Chabriol, relatif au repeuplement. 1822. IV. 161.[3]
— & Baudrillart, J. J. Dictionnaire de la culture des arbres. 1821. IV. 22.[2]
— Labbé, H. & Féburier. Gouvernement des arbres à fruits par l'arqure. 1809. III. 174.[1]
Boscawen, William J. The Puka-tree and its home. 1898. I. 506.[1]
Bosch, H. van den. Waarnemingen omtrent den sulphas chininae. 1824. III. 721.
Bosch, H. J. van den. Verslag over het Internationaal congres voor den landbouw en het boschwezen te Weenen. 1873. IV. 39.[1]
Bosch, Jules. Het caoutchouc-vraagstuk. 1900. III. 230.
Bosch, M. van der MEERSCH. See MEERSCH BOSCH, M. van der.
Bosch, Miguel. Manual de botánica aplicada. 1858. III. 218.[1]

Bosch, Roelof Benjamin van den. Enumeratio plantarum Zeelandiae. 1841. I. 392.
Bosch y Juliá, Miguel. Memoria sobre la inundación del Júcar. 1866. IV. 186.[2]
— Memoria sobre la parte forestal de la Exposicion de Lóndres. 1863. IV. 19.[2]
Bosche e selve della provincia di Cuneo. 1868. IV. 364.
Boschi. See RENAUT, BERTIN & BOSCHI.
I boschi. 1861. IV. 276.[2]
I boschi della Serbia. 1865. IV. 375.[1]
I boschi della Stiria. 1897. IV. 369.
I boschi demaniali ed il loro avvenire. 1899. IV. 277.
I boschi ed il brigantaggio. 1863. IV. 277.
I boschi francesi amministrati dagli ufficiali forestali. 1894. IV. 361.
I boschi in America. 1883. IV. 337.[1]
Boschi incendiati. 1863. IV. 181.[3]
I boschi nei rapporti topografici. 1856. IV. 364.
Boschwol. 1853. IV. 468.[1]
Bosco, J. J. MANLIUS DE. See MANLIUS DE BOSCO, J. J.
Bose. Ueber den Einfluss der Unterlage. 1868. III. 39.
Bose, Adolf Julian. De disquirendo charactere plantarum. 1765. I. 31.
— De motu humorum in plantis vernalis. 1764. I. 162.
Bose, Ernst Gottlob. De generatione hybrida. 1777. I. 245.
— Programma de secretione humorum. 1755. I. 162.
— De indicium in plantis ortu et directione. 1754. I. 103.
— & Bosseck, H. O. De nodis plantarum. 1747. I. 104.
Bose, Heinrich Ludwig. Beiträge zur Waldwerthberechnung. 1863. IV. 256.
— Beschreibung zweier Instrumente zum Nivelliren. 1863. IV. 214.
— Zur Diskussion des Reinertragsbetriebs. 1870. IV. 255.
— Das forstliche Weiserprocent. 1889. IV. 245, 258.
— Zur forstlichen Reinertragstheorie. 1865. IV. 255.
— Statistik der Waldungen. 1865. IV. 351.[1]
— Zur Theorie des forstlichen Reinertrages. 1873. IV. 256.
Bose, Hermann von. Handbuch der Jagd- und Forstgesetzkunde des Königreichs Sachsen. 1857. IV. 322.[
Bose, Karl Adam Heinrich von. Hand-Buch der praktischen Landwirthschaft. 1797. IV. 105.
— Hand-Buch der praktischen Landwirthschaft. 1799. III. 103.
— Neues allgemein praktisches Wörterbuch der Forst- und Jagdwissenschaft. 1797. IV. 22.[2]
— Neues allgemein praktisches Wörterbuch der Forstwissenschaft. 1807. IV. 22.[2]
— Uebersicht der praktischen Holzbehandlung. 1799. IV. 105.
Bose, Kaspar. Calycem Tournefortii explicat. 1733. I. 114.
— De motu plantarum sensus aemulo. 1728. I. 193.[2]
Bose, P. Berechnung der Durchforstungen. 1895. IV. 259.
— Die Bestimmung der Umtriebszeit. 1896. IV. 252.
— Betrachtungen über den Unternehmergewinn. 1889. IV. 261.[1]
— Der Bodenwert als Regulator der Umtriebszeiten. 1894. IV. 258.
— Einiges über die Zubereitung des Bodens. 1851. IV. 148.
— Ueber die Erhöhung des Walderwartungswertes. 1888. IV. 257.
— Ueber Erhöhung des Walderwartungswertes. 1890. IV. 227
— Das forstliche Weiserprocent. 1891. IV. 258.
— Das forstliche Weiserprocent. 1892. IV. 258.
— Die Haltlosigkeit der Bodenreinertragstheorie. 1897. IV. 259.[1]
— Höchster Reinertrag und höchste Rentabilität. 1890. IV. 258.
— Instrument zur Messung der Baumhöhen. 1877. IV. 215.
— Zur Reinertragslehre. 1887. IV. 257.
— Die Rentabilität des Eichenschälwaldes. 1886. IV. 513.
— Richtigstellung der falschen Urteile des Professors Dr. Endres über die Waldertragslehre. 1893. IV. 258.
— Ueber die Unterschiede zwischen dem aussetzenden und jährlichen Betriebe. 1872. IV. 244.
— Der Waldreinertrag. 1891. IV. 258.
— Waldreinertrag und Walderwartungswert. 1887. IV. 257.
— Welche Prozente werfen die in den Hochwaldungen des deutschen Reiches . . . niedergelegten Kapitalien ab. 1888. IV. 261.[1]
— Bei welcher Umtriebszeit erreichen die Holzbestands- resp. Wald-Erwartungswerthe ihr Maximum. 1886. IV. 257.
— Bei welcher Umtriebszeit . . . erreicht deren Gesamt-Walderwartungswert sein Maximum? 1894. IV. 258.

Bose, P. (*continued*).
— Wohin würde es führen, wenn in den Hochwaldungen des Deutschen Reiches . . . die Umtriebszeiten der grössten Bodenerwartungswerthe eingeführt werden sollten. 1886. IV. 261.[1]

Bosisto, Joseph. Abhandlung über Eucalyptus. 1876. IV. 531.[2]

— Abstract of a paper on the yield and uses of volatile oils. 1865. III. 224.[3]

— The indigenous vegetation of Australia. 1887. II. 623.[1]

— Is the Eucalyptus a fever-destroring [*sic*] tree? 1876. IV. 531.[2]

— Kinos. 1897. IV. 534.[1]

— Note on Daviesia latifolia. 1890. III. 475.[1]

Bosker, H. Het Beekberger woud. 1874. IV. 356.[2]

— Taxus baccata. 1884. III. 288.[1]

Boskoop — **Pomologische vereeniging.** See POMOLOGISCHE . . . III. 14.

Bosman, Willem. Nauwkeurige beschryving van de Guinese . . . Slave-Kust. 1704. III. 280.[2]

— A new description of the coast of Guinea. 1704. III. 280.[2]

— Viaggio in Guinea. 1704. III. 280.[2]

— Voyage de Guinée. 1704. III. 280.[2]

Bosnia — **Wissenschaftliche Mittheilungen** . . . See WISSENSCHAFTLICHE . . . I. 28.[1]

Bosnisch-herzegovinisches Landesmuseum. See WISSENSCHAFTLICHE Mittheilungen . . . I. 28.[1]

Bosque, Arturo. Informe sobre la utilidad de plantaciones de Eucaliptus. 1900. IV. 532.[1]

Los bosques y las tempestades. 1888. IV. 548.[1]

Bosredon. Sur un genre singulier de névropathie. 1856. III. 585.[2]

Bosredon, Alexandre de. Manuel du trufficulteur. 1887. III. 361.[1]

Bosredon, Ph. de. Les Ormeaux de Pelvésy. 1886. II. 143.[2]

Boss, Ulr. Praktische Anleitung zur Obstbaumzucht. 1868. III. 145.[1]

Bosscha, J. J. Het vergiftige bestanddeel van Sarcolobus. 1877. III. 694.[1]

Bosscha, Jan. De intensieve Peperkultuur. 1900. III. 343.[2]

— Mieren en schildluizen. 1900. III. 737.

Bossche, Léon van den. Acacia lineata A. Cunn. 1900. III. 465.[2]

— Cytisus nigricans Lin. 1900. III. 474.[2]

— L'Eutaxia myrtifolia. 1900. III. 477.[1]

— Hortus thenensis. 1895. I. 50. .

— Le Metrosideros robusta. 1898. III. 637.[1]

Bosschere, Charles de. Les arbres des promenades urbaines. 1899. III. 212.[1]

— Buddleia Colvillei. 1898. III. 681.[2]

— Chamaecyparis Lawsoniana var. Weisseana. 1897. III. 301.[1]

— Le Cocos insignis Martius. 1886. III. 322.[2]

— Une collection de Conifères. 1898. I. 50.

— Une curieuse hybridation. 1894. III. 506.[1]

— Les Dattiers. 1897. II. 72.[3]

— Deux beaux Conifères. 1898. III. 301,[1] 301.[2]

— L'exposition internationale de Paris. 1895. III. 319,[2] 325,[2] 639.[1]

— Les floralies gantoises de 1893. 1893. III. 330,[3] 749.[1]

— L'hiver 1894–1895 en Belgique. 1895. III. 46.[3]

— Hydrangea paniculata grandiflora à haute tige. 1897. III. 412.[3]

— Leiden, le jardin botanique. 1897. III. 351,[1] 360.[2]

— Magnolia parviflora. 1891. III. 400.[1]

— Les Palmiers. 1898. III. 318.[2]

— Les Palmiers dans la décoration des jardins. 1897. III. 318.

— Le Rhodochiton volubile. 1890. III. 704.[1]

— Thuyopsis dolobrata. 1899. III. 312.[1]

— Une variété de l'Abutilon insigne. 1891. III. 586.[2]

Bosse, J. van. Eenige beschouwingen omtrent de achteruitgang van de Koffiecultuur. 1895. III. 731.

Bosse, J. F. W. Ueber die Befruchtung der Passions-Blumen. 1829. III. 615.[1]

— Bemerkungen über vegetabilische Düngung. 1833. II. 48.[1]

— Beobachtungen über Wachsthum . . . einheimischer Holzarten. 1839. III. 40.

— Beschreibung . . . einiger ausgezeichneten Zierpflanzen. 1835. III. 69.

— Cultur einiger Zierpflanzen. 1827. III. 599.[1]

— Deutzia scabra. 1841. III. 410.[2]

— Einige Bemerkungen über die durch das Absterben . . . einzelner Holzarten . . . entstehenden Lücken. 1824. III. 40.

— Einige Notizen aus dem Grossherz. Garten. 1844. III. 703.[1]

— Erprobtes Mittel zur Abhaltung des Nachtfrostschmetterling. 1833. III. 196.

— Erscheinen gefüllter Blumen. 1841. II. 279.[2]

— Über das Gedeihen der ächten Kastanien. 1833. III. 358.[2]

— Ueber Gruppirung der Zierpflanzen im Freien. 1845. III. 201.

— Ueber das Keimen der Cocos nucifera. 1833. III. 322.[2]

— Über die Kultur der Azaleen. 1826. III. 656.

— Über die Kultur der Cryptostegia. 1833. III. 692.[2]

— Leichte und wohlfeile Art, die bengalischen . . . und Theerosen . . . zu überwintern. 1837. III. 183.[1]

— Methode, mehrere Arten Rhododendra . . . zu durchwintern. 1826. III. 183.[1]

— Mittel gegen Blattläuse. 1833. III. 196.

— Nachricht aus dem Grossherzoglichen Garten zu Oldenburg über die Wirkung des letzten Winters. 1838. III. 45.

— Neuere Zierpflanzen . . . in den letzten sechs Jahren . . . eingeführt. 1829. III. 74.

— Die neuesten Zierpflanzen . . . in den letzen fünf Jahren eingeführt. 1829. III. 74.

— Notizen aus dem Grossherz. Garten zu Oldenburg. 1841. II. 279,[2] *III. 410.[2]*

— Verzeichniss und kurze Beschreibung aller Zierpflanzen . . . seit den letzten sechs Jahren . . . eingeführt. 1846. III. 74.

— Vollständiges Handbuch der Blumengärtnerei. 1829. III. 74.

— Wirkungen des Frostes im Winter 1822/23. 1827. III. 45.

— Über die Wirkungen des Nachtfrostes vom . . . Mai v. J. 1833. III. 45.

Bosseboeuf, François. La structure du pétiole . . . du genre Quercus. 1896. II. 131.[2]

Bosseck, Heinrich Otto. See BOSC, E. G. & BOSSECK, H. O.

— & **Küchelbecker, G. G.** De antheris florum. 1750. I. 116.[1]

Bosshard, Ad. See KRAFT, A. & BOSSHARD, Ad.

Bossi-Federigotti, Giuseppe, conte. Imitazione della natura nel riboschimento. 1866. IV. 165.

— Se il rimettere le selve sui monti possa diminuire la popolazione. 1866. . IV. 277.

— Se lo impedire il dissodamento di certe coste montane. 1866. IV. 286.[3]

Bossin. Catalpa nain. 1850. III. 706.[1]

— Catalpa syringaefolia nana. 1850. III. 706.[1]

— Emploi du Jasmin blanc. 1850. III. 673.[1]

— Sur l'Hortensia bleu. 1872. III. 412.[2]

— Des influences atmosphériques sur quelques végétaux pendant l'hiver de 1846–47. 1847. III. 47.

— Le Néflier à gros fruits. 1869. III. 429.[2]

— Plantation estivale d'arbres. 1864. III. 168.[2]

— Plantes supportant les hivers sur les côtes de la Manche. 1852. III. 47.

Bossler, Ludwig. Flora der Gefässpflanzen in Elsass-Lothringen. 1877. I. 387.

Bossmann, Rudolph. Hülfs-Tabellen zur Berechnung des runden Holzes. 1841. IV. 223.

— Hülfs-Tabellen zur Berechnung des runden und viereckigen Holzes. 1841. IV. 223.

Bosson, A. Mémoire sur l'influence physique du déboisement. 18 . . ? IV. 52.

— Second mémoire en réponse à cette question: Quels sont les changemens que peut occasioner le déboisement de forêts. 1825. IV. 52.[2]

Bossu, Antonin. Traité des plantes médicinales indigènes. 1854. III. 86.

Bossu, N. Nouveaux voyages dans l'Amérique septentrionale. 1771. I. 305.

— Travels through that part of North America formerly called Louisiana. 1771. I. 305.

Bostichi, Bernado DAVANZATI. See DAVANZATI BOSTICHI, Bernado.

Boston journal of natural history. See BOSTON SOCIETY OF NATURAL HISTORY. I. 5.

Boston medical and surgical journal. I. 5.

Boston society of natural history. Anniversary memoirs. Boston journal of natural history. Memoirs. Proceedings. I. 5.

The Bostonian. See The NATIONAL magazine. III. 6.

Boswell, J. W. On the nature, causes and prevention of the dry rot. 1829. IV. 414.[2]
Boswell, John T. On the forms (subspecies or hybrids?) of Pyrus Aria. 1875. II. 312.[1]
Botanic eclectic review. III. 16.
The botanic garden. See DARWIN, Erasmus. 1789. I. 93.
Botanic garden. Ed. by B. Maund. III. 16.
Botanic garden, Calcutta. See ROYAL BOTANIC . . . I. 29.[1]
Botanic garden, Grenada. Annual report. 1897. I. 39.
Botanic garden, Grenada. Bulletin. 1894. I. 39.
Botanic garden, Melbourne. General report of the government botanist. 1853. I. 69.[1]
Botanic gardens, Ceylon. See ROYAL BOTANIC . . . I. 29.[1]
Botánica y productos forestales. See VIDAL Y SOLER, Sebastián. 1887. IV. 21.[3]
Botanical bulletin. See BOTANICAL gazette. I. 5.
Botanical cabinet. III. 16.
Botanical department. Bulletin. I. 7.[1]
Botanical department of the University of Nebraska. Contributions. I. 5.
Botanical descriptions of the species of Cinchonae. 1861. II. 812.
A botanical dictionary. See EATON, Amos. 1816. I. 70.
Botanical dissection of the coffee berry. See DOUGLAS, James. 1725. II. 814.[1]
Botanical excursion in Sutherlandshire. 1828. I. 397.
Botanical extracts from a periodical miscellany . . . entitled "El semanario del nuevo reyno de Granada." 1810. I. 339.[2]
A botanical feature of Khiva: Anabasis. 1874. II. 188.[1]
Botanical garden, Saint Lucia. Annual report. 1897. I. 39.
Botanical gazette. I. 5, V. VII.[1]
Botanical gazette. Henfrey. I. 17.
Botanical grammar and dictionary. See EATON, Amos. 1836. I. 70.
Botanical labels for the herbarium. See COWELL, M. H. 1841. I. 399.
Botanical magazine. Curtis. I. 17.
Botanical magazine. [Tokyo.] I. 28.[1]
Botanical miscellany. I. 17.
Botanical notices. 1871. V. XXI.[1]
The botanical origin of araroba. 1880. III. 467.[1]
Botanical pocket book. See FÖRSTER, T. F. 1840. I. 399.
Botanical register. I. 17.
Botanical review. III. 16. See also DONOVAN, E. O. 1790. I. 93.
Botanical school of Trinity college, Dublin. Notes. I. 17.
Botanical sketches. 1825. I. 397, 533.
Botanical society of America. Publications. I. 5.
Botanical society of Canada. Annals. I. 4.[1]
Botanical society of Edinburgh. Annual report. III. 16.
Botanical society of Edinburgh. Transactions. I. 17.
Botanical society of Pennsylvania. Transactions. I. 5.
The botanical source of araroba. 1878. III. 467.[1]
Botanical source of myrrh. 1899. III. 511.[1]
Botanical station, Dominica, W. I. Annual report. 1892. I. 39.
Botanical station of Barbados. Occasional bulletin. 1891. I. 39.
Botanical survey of India. Records. I. 29.[1]
Botanical tour in . . . Perthshire. See PAMPLIN, W. & IRVINE, Alexander. 1857. I. 400.
Der Botaniker; oder, Compendiöse Bibliothek. 1793. I. 375.
La botanique. 1826. I. 94.
Botanique à l'usage de la jeunesse. See B * * *, Mme. 1845. I. 94.
Botanique biblique. 1862. V. XXV.[1]
Botanique de la jeunesse. 1812. I. 94.
Botanique des dames. 181.? I. 93.
Botanique des enfans. 1800. I. 93.
La botanique et la physiologie végétale. See MARCET, Mrs. Jane. 1829. I. 94.
Botanique practique. Choix des plantes de l'Europe. 1878. III. 66,[1] V. XXVIII.[1]
Botanisch jaarboek. I. 16.
Botanische Abbildungen zur Erläuterung des natürlichen Systems. See BURMEISTER, Hermann & TASCHENBERG, E. L.
Botanische Abhandlungen. Hanstein. I. 11.
Botanische Beobachtungen, und zwar über Entwicklung des Keims. See DIETRICH, F. G. 1799. I. 11.
Der botanische Garten der kaiserlichen Universität zu Dorpat. See WEINMANN, J. A. 1810. I. 41.

Der botanische Garten der Universität zu Halle. See SPRENGEL, Kurt. 1800. I. 45.
Der botanische Garten und das botanische Museum der Universität Zürich. 1897. I. 65.[3]
Botanische Hefte. I. 11.
Botanische Jahrbücher. Engler. I. 11.
Botanische Literaturblätter. See LITERATURBLÄTTER. 1828. I. 1.
Botanische Mittheilungen aus den Tropen. I. 11.
Botanische Unterhaltungen. I. 11. See also WEIZENBECK, G. A. 1784. I. 93.
Botanische Untersuchungen 8. Schwendener . . . dargebracht. 1899. I. 34.
Botanische Zeitung. I. 11.
Botanische Zeitung, welche Recensionen . . . I. 11.
Botanischer Garten der K. k. Universität in Wien. Verzeichnis von HORTUS BOTANICUS UNIVERSITATIS VINDEBONENSIS. 1820. I. 65.[2]
Botanischer Garten der Universität Würzburg. Auswahl von Sämereien. See HORTUS BOTANICUS UNIVERSITATIS LITERARUM WIRCEBURGENSIS. 1841. I. 47.
Botanischer Garten und botanisches Museum zu Berlin. See KÖNIGLICHER BOTANISCHER GARTEN . . . I. 13.
Botanischer Garten und Museum zu Berlin. See KÖNIGLICHER BOTANISCHER . . . I. 49.
Botanischer Garten zu Breslau. See KÖNIGLICH BOTANISCHER . . . I. 13.
Botanischer Jahresbericht. 1874. I. 2.
Botanischer Verein am Mittel- und Niederrhein. Jahresbericht. I. 11.
Botanischer Verein für den Kreis Freiburg und das Land Baden. Mittheilungen. I. 11.
Botanischer Verein für die Provinz Brandenburg und die angrenzenden Länder. Verhandlungen. I. 11.
Botanischer Verein für Gesammtthüringen. Mittheilungen. See GEOGRAPHISCHE GESELLSCHAFT (FÜR THÜRINGEN) ZU JENA. I. 12.
Botanischer Verein für Thüringen. Abhandlungen. Correspondensblatt. See IRMISCHIA. I. 12.
Botanischer Verein in Landshut. Berichte. I. 11.
Botanisches Archiv der Gartenbaugesellschaft des österreichischen Kaiserstaats. I. 27.
Botanisches Centralblatt. 1880. I. 2.
Botanisches Centralblatt für Deutschland. I. 11.
Botanisches Institut in Würzburg. Arbeiten. I. 11.
Botanisches Institut zu Graz. Mittheilungen. I. 27.
Botanisches Institut zu Tübingen. Untersuchungen. See UNTERSUCHUNGEN . . . I. 15.
Botanisches Magazin. See MAGAZIN für die Botanik. I. 26.[1]
Botanisches Museum der Universität Zürich. Mittheilungen. I. 26.[2]
Botanisches Museum zu Hamburg. Bericht. 1884. I. 48.
Botanisches Museum zu Hamburg. Station für Pflanzenschutz. Bericht. III. 11.
Botanisches Taschenbuch. I. 11.
Botanisches Taschenbuch. 1821. I. 1.
Botanisches Wörterbuch. 1795. I. 72.[1]
Botanisk Tidskrift. I. 8.[2]
Botaniska notiser. I. 8.[1]
Botaniske Forening i Kjøbenhavn. Botanisk Tidsskrift. See BOTANISK Tidsskrift. I. 8.[2]
Botaniske Forening i Kjøbenhavn. Festskrift. Meddelelser. I. 8.[2]
Botaniske litteraturblade. 1892. I. 3.[1]
Botanist. III. 16.
Botanist; containing . . . figures of tender and hardy ornamental plants . . . Ed. by B. Maund & J. S. Henslow. 1837. I. 268.
Le Botaniste. I. 21.
The botanist's calendar and pocket flora. 1797. I. 533.
The botanist's guide through . . . Northumberland. See WINCH, N. J. 1805. I. 396.
Botanist's repository. I. 17.
The botanist's vade-mecum. 1855. I. 400. See also WILLIAMS, J. 1855. I. 35.
Botanitcheski geographi. See БОТАНИческий географiи.
Botanitcheski sad. See БОТАНИческiй садъ.
Botanologiae juvenilis mantissa. See EHRHART, Balthasar. 1732. I. 95.
Botanotheca Laurembergiana. See LAUREMBERG, Wilhelm. 1626. V. VIII.[1]
Botanotrophium; seu, Hortus medicus Petri Ricarti. See WIONIUS, Georgius. 1644. I. 56.
Botany of Formosa. 1896. III. 91.[2]

Botany of St. Helena. *See* ROXBURGH, William. 1842. I. 498.

On the botany of Tahiti. 1874. I. 510.[2]

On the botany of the district . . . [bounded by the rivers Cray, Ravensbourne and Thames.] *See* CURREY, Frederick. 1858. I. 400.

The botany of the Kuram and Hariab districts. 1880. I. 474.

Botany of the Rocky Mountains. 1859. I. 323.

Botelho de Lacerda Lobo, Constantino. Memoria sobre a cultura das Vinhas de Portugal. 1790. III. 558.[1]

Botella, Federico de. De cómo nuestro suelo no es tan pobre como se quiere decir. 1886. IV. 276.[2]

Both, L. Kulsvierne og deres nærmeste Omgivelser. 1868. IV. 343.[1]

— Veileder paa Udflugter i Grip Skov. 1876. IV. 343.[1]

— Veileder paa Udflugter i Jægersborg Dyrehave. 1875. IV. 343.[1]

Botigou. Botanique. Relevé de quelques erreurs étymologiques. 1899. I. 76.[2]

Botschaft des Bundesrates . . . betreffend die eidgenössische Oberaufsicht des Bundes über die Forstpolizei. 1897. IV. 294.[1]

Botschaft des katholischen Administrationsrathes des Kantons St. Gallen, den Verkauf der Wälder.... betreffend. 1857. IV. 278.[1]

Botta, Carlo Giuseppe Guglielmo. Storia naturale e medica dell'isola di Corfù. 1798. III. 126.[2]

Botta, Paul Emile. Relation d'un voyage dans l'Yémen. 1841. I. 480.

Botter, A. Kaneelkultuur. 1830. III. 405.[2]

Bottin, Sebastian. Sur la culture de l'Orme. 1806. III. 363.[2]

Bottini, Antonio. Sulla struttura dell' Oliva. 1889. II. 713.[1]

Bottione, Angela Maria. Stirpes, quas vivas pinxit. 1813. I. 265.

Bottler, Max. Exkursions-Flora von Unterfranken. 1882. I. 388.

Bou-Hamma. Le Saucissonier en arbre. 1892. III. 707.[1]

Boubée, Nérée. Bulletin de nouveaux gisemens en France de botanique. 1833. I. 408.

Boubier, Alphonse Maurice. Recherches anatomiques sur l'inflorescence des Cuphea. 1896. II. 608.[2]

— Recherches sur l'anatomie . . . des Bétulacées-Corylacées. 1896. II. 115.[1]

Boucard, Henri. Décadence de la propriété boisée. 1891. IV. 276.[1]

— Dommages causés aux pineraies de la Sologne. 1880. IV. 468.[2]

Boucart. Decadencia de la propiedad forestal. 1891. IV. 361.

Bouchard. Note sur le Melaleuca linariifolia. 1831. III. 636.

Bouchard, A. L'hiver de 1879–80 dans . . . Maine-et-Loire. 1880. III. 48.

Bouchard-Huzard, L. Note bibliographique sur le traité des arbres et arbustes . . . par Duhamel. 1866. III. 1.

Bouchardat, Apollinaire. De l'action des sels ammoniacaux sur la végétation. 1843. I. 157.

— De l'action qu'exercent sur les végétaux les produits . . . qui sont des poisons. 1843. I. 211.

— Sur le condurango. 1870. III. 693.[2]

— De la dégénérescence . . . des Cépages. 1849. III. 555.

— Études sur les cépages de la Bourgogne. 1847. III. 546.

— Études sur les produits des principaux Cépages. 1846. III. 555.

— De l'influence du sol relativement à l'action des poisons. 1846. I. 211.

— De la maladie de la Vigne. 1851. III. 575.[2]

— Monographie des tresseaux ou verreaux. 1851. III. 555.

— Nouveau mémoire sur la maladie de la Vigne. 1851. III. 575.[1]

— Sur les principaux Cépages du midi. 1851. III. 555.

— Rapport sur un mémoire de M. Gerardias. 1857. III. 508.[1]

— Recherches sur la végétation. 1846. I. 147.

— Recherches sur les fonctions des racines. 1846. I. 161.

— Traité de la maladie de la Vigne. 1853. III. 576.

— *See also* DELONDRE, Auguste & BOUCHARDAT, Apollinaire.

Bouchardat, Gustave. Action de l'anhydride acétique sur le linalol. 1893. III. 491,[2] 698.[1]

— Sur l'essence d'Aspic. 1893. III. 698.[1]

— Présence du camphène dans l'essence d'Aspic. 1893. III. 698.[1]

— Sur la présence du sucre de lait dans un suc végétal. 1871. III. 666.[3]

— *See also* VOIRY, R. & BOUCHARDAT, G.

— & Lafont, J. Sur l'essence de Citron. 1885. III. 502.[2]

— & Tardy. Sur les alcools dérivés d'un térébenthène droit, l'eucalyptène. 1895. IV. 533.[2]

— — Sur l'essence d'anis de Russie. 1896. III. 398.[1]

— & Voiry, R. Sur le terpinol. 1888. IV. 531.[2]

Bouché, C. B. & Grothe, Hermann. Ramie, Rheea, China-gras. 1884. III. 381.[2]

Bouché, C. P. Handleiding tot de systematische kennis . . . van bloemen. 1821. III. 76.

Bouché, David Carl Peter. Bemerkungen über die Treiberei von Deutzia. 1849. III. 176.[1]

— Om Culturen af Granattræet. 1835. III. 630.[1]

— Mittheilungen über die Kultur der Granate. 1835. III. 630.[1]

Bouché, Franz. Erfahrungen über die Anwendung der Torferde. 1851. III. 660.[1]

Bouché, J. Der Ursprung des Raphia-Bastes. 1883. III. 330.[2]

— Ueber den Ursprung des Raphia-Bastes. 1883. III. 330.[2]

— Verstell- und verlängerbare Baumstütze. 1885. III. 199.

Bouché, Karl David. Abnormitäten von Acer rubrum. 1878. II. 477.[1]

— Ueber Acer dasycarpum. 1875. III. 536.[1]

— Anweisung, um lebende Vegetabilien . . . nach Europa zu schaffen. 1853. III. 155.

— Über die Anwendung des Corynanthelium Moronoa. 1847. III. 755.[3]

— Appendice sur la culture des Laurinées. 1853. III. 403.[2]

— Aralia-Sämlinge. 1875. II. 647.[2]

— Über die Behandlung der Laurinen. 1853. III. 403.[2]

— Bemerkung über Elaeocarpus cyaneus. 1861. III. 584.[2]

— Bemerkung über giftige Eigenschaften . . . von Robinia. 1877. IV. 524.[1]

— Bemerkungen zur Kultur der Luculia gratissima. 1849. III. 745.

— Beobachtungen über das Erfrieren von Gehölzen. 1861. III. 182.

— Bericht über die amerikanische Preisselbeere. 1876. III. 458,[1] 663.[2]

— Ueber Beschädigung der Saugwurzeln. 1872. III. 182.

— Ueber die Cultur der Cyclantheae. 1857. III. 332.[2]

— Over Doorns of Crataegus-Soorten. 1855. III. 421.[1]

— Über einige schlechte Gewohnheiten beim Verpacken . . . lebender Pflanzen. 1861. III. 155.

— Erfahrungen über das Bewurzeln der Cycadeen-Stämme. 1849. III. 284.[1]

— Eine Fasciation von Lycium chinense. 1878. II. 773.[1]

— Ueber Feinde der Nadelhölzer. 1869. III. 295.[1]

— Fraglicher Fall von Parthenogenesis bei Torreya. 1875. II. 12.[1]

— Gärtnerische Notizen, IV. 1869. III. 295.[1]

— Über die Gattungen Carludovica und Cyclanthus. 1861. III. 332.[2]

— Ueber Gefässe für Palmen. 1860. III. 317.

— Ueber Geschlechtsumwandlung bei Dasylirion. 1875. II. 81.[1]

— Ueber künstliche Befruchtung der Ceratozamia. 1880. III. 313.[1]

— Ueber die Kultur der Cycadeen. 1857. III. 284.[1]

— Mittel gegen die Krankheit des Weinstocks. 1853. III. 576.

— Mittheilungen über die Aussaat . . . der Palmen. 1858. III. 294.[1]

— Mittheilungen über Erschöpfung einiger Pflanzen. 1878. I. 192.[2]

— Monströse Wurzelbildungen der Eiche und Kiefer. 1875. I. 209,[2] IV. 510.

— Ueber Nadelholz-Feinde. 1858. III. 294.[1]

— Ueber das Schlafen von Pimelea. 1874. I. 198.[1]

— Semis et multiplication des Conifères. 1858. III. 294.[1]

— Über die sogenannte Herzfäule bei . . . Pandanus. 1851. III. 313.[1]

— Die Stellung der . . . Blüthen bei Caryota. 1871. II. 65.[2]

— Ueber das Tiefpflanzen von Bäumen. 1880. III. 160.[2]

— Ueber Vermehrung der Encephalartos. 1864. III. 285.[1]

— Die Vermehrung der Pflanzen aus Wurzeln. 1849. III. 158.

— Über die verschiedene Entwickelungsart der Palmenstämme. 1867. II. 62.[2]

— Verschiedene Mittheilungen über Gärtnerei. 1849. III. 183.[1]
— Ueber Vertilgung der schwarzen Fliege. 1862. III. 189.
— Über das Wachsthum der Bambusa verticillata. 1861. II, 60.[1]
— Über Wasser und Luft durchlassende Poren in langen Wurzelstücken der Populus monilifera. 1867. II. 97.[1]
— See also Braun, Alexander & Bouché, D.; Braun, Alexander, Klotzsch, J. F. & Bouché, C. D.; Koch, Karl & Bouché, C. D.
Bouché, Karl Friedrich. Der Königliche Schlossgarten zu Pillnitz. 1899. I. 49.
Bouché, Peter Friedrich. Ueber eine Art des Oculirens mit Holz im Holze. 1837. III. 164.[1]
— Bemerkungen über das Beschneiden der Rosen. 1834. III. 451.[1]
— Naturgeschichte der . . . Garten-Insekten. 1833. III. 188.[2]
Bouché, Pierre. Über die Unzweckmässigkeit des Köpfens der Weidenbäume. 1832. III. 347.
Bouché de Vitray & Desmartis. Mémoire sur la possibilité de transmission de l'oïdium. 1864. III. 577.
Boucher. Inconvénients de certaines feuilles et sciures comme litières. 1894. IV. 558.[1]
Boucher, Georges. Culture de l'Hydrangea paniculata grandiflora. 1899. III. 412.[2]
— Culture des Hortensias. 1897. III. 412.[2]
— Multiplication du Polygonum baldschuanicum. 1900. III. 387.[1]
— & Mottet, S. Les Clématites. 1898. III. 84,[3] 87.
Boucher, H. Las pastas de madera empleadas en la fabrication del papel. 1884. IV. 429.
— Les pâtes de bois employées dans la fabrication du papier. 1884. IV. 429.
Boucher, Pierre. Histoire véritable et naturelle . . . du pays de la Nouvelle France. 1664. III. 261.[2]
Boucher de Crèvecœur, Jules Armand Guillaume. Extrait de la flore d'Abbeville. 1803. I. 406.
— Flore d'Abbeville. 1803. I. 406.
Bouchereau. Sur le Chêne noir ou Tauzin. 1851. II. 129.[2]
Boucherie, Auguste. Conservation des bois. 1857. IV. 418.
— Memoir on the preservation of timber. 1840. IV. 417.
— Mémoire sur la conservation des bois. 1840. IV. 417.
— Note sur la conservation des bois enfouis. 1845. IV. 417.
— Nouvelles recherches sur la conservation des bois. 1841. IV. 417.
— Procédés de conservation & de coloration des bois. 1852. IV. 417.
— Rapport sur un mémoire relatif à la conservation des bois. 1840. IV. 417.
Boucherie, Maurice. Sur l'emploi de l'acide phénique pour la préparation des bois. 1874. IV. 419.
— Note sur la conservation des bois. 1874. IV. 419.
— Observations relatives à la conservation des bois. 1868. IV. 419.
— See also Hatzfeld, A. & Boucherie, Maurice.
Die Boucherie-Holzimprägnation. 1859. IV. 418.
Bouches-du-Rhône — Société d'horticulture et de botanique. See Revue horticole des Bouches-du-Rhône. III. 20.
Bouchez, A. De l'art de déplanter . . . les arbres à fruits de table. 1893. III. 145.[1]
Bouchony, Trone de. Les reboisements de la Seyne. 1861. IV. 163.
Bouchotte Charles. Essai sur la culture du Châtaignier. 1824. III. 358.[1]
— Essais sur la culture du Chincapin. 1833. III. 358.[1]
— Sur un nouveau mode d'opérer les boutures de la Vigne. 1847. III. 548.[1]
Bouchut, E. Sur l'action digestive du suc de Papaya. 1880. III. 617.[1]
— De la dissolution des fausses membranes. 1881. III. 617.[2]
— Sur un ferment digestif contenu dans le suc de Figuier. 1880. III. 370.[1]
— See also Bourgoin, Edme & Bouchut, E.; Wurtz, C. A. & Bouchut, E.
Bouckenooghe, V. Le Coco de mer. 1892. III. 327.[1]
Boucquéau, A. Remarques sur la multiplication des Yuccas. 1852. III. 339.[3]
Boude, E. La culture du Teck en Cochinchine. 1899. IV. 537.[2]
— The forests of Cochin China. 1899. IV. 377.[1]
— Les forêts du Cambodge. 1898. IV. 377.[1]
— Notice sur les forêts de la Cochinchine. 1899. IV. 377.[1]
Boudet, Félix. Fabrication du Kirsch avec de l'eau de Laurier-cerise. 1871. III. 438.[1]

— Falsification du Kirsch. 1865. III. 431.[2]
— See also Felouze, J. & Boudet, Félix.
Boudet, J. P. Extrait d'une mémoire de M. Chevreul. 1811. III. 363.[1]
— Propriétés febrifuges des racines du Cinchona. 1818. III. 721.
— Sucre indigène extrait de la sève du Noyer. 1812. III. 356.[1]
Boudier, Émile. La forêt de Carnelle. 1887. I. 417.
Boudouresques, B. Du Choisya ternata. 1895. II. 400.[2]
Boudt, N. De cortice Geoffraea. 1788. III. 477.[2]
Boué, Ami. Ueber die baumlosen Gegenden. 1851. I. 217.
— Dissertatio inauguralis de methodo floram regionis. 1817. I. 298.
— Geological observations. 1826. I. 217.
— Remarks on the scenery, antiquities . . . of central European Turkey. 1838. I. 449.
— Some observations on the geography . . . of . . . Turkey. 1837. I. 449.
— La Turquie d'Europe. 1840. I. 449.
Bouër, Jean. Guide du chasseur forestier. 189 . ? IV. 22.[2]
Bouffard, A. & Semichon, L. Contribution à l'étude de l'oxydase des raisins. 1898. III. 583.[2]
Bougainville, Louis Antoine de. Voyage autour du monde par la frégate du roi la Boudeuse. 1771. · I. 301.
The Bougainvillea. 1875. III. 388.[1]
Bougarel, Charles. · De l'amygdaline. 1877. II. 272.[1]
Bougon. Etymologie du Sureau. 1899. II. 840.[2]
— Étymologies botaniques. 1897. I. 74.[2]
— Rapport sur les noms des plantes. 1899. I. 74.[1]
Bouillaud, Claude. Note sur les récents progrès du phylloxera. 1876. III. 569.[2]
— Nouvelle note sur les progrès du phylloxera dans . . . la Charente. 1878. III. 571.
Bouillie bordelaise. Composition. 1896. IV. 212.
Bouillon, Frédéric. Propriétés thérapeutiques de l'Eucalyptus globulus. 1872. IV. 532.[2]
Bouillot, C. Araucaria chilensis ou imbricata. 1900. III. 299.[1]
— Carica Papaya. 1900. III. 617.[1]
— Chlorose ou jaunisse des arbres fruitiers. 1900. III. 181.
— La culture du Cacao à l'équateur. 1900. III. 593.[1]
Bouin, P. Remarques . . . sur les inconvéniens de l'abus du thé. 1810. III. 806.
Bouis, Jules. See Pimentel, J. M. d'Oliveira & Bouis, Jules.
Bouis, Jules & Pimentel, J. M. d'Oliveira. Composition de la stéarine végétale. 1857. III. 609.[1]
Bouisson, A. Gustave. Synopsis analytique des plantes . . . des Bouches-du-Rhone. 1878. I. 415.
Bouisson, P. Note sur l'ophthalmie produite par le soufrage. 1863. III. 577.
Boulay, Jacques. Manière de bien cultiver la Vigne. 1712. III. 554.[1]
Boulay, Jean Nicolas, (abbé) Les arbres. 1888. I. 92,[2] 147.
— Études batologiques. 1897. II. 300.[2]
— De la marche à suivre dans l'étude des Rubus. 1893. II. 300.[2]
— Quelques notes sur l'étude des Rubus en France. 1891. II. 303.[2]
— Révision de la flore . . . du nord de la France. 1878. I. 415.
— Ronces vosgiennes. 1864. V. xxvi.[1]
— Les Rubus de la flore française. 1898. II. 304.[1]
— Subdivision de la section Eubatus Fock. 1895. II. 300.[2]
Boulaye, Gabriel Eléonor. See Merlet de la Boulaye, G. E.
Boulaye, J. Seurrat de la. See Seurrat de la Boulaye, J.
Boulduc. Observations et analyses du sucre. 1711. III. 259.[2]
— Remarques sur la nature de la gomme gutte. 1704. III. 668.[2]
Sur le Bouleau à papier. 1828. III. 357.[3]
Le Bouleau comme réserve. 1897. IV. 492.[2]
Bouleau, genre Betula. See Coutance, Amédée. 187 . ? II. 118.[2]
Bouleau mérisier. 1898. IV. 491.[2]
Bouleaux et lapins. 1894. IV. 491.[1]
Bouley, Henri Marie. Sur les expériences faites à Prégny. 1877. III. 570.[1]
— Extrait du rapport de la commission de la Société d'agriculture de Chalon-sur-Saône . . . sur le phylloxera. 1874. III. 566.[1]
— Rapport sur les mesures . . . pour préserver les territoires menacés par le phylloxera. 1874. III. 566.[1]
— Rapport sur les réclamations . . . relatif à l'importation en Algérie de plants d'arbres fruitiers. 1875. III. 200,[2] 560,[2] 563.

Boulger, George Simonds. The beauties of British trees. 1882. I. 393.[1]
— Brambles and briers. 1878. III. 449, *457*.[1]
— British Elms. 1879. II. 143.[1]
— On British Elms. 1879. II. 143.[1]
— Bye-products; utilisation of coppice. 1885. IV. 434.
— Cultural first principles. 1878. IV. 111.[1]
— The dispersal of seeds. 1899. II. 241.[1]
— Economic forestry. 1887. IV. 396.[2]
— The evolution of fruits. 1882. I. 119.
— Familiar trees. 1885. I. 393.
— Hibiscus rosa-sinensis var. schizopetalus. 1879. II. 524.[1]
— Notes preliminary to a proposed flora of Gloucestershire. 1877. I. 403.
— Report of progress . . . flora of Gloucestershire. 1878. I. 403.
— The science and teaching of forestry. 1882. IV. 29.
— The training of our Indian foresters. 1880. IV. 34.[1]
— The uses of plants. 1889. III. 218.
— *See also* BURROWS, A. J. & BOULGER, G. S.
Boullay. Notice historique sur le Figuier. 1844. III. 369.[1]
Boullay, Pierre François Guillaume. Analyse chimique de la coque du Levant. 1812. III. 396.[1]
— Analyse des Amandes douces. 1817. III. 434.[2]
— Considérations nouvelles sur la méthode de déplacement. 1835. III. 480.[1]
— Dissertation sur . . . la Coque du Levant. 1818. II. 206.[2]
— **Boutron-Charbard, A. F.** Examen chimique de la fève de Tonka. 1825. III. 475.[2]
Boullay, Polydore. Revue du bulletin général de thérapeutique. 1832. III. 530.[1]
Boullaye, ARBELTIER DE LA. *See* ARBELTIER DE LA BOULLAYE.
Boullenois, Frédéric de. Conseils aux nouveaux éducateurs de vers à soie. 1842. III. 376.
Boullerot, C. Le Maté. 1897. III. 531.[1]
Boullu, A., *(abbé).* Description d'une Rose nouvelle, R. echinoclada. 1892. II. 293.[2]
— Description d'une variété longipedunculata du Rosa macrocarpa. 1887. II. 296.[1]
— Description de deux Rosiers hybrides. 1885. II. 286.[1]
— Description de quatre Rosiers nouveaux. 1884. II. 286.[1]
— Description du Rosa Sauzeana. 1887. II. 298.[1]
— Sur deux Rosiers nouveaux. 1882. II. 286.[1]
— Deux Rosiers nouveaux pour la flore française. 1879. II. 285.[1]
— Enumération des Rosiers de la flore lyonnaise. 1876. II. 285.[1]
— Evolution des sépales après l'anthèse dans le genre Rosa. 1890. II. 289.[1]
— Hybrides de Rosa gallica. 1897. II. 294.[1]
— Les hybrides de Rosa gallica. 1897. II. 294.[1]
— Note sur quelques plantes hybrides. 1884. II. 286.[1]
— Sur une nouvelle espèce de Rosier. 1882. II. 291.[1]
— Oranges prolifères. 1894. II. 403.[1]
— Rapport sur les observations de [O.] Deveaux. 1878. II. 285,[2] *670*.[1]
— Remarques sur les Rosiers décrits par M. Schmidely. 1880. II. 285.[2]
— Rosa Aunieri Cariot. 1889. II. 291.[2]
— Rosa complicata Gren. 1886. II. 293.[1]
— Rosa echinoclada Boullu. 1894. II. 293.[2]
— Rosa Ozanonii Dés. 1890. II. 297.[1]
— Rosa tomentella L. var. eglandulosa Boullu. 1883. II. 299.[2]
— Rosa ucenensis Boullu. 1888. II. 299.[2]
— Variabilité de Rosa cladoleia. 1890. II. 293.[1]
— Variabilité des aiguillons de Rosa echinoclada. 1894. II. 293.[2]
Boulogne. Extrait d'une communication adressée de Castres. 1830. III. 364.[1]
Bouman, J. Bijdrage tot de vaderlandsche landhuishoudkunde. 1848. III. 106.[1]
Bouniceau. Quelques expériences sur la torsion des troncs d'arbres. 1862. I. 107.[1]
Bouquet, E. Il Castagno. 1897. III. 359.[1]
— L'Eucalyptus et la Wellingtonia nel rimboschimento. 1891. IV. 434,[1] *580*.
Bouquet de la Grye, Amédée. Agitation. 1885. IV. 34.[2]
— L'agriculture et les forêts. 1888. IV. 34.[2]
— L'aménagement par contenance. 1881. IV. 236.
— Les amodiations des forêts de Chênes-Liège. 1890. IV. 517.[2]
— Les arbres à Paris. 1869. III. 212.[1]

— Le Chêne de juin. 1900. IV. 509.
— La disparition du Chêne. 1878. II. 129.[2]
— Éléments de sylviculture. 1870. IV. 109.[1]
— Étude sur les nivellements de précision. 1879. IV. 265, 551.[1]
— Évaluation du revenu cadastral des forêts. 1897. IV. 168.[2]
— Exploitation du Liège. 1880. IV. 516.[2]
— Exploitation du Liège. 1885. IV. 517.[1]
— La flore au point de vue forestier. 1885. IV. 85.[2]
— Les forêts de l'Aube. 1879. IV. 360.
— Le gas d'éclairage au bois. 1874. IV. 433.[2]
— Die Gewinnung des Korkes. 1880. IV. 516.[2]
— Guide du forestier. 1859. IV. 99.[1]
— Guide du garde forestier. 1859. IV. 98.[2]
— Guide pratique et raisonné du garde forestier. 1859. IV. 98.[2]
— Inundaciones y repoblación de montañas. 1877. IV. 185.[2]
— Machine à décortiquer la bourdaine. 1880. IV. 434.
— Procédé d'extraction des graines de Cèdre. 1863. IV. 447.[2]
— Le programme du reboisement de l'Algérie. 1885. IV. 447.[2]
— À propos du transfert des forêts. 1897. IV. 553.[1]
— La question forestière en Roumanie. 1881. IV. 332.[1]
— Rapport . . . sur l'organisation du service forestier en Roumanie. 1876. IV. 294.[2]
— Le reboisement dans la Loire. 1898. IV. 546.[2]
— Les réformes forestières. 1878. IV. 292.
— Le régime forestier appliqué aux bois des communes. 1883. IV. 292.
— Le régime forestier en Italie. 1886. IV. 364.
— El regimen forestal en Italia. 1886. IV. 364.
— Réorganisation du service forestier en Belgique. 1886. IV. 291.[2]
— Reorganización del servicio forestal en Bélgica. 1887. IV. 552.[2]
— La surveillance des forêts. 1872. IV. 292.
— La sylviculture à l'Exposition de 1889. 1889. IV. 20.[2]
— La sylviculture à l'Exposition universelle. 1878. IV. 150.
— Les tarifs de douane. 1891. IV. 285.[1]
— *See also* DUPONT, A. E. & BOUQUET DE LA GRYE, Amédée.
Bouquinat, F. Notice; l'art de planter avec succès. 1890. IV. 153.[1]
Bouquinat, Ferdinand. Traité sur les arbres résineux. 1874. III. 290.
Bourbaud. Sur divers produits . . . d'Australie. 1878. III. 282.[1]
Bourbon, C. Destruction du phylloxéra insectes & cryptogames par le pyrophore insecticide. 1879. III. 760.
Bourcet, Paul. Sur l'absinthine. 1898. III. 754.[2]
— Sur l'absorption de l'iode. 1900. I. 162.[1]
Bourdais, Jules. Traité pratique de la résistance des matériaux. 1859. IV. 410.
Bourde, Paul. L'Olivier en Tunisie; rapport. 1892. III. 676.[1]
— Plan of an inquiry into the merits of Prickly-pear. 1897. III. 624.[2]
— Rapport sur les cultures fruitières et . . . de l'Olivier. 1893. III. 676.[2]
Bourdeau, Louis. Conquête du monde végétal. 1893. III. 99.
Bourdillon, Thomas Fulton. Description of a new species of Ficus. 1900. II. 153.[1]
— Descriptions of some new or rare trees from Travancore. 1898. I. 470.[2]
— Insects attacking Teak. 1899. IV. 537.[1]
— The re-discovery of Strychnos Rheedii. 1895. II. 720.[2]
— Report on the forests of Travancore. 1893. IV. 378.
— Weight and strength of Travancore timbers. 1896. IV. 409.
Bourdon. Compte rendu des produits de l'exploitation. 1837. IV. 382.[1]
— Exploitation des bois. 1837. IV. 382.[2]
Bourdon, Ch. Sur le traitement des Vignes phylloxérées. 1881. III. 572.
Bourdon, Jean Baptiste Isidore. Principes de physiologie comparée. 1830. I. 148.
Bourdon, Louis. Notes sur les cultures comparées du Mûrier. 1837. III. 375.
Bourgade, G. Nouvelle étude sur les Vignes américaines. 1887. III. 556.
Bourgade La Dardye, E. de. Le Paraguay. 1889. III. 269.[2]

Bourgeau. Botanical reports. 1863. I. 311.[2]
Bourgeois. Recherches sur l'emploi du bois de Châtaignier. 1854. IV. 493.[1]
Bourgeois. Observations sur les obstacles qu'il faudrait opposer à l'envahissement des Vignes par le phylloxera. 1874. III. 566.[1]
Bourgeois, A. Sur la végétation d'un Saule creux. 1868. II. 104.[1]
— See also DAMASKINOS, Th. & BOURGEOIS, A.
Bourgeois, Conrad. Le Bombice moine. 1891. IV. 200.
— Deux nouveaux ennemis du Pin Cembro. 1894. IV. 464.[1]
— Tarifs de transport et douaniers. 1899. IV. 285.[1]
— & Rüedi, J. Le Bombyce moine. 1891. IV. 200.
— — Der Nonnenspinner. 1891. IV. 200.
Bourgeois, H. Considérations sur la liberté du commerce des bois. 1831. IV. 277.
Bourgeois, Jules. Quelques mots sur les mœurs de la galéruque de l'Orme. 1875. III. 364.[2]
Bourget, A. Des forêts de l'Algérie. 1855. V. 379.[1]
Bourgne, A. Hygiène des arbres fruitiers. 1896. III. 191.
Bourgoin, Edme & Bouchut, E. Recherches chimiques . . . sur la nature des principes purgatifs du Séné. 1870. III. 470.[1]
— & Verne, Claude. Sur l'existence d'un alcali organique dans le Boldo. 1872. III. 403.[1]
Bourgoin d'Orli, P. H. F. Guide pratique de la culture du Cañer. 1867. III. 592,[1] 726.[2]
Bourguet, Louis. Lettres philosophiques sur la formation des sels. 1729. I. 150.[2]
Bourguignat, Jules René. Catalogue raisonné des plantes . . . de l'Aube. 1856. I. 411.
Bouricius, B. R. C. De particuliere Koffie-cultuur op Java. 1898. III. 731.
Bourke, John G. The folk-foods of the Rio Grande valley. 1895. III. 265.[1]
Bourlet, (abbé). Catalogue des plantes . . . de la ville de Douai. 1847. I. 410.
Bourlier, (Dr.). Cultures d'Acacias australiens. 1894. IV. 521.[1]
— Exploitation des forêts de Chêne-Liége. 1893. IV. 517.[3]
— Les Gommiers en Algérie. 1894. IV. 521.[1]
Bourlier, Ch. Le Ghuidjir et le Tchinguèl-Sâkesey. 1858. III. 245.
Bourn, Joseph H. The evolution and variation of fruit plants. 1890. I. 248.[1]
— Old and new Roses. 1885. III. 450.
Bourne, Edward. De plantarum irritabilitate. 1794. I. 197.[1]
Bourne, H. George. Practical hints on the culture of Cacti. 189.? III. 619.
Bouros, Johann. Dissertatio inauguralis de pharmacologia Graecorum. 1829. III. 238.[2]
— Landerer, Xaver & Earterios, Josef. Griechische Pharmakopöe. 1837. III. 238.[2]
— See also BOΥΡΟΣ, Ιωάννης, ΔΛΝΔΕΡΕΡ, Ξαύριος, & ΣΑΡΤΟΡΙΟΣ Ιωσήφ.
Bourot, & Jean, Ferdinand. Étude sur la digestibilité du beurre de coco. 1896. III. 324.[1]
Bourotte, A. La forêt de Châteauvers. 1893. IV. 249.[1]
— Les pépinières de la Jonchère. 1886. IV. 151.[1]
— Le plateau de Millevaches. 1894. . IV. 104.[1]
— Le reboisement des montagnes dans la Creuse. 1877. IV. 162.
— Les Séquoias. 1887. IV. 484.[2]
Bourquelot, Émile. Sur la composition du grain d'amidon. 1887. I. 140.[1]
— Coussine, cosine et cosotoxine. 1896. III. 424.[2]
— Étude chimique . . . de la graine de Canéficier. 1900. III. 471.[1]
— Sur l'origine de la coloration de certaines gommes. 1897. I. 181.[1]
— Présence d'un ferment analogue à l'émulsine. 1893. I. 207.[1]
— Sur la présence de l'éther méthylsalicylique. 1894. I. 177.
— & Hérissey, Henri. Sur la composition de l'albumen . . . de Caroubier. 1899. III. 472.[1]
— — Sur les ferments solubles produits, pendant la germination. 1900. I. 204.
— — Germination de la graine de Caroubier. 1899. III. 472.[1]
— — Sur l'individualité de la séminase. 1900. II. 322.[1]
— — Sur la pectine de Groseille à maquereau. 1899. III. 414.[1]

— — Sur la pectine du Cynorrhodon. 1899. III. 455.[1]
— — Sur la présence de séminase dans les graines. 1900. I. 204.
— & Lawrent, Jules. Sur la composition des albumens de la fève de Saint-Ignace. 1900. III. 684.[1]
— — Sur la nature des hydrates de carbone . . . de la fève de Saint-Ignace. 1900. III. 684.[1]
— — Sur la nature des hydrates de carbone de réserve de la fève de Saint-Ignace. 1900. III. 684.[1]
Bourrit, O. Instruction élémentaire sur la culture des arbres fruitiers. 1855. III. 145.[3]
Boursier de la Rivière. Pavia de Californie. 1855. III. 536.[1]
Bourwieg, E. W. Abhandlung über den Hausschwamm. 1827. IV. 414.[2]
Bouscasse, D., (or.). Prompte formation des arbres fruitiers. 1859. III. 440.[3]
Bouschet, Henri. Collection de Vignes à suc rouge. 1865. III. 546.
— Moyen de transformer . . . les vignobles menacés. 1874. III. 566.[1]
— Note sur des essais de fécondation de Raisins. 1865. III. 546.
— Production . . . d'une série de cépages à suc coloré. 1865. III. 546.
— Trois nouveaux Muscats. 1872. III. 546.
Bousfield, George. The timber merchant and builder's vade mecum. 1877. IV. 402.[3]
Bousquet, (Dr. med.). Nota sulla provincia di Parana. 1865. IV. 342.[1]
Bousquet, H. L. J. De djamoer-oepas. 1879. III. 735.
Boussière. Notice sur la multiplication des plantes grasses. 1833. III. 157.
— & Jacques, Antoine. Le Platane de Saint-Soupplets. 1839. II. 255.[1]
Boussingault, Jean Baptiste Joseph Dieudonné. Sur l'action délétère . . . du mercure. 1867. I. 211.
— De l'action du salpêtre. 1855. I. 228.[2]
— De l'action du salpêtre. 1856. I. 158.
— Le cacao. 1836. III. 592.[1]
— Ueber den Cacao. 1836 (1837). III. 592,[1] 594.
— Chica, a pigment. 1825. III. 705.
— Sur la composition de la cire du Palmier. 1835. III. 321.[1]
— Sur la composition du lait de l'Arbre de la vache. 1878. III. 367.[2]
— Cultivo del Cacao. 1876. III. 592.[2]
— Sur la culture du Cacaoyer. 1883. III. 592,[1] 595.[1]
— Sur les fonctions des feuilles. 1865. I. 172.
— Des influences météorologiques sur la culture de la Vigne. 1837. III. 554.[2]
— Sur une matière sucrée. 1872. I. 213,[1] III. 585.[2]
— Sur la matière sucrée . . . dans les pétales. 1876. I. 153, 175.
— Sur les matières sucrées contenues dans le fruit du Caféier. 1880. III. 740.[2]
— Memoir concerning the effect which the clearing of land has in diminishing the quantity of water. 1838. IV. 49.[2]
— Sur la nature des gaz produits pendant la décomposition de l'acide carbonique. 1861. I. 172.
— Sur la nature des gaz produits pendant la décomposition de l'acide carbonique. 1862. I. 172.
— On the production of honey-dew. 1872. I. 213,[1] III. 585.[2]
— Recherches chimiques sur la végétation. 1838. I. 150,[2] 157.
— Recherches entreprises pour examiner si les feuilles émettent du gaz azote. 1863. I. 172.
— Recherches sur l'influence que l'azote . . . exerce. 1857. I. 158.
— Recherches sur l'influence que le phosphate de chaux . . . exerce. 1857. I. 158.
— Recherches sur la végétation. 1854. I. 158. .
— Remarques à l'occasion de l'extrait du mémoire de M. G. Ville. 1854. I. 161.
— Researches on the action of foliage. 1865. I. 172.
— Sur la respiration des plantes. 1844. I. 170.
— Sur la rupture de la pellicule des fruits. 1873. I. 150,[1] III. 184.[2]
— Sur la sorbite. 1872. II. 312.[3]
— De la terre végétale. 1859. I. 228.[2]
— De la végétation dans l'obscurité. 1864. III. 40.
— De la végétation dans l'obscurité. 1868. I. 230.
— Ueber die Zusammensetzung des Palmwachses. 1835. III. 321.[1]
— See also MARIANO DE RIVERO & BOUSSINGAULT, J. B.

Boussingault, Jean Baptiste Joseph Dieudonné (*continued*).
— & **Léwy, B.** Mémoire sur la composition de l'air confiné dans la terre végétale. 1853. I. 228.[1]
Boutcher, William. A treatise on forest-trees. 1775. IV. 107.[2]
Bouteiller, Edm. Notes sur quelques Roses · . . . de Provins. 1881. II. 286.[1]
— Notes sur quelques Rosiers . . . de Provins. 1880. II. 285.[2]
Boutelou, Claudio. Tratado del injerto. 1817. III. 160.
— & Estéban. Tratado de las flores. 1804. III. 88.[2]
Boutelou, Estéban. Instrucción sobre el cultivo del Argán. 1870. III. 666.[2]
— Memoria sobre el cultivo de la Vid. 1879. III. 558.[1] ·
— Teoría y práctica del cultivo del ingerto. 1879. I. 208.[2]
— *See also* **Boutelou,** Claudio & Estéban; **Colmeiro,** Miguel & **Boutelou,** Estéban.
Boutelou, Pablo. Memoria acerca de la aclimatación de plantas exóticas. 1842. III. 49.[1]
Boutigny. Observations sur le Daphne Philippi. 1855. II. 602.[1]
Boutigny, P. H. Sur l'origine de l'azote des végétaux. 1848. I. 158.
— *See also* **Hutin, B.** & **Boutigny, P. H.**
Boutigny, Philbert. Traité pratique de la culture du Rosier. 1894. III. 453.[1]
Boutilly, V. Le Caféier de Liberia. 1900. III. 733.[1]
— La culture du Thé. 1897. III. 600.[2]
— Eene Koffieziekte in het eiland Réunion. 1898. III. 736.
— Notice sur la maladie appelée "Coulure du Café." 1898. III. 736.
— Le Thé; sa culture et sa manipulation. 1898. III. 600.[2]
Boutin, A. Analyse chimique des diverses parties de la Vigne.. 1875. III. 567.[1]
— Sur la bourre des bourgeons de la Vigne. 1877. III. 583.[1]
— Sur la composition chimique . . . de la Vigne. 1874. III. 566.[2]
— Sur l'efficacité de la méthode de submersion. 1874. III. 560.[2]
— Études d'analyses comparatives sur diverses variétés de Cépages américains. 1876. III. 560.
— Études d'analyses comparatives sur la Vigne. 1877. III. 570.[2]
— Observations relatives au Phylloxera. 1874. III. 566.[2]
— Des produits industriels . . . du Mahonia Ilicifolia. 1864. III. 395.[1]
— Rapport sur les expériences faites . . . en vue de 'la destruction du phylloxera. 1876. III. 569.[1]
Boutineau, Émile. De la fleur des Rosacées. 1883. II. 256.[2]
— *See also* **Guérard,** Henri & **Boutineau,** Émile.
Boutineau, F. E. *See* **Barthe,** Firmin & **Boutineau,** F. E.
Bouton, A. *See* **Grandeau,** Henry & **Bouton,** A.
Bouton, Louis. Sur le décroissement des forêts à Maurice. 1838. · IV. 378.
— Influence des grandes pluies sur la végétation. 1861. I. 232.[2]
— Medicinal plants . . . of Mauritius. 1857. III. 93.[1] ·
— Sur le mode de répartition de certaines plantes à Maurice. 1861. I. 482.
— Note pour une seconde édition de l'Hortus mauritianus. 1873. I. 482.
— Notes au 8ᵉ et 9ᵉ volume du Prodromus. 1846. I. 483.[1]
— Notes au Prodromus de Decandolle. 1870. I. 482..
— Observations on the different varieties of Zizyphus Jujuba. 1834. II. 500.[1]
— Plantes médicinales de Maurice. 1857. III. 93.[1]
— Tea substitutes of Mauritius. 1861. III. 485.[1]
— Water supply commission. 1871. IV. 168.[2]
Boutron-Charlard, Antoine François. *See* **Boullay, P. F. G.** & **Boutron-Charlard, A. F.; Henry, Ossian** & **Boutron-Charlard, A. F.; Robiquet, P. J.** & **Boutron-Charlard, A. F.**
Boutron-Charlard, Henry & A. F. Examen chimique de l'écorce du Quillaia. 1828. III. 447.[1]
Boutroux, A. Cri d'alarme sur le bois d'industrie. 1870. IV. 281.[1]
Boutry, Maurice. Les ouvriers forestiers. 1892. IV. 311.[1]
Boutteville, Lucien &. Anomalie de structure de la fleur . . . de Pommier. 1869. II. 267.[1]
— De l'existence limitée et de l'extinction des végétaux propagés par division. 1862. I. 248.[2]
— Extinction des variétés végétales propagées par division. 1877. I. 248.[1]

— De la haute antiquité attribuée à quelques fruits. 1861. I. 529.
— Le Melofolium de Pline. 1873. II. 279.[2]
— Note sur les Pommiers. 1869. II. 266.[1]
— & **Hauchecorne,** A. Le cidre. 1875. . III. 428.[2]
Bouvart, Simon. De l'écorçage du Chêne. 1866. IV. 512.
— Notice sur la topographie des forêts domaniales de Mormal. 1875. IV. 360.
Bouveault, L. Sur l'α-acétylfurfurane. 1897. I. 156.
— *See also* **Barbier,** Ph. & **Bouveault, L.**
Bouvet, Georges. Catalogue raisonné des plantes utiles . . . de Maine-et-Loire. 1885. III. 86.
— Note sur quelques Rubus . . . de Maine-et-Loire. 1873. II. 303.[2]
— Plantes rares . . . de Maine-et-Loire. 1874. I. 414.
— Les Rubus de l'Anjou. 1889. · II. 303.[2]
— *See also* **Préaubert,** Ernest & **Bouvet,** Georges.
Bouvet, Maurice. Compte rendu du congrès. — Excursions en forêt. 1899. IV. 556.[1]
— Création de sociétés scolaires forestières. 1899. IV. 541.
— Nos importations en bois d'œuvre. 1897. IV. 557.[1]
— Résultats de la chute de neige du 30 octobre. 1897. IV. 548.[1]
— Simple comparaison. 1898. IV. 555.[2]
— Situation forestière et pastorale du Jura. 1900. IV. 545.[2]
— *See also* **Cardot,** Fernand & **Bouvet,** Maurice; **Roux, E.** & **Bouvet,** Maurice.
Bouvier, James. L'Amandier. 1864. III. 434.[1]
Bouvier, Louis. Flore des Alpes de la Suisse. 1878. I. 436.
— Rosa Clusiana Bouv. 1868. II. 293.[1]
— Les Roses des Alpes. 1875. II. 287.[1]
Bouygues, H. Note sur l'anatomie comparée . . . des Rubées et des Rosées. 1900. II. 257.[1]
— Note sur le péridèrme de la tige aérienne de quelques Potériées. 1900. II. 257.[1]
Bouyssou, J. Le Café du Nuyou. 1899. II. 814.[1]
— Le caoutchouc au Congo français. 1899. III. 230.
— Le Manihot Glaziovii. 1898. III. 520.[2]
— Note sur quelques ennemis du Caféier au Congo. 1899. III. 737.
— Les producteurs laticifères dans le bassin de l'Ogooué. 1899. III. 230.
Bouzek, Josef. Nová odrůda Smrku smutečního. 1887. II. 35.[1]
Bouzige, M. El condurango blanco. 1892. III. 693.[2]
Bove, Giacomo. Patagonia, Terra del Fuoco. 1883. I. 347.
Bové, Nicolas. Observations sur les cultures de l'Égypte. 1834. III. 289.[1]
— Relation abrégée d'un voyage botanique en Égypte. 1834. I. 303, *478*.
Bovey, Henry T. Results of experiments on the strength of White Pine. 1898. IV. 411,[1] *445*.[1]
— On the strength of Douglas Fir. 1895. IV. 410.
— Tests of large timber. 1894. IV. 410.
Bowden, Ambroise. De la 'pourriture sèche. 1819. IV. 414.[2] ·
Bowdich, (*afterwards* Lee, *Mrs.* Sarah). *See* **Bowdich,** *Mrs.* T. E.
Bowdich, Thomas Edward. Excursions in Madeira and Porto Santo. ·1825. I. 497.
— Mission from Cape Coast Castle to Ashantee. 1819. I. 494.
— Voyage de découverte aux Îles Madère. 1825. I. 497.
Bowdich, *Mrs.* Thomas Edward, (*afterwards Mrs.* Lee). On the natural order of plants . . . Anonaceae. 1829. II. 215.[1]
— Trees, plants and flowers. *See* **Lee,** *Mrs.* R. 1854. I. 95.
Bowditch, James H. Forestry notes. 1878. IV. 111.[2]
— Management of Maurice. The general management of Cactuses. 1890. III. 619.
Bowen, George Austin. The leaf as a physical study. 1885. I. 154.
Bower, Frederick Orpen. On the comparative morphology of the leaf. 1885. II. 1.
— On the germination . . . of the seedling of Welwitschia. 1881. II. 55.[2]
— Groningen hos Welwitschia mirabilis. 1881. II. 55.[2]
— On the mode of climbing in the genus Calamus. 1887. II. 65.[2]
— Note on a morphological peculiarity of Cordyline. 1887. · II. 80.[1]
— On the structure . . . of Rhynchopetalum. 1884. II. 845.[1]
— & **Vines,** S. H. A course of practical instruction in botany. 1885. I. 36.[2]

Bowerbank, L. Q. The commercial Quassia. 1862. III. 508.[1]
— On the essential oil of Pimento. 1862. III. 637.[1]
Bowers, Edward A. Present condition of the forests on the public lands. 1891. IV. 338.[1]
— Public timber lands. 1888. IV. 272, 314.[2]
Bowers, Samuel. Report of committee on evergreens and hardy shrubs. 1879. III. 60.
Bowie, J. On the culture of the Wax-berry. 1854. III. 353.[1]
Bowler, W. S. Account of remarkable Palmyra trees. 1834. II. 65.[1]
Bowles, William. Introduccion á la historia natural . . . de España. 1775. I. 419.[2]
— Introduction à l'histoire naturelle . . . de l'Espagne. 1775. I. 419.[2]
— Introduzione alla storia naturale . . . de Spagna. 1775. I. 419.[2]
Bowman. Bowman's guide to Richmond. 1836. I. 533.
Bowman, John Eddowes. On the longevity of the yew. 1837. II. 10.[2]
Bowrey, J. J. Papain and its properties. 1894. III. 618.[1]
— On the physiological action of . . . Urechites suberecta. 1878. III. 691.[2]
— Propriétés du Papayer employé comme fourrage. 1894. III. 618.[1]
— Uréchitoxine. 1878. III. 691.[2]
— Vegetable chemistry. 1884. I. 151.[2]
The Box. 1886. III. 523.[1]
The Box-leaved Holly. 1887. III. 530.[2]
Boxwood, Indian. 1882. IV. 525.
Boxwood substitutes. 1884. IV. 428.[1]
Boyaryshnik. See Боярышникъ.
Boyce, W. L. Prickly Pears as fodder. 1898. III. 624.[2]
Boyceau de la Baraudière, Jacques. Traité du jardinage. 1638. III. 111.
Boyd, A. J. Forest conservancy. 1897. IV. 181.[2]
— Forest conservancy in New South Wales. 1900. IV. 280.[1]
— Forest conservation. 1899. IV. 181.[2]
— Forests and moisture. 1900. IV. 52.
— Male Coffee plants. 1899. III. 733.[1]
— Prickly Pears for stock. 1897. III. 624.[2]
— The production of tall trees. 1900. IV. 65,[1] 124.[2]
— Ramie cultivation. 1898. III. 381.[2]
— Ramie . . . the China-grass. 1897. III. 382.[1]
— Waste in sleeper-getting. 1900. IV. 424.[1]
Boyd, John. The Pollok Wych Elms. 1896. IV. 519.[1]
Boyé, E. Les Alpes-Maritimes. 1888. IV. 361.
— Exploitation des Lièges. 1883. IV. 517.[1]
— Forêt communale de Saint-Martin-Lantosque. 1881. IV. 249.
— Le Var. 1889. IV. 361.
Boyer. Note concernant une Vigne attaquée . . . par l'oïdium. 1858. III. 577.
Boyer, F. De la taille et de la culture du Mûrier. 1838. III. 375.
— & Lebaume, G. de. De la culture du Mûrier. 1845. III. 376.
Boyer, Félix. De la fumure chimique des Vignes. 1871. III. 758.[1]
Boyer, Georges. See VIALA, Pierre & BOYER, Georges.
— & Lambert, F. Sur deux nouvelles maladies du Mûrier. 1893. III. 379.[1]
Boyer de Fonscolombe, E. H. Mémoire sur la destruction . . . des bois dans . . . la Provence. 1819. IV. 275, 282.[2]
Boyer de Fonscolombe, E. L. J. H. Calendrier de faune et de flore. 1845. I. 226.[1]
Boyer de Fonscolombe, E. L. J. H., (sr.). Des insectes nuisibles. 1840. III. 189.
Boyer-Peyreleau, Eugène Édouard. Les Antilles françaises. 1823. III. 266.
Boyle, Mrs. Eleanor Vere. Ros Rosarum ex horto poetarum. 1896. II. 290.[2]
Boyle, J. C. Gouvernements-Koffiecultuur ter Sumatra's westkust. 1894. III. 730.
Boyle, John A. Two members of the Ampelopsis family. 1892. III. 544.[1]
Boyle, Robert. See GREW, Nehemiah & BOYLE, Robert.
Boym, Michael. Flora sinensis. 1656. I. 457, V. xxiii.[2]
Boynton, Margaret Fursman. Observation upon the dissemination of seeds. 1895. II. 253.[1]
Boynton, S. S. Olive culture for California. 1889. III. 676.[1]
— The Olive in America. 1891. III. 676.[1]
— A valuable tree for California. 1890. III. 329.[1]

Boynton, W. D. Ruthless felling of our forests. 1892. IV. 281.[2]
Bozino, Albino. Rimboschimento . . . in Sostegno. 1898. IV. 166.[2]
Bozoli, Giuseppe M. Degli alberi ed arbusti. 1851. III. 88.[1]
Br., H. La production et le commerce du Poivre. 1900. III. 343.[2]
Bra, M. Cultures du Nectria. 1899. III. 195.[2]
Braad, Christ. Hinr. Anmärkningar om Sago-trädet. 1775. III. 284.[2]
— Berättelse om Coffé-planteringen. 1761. III. 732.[2]
— Berigt wegens het teelen van Koffij. 1761. III. 732.[2]
Braam, J. S. van. Een rupsenbeschadiging in Djati culturen. 1899. IV. 537.[1]
Bracciforti, Alberto. Dizionarietto botanico piacentino-latino. 1877. I. 74.[2]
— Flora di Piacenza. 1877. I. 74.[2]
— Flora piacentina. 1877. I. 428.
Brace, E. J. C. The formation . . . of Eucalyptus plantations. 1885. IV. 530.
— The formation . . . of forest-tree nurseries. 1885. IV. 151.[1]
— Monograph on the cultivation of Tea on the Nilagiris. 1880. III. 763.[2]
— On the principal varieties of Pinus sylvestris. 1886. III. 309.[1]
— Weights of forest tree seeds. 1883. IV. 147.[1]
Brace, L. J. K. See GARDINER, John & BRACE, L. J. K.
Braced crotches. 1890. I. 209,[2] III. 428.[1]
Brachmann. Ueber Verwendung des Dynamits zur Sprengung von Buchenstöcken. 1874. IV. 386.
Brachmann, (Forstconducteur). Mittheilungen über einen Frass von Coccus racemosus. 1868. IV. 455.
Brackenridge, Wm. D. List of living plants and seed sent from Chile. 1855. III. 116.[2]
— Notes on the flora of the Sandwich Islands. 1886. I. 509.[2]
Brackett, C. B. Nomenclature. 1897. III. 62.
Brackett, Gustavus Benson. The Apple and how to grow it. 1900. III. 427.[1]
— Division of pomology. 1898. III. 62.
— The evolution of the Grape. 1895. III. 547.
— The Osage Orange as a forest tree. 1882. IV. 519.[1]
— The relative hardiness of seedlings and . . . grafted trees. 1886. III. 43.
Braconnot, Henri. Sur la faculté . . . de laurier-rose d'attraper les insectes. 1834. I. 729.[1]
— De l'influence du sel. 1845. I. 211.
Bradbury, John. Travels in the interior of America. 1817. I. 306.
Braddell, T. Nutmeg culture. 1862. III. 402.[2]
Braddick, John. On the treatment of Cactus Opuntia. 1818. III. 625.[1]
Brader, Ferd. Auswahl der vorzüglichsten Birn- und Apfelsorten. 1889. III. 89.[1]
Bradfer, Maurice. Excursion forestière dans l'Hertogenwald. 1896. IV. 355.[1]
Bradford, Aldens. Cranberries. Plymouth. 1868. III. 663.[2]
Bradke, (Revierförster der Herrschaft von Neuhaus) Ermittelung des Holzgehalts. 1859. IV. 217.
Bradley, C. B. A new study of some problems relating to the giant trees. 1886. III. 50.[2]
Bradley, Joseph. On planting exposed . . . moorland. 1872. III. 42.[1]
Bradley, Richard. Almanach der hoveniers. 1718. III. 123.[1]
— Le calendrier des jardiniers. 1718. III. 123.[1]
— The compleat seedsman's monthly calendar. 1727. III. 156.[1]
— The country gentleman and farmer's monthly director. 1726. III. 108.
— Dictionarium botanicum. 1728. III. 80.
— The fruit garden display'd. 1732. III. 78.[2]
— A general treatise of husbandry and gardening. 1724. III. 108.
— The gentleman and gardener's kalendar. 1718. III. 123.[1]
— Historia plantarum succulentarum. 1716. I. 289.
— New experiments and observations, relating to the generation of plants. 1724. I. 198.
— New improvements of planting. 1717. III. 108.
— Nouvelles observations . . . sur le jardinage. 1717. III. 108.

Bradley, Richard (*continued*).
— Observations and experiments relating to the motion of the sap. 1717. I. 162.
— A philosophical account of the works of nature. 1721. I. 522,¹ *III. 116*.²
— A survey of the ancient husbandry. 1725. *III. 99*, 108.
— Ten practical discourses concerning earth and water. 1727. *I. 157, 526*,¹ III. 35.
— Ten practical discourses concerning the four elements. 1727. *I. 157, 526*,¹ III. 35.
— A true account of the Aloe americana. 1729. III. 620.²
— The virtue and use of coffee. 1721. III. 741.¹
— Der vollkommene Saamen-Händler. 1727. III. 155.
Bradley, William Harrison. Olive culture in the Alpes Maritimes. 1891. III. 676.¹
Bradner, E. A partial catalogue of the flora of Steuben county. 1892. V. XVII.¹
Brady, Antonio & Charles. Successful transport of Ailanthus silkworms to Australia. 1869. III. 507.²
Brady, Charles. The Ailant silkworm. 1868. III. 507.²
— *See also* BRADY, Antonio & Charles.
Brady, Henry Bowman. Notes of a visit to the Dutch government Cinchona plantations. 1885. III. 716.
— On the seed of Dictyoloma peruviana. 1861. II. 405.¹
Braemer, Louis. Les poivres de Guinée. 1896. III. 281.¹
— Les tannoïdes. 1890. I. 183.
Bräninger, Johann Martin. De potus caffe usu et abusu. 1725. III. 741.¹
Braesche. Le traitement des sapinières. 1885. IV. 446.¹
Braeucker, Theodor. Deutschlands wilde Rosen. 1882. II. 284.¹
— 292 deutsche ... Rubus-Arten und Fotmen. 1882. II. 284.¹
Bräuner, (*Forstmeister, Landsberg*). Erträge der forstlichen Vorkultur durch Ackernutzung. 1855. IV. 133.
Braeuner, J. J. Thesaurus sanitatis oder menschlicher Gesundheit. 1713. I. 289.
Bräutigam, Justus. Beiträge zur anatomischen Charakteristik der Rosaceen-Bastarde. 1897. II. 257.¹
Bräutigam, Walter. Ueber das Tiliadin. 1900. III. 586.¹
Bragat, José. Proyecto de una casa para guardas de monte. 1882. IV. 266.¹
Braguier, B. & Maurette. Tableau synoptique des végétaux . . . des Deux-Sèvres. 1842. I. 409.
Braichet, Albert. Aménagement des forêts. 1871. IV. 243.
— Aménagements provisoires dans le canton de Vaud. 1888. IV. 249.²
— Einige Worte über die Abnahme der Wälder. 1876. IV. 281.¹
— Fixation de la possibilité. 1887. IV. 237.
— Forst-Betriebs-Einrichtung. 1871. IV. 243.
— La lunure du Chêne. 1879. IV. 510.
— Der Mondring der Eiche. 1879. IV. 510.
— À propos du déboisement. 1876. IV. 281.¹
Brailsford, William. On some ancient trees. 1884. I. 297.¹
Brainerd, Ezra. The Blackberries of New England. 1900. II. 300.²
— Jones, L. R. & Eggleston, W. W. Flora of Vermont. 1900. I. 317.¹
Brainerd, Jehu. An essay on Pear-blight. 1876. III. 446.¹
Braithwaite, Oldam & Farr. Sur le Daphnidium Cubeba. 1887. III. 406.²
Brames. *See* WHITLEY, BRAMES & MILNE.
Brancaccio, Francesco Maria. De usu et potu chocoltae diatribe. 1664. III. 594.
Branche, Pierre. Jardinier de grande experience. 1692. III. 143.
Branched Palms. 1900. II. 67.¹
Branching Palms. 1889. II. 63.¹
Brande, August Everard. Experiments . . . on the Angustura bark. 1791. III. 503.²
Brande, William Thomas. An account of a vegetable wax from Brazil. 1811. III. 225.
— Chemical experiments on guaiacum. 1806. III. 494.¹
— A manual of pharmacy. 1825. III. 257.²
— Note sur une substance végétale astringente. 1817. III. 237.¹
— Observations on an astringent vegetable substance. 1817. III. 237,¹ 272.¹
Brandegee, *Mrs.* Mary Katherine. Botanical notes. 1889. I. 325.
— Catalogue of the flowering plants . . . of San Francisco. 1891. I. 326.
— Contributions to the knowledge of West American plants. 1891. I. 325.

— Descriptions of some Californian plants. *See* CURRAN, M. K. 1886. II. 278.¹
— The flora of Yo Semite. 1891. I. 325.
— List of the plants described in California. 1886. I. 325.
— Notes on Cactese. 1897. II. 587.²
— Rhamnus californica and its allies. 1890. II. 497.²
— Studies in Ceanothus. 1895. II. 492.²
— Viscainoa geniculata. *See* CURRAN, M. K. 1889. II. 396.¹
Brandegee, Townshend S. An arborescent Polygala. 1890. II. 431.¹
— Cactaceae of the Cape region of Baja California. 1891. II. 587.¹
— A collection of plants from Baja California. 1890. I. 332.
— The Coniferae of the Crestones. 1878. II. 14.¹
— The effect of rain on Fouquiera. 1890. II. 563.¹
— Field notes on the plants of Baja California. 1891. I. 325, 332.
— The flora of southwestern Colorado. 1876. I. 324.
— Flora of the Californian islands. 1890. I. 325.
— Flora of the cape region of Baja California. 1893. I. 332.
— Flora of the Santa Barbara Islands. 1889. I. 325.
— Lavatera insularis. 1896. II. 525.¹
— A new Cottonwood from Baja California. 1890. II. 97.²
— A new Nolina. 1890. II. 84.¹
— New species of plants from Mexico. 1899. I. 333.
— New species of western plants. 1899. II. 469.¹
— A new Tapiria from Baja California. 1900. II. 461.² ·
— Pinus latifolia. 1892. II. 42.²
— The plants of Santa Catalina island. 1890. I. 325.
— Southern extension of California flora. 1893. I. 326.
— The Teton and Yellowstone Park forest reserves. 1899. IV. 341.¹
— Teton forest reserve. 1899. IV. 341.¹
— Timber line in the Sawatch Range. 1880. I. 320, *IV. 78*.¹
— Two new species of Ilex. 1894. II. 462.²
— The vegetation of burns. 1891. I. 325.
— Voyage of the Wahlberg. 1900. I. 333.
— Yellowstone Park forest reserve. 1899. IV. 341.¹
Brandeis, Friedrich. Setzlinge in Körbchen. 1897. IV. 153.¹
Brandelius, Petrus. Remedia guineensia. *See* AFZELIUS, Adam. 1813. III. 93.¹
Brandenburg, Friedrich Wilhelm, *Marggraff zu*. Magdeburgische Holtz- und Jagt-Ordnung. *See* MAGDEBURGISCHE . . . 1686. IV. 319.²
Brandenburg, Rudolf & Brunner, Heinrich. Présence de l'acide succinique dans les raisins verts. 1876. III. 583.¹
— Ueber das Vorkommen der Bernsteinsäure. 1876. III. 5⁸².¹
Brandenburg — Botanischer Verein. *See* BOTANISCHER VEREIN FÜR DIE PROVINZ . . . I. 11.
Brandenstein, von. Beytrag zu den allgemeinen Grundsätzen der Forstökonomie. 1798. IV. 117.
Brandenstein, von, (*Revierförster, Homberg*). Das Buttlar'sche Pflanzverfahren. 1861. IV. 152.
Brander, Axel Emil. *See* ZETTERMANN, A. J. & BRANDER, A. E.
Brander, Fredrik Reinhold. Kort begrepp af naturalhistorien. 1785. I. 83.
Brandes, E. Die Flora Deutschlands. 1846. I. 381.
Brandes, Gustav. Die Blattläuse und der Honigthau. 1893. I. 213.¹
Brandes, Rudolph. Einige Versuche über den Bicuhyba-Balsam. 1833. III. 403.¹
Brandes, Wilhelm. Flora der Provinz Hannover. 1897. I. 390.
Brandis, *Sir* Dietrich. Über die Acanthaceen-Gattung Strobilanthes. 1894. II. 803.²
— Anbau der grossen Bambusen in Deutschafrika. 1899. III. 314.¹
— Auszug eines Briefes . . . Domdamu forests. 1863. I. 473.
— Über die Bambusen von Birma. 1887. II. 58.²
— On the bark of Broussonetia. 1881. III. 368.¹
— Die Beziehungen zwischen Regenfall und Wald in Indien. 1884. IV. 49.¹
— Biltmore Forest in Nord-Carolina. 1894. IV. 340.
— Biological notes on Indian Bamboos. 1894. II. 58.²
— Bürgermeister Krahe, Prummern. 1892. III. 349.
— The Burma Teak forests. 1896. IV. 537.²
— Catalogue of specimens of timber . . . from the government forests in the provinces under the government of India. 1878. IV. 21.²
— Charles Sprague Sargent, The silva of North America. 1893. II. 265.²

— Cleghorn's services to Indian forestry. 1888. IV. 295.[1]
— Combretaceae. 1893. II. 615.[1]
— Comparison between the floras of the eastern and western peninsulas of India. 1891. I. 475.[1]
— On the cultivation . . . of Eucalyptus in northern India. 1876. IV. 530.
— The Deodar forests of the Dhauli valley. 1882. IV. 377.[1]
— Diospyros mollis Griffith. 1900. II. 702.[1]
— On the distribution of forests in India. 1872. V. xxxi.[2]
— Doubtful Burmese Bamboos. 1900. II. 58.[3]
— An enumeration of the Dipterocarpaceae. 1895. II. 559.[1]
— Erythrina indica. 1900. II. 357.[2]
— L'Exposition forestière d'Edimbourg. 1885. IV. 20.[1]
— Die Familie der Dipterocarpaceen und ihre geographische Verbreitung. 1896. II. 559.[1]
— Flowering of the Australian Wattle on the Nīlgiris. 1882. II. 324.[2]
— The forest flora of north-west and central India. 1874. I. 470,[1] IV. 88.[2]
— The forest of the outer north-west Himalaya. 1885. I. 470,[3] IV. 88.[2]
— Forestry in Natal. 1894. IV. 380.[1]
— Forestry in North America. 1890. IV. 338.[1]
— The forests of south India. 1882. IV. 377.[2]
— Les forêts de l'Inde. 1886. IV. 378.
— Les forêts du nordouest de l'Himalaya. 1885 (1886). IV. 88,[2] 378.
— Forsteinrichtung in den Teakwaldungen von Pegu. 1898. IV. 537.[1]
— Forstliche Ausstellung in Edinburgh. 1885. IV. 20.[1]
— Forstliche Verhältnisse aus den britisch-indischen Waldungen. 1872. V. xxxi.[2]
— Forstwirtschaft in Natal. 1894. IV. 380.[1]
— The garden Roses of India. 1887. III. 450.
— On the geographical distribution of forests in India. 1872. V. xxxi.[2]
— Die geographische Verbreitung der Bambusen. 1897. II. 58.[1]
— Gesellig wachsende Bäume. 1894. I. 219.[1]
— Growth of grass and underwood. 1884. I. 218.
— Indian forestry. 1897. IV. 378.
— Indian forests. 1886. IV. 378.
— The Indian species of Anogeissus. 1900. II. 615.[2]
— The Indian species of Dillenia. 1900. II. 541.[2]
— L'industrie du bois de Teck au Siam. 1899. IV. 538.[1]
— The influence of forests on rainfall. 1887. IV. 49.[1]
— Le Japon à l'Exposition forestière d'Edimbourg. 1885. IV. 21.[3]
— Kaulia Babul in Berar. 1898. IV. 521.[1]
— Über die klimatischen Verhältnisse . . . in Britisch Ostindien 1871. I. 470,[1] IV. 88.[2]
— The large Elm of Kulu. 1900. II. 145.[1]
— List of specimens of some of the woods of British Burmah. 1862. IV. 21.[3]
— The management and protection of forests. 1895. IV. 102.
— Memorandum on the demarcation of the public forests in the Madras presidency. 1878. IV. 295,[1] 377.[2]
— Memorandum on the establishment of a central forest school. 1877. IV. 37.[1]
— Memorandum on the forest legislation proposed for British India. 1875. IV. 382.[1]
— Memorandum on the rate of growth of Teak. 1879. IV. 537.[1]
— Memorandum on the supply of railway sleepers of the Himalayan Pines. 1879. IV. 423.[2]
— Memorandum on the valuation surveys lately made. 1879. IV. 262.
— Mittheilungen über den Teakbaum. 1886. III. 697.[2]
— Mittheilungen über Terminalia chebula. 1885. III. 632.[1]
— Mixed Oak and Beech forests of the Spessart. 1894. IV. 119,[1] 248,[2] 544,[2] 560.[3]
— Los montes de Teca . . . de Birmania. 1896. IV. 537.[2]
— Los montes del noroeste del Himalaya. 1886. IV. 378.
— The Muga silk industry. 1880. III. 407.[1]
— Die Nadelhölzer Indiens. 1886. II. 15.[2]
— Über die Namen der Rosen in Indien. 1886. II. 290.[2]
— The " Nanmu " wood of China. 1880. IV. 520.[1]
— Natural coppice. 1900. II. 357.[2]
— A new species of Albizzia. 1900. II. 331.[2]
— Note on the production of Teak timber. 1862. IV. 537.[2]
— Notes on forest management in Germany. 1888. IV. 349.[1]
— Notes on " Indirect influences of forests on rainfall in Madras." 1883. IV. 49.[1]

— Notes on the Burmese varnish. 1876. III. 278.
— Preliminary working plan to the Deoban working circle. 1875. IV. 250.[1]
— Progress of forestry in India. 1884. IV. 279.[2]
— The proposed school of forestry [at Edinburgh]. 1888. IV. 34.[1]
— Pure forests and mixed forests. 1899. IV. 137,[2] V. xxx.[2]
— Regen und Wald in Indien. 1887. IV. 49.[1]
— Remarks on the administrative forest staff of Prussia. 1885. IV. 290.[2]
— Remarks upon the natural order Dipterocarpaceae. 1895. II. 559.[1]
— Report for supplying the forest department in India with specially trained assistants. 1868. IV. 294.[1]
— Report on the Teak forests of Pegu. 1860. IV. 537.[1]
— Reports on the Teak forests in Pegu. 1862. IV. 537.[1]
— The Ringal of the north-western Himalaya. 1885. II. 58.[2]
— Ripening of Deodar seed. 1882. II. 27.[3]
— Sind forests. 1879. IV. 377.[2]
— Sir Richard Strachey and Indian forestry. 1898. IV. 295.[2]
— Ueber specifische Individualität in . . . Blüthezeit. 1889. I. 221.
— El Spessart de Baviera. 1894. IV. 544,[2] 560.[3]
— Suggestions regarding forest administration in Ajmere and Merwara. 1879. IV. 295.[1]
— Suggestions regarding forest administration in Assam. 1879. IV. 295.[1]
— Suggestions regarding forest administration in British Burma. 1876. IV. 295.[1]
— Suggestions regarding forest administration in the Central Provinces. 1876. IV. 295.[1]
— Suggestions regarding forest administration in the Hyderabad assigned districts. 1879. IV. 295.[1]
— Suggestions regarding forest administration in the Madras presidency. 1883. IV. 295.[1]
— Suggestions regarding forest administration in the North-western Provinces and Oudh. 1882. IV. 295.[1]
— Suggestions regarding the arrangement of the forests . . . circle N. W. P. 1879. IV. 250.[1]
— Suggestions regarding the forest survey of Naini Tal protected forests. 1881. IV. 250.[1]
— Suggestions regarding the management of the forests in the Jalpaiguri and Darjeeling districts. 1881. IV. 295.[1]
— Suggestions regarding the management of the forests included in the forest school circle. 1879. IV. 295.[1]
— Suggestions regarding the management of the leased forests of Busáhir. 1881. IV. 250.[1]
— Supplement to Report on forest management. 1873. IV. 113.[1]
— Tabasheer. 1887. II. 59.[1]
— The teaching of forestry. 1890. IV. 29.
— On Teak planting in Bombay. 1890. IV. 576.[2]
— The " Than " tree. 1891. II. 618.[1]
— Training of candidates for the superior staff of the forest service in India. 1883. IV. 37.[1]
— Unterschiede in der Vegetation Vorder- und Hinter-Indiens. 1891. I. 475.[1]
— Utilization of the less valuable trees. 1894. IV. 382.[1]
— Vegetation and country from Narkanda to Pangi. 1879. I. 474.
— Der Vegetation der westlichen Küstenländer von Hinterindien. 1866. I. 474.
— Der Wald des äusseren nordwestlichen Himalaya. 1885. I. 470,[2] IV. 88.[2]
— Der Wald in den Vereinigten Staaten. 1890. IV. 338.[1]
— Über die Waldvegetation des . . . Himalaya. 1884. I. 470,[1] IV. 88.[2]
— Über die Waldvegetation von Ajmere. 1885. I. 470,[1] IV. 88.[2]
— The woods of British Burmah. 1862. IV. 401.[1]
— Working of trans-sarda forests in Kheri, Oudh. 1880. IV. 295.[1]
— Das Zusammenvorkommen von Nadelhölzern und Dipterocarpeen in Indien. 1886. II. 21,[1] 559.[1]
— & Bailey, F. Joint report on the first course . . . at the Central forest school. 1882. IV. 37.[1]
— — Portable forest tramways. 1886. IV. 391.
— & Gilg, Ernst. Dipterocarpaceae. 1895. II. 559.[1]
— Baden-Powell, B. H. & Stenhouse, W. Suggestions regarding the demarcation . . . of the forests in Kulu. 1877. IV. 295.[1]
— Stewart, J. L. & Wood, E. Report upon the Deodar forests of Bussahir. 1685. IV. 448.[1]

Brandis, Sir Dietrich (continued).
— & others. Preliminary working plan of the Sutlej working circle. 1875. IV. 250.[1]
Brandon, Jan Hendrik. Hortus regius honselaerdigensis. 17 . . ? I. 50.
Brandsten, Gustavus Fredericus. Flora gothoburgensis. See WAHLBERG, P. F. 1820. I. 352.
Brandt, Ernst. Nonnulla de parasitis quibusdam phanerogamicis. 1849. II. 173.[2]
Brandt, Johann Friedrich. Einige Worte über die Pflanze, welche den Sternanis liefert. 1838. III. 397.[2]
— Flora berolinensis. 1824. I. 377.
— Tabellarische Uebersicht der officinellen Gewächse. 1829. III. 56.
— & **Ratzeburg,** J. T. C. Deutschlands phanerogamische Giftgewächse. 1828. III. 73.
Brandt, M. G. W. Das Pflanzenleben. 1866. I. 515.
Brandt, Paul. Pharmacognostische Studien über einige . . . Rinden. 1894. III. 260.[1]
Brandt, R. See DRUDE, Oscar & BRANDT, R.
— & **Wittmack,** Ludwig. Cotyledon macrantha rubromarginata. 1881. III. 409.[2]
Brandt, Theodor. Der Obstbau in rauhen Gegenden. 1883. III. 139.
— Der schwedische aufrechtwachsende Bocksdorn. 1886. III. 701.[1]
Brandts, A. Over houtparenchijm. 1855. I. 124.
Brandza, Demetriŭ. Despre vegetaţiunea Romanici. 1880. I. 449.
— Plante noué pentru flora Dobrogeĭ. 1889. I. 536.[1]
— Prodromul floreĭ române. 1879. I. 449.
— Vegetaţiunea Dobrogeĭ. 1884. I. 449.
Brandza, Marcel. Recherches anatomiques sur les hybrides. 1890. I. 100,[1] 246.[1]
— Développement des téguments de la graine. 1891. I. 121.
— Recherches anatomiques sur la structure de l'hybride entre l'Aesculus. 1890. II. 481.[2]
— Recherches sur le développement des téguments séminaux. 1890. I. 121.
Branke, Vladimir J. von. See ВРАНКЕ, В. Ю. фонъ.
Branner, John Casper. The course and growth of the fibrovascular bundles in Palms. 1884. II. 63.[1]
— Notes on the forest trees of the Crowley's Ridge region. 1894. IV. 397.
Brannt, William T. India rubber, gutta-percha. 1900. III. 232.[1]
— A practical treatise on animal and vegetable fats and oils. 1888. III. 225.
Branntwein aus dem Saft der Vogelbeeren. 1849. III. 460.[1]
Branson, A. Northern Peaches. 1898. III. 441.[1]
Branth, J. C. Deichmann. Fyrreskovens undergang paa Læsø. 1872. II. 46.[2]
Branthwaite, F. J. Cutch and its adulterants. 1892. III. 464.[2]
— Report on the sea-borne trade in the timbers of Burma. 1892. IV. 407.[2]
Brants, A. Over het doordringen van hout. 1844. IV. 417.
— Waarnemingen omtrent een schadelijk insekt op Pinus Larix. 1839. IV. 450.
— De wapendrager. 1854. IV. 509.
Brants, L. R. Grenen, Vuren, Dennen en de afkomst daarvan. 1892. IV. 443.[1]
— Is de Zeeden winterhard? 1891. IV. 467.[2]
— De nadeelen van het schrapen onzer bosschen. 1890. IV. 72.
— De rupsen van den nonvlinder. 1891. IV. 549.[2]
— Vermenging met loofhout als middel tot bestrijding van versterf onder Grove Dennen. 1892. IV. 478.
— See also BLIJDENSTEIN, A. J. & BRANTS, L. R.
Branza, D. G. Considérations sur les ovaires infères. 1866. II. 261,[1] 289.[2]
— Note sur plusieurs Roses monstrueuses. 1866. II. 289.[2]
Braquehais. Devis pour la création en Indo-chine d'une cacaoyère. 1899. III. 593.[1]
Bras, Antoine. Catalogue des plantes . . . de l'Aveyron. 1877. I. 415.
Brasavola, Antonio Musa. Examen omnium simplicium. 1536. III. 239.
— Examen omnium simplicium medicamentorum. 1536. I. 277, III. *239*, V. XIV.[1]
Brassart. Les clôtures de haies vives. 1873. III. 213.
Brassart, P. J. Guide pratique pour la culture du Pommier. 1886. III. 462.[2]
Brasse, Léon. Action de la distase du malt sur l'amidon. 1885. I. 140.[2]

— Dissolution de l'amidon dans les feuilles. 1886. I. 176.
Brassel, J. Der Cacao. 1886. III. 595.[1]
— Kaffee. 1885. III. 740.[1]
— Narkotische Nahrungs-, resp. Genussmittel. 1886. III. 595.[1]
— Thee. 1888. III. 607.
Brasseur, Charles. Droit romain de la responsabilité du préposant. 1895. IV. 326.
— Du régime forestier et des bois communaux. 1895. IV. 326.
Brata-Yoeda. Koffij-kultuur. 1871. III. 726.[2]
Brater, K. Forstgesetz vom 28. März 1852. 1855. IV. 318.
Bratranek, F. Theodor. Beiträge zu einer Aesthetik der Pflanzenwelt. 1853. I. 516.
Bratz, Emil. Ueber Strychnin und Brucin. 1891. III. 683.[2]
Braud, F. Tératologie végétale. 1883. II. 121.[2]
Brauer, Andreas von. Von den Rebenstichern. 1767. III. 562.[1]
Braun, von. Pomologischer Bericht über die pfälzische Obst-Ausstellung. 1875. III. 138.
Braun, Alexander Karl Heinrich. Ueber abnorme Anordnung der Schuppen an den Zapfen von Pinus. 1874. II. 39.[2]
— Abnorme Blattbildung von Irina glabra. 1861. II. 488.[2]
— Abnorme Fichtenzapfen. 1875. II. 35.[2]
— Ueber abnorme Umdrehung eines Blattes von Magnolia. 1871. II. 212.[1]
— Apfelfrucht mit Vorblatt. 1876. II. 267.[1]
— Bemerkungen über einige Cycadeen. 1876. II. 3.[1]
— Beschreibungen einiger von J. M. Hildebrandt in Ostafrika entdeckter Pflanzen. 1877. I. 492.[2]
— Betrachtungen über die Erscheinung der Verjüngung. 1851. I. 77.
— Caelebogyne ilicifolia J. Sm. 1861. II. 436.[2]
— Ueber die Cedern im Elsass. 1853. II. 28.[1]
— Cephalotaxus pedunculata Sieb. et Zucc. 1861. II. 8.[2]
— Ueber die Cycadeen. 1855. III. 284.[1]
— On the disposition of the scales in the cones of Firs. 1831. I. 102.
— Eichenähnliche Schwarzerle bei Blankenburg. 1873. II. 116.[2]
— Eine eigenthümliche Missbildung eines Zweiges der Guyava-Baumes. 1871. II. 632.[2]
— Ueber einige . . . Krankheiten der Pflanzen. 1853. III. 193.[2]
— Einige morphologische Eigenthümlichkeiten der Gattung Ribes. 1874. II. 244.[1]
— Ueber einige . . . Pflanzenkrankheiten. 1853. III. 193.[2]
— Einjähriger Sämling von Ailanthus. 1870. II. 413.[2]
— Epiphyllum Hookeri mit fasciirten Luftwurzeln. 1853. II. 593.[2]
— Examen comparatif de la disposition des écailles sur les cônes des Pins. 1831. I. 102.
— Die Frage nach der Gymnospermie der Cycadeen. 1876. II. 3.[2]
— Das Individuum der Pflanze. 1853. I. 99.
— Über den innern Bau der Frucht der Juglandeen. 1871. II. 112.[1]
— Ueber Lepidozamia. 1875. II. 6.[2]
— Über die Lorbeerbäume . . . der Gärten. 1852. III. 403.[2]
— Ueber eine Missbildung von Podocarpus chinensis. 1869. II. 9.[2]
— Mittheilungen über Syringa correlata. 1873. II. 714.[2]
— Ueber die im Kgl. Museum zu Berlin aufbewahrten Pflanzenreste aus altägyptischen Gräbern. 1877. I. 523.
— Neue Beobachtungen an Cytisus Adami. 1873. II. 368.[2]
— Notice sur les Laurinées cultivées. 1858. II. 223.[1]
— Nouvelle observation sur le Caelebogyne. 1862. II. 436.[2]
— The oblique direction of the ligneous fibre. 1854. I. 107.[1]
— Sur la parthénogenèse dans les plantes. 1857. I. 202,[1] II. *436*.[2]
— Ueber Parthenogenesis bei Pflanzen. 1857. I. 202,[1] II. *436*.[2]
— Die Pflanzenreste des ägyptischen Museums. 1877. I. 523, V. x.[1]
— Pinus silvestris L. var. erytranthera Sanio. 1871. II. 46.[2]
— Ueber Polyembryonie bei Coffea arabica. 1870. II. 814.[2]
— Ueber Polyembryonie . . . von Caelebogyne. 1860. II. 436.[2]
— A pozonymegyei Rosa Timeroyi. 1886. II. 299.[2]
— Reflections on the phenomenon of rejuvenescence. 1851. I. 187.
— Rindenstücke des chilenischen Seifenbaums. 1877. II. 281.[1]

— Ueber den Samen. 1878.. I. 120.
— Ueber den schiefen Verlauf der Holzfaser. 1854. I. 107.[1]
— Solanum frutescens. 1853. II. 776.[2]
— Solanum (Leptostemonum) hyporhodium. 1853. II. 776.[2]
— Solanum (Leptostemonum) Karstenii. 1853. II. 777.[1]
— Ueber eine sonderbare Wirkung der diesjährigen Spätfröste auf ... . Rosskastanie. 1861. II. 482.[1]
— Spiraea opulifolia mit gedrehten Stämmen. 1868. I. 107,[1] II. 269.[2]
— Stachelbeerfrucht mit Vorblatt. 1876. II. 245.[1]
— The vegetable individual. 1853. I. 99.
— Die Veränderlichkeit der Zapfen der Fichte. 1876. II. 34.[2]
— Vergleichende Untersuchung über die Ordnung-der Schuppen an den Tannenzapfen. 1831. I. 102.
— Verwachsungen der Blätter bei Taxus tardiva. 1870. II. 10.[1]
— Das Vorkommen getrennter Blumenblätter. 1876. II. 662.[2]
— Ueber zwei ... vom Blitz getroffene Eichen. 1869. IV. 194.
— Ueber zwei von Hildebrandt eingeführte Cycadeen. 1876. II. 3.[1]
— & Ascherson, P. F. A. Dunalia brachystemon. 1861. II. 771.[2]
— & Bouché, C. D. Plantae novae a cl. Hildebrandt ... allatae. 1874. II. 6,[1] 776.[2]
— Klotzsch, J. F. & Bouché, C. Species novae et minus cognitae Horti regii botanici berolinensis. 1851. I. 47.
— & others. Appendix observationum botanicarum. 1872. I. 48.
— — Species novae et emendatae Horti regii botanici berollnensis. 1853. I. 47.
Braun, Ernst. Ueber die Anlage von Schneisensystemen. 1855. IV. 251.[1]
— Die Bewirthschaftung der Gemeinde- und Stiftswaldungen in Hessen. 1874. IV. 286.[2]
— Die cubische Messung und Verrechnung des Stangenholzes. 185.? IV. 213.
— Die cubische Messung und Berechnung des Stangenholzes. 1872. IV. 227.
— Die Entstehung des sauren ... Humus oder Mulms. 1886. IV. 69.
— Die forstliche Grundeintheilung in der Ebene. 1855. IV. 251.[1]
— Ueber den Frostschaden und seine Ursachen. 1867. IV. 66.[2]
— Hülfstafeln zur Bestimmung des Bau- und Werkholzes. 1855. IV. 223.
— Hülfstafeln zur Bestimmung des Cubikinhaltes des Bau- und Werkholzes. 1855. IV. 223.
— Hülfstafeln zur Verwandlung der concreten Holzmaase in summarische Stecken. 1855. IV. 222.
— Die Humussäure in ihrer Beziehung zur Entstehung der festen fossilen Brennstoffe. 1884. IV. 69.
— Das Kommunalforstwesen im Grossherzogthum Hessen. 1881. IV. 308.[2]
— Zur Mycorhiza-Frage. 1889. I. 529.
— Sind kränkliche ... Bestände durch Raupenfrass mehr gefährdet? 1885. IV. 207.
— Der sogenannte rationelle Waldwirth. 1005. IV. 240.
— Staatsforstwirthschaft und Bodenreinertragstheorie. 1879. IV. 256.
— Die Stellung des Forstschutzpersonals ... Hessen. 1858. IV. 290.[1]
— Versumpfung und Entsumpfung. 1872. IV. 69.
— Welche Gesichtspunkte sind bei dem Ankauf von Eicheln zu beobachten? 1866. IV. 506.
— Worauf beruht die Zunahme des Engerlingschadens. 1892. IV. 203.
— Zerstörende Wirkung des Blitzes. 1874. IV. 194.
Braun, Georg. Der angehende Förster und Jäger. 1821. IV. 97.
Braun, Gottlieb. Notes sur l'Herbarium Ruborum germanicorum. 1881. II. 302.[1]
Braun, Heinrich. Beiträge zur Kenntniss einiger Arten ... der Gattung Rosa. 1885. II. 284.[2]
— Über einige in Bayern ... wachsende Formen der Gattung Rosa. 1889. II. 284.[2]
— Ueber einige kritische Pflanzen der Flora von Niederösterreich. 1889. II. 288,[1] 298.[2]
— Rosa Borbasiana n. sp. 1885. II. 291.[2]
— Rosa diversisepala und Rosa Halácsyi. 1884. II. 287.[2]
— Rosa Hirciana n. sp. 1882. II. 295.[1]

— Rosa petrophila Borbás et H. Braun. 1886. II. 297.[1]
— Rosa resinosa Sternberg. 1883. II. 298.[1]
— Rosa saxigena, eine noch unbeschriebene Rosenform. 1882. II. 298.[2]
— Rosa Wettsteinii n. sp. 1885. II. 300.[1]
— Rosae C. D. Dre Woloszczak in agro Leopolitano. 1886. II. 288.[1]
— Salix Heimerli. 1881. II. 107.[2]
— See also HALÁCSY, Eugen von & BRAUN, Heinrich.
Braun, Johann Ludwig. Einige praktische Bemerkungen über die Kultur der Eschen, Erlen. 1795. III. 120.[2]
Braun, Johannes. Botanischer Bericht über die Flora von Kamerun. 1889. I. 491.
Braun, Karl. Beiträge zur Anatomie der Adansonia. 1900. II. 529.[1]
Braun, R. List of medicines exported from Hankow. 1888. III. 273.[2]
Braun, V. H. & others. Carpinus Betulus var. quercifolia. 1896. III. 357.[2]
Braune, A. von. Nachrichten von merkwurdig gestalteten Fichtenbäumen. 1803. II. 37.[1]
Braune, Franz Anton Alexander von. Salzburg und Berchtesgaden. 1821. I. 439.
— Salzburgische Flora. 1797. I. 439.
Brauner, Ignaz Alexander. De Punica Granato. 1836. III. 630.[2]
Brauner, Joh. Wilda träns plantering. 1759. IV. 113.[2]
Braungart, Richard. Hat der schroffe Wechsel, mit welchem der mediterrane ... Wald ... dem Gestein folgt, eine ... physikalische Ursache? 1880. I. 349.
— Die Wissenschaft in der Bodenkunde. 1876. IV. 69.
Braunmüller, E. See REINKE, Johannes & BRAUNMÜLLER, E.
Brauns, (Revierförster). Ansichten über die Bedeutung der Spechte. 1861. IV. 198.[2]
— Einiges über Sägen. 1860. IV. 392.
— Entwässerung. 1860. IV. 143.[2]
Brauns, J. A. Beschreibung eines bequemen Dendrometers. 1805. IV. 231.[1]
Braunschweig, J. D. von. Russland's Weinbau. 1842. III. 551.[2]
— Unsere Holz-Frage. 1843. IV. 404.[1]
Braunschweig — Land- und forstwirthschaftlicher Verein. See LANDWIRTHSCHAFTLICHER ... III. 12.
Braunschweig — Landwirthschaftlicher Central-Verein. See LANDWIRTHSCHAFTLICHER ... III. 12.
Braunschweig — Verein für Land- und Forstwirthschaft ... See LAND- UND FORSTWIRTHSCHAFTLICHER VEREIN ... IV. 10.
Braunschweig — Verein für Naturwissenschaft. See VEREIN ... I. 15.
Braunschweigische landwirthschaftliche Zeitung. III. 11.
Brauwers. See GARREAU, Lazare & BRAUWERS.
Bravais, Auguste. See BRAVAIS, Louis & Auguste; MARTINS, Charles & BRAVAIS, Auguste.
— & Martins, Charles. De la croissance du Chêne et du Frêne. 1845. II. 137,[1] 708.[1]
— — Recherches sur la croissance du Pin sylvestre. 1841. II. 47.[2]
— — Recherches sur la croissance du Pin sylvestre. 1843. II. 137,[1] 708.[1]
Bravais, Louis. Examen organographique des nectaires. 1842. I. 118.[1]
— & August. Essai géométrique sur la symétrie des feuilles. 1837. I. 102.
— — Essai sur la disposition ... des feuilles. 1839. I. 102, I. 102.
— — Essai sur la disposition des feuilles curvisériées. 1837. I. 102.
— — Essai sur la disposition ... des inflorescences. 1837. I. 113.[1]
— — Ueber die geometrische Anordnung der Blätter. 1838. I. 102.
— — Mémoires sur la disposition ... des feuilles. 1838. I. 102.
Bravender, John. On fences. 1845. III. 213.
Bravo, Felipe. See BUZETA, Manuel & BRAVO, Felipe.
Bravy, G. Culture de l'Amandier. 1847. III. 434.[1]
— Culture des arbres fruitiers. 1861. III. 143.
— Note sur les espèces ornementales du genre Hibiscus. 1862. III. 587.[2]
— — Observations sur l'éducation ... des arbres fruitiers. 1846. III. 143.
Bray, Franz Gabriel, Graf von. Botanische Beobachtungen. 1815. II. 100.[1]
— Plantae novae et rariores in Livonia. 1818. I. 360.

Bray, Jean de. La Ramie, plante textile. 1873. III. 381.¹
— La Ramie, son origine. 1873. III. 381.¹
Bray, William L. The geographical distribution of the Frank-
eniaceae. 1898. II. 561.²
— Plant geography of North America. 1900. I. 308.
— On the relation of the flora of the lower Sonoran zone.
1898. I. 327.
— The relations of the North American flora to that of South
America. 1900. I. 308.
— See also ULINE, E. B. & BRAY, W. L.
Brayer, A. Notice sur une nouvelle plante de . . . Rosacées.
1822. II. 264.²
Braza, C. Ueber die Bedeutung der Standortsanalysen. 1881.
IV. 481.
— Die Berücksichtigung des Alters bei der Aufstellung von
Baummassentafeln. 1882. IV. 237.
— Graphische Methode oder Weiserverfahren. 1887. IV.
237.
Brazil —Instituto historico, geographico e ethnographico.
See INSTITUTO . . . I. 7.²
Brazil, MOURA-. See MOURA-BRAZIL.
The Brazil-Nut tree. 1848. III. 631.¹
Brazilian gum-arabic. 1888. III. 478,² 484.¹
The Brazilian process of smoking rubber. 1898. III. 232.¹
Bréal, Émile. Contribution à l'étude de l'alimentation
azotée. 1893. I. 160.
— Fixation de l'azote par les Légumineuses. 1889. II. 321.²
Bréant, Victor & Boitard, M. Traité de la culture-des fleurs
et arbustes. 1855. III. 113.
Bréau, J. L. A. de QUATREFAGES DE. See QUATREFAGES DE
BRÉAU, J. L. A. de.
Bréaudat, L. Sur le mode de formation de l'indigo. 1898.
III. 479.¹
— Nouvelles recherches sur les fonctions diastasiques des
plantes indigofères. 1899. III. 479.¹
Brébisson, L. Alphonse de. Coup d'œil sur la végétation de
la Basse-Normandie. 1828. I. 408.
— Coup d'œil sur la végétation de la Basse-Normandie.
·1829. I. 408.
— Flore de la Normandie. 1836. I. 409.
Brebner, George. See SCOTT, D. H. & BREBNER, George.
Brech, Johann & others. Die Veredlung der Paeonia arborea.
1900. III. 393.¹
Brecher, G. . Ueber Anbau von Acer (Negundo) californicum.
1888. IV. 526.²
— Aus dem Auen-Mittelwalde. 1886. IV. 131.
— Aus dem Auen-(Niederungs-) Mittelwalde. 1879. IV.
131.
— Ueber ein bemerkenswertes Auftreten von Eichen-Schild-
läusen. 1897. IV. 511.
— Ueber Erziehung von Kiefernballen-Pflanzen. 1878. IV.
472.
— Lange Dauer von Rothbuchen-Brückenbelägen. 1893.
IV. 499.
— Ueber Mischhölzer für Kiefern. 1875. IV. 472.
— Oberholz-Nachzucht im Mittelwalde. 1885. IV. 131.
— Ein Steigeapparat. 1896. III. 177.
— Ueber das Verhalten einiger Holzarten. 1897. IV. 185.¹
— Verhütung des Benagens von Schwarzpappeln- und Eschen-
pflanzheistern. 1898. III. 186.²
— Vertilgung der Nonnenraupen. 1890. IV. 200.
Brecht. Bemerkungen über die Beschädigungen der Wal-
dungen bei Ellwangen und Dinkelsbühl. 1840. IV. 206.
— Die Waldfeldwirthschaft in Revier Hohenheim. 1845.
IV. 133.
Breck, Joseph. The flower-garden. 1851. III. 63.¹
— New book of flowers. 1866. III. 63.¹
Breda, Jacques Gisbert Samuel van. Genera et species Orch-
idearum et Asclepiadearum. 1827. II. 735.¹
Breda de Haan, Jacob van. Anatomie van het geslacht Melo-
cactus. 1891. II. 595.²
— Middelen tegen plantenziekten. 1899. III. 180.¹
— Regenval en reboistatie in Deli. 1899. IV. 168.²
— De wortels in het huishouden der plant. .1897. I. 162,
III. 98.¹
Bredemeier. See HILLEBRAND & BREDEMEIER.
Bredemeier, H. Abies bracteata W. Hooker. 1887. III.
296.¹
—Acer palmatum Thbg. var. dissectum roseo pictum. 1886.
I·I. 5.²¸¹
— Akebia quinata Sieb. 1886. III. 393.²
— Einige interessante Coniferen-Zapfen. 1886. II. 13.¹
— Pinus insignis Dougl. 1887. III. 308.¹
Breden, A. Leitfaden für den Obstbau. 1898. III. 147.¹

Bredsdorff, Jakob Hornemann. Haandbog ved botaniske
Excursioner i Egnen om Sorøe. 1834. I. 353.
Bredsted. Dyrkning af Figen- og Morbærtræer. 1878. III.
369,¹ 378.
Bredsted, H. C. Haandbog i dansk Pomologi. 1890. III.
66.²
—Hasselnødden. 1887. III. 357.²
Bredsted, L. En Sygdom hos Pærevildlinger. 1886. III.
446.¹
Bree, W. T. Some account of an aged Yew tree. 1833. II.
10.²
— Some remarks relating to the fall of an aged Ash tree.
1833. II. 708.¹
Breese, O. S. Relation of mining to forestry. 1900. IV.
425.²
Breggen, J. van der. Het conserveeren van hout. 1897.
IV. 421.
—Houtafval. 1897. IV. 428.¹
— Wateropname door bouwmaterialen. 1897. IV. 409.
Bréhaut, Thomas COLLINGS. Cordon training of fruit trees.
See COLLINGS BRÉHAUT, T. 1860. III. 142.
— The modern Peach pruner. 1866. III. 440.³
Brehm, Alfred Edmund & Rossmässler, E. A. Die Thiere des
Waldes. 1864. IV. 90.¹
— — See also ВРЕМЪ, А. и РОССМЕССЛЕРЪ, Е.
Breidenstein, W. Mikroskopische Pflanzenbilder. 1856. I.
89.
Breinig, Peter. Anzucht und Kultur der Choisya ternata.
1893. III. 496.¹
Breitenlohner, J. J. Die Torfmoore. 1864. IV. 439.
Breitenlohner, Jacob. Ueber die Aufforstung der Hochmoore.
1877. IV. 155.¹
—Beiträge zur Untersuchung der standörtlichen Verhältnisse
der Rothbuche. 1878. IV. 495.
— Die Cultur der Korbweide. 1873. III. 348.
— Fortschritte in der Lösung der Waldklimafrage. 1891.
IV. 54.
— Zur Lösung der Waldklimafrage. 1893. IV. 54.
— Die meteorologischen Radialstationen zur Lösung der
Waldklimafrage. 1893. IV. 54.
— See also BÜHM, Josef & BREITENLOHNER, Jakob.
Breiter, Christian August. Hortus Breiterianus. 1817. I. 45.
Breitfeld, Alexander. Der anatomische Bau der Blätter der
Rhododendroideae. 1888. II. 658.³
Breithaupt, H. K. W. Hand- und Lehrbuch der Feldmess-
kunst. 1824. IV. 263.
—Sammlung arithmetischer Uebungsaufgaben. 1826. IV.
58.
Breitling, (Pfarrer). Ueber den Einfluss des Wildlings.
1860. III. 39.
— Influence du sujet sur la greffe. 1860. III. 39.
Breitschwerdt, Hermann. Bäume und Sträucher mit zieren-
den Früchten. 1899. III. 208.¹
— Bismarckia nobilis. 1900. III. 320.²
— Die dendrologischen Neuanpflanzungen in Donaueschingen.
1898. I. 49.
Brelin, Nicolaus. Påfund, som intygar huru sprickor på
bygningstimmer kunna förekommas. 1739. IV. 414.¹
Bremen — Naturwissenschaftlicher Verein. See NATUR-
WISSENSCHAFTLICHER . . . I. 14.
Bremer, A. Alte und seltene Bäume. 1894. II. 37.²
Bremer, Petrus. Somnus plantarum. See LINNÉ, Carl von.
1755. I. 197.²
Bremer, W. A. E. Bemerkungen . . . über die Wirksamkeit
der Rinde des Traubenkirschbaums. 1812. III. 439.¹
Brémond, J. B. L'arboriculture des écoles primaires. 1862.
III. 144.
— Notions élémentaires d'arboriculture. 1860. III. 144.
— Tableau synoptique de la taille des arbres fruitiers. 186 . ?
III. 172.
— Le verger. 1865. III. 172.
Brems, Léopold de HAES-. See HAES-BREMS, Léopold de.
Bremzen, I. See ВРЕМЗЕНЪ, И.
Brendel, Frederick. Flora Peoriana. 1882. I. 315.
— Forests and forest trees. 1859. I. 82.¹
— Historical sketch of the science of botany in North America.
1879. I. 80.¹
— Notes on the flora of southern Florida. 1874. I. 319.
— The Oaks of Illinois. 1859. II. 128.²
— The tree in winter. 1876. I. 294.²
— The trees and shrubs in Illinois. 1859. I. 312, IV. 76.²
— Verzeichniss der in Illinois wildwachsenden . . . Gefäss
pflanzen. 1860. I. 314.

Brenier, H. La culture et l'industrie de la Ramie. 1900. III. 381.[2]

Brennecke, C. Ueber die Baumrodung. 1866. IV. 386.
— Mittel gegen das Einspalten gerodeter Baumstämme. 1862. IV. 383.[2]

Brenner, August Rudolf. De communicatione chemica inter plantas et animalia. 1845. I. 170.

Brenner, Mårten Magnus Wilhelm. Om Alnus glutinosa. 1891. II. 116.[1]
— Alnus glutinosa f. lobulata M. Brenn. 1891. II. 116.[1]
— Anmärkningsvärda nyinkomna växter i Finland. 1888. II. 270.[1]
— Om Betula verrucosa var. birkalensis. 1887. II. 120.[1] — 1888. II. 116,[2] 120.[1]
— Bidrag till kännedom af finska vikens övegetation. 1871. I. 363.
— Dendrologiska kuriosa. 1898. II. 35,[2] 47.[1]
— Egendomliga fall af grenbildning hos Gran. 1896. II. 36.[1]
— Einige Beobachtungen über . . . Formen von Alnus glutinosa (L.) Willd. und A. incana. 1891. II. 115.[2]
— Former af Rubus Idaeus funna i Finland. 1891. II. 308.[1]
— Genomvärta Lärkträdskottar. 1871. II. 32.[2]
— Iakttagelser angående . . . formerna af släktet Alnus. 1891. II. 115.[2]
— Missbildning af Hydrangea hortensis. 1888. II. 241.[1]
— Några ovanliga växtformer från Finland. 1895. II. 47.[1]
— Notiser om Alnus. 1891. II. 115.[2]
— Observationer rörande den nordfinska floran. 1899. I. 367.
— Picea excelsa f. oligoclada n. f. 1895. II. 35.[1]
— Rubus Idaeus L. var. simplicior. 1890. II. 308.[1]

Die Brennmaterialien und ihre Benützung. 1862. IV. 394.

Breñosa, Rafael. Nuevos datos en apoyo de la influencia hidrológica de los montes. 1886. IV. 542.[1]
— Un problema sobre montes. 1870. IV. 251.[2]
— Tablas para la cubicación cilíndrica. 1894. IV. 228.
— See also RIVERO, R. L. del, BREÑOSA, Rafael & CASTEL-LARNAU, J. de.

Brenot, L. De l'accroissement des futaies. 1880. IV. 233, 236.
— De l'accroissement des futaies. 1883. IV. 233.
— De l'amenagement des futaies. 1884. IV. 129.
— Crecimiento del monte alto. 1880. IV. 233.
— De l'Épicéa. 1870. IV. 453.
— La méthode expérimentale appliquée aux forêts. 1892. IV. 234, 443.[1]
— Remarques sur deux variétés d'Épicéa. 1878. II. 34.[2]

Bréon. Note historique sur le Litchi et sa culture. 1849. III. 539.[2]

Bréon, Jean Nicolas. Catalogue des plantes cultivées aux Jardins botanique . . . de l'Île Bourbon. 1820. I. 68.[2]

Brera, Valeriano Luigi. Desiderata. 1825. III. 721.
— Nuovo desideratum di chine vere. 1830. III. 721.
— Delle piante chinifere. 1824. I. 174.

Brereton, John A. Botany of the District of Columbia. 1837. I. 318.
— Florae columbianae prodromus. 1830. I. 318.

Brescia — Ateneo. See ATENEO . . . I. 24.[2]

Brescy, P. de. Ueber die Aufastungen. 1860. IV. 170.
— De l'élagage. 1860. IV. 170.

Breslau — Königlich botanischer Garten. See KÖNIGLICH BOTANISCHER . . . I. 13.

Bresler, Moritz. Generis Asparagi historia. 1826. II. 79.[1]

Bretet, Henry. Note pour servir à l'histoire du Sang-dragon. 1874. III. 336.[2]
— Nouvelles observations sur le Sangdragon. 1876. III. 485.[1]
— Recherches pour servir à l'étude pharmacologique du quinquina. 1884. III. 725.[1]

Bretfeld, Heinrich, Freiherr von. Über Vernarbung und Blattfall. 1879. I. 191.[2]

Bréton, (député, Seine). Rapport fait . . . de loi, tendant à valider deux échanges de bois. 1817. IV. 325.

Breton, (sr). Nouveau guide forestier. 1844. IV. 22.[2]

Breton, André. Méthode graphique pour la détermination du coefficient de forme. 1899. IV. 219.

Breton, Louis. Le budget des forêts en France et à l'étranger. 1893. IV. 292.
— Les Chambarans. 1893. IV. 27.[2]
— La marche rétrograde de la végétation. 1894. IV. 74.[2]
— La marche rétrograde de la végétation forestière. 1893. IV. 74.[2]
— Die militärische Organisation des französischen Forstpersonals. 1894. IV. 293.[1]
— Organisation militaire des chasseurs forestiers. 1894. IV. 293.[1]
— Du rôle des forêts en temps de guerre. 1894. IV. 45.

Breton, Philippe. The bark of the stem of the Pomegranate. 1826. III. 830.[2]

Bretschneider, Carl Beatus. Auch ein Beytrag zur Kenntniss der verderblichen Fichtenraupen. 1798. IV. 208, V. xxxi.[1]

Bretschneider, Emil. Botanical investigations into the materia medica of the ancient Chinese. 1895. III. 273.[2]
— Botanicon sinicum. 1882. I. 81,[2] III. 1.
— The botany of the Chinese classics. 1892. III. 273.[2]
— On Chinese Silkworm trees. 1881. III. 148.[2]
— Early European researches into the flora of China. 1880. I. 81.[3]
— History of European botanical discoveries in China. 1898. I. 81.[3]
— Notes on some botanical questions connected with the export trade of China. 1881. III. 273.[1]
— Plantes de Pékin. 1882. III. 125.
— On the study and value of Chinese botanical works. 1870. I. 81.[3]

Bretschneider, Hermann. Die Anwendung der forstlichen Reinertragslehre. 1884. IV. 257.
— Die Anwendung der forstlichen Reinertragslehre. 1885. IV. 257.
— Aufforstung von durch Bergbau zu Bruche gegangenen Grundstücken. 1895. IV. 167.[2]
— Betrachtungen über die Anwendbarkeit des Lichtungsbetriebes. 1899. IV. 129.
— Die Bretschneider'sche Waldmesstasche. 1891. IV. 214.
— Femelschlagbetrieb contra Kahlschlagbetrieb. 1883. IV. 128.
— Das modificirte Abstandsverfahren. 1893. IV. 258.
— Die Verjüngung, beziehungsweise Wiederaufforstung. 1897. IV. 140.
— Waldbahnen. 1883. IV. 391.
— Was können wir Forstwirthe gegen die Hochwassergefahr thun? 1883. IV. 51.

Bretter, Conrad. Notizen über verschiedene Cultur-Versuche. 1850. IV. 123.[2]

Brettmann. Gewinnung und Verwerthung von Fichten-Schiffsknieen. 1894. IV. 459.[1]

Brettmann. Das Einkellern von Kiefern-Jährlingen. 1884. IV. 477.

Brettschneider, Fr. Eine reinweisse . . . Azalea. 1893. III. 655.
— See also WITTMACK, Ludwig & BRETTSCHNEIDER, F.

Bretzel, Philipp Jakob. See Von den REBENSTICKERN. 1767. III. 162.[1]

Breuil, Henri, (abbé). Dédoublement des feuilles. 1899. I. 145.[1]
— Diverses observations sur le dédoublement. 1898. I. 145.[1]

Brevans, A. de. Indicateur du Jardin des plantes. 1875. I. 59.

Una breve excursione degli alunni. See PICCIOLI, Francesco.

Brevol, Johann Friderich Benedict. De plantis in cultorum memoriam nominatis. See BOERMER, G. R. 1770. I. 76.[1]

Brewer, George S. See HIMING, F. W. & BREWER, G. S.
— A new flora of the neighbourhood of Reigate. 1856. I. 400.

Brewer, William H. On the forests of Sequoia gigantea. 1865. II. 50.[1]
— On the forests of Sequoia (Wellingtonia). 1865. II. 50.[2]
— On rotting wood. 1880. IV. 415.[1]
— Woods and woodlands. 1877. IV. 111.[2]
— Woods and woodlands. 1878. IV. 102.

Brewster, David. On the optical . . . properties of Tabasheer. 1819. II. 59.[1]

Breymann, G. A. Constructionen in Holz. 1851. IV. 423.[1]

Breymann, Karl. Anleitung zum Gebrauche des forstlichen Universal-Instrumentes. 1867. IV. 4.[1]
— Anleitung zur Bestimmung der Formzahlen. 1857. IV. 217.
— Anleitung zur Holzmesskunst. 1868. IV. 214.
— Anleitung zur Waldwerthberechnung. 1855. IV. 254.
— Beiträge zur Holzmesskunst. 1865. IV. 214.
— Beleuchtung der von Herrn Forstrath Dr. Th. Hartig neuerlich angeregten Frage. 1856. IV. 254.
— Das composirte Fachwerk. 1857. IV. 251.[1]
— Die Gesetze des Holzzuwachses. 1852. IV. 232.
— Lehrbuch der niederen Geodäsie. 1854. IV. 264.
— Neigung der Holzriesen. 1869. IV. 391.

Breymann, Karl (*continued*).
— Neue Bestimmungsart des . . . Hauptnutzungs-Ertrages. 1854. IV. 235.²
— Die österreichischen Hochgebirgs-Preisaufforstungen. 1868. IV. 167.¹
— Tafeln für Forst-Ingenieure und Taxatoren. 1859. IV. 230.
— Die Wahrscheinlichkeitsrechnung . . . Abhängigkeit der Holzmassen vom Holzalter. 1867. IV. 217.
Breyn, Jacob. Exoticarum . . . plantarum centuria prima. 1678. I. 287.
— Prodromus fasciculi rariorum plantarum. 1680. I. 287.
Breyn, Johann Philipp. Descriptio fructus Cerei americani. 1752. II. 589.¹
— Varias observationes continens, in jtinere per Italiam. 1712. I. 424.
Breynius. *See* BREYN.
Brez, Jacques. La flore des insectophiles. 1791. III. 188.²
Brézéano, V. S. *See* NICOLEANO, G. N. & BRÉZÉANO, V. S.
Brezol, H. Acclimatement d'essences forestières. 1892. IV. 126.¹
— L'acclimatement du Pitch Pin. 1889. III. 306.²
— L'Arbre à coton soyeux. 1893. III. 589.ᵇ
— L'arbre des Janissaires. 1891. II. 255.¹
— Les coques de cacao. 1889. III. 595.¹
— La culture du Giroflier à Zanzibar. 1891. III. 635.²
— Cultures diverses en Californie et en Floride. 1889. III. 117.¹
— L'exploitation des Acajous au Honduras. 1891. IV. 525.²
— L'indigo. 1890. III. 479.³
— La longévità negli alberi. 1889. I. 295.¹
— La longévité des arbres. 1889. I. 295.¹
— Les plantes de vannerie chez les Indiens. 1892. IV. 429.¹
Briard, Emmanuel. Coup d'œil sur la végétation . . . de Constantine. 1878. I. 485.
Briard, Pierre. Catalogue raisonné des plantes . . . de l'Aube. 1880. I. 416.
Briart, Alphonse. Quelques arbres remarquables du parc de Mariemont. 1883. I. 296.³
Brichet, Octave. Excursion forestière en 1895. 1896. - IV. 357.¹
— Hylesinus. 1900. IV. 205.¹
— L'Hylesinus micans. 1898. IV. 457.
— L'Hylesinus micans. 1899. IV. 457.
— *See also* CRAHAY, N. I. & BRICHET, Octave.
Brick, Carl. Das amerikanische Obst und seine Parasiten. 1899. III. 188.¹
— Beitrag zur Kenntnis . . . einiger Rothölzer. 1889. II. 334.¹ *330.¹*
— Ergänzungen zu meiner·Abhandlung über "Das amerikanische Obst. 1899. III. 188.¹
— Über Nectria cinnabarina. 1893. III. 195.¹
— Seltene Waldbäume in Norddeutschland. 1896. IV. 84.¹
Brickell, John. The natural history of North Carolina. 1737. I. 317.³
Bricogné, A. Les forêts de l'empire ottoman. 1877. IV. 375.³
— La mission forestière en Turquie. 1876. IV. 279.¹
— Timber resources of Turkey in Europe. 1877. IV. 375.²
Bridel, J. B. Manuel pratique du forestier. 1798. V. xxx.¹
Bridgeman, Thomas. The florist's guide. 1835. III. 202.²
— The fruit cultivator's manual. 1857. III. 133.
— The young gardener's assistant. 1844. III. 99.
Bridges, M. C. Catalogue descriptif des Conifères de Californie. 1866. II. 14.¹
Brief instructions in regard to sowing seeds. 1873. IV. 150.
Brief over het zonderling verschijnsel van een volwassen Appel aan een Aalbesieboom. 1759. I. 142.
Brière, W. Le Saule diamant. 1883. II. 106.³
Brierre de Boismont, Alexandre Jacques François & Pottier, A. A. Élémens de botanique. 1825. III. 52.
Briers, Frédéric. Aperçu sur l'élagage. 1870. III. 170.
Brieven van een landman in Pensylvanien. 1784. III. 263.¹
Briganti, Francesco. Nota su talune produzioni fungo: di Castagno. 1861. III. 359.²
— Piante tintorie del regno di Napoli. 1842. III. 236.
— Della sostanza gommosa che geme da das' vecchi tronchi di Querce. 1840. IV. 514.³
Briganti, G. Le coltivazioni agrarie e forestali. 1898. I. 134.¹
Briganti, Vincenzio. Clavis systematis sexualis. 1804. I. 259.

— Descrizione della struttura . . . della mosco che fora le Ulive. 1822. III. 677.¹
— Descrizione di una nuova varietà del Cocos chilensis. 1834.
II. 69.²
— Illustrazione del frutto . . . Zabucajo o Iacapucaya. 1834. II. 612.¹
— Memoria su due piante . . . sotto il nome di Carquexe. 1839. II. 319.¹
— Sulla preparazione della pania . . . del Loranto. 1827. III. 385.¹
— Stirpes rariores . . . in regno neapolitano. 1816. I. 425.
Briggs, Thomas Richard Archer. Flora of Plymouth. 1880. I. 403.
— Pyrus communis Linn. var. Briggsii. 1871. II. 279.¹
— Remarks on Pyrus communis c. cordata. 1887. II. 280.²
— Remarks on Pyrus latifolia Syme. 1888. II. 313.¹
— Rubus adscitus Genev. and Rubus mutabilis. 1871. II. 300.¹
— Rubus erythrinus Genev. 1890. II. 307.¹
— On Rubus ramosus Briggs. 1871. II. 309.²
— Rubus silvaticus W. & N. 1890. II. 310.¹
— Stations of . . . some Plymouth Rubi. 1869. II. 303.¹
Brigham, William Tufts. Arboriculture in Central America. 1886. III. 118.²
— Guatemala, the land of the quetzal. 1887. III. 265.¹
— The Guatemalan forests. 1885. IV. 341.³
— A list of the trees and plants. 1882. I. 39.
— Notes on Hesperomannia. 1869. II. 859.¹
— Les productions végétales du Guatémala. 1887. III. 265.¹
— Results of Mr. Mann's study of Hawaiian flora. 1869. I. 509.²
— & Mann, Horace. Four new genera of Hawaiian plants. *See* BRIGHAM, W. T. 1869. II. 859.¹
Brighenti, Maurizio. Sull' effetto del diboscamento. 1859. IV. 43.
Bright, Tom. The different methods adopted in the measurement of . . . timber. 1898. IV. 215.
— Pole plantations and underwoods. 1888. IV. 132,² *255.*
Bright, William. Bright's single stem . . . system of Grape culture. 1860. III. 550.
Brignoli di Brunnhoff, Giovanni de. Catalogus plantarum Horti botanici Urbinatis. 1811. I. 61.
— Catalogus plantarum in horto bot. R. archigymnasii mutinensis. 1836. I. 63.
— Intorno alla flora degli antichi lettera. 1845. I. 514.¹
— Sopra la genesi degli odori. 1833. I. 282.² ·
— Horti bot. R. archigymnasii mutinensis historia. 1842· I. 63.
— Manipolo di piante nuove. 1862. I. 342.
Brill, (*Oberförster, Alsfeld*). Düngungsversuche in den Pflanzgärten. 1900. IV. 145.
— Zum forstlichen Verhalten der Weymuthskiefer. 1882. IV. 469.
Brilman. Handleiding tot de teelt . . . van den Wijnstok. ·1843. III. 559.¹
— Notenmuskaatseep, Notenmuskaatolie. 1840. III. 402.³
Brinch, Chr. Kræft i Frugttræer. 1893. III. 195.¹
Brincken, Julius von den. Ansichten über die Bewaldung der Steppen des europäischen·Russlands. 1833. I. 301, IV. 157.—1854. I. 338, IV. 80.
— Descriptive memoir of the Imperial forest of Bialowież. 1828. IV. 344.²
— Memoire descriptif sur la forêt impériale de Bialowieża. 1828. IV. 344.²
— Rosprawy o leśnictwie technicznem. 1821. IV. 101.
— Theorie des Staatswaldwesens. 1833. IV. 268.
Brinckmann, Just. Holz-Industrie. 1875. IV. 422.¹
Brinckmeier, Eduard. Die Kalt- und Warmhauspflanzen. 1880. III. 75.¹
— Praktische Anleitung zur Anzucht . . . der Korbweiden. 1888. III. 349.
— Praktische . . . Anleitung zur Kenntniss . . . der Pal-

‸... 1758. I. 206.¹
‸). Führer .für die
‸ Crummendorf.

‸86· III.

1893.

rke

— Intorno alla anatomia delle foglie dell' ".Eucalyptus." 1891. II. 624.²
— Contribuzione all' anatomia delle foglie. .1882. I. 110.
— Per difendersi dalla Peronospora. 1892. III. 580.
— Esperienze per combattere la Peronospora. 1888. III. 580.
— Sopra la generale presenza d'amido nei vasi crivellati. 1875. I. 140.¹
— Sul lavoro della clorofilla nella Vite. 1877. II. 508.¹
— Il mal di cenere . . : negli Agrumi. 1877. III. 498.¹
— Intorno al mal di gomma degli Agrumi. 1878.. III. 498.¹
— Il marciume od il bruco dell' Uva. 1877. III. 577.
— Intorno un organo, di alcuni embrioni vegetali. 1882. I. 123,¹ II. 619.²
— Sopra un organo . . . di alcuni embrioni vegetali. 1882. . I. 123,¹ II. 619.²
— Sulla phytoptosi della Vite. 1876. III. 563.
— Intorno alle probabili ragioni dell' eterofilia nell' Eucalyptus. 1883. II. 624.²
— Rassegna delle principali malattie sviluppatesi sulle piante. 1888. III. 194.
— Intorno alle sostanze minerali nelle foglie. 1888. I. 154.
— See also PATERNÒ, Emanuele & BRIOSI, Giovanni.
Briot, Charles. Abelia triflora. 1870. III. 748.²
— Un arbrisseau à recommander. 1867. III. 477.¹
— Un arbrisseau à recommander. 1868. III. 377.
— Bouturage des Conifères. 1873. III. 294.¹
— Ceanothus azureus minor. 1882. III. 541.¹
— Châtaignier à branches fastigiées. 1866. III. 359.¹ III. 503.¹
— Citrus triptera . . . propre à former des haies. 1878. III. 503.¹
— Cotoneaster Fontanesii. 1867. III. 421.¹
— Crataegus corallina. 1875. III. 421.²
— Culture des Paulownia. 1867. III. 703.²
— Culture du Photinia serrulata. 1872. III. 430.¹
— Daphne japonica. 1866. III. 627.¹
— Deux variétés de Rhododendrons. 1868. III. 658.¹
— Encore le Robinia monophylla. 1869. III. 487.¹
— Evonymus radicans variegata. 1870. II. 468.²
— Fagus caroliniana. 1866. III. 360.¹
— De la greffe et du sujet. 1867. . III. 294.¹
— Gymnocladus canadensis. 1870. III. 478.¹
— Hydrangea paniculata grandiflora. 1868. III. 412.¹
— Kerria japonica grandiflora. 1869. III. 424.¹
— Laurocerasus macrophyllus. 1869. ·III. 437.¹
— Du Ligustrum ovalifolium. 1868. III. 674.¹
— Magnolia Lenné. 1866. III. 400.¹
— Marronnier pyramidal. 1882. III. 537.¹
— Multiplication des Aucubas. 1868. III. 644.²
— Multiplication du Gleditschia Bujoti. 1869. III. 477.¹
— Multiplication du Sambucus glauca. 1868. III. 751.²
— Une nouveauté japonaise. 1866. III. 447.²
— Une nouvelle plante à feuilles persistantes. 1867. III. 525.²
— Phellodendron amurense. 1867. III. 504.¹
— Picea excelsa procumbens. 1878. III. 305.¹
— Les Planera acuminata et Kaki. 1868. III. 366.¹
— Plantation des Magnolias. 1872, III. 397.¹
— Des plantes à feuilles persistantes. 1867. III. 362.¹
— Populus intermedia. 1869. III. 345.¹
— Populus subsemper virens. 1867. III. 640.¹
— Prunus prostrata. 1870. · III. 442.²
— Des Pterocaryas au point de vue de l'ornement. 1870. III. 356.²
— Raphiolepis ovata. 1870. III. 447.²
— Rhododendron Rovellii. 1868. III. 662.¹
— Rhodotypus kerrioides. 1866. III. 447.²
— Sambucus canadensis. 1867. III. 751.²
— Spiraea aquilegifolia Vanhouttei. 1866. III. 462.¹
— Stuartia grandiflora. 1879. III. 597.¹
— Taille des arbres . . à branches opposées. 1868. III. 170.
— Weigelia alba. 1868. III. 749.¹
— Weigelia arborea grandiflora. 1867. III. 749.¹
— & Carrière, E. A. Althaea frutex. 1870. III. 588.²
Briot, Félix. Les Alpes françaises. 1896. IV. 164.¹
— Déposition faite devant la Commission des améliorations agricoles et forestières. 1897. IV. 276.¹
— Quelques considérations sur les acquisitions de terrains communaux. 1883. IV. 276.¹
— La question pastorale dans les Alpes. 1886. IV. 135.¹
— Les règlements des pâturages en Savoie. 1883. IV. 197.¹
— Une statistique alpestre. 1884. IV. 361.¹
Brioude — Comice agricole et Société de viticulture, horti-culture . . . See COMICE . . . III. 19. .

Briquet, John. Sur les caractères carpologiques du genre Heteromorpha. 1896. II. 653.²
— Sur la carpologie . . . du genre Rhyticarpus. 1897. II. 654.¹
— Les colonies végétales xérothermique des Alpes léma-niennes. 1900. I. 438.
— Les concrescences . . . dans l'androcée des Labiées. 1896. II. 762.¹
— Contributions à l'histoire phytogéographique des Alpes occidentales. 1894. I. 438.
— Élément d'une classification du genre Sphacele. 1896. II. 766.²
— Espèces nouvelles ou peu connues de l'Herbier Delessert. 1900. . I. 271.²
— Études de biologie florale dans les Alpes. 1896. I. 240.¹
— Études sur les Cytises des Alpes maritimes. 1894. II. 349.¹
— Examen critique de la théorie phyllodique des feuilles entières chez les Ombellifères. 1897. II. 653.¹
— Fragmenta monographiae Labiatarum. 1889. II. 762.²
— Labiatae. 1897. II. 762.¹
— Labiatae africanae. 1895. II. 762.²
— Labiatae et Verbenaceae Wilczekianae. 1899. II. 752.¹
— Labiées. 1897. II. 762.²
— Les Labiées des Alpes maritimes. 1891. II. 762.¹
— Le Mont Vuache. 1894. I. 438.
— Nachträge. 1894. II. 752.²
— Note sur l'histologie . . . Zombiana. 1896. II. 807.¹
— Note sur les hydathodes foliaires des Scolopia. 1898. II. 573.²
— Note sur un nouveau Sphacele des Antilles. 1897. II. 767.¹
— Notes sur la flore du Massif de Platé. 1895. V. XXII.¹
— Notice bibliographique sur les recherches sur la sève ascendante. 1897. I. 166.
— Nouvelles notes floristiques sur les Alpes lémaniennes. 1899. I. 438.
— Observations critiques sur les conceptions actuelles de l'espèce végétale. 1899. I. 253.²
— Observations sur quelques Flacourtiacées. 1898. ·II. 568.²
— Sur les poches sécrétrices schizo-lysigènes des Myoporacées. 1896. II. 805.¹
— Quelques notes d'herborisations dans le Tyrol. 1896. I. 444.
— Recherches anatomiques sur . . . Phrymacées, Stilboï-dées. 1896. II. 753,¹ 805.¹
— Recherches sur la flore du district savoisien. 1890. I. 437.
— Revisio monographica Verbenacearum, Labiatarum. 1894. II. 752.¹ — 1897. II. 762.²
— Trois plantes nouvelles pour la flore française. 1893. II. 680,¹ 835.²
— Verbenaceae. 1894. II 752.²
— Verbenacearum novarum descriptiones. 1896. II. 752.²
— & Hochreutiner, Georges. Énumération critique des plantes du Brésil méridional. 1899. I. 344.
Briquet, P. Traité thérapeutique du quinquina. 1853. III. 721.
The Brisbane botanic garden. 1875. III. 324,¹ 325.¹
Brisbane botanic garden. Report. 1874. V. IX.¹
Brisbin, James Banks. Trees and tree planting. 1888. III. 99.
Brischke, C. G. A. Abbildungen und Beschreibungen der Blattwespen-Larven. 1855. IV. 92.
— Bericht über die Zucht der Kiefernspinner-Raupen. 1874. IV. 199.²
— Die Blattminirer in Danzig's Umgebung. 1881. III. 190.
— Die Ichneumoniden der Provinzen West-· und Ost-Preussen. 1878. IV. 92.
— Nachträge zu . . . die aus den Spinnerraupen erzogenen thierischen Feinde betreffend. 1869. IV. 199.²
— Resultate der Zuchten forstschädlicher Insecten. 1877. IV. 199.²
— Ueber die Zerstörer der Pappeln. 1873. III. 344.²
Brisse, baron. Sur la prééminence du Chêne-rouvre. 1848. IV. 514.¹
Brisseau-Mirbel, Charles François. See MIRBEL, C. F.
Brisseau-.
Brisson, Théodore Polycarpe. Catalogue des plantes . . . de la Marne. 1884. I. 416.
Bristol medico-chirurgical journal. III. 16.
Bristowe, Lindsay W. & Wright, P. B. The handbook of British Honduras. 1889. IV. 398.¹
British and foreign medico-chirurgical review. I. 17.

British association for the advancement of science. Report. I. 17.
The British Baluchistan forest regulation, 1890. 1890. IV. 307.[2]
The British botanist. *See* CLARKE, S. 1820. I. 397, *524*.[1]
British botany. *See* IRVINE, Alexander. 1855. I. 400.
British Burmah. *See* INDIA — BRITISH BURMAH.
The British dispensatory. *See* PHARMACOPŒA londinensis. 1618. III. 250.[2]
British florist. III. 16. *See also* FLORIST'S JOURNAL. III. 16.
British forest trees; a guide to the beauties. 1843. I. 393.[2]
British forestry. 1894. IV. 357.[2]
The British garden. *See* MURRAY, *Lady* Charlotte. 1799. III. 81.
British Guiana — Crown surveyor. Report on forests. IV. 5.[2]
British Guiana — Royal agricultural & commercial society. *See* TIMEHRI, I. 8.[1]
British homœopathic pharmacopœia. 1882. III. 255.[1]
British medical journal. I. 17.
British pharmaceutical conference. Proceedings. I. 17.
British pharmacopœia. 1864. III. 254.
British Solomon Islands. 1897. III. 282.[1]
The British sylva, and planters' . . . manual. 1851. IV. 108.[2]
Britten, James. Anandrous state of Erica cinerea. 1872. II. 665.[2]
— Arruda's Brazilian plants. 1896. I. 343.
— Bombax Jenmani Oliv. = B. carolinoïdes. 1896. II. 529.[1]
— Catalogue of plants collected [in British East Africa]. 1896. I. 493.
— Contributions to a flora of Berkshire. 1871. V. XXI.[1]
— Flora of Buckinghamshire. 1867. I. 402.
— Flora of High Wycombe. 1875. I. 402.
— The Japanese Andromeda. 1877. II. 675.[1]
— Linociera cotinifolia = Chionanthus virginicus. 1894. II. 706.[1]
— A list of Lincolnshire plants. 1872. I. 402.
— A list of Suffolk plants. 1874. I. 534.[1]
— Mistletoe on the Oak. 1872. II. 179.[1]
— Mundia Kunth v. Mundtia Harv. 1889. II. 430.[1]
— The names of herbes by William Turner. 1881. I. 78.[2]
— On the nomenclature of some Proteaceæ. 1886. II. 158.[2]
— Notes on Hoya. 1898. II. 739.[1]
— Notes on Myrmecodia. 1897. II. 824.[2]
— Notes on Naucleeæ. 1897. II. 807.[1]
— Notes on Rhus. 1900. II. 458.[1]
— The origin of the Rose. 1872. II. 290.[2]
— Palms. 1872. II. 63.[2]
— Plant-lore notes. 1878. I. 518.
— The plants of Welwitsch's Apontamentos. 1895. I. 492.[1]
— A sketch of the botany of Devonshire. 1878. I. 403.
— A sketch of the botany of Hampshire. 1877. I. 403.
— Smith's Georgian plants. 1898. I. 320.
— Two little known Australian Myrtaceæ. 1899. II. 619.[2]
— & Baker, E. G. Houston's Central American Leguminosae. 1897. I. 330.
— — Notes on Ceiba. 1896. II. 529.[2]
— & Holland, Robert. A dictionary of English plant-names. 1878. I. 74.[1]
— & Rendle, A. B. Catalogue of plants collected [in British East Africa]. 1896. I. 493.
— & others. The plants of Milanji, Nyasaland. 1894. I. 493.
Brittinger, Christian. Flora von Ober-Oesterreich. 1862. I. 441.
Britton, *Mrs.* Elisabeth G. Elongation of the inflorescence in Liquidambar. 1887. II. 253.[2]
Britton, Nathaniel Lord. Botanical contributions. 1896. II. 260.[2]
— Botanical gardens. 1897. I. 38.[1]
— The Button-bush, a tree. 1900. II. 811.[1]
— Catalogue of plants found in New Jersey. 1889. I. 315.
— Contributions to Texan botany. 1889. I. 325.
— Descriptions of new North American thorns. 1896. II. 260.[2]
— An enumeration of plants collected by Dr. H. H. Rushy in South America. 1889. I. 330.
— On the general geographical distribution of North American plants. 1891. I. 308.
— The generic name of the Silver-bell trees. 1893. II. 704.[1]
— The genus Hicoria of Rafinesque. 1888. II. 112.[1]
— In the Hickory matter. 1889. II. 112.[1]
— On a hybrid Oak near Keyport. 1882. II. 139.[2]

— Leaf-forms of Populus grandidentata. 1886. II. 97.[2]
— A list of plants collected at Fort Verde. 1888. I. 325.
— A list of state and local floras of the United States and British America. 1889. I. 3.[1]
— New or noteworthy North American phanerogams. 1888. I. 308.
— Note on Quercus Muhlenbergii Engelm. 1886. II. 135.[2]
— Note on the flowers of Populus heterophylla. 1887. II. 97.[2]
— Our conception of " species." 1893. I. 243.[1]
— Peculiarly-lobed leaves in Quercus alba. 1881. II. 132.[2]
— Pinus Banksiana Lamb. 1883. II. 40.[2]
— A preliminary catalogue of the flora of New Jersey. 1881. I. 315.
— On Rusbya, a new genus of Vacciniaceæ. 1893. II. 659.[2]
— A supposed new genus of Anacardiaceæ. 1887. II. 421.[1]
— The use of the generic name Halesia. 1893. II. 704.[1]
— When the leaves appear. 1878. I. 222.[1]
— When the leaves fall. 1878. I. 222.[1]
— *See also* MORONG, Thomas & BRITTON, N. L.
— & Brown, Addison. An illustrated flora of the northern United States. 1896. I. 316.
— & Kearney, T. H., (fr.). An enumeration of the plants collected . . . in southeastern Arizona. 1895. I. 326.
— & Rusby, H. H. A list of plants collected by Miss Mary B. Croft. 1887. I. 325.
— Sterns, E. E. & Poggenburg, J. F. Preliminary catalogue of anthophyta and pteridophyta . . . within 100 miles of New York city. 1888. I. 315.
Britton, Thomas Allen. Dry-rot in timber. 1879. IV. 415.[1]
— A treatise on the origin . . . of dry rot in timber. 1875. IV. 415.[1]
Britton, Wilton Everett. The Button bush. 1898. III. 711.[2]
— Experiments in Chestnut grafting. 1899. III. 358.[2]
— La Galleruca dell' Olmo. 1897. III. 365.[1]
— An observation of the effects of nitrogenous fertilizers on California Privet. 1900. III. 674.[1]
— Our street trees and the Elm-leaf beetle. 1897. III. 365.[1]
— The Strawberry-Raspberry. 1899. III. 458.[2]
— Top-grafting native Chestnut sprouts. 1900. III. 359.[2]
— *See also* JENKINS, E. H. & BRITTON, W. E.
Britzger, Frans Xaver. Introductio in artem botanicam. 1850. I. 89.
Brix, A. Praktischer Schiffbau, Bootsbau. 1892. IV. 425.[2]
Brix, P. Wilh. Untersuchungen über die Heizkraft der wichtigeren Brennstoffe. 1853. IV. 413.[1]
Brizi, Ugo. Sulla causa della " malsania " del Nocciolo. 1897. IV. 492.[1]
— La fersa del Gelso. 1896. III. 379.[2]
— Le malattie crittogamiche della Vite. 1895. III. 581.
— Eine neue Krankheit . . . des Mandelbaumes. 1896. III. 434.[1]
— Una nuova malattia . . . del Mandorlo. 1896. III. 434.[1]
— Ricerche sulla brunissure. 1895. III. 581.
Broadbent, Humphrey. The domestick coffee-man. 1722. III. 222.
Broadhead, Garland Carr. Geographical distribution of certain trees . . . in Missouri and Kansas. 1879. I. 324.
— Quercus heterophylla Michx. 1876. II. 134.[1]
Broadway, Walter E. Cereus peruvianus. 1891. III. 621.[2]
— Colonial notes. 1891. I. 40.
— Couroupita guianensis, Cannon-ball tree. 1891. II. 612.[1]
— Echites symphytocarpa Mey. 1897. III. 688.[1]
— Lagerstroemia reginae Roxb. 1891. III. 629.[2]
— List of indigenous trees and shrubs. 1896. I. 334.
— Manchineel. 1897. III. 445.[1]
— The Mangosteen. 1892. III. 609.[2]
— Norantea guianensis Aubl. 1891. III. 596.[2]
— Plant notes. 1891. I. 40.
— Preliminary list of herbarium specimens. 1895. I. 337.
— Rhabdadenia biflora Muell. Arg. 1897. III. 690.[1]
— West Indies. 1892. III. 64.[1]
Broberg, Sv. P. Flora hallandica. *See* FRIES, E. M. 1817. I. 352.
Broca. *See* PICHON & BROCA.
Brocchi, Giambattista. Giornale delle osservazioni fatte . . . in Egitto. 1841. I. 487.
— Memoria mineralogica sulla valle di Fassa. 1811. I. 439.
Brocchi, Giovanni Battista. *See* BROCCHI, Giambattista.
Broche, Eugène. Note sur les vers à soie. 1859. III. 380.[1]

Brochure eines anonymen Burgers gegen die städtische Forst-wirthschaft. 1851. IV. 278.¹
Brock. Ein deutscher Eibenbestand. 1894. IV. 440.²
— Die Fichtengespinstblattwespe. 1898. IV. 457.
— Gedanken über das seitherige Verschwinden . . . unserer Laubholznutzhölzer. 1879. IV. 137.²
— Der Matthes'sche Höhenmesser. 1884. IV. 265.
— Waldbauliche Betrachtungen nach einem Schneebruch im Laubholz. 1881. IV. 190.
Brock, C. Katechismus des Forstschutz- und Hülfsdienstes. 1897. IV. 98.²
Brockdorff, A. H. von. Die wichtigsten Ursachen d. verminderten Höhe . . . unserer jetzigen Waldbäume. 1837. I. 295.¹
Brockdorff, C. H. J. von. Gedanken zur Errichtung einer Förster-Schule. 1792. IV. 31.
Brocke, Heinrich Christian von. Abhandlung . . . Wie ohne Nachtheil . . . das Wachsthum . . . beschleuniget werden kann? 1774. IV. 116, 169.¹
— Wahre Gründe der physicalischen und experimental allgemeinen Forst-Wissenschaft. 1768. IV. 94.²
— Widerlegung der sogenannten Beurtheilung des . . . M. H. L. von Wedel. 1777. IV. 116.
— Zufällige Gedanken von der Natur . . . der wilden Bäume. 1752. IV. 115.
Brockenfeld. Welche Holzarten eignen sich am besten für die Aufforstung von Moorwiesen? 1892. IV. 70.
Brockett, L. P. The silk industry in America. 1876. III. 378.
Brockhausen, Rudolf. Die Pflanzenwelt Niedersachsens in ihren Beziehungen zur Götterlehre. 1865. I. 517.²
Brockman, W. L. Timber culture. 1874. IV. 111.²
Brockmeier, Heinrich. Über den Einfluss der englischen Weltherrschaft auf die Verbreitung wichtiger Culturgewächse. 1884. I. 242.¹
Brockmüller, H. Verwilderte Pflanzen bei Schwerin. 1880. I. 388.
Brodersen, J. Ueber Pappeln. 1888. III. 344.¹
Brodersen, G. Om Haardførheden af Wellingtonia. 1867. III. 292.
Brodhead, J. R. Documents relative to the colonial history . . . of New York. 1856. III. 263.¹
Brodie. Emploi du curare dans le tétanos. 1859. III. 683.¹
Brodie, Benjamin Collins, (jr.). On the chemical nature of a wax from China. 1848. III. 225.
— An investigation on the chemical nature of wax, II. 1848. III. 225.
Brodiez-Lesaint. Note sur la plantation et la culture du Pin du nord. 1829. IV. 471.
Broeck, Henri van den. Catalogue des plantes . . . d'Anvers. 1883. I. 532.²
Broecker, Gustav. De textura et formatione spinarum. 1849. I. 107.¹
Brögelmann, Wilhelm. Beschreibung der vorzüglichsten neuen Pflanzen. 1812. I. 265:
Broek, J. H. van den. Over de werking van Tinctura Guajaci. 1851. I. 36.²
Broekema, L. Verslag over den landbouw in Nederland. 1887. III. 122.²
Broeker, J. Decoct. cort. Chinae fuscae. 1875. III. 723.
Broekhuijzen, H. P. J. van. De Kinacultuur. 1898. III. 712.³
— Over het verschil van enten en zaailingen in de Kinacultuur. 1897. III. 712.²
Broemel, M. Die deutschen Holzzölle vor 1865. 1883. IV. 284.²
Broener, L. & Suis, A. Atlas de photo-micrographia des plantes médicinales. 1894. III. 260.¹
Brönnimann, F. Die Kataster-Vermessung. 1888. IV. 265.
Broers, Georgii. Responsio ad quaestionem . . . Quid botanici de variis plantarum gemmis . . . observarint. 1833. I. 107.³
Brog-il-hart. See BROILLIARD, Charles.
Brohon, Jean. De stirpibus vel plantis ordine alphabetico digestis epitome. 1541. I. 277.
Broillard, Charles. Accroissement dans la forêt de l'Ebenwald. 1898. IV. 235.¹
— De l'âge d'exploitation des taillis. 1892. IV. 252.
— Alcuni cenni sulla diminuzione dei boschi. 1881. IV. 282.²
— Alpes pastorales. 1896. IV. 135.¹
— Aménagement des forêts jardinées. 1883. IV. 244.
— Aperçu historique de l'opération culturale qui est l'éclaircie. 1899. IV. 175.²

— La Belle-Allée. 1898. IV. 137.¹
— Les bois du Canada. 1897. IV. 337.²
— Branchettes pour fourrage. 1893. IV. 438.²
— Un cas d'élagage efficace. 1897. III. 181.²
— Une catachrèse forestière. 1900. IV. 238.
— Le Chalet brûlé. 1895. IV. 140.
— Du choix des arbres pour les plantations d'alignement. 1896. III. 210.
— De la cîme aux racines. 1898. IV. 131.
— Classement des bois sur pied. 1900. IV. 388.²
— Le code forestier de l'Algérie. 1898. IV. 332,² 379.²
— Comparaison entre l'enseignement donné à l'Académie forestière d'Eberswalde et celui . . . à Nancy. 1895. IV. 30.
— Des conditions favorables au développement du Sapin. 1891 (1892). IV. 169,¹ 444.²
— Des conversions en futaie pleine. 1890. IV. 128.
— Cours d'aménagement des forêts. 1878. IV. 241.
— La crise des bois de feu. 1895. IV. 249.¹
— Décret portant modifications à l'organisation de l'École forestière. 1898. IV. 35.¹
— La disette du bois d'œuvre. 1877. IV. 402.²
— Divisez les grandes coupes. 1897. IV. 382.²
— Les eaux et les forêts. 1898. IV. 52.
— L'éclaircie par le haut. 1897. IV. 175.¹
— Éclaircies. 1899. IV. 175.²
— L'enfantement d'une grande administration. 1899. IV. 25.
— Essai sur la reproduction naturelle de l'Épicéa. 1897. IV. 454.
— État de la sylviculture et enseignement forestier pour préposés en Belgique. 1899. IV. 33.²
— Extension de la culture du Sapin en France. 1894. IV. 444.²
— Forest groundrent. 1899. IV. 259.²
— La forêt d'Ouhans. 1897. IV. 129.
— Forêt domaniale française de Bercé. 1896. IV. 362.
— Les forêts du royaume de Prusse. 1897. IV. 355.¹
— Les formules d'éclaircie. 1896. IV. 175.¹
— The function of the Pines and the Larch in the production of soil. 1877. IV. 69.
— Le gaz de bois. 1899. IV. 433.²
— Grèves de bûcherons. 1892. IV. 311.¹
— Du jardinage. 1883. IV. 237.
— Loi du 21 juillet 1899 . . . l'état de la Grèce. 1899. IV. 332.¹
— Les massifs de Sapin. 1876. IV. 446.¹
— Un petit plan de balivage. 1889. IV. 237.
— De la possibilité par pieds d'arbres. 1883. IV. 237.
— Principles of forest organisation. 1878. IV. 241.
— La production pendant là régénération. 1895. IV. 383.¹
— Les 80 Chênes de Cotta sur le Heinrichsseck. 1898. IV. 102.
— Une question de sylviculture. 1888. IV. 65.¹
— Le reboisement dans la Loire. 1898. IV. 164.¹
— Recherches étymologiques à travers bois. 1897. IV. 23.²
— Régénération graduelle des futaies. 1895. IV. 140.
— Du règlement des exploitations dans une petite sapinière. 18 . ? IV. 446.¹
— Rendement et estimation des taillis. 1893. IV. 258.
— De la réserve dans les taillis sous futaie. 1883. IV. 131.
— Le revenu foncier des forêts. 1899. IV. 259.²
— La révolution des taillis sous futaie. 1893. IV. 252.
— La révolution des taillis sous futaie. 1896. IV. 252.
— Le rôle des Pins et du Mélèze dans la production du sol. 1877. IV. 69.
— Semis naturels. 1898. IV. 140.
— La sylviculture, appliquée à la grande forêt de Chêne de Mormal. 1898. IV. 122.²
— La sylviculture en Hongrie. 1897. IV. 374.²
— Les taillis sous futaie de Toutenant. 1885. IV. 131.
— Thinnings. 1899. IV. 175.²
— Sans titre, suite aux erreurs du contrôle. 1896. IV. 246.
— Le traitement des bois en France. 1881. IV. 122.¹
— Traitement du Chêne. 1897. IV. 508.
— De la transformation des taillis en futaies. 1895. IV. 129.
— Trois erreurs du contrôle. 1894. IV. 246.
— Vieux noms cueillis autour des bois. 1895. IV. 23.²
— See also BAGNERIS, G. & BROILLARD, Charles.
— & Boppe, Lucien. Le recepage des plants feuillus. 1897. IV. 547.¹
— & Cardot, Émile. L'affouage pastoral. 1899. IV. 135.²
— The regulation of pasturage. 1899. IV. 135.²
— & Roulleau, R. Les arbres champêtres de la Mayenne. 1897. IV. 134.²

Broilliard, H. La Vosge, ses forêts, ses forges. 1863. IV. 360.
— & **Serval**, G. La Vosge, ses forêts et ses forges. See **Broilliard**, H. 1863. IV. 360.
Brokes, Barthold Heinrich. Irdisches Vergnügen in Gott. 1721. I. 515.
Bromas, P. Nouveaux tarifs pour la réduction et le toisé des bois. 1835. IV. 222.
Bromelius, Olof. Chloris gothica. 1694. I. 351.
Bromfield, William Arnold. Botanico-topographical map of the Isle of Wight. 1850. I. 400.
— Flora vectensis. 1856. I. 400.
— Letters from Egypt and Syria. 1856. I. 480, *488*.
— A list of plants . . . in the Isle of Wight. 1840. I. 399.
— Note on Tamarix gallica. 1842. II. 562.[3]
— A notice of the localities . . . of some rare British . . . plants. 1836. II. 268.[2]
— The Undercliff of the Isle of Wight. See **Martin**, G. A. 1849. I. 400.
Bromhead, *Sir* Edward French. An attempt to ascertain characters of the botanical alliances. 1838. I. 251.
— Remarks on the affinities of Lythraceae. 1838. II. 428,[2] *608*.[1]
Bromirski, Jan. O uprawach sztucznych w lasach. 1849. IV. 141.
Bromley, T. H. The Big trees of the Yosemite. 1871. II. 51.[1]
Bromo-Kolo. Over de bestrijding van de Koffiebladziekté. 1885. III. 735.
Brondeau, Louis de. Note sur une variété de Chêne. 1843. II. 136.[1]
Brondgeest, P. Q. De invloed van een lagen warmtegraad. 1868. I. 212.
Brongniart, Adolphe Théodore. Considérations sur la flore de la Nouvelle-Calédonie. 1865. I. 508.[3]
— Description de deux genres . . . des Rubiacées. 1865. II. 809.[2]
— De la détermination des orga   des plantes. 1859. I. 99.
— Énumération des genres de plantes cultivés au Muséum. 1843. I. 58.
— Habrothamne élégant. 1844. II. 770.[1]
— Sur l'insertion relative des diverses pièces de chaque verticille floral. 1831. I. 114.[3]
— Instructions concernant la botanique. 1838. I. 353.
— Juanulloa à fleurs orangées. 1841. II. 772.[1]
— Ludovia lancaefolia Ad. Br. Pandaneae Cyclantheae. 1861. II. 76.[3]
— Mémoire sur la famille des Bruniacées. 1826. II. 251.[2]
— Mémoire sur la famille des Rhamnées. 1826. II. 491.[2]
— Mémoire sur la génération et développement de l'embryon. 1827. I. 121.
— Nématanthe de Guillemin. 1842. II. 795.[1]
— Ueber eine neue mexikanische Gattung . . . der Cycadeae. 1846. II. 4.[1]
— Note sur la constitution du cône des Conifères. 1871. II. 19.
— Note sur la formation des nouvelles couches ligneuses. 1852. I. 189.
— Note sur le genre Bikkia. 1866. II. 809.[2]
— Note sur le genre Stephanotis. 1837. II. 742.[3]
— Note sur les fonctions des vaisseaux. 1863. I. 133.
— Note sur quelques Conifères. 1833. II. 12.[2]
— Note sur un nouveau genre de Cycadées du Méxique. 1846. II. 4.[1]
— Note sur un nouveau genre de Légumineuses. 1846. II. 89.[1]
— Notes sur quelques Rubiacées de la Nouvelle-Calédonie. 1865. II. 809.[3]
— Notice sur les Palmiers de la Nouvelle-Calédonie. 1873. II. 62.[1]
— Sur un nouveau genre de la famille des Cyclanthées. 1861. II. 76.[2]
— Nouveaux documents sur la flore de la Nouvelle-Calédonie. 1874. I. 609.[1]
— Nouvelles recherches sur la structure de l'epiderme. 1834. I. 129.[1]
— Observations sur le mode de fécondation . . . des Cistinées. 1831. II. 563.[1]
— Observations sur les Pandanées de la Nouvelle-Calédonie. 1875. II. 56.[1]
— Observations sur un genre . . . de Violacées. 1861. II. 567.[1]
— Palmiers de la Nouvelle-Calédonie. 1873. II. 62.[1]

— Psychotrie à fleurs blanches. 1845. II. 830.[2]
— Quelques observations sur . . . la fécondation dans les Asclépiadées. 1831. II. 736.[1]
— Rapport sur la partie botanique du voyage de M. d'Orbigny. 1834. I. 329.
— Rapport sur les mémoires de M. Payer, relatifs à l'organogénie de la fleur. 1853. I. 114.[2]
— Rapport sur les mémoires relatifs aux vaisseaux laticifères. 1866. I. 136.[1]
— Rapport sur les plantations forestières dans la Sologne. 1852. IV. 359.[2]
— Rapport sur les prix proposés pour la culture des arbres resineux. 184 . ? IV. 41.[1]
— Rapport sur les progrès de la botanique phytographique. 1868. I. 300.
— Rapport sur un mémoire de M. A. Trécul sur la formation des feuilles. 1853. I. 109.[3]
— Rapport sur un mémoire de M. Barnéoud, ayant pour objet le développement de l'ovule. 1846. I. 114.[3]
— Rapport sur un mémoire de M. Courbon. 1860. I. 479.
— Rapport sur un mémoire de M. Decaisne, relatif à . . . Lardizabalées. 1838. II. 200.[2]
— Rapport sur un tableau des limites de la végétation . . . du Canigou. 1844. I. 410.
— Recherches sur l'organisation . . . des Cycadées. 1829. II. 2.[2]
— Recherches sur l'origine des diverses dispositions spirales des feuilles. 1848. I. 102.
— Recherches sur la structure . . . des feuilles. 1830. I. 109,[1] *178*.
— Réflexions . . . sur la méthode naturelle et la classification de Jussieu. 1857. I. 252.
— Spathodée élégante. 1844. II. 790.[2]
— Stéphanote à fleurs nombreuses. 1839. II. 742.[3]
— Sur la structure de l'ovule et de la graine des Cycadées. 1875. II. 3.[1]
— Symplocos coccinea. 1846. III. 670.[1]
— Voyage autour du monde . . . sur la corvette La Coquille. 1829. I. 302.
— *See also.* **Fauché**, **Brongniart**, Adolphe, **Chaubard**, L. A. & **Bory de Saint-Vincent**, J. B. M.
— & **Gris**, Arthur. Description de deux nouveaux genres de Myrtacées. 1863. II. 619.[2]
— — Description de quelques Éléocarpées. 1861. II. 510.[1]
— — Description de quelques plantes . . . de la Nouvelle-Calédonie. 1868. I. 508.[3]
— — Description des Protéacées de la Nouvelle-Calédonie. 1865. II. 158.[3]
— — Descriptions de plusieurs espèces du genre Pittosporum. 1864. II. 248.[1]
— — Descriptions de quelques Dilléniacées. 1864. II. 540.[2]
— — Descriptions de quelques espèces nouvelles . . . de Myrtacées. 1864. II. 619.[2]
— — Descriptions de quelques nouvelles espèces de la Nouvelle-Calédonie. 1865. I. 508.[2]
— — Descriptions de quelques Palmiers du genre Kentia. 1864. II. 69.[3]
— — Fragments d'une flore de la Nouvelle-Calédonie. 1864. I. 508.[2]
— — Note sur deux genres nouveaux de Myrtacées. 1863. II. 619.[2]
— — Note sur le genre Chiratia Montrouzier. 1864. II. 610.[1]
— — Note sur le genre Crossostylis de Forster. 1861. II. 613.[2]
— — Note sur le genre Spermolepis. 1867. II. 633.[1]
— — Note sur le nouveau genre Garnieria. 1871. II. 160.[2]
— — Note sur le nouveau genre Pleurocalyptus. 1867. II. 632.[1]
— — Note sur les Épacridées de la Nouvelle-Calédonie. 1864. II. 688.[1]
— — Note sur quelques Protéacées de la Nouvelle-Calédonie. 1863. II. 158.[3]
— — Note sur un genre nouveau d'Ombellifères. 1861. II. 65.[3]
— — Note sur un nouveau genre de Nyctaginées. 1861. II. 192.[2]
— — Notice sur le genre Soulamea. 1865. II. 416.[1]
— — Notice sur les Saxifragées-Cunoniées. 1862. II. 250.[1]
— — Nouvelle note sur les Conifères néo-calédoniennes. 1866. II. 16.[1]
— — Observations sur diverses plantes . . . de la Nouvelle-Calédonie. 1864. I. 508.[2]

— — Observations sur les Myrtacées Sarcocarpées. 1865. II. 619.[2]

— — Sur le prétendu genre Chiratia. 1866. II. 610.[2]

— — Sur quelques Conifères de la Nouvelle-Calédonie. 1866. II. 16.[1]

— — Sur quelques Ombellifères de la Nouvelle-Calédonie. 1865. II. 648,[2] 650.[2]

— — Révision des Cunonia de la Nouvelle-Calédonie. 1872. II. 250.[2]

— — Ueber die Saxifrageen, Cunoniaceen, Neu-Caledoniens. 1862. II. 250.[1]

— — Supplément aux Myrtacées de la Nouvelle-Calédonie. 1866. II. 619.[2]

— — Supplément aux Ombellifères. 1865. II. 648.[3]

— — Supplément aux Protéacées de la Nouvelle-Calédonie. 1871. II. 159.[2]

— — Sur les Symplocas de la Nouvelle-Calédonie. 1866. II. 703.[2]

— Richard, Achille & Jussieu, Adrien de. Rapport sur un mémoire de M. P. Duchartre. 1845. II. 519.[1]

— —,— Report on a memoir by M. P. Duchartre. 1845. II. 519.

— & others. Rapport sur le concours . . . relativement à l'étude des hybrides végétaux. 1862. I. 245.

Brongniart, Charles J. E. & Cornu, Maxime. Note relative à la destruction de phylloxera. 1880. III. 572.

Bronn, Heinrich Georg. De formis plantarum Leguminosarum. 1822. II. 320.[1]

— Die Verzinsung des Waldkapitals. 1858. IV. 255.

Bronn, Valentinus. Mémoire sur l'utilisation des terrains incultes de l'Ardenne. 1829. IV. 161.[3]

— Ueber die Nothwendigkeit der wissenschaftlichen Ausbildung des Forstmannes. 1832. IV. 29.

— Oratio qua sylvarum et . . . momenta historica exposuit. 1828. IV. 23.[3]

Bronner, Johann Philipp. Die Verbesserung des Weinbaues. 1830. III. 552..

— Der Weinbau in Süddeutschland. 1833. III. 552.

— Die wilden Trauben des Rheinthals. 1857. II. 507.[1]

Bronnert, Emil. See GEROCK, J. E. & BRONNERT, D.

Bronzet. De la possibilité d'élever le Bombyx mori. 1869. III. 148.[2]

De Broodvrucht of Moerbeiachtige boomen. 1884. III. 366.[1]

Brooke, William O'SHAUGHNESSY. See O'SHAUGHNESSY, Sir William BROOKE.

Brookes, Gilbert. The complete British gardener. 1779. III. 109.

Brookes, O. H. Notes on Tea planting in the Andamans. 1882. III. 603.

Brookes, Richard. The general dispensatory. 1753. III. 252.

— Natural history of vegetables. 1763. III. 217.

Brooklyn, N. Y. — Tree planting and fountain society. See TREE . . . III. 8.

Brooks, Henry. Natal. 1876. III. 281.[2]

— Two remarkable Catalpa trees. 1890. III. 787.[1]

— See also DAME, L. L. & BROOKS, Henry.

Brooks, William P. Fruits and flowers of northern Japan. 1890. I. 463.[1]

— Poisonous plants. 1893. III. 59.[3]

Brookshaw, George. Groups of fruit, accurately drawn. 1817. III. 78.[3]

— The horticultural repository. 1823. III. 79.

— Pomona britannica. 1812. III. 78.[3]

Broome, Christopher Edmund. On an abnormal flower of a Penstemon. 1889. II. 273.[1]

Broome, F. N. W. Australia. 1888. III. 283.[1]

Brooshooft, P. De monoseoko in het Koffievraagstuk. 189.? III. 730.

— Vrijzinnig, niet lozunnig! 189.? III. 730.

Broquet, A. Les Cactacées. 1892. II. 586,[3] III. 625.[1]

Brosi, U. Le Champignon des caves. 1877. IV. 415.[1]

— De la conservation des bois. 1876. IV. 420.

— Ueber die Conservirung des Holzes. 1876. IV. 420.

— Einfluss der Imprägnation auf die technischen Eigenschaften des Holzes. 1878. IV. 500.[1]

— Der Hausschwamm. 1877. IV. 415.[1]

— La lunure du Chêne. 1877. IV. 510.

— Der Mondring im Eichenholz. 1877. IV. 510.

— Des propriétés techniques du bois de Hêtre. 1877. IV. 499.

— Die technischen Eigenschaften des . . . Rothbuchenholzes. 1877. IV. 499.

Brosig, A. Ueber die Aufforstung verödeter Hochgebirgsblössen. 1857. IV. 153.[3]

— Mancherlei aus dem Gebiete des Waldbaues. 1857. IV. 153.[2]

Brosig, Max. Die Botanik des älteren Plinius. 1883. I. 530.[3]

Brossard. De la manière de semer et faire pépinières. See DANY, F. 1560. III. 153.

Brosterhuysen, Jan. Catalogus plantarum Horti medici scholae Auriacae. 1647. I. 50.

Brostrøm, C. J. Amerikansk Graaask. 1885. III. 672.[1]

— Bjærgfyrren (Pinus montana). 1887. III. 307.[2]

— Hvorledes befries Laurbærtræer for Skjoldlus? 1890. III. 406.[2]

— Om Plantning af Læbælter. 1888. III. 215.[1]

Brotbeck, Johann Konrad. Theoria physica de plantis. 1656. I. 30.

Brotbequius. See BROTBECK, Johann Kunrad.

Brotero, Felix de Avellar. Compendio de botanica. 1788. I. 83, V. x.[1]

— Descriptions of a new genus . . . Araujia. 1818. II. 580,[1] 736.[1]

— Descriptions of two new species of Erythrina. 1825. II. 356.[1]

— Enumeratio plantarum Lusitaniae rariorum. 1809. II. 359.[1]

— Flora lusitanica. 1804. I. 420.

— Historia natural dos Pinheiros. 1827. IV. 440.[2]

— Phitographia Lusitaniae selectior. 1801. I. 535.

— Phytographia Lusitaniae selectior. 1816. I. 420.

— Principios de agricultura philosophica. 1793. . III. 37.[1]

Brotherson, R. P. Caryopteris Mastacanthus. 1899. III. 695.[2]

Brotherton, Thomas. An account of several curious observations . . . concerning the growth of trees. 1688. I. 187.

Brotherton, Wilfred A. Abies brevifolia. 1900. III. 305.[2]

— The long-leaved creeping Willow. 1892. III. 352.[1]

— Some wild American fruits. 1892. III. 261.[2]

Brotherus, Victor Ferdinand. Anteckningar till Norra Tavastlands flora. 1872. V. xvii.[2]

— Botanische Wanderungen auf die Halbinsel Kola. 1886. I. 364.

Brou, (abbé). Daphne Laureola. 1867. III. 627.[2]

— Jasmin jonquille. 1869. III. 673.[1]

— Jasminum nudiflorum. 1868. III. 673.[1]

— Le Lierre dans les jardins et sur les toits. 1867. III. 642.

— Lonicera Xylosteum. 1868. III. 751.[1]

— Salix subsempervirens. 1867. III. 352.[1]

Brouard. Catalogue des plantes . . . de l'Eure. 1820. I. 407.

Broughton, Arthur. Enchiridion botanicum . . . per insulas britannicas. 1782. I. 395.

— Hortus Eastensis. 1792. I. 39.

Broughton, John. Chemical examination of the bark of the Azadirachta. 1873. III. 511.[2]

— Chemical . . . experiments on living Cinchonae. 1872. III. 722.

— Cinchona cultivation in India. 1872. III. 714.

— On the Chinchona excelsa of Roxburgh. 1868. III. 744.

— The effect of manures on the alcaloidal yield of Cinchonas. 1873. III. 714.

— Influences des engrais sur les Cinchonas. 1873. III. 714.

— Note on hybridism among Cinchonae. 1871. II. 812.

— Reports and letters. 1870. III. 714.

Broun, J. A. Note on Bentinckia Condapana. 1863. II. 65.[1]

Brousmiche, Édouard. Aperçu général de l'histoire naturelle du Tonkin. 1887. I. 469.[1]

Broussais, Ivan. Notice sur la production . . . du liège. 1891. IV. 517.[1]

Brousse. Code forestier. 1827. IV. 324.

Brousse, Paul. Quelques mots sur l'étude des fruits. 1880. I. 119.

Broussonet. Note sur le bois de Rhodes. 1801. III. 694, IV. 536.[1]

Broussonet, Auguste. Elenchus plantarum Horti botanici monspeliensis. 1805. I. 57.

Broussonet, Jean Louis Victor. Corona florae monspeliensis. 1790. I. 406.

Broussonetia à fruit blanc. 1835. III. 367.[2]

Brouwer, P. Mededeeling over Matico. 1852. III. 342.[1]

Brouwer, R. J. Verhandeling over het aanleggen van boom kweekerijen. 1824. III. 153.

Browall, Johan. Discursus de introducenda in scholas . . . Historiae naturalis lectione. 1737. I. 78.[2]
— Examen Epicriseos in Systema plantarum sexuale. 1739. I. 250.
— Specimen de transmutatione specierum. 1745. I. 243.[2]
Brown, A. M. Importance of our forests. 1889. IV. 272.
Brown, A. R. Satinwood, Chloroxylon Swietenia D. C. 1900. IV. 524.[2]
Brown, A. Samler. Report on the . . . condition of the Canary Islands. 1892. III. 132.[1]
Brown, Abbie Farwell. Ceylon Ebony, Diospyros Ebenum Koenig. 1900. IV. 534.[2]
— Effects of fire protection on Sâl forests. 1887. IV. 184.[1]
— List of principal trees . . . in the Ganges division. 1888. I. 470,[2] *IV. 88.*[3]
— Mimusops hexandra Roxb. in Ceylon. 1900. IV. 534.[2]
— Notable trees about Boston. 1900. I. 295.[1]
— Notes on plantations etc. in the Dehra Dun. 1886. IV. 378.
— Seeding of Bamboos. 1886. II. 58.[2]
Brown, Addison. See BRITTON, N. L. & BROWN, Addison.
Brown, Alexander. The Coffee planter's manual. 1880. III. 732.[2]
Brown, Andrew. See DICKESON, M. W. & BROWN, Andrew.
Brown, Arch. J. A few remarks on the cultivation of Coffee in southern India. 1854. III. 732.[1]
Brown, E. Robert. On the formation . . . of young plantations. 1871. IV. 120.
Brown, Edwin. The flora of the district surrounding Tutbury. 1863. I. 401.
Brown, G. R. Notes on the uses, &c., of some native plants in the Port Macquarie district. 1893. III. 283.[1]
— & Rudder, Augustus. Grass-tree gum. 1894. III. 339.[1]
Brown, Georg. De usu corticis peruviani. 1779. III. 720.
Brown, George E. Pinus austriaca as a seaside plant. 1881. IV. 465.[2]
— Seaside plantations. 1879. III. 41.[2]
— The training of young foresters. 1880. IV. 29.
— Woods and their management. 1881. IV. 173.
Brown, Hay. Facts relative to the fecundation of flowers. 1840. III. 50.[2]
— Faits relatifs à la fécondation des fleurs. 1840. III. 50.[3]
Brown, Horace T. & Escombe, F. Static diffusion of gases and liquids. 1900. I. 160.
— & Morris, G. H. A contribution to the chemistry and physiology of foliage leaves. 1893. I. 154.
Brown, J. CAMPBELL-. On the agricultural chemistry of the Tea plantations of India. 1875. III. 603.
Brown, James. The forester. 1847. IV. 108.[1]
— Thick and thin planting of forest trees. 1848. IV. 154.[1]
Brown, John. An account of the . . . resin in the Cortex Eleutheriae. 1722. II. 439.[2]
— De camphora. 1726. III. 233.[1]
Brown, John Alexander HARVIE-. See HARVIE-BROWN, J. A.
Brown, John B. Forests of Indiana. 1900. IV. 339.
Brown, John Croumbie. African fever and culture of the Blue Gum-tree. 1890. IV. 531.[2]
— On the aridity of Spain. 1884. IV. 47.[1]
— On the "Australian bug." 1882. IV. 210.[2]
— A British school of forestry. 1878. IV. 34.[1]
— A British school of forestry. 1879. IV. 34.[1]
— A British school of forestry. 1881. IV. 34.[1]
— A British school of forestry. 1884. IV. 34.[1]
— Edinburgh as a site for a national school of forestry. 1886. IV. 34.[1]
— Efectos importantes de la tala de los montes. 1881. IV. 44.
— On the employment of national funds in the establishment of a national school of forestry. 1886. IV. 34.[1]
— On endeavours . . . to effect the establishment of a national school of forestry in Britain. 1886. IV. 34.[1]
— Finland. 1883. IV. 347.
— Forest botany in Norway. 1884. IV. 79.[2]
— Forest economy in Germany. 1874. IV. 46.[2]
— Forest economy of France. 1874. IV. 276.[1]
— On forest schools. 1878. IV. 34.[1]
— Forestry in Norway. 1884. IV. 344.[1]
— Forestry in the mining districts of the Ural mountains. 1884. IV. 346.
— Forests and forestry in Poland. 1885. IV. 346.
— Forests and forestry of northern Russia. 1884. IV. 346.
— Forests and moisture. 1877. IV. 50.
— Forests in South Africa. 1881. I. 495.
— The forests of England. 1883. IV. 120.

— French forest ordinance of 1669. 1883. IV. 27.[2]
— The French forestry budget. See JOUBAIRE, A. 1879. IV. 27.[2]
— Glances at forestry in Northern Europe. 1879. IV. 113.[1]
— Glances at the forests of Northern Europe. 1879. IV. 342.[2]
— Hydrology of South Africa. 1875. IV. 49,[1] 50.
— On the important geographical effects of the disforesting of mountains. 1881. IV. 44.
— Importanti effetti geografici del diboscamento dei monti. 1881. IV. 44.
— The International forestry exhibition in Edinburgh. 1885. IV. 34.[1]
— Introduction to the study of modern forest economy. 1884. IV. 270.
— Letter relative to the aridity of Spain. 1884. IV. 47.[2]
— Management of crown forests at the Cape of Good Hope. 1887. IV. 280.[1]
— The manufacture of lucifer matches in Sweden. 1884. IV. 428.[1]
— Opinions of continental foresters . . . on the location of a school of forestry. 1878. IV. 34.[1]
— Papers relative to a . . . British national school of forestry. 188.? IV. 34.[1]
— Pine plantations on the sand-wastes of France. 1878. IV. 360, *461.*[1]
— Practicable arrangements . . . of a national school of forestry in Edinburgh. 1886. IV. 34.[1]
— Reboisement in France. 1876. IV. 162.
— Rural primary schools of science . . . forestry. 1879. IV. 34.[1]
— Sand-plains of Belgium. 1885. IV. 160.[2]
— School of forest engineers in Spain. 1886. IV. 35.[1]
— School of forestry at Evois in Finland. 1877. IV. 31.
— The school of forestry in the Escurial in Spain. 1877. IV. 35.[1]
— The school of forestry in the Polytechnic school of Carlsruhe. 1877. IV. 32.
— The school of forestry in the Royal Wurtemburg academy of land and forest economy. 1877. IV. 32.
— On schools of forestry. 1878. IV. 34.[1]
— The schools of forestry in Europe. 1877. IV. 30.[2]
— Schools of forestry in Germany. 1887. IV. 33.[1]
— Treatises on matters pertaining to modern forest science. 1887. IV. 102.
— Water supply of South Africa. 1877. IV. 49.[1]
Brown, John Ednie. On American and Canadian trees. 1871. III. 116.[2]
— Australian forest administration. 1884. IV. 295.[2]
— On the coniferous trees . . . of California. 1875. IV. 14.[1]
— The forest flora of South Australia. 1882. I. 499,[2] *IV. 89.*[3]
— The forests of Western Australia. 1899. IV. 380.[1]
— Forests of Western Australia. 1900. IV. 380.[2]
— A practical treatise on tree culture in South Australia. 1881. IV. 111.[1]
— On the principal timber trees introduced . . . from . . . North America. 1869. III. 78.[1]
— Report on cultivation of Wattles. 1884. IV. 521.[1]
— Report on planting Olives. 1884. III. 676.[1]
— Report on the forests of western Australia. 1896. IV. 380.[2]
— Timber trees of South Australia. 1880. IV. 401.[2]
Brown, John P. Catalogue des plantes . . . de Thoune. 1843. I. 434.
— The Catalpa tree and its importance. 1900. IV. 538.[2]
— Railroad plantations and Catalpa. 1900. IV. 538.[2]
Brown, John R. Notes on Larix leptolepis. 1898. IV. 452.[2]
Brown, Mrs. Margaret Read. The wild flowers of southern and western India. 1868. I. 474.
Brown, Nicholas Edward. Acalypha Sanderi. 1896. II. 435.[2]
— Aeschynanthus marmoratus Moore. 1882. II. 793.[1]
— Aloe insignis × N. E. Brown. 1885. II. 78.[2]
— Aristolochia hians. 1887. III. 386.[2]
— Aristolochia ridicula N. E. Brown n. sp. 1886. II. 183.[1]
— Bauhinia Galpini N. E. Br. 1891. II. 335.[1]
— Bouvardia scabra. 1884. III. 711.[2]
— Cestrum Hartwegii (Dun.) var. pubescens. 1883. II. 770.[2]
— Cleistogamous flowers of Hoya. 1885. II. 739.[1]
— Crassula monticola. 1882. II. 236.[2]
— Crataegus pinnatifida (Bunge) var. major. 1886. II. 263.[1]
— Elaeodendron sphaerophyllum Presl var. pubescens. 1891. II. 467.[1]

— Fertilisation of Hoyas and other Asclepiads. 1885. II. 739.[1]
— Gasteria colubrina N. E. Br. 1877. II. 83.[1]
— Gasteria dicta N. E. B. 1876. II. 83.[1]
— Grevillea annulifera F. v. Muell. 1882. III. 383.[1]
— Hoya Griffithii. 1885. II. 739.[2]
— Hoya lasiantha Korth. 1882. II. 740.[1]
— Hoya linearis (Wall.) var. sikkimensis. 1883. II. 740.[1]
— Hoya longifolia (Wall.) var. Shepherdii. 1885. II. 740.[1]
— Ixora salicifolia (Blume) var. variegata. 1882. II. 821.[1]
— Leptactina tetraloba N. E. Br. 1885. II. 822.[1]
— Lonicera Hildebrandiana. 1898. III. 750.[2]
— Myriocarpa colipensis Liebm. 1887. III. 382.[2]
— New garden Veronicas. 1890. III. 704.[1]
— New plants of 1877. 1878. III. 83.[1]
— Panax fruticosum L. var. multifidum. 1887. II. 651.[2]
— Paraguay Tea. 1892. II. 463.[1]
— Piper ornatum N. E. Brown. 1884. II. 95.[1]
— Piper porphyrophyllum. 1884. II. 95.[1]
— Rooting terminal buds of the Bramble. 1884. II. 306.[1]
— The Stinging tree. 1882. III. 382.[2]
— Three new species of Treculia. 1894. II. 155.[2]
— Vaccinium intermedium Ruthe. 1888. II. 685.[2]
— Variation in Haworthias. 1878. II. 83.[2]
— Veronica cupressoides and its allies. 1888. II. 783.[1]
Brown, Philip. A catalogue of very curious plants. 1779. I. 52.
Brown, R. B. See HUMMEL, J. J. & BROWN, R. B.
Brown, Robert. Asclepiadeae. 1811. II. 735.[1]
— On the Asclepiadeae. 1811. II. 735.[1]
— Über die Asclepiadeen. 1811. II. 735.[1]
— Botanical appendix to Capt. Sturt's expedition. 1849. I. 501.
— The botanical history of Angus. 1871. V. xxi.[1]
— A brief account of microscopical observations . . . on the particles contained in the pollen. 1828. I. 117.[1]
— Character and description of Kingia. 1826. II. 1.
— Characters and descriptions of 3 new species of plants. 1818. I. 457.
— On Cyrtandreae. 1838. II. 792.[1]
— Sur les Cyrtandrées. 1840. II. 792.[1]
— Extracts from Plantae javanicae. 1867. I. 469.[1]
— Genera et species . . . Compositarum. 1867. II. 848.[1]
— Genera et species . . . Leguminosarum. 1867. II. 318.[1]
— Genera et species . . . Myrtacearum. 1867. II. 619.[1]
— Genera et species plantarum . . . in Horto kewensi. 1867. I. 55.
— General remarks . . . on the botany of Terra Australis. 1814. I. 500.
— General view of the botany . . . of Swan River. 1831. I. 500.
— List of new and rare plants collected in Abyssinia. 1814. I. 487.
— List of plants collected on the coasts of Baffin's Bay. 1819. I. 309.[2]
— A manual of botany. 1874. V. x.[1]
— The miscellaneous botanical works. 1866. I. 34.
— Notes and observations on Indian plants. 1867. I. 474.
— Observations . . . on Christian Smith's collection of plants. 1818. I. 491.
— Observations . . . on the herbarium collected by Prof. Christian Smith. 1818. I. 491.
— Observations on the organs . . . of fecundation in Orchideae and Asclepiadeae. 1831. II. 735.[1]
— Observations on the structure . . . of the more remarkable plants collected by . . . Walter Oudney. 1826. I. 483.[1]
— Observations sur . . . Composées. 1878. II. 850.[1]
— Observations sur la famille des Légumineuses. 1827. II. 376.[1]
— Observations sur les organes sexuels . . . dans les Orchidées et les Asclépiadées. 1831. II. 735.[1]
— Sur la pluralité . . . des embryons dans les graines des Coniferes. 1835. II. 18.
— On the plurality . . . of embryos in the seeds of Coniferae. 1835. II. 18.
— Prodromus florae Novae Hollandiae. 1810. I. 500.
— On the Proteaceae of Jussieu. 1811. II. 158.[1]
— Pterocymbium javanicum. 1838. II. 537.[1]
— Pterocymbium with observations on Sterculieae. 1838. II. 537.[1]
— On the relative position of the divisions of stigma and parietal placentae. 1843. I. 117.[2]
— Ueber die Sexualorgane . . . bei den Orchideen und Asclepiadeen. 1831. II. 735.[2]

— Sketches of Caithness. 1860. I. 401.
— Some observations on the . . . Compositae. 1818. II. 847.[2]
— Sur la structure de l'ovule. 1826. I. 121, II. 1.
— Supplementary observations on the fecundation of Orchideae and Asclepiadeae. 1831. II. 735.[2]
— Supplementum primum Prodromi florae Novae Hollandiae. 1810. I. 500, II. 158.[2]
— Vermischte botanische Schriften. 1825. I. 520.[2]
Brown, Robert (of Campster). British Columbian trees. 1873. I. 311.[1]
— The Cedar of British Columbia. 1873. II. 52.[1]
— Descriptions of some . . . species of Oaks from northwest America. 1871. II. 128.[2]
— Distribution géographique des Conifères et des Gnetacées. 1869. II. 13.[1]
— Florula discoana. 1868. I. 309.[1]
— On the geographical distribution of the Coniferae and Gnetaceae. 1869. II. 13.[1]
— Die geographische Verbreitung der Coniferen und Gnetaceen. 1869. II. 13.[1]
— Horae sylvanae. 1869. I. 320, IV. 77.[2]
— A monograph of . . . Thuja . . . Libocedrus. 1868. II. 33,[2] 52.[1]
— Thuya gigantea and Libocedrus decurrens. 1873. II. 33, 52.[2]
— On the vegetable products used by the North-west American Indians. 1868. III. 261.[2]
— The Yellow Cypress. 1873. II. 28.[2]
Brown, Robert (of Liverpool). The botany of the Liverpool district. 1896. I. 535.[1]
Brown, Robert E. Plantation roads and walks. 1865. IV. 389.
Brown, Robert N. A hand book of the trees, shrubs and herbaceous plants . . . in the Madras agri-horticultural society's gardens. 1862. I. 67,[1] 473.
Brown, Samuel. First[–eighth] book of East India plants. 1702. I. 471.
Brown, T. S. An account of some experiments . . . to ascertain the relative stiffness and strength . . . of timber. 1831. IV. 409.
Brown, Thomas. Certain miscellany tracts. 1684. V. xxv.[1]
— Observations upon several plants mention'd in Scripture. 1684. V. xxv.[1]
Brown, Captain Thomas. The book of butterflies. 1832. III. 374.
— Illustrations of the American ornithology. 1835. I. 306.
Brown, Wilham. The application of scientific and practical arboriculture to Canada. 1885. IV. 111.[2]
— Trees and climate. 1869. IV. 53.
Brown, William H. Report of the committee on the drug market. 1874. III. 365.[2]
Browne, Daniel Jay. Remarks on the propagation of the Vine. 1859. III. 548.[1]
— Report on the seeds and cuttings. 1856. III. 117.[1]
— The sylva americana. 1832. I. 304.
— Trees of America, native and foreign. 1846. I. 304, III. 60, V. xvi.[1]
Browne, H. A. Note on sericulture in British Burma. 1871. III. 377.
Browne, J. Harris. The cultivation of the Olive. 1869. III. 676.[1]
Browne, Patrick. The civil and natural history of Jamaica. 1756. I. 334.
Browne, Raymond. Pine timber statistics of " The valley of the Gander." 1885. IV. 337.[2]
Browne, Sir Thomas. Of garlands and coronary. 1835. I. 515.
— Observations on grafting. 1835. III. 160.
— Observations upon several plants mentioned in Scripture. 1835. I. 513.
— Works. 1835. I. 513.
Brownlow, Charles. On the feasibility of a mixed system of open air silk-culture. 1865. III. 148.[1]
— A few agricultural notes . . . in Cachar. 1869. III. 369.[1]
— Note on the Agur, Eagle. 1865. III. 227, 626.[2]
— The Orange groves of Shalla. 1869. III. 499.[2]
— Some hints on the cultivation of Tea. 1863. III. 603.
— The timber trees of Cachar. 1865. IV. 401.[1]
Brož, Ferdinand. Praktische Erfahrungen über die Anwendung der doppelten Buchführung. 1882. IV. 312.
Bruand, A. Causerie sur la forêt de Compiègne. 1900. IV. 556.[1]

Bruand, Léon. L'administration des forêts en Espagne.
1879. IV. 293.[1]
— Notices sur le débit . . . du Châtaignier. 1878. IV. 85.[2]
— & **Gail,** de. Loi forestière du royaume de Hongrie. 1881.
IV. 331.[2]
— & others. Notices sur le débit et les emplois du Châtaignier.
1878. IV. 493.[1]
Bruand, Theophile. Monographie des lepidoptères nuisibles.
1846. III. 189.
Bruant. L'Aubépine toujours fleurie. 1882. III. 422.[1]
Bruce, C. A. An account of the manufacture of the black tea.
1838. III. 601,[1] 602.[1]
— Observations sur la plante à Thé d'Assam. 1839. III.
602.[2]
— Report on the manufacture of tea. 1839. III. 602.[2]
Bruce, C. W. A. Flowering of Strobilanthes in Burma. 1896.
II. 803.[2]
Bruce, *Lady* Elisabeth. Simla flowers. 1897. I. 475.[2]
Bruce, James. Additional articles of natural history. 1808.
I. 486.
— Reisen zur Entdeckung der Quellen des Nil. 1790. I. 486.
— Select specimens of natural history collected in travels to
discover the source of the Nile. 1790. I. 486.
— Some observations upon Myrrh. 1775. III. 280.[1]
— Travels . . . Third edition . . . to which is prefixed a life
of the author. 1790. I. 486.
— Travels to discover the source of the Nile. 1790. I. 486.
— Voyage aux sources du Nil. 1790. I. 486.
Bruce, Robert. An account of the sensitive quality of . . .
Averrhoa. 1785. II. 392.[1]
— Nachricht von der Empfindlichkeit des Baumes Averrhoa.
1785. II. 392.[1]
Bruce-Suttor, A. See SUTTOR, A. BRUCE-.
Bruch, Friedrich Daniel. Observationes . . . de radicis
fruticis Juniperi decocto. 1736. III. 303.[2]
Bruchausen, A. Aanwijzing ter verbetering van de akker-
bouw. 1792. III. 105.
I bruchi. 1863. IV. 209.[1]
Bruchstücke aus dem im bayerischen Hochgebirge geführten
Tagbuch. 1857. IV. 118.
Bruckisch, C. Spiraea ariaefolia Sims. 1899. III. 424.[2]
Brüche, W. & Beckurts, H. A. Experimentelle Untersu-
chungen über . . . Harze und Balsame. 1892. III. 228.[1]
Brücke, Ernst. Ueber die Bewegungen der Mimosa pudica.
1848. II. 372.[2]
— Ueber das Bluten der Rebstockes. 1844. I. 168, *II. 508.*[1]
— Die Intercellularräume des Gelenkwulstes der Mimoso.
1865. II. 372.[2]
— Pflanzenphysiologische Abhandlungen. 1898. I. 148.
Brückmann, Franz Ernst. De Avellana mexicana. 1721.
II. 539.[1]
— Catalogus exhibens appelationis et denominationes om-
nium potus generum. 1722. III. 222.
— Centuriae tertiae epistola itineraria LVI. 1752. V. XIII.[1]
— Centuriae tertiae epistola itineraria LVIII. 1752. V.
XIII.[1]
— Epistola itineraria LXXI. 1738. V. XXVI,[1] XXVI.[2]
— De rarioribus quibusdam fructibus. 1744. III. 219.[1]
— Relatio brevis . . . de Avellana mexicana. 1721. II.
539.[1]
— Specimen . . . exhibens arborem Limbowe-drewo. 1727.
IV. 464.[1]
— Specimen . . . exhibens fruticem Koszodrewina. 1727.
IV. 465.[1]
Brückmann, Urban Friedrich Benedict. Kurze Abhandlung
vom Sego. 1751. III. 327.[1]
— De nuce Been. 1750. III. 244.
Brückner. Wie kann man ganz astfreies Blochholz erziehen?
1867. IV. 171.
Brückner, (*Landsgerichterath*). Die Bejuka-Pflanze. 1839.
III. 685.[1]
Brückner, Adolphus Fridericus. Florae neobrandenburgensis
prodromus. 1803. I. 375.
Brückner, Arthur. De relationibus et analogia formam inter
et vires plantarum medicas. 1850. III. 259.[2]
Brückner, G. Entwurf einer Pflanzen-Geographie Mecklen-
burgs. 1841. I. 380.
Brüel, Friedrich. Über die beste Art, die Wälder anzupflanzen.
1786. IV. 105.
Brüel, E. P. L. Beretning om en Rejse, foretaget i forstviden-
skabeligt Øiemed. 1859. IV. 343.[1]
— Om Bestillingsmændene i Forstetaten. 1870. IV. 310.[1]
— Betragtninger over vort Skovbrugs Administration. 1900.
IV. 288.[2]
— Bidrag til det praktiske Skovbrug. 1900. IV. 113.[2]
— Om Græsning i Skove. 1858. IV. 135.[1]
— Nogle Bemærkninger om de skaanske Skoves . . . Tilstand.
1861. IV. 343.[1]
— Nogle Henstillinger angaaende Skov-Administrationens
Reform. 1896. IV. 288.[2]
— Skovbruget i Sverige. 1867. IV. 344.[1]
Brüel, G. W. Abhandlungen für Freunde der praktischen
Forstwissenschaft. 1802. IV. 242.
— Bidrag til den practiske Forstvidenskab. 1802. IV.
100.[2]
— Udtog af Bidrag til den praktiske Forstvidenskab. 1802.
IV. 100.[2]
Brüel, Ludwig Bang. Om Anwendelse af Naaletræer.. 1890.
III. 291.
Brügger, Christian Georg. Aufzählung neuer Pflanzen-
bastarde. 1882. I. 436.
— Beiträge zur Flora von Galizien, 1. 1860. I. 441.
— Beobachtungen über wildwachsende. 1880. I. 436.
— Beschreibungen neuer Zwischenformen. 1882. I. 436.
— Botanische Mittheilungen. 1882. I. 436.
— Flora churiensis. 1874. I. 436.
— Flora des Poschiavinothales. 1859. I. 435.
— Zur Flora Tirols. 1860. I. 441.
— Krüppelzapfen an der nordischen Fichte. 1873. II. 36.[1]
— Mittheilungen über neue Pflanzenbastarde der Schweizer-
Flora. 1882. I. 436.
— Mittheilungen über neue . . . Pflanzenformen. 1886. I.
437.
— Spicilegium florae Galiciae. 1860. I. 441.
— Wildwachsende Pflanzenbastarde in der Schweiz. 1880.
I. 436.
Bruehl, L. Sur les bois de teinture et leurs extraits. 1890.
III. 236.
Brühl, Paul & **King,** *Sir* George. A century of new and rare
Indian plants. 1896. I. 475.[2]
Bruel, J. Étude sur . . . la fécondation dans le genre For-
sythia. 1890. II. 706.[2]
Brüllow, Friedrich. Botanische Wandkarte. 1855. I. 256.
— Systematische Eintheilung des Pflanzenreichs. 1845. I.
255.
Brüning, Eduard. Über die Harzbalsame. 1900. II. 21,[2]
IV. 445.[2]
— *See also* TSCHIRCH, Alexander & BRÜNING, Eduard.
Brünings, Karl. Das Augustendorfer Moor. 1879. IV.
158.
— Der forstliche . . . Anbau der Hochmoore. 1881. IV.
158.
Brünn — Naturforschender Verein. See NATURFORSCHENDER
. . . I. 28.[1]
Brünner Lehrerverein. See CLUB FÜR NATURKUNDE . . . I.
27.
Brünnich, Martin Thrane. Bibliotheca . . . recensens Da-
niae, Norvegiae, Islandiae. 1783. I. 3.[1]
Bruggen, M., *Baron* van der. Commerce des bourgeons de
résineux. 1900. IV. 180.[2]
— Recrutement du personnel supérieur de l'Administration
des eaux et forêts. 1900. IV. 303.[2]
Brugmans, Sebald Justin. Elenchus plantarum quae in Horto
lugduno-batavo coluntur. 1818. I. 51.[1]
— Orationes duae . . . De accuratiori plantarum indige-
narum notitia. 1787. I. 390.
Brugnatelli, L. Farmacopea ad uso degli speziali. 1802.
III. 256.[1]
Brugsma, B. Een honderd tachtig onderzoekingen . . . van
de Mycorhiza bij de Koffiewortels. 1899. III. 737.
Bruguière, B. Histoire naturelle [de Siam.] 1845. III.
276.[2]
Bruguière, Louis. Le Prunier en France. 1895. III. 433.[1]
Bruhin, P. Thomas A. Aelteste Flora der Schweiz. 1865.
I. 435.
— Beiträge zur Flora Vorarlbergs. 1865. I. 435.
— Clavis ad Caspari Bauhini Pinacem. 1864. I. 78.[2]
— Ueber Farbenabänderungen bei Blüten. 1867. I. 236.[2]
— Flora einsidlensis. 1864. I. 435.
— Zur Flora Wisconsins. 1870. I. 314.
— Die Lawinennoth in der Schweiz. 1888. IV. 188.[2]
— Prodromus florae adventiciae boreali-americanae. 1886.
I. 308.
— Die Rosen New Coeln's. 187.? II. 283.[1]
— Sechsjährige Beobachtungen über die ersten Erscheinungen.
1876. I. 222.[1]
— Uebersicht der Geschichte . . . der Schweizer Floren.
1863. I. 81.[1]

— Vaccinium Novae-Coloniae Bruhin. 1874. II. 686.²
— Vergleichende Flora Wisconsins. 1877. I. 314.
Bruhm, Ernst Gotthelf. Ausführliche Anweisung zu einer
. . . Übersicht des Quadratinhalts jeder aufgegebenen
Fläche. 1816. IV. 263.
— Tabellarische Uebersicht zur Bestimmung des wahren
Werthes . . . des Nutzholzes. 1802. IV. 402.²
Bruhns, F. E. Baumriesen in Schleswig-Holstein. 1875.
I. 296.¹
Bruijning, F. F. De Wonderboom of Christus-palm. 1897.
III. 521.²
Bruinsma, A. E. J. Het boschwezen in Ned. Indië. 1894.
IV. 376.¹
— Een nieuwe methode van uitdunnen. 1897. III. 727.
— Onderzoekingen omtrent de aanwezige houtmassa en . . .
Djati bosschen van Java. 1898. IV. 537.²
— Onderzoekingen omtrent de aanwezige houtmassa en . . .
Djati bosschen van Java. 1899. IV. 537.³
— Open brief aan den heer Cordes. 1895. IV. 377.¹
Bruinsma, Abrahamus Fredericus Anastasius. De Diosma
crenata. 1838. III. 495.²
Bruinsma, H. J. Mededeelingen omtrent eenige bosch pro-
ducten. 1894. III. 275.²
Bruinsma, J. J. Flora frisica. 1840. I. 391.¹
— Iets over de Ceylonsche Koffijbladziekte. 1880. III. 735.
— Koningsnagelen. 1884. III. 635.²
Bruinsma, T. E. J. Opmerkingen naar aanleiding van de voor-
dracht van den heer A. H. Berkhout. 1900. III. 149.
Bruinsma, P. A. Een en ander omtrent Dr. Lotsy's kina on-
derzoekingen. 1900. III. 724.¹
Brukisch, C. Einige empfehlenswerte Bäume und Sträucher.
1900. III. 203.
Brullé, Raoul. Falsifications des huiles d'olive. 1888. III.
679.¹
— Nouveau procédé pour reconnaître la fraude dans les huiles
d'olive. 1890. III. 679.¹
— Nouvelle méthode pour la recherche des huiles d'olive.
1891. III. 679.¹
Bruman, Hendrik. Index plantarum circa Zuollam. 1662.
I. 390.
Brumhard, August. Beiträge zur . . . Schlagstellung im
Buchenhochwalde. 1843. IV. 494.
— Beitrag zur Revision der Lehre von den Durchforstungen.
1841. IV. 173.
— Ueber gemischte Bestände. 1841. IV. 137.¹
— Die Grundsätze der forstlichen Taxations-Lehre. 1835.
IV. 242, 254.
— Ueber die Kultur exotischer Holzarten in deutschen For-
sten. 1828. IV. 125.¹
— Versuch zur Beantwortung der Frage: Ob der Staat die
Holz verbrauchende Industrie . . . unterstützen soll? 1838.
IV. 268.
— Versuch zur Begründung einer zeitgemässen Forststrafge-
setzgebung. 1833. IV. 319.¹
Brummeler, G. W. ten. Getah-pertjah en caoutchouc. 1884.
III. 229.
Brun, Cornelis le. See BRUYN, Cornelis de.
Brunacci, Gaudenzo. De Cina-cina seu pulvere ad febres.
1661. III. 719.
Brunaud, Paul. Liste des plantes . . . à Saintes. 1878.
I. 415.
Brunchorst, Jörgen. Eiendommeligheder ved visse træers
ernæring. 1886. I. 233.²
— Ueber einige Wurzelanschwellungen. 1886. II. 115,²
607.¹
— Die Function der Spitze bei den Richtungsbewegungen der
Wurzeln. 1884. I. 195.²
— Ueber die Knöllchen an den Leguminosenwurzeln. 1885.
II. 321.²
— Maté og Catha. 1890. III. 531,¹ 531.²
— Ueber eine neue . . . Krankheit der Schwarzföhre. 1888.
IV. 466.¹
— Nogle norske skovsygdomme. 1893. IV. 478.
— Nogle sygdomme i de vestlandske träplantninger. 1891.
III. 179.
— Oversigt over de i Norge optrædende . . . plantesygdomme.
1888. III. 179.
— Planter og træer. 1889. I. 235.¹
— Podning- og okuleringsbastarder. 1882. I. 246.¹
— Die Structur der Inhaltskörper in den Zellen einiger Wurze-
lanschwellungen. 1887. I. 104.
— Undersögelse af sygdomme paa kulturplanter. 1888.
III. 179.
— De vigtigste plantesygdomme. 1887. III. 179.

Bruncken, Ernest. Bibliographical notes on Wisconsin forests.
1900. I. 317.¹
— Botanical notes from the Green Bay peninsula. 1900.
I. 317.¹
— On the forest conditions in the vicinity of Milwaukee.
1900. IV. 339.
— North American forests and forestry. 1900. IV. 46,¹
537.¹
— Notes on the distribution of some trees . . . in the vicinity
of Milwaukee. 1900. I. 313, IV. 77.¹
— Notes on the sylva of Milwaukee county. 1900. II. 122.²
— Some remarkable trees in the vicinity of Milwaukee. 1900.
I. 295.¹
Brunel. A memoir, descriptive of the Chinese trade. 1793.
III. 272.²
Brunel, Adolphe. Observations cliniques sur l'Eucalyptus
globulus. 1872. IV. 533,¹
Brunelli, Joannes. De Mannioca ad Ferdinandum Bassium
epistola. 1767. III. 521.¹
Bruner, D. F. Our native Hard Maple. 1895. III. 536.²
— Timber growing. 1894. IV. 112.
Bruner, Lawrence. Insects injurious to young trees. 1890.
III. 187.
— Report on Nebraska insects. 1889. III. 187.
Brunet, A. Ornementation des squares et promenades.
1900. III. 42.¹
Brunet, Louis Ovide, (abbé). On the Canadian species of the
genus Picea. 1866. II. 34.¹
— Catalogue des vegetaux ligneux du Canada. 1867. I.
309,¹ IV. 76.¹
— Histoire des Picea . . . du Canada. 1866. II. 34.¹
— Notice sur le Musée botanique de l'Université Laval.
1867. V. VIII.¹
Brunet, P. O. Catalogue of Canadian woods. 1857. IV.
397.
Brunet, Pierre Alexandre. La science arboricole pour tous.
1895. III. 110.²
Brunet, Raymond. Les incendies dans les Pins maritimes.
1894. IV. 183.¹
— Matières employées pour le liage de la Vigne: 1. L'Osier.
1899. III. 349.
— Le Pin maritime. 187.? IV. 468,¹ V. XXXII.¹
Brunetti, Silvestro. Dissertazione inaugurale sui fenomeni
fisiologici dei vegetabili. 1858. I. 147.
Brunfaut, Jules. La Vigne et le phillloxéra. 1875. III. 759.
Brunfels, Otto. Contrafeyt kreuterbuch. 1530. I. 276.
— In Dioscoridis historiam plantarum certissima adaptatio.
1543. I. 278.
— Herbarium tomis tribus exacto tandem studio. 1530. I.
276.
— Herbarum vivae eicones. 1530. I. 276, V. XIV.²
— Kreuterbuch contrafeyt. 1530. I. 276.
— Novi herbarii tomus II. 1530. I. 276.
— Onomastikon medicinae. 1534. I. 277.
— Tomus herbarii III. 1530. I. 276.
Bruni, Achille. Descrizione botanica delle campagne di Bar-
letta. 1857. I. 427.
Brtini, Gerolamo. Dissertazione sulla potatura de' Gelsi.
1784. III. 373.
Bruning, F. H. Red Cedars. 1887. III. 304.¹
Brunk, T. L. Best varieties of fruits for . . . Texas. 1890.
III. 61.¹
— List of forest and shade trees. 1890. III. 60.
Brunn, Johann Wilhelm. De vasis plantarum. 1800. I.
133.
Brunnemann & Wullstein. Ertrags-Angabe . . . im Peister-
witzer Oderwalde. 1858. IV. 260.¹
Brunner, A. Erfahrungen bei der Anzucht von Kaffeepflan-
zen. 1898. III. 733.¹
Brunner, Charles, (jr.). Sur les bourgeons . . . du Tilleul.
1847. II. 516.¹
— Observations sur l'inflorescence du Tilleul. 1846. II.
516.¹
Brunner, Friedrich & Rehmann. Gäa und Flora der Quellen-
bezirke der Donau. 1851. I. 383, 454.
Brunner, Heinrich. See BRANDENBURG, Rudolf & BRUNNER,
Heinrich.
Brunner, Samuel. Ausflug über Constantinopel nach
Taurien. 1833. I. 478.
— Bericht über die in der Engepromenade bei Bern befindliche
Sammlung von Bäumen. 1828. I. 65.¹
— Betrachtungen über die . . . Cordofanischen Pflanzen.
1843. I. 487.

130 INDEX OF AUTHORS AND TITLES

Brunner, Samuel (continued).
— Botanische Ergebnisse einer Reise nach Senegambien. 1840. I. 490.
— Ueber die Folliculi Pistaciae. 1836. II. 457.²
— Die Gärten von Genua und Neapel. 1842. II. 45.²
— Reise nach Senegambien. 1840. I. 490.
— Streifzug durch das östliche Ligurien. 1828. I. 451.
Brunnhoff, Giovanni de Brignoli di. See Brignoli di Brunnhoff, Giovanni de.
Bruno-Gambini, F. De l'alimentation des végétaux. 1885. I. 159.
Brunotte, Camille Marie Gabriel. Des fruits utiles de Pipéritées. 1889. III. 342.¹
Brunschwig, Hieronymus. The vertuose boke of distyllacyon. 1527. III. 239, V. xxviii.¹
Brunton, John. A catalogue of plants. 1777. I. 52.
Brunton, Thomas Lauder. Handbuch der allgemeinen Pharmakologie. 1885. III. 244.
— A text-book of pharmacology. 1885. III. 244.
— Traité de pharmacologie. 1885. III. 244.
— & Pye, Walter. On the physiological action . . . of Erythrophleum. 1877. III. 476.¹
Brunyer, Abel. Hortus regius blesensis. 1653. I. 56.
Brusati. Catalogus plantarum Horti . . . ticinensis. 1793. I. 61.
Brusse, P. Nog eenige beschouwingen over de Kinacultuur. 1895. III. 717.¹
Brutelette, Blondin de. See Vicq, L. B. E. de & Brutelette, Blondin de.
Brutelle, Charles Louis L'Héritier de. See L'Héritier de Brutelle, C. L.
Bruun, Alfred. Iagttagelser over Løvspring. 1890. I. 223.²
Bruun, J. Efterretning om Trælast-Handelen i Drammen. 1784. IV. 404.¹
Bruxelles—Académie royale des sciences et belles-lettres. See Académie royale des sciences . . . de Belgique. I. 16.
Bruxelles — Congrès de botanique et d'horticulture de 1880. See Congrès . . . I. 16.
Bruxelles — Congrès international d'horticulture. See Congrès . . . III. 15.
Bruxelles — Société royale Linnenne. See Société . . . I. 17.
Bruxelles — Société scientifique. See Société . . . I. 17.
Bruxius, Adam. Balsambüchslein. 1616. III. 244.
Bruylants, Gustave. Recherches sur les résines. 1876. I. 181.¹
Bruyn, Cornelis de. Reizen over Moskovie, door Persie. 1714. III. 272.²
— Travels into Muscovy, Persia. 1714. III. 272.²
— Voyages par la Moscovie, en Perse. 1714. III. 272.²
Bruyn, H. de. Over den tegenwoordigen toestand van den landbouw op Java. 1869. III. 128.
Bruyn, Léon de. Administration des eaux et forêts. 1894. IV. 540.¹
— Discours . . . à l'occasion de l'installation du Conseil supérieur des forêts. 1894. IV. 551.²
— Pâturage. 1894. IV. 555.¹
— Reconstitution du domaine forestier de l'état. 1897. IV. 551.²
— See also Parville, H. de & Bruyn, Léon de.
Bruyn Kops, G. F. de. Lijst van boomen en planten . . . in de residentie Riouw. 1854. I. 467.
— Mededeeling over Laban-Dawon-Lebas. 1862. III. 274.²
— Statistiek van den handel en de scheepvaart. 1869. IV. 407.¹
Bruyning, F. F. Het schaalgehalte van cacao-zaden. 1899. III. 595.¹
— De scheikundige samenstelling der Theebladeren. 1892. III. 608.¹
Bruzeau, Levacher-. See Levacher-Bruzeau.
Bry, Johann Theodor de. Anthologia magna. 1611. ˙I. 284.
— Anthologia Meriana. 1611. I. 284.
— Florilegium novum. 1611. I. 284.
— Florilegium renovatum et auctum. 1611. I. 284.
Bryant, Arthur. The Ash. 1882. IV. 534.²
— Forest trees for shelter. 1871. III. 99, IV. 111.²
Bryant, Charles. A dictionary of the ornamental trees. 1790. I. 263.
— Flora diætetica. 1783. III. 219.¹
— Verzeichniss der zur Nahrung dienenden . . . Pflanzen. 1783. III. 219.¹
Bryant, F. B. The Boxwood forests of Kumaun. 1885. IV. 525.¹
— Wood for beer barrels. 1896. IV. 522.¹
Bryce, J. Annan. Teak; its production. 1884. IV. 537.²

Brykczyński, Josef, Ritter von. Auftreten und Frass des Tannentriebwicklers. 1896. IV. 445.
— O lesie i drzewach przypolnych. 1899. I.˙438,² IV. 87.¹
The Brynderwen Oak. 1899. II. 139.²
Bryophylle Silvestre, (pseud.). Rapport sur un insecte qui attaque les Poiriers. 1873. III. 446.¹
Brzeziński, Józef. Drzewa karłowe bez cięcia. 1898. III. 176.¹
— Kultura ogrodowa w Zaleszczykach. 1898. III. 147.¹
Brzeziński, Kazimierz. Hodowla lasów. 1884. IV. 104.¹
Bschaidner, Joh. Eine bemerkenswerthe Abart der Weissbuche. 1897. IV. 492.¹
Buazé fibre. 1889. III. 514.¹
Bubák, František. Caeoma Fumariae Link. 1899. IV. 486.²
— Flora bohemica, moravica. 1893. I. 443.
— Lejnice nádherná. 1895. II..538.²
Bubani, Pietro. Dunajia. 1888. I. 421.
— Flora Pyrenaea. 1897. I. 423.
— Flora Virgiliana. 1870. I. 514,² V. xxv.¹
— Illustrazioni ulteriori. 1870. V. xxv.²
Buberl, A. Ueber die Bildung von Tochterstämmen. 1885. IV. 66.¹
Buberl, Michael. Bemerkungen zu Aufstellung des Wirthschaftsplanes. 1895. IV. 246.
— Zur bosnisch-herzegowinischen Karstfrage. 1896. IV. 167.²
— Drahtseilförderungen im forstlichen Betriebe. 1884. IV. 391.
— Ueber Ertragstafel-Schätzung. 1897. IV. 259.¹
— Eine neue Sonnendarre. 1881. IV. 148.
— Aus der Praxis der Forstbetriebs-Einrichtung. 1896. IV. 246.
— Die Tachymetrie im Walde. 1883. IV. 265.
Bubner. Ein neues Mittel gegen das Schälen. 1900. IV. 197.¹
Bucci, Gabriel. Discorso della generazione delle piante. 1697. I. 191.¹
Bucco, Giovanni. Di alcune piante adattate per rimboschimenti. 1879. IV. 165.
— Effetti del freddo a Genova. . 1880. III. 49.²
— Fecondazione artificiale . . . della Cycas circinalis. 1870. II. 4.²
Buch. Beretning om Lolland-Falsters Forstmandsforenings Udflugt til Rostocker Heide. 1889. IV. 354.
Buch, Christian Leopold, Freiherr von. Allgemeine Uebersicht der Flora auf den Canarischen Inseln. 1819. I. 497.
— Über Blattnerven und die Gesetze ihrer Vertheilung. 1852. I. 109.²
— Catalogue des plantes . . . trouvées dans les îles Canaries. 1819. I. 497.
— Coup-d'œil sur la flore des îles Canaries. 1819. I. 497.
— Description physique des îles Canaries. 1825. I. 497.
— Les nervures des feuilles et leur distribution. 1852. I. 109.²
— On the nervures of leaves and their distribution. 1852. I. 109.²
— Observations made during a visit to Madeira. 1826. I. 497.
— Physicalische Beschreibung der Canarischen Inseln. 1825. I. 497.
— Reise durch Norwegen und Lappland. 1810. I. 352.
— Resa genom Lappmarken och Sverige. 1810. I. 352.
— On the subtropical zone. 1830. I. 219.²
— Voyage en Norvège et en Laponie. 1810. I. 352.
Buch, Otto. Ueber Sklerenchymzellen. 1870. I. 134.²
Buchan, Alexander. Report on the meteorological observations made at Carnwath. 1875. IV. 47.¹
Buchan, William. Note on the cultivation of the Cinnamon in England. 1842. III. 405.²
Buchanan, D. Coffee-growing in Queensland. 1897. III. 733.¹
— Coffee-growing in the Mackay district. 1897. III. 733.¹
Buchanan, David D. Hedges. 1865. III. 213.
Buchanan, E. M. The Andamans. 1892. IV. 378.
— Forest tramways in the Andamans. 1900. IV. 392.
— The forests of the Upper Burma ruby mines. 1891. I. 475,² IV. 89.¹
Buchanan, (afterwards Hamilton), Francis. See Hamilton, Francis.
Buchanan, George. Report on the present state of the wooden bridge at Montrose. 1873. IV. 424.²
Buchanan, John. Additions to the flora of New Zealand. 1883. II. 567,² 650.²
— On the Alpine flora of New Zealand. 1882. I. 507.
— Botanical notes. 1884. II. 176.¹
— Botanical notes. 1888. II. 408.¹
— On the botany of Kawau Island. 1877. I. 507.

— Campbell Island and its flora. 1884. I. 507.
— On charring timber as a protection from teredo. 1877. IV. 420.
— On Cyttaria purdiei Buch. 1886. IV. 500.²
— On the durability of Matai timber. 1877. IV. 440.¹
— On the flowering plants . . . of Chatham Islands. 1875. I. 507.
— List of plants found on Miramar Peninsula. 1873. I. 507.
— Notes on new species of plants. 1884. I. 507.
— Notes on the flora of . . . Wellington. 1874. I. 507.
— Notice of a new species of Senecio. 1873. II. 865.²
— Résistance à la décomposition de bois de la Nouvelle Zélande. 1877. IV. 440.¹
— Revised descriptions of two . . . New Zealand Panax. 1877. II. 651,¹ 652.¹
— Sketch of the botany of Otago. 1869. I. 506.²
— On some new native plants. 1887. I. 507.
— On some new species of New Zealand plants. 1870. III. 858,² 865.²
— On some new species . . . of New Zealand plants. 1871. I. 507.
— On some plants new to New Zealand. 1882. II. 853.²
— & Kirk, Thomas. List of plants found in . . . Auckland. 1870. I. 507.
Buchanan, Robert. The culture of the Grape. 1852. III. 550.
— A a on the cultivation of the Grape. 1850. III. 549. re tise
Buche, Fr. Anleitung zur Pfirsichzucht. 1891. III. 441.¹
— Der praktische Zwergobstbau. 1897. III. 139.
Buchenau, Franz. Abnorme Blattbildungen. 1891. I. 145.¹
— Eine ältere Beobachtung aus dem Gebiete der Bildungsabweichungen. 1884. II. 289.²
— Ueber den Aufbau des Palmiet-Schilfes. 1893. II. 77.¹
— Ausserordentlicher Fall von vorschreitender Metamorphose bei einer Gartenrose. 1880. II. 289.²
— Beachtenswerthe Blitzschläge in Bäume. 1886. IV. 194.
— Bemerkungen über die Flora von Fürstenau. 1872. I. 386.
— Bemerkungen über Sorbus hybrida. 1856. II. 313.¹
— Bildungsabweichung einer Hülse von Gleditschia. 1888. II. 361.²
— Blitzschlag in eine canadische Pappel. 1879. IV. 194.
— Ueber Blüthenentwickelung bei den Compositen. 1872. II. 850.¹
— Der Blüthenstand von Empetrum. 1862. II. 454.¹
— Die botanischen Produkte der Londoner internationalen Industrie-Austellung. 1863. III. 28.¹
— Die Calabar-Bohne. 1863. II. 376.²
— Ueber Carpinus Betulus forma quercifolia. 1878. II. 120.²
— Eine aus Citrone und Apfelsine gemischte Frucht. 1873. II. 401.²
— Doppelspreitige Laubblätter. 1888. I. 144.²
— Die düngende Wirkung des . . . Wassers. 1883. I. 218.
— Ueber Einheitlichkeit der botanischen Kunstausdrücke. 1893. I. 254.²
— Einige Beobachtungen aus . . . der Pflanzen-Teratologie. 1862. II. 741.²
— Einige Blüthenabnormitäten. Weigela rosea. 1857. II. 834.³
— Empetrum nigrum . . . auf Steingräbern. 1872. II. 454.¹
— Erica T a L. mit getrennten Kronblättern. 1888. II. 669.² etr² Ix
— Fälle von Mischfrüchten. 1877. II. 267.¹
— Ueber einen Fall der Entstehung der eichenblätterigen Form der Hainbuche. 1891. II. 120.²
— Flora der nordwestdeutschen Tiefebene. 1894. V. xx.¹
— Flora der Ostfriesischen Inseln. 1881. I. 532.².
— Flora von Bremen. 1877. I. 387.
— Füllung des Kelches bei einer Rose. 1886. II. 289.²
— Eine grüne Rose von 6 mm Grösse. 1897. II. 290.¹
— Der Hülsenbestand beim Dorfe Buchholz. 1887. II. 463.²
— Ueber eine interessante Füllungserscheinung bei Lagaperia. 1868. II. 84.¹
— Interessantere Bildungsabweichungen. 1871. II. 150,³ 279,⁴ 676,² 714.³
— Juncaceae. 1888. II. 77.¹
— Mächtiger Stamm von Salix Capraea. 1877. II. 105.³
— Merkwürdig veränderte Blüte einer . . . Fuchsia. 1880. II. 643.²
— Mittheilungen über die Flora von Rehburg. 1876. I. 387.
— Mittheilungen über einen interessanten Blitzschlag. 1867. IV. 194.
— Monographia Juncacearum. 1890. II. 77.¹

— Monstrositäten bei Birnen und Feigen. 1871. II. 150,² 279.²
— Zur Morphologie von Hedera Helix. 1864. II. 649.¹
— Morphologische Bemerkungen über einige Acerineen. 1861. II. 477.¹
— Nachträge und Berichtigungen zur Flora bremensis. 1866. I. 385.
— Ueber die Nervatur der Bracteen bei den Linden. 1872. II. 516.¹
— Die Pflanzenwelt der ostfriesischen Inseln. 1889. I. 389.
— Reliquiae Rutenbergianae. 1880. I. 496.
— Der Rost des Getreides und die Mahonien. 1884. III. 395.¹
— Las " semillas brincadoras." 1891. III. 522.³
— Seriales Dedoublement in Papilionaceen-Blüten. 1884. II. 382.²
— Die " springenden Bohnen " aus Mexiko. 1891. III. 522.²
— Die springenden Samen aus Mexiko. 1873. III. 522.¹
— Die Sprossverhältnisse von Ulex. 1860. II. 387.²
— Starke Drehung der Holzfaser an . . . Sambucus nigra. 1874. II. 841.¹
— Tma. 1861. III. 706.²
— Ueberzähliger Organkreis bei Syringa. 1871. II. 714.²
— Die Ulmen im Bremer Walde bei Axstedt. 1899. II. 144.²
— Eine Verbänderung des Stengels bei Jasione. 1892. I. 144.²
— Weitere Beobachtungen an monströsen Birnen. 1873. II. 279.³
— Weitgehende Spaltung der Blätter eines Rhododendron. 1871. II. 676.²
— Zwei interessante Beobachtungen an Topf-Pelargonien. 1899. II. 390.¹
— & Focke, W. O. Gefässpflanzen [von Ostgrönland]. 1874. I. 309.¹
Buchenblock, Leontzi Ursprung von. Abgekürzter . . . Auszug . . . J. G. Beckmanns fürtrefflicher Beschreibung der Holzsaat. 1760. IV. 110.¹
Buchene Waldriesen. 1900. IV. 500.²
Die Buchenholzfrage. 1884. IV. 499.
Der Buchenwald und seine Rentabilität. 1892. IV. 498.
Buchetet, Christian Traugott. Florae dresdensis nomenclator. 1806. I. 75.
Buchetet, Theodoor. Brieven over Frankrijks tuinbouw. 1872. III. 125.
— Les grands arbres dans les villes. 1877. III. 209.
— Lettres sur l'horticulture française. 1872. III. 125.
Buchhave, Rudolph. Afhandling om Caffe. 1790. III. 741.²
— Grunden til Plantelaeren. 1768. I. 83.
Buchheim, Rudolf. Lehrbuch der Arzneimittellehre. 1859. III. 258.
Buchholtz. Das Eichhorn als Waldverderber. 1857. IV. 197.²
Buchholz, (Revierförster). Enthalten die Zapfen von sogenannten Kiefermkusseln tauglichen Samen? 1888. IV. 473.
— Welche Holzarten eignen sich zu Alleebäumen. 1890. IV. 137.¹
Buchinger, J. Sericographis Mohitli. 1867. III. 709.²
Buchmayer, Augustin. Die Correspondenz und Buchhaltung. 1878. IV. 311.²
— Der Forstschutz. 1878. IV. 177.¹
— Zur Stammeichbirung nach Hossfeld's Formel. 1878. IV. 217.²
— & Lischka, Carl. Forst-Schematismus für Mähren und Schlesien. 1874. IV. 369.
Buchner. See also Büchner.
Buchner. Cacao en theobromine. 1844. III. 594.
Buchner, A. Ueber das Anacahuite-Holz. 1861. III. 695.¹
— Sur le bois d'Anacahuite. 1861. III. 695.¹
Buchner, A. W. Verhandeling over de looistoffen. 1831. III. 237.¹
Buchner, Johann Andreas. Chemische Beobachtungen über die grüne Wallnussschale. 1843. II. 114.¹
— Chemische Notiz über die Säfte einiger Cacteen. 1836. III. 620.¹
— Ueber die von Dr. Winckler entdeckte Identität des Bitterstoffs . . . von Esenbeckia mit dem Chinovabitter. 1843. III. 620.¹
— Theorie der . . . Versuche über die Wirkung der Kohle. 1840. I. 208.²
— Toxicologie. 1827. III. 260.²
— Toxicologie. 1827. III. 260.¹
— & Herberger, J. E. Examen de la racine de Berberis. 1831. III. 395.¹

Buchner, Ludwig Andreas. Ueber das ätherische Oel . . . von Abies Reginae Amaliae. 1864. II. 24.²
— Ueber das ätherische Oel von Pinus Pumilio. 1860. IV. 465.¹
— Sur l'arôme de quelques fleurs. 1837. I. 182,² II. 242.¹
— Beiträge zur Geschichte des Berberins. 1864. III. 394.²
— Commentar zur Pharmacopoea germanica. 1872. III. 249.
— Sur l'huile essentielle de Pinus Pumilio. 1860. IV. 465.¹
— Sur l'huile essentielle des fruits d'Abies Reginae Amaliae. 1864. II. 24.¹
— Über einen neuen gelben Farbstoff. 1853. III. 543.¹
— Ueber einen neuen rothen Farbstoff aus der Faulbaumrinde. 1865. III. 543.¹
— Sur un nouveau pigment rouge extrait du Nerprun. 1865. III. 543.¹
— Sur une nouvelle matière colorante jaune. 1853. III. 543.¹
— Ueber den Porst-Kampfer. 1856. III. 653.¹
Buchnerus, Johannes Godofredus. See BÜCHNER, J. G.
Bucholtz, Guil. Heur. Schast. De cortice Hippocastani. 1770. III. 537.²
Buc'hoz, J. P. See BUC'HOZ, Pierre Joseph.
Buc'hoz, Pierre Joseph. Catalogue latin et français de tous les arbres. 1787. I. 263.
— Catalogue latin et françois des arbres et arbustes. 1785. I. 531.¹
— Catalogue latin et françois des arbres et plantes. 1787. I. 263.
— Catalogue latin et françois des plantes vivaces. 1786. III. 86.
— Collection précieuse . . . des fleurs les plus belles. 1776. III. 86.
— Collection précieuse, économique, coloriée. 1772. III. 51.
— Dictionnaire raisonné universel des plantes . . . de la France. 1770. I. 405.
— Dissertation sur l'Abricotier. 1787. III. 435.¹
— Dissertation sur l'Acacia de Constantinople. 1789. II. 331.¹
— Dissertation sur l'anis étoilé. 1788. III. 397.²
— Dissertation sur l'Arbre au pain. 1788. III. 367.¹
— Dissertation sur l'Ipo. 1787. III. 366.¹
— Dissertation sur la Barrington. 1787. II. 611.¹
— Dissertation sur la Brucée. 1788. II. 414.¹
— Dissertation sur la Douce-amère. 1789. III. 701.²
— Dissertation sur la Lagerstroem. 1787. II. 609.²
— Dissertation sur la Vigne. 1789. III. 582.
— Dissertation sur le Cacao. 1787. III. 594.
— Dissertation sur le cachou. 1787. III. 464.¹
— Dissertation sur le Café. 1787. III. 738.
— Dissertation sur le caoutchouc. 1787. III. 518.²
— Dissertation sur le Cèdre du Liban. 1788. III. 27.²
— Dissertation sur le Dillen de l'Inde. 1788. III. 595.²
— Dissertation sur le Durion. 1788. II. 530.¹
— Dissertation sur le Gustave-Auguste. 1787. II. 612.¹
— Dissertation sur le Laurier-Rose. 1804. III. 689.²
— Dissertation sur le Mangostan. 1788. III. 609.¹
— Dissertation . . . sur le Mélèze. 1806. III. 304.²
— Dissertation sur le Myrte. 1804. III. 637.¹
— Dissertation sur le Niota. 1788. II. 736.²
— Dissertation sur le Noisettier de S. Domingue. 1787. II. 448.¹
— Dissertation sur le pain des Hottentots. 1789. III. 286.¹
— Dissertation sur le Pêcher et l'Amandier. 1787. III. 431.²
— Dissertation sur le Putiet. 1787. III. 431.¹
— Dissertation sur le Quassi. 1787. III. 508.²
— Dissertation sur le Quinquina. 1787. III. 720.
— Dissertation sur le Rocoulier. 1788. II. 565.¹
— Dissertation sur le Romarin. 1804. II. 66.¹
— Dissertation sur le Thé. 1787. III. 606.
— Dissertation sur les Roses. 1787. III. 453.²
— Dissertation sur un nouveau genre . . . de Besenval. 1789. II. 869.¹
— Dissertation sur une espèce de Sophore. 1789. III. 384.²
— Dissertation sur une nouvelle espèce d'Aristoloche. 1789. II. 183.¹
— Dissertations sur le Cèdre du Liban. 1805. II. 27,² III. 413,¹ 473.²
— Dissertations sur les Sorbiers et les Viournes. 1804. II. 848,¹ III. 83,² 459,¹ 758.²
— Les dons merveilleux. 1779. I. 262.
— Flore économique des plantes . . . de Paris. 1799. III. 85.
— Le grand jardin de l'univers. 1785. I. 263.
— Sur l'Halésia. 1806. III. 670.²
— Herbier colorié de l'Amérique. 1783. I. 328.

— Herbier colorié du Japon. 1792. I. 461.
— Herbier ou collection des plantes médicinales de la Chine. 1781. III. 91.¹
— Histoire des insectes nuisibles. 1781. III. 188.²
— Histoire naturelle du Thé de la Chine. 1806. III. 606.
— Histoire universelle du règne végétal. 1773. I. 258.
— Le jardin d'Éden. 1783. I. 263.
— Le jardin du roi. 1792. I. 264.
— Laboratoire de flore. 1773. III. 218.²
— Le Laurier et l'Olivier réunis. 1802. III. 406,² 678.²
— Lettre sur l'Arbre de vie. 1806. III. 311.¹
— Lettre sur le Cyprès. 1806. III. 302.²
— Manuel alimentaire des plantes. 1771. III. 51.
— Manuel cosmétique et odoriférant des plantes. 179 . ? III. 51.
— Manuel de médecine pratique. 1771. III. 241.
— Manuel économique des plantes. 1800. III. 51.
— Manuel floréal des plantes. 1800. III. 86.
— Manuel médical et usuel des plantes. 1769. III. 241.
— Manuel tinctorial des plantes. 1800. III. 236.
— Manuel usuel et économique des plantes. 1782. III. 51.
— Manuel vétérinaire des plantes. 1799. III. 55.
— Mémoire sur l'Arbre de neige. 1804. III. 671.²
— Mémoire sur l'Azedarach. 1804. III. 512.²
— Mémoire sur l'Hortensia. 1803. III. 411.²
— Mémoire sur l'Hortensia. 1804. II. 240.²
— Mémoire sur la Melaleuque . . . sur l'Ixora. 1805. III. 83.²
— Mémoire sur le Lilas. 1804. III. 680.¹
— Mémoires sur l'Hortensia et le Cestrau. 1804. III. 83.²
— Méthode de Maupin sur la manière de cultiver la Vigne. 1798. III. 554.²
— Monographie de la Rose. 1804. III. 281,² III. 447.²
— Notice sur la Stramoine en arbre. 1804. II. 771.¹
— Notice sur le Catalpa commun. 1804. III. 706.¹
— Notice sur le Diosma. 1804. III. 504.¹
— Notice sur le Ginkgo ou Noyer du Japon. 1806. III. 286.¹
— Notice sur le Grenadier. 1804. III. 630.¹
— Notice sur le Grewier. 1804. III. 584.¹
— Notice sur le Syringa. 1804. III. 413.¹
— Nouveau traité physique et économique. 1787. I. 263, III. 51.
— Observations aux amateurs et aux jardiniers-fleuristes. 1804. III. 83.²
— Plantes nouvellement découvertes. 1779. I. 262.
— Première [et seconde] centurie des planches enluminées. 1775. I. 262.
— Présens de flore à la nation françoise. 1780. III. 85.
— Quatrième discours . . . De la génération des plantes. 1760. I. 199.
— Réflexions sur le genre du Robinier. 1804. II. 382.¹ III. 486.¹
— The toilet of flora. 1771. III. 218.²
— Toilette de flore. 1771. III. 218.²
— Tournefortius Lotharingiae. 1764. I. 405.
— Traité de la culture des arbres. 1786. IV. 109.¹
— Traité de toutes les plantes . . . 1800. III. 86.
— Traité historique des plantes . . . dans la Lorraine. 1762. I. 405.
— Traité usuel du chocolat. 1812. III. 592.¹
Buchu folia. 1897. III. 495.²
Le Buchu, ses propriétés. 1879. III. 495.²
Buchwald, A. E. Über die Züchtung des Eichen-Seiden-Spinners. 1889. IV. 502.¹
Buchwald, Balthasar Johannes. Analysis Visci. 1753. III. 385.²
Buchwald, Johann von. Specimen medico-practico-botanicum. 1720. III. 165.
Buchwald, Johannes von. Ueber Pfropfversuche mit Monokotyledonen. 1900. III. 165.
— Umwandlung eines Dalbergia-Haines. 1900. IV. 74.²
— Die Verbreitungsmittel der Leguminosen des tropischen Afrika. 1895. II. 322.¹
— Westusambara. 1897. I. 493.
Buchwald, Stefan von. Der Karst und die Karst-Aufforstung. 1893. IV. 167.²
Buck, E. C. A paper on twenty trees of the Simla neighbourhood. 1885. I. 470,² IV. 88.²
— Shrub for slope. 1888. III. 458.²
— The Spanish Chestnut. 1898. III. 359.²
Buckhout, William A. Another economical Maple. 1891. I. 188.
— The failure to cut trees at maturity. 1900. IV. 196.¹
— Forest fires. 1893. IV. 182.¹

— The need of a forest policy in Pennsylvania. 1890. IV. 178.²
— Pinus pungens. 1887. III. 308.²
— Shade trees for street planting. 1900. III. 208.²
— Suggestions for restoring wasted forests. 1890. IV. 161.¹
— The time and the rate of formation of the annual ring. 1900. II. 33,¹ 46,¹ IV. 65.¹
Buckley, S. P. Notes on indigenous trees and shrubs. 1847. III. 202.¹
Buckley, Samuel Botsford. The Black Walnut. 1871. II. 113.¹
— Description of new plants from Texas. 1862. I. 323.
— Description of several new species. 1861. I. 319.
— The Grapes of North America. 1862. II. 505.¹
— Large trees. 1859. II. 211,¹ 255.¹
— Note on the Bartram Oak. 1862. II. 134.¹
— Notes on some of the American Ash trees. 1863. II. 707.¹
— Notice of some large trees in western New York. 1852. I. 295.²
— The nut bearing trees of the South. 1870. III. 264.¹
— The Pecan. 1883. IV. 488.¹
— Quercus Durandii Buckley. 1882. II. 133.²
— Quercus Durandii var. 1883. II. 133.²
— Quercus rubra L. var. texana. 1882. II. 140.²
— Remarks on Dr. Asa Gray's notes on Buckley's new plants of Texas. 1870. I. 323.
— Rhus cotinoides Nutt. 1882. II. 455.²
— Some new Texas plants. 1883. I. 320.
— Ulmus crassifolia Nutt. — Cedar-Elm. 1883. IV. 518.²
Buckley, W. Epiphyllum truncatum and its varieties. 1868. III. 623.¹
— Hybrid truncate Cactuses. 1852. III. 626.¹
— Treatment of the Javanese Rhododendron. 1852. III. 656.
Buckman, James. A botanical guide to the environs of Cheltenham. 1844. I. 399.
— The British Oak. 1863. II. 138.¹
— The geology, archaeology, botany . . . of Cheltenham. 1842. I. 533.
— Our triangle. 1842. I. 533.
— Pyrus domestica. 1874. II. 312.²
— Report . . . botanic garden . . . Royal agricultural college, Cirencester. 1858. I. 55.
— The Wild Service tree. 1870. II. 312.²
Bucknall, Tho. Skip Dyot. The orchardist. 1797. III. 141.
Buckton, George Bowdler. Phylloxera of the Oak. 1887. IV. 511.
Bucquet, Jean Baptiste. Introduction à l'étude des corps naturels. 1773. I. 83.
Buczyński, Stanislaw. Kilka słów do pilnych gospodarzy o pielęgnowaniu i rozmnażaniu drzew owocowych. 1858. III. 134.³
Budd, J. L. Cherry culture. 1874. III. 432.¹
— Cross-fertilization of trees and shrubs. 1893. III. 50.²
— Cut leaved Birch. 1889. III. 357.¹
— Drought-enduring trees. 1890. III. 42.¹
— Early blooming trees and shrubs. 1890. III. 207.³
— Elaeagnus angustifolia. 1889. III. 628.³
— Experiments with new trees and shrubs. 1892. III. 118.¹
— Experiments with . . . north of Europe fruits. 1883. III. 118.¹
— A few desirable ornamental trees and shrubs. 1892. III. 60.
— The future of our native Plums. 1895. III. 433.¹
— Growing forest trees from cuttings. 1869. IV. 546.¹
— Have we two species of native Plums? 1881. III. 433.¹
— History of cross-fertilization. 1893. III. 51.
— Important facts on Russian shrubs and trees. 1889. III. 60.
— Influence of stock on scion. 1880. III. 39.
— Not well known trees and shrubs. 1882. III. 118.¹
— Notes on Ribes and Lonicera. 1888. III. 414, 751.¹
— Orcharding on the open prairies of northern Iowa. 1868. III. 133.
— Ornamentation of home grounds. 1889. III. 203.
— Our native nuts. 1895. III. 134.¹
— Plant breeding. 1880. III. 50.²
— Plants for a trying climate. 1889. III. 42.¹
— Populus alba Bolleana. 1885. III. 345.²
— Populus certinensis. 1890. III. 345.²
— The relation of blossoms to fruit. 1894. III. 174.²
— Report on the Cherry. 1892. III. 432.¹
— Rose hybrids. 1894. III. 451.¹

— Shrubs for the lawn and park. 1899. III. 61.¹
— Shrubs which endure drought. 1890. III. 42.¹
— Some trees and shrubs which deserve special attention. 1892. III. 118.¹
— Stone fruits and their propagation. 1891. III. 430.¹
— The stone fruits in 1893. 1894. III. 430.²
— Trees and shrubs for a trying climate. 1888. III. 42.¹
— Trees & shrubs [from Russia] in flower. 1889. III. 60.
— Trees on prairie farms. 1883. IV. 112.
— Two fine Poplar trees. 1889. III. 344.³
— What do we mean by a hardy tree or plant? 1879. III. 182.
Budd, Thomas. Good order established in Pennsylvania. 1685. III. 262.²
Buddeus, (Medizinal-Rath Dr.). Bemerkungen zu dem Aufsatze [von Metzger]. 1832. III. 136.
— Beobachtungen über die Einwirkungen des Frosts. 1832. III. 182.
Budding. 1841. III. 164.¹
Budding Oranges. 1893. III. 500.¹⁻
Buddingh, S. A. Neerlands Oost Indie. 1859. III. 274.¹
— Theecultuur in Ledok. 1839. III. 601.²
Budesteanu. Les forêts de la Roumanie. 1895. IV. 556.²
Le budget de l'Administration des eaux et forêts. 1895. IV. 552.²
Le budget de l'administration des eaux et forêts. 1897. IV. 552.²
Le budget de l'Administration des eaux et forêts. 1899. IV. 291.²
Le budget de l'Administration des eaux et forêts . . . Discussion à la Chambre. 1895. IV. 552.²
Le budget de l'administration des forêts. 1879. IV. 276.¹
Le budget des eaux et forêts. 1894. IV. 552.²
Le budget des eaux et forêts au Sénat. 1894. IV. 552.²
The budget estimate of the Forest department. 1879. IV. 262.
Buds out of place. 1885. II. 258.²
Budstikken. I. 8.²
Büchner. See also BUCHNER.
Büchner, Johann Andreas Elia. De gummi-resinis kikekunemalo. 1764. III. 244.
— De nuce Juglande. 1743. III. 356.¹
— De Pareira brava. 1744. III. 396.²
— De Pinastro sive Pino sylvestri. 1754. IV. 482.³
— De usu corticis peruviani. 1762. III. 719.
— De usu corticis peruviano chirurgico. 1766. III. 720.
— De virtute corticis peruviani antiphlogistica. 1763. III. 720.
Büchner, Johann Gottfried. De arbore quadam in Voigtlandia. 1737. I. 224.²
— De arbore quadam quavis aestate binis vicibus. 1737. II. 280.¹
— De floribus insueto anni tempore. 1737. I. 224.²
— De germinatione in germine. 1740. I. 234.¹
— De memorabilibus Voigtlandiae. 1741. I. 296.¹
Büchner, Johann Zacharias. De praecipuis usus corticis peruviani contraindicantibus. 1778. III. 720.
Büchner, Phil. Sur la gomme-gutte. 1843. III. 609.¹
— Ueber Gummi-Gutt. 1843. III. 609.¹
Büchsler, St. Galactodendron utile. 1857. III. 367.²
Büsching, Johann Jakob. Beyträge zur praktischen Forstwissenschaft. 1799. IV. 100.³
— Gegründete Beurtheilung . . . über J. G. Beckmanns . . . Schriften. 1765. IV. 100.¹
— Geometrisch-öconomischer Grund-Riss zu einer . . . Verwaltung derer Waldungen. 1762. IV. 239.
— Der kranke Recensent unter einem gesunden Himmelsstrich. 1770. IV. 100.¹
— Kurzgefasster Entwurf der Jägerey. 1756. IV. 115.
Bueck, P. Nomina plantarum . . . in horto illustrissimi comitis G. W. Orlovii cultarum. 1811. I. 41.
Buée, William Urban. A narrative of the successful manner of cultivating the Clove tree. 1797. III. 635.¹
Bühler, (Oberförster, Welsheim). Ueber die beste . . . Methode, kleine Holzpflanzen auf berastem Boden zu pflanzen. 1840. IV. 152.
— Die Eiche im Nadelwald. 1839. IV. 512.
— Der Fichtenspinner in Franken. 1840. IV. 206.
— Ueber Güte . . . des Tannenbrennholzes. 1840. IV. 446.²
— Ueber Moosstreu. 1840. IV. 70.
— Ueber Nadelreisstreu. 1840. IV. 70.
— Ueber Saaten und Pflanzungen in Schutzgräben. 1840. IV. 152.
— Versuche mit amerikanischen Aexten. 1836. IV. 383.²

Bühler, Anton. Antwort an Herrn Professor Dr. Lehr. 1886. IV. 233.
— Beiträge zur schweizerischen Forst-Statistik. 1887. IV. 367.
— Die Bewegung des laufenden Zuwachses. 1886. IV. 233.
— Desiderien zur schweizerischen Forststatistik. 1888. IV. 367.
— Durchforstungsversuche. 1894. IV. 174.
— Über den Einfluss des Mineralkohlen-Bergbaus auf die Forstwirthschaft. 1874. IV. 336.[1]
— Ueber den Einfluss des Verpflanzens auf das Wachsthum der Fichte. 1884. IV. 454.
— Die Forstbenutzung. 1887. IV. 434.
— Forststatistisches aus der Schweiz. 1888. IV. 367.
— Geschichte, Organisation . . . der Centralanstalt für das forstliche Versuchswesen. 1891. IV. 38.[2]
— Die geschichtliche Entwicklung der Waldwirthschaft. 1897. IV. 24.[2]
— Die Hagelbeschädigungen in Württemberg. 1890. IV. 190.
— Die Niederschläge im Walde. 1892. IV. 73.[2]
— Reiseeindrücke in der Schweiz. 1876. IV. 367.
— Statistische Untersuchungen über den deutschen Holzhandel. 1876. IV. 349.[1]
— Streifzüge durch die Heimath der Lärche. 1886. IV. 449.
— Studien nach dem Schneefall vom 16. Februar. 1885. IV. 48.[2]
— Studien über die Baumgrenze im Hochgebirge. 1898. I. 432,[1] IV. 86.[2]
— Studien und Untersuchungen über die Zuwachsverhältnisse in der Schweiz. 1889. IV. 234.
— Untersuchung über die Qualität des . . . Tannen- und Fichtenholzes. 1886. IV. 408.
— Untersuchungen in den früher vom Kanton Aargau angelegten Probeflächen. 1891. IV. 234.
— Untersuchungen in einem Fichtenbestande. 1886. IV. 458.
— Untersuchungen über den Ertrag an Rothbuchen-Laubstreu. 1876. IV. 498.
— Untersuchungen über die Qualität des im . . . Stande erwachsenen Tannen- und Fichtenholzes. 1889. IV. 176.[1]
— Untersuchungen über die Temperatur des Bodens. 1895. IV. 60.[1]
— Untersuchungen über die Verdunstung des Wassers. 1895. IV. 73.[2]
— Untersuchungen über die Wirkung der Deckgitter. 1894. IV. 151.[1]
— Untersuchungen über Schneebruchschaden. 1886. IV. 190.
— Untersuchungen über Sickerwassermengen. 1891. IV. 73.[1]
— Verschulung von Keimpflanzen. 1895. IV. 151.[1]
— Versuche über das Einschlagen der Pflanzen. 1892. IV. 153.[1]
— Versuche über den Einfluss der Pflanzzeit. 1895. IV. 154.[2]
— Der Versuchsgarten im Stadtwalde Adlisberg. 1891. IV. 38.[2]
— Der Wald in der Culturgeschichte. 1885. IV. 24.[1]
— Welche Mittel und Wege führen in der Schweiz dazu, den Material- und Geldertrag der Waldungen möglichst zu steigern. 1885. IV. 278.[2]
— Wildbachschaden. 1898. IV. 187.[2]
— See also BILLWILLER, R. & BÜHLER, Anton R.
— & Flury, Ph. Untersuchungen über die Astreinheit. 1892. IV. 169.[1]
— & others. Berichterstattung . . . Untersuchungen über den Einfluss des Waldes auf . . . Gewässer. 1900. IV. 52.
— — Projet de programme pour la recherche de l'influence de la forêt sur le régime des eaux. 1900. IV. 52.
Bühler, Ernst Christoph Wilhelm. Einige Worte über die Freigebung der Privatwaldungen in Würtemberg. 1833. IV. 286.[1]
— Die Versumpfung der Wälder. 1834. IV. 143.[2]
Bühler, G. L. W. von. Der laufende Schwamm in den Gebäuden. 1845. IV. 414.[2]
Bühler, Otto. Aufforstungs- und Verbauungsarbeiten bei Barèges. 1899. IV. 186.[1]
Bührlen, Gotthardt Ludwig. Untersuchungen über die winterliche Färbung. See MOHL, Hugo von. 1837. I. 185.[3]
Buek, Heinrich Wilhelm. Genera, species et synonyma Candolleana. 1840. I. 77.
Buek, Johann Nicolaus. Verzeichniss von in- und ausländischen Bäumen, Sträuchern, Pflanzen . . . 1779. I. 44.
— & Peters, J. P. Ankündigung einer neuen . . . Pomologie. 1787. III. 70.

Buek, Johann Nicolaus, (jr.). Hortus francofurtanus. 1824. I. 46.
Buek, Johann Peter. Catalogus von Bäumen und Sträuchern. 1790. I. 44.
Bülow, von, (Gutsbesitzer auf Gr. Kelle bei Wittstock). Pomologica. 1839. III. 137.
Bülow, C. W. von. Deutschlands Wälder. 1834. IV. 348.[2]
— Grundzüge der Forstwissenschaft. 1833. IV. 97.
Bülow, Carl von. Forst-Tabellen zur Uebersicht der . . . Forst-Wissenschaft. 1805. IV. 100.[2]
Bülow, Werner von. Die Samoa-Inseln. 1896. III. 283.[2]
Bülow-Rieth, von. Neue Beobachtungen über den Kieferspinner. 1828. IV. 475.
— Neue Beobachtungen über die Nonne. 1831. IV. 200.
Un buen ejemplo. 1892. IV. 541.[2]
Buen y del Cos, Odon de. Apuntes geografico-botánicos sobre la zona central de la peninsula ibérica. 1883. I. 422.
Bünau, von, (Oberförster). Mittheilungen über den Ertrag eines 30 Jahre alten kiefernen Stangenorts. 1851. IV. 480.
Bündnerisches Monatsblatt. IV. 13.[2]
Buenos Aires — Museo nacional. See MUSEO . . . I. 7.[2]
Bürger, Otto. Reisen eines Naturforschers im tropischen Südamerika. 1900. I. 331.[1]
Bürgermeister, Anton. Möglichst vollständige Anweisung zur Vertilgung der Unkräuter. 1843. IV. 210.[2]
Büsgen, Moritz. Bau und Leben unserer Waldbaume. 1897. I. 82,[1] IV. 62.[1]
— Beobachtungen über das Verhalten des Gerbstoffes. 1890. I. 183.
— Zur Biologie der Galle von Hormomyia Fagi. 1895. IV. 497.
— Der Honigtau. 1891. I. 213.[2]
— Rindenknollen der Rotbuche. 1895. II. 126.[1]
— Le tannin dans les plantes. 1892. IV. 13.[3]
Bütow, A. Die Benutzung von Baumhölzern und Waldfrüchten zur Zeit der Pfahlbautenbewohner. 1899. IV. 24.[1]
— Einfluss des Waldes auf die Elektricität. 1898. IV. 54.
— Einiges aus der Geschichte des Waldes. 1898. IV. 26.
— Färbstoffe im Walde. 1896. IV. 439.
— Ein Feind des Buchenwaldes. 1894. IV. 497.
— Gerbstoffpflanzen. 1895. IV. 435.
— Der Haselstrauch. 1890. IV. 492.[1]
— Parasiten im Walde. 1894. IV. 211.[1]
— Rauch und Schnee als Feinde der Pflanzen. 1900. IV. 193.[1]
— Verschiedenerlei Licht. 1899. IV. 68.[1]
— Wälder- und Baum-Anpflanzungen in alter Zeit. 1897. IV. 24.[1]
— Wespen als Raupenfeinde im Walde. 1894. IV. 93.
Buettner, David Siegmund August. Enumeratio methodica plantarum. 1750. I. 291.
Büttner, G. Die Drehkiefer. 1897. II. 47.[1]
— Der Forstbotanische Garten zu Tharandt. 1899. I. 49, IV. 18.[1]
— Die japanische Lärche. 1900. III. 304.[2]
Büttner, I. G. Pflanzen-physiologische Beobachtungen. 1859. I. 195.[1]
Büttner, Richard. Die Congo-Expedition. 1886. I. 492.[1]
— Einige Ergebnisse meiner Reise in Westafrika. 1886. I. 492.[1]
— Zur Flora des Togolaudes. 1893. I. 491.
— Neue Arten von Guinea. 1890. I. 491.
Buff, Heinrich. Sur le développement de l'électricité. 1854. I. 231.[1]
— Ueber die Electricitätserregung. 1854. I. 231.[1]
— Sur l'électricité des plantes. 1854. I. 231.[1]
— On the electricity of plants. 1854. I. 231.[1]
Buffalo society of natural sciences. Bulletin. I. 5.
Buffault, Paul. La forêt de Lespinasse. 1889. IV. 361.
Buffault, Pierre. Acclimatation de divers végétaux. 1897. IV. 127,[1] 545.[1]
— Une erreur historique. La fixation des dunes et Brémontier. 1895. IV. 164.[1]
— Étude sur la côte et les dunes du Médoc. 1894. I. 535, IV. 164,[1] 362.
— La naissance de la forêt des dunes en Médoc. 1896. IV. 146.[1]
— Le régime forestier de 1669 en Béarn. 1900. IV. 28.[1]
— La vigne, croissant spontanément dans . . . Béarn. 1900. II. 873.[3]

Buffevent, de. Observations d'un ancien conservateur des forêts. 1851. IV. 292.
— De l'organisation de l'administration forestière. 1849. IV. 292.
Buffon, Georges Louis Leclerc, comte de. Expériences sur la force du bois. 1742. IV. 409.
— Mémoire sur la conservation . . . des forests. 1741. IV. 180.[2]
— Mémoire sur la culture des forests. 1745. IV. 151.[2]
— A memorial on preserving and repairing forests.. 1741. IV. 180.[2]
— Memorial on the culture of forests. ·1745· IV. 151.[2]
— Moyen facile d'augmenter la solidité . . . du bois. 1740. IV. 416.[2]
— See also DUHAMEL DU MONCEAU, H. L. & BUFFON, G. L. L., comte de.
Buffum, B. C. Cultivated shade and forest trees. 1898. III. 118.[1]
Buhle, Christian Adolph. Die wichtigsten der deutschen Giftpflanzen. 1804. III. 72.
Buhse, Fedor Aleksandrovitch. See BUHSE, Friedrich Alexander..
Buhse, Friedrich Alexander. Abnormer Baum. 1869. I. 209,[1] IV. 476.
— Die Dattelpalme. 1881. III. 328.[2]
— Dendrologischer Leitfaden. 1887. I. 294,[1] III. 68,[1] IV. 80.
— Die Flora des Alburs. 1899. I. 477.[2]
— Palmenpilz. 1869. III. 318.[2]
— Eine Reise durch Transkaukasien. 1855. I. 477.[2]
— Reisebemerkungen aus dem oestlichen Alburgsgebirge. 1861. I. 477.[2]
— Russisch-Lappland und seine Vegetation. 1883. I. 364.
— Uebersicht der naturhistorischen Literatur von Liv-, Kur- und Ehstland. 1854. I. 3.[2]
— Vorläufiger botanischer Bericht über meine Reise durch einen Theil Armeniens. 1848. I. 479.
— Zapfenhäufung. 1866. II. 47.[2]
— See also BOISSIER, Edmond & BUHSE, Fedor; DIERCKE, C. & BUHSE, Friedrich.
Buignet, Henri. Note concernant l'arbre sur lequel vit l'insecte qui produit la cire de Chine. 1859. IV. 535.[1]
— Recherches sur la constitution chimique de la manne. 1868. IV. 536.[1]
— Recherches sur la matière sucrée·. . . dans les fruits. 1860. · I. 179.[1]
— See also BERTHELOT, M. P. E. & BUIGNET, Henri.
Buijn, G. See CHARANTE, W. E. van & BUIJN, G.
Buijsman, M. Erythroxylon Coca Lam. 1898. III. 493.[2]
Builder. IV. 12.[1]
Builder and woodworker. See AMERICAN builder. New York. IV. 3.
Builders' bulletin. IV. 3.
Building. IV. 3.
Building budget. IV. 3.
Buis comme succédané du Quinquina. 1870. III. 523.[1]
Buissman, M. Les Plantes utiles Anacardium. 1899. II. 455.[1]
Buisson. Les fruitières de la Haute-Garonne. 1900. IV. 134.[2]
Buisson, Louis. Étude sur le cundurango de Loja. 1872. III. 692.[2]
Buisson, Maxime. Le Botrytis tenella. 1892. IV. 203.
— See also HIBBERT & BUISSON, Maxime.
Buiteman, G. F. De aaltjesziekte in de Koffie. 1899. III. 737.
— Enten van Koffieboomen. 1899. III. 733.[2]
— Iets over het onderhoud van Koffietuinen. 1899. III. 727.
— Olie tot bestrijding der groene luis. 1899. III. 737.
— Plantwijze systeem Koch. 1899. III. 734.[2]
De **Buitenman**. III. 14.
Buitenzorg — Institut botanique. See INSTITUT · . : I. 29.[1]
Buitenzorg — Jardin botanique. See JARDIN . . . I. 29.[1]
Buitenzorg — 's Lands Plantentuin. See 's LANDS . . . I. 29.[1]
Buitenzorg — 's Lands Plantentuin. Catalogus der Bibliotheek. See CATALOGUS . . . 1887. I. 2.
Buja, Baldassare. Quali misure sarebbero da adottarsi onde conseguire lo scopo della rimboscazione. 1847. IV.·276.[1]
Bujack, Johann Gottlieb. Die geographische Verbreitung des Weinstocks. 1834. II. 506.[2]
Bujon, A. L'écorce du Tilleul. 1875. IV. 528.[1]
Bulard, Charles. Météorologie: sécheresse et inondations. 1882. IV. 53, 184.[1]

Bulbul, JANGALI. See JANGALI BULBUL, (pseud.).
Bulfinger, Geo. Bern. Observationes botanicae. 1761. I. 145.[2]
Bulitch, A. See БУЛИЧЪ, А. ·
Bull. Dipladenia carissima. 1883. III. 687.[2]
Bull, A. Undersøgelse om en Forbedring i det norske Skov-Væsen. 1780. IV. 113.[1]
Bull, B. W. Remarks upon the Cinchona pitaya. 1852. III. 726.[1]
Bull, E. A. Grape-pruning. 1868. III. 549.[1]
Bull, Henry Graves. The Mistletoe in Herefordshire. 1864. II. 177.[2]
— The Mistletoe on the Oak. 1864. II. 179.[1]
— Note on the production of shoots of Cytisus Laburnum . . . from grafts of C. Laburnum coccineum. 1844. II. 368.[1]
— See also Hogg, Robert & BULL, H. G.
Bull, Marcus. Experiments to determine the comparative quantities of heat evolved in the combustion. 1830. IV. 412.[2]
Bull, William. Bignonia magnifica. 1882. III. 705.
— Campsidium filicifolium. 1877. III. 705.
— Chamaedorea formosa. 1876. III. 322.[1]
— Daemonorops palembanicus. 1877. III. 321.[2]
— Double-flowered Epacris. 1876. III. 665.[1]
— Neue Pflanzen. 1882. III. 83.[1]
— Die neuen Aucuba. 1865. III. 644.[2]
— William Bull's Verzeichniss von neuen . . . Pflanzen. 1872. III. 82.
Bulletin; documents officiels, statistique, rapports . . . de missions en France . . . See FRANCE–MINISTÈRE DE L'AGRICULTURE. Bulletin. III. 19.
Bulletin agricole de l'Algérie. III. 27.[1]
Bulletin algérien et tunisien. I. 21.
Bulletin botanique. [Genève.] I. 26.[2]
Bulletin d'arboriculture . . . de Belgique. See CERCLE PROFESSORAL POUR LE PROGRÈS DE L'ARBORICULTURE. III. 15.
Bulletin d'insectologie agricole. III. 19.
Bulletin de pharmacie. I. 21, V. VII.[1]
Bulletin des Neuesten . . . aus der Naturwissenschaft. III. 11.
Bulletin des sciences naturelles et de géologie. 1824. I. 1.
Bulletin des sciences physiques et naturelles en Néerlande. I. 15.
Bulletin économique de l'Indo-Chine. III. 26.[1]
Bulletin général de thérapeutique. I. 21.
Bulletin général et universel des annonces et des nouvelles scientifiques. 1823. I. 1.
Bulletin of pharmacy. See DRUGGIST'S bulletin. III. 3.[1]
Bulletin scientifique de la France et de la Belgique. I. 21.
Bulletin scientifique du département du Nord. See BULLETIN scientifique de la France . . . I. 21.
Bulleyne, William. The booke of simples. 1562. I. 281.
Bulliard, Pierre. Dictionnaire élémentaire de botanique. 1783. I. 69.[2]
— Flora parisiensis. 1776. I. 405.
— Herbier de la France. 1780. I. 405.
— Histoire des plantes médicinales. 1809. III. 85.
— Histoire des plantes vénéneuses . . . de la France. 1784. III. 85.
— Introduction à la flore des environs de Paris. 1776. I. 405.
— Tradado de las plantas venenosas. 1784. III. 85.
Bullock, Charles. Sur l'essence de Gaultheria. 1887. III. 652.[1]
Bulmerincq, M. E. von. Recension der Beiträge zur Kenntniss des russischen Reiches. 1857. IV. 345.
— See also БУЛЬМЕРИНГЪ, М.
Bulytchef, N. P. See БУЛЫЧЕВЪ, Н. П.
Bunbury, Sir Charles James Fox. Arboretum notes. 1889. III. 123.[2]
— Botanical fragments. 1883.· I. 271.[1]
— Botanical notes at Barton & Mildenhall. 1889. III. 123.[1]
— Influence of chemical nature of subsoil. 1883. I. 229.
— List of ferns cultivated in my garden at Barton. 1889. III. 123.[2]
— List of flowering plants and ferns found in . . . Mildenhall. 1889. III. 123,[2] V. XXI.[2]
— Notes on the vegetation of Brazil. 1883. I. 343.
— Notes on the vegetation of Buenos Ayres. 1855. I. 344.
— Notes on the vegetation of the Cape of Good Hope. 1883. I. 495.
— Notes on wild plants found in·. . . Great Barton. 1889. III. 123,[2] V. XXI.[2]

Bunbury, *Sir* Charles James Fox (*continued*).
— Remarks on the botany of Madeira. 1856. I. 497.
— Some characteristics of South American vegetation. 1867. I. 330.
— Die Vegetation von Madeira. 1856. I. 497.
Bunce, Daniel. Guide to the Linnean system of botany. 1851. I. 256.
— Hortus tasmanensis. 1851. I. 501.
Bund, F. Exkursion in die Waldungen der k. k. Reichsdomäne Brandeis. 1856. IV. 370.
Bund, Karl. El cultivo de la Acacia. 1899. IV. 523.²
— L'éducation de l'Acacia. 1899. IV. 523.³
— Az erdei fák némely tulajdonságainak átöröklődéséről. 1899. I. 248,² IV. 75.¹
— Erdőgazdaság szépészeti czélla. 1898. IV. 55.²
— A Késő-tölgy. 1896. II. 136.²
— A Késő-tölgy kizöldülésének ideje. 1895. II. 136.³
— Vázlatok a külföldi erdőgazdaság köréből. 1899. IV. 336.²
— Die Zucht der Akazie. 1899. IV. 523.²
—Tavi, Gusztáv & Vadas, Jenő. Ssakvélemény Budapest székesfőváros erdőgazdaságáról. 1900. IV. 374.²
Bundesgesetz betreffend eidgenössische Oberaufsicht über die Forstpolizei im Hochgebirge. *See* Loi fédérale . . . 1876. IV. 330.
Bunel. Nouveau mode d'ornementation par l'Evonymus japonica. 1880. III. 532.²
Bunge, Alexander von. Alexandri Lehmann Reliquiae botanicae. 1847. I. 456.
— Anabasearum revisio. 1862. II. 187.¹
— Astragaleae; Астрагаловыя. 1880. II. 333,² 376.¹
— Enumeratio Plantaginearum Salsolacearumque centrasiaticarum. 1880. II. 187.¹
— Enumeratio plantarum . . . in China boreali. 1833. I. 458.
— Enumeratio Salsolacearum . . . in Mongolia. 1879. II. 187.¹
— Enumeratio Salsolacearum centrasiaticarum. 1880. II. 187.¹
— Die Gattung Acantholimon Boiss. 1872. II. 696.¹ ·
— Generis Astragali species gerontogeae. 1868. II. 333.²
— Über die Heliotropien der mittelländisch-orientalischen Flor. 1869. II. 750.²
— Historia Anabasearum. 1862. II. 187.¹
— Icones plantarum novarum . . . operis: Alexandri Lehmann Reliquiae. 1847. I. 456.
— Labiatae persicae. 1873. II. 762.²
— Leguminosarum genus novum. 1876. II. 384.¹
— Ueber eine neue Gattung . . . der Zygophyllaceae. 1843. II. 396.¹
— Pflanzen-geographische Betrachtungen über . . . Chenopodiaceen. 1880. II. 187.¹
— Plantarum mongholico-chinensium. 1835. I. 460.¹
— Plantas Abichianas . . . enumeravit. 1858. I. 531.
— Recensio Salsolearum nonnullarum. 1856. II. 187.¹
— Reise im östlichen Theil des Altai-Gebirges. 1830. I. 453.²
— De relatione methodi plantarum naturalis in vires vegetabilium medicinales. 1825. III. 259.²
— Salsolaceae herbarii petropolitani. 1893. II. 187.¹
— Species generis Oxytropis. 1874. II. 376.¹
— Supplementum ad Astragaleas Turkestaniae. 1880. II. 333.²
— Tentamen generis Tamaricum species. 1852. II. 562.²
— Verzeichnis der . . . im östlichen Theile des Altai-Gebirges gesammelten Pflanzen. 1835. I. 453.²
— Weite und enge Verbreitungs-Bezirke einiger Pflanzen. 1874. I. 300.
— *See also* Бунге, A.
Bunge, Gustav. Ueber den Nátrongehalt der Pflanzenaschen. 1874. I. 153.
Bunitzki, K. *See* Бунизкій, K.
Buniva, Michele Francesco. De generatione plantarum. 1788. I. 199.
— Nomenclator Linnaeanus Florae pedemontanae. 1790. I. 424.
Eine buntblättrige Dracaena Rothiana. 1895. III. 337.¹
Bunting, Martha. The structure of the cork tissues in roots. 1898. II. 257.¹
Buntzel. Schutz gegen Feuersgefahr. 1886. IV. 181.²
Bunya-Bunya. Araucaria Bidwilli. 1881. III. 298.¹
Bunyard, George. Fruit farming for profit. 1881. III. 142.
— Ornamental Crabs. 1900. III. 425.¹
— Woods of Kent. 1895. IV. 398.²
—A year's notes on . . . flowering and ornamental shrubs. 1900. III. 203.

Il buon giardiniere. 1826. III. 88.²
Pel buon nome dei nostri oli d'olive. 1895. III. 679.²
Buonafedi, Emilio. Contro la cocciniglia bianca. 1897. III. 191.
— La cultura delle piante australiane. 1892. III. 126.²
Buonaiuti, Giuseppe. Di una varieta' dal Testucchio o Loppo. 1829. II. 478.²
Burbank, L. S. Cultivating Whortleberries. 1878. III. 663.¹
— Remarks on the River Birch and Hackberry. 1877. II. 119,² 142.¹
Burbank, Luther. The oriental nuts. 1891. III. 354.¹
Burbidge, Frederick William. The acclimatisation garden at Paris. 1873. III. 202.¹
— The art of botanical drawing. 1873. I. 37.¹
— Berry-bearing plants. 1874. III. 208.¹
— The Blue Passion flower. 1894. III. 616.¹
— The Chilian Bellflowers. 1896. III. 337.²
— Cocos Weddelliana. 1873. III. 324.²
— The College garden Slipper-wort. 1895. III. 702.²
— Cultivated plants, their propagation. 1877. III. 50,² 153.
— Date Plums. 1880. III. 669.²
— The Date-plums . . . of Japan. 1897. III. 669.²
— The evils of grafting. 1890. I. 208.²
— Fragrant leaves v. sweet-scented flowers. 1898. I. 182, III. 227.
— The fruit-bearing Garrya. 1899. III. 352.²
— Gardens at Fota, Queenstown. 1900. III. 307.²
— Japanese Tree-strangler or Staff tree. 1898. II. 466.²
— Lapageria rosea in fruit. . 1896. III. 337.²
— Mackay's Heath. 1896. II. 667.²
— Malortiea simplex. 1873. III. 331.¹
— The Mistletoe. 1899. III. 385.¹
— A noble Sycomore. 1888. III. 536.¹
— Poinsettia pulcherrima plenissima. 1876. ·III. 518.¹
— The Scarlet Trumpet Honeysuckle. 1888. III. 751.¹
— The Water Lily trees. 1893. III. 399.¹
— Weeping and other Willows. 1899. III. 349.
— Willows v. Bamboos. 1896. III. 349.
Burchardt, S. Ueber die Ausnutzung der Holz-Bestände . . . der Herrschaft Tarnowitz-Neudeck. 1864. IV. 260.²
— Führer für die Exkursion . . . in den Forsten der gräflichen Herrschaft Neudeck. 1864. IV. 353.
— Ueber das Vorkommen des Taxus. 1864. IV. 440.²
Burchardt, Thr H. O. Abhandlung über die Klassifikation der Obstsorten. 1824. III. 70.
— Über die Anpflanzung . . . der . . . Weiden-Arten. 1833. III. 347.
— Beiträge zur Geschichte der Kultur der Haselnüsse. 1833. III. 357.²
— Beiträge zur Kenntniss der Verbreitung unserer Obstarten. 1849. I. 241.²
— Bemerkungen über den Artikel des Grafen von Flotow. 1841. I. 247.
— Über die Erfindung des Abschälens der Rinde. 1833. III. 175.²
— Fortsetzung der Bemerkungen über die Kultur der Haselnüsse. 1833. III. 357.²
— Über die Kultur der Kanadischen Pappel. 1832. ·III. 345.²
— Ueber die neuen Kulturmethoden. 1849. IV. 152.
— Pomologische Bibliothek. 1806. III. 1.
— Über die Wirkungen des Frostes in den harten Wintern von 1823 und 1826. 1828. III. 45·
Burchell, William. A catalogue of trees, shrubs. 1764. I. 521.²
Burchell, William John. Travels in the interior of southern Africa. 1822. I. 494.
— The zoological and botanical index to Travels. 1824. I. 494.
Burck, William. Aanteekeningen op planten. 1891. I. 466.
— De Aristolochia-bloem. 1891. II. 181.¹
— Ueber die Befruchtung der Aristolochia-Blüthe. 1892. II. 181.¹
— Beitraege zur Kenntniss der myrmecophilen Pflanzen. 1891. I. 235.²
— Burck's method of treatment of the Coffee-leaf disease. 1887. III. 736.
— Contributions à la flore de l'Archipel Malais. 1893. I. 466.
— Sur les Diptérocarpées des Indes néerlandaises. 1887. II. 559.¹

— Dispositions des organes dans les fleurs dans le but de favoriser l'auto-fécondation. 1887. II. 343.[1]
— Eenige opmerkingen betreffende het artikel van Trisnobomie. 1897. III. 731.
— Eenige opmerkingen omtrent getah-pertja. 1884. III. 231.
— Over de eigenaardige heterostylie der bloemen van Erytroxylon. 1893. II. 394.[1]
— Getah-pertjah boomen op Java. 1885. III. 149.
— De gouvernements Koffiecultuur. 1897. III. 731.
— Hemileia vastatrix. 1889. III. 736.
— Herbarium en museum van 's Lands plantentuin. 1892. I. 68.[1]
— Over den invloed van het licht op . . . Hemileia. 1889. III. 736.
— Ueber Kleistogamie. 1890. I. 238.
— Over de Koffiebladziekte. 1887. III. 735, 736.
— Over Koffieproductles. 1896. III. 727.
— Minjak Tengkawang. 1886. III. 225.
— Notes biologiques. 1887. I. 238, II. 343.[1]
— Over de oorzaken van den achteruitgang van de gouvernements Koffiecultuur. 1896. III. 731.
— Opmerkingen omtrent de constructie der bloemen in . . . Cinchona. 1884. II. 813.[2]
— Opmerkingen over de onder den naam van Erythroxylon Coca . . . gecultiveerde gewassen. 1890. II. 394.[2]
— Sur l'organisation florale chez quelques Rubiacées. 1883. II. 808.[2]
— Een paar opmerkingen naar aanleiding van het artikel van Dr. Delacroix. 1900. III. 737.
— Planten onder protectie der mieren. 1892. I. 235.[2]
— Proeven ter bestrijding der Koffiebladziekte. 1887. III. 36.
— Rapport omtrent een onderzoek naar de getah-pertja produceerende boomsoorten. 1884. III. 229.
— Rapport sur son exploration . . . à la recherche des espèces d'arbres qui produisent la gutta-percha. 1884. III. 229.
— Relation entre l'hétérostylie dimorphe et . . . trimorphe. 1887. I. 238.
— Sur les Sapotacées des Indes néerlandaises et les origines botaniques de la Gutta-percha. 1885. II. 696,[2] III. 229.
— Selbstbefruchtung bei geoeffneten Blüthen. 1890. I. 238.
— Spaziergänge durch den Botanischen Garten. 1893. I. 68.[1]
— Wandelingen door den Botanischen tuin. 1892. I. 68.[1]
Burckel, Georges. See Koenig, Charles & Burckel, Georges.
Burckhard, Johann Heinrich. Epistola ad . . . Godofredum Guilielmum Leibnitium. 1750. I. 291.
Burckhardt, (Apotheker). Tabellarische Uebersicht über die Blüthezeit. 1846. I. 224.[2]
Burckhardt, Heinrich. Ueber das Ablegen . . . der Rothbuche. 1867. IV. 494.
— Die Akazie zu Schiffsnägeln. 1865. IV. 524.[1]
— Arbeitermangel und die Löhne. 1873. IV. 310.[2]
— Die Aufästung der Waldbäume. 1865. IV. 170.
— Die Aufforstung der Heiden. 1872. IV. 195.
— Ueber den Baumstand. 1846. IV. 494.
— Bemerkungen über den Akazien-Baum. 1849. IV. 523.[1]
— Bemerkungen zur Frage des Zinsfusses. 1879. IV. 256.
— Ein Buchen-Samenjahr in Sicht. 1873. IV. 495.
— Der Buchen- und Eichen-Stockausschlag. 1879. IV. 139.[2]
— Ueber Buchenzucht. 1862. IV. 494.
— Eine Correspondenz aus Hannover. 1871. IV. 290.[2]
— Cubic-Tabellen für Forstmänner. 1860. IV. 224.
— Ueber die Dampfpflugkultur. 1875. IV. 158.
— Ueber Dampfpflugkultur . . . besonders im Forstdistrikte Osterbrook. 1876. IV. 158.
— Der Eibenbaum . . . im Plesswalde. 1885. IV. 440.[1]
— Die Eiche im alten Mast- und Hutwalde. 1879. IV. 507.
— Ueber die Eiche und ihre Mischhölzer. 1862. IV. 505.
— Ueber Eichenzucht. 1862. IV. 505.
— Einige Bemerkungen über das Studium der Forstwissenschaft. 1875. IV. 29.
— Entgegnung auf die . . . gegen das hannoversche Forstwesen gefallenen Aeusserungen. 1868. IV. 290.[2]
— Die Erlencultur in der Lewitz. 1865. IV. 489.[1]
— Die Fichte als Nutzholzbaum im Buchenhochwalde. 1881. IV. 453.
— Die Fichte . . . im Buchenhochwalde. 1872. IV. 138.[1]
— Fichte und Kiefer in Bezug auf Form. 1856. IV. 216,[1] 458, 480.

— Die Formzahl der Buchenbestände. 1845. IV. 497.
— Der Forstdienst in den letzten hundert Jahren. 1872. IV. 26.
— Die Forstkultur in Jütland. 1879. IV. 113.[2]
— Ueber forstliche Ausstellungen. 1876. IV. 19.[1]
— Forstliche Hülfstafeln. 1852. IV. 230.
— Forstliche Reisenotizen besonders über Kiefern- und Erlencultur im Grossherzogthum Mecklenburg-Schwerin. 1865. IV. 489.[1]
— Die forstlichen Verhältnisse des Königreichs Hannover. 1864. IV. 353.
— Ueber Forstnebennutzungen in den hannoverschen Waldungen. 1864. IV. 434.
— Die Gemeinde- und Genossenschaftsforsten in der Provinz Hannover. 1876. IV. 308.[2]
— Handbuch der Holzerziehung. 1855. IV. 106.
— Hannovers Forsten. 1852. IV. 352.
— Das hannoversche Waldstreu-Gesetz. 1863. IV. 320.
— Ueber den hannover'schen Forstdienst. 1863. IV. 290.[1]
— Hülfstafeln für Forsttaxatoren. 1852. IV. 230.
— Indian forests. 1874. IV. 377.[2]
— Aus dem indischen Walde. 1874. IV. 124,[2] 377.[2]
— Die Kiefern-Pflanzcultur mit ballenlosen Jährlingen. 1865. IV. 472.
— Der Lichtungsbetrieb der Buche. 1877. IV. 495.
— Der Lichtungsbetrieb der Buche und Eiche. 1877. IV. 138.[2]
— Der Lichtungsbetrieb der Eiche. 1877. IV. 506.
— Mass, Gewicht und Münze. 1858. IV. 213.
— Das Mastjahr 1875. 1876. IV. 495.
— Mittheilungen über Ertragsergebnisse im Eichen-Lichtungsbetriebe. 1879. IV. 513.
— Moorerde zur Kiefernkultur. 1875. IV. 472.
— Ortstein-Kultur nicht neu! 1862. IV. 68.
— Der Pflanzheister. 1874. IV. 152.
— Die Riesenkiefer . . . als Forstkulturbaum. 1876. IV. 464.[2]
— In Sachen der Waldwerthberechnung. 1861. IV. 255.
— Säen und Pflanzen nach forstlicher Praxis. 1855. IV. 106.
— Der Sal-Baum. 1874. IV. 528.[2]
— Der Schirmbaum als Mittel der Holzerziehung. 1873. IV. 138.[1]
— Die Schutz- oder Sicherheitsstreifen an Eisenbahnen. 1869. IV. 181.[2]
— Das Schutzholz. 1850. IV. 138.[2]
— Das Schutzholz. 1865. IV. 138.[2]
— Die Scutzholzarten und ihre Wirkungsweise. 1881. IV. 139.[1]
— Des semis et des plantations de Mélèze. 1861. IV. 449.
— Zur Tagesfrage: Die Verkürzung der forstwirthschaftlichen Umtriebszeiten. 1865. IV. 251.[2]
— Der Teak-Baum. 1874. IV. 536.[2]
— Die Teakforsten. 1876. IV. 308.[2]
— Vergleichende Untersuchung über Weisstannen- und Fichten-Stangenorte. 1874. IV. 236.
— Vertilgung der Wühlratte. 1874. IV. 198.[1]
— Waldplagen. 1862. IV. 195.[2]
— Der Waldwerth in Beziehung auf Veräusserung. 1860. IV. 253.
— Waldwerthberechnung. 1860. IV. 255.
— Säen und Pflanzen zu Lützburg. 1865. IV 444.[1]
— Aus der Wirthschaft. 1871. IV. 118.
— See also Буркгардтъ, Г.
Burdach, Christian C. T. Das Theebüchlein. 1840. III. 606.
Burdach, Heinrich. Systematisches Handbuch der Obstbaumkrankheiten. 1818. III. 178.
Bureau, Édouard. Artocarpaceae. 1873. II. 145.[1]
— Des Bignoniacées. 1868. III. 704.[2]
— Description du genre nouveau Saldanhaea. 1867. II. 790.[1]
— Description du genre nouveau Schizopsis. 1864. II. 792.
— État actuel des études sur la végétation des colonies françaises. 1895. I. 301.
— Études sur les genres Reyesia et Monttea. 1863. II. 781.[1]
— Extrait d'une lettre de M. Léon Bureau. 1863. III. 321.
— De la famille des Loganiacées. 1856. II. 716.[2]
— Ficus Roxburghii. 1872. II. 153.[1]
— Sur un Figuier à fruits souterrains. 1888. II. 153.[2]
— La flore de Madagascar. 1896. I. 496.
— Sur les fruits du Crescentia Cujete. 1868. II. 787.[2]
— Sur le genre Tanaecium. 1868. II. 791.[2]

Bureau, Édouard (*continued*).
— Lettre [sur des Bignoniacées]. 1869. III. 704.²
— Monographie des Bignoniacées. 1864. II. 784.¹
— Moraceae. 1873. II. 145.¹
— Morées et Artocarpées de la Nouvelle-Calédonie. 1869. II. 145.¹
— Note sur la culture des Bignoniacées. 1868. III. 704.²
— Note sur les Bignoniacées de la Nouvelle-Calédonie. 1862. II. 788,¹ 789.²
— Notes inédites de Pavon sur le Broussonetia. 1871. II. 147.¹
— Notice sur les travaux scientifiques. 1874. V. VII.¹
— Premier aperçu de la végétation du Congo français. 1886. I. 490.
— Sur les premières collections botaniques arrivées du Tonkin. 1886. I. 469.²
— Sur quelques fruits de Bignoniacées. 1868. II. 784.¹
— Quelques observations sur les Loganiacées. 1856. II. 716.²
— Remarques sur la classification des Bignoniacées. 1861. II. 784.¹
— Révision des genres Tynanthus et Lundia. 1867. II. 789,¹ 792.¹
— Révision du genre Catalpa. 1894. II. 786.²
— Valeur des caractères tirés . . . de la tige, pour la classification des Bignoniacées. 1872. II. 784.¹
— & **Franchet, Adrien**. Plantes nouvelles du Thibet. 1891. I. 460.²
— — Premier aperçu de la végétation du Tonkin. 1886. I. 469.²
— & **Schumann, Karl. Bignoniaceae**. 1896. II. 784.²
Burel. Cantua dependens. 1855. III. 694.²
— Note sur un nouvel ennemi du Laurier Rose. 1875. III. 689.²
Burel, A. Calcul de la possibilité. 1884. IV. 237.
— Étude sur la constitution normale des forêts jardinées. 1888. IV. 252.
— Étude sur les taillis composés. 1885. IV. 244.
— Plan de balivage des taillis. 1885. IV. 237.
Buresch, E. Der Schutz des Holzes gegen Fäulniss. 1860. IV. 418.
— Ueber die verschiedenen Verfahrungsarten . . . beim Imprägniren der Hölzer. 1860. IV. 418.
Burg, C. L. van der. De geneesheer in Nederlandsch Indië. 1882. III. 274.²
Burg, E. A. van der. Over het al of niet gepraeformeerd voorkomen van kinidine. 1865. III. 725.¹
— Hager's methode ter quantitatieve bepaling van Kina-alcaloiden. 1870. III. 722.
— De methode van Varrentrapp en Will. 1866. III. 722.
— Onderzoek naar het alkaloïdgehalt der bladeren van Cinchona succirubra. 1865. III. 726.¹
— Opsporing van kinine. 1873. III. 722.
— Opsporing van vreemde kina-alcaloiden. 1879. III. 723.
— Quantitatieve bepaling der kina-alcaloiden. 1870. III. 722.
Burger, A. De l'asséchement du sol. 1877. IV. 50, 73.¹
— Assèchement du sol par les bois résineux. 1869. I. 232,² IV. 73.²
— De l'asséchement du sol par les essences forestières. 1877. I. 232.²
— Du déboisement des campagnes. 1877. IV. 44.
— De la desecacion del suelo. 1877. IV. 73.¹
— Écimage des jeunes Peupliers. 1878. III. 346.¹
— Hygiène de la Vigne. 1878. III. 571.
— Principes de culture . . . du Chêne de marine. 1864. III. 361,² IV. 505.
— Rôle étiologique du déboisement. 1885. IV. 55.¹
Burger, H. Aanmerkingen gehouden op eene reize door eenige districten der Padangsche bovenlanden. 1835. III. 275.¹
Burger, Hugo. Gummi von Macrozamia Fraseri. 1883. III. 285.²
Burger, Johann. Agriculture du royaume Lombardo-Vénitien. 1842. III. 62.²
— Systematische Klassificazion . . . der . . . . Traubenarten. 1837. III. 546.
Burger, Wilhelm. Ueber Dynamit-Stocksprengversuche. 1880. IV. 387.¹
— Tafeln zur Ermittelung des körperlichen Inhaltes runde Hölzer. 1872. IV. 227.¹
— Tafeln zur Ermittelung des Preises metrisch kubirter Hölzer. 1872. IV. 402.²
De burger-boer of land-edelman. 1766. III. 105.

Burgersdijk, Leendert Alexander Johannes. Handleiding tot de beoefening der plantenkunde. 1857. I. 90.
Burgerstein, Alfred. Zur Anatomie des Albizziaholzes. 1894. II. 330.²
— Anatomie des Holzes von Albizzia moluccana. 1894. II. 331.¹
— Aufklärungen über den " Stock im Eisen." 1894. I. 517.²
— Ueber Bau und Wachsthum des Holzes. 1896. I. 126.
— Beiträge zur Kenntniss der Holzstructur der Pomaceen. 1898. II. 257.¹
— Beiträge zur Xylotomie der Pruneen. 1899. II. 257.¹
— Beschaffenheit . . . von Coniferensamen. 1899. III. 294.²
— Biologie und Culturgeschichte des Feigenbaumes. 1894. II. 151.¹
— Das Chlorophyll. 1877. I. 141.
— Einige Hybriden von Sorbus Aucuparia. 1899. II. 312.¹
— Ueber einige physiologische und pathologische Wirkungen des Kampfers. 1885. I. 211.
— A Fügefa. 1894. III. 369.¹
— Die Gattungen der Pomaceen. 1896. II. 257.¹
— Ueber den Keimungsprocess der Samenpflanzen. 1878. I. 203.
— Ueber Lebensdauer . . . der Pflanzen. 1895. I. 192.²
— Materialien zu einer Monographie betreffend die Erscheinungen der Transpiration. 1887. I. 168.
— Ueber Milchbäume. 1880. III. 218.²
— Die Na . . . der Jetztzeit und der Vorwelt. 1878. II. 21.² de höl er
— Ueber den nyctitropischen Bewegungen. 1887. I. 198.
— Pflanzen und Ameisen. 1899. I. 235.²
— Ueber Pflanzenfasern. 1879. III. 234.
— Ueber primäre und secundäre Wirkungen des Regens. 1897. I. 233.¹
— Der " Stock im Eisen." 1893. I. 517.²
— Ueber die Transspiration von Taxuszweigen. 1875. I. 167.
— Ueber die Transspirationsgrösse der Pflanzen. 1897. I. 168.²
— Untersuchungen über das Vorkommen und die Entstehung des Holzstoffes. 1874. I. 175.
— Untersuchungen über die Beziehungen der Nährstoffe zur Transspiration. 1876. I. 167.
— Vergleichend-histologische Untersuchungen des Holzes der Pomaceen. 1895. II. 257.¹
— Vergleichende-anatomische Untersuchung des Fichten- und Lärchenholzes. 1893. II. 17.¹
— Ueber das Verhalten der Gymnospermen-Keimlinge im Lichte und im Dunkeln. 1900. II. 21.²
— Ueber das Wasserbedürfniss der Pflanzen. 1887. I. 186.
— Weitere Untersuchungen über den histologischen Bau des Holzes der Pomaceen. 1896. II. 257.¹
— Welche Vortheile zieht die Sinnpflanze (Mimosa pudica) aus der Reizbarkeit ihrer Blätter? 1898. II. 373.¹
— Xylotomisch-systematische Studien über . . . Pomaceen. 1898. II. 257.¹
Burgess, Henry W. Eidodendron. 1827. I. 296,² 516, II. 137.²
Burgess, J. T. English wild flowers. 1868. I. 402.
Burgess, Robert. Some Iowa plants. 1877. II. 106,² 295.²
Burgess, T. J. W. Notes on the genus Rhus. 1892. II. 458.¹
Burggraf, Johann Philipp. *See* **Burgrave, J. P.**
Burggrave, Johann Philipp. De Malo Sinensi aureo. 1716. III. 501.¹
— De Malo Sinensi aureo. 1722. III. 499.¹
Burgh, N. I. W. V. Hoorn van. *See* **Hoorn van Burgh, N. I. W. V.**
Burghard, E. Die Kultur der Cocos Weddelliana. 1900. III. 324.¹
Burghart, Gottfried Heinrich. Iter sabothicum. 1736. I 373.
Burgmayer. Die Brennholzrechte und ihr Einfluss auf die Nutzholzausbeute. 1898. IV. 333.
Burgoa, Antonio de San Martin y. *See* **San Martin y Burgoa, Antonio de.**
Burgsdorf, Friedrich August Ludwig von. Abhandlung über das Umwerfen und Ausreissen. 1793. IV. 385.²
— Abhandlung über Vortheile vom . . . Anbau einiger . . . Holzarten. 1790. IV. 125.¹
— Abhandlung vom Umwerfen oder Ausroden. 1793. IV. 385.²
— Abhandlung von den eigentlichen Theilen . . . der . . . Forstwissenschaft. 1783. IV. 56.

— Anleitung zur sichern Erziehung . . . der einheimischen und fremden Holzarten. 1787. IV. 105.
— Anviisning til at opelske indenlandske og udenlandske Traearter. 1787. IV. 105.
— Anzeige derjenigen Insekten . . . an der Rothbuche . . . schädlich. 1796. IV. 496.
— Aufmunterung zu sorgfältiger Miterforschung der Verhältnisse . . . bey ihrer Vegetation. 1785. I. 220.[1]
— Bemerkungen auf sejner Reise nach dem Unterharz. 1784. IV. 352.
— Beyträge zur Erweiterung der Forstwissenschaft. 1780. IV. 241.
— Die Büche. 1783. IV. 493.[2]
— Die einheimischen und fremden Eichenarten. 1787. IV. 500.[2]
— Einleitung in die Dendrologie. 1800. IV. 82.
— Forsthandbuch. 1788. IV. 95.
— Herrn von Burgsdorf rühmliche Bemühung zu Beförderung der wilden Baumzucht. 1788. IV. 125.[1]
— Physikalisch-ökonomische Abhandlung von den verschiedenen Knoppern. 1783. IV. 502.[1]
— Rękoksiag lasowy. 1788. IV. 95. — 179.? IV. 99.
— Umiejętnośé lasowa. 1788. IV. 95. — 1809. IV. 99.
— Versuch einer vollständigen Geschichte vorzüglicher Holzarten. 1783. IV. 105.
— Verzeichnis der Insekten an den Eichbäumen. 1796. IV. 509.
— Ueber die in den Waldungen der Kurmark-Brandenburg befindlichen . . . Holzarten. 1786. I. 370, *IV. 81.*
— Ueber den weissblühenden Acazienbaum. 1801. IV. 522.[2]
— *See also* Бургсдорфъ, Ф.
Burgsdorf, L. J. F. von. Schreiben an seinen Vater. 1801. IV. 352.
Burgund, (*Forstinspektor*). Zur Forstarbeiter-Frage. 1864. IV. 310.[2]
— Kurze Beschreibung des Hagelschadens . . . Pless. 1850. IV. 189.[2]
— Notiz für das Forstvereinsheft pro 1852. 1852. IV. 504.
Buri, Eugen. Amyrin; the principal constituent of elemi. 1877. III. 511.[2]
— Ueber den Japantalg. 1879. III. 528.[2]
— *See also* FLÜCKIGER, F. A. & BURI, Eugen.
Buri, Friedrich Carl von. Abhandlung von der Regalität derer Jagten in Teutschland. 1744. IV. 316.
— Behauptete Vorrechte deren alten königlichen Bann-Forste. 1742. IV. 319.[2]
— Drey-Eichisches Beweiss- und Urkunden-Buch. 1742. IV. 319.[2]
Burian, Ferd. Die Anlage eines Weichselrohrgartens. 1881. III. 438.[2]
— Wie noch manche kranke Pflanze gerettet werden kann. 1883. III. 313.[1]
Burian, Hyn. V. Naše české ovoce. 1894. III. 90.[1]
— Pěstování Růží za účelem výroby růžového oleje. 1887. III. 454.[1]
— O plodňování Hruškových květů. 1895. III. 445.[2]
— Růže a její pěstování ve vých Rumelii. 1885. III. 452.
Burkart. Sammlung der wichtigsten europäischen Nutzhölzer. 1880. I. 37,[1] *IV. 13,*[1] *539,*[2] V. VIII.[1]
Burket, Ladislav. Jáhloň; monograf. pojedn. 1882. III. 425.[2]
— Nauka o pěstování ovocných stromů a keřů v tvarech prirozených i umělých. 1889. III. 146.[2]
— Pěstování ovocných stromů a keřů v hrncich a ve kbelích. 1877. III. 146.[2]
Burkill, Isaac Henry. Changes in sex of Willows. 1898. II. 104.[1]
— On a collection of plants from New Britain. 1896. I. 499.
— List of . . . plants occurring in British Central Africa. 1897. I. 493.
— Notes on plants collected in the Aconcagua valleys. *See* FITZGERALD, E. A. 1899. I. 331.
— On some variations in the number of stamens and carpels. 1895. I. 115.[2]
— *See also* WILLIS, J. C. & BURKILL, I. H.
Burkitt, J. H. On the flora of Gloucestershire. 1893. I. 534.[2]
Burlamaque, F. S. L. Monographia do Cafeeiro. 1860. III. 728.[2]
Burlingham, Richard. Instructions to prevent the blight ineident to Peach. 1802. III. 431.[1]
Burma. *See* INDIA — BURMA.

The **Burma** forest act. 1881. IV. 332.[1]
Burma Teak forests. 1897. IV. 537.[2]
Burma. *See* INDIA — BRITISH BURMAH.
Burman, Johannes. Catalogi duo plantarum africanarum. 1737. I. 482, 493.
— Flora malabarica. 1769. I. 77.
— Horti medici amstelaedamensis plantarum usualium catalogus. 1775. I. 51.[1]
— Index alter in omnes tomos Herbarii amboinensis. 1769. I. 77.
— Rariorum africanarum plantarum . . . decas. 1738. I. 482, 493.
— Thesaurus zeylanicus. 1737. I. 476.[1]
Burman, Nicolaus Laurens. Felicis Valle . . . Flora corsicae. 1770. I. 419.[1]
— Flora indica. 1768. I. 471.
— Florae capensis prodromus. 1768. I. 493.
— Specimen botanicum de Geraniis. 1759. II. 389.[2]
Burmannus. *See* BURMAN.
Burmeister, Carlos V. Relación de un viaje á la gobernacion del Chubut. 1883. I. 345.
Burmeister, E. Verhinderung des Benagens junger Obstbäume. 1882. III. 186.[1]
Burmeister, Hermann. Grundriss der Naturgeschichte. 1845. I. 88.
— Handbuch der Naturgeschichte. 1836. I. 255.
— Landschaftliche Bilder Brasiliens. 1853. I. 342.
— Reise durch die La Plata-Staaten. 1861. I. 344.
— & Taschenberg, E. L. Botanische Abbildungen zur Erläuterung des natürlichen Systems. *See* BURMEISTER, Hermann. 1845. I. 88; TASCHENBERG, E. L. 1845. I. 381.
Burn, R. Scott. The practical directory for the improvement of landed property. 1881. III. 110.[1]
Burnaby Lautier, O. A. De Arenboom. 1890. III. 320.[2]
Burnap, W. A. Best three red Grapes. 1899. III. 547.
Burnat, Émile. Flore des Alpes maritimes. 1892. I. 417.
— Notes sur le Rosa ischiana Crépin. 1899. II. 295.[1]
— Rosa subspoliata. 1883. II. 299.[1]
— & Barbey, William. Notes sur un voyage botanique dans les îles Baléares. 1882. I. 423.
— & Gremli, August. Genre Rosa. 1887. II. 288.[2]
— — Observations sur quelques Roses de l'Italie. 1886. II. 286.[2]
— — Les Roses des Alpes maritimes. 1879. II. 285.[2]
Burnett, Gilbert Thomas. An encyclopaedia of useful and ornamental plants. 1852. III. 60.
— Outlines of botany. 1835. I. 87.
Burnett, *Miss* M. A. Plantae utiliores. 1842. III. 52.
Burnetizing. 1859. IV. 418.
Burnham, Stewart H. The Ericaceae in California. 1895. II. 658.[1]
— The genus Ribes in California. 1894. II. **243.**[2]
Burnham Beeches. 1874. II. 126.[1]
Burnip, J. R. *See* PAMMEL, L. H., BURNIP, J. R. & THOMAS, Hannah.
A burnt forest. 1883. IV. 358.[1]
Buro, (*Forstmeister*). Ueber den Anbau und Ertrag der Erle. 1854. IV. 489.[1]
— Beschreibung der zum Fürstenthum Trachenberg gehörigen Forsten. 1857. IV. 353.
— Beschreibung einiger alter Eichen-Baumriesen. 1854. IV. 515.[2]
— Ertrag der Weiss-Erle. 1853. IV. 489.[2]
— Notiz über den Raupenfrass. 1852. IV. 475.
Burr in Pinus sylvestris. 1886. II. 47.[2]
Burrage, J. H. The adhesive discs of Ercilla volubilis. 1892. II. 192.[2]
— On Nuytsia floribunda. 1900. II. 177.[1]
Burrell, E. The Caucasian Walnut. 1888. III. 356.[2]
— Pyrus Sorbus vars. 1888. III. 460.[1]
Burrell, J. & others. Zauschneria californica. 1898. III. 641.[1]
Burri. Neues eidgenössisches Forstgesetz. 1898. IV. 331.[1]
Burrill, Thomas Jonathan. Anthrax of fruit trees. 1881. III. 444.[1]
— The forest-tree plantation of the University of Illinois. 1888. IV. 112.
— The mechanical injuries to trees by cold. 1886. I. 212.
— & McCluer, G. W. The forest tree plantation. 1893. IV. 112.
Burrows, Alfred J. The Ash tree. 1881. IV. 534.[2]
— Autumn tints on forest trees. 1878. III. 207.[1]
— Bark and bark-stripping. 1878. IV. 434.
— Bark and bark stripping. 1879. IV. 434.

Burrows, Alfred J. (*continued*).
— Bark and bark-stripping. 1883. IV. 515.¹
— The construction and maintenance of roads. 1878. IV. 266.²
— On coppice wood. 1878. IV. 132.¹
— Cortezas curtientes y descortezamiento. 1878. IV. 434.
— Cultivation of underwood. 1882. IV. 132.¹
— Dering Wood, Kent. 1879. IV. 358.¹
— Drainage. 1878. IV. 144.¹
— The growth of coppicing. 1879. IV. 132.¹
— The growth of coppicing and underwood. 1879. IV. 132.¹
— The Hazel. 1881. IV. 492.¹
— Hedges, hedge plants. 1879. IV. 134.²
— On layering. 1879. III. 159.¹
— Magnolias and their propagation. 1880. III. 399.¹
— The New forest. 1879. IV. 358.¹
— The Oak. 1880. IV. 507.
— Ornamental forestry. 1878. IV. 137.¹
— On planting. 1878. IV. 142.
— On planting. 1879. IV. 152.
— Planting forest trees. 1879. IV. 152.
— Pruning forest trees. 1879. IV. 171.
— Qualities of timber. 1880. IV. 408.
— Remarks on the thinning and pruning. 1878. IV. 171.
— Roads; their construction. 1883. IV. 267.
— Science for foresters. 1884. IV. 57.
— Science for young foresters. 1879. IV. 57.
— Seaside plantations. 1878. III. 41.²
— Transplanting. 1879. III. 166, 167.
— Tree planting a profitable investment. 1879. IV. 261.²
— On tree seeds, seed-beds and sowing. 1879. IV. 149.¹
— The valuation . . . of timber and coppicing. 1881. IV. 256.
— & **Boulger**, G. S. Epping forest and its future management. 1882. IV. 358.¹
Burson, D. C. Importance of forest tree growing. 1900. IV. 271.¹
Burt, Edward A. The resistance of plants to parasitic fungi. 1899. III. 193.²
Burt, Henry Potter. On the nature and properties of timber. 1853. IV. 408, 417.
Burt, Isabella. Memorials of the Oak-tree. 1860. II. 132.¹
Burtin, François Xavier. Mémoire . . . Quels sont les végétaux indigènes que l'on pourroit substituer . . . aux végétaux exotiques. 1784. III. 270.²
Burton, Richard F. The copal of eastern Africa. 1861. III. 489.²
Burtt, Arthur H. Ueber den Habitus der Coniferen. 1899. II. 18.
Burvenich, Frédéric. Algemeene regels der snoeikunst. 1871. III. 170.
— Angers en zyn boomkweekerijen. 1875. III. 154.¹
— Angers et ses pépinières. 1875. III. 154.¹
— The annual lopping of ornamental trees. 1872. III. 173.¹
— Anthonome du Pommier. 1899. III. 428.²
— Appelroos van Japan. 1894. III. 456.²
— De Appelsnuitkever. 1899. III. 428.²
— Les Aralia. 1894. III. 641.¹
— Un arbre phénomène. 1880. III. 165.¹
— Les arbustes nouveaux de 1889. 1889. III. 77.¹
— Bambusa aurea (Bambou doré). 1876. III. 316.¹
— Een bejaarde Moerbezieboom. 1882. III. 379.¹
— Le Betula alba foliis atropurpureis. 1878. III. 357.¹
— Over het bewaren der greffels. 1869. III. 161.
— Bigarreau pleureur. 1894. III. 432.¹
— De bladluizen van den Perzikboom. 1893. III. 442.¹
— Bloedluis op den Peerboom. 1899. III. 446.²
— De boomgaard. 1872. III. 140.¹
— Un Camellia géant. 1880. II. 551.¹
— Le Cedrus Deodora robusta. 1892. III. 300.¹
— Les chenilles. 1892. III. 389.¹
— Clematis. 1880. III. 389.¹
— Les Conifères pleureurs. 1878. III. 290.
— De la conservation des greffons. 1869. III. 161.
— Culture du Paulownia imperialis. 1872. III. 703.²
— Cupressus Lawsoni stricta. 1888. III. 301.¹
— Dood van een reus. 1887. II. 139.¹
— Enting der boomen. 1890. III. 165.
— Enting van den Peren- op den Appelboom. 1899. III. 445.³
— Les Érables du Japon. 1889. III. 535.¹
— Evenkracht tusschen wortel en takgestel. 1867. I. 106.²
— Les fleurs mellifères. 1888. III. 224.¹
— De fruitboomen aan de gevels. 1878. III. 140.³

— De fruitboomen als struiken geteeld. 1882. III. 140.²
— De fruitboomen langsheen de ijzeren wegen. 1867. III. 211.¹
— De fruithagen. 1867. III. 213..
— Greffage des arbres. 1890. III. 165.
— Greffage du Néflier. 1891. III. 429.²
— Greffage du Poirier sur Pommier. 1899. III. 445.²
— Griffeling van den Mispelboom. 1891. III. 429.²
— De groepen van bontbladerige heestergewassen. 1874. III. 206.²
— Gruppen von Gehölzen mit bunten Blättern. 1874. III. 206.²
— De heestergroepen met afwisselende kleuren. 1877. III. 201, 206.²
— Hiver de 1879-80. 1880. III. 182.
— De honigdragende gewassen. 1888. III. 224.¹
— Het kweeken van vruchtboomen aan de gevels. 1878. III. 140.²
— Le Ligustrum japonicum. 1899. III. 673.²
— De Linde. 1890. III. 585.²
— Magnolia Yulan var. Alexandrina. 1900. III. 400.¹
— Malus floribunda Sieb. 1880. III. 429.¹
— De Marbelaan. 1897. III. 436.¹
— De Marbelaan. 1898. II. 273.²
— Les massifs d'arbustes à contrastes de couleurs. 1877. III. 201, 206.²
— Les massifs d'arbustes à feuillage coloré. 1874. III. 206.²
— Misvorming. 1887. II. 280.¹
— De mot der fruitboomen. 1891. III. 191.
— Un. Mûrier d'un âge mûr. 1882. III. 379.¹
— Nouveau procédé de marcottage de la Vigne. 1867. III. 548.¹
— Nut van den witten Acacia. 1869. IV. 524.¹
— Die Obstbaumzucht an den Giebelmauern. 1876. III. 172.
— Een ongewoon geval van kleuring. 1886. I. 244.³
— De openbare beplantingen. 1887. III. 42.²
— Le Pêcher à feuilles pourpres. 1875. III. 440.¹
— De Perzikboom met purper blad. 1875. III. 440.¹
— De Phytoptus Piri. 1881. III. 446.¹
— Les pigeons perdus ou exposé des moyens de les utiliser par la culture fruitière. 1887. III. 172.
— Les plantations d'alignement. 1887. III. 42.²
— Praktische aanwijzingen over den snoei der fruitboomen. 1862. III. 140.¹
— Le Prunier Myrobolan. 1897. III. 436.¹
— Pruniers de Chine à fleurs doubles. 1875. III. 437.¹
— Puceron lanigère du Poirier. 1899. III. 446.²
— Pucerons du Pêcher. 1893. III. 442.¹
— Pyrus japonica var. Maulei. 1900. III. 420.²
— Recepage annuel de quelques arbres d'ornement. 1872. III. 173.¹
— De renzen in 't plantenrijk. 1894. II. 125.¹
— Een reusenboom. 1884. II. 97.¹
— Rhus Cotinus pendula. 1885. III. 524.¹
— De ringelrups. 1867. III. 190.
— Robinia neo-mexicana. 1897. III. 486.³·
— Rosier à fruit du Japon. 1894. III. 456.²
— De rupsen. 1892. III. 191.
— Snoei der boomen, die men verplant. 1879. III. 170.
— Snoeijen der sieraads-houtgewassen. 1866. III. 170.
— Le Solanum Seaforthianum. 1899. III. 702.¹
— Le Sorbier. 1891. III. 459.¹
— Spiraea Bumalda. 1891. III. 461.¹
— Spiraea multiflora arguta. 1892. III. 460.²
— Le Spiraea Thunbergi. 1876. III. 461.¹
— Le Sureau. 1891. III. 751.²
— Taille des arbres qu'on transplante. 1879. III. 170.
— De la taille des fruitiers. 1877. III. 295.¹
— Teelt van de Paulownia. 1872. III. 703.²
— La teigne des arbres fruitiers. 1891. III. 191.
— Le Tilleul. 1889. III. 585.¹
— De Treurkerseboom. 1894. III. 432.¹
— Utilité de l'Acacia blanc. 1869. IV. 524.¹
— De Vlinderboom. 1876. III. 751.³
— Over de vormen der leiboomen. 1871. III. 214.¹
— Weigelia amabilis Looymansi aurea. 1876. III. 749.¹
— Wijngaardveld. 1880. III. 535.¹
— Winter van 1879-1880. 1880. III. 182.
— Een wonderboom. 1880. III. 165.
— Xanthoceras sorbifolia. 1890. III. 540.²
— De zwitsersche Populier. 1885. III. 345.¹

Burvenich, Jules. Acer platanoides Schwedleri. 1878. III. 535.²
— Acer platanoides Schwedleri, l'Érable plane à feuilles pourpres. 1878. III. 535.²
— Encore l'Aucuba japonica. 1877. III. 645.¹
— Influence du sujet sur la greffe. 1887. III. 40.
— Invloed van den stam op de enttwijg. 1887. III. 40.
— La maladie des pedicelles des raisins. 1886. III. 561.
— Nog iets over Aucuba japonica. 1877. III. 645.¹
— De ziekte der druifsteeltjes. 1886. III. 561.
Burvenich, Octave. Étude sur la cloque du Pêcher. 1879. III. 441.²
— De kweekerijen van Neu-Britz. 1878. III. 154.¹
— Les pépinières de Neu-Britz. 1878. III. 154.¹
— Verhandeling over de kruiziekte des Perzikbooms. 1879. III. 441.²
Bury, N. See Бурый, H.
Busby, Henry. The cultivation of Cocoa. 1886. III. 492.¹
Busby, James. A visit to the principal vineyards of France. 1835. III. 551.² .
Buscalioni, Luigi. Studi sur cristalli di ossalato di calcio. 1895. I. 139.
— See also MATTIROLO, Oreste & BUSCALIONI, Luigi.
— & Fermi, Claudio. Sull' azione coagulante di alcuni succhi vegetali. 1898. I. 178.
— C ri allo studio degli enzimi proteolitici. 1898. I. 178.ont buto
— & Huber, Jacques. Eine neue Theorie der Ameisenpflanzen. 1900. I. 235.²
Busch. See Бурь.
Busch, Heinrich. Untersuchungen über die Frage ob das Licht zu den unmittelbaren Lebensbedingungen der Pflanzen . . . gehört. 1889. I. 174.
Busch, Johann Wilhelm. Blicke in die Bewirthschaftung der Wälder. 1812. IV. 117.
— Ideen für Forstmänner. 1823. IV. 101.
Busch, Nikolai A. See Бушъ, H. A.
Buschan, Georg. Vorgeschichtliche Botanik der Cultur- und Nutzpflanzen. 1895. I. 248.¹
Buschbaum, Heinrich. Flora des Landrosteibezirks Osnabrück. 1879. I. 387.
— Die Gefäss-Pflanzen des Fürstenthums Osnabrück. 1878. I. 387.
Buse. Eine neue selbstregistrierende Kluppe. 1897. IV. 232.
Buser, Othmar. Ueber das Auftreten der Arve in der Ostschweiz. 1898. II. 41.²
Buser, R. Flora orientalis . . . Supplementum. See BOISSIER, Edmond. 1867. I. 449.
Buser, Robert. Salix Caprea × purpurea Wim. 1894. II. 110.²
Bush & Son & Meissner. Catalogue illustré . . . des Vignes américaines. 1875. III. 547.
— Illustrated descriptive catalogue of American Grape-vines. 1875. III. 547.
— Les Vignes américaines. 1875. III. 547.
— Le Viti americane. 1875. III. 547.
Bush, Benjamin Franklin. Distribution of the trees . . . of Jackson county. 1891. I. 320.
— Hybrid Oaks in western Missouri. 1895. II. 129.¹
— A new hybrid Oak in the Indian Territory. 1895. II. 135.¹
— Notes on a list of plants collected in southeastern Missouri. 1894. I. 326.
— Notes on the mound flora of some southern swamps. 1897. I. 319.
— Notes on the mound flora of Atchison county. 1895. V. XVIII.¹
— Quercus Phellos × rubra. 1895. II. 136.¹
— The trees, shrubs and vines of Missouri. 1895. I. 317,² IV. 78,¹ V. XVII.¹
Bush, Frank. Flora of Jackson county. 1882. I. 319, V. XVII.²
Bushnan, John S. Notice of a new Scottish locality for the Linnaea. 1829. II. 835.³
Buss, Ernst. See HEIM, Albert & BUSS, Ernst.
Buss, Frederick. A practical treatise on the Fuchsia. 1883. III. 640.¹
Bussato, Marco. Giardino di agricoltura. 1592. III. 5.²
Bussche, E. F., Freiherr von dem. Untersuchungen über den Einfluss der éclaircie par la haute. 1895. IV. 176.¹
Bussche, Ernst, Freiherr von dem. Der Wald und das öffentliche Wohl. 1892. IV. 45.
Busse, Ch. Fr. H. De Rhoe Toxicodendro et radicante. 1811. III. 528.¹

Busse, E. Die Bestandtheile des Tolubalsams. 1876. III. 482.²
Busse, Walter. Beiträge zur Kenntniss der Morphologie . . . der Weisstanne. 1893. II. 23.¹
— Expedition nach den deutsch-ostafrikanischen Steppen. 1900. I. 493.
— Ueber gerbstoffhaltige Mangroverinden. 1899. IV. 435.
— Ueber Gewürze. 1894. III. 343.¹ — 1895. III. 403.¹ — 1896. III. 403.¹
— Macis. 1896. III. 403.¹
— Muskatnüsse. 1895. III. 403.¹
— Pfeffer. 1894. III. 343.²
— Reisebericht der Expedition · nach den deutsch-ostafrikanischen Steppen. 1900. I. 493.
— See also POLENSKE, Ed. & BUSSE, Walter.
Bussey, Geo. G. & Co. Willow for bat-making. 1898. IV. 488.¹
Bussey institution. Bulletin. I. 5.
Bussy, A. Sur la culture du Cannellier. 1828. III. 405.²
Busti, Paul. Instructions for the cultivation of the Mulberry. 1826. III. 374.
Bustillos, J. Vicente. Yerba-mate chilena. 1865. III. 533.
Bute, John Stuart, earl of. Botanical tables . . . of British plants. 1785. I. 395.
Butler, A. A. The Tripyramid slides of 1885. 1886. IV. 339.
Butler, Edward A. Silkworms. 1888. III. 148.³
Butler, George S. Japanese plums. 1900. III. 433.¹
Butler, James D. & Jones, Winslow. The Cypress of Somma. 1895. II. 30.¹
Butler, W. C. The uses of our native timber. 1886. IV. 397.
Butler, William Mill. Yerba maté tea. 1900. III. 531.¹
Butret, Charles, baron de. Gründlicher Unterricht vom Schnitte der Fruchtbäume. 1795. III. 143.
— Taille raisonnée des arbres fruitiers. 1795. III. 143, V. XXVIII.¹
Butt, E. N. On Chicle gum. 1897. III. 666.³
Butt, J. M. The botanical primer. 1825. I. 397.
Buttats, F. See Буттацъ, Ф.
Butte, Lucien. Action de certaines substances médicamenteuses. 1891. III. 683.²
Butteaud, Édouard. Flore tahitienne. 1891. I. 510.³
Butter and Tallow tree of Sierra Leone. 1897. III. 610.²
Buttlar, Rudolph von. Die Anwendung . . . des v. Buttlar-'schen Culturverfahrens. 1859. IV. 152.
— Das Buttlar'sche . . . Cultur-Verfahren. 1850. IV. 152.
— Die auf dem Elberberger Forst angewendete Forst-Culturmethode. 1847. IV. 152.
— Forstkultur-Verfahren in . . . seinen Folgen zu der Forstwirthschaft. 1853. IV. 118.
— Der forstliche Anbau der Lärchen. 1865. IV. 449.
Buttner. On the culture of bees in forests. 1828. IV. 438. ·
Butz, George C. Co-operative experiment with forest tree seeds. 1900. IV. 545.²
— Experience with evergreens in Pennsylvania. 1893. III. 117,² 298.
— The Peach industry in Pennsylvania. 1899. III. 441.¹
Buurman, W. De Djaticultuur. 1883. IV. 536.³
— Het herwouden met Eucalyptus Globulus. 1884. IV. 168,¹ 652.²
— Teak cultivation in Java. 1883. IV. 536.¹
Buurman van Vreeden, W. Verslag van getah pertja . . produceerende boomen te Tjipetir. 1899. III. 149.
Buvry, L. Anbauversuche mit ausländischen Nutzpflanzen . 1868. III. 45.
Buxbaum, Johann Christian. Enumeratio plantarum . . in agro hallensi. 1721. I. 373.
— Nova plantarum genera. 1728. I. 290.
— Plantae dubiae ad sua genera relatae. 1729. II. 334.²
— Plantarum minus cognitarum centuria. 1728. I. 448.²
Buxin. 1834. III. 523.¹
Buxton, Edward North. Epping forest. 1884. IV. 358.¹
Buxton, Richard. A botanical guide to the flowering plants . . . of Manchester. 1849. I. 400.
Buys, M. Batavia, Buitenzorg en de Preanger. 1891. III 276.¹ .
— Twee jaren op Sumatra's westkust. 1886. III. 275.²
Buysman, Martin. Caoutchouc. 1899. III. 232.¹
— Culture des plantes tropicales . . . en pleine terre. . 1898. III. 49.¹
— The difference between sea and continental climate. 1884. I. 349.
— Over den invloed van het directe zonlicht. 1885. I. 173.

Buysman, Martin (*continued*).
— Ulex europaeus L. 1897. II. 387.²
— Het verschil tusschen kusten en continentaal klimaat. 1884. I. 349.
Buyssens, A. Deux Palmiers nouveaux. 1898. III. 320,¹ *386.*¹
— La gelée et le dégel, leur action sur les végétaux. 1894. III. 182.
— Invloed van vorst en dooi op de gewassen. 1894. III. 182.
Buzareingues, Charles GIROU DE., *See* GIROU DE BUZAREINGUES, Charles.
Buzeta, Manuel & **Bravo,** Felipe. Diccionario geográfico . . . de las Islas Filipinas. 1850. IV. 399.²
Buzonnière, de. De l'influence du choix des graines sur la prospérité des semis de Pins maritimes en Sologne. 1853. IV. 467.¹
Byasson, Henri. Note on Maté or Paraguay Tea. 1878. III. 531.¹,
Byczkowski, Heinrich. Das Verhältniss der Pflanzen zur Atmosphäre. 1846. I. 170.
Bykof, N. L. *See* БЫКОВЪ, Н. Л.
Byll, A. de, **Timmer,** W. & **Reyers,** O. Bericht wegens ontginningen en bebouwingen van woeste gronden. 1784. IV. 159.
Bynoe. On a kind of manna found on Gum trees. 1846. II. 623.²
— Notice sur la Manne de l'Australie heureuse. 1846. II. 623.²
Byrkit, John W. Catalogue and check-list of the trees . . . of America. 1879. IV. 76.¹
Bytchikhin, A. *See* БЫЧИХИНЪ, А.

C. Areca lutescens. 1874. III. 325.²
C. Comisión de repoblación de las dunas del SO. de la Península. 1889. IV. 546.²
C. ¿Con la . . . ed avvicendamento boschivo. 1882. IV. 74.¹ onsoc zione
C. Designazione e trattamento dei boschi. 1882. IV. 270.
C. Distruzione delle ceppaie d'alberi. 1882. IV. 143.¹
C. La grillotalpa. 1882. IV. 92.
C. Insetti nocivi. 1882. IV. 209.²
C. Die Kultur der Weymouthskiefer. 1896. IV. 469.
C. Lidt om Coniferæ. 1855. III. 289.
C. Máquina Ransome para el apeo de los árboles. 1878. IV. 383.²
C. Moro papirifero (Morus papirifera). 1882. III. 368.¹
C. Una nuova pianta resinosa europea. 1882. IV. 460.²
C. Pericolosa concorrenza alla corteccia da concia. 1882. IV. 435.
C. Presupuesto del Ministerio de fomento. 1892. IV. 552.¹
C. Ricchezze boschive nelle provincie Renane. 1881. IV. 349.¹
C. Il rimboschimento delle montagne in Francia. 1864. IV. 162.
" **C.**" Some remarks on the forest report of the Central Provinces. 1896. IV. 378.
C. Steleocoftiria. 1882. IV. 384.²
C. Lo storno (Sturnus vulgaris Linn.). 1882. IV. 90.¹
C. The Willow as a sea-side tree. 1876. III. 41.²
C., de. Myrtacées. *See* CANDOLLE, A. P. de. 1826. II. 618.²
C., A. Does the cutting down of a forest on a hill decrease the quantity of water? 1888. IV. 51.
C., A. Note on uses of Pinus excelsa. 1884. IV. 464.¹
C., A. Vallombrosa and the Royal Italian forest school. 1894. IV. 35.²
C., A. M. C. Sir Charles Bunbury's arboretum. 1885. I. 55.
C., Alph. d. Le Thé découvert dans une province de l'Inde anglaise. *See* CANDOLLE, Alphonse de. 1835. II. 552.¹
C., B. De Ginkgo of Veertig kroonenboom. 1853. III. 286.²
C., B. U. Willow for cricket bats. 1899. IV. 488.¹
C., C. L'art de multiplier la soie. *See* CASTELLET, C. 1760. III. 372.²
C., C. La cuestion de los montes. 1885. IV. 276.²
C., C. Los montes públicos. Discusion del presupuesto de fomento. 1885. IV. 265.
C., C. ¿Que hay sobre desamortizacion forestal? 1878. IV. 276.¹
C., C. El servicio forestal en Argelia. 1885. IV. 295.²
C., C. L. Marasquin français. 1821. III. 436.²
C., D. S. P. Nouveaux systèmes pour protéger et hâter la maturité des fruites. 1880. III. 174.²

C., E. Boisement de terres communales. 1896. IV. 160.²
C., E. Défrichement et boisement. 1896. IV. 282.²
C., E. Garden Ivies. 1887. III. 643.¹
C., E. Les Genêts et les résineux. 1896. IV. 211.¹
C., E. Les haies d'Épicéa. 1896. III. 305,² *IV. 454.*
C., E. L'impôt foncier des propriétés boisées. 1895. IV. 552.²
C., E. Le Lupin et les plantations. 1896. IV. 143.²
C., E. Les plantations des routes. 1897. III. 210.
C., E. Viticulture in New Zealand. 1896. III. 559.²
C., E. M. Plants of the world and where they grow. 1855. I. 95.
C., E. M. Popular geography of plants. 1855. I. 95, 299.
C., E. W. The Stone Pine of Italy. 1875. II. 45.¹
C., Edm. Les arbres et les champs. 1894. III. 210.
C., F. À propos du Châtaignier. 1895. II. 124.¹
C., F. Toujours à propos du Châtaignier. 1896. II. 124.¹
C., F. H. C. De houtsoorten van Halemahera. 1883. IV. 400.¹
C., G. Conservancy of forests in young communities. 1882. IV. 270.
C., G. Effetti del disboscamento dei monti. 1883. IV. 48.¹
C., G. Un esempio da imitare. 1864. IV. 165.
C., G. Olio per illuminazione. *See* COMINOTTI, G. 1881. III. 225.
C., G. Taglio degli alberi coll' elettricità. 1881. IV. 384.¹
C., G., (Dr.). Du déboisement. 1897. IV. 542.¹
C., H. L. The weight of an axe. 1885. IV. 384.¹
C., H. M. Tree myths. 1883. I. 518.
C., J. Une branche de Citronnier sur un Oranger. 1856. II. 402.¹
C., J. Cacti. 1873. III. 619.
C., J. Het derde deel van de Wijse jaer-beschryver. *See* CATS, Jakob. 1661. III. 104.
C., J. Fertilisation of the Coffee flower. 1899. III. 727.
C., J. The Pearly Aloe. 1876. III. 337.¹
C., J. Reboisement de bancs de craie blanche. 1900. IV. 164.²
C., J. Saddle-grafting Rhododendrons. 1880. III. 656.
C., J. A. Fasciation in the Spruce Fir. 1880. II. 36.¹
C., J. C. Deciduous flowering wall plants. 1883. III. 205.¹
C., J. C. Evergreen wall shrubs. 1883. III. 205,¹ *806.*¹
C., J. C. Rhododendrons in different soil. 1884. III. 656.
C., J. C. Summer foliage tints. 1886. III. 205.²
C., J. C. Surface-dressing Rhododendrons. 1886. III. 656.
C., J. E. Oil of Basswood. 1889. III. 586.¹
C., J. M. Natural grafting. 1877. I. 209.¹
C., J. M. Tension in an Oak. 1879. I. 149.²
C., J. V. H. Begrootingen over 100 en 300 bouws woeste gronden bestend om met Koffie te worden beplant. n. d. III. 729.¹
C., J. W. New and beautiful Crotons. 1884. III. 516.¹
C., J. Y. Transplanting large trees at Brooklyn. 1872. III. 167.
C., K. Over het ontstaan . . . van het lopend zwam. 1790. IV. 414.²
C., L. Produits des taillis à longue révolution. 1900. IV. 252.
Č., L. Rozsáhlosť ruských lesních revírů. . *See* L., Č. 1896. IV. 289.¹
C., L. C. Sur l'extraction . . . de l'huile de Rican. 1814. III. 522.¹
C., M. The Cocoanut in Queensland. 1877. III. 322.²
C., M. B. Carica Papaya. 1900. III. 617.¹
C., M. J. Notes on Aesculus glabra. 1883. II. 481.²
C., N. Nouvelles expériences sur la fève du Calabar. 1868. III. 483.²
C., N. *See* C., P. & C., N.
C., N. L. Commerce du bois. 1897. IV. 557.¹
C., O. Forest administration in Oudh. 1893. IV. 295.²
C., O. Note in the regulation of forest concessions in Oudh. 1896. IV. 353.
C., O. On suitable seasons for coppice fellings. 1899. IV. 132.²
C., P. Stray notes from the Arnold Arboretum. 1891. III. 203.
C., P. & C., N. Commerce des bois. 1895. IV. 557.¹
C., R. Procedimientos rápidos en trabajos forestales. 1889. IV. 265.
C., S. Extraordinary irregularity in the growth of Teak. 1898. II. 761.¹
C., S. Ligeras notas sobre reorganización del servicio forestal. 1893. IV. 553.²
C., S. Notas sobre la estadística de la producción forestal. 1892. IV. 363.²

C., S. A. The attraction of bark beetles to damaged trees. 1898. IV. 205.[1]
C., S. A. The fructification of the Deodar. 1898. II. 27.[2]
C., S. A. The insect plague in Deodar pole forests. 1900. IV. 448.[1]
C., S. N. Oil [of] Buchanania latifolia seeds. 1898. III. 524.[1]
C., V. Della diatesi morbosa della Vite. See COLA, Vincenzo. 1857. III. 577.
C., W. Abies Smithiana. 1889. III. 306.[2]
C., W. The Chili Pine. 1889. III. 299.[1]
C., W. The Japan Cedar. 1889. III. 302.[1]
C., W. Picea concolor violacea. 1890. III. 296.[1]
C., W. Picea lasiocarpa. 1889. III. 296.[1]
C., W. Picea Webbiana. 1889. III. 297.[1]
C., W. Pinus patula. 1887. . III. 308.[1]
C., W. The Plum-fruited Yew. 1890. III. 287.[2]
C., W. D. Planting trees in summer. 1876. III. 168.[2]
C., W. G. Grapes with ornamental foliage. 1895. III. 584.[1]
C., . . . Furetage du Hêtre. 1891. IV. 498.
C*** M. D. See DUMONT DE COURSET, G. L. M.
C. A. Purpus und seine Einführungen. 1896. I. 320.
C. G. Rafns förtjenster om Skandinaviens flora. 1841. III. 100.[1]
C. y Sobron, Félix. Plantas medicinales de la república del Uruguay. 1874. III. 65.[3]
Cabanès, Gustave. Les loupes ou broussins. 1900. III. 345.[1]
— Notes de tératologie végétale. 1900. II. 280.[1]
Cabanis, (er.). Essai sur les principes de la greffe. 1804. III. 159.[2]
Cabanis, F. Le Mûrier, ses avantages. 1866. III. 380.[1]
Cabello é Ibañez, Luis. La vérité sur le Phylloxera. 1879. III. 760.
Cabianca, S. Risaliamo alle origini. 1899. IV. 36.[1]
Cabran, de. Manière de bouturer les arbustes. 1846. III. 158.
Cabrera y Diaz, Anatael. Los Dragos de Canarias. 1892. II. 82.[2]
Cacao; planting and curing. 1889. III. 592.[3]
Cacao en chocolade. 1883. III. 595.[1]
Cacao en chocolade. 1884. III. 595.[1]
Cacao-growing in Grenada. 1893. III. 593.[1]
Cacao industry in Grenada. 1900. III. 593.[1]
Cacaocultuur op de alluviale landen in Suriname. 1893. III. 593.[1]
La caccia alle carrughe. 1864. IV. 209.[1]
Cachat, J. Le Houx et le Gui à la fête de Noël. 1900. I. 518.
Cacheux, E. Le jour des arbres. 1895. IV. 541.[1]
Cachin, M. Table of principal species of wood. 1886. IV. 401.[3]
Cactus journal. III. 16.
Cactuses in-doors and out; what is a Cactus? 1890. III. 619.
Cadell, George. The Beech forests of Hesse Nassau. 1893. IV. 354.
— Foreign versus native timber. 1898. IV. 398.[3]
— Forest administration in the canton Vaud. 1890. IV. 294.[1]
— Forestry. 1888. IV. 337.[1]
— Forestry in the canton Vaud. 1886. IV. 367.
— On the preparation of wood specimens. 1893. I. 37.[2] IV. 18.[1]
— Trees. Nobis placeant ante omnia silvae. 1892. I. 295.[1]
Cadet. Mémoire sur les bois de Corse. 1792. IV. 359.[1] 584.[1]
— Observation sur le Marron d'Inde. 1809. III. 537.[2]
Cadet de Gassicourt, Charles Louis Félix. Analyse de l'huile de Carapa. 1819. III. 511.[1]
— Sur l'Andira Harsfieldii. 1811. III. 476.[2]
— Sur le bois de corail. 1815. IV. 396.[1]
— Du caoutchouc. 1825. III. 230.
— Charbon de bois donné comme febrifuge. 1815. IV. 433.[1]
— Dissertations sur les Euphorbiacées. 1824. III. 514.[1]
— Essai sur les végétaux astringens. 1817. III. 237.[1]
— Examen chimique . . . de la noix d'Acajou. 1818. III. 529.[1]
— Sur le Guarana. 1817. III. 539.[2]
— Sur le Malambo. 1815. III. 516.[2]
— Manne observée sur un Saule. 1810. III. 351.[1]

— Matière médicale des Galibis. 1816. III. 268.[1]
— Mémoire sur l'arbre Cirier de la Louisiane. 1803. III. 352.[2]
— Notes extraites d'un mémoire manuscrit de M. B. 1816. III. 272.[2]
— Notice sur la Diosma crenata. 1827. II. 399.[1]
— Sur les pépinières d'Oliviers. 1817. III. 675.[1]
— Thé acclimaté. 1820. III. 600.[1]
— Le Thé est-il plus nuisible qu'utile? 1808. III. 606.
Cadet de Vaux, Antoine Alexis. Dissertation sur le Café. 1806. III. 738.
— Mémoire sur l'application de l'huile aux arbres. 1806. III. 175.[1]
— Nieuwe middelen om de vruchtboomen voor den vorst te beveiligen. 1806. III. 183.[1]
— De la restauration et du gouvernement des arbres à fruits. 1807. III. 143.
Cador, Ludwig. Anatomische Untersuchung der Mateblätter. 1900. III. 270.[2]
Cadura, Richard. Physiologische Anatomie der Knospendecken. 1886. I. 108.[3]
La caduta delle foglie dell' Olivo. 1898. III. 678.[1]
Caels, Theodor Peter. De Beigii plantis qualitate. 1774. III. 270.[2]
Caen — Académie royale des sciences, arts et belles-lettres. See ACADÉMIE . . . I. 20.
Caen — Société royale d'agriculture et de commerce. See SOCIÉTÉ . . . III. 22.
Caesius, Fridericus, Duke of Acquasparta. See CESI, Federico.
Du Café, son origine. See LALOU, (jr.). 1843. III. 739.
Caféiers hybrides. 1900. III. 742.[1]
De caffe, chocolatae . . . usu et abusu. See MEISNER, L. F. 1720. III. 222.
De caffe et chocolatae . . . usu et abusu. See MEISNER, L. F. 1720. III. 222.
Il Caffè, osia brevi e varj discorsi. 1766. III. 738.
Der Caffee, der Ruin der Menschheit. 1827. III. 741.[2]
Caffin. De l'organisation et de la classification naturelle des fruits phanérogames. 1820. I. 119.
Caflisch, J. B. Ein Räthsel der Sphinx. 1891. IV. 23.[2] 331.[1]
Caflisch, Johann Friedrich. Excursions-Flora für das südöstliche Deutschland. 1878. I. 387.
— Übersicht der Flora von Augsburg. 1850. I. 383.
Cagniard-Latour. Étude des effets que l'action de la chaleur peut produire sur les bois. 1851. IV. 408.
Cahier des charges pour la vente . . . des lièges. 1898. IV. 518.[1]
Cahours, Auguste. Recherches sur l'huile de Gaultheria. 1843. III. 652.[1]
— Recherches sur la respiration des fleurs. 1864. I. 170.
— Recherches sur la respiration des fruits. 1864. I. 170.
— Recherches sur le salicylate de méthylène. 1843. III. 652.[1]
— Recherches sur les corps isomères. 1858. III. 635.[1]
Caie. Ueber die Kultur der Eriken. 1841. III. 649.[1]
Caillaud, Frédéric ROMANET DU. See ROMANET DU CAILLAUD, Frédéric.
Caille, A. Du Rosa polyantha. 1879. III. 456.[1]
Cailletet, Luis. Les feuilles des plantes peuvent-elles absorber l'eau liquide? 1871. I. 161.
— De l'influence des divers rayons colorés. 1867. I. 172.
— Sur l'origine du carbone fixé par les végétaux à chlorophylle. 1871. I. 172.
Cailliaud, Frédéric. Voyage à Méroé. See DELILE, A. R. 1827. I. 487.
Caillot, Amédée. Essai chimique sur la térébinthine des Sapins. 1830. IV. 446.[2]
— Note sur l'essence de térébinthine. 1846. III. 227.
Caimi da Sondrio, Pietro. Cenni sulla importanza e coltura dei boschi. 1857. IV. 43.
— Memoria in risposta al quesito additare la migliore . . . maniera per rimettere i boschi. 1847. IV. 165.
— Relazione sopra un progetto di legge forestale. 1862. IV. 327.[2]
Cairns, John. On the Weir Mallee, a water-yielding tree. 1859. IV. 531.[1]
Caise, Albert. Douaniers, forestiers, pompiers. 1876. IV. 292.
Cajander, Aimo Kaarlo. Botanisk exkursionsresa i Wirmo. 1900. II. 101.[1]
— Fenno-Scandian kasvitieteellisestä kaakkoisrajasta. 1900. I. 368.[1]

Cajeu, René. Le Jardin botanique de Buitenzorg. 1899. I. 68.[1]
Cajuput oil. 1857. III. 636.
Cajus, John. De canibus britannicis. 1570. I. 394.
— De rariorum animalium et stirpium historia. 1570. I. 394, V. xx.[2]
Calabash and abortion in cattle. 1894. III. 706.[2]
Calabro, P. I cristalli del Poulsen nelle specie di Erythrina. 1887. II. 356.[2]
Calagius, Andreas. Hortus Doct. L. Scholzii. 1592. I. 42.
Calandrini, Filippo. Prodotti forestali. 1864. IV. 20.[2]
Calani, Aristide. La Lunigiana. 1866. IV. 364.
Calas, Julien. Essences forestières des Pyrénées-Orientales. 1893. III. 271,[1] IV. 122.[1]
— Notice sur les travaux de restauration de terrains en montagne. 1892. IV. 186.[1]
— Le Pin Laricio de Salzmann. 1899. IV. 466.[1]
— La processionnaire du Pin. 1897. IV. 462.[1]
— Recherches sur une variété de Pin Laricio. 1899. IV. 466.[2]
— Restauration et conservation des terrains en montagne. La processionnaire du Pin. 1900. IV. 209.[1]
— Restauration et conservation des terrains en montagne. Le Pin Laricio de Salzmann. 1900. IV. 466.[2]
— Les travaux de restauration de terrains . . . la Tet. 1893. IV. 186.[1]
Calberla, G. Die Trockenheit. 1877. III. 183.[2]
Calcara, Pietro. Sui boschi della Sicilia memoria. 1848. I. 430, IV. 86.[1]
— Descrizione dell' isola di Lampedusa. 1847. I. 431.
— Florula medica siciliana. 1851. III. 88.[2]
— Storia naturale dell' isola di Ustica. 1842. I. 431.
On the calcareous crystals. 1829. I. 138.[2]
Calceolarius, Franciscus. See CALZOLARIUS, Francesco.
Cálculos fallidos. See ** Cálculos fallidos. 1896. IV. 551.[1]
Calcutta — Medical and physical society. See MEDICAL . . . I. 29.[1]
Calcutta — Royal botanic garden. See ROYAL · . . I. 29.[1]
Calcutta journal of natural history. I. 29.[1]
Calcutta review. III. 26.[1]
Caldas, Francisco José de. Semanario de la Nueva Granada. See HUMBOLDT, Alexander von & BONPLAND, Aimé. 1805. I. 328.
Caldas, J. J. de. Description of the genuine Quina Tree or Loxa. 1853. II. 813.[2]
Caldcleugh, Alexander. Travels in South America. 1825. I. 328.
Caldenbach, Christoph. De Lauro. 1670. III. 406.[2]
— De Olea. 1679. III. 678.[1]
— De Palma. 1679. III. 318.[2]
— Problemata oratoria. 1672. I. 515.
— De Vite. 1683. III. 582.
Calderari, Francesco. Manuale pratico per la coltivazione della Vite. 1868. III. 557.[1]
Calderón, Juan B. Estudio sobre el arbusto llamado Sinicuiche. 1886. III. 629.[2]
Calderón, Luis. El Roble de marina. 1877. IV. 514.[1]
Calderón, Salvador. Classificatión geológica de las arcillas y su papel en. 1893. IV. 543.[2]
— Nota preliminar sobre la clasificación geológica de las arcillas. 1893. IV. 543.[2]
Caldesio, Ludovico. Florae faventinae tentamen. 1879. I. 429.
Caldwell, G. C. A comparison of manures. 1885. III. 151.
— Ueber das Paranussöl. 1856. III. 631.[2]
Caledonia, (pseud.). The Chilian Pine. 1892. III. 299.[1]
Caledonian horticultural society. See ROYAL CALEDONIAN . . . III. 18.
Calendrier de flore. See CHASTENAY, Victorine de. 1802. I. 265.
Calendrier de flore; ou, Catalogue des plantes des environs de Noyon. 1829. I. 408.
Calenus, Christoph Gebhard. · Vitis et viticulturae ortum. See CALENUS, Friedrich. 1679. II. 509.[1]
Calenus, Friedrich. Vitis et viticulturae ortum. 1679. II. 509.[1]
California — Agricultural experiment station. See CALIFORNIA, UNIVERSITY OF — COLLEGE OF AGRICULTURE. III. 3.
California — State board of horticulture. Biennial report. III. 3.
California, University of — College of agriculture — Agricultural experiment station. Bulletin. Report. Report of the viticultural work. III. 3.

California academy of natural sciences. Bulletin. Proceedings. I. 5.
California academy of science. See CALIFORNIA ACADEMY OF NATURAL SCIENCES. I. 5.
The California Fan Palm. 1895. II. 75.[2]
California fruit grower. III. 3.
California horticulturist. III. 3.
The California Nutmeg; Torreya. 1875. II. 12.[1]
California Olive industry. 1892. III. 676.[1]
California Palms. 1892. III. 318.[1]
A California Rose bush. 1891. III. 456.[1]
California state board of forestry. Biennial report. Bulletin. IV. 3.
California state board of forestry. Memorial. 1888. IV. 272.
The California White Oak. 1890. II. 135.[1]
Californian Buckthorns used in medicine. 1887. III. 542.[2]
Californian forestry. 1889. I. 320, IV. 78.[1]
Californian giants. 1856. II. 50.[3]
Californian olive oil. 1884. III. 679.[1]
Californie. 1873. II. 509.[1]
Californische reuzenden. 1850. III. 307.[2]
Ein californischer Riesenbaum. 1891. IV. 484.[1]
Calkins, William Wirt. Collection of Florida woods. 1883. IV. 18.[1]
— Notes on some little known Florida trees. 1883. IV. 77.[2]
Calkoen, Hendrik J. van. Planten-atlas. 1897. I. 391.[1]
Call, C. F. Experiments on the strength of timbers at Kandahar. 1880. IV. 410.
Call, Richard Ellsworth. Notes on the native forest trees of eastern Arkansas. 1890. I. 317,[1] IV. 78,[1] V. XVII.[2]
Callard de la Ducquerie, Jean Baptiste. Ager medicus cadomensis. 1714. I. 405.
Callay, Albert Althanase. Catalogue raisonné et descriptif des plantes . . . des Ardennes. 1900. I. 419.[1]
Callcott, Maria. See GRAHAM, Maria.
Callender, Robert. A practical essay on the raising . . . of the Crataegus Oxyacantha. 1785. III. 212.[2]
Calley. Essai d'un catalogue . . . des plantes . . . des Ardennes. 1875. I. 414.
Callias, H. de. Procédé économique d'extraction de la fécule des marrons d'Inde. 1857. III. 538.[1]
Callier, Alfons. Bemerkungen zur Flora silesiaca exsiccata. 1895. I. 399.
— Mitteilung über Alnus glutinosa × incana. 1889. II. 116.[1]
— Notes sur quelques formes de la sect. Gymnothyrsus. 1894. II. 115.[2]
— Über die in Schlesien vorkommenden Formen der Gattung Alnus. 1892. I. 115.[1]
Calloni, Silvio. Note sur la germination des Daphne. 1884. II. 601.[1]
— Notes sur la géographie botanique du Tessin. 1881. I. 436.
— Pistillodie des étamines dans la fleur de Persica. 1881. II. 276.[2]
"Calluna vulgaris" and "Aira caryophyllea" in the United States. 1862. II. 661.[2]
Calmels, Dr. See HARDY, Ernest & CALMELS, G.
— & Gossin, E. De la constitution chimique de la cocaïne. 1885. III. 493.[1]
Calques des dessins de la flore du Mexique de Mociño et Sessé. See CANDOLLE, Alphonse de. 1874. I. 270.
Calvados — Société Linnéenne. See SOCIÉTÉ . . . I. 23.
Calvel, Étienne. Des arbres fruitiers pyramidaux. 1802. III. 163.
— Manuel pratique des plantations. 1804. III. 165.
— Praktisches Handbuch für Baumpflanzungen. 1804. III. 165.
— Recherches . . . sur les moyens pratiques d'accélérer la frutification. 1811. III. 143, 174.[1]
— Traité complet sur les pépinières. 1803. III. 110.[1]
— Trattato completo delle piantonaje. 1803. III. 110.[1]
Calvert, Agnes. The laticiferous tissue in the stem of Hevea. 1887. III. 445.[1]
— & Boodle, L. A. On laticiferous tissue in the pith of Manihot Glaziovii. 1887. III. 447.[2]
Calvert, Albert F. Western Australia. 1894. IV. 401.[2]
Calvert, F. R. I. Valonea; a word of warning. 1892. IV. 502.[2]
Calvert, Frederick CRACE-. Dyes and dyestuffs. 1872. III. 468,[2] 478.[1]
— Oxydation au moyen de l'oxygène condensé dans le charbon. 1867. IV. 431.[2]

— Sur le pouvoir que possèdent plusieurs substances d'arrêter la putréfaction. *See* CRACE–CALVERT, Frederick. 1872. IV. 433.²

— & Ferrand, E. Mémoire sur la végétation. 1843. I. 151.¹

Calvet, A. Note sur la culture de Bambou. 1878. III. 314.¹

Calvi, Giovanni. Commentarium inserviturum historiae Pisani vireti. 1777. I. 61.

Calwer, C. G. Deutschlands Obst- und Beerenfrüchte. 1854. III. 71.

— Landwirthschaftliche und technische Pflanzenkunde Deutschlands. 1852. III. 73.

— Württemberg's Holz- und Straucharten. 1853. I. 371.

Calzolaris, Francesco. Iter Baldi civitatis Veronae montis. 1566. I. 423.

— Iter Baldi Montis. 1566. I. 423.

— Iter in Baldum Montem. 1566. I. 423.

— Il viaggio di Monte Baldo. 1566. I. 423.

Camandona, Carlo. Scoperta di nuove risorse sul territorio piemontese. 1833. III. 115.²

Camara, Manoel ARRUDA DA. *See* ARRUDA DA CAMARA, Manoel.

Camara, Manoel Ferreira da. Ensaio de descripçaõ fizica e economica da Comarca. 1789. III. 268.²

Camarecq, KINDER DE. *See* STARING, W. C. H. & KINDER DE CAMARECQ.

Cambessèdes, Jacques. Description d'un genre nouveau . . . des Hypéricinées. 1830. II. 554.²

— Enumeratio plantarum . . . in insulis Balearibus. 1827. I. 420, 423.

— Mémoire sur la famille des Sapindacées. 1829. II. 483.¹

— Mémoire sur les familles des Ternstroemiacées. 1828. II. 547.¹

— Monographie du genre Spiraea. 1824. II. 314.¹

— Note sur deux genres nouveaux . . . des Sapindacées. 1834. II. 483.¹

— Observations sur l'organisation florale . . . des Capparidées. 1834. II. 229.²

— Plantae rariores quas in India orientali collegit Victor Jacquemont. 1844. I. 472.

— Portulacearum, Crassulacearum . . . synopsis. 1829. II. 250.¹

— Transplanteur Sabatier. 1861. III. 167.

— *See also* SAINT–HILAIRE, A. F. O. P., JUSSIEU, Adrien de & CAMBESSÈDES, Jacques.

Cambiamento di peso e volume delle diverse specie legnose. 1885. IV. 411.²

Camboué. La Vigue à Madagascar. 1893. III. 559.¹

Cambridge philosophical society. Proceedings. Transactions. I. 17.

Cambry, Jacques. Description du département de l'Oise. 1803. I. 406.

— Voyage dans le Finistère. 1799. I. 406.

Camell, P. De faba S. Ignatii. 1700. III. 682.¹

— De igasur, seu nuce vomica. 1700. III. 682.¹

Camellia fruits. 1873. II. 550.²

Camellia-flowered Peach. 1857. III. 439.¹

Camellus, George Joseph. *See* KAMEL, G. J.

Camend, H. Le balivage dans les taillis composés. 1887. IV. 237.

Camera dei deputati . . . Discussione del bilancio . . . per la parte riguardante il servizio forestale. 1864. IV. 293.²

Camera dei deputati. — Discussione del disegno di legge per modificazioni alla legge provinciale e comunale. 1864. IV. 328.

Camera dei deputati. Sunto della discussione . . . sull' estensione di talune disposizioni forestali. 1865. IV. 328.

Camerarius, Elias. De plantis vernis. *See* CAMERARIUS, R. J. 1688. I. 530.²

— Σημειολογία . . . seu, De Betula. 1727. II. 117.¹

Camerarius, Elias Rudolf. Theoria physica de plantis. *See* BROTBECK, J. K. 1656. I. 30.

Camerarius, Georg Albert. Bigam botanicam . . . *See* CAMERARIUS, R. J. 1712. IV. 462.²

Camerarius, Joachim H. Hortus medicus et philosophicus. 1588. I. 282.

— Icones accurate nunc primum delineatae. 1588. I. 282.

— Symbolorum et emblematum centuriae. 1590. I. 515.

— Symbolorum . . . ex re herbaria desumtorum centuria. 1590. I. 515. V. xxv.²

Camerarius, Johann David. Praeludia rei herbariae. *See* MOEGLING, J. L. 1612. I. 30.

— Προγυμνάσματα βοτανολογικά. *See* MOEGLING, J. L. 1612. I. 30.

Camerarius, Rudolf Jakob. Bigam botanicam . . . submittit. 1712. IV. 462.²

— De convenientia plantarum in fructificatione et viribus. 1699. III. 259.¹

— Epistola . . . de sexu plantarum. 1694. I. 198.

— Ueber das Geschlecht der Pflanzen. 1694. I. 198.

— De herba Mimosa seu Sentiente. 1688. II. 372.²

— Opuscula botanici argumenti. 1797. I. 33.

— Oratio de Quercuum gallis. 1695. IV. 509.

— De plantis vernis. 1688. I. 530.²

— De Rubo Idaeo. 1721. III. 458.²

— De plantis vernis. 1688. III. 267.¹

Cameron, Virgin Islands. 1888. III. 267.¹

Cameron, Charles A. Preliminary note on the absorption of selenium. 1880. I. 153.

Cameron, David. On the cultivation of the hardy Heaths. 1848. III. 650.¹

Cameron, John. Catalogue of plants in the Botanical garden, Bangalore. 1880. I. 67.¹

— Forest trees of Mysore and Coorg. 1894. III. 92.²

— The fruits of Mysore. 1889. III. 279.¹

— The Gaelic names of plants. 1879. I. 74.¹

— The Mango. 1876. III. 524.²

Cameron, Peter. List of Scottish Cynipidae. 1885. IV. 511.

Cameron, Roderick. Queen Victoria Niagara Falls Park. 1895. I. 311.¹

Cametti, Ottaviano. Ragionamento sopra la selva contigua alla città di Pisa. 1762. IV. 47.²

Camfield, J. H. *See* MAIDEN, J. H. & CAMFIELD, J. H.

Camille-Jordan, (*député, Ain*). Opinion sur l'affectation des bois de l'état. 1817. IV. 326.

Caminhoá, Joaquim Monteiro. Botanica geral e medica. 1877. I. 91.

— Catalogue des plantes toxiques du Brésil. 1871. III. 65.¹

— Compendio de Botanica geral e medica. 1877. I. 91.

— Elementos de botanica geral e medica. 1877. I. 91.

— Memoria sôbre . . . conservar as plantas. 1873. I. 35.

— Das plantas toxicas do Brasil. 1871. III. 65.¹

Camino equivocado. 1895. IV. 552.¹

Caminos con carriles de madera en los Estados-Unidos. 1886. IV. 424.¹

Camisola, Giuseppe. Florae astese. 1854. I. 427.

Camman, J. P. M. Een studiereis. 1900. III. 139.

Camouilly. La plantation du Café en Nouvelle-Calédonie. 1899. III. 733.¹

Campagne. Restauration et conservation des terrains en montagne. 1900. IV. 188.²

Campagne, C. J. van LOOKEREN. *See* LOOKEREN CAMPAGNE, C. J. van.

Campana. Sur la découverte de l'œuf d'hiver dans les Pyrénées-Orientales. 1880. III. 572.

Campana, Antonio. Catalogus plantarum horti botanici Regii lycei ferrariensis. 1812. I. 62.

— Catalogus plantarum horti botanici Universitatis ferrariensis. 1824. I. 62.

— Farmacopea ferrarese. 1805. III. 256.¹

Campardon. Rapport présenté à la Commission des améliorations agricoles et forestières. 1897. IV. 276.¹

— Restauration . . . des terrains en montagne. *See* BUISSON. 1900. IV. 134.²

Campbell, A. C. Correspondence regarding the qualities of the Walnut wood of Darjeeling. 1846. IV. 400.²

— A descriptive catalogue of the economic products of Chutia Nagpur. 1886. III. 278.

— Note on the culture of the Tea plant at Darjeeling. 1848. III. 602.²

— Notes on Tea cultivation in Assam. 1863. III. 603.

— On the progress of Tea cultivation at Darjeeling. 1859. III. 603.

— A real weeping tree. 1887. III. 655.¹

— & others. Correspondence regarding the "Pooah" fibre. 1848. III. 592.¹

Campbell, Douglas Houghton. Botanical aspects of Jamaica. 1898. I. 337.

— Lectures on the evolution of plants. 1899. I. 249.¹

— A vacation in the Hawaiian Islands. 1892. I. 509.²

Campbell, Dugald. *See* GRAHAM, Thomas, STENHOUSE, John & CAMPBELL, Dugald.

Campbell, F. Maule. The means of protection possessed by plants. 1888. I. 235.¹

Campbell, Francis Alexander. Experiments upon the hardwoods of Australia. 1883. IV. 408, 415.²

— The want of a uniform system in experimenting upon timber. 1887. IV. 415.²

— A year in the New Hebrides. 1874. I. 509.¹

Campbell, Frederick A. Experiments on the tensile strength of a few of the colonial timbers. 1880. IV. 410.
Campbell, James. The Oaks in Dean forest. 1885. IV. 513.
Campbell, James A. Gujarát trees. 1896. III. 278.
Campbell, John T. Age of forest trees. 1885. I. 193.²
— Why certain kinds of timber prevail in certain localities. 1885. I. 240.²
Campbell, Robert. The flora of Montreal Island. 1893. I. 310.
— The flora of the Rocky Mountains. 1900. I. 311.²
Campbell, T. J. Insect pests in the Goalpara District. 1894. III. 192.²
— Notes on the Goálpára forest division. 1896. IV. 378.
Campbell, Walter Scott. Some western plants. 1900. III. 94.²
— See also MAIDEN, J. H. & CAMPBELL, W. S.
Campbell-Brown, J. See BROWN, J. CAMPBELL-.
Campbell-Johnson, A. See JOHNSON, A. CAMPBELL-.
Campbell-Walker, Inches. See WALKER, Inches CAMPBELL-.
Campegius, Symphorianus. See CHAMPIER, Simphorien.
Campen, C. F. H. De landbouw op Halmahera. 1884. III. 128.
Campèrt, J. De groene kleurstof der planten. 1872. III. 236.
Camphor. 1820. III. 233.¹
Camphor. 1895. III. 405.¹
Camphor industry in Florida. 1891. III. 233.¹
Le camphre au Japon. 1893. III. 404.²
Camphuis, S. A. Durali-bast. 1899. III. 689.¹
— Het onderzoek van eenige Indische planten. 1899. III. 275.¹
Camphuys, S. A. See CAMPHUIS, S. A.
Campi, Baldassare & Michele. In dilucidazione e confirmazione maggiore di alcune cose state. 1641. III. 510.²
— — Parere sopra il balsamo. 1639. III. 510.²
— .— Risposta ad alcune objettioni fatte nel libro nostro. 1640. III. 510.²
— — Spicilegio botanico dialogo . . . nel quale si manifesta lo sconosciuto Cinnamomo. 1654. II. 224.²
— — Spicilegio botanico nel quale . . . cinnamomo ⸳delli antichi. 1654. III. 405.²
Campinas — Estação agronomica. See ESTAÇÃO . . , III. 10.¹
Campinas, Instituto agroncmico de. See INSTITUTO AGRO-NOMICO DE CAMPINAS.
Campion, Jules. L'Eucalyptus globulus. 1872. IV. 533.¹
Campo, Enrique del. Cálculo de una sierra forestal. 1877. IV. 256.
— Carbonizacion en hornos portátiles. 1877. IV. 395.
— Del descortezamiento por medio del calor artificial. 1877. IV. 434.
— Los pinares de Guadarrama. 1878. IV. 556.¹
— Los precios de la madera y del hierro. 1888. IV. 403.¹
— Reformas en la Escuela de ingenieros de montes. 1877. IV. 35.¹
Campo, Hermenegildo del. El articulo 33 de las ordenanzas y daños que á su sombra se cometen. 1885. IV. 293.¹
— Bosquejo meteorológico del año 1891. 1892. IV. 542.²
— Estación meteorológica de San Lorenzo del Escorial. 1893. IV. 542.²
— El Montepio forestal. 1899. IV. 554.²
— Notas adicionales al curso de meteorologia. 1896. IV. 542.²
— Noticias sobre el Pino negral ó maritimo. 1888. IV. 436,² 468,¹ 468.²
— Observaciones al libro del Sr. Bentabol. 1900. IV. 542.²
— Dos palabras más sobre el Montepio forestal. 1899. IV. 554.²
— Propiedad de personas jurídicas. 1898. IV. 555.¹
— Repoblaciones . . . en la provincia de Segovia. 1881. IV. 164.²
— Resumen de algunas influencias fisicas de los montes. 1894. IV. 45, 542.¹
— & Miguel del. Cartilla forestal. 1900. IV. 122.²
Campo, Miguel del. Campo forestal. Trabajos de repoblación. 1892. IV. 165.
— Viveros forestales. 1891. IV. 546.¹
— See also CAMPO, Hermenegildo del & Miguel del.
Dal campo al bosco. 1899. IV. 277.
Camps, Carlos de. La poda de verano. 1886. IV. 172.¹
Campuzano, Antonio. Adquisicion de terrenos forestales. 1877. IV. 276.¹
— Cercados forestales. 1881. IV. 146.²
— Sistema de podas de arbolado. 1864. IV. 170.
— Ueber Spaniens Forst-Verhältnisse. 1867. IV. 363.¹

Camus, Edmond Gustave. Catalogue des plantes de France, de Suisse et de Belgique. 1888. I. 417.
— Note sur l'Ophrys arachnitiformis. 1891. II. 108.¹
— Statistique ou catalogue des plantes hybrides. 1898. I. 271.¹
— & Jeanpert, E. H. Faits nouveaux concernant les Saules . . . de Paris. 1898. II. 102.¹
Camus, Giulio. Alcune nuove osservazioni teratologiche. 1888. I. 144.¹
— Anomalie e varietà nella flora del Modenese. 1884. I. 144.¹
— & Penzig, Ottone. Illustrazione dell' erbario estense. 1885. I. 81.¹
Camus, J. B. Nuovo parassita del Paliurus aculeatus. 1888. III. 542.¹
Camus, Jules. Étude de lexicologie botanique. 1884. I. 74.¹
— Di un parassita del Platano. 1889. III. 418.²
— Tératologie du Paliurus. 1883. II. 362,¹ 495.²
Camus de Mézieres, Nicolas le. See LE CAMUS DE MÉZIERES, Nicolas.
Camuzet, J. B. Arbres nouveaux d'ornement. 1845. III. 421,² 437.¹
— Culture et multiplication du Garrya elliptica. 1841. III. 352.²
— Culture et multiplication du Pêcher d'Ispahan. 1841. III. 440.²
— Des différences que certains arbrisseaux présentent dans leur multiplication. 1847. III. 153.
— Érable à grandes feuilles. 1844. III. 534.²
— Ueber die Gattung Robinia. 1835. III. 486.¹
— Mespilus pendula. 1845. III. 421.²
— Un mot sur la multiplication des Noyers. 1848. III. 355.
— Multiplication du Koelreuteria. 1842. III. 539.¹
— Multiplication du Mûrier noir. 1840. III. 375.
— Multiplication du Mûrier noir. 1841. III. 381.¹
— Note sur deux nouvelles variétés du Mûrier. 1833. III. 380.¹
— Note sur la conservation du Mûrier multicaule. 1837. III. 380.¹
— Note sur la floraison de quelques arbres. 1848. I. 244.¹
— Note sur la multiplication du Virgilia. 1841. III. 472.¹
— Note sur le Marronnier à fleurs rouges. 1832. III. 537.¹
— Note sur le Noyer cendré. 1843. III. 354.¹
— Note sur le Sophora japonica pendula. 1836. III. 488.¹
— Note sur le Virgilia lutea. 1841. III. 472.²
— Note sur les qualités des Juglans. 1842. III. 354.¹
— Note sur un Février de la Chine. 1833. III. 477.²
— Note sur une greffe en fente. 1838. III. 164.²
— Notice sur le genre Robinier. 1835. III. 486.¹
— Notice sur la Pavia coccinea. 1839. III. 539.¹
— Nouvelles observations sur le Cytise-Adam. 1833. II. 368.²
— Observations . . . au sujet d'une greffe en fente. 1838. III. 164.²
— Qualités . . . du Mûrier Gasparin. 1842. III. 376.
— Om Slægten Robinia. 1835. III. 486.¹
— Variétés nouvelles . . . du Robinia-pseud-Acacia. 1839. III. 486.²
— & Pépin. Rapport sur deux greffoirs. 1837. III. 160.
Can the nation defend its forests? 1899. IV. 178.¹
Cañada, Nicolás García. See GARCÍA CAÑADA, N. R.
Canada — Botanical society. See BOTANICAL . . . I. 4.¹
Canada — Department of agriculture. Central experimental farm. Bulletin. III. 2.
Canada — Department of agriculture. Experimental farms. Annual report. III. 2.
Canada — Department of the interior. Report of the chief inspector of timber and forestry. IV. 3.
Canada — Geological survey. See GEOLOGICAL . . . I. 4.¹
Canada — Royal society. See ROYAL society . . . I. 4.²
Canada — Société royale. See ROYAL SOCIETY OF CANADA. I. 4.²
Canada lumberman. IV. 3.
Canadian economics. 1885. IV. 271.¹
Canadian forestry. 1885. IV. 337.¹
Canadian forestry association. Report. IV. 3.
Canadian horticulturist. IV. 3.
Canadian Institute, Toronto. Proceedings. Transactions. I. 4.¹
Canadian journal. I. 4.¹
Canadian magazine of politics, science. III. 2.

Canadian monthly and national review. III. 2.
Canadian naturalist and geologist. I. 4.[1]
Canadian record of science. *See* CANADIAN naturalist and geologist. I. 4.[2]
Canadian society of civil engineers. Transactions. IV. 3.
Canadian timber at the International exhibition. 1862. IV. 19.[1]
Die canadische Hemlocks- oder Schierlingstanne. 1895. IV. 484.[2]
The Canara forest case. n. d. IV. 332.[1]
Cañas, A. Presente y porvenir de la agricultura española. 1868. III. 126.[1]
Cañavate, F. O. Cría del gusano de seda. 1891. III. 378.
Cañaveras, R. M. El arbolado público. 1869. III. 126.[1]
Canby, William Marriott. The forest trees of Delaware. 1876. I. 317,[1] *IV.* 77.[2]
— Liquid exudations in Akebia. 1883. I. 169.[1]
— Notes. 1881. I. 317.[1]
— Notes of botanical visits to the lower part of Delaware. 1864. II. 117.[1]
— The trees of Delaware. 1875. I. 317,[1] *IV.* 77.[2]
Cancrin, Franz Ludwig von. Abhandlung von der Anlage und dem Bau einer . . . Pottaschensiedarey. 1791. IV. 395.
— Vollständige Abhandlung von dem Theerbrennen. 1805. IV. 436.[1]
Candargy, C, A. Flore de l'île de Lesbos. 1889. I. 479.
Candargy, Paléologos C. Flore de l'île de Lesbos. 1897. I. 479.
— La végétation de l'île de Lesbos (Mytilène). 1899. I. 479.
Candelillo. 1880. III. 735.
The Candleberry tree: Aleurites trilobata. 1871. III. 514.[2]
Candolle, Alphonse Louis Pierre Pyramus de. Aegicaraceae. 1844. II. 692.[1]
— L'âge d'un arbre a-t-il une influence sur l'époque moyenne de sa feuillaison? 1876. I. 191,[2] 221.
— Ancistrocladaceae. 1864. II. 584.[2]
— Anleitung zum Studium der Botanik. 1835. I. 87.
— Apocynaceae. 1844. II. 721.[2]
— Batidaceae. 1873. II. 114.[2]
— Begoniaceae. 1861. II. 583.[1]
— Begoniaceae. 1864. II. 583.[1]
— Calques des dessins de la flore du Mexique de Mociño et Sessé. 1874. I. 270.
— Calycantheae. 1828. II. 214.[1]
— Campanulaceae. 1839. II. 845.[1]
— Capparideae. 1824. II. 229.[1]
— Des caractères qui distinguent la végétation d'une contrée. 1854. I. 299.
— Sur les causes de l'inégale distribution des plantes rares dans la chaîne des Alpes. 1875. I. 436.
— Sur les causes qui limitent les espèces végétales du côté du nord. 1847. I. 349.
— Ce qui se passe sur la limite géographique d'une espèce. 1898. I. 219.[1]
— On the characters which distinguish the vegetation of a country. 1854. I. 299.
— Le Chérimolia. 1884. II. 216.[1]
— Compositae Wightianae. 1834. II. 849.[1]
— Constitution dans le règne végétal de groupes physiologiques. 1874. I. 217.
— Corylaceae. 1864. II. 115.[1]
— Crypteroniaceae. 1864. II. 610.[1]
— Cupuliferae. 1864. II. 122.[2]
— Cycadaceae. 1864. II. 2.[3]
— Datiscaceae. 1864. II. 583.[1]
— Sur la découverte du Thé. 1835. II. 552.[1]
— Sur deux genres nouveaux confondus. 1842. II. 269. *708.[2]*
— Dipterocarpaceae. 1864. II. 559.[1]
— On the discovery of the Tea plant in a province of British India. 1835. II. 552.[1]
— Distribution géographique des plantes alimentaires. 1836. I. 299.
— Sur la durée relative de la faculté de germer. 1846. I. 527.[1]
— Ebenaceae. 1844. II. 700.[2]
— Des effets différents d'une même température sur une même espèce au nord et au midi. 1875. I. 221, *232.[1]*
— Sur les effets du froid . . . de janvier 1838. 1839 III. 49.[2]
— Empetraceae. 1869. II. 453.[2]
— Étude sur l'espèce. 1862. I. 252, *II. 123.[1]*

— Sur un exemple de conservation . . . de fruits vert dans l'eau salée. 1878. I. 521.[1]
— Sur l'existence de races physiologiques. 1878. I. 244.[2]
— Feuillaison, défeuillaison, effeuillaison. 1878. I. 191.[2]
— Fragment d'un discours sur la géographie botanique. 1834. I. 299.
— Garryaceae. 1869. II. 110.[2]
— Geissolomaceae. 1846. II. 599.[1]
— Géographie botanique raisonnée. 1855. I. 299.
— On germination at different degrees. 1865. I. 203.
— De la germination sous des degrés divers. 1865. I. 203.
— Globulariaceae. 1848. II. 795.[2]
— Les groupes physiologiques dans le règne végétal. 1874. I. 217.
— Grubbiaceae. 1847. II. 170.[1]
— Helwingiaceae. 1864. II. 654.[1]
— Introduction à l'étude de la botanique. 1835. I. 87.
— Lacistemaceae. 1864. II. 95.[2]
— Laws of botanical nomenclature. 1867. I. 253.[2]
— Levelesadés, elvélhullás, levelezés. 1878. I. 191.[2]
— Lobeliaceae. 1839. II. 845.[1]
— Loganiaceae. 1845. II. 716.[1]
— Lois de la nomenclature botanique. 1867. I. 253.[2]
— Lophiraceae. 1864. II. 544.[1]
— Mémoire sur la famille des Anonacées. 1830. II. 215.[1]
— Mémoire sur la famille des Apocynacées. 1844. II. 722.[1]
— Mémoire sur la famille des Bégoniacées. 1859. II. 583.[1]
— Mémoire sur les causes qui déterminent les limites des espèces du règne végétal. 1847. I. 349.
— Mémoire sur les Lobéliacées. 1839. II. 845.[1]
— Sur une mesure . . . de l'un des grands Sequoia. 1866. II. 51.[1]
— Sur la méthode des sommes de température. 1875. I. 221.
— Du mode d'action de la chaleur. 1850. I. 231.[2]
— On the mode of action of heat. 1850. I. 231.[2]
— Monimiaceae. 1869. II. 221.[2]
— Monimiaceae novae. 1865. II. 221.[1]
— Myoporaceae. 1847. II. 805.[1]
— Myristicaceae. 1846. II. 220.[1]
— Myrsineaceae. 1844. II. 845.[1]
— Sur les naturalisations d'espèces végétales. 1850. I. 241.[1]
— On a new character in the fruit of Quercus. 1862. II. 128.[1]
— On a new character observed in the fruit of the Oaks. 1862. II. 128.[1]
— Note additionnelle sur les maladies. 1836. III. 559.[2]
— Note sur l'Anabasis Ammodendron. 1885. III. 387.[2]
— Note sur la famille des Myristicacées. 1855. II. 220.[1]
— Note sur la famille des Santalacées. 1857. II. 168.[1]
— Note sur le genre Weigela de Thunberg. 1839. II. 834.[2]
— Note sur le Quercus castaneaefolia d'Algérie. 1866. II. 136.[1]
— Note sur un nouveau caractère observé dans le fruit des Chênes. 1862. II. 128.[1]
— Notice sur le Jardin botanique de Genève. 1845. I. 65.[1]
— Notice sur les arbres . . . de la Suisse. 1835. I. 432,[1] III. 89,[1] *IV. 86.[2]*
— Nouvelles remarques sur la nomenclature botanique. 1867. I. 253.[2]
— Origin of cultivated plants. 1883. I. *248,[1]* 247.
— Sur l'origine botanique de quelques plantes cultivées. 1887. I. 248.[1]
— L'origine des plante coltivate. 1883. I. 247.
— Origine des plantes cultivées. 1883. I. *248,[2]* 247.
— Sur la particularité de la nervation des feuilles du genre Fagus. 1864. II. 125.[2]
— Penaeaceae. 1846. II. 599.[1]
— La phytographie. 1880. I. 254.[2]
— Plantae quaedam itinerantium sub numeris. 1852. I. 269.
— Platanaceae. 1864. II. 254.[1]
— Quelles sont les meilleures méthodes à employer pour traiter les monographies? 1885. I. 254.[2]
— Réflexions sur les ouvrages généraux de botanique descriptive. 1873. I. 300.
— Regeln der botanischen Nomenklatur. 1867. I. 253.[2]
— On the relative duration of the power to germinate. 1846. I. 527.
— Réponse à diverses questions . . . sur le recueil des Lois de la nomenclature. 1869. V. XII.[1]
— A review of the natural order Myrsineae. 1834. II. 692.[1]
— Salvadoraceae. 1873. II. 472.[2]
— Santalaceae. 1847. II. 167.[1]
— Santalaceae et Myristicaceae. 1860. II. 220.[1]

Candolle, Alphonse Louis Pierre Pyramus de (*continued*).
— Sapotaceae. 1844. II. 696.[2]
— Second . . . mémoire sur la famille des Myrsinéacées. 1841. II. 692.[1]
— Smilacées. 1878. II. 77.[1]
— Stilbaceae. 1848. II. 752.[2]
— Styracaceae. 1844. II. 704.[1]
— Tentative d'expériences sur la question des modifications dans les espèces végétales. 1872. I. 244.[1]
— Le Thé découvert dans une province de l'Inde anglaise. 1835. II. 552.[1]
— Theophrastaceae. 1844. II. 691.[1]
— Der Ursprung der Culturpflanzen. 1883. I. 247.
— Vahea madagascariensis. 1850. II. 727.[2]
— Végétation de la Sierra-Nevada . . . Le Cèdre. 1837. II. 27.[1]
— *See also* CANDOLLE, A. P. de & A. L. P. P. de; LA RIVE, Aug. de & CANDOLLE, A. L. P. P. de; ДЕКАНДОЛЬ, А.
— & Casimir de. Monographiae phanerogamarum. 1878. I. 261.
Candolle, Anne Casimir Pyramus de. Anatomie comparée des feuilles. 1879. I. 110.
— Über die anatomische Structur der Blätter von Cytisus Adami. 1883. II. 368.[2]
— Sur les bractées florifères. 1893. I. 113.[2]
— Cas remarquable de fasciation chez un Sapin. 1889. II. 36.[1]
— Considérations sur l'étude de la phyllotaxic. 1881. I. 102.
— Diagnosen neuer Arten. 1898. II. 94.[2]
— Sur les feuilles peltées. 1899. I. 111.
— On the geographical distribution of the Meliaceae. 1878. II. 419.[1]
— Juglandaceae. 1864. II. 111.[2]
— On latent life in seeds. 1896. I. 527.
— Meliaceae. 1878. II. 419.[1]
— Meliaceae novae. 1894. II. 419.[1]
— Méliacées. 1878. II. 419.[1]
— Mémoire sur la famille des Juglandées. 1862. II. 111.[1]
— Mémoire sur la famille des Pipéracées. 1865. II. 93.[1]
— Myricaceae. 1864. II. 110.[2]
— Nouvelles recherches sur les Pipéracées. 1881. II. 93.[2]
— Observations sur l'enroulement des vrilles. 1877. I. 196.[2]
— Sur les phyllomes hypopeltés. 1897. I. 111.
— Piperaceae. 1869. II. 93.[1]
— Piperaceae. 1891. II. 93.[1]
— Piperaceae africanae et madagascarienses. 1895. II. 94.[1]
— Piperaceae Andreanae. 1897. II. 93.[1]
— Piperaceae bolivianae. 1892. II. 93.[1]
— Piperaceae costaricenses novae. 1890. II. 95.[1]
— Piperaceae novae. 1866. II. 93.[1]
— Piperaceae novae. 1873. II. 93.[1]
— Piperaceae novae. 1898. II. 93.[1]
— Piperaceae Sodiroanae. 1898. II. 93.[1]
— Piperaceae Uleanae e Brasilia. 1900. II. 94.[1]
— Pipéracées. 1893. II. 93.[1]
— Les Pipéracées de l'Ecuador. 1890. II. 93.[1]
— Plantae Lehmannianae in Guatemala. 1889. II. 93.[1]
— De la production . . . du liége dans le Chêne-liége. 1860. II. 140.[1]
— Sur quelques cas d'embryons velus. 1875. II. 419.[1]
— Recherches sur les inflorescences épiphylles. 1890. I. 113.[2]
— Remarques sur la tératologie. 1897. I. 144.[1]
— Théorie de l'angle unique en phyllotaxie. 1865. I. 102.
— Théorie de la feuille. 1868. I. 110.
— Theory of the leaf. 1865. I. 102.
— Three new species of Mexican plants. 1894. I. 332.
Candolle, Augustin Pyramus de. Acerineae. 1824. II. 476.[1]
— Alangieae. 1828. II. 614.[2]
— Ampelideae. 1824. II. 501.[1]
— Anonaceae. 1824. II. 215.[1]
— Aquilarineae. 1825. II. 599.[2]
— Araliaceae. 1830. II. 646.[1]
— Astragalogia nempe Astragali . . . historia. 1802. II. 333.[2]
— Aurantiaceae. 1824. II. 396.[2]
— Bemerkung über die Eintheilung des Gewächsreichs. 1833. I. 251.
— Bemerkungen über die Blätter der Cliffortien. 1824. II. 259.[1]
— Berberideae. 1824. II. 201.[2]
— Bignoniaceae. 1845. II. 784.[1]
— Bixineae. 1824. II. 565.[2]

— Bombaceae. 1824. II. 528.[2]
— Borragineae. 1845. II. 747.[2]
— Borragineae. Tribus IV. Borrageae. 1846. II. 747.
— Botanicon gallicum. 1828. I. 408.
— On the botany of India. 1829. I. 471.
— Bruniaceae. 1825. II. 251.[1]
— Byttneriaceae. 1824. II. 531.[1]
— Cactene. 1828. II. 584.[2]
— Camellieae. 1824. II. 547.[1]
— Caprifoliaceae. 1830. II. 833.[2]
— Catalogue des arbres . . . du Jardin botanique de Genève. 1820. I. 65.[1]
— Catalogus plantarum Horti botanici monspeliensis. 1813. I. 57.
— Celastrineae. 1825. II. 465.[2]
— Chailletiaceae. 1825. II. 432.[2]
— Chlenaceae. 1824. II. 511.[2]
— Collection de mémoires pour servir à l'histoire du règne végétal. 1828. I. 267.
— Columelliaceae. 1839. II. 795.[2]
— Combretaceae. 1828. II. 615.[1]
— Compositae. 1836. II. 848.[1]
— Conjectures sur le nombre total des espèces . . , sur le globe. 1817. I. 298.
— Considérations générales sur les fleurs doubles. 1817. I. 145.[1]
— Considérations sur la phytologie. 1828. I. 33.
— Coriarieae. 1824. II. 454.[1]
— Corneae. 1830. II. 654.[1]
— Crassulaceae. 1828. II. 234.[2]
— Cruciferae. 1824. II. 233.[2]
— Cucurbitaceae. 1828. II. 844.[2]
— Cyrtandraceae. 1845. II. 792.[2]
— Description d'un nouveau genre . . . des Apocynées. 1802. II. 731.[2]
— Description d'un nouveau genre . . . Strophanthus. 1802. II. 731.[2]
— Description d'une nouvelle espèce de Figuier. 1841. II. 153.[1]
— Description du Chailletia. 1811. II. 432.[2]
— Dilleniaceae. 1824. II. 540.[1]
— Dipsaceae. 1830. II. 844.[2]
— Elaeocarpeae. 1824. II. 509.[1]
— Epacrideae. 1839. II. 687.[2]
— Ericaceae. 1839. II. 657.[2]
— Erycibeae. 1845. II. 743.[2]
— Erythroxyleae. 1824. II. 394.[1]
— Essai élémentaire de géographie botanique. 1820. I. 298.
— Essai sur les propriétés médicales des plantes. 1804. III. 259.[2]
— Expériences relatives à l'influence de la lumière. 1800. I. 229.
— Experiments respecting the influence of light. 1800. I. 229.
— Extrait d'un mémoire sur la famille des Joubarbes. 1801. II. 234.[2]
— Extrait d'un mémoire sur le genre Strophanthus. 1802. II. 731.[2]
— Extrait d'un mémoire sur . . . Pictetia. 1825. II. 376.[2]
— Ficoideae. 1828. II. 193.[2]
— Flacourtianeae. 1824. II. 568.[2]
— Flore françoise. *See* LAMARCK, J. B. de. 1778. I. 405.
— Foetquieraceae. 1824. II. 563.[1]
— Frankeniaceae. 1824. II. 561.[1]
— Genres nouveaux . . . des Composées. 1833. II. 848.[1]
— Géographie botanique. 1820. I. 298.
— Ueber die geographische Verbreitung der Compositen. 1840. II. 848.[1]
— Geraniaceae. 1824. II. 389.[1]
— Gesneriaceae. 1839. II. 792.[2]
— Goodenovieae. 1839. II. 846.[2]
— Granateae. 1828. II. 610.[2]
— Halorageae. 1828. II. 646.[1]
— Hamamelideae. 1830. II. 252.[1]
— Hippocastaneae. 1824. II. 480.[2]
— Hippocrateaceae. 1824. II. 471.[2]
— Histoire de la botanique genevoise. 1830. I. 81.[1]
— Homalineae. 1825. II. 568.[1]
— Icones plantarum Galliae rariorum. 1808. II. 669.[1]
— De l'influence de la temperature atmosphérique. 1831. I. 231.[2]
— Instruction pratique sur les collections botaniques. 1820. I. 35.
— Jasmineae. 1844. II. 705.[2]

— Leguminosae. 1825. II. 318.[1]
— Lineae. 1824. II. 392.[2]
— On the longevity of trees. 1831. I. 193.[1]
— Loranthaceae. 1830. II. 172.[1]
— Lythrarieae. 1828. II. 608.[1]
— Magnoliaceae. 1824. II. 208.[2]
— Malpighiaceae. 1824. II. 423.[3]
— Malvaceae. 1824. II. 519.[1]
— Melastomaceae. 1828. II. 634.[2]
— Meliaceae. 1824. II. 418.[2]
— Memoir on the pores and the bark of leaves. 1801. I, 109.[1]
— Mémoire sur la famille des Combrétacées. 1828. II. 615.[1]
— Mémoire sur la famille des Crassulacées. 1828. II. 235.[1]
— Mémoire sur la famille des Loranthacées. 1830. II. 172.[1]
— Mémoire sur la famille des Myrtacées. 1841. II. 618.[3]
— Mémoire sur la famille des Onagraires. 1829. II. 642.[2]
— Mémoire sur la famille des Ternstroemiacées. 1821. II. 542,[2] 547.[1]
— Mémoire sur la fertilisation des dunes. 1803. IV. 145.
— Mémoire sur la géographie des plantes de France. 1817. I. 407.
— Mémoire sur la tribu des Cuspariées. 1822. II. 396.[1]
— Mémoire sur la végétation du Guy. 1801. II. 178.[2]
— Mémoire sur le Cuviera. 1807. II. 810.[1]
— Mémoire sur le Fatioa. 1829. II. 609.[2]
— Mémoire sur les genres Astragalus, Phaca. 1802. II. 318.[1]
— Mémoire sur les genres Connarus et Omphalobium. 1825. II. 316.[2]
— Mémoire sur les pores de l'écorce des feuilles. 1801. I. 109,[1] 191.[1]
— Mémoire sur quelques espèces de Cactées. 1834. II. 585.[1]
— Mémoire sur quelques genres . . . des Buttnèriacées. 1823. II. 531.[1]
— Mémoires sur la famille des Légumineuses. 1825. II. 318.[1]
— Menispermaceae. 1824. II. 205.[2]
— Monographie des Ochnacées et des Simaroubées. 1811. II. 413,[1] 544.[1]
— Myrtaceae. 1828. II. 618.[2]
— Myrtacées. 1826. II. 618.[3]
— Napoleoneae. 1839. II. 611.[1]
— Note botanique sur le Gingko. 1818. II. 7.[2]
— Note sur la cause de la direction des tiges vers la lumière. 1809. I. 194.
— Note sur la division du règne végétal. 1833. I. 251.
— Note sur la monographie des Légumineuses biloculaires. 1800. II. 318.[1]
— Note sur la place . . . des Cucurbitacées. 1825. II. 844.[2]
— Note sur le feuillage des Cliffortia. 1824. II. 259.[1]
— Note sur quelques plantes . . . dans la serre de M. Saladin. 1828. I. 65.[1]
— Notice sur la botanique de l'Inde orientale. 1829. I. 471.
— Notice sur la botanique du Brésil. 1827. I. 341.
— Notice sur la culture de l'Olivier. 1825. III. 675.[1]
— Notice sur la géographie botanique de l'Italie. 1835. I. 426.
— Notice sur la longévité des arbres. 1831. I. 193.[1]
— Notice sur la racine de cainca. 1829. III. 744.[1]
— Notice sur la végétation des plantes parasites. 1830. IV. 173.[2]
— Notice sur les différens genres et espèces . . . confondues sous le nom de Quinquina. 1829. III. 724.[2]
— Notice sur quelques genres . . . de Légumineuses. 1825. II. 318.[1]
— Observation sur une espèce de gomme . . . du Hêtre. 1799. II. 126.[2]
— Observations sur la structure . . . des Composées. 1838. II. 848.[1]
— Observations sur les plantes composées. 1810. II. 847.[2]
— Ochnaceae. 1824. II. 544.[1]
— Olacineae. 1824. II. 170.[1]
— Oleaceae. 1844. II. 705.[2]
— Onagrariae. 1828. II. 642.[2]
— Organographie der Gewächse. 1827. II. 100.[2]
— Organographie végétale. 1827. I. 100.[2]
— Oxalidaceae. 1824. II. 392.[1]
— Papaveraceae. 1824. II. 229.[1]
— Paronychieae. 1828. II. 194.[1]
— Passifloreae. 1828. II. 575.[2]
— Passifloreae Trib. III. Malesherbieae. 1828. II. 575.[1]
— Pflanzen-Physiologie. 1832. I. 148.

— Philadelpheae. 1828. II. 237.[3]
— Physiologie végétale. 1832. I. 148.
— Phytologie ou botanique. 1828. I. 33.
— Pittosporeae. 1824. II. 247.[1]
— Plantarum succulentarum historia. 1799. I. 264.
— Plantes rares du Jardin de Genève. 1829. I. 65.[1]
— Polygaleae. 1824. II. 429.[2]
— The pores and the bark of leaves. 1801. I. 131.[1]
— Portulaceae. 1828. II. 194.[1]
— Premier mémoire sur les lenticelles. 1826. I. 132.[1]
— Programme . . . sur les pépinières . . . de Genève. 1822. III. 153.
— Projet d'une flore physico-géographique de la vallée du Léman. 1821. I. 433.
— De quelques arbres très-anciens. 1831. I. 295.[2]
— Ranunculaceae. 1824. II. 195.[1]
— Rapports sur deux voyages botaniques . . . dans les départemens de l'ouest et du sud-ouest. 1808. I. 407.
— Rapports sur deux voyages botaniques . . . dans les départemens de nord-est et du centre. 1813. I. 407.
— Rapports sur deux voyages botaniques . . . dans les départemens du sud-est et de l'est. 1810. I. 407.
— Rapports sur les voyages botaniques et agronomiques faits dans les départemens de l'empire. 1813. I. 407.
— Recueil de mémoires sur la botanique. 1813. I. 266.
— Regni vegetabilis systema naturale. 1818. I. 259.
— Remarks on two genera of plants to be referred to . . . Rosaceae. 1818. II. 265,[1] 273.[1]
— Réponse à une lettre . . . sur les maladies des Mélèzes. 1835. IV. 450.
— Revue de la famille des Cactées. 1828. II. 585.[1]
— Revue de la famille des Lythraires. 1826. II. 608.[1]
— Revue de la famille des Portulacées. 1828. II. 194.[1]
— Revue de quelques ouvrages . . . sur le genre des Saules. 1832. II. 98.[2]
— Revue sommaire de la famille des Bignoniacées. 1838. II. 784.[1]
— Rhamneae. 1825. II. 491.[2]
— Rhizoboleae. 1824. II. 546.[1]
— Rhizophoreae. 1828. II. 612.[2]
— Rosaceae. 1825. II. 255.[2]
— Roussaeaceae. 1839. II. 237.[2]
— Rubiaceae. 1830. II. 807.[1]
— Rutaceae. 1824. II. 396.[2]
— Samydeae. 1825. II. 568.[2]
— Sapindaceae. 1824. II. 483.[1]
— Saxifragaceae. 1830. II. 237.[2]
— Simarubeae. 1824. II. 413.[1]
— Statistique de la famille des Composées. 1838. II. 848.[1]
— Strophanthus, novum genus. 1804. II. 731.[2]
— Tamariscineae. 1828. II. 561.[2]
— Terebinthaceae. 1825. II. 454.[1]
— Ternstroemiaceae. 1824. II. 547.[1]
— Theoretische Anfangsgründe der Botanik. 1817. I. 254.[2]
— Théorie élémentaire de la botanique. 1813. I. 254.[2]
— Tiliaceae. 1824. II. 512.[1]
— Tremandreae. 1824. II. 429.[1]
— Turneraceae. 1828. II. 574.[2]
— Umbelliferae. 1830. II. 653.[1]
— Valerianeae. 1830. II. 844.[1]
— Vegetable organography. 1827. I. 100.[2]
— Versuch über die Arancikräfte der Pflanzen. 1004. III. 259.[2]
— Versuche über den Einfluss des Lichts. 1800. I. 229.
— Vóchysieae. 1828. II. 428.[2]
— Zygophylleae. 1824. II. 394.[2]
— See also LAMARCK, J. B. de & CANDOLLE, A. P. de.
— & Alphonse de. Monstruosités végétales. 1841. I. 143.
— & Alphonse de. . . . dans le Jardin botanique de Genève. 1821. I. 65.[1]
— — Notices sur les plantes rares cultivées dans le Jardin botanique de Genève. 1821. I. 65.[1]
— — Prodromus systematis naturalis regni vegetabilis. 1824. I. 259.
— — Rapport sur les plantes rares ou nouvelles . . . dans le Jardin de botanique de Genève. 1821. I. 65.[1]
— & Sprengel, Kurt. Elements of the philosophy of plants. 1820. I. 85.
— — Grundzüge der wissenschaftlichen Pflanzenkunde. 1820. I. 85.
Candolle, Casimir de. See CANDOLLE, Anne Casimir Pyramus de.
Candy, Francis H. The new forest as a national school. 1890. IV. 34.[1]

Canellae sive Cinnamomi . . . historia. 1725. II. 224,² III. 405.²
Canelle, J. Genêt saccharifère. 1895. III. 265.¹
Canepario, P. M. De atramentis cuiuscunque generis. 1606. III. 235.²
Canevari, La coltivazione delle piante legnose fruttifere da foglia e da bosco. 1898. IV. 134.²
Canevarius, Demetrius. De ligno sancto commentarium. 1602. III. 494.¹
Canfield, James H. The use and abuse of the forests. 1896. IV. 270.
Cannelin, Th. A. Metsänhoidollinen koetusasema Mustialassa. 1891. IV. 37.²
— Metsänviljelys suomaalla. 1898. IV. 158.
— Metsäpuittemme suhde valoon ja kosteuteen sekä siitä riippuva metsänhoito. 1892. IV. 67.²
— Orava, hyödyllinen eläin metsässä. 1888. IV. 90.²
— Pieniä neuvoja metsänomistajille ja metsänostajille. 1892. IV. 258.
Canneva, G. B. Sulla Calliandra portoricensis. 1893. III. 469.²
— Di una nuova Sensitiva. 1892. III. 482.¹
Canning, A. Colquhoun. On certain peculiarities in the growth of Pine trees. 1861. II. 48.¹
Cannizzaro, Stanislao & Fabris, G. An examination . . . of certain tests for determining the purity of olive oil. 1891. III. 679.¹
Cannon, David. The Corsican Pine. 1894. IV. 465.²
— Culture des arbres exotiques en Sologne. 1900. III. 124.²
— Déodar, Sàl, Sisson et Khair. 1899. IV. 124.²
— L'eau et la forêt en Sologne. 1898. IV. 47.¹
— Éclaircies. 1890. IV. 174.
— Economical Pine planting. 1885. IV. 461.¹
— Forestal notes. Pinus austriaca. 1884. IV. 465.²
— La maladie ronde chez le Pin sylvestre. 1899. IV. 479.
— Manuel du cultivateur de Pins. 1883. IV. 109.²
— Note sur les transports des plants forestiers. 1898. IV. 546.¹
— Le Pin Laricio. 1894. IV. 465.²
— Pinus rigida. 1898. IV. 469.¹
— The Poplars. 1897. III. 344.²
— Le propriétaire planteur. 1887. III. 110.²
— Réflexions sur les éclaircies. 1890. IV. 174.
— & Gazin, A. Une excursion forestière dans l'Est. 1891. IV. 361.
The Cannon-ball tree. 1882. II. 612.¹
Cannstadt, Carl, Freiherr SCHILLING VON. See SCHILLING VON CANNSTADT, Carl, Freiherr.
Canossa, Ottavio di. Sul nuovo progetto di legge forestale. 1897. IV. 329.
Canstatt's Jahresbericht über die Fortschritte in der Pharmacie. See JAHRESBERICHT über die Fortschritte der gesammten Pharmacie. I. 12.
Canstein, Freiherr von. See NEUBAUER, (Dr.) & CANSTEIN, Freiherr von.
Canstein, Philipp, Baron von. Karte von der Verbreitung der nutzbarsten Pflanzen. 1834. I. 299.
Cantani, A. G. Ein besonderer Fall von Verwachsung zweier Fichten. 1857. I. 209,¹ III. 305.¹
— Fälle von Wurzelbildung aus dem Blatte. 1858. I. 103.
Cantani, Arnaldo. Pro sylvis. 1893. IV. 270.
Cante, Modeste. Observation sur la greffe du Mûrier. 1837. III. 375.
Canterbury agricultural and pastoral association's journal. III. 27.¹
Cantieny, G. Verzeichniss der in der Umgegend von Zittau wildwachsenden . . . Pflanzen. 1854. I. 383.
Cantieri inglesi. 1862. IV. 425.¹
Cantin, G. Les maladies de la Vigne. 1900. III. 562.¹
— Le phylloxéra. 1900. III. 575.¹
Cantley, N. Catalogue of plants in the R. bot. gardens, Mauritius. 1880. I. 68.²
— Notes on economic plants. 1886. III. 278.
— Notes on economic plants. 1887. III. 279.¹
— Reports on the forests of the Straits Settlements. 1883. IV. 378.
Canton d'Uri. Urseren. See URSEREN. 1863. IV. 181.¹
Cantoniensis, (pseud.). Henna in China. 1863. III. 630.¹
Un cantonnement de droits d'usage. 1897. IV. 554.²
Cantonnement des bois de la principauté de Chimay. 1878. III. 323.¹
Cantono, Carlo Pietro. Esperienze sull' assorbimento di diversi liquidi. 1841. I. 161.
Cantor, Theodore. General features of Chusan. 1842. I. 458.

Cantu, Giovanni Lorenzo. Note sur l'application de la couleur jaune du Rhus. 1838. III. 236.
Canvane, Peter. A dissertation on the oleum Palmae Christi. 1766. III. 522.¹
Canzler, F. G. Einleitung in die Forstwissenschaft. 1798. IV. 95.
Canzoneri, Francesco. Essai sur le Marronier d'Inde. 1823. III. 537.²
— Saggio sul Castagno d' India. 1823. III. 537.²
Il caoutchouc. 1866. III. 231.
Le Caoutchouc au Guatémala. 1899. III. 368.²
Le caoutchouc ceara au Soudan. 1899. III. 520.²
Caoutchouc en gutta-percha. 1880. III. 229.
The caoutchouc industry in Assam. 1893. III. 231.
De caoutchouc inzamelaars van de Amazone. 1885. III. 229.
Cap, Paul Antoine. De l'influence de l'eau dans l'acte de la germination. 1848. I. 202.²
Capdevila, Mariano. Nutrición de la planta. 1887. IV. 543.¹
Cape Colony. 1888. III. 281.²
Cape Heaths. 1856. III. 650.¹
The Cape Ivy. 1878. III. 756.²
Cape monthly magazine. I. 29.²
Cape of Good Hope — Department of agriculture. Reports of the conservators of forests. See CAPE OF GOON HOPE — SUPERINTENDENT OF WOODS AND FORESTS. IV. 16.²
Cape of Good Hope — Department of lands, mines and agriculture. See CAPE OF GOON HOPE — SUPERINTENDENT OF WOODS AND FORESTS. IV. 16.²
Cape of Good Hope — Inspector of vineyards. 1887. III. 762.
Cape of Good Hope — Phylloxera commission. 1886. III. 762.
Cape of Good Hope — Phylloxera commission. 1886. III. 762.
Cape of Good Hope — Superintendent of woods and forests. Report. IV. 16.²
Cape Sumach. 1898. III. 384.¹
Capelli, Joseph August de. Cortex peruvianus. 1766. III. 720.
Capelle-Lutgen. Les tarifs de transport des bois. 1894. IV. 552.²
Capelli, Carolo. Catalogus stirpium . . . in Regio horto botanico taurinensi. 1821. I. 62.
Caper industry in France. 1898. III. 409.¹
Capgrand-Mothes. Exploitation des Lièges. 1883. IV. 517.¹
— Exploitation du Chêne-Liège. 1886. IV. 517.¹
— Les insectes nuisibles du Chêne-Liège. 1886. IV. 517.¹
— Réponse au rapport de M. Muterse. 1886. IV. 517.¹
Capitain-Gény. De la révolution dans les taillis sous futaie. 1895. IV. 252.
Caplain, Joseph & Doyet, A. Tarif universel et métrique pour le cubage des arbres. 1866. IV. 225.
Capoduro, Marius. De la concrescence en botanique. 1898. II. 137.¹
— Un curieux exemple de concrescence chez le Capparis. 1893. II. 232.¹
— Essai sur les noms patois des plantes. 1896. I. 74.²
Cappeau, Louis Jean Joseph Pierre. Traité de la législation rurale et forestière. 1824. IV. 323.²
Cappel, Anton Friedrich. De nucis vomicae viribus et usu. See NICOLAI, E. A. 1784. III. 684.²
Cappel, Johann Friedrich Ludwig. Verzeichniss der um Helmstädt wildwachsenden Pflanzen. 1784. I. 374.
Cappel, Moritz Anton. Pilati montis historia. 1767. I. 433.
Cappellinus, Severinus Johannis. Dissertationum physicarum de plantis prima. 1684. I. 30.
Cappello, Agostino. Opuscoli scelti scientifici. 1830. I. 426.
Capper, John. Beschreibendes Verzeichniss der auf Ceylon wachsenden Hölzer. 1849. IV. 401.¹
— A descriptive catalogue of the woods of Ceylon. 1849. IV. 401.¹
Cappi, Giulio. La coltivazione dell' Olivo. 1875. III. 675.²
— Sulla necessità d' imboschire le montagne. 1864. IV. 165.
— Rimboschiamo l' Apennino! 1865. IV. 165.
Caprera coltivata dal generale Garibaldi. 1866. IV. 134.²
Caprile, Luisa. Il profumo dei fiori. 1900. III. 227.
Capsadell, L. The complete guide to silk culture. 1883. III. 378.
Captain Newport's discoveries in Virginia. 1860. III. 264.¹
Capuron-Ludeau. Le Liège et sa production. 1894. IV. 518.¹

Capus, Guillaume. Anatomie du tissu conducteur. 1878. I. 118.[1]
— Azalea. 1878. II. 676.[2]
— De l'exploitation . . . des plantes à caoutchouc en Indo-Chine. 1899. III. 149.
— Guide du naturaliste préparateur. 1879. I. 36.[1]
— Indications sur le climat et la végétation du Turkestan. 1883. I. 457.
— Sur l'observation directe du mouvement de l'eau. 1883. I. 165.
— Sur les plantes . . . sauvage ou subspontané dans le Thian-Schan. 1884. III. 272.[3]
— Quelques effets du climat sur la rapidité de croissance. 1883. I. 218.
Caquet, François. Almanach forestier. 1887. IV. 122.[1]
— L'enseignement agricole et forestier en France. 1887. IV. 34.[2]
— La forêt à travers le monde. 1887. I. 218.
— Les parcs forestiers. 1887. IV. 127.[1]
— Une pépinière de plants forestiers. 1887. IV. 151.[1]
— Le Pommier à cidre. 1887. III. 426.[2]
— Les reboisements par l'Acacia. 1886. IV. 523.[3]
— La sylviculture à l'école primaire. 1886. IV. 109.[2]
— Le vade-mecum du forestier. 1883. IV. 99.[1]
Caracas — Sociedad de ciencias fisicas y naturales. See SOCIEDAD . . . I. 8.[1]
Caractères secondaires distinctifs des deux sexes chez le Ginkgo biloba. 1899. II. 8.[1]
Caragana bark. 1894. III. 470.[1]
Caragana for hedging. 1880. III. 469.[2]
Caragana or Pea tree. 1885. III. 469.[2]
Caranti, Biagio. Progetto di legge sottoposto . . . all' esame della Commissione forestale. 1864. IV. 328.
Carbajal, Lino Delvalle. La Patagonia. 1899. I. 345.
Carballo y Sampayo, Diego. Elementos de agricultura. 1795. III. 114.
Carbone, Giovanni Antonio. L' Olivo e l' olio. 1889. III. 676.[1]
Il carbone di Parigi. 1861. IV. 431.[2]
Carbonnières, L. F. E. RAMOND DE, baron. See RAMOND DE CARBONNIÈRES, L. F. E., baron.
— La figue gourreau noir. 1865. III. 369.[2]
Card, Fred Wallace. Bush-fruits. 1898. III. 62.
— The Choke Cherry in cultivation. 1897. III. 443.[2]
— Ornamental shrubs for Nebraska. 1895. III. 61.[1]
— Windbreaks. 1897. III. 215.[2]
Card, Joseph P. The preservation of railway ties. 1887. IV. 420.
— Preservation of timber. 1887. IV. 420.
Cardan, M. Observations on the vegetation of the common Walnut. 1848 (1849). II. 114.[1] III. 355, V. xxvi.[1]
— Observations sur la végétation du Noyer commun. 1848 (1849). III. 355, V. xxvi.[1]
Cardano, Geronimo. See CARDANO, Girolamo.
Cardano, Girolamo. See CARDANO, Girolamo. Les livres intitulez de la subtilité. 1550. V. xv.[1]
— De radice Cina. 1559. III. 338.[1]
— De rerum varietate libri XVII. 1557. III. 217, V. xv.[1]
— De subtilitate libri XXI. 1550. I. 279, V. xv.[1]
Cardanus, Hieronymus. See CARDANUS, Girolamo.
Cardew, F. Report on the forests of Zululand. 1891. IV. 379.[1]
Cardois, Manuel BOEDO Y. See BOEDO Y CARDOIS, Manuel.
Cardoni, Gasparo Martinetti. Pineta e territorio di Ravenna. 1863. II. 45.[1]
Cardoso, João A. (jr.). Contribuição para o estudo da flora d'Africa. 1896. I. 498.
— Enumeração de plantas colhidas nas ilhas de Cabo Verde. 1896. I. 498.
— Plantas medicinaes do archipelago de Cabo Verde. 1893. III. 93.[1]
Cardot, Émile. Améliorations pastorales en Franche-Comté. 1900. IV. 135.[2]
— Compte rendu des excursions de 1896. 1896. IV. 362.
— La culture pastorale. 1898. IV. 135.[1]
— Le déboisement et le reboisement dans les Alpes. 1876. IV. 162.
— Les forêts du royaume de Prusse. 189.? IV. 354.
— Les forêts du royaume de Prusse. 1897. IV. 555.[2]
— La genèse du régime pastoral. 1896. IV. 135.[1]
— De l'origine des inondations. 1882. IV. 51.
— Un problème forestier. 1894. IV. 140.

— Restauration, aménagement et mise en valeur. 1900. IV. 135.[2]
— Statistique forestière de . . . Pontarlier. 1896. IV. 362.
— See also BROILLIARD, Charles & CARDOT, Émile.
Cardot, Fernand. Aliénations de forêts domaniales. 1899. IV. 276,[1] 551.[2]
— Allongement de la révolution dans les taillis. 1897. IV. 551.[1]
— Allongement de la révolution dans les taillis. 1898. IV. 238.
— Droit d'usage dans une forêt communale. 1897. IV. 555.[1]
— Note sur la croissance des taillis sous futaie. 1897. IV. 551.[1]
— Valeur des coupes de taillis sous futaie. 1898. IV. 238.
— de la Haute-Saône. 1899. IV. 551.[1]
— & Bouvet, Maurice. Rendement des forêts communales . . . de la Haute-Saône. 1899. IV. 551.[1]
Cardot, Jules. See DELAMORE, E., RENAULD, F. & CARDOT, J.
The care of newly planted trees. 1893. III. 168.
The care of small tracts of woodland. 1889. IV. 121.
The care of the national forest-reservations. 1893. IV. 178.[2]
The care of young trees. 1889. III. 117.[1]
Carantin. Emploi de la cendre de bois pour prévenir . . . la maladie de la Vigne. 1856. III. 576.
Carey. Utilization of Salei wood for sleepers. 1878. IV. 525.
Carimantrand, Jules. Avenir des plantations de Cacaoyers au Congo. 1899. III. 593.[1]
Carion, J. E. Catalogue raisonné des plantes du dép. de Saône-et-Loire. 1859. I. 412.
— Catalogue raisonné des plantes . . . de Saône-et-Loire. 1865. I. 413.
Cariot, Antoine. Étude des fleurs. 1860. I. 412.
— Flore de la France centrale. 1868. I. 413.
— Le guide du botaniste à la Grande Chartreuse. 1856. I. 411.
— & Saint-Lager, Jean. Botanique élémentaire . . . du Rhône et de la Loire. 1897. I. 418.
Carl. Die Waldeisenbahnen in . . . Alberschweiler. 1893. IV. 392.
Carl, (Oberförster, Bitsch). Ueber die französische Forstverwaltung. 1887. IV. 292.
Carl, Joseph Anton. Botanisch-medicinischer Garten. 1770. III. 55.
— Catalogus plantarum . . . Horti bot. ingolstadt. 1788. I. 44.
Carlander, Christophorus. Horti upsaliensis plantae. See THUNBERG, O. P. 1826. I. 40.
— Quid Linnæo patri debeat medicina. See HEDIN, S. A. 1784. III. 238.[1]
Carles, Pierre Paulin. Antiscorbutiques et jus de · Citron. 1879. III. 502.[2]
— Sur la caractéristique du vin de figue. 1891. III. 370.[1]
— Étude sur les Quinquinas. 1871. III. 722.
— L'huile d'olives. 1898. III. 679.[2]
— Modifications qu'éprouvent les alcaloïdes des écorces de Quinquina. 1870. III. 718.
— Nouvelle espèce d'écorce de Quinquina. 1890. III. 718.
— Pharmacologie des Kolas. 1895. III. 590.[2]
— Sur la pharmacologie des noix de Kola. 1900. III. 591.[1]
— Réparition des alcaloïdes dans les quinquinas. 1873. III. 723.
— Du siège des alcaloïdes dans les écorces de Quinquina. 1875. III. 723.
Carleson, Edvard. See S., J. C. & CARLESON, Edvard.
Carlet, Gaston. Sur le mouvement des étamines dans les Ruta. 1873. II. 410.[2]
— Sur le Tingis du Poirier. 1882. III. 446.[1]
Carleton, M. M. The advantages of Peach culture. 1892. III. 441.[1]
Carlotti, Regulus. De la culture de l'Eucalyptus en Corse. 1866. IV. 529.[2]
— L'Eucalyptus en Corse. 1877. IV. 530.
Carlowitz, von, (Königl. Sächsischer Kammerherr). Verzeichniss einer . . . Sammlung von Weinreben-Sorten. 1844. III. 546.
Carlowitz, Hans Carl von. Sylvicultura oeconomica. 1713. IV. 104.
Carlson, Josef. Om de olika bladformerna hos Hakea Victoriæ. 1886. II. 163.[1]
— Von den verschiedenen Blattformen der Hakea Victoriae. 1886. II. 163.[1]
Carlstén, Andr. Johan. De Phylica. See THUNBERG, C. P. 1804. II. 495.[1]

Carman, E. S. Hardy shrubs. 1883. III. 203.
— The Papaw. 1891. III. 401.[2]
— Paulownia imperialis. 1888. III. 703.[2]
— Rosa rugosa hybrids. 1890. III. 456.[2]
— Salix laurifolia. 1877. / III. 352.[1]
Carmichael. Account of a new mode of thickening hedges. 1832. III. 175.[1]
Carnation-flowered Peach. 1858. III. 439.[2]
Carnauba Palm. 1881. III. 324.[2]
The **Carob** Bean tree. 1878. II. 345.[1]
The **Carob** tree. 1890. II. 345.[1]
Carge. Om Akasie Træets Dyrkning. 1802. IV. 522.[2]
— Om Udplantningen af Nordamerikansk Ahorn. 1802. III. 536.[1]
Caron. Notes on trees introduced into France by Michaux. 1859. I. 241.[2]
Caron, (abbé). Mélanges littéraires et scientifiques. 1838. I. 520.[2]
— Notice sur l'Arbre-à-pin. 1838. III. 283.[2]
— Notice sur l'Indigotier. 1838. III. 479.[1]
— Notice sur la croissance du Bambou. 1838. III. 315.[1]
— Notice sur le caoutchouc. 1838. III. 228.[2]
— Notice sur le Gevuin du Chily. 1838. III. 383.[1]
— Notice sur le Thé. 1838. III. 606.
— Notice sur les ravages du scolyte. 1838. IV. 203.
— Observations sur la longévite . . . de l'Olivier. 1838. II. 713.[1]
— Rapport sur un tronc de Lilas. 1838. III. 680.[1]
Caron, Claude. Traité des bois servans à tous usages. 1676. IV. 98.[2]
Caron, Edouard. Le Thé; culture, récolte. 1861. III. 600.[1]
Caronelli, Pietro. Memoria sugli Ulivi. 1795. III. 675.[1]
Carpenter, George W. Observations and experiments on Peruvian bark. 1829. III. 721.
Carpenter, William B. The microscope and its revelations. 1856. I. 36.[2]
— Popular cyclopaedia of natural science. 1841. I. 94.
— Scripture natural history. 1828. I. 513.
— Vegetable physiology and systematic botany. 1844. I. 88.
Carpenter. IV. 3.
Carpentier, Adolphe. Histoire naturelle des Smilacées. 1869. II. 85,[1] III. 338.[2]
Carpentier, Ernest de. Plantation des terrains crayeux de la Champagne. 1881. IV. 163.
Carpentry and building. IV. 3.
Carpologia mexicana. 1895. III. 265.[1]
Carr, E. D. Flowering plants. 1865. I. 401.
Carr, Ralph. On extensive fissures observed in the stems . . . of the Spruce Fir. 1850. IV. 455.
— On the Silver Alder. 1867. IV. 488.[2]
Carr, Robert. Periodical catalogue of American trees. 1831. V. VIII.[1]
Carradori, Giovacchino. Esperienze ed osservazioni, per dimostrare che le piante assorbiscono il carbonio. 1804. I. 157.
— Esperienze ed osservazioni sulla Sensitiva. 1814. II. 372.[2]
— Esperienze . . . sopra la direzione della plumula. 1803. I. 195.[1]
— Degli organi assorbenti delle radici. 180 . ? I. 160.
— Osservazioni sulle galle . . . dell' Azzeruolo salvatico. 1814. III. 422.[2]
— Parallelo della gomma nostrale con la gomma arabica. 1814. III. 431.[2]
— Del sonno delle piante. 1814. I. 198.
— Sperienze . . . sopra l' irritabilità della lattuga. 1808. I. 197.[1]
— Sulla vitalità delle piante. 1807. I. 192.[2]
Carreau. L'Exposition de sylviculture à Genève. 1896. IV. 21.[1]
Carrelet. Multiplication de l'Aloe. 1879. III. 334.[1]
Carrère, Joseph Barthélemi François. Abhandlung über die Eigenschaften . . . des Nachtschattens. 1780. III. 701.[2]
— Traité des propriétés de la Douce-amère. 1780. III. 701.[2]
Carriage monthly. See COACH-MAKERS' international journal. IV. 3.
Carrichter, Bartholomaeus. Des hochbegahten Herrn Carrichter's . . . Tractaat. 1686. I. 287.
— Horn des Heyls menschlicher Blödigkeit. 1576. I. 282.
— Kräuterbuch. 1575. I. 281.
Carrick, Robert. The present and prospective sources of the timber supplies. 1885. IV. 405.[1]
Carrier, Amans. Sixième lettre, sur la culture des Mûriers. 1834. III. 374.

Carrière, Élie Abel. Abies amabilis. 1867. III. 295.[2]
— Abies concolor fastigiata. 1890. III. 296.[1]
— Abies Gordoniana pumila. 1869. III. 296.[1]
— Abies lasiocarpa pendula. 1890. III. 296.[1]
— Abies Nordmanniana horizontalis. 1887. III. 296.[2]
— Abies Nordmanniana pendula. 1890. III. 296.[2]
— Abies numidica. 1872. III. 296.[1]'
— Sur l'Abies pectinata pyramidata. 1859. III. 296.[2]
— Abricotier de Schiras. 1870. III. 434.[3]
— Abutilon floribundum. 1881. III. 586.[2]
— Acacia verticillata. 1889. III. 466.[1]
— Acalypha Macafeana. 1882. III. 514.[3]
— Acer colchicum tricolor. 1886. III. 534.[2]
— Acer platanoides columnaris. 1878. III. 535.[2]
— Acer Pseudo-Platanus variegatum. 1877. III. 536.[1]
— Actinidia Kolomikta. 1872. III. 595.[2]
— Actinidia volubilis. 1874. III. 595.[2]
— Adenocarpus decorticans. 1883. III. 466.[1]
— Adhatoda cydoniaefolia. 1873. III. 709.[2]
— Aeschynanthus pulcher. 1883. III. 708.[1]
— Aesculus rubicunda Briotii. 1878. III. 537.[1]
— Aesculus rubicunda versicolor. 1874. III. 537.[1]
— De l'affranchissement du Robinier parasol. 1877. III. 487.[1]
— Ailanthus erythrocarpa. 1867. III. 507.[1]
— Sur l'Ailanthus glandulosa. 1872. II. 413.[2]
— Ailantus flavescens. 1865. III. 512.[1]
— Albizzia rosea. 1870. III. 466.[2]
— Amandier à feuilles panachées. 1874. III. 434.[1]
— Amandier à fruits pédonculés. 1864. III. 439.[1]
— L'Amandier nain. 1859. III. 438.[2]
— Amasonia punicea. 1887. III. 695.[2]
— Amorpha pendula. 1870. III. 467.[1]
— Ampelopsis dissecta. 1868. III. 544.[1]
— Ampelopsis palmiloba. 1867. III. 544.[1]
— Ampelopsis tuberosa and napiformis. 1870. III. 544.[3]
— Ampelopsis tuberosa et . . . napiformis. 1870. III. 544.[3]
— Ampelovitis à fruits bleus. 1890. III. 545.[3]
— Ampelovitis Davidi. 1889. III. 584.[1]
— Ampelovitis intermedia. 1891. II. 506.[2]
— Ampelovitis Romaneti. 1892. II. 506.[3]
— Amygdalopsis Lindleyi. 1862. III. 443.[1]
— Amygdalopsis Lindleyi. 1872. II. 277.[2]
— Amygdalus Boissieri. 1879. III. 439.[1]
— Amygdalus Boissierii. 1875. II. 275.[2]
— Amygdalus campaniflora. 1872. III. 440.[L]
— Amygdalus communis flore pleno. 1875. III. 434.[L]
— Amygdalus communis pyramidata. 1872. III. 434.[1]
— Amygdalus monstrosa. 1870. II. 272.[2]
— Amygdalus nana speciosa. 1872. III. 438.[2]
— Amygdalus orientalis. 1867. III. 439.[1]
— Andromeda japonica. 1876. III. 654.[1]
— Andromeda japonica variegata. 1881. III. 654.[1]
— Anomalie d'un raisin Clairette. 1885. II. 507.[3]'
— Anomalie présentée par des Cerises. 1868. II. 272.[1]
— Anomalie présentée par une poire. 1870. II. 279.[2]
— Anomalie présentée par une Poire Bonne-d'Ézée. 1887. II. 280.[1]
— Anomalies présentées par des feuilles de Sciadopytis. 1868. II. 49.[1]
— Aperçu du genre Deutzia. 1873. III. 410.[1]
— Aphelandra cristata. 1887. III. 708.[2]
— Aralia Veitchii. 1874. III. 642.[1]
— Araucaria excelsa speciosissima. 1874. III. 298.[2]
— Arauja albens. 1874. III. 692.[1]
— Arbre de Judée à fleurs blanches. 1862. III. 472.[1]
— Un arbre extraordinairement beau. 1868. III. 480.[2]
— Un arbre fruitier d'ornement. 1867. III. 436.[1]
— Un arbre fruitier méconnu. 1884. III. 584.[1]
— Arbre généalogique du groupe Pêcher. 1865. III. 440.[1]
— Arbre généalogique du groupe Pêcher. 1867. III. 440.[1]
— Un arbre propre à faire des couverts. 1891. III. 418.[2]
— Sur les arbres à employer dans les promenades. 1852. III. 209.
— Les arbres d'avenues et les sols qui leur conviennent. 1892. III. 210.
— Arbres et arbustes nouveaux. 1886. III. 84.[1]
— Les arbres et la civilisation. 185 . ? IV. 43.
— Aria Hostii. 1877. III. 326.[3]
— Armeniaca Davidiana. 1879. III. 430.[2]
— Armeniaca Mume Carr. 1885. III. 438.[2]
— Armeniaca Mume var. Alphandi. 1885. III. 438.[2]

— Aronia densa. 1879. III. 459.²
— Arrosage des arbres. 1889. III. 150.²
— Les arrosages d'hiver. 1890. III. 150.²
— Arthrotaxis Gunneana. 1869. III. 299.²
— Arundinaria falcata. 1876. III. 315.²
— Les Aucubas. 1866. III. 644.²
— Azalea balsaminaeflora. 1882. III. 657.²
— Azalea dianthiflora. 1889. III. 655.
— Azalea dianthiflora. 1891. III. 655.
— Azalea mollis. 1886. III. 660.²
— Azalea obtusa. 1876. III. 659.²
— Azalea viscosa stricta. 1872. III. 662.²
— Les Azalées rustiques. 1885. III. 656.
— Bambou vert glauque. 1861. III. 316.¹
— Bambusa flexuosa. 1870. III. 316.²
— Bambusa heterocycla. 1878. III. 316.¹
— Bambusa Simonii. 1876. III. 315.²
— Bambusa stricta. 1867. III. 316.¹
— Bambusa sulfurea. 1873. III. 316.²
— Bambusa Veitchi. 1888. III. 316.¹
— Bignonia sambucifolia. 1878. III. 707.²
— Biota orientalis. 1855. III. 287,³ 911.²
— Biota orientalis. 1861. III. 311.²
— Biota orientalis argentea. 1872. III. 311.²
— Biota pyramidalis compacta. 1886. III. 311.²
— Un bon modèle de haie vive. 1881. III. 477.¹
— Boronia elatior et polygalaefolis. 1886. III. 495.²
— Boronia megastigma. 1884. III. 496.¹
— Bougainvillea glabra. 1889. III. 388.¹
— Bougainvillea spectabilis. 1888. III. 388.¹
— Du bourgeonnement. 1885. I. 145.¹
— Bouvardia Humboldti corymbiflora. 1879. III. 711.¹
— Bowenia spectabilis. 1870. III. 284.²
— Brosimum Humboldti. 1874. III. 367.²
— Broussin souterrain d'Allante. 1886. III. 507.¹
— Broussonetia Billiardi. 1878. III. 368.¹
— Brugnon monstrueux. 1887. II. 276.²
— Brugnonnier hétérocarpe. 1872. II. 271.²
— Des Bruyères. 1881. III. 650.¹
— Les Bruyères. 1889. III. 650.²
— Buddleia carnea. 1879. III. 681.²
— Buddleia curvifolia. 1867. III. 681.²
— Buddleia curviflora. 1877. III. 681.²
— Buddleia curviflora salicifolia. 1870. III. 681.²
— Buddleia insignis. 1878. III. 681.¹
— Buddleia intermedia. 1873. III. 681.²
— Buddleia intermedia robusta. 1873. III. 681.²
— Buis à branches dressées. 1873. III. 523.¹
— Burchellia capensis. 1886. III. 711.²
— Buxus Fortunei. 1870. III. 522.²
— Cajanus indicus. 1874. III. 469.¹
— Calophaca grandiflora. 1887. III. 469.²
— Camellia Killwingtoniana. 1873. III. 599.¹
— Camoensia maxima. 1887. III. 469.²
— Le Capparis spinosa et sa variété inermis. 1889. III. 408.¹
— Caractères de Rosiers remontants. 1851. III. 448.
— Caractères différentes des Corypha gebanga. 1876. III. 324.¹
— Caractères différentiels de quelques genres de Conifères. 1895. II. 13.¹
— Les Caragana. 1887. III. 469.²
— Carolinea macrocarpa. 1887. III. 589.²
— Carpenteria californica. 1892. III. 409.²
— Carpodetus serratus. 1892. II. 238.²
— Caryopteris mongolica. 1872. III. 695.²
— Cassia floribunda. 1867. III. 471.¹
— Casuarina nodiflora et C. africana. 1869. III. 342.¹
— Casuarina sumatrana. 1889. III. 342.¹
— Catalpa aureo vittata. 1874. III. 706.¹
— Catalpa erubescens. 1869. III. 706.¹
— Ceanothus axillaris. 1876. III. 541.¹
— Ceanothus azureus Élie Carrière. 1887. III. 541.¹
— Ceanothus Lucie Moser. 1874. III. 541.¹
— Ceanothus Marguerite Audusson. 1876. III. 541.¹
— Ceanothus ovatus. 1875. III. 541.²
— Ceanothus ovatus roseus. 1875. III. 541.²
— Ceanotus [sic] americanus sarmentosus. 1869. III. 541.¹
— Un Cèdre en candélabre. 1890. III. 28.¹
— Cedrela sinensis. 1887. III. 512.¹
— Cedrus atlantica fastigiata. 1890. III. 300.¹
— Cedrus Deodara erecta. 1879. III. 300.¹
— Du Cephalotaxus Fortunei à propos des sexes. 1878. II. 8.²

— Cerasus Capuli. 1893. II. 273.³
— Cerasus Chamaecerasus. 1887. III. 436.²
— Cerasus Juliana flore pleno. 1875. III. 435.¹
— Cerasus Lannesiana. 1872. III. 442.²
— Cerasus Pattoniana. 1872. II. 275.¹
— Cerasus persicaefolia. 1869. III. 439.¹
— Cerasus semperflorens. 1877. III. 436.²
— Cerasus serratifolia rosea. 1877. III. 442.²
— Cerasus Sieboldtii. 1866. III. 442.²
— Cerise à collier. 1873. II. 272.¹
— Cerisier à feuilles denticulées. 1864. III. 442.²
— Cerisier commun pleureur. 1888. III. 436.²
— Les Chaenomeles. 1886. III. 419.²
— Chaenomeles alba grandiflora. 1876. III. 420.¹
— Chaenomeles citripoma. 1891. III. 420.¹
— Chaenomeles citripomma. 1876. III. 420.¹
— Les Chaenomeles et leur multiplication. 1884. III. 419.
— Chaenomeles japonica pedunculata. 1869. III. 420.¹
— Chamaecyparis andelyensis. 1869. III. 301.¹
— Chamaecyparis nutkaensis. 1869. III. 301.¹
— Chamaecyparis nutkaensis pyramidalis. 1882. III. 301.
— Chamaecyparis obtusa. 1869. III. 301.¹
— Chamaerops excelsa. 1870. III. 331.²
— Les Chamaerops excelsa, Fortunei. 1868. II. 75.¹
— Chamaerops excelsa gracilis. 1875. III. 331.³
— The Chapel-Oak of Allouville. 1873. II. 138.¹
— Chêne-chapelle d'Allouville. 1873. II. 138.²
— Le Chêne de Fordes. 1861. III. 362.¹
— Les Chênes de l'Europe et de l'Orient. 1870. II. 129.²
— Chênes remarquables . . . des Vosges. 1887. II. 139.¹
— Chionanthes [sic] retardataires. 1875. I. 192.¹
— Du choix des greffons. 1883. III. 162.
— Choix des greffons ou des boutures. 1886. III. 153.
— Cinchona Calisaya. 1873. III. 725.¹
— Circulation de la sève. 1884. I. 165.
— Cissus Davidiana. 1868. III. 545.²
— Cissus elegans. 1876. III. 544.¹
— Cissus Veitchi. 1877. III. 545.¹
— Citrus triptera. 1886. III. 503.¹
— Citrus triptera et Triphasia trifoliata. 1869. III. 503,¹ 508.¹
— Sur la classification des Pêchers. 1864. III. 440.¹
— Classification des Pêchers. 1884. II. 276.¹
— Clematis aethusaefolia. 1869. III. 390.¹
— Clematis balearica. 1874. III. 390.¹
— Clematis indivisa lobata. 1887. III. 390.²
— Clematis indivisa lobata Hooker. 1853. III. 390.³
— Clematis orientalis glauca. 1890. III. 390.²
— Clematis patens Done. var. Helena. 1855. III. 391.²
— Clematis Pellieri. 1880. III. 391.²
— Clematis Pitcheri. 1878. III. 391.²
— Clematis Viticella alba. 1878. III. 392.¹
— Clematis Viticella magnifica. 1876. III. 392.¹
— Clematis Viticella nana. 1869. III. 392.¹
— Clématite bleue veinée. 1860. III. 392.¹
— Clématite Lady Bowill. 1876. III. 391.¹
— Clématite Louise Carrière. 1880. III. 392.¹
— Clématite Madame Émile Sorbet. 1878. III. 391.¹
— Clématite Madame Grangé. 1877. III. 391.¹
— Clématites hybrides Mme. Méline. 1885. III. 389.¹
— Clerodendron Bungei. 1866. III. 696.¹
— Clerodendron imperialis. 1874. III. 696.¹
— Clerodendron serotinum. 1867. III. 696.¹
— Clerodendron speciosum. 1873. III. 696.²
— Clerodendron speciosum. 1890. III. 696.²
— Cocos australis. 1876. III. 322.¹
— A columnar Cypress. 1859. III. 302.²
— Comarouna odorata. 1873. III. 475.²
— Comment se forment les types? 1867. III. 473.²
— Considérations générales sur les Pommiers microcarpes. 1881. III. 425.¹
— Cornus sibirica Gouchaulti. 1888. III. 645.³
— Corset élastique Bénard pour la greffe en écusson. 1887. III. 162.
— Corylopsis spicata. 1869. III. 416.²
— Cotoneaster reflexa. 1870. III. 421.¹
— Crataegus Bruanti. 1884. III. 422.¹
— Crataegus Carrierei. 1883. III. 421.²
— Crataegus coccinea macrocarpa. 1876. III. 421.²
— Crataegus lobata serotina. 1869. III. 429.²
— Crataegus Ludgi. 1876. III. 422.¹
— Crataegus Oxyacantha punicea plena. 1872. III. 422.¹
— Croton Baronne James de Rothschild. 1879. III. 516.¹
— Croton interruptum elegans. 1880. III. 516.¹

Carrière, Élie Abel (*continued*).
— Crotons nouveaux. 1880. III. 516.[1]
— Cryptomeria araucarioides. 1890. III. 302.[1]
— Cryptomeria japonica pyramidata. 1891. III. 302.[1]
— Cryptomeria nigricans. 1870. III. 302.[1]
— Cryptomeria pungens. 1868. III. 302.[1]
— Cryptomeria pungens rubiginosa. 1873. III. 302.[1]
— Culture des Bambous. 1873. III. 314.[1]
— Culture des Chaenomeles. 1887. III. 419.[2]
— Culture des Chamaerops excelsa. 1870. III. 331.[2]
— Culture des Fusains du Japon à feuilles panachées. 1891. III. 532.[2]
— Culture des Guis. 1887. III. 385.[2]
— Culture du Gardenia florida. 1853. III. 744.[2]
— Culture du Robinia hispida. 1890. III. 486.[1]
— Culture du Sapin Pinsapo. 1859. III. 297.[1]
— Cupressus cornuta. 1866. III. 302.[2]
— Cupressus Lambertiana depressa. 1870. III. 302.[2]
— Cupressus Mac-Nabiana. 1870. II. 29.[2]
— Les Cupressus macrocarpa. 1855. III. 302.[2]
— Cycas siamensis. 1881. III. 285.[1]
— Cydonia Bourgeauti. 1872. II. 420.[1]
— Cytisus Adami pendulum. 1870. III. 480.[2]
— Cytisus alba robusta. 1870. III. 474.[1]
— Cytisus Everestianus. 1872. III. 474.[2]
— Cytisus incarnatus. 1872. III. 474.[1]
— Le Cytisus Laburnum est-il vénéneux? 1880. III. 481.[1]
— Cytisus pilosus. 1852. III. 477.[1]
— Cytisus racemosus. 1890. III. 474.[2]
— Cytisus supinus et leucanthus. 1852. III. 474.[1]
— Daphne Mazeli. 1872. II. 601.[2]
— Daphne salicifolia. 1870. III. 627.[1]
— Dasylirion glaucum. 1872. III. 336.[1]
— Decaisnea Fargesii. 1893. II. 201.[1]
— Déplanteuse Henri Chatenay. 1871. III. 167.
— Description d'une nouvelle espèce de Genévrier. 1854. III. 303.[1]
— Description . . . des variétés de Fêchers. 186 . ? III. 430.[2]
— Desmodium japonicum. 1875. II. 354.[1]
— Desmodium penduliflorum. 1873. III. 481.[1]
— Deutzia crenata candidissima plena. 1870. III. 410.[2]
— Des Deutzias. 1877. III. 410.[1]
— Deux Chaenomeles japonica à fleurs blanches. 1889. III. 420.[1]
— Deux Fusains du Japon à recommander. 1887. III. 532.[2]
— Deux mots sur l'Akebia quinata. 1853. III. 393.[1]
— Deux nouveaux Bambous. 1869. III. 314.[1]
— Deux nouvelles espèces de Bambous. 1869. III. 314.[1]
— Deux nouvelles plantes japonaises rustiques. 1877. III. 415.[1]
— Deux nouvelles variétés d'Amandier nain. 1872. III. 438.[1]
— Deux Pilocereus gigantesques. 1890. III. 626.[1]
— Deux rectifications à propos du Ligustrum. 1863. III. 340.[2] 673.[2]
— Deux variétés remarquables du Sureau. 1890. III. 752.[1]
— Développement anormal d'un fruit de Poirier. 1867. II. 279.[2]
— Développement anormal d'une pomme. 1883. II. 267.[1]
— Dichroïsme de deux sortes de cépages. 1884. II. 507.[2]
— Dichroïsme du Grenadier de Legrelle. 1882. III. 630.[2]
— Dichroïsme du Rosa Eglanteria. 1865. III. 455.[2]
— Dichroïsme du Syringa Saugeana. 1876. III. 681.[1]
— Diervilla Middendorfiana. 1854. III. 749.[2]
— Dimensions de quelques espèces de Conifères. 1873. III. 290.
— Dimorphisme d'un Groseillier à grappes. 1895. II. 246.[1]
— Dimorphisme de l'Osmanthus Fortunei. 1864. II. 713.[2]
— Dimorphisme du Brugnon Lord Napier. 1889. II. 276.[1]
— Dimorphisme du Hêtre commun. 1864. II. 126.[1]
— Dimorphisme du Mérisier commun. 1870. II. 273.[1]
— Dimorphisme du Pêcher Madeleine rouge. 1865. II. 276.[1]
— Dimorphisme du Ribes nigrum. 1869. II. 245.[2]
— Dimorphisme du Robinia hispida. 1865. II. 382.[1]
— Dimorphisme du Rosa cannabifolia. 1873. II. 292.[1]
— Dimorphisme et dichroïsme du Betula purpurea. 1885. II. 120.[1]
— Dimorphisme et dichroïsme du Gardenia radicans. 1864. II. 818.[1]
— Dimorphisme présenté par le Laurocerasus. 1863. III. 437.[2]
— Dimorphisme présenté par le Persica versicolor. 1870. III. 440.[1]

— Dimorphismes de l'Evonymus radicans. 1885. III. 533.[1]
— Diosma Wendlandi. 1892. III. 495.[1]
— Diospyros coronaria. 1885. III. 669.[1]
— Diospyros costata. 1870. III. 669.[1]
— Diospyros costata of Carrière. 1870. II. 701.[2]
— Diospyros lycopersicon. 1878. III. 669.[1]
— Diospyros Mazeli. 1874. III. 669.[1]
— Diospyros Roxburghi. 1872. II. 701.[2]
— Diospyros Wieseneri. 1888. III. 669.[2]
— Doit-on tailler les arbres en les plantant. 1884. III. 166, 170.
— Die Doppelveredelung. 1884. III. 162.
— Dracaena Bartetii. 1886. III. 335.
— Dracaena congesta discolor. 1883. III. 335.
— Dracaena Draco. 1869. II. 82.[2]
— Dracaena indivisa Pigny. 1881. III. 335.
— Dracaena Rothiana. 1877. III. 337.[1]
— Dracaenas nouveaux. 1880. III. 334.[2]
— Echeveria retusa. 1876. III. 409.[2]
— Echinocactus multiplex et sa variété cristata. 1876. III. 622.[2]
— Echinocactus Simpsoni. 1877. III. 622.[1]
— Echinopsis scopa. 1875. III. 622.[1]
— Echium fastuosum. 1876. III. 695.[1]
— L'écorce du Spinovitis Davidii. 1891. II. 506.[2]
— Edwardsia grandiflora. 1869. III. 488.[2]
— Effets de la foudre sur un Cerisier. 1852. IV. 193.[2]
— Ein eigenthümliches Pfropfen.' 1875. I. 198,[1] 203.[1]
— Ueber einige Eutacta-Arten aus Neu-Caledonien. 1866. II. 25.[2]
— Ueber einige Varietäten der Cryptomeria. 1885. III. 302.[1]
— Élevage d'arbres difformes. 1887. III. 202.[1]
— Emploi des feuilles du Caféier. 1887. III. 740.[1]
— De l'emploi des racines comme moyen de multiplication. 1852. III. 158.
— Encephalartos Hildebrandi. 1880. III. 285.[2]
— Encore le Citrus triptera. 1886. III. 503.[1]
— Encore le Diospyros costata. 1872. III. 669.[1]
— Encore le Peuplier régénéré. 1865. III. 345.[2]
— Encyclopédie horticole. 1862. III. 31.
— Une énigme végétale, Yucca pendula aurea. 1877. III. 340.[2]
— Enkyanthus himalaïcus. 1888. III. 649.[1]
— Enkyanthus japonicus. 1877. III. 649.[1]
— Entretiens familiers sur l'horticulture. 1860. III. 36.[1]
— Die Entstehung einer Frucht, ohne . . . Blüthe. 1875. II. 280.[1]
— Epiphyllum Gibsoni. 1886. III. 623.[1]
— Epiphyllum Russellianum Gartneri. 1887. III. 625.[2]
— Époque pour la pratique des greffes. 1884. III. 162,
— Érable Négundo à feuilles panachées. 1852. III. 535.[1]
— Érable Sycomore à fruits rouges. 1864. III. 536.[1]
— Érables japonais. 1867. III. 535.[2]
— Erica Faireana. 1880. III. 651.[1]
— Erica ventricosa coccinea minor. 1880. V. xxix.[2]
— Erica Wilmoreana et variétés. 1892. III. 651.[2]
— Erythrina compacta. 1877. III. 476.[1]
— Une espèce qui tend à perdre son caractère spécifique. 1879. III. 442.[2]
— Essai d'une classification . . . du genre Yucca. 1859. II. 86.[2]
— Essai sur l'horticulture japonaise. 1878. III. 175.[2]
— Essai sur quelques Vignes de la Chine. 1886. II. 505.[2]
— Étêtage ou rabattage des gros arbres. 1885. III. 181.[2]
— Étude générale du genre Pommier. 1883. II. 266.[1]
— Des Eucalyptus. 1878. III. 633.[2]
— Eugenia Ugni. 1879. III. 638.[1]
— Euphorbia officinarum. 1875. III. 518.[1]
— Eutacta Rulei polymorpha. 1866. III. 299.[2]
— Evonymus Carrierei. 1881. III. 532.[1]
— Evonymus japonica Duc d'Anjou. 1872. III. 532.[2]
— Evonymus japonica pallens. 1877. III. 532.[2]
— Evonymus japonicus pyramidatus. 1882. III. 532.[2]
— L'Evonymus japonicus. 1888. III. 532.[2]
— Evonymus pulchellus argenteus. 1884. III. 532.[2]
— Evonymus pulchellus foliis variegatis. 1890. III. 532.[2]
— Evonymus radicans comme plante grimpante. 1879. III. 533.[1]
— Evonymus sinensis et . . . microphyllus. 1883. III. 532.[2]
— Excroissance gemmifère du Sequoia sempervirens. 1868. II. 49.[2]

— Excroissances de Sequoia sempervirens. 1869. II. 49.²
— Exemples de variation fournis par le Rhamnus olaeifolius. 1874. III. 543.²
— Exochorda Alberti. 1891. III. 424.¹
— Fait de dimorphisme observé sur le Podocarpus koraiana. 1863. II. 8.²
— Fécondation de l'Araucaria imbricata. 1878. III. 299.¹
— De la fécondation des Chênes. 1870. II. 131.¹
— Fertilisation of the Araucaria. 1879. II. 26.²
— Ficus Cavroni. 1887. III. 370.¹
— Ficus minima. 1885. III. 371.¹
— Figure théorique de l'Evonymus radicans variegata. 1878. III. 533.¹
— Floraison d'un Bambusa Thouarsii. 1875. II. 59.²
— Floraison du Prunus sinensis flore albo pleno. 1853. III. 437.¹
— Floraison du Robinier à une feuille. 1864. III. 487.¹
— Floraison du Sophora japonica pendula. 1876. III. 488.¹
— Floraison et fructification du Pavia californica. 1862. III. 536.²
— Sur le Fontanesia Fortunei. 1859. II. 706.¹
— Le Fontanesia phillyraeoides variegata. 1859. III. 671.²
— Formation de fruits sans fleurs. 1884. II. 278.²
— De la forme des feuilles. 1878. II. 313.¹
— Formes monstrueuses de Citronniers. 1889. II. 402.¹
— Forms of leaves. 1878. II. 313.¹
— Forsythia Fortunei. 1889. III. 672.¹
— Forsythia suspensa. 1861. III. 672.¹
— Fourcroya tuberosa. 1877. III. 341.²
— Fraxinus dimorpha dumosa. 1865. III. 672.¹
— Fraxinus excelsior cucullata. 1867. III. 672.²
— Fraxinus excelsior foliis aureis. 1878. III. 672.²
— Fremontia californica. 1867. III. 591.¹
— Frêne pleureur de Remilly. 1878. III. 672.²
— Fructification au muséum du Cerasus Fontanesiana. 1870. III. 437.¹
— Fructification de l'Evonymus japonicus fastigiatus. 1883. III. 532.²
— Fructification de l'Evonymus radicans variegata. 1876. III. 533.¹
— Fructification des Forsythia. 1889. III. 671.¹
— Fructification du Chaenomeles alba grandiflora. 1887. III. 420.¹
— Fructification du Libocedrus Doniana. 1866. III. 305.¹
— Fructification du Pandanus furcatus. 1881. III. 313.²
— Fructification du Pin de Sabine. 1859. III. 308.²
— Fructification du Robinia coluteoides. 1873. III. 487.¹
— Fructification du Robinia hispida. 1867. III. 486.¹
— Fructification du Sciadopitys verticillata. 1884. II. 49.²
— Fructification du Torreya myristica. 1875. II. 12.¹
— Fruit-bouture. 1880. II. 596.²
— Fruits de Prunier déformés par l'Exoascus. 1886. III. 433.²
— Fuchsia boliviana. 1876. III. 640.¹
— Fuchsia fulgens pumila. 1881. III. 640.¹
— Fuchsia Jean Sysley. 1878. III. 640.¹
— Fuchsia pendula. 1894. III. 640.²
— Fuchsia syringaeflora. 1873. III. 640.¹
— Les Fuchsias à fleurs erigées. 1886. III. 640.¹
— La fumure des arbres. 1887. III. 151.
— Sur le Fusain du Japon. 1864. III. 532.¹
— Fusain du Japon Duc d'Anjou. 1070. III. 502.¹
— Gardenia citriodora. 1886. III. 747.¹
— Garrya macrophylla [sic]. 1870. III. 352.²
— Garrya Thuretii. 1879. III. 352.²
— Garrya Thuretia. 1869. III. 352.²
— Die Gattung Skimmia und deren Arten. 1869. III. 505.²
— Genista Andreana. 1889. III. 475.¹
— Genista hispanica. 1888. III. 477.¹
— Genista tinctoria flore pleno. 1892. III. 477.²
— Glycine de la Chine à fleurs pleines. 1887. III. 490.²
— Des Glycines cultivées comme arbustes. 1878. III. 490.¹
— Glyptostrobus columnaris. 1886. III. 311.¹
— Un grand arbre nanisé. 1874. III. 307.¹
— Le greffage des Châtaigniers. 1887. III. 359.¹
— Greffage des Idesia. 1877. III. 614.²
— Du greffage en vue de hâter la fructification des semis. 1886. III. 162.
— De la greffe à œil poussant. 1852. III. 164.¹
— Greffe de boutons à fruits. 1892. III. 163.¹
— Sur la greffe des Conifères. 1861. III. 294.¹
— Greffe des Fusains à haute tige. 1883. III. 532.¹
— De la greffe en écusson appliquée à la Wisterie. 1859. III. 490.¹

— Greffe en écusson de Pivoines ligneuses. 1883. III. 393.¹
— Greffe en écusson sur vieux bois. 1884. III. 162.
— Greffe en pipiau. 1882. III. 162.
— Une greffe exceptionnelle. 1875. I. 196,¹ 808.¹
— Greffe nourricière d'un Poirier. 1884. III. 162.
— Greffe sur genoux des anciens. 1859. III. 161.
— Greffes sur racines . . . de Pivoines. 1848. III. 393.¹
— Grenadier des Antilles. 1888. III. 630.²
— Grevillea alpestris. 1887. III. 383.¹
— Le gros Châtaignier d'Évian-les-Bains. 1892. II. 125.¹
— Un groupe de Bruyères. 1880. III. 630.¹
— Groupe de nouvelles Clématites hybrides. 1879. III. 389.¹
— Guide pratique du jardinier multiplicateur. 1856. III. 153.
— Les Guis. 1886. II. 179.²
— Une haie de Fuchsias. 1889. III. 640.¹
— Des haies. 1885. III. 214.¹
— Haies défensives et ornementales. 1876. III. 420,¹ 503.¹
— Les baies ornementales. 1890. III. 456.¹
— Halimodendron speciosum. 1876. III. 478.²
— Hamiltonia spectabilis. 1872. III. 744.²
— Hâtiveté phénoménale de floraison. 1875. II. 413,² 834.²
— Heteromorphous Apple tree. 1881. II. 267.¹
— Les Hêtres monstrueux de la forêt de Verzy. 1864. II. 126.²
— Hibiscus chrysanthus. 1888. III. 587.²
— L'hiver de 1890–91. 1891. III. 49.¹
— Ueber den Holunder von Californien. 1854. III. 751.²
— Hortensia japonica Thomas Hoog. 1877. III. 411.²
— Hortensia Madame Mézard. 1870. III. 411.²
— Des Hortensias à fleurs bleues. 1876. III. 411.²
— Un hybride d'Oranger. 1885. III. 501.²
— Hydrangea acuminata. 1874. III. 411.¹
— Hydrangea Impératrice Eugénie. 1868. III. 411.¹
— Hydrangea japonica rosalba. 1866. III. 411.¹
— Hydrangea paniculata grandiflora. 1873. III. 412.¹
— Hypericum calycinum. 1876. III. 610.¹
— Hypericum patulum. 1875. III. 610.¹
— Idesia polycarpa. 1872. III. 614.² — 1888. III. 614.²
— Idesia polycarpa crispa. 1878. III. 614.²
— If de Dowaston. 1861. III. 287.²
— Ilex Aquifolium Madame Briot. 1866. III. 530.¹
— Ilex camelliaefolia. 1887. III. 530.¹
— Ilex Fischeri. 1887. III. 530.¹
— Une importante collection de Lierres. 1890. III. 643.¹
— L'Indigotier à grandes feuilles. 1859. III. 479.²
— L'industrie des pipes en racine de Bruyère. 1888. III. 651.²
— Influence de la greffe. 1892. III. 40.
— De l'influence de la greffe sur le sujet. 1868. III. 39.
— Influence du greffon sur le sujet. 1887. III. 40.
— Influence du sujet sur le greffon. 1865. I. 246.²
— Un intéressant hybride de Pavonia. 1887. III. 522.²
— Introduction en France du Larix Kaempferi. 1856. II. 49.¹
— Jamesia americana. 1874. III. 413.¹
— Japonaiseries. 1889. III. 175.²
— Jasminum affine. 1878. III. 672.¹
— Les Jolis fous de Remilly. 1877. II. 127.¹
— Juglans ailantifolia. 1878. III. 356.¹
— Juglans cordata tenerrima. 1872. III. 354.²
— Juglans intermedia alata. 1865. III. 355.
— Juglans intermedia quadrangulata. 1870. III. 355.
— Juglans longirostris. 1878. III. 354.²
— Juglans regia olivaeformis. 1868. III. 355.
— Juglans regia suberosa. 1876. III. 355.
— Juglans serotina nova. 1869. III. 355.
— Juniperus drupacea. 1853. III. 303.¹
— Justicia quadrifida. 1872. III. 709.²
— Les Kakis. 1889. III. 669.²
— Sur les Kakis japonais. 1880. III. 669.²
— Keteleeria Fortunei. 1866. III. 304.²
— Keteleeria Fortunei. 1887. III. 32.²
— Laburnum Adami polymorphum. 1872. III. 480.²
— Lagerstroemia indica. 1874. III. 629.²
— Lagerstroemia indica. 1888. III. 629.²
— Larix Griffithiana. 1865. III. 304.²
— Laurier-Cerise de Bertin père. 1885. III. 437.²
— Laurocerasus Ottini. 1877. III. 437.²
— Lembotropis nigricans Carlieri. 1891. II. 351.¹
— Leschenaultia Baxteri major. 1886. III. 754.¹
— Libocedrus chilensis. 1867. III. 305.¹
— Libonia penrhosiensis. 1876. III. 709.²

Carrière, Élie Abel (*continued*).
— Lierre parapluie. 1874. III. 642.¹
— Ligustrina amurensis. 1877. III. 680.²
— Ligustrum californicum robustum variegatum. 1877. III. 674.¹
— Ligustrum chinense. 1863. III. 674.¹
— Ligustrum coriaceum. 1874. III. 673.²
— Ligustrum coriaceum. 1888. III. 673.²
— Ligustrum japonicum paniculatum. 1858. III. 673.¹
— Ligustrum ovalifolium aureum. 1862. III. 674.¹
— Ligustrum ovalifolium instabile. 1878. III. 674.¹
— Ligustrum Quihoui. 1869. III. 674.¹
— Des Lilas à fleurs doubles. 1877. III. 681.¹
— Lilas à fleurs doubles. 1883. III. 680.¹
— Des Lilas à petites feuilles. 1883. III. 680.¹
— Des Lilas blancs d'hiver. 1877. III. 680.¹
— Du Lilas dit de Perse. 1878. II. 715.²
— Lonicera brachypoda. 1887. II. 838.²
— Lonicera brachypoda et longiflora. 1862. III. 749.²
— Lonicera Brownii hort. 1856. III. 750.¹
— Sur les Lonicera chinensis et diversifolia. 1866. III. 750.²
— Lonicera fragrantissima. 1873. III. 750.¹
— Lonicera gigantea. 1882. III. 750.¹
— Lonicera longiflora. 1873. III. 750.²
— Lonicera Phylomelae. 1872. III. 750.²
— Lonicera Standishi. 1873. III. 751.¹
— Des'loupes. 1880. I. 213.²
— Luculia gratissima. 1890. III. 745.²
— Le Maclura tricuspidata. 1864. III. 368.²
— Maclura tricuspidata. 1872. III. 368.²
— Magnolia biflora. 1885. III. 400.¹
— Magnolia Campbelli. 1878. III. 399.²
— Magnolia stellata. 1878. III. 400.²
— Magnolia Wieseneri. 1890. III. 400.¹
— Mahaleb cerasifolia. 1872. III. 438.¹
— Les Mahonia. 1854. III. 395.¹
— Mahonia nepalensis. 1853. III. 396.¹
— Malus cerasifera praecox. 1870. III. 425.¹
— Des Malus coronaria et sempervirens. 1877. III. 429.¹
— Malus floribunda. 1870. III. 429.¹
— Malus kaido purpurea. 1877. III. 429.¹
— Malus microcarpa Bertini. 1882. III. 429.¹
— Malus microcarpa coronaria. 1884. III. 429.¹
— Malus microcarpa fastigiata. 1879. III. 429.¹
— Malus microcarpa kermesina. 1885. III. 429.¹
— Malus Ringo. 1874. III. 429.¹
— Malus sibirica coccinea. 1867. III. 425.¹
— Malus spectabilis kaido. 1874. III. 429.²
— Malus Torringo. 1870. III. 429.²
— Marche de la sève dans les végétaux. 1873. I. 164.
— Le Marronnier de Malebranche. 1890. II. 482.²
— Des mastics ou cires à greffer à froid. 1873. III. 162.
— Menispermum canadense macrophyllum. 1876. III. 397.
— Du Merisier à fleurs doubles. 1852. III. 435.¹
— Merisier et Cerisier à fleurs doubles. 1852. III. 435.¹
— Meyenia erecta. 1863. III. 710.¹
— Microcachrys tetragona. 1866. III. 287.²
— Microphoenix Sahuti. 1885. III. 328.¹
— Mistletoe. 1886. II. 179.²
— Modification et extinction des types. 1872. III. 542.²
— Monstruosité. 1875. II. 280.¹
— Monstruosité. 1876. II. 280.¹
— Monstruosité produite par une Poire William. 1882. II. 280.¹
— Montreuil-aux-Pêches. 187.? III. 125, *441*.¹
— A moveable Ivy bower. 1874. III. 642.²
— Multiplication de l'Araucaria excelsa. 1888. III. 298.²
— Multiplication de l'Itea virginica. 1852. III. 412.²
— Multiplication des Chênes verts. 1885. III. 361.²
— Multiplication des Dracénas. 1890. III. 336.¹
— Multiplication des Pivoines en arbre. 1872. III. 393.¹
— Multiplication du Catalpa Kaempferi. 1852. III. 706.¹
— Multiplication du Garrya elliptica. 1856. III. 352.²
— Multiplication du Garrya elliptica. 1856. III. 352.²
— Multiplication du Juglans regia laciniata. 1856. III. 355.
— Sur la multiplication du Pavia californica. 1862. III. 536.²
— Multiplication du Polycarpa Maximowiezii. 1873. III. 614.²
— Multiplication du Pseudolarix Kaempferi. 1872. III. 309.¹
— Multiplication du Robinia Pseudo-Acacia Bessoniana. 1883. III. 487.¹

— Multiplication du Sambucus pendula nova. 1891. III. 752.¹
— Multiplication du Saxe-gothaea. 1862. III. 287,² *903*.¹
— Multiplication du Spiraea ariaefolia. 1856. III. 424.²
— Multiplication du Staphylea colchica. 1876. III. 533.²
— Multiplication du Tilleul argenté. 1891. III. 586.¹
— Multiplication par graines de l'Aralia Sieboldi. 1875. III. 642.¹
— Myrica rubra. 1890. III. 353.²
— Nerium Madoui grandiflorum. 1869. III. 689.²
— Neubeiten aus Japan. 1887. III. 87.
— A new Grape, Spinovitis Davidii. 1891. III. 584.¹
— A new shrub (Ligustrina amurensis). 1877. III. 680.²
— Noix jumelles. 1873. II. 113.²
— Nomenclature des Pêches et des Brugnons. 1862. III. 430.²
— Note sur Keteleeria Fortunei. 1887. II. 32.²
— Note sur l'Abies cilicica. 1856. III. 296.¹
— Note sur la multiplication de l'Akebia. 1856. III. 393.¹
— Notice sur le Bureau de Californie. 1854. III. 751.²
— Notice sur le Torreya myristica. 1854. III. 286,² *288*.²
— Notice sur les Vignes du Soudan. 1881. II. 501.¹
— Notice sur quelques plantes grimpantes. 1855. III. 388.²
— Nouveau Fusain du Japon. 1891. III. 532.²
— Nouveau mode de bouturage . . . du Ficus elastica. 1892. III. 370.²
— Un nouveau progrès dans l'art du greffage. 1886. III. 456.¹
— Un nouveau type de Rosa polyantha. 1892. III. 456.¹
— Une nouveauté ornementale. 1890. III. 533.¹
— Nouveautés japonaises. 1887. III. 87.
— Nouveaux types de Vignes de l'extrême Asie. 1888. II. 505.²
— Les nouveaux Weigelias en 1864. 1864. III. 748.²
— Un nouvel arbre d'ornement. 1867. III. 422.¹
— Nouvel emploi du Fusain du Japon. 1885. III. 532.²
— Nouvelle espèce de Prunier. 1884. III. 433.¹
— Une nouvelle greffe. 1884. III. 162.
— Nouvelle variété de Ligustrum japonicum. 1856. III. 673.²
— Nouvelles espèces de Conifères. 1870. II. 14.¹
— Nouvelles variétés de Ceanothus. 1868. III. 541.¹
— Nouvelles variétés de Cyprès chauves. 1859. III. 310.²
— Nouvelles variétés de Grenadiers à fleurs pleines. 1880. III. 630.¹
— Nouvelles variétés de Weigelias. 1868. III. 748.²
— Noyer à fruits panachés. 1860. III. 355.
— Noyer commun à grappes. 1873. III. 355.
— Noyer de la Saint-Jean. 1867. III. 355.
— Noyer de la Saint-Jean ou tardif. 1860. III. 355.
— Le Noyer et ses variétés. 1861. III. 355.
— Le Noyer gibbeux. 1860. III. 355.
— Noyer intermédiaire à fruits pyriformes. 1863. III. 355.
— Noyer monohétérophylle. 1865. III. 355.
— Oak of Lebanon. 1872. III. 362.²
— Observation relative à la fécondation des Chamaerops. 1870. II. 67.¹
— Observations pratiques sur les greffes des arbres à rameaux pendants. 1857. III. 204.¹
— Observations sur le Thuia gigantea et Pinus Boursieri. 1854, 1853. II. 41,² *52*.²
— Olearia Hastii. 1886. III. 756.¹
— Oranger hermaphrodite. 1885. II. 402.²
— Oranges triples. 1883. II. 403.¹
— Origine de . . . variétés d'arbres à branches pendantes. 1856. III. 470,¹ *674*.¹
— Origine du Noyer fertile. 1882. III. 355.
— Origine du Rosier Manetti. 1883. III. 455.²
— Origine du Yucca quadricolor. 1878. III. 340.¹
— Origine et orthographe de l'Erica Vilmoreana. 1892. III. 651.¹
— Orme et Planera. 1875. II. 143.¹
— Les Osmanthus ilicifolius. 1856. III. 680.¹
— Oxera pulchella. 1890. III. 697.¹
— Padus cornuta. 1890. III. 313.¹
— Une page inédite à propos du Lilas de Perse. 1878. II. 715.²
— Panax sessiliflora. 1874. III. 641.¹
— Pandanus caricosus. 1878. III. 313.¹
— Pandanus flagelliformis. 1866. III. 313.²
— Pandanus furcatus. 1879. III. 313.²
— Pandanus Houlletii. 1868. III. 313.²
— Pandanus Pancheri. 1880. III. 313.¹
— Passiflora Varanzof. 1872. III. 616.²

— Paulownia imperialis. 1873. III. 703.²
— Pêche Montigny ou Pêche amandiforme de Chine. 1861. III. 439.¹
— Pêche plate. 1870. III. 440.¹
— Pêcher d'Ispahan à fleurs doubles. 1853. III. 439.²
— Pêcher douteux ou mixte. 1867. III. 440.¹
— Pêcher pyramidal. 1870. III. 440.¹
— Pêcher pyramidal. 1888. III. 440.¹
— Des Pêchers à fleurs doubles. 1872. III. 440.¹
— Pelargonium lycopodioides. 1874. II. 391.¹
— Pépinières. 1855. III. 154.¹
— Persica Davidiana. 1872. III. 436.²
— Persica striata. 1870. III. 440.¹
— Peuplier Eugène et Peuplier régénéré. 1865. III. 345.²
— Peut-on élaguer les Conifères? 1881. III. 295.¹
— Phénomène de végétation produit par le Stangeria. 1866. II. 6.²
— Phénomène présenté par un Araucaria excelsa. 1885. II. 26.²
— Phénomènes produits par la fécondation artificielle. 1879. II. 89.¹
— Philadelphus Keteléerii. 1866. III. 413.²
— Philadelphus primulaeflorus. 1870. III. 413.¹
— Philadelphus Souvenir de Billiard. 1875. III. 413.²
— Phygelius capensis. 1886. III. 703.²
— Phyllocladus glauca. 1867. III. 287.²
— Physiologie végétale. 1868. II. 267.¹
— Physiologie végétale. 1885. I. 145.¹
— Picea excelsa denudata. 1854. III. 305.¹
— Picea excelsa Raymontii. 1870. III. 305.¹
— Picea excelsa reflexa. 1890. III. 305.¹
— Picea Morinda monstrosa. 1869. III. 306.¹
— Picea Omorika. 1877. III. 305.²
— Picea orientalis nana. 1891. III. 306.¹
— Les Pimelea. 1887. III. 628.¹
— Les Pins de Heldreich et Peuce. 1864. III. 306.²
— Pinus aristata. 1872. III. 306.²
— Pinus austriaca foliis variegatis. 1883. III. 308.¹
— Pinus Grozelierii. 1869. II. 43.²
— Pinus halepensis conglomerata. 1869. III. 307.²
— Pinus pyrenaica. 1867. III. 307.²
— Pinus Strobus umbraculifera. 1869. III. 309.¹
— Pinus sylvestris fastigiata. 1856. III. 309.¹
— Pinus Tamrac. 1869. II. 43.²
— Planera Kaki. 1890. III. 366.¹
— Plantation des Conifères. 1855. III. 291.
— Plante nouvelle (Quercus Libani). 1870. II. 129.²
— Des plantes à feuilles persistantes. 1866. I. 172.
— Plantes japonaises nouvellement introduites. 1869. III. 87.
— Des plantes naturellement jaunes. 1886. III. 206.²
— Plantes nouvelles, rares ou peu connues. 1866. III. 87.
— Les Platanes dans les promenades publiques. 1890. III. 419.¹
— Platanus occidentalis cucullata. 1877. III. 419.¹
— Plumbago capensis alba. 1888. III. 666.¹
— Les Podocarpus neriifolia. 1888. III. 287.²
— Podocytise de Caramanie. 1861. III. 480.²
— Poire Madame von Siebold. 1879. III. 447.¹
— Poirier japonais Docteur Thurber. 1885. III. 444.¹
— Du poison curare. 1872. III. 366.²
— Des Poiriers japonais, porte Mikado. 1878. III. 447.¹
— Polycarpa Maximowiczii. 1868. III. 614.²
— Pommier hétéromorphe. 1881. II. 267.¹
— Pommier pleureur Elisa Rathke. 1892. III. 425.²
— Des Pommiers dits bacciféres. 1877. III. 425.¹
— Pommiers microcarpes à fruits caducs. 1882. III. 425.¹
— Populus Bolleana. 1881. III. 345.¹
— Populus Bolleana. 1891. III. 345.¹
— Le prétendu Tilleul de Remiremont. 1886. II. 145.¹
— Production de noix anomales. 1877. II. 113.²
— Production de raisins sans organe foliacé. 1882. II. 507.²
— Production et fixation des variétés. 1865. I. 247.
— Production spontanée d'un Prunier Myrobalan à feuilles pourpres. 1891. III. 436.¹
— Prolification d'un cône de Wellingtonia. 1887. II. 50.²
— Prolification indéfinée. 1890. II. 680.²
— À propos de greffes disgénères. 1882. III. 165.
— À propos de la fécondation des Araucaria. 1879. II. 26.²
— À propos du Diospyros costata. 1870. II. 701.²
— Prune Kelsey. 1890. III. 443.¹
— Prunier hybride. 1886. III. 437.¹
— Prunier Myrobolan à fleurs roses doubles. 1883. III. 435.²

— Prunier Satsuma. 1894. III. 443.¹
— Pruniers japonais. 1891. III. 443.¹
— Prunus biferum. 1872. III. 432.²
— Prunus Capuli. 1888. III. 435.²
— Prunus Chapronii. 1881. III. 436.²
— Prunus domestica Plantierii. 1884. III. 436.²
— Prunus humilis. 1872. III. 437.¹
— Prunus hybrida. 1886. III. 437.¹
— Prunus insignis. 1870. III. 443.¹
— Prunus japonica. 1873. III. 437.¹
— Prunus japonica flore pleno. 1876. III. 437.¹
— Prunus japonica sphaerica. 1887. III. 437.²
— Prunus japonica sphaerica. 1890. III. 437.²
— Prunus obovalifolia. 1873. III. 439.¹
— Prunus Pissardi. 1881. III. 435.²
— Prunus praecox. 1892. II. 276.²
— Prunus Simonii. 1872. III. 443.¹
— Prunus Simonii. 1886. III. 443.¹
— Prunus Simonii à fruits allongés. 1891. III. 443.¹
— Prunus sinensis. 1874. III. 437.¹
— Prunus sinensis. 1884. III. 437.¹
— Prunus sinensis flore albo pleno. 1855. III. 437.¹
— Prunus susquehana. 1875. III. 442.²
— Prunus tenerrima. 1870. III. 443.¹
— Prunus tomentosa. 1886. III. 443.¹
— Pseudo-Chaenomeles Maulei. 1882. II. 258.²
— Pseudolarix Kaempferi. 1868. III. 309.¹
— Pseudotsuga Douglasiana. 1873. II. 32.²
— Pseudotsuga Lindleyana. 1868. III. 309.²
— Pterostyrax hispidum. 1875. III. 670.²
— Pueraria Thunbergiana. 1891. III. 485.¹
— Punica Granatum maximum rubrum. 1890. III. 630.²
— Pyrus betulaefolia. 1879. III. 444.²
— Pyrus leucocarpa. 1879. III. 447.¹
— Pyrus maulensis. 1873. III. 445.²
— Pyrus Pollveriana. 1885. III. 460.¹
— Pyrus Sieboldi. 1880. III. 447.¹
— Pyrus Simonii. 1872. II. 281.¹
— Quatre nouvelles variétés de Pêchers de Chine. 1863 III. 439.²
— Quelques arbres remarquables à Vichy. 1890. I. 297.²
— Quelques Diospyros. 1885. III. 670.¹
— Quelques Dracaenas nouveaux. 1880. III. 334.²
— Quelques espèces d'Agnus castus. 1870. III. 697.²
— Quelques Eutacta de la Nouvelle-Calédonie. 1866. II. 25.²
— Quelques mots sur les Chaenomeles. 1874. II. 258.²
— Quelques observations à propos de la greffe. 1876. III. 39.
— Quelques observations sur la greffe. 1859. I. 208,¹ II. 262.²
— Quelques observations sur les Bambous. 1873. III. 314.¹
— Sur quelques plantes inédites ou rares. 1866. III. 345,¹ 363.¹
— Quelques plantes lilliputiennes. 1867. III. 205.¹
— Sur quelques variétés de Cèdres du Liban. 1859. III. 300.¹
— Sur quelques variétés de Cryptomeria. 1885. III. 302.¹
— Quelques variétés de Yucca gloriosa. 1880. III. 340.²
— Sur quelques variétés de Yuccas. 1860. III. 340.¹
— Sur quelques variétés naines de Cerisier. 1876. III. 422.¹
— Quercus Libani, type. 1872. III. 362.²
— Quercus Libani vestita. 1877. III. 362.²
— Quercus sessiliflora pendula. 1887. III. 363.¹
— Quercus stricta dumosa. 1881. III. 363.¹
— Quillaja saponaria. 1873. III. 447.¹
— Rajeunissement des arbres. 1890. III. 181.²
— Raphiolepis salicifolia. 1887. III. 447.²
— Réfutation de divers articles de M. le Dr. J. Guyot. 1865. III. 555.
— Remarques au sujet de la théorie de la sève ascendante. 1872. I. 164.
— Retinospora Ellwangeriana. 1869. III. 311.¹
— Retinospora juniperoides. 1869. III. 311.²
— Retinospora leptoclada. 1869. III. 301.²
— Retinospora obtusa nana. 1881. III. 301.²
— Des Rétinospores. 1874. III. 300.²
— Revue des espèces du genre Diervilla. 1852. II. 834.²
— Revue du genre Retinospora. 1880. II. 28.²
— Rhamnus hybridus. 1873. III. 543.¹
— Le Rhamnus incana. 1858. III. 542.²
— Les Rhamnus intermédiaires. 1868. III. 543.²
— Rhamnus macrophyllus. 1876. III. 543.¹
— Rhamnus utilis longifolia. 1876. III. 543.²

Carrière, Élie Abel (*continued*).
— Rhapis flabelliformis. 1872. III. 331.¹
— Rhododendron praecox. 1868. III. 662.¹
— Rhodoleia Championi. 1878. III. 418.¹
— Rhus glabra laciniata. 1863. III. 527.¹
— Rhus Osbeckii. 1867. III. 527.²
— Les Ribes. 1853. III. 414.¹
— Ribes alpinum insigne. 1891. III. 414.¹
— Ribes nigrum spectabile. 1874. III. 415.¹
— Robinia caroliniana. 1872. III. 487.¹
— Robinia coluteoides. 1876. III. 487.¹
— Robinia dissecta. 1875. III. 487.¹
— Sur le Robinia hispida. 1867. III. 486.¹
— Robinia hispida grandiflora. 1872. III. 486.¹
— Robinia inermis pendula. 1867. III. 487.¹
— Robinia Pseudacacia semperflorens. 1875. III. 487.¹
— Robinia Pseudo-acacia Decaisneana. 1863. III. 486.²
— Robinia Pseudoacacia pendula. 1874. III. 487.¹
— Robinia tragacanthoides. 1873. III. 470.¹
— Robinier faux-Acacia monophylle. 1860. III. 486.²
— Robinier parasol Villevielle. 1870. III. 487.¹
— Le roi des Cormiers. 1888. II. 312.²
— Ronce commune sans épines. 1875. III. 458.¹
— Rosa diversifolia. 1874. III. 455.¹
— Rosa dubia. 1868. III. 456.¹
— Rosa Godefroyae. 1886. III. 455.²
— Rosa minutifolia. 1882. II. 296.¹
— Rosa myriantha. 1865. III. 456.¹
— Rosa Pissardi. 1888. III. 456.¹
— Rosa Pissarti. 1880. III. 456.¹
— Rosa polyantha. 1876. III. 456.¹
— Rosa polyantha et ses enfants. 1884. III. 456.¹
— Rosa rugosa. 1890. III. 456.²
— Rosa Ywara. 1876. III. 455.²
— Rose miniature. 1885. III. 456.¹
— Rubus deliciosus. 1882. III. 458.¹
— Rubus rosaefolius coronarius. 1883. III. 459.¹
— Sur la rusticité de quelques arbres conifères. 1853. III. 291.
— Rusticité de quelques Conifères. 1877. III. 292.
— Rusticité des Mahonia. 1854. III. 395.²
— Salix babylonica Salamonii. 1864. III. 351.²
— Salix babylonica Salamonii. 1872. III. 351.²
— Salix Humboldtiana. 1884. III. 352.¹
— Sur le Salix Lambertiana. 1852. III. 352.¹
— Sambucus aurea. 1891. III. 752.¹
— Sambucus Fontenaysii. 1868. III. 751.²
— Sambucus Fontenaysii. 1870. III. 751.²
— Sambucus glauca preparturiens. 1878. III. 751.²
— Sambucus monstruosa compacta. 1877. III. 751.²
— Sambucus nigra semperflorens. 1891. III. 752.¹
— Sambucus racemosa plumosa. 1890. III. 752.²
— Sambucus racemosa spectabilis. 1872. III. 752.²
— Sambucus rosaeflora. 1869. III. 752.²
— Les Saules au point de vue des plantations d'alignement. 1887. III. 349.
— Schizophragma hydrangeoides. 1881. III. 415.²
— Scutellaria Moriciniana. 1872. III. 698.²
— Les sels de cuivre en arboriculture. 1889. III. 197.
— Semis de Sambucus plumosa. 1891. III. 752.²
— Semis et mise à fruit des arbres fruitiers. 1880. III. 144.
— Senecio Ghiesbreghti. 1890. III. 756.²
— Sequoia sempervirens. 1888. III. 310.²
— Sequoia sempervirens variegata. 1890. III. 310.²
— Des sexes dans les Vignes sauvages de l'Extrême-Asie. 1890. II. 506.¹
— Singular instance of dimorphism. 1873. II. 292.¹
— Skimmia Laureola. 1868. III. 506.¹
— Skimmia rubella. 1874. III. 505.²
— Skimmia rubella. 1885. III. 505.²
— Skimmias. 1869. III. 505.²
— Les Skimmias. 1869. III. 505.²
— Des Skimmias. 1880. V. xxix.¹
— Solanum betaceum coccineum. 1881. III. 699.¹
— Solanum jasminoides floribundum. 1885. III. 702.¹
— Solanum macranthum. 1867. III. 702.¹
— Sophora japonica et sa variété. 1890. III. 488.¹
— Sophora japonica hybrida. 1893. III. 488.¹
— Sorbus Aucuparia atropurpurea. 1889. III. 459.²
— Sorbus Aucuparia corallina. 1858. III. 459.¹
— Sparmannia africana flore pleno. 1884. III. 585.¹
— Spinovitis Davidii. 1890. III. 584.¹
— Spinovitis Davidii. 1891. III. 584.¹
— Le Spiraea Boursieri. 1859. III. 424.²

— Spiraea Fortunei paniculata. 1860. III. 461.²
— Spiraea Fortunei paniculata. 1874. III. 461.²
— Spiraea Fortunei rubra. 1882. III. 461.²
— Spiraea sorbifolia var. Pallasii. 1874. III. 459.¹
— Stachyurus paracox. 1869. III. 615.¹
— Staphilea colchica. 1870. III. 533.²
— Stephanotis floribunda. 1874. III. 694.¹
— Sterculia robusta. 1868. III. 591.²
— Stuartia Malachodendron. 1878. III. 596.²
— Styrax japonica. 1880. III. 671.¹
— Styrax japonicum. 1888. II. 705.¹
— Le surgreffage. 1884. III. 162.
— Swainsonia atrococcinea. 1887. III. 489.¹
— Swainsonia Ferrandi alba. 1886. III. 489.¹
— Syringa Emodi. 1876. III. 681.¹
— Syringa hyacinthiflora. 1876. III. 681.¹
— Syringa oblata. 1874. III. 681.¹
— Taille des arbustes. 1888. III. 172.
— Les Tamarix. 1885. III. 612.¹
— Tamarix plumosa. 1868. III. 612.²
— Sur le Tamarix tetrandra. 1855. III. 612.²
— Taxodium distichum flavidum. 1869. III. 311.¹
— Des théories. 1864. I. 245.
— Thermopsis nepalensis. 1868. III. 484.¹
— Thermopsis nepalensis. 1887. III. 484.¹
— Thuia gigantea et autres Conifères. 1853. II. 38,² 52.²
— Thuia Menziesii denudata. 1869. III. 311.¹
— Tilia argentea orbicularis. 1890. III. 586.¹
— Torreya grandis. 1879. II. 12.¹
— Du Torreya nucifera à propos des sexes. 1873. III. 288.²
— Toxicophlaea spectabilis. 1888. III. 686.¹
— Traité générale des Conifères. 1855. II. 12.²
— Du traitement des arbres gelés. 1880. III. 183.¹
— Transformation d'une fleur de Rosier. 1875. II. 289.²
— Transformation de l'Aria vestita. 1866. III. 460.¹
— Transformation du Persica dianthiflora. 1870. III. 440.¹
— Troène du fleuve Amour. 1861. III. 673.²
— Sur trois Amandiers. 1861. III. 430.²
— Trois variétés de Yucca gloriosa à recommander. 1868. III. 340.¹
— Tsuga Roezlii. 1870. II. 53.²
— Ulmus communis ornata. 1858. III. 365.¹
— Ulmus rotundifolia. 1868. III. 365.¹
— De la valeur des bractées dans les cônes des ... Conifères. 1866. II. 19.
— Sur une variété de Cyprès. 1859. III. 302.²
— Sur une variété de Noyer. 1859. III. 355.
— Sur une variété de Pin sylvestre. 1859. III. 309.¹
— Sur une variété de Tsuga Douglasii. 1861. III. 309.²
— Une variété spéciéisée. 1866. III. 307.²
— Variétés de Chaenomeles japonica. 1872. III. 420.¹
— Variétés des Lonicera tatarica. 1868. III. 751.¹
— Sur les variétés du Sophora japonica. 1861. III. 488.¹
— Végétation de la Vigne Yama-Bouto. 1880. III. 545.²
— Vermehrung der Spiraea araefolia Smith. 1856. III. 424.²
— Veronica Godefroyana. 1888. III. 704.²
— Véroniques en arbre. 1884. III. 704.¹
— Viburnum dahuricum. 1865. III. 753.¹
— Viburnum Keteleèri. 1863. III. 753.¹
— La Vigne. 1865. III. 505.
— Vigne à inflorescence terminale spiciforme. 1884. II. 507.²
— Vigne japonaise Yama-Bouto. 1880. III. 545.²
— Vigne Précoce Caplat. 1892. II. 506.¹
— Les Vignes de la Chine. 1885. III. 584.¹
— Les Vignes du Soudan. 1881. III. 584.¹
— Les Vignes sauvages du Kahsmyr. 1882. II. 505.²
— Viorne à grosses têtes. 1858. III. 753.¹
— La Viorne à grosses têtes. 1862. III. 753.¹
— Virgilia lutea longiracemosa. 1869. III. 472.²
— Vitis acuminata. 1890. III. 583.²
— Vitis argyrophylla. 1892. II. 506.¹
— Vitis japonica densifolia. 1888. III. 583.²
— Vitis multifida gracilis. 1891. III. 506.²
— Les Vitis Pseudospina. 1890. III. 505.²
— Vitis pterophora. 1885. III. 544.²
— Vitis Romaneti serotina. 1891. II. 506.²
— Vitis Romaneti serotina. 1892. III. 584.¹
— Vitis rutilans. 1890. III. 584.¹
— Weigela alba. 1877. III. 749.
— Weigela candida. 1879. III. 749.¹
— Weigela excelsa. 1873. III. 748.²
— Weigela floribunda. 1874. III. 749.¹

— Weigela monstruosa. 1878. III. 748.[2]
— Weigelas. 1875. III. 748.[2]
— Des Weigelas. 1875. III. 748.[2]
— Sur le Weigelia alba. 1861. III. 749.[1]
— Wellingtonia gigantea pendula. 1889. III. 310.[2]
— Wellingtonia pyramidata compacta. 1891. III. 310.[2]
— Welwitschia mirabilis. 1886. III. 312.[2]
— Wistaria frutescens nivea. 1875. III. 490.[2]
— Wistaria multijuga. 1891. III. 490.[2]
— Wistaria multijuga alba. 1891. III. 490.[2]
— Wistaria sinensis flore pleno. 1878. III. 490.[2]
— Xanthoceras sorbifolia. 1872. III. 540.[2]
— Le Yucca angustifolia. 1860. III. 340.[1]
— Sur le Yucca angustifolia. 1864. III. 340.[1]
— Le Yucca filamenteux. 1860. III. 340.[1]
— Yucca filifera. 1880. III. 340.[1]
— Yucca filifera. 1884. III. 340.[1]
— Le Yucca flaccida. 1859. III. 340.[1]
— Le Yucca flexilis. 1859. III. 340.[1]
— Un Yucca gloriosa gigantesque. 1877. II. 88.[1]
— Yucca gloriosa longifolia. 1862. III. 340.[1]
— Yucca gloriosa maculata. 1859. III. 340.[1]
— Yucca orchioides. 1861. III. 340.[1]
— Le Yucca pendula. 1859. III. 340.[1]
— Le Yucca stricta. 1859. III. 340.[1]
— Yucca Treculeana. 1869. III. 340.[2]
— Des Yuccas. 1858. III. 339.[2]
— Sur les Yuccas. 1864. III. 339.[2]
— *See also* BRIOT, Charles & CARRIÈRE, E. A.; GENTILHOMME & CARRIÈRE, E. A.
— & André, Édouard. Cedrela sinensis et Pterocaryas. 1886. III. 356,[2] *518*.[1]
— — Cornus florida rosea. 1891. III. 646.[1]
— — Prunus Myrobolana variegata. 1893. III. 436.[1] ·
— & Déséglise, Alfred. Notes sur les vrilles à pelotes de la Vigne-vierge. 1863. II. 504.[1]
La carrière forestière en Prusse. *See* ZUSAMMENSTELLUNG . . . 1882. IV. 33.[1]
Carrington, Benjamin. *See* MIALL, L. C. & CARRINGTON, Benjamin.
Carrington, Noel Thomas & others. The Teignmouth, Dawlish, and Torquay guide. 1828. I. 533.
Carro. · *See* DUPONT & CARRO.
Carro, Jean de. Treatise on the mineral waters of Carlsbad. *See* ORTMANN, Anton. 1842. I. 440.
Carroll, B. R. Historical collections of South Carolina. *See* ASH, Thomas. 1682. III. 263.[2]
Carruth, James H. Centennial catalogue of the plants of Kansas. 1877. I. 224.
Carruthers, G. W. The selection of trees, shrubs, climbers. 1898. III. 203.
Carruthers, J. B. The canker of the Larch. 1891. IV. 451.
— The Larch canker. 1893. IV. 451.
Carruthers, William. Cycads. 1893. III. 284.[2]
— On Cycas Taiwaniana. 1893. II. 4.[1]
— On some species of Oaks from northern China. 1862. II. 130.[2]
— & others. Report of the committee . . . for the purpose of exploring the flora of the Bahamas. 1889. I. 337.
Carse, George B. & Foss, J. H. Florida; its climate, soil. 1882. III. 117.[1]
Carson, Joseph. Illustrations of medical botany. 1847. III. 58.
— Synopsis of the course of lectures on materia medica. 1855. III. 243.
Carspecken, F. Ueber das Auszeichnen des Oberholzes. 1890. IV. 131.
Carsten, H. J. Beplanting onzer duinen. 1890. IV. 160.[2]
— De schadelijke invloed van den strengen winter van 1890/91. 1892. III. 46.[1]
— Uitslag van eenige vergelijkende proefbeplantingen . . . te Hoogeveen in Drenthe. 1892. IV. 119.[2]
— Het vastleggen onzer duinen. 1892. IV. 146.[1] ·
Carstens, Fredrik Carl. Bemærkninger over Alheden og dens Colonier. 1839. IV. 342.[2]
— Bemærkninger over Heden og dens Træplantning. 1844. IV. 156.[1]
— Bemærkninger over Morvilles Berigtigelser. 1840. IV. 343.[1]
— Bemærkninger over Morvilles Ultimatum. 1840. IV. 343.[1]
Carstensen. Forskjelligheder i den anatomiske Bygning af Sporer og Trægrene. 1887. I. 106.[1]
Carstensen, G. H. The conditions for the distribution · of plants. 1888. I. 475.[1]

— Curious instance of abnormal inflorescence of Caesalpinia. 1891. II. 339.[2]
— Doum plants in India. 1891. II. 69.[1]
— A gall on Tamarix dioica. 1891. III. 612.[1]
— A variety of Butea frondosa. 1891. II. 338.[1]
Carta di legno. 1865. IV. 429.
Carta di legno. 1866. IV. 429.
Carta di legno verde. 1863. IV. 429.
Carta forestale d' Italia. 1863. IV. 364.
Carte botanique de la méthode naturelle. *See* DESHAYES, G. P. 1801. I. 259.
Carter, Alice. Notes on pollination. 1892. II. 504.[2]
Carter, Daniel. *See* RUTTER, John & CARTER, Daniel.
Carter, Henry John. A description of the Frankincense tree of Arabia. 1848. II. 416.[2]
Carter, James Madison Gore. A synopsis of the medical botany of Illinois. 1884. III. 62.
— A synopsis of the medical botany of the United States. 1888. III. 63.[1]
Carter, P. J. Forest technical terms. 1887. IV. 23.[2]
— The mensuration of timber. 1889. IV. 218.
— Note on the extraction of timber. 1896. IV. 390.[1]
— Rate of growth of Scotch Pine in Germany. 1889. IV. 481.
— A treatise on the mensuration of timber. 1893. IV. 219.
Cartheuser, C. W. De oleo kajuput. *See* CARTHEUSER, J. F. 1754. III. 636.
Cartheuser, Johann Friedrich. De cassia aromatica. 1753. III. 404.[1]
— De chocolata analepticorum principe. 1763. III. 594.
— De cortice caryophylloide Amboinensi. 1753. III. 405.[1] ·
— De eximia myrrhae genuinæ virtute. 1746. III. 510.[2]
— De genericis quibusdam plantarum principiis. 1754. I. 152.[1]
— De ligno nephritico. 1749. III. 244.
— De oleo kajuput. 1754. III. 636.
— De praecipuis balsamis nativis. 1755. III. 244.
Cartier, F. Essais sur la matière colorante . . . de la Rose de Provins. 1821. II. 294.[1]
— Examen d'une matière particulière du Peuplier noir. 1822. III. 346.[2]
Cartier, Jacques, Roberval, & Alphonse, Jean. Voyages de découverte au Canada. 1843. III. 262.[1]
Cartwright, John. An essay upon the virtues of balm of Gilead. 1760. III. 511.[1] ·
Caruana-Gatto, Alfred, *conte*. Dello stato presente delle nostre cognizioni sulla vegetazione maltese. 1892. I. 452.
Caruana y Martin, Peregrin. Apuntes sobre el Algarrobo y su cultivo. 1841. III. 471.[2]
Caruel, Teodoro. Di alcuni cambiamenti avvenuti nella flora della Toscana. 1866. I. 428.
— Il Castagno d' India dell' Orto botanico di Pisa. 1886. II. 462.[?]
— Classification des fruits. 1886. I. 119.
— On Combretum butyrosum. 1860. II. 616.[2]
— Conspectus familiarum phanerogamarum. 1889. I. 261.
— Contribuzione alla flora delle Galapagos. 1889. I. 510.[2]
— Dubbi sulla funzione vessillare dei fiori. 1892. I. 238.
— Epitome florae Europae. 1892. I. 350.[1]
— L' erborista italiano. 1883. I. 429.
— L' erborista toscano. 1876. I. 428.
— Florula di Montecristo. 1864. I. 427.
— Sulla gimnospermia delle Conifere. 1869. II. 19.
— Sur des granules particuliers du suc laiteux du Figuier. 1865. II. 150.[2]
— Guida del botanico principiante. 1866. I. 90.
— Guida dell' Orto botanico pisano. 1872. I. 64.
— Sulla identità specifica dei tre Ruscus. 1876. II. 84.[2] ·
— Illustratio in hortum siccum Andreae Caesalpini. 1858. I. 270.
— Illustrazione di una Papaiacea poca nota. 1876. II. 582.[2]
— Illustrazione di una Rubiacea, del genere Myrmecodia. 1872. II. 824.[2]
— Una mezza centuria di specie e di generi fondati. 1880. I. 143. ·
— La morfologia vegetale. 1878. I. 101.[1]
— Nota sopra alcuni fiori rivoltati di Faseolacee. 1879. II. 356.[2]
— Nota sul frutto delle Rosacee pomifere. 1879. II. 256.[2]
— Nota sul frutto è sui semi del Cacao. 1886. II. 539.[1] ·
— Observations sur la nature . . . de la pulpe qui entoure les graines dans certain fruits. 1859. I. 119.
— Origine dell' Agrume detto Bizzarria. 1882. II. 402,[1] III. 165.

Caruel, Teodoro (*continued*).
— L'orto e il museo botanico . . . di Pisa. 1874. I. 64.
— Osservazioni fenologiche. 1879. I. 226.[2]
— Pensées sur la taxinomie botanique. 1881. I. 252.·
— Pensieri sulla tassinomia botanica. 1881. I. 252.
— Polygalacearum italicarum conspectus. 1869. II. 430.[2]
— Primi cenni sulla distribuzione geografica degli ordini di piante. 1882. I. 300.
— Prodromo della flora toscana. 1860. I. 427.
— Prospetto generale della flora toscana. 1871. I. 428.
— Statistica botanica della Toscana. 1871. I. 428.
— Struttura delle foglie della Passerina hirsuta. 1869. II. 604.[2]
— Sulla struttura fiorale. 1878. I. 115.[1]
— Sulla struttura fiorale. 1879. I. 252.
— Studi sulla polpa che innaiga i semi. 1864. I. 119.
— Supplemento al Prodromo della flora toscana. 1860. I. 427.
— Una Vite gigantesca. 1878. II. 509.¹
— De la variabilité dans les plantes. 1884. I. 244.[2]
— La vrille de la Vigne. 1868. II. 507.[1]
— *See also* PARLATORE, Filippo & CARUEL, Teodoro.
— & Cazzuola, Ferdinando. Osservazioni sull' influenza della temperatura. 1880. I. 232.[1]
— & Levier, E. Saggio di un calendario florale per Firenze. 1871. I. 226.[2]
— & Mori, Antonio. Esperimenti sull' assorbimento dell' acqua per le foglie. 1877. I. 161.
— — Sulla vaiolatura delle Arancie. 1879. III. 500.[2]
Carus. Les préservatifs véritables contre le choléra-morbus. 1867. IV. 433.[2]
Caruso, Girolamo. Dell' Olivo; monografia. 1883. III. 676.[1]
Carvalho, Carlos de OLIVEIRA. *See* OLIVEIRA CARVALHO, Carlos de.
Carvalho, José Monteiro de. Diccionario portuguez das plantas. 1765. I. 74.[2]
Carver, George W. Cultivation and management of Cacti. 1893. III. 620.¹
— Grafting the Cacti. 1894. III. 620.¹
— *See also* PAMMEL, L. H. & CARVER, G. W.
Carver, Jonathan. Reisen durch die innern Gegenden von Nord-Amerika. 1778. I. 305.
— Three years travels through . . . North-America. 1778. I. 305.
— Three years travels throughout . . . North-America. 1794. III. 261.¹
Cary, Augustus G. Cranberry culture on a western plan. 1891. III. 663.[2]
Cary, Austin. The effect of bad seasons on the growth of trees. 1895. IV. 65.¹
— Forest management in Maine. 1899. IV. 113.¹
— How to apply forestry in Spruce lands. 1898. IV. 460.[2]
— Insect damage to Spruce timber. 1900. IV. 205.¹
A **Carya**-(Hickory) félék meghonosítása. 1895. III. 353.[2]
Casado, Manuel. Las inundaciones y la repoblación. 1891. IV. 47.[2] 542.¹
Casali, Adolfo. I diboscamenti nei monti. 1897. IV. 45.
Casali, Carlo. Appunti sull' eterofillia nelle Caprifogliacee. 1900. II. 834.¹
— Sulla classificazione dei generi Boelia. 1900. II. 319.¹
Casanova, J. N. Essai sur le Madar. 1833. III. 692.¹
Casares, Antonio. Observaciones sobre el cultivo de la Vid en Galicia. 1843. III. 558.¹
Casaretto, Giovanni. Novarum stirpium brasiliensium decades. 1842. I. 342.
Casassa, Antonio. *See* TEXIDOR Y COS, Juan & CASASA, Antonio.
Casaviella, Juan RUIZ. *See* RUIZ CASAVIELLA, Juan.
Case, L. B. The Catalpa. 1882. III. 705.
— On Catalpa. 1884. III. 705.
Case's botanical index. I. 5.
Casey, Comerford. Riviera nature notes illustrated. 1898. I. 430.
Cashew spirit. 1898. III. 524.¹
Casopis českých zahradníků. III. 24.[2]
Casopis jednoty pro lesnictof. IV. 14.
Casopis spolkový pro lesnictof. IV. 14.·
Casos dudosos. 1895. IV. 555.¹
Caspari, Hermann. Beiträge zur Kenntniss des Hautgewebes der Cacteen. 1883. II. 588.¹
Caspari, Karl. Homöopathisches Dispensatorium. 1825. III. 249.
Caspari, P. Flora der Umgebung von Oberlahnstein. 1879. I. 387.

Caspary, Robert. De Abietinearum Carr. floris feminei structura morphologica. 1860. II. 19.
— Eine Alströmer'sche Hängefichte. 1878. II. 34.[2]
— Die alte Linde . . . zu Neuenstadt. 1868. II. 516.[2]
— Eine Apfeldolde mit fünf Früchten. 1873. II. 266.[2]
— Ausscheidung von Nektar . . . bei Chamaedorea desmonocoides. 1856. II. 66.[1]·
— Bemerkungen über die Schutzscheide. 1865. I. 105.
— Beschädigung der Rosskastanienblätter. 1869. III. 537.[1]
— Bewirkt die Sonne Risse in Rinde. 1857. III. 184.[1]
— Ueber Blüthensprosse auf Blättern. 1874. I. 113.[2]
— On the change of the direction of the branches. 1866. I. 149,[2] 194.
— Einige in Preussen vorkommende Spielarten der Kiefer Pinus silvestris. 1882. II. 46.[2]
— Ueber einige Spielarten, die mitten im Verbreitungsgebiet der Stammarten entstanden sind. 1873. I. 244.[1]
— Etwas über die Schutzscheide. 1877. I. 133.
— Ueber Frostspalten. 1855.. I. 212.
— Eine gebänderte Wurzel von Spiraea sorbifolia. 1878. II. 311.¹
— Gebänderte Wurzeln eines Epheustockes. 1882. II. 649.[2]
— Sur les hybrides obtenus par la greffe. 1866. I. 246.[1]
— On hybrids obtained by grafting. 1866. I. 246.¹
— Ein interessanter Blitzschlag. 1863. IV. 193.[2]
— Eine kanadische Pappel von Blitz getroffen. 1862. IV. 193.[2]
— Kegelige Hainbuche. 1882. II. 120.[2]
— Die Krummfichte. 1874. IV. 456.
— Mischlinge die durch Pfropfen entstanden sind. 1865. I. 246.¹
— Mittheilungen über das Verhalten von Pflanzen zu Verwundungen. 1862. I. 207.[2]
— Mittheilungen über vom Blitz getroffene Bäume. 1872. IV. 194.
— On the morphology of the female flower of the Abietineae. 1860. II. 19.
— De nectariis. 1848. I. 118.[2]
— Ueber die Nektarien der Stipulae von Sambucus. 1848. II. 840.[2]
— Neue Untersuchungen über Frostspalten. 1857. I. 212.
— Paulownia imperialis in Königsberg. 1887. III. 703.[2]
— Pinus Abies L. mit gemeinsam aufgewachsenen breiten Nadeln. 1869. II. 36.[1]
— Pinus sylvestris mit auffallend gebildeten Zapfen. 1883. II. 46.[2]
— Split Willow. 1873. II. 104.¹
— Splitter zweierlei Art bei Blitzschlägen. 1863. IV. 193.[2]
— Ueber die Veränderungen der Richtung der Äste. 1866. I. 149,[2] 232.¹
— Ueber die Verbreitung von Laurus nobilis. 1852. II. 225.[2]
— Vorläufige Mittheilungen über die Statistik der Nährpflanzen des Viscum. 1866. II. 179.¹
— Weidenbäume durch einen Erdrutsch zerrissen. 1873. II. 104.¹
— Ueber die Zeiten des Aufbrechens der ersten Blüthen. 1882. I. 225.
— Zwei Schlangentannen. 1882. II. 23.¹
— Ueber zweibeinige Bäume. 1882. I. 106.[2]
Casper. Die Ernährung unserer Waldbäume. 1898. IV. 64.[3]
Ueber die **caspische** Weide. 1872. III. 351.¹
Cassava. 1892. III. 521.¹
Cassebeer, Johann Heinrich & Theobald, G. L. Flora der Wetterau. 1847. I. 382.
Cassel, Franz Peter. Lehrbuch der natürlichen Pflanzenordnung. 1817. I. 259.
— Morphonomia botanica. 1820. I. 98.
— Versuch über die natürlichen Familien der Pflanzen mit Rücksicht auf ihre Heilkraft. 1820. III. 259.[2]
Cassel — Verein für Naturkunde. *See* VEREIN . . . I. 15.
Cassell's magazine. III. 16.
Cassell's popular gardening. III. 16.
Casselmann, Arthur. Chemische Untersuchung der Früchte des Seidelbast's. 1870. II. 602.¹
— Ueber das Frangulin. 1857. III. 543.¹
— Sur la franguline. 1857. III. 543.¹
Cassianus Bassus. Constantini Caesaris selectarum praeceptionum, de agricultura libri viginti. 1538. III. 98.
— Der Feldbaw; oder, Das Buch von der Feldarbeyt. 1538. III. 98.
— Γεωπονικά. De re rustica selectorum libri XX. 1538. III. 98.·

— Γεωπονικά, geoponicorum; sive, De re rustica libri XX. 1538. III. 98.
— Les vingt livres de Constantin Caesar. 1538. III. 98.
Cassier, A. La culture et la préparation de l'indigo. 1900. III. 479.[1]
Cassier's magazine. III. 16.
Cassini, Henri, comte de. Aperçu des genres nouveaux . . . des Synanthérées. 1816. II. 847.[2]
— Description d'un nouveau genre de plantes. 1819. II. 857,[2] 860.[2]
— Description d'un nouveau genre de plantes. 1820. II. 859.[2]
— Description d'une nouvelle espèce de Carlowizia. 1820. II. 854.[1]
— Description d'une nouvelle espèce de Piqueria. 1819. II. 863.[1]
— Description de quatre plantes. 1818. II. 847.[2]
— Description de trois plantes. 1818. II. 847.[2]
— Description des espèces servant de types à quatre genres. 1818. II. 859.[1]
— Description des nouveaux genres Garuleum. 1819. II. 858,[1] 863.[2]
— Sur la famille des Synanthérées. 1813. II. 850.[1]
— Observations sur le Tarchonanthus camphoratus. 1816. II. 867.[1]
— Observations sur les différents modes de la dissémination chez les Synanthérées. 1821. II. 850.[1]
— Opuscules phytologiques. 1826. II. 847.[1]
— Précis d'un second mémoire sur les Synanthérées. 1814. II. 850.[1]
— Précis des observations sur . . . Synanthérées. 1813. II. 850.[1]
— Tableau méthodique des genres . . . des Inulées. 1821. II. 847.[2]
— Tableau méthodique des genres . . . des Lactucées. 1821. II. 847.[2]
— Tableau synoptique des Synanthérées. 1829. II. 848.[1]
Cassini de Thury, C. F. La méridienne de l'Observatoire royal de Paris. See LE MONNIER, L. G. 1744. I. 405.
Cassius, C. Préparations de sulfure de carbone. 1877. III. 560.
Cassone, Felice. Flora medico-farmaceutica. 1847. III. 58.
Castagne, Louis. Catalogue des plantes . . . de Marseille. 1845. I. 410.
— Catalogue des plantes . . . des Bouches-du-Rhône. 1862. I. 412.
— Observations sur le reboisement des montagnes. 1851. IV. 162.
Il Castagno della California. 1865. IV. 527.[2]
Castanea vulgaris; the common Chestnut tree. 1862. II. 123.[2]
Castel, J. La possibilité par pieds d'arbres. 1884. IV. 237.
Castel, P. Enquête sur les vignobles du département de l'Aude. 1888. III. 556.
Castel, René Richard. Botanicòn libros quatuor e carmine gallico. 1797. I. 511.
— Les plantes. Poème. 1797. I. 511.
Castel y Clemente, Cárlos. Algunas consideraciones sobre la estadística forestal. 1884. IV. 336.[1]
— Un año más. 1893. IV. 552.[1]
— Apuntes sobre la ordenación de los alcornocales. 1891. IV. 517.[2]
— Los árboles gigantes. 1885. IV. 484.[2]
— Un aspecto de la cuestion social en relacion con los montes. 1885. IV. 276.[2]
— Cabidas y superficies. 1877. IV. 265.
— Combustibles vegetales. 1880. IV. 431.[2]
— Combustibles vegetales. 1885. IV. 432.[1]
— La combustione, carbonizzazione e distillazione del legno. 1885. IV. 432.[1]
— Conduccion de maderas por el Tajo. 1877. IV. 390.[2]
— En el Congreso. 1892. IV. 548.[1]
— Contestación á la "Revista de Montes y Plantíos." 1889. IV. 553.[1]
— Contestacion al Sr. Montenegro. 1888. IV. 541.
— Correspondencia. 1890. IV. 553.[1]
— Cortezas curtientes. 1888. I. 183, IV. 435.
— Cuatro palabras sobre la enseñanza en la Escuela de ingenieros de montes. 1887. IV. 540.[1]
— La cuestión de los montes en el Senado. 1887. IV. 551.[1]
— El decreto sobre repoblación de montes. 1888. IV. 546.[2]

— Las dehesas boyales. 1887. IV. 551.[2]
— Discurso combatiendo el cap. XIX del presupuesto. 1887. IV. 553.[1]
— Dosificación del tanino. 1893. IV. 558.[1]
— Enfermedades y defectos de las maderas. 1886. IV. 414.[1]
— Sobre la enseñanza teórico-práctica de los ayudantes de montes. 1892. IV. 540.[2]
— La Escuela preparatoria. 1886. IV. 540.[2]
— Estudio sobre la densidad de las maderas. 1879. IV. 411.[2]
— Excursión á la zona superior de la cuenca del Tajo. 1878. IV. 363.[1]
— La explotación de la ignorancia. 1892. IV. 546.[2]
— Identidad del tanino formado en las diversas plantas. 1879. IV. 435.
— Ilegalidad manifesta. 1894. IV. 552.[1]
— Importancia forestal de la Serranía de Ronda. 1897. IV. 556.[2]
— Iniciativa parlamentaria. 1894. IV. 552.[1]
— Instrucciones para el servicio de las ordenaciones de los montes públicos. 1891. IV. 554.[2]
— Landas interiores en España. 1894. IV. 556.[1]
— Memoria . . . sobre el tema; "Determinar el valor intrínseco de las materias curtientes. 1879. I. 183.
— Memoria sobre la influenca de la luna. 1875. I. 233.[2]
— Memoria sobre las condiciones naturales . . . de la península Escandinava. 1883. IV. 342.[2]
— Monografía dasográfica del Haya. 1873. IV. 498.
— Montes de la provincia de Guadalajara. 1883. IV. 363.
— Naturaleza del tanino. 1879. IV. 435.
— Noticia sobre la fundacion . . . de la Escuela especial de ingenieros de montes. 1877. IV. 35.[1]
— A nuestros lectores. 1890. IV. 553.[1]
— Observaciones sobre la concesion de estudios y aprovechamiento de los montes públicos. 1882. IV. 276.[2]
— Ojeada á la sección forestal en la Exposición del campo de marte. 1878. IV. 20.[1]
— Ordenación de los montes públicos. 1890. IV. 550.[1]
— Organización del personal subalterno facultativo de montes. 1893. IV. 553.[2]
— El personal facultativo en los negociados del Ministerio de fomento. 1893. IV. 553.[1]
— Presupuesto para el año 1889-90. 1889. IV. 553.[1]
— Principios generales sobre la conservación de las maderas. 1884. IV. 420.
— La produccion de los montes en Prusia y en España. 1885. IV. 342.[2]
— Proyecto de presupuestos generales del estado. 1891. IV. 553.[2]
— Rectificación del Catálogo de los montes públicos. 1885. IV. 363.[2]
— Reforma del servicio de montes en Filipinas. 1886. IV. 294.[2]
— Repoblación de los montes. 1891. IV. 546.[2]
— Servicio y personal de montes en España. 1886. IV. 293.[1]
— Servicio y personal de montes en España. 1889. IV. 553.[1]
— Servidumbres. 1890. IV. 334.[2]
— Las turbias del Lozoya. 1899. IV. 547.[1]
— Unidad de cubicacion en los productos maderables. 1882. IV. 214.
— See also ARTIGAS Y TEIXIDOR, Primitivo & CASTEL Y CLEMENTE, Cárlos.
Castella, François. See COTTET, Michel & CASTELLA, François.
Castella, Hubert de. Notes d'un vigneron australien. 1883. III. 559.[2]
Castellani, Idraulico. Dell' immediata influenza delle selve sul corso delle acque. 1818. IV. 49.[2]
Castellani, V. Manuale forestale. 1888. IV. 86.[1]
Castellarnau y de Lleopart, Joaquin Maria de. Los cristales de oxalato de calcio en la madera de la Encina. 1887. IV. 503.[2]
— Descripción micrográfica del sistema leñoso. 1894. I. 126, IV. 62.[2]
— Descripción microscópica de la madera del Quercus Jordanae. 1885. II. 134,[2] 872,[2] IV. 503.[2]
— La enseñanza de las ciencias naturales. 1885. IV. 29.
— Estudio micrográfico de la madera de las Coníferas españolas. 1883. II. 17,[1] IV. 443.[2]
— Estudio micrográfico de tallo del Pinsapo. 1880. II. 24,[2] IV. 447.[1]
— Memoria acerca del estudio del sistema leñoso. 1894. I. 126, IV. 62.[2]
— Las taraquédias de los Pinus. 1899. II. 40.[1]
— See also RIVERO, R. L. del, BREÑOSA, Rafael, & CASTELLARNAU, J. de.

Castellet, C. L'art de multiplier la soie. 1760. III. 372.[2]
Castelli, Edmund. Oratio in scholis theologicis habita. 1667. I. 512.
Castelli, Pietro. Exactissima descriptio rariorum . . . plantarum. 1625. I. 284. See also ALDINUS, Tobias. 1625. I. 60.[2]
— Hortus messanensis. 1640. I. 60.[2]
— Opobalsamum, examinatum. 1640. III. 510.[2]
— Opobalsamum triumphans. 1640. III. 510.[2]
— De Smilace aspera sententia. 1652. III. 338.[2]
— Vera e natural effigie delle pianta . . . Granadilla. 1620. II. 577.[1]
Castet. À propos des Eucalyptus. 1893. III. 634.[1]
Castiglioni, Luigi, conte. Storia delle piante forestiere. 1791. IV. 75.[1]
— Viaggio negli Stati Uniti. 1790. I. 305.
Castillo, Emmanuel DRAKE DEL. See DRAKE DEL CASTILLO, Emmanuel.
Castilloa rubber of Central America. 1887. III. 368.[1]
Castillon, comte de. Les Bambous. 1877. III. 314.[1]
— Les Bambous carrés. 1876. III. 316.[1]
— Le Caféier du Japon. 1879. III. 673.[2]
— Deux variétés de Citrus triptera. 1877. III. 503.[1]
— Greffe en couronne ou greffe toulousaine. 1875. III. 162.
— Horticulture japonaise. 1877. III. 159.[1]
— Œufs de Bambous. 1882. III. 314.[2]
— Quelques mots sur les Vignes asiatiques. 1879. III. 545.[2]
Castle, Lewis. Cactaceous plants. 1884. III. 619.
— Petraea volubilis. 1884. III. 697.[1]
Castle, R. Lewis. Chlorosis in fruit trees. 1899. III. 181.[1]
Castle, Thomas. An introduction to . . . botany. 1829. I. 86.
— An introduction to medical botany. 1829. III. 56.
— The Linnean artificial system of botany. 1836. I. 260.
— A synopsis of systematic botany. 1833. I. 255.
— See also BARTON, B. H. & CASTLE, Thomas.
Castleton gardens. 1896. I. 222.[1]
Castleton gardens: notes. 1894. I. 39.
Castlewellan. 1896. I. 55.
Castner, D. S. Elvira. Zwei Vorträge über Obst- und Gartenbau. 1895. III. 32.[1]
The Castor bean in India. 1894. III. 521.[2]
Castrillón, Hernando. Historia y magia natural. 1692. I. 288.
Castro, Ángel FERNANDEZ DE. See FERNANDEZ DE CASTRO, Ángel.
Castro, Arthur URBANO DE. See URBANO DE CASTRO, Arthur.
Castro, Joaquim de AMORIM. See AMORIM CASTRO, Joaquim de.
Castro, Luiz Filippe de. See CINCINNATO DA COSTA, B. C. & CASTRO, L. F. de.
Castro, Mariano LOZANO Y. See LOZANO Y CASTRO, Mariano.
Caswell, George W. Coffee culture in our new islands. 1898. III. 733.[1]
Catalani, JORDANUS. See JORDANUS CATALANI.
Catalog. See also KATALOG.
Catalog der Ausstellungen des K. k. Ackerbau-Ministeriums. 1873. III. 272.[1]
Catalog der Königl. Central-Baumschule zu Köln. 1850. III. 28.[1]
Catalog über die in dem K. k. Lustgarten . . . vorhandnen edlen Obstbäume. 1823. III. 90.[1]
Catalogi duo plantarum africanarum. See BURMAN, Johannes. 1737. I. 493.
Catalogo de las plantas del herbario . . . de la flora forestal. See CERON, Salvador. 1892. I. 464.[1]
Catálogo de los productos . . . en la exposición de Coyoacán. 1895. III. 265.[1]
Catalogo degli alberi ed arbusti. See TENORE, Michele. 1836. I. 63.
Catalogo degli alberi ed arbusti . . . nelle provincie di Terra di Lavoro. Seé PETAGNA, L., TERRONE, G. & TENORE, Michele. 1827. I. 423.
Catalogo della collezione agraria del Real giardino delle piante. See TENORE, Michele. 1815. I. 62.
Catalogo delle Conifere coltivate nel bosco e giardino della villa del Poggiolo. 1885. IV. 18.[2]
Catalogo delle piante che si trovano nel giardino del Marchese Pietro Torregiani. See TORRIGIANI, Pietro. 1822. I. 62.
Catalogo delle piante coltivate a Bibiani. See RIDOLFI, C. 1843. I. 63, III. 297,[3] 541,[2] 633.[2]
Catalogo delle piante coltivate nel giardino del Sig. Federigo Thellusson. 1837. I. 63.

Catalogo delle piante del giardino botanico del Signor Principe de Bisignano. See TENORE, Michele. 1809. I. 61.
Catalogo delle piante . . . del giardino Cattaneo. See CATTANEO, Antonio. 1812. I. 62.
Catalogo delle piante del giardino Feroni di Firenze. 1805. I. 61.
Catalogo delle piante del giardino Sgaravatti. 1870. I. 64.
Catalogo delle piante del Real giardino botanico di Napoli. See TENORE, Michele. 1807. I. 61.
Catalogo delle piante dell' Orto botanico veronese. See POLLINI, Ciro. 1814. I. 62.
Catalogo delle piante esistenti nel giardino della Signora Marchesa di Priero. 1832. I. 62.
Catalogo delle piante esistenti nell' I. e r. giardino di Boboli. See GHERI, G. 1841. I. 63.
Catalogo delle piante vive che esistono nell' Orto botanico-agrario detto dei semplici in Firenze. 1841. I. 63.
Catalogo generale delle piante . . . nel giardino del Comte de Medici Spada. 1857. I. 63.
Catalogo . . . nel R. orto botanico di Napoli. See TENORE, Michele. 1845. I. 63.
Catalogo razonado de los objetos expuestos por el cuerpo de ingenieros de montes. 1885. III. 271,[3] IV. 20.[2]
Catalogo speciale della collezione di alberi fruttiferi . . . della R. società toscana d'orticultura. 1862. III. 29.[1]
Catalogŭ planteloru, gradinei botanice . . . din Bucuresci. See HOFMAN, Ulric. 1866. I. 66.[2]
Catalogue de l'Exposition forestière. 1884. IV. 20.[2]
Catalogue de l'Exposition forestière. 1885. IV. 20.[2]
Catalogue de l'herbier de Syrie. See PUEL, Timothée & MAILLE, Alphonse. 1854. I. 480.
Catalogue de la bibliothèque du Jardin botanique de Buitenzorg. See CATALOGUS der Bibliotheek . . . 1887. I. 2.
Catalogue de la bibliothèque scientifique de [Adrien] de Jussieu. 1857. I. 2.
Catalogue des Agave, Bonapartea, Dasylirion et Fourcroya, . . . au parc de Lyon. 1880. I. 59.
Catalogue des arbres et arbrisseaux, qui se peuvent élever en pleine terre aux environs de Paris. 1735. I. 56.
Catalogue des collections de bois exhibées à l'Exposition universelle de Paris. 1889. IV. 401.[1]
Catalogue des collections exposées . . . à Amsterdam . . . (Algérie — Service des forêts.) 1889. IV. 21.[3]
Catalogue des Conifères connues jusqu'à ce jour. See A CATALOGUE of coniferous plants . . . 1850. II. 12.[3]
Catalogue des Cycadées, Palmiers et Pandanées cultivés au parc de Lyon. 1880.[?] I. 59.
Catalogue des fruits cultivées à Geest St. Remy. 1854. III. 77.[1]
Catalogue des fruits et des plantes (de l'Inde). See ROBILLARD D'ARGENTELLE, L. M. A. 1827. I. 57.
Catalogue des fruits moulés de pressoir . . . des collections de la Société centrale d'horticulture . . . de la Seine-Inférieure. 1882. III. 29.[1]
Catalogue des fruits moulés de table . . . des collections de la Société centrale d'horticulture de la Seine-Inférieure. 1894. III. 29.[1]
Catalogue des insectes nuisibles. See JOLYET, F. 1870. III. 190.
Catalogue des objets exposés par la Direction générale des forêts. 1900. III. 270,[2] IV. 19.[2]
Catalogue des plantes cultivées au Jardin botanique de la Marine royale du Port du Toulon. 1821. I. 57.
Catalogue des plantes cultivées au Jardin de botanique de Toulouse. 1827. I. 57.
Catalogue des plantes cultivées au Jardin du roy. 1653. I. 56.
Catalogue des plantes cultivées dans le jardin de M. Villard . . . près Hyères (Var). 1890. I. 59.
Catalogue des plantes . . . de Dijon. See COLLET, Philibert. 1702. I. 405.
Catalogue des plantes de l'herbier de M. Breumer. 1844. I. 434.
Catalogue des plantes de Provence. See HUET, Edm. 1889. V. XXII.[1]
Catalogue des plantes de serre et d'arbustes . . . de S. M. Guillaume II. 1850. III. 28.[1]
Catalogue des plantes dicotylédones et monocotylédones . . . de la Mayenne. 1838.[·] I. 409.
Catalogue des plantes du Jardin botanique . . . à Pondichéry. See PERROTTET, G. S. 1867. I. 67.[1]
Catalogue des plantes du Jardin botanique de Krzemieniec en Volhynie. See BESSER, Wilibald. 1810. I. 41.
Catalogue des plantes du jardin de . . . A. F. Kvitka. 1823. I. 41.

Catalogue des plantes du Jardin de botanique de Gironde. 18..? I. 56.

Catalogue des plantes du jardin de l'Académie de Rouen. 177.? I. 56.

Catalogue des plantes du jardin des Messieurs les apoticaires. See DESCEMET, Jean. 1741. I. 56.

Catalogue des plantes du Parc colonial et du Jardin botanique . . . à Pondichéry. 1872. I. 67.[1]

Catalogue des plantes exotiques . . . de Monville. 1846. I. 58.

Catalogue des plantes nouvelles ou rares qui figuraient à l'Exposition universelle. 1864. III. 28.[2]

Catalogue des plantes usuelles, avec une explication des principaux termes de botanique. 1754. III. 54.

Catalogue des plantes usuelles du Jardin botanique d'Amiens. See ROBBE. 1867. III. 29.[1]

Catalogue des plantes usuelles, qui se trouvent dans les jardins de botanique de l'Académie. 1782. I. 56.

Catalogue des plantes vasculaires. See ARDOINO, Honoré. 1862. I. 412.

Catalogue des plantes vasculaires de la Charente-Inférieure. See FAYE, Léon. 1850. I. 410.

Catalogue des plus excellens fruits. 1728. III. 84.[1]

Catalogue des Pommes et des Poires du Valais. 1887. III. 89.[1]

Catalogue des produits des colonies françaises. 1867. III. 218.[1]

Catalogue des produits des colonies françaises. 1873. III. 29.[1]

Catalogue des produits des colonies françaises. 1878. III. 218.[1]

Catalogue des Rosiers cultivés au Luxembourg. See HARDY. 1844. III. 448.[2]

Catalogue des végétaux cultivés à la pépinière centrale du gouvernement à Alger. See HARDY, Auguste. 1844. I. 68.[2]

Catalogue des végétaux cultivés au Jardin du gouvernement à l'île de la Réunion. See RICHARD, (Jardinier botaniste). 1856. I. 68.[1]

Catalogue des végétaux et graines disponibles . . . au Jardin d'acclimatation au Hamma. 1862. I. 68.[2]

Catalogue des végétaux ligneux . . . sur le domaine forestier des Barres-Vilmorin. 1878. I. 59, IV. 18.[2]

Catalogue des végétaux . . . récemment introduits. 1880. III. 87.

Catalogue des Vignes de l'ancienne collection du Luxembourg. 1869. III. 546.

Catalogue descriptif des . . . Vignes américaines. See OLIVE, Marius. 1889. III. 547.

Catalogue et prix-courant. 1867. I. 51.[2]

Catalogue explicatif . . . de l'exposition permanente des produits de l'Algérie. 1855. III. 280.[1]

Catalogue général des fruits imités . . . des collections de la Société nationale d'horticulture de France. 1889. III. 29.[1]

Catalogue général des plantes cultivées dans l'établissement de la Société royale d'horticulture de Belgique. 1842. I. 50.

Catalogue méthodique des arbres, arbrisseaux et arbustes cultivés à l'École. 18..? I. 56.

Catalogue méthodique des plantes du Jardin botanique . . . de Strasbourg. See PÉE, Antoine. 1000. I. 47.

Catalogue of American trees, plants and seeds for sale by Stephen F. Mills & Co. 1827. I. 38.[2]

Catalogue of books in the library of the Massachusetts horticultural society. 1854. III. 1.

Catalogue of British plants included in the I. volume of Hooker's British flora. 1836. I. 398.

A catalogue of capital Oak. 1794. IV. 388.[1]

Catalogue of certain succulent plants . . . in the Royal gardens of Kew. 1855. I. 54.

A catalogue of coniferous plants with their synonyms. 1850. II. 12.[1]

Catalogue of exhibits of Malayan produce sent to the Imperial institute. 1893. I. 464.[1]

Catalogue of exhibits of the colony of the Cape of Good Hope. 1884. III. 281.[1]

Catalogue of fruits cultivated in the garden of the Horticultural society. 1826. III. 79.

Catalogue of fruits recommended for cultivation in . . . the United States. 1897. III. 62.

A catalogue of green house, hot house, herbaceous and hardy plants . . . sold . . . at Hackney. 1799. I. 53.

Catalogue of medical plants. See DUNCAN, Andrew. 1826. III. 56.

A catalogue of new and interesting plants, collected in upper Louisiana. See NUTTALL, Thomas. 1813. I. 318.

Catalogue of plants. See RUSSELL, Anna. 1839. I. 399, V. xx.[2]

A catalogue of plants . . . about Geneva. See PETIVER, Jacob. 1702. I. 432.[2]

Catalogue of plants collected in the years 1871–73. See WATSON, Sereno & others. 1874. I. 307.

A catalogue of plants contained in the Royal botanic garden of Glasgow. See HOOKER, Sir W. J. 1825. I. 54.

Catalogue of plants cultivated in the Royal botanical gardens, Calcutta. See ANDERSON, T. 1865. I. 67.[1]

Catalogue of plants &c. &c. in the Dublin society's botanic garden at Glasnevin. 1800. I. 53.

Catalogue of plants found in the neighbourhood of Newbury. See RUSSELL, Anna. 1839. V. xx.[1]

A catalogue of plants growing spontaneously within thirty miles of the city of New York. See TORREY, John. 1819. I. 313.

Catalogue of plants in Abbotsbury gardens. See FOX-STRANGWAYS, Mary, Countess of Ilchester. 1899. I. 55.

A catalogue of plants in the Botanic garden at Liverpool. See ROSCOE, W. 1808. I. 53.

A catalogue of plants in the botanic garden of the Imperial university. 1887. I. 66.[2]

Catalogue of plants in the . . . botanic garden, Sydney. 1857. III. 29.[2] See also MOORE,, Charles. 1857. I. 69.[1]

Catalogue of plants in the herbarium of the College of science. 1886. I. 66,[2] 453.[1]

Catalogue of plants in the Public garden, Bangalore. See NEW, William. 1861. I. 67.[1]

Catalogue of plants in the Royal society's gardens, Queen's Park, Hobart Town. See NEWMAN, F. W. 1857. I. 69.[1]

Catalogue of plants . . . Royal society's gardens, Queen's Park, Hobart Town. See ABBOTT, F. 1865. I. 69.[1]

Catalogue of products of Michigan. See BEAL, W. J. 1876. IV. 397.

Catalogue of scarce plants . . . of London. See COCKFIELD, Joseph. 1813. I. 396.

Catalogue of scientific papers. 1867. I. 2.

A catalogue of the Brompton botanic garden. See SALISBURY, Wilham. 1803. I. 53.

Catalogue of the collections of forest products exhibited by the Northern circle. 1884. III. 278, V. xxix.[2]

Catalogue of the exhibits in the Queensland court. See BAILEY, F. M. 1886. IV. 22.[1]

Catalogue of the exhibits sent from British Guiana. 1884. III. 268.[1]

A catalogue of the exotic plants cultivated in the Mauritius. 1816. I. 68.[1]

Catalogue of the herbarium of the late Dr. Charles C. Parry. See PARRY, Mrs. E. R. 1891. I. 308.

Catalogue of the Indian exhibit. 1884. III. 978, IV. 21.[2]

Catalogue of the library of the Linnean society of London. 1896. I. 3.[1]

Catalogue of the library of the Royal botanic gardens, Kew. 1899. I. 3.[1]

Catalogue of the library of the Royal colonial institute. 1895. III. 1.

Catalogue of the Lindley library. 1898. I. 3.[1]

Catalogue of the local forestry exhibition . . . Kingstown. 1884. III. 267.[1]

Catalogue of the native phænogamous plants and ferns of Kentucky. 1833. I. 318.

Catalogue of the natural and industrial products of New South Wales. 1867. III. 282.[1]

Catalogue of the natural and industrial products of Queensland. 1862. III. 282.[2]

Catalogue of the natural productions and curiosities. See DELACOSTE. 1804. V. viii.[1]

Catalogue of the phænogamous plants of the United States, east of the Mississippi. See MANN, Horace. 1868. I. 307.

Catalogue of the phenogamous plants and the ferns . . . within five miles of Yale college, Ct. See BALDWIN, Ebenezer. 1831. I. 313.

Catalogue of the plants . . . cultivated in the gardens Dalpeth. See HOPKIRK, Thomas. 1813. I. 53.

Catalogue of the plants distributed . . . from the herbaria of Griffith, Falconer and Helfer. See HOOKER, Sir J. D. 1865. I. 474.

A catalogue of the plants growing wild in the environs of London. See CURTIS, William. 1774. I. 395.

Catalogue of the . . . plants of Great Britain. See COXHEAD, Henry. 1842. I. 399.

Catalogue of the plants under cultivation in the Government botanic garden, Adelaide. 1859. I. 69.[1]

Catalogue of the scientific books in the library of the Royal society, London. 1883. I. 2.

Catalogue of the Tokio museum. Natural products. 1879. I. 66.[2]

Catalogue of the United States plants. See PECH, F. 1867. V. XVI.[2]

Catalogue of the valuable botanical library . . . of the late Aylmer Bourke Lambert. See LAMBERT, A. B. Catalogue . . . 1842. I. 2.

Catalogue of trees and shrubs, etc.; Agri-horticultural society's gardens, Lahore. 1876. I. 67.[1]

A catalogue of trees and shrubs growing in the Botanic garden at Edinburgh. 1775. I. 52.

Catalogue of trees, shrubs and herbaceous plants . . . cultivated . . . at Bartram's botanical garden. 1814. I. 38.[2]

A catalogue of trees, shrubs, plants and flowers. 1730. III. 80.

Catalogue of woods exhibited by the state of Amazon. 1893. IV. 19.[1]

Catalogue provisoire publié pour servir à la Flore de la Charente-inférieure. 1840. I. 409.

Catalogue raisonné des collections exposées par l'Administration des forêts. 1867. IV. 20.[1]

Catalogue raisonné des collections exposées par l'administration des forêts. 1878. IV. 2, 20.[1]

Catalogue raisonné des collections exposées par le service des forêts. 1878. IV. 21.[2]

Catalogue raisonné des collections . . . exposés par l'Administration des forêts. 1884. IV. 20.[2]

Catalogue spécial; groupe 5; classe 44; produits . . . des industries forestières de la Hongrie. 1878. IV. 21.[1]

Catalogue spécial accompagné de notices sur les produits . . . de l'Algérie. 1873. III. 280.[1]

Catalogue spécial d'objets forestiers envoyés à l'Exposition de Moscou. 1882. IV. 80.

Catalogue spécial officiel de l'exposition de la République Argentine. 1889. III. 269.[2]

Catalogus arborum et fruticum in Horto edinensi. 1778. I. 52.

Catalogus arborum, fruticum . . . horti medici D. L. Scholzii. See SCHOLZ, Lorenz. 1594. I. 42.

Catalogus der Bibliotheek van 's Lands Plantentuin te Buitenzorg. 1887. I. 2.

Catalogus der Collectie Vorderman. 1895. III. 275.[1]

Catalogue descriptif des fruits adoptés par le Congrès pomologique. 1887. III. 85.

Catalogue du jardin des plantes du Comte Alexis de Razoumoffsky à Gorenki. See FISCHER, F. E. L. von. 1808. I. 41.

Catalogus herbarii J. Ryani. See RYAN, J. 1809. I. 40.

Catalogus horti botanici Societatis physicae turicensis. See ROEMER, J. J. 1802. I. 65.[1]

Catalogus in IV. sectiones divisus rerum naturalium in musaeo exstantium Josephi de Christofori et Georgii Jan. See JAN, Giorgio. 1832. I. 63.

Catalogus Malorum aurantiorum. See RISLER, Josua. 1747. III. 496.[2]

Catalogus plantarum Caesarei regii horti prope Modiciam. See MANETTI, Giuseppe. 1842. I. 63.

Catalogus plantarum circa Scarborough. See TRAVIS, William. 167 . ? (error). I. 394. — 1800. I. 396.

Catalogus plantarum Horti academici landishutani. See SCHRANK, Franz von Paula von. 1805. I. 45.

Catalogus plantarum Horti botanici carolsruhani. See SCHWEYCKERT, J. M. 1791. I. 44.

Catalogus plantarum Horti botanici coloniensis. See BERKENKAMP, W. A. 1816. I. 45.

Catalogus plantarum Horti botanici divionensis. 1808. I. 57.

Catalogus plantarum Horti botanici ducalis, Jenae. See BATSCH, A. J. G. K. 1797. I. 44.

Catalogus plantarum Horti botanici florentini. See PICCIOLI, Antonio. 1829. I. 62.

Catalogus plantarum Horti bot. patavini. See BONATO, J. A. 1811. I. 61.

Catalogus plantarum Horti botanici Regii lycei ferrariensis. See CAMPANA, Antonio. 1812. I. 62.

Catalogus plantarum Horti botanici taurinensis. See BALBIS, G. B. 1807. I. 61.

Catalogus plantarum Horti botanici Universitatis ferrariensis. See CAMPANA, Antonio. 1812. I. 62.

Catalogus plantarum Horti botanici Urbinatis. See BRIGNOLI DI BRUNHHOFF, Giovanni de. 1811. I. 61.

Catalogus plantarum Horti botanici veronensis. See POLLINI, Ciro. 1812. I. 62.

Catalogus plantarum Horti erfurtensis. See BERNHARDI, J. J. 1799. I. 45.

Catalogus plantarum Horti imp. medici petropolitani. 1796. I. 41.

Catalogus plantarum Horti medici oxoniensis. See BOBART, Jakob. 1648. I. 51.[2]

Catalogus plantarum Horti publici amstelodamensis. See CORNELIUS, Hermann. 1661. I. 50.

Catalogus plantarum Horti regii bot. mantovani. 1785. I. 61.

Catalogus plantarum Horti regii bot. ticinensis. 1785. I. 61.

Catalogus plantarum Horti regii modoetiensis. See ROSSI, Johannes. 1826. I. 62.

Catalogus plantarum Horti regii neapolitani. See TENORE, Michele. 1812. I. 62.

Catalogus plantarum Imp. reg. horti botanici mantuani. See CONFIGLIACHI, Luigi. 1816. I. 62.

Catalogus plantarum . . . in agro Calato-Hieronensi collectarum. See ROSSO, E. T. & GERBINO, Xaverio. 1845. I. 431.

Catalogus plantarum . . . in Hortis ducalibus . . . jenensi et belvederensi. See VOIGT, F. S. 1812. I. 45.

Catalogus plantarum . . . in Hortis non procul a Londino. See MILLER, Philip. 1730. I. 52.

Catalogus plantarum in Hortis regiae villae prope Modoetiam. 1813. I. 62.

Catalogus plantarum . . . in Horto botanico bogoriensi. See TEIJSMANN, J. E. & BINNENDIJK, S. 1866. I. 68.[1]

Catalogus plantarum in Horto bot. R. archigymnasii mutinensis. See BRIGNOLI A BRUNNHOFF, Giovanni de. 1836. I. 63.

Catalogus plantarum officinalium. See MILLER, Philip. 1730. I. 52.

Catalogus plantarum officinalium . . . in Horto edinensi. 1778. I. 52.

Catalogus plantarum quae in agro veronensi. See SÉGUIER, J. F. 1745. I. 424.

Catalogus plantarum quae in Horto regio atestino mutinensi. 1813. I. 62.

Catalogus plantarum quae Monachii in horto Regiae academicae scientiarum . . . colebantur. 1814. I. 45.

Catalogus plantarum, quarum semina . . . in Horto regio pillnitziensi servabantur. 1819. I. 45.

Catalogus plantarum scholae botanicae Horti regii parisiensis. See CATALOGUS plantarum singularum . . . 1656. I. 56.

Catalogus plantarum seminum exoticorum. 1653. I. 38.[1]

Catalogus plantarum singularum . . . Horti regii parisiensis. 1656. I. 56.

Catalogus seminum collectorum in Horto botanico-agrario florentino. See TARGIONI-TOZZETTI, Ottaviano. 1818. I. 62.

Catalogus stirpium Horti acad. taurinensis. See BALBIS, G. B. 1811. I. 61.

Catalogus stirpium in exteris regionibus. See RAY, John. 1673. I. 348.[1]

Catalogus stirpium . . . in Regio horto botanico taurinensi. See CAPELLI, Carolo. 1821. I. 62.

Catalogus stirpium . . . taurinensis. See BIROLI, Giovanni. 1813. I. 62.

Catalogus systematicus bibliothecae Horti imperialis botanici petropolitani. 1852. I. 2.

Catalogus van de bibliotheek der Rijkslandbouwschool. 1891. III. 1.

Catalogus van de levende en gedroogde planten . . . ter . . . uitvoerhandeltentoonstelling. 1883. III. 28.[2]

The Catalpa. 1876. III. 706.[1]

The Catalpa. 1890. III. 705.

The Catalpa for economic planting. 1887. IV. 538.[2]

Catania, T. F. Tussur silk culture. 1900. III. 148.[2]

Catania — Accademia Gioenia di scienze naturali. See ACCADEMIA . . . T. 24.[2]

Cate, O. ten. Natuurlijke historie van de meest schadelijke rupsen der Dennen. 1807. IV. 441.

— Verhandeling over de verwoesting door schadelijke dennenrupsen. 1807. IV. 455.

— Over de verwoestingen der rupsen in de dennebosschen. 1807. IV. 441.

— Verwoestingen door dennenrupsen. 1807. IV. 461.[1]

Catechismo di scienze naturali applicate alla selvicoltura. 1861. IV. 57.

Cater, Rowland W. A Cocoanut plantation in Mosquito. 1897. III. 323.[1]

— Coffee-culture in Central America. 1899. III. 728.[1]

Caterpillars attacking Cocoa trees. 1895. III. 593.[2]

Catesby, Mark. Die Beschreibung von Carolina. 1731. I. 317.[2]

— Hortus britanno-americanus. 1763. I. 304, III. 60.
— Hortus Europae americanus. 1763. I. 304, *III*. 60.
— The natural history of Carolina. 1731. I. 317,² V. xvii.²
— *See also* Edwards, G. & Catesby, M.
Cathartine, or the active principle of Senna. 1822. III. 470.¹
Cathelineau, H. L'ouabaïo, poison des Somalis. 1889. III. 685.²
Cathelot, J. Les forêts du Morvan. 1876. IV. 360.
Catholic world. III. 3.
Catlow, Agnes. Popular field botany. 1848. I. 400, 533.
— Popular garden botany. 1849. III. 82.
— Popular greenhouse botany. 1857. III. 82.
Cato, Marcus Porcius. De agricultura. 1472. III. 97.
— Delle cose rustiche opera. 1472. III. 97.
— Libri de re rustica. 1472. III. 97.
— Methodus rustica. 1472. III. 97.
— De re rustica. 1472. III. 97.
— Scriptores rei rusticae. 1470. III. 96.¹
Il **catrame**. 1865. IV. 436.²
Catros, Toussaint Yves. Traité raisonné des arbres fruitiers. 1810. III. 143.
Catros-Gérand. Le Chêne à feuille de Saule. 1898. III. 362.²
— L'hiver 1879–1880 à Bordeaux. 1881. III. 48.
— & Daurel, Joseph. Manuel pratique des jardins. 188. ? III. 113.
Cats, Jakob. Het derde deel van de Wijse jaer-beschryver. 1661. III. 104.
Catta, J. D. Sur les accidents de végétation . . . dans le traitement des Vignes phylloxérées. 1881. III. 572.
— Sur l'action de l'eau, dans les applications de sulfure de carbone. 1880. III. 572.
Cattaneo, Achille. Sul male del Caffé. 1888. III. 736.
— *See also* Garovaglio, Santo & Cattaneo, Achille.
Cattaneo, Antonio. Catalogo delle piante . . . del giardino Cattaneo. 1812. I. 62.
Cattaneo, Giacomo. Della idropisia de' Gelsi. 1767. III. 378.
Cattaneo, Gottardo. Della riacclimazione del Gelso. n. d. III. 372.²
Cattie, J. Th. Hoe de oranje-gele vlekken op de bladeren van Appel of Pereboomen ontstaan. 1877. III. 444.¹
— Hoe sluipwespen den Vijgenboom . . . bevruchten. 1882. II. 151.¹
— Iets over kleuren. 1878. I. 185.¹
— Iets over wortel en stam. 1882. I. 104.
— De processierups. 1875. III. 190.
— De roest van Appel en Pereboomen. 1883. III. 444.¹
— Sneeuw schadelijk, soms doodelijk voor Coniferen. 1893. III. 293.
— Verslag over Lophyrus pini. 1875. IV. 477.
— In welken vorm nemen de planten stikstof uit den grond op. 1876. I. 159.
Cattley, William. Account of a new Psidium. 1822. III. 637.²
Cats Smallenburg, F. van. Iets over het gebruik van Kwik-chloride. 1837. IV. 417.
The Caucasian Walnut. 1888. III. 356.²
Caucat, (*jr.*). Note sur la culture du Clianthus. 1868. III. 472.¹
Cauchin, Vicc. Note sur des Cactées rustiques. 1876. III. 619.
Cauchy, Augustin. Note sur un procédé employé . . . contre la maladie de la Vigne. 1854. III. 576.
Caudaval, Lafon de. *See* Lafon de Caudaval.
Caulfield, Colbert A. On the Poison Oak of California. 1860. III. 527.¹
Caumartin, Cazin de. *See* Cazin de Caumartin.
Caumel, Jean Baptiste. *See* Heribaud-Joseph, *frère*.
Caupenne, Alfredo de Cás-. *See* Cás-Caupenne, Alfredo de.
Causans, *marquis de, (député, Vaucluse)*. Opinion sur l'article 1er du titre XI. du projet de finances. 1817. IV. 326.
Cause, D. H. De koninglycke hovenier. 1676. III. 105.
Delle cause che motivarono una maggiore distruzione di foreste. 1880. IV. 283.¹
Sulle cause della formazione degli anelli legnosi. *See* Die Jahresringe der Pflanzen. 1878. IV. 64.²
Cause of dripping of water from forest trees. 1896. I. 213.²
Cause of the concentric rings in trees. 1841. I. 127.²
Delle cause principali delle grandi piene. 1870. IV. 50.
Causes and effects of forest fires in . : . New Jersey. 1895. IV. 182.²
Causes de la chute de la foudre sur les arbres. 1894. IV. 548.¹

Causes de la chute de la foudre sur les arbres. 1897. IV. 548.²
Causes of the ascent of the sap. 1864. I. 164.
Caussinus, Nicolaus. Polyhistor symbolicus. 1631. I. 515.
Caustier, E. La flore et les forêts de Madagascar. 1896. IV. 380.¹
Cautegril, (*Conservateur des forêts*). Reboisement et aménagement des eaux. 1884. IV. 51.
Cautley, P. F. P. Report on the timber trade of Trieste. 1888. IV. 407.¹
Cauvet, Désiré. Sur l'écorce de racine de Grenadier. 1877. II. 610.¹
— Études sur le rôle des racines. 1861. I. 158, 161.
— Note sur la vrille des Ampélidées. 1864. II. 501.¹
— Note sur la vrille des Ampélidées. 1883. II. 501.²
— Note sur le dégagement de l'acide carbonique par les racines. 1880. I. 161, 170.
— Nouveaux éléments d'histoire naturelle médicale. 1869. III. 59.¹
— Résumé des observations morphologiques . . . sur . . Solanées. 1865. II. 768.¹
— Des Solanées. 1864. III. 698.²
— De la structure du Cytinet. 1870. II. 564.¹
Cauvy, B. Moyens propres à débarasser les Vignes du phylloxera. 1875. III. 568.
— Note sur l'action que la terre des vignobles exerce sur les gaz sulfurés. 1874. III. 566.²
— Note sur le phylloxéra. 1874. III. 759.
— Sur la réinvasion estivale des Vignes phylloxérées. 1879. III. 571.
— Le salut des Vignes. 1874. III. 759.
Cavalcanti, Adolpho Barbalho Uchôa. Relatorio preliminar sobre a extracção da gomma elastica. 1898. III. 229.
Cavalier, Jean. La maladie des Châtaigniers des Cévennes. 1887. III. 359.¹
Le cavallette in Sardegna. 1866. IV. 209.²
Cavallier, Charles. Le Laurier-Rose à Montpellier. 1875. III. 689.¹
— Rapport . . . à suite de la visite faite . . . au jardin de M. Fabre. 1873. II. 401.¹
Cavallini, Filippo. Brevis enumeratio plantarum. 1689. I. 60.²
— Pugillus meliteus. 1689. I. 451.
Cavanagh, Thomas. Noted American trees. 1871. I. 295.¹
Cavanilles, Antonio José. Carta de . . . en respuesta à la que se insertó. 1789. III. 513.³
— Decima dissertatio botanica. De Passiflora. 1790. II. 576.²
— Descripcion de algunas plantas nuevas. 1800. I. 328.
— Descripcion de cinco géneros nuevos. 1799. I. 264.
— Descripcion de las plantas. 1802. I. 84.
— Descripcion de los géneros Aeginetia, Rizoa y Castelia. 1801. II. 810.¹
— Descripcion de los géneros Goodenia y Scaevola. 1799. II. 846.¹
— Descripcion de los géneros nuevos de plantas. 1801. II. 795.¹
— Descripcion del genero Bonplandia. 1800. II. 746.²
— Descripcion del género Buena. 1800. II. 819.¹
— Dissertatio botanica de Sida. 1785. II. 527.¹
— Dobre los estambres de la Parilphoa. 1802. II. 741.¹
— Sobre la fecundacion . . . de Adelia. 1802. II. 437.³
— Del género nuevo Viviania. 1804. II. 392.¹
— De los generos Cephalophora y Tricycla. 1802. II. 191.¹
— In Hakeam et Banksiam observationes. 1801. II. 158.¹
— Icones et descriptiones plantarum . . . in Hispania. 1791. I. 264; 420.
— Del Macrocnemo. 1804. II. 822.³
— Monadelphiae classis dissertationes decem. 1785. I. 263.
— Nona dissertatio botanica. De Banisteria. 1790. II. 423.²
— Note sur quelques plantes qui produisent le Caoutchouc. 1803. II. 147.¹
— Observaciones botánicas. 1799. I. 500.
— Observaciones botánicas. 1800. II. 437,² 741.²
— Observaciones botánicas. 1803. I. 265.
— Observaciones sobre algunos vegetales que producen resina elástica. 1800. II. 147.¹
— Observaciones sobre el suelo, naturales y plantas del Puerto Jackson y Bahia. 1799. II. 158.¹
— Observaciones sobre la historia natural . . . de Valencia. 1795. I. 420, *III*, 126.¹
— Observations in quintum fasciculum D. L'Héritier. 1790. II. 518.³

Cavanilles, Antonio José (*continued*).
— Octava dissertatio botanica Erythroxylon et Malpighiam complectens. 1789. II. 394,¹ *486*.²
— De las plantas que . . . Broussonet colectó. 1801. I. 484.
— Principios elementáles de la botánica. 1802. I. 84.
— Principj elementari di botanica. 1802. I. 84.
— Quarta dissertatio botanica 128 species complectens. 1787. II. 389.²
— Quinta dissertatio botanica. De Sterculia. 1788. II. 531.¹
— Secunda dissertatio botanica. De Malva. 1786. II. 518.²
— Septima dissertatio botanica. 1789. I. 263.
— Sexta dissertatio botanica. 1788. I. 263.
— Suplemento al género Buena. 1800. II. 819.¹
— Tertia dissertatio botanica. De Ruizia. 1787. II. 518.²
— Verzeichniss aller in [seinen] Observaciones sobre el reyno de Valencia erwähnten Pflanzen. 1801. I. 420.
Cavara, Fridiano. Di alcune anomalie riscontrate negli . . . Lonicere. 1886. II. 836.²
— Appunti di patologia vegetale. 1888. III. 194.
— Contributo alla conoscenza dei funghi pomicoli. 1890. III. 194.
— Contributo alla morfologia . . . delle Camelliee. 1897. II. 550.²
— Il   centrale dei fiori maschili del Buxus. 1894. II. 452. corpo
— Intorno al disseccamento dei grappoli della Vite. 1888. III. 580.
— Funghi pomicoli. 1890. III. 194.
— Sul fungo che è causa del " Bitter rot." 1888. III. 580.
— L' insegnamento nell' Istituto forestale di Vallombrosa. 1897. IV. 35.²
— Una malattia dei Limoni. 1894. III. 502.²
— Micocecidii florali del Rhododendron. 1899. III. 658.²
— Über eine neue Pilzkrankheit der Weisstanne. 1897. IV. 445.
— Di un nuovo Acarocecidio della Suaeda fruticosa. 1900. III. 387.²
— Oogenesi nel Pinus Laricio. 1899. II. 44.¹
— Osservazioni morfologiche sulle gimnosperme. 1900. II. 16.²
— Ricerche sullo sviluppo del frutto della Thea. 1898. II. 552.¹
— Studi sul The. 1899. II. 552.¹
— Tumori . . . nel Juniperus phoenicea. 1898. III. 304.¹
— Sulla vera causa della malattia . . . in . . . Ovada. 1888. III. 579.
Cavazza, Domizio. I boschi, le acque montane e l' agricoltura. 1898. IV. 52.
— La lotta contro la Peronospora. 1893. III. 580.
— *See also* Berti, P. & Cavazza, D.
Cave, Charles. Sur un caractère nouveau du genre Rosier. 1863. II. 282.²
— Cours élémentaire de botanique appliquée. 1870. III. 37.¹
— Structure et développement du fruit. 1869. I. 110.
— Sur la zone génératrice des appendices chez les végétaux monocotylédons. 1870. I. 132.¹
— Sur la zone génératrice des appendices végétaux. 1870. I. 132.¹
Cave, Henry William. Golden tips; a description of Ceylon. 1900. III. 604.¹
Caventou, Eugène. Du Carapa touloucouna. 1859. III. 512.¹
— Deuxième mémoire sur les végétaux des familles Méliacées. 1859. II. 420.¹
— De l'écorce de Cail-cédra du Sénégal. 1858. III. 512.¹
— Rapport . . . sur l'écorce de Cail-cédra. 1857. III. 512.²
— Recherches chimiques sur l'écorce du Cail-cédra. 1849. III. 512.²
— *See also* Pelletier, Joseph & Caventou, Eugène.
Caventou, J. B. Examen chimique des fleurs du Cytise. 1817. III. 480.²
— Note sur la véritable origine . . . de l'huile de Croton tiglium. 1825. III. 517.¹
— *See also* François, Caventou, J. B. & Pelletier, Joseph; Pelletier, Joseph & Caventou, J. B.
Caveye, Charles van de. Du boisement des terres incultes. 1898. IV. 160.³
— Sylviculture. 1896. IV. 119.²
Cayeux, Ferd. Les abris en Provence. 1889. III. 215.²
— Ebourgeonnement. 1892. III. 171.

— Greffe-bouture de Sureau. 1889. III. 751.²
— Le Livistona australis. 1888. III. 326.²
— Poplar Parasol de St. Julien. 1888. III. 346.²
Cayeux, Henri. Bauhinia yunnanensis. 1900. II. 336.¹
— Dombeya Cayeuxii. 1898. III. 591.¹
— Le Néflier du Japon au Portugal. 1896. III. 424.¹
— Un redoutable insecte . . . l'Icerya Purchasi. 1898. III. 498.²
— Le Sciadophyllum pulchrum. 1897. III. 644.¹
Caylus, Anne Claude Philippe de Tubières Grimoard de Pestels de Levis de, *comte*. Histoire du rapprochement des végétaux. 1806. I. 33.
Cazalbou. Arbres à caoutchouc. 1898. III. 229.
Cazalis, F. Un Tamaris d'Algérie. 1893. III. 612.¹
Cazalis-Allut, Louis César. Insuccès des remèdes contre la maladie de la Vigne. 1855. III. 576.
— Mélanges de viticulture. 1859. III. 555.
— Œuvres agricoles. 1865. III. 125.
Cazenave. Decouverte du principe de la maladie de la Vigne. 1854. III. 576.
Cazeneuve, Paul. Sur la cannelle dite de Padang. 1875. III. 275.¹
— Sur la défense des Vignes contre la Cochylis. 1897. III. 564.¹
— Nouvelles observations sur l'écorce de Hoang-nau. 1878. III. 684.²
— Sur le traitement des Vignes phylloxérées. 1891. III. 574.
— & Haddon. Sur l'acide cafétannique. 1897. III. 740.²
— & Hugounenq, L. Sur deux principes cristallisés extraits du Santal rouge. 1887. III. 485.²
— Sur l'homoptérocarpine. 1888. III. 485.²
Cazin, F. J. De la culture du Mûrier. 1856. III. 377.
Cazin de Caumartin. Le Chêne des partisans. 1844. II. 138.¹
Cazzuola, Ferdinando. Gli Aceri saccariferi. 1877. III. 534.²
— Alcuni esperimenti fatti sulla durata della facoltà germinativa dei semi. 1877. I. 527.
— Gli Allori. 1877. III. 403.²
— Il Caffè peruviano. 1879. III. 743.¹
— Cultura del The in Italia. 1898. III. 601.¹
— Dizionario di botanica applicata. 1876. III. 29.²
— Circa agli effetti del freddo dell' inverno 1879–80. 1880. III. 49.²
— Il genere Myrica. 1878. III. 353.¹
— Osservazioni sopra alcuni saggi d'acclimatazione. 1876. III. 49.²
— Le piante utili e nocive . . . in Italia. 1880. III. 88.²
— Il Pistacchio, il Terebinto, ed il Lentisco. 1878. III. 525.¹
— Il regno vegetale tessile e tintoriale. 1873. III. 53.
— Relazione di alcuni esperimenti fatti sopra fibre tessili. 1873. III. 234.
— Ricordi circa agli effetti del freddo dell' inverno 1871–72. 1872. III. 49.²
— *See also* Caruel, Teodoro & Cazzuola, Ferdinando.
— & Nencioni, Giuseppe. Il coltivatore di piante ornamentali. 1880. III. 88.¹
Ce que le montagne de mesure. 1899. IV. 91.¹
Ceara rubber. 1898. III. 526.²
Cecconi, Giacomo. Di alcuni casi fitopatologici. 1899. I. 216.¹
— Contribuzione alla conoscenza delle galle . . . di Vallombrosa. 1897. I. 216.¹
— Danni dell' Hylastes trifolii. 1899. III. 192.¹
La cécidomie du Hêtre. 1900. IV. 497.
Cecil, *Mrs.* Alicia (Amherst). *See* Amherst, *Hon.* Alicia Margaret Tyssen.
The Cedar avenue at Dropmore. 1899. III. 300.²
The Cedar of Algeria. 1895. II. 27.²
The Cedar of Central Africa. *See* Central Africa. 1896. II. 27.¹
The Cedar of Goa. 1891. II. 29.²
Of the Cedar of Lebanon. 1733. III. 300,¹ *304*.²
The Cedar of Lebanon. 1868. II. 28.¹
The Cedar of Lebanon. 1892. II. 28.¹
Cedar pavement. 1887. IV. 447.²
Cedar tree of Mount Mlanje. 1896. IV. 447.²
The Cedars at Bayfordbury. 1886. II. 28.¹
The Cedars of Lebanon. 1839. II. 28.¹
Cedars of Lebanon. 1857. II. 28.¹
The Cedars of Lebanon. 1895. II. 28.¹ — 1893. II. 28.²
Cedars of Lebanon at home. 1895. II. 28.¹
Die Ceder vom Libanon. 1839. II. 28.¹
Cederfelt de Simonsen. Om Akasie-Træers Dyrkning. 1802. IV. 522.²

Cederhjelm, Carl Wilhelm, *Baron*. Tal om wilda träns plantering. 1740. IV. 113.[2]
Cedernwaldungen in Afrika. 1894. IV. 447.[2]
Un Cèdre géant. 1897. III. 300.[3]
Cedro del Libano fulminato. 1889. IV. 194.
Cedro diodara. 1882. IV. 447.[2]
Cedrus Deodara nivea. 1899. III. 300.[1]
Celakovský, Ladislav Jos. Über achtzählige Cyklen pentamer veranlagter Blüthen. 1899. I. 115.[2]
— Ueber die allgemeine Entwickelungsgeschichte des Pflanzenreiches. 1868. I. 249.[1]
— Analytická květena Čech, Moravy. 1897. I. 444.
— Beitrag zur Kenntniss der Flora der Athos-Halbinsel. 1888. I. 450.
— Ueber die Blüthenstände der Quercus ilicifolia. 1893. II. 134.[2]
— Ueber die Cupula und den Cupularfruchtknoten. 1874. I. 118.[1]
— Über die Cupula von Fagus und Castanea. 1890. II. 123.[1]
— Über Doppelblätter bei Lonicera Periclymenum. 1894. II. 839.[1]
— Über einige dem phytostatischen Gesetze unterliegende Fälle von Verzweigung. 1898. I. 107.[1]
— Über einige Resultate der botanischen Durchforschung Böhmens. 1882. I. 443.
— Epilog zu meiner Schrift über die Placenten der Angiospermen. 1900. I. 118.[1]
— O fylogenetickém vývoji rostlin jehnědokvětých. 1889. I. 249.[1]
— Die Gymnospermen. 1890. II. 1.
— Zur Gymnospermie der Coniferen. 1879. II. 19.
— Über Herrn A. W. Eichler's Entgegnung auf meine Kritik. 1882. II. 19.
— Über die Inflorescenzen der Borragineen. 1874. II. 747.[2]
— O kladodích Asparagef. 1893. II. 77.[2]
— Zur Kritik der Ansichten von der Fruchtschuppe der Abietineen. 1882. II. 19.
— Eine merkwürdige Culturform von Philadelphus. 1897. II. 242.[1]
— O morfologickém významu kupuly (číšky). 1886. II. 123.[1]
— Ueber die morphologische Bedeutung der Samenknospen. 1874. I. 122.
— Morphologische und biologische Mittheilungen, II. 1893. II. 134.[2]
— Morphologische und biologische Mittheilungen, III. 1893. II. 40.[1]
— Ueber den Nabel der Fruchtschuppen-Apophyse von Pinus. 1893. II. 40.[1]
— Nachtrag zu meiner Schrift über die Gymnospermen. 1898. II. 2.
— O několových kritických formách rostlinných. 1882. II. 4?.[2]
— O nekterych zrůdnostech na Habru a Smrku se objevujících. 1893. II. 36,[1] 121.[1]
— Neue Beiträge zum Verständniss der Fruchtschuppe der Coniferen. 1900. II. 20.[1]
— Neue Beiträge zur Foliolartheorie des Ovulums. 1884. I. 122.
— Nové doklady sympodiálního složení kmene révovitých rostlin. 1904. II. 501.[1]
— Ueber petaloid umgebildete Staubgefässe von Philadelphus. 1898. II. 239,[1] 242.[1]
— Ueber die Pflanzenformationen . . . Böhmens. 1866. I. 441.
— Über den phylogenetischen Entwickelungsgang der Blüthe. 1897. I. 116.[1]
— Ueber ' Placenten und Hemmungsbildungen. 1875. I. 118.[1]
— Prodromus der Flora von Böhmen. 1867. I. 442.
— Prodromus květeny české. 1867. I. 442.
— Das Reductionsgesetz der Blüthen. 1894. I. 115.[2]
— Résumé der Mittheilung über die morphologische Bedeutung der Cupula. 1886. II. 123.[1]
— Réva viná. 1858. II. 507.[1]
— Růže a její příbuzné. 1858. II. 256.[2]
— Stromy jehnědokvěté. 1857. I. 524.[1]
— Teratologische Beiträge zur morphologischen Deutung des Staubgefässes. 1878. I. 116,[2] 145.[1]
— Tvarozpytné rozhledy po oboru botanickém. 1862. I. 99.
— Untersuchungen über die Homologien der generativen Produkte der Fruchtblätter. 1884. I. 118.[1]

— O ústrojnosti květů Welwitschie. 1874. II. 55.[2]
— O útvarech českého rostlinstva. 1866. I. 441.
— Vergleichende Darstellung der Placenten. 1876. . I. 118.[1]
— Die Vermehrung der Sporangien von Ginkgo. 1900. II. 8.[1]
— Ueber den Zusammenhang der fortschreitenden Stufen des Pflanzenreichs. 1839. I. 252.
Celi, Ettore. Lezioni elementari di botanica. 1856. I. 89.
— Lezioni elementari di organografia. 1853. I. 89.
La Cellule. I. 16.
Die **Cellulose** (chemisch bereitete Holzfaser) in ihren Eigenschaften. 1875. IV. 430.
Die **Cellulose-Fabrikation**. 1888. IV. 430.
Cels. Notice historique sur . . . Robinia viscosa. 1804. III. 487.[2]
Cels, François. Catalogue des Agavées, Cactées. 1865. I. 53.
— Catalogue des arbres, arbustes et autres plantes. 1817. I. 57.
— Cereus Bertini Cels. 1865. III. 621.[1]
— Description des variétés du Cereus . . . Pentlandi. 1862. III. 622.[2]
— Note sur le Cereus Bertini. 1863. III. 621.[1]
— Nouveau catalogue général des végétaux. 1832. I. 57.
Cels, Silvestre, & Hallé. Observations sur l'Hedysarum gyrans. 1793. II. 354.[1]
Celsius, Anders. Nya rön om trästängers utwidgande i köld. 1739. IV. 411.[2]
Celsius, Magnus Nicolaus. De plantis. 1647. I. 30.
Celsius, Olof. אהלים: אלהר . . . Agallochum praestantissimum. 1737. I. 513.
— De arbore scientiae boni et mali. 1715. I. 512.
— Botanici sacri exercitatio prima. 1702. I. 512.
— Dissertationes breves. 1745. I. 513.
— Exercitationis de Palma caput primum. 1711. I. 511.
— Hierobotanicon. 1745. I. 513.
— אלון: אלו . . . Terebinthus Judaica. 1738. I. 513.
Celsus, Aurelius Cornelius. De re medica libri octo. 1549. III. 239.
Ceni, Antonio. Guida all' Orto botanico in Padova. 1854. I. 63.
Cenni brevissimi sopra i boschi . . . di Sardegna. *See* F., P. B. 1832. IV. 364.
Cenni sulla vegetazione in Liguria. *See* CHIAPPORI, Agostino. 1874. I. 428.
Cenno illustrativo delle raccolte forestali inviate alla Esposizione . . . in Milano. 1881. IV. 364.
Censký, Franz. Wahrnehmungen, gemacht . . . bei Auftreten und Vernichten der Nonne. 1896. IV. 202.
Il centenario dell' Orto botanico di Palermo. 1894. IV. IX.[1]
Centola, Giacomo. Deliberazione . . . riguardante la memoria dell' ingegnere signor Taiani. 1864. IV. 434.
Central Africa. The Cedar forests of Mount Mlanje. 1896. II. 27.[1]
Central African planter. III. 27.[1]
Central American rubber. 1899. III. 287.[1]
Central-Moor-Commission. Protokolle. IV. 7.
Central provinces of India. *See* INDIA (CENTRAL PROVINCES). IV. 14.
Centralblatt der Land- und Forstwirthschaft in Böhmen. IV. 14.
Centralblatt für Agrikulturchemie. III. 11.
Centralblatt für das gesammte Forstwesen. IV. 14.
Centralblatt für den deutschen Holzhandel. IV. 7.
Centralblatt für die gesammte Landeskultur. *See* CENTRALBLATT der Land . . . IV. 14.
Centralblatt für Holzindustrie. IV. 7.
Centralblatt für Naturwissenschaften . . . I. 11.
Century illustrated monthly magazine. *See* SCRIBNER'S monthly. III. 8.
Die **Cephalotaxus-Arten**. 1884. III. 287.[1]
Cephalotaxus-Arterne. *See* CEPHALOTAXUS-ARTEN. 1884. III. 287.[1]
Cephalotaxus Kaempferi der Gärten. 1858. II. 8.[2]
Cepurus, (*pseud.*). Sound and unsound timber. 1860. IV. 413.[2]
Cera vegetale. 1863. III. 226.[1]
Cérati, (*abbé*). Sur le Genêt. 1766. III. 474.[1]
Cercle botanique du Nord. Journal. III. 19.
Cercle pratique d'horticulture et de botanique . . . de la Seine-Inférieure. Bulletin. III. 19.
Cercle professoral pour le progrès de l'arboriculture en Belgique. Bulletins. III. 15.

168 INDEX OF AUTHORS AND TITLES

Cerdá, Vicente Tortosa y. *See* Tortosa y Cerdá, Vincente.

Cérenville, Henry de. Auszug aus einem Artikel . . . die forstlichen Kulturen in den Seealpen . . . behandelnd. 1863. IV. 162.
— Extrait d'un article . . . relatif à des cultures forestières dans les Alpes maritimes. 1863. IV. 162.
— Merkwürdige Baum-Formen. 1859. I. 297.²
— Singulières formes d'arbres. 1859. I. 297.²

Ceres. III. 10.²

Cereus splendidus Gard. Mag. 1836. III. 622.¹

Cerfberr de Médelsheim, Alphonse. Le cacao et le chocolat. 1867. III. 222, *763*.¹

Cerini, Giuseppe. Dei vantaggi che apporterebbe . . . l'istituzione di società per l'impianto e conservazione dei boschi. 1844. IV. 43.

Cerio, Ignazio & Bellini, Raffaello. Flora dell' isola di Capri. 1900. I. 430.

Céris, A. de. Transplantation d'un Cèdre de trente ans. 1866. III. 167, *300*.²
— Vigne précoce Caplat. 1898. III. 584.¹

Cermak, Johann. Ueber die Tief- und Hochleimung. 1892. IV. 201.

Cerman, Ignaz. Die Waldmast. 1872. IV. 515.¹

Cerna, David. Thevetia Iccotli and its glucoside. 1879. III. 691.²
— La Thevetia Iccotli y sus glucosidos. 1879. III. 691.²

Cerneiro da Silva, João José. *See* Silva, J. J. Cerneiro da.

Cerný, J. V. Cizi stromovi lesné. 1886. IV. 127.²
— Eine Exkursion in die Zbirower Forste. 1879. IV. 371.
— Modřín v lesním hospodářství. 1873. IV. 448.¹
— & Cívárek, F. J. Lesnictvi. 188 . ? IV. 99.²

Ceron, Salvador. Breves apuntes acerca de los perjuicios ocasionados . . . por la desaparicion de masas forestales. 1885. IV. 47.²
— Catalogo de las plantas del herbario . . . de la flora forestal. 1892. I. 464.¹
— Cultivo de las arenas voladoras. 1888. IV. 165.
— Cultivo de las estepas. . . . de Cádiz. 1877. IV. 164.²
— Estudio del Olivo y de la Vid. 1884. III. 558,¹ *676*,¹ IV. *539*.¹
— Industria forestal-agrícola. 1879. III. 53, 271.²
— Memoria sobre la produccion de los montes públicos de Filipinas. 1893. IV. 554.¹

Cerrès, d' Oliver de. *See* Oliver de Cerres, d'.

Certeux, Alphonse. Guide du planteur d'Eucalyptus. 1877. IV. 530.
— Le Néflier du Japon. 1878. III. 423.²

Cerulli-Irelli, Gastone. Contribuzione allo studio della struttura della radice. 1894. I. 104.

Cervantes, Julian. Tablas botanicas. 1825. I. 522.²

Cervantes, Vicente de. Account of the Ule-tree. 1794. II. 147.¹
— Chirostemon novum. 1809. II. 532.²
— Discurso . . . De resina elastica. 1794. II. 147.¹
— Ensayo à la materia médica vegetal de Mexico. 1889. III. 264.²
— Del genero Chirostemon. 1803. II. 532.²

Cés-Caupenne, Alfredo de. La España y la Argelia. 1864. IV. 363,¹ *379*.¹

Cesalpini, Andrea. De plantis libri XVI. 1583. I. 282.

Cesareo-regia accademia di scienze . . . di Padova. Memorie. Nuovi saggi. I. 24.²

Cesari, R. de. A proposito della fiera nazionale. 1895. III. 679.¹

Cesati, Vincenzo, *barone*. Ad commentarium inchoandum de speciebus plantarum Tenoreanis. 1875. II. 420.¹
— Elenco sistematico di alcune piante dei luoghi di Terra Santa. 1866. I. 480.
— Gestaltung und Verhältnisse der Pflanzenwelt in der Lombardei. 1844. I. 427.
— Illustrazione della Brocchia dichotoma. 1873. II. 453.²
— Illustrazione di alcune piante raccolte dal Sig. Prof. Strobel. 1871. I. 346.
— Note botaniche di vario argomento. 1873. II. 453.²
— Die Pflanzenwelt im Gebiete zwischen dem Tessin. 1863. I. 427.
— Saggio su la geografia botanica . . . della Lombardia. 1844. I. 427.
— Passerini, Giovanni & Gibelli, Giuseppe. Compendio della flora italiana. 1867. I. 428.

Cesi, Federico, *Duke of Aqua-Sparta*. Phytosophicarum tabularum ex frontispiciis Naturalis theatri desumpta. 1651. I. 286.

Ceská flora. III. 24.²

České akademie Cisaře Františka Josefa . . . Rozpravy. I. 27.

Ceský vinař. III. 24.²

Cessac, F. de. Catalogue des plantes vasculaires de la Creuse. 1862. I. 412.

The Cestrums (Habrothamnus). 1885. III. 699.¹

Cetti, Giuseppe. Collezione xilologica. 1863. IV. 17.
— Relazione statistica del ripartimento forestale di Sondrio. 1866. IV. 364. -

Ceylon — Royal botanic gardens. *See* Royal . . . I. 29.¹

Ceylon, a general description of the island. 1876. I. 476.²

Ceylon branch of the Royal Asiatic society. *See* Royal Asiatic society . . . I. 29.¹

Ceylon cacao. 1890. III. 595.¹

Ceylon Coca leaves. 1894. III. 493.²

The Ceylon Tree Rhododendron. 1845. III. 657.¹

Ch., E. Enseignement à la base du service administratif forestier de l'Empire britannique des Indes. 1892. IV. 34.²

Chabanne, G. Allamanda Hendersoni Domb. 1900. III. 686.¹
— Hexacentris mysorensis Wight. 1899. III. 710.²
— Tarif ou comptes faits de la valeur progressive d'un hectare. 1831. IV. 254.
— Thunbergia Harrisii Hook. f. 1899. III. 710.²

Chabannes, Ch. de. Lettre sur les incendies . . . en Algerie. 1866. IV. 184.¹

Chabaud, J. B. Un Cyprès mâle. Trois végétaux remarquables. 1876. II. 29.²
— Encephalartos Altensteinii. 1874. III. 285.²
— Floraison d'un Yucca filifera. 1876. III. 340.¹
— Floraison du Dasylirion longifolium. 1876. III. 337.¹
— Floraison en plein air de l'Erythea edulis. 1897. II. 63.²
— Il giardino dei Cocchi sul Golfo Juan. 1883. I. 59.
— Le Jubaea spectabilis. 1882. III. 326.¹
— Note sur une fructification de l'Encephalartos. 1874. III. 285.²
— Phoecilodermis [*sic*] populnea. 1877. III. 590.¹
— Un Poirier légendaire . . . remarquables. 1876. II. 280.²
— Végétaux exotiques . . . dans la région des orangers. 1871. III. 87.
— Viaggio orticolo da Cannes a Nizza. 1882. I. 59.
— Voyage horticole de Cannes à Nice. 1882. I. 59.

Chabert, Alfred. Contribution à la flore de France et de Corse. 1892. II. 134.²
— De l'emploi populaire des plantes sauvages en Savoie. 1895. III. 271.²
— Note sur la flore d'Algérie. 1889. I. 486.
— Observations sur la flore montagneuse du cap Corse. 1882. II. 665.¹
— De Tunis à Tyout. 1897. II. 860.¹
— *See also* Songeon, André & Chabert, Alfred.

Chabert, J. L. Du Huaco et de ses vertus médicinales. 1853. III. 755.²

Chabert, Lefebvre-. *See* Lefebvre-Chabert.

Chaboisseau, Théodore. Course de deux botanistes à la recherche du Genista delphinensis. 1879. II. 360.²
— De l'étude spécifique du genre Rubus. 1863. II. 303.²
— Note sur les Viscum. 1881. II. 180.³
— Notes sur plusieurs espèces. 1863. II. 351.²
— Observations sur . . . Rubus . . . de la Vienne. 1860. II. 303.²

Chabrey, Dominique. Omnium stirpium sciagraphia et icones 1666. I. 286.
— Stirpium icones et sciagraphia. 1666. I. 286.

Chadt, Jan Ev. Cedič, jeho poměr ku tvoření půdy. 1894. IV. 70.
— Z dějin našich lesních stromů. 1892. IV. 87.—1894. I. 438.
— Dřeviny jehličnaté v Čechách. 1894. IV. 87.¹
— Kolonisace v lesích českých. 1893. IV. 28.¹
— Lesní půdoznalectví. 1887. IV. 69.
— Několik přednášek z lesnictví pro rolníky. 1894. IV. 124.¹
— Pěstování porostů. 1898. IV. 124.¹
— Pěstování porostů lesů. 1894. IV. 111,¹ 381.
— Poměr lesních dřevin k stanovisku. 1891. IV. 70.
— Poměr rostlin ku stanovisku. 1891. IV. 69, 87.¹
— Přehled dějin lesů v Čechách v dobách historických dle letopočtu. 1893. IV. 28.¹
— Střídání dřevin. 1891. IV. 74.²
— Tvary lesů o Čechách a jejich poměr smíšení. 1892. IV. 372.
— Tvary porostů (lesů). 1894. IV. 142.
— Vliv hornin na vzrůst lesních dřevin. 1889. IV. 69.
— Zalesňování holin. 1890. IV. 167.²

— Zaleśňování holin. S přídavkem: jak se upevňují sklony (strže). 1890. IV. 547.²
— Zaleśňování pustých holin (stráně). 1892. IV. 167.²
— Žula, její poměr ku tvoření půdy. 1894. IV. 70.
Chailland. Dictionnaire raisonné des eaux et forêts. 1769. IV. 323.²
Chaire departementale d'agriculture du Loiret. · Publication. III. 19.
Chaix, Dominique. Plantae vapincenses. 1786. I. 406.
Chaix, Louis. Geschichte der Bourbon-Rose. 1851. III. 454.²
— Histoire du Rosier île Bourbon.. 1851. III. 454.²
Challan, A. D. J. B. Rapport analytique . . . d'examiner un ouvrage du citoyen Dettemar-Basse. 1801. IV. 522.²
Challis, T. Danger of placing earth round trees. 1875. III. 169.²
Chalmot, J. A. de. Vervolg op Chomels woordenboek. · 1786. III. 30.
Chalon, Jean. Die alten Oelbäume von Blidah in Algerien. 1872. II. 713.²
— Anatomie comparée des tiges ligneuses dicotylédones. 1867. I. 105.
— Les arbres monumentaux en Belgique. 1880. I. 296.²
— Ein Besuch bei den alten Kastanienbäumen des Etna. 1872. II. 124.²
— Cas de virescence du Rosa indica Lindl. 1867. II. 292.²
— Le Chêne de Cortessem. 1871. II. 138.²
— Le Chêne de Liernu. 1871. II. 138.²
— Chorise diplasique du Rosa canina. 1867. II. 289.²
— Détails anatomiques sur le Schinus Molle. 1867. II. 460.²
— Deux cas de prolification dans les Conifères. 1867. II. 19.
— Étude anatomique du Ricinus. 1867. II. 451.¹
— La graine des Légumineuses. 1875. II. 320.²
— Sur le groupement des vaisseaux dans le bois. 1867. I. 125.
— Le Jardin d'essai d'Alger. 1872. I. 68.²
— Das Leben der Pflanzenzelle von W. Hofmeister. 1867. I. 136.²
— Le manteau de la terre. 1868. I. 300.
— Matériaux pour servir à la détermination . . . par l'étude anatomique des tiges. 1867. I. 105.
— Un mot sur la germination du Gui. 1868. II. 179.¹
— Un mot sur la germination du Gui. 1871. II. 179.¹
— Un mot sur une monstruosité de Rosa. 1866. II. 293.¹
— Petites annotations botaniques. 1866. I. 270, II. 293,¹ 524,² 653.¹
— Petites annotations botaniques. 1867. II. 19, 289,² 292,² 451,¹ 460.²
— De la place des gymnospermes. 1869. II. 1.
— Quelques particularités . . . d'Aralia papyrifera. 1866. II. 653.²
— Quelques particularités de l'écorce de Hibiscus syriacus. 1866. II. 524.²
— Revue des Loranthacées. 1870. II. 172.²
— Structure de la cellule végétale. 186.? I. 138.¹
— Les vieux Oliviers de Blidah. 1872. II. 713.²
— Une visite aux Châtaigniers de l'Etna. 1872. II. 124.²
Chaloner, Edward & Fleming. The Mahogany tree. 1850. II. 422,¹ IV. 525.¹
Chalot, Ch. Le Cacaoyer. 1894. III. 593.¹
— Les Cacaoyères au Congo. 1899. III. 763.¹
— Le Cocotier au Congo. 1895. III. 800.¹
— Conservation de la faculté germinative des graines de Cacaoyer. 1899. III. 593.¹
— Sur la culture du Caoutchoutier de Céara. 1898.· III. 520.¹
— Culture du Giroflier. 1898. III. 635.²
— De la culture . . . du Manioc. 1898. III. 521.¹
— Étude sur le Caoutchoutier de Céara. 1897. III. 520.²
— Le Giroflier. 1897. III. 635.²
— Au sujet du Cacaoyer. 1898. III. 593.¹
— Au sujet du Kickxia africana Benth. 1897. III. 688.²
— See also LECOMTE, Henri & CHALOT, Ch.
Chamaedoreas as house plants. 1873. III. 321.²
Chamberet. See CHAUMETON, F. P., CHAMBERET & POIRET, J. L. M.
Chamberlain, Agnes F. The Maple amongst the Algonkian tribes. 1891. IV. 527.²
Chamberlain, Allen. Our forestal resources from an economic standpoint. 1897. IV. 272.
Chamberlain, Charles J. Contribution to the life history of Salix. 1897. II. 104.²
— Oogenesis in Pinus Laricio. 1899. II. 44.¹
— A remarkable macrospore. 1896. II. 104.²
— Winter characters of certain sporangia. 1898. I. 122.

Chamberlain, Houston Stewart. Recherches sur la sève ascendante. 1897. I. 166.
Chamberlain, Joseph Scudder. A comparative study of the styles of Compositae. 1891. II. 850.²
Chamberlaine, William. A practical treatise on the efficacy of Stizolobium. 1792. III. 482.¹
Chamberland, Ch. See JOUBERT, J. & CHAMBERLAND, Ch.
Chamberlayne, John. See The NATURAL history of coffee, thee, chocolate. 1682. III. 221.²
Chambers, R. An olde thrift newly revived. 1612. IV. 119.²
Chambers, William. De Ribes Arabum et ligno Rhodio. 1724. III. 244.
Chambers-Ketchum, Annie. See KETCHUM, Annie CHAMBERS-.
Chambers's Edinburgh journal. I. 17.
Chambers's journal of popular literature. See CHAMBERS's Edinburgh journal. I. 17.
Chambray, marquis de. L'art de cultiver les Pommiers. 1765. III. 426.¹
Chambray, Georges, marquis de. Gemmage du Pin maritime. 1847. IV. 468.¹
—Observations sur la culture du Pin silvestre. 1844. IV. 472.
— Sur le Pin d'Autriche. 1846. IV. 465.¹
— Traité pratique des arbres résineux conifères. 1845. IV. 441.
Chambrelent, Jules François. Assainissement et culture forestière. 1855. IV. 162.
—Assainissement et mise en valeur des landes de Gascogne. 1859. IV. 360.
— Effets de la sécheresse sur les cultures. 1893. III. 183.²
— Fixation des torrents. 1883. IV. 185.¹
— Fixation des torrents. 1886. IV. 163.
— Fixation des torrents. 1893. IV. 186.¹
— Les landes de Gascogne. 1859. IV. 360.
— Mémoire sur l'assainissement et la mise en valeur des landes de Gascogne. 1859. IV. 360.
— Mémoire sur les travaux de desséchement. 1863. III. 125.
— Mise en valeur des landes de Gascogne. 1859. IV. 360.
— Le reboisement et les travaux publics. · 1883. IV. 163.
— La repoblacion de los montes. 1883. IV. 163.
— Des soins de culture à donner aux forêts.· 1883. IV. 163.
Chamier, George. Australian timber. 1887. IV. 401.²
Chamisso, Adalbert von. Arcticae quae supersunt. 1831. I. 455.
— Bemerkungen und Ansichten auf einer Entdeckungs-Reise. 1821. I. 302.
— Melastomaceae americanae. 1836. II. 634.²
— Plantae Ecklonianae: Gentianearum . . . descriptiones. 1833. I. 494.
— Plantae Ecklonianae: Rosaceae. 1831. I. 494.
— Ex plantis in expeditione Romanzoffiana. . . . genera tria. 1820. II. 863.²
— Reise um die Welt mit der Romanzoffischen Entdeckungs-Expedition. 1821. I. 302.
— Spicilegium plantarum . . . praesertim brasiliensium. 1833. I. 341.
—Uebersicht der nutzbarsten und der schädlichsten Gewächse. 1027. III. 70.
— See also SCHLECHTENDAL, D. F. L. von & CHAMISSO, Adalbert von.
— Schlechtendal, D. F.· L. von and others. De plantis in expeditione speculatoria Romanzoffiana observatis. 1826. I. 302.
Champglin, Rouault de. Aperçu d'économie forestière. 1881. IV. 270.
— De l'emploi des mathématiques en sylviculture. 1882. IV. 59.¹
Champier, Simphorien. Campus Elysius Galliae amoenitate refertus. 1533. I. 276, V. XIV.²
— Hortus gallicus. 1533. I. 276, V. XIV.²
Champignons attaquant le Sapin. 1900. IV. 212.
Champion, John George. Remarks on the state of botany in Ceylon.· 1843. I. 476.¹
— The ternstroemiaceous plants of Hong Kong. 1853. II. 547.²
— See also GARDNER, George & CHAMPION, J. G.
—& Bentham, George. Florula hongkongensis. 1851. I. 460.²
Champion, Paul. Fabrication des cordes de Bambou.· 1866 III. 315.¹
— Fabrication du vert de Chine. 1866. III. 542.²

Champion, William. Rough notes on Ceylon scenery. 1841. II. 152.[1]

Champlain, Samuel de. Narrative of a voyage to the West Indies and Mexico. 1859. I. 329.

— Œuvres publiées sous le patronage de l'Université Laval. 1870. III. 261.[2]

Champoiseau. Note sur l'éducation des vers à soie. 1858. III. 377.

Champouillon. Note sur les moyens d'améliorer par culture les vertus de quelques plantes médicinales. 1860. III. 150.[1]

Champs de tir en forêts. Rapport. 1897. IV. 293.[1]

Champsaur, Marie Gabriel Léon. Restauration et conservation des terrains en montagne. 1900. IV. 186.[1]

Champy, P. Flore algérienne. 1844. I. 484.

Chancerel, L. Considérations générales sur les forêts de l'Algérie. 1885. IV. 379.[1]

— L'usufruit des domaines forestiers. 1894. IV. 326, 399.[1]

— De l'usufruit des forêts. 1893. IV. 314.[1]

Le chancre de l'Aune blanc. 1899. IV. 489.[2]

Le chancre des Peupliers du Canada. 1898. IV. 486.[1]

Le chancre du Peuplier. 1899. IV. 485.[2]

Chancre du Robinier Faux Acacia. 1900. IV. 524.[1]

Chandler, Alfred. Camellia britannica. 1825. II. 550.[2]

— & **Booth**, W. B. Illustrations and descriptions of . . . Camellieae. 1831. II. 550.[2]

Chandler, Charles H. Notes and a query concerning the Ericaceae. 1892. II. 659.[1]

Chandler, W. H. Appliancoes . . . for the preservation of wood. 1890. IV. 421.

Chandra Kumar Chatterjee. The Korai Teak forest. 1882. IV. 537.[1]

Changes at the Nancy forest school. 1888. IV. 34.[2]

On **changes** of temperature in plants. 1830. I. 186.

Changing dwarf Pears to standards. 1874. III. 172.

Chanoine d'Avrilly. Du Myzoxile. 1834. III. 427.[1]

Chantelat, A. Catalogue des plantes . . . de la Teste-de-Buch. 1843. I. 410.

Chanthopoulos, S. See ΧΑΝΘΌΠΟΥΛΟΣ, Σ.

Chantin, Auguste. Du rôle de l'électricité. 1892. I. 231.[2]

Chantrier, frères. Croton-und Dracaena-Arten. 1882. III. 334.[2]

Chanvalon, Jean Baptiste Thibault de. Voyage à la Martinique. 1763. I. 334, III. 266.

Le **Chanvre** de Sisal. 1900. III. 341.[1]

Chapais, Jean Charles. The Canadian forester's illustrated guide. 1885. IV. 111,[2] V. xxx.[1]

— Guide illustré du sylviculteur canadien. 1883. V. xxx.[1]

Chapeaux en bois. 1896. IV. 429.[1]

Chapel, Edmond. Le caoutchouc et la gutta percha. 1892. III. 231.

Chapelain, de. Extrait d'une lettre sur le Châtaignier. 1854. IV. 493.[1]

Chapelle, Édouard LAMY DE LA. See LAMY DE LA CHAPELLE, Édouard.

Chapin, F. H. The first ascent of a glacier in Colorado 1887. I. 325.

— Mountaineering in Colorado. 1889. V. xviii.[1]

Chapin, Loring D. Hand-book of plants and fruits. 1843. I. 94.

— The vegetable kingdom. 1843. I. 94.

Chapins lumber reckoner. 1883. IV. 228.

Chapman. Report on the Olive tree . . . of Tuscany. 1896. III. 679.[1]

Chapman, Alvan Wentworth. An enumeration of some plants . . . of Florida. 1878. I. 319.

— Flora of the southern United States. 1860. I. 319.

— Torreya taxifolia Arnott. 1885. II. 12.[1]

Chapman, James. Travels in the interior of South Africa. See SANDERSON, John & ARMITAGE, Edward. 1858. I. 494.

Chapman, Robert. On the cultivation of the Granadilla. 1822. III. 616.[3]

Chapoteaut. Sur un glucoside du Boldo. 1884. III. 403.[3]

Chapotin. Lettre sur quelques médicaments employés à l'Isle-de-France. 1815. III. 617.[1]

Chapotte. L'agriculture et les forêts dans le sud de Madagascar. 1898. IV. 380.[1]

Chappellier, Paul. Note sur culture antiphylloxérique. 1884. III. 573.

— Nouveau système de culture de la Vigne. 188.? III. 572.

Chappuis, Brun. The manual of the Swiss vigneron. 1834. III. 558.[1]

Chaptal, Jean Antoine Claude, comte de. Chemistry applied to agriculture. 1823. III. 36.[3]

— Chimie appliquée à l'agriculture. 1823. III. 36.[3]

— Instructions sur la manière d'extraire le goudron. 179.? IV. 436.[1]

— Observations chimiques sur la couleur jaune . . . des végétaux. 1799. III. 368.[2]

— & others. Theoretisch-praktische Abhandlung über den Weinbau. 1801. III. 554.[2]

— Traité . . . sur la culture de la Vigne. 1801. III. 554.[2]

— A treatise on the culture of the Vine. 1801. III. 554.[2]

— De Vitiis cultura. 1801. III. 554.[2]

Chapters on propagating by a nurseryman. 1886. IV. 149.[2]

Charabot, Eugène. Sur l'évolution des composés terpéniques. 1900. III. 491.[2]

— Genèse des composés terpéniques dans la Lavande. 1900. III. 698.[1]

— Recherches sur le développement progressif de l'essence de Bergamote. 1899. III. 501.[3]

— & **Dupont**, J. & **Pillet**, L. Les huiles essentielles. 1899. I. 182.[1]

Characters of trees. See LAPORT, J. 1793. I. 516.

Charante, W. E. van & **Buijn**, G. Thee kultuur . . . Nederlandsch-Indie. 1876. III. 602.[1]

Charas, Moyse. Histoire naturelle des animaux, des plantes. 1668. I. 286, V. xvi.[1]

— Operum tomus tertius, continens historiam naturalem animalium. 1668. I. 286.

— Pharmacopée royale galénique. 1676. III. 255.[2]

— Pharmacopœa regia galenica et chymica. 1676. III. 255.[2]

— The royal pharmacopœa, galenical. 1676. III. 255.[2]

— Thériaque d'Andromaous avec une description particulière des plantes. 1668. I. 286, V. xvi.[1]

Le **charbon** de bois dans l'Argentine. 1898. IV. 395.

Charbonnier. Note sur l'Oba. 1870. III. 508.[1]

Charcoal for gunpowder. 1877. IV. 492.[1]

Charcoal for gunpowder. 1888. IV. 432.[1]

On **charcoal** from different woods. 1824. IV. 431.[2]

Chardt, Jan. See CHADT, Jan.

Charente — **Société d'horticulture de la**. See SOCIÉTÉ . . . III. 21.

Chareyre, Jules. Sur la formation des cystolithes et leur résorption. 1883. I. 139.

— Nouvelles recherches sur les cystolithes. 1884. I. 139.

— Sur l'origine et la formation trichomatiques de quelques cystolithes. 1883. I. 139.

Charguéraud, A. Degli alberi e arbusti ornamentali da aria aperta. 1898. III. 203.

— Les arbres de la ville de Paris. 1896. III. 210.

— Des arbres et arbrisseaux d'ornement. 1898. III. 173,[1] 203.

— Les arbres et les arbrisseaux dans les jardins. 1897. III. 207.[2]

— Ceinture d'élagage. 1894. III. 171.

— Le cernage des arbres. 1889. III. 166.

— Du choix des arbres les plus convenables pour les plantations d'alignement. 1896. III. 210.

— Le dépérissement des arbres dans Paris. 1893. III. 212.[1]

— Après la gelée. 1891. III. 182.

— Les Hydrangéas à inflorescences énormes. 1897. III. 411.[2]

— Les Marronniers qui refleurissent. 1890. III. 537.[1]

— Note sur une opération concernant l'arboriculture. 1885. III. 171.

— Observations sur quelques arbustes à feuillage. 1892. III. 206.[2]

— Orientation des jeunes arbres transplantés. 1896. III. 168.

— Ornementation arborigène. 1892. III. 203.

— De la plantation. 1885. III. 171.

— Principales conditions favorables à la reprise des arbres. 1888. III. 166.

— Quelques végétaux à écorce colorée. 1894. III. 208.[3]

— Soins à donner aux arbustes rustiques en massifs. 1893. III. 124.[2]

— & **Baltet**, Charles. La taille des arbres et arbrisseaux d'ornement. 1888. III. 171.

Charin, Ed. Le Cassis, culture et usages. 1897. III. 415.[1]

Charlard, Antoine François BOUTRON-. See BOUTRON-CHARLARD, A. F.

Charlemagne, E. La dune de Quiberon. 1898. IV. 146.[1]

— La forêt de Bellême. 1900. IV. 362.

— La forêt de Bercé. 1899. IV. 362.

— La forêt de Bourse. 1898. IV. 362.

— La forêt de Perseigne. 1899. IV. 362.

— La forêt domaniale d'Écouves. 1898. IV. 362.
— La forêt domaniale des Andaines. 1898. IV. 362.
— Les forêts domaniales d'Ille-et-Vilaine. 1900. IV. 362.
— Les forêts domaniales du Finistère. 1897. IV. 362.
— See also DAUBRÉE & CHARLEMAGNE, E.
— & others. Chênes-liége. 1894. IV. 379.²
Charlemagne, Ph. Étude sur l'urgence des travaux de restauration . . . de l'Isère. 1886. IV. 185.²
Charles, E. La nitrification. 1898. IV. 145.
Charleston—Elliott society of natural history. See ELLIOTT . . . I. 5.
Charlevoix, Pierre François Xavier de. Allgemeine Geschichte und Beschreibung von Neu-Frankreich. 1744. III. 261.²
— Description des plantes principales de l'Amérique septentrionale. 1744. I. 305.
— Histoire . . . de la Nouvelle France. 1744. III. 261.²
— Histoire . . . du Japon. 1736. III. 273.²
— History and general description of New France. 1744. III. 262.¹
Charlton, Andrew & others. Correspondence regarding the discovery of the Tea plant of Assam. 1841. II. 552.¹
Charmeux, Constant. Moyen d'obtenir sur les Vignes . . . d'aussi bons raisins. 1859. III. 555.
Charollois, Cl. Instructions pratiques sur la taille . . . des arbres fruitiers. 18 . . ? III. 171.
Charpentier, Paul. Le bois. 1890. IV. 396.²
Charpentier de Cossigny. See COSSIGNY DE PALMA, J. F. C.
La charpie de bois. 1886. IV. 429.
Charrel, J. Traité de la culture du Mûrier. 1840. III. 376.
Charrier, (sr. & jr.). Instruction sur la culture du Mûrier. 1840. III. 375.
Charron, J. Cocos Weddeliana. 1879. III. 324.¹
Charroppin, Georges. Étude sur le Plaqueminier. 1873. II. 701.¹
Charroppin, Paul. Étude sur le Quinquina cuprea. 1883. III. 747.¹
Charsley, Fanny Anne. The wild flowers around Melbourne. 1867. I. 502.
Chartier, Louis. Contrirutions [sic] à la flore de Carcassonne. 1892. I. 417.
Chase, A. W. Timber belts of the Pacific coast. 1874. IV. 336.²
Chase, C. Thurston. The prairie fruit culturist. 1859. III. 133.
Chasiotes, Spyridon. See ΧΑΣΙΩΤΗΣ, Σπυρίδων.
La chasse aux hannetons. 1892. IV. 203.
Chasseloup, F., DUVILLERS-. See DUVILLERS-CHASSELOUP, F.
Chassenon. Mémoire sur l'emploi des baies de Myrtille. 1841. III. 664.¹
Chastaingt, Gabriel. Catalogue des plantes vasculaires des environs de la Chatre. 1883. I. 416.
Description de deux Rosiers de la soussection Caninae hispidae. 1888. II. 286.¹
— Prodrome d'une monographie des Roses d'Indre-et-Loire. 1890. II. 286.¹
— Quelques mots de l'historique des Rosiers. 1883. II. 286.¹
— Résultats d'études nouvelles relatives aux flores rhodologiques . . . de l'Indre. 1890. II. 286.¹
— Variabilité . . . de quelques formes . . . de Rosiers. 1890. II. 286.¹
Chastenay, Victorine de. Calendrier de flore. 1802. I. 265.
Chate, E., (jr.). Culture pratique des Lantanas. 1864. III. 696.²
Chateauvieux, Frédéric Lullin de. Du défrichement des bois. 1836. IV. 362.
Chateauvieux, MICHELI DE. See MICHELI DE CHATEAUVIEUX.
Chatel, Rémy. De la famille des Bixacées. 1880. II. 568.²
Chatel, Victor. Apparition de la maladie de la Vigne. 1861. III. 577.
— Dégâts causés aux végétaux par les acarus. 1875. III. 190.
— Maladie des Poiriers. 1860. III. 419.¹
— Notice sur la maladie de la Vigne. . 1855. III. 576.
— Nouvelles observations sur la maladie de la Vigne. 1863. III. 577.
— Nouvelles recherches sur la Pomme de terre. 1861. III. 577.
Chatelain, E. Agriculture et forêts. Fossés horizontaux. 1900. III. 151.
Chatenay, Abel. Les végétaux ligneux de plein air. 1893. III. 84.²
Chatenay, H. Greffe mixte. 1880. III. 162.
Chatenier, Constant. Esquisse de la flore de Lus-la-Croix-Haute. 1897. I. 418.

Chater, J. J. Aucuba berries poisonous to robins. 1867. III. 644.¹
— Les baies de l'Aucuba sont-elles vénéneuses? 1867. III. 644.²
Chatin, Gaspard Adolphe. Anatomie comparée des végétaux. 1856. I. 100.²
— Anatomie comparée végétale appliquée à la classification. 1840. I. 251.
— Sur l'anatomie des Santalacées. 1857. II. 168.
— De l'appareil spécial de nutrition des espèces parasites phanérogames. 1879. I. 233.²
— L'arbre à cidre dans la prairie. 1898. III. 426.²
— Sur les arbres et arbustes truffiers. 1869. I. 233.²
— Des caractères . . . anatomiques des Cytinées. 1863. II. 181.¹
— Sur les caractères anatomiques des rhizomes. 1859. I. 105.
— Causes de la déhiscence.des anthères. 1870. I. 116.²
— Le Châtaignier. 1870. III. 359.¹
— Le Chêne blanc de Provence. 1873. IV. 503.²
— Le Chêne pubescent et la truffe. 1875. II. 135.¹
— Contribution à la biologie des plantes parasites. 1891. I. 233.²
— Les Erica de la flore de Paris. 1882. II. 664.²
— Essai sur la mesure du degré d'élevation . . . des espèces végétales. 1855. I. 99.
— Sur une essence forestière très-repandue. 1873. IV. 503.²
— Études anatomiques et physiologiques sur les sucs nourriciers. 1860. I. 151.¹
— Études de physiologie végétale. 1845. I. 147.
— Études expérimentales sur l'action des sels. 1852. I. 158.
— Études sur la respiration des fruits. 1864. I. 170.
— Études sur la symétrie générale des organes des végétaux. 1847. I. 99.
— Sur l'existence d'un appareil préhenseur . . . dans les plantes parasites. 1879. I. 233.²
— Existence d'une troisième membrane dans les anthères. 1866. I. 116.²
— De l'existence de fibres corticales. 1865. I. 133.
— Faits généraux de l'anatomie des Loranthées. 1861. II. 173.²
— Formation du genre Dufrenoya. 1860. II. 168,² 169.¹
— La gradation ou perfection des espèces végétales. 1898. I. 529.
— Over Java-Thee. 1853. III. 602.¹
— Localisation des cellules fibreuses dans quelques anthères. 1866. I. 116.²
— Sur une maladie climatérique des Châtaigniers. 1872. III. 359.²
— Maladie de la Vigne. 1854. III. 576.
— Maladie de la Vigne, observations et expériences. 1854. III. 576.
— Mémoire sur les Limnanthées et les Coriariées. 1854. II. 454.¹
— Mémoire sur les Limnanthées et les Coriariées. 1856. II. 454.¹
— De la multiplicité des parties homologues dans ses rapports avec la gradation des végétaux. 1893. I. 253.¹
— Du nombre et de la symétrie des faisceaux fibrovasculaires. 1897. I. 134.¹
— Du nombre et de la symétrie des faisceaux libéro-ligneux du pétiole. 1897. I. 111.
— Du nombre et de la symétrie des faisceaux libérovasculaires du pétiole. 1897. I. 112.¹
— Sur le nombre et la symétrie des faisceaux libéro-ligneux des appendices. 1897. I. 111.
— Note sur l'existence de cellules cristallifères. 1856. I. 133.²
— Notice sur les travaux scientifiques. 1866. V. VII.¹
— Ordre des Thésiacées ou Santalacées. 1860. II. 168.¹
— Organogénie comparée de l'androcée. 1873. I. 116.²
— Le Pin de Riga. 1865. II. 46.²
— Le Pin noir ou Pin d'Autriche. 1867. IV. 466.¹
— Des placentoïdes, nouvel organe des anthères. 1866. I. 116.²
— Les plantes montagnardes de la flore parisienne. 1886. I. 417.
— Des proportions de sucre . . . dans la sève. 1864. I. 175.
— Quelques considérations sur les théories de l'accroissement par couches concentriques. 1840. I. 127.²
— De quelques faits généraux qui se dégagent de l'androgénie comparée. 1874. I. 116.²
— Rapport . . . sur un nouveau procédé de culture du Chêne-Liège. 1882. IV. 516.²

Chatin, Gaspard Adolphe (*continued*).
— Des rapports de l'anatomie des Thésiacées. 1860. II. 168.[1]
— Recherche des rapports entre l'ordre de naissance et l'ordre de déhiscence des étamines. 1854. I. 116.[1]
— Recherches anatomiques . . . sur les sucs nourriciers. 1860. I. 151.[1]
— Recherches de lois . . . qui lient l'avortement des étamines. 1855. I. 116.[1]
— Recherches des lois . . . entre l'ordre de naissance et l'ordre déhiscence des androcées. 1855. I. 116.[1]
— Recherches expérimentales relatives à l'action qu'exercent . . . les sels. 1854. I. 158.
— Recherches sur le développement . . . de l'anthère. 1862. I. 116.[1]
— Remarques sur une réclamation de priorité. 1860. I. 99.
— La respiration des végétaux. 1885. I. 171.
— Signification de l'existence et de la symétrie de l'axe. 1896. I. 100.[2]
— Signification de l'existence et de la symétrie des appendices. 1897. I. 100,[2] 253.[1]
— Signification de l'hermaphrodisme. 1894. I. 253.[1]
— Signification de la localisation des organes. 1893. I. 253.[1]
— Signification de la variété des organes. 1893. I. 253.[1]
— Structure et fonctions de la cloison des logettes de l'anthère. 1866. I. 116.[2]
— Le Terfezia Leonis dans les Landes. 1898. III. 613.[1]
— Thé de Java. 1853. III. 602.[1]
— Sur la tige des Misodendron. 1865. II. 167.[2]
— Sur les types obdiplostémone et diplostémone. 1855. I. 114.[1]
— Sur les types obdiplostémone et diplostémone direct. 1856. I. 116.[1]
— Les Vignes françaises. 1888. III. 561.
— *See also* FILHOL, Édouard & CHATIN, Adolphe.
— & **Filhol**, Édouard. Recherches sur les matières colorantes des feuilles. 1863. I. 185.[1]
— & **Hitier**, H. L'arbre à cidre dans la prairie. 1898. III. 426.[1]
— & others. Des circonstances qui déterminent la production des plantes à fleurs doubles. 1880. I. 145.[2]
Chatin, Joannes. Sur le développement et la structure des glandes foliaires intérieures. 1875. I. 112.[2]
— Études histologiques . . . sur les glandes foliaires. 1875. I. 135.
— Études sur le développement de l'ovule. 1874. I. 122.
— Sur les mouvements périodiques des feuilles dans l'Abies Nordmanniana. 1876. II. 23.[1]
— Observations sur l'anatomie du Tanghinia venenifera. 1873. II. 733.[2]
— On the periodical movements of the leaves in Abies Nordmanniana. 1876. II. 23.[1]
— Recherches pour servir à l'histoire botanique . . . du tanguin de Madagascar. 1873. III. 691.[1]
Chatterjee, CHANDRA KUMAR. *See* CHANDRA KUMAR CHATTERJEE.
Chaubard, Louis Anastase. *See* FAUCHÉ, BRONGNIART, Adolphe, CHAUBARD, L. A. & BORY DE SAINT-VINCENT, J. B. M.
— & **Bory de Saint-Vincent**, J. B. M. Nouvelle flore du Péloponnèse. 1838. I. 449.
Chaudey. Les chablis dans les taillis du Jura. 1897. IV. 518.[1]
Le **chauffeur**. *See* Le TECHNOLOGISTE. III. 23.[1]
Chauffourt, Jacques de. Instruction sur le faict des eaues et forests. 1642. IV. 323.[2]
Chaulmugra oil. *See* MURRAY, J. A. 1893. III. 614.[2]
Chaumeton, François Pierre, **Chamberet** & **Poiret**, J. L. M. Flore médicale. 1814. III. 55.
Chauny — **Société de pomologie et d'arboriculture**. *See* SOCIÉTÉ . . . III. 22.
Chautard, Jules. Classification des bandes d'absorption de la chlorophylle. 1873. I. 141.
— Examen des différences présentées par le spectre de la chlorophylle. 1873. I. 141.
— Influence des rayons de diverses couleurs sur le spectre de la chlorophylle. 1873. I. 141.
— Modifications du spectre de la chlorophylle. 1873. I. 141.
— Recherches sur le spectre de la chlorophylle. 1873. I. 141.
— Recherches sur le spectre de la chlorophylle. 1875. I. 141.
— Recherches sur les raies de la chlorophylle. 1872. I. 141.
Chautauquan. III. 3.

Chauveau, A. Code forestier. 1827. IV. 323.[2]
Chauveaud, L. Gustave. Sur les caractères internes de la graine des Vignes. 1894. II. 506.[1]
— Sur le développement des tubes criblés. 1895. I. 134.[1]
— Mécanisme des mouvements provoqués du Berberis. 1894. II. 202.[2]
— Moyen d'assurer . . . la germination des Vignes. 1894. III. 548.[2]
— Recherches embryogéniques . . . des Euphorbiacées. 1891. I. 136,[1] *II. 455.[1]*
— Recherches sur le mode de formation des tubes criblés. 1896. I. 134.[1]
— Recherches sur le mode de formation des tubes criblés. 1900. I. 104, *134.[2]*
Chauvière. *See* LEMAIRE, Charles & CHAUVIÈRE.
Chauvin, P. S. Le Quinquina colonial. 1886. III. 712.[2]
Chauzit, B. Étude sur l'adaptation au sol des Vignes américaines. 1889. III. 556.
— Les Vignes américaines en terrain gypseux. 1892. III. 557.[1]
Chavánne, Josef. Pflanzen- und Thierleben im tropischen Ur walde Amerika's. 1877. I. 330.
Chavannes, Dan Alex. Sur un cône de Sapin monstrueux. 1846. II. 23.[2]
Chavannes, Édouard. Chamoerops [*sic*] humilis. 1854. II. 67.[1]
— Introduction à la flore helvétique de Mr. Gaudin. 1830. I. 433.
Chavannes de la Giraudière, H. de. Comment on peut cultiver . . . le Mûrier. 1845. III. 376.
Chavée-Leroy. La maladie de la Vigne. 1881. III. 378, *560, 578.*
Chavegrin, A. Mode de nutrition des Cupulifères. 1886. IV. 74.[1]
— Un nouveau service forestier sous les tropiques. 1892. IV. 295.[2]
Chavin. Rapport sur quelques plantes rares . . . à Compesières. 1855. I. 435.
Chazotte, Peter Stephen. Facts and observations on the culture of Vines, Olives. 1821. III. 117.[2]
Cheal, J. Practical fruit culture. 1892. III. 142.
Cheek, A. H. Experiment at propagating plants by leaves. 1846. III. 693.[1]
— On the juice of Euphorbia ligularia. 1854. III. 518.[1]
Cheeseman, Thomas F. On the botany of the Pirongia Mountain. 1880. I. 507.
— On the botany of the Titirangi district. 1872. I. 507.
— Contributions to a flora of the Nelson provincial district. 1882. I. 507.
— Description of a new species of Loranthus. 1881. II. 175.[2]
— Description of a new species of Senecio. 1875. II. 865.[2]
— Description of three new species of Coprosma. 1886. II. 815.[1]
— On the flora of the Kermadec Islands. 1888. I. 508.[1]
— On the flora of the North Cape district. 1897. I. 508.[1]
— The naturalized plants of the Auckland provincial district. 1883. I. 507.
— On the New Zealand species of Coprosma. 1887. II. 815.[1]
— Notes on the fertilization of Knightia. 1882. II. 163.[2]
— Notes on the Three Kings Islands. 1888. I. 508.[1]
— On some hitherto unrecorded plant-stations. 1882. I. 536.[1]
— On some plants new to the New Zealand flora. 1897. I. 508.[1]
— On some recent additions to the New Zealand flora. 1892. I. 508.[1]
Chefdebien, de. Sur l'emploi du sulfure de carbone. 1874. III. 566.[1]
Chefdebien, baron de. Le sulfurie. 1899. III. 582.
Chelchowski, Stanislaw. Flora kwiatowa W. Ks. Poznańskiego. 1887. I. 390.
— Materiały k florje jawnobracznych rastenij Prasznyszskago ujezda. 1886. I. 364.
Cheldraich, Theodoros. *See* ΧΕΛΔΡΑΪΞ, Θεόδωρος.
Chelmicki, St. Zużytkowanie drzewa. 1888. IV. 426.[2]
Chemical analysis of coffee. 1865. III. 740.[2]
— analysis of true oil of Roses. 1831. III. 454.[1]
Chemical gazette. I. 17.
Chemical news. *See* CHEMICAL gazette. I. 17.
Chemical society of London. Journal. Quarterly journal. I. 17.
Chemical society of London. Memoirs. III. 757.[1]
Chemical substances and products of India. 1863. III. 278.
Les **chemins** de fer vicinaux belges. 1900. IV. 285.[1]

Chemins en terrains sablonneux. 1898. IV. 390.[1]
Chemisch-pharmaceutisch archief. I. 15.
Chemisch-pharmaceutisches Central-Blatt. See PHARMACEUTISCHES Central-Blatt. I. 14, III. 13.
Chemische Untersuchung der Tagua-Nuss. 1844. III. 330.[1]
Chemische Untersuchung des Gerbstoffgehalts schweizerischer Lohrinden. 1885. IV. 435.
Chemisches Central-Blatt. See PHARMACEUTISCHES Central-Blatt. I. 14, III. 13.
The Chemist and druggist. I. 18.
Chemnitius, Johannes. Index plantarum circa Brunsvigam. 1652. · I. 372.
Chemnitz — Naturwissenschaftliche Gesellschaft. See NATURWISSENSCHAFTLICHE . . . I. 13.
Le Chêne de Charles-Quint. 1894. IV. 559.[2]
Le Chêne de juin. 1899. · IV. 509.
Chêne de Labes. 1839. II. 138.[1]
Le Chêne de Liernu. 1898. IV. 516.[1]
Chêne dit Hêchelet de Spa. 1859. II. 138.[1]
Le Chêne rouge d'Amérique. 1895. IV. 516.[1]
Chêne rouge d'Amérique, var. ambigua. 1899. IV. 516.[2]
Le Chêne rouge en Ardenne. 1897. IV. 516.[2]
Le Chêne rouge en pépinière. 1898; IV. 516.[2]
Le Chêne scarlet (écarlate), Quercus coccinea. 1855. IV. 503.[1]
Chênes-Liége; notices sur les forêts domaniales de l'Algérie. 1894. · IV. 517.[2]
Cheney, Lellen Sterling. A contribution to the flora of the Lake Superior region. 1893. I. 316.
— Investigations on Pine and Oak wood. 1894. II. 40,[1] 131.[2]
— & True, R. H. On the flora of Madison. 1893. I. 316.
Chenon, L. J. See DASSOW. C. M. & CHENON, L. J.
Chenot. Note sur les moyens de combattre la maladie de la Vigne. 1851. III. 575.[2]
Cher — Société d'agriculture du département . . . See SOCIÉTÉ . . . III. 21.
Cherbourg — Société d'horticulture. See SOCIÉTÉ . . . III. 21.
Cherbourg — Société impériale des sciences naturelles . . . See SOCIÉTÉ . . . I. 23.
Chérbourg — Société nationale académique. See SOCIÉTÉ . . . I. 23.
Chéreau, Achille. Examen des Roses officinales. 1826. III. 454.[1]
— Note pour faire suite à l'examen des Roses officinales. 1830. III. 454.[1]
— Notice sur le jardin des apothicaires à Londres. 1832. I. 522.[1]
— Rapport sur le Journal de pharmacie. 1832. III. 520.[1]
— Remarques sur la queroie. 1829. IV. 503.[1]
— & Guibourt, N. J. B. G. Note sur la maune. 1828. III. 221.[1]
The Cherkley Yews. 1885. II. 11.[1]
Cherler, Johann Heinrich. See BAUHIN, Johann & CHERLER, J. H.
Chernoviz, Pedro Luiz Napoleão. Formulario ou guia medica. 1841. III. 247.[1]
The Cherokee Rose. 1876. III. 455.[2]
The Cherokee Rose. 1888. III. 455.[2]
The Cherokee Rose. 1895. III. 455.[2]
Cherrier, H. de. Projet de règlement forestier algérien. 1861. IV. 295.[2]
— Statistique forestière de la province d'Oran. 1856. IV. 379.[1]
Cherry, Edgar & Co. Redwood and lumbering in California forests. 1884. IV. 382,[2] 434.[1]
Cherry, J. W. The Moreau pattern charcoal kiln. 1894. IV. 395.
Cherry-blossom. 1878. III. 432.[1]
Chervau, M. Une excursion en Macédoine. 1867. IV. 375.[2]
— La Thessalie. 1882. IV. 375.[2]
Cherville, G. de. Le Houx. 1887. III. 530.[1]
Cheshire — Historic society of Lancashire . . . See HISTORIC . . . I. 18.
Chesnecophorus, Johannes. Disputatio physica de plantis. 1621. III. 53.
— Disputatio physica decima nona de plantis. 1626. III. 53.
Chesnel, Adolphe, marquis de. Histoire de la Rose. 1820. III. 443.
— La Rose chez les différents peuples. 1838. III. 448.
Chesnon, C. G. Statistique du département de l'Eure. Botanique. 1846. I. 410.

Chesnut, Victor King. Abrus poisoning. 1897. III. 462.[2]
— The broad-leaf Laurel. 1898. III. 652.[2]
— The Mountain Laurel poisonous. 1898. III. 652.[2]
— Preliminary catalogue of plants poisonous to stock. 1899. III. 63.[1]
— Principal poisonous plants of the United States. 1898. III. 63.[1]
— Some common poisonous plants. 1897. III. 63.[1]
— Thirty poisonous plants of the United States. 1898. III. 63.[1]
Chester, E. G. Note on Pushundi landslip. 1899. IV. 188.
— The tapping of Rubber trees. 1900. III. 370.[2]
Chester, Grace D. Bau und Function der Spaltöffnungen. 1897. · I. 132.[1]
— Sulla struttura e sulla funzione degli stomi. 1897. I. 132.
Chester society of natural science and literature. Annual reports. Proceedings. I. 18.
Chestnut, Victor King. See CHESNUT, V. K.
The Chestnut. 1842. III. 360.[1]
Chestnut flour. 1890. III. 360.[1]
The Chestnut Oak. 1893. III. 362.[2]
The Chestnut-tree. 1890. II. 123.[1]
A Chestnut-tree in Llewellyn Park, New Jersey. 1893. II 123.[2]
Chestnuts, horse and sweet. 1881. II. 125,[1] 481.[1]
Chevalier. See SONNINI, VEILLARD & CHEVALIER.
Chevalier. See also CHEVALIER.
Chevalier, A. Observations sur . . . la matière colorante des baies de Sureau. 1820. III. 752.[1]
— See also PAYEN, Anselme & CHEVALIER.
Chevalier, Auguste. L'Arbre à fausse gutta de la Casamance. 1900. III. 686.[2]
— Catalogue des plantes . . . de Domfront. 1894. I. 535.
— Sur la coagulation des latex des Apocynacées. 1900. II. 722.[2]
— Les cultures indigènes dans l'Afrique occidentale française. 1900. III. 131.[2]
— Deux plantes intéressantes . . . de la Mayenne. 1897. II. 670.[1] ·
— Mon exploration botanique de la Sénégambie. 1900. I. 491.
— Mon exploration botanique du Soudan français. 1900. I. 491.
— Nos connaissances actuelles sur la géographie botanique . . . du Sénégal. 1900. III. 93.[2]
— Recherches et observations sur la flore . . . de Domfront. 1897. I. 418.
— La structure générale . . . des Myricacées. 1898. II. 111.[1]
— La végétation de la région de Tombouctou. 1900. I. 491.
— Les zones . . . de l'Afrique occidentale. 1900. I. 491.
— Les Bougainvillea. 1900. III. 388.[1]
Chevalier, Charles. Aralia elegantissima. 1899. III. 642.[1]
— Les cultures fruitières . . . de Seine-et-Oise. 1890. III. 144.
— L'horticulture au temps des Romains. 1884. III. 32.[2]
Chevalier, E. Notice sur la longévité . . . de quelques arbres 1870. I. 295.[1]
— Restauration et aménagement des forêts. 1806. IV. 109.[1]
Chevalier, Jean Damien. Lettres à M. de Jean. 1752. III. 63.[2]
Chevalier, Ludwig. Der deutsche Mythus in der Pflanzenwelt. 1876. I. 518.
Chevalier. De bladluis van den Perzikboom. 1880. III. 441.[2]
— La grise du Pêcher. 1880. III. 441.[2]
Chevalier, A. & Lassaigne, J. L.
Chevalier, A. & Lassaigne, J. L. Notice sur les graines du faux Ébénier. 1818. III. 480.[2]
Chevalier, Alphonse. Du café chicorée. 1849. III. 739.
— Du Café, son historique. 1862. III. 739.
— Dictionnaire des altérations et falsifications. 1850. III. 213.[2]
— Mémoire sur le chocolat. 1871. III. 594.
— & Pelletan, Gabriel. Note sur le Zanthoxylum des Caraïbes. 1856. III. 506.[1]
— Zanthopicrite. 1827. III. 506.[1]
Chevallier, Auguste & Lassaigne, J. L. Analyse des baies de l'If. 1818. II. 10.[2]
Chevallier, François Fulgis. Flore générale des environs de Paris. 1826. I. 408.
Chevallier, Jean Baptiste Alphonse. Résumé des travaux entrepris sur les fruits du Marronnier d'Inde. 1848. III. 538.[1]
— Richard, Achille & Guillemin, J. A. Dictionnaire des drogues simples et composées. 1827. III. 242.

Chevallier, L., **Duchesne**, Émile & **Reynal**. Mémoire sur l'If. 1855. III. 288.[2]
Chevallier, Louis. Contributions à la flore de la Sarthe. 1890. II. 179.[2]
— Excursion au Puy de Sancy. 1891. I. 417.
— Notes sur la flore du Sahara. 1900. I. 486.
Chevandier, Eugène. Considérations générales sur la culture forestière en France. 1847. IV. 359.[2]
— Note . . . sur la composition élémentaire des différents bois. 1846. IV. 413.[1]
— Note sur les ravages produits en 1848 par l'orgye. 1849. IV. 209.[1]
— Note sur les travaux de reboisement, exécutés dans les Vosges. 1847. IV. 161.[2]
—? Note sur une invasion de l'hylésine piniperda. 1852. IV. 04.
— Rapport sur un mémoire sur les quantités d'eau contenues dans les bois. 1846. IV. 411.[2]
— Recherches sur l'emploi de divers amendements dans la culture des forêts. 1851. IV. 68.
— Recherches sur l'influence de l'eau. 1844. IV. 49.[2]
— Recherches sur la composition . . . des différents bois. 1844. I. 155.
— Réponse à la réclamation de M. Eugène Robert. 1852. IV. 209.[1]
—& **Wertheim**, Guillaume. Die mechanischen Eigenschaftendes Holzes. 1846. IV. 408.
— — Mémoire sur les propriétés mécaniques du bois. 1846. IV. 408.
Chevandier de Valdrome. Rapport . . . relatif au reboisement des montagnes. 1860. IV. 162.
Chevassu, Octave. Arboriculture fruitière. 1892. III. 145.[1]
Chevet. Rapport sur le tapioca de marrons d'Inde. 1859. III. 538.[1]
Chèvre-feuille de Tartarie nain. 1832. III. 751.[1]
Chevreul, Michel Eugène. Sur les cubes ou prismes de M. Robart. 1878. III. 571.
—.Sur la décomposition de l'acide carbonique par la chlorophylle. 1863. I. 172.
— Découverte de l'acide butyrique dans . . . Gingko. 1861. III. 125.
— Enquête sur la situation de l'agriculture en France. 1880. III. 125.
— Examen comparatif d'une cochenille. 1848. III. 620.[1]
— Explication de la zone brune des feuilles du Geranium zonale. 1857. II. 391.[2]
— Mémoire sur le moyen d'analyser plusieurs matières végétales. 1815. I. 156.[1]
— Note. 1852. III. 559.[2]
— Note sur la couleur d'un assez grand nombre de fleurs. 1854. I. 184.
— Observations à propos de la dernière note de M. Trecul relative à la chlorophylle. 1879. I. 141.
— À propos de Letellier et Spéneux. 1866. III. 194.
— À propos de Reiset, Jules. Mémoire sur les dommages causés . . . par le hanneton. 1867. IV. 202.
— Rapport sur un travail de M. Georges Ville. 1855. I. 158.
— Rapport sur un travail de M. Guérin. 1833. I. 180.[2]
— Rapport sur un travail de M. Peluze. 1834. I. 182.[2]
— Recherches chimiques sur la teinture. 1863. III. 236.
— Recherches chimiques sur le bois de Campêche. 1811. II. 363.[1]
— Remarques à l'occasion du rapport sur le mémoire de M. A. Le Play. 1862. I. 153.
— Remarques sur la conversion de l'amidon en dextrine. 1861. I. 140.[1]
— Sur de la soie provenant de vers nourris. 1834. III. 380.[2]
— Sur une des causes de la coloration en rouge des feuilles du Cissus quinquefolia. 1877. II. 504.[2]
Chevrier, J. Roy-. See ROY-CHEVRIER, J.
Chi non risica non rosica. 1854. IV. 364.
Chiamenti, Alessandro. La festa degli alberi. 1899. IV. 42,[1] 45.
— Della fioritura delle piante. 1876. I. 221.
Chiapperi, Agostino. Cenni sulla vegetazione in Liguria. 1874. I. 428.
— La silvicultura in Liguria. 1876. IV. 123.[1]
— Delle vegetazione attuale . . . a Torriglia. 1875. I. 428.
Chiarelli, Francesco Paolo. Discorso (de' vantaggi dello studio della storia naturale di Sicilia). 1789. I. 431.
Chicago botanical garden. First annual report. See BABCOCK, H. H. 1876. I. 39.

Chicago field. IV. 3.
Chicago hardwood record. IV. 3.
Chichester-Hart, H. See HART, H. CHICHESTER-.
Chick, Edith. On the vascular system of . . . Ricinus. 1899. II. 451.[1]
Chickering, John White. A botanical trip in Virginia. 1877. I. 319.
— Catalogue of . . . plants collected . . . in Dakota and Montana. 1878. I. 307.
— Notes on Roan Mountain. 1881. I. 319.
— Our native trees and shrubs. 1871. I. 304.
— A trip to Roan Mountain. 1883. I. 319.
Chicle gum. 1877. III. 666.[2]
Chicoyneau, François. Discours sur les plantes sensitives. 1732. I. 197.[1]
Chifflot, Julien. Sur une inflorescence monstrueuse d'Anthemis. 1899. II. 854.[2]
— La maladie noire des Clématites. 1900. III. 390.[1]
— Maladies des Platanes de la ville de Lyon. 1900. III. 418.[3]
— Des modifications anatomiques . . . de Crataegus . . . par les pucerons. 1899. III. 423.[1]
Chiflet, Joannes Jacobus. Pulvis febrifugus orbis americani. 1653. III. 719.
Chiga bread. 1889. III. 469.[1]
Chijs, J. A. van der. Over twee soorten van Bamboe. 1865. III. 314.[1]
Chilandarec, Sava. Rostlinstvo půlostrova Athonského. 1886. I. 450.
Child, A. L. Annual growth of trees. 1882. I. 127.[2]
— Concentric rings of trees. 1883. I. 128.[1]
Child, Hamilton. Gazetteer of Grafton County, N. H. See FLINT, W. F. 1886. I. 531.[1]
Child, Henry J. Timbers in the Straits Settlements. 1896. IV. 400.[1]
Childs, A. P. The British botanist's field book. 1857. I. 400.
Childs, George. Woodland sketches. See WOODLAND sketches. 1839. I. 393.
Chile — Sociedad cientifica. See SOCIÉTÉ SCIENTIFIQUE DU CHILI. I. 8.[1]
Chile — Universidad. See UNIVERSIDAD . . . I. 8.[1]
The Chile Pine. 1890. III. 299.
Der chilenische immergrüne Nussbaum. See The CHILIAN Nut. 1884. III. 383.[1]
Chilhaud de la Rigaudie, (député, Dordogne). Opinion sur l'article 1er du titre XI. de la loi sur les finances. 1817. IV. 325.
Chili — Société scientifique. See SOCIÉTÉ . . . I. 8.[1]
The Chilian Nut. 1884. III. 383.[1]
Chilly, MALLET DE. See MALLET DE CHILLY.
Chimani, Otto. Untersuchungen über Bau . . . der Milchröhren. 1895. I. 136.[1]
Chiminelli, L. Delle piante dei fiori nel loro rapporti col clima. 1872. III. 43.
China — Notes and queries. See NOTES . . . I. 28.[2]
China cuprea. 1881. III. 747.[1]
China grass or Rameh fibre. 1878. III. 382.[1]
China review. I. 28.[2]
Over **Chinasche** dwergboom kweekerij. 1853. III. 175.[2]
Chinese Bandoline wood. 1897. III. 407.[1]
Chinese coffin-woods. 1879. IV. 399.[1]
Chinese fibres. 1891. III. 273.[2]
Chinese Hemp-Palm. 1881. III. 331.[1]
Chinese insect white wax. 1898. III. 226.[1]
Chinese method of coloring green teas. 1849. III. 606.
The Chinese Red Bud in America. 1898. III. 472.[1]
Chinese repository. I. 28.[2]
Chinese silkworm gut. 1892. III. 417.[3]
The Chinese traveller. 1775. I. 458.
Chinese Varnish-tree. 1881. III. 514.[2]
Chinese white wax. 1893. III. 674,[1] IV. 536.[1]
The Chinese Wistaria. 1893. III. 491.[1]
Chiolini, Carlo. See MORETTI, Giuseppe & CHIOLINI, Carlo.
Chiovenda, Emilio. Contributo alla flora mesopotamica. 1900. I. 479.
— Piante nuove o rare della flora romana. 1898. II. 130.[2]
— See also PIROTTA, Romualdo & CHIOVENDA, Emilio.
Chipman, Marshall Mead. Government forest reservations. 1893. IV. 178.[3]
Chipman, N. P. California, its resources. 1900. III. 264.[1]
Chipman, Walter E. Notes on the flora of the lake region of northeastern Indiana. 1897. I. 316.
Chirat, Ludovic. Étude des fleurs. 1841. I. 94, 409.

Chiricozzi, Vincenzo. Del ·Castagno nella economia rurale. 1894. III. 359.[1]
Chisholm, C. Remarques sur quelques poisons . . . de l'Amérique. 1820. III. 266.
Chisholm, J. & McCorquodale, D. Preservation of timber. 1883. IV. 420.
Chishull, Edmund. Antiquitates asiaticae christianam aeram antecedentes. 1728. III. 509.[2]
Chitier, A. Étude sur les causes du déboisement en Algérie. 1882. IV. 283.[2]
Chittenden, Frank Hurlbut. A destructive borer enemy of Birch trees. 1898. IV. 491.[1]
— The fruit-tree bark-beetle. 1898. III. 187.
— Insect enemies of the White Pine. 1899. IV. 470.[1]
— The larger Apple-tree borers. 1898. III. 428.[2]
— The Rose-chafer. 1895. III. 453.[2]
— Some insects injurious to garden and orchard crops. 1899. III. 187.
— The two-lined Chestnut borer. 1897. III. 358.[2]
— See also TOWNSEND, C. H. T., CHITTENDEN, F. H., COCKERELL, T. D. A. & CRAW, Alexander.
Chitty, F. Culture of Azalea indica. 1865. III. 660.[1]
Chitty, S. C. Botanical dictionary in Tamil language. 1844. I. 75.[2]
Chizzolini, Ing. Meccanica forestale. 1865. IV. 422.[1]
Chłapowski, Dezydery. O rolnictwie. 1875. III. 104.
Chłapowsky, von, (Oberst). Auszug aus einer Abhandlung über Felder-Bepflanzungen. 1828. III. 214.[2]
Chlebodarow, Alexei. Zur Frage: Woher nimmt die Pflanze ihren Stickstoff? 1855. I. 158.
Chloris lugdunensis. See LA TOURRETTE, M. A. L. C. de F. de. 1785. I. 406.
Chloros, Nikolaos A. Forstwissenschaftliche Leistungen der Altgriechen. 1885. IV. 28.[3]
— Waldverhältnisse Griechenlands. 1884. IV. 375.[2]
— See also ΧΛΩΡΌΣ, Νικόλαος Α.
Chmielewsky, V. F. Eine Bemerkung über die von Molisch beschriebenen Proteïnkörper. 1887. II. 594.[1]
Cho, J. Does hydrogen peroxide occur in plants? 1894. I. 154.
Choay, E. See BÉHAL, A. & CHOAY, E.
Chocolate; its character, history and treatment. 1868. III. 594.
Chodat, Robert. Conspectus systematicus generis Monninae. 1896. II. 430.[1]
— Conspectus systematicus generis Xanthophylli. 1896. II. 432.[2]
— Contribution à l'étude des anomalies du bois. 1893. I. 127.[1]
— Dichapetala nova africana. 1895. II. 433.[1]
— Sur la distribution . . . chez les Polygalacées. 1891. II. 429.[2]
— La famille des Krameriacées. 1891. II. 318.[2]
— Maipighiacées. 1892. II. 424.[1]
— Les Malpighiacées du Paraguay. 1891. II. 429.[2]
— Monographia Polygalacearum. 1891. II. 429.[2]
— Notice sur les Polygalacées. 1887. II. 429.[2]
— Sur un nouveau Carpolobia. 1897. II. 430.[1]
— Le noyau cellulaire dans quelques cas de parasitisme. 1900. I. 234.[1]
— Observations tératologiques. 1889. II. 104.[1]
— Sur la place à attribuer au genre Trigoniastrum. 1895. II. 428.[1]
— Polygalaceae. 1891. II. 429.[2]
— Polygalaceae. 1896. II. 429.[2]
— Polygalaceae novae vel parum cognitae. 1893. II. 429.[2]
— Polygalacées. 1889. II. 429.[2]
— A propos du Polygala Galpini. 1896. II. 431.[1]
— Remarques de géographie botanique . . . dans les vallées de Bagnes. 1894. I. 418.
— Sur la structure anormale de la liane Pachyrhizus. 1895. II. 380.[2]
— Tremandraceae. 1896. II. 429.[1]
— & Balicka-Iwanowska, Mrs. G. Remarques sur la structure des Tremandracées. 1893. II. 429.[2]
— & Chuit, Philippe. Étude sur les noix de Kola. 1888. II. 533.[1]
— & Rodrigue, Alice. Le tégument séminal des Polygalacées. 1893. II. 430.[1]
— & Roulet, Charles. Le genre Hewittia. 1893. II. 745.[1]
— & others. Plantae Hasslerianae.' 1898. I. 345.
Chodnew, A. Untersuchung der organischen Säuren in unreifen Zwetschen. 1845. II. 274.[1]
Choiński, Tymot. Urządzenie lasów. 1872. IV. 94.

Choisy, Jacques Denys. Considérations sur la famille des Nyctaginées. 1849. II. 190.[2]
— Convolvulaceae. 1845. II. 743.[2]
— Convolvulaceae orientales. 1833. II. 743.[2]
— Convolvulaceae orientales. 1834. II. 743.[1]
— De Convolvulaceis. 1839. II. 743.[2]
— Description des Guttifères de l'Inde. 1849. II. 552.[2]
— Description des Hydroléacées. 1833. II. 747.[2]
— Du genre Discostigma. 1860. II. 555.[1]
— Guttiferae. 1824. II. 552.[1]
— Mémoire sur la famille des Sélaginées. 1824. II. 778.[2]
— Mémoire sur les familles des Ternstroemiacées. 1855. II. 547.[2]
— Mémoire sur un nouveau genre de Guttifères. 1823. II. 552.[1]
— Note sur le genre Erycibe. 1834. II. 744.[2]
— Note sur les Convolvulacées du Brésil. 1843. II. 745.[1]
— Nyctaginaceae. 1849. II. 190.[2]
— Plantae javanicae. 1858. I. 469.[1]
— Prodromus d'une monographie . . . des Hypéricinées. 1821. II. 552.[1]
— Une promenade au Jardin royal de Kew. 1855. I. 54.
Choix de mémoires sur divers objets d'histoire naturelle . . . See JOURNAL d'histoire naturelle. I. 520.[1]
Choix des essences pour plantations. 1898. IV. 142.
Choix des plantes de la Suisse et de la Savoie. 1878. I. 436.
Choix des plus belles Roses. 1845. III. 448.
Cholnoky, Jenő. A khinai erdőségekről. 1899. I. 457, IV. 87.[3]
Chomel, Noel. Algemeen huishoudelijk-, natuur-, zede-kundig- en konst-woordenboek. 1709. III. 30.
— Dictionnaire économique. 1709. III. 30.
Chomel, Pierre Jean Baptiste. Abrégé de l'histoire des plantes usuelles. 1712. III. 54.
— Storia compendiosa delle piante usuali. 1712. III. 54.
El Chopo de Dijon. 1886. IV. 486.[1]
Choquens. Notice sur l'arboriculture. 1872. III. 145.[1]
Choris, Louis. Voyage pittoresque autour du monde. 1822. I. 302.
Chorlton, William. The American Grape grower's guide. 1860. III. 550.
— The cold grapery from direct American practice. 1853. III. 550.
Choulant, Ludwig. Bibliotheca medico-historica. 1842. I. 2, III. 1.
— Botanische . . . Abbildungen des Mittelalters. 1857. I. 519.[1]
— Handbuch der Bücherkunde für die aeltere Medicin. 1828. III. 1.
Choulette, Sébastien. Synopsis de la flore de Lorraine et d'Alsace. 1845. I. 381.
Chouvet, (sr.). Culture des gros Orangers en caisses. 1892. III. 500.[1]
— Généralités sur le choix . . . des arbres de ligne. 1868. III. 209.
— Note sur la rusticité des Marronniers d'Inde. 1888. III. 537.[1]
— Note sur plusieurs sortes de Tilleuls. 1888. III. 585.[1]
Chrapowitzki. Über die Synthese der Eiweissstoffe. 1888. I. 177.
Chrétien, E. & Th. Guérison de la Vigne atteinte du phylloxera: n. d. III. 564.[2]
Christ, Hermann. Über afrikanische Bestandteile in der Schweizer Flora. 1900. I. 438.
— Allgemeine Ergebnisse aus der systematischen Arbeit am Genus Rosa. 1884. II. 282.[2]
— Die Alpenflora. 1865. I. 435.
— Die Alpenrose. 1877. II. 676.[1]
— An American arboretum in Germany. 1890. I. 49.
— Analytischer Schlüssel . . . des Genus Rosa. 1888. II. 284.[2]
— Beiträge zur Kenntniss europäischer Pinus-Arten. 1867. II. 42.[2]
— Beiträge zur Kenntniss europäischer Pinus-Arten. Die Formen der Pinus sylvestris. 1864. II. 46.[2]
— Beiträge zur Kenntniss europäischer Pinus-Arten. Pinus Peuce. 1865. II. 44.[2]
— Beiträge zur Kenntniss südeuropäischer Pinus-Arten. 1863. II. 39.[2]
— Betula carpathica W. Kit. in der Schweiz. 1898. II. 119.[1]
— Betula Murithii Gaud. 1895. II. 119.[1]
— Un cas d'androgynie dans le genre Pinus. 1894. II. 41.
— The Cedar of Mount Atlas. 1890. II. 27.[1]
— The Cedars of Europe. 1890. III. 299.[1]

Christ, Hermann (*continued*).
— An enemy of the Larch. 1895. IV. 451.
— Le flora de la Suisse et ses origines. 1879. I. 436.
— Die Flora von Engelberg. 1890. I. 437.
— La flore ancienne africaine. 1892. I. 495.
— Die Formenkreise der europäischen Pinus-Arten. 1865. II. 15.[1]
— Forms of some European Conifers. 1896. II. 34,[1] 35.[3]
— Forstbotanische Bemerkungen über das Seesthal. 1895. I. 432,[3] IV. 86.[2]
— Le genre Rosa. 1884. II. 282.[3]
— The great Wurtemberg Linden. 1891. II. 517.[1]
— The home of certain Syringas. 1891. II. 715.[1]
— Indication du Châtaignier. 1895. II. 124.[1]
— Im Jahre 1876 beobachtete Rosenformen. 1877. II. 287.[1]
— Kleine Beiträge zur Schweizerflora. 1891. I. 437.
— Neue und bemerkenswerthe Rosenformen. 1875. II. 287.[1]
— Noch eine merkwürdige Fichte. 1896. II. 35.[2]
— Notiz über die alpine Pflanzendecke des St. Gotthard. 1872. I. 436.
— Ueber die Pflanzendecke des Juragebirges. 1868. I. 435.
— Das Pflanzenleben der Schweiz. 1879. I. 436.
— Ueber Pinus montana auf den Ravellen. 1869. II. 43.[1]
— Rosa. 1887. II. 288.[3]
— Rosa rubiginosa L. 1885. II. 298.[1]
— Rosa sclerophylla Scheutz. 1875. II. 298.[2]
— Rosa trachyphylla Rau. var. pumila. 1885. II. 299.[2]
— Rosae orientales. 1887. II. 288.[3]
— Die Rosen der Schweiz. 1873. II. 286.[2]
— Zur Rosenflora Italiens. 1873. II. 286.[2]
— Rosenformen beobachtet 1875. 1876. II. 287.[1]
— Rosenformen der Schweiz. 1874. II. 286.[3]
— Les Roses des Alpes maritimes. 1876. II. 285.[2]
— Spicilegium canariense. 1888. I. 498.
— Syringa Josikaea, etc. 1891. II. 715.[1]
— Uebersicht der europäischen Abietineen. 1863. II. 15.[1]
— Vegetation der Schweiz. 1891. I. 437.
— Vegetation und Flora der Canarischen Inseln. 1885. I. 498.
— Vegetationsansichten aus den Tessiner Alpen. 1874. I. 436.
— Was ist Rosa hibernica. 1875. II. 295.[1]
Christ, Johann Ludwig. Allgemeines praktisches Gartenbuch. 1814. III. 103.
— Der Baumgärtner auf dem Dorfe. 1792. III. 135.
— Beiträge zum Handbuch. 1794. III. 135.
— Fruitkundig woordenboek. 1832. III. 136.
— Handbuch über die Obstbaumzucht. 1794. III. 135.
— Die Krankheiten . . . der Obstbäume und ihre Abhülfe. 1808. III. 178.
— Von Pflanzung und Wartung der nützlichsten Obstbäume. 1789. III. 135.
— Pomologisches theoretisch-praktisches Handwörterbuch. 1802. III. 136.
— Vollständige Pomologie. 1809. III. 70.
— Von Weinbau. 1793. III. 552.
Christ, P. Observations sur la flore des environs de Bâle. 1855. I. 435.
Christen, T. Der Baumhöhenmassstab. 1891. IV. 231.[2]
— Ein Baumhöhenmassstab. 1892. IV. 216.
— Eine Taxation im Plänterwalde. 1893. IV. 258.
Christensen, Anton. Beiträge zur Untersuchung des Pilocarpins. 1881. III. 504.[3]
— Nogle Analyser af chinabark. 1878. III. 723.
— Sur la Quassiine. 1882. III. 509.[1]
— Ueber Quassiin. 1882. III. 509.[1]
Christensen, C. Landevejs-Poplerne contra Jordbruget. 1891. III. 200.[3]
Christensen, J. P. Magnoliaceerne. 1884. III. 397.[1]
Christian, P. B. Der echte schwedische Boxdorn. 1887. III. 701.[1]
Christian observer. III. 16.
Christiani, Johannes Georg. Ueber die Waldarbeiterverhältnisse auf dem badischen Schwarzwald. 1894. IV. 311.[1]
Christiania — Videnskabs — Selskabet. See Videnskabs. . . . I. 8.[3]
Christiansen, F. Om Skovcultur. 1860. IV. 343.[1]
Christiansen, O. Ueber Forst-Verwaltung. 1834. IV. 272.
Christie, A. Craig. On the occurrence of stipules in Ilex Aquifolium. 1880. II. 463.[2]

Christie, Alexander Turnbull. Sketches of the meteorology . . . of the southern Mahratta country. 1828. I. 471.
Christie, Joh. Om Berberisrusten. 1891. III. 394.[1]
Christie, T. N. Prize essay on Cinchona cultivation. 1883. III. 712.[3]
Christiernin, P. N. En hus-cur emot vattusot. 1754. IV. 482.[2]
Christines, Demetrios. See ΧΡΙΣΤΙΝΗΣ, Δημητριος.
Christison, David. On the difficulty of ascertaining the age of certain species of trees in Uruguay. 1891. I. 193.[2]
— The effects of transplantation on girth-increase. 1893. III. 38.[2]
— A journey in 1867 from Monte Video to San Jorge. 1878. I. 344.
— On the monthly increase in girth of trees. 1889. III. 38.[2]
— A notice of Mr. R. Marsham of Stratton. 1893. III. 38.[2]
— Observations on the annual increase in girth of trees. 1889. III. 38.[2]
— Observations on the girth-increase of trees. 1900. III. 38.[2]
— Observations on the increase in girth of young trees. 1893. III. 38.[2]
— The size, age, and rate of girth-increase. 1893. IV. 65.[1]
— The weekly rate of girth-increase. 1893. III. 38.[2]
— See also Christison, Sir Robert & David.
Christison, G. W. Tea planting in Darjeeling. 1896. III. 604.[1]
Christison, Sir Robert. Ueber die Abkunft . . . des Gummigutts. 1837. III. 609.[1]
— Action de la fève de Calabar sur l'économie. 1855. III. 483.[2]
— Analysis of the vegetable milk of the Hya-hya tree. 1830. III. 691.[1]
— A dispensatory. 1842. III. 254.
— On the exact measurement of trees. 1879. IV. 215, 217.
— Exact progressive measurements. 1882. IV. 233.
— On the Gamboge tree of Siam. 1850. III. 609.[1]
— How lightning strikes trees. 1876. IV. 194.
— Notice of a tree struck by lightning. 1876. IV. 194.
— Observations on a new variety of gamboge. 1847. III. 609.[2]
— Observations on the effects of Cuca. 1876. III. 493.[1]
— De l'origine et de la composition de la gomme-gutte. 1836. III. 608.[2]
— On the properties of the ordeal bean. 1855. III. 476,[2] 483.[3]
— Sur les propriétés du haricot vénéneux. 1855. III. 483.[2]
— On the sources and composition of gamboge. 1836. III. 608.[2]
— A treatise on poisons. 1829. III. 260.[2]
— See also Turner, Edward & Christison, Robert.
— & Graham, Robert. Bestandtheile . . . verschiedener Sorten Gunmigutt. 1836. III. 609.[1]
Christlieb, Wilhelm August. Die sichersten Vortheile bey dem Acker- . . . und Weinbau. 1768. IV. 116.
Christmas trees and flowers. 1889. III. 203.
Christoff, Christo. The Rose industry of Bulgaria. 1889. III. 453.[1]
— Die Rosenindustrie in Bulgarien. 1889. III. 453.[1]
Christy, F. C. Extracts from Diary in Japan. 1878. I. 462.
— Paper upon colonial timber trees. 1874. IV. 401.[2]
Christy, Miller. Preliminary observations on the seasonal variations of elevation in a branch. 1898. I. 150.[1]
Christy, Robert Miller. Notes on the botany of Manitoba. 1887. I. 310.
Christy, Th. Sur la gomme pistache. 1882. III. 526.[1]
Christy, Thomas. Cocain. 1885. III. 493.[1]
— East African rubbers. 1882. III. 229.
— Germination of seeds. 1882. III. 156.[3]
— India rubber plants. 1882. III. 231.
— New commercial plants. 1878. III. 53.
— On vegetable fibres. 1882. III. 234.
— Yarkasura nuts. 1882. III. 268.[1]
— & Co. Drogues vegetales nouvelles. 1890. III. 245.
Chronik des deutschen Forstwesens. IV. 7.
Chronik des Gartenwesens. III. 11.
Chronique agricole et viticole du canton de Vaud. III. 24.[1]
Chronique horticole. Journal. III. 19.
Chrysarobine. 1888. III. 467.[1]
Chuard, E. Observations concernant le mécanisme de l'introduction . . . du cuivre dans les vins. 1887. III. 561.

— Sur les produits de décomposition du carbure de calcium. 1897. III. 575.[1]
— & Porchet, F. Influence des composés cupriques. 1900. I. 229.
Chubbuck, Isaac Y. Up Tripyramid on snow-shoes. 1893. II. 843.[1]
Chuit, Philippe. See CHODAT, Robert & CHUIT, Philippe.
Churawy, Carl. Die Lopresti-Bahn. 1870. IV. 391.
Church, Arthur Herbert. Sur la composition des feuilles blanches et vertes. 1877. I. 153.
— Fleurs de Mahwa. 1887. III. 667.[2]
— Food-grains of India. 1886. III. 278.
— Mahwa flowers. 1886. III. 667.[2]
— Note on Cape tea. 1881. III. 473.[2]
— Researches on colein. 1877. III. 697.[2]
— Sur le thé du Cap. 1881. III. 473.[2]
— Variegated leaves. 1877. I. 153.
— Wild Indigo seed as a famine food. 1898. III. 479.[2]
Churchill, Harry L. Report on the cultivation of Olives. 1896. III. 676.[2]
Churchill, James Morss. See STEPHENSON, John & CHURCHILL, J. M.
Churfürstlich trierische verbesserte neue Wald- und Forst-Ordnung. 1786. IV. 301.
Eines chur-fürstlichen Kunst-Gärtners Garten-Memorial. 1703. III. 121.[1]
Chur-fürstlicher Pfalz Forst- und Wald- auch Weid- Wercks-Jagd- und Fischerey-Ordnung. 1711. IV. 317.[1]
Churfürstlich-mayntzische respektive kurtz verfasst- und erneuerte Wald-Ordnung. 1730. IV. 301.
Churpfältzische Forst-Ordnung. 1744. IV. 317.[2]
Churpfälzische Instruction, wie man bey der Aufnahme der Forst-Garten verfahren solle. 1788. IV. 263.
Chweka, J. Der vollständige Landmann. 1795. IV. 123.[2]
Chys, J. van der. Nederlandsch-koloniale thee versus Engelsche. 1899. III. 608.[1]
Chytil, St. "Candelaberfichte." 1894. IV. 460.[2]
Ciamician & Silber, P. Sur quelques principes des écorces de Coto. 1892. III. 407.[1]
Ciamician, Giacomo Luigi. Destillation des Elemiharzes. 1878. III. 511.[2]
— Ueber die Reductions-Produkte des Elemiharzes. 1878. III. 511.[2]
Ciancio, A. B. PISANI. See PISANI CIANCIO, A. B.
Ciassi, Giovanni Maria. Meditationes de natura plantarum. 1677. I. 30.
Cibot, Achille. Di alcuni alberi utili del Messico. 1866. IV. 398.[1]
Cicatrisation des plaies des arbres. 1896. III. 180.[2]
Cicvárek, F. J. See CERNÝ, J. V. & CICVÁREK, F. J.
Cid, Jerónimo. Memoria sobre la repoblacion . . . de la provincia de Salamanca. 1881. IV. 164.[1]
Cienkowski, L. S. Zur Befruchtung des Juniperus communis. 1853. II. 31.[1]
Ciesielski, Theophil. Untersuchungen über die Abwärtskrümmung der Wurzel. 1872. I. 194.
Cieslar, Adolf. Die Acclimatisation der Douglasfichte. 1889. IV. 454.
— Ueber das Auftreten des Hallimasch. 1896. IV. 212.
— Beiträge zur Kenntniss der Verbreitung der Laubhölzer in Europa. 1890. I. 348,[1] IV. 79.[1]
— Conservation des glands. 1896. IV. 508.
— Ueber Culturversuche im "Grossen Föhrenwalde." 1887. IV. 466.[1]
— Effect of red lead, carbolic acid . . . on germination. 1885, 1886. IV. 65,[2] 148.
— Ueber eine eigenthümliche Rindenbildung an der Fichte. 1894. II. 36.[1]
— Ueber den Einfluss der Grösse der Fichtensamen. 1887. IV. 454.
— Einfluss der Leimringe auf die Gesundheit der Weisstanne. 1893. IV. 445.
— Einfluss der Leimringe auf die Gesundheit der Weisstanne. 1898. IV. 444.[2]
— Ueber den Einfluss verschiedenartiger Entnadelung auf Grösse . . . der Schwarzföhre. 1890. IV. 466.[2]
— Einfluss von Mennige . . . auf die Keimung. Versuche mit Nadelholzsamen. 1885.
— Einfluss wechselnder Feuchtigkeit auf die Keimung. 1885. I. 528,[1] IV. 65,[2] 148.
— Die Erblichkeit des Zuwachsvermögens. 1895. I. 529.
— Ueber die Erblichkeit des Zuwachsvermögens. 1895. I. 529, IV. 75.[1]
— Étude comparative sur l'accroissement . . . de l'Épicéa et du Pseudotsuga. 1898. IV. 235.[1]

— Zur Geschichte der künstlichen Verjüngung. 1888. IV. 24,[1] 148.
— Ueber horstweise Verjüngung. 1884. IV. 139.[1]
— Über den Ligningehalt einiger Nadelhölzer. 1897. II. 871.[1]
— Die Naturwissenschaften im waldbaulichen Unterrichte. 1891. IV. 29.
— Ein neuer Keimkasten. 1890. III. 157.
— Neues aus dem Gebiete der forstlichen Zuchtwahl. 1899. I. 529, IV. 75.[1]
— Die Notwendigkeit der Waldsamencontrole. 1889. III. 157.
— Die Pflanzzeit in ihrem Einfluss. 1892. III. 169,[1] IV. 454, 474.
— Ueber rationelle Weidencultur. 1884. III. 348.
— Recherches sur l'influence du travail mécanique du sol et d'une couverture en mousse, sur la croissance de jeunes Épicéas. 1893. IV. 558.[2]
— Das Rothholz der Fichte. 1896. II. 36.[1]
— La roya del Pino silvestre y su tratamiento. 1899. IV. 559.[2]
— Le Sapin de Douglas. 1889. IV. 484.[1]
— Die Schütte und ihre Bekämpfung. 1899. IV. 559.[2]
— Studien über die Bodenstreu in Schwarzföhrenbeständen. 1897. IV. 466.[2]
— Swoboda's "Samenverteiler." 1887. IV. 149.[1]
— Untersuchungen über den Einfluss der mechanischen Bodenbearbeitung. 1893. IV. 454, 558.[2]
— Vergleichende Studien über Zuwachs . . . von Fichte und Douglastanne. 1898. IV. 235.[1]
— Versuche mit Nadelholzsamen. 1885. I. 528.[1]
— Versuche über Aufbewahrung von Eicheln. 1896. IV. 508.
— Welche Erfahrungen liegen vor über die Beschädigungen der Wälder durch den Rauch? 1899. IV. 193.[1]
— Die Zuchtwahl in der Forstwirthschaft. 1890. I. 529, IV. 75.[1]
— & Kolinek, J. Ueber den Höhenzuwachsgang bei Forstgartenpflanzen. 1886. IV. 233.
De Cijfervruchtboom, de Pawpau. 1853. III. 401.[2]
Il cimento. See GIORNALE toscano di scienze. I. 25.
Cinchona-aanplantingen in de Vereenigde Staten. 1880. III. 712.[2]
Cinchona bark from Jamaica. 1889. III. 718.
Cinchona barks of Java. 1894. III. 725.[1]
Cinchona cultivation in Bengal. 1881. III. 714.
Cinchona cultivation in Bengal. 1896. III. 715.
Cinchona cultivation in British India. 1895. III. 715.
Cinchona cultivation in India. 1889. III. 715.
Cinchona cultivation in Java. 1877. III. 716.
Cinchona-disease in Jamaica. 1890. III. 717.[1]
Cinchona gathering in Peru. 1895. III. 713.[1]
Cinchona in Jamaica. 1880. III. 713.[1]
Cinchona in Jamaica. 1889. III. 713.[1]
The Cinchona plantations of Madras. 1896. III. 715.
Cincinnati society of natural history. Journal. I. 5.
Cincinnato da Costa, Bernardino Camillo. O Portugal vinicola. 1900. III. 547.
— & Castro, L. F. de. Le Portugal au point de vue agricole. 1900. III. 171.[1]
Cinnamomi cortex. 1898. III. 406.[1]
Cinnamon. 1891. III. 405.[1]
Cinnamon culture in Ceylon. 1883. III. 405.[2]
The Cinnamon gardens of Ceylon. 1863. III. 405.[1]
Cinnamon leaves. 1896. III. 405.[1]
La cipollatura del Castagno. 1895. IV. 493.[1]
Circolare del direttore generale di ponti e strade, e delle acque e foreste, e della caccia; ramo forestale. 1838. IV. 304.[2]
Circolari. 1864. IV. 304.[2]
Circolari. 1865. IV. 305.
Circolari. 1866. IV. 305.
Circolari, decisioni e provvedimenti ministeriali. 1863. IV. 304.[2]
Circulaire relative à l'exécution du décret sur la bonification de la pension de retraite. 1899. IV. 311.[2]
Circular for Arbor day. 1899. IV. 42.[1]
Sur la circulation de la sève dans les plantes. 1711. I. 162.
The circulation of sap in trees. 1865. III. 534.[2]
Circulirt der Saft in den Pflanzen oder nicht? 1873. I. 164.
Cire blanche d'insectes. 1898. III. 226.[1]
De la cire d'arbre et des insectes qui se produisent. 1844. III. 225.
Sur la cire du Japon. 1875. III. 527.[2]
Cirillo, Domenico. Ad botanicas institutiones introductio. 1766. I. 83.

Cirillo, Domenico (continued).
— Discorsi accademici. 1789. I. 197.[1]
— De essentialibus nonnullarum plantarum characteribus. 1784. I. 263.
— Fundamenta botanica. 1766. I. 83.
— A letter giving some account of the Manna tree. 1771. IV. 536.[1]
— Del moto e della irritabilità de' vegetabili. 1789. I. 197.[1]
— Plantarum rariorum regni neapolitani fasciculus. 1788. I. 424.
— Tabulae botanicae elementares. 1790. I. 83.
Die Cistus-Röschen. 1885. III. 612.[2]
Citation défectueuse et valable. 1898. IV. 327.
Citerne, Paul Émile. Berbéridées et Erythrospermées. 1892. II. 201,[3] 569,[2] 570.[1]
Citric acid; raw material. 1897. III. 499.[1]
Citron culture in Corsica. 1892. III. 502.[1]
The Citron in commerce. 1894. III. 502.[2]
Der Citronenbaum in Florida. 1889. III. 502.[1]
Citrons in Mogador. 1884. III. 502.[2]
Citrus fruits in Sicily. 1895. III. 499.[1].
The Citrus wood of the ancients. 1859. IV. 447.[2]
Citters, W. van. Iets over duinbeplanting. 1884. IV. 160.[1]
— Ontginning van woeste gronden. 1888. IV. 160.[1]
Civil engineer. London. IV. 12.[1]
Civilingenieur. See Der Ingenieur. IV. 9.
Civinini, Giovanni Domenico. Della storia degli Agrumi. 1734. III. 496.[2]
— Della storia e natura del Caffè. 1731. III. 738, 741.[1]
Civrieux, Larreguy de. See Larreguy de Civrieux.
— ck. Ein Baumriese. 1896. IV. 516.[1]
— ck. Die Holsfrage im Frūstenthum Waldeck. 1858. IV. 274.[1]
— ck. Über die natürliche Verjūngung der Buche. 1895. IV. 496.
Claassen, C. H. De tuinbouw in de Hoeksche Waard. 1898. III. 140.[1]
Claf, Cyriacus Lucas de. De ligni Cotonei natura. 1580. III. 423.[2]
Claire Deville, Charles Joseph Sainte. See Sainte Claire Deville, C. J.
Claire Deville, Henri Saint-. See Saint-Claire Deville, Henri.
Clairville, Joseph Philippe de. Auswahl von Pflanzen und Gestrāuchen. 1796. I. 264.
— Collection choisie de plantes et arbustes. 1796. I. 264.
— Manuel d'herborisation en Suisse. 1811. I. 433.
— Plantes et arbustes d'agrément. 1791. I. 264.
Clapham, A. New hybrid Aucubas. 1875. III. 645.[1]
Clapp, Asahel. A synopsis or systematic catalogue of the . . . medicinal plants of the United States. 1852. III. 62.
Clapperton, Hugh. See Denham, Dixon & Clapperton, Hugh.
Claraz, George. See Heusser, J. C. & Claraz, G.
Clarici, Paolo Bartolomeo. Istoria e coltura delle piante. 1726. III. 115,[1] 126.[1]
Clark. Sur la fabrication de la quinine. 1860. III. 718.
Clark, (of Clark Bros. & Co., Carlisle). The remarkable . . . trees of Cumberland. 1884. I. 297.[1]
Clark, Anna May. The trees of Vermont. 1899. I. 312, IV. 77.[1]
Clark, J. H. Flora of Monmouthshire. 1868. I. 534.[1]
Clark, John. A battle with beetles. 1900. IV. 208.[2]
Clark, Joseph. Catalogue of flowering plants . . . of Cincinnati. 1852. I. 314.
Clark, Matthew. On the judicious planting of trees, and Larch disease. 1884. IV. 451.
Clark, T. Edwards. Ueber den Fichtelit. 1857. II. 48.[1]
Clark, Thomas. On the best collection of Pines and Coniferae. 1890. I. 38.[2]
Clark, Wilham. See Lewis, Meriwether & Clark, William.
Clark, William. An essay on the Larch disease. 1884. IV. 451.
Clark, William Smith. The circulation of sap in plants. 1874. I. 165.
— Observations upon the phenomena of plant life. 1875. I. 165.
— Summary of observations on the circulation of sap. 1874. I. 165.
The Clark Elm. 1890. II. 144.[1]
Clarke, Benjamin. Altingiaceae. 1858. II. 252.[1]
— On the anthers of Columelliaceae and Cucurbitaceae. 1858. II. 795.[2]

— On the floral envelopes of Lauraceae. 1866. II. 223.[2]
— A new arrangement of phanerogamous plants. 1866. I. 252.
— Note on Stilbaceae. 1850. II. 752.[2]
— Notes on the structure of . . . Batideae. 1859. II. 114,[2] 423.[2]
— On the production of varieties. 1857. I. 247.
— On relative position. 1853. I. 117.[2]
— On the structure and affinities of Myricaceae, Plataneae, Altingiaceae, and Chloranthaceae. 1858. I. 99.
— On the structure of the ovary of Marlea. 1850. II. 615.[1]
Clarke, Charles Baron. On Acalypha indica Linn. 1887. II. 435.[2]
— Botanic notes from Darjeeling to Tonglo. 1877. I. 474.
— Cinchona cultivation in Bengal. 1870. III. 714.
— Commelynaceae et Cyrtandraceae bengalenses. 1874. II. 792.[2]
— Compositae indicae. 1876. II. 849.[2]
— Cyrtandreae (Gesneracearum tribus). 1883. II. 792.[2]
— A list of the flowering plants . . . of Andover. 1866. I. 402.
— Note on Gardenia turgida Roxb. 1880. II. 818.[2]
— Oranges in India. 1890. II. 401.[2]
— On the plants of Kohima and Muneypore. 1890. I. 476.[1]
— Report on the Cinchona cultivation in Bengal. 1871. III. 714.
— Report on the cultivation of Cinchona at Darjeeling. 1871. III. 714.
— A revision of the Indian species of Leea. 1881. II. 503.[2]
— & Stapf, Otto. Supplementary note to the flora of British India. 1894. I. 475.[1]
Clarke, Cora H. Galls found near Boston. 1890. I. 214.[2]
Clarke, Frank Wigglesworth. An essay upon the preservation of wood from decay. 1873. IV. 425.[2]
— A trip to North Carolina. 1879. I. 319.
Clarke, George. On the Cocoa-nut of the Seychelles Islands. 1864. II. 70.[2]
— Some further particulars of the Coco de Mer. 1841. II. 70.[2]
Clarke, H. L. The meaning of tree-life. 1894. I. 243.[3]
Clarke, John. A treatise on the Mulberry tree. 1839. III. 375.
Clarke, Robert. Notes on kundoo or tallicoonah oil. 1860. III. 512.[1]
— Notes on the tallicoonah. 1843. III. 512.[1]
— Observations on the Etua-Tree. 1862. II. 789.[1]
— Some further remarks on . . . the oil commonly called croupee. 1860. III. 512.[1]
Clarke, Samuel. A true and faithful account of the four chiefest plantations of the English in America. 1670. III. 261.[1]
Clarke, Stephen. The British botanist. 1820. I. 397, 524.[1]
— Hortus anglicus. 1822. III. 81.
Clarke, William Ambrose. First records of British flowering plants. 1892. I. 534.[2]
Clarke, William Branwhite. Effects of forest vegetation on climate. 1877. IV. 53.
Clarkson, C. F. Mixing forest trees. 1878. IV. 138.[2]
Clarté, Joseph. Le Citronnier du Japon. 1892. III. 503.[1]
— Le Goumi. 1890. III. 629.[1]
Clarus, Julius. Handbuch der speciellen Arzneimittellehre. 1856. III. 258.
Clary, L. R. Catalogue des plantes observées à Daya. 1888. I. 485.
Classen, Insetti che danneggiano i boschi di Migliarino. 1889. IV. 93.
— Notizie sopra la biologia dell' "Hylesinus." 1890. IV. 204.
Classen, Karl. Ueber Waldentwāsserung. 1860. IV. 143.[2]
The classes and orders of the Linnaean system. See Duppa, Richard. 1816. I. 255.
Classification and catalogue of forestry collection. 1894. IV. 18.[2]
Classification de 160 huiles et graisses végétales. See Bernardin, J. de W. 1871. III. 224.[2]
Classification des huiles et des graisses végétales. See Bernardin, J. de W. 1871. III. 224.[2]
Classische Bäume Genf's. See Quelques arbres . . . 1851. I. 297.[2]
Claubry, Henri Gaultier de. See Gaultier de Claubry, Henri.
Claudel & Crochetelle. Influence de quelques substances employées comme engrais sur la germination. 1893. I. 204.
Claudel, Louis. Sur la localisation des matières colorantes. 1890. I. 185.[1]

— Sur les matières colorantes du spermoderme. 1889. I. 185.[1]
—Sur le Quassia africana. 1894. III. 508,[2] 539.[1]
Claudio & Boutelou, Estéban. Razon de. las especies mas raras de árboles y de arbustos . . . de Aranjuez. 1801. I. 60.[1]
Clauditz, (Oberförster zu Meppen). Die Dampfpflugkultur. 1873. IV. 158.
Claudot, Camille. Acción protectora de los montes sobre la caida del granizo. 1896. IV. 542.[3]
— Le commerce extérieur des bois. 1894. IV. 405.[1]
— De la dépréciation des bois de feu. 1895. IV. 431.[2]
— Étude sur la place de production no. 2 installée dans la forêt domaniale de Haye. 1896. IV. 383.[1]
— Influence de l'âge des Sapins sur la puissance germinative. 1894. IV. 147.[1]
— Influence des forêts sur les chutes de grêle. 1896. IV. 54, 542.[3]
— Influencia de los montes en el régimen de las aguas. 1898. IV. 542.[1]
— La méthode du contrôle. 1894. IV. 249.[1]
— Notice historique sur la forêt communale d'Épinal. 1891. IV. 361.
— Du progrès en sylviculture et dans l'utilisation des produits forestiers. 1900. IV. 382.[3]
— Recherches sur la production ligneuse pendant la phase des coupes de régénération. 1895. IV. 234.
— La sylviculture dans les Vosges. 1888. IV. 361.
— Les taxes d'octroi sur les combustibles. 1895. IV. 285.[1]
— Troisième mémoire sur l'influence des éclaircies. 1894. IV. 174.
Claus. Buchen-Bahnschwellen. 1883. IV. 500.[1]
Claus, A. Les Pimelea. 1896. III. 628.[1]
Claus, Karl. Grundzüge der analytischen Phytochemie. 1837. I. 151.[1]
— Localfloren der Wolgagegenden. 1851. I. 361.
— Zur quantitativen Bestimmung des Theeins. 1862. III. 607.
— See also Kraven, K.
Clausen. La Crimée en 1879-1880. 1880. III. 45.
— Greffage des Noyers. 1887. III. 355.
— Une nouvelle greffe. 1880. III. 162.
Clausen, C. H. Om Poppelplantning. 1856. III. 344.[1]
Clausen, E. Ueber das Geschlecht von Cephalotaxus Fortunei. 1882. II. 8.[3]
— Nutzen des Ailantus. 1882. III. 507.[1]
Clausen, H. Beiträge zur Kenntniss der Athmung. 1890. I. 171.
Clauses de la vente des coupes dans les bois des particuliers. 1897. IV. 326.
Clauss, C. Iriartea exorrhiza Mart. und I. altissima. 1867. III. 326.[1]
Clausse. Précis sur l'aménagement et l'administration des forêts et bois nationaux. 1800. IV. 292.
Claussen, chevalier de. Un the Hancornia speciosa. 1856. III. 688.[1]
— Sur le Hancornia speciosa. 1856. III. 688.[1]
— On Papyrus, Bonapartea, and other plants which can furnish fibre for paper-pulp. 1856. IV. 429.
Clauswitz, G. von. Darstellung des Buchen-Hochwaldbetriebes. 1828. IV. 497.
Clautriau, Georges. Les installations botaniques . . . de Java et de Ceylan. 1899. V. IX.[1]
— Nature et signification des alcaloïdes. 1900. I. 178.
— See also Errera, Léo, Maistriau, Ch. & Clautriau, G.
Clavarino, Antonio. Antosmologia. 1897. III. 115,[2] 226.[2]
Clavaud, Armand. Flore de la Gironde. 1881. I. 416.
— Note sur les formes spontanées . . . du genre Prunus. 1884. II. 271.[1]
— Salix alba, fragilis et Russelliana. 1876. II. 100.[1]
Clavé, Jules. Les essences forestières des colonies anglaises. 1862. IV. 19.[3]
— Étude de météorologie forestière. 1875. IV. 53.
— Étude de météorologie forestière. 1877. IV. 59.[2]
— Études d'économie forestière. 1860. IV. 247.[1]
— Études sur l'économie forestière. 1862. IV. 269.
— Forstliche Studien. 1860. IV. 247.[1]
— Le reboisement des Alpes. 1881. IV. 163.
— Le reboisement . . . en France. 1859. IV. 162.
— Om Skovenes meteorologiske Betydning. 1875. IV. 53.
— Die Wiederbewaldung . . . in Frankreich. 1859. IV. 162.
Clave analitica para la determinacion . . . See Conzatti, Cassiano. 1889. V. XVIII.[1]
Clavel de Saint-Geniez. Traité pratique et experimental de botanique. 1855. I, 270.

Clavenna, Jacob Antonius. Clavis Clavennae aperiens naturae thesaurum. 1648. I. 286.
Clavigero, Francesco Saverio. Storia antica del Messico. 1780. III. 264.[2]
Clavijo, José de Viera y. See Viera y Clavijo, José de.
Clavis anglica linguae botanicae. See Berkenhout, John. 1764. I. 69.[3]
Clavis rem harbariam addiscendi. See Nocca, Domenico.
Clay, Cassius M. The preservation of forests. 1883. IV. 178.[1]
Claye, Alfred Durand-. See Durand-Claye, Alfred.
Claye, Louis. Culture des fleurs et des plants aromatiques. 1855. III. 226.[2]
Claypole, Edward Waller. The migration of plants from Europe to America. 1880. I. 241.[2]
— Note on the present condition of the Box Huckleberry. 1884. II. 671.[3]
Clayton, B. F. & Husmann, George. Viticulture in the United States. 1891. III. 551.[1]
Clayton, H. Helm. The Lawrence tornado. 1892. III. 184.[2]
Clebsch, A. Ueber ein Problem der Forstwissenschaft. 1869. IV. 243.
La clef de la botanique. 1796. I. 255.
Clegg, Samuel, (jr.). Seasoning timber. 1852. IV. 416.[1]
Cleghorn, Hugh Francis Clarke. Abstract of experiments on the strength of woods. 1861. IV. 410.
— Address [on forestry]. 1873. IV. 357.[3]
— Avenues. 1861. III. 211.[1]
— Brief account of the Royal forest school at Vallombrosa. 1878. IV. 35.[3]
— Charcoal manufacture. 1861. IV. 394.
— On the distribution of the principal timber trees of India. 1868. IV. 377.[3]
— Dockyard timber. 1861. IV. 519.[1]
— Effects of the gale of 20th Nov. 1856. 1857. III. 184.[1]
— Excursion to the valleys of the Giri, Pabur, and Touse rivers. 1865. I. 474.
— The extension of Tea plantations in India. 1864. III. 603.
— The forests and gardens of South India. 1861. III. 129,[3] IV. 377.[3]
— General index of the plants described and figured in Robert] Wight's . . . Icones. 1856. I. 77.
— Government horticultural garden, Ootacamund. 1858. I. 67.[1]
— Gutta percha in India. 1855. III. 668.[2]
— On the gutta-percha plant of India. 1856. III. 228.[2]
— On the hedge plants of India. 1850. III. 214.[3]
— Hedges. 1861. III. 214.[1]
— Hortus madraspatensis. 1853. I. 67.[1]
— On the introduction of Cinchona trees. 1863. III. 713.[2]
— To make charcoal. 1884. IV. 395.
— Memorandum on the naturalization of Australian plants. 1867. III. 129.[2]
— Memorandum on the timber procurable by the Indus, Swat, and Kabul rivers. 1867. IV. 407.[3]
— Memorandum on the Travancore government garden at Peermade. 1867. I. 67.[1]
— Memorandum upon the Pauchontee. 1858. II. 699.[3]
— Note on the poisonous properties of . . . Andromeda. 1867. III. 653.[2]
— Note on the sand-binding plants. 1856. III. 41.[3]
— Notes of excursions to the higher ranges of the Anamalai Hills. 1861. I. 473.
— Notes on the vegetation of the Sutlej valley. 1865. I. 474.
— Notes upon the Coco-nut tree. 1861. III. 323.[3]
— Notes upon the Coconut tree. 1863. III. 324.[1]
— Notes upon the Pines of the northwest Himalaya. 1867. II. 15.[3]
— Notice of the Cinchona cultivation on the Neilgherry Hills. 1863. III. 713.[3]
— Notice regarding insects injurious to timber trees. 1867. IV. 210.[3]
— Observations on the forest schools of Europe. 1869. IV. 30.[3]
— On the Parchontee, or Indian Gutta tree. 1859. III. 666.[3]
— On the Pauchontee or Indian Guttatree. 1858. II. 699.[3]
— On the poisonous properties of . . Andromeda. 1867. III. 653.[3]
— Remarks on Calysaccion. 1851. III. 610.[1]
— Report on the conservation of forests in India. 1859. IV. 377.[1]

Cleghorn, Hugh Francis Clarke (*continued*).
— Report on the conservation of forests in India. 1860. IV. 181.¹
— Report upon the forests of the Punjab. 1864. IV. 377.²
— Supply of wood-fuel to Indian railways. 1868. IV. 431.¹
— Tea culture in southern India. 1863. III. 603.
— Timber and ornamental woods. 1861. III. 278.
— On the timbers suited for railway sleepers in South India. 1861. IV. 423.²
— On the varieties of Mango fruit. 1861. III. 524.²
— On the varieties of Mango fruit. 1863. III. 525.¹
— & others. Report of the committee . . . to consider the probable effects . . . of the destruction of tropical forests. 1852. IV. 43.
Cleghorn, James. *See* ANDERSON, Thomas & CLEGHORN, James.
Clematis-Hybriden. 1900. III. 389.²
Clematis Viticella und deren Hybriden. 1896. III. 392.¹
Clemen, E. Dendrologische Plaudereien. 1890. II. 675.¹
— Die Ribes-Arten der deutschen Gärten. 1891. II. 243.²
Clemen, R. E. Beobachtungen über das Giftfallen. 1849. I. 213.¹
— *See also* ANTZ, K. C. & CLEMEN, R. E.
Clémenceau. Les arbres fantômes. 1870. III. 535.¹
— Le Cryptomeria elegans, est-il rustique? 1870. III. 302.¹
— Épacris. 1872. III. 665.¹
— Des jardins réguliers dits à la française. 1867. III. 201.
— Philadelphus verrucosus sempervirens. 1866. III. 413.²
— Plantes méritantes nouvelles. 1868. III. 77.
— Spiraea callosa alba. 1868. III. 461.²
Clemens, Cynthius. Disputationes medicae de natura . . . ligni sancti. 1601. III. 494.¹ .
Clémens, F. W. Éthérisation des plantes. 1849. I. 193.²
Clement. *See also* KLEMENT.
Clement, (*Rentmeister, Muskau*). Die Forsten der Standesherrschaft Muskau. 1872. IV. 354.
Clément, A. L. Les plantes mellifères et le nectar. 1898. III. 224.¹
Clement, Asa. Transplanting fruit and forest trees. 1867. III. 117.¹
Clément, Eugène. Manuel forestier. 1851. IV. 107.²
— Semis et plantations d'arbres forestiers. 184 . ? IV. 121.
Clement, M. Handboek voor het boschbestier. 1852. IV. 98.²
Clément-Mullet, J. J. De la culture du Mûrier. 1854. III. 377.
— Études sur les noms arabes de . . . végétaux. 1870. I. 76.¹
Clemente, Cárlos CASTEL Y. *See* CASTEL Y CLEMENTE, Cárlos.
Clemente y Rubio, Simon de Roxas. Ensayo sobre las variedades de la Vid comun. 1807. III. 545.²
— Essai sur les variétés de la Vigne. 1807. III. 545.²
— Plantas que viven espontáneamente in el termino de Titaguas. 1864. I. 421.
— Versuch über die Varietäten des Weinstocks. 1807. III. 545.²
Clementi, Josepho. Sertulum orientale. 1855. I. 479.
Clements, Frederic E. *See* POUND, Roscoe & CLEMENTS, F. E.
Clerc, O. Du pâturage en forêt. 1899. IV. 545.²
— Plantations d'Épicéas. 1900. IV. 559.¹
— Taillis et futaies, accroissements comparés. 1897. IV. 550.¹
Clerc, George Onesime. Catalogus florae mosquensis. 1878. I. 363.
— *See also* КЛЕРЪ, O.
Clerc, Louis. Manuel classique et élémentaire de botanique. 1835. I. 87.
— Manuel de l'amateur de café. 1823. III. 738.
Clerck, Carl Alexander. Nomenclator extemporaneus rerum naturalium. 1759. I. 76.³
Clercq, F. S. A. de. Bijdragen tot de kennis der residentie Ternate. 1890. III. 274.²
— Het eiland Wiak of Biak. 1888. III. 274.²
— Het gebied der Kalana-fat. 1889. III. 282.¹
— Inlandsche plantennamen. 1892. I. 76.¹
— Langs de zuidkust der Macoluer golf. 1889. III. 128.
Clercq, H. de. Les importations de Québracho. 1897. IV. 536.¹
Clerfeyt, J. Le domaine de Westerloo. 1896. IV. 357.¹
Clericus, (*pseud.*). On training and standard Honeysuckle. 1858. III. 749.² .
Clerke, F. W. The preservation of wood from decay. 1883. IV. 420.
Clermont, J. . Sur la présence du bioxyde d'hydrogène. 1875. I. 153. .

Clermont-Ferrand—Académie des sciences, belles-lettres et arts. *See* ACADÉMIE . . . I. 20.
Clermont-Tonnerre, Tillette de. Note sur une variété femelle du Pommier commun. 1825. II. 266.²
Ueber Clerodendron R. Br. 1853. III. 696.¹
Clerzac, DEBERT. *See* DEBERT-CLERZAC.
Cleve, Astrid. Studier öfver några svenska växters groningstid. 1898. I. 188.
Cleve, M. J. Forest-culture in alpine ravines. 1881. IV. 185.²
Cleveland, Horace Wilham Shaler. The culture and management of our native forests. 1882. IV. 112.
— Tree culture. 1881. IV. 281.²
Cleveland, Treadwell. Forest laws in the United States. 1900. IV. 314.²
Clewberg, Christophorus. De רדם arbore sub qua Elias. 1758. I. 513.
Cleyer, Andreas. De Arbore laccifera japanensi. 1686. III. 528.² .
— De Catechu. 1686. II. 324.¹
— Herbarium parvum sinicis vocabulis . . . constans. 1680. I. 75.¹
Clifford, Frederick. Indian Coffee. 1887. III. 732.²
Clifford, M. H. Spread of Loranthus. 1896. II. 175.²
Clifford, T. & A. Topographical . . . description of the parish . . . [in Staffordshire]. *See* CLIFFORD, T. H. 1817. I. 396.
Clifford, Thomas Hugues. Flora tixalliana. 1817. I. 396.
Clift, J. E. On the preservation of timber by creosote. 1851. IV. 417.
Climbing plants in trees. 1885. III. 204.²
Clinton, George W. Preliminary list of plants of Buffalo. 1864. V. XVII.¹
Clipped trees; a reversion. 1900. III. 202.²
Clodius, Christian. Zuverlässige Nachricht von . . . Holtz-Cabinet. 1729. I. 37,³ *IV. 17.*
Cloëz, François Stanislas. Étude chimique de l'Eucalyptol. 1870. IV. 532.²
— Examen chimique des feuilles d'Eucalyptus globulus. 1868. IV. 532.²
— Expériences et observations sur les matières grasses. 1865. I. 182.¹
— Sur l'huile d'Elaeococca. 1876. III. 514.²
— Note sur la matière grasse . . . de l'Arbre à huile de la Chine. 1875. III. 514.²
— Note sur les proportions relatives des alcalis. 1869. I. 53.
— Recherches expérimentales sur la nitrification. 1855. I. 158.
— Remarques sur la décomposition du gaz acide carbonique. 1863. I. 172.
— *See also* FRÉMY, Edmond & CLOËZ, S.
— & Gratiolet, Pierre. Recherches sur la végétation. 1850. I. 147.
— & Guignet, Er. Recherches sur la composition chimique du vert de Chine. 1872. III. 542.¹
Clos, Dominique. Affinité réciproque des genres Rubus et Rosa. 1876. II. 367.¹
— Anomalies végétales. 1877. I. 143.
— Arbres atteints par la foudre. 1886. IV. 194.
— Des arbustes du Chili. 1889. III. 124.²
— Les Arum vulgare Lamk. et italicum. 1895. II. 564.²
— Sur une Asclépiadée à fibres textiles. 1890. III. 692.¹
— Des bourgeons des plantes. 1894. I. 108.²
— Le Cabrillet ou Ehrétie serreté. 1889. III. 695.¹
— Le calice ou le périanthe simple et l'ovaire infère. 1893. I. 115.²
— Des caractères du péricarpe. 1873. I. 119.
— Caractères extérieurs . . . des petits tubercules . . . des Légumineuses. 1896. II. 322.¹
— Des caractères pistillaires du genre Ruscus. 1861. II. 84.²
— Cladodes et axes ailés. 1861. II. 84.²
— De la colonne . . . des Géraniacées, des Malvacées. 1857. II. 519.² .
— Considérations sur la nature du . . . involucre des Malvacées. 1854. II. 519.²
— Contributions à la morphologie du calice. 1884. I. 115.²
— Coup d'œil sur la végétation . . . de l'Aude. 1861. I. 412.
— Coup d'œil sur les principes qui servent de base aux classifications botaniques modernes. 1869. I. 252.
— Du coussinet . . . dans les Cactées. 1860. II. 588.¹
— Du démembrement du genre Hypericum. 1894. II. 556.¹
— Deux nouveaux Pittosporum rustiques. 1900. III. 416.¹

— Deuxième mémoire sur la rhizotaxie. 1852. I. 103.
— De la dimidiation des êtres. 1887. I. 111.
— Discussion d'un principe . . . concernant les bourgeons. 1856. I. 108.[1]
— De la disposition adoptée . . . dans la replantation . . . du Jardin des plantes de Toulouse. 1873. I. 59.
— La double-feuille pédonculaire du Melianthus major. 1899. II. 491.[1]
— Ébauche de la rhizotaxie. 1848. I. 103.
— L'école botanique du Jardin des plantes de Toulouse. 1897. I. 59.
— Des éléments morphologiques des feuilles. 1875. I. 110.
— Essai de tératologie taxinomique. 1871. I. 143.
— Examen critique de la loi dite de balancement organique. 1865. I. 99.
— De l'existence du Betula pubescens. 1873. II. 118.[2]
— Expériences physiologiques sur les boutures droits et renversées. 1862. I. 208,[2] *527*.
— Faits afférents à la vie des organes souterrains des plantes. 1898. II. 322.[1]
— Fascicule d'observations de tératologie. 1859. I. 143.
— D'une fausse dénomination de l' " Aegle sepiaria." 1898. II. 403.[1]
— La feuille florale et l'anthère. 1866. I. 116.[2]
— La feuille florale et le filet staminal. 1877. I. 115.[1]
— La feuille florale et le pistil. 1880. I. 115.[1]
— Des fleurs réellement sessiles. 1858. I. 113.[2]
— Gemmation. 1868. I. 527.
— Genres botaniques de Lamarck. 1896. I. 76.[2]
— Des genres Pavia et Timbalia. 1871. II. 278,[1] *431*.[1]
— Des germinations spontanées. 1868. I. 203, *III. 43*.
— Des glandes dans le genre Hypericum. 1868. II. 556.[1]
— Glanes de faits de morphologie végétale. 1899. I. 111, 114,[1] 118,[1] 144,[1] II. 261,[1] 400,[3] 478,[3] 491,[3] 650,[1] 705,[3] 747.[1]
— De l'Hypericum elatum. 1867. II. 556.[1]
— Importance de la gaîne de la feuille. 1856. I. 108.[1]
— De l'indépendance de certains styles. 1899. I. 118.[1]
— De l'indépendance fréquente des stipules. 1900. I. 112.[1]
— Indépendence, développement . . . des stipules. 1879. I. 108,[1] *112*.[1]
— Indifférence dans la direction des racines. 1874. I. 195.[2]
— Individualité des faisceaux fibro-vasculaires. 1889. I. 134.[1]
— l'influence des plantes sur la civilisation. 1866. IV. 43De
— De l'innocuité des fruits de l'If commun. 1869. III. 288.[2]
— Interprétation de l'anthère. 1897. II. 175.[1]
— Interprétation des parties germinatives du Trapa. 1891. II. 553.[1]
— L'irritabilité du stigmate est-elle un caractère . . . des Bignoniacées? 1869. II. 784.[2]
— Le Jardin des plantes de Toulouse. 1887. I. 59.
— Le Kudzu ou Pueraria. 1890. III. 485.[2]
— Une lacune dans l'histoire de la sexualité végétale. 1887. I. 201.[1]
— Lenticelles et rhizogènes. 1857. I. 132.[1]
— Des liens d'union des organes. 1892. I. 100.[1]
— Lobations ou anomalies de feuilles simples. 1889. I. 145.[1]
— Monographie de la famille des Flacourtianées. 1854. II. 568.[2]
— Monographie de la préfoliation. 1870. I. 110.
— Un mot sur trois espèces de plantes. 1887. II. 602.[1]
— Du nanisme dans le règne végétal. 1889. I. 236.[1]
— Naturalisation d'espèces ligneuses. 1900. IV. 127.[1]
— De la naturalisation . . . des végétaux. 1865. III. 43.
— De la nature préliminaire des sépales du Cobaea. 1899. II. 747.[1]
— Note sur le Zelkova Keaki. 1893. II. 145.[1]
— Nouvel aperçu sur la théorie de l'inflorescence. 1861. I. 113.[2]
— Observations sur le pistil . . . des genres Papaver et Citrus. 1865. II. 401.[2]
— Sur une Orange double. 1866. II. 403.[1]
— De l'orthographe de quelques dénominations de plantes. 1873. II. 140.[2]
— Une page de dendrologie. 1886. I. 295.[1]
— De la part des stipules à l'inflorescence. 1878. I. 113.[2]
— De la partition des axes. 1885. I. 105.
— Partition, entraînement et dichotomie. 1899. I. 114.[1]
— Pétalisation à divers degrés d'appendices. 1899. I. 144.[1]
— Pétioles en lame , . . de l'Acer macrophyllum. 1899. II. 478.[1]
— Phillyrea, Phyllirea, Philyrea. 1890. II. 714.[1]
— Phytostatique du Sorézois bassin méridional. 1895. I. 418.

— La plante au point de vue littéraire. 1868. I. 511.
— Les plantes de l'École de botanique de Toulouse. 1891. III. 49.[1]
— Les plantes de Virgile. 1871. I. 514.[2]
— Le polymorphisme floral. 1894. I. 115.[2]
— De la postfloraison. 1865. I. 115.[1]
— De la postfoliaison. 1867. I. 110.
— Pourrat et son histoire des Cistes. 1858. II. 564.[1]
— Prétendue valeur spécifique du Quercus fastigiata. 1890. II. 135.[2]
— Primefeuilles . . . folio-stipulaires de . Crataegus. 1899. II. 261.[1]
— De la production de lamelles de glace. 1889. I. 212.
— Quelques cas de stérilité de plantes. 1890. II. 204.[2]
— De quelques espèces de Duvauas. 1890. II. 460.[1]
— De quelques faits afférents à la sexualité végétale. 1900. I. 239.[1]
— Quelques faits de carpologie. 1866. I. 119.
— Quelques mots sur la greffe. 1856. III. 435.[1]
— De quelques particularités de l'inflorescence. 1891. II. 653.[2]
— De quelques principes d'organographie végétale. 1872. I. 100.[1]
— De quelques questions afférentes à des plantes brésiliennes. 1872. II. 488.[2]
— De quelques recherches de synonymie, V. 1872. II. 349.[2]
— De la question de priorité dans l'établissement de la famille des Cycadées. 1869. II. 2.[3]
— Des racines caulinaires. 1883. I. 104.
— De la ramification des Éléagnées. 1858. II. 607.[1]
— Recherches sur l'involucre des Synanthérées. 1851. II. 850.[1]
— Récolte de graines de Gingko. 1898. III. 287,[1] IV. 440.[1]
— La région méditerranéenne et le Chêne Kermès. 1899. II. 133.[1]
— Remarques sur la germination du Cocotier. 1861. II. 67.[2]
— Répartition en France des Crataegus. 1890. II. 261.[1]
— Révision comparative de l'herbier . . . de Lapeyrouse. 1857. I. 411, 421.
— Révision d'une des sections du genre Sideritis. 1862. II. 766.[2]
— Révision des tubercules des plantes . . . des Légumineuses. 1893. II. 322.[1]
— Des Sarothamnus Catlierus et Jaubertus. 1872. II. 349.[2]
— Sépales et pétales vaginaux du Lierre. 1899. II. 510.[1]
— Sépales stipulaires. 1859. I. 115.[2]
— Sépales vaginaux du Choisya ternata. 1899. II. 400.[2]
— De la signification du filet de l'étamine. 1876. I. 116.[2]
— Singulier cas de germination des graines d'une Cactée. 1890. II. 597.[2]
— Singulière apparence offerte . . . d'une tige de Chêne. 1884. I. 210,[2] *IV. 510*.
— Solidarité de la botanique et de l'agriculture. 1900. III. 36.[1]
— Des stipules. 1879. I. 112.[1]
— Des stipules et de leur rôle. 1878. I. 111.
— Du stipulium chez les Géraniacées. 1855. II. 256,[2] *320*,[1] *565*.[2]
— De la symétrie des racines dites adventives. 1883. I. 104.
— Tendance de la fleur des Oléinées vers la tétrandrie. 1899. II. 705.[2]
— La tératologie végétale. 1891. I. 144.[1]
— La théorie des soudures en botanique. 1879. I. 100.[1]
— Variations ou anomalies des feuilles composées. 1876. I. 110.
— Variété et anomalie. 1891. I. 244.[2]
— La viviparité dans le règne végétal. 1900. I. 204.
— Les vrilles des Smilax. 1857. II. 85.[1]
— Vrilles foliaires. 1899. I. 111.
Close, C. P. Plant diseases and insect pests. 1900. III. 178.
Closon, Jules. Aphelandra Margaritae. 1885. III. 708.[2]
Clot-Bey, Antoine Barthélémy. Aperçu général sur l'Égypte. 1840. III. 130.[2]
— Einiges über den Gartenbau in Aegypten. 1840. III. 130.[2]
Clouet. Note sur la préparation . . . des Osiers. 1869. III. 347.
Clouet, J. Empoisonnement par les fleurs du Cytise. 1875. III. 481.[1]
Clouth, Franz. Gummi, Guttapercha und Balata. 1899. III. 232.[1]
— Die Kautschuk-Industrie. 1879. III. 231.

The **Clove** as a dye plant. 1894. III. 636.
Clove cultivation. 1893. III. 635.³
Clove industry of Zanzibar. 1893. III. 635.¹
The **Clove** tree. 1888. III. 635.³
Club alpin français. Annuaire. I. 21.
Club alpin suisse. Annuaire. *See* SCHWEIZER ALPEN CLUB. I. 26.³
Club für Naturkunde (Section des Brünner Lehrervereines). Bericht. I. 27.
Clusius, Carolus. Aliquot notae in Garciae Aromatum historiam. 1582. I. 282.
— Appendix cultori plantarum exoticarum necessaria. 1630. III. 116.¹
— Curae posteriores. 1611. I. 284.
— Exoticorum libri decem. 1605. I. 283.
— De nova gummi purgante. 1614. III. 609.¹
— Petit recueil. 1557. III. 239.
— Rariorum aliquot stirpium per Hispanias observatarum historia. 1576. I. 419.¹
— Rariorum aliquot stirpium per Pannoniam . . . observatarum historia. 1583. I. 438.
— Rariorum plantarum historia. 1601. I. 283.
The " **Cluster Pine** " in California. 1890. IV. 467.²
Clute, W. N. The flora of the upper Susquehanna. 1898. I. 316.
Clutius, Augerius. *See* CLUYT, Outger.
Clutterbuck, P. H. Wood-pulp. 1900. IV. 430.
Clutton, John. Pruning Oak timber. 1857. III. 361.²
Clutton, Ralph W. The self-sown Oak-woods of Sussex. 1874. IV. 506.
— The self sown Oak woods of Sussex. 1875. III. 363.¹
Cluyt, D. O. Historia cocci de- Maldiva Lusitanis. 1634. III. 327.¹
— Memoire der vreemder bloombollen, wortelen. 1631. I. 285.¹
— Opuscula duo singularia. 1634. *II. 70,*³ III. 327.¹
Clyers, Andrea. De herba Thée asiaticorum. 1676. III. 604.³
Cnattingius, Jacob. Några iakttagelser rörande löfträden. 1888. I. 296.¹
Coach-makers' international journal. IV. 3.
Coakley, Jean. Histoire naturelle du Thé. *See* LETTSOM, J. C. 1772. III. 605.
Coaz, Johann Wilhelm. Abnorme Rothtannenzapfen. 1883. II. 36.¹
— Arvensamenjahr und Arvenkultur. 1884. IV. 463.³
— Ueber Aufbewahrung . . . des Arvensamens. 1887. IV. 463.²
— Ueber das Auftreten des grauen Lärchenwicklers. 1880. IV. 451.
— Ueber das Auftreten des grauen Lärchenwicklers. 1894. IV. 442.
— Das Blatt und seine Erfärbung. 1880. I. 185.³
— Die bündnerischen Waldungen. 1854. IV. 365.
— La culture des Osiers. 1879. III. 348.
— Du développement des plantes phanérogames sur le terrain abandonné par les glaciers. 1887. I. 220.¹
— Erste Ansiedelung phanerog. Pflanzen auf von Gletschern verlassenem Boden. 1887. I. 220.¹
— Freier Gedankenflug über die Waldungen der Schweizer Alpen. 1864. IV. 366.
— Frostbeschädigungen . . . in der Schweiz. 1884. IV. 191.²
— Der Frostschaden des Winters 1879/80. 1882. IV. 191.³
— Geschichtlich-statistischer Bericht . . . über das Forstwesen in Graubünden. 1869. IV. 366.
— Ueber Klima und Vegetationsverhältnisse von Locarno. 1879. I. 436.
— Die Kultur der Weide. 1879. III. 348, *IV. 487.*¹
— Die Lauinen der Schweizeralpen. 1881. IV. 188.² ·
— Der Lauinenschaden im schweizerischen Hochgebirge. 1889. IV. 188.³
— Mittheilung über Spebälle. 1885. I. 242.³
— Les ouragans du 23 février . . . 1879. 1880. IV. 189.¹
— Der Schneeschaden vom 28./29. September 1885. 1887. IV. 190.
— Die Stürme vom 20. Februar . . . 1879. 1880. IV. 189.¹
— Vorkommen des grauen Lärchenwicklers. 1879. IV. 451.
— Der Wald. 1861. IV. 43.
Ceban, Empedocle. Contribuzione all' anatomia della "Agdestis." 1898. II. 192.²
Cobb, Jonathan Holmes. A manual . . . respecting the growth of the Mulberry tree. 1831. III. 374.
Cobb, N. A. Cause of an important Apple disease. 1898. III. 428.¹

— Letters on the diseases of plants. 1898. III. 180.¹
— A list of plants . . . within thirty miles of Amherst. 1887. I. 315.
— Tylenchus and root-gall. 1890. III. 192.³
Cobban, A. McDonald. A botanical romance. 1896. I. 295.¹
Cobbett, William. The American gardener. 1821. III. 99.
— The woodlands. 1825. IV. 108.¹
Cobelli, Giovanni de. Contribuzione alla flora dei contorni di Rovereto. 1890. I. 429.
— Teratologie del fiore della Crassula lactea. 1877. II. 236.³
Cobelli, Ruggero. Osservazioni sulla fioritura [*sic*]. 1893. II. 242.¹
— La prima e l' ultima fioritura . . . delle flore di Serrada. 1895. I. 430.
Cobres, Joseph Paul von. Deliciae Cobresianae. 1782. I. 1, V. VII.¹
Coca. 1883. III. 492.¹
Coca. 1885. III. 493.¹
'Coca. 1889. III. 493.²
La **Coca.** *See* COCA. 1889. III. 493.
Il **Coca** del Perù. 1865. III. 492.¹
Das **Cocaïn,** ein neues Alkaloid. 1860. III. 492.²
La **Cocaina.** 1885. III. 493.¹
Cocastelli, Adelelmo. Intorno alla coltivazione dell' Ailanto. 1866. III. 506.³
Cocchi, Antonio Coelestino. Dissertatio continens vindicias corticis peruviani. 1750. III. 719.
Cocchi, Igino. Observations sur la culture du Ginko. 1899. III. 287.¹
Cocconi, Girolamo. Contributo alla flora della provincia di Bologna. 1876. I. 428.
— Contributo allo studio dei nettarii mesogamici delle Caprifogliacee. 1888. II. 834.¹
— Flora dei foraggi. 1856. III. 223.¹
— Flora della provincia di Bologna. 1883. I. 429.
Cochet. Notice sur la transplantation de grands Houx. 1838. III. 167.
Cochet, Pierre Charles Marie. *See* COCHET-COCHET.
Cochet-Cochet. Note sur le Rosier Sakoura-Ibara. 1898. III. 456.¹
— Note sur un Rosier hybride. 1897. III. 457.¹
— Notes sur le Rosa laevigata. 1898. III. 455.²
— Rosa laevigata. 1898. III. 455.³
— Les Rosiers en Seine-et-Marne. 1896. III. 453.¹
— & **Mottet,** Séraphin. Les Rosiers. 1897. III. 451.¹
Cochins, F. D. Quelques observations au sujet de la culture du Café libéria. 1898. III. 743.¹
Cochon, F. Alternance des essences dans les forêts. 1846. IV. 74.¹
Cochon, J. Améliorations pastorales et reboisement. 1899. IV. 546.²
— Une fête de l'Épicéa dans le Jura. 1900. IV. 541.
— Forêt des Écollets. 1898. IV. 556.¹
— Sur un phénomène de végétation topiaire. 1900. IV. 558.³
— Sociétés scolaires forestières. 1899. IV. 541.³
— & **Grosjean.** Concours forestier local . . . de Saint-Claude. 1898. IV. 556.¹
Cochran, M. De teelt en bemesting van Klapperboomen. 1900. III. 323.¹
Cochrane, W. J. The cultivation of Osiers . . . 1893. III. 349.
Cockayne, Leonard. On the burning . . . of subalpine scrub. 1899. I. 508.¹
— Descriptions of new species of Astelia, Veronica. 1899. II. 783.¹
— An inquiry into the seedling forms of New Zealand phanerogams. 1899. I. 123.¹
— A sketch of the plant geography of the Waimakariri River basin. 1900. I. 508.²
Cockayne, Oswald. Leechdoms, wortcunning. 1864. I. 292.
Cockerell, Theodore Dru Alison. Abnormal leaves and flowers. 1897. I. 144.¹
— A Date-palm scale insect. 1899. III. 329.¹
— The Evonymus scale in Japan. 1896. III. 532.¹
— Life-zones in New Mexico. '1895. I. 326.
— The lower and middle Sonoran zones. 1900. I. 327.
— Notes on the cochineal insect. 1897. III. 623.³
— The San José scale and its nearest allies. 1897. III. 187.
— Some plants of New Mexico. 1900. II. 198.³
— The validity of the specific name. 1892. I. 254.¹
— *See also* TOWNSEND, C. H. T., CHITTENDEN, F. H., COCKERELL, T. D. A. & CRAW, Alexander.

Cockfield, Joseph. ' Catalogue of scarce plants . . . of London. 1813. I. 396.

Cocks. Products of the Montana of Peru. 1865. III. 268.²

Coclenius, Rudolf. Mirabilium naturae liber. 1625. I. 517.²

The **Coco-de-mer**. 1892. II. 71.¹

Coco-nut butter. 1893. III. 324.¹

The **Coco-palm**. 1857. III. 323.²

Cocoa. 1882. III. 592.²

Cocoa as grown in Trinidad. 1879. III. 592.²

Cocoa in Trinidad, Venezuela. 1898. III. 593.¹

The **cocoa** industry and insect pests. 1887. III. 593.²

Cocoa (or Cacao), Coca, Coco, Cocoa nuts. 1894. I. 72.²

Cocoa-nut and coir·from Lagos. ˙1889. III. 324.¹

Cocoa-nut beetle in Zanzibar. 1879. III. 323.¹

Cocoa-nut butter. 1890. III. 324.¹

Cocoanut cultivation in Samoa. 1897. III. 758.¹

The **Cocoa-nut** Palm. 1851. III. 323.¹

The **Cocoa-nut-tree**. 1894. III. 323.¹

Cocoran, J. St. V. The Altai flora of western Siberia. 1896. I. 454.²

Cocosvezel. 18 . . ? III. 323.¹

Le **Cocotier**, Cocos nucifera. 1900. III. 323.¹

Le **Cocotier** des Séchelles. 1849. II. 70.³

Cocquius, Adrian, Historia . . . sacra plantarum. 1664. I. 512.

—Observationes . . . philologico-physiologicae ad vetus testamentum. 1664. I. 512.

Code des loix des trois mandemens. *See* BOIVE, *Dr.* 1772. IV. 329.

Code des médicamens; ou, Pharmacopée française. *See* CODEX medicamentarius. 1638. III. 255.¹

Le **code** forestier de Madagascar. 1900. IV. 332.²

Code forestier du canton de Fribourg. 1850. IV. 330.

Code forestier du 12 juin 1835. 1835. IV. 330.

Code forestier, suivi de l'ordonnance réglementaire du code de la pêche. 1849. IV. 324.

Code of instructions for the conduct of office and other business. 1885. IV. 307.²

Code of instructions for the conduct of office business. 1877. IV. 307.²

Code pharmaceutique. *See* CODEX medicamentarius. 1638. III. 255.¹

Codes forestier, rural, de la chasse. *See* ROGRON. 1841. IV. 322.²

Codex Augustaeus systematicus venatorio-forestalls. 1792. IV. 321.

Codex medicamentarius. Pharmacopée française. *See* CODEX medicamentarius; seu, Pharmacopœa parisiensis. 1638. III. 255.¹

Codex medicamentarius; seu, Pharmacopœa hispanica. *See* PHARMACOPOEA hispana. 1803. III. 255.²

Codex medicamentarius; seu, Pharmacopœa lusitanica. 1822. III. 250.¹

Codex medicamentarius; seu, Pharmacopœa parisiensis. 1638. III. 255.¹

Codex medicamentarius; sive, Pharmacopœa danica.· *See* PHARMACOPOEA danica. 1772. III. 247.¹

Codex medicamentarius; sive, Pharmacopœa gallica. *See* CODEX medicamentarius; seu, Pharmacopœa parisiensis. 1638. III. 255.¹

Codex medicamentarius; sive, Pharmacopœa suecica. *See* PHARMACOPOEA suecica. 1775. III. 247.¹

Codex medicamentarius hamburgensis. 1835. III. 249.

Codice farmaceutico; ossia, Farmacopea francese. *See* CODEX medicamentarius. 1638. III. 255.¹

Codicele silvic votat în şedinta Senatuluĭ de la 16 Maiŭ 1881. 1885. IV. 332.¹

Codigo pharmaceutico lusitano. *See* CODEX medicamentarius; seu, Pharmacopœa lusitanica. 1822. III. 256.¹

The **Codman** collection of books on landscape gardening. 1899. III. 1, *IV. 2.*

Codornfu, Ricardo. Apuntes relativos á la repoblación forestal de la Sierra de España. 1900. IV. 545.¹

—Atocha; notas sobre su germinación y desarrollo. 1890. IV. 545.²

—Construcción de tablas gráficas. 1894. IV. 542.²·¹

—Notas relativas á la germinación del "Pinus halepensis." 1892. IV. 464.²

—Pinos. Experiencias sobre la germinación. 1889. IV. 464.¹

—La sierra de España y su repoblación forestal. 1897. IV. 547.¹

—Tempestad y avenida en la sierra de Espuña. 1894. IV. 548.¹

Coe, C, a, H. The so-called Florida sea beans. 1894.· II. 164,²·321.ᵉˢ

Coelho, J. A. India-rubber collection at Para. 1896. III. 231.

Coelho de Seabra Silva Telles, Vicente. Memoria sobre a cultura do Ricino. 1791. III. 521.²

—Mémoria sobre o methodo de curar a ferrugem das Oliveiras. 1792. III. 677.¹

Coelln, Johannes von. Specifica Canadensium. *See* LINNÉ, Carl von. 1756. III. 262.¹

Coene, Victor de. Citrus chinensis.˙ 1898. III. 500.²

Coester, Carl. Ueber die anatomischen Charaktere der Mimoseen. 1894. II. 321.¹

Cöthen, VON JENA·. *See* RAMANN, Emil & JENA-CÖTHEN, von.

Coeverden, C. C. L. van. Sumatra's Westkust. 1872. III. 275.¹

On **Coffee**. *See* LINDLEY, John, HOOKER, *Sir* J. D. & others. 1852. V. xxix.²

Coffee at home. 1888. III. 727.

Coffee cultivation at the Gold Coast. 1895. III. 732.²

Coffee cultivation at the Gold Coast. 1897. III. 732.²

Coffee cultivation in Angola. 1894. III. 732.²

Coffee cultivation in British Honduras. 1892. III. 728.¹

Coffee cultivation in the New World. 1893. III. 728.¹

Coffee disease. 1877. III. 735.

Coffee disease. 1878. III. 735.

Coffee-disease. 1881. III. 735.

Coffee-disease in Ceylon. 1879. III. 735.

Coffee diseases. 1897. III. 736.

Coffee enterprise in the East Indies. 1893. III. 732.²

Coffee in America; methods of production. 1893. III. 728.¹

Coffee-leaf disease in central Africa. 1893. III. 736.

The, **Coffee** leaf disease of Ceylon. *See* MORRIS, Daniel. 1880. III. 735.

Coffee leaf miner. 1894. III. 736.

Coffee planting in Lagos. 1896. III. 732.²

Coffin, George W. Forest lands of Maine. 1844. IV. 338.²

Coffin's botanical journal. I. 5.

Cofinas, Georges N. Les forêts et l'administration forestière en Grèce. 1896. IV. 294.²

Coghlan, Timothy Augustine. The timber resources of New South Wales. 1900. IV. 402.¹

Cogho, (*Oberförster, Seitenberg*). Entgegnung auf die Erwiderung des Herrn Oberförsters Lignitz. 1877. IV. 204.

—Ueber Holz-Verbrauch zu Zündhölzchen. 1858. IV. 428.²

—Ueber die Lebensfähigkeit des Fichten-Borkenkäfers. 1874. IV. 204.

—Ueber das Ueberfliegen des Fichten-Borkenkäfers. 1875. IV. 204.

—Ueber die Ueberwinterung der Brut des Bostrychus. 1876, IV. 204.

—Ueber Ursachen der längeren Dauer von Borkenkäfer-Verheerungen. 1875. IV. 204.

—Ueber den Wiederanbau entwaldeter Freilagen. 1877. IV. 158.

Cogniaux, Alfred. Le genre Siolmatra. 1893. II. 844.²

—Melastomaceae. 1883. II. 635.¹

—Melastomaceae. 1889. II. 641.¹

—Melastomaceae. 1891. II. 635.¹

—Melastomaceae et Cucurbitaceae. 1888. II. 634.¹

—Melastomaceae et Cucurbitaceae africanae. 1889. II. 641.¹

—Melastomaceae et Cucurbitaceae portoricenses. 1886. II. 635.¹

—Mélastomacées. 1891. II. 634.²

—Eine neue Melastomaceen-Species. ·1896. II. 638.¹

—New Melastomaceae collected by Miguel Bang. 1896. II. 635.¹

—Notice sur les Mélastomacées austro-américaines. ' 1887. II. 635.¹

—Plantae Lehmannianae . . . Melastomaceae. 1887.· II 635.¹

—Synonymie de l'Heterocentron ‚mexicanum. 1894. II. 637.²

—*See also* SALDANHA DA GAMA, José de & COGNIAUX, Alfred; SCHUMANN, Karl, BAKER, J. G., ROLFE, ʼR. A. & COGNIAUX, Alfred.

Cogrossus, Carolus Franciscus. Della natura . . . della corteccia·del Peru. 1711. III. 719.

Cogswell, W. H. Rhesa. 1886. III. 382.¹

— & **Strettell**, G. W. Paper from vegetable fibres. 1882. III. 235.²

Cohausen, Johann Heinrich. Archeus febrium faber et medicus. 1731. III. 719.

Cohausen, Johann Heinrich (*continued*).
— Neothea; oder, Neu-angerichtete . . . The-Tafel. 1716. III. 222.
— Neothea; or, Nieuwe theetafel. 1719. III. 222.
— Neu-angerichtete medicinische Theetafel. 1750. III. 605.
Cohen, L. Ali. Een woord over den . . . nieuw ontdekten Den, Abies Reginae Amaliae. 1861. III. 297.[1]
Cohn, Ferdinand Julius. Ueber abnorme Kiefer-Nadel- und Zapfenbildung. 1860. IV. 483.[1]
— Anomale Früchte von Citrus Limonum. 1894. II. 403.[2]
— Beitrag zur Geschichte der Botanik. 1882. I. 79.[2]
— Bericht über die Entwicklung der Vegetation. 1851. I. 224.[2]
— Botanische Mittheilungen. 1857. II. 507.[1]
— Contractile Gewebe im Pflanzenreiche. 1861. I. 149.[1]
— On the contractile tissue of plants. 1861. I. 149.[1]
— De cuticula. 1850. I. 129.[1]
— Ueber die Drehung der Baumstämme. 1854. I. 107.[1]
— Einige Worte über die Kiefernkrankheit. 1893. IV. 478.
— Ueber die Einwirkungen des Blitzes. 1853. IV. 193.[2]
— Über die Flora von Westaustralien. 1881. I. 502.
— Fruchtzapfen von Encephalartos Lehmanni. 1892. II. 6.[1]
— Über Gefässe aus Taxusholz. 1889. III. 288.[2]
— Der Haushalt der Pflanzen. 1854. I. 217.
— Ueber die Holzzellen des Weinstockes. 1857. II. 507.[1]
— Ein interessanter Blitzschlag. 1857. IV. 193.[2]
— Zur Lehre vom Wachsthum der Pflanzenzelle. 1850. I. 136.[2]
— Loranthus europaeus L. 1885. II. 176.[1]
— Ueber einen merkwürdigen Blitzschlag. 1855. IV. 193.[2]
— Ueber die Palmen. 1876. II. 63.[2]
— Die Pflanze. 1882. I. 96.
— Ueber den Pflanzenkalender. 1865. IV. 72.
— Zum Pflanzenkalender von Breslau. 1863. I. 225.
— Über · Reizbarkeitserscheinungen der Staubfäden von Opuntia. 1873. II. 596.[2]
— Ueber die Reizleitung bei Mimosa pudica. 1891. III. 373.[1]
— Die Rinde einer Moquilea. 1887. II. 265.[2]
— Symbola ad seminis physiologiam. 1847. I. 179.[1] ·
— Über Tabaschir. 1887. II. 59.[2]
— Der tausendjährige Rosenstock. 1892. II. 290.[1]
— Ueber den Ursprung der schlesischen Flora. 1860. I. 384.
— Ueber die Verbreitung der Pflanzen. 1857. IV. 75.[1]
— Ueber Verunstaltung von Kiefer-Wipfeln durch Insekten. 1862. IV. 476.
— Über das Vorkommen der Eichenmistel in Schlesien. 1870. II. 179.[1]
— Was sich über Wald erzählt. 1863. IV. 75.[1]
— Ueber die Windhose von Mangschütz. 1858. IV. 189.[1]
— *See also* LEBERT, H. & COHN, F; KÖN, Φερδινάνδος.
— & Engler, Adolf. Das botanische Museum der Universität Breslau. 1888. V. VIII.[2]
Coïcou, Edmond. Recherches sur la vrille des Ampélidées. 1882. II. 501.[1]
Coignet, F. Les Kakis du Japon. 1872. III. 669.[1]
Coincy, August de. Ecloga [I.-IV.] plantarum hispanicarum. 1893. I. 423.
— Remarques sur le Juniperus thurifera. 1898. II. 30.[1]
Cointeraux, François. Avis au peuple sur l'économie de son bois. 1806. IV. 431.[1]
Cointrel, Pierre. Catalogue des plantes du Jardin botanique de Lille. 1751. I. 56.
Cola, Vincenzo. Della diatesi morbosa della Vite. 1857. III. 577.
Cola nut. 1881· III. 590.[1]
Cola nut. 1890. III. 590.[2]
Cola nut or Bissy. 1891. III. 590.[1]
Cola nuts of Africa. 1859. III. 590.[1]
Colbatch, *Sir* John. A dissertation concerning Mistletoe. 1719. III. 385.[2]
— Dissertation sur le Guy. 1719. III. 385.[2]
Colberg, Friedrich, *Freiherr* von LÖFFELHOLZ-. *See* LÖFFEL-HOLZ-COLBERG, Friedrich, *Freiherr* von.
Colborne, Robert. A complete English dispensatory. 1753. III. 252.
— The plain English dispensatory. 1753. III. 252.
Colby, George E. Analyses of California Olives. 1898. III. 679.[2]
— Starch in Buckeye fruit. 1896. II. 481.[1]
— *See also* BIOLETTI, F. T. & COLBY, G. E.
— & Dyer, H. L. Investigation of California Oranges. 1891. III. 497.[1]
— & Hilgard, E. W. California Walnuts, Almonds, and Chestnuts. 1896. III. 134.[1]

Coldefy-Dorly. Extrait d'une lettre sur la matière vésicante de l'écorce de Garou. 1825. III. 627.[1]
Colden, Cadwallader. Plantae Coldenghamiae. 1749. I. 313.
— Selections from the scientific correspondence. 1843. I. 307.
Colden, Conwallader. *See* COLDEN, Cadwallader.
Coldstream, John. Marine insects destroyers of wood. 1834. IV. 414.[1]
— On the structure and habits of the Limnoria. 1834. IV. 414.[1]
Coldstream, William. Abstract of experiments with anaesthetic agents on Sensitive plants. 1860. II. 372.[2]
— Memorandum on the economic products . . . in Muzaffargarh district. 1865. III. 278.
— Note on tasar sericulture in the Punjab. 1890. III. 148.[2]
— Notes on fruit culture in Simla. 1894· III. 147.[1]
— On the production of lac. 1881. III. 232.[2]
Cole, S. W. The American fruit book. 1849. III. 133.
Colebrook, John. A venerable Cedar. 1884. II. 28.[1]
Colebrooke, Henry Thomas. On Boswellia. 1827. I. 470,[1] II. 416.[2]
— Description of select Indian plants. 1818. I. 471.
— On the Dryobalanops Camphora . . . 1816. (*By error under* JONES, *Sir* William.) II. 560,[1] V. XXVII.[1]
— On the Indian species of Menispermum. 1822. II. 207.[2]
— On olibanum or frankincense. 1807. II. 416.[2]
— *See also* ROXBURGH, William & COLEBROOKE, H. T.
Colección de leyes . . . relativas al servicio . . . del ramo de montes. 1869. IV. 327.
Coleman, A. The Monterey Pine. 1889. III. 308.[1]
Coleman, N. Catalogue of flowering plants . . . of Michigan. 1874. I. 314.
Coleman, William. Abies Douglasi taxifolia. 1885. III. 309.[2]
— Berry-bearing shrubs. 1886. III. 420.[2]
— The Bracted Silver Fir. 1889. III. 296.[1]
— Coniferen. 1889. III. 293.
— On Conifers. 1889· III. 293.
— Conifers in the west of England. 1889. III. 293.
— The Golden Chinese Arbor-Vitae. 1890. III. 311.[2]
— The Hemlock Firs. 1889. III. 312.[1]
— The Medlar. 1885.· III. 429.[2]
— The Mistleto-Oak in Eastnor. 1878. II. 179.[1]
— The Nepaul Juniper. 1889. III. 304.[1]
— Pawpaw or Custard Apple. 1879. III. 401.[2]
— The Quince. 1886. III. 423.[1]
— The Scotch Fir. 1889. IV. 473.
— Spruces, Firs and Pines, hardy in the west of England. 1889. III. 293.
— Tree notes. 1888. III. 361.[2]
Coleman, William Higgins. Catalogue of the flowering plants . . . of Leicestershire. 1863. I. 533.
— A sketch of the botany of Leicestershire. 1876. I. 403.
— *See also* WEBB, R. H. & COLEMAN, W. H.
Coleman, William Stephen. Our woodlands, heaths and hedges. 1859. I. 393,[1] 533, V. XX.[2]
Colenso, Wilham. On the botany . . . of the North Island. 1869. I. 346.[2]
— On Clianthus puniceus Sol. 1886. II. 346.[1]
— A description of . . . plants from our New Zealand forests. 1880. I. 507.
— A description of . . . plants from our New Zealand forests. 1882. I. 507.
— A description of some . . . indigenous plants. 1885. I. 507.
— Descriptions of a few new indigenous plants. 1883. I. 507.
— Essay on the botany of the North Island. 1865. I. 506,[2] III. 94.[2]
— Excursion in the northern island of New Zealand. 1844. I. 506.[1]
— A further contribution towards . . . the botany of New Zealand. 1884. I. 507.
— In memoriam; an account of visits to . . . the Ruahine mountain. 1884. I. 507.
— Notes and reminiscences of early crossings of . . . Lake Waikaremoana. 1895. I. 508.[1]
— Notes, remarks . . . of two . . . South American plants. 1894. III. 533.[1]
— Tree Ferns of New Zealand. 1887. II. 650.[2]
— On the vegetable food of the ancient New Zealanders. 1881. III. 283.[1]
Colenuci, Pandolfo. Pliniana defensio. 1493.· I. 276.

Colerus, Johannes. Oeconomia ruralis et domestica. 1591.
IV. 115.
Coles, Sherard COWPER-. Some notes on the preserving and
fireproofing of timber. 1899. IV. 421.
Coles, William. Adam in Eden. 1657. I. 286.
— The art of simpling. 1656. I. 286.
Colin. See EDWARDS, Milne & COLIN.
Colin. See GUIGNARD, Léon & COLIN.
Colin, Auguste. Éléments d'arboriculture fruitière. 1891.
III. 145.[1]
Colin, G. Recherches expérimentales sur l'accroissement en
diamètre. 1868. .I. 190.[1]
Colius, Jakob. Syntagma herbarum encomiasticum. 1606.
I. 284.
Colla, Luigi. L' antelogiáta botanico. 1813. I. 85.
— Camelliografia. 1843. II. 550.[3]
— Freyliniae genus. 1830. II. 780.[2]
— Herbarium pedemontanum. 1833. I. 426.
— Hortus ripulensis. 1824. I. 62.
— Mémoire sur une Rubiacée nommé . . . Melanopsidium.
1825. II. 823.[1]
—Observations sur la famille des Rutacées. 1843. II. 396.[2]
— Osservazioni sovra una notizia . . . circa l'Elephantusia.
1842. II. 73.[3]
— Plantae rariores in regionibus chilensibus. 1834. I. 346.
— Storia e descrizione del Cactus senilis. 1838. II. 591.[3]
— Storia e descrizione del Cactus . . . spiraeformia. 1840.
II. 594.[1]
Colladon, Daniel. Effects of lightning on trees. 1880. IV. 194.
— Effects of lightning on trees. 1881. IV. 194.
— Effets de la foudre sur les arbres. 1872. IV. 194.
— Mémoire sur les effets de la foudre sur les arbres. 1872.
IV. 194.
— Peuplier frappé par la foudre. 1880. IV. 194.
Colladon, Louis Théodore Frédéric. Histoire naturelle et
médicale des Casses. 1816. II. 342.[2]
Colladon, Theodor. Adversaria. 1615. I. 284.
Collaert, Adrian. Florilegium ab Hadriano Collaert caelatum.
156 . ? I. 280.
Collantes, Agustin Esteban & Alfaro, Agustin. Diccionario
de agricultura práctica. 1851. III. 31.
Collas, (Dr.). De l'acclimatation du Caroubier. 1864. III.
471.[2]
Collectanea for a flora of Moray. See GORDON, George. 1839.
I. 398.
On collecting, preparing and sowing the seeds of trees. 1833.
III. 156.[1]
Collecting Spruce gum. 1900. III. 306.[1]
Collection de matière médicale . . . par M. François Della
Sudda. 1856. III. 272.[1]
Collection des produits des eaux et forêts du Bas-Canada.
See TACHÉ, J. C. 1862. IV. 19.[1]
Collection des produits forestiers du grand-duché de Finlande.
1867. IV. 19.[1]
A collection of Passion-flowers. See LAWRANCE, Mary. 1799.
II. 576,[2] III. 615.[1]
A collection of rules for the management of forests in the Pun-
jab. 1897. IV. 307.[2]
A collection of rules made by government under the Indian
forest act VII. of 1878. 1894. IV. 307.[3]
College of agriculture. Imperial university of Japan, Bul-
letin. I. 28.[1]
College of science, Imperial university, Japan. Journal.
I. 28.[2]
Collet, Philibert. Catalogue des plantes . . . de Dijon.
1702. I. 405.
Colletias. 1877. III. 541.[3]
Collett, Sir Henry. Notes on some plants of the Himalaya.
1895. I. 475.[2]
— & Hemsley, W. B. On a collection of plants from Upper
Burma. 1891. I. 476.[1]
Collezione di Camelie coltivate nel giardino di Cesare Franc-
chetti. 1855. III. 598.[2]
Collie, R. The influence of bush fires on the distribution of
species. 1888. I. 503.
Collier, A. Experiments in transplanting forest trees. 1851.
III. 167.
Collier, H. Teinture de Quillaya. 1881. III. 447.[1]
Collignon. Essai de bien-public. 1776. IV. 277.
Collignon. Mémoire sur un nouveau mode de culture . . .
de la Vigne. 1850. III. 555.
Collin. Étude microscopique des aliments d'origine végétale.
1899. III. 219.[3] .
— Sur un verglas observé en Floride. 1879. III. 184.[2]

Collin, Andr. Fata botanices in Finlandia. See KALM, Pehr.
1758. I. 80.[1]
Collin, Eugène. Anatomie comparée des feuilles officinales.
1886. I. 110.
— Des Cannelles. 1876. II. 224.[1]
— Caractères anatomiques des poudres officinales. 1890.
III. 260.[1]
—Étude anatomique des poudres officinales. 1890. III. 260.[1]
— Exposition universelle . . . La matière médicale. 1900.
III. 29.[1]
— Falsification du thé en Chine. 1890. III. 608.[1]
— Du Maté ou Thé du Paraguay. 1891. II. 464.[2]
— La matière médicale de la Perse. 1890. III. 279.[2]
— Note sur la poudre de Séné. 1900. III. 470.[2]
— Des poudres de noix vomique. 1892. III. 683.[2]
— Du Thé chinois. 1900. III. 608.[1]
— Sur le vrai et le faux Ko-Sam. 1900. III. 508.[1]
— See also PLANCHON, Gustave & COLLIN, Eugène.
Collin, Nils. Förslag af några Nord-Americas träd. 1822.
III. 119.[2]
Collinet. Formules générales des composés organiques.
1861. I. 151.[1].
Collings Bréhaut, Thomas. See BRÉHAUT, Thomas COLLINGS.
Collingwood, Cuthbert. On Nutmeg and other cultivation in
Singapore. 1869. III. 129,[1] 409.[3]
— Rambles of a naturalist on the shores . . . of the China
sea. 1868. I. 453.[1]
Collins, Henry. Under the Mistletoe. 1890. II. 180.[1]
Collins, J. Geschiedenis . . . van gutta percha. 1885. III.
668.[2]
Collins, James. On the commercial kinds of india-rubber.
1868. III. 231.
— On india-rubber, its history. 1870. III. 231.
— The indiarubber of commerce. 1872. III. 519.[1]
— The Lignaloe-wood of Mexico. 1869. III. 510.[1]
— Materia medica notes. 1872. III. 726.[1]
— Notes on some new . . . vegetable products. 1870. III.
245, 667.[3]
— Report on the caoutchouc of commerce. 1872. III. 229.
Collins, Robert T. The royal Boscobel Oak. 1884. II. 133.[2]
Collins, S. S. See DAME, L. L. & COLLINS, S. S.
Collins, Samuel. Paradise retrieved. 1717. III. 141.
Collinson, T. B. On timber trees of New Zealand. 1851.
IV. 402.[1]
Collman, A. F. The Ash. 1887. III. 672.[1] .
Collodion ter vervanging van entwas. 1886. III. 162.
Colloredo-Mansfeld, Josef von. Eine fürstliche Denkschrift
über Wald und Wasser. 1876. IV. 53.
— Zur Wasser- und Walderhaltungs-Frage. 1876. IV. 50.
Collot. See MARGOTTET & COLLOT.
Collot, Louis. Études morphologiques sur les feuilles. 1876.
I. 110.
— Le phylloxera à Panama. 1879. III. 553.[1]
Collstrop, A. Nogle Oplysninger angaaende impraegnerede
og uimpraegnerede Svellers Holdbarhed. 1900. IV. 424.[2]
Colman, Henry. Treatise on bone manure. 1838. III. 151.
Colman, Norman J. A circular to educational men. 1887.
IV. 30.[1]
— For information of railroad managers. 1887. IV. 424.[1]
— Information to wood consumers. 1887. IV. 420.
Colmar, von. Echinocereus caespitosus. 1883. III. 622.[2]
— Echinopsis Pentlandii var. Cavendishii. 1884. III. 622.[2]
— Ein unbekannter (?) Cactus. 1878. II. 592.[1]
Colmar-Naturhistorische Gesellschaft. See SOCIÉTÉ D'HIS-
TOIRE NATURELLE DE COLMAR. I. 15.
Colmar-Société d'histoire naturelle. See SOCIÉTÉ . . . I. 15.
Colmeiro y Penido, Miguel. Aclimatación del Alerce afri-
cano. 1854. IV. 447.[2]
— Apuntes para la flora de las dos Castillas. 1849. I. 420.
— Árboles y arbustos . . . en el Jardín botánico de Madrid.
1892. I. 60.[2]
— Bosquejo historico . . . del Jardin botánico de Madrid
1875. I. 60.[1]
— La botánica y los botánicos de la península Hispano-Lusi
tana. 1858. I. 3.[2]
— Botanische Erinnerungen an Galicien. 1850. I. 420.
— Catalogo metodico de plantas observadas en Cataluña.
1846. I. 420.
— Catalogus plantarum in Horto botanico barcinonensi.
1844. I. 60.[1]
— Curso de botánica. 1854. I. 89.. .
— Diccionario de los diversos nombres vulgares de muchas
plantas. 1871. I. 74.[3]

Colmeiro y Penido, Miguel (*continued*).
— Ensayo histórico sobre los progresos de la botánica. 1842. I. 81.[1]
— Enumeracion y revision de las plantas de la península hispano-lusitana é islas Baleares. 1885. I. 422.
— Exámen histórico-critico de los trabajos concernientes á la flora hispáno-lusitana. 1870. I. 3.[2]
— Genisteas y Antilídeas de España. 1872. II. 319.[1]
— Influencia del calor y de la luz. 1856. I. 229.
— Investigaciones sobre la antigua madera . . . Alerce. 1852. IV. 447.[2]
— Los jardines botánicos. 1894. I. 38.[2]
— Manual completo de jardineria. 1859. III. 89.[1]
— Naturalizacion del Alerce africano. 1856. III. 299.[2]
— Noticia sucinta de los animales y plantas que mencionó Cervantes en el Quijote. 1895. I. 515.
— Nuevas investigaciones sobre los Alerces. 1852. IV. 447.[2]
— Observaciones hechas en Sevilla sobre la florescencia. 1851. I. 226.[2]
— Observaciones y reflexiones hechas sobre los movimientos de las hojas . . . con motivo del eclipse de sol. 1860. I. 198.
— Pflanzengeographische Schilderung von Catalonien. 1846. I. 420.
— Plantas crasas de España y Portugal. 1874. II. 596.[1]
— Primeras noticias acerca de la vegetación americana. 1892. I. 330.
— Prolificacion observada en dos piñas del Pino doncel (Pinus Pinea). 1873. II. 45.[1]
— Recüerdos botánicos de Galicia; o, Ligeras noticias sobre las plantas observadas de paso en este antiguo reino. 1850. I. 420.
— Resumen de los datos estadísticos concernientes á la vegetación espontánea. 1890. I. 422.
— Rosáceas de España y Portugal. 1873. II. 256.[1]
— **& Boutelou,** Esteban. Exámen de las Encinas . . . que producen bellotas. 1854. II. 129.[2]
Colmenero de Ledesma, Antonio. Chocolata inda. 1631. III. 593.[2]
— Du chocolate. 1631. III. 593.[2]
— Della cioccolata. 1631. III. 593.[2]
— Curioso trattato . . . del chocolate. 1631. III. 593.[2]
— A treatise of the nature and quality of chocolate. 1631. III. 593.[2]
Colnaghi, D. E. Floods and forests. 1883. IV. 185.[1]
— Natural products . . . of Florence. 1888. III. 271.[2]
— Report from Florence on the exhibition of means of combating various Vine diseases. 1887. III. 561.
— Report on the forests, &c., of the province of Belluno. 1889. IV. 364.
Colomb, Georges. Étude anatomique des stipules. 1886. I. 112.[1]
— Note sur l'ochrea des Polygonées. 1886. II. 184.[1]
— Recherches sur les stipules. 1887. I. 112.[1]
Colomb, P. Le Sapin aux Ballons. 1895. IV. 446.[2]
Colombano. Collezione ragionata e fedele delle contraddizioni degli errori di massima botanica. 1800. I. 253.[2]
Colombetti, Giovanni. Della Falsacacia o Robinia. 1833. IV. 523.[1]
Colombian India-rubber. 1890. III. 522.[1]
Colombina, Gasparo. Il bomprovifaccia, per sani et amalati. 1621. I. 284.
Colombo, D. Fernando. Historie . . . dell' Ammiraglio D. Christoforo Colombo. 1571. III. 266.
Colonial, (*pseud.*). Forestry in New South Wales. 1900. IV. 380.[1]
Colonial institute. *See* ROYAL COLONIAL . . . III. 18.
Colonial timber (despatch respecting). *See* HILL, Walter & BAILEY, F. M. 1875. V. xxxi.[2]
Colonna, Fabio. Minus cognitarum plantarum . . . pars. 1616. V. xv.[2]
— Minus cognitarum stirpium aliquot . . . ἔκφρασις. 1616. V. xv.[2]
— Minus cognitarum . . . stirpium ἔκφρασις. 1616. I. 284, V. xv.[2]
— Φυτοβασανος; sive, Plantarum aliquos historia. 1592. I. 283.
Coloquios dos simples. *See* HUERTO, Garcia del. 1563. III. 239.[2]
Colorado —Agricultural experiment station. *See* COLORADO — STATE AGRICULTURAL COLLEGE. III. 3.
Colorado —Forest commissioner. Report. IV. 3.
Colorado — State agricultural college — Agricultural experiment station. Annual report. Bulletin. III. 3.
Colorado — State forest, game and fish commissioner. Biennial report. IV. 3.

Colorado state forestry association. Annual meeting; programme: Proceedings. IV. 3.
Coloration des bois ordinaires en Acajou. 1825. IV. 422.[2]
Coloration du bois. 1896. IV. 422.[2]
The **colouring** of flowers. 1892. I. 185.[1]
Colpaert, Émile. De la Coca. 1862. III. 492.[1]
I **colpevoli.** 1880. IV. 283.[1]
Colson. Lettre . . . au sujet de l'étêtement des Ormes. 1837. III. 363.[2]
Coltivazione artificiale del tartufo. 1866. IV. 439:
Della **coltivazione** del Gelso. *See* FABBRONI, Adamo. 1784. III. 373.
La **coltura** degli Aranci in Algeria. 1898. III. 500.[2]
On **Columba** root. 1830. III. 397.[1]
Columbia College. Contributions from the Herbarium. *See* COLUMBIA UNIVERSITY. I. 519.[1]
Columbia River and Oregon timberman. IV. 3.
Columbia University. Contributions from the Department of botany. I. 519.[1]
Columbian barks. 1880. III. 713.[1]
Columbus horticultural society. Journal. III. 3.
Columella, Lucius Junius Moderatus. Abhandlung von Bäumen. 1523. III. 96.[1]
— Das Ackerwerk. 1472. III. 98.
— L' agricoltura. 1472. III. 98.
— De l' agricoltura libri XII. 1472. III. 98.
— Agricultur oder Ackerbau. 1472. III. 98.
— Los doce libros de agricultura. 1472. III. 98.
— Les douze livres des choses rustieques. 1472. III. 98.
— Of husbandry, in twelve books. 1472. III. 98.
— Om landoekonomi. 1472. III. 98.
— Liber de arbortbus. 1523. III. 96.[1]
— Il libro de gli alberi. 1523. III. 96.[1]
— Opera quae exstant. 1523. III. 96.[1]
— De re rustica libri XII. 1472. III. 98.
— Rerum rusticarum libri. 1472. III. 98.
— Scriptores rei rusticae. 1470. III. 96.[1]
— XII. könyvei, a' Mezei gazdaságról. 1472. III. 98.
— Zwölf Bücher von der Landwirthschaft. 1472. III. 98.
Columna, Fabius. *See* COLONNA, Fabio.
Colvill, William Henry. The Date Palm in Bagdad. 1875. III. 328.[2]
— Palms. 1875. III. 328.[2]
— Some observations on the vegetable productions . . . of Bagdad. 1875. I. 477.[2]
Comanesti, Nicolaus D. GHIKÁ. *See* GHIKÁ-COMANEŞTI, N. D.
Comar, Ferdinand. Préparation de la Myristine. 1859. III. 402.[1]
— Preparazione della Miristina. 1859. III. 402.[1]
Combe, Ad. Les forêts de l'Algérie. 1889. IV. 379.[1]
— Région du Chêne-Liége en Europe. 1889. IV. 517.[2]
Combemale. L'huile d'olives. 1893. III. 679.[2]
— *See also* GAUCHER, E., COMBEMALE & MARESTANG.
Comber, Thomas. The dispersion of British plants. 1874. I. 402.
— Geographical statistics of the extra-British European flora. 1875. I. 349.
— On the world-distribution of British plants. 1874. I. 402.
Combes, Paul. L'aire d'habitat du Palmier nain. 1897. II. 66.[2]
— L'Eucalyptus et ses dérivés. 189 . ? III. 634.[1]
— Quelques notes botaniques sur la Corse. 1899. I. 419.[1]
Combis, Francisco BARCELÓ Y. *See* BARCELÓ Y COMBIS, Francisco.
Combies, de. Traité de la culture des Pêchers. 1745. III. 440.[1]
— A treatise upon the culture of Peach trees. 1745. III. 440.[1]
Combres, Pierre. *See* FLAHAULT, Charles & COMBRES, Pierre.
Combretacea. *See* ALLEMÃO, F. F. 1844. II. 617.[2]
Combs, Robert. Plants collected in the district of Cienfuegos. 1897. I. 337.
— Some Cuban medical plants. 1897. III. 64.[1]
Comercio de maderas. Precios en Valladolid de las maderas de Pino. 1891. IV. 405.[2]
Comes, Orazio. Come provvedere al marciume delle radici. 1884. III. 194.
— La fillosseronosi ed il mal nero della Vite. 1883. III. 561.
— Sulla spontaneità manifestatasi nei Fichi. 1884. III. 370.[1]
— Illustrazione delle piante rappresentate nei dipinti pompeiani. 1879. I. 514.[2]
— Influence de la lumière sur la transpiration. 1880. I. 167.
— Le lave, il terreno vesuviano e la loro vegetazione. 1888. I. 429.

— La luce e la traspirazione. 1880. I. 167.
— Il mal nero della Vite. 1882. III. 578.
— La malattia dei Fichi nel Cilento. 1894. III. 370.¹
— Intorno ad una malattia del Carrubo. 1884. III. 471.²
— Sulla malattia del Nocciuolo. 1885. III. 358.¹
— Il marciume delle radici e la gommosi della Vite. 1884. III. 578.
— Sul marciume delle radici e sulla gommosi della Vite. 1884. III. 578.
— Sulla melata o manna. 1885. III. 179.
— La peronospora della Vite. 1886. III. 194.
— Provvedimenti per combattere la Peronospora. 1885. III. 578.
— Sulla Rhizomorpha necatrix. 1883. III. 578.
— Studii sulla impollinazione in alcune piante. 1874. I. 237.
Comey, Arthur M. See HILL, H. B. & COMEY, A. M.
Comice agricole et Société de viticulture, horticulture . . . de Brioude (Haute-Loire). Bulletin. . III. 19.
Comice de Nancy. Annales. See LE BON cultivateur. III. 19.
Comice horticole de Maine-et-Loire. Travaux. III. 19.
The coming changes with respect to the training and first appointment of forest officers selected in England. 1890. IV. 291.³
Comini, Ludwig von. Die Traubenfäule. 1858. III. 577.
Comino trees of Colombia. 1894. III. 404.¹
Cominotti, G. · Attrezzi americani. 1883. IV. 384.¹
— Le bandite e loro trattamento. 1884. IV. 169.¹
— I boschi del littorale austriaco. 1886. IV. 167.¹
— I boschi della Siberia occidentale. 1882. IV. 376.¹
— Le condizioni forestali del Nuovo Mondo. 1884. IV. 337.¹
— Le condizioni forestali nelle Indie. 1883. IV. 378.
— Fabbisogno dei lavori . . . per eseguire le piantagioni boschive a dimora. 1883. IV. 153.¹
— Fabbisogno dei lavori . . . per favorire la riproduzione naturale nei boschi. 1882. IV. 139.¹
— Fabbisogno dei lavori . . . per la formazione dei semenzai. 1883. IV. 150.
— Fabbisogno dei lavori . . . per le semine boschive. 1882. IV. 149.¹
— Fabbisogno dei lavori preliminari per la formazione dei semenzai. · 1883. IV. 150.
— Fabbisogno per l' escavazione dei fossi. 1883. IV. 146.²
— Le foreste della Russia. 1881. IV. 346.
— Grandezza dei semenzai e piantonai. 1883. IV. 154.¹
— Media quantità di semente necessaria. 1882. IV. 149.¹
— Il morso dei Corymbites ai getti delle Quercie. 1884. IV. 511.
— Numero delle buche. 1883. IV. 154.¹
— Nuovo segone a pancia tirolese. 1890. IV. 393.
— Olio per illuminazione. 1881. III. 225.
— Piante legnose. 1889. IV. 80.¹
— Piante legnose . . . sui punti più elevati della superficie terrestre. 1889. IV. 75.²
— Prontuario pratico . . . 1883. IV. 150.
— Prontuario pratico di stima ad uso del selvicultori. 1882. IV. 110.¹
— Quantità delle piante che possono essere trasportate. 1883. IV. 151.²
— Quantitativo dei semi ritraibili dagli strobili. 1882. IV. 148.
— Rapporti fra la superficie lavorata e la totale nelle semine. 1882. IV. 149.¹
— Il rimboschimento delle Alpi svizzere. 1883. IV. 166.²
— Scuola superiore di agricoltura in Vienna. 1881. IV. 36.²
— Spessore della copertura necessaria ai semi. 1882. IV. 149.¹
— Statistica dei boschi appartenenti all' impero Austro-Ungarico. · 1884. IV. 368.
— Tempo della fruttificazione degli alberi. 1882. IV. 139.²
Comisión corchera catalana. 1893. IV. 559.²
Comisión de rectificación del catálogo. 1892. IV. 363.²
Comisión de repoblación de la cuenca del Jucar. See LARA, Jacinto de. IV. 363.²
La Comisión de repoblación de la cuenca del Segura. 1889. IV. 546.²
Comisión permanente de la Asociación de ingenieros de montes. 1891. IV. 541.¹
Comisión revisora del catálogo de montes públicos. 1890. IV. 363.²
Comisión revisora del catálogo de montes públicos. 1892. IV. 363.²
Comité de Cognac. Station viticole. 1875. III. 567.²

Comité des amis des arbres et des oiseaux. 1897. IV. 541.
Commaille, Antione. Mémoire sur une nouvelle méthode de dosage des matières astringentes. 1864. I. 156.²
— Note sur la composition des cendres. 1863. I. 153.
— Note sur le cuivre normal des végétaux. 1863. I. 153.
Commelin, Jan. The Belgick or Netherlandish Herperides. 1676. III. 496.²
— Catalogus plantarum Horti medici amstelodamensis. 1689. I. 50.
— Catalogus plantarum indigenarum Hollandiae. 1683. I. 390.
— Nederlantschen Hesperides. 1676. III. 496.²
— & Kaspar. Horti medici amstelodamensis . . . plantarum . . . descriptio et icones. 1697. I. 50, 288.
Commelin, Kaspar. Beschryvinge en curieuse afbeeldingen van rare vreemde . . . gewassen. 1701. I. 289.
— Botanographia. 1696. I. 470.²
— Flora malabarica. 1696. I. 470.²
— Horti medici amstelaedamensis plantae rariores. 1706. I. 50.
— Horti medici amstelaedamensis plantarum usualium catalogus. 1715. I. 50.
— Plantarum usualium Horti medici amstelodamensis catalogus. 1698. I. 50.
— Praeludia botanica. 1703. I. 289.
— & Jan. See COMMELIN, Jan & Kaspar.
Comment faire disparaître les coudriers? 1899. IV. 169.²
Comment nos forêts sont protégées! · 1899. IV. 555.¹
Commentaire sur l'ordonnance des eaux et forêts. See JOUSSE, Daniel. 1772. IV. 325.
Commentarii di medicina. III. 23.¹
Commentario della fauna, flora, e gea del Veneto. 1867. I. 428.
Commentatio de.faba St. Iguatii. See HAASE, W. A. 1822. III. 682.²
Le commerce des bois. 1900. IV. 303.²
— · . . . dans la Russie méridionale. 1894. IV. 557.¹
Commerce des bois dans le nord de l'Europe. 1878. IV. 403.²
Le commerce des bois du Canada. 1894. IV. 557.¹
Commerce des bois [en France]. 1895. IV. 557.¹
On the commerce of Mexico. 1867. III. 264.²
The commercial history of a Cinchona plantation. 1878. III. 712.²
Commercial review of the south and west. See DE BOW's review . . . III. 3.
Commercial value of Loxa bark. 1890. III. 725.²
Commercio d' importazione . . . dei principali prodotti boschivi. 1894. IV. 405.²
Commercio d' importazione . . . dei prodotti boschivi in Francia. 1894. IV. 405.¹
Commercio d' importazione e . . . di prodotti forestali tra la Francia e l'Italia. 1865. IV. 405.²
Commercio di legnami in Inghilterra. 1866. IV. 405.¹
Commercio di legnami in Italia. 1866. IV. 405.²
Il commercio e l' industria nella provincia di Cuneo. 1865. IV. 405.²
Commercio internazionale. [Prodotti forestali.] 1863. IV. 402.²
Commercio italiano [dei legnami]. 1865. IV. 405.¹
Commerson, Philibert. See CUSSON, Pierre, GOUAN, Antoine & COMMERSON, Philibert.
Commissâo geographica e geologica, São Páulo (estado de). Brazil. See SÃO PAULO (ESTADO DE), BRAZIL-COMMISSÃO . . . I. 8.¹
La commission des améliorations pastorales. 1898. · IV. 293.¹
La commissione d' imboschimento del Carso. 1892. IV. 167.²
Commissione per lo studio delle condizioni dello stabilimento di Mongiana. 1864. IV. 286.²
Commissioners of woods, forests . . . of the crown. Reports. Special report. IV. 12.¹
Common, J. New roots to old trees. · 1878. III. 164,¹ 181.²
The common Button Bush. 1889. III. 711.²
The common Jasmine. 1896. III. 673.¹
Common sugar existing . . . in the flowers of Rhododendron. 1827. III. 683.¹
Commons, Albert. Bartram's Oak. 1892. II. 134.¹
Von Commun- und Privatwäldern. 1789. IV. 307.² See also MÜLLENKAMPF, F. D. F. 1789. IV. 116.
Communications on different subjects. 1802. III. 118.²
Cómo acaba un pueblo. 1891. IV. 541.

Comolli, Giuseppe. Catalogus plantarum . . . in Horto bot. novocomensi. 1815. I. 62.
— Flora comense. 1834. I. 426.
— Flora comensis. 1826. I. 426.
— Plantarum in lariensi provincia lectarum enumeratio. 1824. I. 426.
— Prodromus florae provinciae comensis. 1824. I. 426.
Compagnie de Bretagne pour une plantation de 100,000 hectares de landes en bois de Pins. 1828. IV. 161.[2]
A companion to Dr. Thornton's lectures on botany. 1816. I. 523.
Companion to the Botanical magazine. I. 18.
Companion to the Glasgow botanic garden. See MURRAY, Stewart. 1840. I. 54.
Companyo, (Dr.). Projet d'organisation du service de santé du canal interocéanique de Panama. 1880. III. 118.[1]
Companyo, Jean Louis. Description de deux nouvelles plantes . . . des Genistées. 1848. II. 349.[2]
— Greffage du Chêne-Liége sur le Chêne-vert. 1848. IV. 516.[3]
— Histoire naturelle . . . des Pyrénées orientales. 1861. I. 412, V. xxii.[1]
— Notice sur les insectes qui ravagent quelques cantons des vignobles. 1839. III. 562.[2]
— Observations sur les insectes nuisibles aux Oliviers. 1858. III. 677.[3]
Comparaison des pavés de bois avec ceux d'asphalte. 1895. IV. 557.[2]
Comparatio nominum plantarum officinalium. See ARENSTORFF, C. F. 1762. III. 72.
Comparative value of wood. 1866. IV. 423.[1]
Comparetti, Andrea. Osservazioni sulle proprietà della china del Brasile. 1794. III. 720.
— Prodromo di fisica vegetabile. 1791. I. 32, 146.
— Riscontri fisico-botanici ad uso clinico. 1793. I. 97.
Comparetti, Pietro. Riflessioni sulle ceppaje ovvero zocche dei boschi di Quercia. 1814. III. 361.[2]
— Saggio sulla coltura e governo de boschi. 1798. IV. 109.[2]
Compendio della storia geografica, naturale . . . del Chile. See MOLINA, G. I. 1776. I. 345.
Compendio di fisiologia vegetale. See TOMMASELLI, Giuseppe. 1880. I. 148.
Compendio di nosologia vegetabile. See MORETTI, Giuseppe. 1839. I. 206,[1] III. 178.[3]
The compleat cyderman. 1754[1] III. 141.
The compleat planter & cyderist. 1685. III. 141.
A compleat system of husbandry. See WORLIDGE, John. 1716. III. 108.
The complete florist. n. d. III. 106.[3]
Compositae aequatorianae. See SODIRO, Aloysius. 189 . ? II. 349.[1]
Composition of ash of young Furze. 1847. II. 387.[3]
Compressed or tablet tea. 1890. III. 607.
Compte-rendu de l'Exposition forestière. 1888. IV. 20.[2]
Compte-rendu des travaux de Congrès viticole de Beaune. 1869? III. 555.
Compte rendu des travaux du Congrès international de pomologie en 1894. 1897. III. 68.[1]
Compte rendu des travaux du service du phylloxera. 1882. III. 573.
Compte rendu du Congrès contre le black-rot. 1896. III. 581.
Compter, (Oberförster). Der heutige Stand der Durchforstungen. 1887. IV. 174.
— Ist der Einfluss der Vorerträge von grösserer Wichtigkeit . . . als jener der Abtriebsertrage? 1887. IV. 257.
Compter, (Waldinspektor, Freudenstadt). Does forestry pay? 1881. IV. 259.[2]
— Rentirt die Waldwirthschaft oder nicht? 1881. IV. 259.[3]
Comstock, F. G. A practical treatise on the culture of silk. 1836. III. 375.
Comstock, John Henry. Report upon cotton insects. 1879. III. 587. See also TRELEASE, William. 1879. I. 238.
Comstock, John Lee. Elements of botany. 183 . ? I. 86.
— The illustrated botany. 1847. I. 95.
— An introduction to the study of botany. 1832. I. 86.
— The young botanist. 1835. I. 94.
Comte, Joseph Achille. Cahiers d'histoire naturelle. 1836. I. 87.
— Introduction au règne végétal. 1834. I. 87.
— Das Pflanzenreich nach A. L. de Jussieu. 1834. I. 87.
Comyn, Tomás de. Estado de las Islas Filipinas en 1810. 1820. IV. 399.[1]

Conceição, José Marianno VELLOSO DA. See VELLOSO DA CONCEIÇÃO, J. M.
Concentrated Mangrove juice for tanning. 1892. III. 632.[1]
Concia delle pelli. 1866. IV. 435.
La concimazione degli alberi fruttiferi. 1899. III. 152.
Concordantia botanica. See WOLF, N. M. von. 1780. I. 77.
I concorsi per la bachicoltura alla scuola Perroncito. 1896. III. 378.
Un concorso a premi per uno studio sulla produzione forestale. 1896. IV. 41.[1]
Las concreciones calizas en la madera de Teck. 1888. IV. 538.[1]
Condamine & Blanchard, C. E. Caractères du Couden. 1868. III. 516.[2]
— Sur l'écorce aromatique du Nin-Dinh. 1868. III. 276.[2]
— — Sur le Haofach. 1889. III. 276.[3]
Condamine, Charles Marie de la. Sur l'arbre du quinquina. 1740. II. 811.[2]
— Mémoire sur une résine élastique. 1755. III. 228.[2]
— Relation abrégée d'un voyage fait dans l'intérieur de l'Amérique méridionale. 1745. I. 328.
Conder, Josiah. Theory of Japanese flower arrangements. 1889. III. 202.[1]
Condition and management of the Brisbane botanic gardens. 1882. V. ix.[1]
Le condizioni forestali della Bosnia e dell' Erzegovina. 1882. IV. 374.[2]
Condogouris. Tableau contenant quelques végétaux indigènes de Chios. 1856. I. 479.
Condon, Thomas. The forest trees of Oregon. 1890. IV. 78.[1]
Conducciones eléctricas de madera endurecida. 1891. IV. 412.[3]
Le condurango. 1871. III. 693.[2]
Le condurango. 1873. III. 693.[2]
Cone of Abies nobilis. 1856. III. 296.[2]
Cones of Abies brachyphylla. 1885. III. 296.[1]
Coneys and Nutmeg trees. 1887. III. 402.[2]
Conférence de l'ordonnance de Louis XIV du mois d'août 1669 sur le fait des eaux et forests. 1725. IV. 323.[2]
Conférence phylloxérique internationale. See ACTES de la 1878. III. 571.
Conferenz über die Organisation des land- und forstwirthschaftlichen Versuchswesens in Österreich. 1873. IV. 541.
Confévron, Le. Le Goumi du Japon. 1895. III.'629.[1]
— Le Staphylier de Colchique. 1895. III. 533.[2]
Configliachi, Luigi. Catalogus plantarum Imp. reg. horti botanici mantuani. 1816. I. 62.
Congdon, Joseph W. Mariposa county as a botanical district. 1891. I. 326.
— New species, principally from Mariposa county. 1899. II. 245.[3]
— See also GREEN, F. H. & CONGDON, J. W.
Congo. See MUSÉE du. See MUSÉE . . . I. 16.
Congrès botanique et d'horticulture de St.-Pétersbourg. Bulletin. I. 9.[3]
Congrès de botanique et d'horticulture de 1880 . . : Bruxelles. Compte rendu. I. 16.
Congrès de botanique . . . Paris . . . 1889. Actes . . I. 21.
Congrès de vignerons. See ACTES du . . . 1843. III. 554.[2]
Congrès de vignerons et de pomologistes. Actes. See ACTES du Congrès . . . 1847. III. 124.[1]
Congrès interdépartemental. Compte-rendu du Congrès . . . tenu à Bordeaux. 1876. III. 759.
Congrès international agricole et forestier. Rapport. See INTERNATIONALER LAND- UND FORSTWIRTHSCHAFTLICHER CONGRESS. IV. 14.
Congrès international d'horticulture . . . Bruxelles. Bulletin. III. 15.
Congrès international de botanique et d'horticulture . . . Amsterdam. Bulletin. I. 15.
Congrès international de botanique et d'horticulture d'Anvers . . . 1885. Actes. I. 16.
Congrès international de botanique et d'horticulture . . . Paris . . . 1878. Comptes rendus. I. 520.[1]
Congrès international de botanique et d'horticulture . . . St. Pétersbourg. Bulletin. I. 9.[3]
Congrès international de botanique . . . Paris. Actes. I. 21.
Congrès international de botanistes, d'horticulteurs . . . Amsterdam. Actes. I. 15.
Congrès international de pomologie. 1863. III. 77.
Congrès international de pomologie en 1894. Compte rendu des travaux. See COMPTE rendu . . . 1897. III. 68.[1]
Congrès international de sylviculture. 1900. IV. 39.[3]

Congrès international de viticulture. 1900. III. 557.[2]
Congrès international des Américanistes. Compte-rendu. III. 11.
Congrès international des rosiéristes. 1900. III. 451.[1]
Congrès international phylloxérique. Programme. 1881. III. 761.
Congrès international phylloxérique de Bordeaux. 1882. III. 573.
Congrès phylloxérique international. Actes. 1877. III. 760.
Congrès pour l'étude des fruits à cidre. 1872. III. 85.
Congrès pour l'étude des fruits à cidre. 1873. V. XXVIII.[1]
Congrès scientifique de France. Sessions. I. 21.
Congrès viticole de Montpellier. 1893. III. 557.[1]
Un Congressiste, (pseud.). Conclusions et vœux du Congrès international de sylviculture. 1900. IV. 29.
Congresso botanico internationale di Genova. Atti. I. 24.[2]
Congresso fillosserico internazionale, Torino. Atti. 1885. III. 761.
Il Congresso forestale e gli ufficiali forestali. 1897. IV. 329.
Congresso internationale botanico . . . Firenze. Atti. I. 24.[2]
Il congresso tra i consorzi di tiro contro la grandine. 1899. IV. 191.[1]
Conhecimento pratico dos medicamentos. See The EDINBURGH new dispensatory. 1786. III. 253.
The conical corky spines of Zanthoxylon. 1893. II. 411.[2]
The conical growth of trees. 1863. I. 106.[2]
On the Coniferae . . . recently introduced. 1869. III. 78.[1]
Le Conifere. 1890. IV. 441.
Conifere . . . nella coltura silvana in Italia. 1883. IV. 441.
De Coniferen. 1852. III. 289.
Coniferen mit goldgelben Nadeln. 1878. III. 290.
Coniferen-Sammlung in Hochfürstlich von Rohan'schen Garten. 1879. I. 66.[1]
Les Conifères du parc de Lovenjoul. 1875. III. 290.
Conifers at Murthly Castle. 1900. III. 293.
Coninck, A. M. C. JONCKINDT. See JONCKINDT CONINCK, A. M. C.
Coninck, C. J. M. JONCKINDT. See JONGKINDT CONINCK, C. J. M.
Coninck, E. de. Dracaena Mooreana. 1873. III. 337.[1]
Coninck, W. OECHSNER DE. See OECHSNER DE CONINCK, W.
Coningh, C. van VRIJBERGHE DE. See VRIJBERGHE DE CONINGH, C. van.
De la connaissance des bois employés dans les arts. 1852. IV. 408.
Connecticut — Agricultural experiment station. Annual report. Bulletin. III. 3.
Connecticut — Storrs (school) agricultural experiment station. Annual report. Bulletin. III. 3.
Connecticut board of agriculture. Annual report. III. 3.
Connecticut forestry association. Leaflet series. IV. 3.
Connell, Arthur. Chemical examination of the Tagua-nut. 1844. III. 330.[1]
— On the Tagua nut. 1844. III. 330.[1]
Connors, Robert. See JACK, Edward & CONNORS, Robert.
Conrad, Abram H. A contribution to the life history of Quercus. 1900. II. 141.[1]
Conrad, Johannes. Über der Herrschaft Tepl. 1837. I. 492.
Conradi. Betrachtungen über die Folgen einer ununterbrochenen Waldwirthschaft. 1828. I. 132.[1]
Conradi, Friedr. Ernst. Tafeln zu Bestimmung des kubischen Inhalts runder und vierkantiger Hölzer. 1842. IV. 223.
— Ein weiterer Beitrag zur Flora von Banjaluka. 1892. II. 179.[2]
Conrath, Paul. Viscum auf Eichen. 1892. II. 179.[2]
Conreur, P. L'exploitation des futaies sur taillis. 1897. IV. 556.[2]
Conseil d'état. 5 juillet 1895. Soumission au régime forestier. 1897. IV. 293.[1]
Conseil supérieur des forêts. 1900. IV. 291.[2]
Consentini, Ferdinando. Saggio di botanica. 1805. I. 84.
Conservacion de las Castañas. 1886. IV. 493.[2]
Conservandae bonae valetudinis praecepta. 1573. III. 240.
Conservation des bois. 1885. IV. 420.
Conservation des bois. See BOUCHERIE, Auguste. 1857. IV. 418.
Conservation des bois sous l'eau. 1898. IV. 421.
Conservation des bois tendres. 1886. IV. 420.
De la conservation des glands. 1896. IV. 508.
Conservation des glands. 1898. IV. 509.
Conservation des graines des résineux. 1899. IV. 148.
Conservation des graines forestières. 1859. IV. 147.[1]
Sur la conservation des herbiers. 1867. I. 520.[1]

Conservation des préparations botaniques. 1881. I. 521.[1]
Conservation des sites et des arbres des routes. 1896. III. 210.
Conservation du bois contre la moisissure. 1885. IV. 420.
Conservation et agrandissement du domaine forestier de l'état. 1895. IV. 551.[2]
Conservatoire des arts et métiers. See CONSERVATOIRE IMPÉRIAL DES ARTS . . . IV. 539.[2]
Conservatoire et jardin botaniques de Genève. Annuaire. I. 26.[2]
Conservatoire (imperial) des arts et métiers. Annales. IV. 539.[2]
Conservazione degli erbari. 1883. V. VIII.[1]
Conservazione dei pali. 1890. IV. 421.
Conservazione dei pali da vite. 1865. IV. 419.
Conservazione dei rami d'innesto. 1865. III. 161.
Conservazione del legname. 1865. IV. 419.
Conservazione del legname. 1885. IV. 420.
Conservazione del legno. 1881. IV. 420.
Conservazione del legno sotto terra. 1863. IV. 418.
Conservazione delle traverse in legno delle ferrovie. 1866. IV. 423.[2]
Conservirung des Holzes. 1857. IV. 418.
Conservirung des Holzes durch Kreosot. 1885. IV. 420.
Considérations générales sur la Liane Gohine. 1899. III. 230.
Considérations générales sur la maladie du Mûrier. See BORDONE, (Dr.). 1865. III. 379.
Considérations sur le tissu des végétaux, au sujet de l'Orange dite bizarrerie. 1836. II. 402.[2]
Consiglio provinciale d'agricoltura pel Tirolo. Bollettino. III. 24.[2]
Consilium de usu herbae et potus Thee. 1708. III. 605, 741.[1]
Consitor, (pseud.). De Koffieluis. 1894. III. 736.
Console, Michelangelo. Anomalien bei Cacteen. 1883. II. 588.[1]
— Myrtillocactus. 1897. II. 589.[2]
— Su taluni casi morfologici . . . delle Cactacee. 1883. II. 588.[1]
Consommation du bois en Angleterre. See MÉLARD, A. 1894. IV. 405.[1]
Il Consorzio del Trasimeno. 1881. IV. 165.
Il Consorzio interprovinciale per il rimboschimento del Murone e del Mombarone. 1895. IV. 166.[1]
Conspectus Horti botanici ducalis jenensis. See BATSCH, A. J. G. K. 1795. I. 44.
Constant, Alexandre. Rhodorhiza florida. 1892. II. 744.[2]
Constantin & Matruchot. Culture d'un champignon lignicole. 1894. IV. 523.[2]
Constantini Caesaris selectarum praeceptionum, de agricultura libri viginti. See CASSIANUS BASSUS. 1538. III. 98.
The Constantinople Nut. 1887. III. 358.[1]
Constitution de la propriété forestière départementale. 1877. IV. 276.[1]
Il consumo del legname negli S. U. d' Inghilterra. 1895. IV. 405.[1]
Il consumo di legname in Germania. 1894. IV. 404.[2]
Il consumo relativo del legno in varî paesi. 1896. IV. 403.[2]
Ai contadini. Sulla malattia dell' Uva. See FRANCESCHINI, F. 1854. III. 576.
Contant, Jacques & Paul. Les divers exercices. 1628. I. 285.[1]
— Les œuvres divisées en cinq traictez. 1628. I. 285.[1]
— Synopsis plantarum indigenarum et exoticarum. 1628. I. 285.[1]
Contarini, Nicolò. Sopra di un gallinsetto delle foglie del Salice. 1852. III. 350.[1]
Conté. Note concernant le développement de l'oïdium. 1869. III. 577.
Conte, Bernardino. Saggio di agraria che versa sopra le cause della decadenza de' boschi. 1795. IV. 276.[2]
Contejean, Charles. Composition du sable des dunes. 1878. IV. 163.
— Enumération des plantes vasculaires des environs de Montbéliard. 1854. I. 411.
— Sur la flore du grés de Fontainebleau. 1876. I. 228.[2]
— Géographie botanique. 1881. I. 228.[2]
— Influence du calcaire. 1875. I. 228.[2]
— De l'influence du terrain. 1874. I. 228.[2]
— Note sur la flore calcifuge. 1877. I 228.[2]
— Pourquoi l'on rencontre quelquefois les plantes du calcaire. 1879. I. 228.[2]
— Quelques faits de dispersion végétale observés en Italie. 1883. I. 429.

Contejean, Charles (*continued*).
— Remarques sur la dispersion des plantes. 1853. I. 228.[1]
— Revue de la flore de Montbéliard. 1890. I. 417.
— La soude dans le sol et dans les végétaux. 1879. I. 153.
— La soude dans les végétaux. 1878. I. 153.
Contemporary review. III. 16.
Contest-Lacour. Des plantes qui peuvent se multiplier par racines. 1872. III. 159.[1]
— Rajeunissement des Cocotiers. 1871. III. 322.[2]
Conti, C. R. Sul pineto ravennate. 1876. IV. 364.
Continental monthly. III. 3.
Continuation der Nürnbergischen Hesperidum. *See* VOLCK-AMER, J. C. 1708. II. 400.[2]
Contius, C. S. Einige Bemerkungen über die mehrere Abnahme der deutschen Forsten. 1805. IV. 282.[1]
Sur le **contre-poison** du Mancenillier. 1822. III. 707.[2]
Contri, Giovanni Francesco. Sulla coltivazione dell' Ulivo. 1850. III. 675.[2]
Contribuciones de Colombia a las ciencias. III. 10.[1]
Contribution foncière des terres incultes. 1898. IV. 285.[1]
A **contribution** towards a complete list of the fauna and flora of Clydesdale. 1876. I. 402.
Contributions à l'histoire naturelle de la Sarthe. 1877. I. 415.
Contributions to the botany of Vermont. I. 5.
Contributions to the Cape oeconomic flora. *See* PAPPE, Ludwig. 1856. III. 93.[1]
Contributions towards a fauna and flora of the county of Cork. *See* POWER, Thomas. 1845. I. 399.
Contribuzioni alla biologia vegetale. I. 24.[2]
La **controprova** all' articolo: Prove di fatto che le piene del fiumi crescono. 1880. IV. 50.
Contzen, Heinrich. Ueber die Bedeutung der Waldstreu. 1870. IV. 71.
— Die Bedeutung des Waldes. 1870. IV. 269.
— Der Einfluss des Waldes. 1868. IV. 43.
— Die ethische und ästhetische **B**edeutung des Waldes. 1870. IV. 55.[2]
— Forstliche Zeitfragen. 1870. IV. 101.
— Die Freiheit des Waldbaues. 1870. IV. 269.
— Die Nationalökonomie. 1868. IV. 101.
— Das Studium der Nationalökonomie. 1869. IV. 29.
— Der Wald im Haushalt der Natur. 1868. IV. 43, 269.
— Die Wichtigkeit der National-Oekonomie. 1859. IV. 269.
— Ein Wort über und für den Wald. 1872. IV. 269.
— Ein Wort über und für den Wald. 1873. IV. 44.
Convention phylloxérique de Berne. 1882. III. 761.
Conversations on botany. *See* FITTON, Elizabeth & S. M. 1817. I. 94.
Conversations on vegetable physiology. *See* MARCET, Mrs. Jane. 1829. I. 94.
Conversations sur la physiologie végétale. *See* MARCET, Mrs. Jane. 1829. I. 94.
Conversion d'un taillis simple en futaie sur taillis. 1899. IV. 129.
Convert & Saint-Lager, Jean. Sexualité des Rhamnus. 1898. II. 497.[1]
Convert, F. & **Degrully**, Léon. Sur les ressources que présente la culture de la Vigne. 1883. III. 559.[1]
Convocatoria y programas para el ingreso en la Escuela especial de ingenieros de montes. 1878. IV. 35.[1]
Conway, Moncure D. Sacred flora. 1870. I. 518.
Conway, William Martin. Climbing and exploration in the Karakoram-Himalayas. 1894. I. 475.[1]
Conwell, W. E. E. Recherches sur les propriétés . . . Croton Tiglium. 1824. III. 517.[1]
Conwentz, Hugo Wilhelm. Alte Bäume im Kreise Elbing. 1890. I. 296.[1]
— Über Antholysen an Rubus Idaeus. 1878. II. 308.[1]
— Ueber aufgelöste . . . Himbeerblüthen. 1878. II. 308.[1]
— Beobachtungen über seltene Waldbäume in Westpreussen. 1895. I. 372.
— Ueber Bienenbäume (Beutkiefern). 1899. IV. 483.[1]
— Bildliche Darstellungen von seltenen . . . Bäumen in Westpreussen. 1899. I. 296.[2]
— Die Eibe in Westpreussen. 1892. II. 11.[1]
— Forstbotanisches Merkbuch. 1900. I. 296.[2]
— Mittheilungen aus den Karthäuser Wäldern. 1897. I. 372.
— Monographie der Baltischen Bernsteinbäume. 1890. II. 18.
— Neue Beobachtungen über das Vorkommen der Eibe. 1898. II. 11.[2]
— Neue Beobachtungen über die Eibe. 1899. II. 11.[2]
— Oehlafens Elenchus plantarum. 1877. I. 80.[2]
— Pelorie von einer Hybriden der Calceolaria crenatiflora. 1882. II. 779.[2]
— Ueber Thyllen und Thyllenähnliche Bildungen. 1889. I. 126.
— Ueber einen untergegangenen Eibenhorst. 1895. II. 11.[2]
— Ueber das Vorkommen der Eisbeere. 1899. II. 313.[2]
Conzatti, Cassiano. Clave analítica para la determinacion de las familias de las plantas . . . en Mexico. 1889. V. XVIII.[1]
— & **Smith**, L. C. Flora sinoptica mexicana. 1895. I. 333.
Cook, A. C. A sketch of the flora of the Canary Islands. 1898. I. 498.
Cook, Albert John. Experiments with insecticides. 1888. III. 196.
— Grape phylloxera. 1875. III. 759.
— The Grape-vine phylloxera. 1878. III. 760.
Cook, Alexander. Notes on the timbers of British North Borneo. 1885. IV. 400.[1]
Cook, James. The three voyages of Captain James Cook round the world. 1821. I. 302.
— A voyage towards the South Pole. 1777. I. 302.
Cook, Moses. The manner of raising . . . forrest-trees. 1676. IV. 107.[2] V. XXX.[1]
Cook, N. Bosques. 1824. IV. 42.[3]
Cook, Orator Fuller. Rubber cultivation for Porto Rico. 1900. III. 149.
Cook, Samuel Edward, (*afterwards* Widdrington). *See* WIDDRINGTON, S. E.
Cooke, E. W. A sculptured Palm seed. 1872. II. 70.[1]
Cooke, George. Seaside shrubs. 1877. III. 41.[3]
Cooke, George H. The forests of New Jersey. 1888. IV. 339.
Cooke, Matthew. Insects injurious to Citrus trees. 1885. III. 488.[1]
— A treatise on the insects injurious to fruit . . . of California and remedies recommended for their extermination. 1881. III. 186.[3]
Cooke, Mordecai Cubitt. Baobab; Adansonia. 1871. III. 589.[1]
— Beech morels. 1871. IV. 496.
— The Beech morels of the southern hemisphere. 1864. II. 127.[2]
— The blue dyes of China and India. 1861. III. 236.
— California Vine disease. 1893. III. 580.
— Clearing nuts. 1878. III. 685.[1]
— Dye-stuffs of India & China. 1861. III. 236.
— Economic products of the Tisso. 1861. III. 468.[1]
— Freaks and marvels of plant life. 1881. I. 96.
— Fungoid diseases of forest trees. 1872. IV. 211.[2]
— Guarana, Paullinia sorbilis. 1871. III. 539.[2]
— Gum olibanum. 1863. III. 509.[3]
— Jassabushit. 1867. IV. 489.[3]
— Juniper fungi. 1878. III. 303.[1]
— A manual of botanic terms. 1862. I. 71.
— A manual of structural botany. 1861. I. 100.[3]
— Materia medica of Baghdad. 1865. III. 278.
— New Indian products at the Exhibition. 1852. III. 278.
— Notes and queries on Asiatic copals. 1864. III. 233.[2]
— Notes on galls. 1861. III. 237.[1]
— Notes on myrabolans. 1863. III. 632.[2]
— Pine wood. 1862. II. 39.[2]
— Pine-wool. 1861. IV. 443.[2]
— The red dye-stuffs of India. 1861. III. 236.
— Report . . . on the gums, resins . . . in the India museum. I. 55, III. 227.
— Report on the oil seeds and oils in the India museum. 1876. III. 224.[2]
— Some parasites of Coniferae. 1878. IV. 442.
— Two Coffee diseases. 1876. III. 735.
— Two medicinal barks from Ceylon. 1872. III. 500,[1] 533.[1]
— Vegetable materia medica sold in the bazaars of Baghdad. 1864. III. 279.[2]
— Vegetable oils & fats of India. 1862. III. 224.[2]
— Vegetable waxes. 1861. III. 226.[1]
— The woodlands. 1879. I. 403.
— Woods of the Indo-Burmese provinces. 1862. IV. 401.[1]
— The yellow dye stuffs of China and India. 1861. III. 236.
Cooke, Theodore. Note on the flora of Mahableshwar. 1887. I. 475.[1]
Coolen, W. A. Iets over het beplanten van wegen. 1877. III. 209.

Cooley, G. E. Notes on movement of water in "Robinia." 1885. II. 383.[1]
Cooley, Robert Allen. Injurious fruit insects. 1900. III. 188.[1]
Coombe wood. 1890. I. 55.
Coomber, Thomas. The Holly and Yew as woodland trees. 1899. II. 11,[2] 463.[2]
— Mistletoe on the Hazel. 1883. II. 179.[2]
— Treatment of trees received during frost. 1895. III. 155.
Cooper. A letter on the manufacture of Maple sugar. 1792. IV. 527.[1]
Cooper, Daniel. Details of the first excursion made this summer by . . . the Botanical society of London. 1838. II. 661.[2]
— Flora metropolitana. 1836. I. 398.
Cooper, Ellwood. Forest culture and Eucalyptus trees. 1876. IV. 529.[2]
— A treatise on Olive culture. 1882. III. 675.[2]
Cooper, H. Stonehewer. Coral lands. 1880. V. xxiv.[2]
Cooper, J. S. The proposed Minnesota national park. 1900. IV. 179.[2]
Cooper, James Graham. Catalogue of plants collected in Washington Territory. 1860. I. 323.
— On the distribution of the forests and trees of North America. 1858. I. 304, IV. 336.[2]
— On the forests and trees of Florida. 1861. V. xvii.[1]
— The forests and trees of northern America. 1861. IV. 45, 544.[1]
— The influence of climate . . . on our trees. 1875. I. 217, IV. 78.
— The Mezquite bean. 1871. II. 379.[1]
— Reprt on the medical flora of Washington territory. 1857. III. 62.
— Report upon the botany of the route . . . explored by I. I. Stevens. 1860. I. 323.
— & Gray, Asa. Botanical report on the route from the Mississippi River to the Pacific Ocean. 1860. I. 323.
Cooper, Joseph. Observations on the Italian Mulberry. 1826. III. 374.
Cooper, Robert T. The re-afforesting of Palestine. 1898. IV. 168.[1]
Cooper, Thomas Henry. The botany of the county of Sussex. 1834. I. 398.
Cooper's Hill règlement du 12 juin 1890. See The PRESENT prospectus . . . 1891. IV. 34.[2]
Coopers' international journal. IV. 3.
Coordes, G. Gehölzbuch. 1882. I. 294,[1] III. 69, IV. 84.[1]
Coorg. See INDIA — COORG.
The Coorg forest manual. 1899. III. 332.[2]
Coote, George. Experiments in pollination of the Peach. 1895. II. 276.[2]
Cop, Marin Johannes. Oratio de botanices . . . necessitudine. 1842. I. 79.[1]
— Uver zoogenoemde eigen warmte bij planten. 1848. I. 186.
The Copaiba tree. 1877. III. 473.[1]
Sur les Copaïfera. 1878. III. 473.[1]
Copal. 1874. III. 489.[2]
A Copal forest. 1882. III. 233.[2]
On the copal of Zanzibar. 1869. III. 489.[2]
Copal-tree of East Africa. 1881. III. 489.[2]
Cope, F. J. See SAUNDERS, William, COPE, F. J. & McMINN, J. M.
Cope, Frank. See PERKIN, A. G. & COPE, Frank.
Cope, J. A. See BELCHILGEN, count & COPE, J. A.
Copeland, D. P. Brief account of how Rubber trees are grown in Assam. 1897. III. 370.[2]
— How Rubber trees are grown in Assam. 1897. III. 370.[1]
Copeland, Edwin Bingham. A biological note on the size of evergreen needles. 1898. II. 21.[1]
— Über den Einfluss von Licht und Temperatur auf den Turgor. 1896. I. 150.[1]
— & Kahlenberg, Louis. The influence of the presence of pure metals. 1900. I. 211.
Copeland, R. Morris. Country life. 1860. III. 99.
Copeland, Ralph. Ein Besuch auf der Insel Trinidad. 1882. I. 498.
Copenhagen — Botaniske Forening. Botanisk Tidsskrift. See BOTANISK Tidsskrift. I. 8.[1]
Copenhagen — Botaniske Forening. Festskrift. Meddelelser. See BOTANISKE . . . I. 8.[1]
Copenhagen — Naturhistorie-Selskabet. See NATURHISTORIE-SELSKABET . . . I. 9.[1]
Copenhagen-Naturhistoriske forening. See NATURHISTORISKE . . . I. 9.[1]

Copenhagen — Société botanique. Journal. See BOTANISK Tidsskrift. I. 8.[2]
Copenhagen — Universitas hafniensis. See UNIVERSITAS . . . I. 9.[1]
Copijn, H. & Koster, A. Duinbeplanting. te Schoorl by Alkmaar. 1898. IV. 160.[2]
Copland, Wyllyam. A boke of the propreties of herbes. 1546. I. 278.
Coppens, Bernard. Terminologie botanique. 1797. I. 70.
Coppice shoots of Dalbergia paniculata. 1888. II. 352.[2]
The coppicing of Cinchonas. 1874. III. 712.[1]
Coppock, W. R. A chapter on mulching. 1860. III. 151.
Copy of a letter addressed to Dawson Turner. See HOOKER, Sir W. J. 1840. I. 853.[1]
Coq, P. P. PETIT-. See PETIT-Coq, P. P.
Coque, J. V. de. The timbers of New South Wales. 1894. IV. 401.[2]
Coquerel, Charles. Déscription des parasites anormaux d'un Figuier. 1855. II. 149.[2]
Coquillett, Daniel William. Report on various methods for destroying scale insects. 1889. III. 196.
Coquito. — Food products. 1882. III. 326.[1]
El corazón rojo en el Haya. 1886. IV. 497.
Corazza, Giovanni. Contribuzione alla flora dei dintorni di Spoleto. 1889. I. 429.
Corbehard, P. P. de. Culture spéciale des Rosiers. 1880. III. 452.
Corbelli, Paolo. Dizionario di floricoltura. 1873. III. 88.[2]
— Il giardiniere medico. 1883. III. 59,[1] 150.[1]
Corbett, P. P. See SEGURA, J. C. & CORDERO, M. D.
Corbett, Lee Cleveland. The development of roots from cuttings. 1897. I. 209.[1]
— Forestry. 1895. IV. 112.
— Elaeagnus hortensis in Dakota. 1893. III. 628.[2]
— Forestry in South Dakota. 1897. IV. 112, 341.[1]
— Four native trees in the Northwest. 1895. IV. 112.
— Influence of groves on moisture. 1897. IV. 52.
— Latitude and plant growth. 1897. I. 219.[1]
— Nursery hints. 1899. III. 153.
— The Papaw, Asimina triloba. 1895. III. 401.[2]
— The reproductive powers of our forests. 1896. IV. 112.
— The rotation of species of trees. 1897. IV. 74.[2]
— Spraying; results of the season. 1900. III. 198.[2]
Corbière, Louis. Nouvelle flore de Normandie. 1893. I. 418.
— & others. Notes sur les plantes distribuées. 1893. I. 418.
Corbos, François. Flora aclensis. 1887. I. 437.
— Flora aclensis. 1893. I. 437.
Corcho mármol de la Cafreria. 1887. IV. 407.[2]
Corcoran, J. St. V. The flora of the Amur littoral. 1895. I. 456.
Corda, August Joseph Carl. Ueber den Bau des Pflanzenstammes. 1830. I. 104.
— Beiträge zur Lehre von der Befruchtung der Pflanzen. 1835. II. 35.[2]
— See also OPIZ, P. M. & CORDA, A. K. J.
Cordeiro, Braulio. Manual do chacareiro brasileiro. n. d. III. 757.[2]
Cordemoy, Camille Jacob de. Monographie du groupe des Chloranthacées. 1862. II. 95.[1]
— Note sur les ovules de deux genres de Dilléniacées. 1859. II. 540.[2]
Cordemoy, Edmond Jacob de. Flore de l'Île de la Réunion. 1895. I. 482.
— Sur le genre Danais Commers. 1871. II. 816.[1]
— Sur un genre nouveau de Composées. 1871. II. 864.[1]
— Note sur les Ambavilles de l'Île de la Réunion. 1868. II. 865.[1]
Cordemoy, Hubert Jacob de. Description d'une Liliacée . . . Cobnia flabelliformis. 1892. II. 80.[1]
— Gommes, résines d'origine exotique. 1899. IV. 437.[1]
— Sur le rôle des tissus secondaires à réserves. 1893. I. 124.
— Sur le second bois primaire de la racine de certaines Liliacées arborescentes. 1893. II. 77.[2]
Cordemoy, Jacob de. Note sur la résine de Courbaril. 1900. II. 364,[2] III. 478.[2]
Cordero, M. D. See SEGURA, J. C. & CORDERO, M. D.
Cordero, Manuel. Memoria sobre el cultivo del Chile. 1870. II. 699.[1]
Cordes, J. W. H. Het artikel van den heer Bruinsma over het boschwezen. 1894. IV. 160.[2]
— Het belang der bosschen in verband met ontginning van heiden en duinen. 1890. IV. 160.[2]

Cordes, J. W. H. (*continued*).
— Een blik op het plantenleven langs Java's strand. 1890. I. 469.[1]
— Het boschgebied op Java's bergen. 1888. IV. 48.[2]
— De Djati-bosschen op Java. 1881. IV. 537.[2]
— Flora en pomona te Batavia. 1889. III. 128.
— Het geslacht Pinus in 't zuidelyk Halfrond. 1867. II. 39.[2]
— Herinneringen aan Sumatra's westkust. 1874. I. 467.
— De leiding der gouvernements-Koffiecultuur. 1892. III. 730.
— Over Oost-Indische houtsoorten. 1888. IV. 400.[1]
— In Pasoeroeans bergen. 1889. I. 469.[1]
— In de Preånger-regentschappen. 1890. I. 469.[1]
— De Rasamalaboom en zijn hout. 1889. IV. 520.[1]
— The Teak forests of Java. 1881. IV. 537.[2]
— Verslag over een onderzoek naar den toestand en de ligging der bosschen . . . van Sumatra's westkust. 1868. IV. 376.[2]
— Eene wandeling in Buitenzorgs plantentuin. 1889. I. 68.[1]
— Een woord naar aanleiding van het artikel: De exploitatie van 's lands bosschen op Java. 1881. IV. 279.[1]
— Het zamenstel der voornaamste Europesche houtsoorten. 1857. I. 124.
Cordes, W.   Beitrag zum Verhalten der Coniferen. 1897. III. 293.
Cordes en fibres de bois. 1900. IV. 429.
Cordienne, Alexandre Joseph.   Notice topo-phytographique . . . du Jura. 1822. I. 433.
— Tableau synoptique d'une classification des plantes. 1822. I. 259.
Cordier, A.   Croissance comparée de diverses espèces d'Eucalyptus. 1874. IV. 529.[2]
— L'Eucalyptus et le Téosinté en Algérie. 1876. III. 633.[2]
— Renseignements sur la rapidité de croissance des Eucalyptus. 1873. IV. 529.[2]
Cordival, E.   Remarques sur l'hiver 1879-1880. 1880. III. 48.
Cordley, A. B.   Some observations on Apple-tree anthracnose. 1900. III.·428.[2]
Córdoba — Academia nacional de ciencias. *See* ACADEMIA . . . I. 7.[2]
Cordonnier, Anatole.   Les engrais pratiques en horticulture. 1895. III. 145,[1] *158*.
Cordus, Euricius.   Botanologicon. 1534. I. 277.
Cordus, Valerius.   Annotationes in Pedacii Dioscoridis . . . libros V. 1561. I. 280.
— Stirpium descriptionis liber quintus. 1563. I. 281, V. xv.[2]
Corenwinder, Benjamin.   Analyse de la châtaigne du Brésil. 1870. III. 631.[2]
— Études sur les feuilles des arbres. 1874. I. 173.
— Études sur les fonctions des racines des végétaux. 1867. I. 161.
— Études sur les fruits oléagineaux des pays tropicaux. 1875. III. 515.[1]
— Études sur les migrations du phosphore. 1860. I. 179.[2]
— Expériences sur les feuilles colorées. 1863. I. 172.
— Expiration nocturne et diurne des feuilles. 1863. I. 170.
— Les feuilles des plantes exhalentelles de l'oxide de carbone? 1865. I. 170.
— Fonctions des feuilles. 1876. I. 173.
— De Kemiri-noot. 1875. III. 515.[1]
— La noix de Bancoul. 1875. III. 515.[1]
— Recherches chimiques sur la végétation. 1864. I. 170.
— Recherches chimiques sur la végétation. 1866. I. 172.
— Recherches chimiques sur la végétation. 1876. I. 173.
— Recherches sur l'assimilation du carbone. 1858. I. 172.
— Recherches sur la composition chimique et les fonctions des feuilles. 1878. I. 173.
— Sur la respiration des végétaux. 1857. I. 170.
— Sur le rôle des racines. 1867. I. 161.
Corinaldi, Jacob.   Sull' analisi del legno Amyris Kafal. 1842. II. 418.[1]
— Cenni sopra alcuni frutti . . . del Cairo. 1835. III. 280.[2]
— Raccolta di scheletri di alcune foglie. 1821. I. 109.[1]
The Cork Oak. 1890. II. 140.[1]
The Cork Oak near Goodwood House. 1880. III. 363.[1]
The Cork tree. 1881. IV. 516.[2]
Cormack, B. G.   On polystelic roots of certain Palms. 1896. II. 63.[2]
Cormack, W. E.   Account of·a journey across·the Island of Newfoundland. 1824. I. 309.[1]
Cormouls-Houlès, Gaston.   Essais de reboisements dans la Montagne-Noire. 1882. IV. 163.
Cormouls-Houlès, Jules.   Exploitation des taillis comme fourrages. 1893. IV. 438.[2]

Cornaggia.   Indurimento del legname. 1864. IV. 419.
Cornalia, Émile Balthazar Marie.   Établissement d'un service de videttes antiphylloxériques en Italie. 1879. III. 571.
Cornalia, Emilio.   Del bruco del Lentisco. 1865. III. 525.[2]
Cornarius, Janus.   Theologiae Vitis viniferae libri tres. 1614. II. 508.[2]
Cornaz, Édouard.   De l'existence de latex chez quelques Érables. 1879. II. 477.[1]
— Existence prés de Neuchâtel du Rosa Sabini. 1893. II. 298.[2]
— Pin d'Autriche avec trois aiguilles. 1897. II. 44.[1]
— Rosa dichroa . . . & R. Lerchii. 1897. II. 287.[2]
— Le Rosa Sabini. 1892. II. 298.[2]
— Roses hybrides de la flore neuchâteloise. 1894. II. 287.[1]
— Salix caesia Vill. var. angustifolia. 1895. II. 105.[2]
Cornaz, Eugène.   Manuel populaire de sylviculture. 1890. IV. 110.[2]
Cornaz, F.   Sur la détermination de la révolution des coupes. 1857. IV. 251.[2]
Cornberg, G. von.   Ueber Lichtungszuwachs an Kiefern. 1885. IV. 481.
Corne, GORGOLE DE.   *See* GORGOLE DE CORNE.
Cornebois, L.   De l'estimation des forêts. 1857. IV.'217.
Cornelis, Louis.   Sur la dessication . . . des plantes. 1873. I. 35.
Cornelissen, Norbert.   De fatis Kamelliae japonicae. 1820. II. 551.[1]
Cornelius, C.   Mittheilungen über . . . grosse Bäume in Westphalen. 1873. I. 295.[1]
Cornelius, Hermann.   Catalogus plantarum Horti publici amstelodamensis. 1651. I. 50.
Cornell university — Agricultural experiment station. *See* NEW YORK — CORNELL UNIVERSITY . . . III. 6.
Cornell university — New York state college of forestry. *See* NEW YORK STATE COLLEGE OF FORESTRY, CORNELL UNIVERSITY. IV. 4.
Cornell s forest-reserve. 1900. IV. 179.[2]
Cornevin, Charles.   Sur l'action de poisons . . . sur la germination. 1891. I. 204.
— Action de poisons sur la germination. 1891. I. 204.
— Étude physiologique sur un toxique des grains . . . de Cotonnier. 1896. III. 587.[2]
— Étude sur les marcs de groseilles. 1892. III. 414.[2]
— Études sur les graines . . . de Ricin. 1897. III. 522.[1]
— Mémoire sur l'empoisonnement par . . . de Cytise. 1886. III. 474.[1]
— Des plantes vénéneuses. 1887. III. 59.[2]
— Recherches sur les Marrons d'Inde. 1895. III. 538.[2]
Cornhill, John.   Blue Hydrangeas. 1885. III. 412.[2]
— Conifer screens and their uses. 1877. III. 214,[2] *215*.[1]
— Crataegus Pyracantha in towns. 1879. III. 443.[2]
— Plants and shrubs grown as standards. 1880. III. 204.[1]
— Propagating Conifers. 1877. III. 294.[1]
— Sea-coast vegetation. 1875. III. 41.[2]
Cornhill magazine. III. 16.
Cornil & Berlioz.   Sur l'empoisonnement par le Jéquirity. 1883. III. 462.[2]
Cornil, Louis.   Transplantation des arbres de moyenne grandeur. 1853. III. 167.
Cornille, A.   Gabriel-.   *See* GOUMAIN-CORNILLE, A.
The Cornish Elm. 1884. III. 365.[1]
Cornu, Ch.   Sur les ferments oxydants de la Vigne. 1899. III. 583.[2] ·
— Traitements cupriques et soufrage de la Vigne. 1900. III. 562.[1]
Cornu, Maxime.   Absorption par l'épiderme des organes aériens. 1882. II. 508,[2] III. 185.[2]
— L'acclimatation végétale en Tunisie. 1897. III. 130.[2]
— Altération des Vignes attaquées par le phylloxera. 1873. III. 565.[2]·
— Anatomie des lésions déterminées sur la Vigne par l'anthracnose. 1878. III. 577.
— Applications de la théorie des germes aux champignons des végétaux. 1880. III. 578.
— Arbres et arbrisseaux à floraison printannière. 1898. III. 207.[2]
— Sur l'arrachage des Vignes phylloxérées. 1877. III. 570.[1]
— Auéun mycélium n'intervient dans la formation . . . des renflements. 1878. III. 571.
— Sur le bouturage d'été. 1895. III. 158.
— Comparaison du Phylloxera vastatrix des galles. 1873. III. 565.[2]
— Crataegus stipulacea. 1899. III. 423.[1]

— Développement des renflements . . . de la Vigne. 1873. III. 565.²
— Émission d'eau liquide par les végétaux. 1897. II. 508.²
— Étude des formes du phylloxera. 1873. III. 565.²
— Étude sur les Péronosporées. 1882. III. 578.
— Études sur la nouvelle maladie de la Vigne. 1874. III. 587.¹
— Études sur le phylloxera. 1873. III. 565.¹
— Études sur le Phylloxera vastatrix. 1879. III. 571.
— Études sur les ravages produits par phylloxera. 1872. III. 565.¹
— Hibernation du phylloxera. 1873. III. 565.²
— Importance de la paroi des cellules. 1878. I. 159.
— Influence des chaleurs printanières sur le Phylloxera. 1874. III. 566.¹
— Lettre à M. Dumas. 1874. III. 567.²
— Maladie causée . . . par une anguillule qui attaque les Rubiacées. 1879. III. 711.¹
— La maladie des Châtaigniers. 1884. IV. 493.¹
— Maladie des taches noires de l'Érable. 1878. III. 534.¹
— Sur une maladie nouvelle qui fait périr les Rubiacées. 1879. III. 711.¹
— Méthode pour assurer la conservation de la vitalité des graines. 1892. III. 154.²
— Méthode suivie pour la recherche de la substance la plus efficace contre le phylloxera. 1874. III. 567.¹
— Le mildew, Peronospora des Vignes. 1880. III. 578.
— Note sur l'identité du phylloxera. 1873. III. 565.¹
— Note sur la formation . . . des renflements déterminés sur la Vigne. 1875. III. 568.
— Note sur la formation des renflements sur les radicelles de la Vigne. 1873. III. 560.
— Note sur la maladie du raisin. 1877. III. 577.
— Note sur la présence de galles phylloxériques. 1875. III. 568.
— Note sur la structure des fruits de l'Argan du Maroc. 1897. II. 697.¹
— Note sur la Tomate en arbre. 1893. III. 699.²
— Note sur le Colea floribunda. 1896. II. 784.¹
— Note sur le phylloxeras hibernants. 1873. III. 565.¹
— Note sur le Quassia africana. 1895. II. 415.¹
— Note sur les altérations déterminées sur la Vigne. 1875. III. 568.
— Note sur les mœurs du phylloxera. 1873. III. 565.²
— Note sur les renflements produits par le phylloxera. 1873. III. 565.²
— Note sur un type nouveau de tiges anomales. 1879. II. 235.¹
— Note sur une forme tératologique de l'Erica cinerea. 1879. II. 666.¹
— Note sur une teigne mineuse . . . du Poirier. 1884. III. 446.¹
— Nouveau procédé de multiplication. 1895. III. 163.¹
— Nouvel exemple de générations alternantes chez les champignons. 1886. IV. 461.¹
— Observations relatives au Phylloxera. 1873. III. 565.¹
— Le Polystigma fulvum Tul. 1886. III. 434.¹
— Prolongation de l'activité végétative des cellules chlorophylliennes. 1881. I. 142.
— À propos de nouvelles plantes à caoutchouc. 1898. III. 229.
— Sur quelques particularités relatives à la forme ailée du phylloxera. 1873. III. 565.²
— Rapport sur le dépérissement . . . des Mûriers. 1883. III. 379.¹
— Remarques sur les accidents causés par l'emploi du sulfure de carbone. 1881. III. 560.
— Les renflements produit par le phylloxera. 1872. III. 565.¹
— Résumé des observations [sur le phylloxera]. 1875. III. 567.²
— La rouille des Pins. 1883. IV. 461.¹
— La stérilité de certains hybrides des Caféiers. 1900. III. 733.¹
— Syringa Emodi à fleurs roses. 1888. III. 681.¹
— Xanthoceras sorbifolia. 1886. III. 540.¹
— See also BRONGNIART, Charles & CORNU, Maxime; GROENLAND, J., CORNU, Maxime & RIVET, Gabriel; NAUDIN, Charles & CORNU, Maxime.
— & Mer, Émile. Recherches sur l'absorption des matières colorantes par les racines. 1880. I. 161.
— & Mouillefert, Pierre. Expériences faites à la Station viticole de Cognac. 1877. III. 703.¹
Cornuault, P. Arbustes à feuillage coloré. 1888. III. 206.²
— Salix divaricata. 1900. II. 108.²

Cornu, Jacques Philippe. Canadensium plantarum . . . historia. 1635. I. 285,³ 305, V. xv.³
Coronado, Daniel E. Annotations sur les Quinquinas . . . de Colombie. . 1878. III. 721.
Coronedi Berti, C. Appunti di botanica bolognese. 1875. I. 423.
Coronel, Luis de LA ESCOSURA Y. See LA ESCOSURA Y CORONEL, Luis de.
Le corps des forestiers. See PEUPION, Auguste. 1882. IV. 292.
Le corps forestier et la direction Lorentz. 1883. IV. 292.
Corre, A. Note sur les gommes du Sénégal. 1876. III. 463.²
Correa, (abbé). Reduction of all the genera of plants contained in the Catalogus . . . of the late Dr. Muhlenberg. 1815. I. 306.
Correa, Alberto. Reseña económica del estado de Tabasco. 1899. III. 265.¹
Correa de Mello, Joaquim C. On a menispermaceous plant, [Burasaia Vitis]. 1875. II. 206.²
— On Myrocarpus frondosus. 1871. II. 374.¹
— & Spruce, Richard. Notes on Papayaceae. 1869. II. 582.¹
Corrêa de Serra, José Francisco. On the Doryanthes. 1800. II. 89.²
— Note sur la valeur du périsperme. 1811. I. 120.
— Observations carpologiques. 1806. I. 118.¹
— Observations sur la famille des Orangers. 1805. II. 396.²
— Observationum carpologicarum fasciculi. 1806. I. 118.¹
— On a submarine forest on the east coast of England. 1799. I. 393.¹
— On two genera of plants belonging to . . . Aurantia. 1800. II. 398,¹ 407.¹
— Vues carpologiques. 1807. I. 118.¹
La corrección de torrentes. 1891. IV. 186.¹
Correns, Carl Erich. Beiträge zur Biologie . . . einiger Blüthen. 1890. I. 115.²
— Zur Biologie und Anatomie der Calceolarienblüthe. 1891. II. 779.²
— Ueber den Einfluss, welchen die Zahl der . . . Pollenkörner auf die Nachkommenschaft hat. 1900. I. 201.²
— G: Mendel's Regel. 1900. I. 246.¹
— Zur Kenntniss der inneren Structur der . . . Zellmembranen. 1892. I. 138.²
— Zur Physiologie der Ranken. 1896. I. 197.¹
— Ueber die Querlamellirung der Bastzellmembranen. 1893. I. 138.²
Correspondance de Fribourg. See KORRESPONDENZ aus Freiburg. 1863. IV. 283.¹
Correspondence connected with the supposed discovery of a Teak forest. 1845. II. 761.¹
Correspondence d'Orient; de l'horticulture en Égypte. See HUSSON, A. 1841. III. 131.¹
Correspondence regarding the cultivation of Mulberry trees. 1882. III. 378.
Correspondence regarding the discovery of the Tea plant of Assam. See CHARLTON, Andrew & others. 1841. III. 552.¹
Correspondence relating to timber on the Chippewa Indian reservations. 1899. IV. 179.²
Correvon, Henry. Alpine plants. 1882. III. 626.²
— Alpine Rhododendron. 1882. III. 655.
— Die alpinen Rhododendron. 1882. III. 655.
— Les arbustes alpins. 1897. III. 205.¹
— Les arbustes saxatiles. 1890. III. 205.¹
— Atlas de la flore alpine. 1899. I. 438.
— The Atragenes. 1894. III. 389.²
— Les Cactées rustiques. 1895. III. 620.¹
— Les Cactus rustiques. 1890. III. 624.¹
— Le Daphné de montagnes. 1892. III. 626.²
— Le dernier de sa race. 1888. II. 864.¹
— Flore coloriée de poche . . . de la Suisse. 1894. I. 438.
— L'hiver à Pallanza. 1891. III. 49.²
— Della insussistenza del genere Retinospora. 1889. III. 300.²
— Der letzte seiner Art. 1888. II. 864.¹
— Linnaea borealis L. 1890. III. 749.²
— Une nouvelle Conifère américaine. 1898. III. 297.¹
— Le Pin d'Arole. 1890. IV. 464.¹
— Pinus Cembra. 1882. II. 41.¹
— Pinus Pinea. 1890. II. 45.¹
— Les plantes des Alpes. 1885. I. 437.
— Les plantes sous bois. 1894. III. 216.
— Protégeons nos forêts. 1897. IV. 181.¹
— Rockery shrubs. 1897. III. 205.¹
— La Rose des Alpes. 1887. III. 655.
— Les Véroniques de la Nouvelle-Zélande. 1896. III. 704.¹

Corrie, A. P. Coffee at Buderim Mountain. 1898. III. 733.[1]
— Timber-getting in Australia. 1898. IV. 383.[2]
Corrispondenza commerciale. 1866. IV. 405.[2]
Corrispondenza scientifica di Roma. I. 25.
Corry, Thomas Hughes. On the development of the pollinium in Asclepias. 1883. II. 736.[1]
— On some points in the structure . . . of the leaves of Pinus silvestris. 1883. II. 40.[1]
— *See also* STEWART, S. A. & CORRY, T. H.
Corsa, William Pinckney. Nut culture in the United States. 1896. III. 62.
La Corse et ses forêts. 1854. IV. 359.[2]
Corsi-Salviati, Bardo. Il re dei Castagni. 1881. II. 125.[1]
The Corsican Pine. 1885. III. 308.[1]
Un corso speciale di selvicoltura all' Istituto agrario di Perugia. 1898. IV. 35.[2]
Corson, Alan W. Sports. 1855. II. 105.[2]
The Corstorphine Sycamore. 1893. II. 480.[1]
Cortambert, Richard. Lettre. 1876. III. 634.[2]
Cortavilla y Sanabria, Diego de. Informacion y pareçer de lo que son Cubebas. n. d. III. 342.[2]
Cortázar, Daniel de. Calculo de altitudes. 1881. IV. 265.
— La resinación en Valladolid. 1878. IV. 436.[2]
Cortés, Santiago. Flora de Colombia. 1897. I. 340.[1]
Cortex radicis Sambuci interior. 1834. III. 752.[1]
Corthum, Johann Karl. Om Ahorn Saftens Benyttelse. 1803. III. 534.[1]
— Catalogus von Bäumen und Sträuchen. 1803. III. 68.[2]
— Handbuch für Gartenfreunde und Blumenliebhaber. 1814. III. 103.
Cortina, Charles Garza. La Chirimoya. 1873. III. 401.[1]
Cortuso, Jacopo Antonio. L' Horto dei simplici di Padova. 1591. *See* PORRO, Girolamo.
Corvetto, *comte* de. Exposé des motifs du projet de loi concernant les engagistes et les échangistes. 1818. IV. 326.
— Exposé des motifs du projet de loi tendant à confirmer deux échanges de bois. 1817. IV. 325.
— Exposé des motifs du projet de loi, tendant à confirmer dix-sept échanges de bois. 1816. IV. 325.
Corvo, ANDRADE CORVO.
A **Corylus** gone wrong. 1886. II. 121.[2]
Cos, Juan TEXIDOR Y. *See* TEXIDOR Y COS, Juan.
Cos, O don de BUEN Y DEL. *See* BUEN Y DEL COS, O don de.
Cose riguardanti gli ufficiali forestali. 1897. IV. 293.[2]
Cosentini, Ferdinando. Colpo d' occhio sulle produzioni vegetali dell' Etna. 1830. I. 431.
— Saggio di topografia botanica . . . l' Arena di Catania. 1824. I. 431.
Cosenza, Raffaele. La legge forestale 20 Giugno 1877. 1878. IV. 328.
Cosmas, *(monachus).* Description des animaux et des plantes des Indes. 1696. III. 277.
Cosmopolitan. III. 3.
Cosmos. *See* LES MONDES. III. 20.
Cosnard, F. Catalogue des plantes cultivées au Jardin botanique . . . de Cayenne. 1828. I. 39.
Cosnier, Ludovico Hieronymo. An morbis chronicis caffé potus? 1751. III. 741.[1]
Cossa, Alfonso. Sull' assorbimento delle radici. 1859. I. 161.
— Composition of the ash . . . of the Lemon tree. 1872. II. 402.[1]
— Sulla composizione delle ceneri . . . del Limone. 1872. II. 402.[1]
Cossigny de Palma, Joseph François Charpentier de. Sur la culture du Muscadier. 1825. III. 402.[1]
— Essai sur la fabrique de l'indigo. 1779. III. 478.[3]
— Lettre sur les arbres à épiceries. 1775. III. 221.[2]
— Memoir . . . on the cultivation . . . of indigo. 1789. III. 479.[1]
Cosson, Ernest Saint-Charles. Appendix Florulae juvenalis. 1859. I. 412.
— Compendium florae atlanticae. 1881. I. 485.
— Considérations générales sur l'Algérie. 1862. III. 130.[1]
— Considérations générales sur la distribution des plantes en Tunisie. 1884. I. 485.
— Considérations générales sur le Sahara algérien et ses cultures. 1859. I. 484.
— Sur les Euphorbes cactoides du Maroc. 1874. II. 441.[2]
— Exploration de la Kroumirie centrale. 1885. I. 485.
— Forêts, bois et broussailles . . . de la Tunisie. 1884. I. 485.
— Illustrationes florae atlanticae. 1882. I. 485.

— Itinéraire d'un voyage botanique en Algérie. 1856. I. 484.
— Liste de plantes observées . . . dans le Sahara. 1855. I. 484.
— Liste des plantes recueillies par M. le Dr. André. 1881. I. 485.
— Note sur l'Acacia gommifère de Tunisie. 1887. II. 328.[2]
— Note sur l'acclimatation de l'Eucalyptus globulus. 1875. IV. 532.[2]
— Note sur l'Euphorbia resinifera. 1871. II. 443.[2]
— Note sur la géographie botanique du Maroc. 1873. I. 485.
— Note sur le Cèdre d'Algérie. 1856. II. 27.[1]
— Notes sur quelques espèces nouvelles d'Algérie. 1856. II. 59.[1]
— Notes sur quelques plantes . . . de Paris. 1848. I. 420.
— Notes sur quelques plantes des Iles Canaries. 1856. I. 497.
— Plantae novae florae atlanticae. 1880. II. 766.[2]
— De quibusdam plantis novis Algeriae australioris. 1859. II. 234.[2]
— Rapport sur un voyage . . . en Algérie. 1852. I. 484.
— Rapport sur un voyage . . . en Algérie. 1855. I. 484.
— Le règne végétal en Algérie. 1879. I. 485.
— Révision du Florae libycae specimen. 1865. I. 484.
— De speciebus generis Polygala . . . Chamaebuxus. 1888. II. 430.[2]
— Species novae maroccanae. 1873. I. 485.
— *See also* RIVIÈRE, Charles, COSSON, Ernest & MICHON, Joseph.
— & **Durieu de Maisonneuve,** M. C. Description d'un genre nouveau . . . des Labiées. 1853. II. 765.[1]
— — Flore d'Algérie. 1846. I. 484.
— N   sur quelques espèces nouvelles d'Algérie. 1855. I. 484.otes
— & **Germain de Saint-Pierre,** Ernest. Flore descriptive et analytique des environs de Paris. 1845. I. 410.
— — Observations sur quelques plantes . . . de Paris. 1840. I. 409.
— — Supplément au Catalogue raisonné des plantes . . . de Paris. 1843. I. 409.
— — Synopsis analytique de la flore des environs de Paris. 1845. I. 410.
— — & **Weddell,** H. A. Introduction à une flore analytique . . . de Paris. 1842. I. 409.
— & **Jamin,** P. De la culture du Dattier. 1855. III. 328.[1]
— — Notes sur les cultures des oasis des Ziban. 1855. III. 130.[1]
— & **Kralik,** Louis. Catalogue des plantes observées en Syrie. 1854. I. 480.
— — Notes sur quelques plantes . . . de Tunis. 1857. I. 48.
— — Sertulum tunetanum. 1857. I. 484.
Cossonnet, A. Pratique raisonnée de la taille des arbres fruitiers. 1849. III. 172.
Le **Cossus** ligniperda. 1895. IV. 549.[2]
Cost of producing White Pine lumber. 1897. IV. 470.[2]
Costa, Achille. La caccia considerata ne' suoi rapporti con l' agricoltura. 1873. III. 95.
— La fillossera in Sardegna. 1883. III. 573.
— Degl' insetti che attaccano l' albero. 1857. III. 189.
— Rapporto sulla malattia delle Viti. 1876. III. 569.[1]
Costa, B. F. da. A cheap and abundant substitute for gutta-percha. 1891. III. 518.[1]
Costa, Bernardino Camillo CINCINNATO DA. *See* CINCINNATO DA COSTA, B. C.
Costa, Joaquín. El arbolado en el Alto Aragón. 1896. IV. 542.[1]
— Arbolado y fiesta del árbol. 1900. IV. 541.
Costa, Oronzo-Gabriele. Degli insetti che vivono sopra l' Ulivo. 1828. III. 677.[1]
Costa de Bastelica, A. M. Reboisement des montagnes. 1866. IV. 50.
Costa de Bastelica, Michel. Les torrents. 1874. IV. 185.[2]
Costa Luz, Luis Caetano Pereira da. Cultura da Oliveira. 1891. III. 679.[1]
Costa-Reghini, Carlo. Freycinetia o Cordylina? 1884. III. 313.[1]
Costa Rica — Instituto físico-geográfico nacional. *See* INSTITUTO . . . I. 7.[2]
Costa Rica — Museo nacional. *See* MUSEO . . . I. 7.[2]
Costa y Cuxart, Antonio Cipriano. Apuntes sobre dos especies nuevas de la flora catalana. 1876. II. 292.[1]
— Arbolado de Barcelona. 1856. III. 126.[1]
— Introduccion á la flora de Cataluña. 1864. I. 421.

— Noticias botánico-agricolas sobre los Pinos de Cataluña. 1857. IV. 463.[1]
— Programa y resúmen de las lecciones de botánica. 1859. I. 90.
Costaeus, Joannes. See Costeo, Giovanni.
Constantin, Julien. Accommodation des plantes aux climats. 1897. III. 44.[1]
— Étude anatomique de l'enracinement d'une branche de Ronce. 1882. II. 305.[2]
— Étude comparée des tiges aériennes et souterraines. 1883. I. 104, 105.
— Influence du séjour sous le sol sur la structure anatomique des tiges. 1883. I. 105.
— Le mythe du Chêne marin. 1899. I. 517.[2] ·
— La nature tropicale. 1899. I. 219.[2]
— Recherches sur l'influence qu'exerce le milieu sur la structure des racines. 1885. I. 104.
— Les végétaux et les milieux cosmiques. 1898. I. 243.[2]
— & Dufour, Léon. Contributions à l'étude de la tige des Lécythidées. 1885. II. 611.[1]
— & Morot, Louis. Sur l'origine des faisceaux libéroligneux . . .. des Cycadées. 1885. II. 3.[1]
Costantini, Girolamo. Il Cadore e i suoi boschi. 1864. IV. 364, 415.[2]
— Le.Cadore et ses forêts. 1864. IV. 364.
Coste, Hippolyte. Cinq plantes nouvelles découvertes dans l'Aveyron. 1896. I. 418.
— Un Ciste hybride nouveau. 1886. II. 564.[2] ·
— Florule du Larzac, du Causse Noir. 1893. I. 418.
— Note sur 150 plantes nouvelles pour l'Aveyron. 1891. I. 417.
— Observations sur quelques plantes de la vallée de l'Ubaye. 1897. I. 418.
— & Soulié, J. Note sur 200 plantes nouvelles pour l'Aveyron. 1897. I. 418.
Coste, Jean François & Willemet, Remi. Botanische . . . Versuche über die vornehmsten einheimischen Pflanzen. 1778. III. 271.[1]
— — Essais botaniques, chimiques et pharmaceutiques. 1778. III. 241, 271.[1]
— — Matière médicale indigène. 1793. III. 85.
Coste, Jean Jacques Cyprien Victor. Les ennemis du phylloxera gallicole. 1880. III. 572.·
Coste, L. Le phylloxéra au Congrès de Montpellier. 1875. III. 759.
— Rapport sur l'état actuel de la maladie de la Vigne. 1876. III. 760.
Coste, P. Considérations sur l'identité des racines et des tiges. 1839. I. 105.
Coste, U. Phytotomie pathologique; étude anatomique de la lésion produite par le phylloxéra. 1877. III. 760.
Coste-Floret, Paul. La culture intensive de la Vigne. 1898. III. 557.[2]
— Les travaux du vignoble, plantations. 1898. III. 557.[2]
Costeo, Giovanni. De universali stirpium natura libri duo. 1578. I. 30, 282.
Coster. De zoogenaamde Atsjin-noten. 1873. III. 524.[1]
Coster, David Jacob. Boomen en bosschen. 1872. I. 82,[?] IV. 84.[?]
— De bouw der plantaardige en dierlyke grondstoffen der derde uitgave der Nederlandsche pharmacopee. 1891. III. 259.[1]
— Inleiding tot de kennis van de plantaardige en dierlyke grondstoffen der Nederlandsche pharmacopee. 1890. III. 259.[1]
— Kunstwoordenboek der zigtbaar bloeiende planten. 1853. I. 71.
— Sur la métamorphose des plantes. 1866. I. 101.[2] ·
— De plantkunde. 1861. I. 90.
— Hoorn, G. H. & Mazure, J. Onderzoek van verdachten Steranijs. 1808. III. 398.[1]
Costerus, J. C. Beginselen der plantkunde. 1881. I. 91.
— Double Nutmegs. 1881. II. 221.[1]
— Kieming van zaden binnen de vrucht. 1898. II. 402.[1]
— Knoppen op een peer. 1897. II. 280.[1]
— 's Lands plantentuin te Buitenzorg. 1894. I. 68.[1]
— Het leven der lenticellen. 1875. I. 132.[1]
— On malformation in Fuchsia globosa. 1890. II. 643.[2]
— Sur la nature des lenticelles. 1875. I. 132.[1]
— Parasitismus in het plantenrijk. 1879. I. 233.[2]
— Les petits points foncés des feuilles des Connarus. 1898. II. 317.[1]
— Staminodie de la corolle dans l'Erica Tetralix. 1891. II. 669.[2]
— Twee vlaggen bij Desmodium tiliaefolium. 1898. II. 354.[1]

Cot, (Dr.). Rapport sur la viticulture. 1891. III. 557.[1]
— La situation vinicole. 1900. III. 557.[2]
Côte ardennaise. 1900. IV. 119.[2]
Coterius, Gabriel. Historia plantarum. 1567. I. 281.
Cotes, E. C. An account of the insects . . . which attack the Tea plant in India. 1895. III. 604.[2]
— Forests versus insects. 1893. IV. 210.[2]
— The locust of N. W. India. 1890. III. 192.[2] ·
— Notes on forest entomology. 1893. IV. 210.[2]
— See also Wood, E. & Cotes, E. C.
Cothenius, Christian Andreas. Dispositio vegetabilium methodica. 1790. I. 251.
Del cotone di Salcio e di Pioppo. 1864. IV. 485.[1]
Cotsworth, M. B. Railway and timber trades' measurer. 1899. IV. 229.
Cotta, Alberto. Escursione ai distretti forestali di Landshut. 1898. IV. 351.[2]
— Sulla formazione degli anelli legnosi. 1898. IV. 62.[3]
— Inaugurazione del busto a Bérenger. 1897. IV. 35.[2]
— Sunto del discorso pronunziato dall' on. Giusso. 1897. IV. 23.[1]
Cotta, August. Einige Mittheilungen über die Erziehung von Eibenpflänzchen. 1857. IV. 440.[1]
— Mancherlei aus dem Gebiete des Waldbaues, III. 1857. IV. 440.[1]
Cotta, Bernhard. Anleitung zum Studium der Geognosie und Geologie. 1842. IV. 61.[1]
— Praktische Geognosie. 1852. IY. 61.[1]
— Geinitz, H. B. & others. Gäa von Sachsen, oder, Physikalisch-geographische . . . Skizze für . . . Sachsen. See Reichenbach, H. G. L. 1843. I. 381.
Cotta, Heinrich. Abriss einer Anweisung zur Vermessung . . . der Waldungen. 1815. IV. 239.
— Anviisning til Skovdyrkningen. 1817. IV. 106.
— Anweisung zum Waldbau. 1817. IV. 106.
— Anweisung zur Forsteinrichtung. 1819. IV. 239.
— Anweisung zur Forst-Einrichtung und Abschätzung. 1820. IV. 239.
— Anweisung zur Waldwerthberechnung. 1818. IV. 252.
— Beilage zum Grundriss der Forstwissenschaft. 1832. IV. 97.
— Einige Worte über den Zweck der Königl. Sächs. Akademie für Forst- und Landwirthe. 1830. IY. 29.
— Entwurf einer Anweisung zur Waldwerthberechnung. 1818. IV. 252.
— Erinnerungen an schwere Zeiten forstlicher Noth. 1870. IV. 190.
— Erläuterung der Forsteinrichtung. 1832. IV. 247.[2]
— Grundriss der Forstwissenschaft. 1832. IV. 97.
— Hülfstafeln für Forstwirthe und Forsttaxatoren. 1821. IV. 229.
— Naturbeobachtungen über die Bewegung und Funktion des Saftes. 1000. I. 160.
— Principes fondamentaux de la science forestière. 1832. IV. 97.
— Rede, gehalten bei Eröffnung der Forstlehranstalt zu Tharandt. 1811. IV. 31.
— Systematische Anleitung zur Taxation der Waldungen. 1804. IV. 239.
— Tables de cubage et d'expériences sur l'accroissement des bois. 1821. IV. 229.
— Tafel 8 zu Heinrich Cotta's Tafeln zur Bestimmung des Inhaltes der runden Hölzer. 1841. IV. 222.
— Tafeln zur Berechnung des Inhalts der runden Hölzer. 1816. IV. 221.
— Tafeln zur Bestimmung des Inhaltes der runden, geschnittenen und behauenen Hölzer. 1816. IV. 221.
— Tafeln zur Bestimmung des Inhaltes der runden Hölzer. 1816. IV. 221.
— Tafeln zur Bestimmung des Inhaltes und Zuwachses der . . . Holzarten. 1819. IV. 216.
— Tafeln zur Bestimmung des Inhalts und Werthes unverarbeiteter Hölzer. 1816. ·IV. 221.
— Unmassgebliche Vorschläge, wie die Fichten- und Kiefernsaaten . . . unternommen werden können. 1833. IV. 441.
— Die Verbindung des Feldbaues mit dem Waldbau. 1819. IV. 132.[2]
— See also Kotta, Генрихъ.
— & Schenkert, F. C. Nachricht über die landesherrliche Forst-Akademie zu Tharand. 1819. IV. 31.
Cotta, Wilhelm. Betrachtungen über die Flugschrift: "Einige Worte über Sachsens Forstbedienten." 1848. IV. 291.[1]
— Einige Worte über Sachsens Wälder. 1848. IV. 355.[1]

Cotta, Wilhelm (*continued*).
— Gedanken betreffs der forstlichen Reformfrage. 1849. IV. 101.
— Weitere Beiträge zu der Aufgabe des forstlichen Ausscbusses. 1849. IV. 291.[1]
Cottage gardener. III. 16.
Die Cotta'schen, Bairischen und Stahl'schen Maassentafeln für Buchen. 1855. IV. 498.
Cotte. Leçons élémentaires d'histoire naturelle. 1787. I. 83.
— Manuel d'histoire naturelle. 1787. I. 83.
Cotter. The flora of the county Cork. 1875. V. xxi.[2]
Cottereau, P. L. See VAVASSEUR, P.; COTTEREAU; P. L. & GILLET DE GRANDMONT, A.
Cotterell, E. Note on guttapercha. 1874. III. 668.[2]
Cottet, Michel. Diagnoses inédites de . . . plantes . . . de la Suisse. 1875. II. 287.[1]
— Enumération des Roses du Valais. 1874. II. 286.[2]
— Note sur le Rosa resinosa Sternb. 1890. II. 298.[1]
— Notes sur le Guide du botaniste dans le canton de Fribourg. 1892. I. 437.
— Quelques considérations sur les motifs qui ont déterminé la publication du Guide du botaniste. 1892. II. 102,[2] 287.[1]
— Quelques nouveaux Saules. 1892. II. 102.[2]
— Roses et Saules . . . nouveaux pour la Suisse. 1891. II. 102,[2] 287.[1]
— & Castella, François. Guide du botaniste dans le canton de Fribourg. 1891. I. 437.
Cottin, Alfred. Culture et taille du Groseillier. 1878. III. 414.[2]
Cotton, Charles. The planter's manual. 1675. III. 141.
Cotton, Frederick. Journal of an expedition over the Annamullay mountains. 1858. IV. 383.[2]
Cotton, Joseph Gustave Stanislas. Étude comparée sur le genre Krameria. 1868. III. 480.[1]
— S. Étude sur la noix d'Argan. 1888. III. 666.[2]
— La traité des gommes au Sénégal. 1893. III. 228.[1]
On the cotton of the ancients. 1827. III. 589.[1]
Cotty, E. Description . . . du Jardin botanique . . . de Tours. 1872. I. 59.
Couanon, Georges. See GASTINE, G. & COUANON, Georges.
— & Salomon, Étienne. Expériences relatives à la désinfection anti-phylloxérique. 1887. III. 574.
— Henneguy, Félix & Salomon, E. Nouvelles expériences relatives à la désinfection antiphylloxérique. 1887. III. 574.
— Michon, Joseph & Salomon, E. Nouvelles expériences relatives à la désinfection antiphylloxérique. 1899. III. 575.[1]
Couard. Note sur la durée des traverses en bois. 1891. V. xxxii.[1]
Coubard D'Aulnay, G. E. Monographie du café. 1832. III. 726.[2]
Couderc, G. Sur les périthèces de l'Uncinula. 1893. III. 580.
Coudure, P. de. Le crédit agricole forestier. 1880. IV. 326.
Coues, Elliott. Notes on Mr. Thomas Meehan's paper on the plants of Lewis and Clark's expedition. 1899. I. 327.
Couleius, A. See COWLEY, Abraham.
Coulet, Paul. Consultation; le commerce des bois du Nord. 1891. IV. 405.[1]
Coulomb, C. A. Expériences relatives à la circulation de la sève. 1799. I. 163.
Coulombier, F. L'arbre à Thé. 1900. III. 600.[2]
Coulon, Louis. Sur l'âge d'une inscription faite dans un arbre. 1853. I. 210.[1]
— Morceau de Sapin avec un fer à cheval. 1867. I. 210,[2] IV. 66.[1]
— Note sur la formation de l'écorce des Sapins coupés. 1847. I. 209.[1]
— Note sur un Sapin blanc sans branches. 1879. II. 23,[1] IV. 66.[1]
Coulon, Paul de. Le Bostriche curvidenté du Sapin blanc. 1896. IV. 445.[2]
— L'éclaircie française. 1895. IV. 175.[1]
— Die französische Durchforstung. 1895. IV. 175.[1]
— Question du cubage. 1899. IV. 215.
— Transport de bois par monorail. 1898. IV. 392.
Coultas, Harland. The fall of the leaves. 1874. III. 207.[1]
— Famous trees. 1872. I. 295.[1]
— The natural history of a Beech twig. 1863. II. 126.[1]
— Observations on the growth of trees. 1859. I. 187.
— The principles of botany. 1854. I. 89.
— What may be learned from a tree. 1859. I. 82.[1]
— The winter life of plants. 1863. I. 217.
Coulter, John. Querci near Hanover, Ind. 1875. II. 128.[2]

Coulter, John Merle. An analytical key to some of the common . . . species of flowering plants. 1900. I. 308.
— On the appearance of the relation of ovary and perianth. 1884. I. 115.[1]
— Botany of western Texas. 1891. I. 326.
— Cactus, Cacti. 1900. III. 620.[1]
— Upon a collection of plants made by Mr. G. C. Neally. 1890. I. 325.
— Geographical distribution of Conifers. 1900. II. 14.[1]
— Geographical distribution of North American Cornaceae. 1891. II. 654.[1]
— List of plants collected by A. B. Donaldson. 1875. I. 324.
— Magnolia acuminata L. 1876. II. 211.[2]
— Manual of the botany . . . of the Rocky Mountain region. 1885. I. 325.
— A new Cornus. 1890. II. 655.[1]
— New or noteworthy Compositae. 1891. II. 849.[1]
— Notes on the fertilization . . . of Conifers. 1897. II. 21.[1]
— Opuntia vulgaris and Rafinesquii. 1876. II. 596.[1]
— The origin of gymnosperms. 1898. II. 2.
— Plant relations. 1899. I. 219.[1]
— Plant structures. 1899. I. 101.[1]
— Preliminary revision of the North American . . . Echinocactus, Cereus and Opuntia. 1896. II. 587.[2]
— Preliminary revision of the North American species of Cactus. 1894. II. 587.[1]
— Some affinities among Cactaceae. 1894. II. 586.[2]
— Some notes on Hypericum. 1886. II. 557.[1]
— See also PORTER, T. C. & COULTER, J. M.
— & Evans, E. M. A revision of North American Cornaceae. 1890. II. 654.[1]
— & Fisher, E. M. Some new North American plants. 1892. II. 185.[2]
— & Rose, J. N. New genus of Umbelliferae. 1894. II. 653.[2]
— Synopsis of North American Pines. 1886. II. 39.[1]
Coulter, M. Stanley. The forest trees of Cass county, Ind. 1876. I. 312, IV. 76.[2]
— The numerical relations existing among the forest trees of Jefferson county, Ind. 1876. I. 312, IV. 76.[2]
— On the size of forest trees in Jefferson county. 1876. I. 312, IV. 76.[2]
Coulter, Stanley. A catalogue of the flowering plants . . . Indiana. 1900. I. 317.[1]
— Contribution to the flora of Indiana. 1897. V. xvii.[1]
— Exceptional growth of a wild Rose. 1897. II. 290.[1]
— The forest trees of Indiana. 1892. IV. 544.[1]
— Histology of the leaf of Taxodium. 1889. II. 51.[2]
— Noteworthy Indiana phanerogams. 1896. V. xvii.[1]
— A report upon certain collections of phanerogams. 1896. V. xvii.[1]
— Some unrecognized forms of native trees. 1900. I. 313.
Coulter, Thomas. Description of a method of cultivating Peach trees. 1802. III. 441.[2]
Councler, Constantin. Ueber den Aschengehalt einjähriger Fichten. 1882. II. 63.[1]
— Ueber den Aschengehalt einjähriger Korbweidenruthen. 1886. II. 104.[1]
— Beiträge zur Chemie des Holzes. 1892. IV. 64.[1]
— Bericht . . . zur Feststellung einer einheitlichen Methode der Gerbstoffbestimmung. 1885. I. 183, IV. 435.
— Ueber Cellulosebestimmungen. 1896. IV. 64.[1]
— Chemische Zusammensetzung des Rothbuchenholzes. 1889. II. 126.[1]
— Deutsches Eichenloh-Extract. 1887. IV. 459.[2]
— Sur le dosage du tannin. 1885. I. 183.
— Eichenholzextract. 1886. IV. 515.[1]
— Einfluss der Witterung auf den Gerbstoffgehalt der Fichtenrinde. 1888. IV. 459.[2]
— Ueber einige . . . Gerbmaterialien. 1884. I. 183, IV. 435.
— Einiges über ausländische Gerbrinden. 1883. IV. 435.
— Ueber den Gehalt dreier auf gleichem Boden erwachsener Nadelbäume. 1884. IV. 64.[1]
— Gerbstoffgehalt des Sumach. 1883. III. 526.[2]
— Gerbstoffgehalt einiger inländischer . . . Rinden. 1884. I. 183, IV. 435.
— Holzfuttermehl und Holzgummi. 1888. IV. 433.[2]
— Mineralstoffgehalt argentinischer Bäume. 1883. III. 636.[2]
— Ueber Quebrachohols. 1882. III. 686.[2]
— Recherches sur le tannin de l'écorce d'Aune. 1882. IV. 489.[1]
— Stickstoffgehalt einiger Waldproducte. 1883. IV. 64.[1]
— Ueber dem Stickstoffgehalt von Hölzern. 1882. I. 155.

— Sur le tannin. 1882. IV. 489.¹
— Untersuchung einiger Streumaterialien. 1883. I. 155, *IV. 71.*
— Untersuchungen über den Gerbstoff der Erlenrinde. 1882. IV. 489.¹
— Untersuchungen über den Gerbstoffgehalt der Eichenrinde. 1882. IV. 515.¹
— Untersuchungen über Waldstreu. 1883. II. 126.²
— Welche Veränderungen des Buchenholzes weist die chemische Analyse nach. 1897. IV. 500.²
— *See also* NOBBE, Friedrich, HÄNLEIN, H. & COUNCLER, Constantin.

Counclerc, C., Sur la saccharification de la gomme. 1893. I. 181.¹

Counsel, E. A. Timber industry of Tasmania. 1898. IV. 407.²

Country gentleman. III. 3.

The country-mans recreation. *See* MASCALL, Leonard. 1654. III. 107.

Coup d'œil sur l'exportation et l'importation des bois en Suisse. *See* UEBERSICHT über die Holz-Ein . . . 1860. IV. 406.¹

Coupar, Robert. Competitive essay on the Larch disease. 1884. IV. 451.
— On the disease in Larch plantations. 1884. IV. 451.
— On the origin and development of ringswell. 1884. *I. 190,¹ IV. 66.¹*
— Reproductiveness of the Larch. 1885. IV. 449.

Coupe Jacques Michel. De la multiplication des arbres résineux. 1796. III. 293.

Coupe des bourgeons et cueillette des cônes. 1896. IV. 196.²

Les coupe-feu. 1894. IV. 547.²

Les coupe-feu dans les peuplements d'Épicéas. 1899. IV. 183.¹

Couper, Archibald S. Recherches sur l'acide salicylique. 1858. III. 652.¹

Couper, William. On the destruction of Apple-trees. 1862. III. 427.²

Couperus, Abrahamus. Berigt aangaande de Gamber. 1780. III. 748.¹

Couperus, G. W. Coffee interests in Java. 1883. III. 730.
— Koffee-aangelegenheden op Java. 1883. III. 730.
— Plantkuilen in Koffietuinen. 1884. III. 734.¹

Couperus, Henry. De Japansche Lakboom. 1897. III. 528.²

Les coupes blanches en Suisse. 1897. IV. 555.¹

Coupes domaniales de 1898. Ventes. 1897. IV. 551.¹

Coupes domaniales de 1899. 1898. IV. 261.¹

Coupes domaniales de 1901. 1900. IV. 331.²

Les coupes du bois de la Cambre. 1896. IV. 274.²

Coupin, Henri. Comment les plantes se défendent. 1898. I. 235.¹
— L'enfer des arbres. 1900. III. 42.²
— Recherches sur l'absorption et le rejet de l'eau par les graines. 1896. I. 162, *804.*
— Sur la structure du micropyle des graines des Légumineuses. 1897. II. 369.¹
— Sur la toxicité des composés chromés. 1899. I. 211.
— Sur la toxicité des composés du sodium. 1900. I. 211.
— Sur la toxicité du chlorure de sodium. 1898. I. 211.
— Les végétaux. Epiphylles. 1899. III. 193.¹
— *See also* TÉODORESCO, E. C. & COUPIN, Henri.

Cour, J. C. LA. *See* LA COUR, J. C.

Courbe, ROUILLÉ-. *See* ROUILLÉ-COURBE.

Courbon, Alfred. Exploration de la Mer Rouge. 1860. I. 488.
— Flore de l'île de Dissée. 1862. I. 488.
— On the toenifuges of . . . Abyssinia. 1862. III. 245.

Courcel, Valentin de. Sur l'Érable à sucre. 1860. IV. 527.¹

Courchet, Lucien. Analyse du mémoire sur les galles du Térébinthe. 1880. HL 526.¹
— Sur les chromoleucites. 1886. I. 185.¹
— Étude sur les galles causées par des aphidiens. 1880. I. 215.¹
— Note sur les Aphides du Térébinthe. 1879. III. 525.¹
— Recherches sur les chromoleucites. 1888. I. 185.¹
— Traité de botanique. 1897. I. 92.

Couret-Villeneuve, Louis Pierre. Description de toutes les plantes . . . dans le jardin botanique . . . à Gand. 1802. I. 49.
— Hortus gandavensis. 1802. I. 49.

Coursur, P. Le Peuplier picard. 1894. IV. 486.¹

Courraut, Louis. Essai sur les propriétés . . . du camphre. 1815. III. 396,¹ *404.²*

Cours élémentaire de botanique forestière. *See* GALMICHE, E. 1880. IV. 85.²

Courset, George Louis Marie DU MONT DE. *See* DU MONT DE COURSET, G. L. M.

Court van der Voort, Pieter de la. *See* DE LA COURT, Pieter.

Courtai, Note sur l'emploi textile du liber du Mûrier. 1854. III. 379.¹

Courtenay. Surrogaat voor chinine. 1883. III. 407.³

Courtenay, J. M. de. The Canada Vine grower. 1866. III. 550.

Courtiller, Auguste. Sur les semis de Vigne. 1857. III. 548.¹

Courtin, Albert. Die Familie der Coniferen. 1833. III. 289.
— On the propagation of Coniferae. 1850. III. 294.¹
— Ueber die Vermehrung der Coniferen. 1850. III. 294.¹
— *See also* PAUL, William & COURTIN, Albert.

Courtois, Jules. Aucuba japonica et Saule pleureur. 1888. III. 351,² 645.¹

Courtois, Richard Joseph. Commentarius in Remberti Dodonaei Pemptades. 1835. I. 78.¹
— De genere Hydrangea commentatio. 1825. II. 240.²
— Magazin d'horticulture. 1833. I. 268.
— Mémoire sur les Tilleuls d'Europe. 1835. II. 515.²
— Responsio . . . "Quaeritur concinna expositio eorum, quae de organorum propagationi . . . innotuerunt." 1822. I. 33.
— *See also* LEJEUNE, A. L. S. & COURTOIS, Richard.

Courtois-Gérard. Manuel pratique du jardinage. 1843. III. 113.
— Note sur le Melia Azedarach. 1842. III. 512.²

Courton, P. de. Nos grandes administrations publiques. 1888. IV. 292.
— La restauration des montagnes. 1888. IV. 163.

Courval, Ernest Alexis, *vicomte* de. Das Aufästen der Waldbäume. 1859. IV. 170.
— Taille et conduite des arbres forestiers. 1859. IV. 170.
— La taille et la conduite progressive des arbres forestiers. 1867. IV. 171.

Courvoisier, Jean Joseph Antoine. Opinion relativement au titre II. de la loi de finances. 1817. IV. 326.

Cousins, M. Preparing and planting fruit and timber seed. 1868. III. 156.¹

Le coût de la réorganisation de l'administration des eaux et forêts. 1898. IV. 291.²

Coutance, Amédée Guillaume Auguste. Bouleau, genre Betula. 187.? II. 118.²
— Histoire du Chêne. 1873. IV. 502.¹
— L'Olivier. 1877. II. 713.¹

Coutant. *See* DEVER & COUTANT.

Coutant, Jacques & Paul. Les divers exercices. 1628. I. 285.¹
— Synopsis plantarum indigenarum et exoticarum. 1628. I. 285.¹

Coutinho, Antonio Xavier Pereira. Botanica florestal. 1886. IV. 86.¹
— Contribuições para o estudo da flora portugueza. 1892. I. 422.
— Curso de silvicultura. 1886. IV. 57.
— Esboço de uma flora lenhosa portugueza. 1886, 1887. I. 419,³ *IV. 86.¹*
— Fructificação of the Cork Oak. 1895. II. 140.⁴
— As Malvaceas de Portugal. 1893. II. 519.¹
— Os Quercus de Portugal. 1888. II. 130.²
— A silvicultura no districto de Bragança. 1882. IV. 363.¹
— Subsidios para o estudo das Salicaceas de Portugal. 1899. II. 95.²

Coutinho, J. M. de SILVA-. *See* SILVA-COUTINHO, J. M. da.

Couto, Vicente, GOMEZ Y. *See* GOMEZ Y COUTO, Vicente.

Coutouly, de, (*consul*). Rapport sur la sylviculture dans la colonie du Cap de Bonne-Espérance. 1889. IV. 379.²

Coutume du bailliage de Troyes. 1715. IV. 324.

Couture, (*abbé*). Mémoire complet sur la culture de l'Olivier. 1783. III. 674.³
— Traité de l'Olivier. 1786. III. 675.¹

Couturier, Edmond. Culture du Pêcher en espalier. 1892. III. 441.¹

Couty, Louis. Sur l'action convulsivante du curare. 1882. III. 683.³
— Des analogues . . . entre le curare et la strychnine. 1882. III. 683.³
— Le Maté et les conserves de viande. 1880. III. 531.¹
— Recherches sur l'action physiologique du maté. 1878. III. 531.¹

Couty, Louis (*continued*).
— *See also* ARSONVAL, A. d' & COUTY, Louis.
— & Lacerda, Antonio de. Comparaison de l'action de divers curares. 1879. III. 683.²
— — Le curare. 1879. III. 683.²
— — Sur un curare des muscles lisses. 1879. III. 683.²
— — Sur un nouveau curare. 1879. III. 685.²
— — Sur l'origine des propriétés toxiques du curare des Indiens. 1879. III. 683.²
— — Des réactions de la zone du cerveau. 1880. III. 683.²
— Guimaraes, A. R. & Niobey. De l'action du café. 1884. III. 742.¹
Couveé, M. M. Album van tien gelithographieerde schetsen. 1860. III. 184.¹
Couverchel, Jean François. Mémoire sur la maturation des fruits. 1821. I. 178.
— Ueber das Reifen der Früchte. 1821. I. 178.
— Traité des fruits. 1839. III. 220.¹
Couvreur, E. Sur la varitaion [*sic*] des substances de réserve. 1895. I. 204.
Covelle, Ernest. Le phylloxéra dans le canton de Genève. 1881. III. 761.
— *See also* MONNIER, Denis & COVELLE, E.
Coventry, B. O. Conversion of a Sissu forest into a Mulberry forest. 1899. I. 241.¹
— Life-history of the "Tun twig borer." 1900. III. 192.²
— A longicorn beetle which attacks Mulberry trees. 1899. III. 380.²
— Yield table for Shisham seedlings at Changa Manga. 1900. IV. 521.²
Coville, Frederick Vernon. The August vegetation of Mount Mazama. 1897. I. 326.
— Botany of the Death Valley expedition. 1892. I. 326.
— Botany of the Yakutat Bay, Alaska. 1895. I. 311.²
— Descriptions of new plants from southern California. 1892. I. 326.
— Directions for collecting specimens. 1895. III. 63.¹
— Forest growth and sheep grazing. 1898. IV. 197.²
— The forests in the vicinity of Crater Lake. 1896. I. 320, IV. 78.¹
— Notes on the plants used by the Klamath Indians. 1897. III. 63.¹
— Ostrya Knowltoni, a new species. 1894. II. 122.²
— The Panamint Indians. 1892. V. xxviii.²
— Papers from the Harriman Alaska expedition, IV. 1900. II. 99.²
— Ribes erythrocarpum. 1896. II. 244.²
— Ribes mescalerium, an undescribed Currant. 1900. II. 245.¹
— The sage plains of Oregon. 1896. I. 326.
— [C. V. *misprint for* F. V.] The Shasta Fir (Abies shastensis). 1897. II. 25.¹
— Sheep grazing in the forest reserves. 1898. IV. 197.²
— The tree Willows of Alaska. 1900. II. 99.²
Covolo, Giovambatista, *conte* del. Discorso della irritabilità d'alcuni fiori. 1764. I. 200.
— A discourse concerning the irritability of some flowers. 1764. I. 200.
— Rede über die Reizbarkeit einiger Blumen. 1764. I. 200.
Cow tree. 1882. III. 367.²
Cowan, B. Trees and shrubs suitable for the seaside. 1884. III. 41.²
Cowan, F. H. Rhododendron maximum in Somerset county. 1899. II. 682.¹
Cowdery, G. S. *See* MAIDEN, J. H., COWDERY, G. S. & DE COQUE, J. V.
Cowell, John. The compleat fruit and flower gardener. 1730. III. 141.
— The curious and profitable gardener. 1730. III. 141.
Cowell, M. H. Botanical labels for the herbarium. 1841. I. 399.
— A floral guide for East Kent. 1839. I. 398.
Cowles, H. C. The ecological relations of the vegetation on the sand dunes of Lake Michigan. 1899. I. 316.
— The physiographic ecology of northern Michigan. 1900. I. 317.¹
— Plant geography of North America, I. 1900. I. 317.¹
Cowley. Historia natural y medica del cafe. 1870. III. 742.¹
Cowley, Abraham. Poemata latina. 1668. I. 511.
Cowley, E. The Breadfruit, Artocarpus incisa. 1898. III. 367.¹
— The Cocoanut, Cocos nucifera. 1898. III. 323.¹
— The Divi divi tree. 1897. III. 468.²
— Papaw (Carica Papaya). 1898. III. 618.¹

— Queensland nuts. 1899. III. 94.²
— A tropical industry. 1897. III. 149.
— West African Oil Palm. 1897. III. 325.¹
Cowley, Luis. El Jaborandi. 1876. III. 505.¹
Cowley, R. Rosa francesa. 1894. III. 689.²
Cownley, A. J. *See* PAUL, B. H. & COWNLEY, A. J.
Cowper-Coles, Sherard. *See* COLES, Sherard COWPER-.
Cox, H. C. M. On the mode of successfully transmitting plants. 1842. III. 155.
— Remarks on . . . woods from central India. 1846. IV. 400.²
Cox, J. C. Fruit culture. 1851. III. 133.
Cox, John. On Coniferae as ornamental plants. 1872. III. 290.
— Coniferous trees in shrubberies. 1869. III. 290.
— On the growth of timber trees. 1870. III. 292.
— Surface dressings for Conifers. 1880. III. 292.
Coxe, Daniel. A description of the English province of Carolana. 1722. III. 263.²
— A way of extracting a volatile salt. 1674. I. 156.¹
Coxe, John Redman. The American dispensatory. 1806. III. 246.
Coxe, Tench. A view of the United States of America. 1794. IV. 271,¹ 527.¹
Coxe, William. A view of the cultivation of fruit trees. 1817. III. 61.¹
Coxhead, Henry. Catalogue of the . . . plants of Great Britain. 1842. I. 399.
Coyte, William Beeston. Hortus botanicus gippovicensis. 1796. I. 53.
— Index plantarum. 1807. I. 77.
Coze, Léon. Histoire naturelle et pharmacologique des médicaments narcotiques. 1853. III. 260.²
Cozzens, Issachar. Examination of the acid of the Rhus glabrum. 1824. II. 459,¹ 840.²
Crab, P. van der. De Molukscbe eilanden. 1862. I. 466.
— and others. Iets over het rijk van Batjan. 1860. III. 274.¹
Crace-Calvert, Frederick. *See* CALVERT, Frederick CRACE-.
Cracking of trees from frost. 1891. III. 182.
Cracovie. *See* CRACOW.
Cracow — Académie des sciences de Cracovie. *See* ACADÉMIE . . . I. 27.
Cracow — Akademie der Wissenschaften in Krakau. *See* ACADÉMIE DES SCIENCES DE CRACOVIE. I. 27.
Cracow — Akademija umiejętności w Krakowie. *See* AKADEMIA . . . I. 27.
Cracow — Towarzystwa ogrodniczego. Biblioteka i zbiory. *See* BIBLIOTEKA . . . I. 326. III. 2.
Craddock, W. H. Paper manufacture in the southern Shan states. 1900. III. 368.¹
Cradwick, Wilham. Budding Orange trees. 1895. III. 500.¹
— Budding Orange trees. 1900. III. 500.²
— Directions for care of young Grape vines. 1896. III. 551.¹
— The Grape industry. 1897. III. 551.¹
— Notes on the cultivation of chocolate. 1895. III. 593.¹
Crahay, Charles. Les Cèdres de Tenied-el-Haad. 1897. II. 27.² IV. 553.²
— A propos de l'Eucalyptus. 1895. IV. 530.
Crahay, Nestor Iris. Des coupes d'amélioration dans les taillis. 1896. IV. 131.
— Emploi du Hêtre pour billes de chemins de fer. 1896. IV. 424.¹
— De l'espacement des plants lors de la création des pinaraies. 1895. IV. 559.¹
— L'excursion à Groenendael. 1896. IV. 357.¹
— Excursion dans les forêts de Frevr. 1892. IV. 357.¹
— Une excursion forestière dans la West-Flandre. 1894. IV. 556.¹
— L'excursion forestière de 1897. 1897. IV. 556.¹
— Le Hêtre. 1896. IV. 496.
— Des incendies de forêts. 1895. IV. 547.²
— De Laroche à St-Jean. 1893. IV. 357.¹
— De Laroche à St.-Jean. 1894. IV. 555.²
— Mitteilungen über Düngungsversuehe. 1900. IV. 145.
— Le parc de Longchamps. 1894. III. 28.²
— Le Peuplier tremble. 1894. IV. 436.²
— Le Pin du Lord Weymouth. 1900. IV. 469.
— La pineraie de Noire Flohay. 1897. IV. 556.¹
— A propos de quelques espèces résineuses de l'Amérique du Nord. 1900. IV. 126.²
— & Blondeau, A. Excursion forestière . . . La forêt de Mormal. 1899. IV. 362, xxxi.²

— & **Bommer**, C. Rapport sur une mission forestière en Suisse. 1897. IV. 555.[5]
— & **Boone**, Alphonse. La coupe des bourgeons de Pin sylvestre. 1897. IV. 548.[2]
— & **Brichet**, Octave. Manuel de cubage des arbres. 1895. IV. 231.[1]
— & **Delacharlerie**, A. De l'élagage des arbres forestiers. 1896. IV. 172.[2]
— & **Marneffe**, Émile de. La culture des résineux en Belgique. 1894. IV. 558.[2]
— — Le Pin sylvestre. 1894. IV. 482.[1]
Craig, B. F. & **Tilden**, W. C. Report on the preservation of wood. 1872. IV. 419.
Craig, James. Improved planters table. 1857. III. 169.[1]
— Is grease injurious to the health of trees? 1872. IV. 198.[1]
— Report on the various Coniferae . . . to resist the attacks of hares. 1872. IV. 198.[1]
Craig, John. Cranberry growing in Nova Scotia. 1899. III. 664.[1]
— Lilac on Privet stock. 1897. III. 680.[2]
— Native Plums. 1900. III. 433.[1]
— Peach culture in Canada. 1898. III. 441.[2]
— Propagation of trees and shrubs from cuttings. 1889. III. 158.
— & **Hume**, H. H. Native Crab Apples and their cultivated varieties. 1900. II. 266.[1]
Craig, William. Aetherisches Aloëöl. 1880. III. 333.[2]
— Huile essentielle d'Aloès. 1880. III. 333.[2]
— The medicinal plants of Scotland. 1877. III. 80.
— Notes on " changed aloin." 1875. III. 333.[2]
Cram, T. J. Decay and preservation of timber. 1873. IV. 419.
— Report upon the decay and preservation of timber. 1871. IV. 419.
Cramb, Alexander. Picea bracteata. 1871. III. 296.[1]
— The Wellingtonia as affected by soils. 1871. III. 310.[1]
— See also EARLEY, William & CRAMB, Alexander.
Cramer, C. A. De usu corticis Chinae febrifugo. See HEINRICI, Heinrich. 1713. III. 719.
Cramer, Carl Eduard. See CRAMER, K. E.
Cramer, J. A. Koffiedrooginrichtingen. 1897. III. 740.[1]
Cramer, Johann Andreas. Anleitung zum Forst-Wesen. 1766. IV. 94.
Cramer, Johann Christian. Dispositio systematica plantarum. 1803. I. 259.
Cramer, Johann Rudolph. De Myrto. 1731. II. 631.[2]
Cramer, Karl Eduard. Bildungsabweichungen. 1864. I. 143.
— Ueber den Gitterrost der Birnbäume. 1876. III. 446.[1]
— See also NÄGELI, Karl & CRAMER, K. E.
Cramoisy. Note sur la destruction du puceron lanigère. 1883. III. 427.[2]
Crampton, A. See LIPPMANN, von & CRAMPTON, A.
The Cranberry bogs of Cape Cod. 1891. III. 663.[2]
Crandall, Albert Rogers. Report on the geology of Menifee county. 1877. IV. 397.
— See also SHALER, N. S. & CRANDALL, A. R.
Crandall, Charles S. Natural reforestation on the mountains of northern Colorado. 1897. I. 531.[1]
— Notes on Plum culture. 1898. II. 272.[1]
— Observations on the relative moisture content of fruit trees. 1898. I. 149.[2]
Crandall, E. S. Two methods of grafting. 1890. III. 163.[1]
Crane, E. W. Cranberry culture. 1874. III. 663.[2]
Cranefield, F. Duration of the growth period in fruit trees. 1900. I. 222.[1]
Crangen, Karl von RIEPENHAUSEN-. See RIEPENHAUSEN-CRANGEN, Karl von.
Die **Cransbeere** oder grossfrüchtige Moosbeere. 1878. III. 663.[2]
Cranston, John. Cultural directions for the Rose. 1857. III. 449.
Crantz, Heinrich Johann Nepomuk von. De duabus Draconis arboribus. 1768. II. 82.[1]
— Institutiones rei herbariae. 1766. I. 257.
— Materia medica et chirurgica. 1762. III. 241.
— Stirpium austriacarum fasciculus. 1762. I. 438.
Cranz, (*Doktor*). Vorschlag auf Brusenfelde über den allgemeinen Anbau der Ebereschen und Apfelbäume. 1824. III. 426.[1]
Cranz, Heinrich Johann Nepomuk von. See CRANTZ, H. J. N. von.
Crasp, T. H. Lifting large trees. 1896. III. 168.[1]

Crasso, G. L. Analyse der Asche der Weinrebe. 1846. III. 582.
— Analyse des cendres de la Vigne. 1846. III. 582.
The **Crataegus** as a town tree. 1890. III. 421.[2]
Crato, E. Gedanken über die Assimilation. 1892. I. 174.
Crausius, R. G. See KRAUSE, R. W.
Craven, E. A remarkable flowering Liana. 1889. I. 496.
Craveri, E. See RIO DE LA LOZA, L. & CRAVERI, E.
Craw, Alexander. See TOWNSEND, C. H. T., CHITTENDEN, F. H., COCKERELL, T. D. A. & CRAW, Alexander.
Craw, William. A few notes on the nursery treatment of Deodar. 1876. IV. 150.
— Short notes on the nursery treatment of Deodar. 1876. IV. 150.
Crawford, F. S. The Apricot disease. 1886. III. 434.[2]
Crawford, J. H. Wild flowers of Scotland. 1897. I. 535.
Crawford, James Coutts. On hedges and hedge plants. 1877. III. 213.
— On New Zealand Coffee. 1877. III. 743.[2]
Crawford, Matthew. Grapes on trees. 1886. III. 550.
Crawfurd, John. Account of the effects of the Piper cubeba. 1818. III. 342.[2]
— On the history and migration of textile and tinctorial plants. 1869. I. 242.[1]
— Migration of cultivated plants. 1861. I. 241.[2]
Crease, Orlando. On Gum anime. 1848. III. 478.[2]
Creation d'un sous-étage dans une pineraie. 1899. IV. 474.
Crécy, H. Étude sur la détermination des Quinquinas. 1879. II. 813.[1]
Credner, A. Daphne. 1887. III. 626.[2]
— Euphorbia jacquiniflora. 1887. III. 518.[1]
— Euphorbia jacquiniflora. 1888. III. 518.[1]
— Lonicera sempervirens. 1888. III. 751.[1]
— Oxera pulchella Labill. 1888. III. 697.[1]
— Paratropia corona-silvae Miq. 1885. III. 644.[1]
— Reinwardtia tetragyna. 1888. III. 492.[1]
— Schubertia grandiflora Mart. 1888. III. 694.[1]
— Wallisia princeps Rgl. 1888. III. 685.[2]
Cree, Gavin. Sur l'élagage des arbres forestiers. 1832. IV. 170.
— On pruning forest-trees. 1832. IV. 170.
— Pruning forest trees. 1847. IV. 170.
Cree, John. Hortus addlestonensis. 1829. I. 54.
Creevy, Caroline A. Flowers of field, hill and swamp. 1897. I. 308.
Cregel, Ernest. De iurisdictione forestali. 1661. IV. 313.
Crell, Johann Friedrich. De cortice Simarouba. 1746. III. 509.[1]
Le **créosotage** des bois. 1894. IV. 557.[2]
Creosoted timber; its preparation and uses. 1900. IV. 421.
Creosoting of timber. 1896. IV. 421.
Creosoting process of Seely. 1870. IV. 419.
Creosoting timber. 1885. IV. 420.
Crépin, François. L'anatomie appliquée à la classification. 1898. I. 253.[1]
— L'Ardenne; sous le rapport de sa végétation. 1863. I. 392.
— Considérations sur quelques faits concernant le genre Rosa. 1889. II. 283.[1]
— Découverte du Rosa moschata Mill. en Arabie. 1889. II. 296.[1]
— La découverte du Rosa Sabini. 1881. II. 298.[1]
— Description d'une nouvelle espèce de Rose américaine. 1875. II. 293.[2]
— Description d'une nouvelle espèce de Rose chinoise. 1896. II. 299.[1]
— Description d'une nouvelle Rose. 1868. II. 293.[1]
— Description d'une nouvelle Rose asiatique. 1888. II. 294.[2]
— Description of some vegetable monstrosities. 1866. I. 143.
— Deux Roses de la flore luxembourgeoise. 1897. II. 285.[1]
— La distribution géographique du Rosa phoenicia. 1892. II. 297.[2]
— La distribution géographique du Rosa stylosa. 1892. II. 299.[1]
— Éléments de botanique à l'usage des jardiniers. 1867. III. 37.[2]
— Études sur les Roses. 1866. II. 283.[1]
— Examen de quelques idées . . . sur le genre Rosa. 1888. II. 282.[1]
— Florule des environs de Han-sur-Lesse. 1873. I. 393.[1]
— Le genre Rosa. 1889. II. 287.[1]
— Grondbegrippen der plantenkunde. 1869. I. 91.
— Guide du botaniste en Belgique. 1878. I. 393.[1]

Crépin, François (*continued*).
— Herbarium of the British Roses. 1865. II. 285.[1]
— Histoire du Rosa multiflora Thunbg. 1876. II. 296.[3]
— Les idées d'un anatomiste sur les espèces du genre Rosa. 1898. II. 283.[1]
— Manuel de la flore de Belgique. 1860. I. 392.
— De la marche de la sève. 1867. I. 164.
— Mes excursions rhodologiques dans les Alpes. 1889. II. 287.[1]
— Sur la nécessité d'une nouvelle monographie des Roses de l'Angleterre. 1894. II. 285.[1]
— Neue Classification der Rosen. 1889. II. 283.[1]
— Note sur la situation des ovaires . . . des Rosa. 1889. II. 289.[1]
— Note sur le Rosa anemonaeflora. 1883. II. 291.[1]
— Note sur les récentes découvertes de Roses. 1882. II. 296.[1]
— Note sur les Rosa Pissarti Carrière. 1881. II. 296,[2] 296.[3]
— Notes sur quelques plantes . . . de la Belgique. 1859. I. 392.
— Notice sur les Roses recueillies dans la province chinoise du Shen-si. 1897. II. 288.[2]
— Nouvelle classification des Roses. 1889. II. 283.[1]
— Une nouvelle Rose du Japon. 1888. III. 457.[1]
— Nouvelles observations sur le Rosa gigantea. 1889. II. 294.[3]
— Nouvelles recherches à faire sur le Rosa obtusifolia. 1887. II. 297.[1]
— Nouvelles remarques sur le Rosa oxyacantha. 1886. II. 297.[1]
— Nouvelles remarques sur les Roses américaines. 1887. II. 283.[1]
— Novae Rosae descriptio. 1888. II. 300.[1]
— Observations sur le Rosa Engelmanni. 1889. II. 293.[1]
— Observations sur le Rosa stellata. 1898. II. 299.[1]
— Observations sur les Roses décrites dans le Supplementum florae orientalis. 1888. II. 288.[2]
— L'obsession de l'individu dans d'étude [*sic*] des Roses. 1893. II. 283.[1]
— L'odeur des glandes dans le genre Rosa. 1889. II. 283.[1]
— Petites annotations à la flore de la Belgique. 1862. I. 392.
— Primitiae monographiae Rosarum. 1869. II. 282.[2]
— Quelques arbres remarquables du parc de Boeckenberg. 1882. I. 296.[3]
— Quelques considérations sur la distribution géografique des Rosa en Scandinavie. 1894. II. 284.[1]
— Quelques mots sur les Roses de l'herbier de Besser. 1893. II. 284.[1]
— Quelques mots sur les Roses de l'herbier du Tarn. 1893. II. 286.[1]
— La question de la priorité des noms spécifiques. 1897. II. 283.[1]
— Recherches à faire pour établir . . . les époques de floraison . . . dans le genre Rosa. 1889. II. 283.[1]
— Recherches sur l'état du développement des grains de pollen . . . du genre Rosa. 1889. II. 289.[1]
— Remarques sur l'inflorescence des Rosa. 1895. II. 289.[1]
— Remarques sur le Rosa oxyodon. 1895. II. 297.[1]
— Sur des restes de Roses. 1888. II. 282.
— Révision des Rosa de l'herbier Babington. 1896. II. 285.[1]
— Révision des Rosa de quelques vieux herbiers suisses. 1897. II. 287.[3]
— Revision des Roses des herbiers de Lejeune. 1896. II. 285.[1]
— Revue de la flore de la Belgique. 1863. I. 392.
— Over de richting der boomen volgens de windstreken. 1869. I. 233.[1]
— Le rôle de la buissonnomanie dans le genre Rosa. 1886. I. 253,[1] *II.* 282.[3]
— Le Rosa algoiensis. 1896. II. 291.[1]
— Rosa Colletti. 1889. II. 293.[1]
— Les Rosa du Yun-nan. 1886. II. 288.[3]
— Rosa Fischeriana Bess. et R. Gorenkensis Bess. 1894. II. 293.[1]
— Rosa sicula? Tratt. var.,maroccana. 1884. II. 299.[1]
— Le Rosa villosa de Linné. 1888. II. 299.[1]
— Rosae americanae. 1896. II. 283.[1]
— Rosae helveticae. 1888. II. 287.[1]
— Rosae hybridae. 1894. II. 283.[1]
— Rosae Synstylae. 1886. II. 282.[2]
— Die Rosen von Tirol und Vorarlberg. 1893. II. 287.[1]
— Les Roses aux prises avec les savants. 1888. II. 283.[1]
— Les Roses de l'herbier de Koch. 1893. II. 284.[3]

— Les Roses de l'herbier de Rau. 1883. II. 284.[2]
— Les Roses de l'île de Thasos. 1892. II. 288.[3]
— Les Roses des îles Canaries. 1887. II. 289.[3]
— Les Roses du Mont Salève. 1894. II. 287.[1]
— Les Roses récoltées par M. Paul Sintenis. 1890. II. 288.[2]
— Les Roses recueillies en Anatolie. 1893. II. 288.[3]
— Les Roses recueillies en Thessalie. 1897. II. 288.[3]
— Les Roses valaisannes. 1892. II. 287.[1]
— A Rózsa növénytani története. 1891. II. 290.[3]
— Sketch of a new classification of Roses. 1889. II. 283.[1]
— En för svenska floran ny Rosa-art. 1893. II. 295.[1]
— Tableau analytique des Roses européennes. 1892. II. 283.[2]
— À travers le pays des Dolomites. 1882. I. 443.
— Sur la valeur . . . d'évolution des sépales après l'anthèse dans le genre Rosa. 1885. II. 289.[1]
— Les variations parallèles. 1897. I. 245.
— *See also* OZANON, Charles & CRÉPIN, François.
Gravet, Frédéric & **Delogne**, C. H. Catalogue de la flore de Belgique. 1872. I. 393.[1]
Crépu, Alex. Descriptions comparatives des Daphne Cneorum. 1855. II. 600.[3]
Crescenti, Francesco. Corso elementare di scienza ed economia silvana. 1866. IV. 99.[1]
Crescenzi, Eduardo de. Sullo scadimento dei boschi nell' Abruzzo ulteriore. 1865. IV. 283.[1]
Crescenzi, Piero de. Vom Ackerbau, Erdwucher und Bawleuten. 1471. III. 97.
— De agricultura, omnibusque plantarum . . . generibus libri. 1471. III. 97.
— Le bon mesnager. 1471. III. 97.
— . . . Epistola commodorum ruralium. 1471. III. 97.
— Liber ruralium commodorum. 1471. III. 97.
— Le livre des profits champêtres. 1471. III. 97.
— Le livre des prouffitz chãpestres. 1471. III. 97.
— La manière d'enter et planter. 1485. III. 98.
— La manière de enter arbres. 1486. III. 98.
— New Feld- und Ackerbau. 1471. III. 97.
— Von dem Nutz der Ding, die in äckeren gebuwt werdē. 1471. III. 97.
— Von dem Nuz der Dinge, die in Ackern gebaut werden. 1471. III. 97.
— De omnibus agriculturæ partibus. 1471. III. 97.
— Opera di agricoltura. 1471. III. 97.
— Opus ruralium commodorum. 1471. III. 97, 757.[3]
— Von Pflanzung der Aeker, Bäume. 1471. III. 97.
— Le quatrième livre du Rustipan. 1864. III. 555.
— Trattato dell' agricoltura. 1471. III. 97.
— Del trattato dell' agricoltura. 1471. III. 97.
Crespi, Alfred. Una enfermedad del Castaño. 1897. III. 359.[3]
Crespi, Alfred J. H. Cocoa and chocolate. 1890. III. 595.[1]
Crespi, Mariano. Trattato della malattia dominante nella vegetazione. 1862. I. 206.[2]
Crespigny, Eyre Champion de. *See* DE CRESPIGNY, E. C.
Cresson, Charles M. Preservation of wood. 187.? IV. 419.
Crested form of Echinopsis scopa. 1875. III. 622.[1]
Creswell, C. F. Report on the elasticity . . . of Eucalyptus. 1882. IV. 410.
Creuzburg, Heinrich. Die Vertilgung der Raupen. 1869. IV. 199.[3]
Crevat, Jules. Mise en éqution d'une pineraie. 1896. IV. 219.
Crévaux, Jules. Observations fournies par un voyage dans l'Amérique équatoriale. 1879. III. 684.[1]
Crèvecœur, Jules Armand Guillaume, **Boucher de**. *See* BOUCHER DE CRÈVECŒUR, Jules Armand Guillaume.
Oriè, Louis Aug. Anatomie et physiologie végétales. 1880. I. 91.
— Essai sur la végétation de l'archipel Chausey. 1876. I. 415.
— Faits pour servir à l'histoire des mouvements chez les végétaux. 1877. I. 194.
— Flore comparée des terrains siliceux. 1878. I. 228.[2]
— Flore comparée du terrain siliceux. 1870. I. 228.[3]
— Note sur un cas fréquent de destruction des feuilles chez l'Hedera. 1874. III. 643.[1]
— Pierre Belon et la nomenclature binaire. 1882. I. 253.[3]
— Rapport sur la maladie des Châtaigniers. 1898. III. 359.[3]
— Rapport sur la maladie des Châtaigniers. 1900. III. 360.[1]
— Rapport sur le dépérissement des Pommiers. 1896. III. 428.[3]

— Des rapports qui existent entre la structure des feuilles du Buxus . . . et l'évolution . . . du Depazea. 1872. III. 523.[1]
— Révision de la flore des Malouines. 1878. I. 347.
— Du rôle des Depazea. 1873. III. 194.
De la Crimée au point de vue forestier. 1855. IV. 348.[1]
Les crimes des Platanes. 1899. III. 419.[1]
The Crimson Camellia-flowered Peach. 1860. III. 439.[2]
Crimson rambler Rose. 1893. III. 456.[1]
Il crine di legno di Tiglio. 1894. IV. 429.
La crisi agrumaria. 1897. IV. 285.[1]
La crisi agrumaria e gli interessi forestali. 1897. IV. 285.[1]
Critic; a fortnightly review of literature. III. 3.
Crivelli, Michele Balsamo. Breve istruzione per allevare la Saturnia yamamai. 1867. IV. 502.[1]
Croatia — Forst-Section der Landwirthschafts-Gesellschaft. See FORST-SECTION . . . IV. 8.
Crochetelle. See CLAUDEL & CROCHETELLE.
Crochetelle, J. Étude chimique sur la chloro[s]e du Poirier. 1895. III. 446.[2]
— See also DUMONT, J. & CROCHETELLE, J.
Crocker, Abraham. A practical essay on raising Apple trees. 1789. III. 426.[1]
Crocker, Charles William. The Wine-Palm. 1862. III. 321.[1]
Crocker, H. See LAPHAM, I. A., KNAPP, J. G. & CROCKER, H.
Crocq, A. J. Tableau synoptique du Jardin des plantes de Bruxelles. 1809. I. 49.
Crocq, Jean Joseph. Recherches sur la maladie de la Vigne. 1854. III. 576.
Croes, J., Engelken, A. M. & F. Kunstmatige droging van Koffie. 1881. III. 739.
Crofton, Mrs. Helen (Milman). See MILMAN, Helen.
Sur la croissance et la durée du Cèdre du Liban. 1848. III. 300.[1]
Croix, SAUVAGES DE LA. See BOISSIER DE LA CROIX DE SAUVAGES.
Croizer, A. A. The work in crossing. 1888. I. 246.[1]
Croizette-Desnoyers, Louis Philippe. Destruction de la larve du haneton. 1888. IV. 203.
— Destruction des vers blancs. 1888. III. 197, IV. 203.
— Effets de l'hiver 1879-1880. 1881. IV. 191.[2]
— Forêt de Fontainebleau; effet de l'hiver 1879-1880. 1881. IV. 191.[2]
— Notice forestière sur les landes de Gascogne. 1874. IV. 360.
— Notice sur le débit . . . des principales espèces de Pins. 1878. IV. 462.[1]
— Notice sur le gemmage du Pin maritime. 1878. IV. 468.[1]
See also DESNOYERS, L. C. 1878. II. 44.[2]
— Notice sur les divers emplois du Hêtre. 1878. IV. 498.
— La sylviculture à l'Exposition universelle. 1878. IV. 20.[1]
Crolas, (Dr.). Phylloxéra et sulfure de carbone. 1888. III. 762.
— & Jobart, F. Traitement des Vignes phylloxérées. 1876. III. 568.
— & Raulin. Traitement de la Vigne par les sels de cuivre. 1886. III. 579.
— & Vermorel, V. Manuel pratique des sulfurages. 1893. III. 762.
Crole, David. Tea, a text book of Tea planting. 1897. III. 604.[1]
Crombie, James Morrison. Braemar. 1861. I. 401.
Crome, Georg Ernest Wilhelm. Der Boden und sein Verhältniss zu den Gewächsen. 1812. I. 228.[1]
— Handbuch der Naturgeschichte für Landwirthe. 1810. III. 35.
Cron, A. Insektenfrass . . . in . . . Schwetzingen. 1863. IV. 207.
Cronberg, Friedrich. De caphura. 1697. III. 233.[1]
Crone, F. Begetmeets Alder. 1865. IV. 494.
Cronemeyer, G. Alphabetical catalogue of plants . . . in the garden of Thomas Hanbury. 1889. I. 64.
— Systematic catalogue of plants . . . in the garden of Thomas Hanbury. 1889. I. 64.
Cronstedt, Carl Joh. Berättelse om frost-fjärilarnas fångande. 1770. III. 188.[2]
— & Adlerheim, Pehr. Resultatan af försöken emot mask på fruktträden. 1770. III. 188.[2]
Croockewit, J. H. Over de zamenstelling van inuline. 1842. I. 175.
Croom, Henry B. Botanical communications. 1834. I. 528,[1] 528,[2] 531.
— A catalogue of plants . . . of New Bern. 1837. I. 318.
— Floral calendar of middle Florida. 1834. I. 528.[2] . . .

— Phenomenon in vegetable life. 1834. I. 528.[1]
— & Loomis, H. Catalogue of plants . . . of Newbern. 1833. I. 318.
Cropp, Frederik Ludwig Christian. Ex itinere in Sylvam Hercyniam. See HALLER, Albert von. 1738. I. 373.
Cropper, R. P. St. Lucia. 1888. III. 267.[1]
Croquevielle. Emploi du sulfate de fer. 1897. III. 581.
Cros, Ulysse. Notes sur la substitution du Lierre à une pelouse de gazon. 1862. III. 642.[2]
Crosfield, George. A calendar of flora composed . . . at Warrington. 1810. I. 396.
Crosnier, Al. JULLIEN-. See JULLIEN-CROSNIER, Al.
Cross, Charles Frederick. Miscellaneous fibres. 1890. III. 235.[1]
— & Bevan, E. J. Report on wood-pulp processes. 1885. IV. 430.
— — Text-book of paper-making. 1900. IV. 430.
— — & Beadle, C. Cellulose. 1895. I. 138.[2]
— & others. Report on Indian fibres. 1887. III. 234.
Cross, Judson N. The Minnesota forestry plan. 1900. IV. 288.[1]
Cross, Robert. The American India-rubber trees at Nilambur. 1882. III. 149.
— The forests of Darien. 1876. I. 333, III. 368.[1]
— Notes on the plants of Peru. 1861. I. 340,[2] II. 812.
— Notes sur les plantes du Pérou. 1861. I. 340.[2]
— Red bark. 1885. III. 726.[1]
— Report of his mission to South America. 1879. III. 712.
— Report on the collecting of seeds . . . of the Chinchonas of Pitayo. 1871. III. 712.[1]
— Report on the collecting of seeds . . . of the India-rubber tree. 1876. I. 333, III. 368.[1]
— Report on the expedition to procure seeds of C. Condaminea. 1862. III. 712.[1]
— Report on the investigation and collecting of plants and seeds of the India-rubber trees. 1878. III. 149, 712.
— Report . . . on the Pitayo Chinchona. 1865. III. 712.
Crossling, Ralph. Evergreen hedges. 1882. III. 214.[2]
Croton-olie. 1883. III. 517.[2]
Crotons. 1870. III. 515.[1]
Les Crotons. 1897. III. 516.[2]
Crouan, P. L. & Hippolyte M. Florule du Finistère. 1867. V. XXII.[1]
Croucher, J. Aspects of vegetation; Mexican Cacti. 1872. II. 78.[2]
— Aspects of vegetation in Nubia. 1872. II. 78.[2]
— The Betel-nut Palm. 1872. II. 64.[2]
— Carludovicas. 1872. III. 332.[1]
— Cereus C. M. Hovey. 1881. III. 621.[1]
— Cereus candicans. 1877. III. 621.[1]
— Cereus serpentinus. 1878. III. 621.[2]
— Cereus-Arten . . . mit scharlachrothen Blumen. 1881. III. 621.[1]
— Corphya [sic] (Livistona) australis. 1872. III. 326.[2]
— Cultivation of Cacti. 1872. III. 619.
— Cycads. 1872. III. 284.[1]
— Disocactus biformis. 1879. III. 625.[2]
— Echinocactus myriostigma. 1874. III. 622.[1]
— Echinocactus ornatus var. Mirbeli. 1873. III. 622.[1]
— Echinocactus unguispinus. 1879. III. 622.[2]
— Echinopsis valida. 1873. III. 623.[2]
— A few good Echinocacti. 1877. III. 622.[1]
— Four free-flowering Cacti. 1878. III. 619.
— Four Opuntias. 1878. III. 624.[1]
— The Gomuti Palm (Arenga saccharifera). 1872. II. 64.[2]
— Leuchtenbergia principis. 1873. III. 623.[1]
— The Lontar Palm. 1872. II. 70.[2]
— Mammillaria elephantidens. 1872. III. 623.[2]
— Mammillaria erecta. 1878. III. 623.[2]
— Mammillaria longimamma. 1878. III. 623.[2]
— Mammillaria sulcolanata. 1874. III. 623.[2]
— Melastoma malabathrica. 1873. III. 638.[2]
— Palm avenue in . . . Rio de Janeiro. 1872. III. 328.[1]
— Palms for the garden. 1872. III. 317.
— Pereskia lychnidiflora. 1878. III. 625.[1]
— Pilocereus fossulatus. 1873. III. 626.[1]
— Pilocereus fossulatus. 1877. III. 626.[1]
— Pilocereus Houlletti. 1878. III. 626.[1]
— Rhipsalis funalis. 1878. III. 625.[1]
— A three-legged Cactus. 1872. III. 622.[1]
— The Tooth-pick Cactus. 1877. III. 622.[1]
— The Turk's Cap. 1877. III. 623.[2]
— Two dwarf Cacti. 1880. III. 622,[1] 623.[2]
— See also JACKSON, J. R. & CROUCHER, J.

Croux. Sur les effets du froid pendant l'hiver 1854–1855. 1855. III. 47.
— Indigotier élégant. 1852. III. 479.²
— Instruction élémentaire sur . . . la taille des arbres fruitiers. 1852. III. 172.
Croux, Gustave. Ligustrum Ibota. 1882. III. 673.²
Crouzel. See JOUÉ & CROUZEL.
Crouzel, Ed. Les parasites du Saule. 1897. III. 350.²
Crow, William Edward. See FORD, Charles, HO KAI & CROW, W. E.
Crownley, A. J. See PAUL, B. H. & CROWNLEY, A. J.
Croy, Friedrich. Ueber die Anwendung der Tachymetrie. 1886. IV. 265.
— Forstliche Baukunde. 1900. IV. 266.¹
— Die Tachymetrie. 1893. IV. 265.
Croy, Raoul, comte de. Avenir forestier de la France. 1853. IV. 275.
— Le Marronnier du 20 mars. 1863. III. 537.¹
Croydon, E. Handbook for Torquay. 1854. I. 533.
Croydon microscopical and natural history club. Proceedings. Report. I. 18.
Croze-Magnan. See GOUFFÉ DE LACOUR & CROZE-MAGNAN.
Crozier, A. A. A dictionary of botanical terms. 1892. I. 71.
— The modification of plants by climate. 1885. I. 218.
— Promising wild fruits. 1890. III. 261.³
— Shrinkage of farm products. 1897. IV. 416.²
— Thornless Honey Locust. 1888. III. 477.³
— A Walnut sport. 1887. II. 113.³
Crozier, F. P. Phylloxéra et sulfure du carbone. 1884. III. 761.
Crüger, Hermann. Abriss der Entwicklungsgeschichte der Blüthe von Couroupita. 1848. II. 612.¹
— Ueber die Befruchtung bei den Orangen. 1851. II. 402.¹
— Botanische Notizen aus Trinidad. 1848. I. 333.¹
— El Cauto. 1857. II. 265.¹
— De duobus Aubletii generibus . . . neglectis. 1847. II. 222,³ 547.¹
— Einige Beiträge zur Kenntniss von sogenannten anomalen Holzbildungen. 1850. I. 126.
— Einiges über die Gewebsveränderungen bei der Fortpflanzung durch Stecklinge. 1860. I. 205.
— Die Entwickelung der Blume von Napoleona. 1860. II. 612.¹
— Zur Entwickelungsgeschichte der Zellenwand. 1855. I. 138.¹
— The fibres of Trinidad. 1862. III. 234.
— Outline of the flora of Trinidad. 1858. I. 338.¹
— Die Primitivfaser. 1854. I. 123.³
— Die Vorläufer. 1856. I. 112.³
— Westindische Fragmente. 1854. I. 123.³ — 1856. I. 112.³ — 1857. II. 265.¹ — 1860. I. 205, II. 612.¹
Crüwell, G. A. Liberian Coffee in Ceylon. 1878. III. 742.³
— & Blacklaw, A. S. Brazil as a Coffee-growing country. 1878. III. 728.³
Crug, Carl. Die Anfertigung forstlicher Terrainkarten. 1878. IV. 265.
— Ueber die Höhenmessung mit Metallbarometern. 1876. IV. 264.
Crugnola, Gaetano. Analogie fra la flora italiana e quella dell' Africa. 1899. I. 430.
— Materiali per la flora dell' Abruzzo teramano. 1900. I. 430.
— La vegetazione al Gran Sasso d'Italia. 1894. I. 430.
Cruickshank, Thomas. The practical planter. 1830. III. 165.
Cruickshanks, James. Forest and fruit tree culture. 1874. III. 117.¹
Cruls, L. Commissão exploradora do planalto central do Brazil. 1894. I. 343.
— Commission d'exploration du plateau central du Brésil. 1894. I. 343.
Cruse, G. L. De Crotonis Tiglii oleo. 1825. III. 517.¹
Cruse, Wilhelm. De Anthospermeis Rubiacearum sectione. 1831. II. 807.¹
— Plantae Ecklonianae: Rubiaceae. 1832. I. 494. .
— De Rubiaceis capensibus. 1825. II. 808.¹
Crusius, Arthur BAUMGARTEN-. See BAUMGARTEN-CRUSIUS, Arthur.
Crusius, C. Borassus flabelliformis. 1900. III. 321.¹
Cruttendon, C. J. Report on the Mijjertheyn tribe of Somalies. 1846. III. 509.²
Crux, Joaquim Luis da. Memoria sobre a cultura do Pinheiro. 1837. IV. 460.²
Crystals in living vegetables. 1831. II. 590.²

Crystals of oxalate of lime in plants. 1828. I. 138.³
Csabai, L. Bougainvillea glabra Sanderiana. 1896. III. 388.¹
Csató, János. Adatok a Juniperus Sabinának hazánkban való elterjedéséhez. 1885. II. 32.¹
— Juniperus Kanitzii. 1886. II. 31.³
— See also BORBAS, Vincenz von & CSATÓ, János.
Csató, Johann von. See CSATO, János.
Cselkó, István. Az Oleanderről. 1897. III. 689.¹
Cserer, Gyula. A Clematis patens. 1899. III. 391.³
— A télen virító Abutilon. 1900. III. 586.³
Cserey, Adolf. Növényhatározó. 1887. I. 446.
Cserny, Győző. A nemes Fűzek mívelése. 1900. III. 349.
Cséti, Ottó. Erdészeti földmérёstan. 1888. IV. 265.
Csiby, Lőrincz. A visfogó gátak vastagságának elmélete és a vissonylagos anyagszükséglet. 1899. IV. 390.³
Cuartero, Octavio. Discusión del presupuesto. Montes. 1892. IV. 553.³
— Las nubes y los árboles. 1892. IV. 542.¹
Cuba, Johannes de. Ortus sanitatis. See ORTUS SANITATIS.
Cuba—Repertorio fisico-natural de la isla.' See REPERTORIO . . . I. 7.³
Cuba Bast. 1856. III. 587.³
Cuba bast. 1857. III. 587.³
Cube, Maximilian von. Die geschichtliche Entwickelung der fürstlich Stolbergischen Forsten. 1893. IV. 26.
Cubebs. 1887. III. 342.²
Cubic-Tabeller. See HOSKIAER, J. 178 .? IV. 220.
Cubières, Simon Louis Pierre, marquis de. Mémoire· sur l'Érable à feuilles de Frêne. 1804. III. 535.¹
— Mémoire sur le Cyprès de la Louisiane. 1809. III. 310.³
— Mémoire sur le Genévrier rouge de Virginie. 1805. III. 304.¹
— Mémoire sur le Magnolier auriculé. 1810. III. 399.³
— Mémoire sur le Tulipier. 1803. III. 398.³
— Mémoire sur les Micocouliers. 1808. III. 363.¹
— Virginische Ahorn. 1804. III. 535.¹
Cuboni, Giuseppe. Appunti sull' anatomia . . . della Vite. 1883. II. 507.³
— Sulla causa della fasciazione nello Spartium. 1894. II. 352,¹ 385.²
— Sulla cosi detta Uva infavata dei colli Laziali. 1889. III. 561.·
— Sulla erinosi nei grappoli della Vite. 1889. III. 561.
— Germinazione di Loidoicea.· 1895. II. 70.²
— Osservazioni anatomiche sugli acini d' Uva. 1890. III. 561.
— Il problema fillosserico in Italia. 1899. III. 762.
— Ricerche sulla formazione dell' amido nelle foglie della Vite. 1885. II. 508.³
— La traspirazione e l' assimilazione. 1887. I. 168, III. 196.
Oudischett suc d'ils guaulds. 1848. IV. 277.
Cürie, P. F. Anleitung die in . . . Deutschland wildwachsenden Pflanzen . . . zu bestimmen. 1823. I. 377, 532.¹
— See also KIOPH.
El Cuerpo de montes francés. 1889. IV. 553.¹
La cuestion de montes con relacion a la provincia de Salamanca. 1886. IV. 276.²
Cugini, Gino. Intorno all' azione dell' etere. 1881. I. 211.
— Descrizione anatomica dell' infiorescenza . . . del Dioon. 1885. II. 5.³
— Il mal nero della Vite. 1883. III. 578.
— Intorno ad una malattia delle Viti. 1886. III. 579.
— Intorno ad un mezzo atto a riconoscere se i semi oleiferi siano ancora capaci di germinare. 1890. I. 203.
— La nuova malattia dell' Uva. 1886. III. 579.·
— Ricerche sul mal nero della Vite. 1881. III. 578.
— Sull' utilità del trattamento dei frutti pomacei col solfato di ferro. 1887. III. 151.·
Cuigneau, (Dr.). Le Chamaerops excelsa. 1869. III. 331.³
Culbertson, Glen. Some notes on the Leguminosae of Siam. 1894. II. 319.¹
Culeron. Emploi pratique du sulfocarbonate de potassium. 1883. III. 573.
Cullen, William. Lectures on the materia medica. 1775. III. 241.
— Traité de matière médicale. 1789. III. 242.
Cullen, William Henry. Flora sidostiensis. 1849. I. 400.
Cullum, Thomas Gery. Florae anglicae specimen. 1775. I. 395.
Culmann. Bericht . . . über die Untersuchung der schweiz. Wildbäche. 1864. IV. 187.¹
— Rapport . . . sur les torrents des Alpes suisses. 1864. IV. 187.¹

Culpeper, Nicholas. Complete herbal. 1652. III. 79.
— Culpeper's complete herbal. 1652. III. 79.
— The English physician. 1652. III. 79.
— Culpeper's English physician. 1652. III. 79.
— Pharmacopoeia londinensis. 1649. III. 251.
— A physicall directory. 1649. III. 251.
Le cultivateur. III. 19.
Cultivation of Cacao. 1890. III. 592.[2]
Cultivation of Cinchona at Darjeeling. 1874. III. 714.
Cultivation of Cinchona in the United States. 1881. III. 712.[2]
Cultivation of Coca in India. 1894. III. 492.[2]
Cultivation of forest trees. 1882. V. xxx.[2]
Cultivation of India rubber in Assam. 1896. III. 370.[2]
Cultivation of Kaurie pine. See McDowALL, A. 1882. V. xxxii.[1]
Cultivation of Lemons in Sicily. 1895. III. 502.[1]
Cultivation of Melocactus humilis. 1897. III. 623.[2]
Cultivation of Osiers. 1893. III. 349.
Cultivation of Tea in Brazil. 1820. III. 601.[1]
The cultivation of the Anise tree. 1886. III. 398.[1]
Cultivation of the Arabian Date Palm in Oudh. 1882. III. 328.[2]
Cultivation of the Castor oil bean. 1877. III. 521.[2]
Cultivation of the Cinchona trees in Java. 1861. III. 715.
Cultivation of the Coco-nut. 1895. III. 323.[1]
The cultivation of the "Eucalyptus globulus" . . . in India 1878. IV. 530.
Cultivation of the Fig. 1878. III. 369.[3]
The cultivation of the Indiarubber tree. 1897. III. 520.[2]
Cultivation of the Oil-Palm. 1880. III. 325.[1]
Cultivation of the Shumac tree in Italy. 1882. III. 527.[1]
Cultivation of the Tea-plant in Assam. 1840. III. 602.[2]
Cultivation of the Thea plant in Anjou. 1874. III. 601.[1]
Cultivation of timber and the preservation of forests. See DUNNELL, M. H. 1874. IV. 271.[2]
The cultivation of useful plants in India. 1876. III. 129.[2]
The cultivator & country gentleman. See COUNTRY gentleman. III. 3.
Cultivo de la Mimbrera. 1882. III. 348.
Cultivo del Café en . . . Chiapas. See ROMERO, Matias. 1874. III. 728.[1]
Cultivo del Cafe en la hacienda de San Antonio. 1891. III. 728.[1]
Cultrera, Paolo. Flora biblica. 1861. I. 513.
Cultrera Teatino, Paolo. Acclimazione degli Eucalitti. 1865. IV. 529.[3]
Zur Cultur der Eiche. 1850. IV. 504.
Ueber die Cultur der Orangen in Australien. 1865. III. 499.[2]
Cultura das plantas que dão a Quina. See GOMES, B. B. 1864. III. 712.[1]
Cultura de Coniferas. 1891. III. 293.
Della cultura degli Agrumi in Italia. 1878. III. 497.[2]
Sulla cultura della Quercia nei piantonai. 1879. IV. 507.
Ueber den Culturbetrieb in den grossh. hessischen Domänen- und Communal-Waldungen. 1863. IV. 118.
Ein Culturbild der Provinz Schlesien. See TRAMNITZ, Adolf. 1869. IV. 353.
Culture de l'Olivier en Perse. 1892. III. 676.[1]
La culture de l'Osier. 1895. III. 349.
Culture de l'Osier. 1896. IV. 487.[1]
Culture de résineux sur résineux. 1899. IV. 145.
Culture des arbres conifères exotiques dans la Grande-Bretagne. 1852. IV. 126.[2]
Culture des arbres fruitiers. 1842. III. 140.[1]
La culture des Cerisiers à Kirsch. See DÉTRIE, L. 1888. III. 436.[1]
Culture des Cinchona à Java. 1873. III. 715.
Culture des Cinchona à la Jamaïque. 1873. III. 713.[1]
Culture des Dipladenia. See Die KULTUR der Dipladenia. 1882. III. 687.[2]
Culture des Quinquinas à la Jamaïque. 1873. III. 713.[1]
Culture des Quinquinas en Bolivie. 1884. III. 713.[1]
Culture du Cacaoyer au Vénézuéla. 1867. III. 592.[2]
La culture du Camphrier en Floride. 1897. III. 404.[1]
Culture du Châtaignier pour la fabrication des cercles. 1899. IV. 493.[1]
La culture du Figuier en Grèce. 1900. III. 369.[2]
Sur la culture du Micooulier. 1848. III. 363.[2]
Culture du Quinquina à Ceylan. 1888. III. 715.
Sur la culture du Quinquina à Java. 1864. III. 715.
La culture du Quinquina à Java et aux Indes. 1883. III. 713.[2]

Culture du Quinquina en Algérie. 1851. III. 717.[1]
Culture du Robinier et de ses variétés. 1899. IV. 523.[2]
Culture du Thé au Brésil. 1851. III. 601.[1]
Culture du Thé en Sicile. 1881. III. 601.[1]
Culture du ver à soie du Chêne en Allemagne. 1892. IV. 502.[1]
De la culture et de l'aménagement des bois. 1853. IV. 101.
La culture forestière en Ardennes. 1898. IV. 119.[3]
The culture of Tea in Brazil. 1855. III. 601.[1]
The culture of the genus Bossiaea. 1850. III. 467.[2]
Culture of the Vine at Mexico. 1830. III. 551.[1]
The culture of the White Mulberry. See Het AANKWEEKEN . . . 1868. III. 377.
Culture of Willows for basket rods. 1885. III. 349.
Cultures au moyen du plantoir de Buttlar. See Die PFLANZUNG. 1859. IV. 152.
Cultures forestières et expériences de la corporation de Binzen. See Ueber das WALDPFLANZEN . . . bei der Genossame Dorf-Binzen. 1865. IV. 366.
Cultures in Nederlandsch Oost-Indië. 1891. III. 129.[1]
Cultus arborum. 1890. I. 517.[1]
Cultuur en bereiding van de Sago. 1887. III. 327.[3]
Cultuur en bereiding van Koffie. 1889. III. 728.[1]
Cultuur en bereiding van Koffie in Amerika. See COFFEE in America. 1893. III. 728.[1]
Cultuur en bereiding van Liberia-Koffie. 1900. III. 743.[1]
Cultuur en bereiding van Rameh. 1883. III. 382.[1]
De cultuur van den Theestruik in het Kangradal. 1884. III. 602.[1]
Culverwell, William. An epitome of the London, Edinburgh and Dublin pharmacopœias. 1851. III. 254.
— & others. Uprooting of Conifers. 1880. III. 151.
— — Uprooting of Conifers, and top-dressing. 1880. III. 151.
Cumberbatch, H. A. Report for the year 1891 on the trade of Adrianople. 1892. III. 583.[2]
Cumming, C. F. Gordon. A Californian forest. 1882. I. 320.
— In the Kauri forests of New Zealand. 1884. III. 297.[2]
— In the Kauri gum fields. 1884. III. 297.[2]
Cumming, George. Japanese dwarf plants at Paris. 1890. III. 176.[1]
Cumming, Joseph George. The Isle of Man; its history. 1848. I. 533, V. xxi.[1]
Cumming, L. & Trott, H. W. Register of plants. 1876. I. 403.
Cumming, William. The pruning of forest trees. 1897. IV. 172.[2]
Cummins, H. A. Botany of Ashanti expedition. 1898. I. 495.
Cummins, L. C. The Walnut and its culture. 1890. III. 355.
Cuní y Martorelli, Miguel. Datos para una flora de los insectos de Cataluña. 1881. I. 239.[1]
— Sobre el desarrollo . . . de la Oceneria. 1889. III. 190.
— Excursion entomologica y botánica a la Cerdaña española. 1881. I. 422.
— Resultado de una exploracion . . . de la Garriga. 1883. I. 422.
Cunitz, Franz. Rhododendron ponticum violaceum-aurantiacum. 1894. III. 662.[1]
Cunningham, Allan. A few general remarks on the vegetation . . . of Terra Australis. 1826. I. 500.
— Florae insularum Novae Zealandiae precursor. 1836. I. 505.[1]
— Notes on the Moreton Bay Pine. 1832. II. 26.[1]
— A specimen of the indigenous botany . . . round Port Jackson. 1825. I. 500.
Cunningham, David Douglas. The causes of fluctuations in turgescence. 1895. I. 150.[1]
— On the phenomena of fertilization in Ficus Roxburghii. 1888. II. 153.[1]
Cunningham, John E. Some observations of Ohio woodlands. 1900. IV. 339.
Cunningham, John F. Some notes upon the forest conditions of Ohio. 1899. IV. 339.
Cunningham, Peter. Two years in New South Wales. 1827. III. 282.[1]
— Zwei Jahre in Neu Südwales. 1827. III. 282.[1]
Cunningham, Robert Oliver. Notes on the natural history of the Strait of Magellan. 1871. I. 347.
— On the occurrence of pleiotaxy of the perianth in Philesia. 1871. II. 84.[2]
— On plants of the Strait of Magellan. 1871. I. 347,

Cuno, Johann Christian. Ode über seinen Garten. 1750.
I. 51.¹
Cupani, Francesco. Catalogus plantarum sicularum. 1692.
I. 430.
— Hortus catholicus. 1696. I. 60.²
— Panphyton siculum. 1713. I. 431.
— Stirpium sicularum icones. 1713. I. 431.
— Syllabus plantarum Siciliae. 1692. I. 430.
— Tabulae Panphytonis siculi. 1713. I. 431.
Cupido, Gaetano. See PEPE, Vincenzo & CUPIDO, Gaetano.
Cuppari, Pietro. Osservazioni sopro due mostruosità. 1844.
II. 596.¹
Cupressus macrocarpa Hartw.; die Monterey-Cypresse in
ihrer Heimat. See The MONTEREY Cypress . . . 1898. II.
29.²
Cupu-assu. 1898. III. 595.¹
Curasson. Le code forestier. 1828. IV. 324.
Curcas-olie. 1883. III. 519.²
Cure da usarsi nell' imballaggio e nella spedizione. 1865.
IV. 151.².
Cure for barked fruit-trees. 1873. III. 180.²
On the cure of the elephantiasis. 1790. III. 462.²
Cure of wounds in Elm-trees. 1831. I. 207,¹ III. 364.¹
Curgenven, J. B. On the use of the oil of Eucalyptus globu-
lus. 1891. IV. 533.²
Curiamo il monte e arricchiremo il piano. 1881. IV. 166.¹
Curie, Paul. Produits résineux du Pin maritime. 1874.
IV. 468.²
Curieuse Nachricht von den . . . Weyden-Rosen. 1747.
III. 349.
Der curieuse Propff- und Oculir-Meister. 1695. III. 159.²
Curieux procédé d'injection du bois. 189L. IV. 409, 421.
Curiöser botanicus. See MUELLER, Samuel. 1687. I. 288.
Curiositez de la nature et de l'art. See BIRON, Claude. 1703.
III. 266.
Curiosities of tree-planting. 1873. III. 34.¹
A curious collection of insects and plants. See MILLER, J. F.
1759. I. 261.
Curious effect of mixing guaiacum with wheat flour. 1820.
III. 494.¹
Curl, S. M. On pituri. 1879. III. 700.¹
Curled leaves. 1889. II. 159.²
Curley, E. Floral calendar. 1869. I. 402.
Curran, Mrs. Mary Katherine. See BRANDEGEE, Mrs. M. K.,
(formerly Mrs. Curran).
The Currant stem girdler. 1895. III. 415.¹
Currey, Frederick. On the botany of the district . . .
[bounded by the rivers Cray, Ravensbourne and Thames].
1858. I. 400.
— Report on vegetable parthenogenesis. 1861. I. 202.¹
Curtel, Georges. Recherches expérimentales . . . chez la
Vigne. 1900. III. 562.¹
— Recherches physiologiques sur la fleur. 1897. I. 148.
— Recherches sur les variations de la transpiration. 1892.
I. 168.
Curten, (sr.). Coup d'œil politique et économique, sur l'état
actuel des bois et forêts en France. 1804. IV. 275.
Curti, G. Istruzione popolare sull' innesto. 1873. III. 162.
Curtis, Carlton C. The anatomy of the stem of Wistaria.
1892. II. 388.²
— A text-book of general botany. 1897. I. 92.
Curtis, Charles. A catalogue of the flowering plants . . . of
Penang. 1894. I. 464,² 466.
— Rubber in Penang. 1899. III. 519.¹
Curtis, Charles E. The manifestation of disease in forest
trees. 1892. IV. 208.²
— Practical forestry. 1898. IV. 121.
— The principles of forestry. 1888. IV. 357.²
Curtis, Henry. Beauties of the Rose. 1850. III. 448.
— Climbing Devoniensis Rose. 1872. III. 455.¹
Curtis, John, (1791-1862). British entomology. 1823. I.
397.
Curtis, John. Effect of loss of bark. 1846. III. 180.¹
— Horsechestnut trees. 1847. II. 482.²
Curtis, Moses A. Botany. 1860. I. 317.¹
— Botany. The woody plants of the state. 1860. I. 317.¹
— Enumeration of plants . . . around Wilmington. 1835.
I. 318.
Curtis, Samuel. A monograph on the genus Camellia. 1819.
II. 550.¹
Curtis, William. A catalogue of certain plants . . . of Settle.
1782. I. 395.
— A catalogue of the British . . . plants cultivated in the
London botanic garden. . . 1783. I. 53.

— A catalogue of the plants growing wild in the environs of
London. 1774. . I. 395.
— Flora londinensis. 1777. I. 395.
— Lectures on botany. 1805. I. 33.
— The subscription catalogue of the Brompton botanic
garden. 1790. I. 53.
Curtiss, Allen Hiram. Catalogue of the . . . plants of
Canada. 1873. I. 314.
— Chápmania and Garberia. 1881. II. 857.²
— The flora of the Florida Keys. 1888. I. 319.
— Fruit growing in Florida. 1888. III. 117.²
— How the Bald Cypress converts lakes into forests. 1888.
II. 51.²
— How the Mangrove forms islands. 1888. II. 614.¹
— Mistletoe parasitic on itself. 1878. II. 177.¹
— North American plants. 1877. I. 307.
Curtis's botanical magazine. See BOTANICAL . . . I. 17.
Curtius, Benedict. Hortorum libri triginta. 1560. I. 511,
III. 96.¹
Curtus, Franciscus. Ad vivium [sic] exprimebat. 1640.
V. XV.²
Ourvo Semmedo, João. Pugillus rerum indicarum. 1722.
I. 200.
Cusa, Salvatore. La Palma nella poesia. 1873. .II. 63.¹
Cusack, Mary Frances. History of the city and county of
Cork. 1875. I. 534.¹ See also COTTER. 1875. V. XXI.²
Cushing, John. The exotic gardener. 1812. III. 150.¹
— Der exotische Gärtner. 1812. III. 150.¹
Cusick, William C. Forest fires in Oregon. 1883. IV. 182.¹
Cusig, Alfred. Bericht über die Schütte. 1854. IV. 475.
— Beschreibung des Verfahrens zur Erziehung von Kiefern-
ballen-Pflanzen. 1876. IV. 472.
— Besprechung der stattgefundenen Bereisung des Patsch-
kau'er Stadtwaldes. 1887. IV. 354.
— Notizen über Pinus rigida. 1852. IV. 468.²
— Ueber den waldbaulichen Werth . . . .der Vorwüchse.
1888, 1889. IV. 138,² 142.
— Welche Arten des Holzverkaufes haben sich für die schle-
sischen Verhältnisse bewährt. 1891. IV. 388.²
— Welchen Einfluss hat die socialpolitische Gesetzgebung
. . . auf die Verhältnisse der Waldarbeiter geübt? 1893.
IV. 311.¹
— Unter welchen Verhältnissen . . .:empfiehlt sich beim
Kahlschlagbetriebe der Ueberhalt. 1898. IV. 130.
— Unter welchen Verhältnissen empfiehlt sich die Erziehung
von Boden-Schutzholz. 1886. IV. 132.¹.
— Unter welchen Verhältnissen sind Birke und Aspe . . .
am Platze. 1897. IV. 486,² 490.²
— Wie ist mit Rücksicht auf die . . . Schüttegefahren die
Bestandsgründung bei der Kiefer zweckmässig zu bewirken.
1894. IV. 478.
— See also DESELAERS, & CUSIG, Alfred; SPANGENBERG &
CUSIG, Alfred.
— & Glaessner, (Oberförster, Breslau). Welche Erfahrungen
sind . . . mit den verschiedenen Durchforstungsmethoden
gemacht worden? 1900. IV. 175.²
— & Salisch, Heinrich von. Inwieweit ist es gerechtfertigt?
. . . einen Wechsel der Holzarten . . . herbeizuführen
1890. IV. 245.
Cusig, Paul. See SPANGENBERG & CUSIG, Paul.
Cusin, Louis. Geonoma Verschaffelti. 1879. III. 325.¹
— Greffage Treyve du Noyer. 1883. III. 355.
— Note sur l'organisation du fruit du Grenadier. 1875. II.
610.¹
— Les Pêchers cultivés en France appartiennentils à plusieurs
espèces? 1879. II. 276.¹
— Persica vulgaris à fruit lisse. 1878. II. 276.¹
— See also MÉHU, Adolphe, SAINT-LAGER, Jean & CUSIN,
Louis.
— & Ansberque, Edme. Herbier de la flore française. 1868.
I. 414.
Cusson, Pierre, Gouan, Antoine & Commerson, Philibert.
Leçons de botanique. 1762. I· 511.
Custer, Jakob Laurenz. Phanerogamische Gewächse des
Rheinthals. 1821. I. 433.
Outanda, Vicente. Flora compendiada de Madrid. 1861.
I. 421.
— & Amo, Mariano del. Manual de botanica descriptiva.
1848. I. 420.
Cutbush, William & son. The Epacris. 1879. III. 665.¹
Cuthill, James. Treatise on the Vine disease. 1855. III. 576.
The Cut-leaved Walnut. 1877. III. 355.
Cutler, Manasseh. An account of some of the vegetable pro-
ductions . . . in this part of America. 1785. I. 305.

Cutting, Hiram A. The forests of Vermont. 1886. IV. 339.
Cuvelier, V. Azalea Vervaeneana. 1886. III. 660.[1]
— Les Boronia. 1891. III. 495.[3]
— Clematis Jackmanni alba. 1888. III. 391.[1]
— Le Rhododendron Boothi. 1881. III. 657.[2]
— Rhododendron Dalhousiae var. Countess of Haddington. 1885. III. 658.[2]
Cuvier, Fr. Examen d'un sel recueilli sur le Réaumuria. 1804. II. 562.[1]
Cuvier, George. Histoire des sciences naturelles. 1841. I. 523.
Cuxart, Antonio Cipriano Costa y. See Costa y Cuxart, A. C.
Cuzaco, P. Le Pin maritime des landes de Gascogne. 1889. IV. 468.[1]
— De l'usufruit dés Pins maritimes. 1875. IV. 468.[1]
Cuzent, Gilbert. De l'Aleurites triloba. 1857. III. 514.[2]
— Arbres de Tahiti. 1857. IV. 402.[1]
— Études sur quelques végétaux de Tahiti. 1857. III. 283.[2]
— Fécule de Pia. 1857. III. 283.[2]
— De la gomme de Mapé. 1857. III. 479.[3]
— De la gomme du Spondias dulcis. 1857. III. 529.[2]
— On Kava or Ava. 1862. III. 343.[1]
— Du Kawa ou Ava de Taïti. 1857. III. 343.[1]
— De la matière colorante rouge ... de Mati. 1857. III. 371.[2]
— Note sur le Kava ou Ava. 1860. III. 343.[1]
— Produits divers. 1857. III. 283.[2]
— De la racine de Kawa. 1861. III. 343.[1]
— Du Ricin. 1857. III. 522.[1]
— Sur le suc de Mapé. 1859. III. 479.[2]
— Du suc gommo-résineux d'Agati. 1857. III. 487.[2]
— Tahiti. 1860. III. 283.[2]
— Du Tamanu, Calophyllum inophyllum. 1857. III. 608.[2]
— On Tamanu resin and oil. 1863. III. 608.[2]
Cybulski, A. K. O zasuszaniu drzewa. 1842. IV. 416.[1]
Cybulski, H. Carica Papaya. 1888. III. 617.[2]
Cycads. 1880. II. 6.[1]
The Cycas. 1897. III. 285.[1]
Cycads at Kew. 1892. III. 284.[2]
Les Cycas revoluta de l'établissement Van Houtte. 1850. II. 4.[3]
Le cyclone du 10 août. 1895. IV. 548.[1]
The cyclopaedia of botany. See New cyclopaedia ... 1868. III. 82.
Cyclopedia of botany. See Goodrich, S. G. 1838. I. 94.
Cynips Malpighi. 1861. IV. 509.
Le Cyprès chauve. See Cypress ... 1893. IV. 484.[2]
A Cypress avenue at Verona. 1889. III. 303.[1]
The Cypress of Montezuma. 1890. II. 52.[1]
Cypress of Noche Triste. 1896. II. 52.[1]
The Cypress-tree of Tule. 1897. II. 52.[1]
Die Cypressen der Alten und Neuen Welt. 1873. III. 302.[1]
Cypresses in tropical Africa. 1892. II. 27.[1]
The Cypresses of Monterey. 1894. II. 29.[2]
Cyriaci, Johann Christoph. Von der Waldwirthschaft. 1798. IV. 177.[1]
Cyrilli, Domenico. See Cirillo, Domenico.
Cyrillus, Dominicus. See Cirillo, Domenico.
Cyrkularz o sadzeniu drzew owocowych żeniącym się. 1809. III. 146.[1]
Cyrus, F. Ueber das Verfahren, den Cereus grandiflorus ... bei Tage zum Blühen zu bringen. 1888. III. 621.[2]
Cytisine. 1871. III. 481.[1]
Czapek, Friedrich. Zur Biologie der holzbewohnenden Pilze. 1899. I. 207.[1]
— Zur Chemie der Holzsubstanz. 1898. I. 156.[1]
— Zur Kenntniss des Milchsaftsystems der Convolvulaceen. 1894. II. 744.[1]
— Zur Lehre von den Wurzelausscheidungen. 1896. I. 162.
— Über die Leitungswege der organischen Baustoffe. 1897. I. 166.
— Über den Nachweis der geotropischen Sensibilität der Wurzelspitze. 1900. I. 196.[1]
— Zur Physiologie des Leptoms der Angiospermen. 1897. I. 166.
— Die plagiotrope Stellung der Seitenwurzeln. 1895. I. 104.
— Über die Richtungsursachen der Seitenwurzeln. 1895. I. 194.
— Ueber die sauren Eigenschaften der Wurzelausscheidungen. 1896. I. 160.
— Untersuchungen über Geotropismus. 1895. I. 196.[1]
— Weitere Beiträge zur Kenntniss der geotropischen Reizbewegungen. 1898. I. 196.[1]
— Über Zusammenwirken von Heliotropismus und Geotropismus. 1895. I. 196.[1]

Czaslavsky, Karel. Statistickotopograficky popis ... panství Zbírov. 1888. IV. 372.
— Statistisch-topographische Beschreibung der ... Domäne Zbírov. 1888. IV. 372.
— & Leske, Fritz. Beschreibung der Exkursionstour ... in den Forsten der Domäne Zbírov. 1888. IV. 372.
— — Popis smeru vycházky ... do lesŭ panství Zhírova. 1888. IV. 372.
Czech, Josef. Ausdauer von Wellingtonia. 1878. III. 310.[1]
— Beitrag zur Kenntniss der Lebensweise des Kiefernmarkkäfers. 1883. IV. 477.
— Deutschlands älteste Eichen. 1900. IV. 516.[1]
— Elateridenfrass an Eichentrieben. 1878. IV. 510.
— Die Forstinsectenschäden. 1890. IV. 210.[1]
— Der grosse Kiefernmarkkäfer in Fichten. 1886. IV. 456.
— Neue Beobachtungen über den Tannenrüsselkäfer. 1889. IV. 445.
— Ein neuer Fichtenschädling. 1880. IV. 456.
— Saperda populnea L. in Weiden. 1878. III. 350.[1]
— Ein wenig bekannter Ulmenschädling. 1887. IV. 518.[2]
Czech, Karl. Ueber die Entstehung der Gallen. 1860. IV. 66.[1]
— Ueber die Funktionen der Stomata. 1869. I. 131.[2]
— Ueber den Hexenbesen an der Rothtanne. 1857. IV. 455.
— Untersuchungen über die Zahlverhältnisse ... der Stomata. 1865. I. 131.[1]
Czspiński, Michal. Powszechne ogrodnictwo obejmujące uwagi nad zakładaniem ogrodów. 1841. III. 165.
— O uprawie Wina w ogrodach. 1874. III. 551.[2]
Czerny, Franz. Znaczenie lasów zwłaszcza w górach. 1878. IV. 44.
Czerwiakowski, Ignaz Raphael. Opisanie roślin. 1849. V. x.[2]
— & Warszewicz, Joseph. Catalogus plantarum ... in Horto botanico cracoviensi. 1864. I. 66.[1]
Czihak, Jakob von. Nahrungsstoffe aus dem Pflanzenreiche. 1853. III. 272.[1]
— & Szabo, Jos. Heil- und Nahrungsmittel. 1863. III. 2'2.[1]
Czihatzky, Anfangs- und Endpunkt der Schaftablängung. 1893. IV. 219.
Czubata, Heinrich. Der Futterwerth der Eicheln. 1880. IV. 515.[1]
Czullick, August. Ueber eine neue Species Catalpa. 1880. III. 706.[1]
Czumpelik, Ed. Sur l'Aloés. 1862. II. 79.[1]
— Untersuchung der Aloë succotrina. 1862. II. 79.[1]
Czy można na Podolu i na Bukowinie uprawiać Winną macicę. 1893. III. 558.[1]

D. De aanbouw van den Caoutchoucboom in Britsch-Indië. 1876. III. 149.
D. Comparaciones. 1892. IV. 552.[2]
D. The destruction of trees by lightning. 1904. IV. 195.[1]
D. Ueber den dreilappigen Ahorn. 1831. II. 478.[1]
D. Einige Worte über Führung der Weisstannen-Schläge. 1840. IV. 444.[1]
D. Heide, Moor und Wald. 1892. IV. 159.
D. Herbaceous and shrubby Clematises. 1887. III. 389.[1]
D. Houtwolindustrie in Nederland. 1886. IV. 429.
D. Hybrid Cistus. 1890. III. 612.[2]
D. Ueber Hydrangea arborescens. 1904. III. 411.[1]
D. New hybrid Rhododendrons. 1877. III. 655.
D. Een nieuwe textiel plant. 1886. III. 587.[2]
D. Le Noyer de Nazareth. 1896. II. 114.[1]
D. Plantation de résineux à fort écartement. 1898. IV. 454.
D. Planting under the shade of trees. 1885. IV. 132.[2]
D. The Purple Virgin's Bower. 1891. III. 392.[1]
D. Rough timber tramway. 1877. IV. 391.
D. Starke Tannen und Fichten. 1873. II. 21.[2]
D. Waarom Teak en geen Djati. 1888. IV. 538.[1]
D. Ypréaux. 1895. V. ix.[2]
D. See also Д.
D., te D. Monumentale boomen ... Doorwerth. 1874. I. 296.[2]
D., van. De Grove Den. 1854. IV. 482.[2]
D., A. Conifers and other evergreens and snow. 1889. III. 185.[1]
D., A. Foliaged deciduous trees. 1886. III. 362.[1]
D., A. Hardy Camellias. 1887. III. 599.[1]
D., A. A lightning-struck tree. 1894. IV. 195.[1]
D., A. Measuring the heights of trees. 1873. IV. 215.
D., A. Notice sur le Magnolia de la Maillardière. 1849. III. 398.[2] 399.[2]

D., A. nouvelle visite au domaine de Gooreynd. 1900. IV. 357Une
D., A. Outdoor Camellias. 1889. III. 599.²
D., A. The Poplars. 1872. III. 345.¹
D., A. Tenacity of life in trees. 1896. III. 180.²
D., A. What makes the best farm hedge? 1851. III. 425.¹
D., A. & others. Ivy on buildings. 1880. III. 642.²
D., C. Contrast of colour in foliage. 1855. III. 205.²
D., C. Exploitation des résineux. 1897. IV. 556.²
D., C. Simple method of transplanting large trees. 1884. III 165.¹
D., La Truffe en Franche-Comté. 1899. IV. 558.¹
D., C. R. S. Daphne indica. 1885. III. 627.²
D., C. R. S. Single Camellias. 1885. III. 599.¹
D., D. Cistuses. 1891. III. 612.²
D., E. Fires caused by Bamboo-friction. 1892. III. 315.²
D., E. Styrax japonica. 1900. III. 671.¹
D., E. E. Wild flowers of South Australia. 1861. I. 502.
D., E. S. An Ash tree on stilts. 1875. II. 708.¹
D., F. Quercus magnifica. 1884. II. 132.²
D., G. Bouturage des plantes par les racines. 1881. III. 158.
D., G. Un Jasmin qui fleurit au mois de janvier. 1881. III. 673.¹
D., G. Le Magango. 1881. III. 589.¹
D., G. Thinning park timber. 1879. III. 202.²
D., G. de. Citrus triptera. 1889. III. 503.¹
D., H. Bassia flowers. 1860. III. 667.¹
D., J. Ueber die Benutzung der Fichtenlohrinde. 1876. IV. 459.²
D., Greenhouse Rhododendrons. 1887. III. 656.
D., Norfolk Island Pine. 1900. III. 298.²
D., Plan of securing single trees in pleasure-grounds. 1846. III. 198.²
D., J. S. C. Cochineal. 1883. III. 624.¹
D., L. Le Dracaena rubra discolor. 1889. III. 334.²
D., L. Le gemmage. 1891. IV. 437.¹
D., M. Sur la production de l'essence de Badiane. 1899. III. 398.¹
D., O. Machine à transplanter les arbres de M. Miller. 1859. III. 167.
D., P. Les conversions dans Le Loiret. 1888. IV. 128.
D., P. Der gemeine Hollunderbaum. 1805. III. 752.¹
D., P. Origine de la Vigne cultivée. 1873. II. 507.¹
D., R. Les Ardisia. 1900. III. 666.¹
D., R. Conifers in boggy soils. 1887. III. 292.
D., R. Crataegus Pyracantha as a standard. 1899. III. 443.²
D., R. Ealing Park. 1884. III. 300.¹
D., R. A fine Wistaria chinensis. 1896. II. 389.¹
D., R. Group of new Azaleas. 1879. III. 660.¹
D., R. A group of new Clematises. 1879. III. 389.¹
D., R. Hardiness of Lapageria rosea. 1879. III. 337.²
D., R. Hybrid Rhododendrons . . . at Ormskirk. 1879. III. 655.
D., R. Le Liège. 1900. IV. 518.¹
D., R. New Fuchsias. 1880. III. 640.¹
D., R. The Mulberry. 1892. II. 154.¹
D., R. Routes fruitières dans le grand-duché de Luxembourg. 1900. III. 211.¹
D., R. E. The forest question in Australia. 1887. IV. 280.¹
D., S. Ampelopsis Veitchi and other wall plants. 1878. III. 204.²
D., U. On the heredity of malformations of Pinus sylvestris. 1895. II. 48.²
D., V. Vitalité des graines de Palmiers. 1897. III. 318.¹
D., W. Berry-bearing Aucubas. 1876. III. 645.¹
D., W. Gum trees of Van Diemen's Land. 1853. II. 623.²
D., W. Napoleona imperialis. 1894. III. 631.²
D., W. Opgave der voornaamste groenblijvende gewassen. 1849. III. 505.²
D., W. Protecting shrubs in winter. 1896. III. 183.²
D'A . . . & Virey, J. J. Histoire naturelle des galles des végétaux. 1820. I. 528.²
Daalen, A. C. van. Welke is de beste tijd voor Dennen planten? 1897. IV. 474.
Dabney, John C. See HICKS, G. H. & DABNEY, J. C.
Dabry de Thiersant, Philibert. Le Caféier de Libéria. See THIERSANT, P. D. de. 1882. III. 742.¹
— The Coffee plant of Liberia. See THIERSANT, P. D. de. 1882. III. 742.¹
— L'Élæococca vernicia. See THIERSANT, P. D. de. 1876. III. 514.¹
— See also SOUBEIRAN, J. L. & DABRY DE THIERSANT, Philibert.

Daccomo, G. & Malaguini. Sur la Cosine. 1898. III. 424.²
Dach. Die Winterpflanzung der Fichten. 1867. III. 305.¹
Dachröden, Friedrich von. Beschreibung von 400 Arten Topfpflanzen. 1831. III. 74.
Da Corogna. De l'influence exercée . . . par les émanations volcaniques. 1866. III. 185.¹
De Dadapziekte van Java. 1894. III. 476.¹
De Dadapziekte van Oost-Java. 1893. III. 476.¹
D'Adda, S. Proposte per modificazione all' attuale legge forestale. 1896. IV. 329.
Dadre, Ernesto. La sericoltura nel Tonkino. 1899. III. 148.²
Daehnert, Theodor Johann Friedrich. De oleo Olivarum. See SCHULZE, J. H. 1740. III. 678.¹
Dänische Gesellschaft der Wissenschaften. See KÖNIGLICHE DÄNISCHE . . . V. VII.¹
Dänische Pharmakopöe. See PHARMACOPOEA danica. 1772. III. 247.¹
Daenzer, F. G. Des Euphorbiacées. 1834. III. 514.¹
Dätzel, Georg Anton. See DÄZEL, G. A.
Däzel, Georg Anton. Anleitung zur Forstwissenschaft. 1802. IV. 96.
— Ueber Forsttaxirung und Ausmittelung des . . . Ertrages. 1793. IV. 239.
— Die Holzzucht, Forstpflege. See DÄZEL, G. A. & GRÜNBERGER, Georg. 1788. IV. 95.
— Die Physiologie der Holzpflanzen. See DÄZEL, G. A. & GRÜNBERGER, Georg. 1788. IV. 95.
— Praktische Anleitung zur Forstwirthschaft. 1788. IV. 95, V. XXXI.¹
— Praktische Anleitung . . . zur Taxirung. 1786. IV. 213.
— Tabellen zur Bestimmung des Geldpreises unbeschlagener Baumstämme. 1798. IV. 402.¹
— Tabellen zur Bestimmung des Inhalts unbeschlagener Baumstämme. 1791. IV. 220.
— Tafeln für Forstmänner zur Bestimmung des Inhaltes der Walzen und Kreisflächen. 1791. IV. 220.
— Vollständige Tabellen zur Bestimmung des Inhalts unbeschlagener Baumstämme. 1791. IV. 216.
— Ueber die zweckmässigste und zuverlässigste Methode grosse Waldungen zu messen. 1799. IV. 216.
— & Grünberger, Georg. Lehrbuch für die pfalzbaierischen Förster. 1788. IV. 95.
Dafert, Franz Wilhelm. De bemesting en het drogen van Koffie. 1898. III. 729.¹
— Considerações a respeito da cultura do Café no Brazil. 1891. III. 728.¹
— Die Düngung des Kaffeebaumes. 1896. III. 728.²
— Erfahrungen über rationellen Kaffeebau. 1896. III. 728.²
— Estrumes artificiaes na cultura do Café. 1896. III. 728.¹
— Estudos sobre o Café. 1894. III. 728.¹
— Ueber die gegenwärtige Lage des Kaffeebaus in Brasilien. 1898. III. 729.¹
— Kleines Handbuch der Bodenkunde. 1885. III. 37.¹
— Kleines Lehrbuch der Bodenkunde. 1885. III. 37.¹
— A phylloxera no estado de S. Paulo. 1896. III. 575.¹
— Principes de culture rationelle du Café au Brésil. 1896. III. 728.²
— Over den tegenwoordigen toestand der Koffiecultuur in Braziliä. 1898. III. 729.¹
— & Lehmann, Ernst. Estudos sobre a cultura do Caféeiro. 1896. III. 728.²
— — Resultados das experiencias da acclimatição. 1893. III. 551.¹
— — Untersuchungen auf dem Gebiete des Kaffeebaus. 1896. III. 728.²
— & Rivinius, L. A seccagem do café I. 1896. III. 740.¹
— — Studien über die Trocknung des Kaffees. 1896. III. 740.¹
Daffner, Franz. Die Voralpenpflanzen. 1893. I. 389.
Dagonet, G. Rapport sur les insectes nuisibles à la Vigne. 1843. III. 562.²
Dagoty, Jacques GAUTIER-. See GAUTIER-DAGOTY, Jacques.
Daguillon, Auguste. Sur les feuilles primordiales des Cupressinées. 1899. II. 18.
— Observations morphologiques sur les . . . Cupressinées. 1899. II. 18.
— Observations sur la structure des feuilles de quelques Coniffères. 1888. II. 18.
— Sur le polymorphisme foliaire des Abiétinées. 1889. II. 18.
— De quelques anomalies foliaires. 1895. I. 145.¹
— Recherches morphologiques sur les feuilles des Coniffères. 1890. II. 18.

Daguin, Arthur. *See* AUBRIOT, L. & DAGUIN, Arthur.

Dahl, Andreas. Observationes botanicae circa systema vegetabilium. 1787. I. 263.

Dahl, Friedrich. Die blumenbesuchenden Vögel. 1900. I. 240.[1]

Dahl, Ove. Botaniske undersøgelser i Søndfjords . . . fjorddistrikter. 1898. V. XIX.[1]

— En gammel Trondhjemsflora af Joachim Irgens. 1891. I. 358.

— Herbarium antiquum danicum. 1892. I. 358.

— Kystvegetationen i Romsdal. 1896. V. XIX.[1]

— Plantegeografiske undersøgelser i ydre Søndmøre. ·1895. V. XIX.[1]

— Om udklængning af skovfrö. 1896. IV. 148.

Dahl, T. Botanisk Lommebog for Skoler. 1861. I. 90.

Dahlberg, Nicolaus E. Metamorphoses plantarum; *See* LINNÉ, Carl von. 1755. I. 243.[2]

Dahlbom, A. G. Anmärkningar om Häggmålet. 1835. III. 439.[1]

Dahlen, H. W. Ueber das Auftreten der Phylloxera. 1877. III. 760.

— Bericht über die . . . unternommene Reise nach den Phylloxerainfektionsheerden des Cantons Neufchâtel. 1879. III. 760.

Dahlerup. De træagtige Pæonier. 1839. III. 392.[1]

Dahlgren, Johan Adolph. De Erica. *See* LINNÉ, Carl von. 1770. II. 663.[2]

Dahll, F. K. G. Rögens skadelige indflydelse. 1896. IV. 193.[1]

Dahlman, G. T. Den färdige trädgårdmästaren. 1728. III. 100.[1]

Dahlmann, Laurent. De conservatione sylvarum in patria. 1741. IV. 179.[2]

Dahlström, K. Vildväxande Pyrus malus och Ulmus montana. . 1878. II. 144.[2] 266.[2]

Dahlström, P. Kubik-Tabeller for rundt Træ. 1868. IV. 226.

— Taxation af Prøveflader i Bøg og Gran. 1870. IV. 255.

Dahmen, Max. Anatomisch-physiologische Untersuchungen über den Funiculus der Samen. 1892. I. 121.

— Recherche de l'albumine. 1892. I. 177.

Dahs, Reuter & Co. Auswahl wertvoller Ziergehölze für Einzelstellung. 1900. III. 203.

Dahuron, René. Il giardiniero francese; overo, Trattato del tagliare. 1692. III. 171.

— Nouveau traité de la taille des arbres fruitiers. 1696. III. 171.

— Tractat vom nützlichen Baum-Beschneiden. 1692. III. 171.

— Traité de la taille des arbres. 1692. III. 106,[1] 171.

— Traité de la taille . . . des melons. 1692. III. 171.

Dai-Nihon-ju-moku shiryaku. 1878. V. XXIII.[2]

Dai Nippon samukai hokoku. IV. 10.[1]

Daiber, J. Taschenbuch der Flora von Württemberg. 1866. I. 386.

Daikuhara, G. On the reserve protein in plants. 1894. I. 179.[2]

Daille, Léon. Note sur l'Uredo viticida. 1880. III. 578.

— Observations relatives à une note de MM. Prillieux et Delacroix. 1894. III. 581.

Dailledouze, J. P. & Jacques, *frères*. Catalogue des arbres . . . dans les pépinières au Petit Saconnex. 1828. I. 65.[1]

Daisy trees. 1897. III. 756.[1]

Daji, Narajan. A new Indian remedy. 1871. III. 506.[2]

Dakin, Rhus Toxicodendron. 1833. III. 528.[1]

Dal, Adolf. Om skoggränsens synkning. 1893. I. 350,[2] IV 79.[1]

Dalbret. Quelques améliorations à faire pour aider à l'affranchissement des arbres. 1843. III. 160.

Daldorph, P. N. Om Skov-Hugst . . . i de Norske Fjæld-Bøyder. 1757. IV. 343.[2]

Dale, Charles William. The history of Glanville's Wootton. 1878. I. 534.[1]

Dale, Samuel. Pharmacologia. 1693. III. 257.[1]

Dale, Thomas. De Paretra brava. 1723. III. 396.[2]

Dalechamps, Jacques. Histoire générale des plantes. 1586. I. 282.

— Historia generalis plantarum. 1554. I. 279.

— Historia generalis plantarum. 1586. I. 282, 530.[2]

Dalgado, D. G. Classificação botanica das plantas e drogas. 1894. III. 59.[1]

— Dalbergia spinosa. 1891. II. 352.[2]

— Flora de Goa e Savantvadi. 1898. III, 92.[2]

— Vires plantarum malabaricarum. 1896. III. 92.[2]

Dalgas, Enrico Mylius. Anvisning til Anlæg af Smaaplantninger. 1875. III. 119.[2]

— The Danish heath-society. 1884. IV. 39.[2]

— Det danske Hedeselskab. 1888. IV. 39.[2]

— Den dybe Reolpløjning. 1872. IV. 143.[1]

— Feldborg Plantage. 1869. IV. 343.[1]

— Geographiske Billeder fra Heden. 1867. IV. 343.[1]

— En Hedereise i Hannover. 1873. IV. 354.

— Hederne i Danmark og deres Tilkultivering. 1878. IV. 156.[2]

— Hedesagens nuværende Standpunkt. 1875. IV. 156.[2]

— Hvilken Betydning have de jydske Heder. 1872. IV. 343.[1]

— De jydske Heder. 1872. IV. 156.[2]

— En Oversigt over Hederne i Jylland. 1866. IV. 343.[1]

— Om plantning i Jylland. 1877. IV. 156.[2]

— Regler for Behandling af Planteskoler. 1884. IV. 150.

— Reisebilleder fra Nordtyskland og Holland. 1889. IV. 356.[3]

— Skov-Kulturer i Jyllands Hedeegne. 1890. IV. 343.[2]

— Société cultivatrice des landes de Danemark. 1893. IV. 39.[3]

— Veiledning ved Træplantning i Hedeegne. 1870. IV. 156.[2]

Dalgas, Gustavo. I rimboscamenti delle montagne. 1881. IV. 165.

Dalgleish, J. Edward. The planting, maintenance . . . of a plantation. 1898. IV. 169.[2]

Dalhousie, *marquess*. Timber and forest trees in the Punjab. 1861. IV. 279.[1]

Dalibard, Thomas François. Florae parisiensis prodromus. 1749. I. 405.

Dalimier, Paul. Sur la présence normale de gaz dans les vaisseaux. 1863. I. 133.

Dall, William Healy. Alaska and its resources. 1870. III. 262.[1]

Dalla Bella, João Antonio. *See* BELLA, João Antonio dalla.

Dallaporta, Niccolo. Prospetto delle piante . . . nell' isola di Cefalonia. 1821. III. 91.[1]

Dalla Torre. *See also* TORRE, dalla.

Dalla Torre, Karl Wilhelm von. Die Alpenflora der österreichischen Alpenländer. 1882. I. 437.

— Die Alpenflora der österreichischen Alpenländer. 1899. I. 438.

— Anleitung zur Beobachtung . . . der Alpenpflanzen. 1882. I. 437.

— Juniperus Sabina L. in den nördlichen Kalkalpen Tirols. 1890. II. 32.[1]

— The tourist's guide to the flora of the Alps. 1882. I. 437.

— Die volksthümlichen Pflanzennamen in Tirol und Vorarlberg. 1895. I. 75.[1]

— Wörterbuch der botanischen Fachausdrücke. 1884. I. 599.[1]

— Die Zoocecidien . . . Tirols und Vorarlbergs. 1893. I. 216.[2]

— & Harms, Hermann. Genera Siphonogamarum ad systema Englerianum conscripta. 1900. I. 77.

— & Sarnthein, Ludwig, *Graf* von. Flora der gefürsteten Grafschaft Tirol. 1900. I. 4,[1] 444.

— — Die Litteratur der Flora von Tirol. 1900. I. 4,[1] 444.

Dallbre, Alexis. Drei empfehlenswerthe Dracaenen. 1875. III. 334.[1]

Dallinger, Prosper. Gesammelte Nachrichten . . . über den Fichtenspinner. 1798. IV. 206.

— Vollständige Geschichte des Borkenkäfers. 1798. IV. 203.

Dalloz, D. & A. Explication de la loi modificative du code forestier. 1860. IV. 326.

Dalloz, Édouard, (*jr.*) & Vergé, Charles. Les codes annotés; code forestier. 1884. IV. 324.

Dalwitz, von, (*Oberforstmeister*) & Wellenberg, (*Oberförster-Candidat*). Geschichte ihrer Cultur. 1864. IV. 353.

— — Promemoria über die forstlichen Verhältnisse der Provinz Preussen. 1864. IV. 353.

Dalman, Olof Johan. Försök at koka socker af svenska Lönnars saft. 1754. III. 535.[2]

Dalmas. Note concernant le maladie de la Vigne. 1852. III. 575.[3]

Dalmer, Moritz. Beiträge zur Morphologie . . . von Ilex Aquifolium. 1897. II. 463.[2]

— Ueber Eisbildung in Pflanzen. 1895. I. 212,

— Ueber die Leitung der Pollenschläuche. 1880. I. 201.[1]

Dalmon, J. Étude sur la busserole et l'arbutine. 1885. III. 648.[3]

Dalmon, Jules & **Gras**, Camille. Promenades botaniques dans la flore parisienne. 1877. I. 415.
Dalrymple-Hay, R. *See* HAY, R. DALRYMPLE-.
Dalton, Henry G. The history of British Guiana. 1855. III. 64.[2]
Dalton, Walter. Opuntia fruit as food. 1890. III. 624.[2]
Dalton, Wilham. Gutta percha. 1849. III. 668.[2]
Daly, William Mahon. Periodical flowering of Strobilanthes Kunthianus. 1894. II. 804.[1]
Dalzell, Nicholas Alexander. Annual report on the Sind forests. 1859. IV. 377.[1]
— On the Antiaris saccidora or Sack tree. 1852. III. 366.[1]
— Catalogue of the indigenous flowering plants of the Bombay Presidency. 1858. I. 473.
— Contributions to the botany of western India. 1850. I. 473.
— New Leguminosae from western India. 1873. II. 319.[1]
— Note on Capparis galeata. 1873. II. 230.[2]
— Observations on the genus Moringa. 1866. II. 234.[2]
— Observations on the influence of forests. 1863. IV. 43.
— Remarks on the genus Moringa. 1866. II. 234.[2]
— & **Gibson**, Alexander. The Bombay flora. 1861. I. 473.
Dam, J. van. De invloed der bosschen op het klimaat. 1890. IV. 54.
Damage done to Himalayan Pines. 1894. IV. 464.[1]
Damart, Max. Sur l'origine de la gomme, dite de Bassora. 1819. III. 592.[1]
Damaskenos, NICOLAOS. *See* NICOLAOS DAMASKENOS.
Damaskinos, Th. & **Bourgeois**, A. Des bourgeons axillaires multiples. 1858. I. 108.[1]
Dambourney, Louis Alexandre. Histoire des plantes, qui servent à la teinture. 1792. III. 236.
— Recueil de procédés . . . sur les teintures solides. 1786. III. 235.[2]
Dame, Lorin Low. Historic trees. 1884. I. 295.[2]
— Our forests. 1881. IV. 281.[2]
— & **Brooks**, Henry. Typical Elms . . . of Massachusetts. 1890. I. 295,[1] II. 144.[1]
— & **Collins**, S. S. Flora of Middlesex county. 1888. I. 315.
Damm, Franz. Camphora. 1834. III. 404.[3]
Dammann, Hermann, (jr.). Beitrag zur Würdigung der Eucalyptus-Arten. 1882. IV. 531.[3]
Dammar from New Caledonia. 1891. III. 297.[3]
Dammar resin. 1899. III. 228.[1]
Dammara australis. 1883. II. 25.[3]
Damme, O. Koffie, thee en chocolade. 187.? III. 222.
Dammer, Udo. Abortion der Stamina bei Philadelphus. 1891. II. 242.[1]
— Anleitung für Pflanzensammler. 1894. I. 36.[1]
— Batidaceae. 1893. II. 114.[2]
— Beiträge zur Kenntnis der Fichtenformen. 1888. II. 35.[1]
— Convolvulaceae. 1897. II. 743.[1]
— Einige Bemerkungen zu dem Mahnrufe des Herrn M. von Sivers. 1895. IV. 474.
— Einige Blütenmissbildungen. 1889. II. 242.[1]
— Ueber einige Fichtenformen. 1889. II. 35.[1]
— Ueber einige Formen der Picea excelsa. 1883. II. 34.[3]
— Die extrafloralen Nectarien an Sambucus nigra. 1890. II. 841.[1]
— Ueber Hyphaene Schatan Bojer. 1900. II. 69.[1]
— Ueber die Keimung der Lodoicea. 1900. II. 70.[2]
— Zur Kenntnis der afrikanischen Brunnichia-Arten. 1899. II. 184.[2].
— Zur Kenntnis der Prevostea alternifolia. 1897. II. 746.[1]
— Zur Kenntnis von Podopterus mexicanus. 1891. II. 186.[1]
— Zur Kenntniss von Batis maritima. 1892. II. 114.[2]
— Nadelhölzer. 1900. III. 291.
— Notizen über einige Pflanzen des Berliner botan. Gartens. 1897. II. 709.[1]
— Palmen. 1900. III. 318.[2]
— Palmensucht und Palmenpflege. 1897. III. 318.[1]
— Picea excelsa var. obovata. 1889. II. 38.[1]
— Picea obovata. 1888. II. 38.[1].
— Polygonaceae. 1893. II. 183.[2]
— Polygonaceen-Studien. 1893. II. 184.[1]
— Seedlings of Oreodoxa regia. 1895. II. 72.[1]
— Theorie der Gartenarbeiten. 1899. III. 36.[1]
— Ueber Verpackung . . . der Palmensamen. 1895. III. 318.[1]
— Ueber das Vorkommen der Symmeria paniculata. 1900. II. 186.[2]
Dampier, William. A new voyage round the world. 1697. I. 301.

Damseaux, Ad. L'azote et la végétation. 1869. I. 159.
— Emploi de la litière des forêts en agriculture. 1896. IV. 438.[1]
— Los humos sulfurosos. 1895. IV. 548.[1]
Dana, C. A. Conifers and their cultivation. 1888. III. 293.
— Une expérience intéressante en sylviculture. 1895. IV. 18.[2]
— An interesting experiment in tree culture. 1895. I. 51,[1] IV. 18.[2]
— The road to the pyramids of Gizeh. 1894. III. 466.[2]
Dana, Marvin. The sacred flower. 1898. II. 290.[2]
Dana, *Mrs.* William Starr. How to know the wild flowers. 1893. I. 316.
Danasi, Lamberto. Comitati forestali provinciali. 1896. IV. 293.[2]
Dancer, Thomas. Catalogue of plants . . . in the botanical garden, Jamaica. 1792. I. 39.
— Some observations respecting the botanical garden. 1804. I. 39.
Danckelmann, Bernhard. Die Ablösung und Regelung der Waldgrundgerechtigkeiten. 1880. IV. 333, 334.[1]
— Die 1893 stattfindende Ermittelung der landwirthschaftlichen Bodenbenutzung . . . und die Forststatistik. 1893. IV. 336.[2]
— Altes und Neues aus dem norddeutschen Fichtenwalde. 1892. IV. 454.
— Anbauversuche mit ausländischen Holzarten. 1884. IV. 25.[2]
— Ausbildung für den Forstverwaltungsdienst im Königreiche Sachsen. 1899. IV. 33.[3]
— Die Betriebsregelung der österreichischen Staatsforsten. 1880. IV. 250.[1]
— Ueber die Bildung der Holzboden-Abtheilungen. 1880. IV. 244.
— Las claras. 1899. IV. 543.[2]
— Die December-Stürme des Jahres 1868. 1871. IV. 189.[1]
— Die deutschen Nutzholzzölle. 1883. IV. 284.[2]
— Ueber Düngungsmittel im Forsthaushalte. 1870. IV. 44.[2]
— Einbringung von Eichen in Buchen-Aufwuchshorste. 1892. IV. 138.[1]
— Ueber den Einfluss der Witterung auf Stärkezuwachs. 1899. I. 190.[2]
— Ueber den Einfluss des Blauwerdens . . . von Kiefernholz. 1897. IV. 482.[2]
— Eisenbahn-Staffeltarife für Grubenholz. 1897. IV. 284.[2]
— Das Ergänzungsgesetz vom 17. Juni 1896 zum bayerischen Forstgesetz. 1899. IV. 319.[1]
— Erweiterung der eidgenössischen Oberaufsicht über die Forstpolizei. 1898. IV. 331.[1]
— Ueber die Erziehung . . . 2jähriger verschulter Kiefern. 1879. IV. 473.
— Festschrift für die fünfzigjährige Jubelfeier der Forstakademie Eberswalde. 1880. IV. 32.
— Les forêts aux États-Unis. 1884. IV. 338.
— Die Forstakademie Eberswalde von 1830 bis 1880. 1880. IV. 32.
— F s -Akademien oder allgemeine Hochschulen? 1872. IV. 308.
— Die forstliche Ausstellung des Deutschen Reiches auf der Wiener Weltausstellung 1873. 1873. IV. 19.[2]
— Die forstlichen Verhältnisse . . . Oldenburg. 1894. IV. 352.
— Forstverwaltung und forstlicher Unterricht in Frankreich. 1876. IV. 292.
— Die 50jährige Jubelfeier der Forstakademie Eberswalde. 1880. IV. 32.
— Ueber die Gebrauchsfähigkeit einiger Holzarten zum Grubenausbau. 1899. IV. 425.[2]
— Ueber Gegenstand und Organisation der forstlichen Statistik. 1873. IV. 336.[1]
— Gemeindewald und Genossenwald. 1881. IV. 274.[1]
— Gemeindewald und Genossenwald. 1882. IV. 308.[1]
— Gerbstoff aus indischen Hölzern. 1898. IV. 435.
— Das Gesetz vom 15. Januar 1892, betreffend die Bewirthschaftung der Privatwaldungen. 1892. IV. 322.[1]
— Ueber die Grenzen des Servitutrechts. 1884. IV. 333.
— Hand-Spaltpflanzung von Kiefernjährlingen. 1889. IV. 473.
— Holzvorrath . . . von Weymouthskiefer. 1898. IV. 471.
— L'idée d'éclaircie en Allemagne. 1899. IV. 68.
— Der Kältewinter 1892/93. 1894. IV. 191.[1]
— Kiefern-Unterbaubetrieb. 1881. IV. 473.
— Kiefern-Zapfenernte. 1869. IV. 472.

— Lichtmessung und Lichtverhältnisse im Walde. 1899. IV. 68, 543.²
— Maikäfervertilgung. 1869. IV. 202.
— Ueber den Masstab für Wärmebedürfnis. 1869. I. 221.
— Ein misslungener Versuch der Insekten-Vertilgung. 1869. IV. 199.²
— The nature and limitation of the servitude. 1884. IV. 333.
— Observations phénologiques. 1898. IV. 73.¹
— Ueber die Organisation des forstlichen Versuchswesens. 1869. IV. 38.¹
— Phänologie der Holzarten. 1898. I. 226,¹ IV. 73.¹
— Physikalische und mechanische Eigenschaften märkischen Kiefernholzes. 1890. II. 48.¹
— Raummeter oder Festmeter als Masseinheit. 1873. IV. 227.
— Rede . . . in der Holzzollfrage. 1882. IV. 284.²
— Regenfreie Eichenrinde. 1892. IV. 513.
— Saatbrett und Pflanzbrett. 1873. IV. 149.¹
— Les salaires des bûcherons en Prusse. 1888. IV. 310.²
— Schutzwaldbestrebungen in der Schweiz. 1895. IV. 181.¹
— Spätfrostbeschädigungen im märkischen Walde. 1898. IV. 192.¹
— Ueber Stufentarife für Holzhauerlöhne. 1888. IV. 310.²
— Die Tarifklassifikation amerikanischer Nutzhölzer. 1897. IV. 284.²
— Die Thermo-Carbolisation. 1884. IV. 420.
— Todtschneiden von Weidenhegern. 1881. III. 350.¹
— Der Verein bayerischer Holzinteressenten. 1898. IV. 274.²
— Versuche mit Reisigfütterung. 1895. III. 223.²
— Die Vertilgung der grossen Kieferraupe. 1870. IV. 476.
— Vorertragstafeln, Sortimentstafeln. 1887. IV. 257.
— Wald und Hochwasser im Flussgebiete der Wupper. 1892. IV. 47.¹
— Waldbauliche Theorien und Reform-Bestrebungen von Gustav Wagener. 1887. IV. 128.
— Waldbrandversicherung. 1897. IV. 182,² 509.¹
— Die Waldverheerungen durch den Orkan . . . 1894. 1897. IV. 189.²
— Waldverwüstung und Waldgesetze in den Vereinigten Staaten. 1884. IV. 338.¹
— Waldwirthschaft, Holzindustrie . . . in Finland. 1885. IV. 114.
— Die Waldwirthschaft im Dienste der Wasserwirthschaft. 1889. IV. 73.¹
— Die Weidenheger im Roer- und Wurmthale. 1879. III. 348.
— Die Weidenheger zu Messdunk. 1874. III. 347.
— Ueber Weidenkultur auf Sandboden. 1869. IV. 487.¹
— Nach welchen Grundsätzen hat bei Ablösung von Waldgrundgerechtigkeiten die Ermittelung des . . . Reinertrags von Forstland . . . stattzufinden. 1889. IV. 333.
— Welches System der Verwaltungsorganisation der Forsten empfiehlt sich am meisten? 1876. IV. 287.
— Wirkung des Buchenwaldes. 1891. IV. 73.¹
— Wünsche des Holzhandels. 1885. IV. 388.¹
— Wurzelknollen an der Schwarzerle. 1869. II. 116.²
Dandenelle, Claës Abraham. De Hermannia. See THUNBERG, C. P. 1794. II. 535.¹
Dandolo, Vincenzo, conte. L'art d'élever les vers à soie. 1819 †† 373
— The art of rearing silk-worms. 1819. III. 373.
— Sui bachi da seta, sui Gelsi. 1815. III. 373.
Dandridge, Danske. American Stuartias. 1900. III. 596.²
— American Viburnums. 1900. III. 753.¹
— An evergreen shrubbery. 1892. III. 206.¹
— Evergreens in winter. 1897. III. 291.
— Neviusia alabamensis. 1900. III. 429.²
— The shrubbery in November. 1891. III. 207.¹
Danĕk, Vincenz, Edler von Esse. Die Forst-Versicherung als Staats-Anstalt. 1893. IV. 284.¹
— Studie über die Ermittelung des Normalvorrathes. 1893. IV. 237, 246.
Dangeard, Pierre Auguste. Les maladies du Pommier. 1892. III. 428,⁴ 446.²
— Le mode d'union de la tige et de la racine. 1888. I. 106.¹
— Le mode d'union de la tige et de la racine. 1890. II. 1.
— Note sur la gaine foliaire des Salicornieae. 1888. II. 187.¹
— Observations sur l'anatomie des Salsoleae. 1888. II. 187.¹
— Recherches sur la structure des Salicornieae. 1888. II. 187.¹
— Recherches sur le mode d'union de la tige et de la racine. 1889. I. 106.¹

— Recherches sur les plantules des Conifères. 1892. II. 19.
— Remarques sur les canaux sécréteurs de l'Araucaria imbricata. 1887. II. 26.²
Dangerous enemies of street trees. 1896. III. 212.¹
A dangerous measure. 1888. IV. 178.¹
Dangerous trees. 1882. III. 34.²
Dangers de l'If pour le gibier. 1894. IV. 558.¹
Dangers de la fabrication des chinois. 1884. III. 501.²
Danhelovsky, Adolf. Abhandlung über die Technik des Holzwaaren-Gewerbes. 1873. IV. 428.¹
— Abtriebs-Ertrag eines slavonischen Stieleichen-Hochwaldes. 1875. IV. 512.
— Aeussere Kennzeichen der Spaltbarkeit des Stieleichen-Holzes. 1875. IV. 506.
— Das b des Weiserprozentes. 1880. IV. 256.
— Handbuch über die Erzeugung und Berechnung des deutschen Fassholzes. 1861. IV. 224.
— Holzmassen-Vorrath der Eichenwälder. 1881. IV. 513.
— Tafeln über Visirmasse, Längen und Stärken des deutschen Binderholzes. 1861. IV. 224, 487.¹
Daniel, Lucien. La chématobie et la greffe du Pommier. 189 . ? III. 163.¹
— Du choix des greffons. 189 . ? III. 163.¹
— Les conditions de réussite des greffes. 1900. I. 246.²
— Étude anatomique sommaire sur les débuts de la soudure dans la greffe. 1895. I. 208.²
— Greffe de quelques monocotylédones sur elles-mêmes. 1899. III. 165.
— La greffe depuis l'antiquité. 1895. III. 163.¹
— Sur la greffe des parties souterraines. 1891. III. 165.
— Sur la greffe des plantes en germination. 1893. III. 163.²
— La greffe et ses applications. 1897. III. 163.¹
— La greffe mixte. 1897. III. 163,¹ 165.
— Influence du sujet sur la postérité du greffon. 1895. I. 529.
— Influence du sujet sur le greffon. 1898. III. 40.
— Influence réciproque du sujet et du greffon. 1899? III. 40.
— Sur les limites de possibilité du greffage. 1900. III. 165.
— Note sur la greffe des arbres fruitiers. 189 . ? III. 163.¹
— Un nouveau procédé de greffage. 1897. III. 163.¹
— Parasites et plantes greffées. 1894. III. 165.
— Le principe de la parenté botanique en fait de greffe. 1900. I. 246.²
— Sur quelques applications . . . de la greffe herbacée. 1894 . ? II. 850.²
— Recherches anatomiques . . . sur les bractées . . . Composées. 1900. II. 850.²
— Recherches anatomiques sur les greffes. 1896. I. 208.²
— Recherches morphologiques . . . sur la greffe. 1894. I. 208.²
— La variation dans la greffe. 1898. I. 246,² 248.²
Daniel-Bekof. See Данiель-Бековъ.
Daniell, William Freeman. On the Cascarilla. 1863. III. 516.¹
— On Coelocline polycarpa. 1857. III. 402.¹
— On the Frankincense tree of west Africa. 1855. III. 475.¹
— On the kola nut of tropical West Africa. 1865. III. 590.¹
— On the natives of Old Callebar. 1846. III. 330,² 483.²
— Notes on some Chinese condiments. 1862. II. 411.⁴
— Notice sur quelques condiments chinois. 1862. II. 411.⁴
— On the Pterocarpus erinaceus. 1855. III. 485.²
— On red Canella bark from the West Indies. 1859. III. 613.²
— Some observations on the copals of West Africa. 1857. III. 473.¹
— On the Synsepalum dulciferum. 1852. III. 669.¹
Danielli, Stefano. Raccolta di quistioni intorno a cose di botanica. 1723. I. 28.²
Daniels, John D. Bougainvilleas. 1870. III. 388.¹
Danker, Herm. Bowenia spectabilis serrulata. 1900. III. 284.²
Danmarks og Norges oeconomiske Magazin. III. 10.²
Dannemann, Adolf. Beitrag zur Kenntniss der Wirkung des Physostigmin. 1891. III. 484.¹
Danni causati dai bruchi. 1863. IV. 209.¹
Danni del diboscamento. 1866. IV. 48.¹
Danni prodotti dal vetriscio . . . Fontainebleau. 1879. IV. 190.
Il danno d'un' inondazione. 1863. IV. 48.¹
Dansey, E. P. A chapter on soils in their bearing on the natural regeneration of Sál. 1886. IV. 529.¹

Dansey, E. P. (continued).
— Impressions of a month in the forests of South Berar. 1888. IV. 378.
— Note on the government forests of Bahraich. 1887. IV. 378.
— The privileges in the Bahraich government forests. 1885. IV. 335.
— On the working of the forests in Bahraich. 1885. IV. 279.²
Dansey, John. Coffee in Queensland. 1898. III. 733.¹
Dansk Haugetidende. See HAVETIDENDE. III. 10.²
Dansk Havebrugs-Tidende. See HAVEBRUGS-TIDENDE. III. 10.²
Dansk Havetidende. See HAVETIDENDE. III. 10.²
Dansk Skovforening. Fællesbestyrelsen. 1894. IV. 315.¹
Dansk Skovforening. Fællesbestyrelsen. Betænkning fra Udvalget om Prismeddelelser. 1896. IV. 404.¹
Dansk Skovforening. Fællesbestyrelsen. Handelsudvalgets Betænkning. 1893. IV. 404.¹
Dansk Skovforening. Fællesbestyrelsen. Toldudvalgets Betænkning. 1894. IV. 284.¹
Dansk Skovforening. Fællesbestyrelsen. Udvalgsbetænkning om Vedtægter for Handelen. 1896. IV. 404.¹
Dansk Skovforening. Fællesbestyrelsens Betænkning fra Dansk Skovforenings Udvalg. 1896. IV. 273.¹
Dansk Skovforening. Fællesbestyrelsens Betænkning fra Udvalget om Opførelse af Skure. 1895. IV. 404.¹
Dansk Tidsskrift. See DANSK Ugeskrift. I. 8.¹
Dansk Ugeskrift. I. 8.¹
Den **danske** Frugthave. 1869. III. 66.²
Det **Danske** Hedeselskab. 1877. IV. 39.²
Danske Hedeselskabet. Beretning. IV. 5.³
Danske Landhuusholdnings-Selskab. See KONGELIGE DANSKE . . . III. 10.²
Danske Videnskabernes Selskab. Oversigt. See KONGELIGE DANSKE . . . I. 9.¹ Skrifter. See KIØBENHAVNSKE SELSKAB . . . I. 8.²
Danty d'Isnard, Antoine. Établissement d'un nouveau genre . . . Evonymoides. 1718. II. 467.¹
— Établissement d'un nouveau genre . . . Monospermalthaea. See ISNARD, A. D. d'. 1723. I. 334.
Dantz, Johann. Tabulae simplicium medicamentorum. 1543. III. 239.
Dany, F. De la manière de semer et faire pépinières. 1560. III. 153.
Danyss, Jean. Destruction des animaux nuisibles. 1894. III. 186.¹
Danzig — Naturforschende Gesellschaft. See NATURFORSCHENDE . . . I, 13.
Daponte, Giovanni Maironi. I tre regni della natura nella provincia Bergamasca. 1823. I. 425.
Dapper, Olfert. Asia; oder, Ausführliche Beschreibung. 1672. I. 452.
— Asia; of, Naukeurige beschryving. 1672. I. 452.
— Beschreibung des Königreichs Persien. 1672. I. 477.¹
— Beschrijving des koningryoks van Persie. 1672. I. 477.¹
— Description de l'Afrique. 1668. I. 482.
— Description exacte des isles de l'archipel. 1688. I. 451.
— Des îles de l'Afrique. 1668. I. 482.
— Naukeurige beschrijving van Asie. 1680. I. 478.
— Naukeurige beschrijvinge der Afrikaensche eylanden. 1668. I. 482, V. xxiv.¹
— Naukeurige beschrijvinge der Afrikaensche eylanden. 1668. I. 482, V. xxiv.¹
— Naukeurige beschryving der eilanden, in de Archipel der middelantsche Zee. 1688. I. 451.
— Umbständliche und eigentliche Beschreibung von Asia. 1680. I. 478.
Dapperen, J. W. van. De "Maragang." 1895. III. 129.¹
Dapsy, Wilhelm. Über die Knoppern. 1855. IV. 502.¹
Darblay. La pâte de bois de France. 1900. IV. 430.
D'Arbois de Jubainville, A. See ARBOIS DE JUBAINVILLE, A. de.
Darboux, Gaston. Sur une galle d' "Ephedra distachya." 1900. II. 54.³
Darby, John. Botany of the southern states. 1841. I. 318.
— A manual of botany . . . of the southern states. 1841. I. 318, V. xvii.³
D'Arcy, W. E. Notes on the preparation of forest working plans. 1892. IV. 250.²
— Portable forest tramways. 1886. IV. 392.
— Preparation of forest working-plans in India. 1892. IV. 250.¹

— Some aspects of forest administration in India. 1890. IV. 295.²
— A timber slide in the Chamba forests. 1886. IV. 390.²
Dardye, E. de BOURGADE LA. See BOURGADE LA DARDYE, E. de.
Darelius, Johan Andreas. Lignum colubrinum. See LINNÉ, Carl von. 1749. III. 684.¹
Dareste, Camille. Note sur l'existence de l'amidou dans les testicules. 1872. I. 201.³
Dargassies. Lettres à Nanine sur la botanique. 1828. I. 94.
D'Argentelle, Louis Marc Antoine ROBILLARD. See ROBILLARD D'ARGENTELLE, L. M. A.
D'Argenville, Antoine Nicolas DEZALLIER. See DEZALLIER D'ARGENVILLE, A. N.
Daries, Peter Johann Andreas. De Amygdalis et oleo amararum aethereo. See LEONHARDI, J. G. 1776. III. 434.²
Dario, Gonzalès. See GUÉRIN, René, DARIO, Gonzalès & GARCIA, Jorge.
To darken Oak. 1892. IV. 422.²
Darley-Mullot. Notice pour la plantation de toutes les espèces d'arbres. 1845. III. 166.
Darling, John. On the preparation of ground for planting. 1858. III. 150.³
— On thinning plantations. 1858. IV. 173.
Darlington, Ralph. The birds, wild flowers . . . of North Wales. 1896. I. 535.
Darlington, William. Additions to the Chester county cabinet of natural science.. 1826. I. 38.³
— Agricultural botany. 1847. III. 62.
— American weeds and useful plants. 1847. III. 62.
— An essay on the development . . . of the external organs. 1839. I. 101.³
— A plea for a national museum and botanic garden. 1841. I. 38.²
— Reliquiae Baldwinianae. See BALDWIN, William. 1843. I. 307.
— Remarks on the Prunus americana. 1828. II. 272.¹
Darluc, Michel. Histoire naturelle de la Provence. 1782. I. 406.
Darolles, Édouard. Le Café sur le marché français. 1891. III. 740.¹
Darrach, (Dr.). Plants appearing in flower in the neighborhood of Philadelphia. 1861. I. 222¹
Darstellung der Abschätzung der Ober-Försterei Hammer. 1828. IV. 247.³
Darstellung der Banater Güter der K. k. priv. österr. Staats-Eisenbahn-Gesellschaft. 1861. IV. 373.
Darstellung der forstlichen Verhältnisse Livlands. 1896. IV. 348.¹
Darstellung der forstlichen Verhältnisse Livlands. 1897. IV. 348.¹
Darstellung der in den Gebirgswaldungen . . . zur Anwendung kommenden Holzbringungsmittel. 1860. IV. 389.
Darstellung der königl. sächs. Staatsforstverwaltung. 1865. IV. 291,¹ 355.³
Darstellung einer einfachen Forstabschätzung. 1825. IV. 254.
Darstellung . . . üblichen Holzverbringung. See DARSTELLUNG der in den Gebirgswaldungen . . . 1860. IV. 389.
Darstellung vorzüglicher ausländischer Bäume und Gesträuche. See KERNER, J. S. von. 1796. I. 293, III. 68,³ IV. 81.³
Dart, E. H. S. Apple trees from seeds. 1889. III. 426.³
— Girdling fruit trees. 1897. III. 175.¹
Darton, Nelson Horatio. Pine Ridge timber. 1899. IV. 341.¹
Daruty de Grandpré, Clément. Compte-rendu d'une brochure, intitulée: "Les forêts de l'Alsace." 1877. IV. 349.¹
— Contributions à la matière médicale de l'Île Maurice. 1887. III. 470.³
— Notes sur la thérapeutique . . . de l'Île Maurice. 1889. III. 279.³
— Plantes médicinales de l'île Maurice. 1886. III. 93.¹
Darwin, Charles Robert. Afændring hos dyrkede Planter. 1871. I. 247.
— Die Bewegungen und Lebensweise der kletternden Pflanzen. 1865. I. 196.²
— The different forms of flowers on plants of the same species. 1877. I. 115,¹ 257.
— Does sea-water kill seeds? 1855. I. 527.
— Effect of salt water on seeds. 1855. I. 527.
— The effects of cross and self fertilisation. 1876. I. 237, 245.

— Über die Entstehung der Arten. 1859. I. 243.[1]
— Journal of researches into the geology and natural history of the various countries visited by H. M. S. Beagle. 1839. I. 303.
— Journal of researches into the natural history . . . of the countries visited. 1839. I. 303.
— Les mouvements et les habitudes des plantes grimpantes. 1865. I. 196.[2]
— On the movements and habits of climbing plants. 1865. I. 196.[1]
— I movimenti e le abitudini delle piante rampicanti. 1865. I. 196.[2]
— Observations on Terra del Fuego. 1841. I. 347.
— Het ontstaan der soorten. 1859. I. 243.[1]
— On the origin of species. 1859. I. 243.[1]
— De l'origine des espèces. 1859. I. 243.[1]
— De la variation des animaux et des plantes à l'état domestique. 1868. I. 247.
— De la variation des animaux et des plantes sous l'action de la domestication. 1868. I. 247.
— The variation of animals and plants under domestication. 1868. I. 247.
— Variazione degli animali e delle piante allo stato domestico. 1868. I. 247.
— Das Variiren der Thiere und Pflanzen im Zustande der Domestication. 1868. I. 247.
— Die verschiedenen Blüthenformen an Pflanzen der nämlichen Art. 1877. I. 115.[1]
— Die Wirkungen der Kreus- und Selbst-Befruchtung. 1876. I. 245.
— & Francis. Das Bewegungsvermögen der Pflanzen. 1880. I. 194.
— — Il potere di movimento nelle piante. 1880. I. 194.
— — The power of movement in plants. 1880. I. 194.
Darwin, Erasmus. Abhandlungen und Bemerkungen über verschiedene naturwissenschaftliche Gegenstände. 1810. .I. 33.
— Gli amori delle piante. 1789. I. 93.
— Les amours des plautes. 1789. I. 93.
— The botanic garden. 1789. I. 93, 527.
— Phytologia. 1800. III. 35.
— Phytonomie. 1800. III. 35.
Darwin, Francis. On the ascent of water in trees. 1896. I. 166.
— Cambridge natural science manuals. 1895. I. 92.
— The elements of botany. 1895. I. 92.
— Etiolation as a phenomenon of adaptation. 1896. III. 40.
— On the glandular bodies on Acacia sphaerocephala. 1877. II. 147,[1] 388.[3]
— Observations on stomata. .1897. I. 168.
— Observations on stomata. 1898. I. 132.[1]
— On the relation between the " bloom " on leaves and the distribution of the stomata. 1887. I. 191,[1] 210.
— Report of a discussion on the ascent of water. 1896. I. 166.
— The theory of the growth of cuttings. 1880. I. 205.
— Ueber das Wachsthum negativ heliotropischer Wurzeln. 1882. I. 195.[1]
— See also DARWIN, C. R. & Francis.
— & Acton, E. H. Practical physiology of plants. 1894. I. 149.[1]
— & Phillips, R. W. On the transpiration-stream in cut branches. 1886. I. 165.
Darwin, Robert Waring. Principia botanica. 1787. I. 83.
Das, LALA THAKUR. See LALA THAKUR DAS.
Dasani, Lamberto. Pro arborum. 1895. IV. 329.
— Il contributo forestale. 1899. IV. 329.
— Sugli effetti della legge forestale 20 Giugno 1877. 1899. IV. 329.
— Pro hominibus. 1896. IV. 329.
— L' insegnamento forestale in Italia. 1896. IV. 35.[2]
— Intorno alla legge forestale. 1896. IV. 329.
— Sul nuovo progetto di legge forestale. 1897. IV. 329.
— Perequazione fondiaria. 1896. IV. 329.
— Piani di coltura . . . pei boschi. 1897. IV. 249.[2]
— Circa la revisione della legge forestale. 1896. IV. 329.
— Per la riforma della legge forestale. 1896. IV. 329.
— Per la riforma della legge forestale. Elenchi di vincolo. 1896. IV. 329.
— Socialismo . . . forestale. 1897. IV. 277.
Dashkof, D. See Дашковъ, Д.
Dasikés nomothesias. See Δασικὴ ѕ νομοθεσίαϛ.
Dassdorff, J. A. Palingenesia; sive, Resurrectio plantarum. See MOEGLING, J. L. . 1683. I. 515.

Dassen, Michael. Ueber die Bewegungen der Pflanzen. 1835. I. 197.[1]
— Onderzoek aangaande de bladbewegingen. 1837. I. 197.[1]
— Onderzoekingen over de verschillende deelen, welke den stengel vormen. 1845. I. 105.
— Onderzoekingen over de vochtbeweging bij planten. 1847. I. 193.[2]
— Onderzoekingen over den . . . stengel. 1847. I. 105.
— Over den stengel der eenzaadlobbige planten. 1848. I. 105.
— Tweede verhandeling over de blad bewegingen. 1844. I. 197.[1]
— Verhandeling ter beantwoording der vrage: Wat weet men . van de bewegingen . . . aan de bladen? 1835. I. 197.[1]
Dassonville, Charles. Action des différents sels sur la structure des plantes. 1898. I. 157.
— Influence des sels minéraux. 1898. I. 229.
Dassow, Carolus Magnus. Nova genera plantarum zeylanicarum. See LINNÉ, Carl von. 1747. I. 476.[2]
— & Chenon, L. J. Nova plantarum genera. See LINNÉ, Carl von. 1747. I. 261.
Dasychira pudibunda. 1895. IV. 549.[2]
Date cultivation in Antigua. 1896. III. 329.[1]
Date cultivation in South Australia. 1895. III. 329.[1]
The Date-palm. 1835. III. 329.[2]
The Date-palm. 1857. III. 329.[2]
The Date Palm. 1894. II. 72.[2]
The Date Palm in Arizona. 1898. III. 329.[1]
The Date palms. 1880. III. 328.[1]
Date planting in Australia. 1893. III. 329.[1]
Date Plums. 1874. III. 669.[1]
Date production in Bussorah. 1898. III. 329.[2]
The Date tree. 1846. III. 329.[2]
Daten über Holz-Production in Österreich. 1882. IV. 406.[2]
Of dates. 1888. III. 329.[2]
Dati statistici della provincia di Como. 1864. IV. 364.
Dato Iradier, Eduardo. La venta de los montes. 1886. IV. 276.[2]
Datos de estadística forestal de Alemania y Austria. 1893. IV. 555.[2]
Datos para la materia médica mexicana. See RAMIREZ, José & others. 1894. III. 265.[1]
Datos recopilados sobre el Cacao. 1900. III. 593.[1]
Datty. Des plantations, de leur nécessité en France. 1805. IV. 161.[1]
Dau. Einige Mittheilungen über Holzpflaster. 1890. IV. 426.[1]
Dau, Becker, Esser & Arnold. Anleitung zur Pflanzung . . . von Strassenbäumen. 1895. III. 210.
Daube, W. Chemische Analysen des Kern- und Splintholzes. 1883. IV. 64.[1]
— Das " naturgemässe Zurückweichen des Waldes " 1881 IV. 74.[2]
— Der Wald und der Wasserstand. 1882. IV. 50.
— Der Wald und die elektrischen Erscheinungen. 1882. IV. 194.
Daubenton. Over de beplanting der zeeduinen enz. 1779. IV. 159.
Daubenton, Louis Jean Marie. Observations sur l'organisation . . . du bois. 1797. I. 100.
— Observations sur les bois du Chêne. 1784. IV. 513.
— Observations sur un grand arbre du Chili. 1787. II. 26.[2]
Daubeny, Charles Giles Bridle. On the action of light upon plants. 1836. I. 229.
— Essay on the trees and shrubs of the ancients. 1865. I. 514.[2]
— Memoir on the degree of selection exercised by plants. 1835. I. 161.
— Memorials of Oxford. 1836. I. 54.
— Oxford botanic garden. 1850. I. 54.
— Sur la proportion relative de soude et de potasse. 1852. I. 152.[2]
— Remarks on the final causes of the sexuality of plants. 1860. I. 199.
— Reply to some comments of M. F. Marcet. 1863. I. 194.
Daubeny, Giles Andrew. The strength and decay of nations. 1899. IV. 45.
Daubrée, & Charlemagne, É. Congrès international de sylviculture. 1900. IV. 3.[9]
Daude, P. Das Feld- und Forst-Polizeigesetz. 1880. IV. 321.
Daudin. Note sur des cônes du Sequoia giganteus. 1873. III. 310.[1]

Daudin (*continued*).
— Note sur des échantillons de bois d'Acacia. 1863. III. 463.[1]
— Note sur quelques plantes volubles. 1865. III. 204.[2]
— Notice sur des plantations forestières et d'agrément faites sur le domaine de Pouilly. 1872. I. 59.
— Notice sur les plantations d'arbres forestiers et d'ornement. 1872. I. 59.
— Premier essai . . . de retarder la floraison prématurée. 1866. III. 175.[2]
Daudin, H. Lettre sur les effets de l'hiver à Boissy. 1880. III. 48.
Daudin, M. H. Le nouveau théâtre d'agriculture. 1864. . III. 113.
Daudirac, François. Dissertation sur l'utilité de la botanique. 1828. III. 238.[1]
Dauer der Keimkraft bei den Cacteen. 1856. II. 588.[2]
Dauerhaftigkeit von Holz. 1871. IV. 413.[2]
Daul, Anton. Illustriertes Handbuch der Kakteenkunde. 1890. III. 619.
Daulat Ram, (*Babu*). Vyakyan-Nisabat Intajam Jauglat Raj Marwar Riyasat Jodhpur. 1886. IV. 26.[2]
Daulat Ram Bimbhat. The dry rakhs of the Punjab. 1882. IV. 378.
D'Aulnay, G. E. Coubard. *See* Coubard d'Aulnay, G. E.
Daum, de. De l'influence du climat sur les époques de la végétation. 1857. I. 220.[3]
Daum, von, (*Regierungs- und Ökonomie-Rath*). Einige Worte zur Kenntniss der Vegetationsverhältnisse . . . von Nizza. 1858. III. 125.
Daum, Franz von. Bemerkungen über die Landwirthschaft . . . in Süd-Frankreich. 1844. III. 119.[1]
Daupley, Cyr Édouard. Étude sur le café. 1867. III. 742.[1]
Daurel, Joseph. Compte rendu de la 28ᵉ session de la Société pomologique de France. 1886. III. 85.
— Compte rendu de la 29ᵉ session de la Société pomologique de France. 1887. III. 85.
— Éléments de viticulture. 1889. III. 556.
— Quelques mots sur les Vignes américaines. 1884. III. 556.
— Résumé du Congrès international phylloxérique. 188.? III. 572.
— Résumé du Congrès national viticole de Bordeaux. 1886. III. 556.
— Traité pratique de viticulture. 1895. III. 557.[1]
— *See also* Catros-Gérand & Daurel, Joseph.
Dauthenay, Henri Louis Mathurin. Acer Negundo californicum aureum. 1898. III. 535.[1]
— Crataegus Oxyacantha inermis. 1900. III. 422.[1]
— Épilogue des effets de l'hiver 1894–95. 1896. III. 49.[1]
— L'Erica Wilmorei et ses variétés. 1900. III. 651.[2]
— Les Géraniums. 1897. III. 491.[2]
— Le Machaerium Tipa. 1900. III. 489.[1]
— Les plantations aux bords de la mer. 1899. III. 42.[1]
— Plantes grimpantes. 1900. III. 205.[1]
— Polygonum baldschuanicum. 1900. II. 186.[1]
— À propos de l'emploi du Sophora. 1899. III. 487.[2]
— Prunier Mirobolan Louis Asselin. 1899. III. 436.[1]
— Rosiers hybrides du Rosa Wichuraiana. 1898. III. 434.[1]
— Singulier cas tératologique sur un Lilas. 1900. III. 714.[2]
— Syringa vulgaris macrostachya. 1899. III. 681.[1]
— De la taille des arbustes d'ornement. 1898. III. 173.[1]
— La taille et la mise à fruits des Kakis. 1900. III. 669.[2]
Dauvesse. Effets produits par l'hiver 1879–1880. 1880. III. 48.
Dauzat. Note concernant une espèce de .ver à soie. 1866. III. 647.[2]
Davaine, C. Recherches sur la pourriture des fruits. 1866. III. 194.
— Recherches sur la pourriture des fruits et des autres parties des végétaux vivants. 1866. III. 194.
Davall, Albert. Araucaria imbricata. 1873. III. 298.[1]
— Le bois de Teck. 1880. IV. 537.[1]
— Courte notice sur les effets de l'hiver 1879–80. 1881. III. 49.[1]
— Les grands Conifères de la Californie. 1870. III. 310.[1]
— Die grossen Nadelholzbäume Kaliforniens. 1870. III. 310.[1]
— Insecte nuisible des Ormes. 1878. III. 364.[1]
— Notices du temps. 1860. I. 227.[1]
— Quelques mots sur le traitement . . . des semences d'arbres. 1864. III. 156.[1]
— Rapport sur les essais qui ont été faits . . . pour l'introduction d'essences étrangères. 1877. IV. 127.[2]
— Schädliches Insekt auf der Ulme. 1878. III. 364.[2]
— Tortrix pinicolana Zeller. 1857. IV. 450.

Davall, J. de. *See* Davall de Joffrey, Edmond.
Davall de Joffrey, Edmond. Arbres remarquables. 1853. I. 297.[2]
— Beobachtungen über den Anbau der Lärche. 1860. IV. 449.
— Ébauche de statistique forestière du canton de Vaud. 1852. IV. 365.
— Eichen-Rinden-Erträge. 1860. IV. 512.
— Eichen-Stammholz-Verkäufe. 1860. IV. 512.
— Ueber einige ausländische Nadelhölzer. 1856. IV. 441.
— Holz-Preise von 1803 & 1860. 1860. IV. 406.[1]
— Mémoire sur la nouvelle méthode de culture forestière. 1846. IV. 152.
— Sur la nouvelle méthode de culture forestière de M. Biermanns. 1846. IV. 152.
— Prix des bois de 1803 & 1860. 1860. IV. 406.[1]
— Produits d'écorce de Chêne. 1860. IV. 512.
— La propagation du Mélèze. 1844. IV. 449.
— De quelle manière peut-on élever des assortiments de bois de fortes dimensions. 1863. IV. 505.
— De quelques Conifères exotiques. 1856. IV. 441.
— A quoi bon? 1859. IV. 309.[1]
— Remarques sur la plantation du Mélèze. 1860. IV. 449.
— Transformation d'un taillis simple en haute futaie. 1858. IV. 128.
— Umwandlung eines Niederwaldes in Hochwald. 1858. IV. 128.
— La vente du bois de Chêne. 1860. IV. 512.
— Was nützt es? 1859. IV. 309.[1]
— In welcher Weise lassen sich starke Holzsortimente erziehen. 1863. IV. 111,[1] 505.
Davans, von. Beschreibung und Bewirthschaftung des . . . Domainenwaldes Hagenschiess. 1859. IV. 118.
— Ist das Aufästen der Waldbäume . . . zulässig oder verwerflich? 1859. IV. 170.
Davanzati Bostichi, Bernardo. Coltivazione toscana delle Viti. 1600. III. 126.[1]
— Toscana coltivazione delle Viti e delli arbori. 1600. III. 126.[1]
— *See also* Soderini, Gioanvettorio & Davanzati Bostichi, Bernardo.
Daveau, Jules. Sur l'aire d'extension du Pin sylvestre dans la Péninsule ibérique. 1894. II. 47.[1]
— Aperçu sur la végétation de l'Alemtejo. 1882. I. 422.
— Choriata spectabilis. 1888. III. 589.[1]
— Cistinées. 1886. II. 563.[2]
— Cistinées du Portugal. 1886. II. 563.[2]
— Cocos odorata. 1893. II. 67.[2]
— Cocos Romanzowiana. 1893. II. 67.[2]
— Contributions pour l'étude de la flore portugaise. 1886. II. 563.[2]
— Le Cupressus glauca de bouture. 1887. III. 302.[2]
— Le Cupressus glauca en Portugal. 1884. III. 302.[2]
— Dichogamie protérandre chez le Kentia . . . Belmoreana. 1896. II. 69.[1]
— Encephalartos cycadifolius. 1888. III. 285.[2]
— Sur une étude de M. E. Gadeceau. 1894. III. 418.[2]
— Euphorbiacées du Portugal. 1885. II. 434.[1]
— Floraison d'un Kentia en Europe. 1891. III. 325.[2]
— La flore littorale du Portugal. 1896. I. 423.
— Fructification du Jubaea spectabilis. 1886. III. 326.[1]
— Jubaea spectabilis. 1889. III. 326.[1]
— Mezoneurum angolense. 1885. III. 481.[2]
— Note sur le Quercus occidentalis. 1899. II. 135.[2]
— Le Palmier nain et le Caroubier en Portugal. 1899. II. 66,[1] 345.[1]
— Les Washingtonia. 1888. III. 332.[1]
Davenport, Charles Benedict. The rôle of water in growth. 1897. I. 188. .
Davenport, George E. Polygamous flowers in Populus. 1878. II. 98.[2]
Davenport, *Sir* Samuel. Olive culture. 1892. III. 676.[1]
Davenport, Samuel Thos. Report on the oil . . . of the Mahwa tree. 1848. III. 667.[2]
Davenport academy of natural sciences. Proceedings. 1869.
David. Arbres de pleine terre, nouveaux. 1845. III. 430.[2]
— Chênes de France nouveaux. 1846. III. 361.[1]
— Des conifères. 1853. III. 305.[1]
— Érables nouveaux ou peu connus. 1845. III. 533.[2]
— Note sur quelques variétés . . . du Sureau commun. 1846. III. 751.[2]
— Ormes nouveaux ou peu connus. 1845. III. 363.[2]
— Revue des Pins cultivés en France. 1852. III. 306.[2]
— Viornes nouvelles ou peu connues. 1845. III. 752.[2]

David, A. L. Note sur les moyens curatifs de la maladie de la Vigne. 1863. III. 577.

David, Antoine. Lettre sur les Oliviers. 1762. III. 674.[2]

√ **David**, Armand. Journal d'un voyage dans le centre de la Chine. 1872. I. 459.

√ — Journal d'un voyage en Mongolie. 1867. I. 460.[1]

√ — Journal de mon troisième voyage . . . dans l'empire chinois. 1875. I. 459.[4]

√ — Natural history of north China. 1873. I. 459.

√ — Notes sur quelques plantes de la Mongolie. 1869. I. 460.[1]

— Quelques renseignements sur l'histoire naturelle de la Chine. 1873. I. 459.

√ — Rapport sur un voyage au Thibet. 1871. I. 460.[1]

— La végétation à Pekin. 1867. I. 460.[1]

David, Eugène. Quelques mots sur le suc des Euphorbes. 1874. III. 517.[2]

David, Georg. Ueber die Milchzellen der Euphorbiaceen. 1872. I. 136.[1]

— Die Wurzellaus des Weinstockes. 1875. III. 567.[1]

David, I. Observations monographiques sur le genre Frêne. 1834. II. 707.[1]

David, Ph., **Foucaud**, Julien & **Vincent**, P. Catalogue des plantes . . . de la Charente-Inférieure. 1878. I. 415.

David, T. W. Edgeworth. *See* ETHERIDGE, Robert, (jr.), DAVID, T. W. E. & GRIMSHAW, J. W.

Davids, (*Oberförster, Wehrstedt*). Die Wipfeldürre übergehaltener Eichen. 1872. IV. 506.

Davids, Eugen. Commentatio ad questionem . . . unde pendet plantarum vegetatio. 1822. I. 157.

— Commentatio de fontibus vegetationis plantarum. 1822. I. 157.

Davidson, Andrew. An account . . . of the Madagascar ordeal poison. 1874. III. 691.[1]

— The Madagascar poison ordeal of 'tangena.' 1874. III. 691.[1]

Davidson, Anstruther. List of plants of Los Angeles county. 1892. I. 326.

— Malvastrum splendidum Kellogg. 1896. II. 525.[2]

Davidson, George. An account of a new species of the Barktree. 1784. II. 811.[2]

— & **Manson**, Marsden. The forestry of California. 189 . ? IV. 46.[1]

Davidson, John. Game versus forestry. 1884. IV. 136.[2]

— On the profitableness of rearing underwood. 1868. IV. 132.[1]

Davidson, Mary M. Silk: its history. 1885. III. 378.

Davidson, William. On the decolorization of Palm oil. 1840. III. 318.[2]

Daviel, A. Pratique des cours d'eau. 1824. IV. 390.[1]

Davies, G. H. The afforestation of Natal. 1900. IV. 169.[1]

Daviss, Hugh. Welsh botanology. 1813. I. 73,[2] 396.

Davies, Richard. Tables of specific gravities. 1749. IV. 411.[1]

Davies, Wilham. Llandeilo-Vawr and its neighbourhood. 1858. I. 533.

Dávila, Alfred de MADRID-. *See* JORDANA Y MORERA, José, MADRID-DÁVILA, Alfredo de & ROBLES, Eduardo de.

Davillé, Ernest. La colonisation française aux Nouvelles Hébrides. 1895. III. 132.[2]

— La culture du Cocotier. 1899. III. 323.[1]

Davin, Gustave. Le Chêne-Liège . . . dans le Var. 1882. IV. 516.[2]

Davin, Vincent. Fructification du Papayer à Marseille. 1900. III. 617.[1]

— Revue de quelques plantes . . . cultivées au Jardin botanique . . . de Marseille. 1897. I. 59, III. 53.

— Voyage botanique et horticole. 1900. III. 29.[1]

Davis, B. W. In White Pine forests. 1894. IV. 470.[2]

Davis, Charles Henry Stanley. A list of the forest trees . . . in Meriden. 1889. IV. 77.[1]

Davis, Charles Thomas. The manufacture of paper. 1886. IV. 430.

Davis, E. W. Japanese trees in Rhode Island. 1893. III. 60.

— A Rhode Island forest. 1891. IV. 155.[2]

Davis, Frederick. Papaïne. 1893. III. 617.[2]

Davis, G. P. A large Amelanchier. 1883. II. 257.[2]

Davis, George S. Pharmacology of the newer materia medica. *See* PHARMACOLOGY . . . I. 6.

— Serenoa serrulata. 1892. III. 331.[1]

Davis, J. F. The Chinese. 1836. III. 216.[1].

Davis, James William & **Lees**, F. A. West Yorkshire. 1878. I. 403, 534.[1]

Davis, John. Fruit culture in the several countries. 1884. III. 132.[2]

Davis, Kary Cadmus. Clematis. 1900. III. 389.[1]

— Clematises in America. 1899. II. 195.[2]

— A review of garden Clematises. 1899. II. 195.[2]

— A taxonomic study of North American Ranunculaceae. 1900. II. 195.[1]

— Wild and garden Paeonies in America. 1900. III. 392.[1]

Davis, Lucius Daniel. Ornamental shrubs for garden . . . planting. 1899. III. 61.[1]

Davis, N. S. & others. Report of the committee on indigenous medical botany. 1848. III. 62.

Davis, Thomas. Copy of a letter relative to the timber . . . of Pines. 1832. IV. 462.[2]

Davis, William T. Hybrid Oaks from Staten Island. 1888. II. 128.[2]

— An interesting discovery. 1888. II. 128.[2]

— Interesting Oaks recently discovered on Staten Island. 1892. II. 132.[2]

— A new hybrid Oak. 1892. II. 132.[2]

— Union of an Oak with a Birch. 1886. I. 209,[1] IV. 490,[2] 502.[2]

— Variations in the rootstock of Smilax glauca. 1891. II. 85.[2]

Davis, Parke & Co. *See* PARKE, DAVIS & Co.

Davodet. Sur un nouveau mode de multiplication du Paulownia. 1848. III. 703.[1]

Davy. Une recette propre à la destruction du phylloxera. 1869. III. 564.[2]

Davy, *Sir* Humphry. An account of some experiments . . . on the constituent parts of certain astringent vegetables. 1803. I. 182.[2]

— Elements of agricultural chemistry. 1819. III. 36.[2]

Davy, John. On carbonic acid as a solvent. 1848. I. 175.

— Miscellaneous observations, chiefly chemical. 1846. II. 386.[1]

— Miscellaneous observations on some tropical plants. 1855. III. 64.[1]

Davy, Joseph Burtt. Acacia. 1900. III. 463.[1]

— Lupinus fallax. 1894. II. 370.[2]

— Notes on Ceanothus. 1896. III. 541.[2]

— Plants hitherto undescribed. 1895. II. 370.[2]

— Shade trees for the region around San Francisco. 1898. III. 208.[2]

— *See also* HILGARD, E. W. & DAVY, J. B.

Davy, Marié. Météorologie et physique agricoles. 1888. III. 36.[1]

Dawany, von. Mittheilung über den Holzmassenertrag der Pyramidenpappel. 1867. IV. 486.[1]

Dawson, Edward Seymour. Cortex Juglandis cinereæ. 1874. III. 354.[1]

Dawson, George Mercer. Forest trees of the far North-west. 1888. I. 311.[1]

— Northern range of the western Service-berry. 1888. II. 257.[2]

— Note on the distribution of . . . trees of British Columbia. 1880. I. 311,[1] IV. 76.[2]

— Timber and ornamental trees for the province of Quebec. 1879. III. 116.[2]

Dawson, Jackson. Andromeda speciosa for forcing. 1891. III. 664.[2]

— Budding and grafting. 1896. III. 163.[1]

— Collecting Kalmias. 1894. III. 652.[2]

— The cultivation of Huckleberries. 1888. III. 652,[2] 663.[1]

— For ornamental planting. 1887. III. 532.[1]

— Propagating Hickories. 1896. III. 353.[2]

— The propagation of Conifers. 1888. III. 294.[2]

— The propagation of Magnolias. 1888. III. 399.[1]

— The propagation of trees and shrubs from seed. 1885. III. 156,[2] IV. 147.[1]

— Propagation of trees from seed. 1885. III. 156,[2] IV. 147.[1]

— Shrubs that are perfectly hardy. 1890. III. 60.

— Summer propagations of shrubs. 1889. III. 158.

— *See also* DOUGLAS, Robert & DAWSON, Jackson.

Dawson, John Wilham. On the destruction and partial reproduction of forests in British North America. 1847. IV. 74.[1]

— The destruction and reproduction of American forests. 1847. IV. 337.[1]

— Notes on the flora of the White Mountains. 1862. I. 314.

— The removal and restoration of forests. 1868. I. 309,[2] IV. 76.[1]

— Ueber das Verschwinden und theilweise Wiedererstehen der Waldungen im britischen Nordamerica. 1847. IV. 74.[1]

Dawson, Maria. " Nitragin " and the nodules of leguminous plants. 1900. II. 322.[1]

Dawson, *Sir* William. Notes on trees on the grounds of Mc-Gill University. 1891. III. 116.[2]
Day, David F. Catalogue of the Niagara flora. 1888. I. 315.
— Catalogue of the . . . plants of the city of Buffalo. 1883. I. 315.
— The plants of Buffalo and its vicinity. 1883. I. 315.
Day, Frank Miles. Microscopic examination of timber with regard to its strength. 1883. IV. 415.[1]
Day, Mary Anna. The local floras of New England. 1899. I. 3.[1]
Dario d' uscita dei legnami dalla Svizzera. 1866. IV. 285.[1]
Deakin, Richard. Flora of the colosseum of Rome. 1855. I. 427.
— The flowering plants of Tunbridge Wells. 1871. I. 402.
— **& Marnock,** Robert. Florigraphia britannica. 1837. I. 398.
Dean, R. Sweet-scented Clematises. 1893. III. 389.[2]
Dean, Richard. Culture of Daphne indica rubra. 1875. III. 627.[2]
— New varieties of Nerium Oleander. 1880. III. 689.[1]
— Passiflora vitifolia. 1878. III. 616.[2]
Dean, William. An historical and descriptive account of Croome d'Abitot. 1824. I. 53.
Deane, *Mrs.* Fannie A. The ethics of the flowers. 1892. I. 516.
— The influence of flowers upon national life. 1888. I. 516.
Deane, Henry & **Maiden,** J. H. The Grey Gum of the North Coast districts. 1896. II. 625.[1]
— — On a new species of Eucalyptus. 1898. II. 625.[2]
— — Observations on the Eucalypts of New South Wales. 1896. II. 623.[1]
— — On the White Ash of southern New South Wales. 1898. II. 624.[1]
Deane, Samuel. The New-England farmer. 1790. III. 30.
Deane, Walter. Flora of the Blue Hills. 1896. I. 316.
— Kalmia latifolia in Vermont. 1899. II. 672.[2]
— The pine grosbeak's attack on the Ashes. 1893. IV. 199.[1]
— A Rhododendron forest in New Hampshire. 1890. II. 682.[1]
— **& Robinson,** B. L. A new Viburnum from Missouri. 1896. II. 843.[2]
Deas, Lizzie. Flower favourites. 1898. V. xxv.[1]
Deb. Emploi de l'Ixora decussata. 1880. III. 745.[1]
De Bary. *See* BARY, de.
Debat, L. Essai sur la constitution de la cellule végétale. 1867. I. 135.[2]
Debate on Sir John Lubbock's motion. 1885. IV. 34.[1]
Debay, A. Les influences du chocolat, du thé. 1864. III. 222.
Debeaux, J. Odon. Catalogue des plantes . . . de Boghar. 1860. I. 484.
— Contributions à la flore de la Chine. 1875. I. 459. — 1876. I. 459. — 1879. I. 459.
— Description d'une espèce nouvelle de Rosa. 1874. II. 285.[2]
— Essai sur la pharmacie . . . des Chinois. 1864. III. 273.[1]
— Une excursion botanique dans la haute Kabylie. 1858. I. 484, V. xxiv.[1]
— Flore de la Kabylie du Djurdjura. 1893. I. 486.
— Florule de Shang-Haï. 1875. I. 459.
— Florule de Tien-Tsin. 1879. I. 459.
— Florule du Tché-Foû. 1876. I. 459.
— Le genre Rosa de la flore agenaise. 1895. II. 286.[2]
— Herborisation faite à Casas-de-Pèna. 1876. II. 309.[2]
— Matériaux pour servir à l'étude monographique des Rosiers . . . dans les Pyrénées-Orientales. 1878. II. 285.[2]
— Nomenclature patoise en idiome gascon des plantes. 1898. I. 522.[2]
— Notes sur plusieurs plantes . . . des Pyrénées-orientales. 1891. II. 286.[1]
— Notes sur quelques plantes . . . de la flore oranaise. 1888. I. 485.
— Observations sur deux espèces du genre Erica. 1876. II. 664.[2]
— Des plantes caractéristiques . . . dans le Roussillon. 1882.. V. xxii.[1]
— Plantes rares . . . d'Aragon. 1894. I. 423.
— Sur quelques matières tinctoriales des Chinois. 1866. III. 236.
— Recherches sur la flore des Pyrénées-Orientales. 1878. I. 415.
— Les régions botaniques de l'arrondissement d'Oran. 1889. I. 486.
— Révision de la flore agenaise. 1898. I. 535.

— Révision des plantes phanérogames de la flore agenaise. 1895. I. 418.
— Rosa nervulosa Gdgr. et Debx. 1887. II. 296.[2]
— Rosa Penchinati Gdgr. et O. Deb. 1888. II. 297.[1]
— Synopsis de la flore de Gibraltar. 1888. I. 422.
— Sur la végétation . . . du littoral de la Chine. 1861. I. 458.
De Bec. The culture and trade in Almonds. 1863. III. 434.[1]
De Bellerive. Le Santal de Juan Fernandes. *See* The SANDAL-WOOD of Juan Fernandes. 1894. II. 169.[2]
Deberitz, E. Anweisung sur Kamellien-Kultur. n. d. III. 599.[1]
Debert-Clerzac. Du fruit de quelques Cactées. 1845. III. 623.[1]
Debey, Matthias Hubert. Annäherung der Blatt- an die Rankenbildung am gem. Holunder. 1846. II. 840.[2]
— Beobachtungen sur Pflanzen-Pathologie und Morphologie. 1846. II. 840.[2]
— Proliferation des Fruchtknotens. 1846. II. 596.[1]
— Umbildung der Achse der Blüthentraube in den Ast. 1846. II. 676.[2]
— Umwandlung des Fruchtknotens in den Ast. 1846. II. 589.[1]
Le **débit** des bois. 1898. IV. 392.
Déboisement. 1897. IV. 281.[1]
Le **déboisement** et les eaux. 1894. IV. 51.
Déboisement et scieries aux États-Unis. *See* DÉBOISEMENT aux États-Unis. 1893. IV. 552.[1]
Debold, Rudolf. Beiträge sur anatomischen Charakteristik der Phaseoleen. 1892. II. 321.[1]
Debonnaire de Gif, *vicomte.* Mémoire sur les avantages . . . du Peuplier blanc. 1834. III. 345.[1]
— Mémoire sur les inconvéniens qui résultent pour l'agriculture de-défrichement des bois. 1814. IV. 42.[2]
De Bow's review of the southern and western states. III. 3.
Debray, Emmanuel Claude. De l'Eucalyptus globulus. 1872. IV. 533.[1]
Debray, Ferdinand. La brunissure chez les végétaux. 1895. III. 581.
— La brunissure en Algérie. 1894. III. 581.
— La destruction des insectes nuisibles. 1898. III. 197.
— Étude comparative des caractères anatomiques . . . des Pipéracées. 1885. II. 93.[2]
— La maladie de la brunissure. 1898. III. 582.
— Nouvelles recherches sur la brunissure. 1895. III. 581.
De Broë, V. E. Sleepers on the North-western railway. 1899. IV. 424.[2]
Debrun-des-Beaumes. Reproduction des tiges des arbres à feuilles persistantes. 1830. III. 295.[1]
De Bruyn, Léon. *See* BRUYN, Léon de.
Deby, Julien. Relation succincte d'un voyage fait aux bords de l'Oostanaula en Géorgie. 1877. I. 319.
Decadencia de la construcción naval en España. 1886. IV. 425.[1]
Decaisne, Joseph. Abelia floribunda. 1847. III. 748.[1]
— Acacia discolor. 1853. III. 464,[2] 465.[1]
— De l'action des gelées tardives. 1847. III. 47.
— Sur les affinités . . . les genres Pseudanthus et Grubbia. 1839. II. 450.[3]
— Akebia quinata. 1853. III. 393.[1]
— Amygdalus nana. 1853. III. 438.[2]
— Arbrisseaux de la Chine. 1851. III. 84.[1]
— Aristolochia lineata Dne. 1854. II. 182.[2]
— Arundinaria falcata. 1848. II. 58.[2]
— Asclepiadeae. 1844. II. 735.[1]
— L'avortement du bourgeon terminal dans les Lilas. 1873. II. 714.[2]
— Bouvardia leiantha. 1851. III. 711.[2]
— Caractères . . . de trois genres nouveaux . . . en Chine. 1873. II. 122,[2] 614.[2]
— Sur les caractères et les affinités des Oliniées. 1877. II. 599.[2]
— Catalogue de la bibliothèque. *See* VESQUE, Julien. 1883. I. 2.
— Sur les Cedrus atlantica et C. Libani. 1852. II. 27.[1]
— Clematis eriostemon Dne. 1852. III. 390.[1]
— Cunonia capensis. 1854. III. 416.[3]
— Cyrtanthera Ghiesbreghtiana. 1848. III. 709.[1]
— Décade de plantes nouvelles. 1877. I. 270.
— Description d'un nouveau genre . . . des Apocynées. 1849. II. 727.[2]
— Description d'un nouveau genre . . . des Monimiées. 1858. II. 221.[2]

— Description des genres Dryinispermum Pseudals et Gyrinopsis du groupe des Aquilariées. 1843. II. 599.²
— On the development of the reproductive organs of the Misseltoe. 1840. II. 178.¹
— Développement du pollen dans le Gui. 1839. II. 178.¹
— Effets du sulfate de fer sur les plantes chlorosées. 1848. III. 181.¹
— Enkyanthus quinqueflorus. 1849. III. 649.¹
— Enumeratio Lardizabalearum. 1839. II. 200.³
— Énumération des diverses espèces de Houx cultivées. 1853. II. 462.³
— Énumération des plantes recueillies par M. Bové dans les deux Arabies. 1834. I. 478.
— Epacris impressa var. fulgens. 1846. III. 665.¹
— Études sur quelques . . . Asclepiadées. 1838. II. 735.¹
— Examen des espèces des genres Bombax et Pachira. 1880. II. 529.¹
— Fagraea zeylanica Tsbg. 1849. III. 682.¹
— Floraison de l'Amherstia nobilis. 1855. III. 466.²
— Florula sinalca. 1834. I. 478.
— Gaultheria coccinea. 1849. III. 652.¹
— Sur le genre Aegotoxicum. 1858. II. 436.¹
— De la greffe herbacée. 1847. III. 163.²
— Sur la gutta-percha de Surinam. 1857. III. 668.¹
— Herbarii timorensis descriptio. 1834. I. 465.
— Houttea pardina Dne. var. calcarata. 1848. II. 792.²
— Introduction et culture des arbres à Quinquina. 1866. III. 713.²
— Le jardin fruitier du Muséum. 1858. III. 85.
— Jasminum nudiflorum. 1852. III. 673.¹
— Kennedya nigricans. 1848. III. 480.¹
— Ueber das krautartige Pfropfen. 1847. III. 163.²
— Kunzea Schaueri. 1854. III. 636.
— Lapageria alba. 1852. III. 337.¹
— Lettre sur le Lilas de Chine. 1878. II. 715.¹
— Lindleya mespiloides. 1854. III. 425.¹
— Liste des plantes recueillies . . . dans la Palestine. 1835. I. 480.
— Lundia acuminata Dne. 1853. III. 707.¹
— Macleania coccinea. 1851. III. 653.¹
— Mémoire concernant la fructification du Gui. 1840. II. 178.¹
— Mémoire sur la famille des Lardizabelées. 1837. II. 200.²
— Mémoire sur la famille des Lardizabalées. 1839. I. 105.
— Mémoire sur la famille des Pomacées. 1874. II. 255.²
— Mémoire sur le développement du pollen . . . du Gui. 1840. II. 178.¹
— Mémoire sur les greffes. 1849. III. 160.
— Miscellanea botanica. 1877. I. 270.
— Mitraria coccinea. 1849. III. 708.¹
— Monochaetum pulchrum. 1848. III. 639.¹
— Monographie des genres Balbisia et Robinsonia. 1834. II. 864.¹ bis.²
— Monographie des genres Ligustrum et Syringa. 1879. II. 711,¹ 774.¹
— Monographie du genre Pentarhaphia. 1846. II. 794.³
— Napoleona Whitfieldii. 1853. II. 612.²
— Note on the floral organogeny of the Pear-tree. 1857. II. 279.¹
— Note sur l'organogénie florale du Poirier. 1857. II. 279.¹
— Note sur la floraison du Cedrele. 1876. III. 512.¹
— Note sur la structure des racines. 1838. I. 103.
— Note sur le climat qu'habite le Cedrus Deodara. 1846. II. 27.²
— Note sur le Libocedrus tetragona. 1853. II. 33.¹
— Note sur le Veronica Andersoni. 1852. III. 704.¹
— Note sur les deux espèces de Nerprun. 1857. II. 497.¹
— Note sur quelques plantes . . . des Théophrastées. 1876. II. 691,²692.¹
— Note sur un nouveau genre de Chicoracées. 1833. II. 855.¹
— Notice sur quelques plantes de la flore d'Égypte. 1835. I. 487.
— Nouvelles espèces de Conifères. 1855. II. 14.¹
— Observations sur les Pomacées. 1871. II. 255,² 256.²
— Observations sur quelques . . . plantes de l'Arabie-Heureuse. 1835. I. 480.
— Observations sur un Diospyros de la Chine. 1870. II. 701.³
— Organographie du Poirier. 1872. II. 279.¹
— Om Plærevarieteternes Afændringsevne . . . fra een Art. 1863. II. 279.¹
— The Paradise Apple. 1869. II. 266.³
— Pécher à fleurs doubles. 1852. III. 439.³

— Pentarhaphia cubensis Dne. 1847. II. 794.³
— Philadelphus mexicanus. 1852. III, 413.³
— Plantaginaceae. 1852. II. 807.¹
— Du Poirier et du cidre. 1880. II. 279.¹
— Le Poirier sauvage. 1870. II. 279.¹
— Premier mémoire sur les greffes. 1847. III. 160.
— Prix Bordin . . . Étude de la structure antomique du pistil. 1868. I. 117.³
— Production d'un tissu anormal dans le Cactus pycnoxiphus. 1858. II. 592.²
— Prunus incana. 1853. III. 437.¹
— Prunus iaponica. 1852. III. 437.¹
— Psammisia penduliflora. 1854. III. 654.³
— Psammisia sarcantha. 1854. III. 654.¹
— Rapport sur un mémoire de M. de Gemini sur le moyen de préserver les bois. 1848. IV. 417.
— Rapport sur une communication de M. le docteur Gannat. 1849. I. 252.
— Recherches sur le Ramie. 1855. III. 382.¹
— Rectification dans la nomenclature de quelques plantes cultivées. 1849. I. 269.
— Remarques sur le sous-ordre des Charianthées. 1846. II. 634.³
— Remarques sur les affinités du genre Helwingia. 1836. II. 656.¹
— Réponse aux critiques de M. Th. Wenzig. 1880. II. 256.¹
— Révision de la nomenclature des Troënes. 1877. II. 711.³
— Revision des Clématites du groupe des tubuleuses. 1880. II. 195.¹
— Rhododendron amoenum. 1854. III. 659.³
— Rhododendron Aucklandii. 1855. III. 659.¹
— Rhododendron glaucum. 1855. III. 659.¹
— Rogiera latifolia. 1853. II. 830,¹ III. 747.²
— Rubus biflorus. 1855. III. 458.¹
— Sur les Sequoia sempervirens et S. gigantea. 1855. III. 309.²
— Sophora secundiflora. 1854. III. 488.¹
— Spirée à feuilles de Prunier. 1846. III. 461.³
— Stiftia chrysantha. 1847. III. 756.³
— Structure and development of the flower . . . of the Pear. 1857. II. 279.¹
— De la variabilité . . . du Poirier. 1863. II. 279,¹ III. 445.¹
— On variability in the Pear-tree. 1863. II. 279.¹
— Voyage autour du monde sur la frégate la Vénus . . . 1846. Botanique. I. 303.
— See also LE MAOUT, Emmanuel & DECAISNE, Joseph; MONTAGNE, J. F. C. & DECAISNE, Joseph; MORREN, Charles & DECAISNE, Joseph.
— & Naudin, Charles. Manuel de l'amateur des jardins. 1862. III. 87.
— & Planchon, J. E. Esquisse d'une monographie des Araliacées. 1854. II. 646.¹
De Candolle, Alphonse P. See CANDOLLE, Alphonse P. de.
Decaux, François. L'avenir du Tamarix articulata. 1895. III. 612.¹
— La Cheimatobia brumata. 1894. III. 191.
— Sur une chenille inédite . . . du Figuier. 1894. III. 370.¹
— La courtilière (Gryllotalpa vulgaris). 1894. IV. 549.³
— Destruction rationnelle des insectes. 1899. III. 192.¹
— Étude des mœurs du ver des pommes. 1897. III. 428.³
— Le fruit de l'Hymenaea Courbaril. 1891. III. 478.¹
— Sur les noix véreuses. 1896. III. 191.
— Notes pour servir à l'étude des insectes nuisibles au Marronnier. 1888. III. 537.³
— Nouvelles observations sur la courtilière. 1894. IV. 549.³
— L'Olivier. 1892. . III. 676.³
— Oriolus galbula, grand destructeur d'insectes. 1897. IV. 91.¹
— Le Pommier, ses principaux ennemis. 1891. III. 428.¹
— Sur les principaux ennemis des Rosiers. 1896. III. 453.³
— Le Tamarix articulé et les moutons algériens. 1895. III. 612.¹
Decaux, J. Note sur une maladie de l'Hydrangea paniculata. 1896. III. 412.³
Decharmes. Note sur la forme hélicoïde dés tiges. 1856. I. 105.²
— See also BERTHEMOT, J. B. & DECHASTELUS, de.
Dechastelus, de. Du Guarana. 1840. III. 539.² ·
Déchauffour de Boisduval, Jean Baptiste Alphonse. See BOISDUVAL, J. B. A. DÉCHAUFFOUR DE.

Dechenaux, A. P. Clé d'analogie en botanique. 1847. I. 252.

Dechesnel, Adolphe. Botanique des poètes, des artistes. 1838. I. 94.

The deciduous Cypress. 1873. III. 311.[1]

The deciduous Cypress. 1890. II. 51.[2]

Deciduous lawn trees. 1853. III. 202.[2]

The deciduous Magnolias. 1891. III. 399.[1]

Deciduous shade trees for private grounds. 1867. III. 208.[2]

Décision du conseil fédéral au sujet des forêts de montagne. See BESCHLUSS des eidg. ·Bundesrathes : . . 1858. IV. 283.[1]

Décision portant création d'un service de reboisement à Madagascar. 1897. IV. 295,[2] 554.

Decisione del Ministero d'agricoltura. — Indennità di trasferta agli agenti boschivi. 1864. IV. 305.

Decisione del Ministero degli interni. 1865. IV. 328.

Decisione del Ministero degli interni. — Taglio di bosco. 1863. IV. 304.[2]

Decisione del Ministero degli interni [concernente la facoltà di nominare . . . gli stipendiati del Comune]. 1863. IV. 304.[2]

Decisione del Ministero dell' interno. — Vendita di piante. 1863. IV. 304.[2]

Decisioni e provvedimenti ministeriali. 1864. IV. 305.

Decisioni e provvedimenti ministeriali. . . . Tassa sui corpi morali e mani-morte. 1863. IV. 285.[1]

Decisioni e provvedimenti ministeriali [concernente l'amministrazione forestale del regno d'Italia]. 1863. IV. 304.[2]

Decken, Karl Claus, Baron von der. Reisen in Ost-Afrika, 1859. See ASCHERSON, Paul & others. 1869. I. 492.[2]

Decker, J. G. Tafeln zur Bestimmung des Inhalts und des Preises runder unbeschlagener Stämme. 1858. · IV. 224.

Deckert, (Forstrath). Der grosse Waldbrand . . . in· dem Klosterreviere Niebeck. 1892. IV. 182.[2]

— Ueber Weidenzucht. 1896. IV. 487.[3]

Déclaration du roi, concernant les grands-maîtres des eaux & forêts. 1784. IV. 325.

Déclaration du roi, donnée à Versailles . . . qui régle la forme dans laquelle . . . les officiers des eaux & forêts. 1756. IV. 325.

Déclaration du roy, donnée à Versailles . . . concernant les amandes des eaux & forêts. 1743. IV. 325.

Déclaration du roy, donnée à Versailles . . . concernant les receveurs généraux des domaines & bois. 1746. IV. 325.

Déclaration du roy, donnée au camp de Bost . . . portant confirmation des privilèges . . . accordés aux grand-maîtres des eaux & forêts. 1746. IV. 325.

Déclaration du roy, portant deffenses de porter ou allumer du feu dans les forests. 1715. IV. 325. -

A declaration of the libertyes of the English nation, principally with respect to forests. 1681. IV. 323.[1]

Décoppet, Maurice. Les joux à croître du canton de Vaud. 1900. IV. 334.[3]

De Coque, J. V. See MAIDEN, J. H. & DE COQUE, J. V.

De Cossigny. Altérations et conservation des bois d'œuvre. 1888. IV. 414.[1]

Découflé. Note sur la multiplication des Pivoines ligneuses. 1833. III. 392.[2]

— Notice sur le moyen d'obtenir promptement des fruits. 1833. III. 174.[1]

Decrept, Alfred. L'arbre vert en Picardie. 1877. IV. 472.

— L'arbre vert en Picardie. · 1885. V. XXXII.[2]

De Crespigny, Eyre Champion. A new London flora. 1877. I. 403.

Décret concernant l'admission à l'École forestière. · 1899. IV. 35.[1]

Décret des 20 août . . . concernant l'établissement d'une nouvelle administration forestière. 1791. IV. 291.[2]

Décret du 10 février 1900 établissant le régime forestier applicable à la colonie de Madagascar. 1900. IV. 280.[1]

Décret relatif au service des forêts en Algérie. · 1898. IV. 332.[2]

Décret relatif aux versements à effectuer à la caisse nationale des retraites . . . des brigadiers et gardes forestiers.· 1897. IV. 311.[2]

Décret réorganisant le service . . . de l'Algérie. 1897. IV. 332.[2]

Décret sur la bonification de la pension de retraite des préposés forestiers communaux. 1899. IV. 311.[3]

I decreti del 31 agosto 1862. 1863. IV. 304.[2]

Decreti, proclami e terminazioni riguardanti ·li doveri del Capitanio al bosco del Montello. 1776. IV. 304.[1]

Decreto ministeriale col quale si stabilisce il programma delle scuole forestali. 1865. IV. 35.[1]

Decreto portante la sistemazione generale della amministrazione dei boschi del 27· Maggio 1811·e successivo decreto . . . 1811. IV. 304.[2]

Decroix, E. Note sur la farine de Cocotier. 1883. III. 324.[1]

— & Grisard, Jules. Sur· le Noyer Pacanier. 1883. III. 353.[3]

Décugis, B. Le Pistachier, culture. 1882. III. 526.[1]

Dědeček, Josef. O pěstování Moruší v jich vlasti. 1873. III. 378.

Dedié, (Oberförster, Zobten). Der Zobtenberg. 1870. IV. 354.

Dedu, N. De l'ame des plantes. 1682. I. 146.

Deegen, Franz, (jr.). Betula alba fol. purpureis. 1878. III. 357.[1]

— Cytisus Laburnum aureus. 1878. III. 480.[2]

— Drei buntfarbige Gehölz-Neuheiten. 1886. III. 206,[2] 365,[3] 534.[1]

— Ulmus campestris elegans. 1879. III. 365.[1]

Deeleman, K. Proeve ter voorkominge van het kankeren der vruchtboomen. 1811. ·III. 193.[2]

Deering, George Charles. Catalogus stirpium. 1738. I. 394.

— Historical account of the town of Nottingham. 1751. I. 533.

Deering, W: H. & Redwood, Boverton. Report on the castor oils. 1894. III. 522.[1]

La défense des forêts de l'Algérie. 1893. IV. 279.[2]·

La défense du vin et le phylloxera. See SAHUT, Félix. 1900. III. 575.[1]

Defert, Carl Friedrich. Die Horizontalaufnahme bei Neumessung der Wälder. 1880. IV. 265.

Defiennés, WATBLED-. See· WATBLED-DEFIENNÉS.

Defiers, Albert. Arabian Coffee. 1889. III. 732.[2]·

— Les Asclépiadées de l'Arabie tropicale. 1896. II. 735.[2]

— Coffea arabica. 1889. III. 732.[2]

— Descriptions de quelques plantes nouvelles ·de l'Arabie. 1895. I. 481.[1]

— Herborisations dans les montagnes . . . d'Aden. 1885. I. 481.[1]

— Note sur un Kalanchoe remarquable. 1893. II. 237.[1]

— Nouvelles contributions à la flore d'Aden. 1887. II. 442.[1]

— Voyage au Yemen. 1889. I. 481.[1]

Deforestation as a cause of mortality. 1894. IV. 55.[1]

Deforestation at Réunion and elsewhere. 1900. IV. 49.[1]

Deforestation in Russia. 1892. IV. 46.[2]

Deformed Fir branch. 1885. II. 36.[1]

Deformed pears. 1871. II. 279.[2]

De Francesco, Nicola. Risposte giuridico-forestali. 1896. IV. 329.

Defranoux & Lervat. Aux vignerons! ·1864. III. 555.

Defrecheux, Albert. Les Chênes d'Amérique en Campine. 1898. · III.·361,[2] IV. 126.[3]

— Le domaine de ·Gooreynd. · 1896. IV. 357.[1]

— Excursion forestière . . Le Mastbosch. 1898. .IV. 357.[1]

— Le lophyre du Pin. 1894. IV. 559.[1]

De Friese, Lafayette Hoyt. Report on a belt of Kentucky timbers. ·1879. IV. 397.

— Report on the timbers of Grayson. 1877. IV. 397.

— Report on the timbers of the district west of the Tennessee River. 1877. IV. 397.

— Report on the timbers of the North Cumberland.· 1877. IV. 397.

— Report ·on the timbers of the Tradewater region. 1877. IV. 397.

Defroom, J. L. F. POTIEZ-. See· POTIEZ-DEFROOM, J. L. F.

Degagny, Charles. Sur le tube pollinique. 1886. I. 201.[2]

Dégâts d'Hylesinus micans. 1898. IV. 457.

Dégâts des larves d'agriotes . . . dans les pépinières. 1898. IV. 151.[2]

Degen, Árpád von. Bemerkungen über einige orientalische Pflanzenarten. 1891. I. 450.

— Ergebnisse einer botanischen Reise nach der Insel Samothrake. 1891. I. 450.

— & Dörfler, Ignaz. Beitrag zur Flora Albaniens und Macedoniens. 1897. I. 451.

Degenhard, M. Erfahrungen in betreff Anpflanzung von Alleebäumen. 1899. III. 210.

— Unterirdische Bewässerung für Strassenbäume. 1900. III. 211.[2]

Dagland, Jean Vincent Yves. Examen de cette question : La sève circule-t-elle. 1800. I. 163.

Degron, Henry. Les Vignes japonaises recueillies sur place. 1900. III. 545.[2]

Degrully. *See* GASTINE & DEGRULLY.

Degrully, Léon. Étude sur la valeur alimentaire du marc de raisin. 1877. III. 583.[1]

— *See also* CONVERT, F. & DEGRULLY, L.

— & Viala, Pierre. Les Vignes américaines. 1884. III. 556.

Dehaut. Remarques sur une communication récente de M. Decaisne. 1863. III. 445.[1]

Dehérain, Pierre Paul. Contributions à l'étude agricole de la Tunisie. 1893. III. 676.[3]

— Cultures dérobées d'automne. 1889. III. 151.

— Sur l'évaporation de l'eau. 1869. I. 167, 172.

— Expériences sur l'influence qu'exerce la lumière électrique. 1881. I. 173.

— Il est rare qu'une découverte dans les sciences physiques ne trouve pas son application en physiologie. 1866. I. 161.

— Influence de la lumière électrique. 1882. I. 230.

— Sur l'influence qu'exercent divers rayons lumineux sur la décomposition de l'acide carbonique. 1869. I. 167, *172*.

— Sur l'intervention de l'azote atmosphérique. 1871. I. 159.

— Le mildew dans le Puy-de-Dôme. 1892. III. 580.

— Nouvelles recherches sur la germination. 1875. I. 203.

— Recherches sur l'absorption de la potasse. 1863. I. 158.

— Recherches sur l'assimilation des substances. 1867. I. 159.

— Recherches sur l'intervention de l'azote. 1873. I. 151.[3]

— El trabajo del suelo y la nitrificación. 1895. IV. 543.[3]

— & Landrin, Ed. Recherches sur la germination. 1874. I. 203.

— & Maquenne, Léon. Sur l'absorption de l'acide carbonique. 1886. I. 173.

— — Sur la décomposition de l'acide carbonique. 1879. I. 173, *230*.

— — Expériences sur la végétation dans des atmosphères riches en acide carbonique. 1881. I. 173.

— — Recherches sur la respiration des feuilles à l'obscurité. 1885. I. 171.

— & Moissan, Henri. Recherches sur l'absorption d'oxygène. 1874. I. 170.

— & Vesque, Julien. Recherches sur l'absorption et l'émission des gaz par les racines. 1877. I. 161.

— — Recherches sur la respiration des racines. 1876. I. 170.

Dehn-Rothfelser, Ernst Abraham. Ein schön Weinbaubuch. 1629. III. 551.[3]

Dehne, Johann Friedrich Anton. Spaziergang von Leipzig nach dem Harze. 1819. I. 376.

Dehnhardt, Friedrich. Sopra alcune piante . . . nel giardino del Signor Conte di Camaldoli Ricciardi. 1836. I. 63.

— Bemerkungen über . . . Morus. 1838. III. 154.[3]

— Catalogus plantarum Horti camaldulensis. 1829. I. 62.

— Notiz über die Kultur der Araucaria. 1838. III. 298.[3]

Dehning, H. Von Bäumen und Wäldern der Lüneburger Heide. 1897. IV. 355.[1]

— Etwas über Lüneburg'sche Forstverhältnisse. 1898. IV. 26.

Dehra Dún-Forest school. *See* FOREST SCHOOL . . . IV. 16.[1]

Dehra Dún forest school. 1885. IV. 37.[1]

Dei, Apelle. Sulla caccia smoderata che . . . si fa agli uccelli. 1866. IV. 209.[3]

— Catalogo ragionato delle piante . . . coltivate. 1868. III. 88.[3]

— Osservazioni sulla benefica influenza che il cosi detto Sambuco-sordo . . . sembra esercitare sulle viti. 1865. III. 559.[3]

Delamba, nouveau narcotique. 1848. III. 260.[3]

Deil, F. *See* MANNHARDT, F. & DEIL, F.

Deiman, Johann Rudolph. Nut van den groei der boomen. 1780. IV. 54.

— & Troostwyk, A. P. van. Verhandeling over het nut van den groei der boomen. 1780. III. 34.[1]

Deinboll. Forest planting in Norway. 1900. IV. 113.[3]

Deines, SCHMIDT-. *See* SCHMIDT-DEINES.

Deiss, E. Extraction du caoutchouc. 1900. III. 232.[3]

— *See also* VIVIER, E. & DEISS, E.

Deistel. Die Stationsanlagen von Buea. 1898. III. 131.[3]

Deitl, Ignaz. Ueber Galiziens Forstwirthschaft. 1850. IV. 123.[3]

Deitz, Trimble & Schroeter. Ueber Fabiana imbricata. 1889. III. 700.[3]

Dejardin, Al. Cam. Du rôle probable de la magnésie. 1887. III. 574, 583.[1]

Dejernon, Romuald. La Vigne en France. 1867. III. 555.

De Jong, A. De ontwouding van Java. *See* JONG, A. de. 1892. IV. 179.[1]

Dekin. Sur le Néflier du Japon. 1819. III. 423.[3]

Dekin, A. & Passy, A. F. Florula bruxellensis. 1814. I. 392.

Dekkers, Johann. Anona Cherimolia. 1895. III. 401.[3]

— Culture du Carica Papaya. 1893. III. 617.[1]

De Klerck, A. W. Lassen's Geschiedenis van den Indischen Archipel. 1852. III. 274.[3]

Dekret des Grossen Bathes betreffend die Ablösung von Waldservituten. 1891. IV. 334.[3]

Dslabarrière. La culture de la Vigne. 1888. III. 553.[3]

— Deux arbres gigantesques. 1891. II. 127,[1] *139*.[1]

— Greffage du Pêcher sur Abricotier. 1890. III. 441.[1]

— Plantation de Bruyères indigènes. 1884. III. 648.[3]

Delabigarre, Peter. On White Mulberry hedges. 1794. III. 373.

Delachanal. *See* VINCENT, Camille & DELACHANAL.

Delachanal, B. Lettre à M. Dumas. 1876. III. 569.[3]

— Lettre à M. Dumas relative aux expériences sur l'emploi du sulfure de carbone. 1876. III. 560.

— Sur les phylloxères des feuilles. 1876. III. 568.

Delacharlerie, A. J. L'exploitation des futaies sur taillis. 1897. IV. 556.[1]

— Quelques mots à propos des futaies sur taillis. 1900. IV. 132.[1]

— *See also* CRAHAY, N. I. & DELACHARLERIE, A.

Delacharlonny, P. MARGUERITE-. *See* MARGUERITE-DELACHARLONNY, P.

Delachaye, B. Abécédaire de flore. 1811. I. 515.

Delacoste. Catalogue of the natural productions and curiosities. 1804. V. VIII.[1]

De la Court, Pieter. Les agremens de la campagne. 1738. III. 105.

— Anmuthigkeiten des Landlebens. 1738. III. 105.

— Bijsondere aenmerkingen over het aanleggen van landhuizen. 1738. III. 105.

De La Croix, Demetrius. *See* LA CROIX, Demetrius de.

Delacroix, G. Le hanneton et sa larve. 1890. IV. 203.

Delacroix, Gaston. Contribution à l'étude du Strophanthus. 1888. III. 732.[1]

Delacroix, Georges. Du café. 1870. III. 742.[1]

— La maladie des Châtaigniers. 1897. III. 359.[1]

— Les maladies du Caféier. 1898. III. 737.

— Les maladies et les ennemis des Caféiers. 1898. III. 737.

— Zicktten van den Koffiboom. 1899. III. 737.

— *See also* PRILLIEUX, E. E. & DELACROIX, Georges.

Delafontaine & Dettwiller. Le chocolat. 1859. III. 594.

Delafosse, Gabriel. Notious élémentaires d'histoire naturelle. 1843. I. 88.

Delaharpe, Jean. Cerises doubles, triples et quadruples. 1868. III. 273.[1]

— Description d'une nouvelle espèce de cochenille parasite du Gui. 1864. III. 385.[1]

— Grappes de Vigne fasciées. 1871. II. 507.[3]

Delaire, Eug. Congrès ampélographique de Bordeaux. 1896. III. 547.

Delaire, L. Floraison du Yucca Treculeana. 1869. III. 340.[1]

Delajoux, Ch. Cytisus racemosus. 1892. III. 474.[3]

Delalande, J. Observations sur les maladies des Caféiers à la Réunion. 1883. III. 735.

— Quelques mots sur les maladies des Caféiers. 1895. III. 736.

Delalande, Jean Marie. Hoedic et Houat. 1850. I. 410.

— Une première excursion botanique dans la Charente Inférieure. 1848. I. 410.

— Une seconde excursion. 1848. I. 410.

Delalande, L. Joseph LEBOUIDRE-. *See* LEBOUIDRE-DELALANDE, L. J.

De la Marre, Louis Gervais. *See* LA MARRE, L. G. de.

Delamore, Ernest, Rsnauld, F. & Cardot, J. Flora miquelonensis. 1884. I. 310.

Delanoye. Traité des productions naturelles. 1831. III. 217.

Delaporte, René. Végétation arborescente à Ceylan. 1899. IV. 89.[1]

Delarbre, Antoine. Flore d'Auvergne. 1795. I. 406.

— Flore de la ci-devant Auvergne. 1795. I. 406.

— Flore de la haute et basse Auvergne. 1795. I. 406.

Delassasseigne, Marie Pierre Léon. Dunes et landes de Gascogne. 1900. IV. 183.[3]

Dela Steyrie, Charles Philibert, C. P. de.

Delastre, Charles Jean Louis. Aperçu statistique de la végétation . . . de la Vienne. 1808. I. 408.

— Flore analytique et descriptive . . . de la Vienne. 1842. I. 409.

— Notice sur deux espèces de plantes. 1842. I. 409.

Delathauwer, L. A. Het belgische kruidboek. 1848. III. 77.

Delaunay, G. Sur les emplois du bois . . . dans l'arrondissement de Bar-sur-Aube. 1889. IV. 383.[1]

— De l'influence de la lune. ·1887. IV. 73.[1]

Delavaud, Charles Eduard. Érable-Sycomore à cotylédons partagés. 1861. II. 480.[1]

— Étude tératologique sur des feuilles de l'Orme. 1861. II. 144.[1]

— Note sur une pluie de sucre. 1858. I. 213.[1]

— Notes sur quelques anomalies . . . végétales. 1858. II. 524,[2] 597.[2]

De Laveleye, Émile. *See* LAVELEYE, Émile de.

De la Vergne. *See* LA VERGNE, de.

Delavie. Note sur l'Araucaria excelsa. 1863. III. 298.[1]

Delavigne, Gislain François. Flore germanique. *See* LA VIGNE, G. F. de. 1801. I. 375, V. XIX.[1]

Delaville, A., (sr.). Cours pratique d'arboriculture fruitière. 1872. III. 144.

Delaware — Agricultural experiment station. *See* DELAWARE COLLEGE. III. 3.

Delaware college — Agricultural experiment station. Annual report. Bulletin. III. 3.

Delbeke, Auguste. La question du lapin au point de vue légal. 1899. IV. 323.[1]

— Dei provedimenti al difetto ed all' eccesso de' boschi. 1793. IV. 276.[1]

Delbet. Des écorces. 1854. IV. 434, 512.

— Des écorces de Chêne. 1854. IV. 512.

Delbos, Joseph. Recherches sur le mode de répartition des végétaux . . . de la Gironde. 1854. I. 411.

Delbrouck, Conrad. Die Pflanzen-Stacheln. 1875. I. 107,[2] 112.[2]

Delcher, Eugène. Recherches historiques et chimiques sur le cacao. 1837. III. 594.

Delchevalerie, G. Un albero fruttifero. 1889. III. 636.

— Der Alkanna oder Hennastrauch. 1874. III. 630.[1]

— Aperçu général sur les végétaux . . . en Égypte. 1881. III. 93.[1]

— Un arbre fruitier de l'Inde. 1889. III. 636.

— Arbrisseaux à fleurs changeantes. 1876. III. 475,[2] 587,[2] 702.[2]

— Catalogue raisonné des plantes ornementales. 1868. III. 7.

— Clerodendron Balfouri. 1867. III. 696.[2]

— Cultures égyptiennes. 1870. III. 131.[1]

— Curiosités horticoles de l'Égypte. 1884. III. 131.[1]

— Le Dattier. 1872. III. 329.[2]

— Encephalartos caffra. 1869. III. 285.[2]

— Flore exotique du Jardin d'acclimatation de Ghézireh. 1871. I. 68.[2]

— Die Fruchtbäume und deren Ertrag in Egypten. 1875. III. 131.[1]

— Le Henné des Égyptiens. 1874. III. 630.[1]

— L'horticulture dans l'Afrique centrale. 1889. III. 131.[1]

— L'horticulture dans le désert égyptien. 1890. III. 131.[1]

— Les jardins arabes de la basse Égypte. 1869. III. 131.[1]

— Les jardins de l'Isthme de Suez. 1870. III. 131.[1]

— Les jardins et les champs de la vallée du Nil. 1870. III. 131.[1]

— Les jardins sur le Lac Majeur. 1881. · I. 64.

— Mémoire sur le bouturage. 1868. III. 158.

— Mémoire sur quelques plantes exotiques . . . en Égypte. 1872. III. 131.[1]

— Sur la multiplication des Euphorbiacées. 1867. · III. 514.[1]

— Note sur le Ceiba pentandrum. 1867. · III. 589,[2] 590.[1]

— Note sur le Sterculia Balanchas. 1868. III. 591.[2]

— Notice sur l'Embrevade. 1873. · III. 469.[1]

— Notice sur l'histoire de l'horticulture en Égypte. ·1881. III. 131.[1]

— Notice sur quelques arbres fruitiers . . . en Égypte. 1875. III. 131.[1]

— Notice sur quelques végétaux d'ornement d'Abyssinie. 1882. I. 489.

— Sur une nouvelle forêt pétrifiée. 1876. I. 488.

— Plantes de serre chaude et tempérée. 186 . ? III. 150.[1]

— Le Poinsettia pulcherrima en Égypte. 1883. III. 518.[1]

— Promenade dans les jardins du Khédive d'Égypte. 1870. III. 131.[1]

— Statistique des arbres fruitiers . . . en Égypte. 1875. III. 131.[1]

— Variétés de Solanum bonariense. 1867. III. 701.[2]

— Sur les végétaux d'ornement . . . en Égypte. 1872. III. 131.[1]

Delden, A. J. W. van. De Liberia-Koffie op Gemampier. 1896. III. 742.[2]

Delden Laërne, K. F. van. Brazil and Java; report on Coffee culture. 1885. III. 727.

— Brasilië en Java; verslag over de Koffiecultuur. 1885. III. 727.

— Le Brésil et Java; rapport sur la culture du Café. 1885. III. 727.

— Koffiecultuur. 1885. III. 730.

— Moet de ontginning van woeste gronden . . . aangemoedigd worden. 1882. III. 729.[2]

Deleau. Mémoire sur la culture des prairies élevées. 1848. III. 125.

Deleau, Paul. Droit romain du contrat litteris; droit français de l'extinction des usages forestiers. 1894. IV. 334.[2]

Delépine, (sr.). Causes premières de la réputation de supériorité acquise aux pépinières d'Angers. 1871. III. 124.[1]

— Note sur la Clématite et ses variétés. 1877. III. 389.[1]

Delesse, Achille Ernest Oscar Joseph. Carte agronomique de Seine-et-Marne. 1879. III. 125.

— Influence du sol sur la composition des cendres. 1881. I. 154.

Delessert, Benjamin. Compositae. 1839. II. 848.[1]

— Icones quas in prodromo . . . descripsit A. P. de Candolle. 1820. I. 266.

— Icones selectae. 1837. II. 318.[1]

— Icones selectae plantarum. 1820. I. 266.

Deleuil, J. B. Hybridation des Yuccas. 1880. III. 340.[1]

Deleuze, Joseph Philippe François. Recherches sur les plantes d'ornement. 1806. I. 241.[2]

Delfs. Bidrag til Ericaeans Cultur. 1847. III. 650.[1]

Delgado, Juan José. Historia general sacro-profana. . . de las islas . . . Filipinas. 1892. III. 274.[1]

— Moción relativa á la enfermedad de los Cocoteros. 1890. III. 323.[2]

Delgado, Tomás GONZALEZ Y. *See* GONZALEZ Y DELGADO, Tomás.

Dalgrange. Les tarifs de transport des bois. 1894. IV. 552.[2]

Le deliberazioni a favore della selvicoltura al congresso di Bruxelles. 1897. IV. 39.[1]

Delić, Stephan. *See* SEUNIK, J. & DELIĆ, Stephan.

Delicado, Francisco. El modo de adoprare il legno de India occidentale. 1529. III. 494.[1]

Delicata, J. C. GRECH. *See* GRECH DELICATA, J. C.

Les délices de la campagne. 1655. III. 104.

Delightful smell on approaching tropical lands. 1836. II. 543.[1]

Delile, Alire Raffeneau. Acclimatisations-Versuche zu Montpellier. 1836. III. 47.

— Annotationes. 1848. I. 58.

— Bericht über den vielstieligen Maulbeerbaum. 1837. III. 380.[2]

— Centurie de plantes d'Afrique. 1827. I. 487.

— Description de l'Égypte. 1813. I. 487.

— Description du Palmier Doum. 1810. II. 69.[1]

— Désignation d'arbres à fruits à importer de Syrie. 1840. III. 93.[1]

— Dissertation sur les effets d'un poison de Java. 1809. III. 682.[2]

— Enumération des plantes recueillies par MM. Ferret et Galinier. 1847. I. 487.

— Ueber die erste Fruchternte von Ginkgo. 1849. III. 286.[2]

— Ueber den ersten fruchttragenden Ginkgo. 1835. · III. 286.[2]

— Essais d'acclimations à Montpellier. 1836. ·III. 47.

— Florae aegyptiacae illustratio. 1813. I. 487.

— Flore d'Égypte. 1813. I. 487.

— Flore d'Égypte. 1824. I. 487.

— Fragments d'une flore de l'Arabie pétrée. 1833. I. 480.

— Greffes insolites. 1839. III. 164.[1]

— Hexades duae plantarum ex Indice seminum Horti . . . monspeliensis. 1847. II. 347.[1]

— Lettre sur le Mûrier multicaule. 1834. III. 380.[2]

— Ueber Maclura aurantiaca. 1836. III. 372.[1]

— Mémoire sur le Doum. 1802. II. 69.[1]

— Mémoire sur le Maclura aurantiaca. 1835. III. 154.[1]

— Mémoire sur les plantes . . . en Égypte. 1813. · I. 487.

— Note sur quelques plantes nouvelles d'Abyssinie. 1843. I. 487.

— Première récolte de fruits du Ginkgo. 1835. III. 286.[2]

— Sur la première récolte de fruits du Ginkgo. 1849. II. 7,[2] III. 286.[2]

Delille, Louis Joseph. Notice sur le culture du Pin. 1812. IV. 460.²

Delimoges, Jules. Mémoire sur l'exploitation forestière des terres de Pagny et Clux. 1877. IV. 360.
— Observations sur le système d'élagage rez tronc. 1877. III. 170.

De Linde, Peter C. Dakota forester and fruit grower. 1887. IV. 112.

Delioux, J. De l'emploi thérapeutique de l'oliban. 1861. III. 509.³

Delisle de Moncel. Mémoire sur le repeuplement. 1791. IV. 161.³

Delius, Adolf. Die Cultur der Wiesen und Grasweiden. 1874. III. 347.

Delius, Henricus Friedericus. Cereus, gelu . . . superstes. 1778. II. 589.¹

Délivrance gratuite de plants aux instituteurs publics. 1898. IV. 541.

Della Fonte, Luigi. Sulle cause probabili della malattia degli Agrumi in Sicilia. 1882. III. 498.¹

Delle Chiaje, Stefano. Flora medica. 1836. III. 57.
— Iconografia ed uso delle piante medicinali. 1824. III. 56.

Dellien, Friedrich. Ueber die systematische Bedeutung der anatomischen Charaktere der Caesalpinien. 1892. II. 318.³

Dellmann, F. Ueber die beste Art hölzerne Fussböden zu präparieren. 1861. IV. 418.
— De la meilleure préparation à faire subir aux planchers en bois. 1861. IV. 418.

Dellon. Restauration et conservation des terrains en montagne. 1900. IV. 186.¹

Délmagyarországi természettudományi társulat. See Ter-mészettudományi füzetek. I. 28.¹

Del Noce, Giuseppe. Trattato istorico . . . delle macchie e foreste del Gran-ducato toscano. 1849. IV. 364.

Delogne, Charles Henri. See Crépin, François, Gravet, Frédéric & Delogne, C. H.

Delondre, Auguste. Ueber die Chinabäume. 1835. III. 717.²
— Essais d'analyse . . . des quinquinas. 1861. III. 722.
— De l'Hymenodictyon excelsum. 1817. III. 744.¹
— Notes de. botanique et d'acclimatation végétale. 1871. III. 712.¹
— Notes de botanique et d'acclimation végétale. 1872 III. 43.
— Notice sur la Chinabäume. 1835. III. 717,² 721, 722.
— De la plantation expérimentale d'Arbres-à-thé dans les Neilgherries. 1871. III. 603.
— Progrès récents de l'acclimatation des Cinchona. 1871. III. 714.
— See also Soubeiran, J. L. & Delondre, Auguste.
— & Bouchardat, Apollinaire. The Cinchona barks. 1854. II. 812.
— — Quinologie. 1854. II. 812.
— & Henry, Ossian. Ueber die Chinabäume. 1835. III. 725.¹
— — Examen chimique . . . Quinquina Calisaya. 1835. III. 725.¹

Delondre, Augustin. See Delondre, Auguste.

Delongchamp, Joseph Alexandre Le Turquier. See Le Tur-quier Delongchamp, J. A.

De Loos, Dirk. Het vet uit de bokkenoten van Suriname. 1879. II. 546.¹

Delorme. Essai d'infection d'une Vigne saine. 1874. III. 567.¹

Dalpierre, Léocade. Traité des bois et forêts. 1829. IV. 109.¹

Delpino, Giacomo Giuseppe Federico. Acacie africane a spine mirmecodiate. 1889. II. 323.¹
— Altri apparecchi dicogamici. 1870. I. 237.
— Anemofilia di Bocconia frutescens. 1890. I. 238.
— Sugli apparecchi della fecondazione nelle piante. 1867. I. 237.
— Apparecchio florale. 1890. II. 853.¹
— Applicazione di nuovi criterii per la classificazione. 1888. I. 253.¹
— Ascidii temporarii di Sterculia. 1889. II. 538.¹
— Biologia delle gimnosperme. 1890. II. 1.
— Causa meccanica della fillotassi quincunciale. 188 . ? I. 102.
— Comparazione biologica di due fiore estreme artica ed an-tartica. 1899. I. 220.¹
— Contribuzione alla teoria della pseudanzia. 1890. II. 556.³

— Contribuzioni alla storia dello sviluppo del regno vegetale. I. Smilacee. 1880. II. 77.¹
— Dicogamia ed omogamia nelle piante. 1876. I. 237.
— Difesa della dottrina dicogamica. 1878. I. 237.
— Dimorfismo nel Noce. 1875. II. 114.¹
— Esposizione della teoria della pseudanzia. 1893. I. 113.³
— Esposizione di una nuova teoria della fillotassi. 1892. I. 102.
— Eterocarpia ed eteromericarpia. 1894. I. 119.
— Fiori doppii. 1887. I. 145.³
— Fiori monocentrici e policentrici. 1889. I. 115.³
— Funzione degli ascidii di Dischidia. 1890. II. 737.³
— Funzione della corolla di Bassia latifolia Roxb. 1890. II. 698.³
— Funzione mirmecofila nel regno vegetale. 1886. I. 235.¹
— Galle quercine mirmecofile. 1889. II. 132.¹
— Sulla impollinazione . . . presso le Conifere. 1872. II. 20.³
— Il nettario florale del Symphoricarpus. 1887. II. 842.¹
— Note ed osservazioni botaniche. 1889. I. 271.¹
— Nuova pianta a nettarii estranuziali. 1889. II. 389.¹
— Osservazioni e note botaniche. 1889. I. 271,¹ II. 132,¹ 323,³ 538.¹ — 1890. II. 698,³ 737,³ 853.¹
— Pensieri sulla biologia vegetale. 1867. I. 252.
— Pensieri sulla metamorfosi. 1891. I. 101.³
— Sulle piante a bicchieri. 1871. II. 546.³
— Piante formicarie. 1899. I. 235.³
— Rapporti tra la evoluzione . . . delle Ranunculacee. 1899. II. 195.¹
— Relazione sull' apparecchio della fecondazione nelle As-clepiadee. 1865. II. 735.¹
— Rivista monografica . . . delle Marcgraviaceae. 1869. II. 546.¹
— Significazione biologica dei nettarostegii florali. 1890. I. 238.
— Studi di geografia botanica. 1897. I. 301.
— Studi fillotassici. 1895. I. 103.
— Studi s   un lignaggio anemofilo delle Composte. 1871. II. 850.³ opra
— Circa la teoria delle spostazioni fillotassiche. 1900. I. 103.
— Teoria generale della fillotassi. 1883. I. 102.
— Ulteriori osservazioni e considerazioni sulla dicogamia. 1868. I. 237.
— Valore morfologico della squama ovulifera delle Abietinae. 1889. II. 19.
— Weitere Bemerkungen über myrmekophile Pflanzen. 1888. I. 235.¹
— See also Bernaroli, U. & Delpino, Federico.

Delponte, Giovanni Battista. Elementi di organografia e fisiologia vegetale. 1871. I. 91.
— Guida allo studio delle piante . . . nell' orto botanico . . . di Torino. 1874. I. 64.
— De polline plantarum. 1841. I. 117.¹
— Stirpium exoticarum . . . pugillus. 1854. I. 269.

Delprino, Michele. La nuova sericoltura. 1867. III. 377.

Delseriés. Société scolaire forestière. — Exposé du but de la société. 1899. IV. 541.

Delville, C. Contribution à l'étude des moyens propres à enrayer la propagation des insectes nuisibles. 1808. IV. 200.
— Mesures préventives contre la reproduction de l'hylobe. 1899. IV. 479.

Del Viscio, Giuseppe. Echi dei boschi garganici. 1897. IV. 48.¹

Demandt, Ph. Drei neue Rubus-Arten. 1892. II. 302.¹

Demaria, P. P. & Leardi, C. Ampelografia della provincia di Alessandria. 1875. III. 557.³

Demarquay. Mémoire sur la résistance des protozoaires aux divers agents de pansement. 1875. IV. 531.¹

Demarteau, Amédée & Émile. Das neue Verkohlungsver-fahren. 1840. IV. 394.

Demarteau, Émile. See Demarteau, Amédée & Émile.

Dematra. Essai d'une monographie des Rosiers . . . de Fribourg. 1818. II. 286.³

Demaude, Armand. Appendice à la notice sur le gemmage des Pins maritimes. 1847. IV. 468.¹
— Du gemmage des Pins. 1851. IV. 468.¹

Dambosz, Stanislaw. Tentamen florae territorii cracoviensis medicae. 1841. I. 591, 440.

Demcker, Robert. Die australischen Gummibäume. 1878. IV. 531.¹

Demeaux. Traitement du diabète sucré. 1861. III. 480.¹

Demel, Josephus Eustachius. · Dissertatio . . . sistens analysin plantarum. 1782. I. 32.

Demerara Greenheart. 1894. IV. 520,[1] 529.[1]

Demersay, Alfred. Étude économique sur le Maté. 1867. III. 531.[1]

— Il Matè. 1865. III. 531.[1]

Demerson, L. La botanique enseignée en 22 leçons. 1825. I. 85.

— Histoire naturelle de la Vigne et du vin. 1826. III. 582.

Demetriadès, Rhainoldos. See ΔΗΜΗΤΡΙΑΔΗΣ, Ῥαινόλδος.

Démidoff, Anatole de. Voyage dans la Russie méridionale. 1840. I. 361.

— Voyage pittoresque et archéologique en Russie. 1840. I. 361.

Demitsch, Wassily. Literarische Studien über die wichtigsten russischen Volksheilmittel. 1888. III. 270.[1]

Demmler, L. Populäres Cubirungsbuch mit Preisberechnungstafeln. 1872. IV. 227.

— Ein praktisches und leicht verständliches Cubirungsbuch. 1872. IV. 227.

Demole-Ador. See FATIO, Victor & DEMOLE-ADOR.

Demonet, Ch. See THIÉRY, E. & DEMONET, Ch.

Démonstrations élémentaires de botanique. See LATOURRETTE, M. A. L. C. de. 1766. I. 83.

Demont, A. Expériences sur la maladie de la Vigne. 1864. III. 577.

Demontzey, Gabriel Louis Prosper. De la correction des torrents. 1890. IV. 164.[1]

— La correction des torrents. 1890. IV. 184.[2]

— Étude économique sur le reboisement des montagnes. 1894. IV. 164.[1]

— Étude sur les travaux de reboisement . . . des montagnes. 1878. IV. 163.

— L'extinction des torrents en France. 1894. IV. 186.[1]

— Sur l'extinction des torrents et le reboisement. 1893: IV. 186.[1]

— Sur la lave du 12 juille 1892. 1892. IV. 186.[1]

— Notice sur les cartes . . . relatifs aux travaux du service du reboisement des montagnes. 1878. IV. 163.

— Quelles expériences a-t-il été fait jusqu'ici à dans le but d'arrêter les ravins et les avalanches? 1890. IV. 184.[2]

— Le reboisement des montagnes. 1891. IV. 164.[1]

— La restauration des terrains en montagne. 1889. IV. 164,[1] 185.[2]

— Studien über die Arbeiten der Wiederbewaldung . . . der Gebirge. 1878. IV. 163.

— The subjection of torrents. 1891. IV. 51.

— Traité pratique du reboisement . . . des montagnes. 1878. IV. 163.

— O upravení bystřin a opětném zalesnění hor. 1890. IV. 184.[2]

— Welche Erfahrungen liegen über Wildbach- und Lawinen-Verbauungen vor? 1890. IV. 184.[2]

— Ueber Wildbachverbauung. 1891. IV. 188.[1]

— See also ДЕМОНЦЕ, П.

Demontzey, Prosper Louis Gabriel. See DEMONTZEY, G. L. P.

Demorlaine, J. La quarrimètre. 1894. IV. 437.[1]

Demouilles. Le Cèdre du Liban du palais du Maréchal. 1866. III. 300.[2]

Demoulin, Mme. Gaspard. Aperçu de la culture des Cactées. 1879. III. 619.

— Catalogue des plantes grasses offertes au jardin botanique de l'état. 1882. I. 521.[2]

— Culture des Euphorbes à tiges succulentes. 1880. III. 517.[2]

Demoussy, Em. Sur l'absorption des sels halogénés du potassium. 1898. I. 162.

— Absorption élective de quelques éléments minéraux. 1898. I. 160.

— Absorption par les plantes de quelques sels solubles. 1899. I. 162.

— Sur l'assimilation des nitrates. 1894. I. 160.

— Les nitrates dans les plantes. 1894. .I. 154.

Demoyen. See FORTUNET & DEMOYEN.

Dempster, George. Report relative to plantations made on the estates at Skibo. 1837. IV. 358.[2]

Demuth, N. See FINGER, E., FRIEDLÄNDER, W. & DEMUTH, N.

— & others. Unterpflanzung einer Kastanien-Allee. 1896. III. 216.

— — Vermehrung der Linden. 1897. III. 585.[1]

Le **dendromètre** Marceau. 1881. IV. 215.

D'Endrophile, (pseud.). Question d'arbres. 1897. III. 210.

Dendrophyle, Hans, (pseud.). Die drei Eichen im Flaachebour. 1877: II. 138.[2]

— Fasciation et enroulement de la tige. 1890. I. 144.[2]

— Phyllomanie. 1890. II. 121.[2]

— Quelques cas de tératologie végétale. 1890. I. 144,[2] II. 121.[2]

— Syncarpie de la Noisette. 1890. II. 121.[2]

Denecourt. Nouvelle carte topographique de la forêt de Fontainebleau. 1887. IV. 361.

Dengel, Stefan. Die Destillation des Pfirsich- und Pflaumengeistes. 1877. III. 431.[2]

— Das Schröpfen der jungen Bäume. 1876. III. 175.[1]

Dengler, Leopold von. Ansichten über die Mittelwaldwirthschaft. 1856. IV. 130.

— Beiträge zur Waldwerthsberechnung. 1857. IV. 255.

— Beitrag zur Kenntniss des Verhaltens der Lerche. 1857. IV. 449.

— Bericht . . . über eine . . . forstliche Reise. 1860. IV. 349.[1]

— Bericht über eine forstliche Reise im badischen Oberlande. 1865. IV. 366.

— Die Buchengallwespe. 1857. IV. 496.

— Die Entwickelung des Forsteinrichtungs- und Abschätzungs-Verfahrens in den Domainen- : . . waldungen des Grossherzogthums Baden. IV. 350.[1]

— Forstliche Reisebilder. 1860. IV. 349,[1] 367.

— Die Kiefern im Hauptsmoor bei Bamberg. 1862. IV. 480.

— Les Pins du Hauptsmoor, prés de Bamberg. 1862. IV. 480.

— Praktische Beispiele. 1857. IV. 255.

— Weg-, Brücken- und Wasserbaukunde. 1863. IV. 266.[1]

— & Landolt, Elias. Zur Charakteristik der Schwarzkiefer. 1861. . IV. 466.[1]

— — Quelques détails sur le Pin noir. 1861. IV. 466.[1]

Denham, Dixon & Clapperton, Hugh. Narrative of travels . . . in northern and central Africa. 1826. I. 483.[1]

— Voyages et découvertes dans le nord . : . de l'Afrique. 1826. I. 483.[1]

Denhardt, (Oberförster, Volpersdorf). Ueber eine alte, starke Rothbuche. 1859. IV. 500.[2]

Denigès, G. Nouvelle méthode pour le dosage de l'acide cyanhydrique. 1894. III. 438.[1]

Deniker, Joseph. Bibliographie des travaux scientifiques. 1895. I. 3.[2]

Deninger, Carl. Analyse der Asche des Holzes von Quercus Robur. 1845. II. 137.[3]

Denings, E. W. The capabilities of New South Wales coast districts for growing Citrus fruits. 1900. IV. 498.[1]

Denis & Rouard. Traité complet de l'horticulture. 1846. III. 113.

Denis, A. See JAUBERT, A., comte & DENIS, A.

Denis, F. A. Lectures sur l'histoire de l'agriculture . . . de Seine-et-Marne. 1880. III. 33.[2]

Denis, Nestor. La forêt de Haye. 1881. IV. 360.

Denis, P. La gestion des forêts de l'état en Prusse. 1883. IV. 274.[2]

— Méthode de cubage de Draudt. 1884. IV. 218.

— Tablas de cubicación forestal de Baviera. 1884. IV. 231.[1]

— Tables de cubage de Bavière. 1884. IV. 231.[1]

Denis, Th. Culture . . : . des Magnolias. 1865. III. 399.[1]

— Destruction certaine et pratique du phylloxera. 186 . ? III. 559.[2]

— Gomphia Theophrasta. 1868. III. 596.[1]

— De la naturalisation . . . des arbres et arbustes à demi rustiques. 1862. III. 43.

— Note sur quelques végétaux . . . à Hyères. 1846. I. 58.

— Nouveau procédé pratique pour garantir les Vignes . . . des gelées. 1892. III. 183.[2]

— De la plantation . . . des arbres d'avenues. 1890. III. 210.

Denison, Sir William Thomas. Account of the analysis, by Dr. Motherwell, of certain woods of Tasmania. 1851. I. 155.

— On the manufacture of potash. 1851. IV. 395.

Denison university; scientific laboratories. Bulletin. I. 5.

Denisse, Étienne. Flore d'Amérique. 1843. I. 329.

Denkschrift betreffend den forstlichen Unterricht in Bayern. 1877. IV. 32.

Denkschrift über die Einrichtung von Prüfungs-Anstalten . . . von Baummaterialien. 1876. IV. 415.[2]

Denkschrift über die Hebung des Obstbaues. 1889. III. 139.

Denkschrift über die Zerstörung der Wälder. See LARDY. 1842. IV. 48.[2]

Denman, J. L. The Vine and its fruit. 1864. III. 554.[1] · ·

Dennert, Eberhard. Anatomie und Chemie des Blumenblatts. 1889. I. 116.¹
— Die anatomische Metamorphose der Blüthenstandaxen. 1887. I. 113.²
— Vergleichende Pflanzenmorphologie. 1894. I. 101.¹
Denning, W. H. Great variety of native woods. 1852. I. 312.
Danning, William. On the decay of Apple trees. 1794. III. 427.¹
Dennis, A. B. Evolution of Plum culture. 1897. III. 433.¹
— Japanese Plums. 1894. III. 443.¹
— The last freeze. 1900. III. 44.¹
— A new era in Iowa Plum culture. 1894. III. 433.¹
— Nut-bearing trees. 1893. III. 134.¹
— Peach culture in Iowa. 1899. III. 441.²
— Prehistoric man and his influence on our native fruit. 1896. III. 50.²
Dennis, Charles. Pruning and lopping town trees. 1879. III. 211.²
— Street-trees. 1878. III. 209.
— Trees and shrubs for densely populated districts. 1878. III. 42.²
Denniston, Goldsmith. Grape culture in Steuben county. 1865. III. 550.
Denniston, R. H. The comparative structure of the barks of certain American Viburnums. 1898. II. 842.²
Dennstedt, August Wilhelm. Das Gewächsreich. 1807. I. 259.
— Hortus belvedereanus. 1820. I. 45.
— Nomenclator botanicus. 1810. I. 77.
— Schlüssel zum Hortus indicus malabaricus. 1818. I. 78.¹
— Weimars Flora. 1800. I. 375.
Denny, O. N. Oregon lumber in China. 1881. IV. 403.²
Denson, I. A catalogue of hardy trees, shrubs . . . in the Botanic garden, Bury St. Edmund's. 1822. I. 53.
Dentan, M. Over de beplanting der zeeduinen. 1779. IV. 159.
Danterghem, Oswald, comte de KERCHOVE DE. See KERCHOVE DE DENTERGHEM, Oswald, comte de.
Dentzsch, C. G. van. Aanteekeningen omtrent proeven . . . met Djatihout. 1855. IV. 537.²
Denyau, Alexander Michael. Oratio panegyrica de plantis. 1695. I. 79.¹
Denys. L'acclimatation de l'Eucalyptus. 1882. IV. 127.¹
Denys, Leon, marquis d'HERVEY SAINT-. See HERVEY SAINT-DENYS, Leon, marquis d'.
Danys, Nicolas Denis. Description géographique et historique des costes de l'Amérique septentrionale. 1672. IV. 396.²
Denzin. Abschluss von der Centralkasse des Sterbekassen-Vereins schlesischer Forst-Beamten. 1866. IV. 310.²
Denzin, A. Allerlei über Reinertrag. 1896. IV. 259.¹
— Ansprechen des Inhalts einzelner stehender Bäume. 1882. IV. 218.
— Zur Kenntniss der Fachwerksmethoden. 1885. IV. 251.¹
— Zur Kenntniss und Würdigung des Massenfachwerks. 188.? IV. 252.
Deodar. 1849. II. 27.¹
Déon, Paul HORSIN-. See HORSIN-DÉON, Paul.
Depelchin, Fernand. Les forêts de la France. 1886. IV. 361.
Dependence of the geographical relations of countries and nations, on the extent and situation of forests. 1844. IV. 43.
Dépérissement de semis d'Épicéa. 1900. IV. 457.
Sur le dépérissement des arbres. See On a DISEASE which has attacked certan Elm trees. 1826. III. 185.¹
Dépérissement du Pin sylvestre en pépinière. 1900. IV. 474.
Déplanche. Catalogue des plantes recueillies à Cayenne. 1859. I. 339.¹
Déplanche, Émile. See VIEILLARD, Eugène & DÉPLANCHE, Émile.
Deplay. Percentage of moisture in green wood. 1896. IV. 412.²
Depth of the frozen ground in Siberia. 1838. I. 453.¹
Derbès. Sur les Pemphigus du Pistacia Terebinthus. 1873. III. 525,¹ IV. 509.
Derbholzgehalte geschichteter Hölzer. 1876. IV. 227.
Dercks, Theodor. De pigmento indico. 1836. III. 479.¹
Dercum, Lorenz Anton. De Rosa. 1751. II. 281.² '
— Theses phytologicae. 1742. I. 31.
— See also BERINGER, J. B. A. & DERCUM, L. A.
Derczen, Johann Dercseny von. Ueber Tokays Weinbau. 1796. III. 558.¹
Dereghat de Villard. Des arbres en pyramides. 1829. III. 172.

Derer, Ignas. Poetica exhibitio Arcis et Horti kismartoniensis. 1828. I. 522.¹
Déresse, Antoine. See RÉVIL, J. & DÉRESSE, Antoine.
Derick, Carrie M. The folk-lore of plants. 1893. I. 518.
Dæring, Henry Nevill. Cacao and India rubber in Mexico. 1899. III. 368,¹ 593.¹
— Le Caoutchouquier du Mexique ou de Panama. 1899. III. 368.²
— Report on the Cultivation of Cacao, Vanilla. 1896. III. 118.²
Derive, Théodore. Flore vénéneuse de la province de Liège. 1839. III. 77.
Dern, H. F. Bemerkung über einen Aufsatz . . . wegen Ginkgo. 1838. III. 286.²
Dern, W. H. Wirkung der vorjährigen Winterwitterung. 1838. III. 45.
De Roo van Westmaas. See ROO VAN WESTMAAS, E. A. de.
Derosne, Bernard. Notice sur le Monésia. 1840. III. 667.¹
— Henry, Ossian & Payen, J. F. Examen chimique . . . de l'écorce de Monésia. 1841. III. 632,¹ 667.¹
— — — Examen chimique et médical du Monésia. 1841. III. 667.²
— — Untersuchung der Monesia-Rinde. 1841. III. 667.²
Derote. Les jardins au Chili et au Pérou. 1862. III. 118,² 119.¹
Derry, Robert. Report on the tapping of the Para rubber trees. 1898. III. 518.²
Derschau, Max von. Einfluss von Kontakt . . . auf rankende Blattstiele. 1894. I. 197.¹
— Über Exoascus deformans. 1897. III. 442.¹
— Die Hilfsmittel der Schling- und Rankenpflanzen. 1894. I. 236.¹
Dérut. Température de coagulation du protoplasma. 1875. I. 136.²
Desacres, DESCOURS-. See DESCOURS-DESACRES.
Desamortizacion de montes en Alava. 1877. IV. 276.¹
De Sarinac, D. The Myrtle and its properties. 1876. III. 637.¹
Désarreglos de un arreglo. 1892. IV. 553.²
Desbarres, L. Sur la migration des principes immédiats. 1879. I. 176.
Desberger, A. F. A. Beschreibende Forst-Insectenkunde. See BECHSTEIN, J. M. 1818. IV. 91.¹
— Charakteristik der Weidenarten Deutschlands. 1831. II. 101.¹
— Ueber Krankheiten und- Gebrechen der Holzgewächse. 1832. IV. 195.²
— Kritische Uebersicht des Ganges der teutschen Forstlitera-tur. 1835. IV. 1.
— See also BEHLEN, Stephan & DESBERGER, F. A.-
Desbois. Les boutures faites au Collodion. 1854. III. 158.
Des Cars, Amédée Joseph, conte. Das Aufästen der Bäume. 1865. IV. 171.
— L'élagage des arbres. 1865. IV. 170.
— A treatise on pruning forest and ornamental trees. 1865. IV. 171.
— Tree pruning. 1865. IV. 171.
— Tree wounds and coal tar. 1883. III. 180.²
Descember. Tableau historique des progrès de la culture des arbres à Odessa. 1833. III. 67.¹
Descemet, Ch. Un erbario del secolo XII. 1887. I. 515.
Descemet, Jean. Catalogue des plantes du jardin des Mes-sieurs les apoticaires. 1741. I. 56.
Descentralización administrativa. 1899. IV. 554.
Deschamps. Sur l'emploi du fruit du Marronnier d'Inde. 1854. III. 538.¹
Deschamps, H. El Eucalipto. 1878. IV. 530.
Des Chênes, Georges. See DES CHESNES, Georges.
Des Chesnes, Georges. Le droit pénal forestier. 1882. IV. 324.
— Essai de commentaire pratique de la loi . . . sur la res-tauration . . . des terrains en montagne. 1886. IV. 163, 185.²
— Une excursion à Porquerolles. 1883. IV. 361.
— Une exploitation de Chênes verts en Provence. 1892. IV. 503.¹
— Valeur nutritive pour le bétail . . . des feuilles, ramilles. 1894. IV. 438.¹
Deschisaux, Pierre. Mémoire pour servir à l'instruction de l'histoire naturelle des plantes de Russie. 1725. I. 41.
Des Cloizeaux, Alfred Louis Olivier. Étude du camphre or-dinaire. 1859. III. 233.¹
Descotils & Berthollet. Observations on the dyeing properties of the Rhenne. See MEMOIRS relative to Egypt. 1800. III. 630.¹

Descours-Desacres. Essais de congélation sur les cidres. 1900. III. 429.[1]
Descourtilz, Jean Théodore. Mémoire sur les Nauchées. 1823. II. 346.[2]
Descourtilz, Michel Étienne. Flore Médicale des Anilltes. 1809. III. 64.[1]
— Flore pittoresque et médicale des Antilles. 1821. III. 64.[1]
— Fruits of St. Domingo. 1809. III. 64.[1]
— Voyages d'un naturaliste. 1809. I. 302.
Descripcion de las plantas. *See* CAVANILLES, A. J. 1802. I. 84.
Descripción del Árbol de la cera. 1831. III. 353.[1]
Description abrégée des plantes usuelles. 1767. III. 54.
A **description** and history of vegetable substances. 1829. III. 52.
Description d'une greffe particulière. 1813. III. 159.[2]
Description des plantes vénéneuses . . . de Neuchâtel. *See* GODET, Charles. 1845. III. 89.[1]
Description des principaux parcs et jardins de l'Europe. 1812. III. 27.[2]
Description des produits forestiers du Japon. *See* HONDA, Seiroku. 1900. IV. 21.[2]
Description du Magnolia-soulangiana. *See* HAMELIN. 1827. II. 212.[1]
Description générale de la forêt des apanages de Nelengsko-Kokovinskaia. *See* YACHNOFF, L. 1899. IV. 347.
Description oder Beschreibung des Holtzes Sassafras. *See* MONARDES, Nicolas. 1613. III. 407.[2]
Description of the Big Black Walnut tree. 1827. IV. 488.[2]
A **description** of the garden and buildings at Kew. 1765. I. 52.
A **description** of the large Black Walnut tree. 1828. II. 113.[1]
Description of the Mammoth tree from California. 1856. II. 50.[2]
A **descriptive** catalogue of rare and curious plants . . . from the East Indies. 1773. I. 471. *See also* MILNE, Colin. 1773. I. 262.
A **descriptive** catalogue of the specimens in the industrial and technological museum. *See* TIMBERS of Victoria. 1877. IV. 401.[2]
Descrizione della privilegiata e premiata ferrovia. 1885. IV. 391.
Descubes, A. Catalogue of maps in the Imperial forest survey office. 1895. IV. 2.
Déséglise, Alfred. Catalogue raisonné . . . des espèces du genre Rosier. 1876. II. 282.[1]
— Description d'un Rosier nouveau pour la flore française. 1878. II. 291.[1]
— Description de plusieurs Rosiers de la flore française. 1880. II. 286.[1]
— Description des Rosa canina, dumalis. 1855. II. 285.[2]
— Descriptions de quelques espèces nouvelles du genre Rosa. 1864. II. 285.[2]
— Descriptions de quelques espèces nouvelles du genre Rosa. 1873. II. 283.[2]
— Descriptions . . . sur plusieurs Rosiers de la flore française. 1880. II. 286.[1]
— Essai monographique sur cent cinq espèces de Rosiers. 1861. II. 285.[2]
— Florula genevensis advena. 1879. I. 436.
— Notes et observations sur . . . plantes de France. 1881. II. 707.[1]
— Notes extraites de l'Énumération des Rosiers. 1874. II. 282.[2]
— Notes extraites de l'Énumération des Rosiers. 1875. II. 282.[2]
— Notes . . . sur quelques plantes de France. 1877. II. 312.[1]
— Observations on Baker's "Review of the British Roses." 1865. II. 285.[1]
— Observations on the different methods proposed for the classification of . . . Rosa. 1865. II. 282.[2]
— Observations sur les Rosa balearica. 1874. II. 283.[2]
— Rapport . . . sur les Rosiers d'Europe. 1874. II. 283.[2]
— Recherches sur l'habitat . . . du Rosa cinnamomea. 1884. II. 293.[1]
— Révision de la section Tomentosa du genre Rosa. 1866. II. 283.[1]
— Revision of the section Tomentosa of the genus Rosa. 1866. II. 283.[2]
— Rosa Bakeri. 1864. II. 291.[2]
— Rosa fraxinifolia. 1855. II. 293.[2]

— Rosiers du centre de la France. 1876. II. 285.[2]
— *See also* CARRIÈRE, E. A. & DÉSÉGLISE, Alfred.
— & Ozanon, Charles. Rosa dilucida Déségl. et Ozan. mss. 1882. II. 293.[1]
Deselaers, (*Oberförster, Reinerz*) & **Cusig,** (*Forstmeister, Kuhbrück*). Das Vorkommen . . . der Rothbuche. 1895. IV. 496.
The **desert** in June. 1889. I. 325.
Des Étangs, Louis. Étude sur la culture des bois résineux. 1865. IV. 441.
— Influence des plantations d'arbres. 1864. IV. 542.[1]
Des Étangs, Stanislas. Sur les bois employés dans les charpentes des anciens édifices. 1847. IV. 493.[1]
— Découverte d'ancienne charpente en Châtaignier. 1843. IV. 493.[1]
— Document sur la culture de la Vigne en Angleterre. 1872. III. 554.[1]
— Liste des noms populaires des plantes. 1845. I. 74.[1]
— Mémoire sur les bois employés dans les charpentes. 1851. IV. 514.[1]
— Note concernant l'absence des bourgeons latéraux sur plusieurs Pinus austriaca. 1870. II. 44.[1]
— Note sur un caractère qui sert à distinguer les Salix cinerea et aurita du S. caprea. 1869. II. 100.[1]
— Note sur un exemplaire de Gui de Chêne. 1870. II. 179.[1]
— Notes sur quelques plantes . . . de l'Aube. 1841. I. 409.
— Trifoliation de diverses espèces ligneuses et herbacées à feuilles opposées. 1872. I. 144.[2]
Desfontaines, Réné Louiche. Catalogus plantarum Horti regii parisiensis. 1804. I. 57.
— Choix de plantes du Corollaire de Tournefort. 1807. I. 348.[2]
— Choix de plantes du corollaire des instituts de Tournefort. 1808. I. 265.
— Commentarii botanici . . . in editione Plinii. 1827. I. 292.
— Description d'un nouveau genre. 1822. II. 725.[1]
— Description d'un nouveau genre de Labiée. 1815. II. 765.[1]
— Description d'un nouveau genre de piante, Spaendoncea. 1795. II. 338.[1]
— Description d'une nouvelle espèce d'Echites. 1819. II. 726.[1]
— Description d'une nouvelle espèce de Papayer. 1802. II. 582.[1]
— Description de quatre nouveaux genres. 1820. I. 266.
— Description de quatre nouveaux genres de plantes. 1818. I. 266.
— Description de trois nouveaux genres. 1819. I. 266.
— Description du genre Diplolaena. 1817. II. 405.[2]
— Dissertation sur la culture . . . du Palmier-dattier. 1799. III. 328.[1]
— Flora atlantica. 1798. I. 483.[2]
— Histoire des arbres et arbrisseaux. 1809. I. 293, III. 83,[2] IV. 85.[1]
— Mémoire sur l'organisation des monocotylédons. 1798. I. 104.
— Mémoire sur le Chêne Ballote. 1797. II. 134.[1]
— Mémoire sur un nouveau genre . . . Ailanthus. 1788. II. 413.[1]
— Note sur les Cierges. 1817. II. 591.[1]
— Nouveau genre de plante; Glossostemon. 1817. II. 534.[1]
— Nouveau genre . . . des Euphorbiacées: Ricinocarpos. 1817. II. 450.[2]
— Nouveau genre . . . des Rubiacées: Ancylanthos. 1818. II. 809.[1]
— Nouveau genre . . . des Térébintacées: Heterodendrum. 1818. II. 486.[2]
— Observations sur l'Érable à fruit cotonneux. 1806. II. 476.[2]
— Observations sur le genre Copaifera. 1821. II. 347.[2]
— Observations sur le genre Gyrostemon. 1822. II. 192.[2]
— Observations sur le genre Royena. 1805. II. 703.[1]
— Observations sur les genres Leucas et Phlomis. 1824. II. 762.[1]
— Plantes rares qui ont fleuri . . . dans les serres du Muséum. 1802. I. 57.
— Précis d'un mémoire de M. Mirbel . . . sur l'anatomie des fleurs. 1807. I. 114.[1]
— Quelques observations et expériences sur la fécondation des plantes. 1832. I. 200.
— Rapport sur un mémoire d'Adrien de Jussieu. 1824. II. 433.[1]
— Rapport sur un mémoire d'Adrien de Jussieu. 1826. II. 306.[2]

— Recherches sur un arbrisseau connu des anciens sous le nom de Lotos de Lybie. 1791. II. 500.[2]
— Supplément au Mémoire sur . . . Chamelaucium. 1819. II. 634.[1]
— Tableau de l'école de botanique. 1804. I. 57.
— Voyage dans les régences de Tunis. 1838. I. 484.
— See also JUSSIEU, A. L. de & DESFONTAINES, Réné: ZUC-CAGNI, Attilio, DESFONTAINES, R. L. & L'HÉRITIER DE BRUTELLE, C. L.
Desforges. Sur quelques procédés de destruction de l'oïdium 1874. III. 560.
Desgenettes, C. ROGER-. See ROGER-DESGENETTES, C.
Desgodets, BABUTY. See BABUTY DESGODETZ.
Desgodins. Sur la reproduction de l'Épicea par boutures. 1845. III. 305.[1]
Deshayes, O. A. Notice sur un Chêne . . . appelé La Cuve. 1826. II. 137.[3]
Deshayes, Gérard Paul. Le botaniste voyageur aux environs de Paris. 1803. I. 406.
— Carte botanique de la méthode naturelle. 1801. I. 259.
— Le vade-mecum du botaniste voyageur aux environs de Paris. 1803. I. 406.
Des Héberts, A. Astrapaea Vallichii. 1861. III. 591.[1]
Des Héberts, Paul. Documents complémentaires sur l'hiver 1879–1880. 1881. III. 48.
— L'hiver de 1864 à Hyères. 1864. III. 48.
Desiderata. See BRERA, V. L. 1825. III. 721.
Desjardins. Herborisations dans l'Hérault. 1879. I. 415.
Desjobert, Ernest. Assainissements. 1900. IV. 144.[1]
— Causerie forestière. 1896. IV. 129.
— Le débit des bois dans les futaies du Bourbonnais. 1893. IV. 383.[1]
— La forêt de Château-Charles. 1893. IV. 361.
— La forêt de Chœurs. 1900. IV. 362.
— La forêt de Dreuille. 1894. IV. 362.
— La forêt de Soulongis. 1891. IV. 361.
— La forêt de Soulongis. 1892. IV. 249.[1]
— La forêt de Tronçais. 1894. IV. 362.
— Les forêts communales de la 20ᵉ conservation. 1892. IV. 361.
— Les forêts de Tronçais et Civrais. 1890. IV. 361.
— Grosbois (Allier). Forêt du grés bigarré. 1892. IV. 27.[2]
— Heures de printemps. 1899. IV. 35.[1]
— Un incendie au long de la voie. 1900. IV. 183.[2]
— Mode de repeuplement en Pin sylvestre. 1894. IV. 362.
— Le sécateur-receveur de Pons. 1891. IV. 172.[1]
— Le Signal de Brion. 1897. IV. 122.[1]
— Three descriptions of the state forest of Tronçais. 1886. IV. 27.[1]
— Trois descriptions de la forêt domaniale de Tronçais. 1886. IV. 27.[2]
Desloch. Der Mittelwald. 1896. IV. 131.
Desloges, R. JARRY-. See JARRY-DESLOGES, R.
Deslongchamps, EUDES-. See EUDES-DESLONGCHAMPS, Eugène.
Deslorme. Dictionnaire portatif du cultivateur. 1828. III. 29.[2]
Desmars, J. Catalogue des plantes . . . de Redon. 1866. I. 413.
Desmartis. Note. 1863. III. 478.[1]
— See also BOUCHÉ DE VITRAY & DESMARTIS.
Desmartis, Téèphe P. Des Peupliers. 1852. III. 344.[1]
Desmazières, Jean Baptiste Henri Joseph. Catalogue des plantes omises dans la Botanographie belgique. 1823. I. 407.
Des Michels. Observations sur la culture . . . des Oliviers. 1829. III. 674.[2]
— Semis des arbres fruitiers. 182 . ? . III. 143.
Des Moulins, Charles. Autonomie réelle du genre Schufia. 1861. II. 643.[1]
— Catalogue raisonné des plantes . . . de la Dordogne. 1839. I. 409.
— Comparaison des départements de la Gironde et de la Dordogne. 1859. I. 412.
— De la connaissance des fruits et des graines. 1861. I. 119.
— Description d'une nouvelle espèce d'Euphorbe. 1830. II. 443.[2]
— Deuxième : . . mémoire relatif aux causes qui paraissent influer . . . sur la croissance. 1847. I. 228.[1]
— Documents relatifs à la faculté germinative conservée. 1846. I. 527.
— État de la végétation sur le Pic du midi. 1844. I. 410.
— Note sur deux ovules de Chêne. 1833. II. 137.[1]
— Note sur une propriété singulière des vrilles de la Vigne-vierge. 1862. II. 504.[1]

— Notes reçues de M. . . . de Paravey sur l'Aralia. 1860. II. 611.[1]
— Notice sur des graines trouvées dans des tombeaux. 1835. I. 527.
— Quatre mémoires. 1862. I. 270.
— Quelques notes à l'occasion d'une publication récente de M. Dominique Clos. 1862. III. 525.[1]
— Rapport . . . sur la maladie du raisin. 1851. III. 575.[2]
— & Lespinasse, Gustave. Plantes rares de la Gironde. 1863. I. 412.
Desmoulins, Ph. Guide pratique du jardinier français. 187. ? III. 113.
Desnoix, Charles Julien. Notice historique sur . . . Logani-acées. 1853. III. 684.[1]
Desnoyers, L. CROIZETTE-. See CROIZETTE-DESNOYERS, L.
Desnoyers, L. CROIZETTE-. The desolation of Central Tunis. 1893. IV. 49.[1]
Desor, Pierre Jean Édouard. Accroissement du tronc des Sapins. 1861. II. 23.[2]
— Du déboisement des forêts. 1869. IV. 283.[1]
— Les effets du déboisement. 1869. IV. 43.
— See also MARTINS, C. F. & DESOR, P. J. E.
Desorthès. Renseignements sur la flore de Tébessa. 1890. I. 486.
Despeissis, J. A. Coffee planting in North-Coast district. 1891. III. 733.[1]
— La culture du Thé dans les Himalayas. 1886. III. 604.[1]
— The handbook of horticulture . . . of western Australia. 1895. III. 116.[1]
— Mechanical application of insecticides. 1891. III. 197.
— Phylloxera of the Vine. 1895. III. 574.
— Phylloxera-resisting vines. 1894. III. 574.
Despetis, L. P. Traité pratique de la culture des Vignes américaines. 1887. III. 556.
Desportes, Baptiste. The Acacia dealbata. 1852. III. 464.[2]
— Cèdre de l'Inde. 1846. III. 300.[1]
— Culture du Magnolia grandiflora. 1847. III. 399.[2]
— Descriptions of ornamental Crabs. 1851. III. 425.[1]
— Effets de la gelée sur les arbres déplantés. 1860. III. 166.
— Fructification à Angers du Néflier . . . du Japon. 1866. III. 423.[2]
— Lettre sur l'état de santé des Camellia cultivés . . . à Angers. 1845. III. 599.[2]
— Malus floribunda. 1866. III. 429.[1]
— To resuscitate trees long out of ground. 1851. III. 155.
— Rhododendron grandiflorum flore pleno. 1847. III. 659.[1]
— Spiraea Reewesiana robusta. 1866. III. 461.[1]
— Taxodium sempervirens. 1850. III. 310.[2]
Desportes, Eugène Henri. De la noix vomique. 1810. III. 684.[2]
Desportes, Henri. De la germination des noyaux. 1866. I. 193,[1] III. 155.[1]
— Multiplication par écusson. 1861. III. 161.
Desportes, Jean Baptiste Réné POUPPÉ. See POUPPÉ-DESPORTES, J. B. R.
Desportes, Narcisse Henri François. Flore de la Sarthe et de la Mayenne. 1838. I. 409.
— Roses cultivées en France. 1828. III. 448.
— Rosetum gallicum. 1828. III. 448.
Desprès, Jules. Causeries sur la montagne. 1872. IV. 44.
— Considérations sur le domaine forestier dans le département des Pyrénées-Orientales. 1860. IV. 909.
Desprez. Rusticité des Dracæna australis et indivisa. 1869. III. 334.[1]
Desprez, Georges. Sur le Chaulmoogra. 1900. III. 614.[2]
Desrousseaux, Louis Auguste Joseph. An ut in plantis . . . perspirationi moderandae inserviat epidermis? 1789. I. 166.
Dessaignes, V. Recherches sur une matière sucrée particulière. 1851. IV. 514.[2]
— Sur la transformation de l'acide malique. 1849. I. 175.
Dessberger. Grundlinien einer vergleichenden Zootomie. 1834. IV. 89.[2]
Dessort, Paul. Du Pin maritime. 1869. IV. 468.[1]
Dessoye. Extrait d'une communication sur la maladie de la Vigne. 1854. III. 576.
Desterro, Fritz MÜLLER-. See MÜLLER, Fritz.
Destrée, C. E. De Exoasceëen. 1896. III. 195.[1]
Destremx, J. J. Elenchus plantarum h. botanici J. J. Destremx. 1806. I. 57.
La destruction des hannetons. 1897. IV. 549.[1]
La destruction des hannetons. 1898. IV. 203.
La destruction des hannetons. 1899. IV. 203.
Destruction du Bombyx processionnaire du Pin. 1897. IV. 209.[2]

La destruction du lapin. 1894. IV. 548.²
The destruction of forests. 1877. IV. 283.² ·
The destruction of forests. 1884. IV. 281.²
Destruction of forests in Madeira. 1851. IV. 283.²
Destruction of mangrove forests. 1884. V. xxx.¹
The destruction of the famous Dragon tree of Teneriffe. 1868. II. 82.¹
Destruction of the gutta percha trees in Singapore. 1857. III. 231.
Desvaux. Lethepar. 1817. III. 632.²
Desvaux. Recherches sur les appareils sécrétoires du nectar. 1826. I. 118.²
Desvaux, Auguste Nicaise. Sur la Belvisia. 1814. II. 612.²
— Sur une espèce nouvelle de Figuier. 1842. II. 153,² 554.¹
— Essai sur les différens genres de fruits. 1813. I. 119.
— Essai sur une classification des principes immédiats des végétaux. 1816. III. 217.
— Flore de l'Anjou. 1827. I. 408.
— De l'Illipe à larges feuilles. 1814. III. 667.²
— Mémoire et observations sur la famille des plantes légumineuses. 1814. II. 318.¹
— Mémoire sur la tribu des Coronillées. 1823. II. 318.¹
— Mémoire sur le genre Varronia. 1808. II. 748.¹
— Nomologie botanique. 1817. I. 98.
— Sur un nouveau Calebassier. 1814. II. 790.¹ᶜ
— Sur une nouvelle espèce du genre Pogonia. 1814. II. 806.²
— Sur la nouvelle famille de plantes fondée sur le genre Tamarix. 1825. II. 561.²
— Observations critiques sur les . . . Rosiers . . . de la France. 1813. II. 285.²
— Observations sur deux nouveaux genres de plantes. 1826. II. 423.¹
— Observations sur l'analyse de l'héderée. 1813. III. 643.¹
— Observations sur la famille des Légumineuses. 1826. II. 318.¹
— Observations sur la famille des Rhodoracées. 1813. II. 657.²
—¹ Observations sur . . . la .poudre . . . de Fragon. 1813. III. 338.¹
— Observations sur les plantes des environs d'Angers. 1818. I. 407.
— Phyllographie. 1809. I. 109.¹ ·
— Précis des caractères de plusieurs genres . . . des Légumineuses. 1813. II. 318.¹
— Précis sur les sucs des végétaux employés pour empoisonner. 1814. III. 260.²
— Quelques observations botaniques faites dans la Haute-Bretagne. 1813. I. 407.
— Remarques sur les différens genres . . . Poiretia et Turpinia. 1813. II. 378,¹ 473.²
— Statistique de Maine et Loire. 1834. I. 408.
— Traité général de botanique. 1838. I. 87.
— Sur un usage singulier . . . relativement au Houx. 1813. IV. 526.¹
Desvaux, Nicaise Augustin. See DESVAUX, A. N.
Désvoidy, A. Jean Baptiste ROBINEAU-. See ROBINEAU-DESVOIDY, A. J. B.
Detection of strychnia. 1856. III. 682.²
Detector, (pseud.). L'Arbre à pluie. 1880. I. 213,² III. 484.²
— Mammillaria Peacockii. 1873. III. 623.²
— Nouvelles plantes grasses. 1873. III. 83.¹
Dethan, Georges. Sur l'Ipécacuanha strié majeur. 1898. III. 747.¹
— & Bertaut, René. Sur une nouvelle variété de Matico. 1897. II. 94.¹
— Sur la présence d'une anomalie dans la structure d'une feuille de Piper angustifolium. 1897. II. 94.¹
Detharding, Georg Christoph. De corticis chinae efficacia. 1746. III. 719.
Detharding, Georg Gustav. Conspectus plantarum Magniducatuum megalopolitanorum. 1773. I. 377.
Detlef. Over het nut van de Palmen. 1860. III. 319.¹
Detlefsen, Emil. Ueber die Biegungselasticität von Pflanzentheilen. 1888. I. 149.²
— Ueber Dickenwachsthum cylindrischer Organe. 1882. I. 190.¹
— Ueber die . . . Gehirnfunction der Wurzelspitzen. ·1882. I. 194.
— Die Lichtabsorption in assimilirenden Blättern. 1888. I. 174.
— Versuch einer mechanischen Erklärung des excentrischen Dickenwachsthums. 1881. I. 105.

Detmer, Wilhelm Alexander. Beiträge zur Theorie des Wurzeldrucks. 1877. I. 168.·
— Beobachtungen über die normale Athmung. 1892. I. 171.
— Der directe und indirecte Einfluss des Lichtes auf die Pflanzenathmung. 1893. · I. 171.
— Ueber die Entstehung stärkeumbildender Fermente. 1883. I. 176.
— Sur la formation des ferments diastatiques. 1883. I. 176.
— Lehrbuch der Pflanzenphysiologie. 1883. I. 148.
— Manuel technique de physiologie végétale. 1888. I. 37.¹
— Die naturwissenschaftlichen Grundlagen der allgemeinen landwirthschaftlichen Bodenkunde. · 1876. IV. 61.¹
— Das pflanzenphysiologische Praktikum. 1888. I. 37.¹
— Pflanzenphysiologische Untersuchungen über Fermentbildung. 1884. I. 176.
— Practical plant physiology. 1888. I. 37.¹
— Vergleichende Physiologie des Keimungsprozesses. 1880. I. 203.
De Toni, G. B. See TONI, G. B. de.
Détrie.. Éclaircies. 1890. IV. 174.
Détrie. La végétation gourmande. 1900. IV. 543.¹
Détrie, L. La culture des Cerisiers à Kirsch. 1888. III. 436.²
— Fixation de l'azote atmosphérique. 1897. IV. 72.
— Influence de l'enlèvement de la couverture du sol. 1893. IV. 72.
— Influence of· the removal of humus. 1893. · IV. 72.
Détrie, V. La culture du Bambou. 1890. III. 314.²
Dettwiller. See DELAFONTAINE & DETTWILLER.
Deu. See MAGNIEN & DEU.
Deusing, Anton. Dissertationes de manna et saccharo. 1659. III. 221.¹
Deussen, Ernst. Sur la composition de l'essence de Santal. 1900. III. 384.²
— Zur Kenntnis des westindischen Sandelholzöles. 1900. III. 384.²
Deutliche Anweisung wie sich bey Anziehung derer Weissen Maulbeerbäume . . . zu verhalten. 1754. III. 372.²
Deutsch, P. Ueber Pflanzen-Erziehung. 1868. III. 154.¹
Deutsch-böhmisches Forstlexikon. 1883. IV. 23.³
Deutsche botanische Gesellschaft. Berichte. I. 11.
Deutsche botanische Monatsschrift. I. 11.
Deutsche chemische Gesellschaft zu Berlin. Berichte. I. 11.
Deutsche dendrologische Gesellschaft. Mittheilungen. I. 11.
Deutsche Forst- und Jagdzeitung. IV. 7.
Die deutsche Forstwirthschaft. 1883. IV. 274.²
Deutsche Forst-Zeitung. IV. 7.
Die deutsche Fruchtgarten. 1816. III. 70.
Deutsche Gärtner-Zeitung. III. 11.
Deutsche Garten- und Obstbau-Zeitung. See SÄCHSISCHE Obstbau-Zeitung. III. 13.
Deutsche Gartenkunst. See DEUTSCHER Garten. III. 11.
Deutsche Garten-Zeitung. See GARTEN-ZEITUNG; Monatsschrift . . . III. 12.
Deutsche geographische Blätter. I. 11.
Deutsche Gesellschaft für Natur- und Völkerkunde Ostasiens. Mittheilungen. I. 28.²
Der deutsche Grosswaldbesitz. 1900. IV. 349.¹
Die deutsche Heide. 1891. IV. 84.¹
Deutsche Obstsorten. See DEUTSCHES Obst-Cabinet. 1840. III. 71.
Deutsche pharmaceutische Gesellschaft. Berichte. I. 11..
Deutsche Pomologen, Obst- und Weinzüchter. Berichte. III. 11.
Deutsche Revue. IV. 539.¹
Der deutsche Wald im deutschen Lied. 1899. IV. 55.²
Deutscher Forst- und Jagd-Kalender. IV. 7.
Deutscher Forstverein. Mittheilungen. IV. 7.
Deutscher Garten. III. 11.
Deutscher Holzhändler-Kalender. See HOLZHÄNDLER . . . IV. 9.
Deutscher naturwissenschaftlich-medicinischer Verein für Böhmen. Sitzungsberichte. See LOTOS; Zeitschrift . . . I. 27.
Deutscher Text des ungarischen Gesetzartikels . . . betreffend . . . gegen die Phylloxera zu ergreifenden Massregeln. 1883. III. 761.
Deutscher wissenschaftlicher Verein zu Santiago. Verhandlungen. I. 7.²
Deutsches Archiv für die Physiologie. See ARCHIV für die Physiologie. I. 10.
Deutsches Kolonialblatt. III. 11, 12.
Deutsches Magazin für Garten- und Blumenkunde. III. 12.
Deutsches Obst-Cabinet. 1840. III. 71.

Deutschlands Flora. 1864. V. xix.²
Deutschlands Giftpflanzen. 1829. III. 73.
Deutschlands Holzhandel nach England. 1840. IV. 404.²
Über Deutschlands holzverschwenderische Missbräuche. 1796. IV. 282.¹
Ueber Deutschlands Holzverschwendung. 1809. IV. 282.¹
Deutschlands Kernobstsorten. See AEHRENTHAL, J. L. Freihert von. 1833. III. 71.
Deutschlands stärkster Eichenbaum. 1886. IV. 515.²
Deutzia Lemoinei und ihre Eltern. 1897. III. 410.¹
Deux Cèdres [à Roissy]. 1897. III. 300.²
Deux fruits intéressants de la région du Nord-Est. See Dumast, P. G. de. 1882. III. 85.
Deux-Sèvres — Société botanique. See Société . . . I. 22.
Deux-Sèvres — Société d'horticulture et d'arboriculture . . . See Société . . . III. 22.
Deux-Sèvres — Société de statistique, sciences . . . See Société . . . I. 23.
Deván, Róbert. Szlavonia öreg tölgyesei. 1889. IV. 513.
Devarenne, Th. Amélioration des sols. 1897. IV. 547.¹
— Un ancien aménagement. 1898. IV. 540.¹
— Cubage des arbres dans les taillis. 189 . ? IV. 213, 550.¹
— Expertise des dommages. 1899. IV. 551.¹
— Le meilleur traitement des taillis sous futaie. 1899. IV. 545.¹
— Note sur l'estimation des taillis en croissance. 189 . ? IV. 258.
— Note sur l'estimation des taillis en croissance. 1897. IV. 551.¹
— Notes forestières. 1899. IV. 102.
— Le pâturage en forêt. 1899. IV. 555.¹
Devastations in the canton of Appenzel. 1822. IV. 188.²
Devastazioni. 1863. IV. 283.¹
Devaux, Henri. Accroissement tangentiel des tissus. 1899. I. 131.¹
— Accroissement tangentiel du péricycle. 1899. I. 190.¹
— Asphyxie spontanée . . . dans les tissus profonds des tiges ligneuses. 1899. I. 206.²
— Étude expérimentale sur l'aération des tissus massifs. 1891. I. 162.
— Origine de la structure des lenticelles. 1898. I. 132.²
— Perméabilité des troncs d'arbres aux gaz. 1897. I. 150.¹
— Porosité des tiges ligneuses. 1895. I. 126.
— Recherches sur les lenticelles. 1900. I. 132.²
— Sur la respiration des cellules à l'intérieur. 1891. I. 171.
Daveen, L. Expériences concernant la nutrition des arbres. 1870. III. 38.¹
—Waarnemingen over de voeding der boomen. 1870. III. 38.¹
Development of a forest policy. 1899. IV. 272.
Development of the trade in Indian-woods. 1882. IV. 407.²
Développement des fougères. 1899. IV. 211.¹
Daventer, M. L. van. Een woord over de toekomst der Koffiecultuur in Brazilie. 1883. III. 728.²
Daventer, S. van. Bijdragen tot de kennis van het landelijk stelsel op Java. 1865. III. 128.
Daver & Coutant. Observations sur une haie de vieux Sureaux. 1841. II. 841.¹
Daville, Charles Joseph SAINTE CLAIRE. See SAINTE CLAIRE DEVILLE, C. J.
Deville, H. See PELLETIER, J. J. & DEVILLE, H.
Deville, Henri Étienne SAINT-CLAIRE. See SAINT-CLAIRE DEVILLE, Henri.
Deville, Nicolas. Histoire des plantes de l'Europe. 1719. I. 290.
— Histoire des plantes de l'Europe. 1762. I. 530.²
Deville, P. Fr. Albéric. La botanique de Jean Jacques Rousseau. 1823. I. 94.
Devincenzi. See SIEMONI, G. C. & DEVINCENZI.
Devis d'une maison de garde. 1864. IV. 266.¹
Devisme. Décrets sur la police forestière. 1791. IV. 292.
Devonshire association for the advancement of science, literature and art. Report. Transactions. I. 18.
De Vos, André. Énumération méthodique des plantes nouvelles. 1875. III. 77.
— Étude sur la naturalisation de quelques végétaux exotiques à la Montagne St.-Pierre. 1872. I. 392.¹
— Flore complète de la Belgique. 1885. I. 393,¹ III. 78.¹
— De l'influence des forêts dans l'économie de la nature. 1886. IV. 44.
— Influenza delle foreste sull' economia della natura. 1886. IV. 44.
— Observations sur la dispersion . . . de quelques plantes . . . de la Meuse. 1866. I. 392.

— De quelques moyens pratiques pour reconnaître les plantes pendant les herborisations. 188 . ? I. 535.
— See also MORREN, Édouard & Vos, André de.
De Vos, C. See Vos, C. de.
De Vriese, Willem Hendrik. See VRIESE, W. H. de.
Dewalque, G. De la propriété de certains arbres de prendre leurs feuilles et leurs fleurs avant les autres. 1852. I. 220.²
Devèvre, Alfred. Les Caoutchoucs africains. 1895. II. 727,² III. 229.
— Liste de plantes récoltées au Congo. 1894. I. 492.¹
— Les plantes utiles du Congo. 1894. III. 93.¹
— Quelques espèces nouvelles du Congo. 1895. II. 175,² 829.¹
— Recherches sur le Cubèbe. 1836. III. 342.¹
— Les Strophanthus du Congo. 1894. II. 732.¹
— & Bordage, Edmond. Sur l'analyse photographique des mouvements des végétaux. 1892. I. 194.
Dewey, Chester. Catalogue of plants found in the county of Berkshire, Ms. 1829. I. 313.
Dewey, Lyster Hoxie. The Camphor tree. 1897. III. 404.¹
— Characteristic vegetation of the desert region. 1892. I. 326.
Dewey, S. B. The Hard Maple. 1900. III. 536.²
De Wildeman, Émile. Icones selectae Horti thenensis. See WILDEMAN, Émile de. 1899. I. 50.
— Sur les nodosités . . . du Clerodendron Bungei. 1893. III. 696.¹
— Notes sur les espèces africaines du genre Kickxia. 1900. II. 727.¹
— Notes sur quelques espèces du genre Coffea L. 1900. II. 814.¹
— Une plante myrmécophile nouvelle. 1897. II. 537.²
— Quelques mots à propos des " Kickxia." 1900. II. 727.¹
— Un Theobroma nouveau. 1899. II. 539.¹
— See also DURAND, Théophile & DE WILDEMAN, Émile.
— & Durand, Théophile. Census plantarum congolensium. 1900. I. 492.¹
— — Contributions à la flore du Congo. 1899. I. 492.¹
— — Illustrations de la flore du Congo. 1898. I. 492.¹
— — Plantae Thonnerianae congolenses. 1900. I. 492.¹
— — Prodrome de la flore belge. 1899. I. 393.¹
De Wolf, John. Cacti in landscape gardening. See WOLF, J. D. 1891. III. 619.
— The English Ivy in the United States. 1887. III. 643.¹
— Hardy Cactuses in the open ground. 1890. III. 624.¹
— Maples from Japan. 1888. III. 534.¹
Dewora, J. V. Monatliche Verrichtungen in der Obstbaumzucht. 1815. III. 136.
Dexbach, Johann Georg. De Cassia cinnamomea. 1700. III. 404.¹
Dexter, Thomas E. Animal and vegetable substances. 1857. III. 217.
Dey. Observations sur quelques espèces de Lyciet. 1849. III. 772.²
Dey, Kanny Loll. The indigenous drugs of India. 1867. III. 278.
— Notes on some Indian drugs. 1882. III. 670,² 698.¹
Dey, KRIPA NATH. See KRIPA NATH DEY.
Deydier, P. Multiplication du Bignonia du Cap. 1866, III. 707.¹
Deynoot, GEVERS. See GEVERS DEYNOOT.
Deyrolle, Théophile. La viticulture dans . . . Caucase. 1899. III. 551.¹
Dézallier d'Argenville, Antoine Joseph. La theorie et la pratique du jardinage: 1711. III. 105; see also LE BLOND, Alexandre. (By error.) 1709. III. 112.
Dézallier d'Argenville, Antoine Nicolas. Dictionnaire du jardinage. 1777. III. 30.
Dezeimeris, Reinhold. D'une cause de dépérissement de la Vigne. 1886. III. 561.
Dharma. De Koffiecultuur als volkscultuur. 1890. III. 730.
Dhers. Le Jujubier. 1868. III. 544.¹
Dialoghi agrarj tenuti in Cavriana. 1788. III. 126.²
Dialogue entre deux anciens administrateurs forestiers. 1804. IV. 292.
Dialogues on botany. See EDGEWORTH, Maria. 1819. I. 94.
Diana. IV. 7.
Diana. See REYNARD, J. & DIANOUS.
Diard. Catalogue raisonné des plantes . . . à Saint Calais. 1852. I. 411.
La Diaspis pentagona. 1894. III. 379.¹
Diaz, Anatael, CABRERA Y. See CABRERA Y DIAZ, Anatael.

Díaz, Juan VILARÓ. *See* VILARÓ DÍAZ, Juan.
Díaz Machado, Juan. Disertación sobre la utilidad de los árboles. 1832. IV. 268.
Díaz Oyuelos, José. Medicion y tasacion de montes. 1880. IV. 256.
— Observaciones al proyecto de ley sobre concesión á los pueblos de terrenos. *See* OYUELOS, J. D. 1887. IV. 327.
— Prontuario forestal. *See* OYUELOS, J. D. 1877. IV. 99.[1]
Díaz Rocafull, Aurelio. Indice de la legislación del ramo de montes. 1881. IV. 327.
— La inspección general de montes de Filipinas. 1899. IV. 554.
— Memoria de repoblación de la provincia de Lérida. 1881. IV. 164.[2]
— Recopilación de las leyes . . . relativas al ramo de montes. 1881. IV. 327.
— Repoblación de los montes de Astúrias. 1881. IV. 164.[2]
— Repoblación de montes en la provincia de Cádiz. 1881. IV. 164.[2]
Dibbetz, D. J. Kina-enten. 1886. III. 716.
— De Koffiebladziekte. 1885. III. 735.
Dibos, Édouard. Culture de la Coca. 1867. III. 492.[1]
Dichtl, P. A. Ergänzungen zu den "Nachträgen zur Flora von Nieder-Österreich." 1883. I. 443.
Dick, Andrew. Remarkable Portugal Laurel tree. 1864. II. 275.[1]
Dick, L. Natuurlijke geschiedenis der schadelijke rupsen. 1841. III. 189.
Dickel, Karl. Das deutsche bürgerliche Recht für Forstmänner. 1900. IV. 317.[1]
Dickenson, F. B. Notes on the flora of Berar. 1892. I. 475.[1]
Dickeson, Montroville Wilson & Brown, Andrew. On the Cypress timber of Mississippi and Louisiana. 1848. IV. 484.[2]
Dickie, George. The botanist's guide to the counties of Aberdeen. 1860. I. 401.
— Contributions to the physiology of fecundation in plants. 1846. I. 200.
— On the effects of the past winter on certain trees in the neighbourhood of Belfast. 1855. III. 46.[3]
— Flora abredonensis. 1838. I. 398.
— A flora of Ulster. 1864. I. 401.
— On the influence of last winter on trees. 1856. III. 46.[3]
Dickins, Frederick Victor & Satow, *Sir* Ernest. Notes of a visit to Hachijô. 1878. I. 462.
Dickinson, F. B. A method for introducing Conifers into Beech forest. 1900. IV. 138.[2]
— Sandal. 1883. IV. 519.[1]
— A tree yielding balsam of copaiba. 1883. III. 227.
Dickinson, Joseph. The flora of Liverpool. 1851. I. 400, 533.
Dicks, John. The new gardener's dictionary. 1771. III. 30.
— Vollständige Gartenkunst. 1771. III. 30.
Dickson, Adam. De l'agriculture des anciens. 1802. III. 32.[2]
Dickson, Alexander. Address to the Botanical society of Edinburgh. 1866. II. 1.
— On the compound nature of the cormophyte. 1858. I. 99.
— On the development of bifoliar spurs . . . in Pinus silvestris. 1886. II. 47.[1]
— On diplostemonous flowers. 1864. I. 114.[2]
— Mémoires sur la fleur des Conifères. 1861. II. 19, 25.[2]
— Note on the embryo of Ruscus. 1870. II. 84.[2]
— Note sur la traduction qui précède, et observations sur la constitution . . . de certaines Abiétinées. 1861. II. 19.
— Note upon the preceding translation: [Baillon, Henri. Organogenic researches.] 1861. II. 19.
— Notice of an abnormal leaf in Prunus Laurocerasus. 1867. II. 274.[2]
— Notice of exhibition of vegetable spirals. 1871. I. 102.
— Observations on some bisexual cones . . . in the Spruce Fir. 1860. II. 36,[1] 871.[1]
— On the occurrence of foliage-leaves in Ruscus. 1883. II. 85.[1]
— On the phylloid shoots of Sciadopitys. 1866. II. 49.[1]
— Sur quelques phases du développement des fleurs femelles du Dammara. 1861. II. 25.[2]
— Remarks on the embryos of the White Water Lily. 1870. II. 72.[2]
— Ruscus androgynus. 1883. II. 85.[1]

— On the septa across the ducts in Bougainvillea. 1882. II. 191.[1]
— On some abnormal cones of Pinus Pinaster. 1870. II. 44.[2]
— On some of the stages of development in the female flower of Dammara australis. 1861. II. 25.[2]
— On the staminal arrangements in . . . Potentilla. 1866. I. 116,[1] II. 268.[2]
— Suggestions on fruit classification. 1871. I. 119.
Dickson, James Hill. The fibre plants of India. 1865. III. 234.
Dikson, R. W. *See* MCDONALD, Alexander, (*pseud.*).
Dickson, Robert. A lecture on the dry rot. 1837. IV. 414.[2]
Dictamen de la comisión, referente al proyecto de ley sobre concesión á los pueblos de terrenos. 1887. IV. 551.[2]
Dictionarium botanicum. *See* REUSS, C. F. 1781. I. 32.
The dictionary of hardy trees and shrubs. 1848. III. 78.[1]
Dictionnaire botanique et pharmaceutique. *See* ALEXANDRE, Nicolas. 1716. III. 241.
Dictionnaire des plantes alimentaires. 1803. III. 219.[1]
Dictionnaire des plantes usuelles, des arbres. 1793. I. 32.
Dictionnaire des sciences médicales. 1812. III. 242.
Dictionnaire des sciences naturelles. 1804. I. 33.
Dictionnaire des sciences naturelles. 1816. I. 33.
Dictionnaire des termes latins, consacrés à l'étude de la botanique. 1798. I. 70.
Dictionnaire du jardinage. *See* DÉZALLIER D'ARGENVILLE, A. N. 1777. III. 30.
Dictionnaire populaire d'agriculture pratique illustré. [Commencé par Gaston Percheron et Paul Dubreuil, continué par Charles Deloncle et Paul Dubreuil.] n. d. III. 30.
Dictionnaire raisonné du jardinier botaniste, fleuriste. n. d. III. 30.
Dictionnaire universel d'agriculture. *See* LA CHENAYE-DES-BOIS. 1751. III. 30.
Dictionnaire universel d'histoire naturelle. 1839. I. 34.
Didier-Mongeot, A. Notions sur la clôture et la plantation des arbres. 1894. III. 124.[3]
Didiera [*sic*] mirabilis. 1898. II. 485.[1]
Didierea mirabilis. 1898. II. 485.[2]
Didion, Mary & Avril. *See* AVRIL, DIDION & MARY.
Didrichsen, A. Om Tornene hos Hura crepitans. 1895. II. 445.[2]
Didrichsen, D. Skovbog. 1803. IV. 103.[1]
Didrichsen, Didrik Ferdinand. Har Linné seet Tingen og havt Syn paa Sagen trods nogen Eftermaal. 1861. I. 112.[2]
— Plantas nonnullas musei Universitatis hauniensis descripsit. 1854. I. 269.
— Remarks on the flora of the Nicobar Islands. 1850. I. 481.[1]
— Samlinger til d. Danske botanikens Historie. 1870. I. 80.[1]
Didron. Rapport sur le bois de construction. 1885. IV. 399.[1]
Diesl, Franz. Die Feldbaumwirthschaft. 1834. IV. 134.[2]
— Kurze Belehrung über die Seidenraupenzucht. 1845. III. 376.
— Lehre von der Baum-Zucht. 1844. III. 115.[3]
Diebl, W. E. Forst-Beschreibung der . . . Allodial-Domaine Pullis in Mähren. 1853. IV. 368.
Dieck, Georg. Die Acclimatisation der Douglasfichte. 1889. IV. 483.[2]
— Acer californicum. 1886. III. 534.[2]
— Die Booth'sche Acclimatisation der Douglasfichte war und ist, ein Hazardspiel! 1890. IV. 483.[2]
— Carrières Étude générale du genre Pommier. 1837. II. 266.[1]
— Aus dem Daba-Thale im kleinen Kaukasus. 1893. II. 23.[1]
— Dendrologische Plaudereien. 1887. II. 13.[1]
— Ein dendrologischer Spaziergang nach dem Kaukasus. 1891. I. 368.[1]
— Zur Frage der Einführung der Douglastanne. 1889. IV. 483.[2]
— Ueber Gehölzvermehrung durch Sommerstecklinge. 1883. III. 158.
— Kann der Wald die Malaria beswingen? 1885. IV. 55.[1]
— National-Arboretums zu Zöschen. 1893. I. 49.
— Ueber neue Gehölzformen. 1883. III. 69.
— Zur Nomenklatur der Koniferen. 1887. II. 13.[1]
— Oel-Rosen. 1896. III. 454.[2]
— Die Oirosen und ihre deutsche Zukunft. 1889. III. 454.[2]
— Pirus heterophylla Rgl. et Schmalh. 1886. II. 280.[2]
— Rubus melanolasius. 1894. II. 308.[2]

— Salix amplexicaulis Boiss. 1893. II. 109.[1]
— Ueber die Ulmen und Negundo. 1882. II. 142,[2] *478*.[1]
— Zwei neue Eschenbastarde. 1886. II. 707.[1]
Diecker, H. R. Kommentar über die gewöhnlichen Regeln der Obstbaumzucht. 1841. III. 137.
— Der Obstgärtner im Zimmer. 1826. III. 136.
Dieckhoff. Die gemischten Eichen- und Kiefern-Culturen. 1879. IV. 472, *507*.
Dieckvoss, August. Die Pernettyen. 1890. III. 653.[2]
— & others. Einiges über die Gattung Elaeagnus. 1894. III. 628.[2]
Diefenbach, Ludwig. Dje Rebenkrankheiten. 1895. III. 562.[1]
Dieffenbach, Ernest. Travels in New Zealand. 1843. I. 506.[1]
Diel, August Friedrich Adrian. Über die Anlegung einer Obstorangerie. 1796. III. 135.
— Systematische Beschreibung der vorzüglichsten . . . Kernobstsorten. 1799. III. 70, *444*.[1]
— Systematisches Verzeichniss der vorzüglichsten . . . Obstsorten. 1818. III. 70.
— Versuch einer systematischen Beschreibung . . . Kernobstsorten. 1799. III. 70, *444*.[1]
Diels, Ludwig. Beiträge zur Kenntnis der Scrophulariaceen Afrikas. 1899. II. 779.[1]
— Die Epharmose der Vegetationsorgane bei Rhus. 1898. II. 458.[1]
— Die Flora von China. 1898. I. 460.[1]
— Stoffwechsel und Structur der Halophyten. 1898. I. 229.
— Vegetations-Biologie von Neu-Seeland. 1896. I. 508.[1]
— See also ENGLER, Adolf & DIELS, Ludwig.
— & others. Die Flora von Central-China. 1900. I. 460.[1]
Die zum Dienst des Forstwesens verstärkte Kraft des Hebels. 1751. IV. 385.[1]
Dienst-Anweisung für die Forsteinrichtungs-Anstalt. 1881. IV. 300.[2]
Dienstanweisung über Forsteinrichtung in den Domänen- . . . waldungen des Grossherzogthums Baden. 1869. IV. *248*,[1] 299.
Dienstanweisung über Vermarkung . . . der Waldungen im Grossherzogthum Baden. 1874. IV. 299.
Das Diensteinkommen . . . der herzoglich braunschweigischen Forstbeamten. 1863. IV. 290.[1]
Das Diensteinkommen der herzoglich nassauischen Forstbeamten. 1863. IV. 290.[2]
Das Diensteinkommen der k. bayerischen Forstbeamten. 1863. IV. 289.[2]
Dienstesinstruktion für den k. bayerischen Förster. 1886. IV. 300.[1]
Dienstesinstruktion für den k. bayer. Forstamtsassistenten. 1886. IV. 300.[2]
Dienstesinstruktion für den k. bayerischen Waldwärter. 1886. IV. 300.[1]
Dienstes-Instruktion für die bayer. Waldaufseher. 1871. IV. 300.[1]
Dienstes-Instruktion für die Forstaufseher in den Gemeinde-, Stiftungs- und Körperschafts-Waldungen. 1871. IV. 300.[1]
Dienstesinstruktion für den k. bayerischen statusmässigen Forstschutzbediensteten. 1886. IV. 300.[2]
Dienstinstruction für die Forstaufseher im k. sächsischen Staats-Forstdienst. 1854. IV. 302.
Dienst-Instruction für die k. baierischen Forstwarte. 1806. IV. 299.
Dienst-Instruction für die k. baierischen Landgerichte. 1806. IV. 299.
Dienst-Instruction für die k. baierischen Oberförster. 1806. IV. 299.
Dienst-Instruction für die k. baierischen Revier-Förster. 1806. IV. 299.
Dienst-Instruction für die k. k. Förster. 1888. IV. 307.[1]
Dienst-Instruction für die k. k. Forst- und Domänen-Verwalter. 1884. IV. 307.[1]
Dienst-Instruction für die k. k. Forstwarte. 1884. IV. 307.[1]
Dienst-Instruction für die k. k. Legstatts-Verwalter. 1884. IV. 307.[1]
Dienst-Instruction für die k. preussischen Oberförster. 1817. IV. 301.
Dienstinstruction für die Oberforstmeister in k. sächsischen Staats-Forstdienst. 1854. IV. 302.
Dienstinstruction für die Revierverwalter (Ober- oder Revierförster) im k. sächsischen Staats-Forstdienst. 1854. IV. 302.
Dienstinstruction für die Waldwärter in den k. sächs. Staatsforsten. 1854. IV. 302.

Dienst-Instruction für einen k. sächs. Forstmeister. 1818. IV. 302.
Dienst-Instruktion für den Oberförster des Kantons Luzern. 1878. IV. 306.
Dienstinstruktion für den Oberforstmeister des Kantons Zürich. 1865. IV. 306.
Dienstinstruktion für die Bannwarte des Kantons Luzern. 1875. IV. 306.
Dienstinstruktion für die Bezirks- und Gemeindebannwarte des Kantons Uri. n. d. IV. 305.
Dienst-Instruktion für die Förster der Staatswaldungen des Kantons Zürich. 1837. IV. 306.
Dienst-Instruktion für die Förster über die Staatswaldungen des Kantons Zürich. 1850. IV. 306.
Dienst-Instruktion für die fürstlich hohenzollern'schen Forstinspektionen. 1883. IV. 302.
Dienst-Instruktion für die fürstlich hohenzollern'schen Forst-Verwaltungen. 1879. IV. 302.
Dienst-Instruktion für die Gemeinds- und Genossenschaftsförster im Kanton Zürich. 1861. IV. 306.
Dienst-Instruktion für die k. preussischen Förster. 1868. IV. 302.
Dienst-Instruktion für die k. preussischen Förster. 1880. IV. 302.
Dienst-Instruktion für die k. preussischen Förster. 1894. IV. 302.
Dienst-Instruktion für die k. preussischen Revierförster. 1817. IV. 301.
Dienst-Instruktion für die k. preussischen Unterförster. 1817. IV. 301.
Dienst-Instruktion für die Kreisförster des Kantons Luzern. 1878. IV. 306.
Dienstinstruktion für Privat-Forstwächter. 1894. IV. 298.[1]
Dienstinstruktion für sämmtliche Waldhüter des Grossherzogthums Baden. 1834. IV. 298.[2]
Dienst-Instruktionen für das k. württembergische Forst-Personal. 1822. IV. 303.[2]
Dienstvorschriften für die Fürstlich fürstenbergische Forstverwaltung. 1865. IV. 299.
Dienstvorschriften für die Fürstlich fürstenbergische Forstverwaltung. 1865. IV. 299.
Dienst-Vorschriften für die Staatsforst-Verwaltung der Fürstenthums Reuss j. L. n. d. IV. 303.[1]
Dieppe — Société d'horticulture de l'arrondissement . . . See SOCIÉTÉ . . . III. 21.
Dierbach, Johann Heinrich. Abhandlung über die Arzneikräfte der Pflanzen. 1831. III. 259.[3]
— Anleitung zum Studium der Botanik. 1820. I. 85.
— Die Arzneimittel des Hippocrates. 1824. III. 238.[3]
— Beiträge zu Deutschlands Flora. 1825. I. 377.
— Bemerkungen über die officinellen Früchte der Eichen. 1834. IV. 502.[1]
— Bemerkungen über die Tamarinden. 1834. III. 489.[1]
— Die botanische Terminologie älterer Zeiten. 1824. V. IX.[1]
— Énumération de quelques plantes qui donnent une matière colorante bleue. 1832. III. 236.
— Flora Apiciana. 1831. I. 514.[1]
— Flora heidelbergensis. 1819. I. 376.
— Flora mythologica. 1833. I. 514.[1]
— Grundriss der . . . ökonomischtechnischen Botanik. 1836. III. 52.
— Handbuch der medicinisch-pharmaceutischen Botanik. 1819. III. 56.
— Die neuesten Entdeckungen in der materia medica. 1828. III. 242.
— Ueber die Pimentsorten des Handels. 1837. III. 404,[1] 637.[1]
— Repertorium botanicum. 1831. I. 2.
— Synopsis materiae medicae. 1841. III. 243.
— Systematische Uebersicht der um Heidelberg wildwachsenden . . . Gewächse. 1827. I. 377.
— Uebersicht einiger Gewächse, welche einen blauen Farbestoff liefern. 1832. III. 236.
— Uebersicht einiger . . . Obstarten. 1831. III. 430.[1]
— Versuch einer systematischen Anordnung der . . . Varietäten des Weinstocks. 1828. III. 546.
— Die Weinrebe. 1838. III. 546.
Diercke, C. & Buhse, Friedrich. Verzeichniss der in der Umgebung Riga's beobachteten Phanerogamen. 1870. I. 363.
Diéreville. Relation du voyage du Port Royal de l'Acadie. 1708. I. 309.[2]
— Voyage du Sieur de Diéreville en Acadie. 1708. I. 309.[2]

Diervilla (Weigela) praecox Lemoine. 1897. III. 749.²
Diesing, Karl Moritz. De nucis vomicae principio -efficaci. 1826. III. 684.²
Diesing, Paul. Beiträge zur Untersuchung von Cacao-Präparaten. 1890. III. 595.¹
Dieskau, Christian Johann Friedrich von. Das regelmässige Versetzen der Bäume. 1776. III. 165.
— Vortheile in der Gärtnerei. 1779. III. 121.¹
Diesskau, C. H. J. E. von. Der besorgte Forstwirth. 1802. IV. 96.
Dieterich, C. F. Neueste Anleitung den Weinstock . . . zu erziehen. 1856. III. 137.
Disterich, Karl. Analyse der Harze. 1900. I. 181.²
— Beiträge zur Charakteristik seltenerer Harze. 1897. I. 181.²
— Ueber das Palmendrachenblut. 1896. III. 321,³ 336.²
Dieterich, Karl Friedrich. Anfangsgründe der Pflanzenkenntniss. 1775. I. 83.
Dieterichs, Ludwig Michael. Observationes de usu corticis peruviani. 1747. III. 719.
Dietlen. Andeutungen in Betreff der dauernden Sicherung eines . . . Eichen-Vorrathes. 1856. IV. 242, 618.
— Instruktion für Gemeinde etc. Wald-Meister. 1840. IV. 303.²
— Die nachhaltige Forstertrags-Ermittlung in Württemberg. 1844. IV. 235.²
— Nadelhölzer und Bewässerung. 1871. IV. 50.
— Ueber die Umwandlung schlechter Nieder- oder Mittelwaldungen in Nadelholzbestände. 1844. IV. 169.²
Dietrich, Albert. Acclimatisationsversuche im Norden. 1854. III. 44.²
— Beiträge zur Cacteenkunde. 1846. II. 586.¹
— Beiträge zur Cacteenkunde. 1848. II. 586.¹
— Beiträge zur Cacteenkunde. 1851. II. 591.²
— Beiträge zur genauern Kenntniss einiger Cactus-Arten. 1839. . II. 591.²
— Bemerkungen über die einheimischen Nutzpflanzen. 1843. III. 73.
— Bericht über zwei neue Zamien. 1851. II. 6.²
— Beschreibung der Calceolaria robusta. 1833. II. 779.²
— Beschreibung der Echinopsis Forbesii. 1849. II. 586.¹
— Beschreibung der Erythrina princeps. 1834. II. 357.²
— Beschreibung der Erythrina rosea. 1834. II. 357.²
— Beschreibung der Mammillaria-Arten. 1841. II. 594.¹
— Beschreibung der Mammillaria Wildii. 1836. II. 595.¹
— Beschreibung der Melaleuca lateritia Nob. 1834. II. 630.¹
— Beschreibung der Opuntia decumbens. 1838. III. 625.¹
— Beschreibung der Sida venosa Nob. 1835. II. 591.¹
— Beschreibung des Cereus nyctícallus. 1834. II. 591.¹
— Beschreibung des Cereus pteranthus. 1834. II. 591.¹
— Beschreibung einer neuen Cactee, Echinopsis Maximiliana. 1846. II. 593.²
— Beschreibung einer neuen Mammillaria. 1840. II. 594.¹
— Beschreibung einer neuen Passionsblume. 1853. II. 579.¹
— Beschreibung eines neuen Echinocactus. 1840. II. 585.
— Beschreibung einiger . . . Cacteen-Blüthen. 1838. II. 585.¹
— Beschreibung einiger noch unbekannter Cacteen. 1844. II. 585.²
— Beschreibung von zwei neuen Begonien. 1847. II. 584.¹
— Beschreibung von zwei neuen Cacteen. 1848. II. 586.¹
— Beschreibung von zwei . . . unbekannten Cactus-Früchten. 1848. II. 589.¹
— Beschreibung zweier neuen Cacteen. 1846. II. 591.²
— Beschreibung zweier neuen Cacteen. 1837. II. 591.²
— Botanik für Gärtner und Gartenfreunde. 1837. I. 268.
— Ueber die deutschen Benennungen der Zapfenbäume. 1842. II. 12.²
— Ueber einige neue Epacris-Varietäten. 1845. III. 664.²
— Flora der Gegend um Berlin. 1841. I. 377.
— Flora marchica. 1841. I. 380.
— Flora regni borussici. 1833. I. 378.
— Handbuch der pharmaceutischen Botanik. 1837. III. 57.
— Ueber die kultivirten Arten der Gattung Citrus. 1853. III. 497.¹
— Kunstwoordenleer der zigtbaar-bloeijende planten. 1829. I. 70.
— Muskatnuss und Muskatblüthe. 1853. III. 402.²
— Die neuholländischen Acacien mit gefiederten Blättern. 1835. . II. 322.²
— Ueber die n·uholländischen Acacien . . . unter . . . Acacia paradoxa. 1833. II. 326.²
— De nyhollandske Acacier med finnede Blade. 1835. II. 322.²

— Ueber die Phylica-Arten des . . . botanischen Gartens. 1839. II. 495.²
— Die Polygaleae vom Vorgebirge der guten Hoffnung. 1834. II. 429.²
— Eine sogenannte grüne Rose. 1856. II. 289.²
— Terminologie der phanerogamischen Pflanzen. 1829. I. '0.
— Theorie von der Gewinnung neuer Varietätin. 1854. III. 50.²
— Zwei neue blühende Cacteen. 1845. II. 591.²
— See also OTTO, Friedrich & DIETRICH, Albert.
Dietrich, C. H. Das Ganze des Gartenbaues. 1802. III. 103.
Dietrich, David Nathanael Friedrich. Abbildungen von mehr als 30,000 Pflanzenarten. 1846. I. 269.
— Deutschlands Flora. 1833. I. 378.
— Deutschlands Giftpflanzen. 1826. III. 73.
— Deutschlands ökonomische Flora. 1841. III. 73.
— Encyclopädie der Pflanzen. 1841. I. 261.
— Flora jenensis. 1826. I. 377.
— Flora medica. 1831. III. 57.
— Flora universalis. 1831. I. 268.
— Forstflora. 1828. IV. 82.
— Handbuch der Botanik. 1828. I. 378.
— Synopsis plantarum. 1839. I. 260.
— Taschenbuch der Arzneigewächse Deutschlands. 1838. III. 73.
— Taschenbuch der ausländischen Arzneigewächse. 1839. III. 57.
— Taschenbuch der pharmaceutisch vegetabilischen Rohwaarenkunde. 1842. III. 86.
— Das Wichtigste aus dem Pflanzenreiche. 1831. I. 86.
Dietrich, E. Oberbau und Betriebsmittel der Schmalspurbahnen. 1889. IV. 392.
Dietrich, Franciszek. Wywód o rozkrzewieniu Drzew Śliwowych. n. d. III. 432.²
Dietrich, Friedrich Gottlieb. Aesthetische Pflanzenkunde. 1812. III. 74.
— Bemerkungen über . . . Diosma. 1806. III. 504.¹
— Beschreibung der vorzüglichen Gärten in und bey Eisenach. 18 8. III. 27.²
— Botanische Beobachtungen, und zwar über Entwicklung des Keims. 1799. I. 123.¹
— Darstellung vorzüglicher Zierpflanzen. 1803. III. 74.
— Über die Entstehung der Mistel. 1830. III. 385.²
— Handbuch der botanischen Lustgärtnerei. 1826. III. 74.
— Handlexicon der Gärtnerei und Botanik. 1829. III. 74.
— Die Linnéischen Geranien für Botaniker. 1801. II. 389,² III. 491.¹
— Modeblumen für Botaniker und Blumenliebhaber. 1801. III. 491.¹—1803. III. 74.
— Nachtrag zu Borckhausens botanischen Wörterbuche. 1816. I. 70.
— Neu entdeckte Pflanzen, ihre Charakteristik. 1802. III. 74.
— Praktischer Gartenbau. 1826. III. 74.
— Verzeichniss einiger ausländischen . . . Bäume und Sträucher welche . . . zu Belvedere . . . geblühet haben. 1795. I. 44.
— Verzeichniss einiger ausländischen Pflanzen welche . . . zu Weimar . . . geblühet haben. 1795. I. 44.
— Vollständiges Lexicon der Gärtnerei. 1802. III. 74.
— Die Weimarsche Flora. 1800. V. xix.¹
— Die Wunder der Pflanzenwelt. 1841. I. 94.
Dietrich, Heinrich & Rossmässler, E. A. Ansichten über Bodendecke im Walde. 1845. IV. 68.
Dietrich, R. F. Pflanzenreich. 1770. I. 257.
Dietrich, L. F. Encyklopädie der gesammten . . . Gartenkunst. 1860. III. 31,
Dietrich, L. L. Handbuch des Gärtners. 1844. III. 31.
— Die Vermehrungsarten der Ziergewächse. 1844. III. 152.
Dietrich, Victor. Étude comparée sur l'acide abiétique et l'acide pimarique. 1883. II. 40.²
Dietrich, Vincens. Das Ganze der Verkohlung. 1847. IV. 304.
Dietz, E. De l'influence des forêts sur les pluies. 1882. IV. 50.
Dietz, Johann Heinrich. Μοσχοκαρυολόγια, id est; Dissertatio . . . de nuce moschata. 1680. III. 758.²
Dietz, Phil. Femelartige Wirtschaft· mit Horsten. 1888. IV. 131.
Dietz, Sándor MÁGÓCSY. See MÁGÓCSY-DIETZ, Sándor.
Dietze, Jindřich. Kotázce pěstění Malin. 1898. III. 458.¹
Diez, Rudolf. Ueber die Knospenlage der Laubblätter. 1887. I. 108.²

Diez de Andino, Julian. Cartilla de selvicultura. 1860. IV. 109.[2]
In difesa delle guardie forestali. 1896. IV. 293.[2]
Difesa e illustrazione delle opere botaniche di Pietro Andrea Mattioli. See MORETTI, Giuseppe. 1844. I. 292.
Of the **different** uses to which the woods of the American forests are applied. 1819. V. XXXI.[2]
Different yield of produce from the two varieties of the Oak. 1885. IV. 515.[1]
Les **différentes** modes de toisé des bois. 1898. IV. 219.
Digby, Kenelme. Discours sur la végétation des plantes. 1661. I. 30.
— A discourse concerning the vegetation of plants. 1661. I. 30.
— Dissertatio de plantarum vegetatione. 1661. I. 30.
Digest of criticisms on the United States pharmacopœia. 1889. III. 247.[1]
Digram, M. The Scrub Oak for hedges. 1881. III. 362.[2]
— Shepherdia canadensis. 1887. III. 629.[1]
Diguet, Léon. Le Jojoba. 1895. III. 523.[1]
Dijon, Philippe, comte de. Opinion sur les bois de l'état. 1817. IV. 325.
Dijon — **Académie des** sciences arts et belles-lettres. See ACADÉMIE . . . I. 20.
Dik, VAN-, (pseud.). See VAN-DIK, (pseud.).
Dillenius, Johann Jakob. Catalogus plantarum sponte circa Gissam nascentium. 1718. I. 372.
— Hortus elthamensis. 1732. I. 52.
Dillmann, C. Die Reblaus (Phylloxera vastatrix). 1875. III. 759.
Dillwyn, Lewis Weston. On the effects of the severe winter of 1837–8. 1839. III. 46.[2]
— Hortus Collinsonianus. 1843. I. 54.
— Materials for a fauna and flora of Swansea. 1848. I. 400.
— Purple Laburnum. 1842. III. 480.[1]
— A review of the references to the Hortus malabaricus. 1839. I. 78.[1]
— Some account of a lusus of the hybrid Cytisus Adami. 1845. II. 368.[1]
— See also TURNER, Dawson & DILLWYN, L. W.
Dimick's log reckoner. 1893. IV. 228.
De la **diminution** des arbres. 1856. IV. 43.
Dimitz, Ludwig. Die Durchforstungsversuche Frankreichs. 1890. IV. 174.
— Forste, Jagd und Fischerei in der Schweiz. 1899. IV. 367.
— Forste und Forstwirthschaft. 1892. IV. 102.
— Die forstliche Organisation . . . in Illyrien. 1885. IV. 28.[1]
— Futterlaub und Futterreisig. 1894. III. 223.[3]
— Der internationale Waldschutz. 1883. IV. 177.[2]
— Katalog der forstlichen Collectiv-Ausstellung Krains. 1873. III. 272.[1]
— Die Motive des Waldschutzes. 1902. IV. 177.[1]
— Die österreichische Cameraltaxe. 1888. IV. 250.[1]
— Oesterreichs Forstwesen 1848–1888. 1890. IV. 28.[2]
— L'organisation forestière . . . en Illyrie. 1885. IV. 28.[1]
— De quelle manière faudrait-il completer l'organisation? 1890. IV. 37.[2]
— Was gehört zur Zwischen- und was zur Haubarkeitsnutzung? 1896. IV. 246.
— In welcher Weise wäre die bisherige Organisation des forstwirthschaftlichen Versuchswesens zu ergänzen. 1890. IV. 37.[2]
Dimmock, Anna Katharina. The insects of Betula in North America. 1885. IV. 490.[2]
Dimmock, George. Fruiting of Akebia in Springfield. 1900. III. 393.[2]
— A trip to Mt. Mitchell. 1877. I. 319.
Dimorphism in plants. 1880. II. 152.[2]—1886. II. 202,[2] 325,[1] 628.[2]
Dineen, Thomas. Tonite applied to clearing land for cultivation. 1879. IV. 386.[2]
Dinger, R. Staatsboschcultuur. 1897. IV. 288.[1]
— Staats-Boschkultuur en partikulier initiatief. 1890. IV. 309.[1]
— De zaailingappels der Luntersche tuinbouwvereeniging. 1896. III. 426.[2]
Dingler, Hermann. Ueber abnorme Ausbildungen des Grasstammes. 1896. II. 58.[2]
— Der Aufbau des Weinstockes. 1885. II. 507.[3]
— Die Bewegung der pflanzlichen Flugorgane. 1889. I. 240.[2]
— Ueber die Bewegung rotirender Flügelfrüchte. 1887. I. 240.[2]

— Ueber eine von den Carolinen stammende Coelococcus-Frucht. 1887. II. 71.[2]
— Correlative Vorgänge in der Euphorbiaceengattung Phyllanthus. 1885. II. 449.[1]
— Die Flachsprosse der Phanerogamen. 1885. I. 105, II. 449.[1]
— Korrelative Vorgänge in der Gattung Phyllanthus. 1884. I. 449.[1]
— Das Rhodopegebirge. 1877. V. XXIII.[1]
— Zum Scheitelwachsthum der Gymnospermen. 1886. II. 1.
— Ueber das Scheitelwachstum des Gymnospermenstammes. 1882. II. 1.
— Die Verbreitung der Zirbelkiefer. 1887. II. 41.[1]
— Ueber Welwitschia mirabilis. 1886. II. 55.[2]
Dingler's polytechnisches Journal. See POLYTECHNISCHES . . . III. 13.
Dini, F n es. Della lupa; malattia degli Ulivi. 1794. III. 677æ' c co
Dinter, Kurt. Botanizing in South-west Africa. 1897. I. 495.
— Germination of Welwitschia. 1898. III. 312.[2]
— How Hyphaene ventricosa protects itself from fire. 1900. II. 69.[2]
— Noterelle botaniche dall' Africa meridionale. 1897. I. 495.
— Une plante rare. 1899. II. 55.[2]
— Vegetation of German southwest Africa. 1900. I. 496.
— The Welwitschia country. 1898. II. 55.[2]
Dionis-du-Séjour. De la manière prompte . . . de multiplier le Mûrier. 1812. III. 373.
Ueber **Dioon** edule Lindl. 1856. III. 285.[1]
Dioscorides, Pedakios, Anazarbeus. Dioscoride Anazarbeo della materia medicinale. 77. I. 273.[1]
— Il Dioscoride dell' . . . M. P. Andrea Matthioli. 77. I. 273.[1]
— Dioscoridis libri octo graece et latine. 77. I. 272.
— Dyoscoridis . . . virtutá simplició medicinaró Liber. 77. I. 272.
— Εύρωπίστα Ped. Dioscoridis Anazarbei. 77. I. 272.
— Des hochberümpten Pedanii Dioscoridis Anazarbei Gründliche und gewisse Beschreibung aller Materien und Gezeugs der Artzney. 77. I. 273.[2]
— Kräuterbuch des uralten und in aller Welt berühmtesten . . . Pedacii Dioscoridis. 77. I. 273.[2]
— De materia medica libri V. 77. I. 273.[1]
— De medicinali materia libri sex. 77. I. 273.[1]
— De medicinali materia libri sex. 77. I. 273.[1]
— Pedacii Dioscoridae Anazarbei de medica materia libri V. 77. I. 272.
— Pedacii Dioscoridis de medicinali materia libri quinq. 77. I. 273.[1]
— Pedacii Dioscoridis de materia medica libri sex. 77. I. 272.
— Di Pedacio Dioscoride Anazarbeo libri cinque della historia e materia medicinale. 77. I. 273.[1]
— Pedacio Dioscorides Anazarbeo Acerca de la materia medicinal. 77. I. 273.[2]
— Pedanii Dioscoridis Anazarbei de medica materia. 77. V. XIV.[1]
— Pharmacorum simplicium, reiq; medicœ libri. 77. V. XIV.[1]
— Simplicium medicamentoru, reiq; medicœ libri. 77. V. XIV.[1]
— Les six livres de Pedacion Dioscoride d'Anazarbe de la matière médicale. 77. I. 273.[2]
Diószegi, Sámuel. Orvosi füvészkönyv mint a magyar füvészkönyv praktika része. 1813. III. 55.
— & **Fazekas,** Mihály. Magyar füvészkönyv melly. 1807. I. 444.
Dippel, C. Die Cultur der Eiche. 1839. IV. 504.
— Abhandlung über ausländische Holzarten. 1821. IV. 125.[1]
Dippel, Leopold. Das Arboretum des Ritterguts Zoeschen. 1886. I. 48.
— Beiträge zur Histologie der Pflanzen. 1865. II. 840.[2]
— Beiträge zur vegetabilischen Zellenbildung. 1858. I. 58.[2]
— Einige Bemerkungen über die Struktur der Zellhülle von Pinus silvestris. 1874. II. 47.[1]
— Einige Bemerkungen zu Dr. Pax. 1893. II. 476.[2]
— Einige Bemerkungen zur Gattung Deutzia. 1894. II. 238.[2]
— Enstehung der Milchsaftgefässe. 1865. I. 135.
— Die Gehölzkunde in Deutschland. 1887. I. 38,[1] III. 32.[1]
— Handbuch der Laubholzkunde. 1889. I. 294,[1] III. 70, IV. 84.[1]

Dippel, Leopold (*continued*).
— Zur Histologie der Coniferen. 1862. II. 16.²
— Die Intercellularsubstanz. 1867. I. 138.¹
— Lonicera fragrantissima und Standishii. 1886. II. 836.¹
— Lonicera Webbiana. 1888. II. 836,¹ *838*.¹
— Das Mikroskop. 1867. I. 36.²
— Die milchsaftführenden Zellen der Hollunderarten. 1865. II. 840.²
— Die neuere Theorie über die feinere Structur der Zellhülle. 1876. I. 138.¹
— Les résultats des observations au microscope font l'essential d'une dissertation histologique. 1863. I. 123.²
— *See also* ДИППЕЛЬ.
Dippel, Ludwig. Beiträge zur Lösung der Frage; " Kommt der Zellmembran bloss ein Wachsthum von Aussen nach Innen zu?" 1851. I. 137.
— Ueber die Entstehung und den Bau der Tüpfel. 1860. I. 124.
Dirección general de agricultura, industria y comercio. Circular. Montes. 1891. IV. 554.
Directions for tree-planting. 1885. III. 166.
Diricq, Jules & Sabatier, E. Mémoire sur le soufre solubilisé dans l'eau. 1870. III. 197.
Diritto amministrativo-forestale. 1864. IV. 327.
Diritto amministrativo-forestale. 1865. IV. 328.
Diritto amministrativo forestale. Commenti agli articoli della legge comuuale 13 Novembre 1859. 1863. IV. 327.
Diritto amministrativo forestale. — Vendita d'immobili. 1863. IV. 327.
Dirks, Fr. Einige Worte über die Freiherrlich von Hake'-schen Gärten in Ohr. 1866. I. 48.
Disappearance of desert plants in Egypt. 1892. I. 489.
Disappearance of forests. 1858. I. 217.
Il disastro della " mosca olearia " nelle Puglie. 1899. III. 678.¹
I disboscamenti nel Tirolo. 1882. IV. 184.²
Il disboscamento dei monti e suoi effetti. 1882. IV. 48.¹
Disciplinar-Gesetze für die Studirenden der K. sächs. Akademie für Forst- und Landwirthe zu Tharand. 1847. IV. 32.
Disciplinar-Gesetze für die Zöglinge der Forst- und landwirth-schaftlichen Lehr-Anstalt in Tharandt. 1833. IV. 31.
Discorso della irritabilità d' alcuni fiori. *See* COVOLO, Giovambatista, *conte* dal. 1764. I. 200.
Discours familier sur le danger de l'usage habituel du café. 1774. III. 741.¹
A discours of husbandrie. *See* HARTLIB, Samuel. 1650. III. .107.
Discours sur les Vignes. *See* HERBERT. 1756. III. 554.¹
Discovery of the genuine Tea plant in Upper Assam. 1835. II. 551.²
Discursos pronunciados en la sesión del día 1º de Agosto de 1895. [Conservación, repoblación.] 1895. IV. 341.²
Discusión en el Congreso de los Diputados sobre el proyecto de presupuesto. 1890. IV. 553.¹
Discusión en el Senado sobre el proyecto de presupuesto. 1890. IV. 553.¹
Discussion d'une interprétation donnée, relativement à l'application de la loi du 9 avril 1898. 1900. IV. 327.
Discussione del progetto di legge forestale; discorsi pronu ½-ciati . . . al Senato. 1877. IV. 328.
Discussione del progetto di legge forestale; discorsi pronun-ciati . . . alla Camera dei deputati. 1877. IV. 328.
A disease-destroying tree. 1873. IV. 533.¹
Disease of Cocoanut Palms in the West Indies. 1888. III. 323.¹
Disease of Pepper plants in Mysore. 1895. III. 343.²
The disease of the Sycamore or Buttonwood tree. 1847. III. 418.²
On a disease which has attacked certain Elm trees. .1826. III. 185.¹
Disegno di legge forestale che modifica quella vigente del 20 Giugno 1877. 1897. IV. 329.
Il disegno di legge per la riforma delle vigenti disposizioni forestali. 1897. IV. 329.
Il disegno di legge per le bonifiche. 1898. IV. 329.
Disegno di legge presentato alla Camera dal Ministro. 1882. IV. 328.
In disem Buch ist der Herbary, oder Kräuterbuch. *See* ORTUS sanitatis. 148 . ? I. 275.²
Disertacion botanica sobre los generos Tovaria. *See* PAVON, José. .1791. I. 264.
Disinfezione dei Gelsi. 1894. III. 379.¹
Disosway, G. P. The big tree of· Monmouth. 1865. II. 211.¹

Dispensatorium brandenburgicum. 1698. III. 248.
Dispensatorium electorale hassiacum. 1806. III. 248.
Dispensatorium medico-pharmaceuticum . . . emissum a Concilio medico electorali palatino. 1764. III. 248.
Dispensatorium pharmaceuticum austriaco-viennense. 1729. III. 256.¹
Dispensatorium pharmaceuticum brunsvicense. 1777. III. .248.
Dispensatorium regium et electorale borusso-brandenburgicum. *See* DISPENSATORIUM brandenburgicum. 1698. III. 248.
The dispensatory of the Royal college of physicians. *See* PHARMACOPOEA londinensis. 1618. III. 250.²
Disposiciones oficiales. 1886. IV. 293.¹
Disposiciones oficiales. 1887. IV. 553.¹
Disposiciones oficiales. 1888. IV. 553.¹
Disposiciones oficiales. 1889. IV. 553.¹
Disposiciones oficiales. 1890. IV. 553.¹
Disposiciones oficiales. Dirección general de administración civil de Filipinas. Montes. 1885. IV. 294.¹
Disposiciones oficiales. Gobierno general de Filipinas. 1885. IV. 294.¹
Disposiciones oficiales relativas á la creación . . . de la inspección facultativa de montes. 1897. IV. 554.
Disposizioni diverse in materia forestale. 1870. IV. 305.
A disputed claim to cut brushwood. 1879. IV. 323.¹
Diss. Pruning and switching hedges. 1886. III.· 214.¹
Dissard, A. La greffe et la taille dans la création des variétés. 1899. III. 40.
Dissel, E. D. van. Bestrijding van schadelijke insekten.· 1899. IV. 208.²
— De humus in het bosch. 1896. IV. 70.
— Mededeelingen omtrent het belang der aanplanting van exotische Coniferen. 1899. IV. 126.²
Dissemination of plants chiefly by their seeds. 1895. I. 241.¹
Dissertatio epistolaris de cole wittnebiano. *See* ·MARTINI. 1751. III. 636.
Dissertation philologique sur les plantes religieuses. *See* AMOREUX, P. J. 1817. I. 513.
Dissertation . . .·. sur l'origine du cachou. *See* AMOREUX, P. J. 1812. III. 463.¹
Dissertation sur le Cacao. *See* BUC'HOZ, P. J. 1787. III. 594.²
Dissertation sur les Pommes d'or des Hespérides. *See* AMOREUX, P. J. 1809. III. 499.¹
Distance à laquelle il faut planter les Peupliers. 1900. IV. 485.²
Distance des boutures de Peupliers en pépinière. 1899. IV. 151.²
La distillazione dei legnami di Ollivier de Rawton. 1884. IV. 433.¹
Distribution des Camellia par couleurs. 1832. III. 597.²
Distribution of colour in flowers. 1892. II. 676.²
Distribuzione di paintine e semi forestali. 1894. IV. 166.¹
Distruzione degli afidi. 1863. IV. 209.¹
Distruzione del legname nei lavori marittimi. 1866.· IV. 425.¹
Dit is de genochlike Garde der suntheyt. *See* ORTUS sanitatis. 148 . ? I. 275.²
Ditain. 1878. III. 686.²
Dittrich, Ludwig. Plantae officinales indigenae. 1835. III. 90.²
Dittmar. Die verbesserte Hacker'sche Verschulungsmaschine. 1889. IV. 153.¹
Dittmer. Kiefernzapfensaat. 1897. IV. 474.
Dittrich, A. Die Correa. 1886. III. 503.¹
— Eucalyptus globulus. 1888. III. 634.²
Dittrich, Gustav & Soucha, Wilhelm. Die über transportable Waldeisenbahnen . . . veranstalteten Versuche. 1889. IV. 391.
Dittrich, J. Ueber kulturwürdige Eucalyptusarten. 1887. III. 634.¹
Dittrich, Johann Georg. Systematisches Handbuch der Obst-kunde. 1837. III. 154.¹
— Die vollkommene Obstbaumschule. 1839. III. 154.¹
Dittweiler, Wilhelm. Lehrbuch der Botanik. 1847. I. 88.
Divald, Adolf. Jelentése Erdély kincstári erdőségeiről. 1871. IV. 373.
— Jelentése Máramaros, Ungh és Liptómegye kincstári erdő-ségeiről. 1871. IV. 373.
— A magyar birodalom álladalmi erdőségei kezelésének eredményei 1867-ig. 1867. IV. 294.¹
— A természettudományok és az erdészet. 1865. IV. 56.
— Was sollte geschehen, um die Forstwirthschaft in Croatien . . . zur Blüthe zu bringen. 1864. IV. 278.¹

— & **Wagner**, Károly. Erdészeti segédtáblák. 1864. IV. 230.

— — Magyar-német · és német-magyar erdészeti műszótár. 1868. IV. 23.[1]

Divald, Béla Adalbert. Adatok a kétféle Csertölgy kérdéséhez. 1887. II. 133.[1]

Dive, Hippolyte. Monographie industrielle . . . du Pin maritime. 1864. IV. 468.[1]

Divers, E. & **Kawakita**. Sur la composition de ·la glu du Japon. 1888. III. 530.[2]

Divers, W. H. Daphne Laureola and Daphne Mezereum. 1897. III. 627.[1]

— A large Yew tree. 1899. II. 11.[2]

Diverses opiniòns sur l'usage d'étêter les arbres. 1842. III. 173.[1]

The **Divi-divi**. 1883. III. 468.[2]

Divisione della Toscana in tre zone per la coltura forestale. 1865. IV. 122.[2]

Divof, P. See Дивовъ, П.

Dixon, G. Handbook to the herbarium. 1845. I. 399.

Dixon, H. H. Fertilization of Pinus silvestris. 1894. II. 48.[1]

— On the germination of seeds. 1893. I. 204.

— Note on the rôle of osmosis in transpiration. 1897. I. 150.[1]

— On the osmotic pressure. 1897. I. 150.[2]

— On the physics of the transpiration current. 1897. I. 168.

— The possible function of the nucleolus in heredity. 1899. I. 248.[1]

— The tensile strength of cell-walls. 1897. I. 138.[2]

— & **Joly**, J. On the ascent of sap. 1894. I. 166.

— — The path of the transpiration-current. 1895. I. 168.

Dixon, J. N. Orchards and insects. 1882. III. 186.[1]

Dixon, R. M. On the size of Mango trees. 1894. II. 456.[2]

— The Strychnine tree. 1894. III. 685.[1]

Dixon, Samuel. The effects of settlement . . . in Australia. 1892. I. 504.

— Remarks on some indigenous shrubs of South Australia. 1886. III. 223.[2]

Dixon, Thomas. Note upon the bark . . . from New Caledonia. 1883. III. 283.[1]

Dixon, W. A. On the chemistry of Australian products. 1884. III. 282.[2]

— On Salt-bush. 1881. III. 387.[2]

Dixson, Hugh. Lemon culture in Italy. 1900. III. 502.[1]

Dizionario delle scienze naturali. See DICTIONNAIRE . . . 1816. I. 33.

Djupedius, Petrus. De Gardenia. See THUNBERG, C. P. 1780. II. 817.[2]

Dlatovski, A. See Длатовскій, A.

Dmitriyef, A. M. See Дмитріевъ, A. M.

Dmitriyef, M. See Дмитріевъ, M.

D не spate the axe. 1866. III. 202.[7]

Dobbie, James J. & **Henderson**, G. G. On a red resin from Dracaena cinnabari. 1883. II. 82.[1]

Dobbs, E. Cyprus. 1885. IV. 375.[2]

Dobel, Karl Friedrich. Neuer Pflanzenkalender. 1835. I. 378.

— Synonymisches Wörterbuch. 1872. III. 72.[2]

Dobeneck. Die Icerya Purchasi-Schildlaus. 1898. III. 192.[1]

Dobroviyanski, B. Zum russischen Waidschongesetz vom 4. April 1888. 1895. IV. 315.[2]

— & others. Causes de variation de l'accroissement. 1889. IV. 65.[1]

Dobrovlyanski, Vasili. See Добровлянскій, B. Я.

Dobrovlianski, B. See DOBROVLYANSKI, B.

Dobrowljonski, B. See DOBROVLYANSKI, B.

Dorowsky, Abt Joseph. Entwurf eines Pflanzensystems. 1802. I. 251.

Dochard. See GRAY, William & DOCHARD.

Dochnahl, Friedrich Jakob. Die allgemeine Centralobstbaumschule. 1848. III. 32.[1]

— Anleitung Holzpflanzen Deutschlands . . . zu erkennen. 1860. I. 371, *IV. 83.*

— Anleitung zur Taxation der Obstbäume. 1870. III. 200.[1]

— Aufstellung aller charakteristischen Merkmale des Weinstocks. 1847. III. 546.

— Die Band- und Flecht-Weiden. 1881. III. 348.

— Bibliotheca hortensis. 1861. III. 1.

— Katechismus des Weinbaues. 1855. III. 552.

— Die Lebensdauer der durch ungeschlechtliche Vermehrung erhaltenen Gewächse. 1844. I. *192,[2] 193.*[1]

— Neues pomologisches System. 1847. III. 71.

— Der sichere Führer in der Obstkunde. 1855. III. 71.

— Über Sortimentslisten für Obstbaumschulen. 1847. III. 71.

— Versuch einer natürlichen Klassifikation der Obstsorten. 1847. III. 71.

— Der Weinbau in allen Gegenden Deutschlands. 1873. III. 553.[1]

Dock, Mira Lloyd. Bartram's garden today. 1896. I. 39.

— The Chestnut in bloom. 1897. III. 358.[2]

— The Dauphin Chestnut. 1896. II. 123.[2]

— The Dauphin Elm. 1896. II. 144.[1]

— Magnolia glauca. 1897. III. 399.[2]

— The Oaks at Paxtang. 1896. II. 132.[2]

— The procession of flowers in Pennsylvania. 1900. I. 317.[1]

— Viburnum dentatum. 1897. III. 753.[1]

Docteur, Anatole. Du Thé et de son acclimatation. 1855. III. 601.[1]

Dr. Hamilton Ramsay's garden, Torquay. 1898. III. 642.[1]

Dr. Hasskarl's mislukte poging tot invoering der Coca-cultuur op Java. 1886. III. 492.[1]

Dr. Leichhardt; papers relative to expedition in search of. See MUELLER, Ferdinand, Baron von. 1859. V. XXIV.[2]

Dr. Mayr on the parasitic fungi of North American forest trees. 1892. IV. 212.

Dr. Neubert's Deutsches Garten-Magazin. See DEUTSCHES Magazin für Garten . . . III. 12.

Documents pour servir à la flore du sud-ouest de la France. 1854. I. 411.

Documents sur une enquête relative à la consommation . . . des écorces à tan. 1861. IV. 399.[1]

Dod, C. Wolley. An Ash tree set on fire by lightning. 1883. IV. 194.

— Cistus. 1885. III. 612.[2]

— Cistus. 1897. III. 612.[2]

— The Gum Cistus. 1888. III. 612.[2]

— Improving Spruce Firs by cutting off their tops. 1879. III. 295.[1]

— Pinus Laricio. 1884. IV. 465.[2]

— Rhododendron ponticum. 1883. III. 657.[1]

— Service-tree beer. 1890. III. 460.[1]

— Sex of Skimmias. 1889. III. 505.[2]

— Veronica parviflora. 1898. III. 704.[2]

Dodart, Dionys. Sur l'affectation de la perpendiculaire . . . dans toutes les tiges. 1703. I. 195.[1]

— Descriptions de quelques plantes nouvelles. 1731. I. 290.

— Mémoires pour servir à l'histoire des plantes. 1676. I. 287.

— Mémoires pour servir à l'histoire naturelle. 1676. I. 287.

— Sur la multiplication des corps vivans. 1703. I. 204.

— Opheldering, waarom de stammen der planten altoos een loodregten stand . . . hebben. 1703. I. 195.[1]

— Second mémoire sur la fécondité des plantes. 1703. I. 204.

Dodd, R. The propagation of plants by leaves. 1848. III. 159.[1]

Dodds, George. Essay on the Larch disease. 1884. IV. 451.

— On the improvement of woods. 1885. IV. 121.

— The plantations on the estate of Wentworth. 1890. IV. 358.[1]

— Suitable trees for various soils. 1884. III. 41.[1]

Dodel-Port, Arnold. Der Übergang des Dicotyledonen-Stengels in die Pfahlwurzel. 1872. I. 524.[1]

— See also Додель-Порть, A.

— & Carolina. Anatomical and physiological atlas of botany. 1878. I. 91.

— — Anatomisch-physiologischer Atlas der Botanik. 1878. I. 91, 523.

Dodel-Port, Carolina. See DODEL-PORT, Arnold & Carolina.

Dodge, Charles Richards. Descriptive catalogue of manufactures from native woods. 1886. IV. 19.[1]

— A descriptive catalogue of useful fiber plants. 1897. III. 235.[1]

— Facts concerning Ramie. 1895. III. 381.[2]

— Office of fiber investigations. 1898. III. 235.[1]

— Recent facts regarding the Ramie industry. 1891. III. 381.[2]

— A report on Sisal Hemp culture. 1891. III. 340.[2]

— A report on the cultivation of Ramie. 1895. III. 381.[2]

— A report on the leaf fibers of the United States. 1893. III. 341.[1]

Dodge, J. R. The Big tree. 1875. II. 51.[1]

Dodoens, Rembert. Appendix variarum et quidem rarissimarum nonnullarum stirpium. 1574. I. 281.

Dodoens, Rembert (*continued*),
— Commentariorum de stirpium historia imaginum tomus secundus. 1553. I. 279.
— Cruydeboeck. 1554. I. 279.
— Florum et coronariarum odoratarumque nonnullarum herbarum historia. 1568. I. 281.
— De frugum historia liber unus. 1552. I. 278.
— Histoire de plantes. 1554. I. 279.
— Historia Vitis vinique et stirpium nonnullarum aliarum. 1580. I. 282, *III. 552.*
— A new herbal or historie of plants. 1554. I. 279.
— A niewe herball. 1554. I. 279.
— Posteriorum trium de stirpium historia commentariorum icones. 1553. I. 279.
— Purgantium aliarumque eo facientium . . . historial libri IV. 1574. I. 281.
— Rams little Dodeon. 1554. I. 279.
— De stirpium historia commentariorum, imagines. 1553. I. 279.
— Stirpium historiae pemptades sex. 1583. I. 282.
— Triorum priorum de stirpium historia commentariorum imagines. 1553. I. 279.
Dodonaea. *See* BOTANISCH jaarboek. I. 16.
Dodson, W. R.   The principal plants of . . . Louisiana. 1896. I. 319.
Dodwell, Arthur **& Rixon,** T. F.   Olympic forest reserve. 1900. IV. 341.[1]
Döbel, Heinrich Wilhelm.   Eröffnete Jäger-Practica. 1746. IV. 115.
— Neueröffnete Jäger-Practica. 1746. IV. 115.
Döbner, Dr. Edward Ph.   Abnormer Fichtenzapfen. 1875. II. 34.[1]
— Ein astloses Fichtenstämmchen. 1872. II. 34.[2]
— Botanik für Forstmänner. 1853. I.[2] 371, *IV. 83.*
— Handbuch der Zoologie. 1862. IV. 90.[1]
— Lehrbuch der Botanik für Forstmänner. 1853. *I. 371,* IV. 61,[2] 83.
— Das Licht in Bezug auf die Wachsthumsverhältnisse. 1859. IV. 67.[2]
Doebner, O. **& Lücker,** E.   Ueber das Guajakharz. 1896. III. 494.[3]
Doederlein, Ludwig.   Die Liu-Kiu-Insel Amami Oschima. 1880. I. 462.
Doehl, C.   Waldungen und Waldwirthschaft. 1876. IV. 269, 874.[1]
Döhner, Theodor.   Über die verderblichen Folgen rücksichtsloser Zerstörung natürlicher Landeszustände. 1851. IV. 43.
Döll.   Die Baumpäonie. 1858. III. 392.[2]
— Notizen über Obst-, Wein- und Pflanzenkultur auf der . . . Krim. 1860. III. 120.[1]
Döll, Johann Christof.   Bemerkungen über die Zygomorphie seitlicher Blüthen. 1859. I. 114.[3]
— Zur Erklärung der Laubknospen der Amentaceen. 1848. I. 107.[2]
— Flora des Grossherzogthums Baden. 1857. I. 384.
— Gramineae 3, Bambusaceae, Hordeaceae. 1880. II. 58.[1]
— Nachrichten über die mit Unrecht der badischen Flora zugeschriebenen Gewächse. 1858. I. 384.
— Pflanzenkunde [von Baden]. 1884. I. 388.
— Rheinische Flora. 1843. I. 381.
Döll, Wilhelm.   Der Rosen-Garten. 1855. III. 448.
Dölts, Johann Christian.   Neue Versuche . . . über einige Pflanzengifte. 1792. III. 260.[3]
Doengingk, Alexander.   Fünf- und- dreissigjährige Beobachtungen über den Beginn . . . der Blüthezeit. 1886. I. 224.[1]
— Tabellarische Uebersicht der . . . gepflanzten und 14 Jahre hindurch beobachteten Gehölze. 1856. III. 44.[3]
— Tableau des observations . . . relativement au degré de froid que peuvent supporter divers arbres. 1856. III. 44.[2]
— Tabular view of the results of fourteen years' observations on the degree of cold borne by various trees. 1856. III. 44.[2]
— Vergleichende Uebersicht der in Russland ausgeführten Beobachtungen über . . . Blüthenentwicklung. 1887. I. 224.[2]
— Zwölfjährige Beobachtungen über . . . Blüthezeit. 1857. I. 223.[3]
Doepping, O.   Chemische Untersuchung der Rinde der Korkeiche. 1843. II. 140.[1]
— Examen chimique de l'écorce de liége. 1843. II. 140.[1]
Dörfling, K. F.   Abhandlung über . . . Gegenstände des Forstwesens. 1808. IV. 100.[3]
Dörfler, Ignaz.   Herbarium normale. 1894. I. 350.[1]
— Eine Lonicera aus Niederösterreich. 1897. II. 838.[1]
— *See also* DEGEN, Árpád von & DÖRFLER, Ignaz.

Doering, Adolfo.   Los constituyentes inorgánicos de algunos árboles. 1875. I. 155.
Döring, Michael.   Diatribe de opobalsamo. 1620. III. 510.[1]
Döring, Wilhelm Ludwig.   Die Königin der Blumen. 1835. II. 290.[2]
Doerr, (*Forstassessor*).   Verwerthung der Fichtenstangen. 1900. IV. 459.[1]
Dörre, F. C. **& Funke,** W.   Der Bezirk Tetschen. 1871. IV. 371.
Dörrien, C. H.   Verzeichniss . . . in den Fürstlich Oranien-Nassauischen Landen wild wachsenden Gewächse. 1777. I. 374.
Doflein, Franz.   Von den Antillen zum fernen Westen. 1900. I. 327, *337.*
Dohms, A. R. L. **& Engelhardt,** H.   Chemistry of Cascara. 1898. III. 543.[2]
— — Composition chimique du Cascara. 1898. III. 543.[2]
— — Some observations regarding kola nuts. 1896. III. 590.[3]
Doisy, C.   Essai sur l'histoire naturelle . . . de la Meuse. 1835. I. 408.
Doit-on faire des fosses pour le reboisement des vieux taillis? 1899. IV. 170.
Doklad . . . *See* ДОКЛАДЪ . . .
Dokoupil, W. V.   Die Bauhölzer. 1876. IV. 423.[1]
Dokutchaeff, V.   *See* ДОКУТЧАУЕВЪ, V. V.
Dokuchaev, V.   *See* ДОКУТЧАУЕВЪ, V. V.
Dokutchayef, V.   Le court contenu des travaux de l'expedition equipée par le Departement forestier. 1894. IV. 346.
— *See also* ДОКУЧАЕВЪ, B. B.
Dold, J. M.   Praktische Anleitung zur Ausmessung des beschlagenen und runden Holzes. n. d. IV. 219.
Dôle — Société d'horticulture.   *See* SOCIÉTÉ . . . III. 21.
Dolene, Fr.   Ein beachtenswerther Baum der Flora Südtirols. 1885. IV. 534.[2]
Doleschall, C. L.   Korte karakterschets der flora van Amboina. 1857. I. 465.
Doleschall, Gabriel.   Physiologia plantarum. 1840. I. 147.
Dolivot, A. E.   Les arbres fruitiers. 1874. III. 144.
— Lettre . . . à M. Alix en réponse à la brochure de M. l'Abbé Lefèvre. 1882. III. 144.
Dolivot, E.   Guide pratique de l'amateur d'arbres fruitiers. 1863. III. 85.
Dollen, van.   *See* ФАНЪ ДОЛЛЕНЪ.
Dolles.   Das Auftreten des Bostrichus bidens. 1885. IV. 477.
— Beobachtungen . . . über Hylobius. 1890. IV. 208.[1]
— Lyda hypotrophica. 1895. IV. 457.
Dolley, Charles Sumner.   The botany of the Bahamas. 1890. I. 337.
— Evil effects of drifting sands along the Jersey coast. 1895. IV. 46.[1]
Dollfuss, Johann Georg.   Cerasologia medica. 1718. III. 432.[2]
Dolliner, Georg.   Enumeratio plantarum . . . in Austria inferiori. 1842. I. 440.
Domáčnost.   *See* HÁJ. IV. 14.
Domänstyrelsens underdåniga utlåtande angående lagstiftning för den enskildes skogshushållning. 1885. IV. 288.[2]
Le domaine forestier de l'état. 1899. IV. 274.[2]
Le domaine forestier et l'enlèvement des feuilles. 1898. IV. 72.
Domaine situé en Campine. 1898. IV. 119.[3]
Dombasle, Christophe Joseph Alexandre MATHIEU DE.   *See* MATHIEU DE DOMBASLE, C. J. A.
D'Ombrain, Henry Honywood.   New variegated Japanese Honeysuckle. 1862. III. 750.[2]
— Roses for amateurs. 1887. III. 450.
Dombrowski, Ernst von.   Die Wildschäden. 1896. IV. 197.[2]
Dombrowski, Raoul, *Ritter* von.   Allgemeine Encyklopädie der gesammten Forst- und Jagdwissenschaften. 1886. IV. 22.[2]
— Collectiv-Ausstellung land- und forstwirthschaftlicher Produkte des Königreichs Böhmen. 1873. III. 272.[1]
— Die Urproduction und Industrie der Land- und Forstwirthschaft. 1869. IV. 269.
Domenech, Bernardo **& Pau,** J. B.   Concordia pharmacopolarum barcinonensium. 1587. III. 240.
Domergue, A.   Huiles d'olive de Tunisie et d'Algérie. 1891. III. 679.[1]
— **& Nicolas,** Cl.   Documents analytiques pour l'étude de thé et du café. 1892. III. 608,[1] 740.[3]
The domestic utility of the Lilac. 1880. III. 681.[2]

Domet, Paul. Examen . . . de l'histoire de la forêt d' Orléans. 1892. IV. 361.
— Histoire de la forêt de Fontainebleau. 1873. IV. 360.
— Les incendies dans la forêt d'Orléans. 1891. IV. 183.[1]
— Produit des Pins sylvestres de la forêt d'Orléans. 1886. IV. 481.
— Recherches sur l'étymologie des noms de lieux de l'ancienne forêt d'Orléans. 1896. IV. 362.
— Statistique forestière . . . du Loiret. 1889. IV. 361.
Domin, Fr. Beiträge zur Forstkultur. 1867. IV. 123.[2]
Dominé. Note sur la préparation de l'huile de Croton tiglium. 1849. III. 517.[1]
Dominica Pimento. 1880. III. 637.[1]
Dominica, W. I. — Botanical station. *See* BOTANICAL . . . 1892. I. 39.
Dominicus, J. D. & Sons. Illustrirtes Handbuch für Sägemüller. 1889. IV. 393.
— Illustrirtes Handbuch über Sägen. 1889. IV. 393.
Domis, D. J. Journaal eener reis van Welerie. 1830. III. 275.[3]
Domis, H. I. De residentie Passoeroeang. 1836. III. 275.[2]
Domis, Hendrik Jacob. Aanteekeningen over het gebergte Tinger. 1832. III. 274.[1]
Domitzer, Johan. Ein neüwes fast hübsch . . . Pflantsbüchlin. 1529. III. 135.
— Ein newes Pflantzbüchlin. 1531. III. 159.[1]
— Pflantzbüchlin. 1531. III. 159.[1]
Dommages causés par le föhn . . . 1900. 1900. IV. 189.[2]
Dommages causés par le gibier dans le canton d'Argovie. *See* WILDSCHADEN. 1858. IV. 196.[2]
Dommages occasionnés par les avalanches à Calanca. 1888. IV. 188.[2]
Dommanget. Code du garde particulier des bois. 1887. IV. 304.[1]
Dommes, Albert. Aphorismen zur Beantwortung der Frage: " Ist durch die zunehmende Steinkohlen-Production . . . ein Rückgang der Brennholzpreise . . . hervorgerufen ? " 1868. IV. 243.
— Beobachtungen über die Schütte der Kiefer. 1856. IV. 475.
— Bericht über die praktische Anwendbarkeit des Presslerschen Messknechtes. 1853. IV. 213.
— Zur Insekten-Vertilgungsfrage. 1874. IV. 199.[2]
— Liparis dispar. 1854. IV. 206.
— Ueber Verhütung des Maikäferfrasses. 1867. IV. 202.
— Ueber Vorkommen des Borkenkäfers. 1877. IV. 455.
Vom **Domogled.** 1871. II. 43.[2]
Domonkos, János. Ampelovitis Davidi. 1890. III. 584.[1]
Dompierre, J. T. Versuch einer Aufzählung der in der Umgebung von München einheimischen . . . Weiden. 1873. II. 101.[2]
Don, David. Additional remarks on Ercilla. 1833. I. 268.
— Additions to some . . . communications on the " Palo de Vaca." 1830. II. 146,[2] 783.[2]
— On the affinities of the Empetreae. 1827. II. 453.[2]
— On the anomalous structure of the leaf of Rosa berberifolia. 1830. II. 297.[1]
— An attempt at a new arrangement of the Ericaceae. 1834. II. 657.[2]
— An attempt at a new classification of the Cichoraceae. 1829. II. 848.[1]
— On the characters . . . of certain genera. 1831. I. 340.[2]
— On the characters of certain groups of the class Personatae. 1835. II. 778.[2]
— On the Coniferae . . . growing in Australia. 1833. II. 16.[1]
— On the connexion which subsists between the calyx and ovarium in . . . Melastomaceae. 1833. II. 635.[1]
— Description de deux nouveaux genres . . . des Conifères. 1838. II. 26.[2]
— Description of a new genus belonging to . . . Scrophularinae. 1827. II. 780.[2]
— Description of a new genus of . . . Bignoniaceae. 1841. II. 787.[1]
— Description of Columnea, Tovaria and Francoa. 1829. II. 795.[2]
— Description of Cowania. 1825. II. 260.[1]
— Description of five new genera of . . . Bignoniaceae. 1823. II. 784.[1]
— A description of the genus Malesherbia. 1827. II. 575.[1]
— Descriptions of five new species of . . . Pinus. 1837. II. 38.[1]
— Descriptions of several new plants from . . . Nepaul. 1821. I. 471.

— Descriptions of some new species of Malesherbia. 1832. I. 268.
— Descriptions of the new genera . . . Compositae. 1833. II. 848.[2]
— Descriptions of two new genera of . . . Coniferae. 1838. II. 26.[2]
— Descriptions of two new genera of Nepaul plants. 1822. II. 792.[2]
— An illustration of the natural . . . Melastomaceae. 1822. II. 634.[2]
— On the Indian Cedar. 1825. IV. 448.[1]
— Sur l'irritabilité du stigmate dans le Pinus Larix. 1828. II. 33.[1]
— On the irritability of the stigma. 1828. II. 33.[1]
— On the leaves used by the Chinese in lining tea-chests. 1825. III. 218.[2]
— A list of plants collected by . . . [C. Fellows]. 1841. I. 478.
— A list of plants collected by Charles Fellows. 1841. I. 478.
— Memoir on the classification . . . of Gnaphalium and Xeranthemum. 1824. II. 847.[2]
— On the modifications of aestivation observable in certain plants. 1837. II. 808.[1]
— A monograph of the family of . . . Cunoniaceae. 1830. II. 250.[1]
— Note on the affinities of the " Palo de Vaca." 1827. II. 46.[2]
— Note on the identity of Polystemon. 1830. II. 250.[1]
— Observations on . . . Cobaeaceae. 1824. II. 746.[2]
— Observations on Philadelpheae and Granateae. 1826. II. 237,[2] 610.[2]
— Observations on . . . Polemoniaceae. 1822. II. 746.[2]
— Observations on the affinities of Vellosia. 1830. I. 268.
— Observations on the characters . . . of Darwinia. 1829. I. 267.
— Observations sur la nouvelle famille des Cobœaceés. 1824. II. 746.[2]
— Sur la plante qui fournit l'écorce de Cascarille. 1832. II. 439.[1]
— Prodromus florae nepalensis. 1825. I. 471.
— Remarks on Azalea, Rhododendron. 1822. II. 657.[2]
— Remarks on the rhubarb of commerce. 1827. II. 25,[1] 473.[1]
— Some remarks on the plant which yields the Cascarilla bark. 1832. II. 439.[2]
— Some remarks on the plant which yields the Cascarilla bark. 1834. III. 516.[1]
— On various plants used as tea. 1825. III. 222.
— *See also* SWEET, Robert & DON, David.
Don, George. Account of several new species of Combretum . . . from Sierra Leone. 1824. I. 490.
— A general system of gardening and botany. 1831. I. 260.
— A review of the genus Combretum. 1827. II. 610.[1]
Donald, James. Notes upon Begonias. 1846. III. 618.[1]
Donald, John. Soils and manures. 184 .? III. 151.
Donaldson, Thomas. The public domain. 1884. IV. 271.[2]
Donarelli, Carlo. Enumeratio seminum ex collectione anni 1834 Horti romani. 1834. I. 63.
Donati, Antonio. Trattato de semplici. 1631. I. 285.[1]
Donato d'Eremita. Vera effigie della Granadiglia. 1619. II. 577.[1]
Die **Donauauen** unterhalb Wien's und ihre Bestände. 1890. IV. 369.
Donceel, Henri DONCKIER DE. *See* DONCKIER DE DONCEEL, Henri.
Donck, Adriaen van der. Beschryvinge van Nieuw-Nederlant. 1655. III. 262.[1]
— The representation of New Netherland. 1655. III. 262.[2]
Donckier, A. Stations géologiques de quelques plantes . . . de Limbourg. 1862. I. 392.
Donckier de Donceel, Henri. *See* DURAND, Théophile & DONCKIER DE DONCEEL, Henri.
Donde Ibarra, Joaquín & **Donde Ruiz**, Juan. Apuntes sobre las plantas de Yucatan. 1873. III. 264.[2]
Donde Ruiz, Juan. *See* DONDE IBARRA, Joaquín & DONDE RUIZ, Juan.
Donders, Frans Cornelis. Over de opstijgende beweging der plastische stoffen. 1868. I. 164.
— Der Stoffwechsel, als Quelle der Eigenwärme. 1847. I. 186.
Doni, G. Considerazioni e proposte relative al regime forestale in Italia. 1865. IV. 277.
Doni, Pergentino. Osservazioni sul progettato imboschimento delle crete senesi. 1866. IV. 165.

Donlan, J. I.   Rubber trees at Mr. Frank T. Holder's.   1896. III. 370.[1]
Donn, James.   Hortus cantabrigiensis.   1796.   I. 53.
Donnadieu, A. L.   Sur les deux espèces de phylloxera.   1887. III. 574.
— Sur la ponte du phylloxéra.   1887.   III. 762.
— Sur quelques points controversés de l'histoire du phylloxera. 1887.   III. 574.
— Les véritables origines de la question phylloxérique.   1887. III. 762.
Donnell, Webb.   Draining land with trees and shrubs.   1897. III. 150.[1]
Donnelly, Edward.   On Theobroma Cacao.   1860.   III. 594.
Donner, (*Oberforstmeister*).   Die harte und weiche Seite der Kiefer.   1875.   IV. 480.
Donnersmarck, Leo Victor Felix HENCKEL VON.   See HENCKEL VON DONNERSMARCK, L. V. F.
Donohoe.   Fruit production in California.   1888.   III. 133.
Donop, L. B. van.   Landbouw-vooruitzichten op Borneo. 1883.   III. 128.
Donos, Victor de MARTRIN-.   See MARTRIN-DONOS, Victor de.
Donovan, Edward O.   The botanical review.   1790.   I. 93.
— Essay on the minute parts of plants.   1789.   I. 97.
Donovan, Michael.   On the nature and combinations of a newly discovered vegetable acid.   1815.   I. 180.[1]
Donzelli, Giuseppe.   Additio apologetica ad suam de opo- balsamo orientali synopsin.   1640.   III. 510.[2]
— Lettera familiare . . . sopra Opobalsamo orientale.   1643. II. 417,[2] *III. 510.*[3]
Doolittle, M. H.   The American Mistletoe.   1876.   II. 177.[1]
Doorman, A. J.   Een en ander over cultuur . . . van den wijngaard.   1887.   III. 553.[2]
Doornik, J. J. F. H. T. MERKUS.   See MERKUS DOORNIK, J. J. F. H. T.
Dopontanus, J.   Onderrichting voor den land en tuinman. 1824.   III. 105.
Doppelmair, G.   The protection of railway tracks.   1886. III. 215.[1]
Die Doppelveredlung.   1891.   III. 163.[1]
Dora, KONDA.   See KONDA DORA.
Doran, A.   Sur les propriétés fébrifuges . . . du Laurier. 1872.   III. 406.[2]
Doran, J.   Grape growing.   1868.   III. 550.
Dorat, Charles.   On the production of balsam of Peru.   1861. III. 482.[1]
D'Orbigny, Charles.   Tableau synoptique du règne végétal. 1834.   I. 260.
Dordogne — Société d'horticulture et d'acclimatation.   See SOCIÉTÉ . . . I. 22.
Dorl.   Ein Wort zur Rentabilität . . . des Laubholz-Misch- waldes.   1895.   IV. 138.[1]
Dorl, H.   Die Blutbuche im Klappenthale.   1877.   II. 127.[2]
Dorly-Coldefy.   See COLDEFY-DORLY.
Dormayer, (*Revierförster*).   Zur Vergleichung der Erfolge der Einzelpflanzung . . . der Fichte.   1855.   IV. 453.
Dorn, Paul.   Der Holz- oder Gebäudeschwamm.   1867.   IV. 415.[1]
— De Hout of Gebouwzwam.   1867.   IV. 415.[1]
Dorner, Herman Bernard.   The resin ducts . . . of Abies and Picea.   1900.   II. 18.
Dorotea, L.   Alcune osservazioni sul tavoliere di Puglia. 1863.   IV. 165.[1]
— Sull' amministrazione delle acque e foreste . . . d'Italia. 1862.   IV. 293.[2]
Dorpat — Universitas imperialis jurjevensis.   See UNIVERSI- TAS . . . I. 10.
Dorpater Naturforscher-Gesellschaft.   Archiv.   Sitzungsbe- richte.   I. 9.[2]
Dorrer, August.   Das Ende der Nonnenkalamität.   1893. IV. 201.
— Das Forsteinrichtungsverfahren in Württemberg.   1880. IV. 248.[2]
— Forstwirthschaftliche Reduktions- und Hülfstabellen. 1871.   IV. 214.
— Ein neues forstliches Messinstrument.   1880.   IV. 215.
— Die Nonne.   1891.   IV. 201.
— Die Regulirung der Waldstreunutzungen.   1874.   IV. 437.[2]
— Ueber die Wahl der Holzarten im Gebiete der schwä- bischen Alb.   1873.   IV. 118.
— Die Waldbeschädigungen durch die Nonne.   1891.   IV. 457.
Dorrien, Charles.   Cultivation of the Paulownia.   1852. III. 703.[2]

Dorrien, Sophus von.   Forests and forestry.   1879.   IV. 102.
— Protection of forests a necessity.   1879.   IV. 45, *178.*[1]
The Dorsst Heath.   1898.   III. 651.[1]
Dorsst natural history and antiquarian field club.   Proceed- ings.   I. 18.
Dorstenius, Johann Daniel.   Rei herbariae commentatio. 1675.   I. 287.
Dorstenius, Theodericus.   Botanicon.   1540.   I. 277.
Dorvault, F. L. M.   L'officine.   1844.   III. 255.[2]
— La oficina de farmacia.   1844.   III. 255.[2]
— Revue pharmaceutique.   1844.   III. 255.[2]
Doryphora, (*pseud.*).   Middelen om de Olmen van den Kouter te behouden.   1887.   III. 364.[2]
— Moyens de conserver les Ormes de la Place d'armes.   1887. III. 364.[2]
Dosage du tannin.   1891.   IV. 435.
Dosch, Ludwig & **Scriba,** J.   Excursions-Flora . . . des Grossherzogthums Hessen.   1878.   I. 387.
— — Flora . . . des Grossherzogthums Hessen.   1873.   I. 387.
Dossie, Robert.   The cultivation of Logwood.   1769.   III. 478.[1]
— The cultivation of Olive trees.   1769.   III. 674.[2]
— Encouragement of the production of silk.   1769.   III. 373.
— Importation of Myrtle wax into England.   1769.   III. 352.[1]
— Of improvements relating to our trade with the British colonies.   1769.   III. 32.[1]
— Memoirs of agriculture.   1768.   III. 123.[2]
— The production of pot-ash.   1769.   V. XXXI.[2]
Dott, David B.   The acid of Willow bark.   1877.   III. 351.[1]
— L'acide lactique.   1877.   III. 351.[1]
Dotzauer, J. O. F.   Ueber Baumpflanzung.   1856.   III. 166.
— Ueber eine merkwürdige Lebensthätigkeit eines Cereus grandiflorus.   1838.   II. 590.[1]
Dotzel.   Statische Betrachtungen über die schmalspurigen Waldeisenbahnen.   1900.·   IV. 392.
Dotzel, K.   Handbuch des forstlichen Wege- und Eisenbahn- baues.   1898.   IV. 267.
Douanes et bois de la zone frontière.   1892.   IV. 285.[1]
Double Blackberries.   1882.   III. 458.[1]
Double Cocoanut (Lodoecia Seychellarum).   1853.   III. 327.[1]
The double Cocoanut of the Seychelles Islands.   1892.   III. 327.[1]
The Double Cocoa-nut Palm.   1867.   II. 70.[2]
Double flore parisienne.   See DUPONT, J. D.   1805.   I. 406.
Double-flowered Blackberries.   1879.   III. 457.[1]
Double-flowered Rhododendron.   1878.   III. 658.[2]
A double-flowered Wistaria.   1872.   III. 490.[2]
The double-flowering Cherry.   1879.   III. 435.[1]
The double flowering pink Bramble.   1878.   III. 458.[1]
Double Lagaperia.   1881.   III. 337.[1]
Doubs — Société d'émulation du departement . . . *See* SOCIÉTÉ . . . I. 23.
Doubs — Société d'horticulture . . . III. 22.
Doubs — Société d'horticulture et d'arboriculture.   See SOCIÉTÉ . . . III. 22.
Doue, Bertrand de.   De l'aménagement et de l'exploitation des bois de Pin.   1861.   IV. 462.[1]
Douette-Richardot, Nicolas.   De la pratique de l'agriculture. 1806.   III. 125.
Douglas, David.   An account of a new species of Pinus. 1827.   II. 42.[1]
— An account of some . . . species of the genus Ribes.   1830. II. 243.[1]
— Beschreibung einer neuen Pinus-Art.   1833.   II. 45.[2]
— Description of a new species of the genus Pinus. ·1833. II. 45.[2]
Douglas, J.   The Boronias. .1890.   III. 495.[1]
— Coniferous trees and the late winter.   1891.   III. 293.
Douglas, James.   Arbor Yemensis fructum Cofè fercus. 1727.   II. 814.[2]
— Botanical dissection of the Coffee berry.   1725.   II. 814.[1]
— Supplement to the description of the Coffee tree.   1727. II. 814.[2]
Douglas, Robert.   Abies Engelmanni and A. Menziesii. 1877.   III. 306.[1]
— Ailanthus as a timber tree.   1882.   IV. 525.
— American coniferous forests.   1893.   IV. 338.[1]
— American Pines.   Hardy evergreens.   1896.   III. 293.
— Beech forests.   1883.   III. 360.[1]
— Care in selecting the seeds of trees.   1890.   III. 156.[2]

— The Catalpa for forest-planting. 1894. IV. 538.²
— The conquering Oak. 1885. IV. 507.
— The Corsican Pine for timber. 1885. IV. 466.¹
— The European Larch, its durability. 1873. IV. 452.¹
— Facts in American forest planting. 1885. IV. 525,¹ 533.²
— Forest tree planting on the prairies. 1888. IV. 112.
— Growing deciduous forest trees from seeds. 1888. III. 156.²
—┬Growth of foreign trees in New Hampshire. 1888. III. 17.¹
— Is the White Pine doomed? 1897. IV. 469.
— Notes on the longevity of coniferous tree seeds. 1888. II. 21.¹
— Ornamental trees in California. 1889. III. 60.
— Our coniferous forests. 1893. IV. 338.¹
— Packing nursery trees. 1885. IV. 151.¹
— Propagation of Conifers from seeds in the open air. 1888. III. 294.²
— Range of the White Spruce. 1884. II. 37.²
— Report on new, rare, and valuable Conifers. 1880. III. 292.
— Succession of forest growths. 1882. IV. 74.¹
— Succession of forest growths. 1889. IV. 74.²
— Succession of forests. 1887. IV. 74.²
— Succession of species in forests. 1875. IV. 74.²
— Thoughts on forestry in California. 1888. IV. 112.
— Tree planting in California. 1888. IV. 112.
— & Dawson, Jackson. When to transplant Conifers. 1894. III. 295.¹
Douglas, T. H. The germination of Conifer-seeds. 1897. III. 294.²
— Vaccinium ovatum as a hedge-plant. 1893. III. 664.¹
— The Weeping Spruce. 1892. II. 37.¹
The Douglas Fir. 1887. IV. 484.¹
The Douglas Fir. 1890. II. 49.¹
The Douglas Fir in Scotland. 1889. IV. 484.¹
The Douglas Spruce. 1897. II. 49.¹
Douglass, Robert. See Douglas, Robert.
Douglass, William. A summary . . . of the British settlements in North-America. 1755. IV. 336.³
Doulcet, A. J. B. L. Mémoire sur la destruction des forêts. 1821. IV. 180.²
Douliot, H. Sur le développement de la tige des Conifères. 1890. II. 18.
— Sur les faisceaux médullaires du Phytolacca. 1885. II. 193.¹
— Influence de la lumière sur le développement du liège. 1889. I. 130, 190.²
— Note sur la formation du périderme. 1888. I. 130.
— Note sur la structure des Crassulacées. 1886. II. 235.¹
— Sur le périderme des Légumineuses. 1888. II. 320.²
— Sur le périderme des Rosacées. 1887. II. 256.²
— Recherches sur la croissance terminale de la tige. 1800. I. 106.¹
— Recherches sur le périderme. 1889. I. 130.
— See also Tieghem, Philippe van & Douliot, H.
Die Doum-Palme, Hyphaene thebaica Mart. 1878. III. 325.²
Doumenjou, Hippolyte. Critique du projet de loi de l'application de l'expropriation. 1877. IV. 276.¹
— Études sur la revision du code forestier. 1883. IV. 163.
— Influence des bois sur l'atmosphère. 1880. IV. 34.
Doumenjou, Jean Bazille. Herborisations sur la Montagne-Noire. 1848. I. 410.
Doumergue, François. Contributions à la flore de Montolieu. 1885. II. 497.¹
— Les hauts plateaux oranais. 1897. I. 486.
— Note sur trois espèces algériennes.¨ 1888.¨ II. 374.²·
— Notes sur quelques plantes . . ; d'Oran. 1896. I. 486.
Doûmet-Adanson, Paul Napoléon. Sur l'Acacia gummifère. 1875. III. 466.¹
— De Biskra à Ouargla. 1893. I. 486.
'— Sur un cas de tératologie . . . de Rosa Fortunei. 1879. II. 293.²
— Description des Figues comestibles. 1870. II. 150.¹
— Evonymus japonica elegans. 1871. III. 532.³
— Sur les forêts de la Corse. 1872. IV. 360.
— Note sur l'Acacia gommifère de la Tunisie. 1874. II. 323,¹ III. 465.¹
— Note sur la floraison du Pilocereus Celsianus. 1879. III. 626.¹
— ̌Note sur un Sapin hybride. 1889. II. 23.¹
— Le Pachira (Carolinea) à fleurs blanches. 1866. II. 530.² — D'une production de rameaux sur des fruits d'Opuntia. 1858. II.¨596.¹

— Rapport sur l'hygroscope à branche de Sapin. 1866. III. 295.²
— Rapport sur une mission botanique¨. . . dans la région sabarienne. 1888. I. 485.
— Une semaine d'herborisation en Corse. 1865. I. 535.
— Souvenir d'une herborisation au Mont Viso. 1861. I. 412.
— L'utilité des arbres. 1889. IV. 164.¹
Doundaké en zijn bast. 1885. III. 747.²
Douteau, Jules J. Flore de Vendée. 1896. I. 418.
— Flore de Vendée; tableaux dichotomiques des plantes vasculaires recueillies en Vendée jusqu'à nos jours. 1896. I. 418.
Douy, J. Nouveau manuel de botanique. 1836. I. 87.
— Physique végétale. 1832. I. 148.
Douzième exposition de plantes de la Société d'agriculture hollandaise. 1859. II. 586.²
The Dovaston Yew. 1900. III. 288.¹
Dove, Heinrich Wilhelm. Über den Zusammenhang der Wärmeveränderungen der Atmosphäre. 1846. I. 231.²
Doveton, John Chadwick. Note on the Dendrocalamus strictus. 1883. IV. 485.¹
Dowden, Richard. Walks after wild flowers. 1852. I. 95, 400.
Dowling, Robert. Brugmansia sanguinea. 1856. III. 700.¹
Downar, N. Enumeratio plantarum circa Mohileviam ad Borysthenem. 1861. I. 362.
Downes, W. H. The Arnold Arboretum. 1898.¨ III. 27.²
Downey, John G. More about Orange culture. 1874. III. 500.¹
Downie, John. Large trees in the western Highlands of Scotland. 1886. I. 297.¹
Downing, Andrew Jackson. The fruits and fruit trees of America. 1845. III. 61.¹
— Rural essays. 1857. III. 117.²
— A treatise on the theory and practice of landscape gardening. 1841. III. 201.
Downing, Charles. Chinese Sand Pear. 1880. III. 447.¹
— Selected fruits from Downing's Fruits and fruit-trees of America. 1871. III. 61.²
— Willows and Willow culture. 1854. III. 347.
Downing, Charles Toogood. On Norfolk Island. 1859. III. 283.¹
Doyet, A. See Caplain, Jh. & Doyet, A.
— dr. Einige Betrachtungen über die Forste . . . des Marsgebirges. 1890. IV. 369.
Draakestein, H. A. van Rheede tot. See Rheede tot Draakestein, H. A. van.
Dracaena Draco (the Dragon tree). 1885. II. 82.²
Dracaena Godseffiana, eine nachdenkliche Geschichte. 1893. III. 336.²
Drack, Ed. Der Obstbau. Ein Leitfaden. 1900. III. 146.¹
Draft forest office and account code. 1876. IV. 295.¹
Dragoblostrmdot paa Teneriffa. 1860. II. 80.³
Dragendorff, Georg. Analysen von Aepfeln. 1881. II. 267.²
— Ueber die Beziehungen zwischen chemischen Bestandtheilen und botanischen Eigenthümlichkeiten. 1879. I. 151.²
— Chemische Analyse der Blätter des Memecylon tinctorium. 1882. II. 639.³
— Chemische Beiträge zur Pomologie. 1878. II. 267.²
— Ueber einen an der Betula . . . vorkommenden Pilz. 1864. IV. 490.¹
— Ueber einige in Turkestan gebräuchliche Heilmittel. 1872. III. 91,¹ 272.²
— Die Heilpflanzen der verschiedenen Völker. 1898. III. 239.
— Die qualitative und quantitative Analyse. 1882. I. 156.¹
— Quantitative Bestimmung des Strychnin. 1866. III. 683.¹
— Zur Volksmedicin Turkestans. 1873. III. 91.¹
— Ueber das wirksame Princip . . . der Sennesblätter. 1866. III. 470.²
— & Kondracki, Eugen. Sur l'Aloès. 1875. III. 333.²
The Dragon tree (Dracaena Draco). 1872. II. 82.¹
The Dragon tree of Ajuda. 1880. II. 82.²
Dragon trees in Madeira. 1888. II. 82.¹
Le Dragonnier et l'allée des Palmiers. 1899. III. 336.²
Dragon's blood. 1893. III. 336.³
Dragon's blood of Africa. 1879. III. 336.²
Dragon's Blood tree of the West Indies. 1893. III. 485.¹
Draguignan — Société d'études scientifiques . . . See Société . . . I. 23.
Die Drahtriesen in Südtirol. 1859. IV. 391.

Die Drahtseilbahn als rationelles Transportmittel. 1884. IV. 391.

Drais, Friedrich Heinrich Georg, *Freyherr* von. Ueber den Lerchenbaum. 1801. IV. 448.[2]

— Nachricht von der Einrichtung der Privat-Forst-Lehranstalt in Schwetzingen. 1807. IV. 31.

— Versuch eines Lehrbuchs der Forstwissenschaft. 1807. IV. 96.

— Weitershausen, *Freiherr* von & **Gatterer**, C. W. J. Abhandlungen vom Lerchenbaum. 1801. IV. 448.[3]

Drake, Daniel. Natural and statistical view of Cincinnati. 1815. *III. 263.[1]

Drake del Castillo, Emmanuel. Contribution à la flore de l'Amérique équatoriale. 1889. I. 330.

— Contributions à l'étude de la flore du Tonkin. 1890. I. 469.[2]

— Sur deux genres de Madagascar . . . des Composées. 1899. II. 849.[2]

— Sur la distribution géographique des Cyrtandrées. 1894. II. 792.[2]

— Flore de la Polynésie française. 1893. I. 509.[2]

— Sur la géographie botanique des Îles de la Société. 1887. I. 510.[2]

— Illustrationes florae insularum maris pacifici. 1886. I. 509.[2]

— Note sur deux genres de Rubiacées. 1898. II. 808.[1]

— Note sur le genre Pyrostria. 1898. II. 829.[1]

— Note sur le Wickstroemia Balansae. 1899. II. 606,[2] 778.[2]

— Note sur les Araliées . . . de l'Afrique orientale. 1897. II. 646.[2]

— Note sur quelques plantes nouvelles. 1896. I. 496.

— Note sur un genre nouveau du Tonkin. 1896. II. 146.[2]

— Note sur une plante nouvelle des Andes. 1892. II. 778.[2]

— Note sur une Thyméléacée nouvelle. 1889. I. 606.[2]

— Remarques sur la flore de la Polynésie. 1890. I. 509.[2]

— Sur les Rubiacées de la flore de Madagascar. 1898. II. 708.[1]

— De la véritable place du genre Fitchia. 1898. II. 857.[2]

— *See also* BAILLON, Henri & DRAKE DE CASTILLO, Emmanuel.

Dralet. Description des Pyrénées. 1813. IV. 359.[2]

— Recherches sur les Chênes à glands doux. 1812. IV. 502.[1]

— Traité de l'aménagement des bois. 1807. IV. 239.

— Traité des délits, des peines et des procédures en matière d'eaux et forêts. 1818. IV. 323.[2]

— Traité des forêts d'arbres résineux. 1807. IV. 239.

— Traité du Hêtre. 1824. IV. 493.[2]

— Traité du régime forestier. 1812. IV. 292.

Draparnaud, Jacques Philippe Raymond. Dissertation sur l'utilité de l'histoire naturelle. 1803. III. 238.[1]

Draper, John William. A treatise on the forces which produce the organization of plants. 1844. I. 147.

Draper, Walter. Gardening in Egypt. 1895. III. 116.[1]

— Le jardinage en Égypte. 1895. III. 116.[1]

Drapiez, Pierre Auguste Joseph. Dictionnaire classique des sciences naturelles. 1837. I. 34.

— Herbier de l'amateur de fleurs. 1828. I. 267.

— Notice sur le Nhandirobe. 1819. II. 844.[3]

Draudt. Baumrodemaschine aus Nassau. 1870. IV. 386.

Draudt, August. Die Ermittelung der Holzmassen, 1860. IV. 217.

Draudt, Eduard. Baumrodemaschine aus Nassau. 1864. IV. 386.

Drayton, John. A view of South Carolina. 1802. I. 318.

Drechsler, Gustav. Ueber den Einfluss, welchen der Feuchtigkeitszustand . . . des Holzes auf die Verkohlung . . . äussert. 1841. IV. 394.

— Die Forsten des Königreichs Hannover. 1851. IV. 352.

Drège, Johann Franz. Catalog südafricanischer getrockneter Pflanzen. 1840. I. 494.

— Catalogus plantarum . . . Africae australioris. 1837. I. 494.

— Vergleichung der von Ecklon und Zeyher und von Drège gesammelten südafrikanischen Pflanzen. 1847. I. 494.

— Zwei pflanzengeographische Documente. 1843. I. 494.

Die drei stärksten Eichen der Mark Brandenburg. 1894. IV. 516.[1]

Dreier, Johann, Focke, W. O. & **Kottmeier**, Johann. Flora bremensis. 1855. I. 383.

300 Jahre alte Buche. 1899. I. 210,[3] IV. 497.

Dreissig, Friedr. Aug. Praktische Behandlung der Hortensia mutabilis. 1812. III. 412.[1]

Dreixhe, N. L'Airelle-myrtille. 1897. IV. 534.[2]

Drejer, Solomon Thomas Nicolai. Elementa phyllologiae. 1840. I. 109.[2]

— Flora excursoria hafniensis. 1838. I. 353.

— Van Mons's Theorie. 1841. I. 247.

Dresden — Gesellschaft für Natur- und Heilkunde. *See* GESELLSCHAFT . . . I. 12.

Dresden — Naturwissenschaftliche Gesellschaft Isis. *See* NATURWISSENSCHAFTLICHE . . . . I. 13.

Dresden — Verein für Erdkunde. *See* VEREIN . . . I. 15.

Dresser, Christopher. On the morphological import of certain vegetable organs. 1860. I. 99.

— The rudiments of botany. 1859. I. 90.

— On the stem or axis as the fundamental organ. 1860. I. 105.

Dressler, Christian. Anweisung zu einer guten . . . Abwartung der Obstgärten. 1804. III. 136.

Dressler, Eugen. Die fiscalischen Sägewerke der Oberförsterei St. Quirin. 1880. IV. 393.

— Die Weisstanne . . . auf dem Vogesensandstein. 1880. IV. 444.[2]

Dreuilhe, Auguste. Les Ménispermées et leurs produits. 1887. III. 396.[1]

Dreves, Johann Friedrich Peter. Botanisches Bilderbuch. 1794. I. 375.

— Getreue Abbildungen und Zergliederungen deutscher Gewächse, von Fr. Dreves & Friedrich Gottlob Hayne. 1794. I. 375.

— & **Hayne**, F. G. Choix de plantes d'Europe. 1802. I. 348.[2]

Drew, W. C. L. Ceanothus. 1878. III. 541.[1]

— Rhododendron occidentale. 1878. III. 661.[1]

Drew log scale. 1897. IV. 229.

Drewsen, J. C. Om Morbærtræet. 1841. III. 376.

Dreyer. Sur une Badiane dangereuse. 1884. III. 398.[1]

Dreyfus, Ludwig, T. Ueber Phylloxerinen. 1889. III. 762.

Driberg, C. E. On the culture of the Cocoanut tree in Ceylon. 1839. III. 322.[2]

Driessche, P. van den. Flore, productions . . . de l'Afrique équatoriale. 1885. III. 131.[1]

Driessen, Petrus. Index plantarum quae in Horto academico groningano, 1820. I. 51.[1]

Driessen Mareeuw, W. P. H. van den. De afscheiding . . . van het alkaloide uit de Kopsia. 1896. II. 727.

— Colorimetrische alkaloide-bepaling. 1896. III. 724.[1]

— Een kleine bijdrage tot de kennis van het Maripavet. 1900. III. 327.[1]

— Onderzoek van cortex Lokri. 1899. III. 478.[2]

Drift, J. van der. Duinbeplanting. 1874. IV. 160.[1]

Driftsplanens Betydning for Skovbrugets Praksis. 1891. IV. 246.

Driver, A. & W. The pomona britannica. 1788. III. 78.[2]

Driz, MOHAMMED BEN. *See* MOHAMMED BEN DRIZ.

Droèze, F. J. HAVER. *See* HAVER DROEZE, F. J.

Droinet, Felix. Allgemeine Betrachtungen über ein neues Verkohlungs-Verfahren. 1839. IV. 327.[1]

Droit de chasse. Compétence divisée. 1900. IV. 327.[1]

Droit de pâture. Compétence divisée. Conseil de préfecture. 1900. IV. 327.[1]

Les droits d'entrée sur les bois. 1895. IV. 552.[2]

Les droits d'entrée sur les bois. Décision au Sénat. 1895. IV. 552.[2]

Droits d'usage dans vingt sept mille arpens de forêts. *See* GEORGEL. IV. 333.

Droits de douane sur les bois. 1900. IV. 285.[1]

Les droits protecteurs sur les bois. 1894. IV. 552.[2]

Droixhe, N. Le Genêt à halai. 1897. IV. 521.[2]

— La tisane de feuilles de Bouleau. 1897. IV. 491.[3]

Dromard. Landes de Gascogne . . . incendies dans les forêts. 1872. IV. 183.[1]

Dromart, Ed. Étude sur les landes de la Gascogne. 1898. IV. 362.

— Mémoire sur la carbonisation des bois. 1876. IV. 394.

— Utilisation de produits d'éclaircie par la carbonisation. 1879. IV. 395.

Dronke, Ad. Abnorme Fruchtbildung bei Prunus Armeniaca. 1862. II. 272.[3]

Dronke, F. Note sur de nouvelles analyses chimiques relatives à la maladie des vers à soie. 1866. III. 380.[1]

Drooping deciduous trees. 1867. III. 204.[1]

Drope, Francis. A short and sure guide in the practice of raising and ordering of fruit-trees. 1672. III. 141.

Dropisch, Bernhard. Holzstoff und Holzcellulose. 1879. IV. 429.

The **Dropmore** pinetum. 1872. I. 55.

Drouard, Ch. Maladie de la Vigne. 1858. III. 577.

Drouet, Henri. Catalogue de la flore des îles Açores. 1866. I. 497.

Drouet, Paul. Notes sommaires sur l'arboriculture . . . aux États-Unis. 1894. III. 116.[2]

Drouin, A. Barême de toisés pour les bois équarris. n. d. IV. 213.

Drouin, R. *See* GAUTIER, Armand & DROUIN, R.

Drouyn de Lhuys. Sur la découverte . . . d'un insect qui attaque la Vigne. 1870. III. 563.

Drown, Solomon. *See* DROWN, William & Solomon.

Drown, William & Solomon. Compendium of agriculture. 1824. III. 99.

Droz. Instruction pour le levé de détail des forêts. 1883. IV. 265.

— Instruction sur la triangulation de IV e ordre. 1882. IV. 265.

— Instruktion für die Detailvermessung der Waldungen. 1883. IV. 265.

— Instruktion für die Triangulation IV. Ordnung. 1882. IV. 265.

Druce, George Claridge. Acer campestre L. 1891. II. 477.²

— The flora of Berkshire. 1897. I. 404.¹

— The flora of Oxfordshire. 1886. I. 403.

Drude, Oscar. Anleitung zu phytophänologischen Beobachtungen. 1882. I. 221.

— Die Anwendung physiologischer Gesetze zur Erklärung der Vegetationslinien. 1876. I. 217.

— Atlas der Pflanzenverbreitung. 1887. I. 301.

— Ausgewählte Beispiele . . . der Fruchtbildung bei den Palmen. 1877. II. 63.¹

— Über die australischen Livistona-Arten. 1893. II. 70.¹

— Ueber den Bau . . . der Gattung Carludovica. 1877. II. 76.¹

— Bemerkungen zur Nomenclatur und Kulturfähigkeit der . . . Palmen. 1882. II. 61.¹

— Bericht über die Isis-Fahrt nach den Central-Karpathen. 1894. I. 446.

— Clethraceae. 1891. II. 657.¹

— Cyclanthaceae. 1889. II. 76.¹

— Cyclanthaceae et Palmae. 1881. II. 61,² 76.¹

— Deutschlands Pflanzengeographie. 1896. I. 389.

— Diapensiaceae. 1889. II. 691.¹

— Die einheitliche Entstehung neuer Pflanzenarten. 1886. I. 243.¹

— Epacridaceae. 1891. II. 688.¹

— Die Ergebnisse der in Sachsen . . . angestellten pflanzenphänologischen Beobachtungen. 1892. I. 225.

— Ericaceae. 1891. II. 638.¹

— Die Florenreiche der Erde. 1884. I. 300.

— Führer durch den botanischen Garten in Dresden. 1894. III. 28.¹

— Ueber die Gattung Trithrinax. 1878. II. 75.¹

— Die geographische Verbreitung der Palmen. 1878. II. 60.²

— Der Haarfilz der Platanen-Blätter. 1889. III. 419.¹

— Handbuch der Pflanzengeographie. 1890. I. 301.

— Ueber die Herkunft der . . . verwendeten Gewächse. 1899. III. 70.

— Manuel de géographie botanique. 1890. I. 301.

— Die natürliche systematische Anordnung der Blüthenpflanzen. 1887. I. 261.

— Palmae. 1889. II. 61.¹

— Die Palmenflora des tropischen Afrika. 1896. II. 62.¹

— Pirolaceae. 1891. II. 657.²

— Über die Principien in der Unterscheidung von Vegetationsformationen. 1890. I. 389.

— Pritchardia Thurstoni F. v. M. et Dr. 1887. II. 74.¹

— Resultate der floristischen Reisen in Sachsen. 1899. I. 390.

— Studien über die Conservirungsmethoden des Holzes. 1889. IV. 420.

— Ueber die Trennung der Palmen Amerika's. 1876. II. 60.²

— Umbelliferae. 1898. II. 653.¹

— Die Unterscheidungsmerkmale der Palmen Howea. 1897. II. 69.¹

— Untersuchungen über klimatische Grenzen exotischer Bäume. 1900. III. 46.¹

— Die Vegetationsformationen . . . der Flora saxonica. 1889. I. 389.

— Das Verfahren der Japaner zur Erzielung langlebiger Zwergformen. 1889. III. 175.²

— Die Vertheilung östlicher Pflanzengenossenschaften in der sächsischen Elbthal-Flora. 1896. I. 389.

— Ueber das Vorkommen der Riesengebirgs-Race von Pinus montana. 1882. II. 45.¹

— Ueber das Vorkommen von Alnus viridis DC. in Sachsen. 1892. II. 117.¹

— *See also* ENGLER, Adolf & DRUDE, Oscar; KOEHNE, Emil; VOCKE, A. & DRUDE, Oscar; WENDLAND, Hermann & DRUDE, Oscar. .

— & Brandt, R. Cocos australis. 1889. III. 322.²

Drümpelmann, Ernst Wilhelm. Flora livonica. 1810. I. 360.

Druery, Charles T. Codiaeum pictum. 1900. II. 439.¹

— Gutta percha. 1900. III. 232.²

— A medicinal Mistleto. 1896. III. 385.¹

— Pollen grains. 1900. I. 117.¹

Druggist's bulletin. III. 3.

Druggists' circular. *See* AMERICAN druggists' circular . . . I. 4.¹

Druman, J. C. Verhandeling over de Castanjeboomen. 1780. III. 358.²

Drummond, Andrew Thomas. The affinities of the tendrils in the Virginian Creeper. 1887. II. 504.²

— Canadian timber trees. 1879. IV. 397,¹ V. xxxi.²

— Distribution . . . in its relation to climate. 1885. I. 309.²

— The distribution . . . of British North American plants. 1887. I. 310.

— The distribution of Canadian forest trees. 1885. I. 309,² IV. 76.²

— Forest preservation in Canada. 1885. IV. 178.¹

— Observations on Canadian geographical botany. 1864. I. 310.

— Our northwest prairies. 1887. I. 320, IV. 78.¹

Drummond, Gregor. Abstract of a memoir on the cultivation of French Pears. 1842. III. 142.

Drummond, H. Useful products of western Australia. 1862. III. 282.²

Drummond, James. On the botany . . . of western Australia. 1853. I. 501.

— Discovery of three remarkable plants in southwest Australia. 1848. I. 501.

— Extracts . . . relating to the botany of Swan River. 1853. I. 501.

Drummond, James L. First steps to botany. 1823. I. 85.

— Observations on natural systems of botany. 1849. I. 252.

Drummond, Malcolm. Report on the cultivation of Citrons or Cedrats. 1891. III. 502.¹

Drummond-Hay. *See* HAY, DRUMMOND-.

The Drumsheugh Rhododendrons. 1864. III. 654.²

Drunken, Ernest. The legislative outlook for forestry in Wisconsin. 1900. IV. 272.

Drury, Heber. Handbook of the Indian flora. 1864. I. 473.

— The useful plants of India. 1858. III. 92.²

Drury, W. D. The book of gardening. 1900. III. 83.²

The dry-rot. 1889. IV. 415.¹

Dry-rot in enclosed timber. 1879. IV. 415.¹

Dry rot in timber. 1884. IV. 420.

Dry rot in timber. 1887. IV. 415.¹

Dryander, Jonas. Bemerkungen über die Gattung Begonia. 1791. II. 583.²

— Botanical description of the Benjamin tree. 1787. II. 704.²

— Botanische Beschreibung von dem Benzoe-Baum. 1787. II. 704.²

— Catalogus bibliothecae historico-naturalis Josephi Banks. 1796. I. 1.

— Desiderata pro Bibliotheca Banksiana. 1790. I. 1.

— Un genera and species of plants which occur twice or three times. 1794. I. 264.

— Observations on the genus of Begonia. 1791. II. 583.¹

Dryfhout, J. F. Wortelschieting. 1760. I. 188.

Drymmer, Karol. Spis roślin, zawartych w XIV tomach "Pamiętnika fizyograficznego." 1898. I. 367.

— Wycieczka botaniczna w północne okolice Augostowskiego. 1887. I. 365.

Drysdale, A. T. Forestry in India. 1884. IV. 378.

— Light grazing in the Berar forests. 1885. IV. 197.²

Drysdale, T. C. Gambier, as a preservative of timber. 1850. III. 748,¹ IV. 417.¹

Dubarle. Cours d'arboriculture. 1868. III. 110.²

Dubbe, Carl. Medicinsk användning af bären af Myrtillus nigra. 1750. III. 664.¹

Dubigadoux & Durieu. Sur la présence de la strophantine dans le Laurier-rose d'Algérie. 1898. III. 689.²

Dublin — Botanical school of Trinity college. *See* BOTANICAL . . . I. 17.

Dublin — Royal Dublin society. *See* ROYAL . . . I. 19.

Dublin review. IV. 539.¹

Dublin university magazine. I. 18.

Dublin university zoological and botanical association. Proceedings. I. 18.

Dubliner Pharmakopöe. *See* PHARMACOPOEA Collegii regii medicorum dublinensis. 1818. III. 254.
Du Bochet, L. L'utilité des forêts. 1898. IV. 271.[1]
Dubois. Charrue forestière. 1860. IV. 143.[1]
Dubois. De la culture des.différentes espèces de Pins. 1823. IV. 460.[3]
Dubois, Alphonse. Les oiseaux de nos forêts. 1898. IV. 91.[1]
— Traité d'entomologie horticole. 1865. III. 189.
Dubois, Constance G. The Torrey Pine. 1898. II. 48.[3]
Du Bois, E., (*jr*.). Bemesting van Koffietuinen. 1900. III. 734.[1]
— Bemesting van Koffietuinen en het weerstandsvermogen der Koffieboomen. 1899. III. 734.[1]
— Bemesting van Koffietuinen met dierlijken en anderen afval der ondernemingen. 1899. III. 734.[1]
— De beteekenis der Leguminosen vor den Koffieplanter. 1900. III. 734.[1]
— Het kalkgehalte onzer Koffiegronden. 1899. III. 731.
— Over de Koffiebladziekte. 1900. III. 737.
— Koffiezaad. 1885. III. 733.[1]
— Over de Mycorhiza van den Koffiewortel. 1899. III. 737.
— Het onderaardsch gedeelte van den Koffieboom. 1899. III. 727.
— Over voortbrenging . . . van Koffie. 1886. III. 740.[1]
— Zaadselectie bij de Koffiecultuur. 1900. III. 733.[3]
Dubois, Fr. Matière médicale indigène. 1848. III. 85.
Dubois, François. Excursion forestière en 1893. 1894. IV. 555.[1]
— Excursion forestière en 1894; 1re journée. 1895. IV. 556.[1]
Dubois, François Noël Alexandre. Méthode éprouvée . . . à connoître les plantes de l'intérieur de la France. 1803. I. 406.
Dubois, G. L'Oxycoccus palustris. 1886. III. 664.[3]
Du Bois, Louis. L'amateur des fruits. 1836. III. 143.
— Considérations culturales sur les futaies de Chêne. 1856. IV. 505.
— Notice sur le Chevalier de Clieu. 1855. III. 739.
— Du Pommier, du Poirier. 1804. III. 444.[1]
— Travaux de reboisement . . . dans le Blésois. 1862. IV. 149,[1] 162.
Dubois de Montpéreux, Frédéric. Voyage autour du Caucase. *See* GODET, Charles. 1840. I. 368.[1]
Dubourg, Jacques BARBEU-. *See* BARBEU-DUBOURG, Jacques.
Du Breuil, Alphonse. Sur l'accroissement . . . de quelques souches. 1848. I. 209.[3]
— Action du soleil couchant sur le tronc. 1851. III. 184.[1]
— Aubépine de Bouquetot. 1849. II. 263.[1]
— Choix des graines . . . fais du semis des Pistachiers. 1856. III. 526.[1]
— Cours d'arboriculture. 1873. III. 144.
— Cours élémentaire . . . d'arboriculture. 1846. III. 110.[1]
— Création et entretien des haies vives. 1856. III. 213.
— Culture des arbres . . . à fruits de table. 1868. III. 144.
— Culture des arbres et arbrisseaux d'ornement. 1875. III. 110.[3]
— Culture perfectionnée . . . du vignoble. 1863. III. 555.
— Effets d'une décortication partielle. 1873. III. 537.[1]
— Expériences relatives à la transplantation des plantes ligneuses. 1877. III. 168.[3]
— Instruction élémentaire.sur la condúite des arbres fruitiers. 1854. III. 143.
— Laps de temps qui doit s'écouler entre la plantation . . . et leur première taille. 1854. III. 172.
— Manuel d'arboriculture des ingénieurs. 1860. III. 110.[3]
— Le Néflier du Japon. 1876. III. 423.[3]
— Neueste Methode des Schnittes . . . der Obstbäume. 1860. III. 137.
— Notes sur deux nouvelles formes applicables aux arbres fruitiers en espaliers. 1842. III. 172.
— Principes généraux d'arboriculture. 1876. III. 36.[1]
— Quelques notes sur l'accroissement des arbres. 1847. I. 187, 189, 297.[3]
— The science and practice of grafting . . . fruit trees. 1854. III. 143.
— The scientific and profitable culture of fruit trees. 1854. III. 143.
— Theoretisch-praktische Anleitung zur Baumzucht. 1846. III. 110.[1]
— Les vignobles et les arbres à fruits. 1875. III. 144.
— Vineyard culture improved. 1863. III. 555.
— *See also* ДЮ БРЕЙЛЬ, А.
Dubreuil, H. Histoire naturelle . . . de quelques . . . Euphorbiacées. 1835. III. 514.[1]

Dubrulle, Louis. Cours d'arboriculture fruitière. 1880. III. 140.[3]
Dubrunfaut. Sur l'influence de la lumière. 1868. I. 230.
— Mémoire sur les sucres. 1849. III. 582.
— Note sur l'inuline. 1856. I. 175.
— Statique de la lumière. 1868. I. 230.
Dubuisson. Mémoire sur les acides natifs du verjus de l'Orange. 1783. II. 402.[1]
Du Buisson, Édouard. L'Île de la Réunion en 1889. 1889. III. 130.[1]
Dubuisson, J. R. Jacquelin. Essai sur les propriétés de la force vitale. 1846. I. 146.
— Plantes usuelles indigènes et exotiques. 1809. III. 51, 55.
Du Buysson, H. Étude historique & botanique de la Coca. 1892. III. 493.[3]
Duby, Jean Étienne. Géographie botanique de l'Espagne. 1854. I. 421.
— Mémoire sur la famille des Primulacées. 1844. II. 695.[3]
— Note sur une maladie des feuilles de la Vigne. 1836. III. 575.[1]
— Primulaceae. 1844. II. 695.[3]
Ducamp, Roger. Administration des forêts des Indes anglaises. 1899. IV. 378.
— L'Association forestière américaine. 1900. IV. 39.[1]
— Construction d'esquifs et de pirogues. 1900. IV. 425.[3] -
— Les forêts des Indes. 1899. IV. 124.[3]
— La houille blanche. 1900. IV. 52.
— Naissance du régime forestier aux États-Unis. 1899. IV. 288.[1]
— Navigabilité de la Loire. 1900. IV. 47.[3]
— Œuvre chinoise. 1900. IV. 283.[3]
— La question forestière en Annam. 1900. IV. 377.[1]
Ducarel, Andrew Coltee. Letter from Dr. Ducarel to Dr. William Watson. 1772. II. 123.[3]
Ducatel, J. T. Outlines of the physical geography of Maryland. 1837. I. 318.
Duchartre, Henri. Observation de feuilles de Marronnier d'Inde hâtivement desséchées. 1888. III. 537.[3]
Duchartre, Pierre Étienne Simon. Aristolochiaceae. 1864. II. 180.[3]
— Botanique phanérogamique. 1862. II. 154.[1]
— Sur un cas de grossissement . . . du Cycas revoluta. 1862. II. 5.[1]
— La décomposition de l'acide carbonique par les feuilles. 1866. I. 172.
— Dernières réflexions au sujet de la production des matières saccharoïdes. 1876. I. 175.
— Dimensions de quelques Palmiers . . . de Kew. 1855. III. 316.[3]
— L'eau de la pluie . . . est-elle absorbée directement? 1860. I. 161.
— Éléments de botanique. 1867. I. 91.
— Époques de végétation pour un même arbre. 1880. II. 482.[1]
— Erythrina (hybr.) Marie Bellanger. 1861. II. 357.[1]
— Examen physiologique des cultures forcées de Lilas. 1860. III. 176.[3]
— Expériences relatives à l'influence de la lumière sur l'enroulement des tiges. 1865. I. 196.[1]
— Expériences sur des boutures droites et renversées. 1854.- I. 208,[1] 527.
— Expériences sur la décoloration des fleurs du Lilas. 1863. II. 716.[1]
— Expériences sur la décoloration des fleurs du Syringa. 1863. II. 716.[1]
— Expériences sur le développement . . . des bourgeons. 1865. I. 108,[1] 232.[1]
— Expériences sur le développement . . . des bourgeons dans la Vigne. 1865. II. 508.[1]
— Famille des Aristolochiées. 1854. II. 180.[3]
— Fleur double d'un Bouvardia. 1884. II. 810.[1]
— Formación del almidón en las hojas. 1886. IV. 543.[1]
— Formation.de.l'amidon dans les feuilles. 1886. IV. 64,[1] 543.[1]
— Sur la géographie botanique des environs de Béziers. 1844. I. 410.
— Inoculation de la panachure par la greffe. 1870. III. 39.
— La maladie des Châtaigniers. 1879. III. 359.[3]
— Manuel général des plantes. Vol. IV. *See* JACQUES, A. & HÉRINCQ, F. Manuel général des plantes. 1847. I. 269.
— Mémoire sur les embryons . . . polycotylés. 1848. I. 122.
— Monographie de la famille des Aristolochiées. 1854. II. 181.[1]

— Monstruosité foliaire et florale d'une Clématite. 1893. II. 196.[1]
— Le Muscadier. 1856. III. 402.[2]
— Note sur des fleurs monstrueuses de Grenadier. 1879. II. 611.[1]
— Note sur deux Roses prolifères. 1887. II. 290.[1]
— Note sur l'enracinement de l'albumen d'un Cycas. 1888. II. 4.[1]
— Note sur l'organogénie . . . des Malvacées. 1844. II. 519.[2]
— Note sur la sécrétion salée du Tamarix gallica. 1861. II. 562.[2]
— Note sur le bois de Phytolacca dioica. 1886. II. 193.[1]
— Note sur les aiguillons du Rosa sericea. 1893. II. 298.[2]
— Note sur les fleurs doubles du Bouvardia leiantha. 1884. III. 711.[2]
— Note sur les ovaires infères . . . des Pomacées. 1891. II. 257.[1]
— Note sur trois fleurs monstrueuses. 1861. II. 294.[1]
— Note sur une feuille monstrueuse de Tilleul. 1857. II. 516.[1]
— Note sur une monstruosité de Rose. 1858. II. 294.[1]
— Note sur une poire monstrueuse. 1879. II. 280.[1]
— Note sur une Rose prolifère. 1886. II. 289.[2]
— Notice sur l'Aristolochia lineata. 1855. III. 386.[2]
— Notice sur le Jardin d'essai ou du Hamma. 1880. I. 68.[2]
— Notiz über die gefüllten Blumen der Bouvardia leiantha Benth. 1884. II. 810.[1]
— Nouvelles observations sur les aiguillons du Rosa sericea. 1893. II. 298.[2]
— Observations sur des Marronniers. 1879. II. 482.[1]
— Observations sur l'accroissement. 1866. I. 191.[1]
— Observations sur l'organogénie de la fleur. 1844. I. 114,[1] 117.[2]
— Observations sur l'organogénie . . . des Malvacées. 1845. II. 519.[2]
— Observations sur l'organogénie florale . . . des Nyctaginées. 1848. II. 190.[2]
— Observations sur la transpiration des plantes pendant la nuit. 1857. I. 166.
— Sur les Orangers cultivés . . . à Roquebrun. 1863. III. 499.[2]
— Origine probable des Poiriers cultivés. 1873. II. 279.[1]
— Pays d'origine de nos principaux végétaux cultivés. 1900. I. 242.[2]
— Pays d'origine de nos principaux végétaux cultivés. 1894. I. 242.[1]
— Présentation de cônes de Sequoia gigantea. 1863. III. 310.[1]
— Sur les prétendues stipules des Aristoloches. 1854. III. 181.[1]
— Prix Bordin. Question . . . Étudier la distribution des vaisseaux du latex. 1861. I. 135.
— Quelques mots sur le développement des boutures courtes de la Vigne. 1865. II. 508.[1]
— Quelques observations relativement à l'influence de la lumière sur la maturation du raisin. 1882. II. 505.[1]
— Quelques remarques sur la théorie de l'extinction par vieillesse. 1869. I. 248.[1]
— Rapport de la Commission d'enquête sur l'hivre de 1879–1880. 1880. III. 48.
— Recherches expérimentales sur la respiration des plantes. 1856. I. 170.
— Recherches expérimentales sur la transpiration des plantes dans les milieux humides. 1858. I. 166.
— Recherches expérimentales sur les rapports des plantes avec l'humidité atmosphérique. 1856. I. 232.[2]
— Recherches expérimentales sur les rapports des plantes avec la rosée. 1861. I. 232.[2]
— Recherches sur la végétation . . . des Aristolochiées. 1854. II. 180.[2]
— Recherches sur les rapports des plantes avec la rosée. 1857. I. 232.[2]
— Sur une soudure de deux rameaux de Vigne. 1856. II. 507.[1]
— Tentamen methodicae divisionis generis Aristolochia. 1854. II. 181.[1]
— Végétation de quelques Marroniers hatifs. 1880. II. 481.[1]
Duchassaing, Pierre. The bark of the Adansonia digitata. 1848. III. 589.[1]
— De l'emploi de l'Adansonia. 1848. III. 589.[1]
— Sur l'emploi de l'écorce d'Adansonia. 1848. III. 589.[1]
Duchassaing, Placide & Walpers, G. W. Plantae novae et minus cognitae in Isthmo panamensi. 1854. III. 589.[1]
Du Chastel, Ferdinand, comte. Des arbres forestiers. 1849. III. 77.
— De l'Orme Pitteurs. 1853. III. 366.[1]
— La plantation des routes en Belgique. 1853. III. 209.

Duchaussoy, H. Végétation comparée de la Somme et du Cher. 1898. I. 535.
Duchemin, E. L'exploitation du Coco. 1898. III. 324.[1]
Duchesne. Note sur les ruptures transversales . . . dans l'écorce . . . de Peuplier de Canada. 1806. III. 345.[2]
Duchesne, A. Le jardinier prévoyant. 1772. III. 112.
Duchesne, Antoine Nicolas. Sur l'arrangement à donner aux grands arbres. 1804. I. 38.[1]
— Manuel de botanique. 1764. III. 85.
Duchesne, Édouard Adolphe. Répertoire des plantes utiles. 1836. III. 52.
Duchesne Émile. Eugenia Michelli. 1900. III. 635.[1]
— Jeunes plantes d'Hevea braziliensis. 1900. III. 519.[1]
— Tecoma Ricasoliana hort. mort. 1900. III. 707.[1]
— See also CHEVALLIER, L., DUCHESNE, Émile & REYNAL.
Duchesne, J. B. Guide de la culture des bois. 1825. IV. 85.[1]
Du Chesne, Josephus QUERCETANUS. See QUERCETANUS DU CHESNE, Josephus.
Duchesne, L. L'industrie de Châtel-Gérard. 1878. IV. 427.[2]
Duchesne, Leger. In Ruellium de stirpibus epitome. 1539. I. 277.
— De stirpibus vel plantis ordine alphabetico digestis epitome. 1539. I. 277.
Duchesne de Bellecourt. Note sur l'écorce de l'arbuste à papier du Japon. 1865. III. 368.[1]
Duchesne-Thoureau, J. De l'amélioration des forêts. 1862. IV. 275.
— Fabrication des sabots. 1861. IV. 428.[2]
— Semis et culture du Pin de Riga. 1866. IV. 472.
Du Choul, Jean. De varia Quercus historia. 1555. II. 132.[1]
Ducie, Henry John Reynolds, 3d earl of Moreton. Castanopsis chrysophylla. 1897. III. 560.[1]
— Effects of geological position on Conifers. 1858. III. 291.
— Remarks on the effects of geological position on certain Coniferae. 1858. III. 291.
Duck, John N. The natural history of Portshead. 1832. I. 398.
— The natural history of Portshead. 1852. V. xxi.[1]
Duckstein. Zur Aufastungsfrage. 1883. IV. 172.[1]
Duckworth, A. S. Insect pests. 1898. III. 187.
Duclaux, Émile. Études sur la nouvelle maladie de la Vigne. 1876. III. 570.[1]
— Sur l'iodure d'amidon. 1872. I. 140.[1]
— Sur la maladie de la Vigne dans le sud-est. 1872. III. 577.
— Pays vignobles atteints par le phylloxera. 1875. III. 568.
— Progrès de la maladie du phylloxera. 1877. III. 570.[2]
— Traitement, par les sulfocarbonates. 1875. III. 568.
Du Colombier, Maurice. Exposition d'une méthode propre à résoudre . . . diverses questions de statistique botanique. 1857. I. 299.
Ducommun, J. C. Taschenbuch für den schweizerischen Botaniker. 1869. I, 435.
Ducommun, Jules. Étude sur les acides cristallisables des Ablétinées. 1883. II. 21.[1]
Ducos, A. Pritchardia filifera. 1876. III. 332.[1]
— Zamia obliqua Regel. 1877. III. 286.[1]
Ducoutdré. Note sur le ver à soie de l'Ailante. 1866. III. 507.[3]
Ducquerie, J. B. CALLARD DE LA. See CALLARD DE LA DUCQUERIE, J. B.
Ducreux, REYNAUD-. See REYNAUD-DUCREUX.
Ducros, L. C. De l'utilisation de divers végétaux de la Lorraine. 1893. III. 507.[2]
Duda, Ladislav. Vrba. 1874. III. 347.
Dudan, M. J. Ueber die Stickstoffquellen der Waldbäume. 1899. IV. 64.[1]
Dudley, Sir Matthew. An account of insects in the barks. 1706. III. 188.[1]
Dudley P. H. The cell-structure of Pinus Strobus. 1885. II. 46.[1]
— Chamaecyparis sphaeroidea Spach. 1887. III. 301.[2]
— Duct formation in Chestnut-wood. 1886. II. 123.[2]
— Fungi which cause decay in timber. 1886. IV. 415.[1]
— The medullary rays of the Tamarack. 1885. II. 33.[2]
— Notes on starch in the Chestnut wood. 1886. II. 123.[2]
— Observations on the structure of Castanea. 1886. II. 124.[2]
— Spiral, or elliptically wound tracheids. 1890. I. 207.[1]
— Structure of certain timber-ties. 1887. IV. 424.[1]
— The structure of Quercus alba. 1886. II. 132.[2]
Dudley, Paul. An account of the method of making sugar from the juice of the Maple tree. 1723. IV. 527.[1]
— An account of the Poyson wood tree. 1723. III. 527.[2].
— Observations on some of the plants in New-England. 1726. III. 263.[1]

Dudley, William Russell. The Big trees of California. 1900. II. 51.[2]
— Cayuga flora. 1886. I. 315.
— Forest reservations. 1896. IV. 179.[1]
— Forestry notes. 1900. IV. 341.[1]
— Lumbering in the Sequoia national park. 1900. IV. 382.[2]
— A preliminary list of the vascular plants of the Lackawanna and Wyoming valleys. 1887. I. 315.
— & **Thurston**, C. O. Additions to the flora of Lackawanna and Wyoming valleys. 1892. I. 316.
— — A catalogue of the flowering plants . . . Lackawanna and Wyoming valleys. 1892. I. 316.
Dudok de Wit, C. Eene inspectie van gebeukerde boomen te Antwerpen. 1867. III. 121.[2]
I due ultimi mesi di vita. 1883. IV. 41.[1]
Dueben, Magnus Wilhelm von. Conspectus vegetationis Scaniae. 1837. I. 353.
— Enumeratio plantarum in regione landscronensi. 1835. I. 353.
— Exkursion i Bohuslän. 1843. I. 354.
— Handbok i Vextrikets naturliga familjer. 1841. III. 52.
Dücker, von. Die forstlichen Verhältnisse der Senne. 1874. IV. 354.
— Die forstlichen Verhältnisse der Wiehen-Gebirges. 1870. IV. 354.
— Zur Frage der Oedlandaufforstungen. 1885. IV. 158.
— Zur Frage der Wasserpflege. 1881. IV. 118, 144.[1]
— Ist die Pflanzung junger Kiefern mit entblösster Wurzel eine empfehlenswerthe Kulturmethode? 1883. IV. 473.
— Zur Wasserpflege im Walde. 1885. IV. 73.[2]
Düssberg, (*Oberförster*). Zur Begründung einiger Wachsthumserscheinungen. 1897. IV. 67.[2]
— Wie erwachsen astreine Kiefern? 1893. IV. 474.
Düsberg, Walter. Embothrium coccineum Forst. 1891. II. 160.[2]
— Skimmia Foremanni. 1890. III. 506.[1]
— Spartium scoparium var. Andreana. 1891. III. 475.[1]
Dümler, Wolfgang Jacob. Erneuerter und vermehrter Baum- und Obstgarten. 1664. III. 135.
Über das **Düngen** der Obstbäume. 1828. III. 151.
Die **düngende** Wirkung des von den Baumkronen abtropfenden Wassers. 1884. IV. 73.[2]
Ueber **Düngung** von Saat- und Pflanz-Schulen. 1855. IV. 144.[1]
Dünkelberg, Friedrich Wilhelm. Der nassauische Weinbau. 1867. III. 553.[1]
Dünnenberger, Eugen. Ueber eine . . . Alcornoco-Rinde. 1900. III. 468.[1]
Duerden, J. E. The Orange tree in Jamaica. 1895. III. 501.[1]
Dürer, B. Forêts et école forestière en Italie. 1875. IV. 35.[1]
— Forstschule und forstliche Zustände in Italien. 1875. IV. 35.[1]
Dürer, Bernardo. Il baco da seta della Quercia giapponese. 1865. IV. 501.[2]
Düring, E. von. Praktische Handgriffe beim Korbweidenbetriebe. 1886. III. 349.
Dürr, F. Julius. Ueber das Keimen . . . der Araucaria Bidwilli. 1865. II. 26,[1] *III. 298.[1]*
Düsing, Carl. Die Regulierung des Geschlechtsverhältnisses. 1884. I. 200.
Duestsch, Ph. Einfluss übermässigen Streusammelns. 1877. IV. 71.
— Ueber die Kosten der Pflanzen-Erziehung. 1877. IV. 150.
— Ueber das Schütten der jungen Kiefern. 1868. IV. 476.
— Ueber die Weymouthskiefer. 1869. IV. 469.
Du Fay, C. F. Observations sur la Sensitive. 1739. II. 372.[2]
Dufay, G. Description . . . du nouveau dendromètre de M. Huet. 1845. IV. 215.
Dufay, Louis. Boisement économique des terrains délaissés. 1899. IV. 546.[1]
Duff, James. On the arboriculture of the county of Kent. 1878. IV. 358.[1]
— Notes of forest travel in Europe. 1884. IV. 342.[2]
— Report on old . . . trees growing on the estates of Bayham Abbey. 1878. I. 297.[1]
Duff, John. The cultivation of Saltbush. 1898. III. 387.[1]
Duffer Blom, G. Over het groote belang van kiezelzuur. 1861. I. 180.[1]
Duffield, G. Double white Lapageria. 1882. III. 337.[2]
Duffort, Louis. See OZANON, Charles & DUFFORT, Louis.

Duffour, Edmond. Note sur le Rhizoctone des arbres. 1862. III. 193.[2]
— Rapport de la Commission départementale de l'Hérault. 1869. III. 758.[2]
Dufft, C. Beiträge zur Flora von Thüringen. 1882. II. 284.[2]
— Beiträge zur Flora von Thüringen. 1883. II. 302.[1]
— Ueber eine neue Form der Rosa venusta. 1880. II. 299.[2]
— Die Rosen in der Umgegend von Rudolstadt. 1882. II. 284.[2]
Dufios, A. & **Hirsch**, A. Landbouwkundige scheikunde. 1844. III. 36.[1]
Dufougeray, (*député, Ille-et-Vilaine*). Opinion sur la dotation de la caisse d'amortissement [bois de l'état]. 1817. IV. 326.
Dufour. Catalogue général de sa pépinière. 1828. I. 65.[1]
Dufour, B. J. Culture du Mûrier. 1863. III. 377.
— Sur la culture du Mûrier sauvageon. 1860. III. 377.
— Nouvelles études et expériences séricicoles. 1863. III. 377.
— Observations pratiques . . . sur la maladie actuelle des vers à soie. 1860. III. 377.
Dufour, Charles. Cyclone de Jougne. 1889. III. 184.[2]
— De la quantité de grêle tombée. 1882. IV. 48.[2]
Dufour, Henri. Note sur quelques effets de la foudre. 1887. IV. 194.
Dufour, Jean. Sur l'ascension du courant de transpiration. 1884. I. 165.
— Beiträge sur Imbibitionstheorie. 1888. I. 161, *IV. 412.[1]*
— Destruction du ver de la Vigne. 1893. III. 564.[1]
— Einige Versuche mit Botrytis tenella. 1892. III. 197.
— Führer des Winzers im Kampf gegen die Reblaus. 1895. III. 574.
— Notice sur quelques mala*?ies de la Vigne. 1888. III.'580.
— Notices microchimiques sur le tissu épidermique. 1887. I. 154.
— La périodicité des phénomènes de la végétation. 1886. I. 191.[1]
— Les Vignes américaines et la situation phylloxérique. 1899. III. 575.[1]
Dufour, L . n, (1782–1865). Sur le Chêne-Tauzin. 1851. IV. 518.[2]
— Coup d'œil topographique sur la ville de Xativa. 1820. I. 420.
— Diagnoses . . . sur quelques plantes d'Espagne. 1860. I. 421.
— On a fluorescent solution from Fraxinus. 1860. II. 708.[2]
— Notice sur la culture de l'Indigotier. 1817. III. 479.[1]
— Sur une solution fluorescente tirée du Fraxinus. 1860. II. 708.[2]
Dufour, Léon. Influence de la lumière sur la forme . . . des feuilles. 1887. I. 111.
— Influence de la lumière sur la structure des feuilles. 1886. I. 110, *230*.
— Influence de la lumière sur le nombre des stomates. 1885. I. 131.[2]
— Influence de la lumière sur les feuilles. 1887. I. 174.
— Les récents travaux sur le tissu assimilateur. 1887. I. 173.
— *See also* COSTANTIN, Julien & DUFOUR, Léon.
— & **Hickel**, Robert. Les ennemis du Pin dans la Champagne crayeuse. 1894. IV. 478.
Dufour, Louis. Cours élémentaire sur les propriétés des végétaux. 1855. III. 52, *217*.
— Propriétés des végétaux et leurs applications. 1861. III. 52.
Dufour, Philippe Sylvestre. Drey neue curieuse Tractätgen von dem Trancke Cafe. 1685. III. 221.[2]
— The manner of making coffee, tea. 1671. III. 221.[2]
— Novi tractatus de potu caphé. 1685. III. 221.[2]
— Tractatus novi de potu caphé. 1685. III. 221.[2]
— Traitez nouveaux & curieux du café. 1685. III. 221.[2]
— De l'usage du caphé, du thé. 1671. III. 221.[2]
Dufournel, A. Du défrichement et du reboisement. 1847. IV. 161.[2]
Dufrené, Hector. La flore sanscrite. 1887. I. 514.[2]
Dufresne, Pierre. Plantes nouvellement introduites par M. J. Linden. 1873. III. 77.
Du Fresnoy. Des propriétés de la plante appelée Rhus radicans. 1788. III. 528.[1]
Dufresnoy. Emploi des terres pyriteuses. 1877. III. 570.[1]
Dufriche, Pierre. Les Dracæna colorés et leurs ennemis. 1891. III. 334.[2]
— Le Ficus elastica et sa multiplication. 1891. III. 370.[2]
— Les Lapageria. 1892. III. 337.[2]
— Le Poinsettia pulcherrima. 1889. III. 518.[1]

Duftschmid, Johann. Die Flora von Oberösterreich. 1870. I. 442.

Dugas des Varennes, (*député, Loire*). Opinion sur la cession des bois dits de l'état. 1817. IV. 325.

Dugast, J. Contribution à l'étude de la Vigne. 1892. III. 583.[2]

— Contribution à l'étude des Raisins d'Algérie. 1892. III. 547.

— & **Poussat**, J. La maturation des raisins en Algérie. 1895. II. 508.[2]

Dugat-Estublier, E. De l'emploi de l'Ailante glanduléux. 1877. III. 507.[2]

Dugdale, William. The history of imbanking and drayning. 1662. III. 150.[2]

Dugés, Alfredo. Descripcion de un género nuevo . . . de las Ramnáceas. 1879. II. 492.[1]

— Ensayo de una clasificacion anatomica de los frutos. 1882. I. 119.

— Flores de Madèra. 1898. II. 174.[1]

Duggar, Benjamin Minge. On the development of the pollen grain . . . in Bignonia venusta. 1899. II. 790.[1]

— Notes on the archesporium and nucleus of Bignonia. 1898. II. 785.[2]

— Some important Pear diseases. 1898. III. 446.[2]

Dugied, P. H. Projet de boisement des Basses-Alpes. 1819. IV. 161.[1]

Dugnani, Giulio. Saggio di botanica. 1775. I. 83.

Dugourd, Justin. Greffage de l'Eucalyptus. 1893. III. 634.[1]

Du Graty, Alfred M. La république du Paraguay. 1862. III. 269.[2]

Dugué. Du suc résineux du Pin maritime. 1844. IV. 467.[2]

Du Guiny. Soins à donner à l'emballage. 1865. III. 155.

— Statistique forestière du département de l'Allier. 1885. IV. 361.

— Traitement des futaies résineuses. 1886. IV. 140.

Du Guiny, A. Incendies des forêts des Maures. 1877. IV. 183.[1]

— L'ouragan du 20 février 1879. 1879. IV. 189.[1]

Du Haide, Johann Baptista. Description géographique . . . de la Chine. 1735. I. 458.

— Gründlicher Unterricht vom Seidenbau. 1753. III. 372.[2]

Du Hamel, H. L. *See* Du Hamel du Monceau, H. L.

Duhamel du Monceau, Henri Louis. Abhandlung von Bäumen, Stauden und Sträuchen. 1755. I. 292, *III. 83,*[2] *IV. 85.*[1]

— Abhandlung von den Lehr-Arten in der Pflanzenkunde. 1758. I. 250.

— Anatomie de la Poire. 1732. II. 279.[1]

— Art du charbonnier. 1761. IV. 393.

— Avis pour le transport par mer des arbres. 1753. III. 154.[2]

— Compendio del tratado sobre siembras y plantios de árboles. 1760. IV. 108.[2]

— Disertacion acerca de los métodos botánicos. 1758. I. 250.

— Dissertation sur les méthodes de botanique. 1758. I. 250.

— Diverses observations sur le Guy. 1742. II. 178.[2]

— Erklärung von Kunst-Wörtern aus der Botanic. 1755. III. 29.[2]

— Expériences pour connaître la force des bois. 1770. IV. 409.

— Expériences sur l'imbibition de différentes qualités de bois de Chêne. 1748. IV. 513.

— De l'exploitation des bois. 1764. IV. 381.

— Von Fällung der Wälder. 1764. IV. 381.

— La fisica degli alberi. 1758. IV. 56.

— Del governo dei boschi. 1764. IV. 381.

— Von der Holz-Saat. 1760. IV. 108.[2]

— De l'importance de l'analogie . . . que les arbres doivent avoir entre eux pour la réussite . . . des greffes. 1732. I. 208.[1]

— Die Kunst des Kohlenbrennens. 1761. IV. 393.

— De la Lande, qu'on nomme aussi Jonc marin. 1762. III. 489.[3]

— Mémoire sur une production monstrueuse du Pommier. 1778. II. 266.[3]

— Natur-Geschichte der Bäume. 1758. IV. 56.

— Onderzoek of verschillende planten. 1761. I. 157.

— La physique des arbres. 1758. IV. 56.

— Sur les plantes qu'on peut élever dans l'eau. 1752. I. 157.

— Pomona gallica; oder, Von Obstbäumen. 1768. III. 84.[2]

— Recherche d'une méthode pour faire réussir les boutures. 1744. III. 157.

— Recherches physiques de la cause du prompt accroissement des plantes. 1731. I. 232.[2]

— Recherches sur la formation des couches ligneuses. 1755. I. 127.[2]

— Recherches sur la réunion des plaies des arbres. 1751. I. 208.[1]

— Recherches sur les causes de la multiplication des espèces de fruits. 1730. III. 39.

— Réflexions et expériences sur la force des bois. 1745. IV. 409.

— Des semis et plantations des arbres. 1760. IV. 108.[2]

— Traité des arbres et arbustes. 1755. I. 292, *III. 83,*[2] *IV. 85.*[1]

— Traité des arbres fruitiers. 1768. III. 84.[1]

— Du transport, de la conservation et de la force des bois. 1767. IV. 381.

— Tratado de las siembras y plantíos de árboles. 1760. IV. 108.[2]

— Tratado del cuidado y aprovechamiento de los montes y bosques. 1764. IV. 381.

— Underretning, om hvorledes Træer . . . best kand forsendes til Søes. 1753. III. 154.[2]

— Vorschläge nach welchen der Transport der Baume . . . über die See zu veranstalten ist. 1753. III. 154.[2]

— & Bidet, Nicolas. Beschreibung der Weinstöcke. 1784. III. 545.[1]

— & Buffon, G. L. L., *comte* de. Observations des différents effets que produisent sur les végétaux les grandes gelées. 1740. I. 211.

— — Recherches de la cause de l'excentricité des couches ligneuses. 1740. I. 127.[1]

Du Hays, Charles. Un mot sur la conduite des arbres forestiers. 1857. IV. 170.

Duile, Joseph. Ueber Verbauung der Wildbäche. 1834. IV. 187.[2]

Duiller, Nicolaus Fatio de. *See* Fatio de Duiller, Nicolaus.

Dujardin, A. *See* Béchamp, M. J. & Dujardin, A.

Dujardin, Felix. Empoisonnement par les feuilles de l'If. 1854. III. 288.[2]

— Sur l'étude microscopique de la cire. 1850. III. 225.

— Flora complète d'Indre et Loire. 1838. I. 409.

— Sur un froid exceptionnel. 1859. III. 48.

— Nouveau manuel complet de l'observateur au microscope. 1842. I. 36.[3]

Dujardin-Beaumetz, Georges Octave. Sur l'Hamamelis virginica. 1884. III. 417.[1]

— Propriétés fébrifuges du Cédron. 1880. III. 509.[1]

— *See also* Beranger-Feraud & Dujardin-Beaumetz.

— & Égasse, Ed. Les plantes médicinales. 1889. III. 59.[1]

— — Des Strophanthus. 1889. III. 690.[1]

— & Restrepo, A. E. Propriétés physiologiques . . . de la cédrine. 1881. III. 508,[2] *509.*[1]

Dulac, Claude. Sur le Boldo. 1874. III. 402.[2]

Dulac, Joseph. L'Aubépine de Garaison. 1886. II. 263.[1]

— Fleurs de Massabieille. 1886. III. 290.[3]

— Flore du département des Hautes-Pyrénées. 1867. I. 413.

— Mélanges botaniques. 1886. I. 417.

— Nom patois de l'Ajonc. 1886. II. 387.[1]

— Nom patois de la Clématite. 1886. II. 195.[3]

Dulière, W. Dosage du santalol. 1896. III. 804.[7]

Dulk, Albert Benno. De resinis praesertim de resina Dammara. 1846. II. 25.[1]

Dulk, L. Untersuchungen der Saatschulpflanzen. 1874. IV. 63.[2]

Dull, A. J. Sterfte in Populieren. 1879. III. 344.[3]

Dulong, J. Analyse chimique du Poivre long. 1825. III. 342.[2]

Dumaine, Claude Jean. The lac insect. 1886. III. 232.[2]

— List of timber trees . . . of the Hazareebaugh Zillah forests. 1871. IV. 401.[1]

— Mode of extracting the oil from the Mowah seed. 1869. III. 667.[1]

— Mode of preparing the cutch. 1869. III. 464.[1]

— Native process of extracting the oil . . . of the Bhaylah. 1869. III. 529.[1]

— Remarks on the wild silk-yielders. 1886. III. 148.[2]

— The Tusser silk worm. 1886. III. 148.[1]

Dumas, A. Calendrier horticole pour le midi de la France. 1867. III. 113.

Dumas, Alexandre. Origine du Pommier. 1868. II. 266.[2]

Dumas, J. Études sur les inondations. 1857. IV. 49.[2]

Dumas, Jean Baptiste André. Analyse des documents adressés à la Commission de phylloxera. 1872. III. 565.[1]

Dumas, Jean Baptiste André (*continued*).
— Sur l'arrivée de phylloxera à Pregny. 1874. III. 567.[2]
— Communication relative à la destruction du phylloxera. 1874. III. 567.[1]
— Études sur le phylloxéra. 1876. III. 760.
— Mémoire sur les moyens de combattre l'invasion du phylloxera. 1874. III. 566.[1] 567.[2]
— Mémoire sur les substances végétales qui se rapprochent du camphre. 1832. III. 224.[1]
— Sur les mesures à prendre . . . concernant la réapparition de phylloxera. 1879. III. 571.
— Note on an experiment by Hervé-Mangon concerning the amount of carbon dioxide. 1869. I. 211.
— Note sur l'emploi des sulfocarbonates alcalins. 1875. III. 568.
— Note sur l'emploi du carbon disulphide. 1858. III. 678.[2]
— Note sur le transport du phosphate de chaux. 1846. I. 175.
— Note sur les sulfocarbonates. 1875. III. 568.
— Observations sur la lettre de M. Aubergier. 1875. III. 568.
— À propos de Marion. 1879. III. 571.
— Rapport sur le mémoire de M. André Jean. 1857. III. 379.[2]
— Rapport sur le mémoire de M. Cauvy. 1874. III. 566.[1]
— Rapport sur les études relatives au phylloxera. 1873. III. 565.[1]
— Rapport sur les mémoires présentés par les délégués de l'Académie. 1875. III. 568.
— Rapport sur un mémoire de M. Albert Le Play relatif à l'origine de la chaux. 1862. I. 153.
— Rapport sur un mémoire de M. Cabours. 1844. III. 652.[1]
— Rapport sur un mémoire de M. le docteur Boucherie. 1841. IV. 417.
— Rapport sur un mémoire de M. Payen, relatif à la composition de la matière ligneuse. 1839. I. 155.
— Remarques concernant la Rapport sur les mesures . . . pour préserver les territoires menacés par le phylloxera. 1874. III. 566.[1]
— Remarques concernant Mouillefert, Expériences sur l'emploi des sulfocarbonates. 1874. III. 566.[2]
— On the substitution of wood for coal. 1870. IV. 433.[2]
— & others. Communication relative à la destruction du phylloxera. 1874. III. 567.[1]
— Mémoires sur le phylloxera. 1875. III. 567.[2]
Dumast, P. G. de. Deux fruits intéressants de la région du Nord-Est. 1882. III. 85.
Dumek, Josef. Několteré druhy ovocného stromoví a krovín, 'které by se u nás s prospěchem dařily. 1887. III. 90.[1]
— Stromoví ovocné. 1886. III. 146.[2]
— Vrba. 1884. III. 348.
Du Mênil, Auguste Peter Julius. Handbuch der Reagentienund Zerlegungslehre. 1837. IV. 60.[2]
— Leer der herkenningsmiddelen voor plantenontleding. 1834. I. 36.[1]
— Die Reagentienlehre für die Pflanzenanalyse. 1834. I. 36.[1]
Duméril. Rapport sur un mémoire de MM. Guérin-Méneville et Perrotet. 1842. III. 734.[2]
— Rapports sur deux mémoires de M. Guérin-Méneville. 1851. III. 677.[2]
Duméril, André Marie Constant. Élémens des sciences naturelles. 1804. I. 84.
— Histoire de la caprification. 1858. II. 150.[2]
— Observation sur la cuticule des plantes. 1859. I. 129.[2]
— Rapport sur les recherches de M. Laurent. 1852. IV. 414.[1]
— Traité élémentaire d'histoire naturelle. 1804. I. 84.
Duméril, Auguste Henri André. Des odeurs. 1843. I. 182.[2]
— Sur des vers à scie du Chêne. 1861. IV. 501.[2]
Du Mesnil, Eugène. Sur le dépérissement des vignobles de la Côte-d'Or. 1876. III. 560.
— Sur l'emploi de l'outil désigné sous le noms de dame. 1874. III. 566.[2]
Dumesnil, Lecoq-. *See* Lecoq-Dumesnil.
Du Mesnil, Nicolas. De l'art d'enter. 1560. III. 159.[2]
Du Molin, Jean Baptiste. Flore poétique ancienne. 1856. I. 514.[2]
Du Moncel, Theodore Achille Louis. Sur la conductibilité électrique des arbres. 1877. IV. 194.
— Deuxième[–septième] note sur la conductibilité électrique des corps ligneux. 1874. IV. 412.[2]
— Recherches sur les transmissions électriques à travers les corps ligneux. 1874. IV. 412.[2]
— De la transmission électrique à travers le sol par l'intermédiaire des arbres. 1877. IV. 194.

Dumont, Arthur. Note relative à l'efficacité de la submersion des Vignes. 1873. III. 565.[2]
— Sur la possibilité d'appliquer la submersion de la Vigne. 1873. III. 565.[1]
— Sur le prix de revient des grandes dérivations d'eau en Italie et en France. 1883. III. 150.[2]
— Recherches sur l'anatomie comparée des Malvacées. 1887. II. 512,[2] 522.[1]
Dumont, Charles. Dictionnaire forestier. 1802. IV. 22.[1]
Dumont, J. & Crochetelle, J. Sur la nitrification des terres de prairie. 1893. I. 229.
Dumont, L. Plantations d'arbres dans les rochers. 1898. IV. 143.[2]
Du Mont, Maxime. L'Arbre à huile de la Chine. 1888. III. 514.[2]
Dumont, W., Schmitz-. *See* Schmitz-Dumont, W.
Dumont d'Urville, Jules Sébastien César. Enumeratio plantarum quas in insulis Archipelagi . . . collegit. 1822. I. 451.
— Flore des Malouines. 1825. I. 347.
Du Mont de Courset, George Louis Marie. Il botanico coltivatore; recata in italiano dall' Ab. Girolamo Romano. 1802. I. 265.
— Die botanische Pflanzkunst nach Dumont-Courset von Christian Gottlieb Berger. 1802. I. 265.
— Le botaniste cultivateur. 1802. I. 265.
— Mémoires sur l'agriculture du Boulonnois. 1784. III. 125.
Dumonteil, Fulbert-. *See* Fulbert-Dumonteil.
Dumontier, F. A. C. Vergiftiging door de vrucht van de Cerbera. 1855. III. 691.[2]
Dumortier, Barthélemy Charles. Analyse des familles des plantes. 1829. I. 260.
— Sur les bases d'un système symétrique . . . des végétaux. 1822. I. 251.
— Boquet du littoral belge. 1869. I. 392.
— Commentations botanicae. 1822. I. 266.
— Discours sur la marche de la classification. 1864. I. 252.
— Discours sur la théorie de la classification. 1865. I. 252.
— Essai carpographique. 1835. I. 119.
— Flora belgica. 1878. I. 393.[1]
— Florula belgica. 1827. I. 392.
— Monographie des espèces du genre Rubus. 1863. II. 302.[2]
— Monographie des Roses de la flore belge. 1863. II. 302.[2]
— Monographie des Roses de la flore belge. 1867. II. 285.[1]
— Monographie des Saules de la flore belge. 1862. II. 102.[1]
— Note sur deux faits de physiologie végétale. 1873. I. 165.
— Notice sur un nouveau genre de plantes, Hulthemia. 1824. II. 297.[1]
— Opuscules de botanique. 1873. I. 270.
— Pomone tournaisienne. 1869. III. 77.
— Quelques genres dédiés à des botanistes belges. 1822. II. 181,[1] 490.[1]
— Recherches sur la structure . . . des animaux et des végétaux. 1832. I. 98.
— Verhandeling over het geslacht der Wilgen. 1825. II. 98.[2]
Du Moulin. Nouvelle méthode pour cultiver toutes sortes d'arbres fruitiers. 1763. III. 143.
— *See also* La Rivière, de & Du Moulin.
Dumoulin, L. J. G. Guide du botaniste dans les environs de Maestricht. 1868. I. 392; V. xx.[1]
Dumoutier, G. Essai sur la pharmacie annamite. 1887. III. 276.[2]
Dunac, Florentin. Contribution à l'étude du genre Actinidia. 1899. II. 540.[2]
Dunal, Michel Felix. Cistineae. 1824. II. 563.[2]
— Considérations sur la nature . . : de quelques-uns des organes de la fleur. 1829. I. 114.[1]
— Considérations sur les fonctions des organes floraux colorés. 1829. I. 237.
— Description du Pinus Salzmanni. 1851. II. 43.[2]
— Description du Planera Richardi. 1843. II. 145.[1]
— Des effets de la gelée. 1848. I. 212.
— Histoire naturelle . . . des Solanum. 1813. II. 774.[2]
— De l'influence minéralogique du sol. 1848. I. 228.[1]
— Monographie de la famille des Anonacées. 1817. II. 215.[1]
— Note sur deux genres . . . des Composées. 1819. II. 858.[1]
— Petit bouquet méditerranéen. 1847. I. 410, 452.
— Solanaceae. 1852. II. 767.[1]
— Solanorum generumque affinium synopsis. 1816. II. 767.[1]
— Vaccineae 1838. II. 657.[1]
— *See also* Fabre, Esprit & Dunal, M. F.

Dunant, C. G. *See* La Roche, Daniel de, Odier, Louis & Dunant, C. G.

Dunbar, John. Abies Nordmanniana. 1899. III. 296.²
— The American and Chinese Fringes. 1899. III. 671.³
— Daphne Mezereum. 1893. II. 602.¹
— Syringa oblata. 1899. III. 681.¹

Duncan, Andrew. Arboriculture. 1877. III. 132.²

Duncan, Andrew (*of Edinburgh*). Catalogue of medical plants. 1826. III. 56.
— Tentamen inaugurale de Swietenia Soymida. 1794. III. 513.¹
— & Lyon. Observations on . . . Calotropis Mudarii. 1829. III. 692.¹

Duncan, Daniel. Avis salutaire à tout le monde. 1705. III. 222.

Duncan, James. Catalogue of plants in the R. bot. garden, Mauritius. 1863. I. 68.²

Duncan, John. Notice of the stoppage of a water pipe by the roots of a tree. 1857. III. 34.¹

Duncan, John Shute. Botanical theology. 1825. I. 511.
— Botano-theology. 1825. I. 511.

Dunglison, Robley. Coffee in Central Africa. 1896. III. 732.²
— New remedies. 1839. III. 242.

Dunker, Johann Heinrich August. Kurzer Beschreibung der gefährlichsten Giftpflanzen. 1796. III. 72.

Dunkers, Michael Wenzeslaus. Kurze doch gründliche Abhandlung über die Kienraupe. 1793. IV. 205.³

Dunlap, J. M. The American Sweet Chestnut. 1896. III. 358.¹

Dunlop, John. *See* Ward, H. M. & Dunlop, John.

Dunn, Malcolm. Cryptogamic plants injurious to forest trees. 1878. IV. 211.²
— Forestry in Scotland. 1898. IV. 359.¹
— On insects injurious to forest trees. 1878. IV. 208.³
— Statistics of Conifers in the British Islands. 1892. III. 293.
— The value in the British Islands of introduced Conifers. 1892. IV. 443.¹

Dunn, S. H. English forests. 1899. I. 516.

Dunn, S. T. Flora of southwest Surrey. 1893. I. 534.²

Dunnell, Mark Hill. American forestry. 1882. IV. 338.¹
— Cultivation of timber. ·1874· IV. 178,¹ 271.³

Duns, John. Biblical natural science. 1863. I. 513.

Dunstall, John. A booke of flowers, fruicts. 1661. I. 286.
— The second booke of flowers. 1661. I. 286.

Dunstan, Wyndham Rowland. Bon or Ban (wild) Réha. 1899. III. 382.¹
— Boswellia serrata. 1900. III. 510.¹
— The chemistry . . . of the Strychnos nux-vomica. 1885. III. 685.¹
— Divi-divi pods. 1899. III. 468.¹
— Edible oils used in India. 1899. III, 225.
— Jingan gum. 1900. III. 524.³
— Madár bast-fibre. 1899. III. 692.³
— On pial or peal gum. 1900. III. 524.¹
— Sur la présence du skatol dans le règne végétal. 1889. III. 363.²
— Report on some Indian gums. 1899. III: 228.¹
— Semla gum. 1900. III. 467.³
— Tari or Teri pods. 1899. III. 469.¹ ·
— *See also* Tubbenrof, Dietbold & Dunstan, W. R. ·
— & Boole, (*Miss*). Sur le principe vésicant de l'huile de Croton. 1896. III. 517.¹
— & Short, F. W. Sur la loganine. 1884. III. 685.¹

Dunster, Henry Peter. The young collector's handybook of botany. 1871. I. 285.

Duparchy. Mémoire sur le déboisement . . . de Saint-Claude. 1898. IV. 546.²

Du Pas, Crispinis. Cognoscite lilia agri quomodo crescant. 16.? I. 512.
— Hortus floridus. 1614. I. 284.

Du Pasquier, L. *See* Heim, Albert, Du Pasquier, L. & Forel, F. A.

Du Pasquier, Max. Les moyens . . . pour opérer le reboisement des pâturages. 1884. IV. 140.

Du Petit, François. Pourfour. Lettres d'un médecin des ·hôpitaux du roy. 1710. III. 238.¹

Du Petit-Thouars, Abel Aubert. Note sur la maladie de la Vigne. 1857. III. 559.²
— Observations faites aux îles Galapagos. 1859. I. 510.³

Du Petit-Thouars, Aubert Aubert. *See* Du Petit-Thouars, L. M. A. A.

Du Petit-Thouars, Louis Marie Aubert Aubert. Sur l'accroissement en diamètre. 1809. I. 189.

— Sur l'accroissement en diamètre du tronc des Dracaenas. 1809. I. 189.
— Caniram. 1806. II. 719.²
— Comparaison spécifique du Passiflora mauritiana. 1805. II. 577.³
— Cours de phytologie ou de botanique générale. 1819. I. 5.
— Sur la distribution des nervures . . . du Marronier d'Inde. 1809. II. 481.²
— Esquisse de la flore de l'isle de Tristan d'Acugna. 1811. I. 498.
— Essais sur l'organisation des plantes. 1806. I. 146, 189.
— Essais sur la végétation. 1809. I. 146.
— Extrait d'un mémoire sur les espèces de Pandanus. 1807. II. 56.³
— Extrait d'une lettre contenant des observations sur les plantes des isles de France. 1801. I. 481.²
— Sur la formation des arbres naturelle ou artificielle. 1823. III. 37,³ *169.²*
— Genera nova madagascariensia. 1806. I. 496.
— Sur la germination du Lecythis. 1809. II. 612.¹
— Histoire d'un morceau de bois. 1815. I. 163.
— Histoire des végétaux recueillis dans les isles australes d'Afrique. 1804. I. 482.
— Histoire des végétaux recueillis sur les isles de France. 1804. I. 481.³
— Mélanges de botanique. 1811. I. 265.
— Mémoire sur la germination du Cycas. 1803. II. 4.¹
— Mémoire sur les propriétés tinctoriales du Danais. 1804. III. 743.²
— Note sur l'origine du Caféyer. 1829. III. 738.
— Notice historique sur la nature . . . de la moelle et du liber. 1810. I. 146.
— Notice historique sur la pépinière du roi au Roule. 1825. III. 32.¹
— Notice historique sur le genre Caniram. 1806. II. 719.²
— Notice sur le Manglier. 1813. II. 614.¹
— Observations botaniques . . . sur le nouveau genre Canavali. 1813. II. 341.¹
— Observations sur la manière dont certains arbres se dépouillent de leur épiderme. 1807. I. 130, *192.²*
— Observations sur les bourgeons du Gleditsia macracantha. 1807. II. 361.²
— Observations sur quelques espèces de Cissampelos. 1809. II. 206.²
— Sur l'organisation végétale. 1809. I. 208,¹ *III. 620.¹*
— Recherches sur le cachou. 1805. III. 464.¹
— Recueil de rapports et de mémoires sur la culture des arbres fruitiers. 1815. III. 143.
— De la terminaison des plantes. 1816. I. 191.¹
— Treizième essai; notice historique sur la nature et les fonctions de la moelle. 1811. I. 128.²
— Le verger français. 1817. III. 143.
— & others. Rapport . . . sur le choix des arbres. 1827. III. 209.

Dupin, (*sr.*). Code forestier. 1828. IV. 324.

Du Pinet, Antoine. L'histoire des plantes. 1561. I. 280.
— Historia plantarum. 1561. I. 280, V. xv.³

Duplaquet, Jean Louis Charles. Les reboisements en Autriche. 1886. IV. 167.²

Duplessis, J. Sur l'étendue de la surface en vahie par le phylloxera dans le Loiret. 1878. III. 571.
— Le phylloxera dans le Loiret. 1879. ·III. 572.
— Sur la présence du phylloxera dans . . . Loir-et-Cher. 1877. III. 570.²

Duplessis, L. L'écorce du Pin d'Alep. 1873. III. 307.²

Duplessy, F. S. Des végétaux résineux. 1802. III. 227.

Duponchel. Le sulfure de charrée et son emploi. 1885. III. 561.
— Duponchel. *See* Moringlane, Duponchel, & Bonastre, J. F.

Duponchel, Adolphe. Le phylloxéra. 1873. III, 759.

Dupont & Carro. Catalogue d'arbres fruitiers et autres . . . composant la pépinière . . . à Kichinoff. 182.? I. 44.¹

Dupont, Adolphe E. Arbres japonais. 1880. IV. 127.¹
— Essai d'étude sur les espèces des arbres fruitiers. 1886. ·III. 428.¹
— Les essences forestières du Japon. 1879.· IV. 399.¹
— Sur les étamines des Légumineuses-Papilonacées. 1833. II. 320.¹
— & Bouquet de la Grye, Amédée. Les bois indigène et étrangers. 1875. IV. 109.²

Du Pont, Andreas. Gymnasium Rosarum. 1819. III. 448.

Dupont, C. Cultur des Morus multicaulis. 1834. III. 380.¹
— Culture du Mûrier multicaule. 1834. III. 380.²

Dupont, E. Les Kakis japonais cultivés. 1880. III. 669.³
— Notes relatives au Kakis cultivés. 1880. III. 669.²
Dupont, Édouard. Élaïs, ou Palmier à huile. 1894. III. 325.¹
Dupont, J. See CHARABOT, Eugène, DUPONT, J. & PILLET, L.
— & **Guerlain, J.** Sur l'essence de Rosas de France. 1896. III. 454.²
Dupont, J. D. Double flore parisienne. 1805. I. 406.
Dupont, P. Les gardes-champêtres de nos récoltes. 1898. IV. 91.¹
— De veldwachters onzer oogsten. 1898. IV. 91.¹
Dupoty, Auguste. Promenades au Muséum. 1851. I. 58.
Duppa, Richard. The classes and orders of the Linnaean system. 1816. I. 255.
Dupré. Causerie sur les bois de la Guyane. 1889. IV. 398.¹
Dupré, August. See THUDICHUM, J. L. W. & DUPRÉ, August.
Du Pré, F. Interprétation du Rubus montanus. 1898. II. 308.²
Dupré, V. See FAIVRE, Ernest & DUPRÉ, V.
Dupré de Saint-Maur. Note sur une expérience relative à la durée des lattes de Pin maritime. 1850. IV. 468.¹
Dupuis, Augustin Noël Aristide. L'Allamanda neriifolia 1859. III. 686.¹
— Les Andromèdes. 1860. III. 646.²
— Arbres d'ornement de pleine terre. 1868. III. 84.¹
— Arbrisseaux et arbustes d'ornement de pleine terre. 1868. III. 84.¹
— L'Azédarach. 1856. III. 512.²
— La Bruyère flamboyante. 1860. III. 651.¹
— Les Bruyères admirable et pendante. 1860. III. 651.²
— Les Casuarina. 1856. III. 342.¹
— Le Chêne. 1858. III. 361.¹
— Les Cierges. 1860. III. 621.²
— Clematis divaricata Jacq. 1856. III. 390.¹
— Clematis florida var. Sieboldii. 1856. III. 390.²
— Clematis patens Dene. 1856. III. 391.¹
— Conifères de pleine terre. 1872. III. 290.
— Les Dillénies. 1876. III. 595.¹
— Le Drimys aromatique. 1860. III. 397.¹
— Les Échinocactus. 1861. III. 622.¹
— L'Echinopsis de Pentland. 1860. III. 622.²
— Épiphylles et Phyllocactes. 1861. III. 623.¹
— Les Érables. 1863. III. 533.²
— Sur une espèce nouvelle de Mahonia. 1860. III. 396.¹
— La Gaulthérie du Canada. 1860. III. 652.¹
— La Gnidienne à feuilles de Bruyère. 1860. III. 628.¹
— Le Gonocalyx pulcher. 1858. III. 663.¹
— Le Goyavier. 1860. III. 637.²
— Le Jujubier. 1859. III. 544.¹
— Lonicera pallida. 1856. III. 750.¹
— Lonicera sempervirens L. 1856. III. 751.¹
— Les Mamillaires. 1861. III. 623.³
— Les migrations des végétaux. 1862. I. 241.³
— Les Myrica. 1859. III. 353.¹
— Noticesur l'Ailante glanduleux. 1862. IV. 525.
— Notice sur la culture de l'Ailante. 1862. IV. 525.
— Nouveau catéchisme d'agriculture. 186.? III. 113.
— Sur l'Ortie blanche. 1864. III. 381.³
— Le règne végétal. 1864. III. 52.
— Les Rhipsalis. 1861. III. 626.¹.
— Le Ricin en arbre. 1861. III. 521.²
— Les Ruscus. 1856. III. 338.¹
— Sur les Sequoia. 1859. III. 309.²
— Le Tulipier. 1860. III. 398.¹
— & **Hérincq,** François. Horticulture. Végétaux d'ornement. 1885. III. 87.
— & **Réveil,** Oscar. Flore médicale usuelle et industrielle. 1887. III. 53.
— **Gérard,** Frédéric, **Réveil,** Oscar & **Hérincq,** François. Le règne végétal. 1864. I. 90.
Dupuis, J. B. P. Tarif pour la réduction du sciage des bois. 1837. IV. 222.
Dupuits de Maconet, (jr.). Lettre . . . sur le Mûrier multicaule. 1835. III. 380.¹
Dupuy, B. Acides organiques. 1894. I. 180.²
— Alcaloïdes. 1887. I. 177.
— Glucosides. 1891. I. 177.
Dupuy, Dominique. Florule du département du Gers. 1847. I. 410.
— Mémoires d'un botaniste. 1868. I. 413.
— Des plants de Vignes américaines. 1880. III. 547.
— Question préliminaire à la culture des arbres fruitiers. 1857. III. 144.
— Traité de la greffe des arbres fruitiers. 1859. III. 161.

Dupuy-Jamain. Pêcher de la Chine à fleurs doubles. 1857. III. 439.²
— Rhus Cotinus purpureus. 1870. III. 524.¹
Duquesne, A. Petit catalogue des plantes . . . autour de Pont-Auderner. 1884. I. 535.
Duquesnel, H. Duboisine. 1881. III. 700.¹
Duquesney, DURAND-. See DURAND-DUQUESNEY.
Duquid. Sur l'Andira inermis. 1886. III. 467.¹
Durability of Oak timber. 1849. IV. 514.¹
The durabilty [sic] of railway sleepers. 1898. IV. 424.¹
Durand. Arbres fruitiers, arbres d'ornement. 187.? I. 58.
Durand. Étude sur l'écorce . . . de Grenadier. 1878. III. 630.²
Durand. Émulsion de l'huile de houille. 1896. III. 538.²
Durand. Medinilla magnifica. 1857. III. 638.²
Durand (of Caen). Sur l'accroissement en diamètre. 1846. I. 189.
— Accroissement en diamètre. 1852. I. 189.
— Sur la direction des tiges. 1846. I. 195.¹
— Mémoire sur un fait singulier de la physiologie des racines. 1845. I. 193.²
— Recherche et fuite de la lumière par les racines. 1845. I. 194.
— Sur la tendance des racines à chercher la bonne terre. 1845. I. 193.³
— & **Manoury** (of Caen). Sur l'accroissement en diamètre. 1852. I. 189.
— — Mémoire sur l'accroissement en diamètre. 1847. I. 189.
Durand, A. Deux nouvelles Cyclanthées. 1893. III. 332.²
Durand, Aristide. Du Genévrier. 1864. III. 303.²
Durand, Elias. On American Tea plants. 1864. II. 492.²
— Plantae Kaneanae groenlandicae. 1856. I. 309.¹
— Plantae Prattenianae californicae. 1855. I. 322.
— Remarks on changing the name of Carya texana. 1861. II. 112.¹
— A sketch of the botany of the basin of the Great Salt Lake. 1860. I. 323.
— Sur les vignes et les vins des États-Unis. 1862. II. 505.¹
— Vites boreali-americanae. 1862. II. 505.¹
— & **Hilgard,** T. C. Botanical report [of the routes in California]. 1855. I. 322.
— — Plantae Heermannianae. 1855. I. 322.
— **James,** T. P. & **Ashmead,** Samuel. Enumeration of the arctic plants. 1864. I. 309.¹
Durand, Elias Judah. A disease of Currant canes. 1897. III. 415.¹
— The embryology of Taxus. 1898. II. 10.²
Durand, Eugène. Note sur le Pin de Salsmann. 1893. II. 43.²
— & **Flahault,** Charles. Les limites de la région méditerranéenne en France. 1886. I. 417.
— & **Guicherd,** J. Culture de la Vigne en Côte-d'Or. 1896. III. 557.¹
Durand, Henry. Note sur l'aménagement des bois taillis. 1861. IV. 132.¹
Durand, J. Arbres fruitiers cultivés chez Durand. n. d. I. 490.
Durand, Jean Baptiste Léonard. Voyage au Sénégal. 1802. I. 490.
Durand, Léon. Rapport de la commission instituée pour l'expérimentation du procédé d'écorçage des bois par la chaleur. 1878. IV. 434.
Durand, M. D. Nuova polvere da cannone. 1866. IV. 431.¹
Durand, Théophile. Catalogue de la flore liégeoise. 1878. I. 393.¹
— Essai d'une monographie des Ronces de Belgique. 1887. II. 302.²
— Index generum phanerogamorum. 1888. I. 261.
— Notes rubologiques. 1890. II. 302.³
— Reliquiae Lecardianae. 1884. I. 490.
— Le Rubus tomentosus Borkh. existe-t-il en Belgique? 1886. II. 310.³
— See also AUTRAN, Eugène & DURAND, Théophile; DE WILDEMAN, Émile & DURAND, Théophile.
— & De **Wildeman,** Émile. Matériaux pour la flore du Congo. 1897. I. 492.¹
— & **Donckier de Donceel,** Henri. Matériaux pour servir à la flore de la province de Liége. 1873. I. 393.¹
— & **Pittier,** Henri. Contributions à l'étude de la flore suisse. 1881. I. 436.
— — & others. Primitiae florae costaricensis. 1891. I. 334.
— & **Schinz,** Hans. Conspectus florae Africae. 1892. I. 483.¹
— — Études sur la flore de . . . Congo. 1895. I. 492.¹

Durand-Olaye, Alfred. Rapport sur le matériel . . . des industries agricoles et forestières. 1880. IV. 102.
Durand-Duquesney. Coup d'œil sur la végétation . . . de Lisieux. 1846. I. 410.
Durande, Jean François. Flore de Bourgogne. 1782. I. 405.
— Notions élémentaires de botanique. 1781. I. 83.
Durando, Gaétan. Excursion à l'établissement forestier d'Aïn-Baïnen. 1878. I. 68.[2]
— Excursion botanique d'Alger à Saïda. 1883. I. 485.
— Note sur une excursion à la forêt de Cèdres de Teniet-el-Haâd. 1882. I. 485.
Durant. Edicts et ordonnances des eaues et forests. *See* EDICTS . . . .1588. IV. 323.[1]
Durante, Castore. Herbario nuovo con figure. 1585. I. 282, V. xv.[2]
— Hortulus sanitatis. 1585. I. 282.
— Il tesoro della sanità. 1586. III. 219.[2]
Durazzo, Ippolito. Catalogue des plantes cultivées dans le jardin de Madame Durazzo de Grimaldi. 1806. I. 61.
— Il Giardino botanico dello Zerbino. 1804. I. 61.
D'Urban, William Samuel Mitchell. Natural history of the neighbourhood of Exeter. 1876. I. 403.
— Natural history . . . South Devon. 1876. I. 403.
Durban botanic society. Report . . . I. 29.[2]
Durchánek, Vítĕslav. Citrus chinensis. 1884. III. 500.[1]
— Latania bourbonica. 1884. III. 327.[1]
— Seaforthia elegans. 1884. III. 319.[2]
Die **Durchforstungen.** 1845. IV. 173.
Über **Durchforstungen.** 1896. IV. 175.[1]
Durchforstungsertrage aus Böhmen. 1853. IV. 175.[2]
Durchforstungsertrage von Saat und Pflanzung. 1853. IV. 175.[2]
Des **durchsuchtigsten** Fürsten und Herrn . . . Herzogen zu Braunschweig . . . erneuertes Forst-Reglement. 1747. IV. 319.[1]
Durchwinterung der Eicheln. 1891. IV. 508.
Dureau, L. Note sur la Châtaigne du Brésil. 1844. III. 631.[1]
Dureau de la Malle, Adolphe Jules César Auguste. Antiquité botanique. 18 . ? II. 706.[2]
— Sur les grands Bambous de l'Inde. 1855. II. 59.[1]
— Histoire du Citronnier. 1851. III. 502.[1]
— Mémoire sur les espèces de Frênes. 1804. II. 706.[2]
— Note on a name used by Pliny. 1856. I. 514.[1]
— Note sur une sorte de torpeur très longue. 1826. I. 192,[2] II. 154.[2]
— Réfutation de l'ouvrage du docteur Fuster. 1846. III. 47.
— Retour d'une variété. 1855. III. 444.[2]
— Serres chaudes des anciens. 1851. III. 150.[1]
Durègne. Sur l'aire de dispersion de l'Arbutus Unedo. 1899. II. 660.[2]
Duren, Eugène de. L'Allamanda violacea Gardn. 1895. III. 686.[1]
— L'Aralia elegantissima. 1876. III. 642.[1]
— L'arbre de la liberté. 1876. II. 97.[1]
— Les Bactris. 1880. II. 65.[1]
— Le Chèvre-feuille. 1883. III. 750.[1]
— Une collection de plantes rares. 1886. I. 50.
— Le Crataegus Pyracantha Lalandei. 1882. III. 443.[2]
— Le Delabechia rupestris Lindl. 1880. III. 590.[1]
— Floraisons automnales. .1899. I. 222.[1]
— Les Fuchsia de pleine terre. 1898. III. 640.[1]
— Le Fuchsia triphylla Pl. 1889. III. 640.[2]
— Les Kalmia. 1883. III. 652.[2]
— Les Kentia Bl. 1877. III. 326.[1]
— Le Luculia gratissima Sweet. 1882. III. 745.[2]
— Le Noyer, Juglans regia L. · 1881. II. 114.[1]
— Le Pandanus Sanderi. 1898. III. 313.[2]
— Une réhabilitation. 1881. III. 490.[3]
Duret, C. Histoire admirable des plantes. 1605. I. 283.
Duret, L. *See* LOREY & DURET, L.
Duret, V. Introduction des Marronniers d'Inde. 1900. II. 481.[2]
Durham — Natural history society of Northumberland . . . *See* NATURAL . : . I. 19.
Durheim, Carl Jakob. Schweizerisches Pflanzen-Idiotikon. 1856. I. 75.[1]
Durieu. *See* DUBIGADOUX & DURIEU.
Durisu, Paul. L'exposition d'horticulture de Gand. 1881. III. 285.[2]
Durieu de Maisonneuve, Michel Charles. Notes détachées sur quelques plantes de la flore de la Gironde. 1855. I. 411.

— Le nouveau jardin des plantes. 1853. I. 58.
— Transformation d'un grain de Raisin en rameau. 1868. II. 507.[2]
— *See also* COSSON, Ernest & DURIEU DE MAISONNEUVE, M. C.
Durival, (*jr.*). De la Vigne. 1777. III. 554.[1]
Durkee, Silas. Morus alba grown from seed of a grafted Morus expansa. 1854. II. 154.[2]
Durmientes de Quebracho colorado. 1899. IV. 424,[2] 586.[1]
Durocher, J. Extrait d'observations sur les rapports qui existent entre la nature minérale. 1848. I. 228.[1]
— Observations relatives à l'influence de la nature du sol. 1849. I. 228.[1]
— *See also* MALAGUTI, F. J. & DUROCHER, J.
Du Roi, Johann Philipp. Beschreibung einer neuen Ahorngattung. 1784. II. 479.[1]
— Dissertatio . . . observationes botanicas sistens. 1771. I. 32.
— Die Harbkesche wilde Baumzucht. 1771. I. 292, III. 63,[1] IV. 81.
Du Rondeau, François. Quelles sont les plantes les plus utiles des Pays-Bas. 1772. III. 270.[2]
Du Roscoat, *vicomte.* Écorçage du Chêne par la vapeur. 1873. IV. 434.
— Écorcement des bois par la chaleur. 1873. IV. 434.
Dursta, Emila. Rośliny ozdobne pojedyńcze czyli solitery. 1892. III. 68.[3]
Durupt, N. De la taille des arbustes à feuilles caduques. 1868. III. 172.
Durvelle, J. P. Fabrication des essences et des parfums. 1893. III. 227.
Duschak, M. Zur Botanik des Talmud. 1870. I. 514.[2]
Duschek, Franz de Paula. Anfangsgründe der Forstwissenschaft. 1808. IV. 61,[2] 99.[2]
Dusén, Karl Fredrik. Bidrag till Härjedalens och Helsinglands flora. 1880. II. 100.[2]
Dusén, Per. Den Eldslandska ögruppens vegetation. 1896. I. 347.
— Die Gefässpflanzen der Magellansländer. 1900. I. 347.
— Ombrägestraktens flora. 1888. I. 357.
— Über die Vegetation der Feuerländischen Inselgruppe. 1896. I. 347.
Du Sert, Fleury Percie. *See* ROSTAING, Léon & Marcel, & DU SERT, F. P.
Dusold. Forstwirthschaftliche Bemerkungen über eine Fohrensaat. 1828. IV. 471.
Duss, R. P. Flore phanérogamique des Antilles françaises. 1897. I. 337.
Dussance, H. China green. 1864. III. 542.[2]
Dussaut, E. Remarques sur le problème de la restauration des montagnes. 1898. IV. 327.[1]
— Remarques sur le projet de loi du régime pastoral. 1899. IV. 135.[1]
Dussaux, L. F. L'Albicocco. 1880. III. 434.[2]
— Dell' innesto digenere. 1881. III. 169.
— Se l' innesto possa recar danno agli alberi. 1881. III. 162.
— De' mezzi di provocare la messa a frutto. 1880. III. 174.[2]
Dussen, J. G. H. van der. Houtkultuur. 1848. IV. 159.
— Iets over het mos der boomen. 1847. III. 193.[1]
— Vriesbarsten bij Beukenboomen. 1848. IV. 496.
Dussuc, Élie. Les ennemies de la Vigne. 1894. III. 561.
Dutailly, Didier Edme Rodolphe Gustave. Sur l'existence de ponctuations criblées. 1874. II. 330.[1]
— Sur les faisceaux diaphragmatiques du Ricin. 1876. II. 451.[1]
— Sur la fleur mâle des Corylus. 1878. II. 121.[2]
— Sur la formation des pelotes adhésives chez une Ampélidée. 1875. II. 504.[2]
— Sur l'inflorescence mâle du Pandanus furcatus. 1882. II. 57.[1]
— Des modifications anatomiques de la tige dans une même plante. 1874. II. 489.[1]
— Morphologie de la fleur mâle du Coudrier. 1878. II. 121.[2]
— Note sur l'inflorescences des Aristoloches. 1874. II. 181.[1]
— Observations organogéniques sur les inflorescences unilatérales des Légumineuses. 1877. II. 320.[1]
— Sur la partition égale du point végétatif chez les Valerianella. 1876. II. 836.[2]
— Un Pirus à graines mucilagineuses. 1898. II. 281.[1]
— Recherches anatomiques . . . sur les Cucurbitacées. 1880. II. 575.[2]
— Recherches sur le développement des Asparaginées. 1897. II. 84.[2]
— De la signification . . . de la vrille de la Vigne vierge. 1868. II. 504.[1]

Dutailly, Didier Edme Rodolphe Gustave (*continued*).
— De la signification . . . de la vrille des Ampélidées. 1873.
II. 501.²
— Sur la signification des cladodes du Ruscus. 1878. II. 84.²
— Des vaisseaux considérés comme remplissant. 1879. I. 135.
Dutch East Indies — **Geneeskundig tijdschrift.** *See* GENEES-
KUNDIG . . . I. 29.¹
Dutch East Indies — **Natuur**- en geneeskundig archief . . .
See NATUUR- . . . I. 29.¹
Dutch East Indies — **Natuurkundige** tijdschrift voor Neder-
landsch-Indië. *See* NATUURKUNDIGE . . . I. 29.¹
Dutch East Indies — **Natuurkundige** vereeniging . . . *See*
NATUURKUNDIGE . . . I. 29.¹
Dutch East Indies — **Tijdschrift** voor land- en tuinbouw . . .
See TIJDSCHRIFT . . . III. 26.²
Dutch East Indies — **Tijdschrift** voor Neerland's Indië. *See*
TIJDSCHRIFT . . . I. 29.²
Duterte. Catalogue des plantes . . . à Alençon. 1884. I.
416.
Du Tertre, Jean Baptiste. Histoire generale des Antilles.
1667. I. 334.
— Histoire générale des isles Saint Christophe. 1654. III. 63.²
Duthie, John Firminger. The botany of the Chitral relief ex-
pedition. 1898. I. 475.²
— Kumaun. 1886. I. 475.¹
— List of north-west Indian plants. 1881. I. 474.
— List of north-west Indian plants. Ranunculaceae to Plan-
tagineae. 1881. I. 474.
— A list of the plants collected on the Pamirs. 1898. I. 477.²
— A list of the trees . . . of Pilibhit. 1899. I. 470.² *IV.*
89.¹
— Notes on some trees and shrubs observed during a . . .
expedition to north-eastern Kumaun. 1885. I. 470.² *IV.*
88.²
— Periodical flowering of Strobilanthes. 1890. II. 803.²
— Plants found in Kumaon, Garhwál. 1882. I. 474.
— Report on a botanical tour in Kashmir. 1893. I. 475.¹
— Report on a botanical tour in Merwára. 1886. I. 475.¹
— A rough list of Indian fodder-yielding trees. 1889. III.
223.²
Duthiers, LACAZE-. *See* LACAZE-DUTHIERS.
Dutoit. Über den Vegetationscharakter der Grajischen Alpen.
1900. I. 438.
— Ueber den Vegetationscharakter von Nord-Wales. 1888.
I. 403.
Dutoit, A. Deux arbres géants. 1887. II. 114,¹ *139.*¹
Dutoit, Benoit Édouard. Histoire naturelle . . . des Eu-
phorbiacées. 1848. III. 514.¹
Dutour, P. *See* Дютуръ, Ц.
Du Trieu de Terdonck, Charles. Notice sur l'Acacia. 1848.
IV. 524.¹
Dutrochet, Henri Joaquim. L'agent immédiat du mouve-
ment vital. 1826. I. 193.²
— De la déviation descendante et ascendante de l'accroisse-
ment. 1835. I. 189.
— Experiments on the temperature of vegetables. 1839. I.
186.
— Extrait des observations sur l'ascension de la sève. 1837.
I. 163.
— Extrait des observations sur la nature . . . du liège.
1837. I. 130.
— Iets over de onvruchtbaarheid. 1831. I. 146.
— De l'inflexion des tiges végétales vers la lumière colorée.
1843. I. 229.
— Mémoire sur les organes aérifères. 1832. I. 169.²
— Mémoires pour servir à l'histoire anatomique . . . des
végétaux. 1837. I. 34.
— Des mouvements révolutifs spontanés. 1843. I. 193,²
197.¹
— Note sur la prétendue circulation des fluides. 1831. I.
163.
— Note sur la substance végétale qui a servi à la fabrication
des toiles. 1837. III. 315.¹
— Nouvelles observations sur la direction des tiges. 1833.
I. 195.²
— Nouvelles recherches sur l'endosmose et l'exosmose. 1828.
I. 146.
— Observation scarpologiques. 1821. I. 121.
— Observations sur la forme . . . des embryons. 1835. I.
121.
— Observations sur la longue persistance de la vie . . . dans
la souche du Pinus Picea. 1833. I. 209.²
— Observations sur les enveloppes de l'embryon. 1820. I.
121.

— Observations sur les variations accidentelles du mode sui-
vant lequel les feuilles sont distribuées. 1834. I. 102.
— Recherches anatomiques et physiologiques. 1824. I. 98,
— Recherches faites . . . sur la chaleur vitale des végétaux.
1839. I. 186.
— Recherches sur l'accroissement et la reproduction des végé-
taux. 1821. I. 121, *187.*
— Recherches sur la chaleur propre des êtres vivans à basse
température. 1840. I. 186.
— Recherches sur la respiration des végétaux. 1836. I. 169.²
— Recherches sur la température propre des végétaux. 1839.
I. 186.
— Recherches sur la volubilité des tiges. 1844. I. 196.¹
— Réponse à la note lue par M. Becquerel. 1839. I. 186.
— Du réveil et du sommeil des plantes. 1836. I. 198.
— De la tendance des végétaux à se diriger vers la lumière.
1837. I. 194.
Dutt, Udoy Chand. The materia medica of the Hindus.
1877. III. 278.
— *See also* KING, George & DUTT, U. C.
Dutt, W. A. Norfolk. 1900. I. 535.
De duurzame Surinaamsche . . . houtsoorten. 1893. IV.
398.¹
Duval, Guillaume. Medical history . . . of Cascarilla. 1846. III. 516.²
Duval. Histoire du Poirier. 1848. III. 445.¹
— Empoisonnement par les fruits de Chèvrefeuille.
1870. III. 751.¹
Duval, (*Jardinier à Chaville*). Greffe Huard ou greffe à la
Pontoise. 1854. III. 161.
— Plantation des arbres à feuilles persistantes. 1855. III.
291.
Duval, A. Recherches chimiques sur la Cascarilla. 1845.
II. 439.²
— Scheikundige onderzoekingen omtrent de cortex Cascarillae.
1845. II. 439.²
Duval, Charles Jeunet. Irlbacher Flora. 1817. I. 376.
Duval, Clotaire. Introduction du Platane en France. 1896.
II. 255,¹ *III. 418.²*
— Maturation des fruits. 1897. I. 179.¹
Duval, Guillaume. Phytologia. 1647. I. 30.
— In phytologiam . . . paraenetica. 1614. I. 30.
Duval, Henri Auguste. Plantae succulentae in Horto alen-
conio. 1819. I. 57.
Duval, Léon. Les Azalées. 1895. III. 657.¹.
— Le Cocos Weddeliana. 1889. III. 324.²
— Culture pratique des Azalées de l'Inde. 1885. III. 656.
— Les cultures de Biskra. 1897. III. 130.²
— Le Cycas néo-calédonica. 1887. III. 285.¹
— Le Dracaena neocaledonica. 1889. III. 335.
Duval, P. N. Traité universel des eaux et forets de France.
1699. IV. 324.
Duval, Raoul. De la propriété forestière en France. 1844.
IV. 275.
Duval-Jouve, Joseph. Sur ce qu'on a appelé les cladodes des
Ruscus. 1876. II. 84.²
— Sur une déformation des tiges du Pinus silvestris. 1858.
II. 47.¹
— Étude histotaxique des cladodes du Ruscus. 1877. II. 84.²
— Étude histotaxique . . . les cladodes des Ruscus. 1876.
II. 84.²
— Notes sur quelques plantes . . . de l'Hérault. 1876. I. 415.
— Notes sur quelques plantes . . . de l'Hérault. 1877.
II. 498.²
— Sur quelques plantes . . . de Montpellier. 1877. II.
499.¹
— Des Salicornia de l'Hérault. 1868. II. 188.²
Duvaure, Antoine. Mémoire sur la culture du Mûrier. 1789.
III. 373.
— Mémoire sur les avantages . . . de la culture du Mûrier.
1790. III. 373.
— Mémoires divers d'agriculture. 1789. III. 125.
Duve, G. C. Vollständige nach dem Decimalmass herech-
nete Tabellen. 1801. IV. 221.
Duve, Jordan. De acceleranda per artem plantarum vegeta-
tione. 1717. III. 176.¹
Duvernay, L. A., (*sr.*). Traité sur la culture du Mûrier.
1843. III. 376.
Duvernoy, Johann Georg. Designatio plantarum circa
Tubingensem arcem. 1722. I. 373.
Duveyrier, Henri. Les Touáreg du Nord. 1864. I. 484.
Duvillers-Chasseloup, F. Un essai sur l'avantage qu'il y
aurait de prendre date des semis . . . et sur l'If. 1842.
II. 10.²
— Note sur quelques arbres foudroyés. 1841. IV. 193.²

Du Vivie, J. De nieuwe en nauwkeurige Nederlandse hovenier. 1721. III. 105.
Duvivier, Ch. La Forêt charbonnière. 1861. IV. 27.[1]
Du Vivier, Olivier. Note sur le Forsythia suspensa. 1858. III. 672.[1]
— Notice sur quelques produits . . . de Palmiers. 1856. III. 319.[1]
— L'Olivier d'Europe. 1858. III. 678.[2]
— Les Oxycoccos. 1857. III. 663.[1]
— De quelques plantes équatoriales et de leurs produits. 1857. III. 319.[1]
— Le Tamarinier. 1858. III. 489.[1]
Duyk. Les huiles essentielles au point de vue chimique. 1896. III. 225.
Dvigubsky, Ivan A. *See* Двигубскій, Ив.
The **Dwarf** Palm of Algeria. 1893. III. 322.[1]
Dwars, D. W. Analysis of the Take-no-ko. 1879. III. 315.[1]
Dwight, Timothy. A statistical account of the towns and parishes in the state of Connecticut. 1811. I. 313.
— Travels in New-England and New-York. 1821. I. 313.
Dyakowski, Bogdan. Nasz las i jego mieszkańcy. 1898. I. 82.[2]
— Rozsiedlanie się roślin dzikich za pośrednictwem człowieka. 1899. I. 241.[2]
Dybdahl, J. A. Jordbær- og vore vigtigste frugtbusk-arter. 1879. III. 66,[2] 147.[2]
— Plantning af Kurv- og Baandpiil. 1873. III. 347.
Dybkowsky, W. & **Pélikan**, Eugène. Recherches physiologiques sur l' action de différents poisons du cœur. 1861. III. 366,[2] 691.[1]
Dybowski, Jean. Les Bananiers et les Palmiers à huile. 1893. II. 68.[2]
— Le Caféier des terres humides. 1898. III. 727.
— Un cas de dimorphisme. 1888. II. 292.[2]
— Sur les conditions culturales en Tunisie. 1899. III. 130.[2]
— Le Dattier. 1890. III. 329.[1]
— Le Girofiler au Congo. 1894. III. 635.[2]
— Les oasis du sud de la province de Constantine. 1889. III. 329.[1]
— Le Papayer. 1894. III. 617.[1]
— Production du caoutchouc. 1897. III. 231.
— & **Fron**, G. L'Eucomia ulmoides. 1899. III. 418.[1]
— Sur une plante à gutta-percha. 1899. III. 418.[1]
— Bertrand, Gabriel & **Phisalix**, C. Le Ko-Sam. 1900. III. 507.[2]
Dybowski, Władysław. Flora Nowogródzka. 1890. I. 365.
— W kwestyi gatunków Głogu na Litwie rosnących. 1900. II. 261.[1]
— Przyczynek do flory nowogrodzkiej. 1899. I. 367.
— Rośliny litewskie w poezyach Adama Mickiewicza. 1898. I. 515.
— Skorowidz do slelnika flory palskiej. 1900. I. 267.
Dyck, Joseph, *Fürst* SALM-REIFFERSCHEID-. *See* SALM-REIFFERSCHEID-DYCK, Joseph, *Fürst*.
Dye plants. 1893. III. 236.
Dyer, Herbert L. *See* COLBY, G. E. & DYER, H. L.
Dyer, Thomas Firminger THISELTON-. The folk-lore of plants. 1889. I. 518.
— Plants in witchcraft. 1889. I. 518.
Dyer, William Turner THISELTON-. Les Acacias australiens aux Indes orientales. 1883. II. 324.[2]
— Die Aloe Bainesii des westlichen Süd-Afrika. 1874. II. 77.[2]
— Aloe Bainesii. 1874. II. 77.[2]
— Aloës Dichotoma. 1874. II. 77.[2]
— Calcareous deposit in Hieronyma. 1887. II. 445.[2]
— Cycads of Indian Peninsula. 1881. II. 4.[1]
— On the determination of three . . . Ternstroemiaceae. 1873. II. 547.[2]
— On the Dipterocarpeae of New Guinea. 1878. II. 559.[1]
— The disputed identity of the Redbark of the Nilgiris. 1885. II. 814.[1]
— Encephalarthos acantha. 1879. II. 5.[2]
— Encephalartos latifrons. 1881. II. 5.[1]
— Flora capensis. 1896. I. 495.
— Flora of tropical Africa. 1897. I. 483.[2]
— On the genus Hoodja. 1877. II. 739.[1]
— Hibiscus rosa-sinensis var. schizopetalus. 1879. II. 524.[1]
— Influence of environment upon plants. 1883. II. 324.[2]
— Larch disease. 1875. IV. 450.
— Myrrh. 1897. III. 511.[1]
— On a new species of Cycas. 1883. II. 4.[1]
— Note on some Indian Dipterocarpeae. 1874. II. 559.[1]

— Note on the cultivation of Sumach in Sicily. 1885. III. 527.[1]
— Note on the fruiting of Wistaria sinensis. 1880. II. 388.[1]
— Note on the origin of Cassia lignea. 1882. III. 405.[1]
— Note on the origin of Cassia lignea. 1884. II. 224.[2]
— Notes on some new economic products. 1884. III. 218.[2]
— Podocarpus pectinatus. 1892. II. 8.[1]
— The Rain-tree of Moyobamba. 1878. II. 377.[2]
— Remarks upon M. Vesque's new species. 1874. . II. 559.[2]
— Report on the botany of Mr. H. O. Forbes's expedition to Timor-Laut. 1886. I. 466.
— A revision of the genera Dryobalanops. 1874. II. 559.[1]
— The sacred tree of Kam-Bam. 1896. II. 715.[2]
— Streblus paper. 1888. III. 381.[1]
— On the structure of the stem of the Screw Pine. 1872. II. 57.[1]
— Tree-Aloes. 1875. II. 77.[2]
— The tree Aloes of South Africa. 1874. II. 77.[2]
— Zamia Fischeri. 1883. II. 7.[1]
— Zamia montana. 1882. II. 7.[1]
— Zamia obliqua. 1882. II. 7.[1]
— Zamia tonkinensis. 1885. II. 7.[2]
— *See also* TRIMEN, Henry & DYER, W. T. THISELTON-.
— & others. Report of the committee . . . on the present state of our knowledge of the zoology and botany of the West India Islands. 1889. I. 337.
Dýk. Theerbrennerei in den Militärgrenz-Waldungen. 1871. IV. 436.[2]
Dyk, van. Iets over de bijen. 1900. III. 129.[1]
— Iets over de Rami-cultuur. 1899. III. 381.[2]
Dykema, H. Bijdrage tot de kennis der verbeteringen in de vaderlandsche landhuishouding. 1852. III. 106.[1]
Dykstra, J. F. Opium, Koffie en nog wat. 1897. III. 727.
Dymock, William. Anthropogonic trees of the Hindu castes. 1887. I. 517.[1]
— Marathi names of plants with a glossary. 1887. I. 75.[2]
— The means of self-protection possessed by plants. 1888. I. 235.[1] ea.
— Sur la myrrhe et le bdellium. 1876. III. 227.
— Naregamia alata. 1888. III. 512.[2]
— Sur le Naregamia alata. 1888. III. 512.[2]
— Note on myrrh. 1876. III. 245.
— Notes on Indian drugs. 1877. III. 278, 409,[1] 470,[2] 493,[2] 504,[2] 511,[1] 515,[1] 519,[2] 520,[1] 534,[2] 586,[2] 589,[1] 603,[2] 610,[2] 651,[1] 692,[2] 707,[1] 708,[2] 709,[1] 745,[1] 746.[1]—1878. III. 327,[1] 394,[2] 405,[1] 489,[1] 511,[1] 544,[2] 591,[1] 591,[2] 592,[1] 609,[1] 630,[1] 691,[1] 696.[1]—1879. III. 466,[1] 632.[1]—1880. III. 517,[1] 518,[1] 690,[1] 695,[1] 702.[1]
— Sacred trees of the Hindus. 1887. I. 517.[1]
— Substances used as incense in the East. 1891. III. 226.[2]
— The vegetable materia medica of western India. 1883. III. 278.
— & **Warden**, C. J. H. Aristolochia indica. 1892. III. 386.[2]
— Picrasma quassioides. 1889. III. 508.[2]
— Picrasma quassioides Benn. 1889. III. 508.[2]
— & **Hooper**, David. Pharmacographia indica. 1890. III. 279.[1]
Om **Dyrkning** af Naaletræer (Coniferæ) i Potter. 1849. III. 291.
Om **Dyrkning** af Pil. 1882. III. 348.
Dzerzhanovski, V. *See* Держановскій, B.
Dziarkowski, H. A. & **Siennicki**, K. Pomnożenie dykcyonarza roślinnego. 1830. I. 93.
Dziędzielewicz, Józef. Krawędź wyżyny podolskiej. 1877. I. 442.
Dziekoński, Bartłomiej. Rolnictwo i ogrodnictwo. 1796. III. 115.[2]
Dziennik ogrodniczy. III. 24.[2]
Dzievulski, L. *See* Дзвянульскій, Л.
Dzikowski. Nouveaux tarifs de cubage des bois. 1861. IV. 224.
—e. Ueber Düngung im Forstbetriebe. 1898. IV. 145.
—e. Forstwirthschaft . . . in Obersteiermark. 1895. IV. 369.
—e—. Bosnischer Eichen-Auwald. 1897. IV. 508.
—e—. Ein dichter Buchenbestand. 1897. IV. 496.
—e—. Hyponomeutafrass in Bosnien. 1897. III. 191.
—e—. Osmanthus. 1894. III. 679.[2]
—e—. Die Panzerkiefer . . . in der Herzegowina. 1897. IV. 464.[2]
E. Aus den Annalen unserer vaterländischen Forstgeschichte. 1887. IV. 26.
E. Cryptomeria elegans. 1889. III. 302.[1]
E. Iets over de teelt van Europeesche vrucht boomen op Java. 1873. III. 147.[1]

E. Removal of trees. 1844. III. 167.
E. Der Sturm vom 1. Juli 1897 in Graubünden. 1897. IV. 189.[2]
E. Die volkswirtschaftliche Bedeutung des Waldes. 1891. IV. 270.
E., v. Over de gewassen en boomen, die niet onbehevig zijn aan de vernielingen door konijnen. 1870. III. 186.[1]
E., A. H. Bouvardias. 1889. III. 711.[1]
E., A. X. Larch, native and foreign. 1885. IV. 449.
E., C. Einiges über die Vermehrung der Zierbäume. 1873. III. 153.
E., C. Einiges über Vermehrung der Paeonia arborea. 1874. III. 393.[1]
E., C. Der Werth der ombrometrischen Beobachtungen. 1897. IV. 60.[1]
E., G. Frühzeitiger Durchforstungsertrag. 1844. IV. 261,[2] 480.
E., H. Curious and historic trees. 1882. I. 297.[1]
E., H. Epping forest. 1882. IV. 358.[1]
E., H. Junipers. 1885. II. 30.[1]
E., H. The Oriental Plane tree. 1885. IV. 520.[2]
E., H. Profitable planting. 1882. IV. 259.[2]
E., H. The sweet Chestnut. 1884. II. 125.[1]
E., H. Trees as artists' models. 1883. I. 516.
E., H. Der Wachholder. 1892. IV. 448.[2]
E., H. Wistman's wood. 1881. IV. 516.[1]
E., H. Woodlands in Sussex and Kent. 1885. IV. 358.[1]
E., H. N. Single Roses. 1880. III. 455.[2]
E., J. Sylva. *See* EVELYN, John. 1664. IV. 107.[2]
E., J. C. Erfahrung von der Wirkung des Blumenstaubes. 1775. I. 245.
E., J. F. Gedanken über die Rosen . . . die Weiden tragen. 1750. III. 350.[1]
E., R. A. De bewerking van guttapercha. 1899. III. 232.[1]
E., R. C. On the tenderness . . . of the Larch in Britain. 1874. III. 304.[2]
E. v. W. De heesterachtige Poelpalm. 1784. II. 71.[2]
E—o. Ueber Standortsansprüche unserer Holzarten. 1895. IV. 70.
The Eagle's Claw Echinocactus. 1879. IV. 529.[1]
Eakin, John R. Rudiments of Grape culture. 1868. III. 550.
Eakins, George. Olive culture. 1898. III. 679.[2]
Ealing Park, Amherstia nobilis. 1849. III. 466.[2]
Eames, Ninetta. Mr. Luther Burbank's nursery. 1896. III. 389.[2]
Eardley-Wilmot, S. *See* WILMOT, S. EARDLEY-.
Earle, Franklin Sumner. The blooming season of Plums. 1898. II. 272.[1]
— *See also* EISEN, Gustav & EARLE, F. S.
Earle, John. English plant names from the 10th to the 15th century. 1880. I. 74.[1]
Earle, Parker. The ripening and preservation of fruits. 1886. III. 173.[2]
Earley, William. Benthamia fragifera. 1880. III. 645.[2]
— Catalpa as a town tree. 1900. III. 706.[1]
— Cotoneaster Simonsii. 1872. III. 421.[1]
— Crataegus tanacetifolia. 1896. II. 263.[2]
— Cydonia Maulei. 1874. III. 420.[2]
— Hardy winter blooming shrubs. 1886. III. 207.[2]
— How should we lop trees? 1874. III. 173.[1]
— The Macartney Rose. 1874. III. 454.[2]
— Support v. restraint, in connection with staking trees. 1874. III. 198.[2]
— & Cramb, Alexander. Aërial roots upon Vines. 1868. II. 508.[1]
Earliest notice of Coca. 1889. III. 493.[1]
Early flora of the Truckee Valley. *See* HILLMAN, F. H. 1894. I. 326.
Early flowering shrubs. 1890. III. 415.[2]
Early flowering shrubs and trees. 1873. III. 207.[2]
Early Oranges. 1893. III. 500.[1]
East African sandal wood. 1898. III. 384.[1]
East India (Chinchona cultivation). Return to an address. 1870. III. 714.
East India (Chinchona plant). Return to an address. 1863. III. 713.[2]
East Indian furniture woods. [Extracts.] 1883. IV. 426.[2]
'**East Indian Walnut.**' 1894. IV. 521.[1]
Eastbourne natural history society. Papers. Transactions. I. 18.
Easter, J. Posoqueria longiflora. 1898. III. 746.[2]

Easterbrook, George. The mode of clearing timber tracts in Russia. 1878. IV. 383.[1]
Eastlea, Walter. The hybridisation of Roses. 1896. III. 453.[1]
Eastwood, Alice. Arctostaphylos as a host plant for Phoradendron. 1900. II. 177.[1]
— The Coniferae of the Santa Lucia Mountains. 1897. II. 14.[2]
— Description of some new species of Californian plants. 1897. V. XVIII.[1]
— On heteromorphic organs of Sequoia sempervirens. 1896. II. 49.[2]
— The Manzanitas of Mt. Tamalpais. 1897. II. 660.[2]
— The Morning Glory bush. 1890. III. 694.[2]
— New species of California plants. 1900. I. 327.
— New species of Pacific coast plants. 1898. II. 258.[2]
— Notes on Cupressus Macnabiana. 1900. II. 29.[1]
— Notes on the plants of San Nicolas Island. 1898. I. 327.
— Pinus Lambertiana on Mt. St. Helena. 1900. II. 42.[3]
— A popular flora of Denver. 1893. I. 326.
— Report on a collection of plants from San Juan county. 1897. I. 326.
— Report on . . . plants from the White Sands of New Mexico. 1897. I. 326.
— Some plants of Mendocino county. 1900. I. 327.
— Studies in the herbarium and the field. 1897. I. 326, 327, II. 660.[1] — 1898. II. 258,[2] 747.[1]
— Two species of Eriodictyon. 1898. II. 747.[1]
Eastwood, B. A complete manual for the cultivation of the Cranberry. 1856. III. 663.[2]
Eaton, Amos. A botanical dictionary. 1816. I. 70.
— Botanical dictionary. 1824. V. IX.[1]
— Botanical grammar and dictionary. 1836. I. 70, V. IX.[1]
— A geological and agricultural survey of Rensselaer county. 1822. III. 117.[2]
— A manual of botany for North America. 1817. I. 306.
— A manual of botany for the northern and middle states. 1817. I. 306.
— A manual of botany for the northern states. 1817. I. 306, V. XVI.[2]
— North American botany. 1817. I. 306.
Eau-de-vie de baies de Sorbier. 1850. III. 459.[1]
Eaux d'égout de Paris. Travaux du comité de défense contre les projets de déboisement. 1879. IV. 180.[2]
Ebbenhout. 1884. IV. 534.[1]
Ebe, J. D. Deutliche und gründliche Anleitung wie man . . . Obstbäume erziehen. 1811. III. 136.
Ebel, (*Privatförster*). Welches ist die beste Methode für die Pflanzung ballenloser Kiefern? 1898. IV. 473.
Ebel, Wilhelm. Zwölf Tage auf Montenegro. 1842. I. 449.
Ebeling, Johann Theodor Philippe Christian. De Quassia et lichene islandico. 1779. III. 508.[2]
Ebeling, Max. Die Saugorgane bei der Keimung. 1884. I. 203.
Ebenhöch, Franz. Die phanerogamen Pflanzen von Koroncsó. 1860. I. 445.
Ebenhof, Alfred WEBER VON, *Ritter*. *See* WEBER VON EBENHOF, Alfred, *Ritter*.
Eberbach, Otto. Der Forstwart. 1900. IV. 98.[2]
Eberdt, Oscar. Ueber das Palissadenparenchym. 1888. I. 124.
— Die Transpiration der Pflanzen. 1889. I. 168.
Eberhard, Julius. Die Durchforstung in reinen Beständen. 1897. IV. 175.[1]
— Die Inhaltsberechnung des Langnutzholzes. 1894. IV. 228.
Eberhardt. Action de l'air sec et de l'air humide. 1900. I. 233.[1]
— Influence du milieu sec et du milieu humide. 1900. I. 233.[1]
— Modifications dans l'écorce primaire. 1899. I. 130. .
Eberhardt, Louis Adolph. Ueber den Japantalg. 1888. III. 526.[2]
Eberle, John. Botanical terminology. 1818. V. IX.[1]
— A treatise of the materia medica. 1822. III. 242.
Eberlin, Peter. Blomsterplanterne i dansk Östgrönland. 1888. I. 309.[1]
Ebermaier, Johann Christoph. Ueber die nothwendige Verbindung der systematischen Pflanzenkunde mit der Pharmacie. 1796. III. 238.[1]
Ebermaier, Karl Heinrich. Dissertatio . . . sistens plantarum Papilionacearum monographiam medicam. 1824. III. 462.[1]
— *See also* NEES VON ESENBECK, T. F. L. & EBERMAIER, C. H.

Ebermann, Louis. Ueber die Vermehrung der Paeonia Mouton. 1839. III. 393.[1]
Ebermayer, Ernst Wilhelm Ferdinand. Die Bedeutung der Wälder. 1876. IV. 50.
— Beobachtungen über Blitzschläge. 1891. IV. 190, *194*.
— Die Beschaffenheit der Waldluft. 1885. IV. 64,[1] *72*.
— The casting of young Pine trees. 1879. IV. 477.
— Dlaczego drzewa leśne nie zawierają azotanów? 1888. I. 155.
— Einfluss der Wälder auf die Bodenfeuchtigkeit. 1900. IV. 52.
— Einfluss des Waldes . . . auf die Bodenfeuchtigkeit. 1889. IV. 51.
— Zum forstlichen Anbau der Lärchen. 1866. IV. 449.
— Die gesammte Lehre der Waldstreu. 1876. IV. 71.
— Graphische Darstellungen über den Gang der . . . Temperatur. 1873. IV. 53.
— Hygienische Bedeutung des Waldes. 1890. IV. 55,[1] 542.[2]
— Influence de la forêt . . . sur le degré d'humidité. 1889. IV. 51.
— Influence hygiénique de la forêt. 1890. IV. 55.[1]
— The influence of forests . . . on the moisture in the earth. 1889. IV. 51.
— Influencia higiénica de los montes. 1890. IV. 542.[2]
— Instruction für die Beobachter der . . . meteorologischen Stationen in Bayern. 1866. IV. 59.[1]
— Instructionen für phänologische . . . Beobachtungen. 1868. IV. 72.
— Klimatische Wirkung des Waldes. 1893. IV. 54.
— Metsä-ilman ja metsämaan ominaisuuksista ja niiden merkityksestä hygienisessä. 1890. IV. 55.[1]
— Mittheilungen über den Kohlensäuregehalt eines bewaldeten und nicht bewaldeten Bodens. 1877. IV. 44.
— La nutrition minérale des arbres des forêts. 1893. I. 160, IV. 70.[1]
— Die physikalischen Einwirkungen des Waldes. 1873. IV. 44, 53.
— Physiologische Chemie der Pflanzen. 1882. I. 152,[1] *IV. 63*.[2]
— La statique chimique des forêts. 1878. IV. 71.
— Studien über das Wasserbedürfniss der Waldbäume. 1884. IV. 73.[2]
— Untersuchungen über die Zahl und Grösse der Blätter. 1882. I. 173, *IV. 63*.[2]
— Untersuchungen über . . . Waldluft. 1886. IV. 54.
— Untersuchungen und Studien über die Ansprüche der Waldbäume. 1893. *I. 160*, IV. 70, *V. xi*.[2]
— Die Waldstreufrage. 1894. IV. 72.
— Warum enthalten die Waldbäume keine Nitrate? 1888. I. 155.
— Welchen Standort . . . verlangt die Lärche. 1864. IV. 449.
— Wie kann man den Einfluss der Wälder auf den Quellenreichthum ermitteln? 1879. IV. 50.
Ebermayer, Theodor. Die Lehren der Forstwissenschaft. 1872. IV. 98.[1]
— Nachtrag zu dem Leitfaden für den Unterricht der Forsteleven. 1872. IV. 98.[1]
Eberswald, SIEGLER VON. *See* SIEGLER VON EBERSWALD.
Eberswalde — **Königliche Forstakademie**. Katalog der Bibliothek. *See* MUNDT, O. 1883. IV. 2.
Ebert, C. Die balsamischen Kiefernadelbäder. 1853. IV. 462.[2]
Eberts. Der Anbau der Kiefer in Hessen. 1900. IV. 26, *474*, *482*.[1]
Eberts, (*Oberförster, Gemünd*). Emploi de la glu pour chenilles contre les dégâts du gibier. 1895. IV. 548.[1]
— Raupenleim als Mittel gegen Wildverbiss. 1895. IV. 548.[2]
Eberts, A. Der Akazienniederwald. 1899. IV. 523.[1]
— Ueber die Leistungsfähigkeit von Waldsortimente. 1875. IV. 388.[1]
— Etwas über die Leistungsfähigkeit von Waldsägen. 1881. IV. 393.
— Ueber Holzverkäufe im Wege des schriftlichen Angebots. 1888. IV. 388.[2]
— Kreisflächentafeln nach Metermaass. 1874. IV. 230.
— Ueber die Leistungen verschiedener Waldsägen. 1878. IV. 393.
— Samenertragsergebniss der wichtigsten Holzarten Preussens. 1875. IV. 438.[1]
— Untersuchungen über Gewicht und Festgehalt der Eichenrinde. 1876. IV. 512.
— Untersuchungen über Holz- und Rinden-Erträge in Weidenheegern. 1876. IV. 487.[1]

— Vergleichende Untersuchungen über die Leistungsfähigkeit des . . . Waldpfluges. 1876. IV. 143.[1]
— Vergleichende Versuche über die Leistungsfähigkeit des . . . Waldpfluges. 1878. · IV. 143.[1]
— Waldbeschädigungen durch Schneeanhang. 1875. IV. 190.
— In welcher Weise lassen sich aus den Staats- und Gemeindewaldungen . . . grössere Reinerträge erzielen? 1888. IV. 245.
— Wiederkehr der Kiefernsamenjahre in Preussen. 1875. IV. 472.
— Ueber die Zweckmässigkeit der Verwendung der Urich'schen Zündnadelsprengschraube. 1878. IV. 386.
Eberts, E. Einiges über die Holzschuhfabrikation in Pommern. 1880. IV. 428.[2]
— Gesetz betreffend die Unfall- und Kranken-Versicherung. 1886. IV. 310.[2]
— Die Holzschuhfabrikation in Frankreich. 1879. IV. 428.[2]
— Waldflächen und Waldertrag in Russland. 1880. IV. 346.
— Zwei neue Keim-Apparate. 1884. III. 156.[1]
Eberts, Eduard. Forstliche Rechtskunde Preussens. 1881. IV. 321.
Eble, Burkard. Die Lehre von den Haaren. 1831. I. 112.[1]
Eble, Mich. Das neue Messbrettchen. 185.? IV. 264.
Eblin, Bernhard. Ueber die Auslaufer bildende Fichte. 1896. II. 37.[1]
— Ueber den durch Faktoren . . . mitbedingten Zerfall unserer Hochgebirgswälder. 1896. I. 432,[1] *IV. 86*.[3]
— Ueber die Waldreste des Averser Oberthales. 1895. I. 432,[1] *IV. 86*.[3]
Ebn Serab. Liber Serapionis aggregatus. 1473. III. 239.
Ebrodensis, (*pseud.*). Ifs et Cèdres. 1900. I. 298.[1]
— Pins et Mélèzes. 1899. I. 298.[1]
Eby, A. Copse culture. 1883. IV. 132.[1]
Eby, S. P. Uses of forests in Lancaster county. 1881. IV. 46.[1]
— Eccentric growth in timber. 1878. II. 35.[2]
Echeandia, Pedro Gregorio. Flora caesaraugustana. 1861. I. 421.
Echegaray, José de. Memoria sobre las causas de la sequía de las provincias de Almeria y Murcia. 1851. IV. 47.[2]
Echegaray, Saile. Determinacion de plantas sanjuaninas. 1875. I. 344.
— Echinocactus Kunzei Först. und Opuntia stricta. 1882. II. 592,[2] 597.[1]
L'Echo forestier. IV. 12.[2]
Echterling, Johann B. H. Verzeichniss der im Fürstenthum Lippe wildwachsenden . . . Pflanzen. 1846. I. 381.
Eck, Heinrich. Zum Artikel im Decemberheft 1884: "Der Eck'sche Numerirhammer." 1885. IV. 387.[3]
Eckard, Eduard Ludwig Albert Valerius. De radice Ratanbiac. 1822. III. 338.[1]
Eckard, C. E., Beedecker, C. & **Lutterberth**, H. Présence de la baryte dans les cendres végétales. .1859. IV. 500.[1]
Eckardt, Theo. Der Flieder. 1900. III. 680.[2]
Eckart, Johann Gottlieb von. Vollständige Experimentalökonomie. 1754. IV. 115.
Eckart, Ulrich. Chemische Untersuchung des . . . Rosenöles. 1891. III. 454.[2]
— Etudes chimiques de l'essence de Roses. 1891. III. 454.[2]
Eckelberg, Johann Gustaf. De reformatioribus classium plantarum. 1804. I. 251.
Eckert, Franz. Ueber die Bestandesmassenermittlung. 1887. IV. 218.
— Lehrbuch der Forstwirtschaft. 1896. IV. 98.[1]
— Die Vegetationsdecke als Modificator des Klimas. 1893. IV. 45.
Eckert, J. P. Some peculiar changes in the colour of the flower of Swainsonia procumbens. 1892. II. 386.[1]
Ecklon, Christian Friedrich. Topographisches Verzeichniss der Pflanzensammlung. 1827. I. 494.
— & **Zeyher**, Carl. Enumeratio plantarum Africae australis. 1835. I. 494.
Eckstein, Karl. Beiträge zur Kenntniss der Gespinnstblattwespen. 1889. IV. 208.[1]
— Die Feinde der Coniferenzapfen. 1888. IV. 442.
— Forstliche Zoologie. 1897. IV. 90.[1]
— Infektionsversuche . . . an Nonnenraupen. 1900. IV. 202.
— Insektenschaden im Walde. 1893. IV. 208.[1]
— Zur Kenntniss der vom grossen Kiefernmarkkäfer verursachten Abbrüche. 1890. IV. 478.
— Die Kiefer . . . und ihre tierischen Schädlinge. 1893. IV. 478.

Eckstein, Karl (*continued*).
— Die Kiefernnadelscheidengallmücke. 1893. IV. 478.
— Der Korbweiden-Blattkäfer. 1890. III. 350.[1]
— Die Lebensweise der Kiefernsaateule. 1896. IV. 479.
— Eine merkwürdige Allee. 1886. IV. 483.[1]
— Pflanzengallen und Gallentiere. 1891. I. 215.[1]
— Versuche über die Vertilgung der Nonne. 1899. IV. 202.
— Werkzeuge zum Leimen. 1892. IV. 199.[2]
Eckstorm. Nochmals " Zur Invaliditäts- und Altersversicherung." 1893. IV. 311.[1]
Des éclaircies. 1896. IV. 175.[1]
Éclaircies dans un peuplement mélangé de Pins sylvestres et d'Épicéas. 1898. IV. 175.[1]
Éclaircissements sur le baume à cochon. 1824. III. 511.[2]
The eclectic and general dispensatory. 1827. III. 246.
Eclectic magazine of foreign literature. I. 5.
Eclectic museum. See ECLECTIC magazine . . . I. 5.
Eclectic review. III. 16.
El Eco de la ganaderia y de la agricultura. III. 23.[1]
L'Eco dei campi e dei boschi. IV. 13.[1]
École d'horticulture de l'état à Vilvorde. 1898. IV. 33.[2]
École des hautes-études. Bibliothèque. I. 520.[1]
L'école du jardinier fleuriste. 1764. III. 112.
L'école forestière anglaise de Cooper's Hill. See PROSPECTUS . . 1888. IV. 34.[1]
École forestière de Nancy. 1894. IV. 540.[2]
L'École nationale d'agriculture de Montpellier. Annales. III. 19.
L'École normale supérieure. Annales. I. 21.
Écoles de sylviculture pour les gardes-forêts. See WALD-BAUSCHULEN. IV. 36.[1]
Le economia forestale nel cantone Ticino. 1873. IV. 367.
Economic and medicinal plants. 1887. III. 64.[1]
Economic plants in the Missouri botanic garden. 1886. I. 39.
Economic plants of Sierra Leone. 1893. III. 93.[1]
Economic tropical horticulture in Northern Queensland. See BERNAYS, L. A. 1880. V. xxviii.[1]
Economical uses of the Birch-tree. 1843. IV. 491.[1]
Economical uses of the Larch. 1843. IV. 452.[1]
Economical uses of the Maple. 1843. III. 534.[1]
Economical uses of the Oak. 1843. IV. 514.[1]
Economical uses of the Willow. 1842. III. 350.[1]
Le economie dello stato e le forniture di legname. 1894. IV. 277.[1]
De Economist. III. 14.
L'Économiste française. III. 19.
L'écorçage des souches de Pins sylvestres abattus. 1899. IV. 479.
L'écorce à tanner. See EICHEN-GERBER-RINDE. 1858. IV. 512.
Une écorce aromatique. 1869. III. 276.[2]
Écorce de Grenadier. 1873. III. 630.[2]
L'écorce de Mimosa tannante. 1892. III. 481.[2]
Écorce de Müsenna. 1852. III. 466.[1]
Écorce du Strychnos nux vomica. 1837. III. 684.[2]
Écorcement des résineux employés dans les houillères. 1899. IV. 387.[1]
Écorchard, E. F. Flore régionale de toutes les plantes . . . de Paris. 1877. I. 415.
— Synopsis de la flore des environs de Paris. 1878. I. 415.
Écorchard, Jean Marie. Histoire du Jardin des plantes de Nantes. 1855. I. 58.
— Nouvelle théorie élémentaire de la botanique. 1876. I. 52.
L'écureuil. 1895. IV. 548.[2]
Eddy, Caspar Wistar. Plantae plandomenses. 1808. I. 313.
Eddy, John Mathewson. In the Redwood's realm. 1893. II. 49.[2]
Ede, W. L'Hydrangea Otaksa monstrosa. 1898. III. 412.[1]
Edel, Eduard. Beitrag zum Baumroden. 1857. IV. 385.[2]
— Der Streuwerth. 1863. IV. 71.
Edel, Julius. Bemerkungen über die Vegetation der Moldau. 1853. I. 440.
Edelhoff, Edwin. Vergleichende Anatomie des Blattes . . . der Olacineen. 1886. II. 170.[2]
Edeling, A. C. J. Botanische wandeling in den omtrek van Bidara-tjina. 1870. I. 466.
Edelkrantz, d'. Descriptions d'un onguent nouveau pour les arbres. 1804. III. 180.[1]
Eder, Carl. Untersuchungen über die Ausscheidung von Wasserdampf. 1875. I. 167.

Edes, Robert T. Therapeutic handbook of the United States pharmacopoeia. 1883. III. 247.[1]
Edge, Thomas J. The cost of fencing timber in Pennsylvania. 1887. IV. 403.[2]
— The forests of our state. 1878. IV. 45.
Edgeworth, Maria. Dialogues on botany. 1819. I. 94.
Edgeworth, Michael Pakenham. Botanico-agricultural account of the protected Sikh states. 1838. I. 472.
— Catalogue of plants found in the Banda district. 1851. I. 473.
— A couple of hours' herborization at Aden. 1847. I. 480.
— Descriptions of some . . . plants from northwestern India. 1851. I. 473.
— Florula mallica. 1862. I. 473.
— Florula of Banda. 1867. I. 474.
— Memoranda regarding two kinds of dyestuffs. 1850. III. 236.
— Pollen. 1877. I. 117.[1]
Edgren, Pehr Adolph. Horti upsaliensis plantae. See THUNBERG, C. P. 1826. I. 40.
— Piper nigrum. See THUNBERG, C. P. 1827. III. 343.[2]
Edible productions of the North American forests. 1840. III. 261.[2]
Edicts et ordonnances, arrests et reglemens des eaües et forests. 1649. IV. 323.[2]
Edicts et ordonnances des eaues et forests. 1588. IV. 323.[1]
Edinburgh — Botanical society. See BOTANICAL . . . I. 17, III. 16.
Edinburgh — Royal botanic garden. See ROYAL BOTANIC GARDEN. I. 55.
Edinburgh — Royal society. See ROYAL . . . I. 20.
Edinburgh field naturalists' and microscopical society. Transactions. See EDINBURGH NATURALISTS' FIELD CLUB. I. 18.
Edinburgh journal of science. I. 18.
Edinburgh medical and surgical journal. I. 18.
Edinburgh medical journal. See EDINBURGH medical and surgical journal. I. 18; The MONTHLY journal of medicine. I. 19.
Edinburgh museum of science and art. List of books, etc., relating to botany and forestry . . . in the library. See LIST . . . 1897. I. 3.[1]
The Edinburgh naturalists' field club. Transactions. I. 18.
Edinburgh new dispensatory. 1786. III. 253.
Edinburgh new philosophical journal. See EDINBURGH philosophical journal. I. 18.
Edinburgh philosophical journal. I. 18.
Edinburgh review. III. 16.
Eding, H. Die Rechtsverhältnisse des Waldes. 1874. IV. 314.[1]
Édit du roi portant réglement pour les offices de grand-maitres. 1784. IV. 325.
Édit du roi, pour autoriser les officiers des maitrises à juger en dernier ressort les causes pour vente de bois. 1783. IV. 325.
Édit du roy, concernant la vente du caffé. 1692. III. 222.
Édit du roy, concernant les receveurs généraux & particuliers des finances & des domaines & bois. 1749. IV. 303.[2]
Édit du roy, donné à Paris . . . portant règlement sur les amandes des eaux & forêts. 1743. IV. 325.
Édit du roy, donné à Paris . . . portant supression de differens offices dans les maltrises des eaux & forêts. 1717. IV. 325.
Édit du roy, donné à Versailles . . . portant supression . . . des chambres de reformation des eaux & forêts. 1704. IV. 324.
Édit du roy, donné à Versailles . . . qui ordonne que les grands-maltres des eaux & forêts. 1745. IV. 324.
Édit du roy portant reglement general pour les eaux & forests. 1681. IV. 324.
Édit du roy, portant suppression des offices de controleurs & inspecteurs generaux des eaux & forêts. 1715. IV. 325.
Édit du roy, portant suppression des offices de contrôlleurs generaux des bois. 1708. IV. 324.
Edkins, G. Verte de Chine. 1857. III. 542.[1]
Edle Kastanien in Kärnten. 1878. IV. 492.[2]
Edler, H. Die Rose. 1882. III. 450.
Edm. Zur Aufbewahrung der Eicheln und Bucheln im Winter. 1883. IV. 148.
Edmonston, Thomas. A flora of Shetland. 1845. I. 399.
— List of phanerogamous plants . . . in the Shetland Islands 1841. I. 399.
Ednie-Brown, John. See BROWN, John EDNIE-.

Education. I. 5.
Edvardsen, Edvard. Bergens beskrivelse 1679–1694. 1868. III. 120.[1]
Edwall, Gustavo. Indice das plantas do herbario da Commissão geographica . . : de S. Paulo. 1896. I. 343.
Edwards, Alphonse MILNE. Les Arbres à gutta-percha. 1898. III. 668.[1]
— De la famille des Solanacées. 1864. II. 767.[2]
— La gutta-percha à la Grande-Comore. 1899. III. 669.[1]
— La gutta-percha recueillie à la Grande Comore. 1899. III. 669.[1]
Edwards, Bryan. Catalogue of . . . plants growing in the Publick botanik garden . . . in the island of Jamaica. 1794. I. 39.
— The history . . . of the British colonies in the West Indies. 1793. III. 266.
— The history . . . of the British West Indies. 1793. III. 266.
— A new atlas of the British West Indies. 1793. III. 266.
Edwards, G. & Catesby, M. Verzameling van uitlandsche en zeldzame vogelen. See CATESBY, Mark. 1731. I. 317.[2]
Edwards, Henri MILNE. Note sur les observations de M. Lecoq de Boisbaudron. 1873. III. 565.[2]
— Rapport sur un mémoire de M. Blaud. 1846. III. 677.[1]
— Rapport sur une note de M. Basin. 1854. III. 563.
— & Colin. De l'influence de la température sur la germination. 1834. I. 202.[2]
— — Sur la respiration des plantes. 1838. I. 169.[2]
— & Vavasseur, P. A manual of materia medica and pharmacy. 1829. III. 242.
— — Manuel de matière médicale. 1829. III. 242.
Edwards, John. The British herbal. 1770. I. 530.[1]
— The British herbal. 1775. I. 262.
— A select collection of 100 plants. 1775. I. 262.
Edwards, Samuel. Adaptation of our varied soils to ever-green culture. 1876. III. 292.
— Timber on the prairies. 1863. III. 117.[2]
— Tree planting for our western prairies. 1871. IV. 111.[2]
Edwards, Sydenham. The new botanic garden. 1812. III. 81.
Edwards, William H. A voyage up the River Amazon. 1847. I. 329.
Edwards's botanical register. See BOTANICAL register. I. 17.
Edwart, A. Kentia Forsteriana. 1872. III. 325.[2]
Edye, John. Description of the sea-ports on the coast of Malabar. 1835. IV. 400.[2]
Eeckhaute, Ernest. De koele serreplanten met bont gebladerte. 1880. III. 206.[2]
— Les plantes de serre froide à feuillage coloré. 1880. III. 206.[2]
Eeden, Frederik Willem van. Aanplanting van nuttige boomsoorten in Nederlandsch Indie. 1884. III. 128.
— Aanplanting van vruchtboomen in Nederlandsch Indië. 1888. III. 147.[1]
— Algemeene beschrijvende catalogus der houtsoorten van Nederlandsch Oost-Indië. 1872. IV. 400,[1] 539.[2]
— Bamboe en Bamboe-industrie. 1889. III. 315.[2]
— Bijdrage tot de kennis van de boomen, die het boomvet . . . voortbrengen. 1883. III. 225.
— Borneo. 1882. III. 276.[1]
— De bosschen van Kennemerland. 1867. IV. 356.[2]
— De Cinchona in Indië. 1879. III. 716.
— Cubeben. 1888. III. 342.[2]
— De Dryaden van Holland. 1856. IV. 356.[2]
— De duinen en bosschen van Kennemerland. 1868. IV. 356.[2]
— Duinplanten. 1869. IV. 160.[1]
— Flora batava. See KOPS, Jan & others. 1800. I. 390.
— De flora der Hollandsche duinen. 1866. I. 391.[1]
— Gedenkschrift bij het 12½ jarig bestaan van het Koloniaal museum. 1884. III. 274.[2]
— Genitripitten van Nederlandsch Indie. 1879. III. 584.[2]
— Gutta percha. 1883. III. 231.
— In 't hart van Kennemerland. 1869. IV. 356.[2]
— Herinneringen aan de Veluwe. 1880. IV. 356.[2]
— Hortus batavus. 1868. III. 77.
— Houtsoorten van Nederlandsch Oost-Indië. 1886. IV. 400.[1]
— De Huiszwam. 1867. IV. 415.[1]
— Kinacultuur op Java. 1873. III. 715.
— De Klimop. 1858. II. 650.[1].
— De kolonien op de Wereldtentoonstelling. 1878. III. 29.[1]
— Kort oversigt van den landbouw . . . in Nederlandsch Oost Indie. 1871. III. 128.

— Een nieuwe kultuur in Nederlandsch Indie. 1884. III. 149.
— Nog iets over Liberia-Koffie. 1880. III. 742.[2]
— Over de nuttige toepassing in de nijverheid van Mahonia Aquifolium. 1865. III. 395.[2]
— De Olieboom van Mogador. 1872. III. 666.[2]
— De omstreken van Alkmaar. 1871. IV. 356.[2]
— Onkruid. Botanische wandelingen. 1886. I. 391.[2]
— Overzicht van den landbouw . . . in Nederlandsch Oost-Indie. 1876. III. 128.
— Plantaardige vetsoorten van Riouw. 1872. III. 224.[2]
— Plantaardige veselstoffen. 1887. III. 234.
— Proeve van een . . . overzicht van de flora der verschillende Hollandsche duinstreken. 1873. I. 391.[2]
— De Raffia Palm. 1889. III. 330.[2]
— Rotans en Palmen van Borneo. 1868. III. 319.[1]
— Tessel. 1868. I. 391.[1]
— West-Indische houtsoorten. 1894. IV. 398.[1]
— See also HARTSEN, F. A. & EEDEN, F. W. van.
Eekhaute, G. van. Le Fuchsia procumbens. Cunn. 1886. III. 640.[2]
Eekhout, G. W. Het een en ander over Kina. 1887. III. 716.
— Kinasaken. 1888. III. 716.
— Het oogsten van inferieure Kinabasten. 1888. III. 718.
— See also MUNDT, G. & EEKHOUT, G. W.
Een ambtenaar, (pseud.). See Eene BIJDRAGE tot verbetering van de Koffij-cultuur. 1892. III. 727.
Een belandstellende, (pseud.). Toekomst van de Koffiecultuur op Kawi. 1899. III. 731.
Een bloemist, (pseud.). De Magnolia's. 1853. III. 399.[1]
Een boomkweeker, (pseud.). Het planten der oostboomen. 1853. III. 139.
Een Planter, (pseud.). Het officieel verslag over de Europeesche landbouwindustrie op Sumatra's westkust. 1894. III. 129.[1]
Een' zee-officier, (pseud.). De cochenille-teelt. 1848. III. 623.[2]
Eenige Coniferen van het Himalaya-Gebergte. 1855. II. 15.[2]
Eenige mededeelingen betreffende de opleiding der technische ambtenaren bij het boschwezen. 1891. IV. 37.[1]
Eenige voorschriften over het poten . . . van vruchtboomen. 1848. III. 139.
Over eenige woudboomen op Java. 1853. IV. 399.[2]
Eepoel, Aug. van. Kentia (Cyphokentia) Lindeni. 1895. III. 326.[2]
Effect of hot water in reviving flowers. 1820. V. XI.[2]
The effect of low temperature. 1853. I. 231.[2]
The effects of forest-clearing. 1842. IV. 49.[2]
Effects of inundation on trees and shrubs. 1875. III. 185.[1]
The effects of lightning on trees. 1895. IV. 195.[1]
The effects of the winter [1894–95] in Ireland. 1895. III. 47.
Effects of vegetation in cities. 1874. III. 34.[2]
Effeuille, (pseud.). 1900. IV. 161.[1]
Effenram, Ed. La mise en valeur des bruyères de la Campine. 1900. IV. 161.[1]
Effets de l'hiver de 1853–1854. See ASCERTAINED effects of the winter . . . 1854. III. 46.[2]
Effets de l'hiver 1879–80 sur la végétation. 1880. III. 46.[1]
Les effets de la foudre sur les diverses essences forestières. See ADRIÄNGIGKEIT der Blitzschläge. 1882. IV. 194.
Les effets de la gelée , . pendant l'hiver 1894–1895. 1895, III. 49.[1]
Effets des gaz s'échappant d'une briqueterie. 1899. IV. 193.[1]
Effetti dei rimboscamenti sulle piene. 1880. IV. 50.
Effetti del diboscamento. 1865. IV. 48.[1]
Effetti del fulmine sugli alberi. 1865. IV. 193.[2]
The effort to acclimate the Camphor tree. 1898. III. 405.[1]
Effront, Jean. Sur la caroubinase. 1897. III. 472.[1]
— Sur un nouvel hydrate de carbone. 1897. III. 472.[1]
— Sur une nouvelle enzyme hydrolytique. 1897. III. 472.[1]
Egasse. Tarif métrique pour la réduction des bois. 1840. IV. 222.
Égasse, Ed. See DUJARDIN-BEAUMETZ & ÉGASSE.
Egeberg. Sammenvokset Grantræ. 1896. I. 209,[1] III. 505.[2].
Egeberg, V. Om Skove og Brændsel. 1761. IV. 280.[1]
Egeberg, W. Betænkning om Frugt- og Urte-Hauger. 1757. III. 134.[1]
Egede, Hans. Beschreibung und Naturgeschichte von Grönland. 1741. I. 308. .
— Description et histoire naturelle du Groenland. 1741. I. 308.
— A description of Greenland. 1741. I. 308.
— Det gamle Grønlands nye Perlustration. 1741. I. 308.

Egeling, C. GULDENSTEEDEN. *See* GULDENSTEEDEN EGEL-
ING, C.
Egendomliga företeelser inom växtriket. *See* LINDBLÓM, A. E.
1846. I. 231.[2]
Egenolph, Christian. Plantarum, arborum, fruticum et her-
barum effigies. 1562. I. 281.
Egerer, J. C. J. F. Die Forstwissenschaft. 1812. IV. 96.
— Grundsätze des Forstrechts. 1818. IV. 313.
Egerton, William S. Ornamental planting for parks. 1896.
III. 202.[1]
Egger, Franz Xavier. Unmassgebliche Bemerkungen über
Waldwerths-berechnungen. 1854. IV. 254.
Eggers, Heinrich Franz Alexander, *Baron.* Die Bahama-
Inseln. 1892. I. 337.
— Et Bessg paa Øen Dominica. 1880. I. 336.
— Botanical exploration of Cuba. 1890. I. 337.
— The flora of St. Croix and the Virgin Islands. 1879. I. 336.
— Flora of the Bahamas. 1888. I. 337.
— Die Insel Tobago. 1893. I. 338.[1]
— Kaffeavlen paa Kuba. 1890. III. 728.[2]
— Kleistogamie einiger westindischer Pflanzen. 1881. II. 816.[2]
— Die Manglares in Ecuador. 1892. II. 614.[1]
— Naturen paa de dansk-vestindiske Øer. 1878. I. 336.
— Plantae novae ecuadorienses. 1898. I. 340.[1]
— Porto-Rico. 1883. I. 336.
— Die Poyales des östlichen Portorico. 1882. I. 336.
— Reise in das Innere von Sto. Domingo. 1888. I. 337.
— Reynosia Griseb. En hidtil ufuld kjendt Slægt. 1878.
II. 496.[2]
— Rhizophora Mangle L. 1878. II. 614.[1]
— St. Croix's Flora. 1876. I. 336.
— Supplement til St. Croix's og Jomfruøernes Flora. 1889.
I. 337.
Eggert, Johann Dietrich. Geoffraeae surinamensis virtus an-
thelmintica. 1791. III. 467.[1]
Eggert, Udo. Die Preisbewegung in den masurischen Forsten.
1884. IV. 26.
Eggler, P. J. Alpenpflanzen der Schweiz. 1878. I. 436.
Eggleston, Willard Webster. Further notes upon the distribu-
tion . . . of Arceuthobium pusillum. 1900. II. 174.[2]
— *See also* BRAINERD, EZRA, JONES, L. R. & EGGLESTON, W. W.
Egidy, Heinrich Eduard von. Der Holzkenner. 1852. IV.
426.[2]
Egleston, Nathaniel Hillyer. Arbor-day. 1886. IV. 41.[2]
— Arbor day. 1896. IV. 42.[1]
— Arbor day leaves. 1891. IV. 42.[1]
— Connection of railroads with forest fires. 1887. IV. 182.[1]
— European schools of forestry. 1881. IV. 30.[2]
— Hand-book of tree-planting. 1884. III. 99.
— Preserving small forests. 1890. IV. 178.[2]
— Report on forestry. 1884. IV. 338.[1]
— Summary of legislation for the preservation of timber.
1888. IV. 178.[1]
— The value and management of government timber lands.
1885. IV. 272.
— The value of our forests. 1881. IV. 44.
— What we owe to the trees. 1882. IV. 270.
Eglinger, Nicolas. Positionum botanico-anatomicarum cen-
turia. 1685. I. 97.
Eglingerus, Christian. Theses ex anatome et botanica im-
primis depromptas . . . Hugoninus. 1711. I. 31.
Egloffstein, Béla, *báró.* Vélemény, mely a magyarországi
erdők benső igazgatását tárgyazza. 1846. IV. 278.[2]
Egnatius, J. B. *See* EGNAZIO, R. B. C.
Egnazio, Giovanni Battiste Cipelli. In Dioscoridem ab
Hermolao Barbaro tralatum annotamenta. 1516. I. 276.
Ehinger, ALLEMANDI-. *See* ALLEMANDI-EHINGER.
Ehle, Nils Herman NILSSON-. *See* NILSSON-EHLE, N. H.
Ehmsen. Die Haubergswirthschaft im Kreise Siegen. 1893.
IV. 134.[1]
Ehrenberg. Alcaloïdes des fèves de Calabar. 1895. III.
484.[1]
Ehrenberg, Christian Gottfried. Beitrag zur Charakteristik
der nordafrikanischen Wüsten. 1827. I. 484.
— Ueber die Manna-Tamariske. 1827. II. 561.[2]
— De Myrrha et Opocalpasi . . . plantis. 1841. I. 268.
— Observations sur la famille des Tamariscinées et sur la
Manne du Tamarisque du Mont Sinai. 1827. II. 561.[1]
— Plantarum cotyledonearum nova genera. 1829. II. 417.[2]
— Ueber das Pollen der Asclepiadeen. 1831. II. 735.[2]
— Symbolae physicae. 1828. I. 267.
Ehrenberg, Fritz. Die Behandlung frisch importirter Cy-
cadeen. 1883. III. 284.[1]
— Der practische Rosenzüchter. 1882. III. 450.

Ehrenberg, Karl August. Beitrag zur Geschichte einiger
mexikanischer Cacteen. 1847. II. 586.[1]
— Mammillaria Schiedeana. 1838. II. 595.[1]
— Mammillaria Wegenerii. 1843. II. 595.[1]
— Eine neue Cacteen-Gattung. 1843. II. 597.[2]
— Neue und seltene Cacteen aus Mexico. 1848. II. 587.[2]
— Ein neuer Cereus. 1846. II. 591.[2]
— Sieben neue Cacteen. 1844. II. 585.[2]
— Vier neue Mammillarien. 1840. II. 594.[1]
— Vierzig neue Mamillarien aus Mexico. 1849. II. 594.[2]
Ehrenfels. Ein Beitrag zur Aufforstungsfrage. 1899. IV.
168.[1]
Ehrenfels, J. M., *Ritter* von. Ueber die Krankheiten . . .
der Frucht- und Gartenbäume. 1795. III. 178.
— Ueber die Verbindung des Feldbaues mit dem Waldbaue.
1830. IV. 132.[2]
Ehrenkreutz, *Baron* von. Neuer hundertjähriger Jagd- und
Forstkalender. 1859. IV. 101.
Ehrenstein, von, (*Forstmeister*). Anfrage: Ob und wie der
Ertrag aus der Durchforstung . . . in Anrechnung kommen
dürfe? 1850. IV. 254.
— Bericht über das Biermanns'sche Kulturverfahren. 1850.
IV. 141.
— Bericht über die Versuche mit . . . Stockholz-Rodema-
schine. 1858. IV. 386.
— Beschreibung der zur . . . Herrschaft Slawentzits gehö-
rigen Forsten. 1855. IV. 352.
— Die Feststellung der Stärke des Raff- und Leseholzes be-
treffend. 1862. IV. 438.[1]
— Ho zanbau mit Rasenasche. 1849. IV. 148.
— Ueber die Holzverkohlung. 1851. IV. 394.
— Mittheilung über langjährige Keimfähigkeit von Kiefer-
saamen. 1846. IV. 472, V. XII.[1]
— Welches ist die zweckmässigste Zeit zur Gestaltung der
Waldstreu-Nutzung? 1852. IV. 437.[2]
Ehret, Georg Dionysius. De arboribus Sassafras dictis.
1759. II. 228.[1]
— A description of the Andrachne. 1768. II. 660.[1]
— De Jasmino? ramo unifloro, pleno. 1759. II. 817.[2]
— Plantae et papiliones rariores. 1748. I. 291.
Ehrhardt. Ueber das Versetzen stärkerer Pflanzen. 1843.
IV. 546.[1]
Ehrhart, Balthasar. Botanologiae juvenilis mantissa. 1732.
I. 35.
— Oekonomische Pflanzenhistorie. 1753. I. 93.
Ehrhart, Friedrich. Anmerkungen über das gewöhnliche
Bepflanzen der Landstrassen mit Bäumen. 1789. III.
208.[2]
— Beiträge zur Naturkunde. 1787. I. 32.
— Bestimmung einiger Bäume und Sträucher. 1787. I. 293.
— Bestimmungen einiger Pflanzen meines Gärtchens. 1787.
II. 389.[2]
— Empfehlung einiger ausländischen Bäume. 1789. III.
72.
— Empfehlung einiger Bäume. 1788. III. 72.
— Meine Beiträge zum Linnéischen Supplemente plantarum.
1787. II. 255.[2]
— Plantae selectae hortuli proprii. 1792. I. 44.
— Rälingis, oder Pflanzengattung. 1787. II. 194.[1]
— Wirkung der Kälte des letzten Winters auf die Bäume.
1790. III. 45.
Ehrlich, Edmund. Die neueste Methode zu einer dauerhaf-
ten Conservirung des Holzes. 1858. IV. 418.
Ehrlich, Hans. Schädliche Forstinsekten. 1890. IV. 208.[1]
— Temperatur-Extreme und die Pflanzen. 1893. IV. 73.[1]
— Die Waldflora in ihren Bezeichnungen. 1891. IV. 55.[2]
Ehrlich, Johann. Ueber die Nr. 47 . . . aufgestellte Frage:
Ob . . . das . . . abfallende Laub das Wachsthum der
Bäume befördere? 1793. IV. 70.
— Abnorme Blattformen an einer Weissbuche.
1899. II. 121.[1]
Ehrmann. Étude du Henné. 1894. III. 630.[1]
Ehrmann, Martin S. Lehrbuch der Pharmacie. 1832. III.
257.[2]
Ehrnström, And. Beskrifning öfver kongl. svenska amtet
Neukloster. 1783. IV. 352.
Eine ehrwürdige Eiche. 1872. IV. 515.[2]
Ueber die Eibe. *See* KORSCHELT, Paul. 1897. II. 11.[2]
Die **Eibe,** Taxus baccata. 1898. III. 288.[1]
Die **Eiche** von Cadenham. 1834. II. 137.[2]
Eichelberg, F. J. A. Methodischer Leitfaden zum Gründ-
lichen Unterricht in der Naturgeschichte. 1840. I. 88.
— Naturgetreue Abbildungen . . . aller in- und ausländi-
schen Gewächse. 1845. III. 52.

Die **Eichen**- und Eichenschälwaldungen. 1885. IV. 513.
Eichene Gerbstoffe. 1874. IV. 515.[1]
Eichen-Gerber-Rinde. 1858. IV. 512.
Eichenrindenernte. 1853. IV. 512.
Die **Eichenrindennutzung.** 1866. IV. 512.
Der **Eichenschälwald** und seine Rentabilität. 1881. IV. 507.
Der **Eichenschälwaldbetrieb** im badischen Odenwald. 1858. IV. 505.
Eichen Stockausschlag in Oesterreich. 1865. IV. 505.
Die **Eichenzucht** betreffend. 1866. IV. 505.
Eichhörnchen-Falle. 1895. IV. 198.[2]
Eichhoff, Fr. Ueber Bewirthschaftung der Eichen-Schäl-Nieder-Waldungen. 1829. IV. 504.
Eichhoff, Wilhelm. Zur Abwehr und Aufklärung " über Fangbäume." 1883. IV. 199.[2]
— Ueber Buchelnsaaten. 1869. IV. 495.
— Zur Entwickelungsgeschichte . . . der Borken- und Rüsselkäfer. 1881. IV. 207.
— Zur Entwicklungsgeschichte . . . der Borken- . . . käfer. 1882. IV. 199.[2]
— Die europäischen Borkenkäfer. 1881. IV. 92.
— Ueber Fangbäume gegen Borken- . . . käfer. 1883. IV. 199.[2]
— Fangknüppel . . . gegen Engerlingfrass. 1882. IV. 203.
— Zur Generation der forstschädlichen Rüssel- und Borken-käfer. 1882. IV. 207.
— Käferschaden nach Aufästungen. 1869. IV. 171.
— Zur Naturgeschichte des grossen braunen Nadelholz-Rüsselkäfers. 1884. IV. 207.
— Die Vertilgung forstschädlicher Borken- . . . käfer. 1882. IV. 199.[2]
— Vorschläge zur Vertilgung verschiedener . . . Kerbtiere. 1892. IV. 199.[3]
Eichholz, Georg. Untersuchungen über den Mechanismus einiger zur Verbreitung von Samen . . . dienender Bewegungsrescheinungen. 1885. I. 240.[2]
Eichhorn, Fritz. Untersuchungen über das Holz der Roteiche. 1895. II. 139.[2]
Eichler, August Wilhelm. Die Ameisenpflanze Myrmecodia echinata Gaud. 1883. II. 824.[1]
— Anona rhizantha n. sp. 1883. II. 216.[1]
— Ueber die Bedeutung der Schuppen an den Fruchtzapfen der Araucarien. 1862. II. 25.[2]
— Ueber Beisprosse ungleicher Qualität. 1881. I. 106.
— Bemerkungen über die Struktur des Holzes. 1864. II. 194.[2]
— Bewegung im Pflanzenreiche. 1864. I. 194.
— Ueber Bildungsabweichungen bei Fichtenzapfen. 1882. II. 34.[1]
— Ueber die Blattstellung einiger Alsodeien. 1870. II. 568.[1]
— Ueber die Blattstellung von Liriodendron. 1881. II. 211.[1]
— Ueber den Blüthenbau der Fumariaceen. 1865. II. 229.[2]
— Blüthendiagramme. 1875. I. 115.[1]
— Capparideae. 1865. II. 229.[1]
— Combretaceae. 1867. II. 615.[2]
— Coniferae. 1889. II. 13.[2]
— Cycadaceae. 1889. II. 2.[1]
— Cycadeae et Coniferae. 1863. II. 2.[2]
— Dilleniaceae. 1803. II. 540.[1]
— Einige Gegenstände aus dem botanischen Museum. 1884. I. 242.[3]
— Entgegnung auf . . . Čelakovský's Kritik meiner Ansicht über die Fruchtschuppe der Abietineen. 1882. II. 19.
— Zur Entwickelungsgeschichte der Palmenblätter. 1885. II. 63.[1]
— Zur Entwickelungsgeschichte des Blattes. 1861. II. 19.
— Excursus morphologicus de formatione florum gymnospermarum. 1863. II. 1.
— On the formation of the flower in the gymnosperms. 1863. II. 1.
— Gnetaceae. 1889. II. 53.[2]
— Zur Kenntniss von Encephalartos Hildebrandtii. 1880. II. 6.[1]
— Lepidozamia Peroffskyana. 1883. II. 6.[2]
— Loranthaceae. 1868. II. 173.[1]
— Magnoliaceae, Winteraceae. 1864. II. 195,[2] 202,[1] 206,[1] 209,[1] 213.[1]
— Menispermaceae americanas digessit. 1864. II. 206.[1]
— Napoleonaceae. 1889. II. 611.[1]
— Ein neues Dioon (Dioon spinulosum). 1883. II. 5.[2]
— Ein neues Vorkommen polycotyledonischer Embryonen. 1867. II. 177.[2]

— Oleaceae et Jasmineae. 1868. II. 705.[2]
— Samen von Ceratozamia mexicana. 1879. II. 4.[1]
— Sind die Coniferen gymnosperm oder nicht? 1873. II. 19.
— Ueber die Struktur des Holzes von Drimys. 1864. II. 194.[2]
T Syllabus der Vorlesungen über Phanerogamenkunde. 1876. I. 256.
— Syllabus der Vorlesungen über specielle . . . Botanik. 1876. I. 256.
— On the systematic position of the natural order Trochodendreae. 1864. II. 194.[2]
— Thilco und Buchenavia. 1866. II. 615.[2]
— Über die Verdickungsweise der Palmenstämme. 1886. II. 63.[1]
— Verdoppelung der Blattspreite bei Michelia. 1886. II. 213.[1]
— Zum Verständniss der Weinrebe. 1881. II. 507.[1]
— Versuch einer Charakteristik der . . . Menispermaceae. 1864. II. 206.[1]
— Violaceae, Sauvagesiaceae, Bixaceae. 1871. II. 544.[1]
— Ueber die weiblichen Blüthen der Coniferen. 1881. II. 19.
— Ueber Welwitschia mirabilis. 1863. II. 55.[1]
— *See* MARTIUS, K. F. P. von, EICHLER, A. W. & URBAN, Ignatz.
Eichler, Bogumir. Ribes alpinum w Siedleckiem. 1892. II. 244.[1]
— Spis roślin jawnopłciowych, rosnących w okolicach miasta Międzyrzeca. 1883. I. 364.
Eichler, G. Tacsonia Van Volxemi. 1886. III. 617.[1]
Eichstadt, Lorenz. An camphora Hippocrati . . . incognita. 1650. III. 233.[1]
Eichstättische Forst- und Holz-Ordnung. 1887. IV. 319.[1]
Eichthal, A. d'. Bordereau des pièces relatives à l'emploi des eaux du canal du Midi. 1878. III. 571.
Eichwald, Eduard von. Naturhistorische Skizze von Lithauen, Volhynien. 1830. I. 360.
— Plantarum novarum vel minus cognitarum . . . in itinere caspio-caucasico. 1831. I. 368.[2]
— Reise auf dem Caspischen Meere und in den Caucasus. 1834. I. 368.[2]
Eickma, B. Over het middel van Kyan tegen dryrot. 1848. IV. 414.[2]
— Over de scheikundige samenstelling van het koude infusum van kina. 1833. III. 722.
Eide, Frederick Carl. Om skadelige Forstinsekter. 1857. IV. 205,[1] 442.
Der **eigenthümliche** Bau . . . der deutschen Waldbäume. 1851. IV. 118.
Das **Eigenthümliche** der Fachwerksmethode. 1853. IV. 251.[1]
Das **eigenthümliche** Verhalten der Buche im Sandboden. 1899. IV. 403.[1]
Die **Eigenthümlichkeiten** der grossen Kiefernwaldungen des nordöstlichen Deutschlands. 1855. IV. 480.
Eigenthümlichkeiten des Taxus. 1850. IV. 440.[1]
Die **Eignung** verschiedener Holzarten zu Telegraphenstangen. 1898. IV. 426.[1]
Eijbergen, H. C. van. Bijdrage tot de kennis van de Kakao-kultuur. 1865. III. 592.[1]
Eijdman, F. H. Verwerking van Kluabast op Java. 1885. III. 718.
Eijken, P. A. A. F. Brucamarine. 1891. III. 507.[2]
Eijkman, Joh. in Frederik. Over de bestanddeelen van Andromeda japonica. 1883. III. 654.[1]
— Een bezoek aan 's Lands plantentuin te Buitenzorg. 1887. I. 68,[1] 522,[1] III. 29.[1]
— Over coffeïne-gehalte der theezaden. 1881. III. 607.
— Over het giftige bestanddeel van Andromeda japonica. 1881. III. 654.[1]
— Poison de l'Andromeda japonica. 1881. III. 654.[1]
— The poisonous constituent of Andromeda japonica. 1881. III. 654.[1]
— Over de quantitatieve bepaling der alcaloïden. 1881. III. 723.
Eijs, J. N. van & **Reinwardt,** C. G. C. Over de eigenschappen en het nut van den Kanadaschen Popel. 1817. III. 346,[1] IV. 486.[1]
Eimbcke, Georg. Flora hamburgensis pharmaceutica. 1822. I. 376, III. 73.
Ein Forstbetriebsleiter, (*pseud.*) Waldexploitationsfragen. 1897. IV. 382.[1]
Einarsem, Haldor. Om Ager- og Skovdyrkning i Island. 1835. IV. 342.[2]

Einarsson, B. Ritgiörd um birkiskóga vidurhald. 1827.
IV. 490.[1]
Eine einfache Kubirungsmethode stehender Bäume. 1869.
IV. 217.
Einfache Rose, durch das Aufsetzen auf eine Centifolie gefüllt
geworden. 1844. III. 39.
Einfluss der deutschen Holzzölle auf den böhmischen Holz-
export. 1887. IV. 284.[2]
Der Einfluss der organischen und anorganischen Nährstoffe.
1850. IV. 68.
Einfluss der Schlagzeit auf die Dauerhaftigkeit der Hölzer.
1859. IV. 413.[2]
Ueber den Einfluss der Wälder auf das Klima. 1851. IV.
52.
Einfluss der Waldungen auf den Boden. 1856. IV. 52.
Einfluss der Zeit des Holzfällens. 1865. IV. 384.[2]
Der Einfluss des Edelreises auf die Unterlage. 1870. III.
39.
Einfluss des Gebirgsforstwesens. 1856. IV. 48.[2]
Ueber den Einfluss des Streuentzugs. See BLEUEL, Georg.
1891. IV. 72, 495.
Einfluss des Waldes auf den Feuchtigkeitsgrad. 1885. IV.
51.
Der Einfluss des Waldes auf die Bodenfeuchtigkeit. 1889.
IV. 51.
Ueber den Einfluss dess Waldes auf die Regenmenge. 1888.
IV. 51.
Der Einfluss des Waldes auf . . ., Gewässer. 1887. IV. 51.
Einführung der China-Cultur in Java. 1855. III. 715.
Ueber die Einführung . . . der zahmen Kastanie. 1845. IV.
492.[2]
Ueber die Einführung des Chinarinden-Baumes. 1857. III.
715.
Ueber die Einführung von Wirthschafts- oder Betriebs-
Charten. 1874. IV. 251.[1]
Eingewachsener Kiefernzapfen. 1881. I. 528.[1]
Einige allgemeine Bemerkungen über die Nadelhölzer. 1850.
III. 289.
Ueber einige alte bekannte . . . Gehölzarten. 1880. III.
69.
Einige Bemerkungen über den Begriff der "Fachwerks-
methoden." 1884. IV. 251.[1]
Einige Bemerkungen über den Zustand . . . des hannover-
schen Forstwesens. 1848. IV. 352.
Einige Bemerkungen über die Verwendung von Weymouths-
kiefernholz. 1883. IV. 471.
Einige in der Erfahrung gegründete Gedanken über die Con-
servation der . . . Holtzungen. See SCHARMER, C. C.
1739. IV. 115.
Einige kurzgefasste Bemerkungen über Holzwuchs. 1799.
IV. 280.[2]
Einige Mittheilungen über die Pflanzung . . . der städtischen
Alleen. 1900. III. 210.
Ueber einige neuere Araliaceen. 1869. III. 641.[1]
Ueber einige Riesen der europäischen Pflanzenwelt. 1869.
I. 295.[1]
Einige Vitis-Arten. 1895. III. 545.[1]
Einige Worte über das Ringeln der Weinrebe. 1859. III.
549.[1]
Einige Worte über die königlich sächsischen Staatsforste.
1831. IV. 291.[1]
Einige Worte über Einführung . . . der Deutzia gracilis.
1857. III. 410.[1]
Einige Worte über Sachsens "Forstbedienten." 1848. IV.
291.[1]
Einige Worte über Sachsens Wälder. See COTTA, Wilhelm.
1848. IV. 355.[1]
Von einigen merkwürdigen Bäumen. 1790. I. 295.[1]
Einiges aus der Praxis bei Verwaltung von Gemeinde-Wal-
dungen. 1888. IV. 308.[2]
Einiges über das forstliche Verhalten des Fichtenbastkäfers.
1845. IV. 455.
Einiges über die Aufstellung der Zuwachstafeln. 1861. IV.
232.
Die einnadelige Kiefer . . . in Italien eingeführt. See LE
PIN à noisette . . . 1880. IV. 464.[1]
Einrichtung der K. k. Forstlehranstalt Mariabrunn. 1866.
IV. 36.[2]
Einrichtungen und Vorschriften . . . zur Verhütung von
Waldbränden. 1894. IV. 182.[2]
Einsiedeln. 1863. IV. 366.
Einsiedeln. 1866. IV. 249.[2]
Einsiedelns Holzausfuhr. 1864. IV. 406.[1]
Eintheilung des Kantons in vier Forstkreise. 1871. IV. 306.

Die Eintheilung grösserer Waldflächen in Wirthschaftsfiguren.
1852. IV. 250.[2]
Einwirkung der Unterlage auf das Edelreis. 1898. III. 40.
Ueber die Einwirkung des Rauches der Silberhütten. 1845.
IV. 192.[1]
Die Einwirkung des zu hohen Temperaturgrades . . . auf den
Wuchs der . . . Holzpflanzen. 1838. IV. 72.
Einzelne. Data aus der Vegetationsentwicklung . . . zu St.
Petersburg. 1854. I. 223.[2]
Eiselen, Johannes. Über den systematischen Wert der
Rhaphiden. 1887. I. 139.
Eisen, Gustav. Biological studies on Figs, Caprifigs. 1896.
II. 151.[1]
— Forms of trees as determined by climatic influences. 1892.
I. 106,[2] 219,[1] 233.[1]
— Native habits of Sequoia gigantea. 1893. II. 50.[1]
— The reciprocal influence of stock. 1891. I. 529.
— & Earle, F. S. Fig culture. 1897. III. 369.[2]
Eisen, S. O. T. Was hat der Wald für eine Bedeutung im
Allgemeinen und in Beziehung auf Bayern? 1875. IV. 46.[2]
Eisen, Theodor. Etwas über das Wachsthum der Kiefer.
1859. IV. 472.
Eisenach, (Sanitätsrath). Flora des Kreises Rotenburg a/F.
1885. I. 532.[2]
Eisenbahnschwellen aus Kiefern- und Pappelholz. 1852.
IV. 423.[2]
Eisengrein, Georg Adolf. Beiträge zur Entwicklungsge-
schichte und Metamorphose des Samenkeimes der Pflanzen.
1851. I. 202.[2]
— Die Familie der Schmetterlingsblüthigen. 1836. II. 320.[1]
Eismann, Gustav. Amherstia nobilis. 1891. III. 466.[2]
— Die Gattung Robinia. 1878. III. 486.[1]
— Das Verjüngen alter Lindenbäume. 1891. III. 181,[2] 585.[1]
Eissenbeiss, Otto. Selbstthätige, directe Befeuchtungsan-
lage der Saugwurzeln. 1885. III. 150.[2]
Eissler, H. Die Bukowinaer Rothbuche. 1883. IV. 500.[1]
Eitel, Carl. Einiges über das Einpacken der Bäume. 1900.
. III. 155.
Eitner, J. F. W. Neue Armen-Pharmakopoe. 1856. III. 249.
Eitner, Wilhelm. Die Fabrication von Eichenholzextract.
1889. IV. 515.[1]
— Die Fichtenrinde als Gerbematerial. 1878. IV. 456.
Ejsmond, A. Z wycieczki botanicznej do puszczy Białowie-
skiej. 1888. I. 565.
Ekama, C. Fondation Teyler. Catalogue. 1885. V. VII.[1]
Ekeberg, Carl Gust. On Ferdinando Noronho. 1761. I.
498.
Ekelund, Daniel. Remedia guineensia. See AFZELIUS,
Adam. 1813. III. 93.[1]
Ekenstein, William ALBERDA VAN. See ALBERDA VAN EKEN-
STEIN, William.
Ekermark, Isaac Vilhelm. Afhandling om de wäxter som i
Bibelen omtalas. See THUNBERG, C. P. 1828. I. 513.
Ekert, Franz. Kubische Holzberechnung zum Privatgebrauch.
1835. IV. 222.
Ekstam, Otto. Beiträge zur Kenntnis der Gefässpflanzen
Spitzbergen's. 1899. I. 358.
— Bidrag till kännedomen om Novajá Semljas. 1894. I. 365.
— Einige blütenbiologische Beobachtungen. 1897. I. 367.
— Neue Beiträge zur Kenntnis der Refässpflanzen Novaja
Semlja's. 1897. I. 367.
Ekström, C. W. Beskrifning öfver Mörkö socken. 1828.
. I. 353.
De l'élagage des arbres languissants. See TREE pruning.
1897. III. 181.[2]
De l'élagage des sapinières. 1895. IV. 558.[2]
Élagage du Peuplier. 1898. IV. 485.[2]
Elben, (Staatsanwalt). Das württembergische Forststrafge-
setz. 1880. IV. 322.[1]
— & Jäger, Ludwig. Das württembergische Forstpolizeige-
setz. 1881. IV. 322.[2]
Elberling, Frederik Carl. Et Bidrag til Hortensiens Historie.
1897. III. 412.[1]
— Elaeagnus longipes Asa Gray. 1897. III. 629.[1]
Elborne, William. Analyse approximate des semences de
Cassia tora. 1888. III. 471.[1]
— Cinchona barks. 1884. III. 712.[2]
— A contribution to the pharmacognosy of Strophantus.
1887. III. 690.[1]
— Jambul. 1888. III. 637.[2]
— Notes on American drugs. 1882. III. 262.[2]
— Remarks on Gnetum. 1895. III. 312.[2]
— A summary of the Cinchona barks of commerce. 1883.
III. 718.

Elbourne, William. See ELBORNE, William.
Elder, Walter. Pittosporum Tobira. 1876. III. 416.[1]
The electric tree of New Guinea. 1885. I. 517.[1]
L'Électricien. III. 19.
E'émens du jardinage utile. 1786. III. 143.
Élémens succincts de la langue et des principes de botanique. See AUBIN, L. C. P. 1803. I. 93.
Éléments de botanique. See HANIN, L. 1809. I. 85.
Elenchus plantarum Borussiae. See MEYER, E. H. F. 1835. I. 378.
Elenchus plantarum hor. botanici J. Car. Dinegro. See VIVIANI, Domenico. .1802. I. 61.
Elenchus plantarum h. botanici J. J. Destremx. See DESTREMX, J. J. 1806. I. 57.
Elenchus plantarum quae in Horto botanici monspeliensis. See BROUSSONET, Auguste. 1805. I. 57.
Elenchus plantarum Horti medici amstelodamensis. See VROLIK, Gerard. 1807. I. 51.[1]
Elenchus plantarum Horti . . . parmensis. See PASCAL. 1802. I. 61.
Elenchus plantarum Horti regii botanici matritensis. 1796. I. 60.[1]
Elenchus plantarum, quae in Horto amstelaedamensi coluntur. See VROLIK, Gerard. 1814. I. 51.[1]
Elenchus plantarum quae in Horto botanico lovaniensi coluntur. 1829. I. 49.
Elenchus plantarum quae in horto . . . Josephi Malabaila de Canal. See NOWODWORSKY, Johann. 1804. I. 65.[2]
Elenchus plantarum quae in Horto lugduno-batavo coluntur. See BRUGMANS, S. J. 1818. I. 51.[1]
Elenchus plantarum, quae in Horto regio botanico matritensi. . . . See LACASCA, Marioano. 1816. I. 60.[1]
Elenco delle Cactee esistenti nel giardino dei Marchesi Bottini. 1877. III. 619.
Elenco delle opere dell' ing. comm. Elia Lombardini. 1883. IV.‘2.
Elenco delle piante . . . nel territorio di Vicenza. See MARZARI-PENCATI, Giuseppe, conte. 1802. I. 425.
Elenco delle principali opere . . . dal comm. Adolfo di Béreriger. 1895. IV. 2.
The Elengi tree. 1899. III. 668.[1]
Eleutherescu, Ion C. Pădurile nóstre. 1881. IV. 375.[1]
Elfstrand, Mårten. Albuminoïdes toxiques . . . de Croton. 1897. III.‘517.[2]
— Brasilianische und paraguayische Drogen. 1897. III. 269.[2]
— Über die Pflanzenfamilie der Solanaceen. 1897. III. 701.[2]
— Salicologiska bidrag. 1892. II. 100.[2]
— Ueber Strychnos lanceolaris. 1898. III. 684.[2]
— Studier öfver alkaloidernas lokalisation företrädesvis inom familjen Loganiaceae. 1895. II. 716.[2]
Elfving, Fredrik Emil Volmar. Anteckningar om kulturväx terna i Finland. 1897. I. 271.[1]
— Det Hj. Hjelts kartor öfver trädslag och buskar i Finland. 1895. I. 350,[2] IV. 81.
— Fagus silvatica i Finland. 1893. II. 126.[1]
— Former af Picea excelsa i Finland. 1893. II. 35.[1]
— Salix rotundifolia och Salix arctica. 1881. II. 100.[2]
— Studien über die Pollenkörner. 1879. I. 117.[1]
— Tillkeimatt viljelyskauti i. III. 50.
— Ueber den Transpirationsstrom. 1884. I. 167.
— Ueber die Wasserleitung im Holz. 1882. I. 165.
Eigenstierna, Nicol Willem. See AFZELIUS, Adam & ELGENSTIERNA, N. W.
O Ели. See O ели.
Elias, (Forstmeister). Zur Ausästung der Eichen. 1872. IV. 506.
— Bericht über die Anwendung des Heyer'schen Hohlbohrers. 1859. IV. 152.
— Besprechung der Bereisung des Trachenberger Reviers. 1886. IV. 354.
— Einige Worte über Hylesinus piniperda. 1854. IV. 475.
— Zur Forstarbeiter-Frage. 1858. IV. 310.[1]
— Haben die Privat-Forstbesitzer in Oberschlesien wirklich nur noch Brennholz zu verkaufen? 1871. IV. 274.[1]
— Die künstliche Düngung. 1897. IV. 144.[2]
— Ueber das Schütten der Kiefer. 1855. IV, 475.
— Uebersicht der Geld- und Holzmassen-Erträge in . . . Distrikten der herzogl. Oberförsterei Kieferstädtel. 1858. IV. 260.[2]
— See also SCHILLING, (Oberförster) & ELIAS, (Oberförster).
Elias, Karl Philipp Friedrich. Analecta ad Sabinae historiam medicophysicam. 1816. III. 304.[1]

Eliasson, Albin Gottfrid. Om sekundära anatomiska förändringar inom fanerogamernas florala region. 1893. I. 113.[2]
— Taprina acerina. 1895. III. 535.[2]
Élie de Beaumont, Jean Baptiste Armand Louis Léonce. L'emploi de la neige . . . à la destruction du phylloxera. 1874. III. 566.[1]
— Note sur l'action d'un vent impétueux. 1856. III. 184.[1]
— Remarque sur l'apparition des premières feuilles de quelques Marronniers. 1855. . II. 482.[1]
— Sur la rupture d'une grande nombre de branches. 1856. III. 184.[2]
Eliot, Charles. Vegetation and scenery in the metropolitan reservations of Boston. 1898. IV. 55.[2]
Elisha Mitchell scientific society. Journal. I. 5.
Elkan, L. See PATZE, C., MEYER, Ernst & ELKAN, L.
Ellacombe, Canon. The weather of the past season. 1897. I. 219.[1]
Ellacombe, Henry Nicholson. Bucklandia populnea. 1883. III. 416.[2]
— Common English names of plants. 1870. I. 74,[1] 522.[1]
— Ellacombe's Yucca. 1879. III. 340.[1]
— Genista praecox. 1882. III. 474.[2]
— The great drought of 1896. 1897. III. 184.[1]
— The great frost of 1895. 1896. III. 47.
— Hardy Yuccas. 1872. III. 339.[2]
— History of the parish of Bitton. 1881. I. 534.[‘]
— Notes on new and rare Yuccas. 1875. III. 339.[2]
— Place names derived from plants. 1889. I. 512.
— The plant-lore and garden-craft of Shakespeare. 1878. I. 515.
— Propagation of Xanthoceras sorbifolia. 1880. · III. 540.[2]
— The species of Yucca. 1876. II. 86.[2]
— The vineyards of Somerset & Gloucestershire. 1893. II. 509.[1]
Ellemeet, De Jonge van. Eine Agaven-Sammlung. 1871. III. 340.[2]
— Énumération des Agave de sa collection. 1871. III. 340.[2]
Ellenberger, Gustav. Beschreibung der Exkursionstour . . . in die Forste der Stiftungs-Domäne Ronov. 1884. IV. 371.
— Popis vycházky Českého lesnického spolku v. Čáslavi do lesů nadačního panství Ronovského. 1884. IV. 371.
— Statisticko-topografický popische nadačního panství Ronova. 1884. IV. 371.
— Statistisch-topographische Beschreibung der Stiftungs-Domäne Ronov. 1884. IV. 371.
Ellenrieder, C. A. M. M. M. von. De semoet graman. 1861. III. 735.
Ellery, R. L. J. On the relation between forest lands and climate in Victoria. 1880. . IV. 49.[1]
Ellinger, H. O. G. En dansk forstmeteorologisk Station.· 1897. IV. 60.[1]
Elliot, George Francis Scott. On the botanical results of the Sierra Leone boundary commission. 1895. I. 491.
— The flora and fauna of Madagascar. 1892. I. 496.
— Flora of Dumfriesshire and Dumfries district. 1891. I. 534.[1]
— Mangroves in Sierra Leone. 1894. II. 614.[1]·
— New and little known Madagascar plants. 1893. I. 496.
— Note on the fertilisation of Musa. 1889. II. 90.[3]
— Notes on a botanical trip in ·Madagascar. 1889. I. 496.
— Notes on a botanical trip in Madagascar. 1091. I. 490.
— Notes on the fertilisation of South African . . . .flowering plants. 1890. I. 240.[1]
— Ornithophilous flowers in South Africa.· 1889. I. 240.[1]
— A revision of the genus Pentas. 1896. II. 826.[1]
— Rubber in Sierra Leone. 1894. III. 371,[2] 688.[2]
— Some economic plants of Sierra Leone. 1893. III. 281.[1]
— & others. The flora of Dumfriesshire. 1896. I. 404.[1]
Elliot, Robert Henry. Coffee planting in Mysore. 1894. III. 732.[2]
Elliot, Walter. On the farinaceous grains . . . in.southern India. 1862. III. 278.
— Flora andhrica. 1859. I. 473.
Elliot, William. The Washington guide. See BRERETON, J. A. 1837. I. 318.
Elliott, C. F. Subordinate forest establishment. 1877. IV. 295.[1]
Elliott, Charles Wyllys. Transplanting large trees. 1852. III. 167.
Elliott, F.R. Elliott's fruit book. 1854. III. 61.[2]
— Hand-book for fruit growers. 1876. III. 133.
— Popular deciduous and evergreen trees. 1868. III. 60.
— The Service berry. 1868. III. 419.[1]
— The western fruit book. 1854. III. 61.[2]

Elliott, J. W. Hardy plants and shrubs. 1896. III. 63.²
Elliott, Stephen. Observations on the genus Glycine. 1818.
II. 388.¹
— A sketch of the botany of South Carolina. 1816. I. 318.
Elliott, W. R. Grenada. 1888. III. 268.¹
Elliott society of natural history of Charleston. Proceedings.
I. 5.
Ellis, J. SALVATOR. See SALVATOR ELLIS, J.
Ellis, John. Account of a method of preventing . . . decay
of Peach trees. 1802. III. 441.²
— An account of some experiments relating to the preserva-
tion of seeds. 1760. III. 154.²
— An account of the plants Halesia and Gardenia. 1761.
II. 704,¹ 818.¹
— Anweisung wie man Saamen und Pflanzen aus Ostindien
. . . über See bringen kann. 1770. III. 155.
— A catalogue of such foreign plants as are worthy of being
encouraged in our American colonies. 1769. III. 261.¹—
1771. III. 62.
— The copy of a letter on a new species of Illicium. 1771.
II. 210.¹
— A copy of a letter with the figure . . . of . . . Loblolly-
Bay. 1771. II. 549.¹
— Description du Mangostan. 1775. II. 554.²
— A description of the Mangastan and the Breadfruit. 1775.
II. 146,¹ 654.²
— Directions for bringing over seeds. 1770. III. 155.
— Directions for bringing over seeds and plants from distant
countries. 1771. III. 155.
— Extracts from An historical account of Coffee. 1774. III.
738.
— Geschichte des Koffees. 1774. III. 738.
— Historical account of Coffee. 1774. II. 814,² III. 738.
— A letter attempting to ascertain the tree that yields the
common varnish. 1757. III. 526.²
— Some additional observations on the method of preserving
seeds from foreign parts. 1773. III. 155.
— On the success of experiments for preserving acorns. 1769.
III. 154.²
Ellis, R. Report on the Mahasu water-catchment area.
1880. IV. 377.¹
Ellis, T. F. Hints on budding. 1900. III. 164.²
Ellis, T. LIBERTADOR. See LIBERTADOR ELLIS, T.
Ellis, William. Von Erbauung des Zimmerholzes. 1738.
IV. 107.²
— The timbertree improved. 1738. IV. 107.²
Ellis, William, (1794-1872). History of Madagascar. 1838.
III. 282.¹
— Three visits to Madagascar. 1858. I. 496.
Ellis, William Smith. Parks and forests of Sussex. 1885.
I. 512.
Ellison, Ralph Carr. On arresting the growth of large trees.
1871. I. 191.¹
— On gathering the cones of resinous trees. 1872. III.
294.¹
— The Giant or Irish Ivy. 1879. III. 643.¹
— The native British Ivy. 1879. III. 642.¹
— On the radiating root-swell. 1871. I. 191.¹
— Summer torch pruning. 1873. III. 170.
— On the tapping of Birch nurses. 1881. IV. 490.¹
— On the terminal stopping . . . by means of torchflame.
1879. IV. 171.
— On the value of the Horse-chestnut. 1880. IV. 527.¹
Ellram, W. Ein Beitrag zur Histochemie verholzter Mem-
branen. 1895. I. 156.¹
Ellwanger, G. H. Ornamental trees, Magnolias. 1875.
III. 399.¹
Ellwanger, Henry Brooks. Old and new Roses. 1883. III.
450.
— The Rose. 1882. III. 450.
The Elm. 1842. II. 143.²
The Elm-leaf beetle. 1896. III. 364.²
Elmgren, Gabriel. Plantarum jamaicensium pugillus. See.
LINNÉ, Carl von. 1759. I. 334.
Elmgren, Johannes. Termini botanici. See LINNÉ, Carl von.
1762. I. 69.²
Elmstedt, Peter. De Blaeria. See THUNBERG, C. P. 1802.
II. 661.²
Éloffe, Arthur. L'art de préparer les plantes. 1862. I. 35.
— Destruction des mousses . . . sur les arbres fruitiers.
1862. III. 175.²
Eloste, P. Sur une maladie de la Vigne. 1894. III. 581.
Élot, Auguste. Culture et préparation du cacao à la Trini-
dad. 1900. III. 593.¹

Elout van Soeterwoude, M. E. T. De handel op onze groote
Oost. 1883. III. 274.²
— Journaal eener reis en bezoek aan de Batjan eilanden.
1881. III. 128.
Éloy, Nicolas François Joseph. Apologie du thé. 1751.
III. 605.
— Examen de la question médico-politique: si l'usage habituel
du caffé est avantageux. 1781. III. 741.²
Éloy, P. M. R. AUCHER-. See AUCHER-ÉLOY, P. M. R.
Els, V. See ЭЛЬС, B.
Elsass-Lothringischer Forstverein. Bericht. IV. 7.
Elsenberger, Leo. Die Palmen an der Küste des Mittel-
meeres. 1887. III. 318.¹
Elsholz, Johann Siegesmund. Flora marchica. 1663. I.
372.
— Garten-Bau. 1666. III. 102.
— Garten-Baw. 1666. III. 102.
— Neu angelegter Garten-Bau. 1666. III. 102.
Elsner, Christian Ludwig Karl. De plantarum nutrimento.
1798. I. 157.
Elsner, Moritz. Flora von Hirschberg. 1837. I. 379.
— Synopsis florae cervimontanae. 1839. I. 379.
Elssner, Gotthold. Anschauungs- und Zeichen-Unterricht
. . . zunächst unserer deutschen Bäume. 185 .? I. 516.
— Naturgeschichtliches Bilderbuch; Inhalt: Bäume. 185 .?
I. 516.
Elst, S. L. W. van der. Beschouwingen over terrassen bij
Koffieaanplantingen. 1874. III. 726.²
— Koffie-zaadbeddingen. 1875. III. 733.¹
— Koffie-zaadbeddingen onder Dadap. 1874. III. 733.¹
— Staats-Koffiecultuur op Java. 1874. III. 729.²
— Terrassen. 1875. III. 726.²
— Uitkomsten van niet beschaduwde Koffietuinen. 1874.
III. 734.²
Elton, Frederick. The African Gum copal tree. 1876. III.
489.²
— L'Arbre à copal. 1876. III. 489.²
Eltz, Carl Friedrich Gottlob. De Toxicodendro. See BOEH-
MER, G. R. 1800. III. 528.¹
Eltzholtz, Ditlev. Wellingtonia gigantea. 1886. III. 290.
Elwert, Johann Kaspar Philipp. Fasciculus plantarum e
Flora Margraviatus baruthini. 1786. I. 374.
Elwes, Henry John. Azorean tea. 1879. III. 607.
— The condition and future of the American forests. 1890.
IV. 178.²
— Notes from a naturalist in Mexico. 1888. I. 332.
Ely, William D. The sap and sugar of the Maple-tree. 1891.
IV. 527.²
L'Embrevade. 1874. III. 469.¹
Emeis, C. Allgemeines über Wald . . . in Schleswig-Hol-
stein. 1873. IV. 118.
— Zur Aufforstungsfrage in schleswig-holsteinischen Haiden.
1881. IV. 158.
— Ueber das naturgemässe Zurückweichen des Waldes in
Schleswig-Holstein. 1881. I. 371, IV. 84.¹
— Die Schrägpflanzung im Forstbetriebe. 1899. IV. 153.²
— Waldbauliche Forschungen. 1875. IV. 69, 118.
— Ueber Zusammenziehung und Niederschlag der Stoffe in
den oberen Bodenschichten. 1893. IV. 70.
Emerich, Gustav Wilhelm Benno. De coffeae facultatibus et
effectibus. 1839. III. 741.²
Emerson, George Barrell. Le Chêne écarlate. 1856. III. 362.¹
— Le Chêne rouge, Quercus rubra. 1851. II. 139.²
— L'Épine ergot de coq. 1851. III. 421.²
— Forest trees. 1859. III. 201.
— Forest trees of Massachusetts. 1841. IV. 397.
— Le Quercitron, Chêne à teinture. 1851. II. 140.²
— Report on the trees and shrubs . . . of Massachusetts.
1846. I. 312, IV. 76.²
Emerson's magazine. See PUTNAM's monthly magazine.
III. 8.
Emery. Empoisonnement par l'écorce du Faux Acacia. 1887.
IV. 524.²
Emery, d'. Nouveau recueil de curiosites. 1688. III. 121.²
Emery, Carlos. Die in Akaziendornen lebenden Ameisen.
1888. V. xxvi.²
— Hormigas de Costa Rica. 1888. V. xxvi.²
Émery, Henri. Le bourgeon du Tulipier. 1888. II. 211.¹
— Études sur le rôle physique de l'eau. 1865. I. 159.
— Influence de l'âge sur la composition des feuilles. 1876.
I. 153, 175.
— De l'influence exercée par le climat. 1879. I. 218.
Emmelhains, J. Die Neuordnung der rheinischen Gemeinde-
forstverwaltung. 1895. IV. 309.¹

Emmerich, A. The culture of forests. 1789. IV. 120.
Emmerich, Georg. Theeologia, ejusque infusum. 1698. III. 605.
Emmerig, A. Erklärung der gebräuchlichsten fremden Pflanzennamen. 1894. I. 76.²
Emmermann. Rapport sur l'introduction d'un aménagement régulier. 1858. IV. 249.²
— Referat über Einführung einer geordneten Forstwirtschaft. 1858. IV. 249.²
Emmert, Friedrich & Segnitz, Gottfried von. Flora von Schweinfurt. 1852. I. 383.
— — Das Florengebiet der Stadt Schweinfurt. 1852. V. XIX.²
Emmet, J. P. Liriodendrine. 1831. III. 398.²
Emmons, Ebenezer. Agriculture of New York. 1846- III. 61.²
— Analysis of [ash of] fruit trees. 1850. III. 37.² See also ANALYSIS of ash of fruit and forest trees. 1850. IV. 543.¹
— The fruit and forest trees. 1849. V. XI.²
Emmrich, Hermann Friedrich. Ueber die Vegetationsverhältnisse von Meiningen. 1851. I. 383.
Émondage des Chênes. 1899. IV. 509.
Emory, William Hemsley. Notes of a military reconnoissance from Fort Leavenworth. 1848. I. 322.
— Notes of travel in California. 1848. I. 322.
— Report on the United States and Mexican boundary survey. 1857. I. 323.
Empeyta, Eugène. Catalogue descriptif des arbres, arbustes . . . en Suisse. 1887. I. 432.¹
Eine empfehlenswerthe Varietät des Nussbaumes. 1875. III. 355.
Emplacements des pépinières. 1895. IV. 546.¹
Emploi de kainite. 1899. IV. 145.
Emploi de l'huile de Chaulmoogra. 1882. III. 614.¹
Emploi de la Bruyère comme fourrage. 1894. III. 649.¹
Emploi de la raupeuleim [sic]. 1900. IV. 200.
Emploi de la sciure de bois dans les moulages. 1885. IV. 431.¹
Emploi de notations uniformes dans les formules de cubage. 1898. IV. 215.
Sur l'emploi des bois d'Eucalyptus comme poteaux. 1879. IV. 531.¹
Emploi des engrais chimiques pour l'Épicéa. 1895. IV. 559.¹
Emploi des feuilles comme fourrage. 1894. IV. 558.¹
Emploi des feuilles de Frêne dans le traitement de la goutte. 1853. IV. 534.²
Emploi des fruits du Prunier Myrobolan. 1900. III. 436.¹
Emploi du bois de Tulipier. 1899. IV. 519.²
Emploi du Hêtre pour billes de chemins de fer. 1896. IV. 424.¹
Emploi du Pin comme bois de chauffage. 1853. IV. 462.²
Emploi du Styrax pour le montage. 1884. III. 417.²
Emploi et durée des traverses de chemin de fer. 1898. IV. 424.¹
Emploi médical des feuilles de Noyer. 1842. III. 356.¹
Empoisonnement par l'ombre de Mancenillier. 1873. III. 519.¹
Empoisonnement par la coque du Levant. 1859. III. 396.¹
Empoisonnement par la fève de Calabar. 1871. III. 483.²
Empoisonnement par le Cytise. 1882. III. 481.¹
Empoisonnement par le Lonicera Xylosteam. 1873. III. 751.¹
Empoisonnement par le Taxus baccata. 1871. III. 288.²
Empoisonnement par les fruits du Gui. 1874. III. 385.²
Empson, Charles. The Cowthorpe Oak. 1842. II. 138.¹
Emsbach, (Kgl. Förster). Ist die Saat oder die Pflanzung bei der Kiefer vorzuziehen? 1889. IV. 473.
— Das Pflanzen und Erziehen von Eichen-Pflänzlingen. 1888. IV. 508.
Emy, A. R. Traité de l'art de la charpenterie. 1837. IV. 422.²
Enajenacion de montes públicos. 1879. IV. 276.²
Enchiridión universale plantarum. See NEWTON, James. 1689. I. 288.
Enckelmann, Heinrich Daniel. Dirdar Ibnsinae Ulmo arbore. See FISCHER, J. A. 1718. III. 365.¹
Enckhausen, F. Die Heideflächen und ihr Nutzungswerth. 1879. IV. 158.
— Der Lupinenbau in Forsten. 1877. IV. 144.²
— Die Macht des Auffrierens. 1876. IV. 191.¹
Encontre, Daniel. Additions à la Flore biblique de Sprengel. 1811. I. 513.
Encore l'h lobe du Pin. 1898. IV. 479.
Encore lesyGenêts. 1896. IV. 211.¹

Encore un moyen de protéger les arbres. 1896. IV. 197.¹
Encouragement of tree-planting in Colorado. 1883. IV. 39.¹
Encyclopaedia Britannica. 1842. I. 34.
Encyclopédie pratique du jardinage. n. d. III. 30.
Ende, Willem Peter van den. Commentatio de methodis botanicis. 1823. I. 251, 266.
— Enarratio et comparatio methodorum plantarum. 1823. I. 251.
Endegeest, Gevers van & others. Toestand van het Haagsche Bosch. 1861. IV. 356.²
Endemann, Max. Ein Beitrag zur Sonnenvermehrung. 1899. III. 158.
Ender, Ernst. Der Garten des Grafen A. S. Uwarow. 1873. II. 34.²
— Die Gattung Franciscea. 1865. III. 698.²
— Verzeichniss von Gehölzen, welche . . . wild wachsen oder im Freien über wintern. 1864. III. 67.²
Enderlin, Florian L. Der Escherwald bei St. Carl. 1898. IV. 167.¹
— Forsteinrichtung im Gebirge. 1892. IV. 246.
— Steuertaxation der Waldungen in Graubünden. 1899. IV. 285.¹
Enderlin, J. F. Die Natur und Eigenschaften des Holzes und seines Bodens. 1767. IV. 61.²
Enders, E. Der Matthes'sche Höhenmesser. 1886. IV. 215.
L'endiguement des torrents en Autriche. 1900. IV. 188.¹
Endlicher, Stephan. Atakta botanika. 1833. I. 268.
— Bemerkungen über die Flora der Südseeinseln. 1836. I. 509,¹ V. XLIV.²
— Catalogus Horti academici vindobonensis. 1842. I. 66.¹
— Enchiridion botanicum. 1841. I. 261.
— Flora posoniensis. 1830. I. 378.
— Genera plantarum. 1836. I. 260.
— Grundzüge einer neuen Theorie der Pflanzenzeugung. 1838. I. 199.
— Liliaceae Endl. 1846. II. 86.²
— Mantissa botanica. 1836. I. 260.
— Die Medicinal-Pflanzen der Österreichischen Pharmakopöe. 1842. III. 57.
— Plantae hortenses. 1843. II. 823.¹
— Prodromus florae norfolkicae. 1833. I. 508.²
— Stirpium australasicarum . . . decades tres. 1838. I. 500, V. XXIV.²
— Stirpium pemptas. 1832. I. 268.
— Synopsis Coniferarum. 1847. II. 12.²
— See also POEPPIG, Eduard F. & ENDLICHER, S. L.
— & Fenzl, Eduard. Novarum stirpium decades. 1839. I. 268.
— Sertum cabulicum. 1836. II. 606.¹
— & Unger, Franz. Grundzüge der Botanik. 1843. I. 88.
— & others. Enumeratio plantarum . . . Novae Hollandiae. 1837. I. 500.
Endrès, Max. Die Besteuerung des Waldes. 1899. IV. 284.¹
— Die O. Heyer'sche Waldertragsregelung. 1893. IV. 237.
— Forsten. 1892. IV. 102.
— Ueber die klimatische . . . Bedeutung des Waldes. 1896. IV. 45.
— Lehrbuch der Waldwertrechnung und Forststatik. 1895. IV. 253.
— Ueber pflanzenphysiologische . . . Forschungsergebnisse im Walde. 1896. IV. 63.²
— Die Productionsfaktoren in der Waldwirthschaft. 1884. IV. 259,² 270.
— Wachsthum und Ertrag der Weymouthskiefer. 1890. IV. 470.²
— Die Waldbenutzung vom 13. bis zu Ende des 18. Jahrhunderts. 1888. IV. 26, 385.¹
— Die Wertberechnung des Mittelwaldes. 1899. IV. 259.¹
Eneroth, Olaf. Bidrag till Europas pomona. 1880. III. 66.²
— Handbok i svensk pomologi. 1864. III. 66.²
La enfermedad de los Castaños. 1889. IV. 493.¹
Engel. L'Oreodoxa oleracea Martius. 1899. II. 72.¹
— (Dr.). Die Gartenflüchtlinge unserer heimischen Flora. 1900. I. 390.
Engel, Alexander. Magyarország faipara és fakereskedése. 1882. IV. 406.²
— See also ЭНГЕЛЬ, А.
— Ungarns Holz-Industrie und Holzhandel. 1882. IV. 406.²
Engel, Franz. Palmae novae columbianae. 1865. II. 61.²
Engel, Louis Charles. Histoire naturelle . . . des médicaments astringents végétaux. 1853. III. 58.
— Influence des climats et de la culture. 1860. III. 238.¹
— Das Leben und Wachsen der Palmen. 1859. II. 63.¹
— La vie et la croissance des Palmiers. 1859. II. 63.²

Engel, Samuel. Der junge Landwirth in Feld und Wald. 1889. III. 115.[2]

Engelberg, Joseph Meinrad von. *See* ROT VON SCHRECKEN-STEIN, Friedrich, *Freiherr* & ENGLEBERG, J. M. von.

Engelbrecht, Theodor. Auswahl der hier zu Lande zu pflanzeuden Obstbäume. 1866. III. 71.

— Deutschlands Apfelsorten. 1889. III. 425.[2]

Engelfeld, V. A. *See* ЭНГЕЛЬФЕЛЬДЪ, B. A.

Engelhard, Karl. Ueber Entwaldung und Hochwässer. 1881. IV. 50.

Engelhardt, Arthur Baron. Beschaffenheit und Wirkung des Hyaenanchin. 1891. III. 522.[2]

Engelhardt, Hermann. *See* DOHME, A. R. L. & ENGEL-HARDT, H.

Engelhardt, Moritz von & Parrot, Friedrich. Reise in die Krym und den Kaukasus. 1815. I. 368.[2]

Engelhardt, P. J. P. Die teutschen Arzneigewächse. 1846. III. 73.

Engelhardt, Robert. Acacia verticillata Willd. 1896. III. 466.[1]

— Andromeda speciosa Michaux. 1896. III. 664.[2]

— Aralia chinensis fol. aureo-variegatis. 1896. III. 641.[2]

— Aristolochien. 1895. III. 386.[1]

— Artocarpus, Cynometra. 1889. III. 220.[1]

— Boronien. 1896. III. 495.[2]

— Bougainvillea. 1894. III. 388.[1]

— Castanea crenata var. Gicust. 1896. III. 358.[2]

— Cercidiphyllum japonicum. 1896. III. 388.[2]

— Cestrum L. 1897. III. 699.[1]

— Clerodendron Bungei Steud. 1891. III. 696.[1]

— Clethra arborea als Kronenbäumchen. 1892. III. 646.[2]

— Cocos australis Mart. 1891. III. 322.[2]

— Einige empfehlenswerte Coniferen. 1896. III. 291.

— Einige seltenere . . . Ziersträucher. 1896. III. 70.

— Elaeocarpus cyanea Sims. 1897. III. 584.[2]

— Empfehlenswerte Zierbäume und sträucher. 1888. III. 70.

— Eurya japonica Tbbg. 1897. III. 596.[2]

— Die Gattung Cassia. 1894. III. 470.[4]

— Die härteren Bambusen. 1891. III. 314.[2]

— Itea virginica L. 1897. III. 413.[1]

— Justicia coccinea Aubl. 1892. III. 709.[2]

— Der Kakaobaum. 1889. III. 592.[2]

— Leiophyllum buxifolium. 1898. III. 653.[1]

— Leucothoë axillaris. 1897. III. 653.[1]

— Libonia floribunda Karl Koch. 1893. III. 709.[2]

— Die Livistona-Arten der Gärten. 1891. III. 326.[2]

— Livistona rotundifolia Mart. 1891. III. 327.[1]

— Lonicera Alberti. 1895. III. 751.[1]

— Myrtus Luma Bara. 1897. III. 637.[1]

— Noch etwas über Habrothamnus. 1887. III. 699.[1]

— Die Pandang oder Schraubenpalmen. 1889. III. 313.[1]

— Ueber Pilzkrankheiten der Phoenix. 1893. III. 318.[2]

— Die Pistasien-Arten. 1889. III. 525.[1]

— Prunus Davidiana. 1894. III. 436.[2]

— Prunus serotina pendula. 1897. III. 442.[1]

— Quercus macranthera. 1897. III. 362.[2]

— Ravenala madagascariensis. 1887. III. 341.[2]

— Reise-Ergebnisse . . . in Süddeutschland und der Schweiz. 1900. I. 49.

— Rhapis humilis Bl. 1891. III. 331.[1]

— Rhododendron dahuricum. 1897. III. 658.[2]

— Rhus Vernix. 1895. III. 528.[2]

— Die schönsten Neuholländer, Pimelea spectabilis. 1890. III. 628.[1]

— Schubertien. 1895. III. 694.[1]

— Smilax-Arten für Parkanlagen. 1895. III. 338.[1]

— Stephanotis floribunda. 1894. III. 694.[1]

— Tecoma radicans Juss. 1886. III. 705.

— Verpflanzen alter Taxus. 1897. III. 288.[1]

— Ein zweiter Flor der Robinia viscosa. 1895. III. 487.[2]

Engelhardt, Wolfgang. Die Nahrung der Pflanzen. 1856. I. 158.

Engelhart, Johan Henric. De Moro alba. 1777. II. 154.[2]

Engelke, (*Oberförster*). Beantwortung der Frage über die mindeste Grösse einer . . . Forstfläche. 1846. IV. 242.

— Bericht über die Ausschlagsfähigkeit . . . von Pinus rigida. 1843. IV. 468.[2]

— Nachricht über die Pinus rigida in Schönbrunn. 1852. IV. 468.[2]

— Stockausschlag an Kiefern. 1842. II. 47.[2]

— Ueber die Waldstreu-Nutzung. 1852. IV. 437.[2]

Engelken, (*Oberförster, Dombrowaka*). Beantwortung der Frage . . . Weidenstecklingspflanzungen im Frühjahr . . . auszuführen. 1853. III. 347.

— Die Nonne . . . im k. Forst-Reviere Dombrowka. 1856. IV. 200.

Engelken, A. M. *See* CROES, J. & ENGELKEN, A. M. & F.

Engelmann, Christoph Wilhelm. Genera plantarum . . . in den russischen Ostseeprovinzen. 1844. I. 361.

Engelmann, G. *See* ЭНГЕЛЬМАНЪ, Г.

Engelmann, George. Abies amabilis. 1880. II. 22.[1]

— Abies (Picea) Engelmanni Parry. 1863. II. 37.[2]

— Abietineae of California. 1880. II. 14.[2]

— The acorns and their germination. 1880. II. 131.[2]

— Additions to the Cactus flora of the territory of the United States. 1863. II. 587.[1]

— Additions to the flora of the United States. 1882. II. 261.[1]

— Agave Parryi. 1879. III. 341.[1]

— Agave Victoriae-Reginae T. Moore. 1880. II. 89.[2]

— The American Junipers of section Sabina. 1877. II: 30.[1]

— The American Spruces. 1879. II. 34.[1]

— De antholysi prodromus. 1832. I. 145.[1]

— The black-fruited Crataegi and a new species. 1882. II. 261.[1]

— Botanical appendix. 1848. I. 322, 331.

— Cactaceae. 1845. II. 586.[2]

— Cactaceae. 1871. II. 587.[1]

— Cactaceae of the . . . boundary. 1859. II. 587.[1]

— Cactaceae of the Ives exploration. 1861. II. 587.[1]

— Cacteae. 1878. II. 587.[1]

— Cacteae of Engelmann and Gray's Plantae Lindheimerianae. 1845. II. 586.[2]

— The Californian Silver Firs. 1879. II. 14,[1] 22,[1] 59.[1]

— Catalpa species. 1880. II. 787.[1]

— Cereus giganteus et C. Thurberi. 1854. II. 589.[2]

— On the character of the vegetation of southwestern Texas. 1851. I. 322.

— Echinocactus Simpsoni. 1876. II. 593.[1]

— Ueber einige nordamerikanische Pinus-Arten. 1863. II. 14.[1]

— Ueber einige nordamerikanische Pinus-Arten. 1865. II. 39.[1]

— Fernere Bemerkungen über Cereus giganteus. 1854. II. 590.[1]

— The flower of the Yucca. 1872. II. 87.[1]

— Fraxinus quadrangulata. 1880. II. 708.[2]

— On the fruit of Viburnum and Cornus. 1866. II. 654.[2]

— Further notes on Cereus giganteus. 1854. II. 589.[2]

— Die Gattung Yukka. 1873. II. 86.[2]

— The genus Pinus. 1880. II. 38.[2]

— Morphology of spines. 1883. I. 107.[2]

— Nachricht von Cereus giganteus Engelm. 1854. II. 590.[1]

— On the nature of the pulp of the Cactus fruit. 1863. II. 588.[1]

— Neuere Mittheilungen über nordamerikanische Cactus-Formen. 1863. II. 587.[1]

— A new Conifer. 1881. II. 53.[1]

— The North American Grapes. 1868. II. 505.[1]

— Notes on Agave. 1875. II. 88.[2]

— Notes on the Cereus giganteus. 1852. II. 587.[1]

— Notes on the Coniferae. 1876. II. 22.[2]

— Notes on the genus Yucca. 1873. II. 86.[2]

— Notes on the Grape-vines of Missouri. 1859. II. 505.[1]

— Notes on western Coniferae. 1882. II. 14.[2]

— The Oaks of the United States. 1876. II. 128.[2]

— About the Oaks of the United States. 1876. II. 128.[2]

— Opuntia subulata Engelm. 1883. II. 597.[1]

— Picea Engelmanni and Picea pungens. 1882. II. 34.[1]

— On Pinus aristata. 1863. II. 14.[1]

— Pinus flexilis James. 1863. II. 42.[1]

— Pinus latisquama n. sp. 1882. II. 42.[2]

— Pinus serotina. 1877. II. 39.[4]

— Remarks on Viburnum and Cornus. 1866. II. 842.[2]

— Report on the botany of the expedition [across the Great Basin of Utah]. 1876. I. 324.

— Revision of the genus Pinus. 1880. II. 38.[2]

— Sketch of the botany of Dr. A. Wislizenus's expedition. 1848. I. 322, 331.

— Some additions to the North American flora. 1881. I. 308.

— Some notes on Yucca. 1882. II. 86.[2]

— On the structure of the fruit . . . of Ribes. 1863. II. 244.[1]

— Synopsis of American Grape vines. 1872. II. 505.[1]

— A synopsis of the American Firs. 1878. II. 22.[1]

— Synopsis of the Cactaceae . . . of the United States. 1856. II. 587.[1]

— The true Grape-vines of the United States. 1872. II. 505.[1]

— Tsuga caroliniana. 1881. II. 53.[1]
— Tsuga Pattoniana and Hookeriana. 1882. II. 53.[1]
— Untersuchungen über die Abietineen. 1868. II. 16.[3]
— Vitality of the seeds of serotinous cones. 1880. II. 40.[3]
— Vitis palmata Vahl. 1883. II. 506.[3]
— Yucca and Hesperaloe. 1871. II. 86.[3]
— See also FARRY, C. C. & ENGELMANN, George.
— & Bigelow, J. M. Description of the Cactaceae collected . . . near the thirty-fifth parallel. 1856. II. 587.[1]
— & Gray, Asa. Plantae Lindheimerianae. 1845. I. 321.
Engelmann, Julius. Das Reichsgesetz betreffend die Unfall- und Krankenversicherung. 1886. IV. 310.[3]
Engelmann, Theodor Wilhelm. Les couleurs non vertes des feuilles. 1888. I. 185.[3]
— Die Farben bunter Laubblätter. 1887. I. 174.
— Recherches sur les relations quantitatives entre l'absorp- tion de la lumière et l'assimilation. 1884. I. 173.
Engelsen, E. Vinstokken og dens Dyrkning. 1898. III. 551.[3]
Engelskjøn, C. Om Petroleum som Middel mod Sygdomme hos Roser. 1890. III. 453.[1]
Engesser, Karl. Flora des südöstlichen Schwarzwaldes. 1852. I. 383.
Engeström, Johan. De Quercu. 1737. II. 132.[1]
Engholm, Jonas Johan. Florula ceilanica. See THUNBERG, C. P. 1825. I. 476.[3]
Engineer, architect . . . See SURVEYOR . . . IV. 5.[1]
Engineering magazine. IV. 3.
Engineering news. See SURVEYOR . . . IV. 5.[1]
Engineers' club of Philadelphia. Proceedings. IV. 3.
England — Royal agricultural society. See ROYAL . . . III. 18.
Engle, H. M. Leaf prints. 1887. I. 521.[1]
— Nut culture. 1895. III. 134.[1]
Engler, Heinrich Gustav Adolf. Anacardiaceae. 1883. II. 454.[3]
— Anacardiaceae. 1896. II. 454.[3]
— Anacardiaceae africanae. 1893. II. 455.[1]
— Aristolochiaceae africanae. 1898. II. 180.[3]
— Balanopsidaceae. 1897. II. 111.[3]
— Ueber Begrenzung . . . der Ochnaceae. 1874. II. 544.[1]
— Beiträge zur Flora des Congogebietes. 1887. I. 492.[1]
— Beiträge zur Flora des südlichen Japan. 1885. I. 463.[1]
— Beiträge zur Flora von Afrika. 1892. I. 483.[1]
— Beiträge zur Flora von Afrika. 1893. II. 171.[3] — 1895. II. 145,[3] 173.[1] — 1898. II. 180.[3] — 1899. II. 206.[1]
— Beiträge zur Flora von Afrika. See LOPRIORE, Giuseppe. 1900. II. 189.[3]
— Beiträge zur Flora von Kamerun. 1886. I. 490.
— Beiträge zur Kenntnis der Sapotaceae. 1890. II. 696.[3]
— Beiträge zur Kenntniss der Antherenbildung. 1875. I. 116.[3]
— Beiträge zur Kenntniss der südamerikanischen Rutaceen. 1873. II. 170,[3] 474.[1]
— Bericht über Kulturversuche in Deutsch-Ostafrika. 1897. III. 131.[3]
— Botanische Jahrbücher. See BOTANISCHE . . . I. 11.
— Brunelliaceae. 1897. II. 250.[1]
— Burseraceae. 1883. II. 416.[1]
— Burseraceae. 1896. II. 416.[1]
— Ueber Cardiogyne africana Bureau. 1897. II. 147.[1]
— Casuarinaceae. 1889. II. 92.[1]
— Chloranthaceae. 1889. II. 95.[1]
— Chlorophora excelsa. 1897. II. 148.[1]
— Clausena anisata. 1900. III. 503.[1]
— Cneoraceae. 1896. II. 396.[3]
— Coriariaceae. 1896. II. 454.[1]
— Corynocarpaceae. 1897. II. 462.[1]
— Crossosomataceae. 1897. II. 255.[3]
— Diagnosen neuer afrikanischer Pflanzenarten. 1897. I. 483.[3]
— Diagnosen neuer Arten und kleinere Mitteilungen. 1895. I. 271.[1]
— Diagnosen neuer Burseraceen und Anacardiaceen. 1881. II. 416,[1] 454.[3]
— Dichapetalaceae. 1896. II. 432.[3]
— Dichapetalaceae africanae. 1897. II. 433.[1]
— Dracaena Sanderiana. 1893. III. 337.[1]
— Drei neue Burseraceae aus Westafrika. 1890. II. 418,[3] 461.[1]
— Ueber einige Guttapercha-Bäume. 1895. I. 499,[3] III. 229.
— Empfehlung der Anlage von Cinchona-Plantagen in Ka- merungebirge. 1895. III. 717.[3]

— Die Entwickelung der Pflanzengeographie. 1899. I. 301.
— Escallonieae et Cunoniaceae. 1871. II. 237.[3]
— Die auf der Expedition S. M. S. Gazelle . . . im malay- ischen Gebiet gesammelten Siphonogamen. 1886. I. 466.
— Über die Familie der Lactoridaceae. 1887. II. 215.[1]
— Über die Familie der Loranthaceen. 1890. II. 172.[1]
— Ueber die Flora der deutschen Schutzländer in Westafrika. 1885. I. 490.
— Über die Flora des Gebirgslandes von Usambara. 1893. I. 492.[3]
— Fouquieriaceae. 1897. II. 563.[1]
— Ueber die geographische Verbreitung der Rutaceen. 1896. II. 397.[1]
— Ueber die geographische Verbreitung der Zygophyllaceen. 1896. II. 395.[1]
— Ueber den Gewürznelkenbau in Zanzibar. 1895. III. 636.
— Guttiferae. 1895. II. 552.[3]
— Guttiferae africanae. 1893. II. 558.[1]
— Guttiferae et Quiinaceae. 1888. II. 547,[1] 552.[3]
— Über die Herkunft des Kinkeliba. 1895. III. 632.[1]
— Herrn M. Dinklage's Beobachtungen über die Raphia- Palmen. 1897. II. 74.[3]
— Ueber die Hochgebirgsflora des tropischen Afrika. 1891. I. 491.
— Icacinaceae. 1896. II. 474.[1]
— Icacinaceae africanae. 1893. II. 474.[1]
— Juglandaceae. 1889. II. 112.[1]
— Koeberliniaceae. 1895. II. 566.[1]
— Lacistemaceae. 1889. II. 95.[1]
— Lactoridaceae. 1891. II. 215.[1]
— Lauraceae africanae. 1899. II. 223.[1]
— Leitneriaceae. 1889. II. 111.[1]
— Liliaceae. 1888. II. 77.[1]
— Loranthaceae. 1889. II. 172.[3]
— Loranthaceae africanae. 1895. II. 173.[1]
— Menispermaceae africanae. 1899. II. 206.[1]
— Monimiaceae africanae. 1899. II. 221.[3]
— Monographieen afrikanischer Pflanzen-Familien. 1898. I. 483.[3]
— Monographische Uebersicht der Gattungen Escallonia. 1870. II. 239.[3]
— Moraceae. 1889. II. 145.[1]
— Moraceae africanae. 1895. II. 145.[3]
— Moraceae (excl. Ficus). 1898. II. 145.[3]
— Über die morphologischen Verhältnisse . . . Gattung Rhus. 1881. II. 454.[3]
— Myricaceae. 1889. II. 111.[1]
— Eine neue Burseraceen-Gattung. 1890. II. 418,[3] 461.[1]
— Eine neue Icacinaceae von Neu-Guinea. 1893. II. 475.[3]
— Eine neue Schinopsis. 1885. II. 460.[1]
— Notizen über die Flora der Marshallinseln. 1895. III. 94.[3]
— Die Nutzpflanzen Ost-Afrikas. 1895. III. 93.[1]
— Ochnaceae africanae. 1893. II. 544.[1]
— Ochnaceae, Anacardiaceae, Sabiaceae. 1876. II. 454,[3] 491,[1] 544,[1] 613.[1]
— Olacaceae. 1889. II. 170.[3]
— Olacaceae africanae. 1893. II. 171.[3]
— Olacineae, Icacineae. 1872. II. 170,[3] 474.[1]
— Opiliaceae. 1897. II. 169.[3]
— Oriza japonica Thunb. 1886. II. 466.[3]
— Passifloraceae africanae. 1892. II. 575.[3]
— Pentaphylacaceae. 1897. II. 462.[1]
— Das Pflanzenreich. 1900. I. 261.
— Die Pflanzenwelt Ost-Afrikas. 1895. V. xxiv.[1]
— Piperaceae. 1889. II. 93.[1]
— Plantae Gürichianae. 1895. I. 495.
— Plantae Marlothianae. 1888. I. 495.
— Populus euphratica Oliv. subsp. Denhardtiorum. 1897. II. 97.[3]
— Proteaceae. 1889. II. 158.[1]
— Quiinaceae. 1895. II. 547.[1]
— Rosaceae africanae. 1893. II. 256.[3]
— Rutaceae. 1896. II. 397.[1]
— Rutaceae africanae. 1897. II. 397.[1]
— Rutaceae, Simarubaceae, Burseraceae. 1874. II. 397,[1] 413,[1] 416.[1]
— Der Saphu-Baum. 1891. III. 510.[1]
— Sapotaceae. 1891. II. 696.[3]
— Saxifragaceae. 1891. II. 237.[3]
— Scheffler's . . . Entdeckungen im östlichen Usambara. 1900. I. 493.

Engler, Heinrich Gustav Adolf (*continued*).
— Scytopetalaceae. 1897. II. 540.[1]
— Simarubaceae. 1896. II. 413.[2]
— Stearodendron oder Allanblackia Stuhlmannii. 1895.
II. 553.[1]
— Studien über die Verwandtschaftsverhältnisse der Ruta-
ceae. 1877. II. 397.[1]
— Ueber die südamerikanischen Escalloniaceen. 1870. II.
237.[2]
— Syllabus der Pflanzenfamilien. 1892. I. 256.
— Syllabus der Vorlesungen über specielle . . . Botanik.
1892. I. 256.
— Die systematische Anordnung der monokotyledoneen An-
giospermen. 1892. I. 253.[1]
— Taxaceae, Typhaceae . . . in Harar et in Somalia . . .
lectae. 1898. I. 490.
— Uebersicht über die botanischen Ergebnisse der [Gazelle]-
Expedition. 1889. I. 303.
— Ulmaceae. 1889. II. 141.[1]
— Urticaceae. 1889. II. 156.[1]
— Ueber die Vegetation des Isergebirges. 1864. II. 102.[2]
— Über die Vegetation des Isergebirges. 1865. I. 385.
— Über die Vegetationsverhältnisse des Ulugurugebirges.
1900. I. 493.
— Über die Vegetationsverhältnisse in den neuen deutsch-
afrikanischen Schutzgebieten. 1885. I. 490.
— Versuch einer Entwicklungsgeschichte der Pflanzenwelt.
1879. I. 300.
— Ueber die Verwendbarkeit des Holzes von Juniperus pro-
cera. 1895. IV. 448.[2]
— Über die Verwerthung anatomischer Merkmale bei . . .
Icacinaceae. 1893. II. 474.[1]
— Verzeichniss der auf der Graf v. Götzenschen Expedition
. . . gesammelten Pflanzen. 1895. I. 493.
— Vorkommen einer . . . Guttiferenart in Deutsch-Ost-
afrika. 1895. III. 608.[1]
— Ueber das Vorkommen von Koso. 1895. II. 264.[2]
— Über die wichtigern Ergebnisse der neuern botanischen
Forschungen im tropischen Afrika. 1894. I. 493.
— Ueber das Wutung-Holz in Shantung. 1897. IV. 538.[1]
— Zygophyllaceae. 1896. II. 395.[1]
— *See also* COHN, Ferdinand & ENGLER, Adolf.
— & Diels, Ludwig. Combretaceae. 1899. II. 615.[2]
— — Uebersicht über . . . Gattungen der Anonaceen. 1900.
II. 215.[2]
— & Drude, Oscar. Die Vegetation der Erde. 1896. I.
301.
— & Harms, Hermann. Bestimmungen wertvoller . . .
Nutzhölzer aus Kilossa. 1897. IV. 401.[1]
— & Prantl, Karl. Die natürlichen Pflanzenfamilien. 1889.
I. 261.
— & others. Beiträge zur Flora von Afrika. 1895. I.
483.[2]
— — Berichte über die botanischen Ergebnisse der Nyassa-
See und Kinga-Gebirgs-Expedition. 1900. I. 493.
— — Diagnosen neuer Arten verschiedener Familien. 1895.
I. 483.[2]
— — Neue Nutzpflanzen Ostafrikas. 1897. III. 93.[2]
— & Volkens, Georg. Ueber das wohlriechende ostafrikanische
Sandelholz. 1895. II. 169.[1]
Engler, Arnold. Die edle Kastanie in der Centralschweiz.
1900. IV. 493.[1]
— Zur Frage der Ausdehnung des eidgen. Forstgebietes.
1894. IV. 278.[2]
— Ueber gemeinsame Holzaufrüstung in Nidwalden. 1895.
IV. 383.[1]
— Eine merkwürdige Fichte. 1896. II. 35.[2]
— El monte y el clima. 1900. IV. 542.[2]
— Eine neue Sämeschine. 1891. IV. 542.[2]
— Stickstoff und Waldvegetation. 1898. IV. 63.[2]
— Wie sollen wir unsere Rottannenbestände verjüngen? 1899.
IV. 459.[1]
— Durch wilde Kaninchen angerichtete Schäden. 1900.
IV. 198.[2]
— Wirtschaftsprincipien für die natürliche Verjüngung der
Waldungen. 1900. IV. 123,[2] 140.
Englerth, Seb. Mitteilungen über Weinbergs-Anlage. 1872.
III. 553.[1]
Englisches Mittel, der Bäume Wachsthum . . . zu befördern.
1803. III. 175.[1]
English, L. W. Notes on the winter-killing of twigs. 1898.
III. 182.
The English arboricultural society. 1885. IV. 40.[2]
English arboricultural society. Transactions. III. 16.

English car timber. 1899. IV. 424.[2]
An English catalogue of the trees and plants in the physicke
garden. *See* BOBART, Jakob.
An English forest. 1890. IV. 358.[1]
On English forestry. 1884. IV. 274.[2]
English forests and forest trees. 1853. I. 393,[2] 511, *IV. 27,*[1]
85.[1]
An English herbal. 15 . . ? I. 276.
English illustrated magazine. III. 16.
The English Oak. 1895. II. 139.[1]
Engrais à employer dans les pépinières. 1899. IV. 145.
Engrais chimiques. Résineux. 1898. IV. 145.
Engrais de pépinière. 1900. IV. 145.
Les engrais verts. Le lupin. 1899. IV. 145.
Engstfeld, E. Ueber die Flora des Sieger Landes. 1856.
I. 383.
Enjubault-la-Roche. Rapport . . . sur les vingt-cinq con-
trats d'échange de la forêt de Senonche. 1792. IV. 275.
Enklaar, E. C. Handboek voor den beoefenaar van den land-
bouw. 1854. III. 106.[1]
— Handleiding tot de kennis der natuur- en landhuishoud-
kunde. 1842. III. 106.[1]
— Nuttige en schadelijke insecten. 1856. III. 95.
— Tuinboek. 1859. III. 106.[1]
— Verhandeling over de wetenschappelijke beoefening van den
landbouw. 1842. III. 35.
Enklaar van Guericke, F. A. Het aanleggen en onderhouden
van Koffietuinen. 1899. III. 727.
— Bemesten van Koffietuinen. 1889. III. 734.[1]
— Bemesting bij dé Kina cultuur. 1900. III. 717.[1]
— Beschouwingen over bemesting van Koffie tuinen. 1896.
III. 734.[1]
— Handleiding bij het onderwijs in de landhuishoudelijke
scheikunde. 1851. III. 36.[2]
— Hervorming der grondslagen van de gouvernements Koffie-
cultuur. 1899. III. 731.
— Is kunstmest hoofdmest of hulpmest? 1899. III. 734.[1]
— Een nieuw stapelprodukt 1877. III. 315.[1]
— Het nut der bijen voor de Koffiecultuur betwijfeld. 1899.
III. 727.
— De teelt van vruchtboomen. 1877. III. 147.[1]
L'enlèvement des feuilles mortes. 1896. IV. 72.
Enlèvement des feuilles mortes dans les bois. 1897. IV. 558.[1]
Les ennemis de l'Épicéa, Chrysomyxa abietis. 1900. IV.
457.
Ennes, Car. Joh. Disputatio medico-botanica exhibens
primitias florae scanicae. *See* LECHE, Johan. 1744. I.
351.
Ennichmann, Zacharias. Historia plantarum generalis. *See*
SCHENCK, J. T. 1656. I. 30.
Enon, H. Étude chimique sur les Oléacées. 1861. II. 705.[2]
Ein enormer Fichtenstamm im Somvixer-Tobel. 1856. II.
37.[1]
Enormous use of Spruce 1893. IV. 452.[2]
Enquête générale sur les incendies de forêts en Algérie. 1866.
IV. 184.[1]
Enquête publiée par la Commission . . . de la Gironde. 1874.
III. 759.
Enquête relative aux effets de l'hiver de 1879–1800. 1880.
IV. 48.
Enquête sur les diverses maladies des arbres résineux. 1877.
IV. 442.
Enquête sur les incendies de forêts dans la region des Maures.
See FARÉ, H. 1869. IV. 183.[1]
Enquête sur les incendies de forêts . . . de Gascogne. *See*
FARÉ, H. 1873. IV. 183.[1]
Enquête sur les vignobles du département de l'Aude. *See*
CASTEL, P. 1888. III. 556.
Enrique de Graef, Juan. Discursos mercuriales. 1755. III.
126.[1]
Enriquez, R. de ZAYAS. *See* ZAYAS ENRIQUEZ, R. de.
Ensayo para la materia médica mexicana. 1889. III. 264.[2]
Enseignement agricole. 1889. IV. 34.[2]
Enseignement forestier. Personnel inférieur. 1897. IV.
540.[2]
Ensign, Edgar T. Forest préservation and tree growing.
1888. IV. 178.[1]
— Forestry in Colorado. 1885. IV. 314,[2] 340.[1]
— Report on the forest conditions of the Rocky Mountains.
1888. IV. 340.[2]
Enslin, Theodor Christian Friedrich. Bibliotheca oeconomica.
1841. III. 1.
— Bibliothek der Forst- und Jagd-Wissenschaft. 1823.
IV. 1.

Het enten van Koffie. 1900. III. 733.²
Entleutner, Anton F. Die immergrünen Ziergehölze von Süd-Tirol. 1891. I. 294,¹ III. 90.¹
— Die periodischen Lebenserscheinungen. 1888. I. 227.²
— Die sommergrünen Ziergehölze von Süd-Tirol. 1892. III. 90.¹
— Die Ziergehölze von Südtirol. 1888. III. 90.¹
Entomological society of London. Transactions. III. 16.
Entomologie appliquée; l'hylésine. 1894. IV. 559.¹
L'entomologie et la sylviculture aux États-Unis. 1899. IV. 205.¹
Entomologie forestière. 1894. IV. 549.²
Entomologie forestière. 1896.· IV. 93.
Entomologie forestière. Le Kermès Strobi. L'hylobe. 1894. IV. 549.²
Entomologie forestière. Le lasiocampe. 1894. IV. 549.²
Entomologie forestière. — Orgyie pudibonde. 1894. IV. 497.
Entomologische Nachrichten. III. 12.
Entomologische Zeitung. IV. 539.¹.
Entreprise de gutta percha et de caouchouc. See GETAH-PERTJAH en caoutchouc-onderneming. 1899. III. 149.
Die Entrindung der Rüstern oder Ulmen. 1859. III. 363.²
Entrup Bavink, T. G. Natuurlijke geschiedenis . . . der schadelijke rupsen. 1841. III. 189.
Die Entstehung blauer Blüthen bei Hortensien. 1897. III. 412.¹
Die Entstehung des Janus-Apfels. 1869. I. 201.²
Die Entwässerung der Gebirgswälder. 1875. IV. 144.¹
Die Entwickelung der Staatsforstwirthschaft im Königreiche Sachsen. 1897. IV. 355.²
Entwurf der Vorschriften betreffend die Holzgehaltsaufnahme von Holzbeständen. 1851. IV. 216.
Entwurf der Vorschriften für die forstwirthschaftliche Einrichtung. 1851. IV. 242, 301.
Entwurf einer Anweisung, betreffend die Aufstellung ·. . . der Wirthschaftspläne. 1876. IV. 248.¹
Entwurf einer Forstorganisation in Württemberg. 1849. IV. 291.¹
Entwurf eines Forst-Gesetzes. 1833. IV. 317.²
Entwurf eines Forst-Gesetzes. 1840. IV. 317.²
Entwurf eines Gesetzes betreffend die Abänderung des Zolltarifs. 1883. IV. 284.²
Entwurf eines Gesetzes betreffend die Bilbung von Waldgenossenschaften. 1868. IV. 308.²
Entwurf eines Gesetzes [für Württemberg] über die Ausübung und Ablösung der Weiderechte. 1868. IV. 333.
Entwurf eines Regulativs, wie es in Rücksicht des Unterrichts der Lehrlinge . . . gehalten werden soll. 1803. IV. 31.
Entwurf zum Regulativ, wie es in Rücksicht des Unterrichts der Lehrlinge . . . gehalten werden könnte und möchte. See GRIESHEIM, L. W. von. 1802. IV. 31.
Entzündung einer Eiche durch einen Blitzschlag. 1885. IV. 511, 5ἱβ¹
Enumeratio alphabetica nominum . . . Palmarum quae in Belgii septentrionalis hortis . . . coluntur. 1860. II. 510.²
Enumeratio plantarum circa Regiomontum Borussorum. See HENCKEL VON DONNERSMARCK, L. V. F. 1817. I. 376.
Enumeratio plantarum horti botanici, Gryphici. See LEDEBOUR, K. F. von. 1806. I. 45.
Enumeratio plantarum Horti botanici regiomontani. See ÖLSCHLÄGER, A. F. 1819. I. 45.
Enumeratio plantarum horti botanici Universitatis . . . christianiensis. See RATHKE, J. 1823. I. 40.
Enumeratio plantarum . . . Nóvae Hollandiae. See ENDLICHER, Stephan & others. 1837. I. 500.
Enumeratio plantarum novarum a cl. Schrenk lectarum. See FISCHER, F. E. L. & MEYER, C. A. 1841. I. 453.²
Enumeratio plantarum quae in horto comitis Alexii a Razumowsky. See REPOWSKY, D. 1804. I. 41.
Enumeratio plantarum quae in Horto lugduno-batavo coluntur. 1831. I. 51.¹
Enum. plantarum quas Reg. hortus calaritanus. See GENNARI, Patrisio. 1872.· I. 64.
Enumeratio plantarum Sueciae. 1830.· I. 353.
Enumeratio seminum ex collectione anni 1834 Horti romani. See DONARELLI, Carlo. 1834. I. 63.
Enumeratio seminum Horti pillnitziensis. 1824. I. 46.
Enumeratio stirpium in Horto academico pisano. 1799. I. 61.
Enumeratio stirpium phanerogamarum . . . in Silesia. See GÜNTHER, C. C., GRABOWSKI, Heinrich & WIMMER, Friedrich. 1824. I. 377.
Épailly. Richesse en tannin des écorces de Chênes-Liéges. 1850. IV. 518.¹

Épernay — Société d'horticulture et de viticulture. See SOCIÉTÉ . . . III. 22.
Epery, René Philippe. Essai sur le Maté. 1883. III. 531.¹
Ephemerides; sive, Observationum medico-physicarum centuriae. See ACADEMIA NATURAE CURIOSORUM. I. 10.
Die Epheu-Formen. 1884. III. 642.²
Épicéas remarquables dans le Toggenbourg. See SCHÖNE Rothtannen. 1864. II. 37.¹
Epistolarum ab eruditis viris ad Alb.· Hallerum.· 1773. I. 520.²
The epitome of the art of husbandry. See BLAGRAVE, Joseph. 1675. III. 107. ·.
Époque d'abatage des arbres. 1899. IV. 385.¹
Époque d'abatage des taillis. 1894. IV. 557.¹
Sur l'époque . . . de la découverte du Café. 17 . . ? III. 738.
Époque de la plantation. 1898. IV. 154.²
Époque de plantation de l'Épicéa. 1898. IV. 454.
Epping forest. 1896. IV. 358.²
Epping forest and county of Essex naturalists' field club. Transactions. I. 18.
Epps, Hahnemann. On the Kola bean. 1889. II. 533.¹
Épremesnil, comte d'. Le Jardin d'essai de Cannes. 1878, I. 59.
— & Sahut, Felix. Effets du froid dans le midi. 1888. III. 49.¹
-er. Die Gewinnung von Eichenholzextract. 1885. IV. 515.¹
Érable remarquable dans le Toggenbourg. 1864. II. 477.¹ See STARKER Ahorn.
The eradication of the Prickly Pear. 1900. III. 624.¹
Erath. Gründliche Anweisung zur Kenntniss . . . der schädlichen Insecten. 1847. III. 189.
Erb. Note relative à un procédé de destruction du phylloxera. ·1872. III. 565.¹
Erb, Josef. Über den Werth der Blattanatomie zur Charakterisirung von Juniperus. · 1897. II. 30.¹
Un' erba che interessa la silvicoltura. 1882. IV. 145.
Erbach-Erbach und Wartenberg, Eberhard, Graf. Ueber Hochwaldwirthschaft in Roth- und Damwild-Thiergärten. 1860. IV. 136.²
Erbe, R. Garrya elliptica. 1886. III. 352.³
Erber, Josef. Ueber die auf der Seestrandskiefer, . . . lebenden schädlichen Insekten. 1865. IV. 464.¹
— Ungeziefer der Seestrandskiefer. 1865. IV. 464.¹
Erbstein, Karl Friedrich Wilhelm. Über Deutschlands holzverschwenderische Missbräuche. See Über DEUTSCHLANDS . . . 1796. IV. 282.¹
Erck, C. Beobachtungen . . . über die Capreaceen. 1889. II. 101.³
— Über die Salices hybridae Ehrhartianae. 1884. II. 101.³
Ercsei, József. Nemes Tordamegye flórája. 1844. I. 445.
Erdelyi, Michael von. Anleitung zur Pflanzenkenntniss. 1835. I. 87.
Erdészeti és gazdászati lapok. See ERDÉSZETI lapok. IV. 14.
Erdészeti kisérletek. IV. 14.
Erdészeti lapok. IV. 14.
Erdészeti rendeletek tára. IV. 14.
Erdészeti segédtáblák. 1883. IV. 230.
Erdészeti zsebnaptár. IV. 14.
Erdinger, Carl. Salix Kerneri. 1865. II. 107.²
— Verzeichnis der in der Umgebung von Krems vorkommenden Gefässpflanzen. 1872. I. 44?
Erdmann, A. Ueber das Huanokin. 1856. III. 722.
Erdmann, Hugo. See WALBAUM, Heinrich & ERDMANN, Hugo.
Erdmann, Julius. Ueber die Concretionen in den Birnen. 1866. II. 280.¹
— Ueber die Constitution des Tannenholzes. 1867. IV. 463.¹
Erdmann, Karl. Die unorganischen Bestandtheile in den Pflanzen. 1855. I. 152.²
— Ueber die unorganischen Bestandtheile von Viscum. · 1855. II. 178.²
Erdmann, Karl Gottfried. Sammlung . . . der Giftpflanzen. 1797. III. 72. ·
— Vermischte botanische Beobachtungen. 1794. I. 264.
— Verschiedenheit der Knopsen. 1794. I. 107.³
Erdmann, O. L. Schets der algemeene warenkennis. 1871. III. 218.²
Erdmann, Richard. Die Grundlehren des rationellen Obstbaues. 1891. III. 146.³
Erdődi, Adolf. Közgazdasági eszmetöredékek az erdészet köréből. 1866. IV. 269.
— Magyarország méregfája. 1867. II. 11.¹
— A termőhelynek a fanövesztésre való befolyásáról. 1867. IV. 67.¹

Az erdőtörvényjavaslat tárgyalása. 1879. IV. 331.²
Eremita, Donato d'. See Donato d' Eremita.
Erfahrungen über Anbau . . . der Schwarz-Erle. 1831. IV. 489.¹
Erfahrungen über das Entstehen der Arten. 1850. III. 50.²
Erfahrungen über den Anbau von Oedungen. 1858. IV. 158.
Erfahrungen über den Holzgehalt der Kiefernbestände.· 1840. IV. 480.
Erfahrungen über den Massengehalt der Commerzialholzsortimente. 1858. IV. 230.
Erfahrungen über den Massen-Vorrath und Zuwachs geschlossener Hochwald-Bestände. 1838. IV. 216.
Erfahrungen über den Schneedruck. 1838. IV. 189.¹
Erfahrungen über die Holzhaltigkeit geschlossener Waldbestände. 1838. IV. 216, 350.¹
Erfahrungen über die schädlichen Eigenschaften des Taxusbaumes. 1807. III. 288.¹
Erfahrungen über Obstbaumdüngung. 1897. III. 152.¹
Erfahrungen und Bemerkungen beim praktischen Forst- und Jagdwesen. See Forst- und Jagd-Archiv. IV. 7.
Erfahrungsmässige Anweisung zur richtigen Kenntniss der Krankheiten der Wald- und Gartenbäume. 1795. III. 178.
Erfahrungssätze über den Torf aus Oberbayern. 1858. IV. 438.³
Erfahrungs-Tafeln für die drei Spessarter Waldkomplexe. 1836. IV. 232.
Erfolge des Ringelns an der Weinrebe. 1859. III. 549.¹
Das Erfrieren der Waldbäume im Winter. 1858. IV. 66.²
Erfurth, Ch. B. Flora von Weimar. 1867. I. 386.
Die Ergänzung und Schulung der Förster für den Staatsforstdienst. 1874. IV. 32.
Ergebniss der Holzsamen-Ernte . . . in Preussen. 1875. IV. 438.¹
Erhaltung der Wälder und Holzmangel. See Kessler. 1839. IV. 281.¹
Erhard, Theodor. Synopsis generum Gomphiae. 1849. II. 545.¹
Erhardt, J. F. Ueber mögliche s zweckmässige und wohlfeile Waldanlagen. 1866. IV. 158.⁹
Erhöhung der Dauer des Buchenholzes. 1865. IV. 499.¹
Erie, Allan. Brazil-wood trees. 1893. III. 468.²
— Cinchona cultivation in Jamaica. 1892. III. 713.¹
— The Cocoanut Palm. ·1894. III. 324.¹
— Culture du Piment à la Jamaïque. 1892. III. 637.²
— The Guaiacum and Cinnamon trees. 1893. II. 224,¹ 395.¹
— Pimento cultivation in Jamaica. ·1892. . III. 637.³
— In a tropical forest. 1892. I. 219.²
Erica; Turnbull's hybrids. 1851. III. ·650.¹
Erica mediterranea found native in Ireland. 1831. II. 667.²
L' Erica pianta a foraggio. 1866. IV. 534.¹
Ericas. 1848. III. 650.¹
La Ericina. 1887. III. 649.¹
Ericsson, Bernhard. Die forstlichen Verhältnisse des Grossfürstentums Finnland. 1896. IV. 348.¹
— Mäntypuiden vikanaisuuksista pohjoisimmassa Suomessa. 1891. IV. 482.²
— Metsien laadusta ja hoidosta Sodankylän metsäpiirissä. 1888. IV. 348.¹
— Porokarjan suhde metsänhoitoon. 1889. IV. 135.¹
Erikson, Gustaf. Dissertatio oeconomica sistens reflexiones nonnullas circa nutritionem vegetabilium. 1815. I. 157.
Erikson, Johan. Om Sorbus scandica. 1900. III. 313.¹ ·.¹
— Studier öfver sandfloran i östra Skåne. 1896. I. 358.
Eriksson, Jakob. Berberisbusken som Bærer . . . af Græsrust. 1897. III. 394.²
— Einige Beobachtungen über den stammbewohnenden Kiefernblasenrost. 1896. IV. 462.¹
— Étude sur le Puccinia Ribis. 1898. III. 415.¹
— Studien über den Hexenbesenrost der Berberitze. 1898. III. 394.²
— Två för Finland nya fröväxter från Åland. 1883. II. 205.¹
— Über das Urmeristen·der Dikotylen-Wurzeln.· 1878. I. 132.²
— Ueber den Vegetationspunkt der· Dikotylen-Wurzeln. 1876. I. 103.
— Was ist in den europäischen Staaten . . . bis jetzt gethan worden, um die Erforschung der · . . . Pflanzenkrankheiten zu befördern? 1890. IV. 177,¹ 196,¹
— Welche Grasarten können· die Berberitze mit Rost anstecken? 1896. III. 394.¹
Érkövy, Adolf. Az 1863. évi aszályosság a magyar alföldön. 1863. III. 183.²

Erläuterung über Zweck und Einrichtung der k. sächs, Forstvermessungs- und Forsttaxations-Arbeiten. 1821. IV. 302.
Erläuterungen zu der Ausstellung der kgl. sächs. Forsteinrichtungsanstalt. 1881. IV. 19.²
Erlangen—Physikalisch-medicinische Societät. See Physikalisch-medicinische . . . I. 14.
Erlenrinde als Gerbmaterial. 1878. IV. 489.²
Ermässigte Tarife für die Beförderung roher Holzmaterialien. 187.? IV. 284.²
Erman, Adolf. Naturhistorischer Atlas. Verzeichniss von Thieren und Pflanzen. 1833. I. 453.¹
— Reise um die Erde durch Nord-Asien. 1833. I. 453.²
— Travels in Siberia. 1833. I. 453.²
Ermel, J. F. De radice Chinae. See Juch, H. P. 1753. III. 338.¹
Ermel, W. K. L. Kraft van. See Kraft van Ermel, W. K. L.
Ermens, G. Aegle marmelos. 1877. III. 495.¹
— L'horticulture en Égypte. 1874. III. 131.¹
Ueber Ermittlung, Einführung, Aufrechterhaltung und Nutzung eines nachhaltigen Materialertrages. 1854. IV. 235.²
Ermunterung und Anweisung zur häufigern Anbauung der Birke. 1799. IV. 490.¹
Ernährung gewisser Bäume durch unterirdische Pilze. 1886. I. 233.²
Erndl, Christian Heinrich. De Flora japonica. 1716. I. 461.
Erndtel, C. H.· Warsavia physice illustrata. 1730. I. 359.
Erneuerte Gesetze für die Studirenden auf der Forstakademie zu Dreissigacker. 1839. IV. 31.
Erneuerter Plan und Statuten der Herz.- Sachsen-gothaischen . . . Societät der Forst- und Jagdkunde. 1812. IV. 40.¹
Ernst, (Forstmeister). Erfolge und Misserfolge . . . in Schleswig-Holstein. 1895. IV. 119.¹
Ernst, von, (Oberförster). Ueber die Anlage eines Saatkampes. 1853. IV. 453.·
— Aufforstung von Haideflächen in der Oberförsterei Quickborn. 1882. IV. 158.·
— Beitrag zur Bestimmung des mittleren Durchmessers der Nadelholzstämme. 1856. IV. 216.
— Bericht über die am 28. und 29. Juni 1861 . . . ausgeführten Exkursionen. 1861. IV. 353.
— Bericht über die vom Schlesischen Forstverein . . . ausgeführten Exkursionen. 1864. IV. 353.
— Entomologische Aphorismen. 1851. IV. 455.
— Die Entwässerung von Forstflächen. 1857. IV. 143.²
— Das forstliche Verhalten der Lärche. 1855. IV. 449.
— Mittheilungen über die forstlichen Verhältnisse des Zobtenberges. 1860. IV. 353.
— Referat über . . . Bradke'schen Baummesser. 1859. IV. 231.²
Ernst, G. Adolph. Amylumkörner in . . . Urticaceen. 1867. III. 382.²
— Ashy crown Cinchona in Venezuela. 1871. III. 725.²
— Ueber das Ausschlagen tropischer Bäume. 1876. I. 221.
— Bemerkungen über die giftigen Eigenschaften der Euphorbia caracasana. 1866. III. 517.³
— Biologische Beobachtungen an Eriodendron. 1885. II. 529.²
— Blausäure in den Früchten von Ximenia. 1867. III. 384.²
— Eine botanische Excursion auf der Insel Margarita. 1886. I. 338.¹
— Botanische Miscellaneen. 1876. II. 377.²
— Botanische Notizen aus Caracas. 1867. III. 64,² 382,² 384,² 465,² 506,¹ 690.¹
— Botanische Notizen aus Venezuela. 1880. IV. 536.¹
— El café de Liberia en Venezuela. 1878. III. 743.¹
— Über das Dickenwacksthum der Adansonia. 1871. II. 529.¹
— Enumeration de las especies de plantas empleadas . . . para el método . . . "embarbascar." 1887. III. 260.²
— Estudios sobre la flore y fauna di Venezuela. 1877. I. 338.¹
— Estudios sobre las deformaciones . . . del árbol de Café. 1878. III. 735.
— La exposición nacional de Venezuela. 1884. III. 267.¹
— Las familias mas importantes del reino vegetal. 1881. III. 64.²
— Über fischvergiftende Pflanzen. 1888. III. 59.²
— Florula chelonesiaca. 1876. I. 338.¹
— Gartenbau in Caracas. 1888. III. 118.²

— Gelber Farbstoff von Xanthoxylum ochroxylum. 1867. III. 506.[1]
— Ueber die giftigen Eigenschaften von Euphorbia caracasana. 1866. III. 517.[2]
— Guachamacá. 1867. III. 690.[1]
— On the Guachamaca. 1870. II. 731.[1]
— El Guachamaca. 1885. II. 728.[1]
— Gummi von Acacia Ouyrarema. 1867. III. 465.[2]
— Hat der Kaffebaum [sic] wirklich dimorphe Blüthen? 1876. II. 814.[2]
— Jottings from a botanical note-book. 1870. I. 338.[1]
— Eine Krankheit des Kaffeebaumes. 1876. III. 735.
— List of Venezuelan woods. 1866. IV. 398.[1]
— Memoria botánica sobre el embarbascar. 1881. III. 260.[2]
— Observaciones botánicas. 1887. I. 338.[1]
— Observaciones aliquot in plantas . . . florae caracasanae. 1874. I. 338.[1]
— On Papaya vulgaris De Cand. 1866. II. 582.[2]
— Pflanzen, welche in Caracas . . . medizinisch benutzt werden. 1865. III. 64.[2]
— Plantas interesantes de la flora caracasana. 1870. I. 338.[1]
— On the plants cultivated . . . in the valley of Caracas. 1867. III. 64.[2]
— Plants used medicinally at Caracas. 1865. III. 64.[2]
— Ueber die Pulpa in den Früchten der Randia. 1867. III. 47.[1]
— Sertulum aturense. 1887. I. 338.[1]
— Some remarks on the poisonous properties of Euphorbia caracasana. 1866. III. 517.[2]
— Studie over de misvormingen . . . van den Koffieboom. 1878. III. 735.
— Studien über die Deformationen . . . des Kaffeebaumes. 1878. III. 735.
— Teratologische Beobachtungen. 1880. I. 143.
— Tropfenausscheidung bei Calliandra Saman. 1876. iI. 377.[2]
— On two cases of laminar enations from · . . . leaves. 1889. II. 457.[1]
— Vargas considerado como botánico. 1877. II. 546.[2]
— Venezuelanisches Buchsbaumholz. 1880. IV. 536.[1]
— Verzeichniss der auf der venezuelanischen Inselgruppe Los Roques . . . beobachteten Pflanzen. 1872. I. 338.[1]
Ernsting, Arthur Konrad. Anfangsgründe der Kräuterwissenschaft. 1748. I. 82.[2]
— Historische und physikalische Beschreibung der Geschlechter der Pflanzen. 1762. I. 257.
— Prima principia botanica. 1748. I. 82.[2]
Ernsts, A. Nizza und Hyères. 1839. I. 409.
Erörterungen über die nächsten Aufgaben des bayerischen Forstwesens. See GANGHOFER, August. 1873. IV. 274.[1]
Errera, Leo. Sur des appareils destinés à démontrer le mécanisme de la turgescence. 1888. I. 131.[1]
— Sur une condition fondamentale d'équilibre des cellules vivantes. 1886. I. 131.
— Une expérience sur l'ascension de la sève. 1886. I. 165.
— Ein Transpirationsversuch. 1886. I. 167.
— & Laurent, Émile. Planches de physiologie végétale. 1897. I. 149.[1]
— Maistriau, Ch. & Clautriau, G. Premières recherches sur la localisation . . . des alcaloïdes. 1887. I. 177.
Errichtung einer Forstschule für das Königreich Italien. 1871. IV. 35.[1]
Errichtung einer schweizerischen Forstschule. 1844. IV. 36.[1]
Ueber die Errichtung von Försterschulen für Preussen. 1886. IV. 33.[1]
Errington. Dyrkning af Camellier. 1850. III. 599.[2]
Errington, R. See JOHNSON, G. W. & ERRINGTON, R.
Errington, Robert. On the Deodar. 1850. III. 300.[1]
— The gardener's note book. 1869. III. 204.[2]
— A list of climbers grown in Calcutta. 1869. III. 204.[2]
— On style and expression in certain trees. 1852. III. 201.
Erslev, Éd. Plantninger paa Skt. Croix. 1882. IV. 532.[2]
Die erste ausführlichere und gedruckte Forstordnung für den Kanton Zürich d. d. vom Jahre 1715. See HOCH-OBERKEITLICHES Mandat . . . 1715. IV. 305.
Erste Fortsetzung der Nachträge und Berichtigungen. 1883. IV. 290.
Erste Gerichtssatzung der Stadt Bern. Art. Forstwesen. 1864. IV. 330.
Ertel, Vasil. Dictionnaire complet de zoologie et de botanique. 1843. I. 522.[2]
Ertrag der Birke als Vornutzung. 1855. IV. 491.[1]

Ertrag der österreichischen Staatsforste 1890. 1893. IV. 262.
Ertrag von Eichenschälholzschlägen von 1853. 1853. IV. 512.
Ertragstafeln, nach den auf den einzelnen Tafeln angegebenen Quellen zusammengestellt. 1899. IV. 238.
Ervin, Éd. Blackberries. 1893. III. 457.[2]
Erxleben, (Landrath und Domherr, Selbelang). Mittel zur vertilgung der Raupen. 1841. III. 196.
Erythea. I. 5.
Erziehung der Buche mit der Hainbuche. 1857. IV. 137.[2]
Über die Erziehung . . . der hochstämmigen Rosenstöcke. 1839. III. 451.[2]
Von der Erziehung gemischter Buchenbestände. 1858. IV. 494.
Erziehung gemischter Hochwaldungen. 1886. IV. 138.[2]
Esami di ammissione nell' Istituto forestale di Vallombrosa. 1894. IV. 35.[2]
Escalafón del Cuerpo de ingenieros de montes. 1895. IV. 553.[2]
Escarpit, J. A. Plantations des grands arbres. 1885. III. 84.[1]
Escayrac de Lauture, comte d'. Die Bäume als Cisternen benutzt. 1853. III. 589.[1]
— Ueber den Baobab. 1853. III. 589.[1]
— Exploration du pays des dattes. 1849. III. 130.[1]
— Flora of the Date country. 1850. III. 328.[1]
— Flore de Soudan: le Baobab. 1853. III. 589.[1]
Esche, J. M. Nog eens de gouvernementskoffiecultuur. 1892. III. 730.
Eschenbach, Johann Friedrich. Diatribe de physiologia seminum. 1777. I. 120.
— Diatribe epistolaris nectariorum usum exhibens. 1776. I. 118.[1]
— Disputatio physica observationum botanicarum specimen. 1784. I. 263.
Escherus, Casparus & others. De variis annonae conservandae methodis. See GESNER, Johann. 1761. III. 174.[1]
Eschke, Ernst Franz. Beiträge zur Vermessung . . . der Forste. 1863. IV. 101.[1]
— Ueber Messung und Cubirung der runden Nutzhölzer. 1851. IV. 223.
Eschscholtz, Johann Friedrich. Descriptiones plantarum novae Californiae. 1826. I. 321.
Eschwege, M. von. Einfluss der Schälzeit auf das Gewicht der Eichen-Lohrinde. 1886. IV. 513.
Escombe, F. Germination of seeds. 1897. I. 204.
— See also BROWN, H. T. & ESCOMBE, F.
Escribano y Pérez, J. M. Pomona de la provincia de Murcia. 1884. III. 89.[1]
Escrivá de Romaní, Rafael. Carta abierta. 1899. IV. 554.[2]
— Cosas del ramo forestal. 1899. IV. 552.[1]
— El Montepio forestal sin intervención del estado. 1899. IV. 554.[2]
Escuela de ingenieros de montes. 1885. IV. 540.[2]
La Escuela de montes en el Congreso pedagógico. 1892. IV. 540.[2]
Escuela del Escorial. 1892. IV. 540.[2]
Escuela especial de ingenieros de montes. 1877. IV. 35.[1]
Escuela especial de ingenieros de montes. 1883. IV. 35.[1]
Escuela especial de ingenieros de montes. 1886. IV. 540.[2]
Escuela especial de ingenieros de montes. Instrucciones. 1896. IV. 541.
Escuela especial de ingenieros de montes. Reglamento. 1896. IV. 541.
La Escuela forestal de la India inglesa. 1885. IV. 541.
Escuela general preparatoria de ingenieros y arquitectos. 1886. IV. 540.[2]
Escuela general preparatoria de ingenieros y arquitectos. 1887. IV. 540.[2]
Escuela práctica de selvicultura. 1889. IV. 540.[2]
Escuela preparatoria para ingenieros y arquitectos. 1886. IV. 540.[2]
Escuelas forestales inglesas. 1892. IV. 540.[2]
On the esculent plants of Van Diemensland. See BACKHOUSE, James. 1833. III. 283.[1]
Escursione degli alunni del R. istituto forestale di Vallombrosa. 1882. IV. 364.
Escursioni e viaggi. 1864. IV. 35.[1]
Esenbeck, NEES von. See NEES VON ESENBECK.
Esencia de trementina. 1890. III. 228.[1]
Esmarch, Heinrich Peter Christian. Anfang . . . einer schleswig'schen Flora. 1789. I. 374.
Esmarch, Lauritz. Historische Nachricht über den Flugsand. 1817. IV. 145.
— Historisk Efterretning om Sandflugten. 1817. IV. 145.

Espejo, Zoilo. Cartilla de agricultura práctica. 1869. III. 114.[2]
— Cultivo de árboles frutales. 1900. III. 145.[1]
Espeut, William Bancroft. The timbers of Jamaica. 1881. IV. 398.[1]
L'Espinasse-Laugeac, vicomte de. La culture de l'Olivier en Tunisie. 1896. III. 676.[2]
Espinosa, Domingo, BELLO Y. See BELLO Y ESPINOSA, Domingo.
Espinouse, A. Du phylloxéra; son traitement. 1874. III. 759.
Espitalier, Silvain. Encore un moyen de salut pour les Vignes phylloxérées. 1874. III. 759.
Esposizione della R. camera di commercio di Genova. 1862. IV. 277.
Esposizione internazionale á Cologna. 1865. IV. 19.[2]
Esposizione nazionale a Firenze. 1862. IV. 20.[3]
Essai de bien-public. See COLLIGNON. 1776. IV. 277.
Essai sur l'agriculture moderne. See NOLIN & BLAVET, J. L. 1755. III. 112.
Essai sur l'histoire naturelle de St. Domingue. See NICOLSON, (père). 1776. I. 334.
Essai sur la minéralogie des Monts-Pyrénées. See PALASSO. 1781. I. 535.[1]
Essai sur la réorganisation du service forestier en France. 1878. IV. 292.
Essai sur la taille des arbres fruitiers. 1812. III. 171.
Essai sur la taille des arbres fruitiers. See PELLETIER DE FRÉPILLON. 1773. III. 171.
Essai sur les Rubus normands. See MALBRANCHE, Alexandre. 1875. II. 303.[2]
Essais d'analyse . . . des quinquinas. See DELONDRE, Auguste. 1861. III. 722.
Les essais de germination. 1895. IV. 545.[2]
Essais de la Station fédérale de contrôle des graines. 1895. III. 157.
Essais sur la culture du Mûrier blanc. See BOLET, L. M. 1766. III. 373.
Essarts et forêts. 1895. IV. 362.
Essay concerning the best methods of pruning fruit-trees. 1732. III. 169.[2]
Essay on the cultivation . . . of Tea in Java. 1841. III. 601.[1]
Essay on the minute parts of plants. See DONOVAN, E. O. 1789. I. 97.
An essay on the natural history of Guiana. See BANCROFT, Edward. 1769. III. 267.[2]
An essay upon the virtues of balm of Gilead. See CARTWRIGHT, John. 1760. III. 511.[1]
Essays on husbandry. See HARTE, Walter. 1764. III. 109.
L'essence d'écorce de Betula lenta. 1884. IV. 491.[2]
Essence de Boldo. 1877. III. 403.[2]
Essence de Rose. 1873. III. 454.[1]
Essences exotiques acclimatées en Allemagne. 1897. IV. 545.[1]
Essences résineuses exotiques. 1900. IV. 126.[2]
Essential oils from . . . Eucalyptus and Melaleuca. 1863. III. 633.[1]
Essential oils from indigenous plants of Victoria. 1865. III. 224.[2]
Essential oils of the Orange tribe. 1895. III. 499.[1]
Essential oils, perfumery, etc. 1877. III. 225.
Esser, Arnold, Dau & Becker. See DAU, BECKER, ESSER & ARNOLD.
Esser, A. Phytelephas macrocarpa. 1861. III. 330.[1]
Esser, J. G. Die Waldberechtigungen in der ehemaligen Grafschaft Dagsburg. 1894. IV. 334.[1]
Esser, Peter. Die Bekämpfung parasitischer Pflanzenkrankheiten. 1892. III. 179.
— Die Entstehung der Blüthen am alten Holze. 1887. I. 113.[2]
Essex agricultural society. Transactions. III. 3.
Essex field club. Transactions. See EPPING FOREST . . . I. 18.
Essex institute. Bulletin. Proceedings. I. 3.
Essex naturalist. See EPPING FOREST . . . I. 18.
Essich, C. F. Beyträge zur forstwissenschaftlichen Mathematik. 1807. IV. 57.
Esslinger, Otto. Bericht über die Schaustellung von Feld- und Forstbahnen zu Osnabrück. 1886. IV. 392.
— Die Festsetzung des Fällungs-Etats. 1887. IV. 237.
— Säelatte für Nadelholzsamen. 1890. IV. 149.[1]
— Ueber die Verwendung von Cellulose zu Möbelverzierungen. 1877. IV. 430.
— Verwerthung des Holzes vom Faulbaumstrauche. 1886. IV. 528.[1]

Essner, Benno Rudolf Gustaf. Ueber den diagnostischen Werth . . . der Markstrahlen bei den Coniferen. 1882. II. 17.[1]
— Ueber den diagnostischen Werth . . . der Markstrahlen bei den Coniferen. 1886. II. 17.[1]
Establishment of forest reservations. 1897. IV. 179.[1]
Establishment of state model forests for Scotland. 1898. IV. 38.[2]
Estação agronomica de Campinas, da republica dos Estados Unidos do Brazil. Relatorio annual. III. 10.[1]
Estacion meteorologica-forestal de San Ildefonso. 1882. IV. 60.[1]
Estaciones meteorológicas de la Escuela forestal de Nancy. 1886. IV. 541.[1]
Estadística de árboles heridos por el rayo. 1892. IV. 548.[1]
Estadística de la producción de los montes publicos. 1866. IV. 363.[1]
Estadística de las semillas adquiridas . . . para la repóblación. 1895. IV. 165.
Estadística de las siembras y plantaciones. 1896. IV. 556.[2]
Estancelin. Observations sur les causes et les effets de la destruction des bois. 1745. IV. 425.[1]
Esteve, Juan Jago. Dictionario de las yervas y plantas medicinales. 1552. III. 88.[2]
Estienne, Charles. L'agricoltura e casa di villa. 1554. IV. 121.
— L'agriculture et maison rustique. 1554. IV. 121.
— Arbustum, fonticulus, spinetum. 1533. I. 276, V. XIV.[2]
— Fünfzehn Bücher von dem Feldbaw. 1554. IV. 121.
— De latinis. See DE LATINIS et graecis nominibus. 1544. I. 71, V. IX.[1]
— Maison rustique; or, The countrie farme. 1554. IV. 121.
— Praedium rusticum. 1554. IV. 121.
— De re hortensi libellus. 1535. I. 277, V. XIV.[2]
— Seminario over plantario. 1540. III. 110.[1]
— Seminarium et plantarium. 1540. III. 110.[1]
— Seminarium sive plantarium. 1537. I. 292.
— Sieben Bücher von dem Feldbaw. 1554. IV. 121.
— Sylva. Frutetum. Collis. 1538. I. 277.
— Vineto. 1537. III. 554.[1]
— Vinetum. 1537. III. 554.[1]
Estländischer Forstverein. Bericht. IV. 6.
Estratto della relazione sulla situazione dell' Impero francese . . . Foreste. 1864. IV. 360.
Estratto di rapporto sulla situazione dell' Impero francese. 1866. IV. 360.
Estrazione della seta dal Gelso. 1865. III. 380.[1]
Estreicher, Aloizy Rafal. Index plantarum in Horto botanico cracoviensi. 1825. I. 66.[1]
— Spis Akacyi w Ogr. botan. krak. 1836. III. 462.[2]
— Spis roślin i nasion od 1. X. 1835 w ogrodzie botanicznym Uniw. Jagiel. 1835. I. 66.[1]
— Spis roślin Ogr. botan. krak. 1825. I. 66.[1]
Estrey, H. MEYNERS D'. See MEYNERS D'ESTREY, H.
Estridge, H. W. Six years in Seychelles. 1885. I. 536.[1]
Estrup, J. B. S. Om Beplantning af Jyllands Heder. 1862. IV. 156.[1]
— Om Skovbrugets Frigjørelse. 1862. IV. 273.[1]
Estublier, E., DUGAT-. See DUGAT-ESTUBLIER, E.
El Estudio. I. 7.[2]
Estudio é informe sobre el Cafe de Costa Rica. 1900. III. 728.[2]
Estudios forestales. See PASCUAL, Agustin. 1852. IV. 287.
Estudo sobre o Café. 1891. III. 740.[2]
Étant donné le projet de transformer une mauvaise prairie en une plantation de Peupliers. 1899. IV. 161.[1]
Étant donnée la situation suivante: Fange d'une trentaine d'hectares. 1900. IV. 143.[2]
Étard, A. Dédoublement de la bande fondamentale des chlorophylles. 1897. I. 142.
— Étude chimique des corps chlorophylliens. 1892. III. 583.[2]
— Méthode d'analyse . . . des extraits chlorophylliens. 1892. I. 142.
— De la présence de plusieurs chlorophylles. 1894. I. 142.
— Des principes qui accompagnent la chlorophylle. 1892. I. 142.
— Recherches sur la strychnine. 1878. III. 683.[2]
— Le spectre des chlorophylles. 1896. I. 142.
État der Forst-, Jagd- und Triftverwaltung. 1893. IV. 291.[1]
État der Forst-Verwaltung der Königreichs Preussen. IV. 7.
État der schweizerischen Forstbeamten mit wissenschaftlicher Bildung. 1895. IV. 13,[2] 294.[1]
État des graines d'arbres, arbrisseaux, plantes. 1779. III. 86, V. XXIII.[1]

État des services des anciens élèves en fonctions dans l'administration des forêts. 1883. IV. 2.
État ·général du personnel de l'administration des forêts. 1855. IV. 292.
Die etatsmässigen Forstflächen. 1892. IV. 261.[1]
Etheridge, Robert. Statistics regarding the size of certain Australian trees. 1876. II. 624.[1]
Etheridge, Robert, (jr.), David, T. W. E. & Grimshaw, J. W. On the occurrence of a submerged forest . . . near Sydney. 1897. I. 499.[3]
Ethnological society of London. Transactions. I. 18.
Étienne, Victor. Botanique. Résumé d'un mémoire sur les éléments corticaux. 1865. I. 130.
Étoilles, Leroy d'. See Leroy d'Étoilles.
Étrennes à tous les amateurs de Café. 1790. III. 738.
L'étrépage. 1897. IV. 558.[1]
Etter, Paul. Ertrag der Mittelwaldungen des thurgauischen Staatsforstreviers Münsterlingen-Kreuzlingen. 1899. IV. 262.
Etti, Carl. Ueber das Bixin. 1874. III. 613.[1]
— Ueber das Bixin. 1878. III. 613.[1]
— Sur la bixine. 1874. III. 613.[1]
— Sur la bixine. 1878. III. 613.[1]
— Sur la Kinoïne. 1878. III. 485.[3]
— Ueber das malabrische Kinogummi. 1878. III. 485.[3]
— Le tannin du Chêne. 1880. IV. 515.[1]
Ettingshausen, Constantin, Freiherr von. Beiträge zur Erforschung der Phylogenie. 1878. I. 249.[3]
— Die Blattskelete der Apetalen. 1858. I. 109.[2]
— Die Blatt-Skelete der Dicotyledonen. 1861. I. 109.[3]
— Über die Blattskelette der Loranthaceen. 1871. II. 173.[2]
— Über Castanea vesca. 1872. II. 124.[1]
— Über fossile Banksia-Arten. 1891. II. 159.[1].
— Über die genetische ·Gliederung der Cap-Flora, 1875. I. 495.
— Die genetische Gliederung der Flora Australiens. 1874. I. 502.
— Über die genetische Gliederung der Flora der Insel Hongkong. 1884. I. 461.
— Über die Nervation der Blätter bei den Celastrineen. 1857. ·II. 465.[3]
— Über die Nervation der Blätter . . . bei den Euphorbiaceen. 1854. II. 434.[3]
— Über die Nervation der Blätter bei . . . Quercus. 1895. II. 131.[3]
— Über die Nervation der Blätter der Papilionaceen. 1854. II. 320.[1]
— Über die Nervation der Bombaceen. 1858. II. 528.[2]
— Photographisches Album der Flora Österreichs. 1864. I. 441.
— Physiographie der Medicinal-Pflanzen. 1862. III. 58. I. 243.[3]
— Zur Theorie der Entwickelung der jetzigen Floren. 1894. I. 243.[3]
— Vorläufige Mittheilungen über phyto-phylogenetische Untersuchungen. 1880. I. 249.[3]
— & Krašan, Franz. Beiträge zur Erforschung der atavistischen Formen. 1888. II. 123.[1]
— — Observations sur l'atavisme des plantes. 1890. I. 249.[3]
— — Résultats des recherches sur l'atavisme des plantes. 1888. II. 123.[1]
— — Untersuchungen über Deformationen. 1891. I. 145,[1] IV. 501.[1]
— — Untersuchungen über Ontogenie und Phylogenie der Pflanzen. 1890. I. 249.[2]
— & Pokorny, Alois. Physiotypia plantarum austriacarum. 1873.[3] I. 442.
Ettmüller, (Ehrenberg). Hochwald oder Mittelwald auf Aueboden? 1883. IV. 131.
Ettorre, Giuliano. Notizie istorico-fisiche su'l Caffe'. 1791. II, 814.[1]
L'Étude de l'écorce. ·1874. I. 130.
Étude sur la carbonisation des bois. See Roux, E. 1870. IV.· 419.
Étude sur le Coccus pé-la. See Rathouis, C. 1880. III. 226.[1]
Étude sur les futaies résineuses de la Champagne. 1897. IV. 461.[1]
Études forestières supérieures. 1898. IV. 33.[3]
Études pratiques d'arboriculture fruitière. 1891. III. 145.[1]
Études sur le Prunier d'Agen. n.d. III. 432.[2]
Etwas für Pflanzschulen. 1856. IV. 150.
Etwas über den Anbau der Fichte. 1833. IV. 452.[3]

Etwas über den Baobab. 1853. II. 528.[3]
Etwas über den Borkenkäfer. See Bernstein, J. G. 1786. IV. 455.
Etwas über den Holzmangel. 1799. IV. 280.[2]
Etwas über die in Deutschland angezogenen . . . amerikanischen Holzarten. 1839. IV. 125.[2]
Etwas über gemischte Bestände. 1844. IV. 137.[1]
Etwas über Standorte . . . der in den Fürstenthümern Hohenlohe und Mergentheim bis jetzt entdeckten wildwachsenden Pflanzen. 1816. I. 376.
Of the etymology, . . . and sacred uses of woods. 1733. IV. 120.
Etzel, F. von. Ueber eine Deputat-Holzberechtigung . . . in der Fürstenwalder Stadtforst. 1870. IV. 274.[1]
— Forsteinrichtungswesen in Frankreich. 1878. IV. 249.[1]
— Eine forstliche Studienreise durch Graubünden und Tessin. 1881. IV. 367.
— Die forstlichen Verhältnisse in der Schweiz. 1879.· IV. 367.
— Aus dem Reichslande. 1876. IV. 349.[3]
— Ueber Waldverwüstung und Holzverschwendung. 1876. IV. 281.[1]
Etzler, August. Isagoge physico-magico-medica. 1631.· I. 285.[2]
Eu. Die ·Lärche als Baum des deutschen Waldes. 1897. IV. 450.
The Eucalypts. 1891. III. 634.[1]
The Eucalypts and decorative ·woods of Tasmania See Perrin, G. S. 1886. IV. 402.[1]
L'Eucalyptus à l'Exposition d'Alger. 1876. IV. 531.[3]
Sull' Eucalyptus amigdalina. 1880. IV. 532.[1]
Eucalyptus coccifera at Powderham Castle. 1879. II. 624.[2]
Eucalyptus culture. 1885.· IV. 530.
A Eucalyptus forest. 1879. II. 624.[2]
The Eucalyptus globulus as a disease-destroying tree. 1874. IV. 533.[1]
L'Eucalyptus nell' Alta Italia e Toscana. 1880. IV. 530.
Eucalyptus oil from Eucalyptus Stuartiana. 1892. IV. 534.[1]
Eucalyptus oil in yellow fever. 1896. IV. 532.[1]
The Eucalyptus plantations of Algeria. ·1874. IV. 529.[2]
Eucalyptus timber for street paving. 1897.· IV. 531.[1]
Eucholz, J. B. Flora Homerica. 1848. I. 514,[1] V. xxv.[1]
Eude. Moyen de tenir . . . en fleurs le Robinia hispida. 1859. III. 486.[1]
— Moyen facile d'avoir toujours le Cytisus albus. 1860. III. 474.[1]
Eudes-Deslongchamps, Eugène. Fruits frondipares de Rosier. 1849. II. 289.[3]
— Une monstruosité de la fleur du Clematis bicolor. 1862. II. 198.[1]
— Note sur plusieurs cas de tératologie . . . sur des Fuchsias. 1858. II. 643.[1]
— Poire monstrueuse. 1849. II. 279.[2]
— Rapport sur une poire monstrueuse. ·1842. II. 279.[3]
Eudes-Deslongchamps, Jacques Amand. Une feuille de Pelargonium zonale. 1864. II. 391.[3]
— Note sur quelques anomalies . . . de Fuschia. 1865. II. 643.[1]
— Orange renfermé dans une autre Orange. 1856. II. 403.
— Remarques relatives aux effets de la décortication ·circulaire. 1929. III. 175.[1]
— Résumé des observations . . . relativement à . . . puceron lanigère. 1830. III. 427.[1]
— Sur le retour du Cytisus Adami vers ses ascendants. 1842. II. 368.[1]
Euen. Aufforstungen von Oedländereien mit Pinus rigida. 1899. IV. 469.
Euen, (Forstrath, Oppeln). See Schilling,· (Oberförster, Bunzlau) & Euen, (Forstrath, Oppeln).
Eulefeld, A. Anlegung von Waldmänteln. 1898. IV. 154.
— Erkrankung von Fichten. 1896. IV. 457.
— Eine forstliche Exkursion in den Vogelsberg. 1899. IV. 351.[3]
— Eine forstliche Studienreise nach·Dänemark. 1898. IV. 343.[3]
— Das Schützen der Waldpflanzen. ·1898. IV.· 197.[1]
— Ueber Schutzmittel gegen Wildbeschädigungen. 1896 IV. 197.[1]
— Die Waldversicherung ·gegen Brand- und Blitzschaden 1898. IV. 182.[3]
Eulenberg.—Mährisch-schlesische Forst-Schule. See Mährisch . . . IV. 15.
Euler. Alte und seltene Bäume. 1893. II. 139.[1]
Euphorbiacea. See Allemão, F. F. 1848. II. 445.[1]

Euphrasén, Bengt Anders. Beskrifning öfver svenska vestindiska ön St. Barthelemy. 1795. I. 335.
— Reise nach der schwedisch-westindischen Insel St. Barthelemi. 1795. I. 335.
Eure — Société d'agriculture, sciences et arts du département . . See Société . . . III. 21.
Eure-et-Loire — Société d'horticulture. See Société . . . III. 21.
Europæus, M. Notis om greniga honhängen af Asp. 1873. II. 98.²
— Salix phylicifolia med öfvergångar mellan ♂ - och ♀ -blommor. 1876. II. 109.¹
The **European** Box Thorn. 1887. III. 701.¹
European forests. 1879. IV. 342.²
European Larch in Massachusetts. 1888. IV. 450.
Eustache. Mode de multiplication applicable aux Échinocactes. 1839. III. 622.¹
Eustratiadès, D. S. Étude expérimentale sur les propriétés . . . de la caféine. 1870. III. 742.¹
Evans, Frank. Lagos. 1888. III. 281.¹
Evans, H. A. The relation of the flora to the geological formations in Lincoln county. 1889. I. 319.
— White and yellow Poplars. 1887. II. 210.²
Evans, John. A tour through part of North Wales. 1800. I. 533, V. xx.²
Evans, Maurice S. The fertilisation of flowers. 1894. I. 240.¹
— See also Wood, J. M. & Evans, M. S.
Evans, Taliesin. Orange culture in California. 1874. III. 500.¹
— Western woodlands. 1871. IV. 336.²
Evans, Walter H.. Cornus Baileyi C. & E. in Oregon. 1891. II. 655.¹
— Notes on the edible berries of Alaska. 1900. III. 262.¹
— The stem of Ephedra. 1888. II. 54.¹
— An undescribed Birch from Alaska. 1899. II. 119.²
— See also Coulter, J. M. & Evans, W. H.
Evans, Sons & Co. The island of Montserrat. 1878. III. 502.²
Evelyn, Charles. The lady's recreation. 1717. III. 108.
Evelyn, John. Kalendarium hortense. 1664. III. 107.
— Pomona. 1664. III. 141.
— Sylva. 1664. IV. 107.²
Evenbly, J. Bericht over het verbeteren van slegte gronden. 1788. IV. 159.
Everdingen, N. van. De kaspische Zandwilg in ons land. 1876. III. 351.¹
Everett, Arthur. Victoria; distribution of forest trees. 1866. I. 499,² IV. 89.¹
Everett, Horace. Ferment of Walnut shucks, etc. 1882. III. 354.²
Evergreen banks. 1876. III. 201.
Evergreen forest trees. 1896. III. 293.
Evergreen shelter. 1877. III. 215.¹
Evergreen trees in forest and woodland. See Evergreen forest trees. 1896. III. 293.
Evers, Georg. Beiträge zur Flora des Trentino. 1896. I. 444.
— Einige südliche Rubusformen. 1895. II. 304.¹
Evershed, Henry. The Cedars of Lebanon. 1877. II. 28.¹
— The Mistletoe. 1883. II. 179.³
— Needwood forest. 1879. IV. 358.¹
— Notes on trees. 1883. III. 123.¹
— Seaside trees and shrubs. 1876. III. 41.²
— Woods and wilds of Shetland. 1884. IV. 120.
— The Yew. 1876. II. 10.¹
Eversmann, Eduard. Die thraenenden Weiden. 1842. III. 350.¹
Every farmer. 1877. III. 3.
1885. évi budapesti országos általános kiállítás; erdészet . . . katalogusa. 1885. IV. 21.¹
Évi 31. 1879. törvényczikk: erdőtörvény. 1879. IV. 331.²
Evon. Extrait d'un rapport sur les semis de Mélèze. 1832. IV. 441.
Sur l'**évonymine**. 1880. III. 532.¹
Ewald, W. & Meinshausen, K. F. Skizzen über die physiognomische Beschaffenheit der Sandgebiete am unteren Oredesh. 1888. I. 362.
Ewart, Alfred J. On contact irritability. 1898. I. 197.¹
— The effects of tropical insolation. 1897. I. 174, 230.
Ewbank, Henry. Rhododendron Auoklandi. 1900. III. 659.¹
— Rosa berberidifolia. 1889. III. 456.²
— Yucca baccata. 1900. III. 340.¹

Ewel & Wiley, H. W. Sur les produits de la Cassave. 1894. III. 521.¹
Ewell, Ervin E. See Spencer, G. L. & Ewell, E. E.
Ewer, Samuel. Manuale sive compendium botanices. 1808. I. 85.
Ewers, Erich. Zur Bestimmung des Alkaloïdgehaltes in der Granatrinde. 1899. III. 631.¹
— Dosage des alcaloïdes dans l'écorce de Grenadier. 1899. III. 631.¹
Ewert, R. Die Vermehrung der winterharten Coniferen. 1890. III. 294.³
Ewig, J. J. Ueber Verderbniss der Waldungen. 1799. IV. 206.
Ewing, G. E. The Cherry Plum as a hedge plant. 1878. III. 435.²
Ewing, Peter. The Glasgow catalogue of native and established plants. 1892. I. 404.¹
Ewing, Thomas J. Gigantic trees in Tasmania. 1879. I. 298.
— & Stutzer. On the cultivation of silk in Tasmania. 1863. III. 507.²
Exactissima descriptio rariorum. See Castelli, Pietro. 1625. I. 284.
Examen d'un ouvrage . . . Illustrationes Theophrasti. See Paulet, J. J. 1816. I. 292.
Examen des avantages résultant de l'emploi de la scie, au lieu de la hache. See Piquet. 1809. IV. 392.
Examen des tiges de Pécher. 1827. III. 442.²
Examen du fragment de bois antique. 1857. II. 16.²
An **example** of an unexpected source for water. 1885. III. 544.²
Das **Excellenz** gräflich Waldstein'sche Forsteinrichtungswesen. 1883. IV. 250.¹
Die **Excellenz** Gustav Hilleprand Freiherr von Prandau'schen Domänen Valpo und Dolnji-Miholjac. 1885. IV. 373.
Excelsior. Een kleine ontnuchtering in zake het enten van Java op Liberia Koffie. 1899. III. 733.²
Excrescences on Sequoia. 1879. II. 50.²
Excursion à la forêt de Compiègne. 1900. IV. 555.¹
Die **Excursion** am 6. August 1860 in die gräflich Buquoi'schen Forste. 1860. IV. 370.
Excursion au domaine des Barres. 1900. I. 60,¹ IV. 18.²
Excursion de prácticas. 1886. IV. 541.¹
Die **Excursion** der vierzehnten Generalversammlung des Böhm. Forstvereins zu Pisek. 1862. IV. 370.
Excursión forêstal [en los Alpes franceses]. 1892. IV. 547.²
Excursion in das königliche Forstrevier Grudschütz. 1868. IV. 353.
Excursion in die Forste der Domäne Binsdorf. 1851. IV. 355.¹
Die **Excursion** in die Tetschner Forste. 1851. IV. 370.
Die **Excursion** in die Waldungen von Schwarzkosteletz. 1858. IV. 370.
Excursionsschrift für die . . . Versammlung des Ysenburg'schen forstwirthlichen Vereins. 1863. IV. 353.
Excursions-Taschenbuch der Flora von Göttingen. 1868. I. 386.
Un **exemple** à suivre. 1898. IV. 546.¹
Les **exemptions** d'impôts . des terrains boisés. 1893. IV. 285.¹
Exercices d'histoire naturelle à l'école . . . du Morbihan. See Aubry de la Mottraie. 1801. I. 406.
The **exhaustion** of guttapercha. 1899. III. 232.¹
Exhaustion of timber in South Australia. 1900. IV. 280.¹
Exhibition lessons on timber-preserving. 1885. IV. 420.
Exhibition of hardy trees and shrubs. 1894. III. 203.
Exigences des oseraies en matières minérales. 1898. IV. 487.²
Die **Exkursion** am 16. August 1858 in die Reviere Buda. 1858. IV. 370.
Exner, G. F. Rapport sur les produits des exploitations et des industries forestières. 1881. IV. 399.¹
Exner, Wilhelm Franz. Anhang . . . Holzmassen-Ermittlung einer Rothbuche. 1875. IV. 499.
— Das Biegen des Holzes. 1876. IV. 422.²
— Das Biegen des Holzes: die Grundlage einer grossen Industrie. 1876. IV. 422.²
— Einfluss der Imprägnirung auf die Festigkeit des Holzes. 1875. IV. 419.
— Fällungsversuche · mit der Dampfquersäge. 1878. IV. 393.
— Grupa lasowa na Wystawie krajowej we Lwowie. 1878. IV. 21.¹
— Die Hausindustrie Oesterreichs. 1890. IV. 407.¹

— Das Holz als Rohstoff für das Kunstgewerbe. 1869. IV. 426.[2]
— Holzbearbeitungs-Maschinen. 1874. IV. 422.[1]
— Die Industrie des Böhmerwaldes. 1872. IV. 406.[2]
— Die Kunsttischlerei vom technologischen Standpunkte. 1870. IV. 426.[2]
— Das Lo-Presti'sche Eisenbahn-Projekt. 1869. IV. 391.
— Maschinenkunde an Forstlehranstalten. 1872. IV. 176.[2]
— Das moderne Transportwesen. 1877. IV. 391.
— Neues über Sparterie. 1876. IV. 487.[1]
— Studien über das Rothbuchenholz. 1875. IV. 499.
— Die technischen Eigenschaften der Hölzer. 1887. IV. 408.
— Versuch einer Theorie der Spaltfestigkeit. 1870. IV. 411.[1]
— Werkzeuge und Maschinen zur Holz-Bearbeitung. 1878. IV. 422.[1]
— Werkzeugmaschinen für Holzbearbeitung. 1874. IV. 422.[1]
— See also MARCHET, Gustav & EXNER, W. F.
— &Lauböck, G. Die mechanische Holzbearbeitung. 1879. IV. 422.[1]
Exorde d'un traité sur . . . Camellias. 1854. III. 599.[2]
Exotic sketches. 1873. I. 219.[2]
Experience, (pseud.). Methods of propagation. 1896. III. 153.
— Plants of the Victorian era. 1897. III. 123.[1]
— Seaside planting. 1899. III. 42.[1]
Une expérience intéressante. 1896. IV. 430.
Expériences au sujet de la ponte de l'hylésine. 1899. IV. 479.
Expériences faites dans la Vigne sud du mas. 1874. III. 759.
Expériences forestières établies en 1897. 1898. IV. 38.[1]
Expériences relatives à l'exploitation de l'écorce de Chêne. See BEITRAG zu den Erfahrungen . . . 1865. IV. 512.
Expériences sur la conservation des graines. 1900. IV. 148.
Expériences sur la production des futaies crues. 1844. IV. 254. See also ERFAHRUNGEN über die Holzhaltigkeit. 1838. IV. 350.[1]
Expériences sur la végétation d'un Chêne. 1899. IV. 516.[1]
Experimental cultivation in Jamaica. 1881. III. 324,[2] 405,[2] 592.[2]
Experimental-Versuche mit Waldsamen. 1855. IV. 141.
Experimente über Gewichts- und Volumenveränderung am Holze der jurassischen Waldbäume. 1883. IV. 412.[1]
Experiments in the treatment of Pear leaf-blight. 1889. III. 444.[1]
The expert gardener. 1640. III. 107.
Explanatory catalogue of a few forest trees. 1886. IV. 78.[1]
Exploitabilité des peuplements résineux. 1899. IV. 252.
Exploitatie van balata in Suriname. 1890. III. 668.[1]
De exploitatie van 's lands bosschen op Java. 1881. IV. 279.[1] See also SCHERMBEEK, A. J. van. 1881. IV. 383.[1]
Exploitation d'une forêt de Pins. See MILLISCHER, J. 1896.
Une exploitation de Bouleaux en Campine. 1898. IV. 491.[1]
Exploitation des bois. See BOURDON. 1837. IV. 382.[1]
L'exploitation des forêts du Congo. 1900. IV. 383.[2]
Exploitation des taillis. Époque. 1898. IV. 385.[1]
L'exploitation des taillis à écorces. 1899. IV. 382.[2]
L'exploitation du bois au Congo. 1897. IV. 556.[2]
L'exploitation du caoutchouc au Soudan français. 1899. III. 229.
L'exploitation inconsidérée des peuplements de Chêne. 1898. IV. 508.
Exploitirung der Wälder in Californien. 1893. IV. 382.[2]
Exportation des bois. See Die HOLZAUSFUHR . . . 1859. IV. 406.[1]
Exportation des bois à Einsiedeln. See EINSIEDELNS Holzausfuhr. 1864. IV. 406.[1]
Exportation des bois de Norwège. 1881. IV. 404.[1]
L'exportation du caoutchouc de l'Indo-Chine. 1900. III. 232.[1]
Exportations [et importations] de bois de la Russie. 1897. IV. 557.[1]
Exposé des motifs du projet de loi concernant les engagistes et les échangistes. See CORVETTO, comte de. 1818. IV. 326.
Exposé sommaire des travaux sur la question du phylloxéra. 1881. III. 761.
Exposición de Filipinas. Colección de artículos publicados en El Globo. See VIDAL Y SOLER, Sebastián. 1887. IV. 21.[2]
Exposición de industrias rurales. 1889. IV. 540.[1]
Exposition de l'Administration des forêts . . . Toulouse. 1887. IV. 20.[2]

Exposition des caractères distinctifs entre le Ribes aureum et le Ribes palmatum. 1831. II. 244.[2]
Exposition forestière. Catalogue . . . Moulins. 1885. IV. 20.[2]
Une exposition forestière au Japon. 1895. IV. 540.[1]
Exposition tunisienne des forêts. 1900. IV. 21.[2]
Exposizione d'insetti. 1865. IV. 92.
Expropriation dans les bois de la principauté de Chimay. 1881. IV. 323.[1]
Extension of the trade in Padauk wood. 1896. IV. 522.[1]
Exterde, Ernst, Baron. Sammlung der wichtigeren oesterreichischen Gesetze . . . im Forst-wesen. 1875. IV. 331.[2]
De l'extinction des torrents. See HUN, L. 1853. IV. 185.[2]
An extract of a letter sent lately to Sir Robert Moray . . . concerning . . . propagating Mulberry trees. 1666. III. 372.[2]
Extract of Chestnut bark. 1893. IV. 493.[1]
Extract of Palmetto. 1895. III. 331.[1]
Extract uit de notulen der Malangsche vereeniging. 1899. III. 731.
Extract uit de Verslagen van Gedeputeerde staten zoo verre aangaat de woeste gronden. 1849. III. 122.[1]
Extraction of gutta-percha from leaves. 1897. III. 668.[2]
Extracto tanífero del Roble. 1888. IV. 515.[1]
Extrait d'anciennes fois forestières. Mesures préventives contre la disette de bois. See AUSZÜGE aus alten Forstgesetzen. Vorsorge . . . 1862. IV. 330.
Extrait d'une autre note sur la fève d'épreuve. 1863. III. 483.[2]
Extrait de la statistique forestière du canton de Berne. See AUSZUG aus der Forst-Statistik des Kantons Bern. 1867. IV. 366.
Extrait du Procès-verbal d'aménagement de la forêt domaniale de Haye. 1867. IV. 248.[2]
Extrait du rapport annuel du Bureau forestier du canton de Zurich. See Aus dem JAHRESBERICHT des Oberforstamtes des Kantons Zürich. 1864. IV. 366.
Extraits d'anciennes lois forestières suisses. See AUSZÜGE aus alten Forstgesetzen. 1861. IV. 330.
Una extralimitación. 1890. IV. 548.[2]
Extraordinary growth of the Bilberry. 1805. II. 686.[1]
Eyber, (Oberförster). Ueber die Cultur der Eichen. 1851. IV. 504.
Eyck, SPRENGER VAN. See SPRENGER VAN EYCK.
Eyck van Zuylichem. Iets over eenige houtsoorten in den omtrek van Maartensdyk. 1858. IV. 126.[2]
— Opmerkingen over eenige boomsoorten. 1873. IV. 448.[2]
Eyk, J. A. van. Invloed van het elektrisch licht op den groei en de ontwikkeling der planten. 1881. I. 231.[2]
— Over een nieuw plantenwas. 1875. III. 226.[1]
— Over het opnemen van de stikstof. 1878. I. 231.[1]
Eykman, Johann Frederik. Over de aetherische olie van de Illicium religiosum. 1881. III. 398.[1]
— De botanical relations of Illicium. 1881. II. 209.[1]
— Ueber den giftigen Bestandtheil . . . von Illicium religiosum. 1880. III. 398.[1]
— Sur l'huile éthérée des feuilles de Bétél. 1890. III. 320.[1]
— Notes phytochimiques. 1888. I. 154.
— Phytochemische Notizen ueber einige japanische Pflanzen. 1883. I. 154.
Eyles, G. Juniperus chinensis aurea. 1875. III. 303.[1]
Eymard, Lacour. Examen chimique de la sève du Bibacier. 1890. II. 264.[1]
Eymard, Nicolas. De la culture du Chêne-Liége. 1845. IV. 516.[2]
Eymard, Sylvain. Quelques mots sur le reboisement . . . des hautes montagnes. 1865. IV. 162.
Eyre, Vincent. Memoranda concerning some seeds sent from Cabul. 1842. III. 92.[2]
Eys, J. N. van. See EIJS, J. N. van & REINWARDT, C. G. C.
Eysel, Johann Philippe. De Agallocho, Paradiesholtz. 1712. II. 600.[1]
— De chocolatae usu et abusu. 1694. III. 594.
— De medicamentis ex malo Cydoniato. 1717. III. 483.[2]
— Die wundernswürdige Weiden-Rosen. 1711. III. 349.
Eysell, H. E. Het aangeprezen middel tegen de oeret. 1885. III. 735.
Eysenhardt, Karl Wilhelm. De accurata plantarum comparatione. 1823. I. 377.
Eysfarth, Christian Siegesmund. De morbis plantarum. 1723. I. 206.[1]
Eysson, Rudolph. Disputatio de Castaneis. 1703. II. 124.[2]
— Silvae Virgilianae prodromus. 1695. I. 514.[1]
Ezquerra, José. Instrucción para el cultivo del Pino maritimo. 18 . . ? IV. 467.[1]

F. Agrandissement du domaine forestier de l'état. 1898. IV. 274.[2]

F. Beitrag zur Kenntniss der schweizerischen Korporations-verhältnisse. 1876. IV. 309.[2]

F. Ueber Blitzschläge im Walde. 1891. IV. 194.

F. Boissier's Almond. 1875. III. 435.[2]

F. Definitive Reinertragsberechnung für das Waldland Böhmens. 1883. IV. 262.

F. Document pouvant servir à l'étude des corporations en Suisse. 1876. IV. 309.[2]

F. Les droits d'entrée sur les bois. 1896. IV. 284.[2]

F. Der Edelkastanien-Wald bei Komotau. 1894. IV. 492.[2]

F. Er det afgjort at Frugttræer altid gjøres bedre og ædlere ved den saakaldte Forædling? 1835. I. 247.

F. Grosse Fichten. 1894. II. 37.[2]

F. Die grossen Nussbäume zu Interlaken. 1894. II. 114.[1]

F. Ein Höhenmesser aus der Praxis. 1885. IV. 215.

F. Planting and management of Quick hedges. 1891. III. 422.[2]

F. Pruning newly planted trees. 1872. III. 170.

F. The ripening of the fruit of the Himalayan Oaks. 1900. II. 132.[1]

F. Ueber Vorrichtungen zur Erziehung einer gleichmässigen Besamung der Saatbeete. 1867. IV. 149.[1]

F. Über den zweckmässigsten Verkauf eines grösseren Nadelholzbestandes. 1897. IV. 259.[2]

F., v. Le ravageur des forêts. 1890. IV. 209.[1]

F., A. A gigantic tree. 1872. I. 296.[1]

F., A. Perzikboomen uit zaad. 1876. III. 441.[1]

F., A. C. The resin of Conifers. 1893. II. 21.[1]

F., B. Bemerkungen über den gegenwärtigen Zustand der Baum- und Bestandesschätzung. 1859. IV. 255.

F., C. Das Vorkommen der Fichte im Gebirge. 1868. IV. 453.

F., C. v. Ueber das die Schutzwaldungen und Waldgenossenschaften betreffende Gesetz. 1877. IV. 321.[1]

F., D. T. The golden-flowered Gooseberry. 1889. IV. 414.[1]

F., D. T. The Paulownia imperialis in Paris. 1887. III. 703.[2]

F., D. T. Two early wall shrubs. 1887. III. 415.[1]

F., E. The effect of pruning on the growth. 1878. IV. 171.

F., E. Una gita alle Tre Fontane. 1881. IV. 530.

F., E. Lettera d' un alpinista. 1880. IV. 283.[1]

F., F. Borkenkäferschaden in Fichten-Stangenholz. 1900. IV. 457.

F., F. Ueber den Schaden, den Ueberschwemmungen an Pflanzen anrichten. 1883. III. 185.[1]

F., F. Wallis. Dröhende Kieferspinner-Invasion. 1897. IV. 209.[1]

F., F. J. de. Cercado de alambre galvanizado. 1881. IV. 146.[2]

F., G. Flowering of Mango trees. 1884. II. 457.[1]

F., G. M. Catalpa wood. 1880. IV. 538.[2]

F., H. N. De achteruitgang der gouvernements Koffie-cultuur. 1899. III. 731.

F., H. N. Beschouwingen naar aanleiding van het eerste Koffie-Congres. 1899. III. 731.

F., H. N. Coffea arabica op Liberia-stam. 1899. III. 727.

F., H. N. Coffea stenophylla. 1899. III. 743.[2]

F., H. N. Het gouvernements Koffiemonopolie. 1899. III. 731.

F., H. N. Groene bemesting in Koffie-tuinen. 1899. III. 734.[1]

F., H. N. Indigofera als groene bemesting in Koffietuinen. 1899. III. 734.[1]

F., H. N. De Koch'sche cultuurwijze. 1899. III. 727.

F., H. N. Een oordeel over cacao. 1899. III. 595.[1]

F., H. N. De opheffing van de gouvernements Koffiecultuur. 1899. III. 731.

F., J. Sophora violacea. 1885. III. 488.[2]

F., J. The Tamarisk. 1886. III. 612.[1]

F., J. G. Wie ist dem Rothwild das Schälen abzugewöhnen? 1886. IV. 196.[2]

F., J. V. Der Wald im Zusammenhange mit der Bevölkerungsvermehrung. 1885. IV. 270.

F., N. Einige Erfahrungen über Pflanzenerziehung. 1900. IV. 151.[2]

F., O. A double-flowered Rhododendron hirsutum. 1896. III. 659.[1]

F., P. Die Akazie als Waldbaum. 1884. IV. 523.[1]

F., P. B. Cenni brevissimi sopra i boschi . . . di Sardegna. 1832. IV. 364.

F., R. Fortune's yellow, or salmon-coloured Rose. 1852. III. 455.[1]

F., R. The white wax insect of China. 1852. IV. 534.[2]

F., S. Eisen- und Stahldraht als Transportmittel. 1872. IV. 391.

F., S. W. Aralia spinosa. 1900. III. 641.[2]

F., S. W. Benthamia fragifera. 1898. III. 645.[1]

F., S. W. Clematis montana. 1897. III. 391.[1]

F., S. W. Clerodendron trichotomum. 1897. III. 696.[2]

F., S. W. Dracaena australis at Tresco. 1895. III. 334.[2]

F., S. W. The Macartney Rose. 1900. III. 454.[2]

F., S. W. Old Olive trees in Majorca. 1899. II. 713.[2]

F., S. W. Rosa laevigata. 1898. III. 455.[2]

F., S. W. Spiraea flagelliformis. 1897. III. 461.[1]

F., S. W. Spiraea Lindleyana. 1896. III. 459.[1]

F., W. Croton undulatum. 1873. III. 515.[2]

F., W. Effect of the winter on evergreens. 1888. III. 44.[1]

F., W. Leycesteria formosa. 1874. III. 749.[2]

F., W. Lithospermum fruticosum. 1872. III. 695.[2]

F., W. Paullinia thalictrifolia. 1873. III. 540.[1]

F., W. Up the Tons. 1891. I. 475.[1]

F., W. Weeping trees in the Fulham nurseries. 1873. III. 204.[1]

F., W. N. Hickory lumber. 1892. IV. 488.[1]

F.-M., J. G. *See* M., J. G. F.-

Fabbisogno dei lavori preliminari per la formazione dei semenzai. *See* COMINOTTI, G. 1883. IV. 150.

Fabbri, O. Calcofilismo del Faggio. 1898. IV. 496.

— Le Querci di Gallipoli-Cognato. 1896. IV. 501.[1]

La fabbricazione dei piammiferi di legno in Francia. 1894. IV. 428.[2]

Fabbricazione del carbone. 1884. IV. 395.

Fabbroni, Adamo. Della coltivazione del Gelso. 1784. III. 373.

Fabbroni, Giovanni. Ricerche sulla quina. 1803. III. 724.[1]

Fabbroni, Joh. Versuch eines Magazins für Beobachtungen . . . über verbrennliche Stoffe. 1798. IV. 412.[2]

Faber, E. Les arbres curieux. 1895. IV. 500.[2]

— Eine interessante Buche. 1895. *II. 127*,[1] IV. 500.[2]

— Der mächtigste Baum der Grossherzogthums Luxemburg. 1895. II. 127.[1].

— Die Rothschwanz-Epidemie. 1897. IV. 497.

— Unsere Baumriesen. 1897. I. 295.[2]

Faber, Ernst. Chinese names of plants identified in Japan. 1892. V. ix.[1]

— General remarks [on Dr. Bretschneider's Botanicon sinicum]. 1892. V. x.[1]

Faber, Johann. Mexicanarum plantarum imagines. 1652. I. 331.

Faber, Johann Matthaeus. Strychnomania. 1677. III. 701.[1]

Faber, Lothar, *Freiherr* von. Ein "Cedernwald" in Deutschland. 1889. IV. 448.[2]

Fáber, Tódor. A Mahagóni-fáról. 1899. III. 513.[1]

Fabiański, Franciszek. Wiadomość o gospodarstwie lasowem, krotko zebrana z dzieł Burgsdorfa. 182 .? IV. 99.[2]

Fabis. *See* WEYN, de & FABIS.

Fabre. Application de l'esprit-de-bois à l'éclairage. 1845. IV. 433.[1]

Fabre. Sur un Cépage américain. 1877. III. 584.[1]

Fabre, A. Comment on peut guérir les Vignes malades. 1876. III. 760.

Fabre, Esprit. Description d'une nouvelle espèce de Spartina. 1850. II. 60.[1]

— & Dunal, M. F. Observations sur les maladies régnantes de la Vigne. 1853. III. 559.[2]

Fabre, Georges. Effets de la congélation sur les végétaux. 1872. I. 212.

— Une nouvelle station du Pin Laricio. 1896. II. 43.[2]

— La processionnaire du Pin dans les Cévennes. 1898. IV. 479.

Fabre, J. P. A. Des habitants des montagnes considérés dans leurs rapport avec le régime forestier. 1849. IV. 269.

Fabre, Jean Henri. Études sur les mœurs du phylloxera. 1880. III. 572.[2]

Fabre, L. A. Les landes de Lannemezan. 1899. IV. 164.[1]

— Le parc et les collections du château de Baleine. 1897. III. 29.[1]

Fabregou, Matthieu. Description des plantes . . . de Paris. 1740. I. 405.

Fabri, Honoré. Tractatus duo, quorum prior est de plantis. 1666. I. 286.

Fabriani, Giovanni. Index plantarum in Horto botanico mutinensi. 1811. I. 61.

Fabricación de la lana de madera. 1886. IV. 429.[1]

Fabricación de las pastas de madera en Norvega. 1882. IV. 429.[2]

Fabricación de tejidos de madera. 1890. IV. 430.

La fabrication de la cocaine aux Indes. 1898. III. 493.[2]

La fabrication du " vieux Chêne." 1899. IV. 557.[2]

Fabrication von Pantoffeln aus Aspenholz. 1879. IV. 486.

Fabricius, Georg Alexander. Tabellen zur Bestimmung des Gehaltes und Preises des beschlagenen und runden Holzes. 1787. IV. 220.

— Tabellen zur Bestimmung des Gehaltes und Preises sowohl des runden als beschlagenen Holzes. 1787. IV. 220.

— Tabellen zur Bestimmung des innern Gehaltes und Preises sowohl des beschlagenen als des runden Holzes. 1787. IV. 220.

Fabricius, Johann. Galandae Montis . . . stirpium enumeratio. 1561. I. 432.[2]

Fabricius, Johannes. Phytologiae. See SCHILLING, J. J. 1752. I. 31.

Fabricius, Philip Konrad. Enumeratio methodica plantarum Horti medici helmstadiensis. 1759. I. 44.

— Oratio de Germanorum in rem herbariam meritis. 1751. I. 80.[2]

— Primitiae florae butisbacensis. 1743. I. 373.

Fabricius, Wolfgang Ambrosinus. 'Ανόρημα Βοτανικόν. 1653. I. 286.

Fabris, G. See CANNIZZARO, Stanislao & FABRIS, G.

Fabry, Johann. Rimaszombat virânya. 1858. I. 445.

Facchini, Francisco. Zur Flora Tirols. 1855. I. 441.

Die Fachwerksmethoden nach ihrer Verschiedenheit. 1841. IV. 250.[2]

De la facilité et des avantages de l'introduction en France de la culture en grand du Coton, du Café. 1830. III. 729.[1]

Faculté des sciences de Marseille. Annales. I. 21.

Fadéieff, A. Mémoire sur quelques expériences tentées dans le but de rendre la poudre de guerre inexplosible. 1844. IV. 432.[1]

Fadyeyef, A. F. See Фадѣевъ, А. Ф.

Fällen der Bäume mittelst Dampf. 1878. IV. 383.[2]

Die Fällung . . . des Holzes im Jachenthale. 1883. IV. 383.[1]

Über die Fällungszeit des Nadelholzes. 1856. IV. 384.[2]

Von Färbepflanzen [um Halle]. 1774. III. 235.[3]

Faermann, L. See Фаерманъ, Л.

Fäsi, J. C. Kurze Anleitung zur Anpflanzung der Akazie 1798. IV. 169.[2]

Faesius, Beatus. De thermoscopio botanico. See GESSNER, Johann. 1755. I. 529.

Fagan, R. A. The Babul meadows of the Sholapur districts. 1884. IV. 521.[1]

— Forest pastures in the Deccan. 1885. IV. 197.[1]

Fagerborg, Andreas. De primordiis botanices. 1808. I. 79.[1]

Faggianelli, A. Des Hêtres monstrueux de la forêt de Verzy. 1864. II. 127.[1]

Faggot, Jacob. Afhandling om avedjande samt utväg til hushållning med skogar. 1750. IV. 287.[1]

— Jämförelse mellan veds och brän-torfs verkan vid kokning. 1748. IV. 412.[2]

— Rön som pröfwar at träwärke icke itändes af eld, när det tilförene sugit något sal fixum. 1739. IV. 416.[2]

Fagon, Guy Crescent. Les qualités du quinquina. 1703. III. 719.

Fagot. Les droits d'entrée sur les bois. 1893. IV. 552.[1]

— La grive. 1894. IV. 544.[1]

Fagraeus, Jonas Theodor. Medicamenta graveolentia. See LINNÉ, Carl von. 1758. III. 241.

Fahlberg, Samuel. Anmärkningar öfver Bomullens planterande. 1790. III. 587.[1]

— Anmärkningar om Silkes-Bomullen. 1790. II. 445,[1] 529.[2]

— Anmärkningar vid åtskilliga westindiska trädarter. 1793. I. 334.[1]

— Utdrag af samlingar til natural-historien öfver ön St. Barthelemi. 1786. III. 64.[1]

Fahle, N. Ferskentraet. 1869. II. 276.[2]

Fahnestock. Rhus glabrum. 1833. III. 527.[1]

Fahnestock, George W. Memoranda of the effects of carburetted hydrogen gas. 1859. III. 185.[1]

Eine fahrbare Winde. 1862. IV. 176.[2]

Fahrner, Georg. Zur Ablösung der Forstservituten. 1876. IV. 333.

— Zwischenfruchtbau in den Hochgebirgswäldern. 1882. IV. 134.[1]

La fainée de 1888 et ses résultats. 1896. IV. 496.

Fairchild, D. L. The uses of Bamboo in Java. 1896. III. 315.[2]

Fairchild, David Grandison. Bordeaux mixture as a fungicide. 1894. III. 198.[1]

— The Lebbek or Siris tree. 1900. III. 466.[2]

— Systematic plant introduction. 1898. I. 242,[1] IV. 125.[1]

— See also HALSTED, B. D. & FAIRCHILD, D. G.

Fairchild, Thomas. The city gardener. 1722. III. 42.[1]

Fairman, Charles E. Ash in basket work. 1887. IV. 534.[1]

Faiseau-Lavanne, J. B. F. Recherches statistiques sur les forêts de la France. 1829. IV. 275.

Fait, Emil. Blahovičnik. 1897. IV. 532.[1]

Faivre, Ernest. See FAIVRE, J. J. A. E.

Faivre, Jean Joseph Augustin Ernest. Considérations sur la variabilité de l'espèce. 1864. I. 244.[1]

— Études physiologiques sur l'effeuillement chez le Mûrier. 1875. II. 154.[2]

— Études physiologiques sur le latex du Mûrier. 1869. II. 155.[1]

— Études sur les cellules spiralées de la fleur du Stenocarpus. 1875. II. 167.[1]

— Expériences sur les effets des plaies de l'écorce. 1869. III. 379.[1]

— Expériences sur les plaies de l'écorce. 1869. II. 154,[2] III. 175.[1]

— Note sur quelques phénomènes physiologiques . . . de Mûrier. 1866. II. 154.[2]

— Nouvelles recherches sur le transport ascendant. 1873. I. 165.

— Observations sur la fécondation du Geonoma. 1873. I. 201.[1]

— Recherches sur la circulation . . . du latex chez le Ficus elastica. 1864. II. 151.[2]

— Recherches sur la circulation . . . du Mûrier. 1865. II. 154.[2]

— Recherches sur le rôle du latex chez le Mûrier. 1869. II. 155.[1]

— Recherches sur les mouvements de la sève à travers l'écorce. 1871. I. 164.

— Résumé d'expériences sur la végétation du Mûrier. 1870. II. 154.[2]

— De la variabilité de l'espèce. 1863. I. 244.[1]

— La variabilité des espèces. 1868. I. 244.[1]

— See also BONNET, G. & FAIVRE, E.

— & Dupré, V. Recherches sur les gaz du Mûrier. 1865. I. 155.

— — Recherches sur les gaz du Mûrier. 1866. III. 583.[1]

Falck, Alfred. Bidrag till kännedomen om den sydsvenska vegetationens ursprung. 1868. V. XVIII.[2]

Falck, Ferdinand August. Übersicht der speciellen Drogenkunde. 1877. III. 259.[1]

Falck, I. W. Bericht wegens de kaneel. 1774. III. 405.[2]

Falco, Friedrich Christian Ernst. De Ratanhia. 1820. III. 338.[1]

Falconer, Hugh. On Edgeworthia. 1845. II. 700.[1]

Memorandum respecting timber trees and materials for fuel. 1848. IV. 431.[1]

— On the Quinine-yielding Cinchonas. 1854. III. 713.[2]

— On a reformed character of the genus Cryptolepis. 1845. II. 737.[1]

— Remarks on Scaevolo Taccada. 1854. III. 754.[1]

— Remarks on the best mode of tapping the Caoutchuc tree of Assam. 1854. III. 148.[1]

— Report on the Teak forests of the Tenasserim Provinces. 1852. IV. 536.[2]

— Report on the Teak plantations of Bengal. 1857. IV. 536.[2]

— Reports on some soap-yielding pods. 1850. III. 290.[1]

Falconer, Randle Wilbraham. Die alte Geschichte der Rose; uebertragen vom Herrn Th. Ed. Nietner. 1839. III. 290.[2]

— The ancient history of the Rose. 1839. II. 290.[2]

— Contributions towards a catalogue of plants . . . of Tenby. 1848. I. 400.

Falconer, William. 1793. I. 264.

Falconer, William (of England). Anderson's Speedwell. 1873. III. 704.[1]

— Croton Hookeri. 1873. III. 515.[2]

— Flower gardening in the Isle of Wight. 1873. III. 83.[1]

— Fremontia californica. 1873. III. 591.[1]

— Menziesias. 1874. III. 649.[1]

Falconer, William (of New York). Early blooming trees and shrubs. 1889. III. 207.[2]

— Midsummer flowering shrubs. 1883. III. 207.[2]

— Pruning shrubs. 1886. III. 172.

— Rhododendrons, the chiefest among shrubs. 1886. III. 656.

Falconer, William (*of New York*) (*continued*).
— Shade and ornamental trees. 1888. III. 117.[1]
— Some Aralias. 1889. III. 641.[1]
— Spring-blooming evergreen shrubs. 1886. III. 206.[1]
Falconnet, H. *See* SEELIGMANN, Th., LAMY-TORRILHON, G. & FALCONNET, H.
Faldermann, Franz. Crataegus sanguinea, Sibirischer Blutdorn. 1837. III. 423.[1]
— Om Ericeernes Formering i England. 1836. III. 646.[2]
— Notice sur le Crataegus sanguinea. 1837. III. 423.[1]
— On the propagation of Zamias. 1826. III. 286.[1]
— Über die Vermehrung der Cycadeen. 1827. III. 284.[1]
— Über die Vermehrung der Ericeen. 1828. III. 646.[2]
Falimierz, Stefanek. Herbarium polonicum. 1534. I. 277.
Falke, T. List of trees and plants growing in the Botanical gardens at Dapooree and Hewra. 1862. I. 67.[1]
Falkenberg, Paul. Vergleichende Untersuchungen über den Bau . . . der Monocotyledonen. 1876. I. 100.[1]
Falkenstein, Julius. *See* GÜSSFELDT, Paul, FALKENSTEIN, Julius & PECHUËL-LOESCHE, Eduard.
Falkman, Ludwig B. Om svenska skogarnas nuwarande tillstånd. 1852. IV. 273.[1]
Falkner, Charles. On the planting and management of forest trees. 1842. IV. 120.
Fallen, Karl Friedrich. De irritabilitate motus caussa in plantis. 1798. I. 197.[1]
Fallenstein, F. Taschenbuch der ökonomischen Pflanzenkunde. 1809. III. 51.
Fallesen, L. S. Chronologisk Samling af de kongelige Forordninger og aabne Breve, Forst- og Jagtvæsenet. 1836. IV. 315.[1]
Fallot, B. Le Noyer et ses produits. 1900. III. 356.[1]
Fallou, Friedrich Albert. Anfangsgründe der Bodenkunde. 1857. IV. 61.[1]
— Die Gebirgsformationen zwischen Mittweida und Rochlitz. 1845. I. 381.
— Grund und Boden des Königreichs Sachsen. 1868. IV. 61.[1]
— Die Hauptbodenarten der Nord- und Ostseeländer. 1875. IV. 61.[1]
— Pedologie. 1862. IV. 61.[1]
Falsan, Albert. Les Alpes françaises; la flore. 1893. I. 418.
Falsches Guajacholz. 1835. III. 494.[2]
Falsification du Pareira-brava. 1874. III. 396.[2]
Falugi, Virgilio. Prosopopoeiae botanicae. 1697. I. 288.
— Prosopopoeiae botanicae. 1705. I. 289.
Familiar lectures on botany. *See* PHELPS, Mrs. A. H. (Lincoln). 1829. I. 86.
Die **Familie** der Palmen. 1878. III. 317.
The **families** of plants. *See* LINNÉ, Carl von. 1787. I. 530.[1]
Familler, Ignaz. Biogenetische Untersuchungen über verkümmerte oder umgebildete Sexualorgane. 1896. I. 115.
A **family-herbal**. 1689. III. 54.
Famine plants in Zululand. 1898. III. 281.[2]
Famine tropicale. 1900. IV. 52.
Famintzin, André Sergbyeevich. Beitrag zur Entwickelung der Sclerenchymfasern von Nerium. 1884. II. 729.[1]
— Beitrag zur Keimblattlehre. 1876. I. 123.[2]
— La décomposition de l'acide carbonique. 1880. I. 173.
— De l'influence de l'intensité de la lumière sur la décomposition de l'acide carbonique. 1880. I. 173.
— Über Knospenbildung bei Phanerogamen. 1886. I. 108.
— Die Wirkung der Intensität des Lichtes auf die Kohlensäurezersetzung. 1880. I. 173.
— Die Zerlegung der Kohlensäure. 1880. I. 173.
— & Borodin, Johann. Sur la formation d'une fécule . . . dans le Bouleau. 1867. II. 118.[2]
— Über transitorische Stärkebildung bei der Birke. 1867. II. 118.[1]
— & Przybytek, D. S. Aschenanalyse des Pollens von Pinus sylvestris. 1886. II. 48.[1]
A famous Chabo-Hiba. 1899. III. 301.[2]
The famous Wistaria at Salt Hill. 1882. II. 389.[1]
Fanchiotti, Carlo. Club alpino italiano . . . Relazione . . . sull' ispezione . . . fatta alle piantagioni. 1880. IV. 165.
— La pastorizia ed il rimboschimento. 1896. IV. 166.[1]
— Prontuario per la cubatura delle piante. 1867. IV. 225.
— Reboisement des forêts. 1875. IV. 165.
— Terre incolte. 1894. IV. 41.[1]
Fangel, (*Forstrath*). Zur Aufforstung der Schleswig'schen Haiden. 1881. IV. 158.
Les fanges des bois communaux de Freyr. 1898. IV. 144.[1]
Fankhauser, Franz. Bericht betreffend Aufstellung eines neuen Wirthschaftsplanes für die bernischen Staatswaldungen. 1866. IV. 249.[2]
— Du départage des bois au moyen de la rise en fil de fer. 1871. IV. 389.
— Die Drahtseilriese. 1872. IV. 391.
— Ueber Entstehung der Lawinen. 1853. IV. 188.[2]
— Gegenwärtiger Zustand des Gemeinde-Forstwesens im Kanton Bern. 1874. IV. 367.
— Guide pratique de sylviculture. 1866. IV. 110.[2]
— Il est indubitable que le parcours est le principal obstacle qui s'oppose au reboisement. 1870. IV. 135.[2]
— Leitfaden für die Bannwartenkurse. 1866. IV. 110.[2]
— Neue Drahtseilriese bei Interlaken. 1873. IV. 391.
— Nouveau lançoir en fil de fer à Interlaken. 1873. IV. 391.
— Quel mode de traitement faut-il adopter pour les pâturages maigres. 1866. IV. 166.[2]
— Quelle est la meilleure manière de transporter le bois dans les forêts de montagne. 1874. IV. 389.
— Quelle serait la conséquence du remaniement du plan d'aménagement des forêts domaniales. 1879. IV. 252.
— Stations forestières d'observations météorologiques. 1875. IV. 59.[2]
— Unzweifelhaft liegt in der Waldweide ein Haupthinderniss für die Wiederverjüngung der Waldungen. 1870. IV. 135.[2]
— Ueber die Ursachen der Entwaldung. 1856. IV. 283.[1]
— Ueber das Vorkommen und Gedeihen der Arve. 1853. IV. 463.[1]
— Welche Bedeutung hat die Umarbeitung des gegenwärtigen Wirthschaftsplanes. 1879. IV. 252.
— Wie sind Magergründe . . . forstwirthschaftlich zu behandeln? 1866. IV. 166.[2]
— Die Wytweiden des Plateau's der Freiberge. 1882. IV. 136.[1]
Fankhauser, Franz, (*jr.*). Adventivwurzeln der Fichte. 1900. II. 37.[1]
— Die Araukarie bei Rheineck. 1896. III. 299.[1]
— Aufforstung von Einzugsgebieten zu verbauender Wildbäche. 1895. IV. 166.[2]
— Die Aufforstungen im Einzugsgebiet der Wildbäche. 1900. IV. 187.[2]
— Ueber Aufforstungen und Verbauungen im mittäglichen Frankreich. 1897. IV. 164.[1]
— Avalanches and their prevention in the Swiss Alps. 1897. IV. 188.[2]
— Die Bedeutung der Aufforstung für . . . Wildwasser. 1897. IV. 167.[2]
— Die Bedeutung der Ziegenwirtschaft. 1887. IV. 184.[1]
— Zur Bekämpfung des Tannenborkenkäfers. 1896. IV. 445.
— Correección de torrentes y repoblaciones. 1900. IV. 548.[1]
— Ueber den Einfluss der Bewaldung auf das Auftreten der Malaria. 1887. IV. 48.[1]
— Einige Erfahrungen betreffend Aufforstungen im Hochgebirge. 1896. IV. 167.[1]
— Zur Empfehlung . . . der Weymouthskiefer. 1899. IV. 471.[1]
— Fabrication de bois pour instruments de musique. 1875. IV. 428.[1]
— Fabrikation des meubles Thonet. 1875. IV. 426.[2]
— Ueber Fabrikation musikalischer Kunsthölzer. 1875. IV. 428.[1]
— Ueber Fabrikation Thonet'scher Möbel. 1875. IV. 426.[2]
— Forstliche Reiseskizzen aus dem mittäglichen Frankreich. 1897. IV. 164.[1]
— Forstliche Reiseskizzen aus Italien. 1885. IV. 364.
— Forstlich-meteorologische Stationen. 1875. IV. 59.[2] . [1]
— Zur Frage der Kahlschläge in Hochlagen. 1900. IV. 130.
— Zur Frage der Vertilgung des Engerlings. 1895. IV. 203.
— Ueber das gegenwärtige Auftreten der "Nonne." 1890. IV. 200.
— Ueber das gegenwärtige Auftreten der Tannen-Triebwickler. 1893. IV. 445.
— Geschichte des bernischen Forstwesens. 1893. IV. 28.[1]
— Der grosse Bergahorn im Melchtal. 1900. II. 480.[1]
— Hasen- oder Mäusefrass? 1895. IV. 198.[2]
— Ueber die Hexenbesen. 1899. IV. 212.
— Die internationale Aktion in Sachen der Bändigung von Wildwassern. 1898. IV. 187.[2]
— L'inventaire des massifs forestiers. 1884. IV. 218.
— Ueber Kahlschläge im Hochgebirge. 1895. IV. 130.
— Der Lammbach. 1896. IV. 187.[2]
— Die neue Friedrich'sche Baummesskluppe. 1884. IV. 331.[2]
— Eine neue Pilzkrankheit der Tanne. 1896. IV. 445.
— Zu einem neuen Bundesgesetz betr. das Forstwesen. 1898. IV. 331.[1]

— Ein neuer Apparat zum Berechnen von Rundholz. 1895. IV. 229.
— Ein neuer Feind unserer Fichtenkulturen. 1898.· IV. 457.
— Les oseraies des bords de l'Elbe. 1876. III. 348.
— Praktische Anleitung zur Bestandesaufnahme. 1884. IV. 218.
— Praktische Anleitung zur Holzmassen-Aufnahme. 1884. IV. 218.
— Schutz der Saaten gegen Vögel und Mäuse. ·1895. IV. 149.²
— The significance of afforestation in . . . correcting torrents. 1897. IV. 167.¹
— Ueber die Trennung von Wald und Weide. 1881. IV. 136.¹
— Ueber das Vorkommen von Buchen-Kopfholzstämmen. 1894. IV. 496.
— Zur Wald- und Wasserfrage. 1900. IV. 52.
— Die Weidenheger der Elbe-Niederungen. 1876. III. 348.
— Auf welche Weise wird der Transport des Holzes aus Gebirgswaldungen . . . vermittelt. 1874. IV. 389.
— Wildbachverbauung und Aufforstung. 1900. IV. 187,² 548.¹
— Die Witterung und der Baumzuwachs. 1898. IV. 73.¹
— Woher kommt es, dass sogenanntes rechtsläufiges Holz schwer spaltbar ist? 1887. IV. 411.¹
— Ueber die Wünschbarkeit einer eidgen. Samenklenganstalt. 1899. IV. 148.
Fankhauser, J. Einfluss mechanischer Kräfte auf das Wachsthum durch Intussusception. 1875. I. 138.¹
— Einiges zur Begründung der Blattstellung. 1877. I. 102.
— Die Entwicklung des Stengels . . . von Ginkgo. 1882. II. 7.²
— Verhältniss verschiedener, organisch verbundener pflanzlicher Sprosse zu einander. 1880. I. 187.
Fanon. Des causes du dépérissement des forêts. 1806. IV. 121.
Fanshaw. Ueber die Kultur der Chorozema-Arten. 1856. III. 472.²
— Treatment of Chorizemas. 1856. III. 472.²
Fant. Dissertatio de Ulricaehamn. See NAEZEN, D. E. 1782. I. 352.
Fant, Carl Georg. Sveriges träd och buskar i vinterdrägt. 1872. I. 294,² IV. 79.²
Fant, Elis M. Betula. See THUNBERG, C. P. 1807. II. 117.¹
Faraday, Michael. On the practical prevention of dry rot. 1833. IV. 416.²
— On pure caoutchouc. 1826. III. 230.
— Some account of the Alstonia teiformis. 1817. III. 670.²
— The substance of a lecture on the practical prevention of dry rot. 1833. IV. 416.²
Farbaky, István Stephan & Hermann, Emil. A több pengével fürészelő gépek munkabirása. 1894. IV. 393.
Faré, H. Enquête sur les incendies de forêts . . . de Gascogne. 1873. IV. 183.¹
— Enquête sur les incendies de forêts .·. . des Maures. 1869. IV. 183.¹
— Rapport sur les forêts de l'état. 1868. IV. 360.
Farin. Catalogue des plantes du Jardin de botanique de Caen. 1781. I. 56.
Farina, Vincenzo. La flora sicula. 1874. I. 431.
Farinas, J. N. Observation sur un développement extraordinaire d'une racine de Peuplier noir. 1835. II. 97.²
Farkaš-Vukotinović, Ljudevit. See VUKOTINOVIČ, Ljudevit FARKAŠ-.
Farlow, John W. Cascara sagrada. 1887. III. 543.²
Farlow, William Gilson. Aecidium on Juniperus virginiana. 1887. III. 304.¹
— On the American Grape-vine mildew. 1874. III. 577.
— The black knot. 1874. III. 431.¹
— On a disease of Olive and Orange trees. 1875 (1874). III. 500,² 677.²
— Diseases of forest trees. ·1879. IV.·211.²
— Diseases of trees likely to follow mechanical injuries. 1891. III. 180.²
— The Gymnosporangia or Cedar-apples. 1880. III. 193.¹
— Notes on some common diseases. 1877. III. 193.¹
— The spread of epidemic diseases in plants. 1884. III. 178.
— White Huckleberries. 1889. II. 685.¹
— White Huckleberries. 1893. III. 663.¹
— & Seymour, A. B. A provisional host-index of the fungi. 1888. III.·193.²
Farmacopea española. See PHARMACOPOEA hispana. 1803. III. 255.²
Farmacopea-formulario universal. 1889.·III. 246.

Farmacopea italiana. 1881. III. 256.¹
Farmacopea ufficiale del regno d'Italia. 1892. III. 256.¹
Farmer, James. Ueber gefüllte Blüthen. 1866. I. 145.²
Farmer, John Bretland. Contributions to the morphology . . . of pulpy fruits. 1889. I. 119.
— On the development of the endocarp in Sambucus. 1888. II. 841.¹
Farmers and forestry. 1888. IV. 178.¹
The farmer's letters to the people of England. See YOUNG, Arthur. 1768. III. 123.¹
Farmers' review. III. 3.
Farnel, Alfred. Studien über den Stocklack. 1899. III. 232.²
Farneti, Rodolfo. Intorno ad una nuova malattia delle Albiococche. 1900. III. 435.¹
— See also MONTEMARTINI, Luigi & FARNETI, Rodolfo.
Faroult, V. Le Ravenala ou Arbre du voyageur. 1891. III. 341.²
— Le Tranes internatus. 1888. III. 286.¹
Farquhar, John K. M. L. Gardens, fields, and wilds of the Hawaiian Islands. 1900. III. 132.²
— Horticulture in Holland. 1899. III. 122.²
— Horticulture in Japan. 1899. III. 127.²
Farquharson, Alfred. On the cultivation of Sambucus nigra. 1835. III.·751.²
Farquharson, James. Count de Cars' book. 1885. IV. 172.¹
— Planting of grassy surfaces. 1884. IV. 142.
Farquharson, Rev. James, (1781–1843). Botanical remarks. 1833. II. 139.²
Farr. See BRAITHWAITE, Oldam & FARR.
Farrer, J. A. Age of trees. 1883. I. 193.²
— Tree lore. 1887. I. 517.¹
Farrington, Ernest A. A clinical materia medica. 1887. III. 244.
Farve, Ernst REVENTLOW-. See REVENTLOW-FARVE, Ernst.
Farwell, Oliver Atkins. The nomenclature of the Spruces and Firs. 1897. II. 34.¹
— Second blooming of Salix humilis. 1886. II. 107.²
Fasch, Augustin Heinric. De myrrha. 1676. III. 511.¹
Fasciated Medlar. 1885. II. 268.¹
Fasciation. 1900. II. 78.¹
Fasciculus plantarum circa Harefield. See BLACKSTONE, John. 1737. I. 394, V. xx.²
Fasciculus plantarum . . . ex horto Kleiniano. See KLEIN, J. T. 1724. I. 43.
Faslem, G. QUAET-. See QUAET-FASLEM, G.
Fassbender, Josef. Die Taxation der Hagelschäden. 1897. III. 179, 800.¹
Fasse, F. Cocos Veddelliana. 1887. III. 324.²
Fassliche Anweisung zum Anbaue . . . der unächten Acacie. See MEDICUS, F. C. 1799. IV. 522.¹
A fastigiate Sugar-Maple. 1894. III. 536.²
Fatio, Victor. Désinfection des véhicules par l'acide sulfureux anhydre. 1880. III. 563.
— État de la question phylloxérique. 1878. III. 571.
— Formes du Phylloxera vastatrix à Pregny. 1875. III. 568.
— Lettre à M. Dumas sur le phylloxera. 1876. III. 568.
— Le phylloxéra. 1877. III. 570.²
— Sur le phylloxera. 1877. III. 570.²
— Sur le traitement des Vignes phylloxérées. 1877. III. 570.
— & Demole-Ador. Rapports sur le traitement des Vignes de Pregny. 1875. III. 569.
— Rapports sur le traitement des Vignes de Pregny.· 1876. III. 570.¹
Fatio de Duiller, Nicolaus. Fruit-walls improved by inclining. 1699. III. 141.
Fatta, Giuseppe. Sui fiori di "Deherainia smaragdina." 1898. II. 691.²
Faubert, J. A. Mémoire instructif sur la manière de tailler les Oliviers. 1830. III. 675.¹
Fauchald, Kr. Forestry in Norway. 1900. IV. 344.¹
Fauché, Brongniart, Adolphe, Chaubard, L. A. & Bory de Saint-Vincent, J. B. M. Expéditiou scientifique de Morée. 1832. I. 448.²
Fauchon, L. J. Sur le Café. 1815. III. 741.²
Faucon, Louis. Sur l'époque à laquelle il conviendrait d'appliquer la submersion aux Vignes. 1873. III. 565.²
— Expérience relative au transport des phylloxeras par le vent. 1879. III. 571.
— Sur la maladie de la Vigne. 1874. III. 577.
— Note concernant les résultats déjà obtenus par le procédé de submersion des Vignes. 1873. III. 565.¹
— Note sur la possibilité d'appliquer la submersion de la Vigne sur une vaste échelle. 1873. III. 759.
— Notes sur la maladie des Vignes. 1871. III. 759.

Faucon, Louis (*continued*).
— Notes sur la maladie des Vignes. 1872. III. 759.
— Observations nouvelles sur le phylloxera. 1872. III. 565.[1]
— Observations relatives aux résultats obtenus . . . concernant le phylloxera. 1873. III. 565.[2]
— Observations sur le réveil du phylloxera. 1873. III. 565.[1]
— Le phylloxéra; submersion des Vignes. 1873. III. 759.
— Le Phylloxera vastatrix. 1873. III. 565.[1]
— Reinseignements sur le phylloxéra. 1873. III. 759.
— Résultat des recherches . . . de trouver l'origine des ré-invasions du phylloxera. 1879. III. 571.
— Résultat des recherches . . . de trouver l'origine des ré-invasions estivales du phylloxera. 1879. III. 571.
— Submersion des Vignes. 1873. III. 759.
— Submersion des Vignes atteintes du phylloxéra. 1873. III. 759.
— Suite des notes sur la nouvelle maladie de la Vigne. 1870. III. 758.[2]
— Traitement par submersion des Vignes. 1871. III. 564.[2]
— Vignes phylloxérées traitées par le sable. 1874. III. 566.[2]
Fauconnet, Charles. Excursions botaniques dans le Bas-Valais. 1872. I. 436.
— Herborisations à Salève. 1867. I. 435.
— Promenades botaniques aux Voirons. 1868. I. 435.
Fauconpret, Félix de. Recherches sur la respiration des végétaux. 1864. I. 170.
Faudel, Friedrich Wilhelm. Bibliographie alsatique. 1874. I. 3.[2]
Faudel, Friedrich Wilhelm. De viticultura richovillana. 1780. III. 552.
Faudrin, Marius. L'arboriculteur fruitier. 1895. III. 145.[1]
— Le bon arboriculteur fruitier. 1869. III. 144.
— La greffe à la portée des classes populaires. 1873. III. 162.
— Note relative à l'emploi des badigeonnages au sulfate de fer. 1885. III. 573.
— Rapport sur l'arboriculture et la viticulture. 1880. III. 124.[1]
— Reconstitution du vignoble. 1882. III. 556.
Faulhaber, Johannes. Tariffa über das kurtz- und lange Brennholtz. 1625. IV. 404.[2]
Fauré, J. Examen analytique des bois de Chêne employés dans la tonnellerie. 1847. IV. 514.[2]
— Examen chimique de l'écorce du Buis. 1830. III. 523.[1]
Faure, L. Rapport présenté à la Commission des améliorations agricoles et forestières. 1897. IV. 159.
Faust, August. Ueber den Farbstoff der Faulbaumrinde. 1869. III. 543.[1]
Faustmann, M. von. Der Bodenwerth und der Durchschnittsertrag. 1870. IV. 255.
— Das Spiegel-Hypsometer. 1856. IV. 215.
— Der Weise'sche Höhenmesser. 1876. IV. 215.
Faut-il émonder une seconde fois ? 1899. IV. 172.[2]
Faut-il regarnir les vides d'un taillis? 1899. IV. 170.
Faut-il repiquer les jeunes Chênes et Hêtres ? 1899. IV. 153.[1]
Fautrat, L. De l'influence comparée des bois feuillus et des bois résineux. 1876. IV. 53.
— Influence comparée des bois feuillus et des bois résineux. 1877. IV. 50.
— Influence des forêts. 1875. IV. 50.
— Influence des forêts sur le climat. 1875. IV. 53.
— De l'influence des forêts sur les courants. 1879. IV. 50.
— Influence du sol et des forêts sur le climat. 1877. IV. 53.
— Observations météorologiques. 1878. IV. 59.[2]
— & **Sartiaux**, A. Ueber den Einfluss der Wälder auf die Regenmenge. 1874. IV. 50.
— De l'influence des forêts sur la quantité de pluie. 1874. IV. 50.
Fauvel, Albert Auguste. Chinese plants in Normandy. 1884. III. 125.
— Le Gui sur l'Aubépine. 1890. II. 179.[2]
— Promenades d'un naturaliste dans l'archipel de Chusan. 1879. I. 459.
— Trip of a naturalist to the Chinese far east. 1876. III. 148.[2]
Faux Acacia. 1835. III. 486.[3]
Favard, J. F. Une Aristoloche hybride. 1897. III. 386.[1]
— Espèces nouvelles de Conifères de l'Amérique occidentale. 1897. II. 14.[2]
— Moyen de prévenir la maladie noire des Clématites. 1899. III. 390.[1]
— Résistance de l'Eucalyptus aux incendies. 1900. IV. 530.
Favard de Langlade, baron, (député, Puy-de-Dôme). Rapport fait . . . sur le projet de loi relatif aux échangistes. 1818. IV. 326.

Favart, Émile, (pseud.). Flowers and plants . . . sketched from nature. 1879. I. 534.[1]
Favero, Luigi. Sul rimboschimento delle montagne. 1849. IV. 165.
— Riserva degli allievi nei boschi. 1852. IV. 242.
— La selva del Montello. 1875. IV. 364.
Favier, Simon-. *See* **Simon-Favier.**
A favore dell' industria e del commercio oleario. 1896. III. 679.[2]
A favore della crisi agrumaria. 1897. IV. 285.[1]
Favrat, Auguste. Catalogue des Ronces du sud-ouest de la Suisse. 1885. II. 304.[1]
— Les Ronces du canton de Vaud. 1881. II. 304.[1]
Favrat, Louis. Note sur quatre hybrides nouveaux. 1890. I. 437.
— Notes sur quelques plantes rares . . . pour la Suisse. 1889. I. 437.
Favre, Émile. Guide du botaniste sur le Simplon. 1875. I. 436.
Favre, Ernest. Recherches sur la fleur femelle du Podocarpus. 1865. II. 9.[2]
— Remarques sur la fleur femelle du Podocarpus sinensis. 1865. II. 9.[2]
Favre, Louis. Observations relatives à la végétation. 1867. I. 227.[1]
Favrot, C. Traité élémentaire d'histoire naturelle pharmaceutique. 1843. III. 57.
Fawcett, J. W. Brief notes on some timber trees of . . . Queensland. 1900. IV. 89.[2]
— Dendrological notes from north-west Durham. 1890. IV. 358.[2]
— Forestry in New South Wales. 1895. IV. 380.[2]
— Some timber trees of Queensland. 1898. IV. 89.[2]
Fawcett, William. Botanical notes on common plants growing in Jamaica. 1888. I. 337.
— A disease in Cocoanut Palms. 1887. III. 323.[1]
— Economic plants. 1891. III. 64.[1]
— Elementary notes on Jamaica plants. 1888. I. 337.
— Elementary notes on planting and care of woodlands. 1896. IV. 113.[1]
— Plants in flower or fruit. 1887. I. 39.[2]
— A provisional list of the . . . plants of Jamaica. 1893. I. 337.
— Report on the Cayman Islands. 1889. I. 337.
— Report on the Coco-nut disease. 1891. III. 323.[2]
— Report on the Coffee leaf fungi. 1893. III. 736.
— Wax Palms of the Andes. 1898. III. 321.[2]
— Wild Olives of Jamaica. 1898. III. 64.[1]
Faxe, Arvid. Beskrifning på dricka, som tilredes af Tallqvistar. 1780. IV. 482.[2]
Faxon, Charles Edward. The silva of North America. *See* **Sargent, C. S.** 1891. I. 305, *IV. 76.[1]*
Fay, Charles E. Through San Luis Park to Sierra Blanca. 1889. II. 45.[1]
Faye, Hervé Auguste Étienne Albans. Sur l'orientation des arbres renversés par les tornados. 1876. III. 184.[1]
— Quels sont les vrais agents chimiques qu'il faut opposer à l'infection miasmatique? 1870. IV. 433.[2]
— Remarques sur quelques particularités du sol des Landes. 1870. I. 228.[2]
— Sur la trombe de Caen. 1875. III. 184.[1]
— Sur la trombe des Hayes. 1875. III. 184.[1]
— Sur le vraie théorie des trombes. 1893. III. 184.[2]
Faye, Léon. Catalogue des plantes vasculaires de la Charente-Inférieure. 1850. I. 410.
Faye, Leopold. Die neue Forstbezirkseintheilung Frankreichs. 1889. IV. 361.
Faymoreau d'Arquistade, A. de. Les grandes exploitations agricoles à Madagascar. 1895. III. 131.[2]
Fayol, Henri. Conservation des bois. 1882. IV. 420.
— Les procédés d'exploitation des mines. 1882. IV. 420.
Fayolle, M. *See* **Villiers, A.** & **Fayolle, M.**
Fazekas, Bálint. Kertünk örökzöldjeiről. 1900. III. 206.[1]
— Szép bogyókkal diszló fák és cserjék. 1896. III. 208.[1]
— A tarka lombú fanemüekről. 1897. III. 207.[1]
Fazekas, Mihály. *See* **Diószeghi, Sámuel** & **Fazekas, Mihály.**
Feast, Samuel. y On the Camellia as a hardy plant. 1849. III. 599.[2]
Featon, E. H. The art album of New Zealand flora. 1889. I. 508.[1]
Féburier, C. Romain. Des espèces, des variétés et des moyens . . . pour conserver et multiplier les dernières. 1825. III. 152.
— Essai sur les phénomènes de la végétation. 1812. *I. 163*, V. xi.[2]

— Extrait de la notice sur les suites de l'élagage. 1828. III. 169.²
— Notice sur l'anatomie végétale. 1824. I. 98.
— Notice sur la moelle. 1812. I. 128.²
— Observations sur la physiologie végétale. 1821. I. 146.
— Précis d'anatomie végétale. 1824. I. 98.
— See also Bosc, L. A. G., Labbé, H. & Féburier.
Fecha memorable. 1898. IV. 541.
Fechner, Gustav Theodor. Nanna. 1848. I. 147.
— Resultate der bis jetzt unternommenen Pflanzenanalysen. 1829. I. 152.¹
Fechner, K. A. Allgemeine Botanik. 1841. I. 88.
— Flora der Oberlausitz. 1849. I. 382.
— Verwachsung zweier Stämme von Pinus sylvestris. 1851. II. 47.²
Fécondité précoce. 1894. IV. 526.²
Fedas, W. W. Lasy slawuckie księcia Romana Sanguszki. 1900. IV. 370.
Fedde, Friedrich. Beiträge zur vergleichenden Anatomie der Solanaceae. 1896. II. 768.¹
— Pflanzengeographische Verbreitung der Gattung Mahonia. 1900. II. 202.¹
— Ueber die Verbreitung von Samen . . . durch Thiere. 1897. I. 241.¹
Feddersen, (*Forstrat*). Die Kiefer und der Maikäfer. 1889. IV. 478.
— Der Maikäfer. 1896. IV. 203.
— Reisebericht . . . über die Untersuchung der Maikäferschäden. 1890. IV. 203.
Feddersen, F. C. Die Möglichkeit einer Nadelholzanlage auf den Haiden Schleswigs. 1860. IV. 156.¹
Fedelissimi, Giambattista. Lexicon herbarum. 1636. I, 285.²
Fédération des sociétés d'horticulture de Belgique. Bulletin. III. 15.
Federici, Antonio & **Serpieri**, A. Saggio di una flora dell' agra urbinate. 187 .? I. 226.²
Federigotti, Giuseppe, *conte* Bossi-. *See* Bossi-Federigotti, Giuseppe, *conte*.
Fedorovitch, F. *See* Федоровичъ, Ф.
Fedosyeyef, S. K. *See* Федосѣевъ, С.
Fedotef, P. *See* Федотьевъ, П.
Fedtschenko, Boris Alexejewitsch. Abies Semenovii mihi. 1898. II. 25.¹
— Liste provisoire des espèces du genre Hedysarum. 1899. II. 363.¹
— Nochmals "Abies Semenovii mihi." 1898. II. 25.¹
— Note sur les Conifères du Turkestan russe. 1899. II. 16.¹
— *See also* Fedtschenko, O. A. & B. A.; Федченко, B. A.
Fedtschenko, Olga Alexandrowna & Boris Alexejewitsch. Ranunculaceen des russischen Turkestan. 1900. II. 196.¹
— *See also* Федченко, О. А. & В. А.
Fée, Antoine Laurent Apollinaire. Bemerkung über den Cytisus der Alten. 1830. II. 350.¹
— Catalogue méthodique des plantes du Jardin botanique . . . de Strasbourg. 1836. I. 47.
— Commentaires sur la botanique . . . de Pline. 1833. I. 78.¹
— Cours d'histoire naturelle pharmaceutique. 1828. III. 63.
— Essai historique et critique sur la phytonymie. 1828. I. 254.²
— Examen de la théorie des rapports botanico-chimiques. 1833. I. 150,²
— Extrait de la Flore de Virgile. 1822. II. 496.²
— Flore de Théocrite. 1832. I. 514.¹
— Flore de Virgile. 1822. II. 496.²
— Histoire du Jardin botanique de Strasbourg. 1836. I. 47.
— L'histoire du Jardin botanique du Strasbourg. 1858. I. 48.
— Sur le Ligustrum des Latins. 1862. II. 711.²
— Sur les Lotos des anciens. 1822. II. 701.²
— Maître Pierre . . . Entretiens sur la botanique. 1835. I. 94.
— Mémoire physiologique . . . sur la Sensitive. 1845. II. 372.¹ — 1846. I. 198.
— Mémoire sur le groupe des Phylliérées. 1834. I. 214.¹ .
— Mimosa pudica L. 1845. II. 372.²
— Notice sur le Cytise des anciens. 1830. II. 350.¹
— Notice sur les plantes dites sommeillantes. 1858. I. 198, II. 396.¹
— Quelques physionomies végétales françaises. 1858. I. 517.²

Feeding experiments with Prickly Pear. 1897. III. 624.²
Feeger, Baltz & **Mücke**, Fritz. Was versteht man unter Femeln und unter Plentern? 1897. IV. 131.
Feeney, Con. Information regarding the Wax-berry plant. 1854. III. 353.¹
Feenstra, Y. Beschouwingen over de ontwikkeling . . . onzer Oost-Indische buiten-bezittingen. 1880. III. 128.
Feestbundel van taal . . . sardrijkskundige bijdragen, aan Dr. P. J. Veth aangeboden. 1894. I. 520.²
Féguaux. Étude sur le Cactus Opuntia. 1859. II. 596.²
Fehling, Hermann von. Les acides de l'huile de noix de Coco. 1845. II. 67,² *III. 323.*²
— Ueber Bestimmung des Gehaltes an Gerbstoff. 1853. III. 237.¹
— Sur le dosage du tannin. 1853. III. 237.¹
— Die Säuren des Cocosnussöls. 1845. II. 67,² *III. 323.*²
— Untersuchung eines Harzes aus dem Copaivabalsam. 1841. III. 473.¹
Fehr, K. F. W. Bericht über die Frage: Ist es rathsam, die Staats-. . . wälder, . . . zu veräussern? 1808. IV. 277.
Feil, Karl Friedrich. Untersuchungen über die Vertheilung der Farben . . . in den Familien der Asperifolien, Primulaceen. *See* Schübler, Gustav. 1831. II. 196.²
Feilberg, L. Holbergs Træ i Fiolstræde. 1882. I. 296.¹
Feilberg, P. Kultur af Baandpil. 1888. III. 349.
Feilberg, P. D. Berberisse med sukkersød Frugt. 1835. III. 395.¹
— Beretning om Berberissen med syd Frugt. 1838. III. 395.¹
— Camelliernes Formering. 1836. III. 599.²
— Erfaringer i Anledning af den Skade, Vinteren 1837 til 1838 foraarsagede paa Træer og Buske. 1840. III. 44.²
— Udvalg af de smukkeste og nyeste Siirplanter. 1837. III. 67.¹
Feilden, H. W. & **Geldart**, H. D. A contribution to the flora of Russian Lapland. 1896. I. 366.
— Notes on a small collection of Spitsbergen plants. 1894. I. 358.
Feist, Aug. Ueber die Schutzeinrichtungen der Laubknospen. 1887. I. 108.²
Feist, Franz. Origine . . . des glucosides des Strophantus. 1900. III. 690.²
— Ursprung . . . der Strophantus-Glycoside. . 1900. III. 690.²
Feist, Karl. Die Ausbildung des Forstpersonales in Baden. 1899. IV. 33.²
Feistmantel, Karl von. Beiträge zur Erörterung der Frage über die finanzielle Umtriebszeit. 1866. IV. 251.²
Feistmantel, Ottokar. Die Theekultur in Britisch-Ost-Indien. 1888. III. 604.¹
Feistmantel, Rudolf, *Ritter* von. Allgemeine Waldbestandestafeln. 1854. IV. 230.
— Anzichten und Gedanken über die Betriebsweise der Hochwälder. 1843. IV. 129.
— Die Forstwissenschaft. 1835. IV. 99.²
— Ueber den Nutzen der Durchforstungen. 1834. IV. 173.
— Die politische Oekonomie mit Rücksicht auf das forstliche Bedürfniss. 1856. IV. 269.
— Die Staatsforste Oesterreichs. 1867. IV. 368.
— Der Streit über die Bewirthschaftung des Wiener Waldes. 1071. IV. 250,¹ 069.
— Ueber das Vorkommen . . . der Tannenbestände. 1841. IV. 446.¹
Feitel, Rudolf. Beiträge zur vergleichenden Anatomie der Laubblätter bei den Campanulaceen. 1900. II. 845.¹
Fejfar, František. Z ruských lesů. 1878. IV. 345.
Fekete, Lajos. Abauj-Torna, Szepes és Gömör vármegyék erdőtenyésztési viszonyai. 1887. I. 446, *IV. 374.*¹
— Beszélgetés az uj erdőtörvényről. 1880. *IV. 331.*²
— Egy szerdülő Sequoia . . . gygantea Endl. hazánkban. 1887. III. 310.¹
— Az erdei vetésről és ültetésről. 1893. IV. 142.
— Erdészeti nyereségszámitástan. 1900. IV. 259.²
— Erdészeti rovartan. 1878. IV. 210.¹
— Erdészeti talajtan. 1882. IV. 61.¹
— Az erdészeti vagy növénytani tekintetben nevezetesebb fafajok tenyészeti határainak megállapitása. 1898. I. 219.¹
— Az erdőfapolásáról és hasznilatáról. 1895. IV. 124.¹
— Erdőértékszámitástan, erdészek, erdőbirtokosok. 1874. IV. 253.
— Az erdők berendezése. 1898. IV. 241.
— Az erdők felujitása. 1898. IV. 140.
— Az erdővédelem körvonalai. 1877. IV. 177.¹

Fekete, Lajos (*continued*).
— A fák görbeségének okairól. 1881. I. 105.
— A fák virágzására és a gyümölcsérésre szükséges melegösszeg. 1869. I. 221.
— Der Flugsand und die Akazie. 1875. IV. 523.[1]
— Hazánk Tölgyesei. 1888. IV. 374.[1]
— Két új Tölgyfajta. 1881. II. 130.[1]
— Közlemények a magyarországi főfanemek tenyészeti határairól és az erdőmivelés köréből. 1875. I. 444.
— A Lúcz és Jegenyefenyő igényeit összehasonlító vizsgálatok ásványi tápanyagok tekintetében. 1881. II. 20.[2]
— A Magyarországon előforduló főbb fanemek csemetéinek termesztése és ültetése. 1889. IV. 124.[1]
— A mezőség kopárainak befásitása. 1876. IV. 167.[1]
— Népszerü erdészeti növénytan. 1900. IV. 87.[1]
— A Quercus conferta Kit. 1886. II. 133.[1]
— A szálalóerdők berendesése. 1897. IV. 131.
— A Tölgy és tenyésztése. 1888. IV. 508.
— A vágásra érett erdő kihasználása. 1898. IV. 382.[2]
— Versuche mit Pinus Pinaster (Ait.) in Ungarn. 1875. IV. 468.[1]
— A Virágos Kőris pusztulása a Bakony vidékén. 1879. III. 672.[2]
— A Vörösfenyő-törzsek görbeségének oka. 1880. II. 33.[1]
— Die Wirkung des heurigen Frostes ... zu Schemnitz. 1876. IV. 191.[2]
— *See also* **Sóltz**, Gyula & **Fekete**, Lajos.
— & **Illés**, Nándor. A köjerdész. 1873. IV. 99.[2]
— & **Mágócsy-Dietz**, Sándor. Erdészeti növénytan. 1891. IV. 87.[1]
— — A fák visszaszerző képességének nyilvánulása erőszakos sérülések folytán. 1891. I. 207.[2]
— — A vörös fenyő és fajai. 1897. IV. 448.[2]
Felber, Theodor. Ein Gang durch den Wald. 1873. IV. 367.
— Leschola. 1899. IV. 438.[1]
— Materielle und ideelle Forderungen an den Wald. 1897. IV. 271.[1]
— Aus der Stadtwaldung Winterthur. 1893. IV. 367.
— Unfallhäufigkeit und Unfallverhütung bei Forst- und Landwirtschaftsarbeiten. 1897. IV. 311.[2]
— Die Versicherungsgesetze und die schweiz. Forstwirtschaft. 1900. IV. 311.[1]
— Was wurde seit dem Bestehen der eidg. Forstgesetzgebung erreicht. 1893. IV. 331.[1]
— Ein Zwergwald im Kánton Appenzell. 1884. II. 36.[2]
Der Feldbaw; oder, Das Buch von der Feldarbeyt. *See* **Casianus Bassus**. 1538. III. 98.
Feldeck, Joseph von. Kern einer vollständigen Haus- und Landwirthschaft. 1717. IV. 115.
Feldfruchtbeschädigung durch Fappelu. 1873. III. 344.[1]
Die Feldjägerfrage im Lichte der Vergangenheit und Gegenwart. 1895. IV. 33.[2]
Feldmann, Bernhard. Dissertatio physico-medica sistens comparationem plantarum et animalium. 1732. I. 31.
Felici, Giovanni Batista. Parere intorno all' uso della cioccolata. 1728. III. 594.
Felix, Johannes Paul. Die fossilen Hölzer West-Indiens. 1883. I. 334.
Fell. Forestry; the pioneer of agriculture. 1884. IV. 270.[1]
Felle, Wilhelm. Liberiakoffie in Palembang. 1895. III. 743.[1]
— Veeljarige waarnemingen ... van een Liberia-Koffie planter. 1894. III. 742.[2]
Fellenberg, L. Rudolph von. Destillation von Pfirsichblättern. 1848. III. 442.[1]
Fellerer, Carl. Beiträge zur Anatomie ... der Begoniaceen. 1892. II. 583.[1]
Felling and trucking in forests. 1886. IV. 392.
Felling of forests causing dryness of climate. 1859. IV. 43.
Felling trees by electricity. 1889. IV. 384.[1]
Felling trees by electricity. 1894. IV. 384.[1]
Fellman, Nils Isak. Plantae vasculares in Lapponia orientali. 1864. I. 362.
Fellmann, Jacob. Index plantarum in Lapponia. 1835. I. 361.
— Index plantarum phanerogamarum in territorio kolaënsi. 1831. I. 360.
Fellner, Robert. Beitrag zur Geschichte des Stadtwaldes von Frankfurt am Main. 1895. IV. 26.
Fellner, Stephan. Die Homerische Flora. 1897. I. 514.[2]
Fellows, Charles. An account of discoveries in Lycia. *See* **Don**, David. 1841. I. 478.
— Travels and researches in Asia Minor. 1852. V. xxiv.[1]
Über den **Felsschlipf** im Lammgraben. 1896. IV. 187.[2]

Felt, Ephraim Porter. Elmleaf-beetle in New York state. 1898. III. 365.[1]
— Illustrated descriptive catalogue of ... insects of New York. 1900. III. 188.[1]
— Insects injurious to forest trees. 1898. IV. 205.[1]
— Insects injurious to Maple trees. 1898. IV. 205.[1]
— 14th.[-15th.] report of the state entomologist ... of New York. 1898. III. 187.
— Shade tree pests in New York state. 1899. III. 188.[1]
Felton, Samuel. On the portraits of English authors on gardening. 1828. III. 33.[1]
Femenías, Juan Joaquin **Rodríguez y**. *See* **Rodríguez y Femenías**, J. J.
Féminier, G. Un cas de tératologie végétale. 1876. II. 665.[2]
Fences and screens in parks and gardens. 1876. III. 213.
Fendrich. Duby rakousko-uherské říše. 1886. II. 130.[1]
— Něco o lípách. 1888. IV. 528.[1]
Fenech y Artélls, Antonio. Los montes públicos de Galicia. 1884. IV. 363.[1]
Fenger, H. F. Om Opdyrkning af Vestjyllands Heder. 1868. IV. 156.[2]
Fenille, P. C. **Varenne-**. *See* **Varenne-Fenille**, P. C.
Fenk, Karl. Der Ausbildungsgang der Forstbeamten in der Schweiz. 1894. IV. 36.[1]
— Einige Zahlen über Kosten der Pflanzenerziehung. 1894. IV. 151.[1]
— Forstgeschichtliches aus dem St. Gallischen Fürstenlande. 1897. IV. 28.[1]
— Mittheilungen über das Auftreten des Nonnenspinners. 1892. IV. 201.
— Ueber unser Forstwesen. 1883. IV. 367.
— Der Wachsthumsgang unsere Waldungen. 1888. IV. 123.[1]
— Der Wäldertausch in St. Gallen. 1898. IV. 309.[2]
Fenn, G., (*jr.*). Bizarrerie sur les Pêches. 1828. II. 276.[2]
— Peach and nectarine in one fruit. 1828. II. 276.[2]
Fennebresque, P. S. Mémoire sur les procédés de boisement ... en Sologne. 1866. IV. 122.[1]
Fennel, Nicolaus. Beschreibung der Blüthen dreier Cactus-Arteh. 1843. II. 585.[1]
— Beschreibung einiger neuen Cacteen. 1847. II. 586.[1]
Fennema, R. Topographische ... beschrijving van ... Sumatra's westkust. 1887. III. 275.[2]
Fenologis notis om vårväxter kring Lund. *See* **Lindblom**, A. E. 1840. I. 223.[1]
Fentener van Vlissingen, P. Onze boomen en heesters. 1896. IV. 84.[2]
Fentzing, Karl. Morphologische ... Untersuchungen der Veränderungen ... durch Rostpilze hervorgerufen. 1892. I. 206.[2]
Fenwick, H. Remarks on some ... products of the Tenasserim provinces. 1850. III. 277.
Fenzi, Emanuele Orazio. Rhododendron. 1876. II. 58.[1]
— Colletia cruciata. 1878. II. 493.[2]
— Dasylirion longifolium. 1890. III. 337.[2]
— La Domenica delle Palme. 1878. III. 328.[2]
— Fioritura del Rhododendron longifolium. 1883. III. 659.[1]
— Ueber die härteren Bambus-Arten. 1872. III. 314.[1]
— Notes on hardy Bamboos. 1872. III. 314.[1]
— Olea fragrans. 1876. III. 680.[1]
— Pritchardia filamentosa Wendl. 1876. III. 332.[1]
— Yucca angustifolia Pursh. 1886. III. 340.[1]
— Yucca filifera Chabaud. 1889. III. 340.[1]
Fenzl, Eduard. Bericht über einige der wichtigsten botanischen Ergebnisse der Bereisung ... von Angola. 1863. I. 491.
— Ueber die Blüthezeit der Paulownia imperialis. 1851. II. 781.[2]
— Darstellung ... vier ... Pflanzen-Gattungen. 1841. II. 784.[2]
— Darstellungen ... neuer ... Gefässpflanzen. 1849. II. 864.[2]
— Diagnoses plantarum orientalium. 1860. I. 479.
— Diagnoses praeviae Pemptadis stirpium aethiopicarum novarum. 1865. I. 488.
— Beitrag im Freien ausdauernde Opuntia-Art. 1873. III. 625.[1]
— Über die Gattung Oxera. 1843. II. 759.[2]
— Illustrationes et descriptiones plantarum novarum Syriae. 1841. I. 480.
— Illustrirte Botanik. 1857. I. 95.
— Über monströse Blüthenbildungen von Rosa. 1848. II. 292.[2]

— Über eine neue Pflanzengattung Arctocalyx. 1848. II. 794.²
— Über eine neue Pflanzengattung . . . der Crescentieen. 1844. II. 789.¹
— Nova quaedam genera et species plantarum. 1849. II. 864.²
— Plantarum generum et specierum novarum decas prima. 1843. II. 333.¹
— Pugillus plantarum novarum Syriae. 1842. I. 480.
— Remarques sur le Cytisus Adami. 1864. II. 368.²
— Ueber die Stellung der Gattung Oxera. 1843. II. 759.¹
— Vier neue Pflanzenarten Süd-Amerikas. 1886. I. 330.
— Vortrag über eine neue Crescentieen-Gattung. 1844. II. 789.¹
— See also ENDLICHER, S. L. & FENZL, Eduard.
Feragen, A. Om Grauens udbredelse paa Furumark. 1892. II. 35.¹
— Om indsamling og udklängning af gran- og furufrö. 1895. IV. 441.
— Paa hvilken maade sörger man bedst for skogens gjenväkst 1894. IV. 156.²
Féraud, BERANGER-. See BERANGER-FERAUD.
Féraud, NÉGREL-. See NÉGREL-FÉRAUD.
Feraud-Giraud, L. J. D. Police des bois. 1861. IV. 275.
Ferber. Raffinage du camphre. 1815. III. 233.¹
Ferber, Johan Eberhard. Hortus agerumensis. 1739. I. 40.
Ferber, Johannes Jacobus. Blomster-almanach för Carlscronas climat. 1771. I. 222.²
— De prolepsi plantarum. See LINNÉ, Carl von. 1760. I. 97.
— See also ULLMARK, Hinricus & FERBER, Johannes Jacobus.
Ferdinandeum für Tirol und Voralberg. Zeitschrift. I. 27.
Ferdinandus, Aloysius. Annotationes de granis tinctorum quae kermes vocant. 1733. IV. 503.²
Ferenczy, Max. Alter Epheu. 1889. II. 650.¹
Feret, André. Les plautes des terrains salés. 1897. I. 229.
Ferguson, Alastair Mackenzie & John. All about Aloe and Ramie fibres. 1890. III. 218.¹
— — All about rubber and gutta-percha. 1882. III. 149.
— — All about the "Coconut Palm." 1885. III. 322.²
— — Ceylon & her planting enterprize. 1885. III. 129.²
— — India rubber and gutta percha. 1882. III. 149.
— Map of the planting districts of Ceylon. 188.? III. 603.
Ferguson, J. H. Kultuurgewassen uit China. 1898. III. 273.²
Ferguson, John. All about the Areca Palm. 1897. III. 320.¹
— The Coffee planter's manual. 1898. III. 732.²
— On the cultivation of Cinchona trees. 1881. III. 712.²
— On the cultivation of the India-rubber trees. 1884. III. 368,¹ 513,² 520.²
— On the Teak plantations at Nelambur. 1881. IV. 536.¹
— See also FERGUSON, A. M. & John.
Ferguson, Margaret C. The development of the egg and fertilization in Pinus Strobus. 1900. II. 46.¹
Ferguson, William. A descriptive list of Ceylon timber trees. 1863. III. 92,¹ IV. 401.¹
— The economical products of the Palmyra Palm. 1864. III. 321.¹
— The Noyau or Noyeau vine or plant. 1885. II. 745.²
— The Palmyra Palm. 1850. III. 320.¹
— Scripture botany of Ceylon. 1859. I. 513.
— The timber trees of Ceylon. 1864. IV. 401.¹
Ferguson, Adam. Notes regarding some plantations upon the estate of Balthayock. 1829. IV. 358.³
Féris, Bazile. See BOCHEFONTAINE, L. T., FÉRIS, Bazile & MARCUS.
Fermi, Claudio. See BUSCALIONI, Luigi & FERMI, Claudio.
Fermin, Philippe. Description générale . . . de Surinam. 1769. III. 267.²
— Histoire naturelle de la Hollande équinoxiale. 1765. I. 531, III. 267.²
— Nieuwe algemeene beschryving . . . van Suriname. 1769. III. 267.²
Ferminger, T. A. C. Method of operating upon stone-fruit trees. 1867. III. 539.¹
Fermond, Charles. Composition organophytogénique des feuilles. 1863. I. 110.
— Conséquences à déduire des défauts d'exastosie. 1863. I. 112.²
— Conséquences à tirer de l'étude des trois formes de l'hécastosie. 1863. I. 110.

— Considérations philosophiques sur les fleurs doubles. 1872. I. 145.²
— Essai de phytomorphie. 1864. I. 99.
— Études comparées des feuilles. 1860. I. 109.²
— Études sur l'évolution des bourgeons. 1863. I. 108.¹
— Études sur le développement des mérithalles. 1854. I. 105.
— Faits pour servir à l'histoire générale de la fécondation. 1857. I. 201.¹
— Mémoire sur la formation des racines de feuilles. 1851. I. 189.
— Note sur la germination du Sapindus divaricatus. 1860. II. 488.²
— Note sur les fruits . . . du Sapindus divaricatus. 1860. II. 488.²
— Note sur les fruits . . . du Sapindus divaricatus. 1861. III. 540.¹
— Observations sur les dédoublements. 1855. I. 144.²
— Observations sur quelques phémomènes présentés par la végétation de la Vigne. 1856. II. 507.¹
— Phytogénie. 1867. I. 99.
— Recherches sur le nombre des parties qui composent les divers cycles hélicoïdaux. 1855. I. 114.²
— Recherches sur le nombre-type des diverses parties. 1861. I. 113.¹
— Du rôle que jouent les périanthes dans l'acte de la fécundation. 1840. I. 200.
Fermont. Considérations sur . . . Sambucus et Viburnum. 1841. II. 833.²
The Fern-leaved Aralia (A. filicifolia). 1877. III. 641.²
The Fern Sumach. 1872. III. 527.¹
Fernald, Charles Henry. Injurious insects. 1888. III. 187.
— See also FORBUSH, É. H. & FERNALD, C. H.
Fernald, Merritt Lyndon. Arceuthobium pusillum. 1900. II. 685.¹
— The distribution of the Bilberries in New England. 1900. II. 685.¹
— The Portland catalogue of Maine plants. 1892. I. 316.
— A revision of the . . . Solanums of the subsection Torvaria. 1900. II. 774.²
— Rubus Idaeus and its variety anomalus. 1900. II. 308.¹
— Some rare and undescribed plants collected by Dr. Edward Palmer at Acapulco, Mexico. 1898. I. 333. ₸
— Some undescribed Mexican phanerogams. 1900. I. 333.
— A synopsis of the Mexican . . . Salvia. 1900. II. 765.²
— Three new western plants. 1899. II. 257.²
— Undescribed plants from western Mexico. 1895. I. 332.
— See also ROBINSON, B. L. & FERNALD, M. L.
Fernand, (Forstwart). Eine starke Tanne. 1869. II. 24.¹
Fernande. The Rose. 1876. II. 290.²
Fernández, Antonio BLANCO Y. See BLANCO Y FERNANDEZ, Antonio.
Fernández, Casildo ASCÁRATE Y. See ASCÁRATE Y FERNÁNDEZ, Casildo.
Fernández, Edward Elias. Appendix series of the Indian forester reports. 189.? IV. 102.
— The Central Provinces forest manual. 1900. IV. 100.¹
— The Dalbergia latifolia. 1877. IV. 521.²
— Deodar in the Dhára Gád valley. 1883. IV. 448.¹
— Forest papers. 1897. IV. 102.
— The formation of concentric rings in wood. 1889. I. 127.²
— Frosts and forests. 1881. III. 50.¹
— Ilme tashrih wa balid dagi wa parwarish Nabatat. 1889. I. 92.
— Memorandum on the season for cutting back for coppice. 1899. IV. 132.²
— Notes for a Manual of sylviculture. 1882. IV. 124.²
— Notes on the utilisation of forests. 1889. IV. 382.¹
— Rough draft of a Manual of Indian sylviculture. 1888. IV. 111.¹
— Tapping Pinus longifolia for resin. 1883. IV. 464.²
— What constitutes a thinning? 1896. IV. 175.¹
— Yield of katha. 1894. III. 464.²
— See also MOIR, E. McA. & FERNANDEZ, E. E.
Fernández de Castro, Ángel. Algo sobre deslindes. 1895. IV. 376.¹
— El catalogo de montes públicos en Filipinas. See CASTRO, A. F. de. 1896. IV. 556.¹
— La comisión especial de ventas y composiciones de terrenos baldios realengos de Filipinas. 1886. IV. 294.²
— Los montes de Filipinas. See CASTRO, A. F. de. 1887. IV. 376.²
— Planes provisionales de aprovechamientos. 1891. IV. 553.²

Fernandez de Castro, Ángel (*continued*).
— Repoblación de dunas. 1900. IV. 547.[1]
— El servicio ordinario. 1897. IV. 553.[2]
— Tabla para calcular en kilogramos el peso del corcho. 1898. IV. 518.[1]
Fernandez de Landa, Joseph ROMERO. *See* ROMERO FERNANDEZ DE LANDA, Joseph.
Fernandez y Jimenez, José María. Tratado de la arboricultura cubana. 1867. IV. 78.[2]
Fernandez y Perez, Juan Zoilo. Catecismo elemental de agricultura práctica. 1856. III. 114.[2]
Fernbach, A. Sur la tannase. 1900. I. 178.
Ferner, Henricus. Ruborum Sueciae . . . *See* ARRHENIUS, J. P. 1839. II. 301.[1]
Fernere Mittheilungen über Wellingtonia. 1855. II. 50.[1]
Fernerweitheres Mandatum, wie und welchergestalten wir es gehalten haben wollen . . . mit Begehr- . . . Verrechnung des Holtzes. 1728. IV. 299.
Fernow, _____ nh _____ Eduard. Address on forestry. 1897. IV. 281.[1]Ber ard
— Adirondack forestry problems. 1900. IV. 272.
— Âge des arbres et des blanchis. 1897. I. 193,[1] IV. 235.[1]
— Age of trees and time of blazing. 1897. I. 193,[2] IV. 235.[1]
— Arbor day planting. 1889. IV. 42.[1]
— The Arizona forests. 1896. I. 320, IV. 78.
— The battle of the forests. 1894. IV. 338.[2]
— Die Bauholzproben der amerikanischen Forstverwaltung. 1891. IV. 415.[2]
— Beginnings of professional forestry in the Adirondacks. 1900. IV. 339.
— The biology of timber trees. 1887. IV. 67.[1]
— The care of our forests. 1888. IV. 272.
— Communal forests. 1890. IV. 308.[1]
— Conditions of forest-growth. 1882. IV. 67.[1]
— Conifers for planting on the plains. 1889. IV. 155.[2]
— Considerations in gathering forestry statistics. 1898. IV. 336.[2]
— Consumption of forest supplies by railroads. 1890. IV. 424.[1]
— A coppice of Pine. 1895. IV. 469.[1]
— Division of forestry. 1898. IV. 271,[1] 338.[2]
— Do forests influence rainfall? 1888. IV. 51.
— Economic conditions antagonistic to a conservative forest policy. 1892. IV. 272.
— Effect of forest-mismanagement on orchards. 1890. IV. 45.
— Effect of turpentine gathering on the timber of Longleaf Pine. 1893. IV. 466.[1]
— European forest management. 1888. IV. 247.[1]
— European state forestry. 1888. IV. 272.[2]
— Exhaustion of soil by trees. 1895. III. 41.[1]
— Facts and figures regarding our forest resources. 1896. IV. 338,[1] 555.[2]
— The failure of foreign trees on American soil. 1887. IV. 124.[2]
— Forest fire legislation. 1896. IV. 182.[1]
— Forest reservation policy. 1897. IV. 179.[1]
— Forestry education in the United States. 1890. IV. 30.[1]
— Forestry for farmers. 1895. IV. 112.
— Forestry in the United States. 1891. IV. 338.[1]
— Forestry in the United States department of agriculture. 1899. IV. 288.[1]
— The forests and deserts of Arizona. 1897. I. 321, IV. 78.[2]
— Forests and floods. 1890. IV. 51.
— Les forêts aux États-Unis. 1899. IV. 113.[1]
— The government timber tests. 1891. IV. 415.[2]
— Growing timber without knots. 1889. IV. 172.[1]
— Hygienic significance of forest air and forest soil. 1893. IV. 54.
— Increasing the durability of timber. 1888. IV. 416.[2]
— Increasing the durability of timber. 1898. IV. 421.
— L'industrie forestière aux États-Unis. 1889. IV. 338.[1]
— Instructions for growing tree seedlings. 1890. IV. 147.[1]
— Is protection against forest fires practicable? 1896. IV. 182.[1]
— Is the White Pine doomed? 1897. IV. 469.
— Is young timber weaker than old? 1895. IV. 410.
— Letter to the Secretary of agriculture regarding forest growth. 1893. IV. 338.[1]
— The Long leaf Pine. 1893. IV. 467.[1]
— Management of the national forest-reservations. 1892. IV. 178.[2]
— Measurements of White Pine. 1894. II. 46.[1]

— New forest law for Italy. 1888. IV. 277.
— The New York state college of forestry. 1898. IV. 30.[1]
— Notes on the climatic influence of forests. 1893. IV. 54.
— Notes on the sanitary significance of forests. 1893. IV. 55.[1]
— Où en est la police forestière chez les nations européennes? 1896. IV. 272.
— Our forestry-problem. 1887. IV. 272.
— Paper on forestry. 1892. IV. 272.
— Planting a tree. 1887. III. 166.
— Planting in waste places. 1883. IV. 153.[1]
— Practicability of an American forest administration. 1891. IV. 288.[1]
— Product of White Pine per acre. 1896. IV. 470.[2]
— The profitableness of forest-culture. 1892. IV. 260.[1]
— Progress in timber physics. 1898. IV. 409.
— The providential functions of government with special reference to natural resources. 1896. IV. 270.
— Recent legislation on state forestry commissions. 1897. IV. 314.[2]
— The relation of forests to farms. 1896. IV. 45.
— Relation of forests to water supplies. 1893. IV. 51.
— The relation of nurserymen to the forestry problem. 1890. IV. 147.[1]
— Report of the Chief of the Division of forestry for 1890. 1891. IV. 338.[1]
— Report on the relation of railroads to forest supplies. 1887. IV. 424.[1]
— Report pro 1892. 1896. IV. 555.[2]
— Report upon the forestry investigations of the U. S. Department of agriculture. 1899. IV. 338.[1]
— Request to educators for coöperation. 1886. IV. 30.[1]
— Les ressources des forêts des États-Unis. 1896. IV. 338.[2]
— Ring-growth in trees. 1888. I. 128.[1]
— La riqueza forestal de los Estados Unidos. 1896. IV. 555.[2]
— Sixty-four millions of dollars. 1891. IV. 338.[1]
— Sketch of the development of the forest policy of Germany. 1883. IV. 26, 274.[2]
— Snow-slides and avalanches. 1888. IV. 188.[2]
— Southern Pine. 1896. IV. 462,[2] 467.[1]
— Sprouting Pines. 1897. II. 39.[1]
— Statement . . . regarding the bill concerning schools of forestry. 1895. IV. 30.[1]
— Strength of "boxed" or "turpentine" timber. 1892. IV. 410, 437.[1]
— Suggestions to the lumbermen of the United States. 1893. IV. 272.
— Summary of mechanical tests on . . . American woods. 1897. IV. 409.
— La sylviculture aux États-Unis. 1896. IV. 555.[2]
— Thinning forests. 1889. IV. 174.
— Timber physics. 1892. IV. 409.
— Tracts on tree topics. 1890. IV. 272.
— The training of professional foresters. 1899. IV. 30.[1]
— Untersuchungen über die Eigenschaften des amerikanischen Keifernholzes. 1896. IV. 462.[2]
— Waldbrände in Nordamerika. 1895. IV. 182.[1]
— What is forestry? 1891. IV. 56.
— What is the forest policy of European nations? 1896. IV. 272.
— White Pine timber supplies. 1897. IV. 470.[2]
— Wood pulp supplies and forestry. 1898. IV. 430.
— Die Zukunft des Forstwesens in Amerika. 1893. IV. 338.[1]
— & others. Forest influences. 1893. IV. 45.
Fernsee, Heinrich WAWRA VON, *Ritter*. *See* WAWRA VON FERNSEE, Heinrich, *Ritter*.
Fernaler, G. Electrische Vorrichtung zum Töten von Insekten. 1892. IV. 200.
Ferrand. Commerce du caoutchouc à Madagascar. 1893. III. 231.
— Exploitation d'une nouvelle variété de caoutchouc. 1893. III. 231.
Ferrand, A. Note sur le Styrax. 1883. III. 417.[2]
Ferrand, E. *See* CALVERT, F. C. & FERRAND, E.
Ferrandi, Consalvi. De Guajacano ligno. 1728. III. 494.[1]
Ferrant, Pfeiffer, Karl & **Podoll,** Adolf. Vermehrung der Buxus. 1898. III. 523.[1]
Ferrara, A. F. Boschi dell' Etna. 1846. I. 430, IV. 86.[1]
Ferrari, Giovanni Battista. Flora; overo, Cultura di fiori. 1633. III. 115.[1]
— Flora; seu, De florum cultura. 1633. III. 115.[1]
— De florum cultura, libri IV. 1633. III. 115.[1]
— Hesperides. 1646. II. 400.[2]

Ferrari, Johann Angelo, *Graf*. Die Forst- und Baumzucht-schädlichen Borkenkäfer. 1867. IV. 92.

Ferrari, P. La festa degli alberi. 1899. IV. 42.[2]

Ferrarini, Antonio. Farmacopea. 1825. III. 256.[1]

Ferraris, Teodoro. Contribuzione allo studio dei miceti degli Agrumi. 1899. III. 501.[1]

— Di un nuovo ifomicete parassita nei frutti di Arancio. 1899. III. 501.[1]

Ferrars, M. H. Description of gear employed for facilitating the transport of timber by land. 1888. IV. 389.

— Journal of a· tour into the Karenee country. 1876. IV. 377.[2]

Ferreira. Emploi thérapeutique du Piscidia. 1887. III. 484.[2]

Ferreira, José Henriques. Memoria sobre a Guaxima. 1789. III. 589.[1]

Ferreira Borges, Joaquim. Essencias florestaes exoticas a utilisar. 1899. IV. 523.[2]

Ferreira da Silva, S. J. Sur une nouvelle réaction de l'ésér-ine. 1893. III. 484.[1]

— Sur une réaction . . . de la cocaïne. 1890. III. 493.[2]

Ferrer, Léon. Enquête sur les Vignes américaines. 1887. III. 556.

— Le mildew. 1888. III. 580.

— Le mildew, moyens de le combattre. 1887. III. 579.

— Note sur divers insectes constatés sur les vignobles. 1889. III. 564.[1]

Ferrer, Miguel RODRIGUEZ-. *See* RODRIGUEZ-FERRER, Miguel.

Ferrer y de Lloret, Javier de. Proyecto de fijación . . . de las dunas . . . de Rosas. 1895. IV. 165.

Ferrero, L. O. Vinificazione dei Fichi. 1884. III. 370.[1]

Ferret, A. & **Galinier**. Voyage en Abyssinie. *See* DELILE, A. R. 1847. I. 487.

Ferri, Alphonsi.· De morbo gallico et ligni sancti natura. 1728.· III. 494.[1]

Ferrière, Émile. Plantes médicinales de la Bourgogne. 1892. III. 86.

Ferris, B. F. Plums. 1896. III. 433.[1]

— Raspberry and Blackberry culture. 1895. III. 457.[2]

— Seedling fruits. 1887. III. 50.[1]

— The three best red Raspberries. 1899. III. 458.[2]

— Trees and fruits for the farm. 1894. III. 118.[1]

Ferris, Jno. C. Forest trees. 1886. III. 118.[1]

— Influence of stock on cion. 1893. III.·40.

— Influences of climate on quality of fruit. 1893. III. 134.[1]

Ferrouillat, Paul. La lutte contre l'oïdium. 1894. III. 581.

— *See also* VIALA, Pierre & FERROUILLAT, Paul.

The **Ferrum** timber company. 1865. IV. 419.

Ferrus. Les forêts à l'île de la Réunion. 1885. IV. 379.[1]

Ferruzza, G. Sulla traspirazione di alcune " Palme e succo-lenti." 1897. I.·168.

Ferry, Jules. La question algérienne. 1892. IV. 279.[2]

Fersman, Jan. O pěstování ovocných stromů se zvl. zřete-lemk českému jihu. 1887. III. 146.[2]

Fertiault, F. Floraison du Lagerstroemia indica. 1848. III. 629.[2]

Fertilisation of Hoya globulosa. 1882. II. 739.[2]

Fertilization of the cultivated Date Palm. 1898. III. 329.[1]

The **fertilization** of the Yucca. 1873. II. 87.[1]

Ferussac, Jean Baptiste Léon d'Audebart, *baron* de. Consid-érations sur les Thérébinthes. 1813. III. 525.[2]

Feser, Jakob. Araucaria imbricata in englischen Gärten. 1899. III. 299.[1]

Fessenden, Thomas G. The new American gardener. 1828. III. 99.

Fessenden's silk manual and practical farmer. III. 3.

Fessmann, S. Handbuch zum Forst-Gesetz für das König-reich Bayern. 1873. IV. 318.

La festa degli alberi. 1899. IV. 42.[1]

La festa degli alberi a Roma. 1899. IV. 42.[1]

La " festa degli alberi " in provincia di Novara. 1899. IV. 42.[1]

Una festa degli alberi modello. 1899. IV. 42.[1]

Fest-Gabe zur Feier der 22. Versammlung deutscher Land-und Forstwirthe. 1861. IV. 40.[1]

Festschrift für die 25. Versammlung deutscher Land- und Forstwirthe zu Dresden. *See* DARSTELLUNG der k. sächs. Staatsforstverwaltung. 1865. IV. 355.[1]

Festschrift für die fünfzigjährige Jubelfeier der Forst-akademie Eberswalde. *See* DANCKELMANN, Bernhard. 1880. IV. 32.

Festschrift zum fünfzigjährigen Jubiläum der·K. land- und forstwirthschaftlichen Akademie Hohenheim. 1868. IV. 32.

Festskrift i Anledning af Hedeselskabets 25-aarige Jubilaeum. 1891. IV. 39.[2]

Fête des arbres. 1900. IV. 42.[2]

Les fêtes des amis des arbres. 1898. IV. 541.

Fetisch, Karl. Verwundete Obstbäume. 1900. III. 180.[2]

— & others. Unterpflanzung eines Buchenwaldes. 1896. III. 216.

Fétu, Anastasie. Enumerațiunea specieloru de plante cul-tivate in Gradina botanica. 1871. I. 522.[1]

Le feu [dans les pineraies]. 1894. IV. 547.[2]

Feuereisen, C. B. Praktische Abhandlungen über . . . Gärt-nerei. 1780. III. 121.[1]

Feuerreusen, Karl Gottlob. Pflanzenorganologie. 1780. I. 32.

Feuerstock, (*Oberförster*). Gelungene Methode der Vermeh-rung der Nadelhölzer durch Stecklinge. 1833. III. 293.

— De la multiplication du Sapin commun par boutures. 1833. III. 293.

Feuille des jeunes naturalistes . . . I. 21.

Feuille succédanée du Thé. 1841. III. 366.[1]

Feuillée, Louis. Beschreibung zur Arseney dienlicher Pflan-zen . . . in den Reichen des mittägigen America. 1714. III. 63.[2]

— Journal des observations . . . sur les côtes orientales de l'Amérique meridionale. 1714. I. 327, III. 63.[2]

Feuilles d'Aesculus Hippocastanum. 1886. III. 538.[2]

Feuller, Karl, *Freyherr* von. Kurzer Entwurf einer . . . An-weisung zu einer . . . Forsthaushaltung. 1785. IV. 95.

Feuser. Die Kultur der Korbweiden. 1872. III. 347.

Feussner. Tortrix viridana. 1874. IV. 510.

De la fève du Calabar. 1863. III. 483.[3]

A few examples of the worst effects of mutilating the branches of timber trees. 1850. III. 170.

A few·notes on the Palmyrah Palm. 1896. IV. 485.[3]

Feye, (*Forstmeister*). Gewitter in den fürstlich Lippe'schen Forsten. 1879. IV. 194.

— Die Hude- und Pflanzwälder. 1875. IV. 135.[1]

Feyerabend, Melchoir Gottlieb. . De Salvia in infuso adhi-·benda. *See* STENTZEL, C. G. 1723. III. 698.[1]

Fiala, Franz. Beiträge zur Flora Bosniens und der Herce-govina. 1899. II. 42.[2]

— Beiträge zur Pflanzengeographie Bosniens. 1893. I. 448.[1]

— Ein botanischer Ausflug in die Klekplanina. 1893. I. 448.[1]

— Die Osječenica und Klekovača planina. 1893. I. 448.[1]

— Zwei interessante Nadelhölzer des bosnischen Waldes. 1893. II. 38.[1]

Fialowski, Ludwig. Über das Herbarium Petri Melii. 1885. I. 81.[2]

Fibig, Johann. Einleitung in die Naturgeschichte des Pflanzenreichs. 1791. I. 83.

Fibra de Palmera. 1885. IV. 485.[1]

Fibre from Lagos. 1889. III. 585.[1]

Fibre industry at the Bahamas. 1889. III. 341.[1]

Fibre of Sterculia guttata. 1849. III. 591.[2]

Fibre of Wikstroemia indica. C. A. Mey. 1897. III. 628.[2]

Fibre productions in the Caicos. 1890. III. 341.[1]

Fibres and fibre plants. 1891. III. 235.[1]

Les fibres de Buazé. *See* Buazé fibre. 1889. III. 514.[1]

Fibres for brushes. 1893. III. 319.[2]

Fibres used for brush making. *See* THURSTON, Edgar. 1892. III. 235.[1]

Ficalho, *conde* de. Apontamentos para o estudo da flora portu-gueza. 1876. I. 421.

— Flora dos Lusiadas. 1880. I. 515.

— Noticia de alguns productos . . . da Africa portugueza. 1878. III. 281.[1]

— Plantas uteis da Africa portugueza. 1884. III. 93.[1]

— & Coutinho, A. X. P. Contribuições para o estudo da flora portugueza. 1899. III. 256.[1]

— As Rosaceas de Portugal. 1899. III. 256.[1]

— & **Hiern**, W. P. On Central African plants. 1881. I. 492.[2]

Fichera, Alfio. *See* LA ROSA FICHERA, Alfio.

Fichner, I. Stamm und Aeste. 1846. III. 137.

Eine Fichte ohne Quirltriebe. 1871. II. 34.[2]

Die **Fichten-Kot-Blattwespe** . . . in Böhmen. 1893. IV. 208.[1]

Fichtennadel-Präparate. 1874. III. 226.[2]

Eine Fichtenpflanzung. 1861. IV. 453.

Ficinus, Heinrich David August. Flora der Gegend um Dresden. 1807. I. 376.

— Rosmarinum. 1725. III. 698.[1]

Fick, R. Untersuchungen über . . . Inosit. 1887. I. 177.
Fickert, K. Über Baumwunden und deren Heilung. 1858.
III. 180.[1]
Il Fico santo dell' isola di Ceylan. 1862. IV. 519.[1]
Ficus elastica. See STEPHENS, A. B. 1898. III. 370.[2]
A Ficus strangling a Mango tree. 1895. II. 149.[2]
Die Fideikommisse in Preussen. 1897. IV. 355.[1]
Fides, (pseud.). Le mandorle, le noci, le nocciole. 1894.
III. 220.[2]
Fieber, Franz Xaver. Symbolische Pflanzen. 1826. I. 515.
Fieder. Ansichten über die Karstbewaldungs-Frage. 1858.
IV. 167.[1]
Fiedler. Die Wichtigkeit des Nutzungsbetriebes in Hochge-
birgsforsten. 1856. IV. 391.
Fiedler, Karl Gustav. Uebersicht der Gewächse des König-
reiches Griechenland. 1840. III. 91.[1]
Fiedler, Karl Wilhelm. Systematisches Handbuch der Forst-
wirthschaft. 1796. IV. 95.
Fiedler, P. J. Die Lösung der Reblausfrage. 1888. III.
574.
Fiedler, Wilhelm & others. Ueber den Schnitt der Wistaria
chinensis. 1895. III. 491.[1]
Fiek, Emil. Botanische Streifzüge in Russland. 1885. I.
364.
— Excursions-Flora für Schlesien. 1889. I. 532.[2]
— & Schube, Th. Resultate der Durchforschung der
schlesischen Phanerogamenflora. 1887. I. 388.
Field, Barron. Geographical memoirs on New South Wales.
1825. I. 500.
Field, E. T. Cocoanut culture in the United States. 1885.
III. 322.[2]
Field, H. C. Notes on Loranthus Fieldii Buchanan. 1885.
II. 176.[1]
Field, Henry. Memoirs historical and illustrative of the
Botanick garden at Chelsea. 1820. I. 53.
Field, Henry M. Cinchona, its action and applications.
1878. III. 721.
Field, Thomas W. Pear culture. 1858. III. 445.[1]
Field. III. 16.
Field and forest. I. 5.
Field Columbian museum. Publications. I. 5.
Field naturalists' club of Victoria. See VICTORIAN naturalist.
I. 30.
Fielder, C. H. On the rise . . . of Tea cultivation in British
India. 1869. III. 603.
— On Tea cultivation in India. 1869. III. 603.
Fielding, Cecil Henry. Memories of Malling and its valley.
1893. I. 534.[2]
Fielding, H. B. & Gardner, George. Sertum plantarum.
1844. I. 269.
Fienga, A. See ALPINI, Giuseppe & FIENGA, A.
Fiera, Baptista. Coena de herbarum virtutibus. 164 . ? I.
285.[1]
Fiesser, G. H. Zur einheitlichen Benennung der Koniferen.
1888. II. 13.[2]
— Die Grossherzoglichen Gärten in Baden-Baden. 1900.
I. 49.
— Poinsettia (Euphorbia) pulcherrima. 1873. III. 518.[1]
— Der praktische Obstbau. 1887. III. 139.
La fiesta del árbol. 1900. IV. 541.
La fiesta del árbol en Barcelona. 1899. IV. 541.
La fièvre ou la malaria. See MAISTRE, Jules. 1899. IV.
55.[1]
Fifteen new forest reservations in the United States. 1893.
IV. 178.[2]
The Fig tree. 1883. III. 369.[2]
Fig-trees. 1821. III. 369.[1]
Figari, Antonio & Husson, A. H. L'exploration scientifique
de l'Égypte. 1896. I. 489.
Figdor, Wilhelm. Zur Anatomie des Stammes der Dammar-
pflanze. 1900. II. 561.[1]
— Ueber eine eigenthümliche Krümmungserscheinung des
Gynophors von Bocconia. 1895. II. 229.[1]
— Experimentelle und histologische Studien über die Er-
scheinung der Verwachsung. 1891. I. 208.[2]
— Untersuchungen über die Erscheinung des Blutungs-
druckes in den Tropen. 1898. II. 169.[1]
— Ueber die Ursachen der Anisophyllie. 1897. I. 111.
Figee, Simon. De akustische methode ter bepaling van den
coefficient van veerkracht. 1877. IV. 415.[1]
— Teak of Djati hout. 1877. IV. 538.[1]
Figert, Ernst. Beiträge zur Kenntniss einiger Pappelarten.
1887. II. 96.[1]
— Botanische Mitteilungen aus Schlesien. 1889. I. 389.
— Botanische Mitteilungen aus Schlesien. 1896. II. 33.[1]
— Hybride der Flora von Liegnitz. 1887. II. 101.[2]
— Salix Caprea L. X pulchra. 1895. II. 106.[1]
Figueiredo, Jeronymo Joaquim de. Flora pharmaceutica e
alimentar portugueza. 1825. III. 88.[2]
Figuier, Louis. Histoire des plantes. 1865. I. 95.
— Historya roślin. 1865. I. 95.
— The vegetable world. 1865. I. 95.
— See also POUMARÈDE, J. A. & FIGUIER, Louis.
Le Figuier. 1899. III. 369.[2]
Figulus, Carolus. Dialogus, qui inscribitur botanomethodus.
1540. I. 277, 530.[2]
Figura, József. Az Eperfa (Morus). 1880. III. 378.
Les figures et pourtraicts des plantes et herbes. 1576. I.
282.
Fiji India rubber. 1898. III. 371,[1] 686,[1] 691.[1]
Fiji ivory nuts. 1897. III. 332.[1]
Fiji rubber. See FIJI India rubber. 1898. III. 686.[2]
Fijnje, J. G. W. Over de boschbeplantingen op de duinen.
1891. IV. 160.[1]
— Nota over de boschbeplantingen. 1889. IV. 164.[1]
Fikenscher, D. J. Christo-Poma. 1674. II. 267.[2]
Fikke, Johann Jakob. See FICK, Johann Jakob.
Filarszky, Nándor. A Luczfenyőnek alakváltozásai. 1900.
II. 35.[2]
Filchner, F. A. Tabellen zur genauen Werthbestimmung ge-
fällter und ungefällter Baumstämme. 1832. IV. 222.
Filet, G. J. De inlandsche plantennamen. 1859. I. 73.[2]
— De planten in den botanischen tuin bij het Groot militair
hospitaal te Weltevreden. 1855. I. 67.[2]
— Plantkundig woordenboek voor Nederlandsch-Indië. 1876.
I. 76.[1]
— Tweede katalogus der in den botanischen tuin . . . te
Weltevreden aangekweekt wordende planten. 1854. I. 67.[2]
Filho, Lacerda. Acção physiologica do urari. 1876. III.
683.[1]
Filhol, Édouard. Composition chimique des Roses de Provins.
1863. III. 454.[1]
— Faits pour servir à l'histoire chimique de la résine copal.
1842. I. 180.[2]
— Note sur la chlorophylle. 1874. I. 141.
— Note sur la composition chimique de l'Arbutus. 1860.
III. 648.[1]
— Note sur les feuilles et les fleurs employées en pharmacie.
1862. III. 245.
— Note sur quelques matières colorantes végétales. 1860.
I. 184, III. 236.
— Nouvelles recherches sur les matières colorantes. 1860.
III. 236.
— Observations sur les matières colorantes des fleurs. 1854.
III. 236.
— Recherches sur la chlorophylle. 1868. I. 141.
— Recherches sur les matières colorantes des fleurs. 1868. I.
184.
— Recherches sur les propriétés chimiques de la chlorophylle.
1865. I. 141.
— See also CHATIN, Adolphe & FILHOL, Édouard.
— & Chatin, Adolphe. Sur les principes immédiats et les
matières colorantes des végétaux. 1863. I. 184.
— Jeanbernat, Ernest & Timbal-Lagrave, Édouard. Ex-
ploration scientifique du massif d'Arbas. See FILHOL,
J. E. (by error) & TIMBAL-LAGRAVE, Édouard. 1875. I.
414.
Fili-Vernay, Claude. De la Vigne, son passé. 1891. III.
557.[1]
Filipecki, Joseph. Observationes circa naturam plantarum.
1781. I. 169.[2]
Filippo, J. D. Laurotetanine, het alcaloid der Tetranthera
citrata. 1898. II. 226.[2]
Filippof, I. See ФИЛИППОВЪ, И.
Filippof, N. See ФИЛИППОВЪ, И.
Filippucci, F. See BALDACCI, A. & FILIPPUCCI, F.
Fillassier, Jean Jacques. Dictionnaire du jardinier françois.
1789. III. 86.
Filleul, G. L'Habrothamnus elegans. 1895. III. 699.[2]
Fillias, Ach. Notice sur les forêts de l'Algérie. 1878. IV.
379.[1]
Filliette, F. Observations sur quelques effets de la gelée du
13 mai 1832. 1832. III. 47.
Fillon, Alphonse. Culture du Chêne-Liége. 1861. IV. 516.[2]
— Mise en valeur des sols pauvres. 1870. IV. 155,[1] 162.
— Le reboisement par les essences résineuses. 1870. IV.
155,[1] 162.
— La silviculture pratique. 1890. IV. 109.[2]

Fillot, Alphonse. Le Chamaecyparis Boursieri filiformis. 1877. III. 301.[1]
— Taxus hibernica. 1875. III. 288.[1]
— Vermenigvuldiging der planten door hare bladeren. 1874. III. 159.[1]
Filly, Carl. Die Wachsthumsbedingungen der Seestrandskiefer. 1873. IV. 467.[2]
La filoxera de la Vid. 1878. III. 570.[2]
Filter, Franz Ernst. De cortice Angusturae. 1791. III. 503.[2]
Financial results of forest administrations. 1898. IV. 259.[2]
Die finanziellen Ergebnisse der Staatsforstverwaltung in Preussen. 1885. IV. 261.[1]
Fincham, John. On the timber used for the masts of ships. 1833. IV. 425.[1]
Fincher, G. W. The Catalpa speciosa. 1889. III. 706.[1]
Finck, Hugo. Apuntes ineditos acerca de algunas plantas del Distrito de Cordoba. 1879. III. 63.[2]
— Cultivation of Cinchona in Mexico. 1871. III. 713.[1]
Finckh, Friedrich Ludwig. Die Cactus, ihre Beschreibung. 1832. III. 618.[1]
Finckh, Hermann. Agaves in New South Wales. 1897. III. 340.[1]
Finckh, Peter Christ von. Ein bewährtes Mittel wider die Holzdieberey. 1765. IV. 313.
Finckh, Robert. Beiträge zur württembergischen Flora. 1872. I. 386.
— Ueber einige neue Entdeckungen in der württembergischen Flora. 1850. I. 383.
Finder, M. Verwendung der Ilex Aquifolium zu Hecken. 1891. III. 530.[1]
A fine Bur Oak. 1890. II. 135.[2]
A fine old Walnut tree. 1882. II. 114.[1]
Fineschi, Anton Maria. Sopra la maniera di coltivare i Mori. 1783. III. 373.
Finger, E. Behandlung der Veredlungen. 1893. III. 163.[1]
— Friedländer, W. & Demuth, N. Veredlung der Blutbuche im Freien. 1891. III. 360.[2]
Finger, Josef. Forststatistische Notizen über die Stiftungsfondsdomäne Ronow. 1853. IV. 370.
Finger, Ladislaus. Holzertrags-Tafeln zur Schätzung der Nadelholz-Hochwälder. 1851. IV. 254.
Finger, Wilhelm. Fünfte praktische Abhandlung aus dem Forstwesen über Hochwald. 1800. IV. 129.
— Practische Abhandlungen ... der Eichen. 1794. IV. 172.
— Praktische Abhandlung über Besaamung. 1794. IV. 140.
— Praktische Abhandlung über die Anlegung neuer Eichelgärten. 1796. IV. 504.
— Praktische Abhandlung vom Schnadeln und Köpfen. 1794. IV. 172.[2]
The fingered Citron. 1890 II. 402.[1]
Fingerhuth, Karl Anton. Einiges zur deutschen Flora. 1829. II. 122,[1] 260.[2]
— Monographia generis Capsici. 1832. II. 760.[2]
— See also BLUFF, M. J. & FINGERHUTH, K. A.
Finistère — Société d'études scientifiques. See SOCIÉTÉ ... I. 23.
Fink (of Fulda). Ueber Anbau der Schwarzkiefer. 1873. IV. 465.[1]
— Noch einiges zur Kenntniss der Schwarzkiefer. 1861. IV. 465.[1]
— & Kalkhof, F. Ueber Entastungen. 1803. IV. 170.
Fink, Bruce. Spermaphyta of the flora of Fayette. 1897. I. 326.
Finkener. Unterscheidung des Ricinusöles. 1886. III. 522.[1]
Finlay. Enfermedad de los Cocoteros. 1882. III. 323.[1]
Finney, George. Evergreens. 1869. III. 292.
Finocchietti, Demetrio Carlo, conte. Industria del legno. 1873. IV. 21.[1]
Finselbach, A. L'anatomie des Kramériacées. 1892. II. 321.[1]
Finska forstföreningen. Meddelanden. IV. 6.
Finsterwalder, J. Verzeichniss der auf Island wachsenden Pflanzen. 1861. I. 356.
Fintelmann, (Dr.). Ueber Anlage ... lebendiger Hecken. 1868. III. 213.
— Hur man kan skydda afhuggna trädstammar för angrepp af insekter. 1855. IV. 418.
— Zur Verhütung des Wurmfrasses im Holze. 1855. IV. 418.
Fintelmann, Axel. Blühen der Paulownia in Norddeutschland. 1899. III. 703.[2]
— Cecidomyia saliciperda. 1882. III. 350.[1]
— Wie kann man den ... jungen Baum am sichersten ... befestigen? 1882. III. 199.

Fintelmann, F. W. L. Ueber die Verbindung der Landwirthschaft mit der Forstwirthschaft. 1834. IV. 133.
Fintelmann, Ferdinand. Bemerkungen über Kirschtreiberei. 1824. III. 431.[2]
— Über die Kultur der blauen Hortensien. 1829. III. 412.[1]
— Mandelbäume mit saftigen Früchten. 1856. II. 272.[2]
Fintelmann, Gustav Adolph. Über das Ankeimen der Samen. 1847. III. 156.[1]
— Anwendung des heissen Wassers zur Vertilgung von Insekten. 1847. III. 197.
— Beiträge zur ... Schwindpocken-Krankheit des Weinstocks. 1839. III. 575.[1]
— Bemerkungen über die gefüllten Blumen. 184 . ? III. 40.
— Beobachtungen über die Temperaturen in der Erde. 1849. II. 183.[1]
— Einige Bemerkungen über Rosen-Okulanten. 1844. III. 452.
— Eintheilung der Fuchsien-Sorten. 1861. III. 639.[2]
— Die Feuchtigkeit der Luft in Beziehung auf das Gedeihen der Pflanzen. 1837. I. 232.[2]
— Ueber Krankheiten der italienischen Pappel. 1858. III. 346.[1]
— Ueber die Kultur der Cocos nucifera. 1838. III. 322.[1]
— Über die lange Dauer des Weidenholzes im Freien. 1853. IV. 487.[2]
— Ueber Nutzbaumpflanzungen. 1856. III. 120.[2]
— Die Pfirsichzucht zu Montreuil bei Paris. 1849. III. 440.[1]
— Weitere Mittheilung über ... Cocos nucifera. 1842. III. 322.[1]
— Die Wildbaumzucht. 1841. III. 101.[1]
Fintelmann, Heinrich Julius. Die Baumbepflanzungen unserer öffentlichen Wege. 1878. III. 209.
— Beobachtungen über die Abweichungen in dem Beginn der Blütezeit der Obstsorten. 1878. I. 225.
— Betrachtungen über die Herbstfärbung. 1887. III. 207.[1]
— Die Epheuvegetation in den baltischen Strandwäldern. 1880. II. 649.[2]
— Über das Für und Wider des Gebrauchs der Heckenscheere. 1884. III. 202.[1]
— Die Königseiche zu Pausin. 1881. II. 138.[1]
— Nochmals Hexenbesen. See HEXENBESEN ... 1886. I. 528.[2]
— Eine Schuppenkiefer. 1881. II. 47.[2]
— Wie schützt man unsere Baumanlagen ... gegen die Verheerungen der Stürme? 1881. III. 184.[2]
Fintelmann, Karl Julius. Anleitung zum zweckmässigen Verpacken verschiedener Obstsorten. 1835. III. 173.[2]
— Beantwortung der Anfrage ... in Betreff der Kellerersel. 1831. III. 188.[2]
— Bemerkungen auf die Mittheilung des Herrn Dr. Lachmann 1835. III. 548.[2]
— Über den diesjährigen Raupenfrass 1831 III 199.[2]
— Einige Worte über Anzucht ... der hochstämmigen Rosen. 1839. III. 451.[2]
— Die Obstbaumzucht. 1839. III. 137.
— Practische Anleitung zur Fruchttreiberei. 1837. III. 176.[1]
— Praktisk Anvisning til Frugtdriveri. 1837. III. 176.[1]
— Vermehrung der Weinstöcke aus Senkreben. 1827. III. 196.
— Vertilgung der Wickler und Stichmaden. 1860. III. 196.
— Vorsichtsmassregeln, welche bei dem Bepflanzen ... mit Obstbäumen ... zu beobachten sind. 1839. III. 137.
— Über zwei, dem Schneeball-Strauch ... schädlichen Insekten. 1847. III. 753.[2]
— See also LENNÉ & FINTELMANN, Carl.
Fintelmann, L. Ueber die Anwendung der Canalwasser-Beieselung. 1876. IV. 144.[2]
— Ueber Baumpflanzungen in den Städten. 1877. III. 42.[2]
— Beiträge zur näheren Bestimmung ... einiger auf der Kiefer ... lebender Lophyren. 1836. IV. 475.
Fioretti, T. MOSTARDI-. See MOSTARDI-FIORETTI, T.
Fiori, Adriano. Ricerche anatomiche sull' ... Hovenia dulcis. 1895. II. 495.[1]
— & Paoletti, Giulio. Iconographia florae italicae. 1895. I. 430.
— & others. Flora analitica d'Italia. 1896. I. 430.
Fiorini-Mazzanti, Elisabetta, contesa. Appendice al Prodromo della flora romana. 1823. I. 425.
— Florula del Colosseo. 1875. I. 428.
Fir and Pine timber. See NOTES on Fir timber. 1874. IV. 443.[1]
Fir timber. 1874. IV. 482.[1]

The **Fire-bush** (Embothrium coccineum). 1876. III. 383.[1]
Fire conservancy in Indian forests. 1883. IV. 184.[1]
A **Fire-tree**. 1895. II. 166.[2]
Fire wounds. 1897. I. 208,[2] *IV. 140.*
Firenze. See FLORENCE.
Firidolfi, Giovanni RICASOLI-. See RICASOLI-FIRIDOLFI, Giovanni.
Firms, L. A., baron d'HOMBRES-. See HOMBRES-FIRMAS, L. A., baron d'.
Firminger, Thomas Augustus Charles. A manual of gardening for Bengal. 1864. III. 92.[2]
— Notes upon Garden-Roses in India. 1874. III. 449.
First catalogues . . . of the Botanical garden of Transsylvania university. See RAFINESQUE-SCHMALTZ, C. S. 1824. I. 38.[1]
The **first** hybrids with Rosa rugosa. 1889. III. 456.[2]
First steps to the British flora. 1855. I. 400.
Firth, J. C. On forest culture. 1875. IV. 380.[2]
— On forest culture. 1879. IV. 124.[2]
Firtsch, Georg. Anatomisch-physiologische Untersuchungen über die Keimpflanze der Dattelpalme. 1886. II. 73.[1]
— Zur Kenntniss der geotropischen Reizbarkeit der Wurzelspitze. 1884. I. 195.[1]
Fiscali, Ferdinand. Deutschlands Forstculturpflanzen. 1856. IV. 83.
— Die schädlichen Forstinsekten. 1857. IV. 92.
Fisch, Carl & **Krause**, E. H. L. Flora von Rostock und Umgegend. 1879. I. 387.
Fisch, Ernst. Beiträge zur Blütenbiologie. 1899. I. 239.[1]
Fischbach, E. von. Welche Wege sind bei der Beweisführung in Betreff der Wohlfahrtswirkungen des Waldes einzuschlagen? 1890. IV. 55.[1]
Fischbach, Heinrich. Einiges über Reinigungshiebe. 1871. IV. 173.
— Einjährige Forchen mit künstlichen Ballen. 1871. IV. 472.
— Ueber die Form der Mischung beim Holzanbau. 1857. IV. 137.[1]
— Eine forstliche Studienreise vor hundert Jahren. 1895. IV. 349.[2]
— Katechismus der Forstbotanik. 1862. IV. 83.
— Ueber die Lockerung des Waldbodens. 1858. IV. 143.[1]
— Ueber die Lockerung des Waldbodens. 1859. IV. 68.
— Mischung von Buche und Fichte eine Gefahr. 1875. IV. 138.[2]
— Aus dem Mittelwald. 1895. IV. 131.
— Über die Pflege der Eiche. 1896. IV. 508.
— Ueber regenfreie Lieferung der Eichengerbrinde. 1891. IV. 434, *513.*
— Die Rotbuche im Mittelwaldbetrieb. 1898. IV. 496.
— Der Wald und dessen Bewirtschaftung. 1884. IV. 107.[1]
— Weisstannen mit hängenden Zweigen. 1880. II. 23.[1]
— Zwei Methoden, die Dämpfe, welche sich bei der Meilerverkohlung . . . bilden, zu benützen. 1856. IV. 394.
Fischbach, Karl von. Allgemeine kleine Ertragstafel. 1873. IV. 236.
— Altes und Neues von der Weisstanne. 1879. IV. 444.[2]
— Anhaltspunkte zur Feststellung des Alters der Nussbäume in Interlaken. 1894. II. 114.[1]
— Ueber die Anlage von Baum-Alleen. 1879. III. 211.[1]
— Ein Beispiel von dem Erfolg der Bodenlockerung. 1877. IV. 69.
— Beiträge zur . . . Geschichte der Flösserei in Schwaben. 1895. IV. 26, *390.[1]*
— Beiträge zur historischen Entwicklung einzelner forstlicher Lehren. 1882. IV. 24.[1]
— Beiträge zur Kenntniss der Weymouthskiefer. 1882. IV. 469.
— Benützung und Züchtung von Unterarten der Waldbäume zu forstlichen Zwecken. 1900. I. 529, *IV. 75.[1]*
— Beschreibung der neueren Imprägnirungsmethode. 1857. IV. 418.
— Die Beseitigung der Waldstreunutzung. 1864. IV. 71.
— Zur besseren Würdigung der Birke. 1892. IV. 490.[2]
— Culture du Sapin blanc. 1863. IV. 444.[1]
— Dänische Praxis und deutsche Theorien in der Buchenwirthschaft. 1897. IV. 496.
— Einige geschichtliche Notizen über die Sägemühlen. 1890. IV. 393.
— Einige Vorschläge zur Waldverschönerung. 1893. IV. 137.[1]
— Die Eisenzölle und Frachttarife in ihrem Einfluss auf die Waldrente. 1879. IV. 284.[1]
— Die Ergänzung des Eichenschälwaldes. 1882. IV. 507.
— Die Familienfideikommisse als Mittel zur Erhaltung des Waldes. 1888. IV. 270.

— Flächeneinheit oder jährliche Schlagfläche. 1877. IV. 236.
— Forst- und Jagdgeschichtliches aus Württemberg. 1894. IV. 24.[1]
— Forstlich-touristische Skizze aus dem südlichen Theil der Krim. 1865. IV. 348.[1]
— Der früheste Vorschlag zur Baumfeldwirthschaft. 1894. IV. 134.[1]
— Zur Geschichte der Durchforstungen. 1890. IV. 174.
— Über die Grenze zwischen relativem und absolutem Waldboden. 1894. IV. 70.
— Haubarkeitsertrag und Normalvorrath. 1882. IV. 257.
— Hintertriebene Haideaufforstung. 1895. IV. 26, *159.*
— Die Hochwasserfrage und der Wald in Preussen. 1897. IV. 47.[1]
— Die Hochwasserfrage und der Wald in Preussen. 1898. IV. 47.[1]
— Die Hügelpflanzung. 1857. IV. 153.[2]
— Ueber die Kosten der Pflanzenerziehung. 1866. IV. 150.
— Der Kostenpunkt bei den Zwischennutzungen. 1880. IV. 252.
— Die Kultur der Weisstanne. 1863. IV. 444.[1]
— Zur Lebensweise des Fichtenborkenkäfers. 1875. IV. 204.
— Lehrbuch der Forstwissenschaft. 1856. IV. 97.
— Die mathematische Grundlage der Reinertragstheorie. 1876. IV. 256.
— Ueber die (muthmassliche) Wasserabnahme. 1882. IV. 51.
— Ueber das Nachtheile des allzutiefen Einsetzens der Fichtenpflänzlinge. 1870. IV. 453.
— Nachträgliches zur Geschichte der Holzconservirung. 1898. IV. 416.[2]
— Eine neue Krankheit der Schwarzkiefer. 1887. IV. 466.[1]
— Die neue Krankheit der Schwarzkiefer. 1890. IV. 466,[1] *470.[1]*
— Eine neue Pflanzlatte. 1884. IV. 153.[1]
— Ueber Nutzholzausbringen. 1883. IV. 237.
— Durch Ostwinde veranlasste Sturmschäden. 1893. IV. 189.[2]
— Praktische Forstwirthschaft. 1880. IV. 107.[1]
— Quelle est la voie à suivre . . .? 1890. IV. 45.
— Die Rechnung mit dem Bodenerwartungswerth der Flächeneinheit. 1876. IV. 256.
— Der Rüsselkäfer vertrieben durch die Schafweide. 1867. IV. 207.
— Die Salweide als Holzart zur Vorkultur. 1896. IV. 488.[1]
— Ueberführung des Eichenschälwaldes. 1898. IV. 74,[2] *509.*
— Variationen an Eichenblättern. 1884. II. 137.[1]
— Ueber das Verhältniss zwischen Haubarkeitsertrag und Normalvorrath. 1881. IV. 236.
— Das Vorkommen der gemeinen Kiefer auf der Jurakalk-Formation. 1866. IV. 472.
— Ueber das im vormaligen Fürstenthum Hohenzollern-Hechingen geltende Forstgesetz. 1896. IV. 321.
— Ueber die Vorzüge des lichteren Bestandesschlusses. 1881. IV. 129.
— Eine Waldvertheilung aus dem Jahre 1740. 1897. IV. 24.[1]
— Zur Weiterentwicklung der Lehre von den Durchforstungen. 1884. IV. 174.
— Ein weiterer Vorschlag zur Verbesserung der Wytweiden. 1882. IV. 116.[1]
— Welche Wege sind bei der Beweisführung in Betreff der Wohlfahrtswirkungen des Waldes einzuschlagen? 1890. IV. 45.
— Die wirthschaftlichen Leistungen . . . bei der Kiefer. 1888. IV. 481.
— Die wirthschaftlichen Leistungen des Voll- und Abtriebsbestandes. 1885. IV. 237.
— Die wirthschaftlichen Leistungen des Voll- und Abtriebsbestandes. 1887. IV. 245.
— Ueber den wirthschaftlichen Nutzen der intensiven Bodenbearbeitung. 1875. IV. 143.[1]
Fischelmayer, Adolph. Bewurzelungsversuche mit chlorophyllarmen Stecklingen. 1881. III. 158.
— Der Ziergehölz-Schnitt in Anlagen. 1890. III. 172.
Fischer, (Schlossgärtner, Simianowitz in Ober-Schlesien). Mittel zur Vertilgung der Schildlaus. 1884. III. 196.
Fischer, A. Mittheilungen über die . . . Studienreise der königl. preuss. Forstakademien. 1882. IV. 354.
— Studienreise der k. preussischen Forst-Akademien. 1882. IV. 354.

Fischer, A. F. Karl von. Über die Vegetationsverhältnisse im südlichen und mittlern Lithauen. 1843. I. 361.
Fischer, Alexandre. Mémoire sur l'accroissement du tronc. 1829. I. 527.
Fischer, Alfred. Beiträge zur Physiologie der Holzgewächse. 1891. I. 160.
— Glycose als Reservestoff der Laubhölzer. 1888. I. 179.[2]
— Studien über die Siebröhren der Dicotylenblätter. 1885. I. 110.
Fischer, Bernhard. Die neueren Arzneimittel ·für Apotheker. 1888. III. 244.
Fischer, C. Bijdragen tot het kweeken van . . . vruchtboomen. 1858. III. 140.[1]
Fischer, C. August. Description de Valence. 1804. I. 420.
Fischer, E. M. The genus Cactus. 1893. II. 586.[2]
Fischer, Edmund. Die Aufforstung des Marchfelder Flugsandbodens. 1885. IV. 146.[1]
Fischer, Eduard. Ueber eine Erkrankung der Rottanne. 1894. IV. 457.
— Ueber Gymnosporangium Sabinae. 1891. III. 194.
— Die Rostkrankheiten der . . . Nadelhölzer. 1900. IV. 442.
— Die Sklerotienkrankheit der Alpenrosen. 1894. III. 657.[1]
— Über die sog. Sklerotien-Krankheiten der Heidelbeere. 1892. III. 657.[1]
— Die Vegetation der Thäler von Lauterbrunnen. 1892. I. 437.
Fischer, Emil. Taschenbuch für Pflanzensammler. 1879. I. 532.[2]
Fischer, Ernst. Album forst- und waidmännischer Denkmale aus dem Grossherzogthum Baden. 1854. IV. 350.[1]
— Das Naphtalin in der Heilkunde. 1883. III. 573.
Fischer, Eugène. Plantes . . . rares de la flore luxembourgeoise. 1882. II. 11.[1]
— Les plantes subspontanées . . de Luxembourg. 1871. I. 392.
Fischer, F. A. Der schnelle Holzberechner. 1841. IV. 223.
Fischer, F. B. See FISCHER, F. E. L. von.
Fischer, Ferdinand. Holzwollemaschine. 1888. IV. 429.
Fischer, Franz. Weswegen haben geworfene Eichen meist keine Pfahlwurzeln? 1873. IV. 510.
Fischer, Friedrich Ernst Ludwig von. The Balsam Poplars. 1841. II. 96.[1]
— Beitrag zur botanischen Systematik. 1812. I. 121.
— Catalogue ·du jardin des plantes du Comte Alexis de Razoumoffsky à Gorenki. 1808. I. 41.
— Index plantarum . . . in Horto botanico imperiali petropolitano. 1824. I. 81.
— Notice sur la Napoleonea imperialis. 1806. II. 612.[2]
— Notiz über den Kaiserl. botanischen Garten zu St. Petersburg. 1844. I. 42.
— Observations sur une graine reçue sous le nom d'Eleodendron argan. 1806. II. 700.[1]
— Synopsis Astragalorum Tragacantharum. 1853. II. 333.[2]
— Ueber die verschiedenen Arten von Balsampappeln. 1841. II. 96.[1]
— Zygophyllaceae. 1833. II. 395.[1]
— See also Фишеръ, Ф. B.
— & Meyer, C. A. Einige Bemerkungen über die Blüthen der Ludolfia. 1840. II. 58.[3]
— — Enumeratio plantarum novarum a cl. Schrenk lectarum. 1841. I. 453.[2]
— — Index seminum quae Hortus botanicus . . . petropolitanus . . . offert. 1835. I. 42.
— — Ueber eine neue Pflanzengattung aus Brasilien. 1841. II. 699.[1]
— — Plantes nouvelles recueillies par M. de Tchihatcheff. 1854. II. 359.[3]
— Sertum petropolitanum. 1846. I. 42.
Fischer, G. A. Rechnende Geometrie. 1826. IV. 58.
— Sammlung der vorzüglichsten Forstrechnungsaufgaben. 1803. IV. 57.
— Sammlung der vorzüglichsten, im Forstwesen vorkommenden Rechnungs-Aufgaben. 1803. IV. 57.
Fischer, Gotthelf. Muséum-Demidoff. 1806. I. 41.
Fischer, H. Die Holzsäge. 1879. IV. 393.
— Ueber die Kultur . . . der Ericaceen. 1861. III. 646.[2]
Fischer, Hans. Ueber Material- und Gelderträge der Weymouthskiefer. 1899. IV. 471.
Fischer, H. n. Vermehrung . . . der Camellia. 1836. III. 599.[2] ei rich
Fischer, Hermann. Die Bearbeitung der Hölzer. 1891. IV. 42.V[2]
Fischer, Hugo. Beiträge zur vergleichenden Morphologie der Pollenkörner. 1890. I. 117.[1]
— Ueber Inulin. 1898. I. 178.

Fischer, J. B. De Thea. 1754. III. 605.
Fischer, J. G. Beschreibung fast aller Gift- und . . . Futtergewächse. 1827. III. 73.
— Die natürliche Anordnung des Gewächsreiches. 1835. I. 87.
— Das Pflanzenreich. 1835. I. 87.
— Die schädlichsten Giftpflanzen Deutschlands. 1835. I. 87.
Fischer, Jan. O výnosu Vejmutovky. 1900. IV. 471.
Fischer, Johann Andreas. Dirdar Ibnsinae Ulmo arbore. 1718. III. 365.[1]
— De potus caffe usu et abusu. See BRÄNINGER, J. M. 1725. III. 741.[1]
Fischer, Johann Bernhard. Agathosma desciscens spec. nova descripta. 1832. II. 398.[2]
Fischer, Johann Leonhard. Versuch einer Naturgeschichte von Livland. 1778. I. 359.
Fischer, Karl. Illustrirtes Handbuch der Obstbaumzucht. 1863. III. 138.
— Der Obstfreund und Obstzüchter. 1866. III. 138.
Fischer, Karl Heinrich. Beitrag zur Kenntniss . . . des Pilocarpin. 1891. III. 505.[1]
Fischer, Karl Hermann. Ein Beitrag zur vergleichenden Anatomie . . . bei Pinus Abies. 1885. II. 35.[2]
— Der Pericykel in den freien Stengelorganen. 1900. I. 128.[2]
Fischer, Levin. Methodus nova herbaria. 1646. I. 285.[2]
Fischer, Ludwig. Der botanische Garten in Bern. 1866. I. 65.[1]
— Flora von Bern. 1855. V. xxII.[2]
— Taschenbuch der Flora von Bern. 1855. I. 435, V. xxII.[2]
— Verzeichniss der Gefässpflanzen des Berner-Oberlandes. 1875. I. 436.
Fischer, Ludwig August. Leitfaden zur systematischen und vollkommen zweckmässigen Einrichtung der Amts-Rechnungen. 1802. IV. 311.[2]
Fischer, M. Růže. 1892. III. 450.
Fischer, Rudolf. Eichenschälwald Betrieb. 1878. IV. 507.
— Die Feldholzzucht. 1878. IV. 134.[2]
— Handbuch für Landwirtschaft, Obst-, Gartenbau. 1881. III. 104.
— Die Korbweidenkultur. 1878. III. 348.
Fischer, Sigmund Kaspar. Lehrbuch der Naturgeschichte. 1842. I. 88.
Fischer, Theobald. Die Dattelpalme. 1881. II. 72.[2]
Fischer-Benzon, Rudolf von. Altdeutsche Gartenflora. 1894. III. 33.[1]
— Zur Geschichte unseres Beerenobstes. 1895. I. 80,[2] III. 33,[1] V. z.[1]
— Untersuchungen über die Torfmoore der Provinz Schleswig-Holstein. 1889. I. 389.
Fischer-Ooster, Carl von. Die Brombeeren der Umgegend von Bern. 1867. II. 304.[1]
— Rubi bernenses. 1907. II. 304.[1]
— Ueber Vegetationszonen . . . in den Alpen. 1848. I. 434.
Fischer von Atzendorf, Salomon. Unterrichteter Hausvater und kluger Gärtner. 1705. III. 102.
Fischer von Waldheim, Alexander. De interna plantarum fabrica. 1820. I. 98.
Fischer von Waldheim, Alexander Alexandrowitsch. Eucalyptus ficifolia. 1891. III. 634.[2]
— Ein weibliche Pyramidenpappel in Warschau. 1887. II. 97.[2]
— See also Фишеръ-фонъ-Вальдгеймъ.
Fischerström, Johan. Anmärkningar om Södra-Halland. 1761. IV. 344.[1]
— Om just-beredningar och garfningsämnen. 1792. III. 237.[1]
— Utkast till beskrifning om Målaren. 1785. I. 352.
Fish, D. T. Advantages of early planting. 1878. IV. 154.[2]
— Arbor-day. 1897. IV. 42.[1]
— Bunches v. tendrils. 1876. II. 508.[1]
— Figs in the open air in the east of England. 1889. III. 369.[2]
— Fruit of Passiflora edulis. 1898. III. 616.[1]
— The hardy-fruit book. 1882. III. 142.
— Hedges and screens. 1883. III. 214.[1]
— Impoverishment of trees on lawns. 1880. III. 41.[1]
— Passiflora edulis and other species. 1898. III. 616.[1]
— Protecting trees from frost. 1874. III. 183.[1]
— To prune, or not to prune. 1882. III. 170.
— The pruning of coniferous trees. 1872. III. 295.[1]
— The pruning of shrubberies. 1872. III. 172.
— The renovation of old trees in the parks. 1878. III. 181.[2]

Fish, D. T. (*continued*).
— The resuscitation of choice trees by top-dressing. 1886. III. 181.²
— Root-pruning. 1889. III. 173.²
— Sanitary properties of Abies Douglasii. 1883. IV. 484.¹
— The spring beauty of coniferous plants. 1881. III. 290.
— The surface culture of forest trees. 1886. IV. 169.¹
— The theory and practice of root-pruning. 1880. III. 173.²
— Top dressing coniferous trees. 1873. III. 292.
— The top-dressing of Coniferae. 1880. III. 151.
Fish, Henry F. On Coca leaves from Erythroxylon. 1863. III. 492.²
Fish, J. Arbres à fruits et utiles des tropiques. 1874. III. 367,¹ 407.²
Fisher, C. P. Notes on the treatment of some European forests. 1900. IV. 113.¹
— & **Smythies**, A. Thinnings in forests. 1896. IV. 175.¹
Fisher, E. M. The genus Caesalpinia. 1893. II. 338.²
— Revision of ... Hoffmanseggia. 1892. II. 363.²
— *See also* COULTER, J. M. & FISHER, E. M.
Fisher, Harry. A summary of the flora of Notts. 1893. I. 534.²
Fisher, Henry M. The Tulip-Poplar and the cigar box industry. 1892. IV. 519.²
Fisher, Jabez. Hardy Grapes. 1894. III. 551.¹
Fisher, O. Notes on the art of growing Roses. 1867. III. 452.
Fisher, Richard Thornton. The Bigtrees of California. 1900. IV. 179.²
Fisher, Roger. Heart of Oak, the British bulwark. 1763. IV. 513.
Fisher, S. I. Observations on the character ... of the European Vine. 1834. III. 551.²
Fisher, William Richard. Afforestation in the British Isles. 1893. IV. 161.¹
— The Conifers at Fampisford Hall. 1900. I. 55.
— Experiments in silk-worm rearing at Berhampur. 1889. III. 148.¹
— Fire conservancy in Sâl forests in the eastern Duars. 1880. IV. 529.¹
— The forest of Essex. 1887. IV. 27.¹
— Forestry in North America. 1891. IV. 337.¹
— Instruction in forestry at Coopers Hill. 1892. IV. 34.²
— The Larch. 1898. IV. 450.
— Lecture on forestry. 1899. IV. 357.²
— Manual of Indian forest botany. 1888. I. 101.¹
— New French law for the prevention of forest fires. 1893. IV. 183.¹
— Note on the destruction of the leaves of Sâl trees. 1881. IV. 528.²
— Notes on the effects of grazing on Sâl forests. 1876. IV. 528.²
— Physiological differences between the Sessile and Pedunculate Oak. 1900. II. 130.²
— Plantations at Kuch Behar. 1882. IV. 377.²
— A plea for Sâl. 1879. IV. 528.²
— Practical forest training grounds for the Coopers Hill college. 1892. IV. 34.²
— Proposed improvements in British forestry. 1898. IV. 275.
— Report on the course of instruction at the Forest school, Dehra Dún. 1888. IV. 37.¹
— Statistical account of French forests. 1894. IV. 362.
— Timber trade in Assam. 1879. IV. 407.²
— A visit to Kuch Behar. 1885. IV. 378.
— *See also* NÖRDLINGER, Hermann & FISHER, W. R.
Fisheries, game and forest law of the state of New York. 1897. IV. 314.²
Fisk, Charles Ezra. The need of better forestry laws. 1896. IV. 179.¹
Fitch, Asa. Report on the noxious ... insects of the state of New York. 1856. III. 186.²
Fitch, Augustus. The shrubs, flowers and plants of California. 1854. I. 322.
— Trees of California and Oregon. 1854. I. 320, IV. 77.²
Fitch, Charles Hall. Woodland of Indian Territory. 1900. IV. 341.²
Fitch, W. G. Le dessin appliqué à la botanique. 1877. I. 516.
Fitch, Walter Hood & **Smith**, W. G. Illustrations of the British flora. 1880. I. 403.
FitzGerald, P. Fuchsia Ricartoni as a hedge plant. 1872. III. 640.²
Fitting, Hans. Geschichte der hallischen Floristik. 1896. I. 80.¹

Fitton, Elizabeth & Sarah Mary. Conversations on botany. 1817. I. 94.
Fitton, William Henry. A geological sketch of the vicinity of Hastings. 1833. I. 533.
Fitz, Albert. Ueber das Traubenkernöl. 1871. II. 508.¹
Fitz, James. The southern Apple and Peach culturist. 1872. III. 133.
FitzGerald, Edward Arthur. The highest Andes. 1899. I. 331.
Fitzgerald, Henry Purefoy. Dictionary of the names of British plants. 1885. I. 76.²
Fitzgerald, Keane. Experiments on checking the ... growth of fruit-trees. 1762. III. 174.¹
Fitzgerald, Philip S. The effects of moisture on Pine. 1883. IV. 462.²
Fitzherbert, S. W. Rhododendrons at Tremough. 1900. III. 656.
Fitz-James, Löwenhjelm, *duchesse* de. Action de la chaux sur les Vignes. 1885. III. 579.
— Grande culture de la Vigne américaine en France. 1881. III. 556.
— La Vigne américaine en Amérique. 1881. III. 550.
— La Vigne américaine en France. 1881. III. 556.
— Les Vignes américaines. 1881. III. 556.
— La viticulture franco-américaine. 1889. III. 556.
Fitzpatrick, Thomas Jefferson. Manual of the flowering plants of Iowa. 1899. I. 327.
— Notes on the flora of northeastern Iowa. 1898. I. 327.
— & M. F. L. Flora of southern Iowa. 1898. I. 327.
— & — The genus Viburnum in Iowa. 1900. II. 842.²
Fivaller de Velaz, José Maria de. Colección de maderas. n. d. IV. 20.²
— Colección de maderas. 1867. I. 37,² IV. 17.
Five hundred Indian plants. *See* STOLZ, C. & PLÆBST, G. 1881. III. 92.²
Die **Fixirung** der Gehölsformen. 1869. I. 248.²
Fjelstrup, S. A. Forsög ... med adskillige Skov-Træers Plantning. 1831. IV. 156.¹
— Min Mening om Plantagerne paa Alheden. 1830. IV. 156.¹
Flacourt, Étienne de. Histoire de la grande isle Madagascar. 1658. I. 496.
Flad, Henry. Wood preservation. 1887. IV. 420.
Flad, Joann Daniel. Natürliche Geschichte des Kirschenwurms. 1775. III. 435.¹
Flagg, Wilson. Beauty of trees. 1868. I. 516.
— The woods and by-ways of New England. 1872. V. xvii.¹
— A year among the trees. 1881. I. 312, V. xvii.¹
Flahault, Charles. L'acclimatation à Hyères. 1900. III. 126.¹
— Sur une carte botanique détaillée de la France. 1894. I. 418.
— Le climat de la Scandinavie. 1880. I. 357.
— La distribution géographique des végétaux dans un coin du Languedoc. 1893. I. 418.
— Essai d'une carte botanique et forestière de la France. 1897. IV. 362.
— La flore de la vallée supérieure du Verdon. 1899. I. 418.
— Sur la formation des matières colorantes. 1879. I. 185.¹
— Note sur les phénomènes périodiques. 1889. I. 221.
— Sur la présence de la matière verte. 1879. I. 141.
— Projet de carte botanique, forestière et agricole de la France. 1894. IV. 362.
— Projet de nomenclature phytogéographique. 1900. I. 301.
— La question forestière. 1891. IV. 281.¹
— La question forestière vue de Collioure. 1895. IV. 47.¹
— Sur les rapports de la radicule avec la tigelle dans l'embryon. 1877. I. 122.
— Recherches sur l'accroissement terminal de la racine. 1878. I. 188.
— Au sujet de la carte botanique forestière et agricole de France. 1896. IV. 362.
— La végétation du Caucase. 1900. I. 370.
— *See also* BONNIER, Gaston & FLAHAULT, Charles; DURAND, Eugène & FLAHAULT, Charles.
— & Combres, Pierre. Sur la flore de la Camargue. 1894. I. 418.
Flamant, Adolphe. Orange culture. 1880. I. 500.¹
Flammarion, Camille. Étude de l'action des diverses radiations du spectre solaire. 1895. I. 230.
— Sur le froid de la nuit du 17 au 18 mai. 1871. III. 48.
Flandin, Ch. Note sur une methode de dépouiller les marron d'Inde de leur principe amer. 1848. III. 538.¹
— Sur la préparation de la fécule de marron d'Inde. 1849. III. 538.¹

Flatt, Károly ALFÖLDI. Bibliotheca botanica. 1891. I. 3.[1]
— Az Északi Egyesült Államok Tölgyei. 1888. II. 128.[2]
— A Ginkgo-fa történetéhez. 1896. III. 287.[1]
— A Jósikafáról, Syringa Josikaea. 1891. II. 715.[2]
— A Syringa Josikaea Biharban. 1886. II. 715.[1]
— A Syringa Josikaea Jacq. fil. faji önállóságáról. 1887. II. 715.[1]
Flavitzki, Flavian. See ФЛАВИЦКІЙ, Ф.
Flechtner, Johannes. Das National-Arboretum zu Zöschen. 1891. I. 49.
Fleck, Hugo. Einige Fingerzeige, welche aus der Gestaltung der Holzverwerthung . . . folgen. 1878. IV. 388.[1]
— Noch einige Worte über die Bruchschäden des Jahres 1868. 1873. IV. 190.
— Ein Wort über Ertragsverhältnisse bei den Durchforstungen. 1875. IV. 175.[2]
Die **Fleckenkrankheit** der Lärche. 1868. IV. 450.
Fleckles, L. Karlsbad. See ORTMANN, Anton. 1838. I. 440.
Fleiner, Albert. Engelberg. See CHRIST, Hermann. 1890. I. 437.
Fleischer, Ant. Bol. Der Fichtenborkenkäfer. 1877. IV. 204.
Fleischer, E. Die Wasch- und Spritzmittel. 1891. III. 197.
Fleischer, Esaias. Forsög til en dansk havebog. 1782. III. 100.[2]
— Forsög til en Undervüsning i det danske og norske Skov-Væsen. 1779. IV. 94.[1]
Fleischer, Frans. Beiträge zur Lehre von dem Keimen. 1851. I. 202.[2]
— Ueber Missbildungen verschiedener Kulturpflanzen. 1862. II. 154.[1]
Fleischer, H. E. Beiträge zur Embryologie der Monokotylen und Dikotylen. 1874. I. 122.
Fleischer, I. Theoph. Enumeratio plantarum . . . in Curonia, Livonia, Esthoniaque. 1829. I. 360.
Fleischer, Johann Gottlieb. Flora der deutschen Ostseeprovinzen. 1839. I. 361.
— Flora von Esth-, Liv- und Kurland. 1839. I. 361.
— S stematisches Verzeichniss der in den Ostseeprovinzen bisyjetzt bekannt gewordenen Phanerogamen. 1830. I. 360.
Fleischer, M. Ueber Einfluss des Bodens auf den Gerbstoff der Eichenrinde. 1880. II. 131.[2]
— Die Thätigkeit der Central-Moor-Kommission. 1882. IV. 158.
Fleischhack, H. Einiges über Paeonia arborea. 1888. III. 393.[1]
Fleischhauer, Johan Jacob. Öconomische Vorschläge die Lüneburger Heyde arthaft zu machen. 1754. IV. 145.
Fleischinger, (Raths-Zimmermeister, Berlin). Bemerkungen über . . . Cactus speciosus. 1824. III. 621.[1]
Fleischmann, A. Die Sonneberger Spielwaaren-Hausindustrie. 1883. IV. 404.[1]
Fleischmann, Andreas. Uebersicht der Flora Krains. 1844. I. 440.
Fleischmann, Johann Martin. Ueber die Erziehung der Maulbeerbäume. 1784. III. 373.
Fleming. See CHALONER, Edward & FLEMING.
Fleming, John. A catalogue of Indian medicinal plants. 1810, 1812. I. 75,[2] III. 92.[1]
— Catalogue raisonné des plantes employées en médecine dans l'Inde. 1812. III. 92.[1]
— On the duration of the life of plants. 1856. I. 192.[2]
— Naamlijst van indische geneeskundige planten. 1812. II. 92.[1]
— On the species of Pine . . . " Dr. Walker's Pouch Fir." 1858. III. 308.[1]
— On a submarine forest in the Firth of Tay. 1823. I. 393.[1]
— Verzeichniss indischer Arzneigewächse. 1810, 1812. I. 75,[2] III. 92.[1]
Flemming, Hanns Friedrich von. Der vollkommene Teutsche Jäger. 1719. IV. 115, V. XXXI.[1]
— Vollkommener deutscher Jäger und Fischer. 1719. IV. 381.
Flemming, Paul. Gesetze, Verordnungen und Instruktionen, welche auf das Forstwesen Bezug haben. 1888. IV. 322.[1]
Fleroff, A. T. Pflanzengeographische Skizzen. 1898. I. 367.
Fletcher, Alice C. The emblematic use of the trees. 1897. I. 517.[2]
Fletcher, James. Practical entomology. 1895. III. 197.
— Recent additions to the list of injurious insects of Canada. 1899. III. 188.[1]

Fletcher, Joseph J. The Macleay memorial volume. 1893. I. 504.
Fletcher, T. C. Wenken voor landbouwers. 1863. III. 106.[1]
Fletcher, T. H. See HANRATTY, M. & FLETCHER, T. H.
Fleurent, E. Recherches sur la constitution des matières albuminoides. 1893. I. 177.
Fleurot. Lettre sur un grand Peuplier à Dijon. 1839. II. 98.[1]
Fleury. Sur la rhamnine. 1841. III. 542.[1]
Fleury, F. P. Considérations sur l'intérêt . . . à maintenir en France une administration forestière. 1818. IV. 275.
Fleury, G. Sur l'écorce de Goyavier. 1878. III. 637.[2]
— Sur la gomme de Grevillea. 1884. III. 383.[1]
— Observations sur la maturation des dattes. 1877. III. 329.[2]
— Sur la recherche du principe actif du Garou. 1879. III. 627.[2]
— Recherches chimiques sur la germination. 1864. I. 203.
— Recherches chimiques sur la germination. 1865. I. 203.
Fleury, V. Produits comparés des taillis et des futaies. 1868. IV. 259.[1]
Fleury Percie du Sert. See ROSTAING, Léon & Marcel & FLEURY PERCIE DU SERT.
Fliche, H. Manuel de botanique forestière. 1873. IV. 85.[1]
Fliche, Paul. Enseignement du droit forestier. 1895. IV. 35.[1]
— Étude sur le Pin Pinier, P. Pinea. 1886. II. 45.[1]
— Étude sur les flores de l'Aube et de l'Yonne. 1894. I. 418.
— Modifications subies par la végétation forestière dans le bassin de la Seine. 1881. I. 404,[2] IV. 85.[2]
— Les naturalisations forestières en France. 1898. IV. 127.[1]
— Note sur des bois soumis à un enfouissement prolongé. 1880. IV. 413.[2]
— Note sur l'Orchestes Quercus. 1878. IV. 510.
— Note sur la présence . . . du Vaccinium Myrtillus L. variété leucocarpum. 1892. II. 686.[2]
— Note sur les formes du genre Ostrya. 1888. II. 122.[2]
— Note sur les tufs du Brabant. 1898. II. 121.[2]
— Note sur une substitution ancienne d'essences forestières aux environs de Nancy. 1886. II. 126.[1]
— Notes pour servir à l'étude de la nervation. 1886. I, 110.
— Notes sur la flore de la Corse. 1889. I. 419.[1]
— Une nouvelle localité d'Ostrya carpinifolia. 1899. II. 122,[2] IV. 492.[1]
— L'Ostrya carpinifolia dans la forêt de Miolans. 1899. IV. 492.[1]
— Le Pin sylvestre (Pinus silvestris L.) dans les dépôts quaternaires. 1889. II. 46.[2]
— Le Pin sylvestre quaternaire. 1900. IV. 483.[1]
— Un reboisement. 1888. I. 404,[1] IV. 485,[2] 163.
— Recherches botaniques et forestières sur un reboisement. 1888. IV. 163.
— Recherches chimiques . . . sur la famille des Ericinées 1889. II. 659.[1]
— Du sol des environs de Fontainebleau. 1876. I. 228.[2]
— De la végétation des tourbières . . . de Troyes. 1876. I. 415.
— Végétation des tourbières . . . de Troyes. 1877. I. 415.
— & Grandeau, Louis. Einfluss der chemischen Zusammensetzung des Bodens auf das Wachsthum der echten Kastanie. 1874. II. 124.[2]
— — De l'influence de la composition chimique du sol. 1873. II. 44,[2] IV. 467.[2]
— — De l'influence de la composition chimique du sol sur la végétation du Châtaignier. 1874. II. 124.[2]
— — Recherches chimiques . . . sur la Bruyère commune. 1884. II. 662.[1]
— — Recherches chimiques sur la composition des feuilles. 1876. I. 153.
— — Recherches chimiques sur la composition des feuilles du Pin noir. 1877. II. 44.[1]
— — Recherches chimiques sur les Papilionacées ligneuses. 1879. II. 321.[2]
Flinck, J. A. Viktis sockens kärlväxter. 1900. I. 368.[1]
Flinders, Matthew. A voyage to Terra Australis. See BROWN, Robert. 1814. I. 500.
Flint, William F. Catalogue [of the plants of Grafton county]. 1886. I. 531.[1]
— Rhus Toxicodendron. 1880. II. 459.[1]
— The trees and shrubs composing the New Hampshire forests. 1885. I. 312, IV. 77.[1]
Flodberg, Johannes Erik & Hedrén, É. De camphora ejusque usu therapeutico. 1834. III. 233.[1]

Floder, Ali. Synopsis plantarum paroeciae Uplandiae Funbø. 1853. I. 355.
Floderus, B. G. O. Bidrag till kännedomen om Salixfloran. 1891. II. 100.[2]
— Salices från Jämtlands fjälltrakter. 1886. II. 100.[2]
Floderus, M. M. & **Krok**, Th. Förteckning öfver Skandinaviska halföns fanerogamer. 1861. I. 356.
Flörke, F. J. Oekonomisch-technologische Encyclopädie. *See* KRÜNITZ, J. G. 1773. III. 30.
Flörke, Heinrich Gustav. Ueber die Abstufungen der Vegetation im salzburgischen Gebirge. 1800. I. 439.
— Einige Bemerkungen über das Unbestimmte der Begriffs der Varietäten. 1810. I. 251.
— Oekonomisch-technologische Encyclopädie. *See* KRÜNITZ, J. G. 1773. III. 30.
Flöystrup, P. Bidrag til Hortensia-Kulturen. 1892. III. 412.[2]
Floh, J. H. Verhandeling over de ziekten der vruchtboomen. 1809. III. 178.
Flor, M. R. Systematisk characteristik over de i Christiania omegn vildvoxende planter. 1817. I. 352.
Flora. I. 11.
Flora anglica; ou, Flore angloise. 1764. I. 395.
Flora austriaca. *See* SCHULTES, J. A. 1794. I. 439.
Flora berolinensis. *See* HECKER, J. J. 1757. I. 373.
Flora bremensis. *See* DREIER, Johann, FOCKE, W. O. & KOTTMEIER, Johann. 1855. I. 383.
Flora; časopis vědeckozahradnický. III. 24.[2]
Flora Columbiana. 1876. I. 319.
Flora complète d'Indre et Loire. *See* DUJARDIN, Félix. 1838. I. 409.
Flora der Gewæchshæuser und Gærten Europas. *See* FLORE des serres . . . III. 15.
Flora domestica. *See* PHILLIPS, Henry. 1823. I. 511, *III. 81*.
Flora en pomona. III. 14.
Flora farmaceutica. *See* NOCCA, Domenico. 1826. III. 56.
Flora fennica. Suomen Kasvisto. *See* LÖNNROT, Elias. 1860. I. 362.
Flora, jaarboekje . . . III. 14.
Flora medica. *See* SPRATT, George. 1829. III. 56.
Flora of Cumberland, Maryland. *See* SHRIVER, Howard. 18 . .? I. 318.
The flora of Liverpool. 1867, 1872. I. 402, V. XXI.[1]
Flora of Marlborough. *See* PRESTON, T. A. 1863. I. 401.
Flora of Nebraska. I. 326.
Flora of St. Vincent and adjacent islets. 1893. I. 337.
Flora of the Blue Hills. *See* DEANE, Walter. 1896. I. 316.
The flora of the Solomon Islands. 1895. II. 57.[2]
The flora of the state of Texas. 1879. I. 324.
Flora paulista. *See* LÖFGREN, Alberto. 1897. I. 343.
Flora repandunensis. *See* WYATT, W. & THORNTON, C. G. 1866. I. 402.
Flora silvestre del cantón de Xalapa. 1899. I. 333.
Flora stuttgardiensis. *See* KERNER, J. S. von. 1786. I. 374.
The flora telegraph. 1836. I. 515.
Flora universalis. 1805. I. 265.
Flora vectiana. *See* SNOOKE, W. D. 1823. I. 397.
Flora wellingtonensis. 1868. I. 402, V. XXI.[1]
Florae anglicae specimen. *See* CULLUM, T. G. 1775. I. 395.
Florae italicae prodromus. *See* TURRA, Antonio. 1780. I. 424.
Florae lusitanicae et brasiliensis specimen. *See* VANDELLI, Domingos. 1788. I. 341.
Florae tyrnaviensis indigenae. *See* HORVATOVSZKY, Sigismund. 1774. I. 444.
Floraison de l'Amherstia nobilis. *See* EALING Park. 1849. III. 466.[2]
Floraison de la Paulownia imperialis. 1859. III. 703.[2]
Floraison du Kentia australis. 1890. III. 326.[1]
Floraison du Metternichia principis. 1852. III. 701.[1]
Floraison du Paulownia à Angers. 1847. III. 703.[1]
Floraison du Paulownia imperialis. 1860. III. 703.[2]
Floraison et fructification du Jubaea spectabilis. 1886. III. 326.[1]
Floral cabinet. III. 16.
Floral magazine. III. 16.
Floral magazine and botanical repository. III. 3.
The floral register. *See* MAUND, Benjamin. 1825. III. 81.
Floral world. III. 16.
Les floralies gantoises de 1898. 1898. III. 513.[2]
Flore analytique du département des Alpes-Maritimes. *See* ARDOINO, Honoré. 1867. I. 413.

Flore de Bourgogne. *See* DURANDE, J. F. 1782. I. 405.
Flore de l'amateur, choix des plantes. 1847. I. 269, III. 87.
Flore de Paris, genera et species. *See* LEFÉBURE, Louis. 1835. I. 409.
Flore des jardins du royaume des Pays-Bas. *See* ANNALES d'horticulture. III. 14.
Flore des serres et des jardins de l'Europe. III. 15.
Flore des serres et jardins de Paris. 1834. III. 86.
Flore du département du Rhone. 1853. I. 411.
Flore n m des plantes. *See* BUC'HOZ, P. J. 1799. III. 8floo o ique
Flore et faune de Virgile. *See* PAULET, J. J. 1824. I. 514.[1]
Florence — Congresso internationale botanico. *See* CONGRESSO . . . I. 24.[2]
Florence — Imperiale museo. *See* IMPERIALE . . . I. 25.
Florence — Real società economica. *See* REALE ACCADEMIA ECONOMICO-AGRARIA DEI GEORGOFILI . . . III. 23.[2]
Florence — Reale accademia economico agraria dei georgofili. *See* REALE . . . III. 23.[2]
Florence — Reale museo di fisica e storia naturale. *See* REALE . . . I. 25.
Floreno, Girolamo. Sull' importanza del mantenimento de' boschi. 1862. IV. 43.
Floret, P., COSTE-. *See* COSTE-FLORET, P.
Floricultural cabinet. III. 16.
Floricultural magazine. III. 16.
Floriculture. 1865. III. 389.
Florida — State agricultural college. Agricultural experiment station. Annual report. Bulletin. III. 3.
Florida agricultural experiment station. *See* FLORIDA — STATE AGRICULTURAL COLLEGE. III. 3.
Florida; its climate, soil . . . *See* CARSE, G. B. & FOSS, J. H. 1882. III. 117.[2]
Florida, its climate, soil, and productions. 1869. III. 117.[2]
See also ADAMS, J. S. 1869. III. 264.[1]
Florida Pines. 1892. II. 44.[1]
Florida state horticultural society. Proceedings. III. 3.
Florida Velvet Bean. 1898. III. 482.[1]
Floridus, MACER. *See* MACER FLORIDUS.
Florin, Isaac. Rön och Anmärkningar om utländska wäxter. *See* GADD, P. A. 1777. III. 120.[1]
Florinus, Frans Philipp. Oeconomus prudens et legalis. 1702. IV. 115.
Florio, Giovanni. Ricerche sperimentali sugl' innesti. 1836. I. 146.
— Intorno alla spiegazione data di un caso singolare d' innesto. 1832. I. 210.[1]
The Florist. III. 16.
The Florist and garden miscellany. *See* The FLORIST. III. 16.
The Florist and horticultural journal. III. 3.
The Florist and pomologist. *See* The FLORIST. III. 16.
The Florist, fruitist . . . *See* The FLORIST. III. 16.
The Florist's exchange. III. 3.
The Florist's journal. III. 16. *See also* BRITISH florist. III. 16.
The Florists' magazine. III. 16.
Florula columbiensis. 1819. I. 318.
Floss, (*Privat-Forstsekretair*), Nachricht über die Veredlung der Ebereschen. 1829. III. 445.[1]
Flossordnung für den fränkischen Wald. 1868. IV. 300.[1]
Flot, Léon. Sur l'origine des tissus dans la feuille. 1900. I. 111, *184*.
— Sur le péricycle interne. 1893. I. 128.[2]
— Recherches sur la structure . . . de la tige des arbres. 1890. I. 126.
— Recherches sur la zone périmedullaire. 1893. I. 129.[1]
— Sur la région tigellaire des arbres. 1889. I. 106.[1]
Flotow, Gustav, *Graf* von. Über einige Behauptungen der Herren van Mons und Poiteau. 1841. I. 247.
— Einige Erläuterungen zu den Anmerkungen . des Herrn Justisrath Burchhard . 1642. I. 247.
— Einige Worte über die van Mons'sche Theorie. 1841. I. 247.
Flotow, Julius von. Ueber den Unterschied zwischen Apfel, Birne und Quitte. 1855. II. 278.[1]
Flourens, Gustave. Tableau des inflorescences. 1863. I. 113.[2]
Flourens, Marie Jean Pierre. Note sur la maladie de la Vigne. 1857. III. 577.
— Note sur un ouvrage par de Martini sur la santonine. 1858. III. 754.[2]
Flower, John. On a portion of the trunk of a Horse-Chestnut. 1878. I. 210,[2] *III. 587*.[1]

Flower, Thomas Bruges. The flora of Wiltshire. 1858. I. 401.[1]
— Flora thanetensis. 1847. I. 399.
The **Flower** garden. III. 3.
The **flower** garden display'd. 1732. III. 80.
Flower lore. 187.[?] I. 518.
Flower lore, December. 1881. I. 518.
The **Flowering** Ash. 1895. III. 672.[2]
The **flowering** Camoensia maxima. 1895. III. 469.[2]
The **Flowering** Dogwood. 1890. II. 655.[1]
Flowering of Camoensia maxima in England. 1894. III. 469.[2]
The **flowering** of seedlings of Dendrocalamus strictus. 1900. II. 60.[1]
Flowering plants. See CARR, E. D. 1865. I. 401.
Flowers and fruits of Australia. 1844. I. 501.
Flowers of Calligonum. 1889. III. 387.[1]
Flowers on midsummer shoots of the Apple. 1899. II. 276.[1]
Floyd, John. An experimental enquiry into the medical properties of the Magnolia. 1806. III. 399.[1]
Floyer, E. A. Note sur quelques plantes utiles. 1894. III. 131.[1]
Ueber die **flüchtigen** Säuren des Oels des Spindelbaums. 1851. II. 468.[1]
Flückiger, Friedrich A. Australische Manna. 1894. III. 710.[2]
— Sur le camphre. 1868. III. 233.[1]
— Ueber Carvol. 1876. III. 511.[1]
— Die Chinarinden. 1883. III. 725.[1]
— The cinchona barks. 1883. III. 725.[1]
— Sur la cire du Hêtre. 1875. IV. 500.[1]
— Contributions to the history of butine. 1870. III. 396,[1] 407.[2]
— Documente zur Geschichte der Pharmacie. 1876. III. 239.
— An Easter holiday in Liguria. 1877. I. 428.
— Sur les écorces de Quinquina. 1867. III. 724.[2]
— Effets d'un froid intense sur le Laurier-cerise. 1880. III. 437.[2]
— Essence de Cananga ou d'Ilang-Ilang. 1881. III. 401.[2]
— Sur l'essence de Roses. 1870. III. 454.[2]
— Experiments on some varieties of camphor. 1874. III. 757.[2]
— Sur les feuilles de Buku ou Buchu. 1874. III. 495.[1]
— Die Frankfurter Liste. 1872. III. 239.
— La gardenine et la résine dikamali. 1877. III. 744.[2]
— Gegenwärtiger Stand unserer Kenntnis des Curare. 1890. III. 683.[2]
— Zur Geschichte des Gewürznelken. 1885. III. 635.[2]
— Zur Geschichte des Buxins. 1869. III. 396,[2] 407.[2]
— Zur Geschichte des Camphers. 1867. III. 404.[2]
— Grundlagen der pharmaceutischen Waarenkunde. 1873. III. 258.
— Grundlagen der Pharmacognosie. 1873. III. 258.
— Grundriss der Pharmakognosie. 1884. III. 259.[1]
— Gummi und Bdellium vom Senegal. 1869. III. 466,[1] 511.[1]
— Sur l'huile de bois. 1876. III. 610.[2]
— L'huile essentielle des feuilles de Buchu. 1880. III. 495.[2]
— Indische Pharmacognosie. 1884. III. 278.
— Lehrbuch der Pharmakognosie des Pflanzenreiches. 1867. III. 258.
— On the manna from Kurdistan. 1872. III. 221.[1]
— Sur la manne de Chêne du Kurdistan. 1872. III. 221.[1]
— Eine merkwürdige Form des Stärkmehles. 1868. II. 623.[2]
— La Mortola. 1886. I. 64, V. VIII.[2]
— Das Nördlinger Register. 1877. III. 239.
— Note on carvol. 1876. III. 511.[1]
— Note on the early history of Canada balsam. 1882. III. 295.[2]
— Note on the "saponin" of Sarsaparilla. 1877. III. 338.[2]
— Notes on Cananga oil or Ilang-ilang oil. 1881. III. 401.[2]
— Notiz über Buchenwachs. 1875. IV. 500.[1]
— Notiz über die Eichenmanna. 1872. III. 221,[1] 362.[1]
— Notiz über sogenanntes Holzöl. 1876. III. 225.[1]
— Notizen über das Canangaöl. 1881. III. 401.[2]
— Notizen über das Saponin der Sarsaparilla. 1877. III. 338.[2]
— Osterferien im Süden. 1889. I. 429.
— Pharmaceutische Chemie. 1879. I. 152.[1]
— Pharmakognosie des Pflanzenreiches. 1867. III. 258.
— Ueber Stärke und Cellulose. 1871. I. 525.

— Sur le stearoptène de l'huile essentielle de muscade. 1874. III. 403.[1]
— The stearoptene of oil of Nutmeg. 1874. III. 403.[1]
— Sur le Storax américain. 1883. III. 418.[1]
— Strychnos Ignatii. 1889. III. 684.[2]
— Über die Verbreitung der Alkaloide in den Strychnos-Arten. 1892. III. 683.[2]
— See also SANSON, A., FLÜCKIGER, F. A. & SPADARO.
— & Buri, Eugen. Koein. 1875. III. 424.[2]
— & Gerock, J. E. Contributions to the knowledge of Catha leaves. 1888. III. 531.[2]
— & Hanbury, Daniel. Histoire des drogues d'origine végétale. 1874. III. 258.
— — Pharmacographia. 1874. III. 258.
— & Meyer, Arthur. Notes on the fruit of Strychnos Iguatii. 1882. III. 684.[2]
Flückiger, G. Bericht ... über die österreichischen Obstbauverhältnisse. 1889. III. 127.[1]
— Rapport ... sur les conditions de l'arboriculture ... en Autriche. 1889. III. 127.[1]
Flühler, Ad. Die Krankheit der Agrumen in Sizilien. 1874. III. 498.[1]
Flügge. Description d'une nouvelle espèce d'Aubépine. 1868. II. 261.[2]
Fluke, N. K. Influence of stock on scion. 1889. III. 40.
— Not well known Conifers. 1888. III. 293.
— Ornamental shrubs. 1893. III. 60.
— Top grafting. 1889. III. 426.[2]
Flüry, Hippolyte. Mémoire sur la culture des Caroubiers. 1844. III. 471.[2]
Flury, Philipp. Die Abrundung der Durchmesser. 1892. IV. 219.
— Berechnung der Holzmasse eines stehenden Bestandes. 1897. IV. 219.
— Einfluss der Berindung auf die Kubirung. 1897. IV. 229.
— Ergebnisse aus Kahlschlägen. 1898. IV. 219.
— Ueber die Gesetzmässigkeit im Wachstumsgange. 1898. IV. 234.
— Die Grundflächenermittelung. 1891. IV. 219.
— Untersuchungen über das spezifische Gewicht des Reisigs. 1892. IV. 387.[2]
— Untersuchungen über das Verhältniss der Reisigmasse. 1892. IV. 387.[2]
— Untersuchungen über die Abnahme des Durchmessers mit der Höhe. 1894. IV. 228.
— Untersuchungen über die Entwickelung der Pflanzen. 1895. III. 38.[2]
— Untersuchungen über die Genauigkeit der Grundflächenermittelung. 1891. IV. 218.
— Untersuchungen über die Genauigkeit der Kubirung liegender Stämme. 1892. IV. 228.
— Untersuchungen über die Verwendbarkeit des arithmetischen Mittelstammes. 1894. IV. 219.
— See also BÜHLER, Anton & FLURY, Ph.
Flygare, Axel & Alner, Federicus Ad. Stirpium in Guinea medicinalium species cognitae. 1817. III. 93.[1]
Flygare, Joannes. De coloniis plantarum. See LINNÉ, Carl von. 1786. I. 241.[1]
Fobe, Fr. Etwas über Euphorbien. 1898. III. 517.[1]
— Euphorbia Hermentiana. 1897. III. 518.[1]
— Opuntia clavarioides Pfeiffer. 1900. III. 624.[1]
Fock, A. See FOKK, A.
Fock, L. C. E. E. Natuur en geneeskundig etymologisch woordenboek. 1855. I. 76.[2]
Focke, Gustav Woldemar. De respiratione vegetabilium. 1833. I. 169.[2]
Focke, H. C. Lijst der planten, welke in de kolonie Suri name gekweekt. 1849. III. 64.[2]
— Nog iets over hout. 1858. IV. 521.[2]
Focke, Ludwig Emil. Leitfaden für den Unterricht in der Botanik. 1846. I. 88.
Focke, Wilhelm Olbers. Anpassungs-Erscheinungen bei einigen Kletterpflanzen. 1875. I. 236.[1]
— Ueber den Artbegriff im Pflanzenreiche. 1877. II. 300.
— Batographische Abhandlungen. 1874. II. 300.[1]
— Batographische Abhandlungen. 1875. II. 300,[2] 305.[2]
— Ueber die Begriffe Species und Varietas. 1875. I. 244.[2]
— Beiträge zur Kenntnis der deutschen Brombeeren. 1868. II. 301.[1]
— Bemerkungen über die Wildrosen ... von Bremen. 1899. II. 285.[1]
— Bemerkungen über einige Rubus-Arten. 1870. II. 300, 308.[2]

Focke, Wilhelm Olbers (continued).
— Eine Birne mit zweierlei Blättern. 1894. II. 279.[1]
— Die Blüthezeiten von Vaccinium Vitis Idaea. 1873. II. 687.[2]
— Die Culturvarietäten der Pflanzen. 1887. I. 248.[1]
— Ueber dichotype Gewächse. 1868. I. 271,[2] 524.[1]
— Über einige Bastarde von Rosa rugosa. 1897. II. 298.[1]
— Einige Bemerkungen über Wald und Haide. 1872. I. 386.
— Über einiga Rosaceeen aus den Hochgebirgen Neuguineas. 1895. II. 309.[1]
— Die Entstehung des zygomorphen Blüthenbaues. 1887. I. 115.[1]
— Eucryphiaceae. 1895. II. 544.[1]
— Der Farbenwechsel der Rosskastanien-Blumen. 1890. II. 482.[2]
— Flora kalkführender Sanddünen. 1893. I. 389.
— Zur Flora von Bremen. 1886. II. 308.[1]
— Zur Flora von Bremen. 1887. II. 284.[2]
— Früchte von Prunus lusitanica. 1877. III. 438.[1]
— Die Herkunft der Vertreter der nordischen Flora. 1890. I. 389.
— Ist Vitis vinifera eine Art oder ein Bastart? 1876. II. 507.[1]
— Über die Keimpflanzen der Stein- und Kernobstgewächse. 1900. II. 257.[1]
— Die Keimung von Kerria. 1892. II. 265.[1]
— Zur Kenntnis einiger ausländischen Rubus-Arten. 1899. II. 300.[2]
— Künstliche Pflanzen-Mischlinge. 1880. II. 300.[2]
— Mehrjährige Samenruhe. 1893. I. 527.
— Meine Brombeer-Studien. 1877. II. 300.[1]
— Nägeli's Einwände gegen die Blumentheorie. 1884. I. 238.
— Über die natürliche Gliederung ... der Gattung Rubus. 1881. II. 300.[2]
— Ueber den Nebenblätter von Exochorda. 1887. II. 264.[1]
— Nebenwurzeln in alten Weidenstämmen. 1877. II. 104.[1]
— Neue Beobachtungen über Artenkreuzung. 1897. I. 239,[1] II. 298.[1]
— Eine neue Rubus-Art aus China. 1897. II. 308.[2]
— Neue Verfälschung von Kamala. 1895. III. 520.[2]
— Die nordwestdeutschen Rubus-Formen. 1885. II. 302.[1]
— Notes on English Rubi. 1890. II. 303.[1]
— Nouvelle falsification du kamala. 1895. III. 520.[2]
— Pflanzenbiologische Skizzen. 1883. I. 271.[2]
— Die Pflanzen-Mischlinge. 1881. I. 271.[2]
— Pinus Mughus Scop. 1877. II. 43.[1]
— Die Pyramidenpappeln. 1883. III. 346.[2]
— Quittenähnliche Aepfel. 1875. II. 267.[1]
— Rosa rugosa × multiflora. 1899. II. 298.[2]
— Rosaceae. 1894. II. 256.[1]
— Rubi americani. 1875. II. 300.[2]
— Rubi australienses. 1875. II. 305.[2]
— Die Rubi der Canaren. 1892. II. 305.[2]
— Die Rubi der Canaren. Rubus Bollei, R. canariensis. 1887. II. 305.[1]
— Rubi nonnulli asiatici. 1877. II. 305.[1]
— Die Rubi Siciliens. 1886. II. 304.[1]
— Rubi species duae novae italicae. 1884. II. 304.[1]
— Rubus. 1885. II. 302.[1]
— Rubus cimbricus n. sp. 1886. II. 306.[2]
— Rubus euprepes n. spec. 1897. II. 307.[1]
— Rubus foliosus × Sprengelii. 1877. II. 307.[1]
— On Rubus Leesii. 1870. II. 308.[2]
— Rubus Leesii Babingt. 1870. II. 308.[2]
— Über Rubus melanolasius. 1896. II. 308.[1]
— Ueber Rubus Menkei. 1894. II. 302.[1]
— Rubus spectabilis × Idaeus. 1891. II. 308.[1]
— Die Rubus-Arten der Antillen. 1890. II. 300.[2]
— Rückschlag bei einer Hortensie. 1897. II. 241.[1]
— Samen der Douglasfichte. 1887. III. 309.[1]
— Short descriptive notes on three Rubi. 1890. II. 303.[1]
— Das Siechthum der Pyramidenpappeln. 1883. III. 346.[2]
— On some hybrid Brambles. 1877. II. 300.[1]
— Spätes Absterben einer vom Blitz getroffenen Eiche. 1879. IV. 194.
— Ein Stück deutschen Urwaldes. 1871. I. 371, IV. 83.
— Synopsis Ruborum Germaniae. 1877. II. 301.[3]
— Die synthetische Methode in der Systematik. 1870. II. 308.[1]
— Thunberg; dissertatio de Rubo. 1892. II. 300.[1]
— Über Unfruchtbarkeit bei Bestäubung mit eigenem Pollen. 1893. I. 239.[1]

— Untersuchungen über die Vegetation des nordwestdeutschen Tieflandes. 1871. I. 386.
— Variationen an gescheckten Hülsen. 1877. II. 463.[2]
— Die Verbreitung beerentragender Pflanzen. 1888. I. 240.[3]
— Die Verbreitung der Pflanzen durch Thiere. 1881. I. 240,[2] 242.[1]
— Ueber die Vermehrung der Weiden. 1873. II. 104.[1]
— Die volksthümlichen Pflanzennamen. 1870. I. 73.[2]
— Vorläufige Mitteilungen über die Verbreitung einiger Brombeeren. 1893. II. 302.[1]
— Die Wanderfähigkeit der Bäume und Sträucher. 1874. I. 241.[2]
— See also BUCHENAU, Franz & FOCKE, W. O.; DREIER, Johann, FOCKE, W. O. & KOTTMEIER, Johann.

Fockel. See ФОКЕЛЬ.

Fockel, E. Eine Säemaschine. 1843. IV. 148.

Focken, H. Contribution à l'histoire des galles. 1889. I. 214.[1]

Fockens, Jacob Wilhelm. Ueber die Luftwurzeln. 1857. I. 103.

Focquereau-Lenfant, J. B. Manuel pratique d'arboriculture fruitière. 1892. III. 145.[1]

Fodder reserves and pastures. 1892. IV. 136.[2]

Fodéré, François Emanuel. Voyage aux Alpes maritimes. 1821. I. 407.

Föhlisch, (Bezirksförster, Ziegelhausen). Bericht über eine forstliche Reise. 1865. IV. 349.[1]

Føhr. Om de forskjellige Træsorters Varighed. 1842. IV. 413.[2]

Fölckel, E. Eine Säemaschine. 1843. IV. 148.

Földes, János. A kései Tölgy. 1892. II. 136.[2]
— A Késői Tölgy (Quercus tardiflora) növekvési viszonyai. 1891. IV. 508.
— A legelő-erdők. 1895. IV. 136.[1]
— Die spätblühende Eiche. 1894. II. 137.[2]
— A Szelid Gesztenye. 1885. IV. 493.[1]
— A szerémi vagy késön virító Tölgy. 1888. II. 136.[2]

Földrajzi közlemények. I. 27.

Om fglgerne af ydre beskadigelser paa træer. 1897. I. 208.[1]

Foelix, Jacques. See VAULX, Charles de & FOELIX, Jacques.

Fölkel, (Oberförster) & **Marks**, (Oberförster, Goschütz). Ueber die Benutzung einjähriger Kiefer-Pflänzlinge. 1849. IV. 472.

Fölkersahm, Baron von. Mittheilungen über den Gemüse- und Gartenbau in Russland. 1853. III. 120.[2]

Die Förderung unseres Forstwesens im XIX. Jahrhundert. 1900. IV. 28.[1]

Förslag till författning rörande dispositionsrätten öfver enskildes skogar. 1875. IV. 315,[1] 344.[2]

Foerste, August F. Abnormal phyllotactic conditions. 1891. II. 498,[2] 707.[1]
— Botanical notes from Bainbridge, Ga. 1893. I. 221.
— On the casting-off of the tips of the branches. 1892. I. 192.[2]
— Curious leaves. 1897. I. 111.
— A curious Rose. 1894. II. 290.[1]
— The identification of trees in winter. 1892. I. 294,[3] IV. 77.[1]
— Large Rhus Toxicodendron. 1883. II. 460.[1]
— Morphological notes. 1883. I. 108.[2]
— The nectar-glands of Apios tuberosa. 1884. I. 192.[1]
— Notes on superposed buds. 1895. I. 108.[2]
— Oaks as weeds. 1894. II. 135.[2]
— On the relation of certain fall to spring blossoming plants. 1892. I. 221.
— The spreading of Raspberry bushes. 1895. II. 306.[1]
— Superposed buds. 1885. I. 108.[2]

Förster, Baron von. Flora excursoria des Regierungsbezirks Aachen. 1878. I. 387.
— Über die Polymorphie der Gattung Rubus. 1879. II. 300.[1]
— See also BEY, de, FOERSTER, A. & MONHEIM, V.

Förster, Carl Friedrich. Beschreibung eines blühenden Cereus Seidelii. 1847. II. 589.[3]
— Beschreibung einiger neuen Cacteen. 1847. II. 586.[1]
— Handbuch der Cacteenkunde. 1846. II. 586.[1]
— Hybris Lorentzii. 1865. III. 621.[1]
— Die Impfungen. 186.? III. 161.
— Neue Cacteen. 1861. II. 586.[3]
— Vorteile der Obstbaumzucht. 1839. III. 137.

Foerster, F. von. Die Korbweidenkultur. 1895. III. 349.

Förster, F. C. & **Beissner**, Ludwig. Der unterweisende Führer durch die gesammte Zier- und Nutzgärtnerei. 1884. III. 104.

Förster, G. R. Aufforstungen im Salzkammergut. 1882. IV. 453.
— Aufforstungen in der Schweiz. 1877. IV. 152.
— Die Central-Anlage für Zirbenpflanzenerziehung. 1888. IV. 463.²
— Das forstliche Transportwesen. 1885. IV. 389.
— Aus dem forstlichen Bauwesen. 1884. IV. 390.²
— Die Fundirung forstlicher Betriebsbauten. 1884. IV. 390.²
— Lawinenverbauungen in der Schweiz. 1877. IV. 188.²
— Motoren für Holzbearbeitungsmaschinen. 1884. IV. 422.¹
— Pilotirungen bei forstlichen Bauwerken. 1884. IV. 390.²
— Riesweg-Anlagen in den Forsten des Salzkammergutes. 1875. IV. 391.
— Von der Standfestigkeit der Holzrechen. 1884. IV. 390.²
— Transportes forestales. 1885. IV. 389.
— Ueber Verbauungen von Wildbächen. 1878. IV. 185.¹
— Wildbäche und Lawinen. 1887. IV. 188.²
Der **Förster**. IV. 7.
Des **Försters** Feierabende. IV. 7.
Ueber **Försterschuren**. 1889. IV. 33.²
Förteckning öfver Skandinaviska halföns fanerogamer. *See* FLODERUS, M. M. & KROK, Th. 1861. I. 356.
Förteckning på wäxterna i Skinskattebergs socken. *See* HISINGER, Wilhelm. 1832. I. 353.
Foëx, Gustave. Catalogue des Vignes américaines et asiatiques. 1881. III. 556.
— Cours complet de viticulture. 1886. III. 556.
— Études sur la réinvasion du phylloxera. 1879. III. 571.
— Manuel pratique de viticulture. 1881. III. 556.
— Mémoire sur les causes de la chlorose chez l'Herbemont. 1882. III. 561.
— Notes relatives aux effets produits par le phylloxera. 1876. III. 570.¹
— La plantation de Vignes. 1890. III. 574.
— Résistance des Vignes américaines. 1880. III. 556.
— Sur la structure comparée des racines des Vignes. 1877. III. 570.¹
— Los viñedos nuevos. 1900. III. 551.¹
— & Ravas, L. Sur l'invasion du Coniothyrium. 1887. III. 5'9.
— & Viala, Pierre. Sur la maladie de la Vigne. 1884. III. 578.
Foëx, H. Informe sobre los escarabajos que destruyen el Cocotero. 1887. III. 323.¹
— Rapport sur les scarabées qui detruisent le Cocotier. 1887. III. 323.¹
Foggia, Amalia Moretti. Florula . . . del bosco Fontana. 1895. I. 430.
Foggo, R. G. Remarks on disease of the Beech. 1862. IV. 496.
Foissac, Maurice. Du camphre. 1866. III. 404.¹
Fokel. *See* FOCKEL.
Fokkens, F. *See* LITH, P. A. van der, SPAAN, A. J. & FOKKENS, F.
Fokker, A. Pertoenjoekan hal segela penjakit hewan jang binasa di tanah Hindoestan. 1890. III. 274.³
Folakowski, Emil. O uprawie Winogradu. 1886. III. 558.²
Folbarri, M. P. Procédé pour rendre le bois incombustible. 1879. IV. 420.
Folcari, Vincenzo. Della naturalizzazione delle piante. 1843. III. 43.
Folchi, Giacomo. Alcune ricerche chimiche su la radice di Salsapariglia. 1824. II. 86.¹
— Descrizione degli esemplari delle Chine-chine. 1830. III. 338.¹
Földi, Janos. Rövid kritika és rajzolat a' Magyar füvésztudományról. 1793. I. 444.
Foley, John. Forestry in Western Australia. 1900. IV. 380.¹
Foley, W. Experimental cultivation of the Tea plant by cuttings. 1878. III. 603.
Folgen der Waldstreunutzung. 1862. IV. 71.
Folgner, Victor Alfred Oswald. Beiträge zur Systematik . . . der Pomaceen. 1897. II. 256.¹
Folia carobae. 1880. III. 706.¹
Foliage effects in autumn. 1873. III. 207.¹
Foliage trees. 1886. III. 202.¹
Folin, Léopold, *marquis* de. Le Jardin d'acclimatation d'Orotava. 1884. III. 29.²
Folkard, Richard, (jr.). Plant lore, legends and lyrics. 1884. I. 518.
Folkerma, D. Een woord over land- en tuinbouw. 1860. III. 122.¹
Folklore of budding and grafting. 1881. III. 162.
Folk-lore record. III. 16.

Folli, Francesco. Dialogo intorno alla cultura delle Vite. 1670. III. 557.³
Follie. Sur les Tilleuls de l'esplanade à Metz. 1872. III. 585.³
Folsom, Justus Watson. Autumnal changes in leaves. 1895. I. 186.
Fonck. Erträge einer Weidenheger-Anlage. 1884. IV. 487.¹
Fonscolombe, E. H. BOYER DE. *See* BOYER DE FONSCOLOMBE, E. H.
Fonscolombe, E. L. J. H. BOYER DE. *See* BOYER DE FONSCOLOMBE, E. L. J. H.
Fonseca, A. A. M. V. Alves PEREIRA DA. *See* PEREIRA DA FONSECA, A. A. M. V. A.
Fonseca Benevides, Antonio Albino. Diccionario de glossologia botanica. 1841. I. 71.
Fonssagrives, Jean. Notice sur le Dahomey. 1900. III. 281.¹
Fontaine. Un nouvel ennemi de la Vigne. 1893. III. 564.¹
Fontaine (*of Aerschot*). Un beau revenu. 1896. IV. 259.¹
Fontaine, G. Réglementation de la récolte des cônes. 1896. IV. 439.
Fontaines, Louis Marie Blanquart de SEPT-. *See* SEPT-FONTAINES, L. M. B. de.
Fontaines Biré, de. Sur un Arbutus Andrachne. 1839. III. 647.²
Fontana, Nicolas. On the Nicobar Isles and the fruit of the Meliori. 1792. II. 56.²
Fontaneilles. Rapport sur une nouvelle espèce de Mûrier. 1829. III. 374.
Fontanelle, Julia. Notiz über den Mudar. 1836. III. 692.¹
Fontenelle. Ueber die Manna vom Berge Sinai. 1838. III. 612.¹
Fontenelle, Jean Sebastian Eugène JULIA DE. *See* JULIA DE FONTENELLE, J. S. E. & TOLLARD, Henri.
Fontenille de Laclotte, Jean Philippe MOUTON-. *See* MOUTON-FONTENILLE DE LACLOTTE, J. P.
Fonteny, Bizot de. *See* BIZOT DE FONTENY.
Fonvert, Am., REINAUD DE. *See* REINAUD DE FONVERT, Am.
Fonvert, Amédée de & **Achintre**, Joseph. Catalogue des plantes . . . d'Aix. 1870. I. 414.
Fonvielle, Wilfrid de. Châtaignier géant en Ecosse. 1863. II. 124.²
— Culture de Thé. 1861. III. 600.³
Foote, Arthur DeWint. Forestry problem of the arid region. 1891. IV. 272.
Foraarsfrostens Indvirkning paa de haardförere Træsorter. 1860. III. 182.
Forbes, A. Reisen in den Indischen Archipel. 1888. III. 274.²
Forbes, Alexander. Short hints on ornamental gardening. 1820. III. 123.²
Forbes, Arthur C. The bark-beetles of the Ash. 1899. III. 672.¹
— Diltish Oaks. 1900. II. 100.¹
— The decay of trees. 1899. I. 206.² -
— Draining woodlands. 1896. III. 150.³
— Drought and newly planted trees. 1896. III. 184.¹
— The education of the forester. 1895. IV. 274.³
— The Elm-bark beetle. 1896. III. 365.¹
— On establishing an experimental forest area in Scotland. 1878. IV. 34.¹
— Felling and planting park timber. 1895. III. 202.¹
— The forest school at Eberswalde. 1893. IV. 33.²
— The formation of plantations. 1893. IV. 142.
— Game coverts and sylviculture. 1900. IV. 136.²
— Ground-game and tree-planting. 1895. IV. 136.²
— On growing timber of clean growth. 1895. IV. 121.
— The home nursery. 1899. IV. 151.²
— How timbers are tested in America. 1895. IV. 419.¹
— On the influence of . . . thinning on the growth of Beech. 1899. IV. 496.
— The leafing of trees. 1899. I. 222.¹
— Management of plantations. 1895. IV. 169.¹
— Management of Scots Fir forests in North Germany. 1893. IV. 482.¹
— The mineral-food of Conifers. 1897. II. 21.¹
— Natural regeneration of Scots Fir woods. 1893. IV. 482.¹
— The natural regeneration of woods. 1895. IV. 140.
— North American Conifers in Germany. 1896. III. 293.
— Our woods and forests. 1898. IV. 121.
— Protection of woods from gales. 1894. IV. 189.¹
— The quality of coniferous timber. 1895. IV. 443.¹
— Season and the growth of trees. 1898. III. 38.² ·
— Types of British woodland. 1896. IV. 121.

Forbes, David. Peruvian Cinchona. 1866. III. 712.[1]
Forbes, Edward. On the connexion between . . . fauna and flora of the British Isles. 1846. I. 399.
— On the Dorsetshire Ulices. 1849. II. 387.[1]
— Notices of botanical excursions in the neighbourhood of Trieste. 1840. I. 447.
— *See also* SPRATT, T. A. B. & FORBES, Edward.
Forbes, Francis. The improvement of waste lands. 1778. IV. 120.
Forbes, Francis Blackwell. On Cudrania triloba. 1883. III. 368.[2]
— On some Chinese species of Oaks. 1884. II. 131.[1]
— On some critical Chinese species of Clematis. 1884. II. 196.[1]
— & **Hemsley,** W. B. Enumeration of all the plants known from China. 1886. I. 459.
— — Systematische Aufzählung der bemerkenswerthesten Zier- und Nutzpflanzen Chinas. 1886. I. 459.
Forbes, G. S. Reports on the fibres of southern India. 1856. III. 234.
Forbes, Henry Ogg. A naturalist's wanderings in the eastern archipelago. 1885. I. 466.
— Notes on Carica Papaya. 1879. II. 582.[2]
Forbes, James. On the cultivation and use of Willows. 1863. III. 347.
— On the management of hedges. 1863. III. 213.
Forbes, James, (1773–1861). A catalogue of the different species of Cacteae. 1837. III. 618.[2]
— Culture des Bruyères. 1837. III. 649.[2]
— Hortus Ericaeus woburnensis. *See* SINCLAIR, George.
— Hortus woburnensis. 1833. I. 54.
— Journal of a horticultural tour through Germany. 1837. III. 119.[1]
— Journal of a horticultural tour through some parts of Flanders. 1823. III. 119.[1]
— Lyngarternes Cultur. 1839. III. 646.[2]
— Pinetum woburnense. 1839. II. 12.[2]
— Salictum woburnense. 1829. II. 98.[2]
Forbes, James David. On the climate of Palestine. 1862. III. 328,[2] *559*.[1]
Forbes, L. A. Report on the Bussorah date season. 1898. III. 329.[2]
Forbes, Robert Humphrey. The Mesquite tree. 1895. III. 485.[1]
Forbes, William. The best method of successfully combining the duties of forester and gamekeeper. 1890. IV. 136.[2]
— The best method of thinning mixed plantations. 1890. IV. 174.
— German forestry or sylviculture. 1895. IV. 119.[1]
— The Pine saw-fly. 1895. IV. 462.[1]
— The preparation of land for an estate nursery. 1898. III. 154.[2]
The **forbidden** fruit. 1888. II. 71.[1]
Forbud for dem, som nyde Udviisning af Hans Kongl. Majest. Skove. 1718. IV. 296.[1]
Forbud om Huggen i Geistlig Godses underliggendis Skowe. 1670. IV. 296.[1]
Forbush, Edward Howe & **Fernald,** C. H. The gypsy moth. 1896. III. 187.
Forcade, de. Notions pratique sur le choix et le classement des bois de marine. 1859. IV. 425.[1]
— Rapport sur les forêts de l'état. 1860. IV. 360.
Force, Peter. Tracts and other papers. 1836. III. 262.[1]
Force de la végétation. 1844. I. 187.
Sur la **force** osmotique des solutions diluées. 1883. I. 150.[1]
Forced flowers for winter. 1887. III. 533.[2]
Forchel, F. Arbres, arbustes et plantes ornementales cultivés . . . entre Cannes et Menton. 1885. I. 271.[1]
Forckel, Fréd. Greffage printanier. 1869. III. 161.
— Snelgriffeling ,by lentetyd. 1869. III. 161.
Ford, Charles. Catalogue of plants in the Government gardens, Hong Kong. 1876. I. 66.[2]
— Ice in Hongkong. 1893. III. 127.[2]
— The Lo-fau-shan Mountains. 1884. I. 459.
— Notes on Cinnamomum Cassia. 1882. III. 405.[1]
— Notes on the vegetation of the West River. 1882. I. 459.
— [Report on] Cassia lignea, Cinnamomum Cassia. 1882. III. 405.[1]
— Report on the effects of the late frosts. 1893. III. 50.[1]
— Rhodoleia Championi. 1879. III. 418.[1]
— *See also* PARKER, E. H. & FORD, Charles.
— **Ho Kai &** Crow, W. E. Notes on Chinese materia medica. 1887. III. 273.[1]
— & others. Gelsemium elegans. 1887. III. 682.[1]
— — Strychnos Ignatii Bergius. 1888. III. 684.[2]

Ford, Henry Chapman. The indigenous shrubs of Santa Barbara county. 1890. I. 320.
— The Lyonothamnus aspleniifolius. 1890. II. 265.[2]
Fordos, Mathurin Joseph. Recherches sur la coloration en vert du bois mort. 1863. I. 155.
Fordyce, C. *See* SMYTHIES, A. & FORDYCE, C.
Foreign forest produce. 1884. IV. 396.[2]
A **foreign** resident. 1882. III. 645.[1]
Foreign seeds and plants collected in Austria. 1900. III. 117.[1]
Foreign seeds and plants imported by the Department of agriculture. 1899. III. 117.[1]
Foreign seeds and plants imported by the Department of agriculture. 1900. III. 117.[1]
Foreign seeds and plants imported by the Section of seed and plant introduction. 1899. III. 117.[1]
Forel, François Alphonse Christian. *See* HEIM, Albert, DU PASQUIER, L. & FOREL, F. A.
Forelsbige Regler for Udførelsen af Omreguleringen af Statsskovene. 1877. IV. 296.[1]
Foreningen til diskussion af landbrugsanliggender. Forhandlinger. III. 10.[2]
Forest, A. De la question du reboisement. 1852. IV. 155.[1]
Forest, H. Du cacao et de ses diverses espèces. 1864. III. 594.
Forest administration under Lord Dufferin. 1889. IV. 295.[1]
The **forest** and chaoe of Malvern. 1881. IV. 358.[1]
Forest and irrigation. 1890. IV. 51.
The **forest** Arcadia of northern New York. 1864. IV. 45.
Forest chart of Switzerland. 1893. IV. 367.
Forest clearing by steam. 1874. IV. 383.[2]
Forest conditions and methods of forest management in Germany. 1899. IV. 248.[2]
Forest conference of Indian forest officers. Report. IV. 16.
Forest conservancy. 1881. IV. 49.[1]
Forest conservancy. Return to an address. 1875. V. XXXI.[1]
Forest conservancy in Bombay. 1885. IV. 279.[2]
Forest conservancy in India. 1881. IV. 295.[1]
Forest conservancy in India. 1893. IV. 181.[2]
Forest conservancy in the catchment area of tanks. 1893. IV. 51.
Forest culture in Germany. 1867. IV. 349.[1]
Forest culture in Minnesota. *See* HODGES, L. B. 1876. IV. 271.[2]
Forest department code. *See* CODE of instructions . . . 1877. IV. 307.[2]
The **forest** department of the Biltmore estate, N. C. 1898. IV. 340.
Forest economy in Sweden. 1880. IV. 288.[2]
Forest fire near Murree. 1887. IV. 184.[1]
Forest fires on the St. Lawrence. 1891. IV. 181.[1]
Forest influences on water flow. 1900. IV. 46.[1]
Forest leaves. IV. 4.
Forest life and forest trees. 1852. IV. 397.
The **forest** manual. 1898. IV. 332.[2]
The **forest** manual of Hyderabad. 1899. IV. 332.[2]
Forest map of the Yakima region. 1883. I. 320, *IV. 340.*
Forest of Salcey. 1878. IV. 358.[1]
Forest officers and their duties. 1878. IV. 27.[1]
Forest organization for beginners. 1885. IV. 241.
The **forest** pavilion at the French exhibition. 1890. IV. 20.[2]
Forest policies of European nations. 1899. IV. 271.[1]
A **forest** policy in suspense. 1897. IV. 272.
The **forest** policy of the Madras government. 1898. IV. 279.[2]
Forest products of Sierra Leone. 1897. IV. 401.[1]
Forest protection and the tariff on lumber. 1883. IV. 284.[1]
The **forest** question in Russia. 1883. IV. 273.[2]
Forest renovation at Mount Macedon. 1886. IV. 169.[1]
Forest report on district and canal arboriculture. 1877.
Forest reservation. 1898. IV. 179.[1]
The **forest** reservation policy. 189 . ? IV. 178.[1]
Forest reservations. 1891. IV. 178.[2]
The **forest** reserves. 1897. IV. 179.[1]
The **forest** resources of the West Australian timber company 1886. IV. 531.[1]
The **Forest** school at Dehra Doon. 1879. IV. 37.[1]
Forest school, Dehra Dün. Progress report. 1885. IV. 37.[1]
Forest school, Dehra Dün. Report. IV. 16.[1]
Forest settlements. 1887. IV. 279.[2]
Forest tree planting in Massachusetts. 1889. IV. 112.
La **foresta** di Epping. 1866. IV. 274.[2]

El **forestal** fotógrafo. *See* Le **forestier** photographe. 1895.
  IV. 541.[1]
Un **forestal,** *(pseud.).* Reformas para el ramo de montes.
  1898. IV. 554.
Foreste [dell' Impero francese]. 1863. IV. 360.
Le **foreste** della Corsica. 1882. IV. 360.
Le **foreste** della Dalmazia. 1865. IV. 374.[2]
Le **foreste** della Finlandia. 1882. IV. 347.
Le **foreste** della Sardegna. 1865. IV. 364.
Le **foreste** demaniali. 1865. IV. 277.
Foreste demaniali della Francia. 1866. IV. 360.
Le **foreste** demaniali in Prussia. 1862. IV. 353.
Le **foreste** demaniali in Russia. 1862. IV. 345.
Le **foreste** in Francia. 1862. IV. 360.
Forestel, X. de. Les plantations commémoratives. 1863.
  III. 34.[1]
A **Forester,** *(pseud.).* Deterioration of Scotch Fir. 1891.
  IV. 473.
Forester. IV. 4.
Forestier, A. Mémoire sur la conservation des bois à la mer.
  1868. IV. 419.
— Préservation des bois contre les attaques du taret. 1867.
  IV. 419.
Forestier, J. Calcul graphique du terme de l'exploitabilité.
  1886. IV. 257.
Forestier, J. C. N. Le Sophora. 1899. III. 487.[2]
Un **forestier d'antan,** *(pseud.).* Souvenirs du cantonnement
  de V. 1893. IV. 292.
— Souvenirs et adieu. 1893. IV. 102.
Le **forestier** photographe. 1895. IV. 37,[2] 541.
Forestry. 1889. IV. 357.[2]
Forestry. 1891. IV. 178.[2]
Forestry. 1893. IV. 401.[2]
Forestry. *See* JOURNAL of forestry. IV. 12.[1]
Forestry commissions. 1888. IV. 288.[1]
The **forestry** committee. 1885. IV. 295.[1]
Forestry for beauty and use. 1900. IV. 102.
Forestry in Colorado. *See* ENSIGN, E. T. 1885. IV. 314,[2]
  340.
Forestry in Europe; reports from the consuls of the United
  States. 1887. IV. 342.[1]
Forestry in its economical bearings. 1873. IV. 269.
Forestry in Massachusetts. 1891. IV. 314,[2] 359.
Forestry in the British Isles. *See* HUTCHINS, D. E. 1900.
  IV. 275.
Forestry in the constitution of the state of New York. 1894.
  IV. 314.[2]
Forestry in the land-grant colleges. 1894. IV. 30.[1]
Forestry in the United States. 1881. IV. 337.[2]
Forestry investigations. 1900. IV. 179.[2]
Forestry manual of the Iowa state horticultural society. 1881.
  IV. 111.[2]
Forestry manual of the Kansas state horticultural society.
  See KANSAS horticultural report. IV. 4.
Forestry of the western states and territories. 1879. IV.
  340.
The **Forestry** school at Cooper's Hill. 1888. IV. 34.[1]
The **Forestry** school in Spain. 1888. IV. 35.[1]
Forests. 1884. IV. 270.
Forests and factories. 1896. IV. 51.
Forests and floods. 1881. IV. 184.[2]
Forests and insanity. 1897. IV. 55.[1]
Forests and rivers. 1895. IV. 51.
The **forest's** foes and friends. 1874. IV. 180.[2]
Forests in the grand duchy of Baden. 1900. IV. 350.[2]
The **forests** of Alaska. 1897. I. 312.
The **forests** of Bosnia and the Herzegovina. 1879. IV. 374.[2]
The **forests** of California. 1888. IV. 178.[1]
The **forests** of Europe. 1884. IV. 342.[2]
Forests of Kaiserwald and Grafenhausen. 1900. IV. 355.[1]
The **forests** of Maine, U. S. A. 1882. IV. 238.[2]
The **forests** of North Carolina. *See* KERR, Dr. 1883. IV.
  339.
Forests of Saxony. 1900. IV. 355.[2]
The **forests** of Siberia. 1894. IV. 376.[1]
The **forests** of the Adirondacks. 1885. IV. 339.
Forests of the Spessart, Bavaria. 1900. IV. 351.[2]
The **forests** on the national domain. 1888. IV. 178.[1]
The **forests** on the public domain. 1890. IV. 178.[2]
Foret. *See* BONDONNEAU, Lucien & FORET.
La **Forêt.** IV. 12.[2]
Pour la **forêt.** 1894. IV. 545.[2]
La **forêt;** conseils aux indigènes. 1883. IV. 124.[2] *See also*
  TROLARD, P. 1883. IV. 168.[2]

Forêt communale de Freyr. 1899. IV. 248.[2]
Une **forêt** de Copal. *See* A COPAL forest. 1882. III. 233.[2]
Forêt de Velours. 1892. IV. 258.
La **forêt** des Minières. 1895. IV. 556.[1]
Forêt disparue. 1895. IV. 552.[1]
Forêt domaniale de Chinon. 1876. IV. 360.
Forêt domaniale de Hertogenwald. 1895. IV. 550.[2]
Forêt du Miroir. 1892. IV. 258.
Forêts. Bibliographie nationale suisse. 1894. IV. 2.
Les **forêts** algériennes. 1899. IV. 379.[2]
Les **forêts** au Concours d'Orléans. 1894. IV. 20.[2]
Les **forêts** au point de vue hygiénique. 1894. IV. 542.[2]
Les **forêts** californiennes. 1899. I. 321, *IV. 78.*[2]
Forêts canadiennes et pâte à papier. 1898. IV. 430.
Forêts, chasse et pêche; section belge. 1897. IV. 357.[1]
Forêts d'Europe et d'Amérique. 1896. IV. 281.[1]
Les **forêts** de Chêne de Roumanie. 1899. IV. 375.[2]
Les **forêts** de l'Algérie. *See* COMBE, Ad. 1889. IV. 379.[1]
Les **forêts** de la Norwège. *See* Die WÄLDER Norwegens.
  1885. IV. 344.[1]
Les **forêts** de la Prusse. 1896. IV. 355.[1]
Les **forêts** de la Suède. 1877. IV. 344.[2]
Les **forêts** de la Tunisie. 1896. IV. 379.[2]
Les **forêts** départementales. 1878. IV. 163.
Les **forêts** du Congo. 1895. IV. 556.[2]
Les **forêts** du monde. 1899. IV. 336.[2]
Les **forêts** en Birmanie. 1899. I. 475,[2] *IV. 89.*[1]
Les **forêts** et l'esthétique. 1898. IV. 55.[2]
Les **forêts** et la chasse [de Serbie]. 1900. IV. 375.[1]
Les **forêts** et le bois aux États-Unis. 1895. IV. 338.[2]
Les **forêts** et les eaux souterraines. 1898. IV. 52.
Les **forêts,** les finances et l'agriculture. *See* TUROT, Paul.
  1866. IV. 275.
Les **forêts** prussiennes. 1894. IV. 555.[2]
Les **forêts** vierges d'Europe. 1871. I. 438, *IV. 79.*[1]
Forfait. Extrait du mémoire sur la marine de Venise. 1845.
  IV. 425.[1]
Forgan, William. The pruning of trees. 1898. IV. 172.[2]
Forget, Jean. Artis signatae designata fallacia. 1633. III.
  259.[1]
Forget, Jules. Archéologie forestière. 1887. IV. 27.[2]
— En plein bois; poésies forestières. 1887. IV. 102.
Formánek, Eduard. Beiträge zur Flora von Albanien. 1895.
  I. 450.
— Beitrag zur Flora des Balkans, Bosporus. 1891. I. 450.
— Beitrag zur Flora des nördlichen Mährens. 1887. II.
  288.[1]
— Beitrag zur Flora . . . Mährens. 1886. I. 443.
— Beitrag zur Flora von Bosnien. 1888. I. 448.[1]
— Beitrag zur Flora von Macedonien. 1898. I. 451.
— Beitrag zur Flora von Serbien. 1890. II. 288.[2]
— Beitrag zur Flora von Serbien und Bulgarien. 1892. I.
  450.
— Beitrag zur Flora von Serbien und Macedonien. 1892.
  I. 450.
— Dritter Beitrag zur Flora von Thessalien. 1897. I. 451.
— Einige neue Arten aus Thessalien. 1897. II. 31.[1]
— Květena Moravy a rakouského Slezska. 1887. I. 443.
— Mährische Rosen. 1885. II. 288.[1]
— Mährische Rubusformen. 1887. II. 304.[2]
— Mährische und schlesische Rubus-Formen. 1887. II.
  304.[2]
— Rosen der Hochgesenkes. 1887. II. 288.[1]
— Teratologisches. 1883. II. 289.[2]
— Teratologisches. 1886. II. 308.[1]
— Zweiter Beitrag zur Flora von Serbien. 1896. I. 451.
De la formation des hydrates de carbone. 1888. I. 177.
Formering af Orangetræer ved Stiklinger. 1855. III. 499.[2]
Om **Formeringen** af Paulownia imperialis. 1843. III. 703.[1]
Formosa camphor. 1866. III. 404.[2]
Formosan camphor. 1893. III. 405.[1]
Forms of Ivy. 1884. III. 642.[2]
Formulaire pharmaceutique des hôpitaux militaires de la
  France. 1870. III. 255.[2]
Fornaini, Antonio. Saggio sopra l'utilità di ben governare,
  e preservar le foreste del sacerdote. 1825. IV. 181.[1]
Fornaini, D. Louis. Dissertation sur la culture des Sapins.
  1813. III. 295.[2]
Fornaini, Luigi. Della coltivazione degli Abeti. 1804. IV.
  444.[1]
Fornaschon, Hermann. Blitzschläge in Bäume. 1895. IV.
  195.[2]
— Mitteilung über den Blitzschlag in eine Eiche. 1894. IV.
  195.[1]

Forné, F. Contribution à l'étude des essences. 1893. III. 636.

Forney. Origine de l'Abricot-Pêche. 1890. III. 434.[2]

Forney, Eugène. Étude des principes généraux de la taille. 1862. III. 170.
— Le jardinier fruitier. 1862. III. 144.
— Note sur les plaies des arbres. 1861. III. 180.[1]
— Notes sur quelques points d'arboriculture. 1877. III. 124.[1]
— Du pincement exagéré. 1860. III. 170.
— La taille des arbres fruitiers. 1862. III. 144.
— De la taille du Poirier. 1867. III. 445.[1]
— La taille du Rosier. 1864. III. 449.
— Taille et culture du Rosier. 1864. III. 449.
— Tree wounds and means of healing them. 1861. III. 180.[1]
— *See also* JAMAIN, Hippolyte & FORNEY, Eugène.

Forni. Delle Chiuse ... nelle vallate della Vallemaggia. 1872. IV. 367.

Forni, F. A. Nota alle Note alsometriche esumate. 1898. IV. 219.
— Note su alcuni esperimenti alsometrici. 1898. IV. 395.
— Notizie sul Corebo bifasciato delle Quercie. 1884. IV. 510.

Forordning angaaende de kongelige Skove. 1781. IV. 296.[1]

Forordning angaaende Sandflugtens Dæmpning. 1792. IV. 296.[1]

Forordning oc Skou-Ordinance i Danmarck. 1670. IV. 296.[1]

Forordning om Bøder for ulovlig Skoufhug. 1676. IV. 296.[1]

Forordning om Oldengield. 1672. IV. 296.[1]

Forordning om Skouf-Hug. 1681. IV. 296.[1]

Forordning om Skovenes Udskiftning. 1805. IV. 296.[1]

Forordning om Skowene til de udlagde Rytter-Gaarde. 1670. IV. 296.[1]

Forordning om ung Skouvs Plantning. 1696. IV. 296.[1]

Forrest, Thomas. Voyage aux Moluques et à la Nouvelle Guinée. 1779. II. 566,[2] III. 405.[1]
— A voyage to New Guinea and the Moluccas. 1779. II. 566,[1] III. 405.[1]

Forresta de Windsor in com. Surrey. 1646. IV. 357;[2] V. XXXI.[2]

Forsander, Johan. De vegetatione Scaniae. 1820. I. 352.
— & others. Aphorismi botanici. *See* AGARDH, C. A. 1817. I. 98, 259.

Forsberg, Carl Pehr. De Cinchona. *See* THUNBERG, C. P. 1811. II. 812.

Forsberg, G. E. Ueber die Geschlechtervertheilung bei Juniperus communis. 1888. II. 31.[1]
— Om könsfördelningen hos Juniperus communis. 1887. II. 31.[1]

Forsbom, Johan. Anmärkningar vid fruktbärande buskars skötsel. *See* HELLENIUS, C. N. 1789. III. 134.[1]

Forschungen auf dem Gebiete der Agrikultur-Physik. I. 11.

Forschungen zur deutschen Landes- und Volkskunde. I. 11.

Forschungsberichte über Lebensmittel. I. 11.

Die **Forschungsreise** S. M. S. "Gazelle" in den Jahren 1874 bis 1876. *See* ENGLER, Adolf. 1889. I. 303.

Forshäll, Johan Henrik. Lärobok i pharmacien. 1836. III. 258.

Forskål, Petrus. Descriptiones animalium ... in itinere orientali. 1775. III. 280.[1]
— Flora aegyptiaco-arabica. 1775. I. 480.
— Icones rerum naturalium ... in itinere orientali. 1776. I. 480.

Forskjellige indberetninger fra de ved statens forstvæsen ansatte funktionærer. 1874. IV. 288.[2]

Forslag til Driftsplanens Udarbejdelse og Benyttelse. 1896. IV. 241.

Forslag til Lov, om Overdragelse af Coloniste derne paa Alheden. 1852. IV. 315.[1]

Forsøg til en Opmuntring for Danske Landmaend, at opelske og plante Skov. 1757. IV. 39.[2]

Forssberg, Gustav Frederik. De pharmacis indigenis. *See* SEGERSTEDT, A. J. 1787. III. 270.[1]

Forssell, Karl Bror Jakob. Anteckningar rörande den s. k. Rubus maximus. 1881. II. 308.[2]

Forsskåhl, Jonas Gustav. Flora, de huiswaardin der bloedelooze dieren. 1757. III. 188.[2]
— Hospita insectorum flora. *See* LINNÉ, Carl von. 1752. I. 256,[2] III. 188.[2]

Forst-, Jagd- und Fischerey-Straf-Regulativ. 1805. IV. 320.

Forst- und Cameralverwaltung des Grossherzogthums Hessen. Mittheilungen. IV. 7.

Forst- und Holznutzung in Bulgarien. 1849. IV. 375.[1]

Forst- und Jagd-Abtheilung der Oekonomischen Neuigkeiten. IV. 14.

Forst- und Jagd-Archiv. IV. 7.

Forst und Jagdbibliothek. *See* ALLGEMEINES öconomisches Forst-Magazin. IV. 6.

Forst- und Jagd-Kalender. Ed. by Zenker. IV. 14.

Forst- und Jagd-Kalender. Leipzig. IV. 7.

Forst- und Jagdkalender für das deutsche Reich. *See* FORST- UND JAGDKALENDER für Preussen. IV. 7.

Forst- und Jagd-Kalender für die österreichisch-ungarische Monarchie. IV. 14.

Forst- und Jagdkalender für Preussen. IV. 7.

Forst- und Jagd-Ordnung für Westpreussen und den Netz-Distrikt. 1805. IV. 301.

Forst- und Jagd-Statistik. 1896. IV. 368.

Forst- und Jagd-Taschenbuch. IV. 14.

Forst- und Jagd-Taschenbuch für das Jahr 1795. IV. 8.

Forst- und landwirthschaftliches Jahrbuch. *See* FORSTWIRTHSCHAFTLICHES Jahrbuch. IV. 8.

Forst- und Waldordnung löbl. Stadt Chur. 1791. IV. 305.

Forst- und Waldungs-Mandat für die Grafschaft Baden. 1793. IV. 298.[2]

Forst-Akademie in Mariabrunn. *See* K. K. FORST-AKADEMIE.

Forst-Amt Lautenstein. Zusammenstellung der Ertrags- und Aufwands-Verhältnisse. 1861. IV. 260.[2]

Forst-Archiv zur Erweiterung der Forst- und Jagd-Wissenschaft. IV. 7.

Der **Forstbeamte**. 188 . ? IV. 29.

Forstbenutzung. 1859. IV. 498.

Forstbetriebs-Einrichtung im Kanton Bern. 1855. IV. 249.[2]

Eine **Forstbetriebs-Einrichtung** in Oesterreich. 1867. IV. 250.[1]

Forstbotanisches Merkbuch. Nachweis der beachtenswerthen ... Bäume ... Westpreussen. 1900. IV. 84.[1]

Forst-Calender; oder. Verzeichniss. *See* ZANTHIER, H. D. von & LASSBERG.

Der **Forstculturbetrieb** in den Staatsforsten Preussens. 1863. IV. 118.

Zur **Forstdienstorganisation** im Königreich Sachsen. 1868. IV. 291.[1]

Die **Forste** der gräflich königsegg'schen Herrschaften Oroszlánkó und Illawa. *See* KÖNIGSEGG gróf Oroszlánköt ... 187 . ? IV. 373.

Über **Forste** und Forstwirtschaft in Rumänien. 1892. IV. 375.[1]

Zur **Forsteinrichtung** der Domänen-Waldungen in dem Herzogthum Gotha. 1894. IV. 248.[2]

Forsteinrichtung der Privatwälder in Russland. 1890. IV. 247.[1]

Forsteinrichtungsoperat vom fränkischen Wald. 1862. IV. 248.[1]

Forsten, Eltio Alegondus. Cedrela febrifuga. 1836. III. 512.[1]

Die **Forsten** der freien und Hansestadt Lübeck. *See* WITTHAUER, J. G. 1857. IV. 353.

Die **Forsten** der Herrschaft Austerlitz. 1859. IV. 368.

Die **Forsten** der Herrschaft Böhmisch-Eisenberg. 1859. IV. 368.

Die **Forsten** der Herrschaft Ungarisch-Brod. 1859. IV. 368.

Forsten in Elsass-Lothringen. 1894. IV. 354.

Forster, A. & **Riechelmann**, R. Sur le dosage de la caféine. 1897. III. 740.[1]

Forster, Edward. Additions to Warner's Plantae woodfordienses. 1784. I. 395.

Forster, Georg. Vom Brodbaum. 1784. II. 146.[1]
— Fasciculus plantarum magellanicarum. 1787. I. 347.
— Florulae insularum australium prodromus. 1786. I. 509.[1]
— Herbarium australe. 1797. I. 500.
— Plantae atlanticae. 1787. I. 497.
— De plantis esculentis insularum Oceani australis. 1786. III. 34.[2]
— De plantis magellanicis et atlanticis commentationes. 1787. I. 347, 497.

Forster, Johann Reinhold. Bemerkungen über Gegenstände der physischen Erdbeschreibung ... auf seiner Reise um die Welt. 1781. I. 302.
— Enchiridion historiae naturali inserviens. 1788. I. 70.
— Flora Americae septentrionalis. 1771. I. 305.
— Method of curing injuries and defects in trees. 1797. III. 180.[1]

—.Observations faites pendant le second voyage de M. Cook. 1778. I. 302.
— Observations made during a voyage around the world. 1778. I. 302.
— Specimen historiae naturalis volgensis. 1768. I. 359.
— & Georg. Beschreibungen der Gattungen von Pflanzen auf einer Reise nach. . . . der Süd-See gesammelt. 1776. I. 509.[1]
— — Characteres generum plantarum quas . . . collegerunt. 1776. I. 509.[1]
Forster, Otto. Mistieto trees. 1883. II. 179.[2]
— Rhododendron myrtifolium. 1899. III. 661.[1]
—Rhododendron Nutalli. 1883. III. 661.[3]
Forster, Thomas Farleigh. See FORSTER, Thomas Furley.
Forster, Thomas Furley. Botanical pocket book. 1840. I. 399.
— Flora tonbrigensis. 1816. I. 396.
— List of the rare plants . . . of Tonbridge Wells. 1801. I. 396.
Forster, Wilhelm Emmanuel. De Aristolochia. See BAIER, J. J. 1719. III. 386.[1]
Die Forst-Geographie und Forst-Statistik. 1833. IV. 336.[1]
Forstgesetz des Kantons Freiburg. See CODE forestier . . . 1850. IV. 330.
Forstgesetz für das Grossherzogthum Baden. 183 . ? IV. 317.[2]
Das Forstgesetz, für das Grossherzogthum Baden. 1836. IV. 317.[2]
Das Forstgesetz, für das Königreich Bayern. 1852. IV. 318.
Das Forstgesetz für das Königreich Bayern. 1853. IV. 318.
Forst-Gesetz für die im Reichsrathe vertretenen Königreiche. 1880. IV. 331.[2]
Das Forstgesetz, Jagdgesetz, die Vorschriften über das Waffentragen. 1864. IV. 331.[2]
Forstgesetz vom 28. März 1852. 1879. IV. 318.
Forstheim, Johann, Ritter PFEIFER VON. See PFEIFER VON FORSTHEIM, Johann, Ritter.
Forst-Instruction für sämtliche publique Wald-Förster des Herzogthums Liefland. 1782. IV. 296.[2]
Forst-Journal. IV. 8.
Forstkalender; oder, Anweisung für die Förster. 1770. IV. 94.
Forst-Kalender; oder, Verzeichniss der Verrichtungen. See KRUTHOFER. 1798. IV. 95.
Forstkatechismus; oder, Lehrbegriff. 1806. IV. 96.
Forstkultur, das v. Butlar'sche Culturverfahren. 1860. IV. 152.
Forst-Kultur-Beobachtungen. 1858. III. 168.[2]
Forstlich-charakteristische Skizze der Waldungen auf dem bunten Sandsteingebirge der Pfalz. 1845. IV. 350.[3]
Forstlich-naturwissenschaftliche Zeitschrift. IV. 8.
Die forstliche Ausstellung des Fürsten Adolf Josef zu Schwarzenberg. 1900. IV. 21.[2]
Forstliche Beilage zum Amtsblatt der Landwirthschafts-Kammer . . . Wiesbaden. See VEREIN NASSAUISCHER LAND-UND FÖRSTWIRTHE. IV. 11.
Forstliche Berichte. IV. 8.
Forstliche Berichte und Miscellen. IV. 8.
Forstliche Berufs-Bildung. 1856. IV. 29.
Ueber forstliche Bestrebungen in Australien. 1902. IV. 380.[2]
Forstliche Bibliographie. See GATTERER, C. W. J. 1796. IV. 1.
Forstliche Blätter; Zeitschrift. IV. 8.
Forstliche Blätter für Würtemberg. IV. 8.
Forstliche Bodenzustände. 1852. IV. 143.[1]
Forstliche Briefe. 1849. IV. 8, 291.[1]
Forstliche Mittheilungen. Ed. by Gwinner. IV. 8.
Forstliche Mittheilungen aus Baden. IV. 8.
Forstliche Mittheilungen aus Java. 1862. IV. 376.[1]
Forstliche Mittheilungen, (Bayern.). IV. 8.
Forstliche Reinerträge. 1858. IV. 255.
Forstliche Reisenotizen, gesammelt im Herbst 1850. 1851. IV. 351.[1]
Forstliche Rundschau. IV. 8.
Forstliche Situation im Kanton Luzern. 1863. IV. 366.
Eine forstliche Studienreise auf den . . . Domänen Teschen. See NEWALD, Johann & GROSSBAUER, Franz. 1875. IV. 369.
Eine forstliche Studienreise . . . Schlesien. 1875. IV. 354.
Forstliche Uebersichtskarte des Königreichs Bayern. 1857. IV. 351.[1]
Forstliche Verhältnisse in Deutsch-Ostafrika. 1892. IV. 379.[2]

Das forstliche Versuchswesen. IV. 8.
Forstliche Zeitschrift. IV. 14.
Forstliche Zeitschrift. Ed. by A. Bernhardt. IV. 8.
Forstliche Zeitschrift für . . . Baden. IV. 8.
Forstliche Zustände in Krain. 1869. IV. 369.
Ueber den forstlichen Theil der Ausstellung im Wiener Augarten. 1858. IV. 21.[1]
Zur forstlichen Unterrichtsfrage. 1873. IV. 29.
Die forstlichen Verhältnisse Holland's. 1884. IV. 356.[2]
Die forstlichen Verhältnisse in Elsass-Lothringen. 1884. IV. 349.[2]
Die forstlichen Verhältnisse Württembergs. 1880. IV. 356.[1]
Forstlicher Verein im badischen Oberlande. Verhandlungen. IV. 8.
Forstliches aus Elsass-Lothringen. 1893. IV. 349.[2]
Forstliches aus Kaukasien. 1897. IV. 348.[1]
Forstliches aus Norwegen. 1890. IV. 344.[1]
Forstliches vom Pavillon Dolfuss. 1894. IV. 123.[2]
Forstliches Wochenblatt. IV. 8.
Forstliches Wörterbuch. 1893. IV. 23.[1]
Forstlig Diskussionsforenings. Forhandlinger. IV. 5.[2]
Forstmagazin. IV. 8.
Der Forstmann; oder, Waldökonome. 1808. IV. 110.[2]
Forst-Ordnung der Churfl. Durchl. in Bayern. See LANDRECHT der churfürstl . . . 1657. IV. 318.
Forst-Ordnung der Fürstenthumben Obern und Nidern Bayrn. See LANDRECHT, Policey . . . 1616. IV. 318.
Forstordnung der Korporation Oberallmeind in Schwyz. 1874. IV. 306.
Forstordnung der Stadt Aarau verfasset. 1785. IV. 305.
Forst-Ordnung des Durchlauchtigsten Fürsten und Herrn, Herrn Carls, Marggrafen zu Baaden. 1723. IV. 317.[1]
Forst-Ordnung für das Herzogthum Oldenburg. 1840. IV. 301.
Forstordnung für den Kanton Graubünden. 1839. IV. 306.
Forst-Ordnung für der Stadt Bern deutsche Lande. 1786. IV. 329.
Forstordnung für die Ritterschaftsgüter. 1878. IV. 297.
Forst-Ordnung für die schlesischen Gebürgsforsten. 1777. IV. 301.
Forstorganisation im Kanton Aargau. 1851. IV. 294.[1]
Forstpolizeiordnung für die Waldungen der Stadt Chur. 1846. IV. 306.
Forstreglement für das Kurländische Gouvernement. 1805. IV. 296.[2]
Die Forstrente in Elsass-Lothringen. 1884. IV. 261.[1]
Forstreservationen in Amerika. 1894. IV. 178.[2]
Das Forstrevier Ertinghausen. See RÖSSING, A. von. IV. 353.
Die Forstrevisions-Protokolle, die Nutzungs- und Kultur-Vorschläge. 1851. IV. 301.
Forst-Rugen-Ordnung für das Grossherzogthum Frankfurt. 1812. IV. 320.
Die Forstschule in Hohenheim. 1855. IV. 32.
Forstschule in Laufenburg. 1802. IV. 36.[1]
Die Forstschule zur nützlichen Pflege des Waldes. 1814. IV. 31.
Zur Forstschulfrage. 1874. IV. 32.
Forstschutz und Strafrecht. 1888. IV. 314.[1]
Forst-Section der Landwirthschafts-Gesellschaft für Croatien und Slavonien. Verhandlungen. IV. 9.
Forst-Section für Mähren und Schlesien. Verhandlungen. IV. 8.
Forststatistik der Schweiz; Kanton Basel-Land. 1855. IV. 365.
Forststatistik der Schweiz; Kanton Genf. 1852. IV. 365.
Forststatistik des Herzogthums Sachsen-Coburg-Gotha. 1860. IV. 355.[2]
Forst-Statistik des Kantons Thurgau. 1860. IV. 365.
Forst-Statistik des Kantons Zürich. 1880. IV. 367.
Zur Forststatistik Frankreichs. 1884. IV. 361.
Forststatistische Mittheilungen aus Bayern. 1869. IV. 351.[1]
See also FORSTVERWALTUNG Bayerns. 1861. IV. 289.[2]
Forststatistische Mittheilungen aus Württemberg. IV. 8.
Forststatistische Uebersicht der Gemeindewälder des Forst-Inspektions-Bezirks Laufenburg. 1855. IV. 365.
Forststatistisches aus Deutschland. 1884. IV. 349.[1]
Forststatistisches aus Württemberg. 1889. IV. 356.[1]
Forststraf-Gesetz, d. d. Braunschweig. 1837. IV. 319.[1]
Forststrafgesetz für das Königreich Hannover. 1847. IV. 320.
Ueber Forsttaxirung und Ausmittelung des . . . Ertrages. See DÄZEL, G. A. 1793. IV. 239.
Forst-Tidende. IV. 5.[2]

Forstverein fur das Grossherzogthum Hessen. Bericht. IV. 8.
Forstverein für Nordtirol. Berichte. IV. 14.
Forst-Verein für Oberösterreich und Salzburg. Berichte. See FORST-VEREIN FÜR ÖSTERREICH . . . IV. 14.
Forst-Verein für Österreich ob der Enns. Berichte. IV. 14.
Forstverein für Tirol und Vorarlberg. Berichte. Mittheilungen. See FÖRSTVEREIN FÜR NORDTIROL. IV. 14.
Forstverein für Westfalen und Niederrhein. Versammlung. IV. 8.
Forstvereine für Niederösterreich, Steiermark . . . Mittheilungen. See NIEDERÖSTERREICHISCHER FORSTVEREIN. IV. 15.
Von der Forst-Verfassung in dem Herzogthum Würtemberg. 1788. IV. 322.[2]
Forstverkehrsblatt. IV. 8.
Die Forstverwaltung Badens. 1857. IV. 289.[2]
Die Forstverwaltung Bayerns. 1844. IV. 289.[2]
Die Forstverwaltung Bayerns. 1861. IV. 289.[2]
Die Forst-Verwaltung der Stadt Schaffhausen. 1858. IV. 365.
Die Forstverwaltung des Fürstenthums Schwarzburg-Sondershausen. 1862. IV. 291.[1]
Forstverwaltung für das Etatsjahr 1899. See ETAT der Forst-Verwaltung: IV. 7.
Forstverwaltungs-Grundsätze. 1892. IV. 287.
Forstwächter-Vertrag. 1894. IV. 298.[1]
Das Forstwesen, die Jagd und Fischerei Bosniens und der Herzegowina. 1896. IV. 374.[2]
Das Forstwesen Frankreichs. 1897. IV. 362.
Das Forstwesen in der Capcolonie. 1888. IV. 379.[2]
Das Forstwesen in Japan. 1896. IV. 376.[2]
Das Forstwesen in Rumänien. 1898. IV. 375.[2]
Forstwesen und Alpwirthschaft, Gesetze. 1877. IV. 330.
Forstwirthe von Mähren und Schlesien. Verhandlungen. See FORST-SECTION FÜR MÄHREN . . . IV. 8.
Die Forstwirthschaft. 1868. IV. 20.[1]
Die Forstwirthschaft auf der erzhersoglichen Kammer Teschen. 1898. IV. 28.[2]
Die Forstwirthschaft des Bukowinaer griechisch-orjentalischen Religionsfonds. 1896. IV. 374.[2]
Die Forstwirthschaft in Russland. 1897. IV. 347.
Die Forstwirthschaft Kroatiens und Slavoniens. 1896. IV. 374.[1]
Forstwirthschaft und Holzhandel in Finland. 1887. IV. 114.
Forstwirthschaftliche Mittheilungen. See FORSTLICHE Mittheilungen, (Bayern). IV. 8.
Forstwirthschaftliches Blatt. IV. 14.
Forstwirthschaftliches Jahrbuch. IV. 8.
Die Forstwirtschaft im Unter-Elsass. 1892. IV. 349.[2]
Forstwissenschaftliche Abhandlungen. IV. 9.
Forstwissenschaftliche Aphorismen. 1835. IV. 117. See also JOCHIMS, P. 1835. IV. 352.
Fortwissenschaftliche Bibliothek. 1874. IV. 102.
Forstwissenschaftliche Hefte. IV. 9.
Forstwissenschaftliche Mittheilungen. IV. 14.
Forstwissenschaftliche Tagesfragen. IV. 9.
Forstwissenschaftliches Centralblatt. See MONATSCHRIFT für das Forst . . . IV. 10.
Forsvar for den Høj- og Velvise Magistrat . . . Brænde-Auctionen angaaende. 1797. IV. 281.[2]
Forsyth, Alexander. The Dogwood and Golden Willow for winter effect. 1881. III. 208.[1]
— The Elm as a Rose-prop. 1880. III. 363.[2]
— Game preserves and fences. 1846. III. 213, 215.[1]
— On Holly-leaf tea. 1853. III. 530.[1]
— Holly tea. 1859. III. 530.[1]
— Leechee fruit. 1873. III. 539.[2]
— Eine neue Methode Pflanzen durch Stecklinge zu vermehren. 1835. III. 157.
— A new method of striking cuttings. 1835. III. 157.
— Paraguay tea. 1866. II. 462.[2]
— Transplanting trees and shrubs. 1865. III. 166.
— Truncheon hedges. 1876. III. 213.
— The Yew tree. 1879. II. 10.[1]
Forsyth, J. S. The first-lines of botany. 1827. I. 255.
Forsyth, William, (jr.) A botanical nomenclator. 1794. I. 77.
— An epitome of Mr. Forsyth's Treatise on the culture . . . of fruit-trees. 1802. III. 141.
— Iagttagelser angaaende Sygdomme . . . paa alle Arter Træer. 1791. III. 178.
— Ueber die Krankheiten und Schäden der Obst- und Forstbäume. 1791. III. 178.
— Über die Kultur und Behandlung der Obst- Bäume. 1802. III. 142.

— Observations on the diseases . . . of fruit and forest trees. 1791. III. 178.
— Observations sur les maladies . . . des arbres fruitiers et forestiers. 1791. III. 178.
— Osservazioni sopra le malattie . . . degli alberi fruttiferi, e di bosco. 1797. III. 178.
— Traité de la culture des arbres fruitiers. 1802. III. 142.
— A treatise on the culture . . . of fruit trees. 1802. III. 141.
The Forsythia as a pillar plant. 1891. III. 672.[1]
Fort, J. A. Des effets physiologiques du café. 1883. III. 742.[1]
Fortemps, Joseph Karl von. Vita plantarum illustrata. 1780. I. 32.
Fortier, Louis. L'École supérieure des forêts. 1894. IV. 34.[2]
— Les forêts algériennes. 1892. IV. 279.[2]
— L'huile de faîne et l'huile d'olive. 1872. III. 678,[2] IV. 500.[1]
— Les taillis et les futaies. 1880. IV. 236.
— La vente et l'exploitation des bois. 1880. IV. 388.[1]
Fortin, C. Sur la greffe de côté. 1860. III. 161.
Fortis, Alberto. Della coltura del Castagno. 1794. III. 358.[2]
Fortnightly review. III. 16.
Fortpflanzung der Fichte durch Stecklinge. 1835. IV. 452.[2]
Fortrinlige nordamerikanske Træer til Lystanlæg. 1835. III. 66.[1]
Fortschritt in der Karstbewaldung. 1867. IV. 167.[1]
Die Fortschritte der Botanik. 1879. I. 2.
Die Fortschritte der Forstcultur in den Vereinigten Staaten. 1885. IV. 112.
Über die Fortschritte der Forsteinrichtung in Bayern. 1842. IV. 247.[2]
Fortune, Robert. Chinese pinnated Berberries. 1852. III. 395.[2]
— The Chinese tree Paeony. 1880. II. 200.[2]
— Communications respecting various seeds and plants . . . of China. 1857. III. 273.[1]
— Ueber Cryptomeria. 1845. II. 29.[1]
— Le Cyprès pleureur de la Chine. 1854. III. 302.[1]
— Découverte du Torreya grandis en Chine. 1857. II. 12.[1]
— Dwarfing of trees. 1847. III. 175.[3]
— Einige Bemerkungen über die Gattung Encyanthus. 1850. II. 663.[1]
— The Enkianthus at Hongkong. 1850. II. 663.[1]
— Experience in the transmission of living plants. 1847. III. 155.
— Der Fundort der Glycine chinensis. 1851. II. 388.[2]
— The Glycine sinensis. 1851. II. 388.[1]
— Iconographie des nouvelles clématides du Japon. 1864. III. 388.[2]
— Introduction of the Tea plant into the United States. 1859. III. 600.[2]
— Introductions [from China and Japan]. 1880. III. 83.[1]
— A journey in search of a new Cedar. 1855. II. 49.[1]
— A journey to the Tea countries of China. 1852. I. 458.
— The Kum-Quat. 1871. III. 502.[1]
— The Kumquat, Citrus japonica. 1870. III. 502.[1]
— Le Kum-Quat ou Citrus japonica. 1874. III. 502.[1]
— Note on a new Forsythia from Peking. 1864. II. 706.[2]
— Note upon Azalea ovata. 1847. III. 661.[1]
— Note upon Daphne Fortuni. 1847. III. 627.[1]
— Notes of a traveller. 1849. I. 458.
— Notes of a traveller. 1851. II. 388.[2]
— Notes on plants introduced from China. 1880. III. 83.[1]
— Notes on some Chinese plants. 1860. I. 458, 111. 82, 91.[1]
— Notes on the Aucubas of Japan. 1864. III. 644.[2]
— Notes on the Cryptomeria japonica. 1848. II. 29.[1]
— Observations on the Kumquat. 1870. III. 502.[1]
— Observations upon the best methods of packing seeds. 1848. III. 154.[2]
— De la plante qui fournit le papier de riz. 1854. III. 644.[4]
— Report upon the Tea plantations in the North Western provinces. 1851. III. 602.[2]
— Report upon the Tea plantations in the Northwestern provinces. 1854. III. 603.
— A residence among the Chinese. 1857. I. 458.. —
— The Rice-paper plant. 1854. III. 644.[1]
— Sketch of a visit to China. 1858. I. 458.
— Skimmia japonica. 1852. III. 505.[2]
— Some account of the Chinese Green Indigo plant. 1857. III. 542.[1]
— Three years' wanderings in . . . China. 1847. I. 458.

— Le Torreya grandis de Fortune. 1857. II. 12.[1]
— Ueber Torreya grandis Fort. 1857. II. 12.[1]
— Torreya grandis Fortune. 1857. II. 12.[1]
— Trauer-Cypresse. 1850. II. 29.[1]
— Two visits to the Tea countries of China. 1853. I. 458.
— Yedo and Peking. 1863. I. 458.
— See also McCARTEE & FORTUNE, Robert.
— & Lindley, John. A further account of Weigela rosea. 1846. III. 749.[1]
Fortune's gelbe Camellia. . 1859. II. 551.[2]
Fortunet & Demoyen. Le Pin d'Alep. 1865. IV. 464.[1]
The Forum. III. 3.
Forwood, William Henry. Geological and botanical report. 1882. I. 324.
Foss, James H. See CARSE G. B. & FOSS, J. H.
Fossa, C. Catalogus plantarum Horti bot. regiensis. 1811. I. 61.
Fossat, Adrien LAGRÈZE-. See LAGRÈZE-FOSSAT, Adrien.
Fossey, J. Le Populus trichocarpa. 1897. III. 346.[2]
Fossier, P. Cime et racines. 1898. IV. 65.[1]
Foster, G. H. Coorg and its timbers. 1892. IV. 378.
Foster, John Wells & Whitney, J. D. Report on the geology of the Lake Superior land district. See WHITNEY, W. D. 1851. I. 314.
Foster, Suel. Catalpa speciosa. 1884. IV. 538.[2]
— Evergreens for the western prairies. 1868. III. 292.
— How to plant Catalpa seed. 1884. IV. 538.[2]
— Our native ornamental trees. 1872· III. 706.[1]
— Value of the Catalpa as a timber tree. 1878. IV. 538.[2]
Foster-Melliar, Andrew. See MELLIAR, A. FOSTER-.
Fothergill, John. A letter to the Medical society. 1757. IV 244.
— Observations on the manna Persicum. 1746. III. 221.[1]
— Some account of the cortex Winteranus. 1776. III. 397.[2]
— Of the use of the cortex peruvianus. 1757. III. 719.
— Works. 1783. I. 263.
La fotografia applicata ai rimboschimenti. 1886. IV. 37.[2]
Foucaud, Julien. Additions à la flore de Corse. 1900. I. 419.[1]
— See also DAVID, Ph., FOUCAUD, Julien & VINCENT, P.; ROUY, Georges & FOUCAUD, Julien.
— & Simon, Eugène. Trois semaines d'herborisations en Corse. 1898. I. 419.[1]
Foucault, Emmanuel de. Description d'une nouvelle espèce de Robinier. 1813. II. 382.[1]
La foudre et les Peupliers. 1896. IV. 195.[1]
Fougeroux de Bondaroy, Auguste Denis. Sur la formation des couches ligneuses. 1789. I. 127.[2]
— Lettre . . . sur le Thuya de Théophraste. 1781. II. 27.[1]
— Mémoire sur l'Abricotier de Sibérie. 1787. II. 277.[1]
— Mémoire sur l'emploi de l'écorce du Platane. 1788. III. 418.[2]
— Mémoire sur le bois de Châtaignier. 1784. IV. 513.
— Mémoire sur le Cyprès. 1786. III. 302.[2]
— Mémoire sur le Thé. 1773. III. 605.
— Mémoire sur les différentes espèces de Peupliers. 1786. III. 344.[1]
— Mémoire sur une excroissance de l'Épine blanche. 1785. III. 422.[2]
— Mémoire sur une nouvelle espèce d'Orme. 1787. II. 144.[2]
— Mémoire sur une plante du Pérou. 1787. II. 792.[1]
— Premier mémoire sur des dessins trouvés sur l'écorce . . . d'un gros Hêtre. 1700. I. 210,[1] IV. 400.
— Second mémoire sur les dessins trouvés dans des bûches de Chêne. 1780. I. 210,[2] IV. 509.
— Sur le Thé. 1773. II. 551.[2]
Fougner, H. Beretning om skovkulturerne ved Aas. 1866. IV. 343.[2]
Foukouba, H. Notes sur la flore du Japon. 1888. III. 127.[2]
Foulk, William. On the cultivation of the Madeira Vaccinium. 1826. III. 664.[1]
Fountain, James. Remarks on the medicinal properties of Witch-Hazel. 1848. III. 417.[1]
Fouqué. Sur les moyens d'employer le sulfure de carbone. 1874. III. 566.[1]
Fouquet. Grondverhandeling over de meststoffen. 1852. III. 151.
Fourcault. Sur la maladie des raisins. 1851. III. 575.[1]
— Note n n n n l'influence fâcheuse des arbres. 1841. III. 34.XOO cer a t
Fourcroy, Antoine François de. Recherches chimiques sur le pollen . . . . du Dattier. 1802. II. 73.[1] V
— & Vauquelin, N. L. Analyse du Tabasheer. 1806. II. 59.[1]
— — Mémoire sur l'existence d'une combinaison de tannin. 1810. I. 182.[2]

Fourcroya longaeva in a garden in the Scilly Isles. 1876. III. 341.[2]
Fourcy, Eugène de. Vade-mecum des herborisations parisiennes. 1859. I. 412.
Foureau, Fernand. Essai de catalogue des noms arabes et berbères de quelques plantes. 1896. I. 76.[1]
Fourier, A. Essai sur la résistance des bois de construction. 1828. IV. 415.[2]
Fournet, G. Traitement des Vignes phylloxérées. 1877. III. 570.[1]
Fournier, E. H. On Coca. 1871. III. 493.[1]
Fournier, Eugène. Asclepiadaceae. 1885. II. 735.[1]
— Sur les Asclépiadées américaines. 1882. II. 735.[1]
— Crataegus, graine du buis. 1880. II. 260.[2]
— Sur deux Asclépiadées du Méxique. 1867. II. 738.[1]
— L'Elaeococca et le phylloxera. 1876. III. 514.[2]
— Encore un mot sur le Cypros. 1865. II. 609.[2]
— Essai d'archéologie botanique. 1870. I. 76.[1]
— De la fécondation dans les phanérogames. 1863. I. 201.[1]
— Flore horticole du Nicaragua. 1876. I. 333.
— Géographie botanique. . . . végétation du Caucase. 1895. I. 370.
— Sur le Ligustrum des anciens. 1865. II. 711.[2]
— Sur les noms anciens du Cyprès. 1867. II. 29.[1]
— Note sur la coloration . . . des fleurs de l'Hortensia. 1867. III. 412.[1]
— Notes sur le genre Albizzia. 1860. II. 330.[2]
— Sur le premier envoi de Edm. Kerber. 1883. I. 332.
— Sur quelques anomalies des Ruscus. 1857. II. 84.[2]
— & Bonnet, Maurice. Sur une monstruosité de Rubus. 1862. II. 305.[2]
Fournier, LAFFAY-. See LAFFAY-FOURNIER.
Fournier, Pierre Nicolas Eugène. Des ténifuges employés en Abyssinie. 1861. III. 280.[2]
Fourquet. Diverses applications de la greffe herbacée. 1829. III. 163.[2]
— Das Pfropfen krautartiger Gewächse. 1829. III. 163.[2]
Fourreau, Jules. Catalogue des plantes . . . du cours du Rhône. 1868. I. 413.
— See also JORDAN, Alexis & FOURREAU, Jules.
Foussat, J. Arboriculture fruitière. 1894. III. 145.[1]
— Une maladie des Clématites à grandes fleurs. 1896. III. 389.[2]
— Le nitrate de soude appliqué comme fumure. 1900. III. 152.
— Origine hybride du Lilas Varin. 1896. II. 715.[1]
— La taille et la non-taille des arbustes. 1900. III. 413.[1]
— Le Virgilier à bois jaune. 1895. III. 472.[2]
Fouv, MASSON-. See MASSON-FOUV.
Fowle, F. C. & others. Correspondence relative to . . . Date tree cultivation. 1863. III. 328.[2]
Fowler, Archibald. Cupressus macrocarpa. 1883. III. 302.[2]
— Notes on Conifers. 1872. III. 290.
— A substitute for the Larch. 1882. IV. 441.
Fowler, James. Arctic plants growing in New Brunswick. 1888. I. 310.
Fox, J. Die Ansucht des Clerodendron Balfouri. 1890. III. 696.[2]
— Clerodendron Balfourianum. 1890. III. 696.[2]
Fox, William Freeman. The Adirondack Black Spruce. 1895. IV. 400.[1]
Fox-Strangways, Mary, Countess of Ilchester. Catalogue of plants in Abbotsbury gardens. 1899. I. 55.
Fp. Ueberwallungserscheinungen. 1889. IV. 66.[1]
Fr., C. Neue Untersuchungen über Hölzer. 1884. IV. 64.[1]
Fr. Fra Paolino da San Bartolomeo Reise nach Ostindien. See WESDIN, J. P. 1796. III. 277.
Fraas, Karl. Geschichte der Landbau- und Forstwissenschaft. 1865. IV. 25.
— Klima und Pflanzenwelt in der Zeit. 1847. I. 217.
— Synopsis plantarum florae classicae. 1845. I. 514.[1]
— Wie wird Waldstreu entbehrlich? 1857. IV. 437.[2]
Über die Frage auf welche Art die Bepflanzung der Landstrassen . . . am sichersten zu erreichen ist. 1827. IV. 209.
Zur Frage der Haideaufforstungen. 1892. IV. 155.[1]
Zur Frage der Jahrringsbildung. 1893. I. 128.[1]
Fragen an die Gemeindebehörden des Kantons St. Gallen, in forstwirthschaftlicher Beziehung. 1833. IV. 365.
Fragen den Weidgang in den Wäldern betreffend. 1799. IV. 305.
Fragmenter om hvad hidtil hos . . . See THAARUP, Frederik. 1796. IV. 281.[2]

Fragoso, Juan. Aromatum fructuum, et simplicium aliquot medicamentorum . . . historia brevis. 1572. I. 281.
— Catalogus simplicium medicamentorum. 1566. I. 281.
— Discursos de las cosas aromaticas. 1572. I. 281.
Frahm, G. Auswahl wertvoller Ziergehölze für Einzelpflanzung. 1900. III. 203.
— Cydonia Maulei Lavall. 1898. III. 420.[2]
Fraissinet, Ch. Guide du magnanier. 1836. III. 375.
Franc, Franz Xaver. Das Antreiben, Bewurzeln . . . der Bäume. 1877. III. 158.
— Veredlung in den Rindenausschnitt. 1877. III. 162.
Franca, *baron* de VILLA-. *See* VILLA-FRANCA, *baron* de.
France, Charles. The Larch disease. 1881. IV. 451.
France, Charles S. The advantage . . . of planting waste lands. 1890. IV. 161.[1]
— Eucalypti. 1899. III. 634.[1]
— Eucalyptus in the Transvaal. 1899. IV. 530.
— Forest conservancy in Canada. 1887. IV. 178.[1]
— Landscape and economic planting. 1890. III. 202.[1]
— Remarks upon Coniferae. 1869. III. 292.
France — **Administration des forêts.** *See* ADMINISTRATION . . . IV. 12.[2]
France — **Congrès scientifique.** *See* CONGRÈS . . . I. 21.
France — **Institut des provinces.** *See* INSTITUT . . . I. 21.
France — **Institut impérial.** *See* ACADÉMIE ROYALE DES SCIENCES. I. 20.
France — **Institut national agranomique.** *See* INSTITUT . . . III. 19.
France — **Institut national des sciences** . . . *See* ACADÉMIE ROYALE DES SCIENCES. I. 20.
France — **Ministère de l'agriculture.** *See* MINISTÈRE . . . IV. 12.[2]
France — **Ministère de l'agriculture.** Bulletin. III. 19.
France — **Ministère de l'agriculture, du commerce** . . . Annales du commerce exterieur. III. 19.
France — **Société botanique.** *See* SOCIÉTÉ . . . I. 22.
France — **Société des agriculteurs.** *See* SOCIÉTÉ . . . III. 22.
France — **Société des antiquaires.** *See* SOCIÉTÉ . . . IV. 13.[1]
France — **Société des viticulteurs.** *See* SOCIÉTÉ . . . III. 22.
France — **Société entomologique.** *See* SOCIÉTÉ . . . III. 22.
France — **Société forestière.** *See* SOCIÉTÉ . . . IV. 13.[1]
France — **Société impériale et centrale d'agriculture.** *See* SOCIÉTÉ ROYALE ET CENTRALE D'AGRICULTURE DE PARIS. III. 22.
France — **Société nationale d'acclimatation.** *See* SOCIÉTÉ IMPÉRIALE ZOOLOGIQUE D'ACCLIMATATION. III. 22.
France — **Société nationale d'agriculture.** *See* SOCIÉTÉ ROYALE ET CENTRALE D'AGRICULTURE DE PARIS. III. 22.
France — **Société nationale d'horticulture.** *See* SOCIÉTÉ ROYALE D'HORTICULTURE DE PARIS. III. 22.
France — **Société d'horticulture.** Catalogue de la bibliothèque. *See* GIBAULT, Georges. Catalogue . . . 1900. III. 2.
France — **Société pomologique.** *See* LA POMOLOGIE française. III. 20.
France — **Société séricicole.** *See* SOCIÉTÉ . . . III. 22.
France — **Société zoologique.** *See* SOCIÉTÉ . . . III. 22.
France — **Syndicat central des agriculteurs.** *See* SYNDICAT . . . III. 23.[1]
La France agricole. III. 19.
La France périra faute de bois. 1865. IV. 275.
Franceschi, Francesco. Erythea edulis at home. 1893. II. 68.[1]
— Erythea edulis at Santa Barbara. 1897. III. 325.[1]
— Erythea [*sic*] armata. 1896. III. 325.[1]
— Euphorbia pulcherrima. 1897. III. 518.[1]
— Le Palmier de l'île de Guadalupé. 1893. II. 68.[2]
— Santa Barbara exotic flora. 1895. I. 39.
— Southern California acclimatizing association. 1900. V. XXVII.[2]
— Trees from South Asia acclimated in Southern California. 1898. III. 61.[1]
Franceschi-Marini, Giovanni Battista. Catalogo delle piante coltivate . . . nel di lui giardino del Preto. 1898. I. 63.
Franceschini, Felice. Alcune osservazioni intorno agli studi sulla fillossera. 1893. III. 762.
— Ai contadini. Sulla malattia dell' Uva. 1854. III. 576.
— Influenza del terreno e del clima sull' azione . . . della fillossera. 1895. III. 762.
— Notizie sulla fillossera delle Viti. 1879. III. 572.
— Studii sulla fillossera della Vite. 1892. III. 762.
Franche-Comté — **Société forestière.** *See* SOCIÉTÉ . . . IV. 13.[1]

Franchet, Adrien. Araliaceae, Cornaceae et Caprifoliaceae novae. 1896. II. 646,[2] 654,[1] 883.[2]
— Les Bambusées à étamines monadelphes. 1890. II. 58.[1]
— Sur les caractères de la distribution géographique des Cyrtandracée de la Chine. 1899. II. 792.[2]
— Carrierea calycina. 1896. II. 570.[1]
— Catalogue des plantes . . . de Tché-fou. 1882. I. 459.
— Compositae novae e flora sinensi. 1896. II. 849.[2]
— Un Decaisnea de la Chine occidentale. 1892. II. 201.[1]
— Descriptions de quelques espèces . . de Rhododendron du Yun-nan. 1887. II. 676.[1]
— Sur deux Oléacées du Yun-nan. 1886. II. 713,[2] 715.[2]
— Dipelta yunnanensis. 1891. II. 835.[1]
— Sur la distribution . . . des Chênes dans l'Asie orientale. 1899. II. 131.[1]
— Essai sur la distribution géographique des plantes . . . de Loir-et-Cher. 1866. I. 413.
— Étude sur les Strophanthus. 1893. II. 732.[1]
— Fargesia, nouveau genre. 1893. II. 60.[1]
— Flore de Loir-et-Cher. 1885. I. 416.
— Jasminum polyanthum. 1891. II. 710.[2]
— Les Lilas, leurs espèces. 1891. II. 714.[2]
— Liste des plantes récoltées pendant le voyage. 1898. I. 536.[1]
— Mission Capus; plantes du Turkestan. 1883. I. 457.
— Les Mutisiacées du Yunnan. 1888. II. 850,[2] 861.[1]
— A new Koelreuteria from western China. 1888. II. 487.[1]
— Note sur deux nouvéaux genres de Bambusées. 1889. II. 58.[2]
— Note sur la végétation de l'île d'Yéso. 1885. I. 463.
— Note sur le Davidia involucrata. 1889. II. 614.[2]
— Note sur le fruit du Strophanthus glaber. 1894. II. 732.[1]
— Note sur quelques collections de plantes de l'Asie orientale. 1896. I. 459.
— Notes sur quelques plantes de France. 1880. II. 296.[1]
— Nouelia insignis. 1889. II. 861.[2]
— Un nouveau Koelreuteria de la Chine. 1888. II. 487.[1]
— Observations sur les Strophanthus. 1898. II. 732.[1]
— Observations sur les Syringa. 1885. II. 714.[2]
— Phanérogamie. 1889. I. 347.
— Plantae Davidianae ex Sinarum imperio. 1883. I. 459.
— Plantae Delavayanae. 1889. I. 459.
— Plantarum sinensium ecloge prima [et secunda]. 1896. I. 459.
— Plantas yunnanenses . . . describit. 1886. I. 459.
— Plantes du voyage au golfe de Tadjourah. 1887. I. 489.
— Plantes du Yun-nan récoltées par l'abbé Delavay. 1885. II. 122,[2] 676.[1]
— Plantes nouvelles de la Chine. 1884. II. 199.[2]
— Plantes nouvelles de la Chine occidentale. 1894. I. 459.
— Plantes nouvelles du Thibet. 1897. II. 342.[1]
— À propos du Ribes Davidi Franch. 1898. II. 243.[2]
— Sur quelques nouveaux Strophanthus. 1893. II. 732.[1]
— Sur quelques plantes de la Chine occidentale. 1895. I. 459.
— Sur quelques plantes . . . du nord de la Chine. 1890. II. 482.[2]
— Rhododendron du Thibet oriental et du Yun-nan. 1886. II. 676.[1]
— Saxifragaceae, Crassulaceae et Combretaceae novae. 1896. I. 459.
— Sertum somalense. 1882. I. 489.
— The species and native habitats of the Lilacs. 1891. II. 714.[2]
— *See also* BUREAU, Édouard & FRANCHET, Adrien.
— & **Savatier**, Ludovic. Enumeratio plantarum in Japonia. 1875. I. 462.
Franchet, L. Les Lespedeza de la Chine occidentale. 1890. II. 389.[2]
Franchi, A. Il ciocco di scopa nella confezione degli sbozzi. 1895. IV. 427.[1]
— Che cosa sia una segheria di sbozzi. 1896. IV. 393.
— L'Erica come pianta industriale. 1896. IV. 534.[1]
— L'estrazione del ciocco d'Erica. 1896. IV. 387,[1] 534.[1]
— L' industria delle pipe di radica. 1895. IV. 427.[2]
— La produzione degli sbozzi d' Erica. 1896. IV. 427.[2]
Franchi, Giuseppe. Manuale del coltivatore. 1857. III. 115.[2]
Franchimont, Antoine Paul Nicolas. Over den bast van Carapa. 1878. III. 512.[1]
— Sur la bétuline. 1879. IV. 491.[1]
— Bijdrage tot de kennis van het ontstaan . . . der zoogenaamde terpeenharsen. 1871. I. 181.[1]
— Sur la cellulose ordinaire. 1879. IV. 430.

— Sur le glucose. 1879. I. 176.
— Zur Kenntniss der Entstehung der Harze. 1871. I. 181.[1]

Francia, Louis. Progressive lessons tending to elucidate the character of trees. 1813. I. 516.

Francis, Ernest E. H. Report of the amount of tannin in certain British Guiana tree barks. 1881. IV. 435.

Francis, George William. Acclimatisation of ... animals and plants. 1862. III. 43.
— British botany illustrated. 1840. I. 399.
— A catalogue of British flowering plants. 1835. I. 398.
— The grammar of botany. 1840. I. 88.
— The little English Flora. 1839. I. 399.

Francis, T. M. The gardener's note book, XX. 1882. III. 158.
— Notes on the propagation of plants by leaves. 1874. III. 159.[1]
— A novel mode of putting down cuttings. 1882. III. 158.

Francisci, Erasmus. Ost- und West-Indischer ... Lust- und Stats-Garten. 1668. III. 217.

Franciscus de Honuphriis. Stirpium nomina in pharmacopolio Minimorum. 1682. III. 240.

Franck, Carl August. Untersuchungen über die Farben der Blüthen. See SCHÜBLER, Gustav. 1825. I. 184.

Franck, Johan (of Upsala). Botanologia. 1877. I. 34, 292.
— Signatur; das ist, Gründtliche. Beschreibung der ... gezeichneten Gewächsen. 1618. I. 284.
— Speculum botanicum. 1638. I. 285.[2]

Franck, V. Les Vosges. 1896. IV. 362.

Franck von Frankenau, Georg. Flore Francica. 1672. I. 287.
— Flora Francica aucta; oder, Vollständiges Kräuter-Lexicon. 1672. I. 287.
— Flora Francica rediviva; oder, Kräuter-Lexicon. 1672. I. 287.
— Lexicon vegetabilium usualium. 1672. I. 287, 530.[2]
— De malo Citreo. 1686. III. 498.[2]

Francke, Georg. See FRANCK VON FRANKENAU, Georg.

Franckenius, Joannes. See FRANCK, Johan (of Upsala).

Francœur, Louis Benjamin. Flore parisienne. 1801. V. 406.

François, Caventou, J. B. & Pelletier, Joseph. Recherches sur les propriétés ... de la racine de kahinça. 1830. III. 744.[1]

François, Auguste. Lettre [sur la culture de l'Oranger à Blidah]. 1876. III. 500.[1]
— Notice sur la culture des Orangers. 1873. III. 497.[1]
— Notice ... sur les Orangeries de Blidah. 1870. III. 499.[2]

François, Jules. Sur les effets produits par l'absence de culture à la surface du sol. 1876. III. 568.
— Sur l'emploi des pyrites. 1876. III. 577.
— Résultats obtenus par l'emploi de la pyrite de fer. 1876. I. 577.

François de Neufchateau, Nicolas Louis, comte. Lettera sopra il Robinier. 1802. IV. 522.[1]
— Lettres sur le Robinier. 1802. IV. 522.[3]
— Plaatsvervangers der koffie. 1808. III. 222.
— Robinia Pseudacacia. 1802. IV. 522.[2]

Francolini, Felice. Avvertenze sulle stime dei boschi. 1856. IV. 254.

Francon, J. A. Tarif de cubage des bois. 1888. IV. 228.

Francox, J. B. Mémoire sur l'importance du Frêne. 1821. IV. 535.[1]

Francus, Johann. See FRANKE, Johann (of Ulm).

Francus, Peter. In laudem Thiae sinensis anacreontica duo. 1685. III. 605.
Le frane nei monti. 1881. IV. 186.[1]
Frane nella Valle di Boalzo. 1888. IV. 186.[2]

Frank, A. & Gruber, I. Tabelle zur Bestimmung der ... Holzgewächse. 1880. I. 371, IV. 83.

Frank, Albert Bernhard. Ueber das Abfallen der Lindenblätter. 1881. III. 585.[2]
— Über die anatomische Bedeutung ... der vegetabilischen Schleime. 1866. I. 134.[2]
— Ueber Assimilation von Stickstoff ... durch Robinia. 1890. II. 383.[1]
— Die Bedeutung der Mykorhiza-Pilze für die gemeine Kiefer. 1894. II. 48.[1]
— Beiträge zur Pflanzenphysiologie. 1868. I. 147.
— Ein Beitrag zur Kenntniss der Gefässbündel. 1864. I. 133.
— Ueber die Bekämpfung der ... Kirschbaumkrankheit im Altenlande. 1887. III. 435.[1]

— Betrachtungen . vom Standpunkt des Land- und Forstwirthes über Zölle. 1880. IV. 284.[2]
— Choroby roślin. 1880. III. 179.
— Ueber den Einfluss des Lichtes auf den bilateralen Bau ... der Thuja. 1873. II. 52.[2]
— Ueber den Einfluss, welchen das Sterilisiren des Erdbodens ... ausübt. 1888. I. 229.
— Ueber einige ... Pflanzenkrankheiten. 1883. III. 179, IV. 486.[2]
— Ueber die einseitige Beschleunigung des Aufblühens einiger kätzchenartigen Inflorescenzen. 1875. II. 104.[1]
— Ueber die Entstehung der Intercellularräume. 1867. I. 136.[2]
— Ueber die Entstehung der Intercellularräume. 1868. I. 123.[2]
— Die Ernährung der Kiefer durch ihre Mykorhiza-Pilze. 1892. I. 234,[1] IV. 74,[1] 543.[2]
— Die Fusicladium- oder Schorfkrankheit. 1899. III. 195.[2]
— Ueber die auf den Gasaustausch bezüglichen Einrichtungen ... der Wurzelknöllchen der Leguminosen. 1892. II. 321.[2]
— Ueber den gegenwärtigen Stand unserer Kenntnisse der Assimilation. 1889. I. 159.
— Ueber die Gummibildung im Holze. 1884. I. 213.[1]
— Sur l'importance des Mycorhizes. 1892. IV. 74.[1]
— Die jetzt herrschende Krankheit der Süsskirschen. 1887. III. 435.[1]
— Ueber die Kirschenfliege. 1891. III. 432.[1]
— Die Krankheiten der Pflanzen. 1880. III. 179.
— Lehrbuch der Botanik. 1892. V. x.[2]
— Lehrbuch der Pflanzenphysiologie. 1890. I. 148.
— Massregeln gegen die Monilia-Krankheit. 1898. III. 436.[2]
— A mézga képződése a fában s ennek élettani jelentősége. 1884. I. 213.[1]
— Mittheilungen über das Clasterosporium. 1900. III. 431.[1]
— Die natürliche wagerechte Richtung von Pflanzentheilen. 1870. I. 195.[1]
— Eine neue Kirschenkrankheit im Altenlande. 1887. III. 435.[1]
— Ueber neue Mycorhiza-Formen. 1887. I. 234.[1]
— Neues über die Mycorhiza der Bäume. 1886. IV. 74.[1]
— La nutrition du Pin par les champignons. 1892. I. 234,[1] IV. 74.[1]
— Pflanzen-Tabellen ... der höheren Gewächse Nord- und Mittel-Deutschlands. 1869. I. 386, 532,[1] V. xix.[2]
— Ueber die physiologische Bedeutung der Mycorhiza. 1888. I. 234.[1]
— Ueber die Pilzsymbiose der Leguminosen. 1889. II. 321.[1]
— Planten-Tabellen ... der Nederlandsche plantensoorten. 1869, 1875. I. 386, 391.[2]
— Ueber die durch die Schwerkraft verursachten Bewegungen. 1868. I. 195.[1]
— Sind die Wurzelanschwellungen der Erlen ... Pilzgallen? 1887. II. 115,[1] 607.[1]
— Tabelle zur Bestimmung der Holzgewächse. 1880. I. 371.
— Tabelle zur Bestimmung der Holzgewächse im winterlichen blattlosen Zustande. 1869. I. 294,[1] IV. 83.
— Untersuchungen über die auf Wurzelsymbiose beruhende Ernährung. 1885. I. 233.[2]
— Ueber die auf Verdauung von Pilzen abzielende Symbiose. 1891. I. 234.[1]
— Ueber den Verlauf der Kirschbaum-Gnomonia-Krankheit. 1891. III. 432.[1]
— Was nützen den Waldbäumen die Wurzelpilze? 1889. I. 529.
— Ueber die auf Wurzelsymbiose beruhende Ernährung. 1885. I. 233.[2]
— Wykład fizyologii roślin. 1890. I. 148.
— & Kottmeier, H. Beobachtungen über einen an Kiefern schädigend auftretenden Pilz. 1898. IV. 479.
— & Krüger, Friedrich. Über die gegenwärtig herrschende Monilia-Epidemie. 1899. III. 431.[1]
— — Die Monilia-Epidemie. 1897. III. 436.[2]
— — Schildkladsch. 1900. III. 192.
— & Otto, Richard. Untersuchungen ueber Stickstoff-Assimilation. 1890. I. 159.
— & Sorauer, Paul. Ochrona roślin. 1892. III. 179.
— — Pflanzenschutz. 1892. III. 179.

Frank, Eugen. Die Hallerdé, ein Spezialdünger für Fichtenpflanzlinge. 1868. IV. 453.
— Zwei starke Ulmen. 1861. II. 143.[2]

Frank, Joseph C. Rastadts Flora. 1830. I. 378.
Frankamp, L. Beknopte verzameling van de resultaten der beschouwingen van ... landbouw. 1853. III. 106.[1]
Franke, G. Der practische Bautischler. 1870. IV. 423.[1]
Franke, Georg. *See* FRANCK VON FRANKENAU, G.
Franke, J. H. Technische Anleitung zu den trigonometrischen Netz- und Koordinaten-Rechnungen. 1889. IV. 265.
Franke, Johann (*of Bautzen*). Hortus Lusatiae. 1594. I. 372.
Franke, Johann (*of Ulm*). Polycresta herba Veronica. 1690. III. 605.
— Le Thé de l'Europe. 1693. III. 605.
— Veronica theézans. 1693. III. 605.
Franke, Johann (*of Upsala*). *See* FRANCK, Johan (*of Upsala*).
Franke, Martin. Beiträge zur Morphologie . V. der Stellaten. 1896. II. 808.[2]
Franke, Max. Beiträge zur Kenntniss der Wurzelverwachsungen. 1881. I. 210,[1] *III. 526,[1] IV. 510.*
— Über die Flora von Messina. 1883. I. 432.[1]
— Qualche nuovo caso di fusione delle radici. 1881. I. 210,[1] *III. 526,[1] IV. 510.*
Frankenau, Georg FRANCK VON. *See* FRANCK VON FRANKENAU, Georg.
Frankenheim, Moritz Ludwig. Ueber die geographische Verbreitung der Acanthaceen. 1848. II. 795.[2]
— Ueber die geographische Verbreitung der Rosaceen. 1843. II. 255.[2]
Frankenhuyzen, D. van. De heidevelden. 1890.· III. 122.[2]
Frankfurt, S. *See* SCHULZE, E. & FRANKFURT, S.
Frankfurt — Naturwissenschaftlicher Verein des Regierungsbezirkes ... *See* NATURWISSENSCHAFTLICHER ... I. 14.
Frankfurter Verein für Geographie und Statistik. Jahresbericht. I. 11.
Frankincense. 1879. III. 509.[2]
Frankl, Joseph. Communication sur le Coca. 1862. III. 492.[2]
Franklin, Alfred. Le café, le thé & le chocolat. 1893. III. 223.[1]
Franklin, John. Narrative of a journey to the shores of the Polar Sea. *See* RICHARDSON, John. 1823. I. 306.
Franklin and Marshall college, Lancaster, Pa. Contributions from the herbarium. I. 519.[1]
Franklin institute of the state of Pennsylvania. Journal III. 3.
Frankreich. Windfallschaden. 1897. IV. 189.[2]
Franquinet, J. L. Observationes ad pharmacopaeam belgicam. 1835. ·III. 250.[1]
Franscini, St. Rapporto sulla memoria reali, della coltura dei boschi. 1835. IV. 365.
Frantz, Ad. Holzdiebstahl und Holzberechtigung. 1853. IV. 320.
Frantz, Alexander. Ueber Leben und Krankheit der Pflanzen. 1856' I. 206.[1]
Frantz-Penzoldt. Sur le Quebracho. 1879.· III. 686.[2]
Frantzius, Alexander von. Über die Urwälder von Costa Rica. 1862. III. 265.[1]
— Ueber die Urwaldungen von Costarica. 1862. III. 265,[1] *IV. 341.[2]*
Franz, Anton. Enumeratio plantarum Horti et agri brèsinensis. 1824. I. 65.[2]
Franz, C. F. Ueber das Schützen der Saatschulpflanzen. 1876. IV. 199.[1]
Franz, F. E. Aufruf ... zur Verhütung der unnützen Verfolgung verschiedener Vögel. 1816. IV. 89.[2]
Franz, Friedrich Christian. Beantwortung der Frage: ·Wie dem Holzmangel vorzubeugen sey? 1795. IV. 116, *280.[2]*
— Erfahrungen und Vorschläge.dem Nutz- und Bauholze ... Härte und Haltung zu geben. 1814. IV. 416.[2]
— Freymüthige Gedanken über die Gebrechen unserer· heutigen Forst- und Landwirthschaft. 1801. IV. 268.
— Ökonomisch-physikalische Vorschläge zur Kultur des Sand- und Sumpfbodens. 1835. IV. 155,[1] *158.·*
— Praktisches Handbuch für Forst- und Bauleute. 1814. IV. 416.[2]
— Schutzmittel für unsere Forsten. 1840. IV. 195.[2]
— Der Spreewald. 1800. IV. 352.
— Versuch über die Rettungsmittel des ... durch den Raupenfrass betroffenen Holzes. 1798. IV. 206.
Franzelin, Jean. Description historique ... de la commune générale de Fiemme. 1779. IV. 362.
Franzmadhes, Matthias Joseph. Betrachtungen über verschiedene Gegenstände des Forstwesens. 1777. IV. 113.[2]
— Gedanken von Vermehrung und Festigkeit des Erlenholzes. 1779. IV. 489.[1]

Der **französische** Forstetat für 1897. 1897. IV. 293.[1] ·
Die **französische** Gesetzgebung wegen Wieder-Bewaldung. 1866. IV. 326.
Französische Pharmakopöe. *See* CODEX medicamentarius. 1638. III. 255.[2]
Franzoja, Giovanni. Disceptatio academica de analysi Smilacis. 1825. II. 85.[2]
Franzoni, Alberto. Le piante fanerogame della Svizzera Insubrica. 1890. I. 437.
Frappier, C. Sur la racine de Jean Lopez. 1867. III. 279,[2] *606.[1]*
Fras, Franz Julius. Kurze Andeutung über die Kirschenart, aus welcher ... Maraschino- Liqueur bereitet wird. 1838. III. 436.[1]
Fraser, Alexander. On the cultivation of Cinchona in· Java. 1862. III. 715.
Fraser, Charles. Journal of a two months' residence on the banks of the rivers Brisbane and Logan. 1830. I. 500.
— Remarks on the botany ... of Swan River. 1830. I. 500.
Fraser, Hugh. ·Abnormal growths on root of Taxodium. 1886. II. 51.[2]
— Edwardsia grandiflora. 1877. III. 488.[2]
— Erica (Calluna) vulgaris Searleyi. 1880. III. 648.[2]
— The genus Colletia. 1891. III. 541.[2]
— Handy book of ornamental Conifers. 1875. III. 78,[1] *290.*
— Hawthorns. 1875. III. 421.[2]
— The Jasmines. 1875. III. 672.[2]
— The Kaurie Pine. 1891. III. 297.[2]
— Ornamental Cherries. 1877. III. 432.[1]
— Ornamental trees and shrubs. 1875. III. 421,[2] *672.[2]*
— Ornamental trees and shrubs, Buxus. 1876. III. 522.[2]
— Ornamental trees and shrubs; Cerasus. 1877. III. 432.[1]
— Ornamental trees and shrubs; Fagus. 1878. III. 360.[1]
— Species and varieties of Beeches. 1878. III. 360.[1]
— Varieties of Box. 1875. III. 522.[2]
Fraser, James Baillie. Notices respecting the Himalaya Mountains. 1820. I. 471.
Fraser, *Sir* Malcolm. Western Australia. 1882. IV. 380.[1]
Fraser, Malcolm. A. C. Western Australian year-book. 1896. III. 283.[1]
Fraser, Thomas Richard. On the characters of the Akazga plant. 1868. II. 720.[1]
— On the Kombi arrow-poison. 1870. III. 690.[2]
— Notes on ... the Calabar poison bean. 1863. III. 483.[2]
— On the physiological action of the Calabar bean. 1866. III. 483.[2]
— The pituri poison of Australia. 1879. III. 700.[1]
— A preliminary notice of the akazga ordeal. 1867. III. 683.[1]
— Recherches experimentales sur l'antagonisme existant entre l'atropine et la fève de Calabar. 1866. III. 483.[2]
— Strophanthus hispidus. 1889. III. 690.[2]
— & **Tillie,** Joseph. Acokanthera Schimperi. 1899. III. 685.[2]
Fraser's Ixora. 1875. III. 745.[1]
Fraser's magazine. III. 16.
Der **Frass** der Nonne. 1853. IV. 475.
Fratscher, (*Oberförster*). Zur Cultur des Faulbaumes. 1887. IV. 528.[1]
Fraude, Georg. Ueber Aspidospermin. 1878. III. 686.[2]
— Sur l'aspidospermine. 1878. III. 686.[2]
— Caractère chimique de l'écorce de Quebracho. 1881. III. 687.[1]
— Notiz über die Erkennung der Quebracho-Rinde. 1881. III. 687.[1]
Frauenfeld, Georg, *Ritter* von. Ueber exotische Pflanzenauswüchse. 1859. I. 214.[1]
— Flora von Neu-Caledonien. 1867. I. 508.[2]
— Die Gallen. 1855. I. 214.[1]
— Die Linsengallen der österreichischen Eichen. 1856. I. 216,[2] *IV. 501.[1]*
— Ueber Pflanzengallen. 1870. I. 214.[1]
— Phylloxera vastatrix. 1872. III. 565.[1]
Fray, J. P. Liste des plantes ... de l'Ain. 1878. I. 415.
Freaks among trees. 1899. I. 295.[2]
Freaks upon flowers, fruits and trees. 1849. III. 123.[2]
Fream, William. Soils and their properties. 1890.· III. 41.[1]
— Analysis of several varieties· of Chestnuts. 1891. III. 358.[2]
Fréard du Castel. L'école du jardinier fleuriste. *See* L'ÉCOLE ... 1764. III. 112.
Freas, P. L. Hardiness of Magnolia grandiflora. 1885.· III. 400.[1]
Fréchou. Sur un nouveau mode de transmission du mildew de la Vigne. 1885. III. 578.

Freda, Pasquale. Sulle colorazioni dei fiori d'Hydrangea. 1877. I. 141, *II.* 241.[1]
Frederickson, Aug. Daniel. Ad Orientem. 1889. I. 453.[1]
Fredericq, C. A. De wilde bloemen. 1882. I. 391.[2]
Frederiksen, K. N. & **Oppermann,** A. Trælasttolden og Skovbruget. 1890. IV. 284.[1]
Frederiksminde Lyst-Anlæg ved Aalborg. *See* SÖDERBERG, W. IV. 343.[1]
Freeman, Edward B. Report on the Plum crop in Bosnia. 1889. III. 433.[2]
— Report on the Plum trade in Bosnia. 1890. III. 433.[1]
— Report on the timber trade of Bosnia. 1892. IV. 407.[1]
— Report on Vine culture in Bosnia. 1892. III. 558.[2]
Freeman, George. On the culture of Eriostemons. 1850. III. 504.[1]
Freeman, Strickland & **Shaw,** J. S. Select specimens of British plants. 1797. I. 396.
Freeman, T. B. Gold Coast. 1888. III. 281.[1]
Freeman-Mitford, Algernou Bertram. *See* MITFORD, A. B. FREEMAN-.
Freese, Heinrich. Das Holzpflaster in Paris. 1891. IV. 426.[1]
Frege, Christian August. Anleitung zur Kentniss der schädlichen ... Pflanzen. 1796. III. 72.
— Gartenflora. 1814. III. 74.
— Versuch einer Klassification der Weinsorten. 1804. III. 545.[2]
— Versuch eines allgemeinen botanischen Handwörterbuchs. 1808. I. 33.
Freiberg, František. Pěstování stromů a keřů ovocných i zdobných. 1896. III. 115.[1]
Freiburg. Eine wertvolle Fichte. 1894. II. 37.[2]
Freiburg — Botanischer Verein. *See* BOTANISCHER VEREIN · FÜR DEN KREIS FREIBURG ... I. 11.
Freiburg i. B. — Gesellschaft für Beförderung der Naturwissenschaften. *See* GESELLSCHAFT ... I. 12.
Freiburg i. B. — Naturforschende Gesellschaft. *See* NATURFORSCHENDE ... I. 13.
Freie ökonomische Gesellschaft zu St. Petersburg. Mittheilungen. *See* KAISERLICHE FREIE ... III. 10.[1]
Freige, Johannes Thomas. Quaestionum medicarum libri. 1558. I. 280.
Freire, Domingos. Sur un alcaloide extrait du fruit-de-loup. 1887. II. 776.[2]
— Les microbes des fleurs. 1899. III. 195.[2]
Freirichs. Empoisonnement par l'Upas tieute. 1864. III. 685.[1]
Freissinet, d', *vicomte* YZARN-. *See* YZARN-FREISSINET D', *vicomte.*
Freitas, Cypriano de. *See* BOCHEFONTAINE & FREITAS, Cypriano de.
Fremond, Ch. Mémoire sur la formation des racines de feuilles. 1851. I. 103.
Frémont, John Charles. Report of the exploring expedition to the Rocky Mountains. 1845. I. 321.
— *See* TORREY, John & FRÉMONT, J. C.
Frémy, Edmond. Action de a chaux sur le tissu utriculaire. 1859. I. 151,[1] 211.
— Caractères distinctifs des fibres ligneuses. 1859. I. 129,[1] 155.
— Sur la composition et le mode de production des gommes. 1860. I. 181.[1]
— Sur la maturation des fruits. 1864. I. 179.[1]
— Maturation des fruits. 1890. I. 179.[1]
— Méthode générale d'analyse du tissu. 1876. I. 156.[2]
— Questions relatives au phylloxera. 1879. III. 571.
— Recherches chimiques sur la composition des cellules végétales. 1859. I. 151,[1] 153.
— Recherches chimiques sur la cuticule. 1859, [I. 151,[1] 153.
— Recherches chimiques sur la matière verte des feuilles. 1860. I. 141.
— Recherches chimiques sur la matière verte des feuilles. 1877. I. 141.
— Recherches chimiques sur la maturation des fruits. 1844. I. 179.[1]
— Recherches chimiques sur le latex. 1860. I. 181.[1]
— Recherches sur la composition chimique des tissus. 1859. I. 153.
— Recherches sur la composition chimique du bois. 1859. I. 155.[1]
— Recherches sur la matière colorante verte. 1860. I. 141.
— Recherches sur les matières gélatineuses. 1847. I. 180.[2]
— Remarques de Frémy à l'occasion de la précédente communication (Payen, Observations). 1859. I. 151.[1]

— Réponse de M. Frémy (à Payen). 1859. I. 151.[1]
— & **Cloëz,** S. Note sur la composition chimique du pollen. 1854. I. 152.[2]
— Note sur les matières colorantes des fleurs. 1854. I. 184.
— & **Terreil,** A. Méthode générale d'analyse immédiate des tissus des végétaux. 1868. I. 156.[2]
— & **Urbain,** V. Études chimiques sur le squelette des végétaux. 1881. I. 154.
French, B. F., (*comp.*). Historical collections of Louisiana. 1846. I. 531.
French, Charles. Botanical trip to the Wimmera. 1888. I. 503.
— A handbook of the destructive insects of Victoria. 1891. III. 192.[2]
— Notes on a new Victorian injurious insect. 1894. III. 192.[2]
— Notes on the natural history of the Western Wimmera. 1889. I. 504.
— *See also* SPENCER, Baldwin & FRENCH, Charles.
French, Frank. Trees. 1900. I. 305.
French, Henry F. Chemical fertilizers. 1876. III. 151.
— Cultivation of Apples. 1850. III. 426.[1]
— Notes upon fruit growing in New Hampshire. 1853. III. 133.
— Transplanting trees in winter.. 1851. III. 167.
French, J. D. W. Forestry annals. 1892. IV. 338.[1]
— The forestry movement in the United States. 1892. IV. 272.
— The forests and the army. 1893. IV. 178.[2]
French, J. M. Maple-sugar making in Vermont. 1886. IV. 527.[1]
French forest budget for 1880. *See* Le BUDGET ... 1879. IV. 276.[1]
French planting of timber on poor soils. 1885. IV. 163.
Frengl, Ludwig. Der Eulenraupenfrass. 1890. IV. 210.[1]
Frentrop, Emanuel. De nuce vomica. 1832. II. 720.[1]
Frenzel, Franz Christoph. Chemie für Forstmänner. 1800. IV. 60.[1]
Frenzel, Fransiskus Justus. Beobachtung über die Haselnusskätzchen. 1803. II. 122.[1]
— Beobachtungen über die Pomologie. 1798. I. 146.
— Von der Luft im Baume. 1804. I. 149.[1]
— Vom Mark in den Pflanzen und Bäumen. 1805. I. 128.[2]
— Physiologische Beobachtungen über den Umlauf des Safts. 1804. I. 163.
Frenzel, Johann Samuel Traugott. Verzeichniss wildwachsender, angebauter ... Holzarten in der Gegend von Wittenberg. 1801. I. 370, *IV. 82.*
— Verzeichniss wild wachsender Pflanzen ... um Wittenberg. 1799. V. xix.[1]
Frépillon, PELLETIER DE. *See* PELLETIER DE FRÉPILLON.
Frere, L. Report on colonial timbers to be used as wine casks. 1900. IV. 427.[1]
Freschi, Gherardo. Sulla coltivazione dei Gelsi. 1852. III. 376.
— Nuovi studii dell' azione del terreno. 1882. I. 229.
Fresenius, Carl Remigius. Sur le bois roux, nouveau combustible. 1868. IV. 500.[1]
— Chemische Untersuchung der wichtigsten Obstarten. 1857. I. 153.
— Lehrbuch der Chemie. 1847. IV. 60.[2]
— Recherches analytiques sur les principaux fruits. 1857. I. 153.
— *See also* WILL, H. & FRESENIUS, C. R.
Fresenius, Georg. Beiträge zur Flora von Abyssinien. 1837. I. 487.
— Beiträge zur Flora von Aegypten. 1834. I. 487.
— Cordiaceae, Heliotropieae et Borragineae. 1857. II. 747.
— Diagnoses generum specierumque ... in Abyssinia. 1838. I. 487.
Fresenius, Heinrich Carl Christian. Abhandlungen über forst- und staatswissenschaftliche Gegenstände. 1811. IV. 100.[2]
— Ganz neue, möglichst kürzeste und leichteste Methode, den körperlichen Inhalt ... zu berechnen. 1817. IV. 222.
— Gründlicher Unterricht. über die Reduction kreisrunder Hölzer. 1812. IV. 221.
— Tabellen zur Reduction aller Hölzer. 1817. IV. 222.
Fresenius, Johann Baptist Georg Wolfgang. Grundriss der Botanik. 1840. I. 88.
— Taschenbuch zum Gebrauche auf botanischen Excursionen in der Umgegend von Frankfurt a/M. 1831. I. 378.
Freshfield, Douglas W. Travels in the central Caucasus and Bashan. 1869. I. 369.

Fressanges, (Dr.). Du reboisement localisé. 1884. IV. 168.[2]

Frestadius, Johannes Abrah. Remedia guineensia. See AFZELIUS, Adam. 1813. III. 93.[1]

Fret, A. Een en ander over 't kweeken van Dracaena's. 1878. III. 334.[2]

— Over de Klimopplant. 1877. III. 642.[2]

Freudenberg, Gotthold. Die bekannteren der bei uns kultivierten Nadelhölzer. 1886. III. 290.

Freudenstein, Otto. Geschichte des Waldeigenthums in der vormaligen Grafschaft Schaumburg. 1879. IV. 26.

Freuler, B. Gedanken zu einem neuen Bundesgesetz über das Forstwesen. 1898. IV. 331.[1]

— Ueber die Nutzungsweise ... der Gemeindegüter im Hochgebirge. 1899. IV. 136.[1]

— Waldbrände im südlichen Tessin. 1900. IV. 184.[1]

Freund, August. Zur Kenntniss des Vogelbeersaftes. 1891. II. 312.[3]

— Recherches sur le suc de baies de Sorbier. 1891. II. 312.[3]

Freund, H. D. Kunst, Gartenrosen während des Winters ... zur Blüte zu bringen. 1830. III. 451.[1]

Frey, Albert. Les pâturages boisés du Jura. 1890. IV. 136.[1]

— Quels sont les avantages ... de l'aménagement des forêts en taillis simple et en taillis composé? 1872. IV. 130.

— Welche Vortheile und Nachtheile gewährt der Mittel- und Niederwaldbetrieb? 1872. IV. 130.

Frey, J. A. Gewichts- und Volumenveränderung verschiedener Holzarten. 1885. IV. 412.[1]

Frey, Johann Jakob. Kleines Handbuch der gemeinnützigsten Wissenschaften. 1832. III. 115.[2]

— Kurze ... Anleitung zum schweizerischen Forstwesen. 1832. IV. 99.[1]

— Rationelle Schweizer. Forstwirthschaft. 1847. IV. 110.[2]

Frey, Ludwig. Ueber die Bedeutungslosigkeit des sogenannten Zuwachsprozents. 1892. IV. 258.

— Ein Beitrag zur Lehre vom Waldwertzunahme-Prozent. 1887. IV. 257.

— Ueber den Einfluss des Streurechens. 1889. IV. 72.

— Ueber Erhöhung der Umtriebszeiten. 1890. IV. 270.*

— Die Festsetzung der Fällungsetats. 1887. IV. 237.

— Forsteinrichtungs- und Ertragsregelungs-Verfahren. 1891. IV. 237.

— Zur Lösung der Waldwerthrechnungsfrage. 1885. IV. 257.

— Die Methode der Tauschwerte. 1891. IV. 258.

— Die Methode der Tauschwerthe. 1888. IV. 257.

— Sind Waldnebenutzungen bei Berechnung des Holzbestandswertes in Anrechnung zu bringen. 1888. IV. 237.

— Der Unternehmergewinn im forstwirtschaftlichen Betrieb. 1893. IV. 258.

— Zur Weiterentwicklung der Lehre von den Durchforstungen. 1886. IV. 174.

— Die Ziele der Forstwirthschaft. 1880. IV. 270.

Freycinet, Casimir. Catalogue raisonné des arbres, arbrisseaux. 18..? I. 56.

Freycinet, Louis de. Voyage autour du monde. See GAUDICHAUD-BEAUPRÉ, Charles. 1826. I. 302.

Freye oekonomische Gesellschaft in St. Petersburg. Abhandlungen. Auswahl oekonomischer Abhandlungen. III. 10.[1]

Freyer, C. F. Die schädlichsten Schmetterlinge Deutschlands. 1839. III. 189.

Freyer, Friedrich Wilhelm. Eenige bijvoegselen ... tot de verhandeling over de ziekten der vruchtboomen. 1809. III. 178.

— Over de schadelijke insecten der ooftboomen. 1809. III. 188.[3]

— Verhandeling over de ziekten der vruchtboomen. 1809. III. 178.

Freyhold, Edmund von. Über Symmetrieverhältnisse und Zygomorphismus der Blüthen. 1874. I. 115.[1]

Freylin, L. de. Catalogue des plantes cultivées dans le Jardin de Buttiglièra (Marengo). 1810. I. 61.

Freyn, Josef. Beiträge zur Kenntniss der Vegetations-Verhältnisse des Brdy-Gebirges. 1873. I. 442.

— Beitrag zur Flora von Bosnien. 1888. I. 448.[1]

— Ueber einige Pflanzen insbesondere der österr.-ungar. Flora. 1876. I. 442.

— Zur Flora von Ober-Steiermark. 1898. I. 444.

— Die Flora von Süd-Istrien. 1898. I. 448.[1]

— Ueber neue ... orientalische Pflanzenarten. 1895. I. 451, 479.

— Neue Pflanzenarten der pyrenäischen Halbinsel. 1893. I. 422.

— Plantae Karoanae. 1889. I. 456.

— Plantae Karoanae dahuricae. 1895. I. 456.

— Plantae novae orientales. 1890. I. 450, 479.

— Ranunculaceae aus dem westlichen Nord-Amerika. 1890. II. 195.[2]

— Weitere Beiträge zur Flora von Steiermark. 1900. II. 305.[1]

Freyss, G. Notes sur la créosote de goudron de Hêtre. 1896. IV. 500.[2]

Freytag, Ferd. Einige neue Erfahrungen ... aus dem Gebiete der Eisenhüttenkunde, Holzverkohlung. 1839. IV. 394.

— Von der vortheilhaftesten Verkohlung des Holzes. 1831. IV. 394.

Freytag, Franz. Kreisflächen für Durchmesser von 0,1 bis 151,2 Centimeter. 1881. IV. 228.

Freytag, Morits. Die schädlichen Bestandteile des Hüttenrauchs. 1882. IV. 192.[2]

— Wissenschaftliches Gutachten über den Einfluss des Hüttenrauchs. 1873. IV. 192.[2]

— Wissenschaftliches Gutachten über den Einfluss, welchen die Hüttenwerke ... ausüben. 1870. IV. 192.[1]

Frezard, A. Le Pin d'Autriche. 1862. IV. 465.[2]

Frezier, Amadée François. Relation du voyage de la Mer du Sud aux côtes du Chily et du Perou. 1716. I. 327.

— A voyage to the South-Sea and along the coasts of Chili and Peru. 1716. I. 327.

Friar Park, Henley. 1899. III. 202.[2]

Fribolin, Friz. Die Arbeiterfrage in Beziehung auf das forstliche Gewerbe. 1874. IV. 310.[2]

— Ueber Aufbereitung ... eichener Astrinde. 1871. IV. 512.

— Ein Beitrag zur Schälwaldfrage. 1891. IV. 508.

— Bericht über eine Reise in verschiedene Eichenschälwald-Gebiete Deutschlands. 1872. IV. 506.

— Der Eichenschälwaldbetrieb. 1876. IV. 506.

— Ueber Einschätzung des Ertrages an Eichengerbrinde. 1869. IV. 512.

— Reisenotizen aus den Waldungen des Oberelsass. 1878. IV. 349.[1]

— Ein Wort über das Vermessen des Eichenstammholzes. 1891. IV. 513.

Friborg, Nicolaus. De usu corticis peruviani medico. See KRATZENSTEIN, C. G. 1773. III. 720.

Fribourg. Arbre colossal. 1900. II. 114.[1]

Fribourg — Société fribourgeoise des sciences naturelles. See SOCIÉTÉ ... I. 27.

Friche-Joset, & Montandon, F. J. Guide du botaniste dans le Sundgau. 1856. I. 411.

— Synopsis de la flore du Jura septentrional. 1856. I. 411.

Frick, R. De l'inosite. 1887. I. 177.

Fricke, (Forstassessor). Buchenderbholzformzahlen. 1891. IV. 498.

— Das Wachsthum der Eiche und Buche. 1892. IV. 495, 508.

— Zuwachsuntersuchungen. 1890. IV. 234.

Fricken, Wilhelm von. Excursionsflora ... Westphalens. 1871. I. 386.

Frickhinger, Albert. See SCHNIZLEIN, Adalbert & FRICKHINGER, Albert.

Frickinger, C. Ueber die nachtheiligen Einwirkungen chemischer Fabriken. 1867. III. 185.[1]

— Ueber die schädliche Einwirkung einer chemischen Fabrik. 1868. III. 185.[2]

Friderich, Karl. Vergleichende Versuche über den Einfluss der Streunutzung. 1887. IV. 71.

Friderich, Samuel. De Camphora. 1771. II. 224.[2]

Friderichsen, Kristian. Beiträge zur Kenntniss der Rubi corylifolii. 1897. II. 300.[2]

— Die Nomenclatur des Rubus thyrsoideus. 1899. II. 310.[2]

— Ueber Rubus. Commimelli. 1896. II. 310.[1]

— Rubus Gelertii. 1886. II. 307.[1]

— & Gelert, Otto. Danmarks og Slesvigs Rubi. 1888. II. 301.[1]

— — Om Rubus commixtus. 1890. II. 306.[2]

— — Rubus commixtus nova subspecies. 1890. II. 306.[2]

— — Les Rubus de Danemark et de Slesvig. 1888. II. 301.[1]

Friderici, Johann Arnold. Guajacan. 1665. III. 494.[1]

Fridolin. Gesetz betreffend den Forstdiebstahl. 1890. IV. 321.

— § 1 des Gesetzes vom 31. März 1837. 1890. IV. 317.[1]

Fridolin, Alexander. Vergleichende Untersuchungen über die Gerbstoffe. 1884. I. 183, III. 631.[1]

Fridrich, A. Beschreibung der Forste der k. Stadt Ung.-Hradisch. 1898. IV. 370.
— Ein neuer Schädling der Laubhölzer. 1896. IV. 212.
Friebe, Wilhelm Christian. Von der Kultur des Weinstocks. 1791. III. 551.²
— Oekonomisch-technische Flora für Liefland. 1805. III, 68.¹
Friedel, Charles. Sur la forme cristalline de la cinchonamine. 1887. III. 747.²
— Forme cristalline de la quercine. 1887. IV. 515.¹
— Rapport sur les travaux de M. A. Haller. 1887. III. 611.²
— Rapport sur les travaux de M. Arnaud. 1887. III. 747.²
Friedel, Ernst. Die alten Weiden von Berlin. 1888. II. 105.¹
Friedel, Jean. Action de la pression totale sur l'assimilation chlorophyllienne. 1900. I. 174.
Friedemann, T. A. Der Frost in seinen Wirkungen auf Holzgewächse. 1829. IV. 66.¹
Friederici, von, (Obrist-Lieutenant). Auszug eines Schreibens aus Surinam. 1792. III. 267.²
Friederici, E. Die Zubereitung der Kakao-Ernte. 1898. III. 593.¹
Friedl, František. Sortiment ovocných druhů pro vých. Cechy. 1891. III. 90.¹
Friedländer, W. See FINGER, E., FRIEDLÄNDER, W. & DEMUTH, N.
Friedrich, G. Ueber einen Blitzstrahl in eine Pappel. 1898. IV. 195.¹
Friedrich, Josef. Über den Einfluss der Witterung. 1897. IV. 73.¹
— Präcisionsxylometer. 1890. IV. 231.²
— Präcisions-Xylometer. 1894. IV. 232.
— Tägliche Durchmesserschwankungen der Zweige. 1899. I. 150.¹
— Le volume des aiguilles d'Épicéa. 1896. IV. 459.¹
— Das Volumen der Fichtennadeln. 1896. IV. 459.¹
— Vorführung des Zuwachsautographen. 1900. IV. 235.¹
— Zuwachsmesser. 1890. IV. 234.
Friedrich, K. Über eine Eigenthümlichkeit der Luftwurzeln von Acanthöriza. 1881. II. 64.¹
Friedrich, Paul Alexander. Die Bäume und Sträucher unserer öffentlichen Anlagen. 1889. I. 294, III. 70.
Friedrich August II., King of Saxony. Flora von Marienbad. 1837. I. 440.
Friedrichsthal, Emanuel, Ritter von. Reise in den südlichen Theilen von Neu-Griechenland. 1838. I. 449.
Friend, Hilderic. Flowers and flower lore. 1884. I. 518.
Fries, Andreas. Die weidenartigen Gewächse in der Gegend von Wertheim. 1864. II. 101.¹
Fries, Elias Magnus. Anlagen till ett kommande års fruktbarbet. 1852. I. 217.
— Anmärkningar öfver Cotula matricarioides. 1852. II. 292.¹
— Anmärkningar öfver de i Sverige växande Pilarterna. 1059. III. 050.¹
— Anmärkningar öfver de i Kapska Pilarterna. 1856. II. 103.¹
— Betula glutinosa. 1841. II. 118.²
— Bidrag till bestämmande af de olika begrepp. 1840. I. 251.
— Bidrag till några Linneanska vexters riktiga bestämmande. 1842. I. 268.
— Bidrag till några svenska vaxters synonymik. 1857. I. 355.
— Botaniska utflygter. 1843. I. 34.
— Commentatio de Salicibus Sueciae. 1832. II. 100.¹
— Conspectus dispositionis Salicum Sueciae. 1825. II. 100.¹
— Conspectus florae Ostrogothicae. 1854. I. 355.
— Corpus florarum provincialium Sueciae. 1835. I. 353.
— Drifning vintertiden af hela exemplar af Syringa. 1841. III. 176.¹
— Flora gevaliensis. See HARTMAN, Carl. 1847. I. 355.
— Flora hallandica. 1817. I. 352.
— Förslag till ett bestämdt betecknings-sätt af de olika begrepp. 1840. I. 251.
— Grunddragen af Aristotelis vextlära. 1842. I. 292.
— Grundzüge von Aristoteles's Pflanzen. 1842. I. 292.
— Kritisk ordbok öfver svenska växtnamnen. 1880. I. 73.¹
— Några anteckningar till Reichenbachs Flora germanica exsiccata. 1845. I. 381.
— Några ord öfver slägt- och artbegreppen. 1852. I. 252.
— Novitiae florae suecicae. 1814. I. 355.
— Nya skandinaviska växter. 1849. I. 355.
— Nya växtfynd vid Upsala. 1842. II. 118.²

— Observationes criticae plantas suecicas illustrantes. 1854. I. 355.
— Öfver parthenogesi hos växterna. 1857. I. 202.¹
— Om Pilplanteringar. 1836. II. 100,¹ III. 350.²
— Plantae vasculares circa Quickjock. See ANDERSSON, N. J. 1844. I. 354.
— Referat af J. G. Agardh. Om växternas stipler. 1849. I. 111.
— Reservation emot en del antagna åsigter öfver åtskilliga svenska vexter. 1844. I. 354.
— Rön öfver vissa vextformers sjelfständighet. 1841. I. 252.
— Ruborum Sueciae disposito. See ARRHENIUS, J. P. 1839. II. 301.¹
— Öfver de i särskilda trakter af Sverige. 1843. I. 354.
— Salix ₙ ₛ *acutifolia funnen i Dalarne. 1840. II. 106, idaph oide
— Stirpes agri femsionensis. 1825. I. 353.
— Strödda anmärkningar öfver några svenska växter. 1840. I. 354.
— Summa vegetabilium Scandinaviae. 1846. I. 355.
— De svenska arterna af slägtet Betula. 1848. II. 117.²
— Svenska Pilarterne. 1840. II. 100.¹
— De i Sverige växande Pilarterna. 1859. III. 350.²
— Tillägg till E. Fries' naturliga växtsystem. 1843. I. 252.
— Vårens antåg. 1839. I. 223.¹
Fries, Elias Peter. Om storax. 1858. III. 417.²
Fries, Theodor Magnus. Anteckningar rörande en i Paris befintlig Linneansk växtsamling. 1861. II. 99.¹
— Beiträge zur Kenntniss der Nadelhölzer Skandinaviens. 1890. II. 15.¹
— Botaniska anteckningar rörande Femsjö socken. 1852. I. 355.
— Egendomliga sammanväxningar hos Barrträd. 1892. I. 209,¹ IV. 66.²
— Ueber eigenthümliche Verwachsungen bei Nadelhölzern. 1892. I. 209,¹ IV. 66.²
— Exemplar i Sverige af Aesculus Hippocastanum. 1857. II. 482.¹
— Farsot hos Norrlands barrskogar. 1857. IV. 211.¹
— Iakttagelser rörande några arktiska växter. 1858. II. 108.²
— Menniskans inflytande på den svenska florans nuvarande sammansättning. 1886. I. 357.
— Notis om groning af Acer platanoides. 1872. II. 479.²
— Om Nowaja Semljas vegetation. 1873. I. 363.
— Nya skandinaviska växter. 1857. II. 38.¹
— Sömnställning hos bladen af Mimosa och Acacia, förorsakad af solförmörkelsen. 1858. I. 198.
— Spridda växtgeografiska bidrag till Skandinaviens flora. 1857. I. 355.
— Strödda bidrag till kännedomen om Skandinaviens Barrträd. 1900. II. 15.¹
— Tillägg till ... Några ord om de ... formerna af Granen. 1867. II. 34.²
Friese, Friedrich Gotthilf. Oeconomisch-technologische Abhandlung über die syrische Seidenpflanze. 1791. III. 373.
Friese, J. R. Grundriss der Phytognosie. 1836. I. 255.
Friese, Johann Bernhard. Disputatio de iure arborum. 1678. IV. 313.
— De jure giutiae. 1701. IV. 013.
Friese, Lafayette Hoyt de. See DE FRIESE, L. H.
Friese, Lorenz. Synonyma und gerecht usslegung der wörter, so man das in der artzny allen Kreutern. 1519. I. 71.
Friesen, F. O. H., Freiherr von. Die volkswirthschaftliche Bedeutung des Baumschnitts. 1880. III. 172.
Friess, Franz. Die grosse Kiefernraupe. 1851. IV. 475.
Frignet, Ernest. Essai sur l'histoire de la blastogénie foliaire. 1846. I. 107.¹
Friktion des Holzes. 1850. IV. 411.²
The Fringe trees. 1894. III. 671.²
The Fringed Hibiscus. 1879. III. 588.¹
Frisch, Friedrich. See BIEBER, Hermann & FRISCH, Friedrich.
Frisch, J. P. Ueber die Verwendung der Valonea. 1877. III. 362.¹
Frisoni, Eduard. Ueber die Verbindung der Pflanzenzellen. See MOHL, Hugo. 1835. I. 123.¹
Fristedt, Robert Fredric. Växtgeographisk skildring af Södra Angermanland. 1857. I. 355.
Frith, R. W. G. See HODGSON, B. H. & FRITH, R. W. G.
Fritsch, A. T. Der preussische Forstbeamte. 1862. IV. 32, 290.²

Fritsch, Ahasver. Corpus juris venatorio-forestalis. 1676. IV. 316.
— Dissertatio juridico-politica de jure plantandi. 1681. IV. 313.
— Dissertationes duae, quarum prior de jure boscandi. 1676. IV. 313.
— Tractatus de regali iure grutiae vulgo Flössrecht. 1668. IV. 313.
Fritsch, Alban. Die historische Entwicklung des Pflanzenlebens im Pöhlberg-Gebiete. 1898. I. 390.
Fritsch, Carl (*of Tilsit*). Ueber die Marklücke der Coniferen. 1886. IV. 62.[1]
— Die Marklücken der Coniferen. 1886. II. 17,[1] 871.[1]
— Die sogenannte "Marklücke" bei den Nadelhölzern. 1886. IV. 62.[1]
Fritsch, Josef. Betrachtungen über die Pappelcultur. 1857. III. 344.[1]
Fritsch, Karl (*of Graz*). Anatomisch-systematische Studien über . . . Rubus. 1887. II. 305.[2]
— Beiträge zur Flora der Balkanhalbinsel. 1895. I. 450.
— Beiträge zur Flora von Salzburg. 1888. I. 443.
— Beiträge zur Kenntniss der Chrysobalanaceen. 1889. II. 256.[1]
— Das botanische Museum . . . der K. k. Universität in Wien. 1894. I. 522.[1]
— Botanisches Museum. 1894. I. 522.[1]
— Ein von C. Mulley . . . gesammelten Rhamnus. 1896. II. 498.[1]
— Caprifoliaceae. 1891. II. 833.[2]
— Die Casuarineen. 1893. II. 92.[1]
— Columelliaceae. 1895. II. 795.[2]
— Ueber die Eigenthümlichkeiten . . . üppig entwickelter Schösslinge des schwarzen Hollunders. 1889. II. 841.[1]
— Ueber einige Licania-Arten. 1892. II. 265.[2]
— Über einige südwestasiatische Prunus-Arten. 1892. II. 271.[2]
— Über einige während der ersten Regnell'schen Expedition gesammelte Gamopetalen. 1898. I. 344.
— Zur Flora von Madagascar. 1890. I. 496.
— Die Gattungen der Caprifoliaceen. 1892. II. 833.[2]
— Ueber die Gattungen der Chrysobalanaceen. 1888. II. 256.[1]
— Gesneriaceae. 1895. II. 792.[2]
— Kletterpflanzen: 1896. I. 236.[1]
— Nomenclatorische Bemerkungen. 1892. I. 254.[1]
— Die Palmen. 1900. II. 64.[1]
— Zur Phylogenie der Gattung Salix. 1888. II. 99.[1]
— Die Rubi Neuseelands. 1886. II. 305.[1]
— Ueber Salix oppositifolia Host. 1894. II. 109.[1]
— Ueber Spiraea. 1889. II. 314.[1]
— Zur Systematik der Gattung Sorbus. 1898. II. 311.[2]
— Zur systematischen Stellung von Sambucus. 1892. II. 840.[2]
— Vorläufige Mittheilung über die Rubus-Flora Salzburgs. 1888. II. 304.[2]
Fritsch, Karl (*of Prag*). Über die absolute Veränderlichkeit der Blüthezeit. 1871. I. 221.
— Anleitung zur Ausführung von Beobachtungen über . . . jährliche Periode. 1850. I. 220.[2]
— Begriff der Phänologie. 1861. I. 220.[1]
— Belaubung . . . der Holzgewächse in Wien. 1862. I. 528.[2]
— Blüthe und Fruchtreife der Holzgewächse in Wien. 1863. I. 529.
— De la dynamique des végétaux. 1864. I. 221.
— Ergebnisse mehrjähriger Beobachtungen über die periodischen Erscheinungen. 1865. I. 227.[2]
— Instruction für phänologische Beobachtungen. 1859. I. 220.[2]
— Kalender der Flora des Horizontes von Prag. 1852. I. 227.[1]
— Kalender der Fruchtreife. 1866. I. 227.[2]
— Nachricht von den in Österreich . . . angestellten phänologischen Beobachtungen. 1860. I. 227.[1]
— Normaler Blüthen-Kalender. 1867. I. 227.[2]
— On the periodical opening and closing of flowers. 1851. I. 198.
— Ueber die periodischen Erscheinungen im Pflanzenreiche. 1845. I. 220.[1]
— Pflanzenphänologische Untersuchungen. 1866. I. 221.
— Phänologische Beobachtungen. 1869. V. XII.[1]
— Ueber phänologische Beobachtungen an . . . der Donau. 1858. I. 227.[1]
— Phänologische Notizen über die Blüthezeit des Roggens. 1862. II. 508.[1]

— Phänologische Studien. 1870. I. 221.
— Phänologische Uebersichten von Oesterreich. 1856. I. 227.[1]
— Resultate aus den Beobachtungen über jene Pflanzen, deren Blumenkronen sich . . . öffnen und schliessen. 1850. I. 198.
— Resultate mehrjähriger Beobachtungen über die Belaubung. 1861. I. 227.[1]
— Resultate mehrjähriger Beobachtungen über jene Pflanzen, deren Blumenkronen sich . . . öffnen und schliessen. 1851. I. 198.
— Thermische Constanten. 1862. I. 227.[2]
— Untersuchungen über das Gesetz des Einflusses der Lufttemperatur. 1858. I. 220.[2]
— Vegetations-Verhältnisse in Österreich. 1854. I. 227.[1]
— Vergleichung der Blüthezeit der Pflanzen von Nord-Amerika und Europa. 1871. I. 22].
— *See also* Boos, Josef & FRITSCH, Karl; QUETELET, Adolphe, LINSTER, Ch. & FRITSCH, Karl.
Fritsch, Karl (*of Tilsit*). *See* FRITSCH, Carl.
Fritsch, P. Über farbige körnige Stoffe. 1884. I.]85.[1]
Fritsch, Peter. De manna. 1677. III. 221.[1]
Fritsche, (*Oberförster*). Aus den rigaschen Stadtforsten. 1881. IV. 144.[1]
— Die Riga'schen Stadtwälder. 1878. IV. 347.
Fritscher, C. Eine neue Veredlungsmethode. 1884. III. 162.
Fritz, Hermann. Die Perioden der Weinerträge. 1881. III. 553.[1]
Fritz, Karl. Herstellung und Pflege der Baumpflanzungen. 1897. III. 210.
Fritz, N. Bladhvepseangreb i Vester-Palsgaard Plantage. 1874. III. 190.
— De danske skadelige Løv- og Frugttræinsekter. 1894. III. 191.
— De danske skadelige Naaletræinsekter. 1892. IV. 549.[1]
— Forstentomologiske Meddelelser. 1873. IV. 205.[1]
— Hvorfor vil Fyrren ikke trives paa de jydske Heder? 1873. IV. 472.
Fritze, Johann Friederich. De usu corticis peruviani . . . experimentando. 1756. III. 719.
Fritze, R. & Ilse, Hugo. Beiträge zur Flora der hohen Tatra. 1870. I. 446.
— — Karpaten-Reise. 1870. I. 446.
Fritzemayer, E. Der Obstbau. 1885. III. 139.
Fritzsche, Carl. Die Brennstoffe und ihre Anwendung. 1843. IV. 412.[2]
Fritzsche, Hermann. Vollständige Abhandlung über den Hausschwamm. 1866. IV. 415.[1]
Fritzsche, Karl Julius Philipp von. Beiträge zur Kenntniss des Pollen. 1832. I. 117.[1]
— De plantarum polline. 1833. I. 117.[1]
— Ueber den Pollen. 1833. I. 117.[1]
— Ueber den Pollen der Pflanzen. 1834. I. 201.[2]
Fritzsche, Louis. Rechtskunde für Forst- und Landwirthe des Königreichs Sachsen. 1847. IV. 322.[1]
Frivaldszky, Imré. Plantae novae turcicae. 1835. I. 449.
— Succinctae diagnoses specierum . . . europaeo-turcicarum. 1835. I. 448.[2]
Frochot, Alexis. Des formes paraboliques appliquées au cubage. 1890. IV. 218.
— Guide théorique et pratique de cubage. 1890. IV. 218.
— Une question de sylviculture. 1867. IV. 382.[1]
— La règle de cubage. 1877. IV. 217.
— Traité de sylviculture. 1877. IV. 109 [2]
Froebel, Otto. Ueber Alpenpflanzen und deren Cultur. 1885. III. 126.[2]
— Lettre de la Suisse. 1880. III. 49.[2]
— Rosa canina L. var. Froebelii Christ. 1892. II. 292.[1]
— Rosa laxa. 1890. III. 455.[2]
Fröbel, Theodor. Bemerkungen über Acacia petiolaris. 1852. III. 465.[2]
— Einiges über Ziergehölze. 1879. III. 89.[1]
Froebel & Comp. Zwei werthvolle Granaten-Varietäten. 1882. III. 630.[2]
Froehner, Albrecht. Die Gattung Coffea und ihre Arten. 1898. II. 814.[1]
— Uebersicht über die Arten der Gattung Coffea. 1896. II. 814.[1]
Frölich, C. F. Botanische Spaziergänge im Kanton Appenzell. 1850. I. 434.
Fröman, Gustaf Alfrid. Om slingringen hos Solanum Dulcamara. 1893. II. 776.[1]
Frömbling, C. Anleitung zur natürlichen Verjüngung des Buchen-Hochwaldes. 1892. IV. 496.

— Ueber das Auftreten der Schütte. 1869. IV. 476.
— Ueber die Bedeutung der Vorbereitungshiebe für die natürliche Buchen-Verjüngung. 1888. IV. 495.
— Ein Beitrag zur Frage über den Werth des Unterbaues. 1886. IV. 129.
— Betrachtungen über die Schütte. 1871. IV. 476.
— Eigenthümliche Erkrankung der Fichte. 1876. IV. 456.
— Der Goldregen. 1886. IV. 521.²
— Die natürliche Verjüngung des Buchen-Hochwaldes. 1892. IV. 496.
— Noch einmal von der Traubeneiche. 1889. IV. 508.
— Nochmals die Traubeneiche. 1887. IV. 507.
— Nochmals über Lichtungszuwachs. 1899. IV. 235.¹
— Saatlatte zu Nadelholz-Saatkämpen. 1871. IV. 149.¹
— Der Ueberhalt im Buchen-Hochwalde. 1887. IV. 495.
— Ueber die Ursachen der Lärchen-Erkrankung. 1889. IV. 451.
— Verschiedene Ursachen der Kiefern-Schütte. 1900. IV. 480.
— Ueber die waldbauliche Bedeutung des Elsterbaumes. 1889. IV. 520.²
— Wie ist den Schädigungen des Agaricus melleus vorzubeugen? 1890. IV. 212.
— Ein Wort zu Gunsten der Traubeneiche. 1886. IV. 507.
Frömbling, Friedrich Wilhelm. Ueber die Absprünge der Fichte. 1825. II. 36.³
— Die Bau- und Brennmaterialvorräthe auf und innerhalbs des vaterländischen Bodens. 1848. IV. 348.²
— Die Feld- und Waldfortifikation für Deutschland. 1844. IV. 46.³
— Fragmente über den Stand der königlich preussischen Domainen-Forst-Verwaltung. 1839. IV. 290.¹
— Fragmente über Vertheilung des Grundeigenthums. 1839. IV. 273.²
— Der Grunewald. 1848. IV. 117.
— Leuchtkugeln über Forst-Literatur. 1839. IV. 268.
— Die naturhistorischen und forstwirthschaftlichen Zustände der Dünen. 1858. IV. 158.
— Vortrag über das nothwendige Waldgesetz. 184.? IV. 43.
— Der Waldanbau. 1848. IV. 141.
— Die Waldfelder. 1848. IV. 133.
Froembling, Walter. Anatomisch-systematische Untersuchung ... der Crotoneen. 1896. II. 435.¹
— Ueber botanische Excursionen ... in Chile. 1895. I. 347.
Die Fröste, ihre verschiedenen Formen. 1864. IV. 66.²
Froger, François. Relation d'un voyage de la Mer du Sud. 1698. I. 301.
— A relation of a voyage ... on the coasts of Africa. 1698. I. 301.
Froggatt, Walter Wilson. Australian case or bag moths. 1900. III. 193.¹
— The entomology of the Grass-trees. 1896. III. 330.¹
— Forest moths. 1897. III. 192.²
— The growth of vegetable galls. 1899. I. 216.²
— Insect pests. 1900. III. 370.¹
— Insects living in Figs. 1900. II. 151.¹
— San José scale. 1898. III. 193.¹
— Scale insects that produce lac. 1900. III. 233.¹
— See also ALLEN, W. J., BLUNNO, M., FROGGATT, W. W. & GUTHRIE, F. B.; BLUNNO, M. & FROGGATT, W. W.
Froidour, Louis de. Instruction pour les ventes des bois du roy. 1668. IV. 303.¹
Frojo, Giuseppe. Del Corylus Avellana. 1865. III. 358.¹
— Sopra una malattia degli Albicocchi. 1868. III. 434.²
From, J. Forsøg med at saae Frø. 1837. III. 156.¹
— Den urteagtige Podning. 1841. III. 163.²
Fromberg, Peter Friedrich Heinrich. Berigt over een scheikundig onderzoek der notenmuskaatschillen. 1856. III. 402.²
— Berigt over een scheikundig onderzoek van muskaatnotenschillen. 1856. III. 402.³
— Over de bestanddeelen der planten. 1847. I. 152.³
— Over cellulose. 1845. I. 137.
— De connexione inter plantarum vitam et partes constituentes. 1847. I. 147.
— Eerste verslag over de uitkomsten der bemesting van Koffijboomen. 1858. III. 733.¹
— Iets over het pectine zuur. 1845. I. 180.¹
— Over den invloed door vermindering ... van houtbosschen uitgeoefend op het klimaat. 1855. IV. 52.
— Landbouwkunde in verband met de natuurkundige wetenschappen. 1847. III. 36.¹
— Nota over de kultuur ... der kakao. 1858. III. 592.¹

— Rapport over harsen van Borneo. 1858. III. 227.
— Uittreksel uit een verslag over de oorzaken der uitsterving van Koffijboomen. 1852. III. 735.
— Verslag over .. soerenbast. 1858. III. 512.¹
— Over het watergehalte in verschillende lucht drooge koffiesoorten. 1852. III. 739.
Fromm. Naturmerkwürdigkeiten. 1830. IV. 486.¹
— Zwei riesige deutsche Pappeln. 1830. II. 98.¹
Fromm, Franz & Kopeczek, Franz. Zur Frage über Veredlung von Camellien. 1872. III. 165.
Frommann. Forstliche Exkursion in den Jaxtkreis. 1844. IV. 356.¹
— Reise-Früchte. 1843. IV. 356.¹
Frommann, Carl Friedrich Wilhelm. Über Beschaffenheit und Umwandlungen der Membran. 1888. I. 137.
— Zur Lehre von der Bildung der Membran von Pflanzenzellen. 1884. I. 138.¹
— Ueber Veränderungen der Membranen der Epidermiszellen ... Pelargonium zonale. 1885. II. 391.³
Frommann, Johann Christian. Quod felix faustumq. 168.? II. 509.¹
Fromme Wünsche, den forstlichen Unterricht betreffend, am Polytechnikum zu Zürich. 1854. IV. 36.¹
Fromme's forstliche Kalender-Tasche. See FROMME's österreichischer Forst-Kalender. IV. 14.
Fromme's österreichischer Forst-Kalender. IV. 14.
Fromme's Österreichisch-ungarischer Gartenkalender. III. 24.²
Frommel, W. & Pfaff, Friedrich. Sammlung von Vorträgen. See WOLF, Theodor. 1879. I. 510.²
Fron, A. L'apiculture en maison forestière. 1898. IV. 439.
Fron, Georges. Recherches anatomiques sur ... Chénopodiacées. 1899. II. 187.¹
— See also DYROWSKI, Jean & FRON, G.
Fronius, Friedrich. Beobachtungen während des Jahres 1855. 1855. I. 227.¹
— Flora von Schässburg. 1858. I. 445.
Fronmuller, C. & Baelz, Erwin. Recherche sur les propriétés de l'écorce de coto. 1879. III. 268.²
Frost, Charles C. See TUCKERMAN, Edward & FROST, C. C.
Frost, Henry R. Elements of the materia medica. 1843. III. 243.
Frost, John. Remarks on the Mustard tree. 1827. I. 513.
Frostschäden des Winters 1870-1871. 1871. III. 45.
Fruchier, Charles. Le Pistachier. 1859. III. 525.¹
Der Fruchtbau im Walde. 1836. IV. 133.
Der fruchtbringenden Gesellschaft Namen. 1646. I. 515.
Fructus, X. Sur la préparation du sirop de bourgeons de Sapin. 1897. IV. 447.¹
Früchte der Tropen. 1898. III. 220.²
Frühauf, Thomas. In welcher Weise lässt sich die Bekämpfung der Peronospora. 1890. III. 580.
Ueber die frühere ... Bewurzelung der Senker. 1833. III. 157.
Frühlings- oder Herbst-Pflanzung? 1857. IV. 154.²
Frugtrædyrkningen hos de gamle Romere. 1852. III. 33.
The fruit and forest trees. See EMMONS, Ebenezer. 1849. V. XI.²
The fruit culture on the Himalaya. 1896. III. 147.¹
Fruit de Passiflora quadrangularis. 1858. II. 581.¹
The fruit garden display'd. See BRADLEY, Richard. 1732. III. 78.²
The fruit-gardener. See GIBSON, J. 1768. III. 141.
Fruit growers' association of Ontario. Report. III. 2.
Fruit growers' association of the province of Quebec. Report. See MONTREAL HORTICULTURAL SOCIETY. III. 2.
Fruit of Lecythis. 1861. II. 612.¹
The fruit of Ptelea trifoliata. 1879. III. 505.²
Fruit of Stephanotis floribunda. 1874. III. 694.¹
Fruit of Torreya myristica. 1875. III. 288.²
Fruit-walls improved by inclining ... See FATIO DE DUILLER, Nicolaus. 1699. III. 141.
The fruiterer's secrets. 1604. III. 173.²
Fruiting of Akebia quinata. 1898. III. 393.³
Fruiting of Brugmansia lutea. 1888. III. 699.²
Fruiting of the common Jasmine. 1884. III. 673.¹
A fruiting stove shrub. 1875. III. 459.¹
Fruits and flowers of Oregon and Washington. III. 3.
Fruits and forest, shade and ornamental trees. See RICHMANN, E. S. 1893. III. 118.¹
Les fruits d'élite, 2 éd. des Actes du Congrès de pomologie. 1882. III. 77.

Les fruits du Caroubier. 1899. III. 472.[1]
The fruits of Egypt. 1886. III. 280.[3]
Fruwirth, C. Der Rindendruck. 1884. IV. 64.[2]
Fry, George. The Fuchsia; its history. 1893. III. 640.[1]
Fry, R. E. On aggregations of proteid in ... Euphorbia. 1890. II. 443.[3]
Fry, Walter G. A catalogue of vegetable substances ... used for tanning leather. 1864. III. 237.[2]
— Notes on tanning substances. 1861. III. 237.[1]
Fua. Note concernant quelques expériences faites avec le cyanure de potassium. 1874. III. 567.[1]
Fuard du Castel. L'école du jardinier fleuriste. See L'ÉCOLE ... 1764. III. 112.
Fuchs, von. See ROTTENBERG, Baron von & FUCHS, von, (Oberförster, Krascheow).
Fuchs, C. A. Untersuchungen über Cytisus Adami. 1898. II. 368.[3]
Fuchs, Christian Joseph. Versuch über den Einfluss des Leuchtgases. 1873. III. 185.[2]
Fuchs, Franz. Ueber einige neue forstschädliche Tipuliden-arten. 1900. IV. 208.[1]
Fuchs, Friedrich. Ungarns Urwälder. 1861. IV. 123.[2] ·
Fuchs, János. A fák görbeségének okairól. 1881. I. 105.
— A Körismag csiráso képessége. 1883. IV. 535.[1]
Fuchs, Josef. Betriebsresultate der ersten Riesweganlage im Salzkammergute. 1875. IV. 391.
Fuchs, Josef. Katalog der Hölzer-Sammlung des allgemeinen Österr. Apotheker-Vereines. 1866. I. 37,[2] IV. 17.'
Fuchs, Joseph. Vollständiges Lehrbuch die Eiche ... zu erziehen. 1824. IV. 504.
Fuchs, Leonhard. Annotationes aliquot herbarum & simplicium. 1532. I. 276.
— Commentaires tres excellens de l'hystoire des plantes. 1542. I. 278.
— De componendorum miscendorumque medicamentorum ratione. 1556. III. 239.
— Histoire des plantes. · 1542. I. 278.
— Histoire generale des plantes et herbes. · 1542. I. 278.
— De historia stirpium commentarii insignes. 1542. .I. 278, 530,[3] V. xv.[1]
— Läbliche Abbildung und Contrafaytung aller Kreuter. 1545. I. 278.
— New Kreüterbüch. 1542. I. 278.
— Den nieuwen herbarius. 1542. I. 278.
— Plantarum effigies. 1545. I. 278.
— Plantarum et stirpium icones. 1545. I. 278.
— Primi de stirpium historia commentariorum tomi vivae imagines. 1545. .I. 278, V. xv.[1]
— Stirpium imagines. 1545. I. 278.
Fuchs, Max. Die geographische Verbreitung des Kaffee-baums. 1885. II. 314.[2]
Fuchs, P. C. A. Untersuchungen über den Bau der Raphidenzelle. 1898. I. 139.
Fuchs, Remacleus. De herbarum notitia, natura atque viribus dialogus. 1544. I. 278.
— Plantarum omnium ... nomenclaturae. 1541. I. 278.
— De plantis antea ignotis. 1542. I. 278.
Fuchs, Theodor. Die Mediterranflora. 1877. I. 228,[3] 428.'
Fuchsia; florists' varieties. 1851. III. 639.[3]
Fuchsier med oprette Blomster. 1886. III. 640.[1]
Fuckel, Leopold. Nassau's Flora. 1856. I. 383.
— Nassau's Flora. 1870. I. 386.
Fucsek, Gyula. Az Eperfa. 1897. III. 378.
Függelék a Magyar gyógyszerkönyvhöz. See MAGYAR gyógyszerkönyv. Pharmacopoea hungarica. 1871. III. 256.[2]
Führer, Georg Ferdinand. Anleitung zur ... Behandlung der Holzungen. 1804. IV. 105.
Führer für die Excursion ... durch das k. Forstrevier Tschiefer. 1896. IV. 355.[1]
Führer für die Excursion ... durch den Schutzbezirke Klodnitz und Lenkau. 1897. IV. 355.[1]
Führer für die Land- und Forstwirthschaft. IV. 9. ·
Führer zu der Excursion in die Görlitzer Haide. 1885. IV. 354.
Führer zur Besichtigung der mündener Lehrforstreviere. See BORGGREVE, Bernard. 1890. IV. 354.
Füldner, Christoph. Die Garten-, Feld- und Wald-Raupen. 1804. IV. 549.'
Fülleborn, Johann Gottlieb. De eximia myrrhae genuinae virtute. See CARTHEUSER, J. F. 1746. III. 510.[3]
Fünfstück, Moritz. Botanischer Taschenatlas. 1894. I. 532.[2]
— Naturgeschichte des Pflanzenreichs. 1885. V. xiii.[2]

Fuentes, Manuel A. La Coca du Pérou. 1866. III. 492.[2]
— Mémoire sur le Coca de Pérou. 1866. III. 492.[2]
Fürnrohr, August Emanuel. Flora ratisbonensis. 1839. I. 380.
— Naturhistorische Topographie von Regensburg. 1838. I. 379.
Fürsorge für den Waldarbeiterstand. 1890. IV. 310.[1]
Fürst, Alexander. Gesetz betreffend den Forstdiebstahl. 1894. IV. 321.
Fürst, Friedrich. Zur Ungleichheit des Stärkenwachsthums. 1899. IV. 235.[1]
— Zur Beseitigung einer unregelmässigen Vertheilung der Altersclassen. 1883. IV. 244.
— Die Düngung der Forstgärten. 1884. IV. 144.[3]
— Die Erziehung von Akazienpflanzen. 1884. IV. 523.[1]
Fürst, Hermann. Die Aufforstung der Nonnenfrassflächen. 1898. IV. 142.
— Das Auftreten der Forleule. 1897. IV. 208.[1]
— Das Auftreten ... der Forstunkräuter. 1895. IV. 211.[1]
— Die Auswahl des richtigen Platzes für Saatkamp. 1890. IV. 234.
— Bedenken auf dem Gebiet der Holzmesskunde. 1896. IV. 234.
— Ein Beitrag zur Unterbau-Frage. 1893. IV. 139.[1]
— Blitzschlag oder Insektenschaden. 1892. IV. 194.
— Chronik der Königl. bayr. Forstlehranstalt Aschaffenburg. 1894. IV. 33.[2]
— Der deutsche Reichsforstverein. 1899. IV. 40.[2]
— Drohende Insektenbeschädigungen. 1889. IV. 208.[1]
— Zur Durchforstungs- und Aufastungs-Praxis. 1895. IV. 172,[2] 175.[1]
— Die Entwickelung der Staatsforstwirtschaft im Königreich Sachsen. 1898. IV. 291.[1]
— Die Erziehung von Pflanzheistern. 1891. IV. 147.[1]
— Eine Exkursion auf den Karst. 1891. IV. 167.[2]
— Eine Exkursion in das Gebiet der Plenterdurchforstung. 1900. IV. 175.[3]
— Das Forstgesetz für das Königreich Bayern. 1885. IV. 319.[1]
— Forstschutz. 1887. IV. 177.[2]
— Zur Frage der Plenterdurchforstung. 1893. IV. 174.
— Die " freie Wirthschaft " im Walde. 1890. IV. 245.
— Die Gründung des deutschen Forstvereins. 1900. IV. 40.[2]
— Die Gründung eines deutschen Reichsforstvereins. 1882. IV. 40.[2]
— Der höhere forstliche Unterricht. 1898. IV. 29.
— Illustriertes Forst- und Jagd-Lexikon. 1888. IV. 22.[2]
— Immer wieder Reinertrag! 1888. IV. 257.
— Aus dem Insektenjahre 1889. 1890. IV. 208.[1]
— Konsequenzen im Kampf um die vortheilhafteste Umtriebszeit. 1892. IV. 252.
— Die Mistel (Viscum album) als forstschädliches Unkraut. 1876. · III. 385.[1]
— Mittel gegen Schneedruckschaden in Buchenjunghölzern. 1882. IV. 495.
— Der Muth'sche Wurzelverschnitt. 1899. IV. 154.[1]
— Das Nachbarrecht bezüglich Wald und Feld. 1897. IV. 314.[1]
— Die Nachzucht der Buche und Eiche. 1897. IV. 496, 508.
— Die Nachzucht der Eiche im Hochwalde. 1888. IV. 508.
— Die Nachzucht der Zirbelkiefer. 1899. IV. 464.[1]
— Die naturgemässe Aufführung der Pflanzung. 1890. IV. 153.[1]
— Die Pflanzensucht im Walde. 1882. IV. 150
— Ueber Pflanzweite. 1893. IV. 154.[1]
— Die Plänterdurchforstung. 1886. IV. 174.
— Plänterwald oder schlagweiser Hochwald. 1885. IV. 128.
— Die rechnerischen Ergebnisse des Lichtwuchsbetriebes. 1890. IV. 258.
— Ueber Schutzwaldungen. 1875. IV. 177.[1]
— Zur Statistik der Waldbrände. 1885. IV. 182.[2]
— Sterben von der Nonne kahlgefressene Fichtenbestände ab. 1890. IV. 456.
— Die Tageslitteratur über die Nonne. 1892. IV. 201.
— Zur Verjüngungs-Praxis. 1898. IV. 140.
— Die Verzinsung unserer Waldkapitale. 1891. IV. 258.
— Die Waldungen in der Umgebung von Aschaffenburg. 1884. IV. 351.[1]
— Wandernde Pflanzkämpe. 1890. IV. 151.[1]
— & Prantl. Der Einfluss des Winters 1879/80. 1880. IV. 191.[3]

Fürst, Johann Evangelist. Über die Benützung unserer Erde als Obstbaumfeld. 1817. III. 136.
Des Fürstenthumbs Newburg Forst- und Holtsordnung. 1577. IV. 318.
Fürstl. braunschw. lüneburgische wolffenbüttelsche theils Forst- und Amts-Cammer-Ordnung. 1729. IV. 319.[1]
Fürstl. Forst-Reglement auch andere Forst-Ordnungen in dem Fürstenthum Blankenburg. 172.? IV. 319.[1]
Die fürstlich schwarzburg-rudolstädtischen Waldforste. 1872. IV. 355.[2]
Das fürstl. Johann Adolf Schwarzenberg'sche Forsteinrichtungsweesen. 1883. IV. 250.[1]
Fürstliche oettingische Jägerey- und Forst-Ordnung. 1682. IV. 318.
Fürstlich-waldeckische Forst- und Jagd- oder Weidewercks-Ordnung. 1741. IV. 319.[2]
Fürth, J. De zwarte schimmel op Succirubra boomen. 1888. III. 717.[2]
Fugger, Eberhard. Die phänologischen Beobachtungen in Salzburg. 1880. I. 227.[2]
Fuhlrott, Karl. Beiträge zur Systematik. 1833. I. 268.
— Ueber Fruchtbildung von Juglans nigra. 1848. II. 112.[2]
— Jussieu's und De Candolle's natürliche Pflanzensysteme. 1829. I. 260, V. XIII.[1]
Fuhr, E. A. Forest devastation. 1900. IV. 281.[1]
Fuhrmann, (Kunst- u. Handels-gärtner, Berlin). Bemerkungen über die Vortheile der Anzucht des Weinstocks aus dem Samen. 1835. III. 548.[1]
— Einige Bemerkungen über Obst-Orangerie. 1830. III. 136.
— Versuche, die Erziehung von Weinstöcken . . . betreffend. 1830. III. 548.[1]
— Über eine dem Wein schädliche Raupe. 1832. III. 562.[2]
Fuiren, Georg. Index plantarum indigenarum. 1662. I. 350.[1]
Fuiren, Thomas. Bibliotheca medica Henrici Fuiren. 1659. III. 1.
Fuji, Kenjiro. On the different views . . . of the flowers of Ginkgo. 1896. II. 8.[1]
— On the nature . . . of so-called "Chichi" of Ginkgo. 1895. II. 8.[1]
— Physiological researches on the sexuality . . . of Pinus densiflora. 1895. II. 41.[3]
Fulbert-Dumonteil. Un Tilleul sans pareil. 1898. II. 517.[1]
Fuldner, Adolf. Ueber Aufbewahrung der Bucheckern. 1881. IV. 495.
— Ueber das Ausfrieren der jungen Pflanzen. 1881. IV. 191.[2]
— Geschichtliche Entwickelung des forstlichen Studiums. 1876. IV. 24.[1] 29.
— Eine Mittheilung über die Wirkung des Schneeschüttelns. 1869. IV. 190.
Fulin, Martin. Bignonia magnifica. 1887. III. 705.
— Camoensia maxima. 1886. III. 469.[3]
— Domací zahrada. 1891. III. 116.[1]
— Druhý květ Ořešáku. 1888. II. 114.[1]
— Květinářství. 1895. III. 116.[1]
— Ovocní oranžerie. 1900. III. 147.[1]
— Pandanus Liaisianus. 1887. III. 313.[2]
— Reinwardia trigyna. 1886. III. 492.[1]
— Srstka Angrešt. 1895. III. 414.[1]
— Syringa vulgaris fl. pleno. 1887. III. 681.[1]
— Xanthoceras sorbifolia Bunge. 1889. III. 540.[2]
Fuller, Andrew S. The best hedge in America. 1892. III. 312.[1]
— The Cilician Silver Fir. 1895. III. 296.[1]
— Cranberry, Vaccinium. 1867. III. 663.[2]
— Extracting Cedar of Lebanon seeds. 1894. III. 300.[3]
— The forest tree culturist. 1866. III. 80, IV. 103.[1]
— A giant English Walnut. 1888. II. 114.[1]
— The Grape culturist. 1864. III. 550.
— Hickories from root cuttings. 1895. III. 353.[2]
— How to graft. 1896. III. 163.[1]
— Hybrid Forsythias. 1886. III. 671.[2]
— Japan Judas tree. 1875. III. 472.[1]
— Kultur der Fruchtsträucher. 1867. III. 147.[3]
— Miniature evergreen trees. 1874. III. 290.
— Miniature gardening; an evergreenery. 1874. III. 290.
— Numbo and Paragon Chestnuts. 1893. III. 358.[3]
— The nut culturist. 1896. III. 134.[1]
— Practical forestry. 1884. IV. 103.[1]
— Ueber Preisselbeeren. 1867. III. 663.[2]
— Propagating plants by grafting. 1868. III. 161.

— Propagation of plants. 1867. III. 153.
— The propagation of plants. 1887. III. 153.
— Select deciduous shrubs and small trees. 1896. III. 203.
— Select small shade and ornamental trees. 1896. III. 203.
— The small fruit culturist. 1867. III. 147.[2]
— About Wistarias. 1875. III. 490.[1]
Fuller, Claude. Forest insects. 1897. IV. 210.[2]
— A gall-making Diaspid. 1898. IV. 531.[1]
— The Orange mussel scale. 1897. III. 501.[1]
— Plant-galls formed by insects. 1897. I. 216.[3]
Fuller, Joseph B. See BECKWITH, Florence, MACAULEY, M. E. & FULLER, J. B.
Fuller, Mary. The national flower. 1889. II. 212.[1]
Fuller, Thomas. Pharmacopoeia domestica. 1723. III. 252.
— Pharmacopoeia extemporanea. 1702. III. 251.
Fulmer, Eduard L. Cell division in Pine seedlings. 1898. II. 40.[3]
Fulton, James Alexander. Peach culture. 1870. III. 441.[1]
Fulton, W. M. Protection from frost. 1900. III. 183.[2]
Fultz, W. S. Wind-breaks and shelter belts. 1893. III. 215.[2]
De la fumée de bois. 1898. IV. 558.[1]
La fumée du bois comme agent de désinfection. 1896. IV. 433.[3]
Fumigation of seeds and plants. 1900. III. 198.[3]
Fumouze, Armand. Sur les tyroglyphus. 1874. III. 563.
La fumure des plantes tropicales. 1896. III. 152.
Funch, Diderich Hansteen. Praktisk Skibbyggerie. 1833. IV. 485,[1] 513.
— Proeve over het eikenhout. 1833. IV. 513.
Funciones de los conservadores. 1889. IV. 553.[1]
Funck, Alb. Die Kultur der Croton in England. 1900. III. 516.[2]
Funck, N. Coup d'œil sur la végétation du Luxembourg. 1855. I. 532.[3]
Funcke, Joseph. Der Waldcultus. 1869. I. 517,[1] II. 517.[1]
On a function of roots. 1864. I. 161.
The Funeral Cypress. 1872. III. 302.[2]
Una funesta malattia negli Agrumi. 1864. III. 498.[1]
Funghi mangerecci. 1888. IV. 439.
Fungi and timber. 1891. I. 207.[1]
Fungous diseases of the Grape. 1897. III. 581.
Funk, (Geh. Regierungsrat). Ueber die Dauer der Hölzer. 1880. IV. 420.
Funk, L., Baron. Beschreibung welchergestalt Theer- und Kohlenöfen einzurichten sind. 1748. IV. 393, 436.[1]
— Beskrifning om tiären och kolugnars inrättande. 1748. IV. 393, 436.[1]
Funke. Einiges über Maclura aurantiaca Nutt. 1870. III. 372.[1]
Funke, (Garten-Direktor). Der botanische Garten . . . des Fürsten von Salm-Dyck. 1828. I. 46.
Funke, Otto. Beiträge zur Kenntnis der Wirkung des Urari. 1859. III. 682.[2]
Funke, W. Exkursion . . . durch die Waldungen der Domäne Daschitz. 1871. IV. 371.
— See also DÖRRE, F. C. & FUNKE, W.
Funke, Walter. Zur landwirthschaftlichen Taxation bei der Ablösung der . . . Weide- und Streurechte. 1875. IV. 333.
Funke, Wilhelm. Borkenkäfer. 1875. IV. 204.
— Die Forstbetriebs-Einrichtung nach Cotta's Prinzip. 1865. IV. 240.
Der Funkenbaum. 1886. IV. 485.[1]
Furbat, G. Culture des Bruyères. 1892. III. 650.[2]
Furber, Robert. A catalogue of curious trees. 1724. III. 80.
— Catalogue of trees. 1727. III. 78.[1]
— Fruits for every month in the year. 1727. III. 78.[2]
Furerius, N. De radice Chinae. 1554. III. 338.[1]
Furlough, (pseud.). Forestry in Japan. 1884. IV. 376.[1]
Furnas. Growth of trees in the West. 1884. IV. 64.[3]
— Wood of Salix cordata, variety vestita. 1884. IV. 488.[1]
Furnas, Robert W. Arbor day. 1888. IV. 42.[1]
— Progress and effects of forest growing. 1898. IV. 112.
— The rings in trees. 1887. IV. 235.[1]
— See also BAKER, F. P. & FURNAS, R. W.
Furniture and decoration. IV. 12.[1]
Furniture gazette. IV. 12.[1]
Furniture journal. IV. 4.
Furniture record. IV. 12.[1]
Furquim d'Almeida, L. De l'exploitation du caoutchouc au Brésil. 1900. III. 230.
Furrer, A. Volkswirthschafts-Lexikon der Schweiz. See CHRIST, Hermann. 1891. I. 437.

Further notes from Ghent. 1883. III. 642.[1]
Further notice regarding the "Pooah." 1848. III. 382.[2]
Further progress of Mr. Jameson's great Tea-planting operations in India. 1848. III. 602.[2]
Furuhjelm, E. J. Nordliga lokaler för Alnus glutinosa. 1886. II. 116.[1]
Fusina, Vincenzo. Quale posse essere una delle maggiori cause producenti l'assorbimento nelle radici. 1871. I. 161.
Fusinieri, Ambrogio. Circa la causa della fusione della neve attorno le piante. 1838. I. 186.
— Degli effetti degli alberi sull' erba. 1841. I. 231.[2]
Fuss, Franz. Unterricht zur Aufnahme, Eintheilung und Abschätzung der Wälder. 1794. IV. 239.
Fuss, Michaele. Flora Transsilvaniae excursoria. 1866. I. 445.
Fuster. Recherches sur le climat de la France. 1844. III. 47.
— Recherches sur les grands hivers de la France. 1841. III. 47.
Futaie, *(pseud.)*. On forest settlement and administration. 1893. IV. 134.[1]
Les futaies et les taillis. 1880. IV. 128.
Futterlaub und Futterlaubwald. 1876. III. 223.[1]
Der **Futterwerth** des Haidekrautes. 1875. III. 649.[1]
La futura organización forestal. 1900. IV. 554.[1]
Fynje, J. G. W. Nota over de boschbeplantingen op de duinen, langs de golf van Gasconje. 1889. IV. 361.
Fysiografiska sällskapets i Lund. *See* LUNDS UNIVERSITETS. I. 519.[1]

—g—. Noë Meurers Abhandlung von forstlicher Oberherrlichkeit. 1892. IV. 24.[1]
G. The Alders. 1878. III. 356.[2]
G. Ueber den Anbau ausländischer Holzarten in Deutschland. 1846. IV. 125.[2]
G. Aphelandra fascinator. 1878. III. 708.[3]
G. Bemesting van Koffietuinen. 1899. III. 734.[1]
G. Beobachtung über die ... Bildung des Jahresringes. 1852. I. 525.
G. Beschützung der Saatschulen. 1892. IV. 203.
G. Birthworts (Aristolochias). 1877. III. 385.[3]
G. The Butcher's Broom. 1879. III. 238.[1]
G. Du cantonnement des droits de pâturage. 1881. IV. 334.[1]
G. Cape Heaths. 1848. III. 650.[1]
G. Tha Cistuses. 1885. III. 612.[2]
G. The Clethras. 1879. III. 646.[2]
G. Cycads. 1873. III. 284.[1]
G. The flowering of the Paulownia. 1885. III. 703.[2]
G. Ueber die forstlichen Verhältnisse des kaukasischen Küstengebietes des Schwarzen Meeres. 1887. IV. 348.[1]
G. Galeworts. 1877. III. 353.[1]
G. Ueber die Heiden (Erica) vom Cap. 1848. III. 650.[1]
G. Die Hochschule für Bodencultur im Parlamente. 1888. IV. 36.[2]
G. The Larch, its disease, value, and uses of wood. 1887. IV. 449.
G. Leuchtöl aus der Seestrandskiefer. 1877. IV. 468.[2]
G. De Liberia-Koffie. 1879. III. 742.[2]
G. A new Maple. 1881. III. 534.[2]
G. New Zealand. 1872. I. 507.
G. Noch ein Wort über das Vermessen des Eichenstammholzes. 1892. IV. 513.
G. Palms in fruit at Kew.. 1879. III. 317.
G. The St. John's-worts. 1886. III. 610.[1]
G. Der Schneedruckschaden im Forstkreise Disentis. 1900. IV. 101.[1]
G. Screw Pines. 1872. III. 313.[1]
G. Select trees and shrubs for outside walls. 1878. III. 205.[1]
G. Shaw Lefevre's English commons and forests. 1894. IV. 323.[1]
G. Ueber die Tauglichkeit der Hainbuche. 1858. IV. 491.[1]
G. Trees and shrubs for autumn effect. 1878. III. 207.[1]
G. Trees for cities and towns. 1872. III. 42.[2]
G. Trees on chalk soils. 1885. III. 41.[1]
G. Ulmus campestris var. umbraculifera. 1887. III. 365.[1]
G. Vegetation in the Philippine Islands. 1873. I. 464.[1]
G. Ueber Waldbewässerung. 1869. IV. 144.[1]
G. Wirtschaftliche Behandlung der Kiefernbestände geringer Bonitätsklasse. 1896. III. 474.

G., A. Adenandra fragrans. 1852. III. 495.[1]
G., A. Bestraten met houtblokjes. 1851. IV. 425.[2]
G., A. Nutrición de las Cupulíferas. 1886. IV. 543.[1]
G., A. Des plantations d'arbres dans Paris. 1860. III. 211.[1]
G., A. H. B. Het Aloë-hout. 1861. IV. 399.[2]
G., A. H. B. De Koessambie of Makassar-olie. 1861. III. 540.[1]
G., A. H. B. De sagueer en de sosootwortel. 1861. III. 222.
G., A. H. B. De Soe-gha van den Indischen archipel. 1861. III. 468.[1]
G., A. H. B. Timmerhoutsoorten van den Indischen archipel. 1861. IV. 399.[2]
G., A. H. B. Zuivering van het suikerrietsap. 1861. III. 591.[1]
G., C. Destilación seca de las maderas. 1898. IV. 558.[1]
G., D. H. R. Dangers from the Pride of China tree. 1894. III. 512.[2]
G., E. La processionnaire du Pin. 1887. IV. 478.
G., E. v. De invloed der bosschen op ket klimaat. 1875. IV. 53.
G., E. v. Koffie-cultuur. 1875. III. 726.[3]
G., E. van. De Sagoboom op Java. 1873. III. 327.[2]
G., F. Clef analytique de la flore d'Auvergne. 1873. I. 414.
G., F. Ein neuer Feind der Eiche. 1856. IV. 509.
G., F. Parasitic trees. 1889. II. 539.[1]
G., F. Shade, cover and shelter. 1898. IV. 68.
G., F. C. Note sur des racines de Grenadier. 1850. III. 630.[2]
G., F. C. V. Wald- Forst- und Jägerey-Lexikon. 1764. IV. 22.[1]
G., G. Éclaircissements relatifs à ... Garou. 1866. III. 627.[1]
G., G. Il frutice della cera. 1864. III. 226.[1]
G., H. von. Beschädigung der Karstculturen durch die Bora. 1891. IV. 189.[2]
G., H. von. Ein dalmatinischer Inselwald. 1868. IV. 374.[2]
G., H. v. Ueber die Nomenclatur einiger Pinus-Arten. 1885. IV. 463.[1]
G., J. W. Zaailing-appels. 1876. III. 426.[1]
G., L. Trees at Arundel. 1873. III. 703.[2]
G., O. Metodo per misurare l' altezza degli alberi. 1890. IV. 216.
G., P. Hardy fruit trees in their ornamental aspect. 1885. III. 203.
G., P. Hedges useful and ornamental. 1886. III. 214.[1]
G., P. Zuwachsgang einer Arve.. 1887. IV. 463.[3]
G., P. B. *See* P., P. B.
G., R. Betrachtungen über Rosa canina. 1890. III. 453.[1]
G., R. Ueber das Vorkommen wurselkranker Fichtenbestände. 1838. IV. 455.
G., S. Close woods or open? 1885. IV. 128.
G., S. Note sur la culture de l'Ailanthe. 1862. IV. 525.[1]
G., S. The uses of the thicket. 1886. IV. 128.
G., T. W. The Macartney Rose. 1886. III. 454.[2]
G., T. W. Scotch Briars. 1886. III. 457.[1]
G., T. W. Single Roses. 1887. III. 455.[1]
G., V. S. Bijzonderheden wegens den Grafensteiner Appel. 1840. III. 426.[1]
G., V. S. Brief over de behandeling ... van de vrucht boomen. 1830. III. 139.
G., W. Autumn-tinted trees and shrubs. 1879. III. 207.[1]
G., W. The best Barberries. 1882. III. 394.[1]
G., W. The Bhotan Cypress. 1885. III. 303.[1]
G., W. The Black Broom. 1887. III. 474.[6]
G., W. The Bougainvillea. 1883. III. 388.[1]
G., W. Broad-leaved Spindle tree. 1881. III. 532.[2]
G., W. The Bunya Bunya tree. 1880. III. 298.[1]
G., W. Ceropegias at Kew. 1880. III. 692.[2]
G., W. Clematis Sieboldi and Jackmani. 1882. III. 389.[1]
G., W. The Crimean Lime. 1887. III. 586.[1]
G., W. Double White Bramble. 1883. III. 458.[1]
G., W. The double Wistaria. 1887. III. 490.[2]
G., W. The Douglas Spruce. 1887. III. 309.[1]
G., W. Dracaenas at Anerley. 1881. III. 334.[2]
G., W. The Dragon tree. 1881. II. 82.[1]
G., W. An edible-fruited Yucca. 1879. III. 340.[1]
G., W. Eugenia Ugni. 1880. III. 638.[1]
G., W. Eurybia Gunni. 1880. III. 756.[1]
G., W. Ficus repens and its fruit. 1882. III. 371.[1]
G., W. Flowering Dogwood. 1882. III. 645.[2]
G., W. The fragrant Olive. 1881. III. 680.[1]
G., W. Fremontia californica. 1882. III. 591.[1]
G., W. Hardy Azaleas. 1886. III. 655.

G., W. Iochroma longiflorum. 1880. III. 700.[3]
G., W. Leycesteria formosa. 1887. III. 749.[2]
G., W. Lindenia rivalis. 1881. III. 745.[2]
G., W. Luculia Pinceana. 1880. III. 745.[2]
G., W. Melastoma malabathrica. 1882. III. 638.[2]
G., W. Eine merkwürdige Rothbuche. 1847. II. 126.[2]
G., W. Mespilus grandiflora. 1882. III. 429.[3]
G., W. New Californian shrub. 1880. III. 409.[2]
G., W. New England Mayflower. 1882. III. 649.[3]
G., W. New evergreen Oak. 1881. III. 362.[1]
G., W. New evergreen Oaks. 1880. III. 361.[1]
G., W. New hardy Passion-flower. 1887. III. 616.[1]
G., W. The Olympian St. John's wort. 1887. III. 610.[1]
G., W. Pentas carnea. 1882. III. 746.[2]
G., W. The Pine Barren Beauty. 1884. II. 691.[1]
G., W. A pretty basket plant. 1881. III. 640.[2]
G., W. Prunus Mume. 1896. III. 438.[2]
G., W. The Purple Gum Cistus. 1887. III. 613.[1]
G., W. The Purple-leaved Cherry Plum. 1887. III. 436.[1]
G., W. Raphiolepis japonica. 1882. III. 447.[2]
G., W. Rhododendron Keysi. 1880. III. 660.[2]
G., W. Rhodotypus kerrioides. 1881. III. 447.[2]
G., W. The Rose Acacia. 1881. III. 486.[1]
G., W. Small-leaved Azara. 1880. III. 614.[1]
G., W. The Tree Paeony. 1887. III. 392.[3]
G., W. Trees and shrubs at Syon. 1880. I. 55.
G., W. Variegated trees and shrubs. 1879. III. 206.[2]
G., W. Weeping Hemlock Spruce. 1887. III. 312.[1]
G., W. Weigela hortensis nivea. 1882. III. 749.[1]
G., W. White-flowered Cytisus purpureus. 1882. III. 474.[1]
G., W. See P., H. & G., W.
G., W. E. Abutilon vitifolium. 1883. III. 587.[1]
G., W. E. Bamboos and half-hardy trees . . . at Fota. 1874. III. 78.[2]
G., W. E. Brownea macrophylla. 1879. III. 468.[1]
G., W. E. Comparative hardiness of hybrid Aralias. 1877. III. 641.[1]
G., W. E. The Mock Oranges. 1879. III. 413.[1]
G., W. E. Remarkable hardy shrubs in Wicklow. 1877. III. 672.[2]
G., W. E. Smaller flowered Mock Oranges. 1884. III. 413.[1]
G., W. E. Two Desfontaineas. 1873. III. 682.[1]
G., W. E. Varieties of Hamamelis. 1884. III. 417.[1]
G., W. E. Winter-blooming deciduous hardy shrubs. 1880. III. 417.[1]
G., W. H. Beaumontia grandiflora. 1887. III. 687.[1]
G., W. H. The Blue and White Leadworts. 1888. III. 666.[1]
G., W. H. Boronias. 1876. III. 495.[3]—1887. III. 495.[2]
G., W. H. The Drooping Glory tree. 1888. III. 696.[1]
G., W. H. Erica of the Ventricosa section. 1889. III. 651.[3]
G., W. H. The Golden vine. 1888. III. 513.[2]
G., W. H. Hibbertias. 1888. III. 596.[1]
G., W. H. Japanese Camellias. 1889. III. 599.[1]
G., W. H. New Cape Heath. 1879. III. 650.[1]
G., W. H. Reinwardtia tetragynum. 1887. III. 492.[1]
G., W. H. Ruellia macrantha. 1887. III. 710.[1]
G., W. H. The Scarlet Mallow. 1888. III. 588.[1]
G., W. H. Schubertia grandiflora. 1887. III. 694.[1]
G., W. H. Soft wooded heaths. 1887. III. 650.[3]
G., W. R. The "Indian Peach." 1885. II. 270.[2]
G., W. R. The "Mocker-nut." 1885. II. 112.[1]
G., W. R. Note on Populus balsamifera L. var. candicans. 1880. II. 97.[1]
G., W. R. Samaras of Maple. 1884. II. 477.[1]
G. . . . Bestrebungen zur Verwerthung der Waldschätze Russlands. 1883. IV. 398.[2]
G . . . t, Fr. Bemærkninger over de haardveddede Vårmhuusplanters Formering. 1845. III. 152.
G . . . t, Fr. Bemerkungen über die Vermehrung bartholziger Warmhauspflanzen. 1845. III. 152.
G-. Die Aufforstung des Karstes. 1885. IV. 167.[2]
G-ê. The cut-leaved Hornbeam. 1879. III. 357.[2]
G-e. Duboisia myoporoides. 1879. III. 700.[1]
G-g. Welche Holzarten eignen sich zu Alleebäumen. 1890. IV. 137.[1]
Gaardboe, A. P. Historiske Efterretninger om Skove i det nordlige Vendsyssel. 1876. IV. 343.[1]
Gabb, William More. Notes on the distribution of the vegetation of Santo Domingo. 1871. I. 336.
Gabbema, Simon Abbes. Friesche lust-gaarde. 1686. III. 105.

Gabe für die Theilnehmer an der Excursion der Forstsection nach dem Wermsdorfer Walde. 1864. IV. 355.[1]
Gabelli, Lucio. Alcune notizie sulla Robinia. 1894. II. 382.[2]
— Sopra un caso . . . di sinfisi fogliare. 1897. I. 145.[1]
— Sulla causa degli adoppiamenti fogliari. 1896. I. 145.[1]
— Considérations sur la floraison des jeunes plantules. 1896. II. 414.[1]
— Considerazioni sulla nervazione fogliare. 1895. I. 111.
— Feuilles dédoublées. 1898. I. 145.[1]
Gablenz, F. A. von. Resultate eines Versuchs zur Erziehung der Eiche. 1848. IV. 504.
Gablitzel. See HABLIZL, K. L.
Gabnay, Ferenc. Die Excentricität der Bäume. 1892. I. 106.[1]
— A tülevelüek excentricitása. 1892. I. 106.[1]
— A tülevelüek virágjának mesterséges termékenyítéséröl. 1899. II. 21.[1]
Gabor. Le Chêne de Turquie. 1894. III. 362.[1]
— Reboisement du bassin du Bourget. 1892. IV. 164.[1]
Gabriel, J. A. Der königliche Wald Hwozd. 1864. IV. 370.
Gabriel, Peter. Kunsterfahrener Blumen-, Küchen- und Baumgärtner. 1755. III. 103.
Gaches. Sur la destruction du phylloxera par . . . maïs rouge. 1876. III. 569.[1]
Gadamer, J. Ueber Koffeinbestimmungen. 1899. III. 260.[1]
Gadd, Pehr Adrian. Afhandling om medel at underhålla och öka skogsväxten i Finland. 1792. III. 120.[1]
— Rön, gjorde vid silkes-afvelens införande i Finland. 1773. III. 373.
— Rön och Anmärkningar om utländska wäxter. 1777. III. 120.[1]
— Underrättelse i träd och skötseln. 1759. IV. 113.[2]
Gadeau de Kerville, Henri. Le Chêne porte-gui de la ferme du bois. 1898. II. 180.[1]
— Les Chênes porte-gui de la Normandie. 1898. II. 180.[1]
— Une Glycine énorme à Rouen. 1895. II. 389.[1]
— Vieux arbres de la Normandie. 1890. I. 297.[2]
— Les vieux arbres de la Normandie. Le Chêne-chapelles. 1891. II. 139.[1]
Gadeceau, Émile. Note sur les Platanes. 1894. II. 254.[2]
Gaede, F. Über die Anlage von Knicks. 1879. III. 214.[2]
Gaede, Heinrich Moritz. Index plantarum Horti botanici leodiensis. 1828. I. 49.
Gaerdt, Heinrich. Die Aufbewahrung frischen Obstes. 1886. III. 173.[3]
— Beitrag zur Vermehrungs-Methode der Fuchsia macrantha. 1849. III. 640.[3]
— Eine desinficirende Pflanze. 1876. IV. 533.[1]
— Drei Blüthensträucher. 1876. III. 471,[1] 629,[2] 666.[1]
— Einiges zur Kultur der Luculia gratissima. 1854. III. 745.[2]
— Gärtnerische Düngerlehre. 1888. III. 151
— Gartentaxator. 1885. III. 200.[1]
— Eine gelbe Blume, Cassia floribunda. 1887. III. 471.[1]
— Pfropfen und Veredeln. 1889. III. 163.[1]
— Ueber Treiberei im Allgemeinen. 1869. III. 176.[3]
— Die Winterblumen. 1884. III. 75.[1]
— & **Wittmack,** Ludwig. Aphelandra tetragona Nees var. imperialis. 1891. II. 797.[2]
Gaertner, Joseph. Adumbrationes plantarum. 1704. I. 061.
— Fragmentum systematicae dispositionis plantarum. 1794. I. 259.
— De fructibus et seminibus plantarum. 1788. I. 118.[1]
Gärtner, Karl Friedrich von. Ueber Bastardbefruchtungen im Pflanzenreich. 1847. I. 245.
— Extraits de l'ouvrage intitulé: Recherches sur la fécondation. 1844. I. 200.
— Methode der künstlichen Bastardbefruchtung. 1849. III. 50.[2]
— Nachricht über Versuche, die Befruchtung einiger Gewächse betreffend. 1826. I. 200.
— Notice sur les expériences concernant la fécondation. 1826. I. 200.
— Supplementum carpologiae. See GAERTNER, Joseph. 1788. I. 118.[1]
— Verhandeling ter beantwoording der vraag: wat leert de ondervinding aangaande het ontstaan van nieuwe soorten. 1838. I. 245.
— Versuche und Beobachtungen über die Bastarderzeugung. 1849. I. 245.
— Versuche und Beobachtungen über die Befruchtungsorgane der vollkommeneren Gewächse. 1844. I. 200.

Gärtner, Philipp Gottfried, **Meyer**, Bernhard & **Scherbius**, Johannes. Oekonomisch-technische Flora der Wetterau. 1799. I. 375.
Gärtner, R. Der deutsche Obstbau. 1884. III. 139.
— Die ersten deutschen Obstbäume in Japan. 1882. III. 147.[1]
— Erziehung, Schnitt . . . der Form- oder Zwergobstbäume. . 1887. III. 139.
— Reisekizzen aus Amerika. 1879. IV. 483.[2]
Gärtnerische Mittheilungen. III. 24.[1]
Gärtnerische Rundschau. III. 24.[2]
Gärtnerisches Zentralblatt. III. 12.
Gaeta, Giuseppe. Catalogo sistematico delle Conifere . . . nel parco di Brolio. 1899. I. 64.
— Catalogo sistematico . . . di Conifere cultivate nel bosco . . . di Moncioni. 1893. I. 64, *III. 291.*
— Conifere. 1892. II. 13.[2]
— Le Conifere coltivate . . . a Moncioni. 1890. I. 64.
— Le Conifere del giardino . . . di Brolio. 1899. III. 291.
— Sulle Conifere più adulte coltivate . . . a Moncioni. 1890. I. 64.
— Sui frutti di Juniperus drupacea. 1899. II. 31.[2]
Gaffron, von. Nota omtrent den getah-pertja boom.. 1858. III. 231.
Gage, John. The Osage Orange as a hedge plant. 1855. III. 372.[1]
Gaglio, Gaetano. Sul contenuto di pilocarpina. 1897. III. 505.[1]
Gagnaire. Greffe du Robinia inermis. 1863. III. 486.[2]
— Libonia floribunda. 1865. III. 709.[3]
— Spirea grandiflora. 1868. III. 424.[1]
— Taille du Fabiana imbriqué. 1859. III. 700.[2]
— Weigelia hortensis nivea. 1866. III. 749.[1]
Gagnaire, (jr.). Elaeagnus rotundifolia. 1870. III. 628.[2]
— Sur la greffe en fente. 1860. III. 161.
— Physianthus albens. 1856. III. 692.[1]
— Une question sur les Platanes. 1878. III. 419.[1]
— Spirea Thunbergii. 1868. III. 461.[1]
— Taille de l'Hibiscus syriacus. 1861. III. 588.[1]
— Taille de la Véronique de Lindley. 1860. III. 704.[2]
— Taille du Jasmin à fleurs nues. 1860. III. 673.[1]
Gagnebin, Abraham. Description du Bouleau nain. 1751. II. 119.[2]
Gagnepain, François. Nouveaux cas tératologiques. 1894. II. 104.[1]
— Nouvelles notes tératologiques. 1894. II. 708.[1]
Gagneraux, L. Code forestier. 1827. IV. 323.[3]
Gahn, Nicolaus. Plantae officinales. *See* LINNÉ, Carl von. 1753. III. 54.
Gaiffier, de & Gouët. Une visite au parc de Baleine. 1878. I. 59.
Gail, de. Un ascenseur forestier. 1894. IV. 172.[2]
— Le bois fondu. 1892. IV. 431.[1]
— Bois fondu et bois durci. 1893. IV. 422.[2]
— Caractères distinctifs du bois des principales essences forestières. 1891. IV. 62.[2]
— La conservation des forêts en Russie. 1890. IV. 273.[2]
— Des exploitations dans les pays neufs. 1892. IV. 382.[1]
— Les forêts du bassin de la Kouban. 1893. IV. 348.[1]
— Mise en valeur des landes danoises. 1893. IV. 156.[2]
— La nonne ou le bombyx moine. 1891. IV. 201.
— Les préférences de la foudre. 1894. IV. 195.[1]
— The preferences of lightning. 1894. IV. 195.[1]
— Recettes utiles; moyens de préserver contre le rouge les jeunes semis de Pins en pépinière. 1893. IV. 478.
— Statistique des forêts domaniales du Danemark. 1890. IV. 343.[2]
— Traitement d'une sapinière. . 1896. IV. 238.
— Traverses de chemin de fer. 1895. IV. 424,[1] 557.[2]
— *See also* BRUAND, Léon & GAIL, de.
Gaillard, D. Sur l'Echinocereus leptacanthus. 1864. III. 622.[2]
— Floraison d'un Cereus hybride. 1864. III. 621.[2]
— Note sur la fructification des Cereus. 1847. III. 620.[2]
Gaillard, F. Populus caroliniana. 1872. III. 345.[1]
Gaillard, Georges. Contribution à l'étude des Roses du Jura. 1898. II. 286.[2]
— Excursion rhodologique au Salève. 1898. II. 299.[1]
— Mélanges rhodologiques. 1899. II. 287.[2]
— Rosa alpina L. × rubrifolia. 1896. II. 297.[1]
Gaillardot, Charles. Note sur le déboisement des montagnes en Syrie. 1857. IV. 49.[1]
Gaillardson, B. Manuel du vigneron en Algérie. 1889. III. 559.[1]

Gaillot's patent automatic torches. 1885. IV. 199.[2]
Gaimard, Paul. Voyages de la commission scientifique du nord. 1843. I. 354.
— Voyages en Scandinavie. 1843. I. 354.
Gain, Edmond. Action de l'eau du sol sur la végétation. 1895. I. 233.[1]
— Sur la germination des graines de Légumineuses. 1897. III. 462.[1]
— Influence de l'humidité du sol sur la végétation. 1893. I. 233.[1]
— The physiological rôle of water in plants. 1895. I. 233.[1]
— Sur une plantule anormale de Quercus pedunculata. 1894. II. 137.[1]
— Recherches relatives à l'influence de la sécheresse. 1895. III. 183.[2]
— Recherches sur le rôle physiologique de l'eau. 1895. I. 233.[1]
Gaines, N. Correa var. brilliant. 1848. III. 503.[1]
Gair. Notice on the cones of Cupressus Lambertiana. 1859. III. 302.[2]
Gal, H. U ein Homologes des Borneocamphers. 1869. III. 611.[2] eber
— Sur un homologue du camphre de Bornéo. 1869. III. 233.[1]
— Recherches sur l'essence d'Alan-gilan. 1873. III. 401.[2]
Galama, S. De plantarum . . . nostratium usu oeconomico. 1822. III. 270.[1]
Galama, S. J. Over het gebruik van kina. 1832. III. 721.
— Verhandeling over het gebruik der kina. 1832. III. 721.
Gale, Leonard D. On the Oaks of the District of Columbia. 1855. II. 128.[2]
Galen, James. Flora of Lancaster county. 1884. I. 315.
Galenus, Klaudios. Opera omnia. 200. I. 274.
— De plenitudine. *See* APULEJUS PLATONICUS. 400. I. 274.
— . . . De simplicium medicamentorum facultatibus libri XI. 200. I. 274.
Galeotti, Henri Guillaume. *See* MARTENS, Martin & GALE- OTTI, H. G.
Galesloot, Jac. P. R. De ooftboom en zijne behandeling. 1877. III. 140.[1]
Galgóczy, Károly. Az erdőségek és a befásitás fontossága Magyarországon. 1877. IV. 48.[2]
Galin. Doccia fredda. 1899. IV. 166.[2]
— "Doman te n' avvedrai!" 1899. IV. 294.[1]
Galinier. *See* FERRET, A. & GALINIER.
Galippe, L. M. V. Sur la présence du cuivre dans le cacao. 1883. III. 595.[1]
— Le sulfate de cuivre et le mildew. 1887. III. 579.
— *See also* BEAUREGARD, Henri & GALIPPE, L. M. V.
Galitzin, Emmanuel de. De la croissance . . . du Bouleau en Russie. 1845. IV. 491.[1]
— De l' écorce de Tilleul. 1845. III. 585.[2]
— Emploi de l'écorce d'Épicea pour l'alimentation. 1847. III. 297.[1]
— De l'état de la végétation des forêts dans le nord de la Sibérie. 1846. IV. 375.[2]
— Des forêts de la Russie. 1847. IV. 345.
— Note concernant un arbre singulier. 1848. IV. 519.[2]
Galjema. Een gevaar voor de Java-Koffie. 1898. III. 731.
— Is verbetering der Javakoffie mogelijk? 1898. III. 731.
Gall, Karl, Baron von. Der Anbau der Weisserle. 1833. IV. 489.[2]
Gallaher, Frank M. Forest experiment station at Santa Monica. 1892. IV. 30.[1]
— Quercus densiflora. 1893. IV. 503.[1]
Gallais, A. Monographie du Cacao. 1827. III. 592.[1]
Gallais, F. Essai de naturalisation des végétaux utiles. 1868. III. 130.[1]
Galland, A. F. PISON-DU-. *See* PISON-DU-GALLAND, A. F.
Galland, Antoine. De l'origine et du progrès du Café. 1699. III. 738.
Gallardo, Angel. La carioquinesis. 1896. I. 137.
— Flores é insectos. 1894. I. 239.[1]
— Notas fitoteratológicas. 1899. I. 144.[1]
— Semillas y frutos. 1896. I. 241.[1]
Gallardo, Carlos R. La industria yerbatera en misiones. 1898. III. 269,[2] 551.[2]
Gallé, Émile. Hamamelis arborea. 1884. III. 417.[1]
Le galle nella flora di alcune province napolitane. *See* LI- COPOLI, Felice. I. 215.[2]
Gallego, Mariano. Mis opiniones acerca . . . la enseñanza del derecho en la Escuela de ingenieros de montes. 1894. IV. 541.[1]
— Modo causa manet, manet efectum. 1892. IV. 551.[2]

— El reglamento de la Escuela de ingenieros de montes. 1891. IV. 540.²
— Réplica. 1892. IV. 552.¹
Gallès, P. La végétation à Madagascar. 1896. I. 496.
Gallesio, Giorgio, *conte.* Gli agrumi dei giardini botanico-agrarii di Firenze. 1839. II. 401.¹
— Orange culture. 1811. III. 496.¹
— Pomona italiana. 1817. III. 88.¹
— Della teoria degl' innesti. 1839. I. 208.¹
— Teoria della riproduzione vegetale. 1813. I. 205, *243.*¹
— Theorie der vegetabilischen Reproduktion. 1813. I. 205, *243.*¹
— Traité du Citrus. 1811. III. 496.¹
Galletley, A. On certain properties of Rosewood. 1886. II. 352.²
— Note on a sweet substance called Manna. 1889. III. 466.²
— Observations on the wood of certain resinproducing trees. 1889. I. 126.
Gallie, George. On the pruning of hardwood trees. 1890. IV. 172.¹
Gallieni, (*governor of Madagascar*). Circulaire relative aux concessions de terrains boisés à Madagascar. 1897. IV. 280.¹
— Forestry in Madagascar. 1899. IV. 380.¹
— L'industrie forestière à Madagascar. 1899. IV. 380.¹
Gallisch, F. A. De Aristotele rei naturalis scriptore. 1776. I. 292.
Gallizioli, Filippo. Dizionario botanico. 1812. I. 72,¹ III. 37.²
— Elementi botanico-agrari. 1809. III. 37.²
Gallo, Agostino. Le vinti giornate dell' agricoltura. 1575. III. 114.²
Gallois, François Narcisse. *See* HARDY, Ernest & GALLOIS, F. N.
— & Hardy, Ernest. Sur les effets toxiques de l'écorce de Mancône. 1875. III. 476.²
— — Sur l'Erythrophloeum guineense. 1877. III. 476.²
— — Sur le poison de l'écorce de Mancône. 1875. III. 476.²
— — Recherches chimiques . . . sur l'écorce de Mancône. 1876. III. 476.²
Gallois, J. Le Phylloxera vastatrix. 1873. III. 565.¹
Gallot, J. B. H. Eugene. Notice sur le débit et les emplois du Sapin. 1878. IV. 399.¹·
— Quelques études forestières dans l'Yonne. 1879. IV. 360.
— & Gast, L. Notice sur le débit et les emplois du Chêne. 1878. IV. 514.¹
Galloway, Beverly Thomas. Die Bekämpfung des Black-rot der Reben. 1889. III. 580.
— Combating the diseases of nursery stock. 1893. III. 198.¹
— Combating the fungous diseases of plants. 1893. III. 193.²
— The effect of spraying with fungicides. 1894. III. 198.¹
— Frosts and freezes as affecting cultivated plants. 1896. III. 182.
— Fungous diseases of the Grape. 1891. III. 580.
— New spraying devices. 1899. III. 198.¹
— Pear leaf blight. 1890. III. 442,¹ V. xxix.²
— Report on the experiments . . . in the treatment of fungus diseases. 1890. III. 196.
— Report on the experiments . . . in the treatment of plant diseases. 1892. III. 196.
— A rust and leaf casting of Pine leaves. 1896. IV. 462.¹
— Spraying for fruit diseases. 1896. III. 198.¹
— Treatment of black-rot of the Grape. 1889. III. 580.
— Treatment of nursery stock for leaf-blight. 1891. III. 196.
— & Woods, A. F. Diseases of shade and ornamental trees. 1897. III. 178.
— — Water as a factor in the growth of plants. 1895. I. 188.¹
Galmiche. Histoire d'une recherche sur l'emploi des engrais chimiques. 1898. IV. 545.²
— Notes pour l'achat et la vente des forêts. 1897. IV. 551.¹
Galmiche, E. Des bouquets de bois résineux. 1893. IV. 169.¹
— Cours élémentaire de botanique forestière. 1880. IV. 85.¹
— Manuel d'économie forestière. 1882. IV. 99.¹
— Du traitement des futaies irrégulières. 1891. IV. 131.
Galpin, Francis William. An account of the flowering plants . . . of Harleston. 1888. I. 534.²

Galpine, John. A synoptical compend of British botany. 1806. I. 396.
Galschiøt, C. Underplantning under stedsegrønne Træer. 1886. III. 216.
Galschiøt. Om Udhugning og Plantning i Lystskove. 1867. III. 202.²
Galvani, Andrea. Sul seccume o macchie delle foglie. 1843. I. 206.¹
Galvani, Antonio. Sopra l' estratto della noce vomica. 1856. III. 682.²
Gama, José de SALDANHA DA. *See* SALDANHA DA GAMA, José de.
Gama, M. J. NOGUEIRA DE. *See* NOGUEIRA DE GAMA, M. J.
Gambia Mahogany. 1890. III. 512.²
Gambia native medicines. 1893. III. 281.¹
Gambier. 1881, 1889, 1890. III. 748.¹
Over de Gambier en Peperkultuur op Riouw. 1854. III. 343,¹ 748.¹
Gambier in British North Borneo. 1893. III. 748.¹
Gambini, F. BRUNO-. *See* BRUNO-GAMBINI, F.
Gamble, James Sykes. Average amount of heart-wood in Sandal. 1884. II. 169.²
— The Bambuseae of British India. 1896. II. 58.²
— Concentric rings in the Mangrove. 1898. I. 128.¹
— The Darjeeling forests. 1876. IV. 377.²
— Description of a new genus of Bamboo. 1890. II. 59.¹
— Description of a new genus of Bamboos. 1890. II. 59.¹
— On the determination of the fungi which attack forest trees in India. 1900. IV. 210.²
— An excursion to Sukmamri Hill. 1885. I. 475.¹
— Experiments on the durability of various woods. 1893. IV. 413.²
— A fore st 's short trip to the Cape peninsula. 1890. IV. 379.¹er²
— A handsome new Burmese Bamboo. 1894. II. 60.²
— Indian Date-Palms. 1889. II. 72.¹
— Is Poinciana elata a wild tree in India? 1900. II. 378.²
— List of the trees . . . found in the Darjeeling district. 1878. I. 470,¹ IV. 88.¹
— Manual of Indian timbers. 1881. I. 470,¹ IV. 88.¹
— Memorandum on the different species of Prosopis. 1879. II. 379.¹
— Mineral deposits in wood. 1888. I. 156.¹
— A new species of Mahogany. 1889. II. 422.¹
— The Nilgiri ' Strobilanthes.' 1888. II. 803.²
— Notes on a forest tour in Bavaria. 1887.. IV. 351.¹
— Notes on a tour in the forests of the Austrian Salzkammergut. 1887. IV. 369.
— Notes on the small Bamboos of the genus Arundinaria. 1888. II. 58.²
— Preliminary list of the trees and shrubs of the Northern Circars. 1885. I. 470,¹ IV. 88.¹
— Preliminary lists of the trees of the ceded districts. 1883. I. 470,¹ IV. 88.²
— The rate of growth of Red Sanders plantations. 1883. IV. 522.¹
— The rate of growth of Sâl. 1879. IV. 528.²
— Rate of growth of Sâl in Chota Nagpore. 1881. IV. 529.¹
— Revised list of the trees and shrubs of the Northern Circars. 1885. I. 470,¹ IV. 88.¹
— Seedlings of Duabanga on old charcoal kilns. 1879. II. 610.¹
— A short account of the forests of the northern forest circle. 1884. IV. 378.
— On the state forests and forest schools of France. 1872. IV. 34,¹ 360.
— The Stinging tree. 1892. III. 382.²
— Stunted forms of trees. 1883. I. 470.¹
— The treatment of Bamboo clumps. 1900. IV. 485.¹
— Woods to be avoided in making tea-boxes. 1883. IV. 427.¹
— *See also* BADEN-POWELL, B. H. & GAMBLE, J. S.; LUSHINGTON, A. W. & GAMBLE, J. S.
Gamet, P. A. Tarif pour le cubage des bois. n. d. IV. 219.
Gamgee, Arthur. *See* MACLAGAN, Douglas & GAMGEE, Arthur.
Gammie, George Alexander. Botanical exploration of Sikkim, Thibet frontier. 1893. I. 475.¹
— A botanical tour in Chamba and Kangra. 1898. I. 475.²
— A botanical tour in Sikkim. 1893. I. 475.¹
— Report on a botanical tour in Sikkim. 1893. I. 475.¹
— Report on a botanical tour in the Lakhimpur district. 1895. I. 476.¹

Gammie, James A. The Cinchona in India. 1898. III. 715.
— Memorandum on Cinchona pruning. 1873. III. 712.[1]
— Vegetation of Sikhim. 1894. I. 475.[1]
— The vegetation of temperate and alpine Sikhim. 1894. I. 475.[1]
Gamper, Max. Beiträge zur Kenntnis der Angosturarinden. 1900. III. 260.[1]
— *See also* HARTWICH, Carl & GAMPER, Max.
Gamrekelof, A. S. *See* Гамрекеловъ, A. C.
Gamwell, S. C. Official guide and handbook to Swansea. 1880. I. 534.[1]
Gand, Gustave. Distribution géographique des arbres en Europe. 1845. I. 348,[1] *IV. 79.*[1]
— Essai sur les stations et habitations des Conifères en Europe. 1840. II. 15.[1]
— Les forêts de l'Europe. 1845. I. 348,[1] *IV. 79.*[1]
— Mémoire sur l'alternance des essences forestières. 1839. IV. 74.[1]
Gand — **Académie. d'horticulture.** *See* SOCIÉTÉ D'HORTI-CULTURE DE GAND. III. 15.
Gand — **Société d'horticulture.** *See* SOCIÉTÉ ... III. 15.
Gand — **Société royale d'agriculture et de botanique.** *See* SOCIÉTÉ ... I. 17.
Gandi, Pietro Casimiro. Della selvicoltura. 1878. IV. 109.[1]
Gandoger, Michael. Catalogue des plantes récoltées ... en Algérie. 1882. I. 485.
— Ce qu'il faut penser des modifications produites dans les plantes par la culture. 1885. II. 297.[1]
— Crataegus lampophylla Gdgr. mss. 1882. II. 262.[1] .
— Decades plantarum novarum. 1874. I. 349. .
— Essai sur une nouvelle classification des Roses. 1876. II. 282.[1]
— Flora Europae terrarumque adjacentium. 1883. I. 349.
— Flore lyonnaise. 1875. I. 414.
— Monographia Rosarum Europae et Orientis. 1892. II. 283.[1]
— Plantes houvelles pour la Suisse. 1876. II. 287,[1] 601.[1]
— Prunus Magnieri Gdgr. mss. 1882. II. 275.[1]
— Rectifications rhodologiques. 1882. II. 283.[1]
— Révision du genre Crataegus. 1871. II. 261.[1].
— Rosae novae Galliam austro-orientalem colentes 1877. II. 285.[1]
— Rosmarinus ligusticus Gdgr. mss. 1883. II. 765.[1]
— Rubus nouveaux avec un essai sur la classification. 1884. II. 303.[1]
— Salices novae. 1881. II. 99.[1]
— Tabulae rhodologicae europaeo-orientales. 1881. II. 282.[1]
Gandolfi, Bartolommeo. Saggio teorico-pratico .sopra gli Ulivi. 1793. III. 678.[1]
Ganeau. Mémoire sur le protoplasma végétal. 1874. I. 136.[1]
Gange, René. Nos sources. 1895. IV. 542.[1]
Ganghofer, August. Bureau für forstliches Versuchswesen. 1875. IV. 383.[1]
— Erörterungen über die nächsten Aufgaben des bayerischen Forstwesens. 1873. IV. 274.[1]
— Das Forstgesetz für das Königreich Bayern. 1880. IV. 318.
— Das forstliche Versuchswesen. 1881. IV. 37.[1]
— Der praktische Holzrechner nach dem Meter-Masse. 1872. IV. 227.
— Der Wald im nationalen Wirthschaftsleben. 1880. IV. 274.[1]
— *See also* Ганггоферъ, A.
Gangloff, Karl. Kurze Beschreibung ... eines praktischen Holz-Berechnungs-Stockes. 1850. IV. 223.
— Uiber [*sic*] Pflanzungen mit künstlichen Ballen. 1855. IV. 152.
Gannal, Jean Nicolas. Préparation des plantes. 1849. I. 35.
Gannett, Henry. Bewirken Anbau und Aufforstung eine Zu-nahme der Niederschläge? 1889. IV. 51.
— Do forests influence rainfall? 1888. IV. 51.
— The forest conditions ... of the state of Washington. 1898. IV. 341.[1]
— Forest fires. 1898. IV. 182.[1]
— The forests of the United States. 1899. IV. 338.[1]
— Is the rainfall increasing upon the plains? 1888. IV. 46.[1]
— The Redwood forest of California. 1899. II. 49.[1]
— The Redwood forest of the Pacific coast. 1899. IV. 484.[1]
— Summary of forestry work in 1899–1900. 1900. IV. 288.[1]
— The " timber line." 1882. I. 308.[1]
— & others. .Classification of lands. 1900. IV. 288.[1]
Ganong, William F. Beiträge zur Kenntniss der Morphologie ... der Cacteen. 1894. II. 588.[1]

— Contributions to a knowledge of the morphology ... of the Cactaceae. .1894. II. 588.[1]
— Upon polyembryony ... in Opuntia. 1898. II. 597.[1]
— Present problems in the anatomy ... of the Cactaceae. 1895. II. 588.[1]
Gansauge, von. Ueber Taxus baccata. 1862. II. 11.[1]
Ganschow, J. Ueber einige einheimische Gewächse, die zur Lieferung von Farbenstoffen geeignet sind. 1868. III. 236.
— Einige kurze Bemerkungen über die gemeine Heidelbeere. 1868. III. 664.[1]
— Die italienische Pappel. 1868. III. 346.[1]
Ganser, Benno. Observationes botanicae cira nutritionem: 18 .. ? I. 157.
Ganss, Woldemar. Die Kokkelskörner. 1870. III. 396.[1]
Ganter. *See* JUNG & GANTER.
Ganter. Forstliche Chronik für ... 1851 bis dahin 1860. 1862. IV. 248.[1]
Gantois, P. Taille des arbres. 1896. III. 171.
Ganzel, (*Dr.*, *Perleberg*). Bemerkungen über die Behandlung des Weinstocks. 1835. III. 552.
Garbaglia, L. Alimentazione delle piante. 1899. IV. 64.[1]
— Concimi artificiali. 1899. IV. 145.
— Sulla conservazione delle ghiande. 1898. IV. 148.
— L'Eucalyptus urnigera. 1898. IV. 534.[1]
— I fermenti nel terreno. 1898. IV. 70.
— Influenza delle foreste sul ... acque. 1898.. IV. 52.
— L'innesto misto. 1898. III. 163.[1]
— La " Liparis monacha " in Svezia. 1898. IV. 202.
Garcelon, G. W. & **Lelong**, B. M. Citrus fruits. 1891. III. 497.[1]
Garcia, Fabian. *See* VESTAL, George & GARCIA, Fabian.
Garcia, Francisco de. Der Kork und dessen Gewinnung. 1859. IV. 518.[1]
Garcia, G. J. de GUILLÉN-. *See* GUILLÉN-GARCIA, G. J. de.
Garcia, Jorge. *See* GUÉRIN, René, DARIO, Gonzalès & GAR-CIA, Jorge.
Garcia Blanco, José. Aprovechamiento del corcho. 1900. IV. 559.[1]
— Efectos fisiológicos del descorche. 1898. IV. 518.[1]
— Formación del corcho segundero. 1897. IV. 518.[1]
Garcia Cañada, Nicolás R. Comentarios á un método de ordenación de montes. *See* CAÑADA, N. G. 1899. IV. 550.[1]
— Reforma de las instrucciones vigentes para la ordenación de los montes. 1899. IV. 550.[1]
Garcia de Tejada, Casimiro de BONA Y. *See* BONA Y GAR-CIA DE TEJADA, Casimiro de.
Garcia Maceira, Antonio. Las agallas. 1896. IV. 548.[1]
— Los árboles en " El Quijote." 1894. IV. 556.[1]
— El Cachón de Camaces. 1890. IV. 544.[1]
— Estudio de la invasión del insecto ... brugo en los roble-dales. 1895. IV. 501.[1]
— Estudio de la invasion .·. del insecto llamado vulgarmente " Lagarta." 1886. IV. 209,[1] 550.[1]
— Hartig, Cotta y Hundeshagen. 1888. IV. 539.[1]
— Insectos. 1891. IV. 550.[1]
— Un Lepidoptero dañoso á los montes de Castilla. 1897. IV. 550.[1]
— Lepidópteros diurnos de interés forestal. 1895. IV. 550.[1]
— Una monstruosidad del brugo. 1892. IV. 544.[1]
— Nueva fase de la entomología práctica. 1895. IV. 548.[1]
— Una nueva teoría sobre la vida. 1888. IV. 543.[1]
— Oruga de librea. 1900. IV. 550.[1]
— La práctica y el empirismo en la entomología forestal. 1897. IV. 548.[1]
— La zona subtropical de los arribes del Duero. 1890.. IV. 544.[1]
Garcia Sans, José. Manual de agricultura. 1861. III. 114.[1]
— Manual de selvicultura práctica. 1863. IV. 109.[1]
— Manual del jardinero. 1865. III. 114.[1]
Garcia y Merino, Manuel. Las epidemias de las plantas en la costa del Perú. 1878. III. 118.
Garcilasso de la Vega, Inca. La Florida del Inca. 1605. III. 263.[1]
— Historia de la Florida. 1605. III. 263.[1]
Garcin, A. G. Contribution à l'étude des péricarpes charnus. 1890. I. 119.
— Sur le fruit des Solanées. 1888. II. 768.[1]
— Du noyau des drupes, histologie et histogénèse. 1890. I. 119.
— Recherches sur l'histogénèse des péricarpes charnus. 1890. I. 119.
— Recherches sur les Apocynées. 1888. II. 722.[1]
— Sur une série d'anomalies du Lonicera Periclymenum. 1889. II. 839.[1]

Garcin, F. Note sur une maladie du raisin. 1877. III. 577.

Garcin, Laurentius. Memoirs . . . containing a description of a new family of plants called Oxyoïdes. 1731. II. 392.[2]
— The settling of a new genus . . . Mangostans. 1735. II. 554.[3]

Le Garcinia Mangostana. See " The MANGOSTEEN." 1895. III. 609.[3]

Garcke, Friedrich August. Abutilon australe Gke. 1861. II. 520.[1]
— Ueber Abutilon erosum Schldl. 1895. II. 521.[2]
— Ueber Achania Poeppigii Spr. 1850. II. 524.[1]
— Über anfechtbare Pflanzennamen. 1891. I. 254.[1]
— Ueber Asterochlaena. 1850. II. 523.[1]
— Aufzählung der abyssinischen Malvaceen. 1882. I. 489.
— Aufzählung der von J. M. Hildebrandt . . . gesammelten Malvaceen. 1883. II. 519.[2]
— Botanische Mittheilungen. 1853. II. 519.[1]
— Über Cassine domingensis. 1890. II. 493.[1]
— Ueber einige Arten der Gattung Anoda. 1887. II. 521.[1]
— Über einige Arten von Melochia. 1890. II. 536.[2]
— Ueber einige ganz unbekannte Malvaceen. 1863. II. 519.[1]
— Ueber einige im Prodromus . . . falsch untergebrachte Pflanzen. 1853. II. 519.[1]
— Über einige Malvaceengattungen. 1896. II. 519.[1]
— Ueber einige unbekannte Arten der Gattung Hermannia. 1864. II. 535.[1]
— Ueber einige unbekannte Pflanzen. 1874. I. 270.
— Einige Worte über die Gattung Hibiscus. 1874. II. 522.[1]
— Flora von Deutschland. 1849. I. 382.
— Flora von Halle. 1848. I. 382.
— Flora von Nord- und Mittel-Deutschland. 1849. I. 382.
— Über die Gattung Abutilon. 1893. II. 520.[1]
— Ueber die Gattung Fugosia Juss. 1860. II. 521.[2]
— Die Gattung Goethea. 1861. II. 521.[2]
— Ueber die Gattung Grewia. 1864. II. 513.[3]
— Die Gattung Malvastrum Asa Gray. 1857. II. 525.[3]
— Ueber die Gattung Pavonia. 1881. II. 526.[1]
— Ueber die Gattungen Solandra und Lagunea. 1853. II. 522,[1] 774.[1]
— Ueber die häufige Verwechselung von Malva coromandeliana. 1853. II. 519.[1]
— Ueber Hibiscus eriocarpus DC. 1857. II. 523.[2]
— Illustrierte Flora von Deutschland. 1849. I. 382.
— Ueber die am Kap der guten Hoffnung vorkommenden Malvaceen. 1864. II. 519.[2]
— Kritische Bemerkungen zu der Familie der Malvaceen. 1849. II. 519.[1]
— Malvaviscus longifolius. 1854. II. 526.[1]
— Ueber Malvaviscus spathulatus. 1853. II. 526.[1]
— Plantae Kegelianae surinamenses. 1849. I. 339.[1]
— Ueber die Stellung von Plagianthus und Hoheria. 1860. II. 524,[3] 526.[3]
— Was ist aus Astropos tomentosus Spr. geworden? 1890. II. 539.[3]
— Ein Wort über Walpers' Repertorium. 1854. II. 519.[1]
— Ueber zwei wenig bekannte Grewia-Arten. 1857. II. 513.[3]
— See also KLOTZSCH, J. F. & GARCKE, August.

Gargon, J. B. Réponse à une question de médecine. 1740. III. 238.[1]

Gargon, Jules. Bibliographie de la technologie chimique. 1893. III. 1.

Gard, M. R. Sur l'origine variable du premier périderme chez les Vitis. 1900. II. 506.[1]
— Sur un point de l'histologie de la tige des Vitis. 1900. II. 506.[1]
— Sur les variations de la structure anatomique . . . des entre-nœuds. 1900. I. 106.[1]

Gard, Maurice. Instructions pour les préposés aux pépinières. 1890. III. 127.[1]

Garden, Alexander. The effects of the Opuntia. 1758. III. 624.[3]

Garden. III. 17.

Garden and field. III. 27.[1]

Garden and forest. III. 3.

Garden companion. III. 17.

The garden companion and florists' guide. See HENFREY, Arthur & others. 1852. III. 82.

Garden egg. 1892. III. 702.[1]

Garden memoranda. Messrs. Jackman & Son's nursery. 1864. III. 390.[2]

Garden oracle. III. 17.

Gardener, C. F. Forestry for the Northwest. 1891. IV. 112.

Gardener; a magazine of horticulture. See The SCOTTISH gardener. III. 18.

Gardeners' and farmers' journal. See UNITED GARDENERS' . . . III. 18.

Gardener's and forester's record. III. 17.

Gardeners' chronicle. III. 17.

Gardeners' gazette. III. 17.

Gardener's magazine. See FLORICULTURAL cabinet. III. 16.

Gardener's magazine. Ed. by J. L. Loudon. III. 17.

Gardeners' magazine of botany. III. 17.

Gardeners' monthly. III. 4.

The gardener's monthly volume. 1847. III. 123.[1]

Gardener's weekly magazine. See FLORICULTURAL cabinet. III. 16.

Gardener's yearbook. III. 17.

Gardening. III. 4.

Gardening illustrated. III. 17.

Gardening world illustrated. III. 17.

Gardening year book. See GARDEN oracle. III. 17.

The gardens of Levens Hall. 1889. III. 202.[3]

Gardeur, A. F. Étude du bassin de la rivière Claire. 1894. IV. 400.[3]

Gardiner, John, & Brace, L. J. K. Provisional list of plants of the Bahama Islands. 1890. I. 337.

Gardiner, Walter. On the constitution of the cell-wall. 1884. I. 138.[1]
— On the continuity of the protoplasm. 1883. I. 137.
— On the general occurrence of tannins. 1883. I. 183.
— On the germination of Acacia sphaerocephala. 1890. II. 328.[1]
— Note on the functions of the secreting hairs . . . of Thunbergia. 1887. II. 805.[1]
— On the physiological significance of water glands. 1884. I. 169.[1]
— See also POTTER, M. C. & GARDINER, Walter.
— & Lynch, R. I. On the secretory hairs on the stem of Thunbergia. 1885. II. 805.[1]

Gardiner, William. Botanical rambles in Braemar. 1845. I. 399.
— The flora of Forfarshire. 1848. I. 400.
— Linnaea borealis, &c., on Ben Beck, Braemar. 1846. II. 835.[3]

Gardini, Francesco Giuseppe. De influxu electricitatis atmosphaericae. 1784. I. 231.[1]

Gardner, Charles F. On the care . . . of small evergreens. 1885. III. 292.
— Conifer growing in northern Iowa. 1882. III. 118.[1]
— Evergreens, desirable, but neglected. 1899. III. 293.
— Evergreens for North Iowa. 1893. III. 293.
— Evergreens for shelter belts. 1894. III. 215.[3]
— Evergreens for the farm. 1896. III. 293.
— Evergreens, transplanting. 1888. III. 295.[1]
— The gathering . . . of Conifer and forest tree seeds. 1895. IV. 145.
— Gooseberry and Currant culture. 1895. III. 414.[1]
— Hedges. 1894. III. 214.[1]
— Nursery management of evergreens. 1896. III. 293.
— Propagation, training and uses of the Conifers. 1886. III. 292.
— Report on forest trees. 1887. IV. 112.
— Trees in northeastern Iowa. 1899. III. 118.[1]

Gardner, D. P. On the action of yellow light. 1844. I. 229.

Gardner, George. The Coffee bug and Coffee mildew. 1849. III. 734.[2]
— Contributions toward a flora of Brazil. 1842. I. 342.
— Contributions towards a flora of Ceylon. 1845. I. 476.[3]
— Description of a new species of Crescentia. 1840. II. 787.[3]
— Descriptions of four new genera. 1843. II. 860.[1]
— Einige allgemeine Bemerkungen über die Flora von Ceylon. 1847. I. 476.[3]
— On the establishment of the genus Mouriria. 1840. I. 329.
— Excursionen in den benachbarten Gebirgen von Rio de Janeiro. 1847. I. 342.
— Mededeeling betreffende eene ziekte der Koffijboomen in Ceylon. 1850. III. 735.
— Observations sur l'origine . . . des fibres ligneuses des tiges de Palmiers. 1840. II. 62.[3]
— Report on the brown scale or Coccus. 1850. III. 735.
— Some general remarks on the flora of Ceylon. 1847. I. 476.[3]
— Some observations on . . . woody fibre of the stems of Palms. 1840. II. 62.[3]

Gardner, George (*continued*).
— Travels in the interior of Brazil. 1846. I. 342.
— Végétation de la province de Rio de Janeiro. 1846. I. 342.
— Die Vegetation des Orgelgebirges. 1846. I. 342.
— La végétation du Brésil. 1848. I. 342.
— The vegetation [of Brazil]. 1846. I. 342.
— The vegetation of Ceylon. 1849. I. 476.²
— *See also* FIELDING, H. B. & GARDNER, George; WIGHT, Robert & GARDNER, George.
— & **Champion**, J. G. Descriptions of some new . . . plants, collected in . . . Hongkong. 1849. I. 460.²
Gardner, John Starkie. On Coniferae. 1881. II. 13.¹
— Some facts about Conifers. 1882. II. 13.¹
Gareiso, Joseph. Synopsis analytique de la flore du Gard. 1847. I. 410.
Garelli, Felice. Manuale di viticoltura. 1878. III. 558.¹
Garey, Thomas A. Orange culture in California. 1882. III. 500.¹
Garfield, Charles W. Forest problems in Michigan. 1900. IV. 272.
Garibaldi, Giuseppe. Notizie sull' isola di Caprera. 1864. IV. 364.
Garidel, Pierre Joseph. Histoire des plantes . . . d'Aix. 1715. I. 405.
— Histoire des plantes qui naissent en Provence. 1715. I. 405.
Garland, John. Berberis asiatica as a hedge plant. 1875. III. 394.¹
— Cotoneaster affinis. 1884. III. 420.¹
— Transplanting Cedars. 1876. III. 299.²
Garlinski, Leon. Sprawozdanie z wyciecski do (lasów) Krechowic i Suchodołu. 1900. IV. 370.
Garman, Harrison. The Elms and their diseases. 1899. III. 365.¹
— The pests of shade and ornamental trees. 1893. III. 187.
Garner, Robert. Natural history of the county of Stafford. 1844. I. 399.
Garnett, Thomas. Observations on a tour through the Highlands. 1800. V. xx.²
Garnier, Ad. Influence de l'hiver 1890–1891. 1892. III. 49.¹
Garnier, Antoine. An Parisinis frequens potus thé frequenti potu café salubrior? 1749. III. 222.
Garnier, Francis. Voyage d'exploration en Indo-Chine. 1873. III. 276.²
Garnier, J. Le pâturage dans les forêts de la haute vallée. 1888. IV. 135.¹
Garnier, L. Étude microscopique . . . poudres de cannelle. 1884. III. 406.¹
Garnier, Max. Quelques Dracaena. 1895. III. 334.²
Garot. Sur du café avarié. 1826. III. 738.
— Observations sur la distillation du Laurier-cerise. 1842. III. 438.¹
— Sur la présence du malate de chaux dans les feuilles du Frêne commun. 1853. IV. 535.²
Garovaglio, Santo. Acclimatation, naturalisation. 1864. III. 49.¹
— Alcuni discorsi sulla botanica. 1862. I. 95.
— Di alcuni nuovi funghi . . . sugli Agrumi. 1875. III. 498.¹
— Sulle attuali condizioni dell' orto botanico della Università di Pavia. 1862. I. 63.
— Discorsi sulla botanica. 1862. I. 95.
— Sulle principali malattie degli Agrumi. 1875. III. 498.¹
— Sulle principali malattie degli Agrumi. 1879. III. 498.¹
— La Vite e i suoi nemici. 1881. III. 560.
— & **Cattaneo**, Achille. Sulla ruggine dell' Abete rosso. 1876. IV. 456.
— Studj sulle dominanti malattie dei Vitigni. 1878. III. 578.
Garraud, Léopold. Études sur les bois de construction. 1863. IV. 423.¹
Garreau, J. Sur la nature de la cuticule. 1850. I. 122.
Garreau, Lazare. Fonctions de la matière azotée. 1860. I. 158.
— On the functions of the nitrogenous matter of plants. 1860. I. 158.
— Mémoire sur la respiration des plantes. 1851. I. 170.
— Nouvelles recherches. 1859. V. xi.²
— Nouvelles recherches sur la respiration des plantes. 1851. I. 170.
— Physique des plantes. 1850. I. 117,² 129.¹
— Recent researches on the respiration of plants. 1851. I. 170.
— Recherches expérimentales. 1859. I. 153, V. xi.²
— Recherches sur l'absorption et l'exhalation. 1850. I. 166.
— Recherches sur l'absorption et l'exhalation 1853. I. 170.
— Recherches sur la distribution des matières minérales. 1859. I. 153.
— De la respiration chez les plantes. 1851. I. 170.
— & **Brauwers**. Recherches sur les formations cellulaires . . . des extrémités radiculaires. 1858. I. 103.
— — Researches on the cellular formations. 1858. I. 103.
Garrigues, F. Les Bambous français. 1890. III. 315.²
— Culture du Bambou. 1879. III. 314.¹
Garrod, Alfred Baring. The essentials of materia medica. 1864. III. 243.
— *See also* BALLARD, Edward & GARROD, A. B.
Garros, F. Sur les matières gommeuses. 1892. II. 273.¹
Garsault, A. G. Notice sur la Réunion. 1900. III. 279.²
Garsault, François Alexandre Pierre de. Description, vertus et usages de 719 plantes. 1767. I. 292.
— Les figures des plantes . . . d'usage en médecine. 1764. III. 54.
Garsed, W. The characters of oil of Akee. 1900. III. 539.¹
Garston, de. Orange cultivation in Sicily. 1896. III. 497.²
Gart der Gesuntheit. *See* ORTUS sanitatis. 148.? I. 275.¹
Der **Garten**. Aarau. III. 24.¹
Ain **garten** der gesunthait. *See* ORTUS sanitatis. 148.? I. 275.¹
Garten- und Blumen-Verein für Hamburg, Altona . . . Archiv. III. 12.
Gartenbau-Gesellschaft. *See* K. k. GARTENBAU-GESELL-SCHAFT.
Gartenbaugesellschaft des österreichischen Kaiserstaates. *See* BOTANISCHES Archiv . . . I. 27.
Gartenbau-Gesellschaft Wien. Verhandlungen. III. 24.²
Gartenbau-Verein für die Königreich Hannover. Zeitschrift. III. 12.
Gartenbau-Zeitschrift für die Centralschweiz. III. 24.¹
Der **Gartenbeobachter**. *See* ANNALEN der Blumisterei. III. 11.
Gartenflora. III. 12.
Der **Gartenfreund**. III. 24.²
Garten-Kalender. III. 12.
Gartenkunst. III. 12.
Garten-Nachrichten. III. 12.
Die **Gartenwelt**. III. 12.
Garten-Zeitung. Ed. by Kurt Sprengel. III. 12.
Garten-Zeitung. Ed. by L. Wittmack & W. Perring. III. 12.
Garthe, (*Oberförster*). Erziehung von Pflänzlingen aus Stock-lohden. 1840. IV. 149.²
Garthe, T. Antheeren der jungen Buchen. 1879. IV. 497.
— Praktisches Mittel zur Erhaltung der von den Mäusen geschälten Buchenpflanzen. 1892. IV. 198.²
Gartig, R. *See* ГАРТИГЪ, P.
Gartner-Tidende. III. 10.²
Gartwig. *See* ГАРТВИГЪ.
Garsoni, Ernesta, *marchesa*. L' inverno 1879–80. 1880. III. 49.²
Gås de leña. 1861. IV. 433.²
Gas illuminante dai trucioli di legno. 1885. IV. 433.²
Gasc, J. P. Mémoire sur l'influence de l'électricité dans la fécondation. 1811. I. 200.
Gascard, Albert. Contribution à l'étude des gommes laques des Indes. 1893. III. 232.²
Gases found in plants. 1868. I. 147.
Gaskell, Alfred. American foresters in Germany. 1900. IV. 349.²
— Forestry schools. 1900. IV. 33.²
Gaskins, James. The farmer's guide. 1838. III. 375.
Gaslini, Cav. Angelo. I prodotti agricoli del tropico. 1896. III. 131.¹
Gaspard, B. Mémoire physiologique sur le Gui. 1827. II. 178.²
Gasparin, de. Mémoire sur la culture de l'Olivier. 1822. III. 675.¹
Gasparin, de. Oak truffles. 1862. IV. 514.²
Gasparin, Adrien de, *comte*. Considérations sur l'extension de la culture des Mûriers. 1833. III. 374.
— Coup d'œil sur l'agriculture de la Sicile. 1840. III. 126.²
— Influence de l'acide phosphorique. 1881. I. 159.
— Influence de la chaleur. 1855. I. 232.¹
— Mémoire sur la radiation solaire. 1853. I. 229.
— Mémoire sur les moyens de déterminer les limites de la culture des Mûriers. 1840. III. 376.
— Observations sur une lettre de M. Charpentier. 1850. III. 741.²
— Rapport sur une note de M. Hardy. 1854. III. 130.¹

Gasparin, Auguste. Note sur les Mûriers multicaules hybrides. 1836. III. 380.²
Gasparin, Paul Joseph de. Sur la constitution . . . des terrains vignobles. 1883. III. 556.
— Note sur l'emploi des superphosphates. ·1882. III. 151.
Gasparis, Aurelio de. Sopra alcune piante a funzione mirmecofoba. 1895. II. 380,¹ 533.²
Gasparrini, Guglielmo. On the caprification of the Fig. 1845. II. 150.²
— Cenno sulla origine dell' embrione. 1846. I. 121.
— Descrizione di un nuovo genere . . . delle Leguminose. 1836. II. 325.¹
— Sulla maturazione e la qualità dei Fichi. 1863. II. 150.²
— Sopra la melata. 1863. I. 213.¹
— Sulla melata dell' Uva. 1865. III. 560.
— Mémoire sur un nouveau genre . . . des Légumineuses. 1836. II. 325.¹
— New observations on some artificial agents which promote the ripening of Figs. 1865. II. 150,² *III. 369.²*
— Note sur l'origine de l'embryon. 1846.· I. 122.
— Notizie sopra una Mortella dell' Australia. 1865. III. 636.¹
— Nouvelles recherches sur quelques points d'anatomie et de physiologie, relatifs au Figuier. 1848. II. 150.²
— Nova genera . . . super nonnullis Fici speciebus. 1844. II. 148.²
— Nuove osservazioni su taluni agenti artifiziali che accelerano la maturazione nel Fico. · 1865. II. 150.²
— Nuove ricerche sopra alcuni punti di anatomia . . . del Fico e Caprifico. 1848. II. 150.²
— Nuove ricerche sulla struttura dei cistomi. 1844. I. 131.¹
— Osservazioni intorno alla struttura delle piante . . . di Boccadifalco. 1832 (1833). I. 62, 63.
— Osservazioni intorno alla struttura dell' arillo. 1843. I. 120.
— Osservazioni ·intorno alla struttura delle gemme . . . dell' Opunzia. 1851. II. 596.¹
— Osservazioni intorno la struttura del frutto dell' Opunzia. 1842. II. 596.¹
— Osservazioni sopra alcune malattie . . . degli Agrumi. 1862. III. 498.¹
— Osservazioni sopra talune modificazioni organiche in alcune cellule vegetali. 1863. I. 129.²
— Osservazioni su le Viti e le Vigne del distretto di Napoli. 185 . ? III. 557.²
— Osservazioni su taluni agenti artificiale che accelerano la maturazione nel fico. 1865. III. 369.²
— Osservazioni sul cammino di un micelio . . . dell' Acacia dealbata. 1865. III. 464.²
— Osservazioni sulla malattia della Vite. 1855. III. 576.
— Osservazioni sulla origine del calice monosepalo. 1863. I. 115.²
— Osservazioni sulla struttura dei tubercoli spongiolari di alcune piante leguminose. 1851. II. 320.¹
— Ricerche sulla natura dei succiatori. 1856. I. 103.
— Ricerche sulla natura del Caprifico. 1845. II. 150.²
— Ricerche sulla origine dell' embrione. 1846. I. 122.
— Ricerche sulla struttura degli stomi. 1842. I. 131.¹
— Struttura dei cistomi del Cereo peruviano. 1842. II. 590.²
Gasper, V. A Paulownia imperialis. 1896. III. 703.²
Gasparini, Gustavo. Il leghbi o vino di Palma. 1666. III. 329.¹
— Sopra un nuovo morbo che attacca i Limoni. 1888. III. 498.¹
Gasquet, de. Mémoire envoyé au concours pour l'établissement de pépinières d'Oliviers. 1825. III. 675.¹
— Mémoire sur la culture de l'Olivier. 1825. III. 675.¹
Gassée, Éd. Aucuba splendida aureo var. 1882. III. 645.¹
Gassendi, Sierre. Opera. 1658. I. 286.
Gasser, Aug. *See* MAIRE, Réné & GASSER, Aug.
— & Maire, Réné. Sur l'influence du calcaire. 1900. I. 229.
Gassicourt, CADET DE. *See* CADET DE GASSICOURT.
Gassmann, Ferdinand. Forstliche Mittheilungen aus dem europäischen Russland. · 1871. IV. 345.
Gast, L. La législation étrangère sur la conservation des forêts. 1876. IV. 314.¹
— Notice sur le Charme. 1878. IV. 492.¹
— *See also* GALLOT, J. B. H. E. & GAST, L.
Gastine, G. Expériences faites pour apprécier la diffusion des vapeurs du sulfure de carbone. 1877. III. 563.
— *See also* MARION, A. F. & GASTINE, G.

— & **Couanon,** Georges. Traitement des Vignes phylloxérées. 1884. III. 761.
— & **Degrully.** Sur la chlorose des· Vignes américaines. 1895. III. 562.¹
Gastrell, William H. S. Report . . . on the agricultural conditions of the Argentine Republic. 1893. III. 551.¹
Gaterau. Description des plantes . . . de Montauban. 1789. I. 406.
Gattenhof, Georg Matthias. Stirpes agri et Horti heidelbergensis. 1782. I. 44.
Gatterer, Christoph Wilhelm Jakob. Abhandlung vom Nutzen und Schaden der Thiere. 1781. IV. 89.²
— Allgemeines Repertorium der forstwissenschaftlichen Literatur. 1796. IV. 1.
— Anleitung den Harz . . . zu bereisen. *See* RÜLING, J. P. 1786. I. 374.
— Authentische Nachricht von dem . . . Brande im wirtembergischen Schwarzwald. 1801. IV. 182.²
— Forstliche Bibliographie. 1796. IV. 1.
— Forstordnungen. 1796. IV. 314.¹
— Literatur des Weinbaues aller Nationen. 1832. III. 545.²
— Materialien zur Kulturgeschichte des Lerchenbaums. 1801. IV. 448.²
— *See also* DRAIS, F. H. G., *Freyherr* von, WEITERSHAUSEN, *Freyherr* von & GATTERER, C. W. J.
Gattinger, August. Botanical fragments. 1884. I. 319.
— Diervilla rivularis. 1888. II. 835.¹
— The medicinal plants of Tennessee. 1894. III. 63.¹
— The Tennessee flora. 1887. I. 319.
— On trees and shrubbery. 1878. III. 60.
Gatto, Alfred, *conte* CARUANA-. *See* CARUANA-GATTO, Alfred, *conte*.
Die **Gattung** Adamia und deren bekannten Arten. 1854. III. 410.¹
Die **Gattung** Azara. 1874. III. 614.¹
Die **Gattungen** der Araliaceen. 1856. III. 641.¹
Gatzemeyer. Einige phänologische Angaben für . . . Tremessen. 1900. I. 528.²
Gaucher, E., **Combemale & Marestang.** Sur l'action physiologique de l'Hedwigia. 1888. III. 511.¹
Gaucher, Louis. Sur le développement de l'ovaire du Punica. 1897. II. 611.¹
— La racine des Euphorbes cactiformes. 1899. II. 442.¹
Gaucher, Nicolas. Der Baumkitt von Heinrich Bauer. 1883. III. 181.²
— Belehrungen über das Ablaktieren, Pfropfen. 1885. III. 153.
— Die Blutlaus . . . 1886. III. 428.¹
— Handbuch der Obstkultur. 1889. III. 139.
— Pomologie des praktischen Obstbaumzüchters. 1894. III. 72.
— Praktischer Obstbau. 1891. III. 139.
— Die rationelle Obstkultur. 1881. III. 138.
— Die Veredelungen. 1885. III. 153, 162.
— *See also* TOMB, H.
Gauchery, Paul. Sur un Melianthus hybride. 1897. II. 491.²
— Notes anatomiques sur quelques Vignes hybrides. 1899. II. 506.¹
— Recherches sur le nanisme végétal. 1890. I. 236.¹
— Recherches sur les hybrides dans le genre Cistus. 1894. II. 504.¹
Gauchet, L. C. F. Danger de l'aliénation des forêts. 1831. IV. 275.
Gaudais (*de Nantes*). Culture de la Vigne. 1866. III. 555.
— Réponse à l'article de M. P. Bounin. 1868. III. 555.
Gaudet, A. Les bois de Saône-et-Loire. 1890. IV. 361.
— La fin d'une pépinière forestière. 1887. IV. 276.¹
Gaudey. Les éboulements du Mont-Dore. 1900. IV. 186.²
Gaudichaud-Beaupré, Charles. Adriana. 1825. II. 436.¹
— Aperçu sur la chimie physiologique. 1847. I. 561.¹
— Descriptions de quelques nouveaux genres. 1824. II. 56.¹
— La flore des îles Malouines. 1825. I. 347.·
— Instructions demandées par M. le docteur Petit. 1849. I. 346.
— Note relativement à . . . communication de M. le docteur Boucherie, sur la vascularité des végétaux. 1841. I. 133.
— Note sur un Pommier. 1852. II. 266.¹
— Notes . . . relatives à la protestation . . . à la suite de la lecture du mémoire de M. de Mirbel . . . Recherches anatomiques. 1843. I. 99.
— Observations on the organogeny of the flower. 1844. I. 114.²

Gaudichaud-Beaupré, Charles (*continued*).
— Observations relatives à une présentation . . . sur l'accroissement en diamètre. 1852. I. 189.
— Observations sur l'ascension de la sève dans une hane. 1836. *I. 163*, II. 503.[2]
— Observations sur quelques points de physiologie et d'anatomie. 1833. I. 104.
— Première note sur la chute des feuilles. 1852. I. 191.[2]
— Premières . . . remarques sur les deux mémoires de M. M. Payen et de Mirbel relatifs à l'organographie. 1846. I. 99, 147.
— Quatrièmes notes relatives à la protestation . . . à la suite de la lecture du mémoire de M. de Mirbel . . . Recherches anatomiques. 1844. I. 123.[3]
— Rapport sur un mémoire de M. Duchartre . . . Observations sur l'organogénie de la fleur. 1844. I. 114.[2]
— Rapport sur un mémoire de MM. Durand et Manoury . . . relatif à l'accroissement en diamètre. 1848. I. 189.
— Recherches anatomiques sur la tige du Ravenala. 1845. II. 91.[3]
— Recherches expérimentales sur la sève ascendante. 1853. I. 164.
— Recherches générales sur l'organographie. 1835. I. 146.
— Recherches générales sur l'organographie. 1841. I. 34.
— Recherches générales sur la physiologie et l'organogénie des végétaux. 1842. I. 98.
— Recherches sur l'accroissement en hauteur. 1847. I. 187.
— Recherches sur l'anatomie . . . des végétaux monocotylés. 1847. I. 99.
— Réfutation de toutes les objections . . . contre les nouveaux principes phytologiques. 1852. I. 189.
— Réfutation des théories établies par M. de Mirbel. 1845. I. 105, *II. 80*.[1]
— Remarques générales sur le rapport qui a été fait . . . sur un mémoire de M. Trécul. 1852. I. 189.
— Remarques générales sur les vaisseaux tubuleux des végétaux. 1841. I. 133.
— Remarques sur la lettre de M. Martius. 1845. II. 62.[2]
— Réplique à une note de M. de Mirbel. 1845. II. 80.[1]
— Réponses aux observations qui nous ont été faites . . . par MM. Ach. Richard, Ad. Brongniart et Ad. de Jusseiu. 1852. I. 189.
— Des sucs séveux acides. 1848. I. 180.[1]
— Voyage autour du monde. 1826. I. 302.
— Voyage autour du monde . . . sur la corvette la Bonite. 1851. I. 303.
Gaudin, A. Sur la préparation d'un lait artificiel. 1871. III. 594.
Gaudin, Charles. Note sur l'origine . . . du Platanus occidentalis. 1858. II. 255.[1]
Gaudin, Jean François Gottlieb Philippe. Etrennes de flore no. 1. 1804. I. 433.
— Flora helvetica. 1828. I. 433.
— Observations sur la direction des feuilles du Houx-frélon. 1809. II. 84.[2]
— Synopsis florae helveticae. 1836. I. 434, V. xxii.[2]
Gaudry, Albert. Recherches scientifiques en Orient. 1855. III. 127.[1]
Gaudry, Louis. Cours pratique d'arboriculture. 1848. III. 143.
Gaudy, Jules. Nos méthodes de culture des arbres fruitiers. 1885. III. 132.[2]
Gauhe, Fr. Note concernant la clématine. 1869. III. 392.[1]
Gaujard, Narcisse. L'arboriculture en Russie. 1869. III. 120.[1]
— Die Aucuba japonica. 1866. III. 644.[2]
— Polymorphisme de l'Ilex Aquifolium. 1872. II. 463.[2]
Gauker, I. *See* Гукеръ, I.
Gaultier, Gabriel. Droit romain de la protection des servitudes par les interdits. Droit français nature. juridique de l'usage forestier. 1894. IV. 334.[2]
— Faculté de droit de Paris. Droit romain: De la protection de servitudes par les interdits. 1894. IV. 314.[1]
Gaultier de Claubry, Henri. De la culture et de la récolte du Liége. 1860. IV. 516.[2]
Gaunersdorfer, Johann. Beiträge zur Kenntniss der Eigenschaften und Entstehung des Kernholzes. 1882. I. 125.
— Einiges über den Einfluss des Menschen auf die Vegetation Europas. 1877. I. 242.[1]
Gausby, Robert. Curious illustration of vegetable morphology. 1863. II. 707.[1]
Gauthier. Analyse de l'épiderme du Bouleau. 1827. IV. 491.[1]

Gauthier, Hugues. Introduction à la connaissance des plautes. 1760. III. 85.
Gautier, Alexandre. Herbier médical. 1822. III. 85.
— Manuel des plantes médicinales. 1822. III. 85.
Gautier, Émile Justin Armand. Sur les catéchines. 1877. III. 748.[1]
— Sur la chlorophylle. 1879. I. 141.
— Gaz combustibles de l'air. 1900. IV. 54.
— Isomères de la phloroglucine. 1880. I. 176.
— Sur l'origine des matières colorantes de la Vigne. 1892. III. 583.[2]
— Les Pommiers de France. 1899. III. 426.[2]
— Remarques à propos d'une note par Prillieux. 1893. III. 581.
— Réponse à M. Trécul et à M. Chevreul relativement à la chlorophylle cristallisée. 1879. I. 141.
— Sur le rôle que jouent les matières humiques. 1897. I. 229.
— & **Drouin, R.** Recherches sur la fixation de l'azote. 1888. I. 159.
— — Remarques sur le mécanisme de la fixation de l'azote. 1892. I. 160.
Gautier, Gaston. Catalogue raisonné de la flore des Pyrénées-orientales. 1897. I. 418.
— Rapport sur l'herborisation . . . au Mont-Allaric. 1888. II. 497.[1]
— Rapport sur l'herborisation . . . aux pinèdes de Boutenac. 1888. II. 564.[1]
Gautier, Joseph. Traité de la taille des grands arbres. 185. ? III. 170.
Gautier-Dagoty, Jacques. Collection des plantes usuelles. 1767. III. 55.[1]
— Plantes purgatives d'usage. 1776. III. 55.
Gautier-Lacroze, J. Flore d'Auvergne. 1876. I. 415.
Gautieri, Giuseppe. Dell' influsso de' boschi. 1814. IV. 42.[2]
— Nozione elementari sui boschi. 1812. IV. 383.[1]
— Prospetto di tutti i concimi europei. 1809. III. 151.
— Quando e come abbiasi a permettere il pacolo ne' boschi. 1813. IV. 135.[3]
— Dei vantaggi e dei danni derivanti dalle capre. 1816. IV. 197.[1]
Gautxet & Lautier. La strychnine, principe actif du m'boundou. 1896. III. 684.[1]
Gawarecki, Zygmunt. Sposoby powiększania urodzajności drzew owocowych. 1892. III. 174.[2]
Gay (*of Médéa*). Sur quelques plantes . . . d'Algérie. 1890. I. 486.
Gay, Claude. Agriculture chilienne. 1862. III. 119.[1]
— Fragments de géographie botanique du Chili. 1856. I. 346.[2]
— Historia fisica y política de Chile. 1845. I. 346.
— Rapport sur un mémoire de M. Édouard de Rivero. 1857. III. 492.[2]
Gay, Henri. Florule de Blida. 1888. I. 486.
— Herborisations algériennes. 1886. II. 273.[1]
— L'Oxyédre des Haouaras. 1888. II. 31.[2]
Gay, J. P. J. Pharmacopée de Montpellier. 1845. III. 255.[2]
Gay, Jacques E. Le Chamaerops excelsa Thunb. 1861. II. 75.[1] *III. 331*.[2]
— Duriaei iter asturicum botanicum. 1836. I. 420.
— Fragment d'une monographie des vraies Büttneriacées. 1823. II. 531.[1]
— Monographie des cinq genres . . . des Lasiopétalées. 1821. II. 531.[1]
— Note sur Chênes-liéges cultivés en Angleterre. 1863. II. 135.[2]
— Note sur la végétation . . . du Chêne. 1857. II. 131.[1]
— Notice sur un Chêne nouveau de la flore de France. 1856. II. 129.[2]
— Note sur une nouvelle espèce de Chêne. 1856. II. 129.[1]
— Station minéralogique du Châtaignier. 1852. II. 124.[2]
— Voyage botanique au Caernarvonshire. 1863. II. 135.[2]
Gay, Paul. Recherches expérimentales sur la valeur nutritive du marron d'Inde. 1896. III. 538.[2]
Gayer, Karl. Beiträge zur Kenntniss der Lärche. 1895. IV. 450.
— Bestockungswandlungen im Spessart. 1876. IV. 118.
— Ueber Buchenmischung im Nadelwald. 1897. IV. 138.[2]
— Ueber Eichenzucht im Spessart. 1874. IV. 506.
— Ueber den Femelschlagbetrieb. 1895. IV. 131.
— Forest utilization. 1863. IV. 381.
— Die Forstbenutzung. 1863. IV. 381.

— Ueber forstliche Versuchsstationen, insbesondere in Bayern. 1867. IV. 38.[1]
— Ueber die gegenwärtigen durch . . . Sturmschäden herbeigeführten Verhältnisse. 1871. IV. 189.[1]
— Der gemischte Wald. 1886. IV. 137.[2]
— Der Kahlschlagbetrieb. 1879. IV. 129.
— Der Köschingerforst in Bayern. 1899. IV. 351.[2]
— Leistung einiger Waldsägen. 1871. IV. 393.
— Die neue Wirthschaftsrichtung in den Staatswaldungen des Spessarts. 1884. IV. 118.
— Der obere bayerische Wald. 1892. IV. 119,[1] 140.
— Das Revier Heinrichsthal im Spessart. 1869. IV. 351.[1]
— Le soutrage. 1896. IV. 72.
— Der Wald im Wechsel der Zeiten. 1889. IV. 270.
— Der Waldbau. 1878. IV. 107.[1]
— Der Waldbesitz ihrer kgl. Hoheiten des Prinzen und der Prinzessin Ludwig von Bayern. 1893. IV. 351,[1] 374.[1]
— Die Waldungen der gräflich v. Seinsheim'schen Familie bei Regensburg. 1900. IV. 351.[2]
— & Kast, Karl. Beiträge zur Ermittelung der Leistungsfähigkeit der Waldsägen. 1896. IV. 393.
— & Mayr, Heinrich. Statistische Erhebungen über die Holzarten . . . in den Staatswaldungen Bayerns. 1897. IV. 351.[2]
Gayffier, Eugène de. Herbier forestier.de la France. 1868. I. 404,[1] IV. 85.[1]
— Reboisement et gazonnement des montagnes. 1877. IV. 162.
Gaylord, Edson. The five most important requisites necessary to successful orcharding. 1898. III. 134.[1]
— Fruit tree protection. 1895. III. 134.[1]
— Top-working to secure hardiness. 1893. III. 183.[2]
Gayon, M. Ulysse. Recherches sur les engrais de la Vigne. 1891. III. 549.[1]
Gayon, Ulysse. Action des vapeurs . . . sur la fermentation des fruits. 1877. I. 179.[1]
— Recherches effectuées en vue de découvrir des organismes parasites du phylloxera. 1881. III. 573.
— See also Millardet, Alexis & Gayon, Ulysse.
— & Millardet, Alexis. Le cuivre, dans la récolte des Vignes. 1886. III. 579.
— — Sur les matières sucrées des Vignes phylloxérées. 1879. III. 560.
Gaytan, Candido. Note sur la matière grasse . . . de Sapotille mammée. 1840. III. 668.[1]
Gazeau, Ch. L'écussonnage du Poirier. sur Pommier franc. 1898. III. 445.[2]
Gazeau, Charles. Nouvelles recherches . . . du Coca. 1870. III. 492.[2]
— Recherches expérimentales . . . de la Coca. 1870. III. 492.[2]
Gazeta liesovodstva. See Газета лѣсоводства.
Gazeta rolnicza. III. 24.[2]
Gazette hebdomadaire de médecine. 1. 21.
Gazette médicale de Paris. I. 21.
Gazetteer of Sikhim. See Gammie, J. 1894. I. 475.[1]
Gazetteer of the Bombay Presidency. Botany. 1886. I. 475.[1]
Gazin. Pasture in the mountains of Savoy. 1885. IV. 135.[1]
Gazin, A. La culture forestière dans la région du Chablais. 1887. IV. 361.
— Introduction des résineux dans les taillis. 1900. IV. 441.
— See also Cannon, David & Gazin, A.
Gazin, E. Quelques considérations sur les forêts vosgiennes. 1889. IV. 361.
Gazzetta chimica italiana. I. 25.
Gazzetta toscana delle scienze medico-fisiche. III. 23.[1]
Gazzetti, Francesco. Cenni sui danni del diboscamento. 1863. III. 506,[2] IV. 281.[1]
— Il diboschimento. 1886. IV. 48.[1]
— Il diboschimento. 1887. IV. 281.[1]
— Relazione sulla coltura dell' Ailanto. 1864. III. 506.[2]
— Il rimboschimento. 188.? IV. 165.
— Selvicoltura. 1887. IV. 281.[1]
— See also Salvagnini, Enrico & Gazetti, Francesco.
Gebhard, C. Beiträge zur der Frage über die . . . Zukunft des Eichenschälwald-Betriebs in Süddeutschland. 1859. IV. 505.
— Die Birke . . . gegen Curculio pini. 1863. IV. 207, 490.[1]
— Einige Bemerkungen zur Pflege der Saat- und Pflanzschulen. 1863. IV. 150.
— Mittheilungen über ein neues Kulturwerkzeug. 1864. IV. 143.[1]
Gebhard, Friedrich. Vollständige Anleitung zur Obstbaumzucht. 1822. III. 136.

Gebhard, Johann Nepomuk. Verzeichniss der . . . in der Steyermark . . . gesammelten Pflanzen. 1821. I. 439.
Gebhardt, J. G. Die schädlichsten Feld-, Wald- . . . Insekten. 1834. IV. 91.[2]
Gebhardt, Matthias. Alangium. 1899. III. 632.[1]
— Die besten Buddleia-Arten. 1898. III. 681.[2]
— Buddleia variabilis Hemsl. 1898. III. 681.[2]
— Buddleia variabilis, un nouveau Buddleia rustique. 1898. III. 681.[1]
— Die buntholzigen Rubus-Arten. 1899. III. 457.[2]
— Carpenteria californica. 1898. III. 410.[1]
— Cornus capitata. 1898. III. 645.[2]
— Lycium pallidum. 1899. III. 701.[1]
— Fosoqueris Aubl. 1899. III. 746.[2]
— Der Schnitt der Spiraeen. 1899. III. 460.[2]
Gebhart, E. Pâturages et forêts dans le Massif central. 1893. IV. 135.[1]
Gebhart, F. De l'extraction du sous-bois. 1897. IV. 140.
— Paturages et forêts. 1890. IV. 164.[1]
— Statistique forestière du . . . Cantal. 1889. IV. 361.
Gebrath, von. Kurze Anleitung zur Holzanbauung. 1781. IV. 105.
— Wie kann man dem über Hand nehmenden Holzmangel abhelfen. 1790. IV. 280.[1]
Ueber den Gebrauch des Hibiscus esculentus. 1835. III. 587.[2]
Von den Gebrechen der Wälder. 1799. IV. 268.
Gebruik van de bladeren der Koffijplant. 1854. III. 739.
Gedanken betreffs der forstlichen Reformfrage. See Cotta, W. 1849. IV. 101.
Gedanken über den Anbau des Erlenholzes. 1797. IV. 488.[2]
Gedanken über Forstwissenschaft und Forstwirthschaft. 1897. IV. 102.
Geddes, Patrick. Chapters in modern botany. 1893. I. 96.
— Entwickelung und Aufgabe der Morphologie. 1885. I. 100.[1]
Über das Gedeihen und die Kultur der Wallnuss- und ächten Kastanien-Bäume. 1827. III. 136.
Gedenkbuch der hundertjährigen Gründung der Königl. ungarischen Berg- und Forstakademie Schemnitz. See A Selmeczi m. k. 1871. IV. 36.[2]
Gedenkbuch der im April 1879 . . . in Oesterreich-Ungarn vollführten Baumpflanzungen. 1879. III. 34.[1]
Gedner, Elias. Ficus genus. See Thunberg, C. P. 1786. II. 148.[1]
Gee, Richard. Famous trees of Hertfordshire. 1877. I. 297.[1]
— Windsor forest. 1884. I. 297.[1]
Gee, W. H. Monograph on fibrous manufactures in the Punjab. 1891. III. 235.[1]
Geel, P. C. van. Sertum botanicum. 1828. I. 267.
Geel, Jan Ladewijk Willem, baron van. Plantarum Belgii confoederati indigenarum spicilegium. 1814. I. 392.
Geering, (Dr.). Ein- und Ausfuhr von Holz. 1897. IV. 406.[2]
Geert, Auguste van, (jr.). L'Abutilon Darwini tessellatum hort. 1877. III. 586.[2]
— Arbres et arbustes nouveaux de pleine terre. 1875. III. 77.[1]
— Le Boronia heterophylla. 1890. III. 495.[2]
— Citrus trifoliata. 1886. III. 503.[1]
— Les corbeilles parterres de Conifères. 1876. III. 290.
— Daphne Genkwa. 1884. III. 627.[1]
— Dracaena Massangeana. 1882. III. 337.[1]
— L'Hibiscus rosa sinensis L. var. fulgidus. 1876. III. 588.[1]
— Hydrangea hortensis var. Thomas Hogg. 1878. III. 411.[2]
— Hypericum Moserianum. 1890. III. 610.[1]
— Iconographie der indischen Azaleen. 1881. III. 660.[1]
— Iconographie des Azalées de l'Inde. 1881. III. 660.[1]
— Iconography of Indian Azaleas. 1881. III. 660.[1]
— Le Jardin d'essai du Hamma. 1883. I. 69.[1]
— Le Phoenix rupicola J. Anderson. 1878. III. 330.[1]
— Les plantes nouvelles de l'année 1878. 1879. III. 516.[1]
— Pseudo-Tsuga (Abies) Douglasi Carr. 1881. III. 309.[2]
— Sur la transplantation des Conifères. 1884. III. 294.[2]
— See also Pynaert, Édouard & Geert, Auguste van.
Geert, Charles van. Observations sur la germination . . . du Gui. 1871. III. 385.[1]
Geerts, A. J. C. Observations on Kinch's list of plants used for food. 1883. III. 273.[2]
— Preliminary catalogue of the Japanese kinds of wood. 1876. IV. 399.[1]

Die gefährlichsten Giftpflanzen Deutschlands. 1837. III. 73.

Geffen, A. MARTINI VAN. See MARTINI VAN GEFFEN, A.

Gefüllt blühende Brombeeren. See DOUBLE-FLOWERED Blackberries. 1879. III. 457.[1]

Die gefülltblühende Kirschpflaume. 1899. III. 436.[1]

Die gefülltblühenden Prunus. 1897. III. 431.[1]

Die gegenwärtig vorhandenen Formen des Trompetenbaumes. 1890. III. 705.

Géhin, Joseph Jean Baptiste. Catalogue des plantes cultivées . . . au . . . Jardin botanique de Metz. 1868. I. 48.

— Notes pour servir à l'histoire des insects nuisibles. 1857. III. 189.

— Quelques essais de sériciculture. 1860. III. 148.[1]

Gehler, Johann Karl. De usu macerationis seminum. 1763. I. 202.[2]

Gehmacher, Arthur. Ueber den anatomischen Bau einige sogenannter Korkhölzer. 1884. -I. 125.

— Structure of wood. 1884. II. 529.[3]

— Untersuchung über den Einfluss des Rindendruckes. 1883. I. 130.

Die Gehölze von Rosenthal's Erben in Wien. 1870. I. 66.[1]

Gehren, von, (Kammerdirector, Ratibor). Bekämpfung der Nonne. 1892. IV. 201.

— & Kühn, (Forstrath, Breslau). Wie stellt sich der Soblesische Forst-Verein zu der . . . Verschmelzung des Reichsforstvereins. 1900. IV. 40.[3]

Gehren, Edmund Franz von. Anleitung zur Waldwerthberechnung. 1835. IV. 252.

— Lehrbuch der Arithmetik und Waldwerthberechnung. 1835. IV. 58.

— Mathematisches Taschenbuch. 1832. IV. 58.

— Ueber die zweckmässigste Abgabe . . . des Holzes. 1840. IV. 290.[1]

Gehret, G. Umwandlung des Niederwaldes in Hochwald. 1846. IV. 128.

Gehrke, Otto. Beiträge zur Kenntniss der Anatomie von Palmenkeimlingen. 1887. II. 63.[1]

Geier, Gustav. See Гейеръ, Густавъ.

Geier, Karl. See Гейеръ, Карлъ.

Geigel, Martin. Bodenergiebigkeit, Bodenerzeugnisse . . . in den Deutschen Staaten. 1881. IV. 349.[1]

Geiger, Franz Xaver. Krankheiten und Feinde der Obstbäume. 1825. III. 178.

— Die Obstbaumzucht. 1804. III. 136.

— Unterricht in der Baumgärtnerey. 1795. III. 135.

— Unterricht in der edlen . . . Kunst die Obstbäume durch Pfropfen zu veredeln. 1806. III. 159.[1]

— Unterricht in der Kunst, die Obstbäume durch Propfen zu veredeln. 1806. III. 159.[2]

Geiger, Hermann. Beiträge zur . . . Kenntnis der Jaborandiblätter. 189 .? III. 505.[1]

— Beiträge zur Kenntnis der Jaborandiblätter. 1897. III. 489,[1] 505.[1]

— Beiträge zur pharmakognostischen . . . Kenntnis der Jaborandiblätter. 1897. II. 409.[3]

Geiger, Philipp Lorenz. Einige Versuche mit der Wurzelrinde von Cornus florida. 1835. III. 646.[1]

— Handbuch der Pharmacie. 1824. III. 257.[2]

— Pharmaceutische Botanik und Pharmacognosie. 1829. III. 56.

— & Mohr, C. F. Pharmacopoea universalis. 1835. III. 245.

Geikie, James. On the buried forests . . . of Scotland. 1865. I. 402.

— Note on the occurrence of drifted trees. 1884. I. 393.[2]

Geilfusius, Bernhard Wilhelm. De Moxa. 1676. III. 754.[1]

Geinitz, H. B. See COTTA, Bernhard, GEINITZ, H. B. & others.

Geiseler. Sur l'acide cyanhydrique . . . du Cerisier à grappes. 1860. III. 439.[1]

Geiseler, Eduard Ferdinand. Crotonis monographiam . . . exhibet. 1807. II. 439.[1]

Geisenheim am Rhein — Kgl. Lehranstalt für Wein-, Obstund Gartenbau. See KGL. LEHRANSTALT . . . III. 12.

Geisenheyner, Louis. Deutsche Pflanzennamen. 1889. I. 73.[2]

— Einige Beobachtungen in der Gegend von Kreuznach. 1890. II. 773.[2]

— Zur epiphytischen Kopfweidenflora. 1895. I. 234.[2]

— Mitteilungen über Ueberpflanzen. 1897. I. 234.[2]

— Populus pyramidalis Rozier. 1885. II. 97.[2]

Geisinger, József. Észleletek a kocsános Tölgy, a Juharfa és közönséges Köris évgyürüinek havi növekvéséről. 1880. I. 127.[2]

Geiss. Zur Aufforstung von Oedländereien. 1897. IV. 167.[2]

Geissler, O. Die Flora von Davos. 1882. I. 436.

Geitel, Carl. Forstdirektor oder Forstdirektion? 1863. IV. 287.

— Gegenwärtiger Zustand . . . der Forsten im Herzogthume Braunschweig. 1858. IV. 351.[2]

Geitner, G. Cupressus Lindleyana W. var. 1863. III. 302.[1]

Gelbblättrige Gehölzpflanzen. 1890. III. 206.[2]

Geldart, Herbert D. Fauna and flora of Norfolk. 1875. V. XXI.[2]

— See also FEILDEN, H. W. & GELDART, H. D.

Gelder, H. van. De kinineproef van Hirschsohn. 1890. III. 723.

De Geldersche bouwhof. 1848. III. 106.[1]

Geldmaker, F. Over het snoeien der vruchtboomen. 1858. III. 172.

— Waarnemingen genezing der druivenziekte. 1858. III. 577.

Gelehrte Anzeigen. See KÖNIGLICHE BAYERISCHE AKADEMIE DER WISSENSCHAFTEN zu MÜNCHEN. I. 13.

Gelert, Otto. Batologische Notizen. 1890. II. 300.[2]

— Brombeeren aus der Provinz Sachsen. 1896. II. 302.[2]

— Die Rubus-Hybriden des [J.] Utsch. 1898. II. 302.[2]

— See also FRIEDERICHSEN, Kristian & GELERT, Otto.

Geleznoff, Nicolas. See GELEZNOW, Nicolas.

Geleznow, Nicolas. Sur l'embryogénie du Mélèze. 1849. II. 32.[3]

— Mémoire sur la quantité . . . de l'eau. 1876. I. 167.

— Sur le mouvement des branches. 1867: I. 149.[3]

— Observations sur le développement des bourgeons. 1851. I. 107.[3]

— Recherches sur la quantité . . . de l'eau dans la tige. 1876. I. 149,[1] 165.

— See also Желѣзновъ, Н.

Gelinek, Tivadar. A bégavölgyi ligeterdők Kocsános Tölgyeinek növekvés-menete. 1880. IV. 507.

Gell, F. A hand-book for use in the jungles of western India. 1863. I. 75.[2]

Gell, Philip Lyttleton. The rubber industry. 1900. III. 230.

Gellatley, John. On the colouring matter of Persian berries. 1858. III. 542,[1] 543.[2]

Geller, P. Eine Schlangenfichte . . . in Ostpreussen. 1889. II. 35.[1]

Gellerstedt, Johan Daniel. Flora paroeciae Bränkyrka. See SILLÉN, N. J. 1827. I. 353.

— Nerikes flora. 1831. I. 353.

Gelm, P. See Гельмъ, П.

Gelmer & Tostrup, Tho. Les forêts et le commerce des bois en Norvège. 1891. IV. 344.[1]

Gelmi, Enrico. Aggiunte alla flora trentina. 1898. I. 444.

— Contribuzione alla flora dell' isola Corfù. 1889. I. 450.

— Il monte Boudone di Trento. 1880: I. 429.

— Neue Standorte einiger selteneren Rosen. 1888. II. 286.[2]

— Prospetto della flora trentina. 1893. I. 430.

— Rosa arvensis Huds. 1884. II. 291.[2]

— Ueber Rosa canina und Rosa glauca. 1890. II.· 294.[2]

— Le Rose del Trentino. 1886. II. 288.[1]

Gelpke, J. H. F. SOLLEWYN. See SOLLEWYN GELPKE, J.H.F.

Gembloux, Claude Charles PIERQUIN DE. See PIERQUIN DE GEMBLOUX, C. C.

Gembloux — Association des anciens élèves . . . See ASSOCIATION . . . III. 15.

Gembloux — L'ingénieur agricole. See ASSOCIATION DES ANCIENS ÉLÈVES . . . III. 15.

Gamböck, Robert. Die Au im oberen Donaugebiet. 1892. I. 443.

Der gemeine Holhunderbaum. See D., P. 1805. III. 752.[1]

Die gemeine Platane in Nordamerika. 1896. II. 255.[1]

Ueber den Gemeinen Akazienbaum. 1858. IV. 523.[1]

Gemeinhardt, Johann Kaspar. Catalogus plantarum circa Lauham. 1724. I. 373.

Gemeinnütziges Handbuch für Forst- und Jagdbediente. 1799. IV. 105.

Gemeinnützliche Mittheilungen über Wein-, Obst- und Gemüsebau. III. 12.

Les gémissements des arbres. 1854. I. 168.

Gemmellaro, Carlo. Cenno sulla vegatasione . . . dell' Etna. 1830. I. 431.

Gemmingen, Karl, Freiherr von. Gedanken über Holzmangel in Würtemberg. 1790. IV. 282.[1]

— Gründliche Anleitung zur Erzeugung . . . vorzüglicher Holzarten. 1799. IV. 105.

Gemminger & Harold, B. von. Scolytidae. 1872. IV. 204.
Gempp, H. W. Maclura aurantiaca Nutt. 1848. III. 372.[1]
Gené. Ueber Bodenbearbeitung in Buchen-Samenschlägen. 1873. IV. 139,[2] V. xxxii.[2]
Genealogie der Europeaansche vruchtboomen. 1815. I. 246.[2]
Géneau de Lamarlière; Leon. Sur l'assimilation comparée. 1892. I. 160.
— Sur la production expérimentale de tiges. 1899. I. 144.[2]
— Recherches physiologiques sur les feuilles. 1892. I. 230, 233.[1]
— Sur la respiration, la transpiration. 1892. I. 171, 233.[1]
Génean de Sainte Gertrude, G. Statistique forestière de l'Allemagne. 1882. IV. 349.[1]
Geneeskundig tijdschrift voor Nederlandsch Indië. I; 29.[1]
Genera plantarum ad familias suas redacta.· See TRINIUS, C. B. 1835. I. 77.
Genera plantarum . . . definita. See WOLF, N. M. von. 1776. I. 258.
A general account of the productions of the nursery-wood. 1733. III. 363.[2]
General catalogue of plants in the . . . botanic garden, Calcutta. 1843. I. 66.[2]
General index of the plants described and figured in [Robert] Wight's . . . Icones. See CLEGHORN, Hugh. 1856. I. 77.
General instructions to forest fire rangers. 1898. IV. 181.[2]
General remarks on the Grape-vine. 1862. III. 546.
General Bestallung vor die Forst-Bedienten.· 1575. IV. 302.
General-Verordnung . . . die Einberufung eines Ausschusses zur Berathung der Abänderung in der Forstverwaltung betr. 1849. IV. 291.[1]
Genersich, Samuel. Catalogus plantarum rariorum Scepusii. 1801. I. 444.
— Florae scepusiensis elenchus. 1798. I. 444.
Geneste. Greffage souterrain. 1893. III. 548.[2]
Genet, E. C. Observations on the disease of the gum trees. 1819. III. 431.[1]
Genet, Lucien GIROD-. See GIROD-GENET, Lucien.
Le Genêt à balais et l'azote de l'air. 1894. IV. 521.[2]
Les Genêts et les Pins sylvestres. 1896. IV. 143.[2]
Genetz, A. T, B. Kansan ja kansakoulun kasvitarhakirja. Kartalla ja kuvilla varustettu. 1894. III. 101.[2]
— Kasvioppi kansakouluja varten. 1894. I. 92.
Genève — Association pour la protection des plantes. See ASSOCIATION . . . I. 26.[1]
Genève — Bibliothèque universelle. See BIBLIOTHÈQUE universelle des sciences. I. 26.[1]
Genève — Conservatoire et jardin botaniques. See CONSERVATOIRE . . . I. 26.[2]
Genève — Institut national genevois. See INSTITUT . . . I. 26.[2]
Genève — Jardin botanique. See JARDIN . . . 1826. I. 65.
Genève — Laboratoire de botanique générale de l'université. See LABORATORIE . . . I. 26.[2]
Genève — Société botanique. See SOCIÉTÉ . . . I. 27.
Genève — Société d'horticulture. See SOCIÉTÉ . . . III. 24.[1]
Genève — Société de physique et d'histoire naturelle. See SOCIÉTÉ . . . I. 27.
Genève — Société des arts. See SOCIÉTÉ . . . III. 24.[2]
Genevier, L. Gaston. Essai monographique sur les Rubus du bassin de la Loire. 1868. II, 303.[2]
— Essai sur quelques . . . Rubus de Maine et Loire. 1860. II. 303.[2]
— Extrait de la florule des environs de Mortagne-sur-Sèvre. 1866. I. 413.
— Monographie des Rubus du bassin de la Loire. 1868. II. 303.[2]
— Observations sur . . . Rubus de l'herbier de T. Bastard. 1863. II. 303.[2]
Genevoix. Préparation de l'huile éthérée de marron d'Inde. 1859. III. 538.[1]·
Le Genévrier de Virginie. See The RED Cedar. 1897. II. 32.[1]
Genke, K. F. G. See ГЕНКЕ, К. Ф. Г.
Genko, N. K. See ГЕНКО, Н. К.
Genlis, Stéphanie Félicité Ducrest de S. - A., comtesse de. La botanika istorica e letteraria. 1810. I. 511.
— Die Botanik der Geschichte und Literatur. 1810. I. 511.
— La botanique historique et littéraire. 1810. I. 511.
— Historical and literary botany. · 1810. I. 511.
— Zuma. 1818. III. 717.[2]
Gennadius, Panagiotes. Sur les dégâts causés en Grèce par l'anthracnose. 1881. III. 578.
— Nouveau procédé pour la destruction du kermès du Figuier. 1880. III. 370.[1]

— Prickly Pear; Opuntia. 1899. III. 624.[2]
— Sur le souffrage de la Vigne en Grèce. 1883. III. 561.
— See also ΓΕΝΝΑΔΙΟΣ, Παναγιώτης.
Gennari, Patrisio. Enum. plantarum quas Reg. hortus calaritanus. 1872. I. 64.
— Flora medica sarda. 1870. III. 88.[2]
— Florula di Caprera. 1870. I. 428.
— Guida dell' Orto botanico . . . di Cagliari. 1874. I. 64.
— L' orto botanico . . . della Real univ. di Cagliari. 1872. I. 64.
— Semina in Regio horti bot. caralitano et per Sardiniae insulam lecta. 1867. I. 63.
Gennep, J. L. van. Djeroek-cultuur in de afdeeling Malang. 1893. III. 497.[2]
Gennep, W. K. van. Over de meest gebruikelijke wijze van den aanleg van dennenbosschen in Nederland. 1842. IV. 471.
— Verhandeling over de meest gebruikelijke wijze van den aanleg van dennenbosschen in Nederland. 1842. IV. 471.
Genoa — Congresso botanico internationale. See CONGRESSO . . . I. 24.[2]
Genoa — Museo civico di storia naturale. See MUSEO . . . I. 25.
Genoa — Reale università. See REALE . . . I. 26.[1]
Genonceaux, L. Rapport sur l'enseignement supérieur de la sylviculture en Allemagne et en Autriche-Hongrie. 1888. IV. 33.[1]
Genootschap ter bevordering van natuur- genees- en heelkunde te Amsterdam. Maandblad. I. 15.
Genossenschaft Flora. Sitzungsberichte. III. 12.
Genova. See GENOA.
Le genre Swainsona et ses espèces. 1859. II. 385.[2]
Gensen, A. See ГЕНЗЕНЪ, A.
Gensert, (Oberförster, Sprottau). Beschreibung des Sprottauer Stadtforstes. 1863. IV. 353.
Gensoul. Emploi du camphre contre la maladie de la Vigne. 1851. III. 575.[2]
Gensoul, J. Lettres . . . sur la culture du Mûrier. 1838. III. 375.
Gensz, Al. Sur l'acide cathartique du Séné. 1894. III. 470.[2]
Genth, Gustav. Doppelte Riefen. 1874. IV. 149.[1]
— Genth's Grundlagen der doppelten Riefen. 1874. IV. 149.[1]
Gentil, A. A. P. Dissertation sur le caffé. 1787. III. 738.
Gentil, Ambroise. Histoire des Roses indigènes de la Sarthe. 1897. II. 286.[2]
— Inventaire général des plantes vasculaires de la Sarthe. 1891. I. 417.
— Nouvelle note. 1897. II. 296.[1]
— Petite flore mancelle. 1884. V. xxii.[1]
— Quelques mots au sujet du Rosa macrantha. 1897. II. 296.[1]
Gentil, François. (Le jardinier solitaire; oder,) Nützliche Unterredungen. 1704. III. 112.
— Le jardinier solitaire; ou, Dialogues. 1704. III. 111.
— Le jardinier solitaire. The solitary or Carthusian gard'ner. 1704. III. 111.
— The retir'd gardener. 1704. III. 111.
Gentilhomme. Note sur les Kirschs. 1868. III. 435.[2]
Gentilhomme & Carrière, E. A. Description des Ericas. 1882. III. 650.[1]
Gentili, G. Monografia sulle piante forestali. 1879. III. 88.[2]
The gentleman and lady's gardener. 1776. III. 109.
The gentleman farmer. See HOME, Henry. 1776. III. 109.
Gentleman's magazine. III. 17.
Gentman, W. Tuin-catechismus voor liefhebbers van tuinen. 1783. III. 105.
Gentner, (Oberförster, Windisch-Marchwitz). Das Absterben der Weisstannen. 1894. IV. 444.[1]
— Die Anzucht der Rothbuche. 1844. IV. 494.
— Schluss-Bericht über die Krankheit der Weisstannen. 1846. IV. 445.
Genty, P. -A. Betula intermedia Thomas var. microphylla Nob. 1891. II. 119.[1]
Gentz, C. Bidrag til Kundskab om Azalea-, Andromeda- og Rhododendron-Arternes Cultur paa Frieland. 1835. III 646.[2]
— Bidrag til Kundskab om den Indflydelse, som Frosten . . . har viist paa adskillige Træer. 1853. III. 44.[2]
Gentz, J, C. Ueber die Anzucht von Jlickoryholz. 1876 III. 353.[2]
— Bidrag til Kundskab om de Sirtræer. 1878. I. 40.

Genuensis. *See* SIMON JANUENSIS.
The genus Agonis. 1886. III. 633.[1]
Gény, CAPITAIN-. *See* CAPITAIN-GÉNY.
Geoffroy, Claude Joseph, (jr.). Observationes de gummi laccae. 1716. III. 232.[1]
— Observations sur la gomme lacque. 1716. III. 232.[2]
— Observations sur la structure & l'usage des principales parties des fleurs. 1714. I. 200.
— Observations sur les vessies qui viennent aux Ormes. 1726. III. 364.[1]
— Sur le Pareira brava. 1712. III. 396.[2]
Geoffroy, Emmanuel; Contribution à l'étude du Robinia Nicou. 1895. III. 481.[2]
—.Rapport de mission à la Martinique et à la Guyane. 1897. III. 268.[1]
— Sur le Robinia Nicou. 1892. III. 481.[3]
Geoffroy, Étienne François. Tractatus de materia medica. 1741. III. 241.
— Traité de la matière medicale. 1741. III. 241.
Geoghegan, J. Silk in India. 1872. III. 148.[1]
Geografisk Tidskrift. I. 8.[2]
Geografiska föreningen. Tidskrift. I. 9.[2]
Geographical journal. *See* ROYAL GEOGRAPHICAL SOCIETY OF LONDON. I. 19.
Geographical magazine. London. *See* OCEAN highways. III. 17.
Geographical society of Australasia. *See* ROYAL GEOGRAPHICAL ... I. 30.
Geographical society of London. *See* ROYAL GEOGRAPHICAL ... I. 19.
Geographische Gesellschaft (für Thüringen) zu Jena. Mit theilungen. I. 12.
Geographische Gesellschaft, [Wien]. *See* KAISERLICH-KÖNIG-LICHE GEOGRAPHISCHE ... I. 27.
Geographische Verbreitung der Cacteen. 1899. II. 586.[2]
Geographische Zeitung. *See* HERTHA. I. 12.
Geographisch-naturhistorische Beschreibung des Herzog-thums Schlesien. 1800. I. 375.
Geographiske Billeder fra Heden. *See* DALGAS, Enrico. 1867. IV. 343.[1]
A geological and agricultural survey of Rensselaer county. *See* EATON, Amos. 1822. III. 117.[2]
Geological and natural history survey of Minnesota. *See* MINNESOTA — GEOLOGICAL ... I. 6.
Geological survey in Kentucky. Report. IV. 539.[1]
Geological survey of Canada. Annual report. I. 4.[2]
Geological survey of Indiana. Report. I. 5.
Geological survey of New Jersey. *See* NEW JERSEY — GEO-LOGICAL ... I. 6.
The geology, archaeology, botany ... of Cheltenham. *See* BUCKMAN, James. 1842. I. 533.
Geology of Ohio. *See* KELLERMAN, W. A. & WERNER, W. C. 1895. I. 531.[1]
Die Geometrie in ihren Grundsätzen ... mit besonderer An-wendung auf ... Forstwissenschaft. 1793. IV. 57.
Geoponika. *See* ΓΕΩΠΟΝΙΚΑ.
Georg, F. A. Institutiones juris forestalis Germanorum. 1802. IV. 316.
Georg, W. Die Pissodes-Arten in ... Lüneburg. 1865. IV. 207.
— Die Vertilgung des Rüsselkäfers. 1865. IV. 237.
Georg-Augusts-Universität ... zu Göttingen. *See* KÖNIG-LICHE GESELLSCHAFT DER WISSENSCHAFTEN ZU GÖTTINGEN. I. 13.
George. Rapport présenté ... à la Sous-commission des améliorations agricoles et forestières. 1897. IV. 276.[1]
Georgel. Droits d'usage dans vingt sept mille arpens de forêts. 1811. IV. 333.
— Mémoire où l'on propose les moyens infallibles de prévenir la ruine totale des forêts nationales. 1802. IV. 180.[1]
Georges. Sur le dosage de la caféine. 1896. III. 740.[1]
— Étude sur le noyau de datte. 1881. III. 329.[1]
— Le vinaigre de Lagmi. 1883. III. 319.[1]
Georges, de. Sur l'emploi des sulfocarbonates. 1877. III. 560.
Georgeson, C. C. The economic plants of Japan. 1891. III. 91.[1]
— The ornamental Cherries of Japan. 1891. III. 432.[1]
Georgi, Johann Gottlieb. Bemerkungen einer Reise im rus-sischen Reiche. 1775. I. 453.[1]
— Cinerum clavellatorum Rossiae ... examen chemicum. 1788. IV. 395.
— Geographisch-physikalische und naturhistorische Beschrei-bung des russischen Reichs. 1797. I. 360.

Georgia — State college of agriculture and mechanic arts — **Georgia experiment station.** Annual report. Bulletin. III. 4.
Georgia agricultural experiment station. *See* GEORGIA — STATE COLLEGE OF AGRICULTURE AND MECHANIC ARTS. III. 4.
Georgi, Andreas Kaspar. Disputatio de nuce vomica. *See* LOSSIUS, Jeremias. 1682. III. 682.[1]
Georgi, Johan Christian. Rön, huru Citron-saft genom frys-ning kan med förmån concentreras. 1774. III. 502.[2]
Georgius, Johann Christoph Samson. De Coffee. 1752. III. 741.[1]
Gepfropfte Zirbelkiefer. 1864. II. 41.[1]
Geppert. Erfahrungen über die Verjüngung der Eichen-bestände. 1887. IV. 507.
Gera, Francesco. Della fecondazione delle piante. 1830. I. 199.
— Sopra una nuova specie di Gelso. 1826. III. 374.
Gérand, CATROS-. *See* CATROS-GÉRAND.
Gérard. Sur les chlostérines végétales. 1892. I. 177.
Gérard & Prédaval. Note sur la fabrication du papier avec l'écorce du Mûrier. 1838. III. 379.[1]
Gerard, Albert. Manuel complet et pratique du cubage des bois. 1884. IV. 228.
Gerard, Alexander & Patrick. Account of part of a journey through the Himalaya Mountains. 1824. I. 471.
Gérard, COURTOIS. *See* COURTOIS-GÉRARD.
Gérard, Frédéric. Notes sur quelques plantes des Vosges. 1890. I. 417.
— Pinus montana Du Roi var. 1890. II. 43.[1]
— Pinus sylvestris L. variétés F. Gérard. 1888. II. 46.[1]
— Rosa Didieri F. Gérard sp. nov. 1886. II. 293.[1]
— Rosa Gabrielis F. Gérard sp. nov. 1885. II. 294.[1]
— Rosa robusta F. Gérard. 1886. II. 298.[1]
— Rubus prasinus Focke forma pseudopsis. 1890. II. 309.[2]
— Salix viridis Fries var. vestita. 1892. II. 110.[1]
— *See* also DUPUIS, Aristide, GÉRARD, Frédéric, REVEIL, Oscar & HÉRINCQ, François; HÉRINCQ, François & GÉRARD, Fr.
Gérard, J. F. An historical ... treatise on Coffee. 1833. III. 738.
Gerard, J. N. The hardiness of Japanese Bamboos. 1891. III. 314.[2]
Gerard, John. Catalogus arborum. 1596. I. 51.[3]
— The herball. 1597. I. 283.
Gerard, Louis. Flora gallo-provincialis. 1761. I. 405.
Gérard, Louis. Précis biographique et bibliographique de l'histoire de la botanique. 1871. I. 79.[3]
— Précis de l'histoire de la botanique. 1871. I. 79.[2]
Gérard [?], P. Le Croton picturatum. 1876. III. 515.[3]
— Le Magnolia de Campbell. 1876. III. 399.[2]
Gerard, Patrick. *See* GERARD, Alexander & Patrick.
Gérard, René. L'anatomie comparée végétale appliquée à la classification. 1884. II. 256.[2]
— La botanique à Lyon. 1896. I. 81.[1]
— Sur les formations anomales des Ménispermées. 1886. II. 206.[1]
— Sur l'oxalate de chaux ... chez le Gui. 1882. II. 179.[2]
— Recherches sur la structure de l'axe au-dessous des feuilles séminales. 1880. I. 123.[1]
— Recherches sur le passage de la racine. 1880. I. 103.
Gérard, W. R. The name Persimmon. 1885. II. 702.[1]
— Origin of the name Sambucus. 1895. IV. 840.[2]
— Plant names of Indian origin. 1896. I. 72.[2]
Gérardin, Léon. Botanika ogólna. 1894. I. 92.
— Herbier des écoles. 1888. I. 256.
— Herbier pour le classement. 1888. I. 256.
Gérardin, Sébastien. Essai de physiologie végétale. 1810. I. 85.
— Tableau élémentaire de botanique. 1805. I. 84.
Gérardin de Mirecourt, Sebastien. Dictionnaire raisonné de botanique. 1817. I. 33.
Gerber, Albert. Ueber die jährliche Korkproduction. 1883. I. 130.
Gerber, Charles. Contribution à l'histoire botanique ... du genre Adansonia. 1895. III. 589.[1]
— Sur le dimorphisme sexuel des fleurs du Romarin. 1900. II. 765.[3]
— Étude comparée de la respiration des graines oléagineuses. 1900. I. 172, 804.
— Étude comparée des quotients d'acides ... pendant la maturation des fruits. 1897. I. 179.[1]
— Étude de la transformation des matières sucrées en huile dans les olives. 1897. III. 679.[2]

— Études anatomiques . . . sur les Cistes de Provence. 1899. II. 564.[1]
— De la fécondation directe chez quelques plantes. 1898. II. 564.[1]
— De l'inflorescence des Liquidambars. 1899. II. 253.[2]
— Principes des méthodes utilisées pour hâter ou pour retarder la maturation des fruits. 1898. I. 179.[2]
— Recherches sur la formation des réserves oléagineuses. 1897. I. 180.[1]
— Recherches sur la maturation des fruits charnus. 1896. I. 179.[1]
— Rôle des tannins. 1897. I. 184.
— Variation de la teneur en acides . . . des fruits. 1898. I. 179.[2]
— Variations du quotient respiratoire dans les fruits charnus acides. 1897. I. 179.[2]

Gerber, Karl. Leitfaden zur Obstbaukunde. 1887. III. 146.[1]

Gerbino, Xaverio. See Rosso, E, T. & Gerbino, Xaverio.

Gerbstoffgehalt verschiedener Eichenrinden. 1865. IV. 514.[1]

Gerder, F. E. See Гердеръ, Ф. Е.

Gerdes. Auszug aus dem Reisebericht . . . über Eichenschalwaldungen. 1866. IV. 506.

Gerdes, F. Baumpflanzungen auf Marschboden. 1883. IV. 146.[1]
— Fixation du sol au bord de la mer du Nord. 1883. IV. 146.[1]
— Die flüchtigen Moorflächen. 1879. IV. 145.
— Die neuen Aufforstungen im Amts-Bezirke Wittmund. 1880. IV. 158.
— Unterbau von Kiefernbeständen. 1881. IV. 473.

Gerding, L. Die Birke als Schutzholz. 1885. IV. 490,[1] 495.
— Einige bei Erziehung von Kiefernbeständen . . . gemachte Beobachtungen. 1886. IV. 481.
— Die Geschichte eines Buchenbestandes. 1886. IV. 495.
— Ueber Haide-, Moor- und Waldbrände in der Lüneburger Haide. 1886. IV. 182.[2]
— Die Heide-, Moor- und Waldbrände. 1896. IV. 182.[2]
— Kahlschlag oder Schirmschlag? 1885. IV. 128.
— Zur Ocularschätzung des Derbholzmassen-Vorrathes. 1891. IV. 219.
— Die Wald-, Heide- und Moorbrände. 1896. IV. 182.[2]

Gerdolle, Heinrich. L'administration forestière allemande en Alsace-Lorraine. 1877. IV. 289.[2]
— Le phylloxéra dans le pays messin. 1900. III. 575.[1]

Geremia, Gioachino. Storia delle varietà delle Uve . . . dell' Etna. 1835. III. 546.
— Vertunno Etneo; overro, Stafulegrafia storia delle varietà delle Uve . . . dell' Etna. 1835. III. 546.

Geremicca, Michele. Sulle cellule del mesotecio dell' Hydrangea Hortensia. 1892. II. 241.[1]
— Il latice ed i vasi laticiferi. 1891. I. 136.[1]

Gergonne, Ueber Ansucht junger Orangenbäume. 1845. III. 499.[2]

Gerhard. Rosa Mariae; eine neue Rosenvarietät. 1833. II. 292.[1]

Gerhardt, Ch. Recherches concernant les alcalis organiques. 1844. I. 152.[2]

Gerhardt, Hermann. Flora von Prenzlau. 1856. I. 383.

Gerhardt, Julius. Verzeichniss der bei Liegnitz vorkommenden . . . Gefässpflanzen 1871 I 386.

Gerhardt, Paul. Handbuch des deutschen Dünenbaues. 1900. IV. 159.

Gerhold. Lattig . . . als Mittel gegen die Engerlinge. 1872. IV. 202.
— Die Schütte der Kiefer. 1872. IV. 476.

Gericke, (Oberförsterkandidat). See Gericke, (Forstmeister).

Gericke, (Forstmeister). Ueber das Alter der deutschen Waldbäume. 1885. I. 527, IV. 65.[1]
— Ueber forstliche Versuchs-Stationen. 1868. IV. 38.[1]
— Ueber Haupt- und Vornutzung. 1883. IV. 237.
— Holz-Zuwachs-Ermittelungen vom Zobtenberge. 1864. IV. 232.
— Das Theeren als Vertilgungsmittel der Raupen. 1870. IV. 476.

Gericke, Peter. De usu medico camphorae . . . 1748. III. 404.[2]

Gering. Güte des Holzes der Scharlacheiche. 1838. IV. 503.[1]

Gerlach, (Forstmeister, Trachenberg). In wie weit ist es erforderlich . . . den Betriebsregulirungs-Arbeiten die Feststellungeines Wegenetzes vorausgehen zu lassen. 1886. IV. 267.

Gerlach, Martin. Baumstudien. 1895. I. 516.

Gerland, Wilhelm. Heidekulturen und Dampfpflug. 1887. IV. 143.[1]

Germain. Notice sur l'emploi en médecine des plantes vertes. 1823. III. 238.[1]

Germain, Ernest. Du collet organique. 1851. I. 105.
— Empreintes de feuilles sur des poires. 1850. II. 279.[2]
— Note sur le gland à trois embryons. 1851. II. 137.[1]

Germain, Félix. Rapport sur le reboisement . . . de la Drôme. 1873. V. xxx.[2]

Germain, Léon. L'affouage communal. 1900. IV. 555.[1]
— Manuel de l'affouagiste. 1897. IV. 334.[2]
— Du partage de l'affouage dans les bois communaux. 1895. IV. 334.[2]
— La question de l'affouage. 1898. IV. 555.[1]

Germain, Rodolphe. L'Eucalyptus à Madagascar. 1888. III. 634.[1]
— Les perles en Nouvelle-Calédonie. 1888. III. 634.[1]

Germain de Saint-Pierre, Ernest. Archives de biologie végétale. 1856. I. 147.
— Caractères des feuilles anomales frondipares. 1860. II. 155.[1]
— Considérations morphologiques sur les ovaires adhérents. 1854. I. 114.[2]
— Curieux mode de reproduction du Rubus fruticosus. 1875. II. 307.[1]
— De la déhiscence des fruits. 1869. I. 119.
— Détermination du collet organique. 1855. I. 120.
— Sur la disposition des feuilles . . . des Rubiacées. 1854. II. 808.[1]
— Essai d'une classification morphologique des fruits. 1869. I. 119.
— Examen de la structure de l'ovule chez le Nerium. 1855. II. 729.[1]
— Fruit adventif sur une cicatrice. 1857. II. 596.[2]
— Guide du botaniste. 1852. I. 35, III. 86.
— De l'hermaphrodisme vrai. 1865. II. 103.[2]
— Histoire iconographique des anomalies. 1855. I. 143.
— L'hybridation d'un Chamaerops humilis par un Dattier. 1870. II. 67.[3]
— De l'influence du déboisement des montagnes. 1856. IV. 49.[3]
— Interprétation morphologique du funicule du raphé. 1855. I. 122.
— Mémoire sur l'individualité des feuilles. 1855. I. 109.[2]
— Mémoire sur la structure . . . de l'ovule. 1855. I. 122.
— Mémoire sur le phénomène de la divulsion. 1855. I. 143.
— On the morphology of the organs called lenticels. 1855. I. 132.[1]
— Note sur divers autres cas tératologiques. 1857. I. 196,[1] II. 497,[2] 596,[3] 631.[2]
— Note sur quelques faits d'expansivité. 1857.. I. 144.[2]
— Note sur une transformation du chaton femelle en rameau persistant. 1857. II. 105.[2]
— Nouveau dictionnaire de botanique. 1870. I. 34.
— Observations relatives à l'étude des lenticelles. 1874. I. 132.[1]
— Observations sur l'état de la végétation. 1857. I. 226.[2]
— Observations sur l'origine et la nature des lenticelles. 1855. I. 132.[1]
— Phénomène de l'expansivité dans les axes. 1860. I. 144.[2]
— Des plantes décoratives rustiques qui conviennent le mieux . . . terraine sec. 1865. III. 42.[1]
— Rameaux à feuilles panachées . . . chez un Rhamnus Alaternus. 1857. II. 497.[2]
— Rapport . . . établissement horticole (pépinières) de André Leroy. 1875. I. 59.
— Recherches sur la morphologie des . . . lenticelles. 1855. I. 132.[1]
— Réponse aux observations de [D.] Cauvet. 1871. I. 164.
— Le sommeil dans le règne végétal. 1869. I. 198.
— Végétation d'un arbre . . . renversé. 1857. I. 196,[1] II. 631.[2]
— See also Cosson, Ernest & Germain de Saint-Pierre, Ernest; Cosson, Ernest, Germain de Saint-Pierre, Ernest & Weddell, H.

German colonies in tropical Africa. 1894. III. 281.[2]
German colonies in tropical Africa and the Pacific. 1896. III. 281,[2] 283.[2]
A German view of the value of the forest. 1896. IV. 270.

Germann, Gottfried Albert. Verzeichniss der Pflanzen des botanischen Gartens der . . . Universität zu Dorpat. 1807. I. 41.

Germann, H. Ueber die Früchte von Myroxylon Pereirae. 1896. III. 482.[2]

Germanos, Nicolaos. ˙ *See* ΓΕΡΜΑΝΟΣ, Νικόλαος.

Germershausen, Christian Friedrich & Manger, H. L. Der Hausvater ·in systematischer Ordnung. 1783. *III. 103,* IV. 116.

La germination des graines forestières. 1897. IV. 545.[2]

Gernet, (*Hofgärtner, Jugenheim*). Ueber Kultur der Rosen. 1870. V. xxix.[1]

— *See also* ACHENBACH, NOACK, R. & GERNET.

Gernet, Carl A. von. Notizen ueber den Bau des Holzkoerpers einiger Chenopodiaceen. 1859. II. 187.[1]

— Ueber die Rindenknollen von Sorbus Aucuparia. 1860. II. 312.[1]

— Xylologische Studien. 1861. I. 125.

— *See also* ГЕРНЕТ, К.

Gernez, D. Sur le pouvoir rotatoire de la rhamnose. 1895. III. 542.[2]

Gernhard, Robert. ˙ Zur Versendung von Sämereien und Pflanzen. 1887. III. 155.

Gernlein. Ueber die Grösse der Werthverminderung haubarer Kiefernbestände durch den Kiefernbaumschwamm. 1899. IV. 479.

Gerock, J. E. Über den Sitz der Alkaloide in Strychnossamen. 1892. III. 684.[1]

— *See also* FLÜCKIGER, F. A. & GEROCK, J. E.; SCHNEEGANS, August & GEROCK, J. E.

— & Bronnert, E. Beitrag zur Anatomie des Stammes von Strychnos. 1894. III. 720.[2]

Gérôme, Joseph. Aristolochia brasiliensis, sa floraison en plein air. 1897. III. 386.[1]

— Cassinia fulvida Hook. et Diplopappus. 1897. III. 755.[1]

— Clerodendron splendens G. Don. 1895. III. 696.[2]

— Le Dattier du Sénégal. 1894. III. 330.[1]

— L'émoussage. 1894. III. 175.[2]

— Heritiera maerophylla. 1894. III. 591.[2]

— Les noms des plantes. 1895. I. 76.[2]

— Sur l'origine curieuse d'un nom horticole. 1897. III. 313.[2]

— Peltostigma pteleoides. 1894. III. 504.[2]

— Solandra grandiflora. 1897. III. 701.[1]

— Trachelospermum jasminoides. 1894. III. 691.[2]

Gerrard, A. W. L'alcaloïde du Duboisia myoporoïdes. 1878. III. 700.[1]

— Sur l'alcaloïde du Jaborandi. 1876. III. 505.[1]

— ⇁ The alkaloïd . . . of Duboisia myoporoïdes. 1878. III. 700.[1]

— Sur la jambosine. 1884. III. 636.

— & Symons, W. H. Ulexine et cytisine. 1890. ˙II. 321.[1]

Gerrard, W. Ulexine. 1886. III. 490.[1]

Gers — Société d'agriculture et d'horticulture. *See* SOCIÉTÉ . . . III. 21.

Gerschel, J. Deutsch-französische und französisch-deutsche Forst-Terminologie. 1876. IV. 23.[1]

— Vocabulaire forestier allemand-français. 1876. ·IV. 23.[2]

Gerson, Joseph. ·De tempore corticis peruviani · . . . exhibendi. *See* MURRAY, J. A. 1776. III. 720.

Gerstäcker. Nordamerikanische Stockrode-Maschinen. 1868. IV. 386.

Gerstäcker, Carl Eduard Adolph. Die Wanderheuschrecke. 1876. III. 190.

Gerstenberg, J. L. J. von. Anleitung zum Gebrauch für diejenigen, die sich zu Cameralisten . . . Forstbeamten bilden wollen. 1792. IV. 57.

Gerstenbergk, Heinrich ·von. Der allzeit fertige Holz-Berechner. 1871. IV. 226.

— Arithmetisches-Examinatorium. 1838. IV. 58.

— Tafeln zur Berechnung der Baumstämme. 1844. IV. 223.

Gerstendörfer, Josef. Die Blätter unserer Abietineen. 1877. II. 17.[2]

Geruch der Philadelphus-Arten nach Gurken. 1889. III. 413.[1]

Gervais, Paul. Note sur le Niauli de la Nouvelle Calédonie. 1866. III. 636.

Gervasi, Nicolo. Bizzarrie botaniche d' alcuni semplicisti di Sicilia. 1673. I. 81.[1]

Gerwig, Friedrich. Die Weisstanne im Schwarzwalde. 1868. IV. 444,[1] *446.*[1]

Gesammtthüringen — Botanischer Verein. Mittheilungen. *See* GEOGRAPHISCHE GESELLSCHAFT (FÜR THÜRINGEN) ZU JENA. I. 12.

Der gesamte Waldbesitz der Stadt Leipzig. 1899. IV. 355.[2]

Geschäfts-Anweisung für das ausübende Forst-Personal. 1851. IV. 301.

Geschäftsanweisung für die Bewirthschaftung der Gemeinde- und Stiftungs-Waldungen der Pfalz. 1885. IV. 300.[2]

Geschäfts-Anweisung für die königlichen Forstkassenrendanten. 1888. IV. 302.

Geschäftsanweisung für die mit der Ausführung von Waldwegebauten . . . beauftragten Forstgeometer. 1864. IV. 302.

Geschäfts-Anweisung für die Oberförster der königlich preussischen Staatsforsten. 1870. IV. 302.

Geschäfts-Anweisung für die Oberförster der königlich preussischen Staatsforsten. 1881. IV. 290.[2]

Geschäfts-Instruktion für die Forstgeometer ·in Kurhessen. 1863. IV. 302.

Zur Geschichte der Durchforstungen. 1832. IV. 172.[2]

Zur Geschichte der Durchforstungen. 1864. IV. 24,[1] *175.*

Geschichte der Entstehung der österreichischen Cameral-Taxationsmethode. 1854. IV. 235.[2]

Geschichte der Heuschrecken. 1753. IV. 205.[2]

Geschichte der österreichischen Land- und Forstwirtschaft. 1899. IV. 28.[2]

Zur Geschichte der Pflanzenwelt. 1854. IV. 75.[1]

Ueber Geschichte . . . der Rose. *See* ACHENBACH, (*Oberconsistorial-Secretair*), NOACK, R. & GERNET, (*Hofgärtner, Jugenheim*). 1870. V. xxix.[1]

Zur Geschichte der Säcularfeier. *See* EMMERT, Friedrich & SEGNITZ, Gottfried von. 1852. V. xix.[2]

Zur Geschichte der Ulme in Frankreich. 1828. II. 142.[2]

Geschichte der Verpflanzung zweier Coniferen. 1865. III. 300,[3] 307.[3]

Zur Geschichte der Waldwerthberechnung. 1841. IV. 254.

Geschichte des Holzflössens besonders in Schwaben. 1792. IV. 390.[1]

Geschichtliche Darstellung der forstlichen Verhältnisse in der Lüneburger Heide. 1891. IV. 354.

Geschichtliche Entwicklung des Waldbauvereins Herisau. 1881. IV. 41.[2]

Geschichtliches und Allgemeines über die Stadt Grünberg i. Schl. und ihren Forst. 1900. III. 355.[1]

Geschichtlich- statistischer Bericht : . . über das Forstwesen in Graubünden. *See* COAZ, Johann. 1869. IV. 366.

Geschiedenis en eigenschappen der gutta-percha. 1884. III. 668.[2]

De geschiedenis van het cultuurstelsel in Nederlandsch Indië. *See* PICCARDT, R. A. S. 1873. III. 128.

Geschwind, Anton. Die Haselfichte in Bosnien. 1884. II. 35.[1]

Geschwind, Rudolf. Erziehung neuer, edler Obstorten. 1880. III. 50.[2]

— Feinde der Rose. 1883. III. 453.[2]

— Ueber die Hybridation der Eichen. 1876. II. 137.[2]

— Die Hybridation der Forstgehölze. 1864. III. 50.[2]

— Die Hybridation und Sämlingszucht der Rosen. 1864. III. 449.

— Kletterrosen. 1881. III. 450.

— Landrosen. 1881. III. ·450.

— Die Mandel, die Pfirsich. · 1880. III. 430.[2]

— Nordlandrosen. 1898. III. 451.[1]

— Das Pfropfen des Himbeerstrauches. 1875. III. 457.[1]

— Plaudereien über die Rose. 1884. III. 450.

— Rosa microphylla Roxb. 1881. III. 455.[2]

— Rosa microphylla Roxb. 1887. III. 456.[1]

— Rosa rugosa. 1877. III. 456.[2]

— Eine Rose der Zukunft. 1889. III. 456.[2]

— ⊢ Die Rose im Winter. 1884. III. 452.

— Die Rose in ihrem Verhalten gegen Kälte. 1880. III. 452.

— Die Rose und der Winter. 1893. III. 450.

— Die schwarze Rose. 1894. III.451.[1]

— Studien über die Bourbonrose. 1900. III. 454.[2]

— Die Variiren der Rosen. 1878.˙ III. 449.

— Ueber die Verwendbarkeit einiger Rosenspecies. 1863. III. 452.

— Verwendungsfähigkeit verkümmerter Nachwüchse. 1865. IV. 169.[2]

Das gesellige und die vereinzelte Vorkommen der deutschen Waldbäume. 1852. I. 371, *IV. 82.*

Gesellschaft der Künste und Wissenschaften in Batavia. Abhandlungen. I. 12.

Gesellschaft der Wissenschaften zu Göttingen. *See* KÖNIGLICHE GESELLSCHAFT . . . I. 13.

Gesellschaft des Vaterländischen Museums in Böhmen. Verhandlungen. III. 24.[2]

Gesellschaft deutscher Naturforscher und Aerzte. Amtlicher Bericht. Tageblatt. Verhandlungen. I. 12.

Gesellschaft für Beförderung ˙der Naturwissenschaften in Freiburg i. B. Beiträge. I. 12.

Gesellschaft für Botanik zu Hamburg. Berichte. I. 12.
Gesellschaft für Erdkunde zu Berlin. Monatsberichte. Verhandlungen. Zeitschrift. I. 12.
Gesellschaft für Natur- und Heilkunde in Dresden. Jahresbericht. I. 12.
Gesellschaft naturforschender Freunde. Beobachtungen. Magazin. Mittheilungen. Neue Schriften. Sitzungsberichte. Verhandlungen. See BERLINISCHE GESELLSCHAFT NATURFORSCHENDER FREUNDE. I. 11.
Gesellschaft zur Beförderung der gesammten Naturwissenschaften zu Marburg. Schriften. I. 12.
Das Gesetz betreffend die Schutzwaldungen. 1878. IV. 321.
Gesetz betreffend Schutzwaldungen. 1875. IV. 321.
Gesetz die Untersuchung . . . der Forst- und Jagdverbrechen in dem Fürstenthume Schwarzburg-Sondershausen. 1841. IV. 322.[1]
Gesetz über den Waffengebrauch der Forst- und Jagdbeamten. 1882. IV. 321.
Gesetz vom 28. Juli 1898 wirksam für das Herzogthum Steiermark betreffend . . . Walderhaltung. 1899. IV. 307.[1]
Gesetze betreffend das Forstwesen und den Feldschutz. See Das FORSTGESETZ . . . 1864. IV. 331.[2]
Gesetze f. die Eleven d. Königl. Forstlehranstalt. 181 . ? IV. 31.
Gesetze und Verordnungen über das Forstwesen im Kanton Solothurn. 1884. IV. 331.[1]
Die Gesetzgebung der Provinz Hannover über Ablösung von Forstservituten. 1877. IV. 334.[1]
Gesetzliche Bestimmungen über Gemeinde-Waldungen. 1893. IV. 321.
Geslin, Baron, BERTRAND. See BERTRAND-GESLIN, Baron.
Gesmold, Wilhelm. Zur Cultur der Hortensien. 1881. III. 412.[2]
— Sollen wir im Herbst oder im Frühjahre unsere Bäume setzen. 1881. III. 168.[2]
— Das Verpacken der Obstbäume. 1880. III. 155.
Gesner, Johann. Dissertationes physicae de vegetabilibus. 1743. I. 97.
— Phytographia sacra generalis. 1759. I. 513.
— Tabulae phytographicae. 1795. I. 264.
— De thermoscopio botanico. 1755. I. 529.
— De variis annonae conservandae methodis. 1761. III. 174.[1]
Gesner, Konrad. Catalogus plantarum latine, graece, germanice & gallice. 1542 (1543). I. 71, 278.
— Descriptio Montis Fracti. 1752. I. 433.
— Epistolarum medicinalium liber IV. 1584. I. 282.
— Historia plantarum et vires. 1541. I. 278.
— Horti Germaniae. 1561. I. 42.
— Opera botanica. 1751. I. 291.
— Conradi Gesneri Philosophi . . . Historiae plantarum fasciculus. 1759. I. 291.
— De rei herbariae scriptoribus. 1552. I. 79.[1]
— De stirpium collectione tabulae. 1587. I. 282.
— Tabulae collectionum . . . per XII. menses. 1553. I. 530.[2]
— Tesauro di Evonomo Filatro. 1558. III. 239.[2]
— Thesaurus Evonymi Philiatri de remediis secretis. 1558. III. 239.[2]
— The treasure of Evonymus. 1558. III. 239.[2]
— & Guilandinus, M. De stirpibus aliquot epistolae V. 1557. I. 280.
— — De stirpium aliquot nominibus. 1557. I. 280.
Gesse, L. A. Notices sur les plantes qui croissent en Suisse. 1817. III. 271.[1]
Gessert, F. Gummiplantage im Nama-Land. 1898. III. 465.[1]
Gessmann, G. W. Die Pflanze im Zauberglauben. 1899. I. 518.
Gessner, (Forstmeister, Carlshof). Führer bei der Excursion durch die Graf Henckel'sche Oberförsterei Halemba. 1894. IV. 354.
Gessner, Johann. See GESNER, Johann.
Gestampfte Nadeln einiger Koniferen als Viehfutter. 1874. III. 223.[1]
Getah-Laboeai, Lagam-olie en Mangkoedoe. 1884. III. 274.[2]
Getah pertja van Borneo. 1854. III. 228.[2]
Getah-pertjah en caoutchouc-onderneming. 1899. III. 149.
Getah pertjah in de westerafdeeling van Borneo. 1853. III. 230.
Gêtaz, Sl. Sapins et Hêtres (Foyards). 1888. IV. 74.[2]
Getzuhn, (Pfarrer, Mensguth bei Ortelsburg). Erfahrung über Vertilgung der grünen Blattlaus. 1838. III. 189.

Geubel, Heinrich Karl. Die physiologische Chemie der Pflanzen. 1845. I. 152.[1]
Geuns, M. van. De cortice Salicis albae. 1778. III. 351.[1]
Geuns, M. van. Caoutchouc en getah-pertja in Nederlandsch-Indië. 1900. III. 149.
Geuns, Steven Jan van. Plantarum Belgii confoederati indigenarum spicilegium. 1788. I. 392.
— Plantarum indigenarum in usum . . . selectarum index. 1800. III. 270.[2]
— Verhandeling over de inlandsche plantgewassen. 1789. III. 270.[2]
Geutebrück, C. A. Kurtze Anweisung wie mit dem Anbau des Holtzes . . . zu Werck zu gehen. 1757. IV. 115.
Gevalin, Johannes Eric. De Protea. See THUNBERG, C. P.
Gevers, D. T. Verhandeling over het snoeien. 1832. III. 169.[2]
Gevers Deynoot, C. S. Algemeen verslag van den staat van den landbouw. 1856. III. 122.[1]
— Algemeen verslag wegens den staat van den landbouw. 1859. IV. 160.[1]
Gevers Deynoot, P. M. E. Flora batava. See KOPS, Jan & others. 1800. I. 390.
— Flora rheno-trajectina. 1843. I. 391.[1]
— Flora van Utrecht. 1843. I. 391.[1]
— & Abeleven, T. H. A. J. Flora noviomagensis. 1848. I. 391.[1] V. xx.[1]
— & Hartsen, F. A. Flora batava. See KOPS, Jan & others. 1800. I. 390.
Gewicht der österr.-ungarischen Hölzer. 1874. IV. 411.[1]
Gewinnung des Kiefernsamens. 1841. IV. 471.
Gewinnung von Kolophonium und Terpentin. 1883. IV. 467.[1]
Geyer. Iets over de Wilgensoorten. 1877. III. 348.
Geyer, Bernhard. Geyer's neuer Messtischapparat. 1881. IV. 265.
Geyer, C. W. Americká obrovská Borovice. 1878. IV. 464.[2]
— Anbau und Pflege derjenigen fremdländischen Laub- und Nadelhölzer. 1872. IV. 125.[2]
— Die Erziehung der Eiche. 1870. IV. 506.
— Die Erziehung der Eichenpflanzbeister. 1865. IV. 505.
— Ořešák černý. 1878. IV. 488.[1]
— Smrk mamutový. 1878. IV. 484.[1]
— Ein Waldfruchtbaum . . . Nordamerikas. 1875. III. 307.[2]
Geyer, Ph. Der Wald im nationalen Wirthschaftsleben. 1879. IV. 274.[1]
Geyler, Hermann Theodore. Bericht über die betheilite Ausbeute der durch die DDr. Noll und Grenacher ausgeführten Reise. 1872. I. 498.
— Ueber Culturversuche mit dem japanischen Lackbaum. 1881. III. 528.[2]
— Exobasidium Lauri. 1874. III. 406.[1]
— Über den Gefässbündelverlauf . . . der Coniferen. 1867. II. 17.[2]
De gezeegende pomoona. See De NATUERLIJCKE. 1663. I. 292.
Ghati, (pseud.?). The grazing question. 1890. IV. 136.[1]
Ghent-Kruidkundig genootschap Dodonaea. See BOTANISCH jaarboek. I. 16.
Ghent — Naturwetenschappelijke genootschap. See NATURA. I. 16.
Gheorghieff, St. Beitrag zur . . . Anatomie der Chenopodiaceen. 1887. II. 187.[1]
Gheri, G. Catalogo delle piante esistenti nell'I. e r. giardino di Boboli. 1841. I. 63.
Ghiká-Comanesti, Nicolaus D. Cinq mois au pays des Somalis. See SCHWEINFURTH, Georg & VOLKENS, Georg 1897. I. 489.
Ghiringhelli, P. Topographisch-statistische Darstellung des Kantons Tessin. 1843. IV. 365.
Ghosha, Protapa Chandra. Some notes on the Soma. 1890. II. 54,[1] 742.[2]
Giacomelli. Le inondazioni della regione Veneta. 1883. IV. 48.[1]
Giacomelli, Angelo. Catalogo delle Cactee. 1842. III. 618.[2]
Giacomini, Giacomo Andrea. Traité philosophique . . . de matière médicale. 1842. III. 243.
Giacomo, Gentile. Monografia sulle piante forestali. 1879 IV. 86.[1]
Giacosa, P. See GIBELLI, Giuseppe & GIACOSA, P.
— & Soave, M. Die Rinde von Xanthoxylon senegalense 1889. III. 506.[1]

Giannazi, Bugalini & **Andrews**. Cundurango. 1874. III. 693.²
Giannini, G. Catologo di piante appennine. 1866. I. 428.
The **Giant** Bamboo. 1892. II. 60.¹
A giant Bay tree. 1900. III. 406.¹
Giant Ivies. 1889. III. 643.¹
Giant trees. .1861. I. 295.¹
A giant Walnut log. 1894. IV. 488.²
Giaquinti, Triultio. Ragguaglio . . . sopra il Balsamo d'Arabia. 1640. II. 417.² *III. 510.²*
Giard, Alfred. La cochenille de San José. 1899. III. 192.¹
— L'Isaria, parasite. . . . du hanneton. 1891. III. 196.
Giardina, Giuseppe. Metodo economico di assiepare un latifondo. 1880. IV. 244.
— Studio; [economia sylvana]. 1869. IV. 255.
I. **Giardini**. *See* Il **GIARDINIERE**. III. 23.¹
·Il **Giardiniere**. III. 23.¹
Il **Giardino** botanico dello Zerbino. *See* DURAZZO, Ippolito. 1804. I. 61.
Gibault. Charme commun pyramidal. 1882. III. 357.²
— Solanum Dulcamara. 1870. III. 701.²
Gibault, Georges. Catalogue de la bibliothèque de la Société nationale d'horticulture de France. 1900. III. 2.
— Les origines de la culture forcée. 1898. III. 177.
— *See also* BOIS, Désiré & GIBAULT, G.
Gibb, (*Minister*). Cultivation of Cinchona in Bolivia. 1885. III. 713.¹
Gibb, Charles. Fruits for the cold north. 1884. III. 61.²
— Hasty notes on trees and shrubs of northern Europe. 1883. III. 119.¹
— The nomenclature of our Russian fruits. 1887. III. 68.¹
— Ornamental and timber trees. 1882. III. 60, *IV. 76.³*
— Ornamental trees in Canada. 1886. III. 60.
— Revised lists of names of . . . some of the fruits . . . from . north-east Europe. 1885. III. 61.²
— On the Russian Apples. . 1884. III. 425.¹
Gibb, G. D. On the examination of the sap of the Sugar Maple tree. 1852. IV. 527.¹
Gibbes, Lewis R. Botany of Edings' Bay. 1857. I. 318.
— A catalogue of the phænogamous plants of Columbia. 1835. I. 318.
Gibbons, William P. The Redwood in the Oakland Hills. 1893. II. 49.²
Gibbs, George. Observations on the dry rot. 1820. IV. 414.².
Gibbs, Wolcott. A disease of certain Japanese shrubs. 1888. III. 178.
Gibelli, Giuseppe. La malattia del Castagno. 1883. III. 359.²
— Di una nuova malattia dei Castagni. 1876. III. 359.²
— Nuovi studii sulla malattia del Castagno. 1882. III. 359.¹
— Osservazioni sopra la malattia dei Gelsi. 1877. III. 379.¹
— Sul Protomyces violaceus. 1872. III. 379.¹
— Der Quebracho colorado. 1873. II. 387.¹
— Di una singolare struttura delle foglie delle Empetracee. 1876. II. 453.²
— Di una struttura singolare delle foglie delle Empetracee. 1876. II. 453.²
— *See also* CESATI, Vincenzo, PASSERINI, Giovanni & GIBELLI, Giuseppe.
— & **Antonielli**, G. Sopra una nuova malattia dei Castagni. 1877. III. 359.²
— & **Giacosa**, P. Le piante medicinali. 187.? III. 59.¹
— & **Pirotta**, Romualdo. Flora del Modenese. 1882. I. 429.
Gibert. *See* MÉRAT & GIBERT.
Gibert, Ernest. Enumeratio plantarum . . . agro montevidensi. 1873. I. 344.
Giboin, N. J. B. Fragmens de physiologie végétale. . 1799' I. 146.
— Fragmention aus der Physiologie der Pflanzen. 1799. I. 146.
Gibourt. On the galls of Terebinthus and Pistacia. 1844. III. 525.¹
Gibson, A. Dipladenia amabilis. 1889. III. 687.²
Gibson, Alexander. Cortex Alstonia scholaris. .1853. III. 686.²
— Forest report for 1844–[50]. 1852. IV. 377.¹
— A handbook to the forests of the Bombay presidency. 1863. IV. 124.¹
— Note on the various vegetable substances used in India for . . . producing intoxication. 1853. III. 667.²
— Report on Teak. 1852. IV. 377.¹
— *See also* DALZELL, N. A. & GIBSON, Alexander.

Gibson, George Stacey. The flora of Essex. 1862. I. 401.
Gibson, H. C. & others. Particulars regarding the yield of tea. 1867. III. 603.
Gibson, J. The fruit-gardener. 1768. III. 141.
Gibson, John. *See* MACOUN, John & GIBSON, John.
Giddings, A. The Miner Plum. 1877. III. 437.¹
— Report of standing committee on evergreens. 1875. III. 292.
Gidon, Ferdinand. Essai sur l'organisation générale . . . des Nyctaginées. 1899. II. 190.²
Gidones, Eugenios. *See* ΓΙΔΩΝΗΣ, Εὐγένιος.
De **Gids** in het plantenrijk. III. 14.
De **Gids**, nieuwe vaderlandsche . . . III. 14.
Giebel, C. G. Die nützlichen Vögel. 1868. IV. 90.²
— *See also* ГИБЕЛЬ, К. Г.
Gielen, Ph. Die Nadelhölzer des Wörlitzer Gartens. 1878. I. 48, *III. 290.*
— Verzeichnis einiger Coniferen, welche im Winter 1875– 1876 . . . ausdauerten. 1878. III. 45.²
Gierlings, Fr. & others. Rapport over de proefnemingen met middelen ter bestrijding der groene luis. 1900. III. 737.
Giers, Petrus. Tankar om Säcker och Sirup af inhemska växter. *See* TROZELIUS, ·C. B. 1771. III. 270.¹
Giersing, N. Om Agerdyrknings- og Forst-Institutet paa Mœrupgaard. 1831. IV. 30.²
Gies, W. J. *See* KIRKWOOD, J. E. & GIES, W. J.
Gies, Wilhelm. Anleitung zum Bestimmen der offenblütigen Gewächse. 1847. I. 382.
— Flora für Schulen. 1873. I. 532.¹
Giesch, A. Coup-d'œil sur l'économie forestière dans le canton du Tessin. 1863. IV. 278.¹
— Dégâts causés par le poids des neiges . . . 1862 à 1863. 1863. IV. 190.
— Description abrégée · d'un dévaloir pour les bois. 1861. IV. 391.
— Die Gemeinds-Souveränität und die Forstwirthschaft. 1862. IV. 278.¹
— Kurze Beschreibung eines Holzriesses. 1861. IV. 391.
— Kurze Uebersicht über das Forstwesen im Kanton Tessin. 1863. IV. 278.¹
— Der Schneedruck . . . 1862 auf 1863. 1863. IV. 190.
— La souveraineté des communes et l'économie forestière. 1862. IV. 278.¹
Gieseler, (*Oberförster*, *Syke*). Die Wurzelfäule der Kiefer. 1879. IV. 477.
Gieseler, Eb. Lehrbuch des Erdbaues. 1880. IV. 266.¹
Giesenhagen, Karl Friedrich Georg. Lehrbuch der Botanik. 1894. V. x.²
— Die radialen Stränge der Cystolithen von Ficus. 1891. II. 151.²
— Das Wachsthum der Cystolithen von Ficus elastica. 1889. II. 151.²
Giêsse, G. A. C. Einige Bemerkungen über die Zuwachsberechnung. 1840. IV. 232.
— Tafeln zur Bestimmung des Kubikinhalts der . . . Hölzer. 1844. IV. 223.
Giessendam, D. W. P. WISBOOM VAN. *See* WISBOOM VAN GIESSENDAM, D. W. P.
Giessler, Rudolf. Die Lokalisation der Oxalsäure. 1892. I. 180.²
Gieswald, Hermann. Über den Hemmungsprozess in der Antherenbildung. 1858. I. 116.¹
Gif, DEBONNAIRE DE, *vicomte*. *See* DEBONNAIRE DE GIF, *vicomte*.
Gifford, John Clayton. Die Ahorn-Zuckerindustrie in Amerika. 1900. IV. 527.²
— Causes and effects of great forest fires. 1895. IV. 182.¹
— Distribution of the White Cedar in New Jersey. 1896. II. 28.²
— The Eucalyptus in the tropics. 1900. IV. 532.¹
— Forest conditions of Cuba. 1900. IV. 342.¹
— Forest fires in New Jersey. 1896. IV. 182.¹
— The forestal conditions . . . of · the coastal plain of New Jersey. 1900. IV. 339.
— Forestry in relation to physical geography. 1898. ·IV. 271.¹
— Forestry in Virginia. 1898. IV. 288.¹
— Forestry on sandy soils. 1899. · IV. 155.²
— Holzflösse auf dem Stillen Ocean. 1899. IV. 391.
— The Locust tree. 1896. IV. 542.¹
— La mise en valeur des terres incultes en Hollande. 1896. IV. 546.²
— Moderne amerikanische Holzhauerei- und Waldwerkzeuge. 1900. IV. 384.¹ · .

— Notes collected during a visit to the forests of Holland, Germany, Switzerland and France. 1897. .IV. 342.²
— Peculiar growth of the flowers in a grafted Laburnum. 1857. II. 369.¹
— The Pine forest of Ravenna. 1900. IV. 468.²
— A preliminary report on the forest conditions of South Jersey. 1895. IV. 339.
— Reforesting waste lands in Holland. 1896. IV. 160,² 546.²
— Report on forest fires for season of 1895. 1896. IV. 182.¹
— Silvicultural prospects of the island of Cuba. 1900. IV. 342.¹
— Waldbrände in Amerika. 1896. IV. 182.¹
— Die Weymouthskiefer in ihrer Heimat. 1898. IV. 471.
— See also VERMEULE, C. C. & GIFFORD, John.
Giftiges Holz. 1884. IV. 64.¹
Zur Giftigkeit des Goldregens. 1884. III. 481.¹
Giftpflanzen. n. d. III. 627.²
Die Giftpflanzen des Elsasses. 1825. III. 73.
Giftpflanzenbuch. 1801. III. 72.
Il gigante della California. 1864. IV. 484.²
The gigantic Chesnut tree of Mount Aetna. 1833. II. 124.²
Gigantic Elm at Schimsheim, Hesse. 1876. II. 143.²
Gigantic Grape Vine. 1858. II. 509.¹
The gigantic Swallow-wort. 1894. III. 692.¹
Gigantische Vegetation in Californien. See CALIFORNIAN gi n s. 1856. II. 50.²
Giggberger, J. A. Ueber Aufforstung in Kiefernkrüppel-Waldungen. 1886. IV. 473.
— Ueber massenhaftes Auftreten ... der Forleule. 1884. IV. 477.
— Zur Schüttekrankheit der Kiefer. 1865. IV. 476.
— Ueber das Vorkommen ... des Kiefernbastkäfers in Fichten. 1873. IV. 456.
Giglioli, Italo. Sulla resistenza di alcuni semi. 1881. I. 527.
Gihoul, L. De bosch-cultuur der Pijn- en Denneboomen. 1847. IV. 441.
— Culture forestière des arbres résineux. 1847. IV. 441.
Gijsberts, A. H. De Kokospalm in de Kapoeas delta. 1891. III. 324.¹
Gil, J. M. Árboles resinosos. 1866. IV. 122.²
Gil y Montaña, José. Cálculos de cubicaciones de maderas. 1858. IV. 224.
Gilardoni, E. Le Chêne de juin. 1895. II. 136.²
— Forêt de Chaux. n. d. IV. 359.¹
Gilbert, Ch. Les poires belges. 1874. III. 445.¹
Gilbert, E. Les plantes magiques et la sorcellerie. 1899. I. 518.
Gilbert, H. Kugelkakteen. 1889. III. 619.
— Wachsthum und Nutzung des Ginsters. 1891. IV. 521.²
Gilbert, Joseph Henry. Sur la formation de la chlorophylle et ses fonctions. 1885. I. 142.
— Note on the conditions of the development ... of chlorophyll. 1885. I. 142.
— See LAWES, J. B. & GILBERT, J. H.; LAWES, J. B., GILBERT, J. H. & PUGH, Evan.
Gilbert, Samuel. The florists vade-mecum. 1682. III. 107.
Gilburt, W. H. On the morphology of vegetable tissues. 1879. I. 128.²
Gilhy, William Hall. Disceptatio ... de mutationibus quas ea, quae e terra gignuntur, aëri inferunt. 1815. I. 169.²
— On the respiration of plants. 1821. I. 169.²
Gilchrist. On the effects of the frost in the winter of 1855. 1856. III. 46.²
Gilchrist, Andrew. On different methods of pruning forest trees. 1873. IV. 171.
— On the influence of arboriculture. 1869. IV. 53.
— On natural coppice wood. 1876. IV. 132.¹
— Oak coppice, its management and treatment. 1874. IV. 506.
— On the planting and maintaining of undercover. 1868. III. 215.¹
— On planting and rearing shrubs. 1873. III. 123.¹
— Planting under covert. 1886. III. 216.
— Practical arboriculture. 1872. III. 123.¹
— On the pruning of Oak coppice. 1872. IV. 506.
— On the rearing of woods profitably where a full stock of game is preserved. 1868. IV. 186.²
— Report on the comparative advantages of the different methods of pruning. 1875. IV. 171.
— On successful planting on exposed land. 1875. III. 42.¹
— On the treatment ... of Oak coppice in Scotland. 1874. IV. 506.

— On the trees best adapted for ... exposed margins. 1868. III. 42.¹
— On trees grown on " Undrained moorband pan." 1872. III. 41.¹
Gilchrist, Wilham. The cultivation of the Scotch Fir and its varieties. 1872. IV. 472.
— On the different ages at which the various sorts of timber trees ... may be ... felled. 1869. IV. 383.²
— On the formation ... of young plantations. 1871. IV. 120.
— On the natural production ... of the Common Silver-Fir. 1875. III. 296.²
— On the planting and maintaining of undercover. 1868. III. 215.¹
— Planting and maintaining of underwood. 1868. III. 215.¹
— Planting of mixed Fir plantations. 1865. IV. 472.
— On practical arboriculture. 1871. III. 123.¹
— On the present state and prospects of arboriculture in Aberdeenshire. 1875. IV. 358.²
— Report on an arboretum at Cluny Castle. 1875. I. 55.
— Report on the Scots Fir. 1872. IV. 472.
— Report on the transplanting of old Thorn hedges. 1868. III. 213.
— On the soils and subsoils. 1876. III. 41.¹
— On the soils best suited for the different kinds of forest trees. 1872. III. 41.¹
— On the thinning of plantations. 1869. IV. 173.
— On the various kinds of trees ... suited for planting within the influence of the seabreeze. 1869. III. 41.¹
Gildas, (frère). L'Eucalyptus dans la campagne romaine. 1875. IV. 529.²
Gildeman, A. See ГИЛЬДЕМАНЪ, A.
Gildemeister, E. See BERTRAM, Julius & GILDEMEISTER, E.
— & Hoffmann, Fr. Die aetherischen Oele. 1899. III. 225.
— — The volatile oils. 1899. III. 225.
Gildner, W. Einiges zur Vermehrung holzartiger Pflanzen. 1877. III. 158.
Giles, W. R. The official ... sources of Pareira brava. 1874. III. 396.²
Gilg, Ernst. Ueber die afrikanischen Kopale. 1895. III. 233.²
— Ueber die Anatomie der Acanthaceengattungen Afromendoucia und Mendoncia. 1893. II. 796.²
— Ueber den anatomischen Bau der Ochnaceae. 1893. II. 544.¹
— Ancistrocladaceae. 1895. II. 584.²
— Camptostylus. 1897. II. 569.¹
— Capparidaceae somalenses. 1897. II. 229.²
— Connaraceae. 1894. II. 316.²
— Connaraceae africanae. 1892. II. 316.²
— Cyrillaceae. 1896. II. 461.²
— Dilleniaceae. 1895. II. 540.¹
— Elaeasnaceae. 1894. II. 607.¹
— Ueber die Gattung Octolepis. 1900. II. 604.²
— Geissolomaceae. 1894. II. 599.¹
— Gentianaceae. 1895. II. 721.¹
— Ueber giftige Strychnos-Arten. 1897. III. 684.¹
— Ueber giftige und unschädliche Strychnos-Arten. 1900. III. 684.¹
— Gonystylaceae. 1897. II. 512.¹
— Kurze Bemerkung über den Strophanthus glabre. 1900. II. 732.²
— Loasaceae. 1894. II. 583.¹
— Loganiaceae africanae. 1893. II. 716.²
— Melastomataceae. 1898. II. 635.¹
— Ochnaceae. 1895. II. 544.¹
— Oliniaceae. 1894. II. 599.¹
— Oliniaceae africanae. 1895. II. 599.¹
— Der ostafrikanische Kopalbaum. 1895. II. 387.¹
— Penaeaceae. 1894. II. 599.¹
— Sapindaceae africanae. 1898. II. 483.²
— Stachyuraceae. 1895. II. 574.²
— Ueber die Stammpflanze des Zanzibar-Kopals. 1895. II. 387,¹ III. 233.²
— Studien über die Verwandtschaftsverhältnisse der Thymelaeales. 1894. II. 600.¹
— Über die systematische Stellung der Gattung Monotes. 1900. II. 560.²
— Thymelaeaceae. 1894. II. 600.¹
— Thymelaeaceae africanae. 1895. II. 600.¹
— Thymelaeaceae somalenses. 1897. II. 604.¹
— Turneraceae. 1894. II. 574.²
— Vitaceae (Ampelidaceae). 1896. II. 501.¹
— Zwei neue Capparidaceengattungen. 1898. II. 230.¹
— Zwei neue Dipterocarpaceen aus Malesien. 1894. II. 561.¹
— See also BRANDIS Sir Dietrich & GILG, Ernst.

Gilibert, Jean Emmanuel. Le calendrier de flore. 1809. I. 222.[2]
— Chloris grodnensis. 1781. I. 359.
— Exercitia phytologica. 1792. I. 348.[2]
— Flora lithuanica. 1781. I. 359.
— Flora litvanica inchoata. 1781. I. 359.
— Histoire des plantes d'Europe. 1798. I. 348.[2]
— Methodi Linneanae botanicae delineatio. 1790. I. 258.
— Synopsis plantarum Horti lugdunensis. 1810. I. 57.
Gilii, F. L. & **Xuarez,** Gaspare. Osservazioni fitologiche sopra alcune piante esotiche. 1789. I. 61.
Gill. A botanical fact. 1854. III. 367.[1]
Gill, Richard. Himalayan Rhododendrons. 1898. III. 657.[1]
Gill, Walter. Arboreal shelter. 1900. III. 215.[2]
— On forest planting. 1900. IV. 153.[2]
Gill, Wilham. The river of golden sand. 1880. III. 226.[1]
Gillain, Gust. Beiträge zur Anatomie der Palmen- und Pandanaceen-Wurzeln. 1900. II. 56,[1] 63.[2]
Gillanders, A. T. Arboreal aphidae. 1899. III. 192.[1]
Gillanders, Alex S. Pruning. 1887. IV. 172.[1]
Gille, A. Welches ist die zweckmässigste Weise zur Verschulung einjähriger Nadelholzpflänzlinge? 1891. IV. 546.[1]
Gille, Arnold. Hortus cassellanus. 1627. III. 27.[1]
Gille, J. B. L'Eucalyptus globulus. 1886. IV. 533.[2]
Gillekens, L. Guillaume. Éléments d'arboriculture forestière. 1891. IV. 107.[1]
— Traité de la taille & de la culture des arbres fruitiers. 1866. III. 140.[1]
Gillemot, G. L. Anpflanzung der Hickorynuss. 1878. III. 354.[1]
— Baumschutz gegen Hasenfrass. 1876. IV. 198.[1]
— Beitrag zur Acclimatisirung neu eingeführter Baumsorten. 1876. III. 485,[1] 614.[2]
— Beitrag zur Veredlung verschiedenartiger Gewächse aufeinander. 1876. III. 165.
— Clerodendron Bungei. 1877. III. 696.[1]
— Einwirkung der Rose Dundee Rambler auf die Unterlage. 1882. III. 39.
— Platanus vulgaris fol. varieg. 1876. III. 419.[1]
Gillemot, Vilmos. A nemes orgona Szaporitása. 1899. III. 680.[2]
Gilles, M. Experimentelle Untersuchungen über Sitz und Verbreitung des Bildungssaftes. 1873. I. 165.
Gillet, Claude Casimir & **Magne,** J. H. Nouvelle flore française. 1863. I. 412, V. xxii.[1]
Gillet de Grandmont, A., **Vavasseur,** P. & **Cottereau,** P. L. See **Vavasseur,** P., **Cottereau,** P. L. & **Gillet de Grandmont,** A.
Gillet de Laumont, Ch. Note sur l'Épicéa-Bosc. 1833. II. 34.[1]
Gillet de Laumont, François Pierre Nicolas. Note sur une variété de Châtaignier. 1834. II. 123.[2]
Gillette, C. P. Cynipids . . . on Oaks common to Iowa. 1890. IV. 501.[1]
— The gall-producing Cynipidae of Iowa. 1892. I. 214.[2]
Gillies, T. B. On the growth of the Cork Oak in Auckland. 1883. IV. 517.[1]
— Notes on the growth of certain trees. 1880. III. 38.[2]
Gillot, A. Sur la carbonisation du bois. 1868. IV. 432.[1]
Gillot, François Xavier. Betula Murithii Gaud. 1895. II. 119.[1]
— Contribution à l'étude de la flore du Beaujolais. 1880. I. 416.
— Étude sur la flore du Beaujolais. 1880. I. 416.
— Étude sur quelques Poiriers sauvages. 1882. II. 278.[2]
— Étude sur un hybride du Mespilus germanica. 1876. II. 268.[2]
— Herborisations dans l'arrondissement de Beaune. 1882. I. 416.
— Herborisations dans le Jura central. 1891. I. 437.
— Note sur la flore du Morvan autunois. 1870. I. 414.
— Note sur la flore du plateau d'Antully. 1879. I. 415.
— Note sur la flore du plateau d'Antully. 1882. I. 416.
— Note sur quelques plantes nouvelles pour la flore de France. 1883. II. 841.[1]
— Notes tératologiques. 1894. I. 144.[1]
— Notice sur la flore de St. Honoré-les-Bains. 1883. I. 416.
— Observations sur la coloration rosée . . . des fleurs normalement blanches. 1893. I. 185.[1]
— Observations sur quelques plantes des Pyrénées. 1894. II. 286.[2]
— Observations sur quelques Rosiers du Cantal. 1891. II. 286.[1]
— Pyrus Achras Bor. forma medioxima. 1884. II. 279.[1]

— Rapport sur les herborisations . . . à Santenay. 1882. I. 416.
— Relations entre la constitution minéralogique et hydrologique. 1896. I. 229.
— Rosa æduensis Déségl. et Gillot. 1882. II. 291.[1]
— Rosa analoga Déségl. 1882. II. 291.[1]
— Rosa latebrosa Déségl. 1882. II. 295.[2]
— Salix Lapponum × phylicifolia. 1891. II. 107.[2]
Gilow, Chr. De planten, as man to seggt un wat's seggen. 1872. I. 518.
Gilpin, William. Forest scenery. 1791. I. 516.
— Remarks on forest scenery. 1791. I. 516, IV. 357.[2]
— Remarks on forest scenery. 1834. I. 393.[2]
Gilsanz, Felipe, **Romero y.** See **Romero y Gilsanz,** Felipe.
Gilson, Eugène. Caractères microscopiques permettant de distinguer le cachou du gambir. 1894. III. 464,[2] 748.[1]
— La subérine et les cellules du liège. 1890. I. 131.[1]
Gilson, Franklin Howard. Trees of Reading, Mass. 1888. I. 295.[2]
Giltay, Eduard. Anatomische Eigentümlichkeiten in Beziehung auf klimatische Umstände. 1886. I. 391.[1]
— Het collenchym. 1882. I. 134.[2]
— Sur le collenchyme. 1882. I. 134.[2]
— Über den directen Einfluss des Pollens. 1893. I. 201.[1]
— Over een eigenaardige structuur van het plasma. 1884. I. 137.
— Einige Winke für zukünftige Besucher des Botanischen Gartens zu Buitenzorg. 1898. I. 37.[3]
— Einiges über das Collenchym. 1881. I. 134.[2]
— Een merkwaardige Kersen-varieteit. 1893. II. 273.[1]
— Eine mekwürdige Kirschen-Varietät. 1893. II. 273.[1]
— Vergleichende Studien über die Stärke der Transpiration. 1897. I. 168.
Gimbert, J. L. Assainissement des terrains marécageux par l'Eucalyptus globulus. 1873. IV. 533.[1]
— Étude sur l'influence des plantations d'Eucalyptus globulus. 1875. IV. 533.[1]
— El Eucalyptus glóbulus. 1870. IV. 532.[2]
— L'Eucalyptus globulus. 1870. IV. 532.[2]
— Sur les sécrétions de la fleur de l'Eucalyptus. 1873. II. 624.[2]
Ginanni, Francesco, conte. Istoria civile e naturale delle pinete ravennati. 1774. IV. 363.[2]
Ginet, N. Traité et tarif général du toisé des bois. 1760. IV. 220.
Gingins de Lassaraz, Frédéric Charles Jean, baron. Histoire naturelle des Lavandes. 1826. II. 764.[1]
— Mémoire sur la famille des Violacées. 1823. II. 566.[2]
— Violarieae. 1824. II. 566.[2]
Gingins-Lassaraz, Frédéric, baron de. See **Gingins de Lassaraz,** F. C. J., baron.
Der **Gingko-Baum.** 1874. III. 287.[1]
The **Gingko-**tree on Boston Common. 1850. II. 8.[1]
Ginkgo biloba in der Handelsgärtnerei von C. Fr. Velten in Speyer. 1896. II. 8.[1]
The **Ginkgo** tree. 1888. III. 287.[1]
Gintl, J. F. Mittheilung über die Anwendung des Biermanns'schen Kulturverfahrens. 1850. IV. 141.
Gintl, Wilhelm Friedrich. Über einen Bestandtheil des Harzes von Ferreira. 1868. II. 358.[1]
— Über einige Bestandtheile von Fraxinus excelsior. 1868. II. 708.[1]
— Présence de l'acide malique dans les feuilles de Fraxinus. 1868. II. 708.[1]
— & **Reinitzer,** Friedrich. Über die Bestandtheile der Blätter von Fraxinus. 1882. II. 708.[1]
Ginzberger, August. Botanische Skizzen aus Dalmatien. 1896. I. 448.[1]
Giobert, Giovanni Antonio. Trattato di agricoltura, fisica e chimica. 1790. III. 35.
Giordano, Antonio. Cenno fisiologico-chimico sulla decolorazione delle foglie. 1835. I. 191.[2]
Giordano, Ferdinando. Memoria su di una nuova specie d'Ibisco. 1833. II. 521.[3]
— Osservazioni sopra una nuova specie di Embothrio. 1837. II. 167.[2]
Giordano, Giuseppe Camillo. Contributo all' illustrazione della flora lucana. 1885. I. 429.
Giornale agrario toscano. III. 23.[3]
Giornale botanico italiano. I. 25.
Giornale d' agricoltura . . . d' Italia. III. 23.[2]
Giornale dei letterati del A. Fabroni. I. 520.[1]
Giornale dell' I. R. Istituto lombardo di scienze. See **Biblioteca.** I. 24.

Giornale delle scienze mediche. III. 23.²
Giornale di economia forestale. IV. 13.¹ — Bolletino forestale. IV. 13.¹
Giornale di fisica chimica e storia naturale. I. 25.
Giornale di scienze naturali ed economiche. I. 25.
Un **giornale** forestale a Varzavia. 1866. IV. 39.³
Giornale toscano di scienze . . . I. 25.
Giornale vinicolo italiano. III. 23.³
Giovene, Giuseppe Maria. Sopra alcune Rose prolifere. 1804. II. 289.²
— Sopra là caduta delle foglie. 1807. I. 191.²
— Descrizione e storia della cocciniglia dell' Ulivo. 1809. III. 677.¹
Giraldés, Joachim Albin Cardozo Cazado. Action exercée . . de la fève du Calabar. 1863. III. 483.²
Giralt, José PLANELLAS. See PLANELLAS GIRALT, José.
Girard, A. Ch. Emploi des feuilles d'arbres dans l'alimentation du bétail. 1892. III. 223.²
— De l'emploi des feuilles d'arbres dans l'alimentation du bétail. 1894. IV. 558.¹
— Emploi des fourrages feuillus dans l'alimentation du bétail. 1892. III. 223.²
— Recherches sur l'emploi des feuilles d'arbres dans l'alimentation du bétail. 1892. III. 223.²
Girard, Aimé. Sur l'accumulation dans le sol des composés cuivriques. 1895. III. 198.¹
— Bornesit, eene nieuwe . . . stof. 1871. III. 231.
— Sur la composition des fruits du Phoenix melanocarpa. 1896. II. 73.³
— Étude sur la cellulose. 1876. I. 155.
— Sur la mesure superficielle des parties souterraines des plantes. 1886. I. 104.
— Note sur un nouveau principe volatil . . . dans le caoutchouc du Gabon. 1868. III. 231.
— Sur un nouveau principe . . . dans le caoutchouc de Bornéo. 1871. III. 231.
— & **Lindet**, L. Recherches sur la composition des raisins des principaux Cépages. 1895. III. 583.²
— — Recherches sur le développement progressif de la grappe de raisin. 1898. II. 508,² III. 583.²
Girard, E. Mémoire sur la maladie ronde du Pin maritime. 1880. IV. 467.²
— Mémoire sur la sylviculture en Sologne. 1881. IV. 122.¹
— Les pineraies de la Sologne. 1881. IV. 122.¹
— Traité de sylviculture pratique en Sologne. 1881. IV. 122.¹
Girard, Frédéric de. Armeriae et Statices generum species nonnullas novas proponit. 1844. II. 696.³
Girard, Heinrich. Grundlagen der Bodenkunde. 1868. IV. 61.¹
Girard, Jules. Les plantes étudiées au microscope. 1872. I. 36.²
— Rośliny pod mikroskopem. 1872. I. 36.²
Girard, Maurice. Catalogue raisonné des animaux utiles. 1878. III. 95.
— Clematis montana grandiflora. 1896. III. 391.¹
— Effets produits par les premiers froids sur les Vignes phylloxérées. 1874. III. 567.¹
— État actuel de l'invasion du phylloxera dans les Charentes. 1874. III. 566.¹
— Sur l'état actuel de l'invasion du phylloxera dans les Charentes. 1874. III. 566.²
— Études sur la maladie de la Vigne. 1876. III. 560.
— Indications générales sur les vignobles des Charentes. 1876. III. 560.
— Influence de la température sur le . . . phylloxera. 1874. III. 567.¹
— Note sur des cocciens qui attaquent les . . . Aurantiacées. 1877. III. 498.¹
— Note sur des galles de Poirier. 1879. III. 446.¹
— Note sur deux insectes nuisibles. 1876. III. 370.¹
— Note sur l'Anthonomus Piri. 1876. III. 446.¹
— Note sur la galéruque de l'Orme. 1878. III. 364.²
— Note sur les Acariens. 1880. III. 190.
— Note sur les carpocapses des fruits. 1877. III. 190.
— Note sur un coccien des Orangers. 1879. III. 500.²
— Note sur un insecte nuisible. 1878. IV. 510.
— Note sur un insecte très nuisible aux Poiriers. 1884. III. 446.¹
— Observations . . . sur la nécessité d'entourer le pied des ceps de Vigne d'un bourrelet de poudres coaltarées. 1875. III. 560.
— Observations [sur le phylloxera]. 1875. III. 568.
— Le phylloxera de la Vigne. 1874. III. 567.²

— Sur quelques expériences de laboratoire. 1874. III. 566.²
— Sur la résistance du phylloxera. 1880. III. 572.
— Les tenthrèdes des Pins. 1881. IV. 461.²
Girardi, Michaelis. De Uva ursina. 1764. III. 648.¹
Girardin & Bidard. Sur la fécule du cacao. 1860. III. 594.
Girardin, Jean. Sur l'ancienneté de l'usage du cidre en Normandie. 1844. III. 428.²
— Sur la bixine. 1852. III. 613.¹
— Examen chimique de la terre prise au pied d'arbres morts. 1847. III. 209.
— Sur la germination de quelques graines antiques. 1849. I. 193.¹
— To guard trees against bares. 1852. III. 186.¹
— Mémoire sur les falsifications qu'on fait subir au rocou. 1836. III. 613.¹
— Nouvelle espèce d'Ajonc. 1850. II. 387.⁷
— Observations sur la végétation du Noyer commun. 1849. II. 114.¹
— Rapport sur un café avarié. 1834. III. 739.
— Rapport sur une poudre destinée à remplacer le café. 1834. III. 739.
— Rapports adressés à M. Henry Barbet. 1834. III. 739.
— & **Juillet**, Jules. Manuale di botanica. 1827. I. 86.
— — Nouveau manuel de botanique. 1827. I. 86.
— — Nouveau manuel de botanique. 1831. I. 148.
— & **Preisser**, F. Sur le cachou épuré du commerce. 1840. III. 463.²
Giraud. Le Café perfectionné. 1846. III. 739.
Giraud, Barthélemy. De l'Ailante glanduleux. 1875. III. 507.¹
Giraud, E. Étude comparative des gommes et des mucilages. 1875. I. 181.¹
— To guard trees against bares. 1852. III. 186.¹
Giraud, Herbert. On the existence of a third tunic. 1839. I. 117.¹
— On the recent doctrines of vegetable embryology. 1840. I. 121.
Giraud, J. E. Floral months of England. 1851. I. 400.
Giraud, Josef. Signalements de quelques espèces nouvelles de Cynipides. 1859. I. 214.¹
Giraud, L. J. D. **Féraud**-. See FÉRAUD-GIRAUD, L. J. D.
Giraud, Paul. De la culture du Néflier du Japon. 1866. III. 423.²
Giraud-Soulavie, J. L. Histoire naturelle de la France méridionale. 1783. I. 406.
Giraudias, Ludovic. Enumération des plantes . . . de Limogne. 1876. I. 415.
Giraudière, A. L. BERTHEREAU DE LA. See BERTHEREAU DE LA GIRAUDIÈRE, A. L.
Giraudière, H. de CHAVANNES DE LA. See CHAVANNES DE LA GIRAUDIÈRE, H. de.
Girdlestone, T. W. A giant Rose bush. 1887. III. 456.¹
— Rosa polyantha. 1887. III. 456.¹
Gireoud, H. Fuchsia triphylla, F. macrantha. 1892. III. 640.²
Girlesio, Francesco. Dissertazione sopra il governo de' boschi. 1791. IV. 122.²
Girod, Paul. Le Jardin botanique de Clermont. 1893. I. 81.¹
Girod-Genet, Lucien. À Madagascar. À travers . bois. 1897. IV. 556.²
— Le service forestier dans la grande île africaine. 1898. IV. 554.¹
Girókuti, Ferenc & **Kozocsa**, Tivadar. A fák alak- és fejlődéstana. 1881. I. 82.²
Gironde — Société d'agriculture du département . . . See SOCIÉTÉ . . . III. 21.
Gironde — Société d'horticulture de la. See SOCIÉTÉ . . . III. 21.
Girou de Buzareingues, Charles. Mémoire sur l'accroissement en grosseur. 1836. I. 189.
— Mémoire sur l'évolution des plantes. 1831. I. 189.
— Mémoire sur l'ordre de distribution des fibres. 1833. I. 104, 133.
— Mémoire sur l'origine . . . de l'écorce. 1834. I. 130.
— Mémoire sur la distribution . . . des fluides. 1836. I. 163.
Girtanner, A. Ein merkwürdiger Blitzschlag. 1881. IV. 194.
Girval, A. de. Observations sur la saison la plus favorable à la plantation des Pins. 1833. III. 306.²
Gisbert, Eladio POMATA Y. See POMATA Y GISBERT, Eladio.
Giseke, Paul Dietrich. Icones plantarum. 1777. I. 262.
— Index Linnaeanus in L. Plukenetii Opera. 1779. I. 77.
— Systemata plantarum recentiora. 1767. I. 250.
— Tabula genealogico-geographica affinitatum plantarum. 1789. I. 251.

Gisler, Nils. Rön och berättelse om båsverns natur. 1756. III. 186.[1]

Gissing, Thomas Waller. Materials for a flora of Wakefield. 1867. I. 402.

La **gita** forestale a Vallombrosa. 1897. IV. 35.[2]

Giurisprudenza amministrativo-forestale. 1863. IV. 327.

Giurisprudenza forestale. 1864. IV. 328.

Giurisprudenza forestale. 1865. IV. 328.

Giurisprudenza forestale. 1866. IV. 328.

Giurisprudenza forestale. 1894. IV. 328.

Una **giusta** rivendicazione di nome. 1896. III. 678.[1]

Givelet, Henri. L'Ailanteet on Bombyx. 1866. III. 506.[2]

Giżycki, Franc. Ogrodnictwo zastosowané do potrzeb ziemianina polskiego. 1866. III. 101.[1]

Gjokić, G. Zur Anatomie der Frucht und des Samens von Viscum. 1896. II. 178.[1]

Glaab, L. Frostbeschädigungen im K. k. bot. Garten zu Salzburg. 1893. III. 50.[1]

Gladstone, John Hall. On essential oils. 1864. I. 182.[1]

Glady, Eug. Sur le Cormier à fruit comestible. 1885. III. 460.[1]

— La Figue à trois récoltes. 1875. III. 369.[2]

Gläsemer, (*Oberförster*). Welche Erfahrungen werden neuerdings mit dem Eichenschälwalde . . . gemacht? 1897. IV. 513.

— Wie ist bei der Umwandelung von Niederwald in Hochwald . . . zu verfahren? 1898. IV. 129.

— See also CUSIG, Alfred & GLAESEMER.

Glanvilla, BARTHOLOMAEUS DE. See BARTHOLOMAEUS DE GLANVILLA.

Glarus. Ablösung von Holzhaurechten. 1896. IV. 334.[2]

— Aufforstungen im Einzugsgebiet der Guppenruns. 1898. IV. 167.[1]

— Dauer von Pfählen aus Hagenbuchenholz. 1896. IV. 492.[1]

— Expropriation von Holzdurchfahrtsrechten. 1898. IV. 334.[2]

— Folgen eines Kahlschlages. 1899. IV. 187.[2]

— Die Gäsiwaldungen. 1896. IV. 367.

— Waldschaden durch einen stürzenden Felsblock. 1896. IV. 187.[2]

Glasenapp, (*Docent*). Schwarz gewordenes Holz. 1874. I. 207.[1]

Glaser, J. Die der Land- und Forstwirthschaft schädlichen und nützlichen Thiere. 1862. IV. 90.[1]

Glaser, L. Alphabetisches Verzeichniss der in den Promenaden . . . um Worms angepflanzten Bäume. 1866. I. 48.

— Landwirthschaftliches Ungeziefer. 1867. III. 190.

Glaser, Ludwig. Taschenwörterbuch für Botaniker. 1885. I. 71.

Glasgow — **Philosophical** society. See PHILOSOPHICAL . . . I. 19.

The **Glasgow** catalogue of native and established plants. See EWING, Peter. 1892. I. 404.[1]

Glashoff, L. F. C. Berichtigung und Anhang zu Georg Ludwig Hartigs Physikalische Versuche. 1846. IV. 413.[1]

Glass, Richard. Wie weit geht die Berechtigung . . . des Staats in Beaufsichtigung . . . Privatholzgrundstücke? 1844. IV. 285.[2]

Glasson, K. E. Analyse der Wallnussasche. 1847. III. 356.[1]

— Analyse des cendres de Noix. 1847. III. 356.[1]

Glasspoole. Cork. 1879. III. 363.[1]

Glatfelter, Noah Miller. Notes on Salix longipes. 1897. II. 108.[2]

— Relations of Salix missouriensis. 1896. II. 108.[1]

— Salix cordata × sericea. 1896. II. 106.[2]

— A study of the relations of Salix nigra. 1894. II. 99.[2]

— A study of the venation . . . of Salix. 1893. II. 99.[1]

Glauber, J. R. Miraculum mundi. 1653. I. 286.

— Pharmacopoea spagyrica. 1654. III. 249.

Glaser, Stanislaus von. Anleitung zur Anlage . . . der Eichenschälwälder. 1864. IV. 505.

— Die Eichenschälwälder. 1864. IV. 505.

— Die Forst-Einrichtung. 1865. IV. 240.

Glavimans, C. J. Verslag wegens de proeven . . . tegen de vervuring van het bout. 1848. IV. 414.[2]

Glawatz, Emil Theodor Eduard. Beitrag zur Kenntnis der Wirkung des Erythrophlœin. 1891. III. 476.[2]

Glazebrooke, T. K. Guide to Southport 1826. I. 397.

Gleadow, F. Conversion of irregular forest into coppice. 1899. IV. 132,[2] 335.[1]

— Coppice with standards in the Vosges. 1898. IV. 131.

— Equilibrium between the crown and the roots. 1899. I. 524.[1]

— The Forest school tour in Jaunsar. 1900. IV. 378.

— Forests and sub-soil waters. 1899. IV. 52.

— Future treatment of Sál forests. 1900. IV. 528.[2]

— Note on the Forest school tour in Oudh. 1899. IV. 378.

— The poisonous plants of Bombay. 1894. III. 519.[2]

— Rate of growth of Bauhinia [*sic*] Vahlii. 1900. II. 336.[1]

— Syllabus of practical work at the Imp. forest school. 1900. IV. 37.[1]

Gleanings from books, on agriculture. 1801. III. 123.[2]

Gleditsch, Georg Friederich. Gründliche Anleitung zum Seidenbau. 1770. III. 373.

Gleditsch, Johann Gottlieb. Abhandlung von Vertilgung der Zug-Heuschrecken. 1754. IV. 205.[2]

— Alphabetisches Verzeichniss der gewöhnlichsten Arzneigewächse. 1769. III. 241.

— Anzeige von einem zwitterblütigen Gewächse. 1787. II. 103.[2]

— Von Anzucht und Eigenschaften der Buche. 1789. IV. 493.[2]

— Ausführliche Instruktion . . . wie . . . der wolletragende Weidenbaum anzubauen. 1789. III. 347.

— Betrachtung des nützlichen Bienenstandes. 1766. III. 224.[1]

— Beytrag zur natürlichen . . . Arzney-Wissenschaft der Weiden. 1789. III. 350.[2]

— Botanica medica. 1788. III. 72.

— Cappadocischer Ahorn. 1785. II. 478.[1]

— Catalogus plantarum . . . in horto Domini de Zieten. 1737. I. 43.

— Consideratio Epicriseos Siegesbeckianae. 1740. I. 250.

— Dissertatio inauguralis de methodo botanica, dubio . . . virtutum in plantis indice. 1742. III. 259.[1]

— Einleitung in die Wissenschaft der . . . Arzneimittel. 1778. III. 257.[2]

— Gedanken über das . . . Abfallen der jungen Zweige von den Roth-Tannen. 1788. IV. 455.

— Gedanken über den . . . Raupenfrass in den Kienheiden der Mark Brandenburg. 1788. IV. 474.

— Gedanken über die Anwendung der selbst wachsenden Hecken. 1766. III. 212.[1]

— Gedanken über etliche Unterschiede des Geschlechts. 1789. I. 199.

— Gedanken und Erfahrungen über den schwarzbraunen haarigten Borkenkäfer. 1788. IV. 474.

— Kurze Anweisung zum Anbau der Baumwollen Weide. 1789. III. 347, 352.[1]

— Kurze Nachricht von einer künstlichen wohlgelungenen Befruchtung. 1765. I. 200.

— Meditationes, de quibusdam differentiis sexus. 1778. I. 200.

— Nachricht von der gewöhnlichen Pflege des Drachenbaumes. 1768. III. 336.[1]

— Naturgeschichte der einheimischen . . . nutzbarsten Pflanzen. 1786. III. 72.

— Neu vermehrte Erläuterung über die . . . Wirkungsfolgen eines . . . Giftcebenstrauchs. 1779. III. 527.[2]

— Neue Bemerkung über das Geschlecht . . . der ächten. Balsampflanze. 1782. II. 418.[1]

— Neue phisicalisch [*sic*] öconomische Beobachtungen über . . . Verpflanzung der bereits erwachsenen Fichten. 1765. IV. 440.[2]

— Neuer Beytrag zur . . . Fortpflanzung der Landeichen. 1789. II. 137.[2]

— Neueste Nachricht von einem schädlichen nordamerikanischen Gewächse. 1789. III. 528.[1]

— Nouvelles expériences concernant les dangereux effets . . . d'une plante de l'Amerique. 1779. III. 527.[2]

— Vom nützlichen Anpflanzen der kleinen Rüster. 1789. III. 365,[1] IV. 513.[2]

— Onderrigting hoe verscheijde inlandsche planten tot leertouwen gebruikt kunnen worden. 1759. III. 237.[1]

— Pflanzenverzeichniss. 1773. III. 68.[2]

— Von der Pflanzung und Wartung des Holzes. 1789. IV. 116.

— Phisicalisch-öconomischer Beytrag zur Erkenntniss der Pflanzen . . . bey denen Lohgerbereyen. 1759. III. 237.[1]

— Physikalisch-ökonomische Betrachtung über den Heideboden in der Mark Brandenburg. 1782. IV. 145.

— De potus cafe abusu. See PLAZ, A. W. 1744. III. 741.[1]

— Praktisch-ökonomische Abhandlung von Aufhebung aller Gemeinheiten. 1790. IV. 332.[2]

— Systema plantarum. 1764. I. 257.

— Systematische Einleitung in die . . . Forstwissenschaft. 1774. IV. 95.

— Untersuchung der Fragen: Welche Art des Forstbetriebes ist . . . die vortheil hafteste? 1790. IV. *187*,¹ 241.

— Vermehrte Abhandlung von dem vermeintlichen Apfelbaume sonder Blüte. 1767. II. 266.¹

— Vermischte Bemerkungen aus der Arzneywissenschaft, Kräuterlehre. 1768. I. 31.

— Vermischte botanische Abhandlungen. 1789. I. 32, IV. 116.

— Vermischte botanische und ökonomische Abhandlungen. 1789. I. 32, IV. 116.

— Vermischte physicalisch-botanisch-öconomische Abhandlungen. 1765. I. 31, *III. 181.*¹

— Versuch eines . . . Beytrages zur Naturgeschichte des Kampferbaumes. 1789. II. 224.²

— Versuch zur [*sic*] Verhältniss der Hölzer. 1789. IV. 407.²

— Vier hinterlassene Abhandlungen das praktische Forst-Wesen betreffend. 1788. IV. 116.

— Vollständige theoretisch-praktische Geschichte aller . . . nützlich befundenen Pflanzen. 1777. III. 51.

— Vorläufige Betrachtungen über, die in der schleimigen Grundmischung . . befindliche mehlige Erde. 1775. I. 139.

— Zufällige Gedanken über den Blumen-Staub. 1789. I. 200.

— Zufällige Gedanken über die Beförderung der . . . Vermehrung des Faulbaums. 1789. IV. 527.²

— Zufällige Gedanken über die Fragen: Durch was für Wege geschiehet die Hauptvermehrung des wilden Holzes. 1765. IV. 146.²

— Zuwachs-Rechnung einer Mastbüche. 1790. IV. 216.

— Von einem zwitterblüthigen Gewächse an den Palmen von . . . Werft oder Saalweiden. 1787. II. 103.²

Gleeson, J. M. Catalogue of plants in the Agri-horticultural society's gardens, Madras. 1884. I. 67.¹

— Catalogue of the trees, shrubs . . . in the gardens of the Agri-horticultural society of Madras. 1898. I. 67.¹

Glehn, Peter von. Flora der Umgebung Dorpats. 1860. I. 362.

— Reisebericht von der Insel Sachalin. 1868. I. 455.

— Verzeichniss der im Witim-Olekma-Lande . . . gesammelten Pflanzen. 1876. I. 454.¹

Gleich, Franz. Der Lieblingsbaum der italienischen Höhenbewohner. 1890. IV. 493.²

Gleichen, Wilhelm Friederich, *Freiherr* von. Auserlesene mikroskopische Entdeckungen. 1777. I. 114.¹

— Découvertes les plus nouvelles dans le règne végétal. 1764. I. 114.¹

— Mikroskopische Untersuchungen und Beobachtungen. 1764. I. 114.¹

— Das neueste aus dem Reiche der Pflanzen. 1764. I. 114.¹

— Observations microscopiques. 1777. I. 114.¹

Gleichmann, H. A. Tafeln zur Bestimmung des Holzgehalts unbeschlagener Stämme. 1851. IV. 223.

Glen, David A. The formation of plantations. 1887. IV. 142.

— Hedges and their management. 1895. III. 214.¹

Glénard, Alexandre & **Bondault**, P. C. Mémoire sur les produits . . . du sang-dragon. 1843. II. 82.¹

Glendinning, Robert. On edgings for garden walks. 1853. II. 214.²

— On transplanting large evergreen trees. 1849. III. 169.¹

Glenk, Robert. Die Untersuchung des Harzes . . . Populus tremuloides. 1889. III. 346.²

Glenny, G. The Linnaea borealis. 1852. III. 749.¹

Glenny, W. W. Willows and Osiers. 1895. IV. 487.²

Gley, E. Sur la toxicité comparée de l'ouabaïne. 1888. III. 685,² 690.²

Gliddon, George R. *See* NOTT, J. C. & GLIDDON, G. R.

Gliemann, Theodor. Geographische Beschreibung von Island. 1824. I. 353.

Glimmann, Gustav. Ueber das Dammarharz. 1896. III. 297.²

Glinka, Edward JANCZEWSKI VON, *Ritter*. *See* JANCZEWSKI VON GLINKA, Edward, *Ritter*.

Gliński, Fr. Kilka słów o puszczy białowieskiej. 1897. IV. 347.

— *See also* ГЛИНСКІЙ, Ф. А.

Glinzer, E. Grundriss der Festigkeitslehre. 1890. IV. 415.²

Glocker, (*Prof.*, *Breslau*). Ueber die Einwirkung der Blausäure. 1828. III. 185.²

— Ueber die Einwirkung des metallischen Quecksilbers. 1828. III. 185.²

— Versuch über die Wirkungen des Lichtes. 1820. I. 229.

Gløersen. Gran ved Fåmunsjöen og i tilgrånsende trakter. 1885. II. 35.¹

— Låbelter om haver. 1886. III. 215.¹

— Skovanlåg og plantning. 1896. IV. 113.²

— Vestlandsgranen og dens indvandringsveie. 1884. II. 34.²

Gløersen, A. T. Indberetning . . . om de af ham i 1864 anstillede skovundersøgelser i Stavanger amt. 1865. IV. 288.²

Gloesener, Michel. Commentatio ad quaestionem . . . qua quaeritur . . . opinionum de fabrica . . . plantarum enumeratio. 1822. I. 79.²

Glogauer Stadtforst. 1878. IV. 354.

Gloger, Constantin W. Lambert. Abhandlungen über . . . den Schutz nützlicher Thiere betreffende Fragen. 1862. IV. 90.¹

— Die Hegung der Höhlenbrüter. 1865. IV. 90.²

— De la nécessité de protéger les animaux utiles. 1863. IV. 90.¹

— Die nützlichsten Freunde der Land- und Forstwirthschaft. 1858. IV. 90.¹

— I più preciosi amici della economia rurale e forestale. 1858. IV. 90.¹

— Schutz den Vögeln! 1880. IV. 90.¹

— Was ist zu thun zur . . . sicheren Verminderung . . . von Ungezieferschäden? 1861. IV. 196.¹

— Zuschrift . . . betreffend die naturgemässe Fürsorge gegen Ungezieferschäden. 1862. IV. 196.¹

Gloger, E. W. B. Hecken-Anpflanzungen gegen das Verwehen . . . durch Schnee. 1856. III. 213.

— Zur Naturgeschichte des Mistels. 1853. II. 178.²

The glory of trees. 1894. I. 516.

A glossary of names of plants from the library of the Cathedral. 1864. I. 74.¹

Glover, F. A. Report on the discovery of the Tea plant in . . . Sylhet. 1857. II. 552.¹

Glover, Thomas. An account of Virginia. 1676. III. 263.²

Gloxin, Benjamin Petrus. Observationes botanicae. 1785. I. 32.

Giu en usage pour préserver les arbres des invasions de chenilles. 1898. IV. 208.¹

Glück. Das Auftreten des Hylesinus micans. 1876. IV. 456.

Glückselig. Der Elbogner Kreis. *See* ORTMANN, Anton. 1842. I. 440.

Gluthorst, Erdmann von. Die Kultur der Georginen. 1842. III. 412.¹

Glycine élégante, Glycine elegans. 1832. III. 486.¹

Ueber **Glycosmis** Corr. *See* The GENUS Glycosmis. 1847. III. 504.²

Gmelch, Franz. Die Bäume und Sträucher der Flora des Isargebietes. 1886. I. 371.

Gmelin, Christian Gottlob. Chemische Untersuchung der ächten Angustura Rinde. 1830. III. 503.²

— Chemische Untersuchung der Seidelbast-Rinde. 1822. III. 627.²

Gmelin, Ferdinand Gottlob von. Beiträge zur Kenntniss der Metamorphose der Gewächse. 1826. I. 101.²

— Historia veneni upas antiar. *See* SCHNELL, Joannes. 1815. III. 168.²

— De plantarum exhalationibus. *See* PALMER, J. L. 1817. I. 169.²

— Ueber das Winden der Pflanzen. 1827. I. 169.¹

Gmelin, Georg Friedrich. De conventia plantarum in fructificatione et viribus. *See* CAMERARIUS, R. J. 1699. III. 259.¹

Gmelin, Johann Friedrich. Abhandlung von den giftigen Gewächsen. 1775. III. 72.

— Abhandlungen über die Wurmtroknis. 1787. IV. 203.

— Allgemeine Geschichte der Pflanzengifte. 1777. III. 260.¹

— Enumeratio stirpium agro tubingensi. 1772. I. 373.

— Historia venenorum vegetabilium Sueviae. 1778. III. 72.

— Irritabilitatem vegetabilium . . . exploratam . . . proponet. . . . 1788. I. 197.¹

— Onomatologia botanica completa. 1772. I. 32.

Gmelin, Johann Georg. De Coffee. *See* GEORGIUS, J. C. S. 1752. III. 741.¹

— Flora sibirica. 1747. I. 453.¹

— De novorum vegetabilium post creationem exortu. 1749. I. 243.²

Gmelin, Karl Christian. Flora badensis alsatica. 1805. I. 376.

— Hortus Magni ducis Badensis carlsruhanus. 1811. I. 45.

Gmelin, Leopold. Handbook of chemistry. 1843. I. 151.²

— Handbuch der Chemie. 1843. I. 151.²

Gmelin, P. F. Die natürlichen Pflanzenfamilien. 1867. I. 256.

Gmelin, Philipp Friedrich. Dissertatio ... fasciculum plantarum patriae urbi ... vicinarum. 1764. III. 72.

— Otia botanica. 1760. I. 261, V. xiii.[1]

— & Böhmer, G. R. Regnum florae. 1788. I. 292.

— — Thesaurus rei herbariae hortensisque. 1788. I. 292, V. xvi.[1]

Gmelin, Samuel Gottlieb. Observationes et descriptiones botanicae. 1768. II. 518.[1]

— De proprietatibus plantarum ex charactere botanico cognoscendis. 1768. III. 259.[1]

— Reise durch Russland. 1770. I. 359.

Gnentzsch, Felix. Ueber radiale Verbindung der Gefässe und des Holzparenchyms. 1888. I. 126.

Gniditsch, Peter. See Ludwig, C. F. & Gniditsch, Peter.

Gnüchtel, H. Ziegner-. See Ziegner-Gnüchtel, H.

Goats, forests and famines. 1884. IV. 197.[1]

Gobanz. Parasitologisches. 1875. IV. 450.

— Rieswerke im Staatsforste Cadino. 1875. IV. 391.

Gobée. Roode mijten op de Thee. 1900. III. 604.[2]

Gobelin, (abbé). Le jardinier royal. 1661. III. 142.

Gobi, Christoph. See Toči, Xp.

Gobin, A. Influence de la lumière. 187.? I. 230.

— Précis élémentaire de sériciculture pratique. 1874. III. 378.

Gobin, Henri. Guide pratique d'entomologie agricole. 1865. III. 189.

Gobley. Bourgeons de Peuplier du Canada. 1868. III. 345.[2]

— Sur les eaux distillées ... d'Oranger. 1866. III. 501.[2]

— Écorce de la racine du Myrica cerifera. 1869. II. 111.[1]

— Écorce de la racine du Ptelea trifoliata. 1869. III. 505.[2]

— Écorce de la racine et moelle de Sassafras. 1868. II. 228.[1]

— Écorce du Betula lenta. 1869. IV. 491.[2]

— Écorce du Cornus florida. 1869. III. 646.[1]

— Écorce du Prunier de Virginie. 1869. III. 443.[2]

— Écorce du Sapin du Canada. 1868. III. 312.[1]

— Écorce du Xanthoxylum fraxineum. 1869. III. 596.[1]

— Fruits du Sumac glabra. 1868. III. 527.[1]

— Racine de l'Hydrangea arborescens. 1869. III. 411.[1]

— Racine du Gelsemium sempervirens. 1869. III. 682.[1]

— Racine et feuilles de la Céanothe. 1869. III. 541.[1]

— Rapport sur les objets de matière médicale. 1868. III. 243.

— Recherches chimiques sur la racine de Kawa. 1860. III. 343.[1]

Gochöcxy, M. A Fügefa müvelése. 1898. III. 369.[2]

Gochet, Léon. Excursion forestière en 1894; 2e journée. 1895. IV. 556.[1]

Godard, L. E. & **Périnet,** Ovide. Tarifs métriques pour la réduction des bois. 1872. IV. 227.

Godeffroy, Richard. Nouveau moyen de colorer le bois en noir. 1880. IV. 422.[2]

— Le tannin de l'Algarobillo. 1879. III. 485.[1]

Godefroy. Note sur l'Abies Fraseri. 1831. III. 296.[1]

— Note sur le Mimosa Julibrissin. 1847. III. 466.[2]

— Notice sur une plante du genre Ceanothus. 1829. III. 541.[1]

— Observations faites à Ville-d'Avray ... sur les effets de la gelée du 13 mai. 1832. III. 47.

Godefroy, F. F. Essai sur la formation des substances végétales. 1818. I. 525.

Godefroy, Richard. See Godeffroy, Richard.

Godefroy, V. Sur la constitution chimique des bois. 1870. I. 155.

— Cours de géologie agricole. 1867. III. 37.[1]

Godefroy-Lebeuf, Alexandre. Lettre [sur le Nipafrutescens]. 1877. III. 327.[2]

— Phoenix canariensis. 1887. III. 328.[1]

— À propos du Cycas siamensis. 1881. III. 285.[1]

— The Tonquinese Mulberry. 1889. III. 380.[1]

Godeheu de Riville. Vertoog over 't rijp maken der Vijgen. 1761. III. 369.[1]

Godemann. See Wörmann & Godemann.

Godet, Alfred. Encore à propos du Châtaignier. 1895. II. 124.[1]

— Encore un mot à propos du Châtaignier. 1897. II. 124.[1]

— La mort du vieux Châtaignier des Cadolles. 1895. III. 359.[1]

— Quelques mots sur les plus gros arbres du pays. 1894. I. 298.[1]

Godet, Charles Henry. Description des plantes vénéneuses ... de Neuchâtel. 1845. III. 89.[2]

— Énumération des végétaux ... de Neuchâtel. 1839. I. 434.

— Énumération des végétaux ... du Jura. 1851. I. 434.

— Essai d'une flore des montagnes du Béchetau. 1840. I. 368.[2]

— Flore du Jura. 1852. I. 411.

— Les plantes vénéneuses. 1845. III. 89.[2]

— Rosa nova italica. 1877. II. 679.[2]

Godet, Paul. À propos du Rhododendron du Creux-du-Van. 1891. II. 679.[2]

Godey's lady's book. See The Lady's book. III. 4.

Godey's magazine. See The Lady's book. III. 4.

Godfrey, Edward K. The island of Nantucket. 1882. I. 315.

Godfrin, Julien. Sur les canaux résineux de la feuille du Sapin. 1892. II. 23.[2]

— Étude histologique sur les téguments séminaux. 1880. I. 120.

— Une m non décrite de bourgeon dans le Sapin. 1894. II. 23. for e

— Recherches sur l'anatomie comparée des cotylédons et de l'albumen. 1884. I. 123.[1]

— Trajet des canaux résineux ... du Sapin. 1894. II. 23.[1]

— & **Noël,** Ch. Atlas manuel de l'histologie des drogues simples. 1887. III. 259.[1]

Godin, Freiherr von. Ueber Eichensucht und Waldverhältnisse in den Niederlanden. 1869. IV. 119.[2]

Godin, Leopold. De camphora. 1823. III. 233.[1]

Godin de Lépinay, Gaston. Noms patois ou vulgaires des plantes de la Corrèze. 1886. I. 74.[3]

Godlewski, Emil. Abhängigkeit der Sauerstoffausscheidung der Blätter von dem Kohlensäuregehalt der Luft. 1874. I. 173.

— Die Art und Weise der Wachsthum retardierenden Lichtwirkung. 1891. I. 191.[1]

— Beiträge zur Kenntniss der Pflanzenathmung. 1882. I. 171.

— Contribution à la théorie de la circulation de la sève. 1885. I. 165.

— Contributions à la connaissance de la respiration. 1882. I. 171.

— Sur la formation des albuminoïdes. 1897. I. 176.

— Influencia de los factores exteriores. 1892. IV. 543.[1]

— Zur Kenntniss der Eiweissbildung aus Nitraten. 1897. I. 178.

— O nasiąkaniu drzew. 1884. IV. 420.

— O powstawaniu i znikaniu skrobi w galeczkach zieleni. 1875. I. 141.

— Ueber die tägliche Periodicität des Längenwachsthums. 1889. I. 191.[1]

— Zur Theorie der Wasserbewegung. 1884. I. 167.

— & **Polzeniusz,** F. Ueber Alkoholbildung bei der intramolecularen Athmung höherer Pflanzen. 1898. I. 178.

Godman, Frederick Du Cane. Natural history of the Azores. 1870. I. 498.[1]

Godron, Dominique Alexandre. Considérations sur les migrations des végétaux. 1852. I. 241.[1]

— Considérations sur les migrations des végétaux. 1853. I. 411.

— Contributions à la flore de France. 1880. I. 34.

— Description d'une nouvelle espèce de Sorbier. 1858. II. 313.[1]

— Essai sur la géographie botanique de la Lorraine. 1861. I. 412.

— Étude sur les bourgeons des Platanes. 1868. II. 254.[2]

— Examen tératologique d'un pied de Rubus caesius. 1876. II. 306.[2]

— Flora Juvenalis. 1853. I. 411.

— Flore de Lorraine. 1843. I. 409.

— Florula Juvenalis. 1853. I. 411.

— Le genre Rubus considéré au point de vue de l'espèce. 1850. II. 300.[1]

— Herborisations autour de Lorient. 1875. I. 414.

— Les Hêtres tortillards des environs de Nancy. 1870. II. 126.[1]

— Des hybrides végétaux considérés au point de vue de leur fécondité. 1863. I. 245.

— De l'hybridité dans le genre Sorbier. 1873. II. 311.[1]

— De l'hybridité dans les végétaux. 1847. I. 245.

— Mélanges de tératologie végétale. 1871. I. 143.

— Mémoire sur les feuilles inéquilatères. 1861. I. 109.[2]

— Les migrations des végétaux ... de la Moselle et de la Meurthe. 1880. I. 416.

— Monographie des Rubus. 1842. II. 303.[2]

— Note sur le Rosa glauca de Villars. 1876. II. 294.³
— Note sur le Sorbus latifolia Pers. 1876. II. 313.¹
— Note sur un hybride du genre Veronica. 1876. II. 782.²
— Note sur une nouvelle espèce d'Hyssope. 1851. II. 764.¹
— Notice historique sur les Jardins des plantes de Pont-à-Mousson et de Nancy. 1872. I. 59.
— Notice sur les explorations botaniques faites en Lorraine. 1875. I. 414.
— Nouvelles expériences sur l'hybridité. 1866. I. 245.
— Nouvelles recherches sur l'hybridité. 1866. I. 245.
— Observations sur les bourgeons . . . des Papilionacées. 1866. II. 320.¹
— Observations sur les bourgeons . . . du Liriodendron. 1861. II. 210.¹
— Observations sur les organes de la végétation du Hedera. 1868. II. 649.²
— Observations sur les Ulex Gallii. 1879. II. 387.¹
— Observations sur quelques axes végétaux constamment définis. 1868. I. 192.¹
— De la pélorie des Pelargonium. 1866. II. 390.¹
— Une promenade botanique aux environs de Benfeld. 1864. II. 661.²
— Quelques notes sur la flore de Montpellier. 1854. I. 411.
— Des races végétales qui doivent leur origine à une monstruosité. 1874. I. 244.¹
— Recherches expérimentales sur l'hybridité. 1862. I. 245.
— Le rôle politique des fleurs. 1879. I. 516.
— De la signification morphologique des différents axes . . . de la Vigne. 1867. II. 507.¹
— Sur les trois floraisons du Wistaria chinensis. 1865. II. 388.³
— De la végétation du Kaiserstuhl. 1863. I. 385.
— *See also* GRENIER, J. C. M. & GODRON, D. A.
Goebel, Carl Friedrich. De tussi convulsiva. 1825. III. 701.³
Göbel, Christian Gottlob. Forstwirthschaftslehre. 1801. IV. 96.
Göbel, H. M. SCHMIDT-. *See* SCHMIDT-GÖBEL, H. M.
Goebel, Karl Christian Traugott Friedemann. Reise in die Steppen des südlichen Russlands. 1837. I. 152,² 361.
— & KUNZE, Gustav. Pharmaceutische Waarenkunde. 1827. III. 257.²
Goebel, Karl Eberhard. Beiträge zur Kenntniss gefüllter Blüthen. 1886. I. 145.²
— Beiträge zur Morphologie . . . des Blattes. 1880. I. 110, *190*.²
— Ueber die Einwirkung des Lichtes auf . . . Kakteen. 1895. II. 588.²
— Zur Entwickelungsgeschichte des unterständigen Fruchtknotens. 1886. I. 118.¹
— Ueber die gegenseitigen Beziehungen der Pflanzenorgane. 1884. I. 100.¹
— Grundzüge der Systematik. 1882. I. 256,
— Ueber Jugendformen von Pflanzen. 1897. I. 101.¹
— Ueber die Luftwurzeln von Sonneratia. 1886. II. 610.²
— On metamorphosis in plants. 1895. I. 101.²
— Organographie der Pflanzen. 1898. I. 101.¹
— Outlines of classification and special morphology of plants. 1882. I. 256.
— Pflanzenbiologische Schilderungen. 1891. I. 219.¹
— Pleospora conglutinata. 1879. III. 203.¹
— On the study of adaptation in plants. 1894. I. 219.¹
— Ueber die Verzweigung dorsiventraler Sprosse. 1882. I. 106.¹
Goeckel, C. F. De quartana et hydrope per corticem peruvianum curatis. *See* HEISTER, E. F. 1740. III. 719.
Göckel, C. L. De Serpentaria virginiana. 1732. III. 386.¹
Göckel, H. *See* TRILLIUS, H. & GÖCKEL, H.
Goeckel, P. C. Meditationes et animadversiones. *See* HEISTER, Lorenz. 1741. I. 250.
Goecker, Paul. Die Waldwollefabrikation. 1876. IV. 482.²
Goedde, August. Die Privatforsten . . und Privat-Forstbeamten Deutschlands. 1886. IV. 308.²
— Der Wildpark. 1881. IV. 126.³
De **goedkoope** landbouwbibliothek. 1900. III. 140.¹
Goegginger, L. Die Kultur der Eriken. 1846. III. 650.¹
Göldi, Emilio Augusto. Eine Naturforscher-Fahrt nach dem Litoral des südlichen Guyana. 1898. I. 344.
— Relatorio sobre a molestia do Caffeiro. 1892. III. 736.
— Studien über die Blutlaus. 1885. III. 427.²
Goelicke, Andreas Ottomar. De balsamo cacao. 1723. III. 594.
— De corticis Chinae usu noxio. 1729. III. 719.
— De impostura corticis Peruviani. 1727. III. 719.

Goelitz. Ueber Vorkommen . . . der Trauben- und der Stieleiche. 1868. IV. 506.
Goeller, Christoph Ludwig. De cinnamomo. 1709. III. 405.¹
Goemans, H. J. Les Aunes comme arbres d'ornement. 1890. III. 356.²
— Le Cercis Siliquastrum. 1890. III. 472.¹
— L'Hyphaene thebaica Mart. 1892. III. 325.²
— Lodoicea Seychellarum germinating. 1890. II. 70.¹
— Le Sutherlandia frutescens R. Br. 1894. III. 488.²
Goeppert, Johann Heinrich Robert. De acidi hydrocyanici vi in plantas. 1827. I. 210.³
— Allgemeine Uebersicht der . . . ausdauernden Bäume und Sträucher. 1850. III. 69, IV. 82.
— Ueber die anatomische Structur einiger Magnoliaceen. 1842. II. 209.¹
— Über Arten und Varietäten der Gattung Citrus. 1879. III. 497.¹
— Ueber den auf- und absteigenden Saft. 1874. I. 165.
— Über die ausländischen Hölzer. 1862. IV. 396.¹
— Bandförmige Zweige . . . der Rothtanne. 1854. IV. 460.¹
— Bäume als historische Monumente. 1871. I. 295.¹
— Bäume als historische Monumente. 1872. IV. 75.¹
— Beiträge zur Geschichte der Gärten. 1864. III. 33.¹
— Beiträge zur Kenntniss der Dracäneen. 1854. II. 81.¹
— Bemerkungen über das Vorkommen des Taxus. 1841. II. 10.³
— Bemerkungen über den anatomischen Bau der Casuarinen. 1841. II. 92.¹
— Bemerkungen über den Bau . . . der Bäume. 1843. IV. 61.²
— Bemerkungen über den Drachenbaum. 1853. II. 82.¹
— Bemerkungen über die Formen der Pinus montana. 1864. II. 43.¹
— Bemerkungen über die Vegetations-Verhältnisse Norwegens. 1860. I. 355.
— Bemerkungen über die Vegetationsverhältnisse Norwegens. 1861. IV. 79.¹
— Beobachtungen über das sogenannte Ueberwallen. 1842. I. 209.³
— Beobachtungen über das Verhalten der Pflanzenwelt während der Sonnenfinsterniss. 1851. I. 198.
— Beobachtungen über die Blüthenzeit . . . zu Breslau. 1831. I. 224.²
— Beobachtungen über die Wachsthumsverhältnisse der Abietineen. 1847. II. 21.²
— Bericht über den gegenwärtigen Zustand des Botanischen Gartens in Breslau. 1868. I. 48.
— Zur Beschaffenheit der Baumwurzeln. 1851. IV. 460.¹
— Beschreibung des botanischen gartens . . . Breslau. 1830. I. 46.
— Ueber bisher unbekannte Vorgänge beim Veredeln. 1872. I. 208,¹ III. 40, IV. 66.³
— Über den blauen Gummibaum. 1877. IV. 533.¹
— Der botanische Garten zu Kew. 1863. V. VIII.²
— Botanische Mittheilungen. 1859. II. 213.²
— Ueber botanische Museen. 1856. V. VIII.²
— Eine botanische Reliquie von Orotava. 1880. II. 82.²
— Chronik alter Bäume und Sträucher in Schlesien. 1846. IV. 82.
— De coniferarum structura anatomica. 1841. II. 16.¹
— Über die Coniferen. 1840. II. 16.²
— Der December 1875 und die Vegetation. 1877. III. 45.
— Sur le développement de la chaleur dans les plantes. 1830. I. 211.
— Über den Einfluss der Kälte. 1883. I. 212.
— Ueber Einführung fremdländischer Holzgewächse. 1881. IV. 125.²
— Ueber Einführung nordamerikanischer Holzgewächse. 1881. IV. 125.²
— Einige Bemerkungen über das Verhalten der Vegetation im letztverflossenen (1870–71) Winter. 1871. III. 45.
— Einige Nachträge zu meinen Skizzen der Urwälder. 1868. I. 371, IV. 83.
— Ueber Einrichtung sogenannter physiologischer Partieen in botanischen . . . Gärten. 1868. I. 46.
— Ueber Einwirkung der Kälte. 1871. I. 212.
— Ueber Einwirkung der Kälte auf die Vegetation. 1872. I. 212.
— Ueber die Einwirkung des Camphers. 1829. I. 210.¹
— Ueber die Einwirkung des Chlors. 1834. III. 83.²
— Ueber die Einwirkung des Frostes. 1875. I. 212.
— Ueber die Einwirkung des regulinischen Quecksilbers. 1830. I. 210.¹

Goeppert, Johann Heinrich Robert (*continued*).
— Ueber Einwirkung niedriger Temperatur. 1879. I. 212.
— Enumeratio Ilicum. 1852. _II. 462.¹
— Zur Erläuterung eines Vortrags über den Bau und das Wachsthum der Bäume. 1843. I. 187.
— Die Erwerbung der Serpentara. 1878. IV. 181.¹
— Ueber die Existenz eines absteigenden Saftes. 1852. V. XI.²
— Ueber die Flora des Böhmerwaldes. 1867. I. 441.
— Om Følgerne af udvendige Beskadigelser paa Træer. 1875. I. 207.¹
— Ueber die Folgen äusserer Verletzungen der Bäume. 1873. III. 40, *180.*³
— Ueber forstbotanische Gärten. 1880. IV. 539.³
— Forstliche Notizen über das schlesische Riesen-Gebirge. 1864. IV. 353.
— Über das Gefrieren, Erfrieren der Pflanzen. 1883. I. 212.
— Geräusch beim Durchschneiden eines Cycadeenzapfens. 1862. II. 6.²
— Ueber die giftigen Pflanzen Schlesiens. 1832. III. 73.
— Ueber Graf Matuschka's Flora Schlesiens. 1877. IV. 63.¹
— Grosse Eiche. 1858. II. 138.¹
— Die grosse Eiche zu Fleischwitz. 1857. II. 138.¹
— Ueber den Häuserschwamm. 1876. IV. 415.¹
— Der Hausschwamm. 1885. IV. 415.¹
— Höhe der Kältegrade, welche die Vegetation überhaupt erträgt. 1871. I. 212.
— Über Holzverwüstung unserer Tage. 1881. IV. 44.
— Ueber einen von ihm ... entdeckten Urwald. 1859. I. 371, *IV. 83.*
— Ueber die Ilices unserer Gärten. 1878. IV. 462.³
— Ueber innere Vorgänge bei dem Veredeln. 1874. I. 208.¹
— Innere Zustände der Bäume nach äusseren Verletzungen. 1873. III. 40, *180,*³ IV. 66.¹
— Ueber Inschriften auf und in lebenden Bäumen. 1868. I. 210,³ IV. 66.¹
— Über Inschriften in Bäumen. 1869. I. 210.³
— Ueber Inschriften und Zeichen in lebenden Bäumen. 1868. I. 210,³ *IV. 66.*¹
— Sur l'irritabilité des filets des étamines du Berberis. 1828. II. 205.³
— Ueber Kien-Bildung. 1846. IV. 483.¹
— Ueber die Knieholz-Kiefer. 1864. IV. 464.³
— Der K. botanische Garten der Universität Breslau. 1857. I. 48.
— Der K. botanische Garten der Universität Breslau in forstbotanischer Hinsicht. 1858. IV. 18.¹
— Liste synonymique des espèces de Hqux. 1852. II. 462.¹
— Luftwurzelbildung bei einheimischen Bäumen. 1878. I. 188.¹
— Mittheilung über die morphologisch-physiologische Partie des Breslauer botanischen Gartens. 1872. IV. 18.¹
— Nachträge zu der Schrift über Inschriften. 1868. I. 210.¹
— Nachträge zur Kenntniss der Coniferenhölzer. 1888. II. 13.²
— Ein Naturspiel, das Zeichen eines Kreuzes. 1868. IV. 6³,¹
— Nonnulla de plantarum nutritione. 1825. I. 157.
— Observations sur les bourrelets ligneux. 1843. I. 209.³
— Die officinellen Gewächse europäischer botanischer Gärten. 1863. I. 48, *III. 58.*
— Die offizinellen und technisch wichtigen Pflanzen unserer Gärten. 1857. I. 47, *III. 58.*
— Particularités de la végétation des Conifères. 1853. IV. 20.²
— Über Pflanzenmetamorphosen. 1877. I. 143.
— Ueber die Pflanzenwelt in dem vergangenen Winter. 1873. III. 182, IV. 72, *V. xii.*²
— Ueber Pinus Pumilio Hk. 1839. II. 43.¹
— Plantas lefiosas que vejetan en los puntos más elevados. 1890. IV. 543.¹
— Polyembryonatie der Thuja orientalis. 1841. II. 52.³
— Sur le principe glacant des fleurs du Magnolier. 1859. II. 213.³
— Recherches sur la structure anatomique des tiges des Casuarina. 1841. II. 92.¹
— Recherches sur la structure ... de quelques Magnoliacées. 1842. II. 209.¹
— Ueber die Reizbarkeit der Staubfäden von Berberis. 1828. II. 205.³
— Ueber das Resonanzbodenholz. 1865. IV. 459.¹
— Ueber das riechende Prinzip in den Blüthen der Magnolia fuscata. 1859. II. 213.¹
— Ueber die Riesen des Pflanzenreiches. 1869. I. 295.¹

— Über das Saftsteigen und über Inschriften. 1880. *I. 210,³* IV. 66,¹ *V. xii.*¹
— Ueber die Schädlichkeit der an Bäumen ... haftenden Pilse. 1882. III. 194.
— Die in Schlesien wildwachsenden offizinellen Pflanzen. 1835. III. 73.
— Ueber den Schutz, welchen die Schneedecke ... gewährt, und über Frostrisse. 1871. IV. 191.¹
— Skizzen zur Kenntniss der Urwälder. 1868. I. 371, *IV. 83.*
— Ueber die sogenannte Auferstehungs-Linde. 1878. II. 516.³
— Die Torstenson-Linde bei Gross-Glogau. 1877. II. 516.¹
— Ueber das Ueberwallen der Coniferenstümpfe. 1853. I. 209.¹
— Ueber die Ueberwallung der Tannenstöcke. 1846. I. 209.³
— Unsere offizinellen Pflanzen. 1883. III. 59.¹
— Ueber die in unsern Gärten kultivirten Ilex-Arten. 1854. II. 462.²
— Über Urwälder Deutschlands. 1865. *I. 371,* 438, IV. 83, *86.*³
— Urwälder in Schlesien und in Böhmen. 1868. I. 371, *IV. 83.*
— Über die Verbreitung der Coniferen in der Schweiz. 1864. II. 15.¹
— Veredelungs-Methode der feineren Gehölze. 1853. III. 161.
— Über das Verhältniss der Pflanzenwelt zur ... Witterung. 1873. *I. 225,* IV. 72, *V. xii.*¹
— Über das Verhalten einer Mimosa pudica. 1862. - II. 373.¹
— Verzeichniss der ... kultivirten Dracaeneen. 1855. II. 77.¹
— Das Vorkommen der Holzgewächse auf den höchsten Punkten. 1877. I. 220.¹
— Vortrag ... über die Vorgänge beim Veredeln der Bäume. 1872. IV. 66.²
— Wachsen Rosen auf Eichen? 1853. III. 161, *458.*
— Über Wachsthumsverhältnisse der Coniferen. 1853. II. 20.¹ — 1854. *III. 291.*
— Ueber die Wärme-Entwickelung in den Pflanzen. 1830. I. 211.
— Über Wärme-Entwickelung in der lebenden Pflanze. 1832. I. 186.
— Wann stirbt die durch Frost getödtete Pflanze? 1871. I. 212.
— Ueber Widerstandsfähigkeit der Pflanzen ... gegen Kälte. 1874. III. 43.
— *See also* PANKEWITZ, Julius von & GÖPPERT, H. R.
Görges, C. Diebauf den Staatswaldungen der ehemaligen Grafschaft Dags urg. 1878. IV. 334.¹
Göring, (*Förster, Birkenfeld*). Bemerkungen über die Stockfäule in Fichtenwaldungen. 1853. IV. 455.
Goeritzius, J. A. De differentia inter Aloën veram. 1737. III. 333.¹
Görlich, Heinrich. Anweisung zur Obstbaumzucht. 1834. III. 137.
— Über die Wickelraupe und ihre Vertilgung. 1834. III. 188.²
Görlitz — Naturforschende Gesellschaft. *See* NATURFORSCHENDE ... I. 13.
Görlitzer Heide. 1875. IV. 354.
Goerner, F. A. Über Ausartung der Pflanzen. 1853. I. 244.¹
— Eine besonders erfolgreiche Methode, von den gelben gefüllten Rosen ... Blumen zu erhalten. 1834. III. 451.³
— Erfahrungen in der Obstbaumzucht. 1839. III. 137.
— Rosa suaveolens zu Hecken. 1861. III. 452.
— Topfrosen schneller zum ... Blühen zu bringen. 1839. III. 451.³
— Der Weissdornzaun. 1856. III. 213, *422.*³
— Ueber die Wirkungen des flüssigen animalischen Düngers. 1856. III. 151.
Goerres, Franz. De acidorum mineralium et Cubebarum facultatibus. 1833. III. 342.³
Goerth, B. Kleine Beobachtungen über die durch fehlerhafte Baumpfähle an Obstbäumen entstandenen Schäden. 1900. III. 199.
Goertz, Johann. Ueber die Chinarinden. 1853. III. 724.¹
Goës, A. von. Vegetationen på St Barthelemy. 1867. I. 336.
Goes, Edmund. Die Holzverwüstungen in Nordamerika. 1898. IV. 281.³
Goeschke, Franz. Acer Wieri laciniatum hort. 1882. III. 536.¹
— Ueber Anpflanzung von Coniferen. 1890. III. 293.

— Bærfrugten. 1885. III. 147.[2]
— Das Beerenobst. 1885. III. 147.[2]
— Beitrag zur Vermehrung der Platanen. 1882. III. 418.[2]
— Bunte Gehölze. 1900. III. 207.[1]
— Ueber buntlaubige Gehölze. 1883. III. 206.[2]
— Castanea pumila Mill. 1885. III. 358.[2]
— Dendrologische Notizen. 1877. III. 69.
— Die Haselnuss. 1887. III. 357.[2]
— Nuttallia cerasiformis. 1885. II. 268.[2]
— Der Obstbau. 1875. III. 138.
— Ogród wiejski. 1878. III. 101.[1]
— Pinus Peuce. 1889. II. 44.[2]
— Sikkim-Rhododendron "Oekonomierath Stoll." 1885. II. 679.[2]
— Der Spitzahorn. 1888. III. 535.[2]
— Die Wassersucht der Ribes. 1880. III. 414.[1]
— Xanthoceras sorbifolia. 1884. III. 540.[2]
— Zamia Heyderi. 1884. II. 7.[1]
Goeschke, J. Prunus Petzoldi C. Koch. 1886. III. 442.[2]
Goeschke, Oscar. Die rationelle Korbweiden-Kultur. 1897. III. 349.
Goessman, Charles A. Action of a special chemical fertilizer on . . . Concord grape. 1882. III. 583.[1]
— On mineral constituents in plant growth. 1882. I. 154.
— On rational fertilization. 1887. III. 151.
Goessman, Charles P. Experiments with Peach trees. 1882. II. 276.[2]
Goethals, J. De snoeikonst der ooft of vruchtboomen. 1734. III. 171.
Goethart, Jan Willem Christiaan. Beiträge zur Kenntniss des Malvaceen-Androeceums. 1890. II. 519.[2]
— De ziekte der Populieren. 1891. III. 344.[2]
Goethe, Hermann. Ampelographisches Wörterbuch. 1876. III. 547.
— Beiträge zur Kultur und Veredlung amerikanischer Reben. 1895. III. 558.[2]
— Bericht über eine zum Studium der Phylloxerafrage . . . unternommene Reise. 1888. III. 574.
— Aus der biologischen Weinbau-Versuchsstation. 1891. III. 558.[2]
— Handbuch der Ampelographie. 1878. III. 547.
— Der Obstbau. 1871. III. 138.
— Die Obstbauuschule. 1869. III. 138.
— Die Phylloxera und ihre Bekämpfung. 1887. III. 574.
— Weinbau-Statistik des Herzogthums Steiermark. 1881. III. 558.[2]
— Der Weingarten. 1873. III. 558.[2]
— Die Wurzellaus des Birnbaumes. 1884. III. 446.[1]
— & Rudolf. Die für den Weinbau Deutschlands . . . wertvollsten Traubensorten. 1873. III. 546.
Goethe, Johann Wolfgang von. Essai sur la métamorphose des plantes. 1790. I. 101.[1]
— Essay on the metamorphosis of plants. 1790. I. 101.[2]
— Die Metamorphose der Pflanzen. 1799. I. 101.[2]
— Zur Naturwissenschaft überhaupt, besonders zur Morphologie. 1817. I. 101.[1]
— Saggio sulla metamorfosi delle piante. 1790. I. 101.[2]
— Versuch die Metamorphose der Pflanzen zu erklären. 1790. I. 101.[1]
— Versuch über die Metamorphose der Pflanze. 1790. I. 101.[1]
Goethe, Rudolph. Beobachtungen über Schildläuse. 1904. III. 190.
— Bericht über die Elsass-Lothringische Landes-Obst-Ausstellung. 1877. III. 138.
— Bericht über eine Reise nach Steiermark. 1889. III. 561.
— Ueber die Blutlaus. 1876. III. 427.[2]
— Ueber das Drehen der Baumstämme. 1888. I. 107.[1]
— Die Frostschäden der Obstbäume. 1883. III. 182.
— Handbuch der Tafeltraubenkultur. 1894. III. 553.[1]
— Hvorledes kan Roddannelse og Vækst bedst fremmes hos nyplantede Frugttræer? 1898. III. 166.
— Instruktion für Strassenpflanzungen. 1878. III. 209.
— Die Kernobstsorten des deutschen Obstbaues. 1890. III. 72.
— Zum Krebs der Apfelbäume. 1884. III. 427.[2]
— Mittheilungen über den Krebs der Apfelbäume. 1877. III. 427.[2]
— Mittheilungen über den schwarzen Brenner. 1878. III. 560.
— Die Obst- und Traubenzucht an Mauern. 1900. III. 139.
— Die Obstverwertung unserer Tage. 1893. III. 174.[1]
— Pomologische Curiositäten. 1881. II. 272.[1]
— Das Wesen der Baumschwämme. 1897. III. 195.[2]

Goethe, W. J. Erythrochiton brasiliense. 1897. III. 504.[1]
— Petrea volubilis. 1897. III. 697.[1]
Goetsbloets, Maria. Note sur le Ledum palustre. 1889. II. 673.[1]
Götterbaum. 1856. III. 506.[2]
Götting, F. Der Obstbau. 1887. III. 139.
Göttingen — Königliche Gesellschaft der Wissenschaften. See KÖNIGLICHE . . . I. 13.
Göttingen — Societas regia scientiarum gottingensis. See SOCIETAS . . . I. 14.
Göttingen—Universität — Botanisches Laboratorium. Untersuchungen. See UNTERSUCHUNGEN . . . I. 15.
Göttingisches Journal der Naturwissenschaften. I. 12.
Götz, A. Zur Publikation des Rubus folio-crispatus. 1894. II. 302.[1]
— Die Rubusflora des Elzthales. 1893. II. 302.[1]
Götz, C. F. von. Die kleinen Feinde des Waldes. 1876. IV. 204.
Goetz, Georg Heinrich. Κηνοφιλος; seu, De eruditis hortorum cultoribus. 1726. III. 32.[1]
Goetz, Georg Max Theodor. Abbildungen der vorzüglichsten in Deutschland einheimischen . . . Giftpflanzen. 1817. III. 72.
Götz, Joh. E. Anweisung zu vortheilhafter Anlegung der Baumschulen. 1787. III. 135.
Goetz, Joseph Michael. Systematica descriptio plantarum exoticarum officinalium. 1818. III. 56.
Götze, Karl. Plumbago capensis. 1886. III. 666.[1]
Goetzee, P. N. Bereiding van kakao in Suriname. 1866. III. 594.
Götzen, G. A., Graf von. Durch Afrika von Ost nach West. 1895. I. 483.[2]
Goetzius, J. C. Sambuci abhorrescentia. 1747. III. 752.[1]
Goeze, Edmund. Die Ampelideen oder Rebenpflanzen. 1888. III. 544.[1]
— Aussaat und Keimung. 1886. I. 204, III. 154.[2]
— Ein Beitrag zur Kenntniss der Orangengewächse. 1874. II. 397,[1] III. 497.[1]
— Die Berberidaceen . . . in unseren Gärten. 1887. III. 393.[1]
— Ein Blick in die Familie der Coniferen. 1878. II. 21.[2]
— Ein Blick in die Pflanzenwelt Portugals. 1869. III. 126.[1]
— Blicke in die Familie der Leguminosen. 1900. III. 462.[1]
— Ein botanischer Privatgarten. 1890. I. 64.
— Catalogue des plantes médicinales . . . de Coimbra. 1868. I. 60.[1]
— Die Cupuliferen. 1887. III. 358.[1]
— Deutsche Pflanzen- und Samenkataloge. 1885. III. 290.
— Die Doum-Palme. 1863. II. 69.[1]
— Die Eiben, Taxaceen. 1884. III. 288.[1]
— Einige weniger bekannte . . . Früchte. 1887. III. 71.
— Empfehlenswerthe Coniferen-Neuheiten. 1888. III. 290.
— Eucalyptus globulus. 1878. IV. 533.[1]
— Die Familie der Cacteen. 1888. III. 626.[1]
— French colonial products in the Palais de l'industrie. 1864. III. 29.[1]
— Die Gattung Brachychiton. 1885. III. 590.[1]
— Die Gattungen Dyckia, Hechtia. 1886. III. 333.[1]
— Zur Geschichte der Kautschukpflanzen. 1899. III. 230.
— Die heilige Citrone von Marokko. 1898. II. 402.[2]
— Die Hickory-Arten. 1885. III. 353.[1]
— Hinweis auf einige noch im October blühender Sträucher. 1890. III. 207.[2]
— Die Hippomane Mancinella L. 1862. II. 445.[1]
— A ilha de S. Miguel. 1867. I. 60,[1] 536.[2]
— Die Insel St. Miguel. 1867. III. 132.[1]
— Kurze Beschreibung einiger Tropenfrüchte. 1864. III. 220.[1]
— Kurze Mittheilungen über die Pflanzenwelt des tropischen Afrika. 1885. I. 490.
— Kurzer Bericht über einige . . . Pflanzen-Arten im Garten zu Kew. 1865. I. 55.
— Die Loranthaceen. 1889. II. 179.[2]
— Die Loranthaceen. 1897. III. 174.[1]
— New introductions. 1891. III. 75.[2]
— Notes from Germany. 1892. III. 75.[2]
— Ueber die öconomische Anwendung verschiedener Baumrinden. 1864. IV. 436.[1]
— Die Palmen und Nadelhölzer. 1884. V. xxv,[1] xxv.[2]
— Die Palmen-Gattung Calamus. 1884. III. 321.[1]
— Pflanzengeographie für Gärtner. 1882. I. 300.
— Die Pflanzenschätze von Südafrika. 1882. I. 218.
— Die Pflanzenwelt Portugals. 1877. I. 421.
— Die portugiesischen Eichenarten. 1886. II. 130.[1]

Goeze, Edmund (*continued*).
— Remarkable gardens of Portugal: Lumiar. 1875. III. 126.[1]
— Syagrus botryophora Mart. 1884. III. 322.[2]
— Tabellarische Uebersicht der wichtigsten Nutzpflanzen. 1883. III. 53.
— Sur la variabilité des espèces. 1868. I. 244.[1]
— Das Vaterland der in Europa angebauten Früchte. 1884. V. xii.[2]
— La végétation de l'île de San Miguel. 1867. III. 132.[1]
— Die Vitis-Arten mit essbaren ... Beeren. 1896. III. 583.[2]
Goeze, Johann August Ephraim. Mikroskopische Beobachtungen einer ... Minirraupe in den Apfelblättern. 1775. III. 427.[1]
Goff, E. S. Cranberries in Wisconsin. 1890. III. 663.[2]
— The domestication of wild fruits. 1888. III. 419.[2]
— Elaegnus multiflora in Wisconsin. 1896. III. 629.[1]
— Flowering and fertilization of native Plums. 1895. II. 272.[1]
— Notes on ornamental trees and shrubs. 1895. III. 61.[1]
— The origin ... of the flowers in the Cherry. 1899. II. 257,[1] *271.*[2]
— The Siberian Pea-tree, Caragana. 1896. III. 470.[1]
— A study of the roots of certain perennial plants. 1897. I. 188.[2]
— Sun-scald and means for its prevention. 1897. III. 184.[1]
— Trees and shrubs at Madison, Wisconsin. 1895. III. 61.[1]
Gogela, Franz. Einige Rosen aus der Umgebung von Friedek. 1892. II. 288.[1]
Gogh, V. W. van. Jaarverslag der Malangsche vereeniging van Koffieplanters. 1899. III. 731.
— Over de oeret plaag. 1897. III. 736.
— Tuin-onderhoud. 1900. III. 732.[1]
Gohren, Fr. Ludwig August Hermann von. Medicorum priscorum de signatura ... doctrina. 1840. III. 259.[2]
Goinbault, Charles. Mémoire sur les Robinia pseudo-acacia. 1837. III. 486.[1]
Going, Maud. With the wild flowers. 1894. I. 96.
Goiran, Agostino. Di alcune galle della Quercia. 1890. IV. 511.
— Alcune notizie sulla flora Veronese. Comunicazione. 1889. II. 701.[2]
— Anarcardiaceae veronenses. 1900. II. 454.[2]
— Appunti botanici. 1880. I. 429.
— Betulaceae veronenses. 1898. II. 115.[1]
— Sopra diverse forme appartenenti ai generi Scolopendrium. 1890. I. 429.
— Due nuove stazioni veronesi per Diospyros. 1896. II. 311,[1] *702.*[1]
— Erbario forestale veronese. 1876. I. 74,[2] *IV. 86.*[1]
— Erborizzazioni ... attraverso i Monti Lessini. 1892. I. 430.
— Sulla estrazione del vischio o pania da Viburnum. 1889. III. 271.[2]
— Sulla inserzione spontanea di una pianta di Quercus Ilex. 1890. I. 209.[2]
— Juglandaceae et Salicaceae veronenses. 1898. II. 95,[1] *112.*[2]
— Nomi volgari adoperati in Italia a designare le principali piante di bosco. 1876. I. 74,[2] *IV. 86.*[1]
— Note di fitografia. 1880. II. 655.[1]
— Note di fitografia e di patologia vegetale. 1878. II. 274.[1]
— Note ed osservazioni botaniche. 1891. I. 429.
— Di una nuova stazione di Viscum laxum. 1890. II. 180.[2]
— Plantae vasculares ... in veronensi provincia. 1874. I. 428.
— Sulla presenza di Diospyros Lotus L. nel Veronese. 1889. II. 701.[3]
— Sulla presenza ... di Evonymus latifolius. 1892. II. 468.[3]
— Sulla presenza di Fraxinus excelsior. 1892. II. 707.[3]
— Sulla presenza in Verona di Spiraea sorbifolia. 1893. II. 311.[1]
— Sulla probabile introduzione ... di Laurus nobilis. 1894. II. 225,[3] *713.*[1]
— Prodromus florae veronensis. 1882. I. 429.
— Sopra la pubblicazione ... Nomi volgari adoperati in Italia. 1877. I. 423, *IV. 86.*[1]
— Stazioni veronesi di Quercus pseudo-Suber. 1890. IV. 136.[1]
— Una varietà di Celtis australis L. 1893. II. 141.[3]
Goizet, Un tramway forestier. 1883. IV. 391.
Goizet, G. De la situation des forêts d'essences mélangées à l'île de la Réunion. 1888. IV. 379.[1]

Gok, Carl Friedrich. Die Wein-Rebe. 1829. II. 505.[1]
— Die Weinrebe und ihre Früchte. 1836. III. 546.
Golberry, Sils Meinrad Xavier. Fragmens d'un voyage en Afrique. 1802. I. 490.
— Reisen durch das westliche Afrika. 1802. I. 490.
Goldbach, Karl Ludwig. Plantae officinales Rossiae. 1823. III. 68.[1]
Goldbeck, von (*Präsident*, *Berlin*). Über die Kultur der Feige. 1827. III. 369.[1]
Goldberg, (*Oberförster in Glauchau*). Die Wasser-, Baum- und Waldwirthschaft. 1891. IV. 51.
Golden, Katherine E. Movement of gases in rhizomes. 1895. I. 162.
Golden, Michael J. Notes on wood shrinkage. 1896. IV. 412.[2]
The **Golden-leaved** Oak of California. 1892. II. 133.[1]
Golden-leaved shrubs and trees. *See* SHRUBS and trees with golden foliage. 1885. III. 206.[2]
Goldenberg, Alfred. Les devoirs de l'État envers les populations forestières. 1870. IV. 269.
— Von den Pflichten des Staates gegen die Forst-Bevölkerungen. 1870. IV. 269.
Goldgelbe Färbungen in Park und Landschaft. 1892. III. 206.[3]
Goldie, John. Description of some ... plants discovered in Canada. 1822. I. 309.[3]
Goldman, C. F. Notenteelt op de Banda-eilanden. 1864. III. 758.[1]
Goldmann, (*Oberförster*). Ueber den Anbau der Kiefer. 1835. IV. 471.
— Mausefrass in einer Kiefernsaat. 1839. IV. 475.
Goldmann, Ignaz. Grundriss der Botanik. 1841. I. 88.
— Lehrbuch der Botanik. 1848. I. 89.
Goldring, W. Azalea odorata. 1890. III. 657.[2]
— The bush Spiraeas. 1894. III. 460.[2]
— The Californian Buckeye. 1894. III. 536.[2]
— The Catalpas or Indian Bean trees. 1889. III. 705.[2]
— The Chinese Chestnut. 1896. III. 540.[2]
— Daphne Blagayana. 1889. III. 627.[1]
— Forsythia suspensa. 1896. III. 672.[1]
— The Forsythias. 1890. III. 672.[1]
— Herbaceous non-climbing Clematises. 1896. III. 390.[1]
— The Irish or Florence Court Yew. 1891. III. 288.[1]
— The Japanese and Chinese Quinces. 1891. III. 419.[2]
— The Monterey Cypress at home. 1896. II. 29.[2]
— A new hardy Magnolia. 1891. III. 400.[3]
— The Nootka Raspberry and others. 1894. III. 457.[2]
— Olearia Haasti. 1891. III. 756.[1]
— Ornamental tree and shrub planting. 1887. III. 203.
— Ornamental Walnut trees. 1896. III. 354.[1]
— Our earliest Lebanon Cedars. 1884. III. 300.[3]
— Planting in connection with buildings. 1881. III. 201.
— The Sea Buckthorn. 1896. III. 629.[1]
— Spring-flowering trees and shrubs. 1890. III. 207.[3]
— Styrax japonica. 1891. III. 671.[1]
— Tree planting on chalk soil. 1889. III. 41.[1]
— The twining Honeysuckles. 1894. III. 750.[1]
Goldschmidt, F. *See* KOBERT & GOLDSCHMIDT, F.
Goldschmiedt, Guido. Notiz über das Vorkommen von Bernsteinsäure. 1882. II. 155.[1]
— *See also* BARTH, Ludwig, *Ritter* von.
Goldsmith, Sophie. Beiträge zur Entwickelungsgeschichte der Fribrovasalmassen. 1876. I. 133.
Golenkin, Mikhail. Beiträge zur Kenntniss der Urticaceen. 1897. II. 145.[1]
— Beitrag zur Entwicklungsgeschichte der Inflorescenzen der Urticaceen. 1894. II. 145.[1]
— Ueber Daphne Sophia Kalenicz. 1899. II. 602.[1]
— Ueber die Entwicklungsgeschichte der Inflorescenzen bei ... Urticaceen. 1894. II. 145.[1]
— *See also* ГОЛЕНКИНЪ, М. И.
Goll, Wenzl. Die Karstaufforstung in Krain. 1898. IV. 167.[2]
Gollan. L'écussonnage du Manguier. 1900. III. 525.[1]
Gollmann, O., Krause, Rudolf & Scheuerlein, Fedor. Heckenpflanzen und Heckenpflanzung. 1898. III. 214.[1]
Gollner, H. Ueber die Festigkeit des Schwarzföhrenholzes. 1881. IV. 466.[2]
Golobardas, Juan Bautista. Compendio sobre el modo de sembrár, plantár. 1817. III. 114.[1]
Golovin, Vasil. *See* ГОЛОВИНЪ, В.
Goltstein, W. van. Het doodvonnis der gouvernements Koffiecultuur. 1890. III. 730.
— Dé gouvernements Koffiecultuur. 1888. III. 730.

De **Gomboomen** in Australie. 1880. IV. 531.[2]
Gomelastiek (Hevea) plantages in Suriname. 1895. III. 518.[2]
Gomelastiek van Borneo en Java. 1854. III. 228.[2]
Gomer, Maxime, *comte* de. De l'amélioration des plantes cultivées. 1870. I. 247.
— Les engrais et les plantations en espalier. 1875. III. 151.
— Étude sur les végétaux et sur leur naturalisation. 1867. III. 43.
— Over meststoffen en leiboomen. 1875. III. 151.
Gomès, Bernardino. Huile purgative d'Anda. 1832. III. 520.[1]
Gomes, Bernardino Antonio, (1769–1823). Ensaio sobre o cinchonino. 1812. III. 721.
— Memoria sobre a Canella do Rio de Janeiro. 1809. II. 566.[2]
— Modo de cultivar a Canelleira. 1809. III. 613.[2]
— Observationes botanico-medicae de . . . Brasiliae plantis. 1803. III. 65.[1]
— Observationes botanico medicae de . . . Brasiliae plantis. 1812. I. 341.
Gomes, Bernardino Antonio, (*jr.*). As Arvores da quina em Cabo Verde. 1876. III. 717.[2]
— Os Cedros do Bussaco. 1871. II. 29.[2]
— As explorações phyto-geographicas da Africa tropical. 1873. I. 491.
— Relação do que existe impresso . . . ácerca da flora e fauna angolense. 1868. I. 4.[1]
— Relatorio sobre o Herbario da Madeira. 1863. I. 497.
— & **Beirão**, C. M. F. da S. Catalogus plantarum horti botanici Medicochirurgicae scholae olisiponensis. 1851. I. 60.[1]
Gomes, Bernardino BARROS. Condições florestaes de Portugal. 1876. IV. 362.
— Cultura das plantas que dão a Quina. 1864. III. 712.[1]
— Étude sur les espèces de Chênes forestiers du Portugal. 1876. II. 129.[3]
— Notice sur les arbres forestiers du Portugal. 1878. *I. 419,[1]* IV. 85,[2] 363.[1]
— Observations forestières durant une excursion à travers la Beira. 1876. IV. 362.
— Relatorio florestal sobre as matas da Machada. 1865. IV. 362.
Gómez, Gabriel. Cultivation and preparation of Coffee. 1894. III. 727.
— Cultivo y beneficio del Café. 1894. III. 727.
Gómez de la Maza, Manuel. Catálogo de las periantiadas cubanas. 1890. I. 337.
— Catálogo de las perigoniadas cubanas. 1894. I. 337.
— Catálogo de plantas Cubanas. 1896. I. 337.
— Diccionario botanico de los nombres vulgares. 1889. I. 73.[1]
— Distribucion de los géneros fanerogámicos cubanos. 1895, I. 337.
— Ensayo de farmacofitologia cubana. 1889. III. 64.[1]
— Florayde Cuba. 1887. I. 336.
— Flora habanera. 1897. I. 337.
— Nociones de botánica sistemática glosología. 1893. I. 337.
— Nombre moderno y clasificacion familiar de las plantas representadas por A. Richard. 1896. I. 337.
— Notas sobre la "List of plants collected in the Bahamas." 1894. I. 337.
— & **Torralbas**, J. I. Flórula fanerogámica del jardin botánico. 1895. I. 39.
Gomez y Couto, Vicente. La Coca. 1876. III. 493.[1]
Gomilevski, Vasilí. *See* Гомилевскій, Василій.
Gomlak, zijne soorten en zijn gebruik. 1882. III. 232.[2]
Sur la **gomme** du Sénégal. 1803. III. 463.[1]
Gomme Mesquite. 1876. III. 485.[1]
Gommes de l'Australie. 1874. III. 463.[2]
Gon Netscher, van der. *See* BLEEKRODE, S. A. & GON NETSCHER, van der.
Gonda, Béla. A Majomkenyérfa. 1872. III. 589.[1]
Gondim, M. R. Observações sobre serviços anti-phylloxericos. 1889. III. 762.
Gondouin, C. Exemples de rechaussements à neuf de vieux arbres d'ornement. 1845. III. 181.[2]
Gongryp, J. R. C. *See* SCHLUCH, P. G., BARNET LYON, G. H. & GONGRYP, J. R. C.
Gonin, Louis. Visite d'un ingénieur suisse aux travaux de reboisement des Alpes françaises. 1890. IV. 164.[1]
Gonnermann. Ueber die Abbisse der Tannen. 1865. IV. 207.

Gonnet, Philippe H. Flore élémentaire de la France. 1847. I. 410.
Gonod d'Artemare, C. Matériaux pour la flore d'Auvergne. 1889. I. 417.
Gontershausen, H. WELCKER VON. *See* WELCKER VON GONTERSHAUSEN, H.
Gontier. Sur une nouvelle Passiflore. 1850. II. 580.[1]
Gonzaga, A. J. H. A alfarrobeira e a alfarroba. 1877. III. 472.[1]
Gonzalez, Eleuterio. Apuntes . . . para la formacion de la flórula de la ciudad de Monterey. 1876. I. 331.
Gonzalez le Linares, Augusto. La celula vegetal. 1878. I. 137.
— Sobre la forma general de los vegetales. 1879. I. 100.[1]
Gonzalez y Delgado, Tomás. Apuntes para la flora cubana. 1867. I. 336.
Good, Peter P. The family flora and materia medica botanica. 1847. III. 58.
A **good** hedge plant. 1874. III. 477.[2]
A **good** tree planter. 1864. III. 166.
Good weeping trees. 1885. III. 204.[2]
Good words. III. 17.
Goodale, George Lincoln. A catalogue of the flowering plants of Maine. 1862. I. 314.
— A course of lectures on forests. 1888. IV. 102.
— Fertilisation and cross-fertilization. 1877. I. 237.
— Hybridisation in plants. 1878. I. 245.
— Physiological botany. 1885. I. 148.
— Pine forestry. 1896. IV. 462.[1]
— The problem of Heather in North America. 1890. II. 662.[1]
— Tropical horticulture. 1898. III. 96.[1]
— Useful plants of the future. 1891. III. 53.
— Wild flowers of America. 1882. I. 308.
— Zukunftsfragen über Nahrungs- und Nutzpflanzen. 1891. III. 53.
— & **Blake**, Joseph. The Portland catalogue of Maine plants. 1868. I. 314.
Goodale, S. L. The Mountain Ash as a stock for Pears. 1849. III. 459.[1]
Goode, George Brown. The beginnings of American science. 1886. V. x.[1]
— The beginnings of natural history in America. 1884. V. x.[1]
Goode, Richard U. Bitter Root forest reserve. 1898. IV. 179.[1]
Goodloe, Daniel R. Grape-culture and wine-making. 1861. III. 150.
Goodrich, Chauncey. The northern fruit culturist. 1849. III. 133.
Goodrich, Samuel Griswold. Cyclopedia of botany. 1838. I. 94.
— Tales about plants. 1839. I. 517.[2]
Goodwin, H. Correspondence accompanying certain specimens of wood from Darjeeling. 1846. IV. 400.[2]
— Memorandum accompanying a piece of Teak from Arracan. 1844. IV. 537.[2]
Goodwyn, H. *See* GOODWIN, H.
Goodwin, W. L. Ringed trees. 1889. IV. 385.[1]
Goos, M. J. Pinus Coulteri Don. 1886. III. 307.[1]
The **Gooseberry growers' register**. III. 17.
Gorbunof, *Mrs.* E. *See* Горбунова, Е.
Gordinier, Herman Camp & **Howe**, E. C. The flora of Rensselaer county. 1894. I. 316.
Gordon, Alexander. *See* MILNE, Colin & GORDON, Alexander.
Gordon, George. An account of the Evergreen Plum of California. 1852. III. 437.[1]
— Amygdalus nana. 1877. III. 438.[2]
— Collectanea for a flora of Moray. 1839. I. 398.
— Ueber die Coniferen auf Japan. 1844. II. 15.[2]
— Coniferous plants. 1841. III. 289.
— Coniferous plants. 1842. III. 293.
— Cotoneasters. 1876. III. 420.[2]
— Cryptomeria japonica. 1845. III. 301.[2]
— Die Daphne-, Seidelbast- oder Kellerhals-Arten. 1876. III. 626.[2]
— The Daphnes. 1876. III. 626.[2]
— Double-flowered Cherries. 1876. II. 270,[2] *III. 432.*[1]
— The hardier kinds of Viburnum. 1874. III. 753.[1]
— Hardy Magnolias. 1876. III. 399.[1]
— Hardy trees and shrubs. 1872. III. 78.[2]
— The hardy varieties of the Gum-Cistus. 1876. III. 612.
— The Himalayan Lilac. 1877. III. 681.[1]
— The Honeysuckles or Loniceras. 1877. III. 750.[1]

Gordon, George (*continued*).
— The Honeysuckles or Woodbines. 1877. III. 749.²
— The Mahonias. 1876. III. 395.²
— The Mistletoe of the ancients. 1872. III. 385.¹
— Notes on Coniferae of Japan. 1844. II. 15.²
— Notes upon some newly-introduced Conifers. 1849. II. 38.²
— Ornamental Pyruses. 1876. III. 425.¹
— Pendulous Conifers. 1876. III. 290.
— The pinetum. 1858. II. 12.²
— Des Pins de la Californie. 1849. II. 38.²
— Pinus cembroides. 1846. II. 41.²
— The Planes. 1872. III. 418.¹
— On raising coniferous plants from seed. 1842. III. 293.
— Upon raising coniferous plants from seed. 1842. III. 293.
— Revue des Conifères rares. 1841. III. 289.
— The shrubby Cinquefoils. 1876. III. 430.¹
— Some account of the Cryptomeria japonica. 1846. III. 301.²
— The Spiraeas. 1877. III. 460.²
— The Sweet Chestnut. 1872. II. 124.¹
— The Western Alls ice. 1877. III. 401.¹
— The Yellow Pine, Pinus ponderosa. 1872. II. 45.¹
— The Yews. 1877. III. 288.¹
— *See also* ROYLE, J. F. & GORDON, George.
Gordon, Henry Doddridge. The history of Harting. 1877. I. 403.
Gordon, J. D. The sandalwood trade and traders of Polynesia. 1862. III. 384.¹
Gordon, James. Abies Douglasii and its precocity. 1878. IV. 483.¹
— Male flowers of Pines. 1879. V. xxv.²
— Trees; their forms and laws of growth. 1883, 1884. I. 106,³ *IV*. 63.²
Gordon, John (*of Swinzie*). Essay on Whin hedges. 1816. III. 489.²
Gordon, Patrick Robertson. *See* BAILEY, F. M. & GORDON, P. R.
Gordon, T. E. Report on a journey from Tehran. 1891. III. 329.¹
Gordon, W. J. Our country's flowers and how to know them. 1891. I. 534.²
Gordyagin, Andrej. *See* Гордягинъ, A.
Gore, *Mrs.* C. F. The Rose fancier's manual. 1838. III. 448.
Gore, Charles. The book of Roses. 1837. III. 448.
Górecki, W. Niszczenie lasów . . . w Polsce. 1874. IV, 283.²
Goret, Maurice. Sur la composition de l'albumen de la graine de Février. 1900. II. 362.¹
Gorgole de Corne. De la manière d'enter. 1580. III. 159.²
— Traicte de la manière de planter. 1560. III. 165.
Gori, Augusto de. *See* GORI PANNILINI, A., *conte* de.
Gori, Pietro. L' amore per i fiori, loro storia. 1894. I. 518.
— Le Rose; loro storia. 1890. III. 450.
Gori Pannilini, Augusto, *conte* de. Sulla legislazione forestale. 1861. IV. 277.
— Risposta al quesito del governo. 1862. IV. 277.
Goriany, Victor. De l'emploi du bois de Tremble. 1893. IV. 487.¹
Gorini, Gemello. Index Bertolonianus. 1867. I. 428.
— Piante industriali. 1878. III. 53.
— Delle piante industriali. 1878. III. 53.
Goritzki, K. S. *See* Горицкій, K. C.
Gorkom, Karel Wessel van. Beiträge zur Kenntniss der Chinakultur auf Java. 1873. III. 715.
— Bericht über die Kultur der Chinarindenbäume. 1867. III. 715.
— Berigt nopens den stand der Kina-kultuur. 1870. III. 15.
— Berigt over 1864, aangaande den toestand der Kinakultuur. 1865. III. 715.
— Bijdrage tot de geschiedenis der Rhamnuskultuur. 1869. III. 542.¹
— Bijdrage tot de kennis der Kina-cultuur op Java. 1867. III. 715.
— Bijdrage tot de kennis van den wortel der Morinda citrifolia. 1867. III. 746.¹
— Een bijdrage tot verbetering van de Koffiecultuur. 1893. III. 727.
— Bijdragen tot de kennis der Kinacultuur. 1872. III. 715.
— Bijdragen tot de kennis der Kinakultuur. 1873. III. 715.
— Ca-ao en vanielje. 1882. III. 592.²
— Die Chinacultur auf Java. 1869. III. 715.
— Chinchona cultivation in Java. 1867. III. 715.
— The cultivation of the Chinchonas . . . in Java. 1869. III. 715.
— Dr. Bureks middelen ter bestrijding van de Koffiebladziekte. 1888. III. 736.
— Eenige opmerkingen, naar aanleiding van Dr. J. E. de Vrij's Verslag. 1874. III. 715.
— De Gambier en eenige andere looistoffen. 1859. III. 237.¹
— Gedachten over landbouw-aangelegenheden op Java. 1899. III. 731.
— De Gouvernements-Kinakultuur. 1888. III. 716.
— De gouvernements Kinakultuur. 1893. III. 716.
— De gouvernements Koffiecultuur. 1890. III. 730.
— De gouvernements Koffiecultuur. 1896. III. 731.
— De gouvernements Koffie-kultuur. 1869. III. 729.²
— A hand-book of Cinchona culture. 1881. III. 712.²
— Iets over de Lantana. 1871. III. 696.²
— Inlandsche landbouw op Java. 1880. III. 128.
— De invloed van het zonlicht op het gehalte van Kinabast. 1892. II. 813.²
— De Java-Kina. 1874. III. 724.²
— De Kina. 1880. III. 716.
— De Kina. 1881. III. 712.²
— Kina. 1883. III. 718.
— Kina. 1888. III. 716.
— De Kina-cultuur. 1887. III. 716.
— Kinakultuur. 1876. III. 716.
— Kinakultuur op Java. 1871. III. 715.
— Kininebereiding op Java. 1896. III. 718.
— Kinologische schetsen. 1892. III. 716.
— Koffie. 1882. III. 727.
— De markt en de toekomst der kina. 1881. III. 718.
— Een nieuwe meststof voor Koffiboomen. 1871. III. 734.¹
— Een nieuwe plaag der Kinaboomen.. 1888. III. 717.²
— Nota over de Kinateelt op Java. 1874. III. 716.
— Note sur la culture du Quinquina à Java. 1874. III. 716.
— Olie tot bestrijding der groene luis. 1899. III. 737.
— De Oost-indische cultures. 1880. III. 128.
— Particuliere Kina-cultuur. 1875. III. 716.
— De positie der Koffiebladziekte of Java. 1889. III. 736.
— De Preanger-regeling der Koffiecultuur. 1880. III. 29.²
— Over de quiniumbereiding van Maier. 1871. III. 722.
— Over de quinium bereiding van Mayer. 1873. III. 718.
— Regenval en reboisatie in Deli. 1898. IV. 168.²
— Scheikundig onderzoek van Himalaya-thee. 1871. III. 607.
— Schets eener handleiding voor de Kinakultuur. 1869. III. 715.
— Specerijen. 1884. III. 221.²
— Thee. 1883. III. 607.
— Vernietiging van insecten. 1900. III. 737.
— Verslag omtrent de Kinakultuur op Java. 1867. III. 715.
— Verslag over . . . scheikundig onderzoek der vruchten van Tangkallak. 1859. III. 407.¹
— Voortkweeking van Kina door enten. 1899. III. 717.¹
— Wetenschappelijke opmerkingen . . . betreffende de Kinacultuur. 1873. III. 716.
— Een woord over de ontwouding van Java. 1874. IV. 283.²
— Een woord over de ontwouding van Java, ter ontginning van gronden. 1874. IV. 279.³
— De wortelziekte der Kina. 1891. III. 717.²
— De siekte der Kinaplant op Java. 1878. III. 717.²
— & Moens, J. C. Bernelot. De uitkomsten der Kinakultuur. 1873. III. 715.
— — Verslag namens de gouvernements-Kina-onderneming. 1875. III. 716.
— — Verslag nopens de gouvernements-Kina-onderneming. 1875. III. 716.
— Pies, D. & Holle, K. F. Voorschriften voor gouvernements-Koffie-kultuur. 1873. III. 729.²
Gorkum, R. van. De landbouw in de bergstreken. 1872. III. 128.
Gorman, Martin W. Eastern part of Washington forest reserve. 1899. IV. 341.¹
— Economic botany of southeastern Alaska. 1896. III. 63.¹
Gorozhankin, Ivan Nikolaevitch. Ueber den Befruchtungsprocess bei Pinus Pumilio. 1883. II. 43.¹
— Zur Kenntniss der Corpuscula bei den Gymnospermen. 1883. II. 1.
— *See also* Горожанкинъ, И. Н.

Gorozhankin, Johann. *See* GOROŽHANKIN, I. N.
Gorriá, Hermenegildo. Volumen de agua que es necesario para el riego de una hectárea de terreno. 1884. IV. 144.[1]
Gorrie, Archibald, (1777–1857). Essay on the nature and quality of soils. 1829. III. 40.[2]
— Some account of a remarkable Spruce Fir tree. 1829. III. 305.[1]
Gorrie, Archibald. Remarks on the planting of the sand-hills on the seacoast. 1893· III. 41.[2]
Gorrie, William. The advantages of planting in groups. 1875. IV. 450.
— The failures of the Larch. 1878. IV. 450.
— Hardiness of Sikkim and other Rhododendrons. 1854. III. 656.
— How to measure the annual growth. 1881. IV. 233.
— Note on the York and Lancaster Rose. 1873. II. 299.[2]
— Notes on New Zealand plants. 1883, 1880. III. 47, 83.[1]
— Rusticité des Rhododendrons du Sikkim. 1854· III. 656.
— The selection of hardy plants. 1880. III. 43.
Gorsse, E. de. Les forêts des Pyrénées. 1894. IV. 362, 556.[1]
— Influence des forêts sur les inondations. 1879. IV. 50.
— Los montes de los Pirineos. 1894. IV. 556.[1]
— Restauration et conservation des terrains en montagne. 1900. IV. 186.[2]
Gorter, David de. Bericht betreffende den Tamarischboom. 1775. II. 562.[2]
— Elementa botanica methodo cl. Linnaei. 1749. I. 82,[1] V. x.[1]
— Flora belgica. 1767. I. 391.[2]
— Flora gebro-zutphanica. 1745. I. 390, 532,[2] V. xx.[1]
— Flora ingrica ex schedis . . . Krascheninnikow. 1761. I. 359.
— Flora 7 provinciarum Belgii foederati. 1781. I. 392.
— Kruidkundige verhandeling over Jerem. XVII. vs. 6. 1774. I. 513.
— Leer de plantkunde. 1782. I. 83.
Gorter, K. Over de van der Moer'sche reactie. 1895. II. 322.[1]
Gorup-Besanez, Eugen Franz Cajetan, *Freiherr* von. Buttersäure in den Früchten des Seifenbaums. 1848. III. 540.[1]
— Ueber die chemischen Bestandtheile der Blätter von Ampelopsis. 1872. II. 504.[2]
— Ueber das Vorkommen eines diastatischen . . . Fermentes. 1874. I. 175.
— & **Will**, Hermann. Fortgesetzte Beobachtungen über peptonbildende Fermente. 1876. I. 175.
— — Sur la présence dans le règne végétal de ferments diastasiques. 1876. I. 176.
Goryaninof, P. *See* ГОРЯНИНОВЪ, П.
Gosché, V. R. The Cork, and its future. 1900. IV. 436.[1]
Goshe, N. *See* ГОШЕ, Н.
Gosling, Audley. Report on the financial . . . condition of Guatemala. 1892. III. 740.[1]
— Report on the School of forestry in Spain. 1888. IV. 35.[1]
Gosse, Louis André. Monographie de l'Erythroxylon Coca. 1861. III. 492.[2]
Gosse, Philipp Henry. The Canadian naturalist. 1840. I. 310.
— Letters from Alabama. 1859. I. 219.
— Wanderings through the conservatories at Kew. 1856. I. 54.
Gosselin, Robert Roland-. *See* ROLAND-GOSSELIN, Robert.
Gosselmann, Carl August. Systematisk förteckning på de i Blekinge . . . fanerogamer. 1861. I. 356.
Gossin, E. *See* CALMELS, G. & GOSSIN, E.
Gossin, Louis. Traité spécial sur les Osiers. 1866. III. 347.
Gossip for the garden. III. 17.
Gott, B. Forest tree-planting. 1883. IV. 44.
Gottesgab st ate forest, Bohemia. 1900. IV. 373.
Gottfriedt, M. R. Merkwürdiger Blitzschlag. 1877. IV. 194.
— Ueberdeckte Wälder bei Riga. 1852. I. 358.
Gottgetreu, Rudolph. Die Hausschwammfrage. 1891. IV. 415.[1]
— Physische und chemische Beschaffenheit der Baumaterialien. 1869. IV. 408.
Gotthard, F. C. Garten-, Feld- und Waldraupen. 1804. III. 188.[2]
Gotthard, Johann Christian. Die Kultur des unächten . . . Akazienbaums. 1796. IV. 522.[1]
Gotthard, Karl. Zur Geschichte märkischer Stadtforsten. 1889. IV. 26.

Gottlieb, Alexius W. Die Sandebenen Ungarns. 1856. IV. 167.[1]
Gottlieb, Emil. Undersøgelse af nogle Vedsorters. 1882. I. 155.
Gottrau, E. de. Épicéa gigantesque à Charmey. 1864. II. 37.[1]
— Riesenfichte in Charmey. 1864. II. 37.[1]
Gottschalck, Jakob. Catalogus plantarum Horti academici Lugduni Batavorum. 1697. I. 50.
Gottschalck, Zacharias. Flora hortensis. 1703. III. 66.[1]
Gottschalk, F. On the volatile oil of Pinus Abies. 1844. IV. 459.[2]
Gottschall, Michael. Anatomisch-systematische Untersuchung des Blattes der Melastomaceen. 1900. II. 635.[1]
Gottsche, Karl Moritz. Bemerkungen sur Inaugural-Dissertation: De Macrozamia Preissii. 1845. II. 3.[1]
Gotz, Antoine. Description du Ginkgo biloba. 1812. II. 7.[2]
— Discours sur les causes du mouvement de la sève. 1802. I. 163.
— Explicacion del sistéma botánico. 1787. V. xiii.[1]
— Explication du système botanique du . . . Linné. 1787. I. 254,[2] V. xiii.[1]
— Flora monspeliaca. 1765. I. 405.
— Herborisations des environs de Montpellier. 1796. I. 406.
— Hortus regius monspeliensis. 1762. I. 56, 405.
— Illustrationes et observationes botanicae. 1773. I. 262.
— Traité de botanique et de matière médicale. 1804. I. 84.
— *See also* CUSSON, Pierre, GOUAN, Antoine & COMMERSON, Philibert.
Gouan, Léon. Sur la Bruyère cylindrique. 1859. III. 651.
— La Bruyère de Bergius. 1859. III. 650.[2]
— Sur la Bruyère laineuse. 1859. III. 651.[1]
— La Bruyère translucide rose. 1859. III. 651.[2]
— Clematis lanuginosa. 1857. III. 391.[1]
— Cotyledon orbiculata. 1857. · III. 650.[2]
— Erica abietina Linné. 1857. III. 650.[2]
— Erica baccans Linné. 1858. III. 650.[2]
— Erica cerinthoïdes. 1857. III. 651.[1]
— Erica seriphiifolia Salisbury. 1858. III. 651.[2]
— Erica ventricosa. 1858. III. 651.[2]
— Erica vestita Thunberg, variété alba. 1857. III. 651.[2]
— Eucalyptus coccifera. 1858. III. 634.[1]
— Les Freycineta. 1857. II. 56.[1]
— Furcroya gigantea Ventenat. 1857. III. 341.[2]
— Groseillier sanguin. 1857. III. 415.[2]
— Melocactus communis. 1857. III. 623.[1]
— Mussaenda macrophylla Wallich. 1857. III. 746.[1]
— Passiflora edulis Sims. 1857. III. 616.[1]
— Rondeletia longiflora Cham. 1858. III. 744.[1·]
Gouault, A. Indigofera alba. 1854. III. 479.[2]
— Lantana mutabilis, croceas et delicatissima. 1852. III. 696.
Goube, J. J. C. Traité de la physique végétale des bois. 1801. IV. 109.[1]
— Traité de la vie et de l'organisation des plantes. 1810. I. 148.
Goudot, Justin. Aulonemia, nouveau genre. 1846. II. 59.[1]
— Cespedesia gen. nov. 1844. II. 544.[1]
— Description d'un nouveau genre . . . Herrania. 1844. II. 535.[2]
— Notice sur une Rubiacée du genre Condaminea. 1844. III. 743.[2]
Gouet. Le Chêne de Banister. 1867. IV. 503.[2]
— Étude sur le Pin Laricio et le Pin maritime. 1870. IV. 465.[2]
— Des semis de Bouleau. 1863. III. 357.[1]
— *See also* GAIFFIER, de & GOUET.
Gouffé de Lacour. De la culture du Mûrier. 1813. III. 373.
— Mémoire sur les végétaux exotiques. 1813. III. 125.
— Tableau des pertes . . . par l'hiver de 1829–30. 1831. III. 47.
— & **Croze-Magnan**. Mémoire sur la culture du Prunier. 1814. III. 432.[2]
— & others. Examen d'un mémoire de M. Victor Gangadi de Corfou. 1813. II. 712.[2]
Gouffé de Troisulle, *chevalier*. Mémoire sur l'Olivier. 1823. III. 675.[1]
Gouget, Eduard. Les forêts de l'arrondissement d'Embrun. 1888. IV. 361.
— Notice géologique et forestière sur la montagne de la Serre. 1878. IV. 360.

Gough, Richard. An account of the Cedar of Libanus. 1788. III. 300.[1]

Gouillon, G. M. & **Gouirand,** G. Sur l'adhérence des bouilles cupriques. 1898. III. 582.

Gouirand, G. *See* GOUILLON, G. M. & GOUIRAND, G.; RAVAZ, L. & GOUIRAND, G.

Goujon. Des bois propres aux construction navales. 1803. IV. 424.[2]

Goujon, J. Acacia Lopbantha. 1872. III. 466.[2]
— Multiplication de l'Exocorda. 1873. III. 424.[1]

Gould, Charles Newton. Jack Oaks in Oklahoma. 1900. II. 135.[2]

Gould, Harris Perley. Notes on spraying and on the San José scale. 1898. III. 198.[1]
— Second report on the San José scale. 1898. III. 198.[1]

Goulin & Labeyrie. Dictionnaire des plantes usuelles. 1794. III. 51.

Goumain-Cornille, A. Épisodes d'un voyage en Savoie ... relatifs à la longévité de certains arbres. 1866. II. 51,[1] 255.[1]
— La Savoie, le Mont Cenis. *See* BOISDUVAL. 1866. I. 413.

Gourbeyre, A. IMBERT-. *See* IMBERT-GOURBEYRE, A.

Gourcy, Conrad, *comte* de. Journal du second voyage agricole en Angleterre. 1849. III. 123.[2]

Gourdon, Jean. Excursion dans la vallée de l'Ariège. 1874. I. 414.

Goureau, Claude Charles. Les insectes nuisibles aux arbres fruitiers. 1861. III. 189.
— Les insectes nuisibles aux arbustes. 1869. III. 190.
— Note pour servir à l'histoire des insectes ... du Genêt épineux. 1847. III. 489.[2]
— Note pour servir à l'histoire du Pissodes pini. 1842. IV. 475.

Gourgue, *comté* de. Consultation sur les causes de l'altération des arbres. 1869. IV. 192.[1]

Gouriet, Édouard. Essai sur la méthode naturelle. 1866. I. 252.

Gourlot, A. Hybrides ... du Lilas de Bretschneider. 1897. III. 680.[2]

Gourrier, A. H. Traité de la culture de l'Olivier. 1881. III. 675.[2]

Goursaud, A. Cubage et estimation des bois. 1866. IV. 214.
— Les landes et les dunes de Gascogne. 1878. IV. 163.

Gout, W. A. C. Bijzonderheden omtrent de voornaamste houtsoorten. 1896. IV. 400.[1]

Gouvernements en particuliere Koffie-cultuur. 1891. III. 730.

De Gouvernements-Kina-Onderneming. 1899. III. 717.[1]

De gouvernements Koffiecultuur. 1888. III. 730.

Gouvernements-Koffiecultuur; rapport. 1889. III. 730.

De gouvernéntskoffiecultuur in de residentie Bezoeki. 1873. III. 729.[1]

Gouvernements Koffiecultuur in de residentie Menado. 1893. III. 730.

De gouvernements-Koffiecultuur op Java. 1895. III. 730.

De gouvernements Koffiecultuur op Java. 1900. III. 732.[1]

Gouvernements-Koffiecultuur ter Sumatra's westkust. Advies. 1893. III. 730.

Gouvernements Koffiecultuur ter Sumatra's westkust. Rapport. 1893. III. 730.

De gouvernements-Koffij-cultuur op Java. 1867. III.729.[2]

Gouvernon, Victor. Notice sur le Sorbier hybride. 1871. II. 313.[1]
— Notice sur le Sorbier hybride. 1885. II. 313.[1]

Govaerts, E. Étude pharmaceutique sur les feuilles ... du Sureau noir. 1881. III. 752.[2]
— Sur les feuilles ... de Noyer. 1879. III. 356.[1]
— Des feuilles ... de Noyer. 1879. III. 356.[1]

Government botanical gardens at Saharanpur and Mussoorie. Report. 1879. I. 522.[1]

Government timber tests. 1891. IV. 415.[2]

The government timber tests. 1895. IV. 416.[1]

Goverts, W. J. Ueber Quercus-Arten mit offener Spaltung. 1894. II. 131.[2]
— Ueber die Verbänderung bei Alnus incana. 1893. II. 117.[1]

Govett, R. H. A bird-killing tree. 1884. II. 191.[2]

Govinda Menon, V. K. The life-history of the insects which attacked the Teak plantations. 1899. IV. 537.[1]

Gow, James E. Effects of a sleet storm on timber. 1899. III. 185.[1]
— Forest trees of Adair county, Iowa. 1899. I. 321, IV. 78.[1]

Gowan, J. *See* SEWARD, A. C. & GOWAN, J.

Gower, William Hugh. Soft-wooded Heaths. 1892. III. 650.[2]

Goyder, G. *See* RENNIE & GOYDER, G.

Gr. Vom gothaischen Thüringerwald. 1864. IV. 355.[2]

Gr. Die Nachtheile des Heide- und Beerkrauts. 1869. IV. 68.

Gr., M. Chineesche planten in verband met Nederlandsch Indië. *See* GRESHOFF, Maurits. 1894. III. 92.[1]

Graaf, G. S. de. Beheer en instandhouding der wildhoutbosschen op Java en Madoera. 1899. IV. 377.[1]
— Boschbouw en landbouw. 1900. IV. 377.[1]
— Moeten zooveel mogelijk alle Djatibosschen blijven bestaan. 1899. IV. 537.[2]

Graaf, N. H. de. Mededeeling over de teelt van Ailanthus. 1862. III. 506.[2]

Graaff, M. H. de. Landbouw, fabrijkswezen ... in Nederland. 1845. III. 122.[1]

Graafland, L. De Koffiecultuur in de Minahassa. 1899. III. 731.

Gräberg, Johann Mart. Fundamentum fructificationis. *See* LINNÉ, Carl von. 1762. I. 242.[2]

Grabner, Leopold. Anfangsgründe der Naturkunde für den Forstmann. 1838. IV. 57.
— Ergebnisse der zur Erforschung der besten Fällungszeit ... angestellten Versuche. 1851. IV. 384.[2]
— Die Forstwirthschaftslehre. 1841. IV. 110.[3]
— Grundzüge der Forstwirthschaftslehre. 1841. IV. 110.[3]
— Tafeln zur Bestimmung des kubischen Inhalts ... Bauholz-Stücke. 1840. IV. 222.

Grabowski, Heinrich. *See* GÜNTHER, C. C., GRABOWSKI, Heinrich & WIMMER, Friedrich; WIMMER, Friedrich & GRABOWSKI, Heinrich.

Grabowski, Heinrich Emanuel. Flora von Ober-Schlesien. 1843. I. 381.

Grace, de. Le jardinier portatif. 1784. III. 112.

Grad, Charles. Les forêts de l'Alsace. 1876. IV. 349.[2]
— Ueber den Grad der Durchforstung. 1888. IV. 174.

Gradenwitz, Salomon. De coffeae vi noxia et salubri. 1841. III. 741.[1]

Grady, M. C. Le bois vulcanisé. 1896. IV. 421.

Graebener, Leopold. Aesculus parviflora. 1899. III. 539.[1]
— Akebia quinata. 1892. III. 393.[1]
— Carludovica palmata. 1900. III. 332.[2]
— Garcinia Mangostana. 1899. III. 609.[2]
— Der Grossherzogliche botanische Hofgarten zu Karlsruhe. 1900. I. 49.
— Gymnocladus dioeca Baill. 1900. III. 478.[1]
— Die Magnolien. 1900. III. 399.[1]
— Planera Keaki Sieb. 1888. III. 366.[1]
— Pseudolarix Kaempferi Gord. 1896. III. 309.[1]
— Rhododendron virgatum. 1887. III. 662.[1]
— Rhus glabra. 1899. III. 527.[2]
— Rubus crataegifolius Bnge. 1897. III. 458.[1]
— Samen an Gingko. 1894. III. 287.[1]
— Samen an Gymnocladus dioicus. 1894. III. 478.[1]
— Eine Schlingpflanze mit essbaren Früchten. 1895, 1897. III. 595.[2]
— Spartium scoparium. 1887. III. 474.[2]
— Der Tulpenbaum. 1891. III. 398.[2]
— Die Vermehrung der Kakteen aus Samen. 1898. III. 620.[1]
— Verzeichniss der Bäume, Sträucher ... der Grossh. Gehölzbaumschule. 1888. III. 28.[1]
— Vorkommen von Adventivknospenbildung an einer Rosskastanie. 1891. II. 482.[2]
— Wenig verbreitete Winterblüher. 1900. III. 474.[1]

Graebner, Paul. Beitrag zur Kenntnis der ... Parthenocissus(Ampelopsis)-Arten. 1900. II. 501.[1]
— Ueber die Bildung natürlicher Vegetationsformationen. 1898. V. xx.[1]
— Zur Flora der Kreise Putzig. 1895. I. 389.
— Die Gattung Linnaea. 1900. II. 834,[1] 835.[2]
— Gliederung der westpreussischen Vegetationsformationen. 1898. I. 390.
— Studien über die norddeutsche Heide. 1895. I. 389, V. xx.[1]
— *See also* ASCHERSON, Paul & GRAEBNER, Paul.

Graef, August. Die Holzbearbeitungsmaschinen. 1877. IV. 422.[1]

Graef, Juan, ENRIQUE DE. *See* ENRIQUE DE GRAEF, Juan.

Gräffinn, Maria Sibijlla. *See* MERIAN, M. S.

Gräflich görtzische Bekanntmachung der schlitzischen Wald- und Forst-Gesetze. 1802. IV. 320.

Graeger. Darstellung von Citronsäure aus Preisselbeeren. 1873. III. 664.²
— Sur la gomme arabique. 1874. III. 463.²
Graells y de la Agüera, Mariano de la Paz. Indicatio plantarum novarum. 1854. I. 421.
— Las plantas y los cambios atmosféricos. 1894. IV. 543.²
— Prontuario filoxérico. 1879. III. 760.
— Ramilletes de plantas españolas. 1859. II. 359.²
Graenicher, Sigmund. The fertilization and insect visitors. 1900. I. 239.²
— The fertilization of Symphoricarpos and Lonicera. 1900. I. 239.²
Grätzel, Adolph. La créosote du goudron de Hêtre. 1882. IV. 500.¹
Graf, B. *See* MOELLER, L. & GRAF, B.
Graf, Bernhard. Zur chemischen Kenntnis des Dammarharzes. 1889. II. 25.²
Graf, Edmund. Waldverwüstung und Murbrüche. 1879. IV. 187.²
Graf, Ferdinand. Die Alpenpflanzen. 1879. I. 436.
— Alpine plants. 1879. I. 436.
Graf, Rainer. Ueber Spiraea decumbens Koch. 1854. II. 315.¹
Graf, Siegmund. De cortice peruviano. 1824. III. 721.
— Die Fieberrinden. 1824. III. 721.
— Versuch einer gedrängten Zusammenstellung der Vegetationsverhältnisse ... Krain. 1837. I. 440.
Grafenberg, Johann Georg SCHENCK VON. *See* SCHENCK VON GRAFENBERG, J. G.
Graff, Eberhard Gottlieb. Preussens Flora. 1809. I. 376.
Graff, *Mme.* Maria Sibilla (Merian). *See* MERIAN, M. S.
Graffen, Fr. Georg von. Der praktische Gärtner. 1822. III. 104.
Graffenauer, Jean Philippe. Traité sur le camphre. 1803. III. 404.²
Graft hybrids. 1899. I. 246.²
Grafting. 1892. III. 163.¹
Grafting. 1900. I. 208.²
Grafting Camellias. 1892. III. 600.¹
Grafting Rhododendrons. 1884. III. 656.
Grafting the Grapevine on the l'Eglantier. 1883. III. 165.
Graham, John. Catalogue of plants collected at Bombay. 1837. I. 472.
— A catalogue of the plants growing in Bombay. 1839. I. 472.
Graham, M. J. Cherries, three best for market. 1899. III. 432.¹
Graham, Maria (*later* Maria CALLCOTT). Journal of a residence in Chile. 1824. III. 65.² ·
— A Scripture herbal. 1842. *See* CALLCOTT, Maria. I. 513.
Graham, Robert. On the botanical origin of gamboge. 1845. III. 609.¹
— Bouvardie brillante; Bouvardia splendens. 1840. II. 10.¹
— Characters of genera, extracted from the British flora. 1830. I. 397.
— List (description) of rare plants which have flowered in the Royal botanic garden, Edinburgh. 1824. I. 53.
— Notes regarding some of the plants observed ... in excursions from Edinburgh. 1836. I. 398.
— Notice of botanical excursions into the highlands of Scotland. 1835. I. 496.
— Notice of plants observed in an excursion. 1830. I. 397.
— Remarks on Dr. Wight's paper regarding ... gamboge. 1838. III. 555.¹
— Remarks on the Gamboge Tree of Ceylon. 1836. II. 555.²
— *See also* CHRISTISON, Robert & GRAHAM, Robert.
Graham, T. H. B. The Orange-tree. 1887. III. 403.¹
Graham, Thomas, Stenhouse, John & Campbell, Dugald. Sur le café et ses succédanés. 1857. III. 739.
Grahe, Ferdinand. Ueber die Chinarinden. 1857. III. 721.
Grahl, Johann Friedrich. Medicamenta quaedam Rossorum domestica. 1790. III. 270.¹
Grahn, Georg. Zusammenstellung der im Gebiete des ehemaligen Königreichs Hannover geltenden Bestimmungen über das Forststrafwesen. 1867. IV. 324.
Graichen, H. L. Ontwerp tot winning van Zaadkoffie. 1900. III. 733.¹
Graine d'Avignon. 1775. III. 542.¹
La graine des Légumineuses. *See* CHALON, Jean. 1875. II. 320.²
Graine du Pin sylvestre. 1894. IV. 482.¹

Graines de Pin sylvestre. 1898. IV. 474.
Sur des graines envoyées du Brésil. 1819. II. 579.¹
Grainville. Note sur un Châtaignier remarquable. 1848. II. 124.²
Gram, Hans. Praktisk Vejledning i Frugtavl. 1898. III. 134.¹
Gram, Jörgen Pedersen. Om Beregning af en Bevoxnings Masse. 1883. IV. 218.
— Om Konstruktion af Normal-Tilvæxtoversigter. 1879. IV. 217.
Gramberg, J. S. G. De Oliepalm van Guinea. 1864. III. 325.¹
— Een tweetal monsters natuurproducten. 1867. III. 611.
Grams. Das Schneiden und Pflanzen der Weidenstecklinge. 1900. IV. 487.²
Granberg. Betula verrucosa med 3–5-klufna blad. 1884. II. 120.¹
Grand. Le royaume de Luang-Prabang. 1899. III. 276.²
Grand Marais, Ambroise VIAUD-. *See* VIAUD-GRAND-MARAIS, Ambroise.
Le Grand Bailli des bois du Hainault. 1897. IV. 27.¹
A grand Plane tree ... at Mottisfont Abbey. 1898. II. 255.²
Grandclément. Sur quelques moyens employés pour combattre les gelées blanches. 1869. III. 183.¹
Grande, José Maria. Memoria sobre a molestia das Vinhas. 1855. III. 576.
Grande microtomo. 1887. IV. 37.²
Grande sega a nastro per legnami duri e teneri. 1886. IV. 393.
Grandeau, Henry. Recherches chimiques sur le Gui. 1878. II. 179.¹
— & Bouton, A. Étude chimique du Gui. 1877. II. 179.⁴
Grandeau, Louis Nicolas. L'azote et la végétation forestière. 1897. IV. 543.²
— Le Cactus inerme. 1898. III. 624.¹
— Chimie et physiologie appliquées. 1878. · IV. 63.²
— Chimie et physiologie appliquées. 1878. IV. 63.¹
— Contribution à l'étude du Caféier. 1898. III. 741.
— L'emploi des jeunes branches ... comme fourrages. 1896. IV. 558.¹
— La forêt et la disette de fourrage. 1893. III. 223.²
— La forêt et la disette des fourrages. 1895. III. 223.²
— De l'influence de l'électricité atmosphérique sur la fructification. 1878. I. 231.¹
— De l'influence de l'électricité atmosphérique sur la nutrition. 1878, 1879. I. 231.¹
— De l'influence de l'électricité atmosphérique sur la végétation. 1878. I. 231.¹
— Le Kentia et sa nourriture. 1890. III. 326.¹
— Note sur les pépinières forestières. 1878. IV. 150.
— Sur la présence du rubidium. 1862. I. 153.
— Las ramillas de los árboles como alimento del ganado. 1892. IV. 438.²
— Recherches expérimentales sur le rôle des matières organiques du sol. 1878. I. 228.²
— Recherches sur le rôle des matières organiques du sol. 1872. I. 159.
— *See also* FLICHE, Paul & GRANDEAU, Louis.
— & Henry, Edmond. Le sol des landes et la végétation du Pin maritime. 1878. II. 44.² IV. 493.¹
Grandgagnage, Charles. Vocabulaire des noms wallons d'animaux, des plantes. 1857. I. 73.²
Grandgeorge. Tarif C. G. no. 1 pour les bois en grumes. n. d. IV. 219.
Delle grandi alluvioni dell' ultimo quadrimestre 1882. 1883. IV. 186.²
Grandidier, Alfred. Du sol et du climat de l'île de Madagascar. 1894. III. 131.²
Una grandiosa ed audace ruberia di alberi nelle foreste americane. 1882. IV. 281.²
Grandjean, (*conservateur des forêts*). Les bostriches. 1878. IV. 204, 549.¹
— Comice agricole de l'arrondissement de · Remiremont. 1868. IV. 360.
Grandjean, C. La dune littorale. 1887. IV. 163.
— Les landes et les dunes de Gascogne. 1896. IV. 362.
Grand-Jean, MONEUZE-. *See* MONEUZE-GRAND-JEAN.
Grandjean, P. La méthode du contrôle de M. Gurnaud. 1885. IV. 244.
Grandmaison, Aubin Louis MILLIN DE. *See* MILLIN DE GRANDMAISON, A. L.

Grandmont, A. *See* VAVASSEUR, P., COTTEREAU, P. L. & GILLET DE GRANDMONT, A.

Grandpré, Clément DARUTY DE. *See* DARUTY DE GRANDPRÉ, Clément.

Grandprey, POULLAIN-. *See* POULLAIN-GRANDPREY.

Grandval, Alexandre & Lajoux, Henri. Dosage de la caféine. 1893. I. 177.

—— Dosage des alcaloïdes. 1893. I. 177.

Grandvoinnet, J. Les Cépages américains. 1900. III. 557.[2]

Grandy, R. E. The timber importer's, timber merchant's and builder's standard guide. 1865. IV. 225.

Granel, Maurice. Note sur l'origine des suçoirs de quelques . . parasites. 1887. II. 169.[4]

— Observations sur les suçoirs de quelques Rhinanthées. 1889. II. 169.[1]

Graner, Friedrich. Der anatomische Bau des Holzes. 1894. *I. 128,*[1] IV. 62.[1]

— Der Boden des deutschen Waldes. 1899. IV. 70.

— Cenni sulla struttura dei legnami. 1894. IV. 62.[2]

— Ueber einige Fragen der vegetabilischen Ernährungslehre. 1895. I. 160.

— Einiges über die Zwangs-Ablösung der -Wald-Servituten. 1873. IV. 333.

— Die Forstbetriebseinrichtung. 1889. IV. 241.

— Forstgesetzgebung und Forstverwaltung. 1892. IV. 287, *314.*[1]

— Die forstliche Unterrichtsfrage. 1892. IV. 29.

— Die forstpolitischen Ziele der Gegenwart. 1887. IV. 270.

— Zur Frage der Forstdiensteseinrichtung mit besonderer Beziehung auf Württemberg. 1894. IV. 291.[2]

— Zur Frage der Organisation des Forstdienstes in Württemberg. 1890. IV. 291.[1]

— Zur Frage nach der Einheit des Betriebsplanes. 1897. IV. 246.

— Die geographische Verbreitung der Holzarten. 1894. I. 301.

— Die geographische Verbreitung der Laub- und Nadelhölzer. 1897. I. 301.

— Der geologische Bau und die Bewaldung des deutschen Landes. 1900. I. 372, *IV. 84.*[1]

— Eine Gesetzesvorlage über die Bewirthschaftung der Gemeinde . . . Waldungen in Württemberg. 1874. IV. 286.[2]

— Eine neue Verordnung über die Forstdienstprüfungen in Württemberg. 1896. IV. 291.[2]

— Noch ein Wort in der Forsteinrichtungsfrage. 1898. IV. 246.

— Die Produktionskosten und die Grundrente. 1872. IV. 255.

— Der Schwarzwald. 1897. IV. 356.[1]

— La struttura anatomica dei legnami. 1894. IV. 62.[2]

— Zuwachs und Altersklassenfaktor in der Ertragsregelung. 1900. IV. 238.

Grange. Tarif C. G. No. 6 spécial pour le cubage des bois de mines. n. d. IV. 219.

Granier. Concours forestier local . . . de Montbéliard. 1899. IV. 546.[2]

Granier, G. La compagnie des forges d'Audincourt. 1882. IV. 395.

— Le façonnage des bois. 1894. IV. 287.[2]

Granit, A. W. Om förekomsten af Barrträd i Syd-Varanger. 1900. II. 15.[1]

— Förekomsten af Betula verrucosa Ehrh. i Pasvigdalen. 1900. II. 120.[1]

— Zoologiska och botaniska smånotiser från Sodankylä. 1898. II. 98.[1]

Granite monthly. III. 4.

Granlund, J. F. Tietoja Suomen maan puiden kasvattamiseesta ja hoidosta. 1891. IV. 104.[1]

Granlund, Wilhelmus. Florae fennicae, pars prior. *See* KALM, Pehr. 1765. I. 259.

Grant, A. N. Templetonia egena. 1898. III. 489.[1]

Grant, Alexander McDonald. The formation of plantations. 1884. IV. 142.

— On the rearing . . . of hardwood plantations. 1887. IV. 138.[1]

Grant, Arthur H. Wellingtonias. 1878. III. 310.[1]

Grant, C. W. Descriptive catalogue of Vines. [c]1859. III. 546.

— Grape-vines. 1864. III. 550.

— Illustrated catalogue of Vines. 1859. III. 546.

Le grant herbier en francoys. *See* ARBOLAYRE. 1485. I. 276, V. XIV.[2]

Grantzow, C. Flora von Uckermark. 1880. I. 388.

Granville, Augustus Bozzi. An account of the . . . properties of the Malambo bark. 1816. III. 516.[2]

The grape culturist. III. 4.

Gras. Recherches sur les causes géologiques de l'action dévastatrice des torrents des Alpes. 1847. IV. 185.[2]

Gras, Albin. Statistique botanique . . . de l'Isère. 1844. I. 410.

Gras, Auguste. Note sur l'histoire du genre Bassia. 1864. II. 187,[2] *698.*[1]

— Sur l'orthographe de quelques noms de plantes. 1860. II. 195.[1]

Gras, Camille. *See* DALMON, Jules & GRAS, Camille.

Graser. Die dänische Buchenbestandspflege. 1899. IV. 496.

Grasmann, Eustach. Beitrag zur Lehre vom Lichtungszuwachs. 1890. IV. *176,*[1] *234.*

— Beobachtungen in Fichtenpflanzbeständen. 1886. IV. 454, *466.*

— Forstliche Excursion in die Kisogwaldungen. 1889. IV. 376.[1]

— Der Kampferbaum. 1893. III. 405.[1]

Ueber **Grasnutzung** im Walde. 1880. IV. 438.[1]

Grass, L. S. De Ceraso pleniflora prolifera. 1676. II. 271.[2]

— De Rosa prolifera. 1676. II. 289.[1]

The **Grass** tree. 1895. III. 339.[1]

Grasser, Georg. Der Wald und seine Bedeutung. 1888. IV. 44.

Grasset & Jeannel. De l'action physiologique de la cocaïne. 1885. III. 493.[1]

Grasset, Ch. de. *See* MILLARDET, Alexis & GRASSET, Ch. de.

Grasset, Eugène de. Acclimatation du Lagerstroemia indica. 1831. III. 629.[2]

Grassmann, Gottfried Ludlof. Ueber die Anlegung der Hecken. 1793. III. 212.[2]

Grassmann, Hermann. Deutsche Pflanzennamen. 1870. I. 73.[2]

Grassmann, Robert. Das Pflanzenleben. 1882. I. 148.

Grateloup, Jean Pierre Sylvestre de. Description d'une nouvelle espèce de Daphné. 1827. II. 601.[2]

— Florula littoralis aquitanica. 1826. I. 408.

Gratiolet, Pierre. *See* CLOËZ, S. & GRATIOLET, Pierre.

Graubünden. 1873. II. 24.[1]

Graubünden — Naturforschende Gesellschaft. *See* NATURFORSCHENDE . . . I. 26.

Graubünden. Waldbrand in Bevers. 1894. IV. 183.[2]

Graulhié. Observations sur l'Azalea liliiflora. 1836. III. 661.[1]

Graumüller, Johann Christian Friedrich. Characteristik der um Jena wildwachsenden Pflanzenarten. 1803. I. 375.

— Diagnose der bekanntesten . . . Pflanzengattungen. 1811. I. 349, *581,*[2] V. XVIII.[1]

— Flora jenensis. 1824. I. 377.

— Flora pharmaceutica jenensis. 1815. III. 72.

— Handbuch der pharmaceutisch-medicinischen Botanik. 1813. III. 55.

— Systematisches Verzeichniss wilder Pflanzen . . . Jena. 1803. I. 375.

— Tabellarische Uebersicht des alten Linnéischen Pflanzensystems. 1811. I. 259.

Gravander, Pehr Olaf. Meditationes circa alimenta Sueciae succedanea. 1805. III. 270.[1]

Gravenhorst, Johannes Andreas Christoph. De Cinchonae corticibus. 1791. III. 720.

Gravereaux, Jules. Roseraie de l'Hay. 1899. V. xxix.[1]

— Roseraie de l'Hay. Catalogue. 1900. III. 451.[1]

Graves, A. J. Nursery management. 1878. III. 154.[1]

Graves, George. Hortus medicus. 1834. III. 57.

— Naturalist's pocket book. 1817. I. 35.

Graves, Henry Solon. Black Hills forest reserve. 1899. IV. 341.[1]

— Damage to timber by acid fumes. 1900. IV. 193.[1]

— The Douglas Spruce of Northern Oregon. 1899. II. 49.[1]

— Practical forestry in the Adirondacks. 1899. IV. 339.

— The practice of forestry by private owners. 1900. IV. 308.[1]

— Working plan for a wood lot. 1899. IV. 247.[1]

— *See also* PINCHOT, Gifford & GRAVES, H. S.

Graves, J. A. An ancient Ash. 1874. II. 708.[1]

Graves, Louis. Catalogue des plantes . . . de l'Oise. 1857. I. 411.

Graves, Robert. A pocket conspectus of the new London and Edinburgh pharmacopœias. 1796. III. 253.

Gravet, Frédéric. *See* CRÉPIN, François, GRAVET, Frédéric & DELOGNE, C. H.

Gravier. Sambucus racemosa. 1889. III. 752.[2]

Gravier, Leon Armand. La culture et la taille des arbres fruitiers. 1900.. III. 145.[1]

Gravis, Auguste. Les anomalies florales du Poirier. 1880. I. 116.[2]

— Les fascies souterraines des Spirées. 1881. II. 314.[1]

— Note sur une fascie des tiges . . . du Spiraea. 1880. II. 315.[2]

— Notice sur quelques faits tératologiques. 1877. II. 280.[1]

Gravure sur bois. 1894. IV. 428.[1]

Gray, Asa. Account of the botanical specimens. (*In* PERRY.) 1856. I. 462.

— Additional note on the genus. Rhytidandra. 1862. II. 615.[1]

— On the affinities of the genus Vavaea. 1854. II. 423,[1] *615.[1]*

— Age of a large California coniferous tree. 1854. II. 50.[2]

— Analogy between the flora of Japan and that of the United States. 1846. I. 462.

— The botanical text-book. 1842. I. 88.

— Botany of the Black Hills of Dakota. 1880. I. 324.

— Catalogue of plants collected east of the Rocky Mountains. 1860. I. 323.

— On the characteristics of the North American flora. 1884. I. 308.

— Characters of new Compositae. 1884. II. 848.[2]

— Characters of new genera and species of plants. 1873. I. 307.

— Characters of new or obscure species of plants . . . South Pacific exploring expedition. 1861. I. 329.

— Characters of new plants of California. 1867. I. 323.

— Characters of some . . . Australian Compositae. .1852. II. 858.[2]

— Characters of some Compositae. 1861. II. 849,[1] *850.[1]*

— Characters of some new . . . Compositae. 1844, 1845. II. 852,[1] 858.[1]

— Characters of some new . . . plants, mostly from Polynesia. 1853. I. 509.[1]

— Characters of some new plants of California. . 1865. I. 323.

— Characters of some new species of Compositae. 1880. II. 849.[1]

— Characters of various new species. 1875. I. 307.

— Chloris boreali-americana. 1846. I. 307.

— On the composition of the plant by phytons. 1850. I. 101.[2]

— Contributions to American botany. 1887. I. 308.

— Contributions to the botany of North America. 1878. I. 307, II. 798.[2]

— A cursory examination of a collection of dried plants made . . . around Wartenberg . . . Mexico. 1861. I. 331.

— Darwiniana. 1876. I. 243.[1]

— Description de. cinq nouveaux genres de plantes de la Polynésie. 1853. I. 509.[1]

— Determination of a collection of plants made in Oregon. 1872. I. 323.

— On the development of the seed-coats of Magnoliaceae. 1856. II. 211.[1]

— Diagnosis of the species of Sandal-wood. 1859. II. 169.[1]

— Diagnostic characters of new species , . . collected in Japan. 1860. V. XXIII.[2]

— Dimorphism of Forsythia. 1873. II. 706.[2]

— Distribution of vegetable species. 1860. I. 300.

— Do varieties wear out? 1875. I. 248.[2]

— Dr. Siebold. Flora japonica. 1840. I. 462.

— Elements of botany. 1836. I. 87.

— Engelmann; notes on the genus Yucca. 1873. II. 86.[2]

— Enumeration of a collection of dried plants made . . . in Lower California. 1861. I. 331.

— Enumeration of the species of plants collected by Dr. C. C. Parry. 1864. I. 323.

— Extract from the concluding part of a Memoir on the botany of Japan. 1860. V. XXIII.[2]

— First lessons in botany. 1857. I. 90.

— Forest geography and archaeology.' 1878. I. 307.

— Généalogie des Wellingtonia. 1872. II. 49.[2]

— Genealogy of the Wellingtonias. 1872. II. 49.[2]

— Genera florae Americae boreali-orientalis illustrata. 1849. I. 307.

— The genera of the plants of the United States. 1849. I. 307, V. XVI.[2]

— The genus Asimina. 1886. II. 216.[2]

— On the genus Garberia. 1880. II. 857.[2]

— Géographie et archéologie forestières de l'Amérique du Nord. 1878. I. 307.

— How plants grow. 1858. I. 90.

— How trees grow tall. 1889. . I. 187.

— Introduction to structural and systematic botany. 1842. I. 88.

— Om de Kaliforniske Kaempetræers Fortid. 1872. II. 49.[2]

— Lessons in botany. 1857. I. 90.

— Linnaea borealis. 1882. II. 835.[2]

— List of the dried plants . . . from Chile. 1855. V. XVIII.[2]

— Lombardy Poplars for lightning-rods. 1878. III. 346.[2]

— The longevity of trees. 1844. I. 193.[1]

— Lonicera grata. 1883. II. 836.[2]

— A manual of the botany of the northern United States. 1848. I. 314.

— Miscellanea. 1878. I. 307.

— Miscellaneous botanical contributions. 1876. I. 324.

— The most arctic timber. 1879. II. 105.[1]

— Neviusia a new genus of Rosaceae. 1857. II. 268.[2]

— A new Fijian Hedyosaria. 1866. II. 222.[1]

— New genera of Arizona, California. 1885. I. 325.

— A new genus of Anonaceae. Richella. 1852. II. 218.[1]

— A new genus of the order Rosaceae. . 1858. II. 268.[2]

— New or little known Polynesian Thymeleae. 1865. II. 600.[1]

— Note on Tetratheca. 1852. II. 429.[1]

— Note on the affinities of the genus Vavaea. 1854. II. 423, *615.[1]*

— Note on the genus Buckleya. 1854. II. 168.[1]

— Notes of a botanical excursion to the mountains of North Carolina. 1842. I. 318.

— Notes on Compositae. 1873. II. 848.[2]

— Notes on Labiatae. 1872. II. 766,[1] *766.[2]*

— Notes on some Compositae. 1881. II. 848.[2]

— Notes on tree growth. 1875. I. 190.[1]

— Notes upon a portion of Dr. Seemann's recent collection . . . in the Feejee Islands. 1861. I. 510.[1]

— Notes upon some Polynesian plants of . . . Loganiaceae. 1859. II. 716.[2]

— Notes upon some Rubiaceae. 1858. II. 808.[1]

— Notes upon the " Description of new plants from Texas by S. B. Buckley." 1863. I. 323.

— Notice of a new genus of . . . Santalaceae. 1846. II. 168.[1]

— Notices of new native plants. 1860. III. 63.[1]

— Novitiae arizonicae. 1882. I. 324.

— Observations sur les rapports qui existent entre la flore du Japon . . . de l'Amérique et d'autres parties de la zone tempérée boreale. 1860. I. 299, V. XXIII.

— Our wild Gooseberries. 1876. II. 243.[2]

— A pilgrimage to Torreya. 1875. II. 12.[1]

— Plantae Fendlerianae novimexicanae. 1849. I. 322.

— Plantae Lindheimerianae. 1850. I. 322.

— Plantae novae Thurberianae. 1854. I. 322.

— Plantae vitienses Seemannianae. 1862. I. 510.[1]

— Plantae Wrightianae texano-neo-mexicanae. · 1852. I. 322,

— Plates . . . to accompany a report on the forest trees of North America. 1891. I. 305.

— The relation of insects to flowers. 1882. I. 238.

— Remarks concerning the flora of North America. .1883. I. 308.

— Remarks on the botany of Japan. 1860. I. 462, V. XXIII.[2]

— Review of the North American . . . Clematis. 1881. II. 195.[2]

— Revision of some polypetalous genera . . . of North America. 1887. I. 308.

— A revision of the genus Forestiera. 1860. · II. 706.[1]

— Revision of the genus Symphoricarpus. · 1875. II. 841.[2]

— Rhododendron (Azalea) Vaseyi. 1883. II. 684.[1]

— School and field book of botany. 1869. I. 256.

— Scientific papers. 1889. I. 34.

— Sequoia and its history. 1872. II. 49.[2]

— On the Sequoias. 1872. II. 49.[2]

— Sertum chihuahuanse. 1886. I. 332.

— A short exposition of the structure of the ovule . . . of Magnolia. 1858. II. 211.[1] .

— Siebold's Flora of Japan. 1840, 1846. I. 462.

— On some plants of . . . Compositae. 1850. II. 850.[1]

— Some remarkable specimens of Kalmia latifolia. 1878. II. 672.[2]

— Species, considered as to variation. 1863. I. 244.[1]

— Synopsis of the genus Pentstemon. 1862. II. 781.[2]

— Synopsis of the species of Hosackia. 1864. II. 363.[2]

— Synoptical flora of North America. 1878. I. 307.

— Tennessee plants. 1880. II. 706.[1]

— Trees and shrubs of Massachusetts. 1875. I. 312.

— Trees of North Carolina. 1860. I. 317,[1] *IV. 77.[2]*

Gray, Asa (*continued*).
— Two new genera of Acanthaceae. 1878. II. 798.²
— Two new genera of Violaceae. 1852. II. 567,¹ 567.²
— United States exploring expedition . . . Botany Phanero-
gamia. 1854. I. 303.
— Use of plants in the economy of nature. 1856. I. 217.
— Vaccinium macrocarpon var. intermedium. 1879. II.
686.¹
— Veatchia nov. gen. Anacardiacearum. 1884. II. 461.²
— On the vegetation of New Mexico. 1852. I. 322.
— On Welwitschia. 1863. II. 55.²
— For what purpose were plants created? 1856. I. 217.
— Wild American Gooseberries. 1876. II. 243.²
— *See also* COOPER, J. G. & GRAY, Asa; ENGELMANN, George
& GRAY, Asa; TORREY, John & GRAY, Asa; TRELEASE,
William & GRAY, Asa.
— & Hooker, J. D. Die Vegetation des Rocky Mountain-
Gebietes. 1882. I. 324.
— — The vegetation of the Rocky Mountain region. 1882.
I. 324.
— & others. Botany [of the Colorado exploring expedition].
1860. I. 323.
Gray, Christopher. A catalogue of trees, shrubs, plants and
flowers. 1755. I. 52.
Gray, G. W. The Redwood. 1883. IV. 484.¹
Gray, J. B. Evergreen trees. 1854. III. 291.
Gray, J. E. & S. F. A natural arrangement of British plants.
1821. I. 397.
Gray, John. An account of the Peruvian or Jesuits bark.
1741. III. 719.
Gray, John C. Essay on forest trees. 1856. IV. 397.
— Essay on orchards reported to the Massachusetts board of
agriculture. 1853. III. 133.
Gray, Moses P. Sugar from the Butternut tree. 1815. III.
354.¹
Gray, Roderick. Account of the mode of planting. 1837.
III. 165.
Gray, Samuel Frederick. A supplement to the pharmaco-
poeias. 1818. III. 254.
Gray, Thomas. On the variation of strength of timber. 1894.
IV. 410.
Gray, William. The botany of the Bombay Presidency.
1886. I. 475.¹
— *See also* POTTS, T. H. & GRAY, William.
Gray, William & Dochard. Travels in western Africa. *See*
HOOKER, *Sir* W. J. 1825. I. 490.
— Voyage dans l'Afrique occidentale. *See* HOOKER, *Sir*
W. J. 1825. I. 490.
Gray, William, (*jr.*). Pelargoniums. 1875. III. 491.²
Gray herbarium of Harvard university. Contributions. I. 5.
Graz — Botanisches Institut. *See* BOTANISCHES . . . I. 27.
Gréa, P. Résultats de la chute de neige du 30 octobre. 1897.
IV. 548.¹
Gréard, Louis. Mémoires concernant le droit de tiers et
danger sur les bois de la province de Normandie. 1737.
IV. 334.¹
The great Araucaria at Dropmore. 1876. III. 299.¹
The great Black Poplar at Dijon. 1884. II. 98.¹
Great Britain — Board of agriculture. Journal. III. 17.
Great Britain — Department of science and art. Calendar
of state papers. Colonial series. III. 17.
Great Britain — Foreign office. Diplomatic and consular
reports. III. 17.
Great Britain — Imperial institute. *See* IMPERIAL . . . III.
17.
Great Britain — Philosophical society. *See* VICTORIA IN-
STITUTE. I. 20.
Great Britain — Royal Asiatic society. *See* ROYAL . . . I. 19.
Great Britain — Royal institution. *See* ROYAL . . . III. 18.
The great Dragon tree. 1872. II. 82.²
The Great Elm of Hampstead. 1895. II. 145.¹
Great frost of 1895 [at Kew]. 1896. III. 47.
The great improvement of commons that are enclosed. 1732.
IV. 120.
The Great Madroña of San Rafael. 1892. II. 660.¹
The Great Oak at Windsor. 1898. II. 139.²
Great snow-fall amongst Olives and Palms. 1871. III. 184.²
The great Wych Elm at Moor Court. 1876. II. 145.¹
The greate herball. *See* ARBOLAYRE. 1485. I. 276.
Gréau. Note sur une variété de Noyer. 1832. III. 355.
— Notice sur le Noyer. 1832. III. 355.
Grebe, Carl Friedrich Augustus. Die Aufforstung von Oed-
ländereien. 1895. IV. 159.
— Aufforstung von Oedländereien. 1896. IV. 159.

— Die Beaufsichtigung der Privatwaldungen von Seiten des
Staates. 1845. IV. 285.²
— Die Betriebs- und Ertragsregulirung der Forsten. 1867.
IV. 240.
— Buchenformzahlen auf Basalt. 1891. IV. 498.
— Der Buchen-Hochwaldbetrieb. 1856. IV. 494.
— De conditionibus ad arborum . . . vitam necessariis. 1841.
I. 147.
— Ueber die Einwirkung der Dürre des Sommers 1868.
1869. IV. 192.¹
— Ergebnisse einer im Herbst 1841 unternommenen forst-
lichen Reise. 1842. IV. 342.¹
— Die Erziehung von Tannen-Pflänzlingen. 1873. IV.
444.²
— Ueber die Erziehung von Weiden. 1843. IV. 487.¹
— Eine Excursion in die Lehrforste der Eisenacher Forst-
schule. 1870. IV. 355.²
— Gebirgskunde, Bodenkunde. 1853. IV. 67.¹
— Die Grossh. sächs. Forstlehranstalt zu Eisenach. 1880.
IV. 32.
— Der Holzanbau auf öden Kalkflächen. 1875. IV. 158.
— Die Kiefer auf . . . Tuchler Haide. 1885. IV. 473.
— Die Lehrforste der Eisenacher Forstschule. 1858. IV.
32.
— Die neuere Harznutzung am Thüringerwalde. 1865. IV.
436.²
— Die Ueberführung des Mittelwaldes in Hochwald. 1872.
IV. 129.
— Untersuchungen über den Lichtungszuwachs im Buchen-
hochwalde. 1887. IV. 498.
— Die Verheerungen der vorjährigen Decemberstürme. 1869.
IV. 189.¹
— Der Waldschutz und die Waldpflege. *See* KÖNIG, Gottlob.
1849. IV. 106.
Grebel. Ueber die Saamen des Evonymus latifolius. 1820.
II. 468.²
Grebner, W. von. *See* Гребнеръ, В. фонъ.
Grebnitzki, A. S. Ueber die jährliche Periode der Stärke-
speicherung. 1884. I. 159, 179,³ 526.²
— *See also* Гребницкiй, A. C.
Grebnitzky, A. *See* GREBNITZKI, A. S.
Grecescu, Demetriu. Catalogul plantelar cultivate in
Gradina botanica din Bucaresci. 1876. I. 66.²
— Conspectul florei românei. 1898. I. 451.
— Plantele indigene din Românica. 1899. V. XXIII.¹
— Plantes de la Macédonie . . . de Monastir. 1899. I. 451.
Grech Delicata, Joanne Carolo. Plantae Melitae lectae.
1849. I. 452.
Greef, H. de. *See* BLEEKER, S. & GREEF, H. de.
Greely, Adolphus Washington. Rubber forests of Nicaragua
and Sierra Leone. 1897. III. 229.
Green, Edward Ernest. Insect pests attacking . . . timber.
1900. IV. 210.²
— Scale insects. 1899. III. 188.¹
— Some caterpillar pests of the Tea plant. 1900. III. 604.²
— Tea-mites. 1900. III. 604.²
— *See also* WILLIS, J. C. & GREEN, E. E.
Green, Frances H. & Congdon, J. W. Analytical class-book
of botany. 1859. I. 90.
Green, G. F. The production of wood-pulp. 1885. IV.
430.
Green, J. Timber suitable for building purposes. 1866.
IV. 423.¹
Green, Jacob. Catalogue of plants indigenous to . . . New
York. 1814. V. XVII.¹
Green, Joseph Reynolds. Action de la lumière sur la diastase.
1897. I. 178.
— On the action of light on diastase. 1897. I. 178.
— Les ferments solubles des végétaux. 1893. I. 177.
— On the germination . . . of the Castor-oil plant. 1891.
II. 451.¹
— On the germination of the pollen-grain. 1894. I. 201.³
— A manual of botany. 1895. I. 92.
— Observations on vegetable proteids. 1885. I. 176.
— On the organs of secretion in the Hypericaceae. 1884·
II. 553.¹
— Researches on the germination of the pollen grain. 1894.
I. 201.³
— The reserve materials of plants. 1894. I. 179.³
— On vegetable ferments. 1893. I. 177.
Green, Samuel Bowdlear. Forestry in Minnesota. 1898.
I. 321, IV. 541.¹
— Ornamental and timber trees . . . in Minnesota. 1892.
III. 63.²

— Russian Willows and Poplars. 1889. III. 344,[1] *349*.
— Russian Willows and Poplars from hard wood cuttings. 1889. III. 344,[1] *349*.
— & Ayres, H. B. Rate of increase on the cutover timber lands of Minnesota. 1896. IV. 234, *540*.
Green, Thomas. The universal herbal. 1820. III. 51.
The Greendale Oak and Welbeck Abbey. 1890. II. 139.[1]
Greene, Edward Lee. The American species of Rhamnus. 1896. II. 497.[1]
— Are Plums and Cherries of one genus? 1891. II. 270.[2]
— Bibliographical notes on American trees. 1897. II. 22,[1] *54*.[1]
— Bibliographical notes on well-known plants. 1887. I. 254.[1]
— The botany of the Cedros Islands. 1887. I. 333.
— California woods in autumn. 1888. III. 60.
— On certain Spiraeaceaè. 1889. II. 314.[1]
— A decade of new Pomaceae. 1899. II. 257,[2] *311*.[2] ·
— Distribution of Rhamnus in America. 1896. II. 497.[1]
— Eclogae botanicae. 1893. I. 308.
— Emendation of the genus Fendlera. 1881. II. 240.[1]
— Flora franciscana. 1891. I. 326.
— The fruit of Garrya. 1889. II. 110.[2]
— The genus Kunzia. 1889. II. 278.[1]
— Historical notes on some Californian trees. 1894. I. 295.[2]
— Manual of the botany of . . . San Francisco Bay. 1894. I. 326.
— Miscellaneous species, new or rare. 1887. I. 325.
— Native shrubs of California. 1889. I. 320.
— New California Compositae. 1882. II. 867.[2]
— New choripetalous exogens. 1899. II. 257.[2]
— New Compositae from New Mexico. 1898. II. 867.[1]
— A new genus of Asteroid Compositae. 1887. II. 858.[1]
— New or noteworthy species. 1887. I. 325.
— New plants of New Mexico and Arizona. 1881. II. 782,[1] 853.[2]
— New plants of the Pacific coast. 1886. II. 185.[2]
— New species, mainly Californian. 1887. I. 325.
— New species of Mexican plants. 1881. II. 245.[2]
— New species of plants from New Mexico. 1881. II. 246.[1]
— New western plants. 1882. II. *89*,[1] 853.[1]
— New western species of Rosa. 1899. II. 283.[1]
— The North American Neilliae. 1889. II. 269.[2]
— Notes on Guadalupe Island. 1886. I. 325.
— Notes on some western Cherries. 1889. II. 270.[2]
— Notes on the botany of Santa Cruz Island. 1887. I. 325.
— Notes on western Oaks. 1889. II. 129.[1]
— Notulae californicae. 1882. II. 744.[2]
— Novitates occidentales. 1893. I. 326.
— Observations on the Compositae. 1893. II. 848.[2]
— Remarks on certain Pentstemons. 1889. I. 325.
— Reprint of Fraser's Catalogue [of new and interesting plants collected in upper Louisiana]. *See* NUTTALL, Thomas. 1813. I. 318.
— Some California Polypetalae. 1886. II. 229.[1]
— Some genera of Rafinesque. 1889. I. 308.
— The specific name of the Texan Cercis. 1891. II. 345.[2]
— Studies in the botany of California [*sic*]. 1886. I. 325.
— A supplementary list of Cedros Island plants. 1887. I. 333.
— Teratological notes. 1889. II. 272.[1]
— Against the using of revertible generic names. 1889. I. 254.[1]
— The vegetation of the summit of Mount Diablo. 1893. II. 498.[1]
— *See also* KELLOGG, Albert & GREENE, E. L.
Greene, F. W. Extraction de la caféine du Guarana. 1877. III. 540.[1]
Greenheart. 1893. IV. 520.[1]
Greenhouse Palms. 1874. III. 317.
Greenhouse Rhododendrons. 1882. III. 660.[2]
Greenhouse Rhododendrons. 1891. III. 655.
Greenhouse Rhododendrons at Christmas. 1891. III. 655.
Greenish, Edw. Extraction de la matière grasse de la noix vomique. 1881. III. 685.[1]
Greenish, Henry George. Canella bark. 1894. II. 566.[2]
— Cape tea. 1881. III. 473.[2]
— Chemische Untersuchung . . . des Nerium odorum. 1881. III. 689.·
— Sur la composition du Nerium odorum. 1881. III. 689.[1]
— Contribution to the chemistry of Nerium odorum. 1881. III. 689.[1]
— Faux Séné d'Alexandrie. 1899. III. 470.[2]
— Spurious Alexandrian senna. 1899. III. 470.[2]
— Untersuchung des Buschthees. 1881. III. 473.[2]
Greenish, Thomas. The histology of araroba. 1880. III. 467.[1]

— Pine or forest wool. 1884. IV. 463.[1]
— Pine or forest wool. 1885. IV. 429.[1]
Greenlee, L. June Roses. 1892. III. 450.
Greenman, Jesse More. Descriptions of new and little known plants from Mexico. 1897. I. 333.
— Diagnoses of new and critical Mexican phanerogams. 1898. I. 333.
— Key to the Mexican species of Liabum. 1897. II. 860.[1]
— New species . . . of Mexican plants. 1900. I. 333.
— Northwestern plants. 1899. II. 265.[1] ·
— Revision of the Mexican and Central American species of Houstonia. 1897. II. 820.[1]
— Some new . . . plants of the Northwest. 1898. II. 315.[1]
— Some new species . . . among the Mexican phanerogams. 1899. I. 333.
— *See also* ROBINSON, B. L. & GREENMAN, J. M.
Green's fruit grower. III. 4.
Greenwich natural history club. Report of the botanical committee. *See* CURREY, Frederick. 1858. I. 400.
Greenwood, F. W. P. A description of the principal fruits of Cuba. 1839. III. 64.[1]
Greenwood, George. Der Baumheber. 1844. III. 167.
— Greenwood's Baumheber. 1844. III. 167.
— The tree-lifter. 1844. III. 167.
Under the Greenwood tree. *See* UNDER . . . 1868. I. 517.[1]
Le greffage des monocotylédones. 1899. III. 165.
Greffe de Châtaignier sur le Chêne. 1840. III. 359.[1]
Greffe de la Pivoine en arbre. 1834. III. 392.[1]
Greffe des Poiriers sur le Sorbier. 1833. III. 445.[1]
Greffe du Caféier. *See* MANÈS, Henri. 1894. III. 733.[1]
Greffe du Lilas sur le Frêne. 1838. III. 680.[1]
De la greffe du Noyer. 1890. III. 355.
De la greffe du Poirier sur Pommier. 1831. III. 445.[1]
Greffe étouffée ou à l'étouffée. 1832. III. 160.
Greffe intergénérique. 1899. III. 165.
De la greffe par approche du Cèdre. 1837. III. 300.[1]
Gregg, Thomas. How to raise fruits. 1880. III. 133.
Gregg, W. H. Anomalous thickening in the roots of Cycas Seemanni. 1887. II. 5.[1]
— A text-book of Indian botany. 1883. I. 256.
Grégoire, Ach. Treuil pour défoncement. 1897. IV. 143,[1] *557*.[1]
Grégoire, Jacques. Hortus pharmaceuticus lutetianus. 1638. I. 56.
Gregori, P. Eine kleine Kritik des Faustmann'schen Spiegel-Hypsometer. 1888. IV. 216.
— Unsere Hochgebirgswaldungen. 1890. IV. 367.
Gregorio, Antonio de. Appunti intorno alla Salvia Sclarea. 1896. II. 414.[1]
— Sulla crisi degli Agrumi. 1897. III. 126.[2]
Gregorius de Regio. De varietate Capsicorum commentarius. 1611. II. 769.[3]
Gregory, Emily L. Comparative anatomy of the filz-like hair-covering. 1886. I. 113.[1]
— Development of cork-wings. 1888. I. 130.
— The pores of the libriform tissue. 1886. I. 125.
Gregory, J. B. To Wilson's Promontory overland. 1886. I. 503.
Gregory, John Walter. The Great Rift Valley. 1896. I. 493.
Gregson, J. P. An injurious beetle in the Chittagong Division. 1000. III. 314.[2]
Gréhant, Louis François Nestor & Peyron, J. Extraction et composition des gaz contenus dans les feuilles aériennes. 1885. I. 151,[1] *154*.
Greifswald — Naturwissenschaftlicher Verein von Neuvorpommern und Rügen. *See* NATURWISSENSCHAFTLICHER . . . I. 14.
Greig, G. The Bánda forests. 1879. IV. 377.[2]
— & others. Forestry in India. 1884. IV. 378.
Greig, Thomas. On injury done to drains by roots of trees. 1876. III. 34.[1]
Greiner, Ludwig. Beiträge zur Kenntniss und Verbesserung des ungarischen Forstwesens. 1839. IV. 373.
— Bizlositva vannak-e erdeink a mostani törvények által? 1845. IV. 181.[1]
— Forst-Statistik des waldreichen Gömörer Comitates in Ungarn. 1873. IV. 373.
— Grundzüge zu dem Forst-Taxationsverfahren . . . auf den herzogl. sachsen-coburg'schen Gütern. 1873. IV. 307.[1]
— Instruktion zur Führung der Forstertrags-Kontrole in . . . Murány und Kapsdorf. 1882. IV. 307.[1]
— Noch einmal über Wallnussbäume. 1865. II. 114.[1]
— Wodurch könnte dem sehr fühlbaren Holzmangel . . . abgeholfen werden? 1845. IV. 283.[2]

Grell, Moritz. Eichenschwelle und Waldsubstanz. 1887. IV. 513.

Grélot, Paul. Sur le faisceau staminal. 1897. I. 116.[2]
— Sur les faisceaux staminaux. 1897. I. 116.[2]
— Sur l'indépendence de certains faisceaux dans la fleur. 1897. I. 115.[2]
— Origine botanique des Caoutchoucs 1899. .III. .230.
— Sur quelques exemples de lignification de l'épiderme placentaire. 1896. I. 118.[1]
— Recherches sur la nervation carpellaire. 1896. I. 118.[1]
— Recherches sur le système libéroligneux floral. 1897. I. 115.[2]

Gremblich, P. Julius. Die Formenreihe der Alpenrosen. 1874. II. 676.[1]
— Der Legföhrenwald. 1893. II. 43.[1]

Gremli, August. Beiträge zur Flora der Schweiz. 1870. I. 436, *II. 304.*[1]
— Beiträge zur Kenntniss der schweizerischen·Brombeeren. 1871. II. 304.[1]
— Excursionsflora der Schweiz. 1867. I. 435.
— The flora of Switzerland. 1867. I. 435.
— Flore analytique de la Suisse. 1867. I. 435.
— Vorarbeiten zu einer Monographie der schweizerischen Brombeeren. 1870. II. 304.[1]
— See also BURNAT, Émile & GREMLI, August.

Grenada — Botanic garden. Annual report. See BOTANIC . . . I. 39.[3]

Grenada — Botanic garden. Bulletin. See BOTANIC . . . I. 39.[3]

Grenier, Jean Charles Marie. Catalogue des plantes . . . du Doubs. 1842. I. 409.
— Contributions à la flore de France. 1876. I. 415.
— Flore de la chaine jurassique. 1865. I. 413.
— Observations sur le Crataegus Azarolus. 1864. II. 261.[1]
— Revue de la flore des Monts Jura. ·1874. I. 414.
— Tableau analytique des familles de la flore de France. 1874. I. 414.
— Thèse de géographique botanique du département du Doubs. 1844. I. 410.
— & Godron, D. A. Flore de France. 1848. I. 410.·

Grenz, Adam. Commentatio de arboribus. 1743. IV. 313.

Greshoff, Maurits. Aanteekeningen over Dempo-lelet. 1891. II. 444.[2]
— Abrus precatorius L. en Adenanthera pavonina. 1900. III. 462,[1] *466.*[1]
— Acacia Farnesiana. 1897. III. 465.[1]
— Agathis loranthifolia Salisb. 1900. III. 297,[2] *611.*[2]
— Aleurites moluccana. 1894. III. 514.[1]
— Anacardium occidentale. 1894. III. 524.[1]
— Antiaris toxicaria Lesch. 1895. III. 366.[2]
— Aperçu du premier rapport du laboratoire chimico-pharmacologique . . . de Buitenzorg. 1891. I. 151.[2]
— Barringtonia speciosa Forst. 1896. III. 631.[1]
— Beschrijving der giftige . . . planten bij de vischvangst in gebruik. 1893. III. 59.[2]
— Bijdrage tot de kennis der Bixakleurstoffen. 1884. III. 613.[1]
— Bixa Orellana. 1895. III. 613.[2]
— Boeloe Ongko. 1890. III. 367.[2]
— Bouea macrophylla Griff. 1897. III. 524.[1]
— Brucea sumatrana Roxb. 1895. III. 507.[2]
— Caesalpinia Sappan. 1896. III. 469.[1]
— Calophyllum inophyllum L. 1895. III. 608.[2]
— Calotropis gigantea. 1897. III. 692.[2]
— Campéche hout in Nederlandsch Indië. 1891. III. 478.[1]
— O het Caoutchouc-surrogaat "Bresk." 1899. III. 232,[2]erp]
— Carica Papaya. 1898. III. 618.[1]
— Carpaïne. 1890. III. 617.[2]
— Cassia alata. 1894. III. 470.[2]
— Cedrela serrata Royle. 1896. III. 512.[1]
— Cerbera Odollam Gaertn. 1895. III. 687.[2]
— Chineesche planten in verband met Nederlandsch Indië. 1894. III. 92.[1]
— Derris elliptica. 1896. III. 475.[1]
— 'Over de deugdelijkheid . . . van papier. 1897. III. 235.[2]
— Eerste[-tweede] verslag van het onderzoek naar de plantenstoffen. 1890. I. 154.
— Eriodendron anfractuosum. 1898. III. 589.[2]
— Euchresta Horsfieldii Benn. 1896. III. 477.[1]
— Eurycoma longiflora. 1896. III. 508.[1]
— Giuta Renghas. 1900. III. 518,[2] 524.[2]
— Over Gondang-was. 1899. III. 371.[2]
— Over Gondangwas. 1899. III. 371.[2]

— Gonystylus Miquelianus. 1897. III. 584.[2]
— Over de handelssoorten van benzoe. 1893. III. 671.[1]
— De herkomst van "Bresk" of "Dead Borneo." 1900. III. 686,[2] 588.[1]
— Hernandia peltata Meissn. 1895. III. 408.[1]
— Iets over de bestand deelen van Assamtheesaad. 1890. III. 607.
— Iets over de vluchtige ·olie der Liberia-koffie-bloemen. 1890. III. 743.[1]
— Indische ooftboomen en veredeling van vruchten. 1894. III. 92.[1]
— Een jaargeld van £100 voor C. Ledger. 1897. III. 718.
— Jatropha curcas. 1900. III. 519.[2]
— Kamfer-productie in Nederl. Indië. 1890. III. 233.[1]
— Over de kenmerken der verschillende handelssoorten cacaobonen. 1893. III. 595.[1]
— Kleinhovia hospita. 1895. III. 591.[2]
— De Kruidnagelteelt in Zanzibar. 1893. III..635.[2]
— Litsaea (Cylicodaphne) sebifera. 1894. III. 407.[1]
— Melaleuca Leucadendron. 1898. III. 636.
— Morinda citrifolia L. 1897. III. 746.[1]
— Moringa pterygosperma Gaertn. 1895. III. 409.[1]
— Eene nieuwe bereidingswijze van gutta-percha. 1892. III. 668.[2]
— Een nieuwe bijdrage tot de kennis der Indische voedings-middelen. 1893. .III. 275.[1]
— Nieuwe vluchtige oliën voor den Europeeschen handel. 1893. III. 225.
— Nota over de kleurstof van Bixa. 1889. III. 613.[1]
— Nuttige Indische planten. 1894. I. 466.
— Nyctanthes arbor-tristis. 1897. III. 674.[2]
— Onderzoek van eenige Nederlandsch Oost Indische plantenstoffen. 1893. III. 275.[1]
— Pangium edule Reinw. 1894. III. 615.[1]
— Papaya-melksap als geneesmiddel. 1893. III. 617.[2]
— Papier-controle. 1897. III. 235.[2]
— Parinarium glaberrimum Hassk. 1894. III. 430.[1]
— Piper Cubeba L. 1897. III. 342.[3]
— Plant-lore. 1899. I. 518.
— Planten en plantenstoffen. 1891. III. 218.[1]
— Plumiera acutifolia Poir. 1895. III. 690.[1]
— Professor Plugges onderzoek der cerberine. 1893. III. 687.[3]
— Pterocarpus indicus. 1896. III. 485.[2]
— Het rapport van Wood·over de bereiding van kinine. 1890. III. 725.[1]
— Rauwolfia sepentina Benth. 1900. III. 690.[1]
— Rhinacanthus communis Nees. 1894. III. 710.[1]
— Samadera indica Gaertn. 1894. III. 509.[1]
— Santalum album L. 1897. ·III. 384.[1]
— Sarcolobus narcoticus Span. ·1895. III. 694.[1]
— Schetsen van nuttige Indische planten. 1894. III. 92.[1]·
— Styrax Benzoin Dryand. 1896. III. 671.[1] ·
— Theezaadolie. 1893. III. 608.[1] ·
— Twee nieuwe verfbasten. 1900. III. 237.[1]
— Untersuchung zweier Farbrinden. 1900. II. 411,[2] *III. 596.*[1]
— ·Vruchtenteelt. .1898. III. 367.[3]
— De waarde van Kola. 1891. III. 590.[2]

Gressenberg, d' ABLAING VAN. See ABLAING VAN GRESSENBERG, d'.

Gressent. L'arboriculture fruitière. 1865. III. 144.
— Einträglicher Obstbau. 1865. III. 144.
— Leçons élémentaires . . . d'arboriculture. 186 .? III. 144.

Gressler, F. G. L. Deutschlands Giftpflanzen. 1853. III. 73.

Grete, A. Untersuchung schweizerischer Gerbrinden. 1891. I. 183, *IV. 435.*
— Untersuchung von Fichtenrinden. 1891. II. 37.[1]·

Grete, E. A. See ZOELLER, Philipp Hugo & GRETE, E. A. The grete herball. See ARBOLAYRE. 1485. I. 276. ·

Grétrant. See GRÉHANT, N. & PETRON, J.

Gretsch. Zur Ertragsregelung der Weisstannen-Femel-oder Plenterwaldungen. 1893. IV. 446.[3]
— 1. Niederschlagsbeschädigungen in den Waldungen des badischen Schwarzwaldes. 1893. IV. 191.[1]
— Ueber die Versicherung der forstwirtschaftlichen Arbeiter im Grossherzogtum Baden. 1895. IV. 311.[1]

Gretschula, Karol. Krótki opis lasów do dóbr hrabstwa Tenczyńskiego należących. 1883. IV. 369.

Gretzler, F. Wie kann der Privatwaldbesitzer seinen Wald am ·vortheilhaftesten benutzen? 1849. IV. 117.

Greve, A. Kurzgefasste Naturgeschichte der schädlichen Insekten. 1810. IV. ·91.[1]

Greve, A. *See* LENNEP, H. H. T. van & GREVE, A.
Greve, D. R. de. Hoe de Koffiebladziekte het eerst . . . werd waargenomen. 1889. III. 736.
Greve, Rudolph. Die falschen Chinarinden. 1891. III. 725.[1]
Greve, V. *See* ГРЕВЕ, В.
Greve, W. R. de. De cultuur . . . van Thee op Java. 1898. III. 602.[1]
— Java-Theens Dyrkning. 1892. III. 602.[1]
Grevelink, Arnold Hermann BISSCHOP. Botanische mede-deelingen. 1858. I. 465.
— Iets over de myrabolams. 1879. III. 632.[2]
— Iets over de West-Indische Kalabas. 1881. III. 706.[2]
— Indische handelsprodukten. 1880. III. 343.[1] — 1881. III. 402,[2] 635.[2]
— Indische houtsoorten. 1881. IV. 400.[1]
— Kruidkundig woordenboekje. 1859. I. 71.
— Kruidnagelen. 1881. III. 635.[2]
— Het leerlooien in Indie. 1880. III. 464.[1]
— Looimiddelen van den lateren tijd. 1880. III. 237.[2]
— De Mahwahboom. 1880. III. 667.[2]
— Mienjak Tangkawang en Mienjak Tangkallah. 1881. III. 407,[1] 611.[2]
— De myrabolam, wat daarvan bekend is. 1880. III. 632.[2]
— Notenmuskaat. 1881. III. 402.[2]
— De Peper. 1880. III. 343.[1]
— De Pinang of Areeknoot. 1876. III. 320.[1]
— Planten van Nederlandsch-Indië. 1883. III. 92.[1]
— De Slijmappel of Belvrucht. 1881. III. 495.[1]
— Voedergewassen voor Indië. 1880. III. 474.[1]
— De West-Indische Stuipboom. 1881. III. 465.[1]
Grevelink, P. W. ALSTORPHIUS. *See* ALSTORPHIUS GREVE-LINK, P. W.
Greville, Robert Kaye. On the botanical characters of British Oaks. 1844. II. 129.[1]
— Flora edinensis. 1824. I. 397.
— New Holland Acacias emitting garlic odor. 1862. II. 323.[2]
Greville-Williams, J. & Müller, Hugo. Sur la production du furfurol. 1873. IV. 432.[2]
Grevillius, Anders Yngve. Anatomiska studier öfver de florala axlarna. 1890. I. 113.[2]
— Einige Untersuchungen über das mechanische System. 1887. I. 134.[2]
— Om fruktbladsförökning hos Aesculus. 1892. II. 482.[1]
— Några egendomliga löfträdsformer från Norrland. 1894. I. 350.[2]
— Undersökningar öfver det mekaniska systemet. 1887. I. 134.[2]
— Über die Zusammensetzung einiger jämtländischer Relict-Formationen. 1895. I. 350,[2] *II. 144,[2] IV. 79.[2]*
Grew, Nehemiah. Anatomia, ed anima delle piante. 1682. I. 97.
— Anatomie vegetabilium primordia. 1672. I. 97. Anatomie des plantes. 1679 (1680). I. 97.
— The anatomy of leaves, flowers. 1682. I. 97.
— The anatomy of plants. 1682. I. 97.
— The anatomy of vegetables begun. 1672. I. 97.
— Comparativa anatomia truncorum. 1675. I. 104.
— The comparative anatomy of trunks. 1675. I. 104.
— Idea historiae phytologicae. 1673. I. 103.
— An idea of a phytological history. 1673. I. 103, V. XI.[1]
— Musaeum Regalis societatis. 1681. I. 52.
— & Boyle, Robert. Raccolta di sperienze . . . sopra il com-battimento risultante dalla mescolanza de' corpi. 1685. I. 182.[1]
— — Recueil d'expériences . . . sur le combat, qui procède du mélange des corps. 1685. I. 182.[1]
Grey-leaved shrubs. 1884. III. 205.[2]
Greyerz, von. Ueber Acclimatisirung exotischer Holzarten. 1845. IV. 127.[1]
— Bericht über Cultur-Versuche in sterilem Sandboden. 1839. IV. 471.
— Ueber Erziehung von Brenn- und Stammholz. 1838. IV. 169.[1]
— Ueber Holztheuerung und Holzmangel. 1838. IV. 282.[2]
— Über das sogenannte Ueberwallen. 1844. I. 32.
— Über das Vorkommen und Verhalten der Kiefern. 1844. II. 46,[1] 117.[2]
— & others. Beaufsichtigung der Privatwaldungen. 1843. IV. 286.[2]
Greyerz, Adolph von. Alpenforstwirthschaft. 1866. IV. 366.
— Ueber den Anbau einheimischer und exotischer Holzarten auf dem bernischen Jura. 1846. IV. 123.[1]

— Bericht über die Waldungen in Sachseln. 1862. IV. 366.
— Les coupes rases & les exploitations jardinatoires. 1870. IV. 128.
— Haut-Unterwald. 1864. IV. 366.
— Ueber die Holzfäule. 1860. IV. 418.
— Holzreisser für Durchforstungsanzeichnungen. 1854. IV. 173.
— Die Kahlschläge und die Pländer-Hiebe. 1870. IV. 128.
— Observations sur l'état d'aménagement des forêts . . . de Fribourg. 1857. IV. 249.[2]
— De la pourriture du bois. 1860. IV. 418.
— Eine Stimme aus dem Walde, über . . . Forst-Organisation im Canton Bern. 1847. IV. 294.[1]
— Die Weymuthskiefer im Berner Oberland. 1867. IV. 469.
Greyers, Emil von. Bericht über die Waldungen der Stadt-gemeinde Solothurn. 1842. IV. 365.
— Gedanken eines wunderlichen Forstmannes. 1860. IV. 101.
— Ueber den gegenwärtigen Zustand der Gemeinde- und Privatwaldungen im Kanton Bern. 1859. IV. 365.
— Ideen über die Verbauungen . . . im Gebirge. 1868. IV. 187.[1]
— Der Kapital-Werth der Staatswälder des Kantons Bern. 1856. IV. 261.[2]
— Über das Leben der Wälder. 1843. IV. 67,[1] 101.
— Un mot sur les endiguements et les reboisements. 1868. IV. 283.[1]
— Nachrichten über die Pflanz-Versuche mit der Pinus mari-. tima. 1855. IV. 467.[1]
— Pensées d'un forestier original. 1860. IV. 101.
— Lê Pin de Weymouth. 1869. IV. 469.
— Quelques idées sur les endiguements . . . dans les mon-tagnes. 1868. IV. 187.[1]
— Rüfi- und Wasser-Runsen-Verbauung. 1856. IV. 187.[1]
— Die Saat- und Baumschule im . . . Löhrwalde. 1855. IV. 150.
— Ein Tag im Stadt-Bremgartenwalde. 1855. IV. 365.
— Ueber Vertheilung und Verwaltung der Gemeinde-Wald-ungen. 1844. IV. 294,[1] 309.[1]
— Waldbesteurung. 1856. IV. 261.[2]
— Die Weymuths-Kiefer. 1869. IV. 469.
— Ein Wort über die Verbauungen und Aufforstungen. 1868. IV. 283.[1]
Greyerz, Walo von. Ueber das Abstossen der Fichten-Zweige. 1860. II. 36.[2]
— Zur Ahorn-, Eschen-, Ulmen- und Lärchen-Kultur. 1860. IV. 123.[1]
— Ueber die Aufastungen. 1860. IV. 170.
— Behandlung reiner Eichenhochwälder. 1846. IV. 504.
— Behandlung reiner Eichenhochwaldungen. 1847. IV. 504.
— Bericht über die Forstschule zu Büren. 1845. IV. 36.[1]
— Betreffend Aufforstungen. 1869. IV. 171
— Zur Borkenkäfer-Angelegenheit. 1860. IV. 204.
— Der Borkenkäfer-Lärm. 1858. IV. 204.
— Des cultures agricoles dans les forêts. 1869. IV. 133.
— Cultures d'Érables, de Frênes. 1860. IV. 123.[1]
— Les cultures des coupes. 1871. IV. 139.[1]
— Le demeste. 1858. IV. 204.
— De l'élagage. 1860. IV. 170.
— Engerling-Frass in Kulturen. 1870. IV. 202.
— Ergebniss einer Aufastung in einer Pflanzung. 1857. IV. 261.[2]
— Ertrag einer 14-jährigen Eschen- und Erlen-Pflanzung. 1874. IV. 236.
— Eschenblättriger Ahorn. 1857. IV. 526.[1]
— Les forêts du Norrland. 1871. IV. 344.[1]
— Forstertrāge einiger Forstverwaltungen des Kantons Aar-gau im Jahre 1857. 1859. IV. 261.[2]
— Forst-Erträge einiger Forstverwaltungen des Kantons Aar-gau im Jahre 1858. 1859. IV. 261.[2]
— Forstliche Regungen im Kanton Glarus. 1853. IV. 365.
— Forstliche Regungen im Kanton Schwyz. 1852. IV. 365.
— Frais des expurgades forestières. 1872. IV. 175.[2]
— Inconvénients des mélanges d'essences trop variées. 1874. IV. 137.[2]
— Influences atmosphériques. 1859. IV. 67.[1]
— Käferfrass in Weisstannenbeständen. 1851. IV. 209.[1]
— Die Kultur der Schlagflächen. 1871. IV. 139.[1]
— Ueber landwirthschaftliche Zwischennutzungen. 1854. IV. 133.

Greyerz, Walo von (*continued*).
— Leitfaden für Bannwarte. 1860. IV. 110.[2]
— Leitfaden für Bannwarten. 1849. IV. 110.[3]
— Lettre de Suède. 1872. IV. 273.[1]
— Die Liebe zum Walde beim Volke. 1849. IV. 55.[2]
— Mittheilungen aus Schweden. 1872. IV. 273.[1]
— Moyen de prolonger la période des cultures. 1860. IV. 152.
— Ueber die natürliche Verjüngung der Wälder. 1868. IV. 139.[1]
— Notice relative aux élagages. 1868. IV. 171.
— Notizen. Aus dem Kanton Glarus. 1853. IV. 365.
— Des Pins de Weymouth. 1860. IV. 469.
— Plantation de l'Épicéa par touffes. 1873. IV. 453.
— Produit d'une plantation de Frênes et d'Aulnes. 1874. IV. 236.
— Produit hâtif du Bouleau dans les cultures. 1859. IV. 490.[1]
— Produits des forêts de quelques arrondissements forestiers du canton d'Argovie. 1859. IV. 261.[2]
— Produits forestiers de quelques administrations forestières du canton d'Argovie. 1859. IV. 261.[1]
— A propos du dermeste. 1860. IV. 204.
— Propositions pour remédier à l'état défectueux des forêts de nos montagnes. 1860. IV. 278.[1]
— Protection des graines contre les souris. 1860. IV. 197.[3]
— Quelques mots sur l'imposition des forêts . . . dans le canton de Berne. 1860. IV. 262.
— Quelques mots sur la chute des pousses de Sapin. 1860. II. 36.[2]
— Une question de régénération forestière. 1873. IV. 169.[3]
— Ravages des vers blancs dans les cultures. 1870. IV. 202.
— La régénération des peuplements. 1868. IV. 139.[1]
— Sur la régénération naturelle des forêts. 1868. IV. 139.[1]
— Die Rothtannen-Büschel-Pflanzung. 1873. IV. 453.
— Schutz der Saamen vor Mäusefrass. 1860. IV. 197.[2]
— Die Unzweckmässigkeit allzu bunter Holzarten-Mischungen. 1874. IV. 137.[2]
— Verlängerung der Frühlings-Kultur-Zeit. 1860. IV. 152.
— Versuche mit der Biermann'schen Kulturmethode. 1846. IV. 152.
— Vornutzung durch die Birke im Waldfelde. 1860. IV. 490.[1]
— Vorschläge zur Hebung der bestehenden Uebelstände. 1860. IV. 278.[1]
— Die Wälder Norrlands. 1871. IV. 344.[1]
— Waldfeldbau. 1849. IV. 133.
— Ueber den Waldfeldbau. 1856. IV. 133.
— Der Waldfeldbau. 1869. IV. 133.
— Waldfelderträge. 1851. IV. 133.
— Die Wald-Verjüngung. 1868. IV. 139.[1]
— Eine Wald-Verjüngungs-Frage. 1873. IV. 169.[2]
— Weisstannen-Pflanzung. 1856. IV. 444.[1]
— Ueber die Weymouths-Kiefer. 1860. IV. 469.
— Witterungs-Einflüsse auf die Waldbestände. 1859. IV. 67.[1]
— Ein Wort über Steuerschatzung der Wälder. 1860. IV. 262.
— & **Bertholet**, Charles. Remarque relative à l'histoire des lançoirs en fil de fer. 1873. IV. 391.
The **Greyish** Bamboo. 1875. III. 316.[1]
Grez, J. de. Bijdrage tot de geschiedenis van de dennen teelt in Noordbrabant. n. d. IV. 27.[1]
Gribble, Henry. The preparation of Japan Tea. 1885. III. 601.[1]
— The preparation of vegetable wax. 1875. III. 226.[1]
Gridley, A. D. A word for evergreens. 1858. III. 306.[1]
Grieb, Richard. Das europäische Oedland. 1898. IV. 155.[2]
— Ueber die lange Lebensdauer der Lärche. 1897. IV. 452.[2]
— Die Nachhaltigkeitsforderung in der früheren und heutigen Forstwirtschaft. 1899. IV. 247.[1]
Griechische Jahreszeiten. See HELDREICH, Theodor von. 1873. I. 449.
Grienwaldt, Franz Joseph. De vita plantarum. 1732. I. 31.
Grieser, F. Aristolochia caudata. 1860. III. 386.[1]
Griesheim, Ludwig Wilhelm von. Aufruf eines praktischen Forstmannes. 1801. IV. 100.[2]
— Cameralistische Grundsätze der . . . Forstwissenschaft. 1778. IV. 95.
— Entwurf zum Regulativ . . . des Unterrichts der Lehrlinge. 1802. IV. 31.

— Handbuch der grundsätzlichen Forstwirthschaft. 1800. IV. 268.
— Handbuch der natürlich grundsätzlichen Forstwirthschaft. 1800. IV. 268.
Griesselich, Ludwig. Deutsches Pflanzenbuch. 1847. III. 73.
— Kleine botanische Schriften. 1836. I. 379.
— Versuch einer Statistik der Flora Badens. 1836. I. 379.
Griessen, Albert. Les Bougainvillea. 1896. III. 388.[1]
— Eugenia malaccensis. 1896. III. 636.
— Le Phylica ericoides. 1893. III. 542.[1]
Grieve, Peter. Aucuba japonica. 1881. III. 645.[1]
— Best time for transplanting. 1876. III. 168.[2]
— Euonymus latifolius. 1882. III. 533.[1]
— Hedges, useful and ornamental. 1882. III. 214.[1]
— A history of variegated Zonal Pelargoniums. 1868. III. 491.[1]
— Indian and other Azaleas. 1883. III. 656.
— Trees near dwellings. 1882. III. 202.[1]
— Yew trees. 1880. III. 288.[1]
Grieve, Symington. Botany [of Scotland]. 1884. I. 534.[2]
— Some notes on Andromeda polifolia. 1900. II. 659.[2]
Griewank, Gustav. Kritische Studien zur Flora Meklenburgs. 1856. I. 383.
Griffen, J. S. Evergreens for shelter. 1900. III. 215.[3]
Griffin. Tanekaba-schors van Nieuw Zeeland. 1884. III. 287.[2]
Griffin, R. B. & **Little**, A. D. Chemistry of paper-making. 1894. IV. 430.
Griffini, L. La legge forestale ed il codice civile. 1897. IV. 329.
Griffit. De zijdewormenteelt. 1883. III. 378.
Griffith, J. W. & **Henfrey**, Arthur. The micrographic dictionary. 1856. I. 34.
Griffith, John Edward. The flora of Anglesey & Carnarvonshire. 1894. I. 404.[1]
Griffith, Robert Eglesfeld. Medical botany. 1847. III. 58.
Griffith, William, (1810–1845). On the Black-dye plant of the Shans. 1844. II. 702.[1] III. 228.[2]
— Ueber den Caoutchouc-Baum des Landes Assam. 1838. III. 370.[2]
— Description de deux genres . . . des Hamamélides. 1836. II. 252.[1]
— Description of two genera of . . . Hamamelideae. 1836. I. 252.[1]
— On the development of the ovulum in Avicennia. 1847. II. 753.[2]
— Sur le développement de l'ovule chez les Avicennia. 1847. II. 753.[2]
— Sur le développement des ovules du Santalum album du Loranthus et du Viscum. 1839. II. 169.[1] 173.[2]
— Extracts from a report on . . . Affghanistan. 1841. I. 477.[1]
— Sur la famille des Rhizophorées. 1838. II. 612.[2]
— On the family of Rhizophoreae. 1836. II. 612.[2]
— Icones plantarum asiaticarum. 1847. I. 472.
— Iets over den Kaoutschoukboom van het Koningrijk Assam. 1838. III. 370.[2]
— Itinerary notes of plants collected in the Khasyah and Bootan Mountains. 1847. I. 452, 472.
— Journals of travels. 1847. I. 452.
— Notes on the botanical geography of the Tenasserim coast. 1847. I. 476.[1]
— Notes on the development of the ovula of Loranthus. 1839. II. 173.[2]
— Notulae ad plantas asiaticas. 1847. I. 472.
— On the ovulum of Santalum. 1845. II. 168,[1] 173.[2]
— On the ovulum of Santalum album. 1839. II. 169.[1].
— The Palms of British East India. 1844. II. 62.[1]
— Palms of British East India. 1850. II. 62.[1]
— Remarks on a collection of plants made at Sadiyá. 1836. I. 475.[2]
— Remarks on a few plants from central India. 1842. I. 472.
— Remarks on Gnetum. 1859. II. 54.[2]
— Report on the Caoutchouc tree of Assam. 1838. III. 370.[2]
— Report on the Hon'ble company's botanic gardens, Calcutta. 1843. I. 66.[2]
— Report on the Tea plant of Upper Assam. 1838. III. 602.[2]
— On the root-parasites referred . . . to Rhizantheae. 1845. II. 180.[1]
— Some account of the botanical collection, brought from the eastward in 1841, by Dr. Cantor. 1855. I. 458.

— On some remarkable plants in the H. C. botanic gardens, Calcutta. 1843. I. 66.²
— Some remarks on the development of pollen. 1836. I. 117.¹
Griffith, William. The Vine and its culture. 1884. III. 551.¹
Griffiths, A. B. Sur la composition des cendres de quelques plautes médicinales. 1900. I. 154.
Griffiths, William Handsel. A system of botanical analysis applied to ... British natural orders. 1870. I. 402.
Griffon, Eduard. L'assimilation chlorophyllienne chez lès plantes d'appartement. 1900. I. 174.
— L'assimilation chlorophyllienne chez les plantes du littoral. 1898. I. 174.
— L'assimilation chlorophyllienne dans la lumière solaire. 1899, 1900. I. 174.
— L'assimilation chlorophyllienne et la coloration. 1899. I. 174, 186.
— Influence de la gelée printanière de 1897. 1897. IV. 191.²
— De l'influence de la gelée printanière de 1897. 1897. IV. 191.²
— Relations entre l'intensité de la coloration verte des feuilles et l'assimilation chlorophyllienne. 1899. I. 174.
Griffon, Étienne. Cours d'arboriculture. 1887. III. 140.²
Grigg, H. B. Chinchona culture. 1880. III. 714.
— Coffee cultivation. 1880. III. 732.²
— Forests [of the Nilagiri district]. 1880. IV. 377.²
— Manual of the Nilagiri district. 1880. III. 129.²
Grigg, T. E. Our Salt-bushes. 1900. III. 387.²
Grignan, G. T. Choisya ternata. 1900. III. 496.¹
— Exposition de Paris. 1900. III. 557,¹ 571,¹ 666.¹
— Quelques Hydrangea. 1898. III. 411.¹
Grignon, Eugène. Étude comparée des caractères anatomiques des Lonicérées et des Astéroïdées. 1884. II. 833.²
Grigolato, Gaetano. Flora medica del Polesine. 1843. III. 88.¹
Grigor, James. Eastern arboretum. 1841. I. 296.²
— Fences. 1874. III. 213.
— On planting within the influence of the sea. 1847. III. 41.²
— Report on Trimingham and Runton plantations. 1847. IV. 358.²
— Transmission of Coniferae from the Himalayas. 1846. III. 154.²
Grigor, John. Arboriculture. 1868. IV. 108.²
— Essay on raising and managing hedges. 1835. III. 212.²
— On forest planting. 1841. IV. 152.
— Observations sur le Pin sylvestre. 1834. IV. 471.
— Remarks on Pinus sylvestris. 1835. IV. 471.
— Report on Larch forests. 1869. IV. 452.¹
— Report on the native Pine forests of Scotland. 1839. IV. 358.²
— Reports on collecting ... the seeds of forest trees. 1832. IV. 147.²
— On varieties of Larch. 1865. III. 304.²
— & others. Essays on the pruning of forest trees. 1839. IV. 170.
Grigor, Robert. Report on plantations of Pinus sylvestris. 1847. IV. 358.²
Grigorieff, A. Zur Anatomie des Phellodendron. 1871. II. 409.²
Grijs, C. F. M. de. Over de bereiding ... der groene Chinesche verfstof lo-kao. 1857. III. 542.¹
Grilli, Marcello. Aristolochia caudata L. 1890. III. 386.¹
— Chorosema ilicifolium var. Pandolfinii. 1886. III. 472.²
— Nuove varietà di Epacris. 1885. III. 665.¹
— Pitecoctenium clematideum Griesb. 1890. III. 707.¹
— Sementa d' alberi fruttiferi. 1883. III. 50.²
— Della sementa degli alberi fruttiferi. 1893. III. 50.²
— Dei soggetti da innesto per il Pesco. 1882. III. 430.²
— Staphylea colchica Stev. 1890. III. 533.²
— Une Vite gigantesca. 1877. III. 509.¹
Grillot. Note sur une variété de Mélèze. 1870. IV. 449.
Grimal. Généralités sur la propriété en Algérie. 1899. IV. 332.²
— Histoire sommaire de l'administration des eaux et forêts en Algérie. 1900. IV. 28.²
Grimaldi, Clemente. Sopra una forma particolare di seccume. 1888. III. 580.
Grimaldi, Domenico. Istruzioni sulla nuova manufattura del olio. 1777. III. 678.¹
— Memoria sulla economia olearia. 1783. III. 678.¹
Grimard, Édouard. La plante. 1864. I. 90.
Grimaud, François Émile. Monographie du camphre. 1855. III. 233.¹

Grimaud, G. Sur quelques faits relatifs au phylloxera. 1874. III. 567.¹
— Traitement par submersion des Vignes. 1874. III. 566.¹
Grimaux, Édouard & Arnaud, Albert. Sur quelques bases homologues de la quinine. 1892. III. 747.²
— Transformation de la cupréine en quinine. 1891. III. 747.²
— & Ruotte, J. Sur l'essence de Sassafras. 1869. III. 408.¹
— Ueber das Sassafrasöl. 1869. III. 408.¹
Grimbert, L. Examen de diverses matières sucrées extraites de dattes. 1889. III. 329.²
Grimblot, A. G. La truffe. 1879. IV. 439.
— La truffe française. 1887. IV. 439.
Grimburg, Carl, *Ritter* GRIMUS VON. *See* GRIMUS VON GRIMBURG, Carl, *Ritter*.
Grimes, D. S. Crooked trees. 1886. III. 202.¹
Grimm, (*Revierförster*). Die landwirthschaftliche Benutzung der Schlagflächen. 1862. IV. 133.
Grimm, J. P. Tabelle, nach welcher man in einer Uebersicht nach ... Länge des Baumschaftes dessen Cubik-Inhalt sogleich ersehen kann. 1829. IV. 222.
Grimm, Jacob. Über frauennamen aus blumen. 1853. I. 515.
Grimm, Johann Friedrich Carl. Synopsis methodica stirpium agri isenacensis. 1767. I. 373.
Grimmann, Johann Nicolaus. De coffee potus usu noxio. *See* ALBERTI, Michael. 1730. III. 741.¹
Grimme, F. W. Flora von Paderborn. 1868. I. 386.
Grimnäs, A. Hvad kan der gjöres for det vestlandske skovväsen? 1890. IV. 273.¹
Grimshaw, J. W. *See* ETHERIDGE, Robert, (*jr.*), DAVID, T. W. Æ. & GRIMSHAW, J. W.
Grimus von Grimburg, Carl, *Ritter*. Beiträge zur Flora Albaniens. 1871. I. 449.
Grimwood, Daniel. A catalogue of greenhouse plants, hardy trees and shrubs. 1783. I. 53.
Grin, (*tr.*). La direction des arbres par le pincement. 1863. III. 440.²
— Le pincement court. 1863. III. 440.²
Grindel, David Hieronymus. Botanisches Taschenbuch für Liv-, Cur- und Ehstland. 1803. I. 360.
— Fasslich dargestellte Anleitung zur Pflanzenkenntniss. 1804. I. 255.
— Pharmaceutische Botanik. 1802. III. 55.
Grindon, Leo. The apple of literature. 1875. II. 267.²
— The Bay and the Laurel. 1876. II. 225.²
— Labdanum, the Cistus, the Anemone. 1876. II. 564.¹
— Mulberries. 1876. II. 154.¹
— The nuts of the Old Testament. 1876. III. 220.¹
— The Pomegranate. 1876. II. 611.¹
— The Rhododendron. 1876. II. 675.²
— The trees at Fulham palace. 1873. I. 55.
Grindon, Leopold Hartley. British and garden botany. 1864. I. 401, III. 88.
— Fruits and fruit-trees. 1885. III. 220.¹
— The Manchester flora. 1859. I. 401.
— Manchester ... walks and wild flowers. 1859. I. 401.
— A manual of British and foreign plants. 1861. I. 401.
— The Shakspere flora. 1883. I. 515.
— Summer rambles in Cheshire. 1864. I. 402.
— Trees of old England. 1868. I. 293.²
Gris, Arthur. Considérations générales sur la structure de l'écorce dans les Éricinées. 1872. II. 653.²
— Mémoire sur la moelle des plantes ligneuses. 1870. I. 129.¹
— Note sur la Rose verte. 1858. II. 293.¹
— Note sur le développement de l'aleurone. 1862. II. 321.²
— Note sur les corps reproducteurs des Cycadées. 1866. II. 3.²
— Note sur les ovules des Cycadées. 1869. II. 3.¹
— Note sur les téguments de la graine du Ricin. 1862. II. 450.²
— Note sur quelques cas de monstruosité. 1858. II. 289.²
— Note sur quelques cas de monstruosité ... sur le Philadelphus. 1858. II. 242.¹
— Nouvelles observations sur la structure et les fonctions des vaisseaux. 1863. I. 133.
— Observations anatomiques et physiologiques sur la moelle. 1869. I. 129.¹
— Recherches anatomiques ... sur la germination. 1864. I. 203.
— Recherches concernant les fonctions des vaisseaux. 1863. I. 133.
— Recherches microscopiques sur la chlorophylle. 1857. I. 140.²

Gris, Arthur (*continued*).
— Recherches pour servir à l'histoire physiologique des arbres. 1866.   I. 147.
— Recherches sur la moelle des végétaux ligneux. 1871. I. 129.[1]
— Remarque sur la fleur femelle des Conifères et des Cycadées.   1865.   II. 1.
— Vivre, c'est en même temps changer et demeurer.   1863. I. 203.
— *See also* BRONGNIART, Adolphe & GRIS, Arthur; GRIS, Eusèbe & Arthur.
Gris, Eusèbe.   De l'action des sels ferrugineux solubles. 1845.   III. 180.[2]
— Addition à une précédente note concernant . . . l'application des sels de fer.   1847.   III. 180.[1]
— Nouvelles expériences sur l'action des composés ferrugineux solubles.   1844.   III. 180.[2]
— & Arthur.   Notes sur l'application des sels de fer.   1849. III. 181.[1]
Grisard, Jules. . L'Acajou à meubles.   1890.   IV. 427.[1]
— L'Aliboufier.   1891.   III. 671.[2]
— L'Araucaria du Chili.   1890.   III. 299.
— L'Arbre du voyageur.   1897.   III. 341.[2]
— Le Balata de la Guyane.   1890.   III. 668.[1]
— Le Baobab. ' 1891.   III. 589.[2]
— Le Benjoin.   1890.   III. 671.[1]
— Le Bois dentelle.   1889.   III. 628.[1]
— Le cacao, propriétés, usages.   1891.   III. 595.[1]
— Le Cajan où Ambrevade.   1895.   III. 469.[1]
— Le Carapa ou Arbre à huile de la Guyane.   1890.   III. 513.[1]
— Le Cedrela sinensis.   1876.   III. 512.[1]
— Le Chêne-Liège.   1889.   IV. 518.
— Citronnier du Japon.   1896.   III. 497.[2]
— Le Courbaril, Copalier d'Amérique.   1889.   III. 478.[2]
— Emploi de l'écorce d'Erythrine.   1893.   III. 476.[1]
— Emploi des Opuntia dans l'alimentation du bétail.   1896. III. 624.[2]
— La fève Tonka.   1894.   III. 475.[2]
— Le fruit de Bela.   1892.   III. 495.[1]
— Le fruit du Canéficier.   ·1894·   III. 471.[1]
— Le fruit du Fusain.   1893.   III. 532.[1]
— Le fruit du Tamarinier.   1894.   III. 489.[1]
— Les fruits des Citrus.   1892.   III. 499.[1]
— Le Gaïac·ou Gayac.   1890.   III. 494.[2]
— Le Genêt à balais.   1890.   III. 475.[1]
— Les gommes du Sénégal.   1894.   III. 463.[2]
— Les Goyaviers.   1888.   III. 637.[2]
— Le Henné des Arabes.   1892.   III. 630.[1]
— L'industrie des laques en Chine.   1893.   III. 529.[1]
— Industrie du sucre d'Érable en Amérique.   1893.   IV. 527.[2]
— Le Jasmin blanc.   1890.   III, 673.[1]
— Le Jujube.   1893.   III. 544.[1]
— Le Karité ou Arbre à beurre d'Afrique.   1891. ·III. 667.[1]
— Le Maïteï.   1894.   III. 533.[1]
— Le Mallotus philippensis.   1894.   III. 520.[2]
— Le Marron d'Inde.   1893.   III. 538.[2]
— Morinda citrifolia.   1896.   III. 746.[1]
— Le Myrte piment ou Poivre de la Jamaïque.   1891.   III. 637.[2]
— Noms vulgaires des diverses espèces d'Eucalyptus.   1876. II. 623.[1]
— Le Paliure épineux.   1894. ' III. 542.[1]
— Le Palmier à ivoire.   1877.   III. 330.[1]
— Produits accessoires du Houx.   1893.   III. 530.[2]
— Propriétés médicinales de l'Ailante.   1892.   III. 507.[1]
— Le Quebracho colorado comme matière tannante.   1894. III. 529.[1]
— Le Quebracho colorado de la République Argentine.   1890. III. 529.[1]
— Ravenala madagascariensis.   1897.   IV. 485.[2]
— Le Ravensara de Madagascar.   1897.   III. 407,[2] IV. 520.[1]
— Récolte du baume du Salvador.   1894.   III. 482.[2]
— Le Solom du Sénégal.   1888.   III. 475.[2]
— Le specie del genere Psidium.   1888.   III. 637.[2]
— Usages économiques du Caroubier.   1894.   III. 472.[1]
— Usages économiques du Manguier.   1894.   III. 525.[1]
— *See also* DECROIX, E. & GRISARD, Jules.
— & Vanden-Berghe, Maximilien.·· Les bois industriels. 1891.   IV. 396.[2]
— Catalogue . . . essences forestières de la Nouvelle-Zélande.   189.?   IV. 89.[2]
— — Cladrastis tinctoria Raf.   1894.   IV. 521.[1]

— — Essences exotiques.   Cladrastide ou Virgilier à bois jaune.   1894.   IV. 521.[2]
— — Le Genêt comme plante textile.   1892.   III. 488.[2]
— — Les Mimosées.   1894.   IV. 521.[1]
— — Les Palmiers utiles.   1887.   III. 319.[2]
— — Les plantes utiles de l'Inde.   1893.   III. 92.[1]
— — La Raffia del Giappone.   1888.   III, 330.[2]
— — Le Raphia Ruffia.   1888.   III. 330.[2]
— & Vilbouchevitch, Jean.   Une plante utile· des déserts salants.   1892.   *II. 188*,[1] IV. 519.[2]
— — Le Saxaoul du Turkestan.   1892.   IV. 519.[2]
Grisard du Saulget.   Résultats de l'hybridation du Cactus . . Ackermanni.   1859.   III. 625.[2]
Grischow, Carl Christoph.   Physikalisch-chemische Untersuchungen über die Athmungen der Gewächse.   1819.   I. 169.[2]
Grisebach, August Heinrich Rudolph.   Avstralien, især i plantegeografisk Henseende.   1872.   I. 502.
— Bemerkungen zu Willkomm's Monographie der europäischen Krummholzkiefern.   1861.   II. 43.[1]
— Beobachtungen über das Wachsthum der Vegetationsorgane.   1845.   I. 187.
— Bericht über die Leistungen' in der Pflanzengeographie. 1841.   I. 299.
— Catalogus plantarum cubensium.   1866.   I. 336.
— Erläuterungen ausgewählter Pflanzen des tropischen Amerikas.   1860.   I. 329.
— Flora of the British West Indies.   1864.   I. 336.
— Gentianaceae.   1845.   II. 721.[1]
— Die geographische Verbreitung der Pflanzen Westindiens. 1865.   I. 336.
— Gesammelte Abhandlungen . . . zur Pflanzengeographie. ' 1880.   I. 300.
— Grundriss der systematischen Botanik.   1854.   I. 256.
— Lysiforholdene i Urskove.   1847.   I. 229.
— Malpighiaceae.   1849;   II. 423.[1]
— Malpighiaceae.   1858.   II. 423.[2]
— Malpighiacearum brasiliensium centuriam recensat.   1839. II.·423.[2]
— Notes on Coutoubea volubilis Mart.   1862.   II. 721.[1]
— Notice sur le genre Rheedia.   1861.   II. 558.[2]
— Novitiae florae panamensis.   1858.   I. 333.
— Plantae Lorentzianae.   1874.   I. 344.
— Plantae Wrightianae.   1860.   I. 336.
— Reise durch Rumelien.   1841.   I. 449.
— Reliquiae Grisebachianae.   1882.   I. 349.
— Report on the contributions to botanical geography.   1841. I. 299. ··
— Smilaceae et Dioscoreae.   1842.   II. 77.[1]
— Spicilegium florae rumelicae. ' 1843.   I. 449.
— Symbolae ad floram argentinam.   1879.   I. 344.
— Zur Systematik der Birken.   1861.   II. 117.[2]
— Systematische Bemerkungen über die . . . Pflanzensammlungen Philippi's und Lechler's im südlichen Chile.   1854. I. 347.
— Systematische Untersuchungen über die Vegetation der Karaiben.   1857.   I. 336.
— La vegetacion de México.   1884.   I. 332.
— Die Vegetation der Erde.   1872.   I. 300.
— La végétation du globe.   1872. · I. 300. ·
— Über den Vegetationscharacter von Hardanger.   1844. 'I. 354.
— Ueber die Vegetationslinien des nordwestlichen Deutschlands.   1847.   I. 382.
— *See also* ГрИзебАхъ, A.
— & Schenk, August.   Iter hungaricum.   1852. · I. 445.
— — Observationes quaedam de plantis . . , in itinere alpino. 1852.   I. 349.
Griselini, Francesco.   ·Instruzione . . . per la coltura de Mori. 1768.   III. 373.
Grisley, Gabriel.   Viridarium Grisley lusitanicum.   1661. I. 419.[2]
— Viridarium lusitanum.   1661.   I. 419.[2]
Grisolia, Filippo.   Foreste e boschi.   1897.   IV. 364.
Grisons.   *See* GRAUBÜNDEN.   1873.   II. 24.[1]
Griveau, Maurice.   Estética de las floras.   1899.   IV. 542.[2]
Grob, Leonhard.   Kurzer praktischer Unterricht in der Obstbaumsucht.   1814.   III. 136.
Groddeck, Gabriel. לבב הלבוב לך לב h. e. Caeremonia Palmarum.   1694.   I. 515.
Groebenschütz, Anton Felix.   De strychnii in neurosibus vi. 1833.   III. 682.[2]
Gröbl, A.   Ein winterlicher Waldbrand im Hochgebirge. 1898.   IV. 182.[2]·-

Groen, Jan van der. Le jardinier du Pays-Bas. 1668. III. 105.
— Le jardinier hollandois. 1668. III. 105.
— Kweekschool voor liefhebbers der hooven en thuynen. 1738. III. 105.
— Den nederlandzen hovenier. 1668. III. 105.
— Der niederländische Gärtner. 1668. III. 105.
— De nieuwe en nauwkeurige neederlandse hovenier. 1753. III. 105.
— Register van alle de soorten van Peeren en Appelen. 1752. III. 75.[2]
Grönelius, Gabriel. Rön och Anmärkningar om utländska wäxter. See GADD, P. A. 1777. III. 120.[1]
Groeneveldt, W. P. & others. Gouvernements Koffiecultuur ter Sumatra's westkust. 1893. III. 730.
Groenewegen, J. H. Piper Cubeba (Bijsoort). 1861. III. 342.[2]
Groenewegen, Jacob Cornelius. Les Cycadées du Jardin botanique d'Amsterdam. 1860. III. 284.[1]
— Een Encephalartos spec. 1855. III. 285.[1]
— Index op de kunstwoordenleer der planten. 1836. I. 70.
— See also MIQUEL, F. A. G. & GROENEWEGEN, J. C.
Groenewegen & Co. Neue Einfuhrungen der Herren Groenewegen. 1867. III. 666.[1]
— Pflanzenverzeichnisse. 1866. III. 693,[2] 745.[1]
Grœnewold, Eme. Contributions à l'étude de l'aloine. 1890. III. 333.[2]
Groening, C. G. Nomenclator Linnaeanus in Elisabeth Blakwell herbarium. 1794. I. 78.[1]
Groenland, Johannes. Abies Nordmanniana. 1866. III. 296.[2]
— L'Arbre à cire du Japon. 1863. III. 527.[2]
— Bouvardia leiantha Benth. 1857. III. 711.[2]
— Sur le Callicarpa purpurea. 1859. III. 695.[2]
— Cassia floribunda. 1858. III. 471.[1]
— Cestrum aurantiacum Lindl. 1858. III. 699.[1]
— Le Cyanophyllum magnificum. 1859. III. 638.[2]
— Deux Butzneriacées. 1860. III. 591.[2]
— Diplacus grandiflorus. 1857. III. 703.[1]
— Le Franciscea à grandes fleurs. 1860. III. 699.[1]
— Sur le Gardenia citriodora. 1859. III. 747.[1]
— Genetyllis tulipifera. 1857. III. 633.[2]
— Hibbertia perfoliata. 1857. III. 596.[1]
— Lagerstroemia indica. 1857. III. 629.[2]
— Leycesteria formosa Wal. 1857. III. 749.[2]
— Mahonia Bealii Fort. 1857. III. 395.[2]
— Mandevilla suaveolens. 1857. III. 689.[1]
— Montanos mollissima. 1857. III. 755.[1]
— La Piméléé élégante. 1859. III. 628.[1]
— Les plantes à feuilles bigarrées. 1862. III. 206.[2]
— Les plantes à feuilles ornementales. 1862. III. 205.[2]
— Quelques mots sur les Yuccas. 1858. III. 339.[2]
— Quercus glabra Thunbg. 1858. III. 362.[1]
— Quisqualis indica. 1858. III. 632.[2]
— Rhododendron Hodgsoni. 1866. III. 659.[1]
— Sparrmannia africana. 1858. III. 585.[1]
— Sphaerostema marmoratum. 1862. III. 400.[2]
— Thea viridis L. et Chirita sinensis. 1858. III. 600.[1]
— Le Thunbergia à feuilles de Laurier. 1860. III. 710.[2]
— Le Welwitschia mirabilis. 1863. II. 55.[2]
Cornu, Maxime & Rivet, Gabriel. Des preparations microscopiques. 1872. I. 36.[2]
Grønlund, Chr. Danske Giftplanter. 1874. III. 67.[1]
— Om Egetræernes Galler. 1892. IV. 501.[1]
— Om Giftplanter. 1877. III. 59.[1]
— Hussvampen. 1888. IV. 415.[1]
— Islands Flora. 1881. I. 357.
— Karakteristik af Plantevæxten paa Island. 1884. I. 357.
— Nogle Løv- og Naaletræers ydre Former. 1889. I. 106.[1]
— Om Planternes Galler. 1899. I. 214.[2]
— Stammens ... anatomiske Bygning hos Nesa theifera. 1872. II. 190.[1]
— Sur la structure anatomique ... du Nesa theifera Oerd. 1872. II. 190.[2]
— Sveriges plantegeografiske Bælter. 1867. I. 356.
Grönvall, Troed Axel Ludvig. Några anteckningar till Skånes flora. 1859. I. 355.
Grösse, Ernst. Taschenbuch der Flora von Nord- und Mitteldeutschland. 1865. I. 385.
Ueber die **grössere** oder geringere Gefahr des Windbruchs. 1835. IV. 189.[1]
Die **grössere** oder geringere Sicherheit des normalen Ertrags des Waldbodens. 1857. IV. 251.[2]
Die **grösste** Tanne der Schwarzwaldes. 1878. II. 24.[1]
Grötzsch. Zur Geschichte und dem Wesen der Baumrodung. 1891. IV. 387.[1]

Groff, George B. Chestnut trees on limestone soil. 1884. III. 358.[2]
Grognier. Recherches historiques ... sur le Mûrier. 1825. III. 374.
Grognot, C. Plantes vasculaires ... de Saône-et-Loire. 1861. I. 412.
Gromaire, E. Notions pratiques d'agriculture. 1888. III. 144.
De **grondslagen** der Plantengeographie. 1848. I. 299.
Grondstoffen voor de papierfabricatie. 1884. III. 380.[1]
Groneman, J. Bladen uit het dagboek van een indisch geneesheer. 1874. I. 466.
Grouen, Damian. Zwei neue Pflanzenarten aus Kärnten. 1881. II. 498.[1]
Gronovius, Jan Fredrik. Camphorae historia. 1715. III. 233. See also SENGUERD, Wolferd. 1715. III. 404.[2]
— Flora orientalis. 1755. I. 478.
— Flora virginica. 1739. I. 305.
Gronovius, Laurentius Theodorus. Auctuarium in Bibliothecam botanicam. 1760. I. 1.
Groom, James. Exhaustive effects of tree roots. 1877. III. 34.[2]
— Ivy a seaside plant. 1882. III. 642.[2]
— Laurel banks in pleasure grounds. 1876. III. 406.[1]
Groom, Percy. On bud-protection in dicotyledons. 1893. I. 108.[1]
— Elementary botany. 1898. I. 92.
— On the extra-floral nectaries of Aleurites. 1894. II. 436.
— On the function of laticiferous tubes. 1889. I. 136,[1] 181.
— On the thorns of Randia dumetorum Lam. 1892. II. 829.[2]
— Ueber den Vegetationspunkt der Phanerogamen. 1885. I. 132.[2]
Grooss, N. Christian. Veiledning ved Behandlingen af Sandflugtstrækningerne i Jylland. 1847. IV. 145, 156.[1]
Groot, J. J. M. de. Vruchtboomen kunstmatig onder bescherming van wÿnen. 1899. I. 235.[2]
De **grootste** boom van de wereld. 1822. II. 149.[2]
Groppler, Robert. Vergleichende Anatomie des Holzes der Magnoliaceen. 1894. II. 209.[1]
Gros. Rapport ... Sur l'aliénation du sol de la forêt de Beaufort. 1791. IV. 275.
Un **gros** Chêne. 1897. IV. 559.[2]
Les **gros** Chênes. 1894. IV. 516.[1]
Grosdemange, Charles. Un cas de dimorphisme. 1893. II. 271.[2]
— Les Ceanothus rustiques. 1893. III. 541.[1]
— Les Cupulifères à feuillage ornemental. 1894. III. 358.
— Deux bonnes greffes. 1897. III. 163.[1]
— Deux Sapindacées remarquables. 1895. II. 483,[1] 487.[1]
— Effet ornemental des fruits du Fusain du Japon. 1897. III. 532.[2]
— Les Érables à feuillage panaché. 1893. III. 534.[1]
— Les Exochorda. 1896. III. 424.[1]
— Formation de la palmette chez le Poirier. 189.? III. 445.[2]
— Les Forsythia. 1893. III. 671.[2]
— Fructification de l'Elaeagnus reflexa. 1897. III. 629.[1]
— Fructification du Cedrela sinensis. 1894. III. 512.[1]
— La Glycine de Chine à fleurs doubles. 1895. III. 491.[1]
— Greffe en placage de côté sous écorce. 1894. III. 163.[1]
— The Griselinias. 1894. III. 646.[2]
— Les Groseilliers à fleurs. 1895. III. 414.[1]
— Les Ligustrina. 1894. III. 680.[2]
— L'Osteomeles anthyllidifolia. 1894. III. 430.[1]
— Le Pitch-Pin. 1897. III. 308.[1]
— Les Pommiers microcarpes d'origine américaine. 1896. III. 429.[1]
— À propos des Griselinia. 1894. III. 646.[2]
— Quelques Papilionacées ligneuses remarquables. 1894. III. 462.[1]
— Recherches sur les caractères ... de Rosiers. 1896. III. 451.[1]
— Remarque sur la floraison du Xanthoceras. 1898. III. 540.
— Les Rosiers grimpants de Suisnes. 1895. III. 451.[1]
— Sciadopitys verticillata. 1895. III. 309.[2]
— The service trees. 1894. III. 459.[1]
— Les Sorbiers. 1894. III. 459.[1]
— Les Sumacs d'ornement. 1893. III. 526.[1]
— Le Symphoricarpus occidentalis. 1894. III. 752.[2]
— Taille des arbustes et arbrisseaux fleurissant. 1897. III. 173.[1]
— Transplantation estivale des Conifères. 1893. III. 295.
— Transplantation estivale des Pivoines en arbre. 1895. III. 393.[1]

Grose, G. H. Note on the oil of the Kurrungah. 1859. III. 484.²
Groser, William H. Scripture natural history. 1888. I. 513.
Grosglik, S. Barwność liści. 1887. I. 185.²
— Kwiaty drzewa Melonowego. 1884. II. 582.²
— Kwiaty i kwiatostany Klonu. 1887. II. 477.¹
— O metodzie badania asymilacyi. 1890. I. 174.
— Nowsze poglądy na budowę przestworów międzykomórkowych. 1886. I. 137.
— O padanie liści. 1888. I. 192.¹
— Zaraza na Wiśnie. 1886. III. 435.¹
— Z życia Jemioły. 1888. II. 179.¹
Grosier, Jean Baptiste Gabriel Alexandre. ·Description générale de la Chine. 1787. I. 458.
— A general description of China. 1787. I. 458.
Grosjean. Forêt de Molinges. 1898. IV. 556.¹
— Notice sur l'industrie du sabotage. 1878. IV. 428.²
— See also COCHON, J. & GROSJEAN.
Grosjean, H. Note sur la destruction de la chématobie. 1896. III. 191.
Grosourdy, Réné de. El médico botánico criollo. 1864. III. 63.²
Gross, (Forstmeister). Anleitung zur künstlichen Erziehung der . . . Waldbaumpflanzen. 1854. IV. 150.
Gross, Fr. Wilhelm. Die Gross- und Urgrossväter der Pflanzenwelt. 1895. IV. 65.¹
— Wälder und Steppen . . . Kostroma. 1891. IV. 346.
Gross, H. Die einfacheren Operationen der praktischen Geometrie. 1879. IV. 265.
Gross, Heinrich. Die wichtigeren Handelspflanzen. 1880. III. 53.
Grossbauer, (Prof.). Ueber die Conservirung des Holzes. 1859. IV. 418.
Grossbauer, Franz von. Die kleinste Fichte- Oesterreichs. 1887. IV. 460.¹
— Die stärkste- Tanne des Kobernauserwaldes. 1875. IV. 24.¹
— Ueber die Stellung des Forstbeamten gegenüber den Holzhandel. 1873. IV. 388.¹
— Weymoutskiefer und Borkenkäfer. 1875. IV. 470.¹
— Das Winkler'sche Taschen-Dendrometer. 1864. IV. 215, 231.³
— See also NEWALD, Johann & GROSSBAUER, Franz.
Der grossblühende Laurustin. 1857. III. 753.¹
Die grossblüthigen Clematis-Arten. 1885. III. 389.¹
Grosse, Ernst. Flora von Aschersleben. 1861. I. 384.
Grosse, Franz. Die Verbreitung der Vegetationsformationen Amerikas. 1899. I. 308.
Grosse, Karl. Leitfaden der Botanik. 1835. I. 87.
Grosse Bäume in Kalifornien. See CALIFORNIAN giants. 1856. II. 50.²
Grosse Birke in Irland. 1831. II. 118.¹
Der grosse centralafrikanische Wald. 1893. IV. 89.¹
Grosse Eiche. 1834.. II. 138.¹
Grosse Eiche am Uetliberg. 1887. II. 139.¹
Die grosse Eiche in Riffersweil. 1890. II. 139.¹
Grosse Eichen. 1887. II. 139.¹
Grosse Eichen in England. 1858. II. 138.¹
Die grosse Linde zu Neuenstadt in Württemberg. 1877. II. 516.²
Grosse Linden. ·1858. II. 516.²
Grosse Nefle. 1835. III. 429.²
Die grosse Sperre im Wildbach Rieulet bei Barèges. · 1899. IV. 187.²
Grosse Tanne in Böhmen. 1858. II. 24.¹
Die grosse Tanne zu Illfingen. 1895. II. 24.¹
Grosse Taunen. 1883. II. 24.¹
Grosser Baum. See Eine MÄCHTIGE Ceder. 1853. II. 50.²
Grosser Waldbrand bei Aachen. 1900. IV. 182.²
Ein grosser Weidenbaum in England. See The LARGEST Willow in England. 1893. IV. 488.¹
Grossgebauer, F. Eigenthümlichkeiten der Wirthschaftsführung in den Höhenbeständen· des Thüringerwaldes. 1867. IV. 118.
— Die grossfälligen Holzerträge. 1865. IV. 243.
Die grossherzoglich hessische Oberförsterei Erbach. See WEITERSHAUSEN, Heinrich, Freiherr von. 1875. IV. 351.¹
Grossherzogthum Berg; kaiserliches Decret die Organisation der Forstverwaltung enthaltend. 1811. IV. 290.¹
Das Grossherzogtum Baden. See DÖLL, J. C. 1884. I. 388.
Grossi, Vincenzo. Nel paese delle Amazzoni. 1897. III. 269.³

Grossinger, Johann Baptist. Universa historia physica regni Hungariae. 1792. I. 444.
Grosskopff, Johann August. Neues und wohl eingerichtetes Forst- Jagd- und Weidewercks-Lexicon. 1759. IV. 22.¹
Grossmann. Der preussische Jäger und Forstbeamte. 1862. IV. 290.²
— Die Rentenrechnung ohne geometrische Reihen. 1886. IV. 257.
— Schwedische Untersuchungen über den Einfluss des Waldes auf das Klima. 1886. IV. 46.²
Grossmann, L. Elementarbuch für den Unterricht in der Botanik. 1843. I. 88.
Grote, Carl Gottlieb. Entwurf der Forstwissenschaft. 1765. IV. 94.
De grote herbarius met al zyn figure. See ORTUS sanitatis. 148 . ? I. 275.²
Den groten herbarius met alden figuren der cruyden. , See ORTUS sanitatis. 148 . ? I. 275.²
Groth, Eric Gustav. Om inhemske träd och buskar. See THUNBERG, C. P. 1821. I. 350.¹
Grothe, D. De bewerking der getah-pertsja. 1859. III. 231.
Grothe, Hermann. Die Gespinnstfasern aus dein Pflanzenreiche. 1879. III. 234.
— See also BOUCHÉ, C. B. & GROTHE, Hermann.
Grothè, Otto. Dienstliche Schreiben des Försters. 1896. IV. 312.
— Sammlung von forstlichen Rechenaufgaben. 1881. IV. 59.¹
Group of Cycas circinalis. 1887. III. 285.¹
Group of Cycas siamensis. 1882. III. 285.¹
Un groupe de Cycas revoluta. 1850. II. 4.³
Un groupe de Cycas . . . 1850. II. 4.³
Un groupe de Yucca Draconis. 1899. III. 340.¹
A grove of Wild Cherry in North Carolina. 1899. II. 277.¹
Groves, Charles Edward. · See STENHOUSE, John & GROVES, C. E.
Groves, Enrico. See GROVES, Henry.
Groves, Henry. The coast flora of Japygia, S. Italy. 1885. I. 429.
— Flora del Sirente. 1880. I. 429.
— Flora della costa meridionale della Terra d'Otranto. 1887. I. 429.
Groves, Thomas B. On kamala. 1872. III. 520.³
Grower, (pseud.). The Tetrathecas. 1894. III. 513.² ·
Growth and manufacture of silk. See RUSH, Richard. 1828. III. 374.
Growth of English timber trees. 1863. IV. 64.²
Growth of Pinus Pinaster. 1884. IV. 64.²
Growth of the Bamboo. 1864. II. 59.²
Growth of the Lemon-scented Gum. 1900. III. 634.²
The growth of the Mistletoe on the Oak. 1871. II. 179.¹
On the growth of the Willow. . 1876. II. 104.²
The growth of trees. 1862. I. 187.
Growth of trees in scoria. soil. 1880. III. 41.¹
The growth of tropical fruits in Madeira. 1897.· III. 132.¹
The growth of Yew trees. 1889. II. 10.³
Grube, A. Strassenbäume. 1899. III. 211.²
Grube, Hermann. Analysis mali Citrei compendiosa. 1668. III. 498.²
— De vita et sanitate plantarum. 1664. I. 30. ·
Gruber, D. See MUSCULUS, Friedrich & GRUBER, D.
Gruber, Friedrich. See WAGENER, P. C. & GRUBER, Friedrich.
Gruber, Hugo. Über die Anatomie des· Holzes von Pinus Larix. 1890. II. 871.¹
Gruber, I. See FRANK, A. & GRUBER, I.
Gruber, Karl. Forststatistik des Komitates Zips. 1873. IV. 373.
Gruber, Michael.· Darstellung der forstschädlichen Insekten. 1842. IV. 92.
Grubs at the roots of Cocoa trees. 1895. III. 593.²
Grude, M. A. Om plantningssagens krav. 1900. IV. 344.¹
— Om skovkultur eller plantning. 1898. IV. 103.²
Grtiger. Beitrag zur Kultur der Wistaria. 1866. III. 490.²
Grün, W. Neu erfundenes Veredlungsverfahren. 1808. III. 162.
Grünberg, (jr.). (Kunst- und Handelsgärtner, Frankfurt a. M,). Uber Camellia Teutonia. 1844. III. 598.¹
Grünberger, Georg. Die Anfangsgründe der Rechenkunst und Messkunst. See DÄZEL, G. A. & GRÜNBERGER, Georg. 1788. IV. 95.
— Einige Ansichten von den Forstwesen in Baiern. 1805. IV. 273.³
— See also DÄZEL, G. A. & GRÜNBERGER, Georg.

Gründliche Anleitung zum Anbau . . . des unächten Accacienbaums. *See* SCHMIDT, J. J. 1797. IV. 522.[2]
Gründliche Anleitung zur Erzeugung . . . vorzüglicher Holzarten. *See* GEMMINGEN, Karl, *Freiherr* von. 1799. IV. 105.
Gründliche Anweisung zur wohleingerichteten Baumschule. 1702. III. 153.
Gründliche Gegen-Information dass der Wildbann in der Drey-Eich über die Franckfurter Waldunge und Felder sich nicht erstrecke. 1738. IV. 319.[2]
Gründliche und sichere Nachricht vom Cafee. *See* LA ROQUE, Jean de. 1717. III. 738.
Gründlicher Bericht von dem uhralten Reichs- und Königs-Forst zur Drey-Eichen. 1736. IV. 348.[2]
Gründlicher Unterricht für den Bürger . . . in der Maulbeerbaum und Seidenraupenzucht. 1829. III. 374.
Grüner, Franz Julius. Ueber den wurzelnden und Gift-Sumach. 1824. III. 528.[1]
Grueno, Joseph. De camphora. 1780. III. 233.[1]
Grüss, Johannes. Beiträge zur Biologie der Knospe. 1892. I. 108.[3]
— Die Diastase im Pflanzenkörper. 1895. I. 177.
— Ueber die Einwirkung der Diastase-Fermente. 1894. I. 177.
— Die Knospenschuppen der Coniferen. 1885. II. 18.
— Über Lösung und Bildung der aus Hemicellulose bestehenden Zellwände. 1896. I. 213.[1]
— Ueber Oxydasen und die Guajakreaction. 1898. I. 157.
— Recherche et rôle de la diastase. 1895. I. 177.
— Studien über Reservecellulose. 1897. I. 179,[1] *II*. 73.[1]
Gruet, P. Mémoire sur la culture du Pécher. 1824. III. 440.[2] IV. 469.
Grütter, E. Zur Würdigung der Weymouthskiefer. 1871. IV. 469.
Grütter, Max Eugen Heinrich. Crataegus brevispina bei Sartowitz. 1896. II. 261.[1]
Grütter, Wilhelm. Ueber den Bau . . . der Samenschalen einiger Lythrarieen. 1893. II. 608.[2]
Grüttner, Fritz. Beiträge zur Chemie der Rinde von Hamamelis virginica. 1898. III. 417.[1]
Grützner, B. Ueber einen krystallisierten Bestandteil der Basanacantha. 1895. III. 711.[1]
Grufberg, Isaac Olaf. Flora anglica. *See* LINNÉ, Carl von. 1754. I. 394.
Grugeon, Alfred. Influence of terminal and axillary buds on the quality of timber. 1865. IV. 414.[1]
Grulich, Oscar. Katalog der Bibliothek der Kaiserlichen leopoldinisch-carolinischen deutschen Akademie der Naturforscher. 1887. I. 2.
Grumbach. *See* ZIMMERMANN, MITTLER & GRUMBACH.
Grundlagen für die Verhandlungen der . . . Commission . . . gegen die Ausbreitung der Nonne. 1890. IV. 200.
Grundner, Fritz. Taschenbuch zu Erdmassen-Berechnungen. 1884. IV. 267.
— Untersuchungen über die Querflächen-Ermittlung der Holzbestände. 1882. IV. 218.
— Die Verwendung von Kupfersoda gegen die Kiefernschütte. 1900. IV. 480.
— *See also* HORN, L. W. & GRUNDNER, Fritz.
— **Schuberg**, Karl & **Schwappach**, Adam. Hilfstafeln zur Inhaltsbestimmung von Bäumen und Beständen der Hauptholzarten. 1898. IV. 231.[1]
Die Grundprincipien der modernen Staatsforstwirthschaft. 1870. IV. 260.
Grundris der Forstwissenschaft. *See* PFEIFFER, von. 1781. IV. 95.
Grundriss der Forstwissenschaft für Vorlesungen. *See* WALTHER, F. L. 1789. IV. 95.
Grundriss der Naturgeschichte. *See* BURMEISTER, Hermann. 1845. I. 88.
Grundsätze der Werths-Bestimmung der Waldungen. *See* SEUTTER, J. G., *Freiherr* von. 1814. IV. 253.
Grundsteuerveranlagung: Klassifikationstarif für die Holzungen. 1872. IV. 261.[1]
Grundy. On the circulation of sap. 1857. I. 164.
— On the structure of the starch granule. 1855. I. 140.[1]
Grundzüge der Buchenfanerziehung. *See* KOENIG, G. 1846. IV. 494.
Grundzüge der Referate für die Versammlung des Schweizerischen Forstvereins in Glarus. 1886. IV. 41.[2]
Grundzüge für die Verwaltung der Staats- und Fondsforste und Domänen (mit Ausnahme der Güter des Bukowina'er griechisch orientalischen Religionsfondes). n. d. IV. 307.[1]
Gruner, A. Ueber das leuchtende Holz. 1870. I. 207.[1]
Gruner, Carl Ernst. Homöopathische Pharmakopöe. 1845. III. 249.

Gruner, Christian Gottfried. De Ledi palustris natura. 1793. III. 653.[1]
Gruner, Heinrich. Kurzer und gründlicher Unterricht in der Obstbaumzucht. 1823. III. 136.
Gruner, Leopold. Zur Characteristik der Boden- und Vegetationsverhältnisse des Steppengebietes. 1872. I. 363.
— Enumeratio plantarum . . . ad flumina Borysthenem et Konkam. 1869. I. 363.
— Zur Kenntniss der Vegetationsverhältnisse von Palna. 1868. I. 362.
— Plantae bakuenses Bruhnsii. 1867. I. 362.
— Schilderung der Vegetationsverhältnisse des östlichen Allentacken. 1862. I. 362.
— Versuch einer Flora Allentackens. 1864. I. 362.
Grunersche Zeitung. IV. 9.
Grunert, Julius Theodor. Bewaldung des Seeufers . . . in Belgien. 1873. IV. 145.
— An Buchen. 1873. IV. 496.
— Der Eichenschälwald im Reg. . . . Trier. 1868. IV. 512.
— Eine eigenthümliche Eichen-Galle. 1877. IV. 510.
— Eigenthümliche Krankheitserscheinungen an Waldbäumen. 1873. IV. 476, 496.
— Einige Erträge der Kiefer, als Treibholz . . . angebaut. 1874. IV. 480.
— Einiges über forstliche Verhältnisse der Schweiz. 1877. IV. 123.[1]
— Der Engerlingsfrass sonst und jetzt. 1878. IV. 203.
— Forstlehre. 1872. IV. 98.[1]
— Die Forstlehrlings- und die Förster-Prüfung in Fragen. 1885. IV. 33.[1]
— Forstmeister- und Oberförster-System. 1877. IV. 287.
— An Kiefern. 1873. IV. 476.
— Der Neuhauser Rückwagen. 1886. IV. 389.
— Der preussische Förster. 1869. IV. 320.
— Der Schneebruch in . . . Tronecken und Morbach. 1875. IV. 190.
— Die staatliche Beschränkung der Gemeinde-Forstverwaltung in Preussen. 1876. IV. 286.[2]
— Die Trierer Lohhecken. 1868. IV. 512.
— Die Waldschutzfrage. 1873. IV. 285.[2]
— Der Wurzeltödter der Eiche. 1877. IV. 510.
Grunert, Oswald. Zu Borggreve's Plenterdurchforstung. 1888. IV. 174.
— Ueber die Zuverlässigkeit . . . Zuwachs mittelst des Pressler'schen Zuwachsbohrers zu bestimmen. 1873. IV. 123.[2]
Gruns, S. J. van. De bast van de Magnolia glauca. 1791. III. 399.[2]
Gruppe. Sur la ditaïne, nouveau succedané de la quinine. 1873. III. 686.[2]
Gruppe von Bambusa aurea. 1891. III. 316.[1]
Grus, Roman. Brzoza jej opisanie. 1891. IV. 490.[2]
— O chorobie młodych Sosen, zwanej osutką. 1891. IV. 478.
— Przypomnienie czynności gospodarskich na każdy miesiąc dla leśnika. 1891. IV. 94.
— Sciółka leśna. 1892. IV. 72.
— Uprawa i pielęgnowanie lasu. 1897. IV. 111.[1]
Grye, Amédée BOUQUET DE LA. *See* BOUQUET DE LA GRYE, Amédée.
Gsaller, Carl. Ein Fall hermaphroditer Blüthen an Salix. 1070. II. 105.[1]
gt. Handelsverträge und Forstwirthschaft. 1900. IV. 271.[1]
Guallart, Eugenio. Aplicaciones del cálculo gráfico. 1897. IV. 542.[2]
— Determinación gráfica de las existencias de los montes. 1896. IV. 550.[1]
— Discusión completa de las soluciones comunes a un sistema lineal. 1900. IV. 542.[2]
— La ordenación de los montes públicos españoles. 1895. IV. 550.[2]
— Pantógrafo-planimetro. 1895. IV. 551.[2]
— Pruebas de la suma y producto según Agustín Cauchy. 1898. IV. 542.[2]
— Trabajos forestales en Salinas. 1895. IV. 543.[2]
Guanabara. I. 7.[2]
The Guarana of Brazil. 1861. III. 539.[2]
Guardiola, Emilio LÓPEZ. *See* LÓPEZ GUARDIOLA, Emilio.
Gubernatis, Angelo de. La mythologie des plantes. 1878. I. 518.
Gubler, Adolphe. Des anomalies aberrantes et régularisantes. 1862. II. 457.[2]
— De l'antagonisme . . . de la belladonne et de la fève de Calabar. 1872. III. 484.[1]

Gubler, Adolphe (*continued*).
— Étude pharmacologique sur la poudre de Goa. 1875. III. 467.[1]
— Étude tératologique sur . . . Pinus Pinea. 1861. II. 45.[1]
— Sur l'Eucalyptus globulus. 1871. IV. 532.[2]
— Fasciation du Cytisus Laburnum. 1860. II. 369.[1]
— " Lime-juice " et antiscorbutiques. 1877. III. 502.[2]
— Note on a Piper, called Jaborandi. 1877. III. 342.[2]
— Note sur le Piper, appelé Jaborandi. 1877. III. 342.[2]
Gudent, Arthur, *Freiherr* von SECKENDORFF-. *See* SECKENDORFF-GUDENT, Arthur, *Freiherr* von.
Guebhard, Ch. Notice géographique et botanique sur la Moldavie. 1849. I. 449.
Guebhart, A. Les Noyers au Val-de-Travers. 1867. III. 355.
Guéguen, Fernand. Recherches sur le tissu collecteur et conducteur. 1900. I. 118.[1]
Gueidan, (*ar.*). Indicateur des semis et travaux de jardins. 189 . ? III. 113.
Güldenstädt, Johann Anton. Reisen durch Russland. 1787. I. 360.
Aus der **Gülich-** und Bergischer Policey-Ordnung. 1761. IV. 319.[2]
Güell, Eduart, TODA Y. *See* TODA Y GÜELL, Eduart.
Guelliot, Maurice Joseph Désiré. Étude sur les Daphnés. 1867. III. 627.[1]
Guelliot, O. Du caféisme chronique. 1885. . III. 742.[1]
Gülzow, Albert. Rosen in Kalifornien. 1894. III. 454.[2]
Gümbel, Friedrich L. Bemerkungen über Forstkulturen. 1832. IV. 140.
— Die Feststellung des nachhaltigen Ertrages. 1834. IV. 235.[1]
— Ueber die Form der Mischung beim Holzanbau. 1857. IV. 141.
— Ueber die richtigere Feststellung des Gesammtalters eines Holzbestandes. 1841. IV. 235.[1]
— Die zahme Kastanie. 1846. IV. 492.[2]
Gümbel, Theodor. Zur Entwicklungsgeschichte von Viscum. 1856. II. 178.[2]
— Der Gipfel des Blüthenbüschels von Prunus Cerasus. 1855. II. 273.[2]
— Ad Viscum album. 1855. II. 178.[2]
Gümbel, W. . Ueber das grünfaule Holz. 1858. I. 206.[2]
Gümbke, Christ Stanislaus. Fundamentum differentiae specificae plantarum. *See* BJÖRNLUND, Benedictus. 1771. I. 250.
Guénard, *baronne* DE MÉRÉ, *Madame*. Les enfans voyageurs. 1819. I. 94.
Günderrode, Friedrich Justinian, *Freiherr* von & Borkhausen, ' M. B. Die Pflaumen. 1804. III. 432.[2]
— — Vorschläge zur Verbreitung des Gemüse- und Obstbaues. 1801. III. 121.[1]
Guénot. Des effets du déboisement dans les Pyrénées. 1896. V. XXIX.[2]
— Des funestes effets du déboisement. 1898. IV. 47.[2]
— Les Pyrénées au Congrès de géographie. 1899. IV. 282.[2]
Guénot, L. Le charançon coupe bourgeons de la Vigne. 1899. III. 564.[2]
— Le pucéron lanigère du Pommier. 1900. III. 428.[2]
— & **Pradel**, Colomb. La pyrale de la Vigne. 1899. III. 564.[1]
Günther, A. *See* ГЮНТЕРЪ, А.
Günther, Alfred. Der Waldarbeiter. 1900. IV. 311.[2]
Günther, Carl Christian, Grabowski, Heinrich & **Wimmer**, Friedrich. Enumeratio stirpium phanerogamarum . . . in Silesia. 1824. I. 377.
Günther, Chr. Aralia papyrifefa var. Neuberti. 1865. III. 644.[1]
Günther, G. Friedrich Carl. Die Ziergewächse . . . bei den Alten. 1861. III. 32.[2]
Guenther, Gustav Biedermann. *See* THIENEMANN, F. A. L. & GUENTHER, G. B.
Günther, Hermann. Botanik; Tabellen zur Bestimmung der . . . angebauten Pflanzen. 1875. I. 387.
— Botanik. Teil I. Morphologie. Systematik. 1875. I. 387.
— Tabellen zur leichten Bestimmung der . . . Blüthenpflanzen Norddeutschlands. 1875. I. 387.
Guenther, Johann & **Bertuch**, Friedrich. Pinakothek der deutschen Giftgewächse. 1840. III. 73.
Günther, N. Beurtheilung der analytischen Methoden . . . zur Bestimmung des in Katechu . . . vorhandenen Gerbstoff's. 1870. I. 183.
Günther, Siegmund. Die Phänologie. 1895. V. XII.[2]

Günther, W. A. Das preussische Gesetz vom 15. April 1878 betr. den Forstdiebstahl. 1878. IV.-321. .
— Die preussische Polizei- und Strafgesetzgebung. 1874. IV. 321.
Günz, J. W. & **Mayenberg**, C. C. De cortice Salicis cortici peruviano substituendo. 1772. III. 350.[2]
Guépin, Jean Pierre. Flore de Maine et Loire. 1830. I. 408, V. XXI.[2]
— Notice sur une flore angevine. 1853. I. 411.
Guéranger, Édouard. Catalogue explicatif des produits agricoles . . . de la Sarthe. 1862. III. 271.[1]
— Floraison du Dasylirium gracile. 1850. III. 336.[1]
— Note sur la mort de deux Pêchers. 1850. III. 441.[2]
— Observations botaniques sur la flore de La Suze. 1868. I. 413.
Guérard, G. de. Conservation des bois. 1890. IV. 421.
— Industrie du bois courbé. 1889. IV. 422.[2]
Guérard, Henri & **Boutineau**, Émile. Tunisie; La Khroumirie. 1892. I. 486, *IV. 379*.[2]
Guerbet, M. Sur la composition de l'essence de Santal. 1900. III. 384.[1]
— Santalène et santalols. 1900. III. 384.[2]
Guercio, Giacomo del. La cocciniglia del Pandanus utilis. 1894. III. 313.[1]
— Intorno ad una nuova infezione del Pero. 1897. III. 446.[2]
— Osservazioni sulla infezione fillosserica. 1892. III. 762.
— Di una speciale alterazione della corteccia della Querce. 1896. IV. 511.
— *See also* TARGIONI-TOZZETTI, Adolfo & GUERCIO, Giacomo del.
— & **Baroni**, Eugenio. La gommosi bacillare delle Viti. 1894. III. 581.
— — Rimedi contro la infezione prodotta sulle Rose. 1894. III. 453.[1]
Gürich, T. Pěstování pomerančovníku. 1886. III. 500.[1]
Guericke, F. A. ENKLAAR VAN. *See* ENKLAAR VAN GUERICKE, F. A.
Guérin, Charles. Expériences sur la germination . . . du Gui. 1890. III. 385.[2]
— Gui de Chêne. 1874. II. 179.[1]
— Implantations de Gui sur Gui. 1896. II. 179.[2]
— Notes sur . . . l'histoire naturelle du Gui. 1892. II. 179.[2]
— Observations biologiques sur le Gui. 1898. II. 180.[1]
Guérin, G. Sur un composé organique, riche en manganèse, retiré du tissu ligneux. 1897. *I. 178*, IV. 433.[1]
Guérin, Jean. Fragmens d'une topographie . . . de Vaucluse. 1807. I. 407.
Guérin, Paul. Culture du Cacaoyer. 1896. III. 593.[1]
— Sur la présence de l'amidon soluble dans les feuilles de Coja. 1897. II. 533.[1]
— Recherches sur la localisation de l'anagyrine. 1895. II. 350.[1]
— Recherches sur le développement du tégument séminal . . . des Graminées. 1899. II. 58.[2]
Guérin, R. Recherches sur les glandes du Rosa rubiginosa. 1874. II. 298.[1]
Guérin, René, Dario, Gonzalès & Garcia, Jorge. Catalogue des produits présentés par . . . Guatémala. 1900: III. 265.[1]
Guérin-Méneville, Félix Édouard. The Ailanthus silkworm and the Ailanthus tree. 1862. III. 507.[2]
— Aperçu sommaire de l'état actuel de l'épidémie des Mûriers. 1862. III. 379.[1]
— Application utile des procédés indiqués pour arrêter les ravages . . . du Dacus. 1852. III. 677.[1]
— Brief note on a Dacus. 1847. III. 677.[1]
— Description d'un nouveau ver à soie du Chêne. 1861. IV. 501.[2]
— Éducation des vers à soie de l'Ailante. 1860. III. 506.[2]
— Éducation en plein air du ver à soie de l'Ailante. 1860. III. 507.[1]
— Éducations hâtives de vers à soie. 1860. III. 377.
— Emploi de l'Ailante pour la fixation des sables. 1861. IV. 525.
— Indication des principales localités où commence à se développer la culture de l'Ailante. 1866. III. 506.[2]
— Introduction d'un nouveau ver à soie de Chine. 1858. III. 507.[1]
— Sur l'introduction en France du ver à soie chinois. 1859. III. 507.[1]
— Sur la maladie de la Vigne. 1872. III. 560.
— Maladie des feuilles de Mûrier. 1858. III. 379.[1]
— La maladie des Vignes. 1853. III. 576.

— Note accompagnant la présentation . . . d' individus vivants . . . de vers à soie du Chêne. 1864. III. 430.[1]
— Note sur diverses espèces du genre Oidium. 1850. III. 193.[2]
— Note sur l'introduction d'une quatrième espèce de ver à soie du Chêne. 1864. IV. 501.[2]
— Note sur la première éducation . . . du ver à soie de l'Ailante. 1860. III. 507.[1]
— Note sur le dommage . . . aux récoltes d' Olives. 1847. III. 677.[2]
— Note sur le ver à soie Tussah. 1855. IV. 501.[2]
— Note sur les moyens . . . de restaurer la graine de vers à soie. 1858. III. 380.[1]
— Note sur les qualités du bois de l'Ailante. 1865. IV. 525.
— Note sur les races de vers à soie du Mûrier. 1859. III. 380.[1]
— Note sur un nouveau sous-genre de Bombycide. 1865. III. 467,[2] 644.[1]
— Note sur un procédé proposé par M. Rozetti. 1851. III. 677.[2]
— Note sur un procédé propre à detruire les vers . . . qui rongent le parenchyme des Olives. 1846. III. 677.[1]
— Note sur une larve de lépidoptère qui dévore les racines de la Pivoine. 1849. III. 393.[1]
— Sur un nouveau ver à soie. 1864. III. 394,[2] 465.[1]
— Une observation sur des Vignes malades. 1854. III. 559.[2]
— Observations pour servir à l'histoire naturelle de l'hylésine piniperde. 1852. IV. 461.[1]
— Observations séricicoles. 1859. III. 379.[1]
— Observations sur la maladie de la Vigne. 1852. III. 575.[2]
— Observations sur la pyrale de la Vigne. 1837. III. 562.[2]
— Observations sur les mœurs . . . des Scolytes des Ormes. 1846. III. 364.[1]
— Observations sur un insecte qui attaque les Olives. 1844. III. 677.[1]
— Le phylloxera n'est pas la cause. 1873. III. 565.[3]
— Rapport . . . sur les progrès de la culture de l'Ailante. 1862. III. 506.[2]
— Rapport . . . sur les travaux . . . pour introduire le ver à soie de l'Aylanthe. 1860. III. 506.[3]
— Recherches sur les maladies des végétaux. 1854. III. 559.[2]
— Sur le ver à soie du Chêne. 1861. IV. 501.[1]
— Sur les vers à soie du Chêne et de l'Ailante. 1861. IV. 501.[2]
— & Perrotet, G. S. Mémoire sur un insect . . . qui ravagent les Cafiers. 1842. III. 734.[2]
Gürke, Maximilian. Die Bedeutung des Ramiekultur. 1899. III. 381.[2]
— Beiträge zur Systematik der Malvaceen. 1892. II. 519.[1]
— Borraginaceae africanae. 1900. II. 747.[2]
— Borraginaceae (Asperifoliaceae). 1897. II. 747.[3]
— Drei neue afrikanische Verbenaceae. 1900. II. 762.[1]
— Ebenaceae. 1891. II. 700.[2]
— Ebenaceae africanae. 1892. II. 700.[3]
— Flacourtiaceae-Oncobeae africanae. 1894. II. 569.[1]
— Ueber den Gerbstoffgehalt einiger Mangroverinden. 1897. III. 631.[2]
— L'intérêt de la culture de la Ramie. 1899. III. 381.[2]
— Labiatae africanae. 1895. II. 762.[3]
— Malvaceae, II. 1892. II. 519.[1]
— Meliaceae africanae. 1892. II. 422.[3]
— Melianthaceae. 1896. II. 491.[1]
— Melianthaceae africanae. 1892. II. 491.[1]
— Notizen über den Anbau . . . der Fasern der Agave-. . . Arten. 1895. III. 235.[1]
— Notizen über die Verwertung der Mangrovenrinden. 1895. III. 631.[2]
— La Ramie. 1899. III. 381.[3]
— Styracaceae. 1891. II. 704.[1]
— Symplocaceae. 1891. II. 703.[1]
— Verbenaceae africanae. 1894. II. 753.[1]
— & Volkens, Georg. Identificierung einiger ostafrikanischer Rinden und Hölzer. 1897. IV. 401.[1]
Gürker, F. Der Obstbaumschnitt. 1828. III. 172.
— Veredlung der Obstbäume. 1828. III. 136.
Guerlain, J. See Dupont, J. & Guerlain, J.
Guernieri, Angelo. L' Ailanto nella provincia di Belluno. 1864. IV. 525.
— Cubazioni dei legnami squadrati e rotondi. 1856. IV. 23.
— Imboschimenti nella provincia di Belluno. 1865. IV. 165.
— Manuale pel commerciante dei legnami. 1862. IV. 405,[2] 408.

Guernsey, A. H. Spare the trees. 1876. IV. 44.
Gürnth, A. Weibliche Forstökonomie. 1807. IV. 438.[2]
Guerpel, H. de. Le Gui sur le Marronnier. 1891. II. 179.[2]
Guerrapain, C. T. Almanach des Roses. 1811. III. 447.[2]
Guerrapain, Th. Notice sur la culture du Sophora. 1809. III. 356,[2] 419,[1] 488.[1]
Guersent. Observation sur le Brucea antidysenterica. 1804. II. 414.[1]
— Observations sur le Sabal d'Adanson. 1804. II. 74.[2]
Guéry. Note sur les effets produits par les gelées . . . sur les Eucalyptus. 1880. III. 633.[2]
Guesde, L. Les colonies françaises; la Guadeloupe. 1900. III. 267.[1]
Guesnet. Note sur la greffe en couronne à œil dormant. 1850. III. 164.[1]
Güssfeldt, Paul. Reise in den Andes von Chile und Argentinien. 1888. I. 330.
— Falkenstein, Julius- & Pechuël-Loesche, Eduard. Die Loango-Expedition. 1879. I. 491.
Güssow, Fritz R. Beiträge zur . . . Anatomie der Araliaceae. 1900. II. 647.[1]
Guettard, Jean Étienne. Mémoire sur la transpiration insensible des plantes. 1752. I. 166:
— Mémoire sur le. caractère spécifique des plantes. 1765. I. 250.
— Mémoire sur les corps glanduleux des plantes. 1749. I. 112.[1]
— Mémoire sur les plantes qu'on peut appeler fausses parasites. 1762. I. 234.[1]
— Mémoires sur différentes parties des sciences. 1768. I. 31.
— Observations sur les plantes. 1747. I. 31, 405.
Güttler, Hermann. Nouveau procédé de carbonisation du bois. 1890. IV. 395.
Gueymard, Émile. Analyse de diverses feuilles. 1864. I. 153.
— Mémoire sur les causes des inondations. 1857. IV. 185.[2]
— Notes sur le reboisement et gazonnement. 186.? IV. 162.
— Sur la nutrition des arbres forestiers. 1863. I. 158.
Gueyraud, F. Emploi d'un pal distributeur. 1876. III. 569.[1]
— Expériences relatives à l'action de l'ammoniaque. 1873. III. 565.[1]
— Sur la régénération des ceps phylloxérés. 1877. III. 570.[1]
— Résultats obtenus dans le traitement des Vignes phylloxérées. 1877. III. 570.[1]
— Traitement par les sulfocarbonates des Vignes d'Orléans. 1877. III. 570.[2]
Guffroy, C. E. L'anatomie végétale au point de vue de la classification. 1898. II. 311.[2]
Guglielmi, Giuseppe. Osservazioni sulla China-china officinale. 1811. III. 338.[1]
Gugnaire, (jr.). Sur la taille des arbustes. 1859. III. 172.
Guia do jardineiro horticultor e lavrador brasileiro. 1853. III. 100.[1]
Guiart, D. L. Classification végétale. 1807. I. 259.
— Exposition d'une nouvelle méthode. 1823. I. 57.
— Nouvelle méthode calquée sur celle de Tournefort. 1823. I. 57.
Las guias de productos forestales en la Argelia. 1886. IV. 285.[3]
Guibert, Victor. Histoire naturelle et médicale. 1861. III. 243.
— See also Heurck, Henri van & Guibert, Victor.
Guibourt, Nicolas Jean Baptiste Gaston. Des baumes du Perou et de Tolu. 1867. III. 627.[1]
— Sur l'écorce de Garou. 1867. III. 627.[1]
— Extrait de la monographie des Quinquinas de M. de Bergen. 1830. III. 717.[1]
— Histoire abrégée des drogues simples. 1822. III. 56.
— Histoire naturelle des drogues simples. 1822. III. 56.
— Sur le kamala, poudre rouge. 1858. III. 520 [1]
— Lettre à M. Félix Boudet sur l'extraction de l'huile de Croton tiglium. 1850. III. 517.[1]
— Mémoire sur l'origine . . . des térébenthines. 1839. III. 227, 859.[2]
— Mémoire sur les résines connues sous les noms de dammar. 1844. III. 227.
— Mémoire sur les sucs astringents. 1847. III. 244.
— Note sur l'Hebradendron cambogioides. 1850. II. 555.[2]
— Note sur l'huile de bois. 1856. III. 610.[2]
— Note sur le nom de Costus. 1819. III. 397,[2] 613.[2]
— Note sur les caractères distinctifs du Quinquina Calisaya. 1836. III. 725.[1]

Guibourt, Nicolas Jean Baptiste Gaston (*continued*).
— Note sur quelques médicaments brésiliens. 1839. III. 269.[1]
— Note sur quelques nouvelles substances apportées d'Amérique. 1846. III. 269.[1]
— Notice sur Félix Louis L'Herminier. 1834. IV. 398.[1]
— Notice sur l'arbre Bebeeru. 1846. III. 407.[1]
— Notice sur l'écorce de Lotour. 1858. III. 670.[2]
— Notice sur la racine de Jean Lopes. 1859. III. 506.[1]
— Observations d'histoire naturelle pharmaceutique. 1831. III. 244.
— Observations sur la classification carpologique. 1848. I. 119.
— Observations sur le duvet des chatons de Peupliers. 1861. III. 345.[1]
— Observations sur le mémoire de M. Canzoneri. 1823. III. 537.[2]
— Observations sur les productions du Méxique. 1866. III. 264.[2]
— On the properties of wood oil. 1859. III: 611.[1]
— Sur le quinquina rouge. 1857. III. 721, 726.[1]
— Storax et styrax liquide. 1856. III. 417,[2] 671.[1]
— Trattato delle droghe semplici. 1822. III. 56.
— *See also* CHÉREAU, Achille & GUIBOURT, N. J. B. G..
Guiburt, N. J. B. G. *See* GUIBOURT, N. J. B. G.
Guichard, Aug. Ch., (*sr.*). Dissertation sur la propriété des arbres des grandes routes. 1834. III. 200,[2] 209.
— Manuel de la police rurale et forestière. 1829. IV. 180.[1]
Guichard, H. Multiplication des Camellias à Nantes. 1889. III. 600.[1]
Guichard, Paul. Histoire chimique des alcaloïdes des quinquinas. 1867. III. 722.
Guichenet. Un mot sur l'Ajonc-épineux. 1840. III. 489.[2]
Guicherd, J. *See* DURAND, Eugène & GUICHERD, J.
Guichet, Maurice. Droit romain; les droits de l'usufruitier dans les bois. 1887. IV. 314.[1]
— Législation de la restauration et de la conservation des terrains en montagne. 1887. IV. 326.
Guida allo studio delle piante ... nell' orto botanico ... di Torino. *See* DELPONTE, G. B. 1874. I. 64.
Guida dell' Orto botanico pisano. *See* CARUEL, Teodoro. 1872. I. 64.
Guide des amateurs et jardiniers. *See* JOURNAL d'horticulture pratique. III. 15.
Le **guide** du cultivateur et du fleuriste. 1825. III. 113.
Guide to Laurel Hill cemetery. 1857. III. 27.[2]
Guide to the Botanical gardens, [Straits Settlements]. 1889. I. 67.[2]
Guidi, Luigi. Collezione xilologica dei prodotti forestali. 1863. IV. 17.
— Di due insetti che danneggiarono i boschi di Quercie. 1869. IV. 509.
— Saggio d' una guida per ... prodotti naturali ... di Pesaro e Urbino. 1871. III. 271.[2]
Guidon. Note sur la floraison du Dracaena Draco. 1854. III. 336.[2]
— Note sur la fructification de l'Urostigmate nuisible. 1866. III. 368.[2]
Guierry, (*abbé*). Sur des graines de plantes et arbres de Chine. 1856. III. 273.[1]
Guignard, Jean Louis Léon. L'appareil sécréteur des Coplfera. 1892. II. 347.[2]
— Les centres cinétiques chez les végétaux. 1897. II. 211.[3]
— Sur certains principes actifs chez les Papayacées. 1894. III. 617.[1]
— Sur la constitution des noyaux sexuels. 1891. I. 527.
— Sur la division du noyau cellulaire. 1883. I. 137.
— Étude histotaxique de quelques espèces de Chêne. 1885. II. 131.[2]
— Examen du Chêne gigantesque de la Balme. 1885. II. 139.[1]
— Sur l'existence ... de l'émulsine dans ... Manihot. 1894. II. 447.[2]
— Sur la formation et la différenciation des éléments sexuels. 1890. I. 201.[1]
— Guide de l'étudiant en Jardin botanique. 1890. I. 530.[1]
— Sur la localisation, dans les Amandes ... des principes qui fournissent l'acide cyanhydrique. 1890. III. 431.[2]
— Localisation des principes actifs chez les Capparidées. 1893. II. 229.[2]
— Sur la localisation des principes actifs chez les Capparidées. 1893. II. 229.[1]
— Sur la localisation des principes actifs chez les Résédacées. 1895. II. 234.[2]

— Sur la localisation ... des principes qui fournissent l'acide cyanhydrique. 1890. II. 275.[1]
— Mémoire sur la fécondation. 1891. I. 201.[1]
— Sur le mode d'union des noyaux sexuels. 1890. I. 201.[1]
— Sur le mode particulier de formation du pollen chez les Magnolia. 1895. II. 211.[2]
— Sur la nature morphologique du phénomène de la fécondation. 1891. I. 201.[1]
— Note sur la structure ... du suspenseur embryonnaire. 1880. II. 320.[2]
— Nouvelles recherches sur la double fécondation. 1900. I. 201.[1]
— Observations sur la structure ... du pollen des Cycadées. 1889. II. 3.[2]
— Observations sur le pollen des Cycadées. 1889. II. 3.[2]
— Observations sur les ovules ... des Cactées. 1886. II. 588.[2]
— Observations sur les Santalacées. 1885. II. 168.[1]
— Sur les organes reproducteurs des hybrides. 1886. I. 246.[1]
— Sur la polyembryonie chez quelques Mimosées. 1881. II. 320.[2]
— Sur quelques phénomènes de la division du noyau cellulaire. 1886. I. 137.
— Recherches d'embryogénie végétale comparée. 1881. II. 320.[2]
— Recherches sur certains principes actifs ... chez les Papayacées. 1894. III. 617.[1]
— Recherches sur la localisation des principes actifs chez les Capparidées. 1893. II. 229.[1]
— Recherches sur le développement de la graine. 1893. I. 121.
— Recherches sur le sac embryonnaire. 1882. I. 122.
— *See also* TIEGHEM, P. E. L. van & GUIGNARD, Léon.
— & Colin. Sur la présence de réservoirs à gomme chez les Rhamnées. 1888. II. 492.[1]
Guignet, Charles Ernest. L'agriculture au Brésil. 1879. III. 269.[1]
— Le bétail ... L'agriculture au Brésil. 1881. III. 119.[1]
— De l'existence de la glycyrrhizine. 1885. I. 176.
— Extraction de la matière verte des feuilles. 1885. I. 142.
— *See also* CLOËZ, S. & GUIGNET, Er.
Guignet, Lazare. Le ramiste. 1890. III. 381.[2]
Guignon, J. H. Le Gui d'après les observateurs. 1898. II. 180.[1]
— À propos du Gui. 1900. II. 180.[1]
Guihéneuf, D. Double-flowered Peaches. 1899. III. 441.[2]
— Le Raphia. 1895. III. 330.[2]
Guilandinus, Melchior. Conjectanea synonymica plantarum. 1600. I. 283.
— Synonymia plantarum. 1608. I. 72.[1]
— *See also* GESNER, Konrad & GUILANDINUS, M.
Guild, W. H., (*jr.*) & Perkins, F. B. The Central park. 1864. III. 27.[2]
Guilding, Lansdown. An account of the Botanic garden in the island of St. Vincent. 1825. I. 39.
Guilford, W. H. The fruit-tree borer. 1894. III. 187.
Guilfoyle, William Robert. Catalogue of plants ... in the Melbourne botanic gardens. 1883. I. 69.[1]
— A botanical tour among the South Sea Islands. 1869. I. 509.[2]
— Fibres from plants. 1894. III. 235.[1]
— A new Victorian Clematis. 1899. II. 197.[1]
Guillard, Jean Claude Achille. Sur la coloration. 1863. I. 521.[1]
— La famille des Urticées. 1861. II. 156.[1]
— Sur la formation ... des organes floraux. 1835. I. 114.[2]
— Une grave lacune de l'anatomie végétale. 1870. I. 110.
— Idée générale de l'inflorescence. 1857. I. 113.[2]
— Sur les mouvements ... de la sève. 1867. I. 164.
— Négation physiologique. 1858. I. 189.
— Observations sur la moelle des plantes ligneuses. 1847. I. 129.[1]
— Singulière composition de la nervure dorsale dans le Cananga. 1868. II. 217.[1]
— *See also* SERINGE, N. C. & GUILLARD, Achille.
Guillard, A. J. Recherches sur l'anatomie ... de la tige. 1878. I. 105.
Guillard, Eugène. L'Olivier et le Mûrier. 1899. III. 378, 677.[1]
Guillaud, J. A. Flore de Bordeaux et du sud-ouest. 1883. I. 416.
Guillaume, (*Dr.*). Notice historique sur les promenades publiques ... de Neuchâtel. 1869. III. 126.[2]
— Le Tilleul du reposoir ou des Druides. 1867. II. 516.[2]

Guillaume, L. La culture des Palmiers dans le Midi. 1893. III. 318.[1]

Guillaume, Louis, (jr.). Développement anormal du Sapin et du Hêtre. 1877. II. 36,[1] IV. 197.[1]

— Lettre de M. le Dr. Christ au sujet des arbres. 1879. III. 42.[1]

— Monstruosité végétale. 1876. II. 280.[1]

— Le Peuplier du Guillery. 1872. II. 96.[2]

Guillebert. Sur un remède employé en Grèce contre la rage. 1857. III. 693.[2]

Guillemard, A. G. Australian forestry. 1882. IV. 280.[1]

— Forest rambles. In California. 1882. IV. 340.[3]

— Forest rambles. In Fiji. 1882. IV. 380.[1]

— Forest rambles. In Lapland. 1882. IV. 344.[3]

— Forest rambles. In Madeira. 1883. IV. 380.[1]

— Forest rambles. In New South Wales. 1883. IV.-380.[1]

— Forest rambles. In Norway. 1883. IV. 344.[1]

— Forest rambles. In Tasmania. 1882. IV. 380.[1]

— Forest rambles. In the Hawaiian Islands. 1883. IV. 380.[2]

— Forest rambles in Denmark. 1883. IV. 343.[2]

— Forest rambles in Finland. 1883. IV. 347.[1]

— Forest rambles in Sweden. 1884. IV. 344.[2]

— The giant Cypresses of Verona. 1883, 1884. II. 30,[1] IV. 448.[1]

Guillemare, A. Acide phyllocyanique. 1898. I. 180.[2]

— Éclairage à l'aide de products extraits des arbres résineux. 1876. IV. 443.[3]

Guillemeau, Jean Louis Marie. Calendrier de flore des environs de Niort. 1801. I. 406.

— Histoire naturelle de la Rose. 1800. III. 447.[2]

Guillemin, Antoine. See GUILLEMIN, J. B. A.

Guillemin, C. M. Développement de la matière verte des végétaux. 1857. I. 140,[2] 195.[1]

Guillemin, H. L'Arctostaphylos officinalis Wimm. 1898. II. 661.[1]

Guillemin, Jean Baptiste Antoine. Considérations sur l'amertume des végétaux. 1832. I. 174.

— Considérations sur l'irrégularité de la corolle des Calceolaria. 1833. II. 779.[3]

— Description de l'arbuste du bdellium. 1833. II. 417.[3]

— Description du Corraea pulchella. 1829. III. 503.[2]

— Description du Dombeya Ameliae. 1831. II. 533.[1]

— Icones lithographicae plantarum Australasiae. 1827. I. 500.

— Note sur la plante qui a servi de type au genre Bobua. 1841. II. 703.[1]

— Observation d'une monstruosité . . . du Lilas. 1828. II. 716.[1]

— Observations sur la nature des organes microscopiques . . . dans le bois des Conifères. 1836. II. 16.[2]

— Observations sur les espèces de Calceolaria. 1829. III. 702.[2]

— Plantes rares ou nouvelles cultivées à Fromont. 1829. III. 754.[1]

— Rapport . . . sur sa mission au Brésil. 1839. III. 600.[1]

— Recherches microscopiques sur le pollen. 1825. I. 116.[2]

— Report of an expedition to Brazil. 1839. III. 600.[1]

— Zephyritis taitensis. 1836. I. 510.[2]

— See also CHEVALLIER, J. B. A., RICHARD, Achille, & GUILLEMIN, J. A.

— Perrottet, Samuel & Richard, Achille. Florae Senegambiae tentamen. 1830. I. 490.

Guillemin, Jules. Amerikanisches Verfahren zur Holzverkohlung. 1858. IV. 394.

Guillén-Garcia, G. J. de. Riqueza perdida. 1894. III. 211.[1]

Guillerna, C. de. La parte forestal de la Exposición general de Filipinas. 1887. IV. 540.[1]

Guillery. De l'influence du déboisement. 1898. IV. 52.

Guillet, Peter, (sr.). Timber merchant's guide. 1823. IV. 222.

Guillier, A. Acacia lophanta. 1866. III. 466.[2]

— Sur la stérilité du Pommier. 1865. III. 267.[1]

Guillochon, L. Des effets du siroco sur certains végétaux. 1900. III. 184.[2]

Guillon. Brunichia cirrhosa. 1879. III. 387.[1]

— Bucklandia populnea. 1880. III. 416.[2]

— Evonymus japonica cristata viridis. 1878. III. 532.[2]

— Franciscea macrantha. 1880. III. 699.[1]

— Greffes hétérogènes. 1881. III. 165, 680.[1]

— Hydrangea paniculata grandiflora. 1881. III. 642.[2]

— Influence du sujet sur le greffon. 1882. III. 39.

— Pterostyrax hispidum. 1881. III. 670.[2]

— Rhamnus obcordata. 1878. III. 543.[2]

— Une vieille plante des plus méritantes. 1882. III. 707.[1]

Guillon, Adolphe. Les amis des arbres. 1893. III. 32.[1]

— Un plaidoyer en faveur des arbres. 1896. IV. 39.[1]

Guillory, (sr.). Les congrès de vignerons français. 1860. III. 555.

— Rapport sur le Congrès de vignerons français de Lyon. 1847. III. 555.

Guilmot, Gustave. Araucaria imbricata Pavon. 1877. III. 299.[1]

Guimaraes, A. R. Sur l'action physiologique du café. 1882. III. 742.[1]

— See also COUTY, Louis, GUIMARAES, A. R. & NIOBEY.

Guimbel. Die Erziehung junger Kastanien. 1845. IV. 492.[3]

Guimpel, Friederich, Otto, Friedrich & Hayne, F. G. Abbildung der fremden . . . Holzarten. 1825. I. 293, III. 69, IV. 88.

— Willdenow, C. L. & Hayne, F. G. Abbildung der deutschen Holzarten. 1815. I. 370, IV. 88.

Guimps, R. de. Les forêts de la Suisse. 1867. IV. 366.

Guindon, PINGUET. See PINGUET-GUINDON.

Guinier, C. L'Industrie de la tournerie. 1878. IV. 427.[1]

Guinier, Ernest. Sur l'accroissement des tiges. 1879. I. 190.[1]

— L'accroissement en épaisseur des tiges. 1891. IV. 65.[1]

— L'accroissement en épaisseur des tiges. Réponse à M. Henry. 1891. IV. 65.[1]

— Aménagement des forêts de montagne. 1878. IV. 244.

— Aménagement des futaies en montagne. 1879. IV. 244.

— Aménagement des futaies résineuses. 1885. IV. 244.

— L'aménagement et le réseau des chemins. 1893. IV. 389.

— Le balivage d'après l'ordonnance réglementaire. 1882. IV. 326.

— Beautés des forêts. 1900. IV. 545.[2]

— Camons forestales. 1880. IV. 267.

— Les chemins forestiers en montagne. 1880. IV. 267, 389.

— Concurrence des bois étrangers. 1890. IV. 405.[1]

— Conservation des beaux arbres. 1893. IV. 137.[1]

— Coupes à blanc étoc dans la vallée de l'Ire. 1899. IV. 282.[2]

— Coupes d'amélioration. 1899. IV. 169.[3]

— Couvert, ombrage, abri. 1897. IV. 67.[2]

— Desideratum. 1899. IV. 70.

— Développement anormal de bourgeons de Hêtre. 1888. II. 126.[2]

— Effets de l'annélation de l'écorce. 1886. III. 175,[1] IV. 66.[1]

— Sur l'émission d'un liquide sucré . . . de l'Oranger. 1893. III. 501.[3]

— Encore le traitement des forêts résineuses. 1885. IV. 237.

— L'esthétique dans le traitement des bois. 1893. IV. 137.[1]

— Étude sur l'Épicéa dans les Alpes. 1877. IV. 452, 458.

— Sur la faculté asséchante des arbres forestiers. 1883. IV. 51.

— Les forêts et les économistes. 1887. IV. 276.[1]

— Forêts et montagnes. 1900. IV. 271.[1]

— Forme des tiges des arbres. 1885. I. 190.[1]

— Le furetage du Hêtre dans les Pyrénées. 1883. IV. 495.

— Importance de l'étude des sciences naturelles pour les forestiers. 1870. IV. 56.

— Influence de la constitution physique du sol sur la régénération . . . de Sapin et Épicéa. 1900. IV. 545.[2]

— Montagnes et forêts. 1900. IV. 271.[1]

— Sur la morphologie des tiges. 1878. I. 105.

— Le mouton. 1897. IV. 197.[2]

— Note sur la culture des pépinières. 1878. IV. 150.

— Note sur la culture du Pin sylvestre. 1879. II. 48.[1]

— Notice sur le tracé d'un réseau de chemins. 1891. IV. 392.[1]

— Nouvelles observations sur les taillis de Hêtre. 1892. IV. 498.

— Parcellaire des forêts en montagne. 1888. IV. 267.[1]

— Les pépinières . . . des Hautes Alpes. 1886. IV. 151.[1]

— Sur les phénomènes de soudure des couches ligneuses. 1885. I. 127,[1] 190.[1]

— Le Pin de l'Andorre. 1900. IV. 465.[1]

— La qualité du bois. 1889. IV. 409.

— Quelques nouvelles observations . . . relatives à l'accroissement. 1886. I. 165.

— Recherches expérimentales sur l'accroissement. 1881. IV. 64.[2]

— Sur la régénération naturelle des futaies. 1884. IV. 129, 139.[2]

Guinier, Ernest (continued).
— Le régime forestier en montagne. 1884. IV. 326.
— Simple observation sur le théorème de l'accroissement. 1881. IV. 233.
— Sur une station remarquable du Rhododendron. 1879. II. 679.[1]
— Le strade forestali sui monti. 1880. IV. 389.
— Taillis sous futaie en montagne. 1894. IV. 131.
— Le terreau des forêts et la tourbe. 1900. IV. 70.
— Sur la théorie de la sève descendante. 1888. I. 166.
— Tracé d'un réseau de chemins en montagne. 1884. IV. 389.
— Traitement de l'Épicéa dans les Alpes. 1896. IV. 454.
Guinier, L. Philosophie de la sylviculture. 1885. IV. 56.
Guinon. See MICHEL & GUINON.
Guiot, L'arpenteur forestier. 1770. IV. 263.
— Kurzgefasstes Forst-Handbuch. 1770. IV. 108.[2]
— Manuel forestier et portatif. 1770. IV. 108.[2]
Guiot, Léonide. Les forêts et les paturages du comté de Nice. 1875. IV. 360.
— Le Mont.Boron. 1871. IV. 360.
Guiraud de Saint-Marsal, baron. La vie des végétaux. 1856. I. 147.
— See also AZÉMAR & GUIRAUD DE SAINT-MARSAL..
Guisan. Observations sur la culture du Giroflier. 1788, III. 613,[2] 686.[1]
Guisan, F. L. Beschreibung des Gewürznelkenbaums. 1797. II. 627.[2]
Guisan, R. La dissémination des plantes. 1888. I. 240.[2]
Guitard, J. Une fleuraison hyémale à Ussat. 1868. I. 221.
Gulbe, L. A. See ГУЛЬБЕ, Л. А.
Guldensteeden Egeling, C. Bepaling van het alcaloidgehalte in extractum strychni. 1890. III. 685.[1]
— Onderzoek van tannas chinini. 1892. III. 724.[1]
Gulf coast record. IV. 4.
Gulia, Gavino. Malta. 1888. III. 272.[2]
— Repertorio botanico maltese. 1855. I. 74,[2] III. 91.[1]
Gulliver, George. Catalogue of plants . . of Banbury. 1841. I. 399.
— The classificatory significance of raphides in Hydrangea. 1880. II. 240.[2]
— On the fibrin and latex of vegetables. 1862. I. 181.
— List of plants which afford raphides. 1877. I. 139, 525.[1]
— On raphides and sphaeraphides. 1863. I. 139.
— On the raphides of Rubiaceae. 1863. II. 808.[1]
Gum animi as connected with the origin of amber. 1825. III. 478.[2]
Gum trees. 1887. III. 634.[1]
Gumbleton, W. E. Abutilon vitifolium. 1894. III. 587.[1]
— Adenocarpus decorticans. 1886. III. 466.[1]
— Buddleia Colvillei. 1893. III. 681.[2]
— Chiogenes serpyllifolia. 1899. III. 649.[1]
— Crataego-mespilus Dardari. 1899. III. 421.[1]
— Deutzia discolor purpurascens. 1899. III. 410.[2]
— Diospyros Kaki. 1891. III. 669.[2]
— Dracaena Doucetti foliis variegatis. 1899. III. 335.[1]
— Dracaenopsis australis at Belgrove. 1893. III. 334.[2]
— Hamamelis Zuccariniana. 1879. III. 417.[1]
— New early-flowering trees and shrubs. 1875. III. 207.[1]
— A new Japanese fruit: Myrica rubra. 1890. III. 353.[2]
— A new Philadelphus, P. Coulteri. 1896. III. 413.[1]
— Nomenclature of Hamamelis. 1890. III. 417.[1]
— Ornamental shrubs in the south of Ireland under severe frost. 1879. III. 46.[2]
— Solanum Pierreanum. 1899. III. 702.[1]
— Xanthoceras sorbifolia. 1892. III. 540.[2]
Gumilla, José. Historie naturelle . . . de l'Orenoque. 1741. III. 267.[1]
— Historia natural . . . del Rio Orinoco. 1741. III. 267.[1]
— El Orinoco ilustrado. 1741. III. 267.[1]
The gums & resins of New Zealand. 1866. III. 267.
Guntau, (Forstmeister, Breslau.) Ein Beitrag zur Beantwortung der Frage: "Welche Einwirkungen üben die Eindeichungen auf den Ertrag der Oderwaldungen aus. 1860. IV. 184.[2]
— Ueber die Erziehung der Fichte. 1853. IV. 453.
— Ueber den Frass von Phalaena Bombyx pinivora. 1854. IV. 475.
— Die Ueberschwemmungen der Oder. 1855. IV. 185.[1]
Gunckel, Friedrich Wilhelm. Sammlung der auf das Forst-, Jagd- und Fischerei-Wesen in Kurhessen Bezug habenden Landes-Ordnungen. 1845. IV. 320.
Gundacker, Karl, Freiherr von Suttner. Die australischen "Wattles." 1881. IV. 520.[2]

Gundlach. Enfermedad de los Cocoteros. 1883. III. 323.[1]
Gunga Parshad. Nabatati Hind. 1874. I. 474.
Gunkel, E. Beiträge zur Rosenflora von Sondershausen. 1884. II. 284.[2]
Gunn, Ronald Campbell. Notes on the Acaciae of Tasmania. 1846. II. 323.[1]
— Observations on the flora of Geelong. 1842. I. 505.
— Richea pandanifolia. 1846. II. 690.[1]
Gunn, W. F. Ross-shire forestry. 1885. IV. 359.[1]
— The woods, forests and forestry of Rossshire. 1885. IV. 359.[1]
Gunnell, Oswald. See PERKIN, A. G. & GUNNELL, Oswald.
Gunner, Niels Dorph. Tentamen oeconomico-botanicum de usu plantarum indigenarum in arte tinctoria. 1773. III. 235.[2]
— Tractatus . . . de divitiis florae danonorwegicae. 1774. III. 270.[1]
Gunnerus, Johann Ernst. Flora norvegica. 1766. I. 351.
Gunning, E. H., Thomson, Robert & Sawyer, A. M. The Tapioca plant. 1897. III. 521.[1]
Gunning, Jan Willem. Bijdrage tot de kennis van brucine. 1857. III. 682.[3]
— Iets over de vetten der palmnoten. 1861. III. 319.[1]
— Opmerkingen naar aanleiding der voordracht . . . van Dr. de Vrij. 1870. III. 722.
— Rapport over Kanarie-olie. 1867. III. 510.[1]
— Scheikundig onderzoek van Minjak sindor. 1864. II. 559,[2] III. 487.[2]
— & Harting, Pieter. Onderzoekingen over de bron der stikstof. 1855. I. 158.
Guppy, Henry Brougham. The dispersal of plants. 1890. I. 481.[1]
Gurnaud, Ad. L'ancienne sylviculture et la nouvelle. 1898. IV. 27.[2]
— L'art forestier et le contrôle. 1887. IV. 245.
— Les bois de l'État et la dette publique. 1866. IV. 261.[2]
— Cahier d'aménagement . . . sur la forêt des Épernons. 1878. IV. 249.[1]
— Conserver les forêts de l'état. 1865. IV. 275.
— Le contrôle. 1880. IV. 236, 244.
— Le contrôle en sylviculture. 1886. IV. 245.
— Le contrôle et le régime forestier. 1886. IV. 237.
— La Double du Périgord. 1895. IV. 362.
— Économie forestière. 1862. IV. 243.
— Étude des forêts du Risoux. 1870. IV. 360.
— Des forêts et de la pratique forestière. 1862. IV. 243.
— Histoire de la sylviculture. 1881. IV. 24,[1] 27.[2]
— Historia de la selviculturá. 1881. IV. 24.[1]
— Lettre à M. Paul Tripier. 1891? IV. 246.
— La lumière, le couvert et l'humus. 1880. IV. 67.[1]
— La lumière, le couvert et l'humus dans la culture forestière. 1880. IV. 244.
— La lumière réfléchie et l'accroissement. 1881. IV. 67.[2]
— Mémoire de la commune de Syam. 1867. IV. 249.[1]
— Mémoire sur l'aménagement des bois de la commune de Syam. 1867. IV. 249.[1]
— Mémoire sur la commune des forêts. 1865. IV. 243.
— Méthode du contrôle. 1886. IV. 237.
— La méthode du contrôle à l'Exposition universelle. 1890. IV. 245.
— La méthode du contrôle dans le taillis composé. 1890. IV. 245.
— La méthode du contrôle et la tradition forestière. 1890. IV. 237.
— Méthode du jardinage. 1883. IV. 237.
— La méthode française et la question forestière. 1885. IV. 244.
— Notice sur les plantations de bois résineux. 1891. IV. 122.[1]
— Notice sur sa formation . . . (Société des amis des arbres). 1894. IV. 1.[1]
— Origine et progrès des méthodes forestières. 1880. IV. 27.[2]
— Le service forestier et le contrôle. 1883. IV. 292.
— Sylviculture française et la méthode du contrôle. 1886. IV. 122.[1]
— La sylviculture française. 1884. IV. 122.[1]
— Traité forestier, pratique manuel. 1890. IV. 99.[1]
— Variations et équilibre de l'accroissement. 1887. IV. 233.
Guryanof, A. See ГУРЬЯНОВЪ, А.
Gusanos de seda del Roble. 1878. III. 148.[2]
Guse, C. Ueber den Anbau der Lärche. 1895. IV. 451.
— Die Anwendung der "Reinertragstheorie." 1899. IV. 238.

— Die Bedeutung der forstlichen Reinerträge. 1876. IV. 236.
— Die Bedeutung der Waldstreu. 1899. IV. 72.
— Beiträge zur Bestimmung des Umtriebsalters. 1879. IV. 252.
— Beiträge zur Entwicklung der Hochwaldwirthschaft. 1879. IV. 129.
— Beiträge zur Forststatistik Russlands. 1883. IV. 346.
— Beitrag zur Vergleichung der Erträge verschiedener Umtriebszeiten. 1878. IV. 252.
— Der Bialowiäschsker Wald. 1879. IV. 345.
— Zur Borkenkäferfrage. 1885. IV. 204.
— Einfluss des Wasserstandes auf die Baumvegetation. 1893. IV. 185.[1]
— Zum Eulenfrass im Regierungsbezirk Gumbinnen. 1872. IV. 207.
— Das forstliche Institut in St. Petersburg. 1884. IV. 31.
— Aus dem Forstschutz. 1876. IV. 177.[1]
— Forstwissenschaftliche Reclame. 1878. IV. 244.
— Gegenfeuer bei Waldbränden. 1894. IV. 182.[2]
— Die Gewinnung von Ahornzucker in Nordamerika. 1897. IV. 527.[2]
— Aus dem Gouvernement Wologda. 1894. IV. 346.
— Die höhere forstliche Ausbildung in Frankreich. 1892. IV. 34.[2]
— Die Kosten der Abwehr des grossen Kiefernspinners. 1892. IV. 478.
— Nachrichten über die frühere preussische Forstverwaltung im jetzigen Königreich Polen. 1890. IV. 24.[2]
— Zu den neuesten Kundgebungen in Sachen Reinertragstheorie. 1897. IV. 259.[1]
— Noch einmal ein Wort für die Rothbuche. 1880. IV. 495.
— Das russische Waldschutzgesetz vom 4. April 1888. 1891. IV. 315.[2]
— Aus dem russischen Norden. 1899. IV. 347.
— Aus den russischen Wäldern. 1872. IV. 345.
— Aus russischen Zeitschriften. 1888. IV. 486.[1]
— Aus Russland. Die Nonne. 1894. IV. 346.
— Aus Russland. Die Wälder im hohen Norden. 1892. IV. 346.
— Aus Russland. Forst-Versammlung in Kasan. 1891. IV. 40.[1]
— In Sachen der Schütte. 1883. IV. 477.
— Le sucre d'Érable. 1896. IV. 527.[2]
— Terrains boisés du nord de la Russie. 1899. IV. 347.
— Le Tremble en Russie. 1888. IV. 486.[2]
— Zur Verteidigung unserer Buchenwälder. 1879. IV. 495.
— Die Verwendung der Fichte zur Unterpflanzung. 1880. IV. 453.
— Wälder oder Gelder? 1877. IV. 236.
— Der Waldreichthum Russlands. 1879. IV. 345.
— Weitere Beiträge zur Kenntniss der forstlichen Verhältnisse Russlands. 1876. IV. 345.
— Der Zuckerahorn. 1896. IV. 527.[2]
Gusmanus, Galeatius. De cortice peruviano. 1767. III. 720.
Gussmann, Karl. Das Beerenbüchlein. 1888. III. 147.[2]
— Zur Geschichte des württembergischen Obstbaues. 1896. III. 33,[1] 139.
— Das Obstbüchlein. 1887. III. 139.
Gussone, Giovanni. Adnotationes ad Catalogum plantarum. 1821. I. 62.
— Catalogus plantarum . . . in regio horto . . . Boccadifalco. 1821. I. 62.
— Enumeratio plantarum . . . in insula Inarime. 1854. I. 427..
— Flora sicula. 1829. II. 188.[2]
— Florae Siculae prodromus. 1827. I. 431.
— Florae Siculae synopsis. 1842. I. 431.
— Notizie sulle isole Linosa, Lampione. 1839. I. 431.
— Plantae rariores, quas in itinere per oras Jonii et Adriatici maris . . . collegit. 1826. I. 451.
— Supplementum ad Florae Siculae prodromum. 1827. I. 431.
— See also TENORE, Michele & GUSSONE, Giovanni.
— & Tenore, Michele. Ragguaglio delle peregrinazioni . . . in alcuni luoghi . . . di Principato Citeriore. 1843. I. 427.
— Traité du cubage des bois. 1840. IV. 222.
Gustave, (frère) & Héribaud-Joseph, (frère). Flore d'Auvergne. 1883. I. 416.
Gustawicz, Bronislaw. O owadach jako szkodnikach drzew owocowych. 1897. III. 191.

Gut. Beleuchtung des neuen Forstgesetzes. 1875. IV. 330.
Gut, J. Ueber den Anbau der Douglas-Tanne. 1877. IV. 483.[1]
— Der Baumwärter. 1877. III. 146.[1]
Gutachten des Ausschusses für die Obstbaumzucht. 1833. III. 94.[2]
Gutachten über den Futterwerth des Laubes. 1857. IV. 438.[1]
Gutachten . . . über die Anwendung der Zimmtrose. 1827. III. 455.[1]
Gutheil, Hermann E. Beschreibung der Wesergegend. 1837. I. 379.
— Grundzüge zu einer Flora von Kreuznach. 1839. I. 380.
Guthnick, K. Die Flora des Faul-, Schwab- und Schwarzhornes. 1832. I. 434.
— Vegetation in Algier. 1856. I. 484.
Guthrie, F. B. Analyses of Prickly Pear. 1900. III. 624.[2]
— The fodder-value of Saltbush. 1898. III. 387.[2]
— The fodder value of a_0m_e of the common scrub plants. 1900. III. 223.[2]
— See also ALLEN, W. J., BLUNNO, M., FROGGATT, W. W. & GUTHRIE, F. B.
Guthrie, Ossian. Remarkable vitality of Willow twigs. 1884. II. 104.[1]
Gutierrez, SAINZ. See SAINZ GUTIERREZ.
Gutmann. Ueber den Nutzen guter Waldwege. 1893. IV. 267.
— Die Stockacher astlose Fichte. 1900. II. 35.[2]
Gutta percha. 1882. III. 229.
Gutta percha; its discovery. 1857. III. 231.
Gutta-percha from leaves. 1895. III. 519,[1] 663.[2]
Gutta-percha of Surinam. 1858. III. 229.
Gutta-shea. 1879. III. 667.[1]
Gutte, (Forstmeister, Oppeln). Das Auftreten der grossen Kiefernraupe. 1858. IV. 475.
— Beitrag zur Ermittelung des Gewichtes einer Klafter-Waldstreu. 1863. IV. 437.[2]
— Beitrag zur Kenntniss über . . . Wurzelbildung der Kiefer. 1857. IV. 483.[1]
— Holzmassen-Ergebniss . . . in der kgl. Oberförsterei Bodland. 1863. IV. 260.[2]
— Kurze Mittheilungen über das Vorkommen der grossen Kiefernraupe. 1856. IV. 206.
— Mittheilungen über das Auftreten der grossen Kiefernraupe. 1857. IV. 475.
— Reale Forst-Erträge . . . in der k. Oberförsterei Budkowitz. 1858. IV. 260.[2]
Guttegom en Benzoë. 1885. III. 609,[1] 671.[1]
Guttenberg, Adolf, Ritter von. Die Aufforstungsbestrebungen des Deutschen und Oesterreichischen Alpenvereines. 1882. IV. 41.[2]
— Die Aufgaben der forstlichen Versuchswesens, III. 1885. IV. 237.
— Die Aufgaben und Ziele der Forstbetriebseinrichtung. 1891. IV. 246.
— Die Aufgaben und Ziele der Forstbetriebseinrichtung der Gegenwart. 1895. IV. 246.
— Die Aufstellung von Ertragstafeln. 1885. IV. 237.
— Die Aufstellung von Holzmassen- und Geldertragstafeln. 1896. IV. 238.
— Ueber den Einfluss des Bestandesschlusses. 1886. IV. 233.
— Entwickelung unserer Forstwirthschaft. 1898. IV. 28.[2]
— Die Forstbetriebseinrichtung. 1896. IV. 246.
— Zur Frage der Revision des Vermögensstandes. 1893. IV. 246.
— Die Heidler'sche patentirte Präcisions-Baummesskluppe. 1889. IV. 231.[2]
— Die Hochwässer des Herbstes 1882. 1883. IV. 187.[2]
— Holzmesskunde. 1887. IV. 214.
— Inwieweit ist bei dem heutigen Stande der Wirthschaft . . . die Forderung strengster Nachhaltigkeit . . . aufrecht zu erhalten. 1890. IV. 245.
— Die Korkeiche in Oesterreich. 1890. IV. 517.[1]
— Die Nachhaltigkeits-Forderung in der Forstwirthschaft. 1890. IV. 245.
— Neue Dendrometer. 1896. IV. 232.
— Neue Grundlagen der Waldwertrechnung? 1892. IV. 258.
— Die Photogrammetrie. 1891. IV. 265.
— Zur Praxis der Waldwertrechnung. 1894. IV. 258.
— Die Reinertrags- und Bestandeswirthschaft. 1885. IV. 244.

Guttenberg, Adolf, *Ritter von (continued).*
— Die Revision des Vermögensstandes in Fideicommiss-
forsten. 1894. IV. 258.
— Ein Rückblick auf die Walderschau . . . in der Bukowina.
1898. IV. 370.
— Das Schneissennetz in Hochgebirgsforsten. 1883. IV.
251.[1]
— Zur Statik des Durchforstungsbetriebes. 1884. IV. 173.
— Vergleichung des Wachsthumsganges der Buche. 1885.
IV. 233.
— Ueber den Wachsthumsgang der Fichte. 1885. IV. 458.
— Die Wachsthumsgesetze des Waldes. 1885. I. 190,[1]
*IV. 64.[2]
— Zur Wahl der Methode bei Massenaufnahmen. 1877.
IV. 217.
— Ueber Waldmisshandlung in unseren Alpenländern. 1896.
IV. 283.[2]
— Unter welchen Verhältnissen ist ein weiter Pflanzverband
zulässig? 1899. IV. 154.[2]
— Zuwachs- und Ertrags-Untersuchungen für die Buche in
Dänemark. 1882. IV. 498.
— Zuwachsleistungen . . . in Fichten-Pflanzbeständen. 1888.
IV. 458.
Guttenberg, Gustave. Botanical guide through the Phipps
conservatories. 1894. I. 39.[1]
Guttenberg, Hermann von. Beiträge zur Kenntniss der in
Südösterreich heimischen Holzarten. 1875. I. 447,[1] *IV. 87.[1]
— Zur Forst- und Jagdstatistik Steiermarks 1895. 1896.
IV. 369.
— Die forstlichen Verhältnisse des Karstes. 1882. IV.
374.[1]
— Ein Schädling der Pinie. 1880. IV. 468.[2]
Guttin, Joseph. Étude sur le Rosa foetida. 1896. II. 293.[2]
— Le genre " Rosa " dans l'Eure. 1894. II. 286.[2]
Guy, Thomas. Formulae used at Guy's hospital. 1818.
III. 254.
— Pharmacopoeia in usum Nosocomii. 1818. III. 254.
— The pharmacopoeia of Guy's hospital. 1818. III. 254.
Guyétant, Sébastien. Catalogue des plantes à fleurs visibles.
. . . du Jura. 1809. I. 407.
Guyettant, C. Memento botanique contenant 11300 noms.
1898. I. 74.[2]
Guyon. Note on a vegetable product employed by the Arabs.
1862. III. 525.[2]
— Note sur le pian. 1853. III. 338.[2]
Guyon, D. Eclosion précoce des œufs déposés . . . par les
œdipodes. 1846. III. 192.[2]
— Invasion de criquets et d'œdipodes. 1845. III. 192.[2]
— Ueber die Ursache der Unfruchtbarkeit der Dattelpalme.
1845. III. 328.[1]
Guyon, E. Remarques relatives à une communication pré-
cédente de M. Ramon de la Sagra. 1870. I. 72.[1]
Guyot. Propriétés vénéneuses du fruit du Redoul. 1858.
III. 523.[1]
Guyot, Charles. Délit forestier. 1897. IV. 327.
— L'enseignement forestier en France. 1898. IV. 35.[1]
— Les forêts lorraines. 1884. IV. 27.[2]
— Les forêts lorraines jusqu'en 1789. 1886. IV. 27.[2]
— La législation forestière en Alsace-Lorraine. 1879. IV.
317.[1]
— La loi sur les accidents du travail. 1899. IV. 311.[2]
— Des lois internationales pour la police des forêts de fron-
tière. 1898. IV. 314.[1]
— Note sur l'installation de l'École forestière à Nancy.
1896. IV. 35.[1]
— La nouvelle législation forestière en Alsace-Lorraine. 1884.
IV. 317.[1]
— Les pensions civiles. 1878. IV. 311.[1]
— Le régime pastoral. 1899. IV. 135.[2]
— Responsabilité en cas d'accident. 1899. IV. 311.[1]
Guyot, Jules. Culture de la Vigne et vinification. 1860.
III. 555.
— Étude des vignobles de France. 1868. III. 555.
— Sur la viticulture dans . . . Charente-Inférieure. 1861.
III. 555.
— Sur la viticulture de l'est. 1863. III. 555.
— Sur la viticulture de l'ouest. 1866. III. 555.
— Sur la viticulture . . . du canton d'Évian. 1868. III.
555.
— Sur la viticulture du centre nord. 1866. III. 555.
— Sur la viticulture du centre sud. 1865. III. 555.
— Sur la viticulture du nord-est. 1864. III. 555.
— Sur la viticulture . . . du Puy-de-Dôme. 1863. III. 555.
— Sur la viticulture du sud-ouest. 1862. III. 555.

Gwinner, N. Uebersicht der Lehrgegenstände . . . des K.
. . . Instituts zu Hohenheim. 1831. IV. 31.
Gwinner, W. G. Die Königlich württembergischen Forst-
dienst-Prüfungen. 1830. IV. 31.
Gw.nner, Wilhelm Heinrich von. Ausserordentlicher Wald-
ertrag und Holzzuwachs. 1836. IV. 260.[1]
— Bericht über die Exkursion nach Tegernsee. 1845. IV.
350.[2]
— Beschreibung . . . der Stadtwaldungen von Stuttgart.
1840. IV. 356.[1]
— Ueber den Einfluss der grossen Trockenheit. 1844. IV.
72.
— Exkursion [in das Engelberger Revier]. 1845. IV. 356.[1]
— Ueber Forstertrag. 1836. IV. 260.[1]
— Forstliche Reisebemerkungen. 1840. IV. 351.[2]
— Forstliche Reiseberichte. 1836. IV. 356.[1]
— Forststatistische Notizen von Württemberg. 1845. IV.
356.[1]
— Gallerie württembergischer Forstleute. 1856. IV. 1.
— Interessante Pflanzgärten. 1845. IV. 149.[2]
— Mittel zur Erhöhung der Holzerzeugung. 1838. IV.
273.[2]
— Notizen über eine forstwirthschaftliche Reise nach Tyrol.
1847. IV. 367.
— Die Pflanzensysteme. 1832. IV. 75.[1]
— Praktische Anleitung . . . zur Holzzucht ausserhalb des
Waldes. 1847. IV. 106, 544.[2]
— Die Samenausklenganstalt zu Schönbronn. 1857. IV.
147.[2]
— Die Verhandlungen in der forstlichen Sektion . . . über das
württembergische Taxationswesen. 1843. IV. 254.
— Versuche über Rindenbenutzung in Böhmen. 1858. IV.
434.
— Waldbau in erweitertem Umfang. 1834. IV. 106.
— Der Waldbau in kurzen Umrissen. 1834. IV. 106.
— Ueber den Wirthschafts- und Kulturbetrieb in den . . .
Oettingen-Wallerstein'schen Waldungen. 1845. IV. 356.[1]
Gyberg, O. E. Om insamling . . . af skogsträdsfrön. 1873.
IV. 148.
Gyldén, C. W. Handledning för skogshushållare i Finland.
1853. IV. 94.
— Samling af författningar rörande landtmäteriet. 1853.
IV. 264.
Gyldenfeldt, W. Ueber die Bestimmung der Formzahl.
1880. IV. 218.
— Die Kagerups-Buche in Gripskov. 1880. II. 127.[1]
— Den kunstige Barkaftagning. 1874. IV. 434.
— En Tilvæxtoversigt for Bøg. 1882. IV. 498.
Gylding, J. Kubiktabel for Cylindere. 1891. IV. 228.
Gyllenband, K. O., *Graf von* UXKULL-. *See* UXKULL-GYLLEN-
BAND, K. O., *Graf von.*
Gyllenståhle, Michael. De regno vegetabili. 1656. I. 30.
Gysin, J. Einiges über Waldvermessung. 1878. IV. 265.
Gyssling, W. Die Auswahl, Lieferung und Prüfung des
Brenn-Materials für Dampferzeugung. 1881. IV. 431.[1]
Gyurgyik, Gyula. Körmöczbányass. k. főbányaváros és a
M. k. bányakincstár között a városi. 1879. IV. 331.[2]

. h . Ueber den Anbau der Lärche. 1842. IV. 449.
–h. Ueber Behacken der Samenschläge. 1878. IV. 139.[2]
H. Abies pectinata Dec. var. fastigiata. 1891. II. 23.[1]
H. Anbauversuche mit der nordischen Fichte. 1889. IV.
454.
H. Bamboos. 1889. III. 314.[2]
H. Om Behandlingen af de danske Statsskove. 1868. IV.
343.[1]
H. Ueber die Benutzung der Erndtwieden. 1859. IV.
196.[2]
H. Beobachtungen über den Schneedruck. 1887. IV. 190.
H. Callistemon rigidus. 1892. III. 633.[2]
H. Chimonanthus fragrans grandiflorus. 1892. III. 401.[1]
H. Evergreen Elaeagnus. 1892. III. 628.[1]
H. Half hours at Kew; Acacias. 1874. III. 463.[1]
H. Hamamelis arborea. 1891. III. 417.[1]
H. Der Holzhandel . . . Obersteiermark. 1883. IV. 406.[2]
H. Holztransport auf Drahtriessen. 1859. IV. 391.
H. Lichtensteig. Dommages causés par les écureuils.
1875. IV. 198.[1]
H. Lichtensteig. Schaden durch Eichhörnchen. 1875.
IV. 198.[1]
H. New theory of the ascent of the sap. 1831. I. 163.
H. Phillyrea Vilmoriniana. 1890. III. 680.[1]
H. Pithecolobium unguiscata. 1894. III. 484.[2]
H. De quelques menus produits des forêts. 1897. IV. 558.[1]

H. Retinosporas. 1892. III. 300.²
H. Schäden an Hochwaldbeständen. 1888. IV. 192.²
H. Ein seltener Baum. 1898. IV. 492.¹
H. Télégraphe des bois. 1889. IV. 391.
H. The trees and shrubs of ancient Greece. 1879. I. 443.²
H. Vorbeugungsmassregeln gegen Schneedruckschaden. 1891. IV. 190.
H. Over de waarde ... van den Eucalyptus. 1889. IV. 530.
H. Ueber die Zunahme von Schnee-Bruch. 1883. IV. 190.
H., Ivan. Nadeel van Populieren, Berken en Sparren. 1872. II. 121.²
H., van. Vermeerdering der Kanadasche Popels. 1872. III. 345.²
H., von. Zur Entwickelung des kgl. württembergischen Staatsforstdienstes. 1897. IV. 291.¹
H., A. Beispiele und Fragen über fremdartige Saftvermischung ... durch Pfropfen. 1851. III. 39.
H., A. Cherry Plum for hedges. 1890. III. 436.¹
H., A. The hardy Smilaxes. 1889. III. 338.¹
H., A. The Musky Rose. 1895. III. 456.¹
H., A. Observations on Viscum album. 1849. II. 178.¹
H., A. G. H. The germination of Sál. See HAMPDEN, A. G. HOBART-.
H., B. The Acacia. 1874. II. 328.¹
H., C. Actinidia volubilis and Kolomikta. 1874. III. 595.²
H., C. Bemerkungen über einige ... Eichenarten. 1835. III. 361.¹
H., C. Ueber die räumliche Eintheilung des Waldes. 1891. IV. 251.¹
H., C. C. M. De Sagoboom op Java. 1892. III. 327.²
H., C. E. De krulloten en het zwart worden der Cacao. 1900. III. 593.²
H., C. R. Propagation of Garrya elliptica. 1875. III. 352.²
H., C. W. Beiträge zur Forstwissenschaft aus der ... Geometrie. See HENNERT, C. W. 1783. IV. 57.
H., C. W. Beyträge zur Forstwissenschaft aus der praktischen Geometrie. See HENNERT, C. W. 1783. IV. 213.
H., C. W. Forest pruning. 1845. IV. 170.
H., D. Epiphyllum truncatum and its varieties. 1850. III. 623.¹
H., D. Ueber Epiphyllum truncatum und dessen Spielarten. 1850. III. 623.¹
H., D. The Oriental Plane in Greece. 1887. II. 255.¹
H., E. Ancient pollard Oaks at Hayes. 1900. III. 363.¹
H., E. Jamaica viewed. See HICKERINGILL, E. 1661. III. 266.
H., F. Berberis Fremonti. 1894. III. 395.²
H., F. The Grand Mesa, West Colorado. 1893. II. 587.¹
H., F. Notes of a visit to Fangi and Lahoul. 1878. I. 474.
H., F. L. von. Weitere Nachricht von guter teutscher Forst-Verfassung. 1789. IV. 348.²
H., G. Ueber die Blattanordnung der Dracaenen. 1889. II. 80.¹
H., G. Der nachhaltige Waldertrag. 1840. IV. 235.³
H., G. Rhodochiton volubile. 1893. III. 704.¹
H., H. Coprosma Baueriana variegata. 1878. III. 743.²
H., H. Bedeutung und Verwendung von Bäumen und Blumen im Alterthum. 1861. I. 511.
H., H. On the hardiness of Himalayan Rhododendrons. 1881. III. 656.
H., H. Method in fire conservancy. 1899. IV. 184.¹
H., H. N. Base of the Grizzly Giant. 1872. II. 51.¹
H., H. N. The beauty of bare branches. 1873. III. 208.¹
H., H. N. The Big barked tree. 1872. II. 51.¹
H., H. N. Carludovica humilis. 1874. III. 332.²
H., H. N. Forestry and poetry. 1876. I. 517,¹ IV. 55.¹
H., H. N. The great Chestnut of Mount Etna. 1872. II. 124.¹
H., H. N. The Monkey's Bread or Baobab tree. 1872. II. 528.³
H., H. N. The Pagoda Fig of India. 1872. II. 153.¹
H., H. N. The Passion-flower. 1872. II. 577.¹
H., H. N. The timber forests of the Andaman Islands. 1872. I. 481.¹
H., H. N. Trees and architecture. 1874. III. 201.
H., H. N. Vegetation in Central Africa. 1873. I. 492.²
H., H. N. The Weeping Willow. 1872. III. 351.²
H., H. N. Worthless Laburnums. 1875. III. 480.¹
H., I. Planting street trees. 1866. III. 208.²
H., J. Bark peeling in Herefordshire. 1878. IV. 507.
H., J. Dipladenias. 1893. III. 687.²
H., J. Een en ander over het enten in de Koffiecultuur. 1898. III. 733.¹

H., J. Eranthemums. 1894. III. 709.¹
H., J. European and American forestry. 1876. IV. 269.
H., J. Madagaskar, het land ... voor de Koffie-cultuur. 1898. III. 732.²
H., J. Nog iets over het enten van Java-Koffie. 1898. III. 733.¹
H., J. The pendulous or long-leaved Crotons. 1880. III. 516.¹
H., J. Timber for pattern work. 1888. IV. 428.¹
H., J. K. Über die Freigebung der Privatwaldungen. 1833. IV. 308.¹
H., J. M. Californian or Mountain Laurel. 1897. III. 408.¹
H., J. Y. The forest of Dean. 1882. IV. 358.¹
H., L. Bemerkungen über Pinus Strobus L. 1837. IV. 469.
H., L. Ueber die Festigkeit einiger Holzarten. 1884. IV. 114.
H., L. Geschichte verschiedener hierländischer Baumwollarten. 1788. III. 345.¹
H., L. Waldweide-Rentabilitäts-Calcul. 1884. IV. 136.¹
H., M. Die Eisenbahnen und die Gefahr der Waldbrände. 1884. IV. 181.²
H., M. Die Forstwirthschaft in Kaukasien. 1883. IV. 114.
H., M. Die Forstwirthschaft in Wolhynien. 1884. IV. 114.
H., M. Jurisprudence. — Dégâts de lapins. 1899. IV. 198.²
H., M. Neue Palmen. 1898. III. 318.²
H., M. E. Transplanting the Holly. 1841. III. 530.¹
H., M. E. Tree-guards. 1843. III. 198.²
H., N. H. Trees and shade. 1874. III. 209.
H., O. Ein neuer afrikanischer Weinstock. 1881. III. 559.¹
H., P. Magnolia parviflora. 1890. III. 400.¹
H., P. v. d. De Koffijkultuur der Padangsche bovenlanden. 1874. III. 729.²
H., P. S. Forest destruction. 1879. IV. 281.²
H., R. Some of the characteristics of soils. 1883. IV. 69.
H., R. S. The woods of Florida. 1848. I. 317.¹
H., S. Einiges über den Eichenkernkäfer. 1851. IV. 509.
H., S. Zur Frage: "Worin liegt der Grund des allmäligen Verschwindens der Eichenwaldungen?" 1853. IV. 504.
H., S. Intensive Forstwirthschaft und ihre Folgen. 1861. IV. 68.
H., S. Kahl- oder Dunkelschlagwirthschaft? 1861. IV. 128.
H., S. Veredeling van Koffie. 1900. III. 733.²
H., S. Wie weit reicht die Wichtigkeit der Wälder? 1851. IV. 49.²
H., S. See also HAYES, Samuel.
H., T. Hamamelis. 1893. III. 417.¹
H., T. Jasminum nudiflorum. 1892. III. 673.¹
H., T. H. Liberian Coffee. 1894. III. 742.³
H., W. Arboriculture in Scotland. 1884. III. 177.¹
H., W. B. Daphne Mezereum. 1889. III. 627.³
H., W. B. Echites peltata. 1875. III. 688.¹
H., W. B. Exochorda grandiflora. 1877. III. 424.¹
H., W. B. The Mock Oranges. 1875. III. 413.¹
H., W. B. Vegetation of the Paramos of New Granada. 1877. III. 856.²
H., W. P. Diospyros Kaki. 1875. III. 669.¹
H., W. P. Diospyros Kaki L. f. var. costata. 1879. III. 669.¹
H., W. T. The new Liberian Coffee. 1876. III. 742.¹
Haack, (Oberforstinspektor). Das Schiffeln oder das Brennen des Waldbodens. 1855. IV. 133.
Haag. Beitrag zu den Erfahrungen über den Wuchs der Weymouthskiefer. 1825. IV. 469.
Haag, G. Ueber horisontale Schutz- oder Sickergräben. 1881. IV. 144.¹
Haage & Schmidt. Antigonon leptopus. 1871. III. 387.¹
— — Neue Palmen. 1881. III. 322.¹
— — Opuntia Raffinesquiana. 1868. III. 625.¹
— — Schizolobium excelsum. 1874. III. 487.²
— — Xerophyta retinarvis. 1877. III. 341.²
— — See also REGEL, Eduard von & HAAGE & SCHMIDT.
Haage, Ferdinand. Haage's Cacteen-Kultur; Handbuch für Cacteenfreunde. 189.? III. 619.
— Haage's culture of Cacti in rooms. 1898. III. 620.¹
— Kakteen-Kultur. 189.? III. 619.
Haagen, G. Die land- und forstwirthschaftliche Unfall- und Krankenversicherung im Königreich Württemberg. 1888. IV. 310.²
Haak, J. Leerboek der plantkunde voor Indië. 1896. I. 92.
— Plantenkunde voor Indie. 1892. I. 92, 466.

Haan, Jacob van BREDA DE. *See* BREDA DE HAAN, Jacob van.

Haan, R. E. de. De druifluis. 1887. III. 574.

Haan, R. W. de. Kort woord over de oorzaken der achteruitgang van de kwaliteit der Java-Koffie. 1868. III. 729.²

Haar, A. A. ter. De vruchtboom. 1896. III. 140.¹

Haarlem — Bataafsche maatschappij der wetenschappen. *See* HOLLANDSCHE MAATSCHAPPIJ DER WETENSCHAPPEN. I. 15.

Haarlem — Hollandsche maatschappij der wetenschappen. *See* HOLLANDSCHE ... I. 15.

Haarlem — Koloniaal museum. *See* KOLONIAAL ... III. 14.

Haarlem — Société hollandaise des sciences. *See* ARCHIVES néerlandaises. I. 15.

Haarmann, A. Eisen und Holz im Eisenbahngeleise. 1892. IV. 424.¹

— Ueber die Verwendung von Eisen und Holz im Eisenbahnoberbau. 1892. IV. 424.¹

Haarmann, Wilhelm. *See* TIEMANN, Ferdinand & HAARMANN, Wilhelm.

Haartman, Carl Daniel von. Dissertatio botanica de Borbonia. *See* THUNBERG, C. P. 1811. II. 336.¹

Haartman, Johannes J. Plantae hybridae. *See* LINNÉ, Carl von. 1751. II. 458.¹

Haas, Friedrich & Rektorýs, Joh. Bereisung grösserer Waldwirthschaften des Auslandes. 1875. IV. 244.

— *See also* REKTORÝS, Johann & HAAS, Friedrich.

Haas, Johann Nep. Der Waldstand im Ersherzogthume Oesterreich. 1846. IV. 368.

Haas, Robert. Die deutsche Seidenzucht. 1852. III. 376.

Haas, W. H. van der. Boschbouw op Java. 1895. IV. 377.¹

— De Djaticultuur. 1894. IV. 536.²

— Eenige waarnemingen omtrent spontane verjonging van den Djati. 1898. IV. 537.¹

— Instandhouding ... van de Wildhoutbosschen in ... Java. 1898. IV. 124.¹

— Nog eens Rameh (Boehmeria nivea) als nevenproduct. 1894. III. 381.²

— Rameh (Boehmeria nivea) als nevenproduct. 1893. III. 381.²

— De toepassing van het uitkap systeem bij de behandeling der Djati. 1899. IV. 537.¹

— Het uitdunnen en uitkappen van de Djatibosschen. 1899. IV. 537.¹

— Een vraag, naar aanleiding van "Eenige waarnemingen." 1898. IV. 537.¹

Haase, Christoph Friedrich. De sexu plantarum. *See* LUDWIG, C. G. 1737. I. 198.

Haase, Johann. Über den Weinbau ... in Mähren. 1873. III. 558.²

Haase, Wilhelm Andreas. Commentatio de faba St. Ignatii. 1822. III. 682.²

Haass, (*Oberförster, Giersdorf*). Das Benutzen des Thaues bei der Aussaat. 1850. IV. 148.

— Einige Worte über das Biermannssche Kulturverfahren. 1855. IV. 141.

— Generelle Beschreibung der Gebirgs-Oberförsterei Hermsdorf. 1858. IV. 353.

— Holzmassen-Nachweis aus dem Riesengebirge. 1854. IV. 235.²

— Die Holzpapier-Fabrik zu Giersdorf. 1852. IV. 429.²

— Der Kalkeinstäuber zur Abwehr der Verwüstungen durch den grossen braunen Rüsselkäfer. 1851. IV. 475.

— Kurzer Bericht über das ... Exkursion in das Gebirgs-Forstrevier Lampersdorf. 1862. IV. 353.

— Ueber die Maulwurfsgrille. 1857. IV. 206.

— Ueber den schwarzen Rüsselkäfer. 1854. IV. 442.

— Die Staarmeise. 1844. IV. 199.¹

— Ueber die Vorbeugungs-Massregeln gegen Schneebruchschaden. 1853. IV. 190.

— Die Zürbelkiefer. 1856. IV. 463.²

— & Pannewitz, Julius von. Einig Worte über das Knieholz. 1862. IV. 464.²

Haass, A. Ist in Schlesien Holznoth vorhande · . 1840. IV. 282.²

Haaxman, P. A., (*jr.*). Landbouw en nijverheid in Nederl. Indië. 1891. III. 274.²

Haaxman, P. J. Aanteekeningen over Jaborandi. 1875. III. 505.¹

— Bijzonderheden over den cortex Bebeeru. 1849 III. 407.¹

— Over Guarana of pasta Guarana. 1868. III. 539.¹

— Over lignum Nyssae. 1879. III. 632.¹

— Nadere bijzonderheden omtrent het oleum cajeputi. 1849. III. 636.

— Over oleum cajeputi. 1849. III. 636.

— Over den oorsprong van zekere O. Indische vruchtjes. 1863. III. 539.¹

— Opzettelijke vervalschingen van scheikundige geneesmiddelen. 1849. III. 259.²

— Over Rhamnus. 1852. III. 542.¹

— & Merck. Quelques mots sur la calabariné. 1878. III. 4⁵4.¹

Habana — Real academia de ciencias médicas, físicas y naturales. *See* REAL ACADEMIA ... I. 7.²

Habeck. Die Vertilgung des Kiefernspinners. 1873. IV. 207.

Habenicht, (*Forstmeister*). Zur Buchenholzfrage. 1888. IV. 499.

— Buchen-Mischbestände. 1893. IV. 496.

— Eine Plänterwald-Form. 1883. IV. 139.²

Habenicht, Bodo. Die analytische Form der Blätter. 1895. I. 111.

Haberer, Joseph V. A list of plants in the vicinity of Utica. 1888. I. 315.

Haberland, Maximilian. Die Riesen-Esche im Thiergarten. 1898. II. 708.¹

Haberlandt, Friedrich. Beiträge zur Frage über die Acclimatisation der Pflanzen. 1864. III. 43.

— Compendium für den arithmetischen Unterricht. 1858. IV. 58.

— Notices sur l'acclimatation des plantes. 1864. III. 43.

— Observations sur l'acclimatation des plantes. 1864. III. 43.

Haberlandt, Gottlieb Johannes Friedrich. Zur Anatomie der Begonien. 1888. II. 583.²

— Anatomisch-physiologische Untersuchungen über das tropische Laubblatt. 1892. I. 168.

— Ueber das Assimilationssystem. 1886. I. 173.

— Ueber Bau und Function der Hydathoden. 1894. I. 132.¹

— Beiträge zur Kenntniss der Lenticellen. 1876. I. 132.¹

— Eine botanische Tropenreise. 1893. I. 466.

— Über den Entleerungsapparat der inneren Drüsen einiger Rutaceen. 1898. II. 397.²

— Die Entwickelungsgeschichte des mechanischen Gewebesystems. 1879. I. 134.²

— Über die Ernährung der Keimlinge ... bei viviparen Mangrovepflanzen. 1893. II. 613.²

— Über die Grösse der Transpiration im feuchten Tropenklima. 1898. I. 168.

— Ueber Jahresringbildung. 1895. I. 128.¹

— Ueber das Markstrahlmeristem von Cytisus Laburnum. 1886. II. 369.¹

— Ueber die Nachweisung der Cellulose im Korkgewebe. 1874. I. 130.

— Ueber die Perception des geotropischen Reizes. 1900. I. 190.¹

— Physiologische Pflanzenanatomie. 1884. I. 101.¹

— Zur physiologischen Anatomie der Milchröhren. 1883. I. 136.¹

— Ueber die Reizbewegungen ... bei Biophytum. 1898. II. 392.¹

— Das reizleitende Gewebsystem der Sinnpflanze. 1890. II. 372.²

— Über Scheitelzellwachsthum. 1881. I. 132.²

— Die Schutzeinrichtungen in der Entwickelung der Keimpflanze. 1877. I. 203.

— Über den tropischen Urwald. 1898. I. 219.²

— Der tropisie urskov. 1898. I. 219.²

— Untersuchungen über die Winterfärbung. 1876. I. 185.²

— Vergleichende Anatomie des assimilatorischen Gewebesystems der Pflanzen. 1881. I. 124.

Haberle, Karl Konstantin. Succ.nota rei herbariae bungaricae ... historia. 1830. I. 81.²

Habermann, Josef. Das Fagin. 1884. II. 126.²

— *See also* HLASIWETZ, Heinrich & HABERMANN, Josef.

Habliz, Karl Ludwig. Description physique de la contrée de la Tauride. *See* Габлицъ. 1785. I. 368.¹

— Physikalische Beschreibung der taurischen Statthalterschaft. *See* Габлицъ. 1785. I. 368.¹

Haché, Hermann. Reiner oder gemischter Hochwald? 1888. IV. 137.²

— Ueber die Verwendung von Holzschwellen. 1888. IV. 424.¹

Hackel, Eduard. Gramineae. 1887. II. 58.¹

— The true grasses. 1887. II. 58.¹

— Verzeichnis der Gräser Japans. 1899. II. 58.¹

— Die Zwerg-Alpenrose. 1900. II. 676.¹

— *See also* MUELLER, Ferdinand, *Baron* von & HACKEL, Eduard.

Hacker, Rudolf. Das forstliche Wirthschaftsbuch. 1898. IV. 246.

— Hacker's vereinfachter Verschulapparat. 1891. IV. 151.¹
— Die Maschine zum Ueberschulen. 1883. IV. 150.
— Ejne Maschine zum Ueberschulen. 1883. IV. 153.¹
— Nestejnodobost rašení Šmrku za možnost jejího praktického použití. 1888. IV. 454.
— Neu·verbesserte Maschine zum Verschulen. 1887. IV. 151.¹
— Příspěvek k poznání života dvou lýkožroutů. 1887. IV. 92.
— Verbesserte Maschine zum Verschulen junger Nadelholzpflanzen. 1886. IV. 151.¹
— Das Verschulen. 1886. IV. 151.¹
— Verschul-Maschinen für Nadelholzpflanzen. 1886. IV. 151.¹
— Die Zuchtwahl bei der Bestandesbegründung. 1886. IV. 75.¹

Hacquet, Balthasar. Mineralogisch-botanische Lustreise. 1780. I. 438, V. xxii.²
— Neueste physikalisch-politische Reisen ... durch die ... nördlichen Karpathen. 1790. I. 444.
— Plantae alpinae carniolicae. 1782. II. 499.¹

Haddington, 6th earl of. See HAMILTON, Thomas, 6th earl of Haddington.

Haddon. See CAZENEUVE, Paul & HADDON.

Hadek, Anton. Kritischer Beitrag zu Kopezky's "Neue Verfahren. 1900. IV. 219.
— Ueber das spezifische Gewicht des welken Buchenlaubes. 1896. IV. 496.
— & Janka, Gabriel. Untersuchungen über die Elasticität ... der österreichischen Bauhölzer. 1900. IV. 411,¹ 459.²

Hadelich, Siegesmund Lebrecht. De Gossipio ... in terris nostris. 1768. III. 218,¹ 345.¹

Hadelich, W. Ueber die Bestandtheile des Guajakharzes. 1862. II. 395.²

Hadi, Saiyid Muhammad. A monograph on dyes ... in the Northwestern Provinces. 1896. III. 237.¹

Hadley, Henricus. De Balsamo peruviano. 1718. III. 482.¹

Hadley, O. M. See TROOP, James & HADLEY, O. M.

Hadwen, Obadiah B. Degeneration of fruits. 1887. I. 249:¹
— A half-century's experience with ornamental tree planting. 1900. III. 202.¹

Haeberlin, Georg Heinrich. Dissertatio theologica, in qua sentenia de generatione plantarum ... ostenditur. 1693. I. 30.

Raeckel, Ernst. A visit to Ceylon. 1883. V. xxiii.²

Haecker, Gottfried Renatus. Lübeckische Flora. 1844. I. 381.

Haedge, J. C. Hortus Magni Duci; Badensis carlsruhanus. 1811. III. 27.²

Haeften, A. M. van. Drie schadelijke insecten voor de dennenbosschen. 1875. IV. 442.
— De pijnboomspinner en de non. 1875. IV. 442?
— Vier schadelijke insecten voor de Dennen. 1875. IV. 442.
— De wintervlinder. 1875. III. 190.

Hägerström, K. P. Åtskilliga former af Quercus Robur. 1887. II. 136.²
— Schwedische Quercus-Formen. 1887. II. 140.¹

Hægtmann, A. Korte Betænkninger om Skov-Væxten. 1700. IV. 155.¹

Hähnle. Ertragsuntersuchungen in Eschenbeständen. 1900. IV. 535.²

Hähnle, E. La costruzione delle strade forestali. 1881. IV. 389.

Hähnle, Eugen. Eucalyptus amygdalina. 1880. III. 634.¹

Hämmerle, J. A. Zur Organisation von Acer Pseudoplatanus. 1900. II. 480.¹

Haene, Ad. d'. Multiplication du Rosier par ... racines. 1872. III. 452.
— Ueber Vermehrung der Rosen durch Wurzelstecklinge. 1872. III. 452.
— Vermenigvuldiging van den Rozelaar door wortels. 1872. III. 452.

Hänel. Mittheilungen über die Erfolge ... im freien Lande kultivirter Pflanzen. 1860. III. 292.

Hänel, (Oberförster). Ueber Baum-Messung. 1867. IV. 215.
— Ueber Maikäferfrass. 1867. IV. 202.
— Notizen über Misch-Holz-Erziehung. 1866. IV. 138.¹

Haenel, Christian Heinrich. De camphora. 1739. III. 233.¹

Haenke, Thaddaeus. Botanische Beobachtungen. 1791. I. 374.

— Introducción a la historia natural ... de Cochabamba. 1900. III. 64.²
— Observationes botanicae in Bohemia. 1786. II. 673.¹
— See also JIRASEK, Johann & HAENKE, Thaddaeus.

Hänlein, von, (Forstmeister zu Ratiborhammer). Ueber Biermanns Kultur-Verfahren. 1856. IV. 141.
— Zur Frage über Entstehung der Schütte. 1867. IV. 476.
— Holz-Ertrags-Resultate aus dem Ratiborer Forst. 1852. IV. 260.¹
— Ueber den Zuwachs gepflanzter ... Bestände. 1852. IV. 141.

Haenlein, F. H. Beiträge zur Entwickelungsgeschichte der Compositenblüthe. 1875. II. 850.¹
— See NOBBE, Friedrich & HAENLEIN, H.; NOBBE, Friedrich, HÄNLEIN, H. & COUNCLER, Constantin.

Haenseler, Felix. Ensayo para una analysis de las aguas de Carratraca. 1817. I. 420.

Häpke, L. Ein merkwürdiger Eibenbaum. 1898. II. 11.²

Häring. Zusammenstellung der Kennzeichen der in Deutschland wachsenden verschiedenen Eichengattungen. 1853. IV. 425,¹ 514.¹

Häring, W. Unsere Wälder und ihr Einfluss auf den Volkscharakter. 1854. IV. 46.²

Haerlin, Albrecht Friedrich. Ueber den Bau der vegetabilischen Zellmembran. See MOHL, Hugo von. 1837. I. 137.

Haertl, Lorenz. De Quassia in specie. 1826. III. 508.²

Haes-Brems, Léopold de. La culture pratique du Pin sylvestre. 1895. IV. 559.¹

Häseler, J. F. Auflösung einer Aufgabe aus der Forstwissenschaft. 1792. IV. 263.

Häussler. Zur Naturgeschichte der Fichte. 1863. IV. 455.
— Der Strauchwuchs an jungen Weisstannen. 1864. IV. 445.

Häussler, C. F. Das forstliche Verhalten der ... Waldbäume. 1839. IV. 82.
— Tabelle über das forstliche· Verhalten der wichtigsten deutschen Waldbäume. 1839. IV. 82.

Haffner, Eugène. L'arbre à gutta-percha au Cambodge. 1898. III. 229.

Hafner, J. Anweisung zum Pflanzen ... der Obstbäume. 1872. III. 121.²

Haga, A. Nederlandsch Nieuw Guinea. 1884. III. 282.¹
— Die Hagelschläge im Kanton Bern. 1835. III. 184.²

Hagelstam. On the regions of perpetual snow in Norway. 1828. I. 353.

Hageman, J. Aanteekeningen over nijverheid ... in oostelijk-Java. 1863. III. 116.¹
— Aanteekeningen over nijverheid ... op ... Madoera. 1863. III. 274.²

Hagemann, Axel. Finmarksbirken. 1889. IV. 490.²
— Spredte bemerkninger om de i Saltdalen vildtvoksende trær og buske. 1888. I. 357.

Hagemeister, August von. Mahnung zur nothwendigen Waldschonung. 1855. IV. 282.¹

Hagen. Ueber das Veredeln von Apfelbäumen. 1860. III. 161.

Hagen, von, (Oberförster). Beschreibung des königlichen Forstreviers Katholisch-Hammer. 1859. IV. 353.
— See also BANDO & HAGEN, von.
— & others. Der waldbauliche Werth ... der Lärche. 1887. IV. 450.

Hagen, Graf von. Über die schnelle Anaucht hochstämmiger Rosen. 1832. III. 452.²

Hagen, Bernhard. Die Pflanzen- und Thierwelt von Deli. 1890. I. 467.
— Een reis naar het Tobahmeer. 1883. I. 467.

Hagen, C. Untersuchungen über die Entwicklung ... der Mesembrianthemen. 1872. II. 193.²

Hagen, Carl. Etwas über das Oculiren. 1861. III. 135.

Hagen, Friederich Wilhelm von. Ueber die Verwüstungen des Borkenkäfers. 1805. IV. 203.

Hagen, Johann Heinrich. Physikalisch-botanische Betrachtungen über die Weidenrosen. 1769. III. 350.²

Hagen, Karl Gottfried. Chloris borussica. 1819. I. 376.
— De plantis in Prussia cultis. 1791. III. 74.
— Preussens Pflanzen. 1818. I. 376.

Hagen, L. See BECKSTRÖM, W. & HAGEN, L.

Hagen, Otto von. Die forstlichen Verhältnisse Preussens. 1867. IV. 353.

Hagena, Karl. Phanerogamen-Flora des Herzogthums Oldenburg. 1869. I. 386.

Hagenaar, R., (jr.). Gallen aan de wortels van Koffieboomen. 1889. III. 736.
— Is er gevaar bij het gebruik van Tjaboetan uit door Koffiebladziekte aangetaste Koffietuinen? 1895. III. 736.

Hagenaar, R., (jr.) (continued).
— Java Koffie op Liberia stam. 1889. III. 733.[1]
— Over Koffie in Palembang. 1894. III. 730.
— Koffiecultuur in Palembang. 1894. III. 730.
— Over Koffiecultuur in Palembang. 1895. III. 731.
— Mannetjes-Koffie. 1886. III. 730.
— Zijn de Koffiebladziekte . . . in Brazilië en op Java identiek? 1889. III. 736.
Hagenbach, Eduard. Optical properties of chlorophyll. 1870. I. 141.
—Untersuchungen über die optischen Eigenschaften des Blattgrüns. 1870. I. 141.
Hagenbach, Karl Friedrich. Nachtrag zur Flora basileensis. 1821. I. 433.
— Tentamen florae ba ileen i³. 1821. I. 433.
Hagendorn, Ehrenfried. De catechu. 1679. III. 464.[1]
— Cynosbatologia. 1681. II. 281.[2]
Hager, Hermann. Commentar zur Pharmacopoea germanica. 1873. III. 249.
— Essai de Café. 1882. III. 740.[2]
— Handbuch der pharmaceutischen Praxis. 1883. III. 259.[1]
— Die neuesten Pharmakopoeen Norddeutschlands. 1855. III. 249.
Hager, J. W. F. Kursgefasster . . . Unterricht von dem Waldbau. 1764. IV. 105.
Haggenmacher, G. A. Reise im Somaliland 1874. 1876. III. 131.[1]
Haggren, Lars Christopher. Beskrifning öfver en skogs-sjö. 1787. II. 47.[2]
Hagström, Anders Johan. Angustura barken. 1792. III. 503.[2]
— Försök, gjorde med den balsam . . . på trädet Populus balsamifera. 1775. III. 345.[3]
— Tvenne års observationer på den tid blomster. 1780. I. 222.[2]
Hagström, Johan Otto. Om Allöf som svinföda. 1747. IV. 489.[1]
— Försök at föda orrar med hvarjehanda örter. 1751. III. 223.[1]
— Rön om de örter och gräs. 1750. III. 223.[1]
— Rön, om nucis vomicae nytta emot rödsot. 1773. III. 684.[1]
— Trenne hus-curer. 1760. III. 270.[1]
Hagstroemer, Andreas Johann. See HAGSTRÖM, A. J.
Hahmann, A. Die Dattelpalme. 1858. II. 73.[1]
Hahn, (Oberforstmeister). Die Aufforstungen in Schleswig-Holstein. 1893. IV. 159.
— Die Buchenverjüngung. 1892. IV. 495.
— Ueber starke Bäume in Schleswig-Holstein. 1889. I. 296.[1]
Hahn, C. W. Gesetz, den Diebstahl an Holz und anderen Waldprodukten betreffend. 1859. IV. 320.
— Das Holzdiebstahl-Gesetz. 1833. IV. 320.
Hahn, Eduard. Pharmacognostische Untersuchung der Adstringens-Rinden. 1892. III. 462.[2]
Hahn, Johann Gottfried. Gemeinnütziges Forst-Taschenbuch. 1809. IV. 117.
Hahn, Johann Joachim. De herbae exoticae Thee infuso. 1722. III. 605.
Hahn, M n. Ein Beitrag zur Borkenkäferfrage. 1885. IV. 204. arti
— Die moderne Holzzucht im Hochwald-Betriebe. 1879. IV. 129.
— Praktische Anleitung zur Bewirthschaftung der Bauern-Waldungen. 1869. IV. 111,[1] 163.[3]
— Die Rasenhügelpflanzung. 1877. IV. 153.[2]
— Schutz der Saatkämpe. 1875. IV. 150.
Hahn, P. D. Viticulture of the colony. 1886. III. 559.[1]
Hahn, Petrus. Δενδρολογία. 1698. I. 82.[1]
— De Platano. 1695. II. 254.[2]
Hahn, W. Exposé über die Besitz- . . . verhältnisse der Joachimsthaler Staatsforste. 1873. IV. 371.
Hahnemann, Samuel. Der Kaffee in seinen Wirkungen. 1803. III. 741.[2]
Haide-Cultur-Verein für Schleswig-Holstein. Vereinsblatt. IV. 9.
Haidinger, Wilhelm. See WÖHLER, FR. & HAIDINGER, W.
Haillant, Nicolas. Flore des Vosges. 1885. I. 74,[1] 417.
Hailstone, T. Catalogue of the rarer plants. 1878. I. 534.[1]
Haimhoffen, Gustav, Ritter von. Beobachtungen über die Blattgalle. 1876. III. 563.
— Beobachtungen über die . . . Pflanzengallen. 1858, I. 214.[1]
— Ueber die Eichengalle von Cynips coriaria. 1867. IV. 509.

Hain, F. H. The practical value of forests to the surface of the country. 1896. IV. 54.
Hainaut — Société des sciences, des arts et des lettres. See SOCIÉTÉ . . . I. 17.
Haines, H. H. Savannah forests in Bengal. 1896. IV. 528.[2]
— See also MANSON, F. B. & HAINES, H. H.
Haines, R. Notes on conessine. 1865. III. 692.[1]
Haite, G. C. Plant studies for artists. 1886. I. 516.
Háj. IV. 14.
Hajdu, János. Levélhullás. 1898. I. 192.[1]
Hájek, Josef. Buxus sempervirens. 1896. III. 523.[1]
— Pěstování Růží ve velkém. 1896. III. 453.[1]
Hakim, ABDUL RAHIM. See ABDUL RAHIM HAKIM.
Hakluyt, Richard. Collection of the early voyages. 1809. I. 302.
Hakubutsukan reppin mokuroku; hensanbu; shokubutsurui. See CATALOGUE of the Tokio museum. 1879. I. 66.[2]
Halácsy, Eugen von. Beiträge zur Brombeerflora Nieder-Oesterreichs. 1886. II. 304.[3]
— Beiträge zur Flora der Balkanhalbinsel. 1890. I. 450.
— Beiträge zur Flora der Landschaft Doris. 1888. I. 450.
— Beitrag zur Flora von Griechenland. 1895. I. 451.
— Botanische Ergebnisse einer . . . Forschungsreise in Griechenland. 1894. I. 450.
— Conspectus florae graecae. 1900. I. 451.
— Flora von Niederösterreich. 1896. I. 444.
— Namensänderungen. 1891. II. 304.[3]
— Neue Brombeerformen aus Oesterreich. 1890. II. 304.[2]
— Ueber eine neue Lonicera. 1896. II. 838.[1]
— Novitäten aus der Flora Albaniens. 1893. II. 844.[2]
— Oesterreichische Brombeeren. 1891. II. 304.[2]
— & Braun, Heinrich. Nachträge zur Flora von Nieder-Oesterreich. 1882. I. 443.
Halaud timber measurer in Hindi. 1874. IV. 227.
Halbey. Ueber das Olibanum. 1898. II. 416.[2]
Haldane, R. C. Subtropical cultivations and climates. 1886. III. 96.[1]
Haldeman, R. J. Preservations of forests. 1872. IV. 178.[1]
Halden, Johann Baptista. Plantarium philosophicum. 1686. I. 30.
Halder, Frans Anton. Beobachtungen über die Temperatur der Vegetabilien. See SCHÜBLER, Gustav. 1826. I. 231.[2]
Hale, Edwin M. Ilex Cassine. 1891. III. 531.[2]
— Intelligence in plants. 1891. II. 504.[2]
— On the toxic . . . qualities of the Cactaceae. 1890. III. 620.[3]
Hale, Eugene. Memorial [presented by Eugene Hale] for the use of the Senate in relation to that part of the Wilson bill which places lumber on the free list. 1894. IV. 284.[1]
Hale, J. H. Apple culture for profit. 1900. III. 427.[1]
— The business side of fruit culture. 1900. III. 134.[1]
— The cultivation and diseases of the Peach. 1888. III. 441.[1]
— Notes on Peach culture. 1895. III. 441.[1]
— Peach culture. 1899. III. 441.[3]
Hale, Joseph. Report on the medical botany of . . . Louisiana. 1853. III. 62.
Hale, Peter M. The woods and timbers of North Carolina. See CURTIS, M. A. 1860. I. 317.[1]
— The woods and timbers of North Carolina. 1883. IV. 397.
Hale, Mrs. Sarah Josepha. Flora's interpreter. 1832. I. 515.
Hale, T. J. Additions to the flora of Wisconsin. 1860. V. XVII.[1]
Hale, Thomas. A compleat body of husbandry. 1756. IV. 544.[2]
Halenius, Jonas P. Plantae rariores camschatoenses. See LINNÉ, Carl von. 1750. I. 454.[3]
Hales, Stephen. Groeijende weegkunde. 1727. I. 162.
— Statica de vegetabili ed analisi dell' aria. 1727. I. 162.
— Statical essays, containing vegetable staticks. 1727. I. 162.
— Statick der Gewächse. 1727. I. 162.
— La statique des végétaux et celle des animaux. 1727. I. 162.
— La statique des végétaux et l'analyse de l'air. 1727. I. 162.
— Vegetable staticks. 1727. I. 162.
Half-hours at Kew. Oaks. 1875. III. 361.[1]
Hall, van. Kokeleko-noten. 1858. III. 631.[2]
Hall, Agnes C. Elements of botany. 1802. I. 84.
Hall, Birger Mårtin. Academisk afhandling om blomstrens honinghus. See LINNÉ, Carl von. 1762. I. 118.[1]
— Nectaria florum. See LINNÉ, Carl von. 1762. I. 118.[1]

Hall, Charles. A concise treatise on ... destroying heath. 1802. III. 81.

Hall, Charles E. Notes on tree measurements. 1891. III. 38.²

— Notes on tree planting at San Jorge. 1893. IV. 113.¹

Hall, Elihu. Notes on the arboreous ... flora of Oregon. 1877. I. 320.

— Plantae texanae. 1873. I. 323.

Hall, Hermann Christian van. Aanteekeningen over Diosma crenata. 1829. II. 399.²

— Antiaris toxicaria Lesch. 1859. II. 146.¹

— Het belang, dat er voor den landbouw gelegen is in de kennis der natuurlijke historie. 1826. III. 35.

— Bijdragen tot de organographie der planten. 1861. I. 111.

— Boombladeren tot veevoeder. 1874. III. 223.¹

— De bosschen van Madera. 1867. I. 498.

— Botanische aanteekeningen. 1849. II. 5,¹ 151.²

— Commentatio de systematibus botanicis. 1821. I. 251.

— Elementa botanica. 1834. I. 87.

— Flora Belgii septentrionalis. 1825. I. 390, V. xx.¹

— Flora van Noord-Nederland. 1825. I. 390.

— Het Garoe-boompje. 1854. III. 627.²

— Gedachten over den honigdauw. 1828. I. 213.¹

— De giftboon van den Calabar. 1865. III. 483.²

— Grondbeginselen der wetenschappelijke landhuishoudkunde. 1865. III. 35.¹

— Handboek der kruidkunde. 1834. I. 87.

— Houtteelt op Java. 1859. IV. 124.¹

— Initia florae groninganae. 1825. I. 390.

— De kruidtuin van 's Rijks hoogere burgerschool te Middelburg. 1871. I. 51.¹

— Lokushara en Arrowroot. 1869. III. 478,² 521.¹

— Nadeel van zwaveldamp. 1853. I. 211.

— Naschrift op de waarneming van A. de Koning. 1827. II. 839.¹

— Natuurlijke geschiedenis van het plantenrijk. 1852. I. 34.

— Nederlandsche werken over de houtteelt. 1848. IV. 1.

— Neerland's plantenschat. 1854. III. 76.

— Nieuwe bijdragen tot de Nederlandsche flora. 1841. I. 391.¹

— Nut der bosschen tot vermeerdering van het water in de duinen. 1871. IV. 160.¹

— Oorzaken der ontaarding van vele gekweekte gewassen. 1851. I. 248.²

— Opmerkingen over de afwisselende tijdperken van ontwikkeling. 1848. I. 187.

— Opmerkingen over eenige plantaardige geneesmiddelen uit Java. 1864. III. 276.¹

— Opmerkingen over het Oostindische Sawoehout. 1846. IV. 534.¹

— Pilocarpus pennatifolius Lem. 1860. II. 409.¹

— Toegepaste kruidkunde. 1857. III. 52.

— Verhandeling over Antoni van Leeuwenhoek. 1834. I. 80.²

— Verhandeling over ... den landbouw in de Nederlandsche West-Indien. 1857. III. 118.²

— De verwoestingen der rupsen in 1829 in Groningen. 1829. III. 188.²

— Verzending van levende planten naar Java. 1842. III. 155.

— Viburnum macrophyllum Thunb. 1859. II. 843.¹

— Waarnemingen over de toeneming der boomen in dikte. 1839. I. 189.

— Het winnen van hars en de in Nederland. 1867. IV. 436.²

— Zandgronden en zandverstuivingen. 1863. IV. 145.

— Ziekte van den Wijnstok. 1852. III. 559.²

— De ziekten der gewassen. 1866. III. 178.

— See also Kops, Jan & Hall, H. C. van.

— & Jacometti, T. M. A. Ooftboomteelt. 1869. III. 140.¹

Hall, I. H. Opuntia Ficus-indica DC. 1877. II. 596.²

Hall, J. J.H. van. Regelen bij het snoeien in acht te nemen. 1874. III. 734.²

— Waarom verbetert hout-kultuur den boden? 1874. III. 1.¹

— Wetenschap en gouvernements Kofficultuur. 1876. III. 729.²

Hall, James. The Blueberry and Thimbleberry. 1877. III. 458,² 663.²

— See also Wright, John & Hall, James.

Hall, John H. On the primary use of ammonia. 1860. I. 158.

Hall, Stephen W. Effects on color of fruits of foreign pollen. 1881. III. 50.²

Hall, Thomas B. A flora of Liverpool. 1839. I. 399.

Hall, Wilham Logan. Forest extension in the middle west. 1900. IV. 155.²

— Notes on Oklohoma [sic]. 1900. IV. 113.¹

— Tree planting in Oklahoma. 1900. IV. 155.²

Hallager, C. B. Charlottenlunds Skovs Fortrin. 1820. IV. 342.²

Hallauer, G. Communication sur une maladie de l'Araucaria. 1892. III. 298.¹

Hallbauer, Max. Düngung der Saatschulen. 1899. IV. 145.

— Edelkastanie und Akazie als Waldbäume. 1896. IV. 492,² 583.²

— Einige praktische Winke aus ... der Pflanzenerziehung. 1889. IV. 147.¹

— Einkeimen von Arvensamen. 1891. IV. 463.²

— Vorkommen der Schlangenfichte. 1891. II. 35.¹

Hallberg, Carl. See Ullgren, O. M. & Hallberg, Carl.

Hallé. See Cels, Silvestre & Hallé.

Halle, Johann Samuel. Die deutsche Giftpflanzen. 1785. III. 72.

Halle, P. E. Herbin de. See Herbin de Halle, P. E.

Halle — Naturforschende Gesellschaft. See Naturforschende ... I. 13.

Halle — Naturwissenschaftlicher Verein. See Naturwissenschaftlicher ... I. 14.

Hallenberg, Georgius. De Dulcamara. See Linné, Carl von. 1771. III. 701.²

Hallensleben, H. Eine konstant verbänderte Esche. 1885. II. 708.¹

Haller, Alb. Sur le camphre de Romarin. 1889. III. 698.¹

— Isomérie du camphols et camphres. 1886. III. 611.²

— See also Heckel, Édouard & Haller, Alb.

Haller, Albert von. Arzneimittellehre der vaterländischen Pflanzen. 1776. III. 89.²

— Bibliotheca botanica. 1771. I. 1.

— Brevis enumeratio stirpium Horti goettingensis. 1743. I. 43.

— Emendationes et auctaria ad Enumerationem stirpium helveticarum. 1742. I. 433.

— Enumeratio methodica stirpium Helvetiae indigenarum. 1742. I. 432.²

— Enumeratio plantarum Horti regii et agri gottingensis. 1753. I. 43.

— Enumeratio stirpium ... in Helvetia rariores. 1760. I. 433.

— Histoire des plantes suisses; ou, Matière médicale. 1776. III. 89.²

— Historia stirpium indigenarum Helvetiae. 1768. I. 433.

— Icones plantarum Helvetiae. 1795. II. 107.²

— Iter helveticum. 1740. I. 432,² V. xxii.²

— Ex itinere in Sylvam Hercyniam. 1738. I. 373.

— Matière médicale, tirée de Haller Historia stirpium. 1776. III. 89.²

— Nomenclator ex Historia plantarum indigenarum Helvetiae. 1769. I. 433.

— Observationes botanicae ex horto et agro gottingensi. 1752. I. 44.

— Opuscula sua botanica. 1749. I. 291.

— Pflichtmässige Relation des neulichen Brandes ... [von Roche]. 1859. IV. 183.²

— De praestantia remediorum vegetabilium. 1752. III. 238.¹

— Rapport officiel sur l'incendie ... de Roche. 1859. IV. 183.²

— Tentamen additamentorum et observationum ad historiam stirpium helveticarum. 1768. I. 433.

— Verzeichniss der in Helvetien wild wachsenden Bäume. 1763. I. 432.¹

Haller, Ch. Notes sur le Coca. 1862. III. 492.²

Haller, Gottfried. Bericht über die ... Sammlung aller an der Rebe lebenden mikroskopischen Tiere. 1880. III. 761.

— Die kleinen Feinde der Phylloxera. 1878. III. 571.

— & Landolt, Elias. Communiqué. 1877. III. 288.¹

— Mittheilungen. 1877. III. 288.¹

Haller, Gottlieb Emanuel von. Bibliothek der Schweizer-Geschichte. 1785. I. 4.¹

— Catalogue raisoné des auteurs qui ont écrit sur l'histoire naturelle de la Suisse. 1772. I. 4.¹

— Dubia ex Caroli Linnaei Fundamentis botanicis. 1751. I. 530.¹

Haller, Gottlieb Emanuel von (*continued*).
— Dubia quaedam ex cl. Linnaei Fundamentis hausta. 1750. I. 291, 530.[2]
— Dubiorum contra sectionem septimam Fundamentorum. 1753. I. 530.[1]
— Epistola qua . . . dubia quaedam ex clarissimi Linnaei Fundamentis hausta offert. 1750. ⁷. 529.
— Nuper proposita dubia. 1752. I. 530.[1]
Haller, Károly. Cydonia japonica. 1896. III. 420.[2]
Haller, Theophilus Emanuel von. *See* HALLER, Gottlieb Emanuel von.
Hallett, Robert. On the cultivation of the American Cranberry. 1822. III. 663.[1]
Halliday, *Sir* Andrew. The West Indies. 1837. III. 64.[1]
Halliday, Robert J. Practical Azalea culture. 1880. III. 660.[1]
— Practical Camellia culture. 1880. III. 599.[2]
Hallier, Ernst. Aedemone mirabilis Kotschy. 1859. II. 330.[1]
— Deutschlands Flora. *See* DEUTSCHLANDS FLORA. 1864. V. xix.[3]
— Ueber einige merkwürdige Störungen in der Holzentwickelung. 1867. I. 127.[1]
— Excursionsbuch. 1874. I. 387, 532.[1]
— Flora der Wartburg. 1879. I. 387.
— De geometricis plantarum rationibus. 1860. I. 34.[1]
— Der Grossherzoglich sächsische botanische Garten zu Jena. 1864. I. 48.
— Die Krankheiten des Kaffeebaumes. 1880. III. 735.
— Ueber Neubildung eigenthümlicher Zellen im Prosenchym von Aedemone. 1864. II..330.[1]
— Die Pestkrankheiten. 1895. III. 195.[1]
— Phytopathologie. 1868. III. 179.
— Eine Pilzkrankheit des Steinobstes. 1876. III. 194.
Hallier, Hans Gottfried. Bausteine zu einer Monographie der Convolvulaceen. 1897. II. 743.[2]
— Beiträge zur Anatomie der Convolvulaceen. 1893. II. 743.[2]
— Betrachtungen über die Verwandtschaftsbeziehungen der Ampelideen. 1896. II. 501.[1]
— Ueber Bombycospermum Presl. 1899. II. 745.[1]
— Die botanische Erforschung Mittelborneos. 1896. V. xxiii.[2]
— Convolvulaceae a Dr. Alfr. Pospischil . . . collectae. 1898. II. 745.[1]
— Convolvulaceae africanae. 1894. II. 744.[1]
— Convolvulaceae in Harrar . . . lectae. 1898. II. 744.[1]
— Zur Convolvulaceenflora Amerika's. 1899. II. 743.[2]
— Dipteropeltis. 1899. II. 744.[2]
— Über Hildebrandtia Vatke. 1898. II. 745.[1]
— Indonesische Acanthaceen. 1897. II. 802.[2]
— Die indonesischen Aeschynanthus-Arten. 1897. II. 793.[1]
— Die indonesischen Clematideen des Herbariums zu Buitenzorg. 1897. II. 196,[1] 872.[2]
— Ueber Kautschuklianen. 1900. II. 721.[2]
— Ueber Leca amabilis und ihre Wasserkelche. 1897. II. 503,[2] 873.[1]
— Neue und bemerkenswerte Pflanzen aus dem malaiisch-papuanischen Inselmeer. 1896. I. 467.
— Ueber Pseuderanthemum metallicum. 1898. II. 796.[1]
— Rapport over de botanische tochten in Borneo's westerafdeeling. 1895. I. 469.[2]
— Sycadenia. 1899. II. 746.[1]
— Systematisch overzicht van de Convolvulaceeën. 1896. II. 743.[2]
— Versuch einer . . . Gliederung der Convolvulaceen. 1893. II. 743.[2]
— Zwei Convolvulacensammlungen. 1898· II. 874.[2]
— & Molengraaff, G. A. F. De Borneo-expeditie-rapport. 1893. I. 469.[2]
Hallische Riesennuss. 1886. III. 357.[1]
Hallman, Daniel Z. Dissertatio . . . de στεφάνῳ ἐξ ἀκανθῶν, corona de spinis. 1757. I. 513.
Hallman, Johannes Gustav. De moxae atque ignis . . . usu. *See* THUNBERG, C. P. 1788. III. 754.[1]
— De Passiflora. *See* LINNÉ, Carl von. 1745. II. 576.[1]
Hallström, K. T. Vergleichend-anatomische Studien über die Samen der Myristicaceen. 1895. II. 220.[2]
Hally, John. How to grow Mistleto. 1876. III. 385.[1]
Halma-Grand. Des conditions physiques et chimiques qui doivent présider à la composition de tout fébrifuge. 1859. III. 344.[1]
Halsted, Byron David. Abnormal Ash leaves. 1888. II. 709.[1]

— Under the Apple tree. 1896. II. 267.[2]
— The climbing mechanism of the Japanese Ampelopsis. 1878. II. 504.[2]
— The Cranberry gall fungus. ·1889· III. 664.[1]
— The Cranberry scald. 1890. III. 664.[1]
— The Cranberry scald. ·1891. III. 664.[1]
— Decay of Quince fruit. 1892. III. 423.[2]
— Effect of forest-management on orchards. 1890. IV. 45.
— The forest in one of its relations to the orchard. 1891. IV. 45, 212.
— Fungous diseases of ornamental plants. 1896. III. 193.[2]
— The genus Rubus. 1886. III. 457.[2]
— Gymnosporangium macropus on Pirus coronaria. 1886. III. 429.[1]
— Injurious and other fungi. 1877. III. 193.[1]
— An investigation of Apple twigs. 1889. II. 267.[2]
— Live covers for country homes. 1900. III. 205.[1]
— Notes upon Epigaea repens. 1891. II. 663.[2]
— Observations upon Barberry flowers. 1889. II. 205.[2]
— Observations upon doubling of flowers. 1890. I. 145.[2]
— Pollen versus rain. 1889. I. 238.
— Reserve food materials in buds. 1890. I. 179.[2]
— Reserve food substances in twigs. 1890. I. 179.[2]
— The rusts of horticultural plants. 1900. III. 193.[2]
— A serious Filbert disease. 1893. III. 358.[1]
— The so-called " grit " in Apple-twigs. 1889. II. 266.[2]
— Some fungus diseases of the Cranberry. 1889. III. 664.[1]
— Sporting in Peaches. ·1898. II. 276.[1]
— The Sycamore blight. 1897. III. 418.[2]
— & Fairchild, D. G. Influence of moisture upon dehiscent fruits. 1891. I. 240.[2]
Halverhout, F. De bevruchting der planten. 1877. I. 201.[1].
Ham, S. P. Boschbouwkundige beschrijving van de residentie Kediric. 1891. IV. 376.[2]
— De proefaanplantingen van caoutchouc . . . leverende houtsoorten te Tjipetir. 1900. III. 149.
Hamann, Anton. Zur Nonnenfrage. 1892. IV. 201.
— Die staatliche Aufsicht bei Fideicommissforsten. 1894. IV. 286.[1]
— Zur Statistik der Staatsforstwirthschaft. 1892. IV. 368.
— Die Verheerungen durch die Kieferschütte. 1899. IV. 480.
Hamberg, Hugo Emanuel. De l'influence des forêts sur le climat de la Suède. 1885. IV. 46.[1]
— Nederbördens mängd på nakna och skogbeväxta åsar i norra Halland. 1886.· IV. 46.[1]
— Om skogarnes inflytande på Sveriges klimat. 1885. IV. 46.[1]
— *See also* ХамбергЪ.
Hamböck, Karol. Nauka praktyczna sadownictwa i przemysłu sadowniczego. 1884. III. 162.
— Welche Zwetschen- und Pflaumensorten eignen sich . . . zum Dörren. 1890. III. 433.[2]
Hamburg — Botanisches Museum. *See* BOTANISCHES . . . 1884. I. 48, III. 11.
Hamburg — Garten- und Blumen-Verein. *See* GARTEN . . . III. 12.
Hamburg — Gesellschaft für Botanik. *See* GESELLSCHAFT . . . I. 12.
Hamburg — Naturwissenschaftlicher Verein. *See* NATURWISSENSCHAFTLICHER . . . I. 14.
Ueber das in Hamburg übliche Kappen der Bäume. ·1793. III. 173.[1]
Hamburger, Emanuel. Salicis triandrae rami monstrosi descriptio. 1842. II. 105.[1]
— Symbolae quaedam ad doctrinam de plantarum metamorphosi. 1842. ·I. 101.[2]
Hamburger Garten- und Blumenzeitung. *See* NEUE allgemeine deutsche Garten- und Blumenzeitung. III. 13.
Hamburgische Pharmakopöe. 1835. III. 249.
Hamburgische wissenschaftliche Anstalten. Beiheft. Jahrbuch. I. 12.
Hamel, H. C. F. Traité sur les maladies des plantes. 1857. III. 178.
Hamelin. Tarif officiel·pour la recette et le classement des bois de construction. 1859. IV. 425.[1]
Hamelin, Fadus Capulinos. 1884. III. 435.[2]
Hamelin, Bon. Description du Magnolia-soulangiana. 1827. II. 212.[2]
— Hybrides obtenues par MM. le baron Thomas Melazzo. 1827. II. 212,[2] 601.[1]

Hamer, H. M. de Witt. *See* Witt Hamer, H. M. de.

Hamerton, James. Arboriculture. 1843. III. 123.[1]

Hamilton, Alexander G. On domatia in certain Australian and other plants. 1896. I. 216.[2]

— On the fertilisation of Clerodendron tomentosum. , 1895. II. 757.[1]

— On the fertilisation of Eupomatia. 1898. II. 217.[2]

— On the fertilisation of some Australian plants. 1895. I. 240.[1]

— On the flora of Mt. Wilson. 1900. I. 505.

— List of . . . New Zealand plants. 1899. I. 508.[1]

— A list of the indigenous plants of the Mudgee district. 1888. I. 503.

— Note on Pittosporum undulatum. 1895. II. 249.[1]

— Notes on the fertilisation of some Australian and other plants. 1898. I. 239.[1].

— Notes on the methods of fertilisation of the Goodeniaceae. 1895. II. 846.[2]

Hamilton, Charles. A description of the Máhwah tree. 1788. II. 698.[1]

Hamilton, Charles Wilham. Notes on the so-called resin canals in Conifers. 1878. II. 17.[2]

Hamilton, E. Botanique de la Bible. 1872. I. 513.

Hamilton, Edward. Dryobalanops Camphora. 1852. III. 611.[1]

— The flora homoeopathica. 1852. III. 58.

Hamilton, Francis. An account of a plant allied to the genus Piper. 1825. II. 95.[1]

— Account of an Indian remedy for the tapeworm. *See* Buchanan, Francis. 1807. III. 630.[1]

— Commentary on the Herbarium amboinense. 1824. I. 464.[2]

— A commentary on the . . . Hortus malabaricus. 1822. I. 471.

— Description of the tree called . . Launzan. *See* Buchanan, Francis. 1798. I. 475,[2] *IV. 88.*[1]

— A journey from Madras. 1807. III. 277.

— Some notices concerning the plants of . . . India. 1823. I. 471.

— Some notices concerning the plants . . . of India. 1826. I. 471.

— & **Maingy**, A. List of Indian timber trees. 1835. IV. 557.[1]

Hamilton, Frédéric. La botanique de la ·Bible. 1871. IV. xxv.[1]

Hamilton, G. J. Essay on woods & plantations. 1820. IV. 120.

Hamilton, John. Notes and statistics of cinchona bark. 1883. III. 718.

— De statistiek van kinabast. 1883. III. 718.

Hamilton, Joshua. Culpeper's English family physician. 1792. III. 253.

Hamilton, Thomas, *6th earl of Haddington*. A short treatise on forest-trees. 1765. III. 123.[2]

Hamilton, William. American Sumach. 1837. III. 468.[1]

— On the American Sumach. 1837. III. 468.[1]

— On the Argemone mexicana, Hura crepitans. 1846. III. 519.[2]

— Bemerkungen über Bocconia frutescens. 1847. III. 408.[1]

— Bocconia frutescens. 1847. III. 408.[1]

— On the Capparis cynophallophora. 1847. III. 408.[2]

— On the commercial ... pioperties of Hymenaea Courbaril. 1847. III. 478.[2]

— On the cultivation . . . of the Myrica cerifera. 1851. III. 353.[1]

— On the gum of the Rhus metopium. 1846. III. 244, 386,[1] 527.[2].

— Om Gummi af Rhus Metopium. 1846. III. 244.

— On the Jamaica Dog-wood. 1845. III. 484.[1]

— On the Malambo bark. 1847. III. 516.[2]

— On the medical and economical properties of Anacardium. 1846. III. 523.[2]

— On the medical . . . properties of Caesalpinia coriaria. 1846. III. 484.[2]

— On the medical . . . properties of Rhizophora. 1847. III. 632.[1]

— On the medical properties of the Piscidia. 1834. III. 484.[1]

— On the medical . . . properties of the Sapindus saponaria. 1848. III. 540.[1]

— On the medicinal properties of the species of Cassia. 1846. III. 470.[1]

— On the Moringa pterygosperma. 1846. III. 409.[1]

— Over de narcotische eigenschappen . . . van Piscidia. 1845. III. 484.[1]

— On the noxious properties of Echites suberecta. 1847. III. 688.[1]

— The oils obtained from the plants indigenous to the Antilles. 1850. III. 519.[1]

— Prodromus plantarum Indiae occidentalis. 1825. I. 335.

— On the properties . . . of Comocladia. 1846. III. 524.[1]

— On the properties of some species of Cathartocarpus. 1846. III. 470.[1]

— On the properties of the Bocconia frutescens. 1847. III. 408,[1] 609.[1]

— On the properties of the Hippomane mancinella. 1846. III. 519.[1]

— Sur les propriétés . . . de Piscidia erythrina. 1845. III. 484.[1]

— Some account of the febrifuge bark . . . El Malambo. 1834. III. 264,[1] *516.*[2]

— On some species of the genus Amyris. 1847. III. 495.[1]

Hamilton association. Journal. I. 5.

Hamlet, William M. The analysis of Prickly Pear. 1889. III. 624.[2]

— On the occurrence of arabin. 1889. III. 624.[1]

Hamm. Mémoire sur les moyens applicables à la destruction du phylloxera. 1880. III. 572.

Hamm. De Wiju. 1868. III. 553.[1]

Hamm, Julius. Der Ausschlagwald. 1896. IV. 132.[2]

— Besprechung einiger forstlichen Fragen. 1897. IV. 119.[1]

— Die Bodendecke im Walde. 1900. IV. 70.

— Die· Forstwirthschaft auf dem Bodenseemolassegebiete. .1879. IV. 350.[1]

— Zur Frage der Durchforstungen im Hochwaldbetriebe. 1882. IV. 173.

— Ueber Holzverwerthung und Kippes. 1879. IV. 388.[1]

— Zur Kiefernfrage. 1896. IV. 474.

— Die Lärche in der Bodenseegegend. 1881. IV. 449.

— Leitsätze für den Mittelwaldbetrieb. 1900. IV. 132.[1]

— Eine Waldexpropriation. 1899. IV. 259.[1]

— Aus den Waldungen des badischen Rheinthales. 1888. IV. 350.[2]

Hamm, W. Grondtrekken der natuurkunde van planten en. dieren. 1857. I. 90.

Hamm, Wilhelm von. Der Fieberheilbaum oder Blaugummi-Baum. 1876. IV. 533.[1]

— Die Sprengcultur. 1877. IV. 143,[1] *386.*

— Stockrodung mittels Dynamitsprengung. 1875. IV. 386.

— Die Wurzellaus der Rebe. 1875. III. 759.

Hamma, Bov-. *See* Bou-Hamma.

Hammar, Olof Niklas. Några anmärkningar rörande carpologien. 1849. I. 119.

Hammarin, Johan Israel, **Almquist**, Johan Magnus & Humble, Adolph Henric. Om utländske träd, buskar och blomster-vixter. *See* Thunberg, C. P. 1820. I. 266.

Hammatt, Edward S. The need of reforestation. 1898. IV. 272.

Hammer, Christopher. Florae norvegicae prodromus. 1791. I. 352.

— Norsk busholdnings kalender. 1772. ·III. 100.[1]

— Samling af botaniske afhandlinger. 1769. I. 31.

Hammer, Friedrich Ludwig. Mémoire sur les arbres. 1802. III. 209.

Hammerbacher, Friedrich. ·*See* Mutschler, C., Hornberger, Richard & Hammerbacher, Friedrich.

Hammerstein, A., *Freiherr* von. Der tropische Landbau. 1886. III. 96.[1]

Hammerstein, Alo. von. Zur Baumhöhenschätzung. 1882. IV. 215.

Hammerstein, C., *Freiherr* von, (*Forstreferendar*). Beiträge zur Buchenschwellenfrage. 1888. IV. 500.[1]

Hammerstein, C., *Freiherr* von, (*Oberforstmeister*). Ueber die ·Bewirthschaftung . . . der Eichenschälwaldungen. 1862. IV. 505.

Hammerstein, E., *Freiherr* von. Die Beaufsichtigung der körperschaftlichen Waldungen. 1851. IV. 285.[1]

— Ueber die Erträge . . . der Eichenschälwaldungen im Hannöverschen. 1847. IV. 514.[2]

Hammon, W. H. Frost;· when to expect it. 1899. III. 183.[1]

Hammond, E. W. Autumn colors in Oregon. 1890. III. 443,[1] *661.*[1]

— Autumn in Oregon. 1889. III. 63.[2]

— The Madroña in winter. 1891. III. 647.[2]

Hammond, Harry. South Carolina; resources. 1883. III. 264.[1]

Hammond, Thomas William. *See* Favart, Émile, (*pseud.*).

Hammr, Jan. O užitku Jalovce obecného. 1890. III. 303.[2]

Hamnerin, Pehr. Vires medicae plantarum quarundam indigenarum. 1737. III. 270.[1]
Hamon. Remarques sur l'Acacia dealbata. 1852. III. 464.[1]
Hamond, W. P., (jr.). Effects of the late winter on coniferous plants. 1854. III. 291.
— Effets de l'hiver 1853–54 sur les arbres conifères. 1854. III. 291.
Hampden, A. G. Hobart-. Effect of the time of felling on the production and development of coppice-shoots. 1892. IV. 132.[2]
— The germination of Sâl. 1896. II. 561.[1]
— The most suitable method of treatment to apply to Sâl. 1899. IV. 528.[2]
— Project for a new timber-catching boom. 1885. IV. 390.[2]
— Report on forest transport works in the Salzkammergut. 1890. IV. 389.
— Report on the transport of sleepers . . . to Dakhpathur. 1886. IV. 390.[2]
Hampe, Ernst. Beobachtungen von Geschlechtsveränderungen an Weiden. 1840. II. 103.[2]
— Flora hercynica. 1873. I. 387.
— Prodromus Florae hercynicae. 1836. I. 379.
Hampel, Julius. Die " italienische " oder Pyramiden-Pappel. 1893. IV. 486.[1]
Hampel, Karl. Einige Gesichtspunkte für die Anordnung freizustellender Gehölze. 1888. III. 202.[1]
— Stadtbäume. 1893. III. 210.
— Ueber die Verschönerung der Städte. 1899. III. 202.[1]
Hampel, Ludwig. Düngungs-Versuche im Forstgarten. 1879. IV. 144.[2]
— Ermittlung des Gewichtes der nordsteirischen Holzarten. 1882. IV. 411.[1]
— Forstlicher Pflanzen-Kalender. 188 .? I. 227,[2] IV. 83.
— Gerbstoff-Untersuchungen. 1878. IV. 435.
— Die Härte einiger Holzarten. 1882. IV. 411.[2]
— Ueber Hagelschäden. 1887. IV. 190.
— Ueber den Harzgehalt des Holzes. 1888. IV. 429.
— Aus dem Hochgebirgs-Köhlereibetriebe. 1879. IV. 395.
— Aus dem Kulturwesen. 1881. IV. 142.
— Ein Normalschlitten zur Holzbringung. 1882. IV. 389.
— Pflege zu dichter Saaten im Pflanzgarten. 1892. IV. 151.[1]
— Project einer transportablen Holzrollbahn. 1878. IV. 391.
— Ueber den Rindenbrand. 1888. IV. 192.[1]
— Soll die Haupt- oder Unterabtheilung als Wirthschaftseinheit gelten? 1897. IV. 246.
— Die Spaltbarkeit des Lärchenholzes. 1888. IV. 452.[1]
— Trockenästungen in Nadelholzforsten. 1894. IV. 172.[2]
— Ueber Verbauungen von Lawinengängen. 1877. IV. 188.[1]
— Die Vereinigung des Wirthschaftlichen mit dem Schönen im Walde. 1898. IV. 137.[1]
— Ueber Verkohlung von Ast- . . . hölzern. 1882. IV. 395.
— Wachsthumsverhältnisse im Urwalde. 1887. IV. 67.[1]
— Wachsthumsverhältnisse im Urwalde. 1891. IV. 67.[2]
— Ueber den Wassergehalt von Holz. 1889. IV. 412.[1]
— Die Weisserle in Mischung. 1884. IV. 489.[2]
Hampel, W. Handbuch der Frucht- und Gemüse-Treiberei. 1885. III. 176.[2]
— Zur Vertilgung der Mäuse. 1883. III. 186.[1]
Hampshire field club. Papers. I. 18.
Hampton, W. C. Descriptive list of the Oaks of Hardin county. 1886. II. 128.[2]
Hamy, Ernest-Théodore. Le Muséum d'histoire naturelle il y a un siècle. 1893. I. 59.
Hanamann, Josef. Die klimatischen Verhältnisse von Lobositz. 1896. IV. 48.[2]
— Mittheilungen der . . . agronomischen Versuchsstation Lobositz. 1881. IV. 134.[1]
Hanausek, Eduard. Ueber Badian, Shikimi. 1888. III. 398.[1]
— Die brasilianische Kaffee-Ausstellung. 1883. III. 739.
— Ueber "erschöpften " . . . Thee. 1893. III. 608.[1]
— Zur Prüfung des Mandelöles. 1883. III. 434.[2]
— Des thés déjà épuisés. 1893. III. 608.[1]
Hanausek, F. F. Botanisches und Praktisches über Kaffee. 1900. III. 740.[1]
Hanausek, Thomas Franz. Zur Abstammung der sogenannten "Tahiti-" Nüsse. 1896. III. 327.[2] ·
— Algarobilla. 1879. II. 873.[1]
— Zur Anatomie der Frucht von Myrospermum. 1878. II. 873.[1] ·

— Zur Anatomie der Tahitinuss. 1893. III. 327.[2]
— Ueber die Bedeutung der Symbiose. 1895. I. 234,[1] IV. 74.[1] ·
— Botanische Mittheilungen. 1879. III. 433.[2]
— Caoba-Frucht. 1878. II. 422.[1]
— Cellulose. 1894. IV. 430.
— Zur Characteristik des Cocablattes. 1885. III. 493.[1]
— Ueber die "Chips." 1896. III. 406.[1]
— Die Entwicklungsgeschichte der Frucht . . . von Coffea. 1890. II. 814.[2]
— Sur un faux macis. 1887. III. 403.[1]
— Folia Boldo. 1880. II. 222.[1]
— Fruta de Burro. 1877. II. 872.[2]
— Goma de Tuna. 1877. II. 874.[1]
— Ueber die Harz- und Oelräume in der Pfefferfrucht. 1886. II. 95.[2]
— Ueber die Harzgänge in den Zapfenschuppen einiger Coniferen. 1879. II. 19.
— Ueber den histologischen Bau der Haselnussschalen. 1892. II. 121.[2]
— Zur Lage der Harzgänge. 1882. I. 135.
— Zur Morphologie der Kaffeebohne. 1894. II. 814.[2]
— Die Nahrungs- und Genussmittel aus dem Pflanzenreiche. 1884. III. 219.[2]
— Ueber eine neue Form der Rosa collina. 1883. II. 293.[1]
— Neue Rosenformen. 1886. II. 288.[1]
— Paraman. 1876. III. 610.[2]
— Pepa de Cola. 1877. II. 873.[2]
— Sur la présence . . . des saponines. 1894. I. 177.
— Quinchonchos. 1878. II. 873.[1]
— Die Raphiafaser. 1885. II. 74.[2]
— Ueber den Samen von Copaifera Jacquini. 1881. II. 347.[2]
— Ueber die Samenhautepidermis der Capsicum-Arten. 1888. II. 769.[2]
— Ueber die Strophantus-Samen. 1887. II. 732.[1]
— Ueber symmetrische . . . nackte Samen von Coffea. 1895. II. 814.[2]
— Die Tahitinuss [Sagus amicarum]. 1880. II. 71.[2]
— Ueber eine unechte Macis. 1887. III. 403.[1]
Hanbury, Daniel. Additional observations on storax. 1863. III. 671.[2]
— On an article imported as Calamba wood. 1851. III. 396.[2]
— Beiträge zur Materia medica China's. 1862. III. 273.[1]
— On the best methods of applying the Calabar bean. 1864. III. 483.[2]
— The botanical origin and country of myrrh. 1873. II. 417,[2] 418,[1] III. 511.[1]
— On the botanical origin of gamboge. 1865. III. 609.[2]
— On Burgundy pitch. 1868. IV. 459.[2]
— On Calabrian manna. 1872. IV. 536.[1]
— Sur un présumé de parthénogénèse dans le Xanthoxylum alatum. 1863. II. 412.[1]
— Chondodendron or Chondrodendron? 1875. II. 206.[1]
— Cinchona or Chinchona? 1875. II. 813.[1]
— Sur la cire de Chine. 1853. III. 527.[3]
— On Cortex Winteranus. 1876. III. 397.[3] ·
— Sur l'écorce de Storax. 1854. III. 417.[3]
— On the febrifuge properties of the Olive. 1854. III. 678.[3]
— Ein grüner chinesischer Farbstoff. 1857. III. 542.[1]
— Historical notes on manna. 1869. III. 221.[1]
— On the insect-white-wax of China. 1853. III. 226.[1]
— Malambo bark. 1860. III. 517.[1]
— Sulla manna di Calabria. 1872. IV. 536.[1]
— On the manufacture of balsam of Peru. 1863. III. 482.[1]
— Memorandum on . . . parthenogenesis in Zanthoxylum alatum. 1863. II. 412.[1]
— Note on Anacahuite wood. 1861. III. 695.[1]
— Note on Cassia moschata. 1863. III. 471.[1] See also Hamburg, Daniel. (By error.) 1863. II. 344,[3] V. xxvi.[3]
— Note on the ordeal bean of Calabar. 1863. III. 483.[2]
— Note on the use of balsam of Peru. 1861. III. 482.[1]
— Note sur le Cassia moschata. 1863. III. 471.[1]
— Note upon a green dye from China. 1857. III. 542.[1]
— Notes on Chinese materia medica. 1862. III. 273.[1]
— Notice sur la fève d'épreuve du Calabar. 1863. III. 483.[1]
— Sur une nouvelle substance appelée wood oil. 1856. III. 610.[2]
— On otto of Rose. 1859. III. 454.[1]
— Pareira brava. 1873. III. 396.[3]
— On Pareira brava. 1873. III. 396.[2]
— On a peculiar camphor from China. 1874. III. 754.[2]

— On the resin of the Norway Spruce Fir. 1850. IV. 459.²
— Über Rosenöl. 1859. III. 454.¹
— On Rottlera tinctoria. 1858. III. 520.¹
— Science papers. 1876. III. 238.²
— On the species of Garcinia which affords gamboge. 1864. II. 555.²
— Storax. 1857. III. 417,² 671.²
— On storax. 1857. III. 417,² 671.²
— Sur le storax. 1857. III. 417.²
— On Storax bark. 1855. III. 671.¹
— On the use of Coffee-leaves in Sumatra. 1854. III. 739.
— On wood oil, a substitute for copaiba. 1856. III. 610.²
— On wurrus. 1853. III. 520.¹
— See also FLÜCKIGER, F. A. & HANBURY, Daniel; HOOKER, Sir W. J. & HANBURY, Daniel.
Hanbury, Frederick Janson & Marshall, E. S. Flora of Kent. 1899. I. 404.¹
Hanbury, Thomas. An ancient Pine at Karasaki. 1894. II. 41.²
— The Kaki. 1893. III. 669.²
Hanbury, William. A complete body of planting and gardening. 1770. III. 81.
— An essay on planting. 1758. III. 35.
Hance, Henry Fletcher. Adversaria in stirpes imprimis Asiae orientalis. 1866. I. 453,¹ 458.
— Analecta dryographica. 1875. II. 123.¹
— Another new Chinese Rhododendron. 1882. II. 682.¹
— Castanea vulgaris Lam. grown in southern China. 1872. II. 123.²
— A Chinese Clethra. 1883. II. 657.¹
— A Chinese Fontanesia. 1879. II. 706.¹
— On a Chinese Maple. 1873. I. 457.
— On a Chinese Screwpine. 1875. II. 57.¹
— A Chinese Stephanandra. 1882. II. 316.¹
— Corolla Pierreana. 1876. I. 469.²
— A decade of new Hong-kong plants. 1882. I. 461.
— Descriptions of four new plants from . . . China. 1865. II. 731.²
— Erica carnea Linn. 1867. II. 664.¹
— Eugenias quattuor novas sinenses ostendit. 1885. II. 626.¹
— Exiguitates carpologicae. 1870. I. 459.
— On the Fagus Castanea of Loureiro's Flora. 1869. II. 121,¹ 125,¹ 153.²
— A few critical, little known . . . plants. 1866. I. 270.
— Florae hongkongensis Προσθήκη. 1872. I. 460.¹
— Florae hongkongensis supplementum. 1872. I. 460.²
— Florae sinicae novitates tres. 1881. II. 175.¹
— A fourth new Hongkong Calamus. 1875. II. 65.¹
— On the fruit of Tecoma grandiflora. 1879. II. 786.¹
— Generis Corni species duas novas . . . proponit. 1881. II. 654.²
— Generis Ruborum speciem novam proponit. 1884. II. 306.¹
— On the huskless Walnuts of North China. 1876. II. 113.¹
— Index of Chinese plants in Journal of botany. 1883. I. 459.
— On Liquidambar formosana Hance. 1867. II. 253.²
— Lysidice. 1867. II. 370.¹
— Manipulus plantarum novarum. 1862. I. 458.
— On a new Araliaceae of uncertain origin. 1881. II. 651.²
— A new Chinese Arundinaria. 1876. II. 58.²
— On a new Chinese Bignoniad. 1872. II. 788.¹
— A new Chinese Bignoniad. 1882. II. 791.¹
— On a new Chinese Caryota. 1879. II. 66.¹
— A new Chinese Hydrangea. 1874. ·II. 240.²
— A new Chinese Maple. 1884. II. 478.¹
— A new Chinese Rhododendron. 1881. II. 680.¹
— A new Chinese Symplocos. 1876. II. 704.¹
— A new Hongkong Anonacea. 1881. II. 218.¹
— A new Hongkong Tephrosia. 1886. II. 386.²
— On a new Indian Oak. 1878. II. 134.²
— A new species of Ardisia. 1884. II. 693.¹
— On a new Symplocos. 1874. II. 703.¹
— Note on Abrus cantoniensis. 1869. II. 322.¹
— Note on Elaeagnus gonyanthes Benth. 1868. II. 607.²
— Note on Quercus Wallichiana Lindl. 1870. II. 141.¹
— Note on Sambucus chinensis. 1869. II. 841.¹
— Note on Spathodea cauda-felina. 1874. II. 788.¹
— Note on the Capparis magna of Loureiro. 1869. II. 232.²
— Note on the genus Amphidonax. 1877. II. 59.¹
— Note on the genus Henslowia Blume. 1868. II. 168.²
— Note on the genus Pygeum Gaertn. 1878. II. 278.¹ .
— Note sur deux espèces du genre Scolopia. 1862. II. 573.²

— Notes on new or little known plants of China. 1849. I. 458.
— Notes on some plants from northern China. 1873. I. 459.
— De nova Pygei specie. 1870. II. 275.¹
— De nova Rhamni specie. 1869. II. 498.¹
— Novam Aristolochiae speciem describit. 1879. II. 183.¹
— Novam Echinocarpi speciem tradit. 1884. II. 511.²
— Novas generis Shoreae species duas proponit. 1878. II. 560.²
— On the Phoenix of the Hongkong flora. 1869. II. 73.²
— On Pierrea, a new genus of Samydaceae. 1877. II. 571.¹
— Pinus Bungeana. 1873. II. 41.¹
— Plantae quattuor novae hongkongenses. 1876. I. 461.
— On Pterocarya stenoptera. 1873. II. 114.²
— On Quercus fissa Champion. 1863. II. 122.²
— Sertulum chinense I.–VI. 1868. I. 459.
— On the Silkworm-oaks of northern China. 1869. IV. 502.¹
— Sketch of the island and flora of Hongkong. 1853. I. 460.²
— On a small collection of plants from Kiukiang. 1874. I. 459.
— The so-called olives of southern China. 1871. III. 510.¹
— On the so-called "Olives" . . . of southern China. 1871. II. 417.¹
— On some Asiatic Corylaceae. 1874. II. 123.¹
— Some Chinese Corylaceae. 1884. II. 123.¹
— On some mountain plants from northern China. 1875. I. 459.
— On some new Malayan Corylaceae. 1878. II. 123.¹
— Spicilegia florae sinensis. 1878. I. 459.
— On Sportella, a new genus of Rosaceae. 1877. II. 278.¹
— Stirpium novarum tetras. 1866. I. 453.¹
— On the structure of the fruit in Punica. 1850. II. 610.²
— Supplementary note on Chinese Silkworm-oaks. 1873. IV. 502.¹
— Symbolae ad floram sinicam. 1861. I. 458.
— Ternio Eugeniarum novarum chinensium. 1871. II. 26.¹
— A third new Chinese Rhododendron. 1884. II. 683.²
— Thorelia. 1877. II. 870.¹
— On three new Chinese Calami. 1874. II. 65.²
— Two additions to the Hongkong flora. 1875. II. 822.¹
— On two Dipterocarpaceae. 1876. II. 559.¹
— Viburnum tomentosum Thunb. in southern China. 1870. II. 843.¹
Hancock, John. The Juríbali. 1834. III. 511.²
— Observations on certain resinous . . . substances found in Guiana. 1829. III. 404.¹
— Observations on quinia. 1829. III. 721.
— Observations on Sarsaparilla. 1829. III. 338.¹
— Observations on the climate . . . of British Guiana. 1835. III. 268.¹
— Observations on the Orayurí or Angustura Bark tree. 1829. II. 407,² III. 503.²
— The properties and preparation of the Rio Negro sarsaparilla. 1829. II. 407,² III. 503.²
— Remarks on the Haiowa. 1838. III. 511.²
— Remarques sur . . . Bonplandia trifoliata. 1828. III. 503.²
Hancock, Thomas. An account of the native oil of Laurel. 1825. III. 403.²
— Personal narrative of the origin . . . of the caoutchouc . . . manufacture in England. 1857. III. 231.
— Remarks on the native oil of Laurel. 1825. III. 403.²
Hand-list of Coniferae grown in the Royal gardens. 1896. I. 55, III. 291.
Hand-list of tender monocotyledons, excluding Orchideae, cultivated in the Royal gardens, Kew. 1897. I. 55.
Hand-list of trees and shrubs grown in Arboretum. 1894. I. 55, III. 78.²
Handatlas sämmtlicher medicinisch-pharmaceutischer Gewächse. 1845. III. 58.
Handboek voor boomkweekerij. 1850. III. 106.²
Handboek voor landbouwers. 1839. III. 105.
Handbok i svenska trädgårds- och blomsterskötseln. See LUNDEQUIST, N. W. 1841. III. 100.²
Handbok i trädgårds-skötseln. See ÖHRGREN, E. M. 1837. III. 100.¹
The handbook of plain botany. 1836. I. 87.
Handbook of useful tables for the lumberman. 1881. IV. 228.²
Hand-books of commercial products; Indian section. 1892. III. 279.¹

Handbuch der Gesetze, Verordnungen und sonstigen Vorschriften für das Forststrafwesen . . . Hessen. 1840. IV. 319.[1]
Handbuch der grundsätzlichen Forstwirthschaft. See GRIESHEIM, L. W. von. 1800. IV. 268.
Handbuch der pharmaceutischen Botanik. See JUCH, K. W. 1804. III. 55.
Handbuch für die Forst- und Cameralverwaltung im Grossherzogthum Hessen. 1883. IV. 290.[1]
Handbuch für Förster und Forstliebhaber. 1794. IV. 95.
Handbuch für Liebhaber englischer Pflanzungen. See ROESSIG, K. G. 1796. III. 74.
Handbuch für praktische Forst- und Jagdkunde. 1796. IV. 22.[2]
Handcross Park. 1883. III. 199.
Handelsblatt für den deutschen Gartenbau. III. 12.
Handelsblatt für Walderzeugnisse. IV. 9.
Das Handels-Museum, Wien. III. 24.[2]
Handleiding tot de kennis . . . der Cactussoorten. 1847. III. 618.[2]
Handleiding tot het verzamelen van kaoutchouk. 1845. III. 230.
Handleiding voor de gouvernements-Koffiekultuur. 1873. III. 729.[2]
Handleiding voor de teelt . . . van de kakao. 1859. III. 592.[1]
Handley, John. Catalogue of plants growing in the Sedbergh district. 1898. I. 535.
Handloss, Heinrich. Beobachtungen über die Nonne. 1892 IV. 201.
— Bestandes-Regenerirung. 1875. IV. 170.
Hands, (Rev.). On the propagation of the Vine. 1842. III. 559.[1]
A handy mode of transplanting. 1872. III. 166.
Die Hanf- oder Tschusan-Palme. 1869. III. 331.[2]
Hangest, G. d'. Du bouturage des arbustes. 1872. III. 158.
Hanham, Frederick. A manual for the park. 1857. I. 54.
Hanin, L. Cours de botanique. 1811. I. 85.
— Eléments de botanique. 1809. I. 85.
— Enumeratio plantarum circa Metas. 1806. I. 376, 406.
— Nouveaux élémens de botanique. 1809. I. 85.
— Voyage dans l'empire de flore. 1800. I. 84.
Hanmann, Christian. De plantis in genere. 1635. I. 30.
Hann, Julius Ferdinand, Hochstetter, F. von & Pokorny, Alois. Allgemeine Erdkunde. See POKORNY, Alois. 1881. I. 218.
Hanna, J. S. Complete ready reckoner and log table. 1897. IV. 229.
Hannaford, Samuel, (jr.). Flora tottoniensis. 1851. I. 400, 533.
— Jottings in Australia. 1856. I. 501.
— The wild flowers of Tasmania. 1866. I. 506.[1]
Hannay, J. Bemerkungen über Aristolochia picta. 1852. III. 386.[2]
— Ueber Myrrhinium atropurpureum. 1852. III. 637.[1]
Hannay, P. S. See HANNAY, S. F.
Hannay, S. F. Further observations on the quality &c. of some of the forest trees . . . of Jeypore. 1848. IV. 400.[2]
— Note on some of the dye stuffs. 1848. III. 236.
— Observations on the quality, &c. of the principal timber trees . . . of Jeypore. 1845. IV. 400.[2]
— On the Rheeas or Nettle grasses. 1850. III. 233.[2]
Hannemann, Ferd. Katechismus der Obstbaumzucht. 1870. III. 138.
Hannemann, Johann Ludwig. Nova et accurata methodus cognoscendi simplicia vegetabilia. 1677. I. 287.
Hannikainen, P. W. Hakkausalan perkauksesta. 1890. IV. 388.[2]
— Hyönteisvahinko Rajajoen kruununmetsissä. 1891. IV. 205.[2]
— Katsaus erinäisiin metsäoloihin sekä metsänhoito-opetukseen Venäjällä. 1893. IV. 31.
— Kauneuden aisti metsänhoidossa. 1893. IV. 55.[2]
— Matkahavaintoja metsänhoidosta ja sen opstuksen aloilta pohjois- ja keski-Euroopan maissa. 1891. IV. 30.[2]
— Metsänhoito-oppi metsän ystäville. 1892. IV. 104.[2]
— Metsänkasvatuksesta, rahvaalle kirjoittanut. 1880. IV. 104.[1]
— Metsien hoidosta. Metsän ystäville kirjoittanut. 1882. IV. 94.
— Mizenkä yleisesti käytetyn säännötön karsintahakkaus on saatava metsille vähemmin turmiolliseksi? 1893. IV. 131.
— Muutama sana kanervakangasten metsistyttamisestä. 1889. IV. 157.

— Muutamia havaintoja metsän uudelleen kasvusta lohkottain hakatessa. 1888. IV. 140.
— Myrskyvahinko metsissä ja mitä voidaan tehdä sen torjumiseksi. 1890. IV. 189.[2]
— Pysyväisten koetussalain tarpeellisuudesta. 1889. IV. 37.[2]
— Vähäisen metsistä. 188 : ? IV. 102.
— See also SONCK, J. G., TIMGREN, G. O. & HANNIKAINEN, P. W.
Hannöverische Anzeigen. See HANNÖVERISCHES Magazin. IV. 9.
Hannöverisches Magazin. IV. 9.
Hannöversche Pharmakopöe. See PHARMACOPOEAS hannoverana. 1819. III. 248.
Hannon, J. D. Flore belge. 1847. I. 392.
Hannover — Gartenbau-Verein. See GARTENBAU-VEREIN . . . III. 12.
Hannover — Naturhistorische Gesellschaft. See NATURHISTORISCHE . . . I. 13.
Hannovers Forsten. See BURCKHARD, Heinrich. 1852. IV. 352.
Hannoversche land- und forstwirthschaftliche Zeitung. IV. 9.
Hannoversches land- und forstwirthschaftliches Vereinsblatt. IV. 9.
Hanocq, Ad. Les trois premières années d'arboriculture pratique. 1900. III. 145.[1]
Hanoteau, Adolphe & Letourneux, Aristide. La Kabylie et les coutumes kabyles. 1872. I. 485.
Hanratty, M. & Fletcher, T. H. Amount of tannin in some astringent substances. 1864. I. 183:
Hauriot, Maurice. Sur la prétendue transformation de la brucine en strychnine. 1883. III. 683.[2]
Hanry, Hippolite. Botanique [du Var]. 1853. I. 535.
Hans, Wilhelm. Abies Eichleri. 1889. III. 297.[1]
Hansen, (bischöflicher Secretär in Trier). Einiges über die ächten Kastanien. 1829. III. 358.[2]
Hansen, A. Havsandene og Landsandene. 1865. IV. 156.[1]
— Kortfattet Udtog af Skovdyrkningslæren. 1865. IV. 94.
— Nogle Bemærkninger om Kulturarbejder paa Lellinge Skovdistrikt. 1870. IV. 343.[1]
Hansen, A. Joergen. Pilens Dyrkning og Anvendelse. 1891. III. 349.
Hansen, Adolph. Ueber Adventivbildungen. 1880. I. 108.[1]
— Ein Beitrag zur Kenntniss des Transpirationsstromes. 1888. I. 166, IV. 418.[2]
— Der Chlorophyllfarbstoff. 1888. I. 142.
— Einiges über Wurzeln und Wasserleitung im Holz. 1884. I. 165.
— Geschichte der Assimilation und Chlorophyllfunction. 1882. I. 173.
— Zur Geschichte und Kritik des Zellenbegriffes. 1897. I. 137.
— Pflanzengeographische Tafeln. 1899. V. XVI.[2]
— On Quebracho bark. 1880. III. 687.[1]
— Die Quebracho-Rinde. 1880. III. 687.[1]
— Ueber Sphärokrystalle. 1888. I. 139.
— Vergleichende Untersuchungen über Adventivbildungen. 1881. I. 108.[1]
— Ueber die Wirkung des Milch-Saftes von Ficus Carica. 1881. III. 370.[1]
Hansen, Anthon P. Nogle Figenarter. 1883. III. 369.[1]
Hansen, C. E. American Conifers in Scandinavia. 1892. III. 293.
Hansen, Carl. Blade af Hortensiens Historie. 1897. III. 412.[1]
— Hække af Stikkelsbærbuske. 1898. III. 414.[2]
— En ny Fare for Frugttrædyrkningen. 1897. III. 191.
— Pinetum danicum. 1892. II. 13,[2] III. 291.
— Rotang-Palmen. 1898. III. 321.[2]
— Skyggepalmen. 1898. III. 318,[2] 324.[2]
Hansen, George. Ceanothus in the landscape of the Sierra Nevada. 1897. II. 492.[2]
— Einige Bemerkungen über die Coniferen. 1885. III. 290.
— Flora of the Sequoia gigantea region. 1896. II. 129.[1]
— Where the big trees grow. 1895. I. 326.
Hansen, J. Forsøg til Forsvar for Gavnligheden af levende Hegn. 1818. III. 212.[2]
Hansén, Jacob. See HEDENBERG, Olaf Anton & HANSÉN, Jacob.
Hansen, Johan Frederik. Et Afsnit af Læren om Skovbrugets Økonomi. 1877. IV. 102.
Hansen, Karl. Læ- og Hegnsplantning paa Marken. 1881. III. 214.[1]
— Om Piledyrkning. 1881. III. 348.
— Om Plantning ved Landeveje. 1882. III. 209.

Hansen, M. L. Kortfattede Vink om Camellia Culturen. 1885. III. 599.[2]
— Mosrosens Formering. 1885. III. 455.[1]
Hansen, N. Naaletræer i Park og Have. 1886. III. 290.
Hansen, Niels Ebbesen. The blossoms of the orchard fruits. 1894. III. 39.
— Field notes on budding. 1893. III. 164.[2]
— Notes on European horticulture. 1895. III. 163.[1]
— Ornamental trees and shrubs. 1893. III. 60.
— Root-killing of Apple trees. ·1899· III. 428.[2]
Hansen, P. C. C. Koffieziekte. 1898. III. 736.
Hansen-Ostenfeld, Carl Emil. See BØRGESEN, F. C. E. & OSTENFELD, C. E. H.
Hansgirg, Anton. Beiträge zur Biologie und Morphologie des Pollens. 1898. I. 117.[1]
— Beiträge zur Kenntniss der Blüthenombrophobie. 1896. I. 239.[1]
— Beiträge zur Kenntniss der Flora von Böhmen. 1883 I. 443.
— Beiträge zur Kenntniss über die Verbreitung der Reizbewegungen. 1890. I. 198.
— Zur Biologie des Pollens. 1897. I. 201.[2]
— Biologische Fragmente. 1893. I. 194.
— Biologische Mittheilungen. 1892. I. 194.
— Botanisches aus der Königgrätzer Gegend. 1881. II. 102.[2]
— Květena okolí Hradce Králové. 1881. I. 443.
— Neue biologische Mittheilungen. 1892. I. 194.
— Neue Untersuchungen über den Gamo- und Karpotropismus. 1897. I. 194.
— Zur Phyllobiologie. 1900. ·I. 219.[2]
— Phytodynamische Untersuchungen. 1890. I. 194.
— Proč se daří stromům jehličnatým v krajinách severnějších lépe než našim stromům lupenatým. 1879. II. 20.[2]
— Ueber die Verbreitung der karpotropischen Nutationskrümmungen. 1890. I. 194.
— Ueber die Verbreitung der reizbaren Staubfäden. 1890. I. 197.[2]
Hanslin, Ulr. Ueber Geldwertung ... der Rinde von alten Eichen. 1855. IV. 512.
— Ueber den Mittelwald-Betrieb. 1856. IV. 130.
Hanson (de Stavanger). Plantation de Saules en Norvège. 1865. III. 347.
Hanstein, Heinrich. Ueber die Bedeutung der Waldstreu. 1862. IV. 71.
— Verbreitung und Wachsthum der Pflanzen. 1859. I. 384.
Hanstein, Johannes von. Über die Absonderung von Schleim und Harz.· 1868. I. 134.[2]
—·Beiträge zur ... Morphologie der Pflanzen. 1882. I. 100,[1] 218.
— Botanische Abhandlungen. See BOTANISCHE ... I. 11.
— De la connexion ... entre la disposition des feuilles et la structure de la sone ligneuse. 1857. I. 109, 127.[2]
— Über einige Beziehungen zwischen Blattstellung und Vertheilung der primären Gefässbündel. 1860. I. 102.
— Die Entwicklung des Keimes der Monokotylen und Dikotylen. 1870. I. 122.
— Forstzeichen in einem Rothbuchenstamm. 1870. I. 210,[2] IV. 496.
— Gesneraceae. 1864. II. 792.[2]
—, Die Gesneraceen des Königlichen Herbariums. 1800. II. 792.[2]
— Eine geweihartige Fasciation eines Eschenzweiges. 1870. II. 707.[2]
— Über gürtelförmige Gefässstrang-Verbindungen. 1858. I. 133.
— Die Milchsaftgefässe. 1864. I. 135.
— Ueber die Organe der Harz- und Schleim-Absonderung in den Laubknospen. 1868. I. 108.[1]
— Organica ab inorganicis differunt. 1863. I. 99.
— Die Parthenogenesis der Caelebogyne. 1877. II. 436.[2]
— Plantarum vascularium folia, caulis. 1848. I. 99.
— Uebersicht des natürlichen Pflanzensystems. 1867. I. 261.
— Untersuchungen über den Bau ... der Baumrinde. 1853. I. 130.
— Versuche über die Leitung des Saftes durch die Rinde. 1860. I. 164.
— Über den Zusammenhang der Blattstellung mit dem Bau des dicotylen Holzringes. 1857. I. 102, 127.[2]
Hantoniensis, (pseud.). Yew trees. 1848. III. 288.[2]
Hanusz, István. ·Alföldünk "magyar fája." 1881. III. 487.[1]

— A Bükkfa. 1899. III. 360.[1]
— Az Eperfa. 1892. III. 378.
— A Füsfa. 1897. III. 349.
— A Leander. 1897. III. 689.[2]
— A magyar Olajfa. 1895. III. 628.[2]
— A növényvilág óriása. 1898. II. 624.[1]
— A Rózsa földrajzi elterjeszkedése. 1894. II. 283.[1]
— A Szelid Gesztenye. 1900. III. 358.[2]
— A Tölgyek földrajzi elterjedése. 1883. II. 128.[1]
Harway, Jonas. An essay on Tea. See HARWAY. (By error.) 1756. III. 605.
Hanzel, Albert. Ueber die Vermehrung unserer Nadelhölzer. 1893. III. 294.[2]
Hapf, Konrad. Bemerkungen über Raupenfrass ... Muskau. 1829. IV. 206.
Hapgood, Bell F. Aromatic leaves in Quercus rubra. 1884. II. 139.[2]
Happe, Andreas Friedrich. Abbildungen ökonomischer Pflanzen. 1792. III. 51.
— Botanica pharmaceutica. 1788. III. 55.
— Flora depicta. 1783. I. 263.
Haračić, Ambros. Sulla vegetazione dell' isola di Lussin. 1890. I. 448.[2]
Harcourt, Helen. Florida fruits and how to raise them. 1886. III. 133.
Harcus, William. South Australia. See SCHOMBURGK, Sir Richard. 1875. I. 502.
Hardcassle, Lucy. An introduction to the elements of the Linnean system. 1830. I. 255.
Hardegger, D. K. von. Der californische Ahorn. 1895. IV. 526.[2]
Hardenberg, C. C. Harsscoorten van Westelyk Borneo. 1858. III. 227.
Hardiness of Rhododendrons. 1895. III. 655.
Harding, A. Conifers at Orton Longueville. 1892. III. 293.
Harding, James Duffield. The park and the forest. 1841. V. xxv.[2]
Harding, William T. Ericaceous beauty. 1885. III. 650.[2]
— Good words for the Prinos and Holly. 1885. III. 529.[2]
— Ligneous marvels. 1877. II. 255.[1]
— Rhus Toxicodendron· versus Ampelopsis japonica. 1883. III. 545.[1]
— Under the Willows at Lichfield. 1882. II. 104.[2]
— Under the Willows at St. Helena. 1883. III. 351.[2]
Harding, E. M., (pseud.). See GOING, Maud.
Hardouin, L. Une variété ... du Chèvrefeuille commun. 1842. II. 839.[1]
— Renou, F. & Leclerc, E. Catalogue des plantes ... du Calvados. 1849. I. 410.
Hardt Aberson, van der. Wat is kanker der boomen? 1875. I. 206.[2]
Hardwich, T. F. Neue fette Säure ... von Bassia latifolia. 1849. III. 667.[2]
— Sur quelques nouveaux acides ... de Bassia latifolia. 1849. III. 667.[2]
— On some new acids ... of the Bassia latifolia. 1849. III. 667.[2]
Hardwicke, Thomas. Narrative of a journey to Sirinagur. 1799. I. 471.
Hardwood. IV. 4.
Hardy. Catalogue des Rosiers cultivés au Luxembourg. 1844. III. 448.
Hardy. Notes on a case of poisoning through ... "Brugmansia." 1890. III. 700.[1]
Hardy, (jr.). Sur la culture du Câprier. 1855. III. 408.[2]
Hardy, Auguste. Catalogue des végétaux cultivés à la pépinière centrale du gouvernement à Alger. 1844. I. 68.[2]
— De la culture du Dattier en Algérie. 1858. III. 328.[2]
— Culture et production de la China-grass. 1872. III. 381.[1]
— L'Eupatoire tinctoriale. 1854. III. 755.[1]
— Fructification du Bambusa spinosa. 1877. III. 316.[1]
— Sur l'introduction ... des Bambous de Chine. 1857. III. 314.[1]
— Klimatologische Bemerkungen über Algerien in Hinsicht auf Cultur. 1847. III. 546.
— Mémoire sur la production comparative de 184 variétés de Vignes. 1871. III. 546.
— Note sur l'Eupatorium levigatum. 1854. III. 755.[1]
— Note sur la culture du Quinquina en Algérie. 1868. III. 717.[2]
— Note sur la situation des dernières plantations. 1863. III. 130.[1]
— Note sur le Thuia de l'Algérie. 1857. IV. 447.[2]

Hardy, Auguste (*continued*).
— Note sur les cultures . . . à El-Aghouat. 1853. III. 130.[1]
— Notes climatologiques sur l'Algérie. 1847. III. 130.[1]
— Rapport sur les opérations de la filature de soie. 1857. III. 379.[2]
— Situation des essais d'acclimatation. 1867. III. 130.[1]
— *See also* MARCHAL, Élie & HARDY, Auguste.
Hardy, Ernest. Sur la composition du Jaborandi. 1875. III. 505.[1]
— Sur la composition du Jaborandi. 1877. III. 505.[1]
— Sur l'essence de Pilocarpus. 1877. III. 505.[1]
— Sur le Jaborandi. 1876. III. 505.[1]
— Sur le Pilocarpus pinnatus. 1876. III. 505.[1]
— Rapport sur l'Inée. 1877. III. 690.[1]
— *See also* GALLOIS, N. & HARDY, Ernest.
— & **Calmels**, G. La Pilocarpine. 1886. III. 505.[1]
— & **Gallois**, F. N. Examen de diverses substances . . . de l'Exposition . . . du Salvador. 1879. III. 265.[2]
—— Sur le principe actif du Strophantus hispidus. 1877. III. 690.[2]
— & **Gallois**, M. Sur l'anagyrine. 1889. III. 467.[1]
—— Note sur l'anagyrine. 1885. III. 467.[1]
Hardy, James. On the effects produced by some insects &c. upon plants. 1850. I. 215.[1]
Hardy, Julian Alexander. Handboek voor boomkweekers. 1853. III. 143.
— Traité de la taille des arbres fruitiers. 1853. III. 143.
Hardy and ornamental Vines. 1887. III. 584.[1]
Hardy Bamboos. 1895. III. 314.[2]
Hardy climbers. 1871. III. 544.[1]
Hardy Eucalypti in India. 1888. III. 634.[1]
Hardy Heaths. 1882. III. 647.[1]
Hardy Japanese and Chinese vines. 1897. III. 545.[2]
A **hardy** Prickly Pear. 1881. III. 625.[1]
Hardy Rhododendrons. 1888. III. 656.
Hardy Rhododendrons. 1894. III. 655.
Hardy shrubs. 1888. III. 78.[2]
Hardy shrubs with berries. 1888. III. 208.[1]
Hardy species of Eucalyptus. 1889. III. 634.[1]
Hardy trees for a trying climate. 1888. III. 42.[1]
Hardy winter-flowering shrubs. 1878. II. 839.[2] *III.* 750.[1]
Hare, Robert. Of sassarubrin. 1837. III. 408.[1]
Die **Harfenfichte** bei Bad Oppelsdorf. 1896. IV. 460.[2]
Hargreaves, A. F. Sur le charbon de bois. 1874. IV. 394.
Haring, Johann. Abnorme Kätschenbildungen bei Salix. 1894. II. 104.[1]
— Floristische Funde aus der Umgebung von Stockerau. 1887. I. 443.
Harington, John E. M. Thé de l'Inde britannique. 1888. III. 604.[1]
Hariot, Louis & Paul. Florule du canton de Méry-sur-Seine. 1874. I. 414.
Hariot, Paul. Sur une algue qui vit dans les racines des Cycadées. 1892. II. 3.[2]
— Les Alisiers. 1899. III. 2.[2]
— Almeidea macropetala. 1896. III. 495.[1]
— Ampelopsis Veitchii hort. 1895. III. 545.[1]
— Les Araucaria. 1895. III. 298.[1]
— Les Aristoloches. 1895. III. 386.[1]
— L'art de greffer. 1898. III. 163.[2]
— Atlas colorié des plantes médicinales. 1900. III. 86.
— Bowenia spectabilis. 1900. III. 284.[2]
— Les Bruyères indigènes. 1898. III. 650.[2]
— Camptosema isopetalum. 1895. III. 469.[2]
— Causerie sur la flore de l'Aube. 1877. I. 415.
— Chorizema varium. 1896. III. 472.[2]
— Colquhounia coccinea. 1895. III. 697.[2]
— Les Cyprès (Cupressus). 1896. III. 302.[1]
— Deux arbustes japonais. 1898. III. 462.[1] *753.*[2]
— Deux plantes intéressantes. 1898. III. 697.[2]
— Flore de Pont-sur-Seine. 1879. I. 415.
— Le genre Pittosporum. 1899. III. 416.[1]
— L g a m insulaire Decsn. et L. Walkeri. 1898. III. 673.[1] u tru
— Liste des plantes vasculaires, observées dans le détroit de Magellan. 1884. I. 347.
— Sur une monstruosité . . . de Poirier. 1892. III. 446.[2]
— Note sur l'Épine de Korolkow. 1892. III. 423.[1]
— Notes pour servir à l'histoire des classifications . . . du genre Ross. 1882. II. 282.[2]
— Le Petrea volubilis L. 1895. III. 697.[1]
— Promenades botaniques dans le Sud-Ouest. 1898. I. 418.
— Promenades botaniques dans le Sud-Ouest. 1899. I. 418.
— Quelques beaux arbres. 1890. I. 297.[2]
— Quelques Cytises. 1900. III. 474.[1]
— Quelques Rosacées intéressantes. 1896. III. 419.[1]
— La Rose capucine. 1893. III. 455.[2]
— Les Saules nains. 1898. III. 349.
— Sequoia, Wellingtonia et Washingtonia. 1894. II. 49.[2]
— Spiraea Millefolium Torrey. 1898. III. 459.[1]
— Des transformations . . . des végétaux. 1889. I. 243.[1]
— Le Welwitschia mirabilis. 1899. II. 55.[2]
— *See also* HARIOT, Louis & Paul.
Hariot, Thomas. Admiranda narratio fida tamen, de commodis . . . Virginiae. 1590. III. 263.[1]
— A brief and true report of the new found land of Virginia. 1590. III. 263.[1]
Harkness, John. Practical Rose growing. 1889. III. 452.
Harl, J. P. Allgemeines alphabetisches Repertorium des Neuesten . . . der Land- und Forstwissenschaft. 1820. IV. 1.
Harlan, Josiah. On the fruits of Cabul and vicinity. 1862. III. 279.[2]
Hårleman, Carl. Tankar om trävärkes bevarande. 1747. IV. 416.[2]
Hårleman, P. Sätt at upodla Måssar. 1758. IV. 156.[2]
Harlequin, N. Nouveau jardin des vertus et propriétés des herbes connues. 1624. I. 284.
Harley, G. Recherches concernant l'action de la strychnine. 1856. III. 682.[2]
Harley, John. On the parasitism of the Mistletoe. 1863. II. 178.[2]
Harlin, Aestanus Eman. De plantis venenatis. *See* THUNBERG, C. P. 1822. III. 59.[2]
Harlin, C. B. F. Die Naturkunde des Obstbaues. 1841. III. 137.
Harlow, S. H. Roots of the Hemlock. 1900. II. 53.[1]
Harmand, F. Juliani. Description des différentes formes du genre Rubus. 1886. II. 303.[2]
Harmant, Antonio d'. Sui vantagi dei boschi. 1883. IV. 44.
Harmens, Gustav. De transpiratione plantarum. 1756. I. 166.
Harms, Hermann. Amaryllidaceae, Leguminosae . . . in Harar et in Somalia . . . lectae. 1897. I. 489.
— Araliaceae. (*In* ENGLER & PRANTL.) 1897. II. 646.[2]
— Araliaceae. (*In* LOESENER.) 1897. II. 649,[1] *651.*[1]
— Araliaceae africanae. 1899. II. 646.[2]
— Über die Arten der Gattung Haematoxylon. 1900. II. 363.[1]
— Ueber die Blüthenverhältnisse der Gattung Garrya. 1897. II. 110.[2]
— Cornaceae. 1898. II. 654.[1]
— Cornaceae-Garryoideae. 1898. II. 110.[2]
— Cornaceae subfam. Alangioideae. 1898. II. 614.[2]
— Cornaceae subfam. Nyssoideae. 1898. II. 614.[2]
— Die Gattungen der Cornaceen. 1897. II. 654.[1]
— Gomortegaceae. 1897. II. 221.[2]
— Zur Kenntnis . . . der Gattung Acanthopanax. 1895. II. 647.[1]
— Zur Kenntnis der Gattungen Aralia und Panax. 1897. II. 646.[2]
— Ueber kultivierte Aralien. 1897. III. 641.[1]
— Leguminosae africanae. 1897. II. 319.[2]
— Malesherbiaceae. 1894. II. 575.[1]
— Meliaceae. 1896. II. 419.[1]
— Meliaceae africanae. 1897. II. 419.[1]
— Zur Morphologie der Ranken . . . bei den Passifloraceen. 1898. II. 576.[1]
— Die Nomenclaturbewegung der letzten Jahre. 1897. V. XII.[1]
— Passifloraceae. 1894. II. 575.[2]
— Passifloraceae africanae. 1899. II. 575.[2]
— Plantae Lehmannianae in Columbia. 1894. II. 575.[1]
— Ueber die Stellung der Gattung Tetracentron. 1897. II. 194.[2]
— Ueber succulente Passifloraceen. 1895. II. 575.[1]
— Über die Verwertung des anatomischen Baues für die Umgrenzung . . . der Passifloraceae. 1893. II. 576.[1]
— Verzeichnis derjenigen Angiospermen-Gattungen . . . eine sichere Stellung . . . nicht zugewiesen. 1897. I. 271.[1]
— Über das Vorkommen durchschnittiger Punkte in den Blättern gewisser Araliaceen. 1895. II. 649.[1]
— Zwei neue Meliaceengattungen. 1897. II. 419.[1]
— *See also* DALLA TORRE, K. W. von & HARMS, Hermann; ENGLER, Adolf & HARMS, Hermann.
— & **Reiche**, C. Plantaginaceae. 1895. III. 807.[1]
Harnack, Friedrich Moritz Erich & **Meyer**, H. Sur les alcaloïdes des feuilles de Jaborandi. 1880. III. 505.[1]

— — Untersuchungen über die Alkaloïde der Jaborandiblätter. 1880. III. 505.[1]
— & Witkowsky, Ludwig. La fève de Calabar. 1877. III. 484.[1]
Harney, Will Wallace. Orange culture. 1887. III. 500.[1]
Harnoth, Franz. Der oberschlesische Muschelkalk. 1895. IV. 70.
Haro. Catalogue des plantes ... de Rome. 1877. I. 428.
Harold, B. von. See GEMMINGER & HAROLD, B. von.
Harper, L. Exposé sur la région du ... Pinus palustris. 1870. II. 44.[1]
Harper, Roland McMillan. Notes on the flora of middle Georgia. 1900. I. 320.
Harper's new monthly magazine. III. 4..
Harpestreng, Henrik. Danske Lägebog. 1244. I. 274.
Harraca. Les Nandinas. 1891. III. 396.[1]
— Note sur le Nandina domestica. 1888. III. 396.[1]
Harraca, J. M. De l'amélioration systématique dans les végé- taux. 1900. I. 248.[1]
— Contribution à l'étude de l'hérédité. 1898. I. 248.[2]
— Observations sur la panachure ... du Laurier-cerise. 1886. II. 275.[1]
Harres. In welcher Jahreszeit soll das Bauholz gefällt werden? 1859. IV. 384.[2]
Harrington, Bernard James. On the sap of the Ash-leaved Maple. 1888. II. 479.[1]
Harrington, F. O. How to save trees that have been barked by rabbits. 1899. III. 186.[2]
— The Persimmon in Iowa. 1900. III. 670.[1]
Harrington, H. H. Analysis of Prickly Pear Cactus. 1889. III. 624.[1]
Harrington,. Mark Walrod. Fauna and flora of Puerto Rico. 1899. I. 337.
— Review of forest meteorological observations. 1893. IV. 54. III. 592.[1]
Harris, A. L. On the mode of cultivating ... cacao. 1845. III. 592.[1]
Harris, E. C. New Zealand flowers. 1900. I. 508.[2]
Harris, J. C. Report on the manufacture of perfumes at Nice. 1890. III. 226.[2]
Harris, J. F. The growing and caring for trees. 1897. III. 134.[1]
Harris, Thaddeus Mason. The natural history of the Bible. 1820. I. 513.
Harris, Thaddeus William. A report on the insects of Massa- chusetts. 1841. III. 186.[1]
— A treatise on some of the insects injurious to vegetation. 1841. III. 186.[2]
— A treatise on some of the insects of New England. 1841. III. 186.[2]
Harris, William. A collecting tour in Jamaica. 1896. I. 337.
— Forestry. 1894. IV. 45.
— Mangosteen. 1888. III. 609.[2]
— The Peach. 1892. III. 441.[1]
— Plant notes. 1889. I. 39.
— Ropes from fibres. 1889. III. 235.[1]
— Silky Oak. 1888. III. 383.[1]
— Timber trees. 1893. IV. 398.[1]
Harris, William Cornwallis. Account of the trees producing myrrh. 1845. III. 511.[1]
— The highlands of Aethiopia. 1844. III. 280.[2]
— On de Planter, som lavere Gummi Myrrhe. 1845. III. 511.[1]
Harrison. Un arbre curieux. 1895. IV. 559.[2]
Harrison, Charles. A treatise on the culture ... of fruit trees. 1823. III. 142.
Harrison, Charles Simmons. The Buffalo berry. 1900. III. 629.[1]
— The Russian Olive. 1900. III. 628.[2]
Harrison, John P. Elements of the materia medica. 1845. III. 243.
Harrison, Jonathan Baxter. Forest interests in Pennsylvania. 1889. IV. 339.
— Forestry. 1886. IV. 178.[1]
— Forestry in New England. 1889. IV. 339.
— Forests and civilisation. 1889. IV. 178.[1]
— The forests and woodlands of New Jersey. 1889. IV. 339.
— Laws alone cannot save our forests. 1888. IV. 178.[1]
— Our forest interests in relation to the American mind. 1893. IV. 272.
— The rocks and soils of Granada. 1896. III. 593.[1]
— The state and the forest. 1892. IV. 184,[2] 272.
— Subjects for attention connected with forestry ... in Massachusetts. 1890. III. 117.[2]
— White Mountain forests. 1893. IV. 889.

Harrison, Joseph. On the cultivation of Camellias. 1830. III. 599.[1]
Harrison, W. H. Maori and other aboriginal manufactures. 1866. IV. 401.[2]
— The Poison Ivy. 1895. III. 528.[1]
Harrison, William Landon. The balsam of Liquidambar styraciflua. 1874. III. 418.[1]
Harrow, H. Propagation of Combretum. 1889. III. 632.[2]
Harrow, R. L. Notes from the Royal botanic garden, Edin- burgh. 1894. I. 55.
— Melia Azedarach var. floribunda. 1889. III. 512.[2]
— Myriocarpa longipes. 1897. III. 382.[2]
— Propagation of Combretum purpureum. 1889. III. 694.[2]
Harrower, William. The different methods of seasoning tim- ber. 1884. IV. 416.[1]
— The Larch bug. 1881. IV. 451.
— On the timber supply of the United States. 1884. IV. 338.[1]
— Tree-planting as an investment in Ireland. 1884. IV. 261.[2]
Harshberger, John William. A botanical excursion to Mex- ico. 1896. I. 531.
— Botanical observations on the Mexican flora. 1899. I. 333.
— The botanists of Philadelphia and their work. 1899. I. 80.[1]
— The Japanese Paulownia. 1900. II. 781.[2]
— The names of the Big tree of California. 1899. II. 50.[1]
— Plants for the sea-shore. 1892. III. 41.[2]
— Some peculiar morphological structures in Paulownia. 1899. II. 781.[2]
— Statistical information concerning the production of fruits and seeds in certain plants. 1898. I. 120, 239.[1] — 1899. I. 201.[1]
— Thermotropic movement of the leaves of Rhododendron. 1900. II. 682.[1]
— The uses of plants among the ancient Peruvians. 1898. III. 493.[2]
— Water storage and conduction in Senecio praecox. 1899. II. 866.[1]
Harsleben, Karl Friedrich. De cortice Winterano. 1760. III. 613.[2]
Harst, C. van der & Bogaardt, A. Berigt wegens aanleg ... van woeste gronden. 1788. IV. 159.
Harst, L. J. van der. Overzicht der voornaamste inlandsche plantensoorten. 1871. I. 391.[2]
— Studien over Taxus baccata. 1884. III. 288.[2]
Barsten, F. A. Recherches sur les matières colorantes des feuilles. 1873. I. 141.
Hart, Edw. Piscidine. 1884. II. 377.[1]
Hart, G. S. Note on the cultivation of the Robinia Pseudo- Acacia in the Simla Hills. 1896. IV. 523.[2]
— Note on the Patiala Western Siwaliks. 1896. IV. 378.
Hart, Henry Chichester. On the botany of the river Suir. 1885. I. 403.
— The flora of Howth. 1887. I. 403.
— Flora of the county Donegal. 1898. I. 535.
— A list of plants found in the Islands of Aran. 1875. I. 402.
— Notes on the plants of some of the mountain ranges of Ire- land. 1884. I. 403.
— On the range of flowering plants ... of Ireland. 1889. I. 404.[1]
— Report on the botany of Sinai. 1885. I. 480.
— Report on the flora of the mountains of Mayo. 1883. I. 403.
— Report on the flora of the Wexford. 1885. I. 403.
— Sikkim and Nepaul Rhododendrons. 1894. III. 656.
— Some account of the fauna and flora of Sinai. 1891. I. 481.[1]
Hart, J. The Bougainvillea. 1880. III. 388.[1]
Hart, James. On the cause of dry-rot in Larch. 1835. IV. 211.[1]
— Directions for preventing Gooseberry and Currant bushes from being infested with vermin. 1835. III. 414.[1]
Hart, John Hinchley. A botanist's ramble in Central Amer- ica. 1886. I. 330.
— Cacao. 1892. III. 593.[1]
— Classified list of plants in the Royal botanic gardens, Trinidad. 1892. III. 27.[2]
— A flowering Bamboo. 1899. III. 316.[2]
— Jamaica. 1888. III. 267.[1]
— A new hybrid Egg-plant. 1895. III. 702.[1]
— Observations on packing and transport of plants. 1900. III. 155.
— Report on forest conservation for the island of Trinidad. 1891. IV. 342.[1]
— Some fungi of the Cacao tree. 1900. III. 593.[2]

INDEX OF AUTHORS AND TITLES

Hart, L. The Black Forest. 1880. IV. 350.[1]
Hart, W. E. Aucuba japonica. 1872. II. 654.[1]
Hart, *Mrs.* W. E. Note on some branching Palms. 1888. II. 63,[1] 73.[2]
Harte, Walter. Essays on husbandry. 1764. III. 109.
Harte Cactus-Arten. 1877. III. 619.
Harteben. L'émondage naturel des Chênes en Alsace. 1897. IV. 559.[2]
Hartenfels, Arnold Friedrich von, (*pseud.*). Neuer Garten-Saal. 1745. III. 74.
Hartert. Die Waldköhlerei in Oberschlesien. 1839. IV. 394.
Harteveld, A. H. De vruchtencultuur in Californie. 1894. III. 134.[1]
Hartig, Ernst. Influenza della stagione dello atterramento sulla durata del legno. 1879. IV. 384.[2]
— Untersuchungen über den Einfluss der Fällung zeit. 1879. IV. 384.[2]
Hartig, Ernst Friedrich. Anweisung zur Aufstellung . . . der jährlichen Forstwirthschaftsplane. 1826. IV. 239.
— Die Forstbetriebs-Einrichtung. 1825. IV. 239.
— Praktische Anleitung zum Baumroden. 1827. IV. 385,[2]
— Praktische Anleitung zum Vermessen. 1828. IV. 263.
Hartig, Friedrich Karl. Die angewandte Forstgeometrie. 1811. IV. 263.
— Ueber die beste Hau-Zeit des Wurzelholzes. 1807. IV. 384.[2]
— Forst- und Jagd-Staatsrecht. 1809. IV. 316.
— Die Forstgeonomie und Lithologie. 1810. IV. 68.
— Gesetze über die Lehre eines Jägerjungen. 1807. IV. 31.
— Die Hoch- und Niederwaldbehandlung. 1808. IV. 100.[1]
— Untersuchung, ob die Hoch- und Niederwaldbehandlung nützlich oder schädlich sey? 1808. IV. 128.
— Vermischte Forstschriften. 1812. IV. 287.
Hartig, Friedrich Karl Theodor. Beschreibung einiger Waldkultur-Instrumente. 1830. IV. 142, 176.[2]
Hartig, Georg Ludwig. Ueber die Ab- oder Einteilung der Forsten. 1830. IV. 250.[2]
— Anleitung zur Berechnung des Geld-Werthes eines taxirten Forstes. 1812. IV. 253.
— Anleitung zur Forst- und Waidmanns-Sprache. 1809. IV. 23.[1]
— Anleitung zur Prüfung der Forstkandidaten. 1818. IV. 31.
— Anleitung zur Vertilgung . . . der Kiefern-Raupen. 1827. IV. 475.
— Anleitung zur wohlfeilen Kultur der Waldblössen. 1826. IV. 140.
— Anweisung zur Holzzucht für Förster. 1791. IV. 105.
— Anweisung zur Taxation der Forste. 1795. IV. 239.
— Anweisung zur Taxation und Beschreibung der Forste. 1795. IV. 239.
— Beitrag zur Lehre von Ablösung der Holz-, Streu- und Weidservituten. 1829. IV. 333.
— Bemerkungen . . . zu des Herrn Professor Dr. Reum's Erfahrungen über Holzpflanzungen. 1829. III. 120.[2]
— Ueber Benutzung des Stockholzes. 1830. IV. 385.[2]
— Ueber die beste Art Nadelholzwaldungen zu verjüngen. 1830. IV. 441.
— Beweiss, dass durch die Ansucht der weissblühenden Acacie . . . Brennholzmangel nicht abgeholfen werden kann. 1798. IV. 280,[1] 524.[1]
— Ueber die Dauer der Hölzer. 1830. IV. 413.[1]
— Einige Bemerkungen zu dem . . . Bericht des Herrn Nieter. 1831. III. 136.
— Entwurf einer allgemeinen Forst- und Jagd-Ordnung. 1833. IV. 320.
— Erfahrungen über die Dauer der Hölzer. 1836. IV. 413.[2]
— Erfahrungstafeln über den Ertrag der Rothbuchen-... Fichten-Hochwaldbestände. 1847. IV. 235.[2]
— Expériences physiques sur les rapports de combustibilité des bois. 1794. IV. 412.[2]
— Forstwirthschaftliche Tabellen. 1807. IV. 311.[2]
— Die Forstwissenschaft. 1831. IV. 97.
— Grundsätze der Forst-Direction. 1803. IV. 287.
— Grundzüge zu einer zweckmässigen Forstorganisation. 1830. IV. 287.
— Gutachten über die Fragen: Welche Holzarten belohnen den Anbau am reichlichsten? 1833. IV. 254.
— Instruction zur la culture du bois. 1791. IV. 105.
— Instruction wornach die Holzkultur . . . betrieben werden soll. 1814. IV. 106.
— Ist ein kurzer oder längerer Umtrieb in den Waldungen vorteilhafter? 1830. IV. 251.[2]

— Kort undervisning om skogens behandling. 1837. IV. 106.
— Kubik-Tabellen für geschnittene, beschlagene und runde Hölzer. 1815. IV. 221.
— Kurze Anleitung zum Unterricht . . . im Forst- und Jagd-wesen. 1827. IV. 97.
— Kurze Belehrung über . . . Kultur des Waldes. 1837. IV. 106.
— Lehrbuch für Förster. 1808. IV. 96.
— Neue Instructionen für die königlich-preussischen Forst-Geometer und Forst-Taxatoren. 1819. IV. 253.
— Noch einige Bemerkungen über . . . Wallnussbäume. 1827. III. 354.[2]
— Noch etwas über die starke Einsaat des Fichten-Saamens. 1829. IV. 452.[2]
— Noch etwas über die Vertilgung der grossen Kienraupe. 1830. IV. 206.
— Opinion sur les questions suivantes: Quelle est l'essence de bois dont la culture est la plus avantageuse? 1833. IV. 254.
— Physikalische Versuche über das Verhältniss der Brenn-barkeit der . . . Wald-Baum-Hölzer. 1794. IV. 412.[1]
— Ueber die platzweisen Fichtensaaten. 1828. IV. 452.[2]
— Om Træers Varighed. 1830. IV. 413.[1]
— Udtog af physikalske Forsøg om Forholdet af de fleste Skovtræers Brændbarhed. 1794. IV. 412.[2]
— Versuche über die Dauer der Hölzer. 1822. IV. 413.[1]
— Versuche und Erfahrungen über die Dauer der Hölzer. 1829. IV. 413.[1]
— Vier Forsttabellen zum Behuf der Förster im Nassauischen. 1808. IV. 117.
— Wahrscheinliche Entstehung der Durchforstungen. 1830. IV. 172.[2]
— & Theodor. Forstliches und forstnaturwissenschaftliches Conversations-Lexikon. 1834. IV. 22.[1]
— & Neufville, J. A. von. Systematische Beschreibung vom Thiergarten-Forste. 1805. IV. 352.
— & others. Abhandlungen über interessante Gegenstände beim Forst- und Jagdwesen. 1830. IV. 101.
Hartig, Robert. Abies pectinata. 1865. IV. 446.[1]
— Abnorm gebildete Eicheln. 1870. II. 131.[2]
— Das Absterben der Fichte nach Nonnenfrass. 1892. IV. 457.
— Der ächte Hausschwamm. 1885. IV. 415.[1]
— Der Ahornkeimlingspilz. 1880. III. 534.[1]
— Die anatomischen Unterscheidungsmerkmale der wichtigeren . . . Hölzer. 1879. I. 125, *IV. 68.[2]*
— Les árboles y el rayo. 1899. IV. 548.[2]
— Les arbres et la foudre. 1899. IV. 195,[1] 548.[2]
— Eine Art der Frostbeschädigung. 1884. IV. 191.[2]
— Das Auftreten der Rhizomorpha. 1870. IV. 442.
— Das Aussetzen der Jahresringe. 1869. I. 127,[2] *IV. 62.[2]*
— Bau und Gewicht des Fichtenholzes. 1898. II. 36.[1]
— Ueber die Bedeutung der Reservestoffe. 1888. I. 159, 79.[1]
— Die Begründung der Pflanzenphys. Abtheilung der forstl. Versuchsstation zu Neustadt-Eberswalde. 1872. IV. 38.[1]
— Beiträge zur Kenntniss der Eichenwurzeltödters. 1900. IV. 511.
— Ein Beitrag zur Eichenästungsfrage. 1879. IV. 507.
— Bemerkungen zu A. Wieler's Abhandlung. 1889. I. 166.
— Ueber die Beschädigung der Coniferen durch Steinkohlen-rauch. 1890. III. 185.
— Beschädigung der Nadelholzsaatbeete. 1883. IV. 442.
— Ueber die Beschädigung . . . durch Hütten-. . . rauch. 1897. IV. 193.[1]
— Zur Beurtheilung der Lebensfähigkeit der durch Raupenfrass entnadelten Kiefern. 1872. IV. 476.
— Ueber die bisherigen Ergebnisse der Anbauversuche mit ausländischen Holzarten. 1892. IV. 126.[1]
— Ueber Blitzbeschädigungen der Waldbäume. 1876. IV. 194.
— Bostrichus bidens in Fichten. 1870. IV. 455.
— Die Buchen-Baumlaus. 1880. IV. 497.
— Die Buchencotyledonen-Krankheit. 1876. IV. 497.
— Die Buchenkeimlingskrankheit. 1879. IV. 497.
— Der Buchenkeimlingspilz. 1880. IV. 497.
— Cæoma pinitorquum A. Br. 1872. IV. 476.
— Cecidomyia? Piceæ n. sp. 1893. IV. 457.
— Cetonia aurata in den . . . Maikäfer-Brutstätten. 1870. IV. 202.
— Coleophora (Tinea) Lutipenella. 1870. IV. 509.
— La coloration rouge et la pourriture sèche. 1888. IV. 415.[1]

— Ueber das Dickenwachsthum der Waldbäume. 1871. IV. 64.²
— Ueber Dickenwachsthum und Jahrringbildung. 1892. I. 128.¹
— Doppelringe als Folge von Spätfrost. 1895. IV. 191.²
— Ueber den Drehwuchs der Kiefer. 1895. II. 47.¹
— Ueber den Eichenkrebs. 1892. IV. 511.
— Der Eichenwurzeltödter. 1880. IV. 510.
— Ueber den Einfluss der Erziehung auf die Beschaffenheit des Holzes der Waldbäume. 1897. IV. 111.¹
— Ueber den Einfluss der Samenproduktion. 1888. I. 200, IV. 65.²
— Ueber den Einfluss des Alters . . . auf die Qualität . . . des Holzes der Rothbuche. 1887. IV. 499.
— Der Einfluss des Baumalters . . : auf die Beschaffenheit des Holzes. 1884. IV. 408.
— Ueber den Einfluss des Hütten- und Steinkohlenrauches. 1897. IV. 193.¹
— Einfluss verschieden starker Ausästung und Entnadelung. 1872. II. 40.¹
— Ueber den Einfluss verschiedener Raupen-Vertilgungsmethoden auf . . . Kiefer. 1871. IV. 476.
— Ueber die Einwirkung des Hütten- . . . .-rauches. 1896. IV. 193.¹
— Ueber den Entwicklungsgang der Fichte. 1892. IV. 458.
— Ueber die Ergebnisse . . . [der] Untersuchungen des anatomischen Baues des Eichenholzes. 1894. II. 137.¹
— Die Erhitzung der Bäume. 1892. IV. 457.
— Das Erkranken und Absterben der Fichte. 1891. IV. 457.
— Das Erkranken und Absterben der Fichte nach der Entnadelung. 1892. IV. 457.
— Erkrankung älterer Weymouthskiefernbestände. 1883. IV. 470.¹
— Die Fällungszeit der Nadelholzbäume im Gebirge. 1889. IV. 385.¹
— Ueber Fäulniss des Holzes. 1877. I. 207.¹
— Das Fichten- und Tannenholz des bayerischen Waldes. 1888. IV. 409.
— Der Fichtenrindenkrebs. 1879. IV. 456.
— Der Fichtenrindenpilz. 1880. IV. 452.²
— Ueber die Folgen der Baumringelung. 1890. I. 166, III. 175.¹
— Frost und Frostkrebs. 1880. I. 212, IV. 66.²
— Die Gasdrucktheorie. 1883. I. 161.
— Das Gefrieren und Erfrieren der Pflanzen. 1882. I. 212.
— Das Holz der deutschen Nadelwaldbäume. 1885. IV. 408, 443.¹
— Ueber das Holz der Normannstanne. 1888. II. 23.¹
— Influence de la production des semences sur l'accroissement. 1888. IV. 65.²
— Innere Frostspalten. 1896. IV. 191.²
— Zur Kenntniss des Wurzelschwammes. 1889. IV. 212.
— Zur Kenntniss von Loranthus . . . und Viscum. 1876. II. 174.¹
— Eine Krankheit der Fichtentriebe. 1890. IV. 456.
— Eine Krankheit der Weisstanne. 1889. IV. 445.
— Eine Krankheitserscheinung der Fichtentriebe. 1891. IV. 457.
— Ueber krebsartige Krankheiten der Rothbuche. 1877. IV. 407.
— Eine krebsartige Rindenkrankheit der Eiche. 1893. IV. 511.
— Die krebsartigen Erkrankungen der Pflanzen. 1889. IV. 212.
— Die krebsartigen Krankheiten der Rothbuche. 1878. IV. 497.
— Der Krebspilz der Laubholzbäume. 1880. IV. 211.²
— Zur Lärchenkrankheit. 1870. IV. 450.
— Die Lärchenkrankheiten. 1880. IV. 451.
— Die Lärchennadelbräune. 1899. IV. 451.
— Lehrbuch der Anatomie und Physiologie der Pflanzen. 1891. I. 92, 148.²
— Lehrbuch der Baumkrankheiten. 1882. IV. 195.²
— Lehrbuch der Pflanzenkrankheiten. 1882. IV. 195.²
— Zur Lehre vom Dickenwachsthum der Waldbäume. 1870. I. 190.¹
— Zur Lehre von der Wasserbewegung. 1883. I. 167.
— Ueber den Lichtstandszuwachs der Kiefer. 1888. IV. 473.¹
— Les maladies des arbres forestiers. 1874. IV. 195.²
— Die Misserfolge beim Anbau der kaspischen Weide. 1872. III. 351.¹
— Mittheilung über Coleosporium Senecionis. 1883. IV. 461.²
— Mittheilungen über Baumkrankheiten. 1875. IV. 211.¹
— Mittheilungen über Pilzkrankheiten der Insecten. 1869. IV. 199.²
— Der Nadelschüttepilz der Lärche. 1895. IV. 451.
— Nepticula (Tinea) Sericopeza Illg. 1870. III. 535.²
— Eine neue Art der Frostbeschädigung. 1883. IV. 191.²
— Neue Beobachtungen über Blitzbeschädigung. 1899. IV. 195.¹
— Ein neuer Keimlingspilz. 1892. IV. 212.
— Ein neuer Parasit der Weisstanne. 1884. IV. 445.
— Ueber neuere Untersuchungen zur Physiologie der Eiche. 1893. II. 137.²
— Die Oberberghauser Weiden-Anlagen. 1889. IV. 487.³
— Ueber den Ort der Saftleitung im Holze. 1889. I. 166, IV. 63.² V. xi.²
— Les parasites des racines. 1888. I. 234.¹
— Die pflanzlichen Wurzelparasiten. 1888. I. 234.¹
— Die durch Pilze erzeugten Krankheiten. 1875. IV. 211.¹
— Der Pressler'sche Zuwachsbohrer. 1869. IV. 232.
— The production of seed in its relation to growth and to the reserve materials in trees. 1888. I. 200, IV. 65.²
— Die Qualität des Nadelholzes. 1885. IV. 408.
— Die Rentabilität der Fichtennutzholz- und Buchenbrennholzwirthschaft im Harze. 1868. IV. 261.¹
— Rhizina undulata Fr. 1892. IV. 212.
— Rhizomorpha (Dematophora) necatrix. 1883. III. 578.
— Ueber Rindenproduction der Kiefer. 1873. IV. 480.
— Die Rothfäule der Fichte. 1877. IV. 456.
— Das Rothholz der Fichte. 1896. II. 36,¹ IV. 558.²
— Septogloeum Hartigianum. 1892. III. 534.²
— Septoria parasitica m. 1893. IV. 457.
— Ueber den Sonnenbrand. 1880. IV. 192.¹
— Sonnenrisse und Frostrisse an der Eiche. 1894. IV. 511.
— Die Spaltung der Oelbäume. 1893. III. 678.¹
— Das specifische Frisch- und Trockengewicht . . . des Kiefernholzes. 1874. II. 48.¹
— Das Studium der Botanik an forstlichen Lehranstalten. 1890. IV. 29.
— Die Tannennadelmotte. 1896. IV. 445.
— Textbook of the diseases of trees. 1882. IV. 195.²
— Timbers and how to know them. 1879. I. 125.
— Tödtung der Bucheckern im Winterlager. 1897. IV. 497.
— Die Unterscheidungsmerkmale der wichtigeren in Deutschland wachsenden Hölzer. 1879. I. 125, IV. 62.²
— Untersuchungen aus dem Forstbotanischen Institut zu München. 1880. IV. 57.
— Untersuchungen des Baues . . . des Eichenholzes. 1895. II. 137.¹
— Untersuchungen des Eichenholzes. 1895. II. 137.¹
— Untersuchungen des Wachsthumsganges der Eiche. 1894. IV. 513.
— Untersuchungen über Blitzschläge. 1897. IV. 195.¹
— Untersuchungen über die Entstehung . . . des Eichenholzes. 1894. II. 137.¹
— Untersuchungen über Wachsthumsgang . . . der Eichenbestände. 1893. IV. 513.
— Ueber die Ursachen excentrischen Wuchses. 1899. I. 524.¹
— Die Veränderungen des Holzkörpers. 1884. I. 125.
— Zur Verbreitung des Lärchenkrebspilzes. 1888. IV. 451.
— Vergleichende Untersuchungen über den Wachsthumsgang . . . der Rothbuche und Eiche. 1865. IV. 232.
— Ueber das Verhältniss des lufttrockenen Zustandes der Hölzer zum absolut trockenen Zustande. 1883. IV. 412.¹
— Ueber das Verhalten der vom Spanner entnadelten Kiefern. 1896. IV. 479.
— Die Verschiedenheiten im Bau des Eichenholzes. 1895. II. 36.¹
— Die Verschiedenheiten in der Qualität . . . des Fichtenholzes. 1892. II. 36.¹
— Ueber die Vertheilung der organischen Substanz . . . in den Bäumen. 1880. I. 147.—1882. I. 167.
— Vertrocknen und Erfrieren der Kiefernzweige. 1892. IV. 478.
— Vervollständigung der Tabelle über den Einfluss des Holzalters. 1883. I. 155, IV. 62.²
— Vorläufige Mittheilungen über Parasiten der Waldbäume. 1873. IV. 211.¹
— Der Wachsthumsgang der Fichte im bayerischen Walde. 1893. IV. 458.
— Wachstumsgang und Holz der Robinie. 1893. IV. 524.²
— Wachsthumsuntersuchungen an Fichten. 1896. IV. 459.¹
— Waldbeschädigung durch ein Eisenwerk. 1897. IV. 457.

Hartig, Robert (*continued*).
— Die Waldbeschädigungen durch die Nonne. 1890. IV. 200.
— Was ist in den europäischen Staaten ... gethan worden . . um die Erforschung der . . . Pflanzenkrankheiten zu fördern. 1890. IV. 195.²
— Ueber die Wasserleitung im Splintholze. 1888. I. 166.
— Wichtige Krankheiten der Waldbäume. 1874. IV. 195.²
— Der Wurzelpilz des Weinstockes. 1883. III. 578.
— Der Wurzeltödter der Eiche. 1876. IV. 510.
— Die Zersetzungserscheinungen des Holzes. 1878. I. 207,¹ *IV. 66,¹ 442, 510.*
— Zersprengen der Eichenrinde. 1880. . I. 149.²
— Das Zersprengen der Hainbuchenrinde. 1883. I. 150.¹
— Zweijährige Rotbuchenausschläge mit Bucheckern. 1889. II. 126.³
— *See also* ГАРТИГЪ, P.
— & Weber, Rudolf. Das Holz der Rothbuche. 1888. II. 126.¹
Hartig, Theodor. Abhandlung über die Verwandlung der polycotyledonischen Pflanzenzelle. 1833. I. 206.²
— Die Aderflügler Deutschlands. 1837. IV. 91.³
— Ueber die Adventiv-Knospen der Lenticellen. 1853. I. 108.¹
— Anatomie und Physiologie der Holzpflanzen. 1878. I. 82,³ *148, IV. 62.*¹
— Die Aschenfliege. 1856. IV. 206.
— Ueber Aufsaugung gefärbter Flüssigkeiten. 1853. I. 164.
— Beiträge zur Entwicklungsgeschichte der Pflanzen. 1843. I. 98.
— Beiträge zur Kenntniss der deutschen Holzpflanzen. 1852. IV. 118.
— Beiträge zur physiologischen Forstbotanik. 1860. I. 164.
— Beiträge zur vergleichenden Anatomie der Holzpflanzen. 1859. I. 124.
— Bericht über gelungene Versuche der Reproduktion neuer Holz- und Rindenschichten. 1844. III. 180.¹
— Ueber die Bewegung des Saftes in den Holzpflanzen. 1858. I. 164. — 1871. I. 164.
— Ueber die Bildung der Knospendeckblätter von Salix und Magnolia. 1855. I. 108.¹
— Ueber Bildung und Befestigung der Dünen. 1830. IV. 145.
— Das Bluten der Bäume. 1872. I. 168.
— Das Bluten der Virgilea lutea. 1877. II. 346.³
— Büschel- und Einzelpflanzung der Fichte. 1855. IV. 453.
— Controversen der Forstwirthschaft. 1853. IV. 129, *242.*
— Ueber das Eindringen der Wurzeln in den Boden. 1866. I. 188.¹
— Ueber den Einfluss der Verdunstung auf Hebung des Pflanzensaftes. 1863. I. 164.
— Ueber das endosmotische Verhalten der Holzfaser. 1863. IV. 412.¹
— Ueber die Entstehung der Markstrahlen. . 1855. I. 124.
— Ueber die Entwickelung des Jahrringes. 1853. I. 127.³
— Entwickelungsgeschichte des Pflanzenkeims. 1858. I. 203.
— Über die Entwicklung des Embryo der Coniferen. 1842. I. 121.
— Über die Entwicklungsfolge und den Bau der Holzfaserwandung. 1870. I. 138.¹
— Expériences sur diverses essences de bois propres aux échalas. 1857. IV. 413.²
— A fák nedvforgásáról. 1871. I. 164.
— Die Familien der Blattwespen und Holzwespen. ·1837. IV. 91.³
— Ueber Fichten-Büschel-Pflanzungen. 1840. IV. 452.²
— Folgen der Ringelung an einer Linde. 1863. I. 164, III. 175.¹
— Folgen der Ringelung an Nadelholz-Aesten. 1863. I. 164, *III. 175.*¹
— Forstliche aphoristische Mittheilungen. 1847. IV. 150.
— Ueber den forstlichen Unterricht an polytechnischen Lehranstalten. 1862. IV. 32.
— Forstwissenschaftliches Examinatorium. 1866. IV. 107.¹
— Freiwilliges Bluten der Hainbuche. 1853. I. 168.
— Das Gerbmehl. 1865. I. 183.
— Ueber den Gerbstoff der Eiche. 1869. III. 362,¹ *IV. 515.*¹
— Hautfrüchtige (birkenartige) Kätzchenträger. 1849. II. 871.²
— Ueber den Herbstsaft der Holzpflanzen. 1858. I. 147.
— Das Insektenleben im Boden der . . . Pflanz-Kämpe. . 1860. IV. 207. ·

— Ueber den Lärchenkrebs. 1872. IV. 450.
— Ueber den Lauf der Wandersäfte.· 1859. I. 164.
— Das Leben der Pflanzenzelle. 1844. I. 136.²
— Ueber das Leuchten das weissfaulen Holzes. 1855. I. 206.²
— Luft-, Boden- und Pflanzen-Kunde. *See* HARTIG, G. L. 1808. IV. 96.
— Ueber die Luftsäcke des Nadelholz-Pollen. 1867. II. 20.²
— Om märgstrålarnes uppkomst. 1855. I. 124.
— Monographie der Betulaceen. 1849. V. XXVI.¹
— Neue Theorie der Befruchtung der Pflanzen. 1842. I. 200.
— Nouveau memoire sur l'aleurone. 1856. I. 175.
— Ueber der Oberhaut der Holzpflanzen. 1853. I. 129.¹
— Ueber die periodischen Schwankungen ·des Wassergehaltes der Bäume. 1871. I. 232.³
— Resultate . . . über Pflanzungen im Spätsommer. 1849. III. 168.²
— Ueber Saftbewegung in den Holzpflanzen. 1868. I. 164.
— Ueber die Schliesshaut des Nadelholz-Tüpfels. 1863. II. 16.³
— Separat-Abdruck aus der 7ten Auflage der Cubiktabellen. 1854. IV. 231.¹
— Ueber das sogenannte Absterben der Haarwurzeln. 1863. I. 188.¹
— Ein Stearopten aus Juniperus virginiana. 1853. II. 32.¹
— System und Anleitung zum Studium der Forstwirthschaftslehre. 1858. IV. 97.
— System und Beschreibung der europäischen Weiden. 1851. II. 100.¹
— Ueber die Thätigkeit des Siebfasergewebes. 1863. I. 164.
— Ueber die Vegetationsperioden der Waldbäume. 1838. I. 175.
— Verdunstung der Zweigspitzen. 1863. I. 166.
— Vergleichende Untersuchungen über den Ertrag der Rothbuche. 1847. IV. 498.
— Vergleichende Untersuchungen über die Organisation des Stammes. 1837. I. 124, *IV. 62.*¹
— Ueber das Verhältniss des Brennwerthes verschiedener Holz- und Torf-Arten. 1855. IV. 413.¹
— Ueber das Verhalten der Blätter zur atmosphärischen Feuchtigkeit. 1865. I. 232.³
— Versuche über Erhöhung der Dauer des Holzes. 1846. IV. 417.
— Vollständige Naturgeschichte der forstlichen Culturpflanzen Deutschlands. 1840. IV. 82.
— Vollständige Naturgeschichte der forstlichen Culturpflanzen Deutschlands. 1851. I. 293, V. XVI.¹
— Ueber die Wachsthumsverhältnisse des Hochwaldes. 1866. IV. 236.
— Weitere Mittheilungen, das Klebermehl . . . betreffend. 1856. I. 175.
— Ueber den Werth der Periodeneintheilung. 1869. IV. 251.³
— Ueber die Wirkung verdünnter Schwefelsäure auf die Ablagerungsschichten der Zellwand. 1855. I. 124.
— Ueber die Zeit des Zuwachses der Baumwurzeln. 1863. I. 188.
— Ueber den Zucker . . . der Nadelhölzer. 1863. II. 20.²
Harting, Pieter. Bijdrage tot de anatomie der Cacteën. 1842. II. 588.¹
— Boomanplanting op het eiland Ascension. 1875. IV. 169.¹
— Het eiland Urk. 1853. I. 391.¹
— Kurk en kurkvorming. 1855. I. 130.
— Mikrochemische onderzoekingen. 1844. I. 187.
— Mikrochemische onderzoekingen over den aard . . . van den plantaardigen celwand. 1846. I. 137.
— Mikrochemische Untersuchungen über die Beschaffenheit . . . des Zellgewebes. 1846. I. 137.
— Mikrometrische Untersuchungen. 1844. I. 187.
— Observations relative à une communication de M. Boussingault. 1872. III. 585.¹
— Over de ontwikkeling der elementaire weefsels. 1844. I. 105.
— De plantengroei in de keerkringsgewesten. 1852. I. 465.
— Recherches concernant l'assimilation de l'azote. 1855. I. 158.
— Recherches microchimiques sur la nature . . . de la paroi des cellules. 1846. I. 137.
— Recherches micrométriques. 1844. I. 187.
— Tegenbedenkingen op het betoog van den heer G. J. Mulder. 1855. I. 158.
— Een wonderboom. 1869. II. 516.²
— De Wonderboom in den Haarlemmerhout. 1853. II. 516.²
— De ziekte der Koffieboomen. 1880. III. 735.
— *See also,* GUNNING, J. W. & HARTING, Pieter.

Hartinger, Anton. Atlas der Alpenflora. 1882. I. 437.
— Endlicher's Paradisus vindobonensis. See SEEMANN, Berthold. (By error.) 1844. I. 269, V. XIII.²
Hartjens, Isaeus Westerveen. De cortice peruviano. 1762. III. 719.
Hartland, Edwin Sidney. The legend of Perseus. 1894. I. 517.²
— Tree-planting at childbirth. 1894. I. 517.²
Hartland, William Baylor. Ozothamnus rosmarinifolius. 1888. III. 755.²
Hartlib, Samuel. A designe for plentie. 1652. III. 140.²
— A discours of husbandrie. 1650. III. 107.
— His legacie; or, An enlargement of the discourse of husbandry. 1650. III. 107.
Hartman, C. V. A valuable fruit tree for the high North. 1895. III. 460.¹
Hartman, Carl. Flora gevaliensis. 1847. I. 355.
— Gefle-traktens vexter. 1847. I. 355.
— Handbok i Skandinaviens flora. See HARTMAN, C. J. 1820. I. 352, 531.
— Landskapet Nerikes flora. 1866. I. 356.
— Skandinaviska halföns fanerogamer. 1864. I. 356, 531.²
Hartman, Carl Johan. Anmärkningar vid Prof. Fries' "Reservation [e]mot." 1845. I. 354.
— Annotationes de plantis scandinavicis herbarii Linnaeani. 1849. I. 355.
— Anteckningar vid de skandinaviska växterna i Linnés herbarium. 1849. I. 355.
— Beskrifning på Äreskutfjället. 1814. I. 352.
— Handbok i Skandinaviens flora. 1820. I. 352, 531.
— De Krameria dissertatio botanico-medica. See THUNBERG, C. P. 1822. III. 480.¹
— Monstrositet i blommorna hos Salix nigricans. 1840. II. 103.²
— Motiver för behandlingen af en del vexter i undertecknads svensk och norsk excursions-flora. 1846. I. 354.
— Olof Rudbecks Lappska vexter. 1841. I. 354.
— Physiographiska observationer under en resa. 1818. I. 352.
— Svensk och norsk excursions-flora. 1846. I. 355, 531.
— Tillägg och rättelser till Handbok i Skandinaviens flora. 1840. I. 354.
— Utkast til populär naturkunnighet. 1836. I. 94.
— Vårens utveckling vid Gefle. 1842. I. 223.¹
Hartman, Robert Wilhelm. Flora gevaliensis. See HARTMAN, Carl. 1847. I. 355.
— Helsinglands cotyledoneae. 1854. I. 355.
Hartmann, (Dr.). Die Haselfichte. 1885. IV. 460.¹
Hartmann, C. Encyclopädisches Wörterbuch der Technologie . . . für Forstleute. 1836. IV. 22.²
— Vollständige Brennmaterialkunde. 1841. IV. 431.¹
Hartmann, Carl. Forst-Culturen in Verbindung mit der Landwirthschaft. 1869. IV. 133.
Hartmann, Ch. Ein Vortrag über Obstkultur. 1875. III. 145.⁴
Hartmann, Christian Friedrich. Tafeln zur Bestimmung des Inhalts und des Preises runder unbeschlagener Stämme. 1865. IV. 225.
Hartmann, E. Sämereien, gesammelt . . . in der Umgebung von Beirut. 1900. I. 480.
Hartmann, Ernst. Ueber die Verbreitung der Ahornarten im Libanon. 1900. II. 477.¹
Hartmann, Franz Xaver. Primae lineae institutionum botanicarum Crantzii. 1766. I. 250.
— Primarum linearum institutionum botanicarum . . . Crantzii editio altera. 1766. I. 250.
Hartmann, Friedrich. Anatomische Vergleichung der Hexenbesen der Weisstanne. 1892. IV. 445.
Hartmann, Hugo. Die Fette. 1864. III. 224.²
Hartmann, Leopold, Freiherr von. Abhandlung von dem Wachsthum und den Krankheiten der Pflanzen. 1774. I. 206.¹
Hartmann, Peter Immanuel. Antinephritica Uvae ursinae virtus. 1778. III. 648.¹
— Circumspectus camphorae . . . usus. 1788. III. 233.¹
— Corticis Angusturae charactere. See HAUPT, C. A. 1791. III. 503.²
— Super Daphnes Gnidii usu. 1780. III. 627.¹
— Iconum botanicarum Gesnerio-Camerarianarum minorum nomenclator Linneanus. 1781. I. 78.¹
— Plantarum prope Francofurtum . . . fasciculus primus. 1767. I. 373.
— De Salice laurea odorata. 1769. III. 352.¹
— Solani Dulcamarae palaiologia Pliniana. 1779. III. 701.²
— Usus corticis peruviani in febribus biliosis. 1790. III. 720.

Hartmann, Samuel Adolf Friedrich. De Pechuri. 1792. III. 403.²
Hartmann, Wilhelm. Dissertatio sistens observationes botanicas de discrimine generico Betulae et Alni. 1801. II. 115,¹ 117.¹
— Observationes botanicae de discrimine . . . Betulae et Alni. 1794. II. 115.¹
Hartog, H. M. Heide-ontginning. 1884. IV. 160.¹
— Maatschappij voor boschkultuur. 1878. IV. 40.²
Hartog, Marcus M. On cortical fibro-vascular bundles. 1889. II. 620.¹
— On the floral organogeny . . . of Brownea. 1888. II. 337,² 383.¹
— On the floral structure . . . of Sapotaceae. 1878. II. 696.²
— Notes on Sapotaceae. 1879. II. 696.²
— Some morphological notes on . . . Thunbergia. 1880. II. 804.¹
Hartogh Heys van Zouteveen, Hermann F. De Reuzenboom van Californie. 1872. II. 51.¹
Hartrodt, A. Die Alkaloide. 1832. I. 175.
Hartsen, On certain coloring matters. 1873. III. 701.²
Hartsen, J. Friederik Antonius. Neuer Stoff in Hedera. 1875. III. 643.¹
— Nouveau principe extrait du Lierre. 1875. III. 643.¹
— Recherches sur l'Eucalyptus globulus. 1875. IV. 533.¹
— Recherches sur le Cypressus pyramidalis. 1876. II. 29.²
— & Eeden, F. W. van. Flora batava. See KOPS, Jan & others. 1800. I. 390.
Hartshorne, Henry. On the relation between organic vigor and sex. 1873. I. 199.
Hartsinck, J. J. Beschrijving van Guiana. 1770. III. 267.²
Hartter, Ferd. Die Guts- und Gemeinde-Waldungen . . . Benediktbeuern. 1869. IV. 25, 318, 351.¹
Hartung, C. A. F. A. Heinrich. De cinchonae speciebus. 1812. III. 721.
Hartung, Georg. Volksnamen Madeiraer Pflanzen. 1856. I. 76.¹
Hartweg. Hortus carlsruhanus. 1825. I. 46, 521,² III. 28.¹
Hartweg, Theodore. Bemerkungen auf einer Reise nach Mexico, Guatemala. 1847. I. 329.
— Journal of a mission to California. 1846. I. 321.
— Notes of a visit to Mexico, Guatemala. 1847. I. 329.
Hartwich, Carl. Ueber einige falsche Chinarinden. 1898. III. 725.¹
— Ueber Gerbstoffkugeln und Ligninkörper in . . . Infectoria-Gallen. 1899. IV. 503.²
— Ueber eine neue Cotorinde. 1899. III. 407.¹
— Die neuen Arzneidrogen. 1897. III. 260.¹
— Ueber den Orlean. 1890. III. 613.¹
— Ueber die Samenschale der Solanaceen. 1896. II. 768.¹
— Tragantähnliches Gummi aus Ostafrika. 1894. III. 592.¹
— See also BECKURTS, H. & HARTWICH, Carl.
— & Gamper, Max Beiträge zur Kenntnis der Angosturarinden. 1900. III. 260.¹
— & Meyer, Gottfried. Beiträge zur Kenntnis der . . . Chinarinden. 1900. III. 725.¹
Hartwich, Otto. Betrachtungen über den Ueberhalt- und Lichtungsbetrieb. 1898. IV. 129.
— Raupenleim. 1896. IV. 200.
Hartwig, George Ludwig. Die Tropenwelt im Thier- und Pflanzenleben. 1860. I. 528.¹
— The tropical world. 1860. I. 528.¹
— See also Гартвигъ.
Hartwig, J. Die Gehölzzucht. 1876. III. 101.² ¹
— Illustriertes Gehölzbuch. 1892. III. 70:
— Praktisches Handbuch der Obstbaumzucht. 1860. III. 138.
— & Rümpler, Theodor. Die Bäume und Sträucher. 1875. III. 69.
Hartwig, Rudolf. Ueber die wirthschaftliche Bedeutung des sogenannten Vorwuchses. 1881. IV. 142.
Hartz, N. Botanisk Rejseberetning fra Vest-Grønland. 1894. I. 309.¹
— Fanerogamer og Karkryptogamer fra Nordøst-Grønland. 1896. I. 309.¹
— Østgrønlands Vegetationsforhold. 1896. I. 309.¹
Hartzen, F. A. de. See HARTSEN, J. F. A.
Harvard college — Astronomical observatory. See ASTRONOMICAL . . . III. 3.
Harvard college — Museum of comparative zoölogy. See MUSEUM . . . III. 6.
Harvard university — Arnold Arboretum. See ARNOLD ARBORETUM. I. 39.

Harvard university — Bussey institution. *See* BUSSEY IN-
STITUTION. I. 5.
Harvard university — Gray herbarium. *See* GRAY HERBA-
RIUM . . . I. 5.
The harvesting of Cinchona bark. 1885. III. 715.
Harvey, Alexander. Observations on the nature . . . of trees.
1847. I. 193.[1]
— Pinea de terra of Spain. 1857. II. 44.[2]
— Trees and their nature. 1856. I. 147.
Harvey, Francis Le Roy. An abnormal form of Carya por-
cina. 1884. II. 112.[2]
— The arboreal flora of Arkansas. 1882 (1883). I. 320, *IV.
73.*[1]
— Curious growth on Gleditschia. 1882. II. 362.[1]
— Forest notes. 1881. I. 320.
— Forest trees of Arkansas. 1882 (1883). I. 320, IV. *73,*[1]
340.
— Forestry notes. 1883. II. 787.[1]
— Notes on forest trees. 1885. I. 320, *IV. 73.*[1]
— Notes upon Maine plants. 1896. V. XVII.[1]
— Some Arkansas trees. 1881. I. 320.
Harvey, J. C. Cultivated Palms in California. 1893. III.
318.[1]
— L'exploitation du caoutchouc de Castilloa. 1900. III. 368.[2]
Harvey, William Henry. Characters of some new genera . . .
discovered . . . in western Australia. 1855. I. 501.
— Description of Christya. 1842. II. 732.[1]
— Descriptions of several new genera of South African plants.
1842. I. 494.
— Fejee Islands and their inhabitants. 1857. I. 510.[1]
— The genera of South African plants. 1838. I. 494.
— On a new genus and two new species. 1859. II. 801.[1]
— Short description of a new genus of . . . Proteaceae. 1847.
II. 160.[2]
— Short directions for drying botanical specimens. 1858.
I. 35.
— Thesaurus capensis. 1859. I. 494.
— Three new species of South African plants. 1859. II.
491,[1] *533.*[1]
— & Sonder, O. W. Flora capensis. 1859. I. 494.
Harvie-Brown, John Alexander. Notes on the Moscar Oaks
of Transylvania. 1879. IV. 373.
Harz. Ueber Heckenpflanzungen. ·1855. III. 213.
Harz, Carl Otto. Ueber das Endosperm von Sagus ami-
carum. 1884. II. 71.[2]
— Landwirthschaftliche Samenkunde. 1885. I. 121.
— Verholzungen bei höheren Pflanzen. 1885. I. 176.
Harz — Naturwissenschaftlicher Verein. *See* NATURWIS-
SENSCHAFTLICHER . . . I. 14.
Harzer, Friedrich. Guttapercha und Kautschuk. 1864.
III. 231.
Harzer Forst-Verein. Verhandlungen. IV. 9.
Has & Snackey. De merkwaardige Geharoeboom. 1881.
I. 298.
Hasack, H. Acalypha Sanderiana. 1899. III. 514.[2]
— Acalypha Sanderiana fl. albo. 1900. III. 514.[1]
— Clerodendron Thomsonae. 1887. III. 696.[1]
Hassaeus, Theodor. Dissertationum . . . philologicarum syl-
loge. 1731. I. 511.
Hasché, Hermann. Ein Beitrag zur Frage: Holz-, Stein- oder
Asphalt-Pflaster. 1887. IV. 426.[1]
Hase, (Oberförster in Eutin). *See* Ueber das in HAMBURG
übliche Kappen der Bäume. 1793. III. 173.[1]
Hase, H. W. Erfahrungen in Bezug auf Obstbaumkultur.
1831. III. 164.[2]
Hasel als Unterholz. ·1865· IV. 492.[1]
Haselberger, Michael. *See* WIESBAUR, J.B. & HASELBERGER,
Michael.
Haselhoff, Emil. Recherches sur la substitution de la stron-
tiane à la chaux. 1895. I. 160.
— *See also* KÖNIG, Johann & HASELHOFF, E.
Hasenclever, Robert. Ueber die Beschädigung der Vegeta-
tion durch saure· Gase. 1879. III. 185.[1]
Hasford, Gustav. Das preussische Feld- und Forst-Polizei-
gesetz. 1881. IV. 321.
Haskell, George. An account of various experiments·for the
production of new . . . Grapes. 1877. III. 550.
Haskin, S. E. Haskinising (vulcanising) for the preservation
of wood. 1897. IV. 421.
— A new process for preserving timber. 1898. IV. 421.
— Vulcanisation du bois. 1896. IV. 421.
Haslinger, Franz. Botanisches Excursionsbuch. (Flora von
Brünn.) 1869. I. 442.

Hassack, Carl. Beiträge zur Kenntnis der Zimmtrinde.
1888. II. 224.[1]
— Cultur und Gewinnung von Thee und Kaffee. 1897. III.
600,[2] *787.*
— Die Ramie. 1899. III. 381.[2]
— Ramie, ein Rohstoff der Textil-Industrie. 1890. III.
381.[2]
— Schönheit und Nutzen der Palmen. 1898. III. 319.[2]
— Untersuchungen über den anatomischen Bau bunter Laub-
blätter. 1886. I. 111, *173.*
Hassall, Arthur Hill. A critical examination of Mohl's views
of the general structure of the pollen granule. 1842. I.
117.[1]
— Food and its adulterations. 1855. III. 219.[2]
Hasse, L. August Wilhelm. Bestimmungstabellen für die
Rosen von Meissen. 1900. II. 285.[1]
— Die Rosen Westfalens. 1891. II. 284.[2]
— Schlüssel zur Einführung in das Studium der mitteleuro-
päischen Rosen. 1895. II. 283.[2]
— Uebersicht zur Bestimmung der· schwäbischen Rosen.
1898. II. 285.[1]
Hasselbom, Nicolaus. Aphorismi de morbis plantárum. 1748.
I. 206.[1]
Hasselman, J. J. Beschouwingen over de partikuliere indus-
trie in vergelijking met het kultuurstelsel. 1863. III. 128.
Hasselquist, Andreas. *Δενδρολογία.. See* HAHN, Petrus.
1698. I. 82.[1]
Hasselquist, Fredric. Iter palaestinum. 1757. I. 479,
V. XXIV.[1]
— Mimosa africana. 1751. II. 331.[1]
— Reise nach Palästina. 1757. I. 479.
— Vires plantarum. *See* LINNÉ, Carl von. 1747. III. 238.[1]
— Voyages and travels in the Levant. 1757. I. 479.
— Voyages dans le Levant. 1757. I. 479, V. XXIV.[1]
Hasselt, A. L. van. Lijst der bout, bamboe . . . van Midden
Sumatra. 1884. III. 275.[1]
— Lijst van hout-, Bamboe- en Rotansoorten van Midden-
Sumatra. 1884. IV. 400.[1]
— & Boerlage, J. G. Bijdragen tot de kennis der flora van
Midden-Sumatra. 1884. I. 467.
Hasselt, Alexander Wilhelm Michael· van. Bijdrage tot· de
kennis der Afrikaansche pijlvergiften. 1872· III. 690.[1]
— Bijdrage tot de kennis . . . van het Curare. 1880. III.
·89.[1]
— Sur les poisons à flèche africains. 1872. III. 690.[1]
— Tweede mededeeling omtrent de Afrikaansche pijlvergiften.
1872. III. 690.[1]
Hasselt, Jan Coenraad van. Brief aan W. de Haan vanuit
Anjer. 1824. I. 468.
— *See also* KUHL, H. & HASSELT, J. C. van.
Hasselt, W. H.· van. Proeven omtrent het planten van
Moerbezieboomen. 1776. III. 173.[1]
Hasskarl, Justus Karl. Aanteekeningen over het nut, door de
bewoners van Java aan eenige planten . . . toegeschreven.
1845. III. 275.[1]
— Adnotationes de plantis Horti bogoriensis. 1845. I. 67·[2]
— Adnotationes de plantis quibusdam javanicis. 1843. I.
468.
— Beiträge zur Flora von Java und Sumatra. 1852. ·II.
494.[2]
— Bemerkungen über einige indische Pflanzen. 1868. I.
474.
— Bemerkungen über einige Pflanzen des Botanischen Gar-
tens zu Buitenzorg. 1856. I. 67.[2]
— Bericht über den Zustand der Chinakultur auf Java. 1861.
III. 715.
— Bijdrage tot de kennis van Zuid Bantam. 1842. I. 468.
— Catalogus plantarum in Horto botanico bogoriensi cul-
tarum alter. 1844. ·I. 67.[2]
— Clavis analytica generum Euphorbiacearum. 1859. II.
433.[2]
— Diplanthera Bnks. et Soland. 1870. II. 788.[1]
— Eenige kritische onderzoekingen van planten in 's Lands
plantentuin te Buitenzorg. 1859. I. 465.
— Ueber einige neue Gattungen der Sapotaceae. 1855. ·II.
·96.[2]
— Genera aliquot nova Horti bot. bogoriensis. 1857. I. 68.[1]
— Horti malabarici clavis nova. 1861. I. 78.[1]
— Hortus bogoriensis descriptus. 1858. I. 68.[1]
— Hortus bogoriensis descriptus. 1858. I. 68.[1]
— Die indischen Euphorbiaceen. 1860. II. 434.[1]
— Ueber Kalmia latifolia L. 1863. II. 672.[2]
— Leguminosarum quarundam javensium descriptiones. 1842.
II. 319.[2]

— Neuer Schlüssel zu Rumph's Herbarium amboinense. 1866. I. 78.²
— Note sur le Soulamea amara. 1863. II. 416.¹
— Over de ontwikkeling van warmte in planten. 1839. I. 186.
— Papilionacearum quarundam javanicarum descriptiones. 1844. II. 319.²
— Plantae javanicae rariores. 1848. I. 468.
— Plantarum . . . e familiis Asclepiadearum et Apocynearum adumbrationes. 1857. II. 722,¹ 735.¹
— Plantarum genera et species . . . javenses. 1842. I. 468.
— Plantarum javanicarum . . . adumbrationes. 1844. I. 468.
— Plantarum rariorum Horti bogoriensis decas. 1838. I. 67.²
— Plantarum rariorum . . . Horti bogoriensis pugillus novus. 1844. I. 67.²
— De planten, door den Heer Noronha . . . opgespoord. 1844. I. 468.
— Polygalaceae praesertim indicae. 1863. II. 429.²
— Retzia. 1855. I. 67.²
— Revisio Euphorbiacearum. 1859. II. 433.²
— Saribus rotundifolius. 1842. II. 70.²
— Tympananthe. 1847. II. 737.²
Dr. Hasskarl's mislukte poging tot invoering der Coca-cultuur op Java. 1886. III. 492.¹
Hast, Carl Fredrik. In genus Echitis observationes. *See* THUNBERG, C. P. 1819. II. 726.¹
Hast, Hermann Rudolf. De Caryophyllis aromaticis. *See* THUNBERG, C. P. 1788. III. 635.²
Hastings, Charles. Illustrations of the natural history of Worcestershire. 1834. I. 398.
Hastings, George Tracy. When increase in thickness begins in our trees. 1900. I. 190.²
— *See also* ROWLEE, W. W. & HASTINGS, G. T.
Hastings, Gerald. The Cactus family. 1890. III. 619.
Hastings, Warren. The Dunkeld Larches. 1887. III. 304.²
Hastrup. Tiltrækning af Azalea. 1889. III. 656.
Hatch, W. H. Investigations and tests of American timber. 1894. IV. 416.¹
Hatch experiment station. *See* MASSACHUSETTS — AGRICULTURAL COLLEGE . . . III. 5.
Hatfield, T. D. Hardy Rhododendrons. 1897. III. 657.¹
— Rhododendrons at Wellesley. 1896. III. 657.¹
— Trees and shrubs for winter effects. 1897. III. 208.²
— The wild Roses. 1895. III. 451.¹
Hathorn, J. G. The culture and manufacture of Tea. 1863. III. 603.
— A few remarks on . . . Tea cultivation . . . in the Himalayan range. 1867. III. 603.
— A hand-book of Darjeeling. 1863. III. 278.
Hatton, W. J. Secrets of Rose culture. 1891. III. 458.¹
Hattori, Hirotaro. *See* INUI, Tamaki, HATTORI, Hirotaro & KUSANO, Shunsuke.
Hatz, Hermann. Beiträge zur Rubusflora des badischen Oberlandes. 1882. II. 302.¹
Hatzel, Adam Heinrich. Grundsätze der Forstpolizey. 1802. IV. 268.
Hatzfeld, A. Sur un nouveau procédé de conservation des bois. 1874. IV. 419.
— & Boucherie, Maurice. Sur un nouveau procédé de conservation du bois. 1874. IV. 419.
Hauk, T. F. Album plantarum . . . circa Conicium 1847 I. 382.
Haubensack, Theodor. Ziersträucher zur Bepflanzung einer Kanaldecke. 1900. III. 42.¹
Hauch, L. A. Kulturverfahren in der Herrschaft Bregentved auf Seeland. 1900. IV. 113.²
— Om Opbevaring af Agern. 1897. IV. 508.
Hauchecorne, A. Le cidre. 1889. III. 429.¹
— *See also* BOUTTEVILLE, L. de & HAUCHECORNE, A.
Hauchecorne, F. W. Die Forstbewirthschaftung in technischer Hinsicht. 1812. IV. 381.
Hauck, Franz. Leitfaden zum Selbst-Studium der . . . Forstwissenschaft. 1898. IV. 111.¹
Hauck, Hieronymus. Das Steigen der Holzpreise. 1860. IV. 402.²
Haucke. Pflugrüster aus 'Rothbuchen. 1884. IV. 499.
Hauenstein, Gottlob. Gründliche Berechnung der Pflanzenzahl. 1835. IV. 154.¹
— Kubik-Tabellen für runde . . . Hölzer. 1844. IV. 154,¹ 223.
Haufe, P. Prunus sinensis fl. albo pl. 1891. II. 437.¹
Haug, (Oberförster). Beitrag zu der Durchforstungsfrage. 1894. IV. 174.
— Beitrag zu der Durchforstungsfrage. 1896. IV. 175.¹
— Zur Durchforstungsfrage. 1897. IV. 459.¹

Haugk, Johannes. Catalogus plantarum Horti academici lugduno-batavi. 1679. I. 50.
Haugvel, P. Plantation des Hêtres. 1894. III. 360.²
— Utilisation des fruits du Rosa rugosa. 1894. III. 456.²
Haukevik, O. S. Et stort Grantra. 1896. II. 37.²
Haumann, Gustav Heinrich. Das Ganze des Seidenbaues. 1829. III. 374.
Hauordnung für die Holzhauer in den k. preussischen Forsten. n. d. IV. 301.
Hau-Ordnung für die kaiserlichen Forsten des Reichslandes Elsass-Lothringen. 1871. IV. 298.²
Haupt, A., (Dr.). Vermehrung des Kgl. Naturalienkabinets. 1893. V. VIII.²
Haupt, Christophorus Gottlieb. Corticis Angusturae characterem. 1791. III. 503.²
Haupt, Herman. On the resistance of timber. 1850. IV. 410.
Haupt-Catalog der Obst- und Gehölzbaumschulen des Ritterguts Zöschen. 1885. III. 28.¹
Hauptmann, August. Insignes aliquot viticulturae errores. 1642. III. 551.²
Hausen, von. *See* ANTRAG, den Erlass eines Waldschutzgesetzes für Sachsen betreffend. 1877. IV. 180.²
Hausen, Emil. Ueber Morphologie und Anatomie der Aloineen. 1900. II. 77.²
Hausen, K. R. Nach den Quellen ausgearbeitete Darstellung des Weinbaues. 1798. III. 552.
Hauser, Johann Jacob. Theses botanico-anatomicae. 1711. I. 31.
Hauser, R. STIERLIN. *See* STIERLIN-HAUSER, R.
Hausmann, Franz, *Baron* von. Flora von Tirol. 1851. I. 440.
Hausmann, Johann Friedrich Ludwig. On the physiognomy of Scandinavia. 1833. I. 353.
— Versuch einer geologischen Begründung des Acker- und Forstwesens. 1825. IV. 60.²
Hausmann, Ulrich. Beiträge zur Kenntniss des Betulins. 1876. IV. 491.¹
— La bétuline. 1876. IV. 491.¹
Hausrath, Hans. Beitrag zur Geschichte der natürlichen Verjüngung. 1891. IV. 26.
— Forstgeschichte der rechtsrheinischen Theile des ehemaligen Bisthums Speyer. 1898. IV. 26.
— Aus den Forstreserven der Vereinigten Staaten. 1900. IV. 179.²
— Zum Vordringen der Kiefer. 1900. II. 47,¹ 136.²
— Die Waldwegbauten des Forstbezirks St. Blasien. 1895. IV. 267.
— Der Wechsel der Holzarten. 1900. IV. 74.²
Haussen, Johann Salomon. Theoretisch-praktische Anweisung zum Plan und Situationszeichnen. 1822. IV. 263.
Haussez, *baron* d'. De l'Acacia. 1844. IV. 524.¹
— Sur l'Acacia. 1845. IV. 524.¹
— De l'amélioration des bois taillis. 1843. IV. 130.
Haussknecht, A. Ueber Manna-Sorten des Orients. 1870. III. 221.¹
Haussknecht, Carl. Ueber das Absterben der Pyramidenpappeln. 1884. III. 346.²
— Floristische Notizen. 1888. II. 97.²
— Floristische Mittheilungen. 1893. II. 117.¹
— Kleinere botanische Mittheilungen. 1890. II. 117.²
— Lonicera Periclymenum in Thüringen? 1891. II. 839.¹
— Pflanzengeschichtliche . . . Beiträge. 1891. II. 273,¹ 274.¹
— Prunus avium × Cerasus. 1891. II. 273.¹
— Prunus Chamaecerasus Jacq. 1891. II. 274.¹
— Rhus Toxicodendron. 1880. II. 460.¹
— Symbolae ad floram graecam. 1893. I. 450.
— Systematische und floristische Notizen. 1895. II. 98.¹
Haut-Laos. 1899. III. 276.²
Haute-Garonne — Société d'horticulture de la. *See* SOCIÉTÉ . . . III. 21.
Haute-Marne — Société horticole, viticole et forestière. *See* SOCIÉTÉ . . . III. 22.
Haute-Saône — Société centrale d'agriculture . . . *See* SOCIÉTÉ . . . III. 20.
Haute-Saône — Société d'agriculture, des sciences . . . *See* SOCIÉTÉ . . . III. 21.
Hautefeuille, Paul. Recherches sur les résines. 1865. III. 227.
Hautes-Alpes — Société d'études. *See* SOCIÉTÉ . . . I. 23.
Hautes-Alpes — Société de secour mutuels des préposés forestiers . . . *See* SOCIÉTÉ . . . IV. 13.¹
Hauteville, de BISEAU D'. *See* BISEAU D'HAUTEVILLE, de.

Havaas, Johan. Floristiske undersøgelser i søndre Bergenhus amt. 1898. I. 358.[2]
Havard, Henry. Dictionnaire de l'ameublement. 1887. IV. 427.[1]
Havard, Valery. Basket-work of the North American Indians. 1890. III. 261.[2]
— The botanical aspect of Pike's Peak. 1893. I. 326.
— Drink plants of the North American Indians. 1896. III. 223.[1]
— Economic notes on the Texano-Mexican flora. 1886. III. 63.[1]
— Food plants of the North American Indians. 1895. III. 63.[1]
— List of plants . . . of western Dakota. 1880. I. 324.
— The Mezquit. 1884. II. 379.[2]
— Report on the flora of . . . Texas. 1885. V. xviii.[1]
— When is Rhus Toxicodendron most active? 1895. III. 528.[1]
Havas, Ágoston. A Lúcsfenyő az alacsony fekvésű helyeken. 1889. IV. 454.
Have-Avis. III. 10.[3]
Havebrugs-Tidende III. 10.[2]
Havelka, Petr. Květena okoli Nového Města. 1896. I. 444.
Havens, Jonathan N. Experiments . . . on the culture of White Thorn. 1798. III. 421.[1]
Haver Droeze, F. J. Eenige aanteekeningen betreffende den houthandel in China. 1896. IV. 407.[1]
— Petroleum en hout uit Nederlandsch Indie. 1897. IV. 407.[2]
Havetidende. III. 10.[2]
Haviland, E. Flowering seasons of Australian plants. 1887. I. 228.[1]
— Occasional notes on the inflorescence and habits of plants . . . of Sydney. 1883. I. 240.[1]
Haviland, G. D. A revision of the tribe Naucleeae. 1897. II. 807.[1]
Haviland, W. C. The Duchess of Oldenburg. 1897. III. 426.[2]
— The Spruce. 1899. III. 305.[1]
Havlik, Friedrich. Zwei neue Hypsometer. 1889. IV. 216.
Havre — Cercle pratique d'horticulture . . . See CERCLE . . . III. 19.
Havre — Société d'horticulture et de botanique. See CERCLE PRATIQUE D'HORTICULTURE . . . DU HAVRE. III. 19.
Hawaiian almanac. III. 27.[1]
Hawaiian annual. See HAWAIIAN almanac. III. 27.[1]
Hawaiian planters' monthly. See PLANTERS' monthly. III. 27.[2]
Hawes. The cultivation of economic plants in central Africa. 1890. III. 131.[1]
Hawes, A. G. S. Report on coffee culture in the Hawaiian Islands. 1897. III. 733.[1]
Hawgood, H. Effect of forests on water supply. 1899. IV. 52.
Hawkes, Henry P. Notes on the vegetable oils of the Madras Presidency. 1859. III. 224.[2]
— Report upon the oils of southern India. 1858. III. 224.[2]
Hawkesworth, John. An account of the voyages undertaken . . . in the southern hemisphere. 1773. I. 301.
Hawkins, Abraham. On raising Lemons and Oranges. 1818. III. 496.[2]
Hawkins, C. K. Manufacture of turpentine and resin in the southern states of America. 1900. IV. 467.[1]
— Turpentine and rosin. 1900. IV. 467.[1]
Hawkins, John. Account of . . . the original quina-quina of Peru. 1797. III. 720.
Hawks, Francis Lister. See AMERICAN forest; or, Uncle Philip's conversations. 1834. I. 304.
Haworth, Adrian Hardy. Dissertatio prima; or, A new arrangement of . . . Mesembryanthemum. 1803. II. 193.[2]
— Dissertatio quinta; sive, Descriptiones viginti-quatuor novarum specierum. 1803. I. 265.
— Dissertatio sexta; sive, Technici botanici. 1803. I. 70.
— Miscellanea naturalia. 1803. I. 265.
— A new arrangement of the genus Aloe. 1804. II. 77.[2]
— Supplementum plantarum succulentarum. 1812. I. 265.
— Synopsis plantarum succulentarum. 1812. I. 265.
Hawranek, C. Ein seltener Wachholderbaum. 1898. IV. 448.[2]
— Verbesserte Holzwollemaschine. 1891. IV. 429.
Hawranek, Ignaz. Dissertatio inaug. chemico-medica de acidis. 1837. I. 180.[1]
Haxthausen, O. Om Dyrkning af Baandpil. 1871. III. 352.[2]
— Den mundenske Tueplantning. 1872. IV. 153.[2]

Hay, David. On the cultivation of native trees. 1873. III. 132.[1]
— The Pine tree in New Zealand. 1869. III. 306.[2]
Hay, G. W. A. DRUMMOND-. Bemerkungen über einige Pflanzen Maroccos. 1833. I. 484.
— Notices of certain plants of Morocco. 1833. I. 484.
Hay, George Upham. The flora of New Brunswick. 1894. I. 311.[1]
Hay, Henry Maurice DRUMMOND-. The comparative hardihood of hardwooded plants. 1882. III. 47.
— Effects of the past winter. 1879. III. 47.
Hay, R. DALRYMPLE. Notes on Pine thinning. 1899. IV. 461.[1]
— The timber trade of New South Wales. 1900. IV. 407.[2]
Hayden, Ferdinand Vandeveer. Catalogue of the collections . . . [in Nebraska and Dakota]. 1875. I. 324.
— Preliminary report of the United States geological survey of Montana. See PORTER, T. C. 1872. I. 323.
Hayden, Walter. Kalmia angustifolia. 1885. III. 652.[2]
Hayek, August von. Neue Rosen- und Rubus-Formen aus Niederösterreich. 1898. II. 288,[2] 305.[1]
Hayes, Augustus Allen. Mineral substance in the center of trees. 1861. I. 155.
— A new species of wax. 1855. III. 226.[1]
Hayes, Charles Willard. An expedition through the Yukon district. 1893. I. 311.[1]
Hayes, Joseph. Sur le Caesalpinia Bonducella. 1862. III. 468.[2]
— Note sur l'Illoupé. 1862. III. 667.[1]
Hayes, Samuel. A practical treatise on planting. 1794. IV. 108.[1]
Hayn, (Oberförster). Mittheilungen über die forstlichen Verhältnisse des Liegnitzer Stadtforstes. 1867. IV. 353.
— Schreiben . . . betreffend die Vertilgung der Maikäfer. 1851. IV. 202.
— Ueber Vertilgung der Maikäfer. 1857. IV. 202.
Hayn, E. Fuchsia triphylla L. 1892. III. 640.[2]
Haynald, Lajos. See HAYNALD, Ludwig.
Haynald, Ludwig. Castanea vulgaris Lam. 1881. II. 124.[1]
— De distributione geographica Castaneae in Hungaria. 1878. II. 124.[1]
— Icones plantarum in S. Scriptura commemoratarum. 1890. I. 513.
— Mily talajon él nálunk a szelid Gesztenyefa? 1877. II. 124.[1]
— Des plantes qui fournissent les gommes. 1894. III. 228.[1]
— A szentirási mézgák és gyanták termőnövényei. 1879. I. 513, III. 227.
— Terem-e vadon Erdélyben a Syringa persica? 1878. II. 115.[2]
Hayne, Arthur P. Olives and olive oils. 1894. III. 676.[2]
Hayne, Friedrich Gottlob. Ueber die Bildung des Zellengewebes. 1828. I. 123.[2] — 1829. I. 136.[2]
— De coloribus corporum naturalium. 1814. I. 184.
— Darstellung und Beschreibung der Arzneigewächse. 1805. III. 55.
— Darstellung und Beschreibung der Arzneygewächse. 1829. III. 56.
— Dendrologische Flora. 1822. I. 293, III. 63,[2] IV. 82.
— Ueber die Gattung Copaifera. 1826. II. 347.[2]
— Ueber die Gattungen Hymenaea, Vouapa. 1827. II. 364,[2] 371,[1] 387.[1]
— Getreue Darstellung . . . der in der Arzneykunde gebräuchlichen Gewächse. 1805. III. 55.
— Ueber die Pflanzen der Gattung Hymenaea. 1828. II. 364.[2]
— Pinus rotundata Link. 1843. IV. 465.
— Pinus sylvestris L. 1843. IV. 482.[1]
— Termini botanici iconibus illustrati. 1799. I. 70.
— See also DREVES, J. F. P. & HAYNE, F. G.; GUIMPEL, Friedrich, OTTO, Friedrich & HAYNE, F. G.; GUIMPEL, Friedrich, WILLDENOW, C. L. & HAYNE, F. G.
Haynes, J. An accurate survey of the Botanic garden at Chelsea. 1751. I. 52.
Haynes, Thomas. An improved system of nursery gardening. 1811. III. 153.
— A treatise on the improved culture of the Strawberry. 1812. III. 142.
Haynes, Wilson G. Cultivation of Basket Willow in the United States. 1852. III. 347.
Hays, W. M. Second growth Pine vs. agriculture. 1900. IV. 469.
Hayward, Joseph. An inquiry into the causes of the fruitfulness . . . of plants. 1834. III. 38.[1]
— The science of horticulture. 1818. III. 35.

Hayward, W. R. The botanist's pocket book. 1872. I. 402, 534.[1]

Hazard, Barclay. Extended range of Quercus densiflora. 1893. II. 133.[2]

Hazen, Henry Allen. Forests and rainfall. 1897. IV. 52.

Hazen, Willem van. Catalogue tant des arbres et plantes étrangères . . . chez Willem van Hazen. 18 . . ? I. 51.[1]

— Welke boomen, graanen . . . zoude men met vrucht in ons land kunnen invoeren? 1779. III. 270.[2]

— Welken zijn de beste middelen om onze landen . . . ten meesten voordeele aan te leggen. 1765. III. 122.[1]

Hazlett, H. Notes on the principal gums and resins. 1872. III. 227.

Hazslinszky, Frigyes Agost. Magyarhon edényes növényei-nek füvészeti kézikönyve. 1872. I. 536.[1]

— Die Sphärien der Rose. 1870. III. 453.[2]

Hazzi, von. Lehrbuch des Seidenbaues für Deutschland. 1826. III. 374.

Hazzi, Joseph. Die echten Ansichten der Waldungen und Förste. 1804. IV. 25, 268.[1]

Hbg., von. Waldbestand . . . in den Vereinigten Staaten. 1893. IV. 112.

The **Headcorn** Oak. 1872. II. 138.[2]

Headley, W. L. Address delivered before the Wayne county agricultural society. 1874. IV. 45.

Heald, Fred de Forest. Contributions to the comparative histology of pulvini. 1894. II. 322.[1]

Heamy, John. P. Creodaphne californica. 1875. III. 408.[1]

Heard, James. Fruit raising for farmers. 1892. III. 133.

Hearle, N. Geographical botany for Indian foresters. 1884. I. 475.[1]

— The grazing question in Jaunsar. 1888. IV. 136.[2]

— A note on an Oak of the N.-W. Himalaya. 1887. II. 139.[2]

— Notes on Box, Alpine Birch. 1883. IV. 378.

— One of nature's coppices. 1900. IV. 528.[2]

— Tour in France. 1895. IV. 362.

Heath, Francis George. Autumnal leaves. 1881. I. 393,[2] III. 207.[1]

— Autumnal leaves. 1882. III. 457.[2]

— Burnham Beeches. 1879. I. 297.[1]

— Our woodland trees. 1878. I. 393.[2]

— Sylvan winter. 1886. I. 516.

— Tree gossip. 1885. I. 96.

— Trees and ferns. 1879. I. 96.

— Trees and lightning. 1884. IV. 194.

Heather as thatch. 1900. III. 649.[1]

Heaths. 1854. III. 650.[2]

Heaton, Samuel. Notes on the winter of 1895 in the Isle of Wight. 1896. III. 47.

— Trees and shrubs in the Isle of Wight. 1898. I. 55.

Heavy woods. 1891. IV. 411.[2]

Hebberling, Max. Ueber die Verwendung der Sägespäne als Futtermittel. 1870. IV. 223.[1]

Hebenstreit, Ernst Benjamin Gottlieb. Caussas [sic] humorum motum in plantis . . . recenset. 1779. I. 163.

— Diatribe de vegetatione hyemali. 1777. I. 32.

Hebenstreit, Johann Christian. De cultura plantarum. See UNGEBAUER, J. R. 1741. III. 103.

— Plantarum aliquot rariorum descriptiones completae. 1763. III. 330.[1]

Hebenstreit, Johann Ernst. De santinuanda Rivinorum industria. See LISCHWITZ, J. C. 1726. I. 250.

— Definitiones plantarum. 1731. I. 290.

— De foetu vegetabili. 1747. I. 121.

— Programma de methodo plantarum ex fructu. 1740. I. 118.[2]

— De sensu externo facultatum in plantis judice. 1730. I. 146.

Hébert, Alexandre. Formation des matières albuminoïdes. 1898. I. 178.

— Sur la présence . . . d'une gomme donnant de la xylose. 1892. I. 181.[1]

— See also LECOMTE, Henri & HÉBERT, Alexandre.

— & **Truffaut**, Georges. Sur l'emploi des engrais en horti-culture. 1898. III. 152.

Hébert, C. J. B. L. Réflexions sur les forêts de la république. 1795. IV. 275.

Hebig, G. J. C. See WAGNER, Christian & HEBIG, G. J. C.

Hebung der Zirbenholzcultur in Tirol. 1900. IV. 463.[2]

Hécart, Gabriel Antoine Joseph. Les bosquets d'agrément. 1808. I. 516.

— Essai sur les qualités . . . des arbres, arbrisseaux. 1794. III. 85.

— Florula hannoniensis. 1836. I. 409.

— Mémoires sur les haies. 1812. III. 212.[2]

Heck, Carl Robert. Ein Beitrag zur Bestandesschätzung. 1899. IV. 219.

— Ueber Bestandeslagerbücher. 1898. IV. 246.

— Ein Düngungs- und Verschulversuch im Forstgarten. 1896. IV. 144.[2]

— Das Genossenschaftswesen in der Forstwirtschaft. 1887. IV. 307.[2]

— Massregeln gegen den Weisstannenkrebs. 1898. IV. 445.

— Die Riesenbuchen des Schurwalds. 1898. IV. 500.[2]

— Der Weisstannenkrebs. 1894. IV. 445.

Hecke, W. Die Forstwirthschaftslehre. 1858. IV. 98.[1]

Heckel, Édouard. De l'action de quelques composés sur la germination des graines. 1875. I. 203.

— De l'action des sels de strychnine. 1879. III. 683.[2]

— De l'action des températures élevées . . . sur la germination. 1880. I. 203.

— Sur l'Araucaria brasiliensis. 1892. III. 298.[1]

— Sur l'arbre africain qui donne le beurre de Galam. 1897. II. 697,[2] III. 667.[1]

— Sur le Barringtonia intermedia. 1885. III. 631.[1]

— Beurre d'Ochoco. 1898. III. 403.[2]

— Le beurre d'Odyendyé. 1898. II. 414.[2]

— Beurre d'Owala. 1898. III. 483.[1]

— Beurre de Bouandjo du Congo français. 1898. III. 608.[2]

— Beurre de Galam ou de Karité. 1898. III. 667.[1]

— Beurre de Kanya. 1898. III. 610.[2]

— Beurre de Kombo du Gabon. 1898. III. 403.[1]

— Beurre de Maloukang. 1898. III. 514.[1]

— Beurre de Staudtia kamerunensis. 1898. III. 403.[1]

— Beurre de touloucouna. 1898. III. 512.[1]

— Sur le beurre et le pain de d'dika. 1893. III. 508.[1]

— Sur le Bunya-Bunya (Araucaria Bidwilli). 1891, II. 26.[1]

— Sur un "Ceratonia Siliqua L." à fleurs . . . hermaphrodites. 1893. II. 345.[1]

— Le Cocotier et ses produits. 1895. III. 324.[1]

— Contribution à l'étude des plantes médicinales . . . de la Côte d'Ivoire. 1900. III. 93.[2]

— Coup-d'œil sur la flore générale de la baie du Prony. 1892. I. 509.[1]

— Les cultures de caoutchouc coloniales. 1898. III. 149.

— Sur deux cas de monstruosité . . . de Citrus. 1879. II. 402.[1]

— Différenciation des mouvements provoqués et spontanés. 1874. II. 202.[2]

— Expériences comparées entre l'action du kola. 1890. III. 590.[2]

— Sur le Fontainea Pancheri. 1872. III. 518.[2]

— Sur la formation des canaux sécréteurs . . . de quelques Guttifères. 1899. II. 553.[1]

— Sur la germination . . . d'Araucaria. 1891. II. 26.[1]

— Sur la germination . . . d'Araucaria Bidwilli. 1892. II. 26.[1]

— Sur la gomme de M' Beppe. 1898. III. 592.[1]

— Sur les graines de l'Ailanthackia. 1899. II. 553.[1]

— Graines grasses. 1898. III. 384,[2] 403,[1] 430,[1] 468,[2] 485,[1] 512,[1] 521,[2] 608,[2] 614.[2]

— Graisse de Krébao où de Chung Bao. 1898. III. 614.[2]

— Du Houille . . . café du Soudan. 1887. III. 483.[1]

— Huile d'Engessang ou d'Essang du Gabon. 1898. III. 521.[2]

— Huile d'Onguéko ou Ongoké. 1898. III. 384.[2]

— De l'huile de Bankoul. 1875. III. 515.[1]

— Huile de Butea frondosa. 1898. III. 468.[2]

— Huile de Carapa de la Guyane. 1898. III. 512.[1]

— Huile de Citron de Mer ou d'Élozy-Zégué. 1898. III. 385.[1]

— Huile de Coula ou de Koumounou. 1898. III. 384.[2]

— Huile de Hongay. 1898. III. 485.[1]

— Huile de Néou du Sénégal. 1898. III. 430.[1]

— De l'influence des acides salicylique . . . sur la germination. 1878. I. 203.

— Sur l'intensité du coloris . . . aux hautes altitudes. 1883. I. 236.[2]

— Sur l'introduction . . . des Araucarias. 1898. III. 298.[1]

— De l'irritabilité des étamines de Berberis. 1874. II. 202.[1]

— De l'irritabilité des étamines. 1873. I. 197.[2]

— Over de Kemiri-olie. 1883. III. 515.[1]

— Des Kolas africains. 1883. III. 590.[2]

— Les Kolas africains. 1893. III. 533,[1] III. 590.[2]

— Le Malgukang ou Ankalaki. 1889. II. 431.[1]

— Un médicament nouveau. 1891. III. 632.[1]

— Du mouvement dans les étamines du Sparmannia. 1874. I. 197,[2] II. 564.[1]

Heckel, Édouard (*continued*).
— Du mouvement dans les stigmates., 1874. I..197.[2]
— Mouvement provoqué dans les étamines de Mahonia. 1874. II. 202.[2]
— Du mouvement provoqué dans les étamines des Synanthérées. 1874. I. 197.[2]
— Sur un nouvel Arbre à gutta-percha. 1885. III. 667.[1]
— Nouvelles observations de tératologie. 1886. I. 144.[1]
— Origine botanique des doundakés d'Afrique. 1885. II. 831.[1]
— Sur le parasitisme du Ximenia. 1899. II. 172.[1]
— Du pilosisme déformant dans quelques végétaux. 1880. I. 143.
— Les plantes medicinales et toxiques de la Guyane. 1897. III. 64.[2]
— Sur la présence . . . des cystolithes dans . . . Exostemma. 1888. II. 816.[2]
— Sur quelques faits remarquables . . . dans la formation secondaire de l'écorce. 1885. I. 130, *II. 851*.[1]
— Sur quelques particularités anatomiques nouvelles dans les graines grasses. 1899. I. 121.
— Recherches sur les graines grasses. 1898. III. 483,[1] 514,[1] 667.[1]
— Recherches sur les graines grasses nouvelles. 1898. III. 225.
— Des relations que présentent les phénomènes de mouvement . . . avec la fécondation. 1878. I. 238.
— Sur la sexualité du Ceratonia. 1892. II. 345.[1]
— Suif de Virola Micheli. 1898. III. 403.[1]
— Sur l'utilisation et les transformations de quelques alcaloïdes. 1890. I. 204.
— Sur les végétaux qui produisent le beurre et le pain d'"o'dika." 1893. III. 508.[1]
— Les végétaux utiles de l'Afrique tropicale. 1887. III. 483.[1]—1889. II. 431.[1]
— & Haller, Alb. Note on Potalia amara. 1877. III. 682.[1]
— & **Schlagdenhauffen**, Fr. Sur le Bakis. 1895. III. 396.[1]
— — Sur le Batjentjor. 1888. III. 756.[2]
— — Du bois piquant de la Guyane française. 1898. III. 506.[2]
— — Du café du Soudan. 1887. III. 483.[1]
— — Sur la constitution . . . du latex concrété de Bassia latifolia. 1889. III. 667.[1]
— — Sur le Copaifera Salikounda. 1893. II. 347.[1]
— — Copaifera salikounda. 1894. III. 473.[1]
— — Sur les deux variétés de Detarium senegalense. 1890. *II. 354*,[2] III. 475.[2]
— — Doundaké and its bark. 1885. III. 747.[2]
— — Du Doundaké et de son écorce. 1885. III. 747.[2]
— — De l'écorce de Bois piquant. 1884. III. 506.[1]
— — De l'écorce de Morinda citrifolia. 1885. III. 746.[1]
— — Étude botanique . . . sur le Connarus africanus. 1897. III. 462.[1]
— — Un faux Kola nouveau. 1888. III. 610.[2]
— — Sur le Févier. 1893. II. 362.[1]
— — Sur le Gaertnera vaginata. 1890. III. 744.[1]
— — Ueber die Gattung Psathura auf der Insel Réunion. 1900. II. 827.[2]
— — Sur une gomme et deux kinos d'Australie. 1890. I. 181.[1]
— — Sur la graine de Ko-Sam. 1900. III. 508.[1]
— — Des graines de Bonduc. 1886. III. 468.[3]
— — Sur les graines de Chaulmoogra. 1885. III. 614.[2]
— — Sur la Gutta-percha de Bassia. 1885. III. 667.[1]
— — De l'huile . . . du Calophyllum. 1876. III. 608.[3]
— — Des Kolas africains. 1883. III. 590.[2]
— — Sur un latex du Bassia latifolia. 1888. III. 667.[2]
— — Du m'boundou. 1881. III. 684.[1]
— — Sur la noix de Kola. 1882. III. 590.[1]
— — Nouvelles recherches sur le doundaké. 1885. II. 831.[1]
— — Nouvelles recherches . . . sur le m'boundou. 1882. III. 684.[2]
— — Sur la présence de la cholestérine. 1886. I. 182.[1]
— — Sur la présence de la lécithine. 1886. I. 176.
— — Sur le produit des laticifères. 1888. III. 231, 668,[1] 669.[1]
— — Sur les Psathura de l'Île de la Réunion. 1900. II. 827.[1]
— De la racine du Danais fragrans. 1885. III. 743.[2]
— Sur les rapports génétiques des matières résineuses. 1892. III. 637,[1] 711,[1] 744.[1]
— Sur la sécrétion des Araucaria. 1887. *II. 25*,[1] III. 208.[1]

— — Sur la sécrétion oléo-gommorésineuse des Araucarias. 1889. II. 25.[3]
— — Sur la sexualité du Caroubier. 1892. II. 345.[1]
— — Sur le Solom. 1889. III. 475.[3]
— — Some African Kolas. 1884. III. 590.[3]
Heckensträucher für Baumschulen, 1880. III. 214.[1]
Hecker, Johann Julius. Einleitung in die Botanik. 1734. I. 82.[2]
— Flora berolinensis. 1757. I. 373.
— Specimen florae berolinensis. 1742. I. 373.
Heckheler, Johann. De potu Theé. *See* MAPPUS, Marcus. 1691. III. 605.
Heckler, Johann Baptist. Der Rheingauer Weinbau. 1844. III. 552.
Hecquet, C. Lidt om den private Træplantning. 1879. IV. 156.[2]
Hector, James. On the geographical botany of New Zealand. 1869. I. 506.[1]
— Notice of a new species of Pomaderris. 1879. II. 496.[2]
— Physical features of the central part of British North America. 1861. I. 310.
Hedde, Aussug aus dem Bericht über den Versuchsgarten in Dar-es-Salam. 1900. III. 131.[2]
Hedemann, Carl von. Das Nothwendigste aus der Forstwissenschaft. 1827. IV. 97.
Hedenberg, Andreas. Stationes plantarum. *See* LINNÉ, Carl von. 1754. I. 228.[1]
Hedenberg, Olaf Anton & Hansén, Jacob. De Aspalatho. *See* THUNBERG, C. P. 1802. II. 333.[1]
Hedenius, J. E. Die Rosskastanien. 1848. III. 538.[1]
Hederström, Hans. Näsby socken i Östergötland. 1757. IV. 344.[1]
Hedeselskabet. 1868. IV. 39.[2]
Fra **Hedeselskabets** Bestyrelse. 1877. IV. 39.[1]
Hedeselskabets Tidsskrift. IV. 5.[2]
Hedges. 1874. III. 213.
Hedges. A premium offered. 1855. III. 213.
Hedges for exposed situations. 1874. III. 213.
Hedin, G. Beskrifning öfver Kräklinge socken. 1754. IV. 344.[1]
Hedin, Sveno Andreas. Quid Linnæo patri debeat medicina. 1784. III. 238.[1]
Hedinger, A. Der Oelbaum. 1886. III. 679.[1]
Hedler, (*Kunstgärtner, Leipzig*). Methode einer schnellen Ansucht der Orangenbäume. 1839. III. 499.[3]
— Über Xanthochymus pictorius Roxb. 1839. II. 555.[2]
Hedley, C. Uses of some Queensland plants. 1889. III. 94.[1]
Hedrén, Adam. De nutritione plantarum. *See* THUNBERG, C. P. 1819. I. 157.
Hedrén, Elis. Examen classis polygamiae. *See* THUNBERG, C. P. 1825. I. 251.
— *See also* FLODBERG, J. E. & HEDRÉN, E.
Hedrich von Wiederhold, E. De groene Koffieluis. 1899. III. 737.
Hedrick, U. P. Tree planting in Utah. 1899. III. 118.[1]
— & others. Prunes in Oregon. 1897. III. 433.[1]
Hedwig, Johann. Von den Ausdünstungswegen der Gewächse. 1793. I. 166.
— Ueber das Bemoosen der Bäume. 1793. III. 193.[1]
— Ueber die beste Methode die Bäume gegen das Erfrieren zu sichern. 1797. III. 182.
— De fibrae vegetabilis et animalis ortu. 1789. I. 32.
— Kann man von dem . . . Abfall der Blätter . . . auf die Strenge . . . des . . . Winters schliessen. 1797. I. 191.[1]
— On the organs of perspiration of plants. 1793. I. 166.
— Sammlung seiner zerstreuten Abhandlungen. 1793. I. 32.
— Vom Stamme der Gewächse. 1797. I. 104.
— Vorschlag, die gänzliche Verwüstung der Tangelwälder von der Kienraupe zu verhüten. 1797. IV. 205.[3]
— Was sind die Blätter und blattartige Uebersüge. 1797. I. 172.
— In wieferne ist die unechte Acacie vermögend, dem Brandhols-Mangel zu steuern? 1797. IV. 522.[1]
Hedwig, Romanus Adolf. Aphorismen über die Gewächskunde. 1800. I. 84.
— Genauere . . . Beschreibung verschiedener Gewächse. 1803. II. 351,[1] 412.[1]
— Genera plantarum. 1806. I. 259.
— Observationum botanicarum fasciculus. 1802. I. 33.
Heeckeren, C. W. van. De Bandoengsche Kininefabriek'. 1899. III. 718.
Heeckeren, G. P. C. van. Over den aanleg en bewerking van woeste gronden. 1836. IV. 159.

Heede, Ad. van den. Acacia platyptera. 1889. III. 463.[2]
— Beaufortia purpurea. 1889. III. 633.[1]
— Les bonnes vieilles plantes. 1889. III. 383,[4] 463,[3] 633.[1]
— Bouturage à l'envers. 1900. III. 158.
— Grevillea Preissi. 1889. III. 383.[1]
— Griselinia macrophilla. 1893. III. 646.[2]
— À propos de la fleur de l'Aristolochia gigas Sturtevanti. 1896. III. 386.[1]
— À propos du Gardenia Stanleyana. 1899. III. 747.[1]
— Rhododendron rubricaule. 1890. III. 662.[1]
Heede, Georges van den. Le Cacaotier. 1892. III. 593.[1]
Heede, Manuel de OSSUNA Y VAN DER. See OSSUNA Y VAN DER HEEDE, Manuel de.
Heer, J. J. BLUMER-. See HEER, Oswald & BLUMER-HEER, J. J.
Heer, Oswald. Analytische Tabellen zur Bestimmung der ... Pflanzengattungen der Schweiz. 1840. I. 434.
— Beiträge zur Pflanzengeographie. 1835. I. 434.
— Der botanische Garten zu Zürich. 1853. I. 65.[1]
— European and North American trees. 1852. III. 131.[2]
— Flora der Schweiz. See HEGETSCHWEILER, Johann. 1840. I. 434.
— Über die Föhren-Arten der Schweiz. 1862. II. 39.[2]
— Zur Geschichte der Ginkgo-artigen Bäume. 1881. II. 7.[2]
— Holzzucht der schweizerischen Gebirgsgegend. 1843. IV. 123.[b]
— Instruction pour la destruction du hanneton. 1843. IV. 202.
— Madeira. 1852. I. 497.
— Ueber die nivale Flora der Schweiz. 1884. I. 437.
— Ueber die obersten Grenzen des ... Lebens in den Schweizeralpen. 1845. I. 434.
— Passiflora Lowei Heer. 1852. II. 579.[1]
— Ueber die periodischen Erscheinungen. 1851. I. 228.[1]
— Pflanzenreste der Pfahlbauten. 1864. I. 242.[1]
— Quelques mots sur les Noyers. 1857. II. 111.[2]
— Der Rentori-Garten in Funchal. 1852. I. 69.[1]
— Über Vaterland und Verbreitung der nützlichsten Nahrungspflanzen. 1847. I. #41,[2] III. 126.[2]
— Die Vegetationsverhältnisse des südöstlichen Theils des Cantons Glarus. 1836. I. 434.
— Ueber Vertreibung und Vertilgung der Laubkäfer. 1843. IV. 202.
— Über die Wallnussbäume. 1857. II. 111.[2]
— & Blumer-Heer, J. J. Über den Kanton Glarus. 1846. I. 434.
— & Regel, Eduard. Index seminum Horti botanici turicensis. 1850. I. 65.[1]
Heer, Otto. Das Kniehols, Pinus Pumillo, betreffend. 1862. IV. 464.[3]
Heering, W. C. A. Über die Assimilationsorgane der Gattung Baccharis. 1899. II. 852.[2]
Heerwagen, (*Kreisforstmeister*). Ueber Waldwerthberechnung. 1859. IV. 255.
Heerwagen, Fritz. Ueber Coniferen und deren Erziehung. 1837. III. 294.[1]
Hees, H. B. van. Antwoord op eenige vragen betreffende het in cultuur brengen van eene Koffie-onderneming. 1874. III. 729.[2]
— Een woord over gouvernements- en particuliere Koffiekultuur. 1873. III. 729.[2]
Heesch, Theodor. Beitrag über die Veredelung der Coniferen. 1851. III. 294.[1]
— Blick auf die Vegetation von Sierra Leone. 1940. I. 490.
Heese, Emil. Cereus amecaensis Heese. 1897. II. 589.[2]
— Echinocactus Grusonii. 1897. III. 622.[1]
Hefele, Carl. Ueber den Einfluss starker Durchforstungen. 1896. IV. 175.[1]
— Ueber den Einfluss verschiedener Durchforstungsgrade. 1897. IV. 176.[1]
— Der Einfluss verschiedener Durchforstungsgrade auf ... Fichtenbestände. 189.? IV. 454.
— Neue Art der Abfeuerung von Sprengschüssen. 1898. IV. 387.[1]
— Neue Bremsvorrichtungen an Handschlitten. 1896. IV. 90.[1]
— Ein Steigapparat. 1896. IV. 172.[2]
— Untersuchungen über die Einwirkung verschiedener Durchforstungsgrade auf ... Fichtenbestände. 1895. IV. 458.
— Die Urichsche Zündnadelsprengschraube. 1894. IV. 387.[1]
— Die Weghauten im kgl. bayr. Forstamte Marquartstein. 1896. IV. 267.
— Der Zehnpfundsche Steigrahmen. 1894. IV. 172.[3]
Heffter, Arthur. Sur les alcaloïdes dés Cactées. 1898. III. 620.[3]
— Ueber Pellote. 1894. III. 620.[2]

Hefti, Thomas. Bemerkungen und Rathschläge zu einem geregelten forstwissenschaftlichen Betriebe. 1859. IV. 166.[2]
Hegardt, Cornelius. Ficus ejusque historia. See LINNÉ, Carl von. 1744. II: 148.[2]
Hegelahr, N. Forlystelser i Heederne. 1788. I. 93.
Hegelmaier, Christof Friedrich. Über androgyne Blüthenstände von Salix. 1866. II. 103.[3]
— Ueber Blüthenentwicklung bei den Salicineen. 1880. II. 96.[1]
— Untersuchungen über die Morphologie des Dikotyledonen-Endosperms. 1885. I. 122.
— Vergleichende Untersuchungen über Entwicklung dikotyledoner Keime. 1878. I. 122.
Heger, (*Förster, Schmiedeberg*). Ueber den Einfluss der Anbaumethode auf ... den Ertrag der Fichte. 1887. IV. 454, 473.
Heger, (*Oberförster*). Zur Frage der Bestimmung des Hiebssatzes. 1887. IV. 245.
Heger, Jens Stephan. Abbildninger af danske oeconomiske Planter. 1828. III. 67.[1]
— Herbarium pharmaceuticum. 1822. III. 67.[1]
Hegetschweiler, Johann Jacob. Beyträge zu einer kritischen Aufzählung der Schweizerpflanzen. 1831. I. 434.
— Flora der Schweiz. 1840. I. 434.
— Flore des plantes vénéneuses de la Suisse. 1849. III. 89.[2]
— Die Giftpflanzen der Schweiz. 1827. III. 89.[2]
— Ueber die helvetischen Arten von Rubus. 1827. II. 304.[1]
— Sammlung von Schweizerpflanzen. 1826. I. 433.
— Versuch über die helvetischen Arten von Rubus. 1829. II. 304.[1]
— Versuch zur Beantwortung der ... Fragen, die Verwüstungen der Obstbäume durch Insekten betreffend. 1833. III. 188.[2]
— Verzeichniss seltener schweizerischer Pflanzen. 1838. I. 434.
Hegler, Robert. Ueber den Einfluss des mechanischen Zugs auf das Wachsthum. 1893. I. 188.[1]
— Histochemische Untersuchungen verholzter Membranen. 1890. I. 126.
— Tallin, ein neues Holzreagens. 1889. I. 37.[1]
Hegner, J. U. Dissertatio Amygdalarum fructus analysin exhibens. See ZWINGER, Theodor. 1703. III. 434.[1]
Hehl, Rudolph Alexander. Von den vegetabilischen Schätzen Brasiliens. 1886. III. 269.[1]
Hehn, Victor. Cultivated Plants and domestic animals. 1870. I. 242.[1]
— Kulturpflanzen und Hausthiere. 1870. I. 242.[1]
— Piante coltivate ed animali domestici. 1870. I. 242.[1]
— The wanderings of plants and animals. 1870. I. 242.[1]
Hehner, Otto. La caféine des feuilles du Caféier. 1880. III. 740.[2]
Heiberg, Axel. Skogsagen, med billeder fra Strand. 1900. IV. 344.[1]
Heicke, C. Alleebäume oder Strassenbäume? 1899. III. 210.
— Die Baumpflanzungen in Strassen der Städte. 1896. III. 210.
— Erfahrungen mit Strassenbäumen. 1900. III. 210.
— Frühjahrspflanzung. 1897. III. 169.[1]
Heicke, Johann Heinrich. Organismus der Staats-Forst-Wirthschaft. 1832. IV. 288.[1]
Heide antginning in Sleeswijk-Holstein 1895. IV. 159.
Der Heidelbeerstrauch ... ein Gerb-Material. 1838. III. 664.[1]
Heidelberg — Naturhistorischer-medicinischer Verein. See NATURHISTORISCHER ... I. 13.
Heiden, Eduard. Die Düngerlehre. 1875. III. 151.
— Lehrbuch der Düngerlehre. 1866. III. 151.
Heiden, Heinrich. Anatomische Charakteristik der Combretaceen. 1893. II. 615.[3]
Heidenreich, (*Dr.*). Das Artrecht der Salix dasyclados. 1874. II. 106.[2]
— Das Artrecht des Rubus suberectus And. 1873. II. 310.[2]
Heider, Adolf. Einiges über die Vegetationsverhältnisse Pamphyliens. 1885. I. 479.
Heidler, Josef. Eine Präcisions-Baummesskluppe. 1889. IV. 231.[2]
Heider, Karl Joseph. Pflanzen und Gebirgsarten von Marienbad. 1837. I. 440.
Heiges, S. B. Tree planting for shade, shelter and profit. 1878. III. 117.[1]
Height of Australian trees. 1868. I. 298.[1]
On the heights of mountains, etc. in Norway. 1845. I. 354.
Heijningen, J. van. Bidoeriwol. 1851. III. 692.[1]

Heijting, J. Gids betreffende de gouvernements Koffiecultuur. 1887. III. 730.
— Handleiding voor de gouvernements Koffiecultuur. 1887. III. 730.
Heike. Das Ablactiren oder Absäugeln. 1850. III. 548.[1]
— Ueber Veredelung des Weinstocks durch Oculation. 1850. III. 548.[1]
— Die Veredelung des Weinstocks durch Stufenpfropfen. 1850. III. 548.[1]
— Ueber die Vermehrung der Gewächse durch Absenken. 1851. III. 159.[1]
— Ueber Vermehrung des Weinstocks. 1850. III. 548.[1]
Heilmann. Schreiben . . . das Hartriegeloel betreffend. 1804. III. 646.[1]
Heilpern, M. Jak żyją rośliny. 1891. I. 92.
— Zasady botaniki. 1899. I. 92.
Heilprin, Angelo. Floras de las regiones templadas y alpinas de los grandes volcanes de México. 1892. I. 332.
— Observations on the flora of northern Yucatan. 1891. V. XVIII.[1]
— The temperate and alpine floras·. . . of Mexico. 1892. I. 332.
Heim, Albert. Ueber Bergstürze. 1882. IV. 187.[1]
— Ueber die Verwitterung im Gebirge. 1879. I. 228.[3]
— & Buss, Ernst. Der Bergsturz von Elm. 1881. IV. 187.[1]
— Du Pasquier, L. & Forel, F. A. Die Gletscherlawine an der Altels. 1895. IV. 188.[2]
Heim, Frédéric. "Balanocarpus acuminatus." 1894. II. 559.[2]
— Deux Richetia nouveaux. 1891. II. 559.[2]
— Développement des vrilles des Smilax. 1892. II. 85.[1]
— Sur une Diptérocarpée aberrante. 1892. II. 560.[1]
— Diptérocarpées nouvelles de Bornéo. 1891. II. 559.[1]
— Sur divers cas d'imbrication et leur explication mécanique. 1894. I. 116,[1] II. 804.[1]
— Sur les faisceaux staminaux des Citrus. 1892. II. 401.[2]
— Sur des fleurs monstrueuses de Fuchsia. 1890. II. 643.[2]
— Sur le genre Leitneria Chapm. 1891. II. 111.[3]
— Sur le genre Pierres. 1891. II. 560.[2]
— Sur un nouveau genre de Diptérocarpacées, Vateriopsis. 1892. II. 561.[1]
— Organogénie florale du "Diospyros Lotus." 1895. II. 702.[1]
— L'ovule de l'Erythroxylon Coca. 1894. II. 394.[1]
— L'ovule de l'Illicium anisatum. 1891. II. 210.[2]
— Sur la polyembryonie chez . . . "Kopsia." 1896. I. 122, II. 787.[1]
— Quelques faits relatifs à la capture d'insects par des fleurs d'Asclépiadacées et d'Apocynacées. 1893. II. 722,[2] 736.[1].
— Recherches sur les Diptérocarpacées. 1892. II. 559.[1].
— Remarques sur les Ancistrocladus. 1892. II. 584.[2]
— Sur un Strophantus entrant dans . . . poison des Moys. 1894. II. 732.[2]
— Sur un type nouveau de Diptérocarpacées. 1893. II. 560.[2]
— Sur un type nouveau de Diptérocarpées. 1890. II. 560.[1]
Heim, Georg Christoph. Deutsche Flora. 1799. I. 375.
— Systematische Classification . . . der Kirschensorten. 1819. III. 431.[2]
Heimans, E. Knoppen. 1897. I. 109.[1]
— Tabel tot het bepalen van boomen en heesters gedurende de wintermaanden. 1897. I. 294,[2] IV. 84.[2]
— Een twygen-collectie. 1899. I. 295.[1]
Die Heimat der süssen Eberesche. 1896. III. 459.[2]
Heimburg, E. von. Beitrag zur Frage der Beforstung öder . . . Sand- und Moorflächen. 1884. IV. 158.
Heimerl, Anton. Beiträge zur Anatomie der Nyctaginaceen-Früchte. 1889. II. 190.[2]
— Beiträge zur Flora Nieder-Oesterreichs. 1882. II. 106.[1]
— Beiträge zur Systematik der Nyctaginaceen. 1897. II. 190.[1]
— Zur Beseitigung der Chlorose. 1891. III. 181.[1]
— Die Bestäubungs-Einrichtungen einiger Nyctaginaceen. 1888. II. 190.[2]
— Ueber Bougainvillea. 1887. III. 181.[2]
— Einiges aus dem Leben unserer Waldbäume. 1898. I. 2, 2.[1]
— Einiges über Blüthenbiologie. 1900. I. 239.[1]
— Über Einlagerung von Calciumoxalat . . . bei Nyctagineen. 1886. II. 190.[2]
— Floristische Beiträge. 1885. II. 348.[1]
— Monographie der Nyctaginaceen. 1900. II. 190.[2]
— Neue Arten von·Nyctaginaceen. 1890. II. 191,[1] 191.[2]
— Nyctaginaceae. 1889. II.·190.[2]

— Phytolaccaceae. 1889. II. 192.[2]
— Rubus brachystemon n. sp. 1882. II. 306.[2]
— Ueber die Schutzmittel der Pflanzen gegen Schneckenfrass. 1889. I. 235.[2]
— Ueber Symbiose. 1891. I. 234.[1]
Hein, Heinrich. Deutschlands Giftpflanzen. 1880. III. 73.
Hein, K. Picea·excelsa Lk. var. virgata. 1899. III. 305.[2]
Heine, H. Ueber die physiologische Function der Stärkescheide. 1885. I. 140.[2]
Heine, Johann Friedrich Ernst. De medicamentis vegetabilibus adstringentibus. 1785. III. 244.
Heinecken, Karl Heinrich von. Nachricht . . . einer vollständigen Sammlung von Obst-Sorten. 1803. III. 70.
Heineken, L. C. A. Einwirkung des Winters 1860-61. 1861. III. 45.
Heinemann, Carl. Bodenrente, Bodenzins . . . gewinn. 1892. IV. 258.
— Ueber den Ertrag der Obstbaumzucht im Walde. 1891. IV. 134.[2]
— Die Obstbaumzucht im Walde. 1885. IV. 134.[2]
— Die Soolweidenbestände. 1887. IV. 488.[1]
— Die Ueberschwemmungen der Saalaue. 1883. IV. 185.[1]
— Ueber die Verjüngung gemischter Buchenhochwaldbestände. 1887. IV. 495.
Heinemann, F. C. Boehmeria argentea. 1861. III. 382.[1]
— Cissus antarctica. 1861. III. 544.[1]
— Clematis; die ausdauernde Waldrebe. 1876. III. 389.[1]
— Der Epheu. 1866. III. 642.[2]
— Die Pflege der Obstbäume. 188 . ? III. 176.[2]
— Selinum decipiens. 1862. III. 644.[2]
— Vitis vinifera fol. var. 1864. III. 584.[1]
Heinig, R. L. Blind root-suckers of the Sunderbans. 1893. I. 171.
— Forest manual of the Andamans. 1900. IV. 100.[1]
— Glossary of the botanic terms. 1899. I. 71.
Heinke, Franz, Freiherr von. Beiträge zur Behandlung . . . der Fruchtbäume. 1798. III. 146.[1]
Heinrich, Herzog von Würtemberg. Einige Erfahrungen in Betreff der elektrischen Anziehungskraft der Bäume. 1829. IV. 193.[2]
Heinrich, Conrad. Die Kultur der Weinrebe. 1880. III. 553.[1]
— Die verschiedenen Methoden, kahle Stellen an Aesten der Formbäume auszufüllen. 1881. III. 138.
Heinricher, Emil. Die Anatomie als Wegweiser für richtige Cultur der Pflanzen. 1884. III. 37.[2]
— Beiträge zur Pflanzenteratologie. 1883. II. 106.[1]
— Ueber einige im Laube dikotyler Pflanzen trockenen Standortes auftretende Einrichtungen. 1885.· I. 110.
— Histologische Differenzierung der pflanzlichen Oberhaut. 1887. I. 129.[2]
— Über isolateralen Blattbau. 1884. I. 110.
— Die Teratologie als Behelf der phylogenetischen Forschung. 1882. I. 249.[2]
Heinrici, De usu corticis Chinae febrifugo. 1713. III. 719.
Heinsius, H. W. Bijdrage tot de kennis der bestuiving. 1890. I. 239.[2]
— Eenige waarnemingen en beschouwingen over de bestuiving van bloemen. 1892. I. 239.[2]
Heinsius, Johann Samuel. De opobalsamo. See SLEVOGT, J. H. 1717. III. 510.[2]
Heintl, Franz, Ritter Edler von. Unterricht über die Obstbaumzucht. 1810. III. 146.[1]
— Der Weinbau des österreichischen Kaiserthums. 1821. III. 558.[1]
Heintz. Eine wahrscheinlich neue Varietät der Rothbuche. 1828. II. 126.[2]
Heints, W. Recherches sur le suc laiteux de l'Arbre de la vache. 1845.· III. 367.[2]
Heintze, Aug. Tre nya skånska former. 1900. II. 245.[1]
Heinzel, Gustav. Einige Notizen über den Saftlauf. 1852. IV. 64.[1]
— De Macrozamia Preissii. 1844. II. 6.[2]
Heinzelmann, F. Die Krankheit der Obstbäume. 1883. III. 179.
— Kurze Anleitung zur Vertilgung der Blutlaus. 1885. III. 427.[2]
Heinzen, Joseph. Die Forst-Verwaltung in .Frankreich. 1808. IV. 299.
Heinzerling, Christian. Die Conservirung des Holzes. 1885. IV. 420.
Heinzerling, F. Die Formen der Pflanzen. 1855. I. 109.[2]·

Heisch. Cacaos, résultats d'analyses. 1879. III. 595.[1]

Heisch, Ch. Falsification du Séné. 1889. III. 470.[2]

Heise, R. Zur Kenntniss des Heidelbeerfarbstoffes. 1894. III. 664.[1]

— Untersuchung des Fettes von Stearodendron. 1895. II. 553.[1]

Heiss, Ludwig. Die Art der Abfindung bei der Ablösung von Forstservituten. 1878. IV. 285,[2] 333.

— Das Auftreten der Nonne. 1890. IV. 200.

— Beitrag zu der Frage: "Kann und darf die Staatsforstwirthschaft keine andere sein als die Privatforstwirthschaft?" 1873. IV. 288.[1]

— Betrachtungen über die Umwandlung von reinen Buchenbeständen. 1881. IV. 137,[2] 495.

— Durchforstungs-Theorie und Praxis. 1886. IV. 174.

— Das Enteignungs-Princip und die Schutzwaldfrage. 1882. IV. 274.[1]

— Das Forstgesetz für das Königreich Bayern. 1885. IV. 319.[1]

— Forstliche Reiseerinnerungen. 1894. IV. 174.

— Gedanken über unseren dermaligen Hochwaldbetrieb. 1874. IV. 129.

— Der Hagenauer Forst. 1872. IV. 349.[2]

— Das Holz und seine Ersatzmittel. 1883. IV. 426.[2]

— Die Organisation der bayer. Forstverwaltung. 1877. IV. 289.[1]

— Studien über Schutzholz. 1874. IV. 139,[1] 170.

— Verdient die horst- und streifenweise oder die Einzeleinsprengung den Vorzug. 1882. IV. 137.[1]

— Der Wald und die Gesetzgebung. 1875. IV. 314.[1]

— Die Waldstreufrage. 1866. IV. 71.

— Welche Lehren sollen wir aus dem neuerlichen Auftreten der Nonne ... ziehen? 1893. IV. 201.

— Worin bestehen die allgemeinen Grundsätze ... zur Heranziehung von Eichenstarkholz. 1876. IV. 506.

Heisse, (Forstmeister). Ueber das Aufasten der Fichte. 1874. IV. 453.

— Pflanzenphysiologisches. 1873. II. 33.[1]

Heister, Elias Friedrich. Oratio de hortorum academicorum utilitate. 1739. I. 38.[1]

— De quartana et hydrope per corticem peruvianum curatis. 1740. III. 719.

Heister, Lorenz. De Aurantiis 1741. III. 499.[1]

— De Cydoniis. 1744. III. 423.[2]

— De foliorum utilitate in constituendis plantarum generibus. 1732. I. 250.

— De generibus plantarum ... potius augendis. 1751. III. 54.

— Index plantarum ... quas ... in hortum Academiae Juliae. 1730. I. 43.

— De manna. 1725. IV. 536.[1]

— Meditationes ... in novum systema botanicum sexuale. 1741. I. 250.

— De nominum plantarum mutatione utili ac noxia. 1741. I. 253.[2]

— De nuce Been. See BRÜCKMANN, U. F. B. 1750. III. 244.

— De Pipere. 1740. II. 93,[3] V. xxvi.[1]

— De Piperodendri arbore florente. 1744. II. 460.[2]

— De Piperodendro, arbore rarissima. 1744. II. 460.[2]

— Programma de studio rei herbariae emandando. 1730. I. 70.[1]

— Systema plantarum generale ex fructificatione. 1748. I. 250.

Heitz, E. Forstregal und Waldrente. 1878. IV. 259.[2]

Ueber den Heizwerth der Brennstoffe. 1861. IV. 413.[1]

Hejberg, P. Betragtninger over ... Gymnospermernes Blomster. 1867. V. xxv.[2]

Hekmeijer, F. Bijdrage tot de scheikundige kennis van het pijlvergif. 1865. III. 683.[1]

— Iets over Strychnos tieute. 1867. III. 685.[1]

— Nog iets over het pijlgif van Borneo. 1867. III. 683.[1]

— Vruchten, drogerijen, geneesmiddelen. 1884. III. 28,[1] 274.[2]

— See also MAYER, P. J. & HEKMEYER, F.

Hekmeyer, F. C. Over het gebruik van de bladeren van den Koffijboom. 1869. III. 739.

Hekmeyer, W. J. E. Kinazaad en nog wat. 1887. III. 716.

— Kleine kinologische mededeelingen. 1887. III. 723.

Helbig, Wolfgang. Sulle origini della vegetazione classica. 1880. I. 429.

Helbing, H. Oil of Eoodia. 1888. III. 504.[1]

Held, Christian August. De tempestivo corticis peruviani usu. 1775. III. 720.

Held, Friedrich. Zur chemischen Charakteristik des Samenmantels Macis ... speziell der sogenannten Bombay-Macis. 189.?. III. 402.[1]

Held, G. F. & Siebdrat, G. A. Criminalgesetzbuch und forststrafrechtliche Bestimmungen für das Königreich Sachsen. 1848. IV. 322.[1]

Held, J. G. van der. De Cacao cultuur in Suriname. 1891. III. 592.[1]

Held, Oskar. Die Clematis und ihre Cultur. 1887. III. 389.[1]

— Die Coniferen unserer Gärten. 1887. III. 290.

— Die im Dienste der Landschaftsgärtnerei stehenden Gehölze. 1887. III. 203.

Held, Ph. Weinbau. 1894. III. 553.[1]

Heldenberg, Fr. G. Praktische Forstkunde. 1828. IV. 97.

Heldenhielm, J. A. Försök, at Förvara unga träd för rättor om vinteren. 1761. III. 184,[1] 186.[1]

Heldmann, C. Oberhessische Flora. 1837. I. 379.

Heldreich, Theodor von. L'Attique au point de vue ... de sa végétation. 1880. I. 449.

— Beispiel von Heterophyllie ... bei Ceratonia. 1882. II. 345.[1]

— Beiträge zur Kenntniss des Vaterlandes ... der Rosskastanie. 1879. II. 113,[2] 126.[1]

— Beobachtungen ... über den Hergang der Keimung bei Phoenix. 1881. II. 73.[1]

— Bericht über die botanischen Ergebnisse einer Bereisung Thessaliens. 1883. I. 449.

— Calendarium florae Atticae. 1873. I. 449.

— Calendarium florae atticae. 1877. I. 227.[2]

— Catalogus systematicus herbarii T. G. Orphanidis. 1877. I. 66.[2]

— Einige Bemerkungen über griechische Arbutus-Arten. 1844. II. 660.[1]

— Die Flora der attischen Ebene. 1873. I. 449.

— Die Flora der Insel Thera. 1899. I. 451.

— Flore de l'île d'Égine. 1898. I. 451, V. xxiii.[1]

— Flore de l'île de Céphalonie. 1883. I. 449.

— Der Keimungsprocess bei der Dumpalme. 1880. II. 69.[1]

— Zur Kenntniss der griechischen Tannen. 1861. II. 24.[2]

— Musinitza. 1880. I. 75.[1]

— Nachträgliches über das wilde Vorkommen der Rosskastanie. 1883. II. 481.[2]

— Ueber die neue arkadische Tanne (Abies Reginae Amaliae). 1860. II. 24.[2]

— Die Nutzpflanzen Griechenlands. 1862. III. 91.[1]

— Pflanzen der attischen Ebene. 1873. I. 449.

— Phänologische Notizen aus Griechenland. 1862. I. 227.[2]

— See also ΧΕΛΔΡΑΪΧ, Θεόδωρος.

Heldring, L. J. De behandeling van den Kaspischen Wilg. 1876. III. 351.[1]

— Salix acutifolia. 1878. III. 351.[1]

Helfer, Johann Wilhelm. Experiments on various trees in Assam. 1838. III. 228.[2]

— Gedruckte ... Schriften über die Tenasserim Provinzen. 1859. III. 278.

Helferich, Johann Alfons Renatus von. Die Forstwirthschaft. 1886. IV. 102.

Helg, Franz Joseph. De botanices systematicae in medicina utilitate. 1770. III. 238.[1]

Helguero, A. de. Un comune rurale modelio. 1899. IV. 309.[1]

— L'Istituto forestale di Vallombrosa. 1898. IV. 35.[2]

— Necessità dei rimboschimenti. 1898. IV. 166.[2]

Helie. Sisteme de M. Linnaeus. 1750. I. 257.

Helin, Arthur. Influence du sujet sur la greffe. 1888. III. 40.

— Invloed van den stam op de griffel. 1888. III. 40.

Helios. See NATURWISSENSCHAFTLICHER VEREIN DES REGIERUNGSBEZIRKES FRANKFURT.

Hellant. Om förekomsten af Tallbötter. 1748. II. 46.[1]

Hellbom, Pehr Johan. Förteckning på phanerogamer ... i Österåkers socken. 1851. I. 355.

Hellenike georgia. See ΕΛΛΗΝΙΚΗ γεωργία.

Hellenius, Carl Niclas. Anmärkningar vid fruktbärande buskars skötsel. 1789. III. 134.[1]

— Beskrifning på ett nytt örteslägte ... Hisingera. 1792. II. 574.[1]

— Beskrifningar öfver tvänne särskilde växter hörande til ört-slägtet Turraea. 1788. II. 422.[1]

— De Evonymo. 1786. II. 467.[2]

— Om Finska allmogens nödbröd. 1782. III. 219.[1]

— Förtekning på finska medical-växter. 1773. III. 68.[1]

Hellenius, Carl Niclas (*continued*).
— De Hippophaë. 1789. II. 607.²
— Hortus Academiae aboënsis. 1779. I. 41.
— Hypericum. *See* LINNÉ, Carl von. 1776. II. 555.²
— Specimen calendarii florae . . . aboënsis. 1786. I. 223.²
— Strödde anmärkningar rörande fruktträns skötsel i Finland. 1789. III. 134.²
Heller, (*Oberförster, Dombrowka*). Einige Worte über die . . . Empfindlichkeit der Fichte. 1841. IV. 452.²
— Um geschlossene . . . Ellern-Bestände . . . zu erlangen. 1843. IV. 488.²
Heller, A. Arthur. Botanical explorations in southern Texas. 1895. I. 326.
— Catalogue of North American plants. 1898. I. 308.
— Corrections and additions to the flora of Minnesota. 1898. V. XVIII.¹
— New and interesting plants from western North America. 1898. I. 327.
— A new Ribes from Idaho. 1897. II. 245.²
— Notes on plants of New Mexico. 1897. II. 241.²
— Observations on the . . . plants of the Hawaiian Islands. 1897. I. 510.¹
— Some changes in nomenclature. 1900. I. 308.
— *See also* SMALL, J. K. & HELLER, A. A.
Heller, F. A. Ueber die sogenannte Drehung der Bäume. 1871. I. 107.¹
Heller, Franz Xaver. Flora wirceburgensis. 1810. I. 376.
— Organa plantarum functioni sexuali inservientia. 1800. I. 114.¹
Heller, Karl Bartholomaeus. Botanika dla szkól. 1870. I. 91.
— Mexikanische Palmen. 1854. III. 319.¹
— Reise-Bericht aus Mexico. 1847. I. 331.
— Reisen in Mexiko. 1853. I. 331.
— Ueber . . . Vegetation besonders von Attika. 1863. V. 449.
— Versuch einer systematisch Aufzählung der in Mexico einheimischen . . . Nutzpflanzen. 1851. III. 264.²
Hellfeld, (*Justirath*). Die seltene Fichte bei Goslar. 1858. II. 34.¹
Hellrung, Karl Ludwig. Atlas der Weinländer in Europa. 1837. III. 551.²
— Karte des Weingebiets in den Zollvereinsstaaten. 1846. III. 552.
Hellsing, Gustaf Henrik. Cassandra calyculata funnen i Sverige. 1900. II. 662.²
— *See also* HELVIGIUS.
Hellwig, (*Forstmeister, Pirmasens*). Die im Handel vorkommenden Gerbemittel. 1883. IV. 435.
Hellwig (*Forstrat*). Welche Erfahrungen sind bei der Umwandlung von Holzbeständen zu Wiesen gemacht. 1887. IV. 245.
— *See also* TÄGER & HELLWIG.
Hellwig, (*Oberförster, Frankenstein*). Einiges über den Engerling-Schaden. 1879. IV. 203.
— Der Plänterbetrieb im Pfälzerwald. 1880. IV. 118.
Hellwig, (*Oberförster, Plietnitz*). Zur Vertilgung der grossen Kiefern-Raupe. 1878. IV. 199.²
Hellwig (*Oberforstmeister*). Die Baummesskluppe mit Registrir-Apparat. 1885. IV. 231.²
— Ergebniss der Holzsamen-Ernte. *See* ERGEBNISS . . . 1875. IV. 438.¹
— Etwas zum Anbau der Weymouthskiefer. 1885. IV. 469.
Hellwig, Christoph von. Compendiöses teutsches und lateinisches Blumen und Kräuterbuch. *See* KRAEUTERMANN, Valentin, (*pseud.*). 1716. I. 289.
— Kompendiöses lexicon exoticorum et materialium. *See* KRAEUTERMANN, Valentin, (*pseud.*). 1730. I. 290.
— Monatliche Kräuter-Lust. 1721. I. 290.
— Thesaurus pharmaceuticus. 1711. III. 248.
Hellwig, F. Resedaceae. 1891. IV. 234.²
Hellwig, M. Lodoicea sechellarum. 1900. III. 327.¹
Helm, Ervin. A magyar erdészegyletröl. 1861. IV. 41.²
Helm, P. *See* ГЕЛЬМЪ, П.
Helmersen, Gregor von. Alexander Lehmann's Reise nach Buchara. 1852. I. 456.³
— Ueber die Nothwendigkeit des Waldschutzes für die schiffbaren Ströme Russlands. 1876. . IV. 180.¹
Helmrich, Karl. Prodromus Florae suidniciensis. 1857. I. 384.
Helms, Joh. Frederiksborgs Amts Plantningsselskab. 1899. IV. 39.²
— & Oppermann, A. Bjærgfyrrens Brændværd og Vægtfylde. 1891. IV. 465.¹

Helms, O. Sydgrønlands Skove. 1895. I. 308, *IV. 76.*¹
Helms, Richard. La flore et la faune de l'Australie occidentale. 1900. V. XXIV.²
Helper, Hinton A. The turpentine and rosin interests of Georgia. 1882. IV. 467.¹
Helvetischer Almanach. IV. 13.²
Helvetius. An extract of a letter to Monsieur Duyvenvoorde. 1717. III. 396.²
Helvetius, Johann Friedrich. Berillus medicus. 1661. III. 53.
— Xystus herbarum. 1661. III. 259.¹
Helvigius. *See also* HELLWIG.
Helvigius, Christoph, (*sr.*). De studii botanici nobilitate oratio. 1666. I. 79.¹
Helvigius, Christoph, (*jr.*). De ligno brasiliensi. 1709. III. 478.¹
— Programma de ortu . . . scientiae botanicae. 1707. I. 79.¹
— De Quinquina europaeorum. 1712. IV. 535.¹
Helweg, L. Acer nikoënse og carpinifolium. 1893. III. 534.¹
— Nogle sjældnere eller nyere Busketplanter. 1896. III. 66.²
— *See also* RASMUSSEN, P. V. & HELWEG, L.
— Sjde Rønnebær. 1891. III. 459.²
— Vinteren 1892–93 og Vegetationen. 1897. III. 44.²
Helwing, Georg Andreas. Flora quasimodogenita. 1712. I. 372.
— Supplementum Florae prussicae. 1726. I. 373.
Hélye, D. Conifères cultivées au Muséum de Paris. 1854. III. 289.
— Effets de l'hiver 1854–55. 1855. III. 47.
— Emploi du Cassia floribunda. 1862. III. 471.¹
— Fructification de l'Abies Kutrow. 1852. III. 306.¹
— Fructification du Pinus excelsa. 1852. III. 307.¹
— Un mot sur le Juniperus virginiana var. pyramidalis. 1861. III. 304.¹
— Pêche Chevreuse. 1862. III. 439.²
— Viburnum dahuricum. 1869. III. 753.¹
Hemlock or Spruce gum. 1875. III. 312.¹
Hemlocks in winter. 1891. III. 312.¹
Hemmendorff, Ernst. Om Ölands vegetation. 1897. I. 358.
Hemmers, S. S. B. Geschichte des schädlichen Blüthenwicklers. 1811. IV. 91.¹
Hemmes, Nicolaus. Stirpes agri fæmsionensis. *See* FRIES, E. M. 1825. I. 353.
Hempel, (*Pfarrer, Zedlitz bei Borna*). Auszug aus einem Schreiben über Pflaumenaussaat. 1828. III. 432.²
Hempel, Charles J. New homoeopathic pharmacopœia. *See* NEW homoeopathic . . . 1850. III. 246.²
Hempel, Georg Carl Ludwig. Der pomologische Zauber-Ring. 1816. III. 174.²
Hempel, Gustav. Die Ästung des Laubholzes. 1895. IV. 172.²
— Die Elektricität im Dienste der Forstwirthschaft. 1883. IV. 384.¹
— Ein forstschädlicher Fäulnisspilz. 1888. IV. 212.
— Zur Geschichte des forstwirthschaftlichen Unterrichtes. 1895. IV. 233.
— Ein neuer Keimapparat. 1879. III. 156.²
— Eine nothwendige Reform auf dem Gebiete der Zuwachsuntersuchungen. 1880. IV. 233.
— Un nuovo fungo dannoso alle foreste. 1888. IV. 212.
— Samenbildung unter anormalen Verhaltnissen. 1880. II. 36.²
— Stainer's Keimapparat. 1877. III. 156.²
— & Wilhelm, Karl. Die Bäume und Sträucher des Waldes. 1889. I. 294,¹ *IV. 87.*¹
— — Die Bergkiefer. 1889. IV. 465.¹
— — A Douglas-fenyő. 1889. IV. 483.¹
— — Die Douglastanne. 1889. IV. 483.²
— — A Fehér Fenyő. 1889. IV. 464.²
— — A Hegyi Fenyő. 1889. IV. 465.¹
— — Die weissrindige Kiefer. 1889. IV. 464.²
Hempel, Johann Gottfried. Pharmaceutisch-chemische Abhandlung über die Natur der Pflanzensäuren. 1794. IV.
Hempel, M. C. Flora; eller, Almeengyldig Haandbog for Blomsteryndere. 1834. III. 67.¹
Hempel, S. Om Behandlingen af de danske Statsskove. 1868. IV. 288.²
Hemsley, William Botting. The Abelias. 1876. III. 748.¹
— Abutilon igneum the sam_e_ as A. insigne. 1878. II. 520.²

— The Admiralty Islands. 1885. I. 499.²
— Agapetes Manni. 1900. II. 659.¹
— Aldabra Islands. 1897. I. 482.
— An apetalous Fuchsia. 1880. II. 643.¹
— The apetalous Fuchsias of South America. 1876. II. 643.¹
— Aristolochia elegans in Africa. 1895. II. 182.¹
— Aristolochia gigas. 1891. II. 182.¹
— The Australian species of Livistona. 1892. II. 70.¹
— Bambusa heterocycla. 1879. III. 316.¹
— The Bermuda Cedar. 1883. II. 30.²
— Bermuda plants in the Sloane collection. 1883. II. 30.²
— The Bermudas. 1885. I. 336.
— Biologia Centrali-Americana. 1879. I. 330.
— Bosquejo de la geografía . . . de la flora de México. 1891. I. 332.
— Bosquejo de la historia de la exploración botánica de México. 1891. I. 80.¹
— Broussonetia papyrifera var. Billiardi. 1879. III. 368.¹
— Buddleia insignis. 1878. III. 681.¹
— The Cactaceae of the Galapagos Islands. 1898. II. 587.²
— Cactaceae of the Galapagos Islands. 1900. II. 587.²
— Calceolaria fuchsiaefolia. 1881. III. 702.²
— The Calceolarias. 1879. III. 702.²
— Ceratozamias. 1876. II. 4.¹
— Chelonespermum and Cassidispermum. 1892. II. 697.²
— The Chinese and Japanese species of Buddleia. 1889. II. 717.¹
— Colossal Fig trees. 1878. II. 149.²
— The common Fig tree. 1883. II. 151.¹
— Concerning Figs. 1886. II. 151.¹
— Coriaria terminalis. 1898. II. 454.²
— A curious Ash. 1879. III. 672.²
— Daphne Blagayana. 1878. III. 627.¹
— The Daphnes of China and Japan. 1878. III. 626.²
— Descriptions of some new plants from eastern Asia. 1895. I. 463.²
— Diagnoses plantarum . . . mexicanarum et centrali-americanarum. 1878. I. 332.
— The different races of Hydrangeas. 1875. II. 240.²
— On the dispersal of plants by oceanic currents. 1885. I. 240.²
— La distribution géographique des plantes. 1877. I. 300, III. 123.²
— Fernando-Noronha. 1885. I. 498.
— The flora of Lord Howe Island. 1896. I. 508.²
— The flora of the Azores. 1898. I. 498.
— The flora of the Tonga. 1895. I. 510.¹
— Freycinetia Banksii. 1878. III. 313.¹
— Fuchsia exoniensis. 1883. III. 640.¹
— Fuchsia triphylla Linneus. 1882. II. 645.²
— Fuchsias. 1875. III. 639.²
— The genus Clematis. 1877. III. 389.¹
— The genus Raphiolepis. 1876. III. 447.²
— The geographical distribution of plants. 1877. I. 300, III. 123.²
— Die geographische Verbreitung der Gartenpflanzen. 1877. I. 300, III. 123.²
— Glossy-leaved Laurustinus. 1879. III. 753.²
— A graceful wall or rock shrub. 1876. III. 481.¹
— Handbook of hardy trees, shrubs. 1872. III. 93.¹
— Hardy Azaleas. 1877. III. 655.
— Hardy Cacti. 1877. III. 619.
— Heveae specierum plurium analyses. 1899. II. 445.¹
— Heveae specierum plurium semina. 1899. II. 445.¹
— Hoffmannia mexicana. 1883. III. 744.²
— Holboellia latifolia Wall. 1878. III. 393.²
— Humming-birds, and the . . . Marcgraviaceae. 1880. II. 546.¹
— Hybrid Cycads. 1883. II. 4.¹
— The Hydrangeas. 1876. III. 411.¹
— Insular floras. 1894. I. 301.
— Juan Fernandes and Masafuera. 1885. I. 510.²
— Juvenile forms of Conifers. 1881. II. 28,² 52.¹
— Lebanon and its Cedars. 1876. II. 28.¹
— Leptospermum lanigerum. 1881. III. 636.
— Liquidambar trees. 1874. II. 253.²
— Mackaya bella. 1879. III. 709.²
— The Magnolias and their allies. 1875. II. 208.²
— Mascarenhasia Curnowiana. 1882. III. 689.¹
— Misletos. 1894. II. 174.¹
— The Mutisias. 1876. III. 755.²
— New and interesting plants from Perak. 1887. I. 464.¹
— New Chinese plants. 1885. I. 459.

— New Solomon Islands plants. 1890. I. 499.²
— Notes on an exhibition of plants from China. 1900. I. 460.¹
— Notes on some Chinese plants, with descriptions of a few new species. 1876. I. 459.
— Notice sur les productions végétales de l'Abyssinie. 1868. I. 488.
— Observations on a botanical collection made by Mr. A. E. Pratt in western China. 1893. I. 459.
— The Ombu. 1879. II. 193.¹
— Opuntia myriacantha. 1900. II. 597.¹
— Oreopanax Sanderianum. 1892. II. 651.¹
— Ornamental Brambles. 1880. III. 457.¹
— An outline of the flora of Sussex. 1875. I. 402.
— Outlines of the geography . . . of the flora of Mexico. 1887. I. 330.
— Panax Mastersianum. 1900. III. 643.²
— The Passion-flowers. 1876. II. 576.²
— Die Passionsblumen. 1876. II. 576.²
— Paulownia Fortunei Hemsley. 1890. II. 781.²
— Pentapterygium rugosum. 1879. III. 653.²
— Planes. 1875. II. 254.²
— The primordial Apple. 1873. II. 425.¹
— Prolonged vitality of the seeds of seashore plants. 1890. II. 528.²
— Recent botanical discoveries in China. 1889. I. 459.— 1891. III. 203.
— Recent botanical discoveries in New Zealand. 1898. I. 508.¹
— Recent writings on Palms. 1878. III. 317.
— On the relations of the Fig and the Caprifig. 1883. II. 151.¹
— Report on present state of knowledge of various insular floras. 1885. I. 301.
— Report on the botanical collections from Christmas Island. 1890. I. 481.²
— Report on the scientific results of the voyage of H. M. S. Challenger. 1885. I. 303.
— Report on the vegetation of Diego Garcia. 1887. I. 481.²
— Rhododendron cinnabarinum. 1879. III. 658.²
— Rhododendron lepidotum. 1879. III. 661.¹
— Rigid-leaved Yucca. 1877. III. 340.¹
— St. Helena. 1885. I. 488.
— The St. John's-worts. 1877. III. 610.¹
— The seed-vessels of Australian trees. 1883. I. 499.¹
— The shrubby Spiraeas with pinnately-divided leaves. 1879. III. 459.¹
— The Silver tree. 1885. II. 164.¹
— A sketch of the history of the botanical exploration of Mexico. 1886. I. 80.¹
— Some ornamental species of Hibiscus. 1879. III. 587.²
— South Trinidad. 1885. I. 498.
— The southeastern Moluccas. 1885. I. 466.
— The species of Fuchsia. 1877. II. 643.¹
— Spindle trees. 1876. III. 532.¹
— Spiraea Aitchisoni Hemsl. n. sp. 1900. II. 311.¹
— Spiraea bracteata Zabel. 1894. II. 314.²
— Sterculia mexicana. 1881. II. 538.²
— The Stuartias. 1878. II. 549.²
— Le Tambor. 1882. III. 521.²
— The "Tambor," a tree yielding purgative oil. 1882. II. 448,¹ III. 521.¹
— A tree Solanum. 1890. II. 778.¹
— The Tristan da Cunha group. 1885. I. 498.
— On two small collections of dried plants from Tibet. 1895. I. 460.²
— Varieties of Lapageria rosea. 1878. III. 337.²
— The various races of garden Fuchsias. 1876. III. 639.¹
— On the vegetable productions of Abyssinia. 1868. I. 488.
— The vegetation of Australia. 1883. I. 503.
— The vegetation of the Galapagos Islands. 1900. I. 510.²
— Weigelas or Diervillas. 1880. III. 748.²
— The White Beam, the Rowan tree. 1881. III. 459.²
— Why Figs cast their fruit. 1883. II. 151.¹
— The Yuccas. 1875. II. 86.¹
— See also COLLETT, Sir Henry & HEMSLEY, W. B.; FORBES, F. B. & HEMSLEY, W. B.; LACE, J. H. & HEMSLEY, W. B. ——— & Sharp, D. Botanical and zoological bibliography of the Lesser Antilles. 1889. I. 519.¹
— & others. Decades kewenses plantarum novarum. 1892. I. 271.¹
———.Flora of the Solomon Islands. 1894. I. 499.²
Henckel von Donnersmarck, Leo Victor Felix. Ueber Andromeda calyculata. See DONNERSMARK, Henckel von. 1819. II. 662.²

Henckel von Donnersmarck, Leo Victor Felix (continued).
— Enumeratio plantarum circa Regiomontum Borussorum. 1817. I. 376.
— Ueber Fuchsia coccinea Ait. 1807. II. 643.[2]
— Index generum. 1803. I. 79, V. ix.[2]
— Lettera sul nettario dei fiori. 1816. I. 118.[1]
— Nomenclator botanicus. 1803. I. 77, V. ix.[2]
— Zur numismatischen Botanik. 1853. I. 511.
Henckelius, Johannes Friederich. De plantis Sinensium. 1733. I. 458.
Hendecourt, vicomte de & others. Écoles à visiter. 1898. IV. 33.[1]
Hendel, Johann Christian. Index generum ad Caroli a Linné Species plantarum. 1806. I. 77, V. ix.[2]
Henderson, (Dr.). Cinchona plantations in Sikkim. 1873. III. 714.
Henderson, Al. Geschichte der Weine der alten und neuen Zeiten. 1833. III. 545.[2]
Henderson, Andrew. See HENDERSON, E. G. & Andrew.
Henderson, Archibald. Timber history from Irish bogs. 1883. IV. 359.[1]
Henderson, Edward George & Andrew. The illustrated bouquet. 1857. III. 82.
Henderson, G. G. See DOBBIE, J. J. & HENDERSON, G. G.
Henderson, George. Cultivation of the Mahogany tree. 1874. III. 513.[1]
— & Hume, A. O. Lahore to Yârkand. 1873. I. 460.[1]
Henderson, Joseph. On the structure of the stigma in Mimulus. 1841. II. 781.[1]
Henderson, L. F. The flora of the Olympics. 1891. I. 325.
— New plants from Idaho. 1900. II. 108.[1]
Henderson, Peter. Henderson's handbook of plants. 1881. III. 63.[1]
Hendricks, H. Girdled Elms. 1892. I. 207,[1] III. 364.[2]
Hendriks, A. K. De houtteelt in de gemeente voorst. 1858. IV. 119.[1]
Hendris, Arn. Jos. Essence de Santal. 1896. III. 584,[2] IV. 447.[2]
Henequen Hemp in Yucatan. 1893. III. 341.[1]
Henfrey, Arthur. Botanical and physiological memoirs. See RAY SOCIETY. I. 19.
— On the development of roots. 1859. I. 103.
— On the development of the ovule of Santalum. 1856. II. 169.[2]
— On the development of vegetable cells. 1846. I. 136.[2]
— An elementary course of botany. 1857. I. 90.
— Outlines of structural and physiological botany. 1847. I. 88.
— Recent discoveries in vegetable embryogeny. 1856. I. 122.
— On the relation of the raphe to the coats of the vegetable ovule. 1858. I. 120.
— The rudiments of botany. 1849. I. 89.
— The vegetation of Europe. 1852. I. 349.
— See also GRIFFITH, J. W. & HENFREY, Arthur.
— & others. The garden companion and florists' guide. 1852. III. 82.
—— New garden plants. 1852. III. 82.
Henke, Karol. Nauka urządzania, szacowania i oceniania lasów. 1846. IV. 240.
— Tabela miąższości wałców, służąca do obrachowania drzewa okrąglawego. 1842. IV. 223.
— See also Генько, К. Ф. Г.
Henkel, (Dr.). See SCHWARZENBACH, (Dr.) & HENKEL, (Dr.).
Henkel, Heinrich. Eine empfehlenswerte Zimmerpalme. 1897. III. 322.[1]
Henkel, Johann Baptist. Handbuch der Pharmacognosie. 1867. III. 258.
— Medizinisch-pharmaceutische Botanik. 1862. III. 58.
— Systematische Characteristik der medicinisch-wichtigen Pflanzenfamilien. 1856. III. 58.
— & Hochstetter, Wilhelm. Synopsis der Nadelhölzer. 1865. II. 13.[1].
Henkel, Johann Friedrich. Flora saturnizans. 1722. I. 520.[2]
Henkel, Jos. Ueber die Butter- und talgartigen Fette. 1864. III. 224.[2]
Henko, N. K. Beiträge zur Statistik der Forsten des europäischen Russlands. See Генько, Н. К. 1888. IV. 346.
— See also Генько, Н. К.
Henley, T. F. Notes on the Pandanus Vacoa. 1843. III. 314.[1]
Henne, A. Untersuchungen über das Wachsthum junger Fichten. 1892. IV. 70.
— Untersuchungen über die Temperatur des Bodens. 1894. IV. 60.[1]

Henne, Samuel David Ludwig. Anweisung wie eine Obstbaumschule ... angelegt ... werden soll. 1770. III. 135.
— Anweisung wie man eine Baumschule von Obstbäumen im Grossen anlegen ... solle. 1770. III. 135.
Hennebergische Wald-, Holtz- und Forst-Ordnung. 1697. IV. 319.[2]
Hennebergischer Holtz-Tax. 1697. IV. 319.[2]
Hennedy, Roger. The Clydesdale flora. 1865. I. 402, 533.
Henneguy, Félix. Effets produits par le sulfure de carbone. 1881. III. 573.
— Sur l'extension du phylloxera à Béziers. 1882. III. 573.
— Observations sur le phylloxera. 1880. III. 572.
— Sur l'œuf d'hiver du phylloxera. 1882. III. 573.
— Sur le phylloxera gallicole. 1882. III. 573.
— Sur les procédés de M. Mandon et de M. Aman-Vigié. 1883. III. 573.
— Rapport sur l'histoire naturelle de l'anthonome du Pommier. 1891. III. 428.[1]
— Résultats obtenus, dans le traitement des Vignes phylloxérées. 1881. III. 573.
— See also COUANON, Georges, HENNEGUY, Félix & SALOMON, E.
Hennepin, Louis. Description de la Louisiane. 1686. III. 263.[2]
Hennert, Carl Wilhelm. Anweisung zur Taxation der Forsten. 1791. IV. 239.
— Beiträge zur Forstwissenschaft aus der ... Geometrie. 1783. IV. 57.
— Bemerkungen auf einer Reise nach Harbke. 1792. IV. 352.
— Beyträge zur Forstwissenschaft aus der ... Geometrie. 1783. IV. 213.
— Kurze Anweisung zu einigen geometrischen Hülfsmitteln. 1789. IV. 250,[1] 263.
— Ueber den Raupenfrass und Windbruch. 1797. IV. 188.[2]
— Verzeichniss derjenigen Bäume, Sträucher ... in den Pflanzungen zu Harbke. 1792. I. 44.
Hennicke, Carl R. Vogelschutz durch Anpflanzungen. 1896. III. 215.[1]
Hennig, C. Étude chimique ... de la gomme kino. 1853. III. 485.[3]
Hennig, Carl. Beiträge zur Begründung des Einflusses der Wälder. 1872. IV. 55.[1]
Henning, Carl. Ueber die Drehung der Baumstämme. 1881. I. 107.[1]
Henning, Ernst. Die Lateralitätsverhältnisse bei den Coniferen. 1887. II. 18.
Henning, Wilhelm. Eine botanische Skizze aus Nordamerica. 1856. I. 314.
Hennings, A. Forst-Rente-Beregnung. 1842. IV. 260.[1]
Hennings, Paul. Ueber Abies Eichleri Lauche = A. Veitchii Lindl. 1890. II. 25.[1]
— Ueber eine auffällige Gallenkrankheit. 1896. III. 295.[2]
— Encephalartos Hildebrandtii. 1890. II. 6.[1]
— Erythrophloeum pubistamineum. 1889. II. 358.[1]
— Eine giftige Kaktee. 1888. IV. 593.[1]
— Der Hausschwamm. 1891. IV. 415.[2]
— Eine neue Blattfleckenkrankheit. 1897. III. 736.
— Ueber Picea Alcockiana und ajanensis. 1889. II. 34.[1]
— Die Septorialkrankheit neuseeländischer Veronicaarten. 1894. III. 704.[1]
— Ueber das Vorkommen von Bulgaria ... an lebenden Eichen. 1894. IV. 511.
Henningson. Rosa sulphurea. 1840. III. 455.[2]
Hennon, V. Géodésie pratique des forêts. 1851. IV. 264.
— Mémoire sur un projet qui tend à sp les arpenteurs-forestiers d'un droit acquis. 1842. IV. 264.
Henry, G. T. H. Beschrijving van de Koffij- en Suiker-cultuur. 1858. III. 729.[1]
Hénon, J. L. Mémoire sur le Mûrier multicaule. 1835. III. 380.[2]
— Notice sur l'établissement d'horticulture de MM. Audibert frères, à Tonelle. 1841. I. 58.
— Poirier Doux. 1842. III. 447.[1]
— Pommier Bronderelle. 1842. III. 425.[2]
— Sur quelques arbres fruitiers. 1838. III. 445.[1]
— Rapports sur les jardins ... de Lyon. 1838. III. 124.[1]
— Sur une variété de Noyers. 1835. II. 113.[1]
— Sur le Wei-Hwa. 1847. III. 488.[1]
Henri, (frère). Cours pratique d'arboriculture fruitière. 1878. III. 144.
Henri, Prince d'Orléans. Du Tonkin aux Indes. See FRANCHET, Adrien. 1898. I. 536.[1]
Henrici, Ant. Alfr. von. Weitere Studien über die Volksheilmittel. 1892. III. 270.[2]

Henrici, Ernst. Kaffeebau im Agome-Gebirge. 1900. III. 733.[1]
— Die Kokospalmen-Aufforstung in Togo. 1900. III. 323.[1]
Henricq, F. Observations critiques sur l'origine des plantes domestiques. 1869. I. 247.
Henrion de Pausey, P. P. N. Des biens communaux et de la police rurale et forestière. 1825. IV. 326.
Henriques, Julio Augusto. Catalogo da flora da ilha de S. Thomé. 1887. I. 491.
— Catalogo de plantas africanas. 1900. I. 493.
— Catalogo de plantas da Africa portugueza. 1889. I. 492.[1]
— Contribuição para a flora africana. 1900. I. 493.
— Contribuição para a flora de Portugal. 1896. I. 423.
— Contribuições para o estudo da flora d'Africa. 1886. I. 491.
— Cupressus glauca. 1885. II. 29.[2]
— Estudos phaenologicos. 1889. I. 226.[2]
— Expedição scientifica à Serra da Estrella. 1883. I. 422.
— Exploração botanica em Portugal por Tournefort. 1890. I. 422.
— Flora de S. Thomé. 1886. I. 491.
— Instrucções praticas para a cultura das plantas que dão a quina. 1880. III. 712.[1]
— O inverno de 1890 . . . em Coimbra. 1891. III. 49.[1]
— Jardim botanico da Universidade de Coimbra. 1876. I. 60.[1]
— Nota sobre a proveniencia do Cupressus glauca. 1885. II. 29.[2]
— Note sur le jardin botanique de l'Université de Coïmbre. 1880. I. 60.[1]
— Observações dos phenomenos periodicos. 1891. I. 226.[2]
— As regiões botanicas de Portugal. 1900. I. 423.
— Subsidios para o conhecimento da flora da Africa occidental. 1899. I. 492.[1]
— A vegetação da Serra do Gerez. 1885. I. 422.
Henriques, Robert. Der Kautschuk und seine Quellen. 1899. III. 232.[1]
— Über Kickxia-Kautschuk. 1899. III. 688.[2]
Henriquet, P. Algunos parasitos del Alcornoque. 1899. IV. 517.[1]
— Le bouillage du liège. 1896. IV. 435.
— La marbrure du Liège. 1897. IV. 517.[1]
— Quelques parasites du Chêne-Liège. 1899. IV. 517.[1]
— Recherches sur les canaux du liège. 1895. II. 140.[2]
Henriquez. Mémoire sur les moyens de multiplier les plantations de bois. 1789. IV. 161.[1]
— Observations impartiales sur l'aménagement des bois du roi. 1781. IV. 241.
Henry. Paeonia Moutan Neumannii Baumann. 1845. III. 392.[2]
Henry. Preuves de l'intervention des ferments organisés dans la décomposition . . . des sols forestiers. 1887. IV. 69.
Henry. See HUET & HENRY.
Henry, Aimé. Beitrag zur Kenntniss der Laubknospen. 1836. I. 107.[2]
— Etwas über Terminalknospe. 1847. I. 107.[2]
— Die Giftpflanzen Deutschlands. 1836. III. 73.
— Knospenbilder. 1847. I. 107.[2]
— & Marquart, Clamor. Ueber abnorme Bildungen des Fruchtknotens der Salix cinerea. 1837. II. 106.[1]
Henry, Augustine. Botanical expedition in Yunnan. 1897. I. 460.[1]
— Chinese names of plants. 1888. I. 73.[2]
— Chinese soap trees. 1896. III. 226.[1]
— A list of plants from Formosa. 1896. I. 463.[2]
— Notes on the flora of Formosa. 1896. I. 463.[2]
— The production of camphor in India. 1897. III. 405.[1]
Henry, B. C. Ling-Nam. 1886. III. 273.[1]
Henry, Edmond. Accroissement des arbres de réserve. 1899. IV. 132.[1] 235.[1]
— L'accroissement en épaisseur des tiges. 1891. IV. 65.[1]
— Atlas d'entomologie forestière. 1892. IV. 93.
— L'azote et la végétation forestière. 1897. I. 160, IV. 70.
— Les cendres des essences principales. 1876. I. 155, IV. 64.[1]
— Le Chêne rouge d'Amérique. 1896. IV. 516.[1]
— Le Chêne rouge en France. 1896. IV. 516.[1]
— La couverture morte des forêts. 1897. IV. 72.
— Destruction des vrillettes. 1893. IV. 209.[1]
— En   un mot sur la processionnaire du Pin. 1898. IV. 479. core
— Étude chimique sur les essences principales. 1876. I. 155, IV. 64.[1]
— Extraction du tannin du bois de Chêne. 1885. IV. 515.[1]
— Les forêts et les eaux souterraines. 1898. IV. 52.
— A Gesstenyefa tannintartalma. 1892. II. 124.[2]

— Die Gewinnung von Tannin aus Eichenholz. 1885. IV. 515.[1]
— La Grapholitha tedella. 1892. IV. 209.[1]
— Influence de l'époque d'abatage sur la production des rejets de Chêne. 1895. IV. 508.
— Influence de la sécheresse de 1893. 1897. IV. 192.[1]
— Influence de la sécheresse . . . en Lorraine. 1894. IV. 192.[1]
— Influence of the season of felling on the production of stoolshoots in the Oak. 1895. IV. 508.
— Influencia de la época de la corta en la producción de brotes de cepa de Roble. 1895. IV. 508.
— Les insectes nuisible au Canada. 1892. III. 187.
— Sur la lunure . . . du Chêne. 1897. II. 137,[1] IV. 511.
— La lutte contre l'Ocneria dispar. 1896. III. 187.
— La maladie des Platanes. 1887. III. 418.[2]
— Mise en valeur de sols pauvres par le boisements. 1899. IV. 164.[1]
— Nitrogen and forest crops. 1898. I. 160.
— Notice explicative de la carte forestière de la région. 1885. IV. 361.
— Poids et composition de la couverture morte des forêts. 1896. IV. 72.
— Sur quelques cochenilles forestières. 1897. IV. 209.[1]
— De quelques essences exotiques. 1900. IV. 127.[1]
— Un reboisement à bon marché. 1900. IV. 142, 164.[2]
— Répartition du tannin dans le bois et l'écorce du Chêne. 1899. IV. 515.[2]
— Répartition du tannin dans les diverses régions du bois de Chêne. 1887. IV. 515.[1]
— Revue des travaux de botanique forestière. 1890. IV. 2.
— Sapins et Épicéas morts de sécheresse dans les Vosges. 1896. IV. 192.[1]
— Le tanin dans le bois. 1896. I. 184.
— Du tanin dans le Châtaignier. 1892. II. 124,[2] IV. 493.[2]
— El tanino de la madera de Roble. 1885. IV. 515.[1]
— La végétation forestière en Lorraine. 1895. IV. 192.[1]
— Les vers de terre en forêt. 1900. I. 235.[1]
— See also GRANDEAU, Louis & HENRY, Edmond.
Henry, Isaac ANDERSON-. On imperfect hybridity. 1872. I. 245.
— Observations on his hybrid Primulas. 1872. II. 678,[1] III. 458.[1]
Henry, James. Reforestation. 1890. IV. 155.[1]
Henry, Louis. Arbres et arbustes attaqués par le puceron lanigère. 1897. III. 421.[1]
— Le Berberis pruinosa Franch. 1900. III. 395.[1]
— Le Buddleia variabilis. 1897. III. 681.[2]
— Cornus Bretschneideri sp. nov. 1899. III. 655.[1]
— Cotoneaster pannosa Franch. 1898. III. 421.[1]
— Le Crataegus coccinea comme sujet. 1898. III. 261.[2]
— Crossings made at the Natural history museum of Paris. 1900. I. 271.[2]
— Un Deutzia nouveau. 1894. III. 410.[2]
— Éléments d'arboriculture fruitière. 1887. III. 144.
— Entretiens sur l'arboriculture fruitière. 1884. III. 140.[2]
— Essais de greffage. 1900. III. 165.
— Étude sur les Lilas. 1899. III. 714.[2]
— Floraison simultanée de quelques arbustes. 1895. I. 226.[2]
— Les Kakis. 1900. III. 669.[2]
— Le Lilas au point de vue horticole. 1899. III. 680.[2]
— Le Lilas de Bretschneider. 1899. III. 680.[2]
— Moyen de reconnaître les sexes du Ginkgo biloba. 1899. IV. 440.[1]
— Multiplication du $Polygonum$ baldschuanicum. 1899. III. 387.[1]
— Note sur les formes intermédiaires entre Néflier et Aubépine. 1899. III. 421.[1]
— Nouveaux Lilas hybrides. 1897. III. 680.[2]
— Un Nuttallia hermaphrodite. 1896. II. 269.[1]
— Onderhoud over de fruitboomteelt. 1884. III. 140.[2]
— Le Parrotia Jacquemontiana. 1898. III. 418.[1]
— Le Peuplier de Boll. 1896. II. 96.[2]
— La Pivoine jaune. 1897. III. 392.[1]
— Plantes nouvelles. 1899. III. 655.[1]
— Le Polygonum baldschuanicum. 1895. III. 387.[1]
— The Scarlet-fruited Thorn as a stock. 1898. III. 421.[2]
— Syringa pubescens Turcz. 1900. III. 681.[1]
— Les Templetonia et les Sophora. 1893. III. 487,[2] 489.[1]
— La vénénosité des Cephalotaxus. 1891. III. 287.[1]
— Le Vitis Coignetiae. 1895. III. 584.[1]
Henry, N. E. Notice sur l'huile de Palme. 1819. III. 318.[1]
— Observations . . . de deux écorces exotiques. 1819. III. 397,[2] 613.[1]

Henry, Ossian. Examen chimique de l'huile d'Illipé. 1835. III. 667.[1]
— Notes sur le Manioc amer. 1834. III. 521.[1]
— Quelques essais analytiques sur une écorce . . . Paraguatan. 1833. III. 743,[2] 747.[1]
— See also DELONDRE, Auguste & HENRY, Ossian; DEROSNE, Bernard, HENRY, Ossian & PAYEN, J. F.
— & **Boutron-Charlard**,· A. F. Recherches sur le principe vénéneux du Manioc amer. 1836. III. 521.[1]
— & **Ollivier**, C. P. Sur le tanguin de Madagascar. 1824. III. 691.[1]
Henry, S. Nouveau moyen de destruction du ver blanc. 188 . ? III. 196.
Henry, Samuel. A new and complete American medical family herbal. 1814. III. 262.[1]
Henschel, August Wilhelm Eduard Theodor. Beobachtungen in Betreff des Sichverwandelns der weiblichen Blüthen der Salix cinerea in männliche. 1831. II. 106.[1]
— Clavis Rumphiana. 1833. I. 78.[1]
— Commentatio de Aristotele botanico. 1824. I. 292.
— Zur Geschichte der botanischen Gärten. 1837. I. 80.[2]
— Von der Sexualität der Pflanzen. 1820. I. 199.
— Ueber die Verwandlung von Pistillen in Antheren bei monströsen Weidenblüthen. 1856· II. 103.[2]
— Vorläufige Nachricht von einigen die Bestäubung der Pflanzen betreffenden Versuchen. 1829. I. 237.
Henschel, Gustav A. O. Entomologische Notizen. 1888. III. 350,[1] IV. 207.
— Erreichung einer einheitlichen Nomenclatur auf dem Gebiete der Entomologie und der Botanik. .1890. IV. 57.
— Der Forstwart. 1883. IV. 98.[1]
— Die " Grasswald- " oder " Schnaidtwirthschaft." 1876. IV. 172.[2]
— Die Insekten-Schädlinge. 1890. III. 191.
— Ist die zu Mycorhizabildungen führende Symbiose an jungen Fichtenpflanzen schädlich? 1887. IV. 456.
— Die Kropfkrankheit der Eiche. 1882. IV. 510.
— Die Lärchenknospen-Gallmücke. 1875. IV. 450.
— Leitfaden zur Bestimmung der schädlichen Forst- und Obstbaum-Insekten. 1861. IV. 210.[1]
— Leitfaden zur leichteren Bestimmung der schädlichen Forst-Insekten. 1861. . IV. 92, 210.[1]
— Ein neuer Förstschädling. 1881. IV. 456.
— Die Nonne in Rücksicht ihrer Bekämpfung. 1891. IV. 201.
— Die Rindenrosen der Esche. 1880. IV. 535.[1]
— Die schädlichen Forst- und Obstbaum-Insekten. 1861. (1895). III. 191, IV. 210.[1]
— Die Seuche der Nonnenraupe. ·1891. IV. 201.
— Tomicus Lipperti n. sp. 1885. IV. 464.[1]
— Die Vernichtung der Reblaus. 1892. III. 574.·
Hensel, Reinhold. Ueber die forstlich schädlichen Nagethiere Schlesiens. 1855. ·IV. 197.[2]
— Die forstschädlichen Nagethiere Schlesiens. 1855. IV. 197.[2]
Hensen, A. See ГЕНЗЕНЪ, А.
Hensen, Alexander H. Het bestbederf bij Cacaoboomen in Ceylon. 1898. III. 593.[2]
— The cultivation of Cocoa. 1882. III. 592.[2]
— Het kweeken der Cacao. 1882. III. 592.[2]
— Liberia-Koffie in Suriname. 1891. III. 742.[2]
Henshall, John. Ueber einige Waldbäume auf Java. 1852. I. 467.
— Memoranda from Java. 1852. I. 467.
— Notizen über einige Waldbäume auf Java. 1852. III. 91.[2]
Henshaw, Henry W.· Indian origin of maple·sugar. 1890. IV. 527.[2]
Henshaw, Samuel. Bibliography of . . . contributions to American economic entomology. 1889. III. 187. ·
— Replanting large trees. 1896. III. 168.[1]
Henslow, George. ·Floral dissections. 1879. I. 403.
— Foliage of Raspberry and Blackberry. 1889. II. 300.[2]
— The frost report on the effects of the severe frosts . . . during the winters 1879–80. 1887. III. 47.
— Hybrid Rhododendrons. 1891. III. 655.
— Medical works of the 14th century. 1899. III. 239.
— The movements of plants. 1896. I. 194.
— Note on thé structure of Genista tinctoria. 1869. II. 361.[1]
— The origin and present distribution of the British flora. 1880. I. 403.
— The origin of floral structures. 1888. I. 115,[1] 233.
— The origin of plant structures. 1895. I. 219.[1]

— On the origin of species in nature. 1898. I. 248.[1]
— On the origin of the so-called scorpioid cyme. 1880. I. 3.
— On the origin of the . . . systems of phyllotaxis. 1875. I. 102.
— The plants of the Bible. · 1895. I. 513.
— On the self-fertilization of plants. 1879. I. 238.
— The student's catalogue of British plants. 1879. I. 403.
— On vernation. 1886. I. 235.[2]
— Yew trees in Berks. 1889. II. 11.[1]
Henslow, John Stevens. British plants . . . in the parish of Hitcham. · 1851. I. 400.
— The cabinet of natural history. 1835. I. 87.
— A catalogue of British plants. · 1829. I. 397.
— Description of two new species of Opuntia. 1837. II. 595.[2]
— A dictionary of botanical terms. 1850. I. 71, III. 29.[2]
— A dictionary of English-Latin terms. 1837. V. IX.[1]
— On the disunion of contiguous layers in the wood. 1837. I. 127.[2]
— · Facts in relation to the reproductive economy of the Mistletoe.· 1833. II. 178.[1]
— Florula keelingensis. 1838. I. 465.
— A notice of the fact . . . sugar candy being produced in the flowers of Rhododendron ponticum.· 1836. II. 683,[1] III. 463.[1]
— The principles of descriptive and physiological botany. 1835. I. 87.
— Scales on a cone of the Spruce Fir. 1840. II. 35.[2]
— On variations in the cotyledons . . . of the Sycamore. 1832. II. 479.[2]
— See also MAUND, Benjamin & HENSLOW, J. S.
— & **Skepper**, Edmund. Flora of Suffolk. 1860. I. 401, V. XXI.[1]
Hensmans, Urbain. Concernant un principe cristallisable . . . du Peupher de Canada. 1839. II. 97.[1]
Hensoldt, H. C.· Tafeln über den Kubikinhalt stehender . . . Stämme. 1838. IV. 222.
Hentig, H. Ueber die Beziehungen zwischen der Stellung der Blätter zum Licht und ihrem inneren Bau. 1882. I. 110, 230.
Hentze, Wilhelm. Bemerkungen über Betula odorata. 1846. II. 117.[2]
— Zur Birkenfrage. 1847. II. 117.[2]
— Ueber einige verkannte Lindenarten. 1867. II. 515.[1]
— Weitere Bemerkungen über die . . . Birkenarten. 1848. II. 117.[2]
Henze, August. Untersuchungen über das specifische Gewicht der verholzten Zellwand. 1883. I. 138.[1]
Hepburn, F. Coffee-growing in Queensland. 1897. III. 733.[1]
Hepp. Ueber Durchforstungen. 1883. IV. 173.
— Ueber die künstliche Verjüngung der Weisstanne.· 1877. IV. 444.[2]
— Die Sumpfkiefer, Pinus uliginosa. 1883. IV. 464.[2]
— Der Weisstannenwickler. 1883. IV. 445.
Heppe, Carl von. Der sich selbst rathende Jäger. 1754. IV. 115, 316.
Heppe, Christian ·Wilhelm von. Einheimisch- und ausländischer wohlredender Jäger. 1763. IV. 22.[1]
Hérail, Jean Joseph Marc. Contributions à l'étude de l'anatomie . . . de la tige. 1885. I. 106.[1]
— Sur l'existence du liber médullaire dans la racine. 1891. I. 104.
— Note sur l'anatomie dè la tige des Strychnos. 1885. II. 720.[1]
— Recherches sur l'anatomie . . . de la tige. 1885. I. 106.[1]
— & **Blottière**, René. Note sur les affinités des Lardizabalées. 1886. II. 200.[2]
— & **Bonnet**, Valère.· Manipulations de botanique médicale et pharmaceutique. 1891. III. 259.[1]
Herald, the botany of the voyage of H. M. S. See SEEMANN, Berthold. 1852. I. 269.
Heraso, Luis. Comisión de repoblación de la cuenca del Lozoya. 1896. IV. 165, 547.[1]
— Estudio sobre la fijación de los dunas. 1890. IV. 545.[2]
— Las inundaciones del Guadalquivir. 1881. IV. 47.[2]
— Memoria acerca de la repoblación de la cuenca del Lozoya. 1895. IV. 165.
— Repoblación de la cuenca del Lozoya. 1896.· IV. 547.[1] 1898. IV. 547.[1]
Héraud, A. Nouveau ·dictionnaire des plantes médicinales. 1875. III. 59.[1]
Hérault, (jr.). Chaulage des arbres par injection. 1864. III. 197.

Hérault — Société d'agriculture du département . . . See SOCIÉTÉ . . . III. 21.
Hérault — Société d'horticulture et d'histoire naturelle. See SOCIÉTÉ D'HORTICULTURE ET DE BOTANIQUE . . . I. 23.
Hérault — Société d'horticulture et de botanique. See SOCIÉTÉ . . . I. 23.
Herb, M. Die Kokospalme. 1890. III. 324.[1]
— Pachystima Canbyi und P. myrsinites. 1891. III. 533.[1]
Herbaceous grafting. 1895. III. 163.[2]
Herbario "Bettfreund." See NIEDERLEIN, Gustav. 1898. V. XVIII.[2]
Herbarium Ammannianum. 17 . . ? I. 288.
Een herbarius. See HERBARIUS. 1484. I. 276.
Herbarius. Aggregator practicus de simplicibus. 1484. I. 275.[1] V. XIV.[2]
Herbarius su teûtsch. See ORTUS sanitatis. 148 . ? I. 275.[2]
Herbarum, arborum, fruticum. See RÖSSLIN, Eucharius. 1533. I. 277.
Herbarum imagines vivae. 1536. I. 277.
Herberger, J. E. See BUCHNER, J. A. & HERBERGER, J. E.
Herbert. Discours sur les Vignes. 1756. III. 554.[1]
Herbert, Auberon. The last bit of natural woodland. 1891. IV. 358.[2]
Herbert, Heinrich. Anatomische Untersuchung . . . der Hippomanen. 1897. II. 435.[1]
Herbert, Heinrich Nicolaus. Auszug . . . aus einer . . . Abhandlung, betreffend die Eigenschaft . . . der bittern Cassawurzel. 1780. III. 521.[1]
— De Cassavae amarae surinamensis radice. 1753. III. 521.[1]
Herbert, William. Amaryllidaceae. 1837. II. 88.[1]
— On hybridization amongst vegetables. 1847. I. 245.
Herbet, Fernand. Manuel de culture . . . du caoutchouc. 1899. III. 149.
Herbich, Franz. Additamentum ad Floram Galiciae. 1831. I. 439.
— Beiträge zur Flora von Galizien. 1860. II. 120.[1]
— Bemerkungen über den bei Krakau wildwachsenden Sarothamnus. 1861. II. 351.[2]
— Flora der Bucovina. 1859. I. 441.
— Zur Geschichte der Betula oycoviensis. 1860. II. 120.[1]
— Pflanzengeografische Bemerkungen über die Wälder Galiziens. 1860. I. 438.
— Przyczynek do geografii roślin w Galicyi. 1865. I. 441.
— Selectus plantarum rariorum Galiciae. 1836. II. 307.[2]
— Stirpes Bucovinae. 1853. I. 440.
— Ueber die Verbreitung der in Galizien . . . wildwachsenden Pflanzen. 1861. I. 441.
L'Herbier Boissier. Bulletin. Mémoires. I. 26.[2]
Herbier élémentaire. See BENOIT, Madame. 1811. III. 85.
Herbiers . . . de la République Argentine. 1889. I. 345.
Herbin de Halle, P. E. Petit manuel forestier. 1824. IV. 323.[2]
— Petit mémorial statistique et administratif des forêts. 1822. IV. 359.[2]
— Traité du cubage des bois. 1812. IV. 221.
Herbolario volgare. See HERBARIUS. 1484. I. 276, V. XIV.[2]
Herbolarium. See HERBARIUS. 1484. I. 275.[2]
Herbst, G. Die grosse Obstbäuser Fichte. 1843. II. 37.[1]
Herburger, G. von. Beschreibung der italienischen Kohlungs-Methode. 1812. IV. 394.
Herculais, Jules KÜNCKEL D'. See KÜNCKEL D'HERCULAIS, Jules.
Herder, Ferdinand Gottfried Theobald Maximilian von. Acer platanoides L. β rubrum. 1867. III. 535.[1] — 1871. III. 365,[1] 535.[2]
— Bemerkungen über die wichtigsten Bäume . . . des K. botanischen Gartens in St. Petersburg. 1864. I. 223.[2]
— Beobachtungen über das Wachsthum der Blätter. 1886. I. 190.[2] — 1893. I. 191.[1]
— Die Blüthenzeiten in St. Petersburg im Frühling 1891. 1891. I. 224.[2]
— Ueber den Einfluss des Klima's auf die Pflanzenwelt. 1872. I. 217.
— Die ersten Periodicitätserscheinungen . . . der Freilandpflanzen bei St. Petersburg. 1873. I. 224.[1]
— Fixation de certaines plantes. 1884. I. 220.
— Die Flora des europäischen Russlands. 1892. I. 366.
— Fontes florae rossicae. 1881. I. 3.[1]
— Labiatae, Plumbagineae . . . in Sibiria orientali collectae. 1887. I. 456.
— Lobeliaceae, Campanulaceae : . . in Sibiria orientali collectae. 1871. I. 456.
— Mittheilungen über die periodische Entwicklung der Pflanzen . . . zu St. Petersburg. 1863. I. 223.[2]

— Die periodische Pflanzenenentwicklung bei St. Petersburg. 1872. I. 224.[1]
— Die periodischen Erscheinungen des Pflanzenlebens bei St. Petersburg. 1868. I. 223.[2]
— Phänologische Beobachtungen bei St. Petersburg. 1880. I. 224.[1]
— Phaenologische Mittheilung. 1886. I. 224.[1]
— Plantae Raddeanae apetalae. 1889. I. 456.
— Plantae Raddeanae monopetalae. 1864. I. 455.
— Die in St. Petersburg befindlichen Herbarien und botanischen Museen. 1893. I. 42.
— Systematisch geordnete Uebersichtstabelle über die periodische Entwicklung. 1870. I. 224.[1]
— Tetratheca ciliata Lindl. 1866. III. 513.[2]
— Vegetationszeiten zu Blieskastel. 1895. I. 225.
— Vegetationszeiten zu Grünstadt. 1893. I. 225.
— Vergleichende Tabelle über die . . . Blüthezeit der wichtigsten Bäume. 1871. I. 222.[2]
— Vergleichende Tabelle über die Blüthezeit einiger Freilandpflanzen . . . St. Petersburg. 1882. I. 224.[1]
— Verzeichniss sämmtlicher botanischen . . . Gärten. 1870. I. 38.[1]
— Verzeichniss von G. Forster's Icones plantarum. 1885. I. 509.[2]
— Viburnum burejaeticum Rgl. et Herd. 1862. II. 843.[1]
— Der Winter 1870-71 und die periodischen Erscheinungen des Pflanzenlebens. 1871. I. 224.[1]
— See also REGEL, Eduard von & HERDER, F. von; REGEL, Eduard von, RACH, Ludwig & HERDER, Ferdinand von; Гердеръ, Ф. Е.
— & Höltzer, H. Systematisch geordnet Uebersichtstabelle über die periodische Entwicklung der Freilandpflanzen. 1875. I. 224.[1]
— Tempora vernationis et frondescentiae. 1875. I. 224.[1]
Herdina, László. A Beszterczebánya szab. kir. bányaváros tulajdonát képező erdőbirtok gazdasági viszonyainak ismertetése. 1895. IV. 374.[1]
Herdman, William Abbott. Handbook to Liverpool. See BROWN, Robert. 1896. I. 535.
Hereafter foloweth the knowledge, properties and the vertues of herbes. 15 . . ? I. 276.
Herefordshire orchards. See BEALE, John. 1657. III. 141.
Hereman, Samuel. Blight on flowers. 1840. III. 189.
Heresbach, Konrad. Foure bookes of husbandrie. 1578. III. 102.
— Rei rusticae libri quatuor. 1570. III. 102.
— The whole art and trade of husbandry. 1578. III. 102.
— The whole art of husbandry. 1578. III. 102.
Herger, J. Ernst. Buntblätterige Eichen. 1875. III. 363.[1]
— Verzeichniss der Eichen-Sammlung. 1875. III. 361.[1]
Herget, Wilhelm Bernhard. Beyträge zur Abwendung des Holzmangels. 1801. IV. 117.
Hergt, Johann Ludwig. Versuch einer Flora von Hadamar. 1822. I. 377.
Herholdt, Johan Daniel. See SCHUMACHER, C. F. & HERHOLDT, J. D.
Héribaud-Joseph, (frère). Analyse descriptive des Rubus du plateau central de la France. 1891. II. 303.[2]
— Plantes nuisibles . . . de l'Auvergne. 1878. III. 86.
— Quelques plantes de la flore d'Auvergne. 1878. V. XXII.[1]
— See also GUSTAVE, (frère) & HÉRIBAUD-JOSEPH, (frère).
Héricart de Thury, Louis Étienne François, vicomte. Bemerkungen über das Pfropfen der Pinus australis. 1837. III. 308.[1]
— Ueber eine Cederncultur im Park von Bologne. 1847. III. 300.[2]
— Sur les dégâts causés par les gelées du mois de mai 1839. 1839. III. 47.
— Histoire d'un vieux Chêne. 1839. II. 138.[1]
— L'If du cimetière du Molay. 1837. II. 10.[2]
— De l'influence des arbres sur la foudre. 1838. IV. 193.[2]
— Légendes du Chêne de Sant-Vigor. 1838. II. 138.[1]
— Note sur un Schubertia disticha. 1832. II. 51.[2]
— Notice historique sur la plantation de la montagne de Saint-Martin-le-Pauvre. 1829. I. 57, IV. 161.[2]
— Notice sur les bois de la Chaussée. 1837. IV. 359.[2]
— Notice sur les collections d'étude de l'École . . . de silviculture. 1838. IV. 34.[2]
— Observations sur les Araucaria imbricata de M. Kersauson. 1846. III. 298.[2]
— Observations sur les ravages exercés par les charançons des Pins sur une plantation de Cèdre. 1847. III. 300.[2]
— Pinus australis greffé. 1837. III. 308.[1]
— Programme d'un prix pour le reboisement des montagnes. 1840. IV. 161.[2]

Héricart de Thury, Louis Étienne François, *vicomte* (*continued*).
— & **Morogues**, *baron* de. Note sur les plantations d'arbres exotiques. *See* NOTE . . . 1832. III. 124.[1]
— & others. Rapport . . . sur un projet de défrichement. 1826. IV. 161.[2]
Héricourt, A. F. d'. L'Ailante glanduleux. 1861. IV. 524.[2]
— Les bois du Canada. 1861. IV. 397.
— Le Cèdre blanc. 1857. IV. 448.[1]
— De l'enlèvement des feuilles mortes. 1858. IV. 71.
Héricourt, C. F. X. ROCHET D'. *See* ROCHET D'HÉRICOURT, C. F. X.
Herigoyen, Karl d'. Wohlgemeinte Andeutungen zur Wald-' wirthschaft. 1854. IV. 118.
Hérincq, François. Acacia ixiophylla. 1851. III. 465.[2]
— De l'acclimatation. 1870. III. 43.
— Des arbres et des boutures renversés. 1860. I. 196.[1]
— Berberis Darwinii. 1867. III. 394.[2]
— Berberis macrophylla, Hookerii et Wallichiana. 1868. III. 395.[2]
— Bignonia Reveili. 1852. III. 705.[1]
— Bignonia speciosa Hook. 1850. III. 706.[2]
— Un bouquet de fleurs de Segres et notamment du Lespedeza bicolor. 1868. III. 389,[1] 481.[1]
— Bouvardia leiantha Bentham. 1851. III. 711.[2]
— Callicarpa purpurea. 1861. III. 695.[2]
— Camellia japonica Linné var. voltaveridiana. 1851. III. 598.[2]
— Le Camellia Sasanqua rosea. 1872. III. 600.[1]
— Cantua Lobbii Hérincq. 1851. III. 694.[2]
— Cassia schinifolia. 1864. III. 471.[1]
— Ceanothus nouveaux, C. papillosus. 1850. III. 541.[2]
— Cereus Roemeri Engelmann. 1865. III. 622.[2]
— Clematis indivisa var. lobata. 1853. III. 390.[2]
— Clematis lanuginosa. 1855. III. 391.[1]
— Colutea rubra. 1852. III. 473.[1]
— Considérations générales sur la culture des Cactées. 1853. III. 618.[2]
— Crowea latifolia. 1857. III. 503.[2]
— Culture et multiplication des Pivoines. 1858. III.-393.[1]
— Cydonia japonica (varietas). 1852. III. 420.[1]
— Description de plusieurs espèces nouvelles du genre Bejaria. 1850. III. 648.[2]
— Deutzia gracilis Zucc. 1851. III. 410.[1]
— Deutzia ignea. 1852. III. 410.[1]
— Diplacus grandiflorus. 1854. III. 703.[1]
— Diplacus hybrides, nouveaux. 1862. III. 703.[1]
— Dissertation sur la végétation. 1867. I. 164.
— Echinopsis Tougardii. 1853. III. 622.[2]
— Enkianthus quinqueflorus. 1859. III. 649.[1]
— Erythrina Bidwillii. 1852. III. 476.[1]
— Exochorda grandiflora. 1867. III. 424.[1]
— Forsythia viridissima. 1852. III. 672.[1]
— Franciscea confertiflora. 1852. III. 699.[1]
— Fructification naturelle d'un Chamaerops excelsa. 1869. II. 75.[1]
— Glycine frutescens var. magnifica. _1855. III. 490.[2]
— De la greffe. 1859. III. 161.
— Les Groseilliers à fleurs jaunes. 1872. III. 414.[1]
— Habrothamnus fasciculatus var. Zephirinae. 1851. III. 699.[2]
— Iochroma grandiflorum. 1863. III. 703.[2]
— Is de Klimop al dan niet schadelijk. 1857. II. 650.[1]
— Jatropha podagrica Hooker. 1858. III. 520.[1]
— Kennedya rubicunda. 1862. III. 480.[1]
— Le Kerria et le Rhodotypus. 1868. III. 424,[2] 447.[2]
— Lasiandra macrantha. 1868. III. 639.[1]
— Le Lierre est-il ou n'est-il pas nuisible. 1857. II. 650.[1]
— Le Lilas blanc d'hiver. 1887. II. 716.[1]
— Luculia gratissima. 1854. III. 745.[2]
— Mahonia japonica. 1855. III. 395.[2]
— Mastic liquide pour greffer. 1856. III. 161.
— Multiplication des Yucca. 1850. III. 161.
— De la multiplication des Yucca. 1867. · III. 339.[2]
— Mutilation des arbres des promenades. 1857. III. 211.[2]
— Il n'y a pas de sève descendante. 1867. I. 164.
— Napoleona Heudelotii Adr. de Juss. 1858. II. 612.[2]
— Note sur le Dion et le Ceratozamia. 1846. III. 284.[1]
— Observations sur les Bougainvillea. 1850. III. 388.[1]
— Observations sur les Diospyros. 1870. III. 701.[2]
— Pandanus utilis var. distichus. 1866. III. 313.[2]
— Petroea volubilis. 1858. III. 697.[1]
— L. i. t. greffer des arbres à feuilles persistantes. 1858. III. reçon 164.[2]

— **Philesia** buxifolia. 1854. III. 337.[2]
— Plantes nouvellement introduites. 1848. III. 87.
— Plantes nouvelles introduites par M. Lindige. 1866. III. 638,[2] 705.[1]
— Plantes nouvelles observées chez M. Cels. 1852. III. 622.[2]
— Pleroma elegans. 1853. III. 639.[1]
— Les Plumbago ou Dentelaires. 1864. III. 666.[2]
— Prunus chinensis flore albo pleno. 1856. III. 437.[1]
— A l'époque faut-il planter les arbres. 1859. III. 168. ᵠue le
— Rhododendron Edgeworthii. 1854. III. 658.[2]
— Rosa anemonæflora Fortune. 1849. III. 454.[2]
— Rosa Banksiæ Rob. Brown. 1851. III. 454.[2]
— Rosa portlandica. 1851. III. 456.[1]
— Rosa rugosa. 1862. III. 436.[2]
— Solanum jasminoides. 1863. III. 702.[1]
— The species of Bejaria. 1850. III. 648.[2]
— Les Spiræa, Spiræa Billardi. 1855. III. 460.[2]
— Swainsona Greyana. 1853. III. 489.[1]
— Le Symplocos japonica. 1867. III. 670.[1]
— Veronica Daniesii. 1851. III. 704.[1]
— La Vigne vierge du Japon. 1868. III. 545.[1]
— Les Weigelia ou Diervilla. 1854. III. 749.[1]
— Widdringtonia cupressoides. 1852. ·III. 299.[2]
— Yucca Treculeana. 1864. II. 88.[1]
— *See also* DUPUIS, Aristide & HÉRINCQ, François; DUPUIS, Aristide; GÉRARD, Frédéric, REVEIL, Oscar & HÉRINCQ, François; JACQUES, Antoine & HÉRINCQ, François; LAVALLÉE, Alphonse & HÉRINCQ, François; NEUMANN, Louis & HÉRINCQ, François.
— & **Gérard**, Fr. Horticulture. 1865. III. 113.
Hering. Abnorme Zweigstellung bei Tannen. 1882. ·II. 23.[2]
Hering, Arthur. Anleitung zur Holzschneidekunst. 1873. IV. 427.[2]
Hering, Constantin. Condensed materia medica. 1877. III. 243.
Hering, Franz. Über Wachsthumscorrelationen. 1896. I. 188.[1]
Hering, Johann Ernst. Discursus politicus de jure sylvae et venationis. 1665. IV. 313.
— De iure sylvae et venatione. 1765. IV. 313.
— De uva. 1666. III. 582.
Hérincq, François, *vicomte*. *See* HÉRINCQ, François.
Hérissant, E. Mœurs et destruction de l'anthonome. n. d. III. 427.[1]
Hérissey, H. *See* BOURQUELOT, Émile & HÉRISSEY, H.
Héritte. Note sur la maladie des Citronniers. 1875. III. 502.[1]
Herlach, (*k. Förster*). Berechnungstabelle des cubic Inhalts aller vorkommenden Stammhölzer. 1842. IV. 223.
Herlandt, A. The relations between the active principles, and the botanical characters of officinal plants. 1879. III. 259.[2]
Herlant, A. Étude sur les principaux produits résineux . . . des Conifères. 1876. IV. 443.[2]
Herlein, (*Oberförster*). Der Fichten-Borken-Käfer. 1878. IV. 204.
Herlitz, Johannes Nicolaus. Horti upsaliensis plantae. *See* THUNBERG, C. P. 1826. I. 40.
Herman, B. R., *Freiherr* von. The camphor industry in Formosa. 1893. III. 405.[1]
— L'industrie du camphre à Formose. 1893. III.·405.[2]
— Die Kampfer-Gewinnung in Formosa. 1893. III. 405.[1]
Hermann, Binger. The United States forest ranger system. 1899. IV. 288.[1]
Hermann, Emil. *See* FARBAKY, István & HERMANN, Emil.
Hermann, Friedrich. Ueber Behämpfung . . . des Trametes 1900. IV. 212.
— Ueber Birken-Aufastung. 1893. IV. 490.[2]
Hermann, Georg Samuel. Bibliotheca Riviniana. 1727. I. 1.
Hermann, Johann Heinrich Gottlieb. Ueber Holzgerech-tigkeiten. 1797. IV. 333.
Hermann, Leonhard David. Von den Weiden-Eich-Rosen. 1711. II. 279,[2] 349.
Hermann, Paul. Characterismi materiae medicae. 1715. I. 289.
— Cynosura materiæ medicæ. 1710. III. 241.
— Floræ lugduno-batavae flores. 1690. I. 50.
— Horti academici lugduno-batavi catalogus. 1687. I. 50.
— Materia medica. 1710. III. 241.
— Musæum zeylanicum. 1717. I. 476.[1]
— Paradisus batavus. 1698. I. 288.

Hermann, R. Ueber das fette Oel des Quittensamens. 1899. III. 423.[2]
— Sur l'huile grasse des semences de Coing. 1899. III. 423.[2]
Hermann, Sebastian. Passion-vine rearing from seed. 1900. III. 615.[2]
Hermans, Jan. Recensio plantarum in horto Joannis Hermanni. 1652. I. 49.
Hermbstaedt, (Geheimer Medizinal-Rath). Bemerkungen zu ... [Oscar Leclerc's] Aufsatze: Reifen der Obst- und Steinfrüchte. 1832. III. 173.[2]
Hermbstädt, Sigismund Friedrich. Anleitung zur Zergliederung der Vegetabilien. 1807. I. 98.
— Chemische Versuche ... über die Darstellung des Zuckers. 1799. III. 220.[2]
— Grundsätze der Experimental-Cameral-Chemie. 1808. IV. 60.[1]
— Versuche und Bemerkungen über das Keimen. 1816. I. 202.[2]
Hermens, F. P. Handbuch der in den königlich-preussischen ... Provinzen am linken Rheinufer bestehenden gesammten Forst-, Jagd- und Fischerei-Gesetzgebung. 1830. IV. 320.
Hermes, (Forstrath, Oppeln). Ueberblick über die ... Entwickelung des Holzverkaufswesens. 1898. IV. 388.[2]
Herminier, Felix Louis l'. See L'HERMINIER, F. L.
Hernandez, Francisco. Cuatro libros de la naturaleza ... de la Nueva España. 1615. III. 264.[2]
— Cuatro libros de la naturaleza ... en la Nueva España. 1615. III. 264.[2]
— Nova plantarum, animalium ... historia in Indiis. 1651. III. 264.[2]
— Opera. 1790. III. 264.[2]
— Quatro libros de la naturaleza ... en la Nueva España. 1615. III. 264.[2]
— Rerum medicarum Novae Hispaniae thesaurus. 1651. III. 264[2]
Hernquist, Pehr. Dissertatio ... genera Tournefortii. 1771. I. 257.
— Kort genwäg til naturaliers kännedom. 1795. I. 255.
Herold. Taschenbuch der teutschen Flora. 1845. I. 381.
Heron, J. S. The Australian fruit garden. 1898. III. 147.[2]
Heron, Mark. The Elm in London. 1886. III. 364.[1]
— The Plane in London. 1885. III. 418.[2]
Herquet, Lothar. Citrus. 1832. III. 497.[1]
— Meine Citrus-Sammlung. 1849. III. 497.[1]
Herr, August. Anleitung zur Botanik. 1827. I. 377.
— Ueber Bewegung in der Pflanzenwelt. 1846. I. 193.[2]
Herre. Ueber Veredlung der Orangen. 1862. III. 497.[1]
Des Herren Perrault, Charras und Dodarts Abhandlungen zur Naturgeschichte. See PERRAULT, Claude, CHARRAS, Moyse & DODART, Dionys. 1757. I. 291.
Herrera, Alfonso. Notes on the Joyote of Mexico. 1873. III. 691.[2]
— El Oyamel. 1873. III. 297.[1]
— Sinonimia vulgar y científica de algunas plantas ... en Méxluo. 1873. I. 72.[3]
— El Yoyote. 1873. III. 691.[2]
— See also MENDOZA, Gumesindo & HERRERA, Alfonso.
— & Villada, M. M. Plantas que existen en México ... para la fabricacion del papel. 1884. III. 235.[2]
Herrera, Antonio de. The general history ... of America. 1725. III. 266.
— Historia general (de las Indias ocidentales). 1601. I. 327.
— Historia general de los hechos de los Castellanos. 1726. III. 266.
Herrera, Gabriel Alonzo de. Agricoltura tratta da diversi ... scrittori. 1513. III. 114.[1]
— Agricultura general. 1513. III. 114.[1]
— Cultivo de árboles. 1777. IV. 122.[2]
— Libro de agricultura. 1513. III. 114.[1]
— Libro di agricoltura. 1513. III. 114.[1]
— Obra de agricultura. 1513. III. 114.[1]
Herreros, Juan. Guardería forestal. 1900. IV. 554.[1]
— El servicio forestal en las islas Filipinas. 1891. IV. 554.[1]
Herrfeld, C. E. Ist die Forstwirthschaft der Privaten von allen Fesseln der Forstpolizey zu entbinden? 1818. IV. 285.[2]
Herrichen, Johann Gottfried. De Thea herba doricum melydrion. 1670? III. 604.[2]
Herrick, Bertha F. The forests and meadows of Mt. Shasta. 1890. I. 325.
Herrick, Francis Hobart. Microscopical examination of wood from the buried forest. See REID, H. F. 1893. I. 311.[2]
— Notes on the flora of Abaco. 1886. I. 335.
Herrin, Charles. Conifers at Dropmore. 1892. III. 293.
— The hardy fruit garden. 1899. III. 163.[2]
— Some methods of grafting. 1899. III. 163.[2]

Herring, T. F. Directions for calculating timber. 18 .. ? IV. 220.
Herrington, A. Spiraea prunifolia fl.-pl. 1898. III. 461.[2]
Herrmann. Ueber Mäusefrass. 1900. IV. 198.[2]
Herrmann, E. Die preussischen Forstkarten. 1898. IV. 266.[1]
Herrmann, G. Fr. Botanischer Kinderfreund. 1806. I. 84.
— Kleines ... Lehrbuch der Botanik. 1806. I. 84.
Herrmann, Johann Friedrich. Calendarium, seu index plantarum ... circa Berolinum. 1810. I. 376.
Herrmann, Johannes. De Rosa. 1762. II. 281.[2]
Herrmann, M. Über Wistaria chinensis. 1881. III. 490.[2]
Herrmann, Rob. Unterirdische Bewässerung von Alleebäumen. 1900. III. 211.[2]
Die Herrschaft Béllye. See ALBRECHT főherczeg ... 1883. IV. 373.
Hersche, Johann. Ablösung von Alpholzbezugsrechten. 1899. IV. 334.[2]
Herschel, Sir J. F. W. A manual of scientific enquiry. See HOOKER, Sir W. J. 1849. I. 35.
Hersey, Edmund. The Basket Willow. 1899. III. 349.
— Facts ... relating to the White Pine. 1896. IV. 470.[1]
— Product of timber per acre. 1896. IV. 259.[1]
— Product of White Pine per acre. 1896. IV. 470.[2]
— The White Pine for timber. 1892. IV. 470.[2]
Die Herstellung der Holzwolle. 1884. IV. 429.[1]
Hertel, J. F. De eo, quod iustum est circa ius glandis legendae. 1736. IV. 313.
Hertel, M. Johann Gottlob. De plantarum transpiratione. 1735. I. 166.
Hertenstein, (Forstmeister). See LANDOLT, Elias, HERTENSTEIN & WEINMANN.
Herter, L. Mitteilungen zur Flora von Württemberg. 1888. I. 388.
Hertfordshire field club. Transactions. See WATFORD NATURAL HISTORY SOCIETY. I. 20.
Hertfordshire natural history society. Transactions. See WATFORD NATURAL HISTORY SOCIETY. I. 20.
Hertha. I. 12.
Hertling, Karl, Baron von. Die Forstwirthschaft auf Java. 1879. IV. 376,[2] 536.[2]
— Rentabiliteit der Djatibosschen. 1896. IV. 537.[2]
Hertwig, Martin. Quod felix faustumq. See FROMMANN, J. C. 168.? II. 509.[1]
Hertz. Ueber ein Paar afrikanische Giftpflanzen. 1856. III. 75.
Hertzer, H. W. Der-Anfang der Blüthe ... bei Wernigerode. 1895. I. 226.[1]
— Grenzmarken der Pflanzenentwicklung. 1895. I. 226.[1]
Hervé-Mangon, Charles François. L'arboretum de Segrez. See MANGON, Hervé. 1882. I. 59.
— Les incondations. 1887. IV. 185.[2]
— Production de la matière verte des feuilles. See MANGON, Hervé. 1861. I. 172.
— Rapport sur un mémoire de M. Alb. Le Plaz. See MANGON, Hervé. 1876. III. 150.[2]
Hervey, Eliphalet Williams. Observations on the colors of flowers. 1899. I. 185.[1]
Hervey Saint-Denys, Leon, marquis d'. Recherches sur l'agriculture et l'horticulture des Chinois. 1850. III. 127.[2]
Hervier, Joseph. Note sur le polymorphisme du Populus tremula. 1896. II. 98.[1]
— Sur quelques plantes d'Espagne. 1892. I. 422.
— Recherches sur la flore de la Loire. 1885. I. 416.
Hervorming der boschcultuur Koffiecultuur op Java. 1890. III. 730.
Herry, Michel Christophe. Catalogue méthodique et classique de tous les arbres ... de l'École impériale. 1809. I. 57, 61.
Herwech, Olof. De praestantia studii historici naturae. 1752. I. 79.[1]
Herwerden, J. D. van. De adressen der Kamers van koophandel ... tegen de concept-cultuurwet. 1866. III. 128.
— Bijdrage tot de kennis van het Tengersch-Gebergte. 1844. III. 275.[3]
— Deorganisatie ... der gouvernements-Koffij-cultuur. 1876. III. 729.[2]
Herwig, Georg. Entwurf einer Forstkunde. 1794. IV. 81.
— Nützliches Handwörterbuch für angehende Forst- und Waidmänner. See NÜTZLICHES ... 1796. IV. 22.[1]
— Wie ist die Beschaffenheit der deutschen Waldungen vortheilhaft. 1796. IV. 116,[2] 348.[1]
Héry. Le Quinquina à la Réunion. 1894. III. 717.[1]

Héry, E.   De l'Acacia de la Nouvelle Hollande.   1872.   III. 463.[1]
— Introduction de l'Acacia decurrens.   1872.   III. 465.[1]
Herzberg, W.   Adansonia-Papier.   1890.   III. 589.[1]
— Analyses qualitative et quantitative du papier.   1893.   III. 235.[2]
— Studien ·über angebliche Baumbastpapiere.   1893.   III. 235.[2]
Herseele, D. van.   Multiplication du Larix Kaempferi.   1872.   III. 309.[1]
— Voortteling van den Larix Kaempferi.   1872.   III. 309.[1]
Hersegovina — **Wissenschaftliche Mittheilungen** . . . *See* WISSENSCHAFTLICHE . . . I. 28.[1]
Herzen, A.   Giardini inglesi e giardini d'Inghilterra.   1890.   III. 123.[2]
— Rimboscamenti e inondazioni.   1890.   IV. 51.
Herzenstein, V. O.   La duración de las traviesas de madera.   1896.   IV. 557.[2]
— Les traverses de chemins de fer.   1896.   IV. 424,[1] 557.[2]
— Les traverses en bois des chemins de fer.   1896.   IV. 557.[2]
— *See also* Герпенштейнъ, B. O.
Herzig, J. & **Schiff**, F.   Studien über die Bestandtheile des Gujakharzes.   1897.   III. 494.[2]
Herzinstein.   *See* HERZENSTEIN, V. O.
Herzog, C.   Angustura und das ätherische Oel derselben.   1858.   III. 504.[1]
Herzog, Michael.   Ueber die Phanerogamen-Flora von Bistritz.   1859.   I. 384.
Herzog, Theodor.   Verzeichniss . . . des Mustersortiments aargauischer Kernobstfrüchte.   1867.   III. 89.[1]
Die herzoglich Coburg'schen Pussten.   1874.   IV. 315.
Die herzoglich nassauischen Forst- und Jagdgesetze.   1845.   IV. 320.
Herzoglich Ratiborer Forsten.   1876.   IV. 354.
Herzogl. sächsische Forst-, Weidwerks-, Wald- und Jagd-Ordnungen.   1774.   IV. 322.[1]
Herzoglich-würtembergische Verordnung, die Fertigung eines Wald-Nutzungs-Etats . . . betr.   1788.   IV. 247.[2]
Der **Herzogthümer** Bremen und Verden Policey-, Teich-, Holtz- und Jagd-Ordnung.   1732.   IV. 319.[2]
Dess **Herzogthumb** Wirtemberg ernewerte Vorst-Ordnung.   *See* NEWE Vorst Ordnung . . . 1540.   IV. 322.
Hesdörffer, Max.   Acacia longifolia Willd.   1900.   III. 465.[1]
— Beitrag zur Ansucht der Citrus.   1886.   III. 497.[1]
— Die Internationale Gartenbau-Ausstellung in Gent.   1899.   III. 78.[1]
— Phyllocactus phyllanthoides Deutsche Kaiserin.   1900.   III. 626.[1]
Hesdörffers Monatshefte für Blumen- und Gartenfreunde.   *See* Die GARTENWELT.   III. 12.
Heske, Franz.   Die Zchen- und Buchennachzucht.   1896.   IV. 129.
— Zur Frage der Loshiebe und Umhauungen.   1898.   IV. 246.
— Wie bewähren sich bisher die üblichen wirthschaftlichen Vorkehrungen gegen Windbruch.   1898-99.   IV. 246.
Hesler.   Hurtig Tiltrækning af Orangetræer.   1842.   III. 499.[2]
Hesperian.   Columbus   I. 5.
Hesperian.   San Francisco   I. 5.
Hesperidum Norimbergensium sive de Malorum Citreorum . . . usu libri IV.   *See* VOLCKAMER, J. C.   1708.   II. 400.[2]
Hess, Carl Friedrich Wilhelm.   Die Entwickelung der Pflanzenkunde in ihren Hauptzügen.   1872.   I. 79.[2]
Hess, C m n s.   Die Hagelschläge in der Schweiz.   1894.   III. 185[4] e
— Über die Pappel alä Blitzableiter.   1896.   IV. 195.[1]
Hess, D.   Der Wald . . . im Kanton Zug.   1871.   IV. 367.
Hess, H.   Der Thüringer Wald in alten Zeiten.   1898.   IV. 26.
Hess, Heinrich.   Ueber die Analogie in Form und Wirkung der Pflanzen.   1851.   III. 259.[2]
Hess, J. Eduard.   Vollständige Cubik- und Quadrat-Tabellen für den Inhalt von . . . Hölzern.   1841.   IV. 223.
Hess, J. G. G.   Beiträge zur Kenntniss der Kultur . . . der unächten Akazie.   1796.   IV. 522.[1]
Hess, J. P.   The most practical way of growing Raspberries.   1898.   III. 457.[2]
Hess, Johann Rudolf.   Theses anatomico-botanicae.   1751.   I. 31.
Hess, Johannes.   Steckbrief der phanerogamischen natürlichen Familien.   1832.   I. 260.
Hess, Karl.   Pflanzenkunde, mit einer vollständigen Flora des germanischen Tieflandes.   1846.   I. 381.

Hess, Richard Alexander.   Der academische Forstgarten bei Giessen.   1878.   IV. 18.[2]
— Aufastung von Eichen.   1879.   IV. 507.
— Ueber Aufastungen in Fichtenstangenhölzern.   1882.   IV. 172.[1]
— Beiträge zur Aufastungsfrage.   1874.   IV. 171.
— Beiträge zur Generation des Hylesinus.   1884.   IV. 204.
— Beiträge zur Theorie . . . der Baum- und Stockrodemaschinen.   1886.   IV. 387.[1]
— Ueber Beschädigung von Kiefern durch Steigeisen.   1882.   IV. 477.
— Comparative Untersuchungen über Baum- und Stockrodung.   1876.   IV. 386.
— Comparative Untersuchungen über die Wirkung von Dungmaterialien.   1878.   IV. 144.[2]
— Comparative Untersuchungen über die Wirkung von Dungmaterialien auf . . . Lärchen.   1879.   IV. 449.
— Comparative Versuche über Baumrodung.   1876.   IV. 386.
— Der Eck'sche Numerir-Hammer.   1884.   IV. 387.[2]
— Die Eigenschaften und das forstliche Verhalten der . . . Holzarten.   1883.   IV. 84.[1]
— Eigenschaften und forstliches Verhalten der . . . Holzarten.   1883.   IV. 84.[1]
— Einfluss der Bodenlockerung.   1875.   IV. 69.
— Ueber die Einwirkung des Steinkohlenrauchs.   1874.   IV. 192.[2]
— Encyklopädie und Methodologie der Forstwissenschaft.   1885.   IV. 98.[2]
— Ueber den Eschenkrebs.   1895.   IV. 535.[2]
— Fang der Raupen des Apfel- une Pflaumenwicklers.   1879.   III. 190.
— Fichtennadelrost.   1876.   IV. 456.
— Forest protection.   1878.   IV. 177.[2]
— Die forstliche Unterrichtsfrage.   1874.   IV. 29.
— Der Forstschutz.   1878.   IV. 177.[2]
— Der forstwissenschaftliche Unterricht an der Universität Giessen.   1881.   IV. 33.[1]
— Frage des Rothschwanzes.   1876.   IV. 497.
— Ueber Gewinnung von Rasenasche.   1879·   IV. 150.
— Ueber die Grösse des Hauspahnverlustes.   1885.   IV. 384.[1]
— Grundriss zu Vorlesungen über Encyklopädie . . . der Forstwissenschaft.   1873.   IV. 56.
— Grundriss zu Vorlesungen über Forstbenutzung.   1876.   IV. 381.
— Der Haselnussbohrer.   1891.   III. 358.[1]
— Hilfsmittel zur Ermittelung des Zuwachses.   1877.   IV. 233.
— Ueber den Kubikinhalt . . . eines Lebensbaumes.   1882.   IV. 484.[2]
— Ueber den Kubikinhalt und Durchschnittszuwachs einer Wellingtonia.   1882.   IV. 484.[1]
— Lebensbilder hervorragender Forstmänner.   1885.   IV: 2.
— Eine merkwürdige Fichte.   1893.   II. 35.[2]
— Mitteilungen über die Wachstumsverhältnisse einer Seekiefer.   1888.   IV. 467.[2]
— Nadeldürre an Kiefern.   1875.   IV. 477.
— I nostri alberi da bosco.   1883.   IV. 84.[1]
— Ueber die Organisation des forstlichen Unterrichts an der Universität Giessen.   1877.   IV. 32.
— Über die' Organisation des forstlichen Versuchswesen.   1869.   IV. 38.[1]
— Rasenasche für Forstgärten.   1875, 1884.   IV. 150.
— Rede, gehalten bei Einweihung des Heyer-Denkmals.   1892.   IV. 2.
— Das Revisionsverfahren der herzoglich gothaischen Forste.   1863.   IV. 248.[1]
— Ueber Saatkämpe und Pflanzbeete.   1866.   IV. 150.
— Schutz der Saatbeete.   1875.   IV. 198.[2]
— Ueber den Umfang und die Bedeutung der Forstwissenschaft.   *See* HESS, Richard & UHICH, Carl.   1882.   IV. 29.
— Untersuchungen über den Einfluss verdünnter Säuren . . . auf die Keimung.   1875.   I. 523,[1] IV. 65,[2] 143.
— Untersuchungen über den Erfolg und Kostenaufwand bei Stocksprengungen mit Pulver.   1881.   IV. 387.[1]
— Untersuchungen über die Schwindungsverhältnisse einiger Holzarten.   1887.   IV. 412.[1]
— Untersuchungen über Ergebnisse bei Durchforstungen von Fichtenstangenhölzern.   1875.   IV. 458, 480.
— Untersuchungen über Formzahlen . . . von Weymouthskiefern.   1875.   IV. 470.[2]
— Vertilgung der Frostspanner durch Brumata-Leim.   1878.   IV. 207.

— Der Waldbau. *See* HEYER, Carl. 1854. IV. 106.
— Ueber Waldschutz und Schutzwald. 1888. IV. 45, *177.*[2]
— Welche Erfahrungen sind in Bezug auf den Unterbau der Eichenhochwaldbestände gemacht worden? 1878. IV. 507.
— Welche Stellung empfiehlt sich für den Forstverein des Grossherzogthums Hessen? 1882. IV. 40.[2]
— & Urich, Carl. Zwei akademische Festreden. 1882. IV. 29.
Hess, V. Ermittlung des Quantitätszuwachsprozentes. 1876. IV. 233.
Hess, W. Bilder aus dem Leben schädlicher . . . Insekten. Die Schmetterlinge. 1881. III. 190.
— Die Feinde des Obstbaues aus dem Tierreiche. 1892. III. 191.
Hesse, F. Lebensweise . . . des grossen Fichtenbastkäfers. 1898. IV. 457.
Hesse, Heinrich. Neue Gartenlust. 1690. III. 102.
— Neue Unterweisung zu dem Blumen-Bau. 1690. III. 102.
— Teutscher Gärtner. 1710. III. 102.
Hesse, Hermann. Bemerkungen über die Härte einiger Coniferen. 1882. III. 292.
Hesse, Oswald. Sur les alcaloïdes de l'écorce de Pao-Péreira. 1877. III. 688.[1]
— Sur les alcaloïdes de l'écorce de Remijia purdieana. 1884. III. 747.[2]
— Ueber die Alkaloïde der Chinarinden. 1877. III. 723.
— Beiträge zur Kenntnis der Chinarinden. 1871. III. 24.[2]
— Beitrag zur Kenntniss des aus Chinarinden darstellbaren . . . Wachses. 1885. III. 723.
— Beitrag zur Kenntniss der Chinarinden. 1876. III. 723.
— Beitrag zur Kenntniss der Chinarinden. 1880. III. 724.[2]
— Ueber Chinicin und Cinchonicin. 1875. III. 723.
— Cinchona alkaloids. 1876. III. 723.
— Ueber Conchinamin. 1881. III. 726.[1]
— Contribution à l'étude des alcaloïdes du Coca. 1888. III. 493.[1]
— Sur l'écorce de Symplocos racemosa. 1879. III. 670.[2]
— Einige Bemerkungen über die javanische Calisaya. · 1874. III. 725.[2]
— Investigation of the Argentine Quebracho drugs. 1882. III. 687.[1]
— Zur Kenntniss der Pereiro-Rinde. 1877. III. 688.[1]
— Sur la matière cireuse des Quinquinas. 1885. III. 723
— Sur la matière grasse ou cireuse des écorces de Quinquina. 1885. III. 723.
— Ueber Physostigmin. 1867. III. 483.[2]
— Physostigmine. 1867. III. 483.[2]
— Ueber Phytosterin und Cholesterin. 1878. III. 484.[1]
— Phytostérine et cholesterine. 1878. III. 484.[1]
— Sur un Quinquina blanc de Payta. 1870. III. 724.[2]
— Sur le Quinquina Calisaya de Java. 1876. III. 725.[2]
— Review of the Cinchona alkaloids. 1877. III. 723.
— Ueber die Rinde von Remija Purdieana. 1884. III. 747.[2]
— Studien über argentinische Quebracho-Droguen. 1882. III. 687.[1]
— Studien über Chinamin. 1881. III. 723.
— Studien über die Alkaloïde der Chinarinden. 1873. III. 723.
— Ueber die weisse Chinarinde von Payta. 1870. III. 724.[2]
— *See also* JOBST, Julius & HESSE, Oswald.
Hesse, Paul. Defensio viginti problematum Melchioris Guilandini. 1562. I. 281.
Hesse, Wilhelm Gottlieb. · Abhandlung über einige meiner Versuche . . . den Holzanbau geschwind wachsender Hölzer betreffend. 1782. ·IV. 116.
— Oekonomische Abhandlung vom Holzanbau. 1779. IV. 116.
Hesse — Forst- und Cameralverwaltung . . . *See* FORST . . . ·IV. 7.
Hesse — Forstverein für das Grossherzogthum. *See* FORSTVEREIN . . . IV. 8.
Hesse-Wartegg, Ernst von. Urwälder und Nutzbäume der hinterindischen Tropen. 1898. IV. 377.[1]
Hessel, Joseph. Ueber die Theerschwelerei in Russland. 1861. IV. 436.[2]
Hesselbarth, Guido. Beiträge zur vergleichenden Anatomie des Holzes. 1879. I. 125.
Hesselgren, Nicolaus L. Pan suecicus. *See* LINNÉ, Carl von. 1749. III. 223.[1]
Hesselius, Johan. De Piceae Pinique silvestris resina. *See* ROBERG, Lars. 1714. IV. 443.[1]

Hesselman, O. A. H. W. Några iakttagelser öfver växternas spridning. 1897. I. 241.[1]
Hesselman, C. Leitfaden der Obstkultur. 1880. III. 138.
Hessenthal, von, *(Oberförster, Nesselgrund).* Nachweisung . . . Abschätzung einer Probefläche von 2 Morgen Weisstannenbestand. 1847. IV. 446.[1]
— Nachweisung der . . . gefundenen Höhen und Stamm-Kreis-Flächen. 1847. IV. 457.
Das hessische Staatsrecht. 1834. IV. 319.[1]
Hessischer Forstverein. · Satzungen. 1875. IV. 40.[2]
Hessischer Forstverein. Verhandlungen. *See* VERSAMMLUNG HESSISCHER FORSTWIRTHE. IV. 11.
Hessler, Hugo. Ueber die Materia Medica des . . . Tscharaka. 1884. III. 239.
Hessler, Robert. Notes on the flora of Lake Cicott. 1896. I. 316.
Heteromorpher Apfelbaum. 1882. II. 266.[2]
Hétet, F. Sur l'accroissement en diamètre. 1859. I. 189.
— Ailantus glandulosa, japansk Fernistræ. 1859. III. 507.[1]
— Emploi de l'écorce de Tartonraire. 1859. III. 628.[2]
— Liste des plantes qui ont résisté en plein air. 1862. III. 48.
— Note sur une nouvelle propriété du Vernis du Japon. 1859. III. 507.[1]
— Recherches expérimentales d'organogénie végétale. 1859. I. 99.
— Recherches expérimentales sur la formation des couches ligneuses dans le Pircunia. 1862. II. 193.[1]
Hetley, *Mrs.* G. B. The native flowers of New Zealand. 1888. · I. 508.[1]
Hêtre phénoménal. 1856. II. 872.[1]
Un **Hêtre** remarquable. 1888. II. 127.[1]
Hetschko, *(Oberförster, Tost).* Beobachtungen über die Schütte der Kiefer. 1856. IV. 475.
— Zur Frage . . . '' Welchen praktischen Erfolg und Einfluss hat das neue Holzdiebstahl-Gesetz? '' 1854. IV. 320.
— Ueber Maikäfer-Schaden. 1856. IV. 202.
— Nadelstreu-Angelegenheit. 1854. IV. 71.
Hetschold, Ed. Ulmenveredlung. 1884. III. 364.[1]
Heucher, Johann Heinrich. Index plantarum horti medici Academiae vitembergensis. 1711. I. 43.
— Novi proventus horti medici Academiae vitembergensis. 1711. I. 289.
— Plantarum historia fabularis. *See* THRYLLITIUS, V. H. 1713. I. 511.
Heudelot. Mémoire sur la culture des Cotonniers. 1833. III. 587.[1]
— Notice sur la culture des Nopals. 1833. III. 623.[2]
Heuffel, J. A. Beiträge zur Kenntniss der in Ungarn . . . Quercus. 1850. II. 872.[1]
— Diagnosen neuer . . . Pflanzen-Arten aus dem Banate. 1858. II. 391.[1]
— De distributione plantarum geographica per comitatum Hungariae pestiensem. 1827. I. 445.
— Enumeratio plantarum in Banatu. 1858. I. 445.
Heufler, Ludwig, *Ritter* von. Ein botanischer Beitrag zum deutschen Sprachschatz. 1852. I. 73.[1]
— Die Golasberge in der Tschitscherei. 1845. I. 447.
— Pinus sylvestris. 1843. II. 46.[1]
— Die Geschichte des Pflanzenreichthums in Tirol. 1842. I. 440.
— *See also* STOTTER, Michael & HEUFLER, Ludwig, *Ritter* von.
Heugel, C. A. Beiträge zur näheren Kenntniss unsrer Weidenarten. 1846. II. 100.[2]
— Bemerkungen und Beiträge zur Flora der Ostsee-Provinzen. 1852. I. 301.
— Ueber die botanische Untersuchung . . . der Weidenarten. 1846. II. 100.[2]
Heukels, Hendrik. Geïllustreerde schoolflora voor Nederland. 1900. I. 391.[2]
— Landbouw flora. 1894. I. 391.[2]
— Schoolflora van Nederland. 1883. I. 391.[2]
Heulot, Émile. Étude sur un Cinchona succirubra. 1873. III. 726.[1]
Heumann, Ch. Sur la quantité d'acide cyanhydrique . . . du Prunus Padus. 1842. III. 439.[1]
Heumen, H. H. van. De Rameh. 1883. III. 381.[1]
Heurck, Henri van. Du Boldo. 1873. II. 222.[1]
— Du Jaborandi. 1875. II. 409.[2]
— Le microscope. 1865. I. 36.[2]
— Notions succinctes sur l'origine . . . des drogues-simples. 1876. III. 258.

Heurck, Henri van (*continued*).
— Observationes botanicae. 1870. I. 270.
— & **Beucker**, J. I. de. Antwerpsche analytische flora. 1861. I. 391,[1] *392*.
— & **Guibert**, Victor. Flore médicale belge. 1864. III. 77.
— & **Wesmael**, Alfred. Prodrome de la flore du Brabant.
1861. I. 392.
Heurlin, E. Summarisk förteckning öfver de meteorologiske observationerne. 1816. I. 223.[1]
Heusden, L. van. De volmaakte timmerman. 1843[1] IV. 423.[1]
Heuser, Justus Georg. Tractatio de eo quod justum est circa jus glandis legendae. 1742. IV. 313.
Heuser, Paul. Einige Bemerkungen über interessante Pflanzen Schlesiens. 1859. I. 384.
Heusinger, Friedrich. Ausführliche Anweisung zur naturgemässen Obstbaumzucht. 1824. III. 136.
Heusinger, Henric. Circa Rhoa Toxicodendron. 1809. III. 528.[1]
Heusler, R. Das Waldkassa-Rechnungswesen im Haushalt der aargauischen Gemeinden. 1900. IV. 294.[1]
Heusser, Jacob Christian & **Claraz**, G. Fragmenta météorologiques . . . de Rio-de-Janeiro. 1859. III. 269.[1]
— — The fruit trees of Brazil. 1862. III. 269.[1]
— — Des principaux produits des provinces brésiliennes de Rio-de-Janeiro. 1859. III. 269.[1]
Heussi, Jacob. Leichtfassliche Anleitung zum Feldmessen. 1863. IV. 264.
Heutsz, P. J. F. van. Dr. Burcks beschouwing over den achteruitgang. 1896. III. 731.
Heuzé, Gustave. Abies cilicica. 1856. III. 296.[1]
— L'agriculture de l'Italie septentrionale. 1864. III. 126.[2]
— La flore au point de vue agricole en France. 1885. III. 113.
— Le Henné. 1888. III. 630.[1]
— Hortensia à fleurs roses et à fleurs bleues. 1856. III. 412.[1]
— Le Jasmin d'Espagne. 1892. II. 710.[1]
— Περὶ Κρότωνος ἡ εἴκεως. 1888. III. 522.[1]
— Les plantes alimentaires. 1872. III. 53.
— Les plantes industrielles. 1859. III. 52.
— Les plantes industrielles. Les plantes oléagineuses. 1871. III. 224.[2]
— The Spanish Jasmine. 1892. II. 710.[1]
— Traitement des Vignes malades. 1853. III. 559.[2]
Hevera, Vincenz. Die Wälder Böhmens. 1876. IV. 167,[1] 181,[1] *878.*[2]
Hewan, Archibald. Notes on the Isere'. 1866. II. 376.[1]
Heward, Robert. Biographical sketch of the late Allen Cunningham. 1842. I. 501, II. 567.[2]
Hewins, Nellie Priscilla. A contribution to a knowledge of the organogeny of the flower . . . of the Caprifoliaceae. 1900. II. 842.[2]
Hewitt, Robert. Coffee; its history. 1872. III. 726.[2]
Hewson, F. Practical observations on the introduction of preservative solutions into railway timber. 1859. IV. 418.
Hexamer. Procédés pour rendre les bois incombustibles. 1899. IV. 421.
Hexenbesen an einer Kiefer. 1886. I. 528.[2]
Hey, *Mrs.* The moral of flowers. 1835. V. xxv.[1]
Hey, C. Ein Erzieher des deutschen Waldes. 1891. IV. 2.
Heyde, O. von der. Forstliche Reisebilder aus Ceylon. 1900. IV. 378.
Heyden, von, (*Dr.*). Statistische Notizen über den vermuthchen Ursprung der . . . linksrheinisch aufgefundenen Reblausinfektionen. 1890. III. 574.
Heyden, M. van. Het enten van Koffie. 1900. III. 733.[2]
Heydenreich, (*Oberlehrer*, *Tilsit*.) Auszug eines Schreibens . . . an den Landrath Herrn Schlenther. 1834. III. 137.
Heyder, Eduard. Die Vorverjüngung der Eiche. 1889. IV. 508.
Heyer, Carl. Anleitung zu forststatistischen Untersuchungen. 1846. IV. 242.
— Aufruf zur Bildung eines forststatistischen Vereins. 1845. IV. 40.[1]
— Encyclopädie der Forstwissenschaft. 1854. IV. 97, 106, *204*.
— Die Hauptmethoden zur Waldertrags-Regelung. 1848. IV. 242.
— Phanerogamen-Flora der grossherzoglichen Provinz Ober-Hessen. 1860. I. 384.
— Die Vortheile und das Verfahren beim Baumroden. 1826. IV. 385.[2]

— Über die Vortheile und das Verfahren beim Baumroden. 1856. IV. 385.[1]
— Der Waldbau. 1854. IV. 106.
— Die Waldertrags-Regelung. 1841. IV. 97, 240.
— *See also* Гаштерь, Карлъ.
Heyer, Eduard. Das Abstecken der Serpentinen beim Waldwegebau. 1876. IV. 266.[2]
— Allgemeine Grundsätze bei . . . Mischbeständen. 1893. IV. 139.[1]
— Anleitung zum Bau von Waldwegen. 1864. IV. 266.[2]
— Aphoristische Mittheilungen aus dem Holzhauereibetrieb. 1872. IV. 171.
— Ueber Aufästen der Bäume. 1872. IV. 171.
— Ueber Aufästung der Nadelholz-Bestände. 1892. IV. 172.[1]
— Ausgleichung der Ab- und Auftragsmassen beim Waldwegebau. 1867. IV. 266.[2]
— Zur Beantwortung der Frage: Welche Erfahrungen sind in Bezug auf den Unterbau der Eichenhochwaldbestände gemacht worden? 1879. IV. 507.
— Beitrag zum reinen und gemischten Eichen-Niederwald. 1884. IV. 507.
— Beitrag zur näheren Würdigung des Flächenfachwerks. 1852. IV. 251.[1]
— Zur Bekämpfung der Nonne. 1891. IV. 201.
— Bemerkungen über Eichenschälwald. 1874. IV. 506.
— Beschädigung der Kiefer durch die Zapfenbrecher. 1883. IV. 477.
— Ueber Bestandsaussonderung. 1867. IV. 255.
— Bodenwerths-Formeln. 1882. IV. 257.
— Conservation des glands. 1883. IV. 148.
— Flächentheilung und Ertragsberechnungs-Formeln. 1859. IV. 236.
— Ueber Forstgärten. 1866. IV. 150.
— Die Holzcultur auf steinigen und felsigen Stellen. 1855. IV. 141.
— Zur Holzmassen-Ermittlung, Bonitirung. 1861. IV. 217, *243*.
— Der Kegelbohrer. 1873. IV. 152, *495*.
— Ueber die Kultur mit ballenlosen Pflanzen. 1866. IV. 152.
— Ueber Messung der Höhen . . . der Bäume. 1870. IV. 217.
— Eine neue Druckmaschine zum Baumroden. 1891. IV. 387.[1]
— Ueber die praktische Ausbildung der Forstdienst-Aspiranten. 1880. IV. 32.
— Ueber die praktische Ausbildung der Forsteleven. 1860. IV. 32.
— Ueber regelmässige gemischte Bestände. 1866. IV. 137.[1]
— Tabelle zum Aufschlagen der Kreisflächen. 1865. IV. 230.
— Tafeln zur Erdmassen-Berechnung. 1879. IV. 265.[2]
— Aus Theorie und Praxis in Betreff der Verjüngung von Eiche mit Buche. 1886. IV. 138.[1]
— Ueberwinterung der Eicheln. 1883. IV. 148.
— Zur Vergleichung der Kosten für Hoch- und Tiefleimen. 1891. IV. 199.[2]
— Ueber das Verhalten des Kiefernspinners. 1890. IV. 478.
— Die Waldertrags-Regelungsverfahren der HH. etc. Dr. Carl Heyer und H. Karl. 1846. IV. 242.
— Waldwerthsberechnung. 1883. IV. 257.
— Wegnetz und Wirthschaftsnetz. 1878. IV. 251.[1]
— Ueber Zubereitung der sogenannten Rasenasche. 1864. IV. 144.[1]
Heyer, Friedrich. Eicheln im Holze. 1885. I. 210.[2]
— Ostbau und Obstnutzung in den Vereinigten Staaten. 1886. III. 133.
— Untersuchungen über das Verhältniss des Geschlechtes bei einhäusigen und zweihäusigen Pflanzen. 1884. I. 238.
Heyer, Gustav. Anleitung zur Waldwerthberechnung. 1865. IV. 253.
— Über die Aufstellung von Holzertragstafeln. 1877. IV. 256.
— Compendio de valoración de montes. 1865. IV. 253.
— De l'effet de la lumière et de l'ombre sur les arbres forestiers. 1852. IV. 57.[2]
— Ueber die Ermittlung der Masse . . . der Holzbestände. 1852. IV. 213.
— Ueber die geographische Verbreitung unserer wichtigsten Waldbäume. 1869. IV. 79.[1]
— Grundsätze für den Entwurf von Holzschadenersatztarifen. 1849. IV. 254.

— Die Hügelpflanzung. 1859. IV. 153.[2]
— Des influences de la lumière et de l'ombre sur les essences forestières. 1852. IV. 67.[2]
— Lehrbuch der forstlichen Bodenkunde. 1856. IV. 57.
— Manuale di stima forestale. 1865. IV..253.
— Die Methoden der forstlichen Rentabilitätsrechnung. 1871. IV. 255.
— Untersuchungen über die Aschenbestandtheile der Kiefer. 1852. II. 47,[2] 186.[2]
— Das Verhalten der Waldbäume gegen Licht und Schatten. 1852. IV. 67.[2]
— Der Waldbau. See HEYER, Carl. 1854. IV. 106.
— Die Waldertrags-Regelung. See HEYER, Carl. 1841. IV. 240.
— See also Гейеръ, Густавъ.
Heyer, J. C. Beschrijving der bereiding van kaneelolie. 1855. III. 406.[1]
Heyer, Karl. See HEYER, Carl.
Heyer, Theodor. Zur Aufastungsfrage. 1893. IV. 172.[1]
Heykál, Ede. Amygdalopsis Lindleyi. 1896. III. 443.[2]
Heyland, J. A. H. Analysis chemica radicis caincae. 1827. III. 743.[2]
Heym. Mittel gegen Engerlinge. 1892. IV. 203.
Heym, A. Kurze Erläuterung der Verhältnisse des Theils des Thüringer Waldes . . . für die Exkursionen gewählt. 1854. IV. 355.[2]
Heymann, V. H. V. Allgemeine Witterungskunde. 1834. IV. 59.[2]
Heymering, G. Surat ilmu hhikmet jang sudah terka rang akan pergunaan dan Kasukaan. 1841. I. 88.
Heyn, Victor. Die Schiffsbauholzflössung aus der Bukowina. 1892. IV. 390.[2]
— Zuwachsverhältnisse in verschiedener Seehöhe. 1886. IV. 454.
Heyne, Benjamin. On the deoxidation of the leaves of Cotyledon. 1815. II. 235.[1]
Heyne, Friedrich Adolf. Pflanzen-Kalender. 1804. I. 375.
Heynhold, E. Ueber das Beschneiden der Kugelakazien. 1888. III. 487.[1]
Heynhold, Gustav. Alphabetische und synonymische Aufzählung der in den Jahren 1840 bis 1846 . . . eingeführten Gewächse. 1840. I. 77. — 1846. III. 74.
— Clavis generum zur Flora von Sachsen. 1843. I. 381.
— Das natürliche Pflanzensystem. 1840. I. 261.
— Nomenclator botanicus hortensis. 1840. I. 77.
— See also HOLL, Friedrich & HEYNHOLD, Gustav.
Heyning, P. M. Eenige opmerkingen over scheefgegroeide boomen. 1898. III. 199.
Heyrowský, Adolf. Weitere Erfahrungen . . . über die Lyda hypotrophica. 1892. IV. 457.
Heyrowsky, C. Die Gewinnung des Lärchen-Terpentins. 1876. IV. 452.[1]
— Vorkommen des Fichtennadelrostes. 1876. IV. 456.
Heyrowsky, Johann. Ausweis des Domainen-Waldbesitzes im Kronlande Böhmen. 1858. IV. 390.
— Forststatistik des Budweiser Kreises. 1850. IV. 370.
— Ueber den Rüsselkäfer (Curculio pini). 1857. IV. 475.
Heyting. Gouvernements Kofficultuur. 1892. III. 730.
Heyting, H. G. Proeve van reorganisatie der gouvernements Koffiecultuur. 1899. III. 731.
Heyting, J. Nota omtrent Liberia-Koffie. 1886. III. 742.[1]
Heywood, A. W. Cape woods and forests. 1886. IV. 379.[2]
Hgn., R. Ueber das gegenseitige Verhalten der Hainbuche und Buche. 1874. IV. 491,[2] 495.
De Hiba Boom van Japan. 1855. II. 53.[1]
Hibberd, James Shirley. The amateur's Rose book. 1864. III. 449.
— The Elm and its insect enemies. 1863. III. 364.[1]
— Étude sur le Pelargonium. 1880. III. 491.[2]
— Familiar garden flowers. 1881. III. 83.[1]
— Field flowers. 1870. I. 402, 534.[1]
— The flowering and fruiting of the Holly. 1877. II. 463.[2]
— The fruiting of the Holly. 1877. II. 463.[2]
— Garden-Ivies. 1870. III. 642.[2]
— Hibberd's Emerald Ivy. 1886. III. 642.[2]
— Hollies. 1886. II. 464.[1]
— The Holly and its varieties. 1880. III. 530.[1]
— The Ivy; a monograph. 1872. III. 642.[2]
— The Ivy in the dictionary. 1875. II. 649.[1]
— Lecture on the Pelargonium. 1880. III. 491.[2]
— New and rare beautiful-leaved plants. 1870. III. 206.[2]
— Notes on the Holly. 1880. III. 530.[1]
— The Pelargonium. 1880. III. 491.[2]

— Report on the varieties of Ivies. 1890. III. 643.[1]
— The Rose book. 1864. III. 449.
— Les Roses du XI Xme siècle. 1882. III. 450.
— Sago palms. 1871. III. 220,[2] 284.[1]
Hibbert & Buist, Robert. The American flower garden directory. 1834. III. 99.[2]
Die Hibbertia-Arten. 1881. III. 595.[2]
Hibsch, Josef Emanuel. Einiges über unsere Ebereschen. 1875. II. 311.[2]
— Salix babylonica L., androgyna et masculina. 1876. II. 105.[2]
Hickel, Robert. Les jardins botaniques des bords du Rhin. 1899. I. 49, V. VIII.[1]
— Note sur quelques insectes nuisibles aux Pins. 1894. IV. 462.[1]
— Le parasite du ver blanc. 1891. IV. 203.
— See also DUFOUR, Léon & HICKEL, Robert.
Hicken, Cristóbal M. La Yerba-mate. 1900. III. 531.[2]
Hickeringill, E. Jamaica viewed. 1661. III. 266.
Hickler. Récolte des graines d'arbres forestiers. 1898. IV. 148.
Hickley, M. E. Rocky mountain Conifers. 1894. III. 293.
Hickman, J. B. Notes on Monterey Conifers. 1896. II. 16.[2]
Hickok, H. T. Eccentric growth of exogenous plants. 1875. I. 105.
Hicks, Edward. Machine for transplanting large trees. 1891. III. 168.[1]
— Transplanting large trees. 1891. III. 168.[1]
Hicks, Gilbert Henry. The germination of seeds. 1900. I. 204.
— Oil-producing seeds. 1896. III. 225.
— Seed control. 1896. III. 157.
— & Dabney, J. C. The superior value of large, heavy seeds. 1897. III. 156.[1]
— & Key, Sothoron. Additional notes on seed testing. 1898. III. 157.
Hicks, Isaac. Large trees on Long Island. 1879. I. 295.[1]
Hicks, John S. The Black or Yellow Locust. 1883. IV. 523.[1]
Hickson, Sydney J. A naturalist in North Celebes. 1889. I. 466.
Hidalgo Tablada, José de. Curso de economía rural española. 1864. III. 114.[2]
— Tratado del cultivo de los árboles frutales. 1871. III. 145.[1]
— Tratado del cultivo del Olivo en España. 1870. III. 675.[2]
Hiebner, Johann Christoph. Horticultura. 1664. III. 102.
Hielscher, Carl. Ueber den jährlichen Bastzuwachs. 1882. I. 130.
Hiepe, Ed. Studien über die Senna. 1900. III. 470.[2]
Hierl, J. C. Abhandlung über die Theorie und den Gebrauch des geradlinigen Transporteurs. 1827. IV. 58.
Hierl, Johann Eduard. Anleitung zur Waldwerths-Berechnung. 1852. IV. 253.
Hiern, William Philip On the African species of the genus Coffea. 1876. II. 814.[1]
— Further notes on Ebenaceae. 1875. II. 701.[1]
— A monograph of Ebenaceae. 1873. II. 700.[2]
— A new genus of Ericaceae from Angola. 1898. II. 670.[2]
— On a new species of Gardenia. 1878. II. 813.[1]
— Notes on Ebenaceae. 1874. II. 700.[2]
— On the peculiarities . . . of Rubiaceae in tropical Africa. 1878. II. 808.[1]
— Third notes on Ebenaceae. 1877. II. 700.[2]
— Two new tropical African Ebenaceae. 1895. II. 700.[2]
— See also FICALHO, conde de & HIERN, W. P.
— & Rendle, A. B. Catalogue of the African plants collected by F. Welwitsch. 1896. I. 492.[1]
— & others. New Somaliland plants. 1899. I. 490.
Hieronymus, Georg. Beiträge zur Kenntnis der europäischen Zoocecidien. 1891. I. 214.[2]
— Erster Beitrag zur Kenntnis der Siphonogamenflora der Argentina. 1897. II. 849.[1]
— Über Caesalpinia Gilliesii. 1882. II. 339.[1]
— Grubbiaceae. 1889. II. 170.[1]
— Icones et descriptiones plantarum . . . in Republica Argentina. 1885. I. 345.
— Myzodendraceae. 1889. II. 167.[2]
— Niederleinia juniperoides. 1879. II. 561.[2]
— Observaciones sobre la vegetacion de la provincia de Tucuman. 1874. II. 344.
— Sobre una planta hibrida nueva formado por el Lycium elongatum . . . y el Lycium oestroides. 1881. II. 772.[2]

Hieronymus, Georg (*continued*).
— Plantae diaphoricae florae argentinae. 1882. III. 65.²
— Plantae Lehmannianae in Columbia. 1895. II. 849.¹
— Plantae Lehmannianae in Guatemala. 1895. I. 330.
— Plantae Stuebelianae. 1896. I. 330.
— Santalaceae. 1889. II. 167.²
— Über seine Untersuchungen einiger Gallen. 1885. I. 214.²
— Sertum patagonicum. 1880. I. 344.
— Sertum sanjuaninum. 1881. I. 344.
— Sobre las Solanageas Lycium argentinum. 1875. II. 772.²
Higbee, Charles H. Hybrid Grapes. 1871. III. 546.
Higgins, John. Notes on Poinsettia. 1893. II. 443.²
High prices for English Oaks. 1892. IV. 405.¹
Highland and agricultural society. Prize essays. Transactions. *See* HIGHLAND SOCIETY OF SCOTLAND. III. 17.
Highland Coffee of Sierra Leone. 1896. III. 743.¹
Highland society of Scotland. Prize essays. III. 17.
Hight, George Ainslie. Rats in nurseries. 1877. IV. 198.¹
— Report on forest administration in Germany. 1894. IV. 289.¹
Higley, Warren. The condition and needs of forestry legislation in the state of New York. 1889. IV. 314.²
Higley, William K. On the microscopic and general character of the Peach tree affected with the "yellows." 1881. III. 441.¹
— The microscopic crystals contained in plants. 1881. I. 139.
— & Raddin, C. S. The flora of Cook county. 1891. I. 316.
Hilaire, A. F. C. P. SAINT-. *See* SAINT-HILAIRE, A. F. C. P.
Hilberer, Jules. Cytisus capitatus L. 1886. II. 350.³
Hilburg, C. Ueber Turgescenzänderungen. 1881. I. 149,² 197.²
Hildebrand, Friedrich Hermann Gustav. Abnorme Blüthe von Sarothamnus. 1862. II. 351.²
— Abweichende Blüthenbildung bei Fuchsia. 1890. II. 643.²
— Anatomische Untersuchungen über . . . Begoniaceen. 1859. II. 583.¹
— Anatomische Untersuchungen über die Farben der Blüthen. 1863. I. 184.
— Bastarde zwischen Chamaedorea Schiedeana und C. Ernesti Augusti. 1890. II. 66.¹
— Der Bau der Coniferenspaltöffnungen. 1860. II. 17.²
— Über die Befruchtung der Salvia-Arten mit Hülfe von Insekten. 1865. II. 765.²
— Über die Befruchtung von Aristolochia. 1866. II. 181.²
— Ueber Bildung von Laubsprossen aus Blüthensprossen bei Opuntia. 1888. II. 596.¹
— Ueber einen Birkenstamm von einem Geisblatt umschlungen. 1867. II. 839.¹
— Ueber Blattrichtung und Blattstellung bei Planera. 1883. II. 145.¹
— Ueber die Blütheneinrichtung von Rhodora. 1881. II. 678.¹
— De caulibus Begoniacearum. 1858. II. 583.¹
— Ueber einige abweichende Birnbildungen. 1885. II. 280.¹
— Einige Beiträge zur Pflanzenteratologie. 1890. II. 520,¹ 643.²
— Einige Beobachtungen an Keimlingen. 1892. I. 123.¹
— Einige Beobachtungen aus dem Gebiete der Pflanzenanatomie. 1861. I. 99.
— Einige Beobachtungen über den Witterungseinfluss. 1883. I. 221.
— Einige biologische Beobachtungen. 1896. II. 84.²
— Einige Experimente . . . über den Einfluss der Unterlage. 1868. I. 529.
— Ueber einige Fälle abnormer Blüthenbildung. 1862. II. 351.²
— Ueber einige Fälle von Abweichungen in der Ausbildung der Geschlechter bei Pflanzen. 1893. II. 134.²
— Ueber einige Fälle von verborgenen Zweigknospen. 1883. I. 103.²
— Über einige Pflanzenbastardierungen. 1889. I. 246.¹
— Ueber einige plötzliche Umänderungen der Pflanzen. 1891. II. 113,² 498.¹
— Ueber die Entwickelung der haarigen Anhänge an Pflanzensamen. 1872. I. 120.
— Auf die an einem Exemplar von Planera Richardi sich zeigenden verschiedenen Grade der Blattstellung. 1884. II. 145.¹
— F. Delpino's Beobachtungen über die Bestäubungsvorrichtungen. 1867. I. 237.

— F. Delpino's weitere Beobachtungen über die Dichogamie. 1870. I. 237.
— Flora von Bonn. 1866. I. 385.
— Ueber die Forsythien. 1894. II. 706.²
— Die Geschlechter-Vertheilung bei den Pflanzen. 1867. I. 237.
— Ueber die Geschlechtsverhältnisse bei den Compositen. 1869. II. 850.²
— Ueber die Heterostylie . . . bei Forsythia. 1894. II. 706.²
— De l'influence du sujet sur la greffe. 1868. I. 529.²
— Ueber die Jugendzustände solcher Pflanzen. 1875. I. 101,¹ 843.²
— Die Lebensverhältnisse der Oxalisarten. 1884. II. 392.²
— Longevity of plants. 1882. I. 193.²
— Ueber eine Missbildung bei Früchten von Passiflora. 1882. II. 578.²
— Ueber die Samen von Acacia melanoxylon. 1883. II. 326.²
— Die Schleuderfrüchte. 1873. I. 119.
— Uebergäng von Blüthen in vegetative Zweige. 1890. II. 520.¹
— Über den unmittelbaren Einfluss der Pflanzenbastardirung. 1867. I. 201.²
— Die Verbreitung der Coniferen. 1861. II. 13.¹
— Die Verbreitungsmittel der Pflanzen. 1873. I. 240.²
— Weitere Beobachtungen über die Bestäubungsverhältnisse. 1869. I. 237.
— Xanthoceras sorbifolia. 1892. II. 490.²
— Ueber die Zunahme des Schauapparates. 1886. I. 145.
— Ueber eine zygomorphe Fuchsia-Blüte. 1899. II. 643.²
Hildebrand, K. Ueber das gelbe und rote Xanthorrhoea-Hars. 1896. III. 339.¹
Hildebrand, Rudolf. Einfluss der Feuchtigkeit auf die Länge von Hölzern. 1889. IV. 412.¹
— Untersuchungen über den Einfluss der Feuchtigkeit auf den Längenzustand von Hölzern. 1889. IV. 412.¹
Hildebrand, J. Cubik-Tabellen für Metermaass. 1871. IV. 226.
Hildebrandt, Johann Ludwig. Auflösung der Preisfrage, welches sind die . . . Mittel, den Wachsthum der Baume in den Forsten . . . zu verbessern. 1777. IV. 116.
Hildebrandt, Johann Maria. Cycas-Samen. 1876. II. 4.¹
— Ueber Drachenblut. 1878. III. 336.²
— Früchte von Raphia vinifera P. Beauv. 1876. II. 74.²
— Über Weihrauch und Myrrhe. 1878. III. 509,¹ 511.¹
Hildegardis de Pinguia. S. Hildegardis abbatissae Opera omnia. 1179. I. 274.
— Physica S. Hildegardis. 1179. I. 274.
Hildegardis, SANTA. *See* HILDEGARDIS DE PINGUIA.
Hildemann, A. *See* ГИЛЬДЕМАНЪ, A.
Hildenhagen. Forstlicher Unterricht in Spanien. 1876. IV. 293.¹
— Die Harzung der Schwarzkiefer. 1875. IV. 436,² 465,² 466.²
Hildesheimer land- und forstwirthschaftliches Vereinsblatt. *See* HANNOVERSCHES land . . . IV. 9.
Hildmann, H. Echinopsis cristata Salm. 1889. II. 593.²
— Empfehlenswerthe Cacteen. 1885. III. 619.
— Neuere und seltene Cacteen. 1885. III. 619.
— Phyllocactus × Franzii. 1892. III. 625.²
— Phyllocactus Hildmanni hort. 1895. III. 625.²
— Phyllocactus kermesinus magnus. 1895. III. 626.¹
— Phyllocactus × Pommer Eschei. 1892. III. 626.¹
Hildreth, Samuel Prescott. Trees of different kinds and their uses. 1826. III. 62.
Hildt, Johann Adolph. Beschreibung in- und ausländischer Holzarten. 1797. I. 37,³ IV. 17, 407,² V. viii.¹
— Sammlung in- und ausländischer Holzarten. 1797. I. 37,² IV. 17, 407.²
Hildwein. Écorce de Dita et ditaïne. 1874. III. 686.²
Hiltenhaus, F. Unsere Gehülfen aus der Vogelwelt. 1897. IV. 91.¹
Hilfstafeln zur Inhaltsbestimmung von Bäumen und Beständen der Hauptholzarten. *See* GRUNDNER, Fritz, SCHUBERG, Karl & SCHWAPPACH, Adam. 1898. IV. 231.¹
Hilgard, Eugene Waldemar. Bench-grafting resistant Vines. 1900. III. 548.²
— Cyanhydric gas as an insecticide. 1887. III. 198.²
— The fertilizing value of Greasewood. 1891. III. 387.²
— Forest trees for California. 1888. IV. 112.
— Forestry. 1890. IV. 112.
— Lecture on the phylloxera. 1876. III. 760.
— List of trees and shrubs in the University grounds. 1890. I. 39.

— The phylloxera in California. 1882. III. 761.
— The phylloxera or Grapevine louse. 1880. III. 761.
— *See also* COLBY, G. E. & HILGARD, E. W.
— & DAVY, J. B. Investigations on the natural vegetation of alkali lands. 1898. I. 229.
Hilgard, Theodore Charles. Exposition of a natural series. 1857. I. 252.
— On the law of phyllotaxis. 1857. I. 102.
— The organic identity of the albumen and endopleura. 1872. I. 120.
— Phyllotaxis. 1856. I. 102.
— *See also* DURAND, Elias & HILGARD, T. C.
Hilger, Albert. Sur la composition de la gomme adragante. 1899. III. 467.²
— Sur l'hespéridine. 1876. III. 501.²
— Neues Vorkommen des Inosits. 1871. I. 175.
— *See also* BAUER, F. E. & HILGER, Albert; JUCKENACK, A. & HILGER, Albert.
— & Juckenack, A. Des alterations provoquées dans . . . café. 1897. III. 740.²
Hill, Ellsworth Jerome. Celtis pumila Pursh. 1900. II. 141.²
— The coast dune flora of Lake Michigan. 1893. I. 316.
— Coontie and Conte. 1892. III. 286,¹ 339.¹
— Flora of the White Lake region. 1900. I. 317.¹
— The Hemlock in eastern Minnesota. 1890. II. 53.¹
— Kalm's St. John's-wort. 1899. II. 557.¹
— A new biennial fruited Oak. 1899. II. 133.²
— Notes on the flora of Chicago. 1896. II. 142.¹
— Notes on western New York woodlands. 1895. IV. 339.
— Oaks in May. 1894. III. 361.¹
— Oecological notes upon the White Pine. 1897. II. 46.¹
— A Peach with a double plumule. 1897. II. 276.²
— Pinus Banksiana at the West. 1890. II. 41.¹
— Prairie woodlands. 1894. IV. 340.²
— Quercus ellipsoidalis in Iowa. 1899. II. 133.²
— The Saguenay region. 1895. I. 311.¹
— The sand dunes of northern Indiana. 1896. I. 316.
— The southern limit of Juniperus Sabina. 1900. II. 32.¹
— A study of Quercus Leana. 1894. II. 135.¹
— Timber-culture in eastern Nebraska. 1892. IV. 112.
— Two noteworthy Oaks. 1898. II. 133.¹
— Vaccinium vacillans with white fruit. 1895. II. 687.¹
— Vitis Labrusca. 1898. II. 506.²
— Wild roses about Chicago. 1894. II. 283.¹
— Winter studies in the Pine Barren flora of Lake Michigan. 1891. III. 63.²
Hill, H. B. Furfurol. 1881. I. 155.
— & Comey, A. M. On the behavior of sound and decayed wood. 1887. IV. 408.
— & Jennings, W. L. On certain products of the dry distillation of wood. 1893. I. 156.¹
Hill, H. C. Note on an inspection of certain forests in the Central Provinces. 1894. IV. 250.¹
— Suggestions for the administration of the forests in Coorg. 1890. IV. 250.²
— Suggestions for the administration . . . of the forests in the Andamans. 1891. IV. 250.¹
— *See also* SEATON, W. J, & HILL, H. C.
Hill, John. Account of a new stain for wood. 1821. III. 355.²
Hill, John, (1716–75). Beschreibung der äusserlichen Theile der Pflanzen. 1781. I. 100.¹
— The British herbal. 1756. III. 81.
— Construction of timber, from its early growth, explained by the microscope. 1770. I. 124.
— Decade di alberi curiosi ed eleganti piante. 1773. I. 262.
— A decade of curious and elegant trees and plants. 1773. I. 262.
— Eden; or, A compleat body of gardening. 1757. III. 109.
— Entwurf eines Lehrgebäudes von Erzeugung der Pflanzen. 1758. I. 199.
— Exotic botany. 1759. I. 261.
— Flora britanica. 1760. I. 395.
— The history of aggregates, or cluster-headed plants. 1772. II. 251.¹
— A history of plants. 1751. I. 83.
— Hortus kewensis. 1768. I. 52.
— Die Kräfte der Salbei. 1778. III. 698.¹
— The origin and production of proliferous flowers. 1759. II. 289.¹
— Outlines of a system of vegetable generation. 1758. I. 199.
— Der Schlaf der Pflanzen. 1757. I. 197.²

— The sleep of plants. 1757. I. 197.²
— Le sommeil des plantes. 1757. I. 197.²
— Il sonno delle piante. 1757. I. 197.²
— Twenty-five new plants rais'd in the Royal garden at Kew. 1773. I. 52.
— The useful family herbal. 1754. III. 80.
— The vegetable system. 1759. I. 83.
Hill, Robert Thomas. Forest conditions of Porto Rico. 1899. IV. 342.¹
— Notes on the forest conditions of Porto Rico. 1899. IV. 342.¹
Hill, T. G. On the roots of Bignonia. 1898. II. 785.²
Hill, Thomas. The arte of gardening. 1568. III. 107.
— The profitable arte of gardening. 1568. III. 107.
Hill, Walter. Botanic gardens, Brisbane. 1880. I. 69.¹
— Catakidozamia, Hill. 1865. II. 6.¹
— Collection of Queensland timbers. 1880. IV. 18.¹
— Timber, &c. on Fraser's Island. 1879. V. xxxi.²
— & Bailey, F. M. Colonial timber (despatch respecting). 1875. V. xxxi.¹
Hillebrand & Bredemeier. Idesia polycarpa. 1890. III. 614.²
Hillebrand, H. Idesia polycarpa Maximow. 1887. III. 614.²
Hillebrand, William. Flora of the Hawaiian Islands. 1888. I. 509.¹
— Die Vegetationsformationen der Sandwich-Inseln. 1888. I. 509.²
Hillenmeyer, H. F. Destruction of trees by coal gas. 1885. III. 185.²
Hiller, Caspar. Paulonia [sic] imperialis. 1887. IV. 538.¹
Hiller, Gottfried Hermann. Ueber Intercellularlücken zwischen den Epidermiszellen der Blüthenblätter. 1884. I. 116.¹
— Untersuchungen über die Epidermis der Blüthenblätter. 1884. I. 116.¹
Hiller, Matthaeus. Hierophyticon. 1725. I. 512.
— De plantis in Scriptura Sacra memoratis decas. 1716. I. 512.
Hiller-Bombien, Otto. Beiträge zur Kenntnis der Geoffroya-rinden. 1892. III. 477.²
— Untersuchungen der Cortex Geoffroyae. 1893. III. 477.²
Hillhouse, Augustus L. Description of the European Olive tree. 1818. III. 675.¹
— An essay on . . . the European Olive-tree. 1818. III. 675.¹
— Olive tree. 1818. III. 675.¹
Hillhouse, William. Bedfordshire plant list. 1877. I. 403.
— Contributions towards a new flora of Bedfordshire. 1876. I. 403.
— Some investigations into the function of tannin. 1887. I. 183.
Hillius, Friedrich Bogislaus. De natura et virtutibus plantarum. *See* WAGNER, G. F. 1688. III. 238.¹
Hillman, Fred Hebard. Early flora of the Truckee Valley. 1894. I. 326.
— Flowers and fruits of common trees. 1900. I. 321.
— Twigs of common trees and shrubs. 1899. I. 295.¹
Hillmann. Die Verwertung des geringsten Kiefern-Durchforstungsholzes. 1900. IV. 482.¹
Hills, William H. Small fruits. 1886. III. 147.²
Hils-Solling-Forst-Verein. Verhandlungen. IV. 9.
Hilsenberg, (Oberförster). Haidekulturen vom vorigen Jahrhundert. 1884. IV. 158.
— Zur Ueberschwemmungs- und Waldfrage. 1884. IV. 51.
Hilt, J. *See* BARBIER, Ph. & HILT, J.
Hiltner, L. Ueber die Keimung gärtnerischer Sämereien. 1899. III. 157.
— Ueber die Ursachen, welche die Grösse . . . der Wurzelknöllchen der Leguminosen bedingen. 1900. II. 322.¹
Himalayan Rubi. 1895. III. 457.²
Himing, F. W. & Brewer, G. S. Wild flowers of Barmouth. 1884. I. 534.²
Himly, Friedrich Carl. De caoutchouk. 1835. III. 230.
Himmel und Erde. I. 12.
Himpel, Stephan. Die Flora der Umgebung von Metz. 1898. I. 390.
Hinckley, M. E. *See* HINKLEY, M. E.
Hincks, Thomas D. On early contributions to the flora of Ireland. 1841. I. 399.
Hincks, Wilham. On chorisis. 1865. I. 115.¹
Hind, William Marsden. Flora of Suffolk. 1889. I. 534.²
Hinderlich, E. The transplantation of Oaks of large size. 1900. III. 168.¹
— Das Verpflanzen starker Eichen. 1900. III. 168.¹

Hinds, Richard Brinsley. Memoirs on geographic botany. 1845. I. 299.
— The physical agents of temperature. 1842. I. 217.
— The regions of vegetation. 1843. I. 299.
— Table of the distribution of the species . . . of De Candolle's " Prodromus." 1842. I. 299.
— & Bentham, George. Remarks on the physical aspect . . . of Hong Kong. 1842. I. 460.[2]
— — Remarks on the vegetation of the Feejee Islands. 1842. I. 510.[1]
Hinds, W. Laying Box edgings. 1882. III. 523.[1]
Hindson, W. R. The Tea industry in Natal. 1896. III. 604.[1]
Hinkert, F. W. Systematisch-geordnetes Handbuch der Pomologie. 1836. III. 71.
Hinkley, M. E. Currants and Gooseberries. 1893. III. 414.[1]
— Evergreens. 1892. III. 293.
— Native evergreens. 1890. III. 293.
L'Hinoki, 1866. IV. 448.[1]
Hinsdale, S. J. Méthode colorimétrique pour le dosage du tannin. 1890. I. 183.
Hinterhuber, Julius. See HINTERHUBER, Rudolf & Julius.
— & Pichlmayr, M. F. Prodromus einer Flora der Herzogthums Salzburg. 1879. I. 442.
Hinterhuber, Rudolf & Julius. Prodromus einer Flora des Kronlandes Salzburg, 1851. I. 440.
Hints on Cocoa planting. 1886. III. 592.[2]
Hintz, Richard. Ueber den mechanischen Bau des Blattrandes. 1889. I. 111.
Hintüber, von. Ferseixnis der im Sollinge . . . waxsenden gefässpflanzen. 1868. I. 386.
Hintüber, von, (Hofrath). Bemerkungen über die Würkungen des Winters 1791–1792. 1794. III. 45.
Hiorth, Johan. Plantae esculentae patriae. See LINNÉ, Carl von. 1752. III. 66.[2]
— Wåra inländska äteliga wäxter. See LINNÉ, Carl von. 1752. III. 66.[2]
Hippel, von. Pinus sylvestris mit hängenden Zweigen. 1866. II. 46.[2]
Hippel, Karl von. Natur und Gemüth. 1867. I. 516.
Hirase, Sakugoro. Études sur la fécondation . . . du Ginkgo. 1815. II. 8.[1]
— Études sur le Ginkgo. 1895. II. 8.[1]
— Notes on the attraction-spheres in . . . Ginkgo. 1894. II. 7.[2]
— Ricerche sul contegno del polline nel Gingko. 1894. II. 7.[2]
— Untersuchungen über das Verhalten des Póllens von Ginkgo. 1894. II. 7.[2]
— See also IKENO, Selitsiro & HIRASE, Sakugoro.
Hirc, Dragutin. Coronilla emeroides Boiss. et Sprunn. 1888. II. 348.[1]
— Flora okolice Bakarske. 1884. I. 443.
— Die Hängefichte in Croatien. 1889. II. 35.[1]
Hirsch, A. See DUFLOS, A. & HIRSCH, A.
Hirsch, Bruno. Die Pharmacopoea germanica. 1873. III. 249.
— Die Prüfung der Arzneimittel. 1875. III. 246.
— Universal-Pharmakopöe. 1887. III. 246.
Hirsch, Vincenz. Veredlungsversuche bei harten Hölzern. 1879. III. 162.
Hirsch, Wilhelm. Untersuchungen über die Entwickelung der Haare bei den Pflanzen. 1900. I. 113.[1]
— Welche Einrichtungen bestehen behufs Ueberführung der . . . Reservestoffe in den Embryo? 1890. I. 204.
Hirschberg, H. Einige Bemerkungen über Jequirity-Samen. 1885. III. 462.[2]
Hirschfeld. Die Bestands-Massenkluppe. 1888. IV. 231.[1]
Hirschfeld, C. C. L. Haandbog om Frugttræers Opelskning. 1788. III. 135.
— Handbuch der Fruchtbaumsucht. 1788. III. 135.
Hirschfeld, Wilhelm. Die Ernährung und das Wachsthum der Pflanzen. 1844. III. 37.[2]
Hirschsohn, Eduard. Beiträge zur Chemie der wichtigern Harze. 1877. I. 181.[1]
— Beitrag zur Kenntniss der Xanthorrhoeaharze. 1884. III. 339.[1]
— Distinctions du goudron de Genévrier. 1895. III. 228.[1]
— Goudron de Pin et goudron de Bouleau. 1893. III. 228.[1]
— Marche à suivre pour déterminer la nature d'une résine. 1877. I. 156.[1]
— Die Unterscheidung des Birkentheers vom Tannentheer. 1893. III. 228.[1]
— Die Unterscheidung des Wachholdertheers. 1895. III. 228.[1]
— Ueber das Verhalten der Harze von Pinus silvestris L. und Picea excelsa Lk. 1885. II. 36,[2] 48.[1]
— Ueber das Vorkommen von Essigsäureester. 1892. III. 295.[2]
Hirscht, Karl. Kakteenkulturen im Hause. 1896. III. 620.[1]
Hirschweh, Hermann. Aldehydbildung in grünen Blättern. 1899. I. 174.
Hirth, F. Storax. 1886. III. 417.[2]
Hirzel. De wijsgeerige landman. 1767. III. 35.
His, Charles. Notice sur les Orangers. 1829. II. 401.[2]
— Notice sur les Pivoines en arbre. 1842. II. 200.[2]
Hisinger, Eduard Victor Eugène. Aecidium Conorum Abietis. 1876. IV. 456.
— Aecidium conorum-abietis Reess. 1878. IV. 442.
— Ceratonia Siliqua blommande i boningsrum. 1883. III. 471.[2]
— Flora fagervikiensis. 1855. I. 362.
— Galläpplebildningar på Quercus ilicifolia. 1894. IV. 503.[2]
— Myrtillus nigra var. pallida. 1883. II. 686.[2]
— Några ord om de . . . formerna af Granen. 1867. II. 34.[2]
— Peridermium Pini. 1876. IV. 470.[1]
Hisinger, Wilhelm. Anteckningar i physick . . . under resor uti Sverige och Norige: 1819. I. 352.
— Förteckning på wäxterna i Skinskattebergs socken. 1832. I. 353.
— Profiler och tabeller öfver de förnämsta bergshöjder . . . i Sverige. 1827. I. 353.
— Tableau de la végétation du Sneehätten. 1841. I. 354.
Histoire de la Société forestière nationale. 1899. IV. 41.[2]
Histoire de la Virginie. See BEVERLY, Robert. 1705. III. 263.[2]
Histoire des découvertes faites . . . dans plusieurs contrées de la Russie. 1779. III. 270.[1]
Histoire des drogues, espiceries. See HUERTO, Garcia del. 1563. III. 240.
Histoire des plantes de l'Europe. 1670. I. 286, 530.[2] See also, DEVILLE, Nicolas. 1719. I. 290 — 1762. I. 530.[2]
Histoire et description de la basse Cochinchine. See IRANG-ROI-DUC. 1863. III. 276.[2]
Histoire générale des plantes. See DALECHAMPS, Jacques. 1586. I. 282.
Histoire naturelle du cacao. See QUELUS, de. 1719. III. 594.
Histoire véritable et naturelle . . . du pays de la Nouvelle France. See BOUCHER, Pierre. 1664. III. 261.[2]
Dell' historia. See HUERTO, Garcia del. 1563. III. 240.
Historia de la sierra. 1889: IV. 393.—
Historia de las yervas, y plantas. 1557. I. 280.
Historia generalis plantarum. See DALECHAMPS, Jacques. 1586. I. 282, 530.[1]
Historia naturalis Brasiliae. See PISO, Willem & MARCGRAF, Georg. 1648. I. 327.
Historic society of Lancashire and Cheshire. Proceedings. Transactions. I. 18.
Historic trees in Switzerland. 1881. I. 297.[2]
Historical magazine . . . America. I. 5.
An historical narrative of the discovery of New Holland. 1786. I. 499.[2]
Historicus, (pseud.). Cocoa; all about it. 1892. III. 595.[1]
Historique de la question des expériences forestières en Hongrie. 1899. IV. 28,[2] 39.[1]
Historische Skizze der Ausbildung der Lehre von der Forstabschätzung. 1828. IV. 242.
Historische verhandelingen over de voornaemste opkomste . . . in de Kempen. 1792. III. 33.[1]
The history and present state of Virginia. See BEVERLY, Robert. 1705. III. 263.[2]
The history of Jamaica. See LONG, Edward. 1774. III. 266.
The history of North America. 1789. III. 261.[1]
A history of the county of Berkshire, Massachusetts. See DEWEY, Chester. 1829. I. 313.
A history of the Rhododendron. 1876. II. 675.[2]
The history of the Rose. 1856. II. 290.[2]
The history of the Tea plant. 1819. III. 606, V. xxix.[2]
The history of Virginia. See BEVERLY, Robert. 1705. III. 263.[2]
Historya naturalna. 1872. I. 96.
Hitchcock, Albert Spear. Another hybrid Oak. 1893. II. 135.[1]

— A catalogue of the anthophyta and pteridophyta of Ames, Iowa. 1891. I. 325.
— Flora of Kansas. 1898. I. 327.
— Key to Kansas trees in their winter condition. 1893. I. 294, *320, IV. 78.*[1]
— A key to the spring flora of Manhattan. 1894. I. 326.
— List of plants collected in the Bahamas. 1893. I. 337.
— A visit to the West Indies. 1891. I..337.
— The woody plants of Manhattan in their winter condition. 1893. I. 294, *320, IV. 78.*[1]
Hitchcock, Edward. A catalogue of plants ... in the vicinity of Amherst college. 1829. I. 313.
— Report on the geology, mineralogy, botany and zoology of Massachusetts. 1833. I. 313.
Hitchcock, Frank Harris. Notes on the plant products of the Philippine Islands. 1899. III. 274.[1]
Hitchcock, J. S. The opening of the buds. 1893. I. 108.[2]
Hitier, H. See CHATIN, Adolphe & HITIER, H.
Hitschmann, Hugo H. Archiv für Landwirthschaft. See SCHMÄL, Jos. 1883. IV. 309.[2]
— Die Land- und Forstwirthschaft in Oesterreich-Ungarn. 1894. IV. 124.[1]
Hitt, Thomas. A treatise of fruit-trees. 1755. III. 141.
— A treatise of husbandry on the improvement of dry and barren lands. 1760. IV. 161.[1]
Hitzemann, Carl. Beiträge zur vergleichenden Anatomie der Ternstroemiaceen, Dilleniaceen. 1886. II. 511,[2] *540,*[2] *547,*[2] *559.*[2]
Hitzer, A. Die Lebensdauer der Pflanzen. 1844. I. 192.[1]
Hitzschold, Edgar. Massenvermehrung wurzelächter Rosen. 1881. III. 452.
Hjaltalin, Oddur Jónsson. Islensk Grasafraeði. 1830. I. 353.
Hjelm, Peter Jacob. Försök på några trä-sorters krympning uti kolnings-hetta. 1780. IV. 394.
— Om et salt utur körsbärssaft. 1788. II. 273.[1]
Hjelm, V. J. P. Stirpes agri femsionensis. See FRIES, E. M. 1825. I. 353.
Hjelt, Hjalmar. Anteckningar från en botanisk resa i Karelen. 1881. I. 364.
— Conspectus florae fennicae. 1888. I. 365.
— Kännedomen om växternas utbredning i Finland. 1891. I. 366.
— Rosa cinnamomea med blommor. 1878. II. 293.[1]
— Tvenne för finska floran nya hybrider. 1885. II. 106.[1]
— See also SAELAN, Thiodolf, KIHLMAN, A. O. & HJELT, H.
— & Hult, Ragnar. Vegetationen och floran i en del af Kemi Lappmark och norra Österbotten. 1885. I. 364.
Hjelt, Otto Eduard August. Försök att bestämma de af Elias Tillandz i hans " Catalogus plantarum " upptagna vexter. 1869. I. 363.
— Naturhistoriens studium: Finland före Linnés tid. See TENGSTRÖM, J. M. 1843. I. 80.[1]
Hjorth, Carolus. Remedia guineensia. See AFZELIUS, Adam. 1813. III. 93.[1]
Hlasiwetz, Heinrich. Über Buchentheer-Kreosot. 1858. III. 494,[2] *IV. 500.*[1]
— Über die Guajakharzsäure. 1861. III. 494.[2]
— Sur les principes immédiats du thé. 1867. III. 607.
— Über das Quercitrin. 1859. I. 175, II. 140.[2]
— Ueber die Rinde der China nova. 1851. III. 710.[2]
— Über die Robinia-Säure. 1854. II. 382.[2]
— See also ROCHLEDER, Friedrich & HLASIWETZ, Heinrich.
— & Habermann, Josef. Ueber das Arbutin. 1875. III. 648.[1]
— — — Sur l'arbutine. 1875. III. 648.[1]
— & Pfaundler, Leopold. Über das Morin und die Moringerbsäure. 1863. II. 148.[1]
Hlawa, Ludwig. Zur Beantwortung der Frage: " Wie können ... weitausgedehnte Culturflächen ... dem Weidebetriebe fortwährend geöffnet ... aufgeforstet werden ?" 1852. IV. 136.[1]
— Habt Acht! Die Borkenkäfergefahr rückt an! 1869. IV. 204.
Hlawa, Vinzenz. Darstellung einer einfachen Abschätzung und Eintheilung der Hoch- und Niederwälder. 1837. IV. 253.
Hlawsa, Anton. Tetropium fuscum et luridum. 1879. IV. 92.
Hlubek, Benjamin. Multiplication du Mélèze par boutures. 1846. III. 304.[2]
Hlubek, Franz Xaver. Betrachtungen über die Bewirthschaftung der Hochwälder. 1844. IV. 129.

— Unterricht in der Maulbeerbaum- und Seidenzucht. 1850. III. 376.
— Versuch einer neuen Charakteristik ... der Rebensorten. 1841. III. 546.
Hn. Zustände und Missbräuche in den Privat- und Gemeindewaldungen Südtyrols. 1858. IV. 123.[2]
Ho Kai. See FORD, Charles, Ho KAI & CROW, W. E.
Hoang-nan, a supposed remedy for leprosy. 1878. III. 684.[2]
Hoare, Clement. A practical treatise on the cultivation of the Grape vine. 1835. III. 553.[2]
Hoare, Henry. Calendar of flowering trees and shrubs. 1900. III. 207.[3]
Hobart-Hampden, A. G. See HAMPDEN, A. G. HOBART-.
Hobbs, Charles E. Botanical hand-book of common local ... names. 1876. I. 72,[2] III. 258.
Hobday, E. Hardy climbers for winter adornment. 1878. III. 204.[2]
— Ivy in the garden. 1875. III. 642.[2]
— Mahonia repens as an edging plant. 1875. III. 396.[1]
Hobe, J. H. von. Freymüthige Gedanken über verschiedene Fehler bey dem Forsthaushalt. 1805. IV. 135.[1]
Hobe, J. W., *Freiherr* von. Anweisung zu einer bessern Holzkultur. 1791. IV. 105.
— Etwas vom Anbau ... der Weiden. 1786. III. 347.
Hobein, Max. Beitrag zur anatomischen Charakteristik der Monimiaceen. 1889. II. 221.[2]
— Über den systematischen Werth der Cystolithen bei den Acanthaceen. 1884. II. 796.[2]
Hobkirk, Charles Codrington Pressick. Huddersfield. 1859. I. 401, V. XXI.[1]
— Notes on Crataegus. 1867. II. 261.[1]
Hoblyn, R. D. British plants. 1851. I. 400.
Hobza, P. Dýchání rostlin, zvláště lesů. 1873. IV. 55.[1]
Hoceja, Javier. Influencias del arbolado. 1882. IV. 44.
Hoch. Forst- und Jagdverhältnisse der Donauauen. 1892. IV. 369.
Hoch, von. Der Hart-Wald. 1876. IV. 349.[2]
Hoch, Friedrich August. Notizen über den Blütenbau der Rebe. 1888. II. 507.[2]
Hoch, Gustav. Die Bekämpfung von Melolontha vulgaris. 1899. IV. 203.
— Der Mittelwald und seine Entstehung. 1898. IV. 131.
— Pygaera anastomosis L. 1897. IV. 210.[1]
Hochfärber, Friedrich. Forst- und landwirthschaftliche Briefe. 1878. III. 151.
Hoch-fürstliche aychstättische Holtz- und Forst-Ordnung. 1689. IV. 318.
Hochfürstl. Brandenburg. onclzsächsische Wald Ordnung. 1692. IV. 319.[2]
Hochfürstl. passauische Anstalten in Holz- und Schwemmwesen. 1788. IV. 318.
Hochfürstl. passauische Forstordnung. 1788. IV. 318.
Hochfürstliche passauische Wald- und Forst-Ordnung. 1762. IV. 299.
Hochhuth, Johann Heinrich. Mittheilungen über den Stand des Gartenwesens zu Kiew. 1844. III. 120.[2]
Eines hochlöblichen Raths der freien Reichsstadt Nürnberg Forst-Ordnung. 1805. IV. 318.
Hoch-oberkeitliche Ordnung ansehend allerhand Missbräuch in Verkauffung des Holtzes. 1733. IV. 305.
Hoch-oberkeitliches Mandat 'betreffend die Versorg- und Beschirmung der Holz und Waldungen. 1715. IV. 305.
Hochreutiner, Bénédict Pierre Georges. Une famille de botanistes. Les Candolle. 1897. I. 81.[1]
— Reliquiae Palisotianae. 1898. I. 491.
— Révision du genre Hibiscus. 1900. II. 522.[1]
— See also BRIQUET, John & HOCHREUTINER, Georges.
Hochstetter, Carl. See SEUBERT, Moritz & HOCHSTETTER, Carl.
Hochstetter, Christian Friedrich. Ueber einige neue Pflanzen aus Abyssinien. 1844. I. 487.
— Die Giftgewächse Deutschlands. 1844. III. 73.
— Naturgeschichte des Pflanzenreichs. 1870. I. 91.
— Nova genera plantarum Africae. 1841. I. 483.[1]
— Plantarum nubicarum nova genera. 1841. II. 438,[1] 760.[1]
— Populäre Botanik. 1831. I. 94, 378.
— Ueber die Priorität ... der Namen Natalia und Rhaganus. 1849. II. 491.[1]
— See also STEUDEL, E. G. & HOCHSTETTER, C. F.
Hochstetter, Ferdinand. Expedition der k. k. Fregatte Novara. 1858. I. 481.[1]
— New Zealand. 1867. I. 506.[2]
Hochstetter, Wilhelm. Araucaria imbricata Pav. 1869. III. 298.[2]

Hochstetter, Wilhelm (*continued*.)
— Die Coniferen oder Nadelhölzer. 1882. II. 13.⁴
— Kritisches Verzeichniss des Coniferen-Herbarium's. 1869. II. 13.¹
— Die sogenannten Retinispora-Arten der Gärten. 1880. II. 28.³
— Wegweiser durch den botanischen Garten der Universität Tübingen. 1860. I. 48.
— *See also* HENKEL, J. B. & HOCHSTETTER, Wilhelm.
Hock, F. Statistische Mittheilungen über die forstwirth-schaftlichen Verhältnisse im Herzogthum Coburg. 1854. IV. 355.²
— Die Waldbesteuerung im Herzogthum Sachsen-Coburg. 1865. IV. 284.¹
Hocquart, E. Le jardinier pratique. 1846. III. 113.
Hocquart, Léopold. Flore du département de Jenmape. 1814. I. 392, V. xx.¹
Hodge, B. Osage Orange for hedges. 1851. III. 372.¹
Hodges, John F. Observations on ... Peruvian matico. 1845. III. 755.¹
Hodges, Leonard Bacon. Facts about forestry. 1883. IV. 112.
— Forest culture in Minnesota. 1876. IV. 271.²
— The forest tree planters' manual. 1879. IV. 103.¹
— The planting of wind-breaks. 1883. IV. 154.²
— Practical suggestions on forest tree planting in Minnesota. 1874. IV. 111.²
— Report of the State forestry association. 1877.. IV. 340.
— Report on forest culture on the main line, first division St. P. & P. R. R. 1875. IV. 340.
Hodgkin, John. Note on "China bicolorata." 1885. III. 747.²
Hodgman, Edwin R. An address delivered ... before the Ornamental tree association. 1876. III. 32.¹
Hodgson, Arthur. Forest and historic trees of Great Britain. 1883, 1884. I. 297,¹ *IV. 85.*¹
Hodgson, Bryan Houghton & Frith, R. W. G. Notes on certain species of silkworms indigenous to India. 1848. III. 611.³
Hodgson, C. M. Teak plantations. 1899. IV. 537.¹,
Hodgson, Christopher Pemberton. A residence at Nagasaki. 1861. I. 462.
Hodgson, E. North or Lake Lancashire. 1874. V. xxi.²
Hodgson, William. Flora of Cumberland. 1898. I. 535.
O hodowaniu Morw. 1856. III. 377.
Hodson, Richard Edmond. Drainage of land. 1886. IV. 144.¹
— The formation ... of plantations. 1885. IV. 121.
Die höchsten Bäume der Erde. 1883. II. 624.¹
Hoechstetter, J. P. De cinnamomo. *See* SCHENCK, J. T. 1670. III. 405.³
Höck, Fernando. Begleitpflanzen der Buche. 1892. II. 126.¹
— Begleitpflanzen der Kiefer. 1893, . I. 389.
— Beiträge zur Morphologie ... der Valerianaceen. 1882. II. 844.¹
— Dipsacaceae. 1891. II. 844.²
— Einige Hauptergebnisse der Pflanzengeographie. 1888. I. 301.
— Ueber einige seltenere Waldbäume Norddeutschlands. 1893. I. 372.
— Der gegenwärtige Stand unserer Kenntnis von der ... Verbreitung der angebauten Nutzpflanzen. 1900. I. 301.
— Grundzüge der Pflanzengeographie. 1897. I. 301.
— Laubwaldflora Norddeutschlands. 1896. I. 389.
— Muthmassliche Gründe für die Verbreitung der Kiefer. 1893. II. 47.¹
— Nadelwaldflora Norddeutschlands. 1893. I. 389.
— Nährpflanzen Mitteleuropas. 1890. I. 242,¹ III. 66.¹
— Pflanzen der Schwarzerlenbestände Norddeutschlands. 1897. I. 390, *II. 116.*¹
— Studien über die geographische Verbreitung der Wald-pflanzen Brandenburgs. 1896. I. 390.
— Zur systematischen Stellung von Sambucus. 1892. II. 840.²
— Ueber Tannenbegleiter. 1895. I. 389.
— Valerianaceae. 1891. II. 844.²
— Die Verbreitung der Kiefer. 1892. . II. 47.¹
— Vergleich der Buchenbegleiter. 1895. II. 125.²
Höck, J. D. A. Ueber die Erziehung des Lerchenbaumes. 1797. IV. 448.²
Hoedt, Josef. Durch Eis zurückgehaltenes Blühen eines Pfir-sichbaumes. 1876. . III. 176.³
Höfer, Ernst, (*jr.*). Notiz über die Behandlung einer Sago-Palme. 1869. III. 285.¹

Hoefer, Ferdinand. Dictionnaire de botanique pratique. 1850. I. 34.
Höfer, Franz & Kronfeld, Moriz. Die Volksnamen der nie-derösterreichischen Pflanzen. 1889. I. 75.¹
Hoefer, Jean Chrétien Ferdinand. Histoire de la botanique. 1872. I. 79.³
— Le monde des bois. 1868. I. 413.
Hoefer, Matthias. Etymologisches Wörterbuch der in Ober-deutschland ... üblichen Mundart. 1815. I. 75.¹
Höffler, C. J. W. Die Staats-Oberaufsicht über das Privat-Waldeigenthum in der preussischen Rheinprovinz. 1862. IV. 286.¹
Hoefft, Franz M. S. V. Catalogue des plantes ... dans le district de Dmitrieff. 1826. . I. 360.
Höfle, Marc Aurel. Die Flora der Bodenseegegend. 1850. I. 383.
— Grundriss der angewandten Botanik. 1851. I. 89.
— Die Pflanzensysteme von Linné. 1845. I. 252.
Höfer, Max. Wald- und Baumkult. 1892. I. 517.³
Hoefling, E. Botanisch- ... lateinisch-deutsch-Wörterbuch. 1844. I. 71.
Hoegberg, J. D. Svensk flora. 1843. I. 354.
Höggrell, E. Empetrum nigrum med hvita bär. 1887. II. 453.³
Högrell, Bengt. Bergjums fanerogamer i blomningsföljd 1887. I. 223 ¹
— Nytt växtställe för Hippophaë rhamnoides. 1888. II. 608.¹
Högström, Pehr. Anmärkningar vid den år 1768 i Väster-botten infallna märkvärdiga vinter. 1764. III. 44.¹
— Om säds och växters friande ifrån köld genom rök. 1757. I. 211.
Höhnel & Wolfbauer. Matière grasse de Vateria. 1886. III. 611.³
Höhnel, Franz, *Ritter* von. Ueber den Ablösungsvorgang der Zweige. 1878. V. xii.¹
— Zur Anatomie der Combretaceen. 1882. II. 615.³
— Anatomische Untersuchungen über einige Secretionsor-gane. 1882. I. 135.
— Über die Art des Auftretens einiger vegetabilischer Roh-stoffe. 1884. III. 485.³
— Beiträge zur Kenntniss der Luft- und Saftbewegung. 1879. I. 165.
— Beiträge zur Pflanzenanatomie und Physiologie. 1882. I. 112,¹ 134,¹ 135, II. 556,¹ 615.²
— Bemerkungen über den Arillus von Ravenala. 1881. II. 91.¹
— La consommation d'eau par les arbres. 1900. IV. 73.³
— Über den Einfluss des Rindendruckes. 1884. I. 130.
— Einige Bemerkungen über die Cuticula. 1878. I. 129.³
— Ueber die Einrichtungen der Blüthen. 1886. I. 238.
— Ueber den etagenförmigen Aufbau einiger Holzkörper. 1884. I. 125.
— Über gefässführende Hölzer mit Harzgängen. 1882. I. 134,¹ 135°
— Die Gerberinden. 1880. IV. 435.
— Ueber das häufige Vorkommen von ... Tracheiden-strängen in Coniferenhölzern. 1879. II. 16.²
— Ueber Harzröhren ... bei Hy ericum. 1882. II. 556.¹
— Histochemische Untersuchungen über das Xylophilin. 1877. I. 176.
— Ueber hystero-lysigene Harzräume. 1882. I. 135.
— Über den Kork und verkorkte Gewebe überhaupt. 1877. I. 130.
— Ueber das Material, welches zur Bildung des arabischen Gummis in der Pflanze dient. 1888. II. 329.¹
— Die Mikroskopie der : .. Faserstoffe. 1887. V. xxviii.¹
— Ueber die nachträgliche Entstehung von Trichomen. 1882. I. 112.³
— Notiz über die Mittellamelle der Holzelemente. 1880. I. 125.
— Die Pflanze und das Licht. 1883. I. 230.
— Ueber pflanzliche Faserstoffe. 1884. III. 234.
— Ueber die Pinkos-Knollen. 1884. IV. 447.³
— Über stockwerkartig aufgebaute Holzkörper. 1884. I. 125.
— Über die Transpirationsgrössen. 1879. V. 72.
— Ueber die Ursache der raschen Verminderung der Filtra-tionsfähigkeit von Zweigen. 1879. I. 167.
— Ueber das Verhalten der vegetabilischen Zellmembran. 1884. I. 138.¹
— Ueber das Wasserbedürfniss der Wälder. 1884. IV. 73.³
— Ueber den Wasserverbrauch der Holzgewächse. 1883. I. 167.
— Weitere Untersuchungen über den Ablösungsvorgang. 1878. V. xii.¹.

Höhnel, Ludwig, *Ritter* von. Discovery of Lakes Rudolf and Stefanie. 1892. I. 492.²
— Zum Rudolph-See und Stephanie-See.' 1892. I. 492.²
Hoehnel, M. De la présence de la dulcite.. 1900. III. 532.¹
— Das Vorkommen von Dulcit. 1900. III. 532.¹
Höinghaus, R. Das neue Feld- und Forst-Polizeigesetz. 1880. IV. 321.
— Das neue Forstdiebstahl-Gesetz. 1878. IV. 321.
— Das neue Gesetz betreffend den Forstdiebstahl. 1878. IV. 321.
— Reichs-Gesetz betreffend die Unfall- und Krankenver-sicherung. 1886. IV. 310.²
Höjer, Axel. Afhandling om de wäxter som i Bibelen omtalas. *See* THUNBERG, C. P. 1828. I. 513.
Hoeller, Ferdinand. Der König und die Königin der Löhr-bäume. 1820. II. 33.¹
Hölscher. Pentapterygium rugosum. 1898.. III. 653.²
Hölscher, Jelto. Aristolochia tricaudata. 1893. III. 386.²
— Bombax macrocarpum. 1896. III. 589.²
— Heterocentron roseum. 1896. III. 638.²
— Ueber die Oelrosencultur in Deutschland. 1894. III. 453.¹
Höltzer, H. *See* HERDER, Ferdinand von & HÖLTZER, H.
Hoelzl, Karl. Ueber die Heil- nnd [*sic*].Zäuberpflanzen der Ruthenen. 1861. III. 90.²
Hönig. Das Verhalten der Haide. 1849. IV. 210.³
— Der Waldbrand in der böhmisch sächsischen Schweiz. 1851. IV. 182.²
Hönig, Gustav. K déjinám Růže. 1897. II. 290.²
— Medinilla magnifica Lindley. 1897. III. 638.¹
Hönlinger, Hans. Ueber den Einfluss der Theuerungspro-centes. 1899. IV. 259.²
— Der Nutzeffect im aussetzenden und jährlichen Betriebe. 1899. IV. 259.¹
— Warum wirthschaften wir im Hochgebirge in höherem Um-triebe als in der Niederung? 1900. IV. 252.
Hoepffner, Nicolaus. Das verkehrte Jahr. 1696. I. 142.
Hörbye, J. Om frostskaden paa barskoven. 1882. IV. 442.
Hörmann, O. *See* LIEBERMANN, C. T. & HÖRMANN, O.
Hörmann, V. Abnorme Baumformen in Folge von Schnee-druck. 1884. IV. 190.
— Tagwurzelbildung an einer alten Schwarzpappel. 1884. IV. 486.¹
Hörter, J. Die besten Setzreben. 1831. III. 552.
Hoesch, E. Der landwirtschaftliche Ostbau. 1883. III. 139.
Höss, Franz. Anfangsgründe der Naturlehre. 1826. IV. 56.²
— Beschreibung der Schwarzföhre. 1825. II. 43.²
— Beschreibung der vorzüglichsten Forstinsecten. 1835. IV. 91.²
— Gemeinfassliche Anleitung die Bäume und Sträuche Oes-terreichs ... zu erkennen. 1830. I. 438, *IV. 86.¹*
— Monographie der Schwarzföhre. 1831. II. 43.⁴
— Die morgenländischen Erdgruben. 1836. IV. 147.²
— Das Nöthigste über den innern Bau der Organe ... in Holzgewächsen. 1833. I. 82,¹ *IV. 61.¹*
Höveler, W. Ueber die Verwerthung des Humus bei der Ernährung. 1892. I. 160.
Hoevell, W. R. van. Bijdrage tot de kennis der Badoeinen. 1845. III. 128.
— De Indische Archipel. 1847. III. 128.
Hoeven, A. PRUYS VAN DER. *See* PRUYS VAN DER HOEVEN, A.
Hoeven, Jan van der. Commentatio de foliorum plantarum ortu, situ, fabrica et functione. 1820. I. 109.¹
— Commentatio ... Qua quaeritur concinna expositio eorum quae de foliorum plantarum ortu ... innotuere? 1820. I. 109.¹
Hoevenaars, J. J. Sur l'identité de la fleur ... Widjåjå Koesoemå. 1898. II. 192.¹
Höybyeg, Welleejus. Dissertatiunculae de coelesti illo cibo, man dicto. 1743. III. 221.¹
Hof, A. C. Untersuchungen über die Topik der Alkaliver-theilung. 1900. I. 178.
Hofacker, Carl. .Das Flossregal besonders in Württemberg. 1844. IV. 390.¹
Hofberg, Herman. Förteckning på sällsyntare vexter funna omkring Södertelje. 1843. I. 354.
— Södermanlands phanerogamer och filices. 1852. I. 355.
Hofer, A. F. Grape culture. 1885. III. 550.
— Grape growing, a simple treatise. 1878. III. 550.
— Grape-growing by the single pole system. 1882. III. 550.
Hofer, Franz Joseph. Abhandlung vom Kaffee. 1781. III. 738.

Hofer, Heinrich. Kurze Anleitung zur praktischen Ausmes-sung und Berechnung von Flächen und Körpern. 1831. IV. 213.
Hoff, E. Planer till Brug ved Underviisningen i Have- og Skovbrugstegning. 1868. IV. 264.
Hoff, J. van & Ottolander, K. J. W. Vruchten-namen. 1879. III. 76.
Hoff, S. Paa egen Erfaring grundet Anviisning til Trædyrk-ning. 1836. III. 119.²
Hoffberg, Carl Fredric. Anvisning till wäxt-rikets kännedom. 1768. I. 83.
Hoffer, Eduard. Beobachtungen über blütenbesuchende Apiden. 1885. II. 431,¹ 776.¹
Hoffer, Raimund. Kautschuk und Guttapercha. 1892. III. 231.
— A practical treatise on caoutchouc. 1883. III. 231.
Hoffman, Antonius. De potu chocolatae. *See* LINNÉ, Carl von. 1765. III. 594.
Hoffmann, Ludwig. Analyse der Asche des Holzes ... der Linde. 1845. III. 586.¹
Hoffmann. Ligustrum japonicum var. Roxburghii. 1898. III. 673.²
Hoffmann, (*Oberförster*). Erfahrungen ... betreffs Erziehung von Kiefern-Beständen. 1885. IV. 481.
— Zur Frage der Erziehung von Kiefernbeständen. 1885. IV. 473.
— Frostschaden bei Kiefern. 1895. IV. 479.
— Ist die Erwartung ... berechtigt ... es liessen sich ledi-glich durch natürliche Besamung genügende Kiefernbestände erziehen? 1890. IV. 481.
— Rodung der Baumstöcke. 1874. IV. 386.
— Ueber die Schüttekrankheit der Kiefer. 1874. IV. 477.
— Zur Schütte-Krankheit der Kiefer. 1888. IV. 478.
— Zur Schüttekrankheit der Kiefer. 1895. IV. 479.
— Die Verjüngung der Kiefer. 1896. IV. 474.
— In welchem Umfange ist der ... Kiefern-Anflug zu nutzen. 1889. IV. 481.
Hoffmann, A. Das Tief- und Flachsetzen der Bäume. 1854. III. 169.²
Hoffmann, Alexander. Die Productionsverhältnisse der königlich-ungarischen Fondsdomänen-Forste. 1873. IV. 406.²
Hoffmann, Boleslaw & others. Schnitt der Kugel-Akazien. 1899. III. 487.²
Hoffmann, Carl. Eine Excursion nach dem Barba-Vulkan in Costa Rica. 1858. I. 333.
— Phänologische Beobachtungen aus Italien. 1878. I. 222.¹
— Phänologische Beobachtungen in Leipzig. 1878. I. 225.
Hoffmann, Christian. Ficus arbor philologice considerata. 1670. II. 149.²
Hoffmann, F. Beobachtungen über die Beschädigungen des Fichtenrüsselkäfers. 1854. IV. 455.
Hoffmann, F. W. Das Obstbuch. 1855. III. 146.²
— Sadownictwo. 1855. III. 146.¹
Hoffmann, Ferdinand. Anleitung zur schnellen Ausmittlung richtiger Einheitspreise für Bauhölzer. 1858. IV. 402.²
— Beiträge zur Kenntnis der Flora von Central-Ost-Afrika. 1889. I. 492.¹
Hoffmann, Friedrich. De Balsamo peruviano. 1703. III. 482.¹
— De Caryophyllis aromaticis. 1701. III. 635.²
— De cortice Cascarillae. 1738. III. 719.
— Disputatio inauguralis medica de china china modo ope-randi. 1704. III. 719.
— Exercitatio medica de Balsamo peruviano. 1703. III. 482.¹
— De manna. 1725. III. 221.¹
— Propemptico ... de chinæ chinæ modo operandi. 1694. III. 719.
— De recto corticis Chinae usu. 1728. III. 719.
— De terebinthina. 1699. IV. 443.¹
— De usu interno camphorae. 1714. III. 233.¹
— *See also* GILDEMEISTER, E. & HOFFMANN, Fr.
Hoffmann, Georg Franz. Deutschlands Flora. 1791. I. 374.
— Dissertatio medica observationes botanicas. 1787. I. 263.
— De fatis et progressibus rei herbariae. 1823. I. 80.¹
— La flore de l'Allemagne. 1791. I. 374.
— Germany's flora. 1791. I. 374.
— Historia Salicum iconibus illustrata. 1785. II. 98.²
— Hortus gottingensis. 1793. I. 44.
— Hortus mosquensis. 1808. I. 41.
— Observationes botanicae. 1787. I. 263.
— Syllabus plantarum officinalium. 1802. III. 55.

Hoffmann, Gottfried Daniel. Observationes circa bombyces. 1757. III. 379.[3]

Hoffmann, Hermann. Amygdalus communis L. 1875. II. 272.[3]

— Areale von Culturpflanzen. 1875. I. 300.

— Ueber das Aufblühen der Gewächse. 1883. I. 221.

— Ein Beitrag zur Lehre von der Vitalität der Samen. 1875. I. 193.[1]

— Bladens ålder hos en del lignoser. 1879. I. 191.[3]

— Ueber die Blätter-Verfärbung. 1878. ·I. 526.[3]

— Ueber Blattdauer. 1878. I. 191.[3]

— Climatologie végétale. 1864. I. 217. ·

— Culturversuche über Variation. 1883. II. 352.[1] — 1884. II. 649.[3] — 1887. . II. 270,[3] 276.[1] — 1892. II. 274.[1]

— Hedera Helix. 1884. II. 649.[3]

— Hexenbesen der Kiefer. 1871. IV. 476.

— Ueber Holzschwamm. 1872. IV. 211.[1]

— Zur Kenntniss der Vegetationsnormalen. 1861. I. 220.[3]

— Zur Kenntniss des Eichenholzes. 1848. II. 137.[1]

— Ueber den klimatischen Coëfficienten der Vegetation. 1859. I. 220.[3]

— Ueber Laubverfärbung. 1883. I. 225.

— Lehrbuch der Botanik. 1857. I. 90.

— Zur Lehre von den thermischen Constanten. 1880. I. 221.

— Mittlere, früheste und späteste Daten der phänologischen Beobachtungen in Giessen. 1895. I. 225.

— Nachträge zur Flora des Mittelrhein-Gebietes. 1879. I. 388.

— Persica vulgaris. 1877. ·II. 276.[1]

— Pflanzenarealstudien in den Mittelrheingegenden. 1867. I. 386.

— Pflanzen-Missbildungen. 1873. II. 113,[3] 330.[1]

— Pflanzenverbreitung und Pflanzenwanderung. 1852. I. 383.

— Pflaumen und Zwetsche. 1892. II. 274.[1]

— Ueber Pfropfen mit Bewurzelung. 1877. III. 165.

— Ueber phaenologische Accommodation. 1890. I. 221.

— Phaenologische Beobachtungen. 1884. I. 225. — 1886. I. 225.

— Phänologische Beobachtungen aus den Jahren. 1879–82. See HOFFMANN, Herman & IHNE, Egon. 1884. I. 222.[3]

— Phänologische Beobachtungen aus Mitteleuropa. 1883. I. 222.[3]

— Phänologische Beobachtungen in Giessen. 1859. I. 225.

— Phänologische Studien. 1885. I. 222.[3] — 1886. II. 272,[1] 481.[3] — 1887. I. 221, IV. 73.[1]

— Phaenologische Untersuchungen. 1887. I. 221.

— Ueber den praktischen Werth phänologischer Beobachtungen. 1889. I. 221.

— Das Problem der thermischen Vegetations-Constanten. 1867. I. 221.

— Prunus; Saatversuche. 1887. II. 270.[3]

— Resultate der wichtigsten pflanzen-phänologischen Beobachtungen in Europa. 1885. I. 222.[3]

— Ringelungsversuche. 1871. I. 140.[1]

— Ueber Rundwerden von Cactus-Stämmen. 1879. II. 588.[1]

— Ueber die Saftwege in den Pflanzen. 1850. I. 164.

— Samenbruch bei der Weinbeere. 1872. III. 560.

— Sarothamnus vulgaris als bodenanzeigende Pflanze. 1883. II. 352.[1]

— Schilderung der deutschen Pflanzenfamilien. 1846. I. 382.

— Ueber das s. g. Erfrieren der Pflanzen. 1865. I. 212.

— Ueber thermische Vegetations-Constanten. 1872. I. 225.

— Untersuchungen über den Pflanzenschlaf. 1850. I. 198.·

— Untersuchungen über künstliche Sempervirenz. 1871. I. 217.

— Untersuchungen zur Klima- und Bodenkunde. 1865. . I. 385, IV. 68, V. züz.[1]

— Die Vegetationsphasen der Rosskastanie. 1886. II. 481.[3]

— Vegetationsseiten in den Jahren 1857–[90]. 1859. I. 224.[3]

— Vergangenheit, Gegenwart . . . des deutschen Waldes. 1877. IV. 26.

— Vergleichende phänologische Karte von Mittel-Europa. 1881. I. 222.[3]

— Vergleichende Studien zur Lehre von der Bodenstetigkeit. 1860. I. 228.[3]

— Witterung und Wachsthum. 1857. I. 232.[1]

— & Ihne, Egon. Beiträge zur Phänologie. 1884. I. 222.[3]

Hoffmann, J. C. Besichtigungs- und Behauungs-Project derer zu . . . Commende Marburg gehörige Waldungen. 1791. IV. 352.

Hoffmann, Jakob Friedrich. Bijdrage ter verklaring van den . . . kruikvorm der bladen. 1840. I. 144,[3] II. 345.[1]

— Drei physiologisch-botanische Abhandlungen. 1828. I. 202.[3]

Hoffmann, Johann. Die Angaben schinesischer und japanischer Naturgeschichten von dem Illicium religiosum 1837. II. 209.[3]

— Bijdragen tot de geschiedenis . . . der Pioenen. 1848. III. 393.[1]

— Notes relating to the history . . . of the Paeony. 1848. III. 393.[1]

— Notice sur l'histoire . . . de Pivoines. 1848. III. 393.[1]

— & Schultes, J. H. Noms indigènes d'un choix de plantes du Japon et de la Chine. 1852. I. 75.[1]

Hoffmann, Johann Adam. De corticis peruviani modo operandi. See NEBEL, W. B. 1740. III. 719.

Hoffmann, Johann Gottfried. Die Berechnung und Benutzung des Bauholzes. 1799. IV. 220.

Hoffmann, Johann Joseph Ignatz. Physik und Mechanik. 1824. IV. 59.[1]

Hoffmann, Johann Moritz. Appendix plantarum . . . Horto medico altdorfino. 1691. I. 43.

— Florae altdorffinae deliciae. 1660. I. 43.

— Florae altdorffinae deliciae sylvestres. 1662. I. 372.

— Florilegium altdorfinum. 1676. I. 43.

— Montis mauritiani . . . descriptio medico-botanica. 1694. I. 372.

Hoffmann, Johannes. Die Forsttaxation. 1823. IV. 239.

Hoffmann, Julius. Die Veredelung des Epiphyllum truncatum. 1857. III. 623.[1]

Hoffmann, Karl. Ueber das Auftreten . . . der Fichten-Gespinnstblattwespe. 1894. IV. 457.

— Unsere Ausschlagforste. 1899. IV. 132.[1]

Hoffmann, Max. Vergleichende Morphologie . . . von Sambucus nigr. 1889. II. 840.[1]

Hoffmann, Otto. Compositae. 1894. II. 848.[3]

— Compositae africanae. 1893. II. 849.[3]

— Compostas da Africa portugueza. 1892. II. 849 [3]

— Plantae Lorentzianae. 1882. I. 345.

— Plantae Mechowianae. 1882. I. 491.

— Sertum plantarum madagascariensium. 1881. I. 496.

Hoffmann, Paul. Ueber Sommerstecklinge von Gesträuchen. 1864. III. 158.

Hoffmann, Philipp. Excursionsflora für die Flussgebiete der Altmühl. 1879. I. 387.

— Prodromus florae eystettensis. 1868. I. 386.

Hoffmann, Robert. Untersuchungen über die Wirkung mechanischer Kräfte auf die Teilung . . . der Zellen. 1885. I. 147.

Hoffmann, Sándor. Alapítványi erdőségek ismertetése. 1873. IV. 373.

— Die Productionsverhältnisse der königlich-ungarischen Fondsdomänen-Forste. 1873. IV. 373.

Hoffmann, T. Butyrum cacao. See MAUCHART, B. D. 1735. III. 594.

Hoffmann, Wilhelm. De strychnio. 1835. III. 682.[3]

Hoffmannsegg, Johann Centurius, Graf von. Catalogus seminum in hortis Comitis de Hoffmannsegg. 1823. I. 46.

— Nachtrag zu dem Preisverzeichnisse der Pflanzen. 1842. I. 47.

— Preisverzeichniss der Pflanzen in seinen Gärten. 1836. I. 47.

— Verzeichniss der Pflanzenkulturen. 1824.· I. 46.

— & Link, H. F. Flore portugaise. 1809. I. 420.

Hoffmeister, Aug. W. Noxious insects of the Cherry and Plum. 1879. III. 431.[1]

— Report on noxious insects. 1880. III. 186.[3]

Hoffmeister, Camill. Ueber ein ·Amygdalusgummi. 1898. II. 272.[1]

Hoffmeister, H. & Joseph. Bericht über die Gewinnung . . . der Eichenlohrinden. 1890. IV. 515.[1]

Hoffmeister, Werner. Briefe aus Indien. 1847. I. 472.

— Travels in Ceylon and continental India. 1847. I. 472.

Hoffschmidt, N. d'. See PICARD, Edmond & HOFFSCHMIDT, N. d'.

Hofstad, Olaf Alfred. Norsk flora. 1891. I. 358.

— Stavanger amts flora. 1891. I. 357.

Hofwenius, Pehr. De mamia. 1681. III. 221.[1]

Hoffy, Alfred. North American pomologist.· 1860. III. 61.[3]

Hofinger, J. Sztuka odmłodnienia starych drzew. 1828. III. 181.²

Hofland, M. Timmerhout op Borneo. 1883. IV. 400.¹

Hofman, Ulric. Catalogŭ planteloru, gradinei botaniœ . . . din Bucuresci. 1866. I. 66.²

Hofman-Bang, Niels E. Bärbuske og buskträr. 1886. III. 208.¹

— Om Dværgfrugttræers Behandling. 1872. III. 134.²

— Om Dværgtræers og Trægrenes Sammenpodning. 1873. III. 162.

— Nogle Bemærkninger om Skovplantning. 1870. IV. 113.²

— Om Trægrenenes Sammenpodning. 1874. III. 162.

— Vejledning til Behandling af Dværg-Æble- og Pæretræer. 1878. III. 134.²

Hofmann, A. Ueber die Arten der Gattung Cassia. 1873. III. 470.¹

Hofmann, August Wilhelm. Note sur deux nouveaux acides volatils . . . de Sorbier. 1859. II. 312.²

— Note sur le quinone. 1863. III. 722.

— Recherches sur la pipéridine. 1881. II. 94.¹

Hofmann, Hermann. Beiträge zur Flora saxonica. 1898. I. 390.

— Rosa Schlimperti. 1898. II. 298.³

Hofmann, J. Flora der Umgebung von Freising. 1857. I. 384.

— Flora von Freysing. 1857. I. 384.

Hofmann, Josef & Zeidler, Josef. Statistik und Geschichte des Gföhler- und Drosserwaldes. 1873. IV. 369.

Hofmann, Karl. Ueber den Eichenschälwald-Betrieb. 1895. IV. 508.

— A practical treatise on the manufacture of paper. 1873. IV. 429.

— Praktisches Handbuch der Papier-Fabrikation. 1873. IV. 429.

— Zusammenstellung der Gesetze, Verordnungen und Staatsverträge über das Forststrafwesen. 1832. IV. 319.¹

Hofmann, Kaspar. De medicamentis officinalibus. 1738. III. 257.¹

Hofmann, Ottmar. Bemerkungen über die Flacherie . . . der Nonnenraupe. 1893. IV. 201.

— Insektentötende Pilze. 1891. IV. 201.

— Die Schlaffsucht . . . der Nonne. 1891. IV. 201.

Hofmann, S. O. See Гофманъ, С. О.

Hofmann, W. Sur le parchemin végétal. 1859. III. 235.¹

Hofmann von Hofmannsthal, Ignaz. Die Caruba di Giudea. 1842. III. 472.¹

Hofmeister, Wilhelm Friedrich Benedict. Ueber die Abwärtskrümmung der . . . Wurzeln. 1868. I. 195.²

— Sur l'ascension de la sève. 1857. I. 164.

— Ueber den Bau der weiblichen Blüthe von Viscum. 1859. II. 178.¹

— Ueber die Befruchtung der Coniferen. 1854. II. 20.¹

— Über die Beugungen saftreicher Pflanzentheile. 1859. I. 149.²

— Sur les directions des parties des végétaux determinées par la pesanteur. 1860. I. 195.²

— Die Entstehung des Embryo. 1849. I. 122.

— Über Entwickelung von Blüthe und Frucht der deutschen Lorantheen. 1860. II. 173.²

— On the fecundation of the Coniferæ. 1854. II. 20.¹

— On the geographical distribution of the Coniferæ on the Himalayan Mountains. 1846. II. 15.²

— Ueber die geographische Verbreitung der Coniferen am Himalayah. 1846. II. 15.²

— Handbuch der physiologischen Botanik. 1865. I. 90.

— Neue Beiträge zur Kenntniss der Embryobildung. 1859. I. 122.

— Neuere Beobachtungen über Embryobildung. 1858. I. 122.

— Nouveaux documents destinés à faire connaître la formation de l'embryon. 1859. I. 122.

— Ueber passive und active Abwärtskrümmung von Wurzeln. 1869. I. 195.²

— Über die durch die Schwerkraft bestimmten Richtungen. 1860. I. 195.²

— Ueber das Steigen des Saftes. 1857. I. 164.

— Zur Uebersicht der Geschichte . . . der Pflanzenbefruchtung. 1856. I. 201.¹

— Vergleichende Untersuchungen der Keimung . . . höherer Kryptogamen. 1862. I. 441.

Hofstädter, P. Gotthard. Vegetationsverhältnisse von Kremsmünster. 1862. I. 441.

Hofstede, H. J. ' Assam-Thee; haar cultuur. 1898. III. 604.¹

Hofstetter, Joh. See **STÄHELIN**, Christoph & **HOFSTETTER**, Joh.

Hogan, F. E., Hogan, John & MacErlean, John. Irish and Scottish Gaelic names of herbs, plants, trees. 1900. I. 74.¹

Hogan, John. See **HOGAN**, F. E., **HOGAN**, John & **MAC-ERLEAN**, John.

Hogendorp, C. S. W., comte de. Coup d'œil sur l'île de Java. 1830. III. 274.¹

— The Molucca islands. 1849. III. 274.¹

Hogendorp, S. W. C., comte de. Beschrijvinge van het eiland Timor. 1781. III. 274.¹

— Beschrijving van het eiland Timor en der nabij gelegen eilanden. 1784. III. 274.¹

— See also **RADERMACHER**, J. C. M. & HOGENDORP, S. W. C., comte de.

Hogg, John. On the ballast-flora of the coast of Durham. 1867. I. 402.

— A catalogue of Sicilian plants. 1842. I. 431.

— On Gebel Haurán, its adjacent districts. 1860. II. 131.¹

— On the geography, geology and vegetation of Sicily. 1830. I. 431.

— On the influence of the climate of Naples. 1834. I. 226.²

— On the natural history . . . of Stockton-on-Tees. 1827. I. 397.

— Observations on some of the classical plants of Sicily. 1834. I. 431.

— On the Rosa rubella of Winch. 1860. II. 298.¹

Hogg, Robert. The Apple and its varieties. 1851. III. 425.²

— British pomology. 1851. III. 425.²

— The fruit manual. 1860. III. 79.

— A new classification of Apples. 1876. III. 425.²

— The vegetable kingdom and its products. 1858. III. 52.

— & Bull, H. G. The Apple and Pear as vintage fruits. 1886. III. 425.²

— — The Herefordshire pomona. 1876. III. 79.

— & Johnson, G. W. The wild flowers of Great Britain. 1863. I. 401.

Hogg, Thomas. On the comparative advantages of cutting large timber by the axe or saw. 1874. IV. 383.²

— Growing Wistarias. 1874. III. 490.¹

— History of Sciadopitys. 1879. III. 309.²

— Introduction of the Cercidiphyllum. 1879. III. 388.²

— Old and remarkable trees on the Hampton Court estate. 1881. I. 297.¹

— Wistarias and their culture. 1874. III. 490.¹

Hogg's weekly instructor. III. 17.

Hohberg, Wolfgang Helmhard, Freiherr von. Georgica curiosa. See **HOHW**, Helmhard. 1682. IV. 115.

— Die mit teutschen Saiten überzogene heilige Kron-Harffe. 1680. V. xxv.²

Die **Hohe** Eiche. 1842. II. 138.¹

Ueber die hohen Holzpreise. 1837. IV. 282.²

Hohenacker, Rudolphus Fridericus. Enumeratio plantarum in territorio elisabethopolensi. 1833. I. 361.

— Enumeratio plantarum . . . per provinciam Talysch. 1838. I. 361, 368.¹

— Höhenprofil und Kärtchen des südwestlichen Theiles von Persien. 1846. I. 477.³

Hohenadel, Wilhelm. Forst- und Jagd-Kalender. 1808. IV. 96.

— Der holzgerechte Förster über Benutzung der Holzarten. 1808. III. 270.²

— Taschenbuch für Forstmaenner. 1823. IV. 222.

Hohenbruck, Arthur, Freiherr von. Der Holzexport Oesterreichs nach den Häfen. 1867. IV. 406.²

— Der Holzexport Oesterreichs nach Westen. 1869. IV. 406.²

— Österreichische land- und forstwirthschaftliche Bibliographie. 1899. IV. 2.

— Tabellen über den Holzhandel. 1869. IV. 402.²

— & Zimmerauer, Friedrich, Ritter von. Der land- und forstwirthschaftliche Unterricht in den im Reichsrathe vertretenen Königreichen und Ländern. 1890. IV. 36,² V. xxix.²

Hohenheim, Aureolus Philippus Theophrastus, BOMBAST VON. See **BOMBAST VON HOHENHEIM**, A. P. T.

Hohenstein, Adolf. Beschreibung des Waldtelegraphen. 1808. . IV. 391.

— Drathriese. 1861. IV. 391.

— Die Drathriese in Südtyrol. 1861. IV. 391.

— Die Eichenschäl-Wirthschaft. 1861. IV. 505.

— Lançoir en fil de fer. 1861. IV. 391.

— Die Pottaschen-Fabrikation. 1856. IV. 395.

— Die Theer-Fabrikation. 1857. IV. 436.¹

— Der Wald sammt dessen wichtigem Einfluss auf das Klima. 1860. IV. 43, 243.

Hohenwarth, Sigmund von. *See* REINER, Joseph & HOHENWARTH, S. von.
Hohes Alter einer Weisstanne. 1861. II. 24.[1]
Hokk'joo Hookoku. Wehonosamagusa. 1808. I. 461.
Hokkyō, Yesukuni. Ya zan sō. n. d. I. 461.
Holandre, Jean Joseph Jacques. Flore de la Moselle. 1829. I. 378.
— Nouvelle flore de la Moselle. 1829. I. 378.
— Observations sur un insecte du Mélèze. 1849. IV. 450.
Holbé. Étude sur les principales Piperacées. 1885. II. 93.[2]
Holck, E. *See* MYLIUS, C. de. & HOLCK, E.
Holden, Louis H. Sur l'Aralia spinosa. 1881. III. 641.[2]
Holder. Account of the effects of the juice of the Papaw tree. 1816. III. 617.[1]
Holdhaus, C. & **Panzer,** R. Denkschrift über die Entwicklung der Seidenzucht. 1864. III. 377.
Hole, Robert Selby. The exudation of gum from ... the Mahua. 1898. III. 667.[2]
— Tannin materials used in the Damoh district. 1900. IV. 435.
Hole, Samuel Reynolds. An apple from Caunton. 1880. II. 267.[1]
— A book about Roses. 1869. III. 449.
— Reynolds Hole's Buch von der Rose. 1869. III. 449.
Holfeld, Anton Franz. Vermischte forstwissenschaftliche Aufsätze. 1826. IV. 101.
Holfert, Johannes. Die Nährschicht der Samenschalen. 1890. I. 121.
— Ueber die primäre Anlage der Wurzeln. 1889. I. 104.
Holkema, Franciscus. De plantengroei der Nederlandsche Noordsee-eilanden. 1870. I. 391.[1]
Holl. Untersuchungen über den Gerbsäuregehalt des Sumachstrauches. 1898. III. 524.[2]
Holl, F. Die Ulme und deren Erziehung. 1897. IV. 518.[2]
— Ueber das Zutagetreten von Baumwurzeln. 1888. IV. 144.[1]
Holl, Ferdinand. Berechnung des Rindenprocentes. 1895. IV. 219.
— Ueber den Einfluss des Baumalters auf den Samen der Fichte. 1887. IV. 454.
— Die Samen einiger nordamerikanischer Nadelholzwaldbäume. 1895. IV. 444.[1]
— Die Stammcubirungsformeln. 1890. IV. 218.
Holl, Friedrich. A list of plants observed in the island of Madeira. 1830. I. 497.
— Verzeichniss der auf der Insel Madeira beobachteten Pflanzen. 1830. I. 497.
— Wörterbuch deutscher Pflanzen-Namen. 1833. I. 73.[1]
— Zapfen, Samen und Keimlinge der Omorika-Fichte. 1893. II. 38.[1]
— & **Heynhold,** Gustav. Flora von Sachsen. 1842. I. 380.
Holland, (*Forstmeister*). Ueber die neuere Entwicklung des Taxationswesens in Württemberg. 1865. IV. 248.[1]
Holland, (*Revierförster*). Ueber die Büschelpflanzung der Fichte. 1853. IV. 453.
Holland, A. Hedera canariensis fol. var. 1891. III. 643.[1]
Holland, F. R. The habitat of the Cherokee Rose. 1888. II. 295.[2]
Holland, Robert. *See* BRITTEN, James & HOLLAND, Robert.
Holland, William J. Ascent of the volcanoes Nantai-san ... and Nasu-take. 1890. I. 463.[1]
Hollandsche maatschappij der wetenschappen te Haarlem. Natuurkundige verhandelingen. Oeconomischen tak. Landbouw. Verhandelingen. I. 15.
Hollandsche maatschappij van landbouw, Lijst der boekwerken voorhanden in de boekerij. *See* LIJST ... 1879. III. 1.
Holle, G. von. Flora von Hannover. 1862. I. 385.
Holle, Gustav. Ueber den anatomischen Bau des Blattes in der Familie der Sapotaceen. 1892. II. 696.[2] ·
— Beiträge zur Anatomie der Saxifragaceen. 1893. II. 237.[2]
— Ueber einige neue Kautschukpflanzen. 1893. III. 668.[1]
Holle, H. G. Ueber den Vegetationspunkt der Angiospermen-Wurzeln. 1876. I. 103.
— Ueber den Vegetationspunkt der Dicotylen-Wurzeln. 1877. I. 103.
Holle, K. F. Over het aanplanten van den Dadelboom in Indië. 1860. III. 328.[1]
— De Arenboom. .1878. III. 320.[2]
— Arenboom. 1879. III. 320.[2]
— Een betere bereiding van aren-lontar. 1893. III. 319.[2]
— Eenige gegevens omtrent den Indischen landbouw. 1894. III. 730.

— De Elaeis guinensis of Oliepalm. 1879. III. 325.[1] — 1880. III. 325.[1]
— Gouvernements-Koffiecultuur ter Sumatra's westkust. 1893. III. 730.
— Iets over bemesting van Koffijtuinen. 1865. III. 734.[1]
— Mishandeling van den Klapper- en Arenpalm. 1864. III. 317.
— Mitra noe tani. 1874. III. 128.
— Opgave van eenige geschikte houtsoorten ... in de bosschen nabij Tjikadjang. 1861. IV. 399.[2]
— Patjoelen in aanplantingen van boom gewassen. 1885. III. 166. ı
— Het planten van boomen langs wegen. 1879. III. 211.[1] —1880. III. 209.
— Proef-handleiding voor de kultuur ... van Koffie. 1862. III. 729.[1]
— Sawo Manila. 1879. III. 666.[2]
— Schaduwboomen. 1879. III. 734.[2]
— Het stekken van Koffie. 1879. III. 733.[1]
— Terrassen in Koffietuinen. 1894. III. 727.
— Terrassen op hellende gronden. 1875. III. 726.[2]
— Toppen van Koffieboomen. 1880. III. 734.[2]
— Veredeling van de Koffij. 1867. III. 733.[2]
— Verslag betreffende de Thee-onderneming Waspada. 1868. III. 602.[1]
— Verslag omtrent de Thee-onderneming Waspada. 1868. III. 602.[1]
— Vrienden en vijanden. 1877. III. 186.[1]
— Het vroege bloeien der Koffieboomen. 1879. III. 727.
— Een vruchtboom. 1878. III. 669.[1]
— Een vruchtboom ... Diospyros Kaki. 1879. III. 669.[2]
— Wetenschap en praktijk, ook met betrekking tot de Koffiekultuur. 1863. III. 726.[2]
— *See also* GORKOM, K. W. van, PLES, D. & HOLLE, K. F.; SCHEFFER, R. H. C. C. & HOLLE, K. F.
Holleben, von. Bereitung von Terpentinöl. 1879. IV. 447.[1]
— Gewinnung von Oel aus Fichtenharz. 1880. IV. 459.[2]
— Ueber die Harznutzung in den fürstlich schwarzburgrudolstädtischen Waldforsten. 1880. IV. 436.[2]
Holleben, C. L. B. von. Die Aufforstung verödeter Muschelkalkberge. 1861. IV. 158.
— Beiträge zur künstlichen Nachzucht der Buche. 1850. IV. 494.
— Beiträge zur Naturgeschichte-des Nonnenspinners. 1840. IV. 200. — 1842. IV. 200.
— Briefliche Notizen. 1845. II. 23.[2]
— Die Königstanne auf dem Wurzelberge. 1879. II. 24.[1]
Holleman, F. A. Het afsterven van jonge dennenbosschen. 1899. IV. 479.
— Beplanting met Plukdennen. 1892. IV. 474.
— Over de doelmatigste wijze van ontginning onzer heidevelden. 1884. IV. 160.[1]
— De oude Lindeboom te Oisterwijk. 1897. II. 517.[1]
Hollick, Arthur. Appendages to the petioles of Liriodendra. 1896. II. 211.[1]
— Notes from Staten Island. 1881. II. 458.[2]
— Observations on the geology and botany of Martha's Vineyard. 1893. I. 316.
— The Old Field Pine in New Jersey. 1897. II. 48.[2]
— Plant distribution as a factor. 1892. I. 316.
— A recent discovery of hybrid Oaks. 1888. II. 134.[1]
— The relation between forestry and geology in New Jersey. 1899. I. 313, *IV.* 77.[1]
Hollies. 1888. III. 530.[1]
Hollings, G. E. & others. Report on fibrous specimens manufactured from the Mdddār. 1854. III. 692.[2]
Hollmann, S. C. De foliorum in plantis perfectioribus mechanismo et usu. 1765. I. 172.
Hollmén, H. Några sällsynta fröväxter från ryska Lappmarken. 1886. II. 101.[1]
— Växtfynd i Finland. 1888. II. 308.[1]
Holloway, James. Planting for timber. 1897. IV. 112.
— Roses for decorative use. 1900. III. 456.[1]
Hollrung, Max. Handbuch der chemischen Mittel gegen Pflanzenkrankheiten. 1898. III. 197.
— Die wichtigsten Obstschädiger. 1898. III. 191.
— *See also* SCHUMANN, Karl & HOLLRUNG, Max.
Hollsten, Jonas. ·Sjutton års observationer på sånings- och skörde-tiden. 1768. IV. 344.[1]
Hollweg. Herbstliches Eindecken der Kiefernkämpe. 1885. IV. 478.
— Zur Schlagführung im Kiefernwalde. 1894. IV. 474.
Holly grove on Seven Mile Beach, N. J. 1897. II. 464.[2]

The Holly-leaved Cherry. 1873. III. 437.[1]
Holm, Carolus Otto. Plantarum brasiliensium. *See* THUNBERG, C. P. 1817. I. 341.
Holm, Georgius Tycho. Prodromus florae danicae. *See* LINNÉ, Carl von. 1757. I. 351.
Holm, John. On cocoa and its manufacture. 1874. III. 595.[1]
Holm, Theodor. Contributions to the flora of Greenland. 1896. I. 309.[2]
— Contributions to the knowledge of the germination of some North American plants. 1890. I. 123.[1]
— The function of the secondary tissues in arborescent monocotyledons. 1894. I. 160.
— Notes on the leaves of Liriodendron. 1890. II. 211.[1]
— Novaja-Zemlia's Vegetation. 1885. I. 364,
— The role of the pericycle in the root of Dracaena. 1894. II. 83.[1]
— Root-tubercles on Ailanthus. 1895. II. 413.[2]
— The seedlings of Jatropha multifida. 1899. II. 227,[2] *446*.[1]
— Third [and fourth] list of additions to the flora of Washington. 1892. V. XVII.[2]
— Third list of additions to the flora of Washington. 1892. II. 133.[2]
— On the validity of some fossil species of Liriodendron. 1895. II. 210.[2]
— La végétation de la Nouvelle-Zemble. 1885. I. 364.
Holm, V. F. Beskrifning af några Salix-former. 1892. II. 100.[2]
Holmberg, Eduardo Ladislao. La flora de la República Argentina. 1895. I. 345.
Holmberger, Petrus. Några vildt-växande svenska örters hushålls-nytta. 1774. III. 270.[1]
— Pan Boum, eller hvilka växter born-boskapen äter eller ratar. 1779. III. 223.[1]
— Rön, om de växter, som ätas eller förkastas af svinkreaturen. 1776. III. 223.[1]
Holmboe, Jens. Notizen über die endozoische Samenverbreitung der Vögel. 1900. I. 241.[1]
Holmboe, O. Underretning om, hvorledes man kand omgaaes med Frugt-Træer i en Have. 1758. III. 134.[1]
Holme, Charles. Catalogue of a collection . . . to illustrate the uses of Bamboo. 1890. III. 315.[2]
— The uses of Bamboo in Japan. 1893. III. 315.[2]
Holmers, C. G. Handledning för skogsskötseln i Norrland. 1877. IV. 288.[2]
— Veiledning i skogens behandling. 1878. IV. 103.[3]
Holmes, Edward Morell. Astringent gum from Mashonaland. 1893. III. 468.[1]
— Catalogue of the collections in the museum of the Pharmaceutical society. 1878. I. 55.
— Ceará Jaborandi. 1894. II. 410.[1]
— Chaulmugra seed. 1900. III. 614.[2]
— Cinchona. 1882. III. 718.
— Cinnamomum Cassia. 1890. III. 405.[1]
— Sur les diverses espèces d'Anis étoilés. 1880. II. 209.[2]
— Duboisia myoporoides. 1878. III. 700.[1]
— Essence de Citron de la Trinité. 1884. III. 499.[1]
— Further notes on vegetable tallow. 1884. III. 407.[1]
— Le Gelsemium sempervirens. 1876. II. 718.[2]
— Guaycuru root. 1879. III. 666.[2]
— On the identity of Goa powder. 1875. III. 471.[1]
— The Jaborandi leaves of commerce. 1895. III. 342,[1] 608.[1]
— Kola nut. 1900. III. 591.[1]
— Kola seeds. 1900. III. 591.[1]
— Lukrabo or Ta-Fung-Tsze. 1885. III. 614.[2]
— Mexican Lign Aloes. 1888. III. 510.[1]
— Myrrh and bdellium. 1898. II. 417,[2] III. 511.[1]
— Myrtus chekan. 1879. III. 635.[1]
— Note on Calabar bean. 1879. III. 484.[1]
— Note on Hedyosmum nutans. 1882. III. 343.[2]
— Note on Shea butter. 1879. III. 667.[1]
— Notes on casual drugs. 1878. III. 521,[2] 608.[2]
— Notes on some American medicinal plants. 1876. III. 695.[1]
— Notes on some Japanese drugs. 1880. III. 273,[2] 431,[2] 504.[2]
— Notes on Star anise. 1889. III. 398.[1]
— Notes on the oil of Akee. 1900. III. 552.[2]
— Notes on the trees yielding myrrh. 1896. III. 511.[1]
— Oil of sandal wood. 1886. III. 225.
— Ouabaio. 1893. III. 685.[2]
— Piptocalyx Moorei Oliv. 1894. III. 403.[2]
— Sur quelques huiles grasses du Japan. 1886. III. 225.
— Remarks on Cinchona Ledgeriana. 1886. II. 813.[2]
— Sur le Séné. 1875. III. 471.[1]

— Some medicinal products from the Straits Settlements 1893. III. 366,[2] *583*.[1]— 1895. III. 275.[1]
— Star-anise. 1880. II. 209.[2]
— Strophantus Nicholsoni, a new species. 1897. II. 732.[2]
— Suif végétal de Singapore. 1883. III. 611.[1]
— Tangkawang fat or vegetable tallow. 1887. III. 225.
— The trees yielding benzoin. 1884. III. 670.[2]
— Tu-chung bark. 1891. III. 418.[1]
— Vegetable tallow from Singapore. 1883. III. 611.[2]
— West Indian Sandal wood oil. 1899. III. 384,[2] *495*.[1]
Holmes, J. A. Occurrence of Abies canadensis and Pinus Strobus. 1884. II. 46,[1] *53*.[1]
— The proposed Appalachian park. 1900. IV. 179.[2]
Holmes, Joseph. On transplanting trees. 1851. III. 167.
Holmes, Samuel. Blackberries. 1900. III. 457.[2]
Holmgreen, August Emil. De for Landbruget . . . nyttige og skadelige Insecter. 1870. IV. 549.[1]
Holmgren, Hjalmar Joseph. Anteckningar öfver vegetationen kring Motala. 1841. I. 354.
— Ruborum Sueciae . . . *See* ARRHENIUS, J. P. 1839. II. 301.[1]
— Tillägg till en . . . afhandling om vegetationen i Motalatrakten. 1843. I. 354.
Holmgren, Karl Albert. Om växtstället "Tryserums s:n, Hornsberg" för Rubus pruinosus. 1886. II. 309.[2]
Hołowkiewicz, Emil. Flora leśna i przemysl drzewny w Galicyi. 1877. IV. 87.[1]
— Las głównym czynnikiem dobrobytu narodowego. 1871. IV. 44.
— Lasy i pastwiska górskie. 1885. IV. 136.[1]
— Obrazy fizyograficzne Galicyi. 1887. IV. 143.[1]
Holst, C. Vegetabilische Seife. 1890. III. 226.[1]
— Vegetabilisches Wachs. 1890. III. 226.[1]
— Die wasser- und milchartigen Getränke. 1890. III. 223.[1]
Holst, E. MØLLER-. *See* MØLLER-HOLST, E.
Holst, Vilh. Om Pileanlæg. 1892. III. 349.
— Resultater af en Piledyrkning. 1899. III. 349.
Holstein, F. A. von. Anvisning for Gaardmændene, . . . til at opelske Skov paa deres Lodder. 1811. IV. 113.[1]
Holster, J. C. *See* JOOSTEN, E. & HOLSTER, J. C.
Holten, Carl Valentin. Bemærkninger om Skovenes Indflydelse. 1867. IV. 53.
Holten, N. Bemærkninger . . . om Fremtids Skovbrug. 1870. IV. 101. .
— Om Fyrren i det danske Skovbrug. 1874. IV. 472.
— Om Nattefrost. 1872. III. 182.
Holtermann, Carl. Beiträge zur Anatomie der Combretaceen. 1893. II. 615.[1]
Holtz, (*Förster, Lindenbusch*). Kurze Anleitung zur Pflanzung der einjährigen Kiefer. 1874. IV. 472.
Holtz, Ludwig. Zur Flora Süd-Russlands. 1879. I. 364.
Holtz-, Mast- und Jagd-Ordnung, für . . . Schlesien. 1750. IV. 301.
Holtzschuhius, Joannes Cosma. Annotationes in Dioscoridem. 1556. I. 279.[2]
Holtzapffel, Charles. Descriptive catalogue of the woods commonly employed . . . for the . . . arts. 1843. IV. 396.[1]
— Turning and mechanical manipulation. 1843. IV. 427.[2]
Holtze, Maurice. Introduced plants in the Northern Territory. 1892. I. 242.[1]
— Narrative of an exploring tour across Melville Island. 1892. I. 304.
Holtze, N. Notes on the fertilisation of some North Australian plants. 1898. I. 240.[1]
Holtzenius, Petrus. Pharmacopoea sive dispensatorium coloniense. 1627. III. 247.[2]
Holtz-Ordnung unser Pfaltz-Graff Carl Philipps. 1760. IV. 317.[2]
Holtz-Ordnung wobey die freydenthal. Holtz-Taxa. 1861. IV. 302.
Holuby, Josef Ludwig. Batographische Notizen. 1875. II. 304.[2]
— Aus der Botanik slovakischer Kinder. 1896. III. 272.[1]
— Ueber die Brombeere . . . bei den Slowaken. 1892. III. 457.[2]
— Die Brombeeren der Flora von Ns. Podhrad. 1873. II. 304.[2]
— Ueber einige auf Pflanzen bezügliche aberglaubische Gebräuche. 1881. I. 518.
— Zur Flora Presburgs. 1870. II. 304.[1]
— Die gewöhnlichsten wildwachsenden Genuszpflanzen des Trencsiner Comitates. 1891. III. 272.[1]
— Der Holler (Sambucus) in der Volksmedizin. 1883. II. 841.[1]

Holuby, Josef Ludwig (*continued*).
— Phanerogame Flora von Nemes-Podhragy. 1866. . I. 445.
— Die Rubi der Ns. Podhragyer-Flora. 1868. II. 304.¹
— Rubus Khekii n. sp. 1891. II. 308.²
— Zusätze zur Flora von Nemes-Podhragy. 1869. I. 446.
— Zwei neue Brombeeren. 1884. II. 304.²
Holway, E. W. D. *See* ARTHUR, J. C., BAILEY, L. H. & HOLWAY, E. W. D.
Holwel, John Zephaniah. A letter giving an account of a new species of Oak. 1772. II. 135.¹
The **Holy** Citron of Morocco. 1891. III. 502.²
Holyoke, Thomas. . The effects of soil upon . . . Apple trees. 1868. III. 426.¹
Holz. Eine starke Fichte. 1859. II. 37.¹
Das **Holz** der sibirischen Lärche. 1891. IV. 452.²
Das **Holz** des Buchsbaumes. 1876. IV. 525.
Die **Holz** producirenden Länder der Erde. 1884. IV. 403.¹
Holz- und Waldordnung für das Königreich Hungarn. 1780. IV. 307.¹
Holzarbeiter. IV. 4.
Die **Holzasche** als Forstgartendünger. 1865. IV. 144.²
Holzaufzug und Drahtseilbahn. 1874. IV. 391.
Die **Holzausfuhr** aus der Schweiz. 1859. IV. 406.¹
Holzbestand und Holzverbrauch in Nordamerika. 1897. IV. 403.²
Der **Holzdiebstahl.** 1841. IV. 196.²
Holzer, Georg. Ueber die physiologische Bedeutung des oxalsaueren Kalkes. 1867. I. 139.
Holzer, Stephan. De camphora. 1780. III. 404.¹
Der **Holzhändler.** *See* Der WESTFÄLISCHE Holzhändler. IV. 11.
Holzhändler-Kalender. IV. 9.
Holzhauer, W. C. Sur l'Eriodictyon californicum. 1881. II. 747.¹
Der **Holzhauereibetrieb** im Kurfürstenthum Hessen. · 1861. IV. 383.¹
Der **Holzhauereibetrieb** . . . in den braunschweigischen Staatsforsten. 1865. IV. 383.¹
Der **Holzhauerei-Betrieb** in den Domanial-Forsten des Herzogthums Sachsen-Gotha. 1861. IV. 383.¹
Holzhauerordnung für die k. württ. Staatswaldungen. · 1882. IV. 303.²
Holzindustrie in Finnland. 1893. IV. 404.¹
Holz-Industrie-Zeitung. *See* ALLGEMEINE Holz-Zeitung. IV. 6.
Holzinger, J. Die Baumschutz-Vorrichtungen. 1887. III. 199.
Holzinger, John M. Determinations of plants collected by J. H. Sandberg. 1896. II. 459.¹
— The range of Amorpha fruticosa. ·1893· II. 333.¹
— Two new species of Idaho plants. 1896. II. 295.²
Der **Holzkonsum** im Kanton Bern. 1885. IV. 406.¹
Ueber **Holzmangel** und Holzausfuhr. 1856. IV. 283.¹
Holzmassegehalt eines Buchenwäldchens. 1870. IV. 498.
Die **Holzmesskluppe**, Patent Otten. 1890. IV. 231.²
Holzner. Ueber die . . . Fütterung mit verkleinertem Holze. 1894. III. 223.¹
Holzner, Georg. Die Beobachtungen über die Schütte der Kiefer. 1877. II. 20,² *IV. 461.*¹
— Die Krystalldrusen in den Blättern des weissen Maulbeer-Baumes. 1867. II. 154.²
— Ueber die Raphiden in den Blättern des Weinstockes. 1866. II. 507.¹
Das **Holzpapier.** 1853. IV. 429.
Ueber **Holzpflanzung** nach Biermanns'scher Art. 1854. . IV. 141.
Holzpreise. 1853. IV. 406.¹
Holzpreiss in den hochfürstlich speierschen Waldungen ober der Queich. 1793. IV. 298.²
Der **Holzrechner.** 1839. IV. 229.
Holzschuler. Erläuterung der natürlichen und künstlichen Systeme in der Botanik. 1841. I. 252.
Holz-Spar-Kunst; ein Buch für Jedermann. 1800. IV. 280.²
Holzstoff-Papier. 1868. IV. 429.²
Holz-Tabellen; Berechnung der kantigen und runden Hölzer . . . in Schweizermass. 1867. IV. 225.
Holztabellen oder Reductionstabellen der runden Holzes nach Cubikfuss. 1836. IV. 222. .
Holz-Taxe des Herzogthums Gotha. 1811. IV. 303.¹
Holz-Taxe für das Amt Grüllenbürg. 1851. IV. 302.
Holz-Taxe für das Forstverwaltungsamt Frauenstein. 1860. IV. 303.¹
Holz-Taxe für das Forstverwaltungsamt Grillenburg. 1859. IV. 303.¹
Holz-Taxe für die herrschaftlichen Forsten . . . des Fürstenthums Schwarzburg-Sondershausen. 1841. IV. 303.¹

Holztaxe ohne Zuschlag der Haulöhne. 1853. IV. 404.²
Der **Holzverkehr** auf dem Schienenwege. 1897. IV. 9, *403.*¹
Ueber **Holzverkohlen.** 1805. IV. 394.
Ueber **Holzverkohlung.** 1829. IV. 394.
Der **Holzwuchs** in nördlichen Schweden. ·1888. IV. 113.²
Ueber **Holzzucht** auf landwirthschaftlichen Gründen. 1862. IV. 123.²
Die **Holzzucht** ausserhalb des Waldes. 1855. III. 101.²
Homann, G. G. J. Flora von Pommern. 1828. I. 378.
Homberg, Wilhelm. Essais pour examiner les sels des plantes. 1702. I. 156.¹
— Experiences sur la germination des plantes. 1730. I. 202.¹
— Observations sur les analyses des plantes. 1704. I. 156.¹
— Sur l'utilité des jardins d'acclimatation. 1704. I. 181.¹
— Observations sur les sels volatils des plantes. 1704. I. 174.
Hombres-Firmas, · Louis Augustin, *baron* d'. Essai sur la croissance des arbres. 1841. IV. 64.²
— Influence de l'ombre du Noyer. 1845. III. 355.
— Notes sur quelques végétaux . . . dans le département du Gard. 1834. III. 271.¹
— Recueil de mémoires et d'observations de physique. 1838. III. 35.
— Relation d'un exemple fort rare de végétation. 1822. II. 714.²
— Sur l'utilité des jardins d'acclimatation. ·1848. I. 58.
— Sur l'utilité des jardins d'acclimatation. · 1849. III. 43.
Hombron. Aperçu sur la · côte nord de l'Australie. 1845. I. 501.
Homburg, Georg Theodor. Ein Beitrag zur Nutzholzwirthschaft. ·1879. IV. 129.
— Begründung der Notwendigkeit einer Reform unserer Buchenwirthschaft. 1891. IV. 495.
— Zur Erklärung des Schüttens der Kiefern. 1852. IV. 475.
— Gedanken über eine . . . Verjüngungsmethode des Buchenhochwaldes. 1857. IV. 494.
— Kurhessens Waldfläche im Jahre 1865. 1867. IV. 353.
— Die Nutzholzwirthschaft im geregelten Hochwald-Ueberhaltbetriebe. 1878. IV. 129, *169.*¹
— Vergleichsberechnung der Rentabilität der beiden Betriebsarten. 1893. IV.-129, *233, 258.*
— Ein weiterer Beitrag zur Nutzholzwirthschaft. 1884. IV. 473.
Home, A. D. Forestry in India. 1884. IV. 378.
Home, *Sir* Everard. On the native cloth and on the Kava. 1847. III. *343.*¹ 363.¹
Home, Henry. The gentleman farmer. 1776. III. 109.
Home of the Redwood. 1897. IV. 382.²
The **home** of the Redwood. 1897. IV. 484.¹
Homergue, John d'. Silk culturist's manual. 1839. III. 375.
Homeyer, von. Beobachtungen an den Coniferen meiner Baumschule. 1887. III. 290.
Homeyer, A. H. *See* WILLDENOW, C. L. & HOMEYER, A. H.
Homeyer, Eugen Ferdinand von. Bemerkungen über die düngende Wirkung des . . . Wassers. 1883. I. 218.
— Die Spechte und ihr Werth in forstlicher Beziehung. 1879. IV. 90,² *199.*¹
Homeyer-Murchin, von. Wie beugt man der Erschöpfung der Bodenkraft in ständigen Baumschulen . . . vor? 1859. IV. 151.¹
Homfray, P. An account of the successful propagation . . . of Mangoe. 1845. III. 524.²
Homma, Juchan. Die forstwirthschaftlichen Verhältnisse des Kronlandes Mähren. 1884. IV. 369.
— Wald und Forstwirtschaft in Mähren. 1897. IV. 369.
L'Hommedieu, Ezra. On ditches and hedges. 1794. III. 212.¹
Hommes, P. J. Bosch-exploitatie "Montferland." 1893. IV. 356.¹
— Verschillende methoden ter bepaling van de opbrengst onser bosschen. 1893. IV. 258.
Honckeny, Gerhard August. Synopsis plantarum Germaniae. 1792. I. 375.
— Vollständiges systematisches Verzeichniss aller Gewächse Teutschlandes. 1782. I. 374.
Honda, Seiroku. Besitzen die Eisfernadeln ein mehrjähriges Wachstum? 1895. II. 40.²
— Description des-produits forestiers du Japon. 1900. IV. 21.³
— Description des zones forestières du Japon. 1900. I. 461, *IV. 87.*²
— Ueber die Entstehung der Verkrümungen [*sic*] an Yotsu-yamaruta. 1895. IV. 448.¹

— Ertragstafel und Zuwachsgesetz für Sugi. 1895. IV. 448.[1]
— Über den Küstenschutzwald. 1897. IV. 188.[1]
— Eine Untersuchungsreihe über den Einfluss der Höhenlage . . . auf die Veränderung des Zuwachses. 1892. IV. 234.
— *See also* LOEW, Oscar & HONDA, Seiroku.

Hongkong — **Botanical and afforestation department.** Annual report. IV. 16.[2]

Honigberger, Johann Martin. Früchte aus dem Morgenlande. 1851. III. 277.
— Thirty-five years in the East. 1851. III. 277.

Honuphrii, FRANCISCUS DE. *See* FRANCISCUS DE HONUPHRIIS.

Hooff, A. Der virginische Tulpenbaum. 1863. III. 398.[2]

Hooftman, P. Alphabetische woordenlijst der . . . kunstwoorden van boomen, planten en bloemen. 1885. I. 71.

Hoogeveen. Beschading van Kokospalmen. 1865. III. 323.[1]

Hooibrenk, Daniel. Darstellung veredelter Pflanzen. 1848. III. 160.
— Ueber den Einfluss des Neigungswinkels der Aeste. 1861. III. 38.[1]

Hooibrink. De Plataan of Plaanboom. 1853. III. 418.[1]

Hooke, Robert. Micrographia. 1665. I. 82.[3]

Hooker, *Sir* Joseph Dalton. Argan oil. 1878. III. 666.[2]
— The Argan tree. 1878. III. 666.
— On Barteria, a new genus of Passifloreae. 1861. II. 569.[3]
— Botany. 1876. I. 523.
— On the botany of Raoul Island. 1857. I. 506.[2]
— The botany of the Antarctic voyage. 1844. I. 303.
— On the Canarian flora. 1878. I. 498.
— On the Castilloa elastica. 1886. II. 147.[1]
— Catalogue of the names of a collection of plants made by Mr. Wm. Stephenson. 1844. I. 506.[3]
— Catalogue of the plants distributed . . . from the herbaria of Griffith, Falconer and Helfer. 1865. I. 55, 474.
— On the Cedars of Lebanon. 1862. II. 27.[1]
— Cleyera Fortunei. 1895. II. 548.[1]
— On the climate and vegetation . . . of East Nepal and the Sikkim. 1852. I. 473, *II. 676.[2]*
— Climate and vegetation of the Himalayas. 1848. I. 472.
— Considérations sur les flores insulaires. 1867. I. 300.
— Cupressus macrocarpa. 1885. II. 29.[2]
— Description of Pleuropetalum. 1846. II. 190.[1]
— Description of some . . . species of Aristolochia. 1865. II. 181.[1]
— Descriptions of two new dilleniaceous plants. 1857. II. 541.[2]
— Les deux Sequoias. 1879. II. 49.[2]
— On the discovery of a variety of the Cedar of Lebanon. 1880. II. 28.[1]
— On the discovery of Phylica arborea. 1875. I. 481.[1]
— Distribution géographique des plantes dans la flore de l'Amérique du Nord. 1878. I. 307.
— The distribution of the North American flora. 1878. I. 307.
— On Dyera. 1882. II. 726.[1]
— Elementos de botanica. 1876. I. 523.
— An enumeration of the plants of the Galapagos Archipelago. 1851. I. 510.[1]
— Des espèces de Cordyline. 1860. II. 79.[2]
— Extracts from the private letters of Dr. Hooker. 1849. I. 472.
— On Fitchia. 1845. II. 857.[2]
— Flora antarctica. 1847. I. 506.[2]
— Flora antarctica. Pt. II. Botany of Fuegia. 1847. I. 347.
— Flora Novae-Zelandiae. 1853. I. 506.[3]
— On the flora of Australia. 1859. I. 502.
— Flora Tasmaniae. 1860. I. 505.
— Florae Tasmaniae epicilegium. 1847. I. 505.
— Forsythia. 1877. II. 706.[2]
— On Fropiera. 1861. II. 573.[1]
— On the growth . . . of the ovarium of Siphonodon. 1837. II. 471.[1]
— Sur la gutta-percha. 1885. III. 668.[3]
— Handbook of the New Zealand flora. 1867. I. 506.[3]
— The Himalayan Hemlock-Spruce. 1886. II. 53.[3]
— Himalayan journals. 1854. I. 473.
— The Himalayan Larch. 1886. II. 33.[3]
— The Himalayan Silver Fir (Abies Webbiana). 1886. II. 25.[1]
— On the Huon Pine and on Microcachrys. 1845. II. 16.[1]
— On the identity of Pinus Peuce. 1855. LL. 44.[3]
— Illustrations of Himalayan plants. 1855. I. 473.

— Illustrations of the floras of the Malayan Archipelago. 1860. I. 465, *483.[1]*
— Insular floras. 1867. I. 300.
— Introductory essay to the Flora of New Zealand. 1853. I. 506.[3]
— Jasminum gracillimum Hook. f. 1881. II. 710.[1]
— Ueber das Klima und die Vegetation . . . von Ost-Nepal und dem Sikkim-Himalaya-Gebirge. 1852. I. 473, *II. 676.[2]*
— Letters . . . giving an account of an ascent of the Atlas. 1871. I. 485.
— A list of Madagascar plants. 1881. I. 496.
— Loranthaceae. Myzodendron. 1846. II. 167.[3]
— On Loxodiscus. 1857. II. 487.[1]
— On Melianthus Trimenianus. 1873. II. 491.[3]
— Mémoire sur l'organisation des Myzodendron. 1846. II. 167.[3]
— Ueber die aus Neu-Seeland und Australien eingeführten Arten der Gattung Cordyline. 1860. II. 79.[3]
— On a new genus . . . of Tasmanian plants. 1853. II. 603,[1] 633.[2]
— Note on the Cider tree. 1844. II. 625.[1]
— Note on the replacement of species in the colonies. 1864. I. 506.[2]
— Notes, chiefly botanical, made during an excursion from Darjiling to Tongló. 1849. I. 472.
— Notes of a tour in the plains of India. 1848. I. 303, *472*.
— Notes on the botany of the Rocky Mountains. 1877. I. 324.
— Notice sur les espèces de Cordyline. 1860. II. 79.[2]
— On Notospartium. 1857. II. 374.[3]
— Observations made when following the grand trunk road across the hills of upper Bengal. 1848. I. 472.
— Observations on some Indian species of Garcinia. 1875. II. 555.[1]
— Observations on the botany of Kerguelen Island. 1879. I. 481.[3]
— On the origination and distribution of species. 1860. I. 505.
— Outlines of the distribution of arctic plants. 1861. I. 220.[1] — 1868. I. 309.[1]
— Des phénomènes généraux de la variation. 1862. I. 244.[1]
— Pinus albicaulis Engelm. 1885. II. 40.[3]
— Pinus edulis. 1886. II. 42.[1]
— Pinus Jeffreyi. 1884. II. 42.[1]
— Pinus Lambertiana. 1885. II. 42.[1]
— Pinus monophylla. 1886. II. 42.[3]
— On the plants . . . of the Cameroons Mountains. 1864. I. 490.
— Plants of the peninsula [of Sinai]. 1871. I. 488.
— Report on seeds and saplings of forest trees. 1868. V. xxix.[1]
— Die Rhododendron des Sikkim. 1849. II. 676.[3]
— The Rhododendrons of Sikkim-Himalaya. 1849. II. 676.[1]
— Les Rhododendrum du Sikkim. 1849. II. 676.[1]
— Rosaceae. 1867. II. 256.[1]
— On seeds and saplings of forest trees. 1868. V. 62,[1] V. xxix.[2]
— The Sikkim Rhododendrons. 1849. II. 676.[1]
— Some account of a new Elaeodendron. 1844. II. 567.[3]
— On the species of Cordyline. 1860. II. 79.[2]
— The student's flora of the British Islands. 1870. I. 402.
— On the subalpine vegetation of Kilima Njaro. 1875. I. 92.[2]
— On three Oaks of Palestine. 1861. II. 131.[1]
— Thuja pendula. 1861. II. 52.[3]
— Torreya californica. 1885. II. 12.[1]
— Tristan d'Acunha. 1847. I. 498.
— On the true Fuchsia coccinea of Aiton. 1869. II. 644.[1]
— The Tumboa of West Africa. 1861. II. 55.[1]
— La végétation des Montagnes Rocheuses. 1877. I. 324.
— On the vegetation of Clarence Peak. 1862. I. 490.
— On the vegetation of the Galapagos Archipelago. 1851. I. 510.[1]
— Végétaux pouvant remplacer la présure. 1883. III. 702.[1]
— Die Verbreitung der nordamerikanischen Flora. 1878. I. 307.
— On Welwitschia. 1863. II. 55.[1]
— *See also* BENTHAM, George & HOOKER, J. D.; GRAY, Asa & HOOKER, J. D.; HOOKER, *Sir* W. J. & *Sir* J. D.; LINDLEY, John, HOOKER, *Sir*. J. D. & others; THWAITES, G. H. K. & HOOKER, *Sir* J. D.; ТУКЕРЪ, I.
— & Ball, John. The Argan tree. 1879. II. 697.[1]
— — Journal of a tour in Marocco. 1878. I. 485.

Hooker, *Sir* Joseph Dalton (*continued*).
— & **Bentham**, George. Flora nigritiana. 1849. I. 490.
— & **Thomson**, Thomas. Description of a new genus of Scrophularineae. 1865. II. 779.[1]
— — On Enkyanthus Himalaicus. 1855. II. 662,[1] 663.[1]
— — Flora indica. 1855. I. 473.
— — On the genus Euptelea. 1864. II. 194.[2]
— — Introductory essay to the Flora indica. 1855. I. 473.
— — On Maddenia and Diplarche. 1854. II. 265,[2] 663.[1]
— — Praecursores ad floram indicam. 1858. I. 473.
— & others. The flora of British India. 1875. I. 474.
Hooker, William. Pomona londinensis. 1818. III. 78.[2]
Hooker, *Sir* William Jackson. Acaciè à ailes planes. Acacia platyptera. 1842. II. 323.[2]
— Additions to the Hortus Kewensis. 1846. I. 54.
— African Oak (or Teak). 1850. II. 448.[1]
— Another Heath found in Ireland. 1835. II. 667.[2]
— Aralia? papyrifera. 1852. II. 652.[2]
— On the Argan-tree of Marocco. 1854. II. 697.[1]
— Aristoloche à fleurs à longue queue. 1840. II. 183.[1]
— Arthrotaxis tetragona. 1843. II. 9.[1]
— Botanical appendix. (*In* Lyon, G. F.) 1825. I. 308.
— Botanical appendix. (*In* Parry, W. E.) 1828. I. 308.
— Botanical characters of a new plant, Isonandra gutta. 1847. III. 668.[2] — 1848. II. 699.[1]
— Botanical extracts from Mr. Low's History of Borneo. 1848. I. 469.[1]
— Botanical illustrations. 1822. I. 98. — 1837. I. 70.
— Botany. (*In* Herschel, J. F. W.) '1849· I. 35.
— Brief descriptions . . . of Dacrydicum elatum. 1843. II. 8,[2] 30.[2]
— The British flora. 1830. I. 397.
— Byttneria heterophylla. 1830. II. 532.[3]
— On the Camphor-tree of Borneo. 1852. II. 560,[1] III. 611.[1]
— The Cannibal's Tomato. 1864. II. 778,[1]
— Catalogue of Mr. Geyer's collection of plants. 1846. I. 321.
— A catalogue of plants contained in the Royal botanic garden of Glasgow. 1825. I. 54.
— Chinese " rice paper." 1850. III. 644.[1]
— On the Chinese rice-paper. 1852. II. 652.[2]
— Copy of a letter addressed to Dawson Turner. 1840. II. 853.[1]
— Coscinium fenestratum. 1853. III. 396.[2]
— Cuba bast in Jamaica. 1856. III. 587.[2]
— Description de l'arbre qui produit le gutta-percha. 1848. II. 699.[2]
— Description of a new melastomaceous plant. 1849. II. 636.[2]
— Description of a new species of Drapetes. 1843. II. 603.[1]
— Description . . . of the Cedron of the Magdalena River. 1850. II. 415.[1]
— Description with a figure, of a new species of Thuja. 1844. II. 33.[2]
— Descriptions and sketches of botanical subjects. (*In* Gray, W. & Dochard.) 1825. I. 490.
— Descriptions botaniques. (*In* Gray, W. & Dochard.) 1825. I. 490.
— Détails sur le papier de Chine. 1850. III. 644.[1]
— Eboe Nut of the Mosquito Shore. 1850. II. 355.[2]
— Erythroxylon Coca. 1836. II. 394.[1]
— Exotic flora. 1823. I. 267.
— Extract of a letter from M. Spanoghe. 1835. II. 146.[1]
— Extraction du toddy. 1850. III. 323.[1]
— On the Fagus antarctica of Forster. 1840. II. 127.[2]
— Figure and description of a new species of Thuja. 1843. II. 33.[2]
— Figure . . . of a new Lisianthus. 1847. II. 721.[1]
— Figure . . . of Castanea chrysophylla. 1843. II. 125.[1]
— Figure . . . of a new species of Araucaria. 1843. II. 26.[1]
— Figures and descriptions of two species of Boehmeria. 1851. II. 156.[2]
— Figures . . . of three species of Podocarpus. 1842. II. 9.[1]
— Figures . . . of two species of Panax. 1843. II. 650.[2]
— Flora boreali-americana. 1833. I. 310.
— Flora scotica. 1821. I. 397.
— Le Garcinia Mangostana. 1855. II. 555.[2]
— On the genus Colliguaja of Molina. 1855. II. 439.[1]
— Ueber das Geschichtliche . . . der Gutta Percha. 1847. III. 668.[2]
— Der grösste Baum der Welt. 1851. II. 624.[1]
— Grosse Bäume in Vandiemensland. 1851. II. 624.[1]
— Du gutta-perca ou percha. 1847. III. 668.[2]
— Sur le gutta percha et la plante qui le produit. 1847. III. 668.[2]
— Inaugural dissertation upon the Cinchonas. 1839. III. 721.

— Journal of a tour in Iceland. 1811. I. 352.
— Over den Kamferboom van Borneo en Sumatra. 1852. III. 611.[1]
— Kew garden museum. 1853. III. 28.[1]
— Kew Gardens. 1847. I. 54.
— Kew gardens museum: Tallow tree. 1852. III. 522,[2] 673.[2]
— On the Kooso, or Brayera. 1850. II. 264.[2]
— List of plants collected by Richard King. 1836. I. 310.
— On Macraea, a new genus of plants from Chile. 1830. II. 860.[1]
— The monster Cactus at Kew. 1845. II. 592.[2]
— Museum of economic botany. 1855. I. 54.
— Museum of the Royal botanic gardens of Kew. 1855. I. 54.
— Die Naturgeschichte der Insel Timor. 1835. II. 146.[1]
— On a new genus of Flacourtianeae. 1844. II. 572.[1]
— On a new genus of . . . Tiliaceae. 1830. II. 514.[1]
— On a new Laurus. 1842. II. 225.[1]
— On a new South-African genus of plants. 1840. II. 604.[2]
— On a new species of Castela. 1830. II. 414.[1]
— On a new species of Thuja and on Podocarpus totara. 1842. II. 10,[1] 33.[2]
— Niger flora. 1849. I. 490.
— Notes on Norway. 1839. I. 354.
— Notes on the botany of H. M. discovery ships Erebus and Terror in the Antarctic voyage. 1843. I. 303.
— Notice concerning Mr. Drummond's collections. 1834. I. 306.
— Notice of a new species of Dammara. 1852. II. 25.[1]
— Notice of the plants collected . . . by Alexander Cruckshanks. 1831. I. 340.[1]
— Notice sur le Napoleona imperialis. 1848. II. 612.[2]
— Occidental Plane. 1856. II. 255.[1]
— On the Palmite of South Africa. 1857. II. 77.[1]
— Piacaba . . . Coquilla nut. 1849. III. 320.[1]
— On Piacaba and Coquilla nuts. 1849. III. 320.[2]
— Plantae Jamesonianae. 1834. II. 846.[1]
— Punciana Gilliesii. 1830. II. 339.[1]
— Report on Kew gardens. *See* Royal gardens at Kew. 1856. I. 54.
— Rice paper of China. 1852. III. 754.[1]
— The Rice paper plant. 1853. III. 644.[1]
— Rosage à fleurs en cloche. 1839. II. 678.[1]
— Simaba Cedron, Cederen fra Magdalene Floden. 1850. II. 415.[2]
— Siphocampylus microstoma. 1848. III. 754.[1]
— Some account of Exothea oblongifolia. 1844. II. 486.[2]
— Some account of the Paraguay Tea. 1842. II. 464.[2]
— Some account of the Vegetable ivory Palm. 1849. II. 73.[2]
— Some account of the Vegetable Ivory Palm. 1850. III. 330.[1]
— On the species of the genus Colletia. 1830. II. 493.[1]
— On the species of the genus Verbena. 1830. II. 761.[1]
— Stillingia sebifera. 1853. III. 522.[1]
— Swietenia Mahagoni. 1830. II. 422.[1]
— Toddymen and toddy implements. 1850. III. 323.[1]
— La Tomate des cannibales. 1864. II. 778.[1]
— & *Sir* J. D. Contributions toward a flora of Van Dieman's Land. 1834. I. 505.
— & **Arnott**, G. A. Walker-. The botany of Captain Beechey's voyage. 1830. I. 302.
— — California. 1830. I. 321.
— — Chili. 1830. I. 346.
— — China. 1830. I. 458.
— — Contributions towards a flora of South America. 1833. I. 329.
— — Kamtschatka. 1830. I. 454.[2]
— — Loo Choo and Bonin. 1830. I. 461.
— — Mexico. 1830. I. 331.
— — Sandwich Islands. 1830. I. 509.[2]
— — Society Islands. 1830. I. 510.[2]
— & **Hanbury**, Daniel. Botanische und pharmakologische Fragen. 1860. III. 245.
Hooker's Icones plantarum. *See* Icones . . . I. 18.
Hooker's journal of botany. *See* Botanical miscellany. I. 17.
Hoop, von der. Nachricht über den Frass des Kiefernspinners. 1861. IV. 476.
— Schutz der Waldungen gegen die von den Eisenbahnen drohende Feuersgefahr. 1858. IV. 182.[2]
— Die Vertilgung des Kiefernspinners. 1861. IV. 207. — 1865. IV. 476.
— Der Waldfeldbau im Grossherzogthum Hessen. 1857. IV. 133.

Hooper, David. Akakia, an ancient eastern medicine. 1900. III. 463.²
— Analysis of the bark of Cassia auriculata. 1893. II. 343.²
— Balsamodendron Berryi. 1890. III. 511.¹
— Bamboo manna. 1900. III. 315.²
— Bamboo manna . . . in the central provinces. 1900. III. 316.²
— The bark-extract . . . of Terminalia Oliveri. 1900. III. 633.¹
— Bark of Ailanthus excelsa. 1895. III. 506.² — 1896. III. 506.²
— The bark of Cleistanthus Collinus. 1898. III. 515.¹
— Bark of Michelia nilagirica. 1888. III. 400.²
— Bark of Rhamnus Wightii. 1888. III. 543.²
— Bragantia Wallichii. 1895. III. 385.²
— Ueber Calophyllum inophyllum. 1889. III. 608.²
— Camphor leaf oil. 1896. III. 233,¹ 405.¹
— Carthagena bark. 1889. III. 712.²
— Du croisement chez les Cinchona. 1889. III. 718.
— Culture du Quinquina dans l'Inde. . 1890. III. 715.
— Damree seeds as medicine for cattle. 1898. III. 707.¹
— An examination of the leaves of Gymnema. 1887. III. 693.¹
— Sur les feuilles d'Adhatoda vasica. 1888. III. 709.²
— Gum barks. 1892. III. 228.¹
— Holigarna and its blistering principle. 1895. III. 524.²
— The hybridisation of Cinchonas. 1889. III. 723.
— Ueber Kreuzung verschiedener Cinchona-Arten. 1889. III. 723.
— Laurel-nut oil. 1889. III. 608.²
— Leaves of the Adhatoda vasica. 1888. III. 709.²
— The mineral concretion of the Teak tree. 1888. III. 697.¹
— On Myristica kino. 1900. III. 402.¹
— A new kino from species of Macaranga. 1900. III. 520.¹
— Notes on the gums, resins. 1888. III. 227.
— Quinological work. 1887. III. 725.¹
— Some drugs of British Sikkim. 1889. III. 279.¹
— Tannin in Indian Oak barks. 1894. IV. 502.¹
— The tannin value of Cassia auriculata Teak. 1899. III. 470.²
— On three natural rubber substitutes. 1899. III. 518.²
— Eine Untersuchung ueber die Bestandteile der Blätter von Gymnema. 1887. III. 693.¹
Hooper, E. D. M. Les forêts de la Jamaique. 1888. I. 337, IV. 342.
— Growth of Bija Sâl. 1883. IV. 528.²
— Large Ber tree in the Central Provinces. 1882. II. 500.¹
— Note on fire-protection. 1883. IV. 184.¹
— Report upon Antigua in relation to forestry. 1888. IV. 342.¹
— Report upon the forests of Grenada and Carriacou. 1887. IV. 342.¹
— Report upon the forests of Honduras. 1887. IV. 342.¹
— Report upon the forests of Jamaica. 1886. IV. 342.¹
— Report upon the forests of St. Lucia. 1887. IV. 342.¹
— Report upon the forests of St. Vincent. 1886. IV. 341.¹
— Report upon the forests of Tabago. 1887. IV. 342.¹
— See also McDowall, A. & Hooper, E. D. M.
Hooper, E. J. Hooper's western fruit book. 1857. III. 61.¹
Hooper, Robert. Observations on the structure and economy of plants. 1797. I. 217.
Hoopes, Josiah. Book of evergreens. 1868. III. 292.
— The Clematis. 1869. III. 389.¹
— Dwarf Conifers. 1871. III. 205,¹ 290.
— Evergreen hedges. 1875. III. 214.¹
— Ivy and its culture. 1875. III. 642.²
— Notes on Conifers. 1875. III. 292.
— The Oaks of America. 1874. III. 361.¹
— Ornamental vines. 1874. III. 204.²
— Pinus koraiensis. 1883. II. 42.¹
— Pinus koraiensis. 1884. III. 307.²
— Propagating evergreens from cuttings. 1868. III. 294.¹
— The Retinisporas. 1870. III. 300.² — 1888. III. 300.²
— Shrub propagation. 1888. III. 153.
— The Yucca. 1883. III. 339.²
Hoorn, G. H. See Coster, D. J., Hoorn, G. H. & Mazure, J.
Hoorn van Burgh, N. I. W. V. Bereiding van Liberia-Koffie. 1899. III. 743.¹
Hooyman, J. Verhandeling over den landbouw . . . van Batavia. 1784. III. 127.²
— Vervolg van den landbouw. 1787. III. 127.²
Hop, Henri. Nouvelle description du Cap de Bonne-Espérance. 1778. III. 353.¹
The Hop Hornbeam. 1890. II. 122.²

Hope, Charles William. How lightning strikes trees. 1885. IV. 194.
— Indian Bamboos. 1897. II. 58.²
— Járul timber. 1885. IV. 529.¹
— Tea-box woods. 1893. IV. 427.¹
Hope, D. T. Abstract of a paper on wood-paving. 1843. IV. 425.²
Hope, Frances Jane. On flowers of trees. 1875. III. 207.¹
Hope, J. Beschrijving van eene Budleia globosa. 1782. II. 717.²
Hope, Thomas Charles. Chemical observations on the flowers of the Camellia. 1845. II. 212,¹ 551.¹
— Observations and experiments on the coloured and colourable matter . . . of plants. 1845. I. 184.
— Tentamen . . . de plantarum motibus. 1787. I. 193.²
Hope Loudon, H. See Suermondt, G. & Hope Loudon, H.
Hopf, J. G. Cupressus pendula Griff. 1854. III. 303.¹
Hopfengärtner. Ein Culturwerkzeug in der Rocktasche. 1866. IV. 176.²
— Theorie und Praxis in der Buchenwirtschaft. 1900. IV. 496.
— Die Weymuthskiefer im Revier Murrhardt. 1866. IV. 469.
Hopffer, Carl. Beschreibung eines neuen Echinocactus. 1842. II. 593.¹ — 1843. II. 592.¹
— Eine neue Mammillarie. 1843. II. 595.¹
Hopfgartner. Eine Ansicht büer [sic] die Geldwerthsberechnung. 1858. IV. 255.
— Die Wald-Servituten und ihre Ablösung. 1852. IV. 334.²
Hopkins, Andrew Delmar. Black holes in wood. 1894. IV. 414.³
— Catalogue of West Virginia . . . tree insects. 1893. III. 187.
— Defects in wood caused by insects. 1894. IV. 414.²
— Divisions of the state as indicated by different kinds of forest trees. 1891. IV. 340.¹
— Forest and shade tree insects. 1891. III. 187.
— Injury to wood by woodpeckers. 1897. IV. 199.¹
— Preliminary report on the insect enemies of forests. 1899. IV. 205.¹
— Report on investigations to determine the cause of unhealthy conditions of the Spruce. 1899. IV. 442.
— Some notes on insect enemies of trees. 1897. III. 187.
— The woodpecker and Bird's-eye Poplar. 1894. IV. 519.³
Hopkinson, John. Report on phenological phenomena. 1890. I. 226.¹
— Report on the rainfall in Hertfordshire. 1894. IV. 195.¹
Hopkirk, Thomas. Catalogue of the plants . . . cultivated in the gardens Dalpeth. 1813. I. 53.
— Flora anomala. 1817. I. 143.
— Flora glottiana. 1813. I. 396.
Hoppe, David Heinrich. Ectypa plantarum ratisbonensium. 1787. I. 374.
— Ueber einige Weidenarten. 1804. II. 100.¹
Dr. D. H. Hoppe's Jubelfeier. See Fürnrohr, A. E. 1839. I. 380.
— Linneische Nahmen zu den Ehretischen Pflanzenabbildungen. 1790. I. 78.¹
— Linneische Trivialnamen zu den Blackwellischen officinellen Pflanzenabbildungen. 1793. I. 78.¹
— Rhododendron germanicum. 1837. II. 680.¹
— Salix purpurea und Salix Helix Linn. 1804. II. 109.¹
— Verzeichniss einiger auf Guiana wachsenden merkwürdigen Pflanzen. 1793. III. 64.²
— Die Weiden, Salices. 1807. II. 100.¹
— & Hornschuch, Friedrich. Journal of a tour to the coast of the Adriatic Sea. 1818. I. 439. — 1823. I. 349.
— — Tagebuch einer Reise nach den Küsten des Adriatischen Meeres. 1818. I. 439.
Hoppe, Eduard. Beiträge zur russischen Forststatistik. 1884. IV. 346.
— Einfluss der Freilandvegetation und Bodenbedeckung auf die Temperatur. 1895. IV. 54.
— Forstmeteorologische Studien im Karstgebiete. 1898. IV. 60.¹
— Regenmessung unter Baumkronen. 1896. IV. 60.¹
— Untersuchungen über den Einfluss der Bestandesdichte auf die Bodenfeuchtigkeit. 1895. IV. 51.
— Untersuchungen über den Einfluss der Bestandesdichte auf die Bodentemperatur. 1897. IV. 52.
— Untersuchungen über die Feuchtigkeit des Lehmbodens. 1900. IV. 52.
— Ueber Veränderungen des Waldbodens. 1898. IV. 70.
— Vergleichende Studie über den Mineralstoffgehalt von Fichte. 1900. I. 526.¹

Hoppe, Friedrich Wilhelm. De balsamo copayba. 1732. III. 473.[1] *See also* NEBEL, Daniel. 1710. III. 473.[1]

Hoppe, Richard. Der Waldsberg . . . und seine forstbotanischen Seltenheiten. 1886. I. 48.

Hoppe, Tobias Konrad. Abhandlung von der Begattung der Pflanzen. 1773. I. 200.

— Antwort-Schreiben auf diejenigen Zweifel, welche . . . J. Fr. Schreiber . . . Zweien Sendschreiben . . . entgegengesetzt. 1748. I. 213,[2] *III. 350.*[1]

— Einige Nachricht von den sogenannten Eichen-, Weiden- und Dornrosen. 1748. I. 214,[1] *III. 350,*[1] *IV. 509.*

— Geraische Flora. 1774. I. 373.

Hora, F. Ueber die gemischte Kultur der Kiefer mit Lärchen. 1864. IV. 138.[1]

— Die Wirkungen der Entnahme der Bodenstreu. 1864. IV. 71.

Hora Adams, W. R. 't Ruitsysteem bij cultures. 1898. III. 727.

Horáček, Karel. Pěstování ovocných stromů. 1871. III. 146.[2]

Horae physicae berolinenses. I. 12.

Horák, Bohuslav. Ergebnisse einer botanischen Reise nach Montenegro. 1899. I. 451.

Horaninow, Paul. Characteres essentiales familiarum. 1847. I. 261.

— Fundamenta botanices. 1841. I. 88.

— Primae lineae systematis naturae. 1834. I. 260.

Horbius, Christianus Johannes. De febrifuga chinae-chinae virtute. 1693. III. 719.

Horizontal trees in Oregon. 1898. I. 517.[2]

Horlacher, E. Die Anwendbarkeit und Verwendung der Nadelreisstreu. 1878. IV. 71.

Horn, Caspar Henry. Von Windbrüchen. 1716. IV. 313.

Horn, F. WINKEL-. *See* WINKEL-HORN, F.

Horn, L. W. Formzahlen und Massentafeln für die Buche. 1898. IV. 499.

— **& Grundner**, Fritz. Buche. 1898. IV. 499.

Horn van den Bos, Henricus Petrus Maria van der. Onderzoek der vrucht van Symphoricarpos. 1873. II. 842.[1]

Hornberger, Karl Richard. Beobachtungen über den Frühsjahrssaft der Birke. 1887. II. 118,[2] *121.*[1]

— Ueber den Einfluss des Waldes auf das Klima. 1888. . IV. 54.

— Grundriss der Meteorologie und Klimatologie. 1891. IV. 60.[1]

— Zur Kenntniss der Vertheilung des Mineralstoffgehalts über den Stammquerschnitt der Rothbuche. 1898. . IV. 500.[2]

— Die Mineralstoffe der wichtigsten Waldsamen. 1884. IV. 64.[1]

— Ueber den Mineralstoffgehalt der Buchel. 1889. II. 126.[2] — 1892. IV. 500.[1]

— *See also* MUTSCHLER, C., HORNBERGER, Richard & HAMMERBACHER, Friedrich.

Horne, John. The islands of the Seychelles group. 1876. III. 279.[2]

— Mauritius. 1888. III. 279.[2]

— Notes on flora of Flat Island. 1886. I. 482.

— A year in Fiji. 1881. III. 283.[2]

Hornemann, E. Nogle Undersøgelser over Massefaktorerne. 1891. IV. 219.

Hornemann, Jens Wilken. Bemærkninger angaaende forskielligheden af vegetationens danske provindser. 1821. I. 353.

— Bemerkungen über die Vegetation der dänischen Provinzen. 1821. I. 353.

— Om Berberissen kan frembringe Kornrust. 1816. III. 394.[1]

— Enumeratio plantarum Horti botanici hafniensis. 1807. I. 40.

— Erörterung . . . ob der Berberizzenstrauch Rost . . . verursacht. 1816. III. 394.[1]

— Over de flora danica. 1838. I. 354.

— Forsøg til en Dansk økonomisk Plantelære. 1796. III. 67.[1]

— Forsøg til en Fortegnelse over de vildvoxende . . Planter i Danmark. 1839. I. 354.

— Hortus regius botanicus hafniensis. 1813. I. 40.

— De indole plantarum guineensium observationes. 1819. I. 490.

— Om den mod Berberissen gjorte Beskyldning. 1816. III. 394.[1]

— Nogle Bemærkninger ved mindre bekiendte officinelle Planter. 1806. III. 55.

— Nomenclatura florae danicae. 1827. I. 353.

— Remarks on the vegetation of the Danish provinces. 1821. I. 353.

— Supplementum Horti botanici. 1813. I. 40.

— Om Universitets botaniske Have. 1822. I. 40.

Horner, Lodewijk. Batoe-eilanden. 1840. I. 467.[1]

Horník, Josef. Drohné ovoce. 1888. III. 147.[1]

— Přehled lesnictví. 1889. IV. 100.[1] .

— Příspěvek k rozmnožování stromů a křovin. 1882. III. 153.

— Vrba košťářská. 1881. III. 348.

Hornschuch, Friedrich. Beschreibung der Melaleuca elegans mihi. 1834. II. 629.[2]

— *See also* HOPPE, D. H. & HORNSCHUCH, Friedrich.

Hornstedt, Claude Frederik. Fructus Javae esculenti. 1786. III. 275.[2]

— Programma quo dissertationem viri . . . C. F. Hornstedt . . . exhibentur. *See* WEIGEL, C. E. 1786. III. 404.[2]

Hornung, Leonhart Friedrich. De Visco. *See* BAIER, J. J. 1706. II. 177.[2]

Hornung, W. A. H. Achteruitgang der Koffie-productie. 1900. III. 732.[1]

— Klappeelevers. 1895. III. 323.[2]

— Een middel tegen zickten . . . der Koffieboomen. 1899. III. 737.

A **horse** poisoned by Oleander. 1881. III. 689.[2]

Horsefield, J. Genista radiata. 1882. III 477.[1]

Horses injuring the bark of trees. 1900. III. 199.

Horsfield, Thomas. Beschrijving van den Gatipboom. 1814. II. 366,[1] III. 479.[2]

— Essay on the geography . . . of the western portion . . . of Java. 1816. I. 468.

— An essay on the Oopas or Poison tree of Java. 1814. III. 366.[2]

— An experimental dissertation on the Rhus Vernix. 1798. III. 526.[2]

— On the Oopas, or Poison-tree of Java. 1814. II. 145.[3]

— Reis naar de oosterstreken van Java. 1814. I. 468.

— Over de rivier van Solo. 1814. I. 468.

— Scheikundige ontleding der vruchten van den Rarak-boom. 1814. III. 540.[1]

— Short acount of the medical plants of Java. 1816. III. 275.[2]

Horsin-Déon, Paul. Sucre de Palmier de Calcutta. 1880. III. 328.[1]

Horst, Christoph. Hortulus medicus. 1610. III. 53.

Horst, Gregor. Herbarium Horstianum. 1630. I. 285.

— De plantis in genere. 1659. I. 30.

Horst, Jacob. Herbarium Horstianum. 1630. III. 240.

— Opusculum de Vite vinifera. 1588. III. 582.

Horst, Johann Daniel. Malva arborescens lutea. 1654. II. 518.[1]

Horstmar, Wilhelm Friedrich Carl August SALM-, *Fürst zu*. *See* SALM-HORSTMAR, W. F. C. A., *Fürst zu*.

Hort, Fenton, J. A. On a supposed new species of Rubus. 1851. II. 308.[1]

Horta, José. El hule en Guatemala. 1899. III. 232.[1]

Sur les **Hortensias** bleus. 1840. III. 412.[1] .

Hortes, Hyacinthe. Quelques vues sur la botanique étudiée dans ses rapports avec l'art pharmaceutique. 1816. III. 259.[2]

Horti beaumontiani . . . catalogus. *See* KIGGELAER, Franciscus. 1690. I. 50.

Horti botanici bononiensis plantae. *See* BERTOLONI, Antonio. 1826. I. 62.

Horti botanici cantabrigiensis catalogus. *See* MARTYN, Thomas. 1794. I. 53.

Horticola, (*pseud.*). The Holly tree. 1854. III. 530.[2]

— The original Red Beech tree. 1866. II. 127.[2]

— Tecoma jasminoides. 1862. III. 707.[1]

L'**Horticulteur** belge. III. 15.

L'**Horticulteur** français. III. 19.

L'**Horticulteur** praticien. III. 15.

L'**Horticulteur** provençal. III. 19.

L'**Horticulteur** universel. Ed. by C. Lemaire. III. 19.

L'**Horticulteur** universel; bulletin. III. 19.

Horticultural art journal. III. 4.

Horticultural, botanical, and economical lexicon. 1792. III. 30.

Horticultural gardens, Lucknow. Report. 1888. I. 67.[1]

Horticultural magazine. *See* ANNALS of horticulture. III. 16.

Horticultural register. . III. 4.

Horticultural register and general magazine. III. 17. .

Horticultural review and botanical magazine. *See* WESTERN horticultural review. III. 9.

Horticultural society of London. Journal. Transactions. III. 17.
Horticulture nouvelle. *See* SOCIÉTÉ D'HORTICULTURE PRATIQUE DU DÉPARTEMENT DU RHÔNE. III. 22.
Horticulturist and journal of rural art. III. 4.
L'Horto dei semplici. *See* PORRO, Girolamo. 1591. V. VII.[2]
Hortolès, (*jr.*). Note sur la greffe des boutons à fruit. 1861. III. 161.
Hortulania. *See* HAVEBRUGS-TIDENDE. III. 10.[2]
Hortulanus, (*pseud.*). Chamaerops excelsa in a Cornish garden. 1877. III. 331.[2]
Hortus, Max. Les cultures spéciales de la Provence. 1897. III. 676.[2]
Hortus academicus gottingensis. Index seminum. 1820. I. 46.
Hortus academicus halensis. Index seminum. 1809. I. 45.
Hortus academicus hauniensis. Index seminum. 1820. I. 40.
Hortus academicus seu botanicus marburgensis. Index seminum. 1822. I. 46.
Hortus academicus . . . Universitatis dorpatensis. Index seminum. 1820. I. 41.
Hortus Amstelodamensis. 1848. I. 51.[2]
Hortus Amstelodamensium botanicus. 1839. I. 51.[1]
Hortus anglicus. *See* CLARKE, Stephen. 1822. III. 81.
Hortus argentoratensis. 1781. I. 44.
Hortus arnoldiensis. *See* STATHAM, S. 1806. I. 53.
Hortus belvedereanus. *See* DENNSTEDT, A. W. 1820. I. 45.
Hortus bengalensis. *See* ROXBURGH, William. 1814. III. 29.[2]
Hortus Bergianus. Acta. I. 8.[1]
De Hortus bogoriensis. 1890. I. 68.[1]
Hortus botanicus academicus lugduno-batavus. 1821. I. 51.[1]
Hortus botanicus Archigymnasii parmensis. Selectus seminum. 1822. I. 62.
Hortus botanicus berolinensis. Index seminum. 1813. I. 45.
Hortus botanicus bononiensis. Semina lecta. 1821. I. 62.
Hortus botanicus gryphicus. Semina. 1820. I. 46.
Hortus botanicus hamburgensis. Semina. 1820. I. 46.
Hortus botanicus heidelbergensis. Delectus seminum. 1833. I. 47.
Hortus botanicus lovaniensis. Selectus seminum. 1836. I. 49.
Hortus botanicus patavinus. Semina. 1824. I. 62.
Hortus botanicus Regii archigymnasii genuensis. Index seminum. 1840. I. 63.
Hortus botanicus Regii musaei physices ac naturalis historiae. Enumeratio seminum. 1836. I. 63.
Hortus botanicus regius monspeliensis. 1827. I. 57.
Hortus botanicus turicensis. Index seminum. 1829. I. 65.[1]
Hortus botanicus Universitatis literarum wirceburgensis. Selectio fructuum et seminum. 1841. I. 47.
Hortus botanicus Universitatis vindebonensis. Delectus seminum. 1820. I. 65.[2]
Hortus botanicus vratislaviensis. Delectus seminum. 1818. I. 45.
Hortus Collinsonianus. *See* DILLWYN, L. W. 1843. I. 54.
Hortus Dyckensis. *See* SALM-REIFFERSCHEID-DYCK, Joseph, Fürst und Altgraf. 1834. I. 47.
Hortus ericaeus woburnensis. *See* SINCLAIR, George.
Hortus Leidensis. *See* HORTUS botanicus academicus . . . 1821. I. 51.[1]
Hortus Magni ducis Badensis carlsruhanus. *See* GMELIN, C. 1811. I. 45.
Hortus Petropolitanus. Acta. I. 9.[2]
Hortus pharmaceüticus lutetianus. *See* GRÉGOIRE, Jacques. 1638. I. 56.
Hortus regiomontanus seminifer. 1820. I. 46.
Hortus regius. *See* VALLOT, Antoine. 1665. I. 56.
Hortus regius Academiae rothomagensis. 1778. I. 56.
Hortus regius botanicus monacensis seminifer. 1821. I. 46.
Hortus regius botanicus neapolitanus. Index seminum. 1823. I. 62.
Hortus regius botanicus panormitanus. Index seminum. 1822. I. 62
Hortus regius monacensis. *See* SCHRANK, Franz von Paula von & MARTIUS, K. F. P. von. 1829. I. 46.
Hortus sanitatis. *See* ORTUS sanitatis.
Hortus thenensis. *See* BOSSCHE, Léon van den. 1895. I. 50.

Hortus universitatis imperialis Petropolitanae. Scripta botanica. I. 9.[2]
Hortus universitatis literarum lipsiensis seminum . . . offert delectum. 1821. I. 46.
Hortus uptonensis. *See* LETTSOM, J. C. 1781. I. 53.
Hortus Vanhoutteanus. *See* HOUTTE, Louis van. 1845. I. 50.
Horvath, Alexis. Beiträge zur Lehre über die Wurzelkraft. 1877. I. 168.
Horváth, Géza de. Rapport annuel de la station phylloxérique hongroise. 1882. III. 573.
Horvath, M. The hardy Clematises. 1899. III. 389.[2]
— The hardy Daphnes. 1899. III. 627.[1]
— Propagating hardy trees and shrubs. 1899. III. 158.
— Shrubs for the seaside. 1898. III. 42.[1]
Horváth, Sándor. Acer saccharinum. 1899. III. 536.[2]
— Adatok az Országos erdészeti egyesület keletkezésének és 20 éves fennállásának történetéhez. 1886. IV. 41.[2]
— A-Szelíd Gesztenyefa. 1900. III. 358.[2]
— Thea chinensis. 1899. III. 600.[2]
Horvatovszky, Sigismund. Florae tyrnaviensis indigenae. 1774. I. 444.
Hosack, David. A catalogue of plants contained in the Botanic garden at Elgin. 1806. I. 38.[2]
— Hortus Elginensis.· 1806. I. 38.[2]
— A statement of facts relative to . . . the Elgin botanic garden. 1811. I. 521.[1]
— Syllabus of a course of lectures on botany. 1795. I. 32.
Hosaeus, A. Analysen von Kiefernfrüchten. 1880. II. 48.[1]
Hosaeus, Arwed. Einige . . . Krankheiten der Bäume. 1892. III. 194.
Hosang, Abondius. Vegetatio. 1773. I. 184.
Hoschedé, Jean Pierre. *See* TOUSSAINT, A. & HOSCHEDÉ, J. P.
Hose, Charles. A nominal list of the flora of Mount Kinabalu. 1896. I. 469.[2]
Hose, J. A. C. Plantae nonnullae florae germanicae. 1799. II. 291.[1]
Hosemann, Johann Fr. Die Pflanzung·der weichen oder geschwindwachsenden Holzgattungen. 1816. IV. 117.
Hoser, Peter. Eine alte Eibe Taxus baccata in Wien. 1899. II. 11.[2]
— Przezrynek do flory wyspy Borkum. 1897. I. 390.
Hosie, Alexander. Report of the cultivation of Boehmeria nivea. 1891. III. 382.[1]
— Three years in western China. 1889. III. 273.[2]
Hosius, (*Forstmeister, Hermsdorf*). Erfahrungen über die Wegenetzlegung. 1892. IV. 267.
Hoskiaer, J. Cubic-Tabeller. 178 .? IV. 220.
— Cubische Tabellen. 178 .? IV. 220.
Hoskins, S. H. Covering amputated limbs. 1884. III. 180.[2]
Hoskins, Thomas H. The Elms of the St. Lawrence Valley. 1892. II. 143.[2]
— The Great Elm at Derby Line. 1892. II. 144.[1]
— Internal decay of forest-trees. 1892. I. 207;[1] IV. 414.[1]·
— Misconception as to forest-growth. 1894. IV. 65.[1]
— The new orcharding. 1892. III. 134.[1]
— Russian shrubs and trees. 1888. III. 68.[1]
Hospodársky obsor. III. 24.[2]
Hossack, A. Cranberry culture in England. 1878. III. 660.[7]
— Pinus insignis. 1878. III. 308.[2]
Hossfeld, Johann Wilhelm. Forsttaxation. 1823. IV. 239.
— Mathematik für Forstmänner. 1821. IV. 58.
— Niedere allgemeine Mathematik. 1819. IV. 58.
— Reformation der Forstwissenschaft. 1820. IV. 101.
— Triumph eines abgelebten Dorfschulmeisters. 1822. IV.. 101.
— Werthsbestimmung der einzelnen Waldprodukte. 1825.. IV. 252.
Host, Nicolaus Thomas. Flora austriaca. 1827. I. 439.
— Sur le Marasquin. 1832. III. 436.[2]
— Salix. 1832. II. 98.[2]
— Synopsis plantarum in Austria. ·1797. I. 439.
Hosten, Jules. Incendies forestiers dans les Landes. 1899. IV. 183.[2]
Hotchkiss, George W. History of the lumber . . . industry of the northwest. 1898. IV. 24;[2] 382.[2]
— Industrial Chicago; the lumber interests. 1894. IV. 403.[2]
L'Hôte, L. Sur la recherche et le dosage de l'alumine. 1887. III. 561.
Ho-tei. Seo-Kwa-Sj'uu. . 1810. III. 91.[2]
Hotton. Manuel de l'élagueur. 1829. IV. 170.

Hotton, Petrus. Sermo academicus, quo rei herbariae historia et fata adumbrantur. 1695. I. 79.[1]
— Thesaurus phytologicus. 1738. I. 291.
Houba, Julien. Les Chênes d'Amérique. 1898. III. 361,[2] IV. 501.[1]
— Les Chênes de l'Amérique. 1887. III. 361.[2]
— Considérations générales sur l'aménagement des bois. 1877. IV. 244.
— Contribution à l'étude des Caryers en Belgique. 1897. IV. 488.[1]
— Contribution à l'histoire du Hêtre. 1896. IV. 496.
— Le corbeau. 1896. IV. 90.[2]
— Les coupe-feu dans les fanges. 1899. IV. 183.[1]
— Drainage des forêts; rapport. 1881. IV. 144.[1]
— Enquête sur les Chênes exotiques. 1898. III. 361,[2] IV. 501.[1]
— L'Épicéa dans les environs de St-Hubert. 1897. IV. 559.[1]
— Les essences exotiques et le gibier. 1899. IV. 197.[1]
— Une excursion dans la forêt de Soignes. 1897. IV. 556.[1]
— Le Pin du Lord Weymouth. 1896. IV. 469, 470.[2]
— Des plantations bordent les routes. 1883. III. 209.
— Les plantations d'Épicéas sur mottes. 1899. IV. 153.[2]
— Projet d'aménagement des bois de Rochefort. 1881. V. xxxi.[1]
— Les sabotiers luxembourgeois. 1896. IV. 428.[2]
— Traitement des forêts en Belgique. 1887. IV. 248.[2]
Houck, Friedrich. De Hyperico. *See* WEDEL, G. W. 1716. III. 609.[2]
Houdaille. Étude sur les propriétés et l'exposition des bois de la Côte d'Ivoire. 1900. IV. 409.
Houdaille, F. Enquête sur le dépérissement . . . de certaines Vignes greffées. 1896. III. 562.[1]
— Météorologie agricole. 189 . ? III. 36.[1]
— & **Mazade,** M. Influence de . . . l'humidité dans le sol sur le développement de la chlorose de la Vigne. 1894. III. 561.
Houdas. Contribution à l'étude du Lierre. 1899. III. 643.[1]
Houdé, A. Nouveau mode de préparation de la spartéine. 1886. III. 475.[1]
Houdoux, Henri. Étude botanique . . . sur la Noix vomique. 1869. III. 683.[1]
Hough, Franklin Benjamin. An address on our schools and our forests. 1881. IV. 30.[1]
— Address on state forest management. 1884. IV. 288.[1]
— I boschi d' America. 1881. IV. 337.
— On the duty of governments in the preservation of forests. 1873. IV. 177.[1]
— Elements of forestry. 1882. IV. 103.[1]
— Experimental plantation of the Eucalyptus, near Rome. 1883. IV. 530.
— A familiar talk about trees. 1883. III. 117,[1] IV. 39.[1]
— Forest tree planting in America. 1884. IV. 39.[1]
— Forestry in America. 1881. IV. 337.[2]
— The forestry of the future. 1882. IV. 271.[2]
— The forestry question. 1884. IV. 338.[1]
— The future policy of forest management. 1885. IV. 272.
— Ueber den gegenwärtigen Zustand der forstlichen Verhältnisse Nordamerikas. 1878. IV. 337.[2]
— On the importance of giving timely attention . . . for the supply of charcoal. 1880. IV. 395.
— Planting trees in school grounds. *See* HOUGH, F. B. & PEASLEE, J. B. 1885. IV. 41.[2]
— Upon the profits of forest culture. 1883. IV. 260.[1]
— Upon the public encouragement of forest tree-planting. 1883. IV. 39.[1]
— Public health interests concerned in the preservation of . . . forests. 1875. IV. 55.[1]
— The relations of woodlands to animal life. 1884. IV. 67.[1]
— Reminiscences of foreign travel. 1882. IV. 342.[2]
— Report upon forestry. 1878. IV. 337.[2]
— The sanitary effects of woodlands. 1884. IV. 55.[1]
— A talk about trees. 1883. IV. 39.[1]
— & **Peaslee,** J. B. Planting trees in school grounds. 1885. IV. 41.[2]
— & others. The proper value and management of government timber lands. 1884. IV. 272.
— Report of the Committee upon forestry. 1880. IV. 271.
Hough, James. Letters on the climate . . . of the Neilgherries. 1829. I. 471.
Hough, Romeyn Beck. The American woods. 1888. I. 38,[1] IV. 18.[1]
— Fruit-trees girdled by mice. 1893. III. 180.[2]
Hough, Walter. Tuna and its uses. 1899. III. 625.[1]

Houghton, John. A discourse of Coffee. 1700. III. 738.
— Husbandry and trade improv'd. 1727. III. 108.
Houlbert, Ch. Phylogénie des Ulmacées. 1899. II. 141.[1]
Houlbert, Constant. Le bois secondaire des Protéacées. 1894. II. 158.[2]
— Étude anatomique du bois secondaire. 1892. I. 126.
— Phénomènes optiques présentés par le bois secondaire. 1893. I. 126.
— Recherches sur la structure comparée du bois secondaire dans les apétales. 1893. I. 126.
— Recherches sur le bois secondaire. 1892. I. 126.
— Recherches sur les propriétés optiques du bois. 1894. I. 126.
— Sur la valeur systématique du bois secondaire. 1893. I. 126.
Houlès, Gaston CORMOULS-. *See* CORMOULS-HOULÉS, Gaston.
Houllet, (R. or B.). Agave attenuata. 1876. III. 341.[1]
— Azalées propres au forçage. 1868. III. 660.[1]
— Bertholletia excelsa. 1867. III. 631.[2]
— Bouturage des plantes grasses dans l'eau. 1880. III. 158.
— Chamaerops excelsa. 1868. III. 331.[2]
— Choisya ternata. 1869. III. 496.[1]
— Clerodendron angustifolium. 1870. III. 696.[1]
— Clerodendron calamitosum. 1867. II. 755.[1]
— Clerodendron Thompsonae. 1867. III. 696.[2]
— Colquhounia tomentosa. 1873. III. 697.[2]
— Columnea erythropaea. 1867. III. 708.[1]
— Disemma Hahnii. 1869. III. 616.[1]
— Epiphyllum Guedneyri. 1875. III. 625.[2]
— Ficus japonica. 1879. III. 871.[1]
— Fremya aurantiaca. 1865. III. 638.[1]
— Freycinetia Banksii. 1872. III. 313.[1]
— Gomphia decora. 1879. III. 596.[1]
— Lucuma deliciosa. 1870. III. 596.[2]
— Macleyana coccinea. 1877. III. 653.[1]
— Mimosa floribunda. 1867. III. 481.[2]
— Myrtus tomentosa. 1879. III. 637.[1]
— Nouvelles espèces de Cactées. 1872. II. 586.[2]
— Passiflora edulis. 1867. III. 616.[1]
— Plumbago coccinea. 1873. III. 666.[2]
— Plumeria tricolor. 1869. III. 690.[1]
— Psycotria [*sic*] leucocephala. 1865. III. 747.[2]
— Quisqualis pubescens. 1874. III. 632.[2]
— Rogiera cordata. 1878. III. 747.[2]
— Tabernaemontana amygdalaefolia. 1879. III. 690.[1]
— Templetonia retusa. 1882. III. 489.[1]
— Theophrasta macrophylla. 1869. III. 665.[2]
— Toxicophlaea Thunbergi. 1880. III. 686.[1]
— Trachycarpus Griffithi. 1879. III. 331.[2]
— Tremandra ericaefolia hirsuta. 1868. III. 513.[2]
— Veronica Traversi. 1882. III. 704.[2]
— Wallichia caryotoides. 1870. III. 332.[1]
— Xanthochymus pictorius. 1881. III. 609.[2]
— Yucca conspicua. 1878. III. 340.[1]
Houlston, J. Garden memoranda, Kew. 1855. III. 317.
— The genus Franciscea. 1854. III. 698.[2]
— Notes on Aphelandras. 1855. III. 708.[2]
Household words. III. 17.
Houssaye, J. G. Monographie du Thé. 1843. III. 606.
— Der Thee, eine Monographie. 1843. III. 606.
Houston, Edwin James. Conditions necessary for the growth of trees. 1885. IV. 67.[1]
— Drainage. 188 . ? IV. 144.[1]
— Outlines of forestry. 1893. IV. 94.
— A plea for the study of elementary forestry. 1894. IV. 30.[1]
Houstoun, William. Reliquiae Houstounianae. 1781. I. 328.
Hout, L. Aufmunterung zur Seidensucht. 1832. III. 374.
— Über die Pflanzung der Maulbeerbäume. 1829. III. 374.
De **Houtbosschen** in Nederlandsch Indie. 1867. IV. 376.[2]
Houten, George van. *See* VAN HOUTEN, George.
Houten, P. J. van. Handleiding voor de Pepercultuur. 1890. III. 343.[2]
— De Peper. 1888. III. 343.[1]
— De Peper, hare teelt en hare beteekenis. 1888. III. 343.[1]
Houten, S. van. Nota betreffende de gouvernements Koffiecultuur. 1892. III. 730.
Houtkunde. *See* HOUTTUYN, Martin. 1773. I. 124; SEFF, J. C. 1773. IV. 17.
Houtte, Louis van. Abricotier de Syrie. 1849. III. 434.[2]
— Areca aurea hort. 1867. III. 324.[1]
— Azalea (indica) striata formosissima. 1847. III. 659.[2]
— Beaucarnea recurvata. 1869. III. 337.[2]

— Courte excursion dans les montagnes des Orgues. 1847. I. 342.
— Escallonia macrantha. .1855. III. 410.²
— Greffes de Camellias. 1851. III. 599.²
— Hortus Vanhoutteanus. 1845. I. 50, V. viii.²
— Múrier blanc à feuilles laciniées. 1851. III. 380.¹
— Nouvelles variétés d'Abutilon venoso-striatum. 1850. III. 587.¹
— Oncosperma Van Houtteanum. 1867. III. 327.²
— Picea alba Link. 1875. III. 305.²
— Pseudolarix Kaempferi Gordon. 1867. II. 49.¹
— See also LEMAIRE, Charles & HOUTTE, Louis van; PLAN-CHON, J. E. & HOUTTE, Louis van.
Houtteelt. ·Veenen. 1859. IV. 119.²
Houttuyn, Martin. Aanmerkinge over de bloemen van den nootenmuskaatboom. 1789. II. 220.²
— Abbildung in- und ausländischer Höltzer. 1773. I. 124.
— Afbeelding van in- en uitlandsche houten. 1773. I. 124.
— De echte Benzoin-boom en Kamferboom van Sumatra. 1784. III. 275.¹
— Houtkunde. 1773. I. 124, V. xi.¹
— Icones lignorum exoticorum et nostratium. 1773. I. 124.
— Natuurlyke historie. 1773. I. 258.
— Het onderscheid der zwarte en witte Peper. · 1784. II. 93.²
— Réprésentation des bois, des arbres & arbrisseaux tant du pays qu'étrangers. 1773. I. 124.
— A representation of inland and foreign wood. 1773. I. 124.
Houwald, Graf. Eine der ältesten ... Eichen Deutschlands. 1896. IV. 516.¹
Un Houx colossal. 1900. IV. 526.¹
Houzeau, Auguste. Observations sur le mode d'essai par teinture. 1868. III. 478.¹
Houzeau de Lehaye, A. Introduction des Bambous en Belgique. 1890. III. 314.²
Hoved-Efterretninger for Eege Skibs Tømmer Leverancer til d. klg. danske Wærft. 17 .. ? IV. 424.²
Hovelacque, Maurice. Sur la formation des coins libériens des Bignoniacées. 1887. II. 784.¹
— Recherches sur l'appareil végétatif des Bignoniacées. 1888. II. 784.²
Hoven, F. J. J. Slingsby van. Flora van 's Hertogenbosch. 1848. I. 391,¹ V. xx.¹
Hoveniers zakboekje. 1833. III. 77.¹
Hovey, Charles M. Arboretum americanum. 1876. I. 39.
— Autumn tints. 1880. III. 632.¹
— The best Philadelphus.' 1875. III. 413.²
— Camellia C. M. Hovey. 1883. III. 599.¹
— The Catalpa as a timber tree. 1880. IV. 538.²
— Catalpa Kaempferi. 1880. III. 706.¹
— The Charter Oak. 1876. II. 132.²
— The fruits of America. 1847. III. 61.²
— Hardy Rhododendrons in New England. 1885. III. 656.
— The Kentucky Coffee tree. 1878. III. 478.¹
— Natural sports. 1875. III. 39.
Hovey, H. C. The largest of Apple trees. 1883. II. 267.²
How, Henry & Rowney, Thomas. Analyse der Asche des Apfelsinenbaums. 1847. III. 501.¹
— — Analyse des cendres de l'Oranger. 1847. III. 501.¹
— — Analysis of the ashes of the Orange tree. 1847. III. 501.¹
How, William. Phytologia britannica. 1650. I. 394.
How Manila hats are made. 1898. III. 319.²
How the Chinese make dwarf trees. 1864. III. 175.²
How the woods and forests affect the rain. 1856. IV. 49.²
How to make palatable food from wood. 1835. III. 219.²
How to spray. 1893. III. 198.¹
How to tell the trees. 1892. I. 305.
How to transplant young trees. 1900. III. 166.
Howard, Charles D. Prussic acid in Wild Cherry leaves. 1898. III. 431.²
Howard, David. Sur l'aricine. 1875. III. 726.¹
— Cinchona cultivation in South America. 1887. III. 713.¹
— Note on aricine. 1875. III. 726.¹
— Notes on cinchona bark. 1880. III. 724.²
Howard, J. A. English and American trees. 1879. III. 60.
Howard, John Eliot. Analysis of Cinchona bark and leaves. 1866. III. 722.
— Sur l'arbre qui produit le quinquina rouge. 1857. II. 14.¹
— On the bark of Gomphosia. 1855. III. 744.¹
— The Calisaya barks of eastern Bolivia. 1869. II. 812.
— On Cinchona Calisaya var. Ledgeriana. 1884. III. 718.
— Cinchona cultivation in Java. 1871. III. 715.

— Cinchona in India. 1879. II. 813.¹
— De Cinchona in Indië. 1879. III. 714.
— Cinchona Ledgeriana. 1879. II. 813.²
— The Cinchona plantations in Java. 1874. III. 716.
— Cinchona trees in India. 1872. III. 714.
— Ueber Cinchona tucujensis Karst. 1872. III. 726.²
— Cinchonas. 1862. III. 718. — 1873. III. 712.¹ — 1880. III. 718.
— Ueber Coca. 1889. III. 493.¹
— On coppicing Cinchonas. 1874. · III. 712.¹
— On the cultivation of Cinchona in the East Indies. 1869. III. 714.
— On the cultivation of the Cinchona plant. 1870. III. 712.¹
— The effect of altitude on the alkaloid of Red bark. 1883. III. 726.¹
— Examination of Pavon's collection of Peruvian barks. 1852. II. 812,¹ III. 724.²
— The fast growing variety of Cinchona. 1878. III. 726.¹
— Fresh exploration of the Calisaya-yielding districts. ·1868. III. 718.
— On the genus Cinchona. 1875. II. 813.¹
— Illustrations of the Nueva Quinologia of Pavon. 1862. II. 812.
— The Mistletoe on the Oak. 1880. II. 180.¹
— Note sur une espèce nouvelle de Cinchona. 1870. II. 814.¹
— Observations on the present state of our knowledge of the genus Cinchona. 1866. II. 812.
— Observations on the specimens of Peruvian barks. 1854. III. 724.²
— Origin of the Calisaya Ledgeriana. 1880. III. 725.²
— Sur l'origine du Quinquina-Calisaya. 1875. II. 813.²
— Sur l'origine du Quinquina-Colombie mou. 1873. II. 813.²
— Presumed hybridization between Cinchona. 1875. II. 813.¹
— The quinology of the East Indian plantations. 1869. II. 812.
— On red bark. 1882. III. 725.¹
— On the red variety of pitayo bark. 1865. III. 726.¹
— Report on the bark and leaves of Cinchona succirubra. 1863. III. 726.¹
— Report to the under secretary of state for India on ... Cinchona succirubra. 1863. III. 718.
— On the root-bark of the Cinchonae. 1865. III. 724.¹
— On the tree producing red Cinchona bark. 1856. II. 814.¹
— See also M'IVOR, W. G. & HOWARD, J. E.
Howard Leland Ossian. The Box-Elder plant-bug. 1898. III. 535.¹
— Danger of importing insect pests. 1898. III. 187.
— The gipsy moth in America. 1897. III. 187.·
— An important enemy to fruit trees. 1893. III. 187.
— Legislation against injurious insects. 1895. III. 197.
— Recent laws against injurious insects in North America. 1898. III. 197.
— Regulations of foreign governments regarding importation of American plants. 1900. III. 197.
— The San José scale in 1896–97. 1898. III. 187.
— The shade-tree insect problem. 1896. III. 187.
— On some scale insects. 1896. III. 187.
— Some scale insects of the orchard. 1895. III. 187.
— Three insect enemies of shade trees. 1896. III. 187.
— The two most abundant Pulvinarias on Maple. 1900. III. 534.¹
— The use of steam apparatus for spraying. · 1897. III. 198.¹
— See also RILEY, C. V. & HOWARD, L. O.
— & Marlatt, C. L. The San José scale. 1896. III. 187.
Howard, Luke. Account of a microscopical investigation of several species of pollen. 1802. III. 181,² 589.²
Howard, N. Sur les Quinquinas de la Nouvelle-Granade. 1893. III. 724.¹
Howard, W. Beautiful leaved plants. See LOWE, E. J. 1861. III. 206.²
Howe, Elliot C. See GORDINIER, H. C. & HOWE, E. C.
Howell, A. M. The pruning of plants. 1900. III. 171.
Howell, H. Rottan en houtsoorten die gebruikt worden tot het vervaardigen van wandel- . . . stokken. 1888. IV. 428.¹
Howell, James. Δενδρολογια. Dodona's grove. 1650. I. 511, V. xxiv.²
— Dendrologia; or, Dodonna's grove. 1650. V. xxiv.²
— Dendrologie; ou, La forest de Dodonne. 1650. V. xxiv.²
Howell, Robert. Catalogue of forest trees ... of Nichols. 1852. I. 312, IV. 76.²

Howell, Thomas. The flora of Mount Hood. 1896. I. 326.
— A flora of northwest America. 1897. I. 327.
— New species of Pacific Coast plants. 1895. II. 245.¹ ˑ
— Scales of Thuya gigantéa 3-ovuled. 1881. II. 52.²
— See also SUKSDORF, W. N. & HOWELL, Thomas.
Howie, Charles. The Great Maple. 1890. II. 480.¹
— See also JEFFREY, John & HOWIE, Charles.
Howison, James. On the Chinese method of propagating fruit-trees. 1808. III. 157.
— Some account of the Elastic gum vine. 1798. III. 230, 691.²
Howison, William. An account of the manufacture of turpentine from the Pinus sylvestris. 1820. IV. 480.
— Short account of the forest trees . . . of Russia. 1825. IV. 404.¹
Howitt, A. W. The Eucalypts of Gippsland. 1891. II. 623.¹
— Note on the occurrence of Eucalyptus maculata. 1897. II. 625.¹
— Notes on the distribution of the Eucalyptus. 1889. II. 623.¹
— On the occurrence of Eucalyptus pulverulenta in Victoria. 1898. II. 625.²
Howitt, Godfrey. Nottinghamshire flora. 1829. I. 397.
— The Nottinghamshire flora. 1839. I, 399.
Howitz, D. Forest protection and tree culture. -1883. IV. 51.
— The value of the Eucalypts as timber trees. 1885. IV. 532.¹
Hoydar, Franz. Statistisch-topographische Beschreibung der . . . Domaine Frauenberg. 1876. IV. 371.
Hoyer, Egbert von. Lehrbuch der vergleichenden mechanischen Technologie. 1878. IV. 422.¹
— Verarbeitung der Metalle und des Holzes. 1878. IV. 422.¹
Hoyer, Karl A. H. Flora der Grafschaft Schaumburg. 1838. I. 379.
— Kurzer aber deutlicher . . . Inbegriff der Obstbaumzucht. 1837. III. 137.
Hoyo, R. del. Repoblaciones. 1879. IV. 164.²
Hoyt, Edward. Evergreen hedges. 1894. III. 214.² ˑ
Hoyt, Edwin. Pruning. 1894. III. 171.
Hrebnitzki, Adam. See Гребницкій, A.
Hromadnik, Hans. Rentabilität der Retortenverkohlung. 1890. IV. 395.
Hruschauer, Franz. Beiträge zur Kenntniss des Einflusses der chemischen Momente im Boden. 1846. I. 228.¹
— Influence de la composition du sol. 1846. I. 228.¹
— See also UNGER, Franz & HRUSCHAUER, Franz.
Hryniewiecki, Boleslaw. Choroby roślin i walka z niemi. 1899. III. 197.
— Die Flora des Urals. 1899. I. 367.
— Nasze lasy. 1900. IV. 347.
— Wpływ światła na kształt i położenie liści. 1899. I. 230.
Hs. Aanvoer van Hollandsche vruchtboomen. 1873. III. 147.¹
Hs. Sonderbar gewachsene Kiefern. 1850. II. 47.¹
Hua, Henri. Sur les collections botaniques faites à la Côte d'Ivoire. 1897. I. 491.
— Les dernières collections de M. Dybowski. 1895. I. 491.
— Deux types intéressants de Capparidacées africaines. 1895. II. 229.²
— Documents nouveaux concernant les Landolphiées. 1900. II. 727.²
— Les feuilles des Caesalpiniées-Cynométrées. 1898. II. 349.¹
— Sur le genre Baissea. 1893. II. 724.¹
— Mocquerysia. 1893. II. 572.¹
— Nouveaux matériaux pour la flore de l'Afrique française. 1897. I. 491.
— Un nouvel arbre à suif du Zanguebar. 1896. II. 553.¹
— De quelques Erythrines d'Afrique. 1898. II. 356.²
— Sur une des sources du caoutchouc du Soudan. 1899. III. 688.²
Huard du Plessis, E., (jr.). Le Noyer; traité de sa culture. 1847. III. 355.
— Traité de la culture du Noyer. 1847. III. 355.
Hub, A. C. Die Douglas-Tanne. 1879. IV. 483.¹
Hub, Karl. Die " Distanztafel." 1890. IV. 265.
— Genauere Bestimmung der Stockhöhe. 1893. IV. 219.
— Der Zoll- oder Centimeterstab als Baumhöhenmesser. 1892. IV. 216.
Hub. IV. 4.
Hubaut, A. Les Marronniers de l'avenue Louise. 1896. III. 210.
— Nos avenues. 1900. III. 210.

Hubbard. Propriétés du Ceanothus americanus. 1837. III. 541.¹
Hubbard, Bela. The lesson of the forest fires. 1895. IV. 182.¹
Hubbard, Ernst. Die Verwerthung der Holzabfälle. 1887. IV. 428.¹
Hubbard, Fred. Trees and rain: 1873. IV. 50.
Hubbard, Henry Guernsey. Bamboo. 1895. IV. 485.¹
— Insects affecting the Orange. 1885. III. 501.¹
— & Pergande, Theodore. A new coccid on Birch. 1898. IV. 491.¹
Hubeny, Joseph. Entwurf einer Waldpolizei- und Waldstraf-ordnung für Ungarn. 1843. IV. 331.¹
— Auf Erfahrungen begründete Anweisung zur schnellen Holz-erziehung. 1836. IV. 110.²
— Forstdienstinstruktion für die erzherzogliche Herrschaft Kiss-Jenő. 1836. IV. 307.¹
— Die vorzüglichsten Ursachen des schlechten Zustandes von vielen ungarischen Forsten. 1835. IV. 373.¹
— Die Waldanlagen von Mezőhegyes. 1834. IV. 373.
— Über die Wichtigkeit . . . der Forstregulirung. 1835. IV. 242.
Huber, (Forstinspektor). Exemplification einer genauen An-schätzung des Holzmaterial-Vorrathes. 187 . ?. IV. 255.
Huber, Candidus. Ankündigung einer natürlichen Holz-Bibliothek. 1792. I. 37,¹ IV. 17.
— Kurzgefasste Naturgeschichte der vorzüglichsten Holz-arten. 1793. IV. 17.
— Naturgeschichte der verschiednen Holzarten in Tabellen. 1804. I. 370, IV. 22.
— Vollständige Naturgeschichte aller in Deutschland ein-heimischen und einiger nationalisirten Baumhölzer. 1804. IV. 82.
— Vollständige Naturgeschichte aller in Deutschland ein-heimischen und nationalisirten Baumhölzer. 1808. I. 370.
Huber, François & Senebier, Jean. Mémoires sur l'influence de l'air . . . dans la germination. 1801. I. 202.²
Huber, Franz Xaver. Hilfs-Tafeln für Bedienstete des Forst- und Baufaches. 1828. IV. 222, 229.
— Tafeln zur Bestimmung der Massengehaltes stehender Waldbäume. 1838. IV. 229.
Huber, Heinrich. Wirthschafts-Regeln des k. Forstrevieres Neuessing. 1886. IV. 248.²
Huber, J. Apontamentos sobre o caucho amazonico. 1900. III. 232.²
Huber, J. C. & Rehm, J. Uebersicht der Flora von Mem-mingen. 1860. I. 384.
Huber, Jacob. Arboretum amazonicum. 1900. I. 340.²
— Beitrag zur Kenntniss der periodischen Wachsthumser-scheinungen bei Hevea. 1898. II. 445.¹
— Sur les campos de l'Amazone inférieur. 1900. I. 344.
— Le " Caucho " Amazonien. 1899. II. 147.² ˑ
— Contribuição á geographia botanica do littoral da Guyana. 1896. I. 339.²
— Duas Sapotaceas novas. 1900. II. 696.²
— Materiaes para a flora amazonica. 1898. I. 344.
— O " Muricy " da Serra do Orgão. 1898. II. 428.²
— Os nossos conhecimentos actuaes sobre as especies de Seringueiras. 1898. II. 445.¹
— Noticia sobre o " Uchi." 1898. II. 393.¹
— Observações histologicas . . . da Wulffia. 1898. II. 868.²
— See also KRAATZ-KOSCHLAU, K. von & HUBER, Jacob.
Huber, Jacques. See BUSCALIONI, Luigi & HUBER, Jacques.
Hubert. Mode de conservation des bois employés. 1874. IV. 419.
Hubert, Ernest. Préposés forestiers. Recrutement. 1899. IV. 291.²
Hubert, Eugène d'. Sur la présence . . . de l'amidon dans le sac embryonnaire des Cactées. 1895. II. 193,² 589.¹
— Recherches sur le sac embryonnaire. 1896. I. 122.
Hubert, F. A. Korte handleiding tot de aankweeking der wilde Pijnboomen. 1825. IV. 471.
— Traité ou méthode de cultiver des Pins sauvages. 1825. IV. 471.
Hubert, K. A. Grundsätze über die Bedeckung . . . des Flug-sandes. 1824. IV. 145.
Huberti, J. C. Abhandlung von dem allgemeinen Holz-Mangel. 1765. IV. 116, 280.¹
Huberty, Jules. Conseils pratiques sur l'économie forestière. 1898. IV. 274.²
— Excursion forestière en 1897. 1897. IV. 556.¹
— Exposition des bois tranchés. 1900. IV. 427.¹
— La forêt de Fontainebleau. 1900. IV. 362.
— La forêt de Soignes. 1894. IV. 555.²

— Les forêts à l'Exposition universelle de Paris. 1900. IV. 20.²
— Le Gui. 1900. II. 180,¹ IV. 811.¹
— L'Hertogenwald belge. 1896. IV. 357.¹
— Le nitrate de soude en sylviculture. 1899. IV. 145.—1900. IV. 145.
— See also MARCHAL, Em. & HUBERTY, Jules.
Huckleberries. 1873. III. 652.²
The Huckleberry and Blueberry. · 1878. III. 419.²
Huckvale, Graily. Timber, plantations, and underwood. 1878. IV. 214.
Hudig, J. Acht dagen in de Koffie-districten van Ceylon. 1876. III. 732.²
— Eenige mededeelingen omtrent de bladziekte der Koffie-boomen op Ceylon. 1877. III. 735.
— Exploitatie van Djattihout. 1875. IV. 537.²
Hudson, C. The giant Betel-nut tree. 1892. III. 320.²
Hudson, E. H. The Olives of San Remo. · 188 . ? III. 679.¹
Hudson, James. The African Hemp. 1894. III. 585.¹
— Allamandas. 1891. III. 686.¹
— Bougainvilleas. 1893. III. 388.²
— Crotons and their culture. 1882. III. 516.¹
— Erica Wilmoreana. 1896. III. 651.²
— The Habrothamnus. 1888. III. 699.¹
— Ixoras. 1892. III. 745.¹
— Magnolia conspicua. 1888. III. 399.²
— The Scarlet Spurge. 1888. III. 518.¹
— Stevensonia grandifolia. 1883. III. 328.¹
Hudson, John. A complete guide to the Lakes. 1843. I. 533.
Hudson, William. Flora anglica. 1762. I. 395.
Huebener, Johan Wilhelm Peter. Einleitung in das Studium der Pflanzenkunde. 1834. I. 87.
— Flora der Umgegend von Hamburg. 1846. I. 381.
— Theoretische Anfangsgründe der wissenschaftlichen Pflanzenkunde. 1835. I. 87.
Hübner, Ferd. Wachsthumsgang der Holzbestände. 1863. IV. 232.—1868. IV. 232.
Huebner, J. G. Pflanzen-Atlas. 1861. I. 90.
— Pflanzenkunde. 1867. I. 91.
Hübsch, Johann. Maclura aurantiaca. 1885. III. 372.¹
Hückel, Eduard. Ueber die Flora der Umgegend von Drohobycz. 1866. I. 441.
— Wyciecska botaniczna w Karpaty Stryjskie. 1868. I. 446.
Hueckl, E. Botanika. 1876. I. 91.
Hüetlin, Gustav. Der Stadtwald vor Freiburg i. B. 1874. IV. 350.¹
Hügel, Carl, Freiherr von. Botanisches Archiv der Gartenbaugesellschaft. 1837. I. 500, V. xxiv.²—See also BOTANISCHES . . . I. 27.
— Kaschmir und das Reich der Siek. 1840. I. 472.
Zur Hügelpflanzung. 1866. IV. 153.²
Hügel's Deodara. 1873. III. 300.¹
Huehnefeld, O. Die Indigofabrikation. 1846. III. 236.
Hülfstabellen zur Bestimmung des Kubikinhaltes runder Hölzer. 1870. IV. 226.
Hülfs-Tafeln zur Berechnung des körperlichen Inhaltes . . . des Bau- und Werkholzes. 1820. IV. 222.
Huell, Q. M. R. VER-. See VER-HUELL, Q. M. R.
Mueller, Karl. Catalogus plantarum quae in Horto regio atestino mutinensi 1820. I. 62.
Hülse (Ilex aquifolium L.). 1872. IV. 526.¹
Huelsen, Rudolf. Ueber die Ergebnisss meiner Excursionen zur Erforschung der Rubus-Formen. 1898. II. 302.²
Hünten, A. Einige Bemerkungen über die Bildung von Wirthschaftsfiguren. 1888. IV. 245.
Hüpsch, von. Beschrijving eenes algemeen nuttigen en beproefden werktuigs . . . schadelijke ongedierten . . . te verdelgen. 1778. III. 196.
Hür heuet an de lustighe inde [ge]nochlighe Gaerde der suntheit. See ORTUS sanitatis. 148 . ? I. 275.²
Huergo, J. M. La viti-vinicultura en la República Argentina. 1898. III. 551.¹
Huerta, Carlos de la TORRE Y. See TORRE Y HUERTA, Carlos de la.
Huerta, Felix de. Estado geográfico . . . de la . . . provincia de San Gregorio Magno. 1855. IV. 399.²
Huerto, Garcia del. Aromatum et simplicium . . . historia. 1563. III. 240.
— Coloquios dos simples. 1563. III. 239.²
— Histoire des drogues, espiceries. 1563. III. 240.
— Dell' historia. 1563. III. 240.
Huet & Henry. Note sur les Cistus olbiensis. 1862. II. 564.¹

Huet, Edm. Catalogue des plantes de Provence. 1889. V. xxii.¹
Huet, G. D. Destruction du kermès. 1891. III. 446.²
— Destruction du puceron lanigère. 1891. III. 428.¹
— Épidémies végétales. 1891. III. 179.
— Expériences sur des chenilles. · 1892. III. 196.
— Nouveau mode de multiplication rapide de la Vigne. 1892. III. 548.²
Huet, L. See LOUISE, E. & HUET, L.
— & Louise, E. Note sur le Mytilaspis pomorum. 1892. III. 428.¹
Huet du Pavillon, A. Note sur diverses plantes . . . dans le département du Var. 1860. .II. 564.²
Huett, J. W. Essay toward a natural history of Lasalle county. 1897. I. 316.
Hüttenbach, H. The cultivation of Liberian Coffee. 1897. III. 743.¹
Hüttenschmidt, C. R. Untersuchungen über die Entwicklung des Korkes und der Borke. See MOHL, Hugo von. 1836. I. 130.
Hüttig, (Gartendirektor at Gothenburg). Vegetationsbilder aus dem Norden. 1870. I. 356.
Hüttig, O. Carica Papaya. 1882. III. 617.¹
— Geschichte des Gartenbaus. 1879. III. 32.²
— Der Obstbau. 1882. III. 139.
— Der Trüffelbau in Frankreich. 1882. IV. 439.
Hüttner, C. von. Gartenflora . . . von San Remo. 1884. III. 88.¹
Hufeland, Christoph Wilhelm. Armen-Pharmakopöe. 1810. III. 248.
Huffel, G. Les arbres et les peuplements forestiers. 1893. IV. 234.
— Le balivage dans les taillis composés. 1886. IV. 382.¹
— Le balivage des coupes de taillis sous futaie. 1891. IV. 237.
— Description forestière du royaume de Prusse. 1894. IV. 354.
— Les éclaircies jardinatoires d'après M. Borggreve. 1887. IV. 174.
— Les forêts de la Roumanie. 1890. IV. 375.¹
— Influence de l'enlèvement de la couverture. 1896. IV. 543.²
— Influence de l'enlèvement de la couverture du sol. 1893. IV. 72.
— Influence de l'enlèvement de la couverture sur la végétation. 1896. IV. 72.
— Influence des forêts sur le climat. 1895. IV. 54.
— Raporte privitore la studiul sumar al padurilor statului. 1890. IV. 375.¹
— Les reboisements dans le royaume de Prusse. 1897. IV. 546.¹
— Les sapinières des Carpathes roumaines. 1894. IV. 375.¹
— Sols forestiers et sols agricoles. 1894. IV. 70.
Hufnagl, Leopold. Anleitung zur Führung des Tagebuches für die forstliche Staatsprüfung. 1895. IV. 36.²
— Die Berechnung der Weiserprocentes. 1898. IV. 259.¹
— Die Betriebseinrichtung. 1893. IV. 241.
— Die Betriebseinrichtung in kleinen Wäldern. 1896. IV. 246.
— Zur Betriebseinrichtungsfrage im Plenterwalde. 1892. IV. 246.
— Die Buchenfrage. 1899. IV. 499.
— Die Grundzüge der wahren Bestandeswirtschaft. 1898. IV. 247.¹
— Ueber natürliche und künstliche Waldeintheilung. 1888. IV. 251.¹
— Eine neue Näherungsmethode zur Bestimmung des Hiebssatzes. 1895. IV. 238.
— Der Plenterwald. 1893. IV. 131.
— Aus der Praxis der Betriebseinrichtung. 1896. IV. 246.
— La question de Hêtre. 1900. IV. 498.
— Die Wahl der Betriebsart im Hochwalde. 1896. IV. 130.
— Was ist der Plenterwald? 1895. IV. 131.
— Das Wirthschaftsziel und der Normalwald. 1890. IV. 245.
— Die Wirthschaftsziele . . . der Betriebseinrichtung. 1898. IV. 246.
Hugel. Sur l'action thérapeutique . . . du Djamboé. 1895. III. 637.²
Huggins, St. Vincent. 1888. III. 267.¹
Hughes, Griffith. The natural history of the Barbados. 1750. I. 334.

Hughes, John. Ceylon Coffee soils and manures. 1879. III. 732.[2]

Hughes, Thomas McKenny. On symmetry in the foliage of a branch of Mulberry. 1896. II. 154.[3]

Hughes, William. The American physitian. 1672. III. 264.[1]

— The compleat vineyard. 1670. III. 553.[2]

Hugi, F. S. Naturhistorische Alpenreise. 1830. V. xxii.[2]

Hugo, August Johannes. Dissertatio ... de variis plantarum methodis. 1711. I. 250.

Hugon, Thomas. Remarks on the silk worms and silks of Assam. 1837. III. 148.[1]

Hugoninus, Abraham. Theses ex anatome et botanica imprimis depromptas. See EGLINGERUS, Christian. 1711. I. 31.

Hugounenq, L. See CAZENEUVE, Paul & HUGOUNENQ, L.

Huguenin, Henri. Sapin géant. 1872. II. 24.[1]

Huguenin, O. Charbonniers bergamasques. 1883. IV. 395.

Hugueny, F. Le coup de foudre de l'île du Rhin. 1869. IV. 194.

Huile d'Anda. 1849. III. 520.[1]

Huile de graine de Fusain. 1863. III. 532.[1]

L'huile de pépins de raisin. 1894. III. 583.[3]

Huin, J. B. Éducation bivoltine du ver à soie du Chêne de Chine. 1882. IV. 502.[1]

Huit jours à Turin; de congressu phylloxerico. 1884. III. 761.

Huizinga, D. Het curare. 1872. III. 683.[1]

Hull, Edmund C. P. Coffee, its physiology, history. 1865. III. 732.[1]

— Coffee planting in southern India. 1865. III. 732.[1]

Hull, Hugh M. Evergreen timber trees of Tasmania. 1881. IV. 402.[1]

Hull, John. The British flora. 1799. I. 396.

— Elements of botany. 1800. I. 84.

Hulle, H. J. van. Altijd de phylloxera. 1886. III. 574.

— Aphelandra fascinator Lind. et André. 1885. III. 708.[2]

— Les Azalées rustiques de Gand. 1877. III. 661.[3]

— Behandeling der versamelings-boomen. 1873. III. 124.[2]

— Beziestruikenteelt in de polders van Noord-holland. 1875. III. 121.[2]

— Boomen dienstig voor openbare plaatsen. 1890. III. 42.[3]

— Boomsnoeistelsel der Belgen. 1866. III. 170.

— De boomteelt. 1864. III. 140.[1]

— De boomteeltkunde op de Haarlemmer tentoonstelling. 1871. III. 121.[2]

— Een boomteeltkundig kijkje in Nederland. 1870. III. 121.[2]

— Chamaecyparis Boursieri. 1890. III. 301.[1]

— Chamaecyparis Boursieri Westermani aurea. 1890. III. 301.[1]

— Le Châtaignier. 1890. III. 359.[1]

— Coup d'œil sur l'arboriculture dans le Danemark. 1876. I. 119.[2]

— Coup d'œil sur l'arboriculture en Néerlande. 1870. III. 121.[2]

— Culture de la Vigne. 1884. III. 553.[3]

— Discours prononcé au Congrès international de pomologie. 1880. III. 33.[1]

— Les écoles d'horticulture. 1899. III. 31.

— L'élagage. 1872. III. 170.

— Encore l'hiver 1879–80. 1880. III. 46.[1]

— Engrais liquides. 1895. III. 152.

— Les Épacris. 1889. III. 665.[1]

— Essences d'arbres propres aux places publiques. 1890. III. 42.[3]

— État actuel de l'horticulture belge. 1874. III. 122.[2]

— Faut-il tailler les arbustes d'ornement? 1877. III. 172.

— Formation des arbres arbres d'ornement. 1873. III. 170.

— Un géant de nos serres. 1881. II. 74.[2]

— Grevillea Forsteri hort. 1898. III. 383.[1]

— Guide arboricole. 1864. III. 140.[1]

— Houtteelt. 1896. IV. 119.[2]

— Importation des Cycas. 1885. III. 284.[3]

— Le jardin botanique de l'Université de Gand. 1871. I. 51.[2]

— De kroonsnoeiing. 1868. III. 170.

— Laurus nobilis. 1886. III. 406.[1]

— Levensduur van sommige planten. 1897. I. 193.[2]

— La Menziésie à feuilles de Germandrée. 1877. III. 649.[1]

— Moet men de sieraadheesters ja of niet snoeien? 1877. III. 172.

— De niet-snoeiing. 1869. III. 170.

— Nogmaals de winter van 1879–80. 1880. III. 46.[1]

— Note sur le Cornus capitata. 1867. III. 645.[2]

— Over het ondiep planten. 1871. III. 169.[2]

— Ormes malades. 1890. III. 364.[2]

— De Palmboomen. 1872. III. 317.

— Pauvres Tilleuls! Leur remplacement. 1883. III. 168.[1]

— Plantes peu profondément. 1871. III. 169.[2]

— Quelques mots concernant la taille raisonnée. 1865. III. 170.

— Roses noires. 1884. III. 450.

— De sleuning. 1872. III. 170.

— Sleuning der kruin en der boomen. 1873. III. 170.

— Sources du malaise des arbres des boulevards. 1890. III. 42.[2]

— Stephanotis floribunda Ad. Brongn. 1885. III. 694.[1]

— Les systèmes de taille d'arbres fruitiers. 1866. III. 172.[1]

— Taille d'été. 1880. III. 170. — 1894. III. 171.

— La taille sur empâtement. 1868. III. 170.

— Thrinax radiata. 1873. III. 331.[1]

— Toestand van België's tuinbouw. 1874. III. 122.[2]

— Toujours le phylloxera. 1886. III. 574.

— Traitement des arbres de collection. 1873. III. 121.[2]

— Une transplantation de grands arbres à Gand. 1883. III. 168.[1]

— Het verduurzamen van hout door koper vitriool. 1884. IV. 420.

— Verplanting van groote boomen te Gent. 1883. III. 168.[1]

— Vloeibare meststoffen. 1895. III. 152.

— Waarom de boomen der stadslanen lijden. 1890. III. 42.[2]

— Een wenk op de boomteelt in Denemarken. 1876. III. 119.[2]

— Zieke Olmen. 1890. III. 364.[2]

— De zickte van het hout. 1881. I. 207.

— Ziekten bij planten. 1877. III. 179.

— Zomersnoei. 1880. III. 170. — 1894. III. 171.

Hulle, Hubert van. Du choix des arbres les plus convenables pour les plantations d'alignement. 1896. III. 210.

— Les Magnolia. 1894. III. 399.[1]

— Rapport sur la sylviculture à l'Exposition ... d'Anvers. 1896. IV. 19.[2]

— Rapport sur le groupe 20, class 64 (sylviculture), de l'Exposition ... d'Anvers. 1896. IV. 19.[2]

Hulme, F. Edward. Bards and blossoms; or, The poetry, history. 1877. I. 511.

— Familiar wild flowers. 1878. I. 403, 534.[1]

Huls, G. F. K. van. De cultuur van overjarige gewassen. 1900. III. 323.[1]

— De Koffiecultuur als volkscultuur. 1899. III. 731.

— De nieuwe regeling van de gouvernements-Koffiecultuur. 1894. III. 730.

— Een nieuwe staats-cultuur. 1899. III. 149.

Hulsebosch, M. L. Q. van LEDDEN. See LEDDEN HULSEBOSCH, M. L. Q. van.

Hult, Ragnar. Alnus glutinosa forma pinnatifida. 1878. II. 116.[1]

— Försök till analytisk behandling af växtformationerna. 1881. I. 218.

— Ueber eine Gruppe von Salix alba L. 1888. II. 104.[2]

— Den nordligaste kulturen af Salix alba i Finland. 1888. III. 351.[1]

— Salix alba 's nordligaste växtplats i Finland. 1888. II. 104.[2]

— Växtgeografiska anteckningar från den finska Lappmarkens skogsregioner. 1898. I. 367.

— See also HJELT, Hjalmar & HULT, Ragnar.

Hulthem, Charles Joseph Emmanuel van. Discours sur l'état ... de l'agriculture ... dans les Pays-Bas. 1817. III. 33.[1]

Hulting, Johan. Några ord om Fagus silvatica. 1899. II. 127.[1]

Humbert, François. Essai monographique sur les Roses ... de la Moselle. 1876. II. 285.[2]

Humbert, Joseph. Sur le désastreux système du défrichement des forêts en France. 1837. IV. 275.

— Quelques considérations sur les excès du déboisement. 1847. IV. 282.[2]

Humble, Adolph Henric. Om utländske träd, buskar och blomstervärxter. See THUNBERG, C. P. 1820. I. 266.

— See also HAMMARIN, Johan Israel, ALMQUIST, Johan Magnus & HUMBLE, Adolph Henric.

Humblot, L. Essai d'introduction de l'Arbre à guttapercha. 1897. III. 668.[1]

Humboldt, Friedrich Heinrich Alexander von. Ansichten der Natur. 1808. I. 217, V. xii.[1]

— Aphorismen aus der chemischen Physiologie der Pflanzen. 1793. I. 150.[2]

— Aspects of nature. 1808. I. 217.
— De Bamboes. 1817. III. 315.[1]
— Ueber die Chinawälder in Südamerika. 1807. II. 812.
— On the Cinchona forests of South America. 1807. II. 812.
— Copie van een brief, geschreven van Cumana. 1801. III. 267.[1]
— De distributione geographica plantarum. 1817. I. 298.
— Le Dragonier d'Orotava. 1852. II. 82.[1]
— On the fecundation of flowers. 1828. I. 236.[2]
— Florae fribergensis specimen. 1793. I. 150.[2]
— Ideen zu einer Physiognomik der Gewächse. 1806. I. 217.
— Sur le lait de l'Arbre de la vache. 1817. I. 181.[2]
— Sul latte dell' Albero della vacca. 1817. I. 181.[2]
— Sur les lois . . . dans la distribution des formes végétales. 1816. I. 298.
— New inquiries into the laws . . . in the distribution of vegetable forms. 1816. I. 298.
— Nouvelles recherches sur les lois. 1816. I. 298.
— Pflanzengeographie. 1817. I. 298.
— Quadri della natura. 1808. I. 217.
— Tableau de la nature. 1808. I. 217.
— Uittreksel uit een brief aan Willdenow. 1802. I. 335.
— Views of nature. 1808. V. XII.[1]
— Vues des Cordillères. 1813. II. 82.[1]
— See also Гумбольтъ, Ф. Г. А. фонъ.
— & Bonpland, Aimé. Essai sur la géographie des plantes. 1805. I. 298.
— — Geografia de las plantas. 1805. I. 328.
— — Géographie des plantes équinoxiales. 1810. I. 328.
— — Ideen zu einer Geographie der Pflanzen. 1805. I. 298.
— — Monographie des Melastomacées. 1816. II. 634.[2]
— — Personal narrative of travels to the equinoctial regions of America. 1808. I. 328.
— — Plantae aequinoctiales. 1808. I. 328.
— — Reis naar de landen bij den equator. 1808. I. 328.
— — Voyage aux régions equinoxiales. 1808. I. 328.
Humboldt. I. 12.
Hume, Allan Octavian. See HENDERSON, George & HUME, A. O.
Hume, Harold Hardrada. Native plants for decorative purposes. 1899. III. 527.[1] — 1900. III. 663.[1]
— Pecan culture; a preliminary report. 1900. III. 354.[1]
— See also CRAIG, John & HUME, H. H.
Hummel, John James. See PERKIN, A. G. & HUMMEL, J. J.
— & Brown, R. B. The dyeing properties of catechin. 1896. III. 464.[2]
— & Perkin, A. G. The tinctorial properties of kaiphal bark. 1897. III. 353.[2]
— — The tinctorial properties of some Indian dyestuffs. 1894. III. 237.[1]
Hummitzsch, Hans. Linné's Pflanzensystem. 18 . . ? I. 255.
Humnicki, Valentin. Catalogue des plantes . . . d'Orléans. 1876. I. 415.
— Catalogue des plantes . . . de Luxeuil. 1876. I. 415.
Humpert, Friedrich. Die Bäume und Sträucher des Bochumer Stadtparkes. 1887. III. 70.
— Die Flora Bochums. 1887. I. 388.
Humphrey, A. G. Expense of planting young trees. 1874. IV. 111.[2]
— The necessity of forest culture in Iowa. 1874. IV. 111.[2]
Humphrey, James Ellis. Amherst trees, an aid to their study. 1897. I. 512.
— Fungous diseases. 1892. III. 193.[2]
— Mildews. 1890. III. 580.
— On some constituents of the cell. 1895. I. 137.
Humphreys, A. G. The relation of forests to agriculture. 1883. IV. 271.[2]
Humphreys, Henry Noel. On the effect of clipped trees. 1850. III. 202.[1]
— The forest of Fontainebleau. 1872. IV. 360.
— Forms of trees in landscape gardening. 1873. I. 516.
— The galery [sic] of exotic flowers. 1855. I. 270.
— Insects injurious to the Elm. 1863. III. 364.[1]
Humusbildung und Bodenkultur. 1887. I. 229.
Hun, L. De l'extinction des torrents. 1853. IV. 185.[2]
— Des inondations. 1856. IV. 19.[2]
Hunault, François Joseph. Discours physique sur les propriétés de la Sauge. 1689. III. 698.[1]
Hundeshagen, Johann Christian. Die Anatomie, der Chemismus und die Physiologie der Pflanzen. 1829. IV. 61.[1]
— Anleitung zum Entwerfen von Bauholz-Anschlägen. 1818. V. 392.
— Die Bodenkunde in land- u. forstwirthschaftlicher Beziehung. 1830. IV. 61.[1]

— Encyclopädie der Forstwissenschaft. 1821. IV. 97.
— Die Forstabschätzung. 1826. IV. 252.
— Forstliche Gewerbslehre. 1821. IV. 97, 239.
— Forstliche Produktionslehre. 1821. IV. 97.
— Forstpolizeilehre. 1821. IV. 268.
— Forstverwaltungslehre. 1821. IV. 239.
— Ueber die Hackwald-Wirthschaft. 1821. IV. 132.[2]
— Lehrbuch der forst- und landwirthschaftlichen Naturkunde. 1827. IV. 56.
— Lehrbuch der Forstpolizei. 1821. IV. 97, 268.
— Methodologie und Grundriss der Forstwissenschaft. 1819. IV. 56.
— Ueber die natürliche Umwandlung der Wälder. 1830. IV. 74.[1]
— Prüfung der Cottaischen Baumfeldwirthschaft. 1820. IV. 132.[2]
— Die Waldweide und Waldstreu. 1830. IV. 70, 135.[1]
Hundius, E. L. Die "Kindertanne." 1848. II. 24.[1]
Hundt, Jos. Tabellen neuesten Systemes zur Kubirung von Stamm- und Blochholz. n. d. IV. 219.
— Universal-Tabelle neuesten Systems. n. d. IV. 219.
Hungary — Mathematische und naturwissenschaftliche Berichte. See MATHEMATISCHE . . . I. 28.[1]
Hungary — Zeitschrift für Natur- und Heilkunde. See ZEITSCHRIFT . . . I. 28.[2]
Hunkiarbeyendian, Rhatchik. Des produits . . . des Menispermées. 1887. III. 396.[1]
Hunnewell, H. H. Hardy Rhododendrons. 1890. III. 656.
— The new Conifers. 1867. III. 292.
— Select lists of trees and shrubs, II. 1881. III. 60.
— A topiary garden. 1899. III. 202.[2]
— The winter-killing of Conifers. 1892. III. 293.
Hunt, R. R. Notes on blowing up snags in the Waikato River with dynamite. 1878. IV. 386.
Hunter, Alexander. The Ahtool Ghaut. 1862. I. 473.
— On the economical uses of the Bamboo. 1859. III. 315.[1]
— The fixed [vegetable] oils of southern India. 1853. III. 224.[1]
— On the Indian woods that have been tried for engraving. 1860. IV. 427.[2]
— The raw products of India. 1859. III. 278.
— On some of the fibrous plants of Madras. 1862. III. 234.
— On the uses of the Bamboo. 1859. III. 315.[1]
— Uses of the Yercum-mudar. 1860. III. 692.[1]
— See also WHITLEY, George, JEPHSON, George & HUNTER, Alexander.
Hunter, Charles. Local medicinal barks. 1883. III. 268.[1]
Hunter, John. Of the heat &c. of animals and vegetables. 1779. I. 186.
— An historical journal of the transactions at Port Jackson. 1793. I. 500.
— Memoranda on vegetation. 1860. I. 34.
Hunter, Robert Edward. A catalogue of plants . . . in Thanet. 1902. V. XX.[2]
— A short description of the isle of Thanet. 1802. V. XX.[2]
Hunter, Thomas. Woods, forests . . . of Perthshire. 1883. I. 297.[1]
Hunter, William. Observations on Nauclea Gambir. 1808. II. 832.[2]
— On the plant Morinda and its uses. 1795. III. 746.[1]
— Remarks on the species of Pepper. 1807. III. 342.[1]
Huntington, J. H. The flowering plants of the White Mountains. 1877. I. 314.
— Reports of the councillors. 1880. II. 682.[1]
— Reports of the councillors for . . . 1881. 1882. II. 40.[2]
Hunt's . . . merchant's magazine. See MERCHANT's magazine. III. 5.
Hunziker, Rudolph. Die Sassaparillae radice. 1835. III. 338.[2]
Huot, L. Ueber das Vorkommen der Eiben. 1841. II. 10.[2]
Hupe, Aug. Thyrsacanthus rutilans. 1884. III. 709.[2]
Hupe, Conrad. Flora des Emslandes. 1877. I. 387, 532.[2]
Huraut, Th. De l'origine du soufre dans les végétaux. 1843. I. 152.[2]
Hurdis, J. L. See JONES, J. M., WEDDERBURN, J. W. & HURDIS, J. L.
Hureaux, Jean Pierre. Histoire des falsifications des substances alimentaires. 1855. III. 218.[2]
Hurlbert, J. B. Description of the chief forest trees of upper Canada. 1863. IV. 76.[1]
— The forests of Canada. 1885. IV. 337.[1]
— The great mixed forests of North America. 1863. IV. 45.
Hurst, C. C. Notes on some experiments in hybridisation. 1900. III. 51.
Hurt, A. B. Mississippi. 1883. IV. 339.

Hurt, T. Transplanting trees at midsummer. 1875. III. 168.²

Hurtig Formering af Ilex. 1842. III. 529.²

Husain ibn 'Abd Allah (Abû 'Alî). *See* IBN SÎNÂ.

The husbandman's fruit-full orchard. *See* The FRUITERER's secrets. 1604. III. 173.²

Husemann, August. Ueber das Cytisin. 1869. *II. 350,*¹ III. 481.¹

— Sur la cytisine. 1869. III. 481.¹

— & Theodor. Die Pflanzenstoffe in chemischer, physiologischer . . . Hinsicht. 1871. III. 258.

— & Marmé, Wilhelm. Sur les alcaloïdes du Faux ébénier. 1865. III. 481.¹

— — Vorläufig Mittheilunge über Cytisin. 1865. III. 481.¹

Husemann, Theodor. Handbuch der gesammten Arzneimittellehre. 1874. III. 258.

— Historische Notiz über das Ditain. 1878. III. 686.²

Huskless Chinese Walnuts. 1876. II. 113.¹

Husmann, George. American Grape growing. 1880. III. 550.

— The cultivation of the native Grape. 1866. III. 550.

— An essay on the culture of the Grape. 1863. III. 550.

— Grape culture . . . in California. 1888. III. 551.¹

— Ornamental tree-planting. 1876. III. 117.²

— The present condition of Grape culture in California. 1899. III. 551.¹

— *See also* CLAYTON, B. F. & HUSMANN, George.

Husnot, Tranquille. Excurson fait par la Société Linnéenne de Normandie. 1875. I. 414.

Hussa, Alois. Beiträge zur Entwicklungsgeschichte der Holzindustrie in der Bukowina. 1897. IV. 407.¹

— Die Entwicklung der Sägegatterconstruction. 1888. IV. 393.

— Holzschälmaschinen. 1884. IV. 429.²

— Die maschinelle Fällung der Bäume. 1888. IV. 384.¹

— Die Rollbahnen im Dienste der Forstwirthschaft. 1890. IV. 392.¹

— Die Schmalspurbahnen. 1894. IV. 392.¹

— Wald, Waldproducte . . . in Kärnten. 1887. IV. 369.

Hussenot. Chardons nancéiens. 1835. I. 409.

Hussey, John. Report on the botany of Barren. 1875. I. 319.

Husson, A. Henry. Correspondence d'Orient; de l'horticulture en Égypte. 1841. III. 131.¹

— *See also* FIGARI, Antonio & HUSSON, A. H.

Husson, C. Action de la fumée des fours à chaux sur les Vignes. 1876. III. 560.

— Le café, la bière et le tabac. 1879. III. 742.¹

— Étude sur le Café, le Thé et les Chicorées. 1879. III. 740.³

Huston, H. A. & Barrett, J. M. Composition of the Persimmon. 1896. III. 670.¹

Hustwick, T. H. Note on Tu-tu. 1884. III. 523.²

Hutchins, David Ernest. Cape national forests. 1900. IV. 380.¹

— Forestry and sylviculture. 1894. IV. 380.¹

— Forestry in the British Isles. 1900. IV. 275.

— The forests of Natal. 1892. IV. 379.³

— The fuel plantations in the Nundydroog forest division. 1881. IV. 377.³

— National forestry. 1900. IV. 275.

— National forests. 1898. IV. 380.¹

— Pine wood at the Cape. 1899. IV. 467.²

— Report on measurements of the growth of Australian trees on the Nilghiris. 1883. III. 129.¹

— Report on the measurement of rates of growth of Casuarina. 1884. IV. 485.¹

— Sandal. 1884. IV. 519.²

— Tree-planting. 1899. III. 131.²

Hutchinson, John. Notes on Beeches. 1875. II. 125.³

— Notes on Chestnuts. 1875. II. 124,¹ *III. 538.*³

— The Olive tree. 1875. II. 713.¹

— Remarkable Lime trees. 1875. II. 516.¹

Hutchinson, S. J. Daphne the beautiful. 1889. III. 626.²

Hutchison, Robert. On the Abies Albertiana. 1880. III. 312.¹

— On the Abies Douglasii. 1873. IV. 483.¹

— On the Abies Menziesii. 1878. III. 306.¹

— On the altitude . . . of the Wellingtonia. 1875. II. 50.¹

— On the best method of rearing . . . live fences. 1865. III. 213.

— On the cause of disease observed on Beech hedges. 1881. IV. 497.

— The cedar of Lebanon. 1890. IV. 448.¹

— On the Cedar of Lebanon. 1893. III. 299.²

— On Cedrus deodara. 1875. III. 300.¹

— On the comparative rise and fall in value . . . of the different varieties of forest timber. 1872. IV. 261.²

— On the conservation of old . . . trees in Britain. 1875. I. 297.¹

— The disastrous gales of season 1881–2. 1885. III. 184.²

— On the economic uses . . . of timber grown in Scotland. 1869. IV. 398.²

— On the effects . . . of the dry seasons of 1868. 1872. III. 42.¹

— On the effects of the severe frost . . . of 1878–79. 1880. III. 47.

— The effects of the severe frost . . . 1879–80. 1882. III. 47.

— On the effects of the severe frost of Dec. 1860. 1863. III. 46.²

— The effects of the severe winter of 1880–1881. 1883. III. 47.

— On the effects of the very dry season of 1868. 1871. III. 183.²

— On the effects of the very dry summer of 1870. 1873. III. 183.²

— On the effects of the very dry summer of 1869. 1872. III. 183.²

— On the effects produced on trees and shrubs by smoke. 1876. III. 185.²

— On forest trees of recent introduction. 1871. IV. 126.²

— Forestry of Scotland. 1879. IV. 359.¹

— On the insects which attack coniferous trees. 1874. IV. 442.

— On the introduction . . . of the newer Coniferae. 1865. III. 292.

— On the literature of Scottish arboriculture. 1875. IV. 2.

— On the most profitable varieties of trees for planting. 1874. III. 344.¹

— On the natural history of beetles and other insects which infest Coniferae. 1874. IV. 442.

— On the old and remarkable Ash trees. 1880. II. 708.¹

— On the old and remarkable Beeches in Scotland. 1881. II. 127.¹

— The old and remarkable Elm trees in Scotland. 1883. II. 143.²

— Old and remarkable Hollies. 1892. II. 463.²

— The old and remarkable Horse-chestnut trees. 1884. II. 482.²

— The old and remarkable Lime trees in Scotland. 1883. II. 517.¹

— On the old and remarkable Oaks in Scotland. 1881. II. 138.²

— On the old and remarkable Spanish Chestnuts. 1879. II. 124.¹

— On the old and remarkable Sycamores. 1880. II. 480.¹

— The old . . . Walnut trees in Scotland. 1884. II. 114.¹

— On the old . . . Yew trees in Scotland. 1890. II. 11.¹

— The Picea grandis. 1883. IV. 444.¹

— On the Picea nobilis. 1879. III. 296.²

— On the Picea Nordmanniana. 1878. III. 296.²

— Picea pectinata (Silver Fir). 1885. IV. 444.¹

— The Pinus insignis. 1882. III. 308.¹

— On the Pinus Pinaster or Cluster Pine. 1876. IV. 467.²

— On the progress of forestry in Scotland. 1881. IV. 359.¹

— On the pruning of the rarer Coniferae. 1868. III. 295.¹

— On the quantity of rain. 1875. IV. 50.

— Report on the pruning of the rarer Coniferae. 1869. III. 295.²

— Report on trees not liable to be destroyed by rabbits. 1869. III. 186.¹

— On some of the summer operations. 1878. IV. 169.¹

— On the species of timber trees suitable to the different soils . . . in Scotland. 1868. IV. 120.

— On the stem and branch pruning of Conifers. 1874. III. 295.¹

— Substitutes for the Larch. 1873. IV. 441.

— On the Taxodium sempervirens. 1877. IV. 484.¹

— The Tay Bridge gale. 1882. III. 184.²

— The time of the year best suited for transplanting Pines. 1868. III. 169,¹ *294.*²

— On transplanting large trees. 1867. III. 167.

— On transplanting trees. 1867. III. 166.

— Trees and shrubs . . . for planting as shelter. 1890. III. 215.²

— On the value of the Corsican, Austrian and Douglas Firs. 1873. IV. 441, 442.¹

— On the varieties of Poplar best suited to ... Scotland. 1871. III. 344.¹
— On the varieties of trees best adapted for planting as shelter. 1881. IV. 154.²
— On the Wellingtonia gigantea. 1873. III. 310.¹
Huteau, H. & Sommier, F. Catalogue des plantes ... de l'Ain. 1894. V. xxii.¹
Huth, Ernst. Ameisen als Pflanzenschutz. 1886. I. 235.¹
— Die Anpassungen der Pflanzen an die Verbreitung durch Thiere. 1881. I. 240.¹
— Beckmann's Catalogus plantarum. 1888. I. 78.¹
— Brennsäfte als Pflanzenschutz. 1890. I. 235.²
— Clavis Commeliniana. 1894. I. 78.¹
— Clavis Riviniana. 1891. I. 78.²
— Dürfen in der botanischen Nomenclatur Genus- und Speciesnamen gleich lautern? 1894. I. 254.¹
— Flora von Frankfurt a. d. Oder. 1880. I. 388, V. xix.²
— Ueber geokarpe, amphikarpe und heterokarpe Pflanzen. 1890. I. 119.
— Die Hakenklimmer. 1888. I. 236.¹
— Heteromericatpie. 1895. I. 120.
— Monographie der Gattung Paeonia. 1892. II. 200.¹
— Myrmekophile und myrmekophobe Pflanzen. 1887. I. 235.¹
— Nachrichten von einer ... pharmazeütischen Flora. 1889. I. 78.²
— Ueber Pepsin-Pflanzen. 1890. III. 245.
— Pflanzenschutz durch Ameisen. 1887. I. 235.¹
— Ranunculaceae japonicae. 1897. II. 196.¹
— Sammlung naturwissenschaftlicher Vorträge. See SAMMLUNG ... I. 14.
— Ueber stammfrüchtige Pflanzen. 1888. I. 113.²
— Systematische Uebersicht der Pflanzen mit Schleuder-Früchten. 1890. I. 119.
— Systematische Uebersicht der Schleuderfrüchte. 1891. I. 240.²
— Der Tabaxir in seiner Bedeutung. 1887. III. 315.¹
— Die Verbreitung der Pflanzen durch die Excremente. 1889. I. 240.²
— Verzeichniss der durch Brennhaare geschützten Pflanzen. 1886. I. 235.²
Huth, J. C. De potu chocolatæ. See MAPPUS, Marcus. 1695. III. 594.
Huth, J. C. Efterretning om Svampenes Oprindelse. 1776. IV. 414.¹
— Nachricht von dem Entstehen des Schwamms. 1776. IV. 414.²
Hutin, B. & Boutigny, P. H. Sur la conservation des bois. ·1848. IV. 417.
Hutstein, J. Ueber Nadelhölzer und deren Härte. 1874. III. 292.
Hutten, Ulrich von. Experience ... du bois dit Guajacum. 1519. III. 492.²
— De Guaiaci medicina. 1519. III. 493.²
— Guaiacum. L'experience ... touchant la medecine du boys dict Guaiacum. 1519. III. 493.²
— Livre sur la maladie française. 1519. III. 493.²
— De morbi gallici curatione. 1519. III. 493.²
— De morbo gallico. 1519. III. 493.²
— Opera quae extant omnia. 1519. III. 493.²
— Of the wood called Guaiacum. 1510. III. 494.¹
— Von der wunderbarlichen Arzney des Holtz Guaiacum. 1519. III. 493.²
Huttenschmid, Gustav Friedrich. Analysis chemica corticis Geoffroyae. 1824. III. 477.¹
Hutton, F. W. The origin of the fauna and flora of New Zealand. 1884. I. 536.¹
Hutton, James. Experiments in planting sand-hills. 1878. III. 41.¹
Hutton, Thomas. Notes on the silkworms of India. 1861. III. 148.¹
— Remarks on certain species of silk-worms. 1857. III. 148.¹
— Remarks on the cultivation of silk in the Australian colonies. 1871. III. 148.²
— Result of experiment for the reclamation of the wild Himalayan silk-worm. 1861. III. 148.¹
Huxmann. Om Opelskningen af Kjerne- og Steenfrugt-Stammer. 1803. III. 134.²
Huyser, P. C. Beschouwingen over ... den achteruitgang der gouvernements Koffiecultuur. 1888. III. 730.
— Bestrijding der Koffiebladziekte. ·1898. III. 736.
Huzard, L. BOUCHARD-. See BOUCHARD-HUZARD, L.
Hvass, Jørgen. Om de visseste Midler til Skovenes Conservation og Fremvæxt i Dannemark. 1761. IV. 272.¹

Hvorledes man kan fremme Valdnøddetræets Væxt. 1842. III. 354.¹
Hy, Felix Charles. Les inflorescences. 1894. I. 113.²
— Sur les Lavandes cultivées dans les jardins. 1898. II. 764.¹
— Sur quelques arbres des genres Salix et Quercus. 1897. II. 104,² 155.¹
— Sur quelques Chênes hybrides observés aux environs d'Angers. 1895. II. 130.²
— Sur quelques végétaux ... dans l'arboretum de G. Allard à Angers. 1886. I. 59.
— Réponse à divers écrits de MM. Bouvet. 1900. II. 286.²
Hyacinthus, P. F. C. Index plantarum Horti botanici melitepsis. 1806. I. 66.²
Hyades, Paul Daniel Jules. Rapport sommaire sur les recherches d'histoire naturelle faites par . la Mission du Cap Horn. 1883. II. 128.¹
Hyams, C. W. The flora of North Carolina. 1899. V. xvii.²
— Medicinal plants ... used in North Carolina. 1898. III. 3.¹
Hyatt, James. Eccentric growth of Rhus Toxicodendron. 1894. II. 460.¹
— Periodicity in vegetation. 1876. I. 221.
Hyatt, T. H. The fruits and fruit trees of Marocco. 1850. III. 280.¹
Hybrid Azaleas. 1831. III. 654.³
Hybrid between Black Current [sic] and Gooseberry. 1892. II. 244.³
Hybrid between Crassula coccinea and Rochea falcata. 1898. III. 409.²
Hybrid coccinea Clematises. 1897. III. 390.¹
Hybrid Firs. 1890. III. 295.²
The hybrid Multiflora Rose Dawson. 1893. III. 456.¹
Hybrid Rhododendron. 1883. II. 679.²
Hybrid Roses. 1895. II. 283.¹
Hybrid Sweet Briar. ·1891· III. 456.¹
Hybrid Tacsonia. 1875. II. 581.²
Hybrid Tacsonia. 1887. III. 616.²
Ueber hybride Rhododendron. 1859. III. 654.²
Hybriden en rieksten van Koffie. 1899. III. 737.
The hybridisation conference. 1899. I. 271.²
Hybrids. 1883. III. 457.³
Hybrids and their raisers. 1899. I. 271.²
Hybrids produced by species of Rhododendron. 1829. III. 654.²
Hyde, James F. C. Plums. 1890. III. 433.¹
Hyde, Thomas. De herbae Cha collectione. 1688. III. 605.
Hyderabad assigned districts. See INDIA — HYDERABAD ...
Hyères — Société d'horticulture et d'agriculture. See SOCIÉTÉ ... III. 22.
Hyett, W. H. On the absorption of liquid solutions. 1843. I. 161.
L'hygiène de la rue et le pavage en bois. 1897. IV. 426.¹
Hylésine. Bois non écorcés. 1898. IV, 205.¹
Hylésine. Dommages. Moyens préventifs. 1899. IV. 479.
L'hylésine du Pin. Arbres-pièges. 1900. IV. 480.
Hylésine piniperde. 1898. IV. 479.
Hyll, Thomas. See HILL, Thomas.
L'hylobie et l'hylésine. 1898. IV. 208.²
Hylonomys, (pseud.). Eenige bedenkingen tegenover "Een vraag naar aanleiding van eenige waarnemingen." 1898. IV. 527.¹
Hyperborean, (pseud.). Ivy hurtful to trees. 1882. III. 642,² IV. 211.¹
Hypnotismus, hervorgerufen durch eine Pflanze. 1889. III. 396.¹
Hypourgeion esoterikon tmema georgias. See ΥΠΟΥΡΓΕΙΟΝ ἐσωτερικῶν τμῆμα γεωργίας.
-i-. Ueber die Blasenroste der Kiefern. 1889. IV. 461.²
-i-. Ceratozamia mexicana. 1876. III. 284.²
-i-. ·Macrozamia plumosa. 1876. III. 286.¹
-i-. Mutisia ilicifolia. 1876. III. 755.³
-i-. Über die Verbreitung der Kiefer in Deutschland. 1896. IV. 483.¹
—i—. Das Alter, die Höhe und Dicke der Bäume. 1891. IV. 65.¹
—i—. Die Bäume des alten Aegyptens. 1890. IV. 89.¹
—i—. Die Behandlung der durch Sturm gelagerten Holzmassen. 1894. IV. 382.²
—i—. Die Beziehungen zwischen der Lage der Laubblätter und der Saugwurzeln. 1891. IV. 73.²
—i—. Ueber den Einfluss der Wärme. 1892. IV. 73.¹
—i—. Der Einfluss des Waldes auf das Klima. 1896. IV. 54.

—i—. Forstliches aus Elsass-Lothringen. 1891. IV. 349.[2]
—i—. Fremdländische Holzarten in Deutschland. 1891. IV. 126.[1]
—i—. Die Geschichte unseres Nadelwaldes. 1891. IV. 75.[1]
—i—. Die Heimat der Rosskastanie. 1898. IV. 527.[2]
—i—. Der japanische Lackbaum. 1887. IV. 526.[1]
—i—. Kennzeichen der inneren Beschaffenheit der Hölzer auf dem Stamme. 1894. IV. 382.[2]
—i—. Land- oder forstwirthschaftliche Benutzung. 1891. IV. 258.
—i—. Die neueren Untersuchungen über die klimatische Bedeutung der Wälder. 1894. IV. 54.
—i—. Die Nonne und ihr Auftreten 1890 in Baiern. 1890. IV. 200.
—i—. Ueber Rauch- und Russbeschädigungen. 1891. IV. 192.[1]
—i—. Die Stechpalme. 1895. IV. 526.[1]
—i—. Die Ursache der Baumlosigkeit der amerikanischen Prairien. 1888. IV. 76.[1]
—i—. Wodurch wird das Baumleben im Norden zurückgedrängt? 1891. IV. 73.[1]
I. Cyrilla racemiflora. 1889. III. 529.[1]
I., (Ingeniero de montes). Las nuevas bases para la clasificación de los montes. 1896. IV. 550.[2]
I., B. Vernieling van levende gewassen door witte mieren. 1899. III. 192.[2]
I., F. Beitrag zur Vermehrung der Rosen. 1876. III. 452.
I., M. De krullenplaag in de Cacao. 1900. III. 593.[3]
I., M. Krullloten van den Cacaoboom in Suriname. 1899. III. 593.[2]
I., W. Amicia zygomeris. 1900. III. 466.[2]
I., W. Chinese method of dwarfing trees. 1846. III. 175.[2]
Iäthenstein, Matthias KALINA VON. See KALINA VON IÄTHENSTEIN, Matthias.
Ibach, C. L. Les Pivoines en arbre. 1862. III. 392.[2]
Ibañez, Joaquin. La Tlatlancuaya de Izucar de Matamoros. 1879. II. 189.[2]
Ibañez, Luis CABELLO f. See CABELLO f IBAÑEZ, Luis.
Ibbotson, Henry. Catalogue of phaenogamous plants of Great Britain. 1848. I. 400.
Ibiza, Blas LÁZARO f. See LÁZARO f IBIZA, Blas.
Ibn Beithar. Elenchus materiae Ibn Beitharis. 1248. I. 274, 530.[2]
— Grosse Zusammenstellung über die Kräfte der bekannten einfachen Heil- und Nahrungsmittel. 1248. I. 274.
— Traité des simples. 1248. I. 274.
Ibn Sinâ. Canon medicinae. See AVICENNA. 1658. III. 240.
— ... Clarissimi ... Abualj Ibn Tsina ... canon medicinae. 428. I. 274.
— Zusammengesetzte Heilmittel der Araber. 428. I. 274.
Ibn Sinâ Albochâri, A. A. A. Avicennae libri in re medica omnes. 1564. III. 240.
Iboога root. 1895. III. 691.[1]
Ibos, Georgios. See*IBOX, Γεώργιος.
Ichimura, Tsutsumi. Pflanzenverbreitung auf dem Tateyama. 1900. I. 463.[1]
Ickstadt, von. De iure forestali. 1748. IV. 313.
Icones arborum fruticum et herbarum exoticarum. 1720. I. 290.
Icones Bogorienses; 1897. I. 29,[1] 68.[1]
Icones florae japonicae. 1900. I. 463.[2]
Icones lignorum exoticorum et nostratium. See HOUTTUYN, Martin. 1773. I. 124.
Icones pictae indo-asiaticae plantarum. See KER, C. H. B. 1818. I. 452.
Icones plantarum. I. 18.
Icones plantarum medicinalium.. See ZORN, Johannes. 1779. III. 55.
Icones plantarum sponte China nascentium. See KER, C. H. B. 1818. I. 452.
Icones stirpium seu plantarum. See LOBEL, Matthias de. 1581. I. 282.
Idaho — Agricultural experiment station. See IDAHO, UNIVERSITY OF.— COLLEGE OF AGRICULTURE. III. 4.
Idaho, University of — College of agriculture — Agricultural experiment station. Annual report. Bulletin. III. 4.
Ide, A. & Bleeker, S. Tuinbouw voor de lagere school. 1895. III. 106.[1]
L'idée forestière aux États-Unis. 1898. IV. 272.
Ideler, G. F. Der Gartenfreund. 1795. III. 30.
— Plan zur Verbesserung der Obstkultur in der Churmark. 1800. III. 135.
Identifications of Guiana timber trees. 1888. IV. 398.[1]

Iets over de aanplanting van caoutchoucboomen. 1876. III. 229.
Iets over de Cananga of Ilang-ilang-wortel. 1881. III. 401.[2]
Iets over de eerste cultuur der Javasche Koffij. 1844. III. 729.[1]
Iets over de Jatropha gossypifolia. 1900. III. 520.[1]
Iets over de teelt van Kapokboomen. 1875. III. 589.[3]
Iets over de uitbreiding der Klapperkultuur. 1859. III. 322.[3]
Iets over het snoeijen van Djati aan planten. 1900. IV. 537.[1]
Iets over Mexico ... uit de reizen van ... Humboldt. 1808. III. 264.[3]
Iets over the Cederhout van Australie. 1880. IV. 401.[2]
Iggulden, W. Mulberries. 1894. III. 378.
Ihering, Hermann von. Die Galläpfel des südbrasilianischen Molho Strauches. 1885. III. 529.[1]
— Das neotropische Florengebiet. 1893. I. 330.
— O territorio da flora neotropical e sua historia. 1893. I. 330.
Ihering, R. von. Pourquoi certains arbres perdent-ils leur feuillage en hiver? 1893. I. 192.[1]
Ihne, Egon. Die ältesten pflanzenphänologischen Beobachtungen. 1892. I. 225.
— Ueber Baumtemperatur. 1884. IV. 63.[2]
— Ueber den Einfluss der geographischen Länge auf die Aufblühzeit. 1894. V. XII.[1]
— Geschichte der pflanzenphänologischen Beobachtungen in Europa. See HOFFMANN, Hermann & IHNE, Egon. 1884. I. 222.[2]
— Karte der Aufblühzeit von Syringa. 1885. II. 716.[1]
— Die norwegischen ... pflanzenphänologischen Beobachtungen. 1885. I. 223.[1]
— Zur Phänologie von Coimbra. 1898. I. 226.[2]
— Phänologische Beobachtungen, Jahrgang 1891–99. 1893. I. 225.
— Ueber die Schwankungen der Aufblühzeit. 1889. I. 221.
— See also HOFFMAN, Hermann & IHNE, Egon.
Ihrig, (Forstmeister, Büdingen). Die Cerreiche ... und die Schwarzkiefer. 1861. IV. 465,[1] 502.[2]
— Ueber Hochwaldwirthschaft in Roth- und Damwild-Thiergärten. 1858. IV. 136.[3]
— Die Kiefer als Hauptholzart in Wildgärten. 1870. IV. 472.
— Untersuchungen über den Werth der Ocular-Taxation. 1861. IV. 214.
— Ueber Vorkommen ... der Pfrieme. 1861. III. 475.[1]
— Ueber Wiederkehr der Mastjahre ... in Buchenhochwaldungen. 1860. IV. 494.
Iinuma, Yokusai. Index to the second edition of Iinuma Yokusai's Sômoku-Dusets. 1873. I. 463.
— Mokuroku. Kusa no bu. 1873. I. 462.
— Sômoku zusetsu. Kankio shintei. 1873. I. 462.
Ijzerhout. 1893. II. 225.[1]
Ijzerman, J. W. & others. Dwars door Sumatra. See KOORDERS, S. H. 1895. I. 467.[2]
Ikeno, Seiitsiro. La comunicazione preliminare sopra la cellula del canale nella Cycas. 1896. II. 5.[1]
— Zur Kenntniss der sog. centrosomähnlichen Körpers im Pollenschlauche der Cycadeen. 1898. II. 3.[3]
— Note préliminaire sur la formation de la cellule de canal chez le Cycas revoluta. 1896. II. 5.[1]
— Gli spermatozoi della Cycas revoluta. 1897. II. 5.[1]
— Untersuchungen über die Entwickelung der Geschlechtsorgane .. : bei Cycas revoluta. 1898. II. 5.[1]
— Vorläufige Mittheilung über die Canalzellbildung bei Cycas revoluta. 1896. II. 5.[1]
— Vorläufige Mittheilung über die Spermatozoiden bei Cycas revoluta. 1897. II. 5.[1]
— & Hirase, Sakugoro. Spermatozoids in gymnosperms. 1897. II. 1.
Ildrewe. The language of flowers. 1865. I. 515.
Ilex Aquifolium (Stechpalme, Pfuebusch). 1852. IV. 463.[3]
Der Ilexstrauch in Oesterreich-Ungarn. 1888. IV. 526.[1]
Illaire, Ulrich von ST. PAUL-. See ST. PAUL-ILLAIRE, Ulrich von.
Ille-et-Vilaine — Société des sciences physiques et naturelles du département ... See SOCIÉTÉ ... I. 23.
Illés, Nándor. Adatok a Cserszömörczéről. 1880. IV. 526.[1]
— Az Akác fájának tartosságáról. 1900. IV. 524.[2]
— Az Ákács értéke és jövője hazánkban. 1870. IV. 523.[1]
— Az Ákács fordaidejének kérdéséhez. 1877. IV. 524.[1]
— Az ákács-paizstetü kérdése Magyarországon. 1896. III. 191.

— Die Akazie in Ungarn. 1891. IV. 524.[1]
— Zur Berechnung des Saatgutes. 1887. IV. 149.[1]
— Zur Berechnung des Samenquantums für Holzsaaten. 1889. IV. 149.[1]
— Die Bewurzelung der Pflanzlinge. 1889. IV. 151.[1]
— A Cser-ssömörczéről. 1877. IV. 526.[1]
— A Csererdőkről. 1869. II. 133.[1]
— Egy érdekes Akácz-állab. 1877. IV. 523.[1]
— Az erdőtenyészet határának feljebb tolásáról magas hegységekben. 1889. IV. 67.[2]
— Erdőtenyésztéstan. 1871. IV. 111.[1]
— A fák rügyei. 1868. I. 105.
— Fanemeink elnevezéséről. 1870. I. 75.[1]
— Fanemek váltakozása az erdőben. 1891. IV. 74.[2]
— A fenyőfajok meghatározásáról. 1870. IV. 441.
— A futóhomok megkötése, befásítása és használata. 1885. IV. 146.[1]
— Hazánk Tölgyfajai. 1870. II. 129.[2]
— Ueber Knoppern. 1872. IV. 509.
— Meglehet-e a Tölgyeink makkját egymástól különböztetni? 1878. II. 130.[1]
— A Szelid Gesztenyéről. 1884. IV. 492.[2]
— A Tengeri-Fenyőről. 1875. IV. 467.[2]
— A Tölgy s annak tenyésztése. 1870. IV. 506.
— Tölgyeink makkja. 1889. II. 130.[2]
— A Tölgyek makkjának megkülömböztetése. 1886. II. 130.[1]
— A Török Mogyóról. 1888. IV. 492.[1]
— A Vörös fenyő tenyésztéséről. 1883. IV. 449.
— *See also* FEKETE, Lajos & ILLÉS, Nándor.
Illiger, Johann Karl Wilhelm. Försök till en ... terminologi för djur- och wäxt- riket. 1800. I. 70.
— Versuch einer ... Terminologie für das Thierreich und Pflanzenreich. 1800. I. 70.
Illinois — Agricultural experiment station. *See* ILLINOIS, UNIVERSITY OF. III. 4.
Illinois — Department of agriculture. Transactions. *See* ILLINOIS STATE AGRICULTURAL SOCIETY. III. 4.
Illinois museum of natural history. Bulletin. *See* ILLINOIS STATE LABORATORY OF NATURAL HISTORY. I. 519.[1]
Illinois state agricultural society. Transactions. III. 4.
Illinois state horticultural society. Transactions. III. 4.
Illinois state laboratory of natural history. Bulletin. I. 519.
Illinois, University of —Agricultural experiment station. Annual report. Bulletin. III. 4.
Illuminating gas from wood. 1896. IV. 433.[2]
Illustrated annual register of rural affairs. *See* RURAL' affairs. III. 8.
The **illustrated** bouquet. *See* HENDERSON, E. G. & Andrew. 1857. III. 82.
Illustrated gardener's guide. *See* ILLUSTRIRTE Berichte ... III. 12.
Illustrated wood-worker. IV. 4.
L'**Illustration** horticole. III. 15.
Illustrierte Flora. III. 25. .
Illustrierte Monatshefte für die Gesamt-Interessen des Gartenbaues. *See* DEUTSCHES Magazin für Garten ... III. 12.
Illustrierte Monatshefte für Obst- und Weinbau. *See* MONATSSCHRIFT für Pomologie. III. 13.
Illustrierte praktische Blätter für den Gartenbau. III. 25.
Illustrierter Forst- und Jagd-Kalender für Liv-, Est- und Kurland. IV. 6.
Illustrierter Führer der Berner-Oberland-Bahnen. *See* FISCHER, Eduard. 1892. I. 437.
Illustrirte Berichte über Gartenbau. III. 12.
Illustrirte Garten-Zeitung. III. 12.
Illustrirter Rosengarten für Rosenfreunde. *See* NESTEL's Rosengarten. III. 13.
Ilmer, Georg. De Tilia. 1669. II. 517.[1]
Imon, Herman. Enumeratio plantarum officinalium Fenniam sponte inhabitantium. 1837. III. 68.[1]
Ilse, (*Forstreferendar, Rappoltsweiler*). Ueber Edelkastanienzucht in Oberelsass. 1898. IV. 493.[1]
Ilse, Hugo. Flora von Mittelthüringen. 1866. I. 385.
— Forstbotanische Wanderung im Thüringer Wald. 1864. I. 385.
— Mittheilungen über die Flora des wilhelmswalder Forstes. 1864. I. 385.
— Notiz über Vaccinium Myrtillo × Vitis idaea. 1865. II. 685.[2]
— *See also* FRITZE, R. & ILSE, Hugo.
Ilsemann, Christian. Ajánlható diszfák és diszcserjék. 1892. III. 203.

— Die Araucarien. 1886. III. 297.[2]
— Beiträge zur Kenntniss ... schöner Gehölzarten. 1886. III. 89.[2]
— Berberis-Arten für den Blumengarten. 1887. III. 394.[1]
— Catalpa speciosa. 1895. III. 706.[2]
— Die Cotoneaster des Arboretums ... zu Ung.-Altenburg. 1884. III. 420.[2]
— Ueber Cydonia japonica. 1882. III. 420.[1]
— Dendrologiai csevegések. 1886. III. 531,[2] 595.[2]
— Dendrologiai jegyzetek a fővárosi kertészet néhány Juharféléjéről. 1897. III. 534.[1]
— Einige neuere .. Gehölze des freien Landes. 1885. III. 70, V. XXVIII.[1]
— Die holzartigen Schlinggewächse. 1885. III. 204.[1]
— A Hydrangea paniculata grandiflora. 1896. III. 412.[2]
— Idesia polycarpa. 1886. III. 614.[2]
— Interessante Gehölze des Arboretums zu Ung. Altenburg. 1888. I. 66.[1]
— Juglans Sieboldiana Maxim. 1886. III. 356.[2]
— Kertjeink Fagyalféléi. 1891. III. 673.[2]
— A legszebb Spiraeák. 1896. III. 460.[2]
— Naše obyčejnější Araucarie. 1896. III. 298.[1]
— Eine neue buntblättrige Konifere. 1887. III. 308.[1]
— Die neuen buntblättrigen Gehölze. 1886. III. 206.[2]
— Nyere og sjældnere Frilands-Trævæxter. 1885. III. 70. V. XXVIII.[1]
— Örökzöld fák és cserjék. I. 'A Rhododendronok. 1899. III. 655.
— Phoenix Roebeleni. 1900. III. 330.[1]
— Die Reichs-Obstausstellung in Wien. 1889. III. 146.[2]
— Der schwedische Bocksdorn. 1886. III. 701.[1]
— Spiraea callosa Froeb. 1900. III. 461.[2]
— Die zum Treiben geeigneten Blüthensträucher. 1886. III. 176.[2]
— Virágzó felfutó cserjéink. 1899. III. 205.[1]
— Welche Massnahmen wären zu ergreifen, um dem ... Einfluss unreeller Baumschulen ... vorzubeugen? 1890. III. 200.[2]
— Zierbäume und Ziersträucher. 1884. III. 89.[2]
Ilsemann, Keresztély. *See* ILSEMANN, Christian.
Im Thurn, Everard Ferdinand. The first ascent of Roraima. 1885. I. 339.[2]
— A journey to Mount Russell in Guiana. 1882. I. 339.[2]
— Memoranda on the Palms of British Guiana. 1884. II. 61.[2]
— Notes on the plants observed during the Roraima expedition. 1884. I. 339.[2]
— The Palms of British Guiana. 1884. II. 61.[2]
Imbert. Leçons de botanique. *See* CUSSON, Pierre, GOUAN, Antoine & COMMERSON, Philibert. 1762. I. 511.
Imbert-Gourbeyre, Antoine. Bidrag til de bittre Pomeransers Pharmacologie. 1853. III. 501.[2]
— Mémoire sur l'action physiologique ... d'oranges amères. 1853. III. 501.[2]
Imboschimento alpino [sul monte Cimolo]. 1881. IV. 166.[1]
Imhof, Eduard. Die Waldgrenze in der Schweiz? 1900. I. 432,[2] *IV. 86.*[2]
Imhoff, A. von. Kurze Darlegung der forstlichen Verhältnisse des Judenbacher Forstes. 1857. IV. 355.[2]
— Imitation of Mahogany. 1826. IV. 426.[2]
Imlay, Gilbert. Nachrichten von dem westlichen Lande der Nordamerikanischen Freistaaten. 1792. I. 021.
— A topographical description of the western territory of North America. 1792. I. 321.
Immergrüne ausdauernde Pflanzen. 1895. III. 206.[1]
Immergrüne Eichen. 1892. III. 361.[1]
Die **immergrünen** Berberis und B. Andreana. 1899. III. 395.[1]
Immisch. Expériences sur la culture des arbres et des arbrisseaux. 1855. III. 124,[1] 173.[2]
Per impedire il tarlari del legno. 1894. IV. 209.[2]
Imperato, Ferrante. Historia naturale. 1599. I. 283.
— Dell' historia naturale. 1599. I. 283.
— Historiae naturalis libri XXIIX. 1599. I. 283.
Imperatorski S.-Peterburgski botanitcheski Sad. *See* HORTUS PETROPOLITANUS. I. 9.
Imperatorski Tomski Universitet. Izvyestia. *See* ИМператорскій Томскій Университетъ. I. 519.[1]
Imperatorski Yurievski Universitet. *See* UNIVERSITAS IMPERIALIS JURIEVENSIS. I. 10.
Imperatorskoye Rossiskoye obshtchestvo sadovodstva v C.-Peterburg. *See* Императорское Россійское общество садоводства в C.-Петербургъ. III. 10.
Imperatorskoye Volno-ekonomitcheskoye obshtchestvo. *See* Императорское Вольно-экономическое общество. IV. 6.

Imperial college of agriculture and dendrology ... Japan. Bulletin. *See* COLLEGE OF AGRICULTURE, IMPERIAL UNIVERSITY OF JAPAN. I. 28.²
Imperial institute of the United Kingdom. Journal. Year book. III. 17.
Imperial instituto fluminense de agricultura. Revista agricola. III. 757.¹
Imperial university of Tokyo, Japan. *See* COLLEGE OF SCIENCE ... I. 28.²
Imperiale museo di Firenze. Annali. I. 25.
Imp. e reale accademia economica agraria dei georgofili di Firenze. *See* REALE ACCADEMIA ECONOMICO-AGRARIA DEI GEORGOFILI. III. 23.²
Imperiale reale istituto veneto di scienze. Atti. I. 25.
Impiego dell' Acacia per la fabbricazione dei cerchi da botte. 1863. IV. 427.¹
Important information regarding the cultivation of Tea in the valley of the Dhoon. 1847. III. 602.²
Una importante innovazione ... fosfati Thomas. 1899. IV. 145.
Importanza della produzione della proprietà forestale dei privati. 1866. IV. 405.²
Importation de bois de Teak. 1894. IV. 538.¹
Importation de bois étrangers. 1898. IV. 405.¹
Importation de coléoptères protecteurs. 1899. IV. 200.
Importation des bois en Belgique. 1894. IV. 404,² 557.¹
Les importations de bois en France. *See* IMPORTATION de bois étrangers. 1898. IV. 405.¹
The imported Elm leaf-beetle. *See* RILEY, C. V. 1885. III. 364.²
Ueber das Imprägniren der Hölzer. 1862. IV. 418.
Impression of a duck found in a tree. 1894. I. 210.¹
The improvement of trees. 1890. I. 248.¹
Imray, John. The useful woods of the island of Dominica. 1862. IV. 398.¹
Inama-Sternegg, Karl Theodor von. Die Familien-Fideikommisse in Oesterreich. 1883. IV. 368.
Inarched Elms. 1890. II. 144.¹
Incarville, d'. Catalogue alphabétique des plantes ... en Chine. 1812. III. 272.²
Ince, Walker H. Cacao at the San Carlos estate. 1896. III. 593.¹
Incendi. 1865. IV. 183.²
Gli incendi di boschi nel 1894. 1895. IV. 181.²
Incendi di foreste. 1864. IV. 183.²
Gl' incendi nelle grandi foreste del Canadà. 1897. IV. 181.²
Incendies. Mesures préventives. 1896. IV. 182.² — 1898. IV. 183.¹
Incendies dans les bois. 1899. IV. 183.¹ — 1900. IV. 183.¹
Incendies de forêts. 1894. IV. 547.³ — 1897. IV. 547.² — 1899. IV. 183.¹ — 1900. IV. 183.¹
Incendies de forêts. Mesures préventives. 1896. IV. 182.²
Des incendies de forêts en Algérie. *See* THIBAULT, R. 1866. V. xxx.¹
Incendies de forêts en 1898. 1899. IV. 183.¹
Incendies de forêts en 1895. 1896. IV. 182.²
Incendies de forêts en 1894. 1895. IV. 547.²
Incendies de forêts en 1897. 1898. IV. 182.²
Incendies de forêts en 1896. 1897. IV. 547.²
Incendies de forêts en 1893. 1894. IV. 547.²
Incendies de forêts en France et en Algerie. 1897. IV. 184.¹
Contre les incendies des forêts en Algérie. *See* Marchand, V. 1897. IV. 184.¹
Gli incendii nelle foreste americane. 1886. IV. 182.¹
Incendio. 1863. IV. 183.² — 1864. IV. 183.²
El incendio de Mindanao. 1889. IV. 547.²
Incendio della Ficuzza. 1865. IV. 183.²
Incense trees of the West Indies. 1898. III. 510,¹ 511,¹ 511.²
Inchaurrandieta, José R. Catálogo de montes públicos. 1891. IV. 363.²
— Contestación á los artículos " Bibliografía " ó " Informe abierto." 1896. IV. 550.¹
— Dehesas boyales. 1889. IV. 553.¹
— Errores observados en la aplicación del método de " Ordenar transformando." 1896. IV. 550.²
— Sobre el impuesto del 10 por 100 para mejoras. 1892. IV. 327.
— Montes de Vélez-Blanco, Vélez-Rubio y Maria. 1891. IV. 554.
— La ordenación de montes públicos en España. 1895. IV. 249.¹
— Planes provisionales de aprovechamiento. 1889. IV. 553.¹
— Repoblación y servicio forestal. 1892. IV. 553.²
— Servicio forestal. 1877. IV. 293.¹

Inchbald, Peter. Llanduino botany. 1864. I. 401.
— Trees and shrubs in the Channel Islands. 1874. III. 78.²
Incombustibilidad en la madera. 1889. IV. 413.¹
Incombustibilità del legno. 1882. IV. 413.¹
Sur les inconvénients de l'exploitation de la litière. *See* FOLGEN der Waldstreunutzung. 1862. IV. 71.
Incoraggiamento al rimboschire nel Belgio. 1863. IV. 160.²
Increasing the durability of timber. 1887. IV. 413.²
Indberetning fra Skovdirektøren. 1883. IV. 343.²
Index horti botanici Universitatis hungaricae. *See* WINTERL, J. J. 1788. I. 55.²
Index of Chinese plants in Journal of botany. *See* HANCE, H. F. 1883. I. 459.
Index op de kunstwoordenleer der planten. *See* GROENEWEGEN, J. C. 1836. I. 70.
Index Palmarum ... in Horto botanico bogoriensi. 1899. I. 68.²
Index plantarum agri cantabrigiensis. *See* RAY, John. 1660. I. 394.
Index plantarum horti bot. Academiae regiae panormitanae. *See* TINEO, Giuseppe. 1790. I. 61.
Index plantarum Horti botanici halensis. *See* JUNGHANS, P. K. 1771. I. 44.
Index plantarum Horti botanici leodiensis. *See* GAEDE, H. M. 1828. I. 49.
Index plantarum Horti botanici Paedagogii regii glauchensis. *See* SCHRADER, C. F. 1772. I. 44.
Index plantarum horti botanici Universitatis vilnensis. *See* JUNDZILL, S. B. 1802. I. 41.
Index plantarum Horti caesarei regii botanici pragensis. *See* KOSTELETZKY, V. F. 1844. I. 66.¹
Index plantarum Horti medici altorfini. *See* VOGEL. 1790. I. 521.²
Index plantarum ... in Horto botanico imperiali petropolitano. *See* FISCHER, F. E. L. von, 1824. I. 41.
Index plantarum in Linnaei Systemae naturae ed. Xᵐᵃ. 1761. I. 76.³
Index plantarum indigenarum ... prope Lugdunum. 1653. I. 390.
Index plantarum officinalium ... in Horto regio edinensi. 1738. I. 52.
Index plantarum quae in Horto academico argentinensi. *See* NESTLER, C. G. 1818. I. 45.
Index plantarum succulentarum in Horto Dyckensi. *See* SALM-REIFFERSCHEID-DYCK, Joseph, Fürst und Altgraf. 1829. I. 46.
Index plantarum ... Van Diemen's Land. *See* BACKHOUSE, James. 1834. I. 505.
Index regni vegetabilis. *See* JACQUIN, N. J. von. 1770. I. 76.²
Index seminario Horti ... *See* VIDAL, A. I. R. 1871. I. 60.¹
Index seminum et plantarum horti botanici Universitatis caesareae mosquensis. 1826. I. 42.
Index seminum et plantarum Horti gryphici. *See* WEIGEL, C. E. 1773. I. 44.
Index seminum quae Hortus botanicus ... petropolitanus ... offert. *See* FISCHER, F. E. L. von & MEYER, C. A. 1835. I. 42; *and* REGEL, E. A. von. 1855. I. 42.
India — Agricultural and horticultural society. *See* AGRICULTURAL ... III. 26.¹
India — Ajmere-Merwara — Forest department. Progress report. IV. 16.¹
India — Andaman Islands — Forest department. Progress report. IV. 16.¹
India — Assam — Forest department. Progress report. IV. 16.¹
India — Baluchistan — Forest department. Progress report. IV. 16.¹
India — Bengal — Forest department. Progress report. Progress report. ... in the lower provinces. Progress report of the forest surveys. IV. 16.¹
India — Bombay Presidency — Forest department. Forest reports. IV. 16.¹
India — Botanical survey. *See* BOTANICAL ... I. 29.¹
India — British Burmah — Forest department. Progress report. IV. 16.¹
India — Burma — Forest department. Progress reports. IV. 16.¹
India — Central provinces — Forest department. Progress report. Report. IV. 16.²
India — Coorg — Forest department. Progress report. IV. 16.¹
India — Forest department. Review of the forest administration. IV. 16.¹

India — Forest survey branch. Progress report. IV. 16.[1]
India — Hyderabad assigned districts — Forest department. Progress report. IV. 16.[2]
India — Lower Burma — Forest department. Progress report. IV. 16.[2]
India — Madras Presidency — Forest department. Report. IV. 16.[1]
India — Mysore — Forest department. Progress reports. IV. 16.[1]
India — North-Western provinces and Oudh — Department of land records and agriculture. Report. IV. 16.[2]
India — North-Western provinces and Oudh — Forest department. Annual progress report. IV. 16.[2]
India — Oudh — Forest department. Annual report. Progress report. IV. 16.[2]
India — Punjab — Forest department. Annual report. Progress report. IV. 16.[2]
India — Scientific memoirs. See SCIENTIFIC . . . I. 29.[1]
India — Upper Burma — Forest department. Progress report. IV. 16.[1]
India rubber. See INDIARUBBER.
Indian agriculturist. III. 26.[1]
Indian annals of medical science. III. 26.[1]
Indian Archipelago — Journal. See JOURNAL . . . I. 29.[1]
Indian coffee. 1837. III. 732.[1]
Indian engineering. IV. 16.[2]
Indian fibres suitable for textile purposes. 1888. III. 234.
The Indian forest act. 1878. IV. 332.[1]
Indian forester. IV. 16.[2]
Indian gardening. III. 26.[1]
Indian gutta percha. 1892. III. 668.[1]
Indian medical gazette. I. 29.[1] III. 26.[1]
Indian turpentines. 1881. IV. 463.[1]
Indian woods for matches. 1898. IV. 429.[1]
Indiana — Agricultural experiment station. See INDIANA-PURDUE UNIVERSITY. III. 4.
Indiana — Geological survey. See GEOLOGICAL . . . I. 5.
Indiana — Purdue university — Agricultural experiment station. Annual report. Bulletin. III. 4.
Indiana academy of science. Proceedings. I. 5.
Indiana department of geology and natural history. See GEOLOGICAL survey of Indiana. I. 5.
Indiana state board of agriculture. Annual report. III. 4.
Indiana state horticultural society. Transactions. III. 4.
India-rubber. 1853. III. 230.
India-rubber. 1876. III. 231.
The indiarubber acclimatisation experiment. 1877. III. 149.
Indiarubber and guttapercha cultivation in Ceylon. 1884. III. 149.
India rubber curtains. 1893. III. 231.
India rubber in Mexico. 1896. III. 368.[1]
India-rubber in Upper Burma. 1888. III. 371.[1]
The indiarubber industry in South America. 1896. III. 668.[1]
India-rubber producing plants. 1875. III. 229.
The India rubber tree. 1889. III. 370.[2]
India rubber world. III. 4.
El indice centesimal. 1893. IV. 550.[2]
Indice de las plantas . . . See ORTEGA, C. G. 1772. I. 60.[1]
Indice general de las obras . . . publicados por la " Revista forestal " y " Revista de montes." 1891. IV. 539.[1]
Indigenous plants of Yoruba-land. 1891. III. 93.[1]
Indigenous vegetable substances. 1862. III. 282.[2]
Indigo. 1820. IV. 479.[1]
Indisch landbouw-genootschap. Tijdschrift. III. 26.[2]
De Indische bij. III. 14.
Der indische Feigenbaum, Asvattha. See RITTER, Karl. 183.? II. 148.[2]
De Indische gids. III. 14.
De Indische mercuur. III. 14.
Indo-Chine — Bulletin économique. See BULLETIN . . . III. 26.[1]
De indole plantarum guineensium.observationes. See HORNEMANN, J. W. 1819. I. 490.
Indophilus, (pseud.). Tea culture in the Hima'syan Mountains. 1852. III. 602.[2]
Indre-et-Loire — Société d'agriculture, sciences, arts . . . See SOCIÉTÉ . . . III. 21.
Om de indtil Udgangen af Aaret 1882 ved Forsøg i Tydskland indvundne Erfaringer om Dyrkning af udenlandske Træsorter. See Über den BISHERIGEN Verlauf. 1884. IV. 125.[2]
Indurimento del legname. 1865. IV. 419. — 1883. IV. 420.
L' industria della fabbricazione degli zoccoli di legno. 1890. IV. 428.[2]

Industria delle resine. 1866. IV. 436.[2]
Industria forestal. 1877. IV. 393.
L'industria serica negli Stati Uniti. 1899. III. 380.[1]
Industrialist. III. 4.
L'industrie de la cellulose en Suède. 1891. IV. 430.[2]
De l'industrie de la cochenille aux Îles Canaries. See BERTHELOT, Sabin. 1851. III. 624.[1]
L'industrie de la pâte de bois au Canada. 1900. IV. 430.
L'industrie de la pâte de bois en Norvège. 1900. IV. 430.
L'industrie de la pâte de bois en Norwège. 1894. IV. 557.[2]
L'industrie des allumettes en Suède. 1900. IV. 429.[1]
L'Industrie du bois de Teck au Siam. 1894. IV. 538.[1]
Industrie du camphre dans la Floride. 1891. III. 404.[2]
L'industrie minière au service de la culture du sol. 1876. IV. 143.[1]
L'industrie séricicole en Annam. 1898. III. 378.
L'Industrie viticole en Russie. 1891. III. 551.[2]
Die industrielle Verwertung des Rothbuchenholzes. See PLIWA, Ernst. 1884. IV. 499.
Les industries du bois en Russie. 1897. IV. 557.[1]
Sur l'infiltration des bois. See Ueber das IMPRÄGNIREN der Hölzer. 1862. IV. 418.
Influence de l'âge des Sapins sur la puissance germinative de leurs graines. 1895. IV. 558.[2]
Influence de la composition des peuplements sur la quantité d'eau contenue dans le sol. See Der WASSERGEHALT . . . 1885. IV. 51.
De l'influence de la constitution géologique sur la distribution des forêts en France. 1860. IV. 68.
Influence de la greffe à propos de la Passiflore Decaisneana. 1880. III. 39, 615.[2]
Influence de la lumière électrique. 1892. I. 230.
Influence des forêts sur le débit des sources. 1894. IV. 542.[1]
Influence des forêts sur les orages à grêle. 1896. IV. 54.
Influence des fumées industrielles. 1898. IV. 193.[1]
Influence du boisement sur le régime des eaux. 1899. IV. 52.
Influence du moment de la coupe sur la durée . . . du bois. See EINFLUSS der Zeit des Holzfällens. 1865. IV. 384.[2]
Influence du porte-greffe sur le greffon. 1897. I. 246.[2]
Influence du soutrage sur . . . Hêtre. 1900. IV. 72.
Influence du sujet sur la greffe. 1869. III. 39.
Influence du sujet sur le greffon. 1896. III. 548.[2]
Influence fâcheuse du Laurier-rose. 1849. III. 689.[2]
The influence of forests on climate. 1865. IV. 53. — 1872. IV. 53.
Influence of forests on rainfall. 1872. IV. 50.
Influence of forests upon the flow of streams. 1886. IV. 51.
The influence of mountain forests. 1889. IV. 51.
The influence of scion on stock. 1887. III. 40.[1]
Influence of stock upon scion. 1879. III. 39.
Influence of the graft upon the roots. 1868. III. 39.
Influence of the scion on its stock. 1857. I. 246.[2]
Influence réciproque de la greffe. See INFLUENCE of the scion on its stock. 1857. I. 246.[2]
Influencia de la temperatura y del viento. 1892. IV. 543.[2]
Influencia de los bosques sobre el clima. 1897. IV. 54.
Influencia de los temblores de tierra. 1892. IV. 543.[1]
Della influenza dei boschi sulla malaria. 1884. IV. 48.[1]
Influenza dei boschi sulle pioggie. 1880. IV. 50.
Influenza dei disboscamenti sulle piene dei fiumi. 1880. IV. 50.
For information of railroad managers. See COLMAN, N. J. 1887. IV. 424.[1]
Informe sobre el estado de las Islas Filipinas. See MAS, Sinibaldo de. 1843. IV. 399.[1]
Ingelrelst, Louis. Les Rhododendrons de Sikkim-Hymalaya. 1858. III. 654.[1]
Ingenhousz, Jan. Über Ernährung der Pflanzen. 1796. I. 157.
— Expériences sur les végétaux. 1779. I. 169.[1]
— Experiments upon vegetables. 1779. I. 169.[2]
— The food of plants. 1796. I. 157.
— Proeve over het voedzel der planten. 1796. I. 157.
— Proeven op plantgewassen. 1779. I. 169.[1]
— Versuche mit Pflanzen. 1779. I. 169.[1]
Der Ingénieur. IV. 9.
L'ingénieur agricole de Gembloux. Journal. See ASSOCIATION DES ANCIENS ÉLÈVES . . . III. 15.
Ingledew, On the culture of the Mango in Mysore. 1842. III. 524.[2]
Ingold, H. Le balai de sorcier et le chancre du Sapin. 1900. IV. 446.[1]
Ingram, B. Root growth under difficulties. 1882. I. 526.[2]

Ingram, C. Timber measurement in Upper Burma. 1886. IV. 228.

Ingram, James. A new method of destroying insects. 1842. III. 196.

Ingram, John. Flora symbolica. 1870. I. 515.

Ingram, W. Evil arising from cramping the roots. 1849. III. 163.

Ingram, William. Elm roots. 1872. II. 144.[2]

Inhalt einer Abhandlung von Fürtrefflichkeit der Gewächse. See MUELLER, Elias. n. d. III. 269.[1]

Inhambane copal. 1888. III. 473.[1]

On the injurious effects of Cedar wood drawers. 1856. IV. 448.[2]

Injurious fungi. 1900. III. 195.[2]

On the injury done to forest trees by wild animals. 1875. IV. 196.[1]

The injury done to forests by sheep and goats. 1890. IV. 197.[2]

Injury to forest vegetation by frost . . . 1895, 1897. III. 50.[1]

The Ink plant. 1871. III. 523.[2]

Inman, Thomas. The causes that determine the fall of leaves. 1848. I. 191.[2]

Inn- und Knyphausen, Edzard, Graf zu. Aus dem Parke in den Wald. 1877. IV. 125.[2]

Innamorati, Giuseppe. La Rosa e sua istoria. 1821. II. 290.[2]

Innewadi yokuqondisa ukutyalwa Kwe-moerbezieboom. See Het AANKWEEKEN . . . 1868. III. 377.

Innes, Cosmo. Notices of early Scotch planting. 1861. IV. 27.[1]

— Some account of early planting in Scotland. 1863. III: 123.[2]

Innsbruck — Naturwissenschaftlich-medizinischer Verein. See NATURWISSENSCHAFTLICH . . . I. 28.[1]

Les inondations et le déboisement. 1895. IV. 542.[1]

Inondations et reboisement. See THOMAS, J. B. 1846. IV. 49.[2]

Sull' inondazione di Messina. 1864. IV. 186.[2]

Inondazioni. 1863. IV. 186.[3] — 1864. IV. 48.[1] — 1866. IV. 186.[2]

Le inondazioni. 1865. IV. 48.[1]

Delle inondazioni su quel di Siena. 1864. IV. 48.[1]

Sull' inopportunità della provvisoria riorganizzazione del personale forestale di Lombardia. 1863. IV. 293.[3]

Inquiries respecting the pollen of vegetables. 1828. I. 201.[2]

An inquiry into the uses . . . of the practice of scraping . . . trees. 1854. III. 175.[3]

Insect pests. 1900. III. 192.[2]

Insect ravages in the Goalpara District. 1899. IV. 550.[1]

Insecte nuisible aux résineux. 1898. IV. 208.[2]

Insecte nuisible (Pyrale des pousses). 1898. IV. 479.

Les insectes dans les oseraies. 1896. IV. 487.[2]

Insectes destructeurs de la Vigne. 1837. III. 562.[2]

Insectes nuisibles à la Vigne. 1837. III. 562.[2]

L' insegnamento della selvicoltura . . . all' Istituto agrario di Perugia. 1898. IV. 35.[2]

L' insegnamento forestale ed i boschi nella Svezia. 1881. IV. 344.[2]

Dell' insegnamento forestale nel Portogallo. 1865. IV. 35.[1]

L' insegnamento forestale nella Svezia. 1881. IV. 30.[2]

Insektenfrass und Saft-Hieb. 1858. IV. 384.[2]

Insektensachen. 1833. IV. 206.

L'Institut. Journal. I. 21.

Institut botanico-géologique colonial de Marseille. Annales. See INSTITUT COLONIAL DE MARSEILLE. I. 21.

Institut botanique de Buitenzorg. Bulletin. I. 29.[1]

Institut botanique de l'Université de Liège. Archives. I. 16.

Institut colonial de Marseille. Annales. I. 21.

Institut des provinces de France. Annales. Mémoires. I. 21.

Institut égyptien. Bulletin. Mémoires. I. 29.[2]

Institut horticole de Fromont. Annales. III. 19.

Institut impérial de France. See ACADÉMIE ROYALE DES SCIENCES. I. 20.

Institut national agronomique de France. Annales. III. 19.

Institut national de France. Mémoires. See ACADÉMIE ROYALE DES SCIENCES. I. 20.

Institut national des sciences (lettres) et arts de France. Mémoires. See ACADÉMIE ROYALE DES SCIENCES. I. 20.

Institut national genevois. Bulletin. I. 26.[2]

Institut Pasteur. Annales. I. 21.

Institut royal grand-ducal de Luxembourg. Publications. See SOCIÉTÉ DES SCIENCES NATURELLES DU GRAND-DUCHÉ DE LUXEMBOURG. I. 16.

Institute of Jamaica. Popular lectures. III. 10.[1]

Institution of civil engineers. Minutes. IV. 12.[1]

Institution of surveyors. Transactions. IV. 12.[1]

O Instituto. Jornal. I. 24.[1]

Instituto agronomico de Campinas. Boletim. III. 757.[1]

Instituto agronomico do estado de São Paulo, Brazil. Relatorio annual. Collecção dos trabalhos agricolas. See ESTAÇÃO AGRONOMICA DE CAMPINAS. III. 10.[1]

Instituto fisico-geografico nacional de Costa Rica. Anales. I. 7.[2]

Instituto historico e geographico brasileiro. See INSTITUTO HISTORICO, GEOGRAPHICO E ETHNOGRAPHICO DO BRAZIL. I. 7.[2]

Instituto historico, geographico e ethnographico do Brazil. Revista. I. 7.[2]

Instituto médico nacional. Anales. See El ESTUDIO. I. 7.[2]

Instrucción formada por un facultativo . . . relativa de las especies y virtudes de la Quina. See MUTIS, J. C. 1792. III. 720.

Instrucción sobre el cultivo del Nopal. 1825. III. 623.[2]

Instrucciones de servicio para el cuerpo de ingenieros de montes. See ALBAREDA, J. L. 1881. IV. 304.[1]

Instrucciones para el régimen de las brigadas de campo. 1896. IV. 554.[1]

Instrucciones para los que deseen seguir la carrera de ingenieros de montes. 1881. IV. 35.[1]

L'Instructeur-jardinier. III. 19.

Instruction betreffend die Einführung der Maass- und Gewichtsordnung für den norddeutschen Bund. 1871. IV. 303.[2]

An instruction book in the art of silk culture. 1882. III. 378.

Instruction des gardes forestiers. See BANNWARTEN-Unterricht. 1858. IV. 36.[1]

Instruction du plantage . . . des Meuriers. See LE ROY, Benigne. 1695. III. 372.[2]

Instruction facile . . . See MORIN, Pierre. 1674. III. 496.[2]

Instruction für das Fachrechnungs-Departement des K. k. Ackerbau-Ministeriums. n. d. IV. 307.[1]

Instruction für den Revierförster im k. sächssl. [sic] Forstdienst. 1818. IV. 302.

Instruction für den Unterförster im k. sächsischen Forstdienst. 181.? IV. 302.

Instruction für die Begrenzung, Vermarkung . . . der österreichischen Staats- und Fondsforste. 1878. IV. 250[1], 285.

Instruction für die Beobachter an den meteorologischen Stationen im preussischen Staate. 1854. IV. 59.[2]

Instruction für den Forstverwaltern . . . und den Holzlegstätten obliegende Verrechnung. n. d. IV. 307.[1]

Instruction für die Förster des Grossherzogthums Baden. 1834. IV. 298.[2]

Instruction für die Forstbetriebs-Einrichtungs-Commissionen des Kurstaates. 1864. IV. 302.

Instruction für die Forstmeister in dem Herzogthum Gotha. 1829. IV. 303.[1]

Instruction für die Holzhauer in den Domanialwaldungen . . . Hessen. 1863. IV. 301. — 1871. IV. 301.

Instruction für die Holzhauer in den Domanialwaldungen des Grossherzogthums Hessen. 1827. IV. 300.[3]

Instruction für die Holzhauer . . . im Forste Umstadt. 1819. IV. 300.[2]

Instruction für die Holzhauer und Setzer in Gemeinds- . . . Waldungen des Forstamts-Bezirks Schwetzingen. 1838. IV. 299.

Instruction für die in [badischen] Gemeinds- und Körperschaftswaldungen arbeitenden Holzhauer. 1836. IV. 298.[2]

Instruction für die in den Domänen- und Gemeinde-Waldungen arbeitenden Holzhauer. 1878. IV. 299.

Instruction für die in den Gemeinds- . . . Waldungen des hiesigen . . . Forstamts-Bezirks [Stockach]. 1837. IV. 299.

Instruction für die in Gemeinde- . . . waldungen des Forstamts-Bezirkes Hüfingen. 1837. IV. 299.

Instruction für die k. bayerischen Forstamts-Actuare. 1854. IV. 300.[1]

Instruction für die k. bayerischen Forstgehülfen. 1854. IV. 300.[1]

Instruction für die k. bayerischen Forst-Inspizirungsbeamten. 1854. IV. 300.[1]

Instruction für die k. bayerischen Forstmeister. 1854. IV. 300.[1]

Instruction für die k. bayerischen Forstwärter. 1854. IV. 300.[1]

Instruction für die k. bayerischen Revierförster. 1854. IV. 300.[1]

Instruction für die k. preuss. Forstgeometer. 1819. IV. 301.

Instruction für die mit der Geldgebarung des Forst- und Domänenwesens betrauten . . . Cassen. n. d. IV. 307.[1]
Instruction für die Rechnungs-Departements der Forst- und Domänen Directionen. n. d. IV. 307.[1]
Instruction für die Revierförster in dem Herzogthum Gotha. 1829. IV. 303.[1]
Instruction für die Unterförster . . . in dem Herzogthume Gotha. 1829. IV. 303.[1]
Instruction für die Waldarbeiter in den sächs. Staatsforstrevieren. 1883. IV. 303.[1]
Instruction für die Waldaufseher. 1854. IV. 300.[1]
Instruction für Forstwirthschafts-Einrichtung. 1830. IV. 299.
Instruction für Holzhauer und Holzsetzer. 1857. IV. 300.[1]
Instruction générale pour les conservateurs, inspecteurs, sous-inspecteurs et gardes généraux. 1821. IV. 303.[1]
Instruction générale sur le service forestier. 1843. IV. 303.[2]
Instruction in the cultivation of the Grape vine. 1892. III. 551.[1]
Instruction, nach welcher bei specieller Abschätzung der k.-preussischen Forsten verfahren werden soll. 1819. IV. 301.
Instruction pour les semis de bois résineux. 1800. IV. 440.[2]
Instruction pour les voyageurs . . . sur la manière de recueillir. 1818. I. 35.
Instruction pratique sur les moyens à employer pour combattre le phylloxera. 1876. III. 568.
Instruction relative aux plans d'aménagement. 1899. IV. 250,[1] 307.[1]
Instruction relative aux travaux décennaux de revision de la gestion forestière. 1899. IV. 234.[2]
Instruction sommaire sur la manière de cultiver les Mûriers. 1755. III. 372.[2]
Instruction sur la greffe des Oliviers. 1854. III. 675.[2]
Instruction sur la manière de planter . . . Gerofliers et Muscardiers. 1772. III. 402,[1] 635.[1]
Instruction sur la manière de semer la graine de Mûrier. 1769. III. 373.
Instruction sur les amenagemens. 1824. IV. 303.[2]
Instruction sur les bois de marine. 1780. V. xxxii.[1]
Instruction sur les bois de marine et leur application. 1859. IV. 425.[1]
Instruction sur les levés topographiques. 1860. IV. 303.[1]
Instruction über Begrenzung . . . Vermessung der . . . Waldungen im Regierungsbezirk Wiesbaden. 1883. IV. 285.
Instruction über Vermessung Aufnahme und Planzeichnung der Waldungen. 1789. IV. 263.
Instruction, wornach die Forst-Taxatoren den Werth der . . . Wald-Grundstücke künftig zu berechnen haben. 1814. IV. 301.
Instruction wornach die Holzkultur . . . betrieben werden soll. See HARTIG, G. L. 1814. IV. 106.
Instruction, wornach die Holzkultur in den k. hannöverschen Forsten betrieben werden soll. 1817. IV. 301.
Instruction zur geschäftlichen Behandlung der Aerarial-Triften im Regenflusse. 1868. IV. 300.[1]
Instruction zur Vornahme der periodischen Revision der Abschätzung . . . der Gemeinds- . . . waldungen. 1846. IV. 299.
Instructiones sur les principaux objets, qui concernent la culture des terres. 1783. IV. 121
Instructions for making final proof on timber culture entries. 1882. IV. 314.[2] See also McFARLAND, N. C. 1882. IV. 155.[1]
Instructions for the collection of test pieces of Pines. 1892. IV. 415.[2]
Instructions pour la destruction des hannetons. 1895. IV. 197.
Instructions pour la semence . . . des Mûriers. 1770. III. 373.
Instructions pour les arbres fruictiers. See TRIQUET, R. 1653. III. 142.
Instructions pour les gardes forestiers . . . des forêts soumises au régime forestier. See INSTRUKTION für die Waldhüter . . . 1851. IV. 306.
Instructions to special agents . . . appointed to prevent timber depredations. 1883. IV. 178,[1] 888.[1]
Instructoriske Bestemmelser for Bestyrelsen af Statens Skove. 1860. IV. 296.[1]
Instructoriske Bestemmelser, som i Henhold til Lov af 8/12 1859 . . . ved Bestyrelsen af Statens Skove. 1890. IV.
Instructoriske Bestemmelser . . . ved Bestyrelsen af Statens Skove og Jagt. 1851. IV. 296.[1]
Instruktion betreffend die Einführung des Metermasses beim Forstbetrieb. 1876. IV. 306.

Instruktion für das k. Forst- und Jagd-Schutzpersonale von Oberfranken. 1858. IV. 300.[1]
Instruktion für definitive . . . Wirthschaftspläne über Staats- : . . . waldungen des Kantons Luzern. 1878. IV. 306.
Instruktion für die Aufseher bei den öffentlichen Arbeiten der Forstfrevier. 1846. IV. 299.
Instruktion für die Aufstellung und Revision von Wirthschaft-pläanen über Gemeinde- . . . wälder des Kantons Zug. 1888. IV. 306.
Instruktion für die Förster der Staatswaldungen. 1833. IV. 306.
Instruktion für die Forstwirthschafts-Einrichtung . . . in Bayern. 1840. IV. 247.[2]
Instruktion für die fürstlich leiningische Förster. 1805. IV. 299.
Instruktion für die fürstlich leiningischen Forstverwalter. 1805. IV. 299.
Instruktion für die fürstlich leiningischen Oberförster. 1805. IV. 299.
Instruktion für die [hessischen] Forstschützen. 1830. IV. 300.[2]
Instruktion für die Holzhauer, Holzsetzer . . . Niederbayern. 1872. IV. 300.[2]
Instruktion für die Holzhauer im Fürstenthume Leiningen. 1805. IV. 299.
Instruktion für die Holzhauer in den Staats- und Mitgebrauchs Waldungen des Kurfürstenthums Hessen. 1858. IV. 301.
Instruktion für die Holzhauer in Staatswaldungen. 1861. IV. 306.
Instruktion für die in den thurgauischen Staatswaldungen angestellten Arbeiter. 1889. IV. 307.[1]
Instruktion für die landesherrlichen Bezirksförster im Grossherzogthum Baden. 1834. IV. 298.[2]
Instruktion [für die Oberforstinspektoren]. 1810. IV. 307.[1]
Instruktion für die Sammlung und Zusammenstellung von Material zu Ertragstafeln. 1873. IV. 236.
Instruktion für die Vermarchung der Waldungen. 1883. IV. 306.
Instruktion für die Vermarkung . . . der grossherzoglich badischen Domänenwaldungen. 1843. IV. 299.
Instruktion für die Vermessung, Abschätzung . . . der Staats- . . . waldungen im Kanton Zürich. 1868. IV. 306.
Instruktion für die Waldhüter in den der Forstverwaltung unterworfenen Waldungen. 1851. IV. 306.
Instruktion für Forstwirthschafts-Einrichtung . . . im Königreich Bayern. 1831. IV. 242.
Instruktion nach welcher die Waldungen vermessen . . . werden sollen. 1783. IV. 263.
Instruktion über die Aufstellung von Wirthschaftsplänen . . . in Unterfranken und Aschaffenburg. 1841. IV. 247.[2]
Instruktion über die Errichtung von provisorischen Waldwirthschafts-Plänen . . . des Kantons Bern. 1878. IV. 306.
Instruktion wie die neue grossherzoglich-badische Forstorganisation in Gang zu setzen ist. 1808. IV. 289.[2]
Instruktion zu Anlegung der Eichelsaat- und Pflanzkämpe. 1811. IV. 504.
Instruktion zur Abschätzung und Einrichtung der Waldungen im Grossherzogthume Baden. 1826. IV. 209.[1]
Instruktion zur Anfertigung der Qualifikations- und Promotionslisten des k. bayerischen Forstpersonals. 1863. IV. 300.[1]
Instruktion zur Behandlung des Forstrügewesens in Oberfranken. 1842. IV. 300.[1]
Instruktion zur Taxation der grossherzoglich badischen Domänen-Waldungen. 1843. IV. 299.
Instruktionen zur Abschätzung und Einrichtung . . . der Domänen- . . . Waldungen im Grossherzogthum Baden. 1858. IV. 299.
Instruktziya . . . See ИНСТРУКЦІЯ . . .
Instrumente zur Messung der Stärke der Bäume. 1858. IV. 231.[2]
Instrux angaaende den 10aarige Revision af Skovregulerings-planerne. 1870. IV. 296.[1]
Insuccès de plantations de Pin sylvestre. 1900. IV. 480.
Insulinde. III. 14.
The Intellectual observer. See RECREATIVE science. I. 19.
Intensieve en extensieve Koffiecultuur. 1888. III. 727.
O intensivnosti lesního hospodářství. 1883. IV. 111.[1]
Die interessantesten Bäume in den Baumschulen von André Leroy. See KOCH, Karl. 1867. I. 58.
An interesting rediscovery. 1891. II. 837.[2]

International forestry exhibition at Edinburgh. 1884. IV. 20.[1]
The International forestry exhibition, Edinburgh. 1884. IV. 20.[1]
International forestry exhibition, Edinburgh. 1887. IV. 20.[1]
International horticultural exhibition . . . London. Report. III. 17.
International woodworker. *See* AMERICAN wood-worker. IV. 3.
Die Internationale Bedeutung der Wälder. 1899. IV. 45.
Internationale Küfer-Zeitung. *See* COOPERS' international journal. IV. 3.
Het internationale Rameh-congres te Parijs. 1900. III. 382.[1]
De Internationale tentoonstelling voor boschkultuur te Edinburg. 1884. IV. 20.[1]
Internationaler Congress der Land- und Forstwirthe. Protokolle. IV. 14.
Internationaler land- und forstwirthschaftlicher Congress, Wien. Bericht. IV. 14.
Internationaler land- und forstwirthschaftlicher Congress zu Wien. 1890. IV. 39.[1]
Internationaler pomologischer Kongress in Wien . . . 1873. Verhandlungen. III. 25.
Internationaler Verband forstlicher Versuchsanstalten. Bericht. Tagesordnung. 1-3 Versammlung. Verzeichniss der Versuchsflächen . . . IV. 5.[2]
Inter-state lumberman. IV. 4.
Introducers of exotic flowers, fruits, etc. 1867. III. 33.[2]
Introduction aux observations sur la physique. V. VII.[2]
Introduction de Conifères rares . . . du Japon en Angleterre. 1862. III. 289.
Introduction du Charme dans les taillis. 1894. IV. 492.[1]
Introduction du Platane d'Orient en France. 1896. II. 255.[2]
The introduction of foreign trees into Great Britain. 1879. IV. 126.[3]
Introduction of the Brazil nut. 1887: III. 631.[2]
On the introduction of the Cinchona or Bark-tree. 1857. III. 713.[1]
Introduction of the culture of Cinchona into Java. *See* EINFÜHRUNG der China-Cultur. 1855. III. 715.
On the introduction of . . . the Deodar. 1854. III. 300.[1]
Introduzione alla raccolta delle leggi forestali. *See* MIRAGLIA, Nicola. 1866. IV. 328.
Introduzione di alberi esotici in Italia. 1882. IV. 127.[1]
Inui, Tamaki, Hattori, Hirotaro & Kusano, Shunsuke. List of plants collected in Mt. Togakushi. 1897. I. 463.[1]
Contra las inundaciones. *See* CONTRA las inundaciones. 1884. IV. 186.[2]
Las inundaciones. 1900. IV. 47.[2]
Invasion de la Nonne dans les forêts de la Bavière. 1890. IV. 200.
Invasions d'hylésines. 1898. IV. 479.
Invención para cortar madera. 1892. IV. 393.
Invernizi, G. B. Sopra il rimboschimento. 1879. IV. 165.
Investigation made . . . of the California Olive industry. 1900. III. 679.[3]
The investigation of the grazing question. 1900. IV. 197.[7]
De invloed der bosschen op het klimaat. 1874. IV. 53.
Invloed van den tijd van het vellen der boomen. *See* EINFLUSS der Zeit des Holzfällens. 1865. IV. 384.[2]
Invloed van het tijdstip voor het vellen van boomen. 1900. IV. 385.[1]
Invloed van het tijdstip, waarop men boomen velt. 1859. IV. 384.[2]
Inzenga, Giuseppe. On the cultivation of Sumach. 1868. III. 527.[1]
— Culture du Sumac en Sicile. 1868. III. 527.[1]
— Manuale pratico della coltivazione del Sommaco. 1874. III. 527.[1]
— Origine singolare di una nuova varietà di Arancio. 1875. II. 402.[2]
Ionian anthology. *See* 'ΙΟΝΙΟΣ ἀνθολογία.
Iosa, G. Influenza delle Carrube sulla secrezione . . . del latte. 1896. III. 472.[1]
Iowa academy of sciences. Proceedings. I. 5.
Iowa agricultural college. Bulletin. III. 4.
Iowa agricultural college — Department of botany. Bulletin. III. 4.
Iowa agricultural college — Department of entomology. Bulletin. III. 4.
Iowa — Agricultural college — Experiment station. Bulletin. III. 4.
Iowa — Agricultural experiment station. *See* IOWA — AGRICULTURAL COLLEGE. III. 4.

Iowa geological survey. Annual report. I. 5.
Iowa state college of agriculture and mechanic arts. Contributions. III. 4.
Iowa state horticultural society. Forestry annual. Forestry bulletin. Forestry manual. IV. 4.
Iowa state horticultural society. Report. Transactions. III. 4.
Ioyelson. *See* ИОЕЛЬСОНЪ.
Iperen, J. van. Over den verbeterden landbouw der Brabanders. 1770. IV. 159.
Ipoh poison. 1895. III. 684.[1]
Ipoh poison of the Malay Peninsula. 1891. III. 366.[2]
Ippolitof, V. P. *See* ИППОЛИТОВЪ, В. П.
Irabien, Francisco URQUIJO DE. *See* URQUIJO DE IRABIEN, Francisco.
Iradier, Eduardo, DATO. *See* DATO IRADIER, Eduardo.
Irang-hoï-duc. Histoire et description de la basse Cochinchine: 1863. III. 276.[3]
Ireland, W. D. Wild silk-yielder in the Akyab district. 1872. III. 148.[2]
Irelli, Gastone CERULLI-. *See* CERULLI-IRELLI, Gastone.
Iriartea gigantea. 1872. III. 326.[1]
Irid, (pseud.). Aralia Veitchii. 1873. III. 642.[1]
Irish, H. C. Comparative phenological notes. 1898. I. 222.[1]
— A revision of the genus Capsicum. 1898. II. 769.[2]
The Irish flora. 1847. I. 399.
The Irish forest problem. 1885. IV. 161.[1]
Irish forester, (pseud.). Rotation of Larch crops. 1885. III. 304.[1]
Irish Furze, Broom and Yew. 1827. I. 393.[1]
Irmisch, Johann Friedrich Thilo. Beiträge zur vergleichenden Morphologie der Pflanzen. 1854. I. 99.
— Bemerkungen über die Auswahl des Stoffes für den botanischen Unterricht. 1849. I. 382.
— Bemerkungen über die Inflorescenzen der . . . Vaccinium-Arten. 1851. II. 431,[1] 658.[2]
— Ueber den Blüthebau von Aesculus Hippocastanum. 1848. II. 481.[3]
— Ueber die Blüthenstände einiger Leguminosen. 1851. II. 320.[1]
— Botanische Mittheilungen. Monströse Birnen. 1858. II. 278.[2]
— Botanische Notizen. 1848. II. 360,[1] 654.[2]
— Einige Beobachtungen an Eucalyptus. 1876. II. 624.[2]
— Einige Beobachtungen über deutsche Eichen. 1847. II. 129.[1]
— Ueber einige Botaniker des 16. Jahrhunderts. 1862. I. 80.[3]
— Ueber einige Pflanzen, bei denen . . . eine ungewöhnlich grosse Anzahl von Sprossanlagen sich bildet. 1876. I. 108.[1]
— Ueber die Keimpflanzen von Rhipsalis Cassytha. 1876. II. 598.[2]
— Notiz über Pyrus decipiens Bechst. 1859. II. 313.[1]
— Rhamnus cathartica und Rh. Frangula. 1855. II. 497.[1]
— Systematisches Verzeichniss der in . . . Theile der Schwarzburgischen Fürstenthümer wildwachsenden . . . Pflanzen. 1846. I. 381.
Irmischia. I. 12.
Irmler, H. Vermehrung von Betula atropurpurea. 1883. III. 357.[1]
Iron-wood. 1897. II. 122.[2]
The Iron-wood tree of Pegu. 1899. III. 491.[1]
On the irritability of the stamina of the Barberry. 1830. II. 202.[2]
Irsengarth, H. F. Gemeinnütziges Compendium theils neu berechneter theils gesammelter Holz-Tabellen. 1809. IV. 221.
Irvine, Alexander. British botany. 1855. I. 400.
— The illustrated handbook of the British plants. 1858. I. 400.
— The London flora. 1838. I. 398.
— *See also* PAMPLIN, W. & IRVINE, Alexander.
Irvine, R. H. A short account of the materia medica of Patna. 1848. III. 277.
Irving, T. T. *See* MACPHAIL, W. M. & IRVING, T. T.
Irwin, (Lieut.). Memoir on the climate . . . of Afghanistan. 1840. III. 279.[2]
Is the Lantana a friend or an enemy? 1896. IV. 536.[2]
Is this the tallest hedge known? 1900. III. 360.[1]
Isaac. Mesures à prendre relativement aux forêts de l'Algérie. 1893. IV. 279.[3]
Isaacs, J. D. Preservation of structural timber. 1896. IV. 421.

Isambert, F. A. Traité de la voirie rurale et urbaine. 1825. III. 200.²
Isayef, A. A. See Исаевъ, A. A.
Isegham, Henri van. Viticulture. 1874. III. 555.
Isenflamm, Jakob Friedrich. Methodus plantarum medicinae clinicae adminiculum. 1764. III. 54.
Isensee, Emil. Elementa nova geographiae . . . medicinalis. 1833. I. 299.
Isère — Société de statistique des sciences naturelles . . . See Société . . . I. 23.
Isert, Paul Erdmann. Reise nach Guinea und den Caribäischen Inseln. 1788. III. 266.
Ishii, J. Mannane . . . in the seeds of Diospyros Kaki. 1894. II. 701.²
— On the occurrence of mucin. 1894. I. 177.
Isidorus Hispalensis. . . . Etymologiarum libri XX. 636. I. 274.
— Opera omnia. 636. I. 274.
Isis. See Naturwissenschaftliche Gesellschaft Isis . . . I. 13.
Isis; maandblad voor natuurwetenschap. See Isis; weekblad . . . I. 15.
Isis; oder, Encyclopädische Zeitung. I. 12.
Isis; weekblad voor natuurwetenschap. I. 15.
Isis; Zeitschrift. I. 12.
The island of Montserrat. See Evans, Sons & Co. 1878. III. 502.²
Islander, (pseud.). The botanical garden of Padua. 1898. I. 64.
Isnard, Antoine Danty d'. See Danty d'Isnard, Antoine.
Isnard, Ch. Effets toxiques du thé. 1865. III. 607.
Issartier, Henri. Culture des arbres fruitiers. 1861. III. 144.
Issler, Emil. Sorbus Mougeotii in den Vogesen. 1898. II. 313.²
Isslieb. Céarine. 1898. III. 324.¹
Ist die Ausübung der Waldweide mit Rindvieh . . . verwerflich? 1868. IV. 135.²
Ist die Camellie eine Gewächshaus-Pflanze? See Is the Camellia a greenhouse plant? 1848. III. 599.²
Ist es besser Gemeindswaldungen zu vertheilen. 1816. IV. 309.¹
Ist es nöthig die Berechnungszeit bei der Ertragsermitelung so weit auszudehnen. 1839. IV. 254.
Istituto botanico dell' Università di Pavia. Atti. I. 25.
Istituto botanico della R. Università di Pisa. Ricerche. I. 25.
Istituto botanico di Roma. See Reale istituto . . . I. 25.
Istituto d'incoraggiamento di agricoltura . . . in Sicilia. See Reale istituto . . . III. 23.²
Istituto d'incoraggiamento . . . di Napoli. See Reale istituto . . . I. 25.²
L' Istituto di esperienze forestali in Giessen. 1882. IV. 38.¹
Per l' Istituto forestale di Vallombrosa. 1898. IV. 96.¹
Istituto lombardo di scienze e lettere. See Reale istituto . . . I. 25.
Istituto tecnico di Bari. See Reale istituto . . . III. 23.²
Istituto tecnico e nautico di Napoli. See Reale istituto . . . III. 23.²
Istituto veneto di scienze. See Imperiale reale istituto . . . I. 25.
Istituzione d' una scuola forestale nel Belgio. 1864. IV. 33.²
Istruzione in esecuzione dei decreti di S. A. I. il principe Vicerà del 27 Maggio e 5 Giugno 1811 sui boschi. 1811. IV. 304.²
Istruzione sul servizio delle guardie forestali del ripartimento di Alessandria. 1865. IV. 309.¹
Istruzione sul sciroppo e zucchero d' Uva. See Olcese, F. J. M. 1810. II. 220.¹
Istruzione sulla compilazione del processo verbale di verificazione dei boschi. 1865. IV. 305.
Istruzioni e circolari. 1863. IV. 304.²
Istruzioni per l' amministrazione forestale. 1874. IV. 305.
Istruzioni per l' amministrazione forestale dello stato. 1879. IV. 305.
Istruzioni per l' amministrazione forestale italiana. 1867. IV. 305.
Istruzioni per l' organizzazione del guardaboschi comunali. 1865. IV. 309.¹
Istruzioni per le guardie e cultura de' Mori. 1767. III. 373.
Istruzioni per le guardie de boschi. 181.? IV. 304.²
Istvánffi, Gyula de. Une visite au jardin botanique . . . de Kolozsvár. 1900. I. 66.¹

Italia — Ministero d' agricoltura, industria e commercio. Bulletino. III. 23.²
Italia agraria e forestale. 1878. III. 271.²
L' Italia agricola. III. 23.²
L' Italia-perde ogni anno notevoli quantità di terreno produtivo. 1880. IV. 48.¹
Italien. . Neues Forstgesetz. 1897. IV. 329.
Italie, L. van. De chemische samenstelling der Macassarolie. 1889. III. 540.²
— Over cortex radicis Rhois aromatic. 1890. III. 527.¹
— Koesambi-noten. 1889. II. 489.²
— Over Kokosnoten. 1890. II. 67.³
— Sur la matière grasse . . . de Calophyllum. 1888. III. 608.²
— Over de vruchten van Terminalia catappa. 1888. III. 632.²
— Over het zaad van Calophyllum. 1888. III. 608.²
Iterson, W. J. D. van. De bebouwing der heidestreken. 1871. IV. 160.¹
— Elzenheggen om beuwland. 1861. III. 356.²
— Handelt men in vele kleistreken verstandig door opgaande boomen zoo streng te weren. 1870. III. 121.²
— Eene ziekte in de Canada's. 1870. III. 345.²
Itier, J. Des cultures et des forêts de la Guyane française. 1845. IV. 398.¹
Ito, Keisuke. A memorial work. See Ito, Tokutaro. 1893. V. viii.¹
— & Kaku, Hika. Koishikawa Shokubutsu-en Somoku Zusetsu. 1881. I. 462.
Itô, Tokutaró. Berberidearum Japoniae conspectus. 1887. II. 201.¹
— On a case of close . . . resemblances in dicotyledons. 1899. II. 437.² 474.¹
— A memorial work. 1893. V. viii.¹
— Plantae sinenses Yoshianae. 1900. I. 460.¹
— Rhizophoreae in Japan. 1899. II. 613.¹
— & Matsumura, Jinzô. Tentamen florae lutchuensis. 1898. I. 463.²
Ivanitzky, Nikolai Aleksandrovich. Catalogue des plantes . . . de Wologda et d'Archangel. 1893. I. 454.¹
— Über die Flora des Gouvernements Wologda. 1882. I. 454.¹
— See also Иваницкій, Н. А.
Ivanof, A. See Ивановъ, A.
Ivanof, M. See Ивановъ, M.
Ivans, G. A. Three best black Grapes for Iowa. 1899. III. 547.
Iverus, Johan Edvard Davidson. Några ej förut namngifna varieteter. 1875. II. 46.²
— Själftuktande Gran. 1898. II. 37.¹
Ives, Joseph C. Report upon the Colorado River of the west, explored in 1857 and 1858. See Gray, Asa & others. 1860. I. 323.
Ivolas, J. Les plantes calcicoles et calcifuges. 1886. I. 229.
— La végétation des causses. 1889. I. 417.
Ivy, Ike. Amelanchier canadensis. 1883. III. 419.²
— A dozen good shrubs. 1883. III. 203.
— Native Spiraeas. 1883. III. 460.²
An Ivy-covered church. 1893. III. 545.¹
Ivy hedges. 1876. III. 642.²
Ivy in the house. 1872. III. 642.²
Ivy screens. 1877. III. 642.²
Ob Ivye. See Объ Ивѣ.
Iwanow, Nicolai. Ueber das aetherische Oel von Ledum. 1876. III. 653.¹
Iwanowska, Mrs. G. Balicka'- See Chodat, Robert & Balicka'-Iwanowska, Mrs. G.
Les Ixora. 1891. III. 745.¹
Izai, József. A vörös Berkenye. 1900. III. 459.²
Izard. Le Quinquina. 1900. III. 712.²
Izawa, Henry. Dwarfing plants in Japan. 1893. III. 176.¹
— Japanese horticulture. 1893. III. 127.²
Izoard, P. A propos du deutocyle foliaire et florifère de l'Aesculus. 1899. II. 482.²
Izslisdovaniya o zapasye. See Изслѣдованія о запасѣ.
Izvletchenie . . . See Извлеченіе . . .

J. Caper plants. 1877. II. 232.¹
J. Echium candicans. 1899. III. 695.¹
— Growth and composition of Furze. 1845. II. 387.²
— Hardy shrubs for forcing. 1891. III. 176.²
— De Koffiehandel. 1869. III. 739.
— Liberia Koffie. 1896. III. 743.¹
J. Méthode naturelle des végétaux. See Jussieu, A. L. de, 1824. I. 251.

J. Notes from the Arnold Arboretum. 1888. III. 203.
J. Reorganización del servicio forestal. 1892. IV. 553.²
J. Die Schädigungen der Stadtbäume. 1900. III. 212.¹
J. Tilia dasystyla. 1888. III. 586.¹
J. Two interesting Willows. 1888. III. 349.
J. See B. & J.
J., A. G. Mishandeling van Koffie-aanplant. 1899. III. 727.
J., B. Het ehten van Koffie. 1897. III. 733.¹
J., B. Palms and their uses, the Wine Palm. 1877. III. 321.³
J., B. The Paraguay Tea. 1877. III. 531.¹
J., C. Ein Besuch auf Bermuda. 1886. I. 336.
J., C. S. De la propriété forestière. 1865. IV. 275.
J., D. S. A tour through the woods and forests of Duff House. 1878. IV. 358.¹
J., E. Une scierie de bois de Teck à Bangkok. 1881. III. 697.²
J., E. Tree Paeonies. 1897. III. 392.²
J., F. Die Forstwirthschaft in Bosnien und der Herzegowina. 1899. IV. 374.²
J., G. Carpenteria californica. 1885. III. 409.²
J., H. Bignonias. 1892. III. 706.²
J., H. A log-lifting machine in use in Burma. 1900. IV. 390.¹
J., J. R. Cape Boxwood. 1887. . IV. 525.
J., J. R. The Clove tree. 1881. III. 635.¹
J., J. R. Notes on articles contributed to the museums of the Royal . . . gardens, Kew. 1887. I. 55.
J., L. De Koffiecultuur in de Palembangsche bovenlanden. 1900. III. 732.¹
J., M. Eene nieuwe Koffiesoort. 1900. III. 728.¹
J., R. J. Teakwood and paper-making in Siam. 1886. III. 697.²
J., R. S. Pinus insignis in Hampshire. 1886. III. 308.²
J., S. The vineyard. 1727. III. 553.²
J., W. The double Poinsettia in Jamaica. 1900. III. 518.¹
J . . . n. Ueber die Moutan-Pflanze. 1833. II. 200.²
Jaager, C. J. de. Een schaduwboom voor Koffie. 1897. III. 484,³ 734.²
Jaap, Otto. Auf Bäumen wachsende Gefässpflanzen. 1898. I. 234.²
— Kopfweiden-Ueberpflanzen. 1896. I. 234.³
— Ueberpflanzen bei Bad Nauheim. 1899. I. 234.²
Het jaar 1894. Berichten uit Suriname. 1895. III. 118.²
Jaarbericht 1899 der Soekaboemische landbouwvereeniging. 1900. III. 129.¹
Jaarverslag der gouvernements Kina-onderneming in de residentie Preanger-Regentschappen. 1900. III. 717.¹
Jaarverslag der Malangsche vereeniging van Koffieplanters. 1900. III. 732.¹
Jaarverslag der Soekaboemische landbouwvereeniging. See JAARBERICHT . . . 1900. III. 129.¹
Jablanczy, Julius. Die amerikanische Rebe als Decorationspflanze. 1892. III. 545.²
— Das Auftreten der Blutlaus des Apfelbaumes. 1897. III. 428.²
— Die Bepflanzung der Strassen mit Obst- und Wildbäumen. 1879. III. 209.
— Zur Cultur der Korbweide. 1882. III. 348.
— Der falsche Mehlthau der Rebe. 1891. III. 580.
— Die Korkveredlung der amerikanischen Rebe. 1890. III. 548.²
— Der Obstbau für den Landmann und Obstzüchter. 1879. III. 146.³
— Obstbaumpflanzungen im Park. 1881. III. 201.
— Der Springwurmwickler. 1881. III. 563.
— Zur Weidencultur. 1878. III. 348.
Jablonski, Paul Ernest. De conditionibus vegetationi necessariis quaedam. . 1832. I. 157.
Sur le Jaborandi du Dr. Coutinho. 1875. III. 505.¹
Jacaby, Felix. Beiträge zur Chemie der Salix-Rinden. 1890. II. 104.¹
Jaccard, A. Sur les Chênes enfouis des marais tourbeux. 1895. I. 432.² — 1896. II. 136.¹
Jaccard, Henri. Catalogue de la flore valaisanne. 1895. I. 438.
— Le Cytisus Laburnum L. à Roche. 1891. III. 369.¹
Jaccard, Paul. Étude géo-botanique. 1900. I. 438.
— Étude géobotanique sur la flore . . . de la Sallanche. 1898. I. 438.
— Influence de la pression des gaz. 1893. I. 150;¹ 188.
— Méthode de détermination de la distribution de la flore alpine. 1900. I. 438.
— Note sur trois cas de tératologie végétale. 1896. II. 54.¹
— Recherches embryologiques sur l'Ephedra. 1894. II. 54.³

Jachtmann, Heinrich. Anweisung wie . . . Feuerungen zur Holzersparung eingerichtet werden können. 1786. IV. 280.¹
Jack, Edward. Forest management in Canada. 1884. IV. 288.¹
— In the forests of northern Wisconsin. 1885. IV. 339.
— Influence of geological formation on forest growths in New Brunswick. 1884. IV. 69, 337.¹
— Recent facts . . . respecting Canadian forestry. 1885. IV. 271.¹
— See also BAILEY, L. W. & JACK, Edward.
— & Connors, Robert. The White Pine. 1883. IV. 469.
Jack, John George. Aesculus parviflora. 1894. III. 538.²
— Arceuthobium pusillum in Massachusetts. 1900. II. 174.²
— Autumnal colors of foliage. 1889. III. 207.¹
— Caragana or Siberian Pea-trees. 1893. III. 469.²
— The care of weak limbs of trees. 1897. III. 199.
— A Clematis borer. 1891. III. 389.²
— Climbing Honeysuckles. 1893. III. 750.¹
— Conifers injured by squirrels. 1889. IV. 442.
— A destructive Cornel saw-fly. 1889. III. 645.¹
— The earliest flowering shrubs. 1894. III. 207.²
— Early deciduous shrubs. 1893. III. 205.²
— Early-flowering Magnolias. 1894. III. 399.¹
— Epigaea repens. 1895. III. 649.²
— L'Érable à sucre. 1889. IV. 527.¹
— Exotic shrubs in Canada. 1890. III. 60.
— A few good shrubs of the hardiest type. 1895. III. 203.
— A few notable shrubs in late November. 1892. III. 208.¹
— Flowering shrubs in mid-August. 1893. III. 207.²
— The fructification of Juniperus. 1893. II. 30.²
— Germinating nuts and acorns. 1895. III. 156.²
— Hardy deciduous Barberries. 1893. III. 394.¹
— Hardy evergreen Hollies and Barberries. 1893. III. 334,¹ 529.²
— The Hazels. 1895. II. 122.¹
— How some half-hardy shrubs survived the winter. 1892. III. 44.¹
— Hybrid Birches. 1895. II. 119.¹
— Late flowers on woody plants. 1893. III. 207.²
— Late ornamental fruits. 1893. III. 208.¹
— Late persisting leaves on trees. 1891. III. 205.²
— Lespedeza bicolor and Lespedeza Sieboldi. 1892. II. 369.²
— Magnolia glauca. 1889. II. 212.¹
— Monœcious or polygamous Poplars and Willows. 1894. II. 96,¹ 104.¹
— Native trees and shrubs about Montreal. 1894. I. 309.²
— A new enemy of the Elm. 1889. III. 364.²
— Notes after a mild winter. 1890. III. 44.¹
— Notes on grafting. 1890. III. 163.
— Notes on Hypericums. 1889. III. 610.¹
— Notes on shrubs. 1890. III. 203. — 1891. III. 430.² — 1892. III. 203.
— Notes on some hardy wild Roses. 1891. III. 450.
— Notes on some injurious insects. 1894. III. 187.
— Notes on the eastern American Spruces. 1897. III. 34.¹
— Notes on the production of maple sugar. 1889. IV. 527.¹
— Notes on trees and shrubs. 1894. III. 203.
— Notes on two troublesome borers. 1892. III. 457,² IV. 525.²
— Noteworthy late-flowering shrubs. 1893. III. 207.²
— Ornamental Currants. 1893. III. 414.¹
— Our trees in ice-storms. 1891. III. 185.¹
— Pikes Peak, Plum Creek, and South Platte reserves. 1900. IV. 341.³
— Prunus tomentosa. 1892. II. 277.²
— Pyrus japonica. 1897. III. 420.²
— September notes on interesting shrubs. 1889. III. 203.
— A sequence of flowering Cherries. 1892. III. 432.¹
— The shrub-garden in November. 1889. III. 208.¹
— Shrubs with conspicuous fruit in August. 1889. III. 208.¹
— Shrubs with conspicuous fruits in July. 1889. III. 208.¹
— Slow-maturing fruits of trees and shrubs. 1893. I. 200.
— Some early Spiraeas. 1891. III. 145.¹
— Some unusual androgynous flowers. 1895. I. 145.¹
— Spiraea discolor var. ariaefolia. 1891. III. 264.²
— Trees for late autumn foliage. 1891. III. 205.²
— A Tulip tree leaf destroyer. 1889. III. 398.²
— Weevils in leguminous tree-seeds. 1891. III. 462.¹
— Wild or single Roses for cultivation. 1893. III. 450.
— A Willow pest. 1897. III. 350.¹
— Winter notes on trees and shrubs. 1890. III. 208.¹
Jack, Joseph Bernhard. Botanische Wanderungen am Bodensee. 1891. I. 389.
— Flora des badischen Kreises Konstanz. 1900. I. 390.

Jack, William. Account of the Lansium. 1825. I. 464.²
— On Cyrtandraceae, a new natural order of plants. 1825. II. 792.³
— Descriptions of Malayan plants. 1820.. I. 464.²
— On the Malayan species of Melastoma. 1825. II. 639.¹
Jackman, A. G. The Clematis. 1900. III. 389.²
— Hybrid Clematis. 1900. III. 389.²
Jackman, George. See MOORE, Thomas & JACKMAN, George.
Jackson. On the cultivation of Roses. 1840. III. 454.¹
Jackson, Benjamin Daydon. A catalogue of plants cultivated in the garden of John Gerard. 1876. I. 78.³
— Daboecia. 1889. II. 662.²
— A glossary of botanic terms. 1900. I. 71.
— Guide to the literature of botany. 1881. I. 2.
— Index kewensis. 1893. I. 77.
— Vegetable technology. 1882. III. 1.
Jackson, Bryan. Osage Orange hedges. 1851. III. 372.¹
Jackson, Charles Loring. On the reduction of camphor to borneol. 1885. III. 611.³
— & Menke, A. E. A new method of preparing borneol. 1883. III. 611.³
Jackson, Charles Thomas. Analysis of the Raspberry bush. 1844. II. 305.²
— Modern methods for the preservation and coloration of wood. 1868. IV. 419.
— Report on the saccharine contents of native American Grapes. 1860. III. 583.¹
— Wax from Rhus succedaneum. 1861. III. 527.²
Jackson, George. Account of Ormosia. 1811. II. 375.¹
Jackson, H. Dendrometers. 1888. IV. 216.
Jackson, H. V. Forest nursery and plantation work. 1898. IV. 151.²
— Forestry operations and the state forest nursery, Gosford. 1897. IV. 380.²
— Pruning ornamental trees. 1898. III. 171.
— The Ramie fibre plant. 1899. III. 381.²
— Ramie, Rhea, or China-grass. 1899. III. 381.²
— Trees for shelter and breakwinds. 1898. III. 215.²
Jackson, J. P. Cherries. 1900. III. 432.¹
— Three best red Raspberries for market. 1899. III. 458.¹
Jackson, James Gray. An account of the empire of Marocco. 1809. III. 279.³
Jackson, John Reader. On the acclimatisation of foreign timber trees. 1878. IV. 126.²
— The African Baobab. 1868. III. 589.¹
— African Tea plants. 1874. III. 222.
— The Algerian Callitris. 1872. III. 299.²
— American Oaks. 1874. II. 128.²
— Boxwood and its substitutes. 1885. IV. 428.¹
— Brooms and brushes. 1885. III. 319.²
— Calcutta botanic garden. 1868. I. 67.¹
— Canes and sticks used in the manufacture of walking sticks. 1888. IV. 428.²
— Le Caoutchouc. 1890. III. 368.¹
— The Chestnut and its uses. 1888. II. 124.¹
— Christmas decorations. 1889. III. 383.²
— Cinchonas. 1869. III. 712.¹
— Cochineal. 1870. III. 624.¹
— Cocoa. 1870. III. 594.
— Cocoa-nut mats and mattings. 1886. III. 324.¹
— Cocoa (Theobroma [sic] Cacao) 1867. III. 594.
— Cocus wood. 1884. II. 338,¹ 437.¹
— Commercial botany. 1890. III. 218.¹
— Cork and its uses. 1865. IV. 518.¹
— The "Dogwoods" used in the manufacture of gunpowder. 1870. IV. 432.¹
— The Dragon tree of Teneriffe. 1868. II. 82.²
— Eucalyptus oil. 1892. IV. 532.¹
— Foreign vegetable products. 1896. III. 218.¹
— Forestry exhibition. 1884. IV. 534.²
— Frankincense (Boswellia Carteri). 1880. II. 416.²
— The genus Araucaria. 1865. III. 298.¹
— On the genus Euphorbia. 1869. III. 517.²
— On the genus Ficus. 1867. II. 149.²
— Germination of Palms. 1870. II. 62.²
— The Gouty-stem tree. 1868. III. 589.²
— Gum Euphorbium. 1882. III. 518.²
— Hemlock Spruce bark extract. 1885. III. 312.²
— India-rubber. 1890. III. 368.¹
— India-rubber and gutta-percha. 1896. III. 229.
— India-rubber plants. 1880. II. 445.¹
— Indian forest administration. 1878. IV. 295.¹
— Indian Laburnum Cassia fistula. 1881. II. 344.¹

— The manufacture of walking-sticks. 1877. IV. 428.¹
— Material para la fabricación de papel. 1892. IV. 430.
— The medicinal properties of the Cow-tree. 1873. III. 367,² 609,¹ 691.¹
— Mexican fibre. 1888. II. 89.¹
— On a new application of wood. 1870. IV. 428.¹
— New facts in economic botany. 1869. III. 523.¹
— New Zealand timber. 1875. IV. 380.²
— Note on the uses of a commercial cane. 1878. III. 316.
— Notes on apparently useful woods. 1863. IV. 396.¹
— Notes on some African vegetable products. 1864. III. 279.³
— Notes on some of the edible fruits of the West Indies. 1864. III. 267.¹
— Notes on the Areca Palm. 1874. III. 320.¹
— Notes on the economic application of barks. 1863. IV. 436.¹
— Notes on the medicinal plants of the Rutaceae. 1873. III. 494.²
— Concerning nuts. 1876. III. 220.¹
— The Olive. 1870. III. 678.²
— On the Owala or Opochala. 1864. III. 483.¹
— Palms and their products. 1896. III. 319.²
— Pepper. 1865. III. 343.²
— The Persimmon. 1871. III. 670.¹
— Pine wool carpets. 1888. IV. 467.¹
— Poisonous properties of Jatropha urens. 1872. III. 382,² 520.¹
— Popular errors in economic botany. 1879. III. 331,¹ 475.¹
— Princewood bark. 1876. III. 695,¹ 744,¹ 744.²
— Products of the Citrus tribe in Sicily. 1897. III. 499.¹
— On the products of the Pea family. 1862. III. 462.²
— Ramee fibre, or China grass. 1868. III. 382.¹
— On the Sack tree of the East Indies. 1869. III. 234.
— Sago. 1871. III. 327.²
— The Screw-pine and its allies. 1868. III. 313.¹
— Some useful . . . varieties of the genus Citrus. 1877. II. 401.¹
— Sources of copal. 1869. III. 233.²
— The Square Bamboo. 1885. III. 316.¹
— The Surinam Quassia. 1881. III. 509.¹
— The Sweet Chestnut. 1885. II. 124.¹
— The Tamarind. 1871. III. 489.¹
— Tea. 1870. III. 607.
— Tea and coffee substitutes. 1890. III. 223.¹
— Tea and its substitutes. 1883. III. 222.
— Tropical fruits in the Kew museum. 1887. III. 220.¹
— On the use of Cocoa. 1870. III. 493.¹
— The uses of some of the Indian species of Bassia. 1878. III. 667.¹
— A valuable African wood. 1885. IV. 520.¹
— Walking sticks. 1877. IV. 428.²
— The Whampoa Bamboo. 1894. III. 315.³
— Wonderful plants 1887. I. 518.
— Zebra wood. 1875. III. 462,¹ 471,² IV. 520,² 521.¹
— & Croucher, J. The Cactus family. 1871. III. 619.
Jackson, Joseph. Catalogue of the . . . plants of Worcester county. 1883. I. 315.
— Flora of Worcester county. 1883. I. 315.
— Through glade and mead. 1894. I. 316.
Jackson, M. A. The pictorial flora. 1840. I. 399.
Jackson, Robert Montgomery Smith. Flora. 1860. I. 014.
Jackson, Robert Tracy. Localized stages in development. 1899. I. 101,¹ 243.²
— Methods of labelling trees and plants. 1888. I. 521.¹
Jacob, Edward. Plantae favershamienses. 1777. I. 395.
Jacob, Georg. Untersuchungen über zweites . . . Blühen. 1890. I. 221.
Jacob, H. 's. De instandhouding der Koffiecultuur. 1899. III. 731.
— Over de stoornis in de ontwikkeling van den Koffieboom. 1896. III. 736.
Jacob, John. West Devon and Cornwall flora. 1836. I. 398.
Jacob, Paul. Les bois de construction et les bois utiles. 1897. IV. 385.¹
— Nos Platânes. 1896. III. 418.²
Jacob-Makoy, L. & Cie. Nouveautés annoncées à Liège. 1865. III. 77.¹
— — Nouveautés de plein air. 1864. III. 77.¹
— — Prix-courant des plantes exotiques. 1866. III. 77.²
Jacobaeus, Johann Adolph. De plantarum structura et vegetatione schedion. 1727. I. 97.
Jacobaeus, Oliger. Museum regium. 1696. I. 40.

Jacobasch, Ernst. Die allmähliche Entwickelung einer ver-
grünten . . . Rose. 1897. II. 290.[1]
— Blitzschlag in vier Bäume. 1890. IV. 194.
— Botanische Mittheilungen. 1887. II. 107.[1]
— Drei interessante Varietäten von Picea vulgaris Lk. 1883.
I. 34.[2]
— Ueber Fasciation. 1895. I. 144.[2]
— Ein grosses Exemplar von Sambucus nigra. 1882. II. 841.[1]
— Reihenfolge des Aufblühens und Umwandlung der Stamina
bei Philadelphus. 1883. II. 242.[1]
— Ueber die Ursache der vermehrten Anzahl der Laubbläter.
1900. I. 145.[1]
— Vergrünte Kätzchen von Salix fragilis. 1887. II. 107.[1]
Jacobi, von. Die Agaveen auf der S. . . . Ausstellung zu
Gent. 1868. III. 340.[2]
— Berichtigung über Agaven. 1872. III. 340.[2]
Jacobi, C. G. Abhandlung . . . die Eichbäume zu säen.
1762. IV. 503.[2]
Jacobi, G. A. von. Über Agaveen. 1869. II. 88.[2]
— Beiträge zur Kakteenkunde. 1856. II. 586.[1]
— Beitrag zur Cakteenkultur. 1854. III. 618.[1]
— Bemerkungen über einige Cacteen. 1848. II. 586.[1]
— Die Ceder im Jacobi'schen Garten. 1868. II. 28.[1]
— Classification des Agavées. 1866. II. 88.[2]
— Echinopsis inermis. 1854. II. 593.[2]
— Einiges über Cacteen. 1851. II. 586.[1]
— Uebersicht einer systematischen Ordnung der Agaven.
1866. II. 88.[2]
— Versuch zu einer systematischen Ordnung der Agaveen.
1864. II. 88.[2]
Jacobi, Johann Gottlieb. Abhandlung von allen . . . Arten,
die Bäume zu vermehren. 1770. III. 152.
— Abhandlung von dem Anbau fremder . . . Bäume und
Stauden. 1770. II. 74.
— Von Anlegung . . . guter Pflanz- und Baumschulen. 1770.
III. 153.
Jacobovics, Anton. Elenchus plantarum officinalium Hun-
gariae. 1835. III. 90.[2]
Jacobs, Heymann. Den cleynen herbarius. 1627. I. 285.[1]
V. xv.[2]
— Den nieuwen kleijnen herbarius. 1627. I. 285.[1]
Jacobs, J. Het familie en kampongleven op Groot Atjeh.
1894. III. 129.[1]
— Melia Azedarach, Linn. 1880. III. 512.[1]
Jacobs, J. C. Iets over het kweeken van Ficus elastica. 1882.
III. 370.[1]
Jacobsen, E. L'essence de Wintergreen. 1883. III. 652.[1]
Jacobsohn, Hermann. Untersuchungen über Muawin. 1892.
III. 476.[1]
Jacobson. Theekultuur; Kroetoe-verdeling. 1871. III.
604.[1]
Jacobson, J. C. & Rothe, Tyge. Description des serres du
Jardin botanique de l'université de Copenhague. 1879.
I. 40.
Jacobson, J. J. L. L. Bijdrage tot de Theecultuur. 1846.
III. 602.[1]
— Handboek voor de kultuur . . . van Thee. 1843. III. 601.[2]
— Handboek voor het sorteren en afpakken van thee. 1843.
III. 606.
— Hand-book for the cultivation . . . of Tea in Java. 1843.
III. 601.[1]
Jacobsthal, J. E. Ueber anomale Vegetationserscheinungen.
1885. I. 221.
Jacometti, T. M. A. See Hall, H. C. van & Jacometti,
T. M. A.
Jacquart, Henri. La cynosbatologie. 1882. II. 282.[2]
Jacquelain. Extraction de la fécule de marrons d'Inde. 1863.
III. 538.[2]
Jacquemart. De la peinture d'histoire naturelle. 1839. I.
37.[1]
Jacquemart, Albert. Flore des dames. 184.? I. 515.
— Flore des dames. Botanique. 1840. I. 94.
Jacquemart, D. A. De l'élévation des droits de douane à l'im-
portation des bois. 1852. IV. 285.[1]
— Reponse aux lettre de M. Michel Chevalier. 1865. IV. 275.
Jacquemart, Frédéric. Rapport sur trente éducations du ver
du Chêne du Japon. 1864. IV. 501.[2]
Jacquemet, Édouard. Étude botanique . . . de l'Ipécacuan-
ha. 1888. II. 828.[1]
Jacquemin. See Peschier, Jacques & Jacquemin.
Jacquemin, Georges. Développement de principes aroma-
tiques. 1897. I. 178, 182.[1]
— Nouvelles observations sur le développement de principes
aromatiques. 1899. I. 178.

Jacquemont, Victor. Voyage dans l'Inde. 1841. I. 472.
Jacques. Conservation du bois. 1881. IV. 420.
Jacques, frères. See Dailledouze, J. P. & Jacques, frères.
Jacques, Antoine A. Adesmie glutineuse. 1839. II. 329.[2]
— Amandier commun à bois jaspé. 1832. III. 434.[1]
— Astrapée visqueuse, Astrapaea viscosa. 1832. II. 533.[1]
— Behandlingen af Lagerstroemia indica. 1842. III. 629.[2]
— Bois-joli à grandes fleurs. 1843. III. 627.[2]
— Bossie à fleurs fauves. 1839. II. 337.[1]
— Catalogue alphabétique des plantes . . . dans les jardins
. . . le duc d'Orléans. 1824. I. 57.
— Catalogue glossologique des arbres . . . aux domaines privés
du roi. 1833. I. 57.
— Cerisier Parmentier à fleurs doubles. 1832. III. 442.[2]
— Conifère nouveau, Biota meldensis. 1855. II. 52.[3]
— Développement de tiges verticales sur les racines de l'Arau-
caria. 1845. III. 297.[2]
— Encore une anomalie du Cytise Adam. 1847. II. 368.[2]
— Epiphyllum articulatum. 1832. III. 626.[1]
— Erable à grandes feuilles. 1845. III. 535.[1]
— Erythrine retournée. 1843. III. 476.[2]
— Floraison du Camellia Kissi. 1847. III. 597.[1]
— Floraison du Cereus obtusus. 1839. III. 621.[2]
— Fructification du Pterocarya caucasica. 1853. III. 356.[2]
— Fructification du Salisburia. 1853. III. 289.[2] 356.[2]
— Le Groseiller [sic] douteux. 1854. III. 414.[2]
— Laurier-Rose de Mabire. 1839. III. 689.[1]
— Marronnier d'Inde à fleurs paniculées. 1846. II. 481.[2]
— Monographie de la famille des Conifères. 1837. III. 289.
— Nérion ou Laurose cuivré. 1841. III. 689.[2]
— Note sur des arbres et arbrisseaux. 1858. I. 270.
— Note sur l'Hydrangea japonica. 1858. III. 411.[2]
— Note sur la germination de quelques Cactées. 1830. II.
587.[1]
— Note sur le Salisburia adiantifolia. 1836. III. 286.[2]
— Note sur quelques espèces rares. 1859. III. 87.
— Note sur quelques plantes rares ou peu connues. 1859.
II. 448,[1] 682.[2]
— Note sur quelques variétés d'arbres verts. 1853. III. 289.
— Note sur quelques variétés de Cereus. 1846. III. 620.[2]
— Note sur un Magnolia probablement nouveau. 1857. III.
400.[2]
— Note sur un Noyer à folioles variable. 1828. II. 113.[2]
— Note sur un Noyer hybride. 1834. III. 355.
— Note sur un Sophora du Japon. 1843. III. 488.[1]
— Note sur une métamorphose d'étamines en pistils dans le
Saule Marceau. 1833. II. 106.[1]
— Notice sur l'Hibiscus syriacus. 1844. III. 588.[1]
— Notice sur plusieurs Cèdres du Liban. 1844. III. 300.[2]
— Nouvelle anomalie remarquée sur le Cytise Adam. 1840.
II. 368.[2]
— Nouvelle variété de Daphné. 1828. II. 601.[2]
— Nouvelles espèces ou variétés de Seringata. 1841. II.
841,[1] III. 751.[1]
— Noyer. 1830. III. 355.[1]
— Observations sur la Clematis florida. 1841. III. 390.[1]
— Orme à feuilles d'ortie. 1832. III. 365.[2]
— Pêcher à fleurs doubles. 1849. III. 439.[2]
— Petite note sur le Tecoma radicans. 1850. III. 705.[1]
— Petite notice sur l'Araucaria Cunninghami. 1845. III.
298.[1]
— Petite notice sur la Lagerstroem. 1842. III. 629.[2]
— Première floraison du Catalpa Bungei. 1855. III. 706.[1]
— Rapport . . . notamment de Spirées, chez M. Billiard.
1859. III. 461.[1]
— Rapport sur quelques feuilles de Noyer. 1842. III. 353.[1]
— Revue des genres . . . cultivés en France. 1837. III. 289.
— Second floraison du Pandanus odoratissimus. 1848. III.
313.[1]
— Sophora du Japon. 1840. III. 488.[1]
— Staphylé du Colchide. 1854. III. 533.[1]
— Trimalium [sic] Fenzl-Endlicher. 1845. III. 543.[2]
— Le Troène à épis. 1862. III. 697.[1]
— See also Boussière & Jacques, Antoine.
— & Hérincq, François. Manuel général des plantes. 1847.
I. 269.
— & others. Note sur un Poirier greffé sur Pommier. 1837.
III. 445.[1]
Jacques, D. H. Orange culture in Florida. 1868. III. 499.[2]
Jacques, George. Experiments with evergreen and other
trees. 1850. I. 207,[1] III. 291.
— Transplanting large trees. 1847. III. 167.
Jacquey, Jules. Des droits d'usage des indigènes dans les
forêts de l'état, en Algérie. 1884. IV. 335.

Jacquin, (jr.). Éclaircissement sur les causes qui produisent des Hortensias bleus. 1843. III. 412.[1]
Jacquin, (sr.). Des hannetons considérés comme insectes nuisibles. 1832. III. 196.
Jacquin, Joseph Franz, Baron von. Eclogae plantarum. 1811. I. 265.
— Sopra il Gingko. 1819. II. 7.[2]
— Ueber den Ginkgo. 1819. II. 7.[2]
— Eine neue Syringa aus Siebenbürgen. 1831. II. 715.[1]
— Der Universitätsgarten in Wien. 1825. I. 65.[2]
Jacquin, Nicolaus Joseph, Baron von. Anleitung zur Pflanzenkenntniss. 1785. I. 83.
— Collectanea ad botanicam. 1786. I. 32.
— Enumeratio stirpium . . . in agro vindobonensi. 1762. I. 438.
— Enumeratio systematica plantarum . . . in insulis caribaeis. 1760. I. 328.
— Florae austriacae . . . icones. 1773. I. 438.
— Fragmenta botanica. 1800. II. 281.[2]
— Fragmenta botanica figuris coloratis illustrata. 1809. I. 265.
— Genitalia Asclepiadearum. 1778. · II. 735.[2]
— Genitalia Asclepiadearum controversa. 1811. II. 735.[2]
— Hortus botanicus vindobonensis. 1770. I. 65.[2]
— Icones plantarum rariorum. 1781. I. 263.
— Index regni vegetabilis. 1770. I. 76.[2]
— Introduzione allo studio dei vegetabili. 1785. I. 83.
— Miscellanea austriaca ad botanicam. 1778. I. 32.
— Observationes botanicae. 1778. I. 262.
— Observationum botanicarum . . . pars I.–IV. 1764. I. 262.
— Oxalis; monographia. 1794. II. 392.[2]
— Plantarum rariorum descriptiones. 1786. I. 328.
— Plantarum rariorum Horti caesarei schoenbrunnensis descriptiones et icones. 1797. I. 65.[2]
— Selectarum stirpium americanarum historia. 1763. I. 328.
— Sideroxylum. 1786. II. 700.[1]
— See also PLAFFART, J. F. & JACQUIN, N. J. Baron von.
Jacqumin, ((Ingénieur). Les traverses de chemins de fer. 1882. IV. 423.[2]
Jacquot, Charles. Les codes. 1861. IV. 324.
— Les codes de la législation forestière. 1861. IV. 324.
Jaczewski, Arthur de. Les formes du black-rot en Russie. 1899. III. 582.
— Eine neue Pilzkrankheit auf Caragana. .1900. III. 470.[1]
— Note sur le black rot du Caucase. 1900. III. 582.
— Über die Pilze, welche . . . " Black-Rot " verursachen. 1900. III. 582.
— Über eine Pilzerkrankung von Casuarina. 1900. III. 342.[1]
Jadart, Henri. Quelques vieux arbres de la contrée. 1900. I. 297.[2]
Jadin, F. The cultivation of gutta-percha. 1898. III. 149.
— La culture des Arbres à gutta-percha. 1898. III. 149.
Jadin, Fernand. Contribution à l'étude des Térébinthacées. 1894. II. 455.[1]
— Localisation de la myrosine. 1900. II. 234,[2] III. 409.[1]
— Observations sur quelques Térébinthacées. 1893. II. 454.[2]
— Recherches sur la structure . . . des Térébinthacées. 1894. II. 455.[1]
— Remarques sur les genres Dobinea et Podoon. 1893, II. 456.[1]
Jaeckle, H. Des produits de la torréfaction du café. ·1898· III. 741.[1]
Jäderholm, Elof. Ueber Salix Lapponum × repens. 1890. II. 107.[2]
— Om Salix Lapponum × repens. 1890. II. 107.[2]
Jäger. Die Anzucht von Holz zu Spazierstöcken. 1879. III. 127.[1]
— Beitrag zur Ausastungsfrage. 1857. IV. 170.
— Beobachtungen über den Ertrag des Hainbuchen-Hochwaldes. 1827. IV. 492.[1]
— Die Forstwirthschaft in Belgien. 1845. IV. 357.[1]
— Ueber das Verhalten der Lärche. 1868. IV. 449.
— Die Waldungen der freien Stadt Frankfurt am Main. 1845. IV. 352.
— Die Waldungen in der Grafschaft Berg. 1845. IV. 356.[2]
— Ueber Zuwachsmehrung. 1857. IV. 175.[2]
Jäger, (Forstamts-Assistent in Zwiefalten). Das Forstkultursystem . . . Biermanns. 1847. IV. 141.
— Über das Kulturverfahren . . . Biermanns. 1847. IV. 141.
Jäger, (Forstdirektor)· Die Eichen, deren Verhalten zum Boden. 1871. IV. 506.

— Ueber den Holzzuwachs. 1872. IV. 233.
— Zur Kritik der finanziellen Forstwissenschaft. 1873. IV. 256, V. xxxi.[1]
— Soll in den Hackwaldungen das Verbrennen der Bodendecke mittelst Schmodens . . . geschehen? 1851. IV. 142.
Jäger, (Revierförster). Beobachtungen bezüglich der Reproductionskraft der Nadelhölzer. 1855. I. 209.[2]
— Ob Forstmeister- oder Oberförstersystem? 1885. IV. 291.[2]
Jäger, Anton. Einige seltene Faserstoffe von Tiliaceen. 1892. III 584.[1]
Jaeger, B. P. Lectures sur l'histoire naturelle d'Haïti. 1830. I. 335.
Jäger, Christian Friedrich. De Cambogiae guttae succo. 1777. III. 668.[2]
— De corticis peruviani in phthisi pulmonali historia. 1779. III. 720.
Jaeger, E. Der einzelne Baum im Landschaftsgarten. 1882. I. 516.
Jäger, F. Abutilon Darwinii mit bunten Blättern. 1877. III. 586.[2]
Jäger, F. P. E. L. Der Hack- und Röderwald. 1835. IV. 133.
Jäger, Friedrich Wilhelm. Erläuterung einiger Hauptgesetze der Natur. 1847. I. 299.
Jäger, Georg von. Beobachtungen über rankende Gewächse. 1862. II. 650.[1]
— Ueber eine Eigenthümlichkeit mancher Gewächse, welche mit der Kugelform . . . zusammenzuhängen scheint. 1854. I. 106,[2] 244.[1]
— Ueber eine krankhafte Veränderung der Blüthenorgane der Weintraube. 1860. II. 508.[1]
— Über das Verhältniss der parasitischen Gewächse zu der Nährpflanze. 1856. II. 178.[2]
Jaeger, Georg Friedrich von. Ueber die Missbildungen der Gewächse. 1814. I. 143.
— De monstrosa folii Phoenicis dactyliferae conformatione. 1841. II. 73.[1]
— Observationes de quibusdam Pini silvestris monstris. 1828. II. 47.[1]
— Transformatio corollae Clematidis. 1829. II. 200.[1]
— Ueber die Wirkungen des Arseniks. 1864. I. 211.
Jäger, H. Beleuchtung der von . . . Helffrich zu Neuwied herausgegebenen Darstellung. 1807. IV. 100.[2]
Jäger, Heinrich. Die Caprification der Feigen in der grossen Cultur. 1883. III. 369.[2]
Jäger, Hermann. Ueber die Abschätzung. 1869. III. 200.[1]
— Ueber das ästhetische Verhältniss vom Stamm zur Krone. 1884. I. 516.
— Allgemeines illustriertes Gartenbuch. 1864. III. 104.
— Amygdalus pumila fl. alb. pl. 1855. III. 437.[1]
— Andeutungen über die Erlangung von Gehölzskenntnis. 1888. I. 78.[2]
— Ueber die Anzucht junger Ziergehölze. 1864. III. 153, 154.[1]
— Die Anzucht von Holz zu Spazierstöcken. 1879. IV. 428.[2]
— Aralia-Arten als Sommer-Freilandpflanzen. 1867. III. 641.[1]
— Die Arten der Gattung Forsythia. 1885. III. 671.[2]
— Aufmunterung zur . . . Anpflanzung von strauchartigem Buxus. 1887. III. 523.[1]
— Ueber die Aushauung vorhandener Holzungen. 1857. III. 202.[2]
— Die Baumschule. 1855. III. 154.[1]
— Behandlung mehrköpfiger Dracänen. 1874. III. 334.[1]
— Beitrag zur Cultur der Ilex. 1868. III. 522.[1]
— Beitrag zur Vermehrung der Gehölze durch krautartige Stecklinge. 1881. III. 158.
— Beitrag zur Vermehrung der Land-Azaleen. 1863. III. 656.
— Die Bekleidung trockener Abhänge. 1870. III. 42.[1]
— Bemerkung über das Verpflanzen sommergrüner Laubgehölze. 1888. III. 169.[1]
— Bemerkungen über den Zierwerth einiger Philadelphus. 1886. III. 413.[1]
— Bemerkungen über die . . . Verwendung der Rosen. ·1882. III. 450.
— Benützung und Werth des Akazienholzes. 1858. IV. 524.[1]
— Ueber die Benutzung des Epheu's. · 1862. III. 642.[2]
— Beobachtungen über den Einfluss der Kälte. 1858. III. 50.[1]
— Beobachtungen über den Einfluss der Kälte auf bereits getriebene und blühende Gehölze. 1874. III. 45.

Jäger, Hermann (*continued*).
— Beobachtungen . . . über die Färbung des Holzes der Blut-
buche. 1873. II. 127.²
— Beobachtungen über Missbildungen. 1849. I. 143.
— Beobachtungen über Winterschutz der Coniferen. 1876.
III. 183.¹
— Ueber das Beschneiden der Gehölze. 1863. III. 172.
— Das Beschneiden der laubabwerfenden Gehölze. 1886.
III. 171.
— Ueber das Beschneiden der Zweige und Wurzeln. 1866.
III. 170.
— Die Boden- und Düngerkunde. 1860. III. 37.¹
— Die Boden- und Düngerkunde für Gartenbau. 1876. III.
151.
— Burchellia capensis R. Br. 1881. III. 711.²
— Chamaecyparis nutkaensis Spach. 1882. III. 301.¹
— Ueber den Charakter . . . der Pflanzungen. 1856. I. 516.
— Clematis Vitalba im Landschaftsgarten. 1887. III. 392.¹
— Coniferen-Schutz gegen Hochwild. 1877. III. 198.²
— Cultur des Jasminum nudiflorum und fruticans. 1860.
III. 672.²
— Cultur und Verwendung der rankenden Lonicera. 1865.
III. 749.²
— Cultur verschiedener Blüthensträucher in Pyramidenform.
1868. III. 204.¹
— Deutsche Bäume und Wälder. 1877. I. 371, *III. 69, IV.
83.*
— Deutsche Riesenbäume. 1851. II. 24.¹
— Die Doppel- und mehrstämmigen Parkbäume. 1869. III.
201.
— Drei Rosen für Gartengebüsche. 1864. III. 449.
— Drei schöne Pflanzen mit hängenden Zweigen. 1857. III.
204.¹
— Eigenthümliche physiologische Erscheinung an Pyrus tor-
minalis. 1843. I. 107,¹ *II. 313.²*
— Einige schöne Rosen. 1883. III. 450.
— Ueber das Entstehen buntblättiger Zweige unter abgebro-
chenen Veredlungen. 1863. III. 39.
— Eine Entstehung von Bäumen mit hängenden Aesten in
Folge der Veredlung. 1864. I. 247.
— Epheulauben im Freien. 1881. III. 642.²
— Erfahrungen über das Gedeihen der Douglastanne. 1880.
IV. 483.¹
— Erfahrungen über die Rückwirkung des Edelreises auf den
Wildling. 1862. III. 39.
— Erythrina Humei. 1857. III. 476.¹
— Die Erziehung von Coniferen. 1870. III. 294.¹
— Erziehung von Spiraea ariaefolia. 1852. III. 460.¹
— Exochorda grandiflora. 1875. III. 424.¹
— Zur Färbung der Blutbuche. 1887. II. 127.²
— Fraxinus heterophylla. 1857. III. 672.²
— Die Frühlingshaide. 1878. III. 650.²
— Gartenkunst und Gärten. 1888. III. 757.¹
— Über das gegenwärtige Siechthum der Pappeln. 1884.
III. 346.²
— Sur la greffe des Cactées épiphytes. 1863. III. 619.
— Ueber Häng- oder Trauerbäume. 1857. III. 204.¹
— Hochstämme von Solanum Capsicastrum. 1867. III.
533,¹ *701.²*
— Der Holzgewinn aus dem Park. 1877. III. 120.¹
— Illustrirtes allgemeines Gartenbuch. 1864. III. 104.
— Immergrüne und halb-immergrüne Gehölze. 1867. III.
205.¹
— Influence de la greffe sur le sujet. 1862. III. 39.
— Jasminum officinale im Freien. 1855. III. 673.¹
— Katechismus der Nutzgärtnerei. 1852. III. 137.
— Katechismus der Rosenzucht. 1882. III. 450.
— Kleine Notizen über Palmensaaten. 1879. III. 317.
— Lagerstroemia indica. 1855. III. 629.²
— Zur Landcultur der Rhododendron. 1880. III. 656.
— Ueber Landesverschönerung. 1873. IV. 136.²
— Eine leichte Vermehrungsart von Azalea pontica. 1859.
III. 656.
— Liegende Gehölzstecklinge. 1868. III. 158.
— Melanoselinum decipiens. 1862. III. 644.²
— Merkwürdige Fichte. 1858. II. 37.¹
— Missbrauch . . . der Coniferen. 1872. III. 290.
— Ueber Misshandlung der Bäume und ihre Folgen. 1875.
III. 170.
— Mittheilungen über die Einwirkung des Winters von 1870–
71. 1871. III. 45.
— Mutterbäume der Trauereiche. 1876. III. 360,¹ *363.¹*
— Ueber die Nachtheile der Veränderung . . . wissenschaft-
licher Pflanzennamen. 1883. I. 254.¹

— Ein neuer Pyramidenbaum. 1874. III. 357.²
— Neuer Veredlungsverband. 1880. III. 162.
— Noch einmal über das Absterben der Pappeln. 1884. III.
46.²
— Nogle Bemaerkninger om Blodbøgen. 1857. II. 127.²
— Die nordamerikanische Moosbeere und ihre Cultur. 1870.
III. 663.²
— Nutzen der Tamarix-Arten zum Abschneiden. 1862. III.
12.¹
— Nutzen des Rindeneinschneidens. 1876. III. 175.¹
— Die Nutzholzpflanzungen. 1877. III. 120,² *IV. 118.*
— Der Obstbau. 1856. III. 137.
— Der Obstbaumschnitt. 1855. III. 137.
— Origine et coloration du Hêtre pourpre. 1857. II. 127.²
— Overvintring af zartere Buske. 1855. III. 183.¹
— Pflanzen, welche . . . frostfrei eingeschlagen durchwintert
werden können. 1860. III. 183.¹
— Ueber die Pflanzung grosser Bäume. 1855. III. 167.
— Ueber das Pfropfen epiphytischer Cacteen. 1863. III.
619.
— Sur la plantation des grands arbres. 1855. III. 167.
— Praktische Andeutungen über Aushauungen. 1880. III.
202.²
— Die Pyramidenbäume. 1862. III. 204.¹
— Ueber Sämlingspflanzen von Thuja Warreana. 1882. II.
52.²
— Die Schädlichkeit der Silberpappel im Garten. 1860. III.
345.¹
— Die schönsten Pflanzen des Blumen- und Landschafts-
gartens. 1873. III. 75.¹
— Ueber die zu städtischen Promenaden in Mitteleuropa am
meisten geeigneten Gehölze. 1883. III. 209.
— Die Stammbäume der Trauerbuche. 1857. III. 360,² *362.²*
— Stammbildung aus Aesten bei Fichten und Tannen. 1884.
II. 18.
— Ueber den Standort . . . der . . . Rhododendron. 1861.
III. 656.
— Stecklingspflanzen von . . . Cupressus funebris. 1882. II.
29.²
— Ueber die Theorie der Uebereinstimmung zwischen den
Blättern und der allgemeinen Form der Bäume. 1856. I.
106.²
— Theorie der Uebereinstimmungen zwischen den Blättern
und der allgemeinen Form der Bäume. 1856. I. 106.²
— Thujopsis borealis Fisch. 1877. III. 301.¹
— Das Treiben abgeschnittener Zweige. 1857. III. 176.¹
— Zur Ueberwinterung fremder immergrüner Gehölze. 1887.
III. 183.²
— Ueberwinterung zärtlicher Sträucher. 1855. III. 183.¹
— Die ungezwungen wachsenden Schlingpflanzen, 1878.
III. 204.²
— Ursprüngliches Vorkommen . . . der Blutbuche. 1857.
II. 127.²
— Ueber das Veredeln der Passifloren. 1843. III. 615.¹
— Veredlung von Weigelia rosea. 1854. III. 748.²
— Verhalten fremder Gehölze . . . bei spätem Frühlingsfrost.
1869. III. 45.
— Vermehrung von Agave geminiflora. 1855. III. 341.¹
— Vermehrung der Sträucher durch Sommerstecklinge. 1852.
III. 158.
— Vermehrung von Gymnocladus canadensis. 1863. II. 478.¹
— Ueber verschiedene Formen von Gehölzpflanzungen. 1856.
III. 201.
— Die Verwendung der Eucalyptus. 1870. III. 633.²
— Ueber die Verwendung der rankenden Lonicera. 1887.
III. 750.¹
— Verwendung von Evonymus radicans. 1868. III. 533,¹ *750.²*
— Verwendung . . . von Nadelwald. 1876. III. 290.
— Die Vorbereitungs- und Versandcultur der immergrünen
Gehölze in Körben. 1864. III. 155.
— Das Vorkeimen der Samen. 1849. III. 156.¹
— Wert . . . der amerikanischen Vitis-Arten im Ziergarten.
1887. III. 545.²
— Wirkung . . . des Niederbiegens von Stämmen. 1880.
III. 174.²
— Die Ziergehölze der Gärten und Parkanlagen. 1865. I.
293, *III. 69, IV. 83.*
— Zwei Ahornarten. 1886. III. 535,¹ *536.¹*
— & Beissner, Ludwig. Die Ziergehölze der Gärten und
Parkanlagen. 1865. I. 293.
Jäger, J. H. Beyträge zur Kenntniss . . . des Borkenkäfers.
1784. IV. 203, *454.*
— Wald-Raupen- und Borkenkäfer-Geschichte. 1798. IV.
206.

Jäger, Johann Philipp Ernst Ludwig. Anleitung zum Betrieb der Privat-Forstwirthschaft. 1848. IV. *106*, 117.
— Erträge der Lärche. 1854. IV. 452.¹
— Das Forstkulturwesen. 1850ˈ IV. 106.
— Die Land- und Forstwirthschaft des Odenwaldes. 1843. IV. 351.²
— Die Polygonometrie. 1860ˈ IV. 264.
Jäger, Louis. Beiträge zur Kenntniss der Endospermbildung . . . von Taxus. 1899. II. 10.²
Jäger, Ludwig. Über die Kosten der künstlichen Bestandesgründung. 1887. IV. 142.
— Vom Mittelwald zum Hochwald. 1889. ˈIV. 128ˈ.
— Das württembergische Gemeindewaldgesetz. 1884. IV. 322.²
— *See also* ELBEN, & JÄGER, Ludwig..
Jaeger, N. H. Kort Anviisning om Maaden, sikkerst at forplante Træer paa, saavel ved Sæden. 1778. III. 152.
Jäger, O. Notiz über die Structur des Endosperms von Coffea. 1881. II. 814.²
Jäger, W. Beitrag zur Literatur über die Einschätzung stehender Bäume und ganzer Bestände. 1853. IV. 216.
— Holzbestands-Regelung und Ertragsermittelung. 1854. IV. 240.
Jägerschmid, E. A. Erste Gründe der Forst-Wissenschaft. 1798. IV. 99,¹ *110*.¹
Jägerschmid, K. F. V. Handbuch für Holztransport- und Flosswesen. 1827. IV. 389.
— Das Murgthal. 1800. IV. 350.¹
— Tabellen zur Bestimmung des kubischen Inhalts der Baumstämme. 1809. IV. 221.
Jäggi, J. Karpologische Sammlung des Schweizerischen Polytechnikums. 1883. III. 513.¹
Jäggi, Jacob. Die Blutbuche zu Buch am Irchel. 1893. II. 127.¹
— Zur Geschichte der Blutbuche. 1892. II. 127.²
Jael, (*pseud.*). British Oaks. 1841. II. 129.¹
— The Manna Oak. 1841. II. 139.²
— The Poplar of the Scripture. 1849. II. 97.²
Jaennicke, Friedrich. Baumhöhenmesser. 1894. IV. 216.
— Ueber städtische Strassenpflanzung. 1899. II. 254.² *III. IV.*⁹
— Studien über die Gattung Platanus. 1892. II. 254.²
Jännicke, W. *See* BLUM, J. & JÄNNICKE, W.
Jännicke, Wilhelm. Ueber abnorm ausgebildete Rebenblätter. 1890. II. 507.³
— Beiträge zur vergleichenden Anatomie der Geraniaceae. 1886. II. 389.¹
— Bildungsabweichungen an Weigelien. 1891. II. 834.²
— Die Entdeckung Amerikas. 1893. I. 242.¹
— Die Gliederung der deutschen Flora. 1888. I. 389.
— Die Sandflora von Mainz. 1889. I. 389.
— *See also* ALTEN, H. & JÄNNICKE, Wilhelm.
Jänsch, Philipp. Leitfaden zum Holzanbau. 1843. IV. 103.²
Jaensch, Theodor. Zur Anatomie einiger Leguminosenhölzer. 1884. II. 320.²
— Über den inneren Bau . . . des Ambatsch. 1883. II. 330.¹
— Nachtrag zur Kenntniss von Herminiera. 1884. II. 330.²
Jäschke. Aufmass einiger starken Kiefern. 1856. IV. 480.
Jäthenstein, Matthias Kalina von. *See* KALINA VON JÄTHENSTEIN, Matthias.
Jafet. The old Seckel Pear. 1880ˈ II. 280.²
Jaffa, Myer Edward. Composition of the Ramie plant. 1891. III. 381.¹
— Composition . . . of the Salt-bushes. 1899. III. 387.²
Jaffa Orange. 1894. III. 501.² — 1896. III. 500.³
Jaffrey, Andrew T. On disease of the Nutmeg trees. 1860. III. 402.¹
— Memorandum on Cinchona pruning. 1873. III. 712.¹
Jagenberg, Ferd. Die Wald-Eisenbahn. 1891. IV. 392.
Jagor, A. Fedor. Reisen in den Philippinen. 1873. III. 127.²
— Singapore-Malacca, Java. 1866. III. 129.¹
Jagt, A. van der. Beschrijving der Kokos of Keelingeilanden. 1832. III. 274.¹
Jahn. Zu " Eine astlose Fichte." 1896. II. 35.²
Jahn, August Friedrich Wilhelm Ernst. Plantas circa Lipsiam nuper inventas describit. 1774. I. 373.
Jahn, Carl Ludwig. Die Holzgewächse des Friedrichshains bei Berlin. 1864. I. 48.
Jahn, Eduard. Holz und Mark an den Grenzen der Jahrestriebe. 1894. I. 126.
Jahn, Emil. Avogat-Birne und Guajava. 1900. III. 407,² *637*.²
— Die Mannigfaltigkeit unserer Acer. 1898. III. 534.¹
— Monochaetum ensiferum. ˈ1899. III.ˈ639.¹

Jahn, Fr., Lucas, Eduard, Oberdieck, J. G. C. Illustriertes Handbuch der Obstkunde. 1859. III. 71.
— — — Systematische Uebersicht der Obstsorten der ersten fünf Bd. 1859. III. 71.
Jahn, G. A. Berechnungstafeln für den Inhalt vierkantiger, walzen- und kegelförmiger Hölzer. 1843. IV. 223.
Jahne, Ludwig. Die chemische Zusammensetzung einiger Waldsamen. 1881. IV. 64.¹
Jahns, E. Sur les alcaloides de la noix d'Arec. 1889. III. 320.¹
— Les alcaloides de la noix d'Arec. 1891. III. 320.¹
— Ueber die Alkaloide der Arekanuss. 1891. III. 320.¹
— Présence de la stachydrine. 1896. III. 501.²
— Das Vorkommen von Stachydrin. 1896. III. 501.²
Jahr, Georg Heinrich Gottlieb. New homœopathic pharmacopœia. 1841. III. 245.
— Nouvelle pharmacopée. 1841. III. 245.
— Nouvelle pharmacopée homœopathique. 1841. III. 245.
Jahrbuch der K. sächs. Akademie für Forst- und Landwirthe zu Tharand. *See* FORSTWIRTHSCHAFTLICHES Jahrbuch. IV. 8.
Jahrbuch der praktischen Pharmacie. I. 12.
Jahrbuch der preussischen Forst- und Jagd-Gesetzgebung. IV. 9.
Jahrbuch der Staats- und Fondsgüter-Verwaltung. IV. 14.
Jahrbuch für Alp- und Forstwirthschaft. IV. 14.
Jahrbuch für das Berg- und Hüttenwesen . . . Sachsen. *See* KALENDER für den . . . Berg- und Hüttenmann. IV. 9.
Jahrbuch für den Berg- und Hüttenmann. *See* KALENDER für den . . . Berg- und Hüttenmann. IV. 9.
Jahrbuch für Gartenkunde. III. 12.
Jahrbuch für Gesetzgebung. IV. 9.
Jahrbuch für Pomologen. *See* TASCHENBUCH für Pomologen. III. 13.
Jahrbuch für praktische Pharmacie. *See* JAHRBUCH der praktischen Pharmacie. I. 12.
Jahrbuch und Personalstatus der königlich preussischen Forstverwaltung. *See* FORST- UND JAGDKALENDER für Preussen. IV. 7.
Jahrbücher der gesammten Forst- und Jagdwissenschaft. IV. 9.
Jahrbücher der Gewächskunde. I. 12.
Jahrbücher für Nationalökonomie. IV. 9.
Jahrbücher für Volks- und Landwirthschaft. *See* ÖKONOMISCHE GESELLSCHAFT IM KÖNIGREICHE SACHSEN. III. 13.
Jahrbücher für wissenschaftliche Botanik. I. 12.
Jahresbericht der forstlich-phänologischen Stationen Deutschlands. 1886. I. 225, IV. 9.
Jahresbericht der K. Forstakademie Eberswalde. ˈ1898. IV. 33.³
Jahresbericht der Pharmacie. *See* JAHRESBERICHT über die Fortschritte der gesammten Pharmacie. I. 12.
Aus dem Jahresbericht des Oberforstamtes des Kantons Zürich. 1864. IV. 366.
Jahresbericht über die Beobachtungs-Ergebnisse . . . Preussen. ˈIV. 9.
Jahresbericht über die Fortschritte der gesammten Pharmacie. I. 12.
Jahresbericht über die Fortschritte der Pharmacognosie. *See* JAHRESBERICHT über die Fortschritte der gesammten Pharmacie. I. 12.
Jahres-Bericht über die Leistungen . . . in der Forstwirtschaft. IV. 9.
Jahresbericht über die Neuerungen . . . auf dem Gebiete des Pflanzenschutzes. III. 12.
Jahres-Bericht zusammengestellt für ausübende Forstmänner. *See* JAHRES-BERICHT über die Leistungen . . . IV. 9.
Jahresbericht über die Fortschritte der Forstwissenschaft. IV. 9.
Jahresheft der böhmischen Forstschule zu Weisswasser. 1857. IV. 36.¹
Die Jahresringe der Pflanzen. 1878. IV. 64.²
Der Jahrring und seine Bedeutung. 1891. IV. 62.²
Jaikrishna Indraji. Sterculia urens as cattle fodder. 1900. III. 592.¹
Jaillard, P. Sur les noyaux de la nèfle du Japon. 1876. III. 423.²
— Observations sur le charbon végétal. 1877. I. 153. III. 155.
Jakimionek, K. Niepłodność drzew owocowych. 1898. IV. 9.
Jakob, N. Die Pflanzenkunde in Verbindung mit . . . Landwirthschaft. 1849. II. 37.²
Jakobsen, Jakob. Havebog for Bønder. 1809. III. 100.¹
Jamaica — Botanical department. ˈ *See* BOTANICAL . . . I. 7.²

Jamaica — Institute of. *See* INSTITUTE . . . III. 10.[1]
Jamaica Cogwood. 1889. III. 544.[1]
Jamaica India rubber. 1888. III. 688.[1] — 1889. III. 688.[1]
Jamaica Walnut. 1894. II. 112.[3]
Jamain, DUPUY-. *See* DUPUY-JAMAIN.
Jamain, Hippolyte & Forney, Eugène. Les Roses. 1873. III. 449.
Jamais, E. Forststatistisches aus Frankreich. 1889. IV. 361.
James, Davis L. *See* WARDER, J. A., & JAMES, D. L. & J. F.
James, E. P. Catalogue of plants . . . Rocky Mountains. 1825. I. 321.
James, Edmund Janes. The government in its relation to the forests. 1888. IV. 272.
James, George B. The preservation of the White Mountain forests. 1893. IV. 178.[2]
James, H. E. M. The Long White Mountain. 1888. II. 456.
James, Isabella. American forests. 1868. IV. 336.[2].
James, Ivor. Handbook for Cardiff. 1891. I. 534.[1]
James, J. Discours historique sur le Jardin . . . d'Amiens. 1858. I. 58.
James, John Wilham. Timber in the tropics; the Teredo. 1891. IV. 414.[3]
— *See also* WARDER, J. A., & JAMES, D. L. & J. F.
James, Robert. Part of a letter concerning some extraordinary effects of lightning. 1744. IV. 193.[1]
— Pharmacopoeia universalis. 1747. III. 252.
James, Thomas Potts. *See* DURAND, Elias, JAMES, T. P. & ASHMEAD, Samuel.
Jameson, Andrew. A method of constructing bee-hives of wood. 1821. IV. 428.[1]
Jameson, Robert. Notes on the natural history . . . of Cerigo. 1836. III. 479,[1] 675.[1]
Jameson, William. Botanic gardens . . . North-western provinces of India. 1855. I. 67.[1]
— Brief notes on the formation of plantations on the canal banks of the N. W. Provinces. 1876. III. 129,[2] IV. 124.[2]
— On the cultivation of Tea in India. 1864. III. 603.
— On the cultivation of Tea in the district of Kangra. 1854. III. 603.·
— Notice of the Tallow tree of China. 1863. III. 522.[1]
— Notice of the vegetation of Pichincha. 1856. I. 339.[2]
— On the physical aspect of the Punjab. 1853. I. 473.
— Remarks on the cultivation of cotton and Tea in India. 1863. III. 603.
— Report on the cultivation . . . of Tea in Kemaon. 1843. III. 602.[2]
— Report on the government Tea plantations in Kumaon. 1843. III. 602.[2]
— Report upon the present condition . . . of Tea cultivation in the North-west provinces. 1857. III. 603.
— Synopsis plantarum aequatoriensium. 1865. I. 330.
— The vegetable productions of the plains of Quito. 1856. I. 340.[1]
— & others. Papers on the Tea factories . . . in Kumaon. 1854. III. 603.
Jamie. Sur la récolte de la gomme-gutte. 1875. III. 609.[1]
Jamieson, James. A new point of resemblance in the respiration of plants and animals. 1879. I. 170.
Jamin. Note sur l'influence de la greffe sur les sujets. 1852. III. 39.
Jamin, Ferdinand. Les fruits à cultiver. 1868. III. 144.
— Du Mûrier noir au point de vue spécifique. 1866. III. 81.[1]
— Rapport sur un mode de traitement des arbres fruitiers. 1877. III. 144.
Jamin, J. Beschädigungen durch Eisanhang in Frankreich. 1879. IV. 190.·
Jamin, J. L. Culture et plantation des arbres fruitiers. 1856. III. 144.
Jamin, P. *See* COSSON, Ernest & JAMIN, P.

Jamin, Victor. Arundinaria Simoni Maximowiczii. 1893. II. 59.[1]
— Sur un Robinia Pseudacacia à floraison anormale. 1900. II. 383.[1]
Jampert, Christian Friedrich. Specimen physiologiae plantarum. 1755. I. 133.
Jamrich, Béla. A Coniferák szaporitása és mivelése. 1898. III. 293.
Jan, Giorgio. Catalogus in IV. sectiones divisus rerum naturalium in musaeo exstantium Josephi de Christofori et Georgii Jan. 1832. I. 63.
— Catalogus plantarum phaenogamarum. 1818. I. 425.
— Elenchus plantarum . . . in Horto ducali botanico parmensi. 1827. I. 62.
Janáček, Anton. Cossus ligniperda L. als Eschenverderber. 1896. IV. 534.[2]
Janczewski von Glinka, Edward, *Ritter*. Botanika systematyczna. 1895. I. 256.
— Czereśnia Jagiellonka. 1898. II. 273.[1]
— Dimorphisme de la Poire. 1898. II. 279.[2]
— Drwupostaciowość gruszek. 1899. II. 280.[1]
— Études comparées sur les tubes cribreux. 1880. I. 134.[1]
— Der Gartenbau in Galizien. 1899. III. 127.[1]
— Odwieczna Jabłoń. 1898. II. 267.[2]
— Sur la pluralité de l'espèce dans le Groseillier a grappes. 1900. II. 243.[2]
— Possukiwania nad powstawaniem korzonków u roślin ziarnowych. 1876. I. 103.
— Possukiwania nad warostem wierzchołkowym korzeni u roślin okrytoziarnowych. 1874. I. 188.
— O rurkach sitkowych u korzeniu roślin okrytoziarnowych. 1874. I. 133.
— Rurki sitkowe. Badania porównawcze. 1880. I. 134.[1]
— Das Spitzenwachsthum der Phanerogamenwurzeln. 1874. I. 103.
— Sur la structure des tubes cribreux. 1878. I. 133.
— Trzy metody hodowli drze owocowych. 1896. III. 147.[1]
— Zapiski pomologiczne. 1879. III. 135.
Jandebeur, S. J. Das Forstgesetz für das Königreich Bayern. 1852. IV. 318.
Jandel, Auguste. La botanique sans maîtres. 1865. I. 413.
Jandrell, R. Will it pay to plant arable land? 1879. IV. 134.[1]
Jandrier, Edm. Caractérisation chimique des fibres végétales. 1890. I. 154.
— Sur la miellée du Platane. 1893. II. 255.[2]
Janeček, Adolf. Der Betrieb und die Verwaltung der Brettsägen. 1886. IV. 393.
Janeczko, M. Die Durchforstung. 1899. IV. 175.[2]·
Janes, Thomas P. Handbook of the state of Georgia. 1876. IV. 397.
— List of woody plants of Georgia. 1876. I. 317,[1] IV. 77.[2]
Jangali Bulbul, (*pseud.*). Technical terms. 1877. IV. 23.[2]
Janitzki, I. *See* ЯНИЦКIЙ, I.
Janka, Gabriel. *See* HADEK, Anton & JANKA, Gabriel.
Janka, Lorenz. De strychneis. 1834. III. 682.[2]
Janka, Victor von. Adnotationes in plantas dacicas. 1860. I. 445.
— Genista Mayeri. 1859. II. 360.[2]
— Genisteae europaeae. 1884. II. 319.[1]
— Leguminoseae europaeae. 1885. II. 319.[1]
— Neue Synonyme zur Flora Europa's. 1866. II. 351.[1]
— Plantarum novarum turcicarum breviarium. 1872. I. 449.
— Syringa Josikaea Jacq. 1885. II. 715.[1]
Jankó, Johann. Abstammung der Platanen. 1890. II. 254.[2]
Jankowski, Edmund. Dobre rady co do sadów dla ziemian a głównie dla włościan. 1898. III. 120.[2]
— Krzew Winny. 1877. III. 551.[2]
— Ogród przy dworze wiejskim. 1888. III. 101.[1]
— Dla ogrodników. Podręcznik dla ogrodników. 1896. III. 101.[1]
— Ogrodnictwo przemysłowe. 1891. III. 101.[2]
— Ogrody na piasku. 1897. III. 41.[2]
— Sad i ogród owocowy. 1878. III. 68.[1]
— Sad przy chacie. 1883. III. 135.
— Wady naszych sadów. 1881. III. 135.
— Zużytkowanie nieużytków. 1885. IV. 167.[2]
Jankowsky, Rudolf. Ein neuer Forstschädling. 1894. IV. 208.[1]
Janmart, Hubert. Le Chicot du Canada. 1894. IV. 521.[2]
— Le tuteur. 1894. III. 199.

Jannack, J. G. Bemerkungen über die Verfahrungsweise . . . bei Aussaaten. 1841. III. 156.[1]
— Ueber Kultur. 1839. III. 626.[2]
— Ueber die Kultur der Gattung Erica. 1839. III. 649.[2]
Janorschke, O. Strassenbäume in Oberschlesien. 1900. III. 210.
— Ziergehölze für Rasenplätze. 1900. III. 203.
— **Pfeiffer**, Karl & **Rehder**, Alfred. Robinia Pseudacacia pyramidalis. 1898. III. 487.[1]
Janovský, František. Beschreibung der Exkursion . . . in die Wälder der kgl. Stadt Tabor. 1887. IV. 371.
— Popis exkurse . . . do lesû kral. města Tábora konané. 1887. IV. 372.
Janse, Jacobus Marinus. Over een aaltjes-ziekte in jonge Koffieplantjes. 1892. III. 736.
— Over eene aaltjes-ziekte in jonge Koffieplantjes, in Tabak en in andere planten. 1892. III. 736.
— Chlorose van cultuurplanten. 1890. III. 181.[1]
— De Dadapziekte van (Oost) Java. 1893. III. 476.[1]
— De la déhiscence du fruit du Muscadier. 1899. II. 220.[2]
— Druppelen. 1891. I. 169.[1]
— Les endophytes radicaux. 1897. I. 234.[1]
— Hoe voeden de planten zich met humus? 1893. I. 234.[1]
— Een kwaal der Koffiebladeren. 1891. III. 736.
— De medewerking der mergstralen aan de waterbeweging. 1885. I. 165.
— Die Mitwirkung der Markstrahlen bei der Wasserbewegung im Holze. 1887. I. 166.
— De Nootmuskaat-cultuur. 1898. III. 402.[2]
— Opstijgende en neerdalende sapstroom. 1891. I. 166.
— De stikstofvoeding van Koffie. 1897. II. 814.[2]
— De voeding der hoogere planten. 1899. I. 160.
— Voorloopig onderzoek van eene ziekte in Theeheesters. 1891. III. 604.[2]
Jansen, H. G. Rapport der beproeving van verschillende buitenlandsche houtsoorten. 1864. IV. 396.[1]
Jansen, R. Die Erziehung von Fichtenpflanzen im Kampe. 1887. IV. 454.
Janson, P. Une nouvelle race de Lilas. 1889. III. 680.[1]
Janssen, (*Landrat*). Die Korbweiden-Cultur . . . im Kreise Heinsberg. 1876. III. 348.
Janssen, Édouard. L'Oranger, ses variétés et sa culture. 1886. III. 500.[1]
— Végétaux d'ornements à feuilles persistantes. 1883. III. 203.[2]
Janssen, J. Fraxinus cultivation and manna production. 1880. III. 672.[1]
Januensis, SIMON. See SIMON JANUENSIS.
Jantisek, (*Förster*). Anbau des Götterbaumes. 1876. IV. 525.[1]
Janzé, de. Phylloxera et bureaucratie. 1887. III. 574.
Japan — Asiatic society. See ASIATIC . . . I. 28.[2]
Japan — College of agriculture, Imperial university. See COLLEGE . . . I. 28.[2]
Japan — College of science, Imperial university. See COLLEGE . . . I. 28.[2]
Japan — Department of agriculture and commerce — Forest bureau. Annual statistical report. IV. 539.[1]
Japan — Notes and queries. See NOTES . . . I. 28.[2]
Japan — Société d'horticulture. See NIHON engei kai zasshi. III. 26.[1]
The **Japan** Lacquer tree. 1889. III. 529.[1]
Japan Plum. 1885. III 443.[1]
The **Japan** society, London. Transactions. III. 17.
Japan varnish. 1861. III. 528.[2]
Japan wax. 1880. III. 526.[2]
Japan wax and varnish. 1900. III. 526.[2]
Japanese botany. 1858. I. 462.
Japanese camphor. 1893. III. 405.[1]
The **Japanese** camphor trade. 1893. III. 405.[1]
Japanese dwarfed trees. 1898. III. 176,[1] #91.
Japanese eccentricities. 1890. III. 176.[1]
Japanese edibles. 1876. III. 273.[2]
The **Japanese** Flowering Apple. 1889. III. 429.[1]
Japanese horticultural society. Journal. See NIHON engei kai zasshi. III. 26.[1]
Japanese Persimmons. 1885. III. 669.[2]
The **Japanese** Plum. 1874. III. 437.[1]
Japanese Tea. 1868. III. 601.[3]
Japanese vegetable wax. 1874. III. 526.[2] — 1875. III. 226.[1]
Japanese Vegetable wax tree. 1874. III. 528.[2]
A **Japanese** Willow tree. 1889. III. 175.[3]
Japanische Baumkünsteleien. 1899. III. 205.[1]
Japanische Gartenbau Gesellschaft. Zeitschrift. See NIHON engei kai zasshi. III. 26.[1]

Japanische Orangen. 1888. III. 497.[1]
Das **japanische** Pflanzenwachs. See JAPANESE vegetable wax. 1874. III. 526.[2]
Die **japanischen** Ahornarten. 1890. III. 534.[1]
Die **japanischen** Diospyros-Arten. 1888. III. 669.[1]
Die **japanischen** Kaki. 1891. III. 669.[2]
Die **japanischen** Zwerg-Koniferen. See JAPANESE dwarfed trees. 1898. III. 176,[1] #91.
Japansche kamferolie. 1885. III. 404.[2]
Japansche Thee. 1885. III. 601.[3]
Japing, (*Forstassessor*). Ueber natürliche Fichtenverjüngung. 1900. IV. 454.
Jaques, George. A practical treatise on the management of fruit trees. 1849. III. 133.
Jarchow, H. Nicholas. Forest fires and how to [prevent] . . . them. 1896. IV. 182.[1]
— Forest planting. 1893. IV. 103.[1]
— Forestry in the state of New York. 1888. IV. 339.
Jardin, Édelstan. Aperçu sur la flore du Gabon. 1890. I. 491.
— Le Caféier et le café. 1895. III. 727.
— Coup d'œil sur la végétation du Gabon. 1891. I. 491.
— Énumération de nouvelles plantes phanérogames. 1874. I. 270.
— Essai d'une flore de l'archipel des Marquises. 1857. I. 510.[2]
— Essai sur l'histoire naturelle de l'archipel de Mendana. 1857. I. 510.[2]
— Herborisations sur la côte occidentale d'Afrique. 1850. I. 490.
— Mémoire sur le Surtarbrandur d'Islande. 1867. IV. 343.[1]
— Le parc national de Yellowstone. 1887. IV. 340.
— Supplément au Zephyritis taitensis de M. Guillemin. 1860. I. 510.[2]
Jardin. III. 19.
Jardin botanique de Buitenzorg. Annales. I. 29.[1]
— Icones Bogorienses. See ICONES Bogorienses. I. 29.[1]
Jardin botanique de Genève. Catalogue des graines. 1826. I. 65.[1]
Le **jardin** botanique de Kew. 1899. III. 29.[1]
Jardin botanique de la ville de Grenoble. "Catalogue des graines récoltées . . ." 1847. I. 58.
— Graines. 1847. I. 58.
Jardin botanique de Lyon. See BONNET, G. 1859. I. 58.
Jardin . . . de Lyon. See BONNET, G. & FAIVRE, E. 1862. I. 58.
Le **jardin** de santé. See ORTUS sanitatis. I. 275.[2]
Jardin-des-plantes de la ville de Bordeaux. Catalogue. 1864. I. 58.
Le **Jardin** du Hamma. See RIVIÈRE, Auguste. 1872. I. 522.[1]
Le **jardin** du Ministère de l'agriculture. 1895. III. 29.[1]
Le **Jardin** fleuriste. 1772. III. 15.
Le **Jardin** senonois. See MONTSAINCT, Thomas. 1604. I. 56.
Le **jardinage**; encyclopédie populaire illustrée. 1898. III. 31.
Le **jardinage** en Amérique. Première traversée. 1898. IV. 131.
Jardine, William. Note regarding the hardiness of some woody plants. 1860. III. 46.[2]
Le jardin real botanicos, Trinidad. Boletin. See ROYAL BOTANIC GARDENS, TRINIDAD. 1888. I. 40.
Le **jardinier** françois. See BONNEFONS, Nicolas de. 1651. III. 111.
Le **jardinier** polonais. See OGRODNIK polski. III. 10.[1]
Jardinier portatif. 1769. III. 106.[2]
Le **jardinier** prévoyant. See DUCHESNE, A. 1772. III. 112.
Le **jardinier** royal. See GOBELIN, (*abbé*). 1661. III. 142.
Le **jardinier** solitaire. See GENTIL, François. 1704. III. 111.
Le **jardinier** suisse. 1787. III. 24.[1]
Les **jardins** néerlandais. 1859. I. 51.[2]
Jaroschka, H. Beitrag zur Kenntniss unserer Borkenkäfer. 1885. IV. 92.
— Xylechinus pilosus Chap. 1889. IV. 456.
Jarrah (Eucalyptus marginata) timber. 1884. IV. 533.[2]
The **Jarrah** of western Australia. 1885. IV. 533.[2]
Jarrah timber. 1890. IV. 533.[2]
The **Jarrah** wood. 1874. IV. 534.[1]
Jarry-Desloges, R. Notes sur les Bégonias ligneux. 1899. III. 618.[1]
Jaschke, Zur Betriebseinrichtung der kleinen Gemeinde-Wälder. 1898. IV. 246.
Jaschke, Robert. De rebus in arboribus inclusis. 1859. I. 210.[1]

Jaschnoff. See YASHNOF, L.
Jaschnow. See YASHNOF, L.
Jaskiewicz, Johann. Pharmaca regni vegetabilis. 1775. III. 257.[2]
De Jasmijn (Jasminium L.). 1853. III. 672.[2]
Jasmund, A. von. Durch Alter und Wuchs merkwürdige Bäume. 1863. II. 138.[1]
Jasmund, Agavia von. Die Verwertung . . . von Garten-, Feld- und Waldfrüchten. 1884. III. 174.[1]
Jastrzębowski, Wojciech. Klucz do ukladu przyrodzonego roślin. 1871. I. 349.
— Ogrodnictwo, podlug wykladu. 1876. III. 101.[1]
Jatta, G. & Savastano, L. L'Anomala Vitis Fabr. 1887. III. 564.[1]
Jaubert, A., *comte.* Sur les Euphorbiacées. 1866. II. 571.[1]
— L'hybridation d'un Chamaerops humilis par un Dattier. 1870. II. 67.[1]
— & Denis, A. Sur la fécondation du Chamoerops. 1867. II. 67.[1]
Jaubert, Hypolyte François, *comte* [de]. La botanique à l'Exposition universelle. 1875. II. 29.[1]
— Sur le dépérissement des arbres de nos promenades. 1857. III. 212.[1]
— Inventaire des cultures de Trianon. 1876. I. 59.
— Les jardins de Naples et l'Île d'Ischia. 1866. I. 63.
— Note sur l'Attalea funifera. 1861. III. 320.[2]
— & Spach, Eduard. Argyrolobia hemisphaerae septentrionalis. 1843. II. 333.[1]
— — Conspectus generis Nitraria. 1850. II. 395.[2]
— — Conspectus subgeneris Armeriastrum. 1843. II. 696.[1]
— — Illustrationes plantarum orientalium. 1842. I. 478.
— — Monographia generis Ebenus. 1843. II. 355.[2]
— — Monographia generis Halimodendron. 1842. II. 363.[2]
Jaubert, Jean Baptiste. Sur le mode d'emploi des sulfocarbonates. 1876. III. 568.
Jaubert de Passa, F. Mémoire sur la culture du Chêne-Liége. 1836. IV. 516.[2]
— Notice sur le Chêne-Liége. 1842. IV. 516.[2]
Jauffret, Louis François. Le panier de fruits. 1807. III. 84.[2]
— Voyage au Jardin des plantes. 1798. I. 56.
Jaume Saint-Hilaire, Jean Henri. Exposition des familles naturelles. 1805. I. 259.
— La flore et la pomone françaises. 1828. *I. 408,* III. 84.[2]
— Flore parisienne. 1835. I. 409.
— Mémoire contenant les expériences . . . sur la croissance des arbres. 1841. I. 187.
— Mémoire sur l'administration . . . des forêts. 1814. IV. 292.
— Mémoire sur la culture du Poivrier noir. 1827. III. 343.[1]
— Mémoire sur le domaine forestier de Rambouillet. 1832. IV. 47.[1]
— Mémoire sur le Thyou ou Thya. See SAINT-HILAIRE, Jaume. 1842. I. 514.[1]
— Mémoire sur les bonnes espèces d'arbres à fruits. See SAINT-HILAIRE, Jaume. 1832. I. 247.
— Mémoire sur les genres Hedysarum et Aeschinomene. 1813. II. 318.[1]
— Mémoire sur les indigofères. 1816. III. 236.
— Mémoire sur une composition chimique, funeste aux vers blancs. See SAINT-HILAIRE, Jaume. 1836. III. 197.
— Observations sur un rapport . . . relatif aux espèces d'arbres exotiques. 1830. IV. 126.[2]
— Plantes de la France. 1805. I. 406.
— Du Poirier et de la grosseur de ses fruits. 1832. III. 445.[1]
— Recueil de mémoires sur l'administration des forêts. 1814. IV. 292.
— Traité des arbres forestiers. 1824. I. 404,[2] *IV. 85.*[1]
— Traité des arbrisseaux et des arbustes. 1825. I. 293, *III. 83,[1] IV. 85.*[1]
Jaussan. Le phylloxera. 1880. III. 572.
Jaussan, Louis. De l'emploi rationnel du sulfure de carbone. 1879. III. 760.
Java-teak. 1894. IV. 538.[1]
Java thee voor Siberie. 1900. III. 608.[1]
Java's Kinacultuur. 1897. III. 717.[1]
Java's Kina-cultuur en Kinine-fabrikatie. 1899. III. 717.[1]
Javillier, M. Note sur l'huile de Croton. 1898. III. 517.[2]
— Sur la pectine du Coing. 1899. III. 423.[2]
Jawein, L. Sur la substance cristallisée du "kamala." 1887. III. 520.[2]
Jean, Ferdinand. See BOUROT & JEAN, Ferdinand.
Jean-Louis, V. D. Documents pour la flore indigène d'Haïti. 1899. I. 337.

Jeanbernat, Ernest. See BAILLET, C., JEANBERNAT, Ernest & TIMBAL-LAGRAVE, Édouard; FILHOL, Édouard, JEANBERNAT, Ernest & TIMBAL-LAGRAVE, Édouard; TIMBAL-LAGRAVE, Édouard & JEANBERNAT, Ernest.
— & Timbal-Lagrave, Édouard. Le Capsir, canton de Montlouis. 1887. I. 417.
— — Le massif du Laurenti. 1879. I. 415.
— — Quelques jours d'herborisation dans les Albères orientales. 1879. I. 415.
Jeanjean, Adrien. Le Châtaignier. 189.? III. 359.[1]
Jeanjean, Al. Note sur une trombe. 1874. III. 184.[1]
Jeannel. See GRASSET & JEANNEL.
Jeannel, J. Le climat du littoral d'après sa végétation. 1890. III. 126.[1]
— Du déboisement. 1891. IV. 45.
— Le déboisement et l'hygiène publique. 1893. IV. 55.[1]
— La dépopulation dans les régions déboisées. 1894. IV. 541.
— Influence des forêts sur la . . . pluie. 1892. IV. 51.
— Note relative à l'influence des racines . . . sur la putrefaction. 1875. I. 234.[2]
— Note sur les jardins du littoral des Alpes-Maritimes. 1881. I. 59.
— Des plantations d'arbres dans l'intérieur des villes. 1872. III. 34.[3]
Jeanpert, Édouard Henri. See CAMUS, G. E. & JEANPERT, E. H.
Jechl, Frans. Ueber die Tilia cucullata Jacq. 1857. II. 517.[2]
Jedlička, Jan. Azalea indica a jeji odrůdy. 1886. III. 660.[1]
— Azalea indica . . . zum Treiben. 1886. III. 660.[1]
— Rhododendron javanicum . . . nebst ihren Hybriden. 1887. III. 655.
— Rhododendron javanicum . . . s jejich mšenci. 1887. III. 655.
Jedlicska, Ferenc. Az Abutilon-félék. 1899. III. 586.[2]
Jedlovský. O pamětihodných stromech. 1878. II. 98.[1]
— Podivně rostlé stromoví. 1805. II. 37.[2]
— O Vrbách. 1878. III. 348.
Jeffrey, John & Howie, Charles. The trees and shrubs of Fife. 1879. I. 297.[1]
Jeffreys, Henry. Practical observations on the use of the 'cubebs. 1821; III. 342.[2]
Jeffreys, Thomas. Du Matico comme hémostatique. 1844. III. 342.[1]
— Remarks on the efficacy of Matico. 1844. III. 342.[1]
Jeffrey's Pine. 1891. II. 42.[1]
Jehan. 'La sciure de bois. 1897. IV. 558.[1]
Jeitter, Johann Melchior. Anleitung zur Taxation. 1794. IV. 239.
— Aufmunterung zum Anbau . . . der Saalweide. 1798. IV. 488.[1]
— Entwurf einer systematischen Belehrung in der . . . Forst- und Jagdkunde. 1830. IV. 97.
— Examinations-Fragen aus der Forst-Wissenschaft. 1820. IV. 101.
— Examinationsfragen zur Selbstprüfung für Forstkandidaten. 1821. IV. 31.
— Die forst- und landwirthschaftliche Wasserbaukunde. 1832. IV. 266.[1]
— Forstlesechsinus. 1805. IV. 96.
— Systematisches Handbuch der . . . Forstwirthschaft. 1789. .IV. 95.
— Versuch einer Knospeplehre. 1825. I. 107.[2]
— Versuch eines Handbuchs der Forstwissenschaft. 1820. IV. 97.
Jekyll, Gertrude. Wood and garden. 1899. III. 124.[1]
Jeleznoff, N. De foetu vegetabili. 1842. I. 121.
Jelinek, A. Ueber die Veredlung . . . der Coniferen. 1882. III. 294.[1]
— Vermehrung der Eriken. 1882. III. 650.[1]
Jelinek, J. W. Die Reform der Obstbaumzucht. 1873. III. 146.[2]
— Reforma sadownictwa. 1873. III. 146.[2]
Jelliffe, Smith Ely. See RUSBY, H. H. & JELLIFFE, S. E.
Jelstrup, Henrik. Om hvorvidt skovkulturer. 1899. IV. 134.[2]
Jena-Cöthen, von. See RAMANN, Emil & JENA-CÖTHEN, von.
Jena — Geographische Gesellschaft. See GEOGRAPHISCHE . . . I. 12.
Jenaische Gesellschaft für Medicin und Naturwissenschaft. Sitzungsberichte. I. 12.
Jenaische Zeitschrift für Medicin und Naturwissenschaft. I. 12.

Jenaische Zeitschrift für Naturwissenschaft. *See* JENAISCHE Zeitschrift für Medicin . . . I. 12.

Jenčič, A. Untersuchungen des Pollens hybrider Pflanzen. 1900. I. 246.[1]

Jenkins, E. H. & Britton, W. E. The protection of shade trees. 1900. III. 212.[1]

Jenkins, Francis. Hints for the management of the Grape vine. 1844. III. 559.[1]

Jenkins, S. E. F. On the manufacture of tannin extracts in Burma. 1899. IV. 435.

Jenkins, Samuel. The Yew tree in Munsley churchyard. 1882. II. 11.[1]

Jenkinson, H. I. Practical guide to North Wales. 1878. I. 403.

Jenkinson, James. A generic and specific description of British plants. 1775. I. 395.

Jenks, Edward W. Viburnum prunifolium. 1877. III. 753.[2]

Jenman, George Samuel. Balata and the Balata industry. 1885. *I. 339,*[2] III. 668.[1]

— British Guiana. 1888. III. 268.[1]

— Collecting rubber. 1899. III. 149.

— Hevea Spruceana. 1883. III. 519.[1]

— The india-rubber . . . trees of British Guiana. 1883. III. 229.

— A journey in search of " Hevea Spruceana." 1882. III. 229.

— Pithecolobium saman. .1879. III. 484.[2]

— Pithecolobium Samman. 1899. III. 484.[2]

— The primæval forests of British Guiana. 1887. I. 339.[2]

— Remarks on the aspect and flora of the Kaieteur Savannah. 1882. I. 339.[2]

— Report on Macwarrieballi. 1888. III. 688.[1]

— Report . . . on some of the india-rubber . . . trees of British Guiana. 1883. III. 229, *231.*

— Report on the fruit resources of British Guiana. 1888. III. 268.[1]

Jenner, Edward. A flora of Tunbridge Wells. 1845. I. 390.

Jenney, Walter P. The mineral wealth . . . and natural resources of the Black Hills of Dakota. 1876. IV. 397.

Jenni-Tschudi. Ueber Waldkultur. 1870. IV. 123.[1]

Jennings, Samuel. Rhea. 1886. III. 382.[1]

Jennings, Walter L. *See* HILL, H. B. & JENNINGS, W. L.

Jenny, Karl. Untersuchungen über die Festigkeit der Hölzer. 1873. IV. 410.

Jensch, F. *See* IEHШЪ, Ф.

Jensen, C. C. Ny-Hollandske Planter. 1895. III. 67.[1]

Jensen, Chr. Kennedya Marryattæ. 1892. III. 480.[1]

Jensen, Christian. Det 200 aarige ægte Kastanjetræe. 1899. II. 125.[1]

Jensen, F. J. C. Dansk Havebog. 1876. III. 100.[2]

— Forsøg til en grundig Veiledning i Frugt- og Kjøkkenhave-Dyrkning. 1845. III. 100.[2]

Jensen, H. H. C. Om Beplantningen af Jyllands Heder. 1861. IV. 156.[1]

Jensen, H. O. Om garvestofmængder i norske barksorter. 1900. I. 184, *IV. 495.*[1]

Jensen, J. L. Berberissens og Kornets Rust. 1885. III. 394.[1]

Jensen, James. Eleagnus as garden plants. 1900. III. 628.[2]

— Transplanting trees during mid-winter. 1898. III. 168.[1]

Jensen, M. Hyldetræet. 1891. III. 752.[2]

Jensen, N. Nogle Meddelelser om Frøstens Indflydelse paa Træer og Buske i Langenøss. 1841. III. 44.[2]

Jensen, J. Daddelpalmen. 1890. III. 329.[1]

Jenssen-Tusch, F. G. von. Die Rolle der Wälder in der Pflanzennatur. 18 . . ? IV. 42.[2]

Jenssen-Tusch, Harald Christian Ludwig von. Navnefortegnelse. 1867. I. 73.[1]

— Nordiske Plantenavne. 1867. I. 73.[1]

Jenssen-Tusch, S. Anbau von Pinus uncinata. 1886. IV. 156.[2]

Jentink. Houtsoorten van Borneo. 1893. IV. 400.[1]

— Houtsoorten van Borneo: lijst van uit de Boven Doeson. 1893. IV. 400.[1]

Jentsch, Frits. Die Arbeiterverhältnisse in der Forstwirthschaft. 1881. IV. 310.[1] — 1882. IV. 310.[2]

— Ueber Bildung von Waldarbeiter-Verbänden. 1881. IV. 310.[2]

— Der deutsche Eichenschälwald. 1899. IV. 509.

— Der Eichenschälwald in den Niederlanden. 1900. IV. 509.

— Der Einfluss der Bodenrente auf die Vertheilung des Bodens. 1890. IV. 270.

— Der Wald und die Staatswirthschaft. 1892. IV. 270.

Jentys, Stef. De l'influence de l'oxygène . . . sur l'accroissement. 1888. I. 187.

— Sur les obstacles à la découverte de la diastase. 1893. I. 177.

Jentzsch, Alfred. Über eine bemerkenswerte Holzstruktur. 1897. I. 242.[2]

— Der Frühlingseinzug des Jahres 1893. 1895. I. 226.[1]

— Nachweis der beachtenswerten . . . Bäume, Sträucher . . . Ostpreussen. 1900. I. 296.[2]

Jenyns, Leonard. On the Bath flora. 1867. I. 402.

Jephson, George. *See* WHITLEY, George, JEPHSON, George & HUNTER, Alexander.

Jepson, Willis Linn. Carpenteria californica. 1897. II. 238.[1]

— The mountain region of Clear Lake. 1893. II. 660.[2]

— Teratological notes. 1894. II. 229.[1]

— On a variety of the western Sumach. 1893. II. 460.[1]

— Vegetation of the summit of Mt. St. Helena. 1899. I. 327.

Jerzykiewicz, Boleslaw. Botanik für die unteren und mittleren Klassen. 1874. I. 91.

— Botanika. 1874. I. 91.

Jespersen, H. K. Om Skovtvang og Skovfrihed. 1863. IV. 273.[1]

Jespersen, J. F. W. Foresatte Studier over Bøgebevoxningernes Pleie. 1890. IV. 495.

— Orienterende Uddrag af Studier over Bøgens Bestandspleje. 1888. IV. 495.

— Om Skovreguleringens Betydning. 1889. IV. 245.

— Studier over Bøgens Bestandspleje. 1890. IV. 495.

Jessen, C. Over het telen van vruchten zonder steenen. 1868. III. 50.[2]

Jessen, Karl Friedrich Wilhelm. Botanik der Gegenwart und Vorzeit. 1865. I. 79.[1]

— Deutsche Excursions-Flora. 1879. I. 387.

— Über die Lebensdauer der Gewächse. 1855. I. 193.[1]

— *See also* PRITZEL, G. & JESSEN, C.

Jessen, N. J. Om Hedeskovdyrkningen i Jylland. 1866. IV. 156.[1]

Jessen, W. & Schmidt, Otto. Feldmessen und Nivelliren. 1879. IV. 265.

Jessenius a Jessen, Johann. De plantis disputatio prior. 1601. I. 30.

Jessop, John. On Lonicera Xylosteum, an addition to the Irish flora. 1857. I. 840.[1]

Jester, Friedrich Ernst. Anleitung zur Kenntniss . . . der Nutzhölzer. 1815. IV. 82, *831.*

Jesup, Henry Griswold. A catalogue of the flowering plants . . . of Hanover. 1891. I. 316.

The Jesup collection of the woods of the United States. 1890. I. 38,[1] *IV. 18.*[1]

Jettmar, J. Düngerlehre des Gärtners. 1891. III. 151.

Das jetzige Gewand der Walderhaltungs-Frage. 1883. IV. 371.

Ueber den jetzigen Stand der Phylloxerafrage. 1879. III. 760.

Jewell, H. W. A pink-flowered form of Rubus triflorus. 1900. II. 310.[2]

Jewitt, Llewellynn. Sherwood forest. 1882. I. 297,[1] *IV. 558.*[1]

Jgr. Ueber die geognostischen . . . Verhältnisse der . . . Frankfurter Stadtwaldungen. 1871. IV. 254.

The Jhand tree (Prosopis spicigera). 1884. II. 379.[2]

Jhering, Hermann. *See* IHERING, H.

Jicamilla. 1898. III. 519.[1]

Jimbo, Kotora & Miyabe, Kingo. Ainu names of Hokkaido plants. 1892. I. 75.[1]

Jimenez, J. B. Sericultura. 1891. III. 378.

Jimenez, José María FERNANDEZ Y. *See* FERNANDEZ Y JIMENEZ, J. M.

Jiménez, Luis. La sierra de las cuatro villas. 1900. IV. 556.[1]

Jiménez, Manuel C. El arbol del Perú. 1873. III. 529.[1]

Jinunia Yokusai. Hong-dso-dzu-rok. 1856. I. 462.

Jirasek, Frans Anton. Beiträge zu einer botanischen Provincial-Nomenclatur. 1806. I. 75.[1]

Jirasek, Johann. Beobachtungen auf Reisen nach dem Riesengebirge. *See* HAENKE, Thaddaeus. 1791. I. 374.

— & Haenke, Thaddaeus. Mineralogische und botanische Bemerkungen auf einer Reise nach dem Riesengebirge. 1788. I. 374.

Joachim, Hans. Verhalten von Fichte und Eiche. 1899. IV. 138.[2]

Joannon, A. Sur un nouveau procédé de dessalement. 1875. IV. 162.

Joannon, Antonin. De l'origine de quelques noms botaniques. 1876. II. 457.²
Jobart, F. See CROLAS & JOBART, F.
Jobert, C. Sur l'action physiologique des strychnées. 1879. III. 683.²
— Falsifications du Maté. 1879. II. 464.¹
— Sur une maladie du Caféier. 1878. III. 735.
— Sur la préparation du curare. 1878. III. 683.²
Jobez, H. Le compas enregistreur. 1896. IV. 232.
— See also BLONAY, H. de, BIOLLEY, H. & JOBEZ, H.
Jobst, Julius. L'écorce de Coto et la cotoine. 1876. III. 407.¹
— Ueber die neueste Importation javanischer Chinarinden. 1872. III. 724.²
— Sur les Quinquinas de Java. 1874. III. 718.
— & Hesse, Oswald. Ueber die Bohne von Calabar. 1864. III. 483.²
— — Dita bark. 1875. III. 686.²
— — Ueber die Ditarinde. 1875. III. 686.²
— — Sur l'écorce de Dita. 1875. III. 686.²
— — Ueber ei ige Bestandtheile der Cotorinden. 1877. III. 407.¹
— — Sur la fève de Calabar. 1864. III. 483.²
— — Sur quelques principes de l'écorce de Coto. 1877. III. 407.¹
Jobst, W. K. Beschreibung der Stat Frankfurt an der Oder. See BECKMANN, J. C. 1676.- I. 372.
Jochim. Auszug aus dem Schreiben ... Empfehlung der Erle. 1828. III. 356.²
Jochims, P. Forstwissenschaftliche Aphorismen. 1835. IV. 352.
Jockin. Bajang-hout (Mak.) Intsia amboinensis. 1893. IV. 521.²
Jodelite. 1893. IV. 421.
Jodin, F. Victor. Action chimique de la lumière. 1864. I. 172.
— Action chimique de la lumière. 1865. I. 230
— Action des vapeurs mercurielles sur les feuilles. 1886. I. 211.
— Culture de plantes dans des dissolutions de matières organiques. 1883. I. 229.
— Études sur l'asphyxie des feuilles. 1865. I. 211.
— Études sur la chlorophylle. 1886. I. 142..
— Recherches sur la germination. 1897. I. 204.
— Recherches sur la glycogénèse. 1877. I. 176.
— Sur la resistance des graines aux températures élevées. 1899. I. 527.
Jodin, Henri. Structure ... de la tige des Borraginées. 1896. II. 748.¹
Jöckel, Ad. Zierbäume und Ziersträucher der Anlagen Dürkheims. 1892. I. 49.
Joelson. See IOEЛЬCOHЬ.
Jönckers, Johann. De usu medico camphorae. See GERIKE, Peter. 1748. III. 404.²
Jöndl, Johann Philipp. Ueber Park-Anlagen und Verschönerung. 1850. I. 147.
Jönsson, Bengt. Bidrag till kännedomen om bladets anatomiska byggnad hos Proteaceerna. 1878. II. 158.²
— Om brännfläckar på växtblad. 1891. III. 184.¹
— Inre blödning hos växten. 1892. I. 169.¹
— Normal förekomst af masurbildning hos slägtet Eucalyptus. 1883. II. 623.²
— Positivt heliotropiska luftrotsfasciationer. 1889. I. 195.¹
— Siebähnliche Poren in den trachealen Xylemelementen. 1892. I. 126.
— Ytterligare bidrag till kännedomen om angiospermernas embryosäcksutveckling. 1881. I. 122.
Jønsson, Helgi. Floraen paa Snæfellsnæs og Omegn. 1899. I. 358.
— Optegnelser fra Vaar- og Vinterexkursioner i Øst-Island. 1895. I. 220.¹
— Studier over Øst-Islands Vegetation. 1895. I. 358.
— Vaar- og Høst-Exkursioner i Island. 1895. I. 358.
— Vegetationen paa Snæfellsnæs. 1900. I. 358.
Jörchel. Uebersicht über den Beitritt von ... Forstbeamten zu dem Sterbekassen-Verein. 1859. IV. 310.²
Jördens, Johann Heinrich. Geschichte der kleinen Fichtenraupe. 1798. IV. 200, 455.
Jörgensen, Alfred. Sympodiale Entwickelung der Wurzel-Achse. 1880. I. 103.
Jørgensen, Eugen. Om floraen i Nord-Reisen. 1894. V. XIX.¹
Jörlin, Engelbert. Partes fructificationis. 1771. I. 69.¹
— Plantae tinctoriae. See LINNÉ, Carl von. 1759- III. 235.³

— Principia botanices illustrata. 1771. I, 69.³
— Specimen ... de usu quarundam plantarum indigenarum. 1769. III. 270.¹
Jösting, H. Die Bedeutung, Verwüstung ... des Waldes. 1896. IV. 72.
— Der Wald, seine Bedeutung, Verwüstung. 1896. IV. 72.
Joffrey, Edmond DAVALL DE. See DAVALL DE JOFFREY, Edmond.
Joffroy. Les terrains argilo-calcaires et le phylloxera. 1877. III. 570.²
Joffroy, H. L'hiver de 1709. 1881. III. 48.
Jogeswar Sur. Notes on Nageswar in the Garo hills. 1883. IV. 528.²
Johanet, Henri & La Briselainne, Ameline de. Recueil annoté des lois ... relatifs à l'agriculture, la viticulture, la sylviculture. 1880. IV. 324.
Johann, Erzherzog von Oestreich. Icones plantarum austriacarum. 1807. I. 439.
Johannsen, R. Allerunderdanigst Klage fra Brændehandler. 1872. IV. 404.¹
— Et Par Ord til Oplysning om hvor man bliver bonnet og paalidelig behandlet. 1873. IV. 404.¹
Johannsen, W. Das Ätherverfahren beim Frühtreiben. 1900. III. 680.²
— Om Amygdalinets og Emulsinets Plads i Mandlerne. 1887. III. 434.²
— Bemærkninger om de hidtil vundne Resultater af Æteriseringsforsøgene. 1897. III. 177.
— Sur la localisation de l'émulsine dans les Amandes. 1887. III. 434.²
— Om Muligheden af at forkorte Planternes Hvileperioder. 1894. I. 191,¹ III. 176.³
— Studier over Planternes periodiske Livsytringer. 1897. I. 178.
Den **Johannsenske** Drivmetode. 1896. III. 176.¹
Johannson, Gustav. Beiträge zur Pharmacognosie einiger ... Rinden. 1891. III. 260.¹
Johanson, Edwin. Beiträge zur Chemie der Eichen-, Weiden-, und Ulmenrinde. 1875. I. 155.
— Bestimmung der Alkaloïde in den Chinarinden. 1879. III. 723.
— Zur chemischen Kenntnis der Fruchtentwicklung von Pirus salicifolia. 1892. II. 281.¹
— Oleum betulae. 1882. IV. 491.¹
— Sur la richesse des baies du Sorbus Aucuparia en acide malique. 1882. II. 312.¹
— Untersuchung über Weidengallen. 1882. II. 104.¹
Johansson, Johannes. De nutritione plantarum. See THUNBERG, C. P. 1819. I. 157.
Johansson, Karl. Hufvuddragen af Gotlands växttopografi. 1897. I. 358.
Johikawa, J. Sur les matières employées au Japon dans le tannage. 1881. III. 237.²
John. On the milky juice, etc. 1815. I. 181.²
— Milky juice of plants. 1815. I. 181.²
John. See FERGUSON, A. M. & JOHN.
John, C. K. Der Raupen- und Insekten-Vertilger. 1831. IV. 199.¹
John, Johann Friedrich. Chemische Tabellen der Pflanzenanalysen. 1814. I. 152.¹
— Dr. John on potash its vegetables. 1817. I. 525.²
— Ueber die Ernährung der Pflanzen. 1819. I. 157.
— Over den oorsprong van de potasch. 1817. I. 152,¹ 525.²
— Recherches sur le tannin ... du Pin. 1806. II. 40.¹
— Welke is de oorsprong der potasch. 1817. I. 152.¹
John, Johann Wilhelm. Versuch mit dem Quassienhols. 1778. III. 568.¹
John, Joseph. Die Schlangenfichte. 1853. IV. 460.¹
John, Karl. Der Raupen- und Insekten-Vertilger. 1831. IV. 206.
John, Václav. Smrk svislý, křivolaký. 1893. II. 35.³
Johnen, Adolf. Allgemeine Beschreibung der Herrschaft Wsetin. 1889. IV. 369.
— Bericht über den ersten forstliche Studien-Reiss. 1881. IV. 349.¹
— Die Cultur der Korbweide in Wsetin. 1884. III. 348.
— Der Lückenhieb. 1884. IV. 137.³
— Niederschlagsmenge und Verdunstung. 1876. IV. 50.
Johns, Charles Alexander. Botanical rambles. 1847. I. 524.¹
— Flora sacra. 1840. I. 513.
— Flowers of the field. 1853. I. 400, 533.²
— The forest trees of Britain. 1847. I. 393,² 533,¹ IV. 95.¹
— Monthly wild flowers. 1860. I. 401.
— A week at the Lizard. 1848. I. 400.

Johns, William. ·Practical botany. 1826. I. 397.
Johns Hopkins university. Circulars. I. 519.¹
Johns Hopkins university. Studies from the biological laboratory. I. 5.
Johnson & Johnson. Kola; a study of its history. 1895. III. 590.²
— — Recent therapeutical notes on the use of papoid. 1890. III. 617.²
Johnson, A. Campbell-. A proposed national arboretum. 1900. I. 29.
Johnson, A. L. Economical designing of timber trestle bridges. 1896. IV. 424.²
Johnson, Andrew. Message from the President of the United States . . . transmitting correspondence in relation to Russian America. See Sumner, Charles. 1868. III. 262.¹
Johnson, Charles Pierpont. British poisonous plants. 1856. III. 80.
— British wild flowers. 1858. I. 401.
— The useful plants of Great Britain. 1862. III. 80.
Johnson, Cuthbert William. The dew of heaven, influence of forests. 1867. IV. 50.
Johnson, Duncan Starr. Notes on the flora . . . of Beaufort, N. C. 1900. I. 320.
Johnson, E. Odal oil. 1856. III. 533.²
Johnson, George. Les forêts du Canada. 1895. IV. 555.¹
— Pulp wood of Canada. 1900. IV. 430.
— La pulpe de bois du Canada. 1900. IV. 337.²
— Rapport sur la richesse forestière du Canada. 1895. IV. 337.²
— Report on the forest wealth of Canada. 1895. IV. 337.² 555.¹
Johnson, George William. The cottage gardeners' dictionary. 1852. III. 82.
— A dictionary of modern gardening. 1847. III. 31.
— The gardeners' dictionary. 1847. III. 31.
— A history of English gardening. 1829. III. 33.¹
— Science and practice of gardening. 1862. III. 38.¹
— See also Hogg, Robert & Johnson, G. W.
— & Errington, R. The Apple, its culture. 1847. III. 426.¹
Johnson, H. S. & Sendtner, O. Chemische Untersuchung verschiedener Pflanzenaschen. 1855. I. 217.
Johnson, Henry. The unsatisfactory nature of the theories . . . for the descent of the radicles. 1829. I. 195.²
Johnson, J. B. & others. Results of investigations on Longleaf Pine. 1892. IV. 467.¹
Johnson, James Yate. Madeira, its climate and scenery. 1885. I. 498.
— Notes on some rare and little-known plants of Madeira. 1857. II. 552.¹
Johnson, L. S. Raspberry and Blackberry culture. 1896. III. 457.¹
Johnson, Laura. Botanical teacher for North America. 1834. I. 306.
Johnson, Laurence. Cephalanthus occidentalis. 1884. III. 711.³
— The eccentricity of the pith of Rhus Toxicodendron. 1876. II. 460.¹
— A manual of the medical botany of North America. 1884. III. 62.
Johnson, R. M. Field memoranda for Tasmanian botanists. 1874. I. 506.¹
Johnson, R. U. Why not more forest preserves? 1894. IV. 178.¹
Johnson, Samuel Wilham. Sur l'assimilation de l'azote par les plantes. 1865. I. 159.
— On the assimilation of complex nitrogenous bodies. 1865. I. 159.
Johnson, Thomas. Descriptio itineris plantarum investigationis ergo suscepti in agrum cantianum. 1632. I. 394.
— Iter plantarum investigationis ergo . . . in agrum cantianum. 1629. I. 394.
— Mercurius botanicus. 1634. I. 394.
— Opuscula omnia botanica. 1847. I. 34, 399.
Johnson, Thomas, (Professor of Botany, Dublin). Arceuthobium Oxycedri. 1888. II. 174.¹
— The nursing of the embryo . . . in Myzodendron. 1889. II. 167.¹
— The sources of rubber. 1899. III. 230.¹
Johnson, W. G. Destructive insects. 1897. III. 187.
Johnson, William Woolsey. Forest leaves. 1884. IV. 112.
Johnston, Alexander. An ingenious mode of transplanting large trees. 1849. III. 167.
Johnston, George. The botany of the eastern borders. 1853. · I. 400.
— A flora of Berwick-upon-Tweed. 1829. I. 397.

Johnston, Sir Harry. See Johnston, Sir Henry Hamilton.
Johnston, Sir Henry Hamilton. Additions to the flora of Mauritius. 1896. I. 482.
— British Central Africa. 1897. I. 493.
— The Kilima-njaro expedition. 1886. I. 492.²
— Der Kongo. 1884. V. xxiv.¹
— Report on the flora of Île des Aigrettes. 1896. I. 482.
— Report on the flora of . . . islands in Mahébourg Bay. 1896. I. 482.
— Report on the flora of Round Island. 1896. I. 482.
— The river Congo. 1884. V. xxiv.¹
Johnston, James. On the most economic uses to which chips . . . may be applied. 1869. IV. 434.
Johnston, James Finlay Weir. Anfangsgründe der praktischen Agrikultur-Chemie. 1842. III. 36.²
— A catechism of agricultural chemistry. 1844. III. 36.²
— Catechismus voor landbouwkundige scheikunde. 1844. III. 36.²
— On the constitution of the resins. 1839. I. 180.²
— Elements of agricultural chemistry. 1842. III. 36.²
— Grondbeginselen der landbouwkundige scheikunde. 1842. III. 36.²
— Handboek over de landbouwstofscheiding. 1842. III. 36.²
— Lectures on agricultural chemistry and geology. 1841. III. 36.²
— Manuel de chimie agricole et de géologie. 1842. III. 36.²
— Traité pratique de chimie et de géologie agricoles. 1842. III. 36.²
Johnston, T. T. The Rose. 1876. II. 290.²
Johnston, W. E. & others. The phylloxera . . . in France. 1882. III. 761.
Johnstone, James. A therapeutic arrangement and syllabus of materia medica. 1837. III. 242.
Johnstone, John. An account of the most approved mode of draining land. 1797. III. 150.²
Johow, Federico. See Johow, Friedrich.
Johow, Friedrich. Ein Ausflug nach der Höhle del Guacharo. 1885. I. 338.¹
— Über Bewegungen, welche die Kurztriebe der Weimuthskiefer . . . ausführen. 1888. II. 46.¹
— Über die Beziehungen einiger Eigenschaften der Laubblätter. 1884. I. 218.
— Zur Biologie der . . . Schau-Apparate. 1884. I. 238.
— Ueber die Brennhaare von Tragia volubilis. 1888. II. 452.¹
— Ueber die chilenische Palme. 1900. II. 69.²
— Über eine eigenthümliche Form von Kleistogamie der Flemmingia. 1888. II. 358.²
— Estudios sobre la flora de las islas de Juan Fernandez. 1896. I. 510.²
— Eine Exkursion nach dem kochenden See auf Dominica. 1884. I. 336.
— Die Mangrove-Sümpfe. 1884. II. 614.¹
— Die obsoleferenden Pflanzen der Tropen. 1885. III. 64.¹
— Über Ornithophilie in der chilenischen Flora. 1898. I. 239.²
— Die phanerogamen Schmarotzerpflanzen. 1890. I. 233.²
— Las plantas de cultivo en Juan Fernández. 1893. III. 283.²
— Vegetationsbilder aus West-Indien und Venezuela, H. 1884. I. 336, II. 614.¹ — 1885. I. 338.¹
Johren, Martin Daniel. Vademecum botanicum. 1710. I. 289.
Jolibois, J. Le Choisya ternata. 1877. III. 496.¹
Joliclœur, H. La pyrale de la Vigne. 1881. III. 563.
Joliisaint, L. Dendrométrie usuelle. 1849. IV. 213.
— Essai practique et raisonné d'aménagement. 1855. IV. 242, 249.³
Jolivet, Er. Notice sur l'emploi de la sciure de bois. 1886. IV. 431.¹
— Notice sur l'emploi du bois dans la fabrication du papier. 1877. IV. 429.
Jollet, T., (jr.). Le Mahonia Aquifolium. 1890. III. 395.²
Jolliet, E., (jr.). Un Orme gigantesque. 1890. II. 144.²
Jolly, A. Les chemins de schlitte. 1891. IV. 389.
— Sledge roads in France and in India. 1891. IV. 389.
Joly. Ueber den Anbau der Sumpfeiche. 1887. IV. 503.²
— Evonymus versicolor. 1870. III. 532.²
— Rückwagen und Rodemaschinen. 1900. IV. 387.¹
Joly, Anton. Bouvardia semperflorens. 1885. III. 711.²
Joly, Charles. See Joly, Victor Charles.
Joly, J. See Dixon, H. H. & Joly, J.
Joly, L. Rapport . . . sur des chemins de vidange. 1845. IV. 389.

Joly, Nicolas. Études sur les maladies des vers à soie.. 1858. III. 705.
— Note sur deux Roses vertes et pleines. 1879. II. 289.²
— Sur une pomme monstrueuse. 1865. II. 267.¹
Joly, P. Alte und seltene Bäume. 1893. II. 139.¹
Joly, Victor Charles. Castagno colossale nell' Isola di Madera. 1887. II. 125.¹
— Congrès international phylloxérique de la Gironde. 1881. III. 761.
— Deux arbres fruitiers remarquables. 1886. II. 267,² 280.²
— Di due alberi giganti del Portogallo. 1886. II. 125,¹ 140.¹
— Les étiquettes horticoles. 1880. I. 38.¹
— Les Eucalyptus. 1886. II. 624.¹
— Les Eucalyptus; leur développement. 1886. IV. 530.
— L' ingiallimento del Pesco. 1895. III. 442.¹
— Nota sopra i giganteschi Eucalyptus. 1885. II. 624.¹
— Note sur deux arbres géants en Portugal. 1886. II. 125,¹ 140.¹
— Note sur l'École d'arboriculture ... de Geisenheim. 1887. III. 32.¹
— Note sur l'enseignement agricole en France. 1886. III. 32.¹
— Note sur l'horticulture en Algérie. 1881. III. 130.²
— Note sur l'horticulture en Espagne. 1883. III. 126.¹
— Note sur l'horticulture en Italie. 1882. III. 126.¹
— Note sur la culture de la Vigne sous verre. 1888. III. 556.
— Note sur la destruction des lapins en Californie. 188 . ? III. 186.¹
— Note sur la jaunisse du Pêcher. 1895. III. 442.¹
— Note sur la production fruitière en Californie. 1891. III. 133.¹
— Note sur la vingtième session de la Société pomologique américaine. 1886. III. 133.
— Note sur la viticulture en Californie. 1884. III. 550.
— Note sur le Palmier de Staoueli. 1886. II. 73.¹
— Note sur le parc de la liberté à Lisbonne. 1888. III. 29.¹
— Note sur le Peuplier du Jardin botanique de Dijon. 1885. II. 98.¹
— Note sur les arbres géants. 1883. II. 51.¹
— Note sur les Eucalyptus géants. 1885. II. 624.¹
— Note sur les orangeries ... de Blidah. 1887. III. 500.¹
— Note sur quelques arbres géants du Portugal. 1893. I. 297.²
— Note sur trois arbres gigantesques. 1888. I. 297.²
— Note sur un Châtaignier colossal. 1887. II. 125.¹
— Note sur un pied de Vigne en Californie. 1887. II. 509.¹
— Note sur une maladie du Pêcher. 1892. III. 442.¹
— Les Orangeries à Blidah. 1888. III. 500.¹
— Wellingtonia dans leur station naturelle. 1883. II. 51.¹
Joly de Lotbinière, H. G. Arbor day. See LOTBINIÈRE, H. G. J. de. 1896. IV. 42.¹
— Culture of the Black Walnut. 1888. III. 354.²
— Forest tree culture. 1881. IV. 111.¹
— Forestry for Canada. 1889. IV. 271.¹
— The forests of Canada. 1878. IV. 337.¹
— The preservation and planting of forest trees in the Dominion of Canada. 1878. IV. 337.¹
— Report on forestry and forests of Canada. 1878. IV. 337.¹
— The returns of forest tree culture. 1882. IV. 259.²
Joylclerc, Nicolas. Cours complet et suivi de botanique. 1795. I. 84.
— Histoire naturelle. See MIRBEL, C. F. B. 1802. I. 33.
— Phytologie universelle. 1799. I. 84.
— Principes de la philosophie du botaniste. 1798. I. 33..
— Principes élémentaires de botanique. 1795. I. 84.
Jolyet, Antoine. Le bombyce du Pin. 1895. IV. 559.²
— Castanoïdes et Bétuloïdes. 1895. II. 115,¹ 185.¹
— Le Chêne de juin. 1899. II. 136.²
— Congrès international des stations de recherches forestières à Lohr et à Bruckenau. 1896. IV. 39.²
— Essais d'acclimatation en Allemagne. 1896. IV. 127.¹
— Expériences ... dans les pineraies de la Champagne. 1895. IV. 479, 559.¹
— Influence de l'espacement des plants. 1899. IV. 67.¹
— Le Pin du Lord Weymouth. 1896. IV. 469.
— Répartition du tannin ... dans le bois d'un Mélèze. 1892. II. 871.¹
Jolyet, F. Bewegungen und Gewohnheiten der kletternden Sträucher. 1880. I. 529.
— Le Bouleau. 1865. IV. 490.¹
— Catalogue des insectes nuisibles ... de la Haute-Saône. 1870. III. 190.

— Effets du froid sur les arbres. 1867. III. 48.
— La forêt des Crochères à la ville d'Auxonne. 1899. IV. 362, 556.¹
— Mouvements et habitudes des arbustes grimpants. 1880. I. 529.
Jomand, Jules. Du café. 1860. III. 742.¹
Jomard. Graine employée dans l'Amérique tropicale ... contre ... la morsure des serpents. 1850. III. 264.¹
— Sur des Grenadiers. 1859. III. 630.¹
Jonquet, Dionys. Hortus. 1659. I. 56.
Jones, A. C. Thea viridis, or Chinese Tea plant. 1877. III. 600.²
Jones, D. The tourist's ... guide to Harlech, Barmouth. 1863. I. 533.²
Jones, Herbert Lyon. Catalogue of the phanerogams and ferns of Licking county. 1892. I. 316.
— A graft hybrid. 1893. I. 246.²
Jones, Hugh. Part of a letter · . . . concerning several observables in Maryland. 1700. III. 263.²
Jones, J. D. Cork Oak. 1895. IV. 517.¹
— & others. Some foreign trees for the southern states. 1895. IV. 124.¹
Jones, John Matthew. On the vegetation of the Bermudas. 1874. I. 336.
— The visitor's guide to Bermuda. 1875. I. 336.
— Wedderburn, J. W. & Hurdis, J. L. The naturalist in Bermuda. 1859. I. 336.
Jones, John Pike. A botanical tour through ... Devon and Cornwall. 1820. I. 397.
— & Kingston, J. F. Flora devoniensis. 1829. I. 397, V. xx.²
Jones, L. R. Arceuthobium pusillum on a new host. 1900. II. 174.³
— See also BRAINERD, Ezra, JONES, L. R. & EGGLESTON, W. W.
— & Orton, W. A. Sap pressure and flow in the Sugar Maple. 1898. II. 480.²
Jones, Marcus Eugene. Contributions to western botany. 1892. I. 326.
— Une excursion botanique au Colorado. 1880. I. 324.
— New plants from Arizona. 1891. II. 258.¹
— New species and notes of Utah plants. 1891. II. 42,¹ 258.¹
— Notes from Utah. 1880. II. 258.¹
Jones, Mrs. N. E. Forestry. 1889. IV. 45.
Jones, Sir William. Botanical observations on select Indian plants. 1795. I. 471.
— A catalogue of Indian plants. 1795. I. 75.²
— The design of a treatise on the plants of India. 1790. III. 277.
Jones, William A. Report upon the reconnaissance of northwestern Wyoming. See PARRY, C. C. 1875. I. 324.
Jones, Winslow. The Planer tree and the Zelkouas. 1884. III. 366.¹
— See also BUTLER, J. D. & JONES, Winslow.
Jonescu, Dimitrie G. La foudre et les arbres. 1896. IV. 195.¹
— Ueber die Ursachen der Blitzschläge in Bäume. 1892. IV. 194.
— Weitere Untersuchungen über die Blitzschläge. 1894. IV. 548.²
Jong, A. de. De ontwouding van Java. See DE JONG, A. 1892. - IV. 279.¹
— Wildhout, contra Djati. 1885. IV. 400.¹
Jong, E. W. de. Heerendiensten in Koffiecultuur. 1885. III. 730.¹
Jong, J. J. de. Cultuur en bereiding van Agave en Rami. 1900. III. 382.¹
Jong, W. de. Verslag der particuliere Thee-onderneming Ledok. 1867. III. 602.¹
Jonghe, J. de. Ueber das Alter des Birnbäumes. 1856. II. 280.¹
— Beknopte aanleiding tot het kweeken van Camellias. 1851. III. 599.²
— Sur la culture de quelques Mélastomacées. 1846. III. 638.¹
— Von der Gattung Luxemburgia, ihren Arten. 1846. II. 544.²
— Du genre Luxemburgia. 1846. II. 544.²
— Longevity of the Pear tree. 1856. II. 280.¹
— Monographie du Pélargonium. 1844. III. 491.¹
— Practische Grundlehren der Cultur von Camellien. 1851. III. 599.²
— Theophrasta imperialis. 1859. III. 667.¹
— Traité de la culture du Camellia. 1851. III. 599.²
— Traité méthodique de la culture du Pélargonium. 1844. III. 491.¹

Jongkindt-Coninck, A. M. C. Die Cercis Siliquastrum . . . zu Leyden. 1874. II. 345.²
— Dictionnaire latin-(grec-)français-anglais-allemand-hollandais des principaux termes employés en botanique. 1894. I. 71, *III. 30.*
Jongkindt Coninck, C. J. M. Het een en ander over de houtteelt in Drente. 1876. IV. 356.²
— Verslag over den landbouw in Nederland. 1876. III. 122.²
— Vijanden en vrienden onser bosschen. 1876. IV. 90.¹
Jonglez de Ligne. Monographie des bois d'ébénisterie. 1864. IV. 427.²
Jonkman, H. F. Vijanden der Koffieplant. 1892. III. 736.
Jonnès, Alexandre MOREAU. DE. See MOREAU DE JONNÈS, Alexandre.
Jonquières, W. von. Ueber das Erscheinen und die Bedeutung der Raseneisensteine. 1853. IV. 68.
Jonston, Johannes. Dendrographias. 1662. I. 292.
— Historiae naturalis de arboribus et plantis libri. 1662. I. 292.
— A history of the wonderful things of nature. 1657. I. 286.
— Notitia regni vegetabilis. 1661. I. 286.
— Thaumatographia naturalis. 1632. I. 285.²
Joor, J. F. The Tamarisk naturalized. 1877. II. 562.²
Joos, Wilhelm. Ueber Cinchonenabbildungen. 1880. I. 813.¹
Joosten, E. Verhandeling over het hakhout. 1821. IV. 132.¹
— & **Holster, J. C.** Over het aanleggen van boomkweekerijen. 1824. III. 154.¹
Jordan, Alexis. Diagnoses d'espèces nouvelles ou méconnues. 1860. II. 199.²
— Notice sur plusieurs plantes nouvelles et autres. 1855. II. 199.²
— Observations sur plusieurs plantes nouvelles. 1846. I. 410.
— De l'origine des diverses variétés ou espèces d'arbres fruitiers. 1852. I. 247.
— Pugillus plantarum novarum. 1851. I. 411.
— Rapport sur l'essai de phytostatique appliqué à la chaine du Jura. 1850. I. 410.
— & **Fourreau, Jules.** Breviarium plantarum novarum. 1866. I. 270.
— — Icones ad floram Europae. 1866. I. 349.
Jordan, CAMILLE-. See CAMILLE-JORDAN.
Jordan, F. T. Ava oder Kava-Kava. 1876. III. 343.¹
— Ueber Goa powder. 1876. III. 468.²
Jordan, G. G. De Amygdalo communi var. amaro. 1834. III. 434.²
Jordan, Karl. Ueber Aphrophora spumaria . . . als Weidenschädling. 1891. III. 350.²
Jordan, Karl Friedrich. Beiträge zur physiologischen Organographie der Blumen. 1887. I. 115.¹
— Die Stellung der Honigbehälter. 1886. I. 115.¹
Jordán, Nicanor. Manual para la extracción . . . de la goma elástica. 1900. III. 230.
Jordan, T. F. Ueber den botanischen Ursprung von Jaborandi. 1875. III. 504.²
Jordana y Morera, José. Aclimatación de plantas leñosas forestales. 1885. IV. 124.²
— La agricultura y los montes de los Estados-Unidos. 1880. IV. 337.²
— Algunas voces forestales. 1900. IV. 23.²
— Aprovechamiento del azúcar de Arce. 1880. IV. 527.¹
— Apuntes bibliografico-forestales. 1873. IV. 1.
— Cómo se mide la madera en el valle de Arán. 1892. IV. 550.¹
— Sobre las especies forestales mas convenientes para repoblar. 1885. IV. 547.¹
— Excursión forestal al noroeste de la isla de Luzón. 1875. IV. 376.²
— Influencia de los bosques en la producción cereal. 1871. IV. 44.
— Las inundaciones y la repoblación de los montes. 1891. IV. 542.¹
— Leyes para la conservacion y fomento del arbolado en los Estados-Unidos. 1879. IV. 314.¹
— Memoria sobre materias curtientes españolas. 1879. IV. 435.
— El monasterio de Piedra. 1887. IV. 363.²
— El Nispero del Japon. 1882. III. 423.²
— Notas sobre los alcornocales. 1884. IV. 517.²
— Noticias forestales de la Argelia. 1881. IV. 379.¹
— Noticias sobre la repoblación . . . . de Zaragoza. 1875. IV. 47.²

— Pesquisas forestales . . . del litoral lusitano. 1897. . IV. 363.¹
— Production du sucre d'Érable aux États-Unis. 1880. IV. 527.¹
— La repoblación forestal. 1894. IV. 47.²
— Repoblaciones forestales en la Argelia. 1886. IV. 547.¹
— Servicio de ordenaciones de los montes públicos. 1891. IV. 304.¹
— Trabajos sobre la flora forestal del archipiélago Filipino. 1886. IV. 544.¹
— & **Morphy, Juan.** Los montes y la colonización en Australia. 1878. IV. 380.¹
— & **Vidal y Soler, Sebastian.** Apuntes sobre los montes y la agricultura norte-americana. 1877. IV. 336.²
— — Les forêts des États-Unis d'Amérique. 1877. IV. 335.²
Madrid-Dávila, Alfredo de & **Robles,** Eduardo de. . La producción agricola y forestal de la Argelia. 1882. IV. 379.¹
Jordana y Morera, Ramon: Bosquejo geográfico . . . del Archipiélago filipino. 1885. I. 464.¹
— El comercio de maderas en Filipinas. 1889. IV. 407.¹
— Estudio forestal acerca de la India Inglesa. 1891. IV. 376.² 378.
— Manual de podas é ingertos de árboles. 1882. III. 114.¹
— Memoria sobre el comercio de maderas en Filipinas. 1894. IV. 407.¹
— Memorias sobre la producción de los montes públicos de Filipinas. 1879. IV. 376.² 399.²
Jordanus Catalani. Mirabilia descripta. 1330. I. 275.¹
Jordens, J. H. G. Opmerkingen gemaakt op eene reis door eenige bosschen in Duitschland. 1855. IV. 348.²
— Verslag over de houtbosschen . . . van Ceram. 1856. IV. 399.²
— Over de voorziening in de behoefte aan masthout . . . uit Nederlandsch Indië. 1858. IV. 399.²
Joret, Charles. Flore populaire de la Normandie. 1887. I. 417.
— Liste des noms de plantes. 1895. I. 74.²
— Les plantes dans l'antiquité. 1897. I. 512.
— La Rose dans l'antiquité et au moyen age. 1892. II. 290.²
Joret, Henri. Le Baobab (Adansonia Lin.) 1887. II. 528.²
— Les Cactées de l'Amérique du Sud. 1887. III. 619.
— Le Caféier. 1888. III. 740.¹
— Les Chênes géants de la forêt de Compiègne. 1893. II. 139.¹
— Le Cocotier commun. 1887. III. 324.¹
— Note sur l'Ambrevade. 1876. III. 469.¹
— La sylviculture tropicale à l'Exposition . . . de Paris. 1889. IV. 20.²
— La Yerba Maté. 1887. III. 531.¹
Jorissen, Armand. Les phénomènes chimiques de la germination. 1886. I. 204.
— Sur la présence de l'acide cyanhydrique. 1894. I. 180.²
— Les propriétés réductrices des graines. 1884. I. 176.
— Recherches sur la germination des graines de Lin. 1884. II. 272.²
— Recherches sur la production de l'acide cyanhydrique. 1884. I. 176. — 1885. I. 180.²
— Du rôle de l'amygdaline pendant la germination. 1883. I. 203.
Jorissenne, Gustave. Le climat et la végétation de l'Isthme de Suez. 1870. I. 488.
— De l'influence du sujet et de la greffe. 1870. III. 39.
— Notice sur le Codiaeum variegatum. 1871. II. 439.¹
— Observations sur la floraison et la fructification du Lierre. 1880. I. 226.¹
Jornal de horticultura pratica. III. 23.¹
Jornal official d' agricultura. III. 23.¹
Josat. Histoire botanique . . . du Thé. 1845. III. 606.
Josch, Eduard. Die Flora von Kärnten. 1853. I. 440.
Jósef, *Erzherzog.* Climatologie comparée. 1888. III. 50.¹
— Egy rendkivül-kemény tél hatása Fiuméban. 1886. III. 50.¹
— Növényhonositási kisérletek Fiuméban. 1885. III. 127.¹
Joseph. See HOFFMEISTER, H. & JOSEPH.
Joseph, (HÉRIBAUD-, *(frère).* See HÉRIBAUD-JOSEPH, *(frère).*
Joseph-Lafosse, Pierre. Études sur les espèces de Bambous. 1867. III. 114.¹
— Note sur le Bambou Montigny. 1866. III. 316.¹
— Notice sur le Chamaerops Fortunei. 1883. III. 331.²
— Notice sur le jardin de M. Hamond. 1875. I. 59.
— Observations sur la germination des graines submergées. 1871. III. 185.¹

Joseph-Lafosse, Pierre (*continued*).
— Le Palmier de la Société Linnéenne de Normandie. 1891. III. 124.²
— Quelques mots sur l'introduction . . . des végétaux à faciès tropical. 1882. III. 125.
Josephsson, Heymann. Praeparator til at befordre en stor Besparelse af Brænde. 1796. IV. 280.²
Joset, FRICHE-. *See* FRICHE-JOSET & MONTANDON, F. J.
Joshi, R. S. Al cultivation, dyeing. 1897. III. 746.¹
Josse-Beauvoir, (*député, Loir-et-Cher*). Opinion sur la vente des bois. 1817. IV. 326.
Josselyn, John. An account of two voyages to New-England. 1674. III. 262.²
— New-Englands rarities. 1672. III. 262.²
Josserand, P. N. La culture du Pommier à cidre. 1890. III. 426.²
Josset, Théophile. Le Châtaignier, sa culture. 18 . . ? III. 358.²
Josst, Franz. Über die Vermehrung der Azalea sinensis. 1851. III. 662.²
Jost, Ludwig. Über die Abhängigkeit des Laubblattes von seiner Assimilationsthätigkeit. 1895. I. 174.
— Beiträge zur Kenntniss der nyctitropischen Bewegungen. 1898. I. 198.
— Ein Beitrag zur Kenntniss der Athmungsorgane. 1887. I. 171.
— Beobachtungen über den zeitlichen Verlauf des secundären Dickenwachsthums der Bäume. 1892. I. 190.²
— Ueber Beziehungen zwischen der Blattentwickelung und der Gefässbildung. 1893. I. 126, *188*.
— Ueber Dickenwachsthum und Jahresrinbildung. 1891. I. 128.¹
— Ueber den Einfluss des Lichtes auf das Knospentreiben der Rothbuche. 1894. II. 127.¹
— Zur Kenntniss der Blüthenentwickelung der Mistel. 1888. II. 178.¹
— Ueber die periodischen Bewegungen der Blätter von Mimosa. 1897. II. 373.¹
— Ueber R. Hartig's Theorie des Dickenwachsthums und der Jahrringbildung. 1892. I. 128.¹
— Die Theorie der Verschiebung seitlicher Organe. 1899. I. 103, *II. 18*.
Jottings respecting the Oak. 1844. II. 138.¹
Jouan, Henri. Coup-d'œil sur la flore de la Basse-Cochinchine. 1866. I. 469.²
— La dispersion des espèces végétales par les courants marins. 1891. I. 241.²
— Notes sur l'archipel Hawaiien. 1872. I. 509.²
— Notes sur les bois de la Nouvelle-Zélande. 1864. IV. 402.¹
— Notes sur quelques animaux et quelques végétaux rencontrés dans les mers australes. 1874. III. 94.²
— Les plantes alimentaires de l'Océanie. 1875. III. 94.²
— Les plantes industrielles de l'Océanie. 1876. III. 94.²
— À propos de la flore de la Polynésie. 1896. I. 509.²
— Quelques arbres remarquables des environs de Cherbourg. 1894. I. 297.²
— Quelques mots sur le peuplement végétal des îles de l'Océanie. 1882. I. 509,² 536.¹
— Recherches sur l'origine . . . de certains végétaux . . . dans les îles du Grand-Océan. 1865. I. 509.²
— Terre-Neuve. 1880. I. 310.
— Une visite à Monterey (Californie). 1886. I. 325.
Jouanet, Alexandre. Mémoire sur les plantations de Paris. 1855. III. 124.¹
Joubaire, A. Forest economy in France. 1879. IV. 27.²
— Glances at forestry in France. 1879. IV. 27.²
— Note sur quelques insectes nuisibles. 1881. IV. 209.¹
— Les réformations forestières sous Colbert. 1879. IV. 27.²
— La rouille du Pin. 1885. IV. 461.²
Joubert. Note sur la dépendance mutuelle des branches et des racines. 1845. I. 524.¹
Joubert, A. Du Haut-Médoc. Observations sur la culture de cette contrée. 1836. III. 554.²
— Rhus Osbeckii. 1870. III. 527.²
Joubert, J. & **Chamberland**, Ch. Note sur la fermentation des fruits. 1876. I. 179.¹
Joubert, P. C. De la greffe. 1839. III. 160.
— De la récolte . . . des graines. 1842. III. 156.¹
— La séminologie générique. 1840. I. 253.²
Joué & **Crouzel**. La bouillie tanno-cuprique. 189 . ? III. 580.
Jouffroy d'Abbans, de. La culture et le traitement de la gutta-percha. 1899. III. 149.

Jougla. Les Pyrénées inconnues. 1880. I. 416.
Jouglard, C. Aurouse et le Pic de Bure par les Échelons. *See* CARDOT, Émile. 1876. IV. 162.
Jouhe, MAYER DE. *See* MAYER DE JOUHE.
Jouhet, Paul. Le nanisme végétal. 1891. I. 236.¹
— Un Oranger de pleine terre. 1891. III. 503.¹
Jouin. Populus angulata Ait. var. cordata. 1898. III. 345.²
Jouin, E. Les arbres & arbustes à feuilles colorées. 1900. III. 207.¹
— Betula alba pendula nana. 1899. III. 357.¹
— Can hybrids be obtained by grafting? 1900. I. 246.²
— Les Ceanothus. 1891. III. 541.¹
— Crataegus leucophlaeos Moench. 1898. III. 423.¹
— Étude sur les Groseilliers d'ornement. 1899. III. 414.¹
— Étude sur les Spirées ligneuses. 1898. III. 460.¹
— Les Frênes à feuilles monophylles. 1899. III. 672.¹
— Les Hêtres. 1899. III. 360.¹
— Hibiscus syriacus et ses variétés. 1899. III. 588.¹
— Multiplication du Sambucus racemosa plumosa. 1892. III. 752.²
— Noyer à cerneau rouge. 1899. III. 355.
— Quelques arbres et arbustes . . . à floraison très précoce. 1899. III. 207.²
— Spartocytisus albus var. durus. 1898. III. 474.¹
— Les Tecoma grandiflora et T. radicans. 1899. III. 705.
— Tilia orbicularis. 1898. III. 586.¹
— Trumpet flowers and their varieties. 1899. III. 705.
— Les variations sexuelles du Nuttallia. 1896. II. 269.¹
Jouin, V. L'hiver 1894–1895 en Alsace-Lorraine. 1895. III. 46.¹
Joulie. Une nouvelle industrie du bois. 1899. IV. 428.²
Joulin, G. Sur l'hélixine. 1891. III. 643.¹
Jourakovsky, V. A. Notice sur les forêts des héritiers du Prince Zacharie Jvanovitch Melikoff. 1897. IV. 348.¹
Jourdain. Mémoire sur l'importance des forêts en France. 1824. IV. 47,¹ 275.
Jourdain, Sylvain. Expériences sur le mode d'action du chloroforme sur l'irritabilitée des étamines des Mahonia. 1870. II. 202.¹
Jourdan, A. J. L. Dictionnaire raisonné . . . des termes usités dans les sciences naturelles. 1834. I. 70.
— Pharmacopée universelle. 1828. III. 245.
— Pharmacopoea universalis. 1828. III. 245.
— The pharmacopoeia universalis. 1828. III. 245.
Jourdan, Pascal. Essai phytographique d'une Chloris vichysoise. 1872. I. 414.
— Flore murale de la ville de Tlemcen. 1866. I. 485.
— Flore rudérale de la ville d'Alger. 1872. I. 485.
— Flore rudérale du tombeau de la Chrétienne. 1867. I. 485.
— Mosaïque de florules rudérales du centre de la France. 1872. I. 414.
Jourdier, Auguste. Voyage agronomique en Russie. 1861. III. 120.²
Journal agricole algérien. III. 27.¹
Journal asiatique. I. 21.
Journal d'agriculture et d'horticulture de la Côte d'Or. III. 19.
Journal d'agriculture pratique. III. 15.
Journal d'agriculture pratique, de jardinage. III. 19.
Journal d'agriculture pratique et d'économie rurale. III. 19.
Journal d'histoire naturelle. I. 520.¹
Journal d'horticulture et des sciences accessoires. *See* SOCIÉTÉ ROYALE D'AGRICULTURE ET DE BOTANIQUE DE GAND. I. 17.
Journal d'horticulture pratique [de la Belgique]. III. 15.
Journal d'horticulture pratique et de jardinage. III. 19.
Journal de botanique. I. 21.
Journal de botanique. Morot. I. 21.
Journal de botanique appliquée. I. 15.
Journal de botanique néerlandaise. I. 15.
Journal de chimie médicale. I. 21.
Journal de l'agriculture. *See* par J. A. Barral. III. 20.
Journal de l'anatomie et de la physiologie. I. 21.
Journal de la physiologie de l'homme. I. 21.
Journal de médecine, chirurgie, pharmacie. I. 21.
Journal de médecine, de chirurgie et de pharmacie militaires. I. 21.
Journal de pharmacie. I. 16.
Journal de pharmacie. *See* BULLETIN de pharmacie. I. 21.
Journal de pharmacie d'Anvers. *See* JOURNAL de pharmacie. I. 16.

Journal de physique, chimie et histoire naturelle. I. 21.
Journal de physique, de chimie. See INTRODUCTION aux observations. V. VII²; OBSERVATIONS et mémoires sur la physique. I. 22.
Journal de vulgarisation de l'horticulture. III. 20.
Journal der Pharmacie für Aerzte und Apotheker. I. 12.
Journal des connaissances usuelles et pratiques. III. 20.
Journal des débats politiques et littéraires. IV. 539.¹
Journal des forêts. IV. 12.²
Journal des mines. IV. 12.²
Journal des observations physiques . . . faites dans l'Amérique méridionale. I. 21.
Journal des rheinländischen Weinbaues. 1827. III. 552, 757.¹
Journal des roses. III. 20.
Journal des savants. I. 21.
Journal des sçavans. See JOURNAL des savants. I. 21.
Journal et flore des jardins. III. 20.
Journal forestier suisse. IV. 13.²
Journal für das Forst-, Jagd- und Fischereywesen. IV. 9.
Journal für das Forst- und Jagdwesen. IV. 9.
Journal für die Botanik. I. 12.
Journal für die Gärtnerey. See JOURNAL für die Gartenkunst. III. 12.
Journal für die Gartenkunst. III. 12.
Journal für Forst-, Bergwerks . . . Sachen. IV. 9.
Journal für praktische Chemie. See JOURNAL für technische . . . III. 12.
Journal für technische und ökonomische Chemie. III. 12.
Journal horticole et viticole. III. 20.
Journal of a horticultural tour through some parts of Flanders. See FORBES, James. 1823. III. 119.¹
The journal of a naturalist. See KNAPP, J. L. 1829. I. 524.¹
The journal of agriculture. See QUARTERLY journal . . . III. 18.
Journal of agriculture and industry of South Australia. III. 27.¹
Journal of American folk-lore. I. 5.
Journal of anatomy and physiology. I. 18.
Journal of applied science. III. 17.
Journal of botany. See BOTANICAL miscellany. I. 17.
Journal of botany British and foreign. I. 18.
Journal of forestry. IV. 12.¹
Journal of horticulture, cottage gardener. See COTTAGE gardener. III. 16.
Journal of literature and science, [Madras]. I. 29.¹
Journal of microscopy and natural science. I. 18.
Journal of mycology. III. 4.
Journal of natural philosophy. I. 18.
Journal of physiology. I. 18.
Journal of progress. IV. 4.
Journal of science. See QUARTERLY journal of science. I. 19.
Journal of science and the arts. See ROYAL INSTITUTION OF GREAT BRITAIN. III. 18.
Journal of the Indian Archipelago and eastern Asia. I. 29.¹
Journal of travel and natural history. I. 18.
Journal suisse d'économie forestière. See JOURNAL forestier suisse. IV. 13.²
Journal universel et hebdomadaire de médecine. I. 22.
Journet, V. Notice sur la direction des arbres en espaliers. 18 . . ? III. 171.
Jousse, Daniel. Commentaire sur l'ordonnance des eaux et forêts. 1772. IV. 325.
Jousselin, M. P. Estudios sobre las maderas. 1855. IV. 418.
Jousset. Du curare au point de vue thérapeutique. 1866. III. 683.¹
Joutel. Journal historique du dernier voyage que feu M. de la Sale fit dans le Golfe de Mexique. 1713. IV. 526.²
Jouve, Joseph DUVAL-. See DUVAL-JOUVE, Joseph.
Jouyne, Z. Reboisement des montagnes. 1850. IV. 155.¹
Jowett, Hooper Albert Dickinson. New glucoside from Willow bark. 1900. III. 351.¹
Jt., R. O., Freiherr von. Vorläufiges Gutachten . . . auf etliche, den Gebrauch der Eichenborke . . . betreffenden Fragen. 1782. III. 237.¹
Juan, George & Ulloa, Antoine de. Voyage historique de l'Amérique méridionale. 1752. III. 268.²
Jubainville, A. d' ARBOIS DE. See ARBOIS DE JUBAINVILLE, A. d'.
Jubiläums-Gartenbau-Ausstellung zu Berlin. 1897. III. 336.²
Jubisch, M. Ueber Kultur . . . der schwarzen Johannisbeere. n. d. III. 415.¹

Jubisch, Max. Geschäftskorrespondenz fur Gärtner. 1897. III. 200.¹
Juch, Carl Wilhelm. See JUCH, K. W.
Juch, Hermann Paul. De radice Chinae. 1753. III. 338.¹
Juch, Karl Wilhelm. Europens vorzüglichere Bedurfnisse des Auslandes. 1800. III. 741.²
— Die Giftpflanzen. 1817. III. 59.²
— Handbuch der pharmaceutischen Botanik. 1804. III. 55.
Juckenack, A. See HILGER, Albert & JUCKENACK, A.
— & Hilger, Albert. Sur le dosage de la caféine. 1897. III. 740.²
— — Studien über die Bestimmung des Coffeins. 1897. III. 740.³
The Judas tree. 1897. III. 472.²
Judeich, Friedrich. See JUDEICH, Johann Friedrich.
Judeich, Johann Friedrich. Aufgabe und Bedeutung der Forsteinrichtung. 1890. IV. 245, 550.²
— Beitrag zur Beurtheilung der durch die Forstwirthschaft verwertheten Arbeitsmenge. 1890. IV. 310.¹
— Beitrag zur Kenntniss der im Königreich Sachsen üblichen Methode der Waldertrags-Regelung. 1861. IV. 248.¹
— Bemerkung zum Kampfe gegen den Fichtenborkenkäfer. 1876. IV. 204.
— Besprechung einiger Forsteinrichtungsfragen. 1885. IV. 244.
— But principal de l'aménagement. 1891. IV. 259.²
— Cionus fraxini. 1869. IV. 535.¹
— Dasychira Stph. (Liparis O.) detrita Esp. 1877. IV. 510.
— Entwickelung des Fichtenborkenkäfers in Aesten. 1876. IV. 456.
— Zur Entwickelungsgeschichte der Borkenkäfer. 1880. IV. 204.
— Excursion durch die Waldungen der Herrschaften Dobrawitz. 1865. IV. 371.
— Die Flügelsäge des . . . Forstmeister Alers. 1869. IV. 171.·
— Die Forsteinrichtung. 1871. IV. 241.
— Die Forstfinanzrechnung. 1866. IV. 255.
— Die Forstwirtschaft auf der Ausstellung zu Wien. 1874. IV. 21.¹
— Die Frage eines Waldschutzgesetzes in Sachsen. 1881. IV. 180.²
— Zur Frage über die finanzielle Umtriebszeit. 1867. IV. 251.²
— Zur Geschichte der Forstakademie Tharand. 1891. IV. 33.¹
— Geschichtliche Beobachtungen über die Fachwerksmethoden. 1879. IV. 252.
— Der Getreidelaufkäfer. 1864. IV. 92.
— Hiebszüge und Bestandeswirthschaft. 1884. IV. 244.
— Eine Hügelpflanzung. 1868. IV. 153.²
— Mittheilungen über Borkenkäfer. 1886. IV. 204.
— Das normale Altersclassenverhältniss im Fehlmelschlagbetriebe. 1891. IV. 246.
— Notiz über den Fichtenborkenkäfer. 1875. IV. 456.
— Notiz über die auf Tharänder Revier gepflanzten indischen Coniferen. 1886. IV. 126.¹
— Notiz über Pseudotsuga Douglasii Carr. 1887. IV. 483.²
— Objeto principal de las ordenaciones. 1890. IV. 550.²
— Ueber die Organisation des forstlichen Versuchswesens. 1871. IV. 38.¹
— Zu § 11 der Bestimmungen über Einführung gleicher Holzsortimente. 1876. IV. 387.²
— Der Streit über den Wiener Wald. 1871. IV. 369.
— Zur Theorie des forstlichen Reinertrages. 1869. IV. 255. — 1873. IV. 256. — 1874. IV. 256. — 1875. IV. 256.
— Das Waldkapital. 1879. IV 256.
— Ueber den Werth der Periodeneintheilung. 1868. IV. 251.¹ — 1870. IV. 251.²
— See also Юдейхъ, Фридрихъ.
— & Nitsche, Hinrich. Lehrbuch der mitteleuropäischen Forstinsektenkunde. 1885. IV. 92.
Judson. See WAIT & JUDSON.
Jühlke, Ferdinand. Aufzählung einiger Bäume und Sträucher . . . in Chiswick. 1853. I. 54.
— Baumriesen bei Wiesbaden.· 1893.· I. 296.¹
— Beiträge zur Naturgeschichte der Forstpflanzen. 1854. III. 69, IV. 83.
— Die botanischen Gärten. 1849. I. 38.¹
— Ueber die Kultur-Essbeere der . . .· Kranbeere. 1873. III. 663.²
— Mittheilungen über die Vegetationsverhältnisse von Buenos-Ayres. 1865. IV. 342.¹
— Ueber die Racen-Verbesserung der Cultur-Pflanzen. ·1870. I. 247.
— See also NEUBERT, Wilhelm & JÜHLKE, Ferdinand.

Juel, Hans Oscar. Die Anatomie der Marcgraviaceen. 1888. II. 546.²
— See also WITTROCK, V. B. & JUEL, H. O.
Jüngst, Ludwig Volrad. Flora der nächsten Umgebungen Bielefelds. 1833. I. 378.
— Flora von Bielefeld. 1837. I. 379.
— Flora Westfalens. 1837. I. 379.
— Kurzer Abriss der Pflanzenkunde. 1833. I. 86.
Jürgens, (sr.). Wie schützt man die Pflanzen . . . gegen die schädliche Einwirkung des Leuchtgases? 1873. III. 185.²
Jürgens, Bruno. Vergleichende microscopisch-pharmacognostische Untersuchungen einiger offizinellen Blätter. 1889. I. 111, III. 860.¹
Jürgens, Carlos. Ueber Kultur und Gewinnung des Mate. 1897. III. 530.²
Jürgens, E. Mittheilungen einiger Erfahrungen über den Schutz der Kulturen. 1895. IV. 197.¹
Juergens, Karl. Etymologisches Fremdwörterbuch der Pflanzenkunde. 1878. I. 76.²
Juergenson, Karl. Beiträge zur Pharmacognosie der Apocyneenrinden. 1889. III. 685.²
Juge, Charles. Méthode de culture propre à combattre le phylloxera. 1874. III. 566.²
— Notice sur l'emploi des terres de la Solfatarre de Pozzuoli. 1874. III. 759.
Juge de St. Martin, Jacques Joseph. Notice des arbres et arbustes . . . dans le Limousin. 1790. I. 293, III. 83.² ·
— Traité de la culture du Chêne. 1788. IV. 504.
Ueber die Jugend von Pflanzen, welche im Alter ihren Verwandten unähnlich. 1877. I. 101.¹
Juglar, (sr.). Le triomphe de l'Acacia. 1808. IV. 524.¹
Jugler, August. Die Eilenriede in alter Zeit. 1884. IV. 26. Jugovitz, Rudolf. Beitrag zur Kenntniss der Zirbe. 1894. IV. 463.²
— Ueber die Lärche. 1896. IV. 450.
— Das Rothholz der Kiefer. 1896. IV. 482.²
Juillet, Jules. See GIRARDIN, Jean & JUILLET, Jules; LECOQ, Henri & JUILLET, Jules.
The Jujube tree. 1878. III. 544.¹
Les Jujubiers. 1899. III. 544.¹
Juliá, Miguel, BOSCH Y. See BOSCH Y JULIÁ, Miguel.
Julia de Fontenelle, Jean Sebastien Eugène & Tollard, Henri. Manuel de l'herboriste. 1828. I. 267.
Julisans, Arnold. De resina elastica cajennensi. 1780. III. 230.
Julian. Rapport sur la plantation d'Anil. 1804. III. 479.¹
Julien. Sur la présence du phylloxera au Auvergne. 1875. III. 568. ·
Julien, A. Aperçu sur le mode de distribution des plantes . . . de Constantine. 1888. I. 485.
— Flore de la région de Constantine. 1894. I. 486.
Julien, Stanislas. Dell' arte di coltivare i Gelsi. 1837. III. 375.
— Chinese cultivation. The Tchouma. 1849. III. 382.¹
— Description des procédés chinois pour la fabrication du papier. 1840. III. 235.¹
— Dissertation on the silk-manufacture. 1849. III. 376.
— Extrait des livres chinois. 1847. IV. 427.²
— Ueber Maulbeerbaumzucht. 1837. III. 375.
— Notes from Chinese sources. 1843. III. 273.¹
— Nouveaux renseignements sur la cire d'arbres. 1840. III. 225.
— Sur la plante textile Tchou-ma. 1857. III. 382.¹
— Procédé des Chinois pour la fabrication de l'encre. 1834. III. 236.
— Résumé des principaux traités chinois sur la culture des Mûriers. 1837. III. 375.
— Sur une substance grasse produit par des insectes. 1840. III. 225.
— Summary of the principal Chinese treatises upon the culture of the Mulberry. 1837. III. 375.
— Verfahren der Chinesen bei der Kultur der Urtica nivea. 1849. III. 382.¹
— & Voisin, (abbé). Sur les climats convenables à la culture du Thé. 1838. III. 600.¹
Julin, Johan. Observationer gorde i Utsjoki Lappmarks prestgård. 1800. I. 223.¹
Jullien, A. La forêt du Mayumbe. 1899. IV. 279.²
Jullien, André. Topographie aller bekannten Weinberge. 1816. III. 551.¹
— Topographie de tous les vignobles connus. 1816. III. 551.¹
Jullien, J. Traitement des Vignes phylloxérées. 1889. III. 574.

Jullien, Jules. Urgence de la régénération de la Vigne. 1875. III. 555.
Jullien, Th. P. La Rose. 1863. III. 449.
Jullien-Crosnier, Al. Catalogue des plantes . . . du Loiret. 1890. I. 535.
— Catalogue systématique de quelques plantes nouvelles pour la flore orléanaise. 1862. I. 412.
Jumelle, Henri Lucien. Sur l'assimilation chlorophyllienne des arbres à feuilles rouges. 1890. I. 174.
— L'assimilation chlorophyllienne des arbres à feuilles rouges. 1891. IV. 64.¹
— Le Cacaoyer. 1899. III. 593.¹
— Sur la constitution du fruit des Graminées. 1888; II. 58.²
— Le Cryptostegia madagascariensis. 1899. III. 692.²
— Sur le dégagement d'oxygène. 1891. I. 174.
— La détermination chimique des . . . cacaos. 1899. III. 595.¹
— L'Erouma de Nouvelle-Calédonie. 1897. III. 520.¹
— Étude anatomique du Cissus gongylodes. 1897. II. 503.¹.
— Le Guidroa, arbre à caoutchouc. 1899. III. 689.¹
— Hevea guyanensis. 1898. III. 519.¹
— Influence comparée des anesthésiques sur l'assimilation. 1890. I. 168. — 1891. IV. 64.¹
— Influence des anesthésiques sur la transpiration. 1890. I. 168.
— Influence des substances minérales. 1889. I. 229.
— Un Landolphia à Caoutchouc de Madagascar. 1899. III. 689.¹
— Le Marsdenia verrucosa. 1900. III. 694.¹
— Les Mascarenhasia à Caoutchouc de Madagascar. 1899. II. 728.²
— Le N'Djembo, liane à caoutchouc du Fernan-Vaz. 1897. II. 727.²
— Nouvelles recherches sur l'assimilation. 1891. I. 174.
— L'Okouendé n'gowa. 1897. III. 687.¹
— Le Piralahy, liane à caoutchouc. 1899. III. 689.¹
— Piralahy rubber. 1899. III. 689.¹
— Les plantes à caoutchouc . . . dans les colonies françaises. 1898. III. 229.
— Le Sakharé. 1897. III. 369.¹
— Sur la structure . . . du Landolphia Foreti. 1898. II. 727.²
Jumilhac. Sur la culture de la Vigne. 1801. III. 554.²
Ju-moku shiryaku Dai Nihon. See DAI NIHON ju-moku shiryaku.
Jumpertz, Karl. De foecundatione plantarum. 1855. I. 200.
Junak. Innenmessungen im Walde. 1900. IV. 266.¹
Jundzill, X. Bonifaciusz Stanislaw. Index plantarum horti botanici Universitatis vilnensis. 1802. I. 41.
— Opisanie roślin w prowincyi W. Xięstwa Litewskiego naturalnie rosnących. 1791. I. 360.
The June-berry, Amelanchier canadensis. 1885. III. 419.²
Jung & Ganter. Les plantations au Tonkin et en Annam. 1899. III. 129.¹
Jung, Georg Sebastian. Χρυσόμηλον; seu, Malum aureum. 1673. III. 423.²
Jung, J. H. Lehrbuch der Forstwirthschaft. 1781. IV. 95.
— Versuch eines Lehrbuches der Forstwirthschaft. 1781. IV. 95.
Jung, Joachim. Doxoscopiae physicae minores. 1662. I. 30.
— Isagoge phytoscopica. 1678. I. 30.
— Opuscula botanico-physica. 1747. I. 31.
Jung, W. Flora des Herzogthums Nassau. 1832. I. 378. ·
Junge, C. Verzeichnis der zum Anbau in der Provinz Brandenburg geeigneten Obstsorten. 1896. III. 74.
Junge, H. Tecoma Smithi. 1896. III. 707.¹ ·
Die jungen Pflanzenforscher. 1836. I. 94.
Junger, E., (jr.) Ueber tricotyledone Embryonen. 1869. I. 123.¹
Junger, Ernst. Azalea indica dialypetala. 1878. III. 680.²
— Botanische Gelegenheitsbemerkungen. 1891. I. 271.²
— Eine neue Form der Rosa gallica. 1863. II. 294.¹
— Notizen aus alten botanischen Büchern. 1878. II. 105,² 270,³ 680.²
— Prunus persica Čelakovský. 1878. II. 270.²
— Salix babylonica mas. 1878. II. 105.³
Jungermann, Ludwig. Catalogus plantarum . . . circa Altorfium noricum. 1615. I. 372.
— Catalogus plantarum . . . in Horto medico altdorphino. 1635. I. 43.
Jungfleisch, Émile Clément. La production de la guttapercha. 1892. III. 229. — 1803. III. 231.

— Sur la production du sulfate de quinine. 1891. III. 718.
— Société d'encouragement pour l'industrie nationale. 1892. III. 668.[2]
— & **Léger**, Edmond. Sur les isoméries optiques de la cinchonine. 1887. III. 723.
Junghans, Philippus Kasparus. Icones plantarum officinalium ad vitam impressae. 1787. III. 627.[2]
— Index plantarum Horti botanici halensis. 1771. I. 44.
Junghuhn, Franz Wilhelm. Aanhangsel tot de vijfde schets, inhoudende diagnosen van onbeschreven planten. 1845. I. 468.
— Appendix diagnosium et adumbrationum plantarum. 1845. I. 468.
— Bericht over de waarde en het alkaloidgehalte van Cinchona Pahudiana. 1863. III. 725.[2]
— Berigt . . . aangaande de op Java gekweekte Groene Indigo planten. 1863. III. 542.[2]
— Berigt . . . aangaande den toestand der. Kinakultuur. 1863. III. 715.
— Berigt omtrent het alkaloidgehalte van . . . Kinaboomen. 1864. III. 722.
— Bijdragen tot de geschiedenis der vulkanen in den Indischen Archipel. 1843. I. 465.
— Brief aan C. L. Blume vanuit Djocjokarta. 1837. I. 465.
— Brieven over Java. 1845. I. 468.
— Geschiedenis van den Kamferboom van Sumatra. 1855. III. 611.[1]
— Inlichtigen over het geschrift van den Heer Blume. 1850. I. 465.
— Java, deszelfs gedaante, bekleeding. 1850. I. 468.
— Java, seine Gestalt, Pflanzendecke. 1850. I. 468.
— Java, zijne gedaante, zijn plantengroei. 1850. I. 468.
— Journey through Java. 1845. I. 468.
— Licht en schaduwbeelden uit de binnenlanden van Jáva. 184 . ? III. 127.[2]
— Nova genera et species plantarum florae javanicae. 1840. I. 468.
— Schetsen, ontworpen op eene nieuwe reis door Java. 1845. I. 468.
— Schilderung der Flora Javas. 1850. I. 468.
— Staat aantoonende de vermeerdering der kinaplanten op Java. 1863. III. 712.[1]
— Statement shewing the increase of the Cinchona plants. 1863. III. 712.[1]
— Terugreis van Java naar Europa. 1851. I. 303.
— Toestand der aangekweekte Kinaboomen. 1857. III. 715.
— Topographische und naturwissenschaftliche Reisen durch Java. 1845. I. 468.
— Uitstapje naar de bosschen van de gebergten Malabar. 1841. I. 468.
— Voorloopige handleiding voor de Proef-kina kultuur. 1859. III. 715.
— Een woord over den boom Sambinoer. 1851. II. 8.[2]
— Yearly reports . . . respecting the condition of Quinine cultivation in Java. 1863. III. 715.
— Der Zustand der angepflanzten Chinabäume. 1857. III. 715.
— & **Vrij**, J. E. de. Die Chinakultur auf Java. 1860. III. 715.
— — The cultivation of the Quina tree in Java. 1860. III. 715.
— — De Kinakultuur op Java. 1860. III. 715.
Jungk, C. L. Observationes botanicae in Floram halensem. 1807. I. 376. V. XIX.[1]
Jungli. Nurseries for Rubber. 1886. IV. 519.[1]
Jungner, Johan Richard. Anpassungen der Pflanzen an das Klima . . . Kamerungebirge. 1891. I. 491.
— Byggnaden af bladen hos några småbladiga fjällväxter of van trädgränsen. 1894. I. 220.[1]
— Ett egendomligt fall af på pollinerande insekter reagerande " skyltning." 1894. II. 824.[1]
— Ett fall af fasciation hos Berberis. 1890. II. 205.[2]
— Ein Fasciationsvorgang der Berberis. 1890. II. 205.[2]
— Några exempel på frukt- och fröspridning. 1894. I. 241.[1]
— Om regnblad, däggblad och snöblad. 1893. I. 233.[1]
— Studien über die Einwirkung des Klimas . . . auf die Gestalt der Früchte. 1894. I. 119.
— Utbildning af droppspetsar hos frukter. 1894. I. 233.[1]
— Wie wirkt träufelndes und fliessendes Wasser auf die Gestaltung des Blattes? 1895. I. 111.
The **Junipers** in Surrey. 1885. II. 31.[1]
Juniperus virginiana tripartita. 1886. IV. 448.[2]
Junker von Langegg, F. A. On the cultivation of Tea . . . in Japan. 1886. III. 601.[2]

— De cultuur enz. van de Thee in Japan. 1886. III. 601.[2]
— Plants in legends. 1890. I. 518.
— Sacred trees. 1890. I. 517.[1]
Junod, Alphonse. Manuel d'arboriculture pratique. 1884. III. 146.[1]
Junod, Henri. See SCHINZ, Hans & JUNOD, Henri.
Junowicz, Rudolf & Kreuz, Johann. Zur Entwicklung der Emergenzen an den Blattstielen von Ribes Grossularia. 1878. II. 245.[1]
Juranyi, Lajos. Ueber den Bau . . . des Pollens bei Ceratozamia. 1872. II. 4.[1]
— Beiträge zur Kenntniss der Pollen-Entwickelung der Cycadeen. 1882. II. 1.
— A Ceratozamia hímsejtjeinek kifejlődéséről. 1870. II. 4.[1]
— Neuere Beiträge zur Kenntniss der Pollenkörner der Cycadeen. 1882. II. 1.
— Ueber den Pollen der Gymnospermen. 1882. II. 1.
— Ujabb adatok a gymnospermák hímporának ismeretéhez. 1882. II. 1.
Jurass, Paul. Laburnum-Arten und -Sorten. 1900. III. 480.[2]
— Niedrigbleibende Spiräen. 1900. III. 460.[2]
— Vermehrung . . . von Staphylea colchica. 1898. III. 533.[2]
Jurie. Des moyens de répression de la pyrale de la Vigne. 1835. III. 562.[2]
Jurine, André. Recherches sur l'organisation des feuilles. 1802. I. 109.[1]
Juritz, C. F. The chemical constitution of some colonial fodder plants and woods. 1892. I. 154.
Jus, H. Les plantes textiles algériennes. 1879. III. 234.
Juslenius, Abraham D. & Torner, Ericus. Centuria plantarum. See LINNÉ, Carl von. 1755. I. 261.
Jussiaume. Cèdre du Liban. 1852. II. 28.[1]
Jussieu, Adrien de. Botanica. 1843. I. 88.
— Die Botanik. 1843. I. 88.
— Botanique. 1843. I. 88.
— Catalogue de la bibliothèque scientifique. See CATALOGUE . . . 1857. I. 2.
— Ueber Cheirostemon platanoïdes. 1851. II. 532.[2]
— Considérations sur la famille des Euphorbiacées. 1823. II. 434.[2]
— Corso elementare di botanica. 1843. I. 88.
— Description d'un genre nouveau nommé Icacina. 1823. II. 474.[2]
— Elementarkurs der Botanik. 1843. I. 88.
— The elements of botany. 1843. I. 88.
— Sur les embryons monocotylédonés. 1839. I. 121.
— De Euphorbiacearum generibus. 1824. II. 433.[1]
— Extrait d'une monographie . . . des Malpighiacées. 1841. II. 424.[1]
— Extrait d'une monographie du genre Phebalium. 1825. II. 409.[1]
— Géographie botanique. 1845. I. 299.
— Malpighiacearum synopsis. 1840. II. 423.[2]
— Mémoire sur le groupe des Méliacées. 1830. II. 418.[2]
— Mémoires sur les Rutacées. 1825. II. 396.[1]
— Monographie de la famille des Malpighiacées. 1843. II. 423.[3]
— Monographie du genre Phebalium. 1825. II. 409.[1]
— Note sur des fleurs monstrueuses . . . d'Erable. 1841. II. 479.[1]
— Note sur l'Oncostemum. 1830. II. 694.[4]
— Note sur la famille des Pénaecées. 1846. II. 599.[1]
— Note sur le Cheirostemon platanoïdes. 1851. II. 532.[2]
— Note sur le genre Napoleona. 1844. II. 612.[2]
— Note sur les remarques de M. Gaudichaud concernant le rapport sur un mémoire de M. Trécul. 1852. I. 189.
— Note sur une espèce nouvelle de Malpighiacée. 1846. II. 427.[1]
— Observations sur quelques plantes du Chili. 1832. I. 346.
— Rapport sur le second voyage en Abyssinie. 1846. I. 487.
— Rapport sur le troisième voyage en Abyssinie. 1851. I. 488.
— Rapport sur un mémoire de M. Gasparrini. 1838. II. 325.[1]
— Rapport sur une note de M. Louis Vilmorin. 1850. III. 489.[2]
— Revue des genres . . . des Ternstroemiacées. 1824. II. 547.[1]
— Tableau général des genres . . . des Euphorbiacées. 1824. II. 433.[1]
— Taxonomie. 1848. I. 252.
— Sur les tiges de diverses hanes. 1841. II. 424.[1]
— See also BRONGNIART, Adolphe, RICHARD, Achille & JUSSIEU, Adrien; SAINT-HILAIRE, A. F. C. P., JUSSIEU, Adrien de & CAMBESSÈDES, Jacques.

Jussieu, Antoine de. Histoire du Cachou. 1722. III. 320.¹
— Histoire du Café. 1716. III. 738.
— Recherches d'un spécifique contre la dysenterie. 1731. III. 509.¹
— Traité des vertus des plantes. 1771. III. 241.
Jussieu, Antoine Laurent de. Exposition d'un nouvel ordre de plantes. 1778. I. 251.
— Sur la famille des plantes Rubiacées. 1820. II. 807.¹
— Sur la famille nouvelle des plantes Polygalées. 1815. II. 429.²
— Genera plantarum. 1789. I. 258.
— Introductio in historiam plantarum. 1789. I. 32.
— An inveteratis alvi fluxibus Simarouba? 1772. III. 509.¹
— Mémoire sur la plante . . . Erica Daboecia. 1802. II. 662.²
— Mémoire sur la réunion de plusieurs genres . . . des Laurinées. 1805. II. 222.²
— Mémoire sur le Cantua. 1804. II. 746.²
— Mémoire sur le Dicliptera et le Blechum. 1807. II. 799.¹
— Mémoire sur le Grewia. 1804. II. 513.²
— Mémoire sur le groupe des Rutacées. 1825. II. 396.²
— Mémoire sur le Melicocca. 1817. II. 487.²
— Mémoire sur le Paullinia. 1804. II. 488.¹
— Mémoire sur les genres de plantes à ajouter . . . aux familles des Primulacées. 1809. I. 265.
— Mémoire sur les genres de plantes à ajouter . . . aux familles des Solanées. 1810. I. 265.
— Mémoire sur les Lobeliacées. 1811. II. 845.¹
— Mémoire sur les Monimiées. 1809. II. 221.²
— Mémoire sur quelques espèces du genre Hypericum. 1804. II. 556.¹
— Mémoire sur une nouvelle espèce de Marcgravia. 1809. II. 546.²
— Méthode naturelle des végétaux. 1824. I. 251.
— Note sur la réunion de plusieurs plantes . . . en un seul genre . . . des Lauriers. 1802. II. 226.¹
— Note sur le calice et la corolle. 1812. I. 114.¹
— Note sur quelques genres anciens. 1819. I. 266.
— Note sur quelques genres de la flore de Cochinchine. 1808. I. 469.²
— Notice historique sur le Muséum d'histoire naturelle. 1802. I. 57.
— Observations on the plant called Erica Daboecia. 1802. II. 662.²
— Observations sur . . . Amarantacées. 1803. II. 189.¹
— Observations sur . . . Nyctaginées. 1803. II. 190.²
— Observations sur . . . Onagraires. 1804. II. 642.²
— Observations sur . . . Verbénacées. 1806. II. 752.²
— Premier . . . mémoire sur les caractères généraux de familles tirés des graines. 1804. I. 118.²
— Premier . . . mémoire sur quelques nouvelles espèces du genre Passiflora. 1805. II. 575.²
— Principes de la méthode. 1824. I. 251.
— Sur le Solanum cornutum du Mexique. 1804. II. 775.²
— & Desfontaines, Réné. Rapport sur un mémoire du citoyen Martin. 1799. III. 118.²
Jussieu, Bernard de. Quaestio medica, an compar animantium et vegetantium perspiratio? 1777. I. 169.¹
Just. Die Unfallversicherung der in land- und forstwirthschaftlichen Betrieben beschäftigten Personen. 1888. IV. 310.²
Just, A. F. Afhandling om de i Danmark voxende Piilearter. 1798. III. 347.
Just, Johann Leopold. Azione della temperatura sulla conservazione della facoltà germinativa dei semi. 1877, 1878. IV. 65,² 148.
— Ueber die Einwirkung höherer Temperaturen auf die . . . Keimfähigkeit der Samen. 1877, 1878. IV. 65,² 148.
— Ueber die Möglichkeit, die . . . verarbeitete Kohlensäure durch Kohlenoxydgas zu ersetzen. 1882. I. 173.
— De la possibilité de remplacer l'acide carbonique . . . par l'oxyde de carbone. 1882. I. 173.
— & others. Botanischer Jahresbericht. See BOTANISCHER . . . 1874. I. 2.
Justander, Johannes Gustaf. Specimen calendarii florae et faunae aboënsis. 1786. I. 223.
— & Tamlander, Z. Observationes historiam plantarum fennicarum illustrantes. 1791. I. 360.
Justen, Joseph. Notes on the properties of wood. 1864. IV. 408.
Justi, Karl Wilhelm. De Thymelaea Mezereo. 1798. III. 627.²
Justice, Sir James. The British gardener's calendar. 1759. III. 109.
— The British gardener's director. 1759. III. 109.
— The Scots gardiners director. 1754. III. 109.

Justitia, (pseud.). On thinning and general management. 1863. IV. 173.
Justus Liebig's Annalen der Chemie. See ANNALEN der Pharmacie. I. 10.
Justus Perthes' geographische Anstalt. Mittheilungen. See MITTHEILUNGEN aus Justus . . . I. 13.
Juta, E. J. W. De ontwikkeling van Suriname. 1891. III. 268.¹
— Opmerkingen betreffende Suriname. 1891. III. 268.¹
Juvelius, Eric. Mémoire sur la distillation de la poix noire. 1823. IV. 462.²

k. Eine Rieseneiche der Niederlausitz. 1897. IV. 516.¹
K. Bamboos. 1883. III. 314.²
K. Beitrag zur Schütte. 1859. IV. 476.
K. Conservirung von Holz in der Erde. 1880. IV. 420.
K. Cultivation of Teak in Java. 1891. IV. 537.²
K. Om Cytisus-Arternes Forædling. 1845. III. 474.¹
K. Ficus quercifolia Roxb. 1899. III. 371.²
K. Die Forstrente in Elsass-Lothringen. 1887. IV. 261.¹
K. Die " Haselfichte." 1884. II. 35.¹
K. Over Koffie in Palembang. 1895. III. 731.
K. Kosten der natürlichen Verjüngung eines Kiefernbestandes. 1895. IV. 474.
K. Ueber Lärchensucht. 1867. IV. 449.
K. Aus dem Leben des Fichtenblattsaugers. 1884. IV. 456.
K. Nochmals die Haselfichte. 1885. II. 35.¹
K. De ontginning onzer woeste gronden. 1862. IV. 160.¹
K. The preservation of wood. 1896. IV. 421.
K. Une question de sylviculture. Cause de variation de l'accroissement des reserves. 1888. IV. 65.¹
K. Die Rentabilität unserer Eichenschälwälder. 1899. IV. 513.
K. Shrubby New Zealand Speedwells. 1887. III. 704.²
K. Starke Weisstannen. 1865. II. 24.¹
K. Vershil in vorm bij bladeren van een en denzelfden boom. 1892. I. 111.
K. (Elsass). Die Weisstanne. 1900. IV. 444.²
K. & St. Ueber den Nutzen des Hollunders. 1890. IV. 538.²
K., van. Iets uit en over de Britsch-Indische landbouwstatistiek. 1886. III. 130.¹
K., A. Ueber Wurzelbeschneiden der Palmen. 1873. III. 284,¹ 517.
K., C. von. Die tellurische Bedeutung der Wälder. 1860. IV. 43.
K., C. F. Geschichte der churmärkschen Forsten. 1789. IV. 25, 352.
K., D. Andromeda (Cassiope) fastigiata. 1885. III. 649.¹
K., D. Purple Box-leaved Milkwort. 1886. III. 514.¹
K., D. The Pyrenean Rose. 1885. III. 456.²
K., D. Shrubby Rock Roses. 1888. III. 612.²
K., D. Single White Moutan Paeony. 1890. III. 392.²
K., D. Zauschneria californica. 1887. III. 641.¹
K., E. Der sibirische Urwald. 1891. IV. 376.¹
K., F. Ein Hollunder . . . zu Lukawitz. 1860. IV. 538.²
K., F. Ein neuer Parasit der Weymouthskiefer. 1898. IV. 470.¹
K., F. Rhizoctonia Strobi. 1898. IV. 470.¹
K., F. Ein starker Bergahorn. 1883. II. 480.¹
K., G. Der Holzverkehr Russlands. 1890. IV. 404.¹
K., G. M. De Appel en Peerenboom. 1851. III. 444.¹
K., H. Acacia Riceana. 1872. III. 465.²
K., H. How to measure the heights of trees. 1884. IV. 215.
K., H. J. van. Bosschen. 1887. IV. 119.²
K., J. Education of foresters in Britain. 1877. IV. 34.⁴
K., J. Frass des Schwammspinners. 1890. IV. 210.¹
K., J. H. Phyllocactus platyrhoides. 1862. III. 626.¹
K., J. J. Ruf eines Würtembergers an seine Landsleute dem einreissenden Holzmangel zu steuern. 1795. IV. 282.¹
K., J. S. J. Die grüne Rose. 1857. III. 455.¹
K., K. A tardy evergreen creeper. 1876. III. 393.²
K., L. Ueber die Gewinnung . . . der Eichenschälrinde. 1885. IV. 513.
K., O. Acclimatation du Mélèze en Belgique. 1897. IV. 558.²
K., P. La gutta-percha. 1899. III. 232.¹
K., S. Zur Naturgeschichte der Linde. 1860. II. 516.²
K., T. Future supplies of timber from abroad. 1885. IV. 405.¹
K., V. E. Trees for towns. 1872. III. 42.²
K., W. Einiges über den Gummibaum. 1870. III. 370.²

K., W. Een rupsenplaag . . . in een Kinaplantsoen. 1897. III. 717.[2]

K., W. Eine Spiräen-Hybride. 1863. III. 461.[2]

K. · · r, F. A. Verhältnisse bei Zugutmachung . . . der Eichen-Rinde. 1853. IV. 512.

K—r, *(Forstmeister zu O—m).* Etwas für Forstmänner und Nichtforstmänner. 1805. IV. 117.

K—r, F. A. Einige Worte über Waldverjüngung. 1852. IV. 139.[1]

Kaán, Károly. Átalakulások az erdei termékek szállító eszközeiben. 1899. IV. 390.[1]

Kaarsen van de baan der Tjampakka sellong. 1854. III. 403.[1]

Kaart over det til Skovdrift benyttede Areal i Danmark. 1888. IV. 343.[2]

Kaas, Clausen. Pilekulturen. 1877. III. 348.

Kaasböl, Hilarius Christoph. De arboribus sodomaeis. 1705. I. 512.

Kabath, Hermann. Flora der Umgegend von Gleiwitz. 1846. I. 381.

Kabeshtof, I. M. *See* Кабештовъ, И. М.

Kabina, János. A Hamvas Kőrisfa. 1878. III. 672.[2]

Kaboth, *(Oberförster).* Ueber Ertrag und Gewicht der Waldstreu. 1863. IV. 437.[2]

— Das Vorkommen der grossen Kiefernraupe. 1855. IV. 475.

Kabsch, Wilhelm. Anatomische und physiologische Beobachtungen über die Reizbarkeit der Geschlechtsorgane. 1861. I. 199.

— Ueber den anatomischen Bau des Holzes von Sucopira Assu. 1863. II. 337.[1]

— Das Pflanzenleben der Erde. 1855. I. 299.

Kachler, J. Über den Perubalsam. 1869. III. 482.[1]

Kachler, Johann. Alphabetisch-tabellarisch-scientifisches Samenverzeichniss. 1839. I. 268, *III. 91.*[1]

— Encyclopädisches Pflanzen-Wörterbuch. 1829. III. 91.[1]

— Grundriss der Pflanzenkunde. 1830. I. 70.

Kačírek, A. Beitrag zur Thiergarten-Waldwirthschaft. 1874. IV. 136.[1]

The **Kadamba** tree. 1894. II. 809.[1]

Kad-handi, *(pseud.).* Castilloa elastica and the western Ghaut forests. 1877. III. 368.[1]

— Famine, forests and sub-soil moisture. ·1880. IV. 485.[1]

— Note on the growth of some introduced trees at the Cape. 1884. III. 131.[2]

— Notes on Sandal. 1878. IV. 519.[1]

— Permanent fire-lines. 1877. IV. 184.[1]

— Sandal-planting in Mysore. 1882. IV. 519.[1]

— Trees at the Cape. 1884. III. 131.[2]

Kadner, Ludwig. Aphorismen über das Bestreben und die Ziele der bayrischen Forstverwaltung. 1879. IV. 118.

— Die Bewirthschaftung und Verjüngung der Fichtelgebirgswaldungen. 1879. IV. 118.

— Die Forstwirthschaftseinrichtung in ·Bayern. 1875. IV. 240.[1]

Källström, Ernst. *See* ANDERSON, Hjalmar & KÄLLSTRÖM, Ernst.

Ueber Kälte, ihre Wirkungen auf Pflanzen. 1838. III. 182.

Kaempfer, Engelbert. Amoenitatum exoticarum . . . fasciculi 5. 1712. I. 461.

— Beschrijving van Japan. 1727. I. 461.

— De beschryving van Japon. 1727. I. 461.

— Description des plantes du Japon & leurs usages. 1736. I. 461.

— Geschichte und Beschreibung von Japan. 1727. I. 461.

— Histoire naturelle . . . de l'empire du Japan. 1727. I. 461.

— The history of Japan. 1727. I. 461.

— Icones selectae plantarum quas in Japonia collegit. 1791. I. 461.

— Relationes botanico-historicae de Palma dactylifera. 1712. II. 72.[1]

Käpler, Melchior · Christian. Erläuterung einiger Sätze über die Beckmannischen Schriften von den Holzsaat. 1779. IV. 105.

— Das ganz unumstössliche Naturzeugniss der besten Abholzungs-Zeit. 1775. IV. 384.[1]

— Zum gemeinen Besten abzielendes Gutachten wie bey dem An- . . . -gang eines Kiefern-Waldes zu verfahren. 1772. IV. 471.

— Gründliche Anleitung zu mehrerer Erkenntniss . . . des Forstwesens. 1764. IV. 105.

— Ueberzeugender Beweiss bey welcher Abholzungszeit die Laub-Holz-Stöcke am besten wieder ausschlagen. .1771. IV. 139.[1]

Käpler, W. H. Holzcultur durch Erfahrung erprobt. 1803. IV. 105, *127.*[1]

— Kleiner Forstcatechismus. 1785. IV. 105.

— Die nöthigsten Vorkenntnisse der Forst- und Jagdwissenschaften. 1803. IV. *31,* 117.

— Der Safthieb. 1804. IV. 384.[2]

— Vermehrter und verbesserter Forstkatechismus. 1785. IV. 105.

Kärnbach, J. Eine botanische Weihnachts-Exkursion in Neu-Guinea. 1893. I. 499.[1]

Kärnbach, Ludwig. Über die Nutzpflanzen . . . in Kaiser-Wilhelmsland. 1893. III. 282.[1]

Kärner, W. Ueber den Abbruch . . . pflanzlicher Behaarung. 1889. I. 113,[1] *235.*[2]

— Das Schälen des Rothwildes. 1880. IV. 196.[2]

Kärnten — Naturhistorisches Landes-Museum. *See* NATURHISTORISCHES . . . I. 28.[1]

Kärntens Forstwirthschaft und Holzindustrie. 1896. IV. 369.

Kärntnerischer Forstverein. Mittheilungen. Rechenschafts-Bericht. IV. 9.

Käser, Friedrich. Die Flora des Avers. 1885, I. 437.

Kässner, B. Der Sägewerk-Techniker. 1881. IV. 393.

Kaeubler, Johannes. Das Forst- und Feldstrafgesetz. 1895. IV. 322.[1]

Kaffeebohnen. 1889. III. 740.[1]

Kafka, Josef. Bambus a jeho moderní upotřebení. 1889. III. 315.[1]

— O Baobabu prstnatém. 1883. III. 589.[1]

— O Brayefe hlistomorné. 1883. III. 424.[2]

— Corynostylis albiflora Lindley. 1889. III. ·613.[2]

— O Hodafe ozdobné. 1884. III. 595.[2]

— O Hortensiích. 1882. III. 411.[1]

— O kapoku celolístečním. 1883. II. 529.[2]

— Květinářství. 1885. III. 116.[1]

— Lesy Tekové. ·1887· III. 697.[2]

— Nový pramen Gutaperdi. 1886. II. 697.[2]

— Odule. 1887. III. 638.[2]

— O Olivě obecné. 1882. III. 679.[1]

— Orleaník barvířský. 1882. III. 566.[1]

— O Palmách. 1886. II. 64.[1]

— Panela vonná. 1886. III. 401.[2]

— Pavonia Makoyana. 1889. III. 587.[1]

— Podstunečník. 1890. III. 586.[2]

— Praktický návod pro zahradníka. 1887. III. 116.[1]

— Rostliny plochovětvé. 1891. I. 106.[1]

— O Sapanech. 1882. III. 468.[1]

— Tupoušek. 1891. III. 638.[2]

— O Vodokleneeh. 1882. III. 418.[2]

— O Weigelii japonské. 1884. III. 749.[1]

— O životě epifytických rostlin Západní Indie. ·1886. I. 234.[2]

— O Zlatoplodě Slívovém. 1883. III. 420.[2]

Kahl, August. Der Buchenhochwald auf dem Vogesensandstein. 1883. IV. 495.

— Einiges über Forsteinrichtungspläne. ·1895. ·IV. 246.

— Forstgeschichtliche Skizzen aus . . . Rappoltsweiler und Reichenweiler. 1894. IV. 26.

— Handbuch für die elsass-lothringischen Förster. 1900. IV. 317.[1]

— Mittheilungen über die forstlichen Verhältnisse in Frankreich. 1897. IV. 293.[1]

Kahl, G. W. Der Reformobstbaum. 1900. III. 139.

Kahle, *(Subrektor, Putlitz).* Über Rosen-Vermehrung. 1834. III. 451.[2]

Kahlenberg, Louis. *See* COPELAND, E. B. & KAHLENBERG, Louis.

Kahlich, Vincenz. Der Tannen-Borkenkäfer. 1865. IV. 445.

Kaibara, Tokushin. Yamato Honzô. 1697. III. 91.[1]

Kaigorodof, Д. *See* Кайгородовъ, Д.

Kaigorodof, Dmitri N. *See* Кайгородовъ, Дм. Н.

Kail, Franz. Praktische Erfahrungen über systematische Eintheilung der Wälder. 1837. III. 534,[1] *IV. 250.*[1]

Kains, Maurice Grenville. Some facts about frost prevention. 1897. III. 183.[1]

Kaiser. Quels principes peut-on établir pour l'organisation d'une police et d'une juridiction forestières cantonales? 1864. IV. 330.

— Welche Grundsätze lassen sich feststellen betreffend eine kantonale Forstpolizei? 1864. IV. 330.

Kaiser, Alfred. Reise durch die Sinai-Halbinsel. ·1889. I. 481.[1] ·

Kaiser, H. Ueber die Erziehung des Normalzustandes eines Waldes. ·1877. IV. 252.

Kaiser, N. J. Forststatistik der Schweiz; Kanton Solothurn. 1852. IV. 365.
Kaiser, Otto. Allgemeine Grundsätze der Eintheilung auf dem Gebiete der Bodenwirthschaft. 1881. IV. 270.
— Aphorismen über Waldwegebau. 1875. IV. 389.
— Beiträge zur Pflege der Bodenwirthschaft. 1883. IV. 73.[1]
— Beitrag zu Thema 4: " Mittheilungen über . . . Methoden der natürlichen Verjüngung der Buchen-Hochwaldungen." 1868. IV. 495.
— Erfahrungen über die Wegenetzlegung. 1873. IV. 251.[1]
— Zur Wasserstandsfrage. 1879. IV. 73.[2]
— Ueber Wegenetzlegung. 1874. IV. 389.
Kaiser, Paul. Ueber die tägliche Periodicität der Dicken-dimensionen. 1879. I. 190.[1]
Kaiserbäume in Mähren. 1879. III. 34.[1]
K. k. Ackerbauministerium. Statistisches Jahrbuch. IV. 14.
K. k. Ackerbauministerium in Wien. Landwirthschaftliches Wochenblatt. Mittheilungen. III. 25.
K. k. Forst-Akademie in Mariabrunn. Jahrbuch. IV. 14.
Die **K. k. Forstakademie Mariabrunn**. 1868. IV. 36.[2]
K. k. Gartenbau-Gesellschaft in Steiermark. Mittheilungen. See K. K. STEIERMÄRKISCHER GARTENBAU-VEREIN. III. 25.
K. k. Gartenbau-Gesellschaft in Wien. See GARTENBAU-GESELLSCHAFT WIEN. III. 24.[2]
K. k. geographische Gesellschaft, [Wien]. Abhandlungen. Mittheilungen. I. 27.
K. k. Mährisch-schlesische Gesellschaft für Ackerbau, Natur- und Landeskunde. Centralblatt. Mittheilungen. III. 25.
K. k. naturhistorisches Hofmuseum, [Wien]. Annalen. I. 27.
K. k. Önologische und pomologische Lehranstalt in Kloster-neuburg. Programme und Jahresberichte. III. 25.
K. k. Österr. Handels-Museum. See HANDELS-MUSEUM. III. 24.[2]
K. k. Steiermärkische Landwirtschafts-Gesellschaft, Graz. Wochenblatt. III. 25.
K. k. Steiermärkischer Gartenbau-Verein. Mittheilungen. III. 25.
K. k. technologisches Gewerbe-Museum in Wien. See TECHNOLOGISCHES . . . IV. 15.
K. k. zoologisch-botanische Gesellschaft in Wien. Festschrift. Verhandlungen. I. 27.
Kaiserlich leopoldinisch-carolinische deutsche Akademie der Naturforscher. Katalog der Bibliothek. See GRULICH, Oscar. 1887. I. 2.
Kaiserliche Akademie der Wissenschaften, [Wien]. Denk-schriften. Sitzungsberichte. I. 27.
Kaiserliche freie ökonomische Gesellschaft zu St. Petersburg. Mittheilungen. III. 10.[1]
Kaiserliche Leopoldino-carolinische deutsche Akademie der Naturforscher. See ACADEMIA NATURAE CURIOSORUM. I. 10.
Der **Kaiserliche Thiergarten** bei Wien. 1866. IV. 368.
Kaiserliches Gesundheitsamt Berlin. Arbeiten. I. 13.
Kaiserliches Gesundheitsamt Berlin. Biologische Abtheilung für Land- und Forstwirthschaft. Arbeiten. IV. 9.
Kaker. Beitrag zur Wurzel-Vermehrung. 1868. III. 159.[1]
Kaku, Hika. See ITO, Keisuke & KAKU, Hika.
Kalberlah, A. Der Bau von Tetrastigma scariosum. 1898. II. 504.[2]
— Das Dickenwachsthum der Eiche. 1895. II. 139.[1]
Kalbruner, Hermann. Sur les fleurs de Tilleul. 1875. III. 585.[2]
Kalbrunner, Hermann. Ueber die Papierfabrication aus Holz. 1854. IV. 429.[2]
Kalchberg, Albert, *Ritter* von. Ueber die Natur . . . der Pflanzenauswüchse. 1828. I. 214.[1]
Kalen, Magnus Vilhelm. See LINDEBERG, C. J. & KALÉN, M. V.
Kalendar. See КАЛЕНДАРЬ.
Kalender, Emil. Anleitung zum Schnitt der Obstbäume. 1874. III. 138.
— Ein Beitrag zur Naturgeschichte der dem Apfelbaum schädlichen Insekten. 1873. III. 427.[2]
— Die Bildung des Honigthau's. 1873. I. 213.[1]
— Die Kultur der Rosen-Kultur. 1873. III. 453.[2]
— Ein gefährlicher Feind der Kirschbäume. 1876. III. 432.[1]
— Der Miesmuschel-Schildträger. 1877. III. 427.[2]
Kalender für den sächsischen Berg- und Hüttenmann. IV. 9.
Kaleniczenko, Jean. Description monographique . . . du genre Crataegus. 1874. II. 260.[2]
— Encore quelques mots sur la Daphné Sophia. 1874. II. 602.[2]
— Quelques mots sur les Daphnés russes. 1849. II. 600.[2]

Die **kalifornische Ceder**. 1871. III. 311.[1]
Die **kalifornische Trauer-Fichte**. 1893. III. 305.[2]
Kalifornskaya SOSNA. See КАЛИФОРНСКАЯ СОСНА.
Kalina von Räthenstein, Matthias. Die Nothhilfe bei Mangel an Futterstroh. 1835. III. 223.[1]
— Der Weisse Maulbeerbaum. 1836. III. 375.
Kalinski, V. See КАЛИНСКІЙ, B.
Kalitsch, von. Zur Aufforstungsfrage in Schleswig-Holstein. 1880. IV. 158.
— See also RAMANN, Emil & KALITSCH, von.
Kalk, Richard. Ergebnisse der Besichtigung schmalspuriger Eisenbahnen. 1885. IV. 391.
— Die Sicherung der Forstgrenzen. 1879. IV. 287.
— Der Zuwachs an Baumquerfläche. 1889. IV. 234.
Kalkhof, F. See FINK & KALKHOF, F.
Kall, Nicolaus Christoph. De duplici plantarum sexu Arabi-bus cognito. 1782. I. 199.
Kállai, Armin. Örökzöld Tölgyfa Nyitramegyében. 1890. II. 132.[1]
Kallenbach. Umspaltung von Prügelholz. 1872. IV. 387.[2]
Kallenbach, (*Oberförster*, *Schotten*). Aphorismen über die Keimkraft der Buchein. 1867. IV. 494.
Kallina, Károly. A Valonea Tölgyfa honosításáról. 1883. IV. 502.[2]
Kallstenius, Johannes Jacobus. Remedia guineensia. See APELIUS, Adam. 1813. III. 93.[1]
Kalm, Pehr. Allmänns anmärkningar wid en krydd- och trä-gårds anläggande. 1754. III. 120.[1]
— Om amerikanska näfwerbåtar. 1753. IV. 491.[1]
— Anmärkningar om vara Furu- och Gran-skogars ömmare wård. 1757. IV. 440.[2]
— Anmärkningar rörande nödvändigheten af Ekskogaruas bättre vård och ans i Finland. 1757. IV. 503.[2]
— Anmärkningar vidfrukt-träns planterande i Finland. 1757. III. 134.[1]
— Apple-träns ans. 1769. III. 426.[1]
— Om Aspens egenskaper och nytta. 1759. IV. 487.[1]
— Beskrifning af der Reise nach dem nördlichen Amerika. 1753. I. 305.
— Beskrifning huru socker göres. 1751. III. 220.[2]
— Beskrifning öfver Eenens egenskaper. 1770. III. 303.[2]
— Beskrifning öfver Swarta Winbärsbuskars nytta. 1772. III. 415.[1]
— Beskrifning om Stickel- eller Krusbärsbuskars ans och nytta. 1757. III. 414.[2]
— Beskrifning på et slags-maskar. 1764. III. 186.[2]
— Beskrifning på hvad sätt dricka göres i Norra America af et slags Gran. 1751. III. 305.[1]
— Beskrifning på norr-americanske Mulbärsträdet. 1776. III. 381.[1]
— Om Caffé och de inhemska växter. 1755. III. 738.
— Om egenskaperne . . . af det americanska Valnöttträdet. 1778. III. 353.[2]
— De Erica vulgari et Pteride aquilina. 1754. III. 648.[1]
— Fata botanices in Finlandia. 1758. I. 80.[1]
— Florae fennicae, pars prior. 1765. I. 359.
— Förtekning på några örter fundna i Bohus-Län. 1743. II. 11.[2]
— Förtekning på någre inhemska färgegräs. 1745. III. 235.[2]
— Genera compendiosa plantarum fennicarum. 1771. I. 359.
— Histoire naturelle et politique de la Pensylvanie. 1768. I. 305.
— Om hvita Valnötträds egenskaper. 1769. III. 353.[2]
— En kärt berättelse om naturliga stället . . . af några växter. 1751. III. 119.[2] 261.[1]
— Korta frågor angående nyttan af våra inländskaväxter. 1753. III. 270.[1]
— Om möjligheten . . . af krydd- och trägårdars anläggande. 1754. III. 270.[1]
— Norr-americanska Svarta Valnötträdets egenskaper. 1767. III. 354.[2]
— Om nyttan af Hallon i hushållningen. 1778. III. 458.[2]
— Oekonomisk beskrifning öfver Björckens egenskaper. 1759. IV. 491.[1]
— Oekonomisk beskrifning öfver vår svenska Hassel. 1759. III. 358.[1]
— Possibilitas varia vegetabilia exotica . . . in Finlandia colendi. 1751. III. 270.[1]
— Reis door Noord Amerika. 1753. I. 305.
— En resa til Norra America. 1753. I. 305.
— Rön och anmärkningar uti natural historien . . . ifrån Norige. 1748. IV. 343.[2]

— Rön, om den americanska så kallade Tupp-sporre Hagtorns nytta. 1773. III. 421.[3]
— Rön om några synnerliga örters nytta. 1747. III. 470.[1]
— Rön vid köldens verkan sistledne vinter. 1761. III. 44.[1]
— Slutelig berättelse om skaller-ormen. 1753. III. 244.
— Trän til häckar. 1756. III. 212.[1]
— Om trän tjenliga til lefvande häckar. 1775. III. 212.[3]
— Travels into North America. 1753. I. 305.
— Wästgötha och bahuslänndska resa. 1746. I. 351.
Kalmár, Tivadar. A Bálványgeszt, vagy Sátoros felleng. 1863. IV. 525.
Kalmuss, F. Die Flora des Elbinger Kreises. 1885. I. 388.
Ueber die kalten Nächte im Monat Mai. 1836. III. 45.
Kaltenbach, Johann Heinrich. Die deutschen Phytophagen. 1856. III. 189.
— Erfahrungen . . . beim Studium der Gattung Rubus. 1845. II. 305.[3]
— Die Feinde des Apfelbaumes. 1858. III. 427.[1]
— Flora des Aachener Beckens. 1843. I. 381.
— Die Pflanzenfeinde aus der Klasse der Insekten. 1874. III. 190, IV. 207.
Kalteyer, Moritz. See KATTEYER, M.
Kalugin, Ivan. See КАЛУГИНЪ, ИВ.
Kambwiri, Harry. An essay on the useful trees of British Central Africa. 1897. III. 281.[3]
Kamel, George Joseph. Descriptiones fruticum et arborum Luzonis. 1704. I. 463.[3]
— Herbarum aliarumque stirpium in insula Luzone. 1704. I. 464.[1]
— Tractatus de plantis philippensibus scandentibus. 1706. I. 464.[1]
Kamenno-stepnoye liesnitchestvo. See КАМЕННО-СТЕПНОЕ лѣсничество.
Kamerling, Z. H. De invloed van het bosch op . . . grond-water. 1900. IV. 52.
— De vroegere en tegenwoordige toestand van handel . . . op Sumatra's westkust. 1895. III. 275.[3]
De Kamferboom op Sumatra. 1871. III. 611.[3]
Kamieński, F. K. Przystosowanie liści do warunków zewnętranych. 1884. I. 236.[1]
Kamm, J. M. Das Gemeinnützigste . . . über die Maulbeer-baum- . . . Zuchts. 1839. V. XXVIII.[3]
Kammerer, Gustav. Zwei Dendrometer von Friedrich und Starke. 1895. IV. 216.
Kamp, (Prof. Dr.). Städtische Verkaufsstellen für deutsches Frischobst. 1896. III. 139.
Kamp, H. A. von. Der Fruchtbain und der Wald. 1829. I. 370, IV. 134.[2]
Der Kampf für die finanzielle Umtriebszeit. 1866. IV. 251.[2]
Der Kampf gegen den Fichtenborkenkäfer. . 1875. IV. 204.
Kampffmeyer, Wilhelm. Der Schälwald und seine Erträge. 1858. IV. 512.
— See also STEINLEIN, O. & KAMPFFMEYER, Wilhelm.
Kamphausen, N. W. Leitfaden zur Zucht des Maulbeer-baumes. 1864. III. 377.
Der Kampherbaum . . . in Japan. 1876. III. 404.[2]
Kamphøvener, Bernhard. Erindringsord til Foredrag over Planternes naturlige Familier. 1840. IV. 75.[1]
— Fortegnelse over de Træer og Buske i det forstbotaniske Anlaeg i Charlottenlund. 1845. I. 40.
Kampmann, F. E., (sr.). De la bêche (stichling). 1863. III. 503.
— Notice sur l'Ile Saint-Marguerite. 1865. I. 413.
Kanadskiya liesniya. See КАНАДСКІЯ лѣсныя.
Kane, Lady. See BAILEY, Katherine.
Kanitz, August. Anthophyta quae in Japonia legit . . . Weiss. 1878. I. 462.
— Die botanischen Resultate der centralasiatischen Expedition des Grafen Béla Széchenyi. 1885. I. 459.
— Geschichte der Botanik in Ungarn. 1863. I. 81.[1]
— Lobeliaceae. 1878. II. 845.[1]
— A növénytani áttekintése. 1887. V. XIII.[1]
— A növénytani gyüjtések eredményei Gróf Széchenyi Béla keletázsiai utjából. 1891. I. 459.
— Pauli Kitaibelii additamenta ad floram hungaricam. 1863. I. 445.
— Plantarum in expeditione speculatoria comitis Béla Széchenyi . . . collectarum enumeratio. 1891. I. 459.
— Plantas Romaniae . . . enumerat. 1879. I. 449.
— Reliquiae Kitaibelianae. 1862. I. 445.
— Die Resultate der botanischen Sammlungen. 1891. I. 459.
— See also ASCHERSON, Paul & KANITZ, August; SCHULZER VON MUEGGENBURG, Stephan, KANITZ, August & KNAPP, J. A.

Kanjilal, Babu UPENDRANATH. See UPENDRANATH KANJILAL, Babu.
Kankelwitz, W. Der Betrieb der Schneidemühlen. 1862. IV. 393.
De kanker van den Cacaoboom. 1899. III. 593.[1]
Kanneborn, E. G. Schicksale des Kaffees. 1844. III. 739.
Kannegiesser, F. A. Die Arten der Rosen. 1805. III. 447.[3]
Kannegiesser, A. Ein Wort über Streu-Nutzung. 1848. IV. 437.[2]
Kanny Lall Dey. See DEY, Kanny Lall.
Kansas — Agricultural experiment station. See KANSAS STATE AGRICULTURAL COLLEGE. III. 4.
Kansas — Commissioner of s . Annual report. Biennial report. IV. 4.
Kansas — Department of forestry and irrigation. Bulletin. IV. 4.
Kansas academy of science. Transactions. I. 5.
Kansas City review of science and industry. I. 5.
Kansas horticultural report. See KANSAS STATE HORTICULTURAL SOCIETY. III. 4.
Kansas horticultural report; forestry department. IV. 4.
Kansas state agricultural college — Experiment station. Annual report. Bulletin. III. 4.
Kansas state board of agriculture. Biennial report. III. 4.
Kansas state horticultural society. Forestry manual. See KANSAS HORTICULTURAL REPORT. IV. 4.
Kansas state horticultural society. Transactions. III. 4.
Kansas state pomological and horticultural society. See KANSAS STATE HORTICULTURAL SOCIETY. III. 4.
Kanton Zürich. Forstgesetze. 1885. IV. 331.[1]
Kantonale Vollziehungsverordnung zum Bundesgesetz betreffend . . . Oberaufsicht über die Forstpolizei. 1880. IV. 330.
Kantonale Vollziehungsverordnung zum Bundesgesetz betreffend . . . Oberaufsicht über den Forst olizei. 1884. IV. 306.
Kapeller, Ferencz, SAÁROSSY. Sep SAÁROSSY-KAPELLER, Ferencz.
Kapff, Jac. De eo, quod circa glandes justum est. 1775. IV. 313.
Kapok. 1896. III. 589.[3]
Kapok of plantenwol. 1884. III. 613.[2]
Kapp, Christian Ehrhard. Motum humorum in plantis cum motu humorum in animalibus comparat. 1763. I. 162.
Kappe, Ernst. Der kleine Botaniker. 1839. I. 380.
Kappler, A. Nederlandsch-Fransche expeditie door . . . Guyana. 1863. I. 339.[1]
Karackson, A. von. Kofhe in Palembang. 1896. III. 731. — 1899. III. 731.
Karamyschew, Alexander de. Dissertatio demonstrans necessitatem promovendae historiae naturalis in Russia. 1766. I. 453.[1]
Karásek, Alfred. O rodu Ebenovníku. 1899. II. 701.[1]
— O šupince na úponkách révy. 1900. II. 507.[2]
Karbasch, R. Zur Praxis der natürlichen Verjüngung. 1895. IV. 140.
Kardos, Árpád. Egy remek kusszónövény. 1900. III. 491.[1]
— Syringa Josikaea újdonságok. 1900. III. 681.[1]
— A valódi Ginkgo-fa. 1900. III. 287.[1]
Karel, John. American Vines in Russia. 1895. III. 762.
Karelin, Gregor. Enumeratio plantarum quas in Turco-mania et Persia boreali legit. 1839. I. 456, 477.[1]
— & Kirilow, Johann. Enumeratio plantarum in desertis Songoriae. 1842. I. 460.[1]
— Enumeratio plantarum . . . in regionibus altaicis . . . collectarum. 1841. I. 453.[2]
Kareltschikoff, S. Zur Entwickelungsgeschichte der Spaltöffnungen. 1866. I. 129.[1]
— Ueber die Vertheilung der Spaltöffnungen. 1866. I. 131.[3]
— Verzeichniss der Pflanzen, bei welchen die Spaltöffnungen auf beiden Blattflächen bemerkt worden sind. 1867. I. 131.[3]
— See also КАРЕЛЬЩИКОВЪ, С.
Karger, Johann. Die Lindenbast-Erzeugung. 1853. III. 585.[3]
Kargin, G. A. See КАРГИНЪ, Г. А.
Karl, H. Anleitung zum Waldwegbau. 1842. IV. 266.[2]
— Ausführliche Abhandlung über die Ermittlung des richtigen Holzbestandalters. 1847. IV. 235.[1]
— Ueber den Ertrag der Weisstanne. 1843. IV. 446.[1]
— Die Forstbetriebs-Regulirung nach der Fachwerks- Methode. 1851. IV. 250.[3]
— Grundsätze einer . . . Forstbetriebs-Regulirungs- Methode. 1838. IV. 240.
— Kritische Beleuchtung der Beiträge zur Lösung einiger volkswirthschaftlichen Widersprüche. 1839. IV. 242.
— Vorschläge zu Waldweide-Ablösungs-Gesetzen. 1840. IV. 333.

Karl, Kraus. *See* TRUXA, Robert & KARL, Kraus.

Karl, Wenzel. Alnus rugosa Sprgl., Haselerle. 1851. II. 117.[1]

Karl August, *Grossherzog von Sachsen-Weimar.* Account of a species of Casuarina. 1819. III. 342.[1]

— Sur une espèce de Casuarina. 1819. III. 342.[1]

Karlinski, Justin. Beiträge zur Phänologie der Hercěgovina. 1895. I. 227.[2]

Karlsruhe — Naturwissenschaftlicher Verein. *See* NATUR-WISSENSCHAFTLICHER . . . I. 14.

Karlsson, G. A. Das Transfusionsgewebe bei den Coniferen. 1887. II. 18.

— Transfusionsvafnaden hos Conifererna. 1887. II. 18.

Karmannaya dendrologiya. *See* КАРМАННАЯ ДЕНДРОЛОГІЯ.

Karmannaya kniza. *See* КАРМАННАЯ КНИГА.

Karmarsch, Karl. Grundriss der mechanischen Technologie. 1837. IV. 421.

— Handbuch der mechanischen Technologie. 1837. IV. 421.

— Die Holzarbeiten in wissenschaftlich-praktischer Darstellung. 1838. IV. 422.[1]

Die **Karnauba-Palme.** 1868. III. 324.[2]

Karo, Ferdynand. Flora okolic Częstochowy. 1881. I. 364.

— Spis rzadszych krajowych roślin . . . w okolicach Lublina. 1883. I. 364.

Karpelles, Ludwig. Über Gallmilben. 1885. IV. 535.[2]

Karpiński, Ignacy. Nowe ogrodnictwo polskie. 1877. III. 120.[1]

Karplus, Hans. Der Holzhandel auf der Jubiläumsausstellung. 1898. IV. 407.[1]

— Tabelle zur Berechnung der Prismenaufläge beim Besäumen. 1895. IV. 392.[2]

Karrer, Friedrich. Ueber das Aufblühen der Gewächse. 1882. I. 225.

— Die Pflanzendecke eines rasirten Waldstücks. 1867. I. 386.

— Vergleichende Untersuchungen über die Flora der vulkanischen Hegauberge. 1881. I. 388.

"**Karri**" wood for pavements. 1893. IV. 532.[2]

Karsch, Anton. Flora der Provinz Westfalen. 1856. I. 383.

— Phanerogamen-Flora der Provinz Westfalen. 1853. I. 383.

Karsch, F. Der Gartenbau bei den Alten. 1880. III. 32.[2]

— Neue Zoocecidien und Cecidozoën. 1880. I. 214.[1]

Karsen, H. T. Java thee. 1893. III. 608.[1]

Karshu. Remarks on the counting of annual rings. 1879. I. 127.[2]

Die **Karstaufforstung** 1895 in . . . Görz und Gradiska. 1896. IV. 167.[2]

Die **Karstaufforstung** 1894 in Görz-Gradisca. 1895. IV. 167.[1]

Die **Karstaufforstung** in Görz . . . 1898. 1899. IV. 167.[2]

Die **Karstaufforstung** in . . . Görz und Gradiska. 1898. IV. 167.[2]

Die **Karstbewaldung** auf der Weltausstellung. 1900. IV. 168.[1]

Karsten. La méthode de culture des Cinchona. 1866. III. 712.[1]

Karsten, C. Vermehrung des Caryophyllus aromaticus. 1867. III. 635.[2]

Karsten, Carl Wilhelm Gustav Hermann. *See* KARSTEN, Hermann.

Karsten, F. C. L. Geschichte der auf den Dünen . . . unternommenen Anpflanzungsversuche. 1804. IV. 145.

Karsten, Georg. Über die Anlage seitlicher Organe bei den Pflanzen. 1886. I. 132.[2]

— Anomalien und Störungen des Klimas. 1884. I. 225.

— Beitrag zur Entwickelungsgeschichte einiger Gnetum-Arten. 1892. II. 54.[2]

— Zur Entwickelungs-Geschichte der Gattung Gnetum. 1893. II. 54.[2]

— Ueber die Mangrovevegetation im Malayischen Archipel. 1890. II. 613.[1]

— Ueber die Mangrove-Vegetation im Malayischen Archipel. 1891. II. 613.[1]

— Morphologische und biologische Untersuchungen über einige Epiphytenformen. 1895. I. 234.[2]

— Notizen über einige mexikanische Pflanzen. 1897. I. 333.

— Untersuchungen über die Gattung Gnetum. 1893. II. 54.[2]

Karsten, Hermann. Ansicht über Saftbewegung. 1870. I. 164.

— Astrocáryum Warszewiczii Krst. 1858. II. 64.[2]

— Auswahl neuer und schönblühender Gewächse Venezuela's. 1848. I. 338.[1]

— Über den Bau der Cecropia peltata. 1854. II. 147.[2]

— Beitrag zur Entwickelungsgeschichte der Loranthaceen. 1852. II. 177.[1]

— Belencita. 1857. II. 229.[2]

— Bentham-Hooker's Genera plantarum und Florae columbianae specimina. 1887. I. 340.[1]

— Beschreibung einer neuen Gattung . . . der Asclepiadeen. 1849. II. 740.[2]

— Beschreibung einiger neuen Pflanzengattungen. 1848. II. 466.[1]

— Ueber die Bewurzelung der Palmen. 1856. II. 62.[2]

— Das Bluten des Rebstocks unter den Tropen. 1848. II. 508.[1]

— Botanische Untersuchungen aus dem physiologischen Laboratorium. 1865. I. 147.

— Der Brodbaum. 1858. III. 367.[1]

— De cella vitali. 1843. I. 136.[2]

— Cinchona L. und Remijia. 1884. II. 813.[1]

— Deutsche Flora. 1880. I. 388.

— Ueber einige Cinchonen Columbiens. 1859. II. 812, 821.[2]

— Einige Euphorbiaceen Columbiens. 1859. II. 434.[1]

— Ueber die Entstehung des Harzes. 1857. I. 181.[1]

— Flora von Deutschland, Oesterreich. 1880. I. 388.

— Florae Columbiae . . . specimina. 1858. I. 340.[1]

— Gesammelte Beiträge zur Anatomie . . . der Pflanzen. 1865. I. 34.

— Zur Geschichte der Botanik. 1870. I. 79.[2]

— Das Geschlechtsleben der Pflanzen. 1860. I. 202.[1]

— Histological researches on the formation . . . of the vegetable cell. 1862. I. 136.[2]

— Histologische Untersuchungen. 1862. I. 136.[2]

— Illustrirtes Repetitorium der pharmaceutisch-medicinischen Botanik. 1886. III. 59.[1]

— Die medicinischen Chinarinden Neu-Granada's. 1858. III. 721.

— Notes on the medicinal Cinchona barks. 1858. III. 721.

— Organographische Betrachtung der Zamia muricata. 1857. II. 7.[1]

— Über Pflanzenkrankheiten, besonders der Orangenbäume. 1861. III. 500.[2]

— Plantae columbianae. 1856. I. 340.[1]

— Plantae Karstenianae ex variis familiis. 1856. I. 340.[1]

— Rathea fibrosa K. 1858. II. 75.[1]

— Reineckia triandra Krst. 1858. II. 75.[1]

— On the sexual life of plants. 1860. I. 202.[1]

— Der Sternanis. 1889. II. 210.[2]

— Die Vegetationsorgane der Palmen. 1847. II. 62.[2]

— De la vie sexuelle des plantes. 1860. I. 202.[1]

— Ueber das Vorkommen der Gerbsäure. 1858. I. 183.

— *See also* RATZEBURG, Christian & KARSTEN, Hermann.

Kartum, K. A. Der Thee und seine Stellvertreter. 1811. III. 606.

Karuna Nidhan Mukerji. Semla gum in Dehra Dún. 1886. III. 467.[2]

Karwacki, Aleksander. O hodowaniu i pielęgnowaniu kwiatów i roślin pokojowych. 1874. III. 150.[2]

— Ogrodnictwo warzywne, drzew owocowych i krzewów jagodowych. 1871. III. 135.

Karyshef, N. *See* КАРЫШЕВ, Н.

Kaselow, G. A. Aucuba japonica. 1873. III. 645.[1]

Kasimir, A. Sur les cristaux chez Opuntia et Pereskia. 1894. II. 588.[2]

Kasper, J. D. Der in der Wald- und Forstwirthschaft . . . unterrichtete Forstbeamte. 1828. IV. 99.[2]

— Der in der Wald- und Jagdwirthschaft . . . unterrichtete Forstbeamte. 1828. IV. 99.[2]

Kassel, E. Over Koffiecultuur in Palembang. 1894. III. 730.

— *See also* SCHUURINGA, H. P. J. & KASSEL, E.

Kassner. Ueber die Bedeutung des Markes der Holzpflanzen. 1888. IV. 63.[2]

— Eigenthümliche Veränderungen im Marke der Holzpflanzen. 1888. IV. 62.[1]

Kassner, Georg Max Julius. Betrachtungen über das Mark der Holzgewächse. 1887. I. 129.[1]

— Ueber die Entstehung . . . des Korkes. 1888. I. 130.

— Der Humus. 1888. IV. 69.

— Ueber das Mark einiger Holzpflanzen. 1884. I. 129.[1]

— Ueber die Verzweigung einer Dracaena. 1889. II. 81.[2]

Kast, J. Die wichtigsten Kulturpflanzen im alten Ägypten. 1894. III. 34.[1]

Kast, Karl. Die horst- und gruppenweise Verjüngung. 1890. IV. 140.
— Ueber den Unterbau. 1889. IV. 169.[1]
— See also GAYER, Karl & KAST, Karl.
Kasthofer, Charles. See KASTHOFER, Karl.
Kasthofer, Karl. Abrégé de sylviculture. 1846. IV. 110.[2]
— Ansichten über die bessere Benutzung des Eigenthums der Burgerschaft von Bern. 1834. IV. 294.[2]
— Ueber Behandlung der Wälder. 1846. IV. 110.[1]
— Bemerkungen auf einer Alpen-Reise über den Brünig, Bragel, Kirenzenberg. 1825. IV. 365.
— Bemerkungen auf einer Alpen-Reise über den Susteu, Gotthard, Bernardin. 1822. IV. 365.
— Bemerkungen über die Bannwälder von Airolo. 1851. IV. 365.
— Bemerkungen über die Forsten des Bernischen Hochgebirgs. 1808. IV. 365.
— Bemerkungen über die Wälder und die Alpen des bernerischen Hochgebürgs. 1816. IV. 123.[1]
— Bericht über die Waldungen der Stadt Biel. 1836. IV. 365.
— Bericht über Kulturversuche mit ausländischen Baumarten. 1851. IV. 127.[1]
— Beschwerdeschrift des Forstmeisters gegen den Regierungsrath . . . der Republik Bern. 1845. IV. 294.[1]
— Betrachtungen über die einheimischen Eisenwerke. 1833. IV. 277.
— I boschi sacri di Airolo. 1847. IV. 365.
— Compendio di selvicoltura. 1846. IV. 110.[1]
— Considérations sur les forges du Jura bernois. 1833. IV. 406.[1]
— Défense du guide dans les forêts. 1829. IV. 101.
— Die Entwaldung der Gebirge. 1850. IV. 281.[1]
— Forstschule für Waldverwalter in Burgdorf. 1845. IV. 36.[1]
— Die Forstverwaltung . . . im bernerschen Hochgebirge. 1850. IV. 294.[1]
— Le guide dans les forêts. 1828. IV. 110.[1]
— Kurzer und gemeinfasslicher Unterricht in der Naturgeschichte der . . . Waldbäume. 1846. IV. 110.[1]
— Der Lehrer im Walde. 1828. IV. 110.[1]
— Memorial über den Bannwald von Andermatt. 1850. IV. 181.[1]
— Die Naturgeschichte . . . einheimischer . . . Holzgewächse . . . Die Weisserle. 1850. IV. 489.[2]
— Riassunto delle osservazioni generali intorno alle condizioni ed al governo dei boschi nel cantone Ticino. 1847. IV. 365.
— Uebersicht der verschiedenen Zweige der Forstwirtschaft. 1850. IV. 294.[1]
— Uebersicht von Erfahrungen . . . über die Alpenwirtschaft und Alpenforstwirtschaft. 1851. IV. 294.[1]
— Versuche und Erfahrungen im Gebiete der Alpenwirthschaft. 1847. IV. 365.
— Das Waldrenten-Verhältniss. 1850. IV. 277.
— Zum Zustand der schweizerischen Forstkultur. 1843. IV. 123.[1]
Kasyanenko, V. See АХМАТОВЪ, М. & КАСЯНЕНКО, В.
Katalog. See also CATALOG.
Katalog der Bibliothek des Königlichen Ministeriums für die landwirthschaftlichen Angelegenheiten. 1877. III. 1.
Katalog der Bibliothek des Vereins zur Beförderung des Gartenbaues in den königl. preussischen Staaten. 1897. III. 1.
Katalog der forstakademischen Bibliothek zu Hann. Münden. 1885. IV. 2.
Katalog der in dem hiesigen Schlossgarten . . . enthaltnen Pflanzen. 1832. I. 47.
Katalog der Lehrmittel der Forstlehranstalt Weisswasser in Böhmen. 1886. IV. 18.[1]
Katalog zur Collectiv-Ausstellung der Fürsten . . . zu Schwarzenberg. 1873. III. 272.[1]
Katalogus a Magyarország erdőgazdaságára vonatkozó magyar és német nyelvü szak-könyvekről. 1896. IV. 2.
Die Katastrophe des im westlichen Böhmen . . . 1872 erfolgten Wolkenbruches. 1873? IV. 190.
Kate Field's Washington. IV. 539.[1]
Kath, or pale cutch. 1891. III. 464.[1]
Kathriner, N. Obwalden. 1897. IV. 167.[1]
— Obwalden. Wegbauten in der Gemeinde Giswyl. 1895. IV. 267.
Kattein, A. F. Der morphologische Werth des Centralcylinders der Wurzel. 1897. I. 104.
Katteyer, Moritz & Neil, W. E. Sur la Sophora speciosa. 1887. II. 384.[2]
— — Sophora speciosa Bentham. 1887. III. 488.[2]

Katzer. Wurzelvermehrung der Cycadeen. 1882. III. 284.[1]
Katzer, Joseph. Systematische Uebersicht der officinellen Pflanzen. 1840. III. 57.
Katzer, Karl. Über die Berechnung des jährlichen Reinertrages. 1895. IV. 258.
— Zum Frasse des Schwammspinners. 1890. IV. 210.[1]
— Leitfaden der Buchführung für Forstverwaltungen. 1892. IV. 312.
Kauenhowen, Willy. Beitrag zur Kenntnis . . . des Spartein. 1892. III. 475.[1]
Kauffman, Levi. Propagation of Grapes by cuttings. 1868. III. 548.[1]
Kauffmann, Karl. Praktische Anleitung zur korrekten Kurven-Absteckung. 1895. IV. 267.
Kauffmann, Nicolaus. Ueber die Bildung des Wickels bei den Asperifolieen. 1871. II. 747.[2]
— Zur Entwickelungsgeschichte der Cacteenstacheln. 1859. II. 588.[1]
— Uber die männliche Blüthe von Casuarina quadrivalvis. 1869. II. 92.[2]
— Ueber die Natur der Stacheln. 1859. I. 112.[2]
— See also КАУФМАНЪ, Н.
Kaufmann, A. Neues Schutzmittel das Holz durch Verdichtung . . . zu schützen. 1863. IV. 418.
— See also КАУФМАНЪ, А.
Kaufmann, Alexander. Der Gartenbau im Mittelalter. 1892. III. 32.[2]
Kaufmann-Bayer, Robert. Schweizer Flora. 1884. I. 437.
Kaunhowen, F. Die Bewaldung Russisch-Turkestans. 1893. IV. 376.[1]
— Zwei seltene Waldbäume. 1894. IV. 520.[2]
The Kauri Pine. 1889. II. 25.[2]
Kauri pine plantation. See McDOWALL, A. & HOOPER, E. D. M. 1885. V. xxxii.[1]
Kauschinger, G. Bemerkungen über das Abfallen der Blätter. 1825. I. 191.[2]
— Die Lehre vom Waldschutz. 1848. IV. 177.[1]
— Protection of woodlands against dangers. 1848. IV. 177.[1]
Die Kautschukproduktion von Brasilien. 1900. III. 232.[1]
Kautzsch, F. O. Beiträge zur Frage der Weisstannenwirthschaft. 1895. IV. 444.[2]
— Zur Forsteinrichtungsfrage. 1896. IV. 246.
— Zur Frage der Begründung von Kiefernbeständen. 1893. IV. 474.
Kautzsch, Otto. Gegen den finanziellen Umtrieb. 1879. IV. 252.
Kawai, Shitaro. Die Unterscheidungsmerkmale der wichtigeren in Japan wachsenden Laubhölzer. 1900. I. 126, 461, IV. 65,[1] 87.[2]
Kawakami, Takiya. Phanerogams of Shōnai. 1895. I. 463.[1]
Kawakita. See DIVERS, E. & KAWAKITA.
Kawalier, A. Über Pinus sylvestris. 1853. II. 48.[1]
— Über Thuja occidentalis. 1854. II. 52.[1]
Kawall, J. H. Chronik phänologischer Beobachtungen in Kurland. 1866. I. 223.[2]
Kawamoura, Seiichi. Notes sur l'acclimation en Chine. 1890. III. 50.[1]
Kay, James. Instrument for measuring the heights of trees. 1869. IV. 215.
— Methods of measuring the heights of trees. 1878. IV. 215. — 1079. IV. 215.
— Old . . . trees in the island of Bute. 1881. I. 297.[1]
— On a new transplanting machine. 1875. III. 167.
— Planting . . . of Beech and Thorn hedges. 1868. III. 213.
— The transplanting machine. 1879. III. 168.[1]
— Transplanting of large trees. 1878. III. 167.
— Transplanting machine. 1879. III. 168.[1]
Kaygorodoff, D. L'appareil pour mesurer la dureté des bois. 1878. IV. 411.[2]
Kay's dendrometer. 1883. IV. 231.[2] — 1884. IV. 215.
Kayser, (Forstmeister, Breslau). See SALISCH, Heinrich von & KAYSER.
— & Salisch, Heinrich von. In welcher Weise sind behufs Erziehung werthvoller Hölzer Kiefernbestände zu begründen. 1886. IV. 473.
Kayser, Georg. Beiträge zur Kenntnis der Entwickelungsgeschichte des Samens. 1893. I. 121.
— Ueber das Verhalten des Nucellus . . . von Croton flavens. 1893. II. 439.[2]
Kaysing, (Oberförster). Ueber die Bewirthschaftung . . . der edlen Kastanie im Elsass. 1876. IV. 492.[1]
— Der Kastanienniederwald. 1884. IV. 492.[1]
Kazitzyn. See КАЗИЦЫНЪ.
Kaznatcheyef, К. А. See КАЗНАЧЕЕВЪ, К. А.

Kearney, Thomas Henry. Buckleya again. 1896. II. 168.[1]
— The liana vegetation of southeastern Virginia. 1897. III. 205.[1]
— New or little known plants of the southern states. 1894. I. 319.
— New or otherwise interesting plants of eastern Tennessee. 1897. I. 319.
— The nomenclature of the genus Büttneria. 1894. II. 214.[1]
Kearney, Thomas Henry, (jr.). The lower austral element. 1900. I. 320.
— The plant covering of Ocracoke Island. 1900. I. 320.
— Plant geography of North America. 1900. I. 320.
— Some new Florida plants. 1894. II. 458.[2]
— See also BRITTON, N. L. & KEARNEY, T. H., (jr.).
Kechelen, George Samuel. De genesi camphorae. 1748. III. 233.[1]
Kecht, J. S. Verbesserter praktischer Weinbau. 1814. III. 552.
— Versuch einer ... Methode, den Weinbau ... zu verbessern. 1814. III. 552.
Keck, Franz Anton. De egregio corticis peruviani effectu. 1782. III. 720.
Keckman, Charles E. Anteckningar om floran i Simo och Kemi socknar. 1896. I. 366.
Keddie, William. Notice of a botanical trip to Ben Lawers. 1861. I. 401.
— A popular guide to the Royal botanic garden of Glasgow. 1861. I. 55.
Kedr. See Кедръ.
Kedzie, Robert Clark. The influence of forest trees on agriculture. 1867. IV. 43.
— Relation of meteorology to forestry in Michigan. 1898. IV. 46.[1]
— & others. Report on the injurious destruction of forest trees in Michigan. 1867. IV. 338.[2]
Keeble, Frederic William. The hanging foliage of certain tropical trees. 1895. I. 233.[1]
— Observations on the Loranthaceae of Ceylon. 1896. II. 174.[1]
Keel, J. J. Kurze Anleitung zur Behandlung der Waldurfgen. 1854. IV. 110.[1]
Keel, Joseph. Anleitung zur Anlage ... der Laub- und Nadelholz-Saatbeete. 1865. IV. 150.
— Der Bannwartenfreund. 1870. IV. 99,[1] 110.[1]
— Bericht über die Prüfungen der Waldungen von Appenzell A. Rh. 1859. IV. 365.
— Denkschrift betreffend ausserordentliche Nutzungen aus den St. Gallischen Staatswaldungen. 1868. IV. 383.[1]
— Gutachten über den Bannwald in Altdorf. 1868. IV. 181.[1]
— Leitfaden zur Betreibung der Eichenschälwirtschaft. 1861. IV. 505.
— Tafeln zur Bestimmung des Kubik-Inhaltes der runden Hölser. 1837. IV. 222.
— Vademecum des Försters. 1869. IV. 226.
Keeler, Harriet Louise. Our native trees. 1900. I. 313, IV. 76.[1]
Keese, John. The floral keepsake. 185 . ? I. 95.
Keffer, Charles Albert. Arbor day; why to plant, what to plant, how to plant. 1888. IV. 42.[1]
— The Banksian Pine in the Nebraska Sand Hills. 1895. IV. 463.[1]
— Black Locust in the West. 1895. IV. 523.[2]
— Black Walnut in the West. 1895. III. 354.[2]
— The Box-elder and the Russian Mulberry. 1894. IV. 519,[1] 526.[2]
— Bull Pine in the West. 1895. IV. 468.[2]
— The Chestnut in the West. 1895. IV. 492.[2]
— Conifers in the West. 1895. III. 293.
— The Cottonwood for forest-planting on the plains. 1894. IV. 486.[1]
— Experimental tree planting in the plains. 1898. IV. 155.[1]
— Forest trees, fruits and vegetables. 1891. III. 118.[1]
— Forestry. 1889. IV. 112.
— Green Ash in the west. 1895. IV. 536.[1]
— The hardy Catalpa in the West. 1894. IV. 538.[1]
— Honey Locust in the West. 1895. III. 477.[2]
— Mature White Pine in Pennsylvania. 1897. IV. 470.[1]
— Notes on the growth of trees in the Agricultural college grounds. 1887. III. 118.[1]
— Prairie forestry and the timber culture law. 1891. IV. 314.[1]
— The Scotch Pine in the West. 1895. IV. 474.
— Second-growth White Pine in Pennsylvania. 1897. IV. 469.

— Tree planting in the western plains. 1896. III. 118.[1]
— Tree planting in waste places. 1897. IV. 155.[2]
— Trees of minor importance for western planting. 1895. IV. 112.
— Wattle tree. 1895. IV. 521.[1]
— The White Elm in the West. 1895. III. 365.[1]
— The White Pine in the West. 1895. IV. 469.
— The Wild Cherry in the West. 1894. III. 442.[2]
— The work of the United States forestry division. 1897. IV. 338.[2]
Der kegelförmige Pflanzspaten. 1830. IV. 152.
Kehding, F. Ueber das Pfeilgift der Karo Batta's. 1897. III. 367.[1]
Kehrer, Eduard. Flora der Heilbronner Stadtmarkung. 1856. I. 384.
— Ein im letzten Drittel des Novembers 1858 durch's Eis zerstörter Wald bei Erbach. 1862. IV. 190.
Kehrig, Henri. La cochenille des Fusains du Japon. 1897. III. 532.[1]
The Kei-apple as a hedge plant. 1897. III. 614.[1]
Keibel, Johan Georg Ludwig. De corticis peruviani usu medico. 1805. III. 720.
Keil, Frans. Phyto-phaenologische Beobachtungen. 1857. I. 227.[1]
Das Keimen der Ceder-Samen. 1844. II. 27.[7]
Keimö, Zufu. n. d. I. 461.[1]
Keiper, Johann. Nachzucht der Eiche. 1893. IV. 508.
— Der Reichswald bei Kaiserslautern. 1895. IV. 351.[1]
Keir, Archibald. Of the method of distilling. 1788. III. 667.[1]
Keir, P. F. Die Laub abwerfenden Bäume mit hängenden Aesten. 1850. III. 204.[1]
— Pendent, or weeping deciduous trees. 1850. III. 204.[1]
— Pendent, or weeping trees. 1850. III. 204.[1]
Keiserling, L. A., Graf. See Кейзерлингъ, Л. А. графъ.
Keiss. See SCHARRER & KEISS.
Keissler, Karl von. Ueber einen androgynen Fichtenzapfen. 1899. II. 36.[1]
— Die Arten der Gattung Daphne. 1898. II. 600.[2]
— Einige neue Missbildungen. 1899. I. 144.[1]
— Einige phänologische Beobachtungen. 1899. I. 227.[2]
— Ueber eine neue Daphne-Art. 1896. II. 602.[2]
— Ueber eine neue Daphne-Art aus Persien. 1897. II. 602.[2]
— Phaenologische Notizen über den Jänner. 1899. I. 227.[2]
— Ueber eine Zweig-Fasciation bei Lonicera. 1899. II. 838.[1]
Keiter, Ernst. Eine Expedition auf Cedernnüsse in Sibirien. 1890. IV. 464.[1]
Keith, Patrick. A botanical lexicon. 1837. I. 147.
— Of the development of the seminal germ. 1815. I. 202.[2]
— On the origin of buds. 1833. I. 107.[2]
— Of the pith of plants. 1839. I. 128.[2]
— A system of physiological botany. 1816. I. 148.
De keizerlijke Paulownia. 1855. II. 781.[2]
Kelaart, Edward Frederick. Flora calpensis. 1846. I. 420.
Kelbel, Waldverheerung durch eine Windhose. 1891. IV. 189.[2]
Kelch, Wilhelm Gottlieb. Flora medica borussica. 1805. III. 72.
Keleti, Károly. Honismertető. See SONTAGH, Nikolauss von.
Kellander, Daniel. De seminibus. 1720. I. 120.
Keller. Forst- und Ackerbau-Chemie. 1847. IV. 63.[2]
Keller, (Forstamtsassessor). Welchen Zweck und welche Bedeutung haben die Durchforstungs- und Reinigungshiebe. 1890. IV. 174.
Keller, (Forstmeister). Beiträge zur Lösung der Frage über Bestandesmischungen. 1884. IV. 137.[2]
Keller, Antonio. Osservazioni fatte sulla malattia delle Uve. 1855. III. 576.[1]
— Principii di botanica. 1856. I. 89.
Keller, C. Zur Aufforstung unproductiver Landflächen in Oesterreich. 1883. IV. 167.[2]
Keller, C. C. Sur le dosage de la caféine dans le thé. 1897. III. 608.[1]
Keller, Conrad. Sur l'arpentage des forêts. 1862. IV. 264.
— Zur Aufforstung unproductiver Landflächen. 1883. IV. 55.[2]
— Beobachtungen auf dem Gebiete der Forstentomologie. 1885. IV. 209.[2]
— Beobachtungen über ... Chermes coccineus. 1883. IV. 209.[2]
— Beobachtungen über den Nonnenfrass. 1890. IV. 200.
— Beobachtungen über die Lebensweise der Tannen-Wurzellaus. 1899. IV. 445.

— Beschädigungen der Eichen durch Gallwespen. 1896. IV. 511.
— Zur Biologie der Chermesarten. 1889. IV. 210.[1]
— Eichenbeschädigungen durch Cynips megaptera. 1896. IV. 511.
— Die Färbungen der Forstinsecten. 1885. IV. 92.
— Concerning the forestal usefulness of millipedes. 1886. IV. 92.
— Die forstliche Bedeutung der Tausendfüssler. 1886. IV. 92.
— Ueber den forstlichen Nutzen der Tausendfüssler. 1886. IV. 92.
— Forstlicher Nutzen der Tausendfüssler. 1886. IV. 92.
— Forstlicher Schaden der Tausendfüsser. 1886. IV. 209.[2]
— Forstzoologische Mitteilungen. 1899. IV. 209.[2]
— Forstzoologischer Excursionsführer. 1897. IV. 90,[1] 208.[1]
— Der Galeriewald. 1897. IV. 446.[1]
— Die Herbstphasen ... der Tannen-Wurzellaus. 1900. IV. 446.[1]
— Humusformen im Gebirge. 1889. IV. 69.
— Insectenschäden im Gebirgswalde. 1885. IV. 210.[1]
— Zur Kenntniss der Pinien-Prozessionsraupe. 1883. IV. 461.[2]
— Die Kosten der Aufforstung der unproductiven Landflächen. 1883. IV. 155.[3]
— Mangrovewaldungen. 1896. IV. 529.[1]
— Neue Forschungsergebnisse über ... Humusdecke. 1890. IV. 69.
— Der Palmenwald. 1896. IV. 75.[3]
— Die Parklandschaft. 1897. IV. 89.[1]
— Ueber Schneedruckbeschädigungen. 1887. IV. 190.
— Thierische Forstbeschädigungen an der Arve. 1890. IV. 464.[1]
— Untersuchungen über die forstliche Bedeutung der Spinnen. 1885. IV. 92.
— Ueber Waldvermessungen. 1862. IV. 264.
— Weitere Beobachtungen über ... Chermes. 1884. IV. 209.[2]
Keller, Franz. See KELLER-LEUZINGER, Franz.
Keller, Heinrich. Kennzeichen von zur Unzeit gepflückten Kiefernzapfen. 1883. IV. 473.
— Pinus sylvestris de Riga. 1881. IV. 473.
Keller, Ida Augusta. The coloring matter of the aril of Celastrus. 1897. II. 467.[1]
— The growth of Viburnum lantanoides. 1899. II. 843.[1]
— Notes on plant monstrosities. 1898. II. 838.[3]
— Notes on the study of the cross-fertilization. 1896. II. 239.[1]
Keller, J. B. Eichenlohgerbung und Schälwaldbetrieb. 1896. IV. 513.
Keller, Jos. B. von. Ueber die Bechsteinschen Rosen. 1886. II. 284.[3]
— Ueber behaarte Rosenpetala. 1884. II. 287.[3]
— Berichtigungen zu Nachträge zur Flora von Niederösterreich. 1882. II. 287.[3]
— Ueber die Flächendrüsigkeit ... bei einzelnen Rosenarten. 1887. II. 295.[3]
— Zur Flora von Niederösterreich. 1882. II. 291.[3]
— Rhodographische Beiträge. 1883. II. 287.[3]
— Rhodologiai adatok. 1888. II. 288.[1]
— Rhodologische Bemerkungen. 1882. II. 287.[3]
— Rhodologische Notizen. 1883. II. 287.[3]
Rosa Braunii n. sp. 1889. II. 901.[1]
— Rosa glanduloso-punctata Opiz. 1882. II. 294.[3]
— Rosa pseudocuspidata Crép. 1881. II. 283.[3]
— Zur Rosa reversa W. K. 1883. II. 298.[1]
— Eine vorläufige Bemerkung aus der Mai-Flora. 1878. II. 287.[3]
— Weitere Beiträge zur Rosenflora von Oberösterreich. 1893. II. 288.[1]
Keller, K. Die Blutlaus. 1885. III. 427.[1]
Keller, Louis. Beiträge zur Flora von Kärnten. 1899. I. 444.
Keller, Matthew. The Grapes and wine of Los Angeles. 1859. III. 550.
Keller, Maximilian. Über die Blühte des Weinstocks. 1826. II. 507.[1]
Keller, Paul. Die Rose. 1885. III. 450.
— Der Weissdornzaun. 1883. II. 214,[1] 422.[2]
Keller, Robert. Beiträge zur Kenntnis der bosnischen Rosen. 1893. II. 288.[1]
— Beiträge zur Kenntnis der wilden Rosen der Grajischen Alpen. 1898? II. 287.[3]
— Beiträge zur Rosenflora des oberen Innthales. 1895. II. 288.[3]

— Beiträge zur schweizerischen Phanerogamenflora. 1890. II. 177,[1] 287.[1] — 1891. II. 287.[1]
— Ueber die central- und südamerikanischen Hyperica. 1898. II. 556.[1]
— Die Coniferenmistel. 1890. II. 177.[3]
— Ueber Erscheinungen des normalen Haarverlustes. 1890. I. 113.[1]
— Flora von Winterthur. 1891. I. 437.
— Hypericum L. 1895. II. 556.[1]
— Rosa gallica L. × R. Jundzilli. 1896. II. 294.[1]
— Die Wasserverdunstung der Pflanzen. 1900. I. 168.
— Wilde Rosen des Kantons Zürich. 1888. II. 287.[1]
— Die wilden Rosen der Kantone St. Gallen. 1897. II. 287.[2]
— Die wilden Rosen der Leventina. 1891. II. 287.[1]
— See also SCHINZ, Hans & KELLER, Robert.
Keller, Wilhelm. Verzeichnis ... der grossen Rosensammlung. 1833. III. 448.
Keller-Leuzinger, Franz. The Amazon and Madeira Rivers. 1874. I. 343, 531.[2]
— Vom Amazonas und Madeira. 1874. I. 343.
— Die nützlichen Gewächse ... des Amazonas. 1874. III. 65.[2]
— Voyage d'exploration sur l'Amazone et le Madeira. 1874. I. 343.
Kellerman, Mrs. Stella (Dennis). Leaf-variation. See KELLERMAN, Mrs. W. A. 1893. I. 111.
— & W. A. See KELLERMAN, W. A. & Mrs. Stella (Dennis).
Kellerman. Culture de l'Arbre à cire. 1857. III. 353.[1]
Kellerman, William Ashbrook. Bibliography of Ohio botany. 1893. I. 3,[1] V. VII.[1]
— The fourth state catalogue of Ohio plants. 1899. I. 316.
— Notes economic ... on the Saw Brier. 1900. II. 85.[2]
— Ohio forest trees. 1895. I. 312, IV. 77.[1]
— An Ohio station for Ampelopsis cordata. 1900. II. 502.[1]
— & Mrs. Stella (Dennis). The non-indigenous flora of Ohio. 1900. I. 317.[1]
— & Swingle, W. T. Branch knot of the Hackberry. 1888. III. 363.[3]
— & Werner, W. C. Catalogue of Ohio plants. 1895. I. 316, 531.[1]
Kellerman, Mrs. William Ashbrook. See KELLERMAN, Mrs. Stella (Dennis).
Kellgren, Anders Gustaf. Om den geografiska utbredningen af Ledum palustre. 1894. II. 673.[1]
— Några observationer öfver trädgränserna. 1893. I. 350,[2] IV. 79.[2]
— Några ord om den skandinaviska Björkregionen. 1894. I. 350,[2] IV. 79.[2]
— De skogbildande trädens utbredning. 1891. I. 350,[2] IV. 79.[2]
Kellner, A. Beobachtungen der Ursachen der sogenannten Fichtenabsprünge. 1862. IV. 197,[3] 455.
— Ueber die im Thüringer Walde vorkommenden Fichtenborkenkäfer. 1880. IV. 456.
Kellner, Carl. Welche Resultate ... bezüglich der Verwendung des Holzes zu chemisch-technischen Zwecken. 1890. IV. 433.[1]
Kellner, Horpacz. Hausratten als Baumverderber. 1876. IV. 198.[1]
Kellner, L. Gründlicher Versuch die Laubholzwaldungen in den möglichst hohen Ertrag zu stellen. 1815. IV. 117.
Kellner, O., Yoshii, T. & Nagaoka, M. Experiments on the cultivation of Lespedeza. 1891. III. 481.[1]
Kellner, W. Die Forstwirthschaft in der Bukowina. 1885. IV. 123.[1]
— Die Forstwirthschaft Tirols. 1886. IV. 124.[1]
Kellogg, Albert. Abies Bridgesi. 1863. II. 53.[2]
— Azalea nudiflora [var. ciliata]. 1854. II. 682.[2]
— Botanical papers. 1877. II. 198.[2]
— Brickelia [sic] multiflora. 1877. II. 854.[1]
— Bridal Honeysuckle. 1861. II. 837.[1]
— California Goat-nut. 1860. II. 453.[2]
— California Marigold shrub. 1861. II. 856.[1]
— Castanea sempervirens. 1854. II. 125.[1]
— Ceanothus cordulatus. 1863. II. 493.[1]
— Ceanothus nevadensis. 1863. II. 493.[1]
— Cedar Island Juniper. Juniperus cedrosiana Kellogg. 1860. II. 30.[2]
— Cupressus fragrans. 1854. II. 29.[1]
— Description of two new species ... from Nevada. 1863. II. 851.[1]
— Description of two new species of plants. 1863. II. 855.[2]
— Descriptions of a new genus. 1875. I. 324.
— Descriptions of new plants from the Pacific states. 1875. I. 324.

Kellogg, Albert (*continued*).
— Descriptions of new plants from the west coast of America. 1875. II. 522.[1]
— Different varieties of Eucalyptus. 1876. II. 623.[1]
— An Ephedra used as tea. 1854. III. 312.[2]
— Forest trees of California. 1882. I. 320, *IV. 78*.[1]
— Four species of Ceanothus. 1854. II. 492.[2]
— The Holly-leaf Buckthorn. 1860. II. 498.[1]
— Idria columnaria. 1860. II. 563.[1]
— Juniperus cerrosianus (Kellogg); Cerros Island Juniper. 1863. II. 30.[2]
— Larrea mexicana. 1863. II. 395.[2]
— Lonicera conjugialis (Kellogg). 1863. II. 837.[1]
— Lonicera intermedia. 1863. II. 838.[2]
— Lonicera pilosa. 1854. II. 838.[1]
— Malvastrum splendidum. 1854. II. 525.[2]
— New plants from Cerros Island. 1863. I. 323.
— Notes and descriptions of some Californian plants. 1877. II. 380.[1]
— Oenothera arborea. 1863. II. 646.[1]
— Parry's Lotus tree. 1890. II. 500.[1]
— Poison Oak and its antidotes. 1862. III. 527.[1]
— Quercus arcoglandis [*sic*]. 1854. II. 132.[2]
— Quercus fulvescens. 1854. II. 133.[1]
— Quercus Morehus (Kellogg), Abram's Oak. 1863. II. 135.[2]
— Quercus Ransomi. 1854. II. 133.[2]
— Rhamnus ilicifolius (Kellogg), Hollyleaf Buckthorn. 1860. II. 498.[1]
— Rhododendron maximum. 1860. III. 661.[2]
— Ribes balsamifera. 1863. II. 244.[2]
— On some new species of Californian plants. 1877. II. 238.[2]
— The tree Primrose or False Fuchsia. 1860. II. 646.[1]
— Trixis californica. 1863. II. 867.[1]
— Virgin's Bower. Clematis lasiantha. 1863. II. 198.[2]
— Washoe Tea tree. 1860. II. 493.[1]
— *See also* VEATCH, J. A. & KELLOGG, Albert.
— & Behr, H. H. Taxodium giganteum. 1854. II. 50.[1]
— & Greene, E. L. Illustrations of West American Oaks. 1889. II. 129.[1]
Kelly, Charles R. Directions for transplanting large trees. 1873. III. 167.
Kelly, Thomas. Taranaki Forest and forest farming. 1877. IV. 124.[2]
Kelsey, F. D. Bark within a tree trunk. 1896. I. 127.[1]
Kembter, A. Veterum scriptorum de re rustica praecepta. 1760. III. 116.[2]
Kemmerich, Diet. H. De iure foresti nobilibus imperii immediatis quoque competente. 1736. IV. 316.
Kemmler, Karl Albert. *See* MARTENS, Georg von & KEMMLER, K. A.
Kemp, A. S. Boscobel and the Royal Oak. 1878. II. 138.[1]
Kemp, James Forman. Notes on the winter flora of Bermuda. 1885. I. 336.
Kemp, John C. On the best method of maintaining the supply of Teak. 1885. IV. 537.[2]
Kemp, P. H. van der. Biliton-opstellen. 1886. III. 274.[2]
— De regeling der statistiek bij de gouvernements -Koffiecultuur. 1881. III. 729.[2]
— De registreering der gereserveerde gronden. 1881. III. 729.[2]
Kemp, W. J. Cinchona in the Nilgiris. 1884. III. 718.
— De oorzaken van het mislukken der Kinacultuur in zuidelijk Indië. 1884. III. 714.
Kemp, William. An account of some seeds, buried. 1844. I. 527.
Kempe, Anders Pehrson. Den anatomerade Granen. 1671. IV. 459.[2]
Kempe, J. Plants indigenous to . . . Hermannsburg. 1880. I. 502.
Kempthorne, G. B. Description of the Frankincense tree. 1845. II. 416.[1]
Kempton, Harold Bigelow. Norway Spruce for profit on the plains. 1900. IV. 454.
Kendo, T. A. Treatise on silk and Tea culture. 1870. III. 377, 600.[2]
Kennedy, George W. Arbutine du Kalmia latifolia. 1875. III. 652.[2]
— Huile essentielle du Betula lenta. 1882. IV. 491.[3]
— Oleum Betulae lentae. 1882. IV. 491.[2]
Kennedy, J. F. The food-value of fruits. 1894. III. 220.[2]
— Food value of nuts. 1898. III. 220.[2]
Kennedy, John. A treatise upon planting, gardening. 1776. III. 109.

Kennedy, Patrick Beveridge. Saltbushes. 1900. III. 387.[2]
Kennedy, S. E. The Cornel Cherry. 1892. III. 645.[1]
The **Kennedyas.** 1885. III. 480.[1]
Kennion, Edward. An essay on trees·in landscape. 1815. III. 202.[2]
Kennis, P. H. Koffiecultuur. 1900. III. 727.
Zur **Kenntniss** der Torf bewohnenden Föhren. 1889. IV. 463.[1]
Kenntniss derjenigen Pflanzen . . . Färbern zum Nutzen. *See* Reuss, C. F. 1776. III. 235.[2]
Die **Kennzeichen** guter Saateicheln. 1849. IV. 504.
Kenrick, William. The American silk grower's guide. 1835. III. 375.
— Des americanischen Seidebauers Anweisung. 1835. III. 375.
— The new American orchardist. 1833. III. 133.
— Silk and the Chinese Mulberry. 1834. III. 380.[2]
Kent, Adolphus Henry. Conifers and Taxads. 1893. II. 13.[2]
— A manual of the Coniferae. 1881. II. 13,[1] V. xxv.[1]
— Manuale dei Coniferi. 1881. V. xxv.[1]
— Ulex strictus. 1862. III. 490.[1]
— Veitch's manual of the Coniferae. 1881. II. 13.[1]
Kent, Elizabeth. Sylvan sketches. 1825. I. 393.[1]
Kent, T. On the extract of Mimosa bark. 1824. III. 481.[2]
Kentia Casterburyana. 1892. III. 326.[1]
Kentish, Richard. Experiments . . . on a new species of bark. 1784. III. 720.
Kentzmann, Theophilus. Tabula locum et tempus, quibus uberius plantae . . . vigent. 1659. V. XVI.[1]
Kentucky — State college — Kentucky agricultural experiment station. Annual report. Bulletin. III. 4
Kentucky agricultural experiment station. *See* KENTUCKY — STATE COLLEGE. III. 4.
Kentucky Coffee tree. 1896. III. 363.[1]
Kenyon, O. A. Seedling fruits. 1887. III. 50.[2]
K'Eogh, John. Botanologia universalis hibernica. 1735. III. 79.
Keppen, F. *See* Кеппенъ, Θ.
Ker, Charles Henry Bellenden. Icones pictae indo-asiaticae plantarum. 1818. I. 452.
— Icones plantarum sponte China nascentium. 1818. I. 452.[2]
Ker, John Bellenden. Carica Papaya foemina. 1820. II. 582.[1]
— Recensio plantarum hucusque in Repositorio botanicorum depictarum. 1801. I. 265.
Kerarmel, Philippe. De l'impérieuse nécessité du reboisement. 1844. IV. 161.[3]
Kerber, Edmund. Un coup d'œil sur Cordova. 1883. I. 332.
— Jacaratia conica n. sp. 1883. II. 582.[2]
— Rückblick auf Cordoba. 1883. I. 332.
— Ueber die untere Niveaugrense des Eichen- und Kiefernwaldes am Vulkan von Colima. 1882. J. 331.
Kerbert, Coenraad. *See* MOLKENBOER, J. H. & KERBERT, C.
Kerchove de Denterghem, Oswald, comte de. L'Acalypha Sanderi. ·1898. III. 514.[3]
— Les Araucaria. 1877 III. 297.[2]
— Eine Auswahl von 40 der schönsten Palmen. 1878. III. 317.
— Culture du Pin sylvestre dans les terrains sablonneux. 1895. IV. 559.[1]
— Les Cupressus. 1896. II. 29.[1].
— Description des ·quarante chromolithographies. 1878. III. 317.
— Le Dracaena Goldieana. 1878. III. 336.[2]
— Les Grenadiers à fleurs doubles. 1886. III. 630.[2]
— Le Magnolia Lennei hort. 1875. III. 400.[1]
— Les Palmiers. 1878. II. 61.[1]
— À propos d'Ypréaux. 1895. V. IX.[2]
— & Pynaert, Édouard. Les Kentia. 1885. III. 326.[1]
Kerckhoff, P. J. van. Mededeeling van eenige proeven omtrent ... china-alkaloiden. 1870. III. 722.
Kerkhoven, A. E. De Goentoer na vijftig jaren rust. 1898. I. 469.[1]
— Houtsoorten·... geschikt voor theekisten. 1895. IV. 427.[1]
Le kermès de San José. 1898. ·III. 191.
Le kermès du Hêtre. 1894. IV. 497.
Kern, Eduard. Über Caeoma pinitorquum A. Br. 1884. IV. 461.[2]
— *See also* Керпъ, S. 3.
Kern, H. Die Erstellung einer neuen Nussbaumallee. 1879. III. 355.

Kern, Maximilian G. Forest tree culture on Kansas prairies. 1879. IV. 111.²
— The relation of railroads to forest supplies. 1887. IV. 272.
Kerndt, Carolus Huldericus Theodorus. De fructibus Asparagi et Bixae. 1849. III. 613.¹
Kerner, Anton Joseph, Ritter. See KERNER VON MARILAUN, A. J. Ritter.
Kerner, Johann Simon von. Abbildungen aller oekonomischen Pflanzen. 1786. III. 51.
— Beobachtungen über die beweglichen Blätter der Süssklee-pflanze. 1784. II. 354.¹
— Beschreibung und Abbildung der Bäume . . . in dem Herzogthum Wirtemberg. 1783. I. 370.
— Darstellung vorzüglicher ausländicher Baeume und Gestraeuche. 1796. I. 293, III. 68,² IV. 81.²
— Figures des plantes économiques. 1786. III. 51.
— Flora stuttgardiensis. 1786. I. 374.
— Genera plantarum selectarum. 1811. I. 265.
— Handlungs-Produkte aus dem Pflanzenreich. 1781. III. 217.
— Hortus sempervirens. 1795. I. 264.
— Icones plantarum selectiorum. 1802. I. 265.
— Le Raisin. 1803. III. 545.³
Kerner, Josef. Beiträge zur Flora Niederösterreichs. 1874. I. 442.
— Bemerkungen über Salixaffinis. 1863. II. 104.²
— Drei neue Bürger der Flora Nieder-Oesterreichs. 1865. II. 105.²
— Salicologische Mittheilungen. 1864. II. 107.²
— ✕ Salix Erdingeri. 1861. II. 107.¹
— ✕ Salix hircina. 1864. II. 107.²
— ✕ Salix retusoides. 1862. II. 109.²
— Salix Fenzliana . . . in Fruchtblüthen. 1874. II. 107.¹
— See also KERNER VON MARILAUN, Anton, Ritter & KERNER, Josef.
Kerner, Justinus. Eine noch wenig bekannte Benutzung der . . . Holderblüthe. 1857. III. 752.¹
Kerner von Marilaun, Anton Joseph. Die Abhängigkeit der Pflanzengestalt von Klima. 1869. I. 217, II. 350.³
— Die Alpenwirthschaft in Tirol. 1866. IV. 123.¹
— Die Aufforstung des Flugsandes. 1865. IV. 145.
— Der Bakonyerwald. 1856. I. 441.
— Die Bedeutung der Dichogamie. 1890. I. 238.
— Beitrag zur Flora von Ostafrika. 1897. I. 493.
— Beschreibungen neuer Pflanzenarten der österreichischen Flora. 1869. I. 442.
— Der botanische Garten der Universität zu Innsbruck. 1863. I. 66.¹
— Ueber botanische Nomenclatur. 1863. II. 349.²
— Die botanischen Gärten. 1874. I. 38.¹
— Ueber Coniferen-Bastarte. 1867. II. 13.¹
— Ueber die Cytisus-Arten der Gruppe Tubocytisus. 1863. II. 340.³
— Decem novae species Ruborum tirolensium. 1870, 1871. I. 270, II. 304.¹
— Descriptiones plantarum . . . florae hungaricae. 1863. I. 445.
— Descriptiones plantarum novarum. 1866. I. 441.
— Descriptiones Salicum novarum florae tirolensis. 1864. II. 102.²
— Die Eichen des mittleren und östlichen Ungarns. 1876. II. 136.²
— Der Einfluss der Winde auf die Verbreitung der Samen. 1871. I. 240.¹
— Flowers and their unbidden guests. 1876. I. 237.
— Die Folgen der Wald-Devastation in Tyrol. 1863. IV. 283.²
— Die Formationen immergrüner Ericineen. 1860. II. 658.¹
— Die Früchte der Linnaea. 1872. II. 835.²
— Gefüllte Alpenrosen. 1865. II. 679.¹
— Gute und schlechte Arten. 1865. I. 530.¹
— Das Hochkar. 1857. I. 441.
— The natural history of plants. 1887. I. 92.
— Die Nebenblätter der Lonicera etrusca. 1893. II. 837.¹
— Ueber eine neue Weide. 1853. II. 110.³
— Niederösterreichische Pflanzennamen. 1855. I. 75.¹
— Niederösterreichische Weiden. 1860. II. 102.²
— Novae plantarum species. 1871. II. 304.²
— Novae plantarum species in Himalajae-montibus. 1870. I. 474.
— Novae plantarum species Tiroliae. 1870. I. 270, 530,¹ IV. 498.¹
— Die obere Rothbuchengrenze in den Alpen. 1863. II. 125.²

— Obere Stieleichengrenze in den österreichischen Alpen. 1868. II. 136.¹
— Oesterreichs waldlose Gebiete. 1863. IV. 367.
— Phänologische Beobachtungen auf der Margaretheninsel. 1858. I. 227.¹
— Pflanzenleben. 1887. I. 92.
— Das Pflanzenleben der Donauländer. 1863. I. 441.
— De la protection du pollen contre les intempéries. 1873. I. 237.
— On the protection of pollen. 1873. I. 237.
— Quercus filipendula, pendulina, fructipéndula. 1868. II. 136.¹
— Regionsgrenzen . . . der Fichte. 1865. II. 34.²
— Salix pentandra alba. 1858. II. 108.²
— Schedae ad floram exsiccatam austro-hungaricam. 1881. I. 443.
— Die Schutzmittel der Blüthen gegen unberufene Gäste. 1876. I. 237.
— Die Schutzmittel des Pollens. 1873. I. 237.
— Symbiosis and its effects. 1896. I. 234,¹ IV. 74.¹
— Vegetations-Verhältniss des mittleren und östlichen Ungarn. 1878. I. 446.
— Die Vegetations-Verhältnisse . . . Ungarns. 1867. I. 445.
— Veränderung der Gestalt durch schmarotzende Sporenpflanzen. 1892. III. 195.¹
— La vita delle piante. 1887. I. 92.
— Vorläufige Mittheilungen über . . . Asyngamie. 1875. I. 237.
— Wachsthumsbedingungen der Zirbe. 1866. II. 41.¹
— Die Wälder des ungarischen Tieflandes. 1861. I. 444.
— & Kerner, Josef. Herbarium österreichischer Weiden. 1863. II. 102.³
— — Salix Mielichhoferi Saut. 1867. II. 108.¹
Kerr, A. Hybrid Rhododendrons. 1875. III. 655.
Kerr, Graham. The botany of the Pilcamayo expedition. 1896. I. 345.
Kerr, James. An account of the tree producing the terra japonica. 1776. III. 464.¹
— Natural history of the insect which produces the gum lacca. 1782. III. 232.³
Kerr, Lord Mark. Memo. on the Delhi store. 1876. IV. 48.¹
— Sanitary notes in Poona. 1876. IV. 48.¹
Kerr, Dr. Washington Caruthers. The forests of North Carolina. 1883. IV. 339.
Kerremans, Charles. L'entomologie au point de vue économique. 1898. IV. 208.²
Kerris. Rapport sur l'exploration forestière du cercle de la Calle. 1842. IV. 379.¹
Kerssenbruch, E. von. Versuche . . . Eichen in Baumschulen . . . zu erziehen. 1801. IV. 504.
Kerstein, Johan Gottfried Sylvester. Universalmaass für alle Geschäfte des praktischen Lebens. 1810. IV. 213.
Kersten, G. A. & Linke, J. R. Atlas der Giftpflanzen. 1868. III. 59.¹
Kerstens, Johann Christian. Primitiae florae holsaticae. See WEBER, G. H. 1780. I. 374.
Kersting, Hermann. Die Forst-, Jagd- und Fischerei-Vergehen nach kurhessischem Rechte. 1854. IV. 320.
A Kert. III. 25.
Kertészeti lapok. III. 25.
Kervert, H. J. Gemengde Djatibosschen. 1900. IV. 537.¹
Kerville, Henri GADEAU DE. See GADEAU DE KERVILLE, Henri.
Kervyn, H. Des plantations dans les Flandres. 1848. III. 122.³
Kerwel. Beschreibung eines Potaschenwerkes. 1735. IV. 395.
Keshavanand. Fructification of the Kharshu Oak. 1891. II. 139.³
— Note on the germination of the Kharshu acorn. 1891. II. 139.³
Kessel, Friedrich. Sur la cire du Ficus gummiflua. 1878. III. 371.²
— Ueber das Wachs von Ficus gummiflua. 1878. III. 371.²
— Over het was van Ficus gummiflua. 1878. III. 371.²
— Wax of Ficus gummiflua. 1878. III. 371.²
Kesselmeyer, Johann. De quorundam vegetabilium principio nutriente. 1759. I. 157.
Kessler. Erhaltung der Wälder und Holzmangel. 1839. IV. 281.¹
Kessler, A. Een en ander over Kina. 1886. III. 716.
— De Koffiecultuur in Brazilie. 1884. III. 728.²
Kessler, G. E. Catalpa. 1891. IV. 538.² ²
— Forestry on the prairies. 1891. IV. 155.²

Kessler, Hermann Friedrich. Das älteste und erste Herbarium Deutschlands. 1870. I. 80.²
— Die Ausbreitung der Reblauskrankheit. 1892. III. 574.
— Beobachtungen an dem Blattfloh Triosa. 1894. III. 406.²
— Beobachtungen an der Reblaus. 1886. III. 574.
— Beobachtungen über Galeruca Viburni. 1889. III. 753.¹
— Drei kleine entomologische Abhandlungen. 1894. III. 750.¹
— Einige Beobachtungen aus der Entwickelungsgeschichte von Psylla fraxini. 1894. IV. 535.²
— Die Entwickelungs-... geschichte der Blutlaus. 1885. III. 427.²
— Die Entwickelungs-... geschichte der Gallwespe Cynips calicis. 1895. IV. 511.
— Die Entwickelungs-... geschichte von Pemphigus lonicerae. 1894. III. 750.¹
— Die Entwickelungs-... geschichte von Schizoneura corni. 1883. III. 645.¹
— Erörterungen über die Reblaus. 1889. III. 762.
— Die Lebensgeschichte der auf Ulmus ... vorkommenden Aphiden-Arten. 1878. III. 364.²
— Der Melonenbaum. 1863. · III. 617.¹
— Neue Beobachtungen ... an den auf Ulmus campestris L. vorkommenden Aphiden-Arten. 1880. III. 364.²
— Die auf Populus ... vorkommenden Aphiden-Arten. 1881. III. 344.²
— Richtigstellungen ... betreffend Beobachtungen ... über die Reblaus. 1890. III. 762.
— Die Ungefährlichkeit ... der Blutlaus. 1889. III. 428.¹
— Ueber die Verwandlung der ungeflügelten Rebläuse. 1889. III. 762.
— Weitere Beobachtungen-... über die Reblaus. 1888. III. 762.
— Weiterer Beitrag zur Kenntniss der Blutlaus. 1886. III. 428.¹.
Kessler, W. Rameh. 1885. III. 381.¹
Kessler, Wilhelm. Ueber die Aufforstung von Oedländereien. 1883. IV. 158.
— Bemestingsproeven. 1899. III. 734.¹
— Beobachtungen und Schilderungen von einer Reise durch Mexiko und Nordamerika. 1889. IV. 337.¹
— Les forêts d'Algérie jugées par un étranger. 1895. IV. 379.²
— Zur Geschichte der kaukasischen Wälder. 1881. IV. 348.¹
— Aus dem Kaukasus. 1890. IV. 348.¹
— Wald- und Forstwirthschaft in Algerien. 1895. IV. 379.²
— Wald und Waldzerstörung auf dem westlichen Kontinent. 1890. I. 308.
— Das Waldkleid des westlichen Continentes. 1890. I. 308.
Kesterčanek, Franz Xaver.· Eine abnorme Zapfenbildung der Pinus sylvestris. 1880. II. 47.²
— Dendrometrija. 1881. IV. 218.
— Die forstlichen Verhältnisse Serbiens. 1883. IV. 375.¹
— Die forstwirthschaftlichen Verhältnisse Bulgariens. 1884. IV. 375.¹
— Das specifische Gewicht diverser in Obercroatien ... heimischer Holzarten. 1880. IV. 411.¹
— Sporer's Taschendendrometer. 1881. IV. 215.
Kestner, Auguste Scheurer-. See Scheurer-Kestner, Auguste.
Ketchum, Annie Chambers-. Lotos-eating. 1886. III. 220.¹
Keteleer. Arthrotaxis selaginoides et A. laxifolia. 1869. III. 299.²
— Cryptomeria elegans. 1869. III. 302.¹
— Notes sur la rusticité de quelques Azalées indiennes. 1871. III. 48.
— Observations sur l'hiver 1870–71. 1870. III. 660.¹
Keteleer, J. B. Description sommaire de quelques Camellia nouveaux. 1832. III. 597.²
Keteleer's Guelder Rose. 1875. III. 753.¹
Kettlitz, F. & others. Verzeichniss einiger Coniferen. 1890. III. 294.²
Kettner, J. F. von. Darstellung der badischen Forst-Administration. 1820. IV. 289.²
— Organische Formen einer zweckmässigen Forst-Verfassung. 1807. IV. 287.
Kettner, W. F. von. Die badische Forstorganisation. 1851.. IV. 289.²
— Beiträge zur Nutzholzwirthschaft. 1846. IV. 117.
— Beschreibung des badischen Murg- und Oosthales. 1843. IV. 350.¹

Keudell, J. Geschichte des Forst- und Jagdwesens von Teutschland. 1837. IV. 25.
Keussler, Eduard. Untersuchung ... der Sennesblätter. 1878. III. 470.²
Kew. 1897. I. 55.
Kew — Royal botanic gardens. Catalogue of the library. See Catalogue ... 1899. I. 3.¹
Kew — Royal gardens. See Royal Gardens ... 1886. I. 38.¹
Kew and its work. 1891. II. 75.¹
Kew bulletin of miscellaneous information. I. 18.
Kew guild. III. 17.
Kexel, Hugo. Apatomie der Laubblätter ... der Hypericaceae. 1896. II. 553.¹
Key, G. Vademecum voor den houtkooper. 1883. IV. 403.¹
Key, L. Ueber Laubfärbungen: 1890. IV. 63.²
Key, Sothoron. See Hicks, G. H. & Key, Sothoron.
A key to the ... plants occurring in the northern United States. See Macbride, T. H. 1898. · I. 316.
Keys, I. W. N. Flora of Devon and Cornwall. 1866. I. 402.
Keys, James. See Bailey, F. M. & Keys, James.
Keyser, Georg Adam. Wie ist dem so sehr einreissenden Holzmangel vorzubeugen. 1794. IV. 158.
— See also Adam, Georg & Keyser, G. A.
— & Adam, Georg. Ueber die Veredlung des Obstes. 1800. I. 246.²
Keyser, J. G. Guajacan. See Friderici, J. A. 1665. III. 494.¹
Keyworth. Empoisonnement par la strychnine. 1870. III. 483.²
Khasiotes, Spyridon. See ΧΑΣΙΩΤΗΣ, Σπυρίδων.
Khat, Cafta, or Arabian Tea. 1883. III. 531.²
Khat, Cafta, Thé d'Arabie. See Khat, Cafta, or Arabian Tea. 1883. III. 531.²
The Khât plant. 1843. III. 531.²
Kheldraich, Theodoros. See ΧΕΛΔΡΑΙΧ, Θεόδωρος.
Khloros, Nicholas. See Χλωρὸς, Νικόλαος.
Kholodkovski, N. See Холодковскiй, Н.
Khorvat, A. See Хорватъ, А.
Khouri, Joseph. Contribution à l'étude ... du Goyavier. 1895.· III. 637.²
Khristines, Demetrios. See Χριστίνης, Δημήτριος.
Khrushchof, J. See Хрущевъ, Я.
Kiär, Frantz Casper. Professor Christen Smiths Dagbog. 1889. I.·498.
Kiär, Thorvald. Vore privatskove. 1898. IV. 282.¹
Kiaerskou, Hjalmar. . Enumeratio Myrtacearum brasiliensium. 1893. II. 619.¹
— Myrtaceae ex India occidentali. 1889. II. 619.¹
Kickx, Jean, (1775–1831). Flora bruxellensis. 1812. I. 392.
Kickx, Jean, (1803–1864). Accurata descriptio plantarum officinalium. 1827. III. 77.
— Commentatio ... Detur accurata descriptio plantarum officinalium ... in agro lovaniensi. 1827. III. 270.²
— Esquisse sur les ouvrages de quelques anciens naturalistes belges. 184.? I. 523.
— Sur le genre Aristoloche. 1839. II. 182.¹
— Note sur une ascidie accidentelle du Rosier. 1851. II. 289.²
— Relation d'une promenade botanique ... dans la Campine. 1835. I. 392.
Kickx, Jean Jacques. Un ennemi du Peuplier de Canada. 1878. III. 345.²
— Notice sur les ascidies tératologiques. 1863.. I. 144.²
— Een vijand van den Canadapopulier. 1878. III. 345.²
Kidder, F. E. Experiments on the fatigue of small Spruce beams. 1882. . IV. 459.²
— Experiments on the strength and stiffness of small Spruce beams. 1881. IV. 459.²
— What coefficients should · be adopted for the transverse strength of timber? 1894. IV. 416.¹
Kidder, Jerome H. Contributions to the natural history of Kerguelen Island. 1875. I. 481.¹
Kidston, Thomas. Ringbarking in western New South Wales. 1894. IV. 385.¹
Kiefer, Ch. Culture de la truffe. 1887. IV. 439.
Kieffer, Jean Jacques, (abbé). Les acarocécidies de Lorraine. 1891. I. 215.²
— Beschreibung neuer Gallmücken. 1886. IV. 490.²
— Les coléoptérocécidies de Lorraine. 1891. I. 215.²
— Les diptérocécidies de Lorraine. 1890. I. 215.²
— Les helminthocécidies de Lorraine. 1891. I. 215.²

— Les hémiptérocécidies de Lorraine. 1891. I. 215.[2]
— Herborisations de Strobelberger à Montpellier. 1881. I. 416.
— Les lépidoptérocécidies de Lorraine. 1891. I. 215.[2]
— Ueber lothringische . . . Phytoptocecidien. 1885. I. 215.[1]
— Mycocécidies de Lorraine. 1892. III. 195.
— Synopse des cécidomyies d'Europe. 1898. I. 214.[2]
Kiehl, Georg Friedrich Wilhelm. De Cassiae speciebus officinalibus. *See* RBIL, J. C. 1801. III. 470.[1]
Kielmann, C. E. Ueber die Waldstreu . . . nebst einem Beitrag zur Monographie der Bergkiefer. . 1843. II. 43,[1] *IV. 70.*
Kielmeyer, Karl Friedrich von. 'Characteristice et descriptiones . . . plantarum Horti academici tubingensis. 1814. I. 266.
— De effectibus arsenici. 1808. I. 210.[2]
— Observata quaedam de materierum . . . in germinationem efficientia. 1805. I. 202.[2]
— Observata quaedam de vegetatione in regionibus alpinis. 1804. I. 219.[2]
— Observationes quaedam chemicae de acredine. 1805. I. 150.[2]
Kielstädt, [?], K. E. *See* КЪЛЬШТЕТЪ, К. Е.
Kielstra, E. B. De Kofficultuur . . . van Sumatra. 1888. III. 730.
Kienast, Gustav Adolf Hermann. Ueber die Entwicklung der Oelbehälter . . . von Hypericum. 1885. II. 556.[1]
Kiene. Ein weissblühendes Rhododendron ferrugineum. 1835. II. 679.[1]
Kienitz, Max. Die Akazie in Norddeutschland. 1900. IV. 523.[2]
— Angaben über die Aufastung der Waldbäume. 1876. IV. 171.
— Ueber die Aufastung der Waldbäume. 1878. IV. 171.
— Ueber Ausführung von Keimproben. 1880. III. 156.[3]
— Der Baum als Element des Waldes. 1880. IV. 57.
— Beobachtungen an zu tief gepflanzten, jungen Eichen. 1894. IV. 508.
— Beobachtungen über die Zapfenmenge an Kiefern. 1881. II. 48.[1]
— Die in Deutschland wild wachsenden Ulmenarten. 1882. II. 143.[1]
— Einfluss der Gewinnungsart der Kiefernsamen auf die Keimthätigkeit. 1880. IV. 473.
— Einfluss der Lage gesäter Eicheln. 1882. I. 203, *IV. 149,[1] 507.*
— Einfluss niederer Wärmegrade auf die Holzgewächse. 1881. IV. 191.[2]
— Einiges über neuere Keimapparate. 1880. III. 156.[2]
— Die Entstehung der Markflecke. 1883. I. 125.
— Ueber Formen und Abarten heimischer Waldbäume. 1879. I. 244,[2] 371, IV. 83.
— Schlüssel zum Bestimmen der . . . Hölzer. 1880. I. 371, *IV. 99.*
— Schlüssel zum Bestimmen der wichtigsten in Deutschland cultivirten Hölzer. 1879. I. 125, *IV. 62.[2]*
— Vergleichende Keimversuche mit Waldbaum-Samen. 1879. I. 213, *IV. 72, 147.[1]*
— Ueber die Verjüngung der Kiefer. 1878. IV. 472.
— Versuche über die Bekämpfung der Kiefernschütte. 1900. IV. 480.
— Ueber die Zwieselbildung der Buche. 1887. II. 126.[1]
— *See also* WEIDEMANN & KIENITZ, MAX.
Kierski, R. Quercus sessiliflora var. laciniata. 1898. III. 363.[1]
Kiesal. Soo-kwa-rjak-guwa-siki. 1814. I. 37.[1]
Kieser, Dieterich Georg. Aphorismen aus der Physiologie der Pflanzen. 1808. I. 146.
— Elemente der Phytonomie. 1815. I. 100.[2]
— Grundzüge der Anatomie der Pflanzen. 1815. I. 100.[2]
— Mémoire sur l'organisation des plantes. 1814. I. 98, V. XI.[1]
— Mémoire sur l'organisation des plantes qui a ramporté le prix. 1812. I. 85.
— Réponse à la question physique. 1814. V. XI.[1]
— Über die ursprüngliche . . . Form der Pflanzenzellen. 1818. I. 136.[1]
Kieseritzky, Gottfried Wilhelm. De ratione, quae inter systema plantarum naturale earumque vires medicinales obtinet. 1826. III. 259.[2]
Kiesler, Carl. Kubiktabellen für runde, geschnittene und beschlagene Hölzer. 1884. IV. 228.
— Kubiktabellen für runde Hölzer. 1884. IV. 228.
Kiesling, Christian Gotthilf. De succis plantarum. 1752. I. 162.

Kiessler, R. Flora der Umgegend von Stendal. 1871. I. 386.
Kievits, J. H. Een en ander over Peperkultuur. 1891. III. 343.[2]
— Het kweeken van Liberia-Koffie. 1891. III. 742.[2]
— Nadere opmerkingen over de cultuur van Cacao. 1893. III. 593.[1]
— Het nut van terrassen. 1893. III. 727.
— Eene paar opmerkingen over de cultuur . . . van cacao. 1893. III. 593.[1]
— Schaduw boomen. 1891. III. 734.[2]
— Vruchtboomen en Badjings. 1894. III. 130.[1]
— Waar gaan we heen. 1891. III. 129.[1]
Kievskoye obshtchestvo estestvoispytatelei. *See* КIEBCKOE общество естествоиспытателей.
Kiggelaer, Franciscus. Horti beaumontiani . . . catalogus. 1690. I. 50.
Kihlman, Alfred Oswald. Anteckningar om floran i Inari Lappmark. 1885. I. 364.
— Beobachtungen über die periodischen Erscheinungen des Pflanzenlebens in Finnland. 1886. I. 224.[2]
— Ett besök på Solovetska öarne. 1890. II. 33.[2]
— De finska formerna af slägtet Rosa. 1894. II. 284.[1]
— Finska Salix-hybrider. 1886. II. 101.[1]
— Förekomsten af Dryas i Kuusamo. 1894. II. 263.[2]
— Förslag till ett noggrant utforskande af växternas utbredning . . . i Finland. 1891. I. 366.
— Hybrider med Salix phylicaefolia. 1886. II. 109.[1]
— Iakttagelser öfver . . . Salix-hybrider. 1886. II. 101.[1]
— Nordiska kärlväxtformer. 1893. II. 100.[2]
— Nordiska Salix-former. 1893. II. 100.[2]
— Pflanzenbiologische Studien aus Russisch Lappland. 1890. I. 365.
— Photographien einiger uralter Bäume. 1891. I. 296.[1]
— Salix Caprea × nigricans i Finland. 1886. II. 105.[2]
— Uråldriga träd i Onega Karelen. 1891. I. 296.[1]
— *See also* SAELAN, Thiodolf, KIHLMAN, A. O. & HJELT, H.
Kihlmann, J. H. Chinesiska théet. 1830. III. 606.
— Kaffé. 1828. III. 738.
Kilian. Einiges über den Ginkgo. 1841. III. 286.[2]
Kiliani, H. Ueber den Milchsaft von Antiaris toxicaria. 1896. III. 366.[2]
Kiliani, Heinrich. Ueber arabisches Gummi. 1882. III. 463.[1]
— Sur la gomme arabique. 1882. III. 463.[2]
Kiljander, L. G. Kansakoulun kasvioppi. 1893. I. 92.
Killebrew, Joseph Buckner. The forests of Tennessee. 1897. IV. 340.
Killias, Eduard. Die Flora des Unterengadins. 1887. I. 437.
— Nachtrag zu Alex. Moritzis Verzeichniss der Pflanzen Graubündens. 1856. I. 435.
— Riesige Rothtanne bei Malans. 1890. II. 37.[2]
— Riesige Weisstanne in Val Fargara. 1889. II. 24.[2]
Kilmer, Fred. B. The alkaloids of kola. 1896. III. 590.[2]
— Collecting juice of Papaw. 1897. III. 618.[1]
— Kola; the history of. 1895. III. 590.[2]
— Kola and kolanin. 1896. III. 590.[2]
— Kola nuts. 1896. III. 590.[1]
— Pharmacological notes on kola. 1896. III. 590.[2]
Kilshtet, K. E. *See* КЪЛЬШТЕТЪ, К. Е.
Kimball, E. D. Acorns in trees. 1894. I. 235.[1]
Kina-cultuur. 1875. III. 725.[2]
De **Kina**-cultuur in Bolivia. *See* CULTURE des Quinquinas. 1884. III. 713.[2]
Over de **Kinakina.** 1806. III. 399.[2]
Over **Kina kultuur.** 1880. III. 713.[1]
De **Kina**-kultuur in Indië. 1878. III. 714.
De **Kinakultuur** op Java beoordeeld in den vreemden. 1862. III. 715.
Kinch, Edward. List of plants used for food . . . in Japan. 1883. III. 273.[2]
Kindberg, Nils Conrad. Östgöta flora. 1861. I. 356.
— Tillägg till Östgöta flora. 1861. I. 356.
Kinder de Camarecq. *See* STARING, W. C. H. & KINDER DE CAMARECQ.
King, Clarence. Report of the geological exploration of the fortieth parallel. *See* WATSON, Sereno. 1871. I. 323.
King, David. Horticulture. 1891. III. 117.[1]
King, F. H. Influence of north and south slopes on the temperature of the trunks. 1896. I. 187.
— Irrigation and drainage. 1899. III. 151.
— The soil; its nature. 1895. III. 41.[1]

King, G. T. A good tree for the South. 1890. III. 409.[1]
King, George. 14th annual report of the government Cinchona plantation in British Sikkim. 1877. III. 714.
— The Anonaceae of British India. 1893. II. 215.[1]
— Cinchona cultivation in Bengal. 1872. III. 714.
— Cinchona cultivation in British Sikkim. 1873. III. 714.
— Cinchona cultivation in Java. 1880. III. 716.
— Cinchona febrifuge. 1877. III. 726.[1]
— Descriptions of some new Indian trees. 1897.. I. 470.[2]
— Directions for sowing Pithecolobium. 1882. III. 484.[2]
— The fertilization of Ficus hispida. 1887. II. 152.[1]
— The gardener's note book. 1882. III. 484.[2]
— A guide to the Royal botanic garden, Calcutta. 1895. I. 67.[1]
— The Indo-Malayan species of Quercus and Castanopsis. 1889. II. 123.[1]
— Le Jardin botanique de Calcutta. 1895. I. 67.[1]
— List of the plants of Garhwál. 1882. I. 474.
— List of the principal plants growing in the Bengal Presidency and Assam. 1877. I. 474.
— The Magnoliaceae of British India. 1891. II. 209.[1]
— A manual of Cinchona cultivation in India. 1876. III. 714.
— Materials for a flora of the Malayan peninsula. 1889. I. 464.[2]
— Note on a sport in Paritium tricuspe. 1877. II. 524.[2]
— Notes on the Indian species of Vitis. 1897. II. 501.[1]
— Observations on the genus Ficus. 1888. II. 149.[1]
— Remarks on the pruning of Tea. 1872. III. 603.
— Report on the Dehra Dun forests. 1871. IV. 377.[2]
— Sketch of the flora of Rajputana. 1879. I. 474.
— On some Indian species of Canarium. 1893. II. 417.[1]
— On some new species of Ficus from New Guinea. 1887. II. 149.[1]
— On some new species of Ficus from Sumatra.. 1888. II. 149.[1]
— The species of Artocarpus indigenous to British India. 1889. II. 146.[1]
— The species of Ficus of the Indo-Malayan ... countries. 1888. II. 149.[1]
— On the species of Loranthus indigenous to Perak. 1888. II. 175.[1]
— The species of Myristica of British India. 1891. II. 220.[1]
— Systematic botany for Indian foresters. 1809. IV. 29.
— On two new species of Ilex. 1886. II. 463.[1]
— See also BRÜHL, Paul & KING, Sir George.
— & DUTT, U. C. A glossary of Indian plants. 1877. I. 75.[2]
— & PRAIN, David. Descriptions of some new plants from ... India. 1898. I. 476.[1]
— — Some new plants from eastern India. 1898. I. 476.[1]
King, J. C. Technics of forestry. 1878. IV. 176.[2]
— Waste in timber-felling. 1885. IV. 384.[1]
King, John. The American dispensatory. 1852. III. 246.
— The American eclectic dispensatory. 1852. III. 246.
— The eclectic dispensatory of the United States. 1852. III. 246.
— King's American dispensatory. 1852. III. 246.
King, Mark. Poisonous plants. 1898. III. 260.[2]
King, Mitchell. Cultivation of the Olive in the southern states. 1847. III. 675.[2]
King, Phillip Parker. Narrative of a survey of ... Australia. 1826. I. 500.
King, R. A. D. Individual effort in preserving ... our trees. 1883. IV. 177.[2]
King, W. R. Report on the relative merit of various stocks for the Orange. 1891. III. 500.[1]
Kingsley, R. G. Hardy Cacti. 1877. III. 619.
Kingsley, R. I. Botanical notes; plants new to Nelson district. 1895. I. 508.[1]
— Notes on the Wangapeka valley. 1898. I. 508.[1]
Kingston, J. F. See JONES, J. P. & KINGSTON, J. F.; TURTON, William & KINGSTON, J. F.
Kinkélibah. 1897. III. 632.[1]
Kinney, Abbot. Eucalyptus. 1895. II. 623.[1]
— Eucalyptus. In JONES, J. D. & others. 1895. IV. 530.
— Forest and water. 1900. IV. 52.
— Forest conditions in California. 1897. I. 321, IV. 341.[1]
— Forest destruction and stream flow. 1898. IV. 46.[1]
— Forestry in California. 1888. IV. 340.
— Forests and fruit growers. 1885. IV. 46.[1]
— The forests of Los Angeles, San Diego. 1888. IV. 340.
— Sabal Palmetto. 1892. III. 331.[1]
Kinney, L. F. Sunlight and fruit buds. 1896. I. 230.
Kino from Myristica malabarica. 1897. III. 403.[1]

Kinoshita, Y. On the assimilation of nitrogen. 1894. I. 160.
Kinzel, Wilhelm. Beitrag zur Flora der Insel Rügen. 1891. I. 389.
Kiøbenhavnske Selskab af Lærdoms og Videnskabs Elskere. Skrifter. I. 8.[2]
Kippist, Richard. On Acradenia. 1854. II. 397.[2]
— On the existence of spiral cells in ... Acanthaceae. 1845. II. 796.[2]
— On Jansonia. 1851. II. 366.[1]
— Notice of two ... species of Genetyllis. 1857. II. 622.[1]
Kirby, Elizabeth. See KIRBY, Mary & Elizabeth.
Kirby, Francis. Letter to John Winthrop, jr. 1846. III. 32.[2]
Kirby, Mary. A flora of Leicestershire. 1848. I. 400.
— & Elizabeth. Chapters on trees. 1873. I. 82.[2]
— — Talks about trees. 1873. I. 82.[1]
Kirby, William. Sandal wood. 1886. III. 384.[1]
Kirchhoff, Alfred. Die Idee der Pflanzen-Metamorphose. 1867. I. 101.[2]
— Pflanzen- und Tierverbreitung. 1899. I. 301.
— Schulbotanik. 1865. I. 90.
Kirchhoff, Theodor. Californisches Yucca-Papier. 1877. III. 339.[2]
Kirchmaier, Georg Kaspar. De arte propagandi Vites. 1697. III. 548.[1]
— De Coralio, Balsamo et Saccharo. 1661. I. 286.
— Georg Holyk verneuertes und vermehrtes dreifaches Gartenbüchlein. 1693. III. 102.
— De raris atq; admirandis arboribus. 1660. I. 295.[1]
Kirchmaier, Karl Christian. De usu et abusu potus calidi cum herba Thee. See THILE, Johann. 1690. III. 605.
Kirchner. Ueber Forchensaaten. 1840. IV. 471.
— Ueber Heidestreunutzung. 1843. IV. 437.[2]
— Die Verwaltung der Kaiserl. russischen Staatsforsten. 1884. IV. 289.[1]
Kirchner, (Oberförster, Rogelwitz). Besprechung der Eichenfrage. 1886. IV. 507.
— Betrübendes aus dem Walde. 1884. IV. 489,[1] 535.[2]
— Die Kraut-Eiche. 1884. IV. 507.
— Zusammenstellung der Resultate, welche durch Verkauf des ... Kiefern-Derbholzes ... erzielt sind. 1874. IV. 261.[2]
Kirchner, Emil Otto Oskar. Über das Absterben junger Cytisus-Pflanzen. 1892. III. 474.[1]
— Beiträge zur Biologie der Blüten. 1890. I. 238.
— Die botanischen Schriften des Theophrastus. 1874. I. 530.[2]
— Ueber einige irrtümlich für windblütig gehaltene Pflanzen. 1893. I. 239.[1]
— Ueber die Empfindlichkeit der Wurzelspitze. 1882. I. 195.[2]
— Die Feige und ihre Befruchtung. 1898. II. 151.[1]
— Über die kernlose Mispel. 1900. II. 268.[2]
— Die Krankheiten und Beschädigungen unserer landwirtschaftlichen Kulturpflanzen. 1890. III. 179.
— Mitteilungen über die Bestäubungseinrichtungen der Blüten. 1900. II. 232.[1]
— Neue Beobachtungen über die Bestäubungs-Einrichtungen einheimischer Pflanzen. 1886. I. 239.[1]
— De Theophrasti Eresii libris phytologicis. 1874. I. 530.[2]
— Zum Wachsthum decapitirter Wurzeln. 1883. I. 195.[2]
Kirchner, Ernst. Schulbotanik. 1831. I. 86.
Kirchner, G. Das Arboretum der prinzlichen Parkes zu Muskau. 1859. I. 48.
— Die buntblätterigen Gehölze des Arboretum zu Muskau. 1864. III. 206.[2]
— Ueber die Cultur ... der ausdauernden Myricaceen. 1864. III. 352.[2]
— Notizen über ... Gehölze des Arboretum zu Muskau. 1866. II. 245,[2] 246,[1] 268.[1]
— Ueber Philadelphus undulatus. 1866. III. 413.[1]
— Ueberwinterung zarter Gehölze. 1863. III. 183.[1]
— Ueber die Veränderlichkeit der Blattform einiger Lonicereae. 1864. III. 750.[2].
— Die Vermehrung der kalifornischen Ross-Kastanie. 1863. III. 536.[2]
— Die Wirkungen des Winters von 1863–64. 1866. III. 292.
— Eine Zusammenstellung der Gehölze ... in Park zu Muskau. 1863. I. 48.
— See PETZOLD, E. & KIRCHNER, G.
Kirchner, Leopold. Zur Amerling'schen Functionstabelle über Forstinsecten. 1860. IV. 210.[1]
— Die Gallenauswüchse des budweiser Kreises. 1855. I. 16.[2]
— Die Harzgallen der Nadelhölzer. 1856. IV. 442.

Kirchner, Ludwig. Kurzer Entwurf eines praktischen Handbuches der Forstökonomie. 1807. IV. 103.[2]
Kirchner, Paul. Riesen-Eichen. 1899. II. 139.[2]
Kirillow, Peter. Die Loniceren des Russischen Reiches. 1849. II. 835.[2]
Kirilow, Johann. See KARELIN, Gregor & KIRILOW, Johann.
Kirk, John. On the Copal of Zanzibar. 1871. II. 387,[1] III. *233*.[2]
— Letter . . . relative to the country near Lake Shirwa. 1860. I. 492.[1]
— On a new dye-wood of the genus Cudranea. 1867. III. 368.[2]
— Notice of Egyptian plants. 1858. I. 488.
— On the Palms of east tropical Africa. 1865. II. 62.[1]
Kirk, Thomas. An account of an undescribed Pittosporum. 1871. II. 175,[2] *249*.[1]
— An account of the Puka. 1870. II. 650.[2]
— Additional contributions to the flora of the Nelson provincial district. 1886. I. 507.
— Botanical notes. 1884. I. 507.
— On the botany of Antipodes Island. 1891. I. 508.[1]
— On the botany . . . of Great Omaha. 1873. I. 507.
— On the botany of the antarctic islands. 1891. I. 510.[2]
— On the botany of the Bluff Hill. 1878. I. 507.
— On the botany of the Great Barrier Island. 1869. I. 506.[2]
— On the botany of the northern part . . . of Auckland. 1871. I. 507.
— On the botany of the Snares. 1891. I. 508.[1]
— On the botany of the Thames gold-fields. 1870. I. 506.[2]
— On Carmichaelia, Corallospartium. 1897. II. 320.[1]
— A comparison of the indigenous floras of the British Islands and New Zealand. 1872. I. 507.
— Contributions to the botany of Otago. 1878. I. 507.
— Cordyline Banksii on Stewart Island. 1895. II. 80.[1]
— Description of a new Pine. 1884. II. 9.[1]
— Description of a new species of Drimys. 1898. II. 209.[2]
— Description of a new species of Fagus. 1885. II. 127.[1]
— Description of a new species of Pimelea. 1894. II. 606.[1]
— Description of a new species of Senecio. 1883. II. 865.[2]
— Description of new plants collected on Stewart Island. 1884. II. 862.[2]
— Descriptions of new flowering plants. 1880. I. 507.
— Descriptions of new plants. 1871. I. 507. — 1877. I. 507.
— Descriptions of new plants from . . . Port Nicholson. 1892. II. 815.[1]
— Descriptions of . . . plants from the Upper Waimakariri. 1895. I. 508.[1]
— Descriptions of two new species of Veronica. 1877. II. 783.[2]
— The displacement of species in New Zealand. 1896. I. 508.[1]
— An enumeration of recent additions to the New Zealand flora. 1878. I. 507.
— On Epacris purpurascens Br. 1870. II. 689.[2]
— On the flora of the isthmus of Auckland. 1871. I. 507.
— On the flowering plants of Stewart Island. 1885. I. 507.
— Forest flora of New Zealand. 1889. I. 506,[1] IV. *89*.[2]
— On the habit of the Rata. 1872. II. 636.[2]
— On heterostyled trimorphic flowers in . . . Fuchsias. 1893. II. 643.[1]
— On the history of botany in Otago. 1897. I. 508.[1]
— On the macrocephalous Olearias. 1891. II. 861.[2]
— Native forests and the state of the timber-trade. 1885. IV. 380.[2]
— On the naturalized plants of Port Nicholson. 1878. I. 507.
— On a new Mistletoe. 1892. II. 177.[1]
— New species of Carmichaelia. 1884. II. 342.[1]
— On the New Zealand Olives. 1882. II. 712.[1]
— On the New Zealand species of Phyllocladus. 1878. II. 9.[1]
— On the New Zealand species of Pittosporum. 1872. II. 248.[1]
— Notes and suggestions on the utilisation of certain neglected New Zealand timbers. 1879. IV. 402.[1]
— Notes on Carmichaelia. 1884. II. 342.[1]
— Notes on certain New Zealand plants. 1871. I. 507.
— Notes on certain Veronicas. 1896. II. 783.[1]
— Notes on indigenous materials for . . . paper. 1874. III. 34.[1]
— Notes on Mr. Hamilton's collection of Okarito plants. 1879. I. 507.
— Notes on Panax lineare. 1877. II. 650.[2]

— Notes on plants observed during a visit to the north of Auckland. 1869. I. 506.[2]
— Notes on the botany of the East Cape district. 1897. I. 508.[1]
— Notes on the botany of Waiheke. 1879. I. 507.
— Notes on the botany of . . . Waikato district. 1871. I. 507.
— Notes on the flora of . . . North Island. 1873. I. 507.
— Notes on the New Zealand Beeches. 1885. II. 127.[2]
— Notes on the plants best adapted for the reclamation of sand wastes. 1874. IV. 169.[1]
— Notes on three dried specimens of Matai. 1878. IV. 440.[1]
— Notice of an undescribed species of Cordyline. 1874. II. 80.[1]
— Notice of the occurrence of an undescribed Palm-lily. 1896. II. 79.[2]
— Olearias of New Zealand. 1893. II. 861.[2]
— Podocarpus spicata R. Brown. 1889. IV. 440.[1]
— On the Punui of Stewart Island. 1885. II. 647.[2]
— Quelques mots encore sur les Palmiers de l'Afrique. 1865. II. 62.[1]
— On a remarkable instance of double parasitism in Loranthaceae. 1876. II. 174.[1]
— Remarks on Paratrophis heterophylla. 1897. II. 155.[1]
— Report on native forests. 1885. IV. 407.[2]
— Report on the durability of New Zealand timbers. 1875. IV. 413.[2]
— A revised arrangement . . . of Dacrydium. 1878. II. 8.[2]
— A revision of . . . species of Hymenanthera. 1896. II. 567.[2]
— Strathmore weed. 1900. III. 628.[1]
— The students' flora of New Zealand. 1899. I. 508.[1]
— See also BUCHANAN, John & KIRK, Thomas.
Kirkby, William. A contribution to the knowledge of the Venezuelan Sandal-wood tree. 1886. II. 169,[1] III. 225.
— Note on kamala. 1884. III. 520.[2]
— Sandal wood. 1886. II. 169,[1] III. 384.[1]
— Some observations upon insects that prey upon timber. 1800. IV. 208.[2]
Kirkwood, Alexander. Papers and reports upon forestry. 1893. IV. 102.
— Report of the Royal commission on forest reservation. 1893. IV. 102.
Kirkwood, J. E. & Gies, W. J. The composition of the endosperm and milk of the Cocoanut. 1900. II. 67.[2]
Kirmsse, Ernst. Beiträge zur . . . Kenntniss der Pasta Guarana. 1897. III. 540.[1]
Kirpitchnikof, D. See Кирпичниковъ, Д.
Kirschleger, Friedrich. Essai historique de la tératologie. 1845. I. 143.
— Essai sur les folioles carpiques. 1846. I. 117.[2]
— Flore d'Alsace. 1852. I. 383.
— Flore vogéso-rhénane. 1870. I. 386.
— Liste des plantes . . . d'Alsace et des Vosges. 1826. I. 377.
— Lonicera Caprifolium var. apetala. 1848. II. 837.[1]
— La métamorphose des plantes. 1865. I. 101.[2]
— Le monde végétal. 1866. I. 511.
— Note sur les Rubus monstrueux. 1862. II. 305.[2]
— Notices botaniques. 1840. II. 289.[2] — 1845. I. 143.
— Notices sur quelques faits de tératologie. 1840. I. 143.
— Prodrome de la flore d'Alsace. 1836. I. 379.
— Statistique de la flore d'Alsace. 1831. I. 378.
— Statistique végétale des environs de Strasbourg. 1845. I. 381.
— Tératologie végétale. 1864. I. 143.
— Sur la valeur morphologique de l'écaille dans le cône des Conifères. 1866. II. 19.
Kirschlorbeer. 1889. II. 274.[2]
Die **Kirschpflaume**, Prunus Myrobalana. 1900. II. 273.[2]
Kirsten, Andreas Jakob. De Areca Indorum. 1739. II. 64.[1]
Kirsten, J. J. Exercitatio de Styrace. 1736. II. 704.[2]
Kirsten, Rudolph. Aulacophyllum Skinneri. 1898. III 286.[1]
— Die Cycadeen im Friedrich-Wilhelm-Garten. 1898. III. 284.[2]
Kirtikar, K. R. The folklore of Indian plants. 1888. I. 518.
— Indian flowers. 1892. III. 203.
— Note on a recent paper . . . on the Mango. 1886. III. 525.[1]
— A note on Pandanus odoratissimus. 1886. II. 57.[2]
— The poisonous plants of Bombay. 1892. III. 521.[1]
Kirtland, Jared Potter. Diseased condition of Peach trees. 1852. III. 441.[2]
— The Magnoliaceae. 1867. III. 397.[1]

Kirwan, Charles de. Des aptitudes végétatives spéciales du Pin noir. 1881. IV. 466.[1]
— Les arbres et les bois des cinq parties du monde. 1870. I. 300.
— Les arbres japonais. 1892. IV. 87.[2]
— L'art d'être propriétaire de bois. 1894. IV. 246, 547.[1]
— L'art forestier français à l'Exposition universelle. 1878. IV. 20.[1]
— Bibliographie de l'exposition forestière de 1878. 1879. IV. 2.
— Du buttage. 1871. III. 166.
— Conifères, indigènes et exotiques. 1867. III. 289.
— Les Conifères indigènes et exotiques. 1867. IV. 441.
— Le couvert et la couverture du sol forestier. 1880. IV. 71.
— De l'écorcement artificiel des bois par la vapeur. 1877. IV. 434.
— De l'époque préférable pour la plantation des Conifères. 1884. III. 294.[2]
— Études forestières; de l'exploitabilité. 1888. IV. 382.[1]
— Études forestières; de l'exploitabilité . . . de leur différents modes. 1887. IV. 245.
— L'Eucalyptus des pays froids. 1898. IV. 534.[1]
— L'Eucalyptus globulus. 1865. IV. 532.[2]
— El Eucalyptus y los pantanos. 1882. IV. 530.
— L'exploitation des forêts. 1898. IV. 556.[2]
— L'exploitation des forêts et la fabrication de la pâte à papier. 1899. IV. 430.
— Une exposition forestière improvisée en Auvergne. 1880. IV. 20.[1]
— Flore forestière illustrée. 1872. I. 404,[2] IV. 79,[1] 85.[1]
— Les forêts du Japon. 1891. IV. 376.[1]
— La France forestière. 1869. IV. 27.[2]
— De l'influence des forêts sur les eaux. 1899. IV. 52.
— Influence of forests on subterranean waters. 1899. IV. 52.
— Le Kaki du Japon. 1898. IV. 534.[2]
— La lumière et l'humus en sylviculture. 1881. IV. 67.[1]
— Montagnes et torrents. 1882. IV. 184.[2]
— Notice sur l'industrie des écorces à tan. 1878. IV. 435.
— Le pavillon forestier du Trocadéro. 1889. IV. 20.[2]
— Les Peupliers. 1866. IV. 485.[1]
— Le plantoir-tarière. 1877. IV. 152.
— De quelques Conifères rares. 1863. IV. 441. — 1865. III. 292.
— Reboisement des terres ruinées ou incultes. 1874. IV. 162.
— Du relèvement de la propriété forestière. 1895. IV. 556.[2]
— Sciadopitys verticillata. 1867. IV. 484.[1]
— Sols, climats, altitudes. 1881. IV. 67.[1]
— Les trois types du Pin sylvestre. 1866. IV. 472.
— Le Tulipier de Virginie. 1893. IV. 519.[2]
Kiseljak, Vladimir. Nauk o čuvanjû šumah. 1883. IV. 177.[2]
Kiss, Ferenc. A Fehér Nyarfa. 1894. IV. 486.[1]
Kissa, N. W. Kropfmaserbildung bei Pirus. 1900. II. 267.[1]
Kissling, P. B. Beiträge zur Kenntniss des Einflusses der chemischen Lichtintensität. 1895. I. 230.
Kitaibel, Paul. Plantae Horti botanici pesthiensis. 1809. I. 65.[2]
— Plantae horti botanici Regiae universitatis hung. 1812. I. 65.[2]
— See also WALDSTEIN, F. A., Graf von & KITAIBEL, Paul.
Kitao, Diro. Über Schwinden und Quellen der Hölzer. 1897. IV. 412.[2]
Kitchener, Frances Anna. A year's botany. 1874. I. 402.
Kitley, John. Removing Araucarias. 1868. III. 167.
Kittary, M. See KHTTAPH, M.
Kittel, Martin Baldwin. Die offenblüthigen Pflanzen . . . von Aschaffenburg. 1871. I. 386.
— Taschenbuch der Flora Deutschlands. 1837. I. 532.[1]— 1847. I. 382.
— Zur Viscum-Frage. 1849. II. 178.[1]
Rittl, Ernst. Ueber Entwaldungen und Hochwässer. 1890. IV. 51.
Kittlitz, Friedrich Heinrich von. Twenty-four views of the vegetation of the coasts and islands of the Pacific. 1844. I. 321.
— Vegetations-Ansichten. 1854. I. 440.
— Vierundzwanzig Vegetations-Ansichten von Küstenlandern und Inseln des Stillen Oceans. 1844. I. 321.
Kitto, John. Palestine. 1841. I. 480.
Kius, Otto. Das Forstwesen Thüringens im . . . Jahrhundert. 1868. IV. 25.

Kiwirikko, K. E. See STENROOS, K. E.
Kiyowara Shigeomi. 1823. I. 461.
Kjær, H. H. C. Anviisning til Hedebeplantning. 1867. III. 119.[2]
Kjærbølling, Niels. Om den hensigtsmæssige Anvendelse og Vedligeholdelse af Buskpartierne. 1844. III. 119.[2]
— Hvad er hensigtsmæssigst til Opelskning, enten haarde eller bløde Træarter? 1844. IV. 113.[1]
— Hvilken Jordbund passer bedst for de forskjellige Træarter? 1844. III. 40.
— Om Hyldebusken. 1846. III. 752.[1]
— Iagttagelser over de Virkninger, Vinteren 1837–38 har havt paa adskillige Træer og Buske. 1839. III. 44.[1]
— Kirsebærtræet. 1846. II. 273.[1]
— Planternes kunstige Formeringsmaader. 1845. III. 152.
— Siirtræer og blomstrende Buske. 1844. III. 204.[1]
— Om Slynge- eller Rankeplanter. 1846. III. 204.[2]
— Ere Træerne om Vinteren ganske saftløse? 1847. I. 164.
— De vigtigste Regler for Træ-Beskjæringen. 1847. III. 172.
Kjellborg, J. F. Flora paroeciae Bränkyrka. See SILLÉN, N. J. 1827. I. 353.
Kjellenberg, Fredrik U. Examen classis dioeciae. See THUNBERG, C. P. 1825. I. 251.
Kjellman, Frans Reinhold. De fanerogama vaxternas meristem. 1892. I. 132.[2]
— Några tillägg till kännedomen om Spetsbergens plantae vasculares. 1874. II. 119.[2]
— Organografiska meddelanden. 1900. II. 708.[1]
— Om växtligheten på Sibiriens nordkust. 1879. I. 454.[1]
Kjellmark, Knut. Några anmärkningsvärda Salix- och Betulaformer. 1895. II. 107,[1] 118.[1]
Kjøbenhavn. See COPENHAGEN.
Kl. Merkwürdige Eiche. 1828. II. 137.[2]
— Ueber die officinelle Kräfte . : . der Besenpfrieme. 1827. III. 475.[2]
Kl., Fr. See KLOTZSCH, FR.
Klase, Laurentius Mag. De Betula nana. See LINNÉ, Carl von. 1743. II. 119.[2]
Klason, Peter. Sur l'huile essentielle de bois de Sapin. 1900. IV. 460.[1]
Klasson. See KRACCOH.[2]
Klatt, Friedrich Wilhelm. Amerikanische Compositen. 1896. II. 858.[1]
— Ueber die Arten der Gattung Rhamnus. 1858. II. 496.[2]
— Ueber die Arten der Gattung Rhamnus . . . in dem Booth'schen Garten. 1858. II. 496.[2]
— Beiträge zur Kenntniss der Compositen. 1884. II. 849.[1]
— Beiträge zur Kenntniss der Compositen Südafrika's. 1879. I. 495.
— Berichtigungen zu einigen von C. G. Pringle . . . gesammelten Compositen. 1893. II. 849.[1]
— Compositae. 1892. II. 848.[2]
— Die Compositae des Herbarium Schlagintweit. 1880. II. 849.[2]
— Compositae Hildebrandtianae. 1890. II. 849.[2]
— Compositae Hildebrandtianae 'et Humblotianae. 1892. II. 849.[2]
— Compositae Mechowianae. 1892. II. 849.[1]
— Compositae novae Costaricenses. 1895. II. 849.[1]
— Determinationes . . . Compositarum. 1885. II. 848.[2]
— Die von Dr. Fr. Stuhlmann . . . gesammelten Compositen. 1891. II. 849.[2]
— Die von E. Ule . . . gesammelten Compositen. 1892. II. 849.[1]
— Flora des Herzogthums Lauenberg. 1865. I. 385.
— Die von Frau Amalia Dietrich . . . gesammelten Compositen. 1892. II. 850.[1]
— Ueber die Gattung Cornus Tourn. 1862. III. 645.[1]
— Ueber die Gattung Sekelblume. 1858. II. 492.[2]
— Neue Compositen aus dem Wiener Herbarium. 1894. II. 849.[1]
— Neue Compositen, in dem Herbar des Herrn Francaville. 1882. II. 848.[1]
— Norddeutsche Anlagen-Flora. 1865. I. 293, III. 69.
— Plantae Lehmannianae in Guatemala. 1887. II. 849.[1]
— Plantae Muellerianae. Pittosporeae. 1856. II. 247.[1]
— Sur   s Composées des colonies françaises. 1873. II. 848 quelque
Klaudyan, Nicolaus. Knieha lekarska kteraz slowe herbarz. 1517. I. 276.
Klauprecht, Johann Ludwig. Ebene Trigonometrie. 1823. IV. 58.
— Forstliche Statistik des Spessarts. 1826. IV. 350.[2]

— Die Holzmesskunst. 1842. IV. 213.
— Die Lehre vom Klima. 1840. IV. 59.²
— Sendschreiben an die Herrn Redaktoren der forstlichen Zeitschrift für Baden.· 1838. IV. 350.¹
Klaus, K. · See Клаусъ, K.
Klebahn, Heinrich. Bemerkungen über Gymnosporangium confusum. 1892. III. 422.³
— Beobachtungen und Streitfragen über die Blasenroste. 1888. IV. 470.¹
— Einige Wirkungen der Dürre des Frühjahres, 1893. 1894. III. 183.²
— Ueber die Formen und den Wirthswechsel der Blasenroste der Kiefern. 1890. IV. 461.²
— Kulturversuche mit heteröcischen Uredineen. 1892. III. 195.¹
— Die Rindenporen. 1884. I. 132.²
— Über den Rindenrost der Weymouthskiefer. 1888. IV. 470.¹
— Ueber die Structur . . . der Lenticellen. 1883. I. 132.²
— Vorläufige Mitteilung über den Wirtswechsel der Kronenroste. 1893. III. 414.²
— Weitere Beobachtungen über die Blasenroste der Kiefern. 1888. IV. 461.²
— Ueber Wurzelanlagen unter Lenticellen bei Herminiera. 1891. II. 930.² 776.³
— Zwei vermutlich durch Nematoden erzeugte Pflanzenkrankheiten. 1891. III. 389.³
Kleberg. Die Benutzung der Cacteen. 1847. III. 620.¹
Klebs, Georg. Beiträge zur Morphologie . . . der Keimung. 1885. I. 204.
Klee, W. G. Culture of the Black Wattle. 1891. III. 465.¹
— Culture of the Date. 1883. III. 328.²
— See also VAN DEMAN, H. E., REASONER, P. W. & KLEE, W. G.
Kleeberg, Christian August. Ueber die Lebensverhältnisse der Cacteen. 1847. II. 588.³
— Die Markstrahlen der Coniferen. 1885. II. 17.¹
Kleemann, A. Wistaria polystachya. 1897. III. 491.¹
Kleemann, C. H. Allgemeines Handbuch des Gartenbaues. 1854. III. 104.
Kleiber, Albert. Versuche zur Bestimmung des Gehalts . . . an Zellwandbestandteilen. 1900. I. 138.²
Klein. Echinocactus Buckii Klein. 1859. II. 593.¹
Klein. See PAUL, George & KLEIN.
Klein, B. Einiges über Schalwald. 1886. IV. 507.
— Zur Frage über die elektrischen Ströme in Pflanzen. 1898. I. 231.²
Klein, C. von. Abhandlungen und Versuche über die Ratanhia. 1819. III. 480.¹
Klein, Edmund. Zur Frage der Wälderbesteuerung. 1870. IV. 285.²
Klein, Ferdinand. Beiträge zur physikalisch-technologischen Kenntniss des Holzes. 1888. IV. 411.²
— Die Formeln zu den Cotta'schen Waldwerthberechnungs-Tafeln. 1823. IV. 58, 265.
— Ueber Verkohlung des Holzes. 1836. IV. 394.
Klein, Gyula. See KLEIN, Julius.
Klein, J. J. Forst-Handbuch. 1826. IV. 106.·
Klein, Jakob Theodor. Fasciculus plantarum . . . ex horto. 1722. I. 43.
— Fasciculus plantarum . . . ex horto Kleiniano. 1724. I. 43.
— Plantarum rariorum et exoticarum in horto Kleiniano. 1748. I. 44.
— An Tithymaloides; frutescens. 1730. I. 290, II. 865.²
Klein, Johann Konrad. De Junipero. See BAIER, J. J. (By error.) 1719. III. 303.³ V. XXVIII.²
Klein, Julius. Az Ailanthus-fák. 1871. III. 507.¹
— Zur Anatomie junger Coniferen-Wurzeln. 1872. II. 17.²
— Ueber Bildungsabweichungen an Blättern. 1891. I. 111.
— A Cinchona vagy China fák. 1871. III. 718.
— A Fenyőfák gyökerének fejlődéséről. 1876. II. 17.²
— Hazánk Orgonafájának . . . egy új termőhelye. 1881. III. 715.¹
— Über die Keimung von Gleditschia. 1877. II. 361.³
— Zur Kenntniss von Robinia. 1880. II. 382.²
— Ein neuer Standort von Syringa Josikaea. 1881. II. 715.¹
— A télen és nyáron vágott fák megkülömböztetése. 1876. IV. 384.²
— Untersuchungen über Bildungsabweichungen an Blättern. 1892. I. 144.¹
— A Vadgesztenye hazája. 1880. II. 481.³
— & Szabó, Franz. Zur Kenntniss der Wurzeln von Aesculus. 1880. II. 482.¹
Klein, Ludwig. Die Physiognomie der mitteleuropäischen Waldbäume. 1900. I. 516.

Klein, M. Erfahrungen vom sibirischen Erbsen-Baum. 1776. III. 470.¹
Klein, O. Sur l'huile de Curcas. 1899. III. 519.³
Klein, Otto. Beiträge zur Anatomie der Inflorescenzaxen. 1886. I. 113.²
Kleine Aufsätze über verschiedene zum Forstwesen gehörige interessante Gegenstände. 1795. IV. 123.³
Kleine forstliche Reiseerinnerungen. 1867. IV. 118.
Die kleine Kiefernblattwespe. 1862. IV. 476.
Kleine Naturgeschichte der in Deutschland einheimischen Bäume. 1811. I. 531.
Kleine Raths-Verordnung betreffend die Bewirthschaftung der Wälder. 1822. IV. 306.
Kleines Holzrechen-Taschenbuch. 1884. IV. 228.
Kleinschmidt. Analyse der Asche der Eicheln. 1844. II. 137.²
Kleinstück, O. Emploi thérapeutique des feuilles de Bétel. 1887. III. 342.¹
Kleiser, von. Eine forstliche Reise ins Königreich Hannover. 1865. IV. 353.
Kleiser, C. von. Ueber den Stock- und Wurzel-Ausschlag der Buche. 1837. IV. 493.²
Kleiser, K. von. Erwiederung dem anonymen Verfasser der Broschüre " Die badische Forstorganisation." 1852. IV. 289.²
— Die Forstorganisation in Baden. 1851. IV. 289.¹
Klekner, Alajos. Az erdőtörvény magyarázata. 1881. IV. 331.¹
Klemann, (Hofgärtner). Über die Kultur der Eriken. 1828. III. 649.²
Klement. See also CLEMENT.
Klement, E. De Bignonia Catalpa. 1834. III. 706.¹
Klemm, Johann Konrad. De Olea. 1679. III. 713.¹
Klemm, Paul. Über den Bau der beblätterten Zweige der Cupressineen. 1886. II. 18.
— Desorganisationserscheinungen der Zelle. 1895. I. 137.
Klencke. Die Cultur des Maulbeerbaumes. 1849. III. 376.
Klencke, Philipp Friedrich Hermann. Gutta percha. 1848. III. 230.
Kler, Onisim Egorovitch. See CLERC, G. O.; Клеръ, O.
Klerck, A. W. de. See DE KLERCK, A. W.
Klercker, John Echard Fredrik. af. En bastard mellan Vaccinium Myrtillus och Vaccinium Vitis Idæa. 1894. II. 686.¹
Kletke, G. M. Gesetz den Diebstahl an Holz und anderen Waldprodukten betreffend. 1855. IV. 320.
— Gesetz vom 2. Juni 1852, den Diebstahl an Holz . . . betreffend. 1855. IV. 320.
— Das Holzdiebstahl-Gesetz vom 7. Juni 1821. 1846. IV. 320.
Klett, Christian. Ueber die schwarze Weide. 1872. IV. 487.¹
Klett, Gustav Theodor & Richter, H. E. F. Flora der phanerogamischen Gewächse der Umgegend von Leipzig. 1830. I. 378.
Klette, Oskar. Die Darlegung einfacher Grundsätze für den Privatwaldbetrieb in Sachsen. 1890. IV. 118, 308.³
— Die Stellung der in land- und forstwirthschaftlichen Betrieben beschäftigten Personen. 1886. IV. 310.³
Kliefoth, A. Beobachtungen über die Entwickelung der Pflanzen. 1892. I. 225.
Kliem, Wilhelm. Rubus phoenicolasius. 1892. III. 459.¹
Klier, Emil. Menge der Flachschindel und Dauben . . . aus einem Rundholze. 1873. IV. 428.⁴
Klier, Jakob. Anleitung zur Kultur der Pelargonien. 1826. III. 491.¹
— Anleitung zur Kultur . . . der Rosa reclinata. 1843. III. 456.²
Der klimatische Einfluss des Waldes. 1890. IV. 54.
Klimatischer Einfluss der Waldungen. See NÖRDLINGER, Hermann. 1862. IV. 53.
Klimatologische und phänologische Beobachtungen . . . im Canton Bern. See PRÄNOLOGISCHE . . . 1877. II. 227.¹
Klimatologische und phaenologische Beobachtungen . . . im Kanton Bern, 1882. See RÄZ, (Forstdirektor). 1883. I. 227.¹
Kling, Johann Peter. Vorschriftsmässige Behandlung der Domänen-Waldungen in der Churpfalz. 1791. IV. 247.²
Klinge, Johannes Christof. Über eine eigentümliche Anpassung bei weissblühenden Farbenvarietäten. 1896. I. 236,² 244.²
— Flora von Est-, Liv- und Curland. 1882. I. 364.
— Die Holzgewächse von Est-, Liv- und Curland. 1883. III. 67.²
— Die· vegetativen . . . Verhältnisse der Nordküste der kurischen Halbinsel. 1886. I. 365.

Klingen, I. *See* Клингенъ, И.
Klinggräff, Carl Julius von. Flora von Preussen. 1848. I. 382.
— Palästina und seine Vegetation. 1880. I. 480.
— Die Vegetationsverhältnisse der Provinz Preussen. 1866. I. 385.
— Ueber die Verbreitung einiger Holzpflanzen in der Provinz Preussen. 1862. I. 371.
Klinggräff, Hugo von. Die in der Umgegend von Agram in Croatien vorkommenden Pflanzen. 1862. I. 447.
— Versuch einer topographischen Flora der Provinz Westpreussen. 1881. I. 388.
— Ueber die westpreussischen Formen von Juniperus communis. 1882. II. 31.[1]
Klingner, (*Forstmeister*). Die Harzscharr-Gerechtsame. 1872. IV. 436.[2]
— Die Waldkultur in der Grafschaft Henneberg. 1877. IV. 26.
— & **Thiem**, (*Oberförster, Seitenberg*). Ansichten der königlichen Forstbeamten . . . über die Beibehaltung eines modificirten Plänterbetriebes. 1849. IV. 130.
Klingsohr, Johann Georg Wilhelm. De Geoffroea inermi ejusque cortice. 1788. III. 467.[1]
Klinkhardt, C. H. Betrachtung des Pflanzenreichs. 1828. I. 146.
Klinsmann, Ernst Ferdinand. Clavis Breyniana. 1855. I. 78.[1]
— Clavis Dilleniana ad Hortum elthamensem. 1856. I. 78.[1]
— Ueber einige . . . mitgebrachte Früchte. 1864. I. 270.
— De Emetino et Cephaeli Ipecacuanha. 1823. III. 244.
— Novitia atque defectus florae gedanensis. 1843. I. 381.
Klipp, O. L'age des grands Sequoia gigantea. 1879. II. 51.[1]
— L'Attalea Maripa Mart. 1884. III. 327.[1]
— De bladluis van den Peerboom. 1883. III. 446.[1]
— Le charançon du Peuplier. 1875. III. 344.[2]
— Les Conifères en Campine. 1884. IV. 441.
— Des Conifères exotiques rustiques. 1886. III. 290.
— Le Cytisus nigricans L. 1900. III. 474.[1]
— De l'enlèvement des Sabines. 1877. III. 304.[1]
— Juniperus Sabina. 1877. III. 304.[1]
— De kever der Frambozen. 1876. III. 458.[2]
— De Kever des Populiers. 1875. III. 344.[2]
— Le Maximiliana regia Mart. 1892. III. 327.[1]
— Le Merelinde de Vosselare. 1896. II. 517.[1]
— Le Phoenix tenuis hort. 1882. III. 328.[1]
— Le scarabée du Framboisier. 1876. III. 458.[2]
— Syn n m de quelques espèces de Conifères. 1886. II. 13.[1] o y ie
— Le Tabernaemontana. 1882. III. 690.[2]
— Le Tacsonia Volxemi. 1883. III. 617.[1]
— Le tigre du Poirier. 1883. III. 446.[1]
Klippart, John H. The principles and practice of land drainage. 1862. III. 150.[2]
Klippel, H. Anleitung zur Kenntniss der Holzgewächse. 1855. IV. 83.
Klipphausen. *See* Ziegler, H. von, Klipphausen & Miessler, Otto.
Klipstein, Schaden durch Engerlinge. 1886. IV. 203.
Klipstein. Johannes Christian Gottlob. De nectariis plantarum. 1784. I. 118.[1]
Klipstein, Philipp Engel. Versuch einer Anweisung zur Forst-Betriebs-Regulirung. 1823. IV. 239.
— Der Waldfeldbau. 1850. IV. 133.
Klitzing, H. Die Gattung Ulmus. 1886. III. 364.[1]
Klöbisch, R. L. Deutsche Waldbäume und ihre Physiognomie. 1857. I. 371, 516.
Klöckner. Die Forsten des Lehngutes Walachisch-Meseritsch. 1861. IV. 368.
Klöckner, Rud. Die "tausendjährige" Eiche. 1895. IV. 516.[1]
Kloeppel, Johannes. Ueber Secretbehälter bei Büttneriaceen. 1885. II. 531.[2]
Kloete Nortier, H. Aanteekeningen op eenige inlandsche geneesmiddelen op Java. 1860. II. 276.[1]
— Catechismus der plantkunde. *See* Nortier, H. K. 1848. I. 89.
— Cortex en extractum Monesiae. 1856. II. 698.[2]
— Cortex Melambo sive Malambo. 1853. III. 517.[1]
— Een mikroskopisch verschijnsel van den Kinabast. 1855. II. 813.[1]
— Over de zoogenaamde Quinquina des iles de Lagos. 1857. II. 812.
Klopfer, (*Oberförster, Primkenau*). *See* Maerker, C. & Klopfer.

Klose, R. Die Korbweiden. 1892. III. 349.[1]
Kloss, P. Clematis montana. 1890. III. 391.[1]
Klosterneuburg — **K. k. önologische und pomologische Lehranstalt**. *See* K. k. önologischen . . . III. 25.
Klotz, (*Forstmeister, Karlsruhe*). Entgegnung auf die von dem Herrn Forst-Inspektor v. Ehrenstein . . . aufgestellte Frage. 1851. IV. 254.
— Ueber die Nothwendigkeit der Forst-Kulturen. 1835. IV. 141.
— Ueber die Nothwendigkeit der Forst-Kulturen . . . vorzüglich in Privatwaldungen. 1847. IV. 141.
— Versuch einer Beantwortung der 5ten . . . vom Oberförster Engelke aufgestellten Frage. 1851. IV. 242.
Klotz, K. Ueber das Drehen der Baumstämme. 1861. I. 107.[1]
— Sur la torsion des troncs d'arbres. 1861. I. 107.[1]
Klotz, M. von. Ueber Einrichtung . . . der Samendarre. 1842. IV. 147.[2]
Klotz, P. A. F. Anleitung zur Bewirthschaftung und Benutzung der Forsten. 1824. IV. 239.
— Ueber die zweckmässige Bildung der Jäger. 1828. IV. 31.
Klotzsch, Johann Friedrich. Ueber die Abstammung der . . . rothen Chinarinde. 1858. II. 814.[1]
— Additamenta . . . in tribus Clavaefloras . . . Ericae. 1838. II. 664.[1]
— Die Aristolochiaceae des Berliner Herbariums. 1859. II. 180.[2]
— Begoniaceae novae. 1855. II. 583.[1]
— Ueber Begoniaceen-Gattungen. 1854. II. 583.[b]
— Begoniaceen-Gattungen und Arten. 1855. II. 583.[1]
— Beiträge zu einer Flora der Aequinoctial-Gegenden der neuen Welt. 1844. II. 329.
— Beiträge zur Nutzanwendung der im Brittischen Gujana wildwachsenden Pflanzen. 1844. III. 268.[1]
— Bemerkungen des Hrn. Dr. H. Karsten zu . . . Pflanzen aus Columbien. 1846. I. 339.[2]
— Bemerkungen zur Gattung Grubbia. 1839. III. 170.[1]
— Beschreibung der Protea Mundii. 1838. II. 166.[1]
— Beschreibung einer neuen mexikanischen Pflanze. 1841. II. 236.[1]
— Beschreibung zweier neuen Euphorbien aus Mexico. 1834. II. 441.[3]
— Drei Arten der Gesneriaceen-Gattung Rytidophyllum. 1852. II. 795.[1]
— Ueber einige neue . . . Pflanzen. 1851. II. 771.[1]
— Enumeration of the Euphorbiaceae of . . . Panama. 1852. II. 434.[1]
— Die Ericeae mit bleibender Blumenkrone. 1838. II. 657.[2]
— Ericearum a . . . Chamisso descriptarum pars addita. 1833. II. 657.[1]–1838. II. 664.[1]
— Ericearum genera et species. 1838. II. 657.[2]
— Euphorbiaceae. 1852. III. 434.[1]
— Euphorbiaceae Juss. 1844. II. 434.[2]
— Die Existenz-Dauer der Gewächse. 1856. I. 193.[1]
— Ueber die Gattung Centradenia. 1851. II. 636.[2]
— Die Gattung Trewia L. 1841. II. 452.[1]
— Heliotropium submolle. 1852. II. 751.[1]
— Das Individuum der Pflanze. 1856. I. 99.
— Linné's natürliche Pflanzenklasse Tricoccae des Berliner Herbarium's im Allgemeinen und die natürliche Ordnung Euphorbiaceae insbesondere. 1859. II. 433.[2]
— Nachschrift zur Frage: Altern die Pflanzensorten? 1857. I. 205, 248.[2]
— Eine neue Gattung der Acanthaceae. 1839. II. 797.[2]
— Neue . . . südamerikanische Euphorbiaceen-Gattungen. 1841. II. 433.[2]
— Novum genus Bixacearum. 1854. II. 573.[2]
— Ueber die Nutzanwendung der Bastarde. 1856. I. 245.
— Ueber die Nutzanwendung der Pflanzen-Bastarde. 1854. I. 245.
— Olinia Thunbg. eine capische Gattung. 1836. II. 599.[2]
— Pentagonaster, eine neue Pflanzengattung. 1836. II. 628.[1]
— Die Pfirsich (Amygdalus Persica), die Mandel. 1858. II. 276.[1]
— Pflanzen-Abbildungen . . . zur Erkenntniss officineller Gewächse. 1838. III. 57.
— Die Pflanzen-Namen. 1856. I. 253.[2]
— Philipp Schönlein's botanischer Nachlass. 1856, 1857. I. 483,[1] 497.
— Ueber Pollenkreuzung der Mandel, Pfirsich. 1856. II. 276.[1]
— De Proteaceis americanis. 1841. II. 158.[2]

— Sur les pseudo-stearoptènes. 1852. III. 225.
— Ueber die seit dem Jahre 1851 bekannt gewordenen Arbeiten der ... Bicornes. 1857. II. 658.[1]
— Sida Sellowiana. 1836. II. 521.[1]
— Studien über die natürliche Klasse Bicornes. 1851. II. 657.[2]
— Eine synoptische Aufzählung der Arten von Myroxylon. 1857. II. 374.[2]
— Tuckermania. 1841. II. 453.[2]
— Vorläufige Nachricht über die Einwirkung der Knospendecken auf die Entwicklung der Rinde. 1847. I. 130.
— Zwei neue Rohrpalmen aus Guatemala. 1852. II. 61.[1]
— See also BRAUN, A., KLOTZSCH, J. F. & BOUCHÉ, C.; LINK, H. F., KLOTZSCH, Friedrich & OTTO, Friedrich.
— & Garcke, August. Die botanischen Ergebnisse der Reise des Prinzen Waldemar von Preussen. 1862. I. 473.
— & Otto, Friedrich. Ueber Datura arborea und suaveolens. 1841. II. 771.[1]
Kluk, Christoph. Dykcyonarz roślinny. 1785. I. 32.
— Roślin potrzebnych, wygodnych, osobliwie krajowych. 1777. I. 359, III. 101.[1]
Klunge. Recherche de l'Aloès. 1880. III. 333.[1]
Klunzinger, Carl Benjamin. Die vegetation der egyptischarabischen Wüste. 1878. I. 488.
Klynton, Ch. De la théorie actuelle de la science agricole. 1828. III. 35.
Kmet, Andreas. Ein neuer Standort der Rosa reversa. 1884. II. 298.[1]
— Rosa reversa W. Kit. 1884. II. 287.[2]
Kmiotek, Bruno. Siedelung und Waldwirtschaft im Salzforst. 1900. IV. 27.[1]
Kn. Die Weisserle als Vorbau-, Schutz- und Treibholz. 1896. IV. 489.[3]
Knabe, C. A. Pflanzenphysiognomische Skizzen aus dem südwestlichen Finnland. 1896. I. 366.
Knabe, Michael. Hortipomolegium. 1621. III. 135.
Knaf, Joseph. Etwas über Giftpflanzen ... der Papilionaceen. 1852. III. 462.[3]
Knaggs, Walter. Remarks on the adaptability of the soil ... of the Malayan Peninsula for the cultivation of Tea. 1878. III. 601.[2]
Knallendes Aufspringen einer Palmenscheide. 1862. II. 63.[2]
Knapp, F. H. The botanical chart of British flowering plants. 1846. I. 399.
Knapp, Frederick N. Fertilizers: Agricultural. 1888. III. 151.
Knapp, Friedrich. Mittheilungen aus der cubanischen Pflanzenwelt. 1877. I. 336.
— Mittheilungen aus der cubanischen Thier- und Pflanzenwelt. 1877. I. 336.
Knapp, J. G. Coniferae of the Rocky Mountains. 1872. II. 14.[1]
— See also LAPHAM, I. A., KNAPP, J. G. & CROCKER, H.
Knapp, John Leonard. The journal of a naturalist. 1829. I. 524.[1]
Knapp, Josef Armin. Die bisher bekannten Pflanzen Galiziens. 1872. I. 442.
— Die Heimat der Syringa persica L. 1889. II. 715.[2]
— Prodromus florae comitatus nitriensis. 1865. I. 445.
— See also SCHULZER VON MUEGGENBURG, Stephan, KANITZ, August & KNAPP, J. A.
Knappe, (Oberförster, Giersdorf). Ueber den Einfluss des Heidekrautes. 1865. IV. 210.[2]
— Ueber eine Fichte im ... Reyier Heinzendorf. 1865. IV. 460.[1]
— Ueber das Vorkommen von Taxus baccata. 1866. IV. 440.[1]
Knappe, (Oberförster, Neustadt). Etwas über die Benutzung des Lindenbastes. 1853. IV. 528.[1]
— Kiefer mit getheiltem Stamm. 1842. IV. 483.[1]
— Massen-Ergebniss von ... Tannen-Stämmen. 1853. IV. 446.[1]
— Mittel, die Entstehung des Grases ... zu verhüten. 1847. IV. 149.[2]
— Nähere Beschreibung der abnormen Tanne. 1844. IV. 447.[1]
— Neue Bemerkungen über das Befressen der jungen Lärchenbaumbestände. 1854. IV. 450.
— Tanne mit abnorm verdicktem Stamm. 1842. IV. 447.[1]
— Tanne mit zweitem jungen Stamm. 1842. IV. 447.[1]
— Zwei Fichten. 1842. IV. 460.[1]
Knaurs and burrs. 1888. I. 213.[1]
Knaus, Carl. Ueber die Mittel, um die Waldstreu ... entbehrlich zu machen. 1839. IV. 437.[3]

Knaut, Christian. Dissertatio ... de variis doctrinam plantarum tradendi variorum methodis. 1705. I. 289.
— Methodus plantarum genuina. 1716. I. 289.
Knauth, (Oberförster). Tagebuch, geführt auf einer forstlichen Reise. 1854. IV. 352.
Knauth, Christoph. Enumeratio plantarum circa Halam Saxonum. 1687. I. 372.
— Herbarium hallense. 1687. I. 372.
Knauth, Hans. Die Aufforstung der Laubholzkrüppelbestände im Spessart. 1889. IV. 159, 170.
— Zur Technik des Buchen-Unterbaues. 1897. IV. 496.
— Waldwegbau und Terrainstudien. 1896. IV. 267.
Knebel. Gutachten über die Ausführung von Waldschutz-Anlagen. 1880. IV. 274.[1]
Knebel. Über die Manna liefernden Gewächse. 1865. III. 221.[1]
Knebel, E. Composition chimique de la noix de Kola. 1893. III. 590.[2]
Kneeland, Samuel. Note on Wellingtonia gigantea. 1856. II. 50.[2]
Kneifl, Reginald. Das Pflanzenreich. 1819. I. 255.
Knepper. Over den stand van het enten op de onderneming Klein-Getas. 1898. III. 743.[1]
Knerr, E. B. Notes on a variety of Ampelopsis quinquefolia. 1893. II. 504.[2]
Knersch, W. Ein sehr starker Wachholderbaum. 1896. IV. 448.[2]
Knieha lekarska kteraz slowe herbarz. See KLAUDYAN, Nicolaus. 1517. I. 276.
Kniep, Ernst. Der deutsche Wald. 1894. I. 372.
Knieskern, P. D. A catalogue of plants ... of Monmouth and Ocean. 1857. I. 314.
Knight, (Prof.). University extension manuals. See GEDDES, Patrick. 1893. I. 96.
Knight, H. Paulownia imperialis. 1877. III. 743.[1]
Knight, Horace. Grafting the Mango tree. 1900. III. 525.[1]
Knight, Joseph. On the cultivation of ... Proteeae. 1809. II. 158.[1]
— & Perry. A synopsis of the coniferous plants. 1850. II. 18,[1] III. 289.
— — Uebersicht der Coniferen. 1850. III. 289.
Knight, Thomas Andrew. Account of some experiments on the descent of the sap. 1803. I. 163.
— Account of two methods of grafting. 1812. III. 159.[1]
— On the action of detached leaves. 1816. I. 172.
— On the advantage of grafting Walnut, Mulberry. 1812. III. 164.[2]
— On the best mode of pruning ... the Mulberry tree. 1820. III. 373.
— On the causes which influence the direction of the growth of roots. 1811. I. 195.[1]
— On the comparative influence of male and female parents on their offspring. 1809. I. 248.[1]
— Upon the culture of the Prunus Pseudo-Cerasus. 1830. III. 442.[2]
— On the difference between spring and winter felled timber. 1820. IV. 384.[2]
— On the direction of the radicle. 1806. I. 195.[1]
— On the effects of different kinds of stocks in grafting. 1818. III. 39.
— Experiments and observations on the motion of the sap. 1804. I. 163.
— Upon the extent of expansion and contraction of timber. 1817. IV. 411.[3]
— On facilitating the emission of roots from layers. 1812. III. 159.[1]
— On the formation of the bark of trees. 1807. I. 130.
— Ueber die Fortpflanzung der Bäume durch Schösslinge. 1838. I. 208.[2]
— Ueber die Fortpflanzung ... Stecklinge. 1838. I. 208.[2]
— Upon grafting the Walnut tree. 1833. III. 355.
— On the inconvertibility of bark into alburnum. 1808. I. 130.
— On the inverted action of the alburnous vessels. 1806. I. 163.
— On the motions of the tendrils of plants. 1812. I. 196.[1]
— Nachricht von einigen Versuchen über das Absteigen des Saftes. 1804. I. 163.
— Über die Neubildung von Knospen. 1805. I. 107.[1]
— A new and expeditious mode of budding. 1812. III. 164.[1]
— Notice of a new variety of Ulmus suberosa. 1824. II. 144,[1] III. 160.
— Observations on the Flat Peach of China. 1824. III. 439.[1]

Knight, Thomas Andrew (*continued*).
— Observations on the grafting of trees. 1795. III. 164.²
— On the office of the heart-wood of trees. 1818. I. 163.
— On the origin and formation of roots. 1809. I. 103.
— On the origin and office of the alburnum. 1806. I. 163.
— On the parts of trees primarily impaired by age. 1810. I. 206.²
— Sur un Pêcher né d'un Amandier. 1820. II. 271.²
— Physiological observations upon the effects of partial decortication. 1822. III. 174.²
— Pomona herefordiensis. 1811. III. 425.¹
— On the propagation of the Mulberry tree. 1818. III. 373.
— On the propagation of trees by cuttings in summer. .1838. I. 208.²
— Upon the pruning and management of transplanted standard trees. 1820. III. 165.
— Ueber die Rankenbewegungen der Pflanzen. 1812. I. 196.²
— On the reproduction of buds. 1805. I. 107.²
— Über die Richtung der jungen Wurzel. 1806. I. 195.
— Sechs pflanzenphysiologische Abhandlungen. 1895. I. 147.
— A selection from the physiological and horticultural papers. 1841. III. 35.
— Some doubts relative to the efficacy of Mr. Forsyth's plaister. 1802. III. 181.²
— Concerning the state in which the true sap of trees is deposited during winter. 1805. I. 179.²
— A treatise on the culture of the Apple. 1797. III. 426.¹
— Über die umgekehrte Wirkung der Splintgefässe. 1806. I. 163.
— Ueber die Ursachen, die auf Richtung . . . der Wurzel einwirken. 1811. I. 195.²
— On the want of permanence of character in varieties. 1818. I. 244.²
Knight, William. Outlines of botany. 1828. I. 86.
Kniphof, Johann Hieronymus. Botanica in originali. 1747. I. 291.
— Botanica in originali; das ist, Lebendig Kräuter-Buch. 1734. III. 74.
— Botanica in originali pharmaceutica. 1733. III. 54.
— Examen succedaneorum . . . corticis peruviani. 1747. III. 244.
— De radice Chinae. 1753. III. 338.¹
Knipping, (*Oberförster*). Ueber die forstwirthschaftlichen Einrichtungen. . . . gegen Feuersgefahr. 1860. IV. 182.²
Knobel, Edward. A guide to find the names of all wild-growing trees and shrubs of New England. 1894. I. 312, *IV*. 77.¹
Knobelsdorff, *baron de*. Floraison d'une plante mâle de Cycas revoluta. 1860. III. 285.¹
Knoblauch, Emil Friedrich. Anatomie des Holzes der Laurineen. 1888. .II. 223.²
— Zur Kenntniss einiger Oleaceen-Genera. 1895. II. 705.²
— Oleaceae. 1895. II. 705.²
— Oleaceae africanae. 1893. II. 705.²
— Salvadoraceae. 1895. II. 472.²
Knoch, A. Holzfussboden und Bauholz. 1893. IV. 423.²
Knohll, Johann Paul. Klein Vitikulturbüchlein. 1663. III. 551.²
Knoke, Eberhard Theodor August Karl. Beitrag zur Kenntnis der Wirkung des Strychnin. 1898. III. 684.¹
Knoll, Paul. *See* KNOLL, J. P.
Knolle, Fryderyk. Katechizm leśny lub nauka krótka dla borowych. 1808. IV. 103.²
Knonau, MEYER VON. *See* MEYER VON KNONAU.
Knoop, Jacob. Remarkable trees in Ohio. 1848. II. 135.¹
Knoop, Johann Hermann. Beknopte huishoudelyke hovenier. 1757. III. 105.
— Beschouwende en werkdadige hovenier-konst. 1753. III. 105.
— Beschrijving . . . van de beste soorten van Appelen en Peeren. 1758. III. 75.²
— Beschrijving van plantagie-gewassen. 1763. III. 75.²
— Dendrologia. 1763. III. 75.²
— Frguctoloia. 1763. III. 76.
— Fructologie; ou, Description. 1763. III. 76.
— Pomologia; das ist, Beschreibungen . . . der Aepfel und Birnen. 1758. III. 75.²
— Pomologia; dat is, Beschryvingen. 1758. III. 75.²
— Pomologie; ou, Description . . . de Pommes et Poires. 1758. III. 75.²
Knop, Wilhelm. Chemische Untersuchungen ueber die Ernährung. 1864. I. 158.
— Der Kreislauf des Stoffs. 1868. III. 37.¹

Die **Knopper** als Forstprodukt und als Handelswaare. 1864. IV. 514.²
Knorr, (*Oberförster*). Ueber Anbruchholzerträge. 1868. IV. 171.
— Ueber intensive und extensive Forstwirthschaft. 1866. IV. 118.
Knorr, August. Die Betriebsarten. 1869. IV. 128.
— Die Forstakademie in Münden. 1891. IV. 33.²
— Aus forstlicher Theorie und Praxis. 1878. IV. 102.
— Ueber das Gesetzliche in den Verhältnissen der Holzpreise. 1866. IV. 388.¹
— Mittelwald- und Plänterwaldformen. 1874. IV. 130.
— Aus Theorie und Praxis. 1876. IV. 102.
— Ueber die Trennung der Haupt- und Zwischennutzungs-Erträge. 1878. IV. 244.
— Der Weg aus der Betriebsartenwirthschaft in die Holzartenwirthschaft. 1866. IV. 137.²
Knorr, E. A. Die heiligen Haine der Germanen. 1892. IV. 26.
— Studien über die Buchen-Wirthschaft. 1863. IV. 494.
— Zur Theorie und Praxis. 1864. IV. 494.
— Die Waldwirthschaft der Deutschen. 1891. IV. 26.
Knorr, Georg Wolfgang. Thesaurus rei herbariae hortensisque. *See* GMELIN, P. F. & BÖHMER, G. R. 1788. I. 292.
Knorre, P. *See* KNOPPE, II.
Knorr. Patriotische Aufmunterung im Chur-Trierischen zur Ansaat der Nadelholzes. 1792. IV. 40.¹
Knotek, Johann. Beitrag zur Biologie einiger Borkenkäfer. 1897. IV. 204.
— Die bosnisch-hercegovinischen Borkenkäfer. 1894. IV. 549.¹
— Die Brutgänge des Eichenkernkäfers. 1896. IV. 511.
— Die krummzähnigen Tannenborkenkäfer. 1899. IV. 445.
Knowledge. III. 17.
Knowles, Etta L. The curl of Peach leaves. 1887. III. 442.¹
— Structure and distribution of resin passages of the White Pine. 1886. II. 46.¹
Knowles, George Beauchamp & Westcott, Frederic. Observations on the custom of administering the tanghin. 1838. III. 691.¹
Knowles, Gilbert. Materia medica botanica. 1723. III. 241.
Knowles, John. An inquiry into the means which have been taken to preserve the British navy. 1821. IV. 416.²
— Recherches sur les moyens employés dans la marine anglaise pour la conservation des bois. 1821. IV. 416.²
Knowlton, Frank Hall. Additions to the flora of Washington. 1886. II. 132,¹ V. XVII.²
— Directions for collecting . . . plants. 1891. I. 36.¹
— The Elephant Tree. 1897. II. 461.²
— The Torch Tree. 1899. II. 563.¹
Knox, Alexander. History of the county of Down. 1875. I. 534.¹
Knox, G. W. The Umbrella China tree. 1885. III. 512.²
Knox, John P. A historical account of St. Thomas, W. I. 1852. I. 335.
Knox, Richard. Ceylanische Reisebeschreibung. 1681. III. 279.¹
— An historical relation of the island Ceylon. 1681. III, 279.¹
— Relation du voyage de l'isle de Ceylan. 1681. III. 279.¹
Knüsel. Beitrag zur Lösung der Waldsteuerfrage im Kanton Luzern. 1897. IV. 278.²
— Seltener Fall einer Kopulation. 1889. I. 209.²
Knutberg, Carl. Sätt, att förvara golf och allehanda träbyggnader från röta och svamp-växt. 1754. IV. 414.²
Knuth, Paul. Bloemen en insecten op Helgoland. 1896. II. 839.¹
— Bloemenbiologische aanteekeningen. 1898. I. 239.¹
— Bloemenbiologische bijdragen. 1897. I. 240.¹
— Bloemenbiologische mededeelingen uit de tropische gewesten. 1898. II. 823.²
— Bloemenbiologische waarnemingen in Thüringen. 1895. I. 240.¹
— Bloemenbiologische waarnemingen op . . . Capri. 1893. I. 239.²
— Bloemenbiologische waarnemingen op . . . Rügen. 1897. I. 240.¹
— Blütenbiologische Beobachtungen auf . . . Capri. 1893. I. 239.²
— Blütenbiologische Beobachtungen auf . . . Rügen. 1897. I. 240.¹

— Blütenbiologische Beobachtungen in Thüringen. 1895. I. 240.[1]
— Blütenbiologische Herbstbeobachtungen. 1892. I. 238.
— Blumen und Insekten. 1894. I. 239.[2]
— Einige Bemerkungen meine Flora von Schleswig-Holstein betreffend. 1888. V. xx.[1]
— Die Fichte, ein ehemaliger Waldbaum Schleswig-Holsteins. 1891. II. 35.[1]
— Flora der Provinz Schleswig-Holstein. 1887. V. xx.[1]
— Gab es früher Wälder auf Sylt? 1889. I. 371, IV. 84.[1]
— Grundriss der Blüten-Biologie. 1894. I. 239.[1]
— Grundzüge der Entwicklungsgeschichte der Pflanzenwelt in Schleswig-Holstein. 1891. I. 389.
— Handbuch der Blütenbiologie. 1898. I. 239.[1]
— Nachuntersuchung der Blüteneinrichtung von Lonicera Periclymenum. 1894. II. 839.[1]
— Ueber den Nachweis von Nektarien auf chemischem Wege 1898. I. 118,[2] 157.
— Die Pflanzenwelt der nordfriesischen Inseln. 1891. I. 389.
— Phänologische Beobachtungen. 1892. I. 225, II. 126.[2]
— Phänologische Beobachtungen . . . im Jahre 1892. 1893. .I. 225.
— Phaenologische Beobachtungen . . . im Jahre 1897. 1898. I. 226.[1]
— Schulflora der Provinz Schleswig-Holstein. 1888. V. xx[1]
Knutzen, H. D. Om Beplantningen af Jyllands Heder. 1861. IV. 156.[1]
— De jydske Heders Opdyrkning. 1867. IV. 156.[2]
— Opmuntrende Veiledning i Træcultur. 1864. IV. 156.[1]
— Om Plantning af Træer og Buske. 1859. III. 166.
— Poppeldyrkning. 1871. III. 344.[1]
— Træplantningens Betydning for Jyllands Hedeegne. 1876. IV. 156.[2]
Kny, Carl Ignatz Leopold. Die Abhängigkeit der Chlorophyllfunction. 1897. I. 142.
— Eine Abnormität in der Abgrenzung der Jahresringe. 1890. I. 128.[1]
— Anatomie des Holzes von Pinus silvestris. 1884. II. 47.[1]
— Ueber die Anpassung der Laubblätter. 1885. I. 236.[1]
— Ueber die Anpassung von Pflanzen . . . an die Aufnahme tropfbarflüssigen Wassers. 1886. I. 161.
— Ueber die Aufnahme tropfbar-flüssigen Wassers durch winterlich-entlaubte Zweige. 1895. I. 162.
— Ein Beitrag zur Entwickelungsgeschichte der "Tracheïden." 1886. I. 125.
— Ein Beitrag zur Kenntniss der Markstrahlen. 1890. I. 126.
— Botanische Wandtafeln. 1874. I. 270.
— On correlation in the growth of roots and shoots. 1894. I. 188.
— Dickenwachsthum des Holzkörpers. 1877. I. 190.[1]
— Ueber das Dickenwachsthum des Holzkörpers. 1882. I. 190.[1]
— Einfluss der Leuchtgases auf die Baumvegetation. 1871. III. 185.[2]
— Ueber den Einfluss von Zug und Druck auf die Richtung der Scheidewände. 1896. I. 132.[2]
— Ueber einige Abweichungen im Bau des Leitbündels. 1882. I. 134.[1]
— Ueber einige Versuche . . . ob der auf Samen einwirkende Frost die Entwickelung . . . beeinflusst. 1887. I. 204.
— Ueber die Flora oceanischer Inseln. 1907. I. 000.
— Die Gärten des Lago Maggiore. 1882. I. 64.
— Les jardins du Lago Maggiore. 1882. I. 64.
— Ueber Krystallbildung beim Kalkoxalat. 1887. I. 139.
— Über künstliche Verdoppelung des Leitbündel-Kreises. 1877. I. 127.[1] .
— Ueber Laubfärbungen. 1889. V. xii.[1]
— Note sur l'adaptation du feuillage. 1885. I. 236.[1]
— Ueber den Ort der Nährstoff-Aufnahme durch die Wurzel. 1898. I. 162.
— Umkehrversuche mit Ampelopsis. 1889. I. 196.[1]
— Ueber die Verdoppelung des Jahresringes. 1879. I. 127.[2]
— Ein Versuch zur Blattstellungs-Lehre. 1887. I. 103.
— Ueber den Widerstand, welchen die Laubblätter . . . der Wirkung eines sie treffenden Stosses entgegensetzen. 1885. I. 236.[2]
— Über die zenithwärts gerichtete Verschiebung der Achselknospen. 1876. I. 195.[2]
— Ueber das Zustandekommen der Membranfalten. 1893. I. 138.[2]
Knyf, Willem Jan. . Goylandiae libri duo. 1621. I. 390.
Knyphausen, Edsard, Graf zu INN- UND. See INN- UND KNYPHAUSEN, Edsard, Graf zu.

Kob, Johann Andreas. Die wahre Ursache der Baumtrockniss. 1786. IV. 203.
Kobell, Fr. von. Ueber Pflanzensagen und Pflanzensymbolik. 1875. I. 518.
Kobelt. Appenzell-i.-Rh. .Der Schutzwald. 1897. IV. 181.[1]
Koberstein, Carl August. Ueber die in Sage . . . gangbare Vorstellung von dem Fortleben . . . in der Pflanzenwelt. 1849. I. 517.[2]
Kobert. Ueber Abrus precatorius L. 1890. III. 462.[2]
Kobert. See BIELKIN, W. W., KOBERT & PACHORUKOFF.
— & Goldschmidt, F. Un succedané du Polygala. 1886. III. 447.[1]
Kobsa, Rudolf. Die Photogrammetrie oder Bildmesskunst. 1892. IV. 246.
Kobus, J. D. Flora van Wageningen. 1886. I. 391.[2]
Koch. Beobachtungen über das Vorkommen . . . des Hexenbesens . . . auf der Weisstanne. 1891. IV. 445.
— Zur Frage: Ob durch das Ueberhalten junger Eichen . . . Eichenstarkholz erzogen werden könne. 1869. IV. 506.
— Kurze Unterweisung für Waldbauschüler. 1869. IV. 18.
Koch, Wheeler & Tollens. Sur la gomme de bois. 1890. I. 156.[1]
Koch, (Forstassessor). Fernere Beiträge zur Beurtheilung der Umtriebszeit der Kiefer. 1890. IV. 481.
Koch, (Garteninspektor). Naar og hvorledes skal man knibe Frugttræerne. 1876. III. 134.
Koch, (Oberförster). Auch einige Worte über d. Auslichten der jungen Fichtenbestände. 1842. IV. 452.[2]
— Ueber Eichencultur. 1857. IV. 505.
Koch, A. F. Beitrag zur Physiologie der Pflanzen. 1853. III. 164.[2]
Koch, Albert Carl. Einige Bemerkungen über in den Urwäldern . . . Nord-Amerika's stattfindende forstlichen Verhältnisse. 1850. IV. 336.[2]
Koch, Alfred. Untersuchungen über . . . Rebenmüdigkeit. 1899. III. 549.[1]
Koch, Elers. Brahetrolleborg Skovdistrikt. 1892. IV. 24.[2]
Koch, Friedrich. Experimentelle Prüfung des Holzgummi. 1886. I. 155.
— Die Weissbuche bei Burg-Schlitz. 1851. II. 120.[2]
Koch, Friedrich Wilhelm. Das schnelle Anschwellen der Gebirgswässer. 1883. IV. 185.[1]
Koch, H. A. Kubiktafel für runde Træstammer. 1885. IV. 228.
Koch, H. P. G. Om Falsters Vegetation. 1862. I. 356.
Koch, Heinrich. Kurze Abhandlung der . . . Pflanzen durch deren unvorsichtigen Gebrauch . . . grosser Schade . . . veranlasset werden kann. 1774. III. 89.[1]
— Kurze Abhandlung von dem oekonomischen . . . Gebrauch der inn-ländischen Bäume. 1774. III. 89.[1]
Koch, Hermann. Beiträge zur Anatomie der Gattung Cinchona. 1884. II. 813.[1]
Koch, J. von. Ueber die Ansicht der Zirbelkiefer. 1879. IV. 463.[2]
Koch, Johann Friedrich Wilhelm. Botanisches Handbuch. 1797. I. 84, V. x.[1]
Koch, Jørgen. Hyldebusken og dens Frugt. 1900. III. 752.[2]
Koch, Julius. Kleine Holzindustrien im südlichen Böhmen. 1868. IV. 428.[1]
— Die Verkleinerung des Brennholzes mittelst Maschinen. 1868. IV. 431.[2]
Koch, Karl Heinrich Emil. Acacia pulchella R. Br. et ses congénères. 1858. II. 322.[2]
— Acacia pulchella R. Br. und die Verwandtea. 1858. II. 322.[2]
— Die ächten Drachenbäume. 1861. II. 81.[1]
— Die Aepfelbäume. 1873. II. 266.[1]
— Die Agaveen. 1860. II. 88.[2]
— Agaveen-Studien. 1865. II. 88.[2]
— Die Akazien aus der Abtheilung der Pulchellae. 1858. II. 322.[2]
— Der amerikanische . . . Mondsame. 1862. III. 397.[1]
— Amherstia nobilis Wall. in Blüthe. 1861. III. 466.[1]
— Amsterdamer Agaveen-Studien. 1865. II. 88.[2]
— Amygdalopsis Carr. 1863. II. 277.[2]
— Ueber Anzucht . . . von Rosen. 1860. III. 452.
— Die Apfelgehölze. 1861. II. 266.[1]
— Aralia Leroana C. Koch. 1864. II. 647.[2]
— Die Araliaceen im Allgemeinen. 1859. II. 646.[1]
— Die Arten der Gattung Dracaena. 1871. II. 81.[2]
— Astrapaea Wallichii. 1854. III. 591.[1]
— Astrocaryum Borsigianum. 1859. II. 72.[1]

Koch, Karl Heinrich Emil (*continued*).
— Azalea sinensis Lodd. und mollis. 1872. III. 655.
— Die Bäume und Sträucher des alten Griechenlands. 1879. I. 514.[2]
— Über die Bambuseen aus China und Japan. 1876. II. 58.[1]
— Der Baum der türkischen Pfeifenröhre. 1860. IV. 428.[2]
— Die Baumschulen von André Leroy. 1864. I. 58.
— Die Baumschulen von Simon-Louis frères in Metz. 1872. I. 43.
— De bedste Arter af Slægten Philadelphus. 1860. III. 413.[1]
— Die Befruchtung bei der Weinrebe. 1867. II. 508.[1]
— Die Behandlung der Citronen- und Orangenbäume. 1860. III. 497.[1]
— Die beiden bereiften Weiden. 1871. II. 99.[1]
— Die beiden deutschen Eichen. 1872. III. 361.[1]
— Beiträge zu einer Flora des Orientes. 1848. I. 479.
— Beiträge zur Flora des nördlichen Küstenlandes von Kleinasien. 1847. I. 478.
— Beiträge zur Kenntniss der Flora des kaukasischen Isthmus. 1851. I. 368.[2]
— Ein Beitrag über die gegenseitige Annahme ... bei der Veredelung. 1867. III. 165.
— Bericht über die Frühjahrsausstellung. 1856. III. 75.[1]
— Bericht über die im letzten Jahre eingeführten Pflanzen. 1872. III. 75.[1]
— Beschorneria yuccoides der Gärten. 1864. II. 89.[2]
— Bildende Gartenkunst. 1859. I. 516.
— Blattpflanzen aus der Familie der Solanaceen. 1860. III. 698.[2]
— Die Blattpflanzen des Warmhauses. 1867. III. 205.[1]
— Die blaue Hortensie. 1872. III. 412.[2]
— Ueber blaue Hortensien. 1872. III. 412.[2]
— Blendlinge aus dem Geschlechte der Spiersträucher. 1860. III. 460.[1]
— Eine blühende Cycas revoluta. 1861. III. 284.[2]
— Blühende Palmen des Berliner bot. Gartens. 1864. III. 317.
— Der Borsig'sche Garten in Moabit. 1860. III. 643.[1]
— Bourbon- und Manetti-Rose. 1866. III. 449.
— Buntblättrige Taxus. 1868. III. 288.[1]
— Die Camaren Brasilien's. 1858. II. 758.[1]
— Cataleuca rubicunda und Pinckneya ionantha. 1859. II. 887,[1] 862.[2]
— Catalogus plantarum ... in itinere per Caucasum, Georgiam. 1841. I. 368.[2]
— Die Cedern; eine monographische Skizze. 1867. III. 299.[1]
— Charles van Geert's Catalogue ... des Conifères. 1863. III. 289.
— Ueber Chaussée- und Wege-Bepflanzung. 1867. III. 211.[1]
— Die chinesische Zwerg-Orange. 1864. III. 499.[2]
— Die Choné'schen [*sic*] Azaleen. 1866. III. 654.[2]
— Cinchona succirubra. 1862. II. 814.[1]
— Clavija speciosa C. Koch et Lind. 1867. II. 691.[2]
— Colea Commersonii DC. 1860. III. 706.[2]
— Cordyline nutans. 1868. III. 335.
— Cordyline Regelii C. Koch. 1865. II. 80.[2]
— Cordyline superbiens C. Koch. 1859. II. 80.[1]
— Cordylinen im Allgemeinen. 1860. III. 334.[1]
— Cornus (thelicrania) ignorata. 1867. II. 654.[2]
— Crescentia macrophylla. 1862. III. 704.[2]
— Cytisus Adami. 1865. II. 368.[1]
— Ueber Dasylirien. 1869. III. 336.[1]
— Les Dasylirion et les Puya. 1865. III. 336.[1]
— Dendrologie. 1869. I. 293, *III. 69, IV. 88.*
— Die deutschen Obstgehölze. 1876. I. 294,[1] *III. 69.*
— Dicotyleae novae et criticae. 1855. I. 47.
— Les Diervilla et les Weigela. 1868. III. 748.[2]
— Die Diervillen und Weigelen. 1868. III. 748.[2]
— Ueber Doppelfrüchte der Apfelsinen. 1871. II. 403.[1]
— Die D henbäume aus der Terminalis-Gruppe. 1871. II. 79.[2] raq
— Ueber Drachenbäume oder Dracänen. 1858. II. 77.[1]
— Drei allgemein verkannte Kiefern. 1875. II. 39.[2]
— Drei Blattpflanzen des Warmhauses. 1864. III. 638.[1]
— Drei zu empfehlende Pflanzen. 1860. III. 481,[2] 685,[1] 696.[1]
— Die edele Amherstie. 1858.
— Die Edelrosen der alten und neuen Zeit. 1877. II. 290.[2]
— Einfluss des Edelreises auf die Unterlage. 1866. I. 529.
— Ueber den Einfluss des Pfropfreises auf die Unterlage. 1870. III. 39.

— Ueber einige Araliaceen. 1859. II. 646.[1]
— Ueber einige blühende Cycadeen. 1860. III. 284.[1]
— Ueber einige blühende Pflanzen des Botanischen Gartens in Berlin. 1863. III. 626.[2]
— Einige grosse Bäume. 1867. I. 296.[1]
— Einige Nachträge zur Trauerweide. 1872. II. 104.[2]
— Einige neue Pflanzen aus der Linden'schen Gärtnerei. 1857. III. 77.
— Ueber einige Weisstannen. 1864. III. 295.[2]
— Ueber einige weniger bekannte Formen von Sträuchern. 1857. III. 69.
— Einige Worte über das Kombiniren der Samen. 1872. I. 203, *III. 164.*[2]
— Einige Worte über den Melonenbaum. 1864. III. 617.[1]
— Einige Worte über die Krim. 1853. III. 120.[2]
— Einige Worte über die Tonel'schen Agaveen in Gent. 1862. II. 88.[2]
— Einiges über Dracäneen. 1871. II. 81.[2]
— Einiges über Zapfenträger oder Koniferen. 1857. II. 8.[2]
— Die Elfenbeinpflanze. 1855. III. 330.[1]
— Die Entstehung der Arten und der Darwinismus. 1872. I. 243.[1]
— Die Feigenbäume Aegyptens. 1872. III. 369.[2]
— Ferdinanda eminens Lag. 1858. II. 857.[2]
— Formen der Entwickelung bei den höheren Pflanzen. 1872. I. 101.[1]
— Ueber Fourcraea, besonders F. Bedinghausi. 1863. II. 89.[2]
— Die Frucht und ihre Bildung. 1872. I. 119.
— Die in den Gärten befindlichen Tamarisken. 1862. III. 612.[1]
— Die Gärten Braunschweigs. 1872. I. 48.
— Galphimia hirsuta. 1857. III. 513.[2]
— Gehen Mandeln in Pfirsiche ... über? 1856. II. 276.[b]
— Le genre Berberis. 1862. II. 201.[2]
— Geschichte der Biota pendula. 1861. III. 311.[2]
— Geschichtliches über die Verbreitung des Gingkobaumes. 1855. III. 286.[2]
— Das Geschlecht der Orangen. 1865. II. 401.[1]
— Getriebener weisser Flieder. 1861. III. 680.[1]
— Über Glyptostrobus heterophyllus. 1862. II. 30.[1]
— Über eine hängende Weide. 1853. III. 352.[1]
— Die Halesien; Gehölze für Anlagen. 1858. II. 704.[1]
— Hedera colchica C. Koch. 1867. II. 649.[1]
— Die Heidelsträucher ... der Kordilleren. 1859. II. 673.[2]
— Die Herbstfärbung der Wälder in Nord-Amerika. 1876. I. 304.
— Heteropterys undulata. 1860. III. 513.[2]
— Hippomane longifolia. 1860. III. 519.[1]
— Holzstücke einer Eiche mit Inschrift. 1870. I. 210,[2] *IV. 509.*
— Hortus dendrologicus. 1853. I. 77, *III. 69.*
— Hybrid Spiraeas. 1863. III. 513.[2]
— Inga rhoifolia Willd. .... ein warmer Blüthenstrauch. 1858. III. 686.[1]
— Ueber Inschriften in Bäumen. 1869. I. 210.[2]
— Die interessantesten Bäume in den Baumschulen von André Leroy. 1867. I. 58.
— Ivoy's Ameliorationen au Pisan. 1864. III. 125.
— Die Ixoren und Pavetten. 1866. III. 745.[1]
— J. G. Veitch's japanische Nadelhölzer oder Coniferen. 1861. II. 15.[2]
— Die japanische Quitte. 1861. III. 420.[1]
— Kassien als Blüthensträucher. 1861. III. 470.[1]
— Die Kernobstgehölze. 1861. II. 278.[1]
— Die Konradskräuter. 1859. II. 556.[1]
— Die Kultur der Kokospalme. 1867. III. 322.[2]
— Der kurze Wurzelschnitt. 1867. III. 173.[2]
— Lantana Camara et ses espèces congénères. 1858. II. 758.[1]
— Ueber Lebensbäume. 1857. III. 311.[1]
— Libonia floribunda C. Koch. 1863. II. 800.[1]
— Die Linden. 1865. II. 515.[1]
— Die Loganiaceen. 1860. III. 682.[1]
— Lonicera (Xylosteum) caprifolioides. 1871. II. 837.[2]
— Malus floribunda. 1865. II. 296.[1]
— Ueber Mirabelle, Myrobalane. 1862. II. 270.[2]
— Die Mispel- und Dorn-Arten. 1862. II. 260.[2]
— Ueber Missbildung einer Rosenblüthe. 1866. II. 289.[2]
— Mittheilungen über neuere und neueste Pflanzen. 1866. III. 75.[1]
— Die Mondblumen oder Yukken. 1873. III. 339.[2]
— Monochaetum Candolleanum. 1860. III. 639.[1]
— Monographie du genre Aesculus. 1855. III. 536.[2]

— Montanoa und Uhdea. 1864. II. 856.[1]
— Das natürliche System des Pflanzenreichs. 1839. I. 260.
— Neue Rhododendren. 1863. III. 654.[3]
— Neue Waldreben-Blendlinge. 1864. III. 388.[2]
— Ein neuer Pappelblendling. 1865. II. 96.[1]
— Die neuesten Pflanzen. 1868. III. 75.[1]
— Die neuesten Schlingpflanzen. 1863. III. 204.[2]
— Die neuesten Seidel'schen Alpenrosen. 1864. III. 654.[2]
— Die neuesten Untersuchungen über Zapfenträger. 1873. II. 16.[2]
— Die. Neuholländer aus der Gruppe der holzfrüchtigen Myrtaceen. 1859. II. 619.[3]
— Die neuholländischen Gummibäume. 1872. III. 633.[2]
— Die neuholländischen Reiherbüsche. 1863. II. 621.[1]
— Die neuseeländischen Cordylinen. 1860. II. 79,[2] 83.[1]
— Notice sur le genre Philadelphus. 1859. III. 413.[1]
— Notice sur le Libonia floribunda C. Koch. 1863. II. 800.[1]
— Notice sur les espèces du genre Pyrus. 1861. II. 278.[1]
— Die nützlichen Gehölze unserer Gewächshäuser. 1860. III. 69.
— Der Obstbau im Deutschen Reiche. 1877. III. 120,[2] 138.
— Ueber Palmen im Allgemeinen. 1858. II. 65.[2]
— Pandanus Boucheanus C. Koch und reflexus Hort. 1858. II. 56.[2]
— Der Papau.. 1872. III. 401.[2]
— Paritium elatum G. Don. 1861. III. 587.[2]
— Die Pfeifensträucher. 1859. III. 413.[1]
— Die Pflanzen mit bunten Blättern. 1862. III. 206.[2]
— Über die Physiognomie der Pflanzenwelt im nördlichen Oriente. 1851. I. 479.
— De phytochemia. 1834 (by error 1804). I. 150.[2]
— Pinus Peuce . . . und P. leucodermis. 1865. II. 39.[2]
— Plantae variae novae. 1854. I. 47, 269.
— Plantes nouvelles. 1865. III. 75.[1]
— Pomaceae, Acerineae et Berberideae. 1863. II. 201,[2] 256,[1] 476.[1]
— Die Pomaceen und ihre . . . Eintheilung. 1861. II. 255.[2]
— Die Prachtsträucher (Habrothamnus). 1862. II. 770.[1]
— Quelques mots sur les Agavées de M. Tonel. 1862. II. 88.[2]
— Reise durch Russland nach dem kaukasischen Isthmus. 1842. I. 368.[2]
— Retinospora leptoclada. 1869. III. 301.[2]
— Les Ribes sanguineum Pursh et aureum. 1863. III. 413.[2]
— Die Riesen-Wellingtonie. 1855. II. 50.[1]
— Rosa Ibara C. Koch. 1867. II. 295.[1]
— Rosa Wichurae C. Koch. 1869. III. 456.[1]
— Die Rosskastanie mit gefüllten Blüthen. 1863. II. 481.[2]
— Über Rosskastanien und Pavien. 1855. III. 536.[2]
— Die roth- und gelb-blühende Johannisbeere. 1863. III. 413.[2]
— Über Roupalen (Rhopalen.) 1861. III. 383.[2]
— Die Rüstern, eine monographische Skizze. 1872. III. 363.[2]
— Sanchezia nobilis Hook. 1868. III. 710.[1]
— Die Sauerdorn-Arten des freien Landes. 1861. III. 393.[2]
— Die Sauraujen (Sauravien) im Allgemeinen. 1862. II. 543.[1]
— Die Schlingpflanzen . . . aus dem Geschlechte der Loniceren. 1867. II. 836.[1]
— Die Schlingpflanzen oder Lianen. 1860. III. 204.[2]
— Der Schloss-Garten von Augny. 1872. I. 48.
— Die Schönmützen. 1868. III. 633.[2]
— Die schönsten Pfeifensträucher. 1860. III. 413.[1]
— Scutellaria Mociniana Benth. 1860. III. 698.[2]
— Die Sechellen-Nuss. 1866. II. 71.[1]
— Sørge-eller Taarepil. 1871. II. 99.[1]
— Ueber Spiersträucher im Allgemeinen. 1857. III. 460.[2]
— Spiraea expansa Wall. 1853. II. 315.[1]
— Spiraea flabellata Bert. 1853. II. 315.[1]
— Spiraea pikoviensis Bess. 1853. II. 315.[2]
— Stachel- und Johannisbeeren. 1867. II. 243.[1]
— Sterculia Balanghas. 1860. III. 591.[2]
— Die strauchartigen Spiräen. 1854. II. 314.[1]
— Sturtia gossypioides. 1860. III. 587.[1]
— Die Südküste der Krim. 1855. I. 369, III. 120.[2]
— Die technisch-officinellen Pflanzen in den Gewächshäusern. 1863. III. 52.
— Theophrasta und Clavija. 1859. II. 691.[1]
— Tilia euchlora C. Koch. 1867. II. 517.[1]
— Die Trauer-Hasel. 1867. III. 357.[2]
— Die Trauer- oder Thränenweiden. 1871. II. 99.[1]
— Tupidanthus Pückleri. 1859. II. 653.[1]
— Uebersicht der in der neuesten Zeit eingeführten Pflanzen. 1867. III. 75.[1]

— Uebt bei Kreuzungen der fremde Pollenschlauch . . . Einfluss auch auf die Mutterpflanze aus? 1862. III. 165.
— Der unbewehrte Angelikabaum. 1861. II. 647.[2]
— Ueber Verbesserung des Bodens durch Dungstoffe. 1866. III. 151.
— Die Veredelung der Gehölze. 1867. III. 161.
— Verhandlungen über Vermehrung . . . der Rosen. 1861. II. 452.
— Vermehrung von Blüthensträuchern durch Augen. 1863. III. 158.
— Zur Verständigung über die Bildung des unteren Fruchtknotens. 1871. II. 278.[2]
— Viburnum Awabuki Hort. Berol. 1867. II. 843.[2]
— Vorlesungen über Dendrologie. 1875. I. 82.[2]
— Die Waldreben der Gärten. 1860. II. 195.[1]
— Der Waru in Ostindien. 1861. III. 588.[2]
— Die Weissdorn-Arten. 1857. III. 421.[1]
— Die Weissdorn- und Mispel-Arten. 1853. II. 260.[2]
— Wohlriechende Dracänen aus Brasilien. 1858. II. 79.[2]
— Der wohlriechende Stechapfel. 1866. III. 700.[1]
— Die Wurzel und ihr Verhalten beim Blühen. 1868. I. 188.[1]
— Xanthorrhoea. 1860. III. 339.[1]
— Zusammenstellung der . . . Dracäneen. 1867. II. 79,[2] 81.[2]
— Ueber zwei blühende Pflanzen des botanischen Gartens. 1860. III. 400.[2]
— Zwei Euphorbiaceen, als Blattpflanzen. 1859. II. 435.[2]
— See also LORBERG, Max & KOCH, Karl; LUCAS, Eduard & KOCH, K.
— & Bouché, C. D. Abutilon planiflorum. 1857. II. 520.[2]
— & Pasewaldt. Argyranthemum pinnatifidum Webb. 1857. II. 854.[2]
— Die chinesischen oder indischen Azaleen. 1857. III. 654.[2]
— & Reinecke. Die Franciscéen der Gärten. 1857. III. 698.[2]
— & Rom, von. Die Weide. 1878. III. 351.[1]
— & Siegling. Einiges über Swainsonen. 1857. III. 489.[1]
Koch, Ludwig. Ueber Bau und Wachstum der Sprossspitze. 1891. I. 132.[2]
— Mikrotechnische Mittheilungen. 1892. I. 37.[1]
— Die Paraffineinbettung. 1890. I. 37.[1]
— Die vegetative Verzweigung der höheren Gewächse. 1893. I. 108.[2]
Koch, Max. A list of plants collected on Mt. Lyndhurst Run. 1898. I. 505.
— Supplementary list of plants from Mount Lyndhurst Run. 1900. I. 505.
Koch, Wilhelm Daniel Joseph. Bemerkungen über die Gattung Rosa. 1832. II. 101.[1]
— Bemerkungen über einige deutsche Weidenarten. 1820. II. 101.[1]
— Ueber die europäischen Föhrenarten. 1845. II. 871.[1] I. 379.
— Index generum, plantae specierum et synonymorum. 1837. I. 379.
— Register der Gattungen, Arten und Synonyme. 1837. I. 379.
— De Salicibus europaeis commentatio. 1828. II. 100.[1]
— Ueber Salix versifolia. 1832. II. 110.[1]
— Die specifischen Unterschiede von Pinus sylvestris und P. Pumilio. 1841. II. 39.[1]
— Synopsis der deutschen und schweizer Flora. 1837. I. 379.
— Synopsis florae germanicae et helveticae. 1837. I. 379. V. XIX.[2]
— Taschenbuch der deutschen und schweizer-Flora. 1838. I. 379.
— & Treviranus, C. L. Ueber einige Rosen. 1832. II. 284.[1]
— & Ziz, J. B. Catalogus plantarum . . . in ditione florae Palatinatus. 1814. I. 376.
Koch-Steenfeld, J. E. von. Beitrag zur Geschichte der Forstwirthschaft im Herzogthum Salzburg. 1816. IV. 28.[1]
Kochanowski, C. Einiges über die Waldflora Galiziens. 1885. IV. 369.
Kochs, J. Beiträge zur Einwirkung der Schildläuse. 1900. III. 192.[1]
Kochs, Julius. Ueber die Gattung Thea. 1900. II. 550.[2]
Koderle, Joh. K. Grundsätze der künstlichen Düngung. 1865. IV. 144.[2]
— Die Kernfäule. 1866. IV. 211.[1]
— Des Kulturbodens Beschaffenheit im Saatschulbetriebe. 1871. IV. 150.
— Ein neuer forstlicher Saatregulator. 1866. IV. 149.[1]

Koderle, Joh. K. (*continued*).
— Ein neues hydraulisches Holztransportsystem. 1864. IV. 391.
— Des Samen's Bedeutung. 1869. IV. 148.
— Wasser, Luft und Licht und die Saatschule. 1871. IV. 150.
Koebele, Albert. Report of a trip to Australia. 1890. III. 196.
Köbert, Hermann. Der zahme Oelbaum. 1894. II. 713.[2]
Koehl. Studien über Moorkulturen. 1894. IV. 155.[1]
Koehler. Essai des feuilles de Coca. 1888. III. 493.[1]
Köhler, (*Oberförster*, *Nienburg*). Ueber Aufforstung von Haideflächen. 1884. IV. 158.
Koehler, von (*Forstverwalter*). Ueber Waldfeldbau in Oberschwaben. 1898. IV. 134.[1]
Koehler, August. Practical botany. 1876. I. 256.
Koehler, Chr. Der Normalvorrath. 189.? IV: 258. — 1896. IV. 259.[1]
Köhler, Fr. Untersuchungen über ... Weintrauben-Arten Württembergs. 1826. III. 546.
Köhler, Fr. Eugen. Köhler's Medizinal-Pflanzen. 1883. III. 59.[1]
Köhler, Franz Joseph. Untersuchungen über die Vertheilung der Farben. See SCHÜBLER, Gustav. 1831. I. 182,[2] *184*.
Koehler, Hugo. Ueber Acclimatisation subtropischer Pflanzen. 1893. III. 44.[1]
— Akklimatisationsbericht. 1892. III. 183.[2]
— Dracaena indivisa × Yucca Smethiana. 1896. II. 80.[2]
— Die Frostschäden des Winters 1894–95. 1895. III. 46.[1]
— Die Frostschäden des Winters 1894/[97]. 1895. III. 50.[1]
— Die Pflanzenwelt und das Klima Europas. 1892. I. 232.[2]
— Die Verluste von Pflanzen im Winter 1892–91. 1891. III. 46.[1]
— Die Winterschäden 1893–94. 1894. III. 46.[1]
— and others. Erwiderung auf den Artikel des Herrn John Booth. 1892. IV. 483.[2]
Köhler, J. G. W. Beobachtungen über den Rinden- oder Borkenkäfer. 1793. IV. 203.
Köhler, J. H. R. Iets over eenige houtsoorten van de Lampongsche distrikten. 1855. IV. 399.[1]
Köhler, J. M. Alphabetisch geordnetes Namens-Verzeichniss der ... Pflanzenarten in der Schweiz. 1850. I. 434.
Köhler, K. See RASCH, Gustav & KÖHLER, K.
Köhler, Oscar. Beiträge zur chemischen Kenntnis der Myrrhe 1890. III. 511.[1]
— Contribution à l'étude chimique de la myrrhe. 1890. III. 511.[1]
Köhler-Ordnung für die gräflich wernigerodischen Forsten. 1835. IV. 301.[2]
Koehne, Bernhard Adalbert Emil. Americani generis Cupheae species. 1873. II. 608.[2]
— Ueber anatomische Merkmale bei Berberis-Arten. 1899. II, 202.[2]
— Ueber die asiatischen Buchen. 1895. II. 125.[2]
— Auflösung von Blattpaaren bei Lagerstroemia. 1881. II. 608.[2]
— Bemerkungen über die Gattung Cuphea. 1873. II. 608.[2]
— Bemerkungen über die Vitaceen. 1892. II. 501.[1]
— Bemerkungen zu J. Bornmüllers Aufsatz über Crataegus tanacetifolia. 1892. II. 263.[2]
— Berichtigung der von D. P. Barcianu gemachten Angaben. 1875. II. 608.[2]
— Cornus brachypoda C. A. Mey. 1897. II. 655.[1]
— Deutsche Dendrologie. 1893. I. 294,[1] *III. 70, IV. 84*.[1]
— Ueber einige Cornus-Arten. 1896. II. 655.[1]
— Ueber einige Fraxinus-Arten. 1899. II. 707.[1]
— Die Gattungen der Pomaceen. 1890. II. 256.[1] — 1891. II. 256.[1]
— Glossopetalon meionandrum n. sp. 1894. II. 469.[1]
— Zur Kenntnis der Gattung Buxus. 1896. II. 452.[2] ·
— Kleine Bemerkungen über Aesculus. 1892. II. 481.[1]
— Lonicera Alberti Regel, seit Jahren bekannt. 1890. II. 839.[2]
— Lythraceae. 1877. II. 608.[1] — 1893. II. 608.[1]
— Lythraceae adjectis specierum ... extraamericanarum descriptionibus. 1887. II. 608.[1]
— Lythraceae monographice describuntur. 1881. II. 608.[1]
— Lythraceae novae. 1900. II. 608.[1]
— Micromeles alnifolia. 1892. II. 311.[2]
— Ueber neuere Pflanzen. 1894. I. 294.[1]
— Noch zu Prunus Myrobalana. 1900. I. 246.[2]
— Philadelphus. 1896. II. 242.[1]
— Prunus Pissardi. 1892. III. 436.[1]
— Quercus Gambeli Nutt. 1895. II. 134.[1]

— Uebersicht der ... Lycium-Arten. . 1892. II. 772.[2]
— Verwachsung der Keimblätter von Aesculus. 1896. II. 482.[1]
— Vier neue Holzgewächse. 1899. I. 294,[1] *III. 70*.
— Ueber das Vorkommen von Papillen und oberseitigen Spaltöffnungen auf Blättern. 1899. I. 111, *132*.[1]
— Ueber Zellhautfalten in der Epidermis von Blumenblättern. 1884. I. 116.[1]
— Zwei neue Gehölzarten. 1896. II. 270,[1] *347*.[1]
— See also KOOPMANN, Karl & KOEHNE, Emil.
— Vocke, A. & Drude, Oscar. Der schwedische Bocksdorn. 1892. III. 701.[1]
Kölbing, F. W. Flora der Oberlausitz. 1828. I. 378.
Koelderer, Johann Georg. Viscum plerarumque arborum plantam parasiticam. 1747. III. 385.[1]
Koeler, George Louis. Lettre à Monsieur Ventenat sur les boutons. 1805. I. 106.[1]
Kölges, B. Oenologie. 1841. III. 552.
Koelle, Johann Ludwig Christian. Flora des Fürstenthums Bayreuth. 1798. I. 375.
Kölle, Rudolf. Analyse der Asche von Taxus. 1870. II. 10.[1]
Kölle, W. & Co. Rosen-Garten-Kalender. 1883. III. 450.
Kölle, Wilhelm. Zwei neue Abutilon's. 1867. III. 586.[2]
Kölliker, Rudolph Albert. On the action of urari. 1856. III. 682.[2]
— Note sur l'action du curare. 1856. ·III. 682.[2]
— Observations on the poison of the Upas Antiar. 1857. III. 366.[2]
— Verzeichniss der phanerogamischen Gewächse des Kantons Zürich. 1830. I. 433. — 1839. I. 434.
— & Pélikan, Eugène. Physiologisch-toxikologischen Untersuchungen über ... Tanghinia venenifera. 1858. III. 691[1]
Köllsch, Carl. Die Baumaterialienkunde. 1861. IV. 423.[1]
Kölpin, Alexander Bernhard. Commentatiб botanico-physica de stylo eiusque differentiis externis. 1764. I. 117.[2]
— Florae gryphicae supplementum. 1769. I. 373.
— Praktische Bemerkungen über den Gebrauch der Sibirischen Schneerose. 1779. III. 658.[1] ·
Koelreuter, Johann Theophilus. De antherarum pulvere. 1806. I. 116.[3]
— Lycia hybrida. 1780. II. 772.[2]
— Malvacei ordinis plantae novae hybridae. 1786. II. 518.[1]
— Observationes quaedam circa vera stigmata ... Periplocae. 1797. II. 741.[2]
Koelreuter, Joseph Gottlieb. Account of the observations on the irritability of the stamens of Berberis. 1790. II. 205.[2]
— Historie der Versuche, welche ... über das Geschlecht der Pflanzen angestellt. 1775. I. 199.
— De insectis coleopteris, nec non de plantis. 1755. II. 460,[1] *709*.[1]
— Nouvelles observations ... sur l'irritabilité des étamines de l'Epine-vinette. .1790. II. 205.[3]
— Vorläufige Nachricht von einigen das Geschlecht der Pflanzen betreffenden Versuchen. 1761. I. 199.
Koene, Johann Rottger. Abhandlung über Form und Bedeutung der Pflanzennamen. 1840. I. 73.[3]
Koenemann, R. Solanum Wendlandii. 1899. III. 702.[1]
König. See also KONIG.
König, (*Dr.*, *Schatzrath in Hannover*). Aphoristische Rückblicke auf die Geschichte des Waldes. 1873. IV. 24.[1]
Koenig, (*sr.*). Notice sur le Mélèze. 1840. IV. 449.
König, A. Der Baumwuchs und der Grundwasserstand. 1886. IV. 378.[2]
— Einige Zuwachsuntersuchungen in vollen ... Fichtenbeständen. 1888. IV. 458.
— Die Kiefer im Buchen-Unterwuchse. 1885. IV. 481.
— Ueber den Lichtzuwachs insbesondere der Buche. 1886. IV. 498.
— Ueber die Naturverjüngung der Kiefer. 1890. IV. 481.
— Ueber die Schlagführung im Buchensamenwalde. 1888. IV. 495.
— Zur Umbaufrage. 1884. IV. 481.
— Wirkungen des Unterbaus auf den Wuchs des Eichenoberholzes. 1887. IV. 507.
— Wuchsleistung eingesprengter Lärchen. 1890. IV. 450.
— See also BORGGREVE, Bernard & KÖNIG, A.
Koenig, Charles. Arbres et arbustes gelés pendant l'hiver de 1879–80. 1880. III. 46.[1]
— & Burckel, G. Plantes ligneuses indigènes de l'Alsace. 1888. I. 371.
König, Chr. Die Altersklassen und ihre Bedeutung. 1900. IV.130.

König, Clemens. Pinus montana. 1892. II. 43.[1]
— Untersuchungen über die Theorie der wechselnden kontinentalen und insularen Klimate. 1883. I. 218.
— Die Zahl der im Königreiche Sachsen heimischen ... Blütenpflanzen. 1892. I. 389.
König, E. F. C. Beschreibung und Abbildung der nützlichsten Geräthe. 1847. IV. 176.[2]
Koenig, Emanuel, (sr.). Regnum vegetabile. 1680. I. 30.
— Spicilegium botanicum et anatomicum. 1703. I. 250.
König, F. W. Beyträge zur practischen Forst- und Flosshandels-Wissenschaft. 1790. IV. 382,[1] V. XXXI.[2]
— Bruchstücke des in- und ausländischen Flossholzhandels in dem Herzogthum Würtemberg. 1785. IV. 404.[2]
König, Franz. Studien über die Desinfection der Pflanzen. 1882. III. 196, 563.
König, Gottlob. Allgemeine Waldschätzungs-Tafeln. 1840. IV. 254.
— Anleitung zur Holztaxation. 1813. IV. 239.
— Die Forstbenutzung. 1851. IV. 381.
— Die Forst-Mathematik. 1835. IV. 58.
— Forsttafeln zur Ausmessung ... und Werthschätzung aufbereiteter Hölzer. 1842. IV. 229.
— Grundzüge der Buchenanerziehung. 1846. IV. 494.
— Ueber die Holzberechtigungen in den Forsten des hannoverschen Oberharzes. 1876. IV. 334.[1]
— Hülfstafeln der Forstmathematik zur Ausmessung. 1842. IV. 229.
— Mittheilungen von dem Forst-Einrichtungs-Wesen im Grossherzogthum Weimar. 181.? V. 247.[2]
— Die Waldpflege. 1849. IV. 106, V. XXX.[1]
— Der Waldschutz und die Waldpflege. 1849. IV. 106.
— Zuverlässige und allgemein brauchbare Holztaxations-Tafeln. 1813. IV. 221.
— See also KEHRE, T.
König, Johann. Sammlung praktischer Erfahrungen aus der Forstwissenschaft. 1820. IV. 123.[2]
— Nachtrag zu [Ferd. Storps] Versuchen. 1883. I. 211.
— & Haselhoff, Emil. Schädlichkeit der Stickstoffsäuren. 1894. I. 211.
König, Johann Gerhard. Auszüge merkwürdiger ... Briefe des seligen D. J. G. König. 1791. I. 471.
— Kurze Beschreibung des Baumes, welcher die ... beschriebenen Nüsse trägt. 1784. II. 423.[2]
— De remediorum indigenorum ... efficacia. 1773. III. 277.
Koenig, Karl Dietrich Eberhard. See KONIG, Charles.
Koenig, Paul. Histoire de la question forestière dans l'Inde. 1896. IV. 28.[2]
König-Warthausen, Richard, Baron. Merkwürdiger Blitzschlag im Jahre 1854. 1852. IV. 193.[2]
Könige, Aloys Albrecht von. Entwurf eines Grundrisses der Forstwissenschaft. 1831. IV. 97.
— Von dem nachhaltigen Ertrage der Waldungen. 1828. IV. 242, 254.
Königlich Allerhöchste Verordnung, die Organisation der Staats-Forstverwaltung in Bayern betreffend. 1887. IV. 290.[1]
Königlich baierische botanische Gesellschaft in Regensburg. Denkschriften. I. 13.
Königlich böhmische Gesellschaft der Wissenschaften. Abhandlungen. Sitzungsberichte. I. 27.
Königlich Dänische Gesellschaft der Wissenschaften. Schriften. V. VII.[1]
Königlich dännemark-holsteinische Holz- u. Jagd-Verordnung. 1737. IV. 315.[1]
Königlich französisches Forst-Gesetz. 1828. IV. 326.
(Königlich) physikalisch-ökonomische Gesellschaft zu Königsberg. Schriften. I. 13.
Königlich preussische Akademie der Wissenschaften zu Berlin. Abhandlungen. Bericht. Monatsberichte. Sitzungsberichte. See KÖNIGLICHE AKADEMIE DER WISSENSCHAFTEN zu BERLIN. I. 13.
Königlich preussische Verordnung, die Verbindung einer systematischen Eintheilung. 1788. IV. 247,[2] 319.[2]
Königlich preussisches Circulare die Behandlung der Schläge und Blössen. 1788. IV. 134,[2] 139.[1]
Königlich prinsliche Forstreviere Seitenberg u. Schnellenstein. 1880. IV. 354.
Königlich sächsische Akademie für Forst- und Landwirthe zu Tharandt. 1830. IV. 31.
Königlich sächsische Gesellschaft der Wissenschaften. Abhandlungen. Berichte. I. 13.
Königlich schwedische Akademie der Wissenschaften. Jahresberichte. See KÖNGL. (SVENSKA) VETENSKAPS AKADEMIEN. 1822. I. 1.

Die königlich würtembergischen Forstdienstprüfungen. 1836. IV. 31.
Die Königlich württembergische Lehranstalt für Land- und Forstwirthschaft in Hohenheim. 1842. IV. 31.
Königliche Akademie der Wissenschaften zu Berlin. Sammlung. I. 13.
Königliche (bayerische) Akademie der Wissenschaften zu München. Abhandlungen. Denkschriften. Gelehrte Anzeigen. Sitzungsberichte. I. 13.
(Königliche) Gesellschaft der Wissenschaften zu Göttingen. Abhandlungen. Nachrichten. I. 13.
Königliche Holtz-Ordnung in Schleswig, Holstein. 1671. IV. 296.[1]
Königliche landwirthschaftliche Hochschule in Berlin. Führer durch die vegetabilische Abtheilung. See WITTMACK, Ludwig. 1886. III. 28.[1]
Königliche Lehranstalt für Wein-, Obst- und Gartenbau zu Geisenheim am Rhein. Berichte. III. 12.
Königliche Oberförsterei Scheidelwitz. 1847. IV. 352.
Königliche technische Versuchsanstalten zu Berlin. Mittheilungen. IV. 9.
Die Königliche württembergische Lehranstalt für Land- und Forstwirthschaft zu Hohenheim. 1838. IV. 31.
Die mit der Königlichen Forstschule zu Gross-Schönebeck verbundene "Willelmstiftung." 1889. IV. 33.[2]
Königlicher bot. Garten der Universität Breslau. Auswahl von Sämereien. See HORTUS BOTANICUS VRATISLAVIENSIS. 1818. I. 45.
Königlicher botanischer Garten und botanisches Museum zu Berlin. Jahrbuch. I. 13.
— Notisblatt. 1895. I. 49.
(Königlicher) botanischer Garten zu Breslau. Arbeiten. I. 13.
Königlicher Würtembergischer landwirthschafter Verein. Correspondenzblatt. III. 12.
Königliches landwirthschaftliches Museum, Berlin. Allgemeiner Katalog. See WITTMACK, Ludwig. 1869. III. 28.[1]
Königsberg — Königliche physikalisch-ökonomische Gesellschaft. See KÖNIGLICH ... I. 13.
Königsberger land- und forstwirthschaftliche Zeitung. See LAND ... IV. 10.
Königsberger naturwissenschaftliche Unterhaltungen. I. 13.
Königsdörfer, Georg Odo. Tabellen zur Berechnung des cub. Inhalts von geschnittenen ... Hölzern. 1873. IV. 190.
Königsegg gróf Oroszlánkói és Illavai uradalmainak erdei Magyarországon. 1871. IV. 373.
Koepert, Otto. Ueber Wachsthum ... der Krystalle. 1885. I. 139.
Köpff, Friedrich. Ueber die anatomischen Charaktere der Dalbergieen. 1892. II. 321.[1]
Koeppen, Friedrich Theodor. Geographische Verbreitung der Holzgewächse des europäischen Russlands und des Kaukasus. 1888. I. 359, IV. 80.
— Ueber die Heuschrecken in Südrussland. 1866. III. 189.
— Die schädlichen Insekten Russlands. 1880. III. 190.
— See also КЕППЕНЪ, Ѳ.
Koeppen, Martin. Ueber das Verhalten der Rinde unserer Laubbäume. 1889. I. 527.
Koeppen, Pet. von. Ueber Pflanzen-Acclimatisirung in Russland. 1856. III. 44.[2]
— Ueber den Wald- und Wasser-Vorrath im Gebiete der ... Wolga. 1841. IV. 46,[2] 344.[2]
— See also КЕППЕНЪ, П.
Koeppen, Wladimir. Waerme und Pflanzenwachsthum. 1871. I. 232.[1]
Koerber, Hylesinus crenatus. 1875. IV. 204.
Körber, (Breslau). Die Flechtenvegetation der Nadelhölzer. 1871. IV. 210.[2]
Körber, J. Die Stuken-Sprengung. 1861. IV. 386.
Körndörfer, Johann Peter. Der praktische Forstmann. 1791. IV. 239.
Körner, Friedrich. Im Walde. 188.? IV. 102.
Koerner, G. See BOHRINGER & KOERNER.
Körnicke. Die autogenetische und heterogenetische Befruchtung bei den Pflanzen. 1890. I. 238.
Körnicke, Friedrich. Beitrag zur Flora der Provinz Preussen. 1863. I. 385.
— Eupatorium Weinmannianum. 1858. II. 857.[1]
— Notizen zur Gattung Deutzia. 1867. II. 238,[2] 241.[7]
— Spiraea media Schmidt. 1863. II. 315.[1]
— See also REGEL, Eduard von & KÖRNICKE.
Koernicke, Max. Ueber die spiraligen Verdickungsleisten. 1899. I. 134.[1]
Körper, G. Ueber das Veredeln alter Bäume. 1900. III. 163.[2]

Körte, Franz. Der Catholikometer. 1815. IV. 231.[1]
— Katholikometret. 1815. IV. 231.[1]
— *See also* SCHWEIGGER, A. F. & KÖRTE, Franz.
Køster, Fr. Formering 'af Sirtræer og Buske. 1892. III. 158.
Koestlin, Charles Henri. Lettres sur l'histoire naturelle de l'isle d'Elbe. 1780. I. 424.
Vom Koffe. 1774. III. 738.[1]
Koffieaaltje, (*pseud.*). Tegenwoordige toestand der Java-Koffie cultuur. 1899. III. 731.
Koffiebladziekte. 1887. III. 735.
Koffieboer, (*pseud.*). Achteruitgang der Koffie-cultuur. 1900. III. 732.[1]
— Meting van den vochtigheidstoestand der lucht. 1900. III. 728.[1]
De Koffiecultuur der inlandsche bevolking op Java. 1897. III. 731.
De Koffiecultuur in de Minahassa. 1877. III. 729.[2]
De Koffiegids. III. 26.[2]
Koffiehybriden. 1893. III. 742.[2]
De Koffie-oogst van Brazilie. 1899. III. 729.[1]
Het Koffieplanten in den ouden ... op Ceylon. 1880. III. 732.[2]
De Koffie-productie. 1896. III. 728.[2]
De Koffieproductie in Brazilie. 1897. III. 728.[2]
De Koffieteelt. 1877. III. 728.[2]
De Koffieteelt in Liberia. 1883. III. 732.[2]
Koffie-tentoonstelling te Rio-Janeiro. 1883. III. 728.[2]
De Koffieziekte in Brazilie. 1887. III. 735.
De Koffij. 1861. III. 739.
De Koffijkultuur in Nederlandsch Oost-Indie. 1862. III. 729.[1]
Kohl. Die Verbreitung der Buche. 1852. II. 125.[2]
Kohl, Friedrich Georg. Anatomisch-physiologische Unter-suchung der Kalksalze und Kieselsäure. 1889. I. 154.
— Die assimilatorische Energie der blauen und violetten Strahlen. 1897. I. 174.
— Die assimilatorische Energie des blauen Lichtes. 1897. I. 174.
— Beitrag zur Kenntniss des Windens der Pflanzen. 1884. I. 196.[2]
— Dimorphismus der Plasmaverbindungen. 1900. I. 137.
— Excursions-Flora für Mitteldeutschland. 1896. I. 389.
— Die officinellen Pflanzen der Pharmacopoea germanica. 1891. III. 59.[1]
— Vergleichende Untersuchung über den Bau des Holzes der Oleaceen. 1881. II. 705.[2]
— Zur Wasserleitungsfrage. 1885. I. 165.
Kohl, Otto. Taschenwörterbuch der botanischen Kunstaus-drücke. 1883. III. 30.
Kohlbrugge, G. Handboek voor landeigenaars. 1858. III. 106.[1]
Köhler. Mittheilungen über das Saponin. 1872. III. 447.[1]
Köhler, J. M. Die wichtigsten Kernobstorten des Kantons Zürich. 1864. III. 89.[1]
Kohlhaas, Johann Jacob. Giftpflanzen auf Stein abgedruckt. 1805. III. 59.[2]
Kohli, Otto. Zur Geschichte der natürlichen Verjüngung der Buche. 1873. IV. 495.
Kohli, P. Anleitung zur Abschätzung stehender Kiefern. 1861. IV. 217, 480.
— Sammlung der preussischen Forst- und Jagd-Gesetze. 1884. IV. 321.
Kohlmann, Benno. Vergleichende Uebersicht der Pharma-copoea Germaniae. 1867. III. 249.
Kohlmann, W. Kubiktabellen über beschnittene und be-schlagene Hölzer. 1862. IV. 224.[2]
— Kubiktabellen über geschnittene und beschlagene Hölzer. 1862. IV. 224.[2]
— Kubiktabellen über runde, geschnittene und beschlagene Hölzer. 1862. IV. 224.[2]
— Kubiktabellen über runde Hölzer. 1862. IV. 224.[1]
— Kubiktabellen über runde und geschnittene Hölzer. 1862. IV. 225.[1]
— Tavole cubiche di legni rotondi. 1862. IV. 225.[1]
— Tavole cubiche di legni rotondi, tagliate e sgrossati. 1862. IV. 225.[2]
— Tavole cubiche di legni segati e tagliati. 1862. IV. 225.[1]
— *See also* КОЛЬМАНЪ, B.
Kohlrausch. Merkwürdiger Blitzschlag. 1878. IV. 194.
Die Kohlung in den Banater Montanforsten. 1861. IV. 394.
Kohn, Ch. Histoire ancienne de la Vigne. 1898. V. xxix.[2]
Kohn, Karl. Schrauben von Tannenholzästen. 1851. IV. 446.[2]

Kohout, Wilhelm. Die Misswirthschaft in den amerikan-ischen Forsten. 1897. IV. 281.[2]
Koide, F. Untersuchungen ueber das Klemmen der technisch wichtigsten japanischen Holzarten. 1895. IV. 412.[1]
Koivupuiden hakkaus havumetsistä. 1891. IV. 490.[2]
Koja, K. Die Forsten der Herrschaft Lukow. 1860. IV. 368.
Koker, Aegidius van. Plantarum usualium Horti medici haarlemensis. 1702. I. 50.
Kokosnootvezels. 1883. III. 324.[1]
Kokos-olie. 1884. III. 324.[1]
Die Kokospalme der Sechellen. *See* LE COCOTIER des Séchelles. 1849. II. 70.[2]
Kokovtzof, D. *See* КОКОВЦОВЪ, Д.
Kolaczek, Erwin. Lehrbuch der Botanik. 1856. I. 90.
Kolb, J. N. Bromatologie. 1829. III. 219.[1]
Kolb, Max. Die älteste Eibe. 1887. II. 11.[1]
— Camellia euryoides. 1867. III. 597.[1]
— Die europäischen und überseeischen Alpenpflanzen. 1890. I. 535.
— Der Gourunussbaum. 1868. III. 590.[1]
— Hibiscus speciosus. 1866. III. 588.[1]
— Der K. botanische Garten in München. 1867. I. 48.
— Neue und empfehlenswerte Pflanzen. 1883. III. 75.[L]
— Pirus P. Scheideckéri. 1887. III. 429.[1]
— Quisqualis pubescens. 1868. III. 632.[2]
— Quisqualis sinensis Lindl. 1876. III. 632.[2]
— Smilax aspera L. var. punctata. 1871. II. 85.[2]
— Theorie des Gartenbaues. 1877. III. 36.[1]
— Thunbergia Harrisii Hook. 1888. III. 710.[2]
— Das Wichtigste aus der Theorie des Gartenbaues. 1879. III. 36.[1]
Kolb, Oscar von. Ueber eine abnorme Wurzelanschwellung bei Cupressus sempervirens. 1896. II. 30.[1]
Kolbani, Paul. Ungarische Giftpflanzen. 1791. III. 90.[2]
Kolbe, J. H. Anweisung, dem Weinstocke den höchsten Nutzen abzugewinnen. 1826. III. 552.
Kolbe, Peter. Beschreibung des Vorgebirgs der Guten Hoff-nung. 1719. I. 493. V. xxiv.[1]
— Description du Cap de Bonne-Espérance. 1719. I. 493.
— Naaukeurige en uitvoerige beschrijving van de Kaap de Goede Hoop. 1719. I. 493.
Kolbenheyer, K. Vorarbeiten zu einer Flora von Teschen und Bielitz. 1862. I. 441.
Die kolchische Pimpernuss. 1884. III. 533.[2]
Kolenati, Friedrich A. Ueber die in Grusien einheimischen Reben. 1846. II. 505.[2]
— Die Höhenflora des Altvaters. 1860. V. xxiii.[1]
— Versuch einer systematischen Anordnung der in Grusien einheimischen Reben. 1846. II. 505.[2]
Kolesof, A. *See* КОЛЕСОВ, А.
Kolinek, J. *See* CIESLAR, Adolf & KOLINEK, J.
Koljo, Johannes. Histologisch-pharmacognostische Unter-suchung von Pichi. 1891. III. 700.[1]
Kolkwitz, R. Beiträge zur Mechanik des Windens. 1895. I. 196.[2]
— Untersuchungen über Plasmolyse. 1896. I. 129.[1]
Kollar, Vincenz. Die adlerbraune oder Waldstroh-Eule. 185.? III. 562.[2]
— Ueber Agrilus viridis Kiesew. 1858. IV. 488.[1]
— Beiträge zur Naturgeschichte des grossen Fichten-Bast-käfers. 1858. IV. 455.
— Beitrag zur Geschichte schädlicher Heuschrecken. 1858. III. 189.
— Beitrag zur Kenntniss über ... Callidium russicum. 1857. III. 303.[1]
— Beitrag zur Naturgeschichte des Bostrichus curvidens. 1857. IV. 442.
— Ueber einen bisher noch nicht beobachteten Feind des Weinstockes. 1850. III. 562.[2]
— Nachtrag zur Naturgeschichte der Cerr-Eichen-Blattwespe. 1851. IV. 502.[2]
— Naturgeschichte der schädlichen Insecten. 1837. IV. 91.[2]
— Naturgeschichte der Zerr-Eichen-Saummücke. 1849. IV. 502.[2]
— Zur Naturgeschichte des Ulmen-Blattkäfer. 1858. III. 64.[1]
— Naturgeschichte eines in den Gallen von Tamarix. 1858. III. 612.[1]
— Neuere Beobachtungen über den Wein-Wickler. 1852. III. 563.
— Ueber springende Cynips-Gallen auf Quercus Cerris. 1857. IV. 502.[2]

— Die Tamarisken-Gallmücke. 1858. III. 612.¹
— A treatise on insects injurious to gardeners. 1837. IV. 91.²
— Ueber Weinbeschädigung durch einen kleinen Nachtfalter. 1850. III. 562.²
— Über zwei der Schwarzföhre . . . schädliche Insekten. 1852. IV. 466.¹
Kollberg, J. H. Den kongel. Planteskole ved Thisted. 1833. I. 40.
Kollen, J. Landbouwscheikunde. 1895. III. 37.¹
Koller, E. Ludwig. Allgemeiner Beweis des . . . Verhaltens des laufenden . . . Zuwachses. 1887. IV. 234.
— Analytische Untersuchung über die Zuwachscurven. 1886. IV. 233.
— Beweis des Satzes, dass beim Höhenmessen dann der kleinste Fehler . . . begangen wird. 188 . ? IV. 215.
— Die S mmz und ihre analytische Deduction. 1887. IV. 257.¹a ahl
— Vergleichung der Resultate verschiedener Methoden der Holzmassen-Aufnahmen. 188 . ? IV. 218.
— Ueber Wertsclasseneintheilung. 1892. IV. 388.²
— Ueber einen wichtigen Zusammenhang der Formzahl mit den Zuwachsprocenten. 1889. IV. 234.
Koller, Johann Baptist Cajetan. Grundzüge der Botanik. 1854. I. 89.
— Die Palmen als Schönheiten. 1857. III. 317.
— Die Waldungen und deren Einfluss auf den menschlichen Zustand. 1855. IV. 43.
Kollewyn, N. Over boschcultuur. 1900. IV. 124.¹
Kollmann, T. Anleitung zur Konservirung der Pflanzen. 1875. I. 35.
Kolmovski, A. I. See КОЛМОВСКІЙ, А. И.
Kolo, BROMO-. See BROMO-KOLO.
Koloniaal museum te Haarlem. Beschrijvende catalogus. 1880. III. 757.¹
Koloniaal museum te Haarlem. Bulletin. III. 14, 757.¹
De koloniaal-radicalen en het cultuur-stelsel. 1862. III. 128.
Koloniaal verslag. See VERSLAG van het beheer. 1857. IV. 124.¹
Kolophonios, NIKANDROS. See NIKANDROS KOLOPHONIOS.
Koltz. Das Levret'sche Verfahren zur Erziehung der Eichensämlinge. 1881. IV. 507.
Koltz, (Oberförster). Einführung des Wachsstrauches in Belgien. 1861. III. 353.¹
— Kultur und Vermehrung der Wellingtonia. 1864. III. 310.¹
Koltz, Jean Pierre Joseph. Le balai de sorcier sur le Pin Weymouth. 1890. IV. 470.¹
— Dendrologie luxembourgeoise. 1875. I. 294,¹ III. 77,¹ IV. 84.²
— Guide du botaniste . . . Grand-duché de Luxembourg. 1877. I. 393.¹
— Guide pratique de la culture du Saule. 1867. III. 347.
— Prodrome de la flore du Grand-duché de Luxembourg. 1873. I. 393.¹
— Traitement du Chêne en taillis à écorces. 1859. IV. 505.
Kolyadin, S. See КОЛЯДИНЪ, С. .
Kolyupanof, N. See КОЛЮПАНОВЪ, Н.
Komarof, Vladimir. See КОМАРОВЪ, В.
Komaroff, Catherine. Remarques sur quelques structures foliaires. 1897. I. 111.
Komitén för utarbetande af förslag till ny allmän skogslag for Finland. 1880. IV. 289.¹
Komitsch, Hermann. Cestrum aurantiacum Lindl. 1897. III. 699.¹
Kommers, P. A. Proeve om door waterbesproeijing woeste gron n in cultuur te brengen. 1854. III. 150.¹
Kommissionen til undersøgelse M. V. af almindingsforholdene i Nordre Throndhjems amt. 1866. IV. 247.¹
Kommissionen för undersökning af forhållandena inom kronoskogarne i Finland. 1872. IV. 289.¹
Konardof, S. See КОНАРДОВЪ, С.
Konda Dora. Note on the advisability of applying the method of coppice with standards. 1886. IV. 131.
Kondakow, Iwan & Schatz, N. Recherches sur les principes immédiats du Cousso. 1900. III. 424.²
— Untersuchung der Bestandteile von Flores Kusso. 1900. III. 424.²
Kondor, Vilmos. Az 1890. évi bécsi Ált. gazdasági és erdészeti kiállítás erdészeti csoportja. 1891. IV. 21.¹
Kondracki, Eugen. Beitrag zur Kenntniss der Aloe. 1874. III. 333.¹
— See also DRAGENDORFF, Georg & KONDRACKI, Eugen.
Kondyles, Panagiotes. See ΚΟΝΔΥΛΗΣ, Παναγιώτης.

Kong Friderich den Fierdes allernaadigste Forordninger og aabne Breve. 1710. IV. 296.¹
Kongelige Danske Landhuusholdnings-Selskab. Skrifter. III. 10.³
Kongelige Danske Videnskabernes Selskab. Oversigt. I. 9.¹
Kongelige Danske Videnskabernes Selskab. Skrifter. See KIØBENHAVNSKE SELSKAB . . . I. 8.³
Kongelige norske (Frederiks) universitet. Programm. I. 8.¹
Kongelige norske videnskabers-selskab. Skrifter. I. 8.²
Kongelige Videnskabernes Selskab. Skrifter. See KIØBENHAVNSKE SELSKAB . . . I. 8.³
Kongliga fysiografiska sällskapets i Lund. Handlingar. See LUNDS UNIVERSITETS. I. 519.²
Kongliga svenska landtbruks-academien. Annaler. III. 10,² V. XXVII.¹
Kongliga svenska vetenskaps academien. Bihang. Handlingar. Öfversigt. I. 8.¹
Kongliga (svenska) Vetenskaps akademien. Årsberättelse. 1822. I. 1.
Kongliga svenska vetenskaps-akademien. Meddelanden. See HORTUS BERGIANUS. I. 8.¹
Konig. See also KÖNIG.
König, Charles. On Aegiceras fragrans (Rhizophora corniculata Linn.). 1805. II. 692.¹
— Blighiae, novi . . generis descriptio. 1806. II. 484.²
— A few botanical observations. 1805. I. 33.
— Observations on the Durion. 1804. II. 530.¹
— Some account of the Sago Palm. 1805. II. 71.²
— Tracts relative to botany. 1805. I. 265.
Koning, A. de. Eene wanschapenheid der bloemen van Lonicera Periclymenum. 1827. II. 839.¹
Koning, I. de. Iets over het extractum foliorum Herb. Haederae. 1828. III. 643.¹
Koning, Peter. De cortice Salicis albae. 1778. III. 351.¹
Koningsberger, Jacob Christiaan. Dierlijke vijanden der Koffiecultuur. 1895. III. 736.
— De dierlijke vijanden der Koffiecultuur op Java, 1897. III. 736.
— Dierlijke vijanden van den landbouw. 1895. III. 192.²
— Eerste overzicht der schadelijke . . . insecten van Java. 1898. III. 192.²
— De engerlingen (Oereto). 1897. III. 736.
— Inleiding tot de systematiek der phanerogamen. 1893. I. 256.
— Insekten op de Thee in Engelsch-Indië. 1898. III. 604.²
— 's Lands plantentuin te Buitenzorg. 1898. I. 68.²
— Een naderend gevaar voor de Dadap. 1897. III. 476.¹
— Nog eens de ziekten der Thee in Engelsch Indië. 1899. III. 604.²
— Recherches sur la formation de l'amidon. 1893. I. 140.²
— De rupsenplaag in Kediri. 1897. III. 736.
— De San-José schildluis. 1899. III. 192.¹
— De slakrupsen (Rupsen der Limacodidae). 1897. III. 736.
— De witte mieren. 1899. III. 192.²
Koninklijk nederlandsch instituut van wetenschappen, letterkunde . . . te Amsterdam. Het instituut. Verhandelingen. I. 15.
Koninklijk-nederlandsche instituut van wetenschappen, letterkunde . . . Tijdschrift voor de wis- en natuurkundige wetenschappen. See TIJDSCHRIFT . . . I. 16.
Koninklijke akademie van wetenschappen. Verhandelingen. Verslagen. I. 16.
Koninklijke Nederlandsche maatschappij tot aanmoediging van den tuinbouw. Jaarboek. III. 14.
Konontchuk, P. I. Die örtliche und einseitige Hartringigkeit der Kiefer und Fichte. See КОНОНЧУКЪ, П. И. 1888. V. 482.¹
Konow, Friedrich Wilhelm. Botanische Miscellen. 1882. II. 840.¹
Konrad von Megenberg. Das Buch der Natur. 1350. I. 275.
— Hye nach volget das puch der natur. 1350. I. 275.
— Naturbuch, vonn nutz, eigenschaft. 1350. I. 275.
Konservirung von Holz in der Erde. 1884. IV. 426.¹
Konshin, A. J. See КОНШИНЪ, А. Ю.
Konstmesten opgegeven door de respective departementen des oeconomischen taks. n. d. III. 151.
Kontopulos, Konstantin. De physiologia plantarum. 1848. I. 147.
Kontoyevski. See КОНТОЕВСКІЙ.
Konvalinka, Joseph George. How to improve the climate of the United States. 1889. III. 215,² IV. 46.¹

Koopman, W. N. De virtute medica foliorum Juglandis. 1845. III. 356.[1]

Koopmann, B. Ferghana's Baum- und Strauch-Vegetation. 1881. I. 456.

Koopmann, Karl. Abies concolor violacea. 1895. III. 296.[1]

— Begründung des Schnittes der Gehölze. 1900. III. 171.

— Beobachtungen über das Aushalten zarterer Gehölze. 1880. III. 50.[1]

— Bericht über den Besuch einiger Reblaus-Infektionsherde. 1889. III. 574.

— Biota orientalis L. in Central-Asien. 1881. II. 52.[2]

— Das Bluten des Eschen-Ahorns. 1880. II. 479.[1]

— Elementarlehren aus dem Gebiete des Baumschnitts. 1896. III. 171.

— Mittheilungen aus Mittel-Asien. 1879. I. 457.

— Picea excelsa mutabilis. 1899. III. 305.[2]

— Pterostyrax hispida. 1899. III. 670.[2]

— Rosen; ihre Klassifikation. 1900. III. 451.[1]

— Turkestans Anstalt für Forst- und Obst-Kultur. 1882. IV. 37.[1]

— Vermehrung der Abietineen aus Stecklingen. 1899. III. 294.[2]

— Der Zwergobstbau. 1899. III. 139.

— & **Koehne, Emil.** Prunus prostrata Labill. var. concolor Boiss. 1895. II. 276.[2]

— & **Wittmack, Ludwig.** Boretta (Dabeocia [sic.]) cantabrica. 1898. II. 662.[1]

Koorders, Sijfert Hendrik. Bemerkungen über den Werth einheimischer Namen von javanesischen Waldbäumen. 1895. I. 76,[1] IV. 88.[1]

— Beobachtungen über spontane Neubewaldung auf Java. 1895. I. 467, IV. 88.[1]

— Beoordeeling der vruchtbaarheid van bosch gronden. 1893. IV. 61.[2]

— Bijdragen tot de kennis der boomflora van Java. 1892. I. 467, IV. 88.[1]

— Biologische Notiz über immergrüne und periodisch laubabwerfende Bäume in Java. 1898. I. 192.[1]

— Ueber die Blüthenknospen-Hydathoden. 1897. I. 132,[1] 169.[1]

— Boschproducten van Australie, Amerika. 1892. III. 29.[1]

— Botanische herkomst van Oost Indische Ijzerhoutsoorten. 1899. IV. 400.[2]

— Cultuur van Sono-Kling. 1892. III. 475.[1]

— Eenvoudige botanische determineer tabellen voor eenige ... boomsoorten der Djatibosschen van Java. 1900. I. 467, IV. 88.[1]

— Goenoeng Moerija. 1887. I. 469.[1]

— Handleiding voor het verzamelen van herbarium. 1894. I. 36.[1]

— Herbewouding ... in Algerie en Spanje. 1898. IV. 165.

— Herbewouding met inheemsche ... houtsoorten. 1892. IV. 168.[1]

— Iets over de aanleiding tot ... het onderzoek naar de boschboomflora van Java. 1894. I. 467, IV. 88.[1]

— Iets over spontane reboisatie. 1894. IV. 168.[1]

— Iets over spontane reboisatie ... op het Midangan Gebergte. 1895. I. 466.

— De kiemontwikkeling van Tectona. 1890. II. 761,[1] V. xxvii.[2]

— De Koffiesoorten der boschboomflora op Java. 1900. II. 814.[1]

— De Koffiesoorten der boschboomflora van Java. 1899. II. 814.[1]

— Die Kultur des Sono-Kling-Baumes. 1894. IV. 521.[2]

— Lijst der phanerogamen-geslachten van den Maleischen Archipel. 1896. I. 467.

— Looistof-basten ... van Nederlandsch-Indië. 1893. III. 237.[2]

— Losse schetsen der vegetatie van equatoriaal Sumatra. 1895. I. 467.[1]

— Morphologische und physiologische Embryologie von Tectona. 1896. II. 761.[1]

— Een nieuwe Koffiesoort. 1900. II. 814.[1]

— Nota over Boeasa-hout. 1895. IV. 529.[1]

— Nota over de waarde van inlandsche namen van Javaansche woudboomen. 1876. I. 76,[1] IV. 88.[1]

— A note on Sandalwood. 1892. IV. 519.[2]

— A note on the propagation of Blackwood. 1894. IV. 521.[2]

— Plantkundig woordenboek voor de boomen van Java. 1894. I. 76,[1] IV. 88,[1] 400.[1]

— Ringen van boomen. 1893. III. 175.[1]

— Over de samenstelling van eenige bosschen in de residentie Madioen. 1894. I. 467, IV. 88.[1]

— Santalhout. 1892. IV. 519.[2]

— Sono-Kling en Sono-Kembang. 1894. III. 475,[1] 485.[2]

— Spezifieke gewichten van de Djati houtvarieteeten. 1892. IV. 538.[1]

— Spontane en kunstmatige reboisatie. 1896. IV. 168.[2]

— Het verduurzamen van hout. 1893. IV. 421.

— Verslag eener botanische dienstreis door de Minahasa. 1898. I. 467.

— Verslag van eene dienstreis naar de Karimondjawa eilanden. 1889. I. 466.

— Over de waarde van Albizzia moluccana Miq. 1894. IV. 521.[1]

— Waarnemingen over spontane reboisatie op Java. 1894. I. 467, IV. 88,[1] 140.

— In het wild groeiende Koffieboomen op Java. 1900. II. 814.[1]

— Wildernis in één 6 jaar geleden verlaten fort op Java. 1899. IV. 140.

— Zakflora voor Java. 1892. I. 467, IV. 88.[1]

— Over de zamenstelling van eenige bosschen in de residentie Madioen. 1894. IV. 377.[1]

— Een zeer goedkoop middel tot herbewouding. 1894. IV. 168.[1]

— See also **Boerlage, J. G. & Koorders, S. H.**

— & **Valeton**, Theodoric. Aphanomyrtus Miquel. 1898. II. 620.[2]

— — Bijdragen tot de kennis der boomsoorten van Java. 1894. I. 467, IV. 88.[1]

— — Diagnosen neuer Phanerogamen von Java. 1899. I. 469.[1]

Kooreman, P. J. De gouvernementskoffiecultuur ter Sumatra's westkust. 1900. III. 732.[1]

Kopecký, Karel. Análytická květena okolí města Rychnova nad Kněžnou. 1888. I. 443.

Kopeczek, Franz. See **Fromm, Franz & Kopeczek, Franz.**

Kopetzky, D. E. Die Walddesolazionen. 1873. IV. 44.

Kopezky, Richard. Ueber Bestandesmassenaufnahmen im Urwälde. 1899. IV. 219.

— Die Holzconservierung. 1891. IV. 421.

— Ueber Massenaufnahmen in Versuchsbeständen. 1891. IV. 219.

— Neue Verfahren der Bestandsmassen-Ermittlung. 1899. IV. 219.

— Ueber die nichtmessbaren Niederschlägen. 1899. IV. 54.

— Wald und Niederschläge. 1899. IV. 54.

Kophina, Georgio N. See **Kôфina, Г. N.**

Kopp, E. Sur le benjoin. 1844. III. 671.[1]

— Recherches sur l'acide cinnamique. 1845. III. 482.[1]

Kopp, J. Anbauversuche mit exotischen Holzarten. 1864. IV. 127.[1]

— Anleitung zum Waldbau. 1875. IV. 110.[2]

— Anleitung zur Drainage. 1864. IV. 144.[1]

— Bericht ... über die gegenwärtigen forstlichen Zustände im Amte Entlebuch. 1870. IV. 366.

— Einige Regeln über Waldwirthschaft. 1863. IV. 123.[1]

— Einladung zur Bestellung von Samen exotischer Holzarten. 1869. IV. 127.[1]

— Essais de culture d'essences exotiques. 1864. IV. 127.[1]

— Die forstlichen Verhältnisse des Entlebuches. 1866. IV. 366.

— Graines d'essences exotiques. 1869. IV. 127.[1]

— Künstliche Mittel zur Beförderung der Keimung. 1868. IV. 147.[2]

— Mitteilungen über die forstlichen Zustände im Thurgau. 1852. IV. 365.

— Moyens artificiels d'activer la faculté germinatrice. 1868. IV. 147.[2]

— Notizen über Waldtheilungen im Kanton Luzern. 1866. IV. 309.[1]

— Pépinières et bâtardières. 1862. IV. 150.

— Quel est ... le meilleur système de traitement à introduire dans les forêts particulières morcelées. 1877. IV. 309.[2]

— Quelles sont les mesures qui pourraient être prises pour engager les cantons montagneux à traiter leurs forêts d'une manière rationnelle? 1870. IV. 41.[2]

— Saat- und Pflanzschulen. 1862. IV. 150.

— Die Waldtheilungsfrage der Corporation Pfaffnau. 1867. IV. 278.[1]

— Welche Massregeln können ergriffen werden, um die Gebirgskantone zu einer angemessenen Behandlung ihrer Waldungen zu bewegen? 1870. IV. 41.[2]

— Welchem Wirthschaftssystem ist bei den stark parzellirten Privatwaldungen ... der Vorzug zu geben. 1877. IV. 309.[2]

— & **Bertholet**, Charles. Anbauversuche mit exotischen Holzarten. 1865. IV. 127.[1]
— — Essais de cultures d'essences exotiques. 1865. IV. 127.[1]
Koppe, A. Behandlung [der Roupalen]. 1861. III. 383.[2]
— Ueber Dracaena-Arten. 1861. III. 334.[1]
Koppe, Karl. Standorte in und bei Soest wachsender Pflanzen. 1859. I. 384.
Koppel. See ORENSTEIN & KOPPEL.
Die **Koppel'sche** Patent-Waldbahn. 1886. IV. 391.
Kops, Jan. Index plantarum . . . in Horto rheno-trajectino. 1823. I. 51.[1]
— Onderzoek wegens de middelen tegen schadelijke dennen-insecten, etc. 1808. IV. 441.
— Opgaaf van werken over den landbouw door Nederlanders geschreven. 1808. III. 33.[1]
— Overzicht van den staat der voornaamste gewassen in Nederland. 1841. III. 122.[1]
— Staat van den landbouw in het koningrijk der Nederlanden. 1813. III. 122.[1]
— Tegenwoordige staat der duinen in den Lande van Voorne. 1805. IV. 159.
— Verhandeling, bevattende overzicht van den staat der voornaamste gewassen in Nederland. 1841. III. 122.[1]
— & **Hall**, H. C. van. Flora batava. See KOPS, Jan & others.
— 1800. I. 390.
— & **Trappen**, J. E. van der. Flora batava. See KOPS, Jan & others. 1800. I. 390.
— & others. Flora batava. 1800. I. 390.
Kops, G. F. de BRUYN. See BRUYN KOPS, G. F. de.
Kops, W. P. Verslag eener proeve . . . weegens het beplanten van . . . duingrond. 1801. IV. 159.
Koptef. See КОПТЕВЪ.
Koptjef, A. Eine russisch-asiatische Forst-Beschreibung. 1858. IV. 376.[1]
Die **Korbweidencultur** der königl. ung. Staatsbahnen. 1883. III. 348.
Kořenský, Josef. Z botanických zahrad tropických krajů. 1896. I. 36.[1]
— V čajovém kraji. 1896. III. 600.[2]
— Posvátné stromy na Ceyloně. 1898. I. 298.
— Zavádění cizokrajných rostlin na Kavkaze. 1899. III. 120.[2]
Kořešník, Moriz. Beitrag zur Erziehung der Weisskiefer-Bestände. 1871. IV. 430.
— Erinnerung an zwei alte Bekannte. 1875. IV. 477.
Korf, baron. See КОРФЪ, барона.
Korinek, Franz. Praktische Erfahrungen über das Hochpflanzen der Bäume. 1873. III. 169.[1]
Koristka, Karel. Lesy dle držebnosti a druhů stromových. 1885. IV. 371.
— Lesy v Čechách dle držebnosti a druhů stromových. 1887. IV. 371.
— Mají-li zůstati menší lesy obecní neporušeny a celistvy. 1899. IV. 308.[1]
— Die natürlichen Gebiete von Böhmen. 1885. IV. 371.
— Přirozené krajiny Čech. 1885. IV. 371.
— Způsob těžení, hospodaření a ošetřo vání lesa. 1885. IV. 124.[1]
Korkeiche und Korkindustrie. 1867. IV. 516.[2]
Kornauth, E. Die chemische Zusammensetzung der ausgelaugten Fichtenlohe. 1884. IV. 460.[1]
Kornauth, Hans. Beiträge zu dem Verhältnisse zwischen Herbstholz und Frühlingsholz . . . der Coniferen. 1882. II. 17.[1]
Kornauth, Karl. Die Bekämpfung von Mäuseplagen. 1893. IV. 198.[2]
— See also WACHTL, F. A. & KORNAUTH, Karl.
Korneven, K. See КОРНЕВЕНЪ, К.
Kornhuber, A. Eine Schildlaus . . . auf Robinia Pseudacacia. 1899. IV. 524.[b]
Kornhuber, Andreas. Alte Parallelen zu neuen Angaben. 1889. II. 179.[2]
— Botanische Ausflüge in die Sumpfniederung des "Wasen." 1886. I. 446.
Korrespondenz aus dem Kanton Thurgau. 1852. IV. 365.
Korrespondenz aus Freiburg. 1863. IV. 283.[1]
Korsch, D. V. Die Waldschutzgesetze Russlands. See КОРЧЪ, Д. В. 1888. IV. 315.[2]
— See also КОРЧЪ, Д. В.
Korschel, F. Flora von Burg. 1856. I. 383.
Korschelt, O. & **Yoshida**, Hikorokuro. The chemistry of Japanese lacquer. 1885. III. 232.[2]
Korschelt, Paul. Ueber die Eibe. (Programm.) 1897. II. 11.[1]

— Ueber die Eibe. (*Tharand. Forstw. Jahrb.*) 1897. II. 11.[2]
— Zur Frage über das Scheitelwachsthum. 1883. I. 132.[2]
Kort Anvisning om Maaden . . . See JAEGER, N. H. 1778. III. 152.
Kort anvisning att anlägga trädgårdar. 1843. III. 100.[1]
Kort overzigt van eenige der meest gebruikelijke kruidkundige stelsels. 1849. I. 252.
Korte schets van het eiland Banka. 1846. I. 465.
Korte vergelijking van de Thee-cultuur in China. 1844. III. 601.[2]
Korte verhandeling van de boomen. See SERVAIS, G. J. de. 1789. III. 75,[2] IV. 84.[1]
Korth, J. W. D. Oekonomisch-technologische Encyclopädie. See KRÜNITZ, J. G. 1773. III. 30.
Korthals, Peter Wilhelm. Aanteekeningen over Borneo's zuid oostkust. 1837. I. 469.[1]
— Aanteekeningen over de vijftig Kotta's. 1835. III. 127.[2]
— Aanteekeningen over eenige soorten van Loranthus. 1836. II. 173.[2]
— Bijdrage tot de kennis der Chrysobalaneae. 1854. II. 256.[1]
— Bijdrage tot de kennis der Indische Magnoliaceae. 1851. II. 208.[2]
— Bijdrage tot de kennis der Indische Melastomaceae. 1839. II. 635.[1]
— Bijdrage tot de kennis der Myrtaceae. 1848. II. 619.[1]
— Bijdrage tot de kennis der Ranunculaceae. 1848. II. 195.[1]
— Bijdrage tot de kennis der Tristroemiaceae. 1839. II. 547.[1]
— Bijdragen tot de geslachten Cleisocratera. 1839. II. 269,[1] 589,[2] 588.[1]
— Bijdragen tot de geslachten Cratoxylon. 1839. II. 554.[2]
— Bijdragen tot de geslachten Salacia en Hippocratea. 1839. II. 471.[2]
— Bijdragen tot de kennis der Eiken. 1839. II. 131.[1]
— Blik op de natuurlijke gesteldheid . . . van Sumatra. 1848. I. 467.
— Over eenige soorten van . . . Dipterocarpeae. 1839. II. 559.[1]
— Over eenige soorten van het geslacht Bauhinia. 1839. II. 334.[2]
— Sur le genre Tupeia. 1838. II. 168.[2]
— Over het geslacht Nauclea. 1839. II. 807.[1]
— Over het geslacht Tupeia. 1838. II. 168.[2]
— Over de geslachten Praravinia en Omphacarpus. 1839. II. 513,[2] 827.[2]
— De groeiplaats van Dipterocarpus Baudii. 1848. II. 559.[2]
— Kruidkunde. 1839. I. 465.
— Note sur la coloration de la fleur de l'Hibiscus mutabilis. 1838. II. 523.[2]
— Observationes de Naucleis indicis. 1839. II. 807.[1]
— Over het omhulsel van het stigma der Scaevolaceae. 1837. II. 846.[2]
— Opmerkingen over Gnetum. 1837. II. 1.
— Overzicht der Rubiaceën van de Nederlandsch Oostindische Koloniën. 1851. II. 807.[2]
— Overzigt der Magnoliaceae en Rubiaceae van de Nederlandsch-oostindische kolonien. 1851. II. 208,[2] 807.[2]
— Overzigt der Sterculiaceae. 1848. II. 531.[2]
— Remarques sur quelques espèces de Loranthus. 1838. II. 175.[1]
— Topographische schets van een gedeelte van Sumatra. 1847. I. 467.
— Uittreksel uit eenen brief aan H. C. van Hall. 1837. I. 465.
— Uittreksels uit brieven aan H. C. van Hall. 1836. I. 467.
— Uittreksels uit eenen brief aan . . . C. L. Blume. 1834. I. 467.
— Verhandeling over de op Java . . . verzamelde Loranthaceae. 1839. II. 173.[1]
— Waarnemingen aangaande den berg Gédé. 1848. I. 468.
— See also OORT, P. van & KORTHALS, P. W
Kortum, Karl Arnold. Der Thee und seine Stellvertreter. 1811. III. 222.
Korzhinski, Sergius Ivanovich. Über die Entstehung und das Schicksal der Eichenwälder im mittleren Russland. 1891. I. 359, II. 130,[2] IV. 81.
— Fragmenta florae Turkestaniae. 1898. I. 457.
— Plantas amurenses . . . describit. 1893. I. 456.
— Tentamen florae Rossiae orientalis. 1898. I. 367.
— See also КОРЖИНСКІЙ, С. И.

Kosch, Josef. Die Baumschule L. Späth in Rixdorf. 1892. III. 154.²

Koschewnikoff, D. Beiträge zur Flora des Tambowschen Gouvernemehts [sic]. 1876. I. 363.

Koschlau, K. von KRAATZ-. See KRAATZ-KOSCHLAU, K. von.

Koschny, T. F. Eine Ertragsberechnung für eine Castilloa-Kautschukplantage. 1899. III. 368.²
— Die Kautschukproduktion in Mittelamerika. 1900. III. 368.²

Kosler, Franz. Kubik-Tafeln für stehende runde Hölzer. 1864. IV. 225.
— Kubik-Tafeln für Walzen und abgestumpfte Kegel. 1863. IV. 225.

Kosmahl. Ein Beitrag zur Frage: " Ueber Auflockerung des Waldbodens." 1863. IV. 143.¹

Kosmahl, A. Durch Cladosporium herbarum getödtete Pflanzen von Pinus rigida. 1892. IV. 469.¹
— Die Fichtennadelröthe. 1889. IV. 456.
— Ist der Agaricus melleus Saprophyt? 1887. IV. 211.²
— Ueber parasitische Pilze im Walde. 1893. IV. 212.

Kosmann, Constant Philippe. Études sur l'ozone exhalé par les plantes. 1862. I. 172.
— Études sur les ferments. 1875. I. 175.
— The ferments contained in plants. 1877. I. 176.
— Nouvelles recherches sur les ferments. 1877. I. 176.
— Recherches sur la nature d'Aloès. 1861. III. 333.¹
— Recherches sur la résine du Bouleau. 1854. IV. 491.¹

Kosmos. I. 13.

Kosmos, [Lwów]. I. 27.

Kosmovski, K. A. See KOCMOBCKIЙ, K. A.

Kospoth, Freiherr von. Sammlung von Holzarten. 1801. IV. 17.

Kossel, A. Sur un nouvel alcaloïde du thé. 1889. III. 607.

Kosteletzky, Vincenz Franz. Allgemeine medizinisch-pharmazeutische Flora. 1831. III. 57.
— Clavis analytica in floram Bohemiae. 1824. I. 439.
— Flora pragensis. 1837. I. 440.
— Index plantarum Horti caesarei regii botanici pragensis. 1844. I. 66.¹

Kosten und Erträge der Weidencultur. 1883. IV. 487.¹

Kostenaufwand für Pflanzungen. 1852. IV. 152.

Koster, A. See COPLIN, H. & KOSTER, A.

Koster, Henry. Reisen in Brasilien. 1816. III. 269.¹
— Travels in Brazil. 1816. III. 269.¹

Kostes, N. See KΩΣTHΣ, N.

Kostka, J. B. Zur Eierablage der Nonne. 1892. IV. 201.

Kostyayef, A. V. See KOCTЯEBЪ, A. B.

Kosyanenko, V. See AXMATOBЪ, M. & KOCЯHEHKO, B.

Kotal, Čeněk. Čajovník čínský. 1875. II. 552.¹
— Cesmina evropská. 1879. III. 530.¹
— O Chinových stromech. 1873. III. 718.
— Cykasovité rostliny čili palmy kiškonosné. 1876. III. 284.¹
— Guttaperča. 1873. III. 231.
— O hřebíčku. 1873. III. 635.¹
— Jaruma a Karatasy. 1875. III. 368.²
1 Krajina s Chlebofi čili Stromy chlebodajnými. 1878. II. —46.¹
— O Muškátovém stromě. 1873. III. 403.¹
— Palma datlová a její plody. 1879. III. 329.²
— O Pepři. 1873. III. 343.¹
— Rostliny hořkoňovité. 1878. III. 506.¹
— Ságovník obecný. 1874. III. 327.²
— Stiftie zlatokvětá. 1875. III. 756.²

Koten, H. J. van. De Liberische Koffieboom. 1878. III. 742.¹

Kotowicz, A. Częściowy spis roślin jawnopłciowych z okolicy Biecza. 1874. I. 442.
— Spis roślin jawnopłciowych, zbieranych w. okolicy Biecza 1875. I. 442.

Kotschy, Theodor. Aus dem Bulghar Dagh. 1856. I. 479.
— Les Chênes de l'Europe et de l'Orient. 1858. II. 128.¹
— Ueber Cypern; zwei Briefe. 1862. I. 452.
— Die Eichen Europa's und des Orient's. 1858. II. 128.¹
— Kigelia pinnata De Cand. 1856. II. 789.¹
— Der Libanon und seine Alpenflora. 1864. I. 480.
— Mittheilungen aus den Nilgegenden. 1864. I. 488.
— Eine neue Gardenia vom westlichen Nilarm. 1865. II. 818.²
— Eine neue Leguminose vom weissen Nil. 1858. II. 330.¹
— Plantae Arabiae in ditionibus Halebschas. 1865. I. 480.
— Plantae Binderianae nilotico-aethiopicae. 1865. I. 488.
— De plantis nilotico-aethiopicis Knoblecherianis. 1864. I. 488.

— Reise in den cilicischen Taurus. 1858. I. 479.
— Ueber Reisen und Sammlungen ... in der asiatischen Türkei. 1864. I. 479.
— Die Sommerflora des Antilibanon. 1864. I. 480.
— Die Sommerflora des Antilibanon und hohen Hermon. 1864. I. 480.
— Topographische Skizze des Bulghar Dagh. 1857. I. 479.
— Ueberblick der Vegetation Mexico's. 1852. I. 331.
— Umrisse aus den Uferländern des weissen Nil. 1858. I. 488.
— Umrisse von Südpalästina. 1861. I. 480.
— Die Vegetation ... auf dem Isthmus von Suez. 1858. I. 488.
— Der westliche Elbrus bei Teheran. 1861. I. 477.²
— See also ANTOINE, Franz & KOTSCHY, Theodor; UNGER, Franz & KOTSCHY, Theodor.
— & Peyritsch, Johann. Plantae Tinneanae. 1867. I. 488, II. 818.

Kotta, G. See KOTTA, ГENPИXЪ.

Kottmeier, (Forstcandidat). Eine Trauertanne. 1882. II. 23.¹

Kottmeier, Hermann. Die Aufforstung der Oed- und Ackerländereien. 1898. IV. 159.
— Cylinder-Fassfabrik-Gesellschaft. 1894. IV. 427,¹ 499.
— Kurzer Leitfaden zum forstlichen Unterricht. 1888. IV. 98,² 107.¹
— Ueber eine neue Krankheitserscheinung von Kiefernwurzeln. 1900. IV. 480.
— See also FRANK, A. B. & KOTTMEIER, H.

Kottmeier, Johann. See DREIER, Johann, FOCKE, W. O. & KOTTMEIER, Johann.

Kottwitz, Freiherr von. Berichterstattung der Ergebnisse vollzogener Anbauungs-Versuche. 1837. III. 121.¹
— Über ein Mittel, die Tragbarkeit des Weins zu erhöhen. 1829. III. 552.

Kotula, Bolesław. Distributio plantarum vasculosarum in montibus Tatricis. 1889. I. 446.
— Rozmieszczenie roślin naczyniowych w Tatrach. 1889. I. 446.
— Spis roślin naczyniowych z okolicy Przemyśla. 1880. I. 442.
— Ueber die Verbreitung der Gefässpflanzen in der Tatra. 1892. I. 446.

Kotz, B. W. Skizze einer Forsteinrichtung. 1872. IV. 241.

Kotz, J. V. De generibus plantarum. 1776. I. 251.

Kotzebue, Otto von. Entdeckungs-Reise in die Süd-See. 1821. I. 302, V. XVI.²
— A voyage of discovery into the South Sea. 1821. V. XVI.²

Kotzi, Ignaz Valentin. De generibus plantarum. 1776. I. 262.

Kovalevsky, A. Ueber das Vorkommen des Metastyrols. 1861. III. 321.¹

Kovařík, Jan. Křovité, vytrvalé Daphne. 1895. III. 627.¹

Kováts, Béla. Összehasonlitó kísérletek a Mikulás-féle ültetéssel. 1900. IV. 153.²

Kovatsch, Martin. Das obere Fellagebiet im Kanalthale in Kärnten. 1881. IV. 187.²

Kowallek. Ueber Anpflanzungen in Neu-Anlagen. 1885. III. 166.

Koyen. Mittel gegen die Schütte der Kiefernjährlinge. 1885. IV. 477.

Kozai, Y. Researches on the ... constituents of Bamboo shoots. 1890. II. 59.²
— Researches on the manufacture of various kinds of tea. 1890. III. 607.

Kozak a Prachien, J. S. Septimanae horologii macrocosmi liber quartus de vegetabilium speciebus. 1640. I. 285.²

Kozarac, Josef. Ueber Ausläuterungen ... in den slavonischen Eichenwäldern. 1899. IV. 509.
— Aus dem Eschenwalde. 1895. IV. 535.²
— Zur Wiederverjüngung der slavonischen Save-Eichenwälder. 1886. IV. 507.

Koželnik, Moriz. Die Aufzucht der Lärche. 1896. IV. 450.
— Die Bestandespflege mittelst der Lichtung. 1898. IV. 169,² 246.
— Die Holzzucht von ... Dr. Bernard Borggreve. 1893. IV. 119.¹
— Ein Mahnruf dem Forstcultivator! 1890. IV. 153.¹
— Die naturgemässe Ausführung der Pflanzung. 1891. IV. 454.
— Eine neue Methode der Lochpflanzung. 1887. IV. 153.¹
— Die neue Pflanzungsmethode im Walde! 1888. IV. 153.¹
— La nouvelle méthode de plantation forestière. 1888. IV. 153.¹

— Die Pflanzung von Heistern. 1896. IV. 153.[1]
— Der Solinger Spaten. 1893. IV. 153.[1]
— Der Vortheil des Zurückhaltens der Vegetation. 1894. IV. 154.[2]
— Die waldbaulich wirthschaftliche Bedeutung der Bestandesbegründung durch Pflanzung. 1890. IV. 142.
Kozhevnikof, D. See Кожевниковъ, Д. и Цингеръ, В.
Kozłowski, Wł. O powstawaniu i przyszłości lasów Dębowych na granicach obszaru leśnego w Rosyi. 1891. I. 359, IV. 81.
— Praenoszenie się ciał przyswojonych w roślinach. 1899. I. 178.
— Przyczynek do wyjaśnienia związku pomiędzy budową roślin i gieograficznem ich rozmieszczeniem. 1891. I. 218.
— Wpływ elektryczności i magnetyzmu. 1896. I. 231.[1]
Kozocsa, Tivadar. See Girókuti, Ferenc & Kozocsa, Tivadar.
Kr. Die Douglastanne. 1892. IV. 483.[2]
Kraatz-Koschlau, K. von & Huber, Jacob. Zwischen Ocean und Guamá. 1900. I. 344.
Krabbe, Gustav. Ein Beitrag zur Kenntniss der Structur ... vegetabilischer Zellhäute. 1887. I. 138.[1]
— Über die Beziehungen der Rindenspannung zur Bildung der Jahrringe. 1882. I. 127.[2]
— Über den Einfluss der Temperatur auf die osmotischen Processe lebender Zellen. 1896. I. 232.[2]
— Einige Anmerkungen zu den neuesten Erklärungsversuchen der Jahrringbildung. 1887. I. 128.[1]
— Zur Frage nach der Funktion der Wurzelspitze. 1883. I. 195.[2]
— Das gleitende Wachsthum bei der Gewebebildung. 1886. I. 124, 187.
— Zur Kenntniss der fixen Lichtlage. 1889. I. 230.
— Ueber die Wachsthum des Verdickungsringes. 1884. I. 190.[1]
— See also Schwendener, Simon & Krabbe, Gustav.
Kraehe, J. C. De oleo Terebinthinae. 1806. III. 525.[2]
Krämer, A. Die Thätigkeit der Gesetzgebung ... in der Schweiz zur Abwehr ... der Phylloxera. 1880. III. 572.
Kraemer, H. Scheikundige onderzoeking van den cortex Sambuci interior. 1845. III. 752.[1]
Krämer, Henry. Formation et recherche microchimique des mucilages végétaux. 1898. I. 178.
— Note on the origin of tannin in galls.· 1900. I. 184.
Kränzlin, F. Daphne Laureola L. winterhart. 1886. III. 627.[2]
— Die Verbreitung der Arten der Gattung Euphorbia. 1876. II. 441.[2]
Kraepelin, Karl Mathias Friedrich. Excursionsflora für Nord- und Mitteldeutschland. 1887. I. 387, 532.[2]
— Neue Pedipalpen ... des Hamburger Museums. 1898. II. 743.[2]
Kraetzl, Fr. Die Buchlauer Linde. 1898. IV. 528.[1]
Kraetzl, Franz. Das Fürstenthum Liechtenstein. 1873. IV. 368.
— Schematismus des ... Liechtenstein'schen Forstbesitzes. 1873. IV. 368.
— Statistische Übersicht des ... Liechtenstein'schen Güterbesitzes. 1873. IV. 368.
— Die süsse Eberesche. 1890. III. 459.[2]
— Die süsse Eberesche, ein ... Gehirzobst. 1885. IV. 520.[2]
Krätzschmar, L. See Reinke, Johannes & Krätzschmar, L.
Kraeutermann, Valentinus, (pseud.).. See Hellwig, Christoph von.
Kraft, (Forstmeister in Hannover). Zur Entwässerungsfrage. 1875. IV. 144.[1]
Kraft, A. See Mühlberg; F. & Kraft, A.
— & Bosshard, Ad. Die Kultur der Zwergobstbäume. 1888. III. 146.[1]
Kraft, Gustav. Zur Aesthetik der Park- und Waldwirthschaft. 1895. IV. 55.[2]
— Die Aestung der Buche. 1874. IV. 495.
— Ueber die Anrechnung der Totalitätsnutzungen auf den Abnutzungssatz. 1877. IV. 236.
— Beiträge zur Durchforstungs- und Lichtungsfrage. 1889. IV. 174.
— Beiträge zur forstlichen Statik. 1887. IV. 257.
— Beiträge zur forstlichen Wasserbaukunde. 1863. IV. 266.[1]
— Beiträge zur forstlichen Zuwachsrechnung. 1885. IV. 245.
— Beiträge zur Lehre von den Durchforstungen. 1884. IV. 173.
— Ueber die Berechnung der durch Hüttenrauch veranlassten Schädigung. 1887. IV. 192.[2]

— Beschädigungen durch Curculio ... Hercyniae. 1862. IV. 207.
— Zur Bestandeserziehung etc., mit besonderer Rücksicht auf die Eiche. 1873. IV. 506.
— Ueber die Beziehungen des Bodenerwartungswerthes ... zur Reinertragslehre. 1890. IV. 245.
— Ueber die Bildung des Abnutzungssatzes. 1875. IV. 236.
— Ueber die biologischen Grundlagen der Bestandeserziehung. 1897. IV. 169.[2]
— Die Durchforstungsfrage. 1886. IV. 174.
— Die Durchforstungsfrage. 1892. IV. 174.
— Ueber einige gewerbliche Eigenthümlichkeiten der Forstwirthschaft. 1871. IV. 255.
— Ueber die Ergebnisse des ... Buchenhochwaldbetriebes. 1876. IV. 498.
— Ueber die Erhaltung ... der Waldbodenkraft. 1863. IV. 68.
— Zur Erinnerung an den Forstdirector Dr. ... Burckhardt. 1880. IV. 2.
— Ueber die Ertragsregelung des Mittelwaldes. 1868. IV. 236.
— Zur Erziehung der Eiche. 1894. IV. 508.
— Die Fichte etc. im Buchenhochwalde. 1880. IV. 138.[1]
— Forstdirektor Dr. Burckhardt. 1880. IV. 2.
— Ueber forstlichen Zuwachsrechnung. 1891. IV. 234.
— Zur Lehre von den forstlichen Geldertrags- und Waldwerths-Anschlägen. 1873. IV. 256.
— Ueber die Materialerträge etc. des Eichen-Lichtungsbetriebes. 1879. IV. 513.
— Zur natürlichen Verjüngung der Buche. 1892. IV. 496.
— Ueber die normalen Betriebsflächen bei der Vorverjüngung. 1875. IV. 496.
— Ueber Ortssteinkulturen. 1891. IV. 155.[1]
— Ueber die Pflege der Stammform. 1893. IV. 169.[1]
— Zur Praxis der Waldwerthrechnung. 1882. IV. 257.
— Ueber die rechnungsmässige Behandlung der Stangen-Nutzhölzer. 1874. IV. 236.
— Ueber die Regelung der Abnutzung im Mittelwalde. 1887. IV. 131, 257.
— Zur Regelung des Plänterwaldes. 1892. IV. 130.
— Zur Reinertragslehre. 1887. IV. 257.
— Ueber die Sonderung der Abnutzungssätze. 1886. IV, 245.
— Zur Sperrwuchsfrage. 1891. IV. 169.[1]
— Ueber die Theilung gemeinschaftlicher Forsten in der Provinz Hannover. 1876. IV. 308.[2]
— Zur Theorie der forstlichen Zuwachsrechnung. 1872. IV. 233.
— Zur Verjüngungs-Praxis. 1893. IV. 140.
— Ueber die Verwendung von Wasserapparaten zu Derbghaltsversuchen. 1875. IV. 214.
— Zur Waldbodenpflege. 1893. IV. 70.
— Zur Waldwerthberechnung und forstlichen Statik. 1866. IV. 255.
— Zum Weiserprocent. 1874. IV. 256.
Kraft, Johann. Anmærkninger over Træernes Natur. 1754. I. 146.
— Pomona austriaca; Abhandlung. 1792. III. 90.[1]
— Pomona austriaca; ou, Arbres fruitiers. 1792. III. 90.[1]
— Verzeichniss der verschiedenen ... meistgeschätztesten Gattungen von Obstbäumen. 1786. III. 90.[1]
Kraft van Ermel, W. K. L. De Koffiecultuur in ... Palembang. 1892. III. 730.
Krag, J. A. Om anlæg af hovedbestand paa vore skovkarter. 1883. IV. 265.
— Bidrag til det norske skovvaesens historie. 1880. IV. 24.[1]
— Om driftsplaners praktiske anvendelse. 1887. IV. 245.
— Om elgens skadelighed. 1893. IV. 197.[2]
— Om grafisk fremstilling af skoves tilvækst. 1888. IV. 234.
— Historisk oversigt over europäiske landes skovväsen. 1889. IV. 24.[2]
— Iagttagelser vedkommende granfröet. 1885. IV. 454.
— Indberetning om den offentlige skovdrift i Namdalen. 1895. IV. 344.[1]
— Lidt om indförelse af hugst- og husholdningsplaner. 1881. IV. 244.
— Nogle vaktagelser om barträfröet. 1882. IV. 441.
— Oversigt over Schweiz's skovväsen. 1895. IV. 367.
— Om skovtaxation. 1895. IV. 258.
— Stipendieberetning ang. svenske skovforhold. 1891. IV. 344.[1]
— Värnskovloven i Namdalen. 1895. IV. 296.[1]
— Vore skoves tilbagegang. 1884. IV. 24.[1]

Krah, Friedrich Wilhelm. Ueber die Vertheilung der parenchymatischen Elemente im Xylem und Phloem. 1883. I. 125.

Krahe. Korbweiden-Cultur und Korbflecht-Industrie. 1877. IV. 487.[1]
— Zur Korbweidenkultur. 1882. IV. 487.[1]

Krahe, J. A. Enger . . . Pflanzenverband in Korbweidenanlagen? 1885. III. 349.
— Der Feldbau in Korbweidenanlagen. 1891. III. 349.
— Handboek der rationeele Teenencultuur. 1879. III. 348.
— Die Korbweiden-Kultur. 1879. III. 348.
— Versuche in Korbweiden-Kulturen. 1882. III. 348.

Krahe, L. I. See Краа, Л. I.

Krainisch-Küstenländischer Forstverein. Mittheilungen. IV. 14.

Krajenbrink, J. A. Over de Kroeing boomen. 1862. III. 610.[1]

Krakau. See CRACOW.

Krakowie. See CRACOW.

Kralik, Louis. Oel aus den Früchten des Argan-Baums. 1854. III. 666.[2]
— See also COSSON, Ernest & KRALIK, Louis.
— & Baillon, J. Catalogue des espèces dont se composent les reliquiae Mailleanae. 1867. I. 58.
— — Catalogue des reliquiae Mailleanae. 1867. I. 58.

Kralitz, Heinrich. Catalogus plantarum Horti academici lugduno-batavi. See VOORST, Adolph van. 1633. I. 50.

Kralovské české společnosti náuk v Prase. See KÖNIGLICHE BÖHMISCHE GESELLSCHAFT DER WISSENSCHAFTEN. I. 27.

Kramer. Forstkatechismus, für Anfänger der Forstwissenschaft. 1797. IV. 95.

Kramer, Arno. Beiträge zur Kenntnis der Entwickelungsgeschichte . . . der Fruchtblätter der Cupressineen. 1885. II. 19.

Kramer, Ernst. Das Verhalten der Waldstreu- und Moosdecken. 1883. IV. 71.

Kramer, Frans August. Phanerogamen-Flora von Chemnitz. 1875. I. 387, V. XIX.[1]
— Phytophänologische Beobachtungen. 1887. I. 225.

Kramer, J. A. Waterglas als middel tegen de bloedluis. 1864. III. 189.

Kramer, Johann Georg Heinrich. Tentamen botanicum. 1728. I. 290.

Kramer, Otto Christoph. Tabellen worin der cubische Gehalt eines jeden Stammes . . . ausgerechnet zu finden. 1786. IV. 220.

Kramer, Wilhelm Heinrich. Elenchus vegetabilium . . . per Austriam inferiorem observatorum. 1756. I. 438.

Kramers, J. G. Over bemesting van Koffietuinen. 1899. III. 734.[1]
— Bemestingsproeven . . . voor de Koffiecultuur. 1899. III. 731.
— Over het enten der Koffie. 1900. III. 733.[2]
— De met het enten in de Koffie. 1899. III. 733.[2]
— De met het enten in de Koffie tot nog toe verkregen uitkomsten. 1900. III. 733.[2]
— De stikstofbindende en stikstofvrijmakende bacterien. 1899. III. 734.[1]
— Tweede verslag omtrent de proeftuinen en andere mededeelingen over Koffie. 1900. III. 732.[1]
— Verslag omtrent de bemestingsproeven. 1899. III. 734.[1]
— Verslag omtrent de bemestingsproeven . . . 1900. III. 734.[1] (Koffie-proefstation.)
— Verslag omtrent de proeftuinen en andere mededeelingen over Koffie. 1899. III. 731.
— Waarnemingen . . . naar aanleiding van eene reis in de Koffie. 1898. III. 731.

Krampen, Wilhelm. Clematis Viticella venosa. 1861. III. 392.[1]

Ueber die **Krankheit** der Pyramidenpappel. 1877. III. 346.[2]

Die **Kranz-Spieren** (Stephanandra). 1899. III. 462.[1]

Krašan, Franz. Über die Bedeutung der gegenwärtigen Verticalzonen der Pflanzen. 1883. I. 218.
— Beiträge zur Entwicklungsgeschichte der mitteleuropäischen Eichenformen. 1886. II. 130.[2]
— Beiträge zur Flora . . . von Görz. 1863. I. 447.
— Beiträge zur Kenntniss des Wachsthums der Pflanzen. 1873. I. 187.
— Beiträge zur Phanerogamen-Flora Steiermarks. 1891. I. 443.
— Beiträge zur Phanerogamen-Flora von Steiermark. . 1885. II. 135.[1]
— Beobachtungen über den Einfluss standörtlicher Verhältnisse. 1895. I. 244.[1]
— Die Berghaide der südöstlichen Kalkalpen. 1883. I. 443.
— Ueber continuirliche und sprungweise Variation. 1888. I. 243.[1]
— Ergänzungen . . . über das Vorkommen steirischer Pflanzenarten. 1900. I. 444.
— Ergebnisse der neuesten Untersuchungen über die Formelemente der Pflanzen. 1891. I. 243.[2]
— Fragmente aus der Flora von Steiermark. 1894. I. 443.
— Ueber die geothermischen Verhältnisse des Bodens. 1884. I. 218.
— Zur Geschichte der Formentwicklung der roburoiden Eichen. 1887. II. 131.[2]
— Die Haupttypen der Blüthenstände europ. Rubusarten. 1863. II. 305.[1]
— Kalk und Dolomit in ihrem Einflusse. 1889. I. 229.
— Pflanzenphänologische Beobachtungen. 1868. I. 227.[2]
— Über regressive Formerscheinungen bei Quercus sessiliflora. 1887. II. 140.[1]
— Untersuchungen über die Ursachen der Abänderung der Pflanzen. 1884. I. 243.[1]
— Ueber die Ursachen der Haarbildung. 1887. I. 113.[1]
— Vergleichende Uebersicht der Vegetationsverhältnisse der Grafschaften Görz und Gradisca. 1880. I. 448.
— Versuch die Polymorphie der Gattung Rubus zu erklären. · 1865. II. 300.[1]
— See also ETTINGSHAUSEN, Constantin, Baron von & KRAŠAN, Franz.

O **Krasilnom** Dub. See O Красильномъ Дубѣ.

Krasnof, Andrei Nikolaevitch. Notices sur la végétation de l'Altay. 1886. I. 457.
— Versuch einer Entwickelungsgeschichte der Pflanzenwelt im Central-Thian-Schan. See Красновъ, А. Н. 1888.· I. 457.
— See also Красновъ, А. Н.

Krasper, K. L. E. Kurzer Grundriss der . . . nothwendigsten botanischen Ausdrücke. 1845. I. 71.

Krasser, Fridolin. Bemerkungen über die Phylogenie von Platanus. 1889. II. 254.[2]
— Bemerkungen zur Systematik der Buchen. 1896. II. 127.[2]
— Zur Kenntniss der Heterophyllie. 1887. I. 111.
— Melastomataceae. 1893. II. 634.[3]
— Ueber den Polymorphismus . . . von Liriodendron. 1890. II. 211.[1]
— Zerklüftetes Xylem bei Clematis Vitalba. 1887. · II. 200.[1]

Krassow, C. K. A., Freiherr von & Leyde; Eduard. Lehrbuch der Botanik. 1836. I. 87.

Krasuski, József. O reformie leśnej rządowej w Królestwie polskiem. 1878. IV. 289.[1]

Kratkoye nastavleniye. See Краткое наставленіе.

Kratkoye opisaniye. See Краткое описаніе.

Kratkoye ponyatiye. See Краткое понятіе.

Kratkoye soderzhaniye. See Краткое содержаніе.

Krátký, Franz. Forstliche Verhältnisse Transkaukasiens. 1885. IV. 348.[1]
— Eine kaukasische Forstwirthschaft. · 1877. IV. 348.[1]
— Die Forstpolizei. Die " Schöne Eiche." 1897. IV. 516.[1]

Kratochwil, Karl. Damiana. 1883. III. 615.[1]

Kratzenstein, Christian Gottlieb. De ligni Quassiae usu medico. 1775. III. 508.[2]
— De usu corticis peruviani medico. 1773. III. 720.

Kratzmann, Eduard Joseph. De Coniferis usitatis. 1835. IV. 443.[1]
— De semine plantarum. 1838. I. 120.

Kratzschmar, Julius. Ueber Bouvardia. 1874. III. 711.[1]

Krauer, Johann Georg. Prodromus Florae lucernensis. 1824. I. 433.

Kraus, Carl. See KRAUS, Karl.

Kraus, Gregor. Ueber Alter . . . ostgrönländischer Holzgewächse. 1873. I. 193,[1] 303.
— Über den Bau der Cycadeenfiedern. 1865. II. 3.[1]
— Über den Bau trockner Pericarpien. 1866. I. 119.
— Ueber die Bestandtheile des Chlorophyllfarbstoffs. 1872. I. 525.
— Ueber die Bevölkerung Europas mit fremden Pflanzen. 1893. V. XII.[1]
— Beziehungen des Gerbstoffs zu den Secretbehältern. 1883. I. 183.
— Ueber Blüthenwärme bei Cycadeen. 1896. II. 3,[1] 63.[2]
— Der botanische Garten der Universität Halle. 1888. V. VIII.[1]
— Botanische Mittheilungen. 1885. II. 40.[3]
— Über eigenthümliche Sphaerokrystalle in . . . Cocculus. 1872. II. 207.[2]

— Einige Bemerkungen über Alter. 1873. I. 193,[1] 217.
— Einige Bemerkungen über die Erscheinung der Sommer-Dürre. 1873. III. 183.[2]
— Einige Beobachtungen über das Vorkommen des Inulins. 1875. I. 175.
— Einige Beobachtungen über den Einfluss des Lichts. 1869. I. 141.
— Einige Beobachtungen über die winterliche Färbung immergrüner Gewächse. 1872. I. 185.[2]
— Die Entstehung der Farbstoffkörper in den Beeren von Solanum Pseudocapsicum. 1872. III. 702.[1]
— Über Entstehungsweise des Gummi arabicum. 1884. II. 323.[2]
— Geschichte der Pflanzeneinführungen. 1894. I. 242.[1]
— Die Gewebespannung des Stammes. 1867. I. 149.[2]
— Grundlinien zu einer Physiologie des Gerbstoffes. 1889. I. 183.
— Die immergrüne Vegetation Italiens im Winter 1879/80. 1880. III. 49.[2]
— Über Inulin bei den Violaceen. 1879. II. 567.[1]
— Die jährliche Korkproduction. 1884. I. 130.
⇒ — Ueber das Kalkoxalat der Baumrinden. 1891. I. 156.[1]
— Zur Kenntniss der Chlorophyllfarbstoffe. 1872. I. 525.
— Eine kurze Mittheilung über Imbibition organisirter Körper. 1879. IV. 412.[1]
— Das Längenwachsthum der Bambusrohre. 1895. II. 59.[2]
— Die Lebensdauer der immergrünen Blätter. 1880. I. 191.[1]
— Mikroskopische Untersuchungen über . . . Nadelhölzer. 1864. II. 16.[1]
— Ueber das nächtliche Verhalten der Rindenspannung. 1871. I. 149.[1]
— Sur l'oxalate de chaux des écorces d'arbres. 1891. I. 156.[1]
— Physiologisches aus den Tropen. 1895. I. 150,[1] II. 59.[2] — 1896. II. 3,[2] 63.[2]
— Die Rolle der Gerbstoffe. 1884. I. 183.
— Die Schwellungsperiode an tropischen Bäumen. 1895. I. 150.[1]
— Ueber Stoffwechsel bei den Crassulaceen. 1886. II. 235.[1]
— Über das tägliche Wachsthum der Früchte. 1883. I. 179.[1]
— Ueber den täglichen Stoffwechsel im Zellsaft. 1882. I. 176.
— La tension du tissu. 1867. I. 149.[2]
— Treibhölzer. 1874. I. 242.[2]
— Untersuchungen von Treibhölzern aus Nowaja-Semlja. 1872. I. 242.[2]
— Über die Ursachen der Formänderungen etiolirender Pflanzen. 1869. III. 181.[1]
— Die Verdünnung geschüttelter Sprosse. 1881. I. 287.
— Versuche mit Pflanzen im farbigen Licht. 1876. I. 185.[1]
— Über die Vertheilung und Bedeutung des Wassers. 1877. I. 187.
— Vorkommen von Stärkemehl in den Siebröhren. 1873. I. 140.[1]
— Ueber die Wasservertheilung. 1879. I. 149.[1]
— Über die winterliche Färbung. 1874. I. 185.[2]
Kraus, Jo. Georg. De dominio arborum turbine deiectarum. 1736. IV. 313.
Kraus, Karl. Ueber amphotere Reaktion der Pflanzensäfte. 1885. I. 156.[1]
— Ueber Ausscheidung der Schutzholz bildenden Substanz. 1884. I. 207.[2]
— Ueber Blutung aus parenchymatischen Geweben. 1885. I. 169.[1]
— Zur Kenntniss der Periodizität der Blutungserscheinungen der Pflanzen. 1886. I. 169.[1]
— Untersuchungen über den Säftedruck. 1882. I. 168.
— Untersuchungen zum Heliotropismus von Hedera. 1880. II. 650.[1]
— Ueber Verbreitung und Nachweis des Blutungsdrucks der Wurzeln. 1882. I. 168.
— Vorläufige Notiz, den Heliotropismus . . . von Hedera betreffend. 1881. II. 650.[1]
Kraus, M. Ueber die einheimischen Giftpflanzen. 1887. III. 74.
Krause. Ueber die forstlichen Verhältnisse der Oberförsterei Rehhof. 1899. IV. 355.[1]
— See also Крауѕе, A.
Krause, A. Deutsch-russisches Forstwörterbuch. 1889. IV. 23.[2]
— See also Крауѕе, A.
Krause, C. G. Die Holz-Taxation. 183.? IV. 213.
Krause, C. G. R. Anleitung zur Behandlung des Mittelwaldes. 1829. IV. 130.
Krause, Christian Ludwig. Catalogus arborum, fruticum et herbarum. 1753. I. 44.

— Funfzigjährig-erfahrungsmässiger Unterricht von der Gärtnerey. 1773. III. 103.
Krause, Ernst, (1839–1903). Die botanische Systematik. 1866. I. 252.
— Die Platanus; ein Sinnbild des beitern Lebensgenusses. 1868. II. 254.[2]
Krause, Ernst H. L. Ueber das·angebliche Indigenat der Pinus Mughus in den Vogesen. 1894. II. 43.[1]
— Beitrag zur Kenntnis der Verbreitung der Kiefer in Norddeutschland. 1890. II. 46.[2]
— Die Brombeeren der Provinz Westpreussen dargestellt nach dem Herbariumsmaterial des Provincial-Museums zu Danzig. 1898. II. 302.[2]
— Die Brombeeren im Herbarium des Naturhistorischen Vereins. 1900. II. 302.[2]
— Die elsässischen Brombeerarten. 1897. V. XXVI.[2]
— Flora der Insel St. Vincent. 1892. I. 498.
— Florengeschichtliches Material aus den brandenburgischen Holz- und Forstgesetzen. 1895. IV. 26.
— Floristische Notizen. 1897. I. 390.
— Die fremden Bäume und Gesträuche der Rostocker Anlagen. 1890. I. 49.
— Die Heide. 1892. I. 350,[1] II. 662.[1]
— Historisch-geographische Bedeutung der Begleitpflanzen der Kiefer. 1893. I. 389.
— Neue Erklärung der ·schwankenden Westgrense der mitteleuropäischen Nadelhölzer. 1893. IV. 79.[1]
— Nova synopsis Ruborum Germaniae et Virginiae. 1899. II. 300.[1]
— Pflanzengeographische Bemerkung über Ilex Aquifolium. 1894. II. 463.[2]
— Pflanzengeographische Uebersicht der Flora von Mecklenburg. 1884. I. 388.
— Rubi berolinenses. 1885. II. 302.[1]
— Ueber die Rubi corylifolii. 1888. II. 302.[1]
— Rubi rostochienus. 1880. II. 302.[1]
— Die Rubi suberecti des mittleren Norddeutschland. 1886. II. 302.[1]
— Spuren einer ehemaligen grösseren Verbreitung der Edeltanne auf den deutschen Gebirgen. 1895. II. 23.[1]
— Synopsis . . . specierum Ruborum moriferorum. 1893. II. 300.[2]
— Urkundliche Nachrichten über Bäume. 1892. IV. 26.
— Veränderung der Ausdehnung der Wälder um Rostock. 1883. I. 371, IV. 84.[1]
— Ueber das Wachsthum der Mangroven. 1885. II. 614.[1]
— Die Waldbäume. 1893. I. 371.
— Die Westgrenze der Kiefer auf dem linken Elbufer. 1891. II. 47.[1]
— See also Fisch, Carl & Krause, E. H. L.
Krause, G. C. A. Der Dünenbau. 1850. IV. 158.
Krause, George Friedrich. Ueber die Ablösung der Servituten. 1833. IV. 333.
— Anleitung zur Abschätzung . . . der Forstgrundstücke. 1812. IV. 252.
— Compendium der höhern Forstwissenschaften. 1824. IV. 288.[1]
— Compendium der niederen Forstwissenschaften. 1806. IV. 96.
— Ueber die Forst-Gesetzgebung in Deutschland. 1834. IV. 316.
— Handbuch der mathematischen Forstwissenschaften. 1900. IV. 57.
— See also Крауѕе, Г. Ф.
Krause, H. L. Bastarde des Rubus Idaeus. 1891. II. 308.[1]
Krause, Hermann Kunz-. See Kunz-Krause Hermann.
Krause, Julius. Abnorme Fruchtbildung bei Buchen. 1883. II. 126.[1]
Krause, K. E. H. Blitzschläge in Bäume. 1891. IV. 194.
— Blitzschlag in Kiefern. 1888. IV. 194.
— Epheu-Aussaat durch Stare. 1891. I. 240,[2] II. 650.[1]
— Zur Flora von Rostock. 1883. ·I. 388.
Krause, Károly. A Lucrefenyő tenyésztésének kérdése őslucrefenyvesekben szersett tapasztalatok alapján. 1898. IV. 454.
Krause, L. Kultur- und Schlingpflanzen. 1846. III. 204.[2]
— Vermehrung der Schlingpflanzen durch Stecklinge. 1845. III. 158.
Krause, Ludwig. Die beiden wilden Taxusbäume bei Rostock. 1885. II. 11.[1]
Krause, Ludwig Philipp. Der kluge und sorgfältige Gärtner. 1738. III. 103.
Krause, M. See Weiss, J. E., Krause, M. & Bleibinhaus, J.

Krause, Rudolf. *See* GOLLMANN, O., KRAUSE, Rudolf & SCHEUERLEIN, Fedor.
Krause, Rudolf Wilhelm. De naturae in regno vegetabili lusibus. 1706. I. 243.[2]
— De signaturis vegetabilium. 1697. III. 259.[1]
Krausold, Johann Friedrich. De Sabina. *See* WEDEL, G. W. 1707. III. 304.[1]
Krauss, (*Dr.*). Über einige essbare Früchte des Natallandes. 1843. III. 281.[2]
Krauss, A. Hand-Heckenschneide-Apparat. 1880. III. 214.[1]
Krauss, F. M. Die Ermittelung des nachhaltigen Ertrags der Wälder. 1848. IV. 253.
Krauss, Ferdinand. Beiträge zur Flora des Cap- und Natal-landes. 1844. I. 494.
— Pflanzen des Cap- und Natal-Landes. 1844. I. 494.
— Ueber die Verwachsung von Bäumen. 1884. IV. 66.[2]
Krauss, Gregor. Verzeichniss von in- und ausländischen Pflanzen . . . im Grossherzogl. Residenzgarten in Würzburg. 1812. I. 45.
Krauss, Johann Carl. Afbeeldingen der fraaiste . . . boomen en heesters. 1802. I. 293, *III. 75.[2]*
Krauss, Otto. Brownea grandiceps Jacq. 1899. III. 468.[1]
— Empfehlenswerte Schlinggewächss. 1900. III. 203.[1]
— Erythrina crista-galli L. 1899. III. 476.[1]
— Hydrangea paniculata. 1898. III. 412.[2]
— Tropische Aristolochien. 1898. III. 386.[1]
— Die Weigelien. 1897. III. 749.[1]
— Ein wertvoller Frühblüher. 1899. III. 436.[2]
Krausse, (*Revierverwalter*). Das Beschneiden der Pfahl-wurzeln an einjährigen Kiefern. 1876. IV. 472.
Krausz, Géza. Selmecz-Bélabánya szab. kir. város erdészete. 1900. IV. 374.[2]
Kraut, K. Ueber den Perubalsam. 1869. III. 482.[2]
Krause, A. *See* Крауsе, Г.
Krause, G. F. *See* Крауsе, Г. Ф.
Kravtchinski, D. Zur Kritik der Untersuchungsmethoden in der jetzigen Waldbaulehre. 1879. IV. 118.
— *See also* Кравчинскій, Дм.
Krayenhoff, Cornelis Johannes. Proefkundige beschouwing van den aart, hoedanigheid en sterkte van timmerhóut. 1762. IV. 407.[2]
Krebel, Rudolf. Russlands naturhistorische und medicinische Literatur. 1847. I. 3.[1]
Krebs, C. F. W. Anleitung zur Betriebs-Regulierung der Hochwaldungen. 1876. IV. 217, *244.*
Krebs, Christian Gotthelf. Ansichten von der Behandlung der Erdrinde. 1822. IV. 132.[1]
Krebs, F. L. Vollständige Beschreibung . . . der sämmt-lichen Holzarten. 1826. IV. 82.
Krebs, H. J. Et Bidrag til St. Thomás' Flora. 1847. I. 335.
— Catalogue of plants found on the island of St. Thomas, W. I. 1852. I. 335.
Krebs, Philipp Helfricus. Fasciculus quaestionum miscel-lanearum in theoria et praxi maxime utilium. 1700. IV. 313.
— Tractatus politico-juridicus de ligno. 1700. IV. 313.
Krebs, Wilhelm. Beitrag zur Flora der Inseln im Erié See. 1892. I. 316.
Kredba, P. V. Pěstování Vrby košíkářské. 1895. III. 349.
Kregting, A. J. von. Mathematische Beiträge zur Forst-wissenschaft. 1788. IV. 57, 213.
Kreisschreiben an die Vorsteherschaften der waldbesitzenden Gemeinden. 1838. IV. 306.
Kreisschreiben des Departements der Staatswirthschaft . . . betreffend Erwerbungen von Gemeinwäldern. 1877. IV. 306.
Kreisschreiben des Departements der Staatswirthschaft . . . betreffend Holzschläge. 1872. IV. 306.
Kreitscheck, Joseph. Praktischer Unterricht zur kubischen Berechnung . . . aller Baumholzgattungen. 1794. IV. 220.
— Vermehrter . . . Unterricht zur kubischen Berechnung und Schätzung aller Bau- und Werkholzgattungen. 1794. IV. 220.
Krelage, J. H. Tuinbouwonderwijs van rijkswege. 1895. III. 32.[1]
Kremel, A. Über den Nachweiss der Aloe in Gemischen. 1895. III. 333.[3]
— Sur la recherche de l'Aloès dans les mélanges. 1895. III. 333.[1]
Kremer, Aleksander. O znaczeniu drzew. 1872. IV. 44.
Kremer, J. P. Description du Populus euphratica. 1866. II. 97.[2]
— De la sexualité et de l'hybridité des plantes. 1852. I. 245.

Kremla, H. Ueber Verschiedenheiten im Aschen-, Kalk- und Magnesiagehalt . . . der Rebe. 1896. III. 545.[2]
Kresling, Karl. Beiträge zur Chemie des Blüthenstaubes. 1891. *I. 585,[1] II. 48.[1]*
— Composition chimique du pollen du Pin sylvestre. 1891. II. 48.[1]
Kress, (*Perleberg*). Über das Blaublühen der Hortensien. 1832. III. 412.[1]
Kress, Franz. Die grosse Kieferraupe Phalaena. 1868. IV. 210.[1]
Kresse, Gottfried. De Sycomoro. *See* MEYER, G. A. 1694. I. 512.
Kretzschmar, Eduard. Südafrikanische Skizzen. 1853. III. 281.[2]
Kretzschmer, Peter. Entwurf, wie ein gewisses Holz . . . besser zu nutzen sey. 1744. IV. 247.[2]
— Öconomische Vorschläge, wie das Holz zu vermehren. 1744. IV. 115.
Kreusler, U. Assimilation . . . der Pflanzen. 1887. I. 171.
— Beobachtungen über Assimilation. 1890. I. 174.
— Beobachtungen über die Kohlensäure-Aufnahme. 1887. I. 174.
— Über Kohlensäure-Einnahme und -Ausgabe. 1890. I. 171.
— Über eine Methode zur Beobachtung der Assimilation. 1885. I. 173.
Kreuter, Franz. Die Forst- und Landwirthschaft. 1859. III. 213,[1] *IV. 357.*
Das Kreuterbuch oder Herbarius. *See* ORTUS sanitatis. 148. ? I. 275.[2]
Kreutterbuch vonn aller Kreuter, Bäum. *See* RÖSSLIN, Eucharius. 1533. I. 276.
Kreutzburg, Fr. Ueber das künstliche Färben der Horten-sien. 1865. III. 412.[1]
Kreutzer, Karl Joseph. Anthochronologion plantarum Euro-pae. 1840. I. 222.[2]
— Blüthen-Kalender. 1840. I. 227.[1]
— Blütenkalender der Pflanzen des mittlern Europa. 1840. I. 222.[2]
— Das Herbar. 1864. I. 35.
— Oesterreichs Giftgewächse. 1838. III. 90.[2]
— Prodromus florae vindobonensis. 1840. I. 440.
— Taschenbuch der Flora Wiens. 1852. I. 440.
Kreutzwald, Martin Joseph. De utilitate foliorum Juglandis regiae. 1842. III. 356.[1]
Kreuz, Johann. Beiträge zur Entwicklungsgeschichte der Harzgänge einiger Coniferen. 1877. III. 17.[2]
— Zu den Bemerkungen . . . A. Tomaschek's. 1881. III. 545.[1]
— Entwicklung der Lenticellen an . . . Ampelopsis. 1881. II. 504.[1]
— Das gehöften Tüpfel des Xylems. 1878. I. 125.
— *See also* JUNOWICZ, Johann & KRUEZ, Johann.
Kreuzberg, Gotth. Die Kunst Blumen und Bäumchen in 2 Zoll hohen Töpfchen zu ziehen. 1851. III. 175.[2]
Kreyenberg, E. Neue Pflanzenarten im Botanischen Garten zu Buitenzorg. 1876. IV. 62.[2]
Kreysig, Georg Christoph. Bibliotheca scriptorum venati-corum. 1750. IV. 1.
— De venatione, aucupio, sylvis. 1750. IV. 313.
Krichauff, F. On the timber supply of Australia. 1878. IV. 380.[1]
Krichauff, F. Annäherung oder Rückkehr hybrider Pflan-zen zur Art. 1848. I. 245.
— Nachrichten von den Nikobaren. 1847. I. 481.[1]
— Uddrag af de paa Nicobar-Öerne . . . anstillede Under-søgelser. 1847. I. 481.[1]
Krichler, F. Die immergrüne Eiche (Quercus Ilex L.). 1892. IV. 503.[1]
Krick, Fr. Ueber die Rindenknollen der Rotbuche. 1891. I. 213,[2] *II. 126,[1] II'. 497.*
Kriegelstein, Carl BINDER VON, *Freiherr*. *See* BINDER VON KRIEGELSTEIN; Carl, *Freiherr*.
Krieger, Maximilian. Neu-Guinea. 1899. I. 499.[2]
Krieger, W. Ueber zwei sehr empfehlenswerthe Sträucher. 1871. III. 481,[1] *527.[1]*
Kriegsheim, C. K. von. Forstwirthschaftliche Bemerkungen. 1806. IV. 100.[2]
Kriegsheim, Christoph. Zur nähern Beleuchtung und Ver-besserung der est- und liständischen Forsten. 1797. IV. 347.
Krieken, A. van. Nieuwe cuituurgewassen. 1899. III. 129.[1]
— Schaduwboomen in Koffietuinen. 1897. III. 734.[2]

Kriner, Alfred. Zur Anbauwürdigkeit der Birke. 1895. IV. 490.²
— Zum Reinigungshiebe im Nadelholzhochwalde. 1895. IV. 175.¹
Krinos, S. D. See ΚΡΙΝΟΣ, Σ. Δ.
Kripa Nath Dey. Sāl in the Saharanpur forests. 1882. IV. 529.¹
Krishnamachari, K. S. Erythroxylon monogynum leaves. 1900. III. 493.²
Kristelli, Hermann, Ritter, SCHRÖTTER VON. See SCHRÖTTER VON KRISTELLI, Hermann, Ritter.
Kristtornen. Holly. 1894. II. 463.²
Kritchagin, N. See КРИЧАГИНЪ, Н.
Kritische Beleuchtung des Neuesten im Forst- und Jagd-Wesen. IV. 15.
Kritische Blätter für Forst- und Jagdwissenschaft. IV. 10.
Kritische Zeitschrift für Chemie. I. 13.
Krocker, Anton Johann. Flora silesiaca renovata. 1787. I. 374.
— De plantarum epidermide. 1800. I. 129.¹
Krocker, Hermann. De plantarum epidermide observationes. 1833. I. 129.¹
Kročzak, Eduard. Beschreibung der Herrschaft Boskowitz. 1864. IV. 368.
Kroeber, Heinrich. Ueber die Ruta graveolens L. 1830. II. 410.²
Krölling, August. Veredelungen mit Kronen und Aesten. 1889. III. 163.¹
Krömmelbein. Ueber die Züchtung der Lärche. 1888. IV. 450.
Kröncke, C. Untersuchungen über den Werth des Holzes, und die Wichtigkeit der Holzersparung. 1806. IV. 280.¹ über
Kröningssvärd, Carl Gustaf. Flora dalekarlica. 1843. I. 354.
Krösl, Hans. Allgemeine Beschreibung der Stadt Mähr.-Schönberger Forste. 1890. IV. 369.
Kröyer, C. K. De sexualitate plantarum ante Linnaeum. 1761. I. 199.
Krog, N. E. Om havningen og skovbruget. 1892. IV. 135.¹
— Hvorledes maa plukningshugst foretages for at kunne kaldes rationel? 1898. IV. 129.
— Lidt om skovkulturerne paa Strand. 1897. IV. 344.¹
— Om Norges offentlige og private skove. 1892. IV. 344.¹
— Om tilvirkning af enerolje. 1893. III. 303.²
Krogh, von. Kort Undervisning f. Forstbetienterne. 1800. IV. 94.
Krohn. De mindre private Skoves Betydning. 1882. IV. 308.¹
Krohn, (Oberförster). Die preussische Forst-Verwaltung. 1867. IV. 290.²
— Die Vertilgung des Maikäfers. 1864. IV. 202.
— Der Werth der Waldstreu. 1864. IV 71
Krohn, (Forstmeister, Breslau). Das Aufästen der Bäume. 1872. IV. 171.
Krohne. See ZANTHIER, H. D. von & KROHNE.
Krok, C. Levensläer der plant. 1877. I. 217.
Krok, Th. Förteckning öfver Skandinaviska halföns fanero-gamer. See FLODERUS, M. M. & KROK, Th. 1861. I. 356.
Król, Z. Roślinność na granicsnym pasie wyżyny podol skiej. 1878. I. 442.
Krombach, Johann Heinrich Wilhelm. Flore du Grand-duché de Luxembourg. 1875. I. 393.¹
Krombholz, Julius Vincenz. Topographisches Taschenbuch von Prag. See KOSTELEZKY, V. F. 1837. I. 440.
Kromer, Nicolai. Studien über die Convolvulaceenglycoside. 1892. III. 694.²
Kronecker, Carl Ernst. De usu corticis peruviani chirur-gico. See BÜCHNER, J. A. E. 1766. III. 720.²
Kronfeld, Moriz. Aquifoliaceae. 1897. II. 462.²
— Beiträge zur Kenntnis des [sic] Walnuss. 1888. II. 113.²
— Bemerkungen über Coniferen. 1889. II. 16.²
— Bemerkungen über volksthümliche Pflanzennamen. 1886. I. 75.¹
— Die Benennungen der Waldrebe in Niederösterreich. 1886. II. 200.¹
— Zur Biologie der zahmen Rebe. 1889. II. 508.²
— Ueber das Doppelblatt. 1887. I. 144.²
— Hat Goethe das Ergrünen der Coniferenkeimlinge im Dunklen entdeckt? 1887. II. 21.¹
— Die Maria-Theresia-Palme. 1890. II. 68.¹
— Mimosa pudica während einer Eisenbahnfahrt. 1886. II. 373.¹

— Polyphyllie bei der Gemeinen und der Krummholzkiefer. 1889. IV. 463.¹
— Polyphyllie bei Pinus Mughus Scop. und Pinus silves-tris L. 1888. II. 40.¹
— Riesenweinstöcke. 1890. II. 509.¹
— Studien über die Verbreitungsmittel der Pflanzen. 1900. I. 241.¹
— See also HÖFER, Franz & KRONFELD, Moriz.
Das Kronland Salzburg. 1851. IV. 368.
Krook, J. C. Handboek tot het aanleggen . . . van tuinen. 1872. III. 106.¹
Krook, J. J. Einiges über die Behandlung der . . . Cacteen. 1855. III. 619.
— Handboek tot de kennis . . . van alle . . . Cactus-soorten. 1854. III. 618.²
— Handboek zur Kenntnis . . . aller . . . Cacteen. 1854. III. 618.² — 1855. II. 586.¹
— Kenntnis . . . aller . . . Cacteen. 1854. III. 618.²
Kropatsch, Louis. Sweet Chestnut in Austria. 1896. II. 124.¹
Kropff, Carl Philipp von. System und Grundsätze . . . bey Vermessung. 1807. IV. 96.
Kropp. Welche Eschen bleiben am längsten im grünen Schmuck? 1885. II. 707.¹
Kropp, (Revierförster). Das Beschneiden der Pflanzheister. 1865. IV. 154.¹
— Ueber Entwässerungen. 1866. IV. 144.¹
Kros, Simon Petrus. Dissertatio botanica inauguralis de Spira. 1845. I. 34.
Krosok. Koffie-reserve en terrein-keuze. 1888. III. 727.
— Koffiereserve en Zaadkoffie. 1890. III. 727.
Kruber, V. See КРУБЕРЪ, В.
Kruch, Osvaldo. Le Conifere della flora italiana. 1897. II. 16.²
— L' epidermide mucilägginosa nelle foglie. 1897. I. 111.
— Ricerche anatomiche . . . sulla Phytolacca. 1894. II. 193.¹
— Ricerche morfologiche . . . sugli sferoidi . . . di alcune Fitolacce. 1898. II. 193.¹
De Krudtlade vermehret. 1602. I. 283.
Krüger, (Kirchen-Kassen-Rendant, Lübbenau). Das Aus-pflanzen der Justicia speciosa. 1842. III. 709.³
Krüger, (Oberförster, Peisterwitz). Aufmass von 6 Eichen. 1856. IV. 512.
— Tabellarische Uebersicht einiger starken Stämme. 1851. IV. 82.
Krüger, Carl. Kultur der Daubentonia Tripetiana. 1847. III. 487.²
Krüger, Caspar Bernhard. Richtig berechnete Tabellen über stehendes Holz. 1790. IV. 229.
Krüger, E. Ueber das Verhalten von Pinus rigida . . . in der Oberförsterei Jädkemühl. 1888. IV. 468.²
Krüger, Friedrich. Ueber die Wandverdickungen der Cam-biumzellen. 1892. I. 126.
— See also FRANK, A. B. & KRÜGER, Friedrich.
Krüger, Johann Friedrich. Kleines Handwörterbuch der botanischen Kunstsprache. 1833. I. 70.
— Lateinisch-deutsches Handwörterbuch der botanischen Kunstsprache. 1833. I. 70.
— Das Pflanzenreich. 1835. I. 268.
Krüger, Johann Gottlob. De cortice peruviano eiusque usu. 1757. III. 719.
— Gedanken vom Kaffee, Thee. 1743. III. 605.
— Traité du Caffé, du Thé et du Tabac. 1743. III. 605.
— Trattato del Caffè e del Tabacco. 1743. III. 605.
Krüger, Marcus Salomonides. Bibliographica botanica. 1841. I. 2.
— Die Botanik in drei Lehrstufen. 1844. I. 255.
Krüger, Otto. Beitrag zur Kenntniss der sogenannten anomalen Holzbildungen. 1884. I. 127.¹
Krüger, Richard. Die Lehre von den Brennmaterialien. 1883. IV. 413.¹
Krüger, V. See КРЮГЕРЪ, В.
Krünitz, J. G. Oeconomische Encyclopädie. 1773. III. 30.
— Oekonomisch-technologische Encyclopädie. 1773. III. 30.
Krug, A. Practische Geodäsie. 1865. IV. 264.
Kruhöffer, E. W. Et Bidrag til Rødellens Karakteristik. 1871. IV. 489.¹
— Om Græsning i Skovene. 1873. IV. 135.¹
— Lidt Forstøkonomi. 1894. IV. 94.¹
— Et Par Ord om Skovgrundens rette Benyttelse. 1864. IV. 113.²
— Rønnebærtræet. 1867. III. 459.²
— Unsere weichen Laubhölzer. 1895. IV. 169.²

Kruidkundig genootschap Dodonaea te Gent. Botanisch jaarboek. *See* BOTANISCH JAARBOEK, I. 16.

Eenige kruidkundige merkwaardigheden der natuur in Zuidelijk Amerika. 1811. III. 269.[2]

Kruijder, C. A. C. *See* MARCK, J. L. B. van der & KRUIJDER, C. A. C.

Kruilov, Porfirii Nikitich. *See* KRYLOF, P. N.

Krull. Ueber den Zunderschwamm. 1892. IV. 497. De krulloten. 1900. III. 593.[2]

Krullotenziekte. 1900. III. 593.[2]

Krumm, Paul. Zur Anatomie einiger Keimblätter. 1889. I. 123.[1]

Krupa, J. Stosunki florystyczne do rzecza Soly. 1879. I. 442.
— Wykaz roślin zebranych w obrębie W. Ks. Krakowskiego. 1877. I. 442.

Krupper, Wenz. Ein Spaziergang durch den prinzlich Stigliano-Colonna'schen Garten in Neapel. 1872. I. 64.

Krupski. Krótki spis roślin dla zaczynających. 1846. I. 381.

Kruse. Nogle Iagttagelser af Frostens Virkninger. 1855. III. 44.[2]

Kruse, C. A. J. Alleebäume und Gasleitungen. 1869. III. 185.[2]
— De Wijnstok in onze tuinen. 1877. III. 553.[2]

Kruse, Friedrich. Botanisches Taschenbuch. 1887. I. 388.

Kruseman, E. L. Het onderhoud van Koffietuinen gedurende den Oost-moessou. 1899. III. 731.

Krusenstern, Adam Johann von. Reise um die Welt. 1810. I. 302.

Kruskal, Nicolai. Ueber einige Saponinsubstanzen. 1890. I. 177, *III. 226.*[1]

Kruthofer. Forst-Kalender; oder, Verzeichniss der Verrichtungen. 1798. IV. 95.

Krutina. Die K. Heyersche Waldertragsregelung. 1894. IV. 248.[2]
— Ueber Mittelwaldwirthschaft in Baden. 1879. IV. 131.

Krutina, Friedrich. Die badische Forstverwaltung.. 1891. IV. 350.[2]
— Die Bewirthschaftung der Gemeinde-... waldungen in Baden. 1874. IV. 286.[2]
— Ueber die Einführung des Metermasses in der Forstverwaltung. 1871. IV. 226.
— Die Gemeinde-Forstverwaltung im Grossherzogthum Baden. 1874. IV. 308.[2]

Krutitzki, P, Ya. *See* КРУТИЦКІЙ, П. Я.

Krutzsch, Hermann. Beobachtungen über die Temperatur der Luft im Walde. 1859. IV. 53.
— Ueber den Einfluss der Waldungen. 1855. IV. 49.[2]
— Die geognostischen und klimatischen Verhältnisse der Umgegend Tharands. 1866. IV. 355.[2]
— Untersuchung über die Temperatur der Bäume. 1854. I. 529.
— Untersuchungen über die Waldstreu. 1850. IV. 71.

Krutzsch, Karl Lebrecht. Auch einige Worte über forstwissenschaftliche Bildung. 1820. IV. 29.
— Gebirgs- und Bodenkunde. 1827. IV. 61.[1]
— Geht der Borkenkäfer nur kranke, oder geht er auch gesunde Bäume an? 1825. IV. 203.
— Leitfaden bei dem physikalisch-chemischen Unterricht. 1819. IV. 60.[2]

Krylof, A. *See* КРЫЛОВЪ, А.

Krylof, Porfirii Nikitich. *See* КРЫЛОВЪ, П. Н.

Kryspin, C. G. Die Anfänge der österreichischen Forstgeschichte. 1895. IV. 28.[2]

Kubel, W. Sur la coniférine. 1866. II. 20.[1]

Kubik-Tabellen für den Holz-Handel. 1825. IV. 402.[2]

Kubik-Tafeln zum Gebrauch bei den Holz-Abgaben. 1822. IV. 222.

Kubinyi, Ágoston. Magyarországi mérges növények. 1842. III. 90.[1]

Kubische Holzberechnung runder Stämme. 1841. IV. 222.

Kubly, Melchior. Beitrag zur chemischen Kenntniss der Rinde von Rhamnus Frangula. 1866. II. 543.[1]

Kudrna, Josef. O tvaru a obsahu Smrku. 1900. IV. 459.[1]

Küchelbecker, Georg Gottlob. De spinis plantarum. 1756. I. 107.[1]
— *See also* BOSSECK, H. O. & KÜCHELBECKER, G. G.

Küchenmeister, Friedrich. Tabelle zum Selbstunterricht im Veredeln der Obstbäume. 1879. III. 162.

Küchenmeister, Gottlob Friedrich Heinrich. Ueber die Blume Schuschan. 1860. II. 290.[2]
— The flower Shushan. 1860. II. 290.[2]

Küchler, Die Wälder von Alpnach und das neue Forstgesetz. 1878. IV. 330.

Küffner, Friederich. Architectura vi v-arboreo-neo-synemphyteutica. 1716. III. 101.[2]

Kügler, Karl. Ueber den Kork von Quercus Suber. 1884. II. 140.[2]
— Ueber das Suberin. 1884. II. 140.[2]

Kühling, L. Verzeichniss der in Bromberg's Umgegend wild wachsenden... Pflanzen. 1866. I. 385.

Kühn, (*Forstrath, Breslau*). *See* GEHREN, VON (*Kammerdirector, Ratibor*) & KÜHN (*Forstrath, Breslau*).

Kühn, B. L. Zur Bekämpfung der ausländischen Konkurrenz im Obsthandel. 1897. III. 139.
— Die Monstre-Veredelungen. 1889. III. 163.[1]
— Die Resultate der letztjährigen Obstausstellungen. 1887. III. 139.
— Welche Zwetschen- und Pflaumensorten eignen sich... zum Dörren. 1890. III. 433.[2]
— Unter welchen Verhältnissen ist der Anbau von Zwetschen... lohnend? 1890. III. 433.[1]

Kühn, H. Einiges über Vermehrung der Coniferen. 1873. III. 294.[1]
— Einiges über Vermehrung der Ilex. 1873. III. 529.[2]

Kühn, Julius. Die Krankheiten der Kulturgewächse. 1858. III. 178.
— Über die Nothwendigkeit eines Verbotes... des Berberitzen-Strauches. 1875. III. 393.[1]

Kuehn, K. G. De extractis vegetabilium Garayanis. 1799. III. 244.
— Febrifuga remedia. 1810. III. 244.

Kühn, Oskar. Mittheilungen über das... Verfahren für Berechnung der gelegentlich des Eisenbahnbaues... zu leistenden Entschädigungen. 1873. IV. 256.
— Mittheilungen über einen Frass von Otio rhynchus äter. 1869. IV. 455.

Kühnau, W. Vom Zwergjasmin. 1884. III. 413.[1]

Kühne, (*Kunstgärtner, Charlottenburg*). Andeutungen über Weintreiberei. 1835. III. 552.

Kühne, Johann Gottfried. Vollständige Nachricht von der Chocolate. 1717. III. 594.

Kükenthal, Georg. Floristisches aus Süd-Thüringen. 1895. II. 294.[2]

Kümpel, J. Kaffee. 1900. III. 728.[1]

Künckel, J. Les Lepidoptères... destructeurs des Oranges. 1875. III. 500.[2]

Künckel d'Herculais, Jules. Histoire de la cochenille vivant sur les racines du Palmier. 1878. III. 318.[2]

Kündig, Jakob. *See* PRANTL, Karl & KÜNDIG, Jakob.

Künigl, *Graf.* Die Hochwasserkatastrophe... in Tirol. 1883. IV. 48.[2]
— Kahlschlag oder Plänterschlag. 1883. IV. 128.

Künstler, G. A. Beiträge zur Kenntniss der... schädlichen Insekten. 1864. III. 189.

Künstler, Gustav. Die unseren Kulturpflanzen schädlichen Insekten. 1871. III. 190.

Künzer. Ueber den Einfluss des Waldes auf... Gewitter. 1879. IV. 46.[2]
— Klimatologisch-phaenologische Beobachtungen. 1887. I. 225.

Kürsner, Christian. De potu Theae. *See* WALDSCHMIEDT, J. J. 1685. III. 605.

Küstenmacher, M. Beiträge zur Kenntniss der Gallenbildung. 1894. I. 214.[1]

Küster, Ernst. Die anatomischen Charaktere der Chrysobalaneen. 1897. II. 257.[1]
— Bemerkungen über die Anatomie der Eichen. 1900. II. 131.[2]
— Ueber Kieselablagerungen im Pflanzenkörper. 1897. I. 178.
— Über Stammverwachsungen. 1899. I. 209.[2]
— Über das Wachstum der Knospen. 1898. I. 109.[1]

Küttner, W. Tafeln zur Inhaltsbestimmung runder und vierkantig bearbeiteter Hölzer. 1871. IV. 226.

Kützing, Friedrich Traugott. Grundzüge der philosophischen Botanik. 1851. I. 89.
— Ueber den Maticocampher. 1883. III. 342.[1]
— Sur le camphre de Matico. 1883. III. 342.[1]

Kuhl, Heinrich & Hasselt, J. K. van. Brief aan de Heeren F. Nees en W. de Haan. 1821. I. 497.
— Brief uit Tjichanjavar. 1822. I. 464.[2]

Kuhla, Fritz. Ueber Entstehung und Verbreitung des Phelloderms. 1897. I. 131.[1]
— Die Plasmaverbindungen bei Viscum. 1900. II. 178.[1]

Kuhn, Franciszek Ksawery. Krótki zbiór praktycznej nauki o hodowaniu Drzewa Morwowego. 1843. III. 376.
— Krótko zebrana praktyczna nauka o pielęgnowaniu Drzew Morwowych. 1859. III. 377.
— Praktyczna nauka hodowania Drzewa Morwowego. 1859. III. 377.

Kuhn, J. Friedrich. Das preussische Forst- und Jagdrecht. 1840. IV. 320.
Kuhn, Johann Melchior. Abhandlung von der höchstnöthigen Conservation des Holzes. 1764. IV. 116.
— Gründlich erprobte Anweisung zur Holz-Cultur. 1761. IV. 104.²
Kuhn, Max. Rhododendron im Tatragebirge. 1864. II. 680.¹
Kuijk, G. A. Het Pinetum Schoberianum. 1898. I. 51.²
Kuinneth, Georg Friedrich. De faba St. Ignatii. 1802. III. 682.²
Kujawa, Heinrich von. Ueber die Anlage von Cämpen zur Erziehung von Kiefern-Ballenpflanzen. 1880. IV. 473.
— Zur Borkenkäfer-Frage. 1875. IV. 204.
— Erläuterungs-Bericht für die Ausstellung von Gegenständen des Forst- und Jagdwesens . . . in Halle. 1881. IV. 19.²
— Ueber die natürliche Verjüngung des Waldes. 1874. IV. 139.²
— Ein offenes Wort an die Privat-Forstbesitzer. 1875. IV. 308.²
— Das Pflug-Cultur-Verfahren. 1873. IV. 143.¹
Kulagin, Nicolai Mikhailovitch. See Кулагинъ, Н. М.
Kulisch, P. Beiträge zur Kenntniss der chemischen Zusammensetzung der Äpfel und Birnen. 1892. III. 444.²
— Untersuchungen über das Nachreifen der Äpfel 1892. I. 179.¹
Kulisher, M. See Кулишеръ, М.
Kull, Rudolf. Der schweizerische Obstgarten. 1869. III. 145.²
Kullberg, Daniel. De affinitate generum plantarum. 1796. I. 251.
Kulmus, Johann Adam. De literis in ligno Fagi. 1730. I. 210.¹ IV. 496.²
Kulmus, Johannes Ernst. De literis in ligno Fagi. See KULMUS, J. A. 1730. I. 210.¹ IV. 496.²
The **Kulni** export works, Jaunsar division. 1900. IV. 390.¹
Kulse, (Revierförster in Nesigode). Nachweisung der in den Saatkämpen des . . . erzogenen Holz-Pflanzen. 1860. IV. 150.
— Uebersicht der im . . . Forstrevier Nesigode befindlichen Pflanzen. 1858. IV. 150.
Ueber die **Kultur** der Allamanda-Arten. 1853. III. 686.¹
Kultur der Andromeda floribunda. 1847. III. 654.¹
Die **Kultur** der Dipladenia. 1882. III. 687.²
Die **Kultur** der Korbweide zu Aisne. 1889. III. 349.
Kultur der Parfümpflanzen. 1868. III. 226.²
Ueber die **Kultur** der zahmen Kastanie. 1865. IV. 492.²
Die **Kultur** des Kastanienbaumes. 1809. III. 358.²
Zur **Kultur** des Pulverholzes. 1886. IV. 528.¹
Ueber die **Kultur** des Zuckerahorns. 1801. IV. 526.²
Kultur und Eigenschaften des Anacardium. 1846. III. 523.²
Kultur und Vermehrung der Salisburia. 1855. III. 286.²
Kultur-Beobachtungen. 1858. IV. 150.
Kulturwerkzeuge 1857 IV 176.²
Kumar Chatterjee, CHANDRA. See CHANDRA KUMAR CHATTERJEE.
Kumm, Paul. Bemerkenswerthe Bäume . . . Pr. Stargard. 1896. I. 296.²
Kummer, Franz. Beitrag zu den Hooker'schen Sikkim-Himalaya-Rhododendren. 1852. II. 676.²
— Chinesische Gärten. 1851. III. 127.²
— Einiges über Pelargonien. 1852. III. 491.¹
Kummer, Paul. Deutsche Blumenwelt in Characterbildern. 1879. I. 388.
— Das Leben der Pflanze. 1870. I. 95.
— Das Räthsel der Mycorhiza. 1885. I. 529.
Der **Kumquat**. 1869. III. 502.¹
The **Kumquat**. 1874. III. 502.¹
Kundmann, Johannes Christian. De nucibus Juglandibus. 1740. II. 112.²
— Vitis ad ingentem magnitudinem . . . producta. 1744. II. 509.¹ III. 549.¹
Kuneman, Julius. De gouvernements Koffiecultuur op Java. 1890. III. 730.
— Een Koffieproefstatje. 1892. III. 730.
Kunhya, LAL RAI BAHADUR. See LAL RAI BAHADUR KUNHYA.
Kunisch, Emanuel Hermann. Ueber die tödtliche Einwirkung niederer Temperaturen. 1880. I. 212.
Kunitzki, B. A. Botanische und waldbauliche Beschreibung der Espe. See Куницкій, B. 1888. IV. 486.¹
— See also Куницкій, B. A.
Kunkele, Theodor. Ueber Strangbildungen im Marke von Alnus glutinosa. 1897. II. 116.²
Kunkler, Adolphe de. Nouveautés d'origine italienne. 1884. III. 88.²

Kunse, W. Sur la séparation et le dosage des alcaloïdes du cacao. 1895. III. 595.¹
Kunshtchikof. See Кұнщиковъ.
Die **Kunst** rohe und kalcinirte Pottasche zu machen. 1780. IV. 395.
Das **Kunstholzhandwerk** . . . Berchtesgaden. 1859. IV. 428.¹
Kunstmatig schillen van eikenhout. 1876. IV. 514.¹
Kunstmatige bevruchting van Koffie. 1885. III. 727.
Kunszt, János. Az Áfonya fajai. 1900. III. 663.¹
— Három Berkenye fajta. 1898. III. 459.²
Kunth, Karl Sigismund. Sur les affinités du genre Stilbe. 1832. II. 760.²
— Anleitung zur Kenntniss sämmtlicher in der Pharmacopoea borussica. 1834. III. 57.
— Bemerkungen über die Familie der Piperaceen. 1839. II. 92.²
— Büttneriaceae. 1822. II. 531.¹
— Ueber einige Aublet'sche Pflanzengattungen. 1833. I. 338.²
— Einige Bemerkungen über Blattstellung. 1843. I. 102.
— Enumeratio plantarum omnium. 1833. I. 260.
— Enumeratio synoptica Ficus specierum. 1846. II. 148.²
— Enumeratio vegetabilium circa Berolinum. 1813. I. 376.
— Ueber die Familie der Dioscorineen. 1850. II. 90.²
— Flora berolinensis. 1813. I. 376.
— Flora berolinensis . . . secundum familias naturales disposita. 1838. I. 379.
— Ueber die Gattung Sympieza Lichtenst. 1832. II. 684.¹
— Sur le genre Saccellium. 1824. II. 751.²
— Handboek der botanie. 1831. I. 255.
— Handbuch der Botanik. 1831. I. 255.
— Lehrbuch der Botanik. 1847. I. 89.
— Malvaceae, Büttneriaceae, Tiliaceae. 1822. II. 565.²
— Mimoses . . . du Nouveau continent. 1819. II. 318.²
— Nachträgliche Bemerkungen über . . . Smilacineen. 1850. II. 77.¹
— Über die natürliche Gruppe der Liliaceen. 1844. II. 77.¹
— Ueber die natürliche Pflanzengruppe der Buddlejeae. 1846. II. 716.¹
— Ueber eine neue Gattung . . . der Nyctagineen. 1832. II. 191.²
— Note sur le genre Bauhinia de Linné. 1824. II. 334.¹·
— Note sur le genre Piper. 1818. II. 93.²
— Notice sur le genre Bambusa. 1822. II. 59.¹
— Notice sur les genres Myrtus et Eugenia. 1823. II. 618.²
— Sur une nouvelle espèce de Cupania. 1824. II. 485.¹
— Nova genera et species plantarum. 1815. I. 328.
— Observations sur la famille des Pipéracées. 1839. II. 92.¹
— Plantae novae Horti regii botanici berolinensis. 1814. I. 47.
— Recherches sur les plantes trouvées dans les tombeaux égyptiens. 1826. I. 81.¹
— Révision de la famille des Bignoniacées. 1818. II. 784.¹
— Révision des Graminées. 1829. II. 58.¹
— Species novae et emendatae. 1845. I. 47.
— Synonyma ad plantas Humboldtianas. 1830. I. 329.
— Synopsis plantarum . . . ad plagam aequinoctialem orbis novi. 1822. I. 328.
— Terebinthacearum genera. 1824. II. 454.²
— Ueber die Thymeleaen. 1830. II. 599.¹ 599.²
— Ueber die Verwandtschaft der Gattung Stilbe. 1832. II. 760.²
— Ueber die Willdenow'sche Gattung Omphalococca. 1832. II. 753.²
Kuntze. Versuche mit der . . . Zündnadel-Sprengschraube. 1878. IV. 386.
Kuntze, Dieterich Eberhard. Anweisung zum Anbau des Nadelholzes. 1788. IV. 140, 440.³
Kuntze, Georg. Beiträge zur . . . Anatomie der Malvaceen. 1891. II. 519.²
Kuntze, Karl Eduard Otto. See KUNTZE, Otto.
Kuntze, Karl Ernst Otto. See KUNTZE, Otto.
Kuntze, Otto. Bemerkungen über Vitaceen. 1893. II. 501.¹
— Les besoins de la nomenclature botanique. 1895. I. 254.¹
— Die Chinarindenbäume. 1877. III. 718.
— Cinchona; Arten; Hybriden. 1878. II. 813.¹
— Cinchona Ledgeriana a hybrid. 1883. II. 813.¹
— Enumeración de las plantas. 1896. I. 345.
— Um die Erde. 1881. I. 303.
— Fünfter Beitrag zur Cinchonaforschung. 1880. II. 813.¹
— Linnaea or Obolaria? 1894. II. 835.¹
— Methodik der Speciesbeschreibung und Rubus. 1879. II. 300.¹

Kuntze, Otto (*continued*).
— Monographie der Gattung Cinchona. 1878. II. 813.[1]
— Monographie der Gattung 'Clematis. 1885. II. 195.[2]
— Nachträge zur Clematis-Monographie. 1887. II. 195.[2]
— Plantae orientali-rossicae. 1887. I. 457.
— Plantae Pehuelianae hereroenses. 1886. I. 495.
— Reform deutscher Brombeeren. 1867. II. 301.[2]
— Revisio generum plantarum. 1891. I. 254.[1]
— Richtige Gartenpflanzennamen, Saribus. 1899. II. 70.[1]
— Die Schutzmittel der Pflanzen gegen Thiere. 1877. I. 235.[1]
— Taschen-Flora von Leipzig. 1867. I. 386.
— Vorläufiger Bericht über Cinchonastudien. 1877. II. 813.[1]
— & **Post**, Tom von. Nomenklatorische Revision höherer Pflanzengruppen. 1900. I. 254.[1]
— & **Wittmack**, Ludwig. Fuchsia Garleppiana. 1893. II. 644.[1]
Kuntzmann, (*Hofrath Dr.*). Beobachtungen über Obst-Orangerie. 1829. III. 136.
Kunz, Ignatz. Das Forst- und Jagdwesen auf den Staats- und Fonds-Gütern Galiziens. 1845. IV. 368.
Kunz-Krause, Hermann. Beiträge zur Kenntnis der Fabiana imbricata. 1899. III. 700.[2]
— Beiträge zur Kenntnis der Ilex paraguayensis. 1893. III. 531.[1]
— Étude sur Ilex paraguayensis. 1893, 1894. III. 531,[1] 700.[2]
Kunze, Gustav. Chloris austro-hispanica. 1846. I. 420.
— Einige Fälle von Umwandlungen der Nebenaxen in Haupt-axen bei den Abietineen. 1851. II. 17.[2]
— Pugillus primus . . . plantarum adhuc ineditarum. 1842. I. 47.
— *See also* GOEBEL, K. C. T. F. & KUNZE, Gustav.
Kunze, Max Friedrich. Ueber die Abhängigkeit der Holz-preise. 1868. IV. 388.[1]
— Die absoluten Formzahlen der Fichte. 1899. IV. 459.[1]
— Die absoluten Formzahlen der Gemeinen Kiefer. 1886. IV. 482.[1]
— Aechte Schaft- und Baumformzahlen . . . der Fichte. 1888. IV. 458.
— Anleitung zur Aufnahme des Holzgehaltes. 1886. IV. 218.
— Beiträge zur Holzmesskunde. 1886. IV. 233.
— Beiträge zur Kenntniss der Derbgehalte der im Schicht-masse eingelegten Holzsortimente. 1876. IV. 387.[2]
— Beiträge zur Kenntniss der Rothbuche. 1890. IV. 498.
— Beiträge zur Kenntniss . . . der Weymouthskiefer. 1900. IV. 469.[1]
— Beiträge zur Kenntniss des Ertrages der Fichte. 1878. IV. 458.
— Beiträge zur Kenntniss des Ertrages der Gemeinen Kiefer. 1890. IV. 481.
— Drainirung im Walde. 1864. IV. 144.[1]
— Ueber Durchforstungserträge. 1852. IV. 175.[2]
— Ueber den Einfluss der Anbaumethode auf den Ertrag der Gemeinen Kiefer. 1882. IV. 481.
— Ueber den Einfluss der Anbaumethode auf . . . Fichte. 1889. IV. 458.
— Ueber den Einfluss der Laub- und Nadelholzwaldungen auf die Temperatur. 1877. IV. 53.
— Ueber den Einfluss des Waldes auf die Regenmenge. 1876. IV. 50.
— Ueber den Einfluss verschiedener Durchforstungsgrade. auf . . . Fichte. 1884. IV. 458.
— Ueber den Einfluss verschiedener Durchforstungsgrade auf . . Kiefer. 1884. IV. 481.
— Ueber den Einfluss verschiedener Durchforstungsgrade auf . . . Kiefer und Fichte. 1890. IV. 176.[1]
— Ueber den Einfluss verschiedener Durchforstungsgrade auf . . . Rothbuche. 1884. IV. 498.
— Ueber den Einfluss verschiedener Durchforstungsgrade. auf . . . Waldbestände. 1894. IV. 175.[1]
— Ueber die Einwirkung des Streurechens auf den Massen-zuwachs der Fichte. 1881. IV. 458.
— Die Formzahlen der g m n n Fichte. 1889. IV. 458.
— Die Formzahlen der Gemeinen Kiefer. 1881. IV. 481. — 1889. IV. 481.
— Ueber die Genauigkeit der Bestandesmassenermittelung. 1884. IV. 218.
— Hilfstafeln für Holzmassen-Aufnahmen. 1884. IV. 231.[1]
— Ueber die Inhaltsberechnung . . . der Fichte. 1894. IV. 58.
— Ueber die Inhaltsberechnung des Langnutzholzes. 1892. IV. 482.[1]
— Zur Kenntniss des Ertrages der Gemeinen Kiefer. 1876. IV. 481.
— Lehrbuch der Holzmesskunst. 1873. IV. 214.
— Massentafel für Nadelholzklötze. 1870. IV. 226.
— Neue Methode zur raschen Berechnung der unächten Schaftformzahlen. 1891. IV. 219.
— Eine neue Methode zur raschen Berechnung der unächten· Schaftformzahlen gefällter Kiefern. 1890. IV. 481.
— Siebenstellige Kreisflächen für alle Durchmesser. 1868. IV. 230.
— Untersuchungen über den Festgehalt . . . der Fichtenrinde. 1875. IV. 458.
— Untersuchungen über den Grad der Genauigkeit, welcher bei Holzmassenaufnahmen . . . zu erreichen ist. 1879. IV. 217.
— Untersuchungen über die Genauigkeit, die bei Holzmassen-aufnahmen . . . zu erreichen ist. 1893. IV. 219.
— Vergleichende Untersuchungen über den Einfluss der Auf-astung auf den Zuwachs . . . junger Kiefern. 1875. IV. 480.
— Die wichtigsten Formeln der Zins- und Rentenrechnung. 1872. IV. 59.[1]
— Ueber den Zusammenhang der unächten mit der absoluten Formzahl. 1874. IV. 256.
— Ueber den Zusammenhang zwischen Durchmesser- und Volum-Zuwachsprozent bei der Fichte. 1900. IV. 459.[1]
— Zur Zuwachsschätzung an stehenden Stämmen. 1888. IV. 234.
— *See also* BÖHMERLE, Karl, KUNZE, M. F. & SCHUBERG, Karl; PRESSLER, M. R. & KUNZE, Max; КУНЦЕ, Максъ.
Kunze, Oskar E. Kleine Laubholzkunde. 1899. I. 294,[2] III. 70.
Kunzé, Richard Ernest. Cactus; its history. 1875. III. 620.[2]
— Cardinal points in the study of medical botany. 1881. III. 238.[2]
— Cereus grandiflorus and Cereus Bonplandii. 1876. III. 621.[1]
— Cereus nycticalus. 1884. II. 591.[1]
— The germination and vitality of seeds. 1882. I. 193.[1]
Kuperus van Oosterlittens, D. J. Mededeelingen: Vrucht-boomen, bevordering der vruchtbaarheid. 1871. III. 174.[2]
Kupfer, Karl August. Beiträge zum Forst- und Jagdwesen. 1819. IV. 117.
— Die praktische, auf Erfahrung gegründete Holzzucht. 1821. IV. 106.
— Winke für Forstmänner. 1812. IV. 96.
Kupferatlas der vorzüglichsten Handelspflanzen. 1839. III. 52.
Ueber die **Kupferkalkbrühe** oder Bordelaiserbrühe. 1900. III. 195.[1]
Kupffer, Karl R. Beitrag zur Flora der Insel Runö. · 1896. I. 366.
— Beitrag zur Kenntnis der Gefässpflanzenflora Kurlands. 1899. I. 367.
— Verzeichniss seltener Pflanzen Liv- und Kurlands. 1895. I. 366.
Kupfferschlaeger, Isidore. Conservation des bois. 1886. IV. 420.
Kuphaldt. Die Flora von Plön. 1863. I. 385.
Kuphaldt, G. Rhododendron catawbiense, Azalea pontica. 1887. III. 395,[1] 656.
Kurdyumof, V. *See* КУРДЮМОВЪ, В.
Kuriger. Forstliche Reisenotizen aus Frankreich. 1881. IV. 360.
Kuris, Iv. *See* КУРИСЪ, Ив.
Kurr, Johann Gottlob von. Über Cytisus Adami. 1865. II. 368.[1]
— Grundzüge der ökonomisch-technischen Mineralogie. 1836. IV. 61.[1]
— Untersuchungen über die Bedeutung der Nektarien. *See* SCHÜBLER, Gustav. 1832. I. 237.
— Untersuchungen über die Bedeutung der Nektarien. 1833. I. 118.[2]
Kurtz, C. Das Forstdiebstahls-Gesetz. 1880. IV. 321.
Kurtz, Federico. Aufzählung der . . . in Westsibirien ge-sammelten Pflanzen. 1879. I. 454.[1]
— Bericht über zwei Reisen zum Gebiet des oberen Rio Salado. 1894. I. 345.·
— Collectanea ad floram argentinam. 1900. I. 345.
— Dos viajes botánicos al Rio Salado. 1892. I. 345.
— Enumeración de las plantas . . de Mendoza. 1897. I. 345.
— Essai d'une bibliographie botanique de l'Argentine. 1900. I. 3.[1]

— Die Flora der Tschuktschenhalbinsel. 1895. I. 454.²
— Die Flora des Chilcatgebietes. 1895. I. 312.
— Informe preliminar de un viaje botánico . . . en las provincias de Córdoba. 1886. I. 345.
— Die kleinen Blüthen von Halesia tetraptera L. 1875. II. 704.²
— Phyllodie (Rückschlag in Laubblätter) der Kelchblätter von Rubus. 1876. II. 305.²
— Ueber einen selten schönen Fall von Phyllodie an Rubus. 1876. II. 305.²
— Sértum eordobense. 1893. I. 345.
Kurts, Fritz. See Kurtz, Federico.
Kurtz, H. Kaffeeschädlinge im Togogebiet. 1897. III. 736.
Kurtze doch best-gegründete Nachricht, was es mit dem . . . Reichs-Wald . . . für eine ; . . Bewandnüs habe. 1748. IV. 25.
Kurtze Unterweisung die Obstbäume recht zu beschneiden. 1714. III. 171.
Kurtzer Begriff der edlen Jägerey. 1730. IV. 115.
Kurtzer doch gründlicher Begriff der edlen Jägerey. 1730. IV. 115.
Kurz, Sulpiz. On the affinity and position of Ryparia. 1873. II. 573.²
— Bamboo and its use. 1876. II. 58,¹ III. 315.¹
— Le Bambou et ses divers emplois. 1876. III. 315.¹
— Eine Bemerkung über Inodaphnis. 1872. II. 366.¹
— Bemerkungen über die Arten von Pandanus. 1869. II. 56.²
— Beschreibung von 4 neuen indischen Euphorbiaceen. 1875. II. 434.¹
— Contributions towards a knowledge of the Burmese flora. 1874. I. 476.¹
— Description of a new Sikkim Vine. 1874. II. 503.²
— Description of a new species of Tetramerista. 1875. II. 550.¹
— Descriptions of a few Indian plants. 1874. I. 474.
— Descriptions of new Indian plants. 1875. I. 474.
— Descriptions of new plants from the Nicobar Islands. 1875. I. 481.¹
— Descriptions of three new species of Porana. 1873. II. 746.¹
— Eenige kruidkundige mededeelingen. 1865. I. 466.
— Ueber einige neue . . . indische Pflanzen. 1870. I. 474.
— Enumeration of Burmese Palms. 1874. II. 62.¹
— On the euphorbiaceous genus Capellenia. 1867. II. 441.¹
— On a few new plants from Yunan. 1873. I. 459.
— Forest flora of British Burma. 1877. I. 475,¹ IV. 83.²
— General key to the Burmese trees. 1875. I. 475,¹ IV. 83.²
— Gnetum Brunonianum. 1872. II. 55.¹
— Korte schets der vegetatie van het eiland Bangka. 1864. I. 466.
— List of Burmese forest trees. 1875. I. 175,¹ IV. 83.²
— Lord Mayo's tree. 1875. II. 789.¹
— Eine neue Art von Gironniera. 1872. II. 142.¹
— New Burmese plants. 1872. I. 476.¹
— On a new genus of Moraceae. 1865. II. 155.²
— Note on the Indian species of Crataeva. 1874. II. 232.²
— Notes on a few new Oaks from India. 1875. II. 131.¹
— Eine Notize über Tetranthera ochrascens. 1872. II. 226.²
— Observationes de quibusdam Pandaneis. 1865. II. 36.¹
— Pachygone dasycarpa. 1870. II. 208.¹
— Pinus Latteri Mason. 1872. II. 42.²
— Plantae nonnullae novae Indiae orientalis. 1867. I. 474.
— Preliminary report on the forest and other vegetation of Pegu. 1875. I. 476.¹
— Remarks on the species of Pandanus. 1869. II. 56.²
— Report on the vegetation of the Andaman Islands. 1870. I. 481.¹
— Revision of the Indian Screwpines. 1867. II. 56.¹
— A sketch of the vegetation of the Nicobar Islands. 1876. I. 481.¹
— Skizze der Vegetation der Insel Bangka. 1866. I. 466.
— On some new or imperfectly known Indian plants. 1870. I. 474.
— On the species of Glycosmis. 1876. II. 407.¹
— On two new species of Heritiera. 1874. II. 535.¹
Kurze Anleitung zur Bekämpfung des Fichtenborkenkäfers. 1875. IV. 456.
Kurze Anleitung zur Erziehung . . . des Maulbeerbaums. 1851. III. 376.
Kurze Anleitung zur Erziehung und Pflege der Obstbäume. 1844. III. 137.

Kurze Anleitung zur Holzanbauung. See Gebrath, von. 1781. IV. 105.
Kurze Anleitung zur Pflanzung . . . des Holzes. 1768. IV. 110.¹
Kurze Anleitung zur Vermehrung und Ersparung des Holzes. 1845. IV. 117, 281.¹
Kurze Anweisung für Landleute zur Erziehung gesunder und fruchttragender Obstbäume. 1830. III. 136.
Kurze Belehrung über den Anbau des unächten Akasienbaums. 1797. IV. 522.²
Kurze Beschreibung der forstlich-statistischen Verhältnisse der Comune Stadt Pisek. 1861. IV. 370.
Kurze Beschreibung der forstlich-statistischen Verhältnisse der Domaine Rothenhaus. See Schröder, Romeo. 1860. IV. 370.
Kurze Beschreibung der Korbweidenanlagen zu Messduk. 1872. IV. 487.¹
Kurze Beschreibung einiger interessanten Gewächshauspflanzen. 1837. III. 74.
Kurze Darlegung der forstlichen Verhältnisse des Judenbacher Forstes. See Imhoff, A. von. 1857. IV. 355.²
Kurze Darstellung nebst einer vollständigen Tabelle, zur . . . Bestimmung der Geld-Preise. See Räthel, J. N. 1802. IV. 221.
Kurze geographisch-statistische Darstellung der Kantone Uri und Unterwalden. 1805. IV. 364.
Kurze geographisch-statistische Darstellung des Kantons Freiburg. 1810. IV. 365.
Kurze geographisch-statistische Darstellung des Kantons Glarus. 1809. IV. 365.
Kurze Notizen. 1853. I. 297.²
Kurze praktische Anweisung zum Forstwesen. See Paulsen, J. C. 1795. IV. 239.
Kurze und möglichst vollständige Belehrung. See Otte, Karl. 1813. IV. 140.
Kurzer Abriss der Forstwissenschaft für junge Förster. 1790. IV. 95.
Kurzer doch gründlicher Unterricht . . . Pflanzung des Maulbeer-Baums. 1780. III. 373.
Kurzer systematischer Grundriss der practischen Forstwissenschaft. See Zanthier, H. D. von. 1764. IV. 94.
Kurzer Ueberblick über die verschiedenen Eigenthümlichkeiten unserer Forsthölzer. 1857. IV. 67.¹
Kurzer und fasslicher Unterricht zur Anlegung . . . der Baum-, Küchen- und Hopfengärten. 1792. III. 146.
Kurzgefasste Beschreibung sämmtlicher Kunstwörter des Jagd- und Forstwesens. 1803. IV. 23.¹
Kurzgefasste Naturgeschichte der schädlichsten Waldinsekten. 1800. IV. 206.
Kusano, Shunsuke. See Inui, Tamaki, Hattori, Hirotaro & Kusano, Shunsuke.
Kusnezow, Nicolai Ivanovitch. See Kuznezof, N. I.
Kuss. Restauration et conservation des terrains en montagne. 1900. IV. 186.²
— Restauration et conservation des terrains en montagne; les torrents glaciaires. 1900. IV. 186.²
Kuss, C. La catastrophe de Saint-Gervais. 1899. IV. 186.¹
Kutsch, (Forstassessor). Die Stellung des Buchenhochwaldes im deutschen Nationalvermögen. 1898. IV. 499.
Kutsomitopulos, Demetrius. Beitrag zur Kenntniss des deutschen und österr. Forsthäume. 1869. III. 435.¹
Kutter. In wie fern kann die Wirthschaftseinrichtung durch die Flächeneintheilung . . . in Anwendung gebracht werden? 1844. IV. 242.
Kutter, Ing. Von den mathematischen Gesetzen, welche sich beim Wachsthum . . . finden lassen. 1869. IV. 232.
Kutter, W. R. Auf welche Weise lassen sich die Waldtheilungen . . . ausführen? 1844. IV. 309.¹
Kutuzof, V. N. Deutsch-russisch-französisches und französisch-russisch-deutsches forsttechnisches Wörterbuch. See Кутузовъ, В. Н. 1896. IV. 23.²
— See also Кутузовъ, В. Н.
Kuyper, J. A. B. Eerste naamlijst van zigtbaarbloijende plaanten . . . in de omstreken van Breda. 1826. I. 391.¹
Kuzmintchef, P. See Кузминчевъ, П.
Kuznetzof, Nicolai Ivanovitch. Beiträge zur Flora caucasica. 1892. II. 497.¹
— Diervilla Wagneri nihi. 1899. III. 749.²
— Die russischen Steppen. 1896. I. 366.
— Die Vegetation und die Gewässer des europäischen Russlands. 1900. I. 368.¹
— Zwei neue Rhamnus-Formen. 1892. II. 497.¹
— See also Кузнецовъ, Н.

Kvassay, Jenő. Gonolobus condurango. 1873. III. 693.²
— A Hársfa leveleinek cukortartalma. 1872. II. 516.¹
Kvassay, E. de. Note concernant le phylloxera en Hongrie. 1876. III. 569.²
Květon, J. Ovocné stromy a keře v krasosadech. 1881. III. 203.
Kviakowska, J. von. Erste Anfangsgründe der Botanik. 1823. I. 85.
Kwasnick, W. Sur l'huile essentielle de Kuro-moji. 1892. III. 406.²
Kwa-wi. Livres Kwa-wi traduits du japonais. 1873. I. 462.
Kyber, David. Lexicon rei herbariae trilingue. 1553. I. 72.¹
Kylburg, August. Handbuch der preussischen Forst- und Jagd-Gesetze. 1873. IV. 302, 320.
Kyle, Juan J. J. La Yerba Mate de Caa-Guazú. 1877. III. 531.¹
Kylling, Peter. Viridarium danicum. 1688. I. 351.
Kynaston, E. R. Obst für Alle. 1882. III. 139.
Kyriakos, Georgios. See ΚΥΡΙΑΚΟΣ, Γεωργιος.
Kytmanof, A. I. See КЫТМАНОВЪ, А. И.

-l. Holzpräparate. 1888. IV. 18.¹
L. Abelia uniflora. 1900. III. 748.²
L. Amorpha canescens. 1900. III. 467.¹
L. Ueber den Anbau der Erle. 1869. IV. 488.²
L. Un ancien domaine forestier du Hainaut. 1899. IV. 357.¹
L. Das Auftreten des Kiefernmark- und Bastkäfers. 1896. IV. 479.
L. Australian Beef-wood. 1881. III. 342.¹
L. Barked Rhododendron stem. 1857. III. 180.¹
L. Der Baumhöhenmesser von Christen. 1892. IV. 216.
L. Den bedste Tid til Udsæd af forskjellige Sorter Træfrø. 1870. III. 156.¹
L. Christen's patent dendrometer. 1892. IV. 216.
L. Duinbeplanting in Nederland. 1897. IV. 160.²
L. Die Eibe in der Vorzeit der skandinavischen Länder. 1898. II. 871.¹
L. Sur l'emploi du bois de Cocotier. 1893. III. 324.¹
L. Ueber forstliche Bildung und forstliche Examen. 1853. IV. 36.¹
L. Glarus. Ausscheidung von Wald und Weide. 1896. IV. 136.¹
L. Over de gouvernements Peperkultuur op Java. 1862. III. 343.¹
L. Grosse Eiche bei Žitomišljić. 1897. IV. 516.¹
L. Hardy trees and shrubs in fruit. 1900. III. 208.¹
L. Hypericum Kalmianum. 1900. III. 610.¹
L. Is de Liberia-Koffie als gouvernementscultuur wenschelijk te achten? 1887. III. 743.¹
L. List of 153 trees. See LOCKWOOD, G. 1876. I. 470.¹
L. Misslingen der Schwarzkiefer-Saaten. 1866. IV. 465.²
L. Nogle Bemærkningen de danske Statsskove vedkommende. 1854. IV. 343.¹
L. Sambucus pubens maxima. 1900. III. 751.²
L. De Sandelboom. 1888. IV. 519.²
L. Om Virkningen af den forløbne Vinter paa forskjellige Planter. 1855. III. 44.²
L. Vitis gongylodes. 1876. III. 544.¹
L. Ein Wort zum Schutze des Tannenhehers. 1889. IV. 90.¹
L., von. Ueber den Anbau des Lerchenholzes. 1791. IV. 448.¹
L., A. Den forløbne Vinters Indvirkning paa forskjellige træagtige Planter. 1853. III. 44.²
L., A. Traité sur la nature chimique. See LATOUCHE, A. 1855. III. 739.
L., B. de. Le Marronnier du 20 mars. 1864. II. 482.¹
L., B. von. Versuch eines theoretischen Beweises der Zuverlässigkeit der . . . neuen Holz-Taxations-Methode. 1803. IV. 253.
L., B. F. The English Ivy wild. 1878. II. 649.²
L., C. The Lucombe Oak and seed-sowing. 1894. III. 162.
L., C. Rozsáhlost ruských lesních revírů. 1896. IV. 289.¹
L., Ch. Spiraea prunifolia with double flowers. 1847. II. 315.¹
L., E. A. La nouvelle maison de campagne. See A., L. E. 1854. III. 113.
L., E. A. M. The Mistletoe. 1881. II. 180.¹
L., E. L. Corners in an old-fashioned garden. 1892. III. 750.²
L., F. A. Dripping of water from trees. 1896. I. 169.¹

L., G. India rubber for grafting. 1845. III. 160.
L., G. May I give my Conifers guano? 1858. III. 291.
L., G. Untersuchung der technischen Eigenschaften der Bauhölzer. 1883. IV. 408.
L., J. Abrégé pour les arbres nains et autres. See LAURENT, J. 1675. III. 143.
L., J. Euphorbia canariensis. 1898. II. 442.¹
L., J. Greffe des tiges herbacées des Rosiers. 1851. III. 452.
L., J. P. Forestry at home and abroad. See LESLEY, J. P. 1880. IV. 336.¹
L., J. R. Pyrus americana DC. 1877. II. 311.²
L., J. W. Some notably large trees. 1884. I. 295.²
L., K. Die Waldbienenzucht in Russland. 1883. IV. 439.
L., L. Le Café; opuscule poëtique. 1831. III. 738.
L., L. A graceful trailer. 1882. III. 339.¹
L., R. I. The American Crab. 1881. III. 429.¹
L., R. I. Crataegus Oxyacantha var. borrida. 1898. III. 422.¹
L., R. I. Cunonia capensis. 1881. III. 416.²
L., R. I. The cut-leaved Bramble. 1882. III. 458.²
L., R. I. Dillenia speciosa. 1881. III. 595.²
L., R. I. Leptospermum scoparium grandiflorum. 1897. III. 636.
L., R. I. Winter's Bark. 1882. III. 397.¹
L., R. J. Arctotis aspera var. arborescens. 1883. III. 754.¹
L., R. J. The Caper plant. 1881. III. 408.²
L., R. J. The Hand-flower tree. 1881. III. 590.¹
L., S. Koelreuteria paniculata. 1900. III. 539.²
L., S. de. L'Aulne blanc. 1900. IV. 489.²
L., S. de. Les gelées . . . en Flandre et en Ardenne. 1900. IV. 192.¹
L., S. de. L'Orme de Sully. 1900. IV. 518.²
L., S. de. Le Pin Laricio. 1896. IV. 466.²
L., S. de. Quelques gros arbres de la France. 1898. IV. 85.²
L., S. de. Résistance des résineaux à la gelée. 1896. III. 293.
L., S. D. Diminuiamo i danni della mosca olearia. 1899. III. 678.¹
L., V. La fécondation artificelle de la Vigne. 1894. III. 54.²
L., V. La greffe bout à bout. 1895. III. 163.¹
L., W. H. Foliation. 1876. I. 222.¹
L., W. H. Separation of sexes in trees. 1877. I. 200.
L. T., A. Situation forestière en Russie. See LE TELLIER, Augustin. 1894. IV. 346.
L . . . . n. Wald und Waldwirthschaft in Russland. 1886. IV. 114.
L.—r. Lückenhieb oder Besamungsschlag? 1888. IV. 128.
L*, M. F.** Abrégé élémentaire des principes de botanique. 1807. I. 84.
L*, S.** Ueber Anbau . . . der . . . Kaffeh-Ersatzmittel. 1808. III. 454.¹
Laag, J. ter. Ziekte in de Populieren. 1877. III. 344.²
La Baïsse, de. Dissertation sur la circulation de la sève. 1733. I. 162.
Laban, F. C. Flora der Umgegend von Hamburg und Altona. 1865. I. 385.
— Flora des Herzogthums Holstein. 1866. I. 385.
— Garten-Flora für Norddeutschland. 1867. I. 270, III. 169.
La Barre, Gaston de. Notice sur la culture de l'Osier en France. 19 . . ? III. 349.
Labarthe, B. S. Étude sur la cueilletté . . . des matières résineuses. 1874. IV. 437.¹
Labat, Jean Baptiste. Nouveau voyage aux isles de l'Amérique. 1722. III. 266.
— Nouvelle relation de l'Afrique occidentale. 1728. I. 490.
Labat, Léon. De l'irritabilité des plantes. 1834. I. 197.¹
Labau. Guérison des Vignes phylloxérées. 1878. III. 571.
Labbé, H. See BOSC, L. A. G., LABBÉ, H. & FÉBURIER.
Labbé, Henry. See BÉNARDEAU, Fabien & LABBÉ, Henry.
— & **Bénardeau, Fabien.** Notice sur le rôle . . . de la photographie dans le service du reboisement. 1886. I. 37,² IV. 163.
Labeyrie. See GOULIN & LABEYRIE.
Labhart-Luatz. Mittheilungen aus Manila. 1873. III. 321.¹
— Riesenbäume in Californien. 1869. II. 51,¹ V. xxv.²
— Die Riesenpedern Californiens. 1869. II. 51,¹ V. xxv.²
Labillardière, Jacques Julien Houton de. Sur le Cocotier des Maldives. 1807. II. 70.²
— Icones plantarum Syriae rariorum. 1791. I. 480.
— Mémoire sur deux espèces di Litchi. 1806. II. 487.¹
— Mémoire sur le Palmier Nipa. 1819. II. 71.²

— Mémoire sur le Sagoutier des Moluques. 1801. II. 61.[2]
— Mémoire sur un nouveau genre de Palmier. 1809. II. 74.[1]
— Mémoire sur un nouveau genre (l'Areng à sucre). 1803. II. 64.[2]
— Novae Hollandiae plantarum specimen. 1804. I. 500.
— Relation du voyage à la recherche de La Pérouse. 1799. I. 302.
— Sertum austro-caledonicum. 1824. I. 508.[2]
La Blanchère, Henri de. Les oiseaux utiles et les oiseaux nuisibles. 1875. IV. 198.[2]
— Les ravageurs des forêts. 1866. IV. 92.
— Les ravageurs des vergers et des Vignes. 1876. III. 570.[1]
— & Robert, Eugène. Les ravageurs des forêts et des arbres d'alignement. 1876. IV. 92.
La Blanchère, Pierre René Henri Moullin Du Coudray de. See La Blanchère, Henri de.
Labollita, Gioacchino. Idee generali per regolamenti sulla economia delle capre. 1867. IV. 135,[2] 328.
Laboratoire de botanique générale de l'université de Genève. Bulletin. I. 26.[2]
Laboratorio botanico della R. Università di Siena. Bulletino. I. 25.
Laboratorio di botanica crittogamica presso la R. università di Pavia. Archivio. III. 23.[2]
Laboratorium für Waarenkunde an der Wiener Handels-Akademie. Mittheilungen. III. 25.
Laborde, Eugène. Étude . . . des Murrays. 1898. III. 504.[2]
Laborde, J. Étude des écorces de coto. 1886. III. 260.[1]
La Borde, Roger de. Le Pommier et le cidre. 1896. III. 426.[2]
Laborie. Contribution à la flore du département du Tarn. 1889. I. 417.
— Sur le mode de végétation du Jujubier. 1887. II. 500.[1]
— Sur les variations anatomiques . . . des rameaux. 1883. I. 105.
Laborie, E. Sur l'anatomie des pédoncules. 1884. I. 113.[2]
Laborie, P. J. The Coffee planter of Saint Domingo. 1798. III. 728.[2]
— Cultivo del Cafeto. 1809. III. 726.[2]
Laborier, (abbé). Procédés nouveaux pour cultiver la Vigne. 1882. III. 556.
Laboulbène, Alexandre. Essai d'une théorie sur la production des diverses galles. 1892. I. 214.[1]
— Sur un insecte coléoptère attaquant les Vignes. 1890. III. 564.[1]
— Métamorphoses de la Cécidomyie du Buis. 1873. III. 523.[1]
Labourasse, H. Xylométrie usuelle. n. d. IV. 220.
Labouret, J. Culture des Cactées. 1855. III. 619.
— Monographie de la famille des Cactées. 1858. II. 586.[1]
— Note relative à un caractère du genre Mamillaria. 1854. II. 594.[2]
— Note sur un caractère différentiel des Cactées. 1855. II. 588.[1]
— Sur quelques Cactées nouvelles. 1855. II. 586.[1]
La Bourgoulière, A. J. de. Théorème sur l'accroissement des massifs forestiers. 1881. IV. 233.
The Labrador Tea plant. 1878. III. 653.[1]
Labram, J. David. Sammlung der Zierpflanzen. 1835. III. 89.[2]
Labrie, A. R. P. À Seringueira. 1873. III. 519.[1]
La Bretonnerie, de. L'école du jardin fruitier. 1784. III. 143.
La Brillantais, Marion de. Quelques observations sur l'approvisionnement des bois. 1827. IV. 425.[1]
La Briselainne, Ameline de. See Johanet, Henri & La Brise-lainne, Ameline de.
La Brosse, Guy de. Catalogue des plantes . . . au Jardin royal. 1641. I. 56.
— Description du Jardin royal des plantes . . . à Paris. 1636. I. 56.
— Icones plantarum Horti regii parisiensis. 163.? I. 56.
— De la nature, vertu et utilité des plantes. 1628. I. 285.[1]
— Reliquiae operis historici plantarum in Horto regio parisiensi. 163.? I. 56.
La Brousse, de. Mélanges d'agriculture. 1789. III. 125.
— A methodical treatise on the cultivation of the Mulberry tree. 1789. III. 373.
— Des Mûriers. 1789. III. 373.
— Traité de la culture du Figuier. 1774. III. 369.[1]
— Traité sur l'Olivier. 1789. III. 675.[1]
— Traité sur le Figuier. 1774. III. 369.[b]
A Laburnum walk. 1900. III. 480.[2]

Laby, E. Pée-. See Pée-Laby, E.
Labzin, N. F. See Лабзинъ, Н. Ф.
Lac, J. L. Alléon du. See Alléon du Lac, J. L.
The Lac industry of Assam. 1900. III. 232.[2]
Lacaille, Hippolyte. Culture du Pommier. 1886. III. 426.[2]
— Rapport sur l'exposition et le congrès de l'Association pomologique de l'Ouest. 1887. III. 85.
Lacanal. Sur les Épiphylles. 1861. II. 593.[2]
— Floraison des Cerei acifer et Roemeri. 1860. III. 621.[1]
Lacaze-Duthiers, F. G. H. Recherches pour servir à l'histoire des galles. 1853. I. 214.[1]
— & Riche, Alfred. Recherches sur l'alimentation des insectes gallicoles. 1853. I. 214.[1]
Lacaze-Duthiers, Felix Joseph Henri de. Address on scientific terminology and nomenclature. 1893. I. 71.
Lacerda, J. H. & Hemsley, W. B. A sketch of the vegetation of British Baluchistan. 1891. I. 477.[2]
Lacerda, Antonio de. See Couty, Louis & Lacerda, Antonio de.
Lacerda, Augusto de Abreu. See Abreu Lacerda, Augusto de.
Lacerda, João Baptista de. Sur l'action toxique du suc de Manioc. 1881. III. 521.[1]
Lacerda Lobo, Constantino Botelho de. See Botelho de Lacerda Lobo, Constantino.
La Chapelle, A. H. de. Nâgra för Finlands flora nya barlastväxter. 1891. II. 361.[1]
La Chapelle, Charles de. La Rose et le Rosier. 1882. III. 450.
La Chataigneraye, de, (abbé). La connoissance parfaite des arbres fruitiers. 1692. III. 143.
Lachaume, Jean. Le Rosier. 1874. III. 449.
Lachaume, Jules. Agricultor cubano: Plantas textiles. 1888. III. 235.[1]
— Mangifera maritima. 1870. III. 525.[1]
— Méthode élémentaire pour tailler . . . les Pêchers. 1857. III. 440.[1]
— Moyen d'obtenir deux floraisons du Magnolia grandiflora. 1857. III. 399.[2]
— Moyen d'obtenir deux floraisons successives du Magnolia grandiflora. 1857. III. 399.[2]
— Sur la rusticité des Mahonias du Japon. 1857. III. 395.[2]
Lachausse, J. X. E. P. Acacias officinalis historia. See Spielmann, J. R. 1768. III. 443.[1]
La Chenal, Werner de. Observationes botanico-medicae. 1776. II. 262.[1]
— Specimen inaugurale observationum botanicarum. 1759. I. 97, 433.
La Chenaye-des-Bois. Dictionnaire universel d'agriculture et de jardinage. 1751. III. 30.
Lachénès, Bertrand. See Besnou, Léon & Lachénée, Bertrand.
Lachenmeyer, Johann C. Untersuchungen über die Farbenveränderungen der Blüthen. See Schübler, Gustav. 1833. I. 184.
Lachmann. Eine monströse Birne. 1860. II. 279.[2]
— Ueber die Summe der Wärme, welche nötig ist, die Lebensthätigkeit . . . zu erwecken. 1857. IV. 72.
Lachmann, (Secretair des Vereins zur Förderung des Gartenbaues in Braunschweig). Mittheilung . . . über die Apfelblattlaus. 1841. III. 427.[1]
Lachmann, Heinrich Wilhelm Ludolph. Flora brunsvicensis. 1827. I. 377.
Lachmann, Paul. Note sur les folioles ascidiées d'un Staphylea pinnata. 1886. II. 473.[2]
— Notice sur le Jardin botanique de Buitenzorg. 1885. I. 68.[1]
Lachmann, W. Die Entwickelung der Vegetation durch die Wärme. 1855. I. 224.[2]
Lachomette, P. de. Une nouvelle variété de Mélèze. 1869. IV. 449.
Lachot, Henry. Flore de l'arrondissement de Semur. 1885. I. 417.
Lacipière, P. Leopold. Des émétiques végétaux. 1854. III. 245.
Lackawanna institute of history and science. Proceedings. I. 5.
Lackner, Carl. Ueber die Orangen. 1881. III. 497.[1]
Lackowitz, Wilhelm. Flora von Berlin. 1868. I. 386, 532.[1]
— Flora von Nord- und Mittel-Deutschland. 1879. I. 388.
Laclotte, Marie Jacques Philippe, Mouton-Fontenille de. See Mouton-Fontenille de Laclotte, J. P.
Lacoizqueta, José María de. Catálogo de las plantas . . . de Vertizarana. 1884. I. 422.

La Condamine, Charles Marie de. Sur l'arbre du Quinquina. 1740. III. 719.
Lacoste, C.. Cours d'herborisation. 1871. I. 35.
— La flore française vulgarisée. 1868. I. 413.
Lacouperie, l'errien de. The tree of life. 1887. I. 514.¹
Lacour. Sur le Maté. 1870. III. 531.¹
Lacour, CONTEST-. See CONTEST-LACOUR.
Lacour, Eymard. See RENARD, Ernest & LACOUR, Eymard.
Lacour, GOUFFÉ DE. See GOUFFÉ DE LACOUR.
La Cour, J. C. Om Hedernes Benyttelse. 1866. IV. 156.¹
— Om Opdyrkning af Vestjyllands Heder. 1868. IV. 156.²
La Cour, Paul. Skovenes Indflydelse paa Varmen. 1870-IV. 53.
La Court, W. de. Iets over de Amerikäansche Eiken. 1889. IV. 501.¹
La Croix, Demetrius de, (pseud. of MacEncroe). Connubia florum. 1728. I. 198.
— Les mariages des fleurs. 1728. I. 198.
Lacroix, Louis Sosthène Veyron. Nouveaux faits constatés relativement à l'histoire de la botanique ... de la Vienne. 1857. I. 411.
Lacroix, S. de. Influence des verres colorés. 1853. I. 229.
Lacroze, J. GAUTIER-. See GAUTIER-LACROZE, J.
Lade. Zur Frage gleichzeitigen Anbaues der Eiche und Buche. 1897. IV. 138.¹
Lade, Ed. von. Der Obst-und Gartenbau in Monrepos. 1893. III. 121.¹
Lademann, Johann Matthias Friedrich. De systematibus plantarum. 1785. I. 251.
Ladenburg, Albert. Sur les alcaloïdes ... de la Belladone. 1880. III. 700.¹
La Devansaye, Alphonse de. Dimorphantus mandschuricus. 1873. III. 641.¹
— Emploi de la tannée. 1874. III. 595.¹.
— Exposition internationale d'horticulture de Belgique. 1876. III. 77.¹
— Introduction de nouveaux Pritchardia. 1874. III. 332.¹
— Palmiers, les Coryphinées. 1875. III. 317.
— Palmiers nouveaux. 1873. III. 317.
— Les Palmiers nouveaux. 1876. III. 317.
— Palmiers qu'il convient de cultiver dans l'eau. 1874. III. 317.
— Sur quelques genres de Palmiers. 1874. III. 317.
— Sur quelques Palmiers nouveaux. 1774. III. 317.
The Ladies' floral cabinet. III. 4.
Ladoucette. Deboisement et reboisement. 1845. IV. 43.
— Sur la proposition de défricher les forêts. 1836. IV. 275.
Ladureau, Albert. Note sur la composition ... des farines de Cocotier. 1879. III. 319.¹
— Du rôle des corps gras dans la germination. 1880. I. 203.
The Lady's book. III. 4.
Laece boc (Leech book). 1865. III. 243.
Läis, E. D. Die Stock- und Vogteiguts-Besitzer der Eifel ... wider ihre Gemeinden. 1830. IV. 333.
Laemmerhirt, Otto. Die Obstverwertung. 1885. III. 174.¹
— Ueber die Ursachen der Unfruchtbarkeit der Obstbäume. 1881. III. 138, 174.²
— Die wichtigsten Obstbaumschädlinge. 1898. III. 191.
Lärchen in Graubündten. 1886. IV. 452.¹
Laërne, K. F. van DELDEN. See DELDEN LAËRNE, K. F. van.
La Escoura y Coronel, Luis de. Breves consideraciones sobre estática quimica forestal. 1879. IV. 60,¹ 63.²
— Manual del capataz de cultivos. 1877. IV. 99,¹ 109.²
Laestadius, Lars Levi. Beskrifning öfver några sällsyntare växter från norra delarne af Sverige. 1824. I. 353.
— Bidrag till kännedomen om växtligheten i Torneå Lappmark. 1860. I. 355.
— Botaniska anmärkningar, gjorda i Lappmarken. 1822. I. 353.
— Loca parallela plantarum. 1839. I. 244.¹
Laet, Joannes de. Beschrijvinghe van West-Indien. 1630. III. 266.
— L'histoire du nouveau monde. 1630. III. 266.
— Novus orbis. III. 266.
Laey, D. de. L'Aubépine comme sujet du Poirier. 1883. III. 422.²
— De Hagedoorn als entstam voor de Peren. 1883. III. 422.³
Lafarge, J. A. BAUDET-. See BAUDET-LAFARGE, J. A.
Lafargue, Eug. Quelques considérations ... sur les racines du Viscum. 1847. II. 178.¹
Lafaurie, J. Sur un procédé de préparation du sulfure de carbone. 1880. III. 572.

Laffay-Fournier. Moyen de faire fructifier les Camellia. 1830. III. 599.¹
Laffemas, Barthélemy de. La façon de faire. 1877. III. 378.
Laffon, J. C. Flora des Cantons Schaffhausen. 1847. I. 434.
Laffont, Marc. Analyse de l'action physiologique de la cocaïne. 1887. III. 493.¹
Lafitau, Joseph François. Mœurs des sauvages Ameriquains. 1724. IV. 527.¹
Lafitte, Prosper de. Le badigeonnage des Vignes phylloxérées. 1887. III. 574.
— Les badigeonnages et les charrues sulfureuses. 1885. III. 561.
— Sur les causes de réinvasion des vignobles phylloxérées. 1879. III. 571.
— Sur la défense de la Vigne. 1886. III. 574.
— Discours sur le phylloxéra. 1878. III. 760.
— Sur les élevages de phylloxera en tubes. 1885. III. 573.
— Sur l'emploi des huiles lourdes de houille. 1882. III. 573.
— Sur l'emploi du bitume de Judée. 1882. III. 561.
— Sur l'emploi du sulfate de cuivre pour la destruction du mildew. 1884. III. 578.
— Essai sur la destruction de l'œuf d'hiver du phylloxéra. 1879. III. 760.
— Sur l'essaimage du phylloxera. 1880. III. 572.
— Sur l'histoire du phylloxera de la Vigne. 1887. III. 574.
— L'œuf d'hiver du phylloxera. 1879. III. 571.
— Sur l'œuf d'hiver du phylloxera. 1881. III. 573.
— L'œuf d'hiver du phylloxera. 1887. III. 574.
— Quatre ans de luttes pour nos Vignes. 1883. III. 761.
— Recherches expérimentales sur la marche, dans les tissus de la Vigne, d'un liquide. 1883. II. 508.²
— Une tête de jacquez, greffée. 1879. III. 548.²
— Sur les traitements des Vignes par le sulfure dé carbone. 1880. III. 560. — 1885. III. 561.
Lafon de Caudaval. Nouveau mode de greffage algérien. 1864. III. 161.
Lafond, A. Fixation des dunes. 1900. IV. 186.³
— Projet d'aménagement ... des forêts de Chênes-Liège. 1896. IV. 518.¹
Lafons, Alexandre de, baron de Melicocq. Des arbres et des arbrisseaux designés ... sous le nom de mort-bois. 1859. IV. 23,¹ 388.²
— Du bois d'If. 1857. IV. 440.¹
— De la culture de la Vigne en grand. 1858. III. 555.
— Sur la culture du Mûrier blanc. 1856. III. 377.
— Encoré un mot sur la pélorie du Linaria. 1859. II. 687.²
— Encore un mot sur le Buis. 1856. II. 453.¹
— Les forêts du nord de la France. 1860. IV. 27.¹
— Note sur les Pêchers. 1865. III. 440.²
— Note sur le Vaccinium Myrtillus et Vitis Idaea. 1858. II. 685.¹
— Prodrome de la flore des arrondissements de Laon. 1839. I. 409.
Lafont, J. See BOUCHARDAT, G. & LAFONT, J.
La Fontaine, Pe. Poeme du quinquina. 1682. III. 719.
La Fontaine, Alphonse de. Effets des grands froids de l'hiver 1879 à 1880. 1881. III. 46.¹
Laforcade. Fructification ... du Maclura. 1867. III. 372.¹
— La science pittoresque. 1899. IV. 362.
Laforest, L. Nos forêts et leurs hôtes. 188.? I. 404.²
Lafosse, Pierre JOSEPH-. See JOSEPH-LAFOSSE, Pierre.
Lag. Le Jujubier. 1892. III. 544.¹
— Le " Kaki du Japon." 1891. III. 669.²
— Le Mûrier de la Chine. 1892. III. 368.¹
Lagalisserie, P. de. See LEGUAY, Léon & LAGALISSERIE, P. de.
La Garde, Th., comte de. Le reboisement des landes du Périgord. 1878. IV. 163.
Lagardette, Eugène. Anthyllis barba Jovis. 1857. III. 467.¹
— Les Cistus indigènes. 1857. II. 564.¹
— Lavatera arborea. 1857. III. 588.²
La Gardie, Eva de. Beskrifning på tvål. 1752. III. 226.¹
Lagasca y Segura, Mariano. Amenidades naturales de las Españas. 1811. I. 33.
— Disertacion sobre un orden nuevo ... de las Compuestas. 1811. III. 847.²
— Elenchus plantarum ... in Horto regio botanico matritensi. 1816. I. 60.¹
— Genera et species plantarum. 1816. I. 266.
— Memoria sobre las plantas Barrilleras de España. 1817. I. 420.

— & Rodriguez, Joseph. Descripcion de algunas plantas del Real jardin botánico. 1801. I. 60.[1]
— — — Descripciones de algunas plantas nuevas. 1802. II. 731.[1]
— — — De las plantas que . . . Broussonet colectó. 1803. I. 484.
Die Lage der Forstwirthschaft in Bosnien und der Herzegowina. 1894. IV. 374.[2]
Lager, Jean SAINT-. See SAINT-LAGER, Jean.
Lagerheim, Carl & Sjögren, Gustaf. Botaniska anteckningar under en resa . . . till fjället Snasahögen. 1845. I. 354.
Lagerheim, Gustaf. Über das Auftreten von Chrysomyxa Rhododendri. 1894. III. 657.[1]
— Beiträge zu einer Monographie der Salix-Parasiten. 1894. III. 250.[2]
— Zur Biologie der Jochroma macrocalyx Benth. 1891. II. 772.[1]
— Einige neue Acarocecidien und Acarodomatien. 1892. II. 768.[1]
— Erineum-Bildungen an Solanaceen. 1892. II. 768.[1]
— Die "Mancha" der Kakaobäume. 1892. III. 593.[3]
— Monographie der ecuadorianischen . . . Brugmansia. 1895. II. 771.[1]
— Eine neue, goldgelbe Brugmansia (B. aurea Lagerh.). 1893. II. 771.[1]
— Sur un nouveau parasite dangereux de la Vigne. 1890. III. 580.
— Pflanzenpathologische Mitteilungen aus Ecuador. 1892. III. 593.[2]
— Ueber ein Phytoptocecidium an . . . Opuntia. 1892. III. 625.[1]
— Die Siempreviva von Quito. 1893. II. 236.[1]
Lagerheim, N. G. Nya acarodomatier. 1890. I. 215.[1]
Lagerheim, Nils. Några vextställen för Westergötland. 1844. II. 116.[2]
Lagerstedt, Nils Gerhard Wilhelm. Teratologiskt meddelande om Azalea indica och Berberis. 1881. II. 205,[1] 680.[2]
Lagger & Puget. Description de nouvelles Roses. 1874. II. 287.[1]
— — Description de nouvelles Roses . . . trouvées par M. de La Soie. 1873. II. 286.[2]
Lagger, Fr. Die Flora vom Kanton Freiburg. 1841. I. 434.
Laghius, Thomas. De rubentibus lignorum cineribus. 1747. I. 154.
La Gironière, Paul de. Aventures . . . aux Îles Philippines. 1855. III. 274.[1]
Lagos Palm Oil. 1892. III. 325.[1]
Lagos rubber. 1888. III. 371.[2]
Lagrave, Édouard TIMBAL-. See TIMBAL-LAGRAVE, Édouard.
Lagrèze-Fossat, Adrien. Flore de Tarn et Garonne. 1847. I. 410.
Notes sur des fentes observées sur le tube du calice du Grosseillier. 1859. II. 244.[1]
— Notes sur les feuilles de l'Aloe fruticosa. 1855. II. 78.[1]
— Notice géologico-botanique sur l'arrondissement de Moissac. 1838. I. 409.
La Groye, Menard de. Note sur un effet . . . que présente la coupe transversale. 1826. II. 44.[2]
Laguarrigue. Valeur et débit du Buis. 1896. IV. 525.
Laguerre, J. N. Essai sur le Café. 1010. III. 738.
Laguesse, J. B. Alphonse. Promenades botaniques. 1877. I. 415.
— Promenades botaniques en Bourgogne. 1880. I. 416.
Laguna, Andrés de. Annotationes in Dioscoridem. 1554. I. 279.
— Pedanio Dioscorides Anazarbeo Acerca de la materia medicinal y de los venenos mortíferos. 1554. I. 279.
Laguna, Maximo. See LAGUNA Y VILLANUEVA, Maximo.
Laguna y Villanueva, Maximo. Abetos y Pinsapos. 1869. II. 22.[1]
— El Abies Pinsapo. 1880. IV. 447.[1]
— Agallas de los Robles. 1880. IV. 518.[2]
— El Alcornoque. 1883. IV. 517.[3]
— Apuntes sobre un nuevo Roble . . . de la flora de Filipinas. 1875. II. 134.[2]
— Caracteres de la flora española. 1884. IV. 86.[1]
— Caracteres de la flora española; discurso pronunciado. 1884. I. 422.
— Comision de la flora forestal española. 1870. I. 419,[1] IV. 85.[2]
— Coniferas y Amentáceas españolas. 1878. I. 419,[2] IV. 85.[1]
— La Coscoja. 1883. IV. 503.[1]

— Cupresíneas. Género Juniperus. 1880. IV. 448.[2]
— Descripción y apreciación del Palmeral de Elche. 1900. III. 329.[1]
— La Encina. 1883. IV. 503.[1]
— Excursión forestal por los imperios de Austria y Rusia. 1866. IV. 345, 367.
— La flora americana. 1892. I. 330, IV. 76.[1]
— Flora forestal española. 1883. I. 419.[2]
— Un folleto forestal del Sr. Barros Gomes. 1877. IV. 502.[2]
— Género "Abies." 1880. IV. 444.[2]
— Les hybrides du genre Chêne. 1881. II. 130.[1]
— Memoria de reconocimiento de la Sierra de Guadarráma. 1864. IV. 164,[2] 363.[1]
— Un Mesto italiano y varios Mestos españoles. 1881. II. 30.[1]
— Montes y plantas. 1891. IV. 86,[1] 102.
— Nota fenológica. 1897. IV. 543.[2]
— Observaciones sobre las temperaturas minimas que pueden soportar los vegetales. 1872. III. 43.
— Un pedazo de Sierra-Morena. 1868. IV. 363.[1]
— Pinos. 1870. II. 39.[2]
— El Pinsapar de Ronda. 1868. II. 24,[2] IV. 363.[1]
— Les Pinsapos de Ronda. 1868. II. 24.[2]
— Pinus. 1878. IV. 463.[1]
— El P. halepensis . . . y el P. pinaster. 1880. IV. 461.[1]
— Pinus Laricio. 1880. IV. 465.[2]
— Pinus montana. 1880. IV. 464.[2]
— El Quejigo y la Quejigueta. 1879. IV. 502.[2]
— Quercus (Ciclobalanus [sic]) Jordanae. 1875. II. 134.[2]
— El Roble (Quercus Jordanae) de la flora de Filipinas. 1875. II. 134.[2]
— Taxineas. Género Taxus. 1881. IV. 440.[2]
— El Valle Iruelas. 1879. IV. 363.[1]
— & Avila, Pedro de. Flora forestal española. 1875. IV. 85.[2]
— — Pinus sylvestris. 1879. IV. 480.
— — & Satorras, Luis. Memoria de reconocimiento de los montes de Sierra Bullones. 1861. IV. 363.[1]
Lagune, von, (Forstrath). Ueber die Korkeichenwälder Afrika's. 1866. IV. 517.[2]
Lagusi, Vincenzo. Erbuario italo-siciliano. 1743. I. 291, II. 88.[1]
La Harpe, Jean de. See DELAHARPE, Jean.
Lahaye. Rapport sur le régime forestier de la Cochinchine. 1883. IV. 377.[1]
Lahaye, P. M. Sur les maladies des fruits. 1866. III. 178.
— Traité sur les causes des maladies organiques. 1862. III. 178.
— Das Verhältniss der Frucht zum Baum. 1866. III. 178.
Lahérard. Clematis barbellata Edgeworth. 1858. III. 390.[1]
La Hire, Jean Nicolas de. Explication physique de la direction . . . des tiges. 1709. I. 195.[1]
— Observation sur les Figues. 1714. II. 150.[1]
Lahontan, Jean, baron de. Memoires de l'Amérique Septentrionale. 1703. III. 261.[1]
— Nouveaux voyages dans l'Amérique Septentrionale. 1703. III. 261.[1]
Laicharding, Johann Nepomuk. Manuale botanicum. 1794. I. 348.[2]
— Vegetabilia europeae. 1790. I. 348.[2]
Laidley, Theodore Thaddeus Sobieski. Strength of wood grown on the Pacific slope. 1881. IV. 410.
L'Aigue, Étienne de. In omnes Plinii Secundi Naturalis historiae libros commentaria. 1530. I. 276.
Lailler, A. Nouveaux faits pour servir à l'histoire de l'huile d'olive. 1865. III. 678.[2]
Laine végétale tirée des feuilles du Pin sylvestre. 1853. IV. 482.[1]
Lair, Pierre Aimé. Description des jardins de Couret. 1814. I. 57.
Laird, J. L. On coomrie cultivation. 1876. IV. 133.
Laire, G. de. La coniferina. 1878. IV. 443.[3]
— Recolecion de la coniferina. 1878. IV. 443.[3]
— Récolte de la coniférine. 1878. IV. 443.[3]
Laisné, O. Traitement de la chlorose. 1887. III. 181.[1]
Laisney, Louis. Dissertation sur quelques plantes vénéneuses. 1806. III. 53.[2]
Laitre, vicomte de. Observations au sujet d'un article de M. Broilliard. 1895. IV. 246.
— Réponse à l'article "Le Chalet-Brûlé." 1896. IV. 140.
Lajara Belda, Vincente. Habla la ciencia. 1897. IV. 542.[1]
Lajard, Félix. Recherches sur le culte du Cyprès. 1847. II. 29.[2]

Lajoux, Henri. *See* GRANDVAL, Alexandre & LAJOUX, Henri.

Lakanal. Notice sur différents essais faits pour introduire aux États-Unis la culture de la Vigne. 1836. III. 549,[2] 675.[1]

Lake, E. R. Prune culture in the Pacific northwest. 1895. III. 433.[1]

Lake, W. F. The Spiraeas. 1890. III. 460.[2]

Lake Bigler forestry commission. Report. 1884. IV. 340.

Lakowitz, Wilhelm. Ein aussterbender Nadelbaum der europäischen Waldflora. 1897. II. 38.[1]

Lal Rai Bahadur Kunhya. Useful rules and tables relating to measurement of timber. 1869. IV. 226.

— & others. Deodar versus steel sleepers. 1888. IV. 424.[1]

Lala Thakur Das. Isharat Naqual Bandi, Punjaub. 1874. III. 129.[2]

Lalanne, Gaston. Recherches sur les caractères anatomiques des feuilles persistantes. 1890. I. 111.

— Recherches sur les cristaux minéraux des feuilles de Citrus. 1892. II. 401.[2]

La Laurencie, de. Pratique de plantation et greffage. 1895. III. 557.[1]

La Laurencie, L. de. La carrière forestière en Prusse. 1883. IV. 290.[1]

— Les forêts de l'Espagne. 1889. IV. 363.[1]

Lalesque, Fernand. Arcachon, ville d'été, ville d'hiver. 1886. I. 417.

Laliman, E. À messieurs les viticulteurs. 1888. III. 760.

Laliman, Léopold. Étude sur les divers phylloxéra. 1871. III. 759.

— Études sur les divers travaux phylloxériques. 1879. III. 572.

— Greffage par soudure naturelle. 1877. III. 162.

— Sur un insecte destructeur du phylloxera. 1877. III. 570.[1]

— Sur le phylloxera gallicole. 1880. III. 572.

— Sur le Phylloxera vastatrix. 1872. III. 564.[2]

— Résultat d'observations faites sur des Vignes. 1876. III. 563.

Lallemand, Alex. Sur la composition de quelques essences. 1859. III. 611.[1]

— Étude sur la composition de quelques essences. 1859. III. 611.[1]

— Untersuchungen über einige flüchtige Oele. 1859. III. 611.[1]

Lallemand, Ch. Sur quelques doutes émis au sujet des lois du Colonel Goulier. 1897. IV. 265.

Lallemant, Julius Leopold Eduard AVÉ-. *See* AVÉ-LALLEMANT, J. L. E.

Lallemant, Robert Christian Bernhard Avé. Die Benutzung der Palmen. 1861. III. 319.[1]

Lalou, (jr.). Du Café, son origine. 1843. III. 739.

Lalouette. Forêt domaniale d'Eawy. 1865. IV. 360.

La Loyère, *vicomte* de. Du phylloxéra en 1880. 1880. III. 761.

— & Muntz. Sur la production d'huiles sulfurées. 1878. III. 197.

— — Sur la production de combinaisons organiques sulfurées. 1878. III. 197.

La Mance, Lora S. A pretty native vine. 1892. III. 616.[1]

Lamarche, C. Eucalyptus urnigera. 1898. IV. 534.[1]

Lamarck, Jean Baptiste Antoine Pierre Monnet, *chevalier* de. Sur le Calodendrum. 1792. II. 400.[2]

— Flore françoise. 1778. I. 405.

— Sur le genre des Acacies. 1792. II. 325.[2]

— Mémoire sur le genre du Muscadier. 1791. II. 220.[1]

— Mémoire sur les classes les plus convenables à établir parmi les végétaux. 1788. I. 251.

— Mémoire sur un nouveau genre . . . Brucea. 1787. II. 414,[1] 455.[2]

— Sur une nouvelle espèce de Loranthe. 1792. II. 175.[1]

— Sur une nouvelle espèce de Vantane. 1792. II. 394.[1]

— Observations [sur l'Acacie oblique]. 1792. II. 328.[1]

— Sur les ouvrages généraux en histoire naturelle. 1792. I. 264.

— & Candolle, A. P. de. Synopsis plantarum in flora gallica. 1806. I. 406.

— & Mirbel, C. F. Brisseau de. Histoire naturelle des végétaux. 1802. I. 259.

— — Storia naturale dei vegetabili. 1802. I. 259.

— & Poiret, J. L. M. Encyclopédie méthodique . . . Botanique. 1783. I. 32.

— — Tableau encyclopédique . . . Botanique. 1791. I. 32.

Lamarlière, Leon GÉNEAU DE. *See* GÉNEAU DE LAMARLIÈRE, Leon.

Lamarque, G. Culture des Gardenias. 1892. III. 744.[1]

La Marre, Louis Gervais de. Historique de la création d'une richesse millionnaire par la culture des Pins. 1827. IV. 121.

— Mémoire sur la culture des Pins. 1820. IV. 121.

— Traité pratique de la culture des Pins. 1820. IV. 121.

Lamattina, Cav. Luigi. L'agricoltura colla scienza. 1878. III. 115.[2]

— Sulla assimilazione dell' azoto. 1881. I. 173.

Lamayran & others. Expériences relatives à l'écorce du Marronnier d'Inde. 1809. III. 537.[2]

Lamb, Frank Haines. Forest conditions in western Washington. 1898. IV. 341.[1]

— A new pest of the Monterey Pine. 1898. II. 45,[2] III. 308.[2]

— Root suckers on Douglas Fir. 1899. II. 49.[1]

— Timber wealth of Pacific North America. 1898. IV. 337.[1] — 1899. IV. 403.[1]

Lambergen, Tiberius. Oratio inauguralis, exhibens encomia botanices. 1754. III. 238.[1]

Lambert. Nouveau procédé de bouturage. 1855. III. 158.

Lambert & Reiter. Buntblätterige Birne. 1880. III. 445.[1]

Lambert, A. The ceremonial use of flowers. 1878. I. 515.

— Beschreibung der Hyaenanche globosa. 1797. II. 452.[1]

— Catalogue of the valuable botanical library. 1842. I. 2.

— Description of a species of Psidium. 1815. III. 632.[3]

— Description of the genus Cinchona. 1797. II. 811.[2]

— A description of the genus Pinus. 1803. II. 12.[1]

— An illustration of the genus Cinchona. *See* RUIZ LOPEZ, Hipolito. 1805. III. 386.[1]

— An illustration of the genus Cinchona comprising descriptions. 1821. II. 812.

— On a new species of Pinus. 1806. II. 45.[1]

Lambert, Ernest. Eucalyptus. 1872. IV. 529.[2]

— Eucalyptus . . . son role en Algérie. 1863. IV. 531.[1]

— Exploitation des forêts de Chêne-liège. 1860. IV. 379,[1] 517,[1] 536.[1]

— De l'Olivier en Algérie. 1860. III. 675.[2]

Lambert, Étienne. Des cannelles. 1888. III. 403.[2]

Lambert, F. Essai d'une comparaison entre le Mûrier. 1892. III. 380.[1]

— *See also* BOYER, G. & LAMBERT, F.

Lambert, Henry. Forests and forestry in Europe and America. 1893. IV. 288.[1]

Lambert, Lucien. Le commerce des églantiers. 1889. IV. 439.

— Les morts-bois. Le Cornouiller. 1890. IV. 534.[1]

— Le sanglier. 1887. IV. 90.[1]

Lambert, N. Hydrangea Otaksa monstrosa. 1898. III. 412.[1]

Lambert, Wilhelm. De geographia plantarum in Wetteravia et Marchia. 1849. I. 382.

Lambertye, Léonce, *comte* de. Catalogue raisonné des plantes . . . de la Marne. 1846. I. 410.

— Conseils sur le choix . . . des arbres fruitiers. 1895. III. 145.[1]

— Eléments de jardinage. 1873. III. 113.

— Le Figuier de Roscoff. 1874. II. 151.[1]

— Nouvelles observations sur l'emploi de la greffe. 1833. III. 164.[1]

— Les plantes à feuilles ornementales. 1865. III. 205.[2]

Lambillion, L. J. L. Maladie des Chênes. 1900. IV. 511.

Lambin, Émile. La cathédrale et la forêt. 1899. I. 516.

— Les églises des environs de Paris. 1896. I. 516.

— La flore des grandes cathédrales de France. 1897. I. 516.

— La flore gothique. 1893. I. 516.

— Le Peuplier régénéré. 1873. III. 345.[1]

Lamborn, Robert H. A Florida Live Oak. 1892. II. 141.[1]

— The knees of the Bald Cypress. 1890. II. 51.[2]

— The Körner Oak. 1891. II. 139.[1]

Lambot-Miraval. Quelques uns des moyens de remédier aux effets désastreux du déboisement. 1856. IV. 162.

Lambert. III. 162.

Lambry. Exposé d'un moyen mis en pratique pour empêcher la Vigne. 1817. III. 559.[2]

Lamesan, *Freiherr* von. Die Wälder und die Waldnutzungen in Finland. 1884. IV. 347.

Lamey, A. Le Chêne-Liège. 1893. IV. 517.[1]

— Le Chêne-Liège en Algérie. 1879. IV. 517.[2]

— Les insectes nuisibles au Chêne Liège. 1886. IV. 517.[1]

— Note sur deux insectes destructeurs du Liège. 1877. IV. 517.[1]

Lameson. *See* MEAUME, Édouard & LA MÉNARDIÈRE, C. de.

La Ménardière, C. de. *See* MEAUME, Édouard & LA MÉNARDIÈRE, C. de.

Lamic, Joseph. Note sur quelques plantes des environs de Toulouse. 1897. II. 177,² *180*.¹
— Une plante nouvelle pour la . . . Haute-Garonne. 1897. II. 564.¹
— Quelques auomalies [*sic*] végétales. 1896. II. 290.¹·
— La région florale du sud-ouest de la France. 1899. I. 418.
Lammers, G. TOEKAMP. *See* TOEKAMP LAMMERS, G.
Lammotte, Martial. *See* LAMOTTE, Martial.
Lamothe, de. Régénération des forêts résineuses. 1885. IV. 139.²
Lamotte, L. Traité élémentaire d'arpentage. 1845. IV. 213.
Lamotte, Martial. Catalogue des plantes . . . de l'Europe. 1847. I. 349.
— Notes sur quelque plantes nouvelles du plateau central de la France. 1855. I. 411.
— Prodrome de la flore du plateau central de la France. 1877. I. 415.
— *See also* LECOQ, Henri & LAMOTTE, Martial.
Lamounette, B. Recherches sur l'origine . . . du liber in-terne. 1890. I. 131,¹ V. XI.¹
Lamouroux, Justin P. Compendio di botanica. 1826. I. 86.
— Iconographie des familles végétales. 1828. I. 255.
— Résumé complet de botanique. 1826. I. 86.
— Résumé de phytographic. 1828. I. 260.
Lampe, Paul. Zur Kenntniss des Baues . . . saftiger Früchte. 1886. I. 119.
Lampe, Robert. Die " Aestung " als Bestandes- und Baum-pflege. 1880. IV. 171.
— Antikritik. 1869, IV. 498.
— " Der Blitz als Waldverderber." 1874. IV. 194.
— Die Forstdienstorganisations-Frage. 1871. IV. 287.
— " Künstliche " oder " natürliche " Verjüngung. 1865. IV. 139,¹ 141.
— Zur Lehre vom Unter- bez. Zwischenbau der Eiche mit der Fichte. 1880. IV. 507.
— In Sachen: " Künstliche " oder " natürliche " Verjüngung. 1867. IV. 139.¹
— Versuch die Buchen-Hochwald-Wirthschaft mit . . . Finanz-Rechnung in Einklang zu bringen. 1868. IV. 498.
De **Lampongsche** districten. 1852. III. 275.¹
Lamson-Scribner, Frank. *See* SCRIBNER, Frank LAMSON-.
Lamy, (*inspecteur des forêts*). Notice sur la récolte des graines de Pin d'Auvergne. 1885. IV. 465.²
Lamy, VIVENOT-. *See* VIVENOT-LAMY.
Lamy de la Chapelle, Édouard. Sur un cas remarquable de vie ralentie chez un arbre fruitier. 1881. I. 192.¹
— Essai monographique sur le Chataignier. 1860. III. 358.²
— Flore de la Haute-Vienne. 1856. I. 411.
Lamy-Torrilhon, G. *See* SEELIGMANN, Th., LAMY-TORRILHON, G. & FALCONNET, H.
Lana vegetal. 1889. IV. 429.¹
Lana vegetale. 1889. IV. 429.¹
Lancashire — Historic society. *See* HISTORIC . . . I. 18.
Lancaster, Pa. — Franklin and Marshall college. *See* FRANK-LIN . . . I. 519.¹
The **Lancet**. I. 18.
Lancewood spars. 1889. IV. 520.¹
Lançon, R. L'agriculture . . . de Vaucluse. 1855. III. 377.
The **Land** magazine. IV. 539.¹
Der **Land**- und Forstwirth. *See* Der ÖSTERREICHISCHE Forst-wirth IV 15
Die **Land**- und Forstwirthschaft des Fürstenthums Schwarz-burg-Sondershausen. 1862. IV. 25.
Die **Land**- und forstwirthschaftliche Akademie Hohenheim. 1869. IV. 32.
Land- und forstwirthschaftliche Unterrichts-Zeitung. IV. 15.
Das **land**- und forstwirthschaftliche Versuchswesen in dem im Reichsrathe vertretenen . . . Ländern. 1890. IV. 38.²
Land- und forstwirthschaftliche Zeitschrift für Braunschweig. IV. 10.
Land- und forstwirthschaftliche Zeitung . . . Preussen. IV. 10.
Die **Land**- und forstwirthschaftlichen Lehranstalten Oester-reichs. 1879. IV. 36.²
Land- und forstwirthschaftlicher Verein zu Braunschweig. Mittheilungen. IV. 10.
Land- und forstwirthschaftlicher Verwaltungskalender. IV. 15.
The **Land** we love. III. 4.
Landa, Joseph ROMERO FERNANDEZ DE. *See* ROMERO FERNAN-DEZ DE LANDA, Joseph.
Landau, G. Die Waldungen zu halbem Gebrauche in Kurbes-sen. 1855. IV. 25.

Landau, Wilhelm. Vegetationsbilder aus Sizilien. 1879. I. 431.
Landbouw-courant. *See* ALGEMEÉNE landhuishoudelijke courant. III. 14.
Over de **landbouw**-produkten der Lampongs. 1862. III. 275.¹
Landbuch des Kantons Appenzell. 1837. IV. 306.
Lande, Félicien & **Léveillé**, Hector. Evonymus europaeus à fruits blancs. 1895. II. 468.¹
The **landed** gentlemen's useful companion. *See* LANGLEY, Batty. 1728. ·IV. 120.
Landerer, Xaver. Athens Alleen. 1861. III. 209.
— Botanische Mittheilungen. 1859. .III. 454.¹
— Botanische Mitteilungen aus Griechenland. 1857. III. 91.¹
— Botanische Notizen aus Griechenland. 1853. III. 272.¹
— On Cassia fistula. 1852. III. 471.¹
— On Cornus mascula. 1853. III. 646.¹
— On Cyprian Labdanum. 1852. III. 612.²
— Das Einsammeln der Wallaniden. ·1861. IV. 502.²
— Die Feigen . . . in Griechenland. 1857. III. 370.¹
— Ueber die Forstgewächse in Griechenland. 1857. I. 448,² *IV. 87.*¹
— Die Giftpflanzen Griechenlands. 1854. III. 272.¹
— Die in Griechenland vorkommenden Arzneipflanzen. 1862. III. 91.¹
— Ueber die in Griechenland vorkommenden Fruchtbäume. 1856. III. 91.¹
— Krankheiten der Olivenbäume. 1854. III. 677.²
— Labdanum creticum. 1851. III. 612.²
— Ein leuchtender Platanenbaum. 1857. I. 206.¹
— Sur une méthode de conserver le raisin en Orient. 1851. III. 582.
— Die neue arkadische Tanne. 1861. II. 24.²
— Note sur Olive culture . . . in Greece. 1877. III. 679.¹·
— Note sur le Cassia fistula. 1852. III. 471.¹
— Ueber die Olivenkultur . . . in Griechenland. 1877.· III. 679.¹
— Ueber das orientalische Rosenöl. 1859. III. 454.¹
— Pharmaceutical notes on the Cornelian Cherry. 1860. III. 646.¹
— Pharmacologische berigten. 1852. III. 272.¹
— Pistacia Lentiscus. 1861. III. 525.³
— Sur la préparation de l'huile de Roses. 1851. III. 454.¹
— Quercus coccifera und dessen Schildläuse. 1856. IV. 503.¹
— Over de scherpe zelfstandigheid van het melksap der Vijgen. 1844. III. 370.¹
— On Senna. 1846. III. 470.¹
— Ueber den Stamm der . . . Dattelpalme. 1859. II. 72.²
— On Tamarinds. 1846. III. 489.¹
— Wallaniden-Sammlung im Oriente. 1862. IV. 502.²
— Weinbau in Griechenland. 1862. III. 558.²
— Ueber die Weinbeeren-Pflanzungen. 1856. III. 558.²
— Zizyphus-Früchte des Orients. 1862. III. 544,¹ *666.²*
— Zusammenstellung der Forstgewächse in· Griechenland. 1861. I. 448,² *IV. 87.*¹
— Zusammenstellung der in Griechenland sich findenden Fruchtbäume. 1862. III. 91.¹
— *See also* BOUROS, Johannes, LANDERER, Xaver & SARTO-RIOS, Josef; ΛÁΝΔΕΡΕΡ, Ξαυέριος.
Landers, A. H.· Memorandum on the . . . products of the Shaan scuatry. 1843. III. 977.
— & **Warwick**, William. Correspondence relative to a black vegetable dye. 1843. III. 236.
Landes, Gaston. La culture du Cacaoyer à la Martinique. 1900. III. 593.¹·
— Sur le cyclone de la Martinique. 1892. III. 184.²
— Les insects qui attaquent le Cacaoyer. 1900. III. 593.²
— Notice sur la Martinique. 1900. III. 267.¹·
— Le Solanum torvum. 1899. III. 702.¹
Landes de Gascogne . . . incendies dans les forêts. *See* DROMARD. 1872. IV. 183.¹·
Les **landes** françaises. 1896. IV. 160.²
Landesverordnung, die Cultur der Forsten betreffend.· 1793. IV. 301.
Landgräflich hessische Forst-Ordnung. 1776. IV. 319.¹
Landgräflich hessische. Verordnung . . . die Holzhauer be-treffend. 1773. IV. 300.²
Landgraf, Josef. Papier-Holz contra Säge- und Rund-Holz. 1897. IV. 430.
Landgrebe, ·Georg. Ueber das Licht. 1834. I. 184.
— On the relations of colour and smell. 1834. I. 184.
Landhuishoudelijke courant. *See* ALGEMEENE landhuis-hou-delijke . . . III. 14.

Landmandsblade. III. 10.²
Landoeconomiske Tidender. III. 10.¹
Landois, Hermann. Die westfälischen . . . Pflanzennamen.
1882. I. 73.²
Landolt, Elias. L'agriculture; la culture des alpages et des
forêts dans les hautes montagnes. 1867. IV. 366.
— Altes und Neues aus der Forstwirthschaft. 1880. .IV.
278.²
—'Ueber die' angeregte Umgestaltung der Forstwirthschaft.
1885. IV. 110.³
— Sur l'arpentage des forêts. 1862. IV. 264.
— L'arpentage des forêts dans les hautes régions. 1878. . IV.
265.
— Ueber die Aufästung der Waldbäume. 1881. IV. 171.
— Die Aufastungen in den Hochwaldbeständen. 1878. IV.
171.
— Auszug aus dem Bericht über die Untersuchung der Ge-
birgswaldungen. 1862. IV. 278.¹
— Avons-nous en perspective la hausse ou la baisse dans les
prix des bois? 1862. IV. 406.¹
— Die Bäche, Schneelawinen. 1886. IV. 188.²
— Die Behandlung der ertraglosen Flächen. 1886. IV. 245.
— Beiträge zur Kenntniss der schweizerischen Waldzustände.
1870. IV. 366.
— Ein Beitrag zur Lösung der Frage betreffend die Wahl der
Umtriebszeit. 1870. IV. 251.²
— Die Benutzung der Gemeinds- und Korporations-Wald-
ungen im Kanton Zürich. 1866. IV. 334.²
— Ueber die Berechnung des Ertrages der Waldungen. 1863.
IV. 236.
— Die Berechnung des Werthes von Boden.· 1872. ' IV. 255.
— Bericht über das Hochgewitter am Rhein. 1881. IV.
190. — 1882. IV. 48.¹
— Bericht über die Gruppen 27 und 28: Forstwirthschaft.
1884. IV. 21.¹
— Bericht . . . über die Untersuchung der Hochgebirgswal-
dungen in den Kantonen Glarus. 1860. IV. 366.
— Bericht . . . über die Untersuchung der Hochgebirgswal-
dungen in den Kantonen Tessin. 1860. IV. 366.
— Bericht . . . über die Untersuchung der schweiz. Hochge-
birgswaldungen . . . 1860. 1862. IV. 366.
— Bericht über die Untersuchung der Waldungen . . . des
obern Tössthales. 1875. IV. 367.
— Bericht über Gruppe II, Forstwirthschaft. 1874. IV.
20.¹
— Bericht zum Entwurf eines eidgenössischen Forstgesetzes.
1876. IV. 330.
— Die Beschaffung von Samen. 1872. IV. 148.
— Die Beziehungen der Zwischennutzungen zum nachhalt-
igen Ertrag. 1888. IV. 245.
— I boschi ed il loro stato nelle montagne. 1863. IV. 366.
— Brennholzpreise. 1873. IV. 406.¹
— Die Buche, Fagus sylvatica. 1861. IV. 494.
— Die Bundesverfassung in ihren Beziehungen zur Forst- und
Landwirthschaft. 1872. IV. 330.
— Sur le calcul de la possibilité des forêts. 1863. IV. 236.
— Calcul de la valeur du sol. 1872. IV. 255.
— Canton de Berne. 1863. IV. 330.
— Canton de Saint-Gall. 1863. IV. 330.
— Ce que les forestiers peuvent faire en présence de la disette
de fourrage. 1865. IV. 135.¹
— Comment faut-il procéder aux recherches sur la marche de
l'accroissement. 1872. IV. 233.
— De la conservation du Sapin blanc et du Hêtre. 1877. IV.
129.
— Le contrôle des surfaces suffit-il pour assurer le maintien du
produit soutenu? 1870. IV.·236.
— Convient-il de faire les enchères de bois dans la forêt.
1867. IV. 388.¹
— Convient-il de reboiser les prés-marais et prairies? 1867.
IV. 166.²
— Dégâts causés par les écureuils. 1861. IV. 197.²
— Le dendromètre portatif perfectionné de Winkler. 1864.
IV. 215.
— Devons-nous aussi établir en Suisse un système complet
d'observations et d'expériences forestières? 1874. IV. 8.²
— Un document pour la solution des questions relatives au
choix de la révolution des forêts. 1870. IV. 251.³
— Von der Durchforstung der Bestände. 1885. IV. 174.
— Ueber die Durchforstungen. 1866. IV. 173.
— Ueber Durchforstungen. 1881. IV. 173. — 1887. IV. 174.
— Ueber Durchforstungen und Durchforstungserträge. 1876.
IV. 173.
— Des éclaircies. 1866. IV. 173.

— Des éclaircies et de leurs produits. 1876. IV. 173.
— L'économie forestière et le budget de la Confédération
suisse. 1863. IV. 278.¹
— L'économie forestière fait-elle des progrès en Suisse? 1862. ·
·IV. 278.¹
— Eibenholzverkäufe nach Indien. 1861. IV. 440.¹
— Die Eichenwälder in Slavonien. 1874. IV. 512.
— Einiges über die Holzernte. 1885. IV. 384.¹
— De l'élagage des futaies. 1878. IV. 171.
— L'endiguement des torrents. 1871. IV. 187.¹
— Ueber die Entfernung der Waldpflanzen. 1892. IV. 142.
— Ueber Ergänzung und Pflege der Jungwüchse. 1884.
IV. 169.¹
— Ueber die Erhaltung der Weisstannne und Buche. 1877.
IV. 129.
— Von der Ermittelung des Waldwerthes. 1862. IV. 255.
— Die Erziehung von starkem Bau-, Säg- und Nutzholz.
1890. IV. 123.²
— Aus dem Expertenbericht betreffend die Aufforstung des
Regengebiets der Brienzer Waldbäche. 1866. IV. 166.²
— Exportation de bois d'If en Inde. 1861. IV. 440.¹
— Extrait du rapport des experts touchant le reboisement du
bassin de réception des torrents de Brienz. 1866. IV. 166.²
— Extrait du rapport sur l'expertise de forêts des hautes mon-
tagnes. 1862. IV. 278.¹
— Faut-il changer les essences de nos forêts? 1876. IV.
74.²
— Festschrift zum fünfzigjährigen Jubiläum des Schweizer-
ischen Forstvereins. 1893. IV. 41.²
— Zur Förderung der Privatforstwirthschaft. 1883. IV.
309.²
— La forêt; manière de la rajeunir. 1866. IV. 110.²
— La forêt dans ses rapports avec la satisfaction des besoins
de la vie matérielle. 1864. IV. 278.¹
— La forêt du Kirchenwald, près de Schwytz. 1866. IV.
366.
— Les forêts de Chênes en Esclavonie. 1874. IV. 512. ·
— Les forêts des Alpes et du Jura. 1863. IV. 366.
— Les forêts . . . du bassin supérieur de la Toess. 1875. IV.
367.
— Die forstliche Betriebslehre. 1892. IV. 241.
— Ueber forstliche Taxation- u. Betriebsregulirung. 1856.
IV. 242.
— Die forstlichen Zustände in den Alpen. 1863. IV. 366.
— Die Forstwirthschaft und das Budget der schweizerischen
Eidgenossenschaft. 1863. IV. 278.¹
— Genügt die Flächenkontrolle zur Sicherung der Nach-
haltigkeit? 1870. IV. 236.
— Ueber die Geschichte der Waldungen. 1858. IV. 24.¹
— Gesetz betreffend die eidgenössische Oberaufsicht über die
Forstpolizei im Hochgebirge. 1876. IV. 330.
— Die Grundzüge der schweizerischen Forstgesetzgebung.
1868. IV. 330.
— Le Hêtre (Fagus sylvatica). 1861. IV. 494.
— Inondations . . . juin 1876. 1876. IV. 187.¹
— L'introduction d'une meilleure économie forestière est-elle
réellement nécessaire. 1867. IV. 278.¹
— Ist die Einführung einer bessern Forstwirthschaft wirklich
nothwendig und lohnend? 1867. IV. 278.¹
— Ist in unsern Wäldern ein Wechsel in den Holzarten
nöthig? 1876. IV. 74.²
— Kanton Bern. 1863. IV. 330.
— Kanton St. Gallen. 1863. IV. 330.
— Der Kirchenwald bei Schwytz. 1866. IV. 366.
— Die Lärche. 1861. IV. 449.
— Ueber Land-, Alp- und Forstwirthschaft im Hochgebirge.
1867. IV. 366.
— De la législation forestière en Suisse. 1870. IV. 330.
— Levé de matériaux pour l'établissement de tables d'expéri-
ences. 1876. IV. 244.
— Der Lichtungszuwachs. 1881. IV. 175.²
— Des lisières de forêts de long des cours d'eau. 1874. IV.
187.¹
— Loi concernant la haute surveillance en matière de police
forestière dans les hautes montagnes. 1876. IV. 330.
— Macht das schweizerische Forstwesen Fortschritte? 1862.
IV. 278.¹
— Matériaux relatifs à l'étude de l'économie forestière en
Suisse. 1870. IV. 366.
— Le Mélèze. 1861. IV. 449.
— Les mesures métriques dans leur rapports avec l'économie
forestière. 1871. IV. 214.
— Das Metermass und seine Beziehungen zur Forstwirth-
schaft. 1871. IV. 214.

— Mittel zur Förderung des Forstwesens. 1863. IV. 278.¹
— Die Mittelwaldungen und deren Bewirthschaftung. 1892. IV. 131.
— Moyens de faire progresser l'économie forestière. 1863. IV. 278.¹
— Moyens de garantir le produit soutenu. 1864. IV. 243.
— Müssen die Holzversteigerungen im Wald abgehalten werden. 1867. IV. 388.¹
— Nachrichten über die Schweiz. Forstschule in Zürich. 1857. IV. 36.¹
— Die neuen Durchforstungs-Theorien. 1888. IV. 174.
— Niederschlagsmengen auf den Regenstationen des Kantons Zürich. 1890. IV. 48.²
— Notre économie forestière privée. 1872. IV. 309.¹ .
— Der Notstand der schweizerischen Landwirtschaft. 1893. IV. 278.²
— Nouvelles de l'École forestière fédérale à Zurich. 1857. IV. 36.¹
— Un partage de forêt. 1877. IV. 330.
— Les peuplements purs et les peuplements mélangés. 1865. IV. 137.¹
— Ueber Pflanzenerziehung. 1879. IV. 146.²
— Die Pflege der jungen Bestände. 1863. IV..169.¹
— Plänter- oder schlagweise Behandlung des Hochwaldes. 1890. IV. 128.
— Principes fondamentaux de la législation forestière suisse. 1868. IV. 330.
— Die Privatforstwirthschaft. 1890. IV. 309.²
— Die Privatwaldungen und deren Stellung zur forstlichen Gesetzgebung. 1886. IV. 309.²
— Prix des bois d'affouage. 1873. IV. 406.¹
— De la production des graines. 1872. IV. 148.
— De la production des plantons. 1879. IV. 146.²
— Le projet de constitution fédérale dans ses rapports avec l'économie forestière et l'agriculture. 1872. IV. 330.
— Die provisorischen Wirthschaftspläne. 1880. IV. 244.
— Prüfung der Festigkeit und Elastizität der Bauhölzer. 1884. IV. 410.
— Quel est l'état actuel de notre économie forestière? 1865. IV. 278.¹
— Quelle est la manière . . . de reboiser nos coupes. 1878. IV. 139.²
— Quelle est la valeur comparative des bois d'Épicéa ou de Sapin. 1863.. IV. 446.²
— Quelles essences forestières devons-nous favoriser. 1873. IV. 123.¹
— Pour quelles raisons les forestiers favorisent-ils la transformation des taillis composés en futaies. 1864. IV. 128.
— Le rajeunissement de nos forêts. 1879. IV. 139.²
— Rapport . . . sur l'expertise des forêts dans les régions élevées des cantons de Glaris. 1860. IV. 366.
— Rapport . . . sur l'expertise des forêts dans les régions élevées des cantons de Tessin. 1860. IV. 366.
— Rapport sur le projet de loi forestière fédérale. 1876. IV. 330.
— Rapport . . . sur les forêts des hautes montagnes de la Suisse . . 1860. 1962. IV. 366.
— Rapporto . . . sulle foreste delle alte montagne della Svizzera. 1862. IV. 366.
— Les ravages des inondations en Suisse. 1869. IV. 48.²
— Le reboisement des montagnes en Suisse. 1890. IV. 166.²
— De la régénération des forêts alpestres. 1878. IV. 139.²
— Reine oder gemischte Bestände. 1865. IV. 137.¹
— Répartition du produit des forêts de communes et de corporations dans le canton de Zurich. 1866. IV. 334.²
— Ueber das Sammeln von Material zu Erfahrungstafeln. 1876. IV. 244.
— Schädlichkeit der Eichhörnchen. 1861. IV. 197.¹
— Schlagweiser- oder Plänterbetrieb. 1884. IV. 128.
— Ueber die schweizerische Forstgesetzgebung. 1870. IV. 330.
— Die schweizerische Landesausstellung in Zürich. 1883. III. 271.³
— Ueber die Sicherstellung der Nachhaltigkeit. 1864. IV. 243.
— Ueber die Sicherung der Nachhaltigkeit. 1889. IV. 245.
— Sind die in den Waldungen liegenden kleinen Wiesen- und Riedtflächen aufzuforsten? 1867. IV. 166.²
— Sollen die Stöcke bei der Fällung des Holzes gerodet werden oder nicht? 1892. IV. 387.¹

— Steht ein Steigen oder ein Fallen der Holzpreise in Aussicht? 1862. IV. 406.¹
— Tafeln zur Ermittlung des Kubikinhaltes liegender, entgipfelter Baumstämme. 1868. IV. 226. .
— Taxation de la valeur des forêts. 1862. IV. 255.
— Taxation des forêts pour la perception de l'impôt. 1862. IV. 255.
— Traitement des jeunes boisés. 1863. IV. 169.¹
— Die Ueberständer — Waldrechter — im Hochwald. 1887. IV. 130.
— Umtriebszeit und Verzinsung des Waldkapitals. 1891. IV. 252.
— Unsere Aufgabe auf dem Gebiete des forstlichen Versuchswesens. 1874. IV. 38.¹
— Ueber unsere Privatforstwirthschaft. 1872. IV. 309.²
— Unsere Privatforstwirthschaft. 1883. IV. 309.¹
— Sur les ventes de bois. 1864. IV. 388.¹
— Die Verbauung der Wildbäche. 1871. IV. 187.¹
— Ueber die Verjüngung der Hochgebirgswälder. 1878. IV. 139.²
— Ueber die Verjüngung der Hochwälder. 1891. IV. 140.
— Die Verjüngung unserer Waldungen. 1879. IV. 139.¹
— Verkauf der Staatswaldungen . . . im Kanton Aargau. 1889. IV. 278.²
— Ueber den Verkauf des Holzes. 1864. IV. 388.¹
— Der Verkehr der Staatsforstbeamten. 1893. IV. 294.¹
— Die Vermessung der Hochgebirgswaldungen. 1878. IV. 265.
— Ueber Vermessung der Waldungen. 1862. IV. 264.
— Die Vermessung der Waldungen. 1871. IV. 264.
— Vices essentiels de l'économie forestière en Suisse. 1861. IV. 278.¹
— Die wässerigen Niederschläge. 1864. IV. 73.¹
— Ueber die Wahl der Umtriebszeit. 1888. IV. 252.
— Der Wald in Haushalt der Natur und des Menschen. 1870. IV. 44.
— Der Wald in seinen Beziehungen zur Befriedigung der Bedürfnisse des täglichen Lebens. 1864. IV. 269, 278.¹
— Der Wald, seine Verjüngung, Pflege. 1866. IV. 110.²
— Der Wald und die Alpen. 1881. IV. 367.
— Die Waldeisenbahnen. 1886. IV. 392.
— Die Waldgenossenschaften im Kanton Zürich. 1891. IV. 309.²
— Die Waldstreifen längs der Bäche und Flüsse. 1874. IV. 187.¹
— Eine Waldtheilung. 1877. IV. 330.
— Die Waldungen . . . des obern Tössthales. 1875. IV. 367.
— Warum begünstigen die Forstmänner die Umwandlungen der Mittelwaldungen in Hochwald. 1864. IV. 128.
— Was kann der Forstwirth bei dem drohenden Futter- und Streumangel . . . thun? 1865. IV. 135.²
— Die Wasserverheerungen in der Schweiz. 1869. IV. 48.¹
— Die Wasserverheerungen vom . . . Juni 1876. 1876. IV. 187.¹
— Welche Erfahrungen liegen über Wildbach- und Lawinenverbauungen vor? 1890. IV. 184.²
— Welche Erfahrungen liegen über Wildbach- und Lawinenverbauungen vor? 1891. IV. 187.¹
— Welche Holzarten sollen wir beim Anbau . . . begünstigen? 1873. IV. 123.¹
— In welcher Richtung sollen bei den Reihenpflanzungen die Reihen laufen? 1866. IV. 154.¹
— Die wesentlichsten Gebrechen des schweizer. Forstwesens. 1861. IV. 278.¹
— Wie ist bei der Erforschung des Zuwachsganges unserer Wälder vorzugehen? 1872. IV. 233.
— Wie ist das Gebiet der Berge und Wildbäche forstwirthschaftlich zu behandeln? 1868. IV. 187.¹
— Wie können wir unsere Schläge . . . in Bestand bringen? 1878. IV. 139.²
— Wie steht es mit unserm Forstwesen? 1865.. IV. 278.¹
— Wie verhalten sich die Gebrauchswerthe des Fichten- und des Weisstannenholzes? 1863. IV. 446.²
— Wie weit haben wir bei der Wahl der Umtriebszeit der Verzinsung . . . Rechnung zu tragen? 1891. IV. 252.
— Wie weit soll und darf die Krediertheilung für die Holzkäufer gehen? 1892. IV. 388.²
— Das Winkler'sche Taschendendrometer. 1864. IV. 215.
— Zürich. 1861. IV. 330.
— Zürich. 1866. IV. 366.
— Die Zusammenlegung stark getheilter Privatwaldungen. 1892. IV. 309.²
— See also DENGLER, Leopold & LANDOLT, Elias; HALLER, G. & LANDOLT, Elias.

Landolt, Elias (*continued*).
— & **Bertholet**, Charles. Coup d'œil en arrière. 1873. IV. 278.[2]
—— Qu'y a-t-il à faire pour les progrès de l'économie forestière en Suisse. 1872. IV. 278.[3]
— **Hertenstein**, (*Forstmeister*) & **Weinmann**, (*Oberförster*). Beschreibung und Wirthschaftsplan über die Stadtwaldungen von Winterthur. 1862. IV. 366.
Landowski. Le lait ou suc d'Alvelos. 1886. III. 518.[1]
Landoz, Johann. Verzeichniss der Pflanzen um Klausenburg. 1844. I. 445.
Landré, W. J. N. Tuinbouw-belangen. 1890. III. 122.[2]
Landrecht der churfürstl. Du. in Bayern. 1657. IV. 318.
Landrecht, Policey; Gerichts-, Malefitz- und andere Ordnungen der Fürstenthumben Obern und Niedern Bayern. 1616. IV. 318.
Landreth; Burnet. Address delivered before the American forestry association. 1876. IV. 271.[2]
— An address delivered before the American forestry association. 1878. IV. 271.[2]
— The American Poplar. 1878. IV. 519.[2]
— Forest planting in Virginia. 1888. IV. 112.
— Suggestive curriculum for a forest school. 1890. IV. 30.[1]
Landrin, A. Quelques monstruosités végétales. 1865. I. 143.
Landrin, Armand. Notice ... sur les travaux relatifs à la coloration des végétaux. 1859. I. 2.
Landrin, Ed. De l'analyse des quinquinas.' 1889. III. 726.[1]
— Sur la composition de quelques sortes de Quinquinas. 1890. III. 723.
— De la falsification du poivre. 1884. III. 679.[1]
— *See also* DEHÉRAIN, P. P. & LANDRIN, Ed.; MOISSAN, Henri & LANDRIN, Ed.
's **Lands plantentuin**. *See* INSTITUT BOTANIQUE DE BUITENZORG. I. 29.[1]
's **Lands Plantentuin**, [Buitenzorg] Mededeelingen. I. 29.[1]
's **Lands plantentuin te** Buitenzorg. Verslag omtrent den staat. 1874. I. 68.[1]
Landsberg, Adolf. Der Kauf von Holz auf dem Stamme. 1900. IV. 388.[2]
Landsberg, M. Pharmacographia Euphorbiacearum. 1831. III. 514.[1]
Landsborough, David. Australian and New Zealand plants in Arran. 1886. III. 123.[2]
— Australian and New Zealand trees in Arran. 1889. I. 55.
— Australian and other foreign trees and plants in Arran. 1896. I. 55.
— Australian plants in Arran. 1876. I. 55.
— Pyrus Aria and its varieties in Arran.' 1900. II. 312.[1]
Landsborough, Wilham. Journal of an expedition from Carpentaria. 1862. *See* MUELLER, Ferdinand, *Baron* von. 1862. I. 502.
Landscape in connection with tree planting. 1857. III. 201.
Landshut — Botanischer Verein. *See* BOTANISCHER ... I. 11.
Die **Landwirthschaft** im Regierungsbezirk Oberbayern. 1885. IV. 351.[1]
Die **Landwirthschaft** und das Forstwesen im Fürstenthume Braunschweig. *See* MENGEN, F. A. 1858. IV. 351.[2]
Landwirthschaftliche Hochschule in Berlin. *See* KÖNIGLICHE landwirthschaftliche ...
Landwirthschaftliche Jahrbücher. III. 12.
Landwirthschaftliche Mitteilungen für Steiermark. *See* K. K. STEIERMÄRKISCHE LANDWIRTSCHAFTS-GESELLSCHAFT. III. 25.
Die **landwirthschaftlichen** Versuchs-Stationen. III. 12.
Landwirthschaftlicher Central-Verein des Herzogthums Braunschweig. Mittheilungen. III. 12.
Landwirthschaftliches Museum, Berlin. *See* KÖNIGLICHES landwirthschaftliches ...
Landwirthschaftliches Wochenblatt. IV. 15.
Das **Landwirthschaftsrecht** im sächsischen Weinbau. 1840. III. 552.
Lanessan, Jean Louis de. Des caractères botaniques du Duboisia myoporoïdes. 1878. II. 771.[2]
— Sur la disposition des faisceaux dans les Conifères. 1875. II. 17.[3]
— Flore de Paris. 1884. I. 416.
— Gamboge. 1872. III. 609.[2]
— Du genre Garcinia. 1871. II. 555.[1]
— Introduction à la botanique; le Sapin. 1885. I. 82,[2] *II. 83*.[1]
— Manuel d'histoire naturelle médicale. 1879. III. 59.[1]
— Mémoire sur le genre Garcina. 1872. II. 555.[1]
— Observations organogéniques ... sur les appendices foliaires des Rubiacées. 1877. II. 808.[1]

— Observations sur la disposition des faisceaux fibrovasculaires dans les feuilles. 1874. I. 110.
— Observations sur la structure ... des canaux à kino dans le Pterocarpus. 1877. II. 338,[1] *380*.[2]
— Observations sur la structure des étamines .. : dans les Rubiacées. 1874. II. 808.[1]
— Observations sur le développement des anthères. 1874. II. 314.[1]
— Les plantes utiles des colonies françaises. 1886. III. 53.
— Recherches sur le développement des faisceaux. 1878. I. 133.
— Sur la structure de l'écorce du Drimys Winteri. 1876. II. 209.[2]
— Sur la structure de la graine du Garcinia. 1875. II. 555.[2]
— Sur la structure des sépales du Calluna. 1874. II. 662.[1]
— Sur la structure et le développement des Pareira-brava. 1877. II. 206.[1]
Lanfossi, Paolo. Saggio di storia naturale dei contorni di Mantova. 1827. I. 426.
Lanfrey. Expériences sur la destruction du phylloxera. 1899. III. 575.[1]
Lang. Ueber die Ansucht ... einjähriger Kiefernballenpflanzen. 1879. IV. 473.
Lang, (*Forstrath, Stuttgart*). Zur Tanne im Schwarzwalde. 1872. IV. 444.[1]
Lang, Adolph Franz. Enumeratio plantarum in Hungaria. 1822. I. 445, V. XXIII.[1]
— Specierum novarum et varietatum notabiliorum. 1824. I. 445.
Lang, Georg. Das Auftreten des Kiefernspanners. 1898. IV. 479.
— Raupenfrass durch Kiefernspinner. 1891. IV. 208.[1]
Lang, O. & others. Résultats des diverses expériences ... sur l'Acajou. 1858. IV. 408.
Lang, Otto Friedrich. Ueber die Gattung Cytisus. 1843. II. 349.[2]
Lang, Thomas. Kilmarnock Weeping Willow. '1853' III. 351.[3]
Lang, Wilhelm. Ueber Welwitschia mirabilis. 1886. III. 312.[3]
Lang, William H. Studies in the development ... of Cycadean sporangia. 1897. II. 3.[2]
Langdon, Fanny E. A study of Epigaea repens. 1894. II. 663.[2]
Lange, (*Dr.*). Beiträge zur Kenntniss der Acidität des Zell-'saftes. 1886. I. 180.[2]
Lange, (*Oberförster, Friedrichsruh*). Ueber die Verwendung des Buchenholzes zu Bauzwecken. 1888. IV. 500.[1]
Lange, (*Oberforstverwalter*). Beschreibung von einigen ... Lerchen-Bäumen. 1851. II. 33.[1]
Lange, A. Nogle sjældnere Træer og Buske. 1897. III. 66.[3]
Lange, Axel. Rubus phoeniculasius Maxim. 1898. III. 459.[1]
Lange, Daniel. Catalogus der Gewächse ... in dem Lastropischen Garten. 1707. I. 43.
Lange, E. Reichsgesetz betreffend die Unfall- und Kranken-Versicherung. 1886. IV. 310.[2]
Lange, Friedrich Wilhelm. Das Streu-, Laub- und Moos-Rechen. 1841. IV. 333, 457.[1]
Lange, G. A. de. Geschiedenis van de Koffiecultuur op Java. 1890. III. 730.
Lange, Herrmann. Imprägnirung des Buchenholzes. 1895. IV. 499.
Lange, Johan. Arboretum Scandinavicum. 1883. I. 350,[2] *IV. 79*.[2]
— Bemærkninger om de ... Karplanter fra Vestkysten af Grønland. 1890. I. 309.[1]
— Bemærkninger om de ... Planter paa Østkysten af Grønland. 1889. I. 309.[1]
— Bemærkninger om de to indenlandske Hvidtørn. 1895. II. 261.[1]
— Bemærkninger ved ... Supplementhæfte til Flora danica. 1874. I. 357, V. XVIII.[1]
— Bemærkninger ved det 48de Hæfte af Flora danica. 1871. I. 356.
— Bemærkninger ved det 49de Hæfte af Flora danica. 1871. I. 357.
— Bemærkninger ved det 50de Hæfte af Flora danica. 1880. II. 107.[1]
— Beretning om Universitets botaniske Have. 1874. I. 40.
— Bidrag til de i Danmark dyrkede Frilandstræers Naturhistorie. 1885. I. 294,[1] *III. 86*,[1] *IV. 79*.[2]
— Bidrag til Spørgsmaalet "om Mangel paa Farverigdom." 1873. III. 201.

— Conspectus florae groenlandicae. 1880. I. 309.[1]
— Descriptio ... plantarum ... praecipue e Flora hispanica. 1864. I. 421.
— Diagnoses plantarum peninsulae ibericae. 1877. I. 421.
— Erindringer fra Universitetet botaniske Have. 1875. I. 40.
— Om Forekomsten af Taxtræet ... i Danmark. 1866. II. 11.[1]
— Fortegnelse over de i Veterinair- og Landbohøjskolens Have ... dyrkede Frilandstræer og Buske. 1871. I. 40.
— Haandbog i den danske Flora. 1851. I. 355.
— Iagttagelser over Løvspring, Blomstring. 1873. I. 223.[1]
— Om nogle danske Planters Fordeling. 1849. I. 355.
— Nogle yderligere Bemærkninger om hængende Pile. 1872. III. 347.
— Nomenclator florae danicae. 1887. I. 357.
— Nye bidrag til Spaniens flora. 1893. I. 423.
— Observations sur la feuillaison, la floraison. 1873. I. 223.[1]
— Observations sur les espèces ... dans la 48e livraison de la Flora danica. 1871. I. 356.
— Oversigt over de europæiske Arter af Naaletræernes. 1877. II. 15.[1]
— Oversigt over de til de Koglebærende ... hørende Slægter. 1887. II. 13.[2]
— Oversigt over Grønlands Planter. 1857. I. 309.[1]
— Pugillus plantarum imprimis hispanicarum. 1860. I. 421.
— Remarques sur la ... livraison supplémentaire de la Flora danica. 1874. I. 357.
— Remarques sur la 49e livraison de la Flora danica. 1877. I. 357.
— Remarques sur la 50e livraison de la Flora danica. 1880. II. 107.[1]
— Revisio specierum generis Crataegi. 1897. II. 260.[2]
— Slægten Crataegus. 1885. III. 421.[2]
— Om store Træer. 1882. I. 295.[4]
— Studien über Grönlands Flora. 1880. I. 309.[1]
— Studier til Grønlands Flora. 1880. I. 309.[1]
— Tornblad (Ulex) som Fodervæxt. 1856. III. 490.[1]
— Om Tornene hos Crataegus. 1895. III. 261.[1]
— Udvalg af de i Kjøbenhavns botaniske Haves Frøfortegnelser ... beskrevne nye Arter. 1872. I. 40.
— Udvalg af de ... i Universitetets botaniske o. fl. andre Haver dyrkede nye Arter. 1872. I. 40.
— Vejviser i Universitetets nye botaniske Have. 1875. I. 40.
— Vinteren 1892–93 og Vegetationen. 1894. III. 44.[3]
— See also LIEBMANN, F. M. & LANGE, Johan; WILLKOMM, Moritz & LANGE, Johan.
Lange, Morten Thomsen. Om Forandringen af Danmarks Plantevext. 1859. I. 355.
— Den sydfynske Øgaards Vegetation. 1857. I. 355.
Lange, Theodor. Allgemeines Gartenbuch. 1895. III. 104.
— Beiträge zur Kenntniss der Entwicklung der Gefässe. 1891. I. 126.
Lange, Walther. Das Holz als Baumaterial. 1879. IV. 408.
Lange, Willy. Fagus silvatica atropurpurea. 1888. III. 360.[1]
Langegg, F. A. JUNKER VON. See JUNKER VON LANGEGG, F. A.
Langenbach. Phil. Cultur der Manna-Esche. 1872. III. 672.[2]
Langenbacher, F. L. Heidler's Präcisions-Baummesskluppe. 1889. IV. 231.[2]
— & Nossek, E. A. Die Kubierung des Holzes im liegenden Zustande. 1889. IV. 228.
Langenbacher, Ferdinand. Breymann's neue Methode ein ... Polygon zum Schlusse zu bringen. 1868. IV. 264.
— Der Dendrometer von Rueprecht. 1889. IV. 216.
— Der Dendrometer von Sanaville. 1870. IV. 215.
— Form des Baumschaftes. 1888. IV. 218.
— Forstmathematik. 1875. IV. 59.[1]
— Interpolation bei Holzzuwachs- und Massenreihen. 1873. IV. 256.
— See also SCHWARZER, Guido von & LANGENBACHER, Ferdinand.
Langer, Carl. Die Vegetationsformen des Kaplandes. 187.? I. 495.
Langer, Carl A. Beobachtungen über die sogenannten Wasserporen. 1879. I. 169.[1]
Langerfeldt, (Forstgehülfe). Forstgeschichte des Herzogthums Braunschweig. 1858. IV. 25.
Langethal, Christian Eduard. Beschreibung der Gewächse Deutschlands. 1858. I. 384.

— Die Gewächse des nördlichen Deutschlands. 1843. I. 381.
— Kalender der heimischen Pflanzen. 1868. I. 225, 295.[1]
— Der Obstbau. 1876. III. 101.[2]
— Terminologie der beschreibenden Botanik. 1845. I. 71.
— See also SCHLECHTENDAL, D. F. L. von, LANGETHAL, C. E. & SCHENK, Ernst.
Langford, T. Instructions to raise all sorts of fruit trees. 1681. III. 141.
Langfurth. Falsification des semences d'anis. 1881. III. 398.[1]
Langguth, Georg August. Cortice peruviano medicina adversus febrem. 1758. III. 719.
— De nucis vomicae virtute medicae. 1771. III. 682.[2]
Langguth, M. G. A. & Pitschel, F. L. Antiquitates plantarum feralium. 1738. I. 514.[1]
Langham, William. The garden of health. 1579. I. 282, V. xv.[2]
Langheinrich, Georg Nikolaus. De sensu plantarum. 1672. I. 193.[2]
Langkavel, Bernhard. Botanik der späteren Griechen. 1866. I. 514.[3]
— Drei alte norddeutsche Rosenstöcke. 1899. II. 290.[1]
Langlade, FAVARD DE. See FAVARD DE LANGLADE.
Langlassé, Eugène. Emploi des Bambous en Malaisie. 1897. III. 316.[2]
— Notes sur le Cocotier. 1895. III. 323.[1]
— Les Palmiers utiles. 1896. III. 91,[2] 319.[2]
Langlès, Louis. Recherches sur la découverte de l'essence de Rose. 1804. III. 454.[1]
Langley, Batty. The landed gentlemen's useful companion. 1728. IV. 120.
— New principles of gardening. 1728. III. 108.
— Pomona. 1729. III. 141.
— A sure method of improving estates by plantations of Oak, Elm. 1728. IV. 120.
Langley, J. N. On the structure of secretory cells. 1884. I. 135.
Langlois. Examen chimique de la séve. 1843. I. 152.[2]
— Rapport relatif à ... la fécule des marrons d'Inde. 1849. III. 538.[1]
Langlois, Auguste Barthélemy. Catalogue provisoire de plantes ... de la basse-Louisiane. 1877. I. 319.
Langlois, P. & Richet, Ch. Influence de la temperature organique sur les convulsions de la cocaine. 1888. III. 493.[1]
Langmann, Johann Friedrich. Flora der beiden Grossherzogthümer Mecklenburg. 1841. I. 380.
— Flora von Nord- und Mitteldeutschland. 1876. I. 383.
Langner. Über abnorme Embryonen bei Leguminosen. 1874. II. 320.[2]
— Über Abnormitäten bei dicotylen Samen. 1875. II. 320.[2]
— Ueber die Familie der Compositen in Neuholland. 1870. II. 850.[1]
— Ueber die Gattung Eucalyptus. 1869. II. 623.[1]
Langsdorf, Karl Christian. Arithmetische Abhandlungen über ... forstwirthschaftliche Fragen. 1810. IV. 57.
Langsdorff, Georg Heinrich von. Bemerkungen auf einer Reise um die Welt. 1812. I. 302.
Langstedt, Friedrich Ludwig. Allgemeines botanisches Repertorium. 1801. I. 265.
— Auszug aus D. John Coakley Lettsom's Abhandlung über den Thee. 1800. III. 606, 733.
— Thee, Kaffee und Zucker. 1800. III. 606, 733.
Lanicca. Definition des Plänter- und Femelbetriebes. 1882. IV. 139.[2]
Lanier, T. Introduction ... du Chêne dans les taillis. 1861. IV. 505.
Lankester, Edwin. Memorials of John Ray. 1846. I. 520.[3]
— Remarks on Du Petit Thouars's theory of the origin of wood. 1840. I. 124.
— Report of lectures on ... plants yielding food. 1845. III. 219.[2]
— Vegetable substances used for the food of man. 1840. III. 219.[2]
Lankester, Mrs. Phoebe. The Mistletoe and parasitic plants. 1863. II. 179.[1]
— Wild flowers worth notice. 1861. I. 401, 533.
Lankhorst, A. M. De camphora. 1829. III. 233,[1] 611.[1]
Lannes. Catalogue des plantes ... des Hautes-Alpes. 1885. I. 416.
Lannoy, de. Un Dattier propre à la région méditerranéenne. 1877. III. 328.[2]

Lanoir, G. Sur une cause possible des incendies de forêts. 1899. IV. 183.[1]
— Les incendies de forêts. 1899. IV. 183.[1]
— La question forestière dans la chaîne saharienne en Algérie. 1894. IV. 283.[2]
Lans, P. C. Rozengain. 1872. III. 274.[3]
Lanternier, J. F. Traité pratique forestier. 1839. IV. 99.[1]
Lantzius-Béninga, Bojung Scato Georg. Beiträge zur Kenntniss der Flora Ostfrieslands. 1849. I. 382.
— Die unterscheidenden Merkmale der deutschen Pflanzenfamilien. 1866. I. 385.
Lanza, Domenico. Note di biologia fiorale. 1894. I. 239.[1]
— La struttura delle foglie nelle Aloineae. 1890. II. 78.[1]
Lanza, Gaetano. Transverse strength of timber. 1883. IV. 410.
Lanzillotti, Leopold. Compendio di botanica. 1863. I. 90.
Lanzoni, Giuseppe. Citrologia. 1690. II. 400.[2]
Lao tea. 1892. III. 608.[1]
Lapa, A. Papstein-. See Papstein-Lapa, A.
Lapa, João Ignacio Ferreira & others. Influence du gemmage sur les Pins. 1881. IV. 436.[3]
— Relatorio . . . influencia da resinagem no Pinhal de Leiria. 1881. IV. 436.[1]
Lapasse, R. de. Gui sur le Chêne. 1900. IV. 519.[2]
— Une invasion de kermès du Chêne. 1896. IV. 511.
— Le Pin à goudron. 1898. IV. 469.
Łapczyński, Kasimierz. Flora Litwy w "Panu Tadeuszu." 1894. I. 515.
— Flora rzeczpospolitej Costa Rica. 1890. I. 334.
— Kilka szczególów o roślinności jawnokwiatowej niziny ciechocińskiej. 1880. I. 442.
— Rośliny jednokwiatowe w Lubelskiem. 1880. I. 364. .
— Wiadomość o zielniku nadbajkalskim Józefa Łaganowskiego. 1886. I. 456.
— Wierzba ostrolistna na odsepiskach wiślanych. 1892. II. 104.[2]
La Perre de Roo. Sur l'emploi des déchets de lin contre le phylloxera. 1874. III. 568.[2]
Lapeyrère. Le Mussaenda borbonica nob. 1888. III. 744.[1]
La Peyrouse, Philippe Picot de. Descriptions de quelques plantes des Pyrénées. 1782. I. 405.
— Figures de la flore de Pyrénées. 1795. I. 406.
— Histoire abrégée des plantes des Pyrénées. 1813. I. 407.
— Mémoire sur la mortalité des Ormes. 1788. III. 364.[1]
Lapeyrouse, Zéphirin de. Essai sur les fleurs à enveloppe unique. 1830. I. 268.
Lapham, Increase Allen. A catalogue of plants found in the vicinity of Milwaukee. 1838. I. 313.
— On the classifications of plants. 1872. I. 252.
— The forest trees of Wisconsin. 1854. I. 312, IV. 76.[3]
— Plants of Wisconsin. 1850. I. 314.
— **Knapp,** J. G. & **Crocker,** H. Report on the disastrous effects of the destruction of forest trees. 1867. IV. 45.
Lapin, Abel. Zur Pharmakologie der Camphergruppe. 1893. III. 233.[1]
Le lapin devant la législature. 1897. IV. 548.[1]
La Pinardière, L. de. The gutta-percha industry. 1894. III. 668.[2]
— L'industrie de la gutta-percha. 1894. III. 668.[2]
Lapine, N. Zum Krebs der Apfelbäume. 1892. III. 428.[1]
La Plata — Museo. See Museo . . . I. 7.[2]
La Plata — Revista de la facultad de agronomia y veterinaria. See Revista . . . I. 8.[1]
Lapommeraie, Christophe Jérôme Barthélemy-. See Barthélemy-Lapommeraie, C. J.
Laport, J. Characters of trees. 1793. I. 516.
Lapparent, Henri de. Assainissement et désinfection des cales de navire. 1863. IV. 418.
— Conservation des bois. 186 . ? IV. 418.
— Du dépérissement des coques des navires en bois. 1862. IV. 418.
— An essay on the prevention of decay in timber for ship-building. 1862. IV. 418.
La Quintinie, Jean de. The compleat gard'ner. 1690. III. 111.
— Instruction pour les jardins fruitiers. 1690. III. 111.
— Le parfait jardinier. 1690. III. 111.
— Traité de la culture des Orangers. 1690. III. 499.[1]
— Trattato del taglio de gl' alberi fruttiferi. 1697. III. 171.
La R., F. de. Un nouveau modèle de compas forestier. 1888. IV. 231.[3]
Lara, Jacinto de. Comisión de repoblación de la cuenca del Jucar. 1895. IV. 165.
Lara, José María Perez. See Perez Lara, J. M.

Lara, Rafael Manrique de. El cultivo del Naranjo. 1891. III. 500.[1]
Larbalétrier, A. Hannetons. 1895. IV. 549.[1]
Larbalétrier, Albert. Ampelopsis Veitchi. 1889. III. 545.[1]
— Jubaea spectabilis. 1892. III. 326.[1]
— Manuel d'essais pratique de chimie horticole. 1898. III. 37.[1]
— La Sensitive ou Mimeuse pudique. 1891. II. 373.[1]
L'Arbousset, Laurent de. Cours de sériciculture pratique. 1893. III. 378.
Larch disease. 1894. IV. 451.
Larché, Thébat-. See Thébat-Larché.
Lardier, J. S. Lois fondamentales de la nature. 1825. III. 113.
Lardner, H. H. Manual on cultivation and preparation for export. 1890. III. 116.[1]
Lardy. Denkschrift über die Zerstörung der Wälder. 1842. IV. 48.[2]
— Mémoire sur les devastations des forêts. 1842. IV. 166,[2] 231.[1]
— Réponse aux questions . . . relativement aux forêts du Canton de Vaud. 184 . ? IV. 277.
Lardy, Charles. Instruction sur les cultures forestières. 1837. IV. 110.[1]
L'Arganier du Maroc en Algérie. 1895. III. 667.[1]
Large, Pierre. Classement des meilleures variétés de Rosiers. 1897. III. 451.[1]
Large Cotton tree in Palamow. 1882. II. 529.[3]
The large-flowered Rose Acacia. See*** The large-flowered Rose Acacia. 1891. III. 486.[3]
The Large flowered Tecoma. 1848. III. 705.
A large Ivy tree. 1873. II. 650.[1]
A large specimen of Euphorbia abyssinica. 1896. III. 517.[2]
The large Walnut tree at Mintmore. 1877. II. 114.[1]
The large white Japan Quince. 1878. III. 420.[1]
The largest Willow in England. 1893. IV. 488.[1]
The largest Willow tree in England. 1893. II. 105.[1]
Laria, Eugen. Cubik-Tabellen zur Berechnung des Cubikinhaltes der Rundhölzer. 1889. IV. 228.
— Die Handels-Usancen im Welt-Holz-Handel. 1889. IV. 403.[1]
— Die Holzvermessung und Berechnung im Welt-Holzhandel. 1890. IV. 228.
La Rive, Aug. de & **Candolle,** Alphonse de. On the relative conductibility for caloric of different woods. 1830. IV. 412.[2]
La Rivière, J. & **Du Moulin.** Méthode pour bien cultiver les arbres à fruit. 1738. III. 143.
Larivière, F. Des Quinquinas. 1847. III. 721.
Larivière, Oscar. Les Jasmins. 1865. III. 672.[2]
Larkins, T. P. Correspondence relative to the discovery of the Tea plant in Sylhet. 1857. II. 552.[1]
Larminat, V. de. Les forêts de Chêne vert. 1893. IV. 503.[2]
La Roche, Daniel de, **Odier,** Louis & **Dunant,** C. G. Pharmacopoea genevensis. 1780. III. 256.[1]
La Rochemacé, Félix de. Le Pin laricio et le Cèdre. 1876. III. 294.[1]
— De la préservation hivernale de l'Eucalyptus. 1884. III. 633.[3]
Laroque, F. Sur la forme du tronc. 1869. I. 105.
La Roque, Jean de. Abhandlung vom Caffe. 1717. III. 738.
— Gründliche und sichere Nachricht vom Cafee. 1717. III. 738.
— Viaggio nell' Arabia Felice. 1716. III. 738.
— Voyage de l'Arabie Heureuse. 1716. III. 738.
— A voyage to Arabia Fœlix. 1716. III. 738.
— A voyage to Arabia the happy. 1716. III. 738.
La Rosa Fichera, Alfio. Nuovo organico forestale pel regno d' Italia. 1862. IV. 293.[2]
— Il rinnovamento dei boschi dell' Etna. 1863. IV. 165.
— Il risorgimento dei boschi in Italia. 1862. IV. 277.
— Studii sulla flora della Cava Catalana Etnea. See Fichera, Alfio. 1891. I. 535.
La Roy, de. Notice sur des essais comparatifs de transplantation d'arbres fruitiers. 1864. III. 168.[3]
Larrabee, W. H. Some curious vegetable growths. 1883. I. 106.[2]
Larreátegui, Joseph Denis. Descripciones de plantas. 1795. II. 532.[3]
— Description botanique du Chiranthodendron. 1795. II. 532.[3]
Larreguy de Civrieux, Sur l'invasion du mildew dans . . . la Touraine. 1885. III. 579.
Larsen, C. V. Naaletraeformering. 1891. III. 294.[2]
— Nytten af Pilevidier som Pakkemiddel. 1887. III. 349.

Larsen, Einar. Om coniferin og vanillin. 1882. I. 176.
Larsen, L. P. Om nogle Træer og Buske. som . . . have ud-
holdt en Kulde hvor Quigsølvet frøs. 1836. III. 44.[1]
Lársen, P. Jasminum nudiflorum. 1887. III. 673.[4]
Larsson, Lars Magnus. Flora öfver Wermland och Dale-
karlen. 1859. I. 355.
— Öfversigt af de . . . arter af slägtet Betula. 1857. II. 117.[2]
— Öfversigt af Sveriges vigtigare fanerogama växtslägten.
1877. V. xviii.[2]
— Symbolae ad Floram Daliae. 1851. I. 355.
Larter, C. E. Manual of the flora of Torquay. 1900. I. 535.
La Rue, de, (abbé). Recherches historiques sur l'histoire de la
botanique à Caen. 1824. I. 81.[1]
La Rue, Adolphe de. L'administration forestière modifiée.
1862. IV. 269.
— Entomologie forestière. 1838. IV. 91.[2]
— Mémoire sur les forêts [de la Turquie]. 18 . . ? IV. 375.[2]
— Notions élémentaires sur l'exploitation des bois. 1886.
IV. 382.[1]
La Rue, Eugène de. Beitrag zur Histologie der Coniferen-
Markscheide. 1873. II. 16.[2]
— Observations sur la phyllomorphose du Syringa. 1872.
II. 716.[1]
— See also Делярко, Е.
La Rue, Hubert. Petit manuel d'agriculture, d'horticulture.
1878. III. 99.
La Rue, Warren de & Müller, Hugo. Ueber das Harz der
Ficus rubiginosa. 1859. III. 371.[2]
— — On the resin of Ficus rubiginosa. 1859. III. 371.[2]
— Sur la résine de Ficus rubiginosa. 1859. III. 371.[2]
Larzillière, F. De l'administration et de la jouissance des
forêts communales. 1876. IV. 326.
— Les forêts de la Meuse. 1887. IV. 361.
— Notice sur l'Aune, du Bouleau. 1878. IV. 85.[2]
— Notice sur le débit des bois de feu. 1878. IV. 387,[2] 395.
— Quelques mots sur l'origine du cantonnement des droits
d'usage. 1877. IV. 334.[1]
Las, de. Phytographie universelle. 1783. I. 254.[1]
Lasausse. See Petit de La Laussate, Sauveur.
Lascaris, marchese. Dell' uso il più proficuo pe' sudditi d. S.
M. degli alberi torti. 1823. IV. 382.[1]
Lascelles, Gerald. A brief history of the arboriculture of the
New forest. 1895. IV. 358.[2]
— The New forest. 1895. IV. 358.[1]
Lascelles-Scott, Wentworth. Sur les graines de Jambul.
1886. III. 637.[2]
Lasch, Wilhelm. Aufzählung der in der Provinz Branden-
burg . . . wildwachsenden Bastard-Pflanzen. 1857. I. 384.
— Beitrag zur Kenntniss der Varietäten . . . einheimischer
Gewächse. 1831. II. 284.[1]
— Beitrag zur Kenntniss . . . einheimischer Gewächse. Cra-
taegus. 1830. II. 260.[2]
— Über die um Driesen wildwachsenden Weidenformen.
1832. II. 101.[1]
— Die Eichenformen der märkischen Wälder. 1857. II. 129.[1]
— Ueber die Pulsatillen der Mark Brandenburg. 1828. II.
101.[1]
— Die Rubusformen . . . um Driesen. 1833. II. 301.[2]
— Ueber die Trennung der Erträge in Abtriebs- und Zwischen-
nutzung. 1881. IV. 236.
Lasègue, A. Musée botanique de M. Benjamin Delessert.
1845. I. 58.
El " Lasiocampa Pini " L. 1895. IV. 559.[1]
Laslett, Thomas. Timber. 1887. IV. 396.[1]
— Timber and timber trees. 1875. IV. 396.[1]
— See also Ласлетъ.
Lasnet. Plantes médicinales du Sénégal. 1900. III. 93.[2]
— & others. Une mission au Sénégal. 1900. I. 491.
Lasnet, (Dr.). Notes sur la pharmacopée des Sakalaves.
1900. III. 282.[1]
Lasnier. Sur le parasitisme du Gui. 1869. II. 179.[1] .
La Soie, de. Observations sur le Gui. 1873. II. 179.[1]
— Roses nouvelles des environs de Bovernier. 1874. II.
287.[1]
La Sourdette. Note sur le moyen propre à prévenir le déve-
loppement de l'oïdium. 1853. III. 576.
Z lasów południowo-zachodniego kraju. 1899. IV. 347.
Laspeyres, Heinrich. Ein alter Weymouthskiefernbestand.
1896. IV. 469.
— Aufforstungsbestrebungen in Spanien. 1898. IV. 165.
— Ausschlagfähigkeit der Pinus rigida. 1898. II. 45.[2]
— Die Eichenblättrigkeit der Hainbuche. 1897. IV. 492.[1]
— Der Einfluss der Streunutzung. 1898. IV. 72, 474, 488.[1]
— Erlen-Ertragstafeln. 1899. IV. 489.[1]

— Forstliches aus Deutsch-Ostafrika. 1898. IV. 379.[2]
— Vom modifizierten Buchenhochwaldbetriebe. 1896. IV.
496.
— Ein neues französisches Gesetz zur Verhütung von Wald-
bränden. 1895. IV. 183.[2]
— Ein neues Verfahren der Holzimprägnirung. 1899. IV.
421.
— Das Verfahren Nodon-Bretonneau zum Senilisiren des
Holzes. 1900. IV. 421.
— Versuche über die Verwendbarkeit verschiedener Holzarten
als Grubenholz. 1900. IV. 425.[2]
Lassaigne, J. L. Sur l'analyse chimique du bois de Naghas.
1824. III. 610.[2]
— Analyse des fruits du Corossolier. 1819. II. 216.[1]
— Examen d'une matière blanche deposée sur les feuilles du
Fusain. 1818. III. 532.[1]
— Mémoire sur le mode de transporte des phosphate et car-
bonate de chaux. 1849. V. xi.[2]
— Sur le mode de transport des phosphate . . . de chaux.
1849. I. 175.
— Recherches sur l'action qu'exercent les sels de fer dans l'acte
de la germination. 1852. I. 202.[2]
— See also Chevallier, A. & Lassaigne, J. L.
Lassaraz, Frédéric Charles Jean, baron Gingins de. See
Gingins de Lassaraz, F. C. J., baron.
Lassaulx, von. Ankeimen und Aussaat von Lärchensamen.
1873. IV. 449.
Lassaulx, C. von. Die Bekämpfung der Reblaus. 1893.
III. 574.
Lassberg. See Zanthier, H. D. von & Lassberg.
Lasseaux. Lettre de l'Uruguay. 1868. IV. 529.[2]
Lassen, A. Zeiner-. See Zeiner-Lassen, A.
Lassimonne, S. E. Mespilus Smithii. 1899. II. 268.[2]
— Le Néflier de Bronvaux. 1900. II. 260.[1]
— Principes de topographie botanique. 1892. I. 301.
— Sur une Rose monstrueuse. 1898. II. 290.[1]
Lassobe. Guide du teinturier moderne. 1826. III. 463.[1]
— Notice sur le bablah. 1827. III. 463.[1]
The last of its race. 1898. II. 864.[1]
Lasteyrie, Charles Philibert de. Du Pastel, de l'Indigotier.
1811. III. 479.[1]
Lastours, de, (député, Tarn). Opinion sur l'emprunt et la
vente des bois de l'état. 1817. IV. 325.
Lastri, Marco. Biblioteca georgica. 1787. III. 1.
— Corso di agricoltura pratica. 1834. III. 115.[2]
Latapie, François de Paula A. Hortus burdigalensis. 1784.
I. 56.
Lataste, Fernand. Contagiosité . . . de la maladie tubercu-
leuse de la Vigne. 1896. III. 562.[1]
— Traitement des Vignes margarodées. 1895. III. 562.[1]
A late fruiting Hawthorn. 1875. III. 429.[2]
Laterrade, Charles. Compte rendu des travaux . . . pour
l'étude de la maladie de la Vigne. 1852. III. 575.[2]
— Observations relatives à l'accroissement en diamètre.
1853. I. 189.
— Observations sur l'Agave geminiflora. 1849. II. 89.[1]
Laterrade, Jean François. Flore bordelaise. 1811. I. 407.
— Note sur le Cierge triangulaire. 1847. II. 591.[2]
— De quelques espèces nouvelles pour la Flore Bordelaise.
1835. II. 309.[1]
The latest forest legislation. 1897. IV. 179.[1]
Lathrop, H. W. Forestry. 1900. IV. 112.
— Forestry. 1889. IV. 112.
— Propagation by slips and cuttings. 1889. III. 158.
Latimer, S. F. Botanic garden, Teneriffe. 1888. II. 82.[1]
Latini, Vincenzo. See Viale, Benedetto & Latini, Vin-
cenzo.
De latinis et graecis nominibus arborum, fruticum. 1544.
I. 71, V. ix.[1]
Latouche, A. Traité sur la nature chimique . . . du café.
1855. III. 739.
Latour. Mémoire sur le Laurier rose. 1857. III. 689.[2]
Latour, Cagniard-. See Cagniard-Latour.
Latour, E. Verdier-. See Verdier-Latour, E.
Latour, G. de. Observations sur le Cupressus disticha nigra.
1863. III. 310.[2]
Latour-Marliac. Bambusa Castilloni. 1886. III. 316.[1]
Latourette, J. F. B. Hilaire de. Flore de l'ancien Velay.
1848. I. 410.
La Tourrette, Marc Antoine Louis Claret de Fleurieu de.
Chloris lugdunensis. 1785. I. 406.
— Démonstrations élémentaires de botanique. 1766. I.
83.
— Voyage au Mont-Pilat. 1770. I. 405.

La Tramblais, de. Note sur une espèce de poire originaire du Berry. 1862. III. 445.[1]

Latrobe, Christian Ignatius. Journal of a visit to South Africa. 1818. V. xxiv.[2]

Il latte di Sandis. 1865. III. 367.[2]

Latter, Thomas. *See* MACTIER, T. B. & LATTER, Thomas.

— & others. Extract of report on the Teak forests. 1848. IV. 537.[1]

Lattorff, Hermann von. Die Entwaldung unserer Gegenden. 1858. IV. 46.[2]

La Tunisie. Agriculture, industrie, commerce. 1896. III. 130.[3]

Lau, Behrend. Beitrag zur Kenntnis der Wirkung des Strychnins. 1886. III. 683.[2]

Laub, F. Udryddelsen af Oldenborrer. 1890. IV. 549.[1]

Laub-, Raff- und Leseholz-Ordnung für . . . Schwarzburg-Sondershausen. 1841. IV. 322.[1]

Laubach, Herman, *Graf* zu SOLMS-. *See* SOLMS-LAUBACH, Herman, *Graf* zu.

Laubert. Mémoire pour servir à l'histoire . . . de Quinquina. 1810. II. 812.

Laubert, Charles Jean. Mémoire pour servir à l'histoire des différentes espèces de quinquina. 1810. III. 724.[1]

— Quelque essai sur la racine de Quinquina. 1819. III. 724.[1]

— Recherches botaniques . . . sur le Quinquina. 1816. III. 721.

Laubhölzer . . . des Hochfürstlich von Rohan'schen Garten. 1879. I. 66.[1]

Zum Laubholz-Niederwald-Betrieb. 1858. IV. 132.[1]

Laubinger, Adolf. Das Gesetz über die Ablösung von Holzberechtigungen. 1877. IV. 334.[1]

— Das Gesetz vom 13. Juni 1873 über die Abstellung von Forstservituten. 1877. IV. 334.[1]

Lauboeck, G. Die Holz verarbeitende Hausindustrie Oesterreichs. 1900. IV. 407.[1]

— Die technischen Eigenschaften des Ailanthusholzes. 1885. IV. 525.[3]

— *See also* EXNER, W. F. & LAUBÖCK, G.

Die Laubstreu. *See* TÜRCKHEIM, von. 1877. IV. 71.

Lauche. Eugenia Ugni . . . Myrtus filifolia. 1857. III. 637,[1] 638.[1]

Lauche, Wilhelm. Abies Eichleri Lauche. 1882. II. 25.[1]

— Actinidia polygama. 1879. III. 595.[2]

— Beiträge zur Palmenzucht. 1858. III. 317.

— Deutsche Dendrologie. 1880. I. 294,[1] *III. 69, IV. 83.*

— Deutsche Pomologie. 1882. III. 71.

— Einige Notizen über den Frostschaden im Winter 1879–80. 1880. III. 46.[1]

— Einige Worte über die . . . kultivirten Palmen. 1856. III. 317.

— Einiges über Palmen. 1858. III. 317.

— Erster Ergänzungsband zu Lucas und Oberdieck's Handbuch der Obstkunde. 1883. III. 71.

— Evonymus Koopmannii Lauche. Turkestan. 1883. II. 468.[2]

— Handbuch des Obstbaues. 1881. III. 138.

— Macrozamia Paulo-Guilielma. 1881. II. 2.[2]

— Eine neue Bignoniacee des freien Landes. 1881. II. 788.[2]

— Eine neue Silberpappel aus Turkestan. 1878. II. 96.[2]

— Ostryopsis Davidiana Decne. 1881. II. 122.[2]

— Der ussurische Birnbaum. 1879. III. 447.[1]

— & Wittmack, Ludwig. Die Entwickelung der Birne und des Apfels. 1879. II. 278.[2]

Lauder-Lindsay, William. *See* LINDSAY, William LAUDER-.

Laue, Gotthelf Moritz. De radice caincae. 1827. III. 744.[1]

Laugeac, *vicomte* de L'ESPINASSE-. *See* L'ESPINASSE-LAUGEAC, *vicomte* de.

Laugier. Sur les chenilles des fleurs de Citronnier. 1883. III. 502.[2]

— Désinfection des végétaux d'ornement. 1883. III. 155.

Laugier, André. Examen chimique de la résine jaune du Xanthorhea. 1810. III. 339.[1]

Laugier, E. Résultats de traitement . . . dans les Alpes-Maritimes, en vue de la destruction du phylloxera. 1882. III. 573.

— Résultats fournis par les traitements des Vignes phylloxérées. 1883. III. 573.

— Résultats obtenus, dans les Vignes phylloxérées. 1881. III. 572.

Laujoulet. Deux nouvelles variétés d'Amandiers. 1862. III. 434.[1]

— Taille et culture de la Vigne. 1866? III. 555.

— Taille et culture des arbres fruitiers. 1865. III. 144.

Laumont, GILLET DE. *See* GILLET DE LAUMONT.

Lauprecht, Gustav. Aus dem A-B-C des Mittelwaldes. 1873. IV. 130.

— Buchen- und Eichen-Samenjahre. 1875. II. 126,[2] *137.*[3]

— Ein Buchen-Plänterwald. 1868. IV. 498.

— Erfahrungen aus dem Eichsfeld über . . . Buche. 1866. IV. 499.

— Etwas über die Aufästungserträge. 1871. IV. 171.

— Etwas über Saftthätigkeit in deutschen Laubholzbäumen. 1871. I. 164, *IV. 63.*[1]

— Aus dem Mühlhauser Mittelwalde. 1871. IV. 26, *243.*[1]

— Umfangreiche Durchforstungs-Erträge eines Buchenhochwaldes. 1872., IV. 498.

— Vermehrung des Buchenzopfreisigs. 1866. IV. 498.

— Wirkliche Durchforstungs-Erträge aus Buchen-Hochwaldungen. 1868. IV. 498.

Laurand, Pierre. Estimation des arbres par une nouvelle règle. 1895. IV. 258.

Laure. Expériences faites sur l'écorcement des arbres. 1842. IV. 434.

Laure, Henri. Effet anormal de plusieurs greffes. 1845. III. 164.[2]

— Guide des cultivateurs du midi. · 1854. III. 31.

— Note sur la greffe d'hiver. 1859. III. 161.

— Nouveau procédé pour obtenir de suite la germination des noyaux osseux. · 1842. III. 156.[1]

Laureau, J. Sur le pouvoir absorbant du charbon de bois. 1876. III. 569.[2]

Laurel Cherries. 1900. III. 437.[2]

Laurell, Fredrik. Schematisk öfversikt öfver de . . . genuskaraktererna . . . Koniferer. 1891. II. 13.[2]

Laurels and Laurels. 1889. III. 437.[2] ·

Lauremberg, Peter. Horticultura libris II. 1632. III.·102.

— Botanotheca Laurembergiana. 1626. I. 35.

Lauremberg, Wilhelm. Botanotheca. 1626. I. 35, V. VIII.[1]

Lauren, L. L. Pari sanaa metsänhävityksestä. 1874. IV. 281.[1]

Lauren, Walter. Om särskiljandet af äkta och falsk Stjärnanis. 1896. III. 398.[1]

— Växtförhållandena i gränstrakterna mellan mellersta och södra Österbotten. 1896. I. 367.

Laurence, John. The clergy-man's recreation. 1714. III. 108.

— The fruit-garden kalendar. 1718. III. 141.

— The gentleman's recreation. 1716. III. 108.

— A letter . . . particularly relating to variegated greens. 1717. III. 206.[1]

— A new system of agriculture. 1726. III.·108.

Laurent, (Dr.). Classification des Cerises. 1860. III. 431.[2]

Laurent, Auguste. Sur les acides pimarique. 1839. II. 44.[2]

— Composés de la créosote. 1841. IV. 432.[1]

— Mouvements spontanés des granules. 1847. II. 508.[1]

— Note sur la créosote. 1844. IV. 432.[1]

— Note sur les acides des Pins. 1845. ·IV. 462.[2]

— Sur les tannins et les glucosamides. 1852. I. 175.

Laurent, Émile. Le Bas-Congo, sa flore. 1894. III. 131.[1]

— Le Caféier et sa culture au Congo. 1898. III. 732.[2]

— Les Caféiers sauvages du Congo. 1898. II. 814.[1]

— Essais relatifs à la dispersion du Gui en Belgique. 1899. II. 180.[1]

— Expériences sur l'absence de bactéries. 1890. I. 159.

— Expériences sur la réduction des nitrates. 1891. I. 160.

— La flore [du Congo]. 1897. I. 492.[1]

— Les forêts du Congo. 1897. IV. 379.[2]

— Guide de la section congolaise à l'Exposition de Bruxelles-Tervueren. 1897.· IV. 379.[2]

— Sur le microbe des nodosités des Legumineuses. 1891. II. 321.[1]

— Les microbes du'sol. 1886. I. 159.

— Notes sur quelques fleurs anomales. 1884. II. 276,[2] *644.*[2]

— Sur l'origine des variétés panachées. 1900. I. 245, *III. 181.*[1]

— De wilde Koffieboom van den Congo. 1898. II. 815.[1]

— *See also* ERRERA, Léo & LAURENT, Émile; SCHLOESING, Théophile, (*jr.*) & LAURENT, Émile.

Latreute, J. Abrégé pour les arbres nains et autres. 1675. III. 143.

Laurent, Jules. Absorption des hydrates de carbone par les racines. 1898. I. 162.

— Sur l'absorption des matières organiques par les racines. 1897. I. 162.

— *See also* BELLEVOYE, Ad. & LAURENT, Jules; BOURQUELOT, Ém. & LAURENT, Jules; BOURQUELOT, Émile & LAURENT, Jules.

Laurent, L. Recherches et résultats d'observations de mœurs des animaux nuisibles aux . . . bois. 1850. IV. 414.[1]
Laurent, Paul. De l'alternance des essences forestières. 1850. IV. 139.[1]
— De l'influence de la culture. 1838. IV. 43.
— Précis du cours de constructions. 1840. IV. 266.[1]
— Du produit des futaies pleines éclaircies. 1849. IV. 259.[2]
— Routes forestières. 1846. IV. 266.[3]
— Des scieries de l'administration forestière. 1848. IV. 392.
— Taux du placement du capital engagé dans les forêts de l'état. 1851. IV. 261.[3]
— Transport des bois. 1846. IV. 389.
Laurentius. Neue Coniferen. 1868. III. 290.
Le Laurier et l'Olivier réunis. See BUC'HOZ, P. J. 1802. III. 406,[3] 678.[3]
Laurinea. See ALLEMÃO, F. F. 1848. II. 226.[2]
Laurop, Christian Peter. Ueber den Anbau der Birke. 1796. IV. 490.[1]
— Archiv der Forst- und Jagdgesetzgebung. 1827. IV. 316.
— Briefe eines in Deutschland reisenden Forstmannes. 1802. IV. 348.[3]
— Etwas über die Kultur . . . der Kiefer. 1799. IV. 471.
— Das Forst- und Jagdwesen . . . Deutschlands. 1843. IV. 25.
— Die Forstdirektion für angehende und ausübende Forst-männer und Cameralisten. 1823. IV. 287.
— Forstordnungen. 1830. IV. 314.[1]
— Ueber Forstwirthschaft. 1796. IV. 105.
— Freimüthige Gedanken über den Holzmangel. 1798. IV. 282.[1]
— Grundsätze der Forstbenutzung. 1810. IV. 381.
— Grundsätze des Forstschutzes. 1811. IV. 177.[1]
— Die Grundsätze des Forstschutzes. 1833. IV. 177.[1]
— Grundsätze . . . Holzzucht. 1804. IV. 105.
— Handbuch der Forst- und Jagdliteratur. 1830. IV. 1.
— Die Hiebs- und Culturlehre der Waldungen. 1816. IV. 106.
— Ideal einer vollkommenen Forstverfassung. 1801. IV. 287.
— Om Opelskning af Birketræer. 1796. IV. 490.[1]
— Die Staats-Forstwirthschafts-Lehre. 1818. IV. 288.[1]
— Der Waldbau für . . . Forstmänner. 1822. IV. 106.
— See also BEHLEN, Stephan & LAUROP, C. P.
Laus, Heinrich & Schierl, Adalbert. Pflanzenformationen . . . im südlichen Mähren. 1900. I. 444.
Lausanne — Société des sciences physiques. See SOCIÉTÉ . . . I. 520.[1]
Laussaulx, von, (Bürgermeister). Vorschläge zur Beseitigung des Waldnothstandes in der Rheinprovinz. 1891. IV. 308.[1]
Lauterbach, Carl. Untersuchungen über Bau . . . der Sekretbehälter bei den Cacteen. 1889. II. 588.[2]
— See also SCHUMANN, Karl & LAUTERBACH, Karl.
Lauterbach, Reinhold. Buch- und Rechnungsführung für ein . . . Privatforstrevier. 1886. IV. 012.
— Erfahrungen über die Bewährung von Säemaschinen. 1890. IV. 149.[1]
Lauterborn, Robert. Pflanzenphänologische Beobachtungen. 1893. I. 225.
Lauterburg. Influence exercée par les forêts sur le régime des eaux. 1876. IV. 50.
Lauterburg, Robert. Ueber den Einfluss der Wälder. 1877. IV. 43.[3]
Lauterer, Joseph. Anatomical . . . researches on the parasitic phanerogams of Queensland. 1895. II. 175.[3]
— Bunya Bunya nuts. 1895. III. 298.[1]
— Caffein-yielding plants. 1895. III. 223.[1]
— Chemical affinities between Rutaceae and Umbelliferae. 1897. II. 397.[1]
— Excursions-Flora für Freiburg. 1874. I. 387.
— Gums of Eucalypts and Angophoras. 1892. IV. 532.[1]
— Native medicinal plants of Queensland. 1894. III. 94.[1]
— New investigations on rickets and Macrozamia. 1899. III. 285.[3]
— Occurrence of saponin in Australian Acacias. 1897. II. 23.[3]
— Queensland native astringent medicines. 1895. III. 283.[1]
— On the resin of Araucaria Bidwilli. 1895. II. 26.[1]
— The Sassafras trees of Queensland. 1895. III. 403.[3]
Lauth, Gustav. See VILLARS, Dominique, LAUTH, Gustav & NESTLER, A.
Lauth, Thomas. De Acere. 1781. II. 476.[1]
Lautier. See GAUXTET & LAUTIER.

Lautier, O. A. BURNABY. See BURNABY LAUTIER, O. A.
Lauture, comte d'ESCAYRAC DE. See ESCAYRAC DE LAUTURE, comte d'.
Lauvergne, Hubert. Géographie botanique du port de Toulon. 1829. I. 408.
Lauzanne, H. de. Chamaerops excelsa naturalisé. 1884. III. 331.[3]
— Végétaux exotiques acclimatés en Bretagne. 1885. I. 59.
Laval, E. de. Réclamation de priorité, à propos de l'emploi du sulfure de carbone. 1873. III. 565.[3]
Laval, Jean. Un dendromètre économique. 1897. IV. 550.[1]
Lavalle, Jean. Arbres remarquables; Peuplier de l'Arquebuse. 1853. II. 98.[1]
— Catalogue général des plantes cultivées . . . de Dijon. 1854. I. 58.
— Histoire et statistique de la Vigne. 1855. III. 555.
— Peuplier de l'Arquebuse. 1853. II. 98.[1]
Lavallée, Alphonse. Akebia quinata. 1869. III. 393.[1]
— Arboretum segrezianum; énumération. 1876. I. 59, III. 84.[1]
— Arboretum segrezianum; icones. 1880. I. 59, III. 84.[1]
— Les arbres et arbustes exotiques. 187.? III. 84.[1]
— Les Clématites à grandes fleurs. 1884. III. 389.[1]
— Les Clématites à grandes fleurs Clematides megalanthes. 1884. II. 195.[1]
— Cornus florida L. 1863. III. 645.[3]
— Sur deux variétés de Noyer. 1882. III. 356,[3] 359.[1]
— Des haies et des abris. 1863. III. 213.
— Monographie du Passiflora coerulea. 1864. III. 615.[3]
— Note sur le Passiflora coerulea. 1864. III. 615.[3]
— Notes et observations sur des arbres et arbustes. 1879. III. 84.[1]
— Les nouveaux Conifères du Colorado et de la Californie. 1874. II. 14.[1]
— Des plantes à effet pittoresque. 1863. III. 203.
— Rosa viridiflora. 1856. III. 455.[1]
— Les Vignes asiatiques et le phylloxera. 1878. III. 571.
— & Hérincq, François. Observations sur l'effet des froids pendant l'hiver de 1859–60. 1860. III. 48.
Lavallée, Robert. Note sur le Carpenteria californica. 1884. III. 409.[2]
Lavanne, J. B. F. FAISEAU-. See FAISEAU-LAVANNE, J. B. F.
Lavedan, Antonio. Tratado de los usos, abusos, propiedades y virtudes del tabaco, café, té. 1796. III. 222.
Laveleye, Émile de. De landbouw in Nederland. 1864. III. 122.[2]
— De landbouwkunst in de Nederlanden. 1866. III. 122.[2]
— De landbouwkunst in de Nederlanden en Belgie. 1866. III. 122.[2]
Lavenir, C. Les haies, leur utilité. 1899. III. 214.[1]
— Des haies ornementales. 1899. III. 214.[1]
— La potatura dei Lillac. 1899. III. 680.[3]
— Le siepi, loro utilità. 1899. III. 214.[1]
Taille des Lilas. 1899. III. 680.[2]
Laveran, A. The influence of Eucalyptus plantations. 1893. IV. 532.[1]
La Vergne, de. Emploi du coaltar et des sulfocarbonates. 1876. III. 568.
— Sur un moyen de préserver les Vignes. 1874. III. 565.[1]
— Note sur le traitement économique des Vignes phylloxérées. 1876. III. 569.[3]
— Note sur un appareil pour le soufrage des Vignes. 1857. III. 577.
— Résultats obtenus par l'application du sulfocarbonate de potassium. 1878. III. 571.
La Vergne, F. de. Guide du soufreur de Vignes. 1858. III. 577.
— Mémoire sur la maladie de la Vigne. 1853. III. 576.
— Théorie du soufrage de la Vigne. 1858. III. 577.
Lavergne, Gaston. Nouvelle bouillie contre le mildiou et le black rot. 1897. III. 581.
— Observaciones sobre algunas enfermedades de la Vid. 1900. III. 562.[1]
— Rapport sur des expériences pour le traitement du black-rot. 1897. III. 581.
— Rapport sur le black-rot dans l'Armagnac. 1896. III. 581.
La Vergne, Louis Gabriel Léonce Guilbaud, comte de. Instruction pratique . . . contre le phylloxéra. 1874. III. 759.
— Maladie nouvelle de la Vigne. 1869. III. 758.[3]
Lavignac, Hector. La destruction des maladies des Vignes. 1890. III. 561.
— À MM. les membres de la Chambre d'agriculture du Board forestier. 1885. III. 125.

La Vigne, Gislain François de. *See* DELAVIGNE, G. F.
Lavigne, P. & Léon, J. Géographie botanique. Une excursion botanique dans . . . l'Ariège. 1870. I. 414.
Laviña, F. Conclusiones acordadas por el congreso contra la inundaciones de Murcia. 1885. IV. 47.²
Lavina, Fernando WEYLER Y. *See* WEYLER Y LAVINA, Fernando.
Lavini, Giuseppe. Continuazione sopra le richerche fisico-chimiche de' prodotti del Prunus Lauro-cerasus. 1820. III. 438.¹
— Suite des recherches physico-chimiques sur les produits du Laurier-cerise. 1820. III. 438.¹
Lavison, RUFZ DE. *See* RUFZ DE LAVISON.
Lavizzari, Luigi. Dimensioni di alcune piante. 1859. I. 297.²
— Escursioni nel cantone Ticino. 1859. I. 435.
— Il monte Generoso ed i suoi dintorni. 1869. I. 435.
Lavori della Commissione forestale. 1864. IV. 293.²
Lavori statistici. 1864. IV. 364.
Lavotha, Albert. A Havasi Fenyő . . . ismertetéséhez. 1883. IV. 463.³
— A Lúczfenyő. 1882. II. 34.³
Lavy, Jean. État général des végétaux originaires. 1830. I. 217.
— Genera plantarum subalpinam regionem exornantium. 1802. I. 424.
— Phyllographie piémontaise. 1816. I. 425.
— Stationes plantarum Pedemontio indigenarum. 1801. I. 424.
Law, A. F. G. Cyprus. 1888. III. 272.³
Law, John. Catalogue . . . of the Sheffield botanical gardens. 1849. I. 54.
Law, William. The history of Coffee. 1850. III. 739.
A law of heredity. 1897. I. 248.³
Lawes, John Bennet. Report upon some experiments undertaken at the suggestion of Professor Lindley. 1851. I. 166.
— & Gilbert, J. H. On the present position of the question of the sources of the nitrogen. 1890. I. 159.
— — & Pugh, Evan. Assimilation de l'azote par les végétaux. 1862. I. 158.
— — — On the sources of the nitrogen. 1862. I. 158.
Lawford, A. C. On the cultivation of the Orange. 1889. III. 497.²
— Essays on viticulture and fruit culture in California. 1889. III. 133.
— On the growth and preparation of raisins. 1889. III. 551.¹
Lawrance, Mary. A collection of Passion-flowers. 1799. II. 576,² *III. 615.¹*
— A collection of Roses from nature. 1799. III. 447.²
Lawrence, Rosewell B. Bandai-san, Miomote. 1893. I. 463.¹
— Camel's Rump and the Rangeley Lake Mountains. 1886. I. 315.
— The Giant's Stairs. 1883. I. 315.
— Middlesex Fells [Mass.]. 1886. I. 315.
Laws of the Hawaiian Islands relating to agriculture and forestry. 1893. IV. 332.²
Laws respecting the sale of public lands, woods and forests. 1896. IV. 314.¹
Lawson. An abstract of several sorts of trees . . . of North America. 1733. III. 261.¹
Lawson. Report on Larches raised from seed. 1837. III. 304.²
Lawson, A. A. Some observations on . . . the karyokinetic spindle in . . . Cobaea. 1898. II. 747.¹
Lawson, Charles. On the introduction of Pinus uncinata. 1839. III. 306.²
— On the Pinus austriaca. 1837. IV. 465.¹
Lawson, G. Palm trees. 1855. III. 319.¹
Lawson, George. On Calluna in America. 1866. II. 661.²
— Celastrus scandens Linn. 1860. II. 467.¹
— Contributions to microscopical analysis. 1860. II. 467.¹
— On the Ericaceae of Canada. 1873. II. 658.¹
— On the geographical range . . . of Canadian Rubi. 1876. II. 300.¹
— On Macadamia. 1860. II. 164.³
— A new locality in Scotland for Ruscus. 1846. II. 84.²
— Note on Comptonia asplenifolia and Myrica. 1884. II. 111.¹
— Note on the leaves of Ulex. 1864. II. 387.¹
— On the occurrence of " cinchonaceous glands" in Galiaceae. 1854. II. 808.¹
— Remarks on Myrica cerifera. 1864. III. 353.¹

— Remarks on some fibrous plants of Canada. 1862. III. 234.
— Remarks on . . . the Canadian Spruces. 1897. II. 34.¹
— Remarks on the flora of the northern shores of America. 1888. I. 310.
— Revision of the Canadian Ranunculaceae. 1885. II. 195.²
— Some account of plants collected in the counties of Leeds. 1863. I. 310, V. XVII.¹
Lawson, John. Allerneueste Beschreibung von Karolina. 1709. III. 263.³
— The history of Carolina. 1709. III. 263.³
— A new voyage to Carolina. 1709. III. 263.³
Lawson, Marmaduke Alexander. Notes on a botanical tour in Travancore. 1894. I. 475.³
Lawson, Peter & Son. The agriculturist's manual. 1836. III. 66.¹
— List of plants of the Fir tribe. 1851. III. 289.
— — The pomologist's manual. 1866. III. 79.
— Synopsis of the vegetable products of Scotland. 1852. III. 271.¹
— & Sons. List of ornamental and rare forest trees. 1850. III. 28.³
Lawson, William. A new orchard and garden. 1618. III. 140.³
— A way to get wealth. 1618. III. 140.³
Lawson's Pinetum britannicum. *See* RAVENSCROFT, Edward. 1884. V. XXV.¹
Lawton, William. Rubus laciniatus. 1860. III. 458.³
Laxmann, Erich. Koelreuteria paniculata, novum plantarum genus. 1772. II. 487.¹
— Novae plantarum species. 1771. II. 315,³ 342.¹
— Sibirische Briefe. 1769. I. 453.¹
Lay, George Tradescant. A few hints regarding Chinese agriculture. 1844. III. 376.
Layard, G. The Cocorite Palm. 1887. II. 71.³
Layau, G. E. Forest culture. 1900. IV. 181.³
Laydeker, J. Compte rendu: 1° Des travaux du reboisement. 1868. IV. 162.
Layé, G. Une bonne plante à feuillage ornemental. 1898. III. 755.¹
Layens, Georges de. *See* BONNIER, Gaston & LAYENS, Georges de.
Layman, W. Precursor to an exposé on forest trees and timber. 1813. IV. 425.¹
Lázár, Jakab. Erdészeti kézikönyv. 1874. IV. 99.³
— Észrevételek as oly kevéssé méltányolt Jegenyefenyőről. 1868. IV. 444.¹
Lázaro, D. B. Historia de la flora ibérica. 1886. I. 81.¹
Lázaro é Ibiza, Blas. Botanica descriptiva. 1896. I. 423.
— Contribuciones à la flora de la peninsula ibérica. 1893. I. 423.
— El problema de las inundaciones. 1884. IV. 47.³
— Regiones botánicas de la peninsula ibérica. 1895. I. 423.
— La suspensión periódica de la vegetación. 1886. IV. 543.¹
— & Andrés y Tubilla, Tomás. Revista critica de las Malvacéas españolas. 1881. II. 519.¹
Lazenby, W. R. & Werner, W. C. Supplementary list to the plants of Ohio. 1890. I. 315.
Lazurianu, L. A. Studiu asupra creşterei arborilor şi a masivelor lemnoase. 1891. IV. 234.
Lazzoni, Beniamino. Tignola dell' Uva. 1895. III. 564.¹
Ldr. Die " schönen Buchen" bei Stixenstein. 1896. IV. 500.³
Ldr. Die Vestenhofer Föhre. 1896. IV. 483.¹
Lea, Sheridan. Le ferment coagulant des graines du Withania. 1885. III. 702.¹
— Sur une présure contenue dans . . . Withania. 1884. III. 702.²
Lea, Thomas Gibson. Catalogue of plants . . . of Cincinnati. 1849. I. 314.
Leach, W. C. Hardy climbing and trailing plants. 1893. III. 205.¹
Leache, Miguel MARTINEZ Y. *See* MARTINEZ Y LEACHE, Miguel.
Leardi, C. *See* DEMARIA, P. P. & LEARDI, C.
Learned, J. E. Forests as playgrounds. 1887. IV. 178.¹
Leasing state forest lands. 1888. IV. 178.¹
Leaves of trees as fodder. 1898. III. 223.³
Leavitt, R. Y. The nutrition of humus-plants. 1900. I. 234.¹
Leavitt, Robert Greenleaf. Reversions in Berberis and Sagittaria. 1900. II. 202.³
Lebaron, William. The lesser Apple leaf-folder. 1871. III. 427.¹

Lebas, E. Acer Negundo variegatum. 1877. III. 535.[1]
— Acer Wagneri laciniatum. 1868. III. 536.[1]
— Allamanda Wardleyana. 1877. III. 686.[1]
— Alnus barbata. 1866. III. 356.[2]
— Alnus subcordata et Alnus Vilmoreana. 1866. III. 356.[2]
— Ampelopsis citrulloides. 1875. III. 544.[1]
— Un arbre doublement utile. 1868. III. 751.[2]
— Atraphraxis spinosa. 1870. III. 387.[1]
— Berberis pallida. 1878. III. 396.[1]
— Berberis stenophylla. 1874. III. 395.[1]
— Cornus Thelicanis. 1875. III. 645.[2]
— Crataegus latifolia. 1869. III. 423.[1]
— Culture du Daubentonia punicea. 1869. III. 487.[2]
— Cytisus elegans. 1881. III. 474.[1]
— Desmodium penduliflorum. 1869. III. 481.[1]
— Deux faits très-remarquables de dimorphisme. 1866. II. 103.[1]
— Deux mots sur le Bambusa Fortunei variegata. 1866. III. 316.[1]
— Deux nouvelles variétés de Frêne à fleurs. 1876. III. 672.[1]
— Le Dragonnier de l'Orotava. 1868. III. 336.[2]
— Forsythia Fortunei. 1869. III. 672.[1]
— Fuchsia Ricartoni. 1877. III. 640.[2]
— Jubaea spectabilis. 1879. III. 326.[1]
— Maackia amurensis. 1880. III. 472.[2]
— Multiplication de l'Indigofera Dosua. 1875. III. 479.[2]
— Multiplication des Chênes à feuilles persistantes. 1874. III. 361.[2]
— Multiplication du Populus grandidentata. 1868. III. 345.[1]
— Multiplication par graines des Weigelas. 1875. III. 541.[1] 748.[2]
— Nouveau mode de culture des Weigelas. 1876. III. 748.[2]
— Noyer pleureur. 1870. III. 355.
— Pêcher à feuilles pourpres. 1876. III. 440.[1]
— Plantes nouvelles ou pas assez connues. 1873. III. 87.
— Poinciana Gilliesii. 1870. III. 469.[1]
— Prunus tomentosa. 1875. III. 443.[1]
— De quelques Fusains du Japon. 1872. III. 532.[2]
— Quelques observations sur la fécondité des Aucuba. 1867. III. 644.[1]
— Ravenia rosea. 1880. III. 505.[2]
— Rhamnus castaneifolius. 1867. III. 543.[1]
— Rhododendron formosum. 1877. III. 659.[1]
— Robinia Pseudo-acacia monophylla. 1868. III. 487.[1]
— Robinia viscosa rubiginosa. 1874. III. 487.[2]
— Rosier Manetti. 1875. III. 455.[2]
— Salix nigra. 1868. III. 352.[1]
— Sambucus nigra flore pleno. 1876. III. 751.[2]
— Sambucus pyramidata. 1884. III. 752.[1]
— Des semis de Lierre. 1879. III. 642.[2]
— Two new varieties of Flowering Ash. 1876. III. 672.[1]
— Des variétés de Chaenomeles japonica. 1868. III. 420.[1]
— Des Viburnum cotinifolium et multratum. 1870. III. 753.[1]
— Viburnum pyrifolium. 1869. III. 753.[2]
— Vitex robusta. 1869. III. 697.[2]
— Weigela alba. 1876. III. 749.[1]
— *See also* VERLOT, Bernard & LEBAS, E.
Lebaume, G. de. *See* BOYER, F. & LÉBAUME, G. de.
Lebaud. Manuel de l'herboriste. 1825. III. 85.
Le Bèle, Jules L. The Clematises. 1896. III. 389.[2]
— Les Clématites. 1896. III. 389.[2]
— Note sur le Pin pleureur de l'Himalaya. 1863. III. 307.[1]
Le Berryais, Louis René. Abrégé du Traité des jardins. 1791. III. 86.
— Traité de l'orangerie. 1788.. III. 150.[1]
— Traité des jardins. 1775. III. 112.
Lebert, H. & **Cohn**, F. Ueber die Fäule der Cactusstämme. 1875. III. 620.[1]
— — Sur une nouvelle espèce de Peronospora. 1870. III. 620.[1]
Lebeuf. Sur une nouvelle maladie du Figuier. 1863. III. 370.[1]
Lebeuf, Alexandre GODEFROY-. *See* GODEFROY-LEBEUF, Alexandre.
Le Bœuf, Ferdinand. Recherches sur la saponine. 1850. III. 447.[1]
Lebl, M. Gemüse- und Obstgärtnerei. 1892. III. 139.
— Illustrierter Rosengarten. 1879. III. 449.
— Rosenbuch. 1895. III. 213.[1]
— *See also* MÜLLER, J. B. & LEBL, M.
Leblanc, TRIPET-. *See* TRIPET-LEBLANC.

Leblois, A. Production de thylles. 1887. II. 414.[1]
— Recherches sur l'origine . . . des canaux sécréteurs. 1887. I. 135.
Leblond. Mémoire sur la culture du Rocouyer. 1803. III. 613.[1]
Le Blond, Alexandre. Die Gärtnerei in ihrer Theorie und Praxis. 1709. III. 112.
— Neu eröffnete Gärtner-Akademie. *See* L'ÉCOLE du jardinier . . . 1764. III. 112.
— La théorie et la pratique du jardinage. *See* DEZALLIER D'ARGENVILLE, A. J. 1709. III. 112.
— The theory and practice of gardening. 1709. III. 112.
Leblond, Charles & **Rendu**, Victor. Botanique. 1834. I. 87.
Leblond, E. Étude physiologique . . . de la caféine. 1883. III. 742.[1]
Le Blond, F. F. Études spéciales sur les fruits de la Guyane. 1855. III. 268.[2]
— Études sur les fruits. 1855. III. 268.[1]
Leblond, Jean Baptiste.· Description abrégée de la Guyane française. 1814. III. 267.[2]
— Mémoire sur le Poivrier. 1806. III. 343.[1]
— Observations sur le Cannelier de la Guiane. 1801. III. 513.[2]
— Observations sur le Cannelier de la Guyane. 1795. II. 506.[1]
Le Bon, Alexis. Les forêts de l'état. 1865. IV. 269, 275.
Lebouidre-Delalande, L. Joseph. Leçons à ma fille sur la botanique. 1834. I. 94.
— Traité élémentaire de physiologie végétale. 1845. I. 148.
Lebret, Georges. Réponse au vœu émis par la Société forestière de Franche-Comté. 1899. IV. 555.[1]
Lebret, Isidore. Notice sur l'Hippophae rhamnoides. 1821. III. 629.[1]
Lebreton, F. Manuel de botanique. 1787. I. 83.
Le Brocq, Philip. A description, with notes, of certain methods of planting . . . fruit-trees. 1786. III. 141.
Lebrün. Praktisches Handbuch der Kutschenfabrikation. 1834. IV. 427.[1]
— Der vollkommene Stellmacher. 1834. IV. 427.[1]
Lebrun, Émile. Lé Baobab. 1900. II. 529.[1]
— Le Brosimum Galactodendron. 1899. III. 367.[2]
— Datura suaveolens. 1900. III. 700.[1]
— Le Leca amabilis. 1897. III. 544.[2]
— Une nouvelle essence à caoutchouc du Congo. 1900. III. 370.[2]
— Pavia alba. 1900. III. 539.[1]
— Rhus glabra. 1900. III. 527.[2]
— Les Wistaria. 1898. III. 490.[2]
Lebrun, Georges. Les arbustes à floraison automnale. 1889. III. 207.[2]
— Plantations ornementales dans les terrains calcaires. 1889. III. 41.[1]
— Le Poinciana Gilliesii. 1891. III. 469.[1]
Le Bruyn, Cornells. *See* BRUYN, Cornells de.
Lebscher, G. La marche de l'absorption des principes nutritifs. 1888. I. 159.
Le Camus de Mézières, Nicolas. Traité de la force des bois. 1782. IV. 409.
— *See also* BABUTI DESGODETZ & LE CAMUS DE MÉZIERES.
Le Canu, Louis René. Étude sur les raisins. 1868. III. 583.[1]
Lécard, Th. Notice sur les Vignes du Soudan. 1881. III. 559.[1]
Lécarlier. Verandering van vruchten. 1806. I. 246.[2]
Lecart, A. Les éléments de la production ligneuse. 1891. IV. 84.[1]
— *See also* BERGER, L. & LECART, A.
Lecart, Alphonse. Conservation et agrandissement du domaine forestier de l'état. 1894. IV. 551.[2]
Lechartier, G. De l'emploi des engrais potassiques en Bretagne. 1884. III. 151.
— Sur l'incinération des matières végétales. 1889. I. 156.[2]
— & **Bellamy**, F. Action des vapeurs . . . sur la fermentation des fruits. 1877. I. 179.[1]
— — Étude sur les gaz produits par les fruits. 1869. I. 179.[1]
— — — De la fermentation des fruits. 1869. I. 179.[1]
— — De la fermentation des pommes et des poires. 1875. I. 179.[1]
— Sur la présence du zinc . . . dans les végétaux. 1877. I. 153.
Leche, Johan. Disputatio medico-botanica exhibens primitias florae scanicae. 1744. I. 351.
— Förteckning öfver de raraste växter i Skåne. 1744. I. 351.
— Horungs-daggens historia. 1762. I. 351.[2]
— Underrättelse, om wilda träns och buskars plantering. 1764. IV. 113.[1]

Lechevalier. Moyen de faciliter la reprise des arbres. 1859. III. 166.

Lechler, Wilibald. Berberides Americae australis. 1857. II. 201.[2]
— Supplement zur Flora von Würtemberg. 1844. I. 381.
— Vergleichung des schweizerischen Jura. 1850. I. 383.

Leclerc. Sur l'emploi du bitume de Judée. 1882. III. 561.

Leclerc, A. Recherches sur la germination. 1875. I. 203.
— De la transpiration dans les végétaux. 1883. I. 167.

Leclerc, E. Addition . . . sur les parties sensibles . . . des plantes. 1855. I. 197.[2]
— De la caprification. 1858. II. 150.[2]
— Influence de l'électricité sur . . . la Sensitive. 1854. II. 372.[1]
— Nouvelles observations concernant le système nerveux des plantes. 1853. I. 122.
— *See also* HARDOUIN, L., RENOU, F. & LECLERC, E.

Leclerc, F. Nouveau traité de la taille des arbres. 1865. III. 172.

Leclerc, François. Goethe et le livre de la métamorphose des plantes. 1872. I. 101.[1]
— Un mot sur la théorie du mouvement de la sève. 1874. I. 165.
— Recherches physiologiques . . . sur le mouvement des végétaux. 1859. I. 194.
— De la segmentation dans les végétaux. 1874. I. 101.[2]
— Théorie de l'anaphytose. 1870. I. 101.[2]

Leclerc, J. Matériel et procédés des exploitations. 1868. IV. 381.

Leclerc, J. & others. Assainissement des terrains fangeux. 1900. IV. 144.[1]

Le Clerc, Louis. Culture et multiplication du Dracaena. 1889. III. 334.[2]
— Plantes nouvelles. 1893. II. 76,[1] 651.[1]
— Rusticité de quelques végétaux. 1860. III. 48.
— Les Vignes malades. 1853. III. 559.[2]

Leclerc du Sablon, Mathieu. Sur l'anatomie de la tige de la Glycine. 1893. II. 388.[2]
— Sur un cas de la chute des feuilles. 1885. I. 192,[1] II. 274.[2]
— Sur un cas pathologique. 1889. III. 465.[2]
— Sur les causes anatomiques de l'enroulement des vrilles. 1886. I. 196.[2]
— Sur la chute des feuilles marcescentes. 1884. I. 191.[2]
— Sur la déhiscence des anthères. 1884. I. 116.[2]
— Sur la déhiscence des fruits secs. 1883. I. 119.
— Sur la dextrine considérée comme matière de réserve. 1899. I. 180.[1]
— Sur la digestion de l'albumen du Dattier. 1897. II. 73.[1]
— Sur la digestion de l'amidou. 1898. I. 178.
— Sur la digestion des albumens gélatineux. 1895. I. 177, 204.
— Sur la formation des réserves non azotées de la noix. 1896. II. 113,[1] 278.[2]
— Sur la germination des Amandes. 1897. III. 272.[2]
— De l'influence des gelées sur les mouvements de la sève. 1886. I. 165, 212.
— Sur une maladie du Platane. 1892. III. 418.[2]
— Observations anatomiques sur la chute de certaines branches du Peuplier blanc. 1886. I. 192,[2] II. 96.[2]
— Recherches sur l'enroulement des vrilles. 1887. I. 197.[1]
— Recherches sur la déhiscence des fruits à péricarpe sec. 1884. I. 119.
— Recherches sur la structure . . . des anthères. 1885. I. 116.[2]
— Sur les réserves oléagineuses de la noix. 1897. II. 114.[1]
— Sur les suçoirs des Rhinanthées et des Santalacées. 1887. II. 168.[1]
— Sur la symétrie foliaire chez les Eucalyptus. 1885. II. 623.[2]
— Sur la tige de la Glycine. 1883. II. 388.[2]

Leclerc-Thouin, Oscar. Considérations relatives aux effets de la gelée. 1840. III. 182.
— Considérations sur l'étude des races végétales. 1842. III. 43.
— Description de la greffe-Kew. 1829. III. 160.
— Sur l'influence des feuilles de la Vigne. 1843. II. 508.[1]
— Influence des feuilles sur la maturation du raisin. 1843. II. 508.[1]
— Des marcottes. 1841. III. 159.[1]
— Note sur un cas particulier de décortication annulaire. 1843. III. 175.[1]
— Das Reifen der Obst- und Steinfrüchte. 1832. III. 173.[3]

Leclercq, J. T. Nouveau calculateur. 1859. IV. 224.

Leclère, Adhémar. Les plantations de Poivriers au Cambodge. 1899. III. 343.[2]

Leclère, L. Cantua dependens Pers. 1858. III. 694.[3]

Le Clerq, J. Des plantes médicinales de l'île de la Réunion. 1864. III. 93.[1]

L'Écluse, A. de. Le Black-Rot et son traitement. 1891. III. 580.
— Le traitement du black-rot. 1891. III. 580.

Lecœur, E. L'anthonome du Pommier. 1891. III. 428.[1]
— La chématobie hiémale du Pommier. 1892. III. 428.[1]

Lecomte, C. AUBRY-. *See* AUBRY-LECOMTE, C.

Lecomte, Henri. Les arbres à gutta percha. 1899. III. 230.
— Le café, culture, manipulation. 1899. III. 727.
— Contribution à l'étude du liber. 1889. I. 130.
— La culture du Cacaoyer. 1897. III. 593.[1]
— Effets produits par la décortication annulaire. 1887. I. 192.[2]
— Sur la formation du pollen chez les Anonacées. 1896. II. 215.[2]
— Le Kickxia africana Benth. 1897. III. 688.[3]
— Le Kickxia africana Benth. au Congo français. 1897. III. 688.[3]
— Sur la mesure de l'absorption de l'eau par les racines. 1894. I. 162, II. 155.[1]
— La production agricole & forestière. 1900. III. 218.[1]
— Les produits végétaux du Congo français. 1894. III. 281.[1]
— Sur quelques points de l'anatomie . . . des Casuarinées. 1886. II. 92.[1]
— La Ramie. 1890. III. 381.[2]
— Sur le rôle du liber. 1890. I. 131.[1]
— Les textiles végétaux. 1893. III. 235.[1]
— Les textiles végétaux des colonies. 1896. III. 235.[1]
— *See also* TIEGHEM, Philippe van & LECOMTE, Henri.
— & Chalot, Ch. Le Cacaoyer et sa culture. 1897. III. 593.[1]
— & Hébart, Alexandre. Sur les graines de Coula. 1894. II. 170.[2]
— — Sur les graines de coula du Congo. 1895. III. 590.[1]
— — Sur les graines de Moábi. 1895. I. 154.

Lecomte, Louis. L'Hazondrano. 1899. III. 688.[2]

Leconet. Note sur les semences de Pignon d'Inde. 1852. III. 519.[2]

Leçons de botanique. *See* CUSSON, Pierre, GOUAN, Antoine & COMMERSON, Philibert. 1762. I. 511.

Leconte, Amédée Henri. Emploi du café en thérapeutique. 1859. III. 742.[1]

Leconte, J. L. Grammaire horticole. 1889. III. 110.[2]

Le Conte, John. American Grape-vines of the Atlantic States. 1858. II. 505.[1]
— Description of a new species of Pacane nut. 1854. II. 112.[3]
— An enumeration of the Vines of North America. 1854. II. 505.[1]
— Notes on Magnolia pyramidata. 1856. II. 212.[3]

Le Conte, Joseph. The flora of the coast islands of California. 1887. I. 325.

Lecoq. Note sur le Thé. 1844. III. 606.

Le Coq, G. Pandanus D'Haenei. 1884. III. 313.[2]

Lecoq, Henri. Botanique populaire. 1862. I. 90.
— Budleia [sic] madagascariensis. 1863. III. 682.[1]
— Études sur la géographie botanique de l'Europe. 1854. I. 349.
— De la fécondation indirecte. 1862. I. 201.[1]
— De la fécondation naturelle et artificielle. 1845. I. 237, III. 50.[1]
— De la génération alternante. 1856. I. 202.[1]
— Sur l'hybridation des Groseilliers. 1848. II. 243.[1]
— De l'influence de la Sabine. 1851. III. 304.[1]
— Von der natürlichen und künstlichen Befruchtung. 1845. I. 237, III. 50.[2]
— Note sur l'étendue de l'aire moyenne . . . des espèces végétales. 1857. I. 299.
— Note sur une manière de greffer pour hâter la fructification. 1844. III. 164.[1]
— Précis élémentaire de botanique. 1828. I. 85.
— De la préparation des herbiers. 1829. I. 35.
— Quelques reflexions sur l'élagage des arbres. 1836. III. 169.[1]
— Recherches sur la reproduction des végétaux. 1827. I. 236.[1]
— La vie des fleurs. 1861. I. 217.
— & Juillet, Jules. Dictionnaire raisonné des termes de botanique. 1831. I. 70.
— & Lamotte, Martial. Catalogue raisonné des plantes vasculaires du plateau central de la France. 1847. I. 410.

Lecoq, L. M. De la culture du Thé. 1845. III. 601.[1]
Lecoq de Boisbaudran, François. Sur l'attaque du phylloxera · par le sulfure de carbone. 1874. III. 566.[1]
— Effets que le sulfure de carbone . . . paraît sur la Vigne. 1873. III. 565.[1]
— Formation des glaçons. 1870. I. 212.
Lecoq de Boisbaudran, Paul Émile. *See* LECOQ DE BOISBAUDRAN, François.
Lecoq-Dumesnil. *See* VERLOT, Bernard & LECOQ-DUMESNIL.
Le Court, Benoît. *See* CURTIUS, Benedictus.
Lecouteux, Édouard. Traité élémentaire de l'agriculture du département de la Seine. 1840. III. 113.
Lecoy, A. The forest question in New Zealand. 1879. IV. 280.[1]
Ledden Hulsebosch, M. L. Q. van. Iets over assimilatie en stofwisseling. 1877. I. 176.
— Koffiesurrogaten. 1899. III. 740.[1]
— Nog eens zwarte Rozen. 1877. III. 449.
— De zwarte! Roos. 1876. III. 449.
Leddet, Pierre. Des dégrèvements d'impôt. 1898. IV. 164.[1]
Ledebour, Karl Friedrich von. Commentarius in J. G. Gmelini Floram sibiricam. 1841. I. 453.[2]
— Decades sex plantarum novarum in imperio rossico. 1814, 1815. I. 360, II. 296.[1]
— Enumeratio plantarum horti botanici Gryphici: 1806. I. 45.
— Flora altaica. 1829. I. 453.[2]
— Flora rossica. 1842. I. 361.
— Icones plantarum novarum . . . floram rossicam . . . illustrantes. 1829. I. 360.
— Index seminum Horti academici dorpatensis. 1822. I. 41.
— Reise durch das Altai-Gebirge. 1829. I. 453.[2]
— & **Adlerstam**, J. P. Dissertatio botanica sistens plantarum domingensium decadem. 1805. I. 335.
Ledebur, A. Die Verarbeitung des Holzes. 1881. IV. 422.[1]
Ledeganck, K. Recherches histo-chimiques sur la chute automnale des feuilles. 1871. I. 191.[2]
Leder, Hans. Les forêts de la Sibérie. 1894. IV. 376.[1]
— Wald, Wild und Jagd in Sibirien. 1894. IV. 376.[1]
Ledermüller, Martin Frobenius. Amusement microscopique. 1759. I. 97.
— Mikroskopische Gemüths- und Augenergötzungen. 1759. · I. 97.
— Physikalisch-mikroskopische Zergliederung . . . einer . . . Winterknospe des Hippocastani. 1764. II. 481.[1]
Ledesma, Antonio COLMENERO DE. *See* COLMENERO DE LEDESMA, Antonio.
Ledien, Franz. Araucaria imbricata in Deutschland. 1899. III. 299.[1]
— Bambusa nana Roxb. 1899. III. 316.[1]
— Ueber Düngungsversuche mit Eriken. 1897. III. 650.[2]
— Fendlera rupicola. 1899. III. 411.[1]
— Ueber die Keimung der Kokosnuss. 1900. . II. 67.[2]
— Picea pungens var. 1891. III. 306.[1]
— D e Verwendung der winterharten Rhododendron. 1900. III.i656.
— Ueber winterharte Rhododendron. 1898. III. 655.
— Winterharte Rhododendron. 1899. III. 655.
— Wirkungen des Winters 1894-95. 1895. III. 46.[1]
Ledig, Bernhard. Beitrag zur Kenntniss der Gummicanäle. 1881. II. 531.[2]
Le Docte, Henri. Mémoire sur la chimie et la physiologie végétales. 1849. I. 147.
Ledos, Carlos. Tratado que comprende el cultivo del Café. 1847. III. 100.[1]
Le Dru, André Pierre. Reise nach den Inseln Teneriffa. 1810. I. 335.
— Voyage aux iles de Ténériffe. 1810. I. 335.
Leduc, Aug. De l'accroissement des tiges de Cocotier. 1873. II. 67.[2]
Le Duc, Philibert. Boisement du département de l'Ain. 1856. IV. 162, 359.[1]
— Œuvres agronomiques et forestières de Varenne de Fenille. 1869. IV. 1.
Le Dulx, G. P. De Calappus-boomen als . . . afleiders van den bliksem. 1790. III. 323.[2]
— De Cokos . . . afleiders van de blixem. 1792. III. 323.[2]
Ledward, W. J. The trees of the Bible. 1895. I. 513.
Lee, Arthur. De cortice peruviano. 1764. III. 720.
Lee, Benjamin. The importance of the woodland areas. 1896. IV. 46.[1]
Lee, Charles Alfred. A catalogue of the medicinal plants. 1848. III. 62.

Lee, James. Catalogue of plants and seeds. 1774. I. 52.
— An introduction to botany. 1760. I. 83.
— Termini botanici. 1813. I. 70.
Lee, John R. Plants of the Kenmuir district of the Clyde. 1896. V. xxi.[2]
Lee, *Mrs.* Robert Bowdich. *See* BOWDICH, *Mrs.* T. E.
Leeds, Josiah W. The derivation of Persimmon. 1885. II. 702.[1]
Leefe, J. Ewbank. An arrangement of the British Willows. 1871. II. 102.[1]
— Dr. Anderson's remarks on the Willows. 1870. II. 102.[1]
— On the groups Triandrae and Fragiles of the genus Salix. 1844. II. 100.[1]
— On hybridity in Salix. 1871. II. 99.[1]
— Remarks on some curious metamorphoses of the pistil of Salix caprea. 1844. II. 103.[2]
— Salix Pontederana Schl? 1872. II. 109.[1]
— On Salix Trevirani Spreng. 1878. II. 108.[1]
Leemans, J. F. & **Wenckebach**. Rapport op het tweede deel van het Algemeen rapport . . . wegens de duinen. 1804. IV. 159.
Leembruggen, C. J. van. De cultuur van rottan. 1899. III. 321.[1]
Leembruggen, W. G. Een en ander over caoutchouc-cultuur. 1900. III. 149.
— Eenige aanteekeningen omtrent . . . Toelang Bawang. 1894. III. 129.[1]
— Eenige mededeelingen omtrent . . . caoutchouc-liänen. 1900. III. 230.
— Eenige mededeelingen over . . . caoutchouc-liänen. 1899. III. 230.
— De mechanische caoutchouc winning uit basten. 1900. III. 232.[2]
Leenderts, C. J. Van Atjeh's stranden tot de koraal rotsen van Nieuw Guinea. 1890. . III. 282.[1]
Leenderts, Janus Matthia. Responsio ad questionem: Quid botanici de variis plantarum gemmis . . . observarint. 1835. I. 107.[2]
Leent, P. J. van. Poisons des flèches des naturels de Bornéo. 1866. III. 276.[1]
Leeraarskring tot volmaaktere boomteeltkunde in België. Tijdschrift. III. 15.
Leers, Joannes Daniel. Flora herbornensis. 1775. I. 374.
Leersum, P. van. Bericht omtrent de gouvernements Kina-onderneming. 1893. III. 716.
— Bericht omtrent de gouvernements Kinaonderneming. 1899. III. 717.[1]
— Een en ander over het oogsten van Kinabast. 1895. III. 712.[2]
— De gouvernements Kina-cultuur 1899. 1900. III. 717.[1]
— Hooge alkaloidgehalten van verschillende Kina-enten. 1891. III. 723.
— Iets over de wortelziekte der Kinaboomen. 1891. III. 717.[2]
— Over den invloed, dien de Cinchona succirubra onderstam . . . Ledgeriana . . . uitoefenen. 1899. III. 717.[1]
— Invloed van kunstmatige droging op het alcaloïde gehalte van Cinchona succirubra-bast. 1895. III. 726.[1]
— Over den invloed van vorst op het alkaloïdegehalte der Kina boomen. 1891. III. 723.
— Kinologische studien. 1889. III. 723. — 1890. III. 723.
— Verslag omtrent de gouvernements Kinaonderneming. 1900. III. 717.[1]
— Verslag over de gouvernements-Kinaonderneming. 1893. III. 717.[1]
Lees, Edwin. On the acceleration of the frondescence. 1848. I. 226.[1]
— Botanical looker-out among the wild flowers . . . of England and Wales. 1842. I. 399.
— The botany of the Malvern Hills. 1843. I. 399.
— The botany of Worcestershire. 1867. I. 402.
— On certain forms or species of fruticose Brambles. 1848. II. 303.[1]
— Comments on some observations . . . on the genus Rubus. 1845. II. 300.[1]
— A descriptive list of the British Rubi. 1853. II. 303.[1]
— The forest and chace of Malvern. 1870. I. 393,[2] V. xx.[2] — 1882. I. 297.[1]
— On the Glastonbury or Holy Thorn. 1875. II. 263.[1]
— The Hawthorn. 1875. II. 263.[1]
— The Lime or Linden tree in Worcestershire. 1874. II. 516.[2]
— New localities for Mistletoe on the Oak. 1851. II. 178.[2]
— Note on Rubus nitidus. 1849. II. 309.[1]

Lees, Edwin (*continued*).
— Note on the genus Tilia. 1842. II. 515.[2]
— Notes of old and curious Wych Elms. 1874. II. 145.[1]
— Notes on remarkable Elms. 1874. II. 143.[2]
— Notes on the Alder. 1874. II. 116.[2]
— Notes on the Ash. 1874. II. 708.[1]
— Notes upon old Oaks. 1875. II. 138.[2]
— Old and remarkable Yews. 1874. II. 11.[1]
— Old Maples. 1876. II. 477.[2]
— Old trees: Willows. 1874. II. 104.[2]
— An old Yew tree. 1878. II. 11.[1]
— Remarks on the mode of growth of the British fruticose Rubi. 1844. II. 302.[2]
— Remarks on the " Rubus leucostachys." 1848. II. 303.[1]
— Resuscitation of old trees. 1878. III. 181.[2]
— Trees within trees. 1876. I. 234.[2]
— Worcestershire Rubi. 1867. II. 303.[1]
Lees, Frederic Arnold. Botany and outline flora of Lincolnshire. 1892. I. 534.[2]
— The flora of West Yorkshire. 1888. I. 404.[1]
— A summary of comital plant-distribution. 1878. I. 403.
— *See also* DAVIS, J. W. & LEES, F. A.
Lees, Wilham Nassau. Tea cultivation . . . in India. 1863. III. 633.
Leete, F. A. Germination of Kharshu. 1894. IV. 516.[2]
— Notes on Assina. 1900. IV. 529.[2]
— Notes on Sál forests. 1900. IV. 528.[2]
— Wire rope-way. 1900. IV. 392.
Leeuwenhoek, Anton van. An abstract of a letter to Mr. R. H. concerning the appearances of several woods. 1683. I. 124.
— Arcana naturae. 1695. I. 97.
— An extract of a letter containing . . . observations on the seeds of Cotton, Palm. 1693. I. 120.
— A letter concerning cochineel. 1705. III. 624.[1]
— A letter concerning the barks of trees. 1706. I. 130.
— Microscopical observations on the cortex peruvianus. 1708. II. 813.[1]
— Microscopical observations on the seeds of several East-India plants. 1708. III. 277.
— Observations upon the seeds of plants. 1723. I. 120.
— Opera omnia. 1695. I. 97.
— The select works. 1695. I. 97.
— Sendbrieven over verschejjden verborgenheden der natuur. 1718. I. 97.
Lefebre, A. De oeretplaag in de Koffietuinen. 1899. III. 737.
Lefébure, E. A. Expériences sur la germination des plantes. 1801. I. 202.[2]
Lefébure, Louis F. H. Atlas botanique. 1817. I. 259.
— Concordance des trois systèmes de Tournefort, Linnaeus et Jussieu. 1816. I. 407.
— Discours sur le principe essentiel de l'ordre . . . en botanique. 1812. I. 251.
— Flore de Paris, genera et species. 1835. I. 409.
— Méthode signalementaire pour servir à l'étude du nom des plantes. 1814. I. 259, 266.
— Sur une nouvelle classification des plantes. 1835. I. 251.
— Reponse à l'auteur anonyme des Observations. 1821. I. 529.[2]
— Système floral. Flore française. 1821. I. 407.
— Le vrai système des fleurs. 1817. I. 251.
— & Leforestier, C. Album floral des plantes indigènes de France. 1829. I. 408.
Lefebvre. Observations sur les mans et les hannetons. 1791. III. 188.[2]
Lefebvre. Rapport . . . par . . . président d'une commission scientifique en Abyssinie. 1844. I. 487.
Lefebvre, A. Le Cornouiller. 1896. III. 646.[1]
Lefebvre, Arsène. Nomenclatura botanica para el curso de farmacologia. 1888. III. 59.[1]
— Rusticité des Dracaena indivisa. 1881. III. 335.
Lefebvre, Charles. Conflit entre bûcherons et marchands. 1893. IV. 311.[2]
— Éclaircies. 1889. IV. 174.
— L'invasion des cynips. 1887. IV. 511.
— Mélange des essences. 1888. IV. 138.[2]
— Mission en Suisse. Organisation forestière du canton de Berne. 1896. IV. 294.[1]
— Le Pin sylvestre dans les forêts d'Orléans. 1885. IV. 4[2]1.
— Question de l'alternance. 1890. IV. 74.[2]
— La question de l'alternance Documents. 1890. IV. 74.[2]
— Semis et plantations. 1892. IV. 142.

— Sylviculture, origines, les anciennes ordonnances. 1894. IV. 24,[1] 87.[2]
— Travaux d'amélioration dans les taillis. 1886. IV. 128.
Lefebvre, Georges. Plantations d'alignement. 1897. III. 84.[2]
Lefebvre, Henri. Les forêts de l'Algérie. 1900. IV. 379.[2]
— Les incendies de forêts eri 1881. 1882. IV. 184.[1]
— Notice sur les forêts de Cèdre. *See* LEVEL & LEFEBVRE, Henri. 1894. IV. 379.[1]
— *See also* LÉVEILLÉ, J. H. & LEFEBVRE, Henri.
Lefebvre, J. G. Les forêts de l'Europe et de l'Amérique. 1876. IV. 244.
— Guide théorique et pratique du négociant en bois. n. d. IV. 220.
— Nouveau guide international théorique et pratique du négociant en bois. n. d. IV. 220.
Lefebvre, Léopold. Essai sur les analogies botaniques. 1860. V. xxviii.[2]
Lefebvre-Chabert. Mémoire traitant de la guérison complète . . . de la Vigne. 1854. III. 559.[2]
Lefeuvre. Étude sur les huiles de bois. 1900. III. 610.[2]
— Étude sur les matières colorantes du Cây-gia. 1900. III. 632.[1]
— L'huile de Cây-tròm. 1900. III. 591.[2]
— L'huile de Mu-u. 1900. III. 608.[1]
Lefeuvre-Meaulle. Commerce du bois de Teck. 1897. IV. 538.[1]
Lefèvre, (*abbé*). Du cassement des rameaux. 188.? III. 172.
— Conseils sur le choix et la forme des arbres. 1882. III. 144.
— Exposé critique du traitement de la branche à fruit. 1890. III. 144.
— Le Poirier martyr. 1886. III. 445.[2]
— Un succès à Nancy sur les arbres à branches renversées. 1886. III. 174.[2]
— Trois erreurs en arboriculture. 1883. III. 144.
— Le verger. 1886. III. 144.
Lefèvre, André. Les parcs et les jardins. 1882. III. 27.[2]
Lefèvre, Édouard. Aperçu général sur la végétation de la Basse-Cochinchine. 1866. I. 469.[2]
— Aperçu sur la flore . . . de Chartres. 1859. I. 412.
— Statistique scientifique [d'Eure-et-Loir]. 1866. I. 413.
Lefevre, G. SHAW-. English commons and forests. 1894. IV. 358.[2]
Le Fèvre, Jean François. De natura, usu & abusu caffé, thé. 1726. III. 222.
Lefèvre, L. V. Examen de l'Essai sur les Rubus normands. 1877. II. 303.[2]
— Observations sur le Rubus plicatus. 1876. II. 309.[2]
— Reproduction des Rubus. 1877. II. 306.[1]
Lefferts, Walter. The practical value of forests to the surface of the country. 1895. IV. 54.
Leffler, Johan Anders. Anmälan af en ny skandinavisk Rosa-art. 1874. II. 295.[1]
— Anmärkningar vid N. J. Scheutz' "Studier." 1872. II. 283.[2]
— Beriktigande [af en uppgift om förekomsten af Rosa pubescens]. 1872. II. 297.[2]
— Ett nytt arbete af N. J. Scheutz' öfver de skandinaviska Rosorna. 1873. II. 284.[1]
— Öfversigt af den skandinaviska halföns anmärkningsvärdare Rosaformer. 1888. II. 284.[1]
— Om Sveriges Rosa-arter. 1871. II. 283.[2]
Leflèvre, L. Plantations aux bords de la mer. 1899. III. 42.[1]
Leforestier, C. *See* LÉFÉBURE, Louis & LEFORESTIER, C.
Lefort, J. Études sur les huiles grasses végétales. 1852. I. 182.[1]
Lefort, Jh. Variations du prix du bois en France. 1876. IV. 405.[1]
Lefort, Jules. Mémoire sur les graines de Nerprun. 1866. III. 542.[2]
— Nouvelles observations sur les principes colorants des Nerpruns. 1868. III. 542.[2]
Lefour. Sol et engrais. 1897. III. 152.
Lefranc, Edmond. Botanique du département d'Eure-et-Loiré. 1867. I. 413.
— La Calle, topographie, botanique. 1865. I. 484.
— Catalogue des plantes . . . de la Calle. 1862. I. 484.
Le Francq van Berkhey, Jan. *See* BERKHEY, Jan LE FRANCQ VAN.
Lefroy, Sir John Henry. The botany of Bermuda. 1884. I. 336.

Le Gall. Flore de Morbihan. 1852. I. 411.
Legati, Lorenzo. Agriomeleis. 1667. II. 267.²
— Chrysomeleida. 1667. II. 402.¹
— Nea Casta. 1767. II. 124.²
Legeler, W. Die praktische Messkunst. 1877. III. 200.¹
Le Gendre, (curé d'Henonville). Baumgärtnerei. 1652. III. 142.
— La manière de cultiver les arbres fruitiers. 1652. III. 142.
— Oeffening der vrugtboomen. 1652. III. 142.
Le Gendre, Charles. Contribution à l'histoire du Gui. 1900. II. 180.¹
— Note sur le Gui. 1898. II. 180.¹
— À propos de tératologie végétale. 1893. II. 352.¹
Legends of trees. See LEGENDS respecting trees. 1847. I. 517.¹
Legends respecting trees. 1844. I. 517.¹ — 1847. I. 517.¹
— See also JUNGFLEISCH, E. & LÉGER, Edmond.
Léger, Edmond. Sur les aloïnes. 1897. III. 333.²
Léger, Louis Jules. Note sur des germinations anormales d'Acer platanoïdes. 1889. II. 479.²
— Recherches sur l'appareil végétatif des Papavéracées. 1894. II. 229.¹
— Recherches sur l'origine . . . des éléments libériens. 1897. I. 131.¹
Léger, L. SAINT-. See BELLAIR, Georges & SAINT-LÉGER, L.
Legge, decreto e regolamento forestale. 1878. IV. 328.
La legge forestale alla Camera. 1897. IV. 329.¹
Una legge non eseguita. 1881. IV. 328.
Legislación. 1892. IV. 555.¹
Législation sur les eaux et forêts. 1874. IV. 332.²
Legler, G. H. Hydrotechnische Mittheilungen über Linth-korrektion. 1868. IV. 187.¹
— Die Verbauung der Rüfirunse. 1855. IV. 187.¹
Del legname da costruzione in Inghilterra. 1862. IV. 423.¹
Il legno campeggio. 1865. IV. 62.¹
Il legno di Gaïac. 1865. IV. 524.²
Legrand, A. Expériences concernant l'action . . . de noix vomique. 1853. III. 682.²
Le Grand, Antoine. Essai sur la géographie botanique de l'Aube. 1859. I. 412.
— Note sur quelques plantes critiques. 1881. II. 306.²
— Observations critiques sur les Fumaria media. 1892. II. 351.²
— Statistique botanique du Forez. 1873. I. 414.
Legrand, Aug. Tables métriques pour le cubage des bois. n. d. IV. 220.
Legrand, Charles & Vattier, Charles. La région forestière australe du Chili. 1892. IV. 342.¹
Le Grand, O. Le Rosa gallica en Berry. 1895.' II. 294.¹
Legrand, Victor. Mémoire pour servir à l'établissement des bases d'une exploitation . . . en Algérie. 1855. IV. 383.²
— Mémoire sur les richesses forestières de l'Algérie. 1854. IV. 379.¹
— Rapport sur le reboisement des montagnes. 1848. IV. 161.²
Legré, Ludovic. La botanique en Provence. 1900. I. 81,¹ 523.
— Le Styrax officinale en France. 1897. II. 705.¹
Legrelle, A. Rapport . . . Jardin des plantes de Mont-pellier. 1893. I. 59.
Le Grix, E. Une excursion forestière dans l'inspection de Lorris. 1876. IV. 360.
Legros, G. Fuchsia Riccartoni. 1896. III. 640.²
— Rosier multiflore main remontant. 1895. III. 456.¹
— Rusticité du Caryopteris Mastacanthus. 1895. III. 695.²
Leguat, François. Voyage et avantures de François Leguat. 1708. III. 217.
Leguay, Léon. Culture du Camellia.' 1853. III, 598.²
— Nouveau mode de plantation des grands arbres. 1851. III. 167.
— & Lagalisserie, P. de.' Culture des Azalées. 1853. III. 659.²
Legué, Léon. Catalogue des plantes . . . de Mondoubleau. 1891. I. 417.
— Notes pour servir à la revision de la flore du Maine. 1881. I. 416.
Le Guen, P. Effets du wolfram sur les fontes au charbon de bois. 1864. IV. 431.²
Leguisamon, Honorio. Yerba-Mate. 1877. III. 530.²
Leguminosa. See ALLEMÃO, F. F. 1847.— II. 374.¹ — 1848. II. 374.¹

Le Hardy de Beaulieu, Camille. Le phylloxéra et les Vignes américaines. 1874. III. 759.
Lehaye, A. HOUZEAU DE. See HOUZEAU DE LEHAYE, A.
Le Héricher, Édouard. Essai sur la flore populaire de Nor-mandie. 1857. I. 74,¹ V. IX.²
Lehfeld, Paul. Die Holzbaukunst. 1880. IV. 423.²
Lehmann. Gedancken über die Wälder. 1774. IV. 113.²
Lehmann, (Forstmeister). Der Kiefern-Rüsselkäfer. 1858. IV. 475.
Lehmann, Adolf. Vergleichende Untersuchungen einiger Catechu- und Gambir-Propsn. 1830. III. 463,¹ 748.¹
Lehmann, C. Der Raupenswinger. 1830. IV. 206.
Lehmann, Christian. Historischer Schauplatz derer . . . Merkwürdigkeiten in dem meissnischen Obererzgebirge. See PATSCHKE, Wolfgang. 1699. I. 372.
Lehmann, Eduard. Ueber das Amygdalin. 1874. III. 419.²
— Beitrag zur Kenntniss der Flora Kurlands. 1859. I. 362.
— Ein Beitrag zür vergleichenden Untersuchung über Vor-kommen . . . des Amygdalins. 1885. III. 419.²
— Flora von Polnisch-Livland. 1895. I. 366.
— Pharmakognostisch-chemische Untersuchungen über die Periploca. 1897. III. 694.¹
— Die sibirischen Cedernüsse. 1890. II. 41.¹
— Sur le sucre . . . des amandes de quelques Rosacées. 1874. III. 419.¹
Lehmann, Ernst. See DAFERT, F. W. & LEHMANN, Ernst.
Lehmann, F. C. Ein Ausflug nach dem Krater des Rucu-Pichincha. 1884. I. 340.¹
— Neue Hybriden von Dracaenen. 1876. III. 334.²
Lehmann, J. H. Von der besten Art Holzkohlen zu brennen. 1774. IV. 394.
Lehmann, János. A Tölgy-, Bükk- és Gesztenyefa geológiája. 1886. I. 348.¹
Lehmann, Johann Christian. De Balsamo peruviano nigro. 1707. III. 482.¹
— Utilitatis physicae verae specim. 6, s. artis lucrandi lignum. 1735. IV. 280.¹
Lehmann, Johann Friedrich. Primae lineae florae herbi-polensis. 1809. I. 376.
Lehmann, Johann Georg Christian. Annotationes botanicae e Delectu seminum Horti botanici hamburgensis. 1836. I. 47.
— Asperifoliae Linn. 1844. II. 750.²
— Auszug aus dem Protokolle über die im Hamburgischen bot. Garten zum Blühen gebrachten . . . Pflanzen. 1850. II. 327,² 645.¹
— Auszug aus dem Protokolle über die im Hamburgischen bot. Garten . . . bestimmten Pflanzen. 1851. II. 542.¹
— Beschreibung einiger neuen . . . Pflanzen. 1817. II. 750.²
— Ueber die Cycadeen des südlichen Afrika. 1834. II. 2.
— Cyclopia tenuifolia. 1830. II. 349.¹
— Entgegnung auf die letzte Schrift der Herrn Gebrüder Booth. 1834. III. 448.
— Icones . . . minus cognitarum stirpium. 1821. II. 749,² 750.²
— Monographia generis Potentillarum. 1820. II. 270.¹
— Novarum et minus cognitarum stirpium pugillus. 1828. I. 46.
— Plantae aliquot novae in Horto hamburgensium botanico. 1831. I. 46.
— Plantae e familia Asperifoliarum nuciferae. 1818. II. 747.²
— Plantae preissianae. 1844. I. 501.
— Plantas quasdam novas in Horto hamburgensium botanico cultas descripsit. 1830. II. 349.¹
— De plantis Cycadeis. 1834. II. 2.
— Pugillus plantarum in Botanico Hamburgensium horto. 1829. I. 46.
— Revisio Potentillarum. 1856. II. 270.¹
Lehmann, Julius. Du café au point de vue chimico-physio-logique. 1853. III. 742.¹
— Sur le café considéré comme boisson. 1853. III. 742.¹
— Ueber den Kaffee als Getränk. 1853. III. 742.¹
Lehmann, Karl Heinrich. De convenientia plantarum in habitu et viribus. 1831. III. 259.²
Lehn. Carbolsäure im Dienste der Forstwirthschaft. 1886. IV. 196.¹
— Rothbuchenholz zu Bauzwecken. 1886. IV. 499.
Lehner, W. Zur Bekämpfung des Hylobius. 1900. IV. 208.¹
Lehnert. Über Alnus incana DC. 1849. II. 116.²
— Ueber Juniperus communis L. 1849. II. 31.¹

Lehnpfuhl, (*Oberförster*). Dünenwanderung und Dünenwald. 1892. IV. 185.[1]
— Die Formhöhe und ihre Bedeutung für Baumcubirung. 1885. IV. 213.
— Zur Frage der Holztaxen-Bildung. 1888. IV. 388.[2]
— Mineraldünger als Kulturmittel. 1893. IV. 144.[2]
— Unterschiede in der Entwicklung der beiden deutschen Eichenarten. 1883. II. 137.[1]
Lehr, Georg Philipp. De Olea europaea. 1779. II. 712.[2]
Lehr, Julius. Beiträge zur Statistik der Preise. 1885. IV. 403,[1] *404*.[2]
— Die Bodenrente. 1871. IV. 255.
— Der Bodenwerth der Nachhaltswaldes. 1883. IV. 257.
— Die deutschen Holzzölle. 1883. IV. 284.[2]
— Ueber einige neuere Erscheinungen im Gebiete des forstlichen Unterrichtswesens. 1875. IV. 29.
— Forstpolitik. 1887. IV. 270.
— Zur Frage der deutschen Holzzölle. 1881. IV. 284.[2]
— Laufender und Durchschnittszuwachs. 1887. IV. 233.
— Laufender Zuwachs und Durchschnittszuwachs. 1886. IV. 233.
— Die "nationalökonomische" Umtriebszeit. 1870. IV. 251.[2]
— Die neuen deutschen Holzzölle. 1878. IV. 284.[2]
— Waldreinertrag und Walderwartungswert. 1887. IV. 257.
— Waldwertrechnung und Statik. 1887. IV. 257.
Lehr, W. See **WOHLFARTH & LEHR,** W.
Lehranstalt für Wein-, Obst- und Gartenbau zu Geisenheim am Rhein. See **KÖNIGLICHE** Lehranstalt . . .
Die **Lehre** vom Nivellement. 1838. IV. 264.
Die **Lehre** vom Standorte der Waldbäume. 1856. IV. 67.[1]
Die **Lehre** von der Forstforstung. 1855. IV. 173.
Leiberg, John B. Bitterroot forest reserve. 1899. IV. 341.[1]
— Bitterroot forest reserve. 1900. IV. 341.[1]
— Cascade Range forest reserve. 1900. IV. 341.[2]
— Effect of forest destruction on mineral resources. 1898. IV. 46.[1]
— General report on a botanical survey of the Cœur d'Alene Mountains. 1897. I. 327.
— Present condition of the forested areas in northern Idaho. 1899. IV. 341.[1]
— Priest River forest reserve. 1899. IV. 341.[1]
— San Bernardino forest reserve. 1899. IV. 341.[1]
— San Gabriel forest reserve. 1899. IV. 341.[1]
— San Jacinto forest reserve. 1899. IV. 341.[1]
Leibitzer, Johann. Der Gartenbau. 1831. III. 116.[1]
— Praktisches Handbuch der Obstbaumzucht. 1804. III. 136.
— Praktisches Handbuch der Zwergbaumzucht. 1804. III. 146.[1]
— Vollständiges Handbuch der Obstbaumzucht. 1798. III. 146.[1]
Leibnitz, Anton. Fragen und Antworten das Forstwesen betreffend. 1793. IV. 116.
Leibold, Friedrich Ernst. Einiges über das Vorgebirge der Guten Hoffnung. 1839. I. 494.
Leichhardt, Ludwig. Journal of an overland expedition in Australia. 1847. I. 501.
— Scientific excursions in New Holland. 1845. I. 501.
— Tagebuch einer Landreise in Australien. 1847. I. 501.
Leichsenring, Max. Ueber Flores Koso. 1894. III. 424.[2]
Leiδbeinandi reglur um meδferδ og notkun skóga. 1896. IV. 113.[2]
Leidy, Joseph. Report . . . on some of the insects injurious to our shade trees. 1862. III. 186.[2]
Leigh, Charles. The natural history of Lancashire. 1700. I. 394, V. xx.[2]
Leighton, William Allport. A flora of Shropshire. 1841. I. 399.
— On the gland of the phyllodium of Acacia magnifica. 1865. II. 326.[2]
— Hints towards a new specific character in the Willows. 1843. II. 103.[1]
— Notes on Shropshire Rubi. 1848. II. 303.[1]
— Notes on the genus Tilia. 1842. II. 515.[2]
Leimsnstoll, Ch. Obstbaumpflege. 1870. III. 138.
Leimer, Franz. Die Flora von Augsburg. 1843. I. 383.
Leinböck, Johann George. Die Forstwirthschaft. 1834. IV. 97.
Leincker, Johann Sigismund. De cortice Simarouba. See **CRELL,** J. F. 1746. III. 509.[1]
— Horti medici helmstadiensis praestantia. 1746. I. 44.
Leingre. L'Eucalyptus globulus. 1875. IV. 532.[2]

Leinweber, Conrad. Ein sehr alter Baum von Cornus mas. 1865. II. 655.[2]
Leipzig — Naturforschende Gesellschaft. See **NATURFORSCHENDE** . . . I. 13.
Leirion, (*pseud.*). Mistletos of the olden times. 1894. I. 518.
Leis. Ueber Laubstreu. 1840. IV. 70.
Leisering, Bruno. Ueber die Entwicklungsgeschichte des interxylären Leptoms bei den Dicotyledonen. 1899. I. 124.
— Ueber die Korkbildung bei den Chenopodiaceen. 1899. II. 187.[2]
Leisewitz, Wilhelm. Die Obstbaum-Blattminiermotte. 1899. III. 192.[1]
— Über die schwarze Kirschblattwespe. 1899. III. 435.[2]
Leisler, J. P. A. Nachträge zu Bechsteins Naturgeschichte. 1812. IV. 56.
Leisterer. Verkauf von Handelsholz auf dem Stamme. 1880. IV. 388.[1]
Leisterer, (*Oberförster, Neuselle*). Zur forstlichen Naturgeschichte der Baumknospen. 1855. I. 108.[1]
— Zur forstlichen Naturgeschichte der Baumwurzel. 1855. I. 188, *IV. 64*.[2]
The **Leisure** hour. III. 17.
Leitersberger, Joh. De jure venatorio-forestali. 1722. IV. 313.
Leitfaden für die Excursionen der 1. deutschen Forstversammlung zu Braunschweig. 1870. IV. 351.[2]
Leitgeb, Hubert. Beiträge zur Physiologie der Spaltöffnungsapparate. 1886. I. 171.
— Die Haftwurzeln des Epheu. 1858. II. 649.[2]
— Ueber Sphärite. 1888. I. 139.
— See also **NÄGELI,** Carl & **LEITGEB,** Hubert.
Leitpunkte zum Referat über die Aufstellung provisorischer Wirthschaftspläne in Gebirgsgegenden. 1877. IV. 249.[2]
Die **Leitung** und Kontrole des technischen Betriebs in den Staatsforsten. 1849. IV. 288.[1]
Le Janne, Eugène François Marie. Des curares. 1881. II. 720.[1]
Lejeaille. Note sur la greffe du Symphoricarpos. 1846. III. 152.
Lejeune, Alexandre Louis Simon. Flore des environs de Spa. 1811. I. 392.
— Remarques critiques sur le mémoire de Rob. Courtois. 1839. I. 78.[1]
— Revue de la Flore des environs de Spa. 1824. I. 392.
— & **Courtois,** Richard. Choix de plantes de la Belgique. 1826. I. 392.
— Compendium floræ belgicæ. 1828. I. 392.
Lejeune, C. Sur les rapports qui existent entre la forme du tube calycinal et la plénitude de la fleur. 1861. II. 289.[1]
Le Jolis, Auguste François. Fiori mostruosi di Yucca gloriosa. 1887. II. 88.[1]
— Fleurs anormales de Cytisus Laburnum. 1882. II. 369.[1]
— De l'influence chimique des terrains. 1860. I. 228.[2]
— Note sur des fleurs anormales de Cytisus Adami. 1859. II. 368.[1]
— Observations sur les Ulex des environs de Cherbourg. 1852. II. 387.[1]
— Observations sur quelques plantes . . . de Cherbourg. 1847. V. xxi.[2]
— Sur l'origine des plantes cultivées. 1861. I. 241.[2]
— Phénomène observé sur un Rosier capucine. 1852. II. 289.[2]
— Plantes vasculaires des environs de Cherbourg. 1860. I. 412.
— De la reduction des flores locales. 1874. I. 414.
— Ulex europaeus et ses formes. 1880. II. 387.[2]
Lejourdan, A. L'Azerolier. 1856. III. 421.[2]
Lejourdan, Alfred. De la maladie noire des plantes. 1864. III. 194.
Lekow, von, (*Forstverwalter, Ezerés*). Der sogenannte "Ringelwald." 1862. IV. 494.
Leland, C. G. The Ash tree. 1862. II. 707.[1]
Lelbach. Ueber den Einfluss des Aufastens der Nadelhölzer. 1859. IV. 170.
Le Lectier. Catalogue des arbres. 1628. *I. 56*, III. 84,[2] *V. viii*.[2]
Lelieur. De la culture du Rosier. 1811. III. 451.[1]
— Mémoire sur les maladies des arbres fruitiers. 1811. III. 178.
Lelieur, *comte.* La pomone françoise. 1817? III. 143.
Lelievre, J. F. Nouveau jardinier de la Louisiane. 1838. III. 99.
Lelo, SOETAN MARADJO. See **SOETAN MARADJO LELO.**
Lelong, (*Dr.*). La Coca du Pérou. 1883. III, 493.[1]

Lelong, B. M. Budding. 1892. III. 164.[1]
— Culture of the Citrus in California. 1900. III. 498.[1]
— Foreign varieties of the Olive. 1889. III. 676.[1]
— Investigation made . . . of the California Olive industry. 1900. III. 677.[1]
— The Olive in California. 1888. III. 676.[1]
— The orange crop, gathering, curing. 1888. III. 501.[2]
— Oranges; curing and packing. 1888. III. 501.[3]
— Propagation. 1892. III. 153.
— A . . . s on Citrus culture in California. 1888. III. 497.streati e
— *See also* GARCELON, G. W. & LELONG, B. M.
Lélut, Louis François. Code forestier. De la distribution de l'affouage. 1851. IV. 334.[1]
— Rapport . . . le projet de loi relatif au défrichement des bois des particuliers. 1857. IV. 275.
Lemaire, (*inspecteur des forêts*). Notice sur des semis de Pin sylvestre. 1870. IV. 472.
Lemaire, Adrien. De la détermination histologique des feuilles médicinales. 1882. III. 259.[3]
— De la lignification de quelques membranes épidermiques. 1882. I. 129.[3]
— De la lignification de quelques membranes épidermiques. 1883. II. 1.
— Recherches sur l'origine . . . des racines latérales. 1886. I. 104.
Lemaire, Charles Antoine. Abricotier de Syrie. 1848. III. 434.[3]
— Abutilon à fleurs striées. 1841. II. 521.[1]
— Abutilon à fleurs veinées. 1845. II. 521.[1]
— Abutilon de Bedford. 1844. II. 520.[1]
— Acacie à feuilles glauques. 1841. II. 325.[3]
— Aesculus Hippocastanum. 1856. III. 537.[1]
— De l'Aloès socotrin. 1857. III. 333.[1]
— Anhalonie prismatique. 1839. II. 589.[1]
— L'Arec sapide. 1860. III. 326.[3]
— Aristoloche à fleurs labellées. 1839. II. 182.[1]
— Azalée à grandes fleurs blanches de souchet. 1842. II. 680.[3]
— Azalée de l'Inde à fleurs pleines. 1843. III. 659.[3]
— Badiane de la Floride. 1844. II. 210.[1]
— Badiane sacrée ou des Pagodes. 1844. II. 210.[1]
— Beaucarnea, eine neue Gattung. 1861. II. 84.[1]
— Begonia fuchsioides. 1847. II. 583.[3]
— Beschreibung einiger neuen . . . Cacteen. 1838. II. 585.[3]
— Bignone à fleurs charmantes. 1842. II. 787.[1]
— Blabérope à feuilles soyeuses. 1845. II. 723.[3]
— Bossieue à tiges grêles. 1842. II. 336.[3]
— Brachysème de Cels. 1844. II. 337.[1]
— Brownée à fleurs coccinées. 1843. II. 337.[3]
— Bruyère de Banks. 1842. II. 665.[1]
— Cactearum aliquot novarum . . . descriptio. 1838. II. 585.[1]
— Cactearum genera nova speciesque novae. 1839. II. 585.[3]
— Des Cactées. 1860. II. 589.[1]
— Sur les Cactées. 1862. II. 586.[2] — 1863. III. 619.
— Les Cactées. 1868. III. 619.
— Cactées nouvelles. 1858. III. 586.[1]
— Calectasie à fleurs bleues. 1841. II. 79.[3]
— Calotropide gigantesque. 1844. II. 736.[4]
— Camellia Dunlap, White Warratah. 1844. III. 598.[1]
— Canavalie de Gaudichaud. 1843. III. 341.[1]
— Caractères génériques du Mamillaria. 1856. II. 594.[3]
— Carludovique porte-cordes. 1845. II. 76.[1]
— Sur le Cereus lombricoides. 1865. III. 626.[1]
— Le Cereus olivaceus Nob. est-il le Cereus eburneus. 1860. II. 590.[3]
— Cestrum à fleurs roses. 1844. II. 770.[3]
— Chalet à rameaux réfléchis. 1843. III. 607.[3]
— Chèvrefeuille de Ledebour. 1844. II. 838.[3]
— Chorisème à feuilles variables var. 1843. II. 346.[3]
— Chorozème à feuilles en bœur. 1841. II. 346.[1]
— Chorozème à feuilles variables. 1839. II. 346.[1]
— Cierge de Russel. 1839. II. 591.[1]
— Clématite des montagnes var. à feuilles et à fleurs glabres. 1843. II. 198.[3]
— Clérodendre à fleurs brillantes. 1844. II. 756.[3]
— Clitorie de Ternate. 1843. II. 347.[1]
— Comment s'opère la fécondation chez l'Encephalartus? 1863. II. 5.[2]
— D'un cône mâle du Dion edule. 1863. II. 5.[1]
— Congo & Belgique. 1894. III. 281.[3]
— Des Conifères. 1854. II. 50.[1]
— Considérations générales sur la famille des Mélastomacées. 1853. III. 638.[1]
— Corrée à longues fleurs. 1842. III. 503.[1]
— Culture des espèces du genre Allamanda. 1865. III. 686.[1]
— Culture des Lantana. 1844. III. 696.[3]
— Culture du Ribes sanguineum. 1841. III. 415.[3]
— Curieux exemple de morphologie végétale. 1854. II. 174.[1]
— Cycas Ruminiana. 1864. II. 5.[1]
— Cytise à rameaux grêles. 1844. II. 350.[3]
— Du défrichement des landes. 1857. IV. 160.[3]
— Delairée à fleurs odorantes. 1845. II. 865.[3]
— Dépouillement précoce des arbres dans les plantations publiques. 1864. III. 211.[3]
— Deutzie crénelée. Deutzia crenata. 1839. II. 239.[1]
— Sur deux arbrisseaux . . . de Cuba. 1854. II. 752.[1] 771.[3]
— Deux espèces nouvelles d'Encephalartus. 1867. II. 5.[3]
— Dierville à grandes fleurs. 1839. II. 834.[3]
— Diplolène de Dampier. 1844. II. 405.[3]
— Distemma carinatum. 1847. III. 615.[1]
— Durée de la faculté germinative chez les Cactées. 1855. III. 619.
— Échévérie à feuilles pulvérulentes. 1845. II. 236.[1]
— Echinocacte port-alènes. 1841. II. 592.[1]
— Echinocactus horizonthalonius. 1866. III. 622.[1]
— Empoisonnement par les baies du Gui. 1867. III. 385.[3]
— Encore l'Inga superbiens. 1854. II. 366.[1]
— Énumération synonymique des genres et des espèces . . . des Cycadées. 1869. II. 2.[3]
— Sur les Épiphylles. 1861. II. 593.[3]
— Eriobotrye du Japon. 1842. II. 264.[1]
— Erythrina (hybr.) Marie Bellanger. 1861. III. 475.[3]
— Erythrochite brésilien. 1843. II. 406.[1]
— Espèces nouvelles (?) d'Agave. 1864. II. 88.[3]
— Etymologie du genre Chorozema. 1861. II. 345.[3]
— Exemple d'une germination hâtive. 1851. II. 592.[3]
— Des feuilles chez les Cactacées. 1855. II. 588.[1]
— Figuier à stipules persistantes. 1843. II. 152.[3]
— Figuier caoutchouc. 1845. II. 151.[3]
— Fita-Roya patagonica. 1854. II. 30.[1]
— Floraison de l'Echeveria linguaefolia. 1864. II. 235.[3]
— Floraison . . . de la Fourcroya longaeva. 1863. III. 341.[3]
— Floraison du Cereus chiloensis. 1864. III. 621.[1]
— Floraison du Cereus chiloensis Colla. 1864. II. 589.[3]
— Floraison du Cereus leptacanthus? 1856. III. 622.[3]
— Floraison du Cereus rostratus. 1854. III. 621.[1]
— Floraison du Lonicera brachypoda var. aureo-reticulata. 1869. III. 750.[3]
— Francisque larges feuilles. 1844. II. 769.[3]
— Frangipanier à fleurs carnées. 1844. II. 730.[3]
— Fructification de l'Encephalartus Lehmanni. 1869. III. 285.[3]
— Fructification du Cereus Martini. 1869. III. 621.[3]
— Fuchsia à fleurs en corymbes. 1841. II. 644.[1]
— Garrya à feuilles elliptiques. 1841. II. 110.[3]
— Le genre Encephalartus. 1864. III. 285.[1]
— Du genre Nopalea (Cactaceae). 1852. II. 595.[3]
— Genre nouveau de la famille des Asparagacées: Beaucarnea. 1861. II. 84.[1]
— Du genre Phyllocactus. 1861. II. 597.[3]
— Le genre Phyllocactus. 1864. II. 597.[3]
— Genre Pilocereus Lem. 1839. II. 598.[1]
— Genre Plumiera. 1869. II. 730.[3]
— Du genre Rochea DC. 1869. III. 237.[1]
— Genre Strelitzia. 1863. II. 91.[3]
— Du genre Yucca. 1866. II. 86.[3]
— Des genres Calpicarpum et Kopsia. 1865. II. 727.[1]
— Des genres Camellia, Rhododendrum. 1844. III. 86.
— Les genres Dipladenia et Cylicadenia. 1863. II. 725.[3]
— Les genres Epiphyllum et Schlumbergera. 1861. II. 597.[3]
— Gilibertia à feuilles palmées. 1843. II. 653.[1]
— Ginorie d'Amérique. 1845. II. 609.[1]
— Gompholobe à feuilles-multiformes. 1839. II. 362.[3]
— Du greffage en hiver. 1859. III. 161.
— Greffage multiple des plantes grimpantes. 1865. III. 615.[1]
— Grevillée de Thelemann. 1845. III. 383.[3]
— Groseillier à fleurs pourpres. 1845. II. 246.[3]
— Hardenbergie à grandes feuilles. 1844. II. 367.[1]
— Hariote à articles alternes. 1841. II. 599.[1]
— Hermaphroditisme chez l'Aucuba. 1866. III. 644.[3]
— Histoire, caractères . . . du genre Anhalonium. 1869. II. 589.[1]

Lemaire, Charles Antoine (*continued*).
— Histoire, espèces . . . du genre Echeveria. 1863. III. 409.[1]
— Histoire et révision du genre Pilocereus. 1862. II. 598.[1]
— Hovée à feuilles pointues. 1839. II. 364.[1]
— Iconographie descriptive des Cactées. 1841. II. 585.[2]
— De l'identité générique du Cereus giganteus. 1862. II. 590.[1]
— Indigotier de Zeyher. 1843. II. 365.[2]
— Inga d'Harris. 1839. II. 340.[1]
— Introduction en Europe du Lodoicea. 1854. III. 327.[1]
— Ipomée de Lear. 1841. II. 745.[2]
— De l'irritabilité staminale chez les Mamillariae? 1863. II. 594.[2]
— Jambosier à fleurs et à fruits pourprés. 1839. II. 628.[1]
— Juglans regia var. praeparturiens. 1848. III. 355.
— Kennédye de Madame Marryat. 1844. II. 367.[2]
— Ketmie à feuilles très découpées. 1841. II. 521.[2]
— Laine et crin végétals. 1855. II. 598.[1]
— Lalage ornée. 1845. II. 336.[2]
— Du Lierre, considéré jardiniquement. 1862. III. 642.[2]
— Lilas de Libert. 1847. III. 681.[1]
— Lophocaulie (Lophocaulia). 1868. II. 588.[1]
— Luculie charmante. 1843. II. 822.[2]
— Macleane à longues fleurs. 1845. II. 674.[1]
— Magnificence florale des Cierges grimpants. 1865. III. 621.[1]
— Magnolia de Lenné. 1854. II. 212.[1]
— Mahernie glabre. 1859. III. 591.[2]
— Mammillaire à dents d'éléphant. 1839. II. 594.[2]
— Manguier de l'Inde. 1842. II. 456.[2]
— Manuel de l'amateur de Cactus. 1845. III. 618.[2]
— Medinilla Sieboldiana. 1853. II. 638.[2]
— Médinillier à feuilles rouges. 1844. II. 638.[2]
— Mélastome à gros fruits. 1845. II. 639.[1]
— Mélocacte de Lemaire. 1839. II. 595.[1]
— Mimose à squames appliquées. 1845. II. 371.[2]
— Miscellanées. 1845. III. 86.
— Monstruosité prolifique d'une Rose. 1863. II. 289.[2]
— Morrenia odorata Hortul. 1844. II. 742.[1]
— D'un mot nouveau . . . tyléole, tyleola. 1862. II. 588.[1]
— Un mot sur le Catalpa Kaempferi. 1869. III. 706.[1]
— Un mot sur le genre Beaucarnea. 1862. II. 84.[1]
— Un mot sur les espèces de Loranthus. 1869. III. 385.[1]
— Multiplication . . . de l'Habrothamnus elegans. 1845. III. 699.[2]
— Da la multiplication des végétaux par . . . racines. 1859. III. 158.[3]
— Nerium odorum. 1845. III. 689.[1]
— Notice rectificative au sujet du Ferdinanda. 1858. III. 755.[1]
— Notice sur la Weigelia rosea. 1847. III. 749.[1]
— Nouveau genre de la famille des Crassulacées. 1851. II. 236.[1]
— Nouveau mode de culture des Cactées. 1863. III. 619.
— Nouveaux arbres verts d'ornement. 1851. I. 293, *III. 84*.[1]
— Nouvelle espèce d'Anhalonium. 1859. II. 589.[1]
— Nouvelle plante de la flore brésilienne. 1854. II. 648.[2]
— D'une nouvelle soie. 1857. IV. 501.[3]
— Nouvelles espèces à ajouter au genre Pilocereus. 1866. II. 598.[1]
— Observations diagnostico-nomenclaturales sur les Euphorbes charnues du Cap. 1855. II. 441.[1]
— Observations diverses sur les Cactées. 1864. II. 586.[2]
— Observations sur le Carludovica. 1855. II. 76.[1]
— Observations sur le genre Aristolochia. 1856. II. 181.[1]
— Observations sur le genre Vellozia. 1865. II. 90.[2]
— D'un organe nouveau chez les Cactées-Opuntiées. 1862. II. 596.[1]
— Origine rectifiée du Berberis Neuberti. 1855. III. 395.[1]
— Ovaires de Cactées metamorphosés en rameaux. 1867. II. 588.[2]
— Oxyanthus longiflorus hortul. 1845. II. 816.[2]
— Parallèle morphologique entre les Euphorbes charnues et les Cactées. 1857. II. 434,[2] 588.[1]
— Le parasitisme n'existe pas dans les Cactées. 1864. II. 588.[2]
— Passiflore à feuilles dentées en scie. 1841. II. 580.[2]
— Paulownie de l'Impératrice. 1843. II. 781.[2]
— Pécher d'Ispahan. 1841. III. 439.[1]
— Pentapterygium rugosum. 1861. III. 653.[2]
— Du Phyllocactus anguliger. 1865. III. 625.[2]
— Piptanthe du Népaul. 1839. II. 377.[1]

— Pivoine en arbre var. papaveracée. 1842. III. 392.[2]
— De la plantation . . . d'arbres à gutta-percha. 1858. III. 149.
— Plantes diverses recommandées. 1851. I. 269.
— Les plantes grasses autres que les Cactées. 1869. III. 87.
— Plantes nouvelles. 1854. I. 269.
— Plantes recommandées. 1854. III. 87.
— Platycarya strobilacea Sieb. et Zucc. 1848. II. 114.[2]
— Plumiéria à feuilles acuminées. 1843. II. 730.[2]
— Podolobe à feuilles en croix. 1844. II. 375.[2]
— Une prétendue Cactée d'Afrique. 1865. II. 443.[2]
— D'un procédé nouveau de propagation par boutures. 1841. III. 157.
— Prolification du Bryophyllum cochleatum. 1860. II. 237.[1]
— Prunier drap d'or. 1848. III. 436.[2]
— Quatre Cactacées nouvelles. 1864. II. 586.[2]
— De quatre Cactacées nouvelles. 1865. II. 586.[2]
— Quelle est la plus belle plante. 1845. III. 745.[2]
— De quelques espèces d'Euphorbes charnues. 1857. II. 441.[2]
— Quelques mots encore au sujet . . . de l'Aloès de Soccotora. 1860. III. 333.[1]
— Quelques mots encore au sujet du Sequoia gigantea. 1860. III. 310.[1]
— Quelques observations sur les Palmiers. 1855. II. 71.[1]
— Radication adventive chez certaines Aloéees. 1862. III. 333.[1]
— Rectification synonymique. 1854. II. 9.[2]
— Rectification synonymique au sujet . . . de Tacsonia. 1869. II. 581.[1]
— Rectifications synonymiques. 1854. II. 802.[1]
— Le rédacteur du Jardin fleuriste . . . au sujet de l'Inga ferruginea. 1853. II. 366.[1]
— Revendication de priorité nominale. 1854. II. 612.[2]
— Rhododendrum Championae. 1852. II. 678.[2]
— Rhodostome à feuilles de Gardenia. 1845. II. 825.[2]
— Die Robinia Pseudacacia L. 1865. II. 382.[2]
— Rondélétie à longues fleurs. 1843. II. 820.[1]
— Rosa Fortuneana varietas? 1854. II. 293.[2]
— Rosage Morel. 1843. III. 661.[3]
— Saillie des baies chez les Mélocactes. 1860. II. 595.[2]
— Schlumbergera (Nouveau genre). 1858. II. 597.[2]
— Solanum quitoense Hortul. 1844. II. 777.[1]
— Sollye à feuilles linéaires. 1842. II. 249.[2]
— Spiraea Douglasii. 1846. III. 461.[1]
— Spiraea prunifolia flore pleno. 1847. II. 461.[2]
— Strobilanthe à feuilles auriculées. 1845. II. 803.[2]
— Strophanthe à rameaux dichotomes. 1841. II. 732.[1]
— Stuartie à cinq styles. 1842. II. 549.[2]
— Tabernaemontana dichotoma. 1842. II. 733.[1]
— Tecoma digitata. 1844. II. 790.[1]
— Thuiopsis dolabrata. 1857. II. 53.[1]
— Thunbergie de Hawtayne. 1839. II. 801.[2]
— Toxication de l'If. 1869. III. 288.[2]
— Tristanie à grandes feuilles. 1845. II. 633.[2]
— Tylophore à fleurs juanatres. 1844. II. 743.[1]
— Variétés d'Epacris (hybrides). 1845. III. 665.[1]
— Véronique élégante. 1845. II. 783.[2]
— Weigelia rosea. 1849. III. 749.[1]
— Zichye de Baumann. 1845. II. 366.[2]
— & Chauvière. Traité de la culture des Geranium. 1842. III. 125.
— & Houtte, Louis van. Cantua buxifolia. 1848. III. 694.[2]

Lemaire, H. Le Tulipier de Virginie. 1894. IV. 519.[1]
Lemaire-Lisancourt. Existe-t-il un principe purgatif dans les Légumineuses? 1814. III. 462.[1]
— Notions générales et remarques particulières sur la physique végétale. 1813. I. 146.
— Sur la polychromie des corolles et des bractées. 1824. I. 184.
Lemaistre. Notice sur un moyen de préserver de tout incendie les . . . bois de la marine. 1844. IV. 417.
Léman, Dominique Sébastian. Note sur plusieurs espèces nouvelles de Rosiers. 1818. III. 285.[2]
Le Maout, Emmanuel. Atlas élémentaire de botanique. 1846. I. 88.
— Leçons élémentaires de botanique. 1844. I. 88.
— & **Decaisne**, Joseph. Flore élémentaire des jardins. 1855. I. 270.
— — A general system of botany. 1868. I. 261.
— — Traité général de botanique. 1868. I. 261.
Lemarchand, F. O. Sleeper slide. 1888. IV. 390.[2]

Lemarié, A. Itinéraire botanique dans l'Île de Ré. 1861. I. 412.

Lemarié, Charles Antoine. Note sur deux arbres à huile du Tonkin. 1899. III. 514.[2]

Le Marois, P. Les accidents du travail. 1900. IV. 311.[2]

Lemberg, Eduard. Die Weymouthskiefer. 1875. IV. 469.

— See also MICKLITZ, Robert & LEMBERG, Eduard.

Lemcke, G. W. An den edlen Lerchenbaum. 1828. II. 33.[1]

— Ueber den Lerchenbaum. 1829. IV. 448.[1]

Lemés, Albert. Encore le Gui du Chêne. 1896. II. 179.[2]

Lemés, E. Résumé historique des travaux de la Société d'horticulture de l'Orne. 1899. III. 33.[2]

Lemés, Félix. Traité sur les différents cubages des bois. 1889. IV. 214.

Lemés, H. Un Hêtre curieux. 1890. II. 127.[1]

Lemeray. De la brûlure des jeunes pousses du Poirier. 1888. III. 446.[2]

Lemery, (jr.). Dat de planten inderdaad ijzer inhouden. 1707. I. 152.[1]

— Que les plantes contiennent réellement du fer. 1707. I. 152.[1]

Lemery, Nicolas. Du camphre. 1706. III. 233.[1]

— Dictionnaire ou traité universel des drogues simples. 1698. III. 240.

— Dictionnaire universel des drogues simples. 1698. III. 240.

— Disionario overo trattato universale delle droghe semplici. 1698. III. 241.

— Nouveau dictionnaire revu. 1698. III. 240.

— Vollständiges Materialen-Lexicon. 1698. III. 240.

— Woordenboek of algemeene verhandeling der enkele droogerijen. 1698. III. 241.

Le Meulais, A. Les vieux Ifs des environs de Vire. 1892. II. 11.[1]

Le Mière. La maladie sur les Cocotiers. 1889. III. 323.[1]

Lemke, E. Das Alter von Salix alba L. 1886. II. 105.[1]

Lemmon, John Gill. Âge de vieux Sequoias. 1879. II. 51.[1]

— The Big trees. 1878. II. 50.[1]

— Cone-bearers of California. 1890. II. 14.[1]

— Conifers of the Pacific slope. 1897. II. 14.[2]

— Forest endowment of Pacific slope. 1900. IV. 341.[1]

— Forest fires. 1889. IV. 182.[1]

— Hand-book of West-American Cone-bearers. 1892. II. 14.[2]

— Concerning Keteleeria Carrière. 1889. II. 32.[1]

— New Californian plants. 1889. II. 277,[1] 680.[2]

— Notes on cone-bearers of north-west America. 1892. II. 9.[1] 3

— Notes on West American Coniferae. 1893. II. 14.[2]

— Orange-flavored Pine, Pinus Jeffreyi variety. 189.? II. 4.[2] 1

— Pines of the Pacific slope. 1888. II. 39.[1]

— Pinus arizonica. 1881. II. 40.[2]

— Revision of Broken-cone Pines. 1889. II 45.[1]

— Three West-American Conifers. 1897. II. 14.[2]

Lemnius, Levinus. An herbal for the Bible. 1566. I. 512.

— Herbarum atque arborum . . . in Bibliis passim obviae . . . explicatio. 1566. I. 512, V. xxv.[1]

— Similitudinum ac parabolarum quae in Bibliis ex herbis . . . desumuntur . . . explicatio. 1566. I. 512.

Lemoine. Sur l'organisation . . . de l'Aspidiotus du Lau-riei-rose. 1896. III. 600.[2]

— Procédé chimique pour la décortication des graines. 1862. III. 517.[1]

Lemoine, Émile, (jr.). Die Abstammung der kultivierten Bouvardien. 1891. III.711.[1]

— Carpenteria californica. 1884. III. 409.[2]

— Deutzia corymbiflora. 1888. II. 238,[2] III. 410.[2]

— Les hybrides du Lilas commun. 1900. III. 680.[2]

— Hybrids between the common Lilac. 1900. III. 680.[2]

— The Lilacs. 1891. III. 680.[2]

— Les Lilas doubles. 1892. III. 680.[2]

— Origin of the Bouvardias. 1891. III. 711.[1]

— De l'origine des Bouvardia cultivés. 1891. III.711.[1]

Le Moine, Guillaume. Opobalsamum declaratum. See LINNÉ, Carl von. 1764. I. 418,[1] III. 510.[2] — 1769. II. 417.[1]

Lemoine, H. Une plante oubliée, l'Ononis fruticosa. 1900. III. 483.[1]

Lemoine, Léonor. Cours complet sur la taille du Pécher. 1804. III. 171.

— Cours de culture des arbres à fruit. 1801. III. 143.

— Leçons . . . sur la plantation . . . des arbres à fruits. 1828. III. 143.

Lemoine, Victor. Atlas des caractères spécifiques des plantes de la flore parisienne. 1880. I. 416.

— Communication sur le Phylloxéra du Chêne. 1884. IV. 511.

— Deutzia corymbiflora. 1898. II. 238.[2]

— Eine neue Rasse von Syringen. 1889. III. 681.[1]

— A new race of Lilacs. 1889. III. 681.[1]

— Note sur les Pélargoniums a grandes fleurs. 1884. III. 491.[2]

Le Moine, Wilhelmus. See LE MOINE, Guillaume.

Lemoine's new double Lilac. 1881. III. 681.[1]

Lemon. Description de plusieurs Pélargoniums nouveaux. 1834. III. 491.[1]

— Liste des plus beaux Pelargonium. 1832. III. 491.[1]

Lemon, Sir Charles. Remarks on the growth of a peculiar Fir. 1835. II. 44.[2]

Lemon and Lime trees as hedge plants. 1896. III. 502.[1]

Lemonnier, C. See ROUSSEAU, Louis & LEMONNIER, C.

Le Monnier, G.. Recherches sur la nervation de la graine. 1872. I. 120.

Le Monnier, Georges. Sur un champignon parasite de la Vigne. 1881. III. 578.

— Notice sur le mildiou et son traitement. 1887. III. 579.

Lemonnier, Louis Guillaume. Lettre sur la cultivation du Café. 1773. III. 726.[2]

— Observations d'histoire naturelle faites dans les provinces méridionales de la France. 1744. I. 405.

Lemons at Massa-Lubrense. 1895. III. 502.[1]

Lemos, E. Braziel en Java-Koffie. 1883. III. 728.[2]

— De Koffie-quaestie. 1883. III. 728.[2]

Le Moult. Le parasite du hanneton. 1890. III. 196. — 1891. III. 196, IV. 203.

Le Moyne de Morgues, Jacques. Brevis narratio eorum quae in Florida Americae : . . acciderunt. 1591. III. 263.[1]

Lemport, E. Ueber das Pepton der süssen Mandeln. 1897. III. 434.[2]

— La peptone des Amandes douces. 1897. III. 434.[2]

Lend a hand; a record of progress. 1874. IV. 539.[1]

Lende, Ede. Körmöcz sz. k. főbányaváros tulajdonát képező fekvőségek gazdasági viszonyainak ismertetése. 1887. IV. 374.[1]

Lendenfeld, Robert von. Recent changes in the forest-flora . . . of New South Wales. 1886. I. 499,[2] IV. 89.[2]

Lenecek, Ottokar. Über folia cucullata bei Ulmus. 1894. II. 143.[1]

— Ueber eine merkwürdige Verwachsung eines Baumastes. 1890. I. 209.[2]

— Über schildförmige . . . Lindenblätter. 1893. II. 516.[1]

Lenfant, J. B. FOCQUEREAU-. See FOCQUEREAU-LENFANT, J. B.

Lengefeld, Carl von. Anmerkungen von denen . . . drey Arten Nadel-Hölzern. 1762. IV. 440.[2]

Lengerke, Alexander von. Anleitung zur Anlage . . . der lebendigen Hecken. 1846. III. 213.

— Anleitung zur Anlage . . . lebendiger Hecken. 1846. III. 213.

Lengerke, August von. Die Bildung der Haftballen an . . . Ampelopsis. 1885. II. 504.[1]

Lenné, (Gutsbesitzer, Hannef a. Rh.). Kalk . . . für den Weinstock. 1835. III. 549.[1]

— Vorschrift zum Weinbau. 1833. III. 552.

— See also WERKMEISTER, R. & LENNÉ.

— & Fintelmann, Carl. Ueber die Behandlung . . . der vom Frost beschädigten Obstbäume. 1830. III. 183.[1]

— & others. Handbibliothek für Gärtner. 1837. III. 104.

Lenné, Peter Joseph. Über die Wichtigkeit der Anzucht von Maulbeerbäumen. 1844. III. 376.

Lennep, H. H. T. van. De achteruitgang der Koffieproductie. 1900. III. 732.[1]

— Achteruitgang der Koffieproductie. 1900. III. 733.[1]

— Achteruitgang onzer Koffie. 1900. III. 733.[2]

— Hybridisatie van Koffie. 1899. III. 733.[2]

— De sterretjes kwaal in de Koffie. 1900. III. 737.

— De sterretjesbloei aan de Koffieboomen. 1900. III. 737.

— Tuin-onderhoud. 1899. III. 727.

— Het verzwakken der Koffieaanplantingen. 1897. III. 733.[1]

— Voordracht over Liberiakoffie. 1899. III. 743.[1]

— & Greve, A. Rapport ter beraming der middelen om krachtiger zaadkoffie te verkrijgen. 1898. III. 733.[2]

Lennep, R. J. van. On the cultivation of the Fig-tree in Syria. 1863. III. 264.[1]

Lenoir, B. A. Traité de la culture de la Vigne. 1828. III. 554.[1]

— Trattato della coltivazione della Vite. 1828. III. 554.[1]

Lenormant, François. Note sur quelques représentations antiques du Chamaerops humilis. 1856. II. 67.[1]

Lens, Adrien Jacques de. *See* MÉRAT, F. V. & LENS, A. J. de.

Lenssen, Ernst. Analyse des baies d'Épine-vinette. 1873. III. 395.[2]

Lent. Zur Ertragsregelung des Mittelwaldes. 1887. IV. 245.

Lenticchia, Attilio. Peregrinazioni nei giardini della Tremezzina. 1900. I. 64.

— Variazioni morfologiche di vegetali. 1896. I. 430.

Lentner, Johann Gottfried. Taschenbüchlein der Forstsprache. 1833. IV. 23.[1]

Lentz. Beschreibung und Maassangaben einer ungewöhnlich grossen Fichte. 1849. IV. 460.[1]

Lenz, A. F. Die Wild-Baumzucht. 1843. *I. 293,* III. 69, 101,[1] *IV. 106.*

Lenz, H. Wykaz roślin jawnopłciowych z okolicy Niwry. 1868. I. 442.

Lenz, Harald Othmar. Botanik der alten Griechen und Römer. 1859. I. 514.[2]

— Gemeinnützige Naturgeschichte. 1838. I. 255.

Lenz, Heinrich Oskar. Uebersicht der lübeckischen Flora. 1869. I. 386.

Lenz, W. Zur anatomischen Unterscheidung der Früchte von Illicium. 1899. II. 210.[1]

Lenz, Wilhelm. Examination of powdered Senna leaves. 1883. III. 470.[2]

Leo, Johannes Africanus. Beschreibung von Afrika. 1556. I. 482.

— Della descrittione dell' Africa. 1556. I. 482.

— Geographical historie of Africa. 1556. I. 482.

— Historicale description de l'Afrique. 1556. I. 482.

— De totius Africae descriptione libri IX. 1556. I. 482.

Leo, Julius. Botanische Kunstsprache. 1826. I. 70.

— Taschenbuch der Arzneipflanzen. 1826. III. 56.

Leo, Ottomar Victor. Beibehaltung oder Veräusserung der Staatswaldungen. 1870. IV. 269.

— Die Eiche als Hochwaldbaum. 1866. IV. 506.

— Ueber die Einrichtung der Forststatistik. 1873. IV. 349.[1]

— Über die Einrichtung der Forststatistik im Deutschen Reiche. 1873. IV. 336,[1] 349.[1]

— Forststatistik über Deutschland und Oesterreich-Ungarn. 1874. IV. 349,[1] *388.*

— Zur Forstwirthschaftspolitik. 1875. IV. 269.

— Geschichtliches über Waldbau. 1871. IV. 26.

— Grosse oder kleine Forstreviere? 1876. IV. 287.

— Plan für die Einrichtung der Forststatistik. 1874. IV. 349.[1]

— Versuch einer geschichtlichen Entwicklung der natürlichen Verjüngung beim Nadelholze. 1872. IV. 139.[2]

— Die Verwendung der Eiche zum Schiffsbau. 1868. IV. 514.[1]

— Die Verwendung des Holzes zu Papierzeug. 1868. IV. 429.

— Von der Wahl der Holzart in Wildgärten. 1868. IV. 136.[2]

— Die waldbauliche . . . Bedeutung der Birke als Mischungsholzart. 1868. IV. 490.[1]

Leo, Wilhelm. Die Brennmaterialien-Lehre. 1860. IV. 394, 431.[1]

Leobschützer Buchwald. 1885. IV. 354.

Léon, Henry. La végétation orientale en Occident. 1886. I. 241.[2]

Léon, Isidore. Recherches nouvelles sur la cause du mouvement spiral des tiges volubiles. 1858. I. 196.[1]

Léon, J. *See* LAVIGNE, P. & LÉON, J.

Léon, Jules. Flore landaise. 1876. I. 415.

Léon, Nicolás. Biblioteca botánico-mexicana. 1895. I. 3.[1]

Leonard. Action de la lumière sur la production de l'amygdaline. 1877. II. 274.[2]

Leonard, H. S. A few notes on rock-gardens. 1896 III. 205.[1]

Leonard, I. A. Sur l'essence de Gaultheria procumbens. 1884. III. 652.[1]

Leonardi, Gustavo. Elenco dei fitoptidi europei. 1894. I. 214.[2]

— *See also* BERLESE, Antonio & LEONARDI, Gustavo; LUNARDONI, Agostino & LEONARDI, Gustavo.

Leonhard, Ch. Pflanzenphänologische Beobachtungen. 1893. I. 225.

Leonhard, Michael. Beiträge zur Anatomie der Apocynaceen. 1891. II. 722.[1]

Leonhardi, Friedrich Gottlob. Beschreibung wie man in Dännemark den Flugsand dämpfet. 1803. IV. 145.

— Ueber die Erziehung . . . der Pappeln. 1798. III. 344.[1]

— Der Förster und Jäger. 1810. IV. 96.

— Forstwirthschaftliche Briefe. 1789. IV. 95.

— Monatliche Übersicht der Forst- und Jagdwirthschaft. 1806. IV. 96.

— Symbolae ad historiam agriculturae . . . Germanorum. 1790. III. 33.[1]

— Von dem Zuckerahorn. 1804. IV. 526.[2]

Leonhardi, G. Das Poschiavinothal: *See* BRÜGGER, C. G. 1859. I. 435.

Leonhardi, Hermann, *Freiherr* von. Beschreibung eines Apfelzwillings. 1861. II. 267.[1]

— Ueber missgebildete Blätter von Syringa. 1864. II. 716.[1]

— Eine morphologisch interessante Rosenblüthe. 1865. II. 289.[2]

— Pflanzenmorphologische Bemerkungen. 1862. II. 154.[2]

— Zwei neuere Fälle von Apfelzwillingen. 1864. II. 267.[1]

Leonhardi, J. G. De Amygdalis et oleo amararum aethereo. 1776. III. 434.[2]

— Plantas circa Lipsiam nuper inventas describit. *See* JAHN, A. F. W. E. 1774. I. 373.

Leoniceno, Nicolo. Opuscula. 1532. I. 276.

— De Plinii et aliorum medicorum erroribus. 1492. I. 276, V. XIV.[2]

— De Plinii, & plurium aliorū medicorum in medicina erroribus. 1492. V. XIV.[2]

Leontef, A. *See* ЛЕОНТЬЕВЪ, А.

Leopold, C. Anteckningar öfver vegetationen i Sahalahti. 1880. I. 364.

Leopold, Johann Dietrich. Deliciae sylvestres florae ulmensis. 1728. I. 373.

— *Σημαλογία* . . . seu, De Betula. *See* CAMERARIUS, Elias. 1727. II. 117.[1]

Leopold, Johann Georg. Nützliche . . . Einleitung zu der Landwirthschaft. 1750. IV. 115.

— *See* ACADEMIA NATURAE CURIOSORUM. I. 10.

Leopoldinisch-carolinische Academie der Naturforscher. Leopoldina. Verhandlungen. *See* ACADEMIA NATURAE CURIOSORUM. I. 10.

Leopoldinisch-carolinische deutsche Akademie. *See* KAISERLICH LEOPOLDINISCH-CAROLINISCHE . . .

Lepage. Sur une éducation remarquable de vers à soie. 1869. III. 380.[1]

Lepage, P. H. Expériences pour servir à l'histoire chimicopharmaceutique des feuilles de Laurier-cerise. 1848. III. 431.[2]

— Note sur une substance extraite des écorces de Hêtre. 1847. IV. 500.[1]

— Quelques faits pour servir à l'histoire . . . du marron d'Inde. 1854. III. 538.[1]

Lepage, Richard C. Papers on the plant Gynocardia. 1878. III. 614.[1]

Le Page du Pratz. Histoire de la Louisiane. 1758. I. 317.[2]

— The history of Louisiana. 1758. I. 317.[2]—1763. III. 62.

Le Paute. Le bois de Vincennes en 1883. 1884. IV. 137.[1]

— Règle dendrométrique et dendroscopique. 1888. III. 202.[1]

Lepechin, Iwan. Tagebuch der Reise durch verschiedene Provinzen des Russischen Reiches. 1774. I. 41, 359.

— *See also* ЛЕПЕХИНЪ, Ия.

Le Peintre, Alexandre. Reboisement et mise en valeur des terres incultes. 1862. IV. 162.

Le Père. Notes on the state forest of Lyons. 1893. IV. 361.

Lepère, Alexis. Die Kultur des Pfirsichbaumes. 1846. III. 440.[2]

— Pratique raisonnée de la taille du Pêcher. 1846. III. 440.[2]

Lépervanche, Paul & Trouette, Émile. Naturalisation de végétaux à l'Île de la Réunion. 1876. III. 130.[1]

Lépinay, Gaston GODIN DE. *See* GODIN DE LÉPINAY, Gaston.

Lépine, Jules. Azadirachta indica (A. de Jussieu), Tamoul. 1861. III. 511.[2]

— Butea frondosa. 1861. III. 468.[1]

— Calophyllum indophyllum. 1861. III. 608.[2]

— Cassuvium pomiferum. 1861. III. 523.[2]

— Jatropha glauca. 1861. III. 519.[2]

— Mesua ferrea. 1861. III. 610.[2]

— Nomenclature des objets envoyés . . . de Pondichéry. 1858. III. 276.[2]

— Note sur l'usage de l'Aeschynomene aspera. 1862. II. 330.[1]

— Note sur la gomme de Cocotier. 1860. II. 67.[2]

— Note sur le Casuarina equisetifolia. 1857. II. 92.[2]

— Note sur le Veppamarum Vembou. 1861. III. 511.[2]
— Notes sur quelques huiles . . . du sud de l'Inde. 1861. III. 224.[2]
— Pongamia glabra. 1861. III. 484.[3]
— Putrangiva Roxburghii. 1861. III. 521.[2]
— Recherches sur quelques plantes alimentaires de Tahiti. 1857. II. 146,[2] III. 367.[1]
— Semecarpus anacardium. 1861. III. 529.[1]
— Sterculia foetida. 1861. III. 592.[1]
Le Play. Grundsätze welche, die Eisenhüttenwerke mit Holz-Betrieb . . . befolgen müssen. 1854. IV. 431.[1]
Lepper, C. H. The Mulberry tree as a source of food. 1881. III. 380.[1]
Leppert, Wladyslaw. W kwestyi lasów. 1878. IV. 102.
Leppett tea. 1896. III. 608.[1]
Leppmann, Arminius. Specimen exhibens notas historicas circa medicamina. 1849. III. 238.[2]
Le Prevost, Auguste. Mémoire sur les plantations en massif. 1818. IV. 154.[1]
Leprieur. Extrait d'une note sur l'huile de Lentisque. 1860. III. 525.[2]
Leprince. Sur la cascarine. 1892. III. 543.[2]
— Contribution à l'étude . . . du Rhamnus Purshiana. 1899. III. 543.[2]
Lsquet, J. Fernand, (jr.). Les arbres rebelles à la taille. 1894. III. 171.
— L'art de faire fleurir les plantes par le bouturage. 1891. III. 158.
— L'art de faire fleurir les plantes par le greffage. 1892. III. 163.[1]
— Le Cobáea scandens dans le nord de la France. 1894. III. 694.[2]
— Erica carnea et Veltheimia. 1892. III. 650.[2]
— Les fleurs changeantes. 1890. I. 185.
— Fleurs sur le vieux bois. 1890. III. 587.[1]
— Indigofera speciosa. 1891. III. 479.[2]
— Influence de la taille sur la floraison. 1894. III. 173.[1]
— Influence de la taille sur la floraison; les végétaux qu'on ne taille point. 1894. III. 173.[1]
— Les plantes de la Nouvelle-Hollande. 1900. III. 94.[2]
— Sericobonia ignea. 1898. III. 709.[2]
Lerch. Ueber Benützung und Verwerthung der Rosskastanien. 1855. IV. 527.[2]
Lerch, Julius. Rosa dichroa. 1872. II. 293.[1]
Lerch, Otto. Forestry [of the hills of Louisiana]. 1893. IV. 340.
Lerche, Johann Jakob. Descriptio plantarum . . . astrachanensium et Persiae. 1773. I. 477.[1]
Leresche, Louis & Levier, Émile. Deux excursions botaniques dans le nord de l'Espagne. 1880. I. 422.
Lerius, Joannes. Historia navigationis in Brasiliam. 1586. I. 327, 531.
Lermier, J. Observations sur le déboisement. 1844. IV. 47,[1] 161.[1]
— Observations sur le reboisement en France. 1848. IV. 161.[1]
Lerolle, Léon. Sur la place à donner aux gymnospermes. 1875. II. 1.
— Place des gymnospermes dans la classification naturelle. 1875. II. 1.
Le Rouge, Dom. Principes du cultivateur. 1773. III. 112.
Leroux, L. J. Recherches sur l'éclosion de l'œuf . . . du phylloxera. 1895. III. 574.
Leroux, S. C. Ampélographie des cépages, indigènes. 1893. II. 505.[1]
Leroy. Mémoire sur la culture des arbres de haute futaie. n. d. IV. 129.
Leroy. Crataegin. 1841. III. 423.[1]
— Note sur le fruit du Myroxylum toluiferum. 1847. III. 482.[1]
— Notice sur le traitement des Ormes. 1834. III. 364.[1]
Leroy, A. Note sur la culture indigène des . . . Thés à Angers. 1837. III. 601.[1]
Le Roy, Alphonse. Notice sur le Jardin botanique de Liège. 1867. I. 50.
Leroy, Alphonse Vincent Louis Antoine. Mémoire sur le kinkina français. 1808. III. 720.
Leroy, André. Acacia julibrissin. 1866. III. 466.[1]
— Æbletraets Historie. 1873. III. 299.[3]
— Le Cèdre de l'Atlas. 1866. III. 299.[3]
— Descriptive catalogue. 1856. I. 58.
— Dictionnaire de pomologie. 1867. III. 85.
— Emballage pour les envois lointains. 1862. III. 155.
— Époque de floraison des Rhododendrons. 1867. III. 654.[3]

— Erythrina crista galli. 1866. III. 476.[1]
— Espèces ou variétés d'arbres ou d'arbrisseaux. 1844. III. 84.[1]
— De la greffe des Magnolia. 1862. III. 399.[1]
— De la greffe du Noyer. 1864. III. 355.
— Grenadier Legrellii. 1867. III. 630.[1]
— Histoire du Poirier. 1867. II. 280.[1]
— Histoire du Pommier. 1873. II. 267.[2]
— De l'importance du choix des rameaux pour les greffes. 1859. III. 161.
— Maclura aurantiaca. 1868. III. 372.[1]
— Magnolia grandiflora anglorum. 1866. III. 399.[2]
— Moyen d'obtenir une seconde floraison du Glycine. 1866. III. 490.[2]
— Note sur l'Andromeda formosa. 1864. III. 654.[1]
— Note sur les greffes des arbres à fruits. 1859. III. 161.
— Pæretraets Historie. 1867. II. 280.[3]
— Plantation des Magnolia grandiflora. 1850. III. 399.[3]
— Populus fastigiata. 1867. III. 346.[1]
— Rhododendron Rovellii. 1867. III. 662.[1]
— Taille des arbustes qui fleurissent au printemps. 1863. III. 172.[3]
— Taille des arbustes qui fleurissent en avril. 1863. III. 172.[3]
Leroy, Arnould. Culture de végétaux exotiques. 1888. III. 130.[3]
— Culture et propagation de végétaux en Algérie. 1894. III. 130.[3]
— Cultures de végétaux exotiques à Oran. 1896. III. 130,[3] 25.[1]
— Sur la fructification d'un Cocotier. 1896. III. 322.[1]
— Fructification du Cocos Datil. 1896. III. 322.[1]
— Le Maté, Thé du Paraguay. 1890. III. 531.[1]
— Le Saxaoul. 1890. III. 387.[2]
Le Roy, Benigne. Instruction du plantage . . . des Meuriers. 1695. III. 253.[2]
Leroy; Chavée-. See Chavée-Leroy.
Le Roy, G. A. Recherche de la sciure de bois dans les farines. 1898. IV. 431.[1]
Le Roy, J. J. De kleuren der bloem. 1880. I. 185.[1]
Leroy, Julien David. Mémoire sur les travaux qui on rapport à l'exploitation de la mâture dans les Pyrennées. 1776. IV. 388.[2]
Leroy, Louis. Les Andromèdes. 1881. III. 647.[1]
Leroy, V. Notice sur la culture de la Vigne. 1851. III. 555.
Leroy d'Étoilles. Action de la santonine. 1858. III. 754.[2]
Le Roy-Mabille. La maladie de la Vigne. 1857. III. 577.
Lervat. See Defranoux & Lervat.
Léry, Jean de. Histoire d'un voyage fait en . . . Bresil. 1578. III. 268.[2]
— Historia navigationis in Brasiliam. 1578. III. 268.[2]
— Historie van een reijse . . . in den lande van Bresillien. 1578. III. 268.[2]
— See also Benzoni, Girolamo & Léry, Jean de.
Lesacher, E. & Mareschal, A. A. Nouvelle botanique médicale. 1876. III. 86.
Lesage, E. Traité pour le cubage des bois. 1861. IV. 224.
Lesage, Pierre. Les arbres nourriciers du Gui. 1894. III. 179.[3]
— Contributions à l'étude de la différenciation de l'endoderme. 1891. I. 131.[1]
— Sur la différenciation du liber dans la racine. 1891. I. 104.
— Influence du bord de la mer sur la structure des feuilles. 1889. I. 218.
— Sur les rapports des palisades dans les feuilles avec la transpiration. 1894. I. 171.
— Recherches expérimentales sur les modifications des feuilles. 1890. I. 229.
Lesaint, Brodiez-. See Brodiez-Lesaint.
Lesbazeilles, Eugène. Les forêts. 1884. IV. 102.
Leschenault de la Tour, Jean Baptiste Louis Claude Théodore. Extrait d'une lettre . . . sur quelques espèces d'Orties. 1820. III. 382.[3]
— Mémoire sur le Strychnos tieute. 1810. III. 366,[2] 476,[2] 685.[1]
— Notice sur la végétation de la Nouvelle-Hollande. 1811. I. 500.
— Notice sur la végétation de la Nouvelle-Hollande et . . . de Diémen. 1816. I. 500.
— Notice sur le Cannellier. 1821. III. 405.[2]
— Notice sur le Cocotier et sur ses produits. 1824. III. 323.[2]
— Notice sur une nouvelle espèce de Vinetier. 1822. II. 205.[1]

Leschevin, C. L. Physiologie végétale. 1825. I. 148.
Lescuyer, O. Abricotier Mume. 1869. III. 438.[2]
— Abutilon malvaeflorum. 1867. III. 586.[2]
— Aeschynanthus tricolor. 1859. III. 708.[1]
— Allamanda neriifolia. 1861. III. 686.[1]
— Antigonon leptopus. 1870. III. 387.[1]
— Arbres et arbustes nouveaux de pleine terre. 1860. III. 461.[2]
— Aristolochia floribunda. 1869. III. 386.[1]
— Begonia incarnata. 1866. III. 618.[1]
— Berberidopsis corallina. 1863. III. 614.[1]
— Bignonia Chamberlaynii. 1861. III. 704.[2]
— Bignonia jasminoides splendida. 1863. III. 707.[1]
— Bouvardia nouveaux. 1865. III. 711.[2]
— Brachysema speciosa. 1864. III. 468.[1]
— Centradenia grandifolia. 1861. III. 638.[1]
— Chamaecerasus Standishi. 1862. III. 751.[1]
— Chameranthemum Beyrichii variegata. 1867. III. 709.[1]
— Clematis Jackmanni. 1872. III. 390.[2]
— Cobaea penduliflora. 1870. III. 694.[2]
— Le Cupressus fastigiata cereiformis. 1859. III. 303.[1]
— Dalechampia Roesliana. 1869. III. 517.[2]
— Desfontainea spinosa. 1855. III. 682.[1]
— Elaeocarpus lanceolatus de Blume. 1862. III. 584.[2]
— Les Epiphyllum, Epiphyllum truncatum. 1862. III. 623.[1]
— Eranthemum cinnabarinum variété ocellata. 1872. III. 710.[1]
— Erythrina ornata. 1866. III. 476.[1]
— Franciscea calycina. 1863. III. 699.[1]
— Le Fremontia californica. 1868. III. 591.[1]
— Garrya elliptica. 1865. III. 352.[2]
— Genetyllis fuchsioides. 1864. III. 633.[2]
— Gomphia Theophrasta. 1872. III. 596.[1]
— Hexacentris mysorensis. 1855. III. 710.[2]
— Hibiscus Cooperii. 1864. III. 588.[1]
— Hortensia ou Hydrangea nouveaux. 1868. III. 411.[1]
— Les Kennedya. 1855. III. 479.[2]
— Lapageria rosea. 1864. III. 337.[2]
— Lespedeza bicolor. 1869. III. 481.[1]
— Libonia floribunda. 1865. III. 709.[1]
— Maackia amurensis. 1872. III. 472.[2]
— Les Magnolia. 1854. III. 400.[1]
— Pandanus Porteanus. 1866. III. 313.[2]
— Pavia californica. 1867. III. 536.[2]
— Plagianthus Lyallii. 1872. III. 587.[1]
— Les plantations et les arbres de la ville de Paris. 1858. III. 209.
— Platycrater arguta. 1870. III. 413.[1]
— Rhododendron Maddeni. 1865. III. 661.[1]
— Rhododendrum glaucum. 1859. III. 659.[1]
— Rhus glabra laciniata. 1868. III. 527.[1]
— Robinia Decaisneana. 1865. III. 487.[1]
— Sanchezia nobilis. 1867. III. 710.[1]
— Spiraea grandiflora. 1855. III. 424.[1]
— Stenocarpus Cunninghami Hooker. 1864. III. 384.[1]
— Tacsonia eriantha. 1870. III. 616.[2]
— Ungnadia speciosa. 1865. III. 540.[1]
— Weigelia Lavallei. 1870. III. 749.[1]
— Weigelia Lowii. 1870. III. 749.[1]
— Yucca filamentosa meldensis. 1862. III. 340.[1]
Die Lessaholznutzung als Hilfsmittel. 1868. IV. 171.
Lesenger. Aphelandra aurantiaca Lindl. 1862. III. 708.[2]
Le Seurre de la Bellerie. Description du vignoble de Garaubaud. 1669. III. 554.[1]
Leske, Fritz. See CZSALAVSKY, Karel & LESKE, Fritz.
Leske, Nathanael Gottfried. Animadversiones in structuram ac figuram foliorum. See POHL, J. E. 1771. I. 109.[1]
— Reise durch Sachsen. 1785. I. 374.
Lesley, Joseph Peter. Forestry at home and abroad. 1880. IV. 336.[1]
Lesne, A. Les plantations de Cactées. 1899. III. 620.[1]
Lesni obzor. See HÁJ. IV. 14.
Z lesovny. See HÁJ. IV. 14.
Lesparre, duc de. Phylloxera et plants américains. 1893. III. 762.
Lespiault, Gaston. Des déboisements américains. 1883. IV. 46.[1]
Lespiault, Maurice. Les Vignes américaines . . . de la France. 1881. III. 547.
Lespinasse, Gustave. Rapport sur les herborisations . . . au Cap Ferret. 1859. I. 412.
— Rapport sur une excursion faite. 1859. I. 412.
— See also DESMOULINS, Charles & LESPINASSE, Gustave.

Lesquereux, Charles Leo. Botanical and palæontological report . . . of Arkansas. 1860. V. XVII.[2]
Lesseck, Johann Karl. Kluger und vorsichtiger Förster. 1781. IV. 105.
Lesseh. Ueber Hoya carnosa. 1858. III. 693.[1]
Lesser, C. Die Pflege des Obstbaumes in Norddeutschland. 1895. III. 139.
Lesser, Paul. Mitteilungen aus dem Kew-Garten. 1891. II. 28.[2]
Lesserteur, E. C. Le Hoàng-Nàn. 1879. III. 681.[2]
Lessing, Christian Friedrich. Beitrag zur Flora des südlichen Urals. 1835. I. 361, II. 187.[1]
— Reise durch Norwegen nach den Loffoden. 1831. . I. 353.
— Synanthereae. 1831. II. 848.[1]
— De Synanthereis Herbarii regii. . 1829. II. 848.[1]
— Synopsis generum Compositarum. 1832. II. 848.[1]
Lessing, M. B. Handbuch der praktischen Arzneimittellehre. See SOBERNHEIM, J. F. 1836. III. 258.
Lesson, Réné Primivère. Flore rochefortine. 1835. I. 409.
— General observations on natural history . . . in New South Wales. 1828. I. 500.
— Observations générales sur l'histoire naturelle. 1826. I. 347.
— Voyage autour du monde. 1838. I. 303.
The lessons of erosion due to forest destruction. 1896. IV. 184.[2]
Lestiboudois, François Joseph. Botanographie belgique. 1781. I. 392.
— Botanographie universelle. 1827. I. 259.
Lestiboudois, Thémistocle. Botanographie belgique; ou. Flore. 1827. I. 392.
— Botanographie élémentaire. 1826. I. 85.
— Carpographie anatomique. 1853. I. 119.
— Dicotylédonés hétérogènes. 1872. I. 127.[1]
— Études sur l'anatomie- . . . des végétaux. 1840. I. 34.
— De l'existence des liquides . . . dans les vaisseaux trachéens. 1865. I. 133.
— Memoir on the structure of the monocotyledones. 1824. I. 98.
— Mémoire sur l'écorce des dicotylédonés. 1860. I. 130.
— Mémoire sur la structure des Cycadées. 1860. II. 3.[2]
— Note sur la structure de l'Hoya carnosa. 1865. II. 739.[2]
— Note sur la structure générale des végétaux. 1869. I. 100.[1]
— Note sur la vrille des Ampélidées. 1865. II. 501.[1]
— Note sur les épines. 1863. I. 107,[2] 112.[2]
— Note sur les tissus élémentaires. 1863. I. 123.[2]
— Note sur les vaisseaux du latex. 1863. I. 135.
— Note sur les vaisseaux propres . . . des Campanulacées. 1865. II. 845.[1]
— Note sur les vrilles des genres Vitis et Cissus. 1857. II. 501.[1]
— Phyllotaxie anatomique. 1848. I. 102.
— Sur quelques hanes anomales. 1873. I. 127.[1]
— Remarks on the vessels of the latex. 1863. I. 135.
— Structure comparée des tiges des végétaux. 1854. I. 105.
— Structure des hétérogènes. 1872. I. 127.[1]
— De la vrille des Cucurbitacées. 1857. II. 844.[2]
Lestrange, H., baron de. Étude sur la sylviculture. 1893. IV. 109.[2]
Z lešů a luhů. See HÁJ. IV. 14.
Lesure. Arbres fruitiers le long des routes. 1895. III. 211.[1]
— Encore les Peupliers régénérés. 1897. III. 344,[2] 345.[2]
— Le Peuplier régénéré. 1896. IV. 486.[f]
Létacq, A. L. Les Cyprès chauves de Vervaines. 1898. III. 311.[1]
— Sur une fascie presentée par le Frêne. 1897. II. 708.[1]
— Sur une fascie présentée par le Salix alba. 1897. II. 104.[2]
— Sur un Gui à tige gigantesque. 1897. II. 177.[2]
— Note sur le Gui de Chêne. 1890. II. 179.[2]
— Remarques sur l'article précédent. 1890. III. 385.[2]
Il patinage fresco e sua azione nel terreno. 1879. V. 144.[2]
Lételié. Introduction et culture des Palmiers. 1865. III. 317.
— Note sur l'Acacia dealbata. 1854. III. 464.[2]
— Les Palmiers rustiques. 1866. III. 317.
Letellier. Addition à une précédente communication sur la maladie de la Vigne. 1851. III. 575.[2]
— Note relative à un liquide à employer contre le phylloxera. 1873. III. 565.[1]
— Nouvelle note sur le traitement des Vignes malades. 1855. III. 559.[2]
— Observations concernant la maladie de la Vigne. 1852. III. 575.[2]

Le Tellier. L'Exposition forestière d'Edimbourg. 1884. IV. 20.[1]
— Exposition internationale forestière à Edimbourg. 1884. IV. 40.[2]
— Les produits des forêts de l'Inde. 1878. IV. 21.[2]
Letellier, Augustin. Essai de statique végétale. 1892. I. 196.[1]
— Les forêts aux États-Unis en 1893. 1895. IV. 338.[2]
— Forêts de la région méridionale des États-Unis. 1886. IV. 340.
— L'industrie du camphre à Formose. 1894. IV. 520.[1]
— Le Kauri de New-Zeeland. 1896. IV. 447.[2]
— Montes de la regióñ meridional de los Estados Unidos. 1886. IV. 340.
— Situation forestière en Russie. 1894. IV. 346.
— La sylviculture aux États-Unis. 1891. IV. 338.[1]
— & son. The Poplars. 1895. III. 344.[2]
— **& Spêneux.** Note sur la pourriture des fruits. 1866. III. 194.
Letheby, H. The decay of timber and its prevention. 1860. IV. 144.[1]
Letourneux, Aristide. Catalogue des arbres . . . de l'Algérie. 187 . ? I. 483.[2]
— Étude botanique sur la Kabylie. 1871. I. 485.[1]
— Flore de la Kabylie. 1871. I. 485.
— Note sur un voyage botanique à Tripoli. 1889. I. 486.
— Rapport sur une mission botanique . . . dans le nord . . . de la Tunisie. 1887. I. 485.
— Voyage botanique en Tunisie. 1886. I. 485.
— *See also* HANOTEAU, Adolphe & LETOURNEUX, Aristide.
Letourneux, H. Lettres à Nanine sur la botanique. 1827. I. 94.
Letourneux, P. Mémoire sur les avantages . . . des plantations de Mélèzes. 1845. IV. 449.
Letrone, Paul. Étude sur le pollen du Pin maritime. 1850. IV. 468.[1]
— Nouveau rapport . . . sur l'état présent de la culture du Mûrier. 1845. III. 376.
Letter, G. de. La Société royale Linnéenne de Bruxelles. 1900. I. 80.[2]
Letter from the Secretary of agriculture . . . in relation to investigation . . . in the planting of native Pine seed. 1894. IV. 461.[1]
Letter from the Secretary of the interior . . . relating to cutting and removing timber. 1895. IV. 178.[2]
Letters, reports, etc., on the subject of the establishment of a school of forestry. 1880. IV. 30.[1]
Lettre à M. de Rocheplate, en réponse à son Mémoire. 1787. IV. 291.[2]
Lettre à M. Le Monnier sur la culture du Café. *See* LETTSOM, J. C. 1773. III. 726.[2]
Lettre de M. le Ministre de l'agriculture . . . au sujet de la prohibition . . . des raisins frais. 1875. III. 200.[1]
Lettre du Bostangi-Bachi de Fourtou. *See* ROLAND (de Fourtou). 1804. III. 153.
Lettre sur l'Hortensia. 179 . ? III. 412.[1]
Lettre sur les arbres à épiceries. *See* COSSIGNY DE PALMA, J. F. C. de. 1775. III. 221.[1]
Lettre sur les Oliviers. *See* DAVID, Antoine. 1762. III. 674.[2]
Lettres d'un médecin des hôpitaux du roy. *See* DU PETIT, F. P. 1710. III. 238.[1]
Lettres édifiantes et curieuses écrites des missions etrangères. 1780. III. 217.
Lettres patentes du roi, portant que la délivrance des coupes ordinaires des bois taillis. 1773. IV. 325.
Lettres patentes du roi, qui ordonnent la prise de possession par Jean Vincent René, de l'administration des domaines & bois. 1778. IV. 325.
Lettres patentes du roi sur un décret de l'Assemblée nationale concernant les délits qui se commettent dans les forêts & bois. 1789. IV. 325.
Lettsom, John Coakley. Geschichte des Thees und Koffees. 1772. III. 605.
— Histoire naturelle du Thé. 1772. III. 605.
— History of the origin of medicine. 1778. III. 238.[2]
— Hortus uptonensis. 1781. I. 53.
— Lettre à M. Le Monnier sur la culture du Café. 1773. III. 726.[2]
— Natural history of the Tea-tree. 1772. III. 605.
— Naturalist's and traveller's companion. 1772. I. 35.
— Le voyageur naturaliste. 1772. I. 35.
— Works of John Fothergill. *See* FOTHERGILL, John. 1783. 263.

Le Turquier Delongchamp, Joseph Alexandre. Flore des environs de Rouen. 1816. I. 407.
Le Tussac. Sur le Brosimum Alicastrum de la Jamaïque. 1807. III. 367.[2]
Leuchs, Johann Carl. Over de aankweeking van nuttige gewassen. 1820. III. 122.[1]
— Anleitung zur Eingewöhnung . . . ausländischer Pflanzen. 1821. III. 43.
— Darstellung der Mittel zur Abhaltung, Vertilgung . . . aller schädlichen Thiere. 1823. IV. 196.[1]
— Welke zijn de algemeene regelen, volgens welke men vooraf beoordeelen kan . . . de aankweeking. 1821. III. 46.[1]
Leuchsenring. Sur l'introduction et la culture du Pin noir d'Autriche. 1855. IV. 465.[1]
Leuchtweiss, A. Untersuchung mehrerer Mannasorten. 1845. IV. 536.[1]
Leue, Adolph. Carriage timber. 1889. IV. 427.[1]
— Forestal experiment stations. 1884. IV. 37.[2]
— Forestal experiment stations in Germany. 1883. IV. 38.[1]
— Gen. Thomas L. Young's White or American Elm. 1887. II. 144.[1]
Leunis, Johannes. Analytischer Leitfaden für den . . . Unterricht in der Naturgeschichte. 1853. I. 89.
— Synopsis der Pflanzenkunde. 1847. I. 89, 382.
Leupold, Bernhard Georg. Beitrag zur Kenntniss . . . des Punicin. 1891. III. 631.[1]
Leuthner, A. Ueber die Gewinnung . . . des Zirbensamens. 1885. IV. 463.[1]
Leutz. Verzeichnis der . . . botanischen Publikationen für . . . Baden. 1885. I. 3.[2]
Leuwenhoek, Antoon van. A letter concerning the seeds of oranges. 1704. II. 401.[2]
Leuzinger, A. Eigenart einer forstlichen Dienstbarkeit. 1894. IV. 334.[2]
Leuzinger, Franz KELLER-. *See* KELLER-LEUZINGER, Franz.
Levacher-Bruzeau. Rapport . . . sur la situation de la pépinière centrale du gouvernement d'Alger. 1846. I. 68.[1]
Le Vaillant, François. Reise in das Innre von Afrika. 1790. I. 494.
— Second voyage dans l'intérieur de l'Afrique. 1790. I. 494, V. XXIV.[2]
— Travels into the interior parts of Africa. 1790. I. 494.
— Voyage dans l'intérieur de l'Afrique. 1790. I. 494, V. XXIV.[2]
Levallois, Alb. Activité optique de la cellulose. 1884. I. 138.[1]
— Sur les caractères des huiles d'olive. 1887. III. 679.[1]
— Dessiccation des plantes. 1885. I. 521.[1]
— Sur le dosage des essences parfumées. 1884. I. 182.[1]
Levanovski, N. *See* ЛЕВАНОВСКIЙ, H.
Levavasseur, T., (jr.). Traité pratique du boisement . . . des montagnes. 1878. IV. 163, V. xxx.[2]
— *See also* ЛЕВАВАСЕРЪ, T., сынъ.
Levée, G., (sr.). Multiplication des Aralias par la greffe. 1894. III. 641.[1]
Léveillé, Augustin Abel Hector. L'Abrus precatorius. 1892. III. 462.[2]
— Les Acacia. 1899. III. 463.[2]
— Aperçu sur la flore du midi de l'Inde. 1889. I. 475.[1]
— Curieux effet de l'électricité. 1892. II. 386.[1]
— Curieux phénomène présenté par le Mangifera. 1891. II. 457.[1]
— Deux plantes médicinales. 1892. III. 465,[1] 520.[1]
— Espèces végétales communes à la France et à l'Inde. 1891. I. 417, 475.[1]
— Essai d'un catalogue critique des espèces végétales . . . de l'Inde française. 1892. I. 470.[1]
— L'Evonymus leucocarpos. 1891. III. 468.[1]
— La noix de Coco et ses propriétés. 1893. III. 324.[1]
— Note sur la différence des phyllodes d'Eucalyptus. 1891. II. 326,[2] 624.[2]
— Notes de biologie végétale. 1892. I. 206.[2]
— Une nouvelle conception de la greffe. 1897. I. 208.[2]
— Les Palmiers. 1892. II. 64.[1]
— Les plantes à mouvement. 1889. I. 194, III. 130.[1]
— Les plantes curieuses, utiles . . . de l'Inde. 1892. III. 92.[1]
— Quelques usages pratiques de plantes de l'Inde. 1893. III. 279.[1]
— Supplément à la flore de la Mayenne. 1895. I. 418.
— *See also* LANDE, Félicien & LÉVEILLÉ, Hector.
Léveillé, Jean H. Les Palmiers à branches dans l'Inde. 1891. II. 63.[1]
Léveillé, Joseph Henri. Observations médicales et énumération des plantes recueillies en Tauride. 1842. I. 368.[2]
— Recherches sur la maladie des Vignes. 1851. III. 575.[2]

Level. Notice sur les forêts de Cèdre. *See* LEVEL & LEFEBVRE, Henri. 1894. IV. 379.[2]
— & Lefebvre, Henri. Les forêts de Cèdre. 1894. IV. 379.[1]
Levenau, J. A. von. Wichtiger Beitrag zu einer allgemeinen Oekonomie des Holzes. 1823. IV. 426.[1]
Levende en groeijende bruggen. 1855. III. 370.[2]
De levende natuur. I. 520.[1]
Levesque, J. Le Poirier, sa culture. 1879. III. 445.[1]
Levi, M. G. Della maniera di formare . . . gli erbari. 1819. I. 35.
Levickzky, Albert. Az amerikai Diófa tenyésztéséről. 1892. IV. 488.[1]
Levier, Émile. À travers le Caucase. 1894. I. 369.
— *See also* CARUEL, Teodoro & LEVIER, E.; LERESCHE, Louis & LEVIER, Émile; SOMMIER, Stefano & LEVIER, Émile.
— & Sommier, Stefano. Addenda ad floram Etruriae. 1891. I. 430.
Levitof, I. *See* ЛЕВИТОВЪ, И.
Levret. De l'abatage des arbres au moyen de machines. 1878. IV. 383.[2]
Levret, H. Note sur . . . le développement des racines latérales du Chêne. 1878. IV. 507.
— El Oecidium ó Peridermium pini var. corticola. 1885. IV. 478.
— L'Oecidium ou Peridermium pini, varietas corticola. 1885. IV. 478.
Lévrier, Xavier. De l'influence du sujet sur le greffon. 1884. III. 39.
— Des plantations commerciales. 1889. III. 144.
— Quelques anomalies végétales. 1897. I. 528.[2]
Lévy, Albert. L'actinomètre Arago-Davy. 1877. II. 508.[1]
— L'actinometro Arago-Davy. 1877. II. 508.[1]
— Note concernant les expériences . . . au sujet de l'influence de la lumière sur la maturation des raisins. 1881. II. 508.[1]
— Note sur un appareil ayant servi à étudier l'influence de la lumière sur la maturation des raisins. 1880. II. 508.[1]
Lévy, Paul. Lianas, or tropical climbers. 1869. I. 236.[1]
— Note sur la coupe de l'Acajou. 1871. III. 513.[1]
— Note sur la culture de l'Indigotier. 1870. III. 479.[1]
— Note sur la culture du Rocou. 1870. III. 613.[1]
— Note sur la récolte du Caoutchouc. 1870. III. 368.[1]
— Notes sur les lianes. 1869. I. 236.[1]
Lewenhaimb, Philipp Jakob Sachs von. *See* SACHS VON LEWENHAIMB, P. J.
Lewes, George Henry. Aristoteles. 1865. I. 292.
Lewin, L. Anhalonium Lewinii. 1888. III. 620.[2]
— Ueber Anhalonium Lewinii. 1888. III. 620.[1]
— Ueber Anhalonium Lewinii und andere giftige Cacteen. 1894. III. 620.[2]
— Les feuilles d'Uva ursi et l'arbutine. 1884. III. 648.[2]
— Die Pfeilgifte. 1894. III. 260.[1]
— Ueber die toxicologische Stellung der Raphiden. 1900. I. 139.
Lewin, Louis. Ueber Areca Catechu. 1889. III. 320,[1] 342.[1]
— Beiträge zur Kenntnis einiger Acokanthera- und Carissa-Arten. 1893. II. 722,[1] 724.[2]
— Om Beteltygningen. 1889. III. 342.[2]
— Sur le Kava. 1886. III. 343.[1]
— Ueber Piper methysticum. 1886. III. 343.[1]
Lewinthal, Moritz. Über das Gummigutti. 1900. III. 609.[1]
Lewis. An easy way of raising fruit-trees. 1673. III. 159.[1]
Lewis, Elias. The longevity of trees. 1873. I. 193.[1]
Lewis, F. J. Formation of an irregular endodermis in . . . Ruscus. 1900. II. 84.[1]
Lewis, Grace Anna. Double-flowered Horse-Chestnut. 1889. II. 482.[1]
Lewis, I. W. P. Letter . . . upon wooden railroads. 1845. IV. 423.[2]
Lewis, James S. Forest trees and shrubs of Hingham. 1868. I. 312, IV. 76.[1]
Lewis, John C. The care of trees on the streets of cities. 1899. III. 210.
— The Rodman Buttwood tree. 1897. II. 211.[1]
— Tree life on our city streets. 1899. III. 208.[1]
Lewis, Meriwether & Clark, William. Travels to the source of the Missouri River. 1814. I. 321.
Lewis, Samuel. Sierra Leone. 1888. III. 281.[1]
Lewis, W. H. Colorado evergreens in central Iowa. 1891. III. 293.
Lewis, William. A complete dictionary of the whole materia medica. 1761. III. 257.[1]
— An experimental history of the materia medica. 1761. III. 257.[1]

— Experiments and observations on American potashes. 1767. IV. 395.
— The new dispensatory. 1753. III. 252.
Lewkowitsch, J. Chemical analysis of oils, fats, waxes. 1895. III. 225.
Lewy, B. Examen de la résine de Maynas. 1844. III. 608.[2]
— Note sur le Cédron. 1851. III. 509.[1]
— *See also* BOUSSINGAULT, J. B. & LÉWY, B.
Lewy, M. B. Exposé des observations faites dans la Nouvelle-Grenade. 1851. I. 339.[2]
Lexarza, Juan. *See* LLAVE, Pablo de la & LEXARZA, Juan.
Lexikon des Kleidermachers. 1895. IV. 289.[2]
Ley, Augustin. Additions to, the Flora of Herefordshire. 1894. I. 535.
— Herefordshire Rubi. 1896. II. 303.[1]
— A new form of Pyrus. 1895. II. 313.[1]
— Pyrus minima Ley. 1897. II. 313.[1]
— Records of Herefordshire plants. 1894. I. 535.
— Two new Bramble forms. 1894. II. 303.[1]
— Two new British Rubi. 1893. II. 303.[1]
— *See also* PURCHAS, W. H. & LEY, Augustin.
Ley, Wilhelm. Ueber Rubus concolor Ley. 1845. II. 301.[2]
Ley de repoblaciones italiana. 1877. IV. 165.
Ley para la repoblación ó fijación de los terrenos montuosos. 1888. IV. 328.
Leybold, Federico. Ein Ausflug nach den Argentinischen Pampas. 1873. V. XVIII.[1]
— Escursion a las pampas arjentinas. 1873. I. 344, V. XVIII.[2]
Leybold, Friedrich. Daphne petraea, eine neue Pflanze der Tyroler Alpen. 1853. II. 602.[2]
— Salicineae. 1855. II. 99.[2]
— Stirpium in Alpibus orientali-australibus. 1855. I. 441, II. 602.[2]
Leycester, W. On a new mode of grafting. 1838. III. 160.
Leyde, Eduard. *See* KRASSOW, C. K. A., *Freiherr* von & LEYDE, Eduard.
Leydekkers, C. Over de kroonsnoeiing. 1888. III. 170.
Leyden-Musée botanique. *See* MUSÉE . . . I. 16.
Leyden — Museum botanicum lugduno-batavum. *See* MUSEUM . . . I. 16.
Leyendecker, Franz. Die Blätter unserer Laubbäume. 1864. I. 110.
Leysar, Friedrich Wilhelm von. Flora halensis. 1761. I. 373.
Leyswood. 1888. III. 311.[2]
Leythäuser. Ein Beitrag zur Wasserfrage. 1892. IV. 73.[2]
— Die Kiefernspanner-Kalamität. 1897. IV. 479.
Leythäuser, Max. Die Forst-Wissenschaft. 1876. IV. 98.[1]
Lezé, R. Culture et industrie du Café au Brésil. 1892. III. 728.[2]
Le lezioni dei grandi disastri. 1882. IV. 48.[1]
Lhérault, Louis. Culture du Figuier blanc d'Argenteuil. 1872. III. 369.[2]
L'Héritier de Brutelle, Charles Louis. Cadia, nouveau genre de plante. 1795. II. 338.[2]
— Cornus; specimen botanicum. 1788. II. 654.[2]
— Die Gattung Calligonum. 1791. II. 184.[2]
— Die Gattung Symplocos. 1791. II. 703.[1]
— On the genus of Calligonum. 1791. II. 184.[2]
— On the genus of Symplocos. 1791. II. 703.[1]
— Geraniologia. 1787. II. 389.[1]
— Mémoire sur les effets du froid de ventose. 1798. III. 47.
— Sertum anglicum. 1788. I. 53.
— Stirpes novae. 1784. I. 263, V. XIII.[2]
— *See also* ZUCCAGNI, Attilio, DESFONTAINES, R. L. & L'HÉRITIER DE BRUTELLE, C. L.
L'Herminier, Felix Louis. Nomenclature synonymique, créole et botanique des arbres. 1834. I. 334.
— Relation de l'histoire naturelle médicale . . . de la Guadeloupe. 1817. II. 266.
L'Herminier, Ferdinand J. Examen du bois jaune des montagnes de la Guadeloupe. 1833. III. 747.[1]
— Résumé des observations faites sur plusieurs espèces d'Indigofère. 1833. III. 479.[1]
L'Hommedieu, John. Method of curing diseases of fruit trees. 1799. III. 180.[1]
L'Horme, A. de. Catalogue des plantes cultivées au Jardin botanique . . . de la Martinique. 1787. I. 39.
L'Hoste & Astruc. Rapport de la commission nommée pour . . . sur les territoires des communes de Creney. 1828. IV. 359.[2]
L'Hote, Louis. Sur la recherche . . . de l'alumine dans le vin. 1887. III. 583.[1]

Lhotsky, Johann. Journey from Sydney to the Australian Alps. 1835. I. 500.
— D'un moyen nouveau d'introduire dans les serres des Palmiers de haute taille. 1840. III. 316.[2]
— On a new method of introducing Palms of large size into hot-houses. 1840. III. 316.[2]
Lhuys, DROUYN DE. See DROUYN DE LHUYS.
Liais, Emmanuel. Le climat et le géographie botanique du Brésil. 1872. I. 343.
— Climats, geologie . . . du Brésil. 1872. I. 343.
Lianvaux. Note sur les nouvelles variétés de Théyers. 1855. III. 601.[1]
Liaskovski, V. See ЛИСКОВСКІЙ, B.
Liaudet, Philipp. Memoranda der medicinischen Botanik. 1851. III. 58.
Libassi, P. I. Catalogo ragionato delle piante . . . nel . . . giardino di Sant' Antonio in Malta. 1870. I. 66.[2] ·
Liber aggregationis. 1481? I. 275.[2]
Libaut, Jan. See STEVENS, Kaerle & LIBAUT, Jan.
Liberia-Koffie. 1883. III. 742.[2]
Liberian Coffee. 1877. III. 742.[2] — 1890. III. 743.[1] — 1895. III. 743.[1]
Liberian Coffee at the Straits Settlements. 1888. III. 743.[1]
Liberian Coffee in the Malay native states. 1892. III. 743.[1]
Libertador Ellis, T. Eenige harde . . . Surinaamsche hout-soorten. 1891. IV. 398.[1]
— De ziekte -. . . der cacao-noten in Suriname. 1889. III. 593.[1]
Liborius, P. Sur la rhinocanthine. 1881. II. 802.[2]
Liboschitz, Joseph. Tableau botanique des genres observés en Russie. 1814. I. 360.
— See also ЛЮБОШИЦЪ, О. & ТРИНІУСЪ, К.
— & **Trinius**, Karl. Flore des environs de St. Pétersbourg et de Moscou. 1811. I. 360.
Liboszyc, Józef. Opisanie jadowitych roślin w Litwie. 1805. III. 90.[2]
Libri de re rustica. See SCRIPTORES rei rusticae. 1470. III. 96.[2]
Liburnau, LORENZ VON. See LORENZ VON LIBURNAU.
Licer, G. Rimboschimento. 1882. IV. 166.[1]
Licer, Giuseppe. Memoria sugli eccessi forestali. 1866. IV. 181.[1]
Liche, Carle. Man-eating tree of Madagascar. 1881. I. 517.[1]
Lichinger, Friedrich. Die officinellen Croton- und Diosmeen-rinden. 1889. III. 495,[1] 516.[2]
Licht. Aufmunterung zum Seidenbau an der Mosel. 1835. III. 375.
Licht, (Hauptmann). Régime militaire des forestiers en Allemagne. 1894. IV. 289.[2]
Licht, Hermann. Erinnerungen aus Eisgrub. 1882. III. 168.[1]
— Die Vegetation von Meran. 1891. I. 66.[1]
Die **Lichtbetriebsfrage** in den Nadelhölzaern. 1882. IV. 173.
Lichtenberg, H. H. Kort Veiledning til Træplantning. 1861. IV. 103.[1]
Lichtensteig. 1865. II. 516.[3]
Lichtenstein (Geheimer Medizinal-Rath). Auszug aus den Berichten des Herrn Professor von Kunitsch. 1834. III. 436.[3]
Lichtenstein, August Gerhard Gottfried. Index alphabeticus generum. 1814. I. 77, 259, V. IX.[2]
Lichtenstein, Georg Rudolf. Anleitung zur medicinischen Kräuterkunde. 1782. III. 55.
Lichtenstein, Jules. Biologie du puceron des Lataniers. 1882. III. 318.[2]
— Les Cépages américains. 1874.· III. 759.
— Complément de l'évolution biologique des pucerons des galles du Peuplier. 1880. III. 344.[2]
— Confirmation nouvelle des migrations phylloxériennes. 1876. III. 569.[1]
— Sur l'emploi du sable dans le traitement des Vignes. 1874. III. 566.[1]
— Sur l'état actuel de la question du phylloxéra. 1873. III. 565.[2]
— Évolution biologique du puceron de l'Aulne. 1881. IV. 488.[2]
— Histoire du phylloxera. 1878. III. 571.
— Sur l'invasion de phylloxeras ailés. 1876. III. 569.[1]
— Lettre à M. le directeur du Messager agricole. 1883. III. 364.[5]
— Métamorphose du puceron . . . du Peuplier noir. 1880. III. 346.[1]
— Métamorphose et sexués du puceron du Peuplier. 1878. III. 344.[2]

— Migration des pucerons des galles du Lentisque. 1878. III. 525.[2]
— Migration du puceron du Peuplier. 1881. III. 344.[2]
— Les migrations des pucerons confirmées. 1883. III. 364.[2]
— Sur les migrations du Phylloxera du Chêne. 1875. IV. 510.
— Les migrations du puceron . . . de l'Ormeau. 1882. III. 365.[2]
— Monographie des pucerons du Peuplier. 1885. III. 344.[2]
— Sur un moyen pour empêcher l'irruption du Phylloxera. 1870. III. 564.[2] ·
— Notes pour servir à l'histoire des insectes du genre phyllox-éra. 1876. III. 760.
— Notes pour servir à l'histoire du genre Phylloxera. 1875. IV. 510.
— Sur un nouvel insecte du genre Phylloxera. 1884. III. 350.[1]
— Observations à propos de la communication récente de M. Balbiani. 1874.· III. 567,[1] IV. 510.
— Observations pour servir à l'étude du phylloxera. 1880. III. 572.
— Sur l'œuf d'hiver du phylloxera. 1881. III. 572.
— Sur les œufs des phylloxeras. 1876. III. 568. ·
— Le phylloxera. 1880. III. 572.
— Sur le phylloxera issu de l'œuf d'hiver. 1876. III. 568.
— Sur un procédé de destruction du phylloxeron. 1872. III. 565.[1]
— Le puceron vrai de la Vigne. 1882. III. 563.
— Les pucerons des Ormeaux. 1879. III. 364.[2]
— Les pucerons des Peupliers. 1885. III. 344.[2]
— Les pucerons du Térébinthe. 1879. III. 526.[1]
— Sur quelques nouveaux points de l'histoire naturelle du Phylloxera. 1874. III. 566.[1]
— Quelques observations sur les Phylloxeras de la Savoie. 1882. IV. 510.
— Sur la rapidité de la reproduction du phylloxera. 1873. III. 565.[1]
— Rectification à une note précédente. 1875. IV. 510.
— Réponse à M. Balbiani. 1876. III. 569.[1]
— See also PLANCHON, J. E. & LICHTENSTEIN, Jules.
— & **Mayet**, Valéry. Etude sur le gribouri ou écrivain de la Vigne. 1879. III. 563.
Lichtenstein, Wilhelm Auguste Jules. See LICHTENSTEIN, J.
Lichtlin, Jn. Jph. Thre. Table de cubage des bois. 1844. IV. 223.
Der **Lichtungszuwachs** und seine Bedeutung. · 1889. IV. 234.
Licopoli, Gaetano. Sopra alcune glandole della Tecoma. 1870. II. 786.[2]
— Sull' anatomia . . . del frutto nell' Anona. 1884. II. 215,[2] 216,[1] 217.[1]
— Sul frutto del Melarancio. 1876. II. 402.[1]
— Sul frutto dell' uva. 1875. II. 508.[1] III. 583.[1]
— Sul fusto del Cissus acida. 1872.· II. 502.[2]
— Le galle nella flora di alcune province napolitane. 1877. I. 215.[2]
— Sulla natura morfologica della fovilla. 1873. I. 524.[2]
— Osservazioni sul fusto della Wisteria. 1871. II. 388.[2]
— Osservazioni teratologiche sul fiore del Melianthus major. 1867. II. 491.[2]
— Ricerche anatomiche · sulla Chamærops. 1882. II. 63.[1]
— Ricerche micro-fito-chimiche sul frutto dell' Uva. 1876. II. 507.[1]
— Ricerche microscopiche sulla origine . . . di alcune granu-lazioni esistenti nella polpa. 1864. I. 119, II. 256.[2]
— Gli stomi e le glandole delle piante. 1879. I. 112,[2] 131.[2]
— Sulla struttura del fusto della Wisteria. 1872. II. 388.[2]
— See also PASQUALE, G. A. & LICOPOLI, Gaetano.
Lidbeck, Andreas. De plantis in Suecorum memoriam nomi-natis. 1792. I. 511.
Lidbeck, Eric Gustaf. Anmärkningar om Skånska climatet. 1751. III. 119.[2]
— Anmärkningar vid Skånska flyg-sandstracterne. 1759. IV. 156.[2]
— Berättelse om en i ett träd invuxen inskärning. 1771. I. 210.[1]
— De Betula Alno. 1779. II. 116.[1]
— De Moro alba. See ENGELHART. 1777. II. 154.[2]
— Observations circa horticulturam academicam. 1791. III. 120.[2]
— Rön och anmärkningar vid Mullbärs-träns uppdragande af sina frön. 1754. III. 372.[2]

Lidbeck, Eric Gustaf (*continued*).
— De silvicultura Scaniae. 1757. IV. 113.²
— Tal om planteringer. 1766. III. 165, *IV. 113.*²
— Uplysning angående Jacob Kavaus hemlige konster. 1747. IV. 491.¹
— De utilitate plantationum arborum. 1768. III. 100,¹ *IV. 113.*²
Lidén, Johan. Examen classis monoeciae. *See* THUNBERG, C. P. 1825. I. 251.
Lidforss, Bengt. Batologiska iakttagelser. 1899. II. 301.²
— Zur Biologie des Pollens. 1896. I. 201.²
— Ueber den Chemotropismus der Pollenschläuche. 1899. I. 201.²
— Zur Physiologie . . . der wintergrünen Flora. 1896. I. 178.
Lidof, A. P. *See* ЛИДОВЪ, A. П.
Lieb, E. Lagerstroemia indica. 1900. III. 629.¹
Liebe, Theodor. Die Elemente der Morphologie. 1868. I. 100.¹
— Über die geographische Verbreitung der Schmarotzerpflanzen. 1869. I. 233.²
— Grundriss der speciellen Botanik. 1866. I. 256, V. XIII.¹
Liebel, Robert. Die Zoocecidien. 1886. I. 215.¹
— Die Zoocecidien . . . Lothringens. 1892. I. 215.¹
Liebenberg, von, (*Professor*). Der Eichenwurzeltödter. 1881. IV. 510.
— Phytophthora Fagi. 1882. IV. 497.
— Le rosellinia (Rhizoctonia) guereina. 1881. IV. 510.
Liebenberg, A., *Ritter* von. Untersuchungen über die Rolle des Kalkes bei der Keimung. 1882. I. 203.
Liebermann, Carl Theodor & Hörmann, O. Sur le glucoside des graines d'Avignon. 1878. III. 543.²
— — Ueber das Glykosid der Gelbbeeren. 1878. III. 543.²
Liebermann, Leo. Caractères analytiques de la gomme arabique. 1893. I. 181.¹
— Az erdők befolyása az aszályra. 1894. IV. 54.
Liebert, von, (*Generalmajor*). Kautschuk von Deutsch-Ostafrika. 1900. III. 230. ·
Liebezeit, J. Adam. Der meissnische Weinbau. 1798. III. 552.
Liebhaber, E. A. W. von. Ankündigung einer Gesellschaft forstwissenschaftlicher Freunde. 1822. IV. 40.¹
— Anleitung zur forstwissenschaftlichen Messkunde. 1806. IV. 263.
— Hülfstafeln zur forstwissenschaftlichen Messkunde. 1806. IV. 229.
— Ueber das Verhältniss der Brennbarkeit der Hölzer. 1806. IV. 412.²
— Ueber den Zuwachs der Waldungen. 1804. IV. 232.
Liebhaber des Seiden Baues, (*pseud.*). Deutliche Anweisung, wie mit Säung des Maulbeer-Saamens . . . ·zu verfahren. 1751. III. 372.²
Liebich. Ueber den Anbau des Acer Negundo. · 1834. III. 535.¹
Liebich, Christoph. Die Altenburger 4. Preisfrage: "Wie weit geht die Berechtigung . . . des Staates in Beaufsichtigung . . . der Privatholz-Grundstücke?" 1844. IV. 255.²
— Bodenstatik für Forst- und Landwirthschaft. 1855. IV. 68.
— Bodenstatik für Forst- und Landwirthschaft. 1859. IV. 123.³
— Ueber Bodenstatik für Forst- und Landwirthschaft. 1857. IV. 68.
— Compendium der Forstwissenschaft. 1854. IV. 99.² ·
— Compendium des Waldbaues. 1855. IV. 111.¹
— Die Durchforstungen. 1845. IV. 173.
— Eröffnungs-Rede als Docent. 1849. IV. 101.
— Die Forstbetriebs-Regulirung. 1836. IV. 240.
— Forst-Katechismus. 1869. IV. 99.²
— Die Forst-Regulirung der Herrschaft Krzeestitz. 1826. IV. 249.²
— Die Forstwissenschaft nach der Prager Lehre. 1859. IV. 101.
— Handbuch für Forsttaxatoren. 1830. IV. 240.
— Der höchste nachhaltige Forstertrag. 1827. IV. 254.
— Der Maulbeerbaum als Waldbaum. 1859. III. 377.
— Der Maulbeerbaum als Waldbaum und als Grundlage des . . . Seidenbaues. 1859. IV. 519.¹
— Die Reformation des Waldbaues. 1844. IV. 111.¹
— Ueber Sinn und Wesen der periodischen Durchforstungen. 1843. IV. 173.
— Ueber die Ursachen der Insectenverheerungen. 1852. IV. 209.²
— Der Waldbau nach neuen Grundsätzen. 1834. IV. 110,² *133.*

Liebig, Justus, *Freiherr* von. Sulla analisi delle foglie del Gelso. 184 . ? II. 154.²
— De bewerktuigde scheikunde toegepast op landbouwkunde en physiologie. 1840. III. 36.³
— Chemistry in its application to agriculture. 1840. III. 36.¹
— La chimica applicata all' agricoltura. 1840. III. 36.³
— Chimie organique appliquée. 1840. III. 36.²
— De grondslagen der landbouwscheikunde. 1855. III. 37.¹
— Die Grundsätze der Agricultur-Chemie. 1855. III. 37.¹
— Herr Dr. Emil Wolff in Hohenheim. 1855. III. 37.¹
— Die organische Chemie. 1840. III. 36.³
— Die Pflanze. 1862. I. 147.
— Principles of agricultural chemistry. 1855? III. 37.¹
— & others. Die Cajeput-Bäume des Rumphius. 1835. III. 636.
— — Chirostemon platanoides. 1835. III. 590.¹
— — Dattelbaumgummi. 1832. III. 329.¹
— Zusammensetzung der Milch des Kuhbaums. 1840. III. 608.²
Lieblein, Franz Kaspar. Flora fuldensis. 1784. I. 374.
Liebmann, Frederik Michael. Americas berusende eller inciterende Planter. 1840. III. 62.
— Americas Egevegetation, etc. 1852. II. 128.²
— Amerikanische Eichen. 1855. II. 129.¹
— Om anomala trädbildningar. 1851. I. 127.¹
— Bidrag til Meliosmeernes Familie. 1850. II. 490.²
— Cacaoplanten. 1851. III. 594.
— Central-Americas Palmeformer. 1845.· II. 61.¹
— Chastoptelea. 1850. II. 142.³
— Chênes de l'Amérique tropicale. 1869. II. 129.¹
— Om Egeslægten i America. 1854. II. 128.²
— Mexicos og Central-Americas Rubi. 1852. II. 300.³
— Mexicos og Central-Amerikas neldeagtige Planter. 1851. II. 156.¹
— N og le Ord om Befrugtningen hos Cycadeerne. 1849. II. 3.¹ °¹
— Novorum plantarum mexicanarum generum decas. 1854. I. 331.
— To nye Arter af Slægten Castelia. 1853. II. 414.¹
— To nye Valnødarter fra Mexico. 1850. II. 111.²
— Eine pflanzengeographische Schilderung des Vulkans Orizaba. 1843. I. 331.
— Philetaeria en ny anomal Slaegt. 1850. II. 563.¹
— Plantarum species novae in indice seminum Horti hauniensis. 1853. I. 40.
— En plantengeographisk Skildering af Vulcanen Orizaba: 1843. I. 331.
— Die Quercus- oder Eichen Vegetation von Amerika. 1852. II. 128.¹
— De Quercus of Eikenvegetatie in Amerika. 1852. II. 128.¹
— Skildring af det mejicanske tierra frias Vegetation. 1842. I. 331.
— & Lange, Johan. Icones plantarum . . . in regnis Sueciae. 1853. I. 355.
Liebreich, O. La strychnine comme antidote du chloral. 1870. III. 683.¹
Liebus. Zeitgemässe Betrachtungen über die Waldarbeiterfrage. 1898. IV. 310.¹
Liebus, Béla. Die Köhlerei als Regiezweig der Forstverwaltung. 1897. IV. 395.
— Die Mimicry und ihre Bedeutung. 1898. IV. 67.²
Liechti. Wie kann in den Hochgebirgswaldungen ein geordneter Forstungsbetrieb eingeführt werden? 1887. IV. 174.
Liechti, H. Zur Fichtenbüschelpflanzung. 1873. IV. 453.
— Sur la plantation en bouquets. 1873. IV. 453.
— Dans quels cas le mode du jardinage doit-il être conservé? 1874. IV. 128.
— Unter welchen Umständen muss die Plänterwirthschaft an die Stelle des regelmässigen Schlagbetriebes . . . treten? 1874. IV. 128.
Liechti, Paul Robert. Studien über die Fruchtschalen der Garcinia. 1891. II. 555,³ III. 609.³
Das Lied von der Nonne. 1892. IV. 201.
Liedbeck, Pehr Jacob. Horti upsaliensis plantae. *See* THUNBERG, C. P. 1826. I. 40.
— De Pipere Cubeba. 1827. III. 342.³ ·
Liégard, Auguste. Flore de Bretagne. 1879. I. 415.
Liège — Institut botanique de l'Université. *See* INSTITUT . . . I. 16.
Liège — Société royale des sciences. *See* SOCIÉTÉ . . . I. 17.
Liegel, Georg. Anweisung, mit welchen Sorten verschiedene Obstbaum-Anlagen besetzt werden sollen. 1822. III. 146.¹

— Beschreibung neuer Obstsorten. 1851. III. 71.
— Botanische und pomologische Characteristik . . . des Pflaumenbaumes. 1836. III. 432.[2]
— Ueber die Geschlechts-Charaktere der Pflaume. 1837. III. 432.[2]
— Kurze Anleitung zur Beschreibung des Obstbaumes. 1844. III. 71.
— Kurze Geschichte des Pflaumenbaumes. 1836. III. 432.[2]
— Die Pflaumen. 1851. III. 432.[2]
— Pomologische Beschreibung von zwei seltenen Pflaumenarten. 1848. II. 270.[2]
— Die pomologische Kunstsprache. 1826. III. 29,[2] 70.
— Systematische Anleitung zur Kenntnis der Pflaumen. 1838. III. 432.[2]
— Systematische Anleitung zur Kenntnis . . . des Kern-, Stein-, Schalen- und Beeren-Obstes. 1825. III. 90.[1]
— Uebersicht der Pflaumen. 1847. III. 432.[2]
— Vollständige Uebersicht aller . . . Pflaumen. 1861. III: 432.[2]
Liegelsteiner, Georg. Wohl fundirter Zwerg-Baum. 1702. III. 135.
Liegnitzer Stadtforst. 1881. IV. 354.
Liehr. Das Forstversorgungswesen. 1884. IV. 290.[3]
Liénard, E. Une excentricité végétale. 1874. II. 708.[1]
Liébard, F. Études sur les insectes nuisibles aux Pins sylvestres. n. d. IV. 474.
Lienau, W. Die phanerogamischen Pflanzen der Fürstenthums Lübeck. 1863. I. 385.
Lienhart, Constant. Recherches . . . sur le camphre monobromé. 1875. III. 404.[3]
Liesa . . . See Лѣса. . .
Liesnoi . . . See Лѣсной. . .
Lissokhozyaistvenny . . . See Лѣсохозяйственный. . .
Lissopromyshlennik. See Лѣсопромышленникъ.
O liesorazvedeni . . . See O лѣсоразведенiи . . .
Lietze, Adolf. Coffea liberica. 1879. III. 743.[1]
— Ueber den Gartenbau in Brasilien. 1882. III. 119.[1]
— Misteln (Loranthus) an Telegraphendrähten. 1888. II. 175.[2]
— Veredlung der Kaffeerace. 1879. III. 728.[2]
— Versendung von schnell verderbenden Samen. 1884. III. 154.[3]
Lieven, Charles. Le Rosier multiflore nain remontant. 1896. III. 456.[1]
Lieventhal. See Wurthner, Lieventhal & Weyrich, Rudolf.
Lièvre, Anton Val de. See Val de Lièvre, Anton.
Life among the loggers. 1851. IV. 382.[1]
Life of Asa G. Sheldon: Wilmington farmer. 1862. III. 117.[1]
Ligar, Charles W. Grass tree. 1866. III. 339.[1]
Liger, Louis. The compleat florist. 1704. III. 112.
— Culture parfaite des jardins fruitiers. 1743. III. 143.
— Économie générale de la campagne. 1700. III. 111.
— Historischer und verständiger Blumen-Gärtner. 1704. III. 112.
— Le jardinier fleuriste et historiographe. 1704. III. 112.
— The manner of planting . . . most kinds of flowers. 1704. III. 112.
— Le nouveau théâtre d'agriculture. 1712. III. 112.
— La nouvelle maison rustique. 1700. III. 111.
— Oeconomie générale. 1700. III. 111.
Lightfoot, John. Flora scotica. 1777. I. 395.
Ligman, Jan. Z dziedziny gospodarstwa leśnego. 1900. IV. 370.
Lignaloe wood. 1899. III. 584,[2] 626.[2]
Ligne, Jonglez de. See Jonglez de Ligne.
Lignier, Octave. Contributions à la connaissance du bouton floral mâle de Chamaedorea elegans. 1890. III. 84.
— Contributions à la nomenclature des tissus secondaires. 1895. I. 124.
— Sur la décortication des tiges de Calycanthées. 1890. I. 192.[2]
— Développement comparé du boyau pollinique. 1892. II. 92.[1]
— Dissémination . . . du Viscum album sur le Pinus sylvestris. 1899. II. 180.[1]
— De la forme du système libéro-ligneux foliaire. 1890. I. 111.
— La graine et le fruit des Calycanthées. 1891. II. 214.[1]
— De l'importance du système libéro-ligneux foliaire. 1888. I. 111.
— De l'influence que la symétrie de la tige exerce sur la distribution . . . de ses faisceaux. 1890. I. 106.[1]
— La nervation des Cycadacées. 1895. II. 3.[1]
— La nervation . . . des folioles de Cycas. 1892. II. 4.[1]
— Note relative à des protubérances observées sur des branches de Biota. 1888. II. 52.[1]
— Observations sur la structure des Lécythidées. 1887. II. 611.[1]
— À propos de la nervation . . . de Cycas siamensis. 1894. II. 5.[1]
— Sur quelques faits intéressants pour la flore du Calvados et la biologie végétale. 1893. I. 226.[2]
— Recherches sur l'anatomie comparée des Calycanthées. 1886. III. 214,[1] 620.[1]
— Recherches sur l'anatomie . . . des Lécythidées. 1890. II. 611.[1]
— Recherches sur les massifs libéro-ligneux de la tige des Calycanthées. 1884. II. 214.[1]
— Sur la valeur morphologique des massifs libéro-ligneux corticaux des tiges des Calycanthées. 1884. II. 214.[1]
Lignières, J. Rapport sur l'évolution du puceron lanigère. 1895. III. 428.[2]
Lignitz, (Oberförster zu Nesselgrund). Die Ausbildung für den königlich preussischen Forst-Verwaltungsdienst. 1883. IV. 33.[1]
— Erwiderung auf die Abhandlung des Dr. Cogho. 1876. IV. 204.
— Nachfrage nach Aspenholz. 1886. IV. 486.[2]
Ligon, Richard. A true & exact history of the island of Barbados. 1657. I. 334, III. 266.
Ligtvoet. Voordracht over Koffie. 1898. III. 727.
Ligue du reboisement de l'Algérie. Bulletin. IV. 16.[2]
Lijst der boekwerken voorhanden in de boekerij der Hollandsche maatschappij van landbouw. 1879. III. 1.
Lijst der voornaamste houtsoorten . . . der residentie Padang. 1868. IV. 399.[2]
Lilas Josikaea. 1834. III. 681.[1]
Lilienfeld-Alp, A. von. Erwägungen über den Antrag . . . auf Versuche mit einer Wald-Grund-Einschätzung. 1878. IV. 260.[1]
Lilja, Nils. Enumeratio specierum . . . generis Lupini. 1844. II. 370.[2]
— Flora öfver Sveriges odlade vexter. 1839. I. 354.
— Handbok i de odlade växternas flora. 1842. III. 100.[1]
— Observationes botanicae. Salix. 1843. II. 110.[1]
— Skånes flora. 1838. I. 354.
— Växter funna i Skåne sommaren 1844. 1844. II. 649.[1]
— Växtfynd i trakten af Billinge. 1843. II. 297.[1]
Liljeblad, Samuel. Svenska oert-slagen. 1792. I. 352.
— Utkast til en svensk flora. 1792. I. 352.
— & Lönberg, E. G. Ratio plantas in sedecim classes disponendi. 1796. I. 251.
Liljenroth, Frans. Anmärkningar om växternas födande ämnen. 1797. I. 352.
Liljevalch, Peter Olof. Om inskrifter i lefvande träd. See Agardh, C. A. 1829. I. 210.[1]
Lille — Société d'amateurs des sciences, de l'agriculture . . . See Société . . . I. 22.
Lille — Société des sciences, de l'agriculture . . . See Société d'Amateurs des sciences . . . I. 22.
Lillie, Charles. The British perfumer. 1822. III. 226.[2]
Lilliehöök, E. G. Ljungens utdöende på Svältorna. 1857. III. 648.[2]
Lilly, Alfred T. The silk industry of the United States. 1875. III. 378.
Limbourg, de, (jr.). Essais à faire pour se procurer plus facilement des bois de construction pour la marine. 1783. IV. 424.[2]
Limbourg, Robert de. Dissertation sur la question: Quelle est l'influence de l'air sur les végétaux? 1758. I. 169.[2]
Limburg-Stirum, comte de & others. Domaine inculte communal. 1890. IV. 40.[2]
The lime-juice industry. 1893. III. 502.[1]
Lime trees. 1884. IV. 528.[1]
Limes. 1892. III. 502.[1]
Limonius, G. Sur l'écorce de Piscidia erythrina. 1884. III. 484.[2]
— Note sur l'écorce de Cascara sagrada. 1885. III. 543.[2]
— Sur la Piscidia erythrina. 1884. III. 484.[2]
Limousin, Henri Bocquillon. See Bocquillon-Limousin, Henri.
Limousin, S. Note sur le pichi du Chili. 1886. III. 700.[2]
Limprecht, J. E. S. Das Abwerfen der Knospen bei den Camellien. 1831. III. 599.[1]
Limprecht, Johannis Adamus. De floribus insueto anni tempore. 1752. I. 224.[2]
Lin-a-loa. — Woods and timbers. 1880. IV. 525.
Linares, Augusto Gonzalez de. See Gonzalez de Linares, Augusto.

Lincke, Johann Rudolf. Deutschlands Flora. 1840. I. 380.

Linckius, Johannes Heinrich. Arbor Caffe Lipsiae florens. 1747. III. 726.[1]

Lincoln, Mrs. Almira (Hart). See PHELPS, Mrs. Almira (Hart) Lincoln.

Lincoln, B. Remarks on the cultivation of the Oak. 1838. IV. 500.[2]

Lincoln, Benjamin. A letter to . . . James Warren, relating to the ingrafting of fruit-trees. 1780. I. 189.

Lindau, Gustav. Acanthaceae. 1895. II. 796.[1]
— Acanthaceae africanae. 1893. II. 796.[2]
— Acanthaceae americanae. 1895. II. 796.[1]
— Acanthaceae americanae et asiaticae. 1897. II. 796.[1]
— Acanthaceae papuanae. 1895. II. 796.[2]
— Acanthaceae somalenses. 1897. II. 796.[2]
— Beiträge zur argentinischen Flora. 1895. I. 345.
— Beiträge zur Systematik der Acanthaceen. 1894. II. 796.[1]
— Einige neue Acanthaceen. 1898. II. 796.[1]
— Zur Entwicklungsgeschichte einiger Samen. 1891. II. 185,[1] 498.[1]
— Der Epheukrebs. 1894. III. 643.[1]
— Monographia generis Coccolobae. 1891. II. 185.[1]
— Ord. Acanthaceae. 1900. II. 796.[1]
— Übersicht über die . . . Arten der . . . Thunbergia. 1893. II. 804.[2]
— Xantheranthemum und Pseuderanthemum. 1893. II. 802.[1]
— Zwei neue Polygonaceen. 1895. II. 183.[2]

Lindberg, G. A. Cereus (Echinocereus) tuberosus. 1886. II. 593.[1]
— Echinocereus caespitosus Engelmann. 1884. II. 593.[1]
— Eine Erleichterung beim Umpflanzen sehr stacheliger Cacteen. 1883. III. 619.
— Lepismium dissimile G. A. Lindberg. 1890. II. 598.[2]
— Eine merkwürdige Euphorbia. 1888. II. 442.[1]
— Rhipsalideen. 1883. III. 626.[1]
— Rhipsaliden und Rhipsalis crispata. 1882. III. 626.[3]
— Rhipsalis (Lepismium?) dissimilis. 1891. III. 626.[1]
— Rhipsalis pulvinigera. 1889. II. 599.[1]
— Rhipsalis puniceodiscus. 1893. II. 599.[1]
— Rhipsalis Regnellii. 1890. II. 599.[1]
— Rhipsalis trigona Pfr. 1891. II. 599.[1]
— Rhipsalis Warmingiana K. Schum. 1892. II. 599.[1]

Lindberg, Harald. Anmärkningsvärda mossor och fanerogamer från Finland. 1896. II. 136.[1]
— Anmärkningsvärda växter från Finland. 1891. II. 673.[1]
— Anmärkningsvärda växtfynd på Karelska näset. 1900. II. 105.[1]
— Eräs rikas turvelöytö Joroisten pitäjässä Savossa. 1899. I. 367.
— Fanerogamer från Karelska näset. 1896. I. 367.
— Om hallonmasken. 1894. III. 458.[2]
— Några för finska floraområdet nya fanerogamer. 1895. II. 115.[1]
— Sjomen Suoviljelysyhdistykselle lähetettyjen turvenäytteiden tutkimus. 1897. I. 367.
— Suomen turvesuot. 1900. I. 368.[1]
— Tre för finska floran nya fanerogamer. 1896. II. 101.[1]
— Växtlokaler i Finland. 1891. II. 105.[2]

Lindberg, Sextus Otto. Abnorma frukter af En. 1881. II. 31.[1]
— Beskrifning af Myrtillus nigra var. pallida. 1879. II. 686.[2]
— Botaniska iakttagelser i Finland. 1878. II. 31.[1]
— En hermafrodit buske af Salix phylicifolia. 1881. II. '09.[1]
— Missbildning af Alfrukter. 1871. II. 115.[1]
— Pinus pichta's förökning. 1878. III. 297.[1]
— Plantae nonnullae Horti botanici helsingforsiensis. 1871. I. 42, V. VIII.[1]
— Om skidans natur hos Cruciferae och Papaveraceae. 1871. I. 2[2] 9.[1]
— Uppgiften om förekomsten af Taxus. 1881. II. 11.[1]
— Uppgifterna om Cuscuta. 1881. III. 193.[1]

Lindblom, Alexis Eduard. Om afsöndring af en sockerhaltig saft från bladen af Tilia. 1846. II. 517.[1]
— Anmärkning till Fries, El. Vårens antåg. 1839. I. 220.[2]
— Anteckningar öfver vårens utveckling. 1844. I. 223.[1]
— Beriktigande af Dr. Beilschmieds uppfattning. 1845. II. 143.[1]
— Bidrag till Blekings Flora. 1830. I. 353.
— Botaniska Upsater. 1838. I. 34.

— Egendomliga företeelser inom växtriket. 1846. I. 231.[2]
— Fenologisk notis om vårväxter kring Lund. 1840. I. 223.[1]
— Fytografiska anmärkningar. 1845. II. 301.[1]
— In geographicam plantarum intra Sueciam distributionem adnotata. 1835. I. 353.
— Novitiae florae suecicae. See FRIES, E. M. 1814. I. 352.
— Stirpes agri rotnoviensis. 1826. I. 353.
— Strödda anteckningar öfver Norges vegetationsförhållander. 1842. I. 354.
— Om tillväxthastigheten hos Adansonia. 1844. II. 529.[1]
— Växtfynd i Blekinge, Sverige. 1840. II. 301.[1]

Lindbom, Olavus. Remedia guineensia. See AFZELIUS, Adam. 1813. III. 93.[1]

Linde, Eduard. Ueber Carpain. 1893. III. 617.[2]

Lindeberg, Carl Johan. Exkursioner i norra Halland. 1850, I. 355.
— Fortsatta excursioner i Norge. 1855. I. 355.
— Fortsatta exkursioner i Bohus län. 1854. II. 301.[1]
— Genmäle [till C. F. Areschoug's Recension]. 1887. II. 301.[1]
— Herbarium Ruborum Scandinaviae. 1882. II. 301.[1]
— Novitiae florae Scandinavicae. 1858. I. 355, II. 119,[1] 310.[2]
— Ruborum Sueciae . . . See ARRHENIUS, J. P. 1839. II. 301.[1]
— Vextarter från vestra skärgården. 1852. II. 517.[2]
— & **Kalén,** M. V. Plantarum vascularium in regione Maeleri. 1848. I. 355.

Lindegaard, P. Om Viinstokkens Dyrkning. 1826. III. 551.[2]

Lindeman, H. Bemesting van Cacaoboomen. n. d. III. 592.[1]

Lindemann, Moritz. Mitteilungen über den bayrischen Wald. 1885. IV. 351.[1]

Lindemann, Waldstreu-Nutzung am vordern Hardtgebirge. 1858. IV. 71.

Lindemann, Eduard von. Flora chersonensis. 1881 I. 369.
— Florula elisabethgradensis. 1867. I. 362.
— Index plantarum . . . in variis Rossiae provinciis. 1860. I. 362.
— Index plantarum usualium florae chersonensis. See Линдеманъ, Э. 1872. III. 68.[1]
— Nova revisio florae kurskianae. 1865. I. 362.
— Prodromus florarum Tschernigovianae. 1850. I. 361.
— Uebersicht der bisher in Bessarabien aufgefundenen Spermatophyten. 1880. I. 364.
— Verzeichniss derjenigen Pflanzenarten . . . aus der Flora rossica auszuscheiden. 1867. I. 311.[2]
— See also Линдеманъ, Э.

Lindemann, Johann Godofred Ludwig. De cortice peruviano eiusque . . . usu. See KRÜGER, J. G. 1757. III. 719.

Lindemann, Karl Eduardovich. Beitraege zur Kenntniss der Borkenkäfer Russlands. 1875. IV. 549.[1]
— Monographie der Borkenkaefer Russlands. 1876. IV. 549.[1]
— Tomicus typographus. 1882. IV. 456.

Lindemuth, Hugo. Die Baumschule und der Obstbau. 1882. III. 139.
— Ueber ein botanisch interessante Birnensorte. 1888. II. 280.[1]
— Handbuch des Obstbaues. 1883. III. 139.
— Die Impfversuche mit buntblättrigen Malvaceen. 1873. I. 529.
— Die Kultur des kleinblätterigen Epheu. 1894. III. 643.[1]
— Ueber vegetative Bastarderzeugung durch Impfung. 1878. I. 246.[1]
— Versuche und Betrachtungen über das Propfen. 1900. III. 165.
— Wert, Umfang und Behandlung des Obstbaues. 1896. III. 139.

Linden, Cort van der & others. Staats en particuliere bemoeiing bij ontginning der woeste gronden. 1892. IV. 160.[2]

Linden, Jean Jules. Hortus Lindenianus. 1859. I. 50.
— Introductions nouvelles à Bruxelles. 1865. III. 77.
— Neue Linden'sche-Pflanzen. 1859. I. 50.
— Die neuesten Einführungen des Herrn J. Linden. 1880. III. 77.
— Plantes introduites . . . par l'établissement J. Linden. 1881. III. 78.[1]
— Plantes nouvelles. 1857. III. 77. — 1867. III. 77.
— Plantes nouvelles récemment introduites. 1866. III. 77.
— Relation d'un voyage scientifique. 1846. I. 329.

— *See also* PLANCHON, J. E. & LINDEN, J.
— & Planchon, J. E. Troisième voyage de J. Linden. 1863. V. XVIII.[1]
Linden, John. Intressanta växtfynd i Karelen. 1891. II. 109.[1]
Linden, Lucien & Rodigas, Émile. Arbres annonçant la pluie. 1890. II. 313.[1]
— — Le Clidemia vittata. 1897. III. 633.[1]
— — Un Peuplier phénoménal. 1885. I. 188.
Lindenau, *Graf* von. Aussug aus dem Schreiben Sr. Excellens ... Grafen von Lindenau. 1829. III. 136.
Lindenblüthen als Handelswaare. 1864. III. 585.[2]
Lindenthal, L. W. Forstwissenschaftlicher Versuch über die Kiefern-Saaten. 1800. IV. 471.
Linder, Johann. Flora wiksbergensis. 1716. I. 351.
— Svenska färgakonst med inländske örter. 1720. III. 235.[2]
Lindermayer, Anton. Euboea; eine naturhistorische Skizze. 1855. I. 449.
Lindern, Franz Balthazar von. Hortus alsaticus. 1747. I. 373.
— Tournefortius alsaticus. 1728. I. 373.
Lindet, L. Caractérisation et séparation des principaux acides. 1896. I. 180.[2]
— Sur le développement ... de la pomme à cidre. 1893. II. 267.[2]
— Sur l'oxydation du tanin de la pomme à cidre. 1895. II. 267.[2]
— Recherches sur le développement ... de la pomme à cidre. 1893. II. 267.[2]
— Sur des Vignes japonaises ... à Damigny. 1896. III. 557.[2]
— *See also* GIRARD, Aimé & LINDET, L.
Lindgren, Erik. Erica carnea (herbacea) coccinea. 1897. III. 651.[1]
Lindgren, S. J. Beriktigande till hans växtgeografiska notiser från Kinnekulle. 1841. II. 117.[1]
— Växtgeografiska notiser från Kinnekulle. 1841. I. 354.
Lindheimer, Ferdinand. Aufsätze und Abhandlungen ... in Texas. 1879. I. 324.
— Die Cypresse im westlichen Texas. 1879. II. 51.[2]
— Pflanzengeographische Uebersicht von Texas. 1846. I. 321.
— Eine Uebersicht der Flora von Texas. 1879. I. 324.
Lindley, George. A guide to the orchard and fruit garden. 1831. III. 79.
— A guide to the orchard and kitchen garden. 1831. III. 79.
Lindley, John. Abies. 1833. I. 268.
— Abies Kaempferi. 1854. II. 49.[1]
— Abies Khutrow. 1841. II. 38.[2]
— An account of a remarkable instance of anomalous structure. 1831. I. 210.[1]
— Amygdalus Persica; double crimson Peach. 1848. II. 276.[2]
— Aphelandra lateritia. 1854. II. 797.[1]
— Aphorismes de physiologie végétale et de botanique. 1835. I. 87.
— Argyreia festiva. 1841. III. 694.[2]
— Bemerkungen über die Vegetation ... am Schwanen-Fluss. 1839. I. 500.
— Bemerkungen über ... Pomaceen. 1822. II. 255.[2]
— Berberis Fortuni nov. sp. 1846. II. 203.[2]
— Botanik für Damen. 1834. I. 94.
— Bouvardia Cavanillesii. 1848. III. 711.[1]
— Bouvardie à trois feuilles var. brillante. 1840. II. 810.[1]
— Calectasia cyanea. 1841. III. 334.[1]
— Callistemon brachyandrum. 1849. III. 633.[1]
— Chrysorhoë; a new genus. 1836. II. 634.[1]
— The close-headed Bejaria. 1848. III. 648.[2]
— Cocuspalme in Frucht. 1863. III. 322.[2]
— Collectanea botanica. 1821. I. 266.
— Colletia serratifolia. 1844. III. 541.[2]
— Coniferen die von Herrn J. G. Veitch in Japan entdeckt worden sind. 1861. II. 15.[2]
— Conifères rares ou nouvelles. 1861. II. 15.[2]
— Convolvulus floridus. 1840. III. 694.[2]
— Cupressus Macnabiana. 1855. III. 302.[2]
— Dammara obtusa. 1851. III. 297.[2]
— Descriptive botany. 1858. I. 254.[2]
— Digitalium monographia. 1821. II. 780.[1]
— Dion edule. 1843. II. 5.[1]
— The dwarf Cocoa-nut of Ceylon. 1861. III. 322.[2]
— The dwarf Cocoanut Palm at Syon. 1862. III. 322.[2]
— Einleitung in das natürliche System der Botanik. 1830. I. 260.
— Elements of botany. 1830. I. 86.
— Empfehlenswerthe oder neue Pflanzen. 1861. II. 15.[2]
— Esquisses des premiers principes d'horticulture. 1832. III. 35.
— Exochorda grandiflora. 1858. II. 264.[1]
— Flora medica. 1838. III. 57.
— Flowering of the dwarf Coconut at Syon. 1862. III. 322.[2]
— Fortunaea chinensis. 1846. II. 114.[2]
— Fortunea sinensis. 1846. II. 114.[2]
— Fructification anomale du Pêcher à fleurs doubles. 1848. II. 276.[2]
— Fructification du Cocotier en Angleterre. 1863. III. 322.[2]
— Fruiting of the dwarf Coco-nut at Syon. 1863. III. 322.[2]
— Fuchsia paniculata. 1856. II. 643.[2]
— Garrya elliptica. 1834. I. 86.
— Garrya elliptica. 1840. II. 110.[2]
— Garrya laurifolia. 1840. III. 352.[2]
— A glossary of technical terms used in botany. 1848. I. 71, V. IX.[1]
— The glowing Bejaria. 1848. III. 648.[2]
— Grondbeginselen der horticultuur. 1832. III. 35.
— Grundzüge der Anfangsgründe der Botanik. 1830. I. 86.
— Hauptgrundsätze des Gartenbaus. 1832. III. 35.
— Hedaroma tulipiferum. 1854. II. 622.[2]
— Horse Chestnut poisonous. 1839. III. 536.[2]
— Hoya à feuilles coriacées. 1839. II. 740.[1]
— Hypocalymna angustifolium. 1843. III. 635.[1]
— Ilex Fortuni. 1857. II. 464.[1]
— Instructions for packing living plants in foreign countries. 1823. III. 155.
— An introduction to botany. 1832. I. 86.
— An introduction to the natural system of botany. 1830. I. 260.
— Juniperus pyriformis. 1855. II. 32.[1]
— A key to structural, physiological and systematical botany. 1835. I. 87.
— Ladies' botany. 1834. I. 94.
— Lemonie charmante. 1840. II. 410.[1]
— Leptodermis lanceolata. 1839. III. 745.[2]
— Liste systématique ... de ... plantes de l'intérieur de la Nouvelle-Hollande. 1841. I. 500.
— The Long-flowered Hornberry. 1848. II. 684.[2]
— Medical and oeconomical botany. 1849. III. 52.
— Memoranda concerning some new plants. 1849. III. 82.
— Memorandum concerning ... vegetable transformation. 1850. II. 493.[2]
— Mexican Oaks recently introduced. 1840. III. 361.[1]
— Mexican Pines. 1839. II. 39.[1]
— Monographie du genre Rosier. 1820. II. 282.[1]
— Myoporum ascendens. 1844. III. 710.[2]
— Nachricht über Rhododendron alta-clerense. 1831. II. 670.[2]
— New plants. 1861. II. 15.[2]
— New plants, etc. from the Society's garden. 1846. I. 54.
— Nixus plantarum. 1833. I. 260.
— Nixus plantarum; die Stämme des Gewächsreiches. 1833. I. 260.
— A note on Chorozema varium. 1842. II. 346.[2]
— A note upon the genus Sarcobatus. 1845. II. 188.[2]
— Notice of five varieties of Pears. 1830. III. 444.[2]
— A notice ... of Rhododendron inhabiting Borneo. 1848. II. 676.[2]
— Notices of certain ornamental plants. 1832. III. 82. — 1851. III. 82.
— Notices of new or rare garden plants. 1853. III. 82.
— Sur la nouvelle famille des Garryacées. 1834. II. 110.[2]
— Oaks of Koordistan. 1840. II. 131.[1]
— Observations on the natural group ... Pomaceae. 1822. II. 255.[2]
— Observations upon the effects produced ... by the frost ... in the winter of 1837-8. 1839. III. 46.[2]
— The ornamental flower-garden and shrubbery. 185.? I. 269.
— An outline of the first principles of botany. 1830. I. 86.
— An outline of the first principles of horticulture. 1832. III. 35.
— Passiflora cinnabarina. 1855. II. 578.[1]
— Passiflora kermesina. 1833. II. 579.[1]
— Pins nouveaux du Mexique. 1839. II. 39.[1]
— Pinus Gordoniana Hart. 1847. II. 43.[1]
— Pinus lophosperma. 1860. II. 48.[2]
— Pinus Royleana. 1855. II. 41.[2]

Lindley, John (*continued*).
— Planera acuminata. 1862. II. 145.[1]
— Pomologia britannica. 1828. III. 79.
— The pomological magazine. 1828. III. 79.
— On the principal questions . . . in the philosophy of botany. 1833. I. 79.[1]
— Principes de botanique. 1830. I. 86.
— Principles of horticulture. 1858. III. 36.[1]
— Prunus Pseudocerasus? 1845. III. 442.[2]
— Pyrus floribunda. 1826. II. 312.[2]
— Quelques mots sur l'Eugenia Ugni. 1857. III. 638.[1]
— Report . . . new or rare plants . . . Horticultural society, Chiswick. 1825. I. 54.
— Report upon the effect produced . . . by the frost . . . of April 29th. 1826. III. 46.[2]
— Report upon the new or rare plants. 1825. I. 267.
— Revue des espèces de Berberis cultivées. 1850. II. 201.[2]
— Rhododendron Fortuni. 1859. II. 679.[2]
— Rhynchospermum jasminoides. 1846. III. 691.[2]
— Rogiera urophylla. 1857. II. 830.[1]
— Rondeletia anomala. 1855. II. 830.[1]
— Rosa Ruga. 1830. II. 298.[1]
— Rosarum monographia. 1820. II. 282.[1]
— The Sack tree. 1846. III. 366.[1]
— The Sapucaya nuts of commerce. 1862. III. 631.[7]
— A short account of . . . evergreen Berberries. 1850. II. 201.[1]
— A sketch of the principal tropical fruits which are likely to be worth cultivating in England for the dessert. 1824. III. 220.[1]
— A sketch of the vegetation of the Swan River colony. 1839. I. 500.
— The Small-leaved Thibaudia. 1848. II. 684.[2]
— Some considerations upon the cultivation of fruit trees. 1831. III. 142.
— Swammerdamia antennaria. 1849. III. 755.[2]
— Swan River; sketch of the vegetation. 1839. I. 500.
— On symmetry of vegetation. 1854. I. 99.
— A synopsis of the British flora. 1829. I. 397, 533.
— Syringa oblata. 1859. II. 715.[2]
— Taxus Lindleyana. 1855. II. 11.[2]
— Théorie de l'horticulture. 1840. III. 35.
— Theorie der Gärtnerei. 1840. III. 35.
— Theorie der Gartenkunde. 1840. III. 35.
— The theory and practice of horticulture. 1840. III. 35.
— The theory of horticulture. 1840. III. 35.
— Thuja ē rameaux filiformes. Thuja filiformis. 1842. II. 52.[2]
— Thujopsis laetevirens. 1862. II. 53.[1]
— Vaccinium rugosum. 1860. II. 674.[2]
— The vegetable kingdom. 1846. I. 261.
— Verticordia densiflora. 1843. III. 638.[1]
— Über das Wachsthum der Bäume. 1831. I. 210.[1]
— Wellingtonia gigantea. 1853. II. 50.[1]
— Wellingtonia gigantea Lindl. 1853. II. 50.[1]
— The white-lipped Vaccinium. 1848. II. 686.[1]
— *See also* Линдлей, I.
— *See also* FORTUNE, Robert & LINDLEY, John.
— & Moore, Thomas. The treasury of botany. 1866. I. 34, V. VIII.[1]
— & Paxton, Joseph. Gleanings and original memoranda. 1850. III. 82.
—— The Kamtchatka Rhodotham. 1850. II. 681.[1]
—— The Oval and the Pallid Hoyas. 1850. II. 739.[1]
— & Smith, John. Saxo-gothaea conspicua. 1851. II. 10.[1]
— & Smith, John. Floraison du Cocotier en Angleterre. 1862. III. 322.[1]
— Hooker, Sir J. D. & others. On Coffee, its substitutes. 1852. V. XXIX.[2]
Lindley library. Catalogue. *See* CATALOGUE . . . 1898. I. 3.[1]
Lindman, Carl Axel Magnus. Beiträge zur Palmenflora Süd-amerikas. 1900. II. 61.[2]
— Bidrag till kännedomen om skandinaviska fjellväxternas blomning. 1887. I. 239.[2]
— Castanea sativa Mill. mit Honigblumen. 1895. II. 124.[2]
— Om drifved . . . vid Norges kuster. 1883. I. 242.[2]
— Einige neue brasilianische Cyolanthaceen. 1900. II. 76.[1]
— Einige Notizen über Viscum. 1890. II. 178.[1]
— Karlväxtfloran på Visby ruiner. 1895. I. 358.
— Leguminosae austro-americanae. 1898. II. 319.[1]
— Några variationer hos Vaccinium uliginosum. 1892. II. 687.[1]
— Om postflorationen och dess betydelse. 1884. I. 238.
— Växtligheten på Madeira. 1886. I. 498.

— Vegetationen i Rio Grande do Sul. 1900. I. 344.
Lindner, Daniel. De Tilia. *See* ILMER, Georg. 1669. II. 517.[1]
Lindner, J. T. Die Holzordnung Churfürst Augusts vom Jahre 1560. 1840. IV. 321.
Lindo, J. A. On some Japanese woods. 1876. IV. 399.[1]
Lindroth, André Bernh. De nutritione plantarum. *See* THUNBERG, C. P. 1819. I. 157.
Lindroth, Johan Ivar. Alnus incana f. monstrosa från Ment-sälä. 1898. II. 117.[1]
Lindsay, Archibald. Dissertatio inauguralis, de plantarum incrementi causis. 1781. I. 32.
Lindsay, John, (about 1790). An account of the Quassia poly-gama. 1794. II. 415,[2] 816.[2]
Lindsay, John. Ormiston Hall; its Yew-tree. 1891. II. 11.[1]
— On Yews. 1886. II. 11.[1]
Lindsay, Lauder. The flora of Iceland. 1861. I. 356.
Lindsay, Robert. Heterophylly in New Zealand Veronicas. 1899. II. 783.[1]
— On the New Zealand Veronicas. 1893. III. 704.[1]
— New Zealand Veronicas. 1894. III. 704.[1]
— Poisoning of sheep by Pieris floribunda. 1893. III. 654.[1]
— Veronica Lindsayi. 1898. III. 704.[2]
Lindsay, William LAUDER-. On the conservation of forests in New Zealand. 1868. IV. 181.[1]
— Contributions to New Zealand botany. 1868. I. 506.[2]
— On the economical value . . . of the forest-trees of New Zealand. 1868. III. 283.[1]
— Growth in Britain of the New Zealand Kowhai. 1879. III. 488.[2]
— Notes on some Compositae of Otago. 1869. I. 506.[2]
— Notes on some plants of Otago, New Zealand. 1868. I. 506.[2] — 1869. I. 506.[2]
— Remarks on the flora of Otago. 1865. I. 506.[2]
— On the Toot plant. 1865. III. 523.[2]
— On the " toot-poison " of New Zealand. 1863. III. 523.[2]
Lindsay, N. A. A spurious Elaeagnus longipes. 1892. III. 629.[1]
Lindwall, Johannes. Observationes in materiam medicam. *See* LINNÉ, Carl von. 1772. III. 241.
Linéard, E. Une excentricité végétale. 1874. I. 234.[2]
Linge, van. Waar wordt het alkaloid gevormd? 1900. III. 724.[1]
Lingenfelder, Ph. Die Kirschfliege. 1866. III. 435.[1]
— Merulius lacrimans. 1874. IV. 415.[1]
Lingke, Wilhelm Friedrich. Bemerkungen über die Wurm-trockniss. 1799. IV. 203.
— Erfahrungen . . . bey der Schwarzholzsaat. 1795. IV. 140, 148, 440.
Link, G. F. Einige Bemerkungen über den Standort. 1795. I. 228.[1]
Link, Heinrich Friedrich. Abietinae Horti regii. 1841. II. 12.[1]
— Über Akklimatisirung der Gewächse. 1835. III. 43.
— Anatomia plantarum iconibus illustrata. 1843. I. 99.
— Anatomie d'une branche de Pinus Strobus. 1836. II. 46.[1]
— Anatomie der Pflanzen in Abbildungen. 1843. I. 99.
— Anatomisch-botanische Abbildungen. 1837. I. 98.
— Ueber das Anwachsen von Theilen in den Pflanzen. 1838. I. 189.
— Ausgewählte anatomisch-botanische Abbildungen. 1839. I. 98.
— Beiträge zur botanischen Geographie des südlichen Europa. 1836. I. 349.
— Bemerkungen auf einer Reise durch Frankreich. 1799. I. 420.
— Bemerkungen über den Bau des Stammes der Dattelpalme. 1845. II. 72.[2]
— Bemerkungen über die natürlichen Ordnungen der Ge-wächse. 1822. I. 251.
— Der botanische Garten bei Berlin. 1820. I. 266.
— Ueber Chamaedorea Schiedeana. 1834. II. 66.[2]
— Dissertatio de vasis plantarum. 1805. I. 133.
— Dissertationes botanicae. 1795. I. 133.
— Einige Bemerkungen über die Vegetation von Dalmatien. 1845. I. 447.
— Einige Bemerkungen über die Wirkungen des Frostes auf die Gewächse im Winter, 1822–1823. 1824. III. 45.
— Elementa philosophiae botanicae. 1824. I. 85.
— Enumeratio plantarum Horti regii botanici berolinensis altera. 1821. I. 46.
— Erinnerung an die grosse Linde bei Neustadt. 1850. II. 516.[2]
— Etwas über die Geschichte der Gärten. 1844. III. 32.[2]

— Ueber die Familie Pinus. 1827. II. 39.[1]
— Ueber die Gattung Phillyrea. 1818. II. 714.[1]
— Grundlehren der Anatomie und Physiologie der Pflanzen. 1807. I. 84.
— Grundlehren der Kräuterkunde. 1824. I. 85.
— Handbuch zur Erkennung der . . . Gewächse. 1829. I. 55.
— De Helianthemi genere observationes. 1806. II. 564.[1]
— Hortus regius botanicus berolinensis. 1827. I, 46.
— Icones anatomico-botanicae. 1837. I. 98.
— Icones selectae anatomico-botanicae. 1839. I. 98.
— Kritische Bemerkungen . . . zu Kurt Sprengel's Werk über den Bau . . . der Gewächse. 1812. I. 33.
— Mammillaria. Spartanthus. 1823. II. 385,[1] 594.[1]
— Philosophiae botanicae novae. 1798. I. 254.[2]
— Recherches sur l'accroissement végétal et la greffe. 1850. I. 208.[1]
— Recherches sur l'anatomie des plantes. 1812. I. 98.
— Revisio Abietinarum Horti regii. 1847. II. 12.[1]
— Some material for the illustration of the botanical geography of the southwestern parts of Europe. 1805. I. 348.[2]
— Ueber die Stellung der Cycadeen. 1845. II. 2.[1]
— De structura caulis plantarum monocotylearum. 1834. I. 104.
— Symbolae ad floram graecam. 1835. I. 449.
— Sur les trachées des plantes. 1831. I. 133, 163.
— Travels in Portugal and through France. 1799. I. 420.
— Vegetabilia saxo calcareo propria. 1789. I. 228.[1]
— Vertheilung der Waldbäume in Europa. 1849. I. 348,[1] IV. 79.[1]
— Vorlesungen über die Kräuterkunde. 1843. I. 88.
— Voyage en Portugal. 1799. I. 420.
— Über Wachsen und Anwachsen im Pflanzenreiche. 1850. I. 208.[1]
— Zusammengestellte Uebersicht der drei Abhandlungen über die Gefässe der Pflanzen. 1809. I. 133.
— See also HOFFMANNSEGG, J. C., Graf von & LINK, H. F.
— & Otto, Friedrich. Abbildungen auserlesener Gewächse des Königlichen botanischen Gartens zu Berlin. 1820. I. 45.
— — Abbildungen neuer und seltener Gewächse des Königl. botanischen Gartens zu Berlin. 1828. I. 46.
— — Beschreibung . . . einer neuen Passionsblume. 1826. II. 579.[1]
— — Über die Gattungen Melocactus. 1827. II. 584.[2]
— — Icones plantarum rariorum Horti regii botanici berolinensis. 1828. I. 46.
— — Icones plantarum selectarum Horti regii botanici berolinensis. 1820. I. 45.
— — Über eine neue Cactus-Art, Echinocactus oxygonus. 1830. II. 593.[2]
— — Verzeichniss der Cacteen des Berliner Bot. Gartens. 1830. II. 585.[1]
— Klotzsch, Friedrich & Otto, Friedrich. Abbildung seltener Pflanzen der Königl. botanischen Gartens zu Berlin. 1841. I. 47.
— — — Icones plantarum rariorum Horti regii botanici berolinensis. 1841. I. 47.
Link, H. J. Bericht über ein Referat . . . den Rosenstock am Dom zu Hildesheim. 1829. II. 290.[1]
Linke, August. Beiträge zur Kakteenkunde. 1858. II. 586.[1]
— Bemerkungen über das Variiren der Cacteen. 1850. II. 586.[1]
— Beschreibung von einigen Cacteen. 1848. II. 586.[1]
— Zur Kacteenkunde. 1857. II. 586.[1]
— Kurze Erwiederung auf meine Bemerkungen über das Variiren der Cacteen. 1852. II. 586.[1]
— Sechs neue Kakteen. 1857. II. 586.[1]
Linke, Johann Rudolf. Analytischer Pflanzenschlüssel. 1863. I. 385.
— Atlas der officinellen Pflanzen sämmtlicher Pharmacopoeen. 1850. III. 58.
— See also KERSTEN, G. A. & LINKE, J. R.
Linnaea. I. 13.
Linnaean association of Pennsylvania college. Literary record. I. 6.
Linnean society of London. Journal. Proceedings. Transactions. 1. 18.
Linnean society of New South Wales. Proceedings. I. 29.[2]
Linné, Carl von. Academisk afhandling om blomstrens honinghus. . 1778. I. 118.[1]
— Amoenitates academicas. 1749. I. 31.
— Arboretum suecicum. 1759. I. 350.[1] III. 66,[1] 119,[1] IV. 79.[1]

— Auctores botanici. 1759. I. 79.[1]
— Auserlesene Abhandlungen. 1749. I. 31.
— De Betula nana. 1743. II. 119.[1]
— Bibliotheca botanica. 1736. I. 1.
— Botanici et mineralogici publici fundamenta botanica. 1741. I. 31.
— Botaniska ord. 1762. I. 69.[2]
— Calceolaria pinnata, en rar växt. 1770. II. 779.[2]
— The calendar of flora. 1756. I. 222.[2]
— Calendarium florae. 1756. I. 222.[2]
— Calendrier de flore. 1756. I. 222.[2]
— Centuria plantarum. 1755. I. 261.
— Classes plantarum. 1738. I. 257.
— Classis Palmarum. 1736. II. 60.[2]
— Collectio epistolarum quas . . . scripsit. 1792. I. 520.[2]
— Die coloniis plantarum. 1786. I. 241.[1]
— Corollarium generum plantarum. 1737. I. 257.
— Cortex peruvianus. 1758. III. 719.
— De cortice peruviano pars prior. 1758. III. 719.
— Critica botanica. 1737. I. 253.[2]
— Cycas proposita. 1778. II. 4.[1]
— Decas . . . plantarum rariorum Horti upsaliensis. 1762. II. 234,[1] 396.[1]
— Decem plantarum genera. 1746. I. 261.
— Disquisitio de quaestione . . . sexum plantarum . . . vel corroborare vel impugnare. 1760. I. 199.
— De Dulcamara. 1771. III. 701.[1]
— De Erica. 1770. II. 663.[1]
— Erica Sparrmanni. 1778. II. 669.[1]
— Euphorbia ejusque historia naturalis. 1752. II. 441.[2]
— Exercitatio botanico-physica de nuptiis. 1828. I. 199.
— Explicacion de la filosofia y fundamentos botanicos de Linneo. 1751. I. 250.
— The families of plants. 1787. I. 257. — 1787. I. 530.[1]
— Ficus ejusque historia. 1744. II. 148.[2]
— Flora Åkeröensis. 1769. I. 351.
— Flora alpina. 1756. I. 219.[2]
— Flora anglica. 1754. I. 394.
— Flora belgica. 1760. I. 391.[2]
— Flora capensis. 1759. I. 493.
— Flora dalekarlica. 1873. I. 357.
— Flora jamaicensis. 1759. I. 334.
— Flora lapponica. 1737. I. 351.
— Flora monspeliensis. 1756. I. 405.
— Flora oeconomica. 1748. III. 66.[2]
— Flora palaestina. 1756. I. 479.
— Flora suecica. 1745. I. 351.
— Flora zeylanica. 1747. I. 476.[1]
— Florula lapponica. 1738. I. 351.
— Förtekning, af de färgegräs. 1742. III. 235.[1]
— On the foliation of trees. 1753. I. 222.[2]
— Fructus esculenti. 1763. III. 219.[1]
— Frutetum suecicum. 1758. I. 350.[1]
— Fundamenta botanica. 1736. I. 254.[1]
— Fundamentum fructificationis. 1762. I. 243.[1]
— Gattungen der Pflanzen. 1737. I. 257.
— Gemmae arborum. 1749. I. 107.[2]
— Genera plantarum. 1737. I. 257.
— A general system of nature. 1735. I. 257.
— Herbarium amboinense. 1754. I. 464.[2]
— Horticultura academica. 1754. III. 120.[1]
— Hortus Cliffortianus. 1737. I. 50.
— Hortus upsaliensis. 1745. I. 40.
— Hortus upsaliensis; exhibens plantas exoticas. 1748. I. 40.
— Hospita insectorum flora. 1752. I. 236,[1] III. 188.[2]
— Hushållsnyttan af de . . . wildt wäxande örter. 1748. III. 66.[2]
— Hypericum. 1776. II. 555.[2]
— Incrementa botanices. 1753. I. 79.[1]
— Inledning i ört-riket efter Systema naturae. 1735. I. 256.
— Instructio peregrinatoris. 1759. I. 35.
— Iter in Chinam. 1768. I. 452.
— Lachesis lapponica. 1811. I. 352.
— De Lavandula. 1780. II. 764.[1]
— De Ledo palustri. 1775. III. 653.[1]
— Ledum palustre. 1785. III. 653.[1]
— Lignum colubrinum. 1749. III. 684.[1]
— Lignum Quassiae. 1763. III. 508.[2]
— Mantissa plantarum. 1767. I. 258.
— Materia medica liber I. de plantis. 1749. III. 241.
— Materia medica per regna tria naturae. 1749. III. 241.
— Medicamenta graveolentia. 1758. III. 241.

Linné, Carl von (continued).
— Medicamenta purgantia. 1775. III. 241.
— Metamorphoses plantarum. 1755. I. 243.[2]
— Methodus sexualis. 1737. I. 257.
— Miscellaneous tracts. 1749. I. 31.
— Nectaria florum. 1762. I. 118.[1]
— Nitraria planta obscura explicata. 1761. II. 395.[2]
— Nomenclator botanicus. 1759. I. 72.[1]
— Nova genera plantarum zeylanicarum. 1747. I. 476.[2]
— Nova plantarum genera. 1747. I. 261.
— Observationes in materiam medicam. 1772. III. 241.
— Öländska och gothländska resa. 1745. I. 351.
— Opera varia. 1758. I. 31, 520,[3] V. VII.[2]
— Opobalsamum declaratum. 1764. II. 418,[1] III. 510.[2] — 1769. II. 417.[3]
— Oratio de necessitate peregrinationum intra patriam. 1741. I. 298.
— Oratio, qua peregrinationum intra patriam asseritur necessitas. 1741. I. 298.
— An oration concerning the necessity of travelling in one's own country. 1741. I. 298.
— På de medicinal wäxter som i apothequen bewaras. 1741. III. 270.[1]
— Pan succicus. 1749. III. 223.[1]
— Pan suecus. 1749. III. 223.[1]
— Parte práctica de botánica. 1779. V. XIII.[1]
— De Passiflora. 1745. II. 576.[2]
— Petiveria, en americansk växt. 1744. II. 193.[1]
— Pflanzenphilosophie im Auszuge. 1751. I. 250.
— Pflanzensystem nach seinen Klassen. 1774. I. 258.
— Philosophia botanica. 1751. I. 250.
— Philosophie botanique.' 1751. I. 250.
— Plantae camschatoenses rariores. 1750. I. 454.[2]
— Plantae esculentae patriae. 1752. III. 66.[2]
— Plantae hybridae. 1751. II. 458.[1]
— Plantae officinales. 1753. III. 54.
— Plantae rariores africanae. 1760. I. 493.
— Plantae rariores camschatoenses. 1750. I. 454.[2]
— Plantae surinamenses. 1775. III. 338.[2]
— Plantae tinctoriae. 1759. III. 235.[1]
— Plantarum jamaicensium pugillus. 1759. I. 334.
— Plantarum rariorum Horti upsaliensis fasciculus. 1767. II. 313.[1]
— De potu chocolatae. 1765.' III. 594.
— Potus coffeae. 1761. III. 741.[1]
— Potus Theae. 1765. III. 605.
— Praelectiones in ordines naturales plantarum. 1792. I. 258.
— Prodromus florae danicae. 1757. I. 351.
— De prolepsi plantarum. 1766. I. 97.
— Purgantia indigena. 1766. III. 270.[1]
— Rariora Norvegiae. 1768. I. 351.
— Reisen durch das Königreich Schweden. 1751. I. 351.
— Reisen durch Oeland und Gothland. 1751. I. 351.
— Reisen durch Westgothland. 1747. I. 351.
— Das Ritter C. von Linné Auserlesene Abhandlungen. 1749. I. 31.
— Rön om wäxters plantering. 1739. III. 119.[2]
— Samling af et hundrade wäxter . . . på Gothland. 1741. I. 351.
— Select dissertations. 1749. I. 31.
— Selectae ex Amoenitatibus academicis dissertationes. 1749. I. 31.
— Sida florum capitulis pedunculatis. 1749. II. 527.[1]
— Sistema de los vegetables. 1779. V. XIII.[1]
— Skånska resa. 1751. I. 351.
— Somnus plantarum. 1755. I. 197.[2]
— Species plantarum. 1753. I. 257.
— Specifica Canadensium. 1756. III. 262.[1]
— Sponsalia plantarum. 1746. I. 198.
— Stationes plantarum. 1754. I. 228.[1]
— Supplementum plantarum Systematis vegetabilium. 1774. I. 258.
— Svensk coccinell. 1759. III. 648.[1]
— A system of vegetables. 1774. I. 258.
— Systema, Genera, Species plantarum uno volumine. 1835. I. 260.
— Systema naturae. 1735. I. 256.
— Systema plantarum Europae. 1785. I. 348.[2]
— Systema plantarum secundum classes. 1779. I. 258, V. XIII.[1]
— Systema vegetabilium. 1774. I. 258, 530,[1] V. XIII.[1]
— Système de la nature. 1735. I. 256.
— Système des plantes. 1774. I. 258.
— Système sexuel des végétaux. 1774. I. 258, V. XIII.[1]

— Tankar om nyttiga växters planterande. 1754. III. 120.[1]
— Tentamen supplementi systematis vegetabilium. 1774. I. 258.
— Termini botanici. 1762. I. 69,[2] V. IX.[1]
— Termini botanici. 1781. I. 69.[2]
— Vernatio arborum. 1753. I. 222.[2]
— Vires plantarum. 1747. III. 238.[1]
— Viridarium Cliffortianum. 1737. I. 50.
— Vollständiges deutsches Pflanzensystem. 1774. I. 258.
— Vollständiges Natursystem. 1735. I. 256.
— Vollständiges Pflanzensystem. 1774. I. 258.
— Wåra inländska äteliga wäxter. 1752. III. 66.[2]
— Wästgöta-resa. 1747. I. 351.
Linney, William M. Report on the botany of Madison. 1882. I. 319.
— Report on the timbers of Boyle and Mercer counties. 1879. IV. 397.
Linocier, Geofroy. Histoire des plantes aromatiques. 1619. I. 284.
— Histoire des plantes nouvellement trouvées en isle de Virginie. 1619. I. 305.
Linossier, G. A propos de l'action de l'oxyde de carbone sur la germination. 1889. I. 204.
Linsbauer, Karl. Zur Anatomie der Vegetationsorgane von Cassiope. 1900. II. 662.[1]
— See also LINSBAUER, Ludwig & Karl.
Linsbauer, Ludwig. Beiträge zur . . . Anatomie der Caprifoliaceen. 1896. II. 834.[1]
— Ueber die Nebenblätter von Evonymus. 1893. II. 467.[1]
— & Karl. Einige teratologische Befunde an Lonicera. 1900. II. 840.[1]
Linschotten, Jan Huyghen van. Discours of voyages into the Easte and West Indies. 1598. I. 470.[2]
— Discours of voyages into the East and West Indies. 1596. III. 277.
— Itinerario, voyage . . . naer oost ofte Portugaels Indien. 1596. III. 277.
— Itinerarium, ofte schipvaert naer Oost ofte Portugaels Indien. 1596. III. 277.
— Navigatio ac itinerarium in orientalem sive Lusitanorum Indiam. 1596. III. 277.
Linsser, Carl. Die periodischen Erscheinungen des Pflanzenlebens. 1867. I. 221.
— Untersuchungen über die periodischen Lebenserscheinungen der Pflanzen. 1869. I. 221.
Linster, Ch. See QUETELET, Adolphe, LINSTER, Ch. & FRITSCH, Karl.
Linstow, C. H. von. Til Publikum. 1791. IV. 288.[3]
Lintner, (Oberförster, Kölmchen). Massen- und Geld-Ertrag eines . . . Weiden-Werders. 1857. IV. 487.[2]
Lintner, Joseph Albert. A destructive Elm-tree bark-borer. 1893. III. 365.[1]
— The San José scale. 1895. III. 187.
Linton, Edward Francis. British Salices. 1895. II. 102.[1]
— Experiments in cross-fertilisation of Salices. 1898. II. 104.[1]
— Flora of Bournemouth. . 1900? I. 404.[1]
— The genus Rubus in the supplement . . . of English botany. 1895. II. 303.[1]
— A new British Rubus. 1887. II. 308.[2]
— A new British Rubus. 1894. II. 310.[1]
— The Salix lists in the " London catalogue." 1896. II. 102.[1]
— Two new Willow-hybrids. 1894. II. 102.[1]
— Two Willow hybrids. 1894. II. 102.[1]
— & W. R. British Willows. 1896. II. 102.[1]
— Some Scottish Willows. 1892. II. 102.[1]
Linton, William Richardson. A new Rubus. 1892. II. 307.[1]
— Some Scotch Willow hybrids. 1897. II. 102.[1]
Lintz, Louis. Dissertations forestières. 1808. IV. 100.[2]
Lintz, Ludwig. Die Grenze zwischen der Feld- und Waldkultur. 1821. IV. 46,[2] 132.[1]
— Ueber die Regulirung einer Holz-Taxe. 1816. IV. 402.[2]
— Vertheidigung des höchst-nachhaltigen Forst-Natural-Ertrags. 1824. IV. 253, 288.[1]
Linz, (Oberförster, Crummendorf). Zusammenstellung des Material- und Geld-Ertrages . . . in dem kgl. Charité-Forstrevier Prieborn. 1863. IV. 260.[2]
Linz, T. See SIERACKOWSKY, von & LINZ, T.
Linzbauer, F. X. A Magyar királyi pesti egyetem növénykertenék jelen állapota. 1866. I. 66.[1]
Liocourt, F. de. De l'aménagement des sapinières. 1898. IV. 555.[1]
— Du calcul de la possibilité. 1893. IV. 246.

Lion, H. J. De kultuur van den Klapper boom. 1855. III. 322.²

Lionetti, G. La cura della Vigna. 1897. III. 562.¹

Lions, A. Essai sur les végétaux utiles . . . des Bouches-du-Rhône. 1863. III. 86.

Liotard, Ernest. Étude sur le Kousso. 1888. III. 424.²

Liotard, L. Memorandum on dyes of Indian growth. 1881. III. 236.

— Memorandum on materials . . . for the manufacture of paper. 1880. III. 235.²

— Memorandum on silk in India. 1883. III. 148.²

Liotard, Pierre Victorin. La fécondation artificielle de la Vigne. 1895. III. 549.¹

Liouville, E. Conversions dangereuses. 1895. IV. 249.¹

— Les taillis des Ardennes. 1897. IV. 129.

— Le ver gris (Agrotis segetum). 1889. IV. 209.¹

Liouville, Henry. See VOISIN, Auguste & LIOUVILLE, Henry.

Le **Liparis** monacha en Suède. 1898. IV. 202.

Liperi, Francesco de. Notizie sulla condizione der boschi . . . di Tempio Pausania. 1864. IV. 364.

Lipiński. Wycieczka do lasów miejskich w Brzuchowicach. 1899. IV. 370.

Lipowitz, A. Anleitung zur Conservation des Holzes. 1841. IV. 417.

Lipp, Franz Joseph. Εγχειρίδιον βοτανικόν. 1765. I. 522, ² V. XIII.¹

— Enchiridium botanicum. 1765. V. XIII.¹

Lippai, János. Posoni kert. 1664. I. 65.²

Lippert, Christian. Danni prodotti dal Visco. 1878. IV. 210.²

— Project einer Rollbahn für den Transport von Holz. 1878. IV. 391.

— Viscum album als Nutzholzverderber. 1878. IV. 210.²

Lippert, J. Die wilden Pflanzen der Heimath. 1874. IV. 442.

Lippincot, Joseph Barlow. Grandeur in an American forest. 1900. IV. 179.²

Lippincott's magazine of literature. III. 4.

Lippmann, von & **Crampton**, A. Présence de l'acide borique. 1889. I. 180.²

Lippold, (*Pfarrer und Professor*). Auszug aus dem Berichte des Herrn Soulange-Bodin. 1834. III. 427.¹

Lips, Eduard von. Ein Beitrag zum Stockroden. 1857. IV. 385.¹

— Ein Beitrag zur Rüsselkäferfrage. 1858. IV. 207.

— Der grosse Rüsselkäfer. 1854. IV. 209.²

— Die Schule des Waldbaues. 1859. IV. 107.¹

— Der Spessart. 1852. IV. 350.²

Lipscombe, William. What arable lands is it advisable to plant? 1880. IV. 134.¹

Lipski, Vladimir. Contributio ad floram Asiae mediae. 1900. I. 457.

— *Florae caucasicae imprimis colchicae novitates* 1897. I. 370.

— *See also* Липский, B.

Liquidambar. 1888. IV. 520.¹

Liquidambar d'Amérique. 1874. III. 418.¹

Liron d'Airoles, Jules de. Anomalies végétales et maladies de la sève. 1862. I. 244.¹

— Catalogue des arbres à fruits . . . des Révérends Pères Chartreux. 1862. I. 58.

— Sur le Chêne-Liége. 1856. IV. 516.²

— Influence réciproque du sujet et de la greffe. 1864. I. 246.²

— Liste . . . des variétés du Poirier. 1859. III. 444.²

— Notice pomologique. 1854. III. 85.

— Notice pomologique; description des poires. 1858. III. 444.²

— Les Poiriers les plus précieux. 1861. III. 444.²

Lisancourt, LEMAIRE-. *See* LEMAIRE-LISANCOURT.

Lisboa, Balthazar da SILVA. *See* SILVA LISBOA, Balthazar da.

Lisboa, José Camillo. Hereditary disease of the branches . . . of Ficus Tsiela. 1892. III. 371.²

— Some plants undescribed in the "Bombay flora." 1878. I. 474.

— Useful plants of the Bombay Presidency. 1886. III. 92.²

Lisboa — Academia real das sciencias. *See* ACADEMIA . . . I. 24,¹ III. 23.¹

Lischka, Carl. *See* BUCHMAYER, Aug. & LISCHKA, Carl.

Lischwiz, Johann-Christoph. Biga orationum. 1739. II. 577.¹

— De continuanda Rivinorum industriâ. 1726. I. 250.

— Dissertatio, sistens plantas anthelminticas. 1742. III. 54.

— Observationes botanicae de variis naturae lusibus. 1733. I. 142.

— Plantae diureticae. 1739. III. 54.

— De plantis diaphoreticis et sudoriferis. 1734. III. 54.

Lishin, I. A. *See* Лишин, И. А.

Lisitzyn, P. A. *See* Лисицынъ, П. А.

L'**Isle**, E. B. MARIÉ DE. *See* MARIÉ DE L'ISLE, E. B.

L'**Isle**, Edward. Observations in husbandry. 1757. III. 123.¹

L'**Isle**, Thiollière de. Traitement de Vignes phylloxérées. 1879. III. 760.

Lismanes, Michael. *See* ΛΙΣΜΑΝΗΣ, Μιχαήλ.

Lisner, Karl Friedrich. De Ulmi campestris virtute medica. 1817. III. 365.²

Lisnevski, V. I. *See* Лиснeвскiй, B. И.

Lissander, Anders. Anmärkningar vid svenska trägårds-skötseln. 1768. III. 119.¹

List, Friedrich Ludwig. Plantae Lithuaniae. 1837. II. 101.¹

— Spicilegium botanicum, continens stirpes nuperrime in Lithuania detectas. 1828. I. 378.

List and description of Borneo woods. *See* MACLEAN, James. 1886. IV. 400.¹

List hospodařský. III. 25.

List of books, &c., relating to botany and forestry in the Edinburgh museum of science. 1897. IV. 2.

List of books, etc., relating to botany and forestry . . . in the library of the museum [Edinburgh]. 1897. I. 3.¹

List of Chinese medicines. *See* MORGAN, F. A. 1889. III. 273.²

List of drugs grown in the Botanical gardens, Gunesh Khind, Poona. *See* WOODROW, G. M. 1876. I. 67.¹

List of flowering plants. 1872. V. XXI.¹

List of forest technical terms. 1887. IV. 23.²

List of fruits cultivated in the gardens. 1887. III. 64.¹

List of hybrid grafts exhibited at Chiswick. 1900. III. 165.

List of large, old and interesting trees. 1892. I. 295.²

List of maps and publications relating to forest administration . . . of India. 1878. IV. 2.

List of medicinal and poisonous plants . . . of Edinburgh. *See* BALFOUR, J. H. 1859. I. 55.

List of 153 trees and shrubs. *See* LOCKWOOD, G. 1876. IV. 89.¹

List of Palms cultivated in . . . Jamaica. 1890. II. 61.¹

List of Palms cultivated in the Royal gardens, Kew. 1884. III. 317.

List of plants and seeds, wanted from China. 1789. III. 154.¹

List of plants cultivated . . . at Milburn Tower, near Edinburgh. *See* LISTON, R. 1817. I. 53.

A list of plants hardy in the garden at Castlewellan, Co. Down. *See* ANNESLEY, Lord. 1890. I. 55.

List of plants in the Botanic gardens, British Guiana. 1885. I. 40.

List of pteridophyta and spermatophyta . . . in northeastern North America. 1893. I. 316.

List of publications relating to forestry in the department library. 1898. IV. 2.

List of published names of plants introduced. *See* NEW garden plants. 1899. III. 93.

A list of South African indigenous plants. *See* PAPPE, Ludwig. 1847. III. 93.²

List of specimens of Indian woods. 1880. IV. 18.¹

List of the Burmese names of trees and plants given in Kurz's Forest flora. 1895. I. 75,² IV. 89.¹

List of the more important woods of the United States. 1899. IV. 398.¹

List of the principal hybrid plants exhibited. 1900. I. 271.²

List of the principal tea districts in China. 185.? III. 607.

List of the rare plants . . . of Tonbridge Wells. *See* FORSTER, T. F. 1801. I. 396.

List of timber and shade trees cultivated in the gardens [Jamaica]. 1888. IV. 398.¹

A list of trees and plants growing in the Botanical gardens at Dapooree and Hewra. *See* FALKE, T. 1862. I. 67.²

A list of trees growing at Greendale. 1896. I. 55.

A list of trees, shrubs, plants . . . in the Madras agri-horticultural society's garden. 186.? I. 67.¹

Lista, Ramón. La Patagonia andina. 1896. I. 345.

— Plantas patagónicas. 1896. I. 345.

Lista de nombres . . . de árboles y arbustos propios para repoblar. *See* ALTAMIRANO, Fernando & RAMÍREZ, José. 1894. IV. 78,² 113.¹

Lista de nombres vulgares y botánicos de árboles. *See* ALTAMIRANO, Fernando & RAMÍREZ, José. 1894. I. 331.

Liste de végétaux ligneux, classés. 1886. III. 41.[1]

Liste der in der deutschen Flora enthaltenen Gefässpflanzen. 1849. I. 532.[1]—1866. I. 385.

Liste générale des fruits adoptés par le Congrès pomologique. 1900. V. XXVIII.[1]

Liste systématique des plantes publiées. 1877. I. 415. ⟨

Lister, Joseph Storr. Report on the extent . . . of the forests of the Transkei and East Griqualand. 1893. IV. 380.[1]

Lister, Martin. An account of the nature . . . of the juices. 1698. I. 150.[2]

— An extract from a letter . . . about kermes. ·1672. III. 624.[1]

— Extracts of divers letters touching some inquiries and experiments of the motion of sap in trees. 1671. I. 162.

— A letter . . . containing an ingenious account of veins. 1671. I. 133.

— Observations on the making of cochineal. 1688. III. 624.[1]

Liston, R. List of plants cultivated . . . at Milburn Tower, near Edinburgh. 1817. I. 53.

Listvennya . . . *See* ЛИСТВЕННЯ . . .

Listy pomologické. *See* LISTY zahradnicke. III. 25.

Listy zahradnice. III. 25.

Litchfield, E. · Memorandum on the forests met with on the roads between Almorah aad [*sic*] Joshimath. 1882. IV. 377.[2]

Literärische Berichte für Forstmänner. 1832. IV. 1, *10*.

Literary and historical society of Quebec. Historical documents. I. 4.[2]

Literary and philosophical society of Liverpool. Proceedings. I. 18.

Literary and philosophical society of Manchester. Memoirs. Proceedings. I. 18.

The **Literary** world. I. 18.

Die **Literatur** der letzten sieben Jahre (1866–72) aus dem Gesammtgebiete der Land- und Forstwirthschaft. 1873. IV. 2.

Literaturberichte zur Flora. *See* LITERATURBLÄTTER . . . 1828. I. 1.

Literaturblätter für reine und angewandte Botanik. 1828. I. 1.

Lith, P. A. van der. Nederlandsch Oost Indie. 1875. III. 274.[2]

— **Spaan,** A. J. & **Fokkens,** F. Encyclopedie van Nederlandsch Indiê. 1894. I. 34.

Littell's living age. III. 5.

Little, A. D. *See* GRIFFIN, R. B. & LITTLE, A. D.

Little, George. Catalogue of ores, rocks and woods. 1878. IV. 397.

Little, James. The timber supply question . . . of America. 1876. IV. 403.[1]

Little, R. Diseases of the Nutmeg tree. 1849. III. 402.[2]

Little, William. Alarming destruction of American forests. 1883. IV. 46,[1] 281.[2]

— Fires in American forests. 1884. IV. 182.[1]

— The history of Warren. 1870. I. 531.[1]

— Letter . . . objecting " To get rid of the timber." 1890. IV. 271.[1]

— The tariff on lumber. 1883. IV. 284.[1]

— Timber and the tariff. 1882. IV. 284.[1]

For little-known trees. 1896. IV. 270.

Litvinof, D. I. *See* ЛИТВИНОВЪ, Д. И.

Litwinow, D. I. *See* ЛИТВИНОВЪ, Д. I.

Liubimenko, V. N. *See* ЛЮБИМЕНКО, В. Н.

Liubomudrof. *See* ЛЮБОМУДРОВЪ.

Livache, Ach. Recherches sur la nature des gaz contenus dans les tissus des fruits. 1877. I. 151,[2] 179.[1]

The **Live** Oak at Drayton Manor. 1895. II. 141.[1]

Liverpool — Literary and philosophical society. *See* LITERARY . . . I. 18.

Liversidge, Archibald. L'alcaloïde de la piturie. 1881. III. 700.[1]

— The alkaloid from pituric. 1881. III. 700.[1]

Livet, Léon, *marquis de* BARVILLE DE. *See* BARVILLE DE LIVET, Léon, *marquis de.*

Livingston, John S. On the aesthetic effects of chloroform . . . on Sensitive plants. 1860. II. 372.[2]

— Expériences sur les effets des gaz narcotiques. 1860. I. 211.

— Experiments on the effects of narcotic . . . gases. 1860. I. 211.

Livingston, Robert R. On the effects of the shade of trees upon vegetation. 1794. III. 34.[3]

Livingstone, John. Account of the method of dwarfing trees. 1822. III. 175.[1]

Livre nouveau de fleurs tres vtil. 1625. I. 284.

Lizasoaín, Juan. El servicio ordinario. 1898. IV. 554.

Lizasoaín, Manuel. Tablas para la cubicación cilíndrica. 1895. IV. 229.

Lizius, Maximilian. Handbuch der forstlichen Baukunde. 1896. IV. 266.[2]

— Taschenbuch für Berechnung des Cubikinhaltes von Rundhölzern. 1890. IV. 228.

— Wald-, Wild- und Waidmannsbilder aus dem Hochgebirge. 1887. IV. 29.

Ljundberg, Nicol. Joh. De plantis venenatis. *See* THUNBERG, C. P. 1822. III. 59.[2]

Ljungström, Ernst Leopold. Om bladets bygnad hos några Ericineer. 1882. II. 658.[2]

Ll, A. Ivy not injurious to trees. 1876. II. 650.[1]

Ll., P. Des Waldes Nutzen für die Landwirthschaft. 1883. IV. 270.

Llandudno botany. *See* INCHBALD, P. 1864. I. 401.

Llanos, Antonio. Fragmentos de algunas plantas de Filipinas. 1851. I. 464.[1]

— Nuevo apéndice ó suplemento a la Flora de Filipinas. 1859. I. 464.[1]

Llanos, Blas. Memoria sobre los medios de mejorar el clima de Madrid. 1825. IV. 47.[2]

Llanos, F__n Antonio. Columniferae. Sterculiae. 1857. II. 444.[2] ra s

— Nueva descripcion del Pasac. 1873. II. 699.[1]

— El Pino de los montes del Mancayan. 1875. II. 39.[2]

Llansó, Jaime. Catecismo de agricultura. 1850. III. 114.[2]

Llauradó, Andrés. La navegación interior en España. 1891. IV. 542.[1]

— Las queserías pirenaicas francesas. 1888. IV. 551.[1]

— Repoblaciones forestales. 1892. IV. 547.[1]

Llave, Pablo de la. Descripcion de algunos géneros . . . de vegetales. 1884. II. 416.[3]

— & **Lexarza,** Juan. Novorum vegetabilium descriptiones. 1824. I. 331.

Lleopart, Joaquin Maria de CASTELLARNAU Y DE. *See* CASTELLARNAU I DE LLEOPART, J. M. de.

Llewelyn, *Sir* John T. D. Hardy Rhododendrons and Azaleas. 1894. III. 655.

— Rhododendrons near Swansea. 1882. ·III. ·655·

Lloret, Javier de FERRER Y DE. *See* FERRER Y DE LLORET, Javier de.

Lloyd, Curtis Gates & J. U. Berberidaceae. 1878. III. 394.[2]

Lloyd, Francis Ernest. On an abnormal cone in the Douglas Spruce. 1898. II. 49.[1]

— The Douglas Spruce, Pseudotsuga taxifólia. 1900. II. 49.[1]

— The Garry Oak. 1894. II. 134.[1]

— Quercus californica. 1896. II. 134.[2]

— The seeds and seedlings of the Hemlock. 1900. II. 53.[1]

— Teratological notes. 1895. II. 134.[1]

Lloyd, G. N. Botanical terminology. 1826. I. 70.

Lloyd, James. Flore de l'ouest de la France. 1854. I. 411, V. XXI.[2]

— Flore de la Loire-Inférieure. 1844. I. 410.

Lloyd, John Uri & C. G. Drugs and medicines of North America. 1884. III. 62.

Lm., F. Ueber das Auftreten von Bostrichus lineatus. 1869. IV. 204.

Loaisel, Lettre [sur la transplantation des arbres en sève.] 1839. III. 168.[2]

Loarer. Sur le Sapindus emarginata. 1860. III. 540.[1]

Loarer, Ed. L'Himalaya ses productions naturelles. 1868. I. 474, *III. 603.*

Lobarzewski, Hyacynt Jan Kanty. Anschauung der Wirtschaftsgesellschaft über eine Forstschule für Galizien. 1850. IV. 36.[1]

— Zdanie Tow. gospod. o . . . szkole leśniczej dla Galicyi. 1850. IV. 36.[1]

Lobel, Matthias de. Balsami, opobalsami . . . explanatio. 1598. III. 510.[1]

— In G. Rondelletii methodicam pharmaceuticam officinam animadversiones. 1605. I. 283.

— Icones stirpium seu plantarum. 1581. I. 282.

— Kruydtboeck. 1576. I. 282.

— Plantarum seu stirpium historia. 1576. I. 282.

— Plantarum seu stirpium icones. 1581. I. 282.

— Stirpium illustrationeš. 1655. I. 286.

— *See also* PENA, Pierre & LOBEL, Mathias de.

Loberdos, Joannes. *See* ΛOBΕΡΔOΣ, Ἰωάννης.
Lobkowitz, Ludwig, *Freiherr* von. Practische Anweisung zur Forstwissenschaft. 1802. IV. 96.
Lobley, James Logan. Hampstead Hill. 1889. I. 534.[1]
Lobo, Constantino BOTELHO DE LACERDA. *See* BOTELHO DE LACERDA LOBO, Constantino.
Locatelli, Michelangelo. Sulla corrente malattia de' Gelsi. 1773. III. 379.[1]
Loch, James. Report on young plantations. 1845. IV. 358.[2]
Lochman, Charles. Photographs of medicinal and economic plants. 1898. III. 53.
Lochner, Michael Friedrich. Nerium sive Rhododaphne veterum. 1716. II. 728.[2]
— De novis et exoticis thee et cafe succedaneis. 1717. III. 222.
— Schediasma de Parreira brava. 1719. III. 396.[2]
Lock, Charles George Warnford. Coffee; its culture. 1888. III. 727.
— Notes on some neglected fibres. 1880. III. 234.
Lock, H. C. The pruning of forest trees. 1898. IV. 172.[2]
Locke, John. Observations upon the growth and culture of Vines and Olives. 1766. III. 116.[2]
— Outlines of botany. 1819. I. 85.
Locke, Robert. Report on lately introduced Coniferae. 1849. III. 289.
— Report on recently introduced Coniferae. 1845. III. 289.
Lockhart, A. D. A description of the fibrous plants of Dominica. 1885. III. 234.
Lockhart, David. Observations on the Cow-tree of the Caraccas. 1827. II. 146,[2] *III. 402*.[1]
Lockhart, *Sir* Simon Macdonald. On plantations on the estate of Carnwath. 1878. IV. 358.[2]
Lockwood, G. List of 153 trees . . . in the Monghyr district. 1876. I. 470,[1] *IV. 89*.[2]
Lockwood, Samuel. The Maple leaf-scale. 1886. III. 534.[1]
— Salix crispa — S. babylonica. 1875. II. 105.[2]
Locqueneuille, SCARSEZ DE. *See* SCARSEZ DE LOCQUENEUILLE. The Locust tree. 1890. II. 383.[1]
Loddiges, Conrad. Catalogue of plants. 1777. I. 52.
— A catalogue of plants and seeds. 1777. I. 52.
— & Sons. Botanical cabinet. *See* BOTANICAL . . . III. 16.
— — Palms, etc., in the collection of Conrad Loddiges and Sons. 1845. III. 316.[2]
Lodeman, Ernest Gustavus. Black-knot of Plums and Cherries. 1894. III. 431.[1]
— Dwarf Apples. 1896. III. 426.[2]
— The grafting of Grapes. 1894. III. 548.[2]
— The Pecan. 1891. III. 354.[1]
— Poisoning from Rhus. 1895. III. 528.[1]
— Pruning and training of Grapes. 1897. III. 549.[1]
— Some Grape troubles of western New York. 1894. III. 551.
— Spray calendar. 1895. III. 198.[1]
— The spraying of orchards. 1895. III. 198.[1]
— The spraying of plants. 1896. III. 198.[1]
Loder, E. C. Echinocereus gonacanthus. 1882. III. 622.[2]
Loder, Justus Christian. De Taxo baccata Linn. 1794. III. 288.[1]
Lodge, James Lee. Coffee; history, growth. 1894. III. 740.[1]
Lodge, William C. Among the Peaches. 1870. III. 441.[1]
Ueber **Lodoicea** Sechellarum. 1865. II. 70.[2]
Loebe, William. Encyclopädie der gesammten Landwirthschaft. 1850. IV. 22.[2]
— Landwirthschaftliche Flora Deutschlands. 1861. III. 73.
— Naturgeschichte für Landwirthe, Gärtner. 1852. III. 499.[2]
Loebel, Friedrich. Ueber Anzucht von Orangenbäumchen. 1852. III. 499.[2]
— Ficus barbata Wall. 1854. III. 371.[2]
— Kultur-Bemerkungen über Paulownia. 1853. III. 703.[1]
— Sur la multiplication du Ginko. 1855. III. 286.[2]
— Ueber das Pflanzen der Bäume. 1853. III. 166.
— Das Veredeln der Gehölze. 1855. III. 161.
— Ueber Vermehrung . . . der Daphne-Arten. 1855. III. 626.[2]
— Ueber Vermehrung der Gingko. 1855. III. 286.[2]
— Ueber Vermehrung . . . der Mitraria. 1855. III. 708.[2]
— Veronica Andersonii. 1855. III. 704.[1]
Loeber, G. A. Die Heiligkeit des Oelbaums in Attika. 1857. II. 713.[2]
Loebisch, W. F. Die neueren Arzneimittel. 1883. III. 244.

Loebl, Otto. Anatomie der Laubblätter. 1888. I. 111.
Löbner, Max. Eine alte Eibe in der Schweiz. 1899. II. 11.[2]
— Der Zwerg-Obstbaum. 1899. III. 139.
Lödman, Magnus Lars. Om trän och buskar i allmänhet. *See* TROZELIUS, C. B. 1781. I. 531.
Löfberg, N. Novitiae florae suecicae. *See* FRIES, E. M. 1814. I. 352.
Löffelholz-Colberg, Friedrich, *Freiherr* von. Ueber den Anbau der Weymuthskiefer. 1832. IV. 469.
— Die Bedeutung und Wichtigkeit des Waldes. 1872. IV. 44.
— Beitrag zu einer kritischen Nachweisung über die Schüttekrankheit. 1865. IV. 476.
— Forstliche Chrestomathie. 1866. IV. 1.
— Gedenkbuch an die sechste Versammlung der Land- und Forstwirthe. 1843. IV. 101.
— Praktische Anweisung zum Holzanbau. 1832. IV. 141.
— Kultur und Veredelung der Setzlinge. 1854. III. 548.[1]
Löffler, Karl. Der Anbau der Korb- und Bandweide. 1862. III. 347.
— Anleitung zur Maulbeerbaumzucht. 1861. III. 377.
— Anleitung zur Obstbaum-Spalierzucht. 1860. III. 138.
— Die Höhlenbrüter. 1883. IV. 90.[2]
Loefgren, Alberto. Da colheita e do preparo das plantas. 1897. I. 36.[1]
— Contribuições para a botanica paulista. 1890. I. 343.
— Ensaio para uma distribuição dos vegetaes . . . de S. Paulo. 1896. I. 343.
— Ensaio para uma synonimia dos nomes populares das plantas . . . de S. Paulo. 1894. I. 73.[1]
— Flora paulista. 1897. I. 343.
Loefling, Peter. An abstract of the most useful and necessary articles mentioned . . . in his Travels. 1758. I. 328.
— Gemmae arborum. *See* LINNÉ, Carl von. 1749. I. 107.[2]
— Iter hispanicum. 1758. I. 328.
— Observaciones de historia natural hechas en Españas y en América. 1801. I. 420.
— Reise nach den spanischen Ländern. 1758. I. 328.
Löhnis, F. B. Het bosch in de huishouding van den staat. 1895. IV. 270.
— Boschcultuur in Nederland. 1880. IV. 356.[2]
— Boschvennootschappen op de Veluwe. 1896. IV. 356.[1]
— De Deensche Heide-maatschappij. 1886. IV. 156.[2]
— Gemeente-bosschen. 1890. IV. 356.[2]
— Iets over Amerikaansche Dennen. 1889. IV. 441.
— De lupinen als middel. 1897. IV. 144.[2]
— Ontginning van heidevelden. 1886. IV. 160.[1]
— Populieren en Wilgen . . . voor de klompenmakerij. 1890. III. 344.[1]
— Poten van Larix in akkermaalsbosch. 1889. IV. 451.
— Snoeien van loofboomen langs wegen. 1889. III. 211.[2]
— De Spechten. 1880. IV. 90.[2]
— Verhandeling over de houtcultuur en de bosschen in Drenthe. 1885. IV. 356.[2]
— Het vraagstuk der heide ontginning. 1887. IV. 119.[2]
Loehr, Matthias Joseph. Botanischer Führer zur Flora von Köln. 1860. I. 384.
— Enumeratio der Flora von Deutschland. 1852. I. 383.
— Flora von Coblenz. 1838. I. 379.
— Taschenbuch der Flora von Trier. 1844. I. 381.
Lönberg, Erich Gustav. *See* LILJEBLAD, Samuel & LÖNBERG, E. G.
Lönn, P. von. Ueber den ökonomischen Gebrauch der Samenkörner des Zwergmandelbaumes. 1857. III. 434.[2]
Lönnberg, Einar. Några ord om Floridas växtvärld. 1894. I. 319.
Lönnrot, Elias. Flora fennica. Suomen Kasvisto. 1860. I. 362.
— Kasvikon oppisanoja. 1858. I. 71.
Lönqvist, Knut Johan. Berättelse om en botanisk resa i östra Småland. 1882. I. 357.
Lönqvist, Nils Johan. De cortice peruviano. *See* ROSÉN, Eberhard. 1744. III. 719.
Lösch, A. Dosage du thé dans les feuilles de Thé. 1887. III. 607.
— Zur quantitativen Bestimmung des Theïns. 1887. III. 607.
Ueber **Löschanstalten** bei Waldbränden. 1856. IV. 183.[2]
Loesche, Eduard PECHUËL-. *See* PECHUËL-LOESCHE, Eduard.
Loesche, Gustav Eduard. De causis naturae chemicae . . . plantarum. 1843. I. 151.[1]
— Das vegetabilische Leben und die chemische Affinität. 1844. I. 151.[1]

Löscher, Eduard. Jatropha multifida. 1851. III. 520.¹
— Ein monströser Blüthenstand der Rosa muscosa. 1850.
II. 292.²
Loescher, Martin Gotthelf. Balsamum de Mecca. 1726.
III. 510.²
Löseke, Johann Ludwig Leberecht. Materia medica. 1785.
III. 241.
Loeselius, Johannes. Flora prussica. 1703. I. 372.
— Plantas in Borussia . . . divulgo. 1654. I. 372.
Loesener, Theodor. Aquifoliaceae, Stechpalmenfamilie.
1893. II. 462.²
— Beiträge zur Kenntnis der Mateipflanzen. 1896. II. 463.¹
— Bemerkungen zu vorstehendem Aufsatze.¹. . . und Nach-
träge . . . über Mate. 1897. II. 464.¹
— Ueber die Benennung zweier nord-amerikanischer Ilices.
1891. II. 462.²
— Celastraceae. 1896. II. 465.²
— Celastraceae africanae. 1893. II. 465.²
— Celastraceae novae. 1900. II. 467.²
— Ueber einige neue Pflanzenarten aus Brasilien. 1889. I.
343.
— Über die geographische Verbreitung einiger Celastraceen.
1898. II. 465.²
— Hippocrateaceae. 1896. II. 471.²
— Hippocrateaceae africanae. 1895. II. 471.²
— Ueber Ilex paraguariensis. 1895. II. 464.¹
— Ueber Mate oder Paraguay-Thee. 1897. II. 463.¹
— Zur Mateangelegenheit. 1892. II. 464.²
— Plantae Selerianae. 1894. I. 332.
— Ueber eine Verbenacee mit stachligen Blättern. 1897.
II. 754.²
— Ueber das Vorkommen von Domatien bei . . . Ilex.
1893. II. 463.¹
— Vorstudien zu einer Monographie der Aquifoliaceen. 1890.
II. 462.²
— & others. Beiträge zur Kenntnis der Flora von Central-
Amerika. 1897. I. 330.
Loeser, J. Praktische Pflanzenkunde für deutsche Schulen.
1877. I. 387.
Løvendal, Emil Adolph. De danske Barkbiller. 1898. IV.
549.¹
— Indberetning . . . angaaende forskellige Barkbillers Fore-
komst. 1892. IV. 549.¹
— Fra Insekternes Verden. 1895. III. 191.
Løvenskjold, E. C. F. Nogle Bemærkninger de danske
Statsskove vedkommende. 1854. IV. 273.¹
Om Løvhytters Anlæg og Beplantning. 1837. III. 204.¹
Löw, C. A. Naturgeschichte aller . . . schädlichen Insekten.
1844. III. 189.
Loew, Ernst. Anfänge epiphytischer Lebensweise. 1892.
I. 234.²
— Beiträge zur blütenbiologischen Statistik. 1890. I. 238.
— Beobachtungen über den Blumenbesuch von Insekten.
1884. I. 239.¹
— Blütenbiologische Floristik. 1894. I. 239.¹
— Blüthenbiologische Beiträge. 1891. I. 238.
— De Casuarinearum caulis foliique evolutione. 1865. II.
92.¹
— Einführung in die Blütenbiologie. 1895. I. 239.¹
— Ueber die Metamorphose vegetativer Sprossanlagen in
Blüthen bei Viscum. 1890. II. 178.¹
— Notiz über die Bestäubungseinrichtungen von Viscum.
1890. II. 179.²
Löw, Franz. Beiträge zur Kenntniss der Gallmücken. 1874.
I. 216.¹
— Beiträge zur Kenntniss der Milbengallen. 1879. I. 216.²
— Beiträge zur Naturgeschichte der Gallmilben. 1874. I.
216.²
— Bemerkungen über die Fichtengallenläuse. 1885. IV. 456.
— Beschreibung neuer Milbengallen. 1880. I. 216.²
— Ueber Diaspis visci Schrank. 1872. III. 385.¹
— Die forstliche Bedeutung der Spinnen. 1895. II. 92.
— Ueber Milbengallen der Wiener-Gegend. 1874. I. 216.¹
— Mittheilungen über Phytoptocecidien. 1882. I. 216.²
— Zur näheren Kenntniss zweier Pemphiginen. 1880. III.
364.¹
— Ueber neue Gallmücken. 1874. I. 216.¹
— Ueber neue . . . Phytoptocecidien. 1886. I. 216.²
— Norwegische Phytopto- und Entomocecidien. 1888. I.
215.²
Löw, Immanuel. Aramaeische Pflanzennamen. 1881. I.
76.¹

Loew, Karl Friedrich. Epistola ad botanicos : . . de flora
pannonica. 1739. I. 444.
Loew, O. Sur l'élaboration des nitrates dans la plante. 1890.
I. 159.
— Ueber Formose. 1887. I. 177.
— Ueber die Verarbeitung der salpetersauren Salze. 1890.
I. 159.
Loew, Oscar & Honda, Seiroku. Ueber den Einfluss wech-
selender Mengen von Kalk und Magnesia auf . . . Nadel-
bäume. 1895. II. 21.¹
Loew, Oscar Carl Benedikt. The physiological rôle of
mineral nutrients. 1899. I. 160.
Loewe, Johann Karl Christian. Handbuch der . . . Kräu-
terkunde. 1787. I. 83.
Loewe, Jul. Sur des tannins de diverses origines. 1876.
III. 237.²
Löwenfeld, Franz, Ritter von. Der Karst und seine Wieder-
bewaldung. 1865. IV. 167.¹
— Das Uebermassgeben beim Klaftern des Holzes. 1861.
IV. 388.¹
Löwenhjelm, C. G. Observationer på växter 1848. 1850.
I. 223.¹
— Samtidiga observationer på växter. 1851. I. 223.¹
Löwis, Andreas von. Abhandlungen über die Naturgeschichte
der in Livland wildwachsenden Holzarten. 1821? IV. 79.¹
— Anleitung zur Forstwirthschaft für Livland. 1814. IV.
103.²
— Ueber die Benutzung der Weisseller. 1839. IV. 489.²
— Ueber die ehemalige Verbreitung der Eichen in Liv- und
Ehstland. 1824. II. 129.¹
— Vorschlag zum Anbau von Eichen. 1834. IV. 114, 504.
Lo Forte, G. Di alcuni apparecchi di disseminazione. 1895.
I. 241.¹
Logan, James. Experimenta . . . de plantarum generatione.
1739. I. 198.
— Experiments . . . on the generation of plants. 1739. I.
198.
— Some experiments concerning the impregnation of the
seeds. 1738. I. 200.
— Versuche und Gedanken von der Erzeugung der Pflanzen.
1738. I. 200.
Logan, James Richardson. Sago. 1849. III. 327.²
Logothetes, A. See ΛΟΓΟΘΕΤΗΣ, Α.
Lohage, A. Über Conservirung der Hölzer. 1871. IV.
419.
Lohde, Georg. Ueber die Entwicklungsgeschichte und den
Bau einiger Samenschalen. 1874. I. 120.
Lohekultur und Mineralgerbung. 1878. IV. 435.
Lohmann, C. J. E. See ROMBURGH, Pieter van & LOHMANN,
C. J. E.
Lohmeier, Johann Andreas. De herbae exoticae Thee in-
fuso. See HAHN, J. J. 1722. III. 605.
Lohrindengewinnung in Baiern. 1893. IV. 515.²
Loi ayant pour objet le règlement des indemnités dues aux
communes . . . dans le département de Constantine. 1897.
IV. 332.²
Loi déclarant d'utilité publique des travaux . . . dans le bassin
du Gardon. 1898. IV. 327.
Loi déclarant d'utilité publique des travaux . . . dans le péri-
mètre du Drac inférieur. 1898. IV. 327.
Loi du 31 janvier 1873 sur les forêts. 1873. IV. 330.
Loi fédérale concernant la haute surveillance de la confédéra-
tion sur la police des forêts. 1876. IV. 294,¹ 330.
Loi forestière . . . Neuchâtel. 1869. IV. 330.
Loi portant abrogation de l'article 153 et modification de l'ar-
ticle 154. 1898. IV. 327.
Loi portant modification des articles 31 et 103. 1898. IV.
327.
Loi sur l'administration forestière. 1791. IV. 325.
Loi sur le commerce des bourgeons de résineux. 1900. IV.
323.¹
La loi sur les accidents du travail. 1899. IV. 554.²
Loi 31 de 1879 sur les forêts. 1899. IV. 331.²
Loidis, (pseud.). The Cowthorpe Oak. 1895. II. 139.²
Loir-et-Cher — Société d'agriculture du département . . .
See SOCIÉTÉ . . . III. 21.
Loire — Société d'agriculture, industrie, sciences . . . See
SOCIÉTÉ . . . III. 21.
Loiret — Chaire départementale d'agriculture. See CHAIRE
. . . III. 19.
Lois du 28 juillet 1860 et du 8 juin 1864, sur le reboisement.
1870. IV. 326.
Loiseau. De la greffe . . . d'obtenir des sujets mixtes.
1860. III 161.

— Greffe en fente renversée. 1862. III. 161.
— Sur un moyen de greffer en fente. 1850. III. 160.
— Note relative à la greffe herbacée. 1858. III. 163.[2]
— Note sur des Mûriers obtenus par la greffe. 1859. III. 377.[1]
— Note sur les avantages de la position inclinée . . . dans les boutures. 1858. III. 158.
— Verfahren zum Pfropfen in den Spalt. 1850. III. 160.
Loiseau, Henri. Culture pratique de la Vigne. 189.? III. 557.[1]
— Multiplication de la Vigne. n. d. III. 548.[1]
— Le Rosier; culture. 189.? III. 450.
Loisel. Note sur la culture du Pin piquant. 1836. III. 308.[2]
Loiseleur-Deslongchamps, Jean Louis Auguste. Avantage des Rosiers francs de pied. 1845. III. 452.
— Sur les avantages qu'on pourrait retirer de cultiver certaines variétés de Vignes. 1828. III. 554.[2]
— Considérations sur le Mûrier multicaule. 1836. III. 380.[2]
— Considerations sur les boutures des arbres. 1846. IV. 149.[2]
— Essai sur l'histoire des Mûriers. 1824. III. 374.
— Essai sur la culture des Vignes. 1849. III. 555.
— Flora gallica. 1806. .I. 407.
— Flore générale de France. 1828. I. 408.
— Geschichte der Ceder vom Libanon. 1837. III. 300.[2]
— Des greffes et des boutures forcées . . . des Roses. 184.? III. 451.[1]
— Herbier général de l'amateur. 1816. I. 266.
— Histoire du Cèdre du Liban. 1837. III. 300.[2]
— Manuel des plantes usuelles indigènes. 1819. III. 85.
— Multiplication des Rosiers par la greffe. 1853. III. 452.
— Mûrier. 1824. III. 374.
— Mûriers et vers à soie. 1832. III. 374.
— Neue Bemerkungen über den Süsskirschbaum. 1850. IV. 520.[2]
— Note historique sur le Ginkgo. 1834. III. 286.[2]
— Note sur les bordures de Bruyères. 1847. II. 715.[2]
— Note sur une manière . . . de greffer la Vigne. 1835. III. 548.[1]
— Notice sur le Chêne Vélani. 1846. II. 140,[2] IV. 502.[2]
— Notice sur le Cytise des Alpes. 1846. III. 480.[2]
— Notice sur le Saule-Marceau. 1833. III. 351.[2]
— Notice sur les plantes à ajouter à la Flore de France. 1809. I. 407.
— Nouveau voyage dans l'empire de flore. 1817. I. 85.
— Nouvel herbier de l'amateur. 1816. I. 266.
— Nouvelles observations sur le Merisier. 1850. IV. 520.[1]
— Observations . . . sur l'accroissement en grosseur d'arbres. 1845. III. 38.[1]
— Quelques considérations sur les Pins. 1843. IV. 462.[1]
— Rapport fait . . . sur la pépinière de Mûriers. 1829. III. 374.
— Rapport sur l'appareil . . . pour faciliter la reprise des boutures. 1843. III. 157.
— Rapport sur la culture du Mûrier. 1836. III. 375.
— Rapport sur la greffe du Châtaignier. 1839. III. 359.[1]
— Sur les recherches à faire de quelques arbres de l'Algérie. 1844. III. 280.[1]
— Recherches historiques . . . sur le Cèdre du Liban. 1814. II. 38.[1]
— Recherches . . . sur l'emploi de plusieurs plantes de France. 1819. III. 271.[1]
— Recherches sur l'histoire des Cyprès. 1834. II. 39.[2]
— Recherches sur l'histoire des Cyprès et note historique. 1834. II. 29,[2] III. 286.[2]
— La Rose; son histoire. 1844. III. 448.
— Roseraies et promenades horticulturales. 1846. III. 448.
Loiselle, A. Les Cécidies des environs de Lisieux. 1900. I. 215.[3]
Loitard, Ernest. See Nivière, Gustave & Loitard, Ernest.
Loixelier. Le nouveau parfait vigneron. 1836. III. 554.[2]
Lojacono, Fr. Ancora sulla modalità del taglio degli alberi. 1899. IV. 384.[1]
— Modalità del taglio degli alberi. 1898. IV. 384.[1]
Lojacono-Pojero, Michele. Flora sicula. 1888. I. 432,[1] V. xxii.[2]
— Sulla influenza dell' esposizione considerata sulla vegetazione delle alte montagne di Sicilia. 1879. I. 432,[1] V. xxii.[2]
— Le isole Eolie e la loro vegetazione. 1878. I. 431, V. xxii.[2]

— Sulla Rosa moschata Mill. in Sicilia. See Pojero, M. L. 1888. II. 296.[2]
— Schizzo orografico della Sicilia. See Pojero, Lojacono. 1890. I. 432,[1] IV. 86,[1] V. xxii.[2]
— Sulla Vasconcellea monoica. 1878. II. 582.[1]
Lojander, Hugo. Beiträge zur Kenntnis des Drachenblutes. 1887. II. 81,[2] III. 321.[1]
Lokale Erfahrungen über die Nachzucht der Tanne. 1881. IV. 444.[2]
Lolland-Falsters Forstmandsforenings Møde. Forhandlinger. III. 10.[2]
Lollesgaard, Svend. Forsøg med Træer og Buske i Chicago. 1889. III. 44.[1]
Lomakin, A. A. See Ломакинъ, A. A.
Lombard. Culture de l'Arbre à thé dans l'Inde anglaise. 1864. III. 603.
Lombard, F. Boussole-dendromètre. 1898. IV. 235.[1]
Lombardo-Veneto — Annali delle scienze del regno. See Annali . . . I. 24.[2]
The Lombardy Poplar. 1883. III. 346.[2]
Lomet, baron. Mémoire sur les eaux minérales . . . des Pyrénées. 1795. IV. 47.[1]
Lomikovski. See Ломиковскій.
Lommatzsch, W. Beobachtungen über den Fichtenritzenschorf. 1890. IV. 456.
— Frostschäden. 1896. IV. 191.[2]
— Kleine waldbauliche Mittheilungen. 1892. IV. 489.[1]
— Was kann der Forstmann zur Erhaltung der Schönheit des Waldes thun? 1890. IV. 137.[1]
— Zwischennutzungserträge. 1888. IV. 245.
Lommler, G. Die neuesten Arbeiten über die Coniferen. 1844. II. 12.[2]
Łomnicki, Jarosław. Czy Cis już w Polsce wytępiony? 1900. II. 11.[2]
Londerseel, Assuwerus van. Icones animalium et plantarum. 1625. I. 285.[1]
Londes, Friedrich Wilhelm. Grundriss zu Vorlesungen über Forst- und öconomische Botanik. 1802. IV. 75.[1]
— Handbuch der Botanik. 1804. I. 84.
— Verzeichniss der um Göttingen wildwachsenden Pflanzen. 1805. I. 375.
Londet. Élagages des arbres de futaie. 1869. III. 170.
— Maladie de la Vigne . . . Oïdium. 1852. III. 575.[1]
— Ravages des bostriches sur les Poiriers. 1871. III. 446.[1]
London — Chemical society. See Chemical . . . I. 17.
London — Entomological society. See Entomological . . . III. 16.
London — Ethnological society. See Ethnological . . . I. 18.
London — Horticultural society. See Horticultural . . . III. 17.
London — International horticultural exhibition. See International . . . III. 17.
London — Japan society. See The Japan . . . III. 17.
London — Linnean society. See Linnean . . . I. 18.
London — Linnean society. Catalogue of the library. See Catalogue . . . 1896. I. 3.[1]
London — Medico botanical society. See Medico-botanical . . . I. 19.
London — Microscopical society. See Microscopic journal. III. 18, and Microscopical society . . . I. 19.
London — Royal geographical society. See Royal . . . I. 19.
London — Royal society. See Royal . . . I. 20.
London — Royal society. Catalogue of scientific papers. See Catalogue . . . 1867. I. 2.
London — Royal society. Catalogue of the scientific books in the library. See Catalogue . . . 1883. I. 2.
London — Société française d'horticulture. See Société . . . III. 18.
London — Society instituted at London for the encouragement of arts . . . See Society . . . III. 18.
London — Statistical society. See Statistical . . . III. 18.
London and Edinburgh philosophical magazine. See Philosophical magazine. I. 19.
The London catalogue of British plants. See Watson, H. C. 1844. I. 399.
London, Edinburgh & Dublin philosophical magazine. See Philosophical magazine. I. 19.
The London graphic. III. 17.
London journal of botany. See Botanical miscellany. I. 17.
London medical and physical journal. See Medical and physical journal. I. 19.
London medical journal. I. 18.

London medical record. I. 18.
The **[London]** times. III. 17.
London tree-ghosts. 1898. I. 517.[2]
London trees and their treatment. 1895. III. 42.[2]
Londoner Pharmakopöe. See PHARMACOPOEA londinensis. 1618. III. 250.[2]
Long, Edward. The history of Jamaica. 1774. III. 266.
Long, Elias A. Air layering. 1896. III. 159.[1]
— Do you summer mulch? 1896. III. 152.
— Extremes in tree pruning. 1896. III. 171.
— Oaks for ornament. 1896. III. 361.[1]
— Ornamental gardening for Americans. 1885. III. 63.[1]
— Plant more Oak trees. 1896. III. 361.[1]
— The poison Ivy and other so-called "Ivies." 1896. III. 527.[2]
— Protecting hardy shrubs in the winter. 1896. III. 183.[2]
— Repairing a broken Beech tree. 1896. III. 180.[2]
— Suggestions on tree pruning. 1896. III. 171.
— Transplanting large trees. 1896. III. 168.[1]
— Trees and drain tiles. 1896. III. 34.[2]
— Trees that become barked. 1896. III. 180.[2]
Long, Ellen Call. Silk farming. 1884. III. 378.
Long, H. L. Some enquiry concerning the Quercus. 1839. I. 514.[1]
Long, J. The indigenous plants of Bengal. 1857. III. 92.[1]
Longchamps, Edmond de SELYS. See SELYS-LONGCHAMPS, Edmond de.
Longévité du mélèze. 1897. II. 33.[2]
Longevity of the Larch. 1897. II. 33.[2]
Longman's magazine. III. 17.
Longo, Biagio. Intorno ai canali delle Opunzie. 1898. II. 596.[1]
— Contributo allo studio degl' idioblasti muciferi delle Cactee. 1898. II. 588.[3]
— Contributo allo studio della mucilaggine delle Cactee. 1896. II. 588.[3]
— Contribuzione alla flora della Valle del Lao. 1893. I. 430.
— Osservazioni sulle Calycanthaceae. 1900. II. 214.[1]
Longstreth, C. H. Forestry in southern Kansas. 1878. III. 118.[1]
Longuet, R. La pharmacopée chinoise. 1884. III. 256.[2]
Longworth, N. On the culture of the Grape. 1848. III. 549.[2]
Lonitzer, Adam. Botanicon. 1551. I. 278.[2]
— Kreuterbuch. 1557. I. 280, V. xv.[1]
— Naturalis historiae opus novum. 1551. I. 278.
— Nöthige Zugabe, darinnen die neueste und nützalichste Observationen. 1557. I. 280.
— De plantarum . . . descriptione, natura et viribus. 1551. I. 278.
— Vollständiges Kräuterbuch. 1557. I. 280, V. xv.[1]
Lonitzer, Johann. In Dioscoridae Anazarbei de re medica libros . . . scholia nova. 1543. I. 278.
Lonkay, Antal. Fenyőfáink. 1897. III. 291.
Loño, José. Del cultivo de los Pinos. 1866. IV. 460.[2]
Le **Lontar**; Palmyra Palm. See The PALMYRA Palm. 1851. III. 321.[1]
Loo, Augustin. Auctores botanici. See LINNÉ, Carl von. 1759. I. 79.[1]
Loo, D. J. SANDERS VAN. See SANDERS VAN LOO, D. J.
Looistoffen. 1889. III. 237.[2]
Lookeren Campagne, C. J. van. Verslag omtrent onderzoekingen over indigo. 1893. III. 479.[2]
Loomis, H. The Diospyros Kaki. 1878. III. 669.[1]
— See also CROOM, H. B. & LOOMIS, H.
Loos, Curt. Beitrag zur Kenntniss der Lebensweise der Lärchentriebmotte. 1898. III. 304.[2]
— Bemerkungen zu einigen gefiederten Vertilgern der Lärchenminirmotteneräupchen. 1896. IV. 451.
— Einige Beobachtungen über Coleophora laricella. 1891. IV. 451.
Loos, Dirk de. Caoutchouc en guttapercha. 1887. III. 229.
— Kaoutchouc en gutta-percha. 1865. III. 231.
— Onderzoek der Mangistan-schillen. 1881. III. 609.[2]
— Onderzoek van plantaardige vetten. 1884. III. 225.
— Oost-Indische vetten. 1878. III. 225.
— Papaïne. 1882. III. 617.[2]
— Vetten, was, aetherische olien. 1884. III. 274.[2]
— Voortbrengselen van Nederlandsch West Indië. 1893. III. 267.[1]
— Voortbrengselen van Surinam. 1879. III. 268.[1]
— Ylang-Ylang olie. 1881. III. 401.[2]
Loosjes, Adrian. Flora harlemica. 1779. I. 390.
Lopatecki, M. de. The trees of British Columbia. 1889. IV. 397.
— The Willows of British Columbia. 1888. II. 99.[2]

Lopes Mendes, A. Matta do Bussaco. 1877. I. 60.[1]
Lopez, Alejandro. Tratado del marco valenciano de las maderas. 1871. IV. 226.
Lopez, Hipólito RUIZ. See RUIZ LOPEZ, Hipólito & PAVON, Josef.
Lopez, J. A. & **Martinez Robles**, F. A. Memoria sobre la pertenencia . . . de los montes de Toledo. 1821. IV. 363.[1]
Lópes Guardiola, Emilio. Cultivo intensivo de la Vid. 1900. III. 558.[1]
Lopez y Lopez, Matias. Breve narración y apuntes acerca . . . del café. 1870. III. 739.
Lophyre du Pin. 1900. IV. 480.
Loppinet, F. Les ouvrages défensifs de la forêt de Varennes-en-Argonne. 1892. IV. 27.[2]
Lo-Presti's Holz-Eisenbahn. 1869. IV. 391.
Lopriore, G. Vorläufige Mittheilung über die Regeneration gespaltener Stammspitzen. 1895. I. 132.[2]
Lopriore, Guiseppe. Amarantaceae africanae. 1900. II. 189.[2]
— Amarantaceae . . . in Somalia et in Harrar lectae. 1900. II. 189.[1]
— Amarantaceae novae. 1900. II. 189.[2]
— Ueber die Regeneration gespaltener Wurzeln. 1896. I. 104.
The **Loquat**. 1899. III. 424.[1]
Loqueneuille, SCARSEZ DE. See SCARSEZ DE LOQUENEUILLE.
Loquex, (abbé). Histoire naturelle de la Morée. 1806. III. 498.[1]
Lorberg, H. Zwei Verzeichnisse seiner Rosensammlung. 1852. III. 448.
Lorberg, Max. Die letzten Frühjahrsfröste. 1874. III. 45.
— & **Koch**, Karl. Die holländische Linde. 1867. III. 586.[1]
Lorch, H. G. Cacao en zijn kultuur. 1889. III. 592.[2]
Lord, O. M. Our native Plum. 1896. III. 433.[1]
— Seedling Apples. 1899. III. 426.[1]
Lord, William Barry. The silkworm book. 1867. III. 148.[1]
The **lords** of the forest. 1883. I. 295.[1]
Lorek, C. G. Flora prussica. 1826. I. 377.
Lorent, J. A. Wanderungen im Morgenlande. 1845. I. 478.
Lorente, Vicente Alfonso. Carta sobre las observaciones botanicas que ha publicado D. A. J. Cavanilles. 1797. I. 264.
— Nova generum polygamiae classificatio. 1796. I. 264.
— Systema botanicum Linnaeano-anomalisticum. 1799. I. 264.
Lorentz. Notice sur le Pin maritime. 1842. IV. 467.[1]
Lorentz, Bernard. Cours élémentaire de culture des bois. 1837. IV. 109.[1]
Lorentz, Paul Guenther. Einige Bemerkungen über einen Theil der Provinz Entre-Rios. 1876. I. 344.
— Ferienreise eines argentinischen Gymnasial-Schullehrers. 1876. V. XVIII.[2]
— Flore argentine. 1876. I. 344.
— Informe científico sobre el resultado de los viajes . . . botánicas. 1875. I. 344.
— Notizen aus Argentinien. 1880. I. 344.
— Reiseskizzen aus Argentinien. 1875. V. XVIII.[2]
— Reiseskizzen aus Argentinien; aus dem Gran Chacó. 1877. V. XVIII.[2]
— La vegetacion del nordeste de la provincia de Entre-Rios. 1878. I. 344.
— Vegetations-Verhältnisse Argentiniens. 1876. I. 344.
— Vegetations-Verhältnisse der Argentinischen Republik. 1876. I. 344.
— & **Niederlein**, Gustav. Informe oficial de la comision científica . . . de la expedicion al Rio Negro. 1881. I. 344.
— & **Stelzner**, A. Ein Winterausflug nach dem Norden der Sierra von Córdoba. 1875. V. XVIII.[2]
Lorenz. Ueber Erziehung der Aristolochia Sipho. 1880. III. 386.[2]
Lorenz, (Oberförster, Baldowitz) & others. Mittheilungen über Waldbeschädigungen. 1887. IV. 196.[1]
— Waldbeschädigungen durch Naturereignisse. 1888. IV. 207.
Lorenz, (Oberförster, Lauterbach). Erfahrungen über Bewirthschaftung von Eichenschälwaldungen. 1856. IV. 505.
— Keimkraft des Fichtensaamens. 1817. IV. 453.
— Material- und Geld-Ertrags-Resultat . . . im Lauterbacher Forst. 1857. IV. 260.[2]
— Nachweis der stattgefundenen Verkaufspreise für Eichene Spiegelrinde. 1847. IV. 514.[2]
— Notizen über das Schütten der Kiefern. 1852. IV. 475.

Lorenz, (Revierförster). Das schädliche Auftreten des Harz-Rüsselkäfers. 1863. IV. 455.
Lorenz, J. B. Handbuch für Förster. 1802. IV. 109.[1]
— Manuel du forestier. 1802. IV. 109.[1]
Lorenz, Johann Friedrich. Grundriss der theoretischen und praktischen Botanik. 1781. I. 83.
Lorenz, P. Hydrangea paniculata grandiflora in Hochstammform. 1890. III. 412.[2]
Lorenz von Liburnau, Heinrich, Ritter. Zur Frage der Waldweide in den Alpen. 1896. IV. 136.[1]
— J. Wiesners " Untersuchungen über den Lichtgenuss der Pflanzen." 1895. IV. 67.[2]
— Neuere Untersuchungen über das photochemische Klima. 1899. IV. 73.[1]
Lorenz von Liburnau, Josef Roman, Ritter. Anschauung, Uebung . . . mit Bezug auf den land- und forstwirthschaftlichen Unterricht. 1877. IV. 29.
— Ueber Bedeutung und Vertretung der land- und forstwirthschaftlichen Meteorologie. 1877. IV. 59.[2]
— Bericht über die Bedingungen der Aufforstung . . . des croatischen Karstgebirges. 1860. IV. 167.[1]
— Bericht . . . über die Frage: Wie können die meteorologischen Institute sich . . . förderlich erweisen? 1879. IV. 59.[2]
— Entwurf eines Programmes für forstlich-meteorologische Beobachtungen in Oesterreich. 1877. IV. 59.[2]
— Das Forstwesen auf der Wiener Weltausstellung. 1874. IV. 21.[1]
— Die geologischen Verhältnisse von Grund und Boden. 1883. IV. 61.[2]
— Die höchste Stufe des land- und forstwirthschaftlichen Unterrichtes. 1874. IV. 29, 36.[2]
— Nachrichten über den forstlich-meteorologischen Beobachtungszweig. 1878. IV. 59.[2]
— Resultate forstlich meteorologischer Beobachtungen. 1890. IV. 60.[1]
— Wald, Klima und Wasser. 1878. IV. 44.
— Ueber die Wohlfahrts-Wirkungen des Waldes. 1889. IV. 45.
— & Rothe, C. Lehrbuch der Klimatologie. 1874. IV. 72.
— & Wessely, Josef. Die Bodencultur-Verhältnisse Oesterreichs. 1868. IV. 368.
— — Skizzen des land- und forstwirthschaftlichen Betriebes. 1868. IV. 368.
— & others. Beiträge zur Physik des Waldes. 1883. IV. 57.
Lorenzana, Maximo. Cultivo de la Quina. 1880. III. 712.[2]
Lorenzi, Bartolommeo. Della coltivazione del Salice viminale. 1807. III. 352.[1]
Lorenzo, Roberto. Le piante a fusto legnoso . . . di Cuneo. 1889. I. 423, IV. 86.[1]
Loret, Henri. Glanes d'un botaniste. 1859. I. 412.
— L'herbier de la Lozère et M. Prost. 1802. I. 412.
— Juniperus Oxycedrus L. varietas. 1855. II. 31.[2]
— Mes herborisations au Bousquet d'Orb. 1864. I. 413.
— Observations critiques . . . sur plusieurs plantes montpelliéraines. 1874. II. 564.[1]
— Plantes nouvelles pour la Gard. 1880. I. 416.
— Promenades botaniques dans . . . Saint-Pons-de-Thomière. 1866. II. 564.[1]
— Des régions botaniques de l'Hérault. 1872. I. 414.
— See also Timbal-Lagrave, Édouard & Loret, Henri.
— & Barrandon, Auguste. Flore de Montpellier. 1876. I. 415.
Loret, Victor. Le Cédratier dans l'antiquité. 1889. II. 402.[1]
— Études de droguerie égyptienne. 1894. III. 280.[2]
— La flore pharaonique. 1887. I. 514.[2] — 1888. I. 82.[1]
— Recherches sur plusieurs plantes connues des anciens Égyptiens. 1886. I. 514.[2]
Lorey & Duret, L. Catalogue des plantes . . . de la Côte d'Or. 1831. I. 407.
— — Flore de la Côte d'Or, 1831. I. 408.
Lorey, Karl Julius Tuisko. Ein alter Weymuthskiefernbestand. 1898. IV. 471.
— Die Altersbestimmung in Weisstannenbeständen. 1882. IV. 446.[1]
— Anbauversuche mit fremdländischen Holzarten. .1897. V. 126.[1]
— Auftreten des Eichenwurzeltödters. 1890. IV. 511.
— Ueber Baummassentafeln. 1882. IV. 218.
— Baummassen-Tafeln für Fichten-Derbholz. 1882. IV. 458.

— Durchforstungs-Theorie und -Praxis. 1891. IV. 174.
— Einiges von unseren Weisstannen. 1897. IV. 446.[2]
— Ertragstafeln für die Fichte. 1899. IV. 459.[1]
— Ertragstafeln für die Weisstanne. 1884. IV. 446.[1]
— Ertragsuntersuchungen in Fichtenbeständen. 1884. IV. 458.
— Der forstliche Unterricht in Württemberg. 1880. IV. 32.
— Das forstliche Weiserprozent von H. L. Bose 1890. IV. 245.
— Die forstlichen Versuchsanstalten. 1899. IV. 38.[1]
— Forstlicher Unterricht. 1888. IV. 29.
— Handbuch der Forstwissenschaft. 1887. IV. 98.[2]
— Die Plenterdurchforstung. 1888. IV. 174.
— Ueber Probestämme. 1877. IV. 217.
— Ueber Stammanalysen. 1880. IV. 64.[2] 218.
— Waldbau. 1888. IV. 118.
Lorgus, Alwin. Die Kultur des Epiphyllum truncatum. 1885. III. 623.[1]
Loring, George B. Forest condition of Ohio. 1884. IV. 339.
— Forestry in the United States. 1883. IV. 338.[1]
Lorinser, Gustav. Botanisches Excursionsbuch für die deutsch-österreichischen Kronländer. 1854. I. 441.
— & Friedrich. Taschenbuch der Flora Deutschlands. 1847. I. 382.
Lortet, Louis. Sur une anomalie de l'Erica multiflora. 1859. II. 668.[1]
Lortet, Pierre. Propagation de la culture du Mûrier. 1842. III. 376.
Loschge, Friedrich Heinrich. Naturgeschichte der Forl- oder Kieferraupe. 1785. IV. 474.
Loscos y Bernal, Francisco & Pardo y Sastrón, José. Serie imperfecta de las plantas aragonesas espontáneas. 1863. I. 421.
— — Series inconfecta plantarum indigenarum Aragoniae. 1863. I. 421.
Lossen, W. Ueber das Cocaïn. 1865. III. 492.[2]
Lossing, Benson J. American historical trees. 1862. I. 295.[2]
Lossius, Franz Anton. Die Kunst des Feldmessens. 1834. IV. 263.
Lossius, Jeremias. Disputatio de nuce vomica. 1682. III. 682.[1]
Lotar. Anatomie comparée . . . des Cucurbitacées. 1882. II. 844.[3]
Lotbinière, H. G. Joly de. See Joly de Lotbinière, H. G.
Loth, Gaston. Les forêts et la question du reboisement en Tunisie. 1896. IV. 168.[2]
Lothelier, A. D. Essai sur la détermination de la valeur . . . de quelques piquants. 1894. I. 113.[1]
— Influence de l'éclairement sur la production des piquants. 1891. I. 236.[2]
— Influence de l'état hygrométrique de l'air sur la production des piquants. 1890. I. 218, 236.[4]
— Observations sur la piquants. 1888. I. 107.[2]
— Recherches sur les plantes à piquants. 1893. I. 107.[2]
Loti, Ignazio. Il bosco e il lago Lapisino. 1771. IV. 363.[2]
Lotichius, C. A. See Wohmann, W., Neubauer, C. & Lotichius, C. A.
Lotos; Jahrbuch für Naturwissenschaft. See Lotos; Zeitschrift . . . I. 27.
Lotos; Zeitschrift für Natur-Wissenschaften. I. 27.
Lotspeich, D. W. Peach culture in northern Iowa. 1894. III. 441.[1]
Lotsy, Johannes Paulus. Contributions to the life-history of the genus Gnetum. 1899. II. 55.[1]
— Een en ander over reservevoedsel. 1898. I. 180.[1]
— The formation of the so-called Cypress-knees. 1893. II. 52.[1]
— De localisatie van het alcaloïd in Cinchona. 1897. III. 724.[1]
— Localisation . . . of the alcaloid in Cinchona. 1900. III. 724.[1]
— Die Localisationen des Alkaloïds in Cinchona. 1897. III. 724.[1]
— Physiologische proeven genomen met Cinchona succirubra. 1899. III. 726.[2]
— Resultate einer Untersuchung über die Embryologie von Gnetum Gnemon. 1898. II. 55.[1]
— Some Euphorbiaceae from Guatemala. 1895. II. 434.[1]
Lotteri, Frédéric. Report of the committee of economical arts. 1857. III. 380.[1]
— Utilisation des branches des Mûriers. 1855. III. 379.[2]
Die Lotuspflaumen. 1869. III. 669.[1]

Lotz, J. C. Tabellen zur schnellen Bestimmung des Würfel-
gehaltes von Rundhölzern. 1809. IV. 221.
Lotz, J. F. Beyträge zu den Grundsätzen einer Forstordnung
vorzüglich für die in der Seulberger Mark. 1804. IV. 286.
Lotze, G. Sur l'essence de cannelle de Chine. 1886. III.
405.[1]
Loubat, Alphonse. The American vine dresser's guide.
1827. III. 549.[2]
Loubeiro, Francisco. Expériences concernant le bois de
l'Eucalyptus globulus. 1881. IV. 532.[2]
Loubet, L. Lettre . . . à M. le marquis de l'Espine . . .
sur la maladie de la Vigne. 1872. IV. 759.
Loubié, Henri. Le Chêne de juin. 1897. IV. 559.[2]
— Les essences forestières. 1897. IV. 85.[2]
— Les essences forestières; essences résineuses. 1897. IV.
441.
Loudon, H. Hope. *See* Suermondt, G. & Hope Loudon, H.
Loudon, *Mrs.* Jane (Webb). British wild flowers. 1844.
I. 399.
— The first book of botany. 1841. I. 88.
— The ladies companion to the flower-garden. 1841. III.
82.
— The ladies' flower garden. 1848. III. 82.
— Tales about plants. 1846. I. 94.
Loudon, John Claudius. Arboretum et fruticetum britanni-
cum. 1838. I. 293, *III. 78*,[1] *IV. 84*.[2]
— Bemerkungen über . . . Coniferae. 1839. III. 289.
— Derby arboretum. 1840. I. 54.
— An encyclopædia of gardening. 1822. III. 31.
— An encyclopædia of plants. 1829. I. 267.
— An encyclopædia of trees and shrubs. 1841. I. 293,
III. 78,[1] *IV. 84*,[2] V. xvi.[1]
— Encyclopädie des Gartenwesens. 1822. III. 31.
— Hortus britannicus. 1830. III. 82.
— Hortus lignosus londinensis. 1838. I. 54.
— Observations on the formation . . . of . . . plantations.
1804. III. 165.
— The suburban horticulturist. 1842. III. 110.[1]
— Trees and shrubs; an abridgement. 1841. I. 293, *III.
78*,[1] *IV. 84*.[2]
Louesse. Note sur l'Opuntia Rafinesquiana. 1870. III.
625.[1]
— Les Opuntia Rafinesquiana et vulgaris. 1870. III. 625.[1]
Louis, Michel. Emploi d'une poudre contre la maladie de la
Vigne. 1857. III. 577.
Louis, Simon-. *frères. See* Simon-Louis, frères.
Louis, V. D. Jean-. *See* Jean-Louis, V. D.
Louise, E. *See* Huet, L. & Louise, E.
— & Huet, L. Sur un parasite du Pommier. 1891. III.
428.[1]
Louisiana — Sugar experiment station. *See* Louisiana
state university . . . III. 5.
Louisiana agricultural experiment stations. *See* Louisiana
state university . . . III. 5.
**Louisiana state university and Agricultural and mechanical
college — Agricultural experiment stations.** Annual report.
Bulletin. Geology and agriculture. Special bulletin. III. 5.
Lounsberry, Alice. A guide to the trees. 1900. IV. 76,[1]
V. xvi.[1]
— A guide to the wild flowers. 1899. I. 308.
Loureiro, João de. Descripção botanica das Cubebas medi-
cinaes. 1799. II. 94.[1]
— Flora cochinchinensis. 1790. I. 469.[2]
— Memoria sobre a natureza . . . do Páo de Aguila. 1797.
II. 600.[3]
— On the nature . . . of Agallochum. 1797. II. 600.[3]
— Da trasplantação das arvores mais uteis. 1789. III. 43.
Loureiro, José, Marques. *See* Marques Loureiro, José.
Lourme. Rapport sur les travaux de la Commission de la
gutta-percha. 1899. III. 149.
Lourmel, Frédéric Henri Lenormand de. Mise en valeur des
landes de Bretagne. 1853. IV. 162.
Loury. Aristolochia tricaudata. 1872. III. 386.[2]
Lous, Karl. Sammenvoksede Granträr. 1885. II. 36.[2]
Loutreul, L. Des prétendues influences de la lune. 1899.
I. 518.
Louvet. Note sur un régime de Palmier nain. 1862. III.
322.[1]
Louvet, Albéric. Études sur le mode de production de la
gomme arabique. 1876. III. 463.[1]
Louyet. Note sur les applications d'un des produits de la
distillation de la résine commune. 1848. IV. 468.[1]
Louyet, P. Note sur l'absorption des poisons métalliques.
1845. I. 211.

Louzier, R. Causeries sur le Brésil. 1897. I. 344.
Lov angaaende overdragelse til staten af skove tilhørende
offentlige fonds M. V. 1874. IV. 315.[1]
Lov angaaende Sandflugtens Dæmpning. 1867. IV. 315.[1]
Lov angaaende Sandflugtsstrækningers Behandling. 1857.
IV. 315.[1]
Lov indeholdene bestemmelser om almindingsskove. 1857.
IV. 315.[1]
Lov om Foranstaltninger med Oldenborren. 1899. IV.
315.[1]
Lov om Foranstaltninger mod Oldenborrer. 1887. IV. 315.[1]
Lov om Sandflugtens Dæmpning. 1852. IV. 315.[1]
Lov om skovvæsenet. 1863. IV. 315.[1]
Lov om Statsskovenes Bestyrelse. 1851. IV. 315.[1]
Lovegrove, W. H. Notes on Dendrocalamus strictus. 1900.
IV. 485.[1]
Lovell, G. W. Notes on transplanting. 1855. III. 166.
Lovell, George. Berberis japonica. 1857. III. 396.[1]
— On the management of forest-trees. 1849. IV. 120.
— Movement of the sap of trees. 1853. I. 164.
— Rhododendrons. 1859. III. 656.
— Some observations on the growth . . . of the wood of
plants. 1849. III. 43, 174.[2]
Lovell, J. H. The insect-visitors of flowers. 1898. II. 654,[2]
671.[3]
Lovell, Robert. Enchiridion botanicum. 1659. I. 286.
— Παμβοτανολογία. 1659. I. 286.
Lovén, Fredrik. Das Wachsthum der Kiefer und Fichte.
1891. IV. 458, 481.
Lovén, Hedvig. Om utvecklingen af de sekundära kärlknip-
pena hos Dracaena och Yucca. 1887. II. 81,[3] 87.[1]
Lovén, Sven Ludvig. Stirpes agri femsionensis. *See* Fries,
E. M. 1825. I. 353.
Lovéna. *See* Hái. IV. 14 .
Loverde, J. de. Un parasite universel. 1900. IV. 212.
The lover's tree. 1841. I. 210.[1]
Lovett, J. T. The Carolina Poplar. 1875. III. 345.[2]
Lovink, H. J. Beschrijving van eenige insecten nadeelig voor
de houtteelt. 1893. IV. 442, 649.[2]
— Bosschen en boschbedrijf in Nederland. 1896. IV. 119.[3]
— Een en ander over het " dennenschot." 1890. IV. 478.
— De Eik. 1891. IV. 513.
— Over het gebruik van hulpmeststoffen bij de houtteelt.
1892. IV. 144.[2]
— Is het spitten van akkermáalshout na elken hak aanbeve-
lenswaardig? 1891. IV. 388.[2]
— Onze Nederlandsche schorshandel. 1898. IV. 435.
— Rapport omtrent eene proeve tot verbetering der gronden
in den " Koegraspolder." 1894. IV. 160.[2]
— Schade, die door eekhorentjes in grove dennenbosschen
kan aangericht worden. 1896. IV. 479.
— Stedelijke beplantingen. 1891. III. 42.[2]
— Twee gevaarlijke vijanden van jonge dennenbosschen.
1895. IV. 479.
— Verslag betreffende de duinbeplanting in Jutland. 1894.
IV. 156.[2]
— *See also* Blijdenstein, A. J. & Lovink, H. J.; Ritzema
Bos, J. & Lovink, H. J.
— & Ritzema Bos, J. De rupsen van het geslacht Retinia.
1897. III. 191.
— — Schade in jonge dennenbosschen. 1897. IV. 479.
Lovisa Ulrika, *Queen of Sweden*. Silke från silkesmaskar upp-
född . . . medsvenska Mullbärsblad. 1753. III. 372.[2]
Low, Albert Peter. Trees and other plants [of the Labrador
peninsula]. 1896. I. 311.[1]
Low, C. R. The Cocoa-nut Palm and its uses. 1873. III.
324.[1]
Low, Hugh. Sarawak. 1848. III. 276.[1]
Low, James. A dissertation on the soil & agriculture . . . of
Penang. 1836. III. 129.[1]
Lowe, Edward Joseph. Beautiful leaved plants. 1861.
III. 206.[1]
— Les plantes à feuillage coloré. 1861. III. 206.[1]
Lowe, John. On an abnormality in the flowers of Salix An-
dersoniana. 1856. II. 108.[3] — 1858. II. 103.[2]
— The age and growth of Yew trees. 1891. II. 10.[3]
— Sur le dosage du tannin dans l'écorce de Chêne. 1868.
IV. 515.[1]
— On the homologies of the floral organs. 1861. I. 114.[3]
— Rapid growth in a Yew tree. 1898. III. 288.[1]
— Remarkable formation of a stem-root in a Willow. 1853.
I. 188.
— The Yew-trees of Great Britain and Ireland. 1897. II.
11.[1]

Lowe, Richard Thomas. On Chamaemeles coriacea. 1829. II. 259.[1]
— Florulae salvagicae tentamen. 1869. I. 498.
— A list of plants observed . . . at Mogador. 1861. I. 484.
— A manual flora of Madeira. 1868. I. 498.
— Notes and observations on . . . plants observed in the island of Madeira. 1834. I. 497.
— Novitiae florae maderensis. 1838. I. 497.
— Primitiae faunae et florae Maderae. 1831. I. 497.
— Primitiae . . . faunae et florae Maderae. 1851. I. 497.
— S m account of the fruits . . . of Madeira. 1866. III. 282[1] e
— Species plantarum maderensium quaedam. 1856. I. 497.
Lowe, V. H. A fumigator for small orchard trees. 1900. III. 198.[2]
— Spraying experiments with kerosene oil. 1900. III. 198.[2]
Lowe, W. E. B. Wych-hazel or Wych-elm? 1900. II. 145.[1]
Lowe, William Henry. Observations on Polyommatus Artaxerxes. 1856. III. 192.[2]
Lowell, John. Some slight notices of the Larch tree. 1822. III. 758.[1]
Lowell, Percival. A visit to Shirane San. 1888. I. 463.[1]
Lower Burma. See India — Lower Burma.
Lowndes, John. The Coffee-planter. 1807. III. 728.[2]
Lowne, Benjamin Thompson. Natural history of Great Yarmouth. 1863. I. 401.
— On the vegetation of the . . . shores of the Dead Sea. 1867. I. 480.
Lowrie, A. E. Forest protection in Ajmere. 1885. IV. 181.[2]
— Kumri Teak plantations. 1898. IV. 537.[1]
— Sâl butter. 1889. III. 611.[2]
Lowrie, A. G. Effects of the late drought. 1900. IV. 192.[1]
Lowrie, J. The home of Caryota urens. 1898. II. 66.[1]
— The home of Lagerstroemia Flos-reginae. 1894. II. 609.[2]
— Seeding of the Bamboo. 1891. II. 59.[3]
— Seeding of the Great Bamboo. 1900. II. 59.[2]
Lowther, Marcus. Yuccas in the Isle of Wight. 1879. III. 340.[2]
Lowther, R. Remarks on the useful property of Aristolochia indica. 1846. III. 386.[3]
Lowther, W. H. On the mischievous increase of a gigantic . . . Solanum. 1861. II. 778.[1]
— On the natural productions of the vale of Kashmere. 1854. III. 277.
— Note on the rusot. 1857. III. 394.[3]
— Notes on the flora of Bourbon. 1861. I. 482.
— Notes on the flora of Southern Africa. 1863. I. 494.
— Notes on the Palm, Sagus Ruffia. 1861. III. 330.[2]
— Particulars regarding certain specimens . . . for the garden and museum of the Society. 1859. III. 278.
— Tentative de boisement aux États-Unis. 1892. IV. 155.[1]
Loza, L. Rio de la. See Rio de la Loza, L.
Loza, Manuel Rio de la. See Vega, J. M. L. de la & Loza, Manuel Rio de la.
Loza y Miranda, Francisco Rio de la. See Rio de la Loza y Miranda, Francisco.
Lozada, Manuel Gutierrez. Liquidambar. 1870. III. 417.[2]
Lozano, Eusebio Sánchez y. See Sánchez y Lozano, Eusebio.
Lozano, Pedro. Descripcion chorografica . . . de las . . . provincias del Gran Chaco, Gualamba. 1733. I. 419.[2]
— Historia de la Compañia de Jesus. 1754. III. 305.[1]
Lozano y Castro, Mariano. Estudio químico de la corteza de Boconia. 1893. III. 408.[2]
Loze, Edmond. Le Bambou. 1891. III. 314.[2]
— De l'influence des sols boisés sur les climats. 1892. IV. 54.
— Le Péguère de Cauterets. 1896. IV. 186.[1]

Lozère — Société d'agriculture, industrie, sciences . . . See Société . . . III. 21.
Lozet, Julien, (jr.). Du choix des arbres les plus convenables pour les plantations d'alignement. 1896. III. 210.
Lr. Weinfässer aus Lärchenholz. 1894. IV. 427.[1]
Luatz, Labhart-. See Labhart-Luatz.
Lubach, D. Over schadelijke vlinders. 1888. III. 190.
Lubbers, L. Aeschynanthus pulcher G. Don. 1892. III. 708.[1]
— Bryophyllum calycinum Roxb. 1898. III. 409.[1]
— Dracaena lineata var. Doucetti. 1893. III. 335.[2]
— Effets de l'hiver 1890–91. 1891. III. 46.[2]
— Effets des émanations du chlorure de chaux au Jardin botanique de Bruxelles. 1871. III. 185.[2]
Lubbers, M. Catalogue de plantes rares . . . au palais de San Donato. 1880. I. 64.
Lubbock, Sir John. Blumen und Insecten in ihrer Wechselbeziehung. 1875. I. 239.[2]
— On British wild flowers considered in relation to insects. 1875. I. 239,[2] 529.
— On buds and stipules. 1899. I. 109.[1]
— On certain relations between plants and insects. 1877. I. 237.
— A contribution to our knowledge of seedlings. 1892. I. 123,[1] V. xi.[1]
— Les feuilles et les lois de leurs formes. 1890. I. 111.
— Flowers, fruits and leaves. 1886. I. 218.
— Flowers, fruits and trees. 1886. I. 218.
— On the form of the leaf of Viburnum. 1891. II. 842.[2]
— On the fruit and seed of the Juglandeae. 1891. II. 112.[1]
— On fruits and seeds. 1881. I. 240.[3]
— Les insectes et les fleurs sauvages. 1875. I. 529.
— On leaves. 1885. I. 110.
— Phytobiological observations on . . . seedlings. 1887. I. 123,[1] 218.
— On stipules. 1891. I. 112.[1]
— Winter buds. 1898. III. 18.[1]
— See also Леббокъ.
Lubbock, Richard. Observations on the fauna of Norfolk. 1845. V. xxi.[1]
Lubelski. Sur la culture et les falsifications du thé. 1890. III. 608.[1]
Luca, Sebastiano de. Action de la terre volcanique . . . sur les maladies de la Vigne. 1873. III. 560.
— Sur la fermentation alcoolique . . . des fruits. 1876. I. 176.
— Recherches chimiques sur l'essence de Citrus Lumia. 1860. III. 502.[2]
— Recherches chimiques sur l'essence de mandarine. 1857. III. 502.[2]
— Recherches chimiques sur les éléments minéraux. 1861. I. 153.
— Recherches chimiques tendant à démontrer la production de l'alcool. 1878. I. 176.
— Recherches sur l'essence de Citrus Lumia. 1860. III. 502.[2]
— Recherches sur la formation de la matière grasse dans les Olives. 1861. II. 713.[1]
— See also Bertagnini, Cesare & Luca, S. de.
— & Ubaldini, Giuseppe. Recherches chimiques sur le Myrte d'Australie. 1865. III. 636.
— — Recherches chimiques sur . . . Stigmaphyllon jatrophaefolium. 1864. III. 513.[2]
Lucas, Carl. Flora der Umgegend der Stadt Konitz. 1866. I. 386.
— Verzeichniss der um Hinzenberg wachsenden Pflanzen. 1862. I. 362.
Lucas, Eduard. Abbildungen württembergischer Obstsorten. 1858. III. 71.
— Abbildungen württembergischer Obstsorten . . . Steinobstfrüchte. 1861. III. 71.
— Auswahl werthvoller Obstsorten. 1871. III. 71.
— Die Bepflanzung der Eisenbahndämme. 1870. III. 138.
— Die Beschädigung unserer Obstbäume durch Schneedruck. 1868. III. 184.[2]
— Einleitung in das Studium der Pomologie. 1877. III. 71.
— Fortgesetzte Beobachtungen über die Wirkung der Kohle auf die Vegetation. 1841. III. 40.
— Die Gemeindebaumschule. 1852. III. 154.[1]
— Hebung der Obstkultur. 1855. III. 137.
— Kaltflüssiges Baumwachs. 1857. III. 161.
— Die Kernobstsorten Württembergs. 1854. III. 71.
— Die Kreis- oder Bezirksbaumschule. 1852. III. 154.[1]
— Kurze Anleitung zur Obstkultur. 1866. III. 138.

Lucas, Eduard (*continued*).
— Kurze Darstellung des Baumschnitts. 1879. III. 172.
— Die Lehre vom Baumschnitt. 1879. III. 172.
— Leitfaden für angehende Pomologen. 1879. III. 71.
— Leitfaden zum Bestimmen der Obstsorten. 1863. III. 71.
— Sur un mastic liquide à froid. 1857. III. 161.
— Das Obst und seine Verwertung. 1856. III. 174.[1]
— Der Obstbau an Staats- und Gemeindestrassen. 1881. III. 211.[1]
— Obstbau auf dem Lande. 1848. III. 137.
— Die Obstbenutzung. 1856. III. 174.[1]
— Die Pfirsiche und Nectarinen. 1870. III. 430.[2]
— Resultate der bisherigen Versuche über die Anwendung der Kohle zur Vermehrung durch Stecklinge. 1840. III. 157.
— Résultats des expériences sur l'emploi du charbon pour multiplication des plantes. 1840. III. 157.
— Schutz der Obstbäume gegen Krankheiten. 1879. III. 179.
— Zum Schutz unserer Weinreben. 1882. III. 573.
— Vollständiges Handbuch der Obstkultur. 1881. III. 138.
— Die wichtigsten Veredlungsarten. 1871. III. 162.
— *See also* JAHN, Fr., LUCAS, Eduard, OBERDIECK, J. G. C.; OBERDIECK, J. G. C. & LUCAS, Eduard.
— & **Koch,** K. Der Ausfall der Obsternte. 1874. III. 138.
— & **Medicus,** Friedrich. Die Lehre vom Obstbau. 1844. III. 137.
— — Die Lehre von der Obstbaumzucht. 1844. III. 137.
— — Sadownictwo zasadzające się na prostych prawach. 1844. III. 137.
Lucas, Fr. Die wertvollsten Tafeläpfel. 1893. III. 425.[2]
— Die wertvollsten Tafelbirnen. 1894. III. 445.[1]
Lucas, Pierre Hippolyte. Carpocapsa Deshaisiana. 1858. III. 522.[2]
— Observations sur la manière de vivre d'un nouvelle espèce de Carpocapsa. 1858. III. 188.[1]
Lucca — Reale accademia lucchese di scienze. *See* REALE . . . I. 25.
Luce, Johann Wilhelm Ludwig von. Topographische Nachrichten von der Insel Oesel. 1823. I. 360.
Lucet, Émile. De la foliole et des glandes de l'Ailantus. 1884. II. 413.[2]
— Insectologie agricole. 1898. III. 453.[2]
— Tératologie végétale. 1897. II. 290.[1]
Luchini, Odoardo. La istituzione dell' Arbor day in Italia. 1898. IV. 42.[2]
Luck, E. Sur la decomposition de l'acide carbonique par le Gui. 1851. II. 178.[2]
— Ueber die Fähigkeit von Viscum . . . Kohlensäure zu zersetzen. 1851. II. 178.[2]
Lucknow — Horticultural gardens. *See* HORTICULTURAL GARDENS . . . 1888. I. 67.[1]
The **Lucombe** Oak. 1900. III. 362.[2]
Lucot, Alexis. Emblêmes de flore et des végétaux. 1819. II. 515.
Lucy, A. Lettre sur l'Eucalyptus globulus. 1873. III. 634.[2]
Lucy, Ad. Essais de plantation d'arbres. 1860. III. 201.
Ludeau, CAPURON-. *See* CAPURON-LUDEAU.
Ludeking, E. W. A. Natuur en geneeskundige topographische schets der assistent-residentie Agam. 1860. I. 467.
Luden, Karl. Die Lehre von den Servituten. 1837. IV. 333.
Ludlam, Alfred. On the cultivation . . . of trees and plants. 1869. III. 132.[2]
— Essay on the cultivation and acclimatization. 1865. III. 50.[1]
Ludloff, K. Forstliches aus dem Staate Washington. 1899. IV. 341.[1]
— Wälder und Waldriesen im Staate Washington. 1891. IV. 340.
— Die wichtigsten Holzarten des Waldstaates Washington. 1898. IV. 341.[1]
Ludlow, William. Report of a reconnaissance of the Black Hills of Dakota. *See* COULTER, J. M. 1875. I. 324; WINCHELL, N. H. 1875. I. 320.
Ludolf, (*Königl. Geheimer Ober-Finanzrath*). Beschreibung eines horizontalen Frucht-Spaliers. 1824. III. 171.
Ludolff, Hieronymus. De fabis coffee. 1724. III. 741.[1]
Ludolff, Michael Matthias. Catalogus plantarum. 1746. III. 54.
Ludwig, (*Professor*). Massenhafte Vegetation des Kiefernblusenrostes. 1879. IV. 477.

Ludwig, Christian Friedrich. Delectus opusculorum ad scientiam naturalem spectantium. 1790. I. 1.
— Handbuch der Botanik. 1800. I. 84.
— Die neuere wilde Baumzucht. 1783. III. 68,[2] *IV. 81.*[1]
— De plantarum munimentis. 1776. I. 235.[2]
— & **Gaditsch,** Peter. De pulvera antherarum. 1778. I. 116.[2]
Ludwig, Christian Gottlieb. Aphorismi botanici. 1738. I. 31.
— De colore plantarum. 1756. I. 184.
— De colore plantarum species distinguente. 1759. I. 250.
— Definitiones generum plantarum. 1737. I. 257.
— Definitiones plantarum. 1737. I. 257.
— Ectypa vegetabilium. 1760. III. 54.
— De elaboratione succorum. 1768. I. 162.
— Institutiones historico-physicae regni vegetabilis. 1742. I. 82.[2]
— De minuendis plantarum generibus. 1737. I. 250.
— De minuendis plantarum speciebus. 1740. I. 250.
— Observationes in methodum plantarum sexualem. 1739. I. 250.
— De plantarum viribus medicis. 1772. III. 238.[1]
— De plantarum viribus specificis. 1772. III. 238.[1]
— De rei herbariae studio et usu. 1768. I. 78.[2]
— De sensu externo facultatum in plantis judice. *See* HEBENSTREIT, J. E. 1730. I. 146.
— De sexu plantarum. 1737. I. 198.
— De viribus plantarum cultura mutatis. 1772. III. 238.[1]
Ludwig, Ernst. *See* VRIJ, J. E. de & LUDWIG, Ernst.
Ludwig, F. Beiträge zur thüringischen Volksbotanik. 1883. III. 345.[1]
— Beobachtungen über Schleimflüsse der Bäume. 1899. III. 195.[2]
— Ueber einige Rost- und Brandpilze Australiens. 1893. III. 465.[2]
— Ein neuer Pilzfluss der Waldbäume. 1893. IV. 497.
— Noch einmal die Schraubenflieger. 1888. I. 240.[2]
— Zur Verbreitung der Pilzflüsse der Bäume. 1899. III. 195.[2]
Ludwig, F. K. Der Spessart und seine Benutzung. 1805. IV. 350.
Ludwig, Friedrich. Ueber Alkoholgährung und Schleimfluss lebender Bäume. 1886. I. 206,[2] *IV. 511.*
— Zur Biologie der Apocyneen. 1881. II. 728.[2]
— Biologische Mittheilungen. I. 1892. II. 602.[1]
— Ueber brasilianische . . . Feigenwespen. 1886. II. 149.[2]
— Ein eigener Fall von Adynamandrie. 1892. II. 602.[1]
— Über einen eigentümlichen Farbenwechsel in dem Blütenstande von Spiraea opulifolia. 1884. II. 269.[2]
— Ein neuer Standort von Ulex europaeus L. 1886. II. 387.[2]
— On self-sterility. 1900. II. 602.[1]
Ludwig, Fritz. Die Befruchtung der Pflanzen. 1867. I. 237.
Ludwig, H. Ueber die Bestandtheile einiger Mannasorten. 1870. III. 221.[1]
— Mannes d'Orient. 1870. III. 221.[1]
— Ueber Pflanzenwächs. 1872. I. 526.[2]
Ludwig, Hub. Die Cultur der Eiche. 1883. IV. 507.
— Resultate verschiedener Methoden der Erziehung von Eichensämlingen. 1892. IV. 507.
Ludwig, P. J. Buchenstamm mit Inschriften. 1861. I. 210,[1] *IV. 496.*
Ludwig, Wilhelm Carl Ernst. De corticis peruviani usu. 1795. III. 720.
Lübeck, Christoph. Nachricht über . . . blühende weibliche Sago-Palme. 1828. III. 285.[1]
Lueben, August. Anweisung zu einem methodischen Unterricht in der Pflanzenkunde. 1832. I. 255.
— Die Hauptformen der äussern Pflanzenorgane. 1846. I. 99.
Lücker, E. *See* DOEBNER, O. & LÜCKER, E.
Lüder, (*Probst*). Ueber die Eszäunungen. 1791. III. 212.[2]
Lueder, Franz Hermann Heinrich. Botanischpraktische Lustgärtnerey. 1783. III. 74.
Lueders, Friedrich Wilhelm Anton. Nomenclator botanicus stirpium brandenburgicarum. 1786. I. 314.
Lueders, Herman Frederick. The vegetation of the town Prairie du Sac. 1895. I. 316.
Lüders, Philippe Ernst. Der Hecken- u. Weiden-Bau. 1784. III. 212,[1] 346.[2]
Luedersdorff, Friedrich Wilhelm. Das Auftrocknen der Pflanzen fürs Herbarium. 1827. I. 35.
— The solution and reproduction of india rubber. 1832. III. 230.

Luedgers, Max Stanislaus Joseph. De medicamento novantiquo Tebaschir dicto. 1791. III. 315.[1]
Lüdicke, Herrmann. Verzeichniss von Gewaechshauspflanzen . . . zu St. Petersburg auf der Apotheker-Insel. 1845. I. 42.
Lüdtke, Franz. Beiträge zur Kenntniss der Aleuronkörner. 1889. I. 140.[2]
Lüdtke, H. Die Eiben Taxus in Tzschocha. 1897. II. 11.[2]
Lüdy, Fritz. Ueber die Handelssorten der Benzoë. 1893. III. 671.[1]
— Studien über die Sumatrabenzoë. 1893. III. 671.[1]
Luehmann, J. George. Description of a new Australian Labiate plant. 1899. II. 763.[2]
— Reliquiae Muellerianae. 1897. I. 505.
— A short dichotomous key to . . . Eucalyptus. 1898. II. 623.[1]
Lüke. Zur Lyda-Kalamität. 1900. IV. 480.
Lüneburg — Naturwissenschaftlicher Verein für das Fürstenthum . . . *See* NATURWISSENSCHAFTLICHER . . . I. 14.
Lüneburger Forstverein. Bericht. IV. 10.
Lünen, L. von. Des Försters Rechenknecht. 1876. IV. 59.[1]
Luerssen, Christian. Zur Controverse über die Einzelligkeit . . . des Pollens der Onagrarien. 1868. II. 115.[1]
— Die Doppeltanne des Berliner Weihnachtsmarktes. 1887. II. 35.[1]
— Die Einführung japanischer Waldbäume. 1886. IV. 126.[1]
— Forstbotanik. 1888. IV. 84.[1]
— Grundzüge der Botanik. 1877. V. x.[2]
— Handbuch der systematischen Botanik. 1879. III. 59.[1]
— Die Pflanzen der Pharmacopoea germanica. 1883. III. 59.[1]
Lüth, Ludwig. Diospyros Kaki, die Persimone. 1896. III. 669.[2]
Luetke, Friedrich. Voyage autour du monde. 1835. I. 303.
Lütken, A. Nord.og Syd. *See* ULDALL, F. P. & BØRGESEN, F. 1898. I. 337.
Lütken, Christian. *See* LÜTKEN, Christopher.
Lütken, Christian Frederik. Almeenfattelige Naturskildringer. 1863. I. 95.
— Dijmphna-Togtets zoologisk botaniske Udbytte. *See* HOLM, Theodor. 1885. I. 364.
Lütken, Christopher. Om de af Dr. Boucherie foreslaaede Midler. 1860. IV. 418.
— Den Langenske Forstordning. 1899. IV. 296.[2]
— Multiplicationstabel for Stammetværsnitsarealer. 1879. IV. 230.
— Præparater til Belysning af Tilvæxtgangen. 1872. IV. 233.
— Die Scheerenkluppe (saksklup). 1878. IV. 231.[2]
— Om Skovdyrkning i det vestlige Jylland. 1865. IV. 343.[1]
— Statistisk Beskrivelse af de danske Statsskove. 1870. IV. 343.[1]
— Om Statsskovenes Salg. 1868. IV. 273.[1]
Lüttwitz, *Freiherr* von. Durchforstungs-Ertrag. 1857. IV. 260.[1]
— Ein junger starker Eichbaum! 1857. IV. 515.[2]
— *See also* BLANKENBURG, von (*Oberförster, Kottwitz*) & LÜTTWITZ, *Baron* von (*Oberförster, Nimkau*).
Lugger, Otto. Insects affecting Poplars and Willows. 1889. III. 344,[1] 550.[1]
— Insects injurious in 1895. 1896. III. 187.
— Oak caterpillars. 1890. IV. 501.[1]
Lui, SELIGMAN-. *See* SELIGMAN-LUI.
Luigioni, A. Appunti sul taglio delle macchie. 1899. IV. 135.[1]
Luisinus, Aloysius. Aphrodisiacus. 1728. III. 494.[1]
— Liber de morbo gallico. 1535. III. 494.[1]
— De morbo gallico omnia quæ extant. 1535. III. 494.[1]
Luiset, Gabriel, (ed.). Classification des fruits du genre Pêcher. 1861. III. 439.[2]
Luja, Éd. Fagus sylvatica Zlatia. 1894. II. 216.[1]
Lukácsy, Sándor. A fatenyésztés. 1871. III. 115.[2]
— A magyar alföld befásitása. 1854. IV. 167.[1]
Lukáš, František. Slechtění Růží. 1900. III. 453.[1]
Lukas, Franz. Beiträge zur Kenntniss der absoluten Festigkeit. 1882. I. 149.[1]
— Vergleichende Untersuchungen an der Epidermis der Blüthenhüllen bei Ribes. 1894. II. 244.[1]
Lukens, T. P. Forest protection and restoration. 1900. IV. 155.[2]
— The restoration of mountain covering. 1899. IV. 155.[2]
Luker & Smith. Catalogue of hardy trees and shrubs, greenhouse and stove plants. 1783. I. 53.

Lukmanoff, Athanase de. Nomenclature . . . des Cannellierss. 1889. II. 224.[1]
Łukaʹski, Józef. Krótki zarys historyi leśnictwa w W. K. Poznańskiem. 1900. IV. 27.[1]
Lukrabo seeds. 1878. III. 614.[2]
Lumber. *See* SAW-MILL gazette. IV. 5.[1]
Lumber review. IV. 4.
Lumber trade gazette. IV. 4.
Lumber trade journal. IV. 4.
The lumber trade of Toledo. 1867. IV. 405.[2]
Lumber weights. 1898. IV. 411.[2]
Lumber worker. IV. 4.
Lumber world. IV. 4.
Lumbering and forestry. 1893. IV. 382.[2]
Lumberman and forester. 1894. IV. 178.[2]
Lumberman's gazette. IV. 4.
Lumberman's review. IV. 4.
Lumia, Corrado. Del miscuglio gassoso contenuto nel sicono del Fico. 1889. II. 151.[1]
Luminare maius. *See* MANLIUS DE BOSCO, J. J. 1528. III. 757.[2]
On the luminosity of ashes of wood. 1821. I. 154.
Luminous plants. 1824. I. 206.[2]
Lummis, W. D. F. The Aboretum [*sic*]. 1881. III. 27.[2]
Lumnitzer, Stephan. Flora posoniensis. 1791. I. 374.
Lumsdaine, J. Cultivation of Nutmegs. 1851. III. 402,[1] 635.[2]
— Report on the cultivation of spices at Bencoolen. 1822. III. 127.[2]
Lunan, John. Hortus jamaicensis. 1814. I. 335.
Lunardoni, Agostino. Alcunché sulla questione forestale. 1898. IV. 277.
— L'Associazione italiana " Pro Montibus." 1897. IV. 41.[1]
— I boschi di Cappadocia ed il loro avvenire. 1899. IV. 364.
— Coltivate il Bagolaro. 1896. IV. 518.[1]
— La coltivazione delle patate negli appezzamenti boschivi. 1894. IV. 134.[1]
— Come si conservano le ghiande. 1894. IV. 148.
— Come si piantano le Quercie? 1895. IV. 508.
— L'escursione scientifico-forestale . . . nei domini slesiani dell'arciduca Alberto. 1881. IV. 369.
— Il fosfato Thomas. 1895. IV. 144.[2]
— L'importazione . . . dei prodotti . . . e forestali. 1895. IV. 406.[2]
— I lavori di rinsaldamento . . . in provincia d'Aquila. 1898. IV. 166.[2]
— Manualetto popolare di selvicoltura. 1887. IV. 110.[1]
— Da Monasterace a Serra San Bruno. 1886. IV. 364.
— Un nuovo apparecchio germinatore. 1880. IV. 147.[1]
— Quando e come si piantano i Pini silvestri. 1894. IV. 474.
— I querceti della Slavonia. 1885. IV. 373.
— La questione forestale in Sardegna. 1899. IV. 277.
— Rimboschiamo! 1895. IV. 166.[1]
— Seminiamo e piantiamo la Robinia. 1895. IV. 523.[2]
— La sistemazione dei torrenti . . . di Aquila. 1895. IV. 186.[2]
— Pro sylvis. 1894. IV. 41.[1]
— La tenuta alberese ed il suo avvenire. 1898. IV. 364.
— La " Tribuna " e l'Amministrazione forestale. 1894. IV. 293.[2]
— Pro Vallombrosa. 1895. IV. 35.[3]
— & Leonardi, Gustavo. Gli insetti nocivi ai nostri orti. 1889. III. 191.
Lunaret, Léon de. Fructification· du Zamia caffra. 1880. III. 285.[1]
Lund, Anders Axel Wilhelm. Om Westervikstraktens Björnballonarter. 1877. II. 301.[1]
— Winmærdy-florans phanerogamer. 1863. I. 356.
Lund, Gabriel. Rön om sjukdomen·noma. 1765. III. 720.
Lund, Johan Jakob Georg. De oleo Crotonis. 1831. III. 517.[1]
Lund, N. Nogle indenlandske . . . Kiendsgierninger. 1802. IV. 156.[1]
— Nogle vigtige Regler for Opelskning af Træer. 1802. III. 156.[1]
— Om Slesten Lynette og Dyrkning. 1802. IV. 526.[2]
Lund, Niels Tønder. Om den rette Quassia amara. 1791. III. 508.[1]
— Von der wahren und falschen Quassia amara. 1791. III. 508.[2]
Lund, Nils. Haandbog i Christianias phanerogame flora. 1846. I. 355.
— Reise igjennem Nordlandene. 1842. I. 354.

Lund, Peter Wilhelm. Bemærkninger over de almindelige Vej- og Ukrudtsplanter i Brasilien. 1838. I. 341.
— Bemærkninger over Vegetationen paa de indre Høisletter af Brasilien. 1834. I. 341.
Lund, Samsöe. Observations sur le calice des Composées. 1874. II. 850.[1]
— Fra udenlandske botaniske Haver. 1885. I. 64.
Lund—Kongl. fysiografiska sällskapets. See LUNDS UNIVERSITETS. I. 519.[2]
Lund—Regia societas physiographica. See LUNDS UNIVERSITETS. I. 519.[2]
Lundberg, Peder. Den rette Have-Dyrkning. 1762. III. 100.[1]
Lundequist, Nicolaus Guilielmus. See LUNDEQUIST, Nils Wilhelm.
Lundequist, Nils Wilhelm. Handbok i svenska trädgårds- och blomsterskötseln. 1841. III. 100.[2]
— **Kjellborg,** J. F. & **Gellerstedt,** J. D. Flora paroeciae Bränkyrka. See SILLÉN, N. J. 1827. I. 353.
Lundman, Pehr. Disputatio medica inauguralis de Junipero. 1727. III. 303.[2]
Lundmark, Johannes Daniel. Beskrifning på et nytt svenskt träd, Betula pinnata. 1790. II. 116.[2]
— De Lavandula. See LINNÉ, Carl von. 1780. II. 764.[1]
— De usu Linnaeae medico. See ACREL, J. G. 1788. III. 749.[2]
Lunds universitets. Års-skrift. I. 519.[2]
Lundström, Anders. Beskrifning om frukt-träds uppdragning af kärnor. 1833. III. 134.[3]
— Handbok i trädgårds-skötseln. 1831. III. 100.[1]
Lundström, Axel Nicolaus. Die Anpassungen der Pflanzen an Regen. 1884. I. 232.[2]
— Die Anpassungen der Pflanzen an Thiere. 1887. I. 235.[1]
— Einige neuere Untersuchungen über Domatien. 1890. I. 235.[1]
— Om formförändringar hos åtskilliga lignoser. 1888. I. 244.[2]
— Gallbildningar hos nordliga Salix-arter. 1891. III. 350.[2]
— Om Jenissej-strändernas Salix-flora. 1888. II. 103.[1]
— Kritische Bemerkungen über die Weiden Nowaja Semljas. 1877. II. 103.[1]
— Nyare undersökningar öfver domatier. 1889. I. 235.[1]
— Pflanzenbiologische Studien. 1884. I. 232.[2]—1887. I. 235.[1]
— Om regnuppfångande växter. 1889. I. 232.[2]
— Om Salix finmarkica. 1876. II. 107.[1]
— Ueber die Salixflora der Jenissej-Ufer. 1888. II. 103.[1]
— Studier öfver slägtet Salix. 1875. II. 103.[2]
— Om symbiotiska växtbildningar. 1886. I. 234.[2]
— Tvenne anmärkningsvärda växtfynd. 1886. II. 107.[2]
Lundy, John Patterson. Forestry at home and abroad. 188.? IV. 44.
— Main cause of destructive floods. 1889. IV. 51.
Lunge, George & **Steinkauler,** Th. Sur un nouveau carbure d'hydrogène fourni par le Sequoia gigantea. 1880. II. 50.[2]
—— Sur un nouvel hydrocarbure du Séquoia gigantea. 1881. II.'50.[3]
Lunteren, D. & H. van. See LUNTEREN, H. & D. van.
Lunteren, H. & D. van. Catalogus van in den open grond overwinterende boomen en heesters. 1819. I. 51.[1]
— Catalogus van kast en oranjerey-gewassen. 1819. I. 5[1].[1]
La lunure du Chêne. 1897. IV. 511.
Lupieri, G. B. Osservazioni sui boschi della Carnia. 180.? IV. 363.[2]
Lupin, Friedrich von. Die Gärten. 1820. I. 45.
Lupke, R. Sur le rôle du potassium. 1890. I. 159.
Lupo, Michele del. Pomologia artificiale secondo il sistema Garnier-Valletti. 1891. III. 29,[1] 88.[1]
Luquet, J. Adenocalymna nitidum. 1891. III. 704.[3]
— Amherstia nobilis. 1889. III. 466.[2]
— Ardisia crispa. 1893. III. 666.[1]
— Burchellia capensis. 1892. III. 711.[2]
— Le Cedrela sinensis. 1890. III. 512.[1]
— Le Chrysophyllum macrophyllum. 1891. III. 667.[1]
— Crataegus populifolia. 1900. III. 423.[1]
— Le genre Leschenaultia. 1889. III. 754.[1]
— Le Gomphia Theophrasta. 1889. III. 596.[1]
— Le Grewia d'Occident. 1891. III. 585.[1]
— Heritiera macrophylla. 1891. III. 591.[3]
— L'Holboellia latifolia. 1888. III. 393.[2]
— Hovea Celsii. 1890. III. 478.[1]
— Howardia caracasensis. 1891. III. 746.[2]

— Un Hydrangea grimpant. 1898. III. 412.[2]
— Hypericum Moserianum. 1888. III. 610.[1]
— Le Kopsia fruticosa. 1891. III. 688.[2]
— Les Lagerstroemia. 1891. III. 629.[3]
— Lemonia spectabilis. 1890. III. 505.[2]
— À propos des Crataegus. 1890. III. 422.[1]
— Le Pterocaryer du Caucase. 1888. III. 356.[2]
— Robinia neo-mexicana. 1899. III. 486.[2]
— Les Skimmia. 1890. III. 505.[2]
— Uraria picta. 1891. III. 490.[1]
— Le Xanthoceras sorbifolia. 1890. ·III. 540.[2]
Lursenius, Philipp Sylvester. De cortice peruviano. 1751. III. 719.
Lusek, P. H. von. Forstliche Beiträge zur Topographie der Domänen Reichenberg. 1838. IV. 370.
Lush, Charles. Note on the identity of three described species of Acacia. 1841. II. 331.[1]
Lushington, Alfred Wyndham. Annual rings in the Nim tree. 1898. II. 421.[3]
— Babul in Guntur. 1896. IV. 521.[1]
— Connection between the roots and leaves of Palms. 1900. II. 63.[2]
— Land reafforested through . . . Prickly Pear. 1893. IV. 529.[1]
— The Palmyra Palm. 1898. II. 65.[1]
— Palmyras.- 1896. IV. 485.[2]
— The qualities of good saws. 1892. IV. 393.
— Timber carting in Surrey. 1892. IV. 389.
— & **Gamble,** J. S. Are the rings of 'Avicennia' wood annual? 1893. II. 753.[2]
Lushington, P. M. Notes on the Sandal tree in southern India. 1900. IV. 519.[2]
— Production of and trade in Teak wood. 1897. III. 697.[2]
Lussana, Filippo. Il Caffè. 1872. III. 739.
— La storia antica del Caffè. 1884. III. 727.
Lusseau, H. Arbustes de pleine terre nouveaux. 1891. III. 84.[1]
— Plantes peu connues à . . . introduire dans le midi. 1892. III. 87.
Lustgärten unn pflantzungen. 1531. \III. 101.[2]
Lutgen, CAPELLE. See CAPELLE-LUTGEN.
Lutgens, G. N. Über Pensylvanien. 1799. IV. 397.
Luther. Dissert. an potus Theae exsiccandi virtute potent. 1702. III. 605.
Luther. Ueber die Feinde der grossen Kiefernraupe. · 1888. IV. 478.
Luther, J. M. De praestantia ligni Quassiae observatio. 1779. III. 508.[3]
— De venenis vegetabilibus in genere. 1792. III. 72.
Lutterkorth, H. See ECKARD, G. E., BOEDECKER, C. & LUTTERKORTH, H.
Lutz, Gotthilf. Die oblito-schizogenen Secretbehälter der Myrtaceen. 1895. III. 620.[1]
Lutz, K. G. Beiträge zur Physiologie der Holzgewächse. 1895. I. 148, 188, 190.[2]
— Das Sapokarbol. 1886. III. 428.[1]
Lutz, Louis Charles. Les cultures de Quinquinas. 1897. III. 712.[2]
— Sur deux Roses prolifères. 1898. II. 290.[1]
— Étude de la gommose chez l'Aralia spinosa. ·1896. II. 648.[1]
— Heritiera littoralis. ‚1898. II. 535.[1]
— Isonandra Gutta. 1898. III. 668.[3]·[1]
— Sur la marche de la gommose dans les Acacias. 1895. II. 323.[2]
— Sur la nutrition azotée. 1898. I. 160.
— Sur la présence . . . dans . . . l'Eriobotrya japonica des principes fournissant l'acide cyanhydrique. 1897. II. 264.[1]
— Sur la présence . . . dans les . . . Pomacées, des principes fournissant l'acide cyanhydrique. 1897. II. 257.[1]
— On the presence . . . in certain pomaceous seeds of the principles producing cyanhydric acid. 1897. II. 257.[1]
— Recherche sur la gommose de l'Aralia spinosa. ·1897. II. 648.[1]
— Recherches sur la nutrition des végétaux à l'aide de substances azotées. 1898. I. 160.
Lutze, Günther. Beiträge zur Flora von Thüringen. 1885. II. 284.[3]
— Flora von Nord-Thüringen. 1892. V. xx.[1]
— Zur Geschichte und Kultur der Blutbuchen. 1892. II. 127.[2]
— Viscum album auf Rosa dumetorum. 1891. II. 179.[2]
Luut, Carl Johan. Flora åkeröensis. See LINNÉ, Carl von. 1769. I. 331.

Luxembourg — Institut royal grand-ducal. *See* Société ĎES SCIENCES NATURELLES DU GRAND-DUCHÉ DE LUXEMBOURG. . 16.

Luxembourg — Société botanique du grand-duché . . . *See* Société . . . I. 16.

Luxembourg — Société des sciences naturelles du grand-duché . . . *See* Société . . . I. 16.

Luxford, George. A. flora . . . of Reigate. 1838. I. 398.

— Notes on the Baobab tree. 1843. II. 529.¹

Luz, Luis Caetano Pereira da Costa. *See* Costa Luz, L. C. P. da.

Luzernerische Forstordnung. 1764. IV. 305.

Luzernische Harzer-Ordnung. 1650. IV. 305.—1751. IV. 305.—1775. IV. 305.

Luzernerische Holzausfuhr-Ordnung. 1775. IV. 406.¹

Luzernerische Verordnung über Kauf und Verkauf der Häute und Felle und in Betreff des Lohmehls. 1756. IV. 305.

Luzernerischer Holzhandel. 1797. IV. 406.¹

Luzernisches Holzausfuhr-Verbot. 1766. IV. 406.¹

Lussiczky, Anton. De vita plantarum. 1842. I. 147.

Lvoff, Th. La gomme de Mélèze. 1858. IV. 452.¹

Lyall, David. Account of the botanical collections. 1864. I. 307.

— Notes on the distribution of the principal trees . . . between the Gulf of Georgia and the Rocky Mountains. 1864. I. 311.¹

Lyceum of natural history of New York. Annals. I. 6.

La lyde champêtre. 1898. IV. 462.¹

Lye, James. On the cross-fertilisation of the Fuchsia. 1900. III. 640.¹

Lyman, C. W. The paper industry and forests. 1900. IV. 430.

Lyman, John Dearborn. An experimental grove of White Pine. 1896. IV. 469.

— A paper on forestry. 1895. IV. 112.

— Practical forestry. 1892. IV. 469.

Lynch, Robert Irwin. Aphelandra cristata. 1889. III. 708.²

— On branch tubers . . . of Vitis gongylodes. 1880. II. 503.¹

— Capparis spinosa. 1886. III. 408.²

— Chrysanthemums. 1884. III. 755.¹

— The evolution of plants. 1900. I. 248.¹

— Fruiting of Ampelopsis Veitchii. 1880. III. 545.¹

— The hardy species of Smilax. 1899. III. 338.¹

— Leonotis Leonurus. 1883. III. 698.¹

— On the mechanism for the fertilization of Meyenia. 1880. I. 804.¹

— Mutisia decurrens. 1883. III. 755.¹

— Myoporum parvifolium. 1883. III. 710.²

— Note on the Blimbing. 1878. II. 392.¹

— Note on the disarticulation of branches. 1878. I. 192.¹

— On the seed-structure . . . of Pahira. 1880. II. 530.²

— Yucca guatemalensis. 1893. II. 88.¹

— *See also* Gardiner, Walter & Lynch, R. I.

Lynden, W. J. E. van. Over de Acacia. 1834. IV. 523.¹

Lyon. Éléments de procédure à l'usage des agents forestiers. 1863. IV. 326.

Lyon. Traitement des futaies. 1868. IV. 129.

Lyon. *See* Duncan, Andrew & Lyon.

Lyon, (*inspecteur de forêts*). Des servitudes de passage. 1867. IV. 334.¹

Lyon, G. H. Barnet. *See* Barnet Lyon, G. H.

Lyon, George Francis. A brief narrative of an unsuccessful attempt to reach Repulse Bay. *See* Hooker, Sir W. J. 1825. I. 308.

Lyon, Patrick. A treatise on the physiology . . . of trees. 1816. I. 146.

Lyon, T. T. Catalogue of fruits of the Michigan state horticultural society. 1879. III. 61.³

— Report on the adaptation of Russian and other fruits. 1888. III. 133.

— The so-called hardy Catalpa. 1886. III. 706.¹

Lyon, W. L. The flora of our south-western archipelago. 1886. I. 336.

Lyon, William S. Australian trees in California. 1890. III. 60.

Lyon — Académie royale des sciences, belles-lettres et arts. *See* Académie . . . I. 20.

Lyon-horticole. III. 20.

Lyon — Société botanique. *See* Société . . . I. 20.

Lyon — Société Linnéenne. *See* Société . . . I. 23.

Lyon — Société royale d'agriculture, histoire naturelle . . . *See* Société . . . I. 24.¹

Lyon — Université. *See* Université . . . I. 24.¹

Lyonet, Pierre. Traité anatomique de la chenille, qui ronge le bois de Saule. 1762. III. 350.¹

Lyonnet. Observations sur les semis et les plantations de quelques arbres utiles. 1815. IV. 121.

Lyons, (*Dublin*). Forestry in Europe and America. 1884. IV. 336.¹

Lyons, Albert Brown. Sur les feuilles de Coca. 1886. III. 493.¹

— Medicinal plants indigenous in Michigan. 1878. III. 62.

— Plant names, scientific and popular. 1900. I. 72.²

Lyons, Israel, (*jr.*). Fasciculus plantarum circa Cantabrigiam. 1763. I. 395.

Lyons, R. D. Forest areas in Europe and America. 1884. IV. 403.¹

— Forestry in connection with agriculture and industry. 1884. IV. 161.¹

— Forestry in Europe and America. 1884. IV. 403.¹

— Re-afforesting of Ireland. 1883. IV. 161.¹

Le lysol. 1891. III. 197.

— m. Die Entwickelung des forstlichen Versuchswesens in Österreich. 1891. IV. 38.²

—m. Forst- und landwirtschaftliche Verhältnisse in Japan. 1892. IV. 376.²

—m. Land- und forstwirtschaftliche Verhältnisse im Kaukasus. 1893. IV. 348.¹

—m. Die Ölwälder etc. auf Korfu. 1891. III. 679.¹

—m. Über das rasche, gründliche Austrocknen der Nutzhölzer. 1895. IV. 416.²

—m. Resultate von Versuchen über die Dauerhaftigkeit imprägnirter Hölzer. 1894. IV. 421.

—m. Die Verwertung der Waldschätze in Siebenbürgen. 1892. IV. 407.¹

—m. Waldungen und Holz-Industrie Bosniens. 1891. IV. 374.²

— m. Waldwirtschaft und Bewaldungsverhältnisse der Erde. 1891. IV. 336.²

—m—. Wald und Waldwirthschaft in Japan. 1890. IV. 376.¹

M. Aanwijzingen over de voortteling der gewassen. 1846. III. 38.²

M. Allgemeine Sätze über die Pflanzenwelt. 1800. I. 146.

M. Das Beschneiden und Aufästen der Waldbäume. 1881. IV. 172.¹

   Conifer grafting. 1885. III. 294.²

   Delabechea rupestris. 1880. II. 532.¹

   The Douglas Fir. 1896. IV. 483.²

M. Einiges über Laubholz-Vorbauhorste. 1887. IV. 142.

M. Die Exkursion in die fürstlich Kinsky'schen Forste. 1856. IV. 370.

M. Exposition universelle de 1900 . . . Données statistiques officielles sur les forêts de France. 1900. IV. 556.¹

M. Forest administration in Madras. 1883. IV. 295.¹

M. Les forêts de la Bavière. 1894. IV. 351.¹

M. Forststatisches aus Bayern. 1894. IV. 351,¹ 555.²

M. Der französische Holzhandel. 1900. IV. 405.²

M. Französisches Forstwesen. 1899. IV. 362.

M. Het groote nut van het aankalken van vruchtboomen. 1900. III. 140.¹

M. Hibiscus rosa sinensis. 1887. III. 588.¹

M. Der Holzhandel Triests. 1898. IV. 407.¹

M. Die Holzschätzung in Absicht auf Masse. 1855. IV. 254.

M. Over het bout van de Robinia Pseudoacacia. 1846. IV. 524.¹

M. Iets over roofbouw en krulloten. 1900. III. 593.²

M. Die Kirschenkrankheit im Altenlande. 1888. III. 435.²

M. Leuthner's Zirkelkluppe. 1890. IV. 231.²

M. Lindenia rivalis. 1881. II. 822.¹

M. The litter of woods. 1876. IV. 71.

M. Los montes de Baviera. 1894. IV. 555.²

M. Über die natürliche Verjüngung der Kiefer. 1895. IV. 474.

   Een niet geind millioen. n. d. III. 725.²

   Note sur les Franciscea. 1848. III. 698.²

   Notwendigkeit der Waldungen. 1897. IV. 52.

   The old Oaks at Thoresby. 1879. II. 138.²

   Pile til Vidier og Fletning. 1870. III. 350.²

   Pine needles. 1885. II. 40.¹

M. Sacred botany. 1850. I. 513.

M. The seeding of Camellia. 1900. III. 600.¹

Eine Silberpappel (Populus alba). 1854. IV. 486.[1]
Terrainbewegungen bei Corticiasca. 1895. IV. 187.[2]
De Thee-cultuur in den Kaukasus. 1890. III. 601.[1]
Transplanting trees and shrubs. 1884. III. 166.
Vorkeimen von Arvensamen. 1896. IV. 464.[1]
M., Waldschutz und Aufforstung in Frankreich. 1900. IV.
464.[2]
M., Weeping trees. 1884. III. 204.[2]
M. Eine Weisstanne von seltener Höhe. 1846. II. 24.[1]
M., A. Aus dem Bakonyerwalde. 1890. IV. 374.[1]
M., A. Bern. Waldbrand im Gadmenthal. 1898. IV.
184.[1]
M., A. The best Conifers for Great Britain. 1874. III.
292.
M., A. Best Cypresses for Britain. 1874. III. 290.
M., A. Le bois d'If. 1894. IV. 558.[1]
M., A. The evergreen Cypress (Cupressus sempervirens).
1871. II. 29.[1]
M., A. La fabrication des allumettes en 1891. 1894. IV.
429.
M., A. Forest scenery in British Columbia. 1873. I. 311.[1]
M., A. The Monterey Cypress. 1872. III. 302.[2]
M., A. Notes on Conifers. 1866. III. 289.
M., A. Trees of the Rocky Mountains. 1873. I. 320, IV.
77.[2]
M., A. B. The Eucalyptus. 1872. III. 633.[2]
M., A. F. Note sur la floraison du Dracaena Goldieana.
See MARION, A. F. 1881. II. 82.[2]
M., B. Blackberries. 1875. II. 306.[1]
M., B. The Catalpa. 1874. II. 786.[2]
M., B. The folklore of the Elder. 1876. II. 840.[1]
M., B. Mistleto as medicine. 1874. III. 385.[1]
M., B. Productos del Pino maritimo. 1885. IV. 468.[1]
M., B. Rosemary. 1875. II. 765.[3]
M., B. Terpentyna. 1884. III. 227.
M., B. The Traveller's Joy. 1875. II. 200.[1]
M., B. The Tulip tree. 1874. II. 210.[2]
M., C. The Areca Palms. 1880. III. 320.[1]
M., C. The Passion-flowers. 1880. III. 615.[2]
M., C. The Scarlet berried Elder. 1879. III. 752.[3] .
M., D. Canary rose woods. 1893. III. 694.[2]
M., D. Cherimoyer. 1887. III. 401.[1]
M., D. Fibre plants. 1887. III. 234.
M., D. The gardeners labyrinth. See MOUNTAINE, Dydy-
mus. 1651. III. 107.
M., D. Instance of teratology in the Brinjai or Egg-plant.
1889. II. 777.[1]
M., D. Mentmore, Buckinghamshire. 1879. IV. 358.[1]
M., D. Oil of Ben. 1887. III. 409.[1]
M., D. de. Las maravillas y la riqueza de la tierra. 1859.
I. 95.
M., E. Berberidopsis corallina. 1894. III. 614.[1]
M., E. De la greffe du Châtaignier sur le Chêne. 1881.
III. 359.[1]
M., E. Ivies. 1889. III. 643.[1]
M., E. L'oiseau semeur. 1893. IV. 74.[1]
M., E. Pyrus japonica as a hedge plant. 1894. III. 420.[2]
M., E. Rendement d'un massif d'Épicéas. 1899. IV.
459,[1] 559.[1]
M., E. M. Forest trees. 1855. I. 511.
M., F. Zur Kultur der Weigelia rosea. 1855. III. 749.[1]
M., F. de. Die Cubikinhalts-Bestimmung der Stammhölzer.
1857. IV. 223.
M., F. d. Die Ermittlung des Holzertrages der Forste.
1855. IV. 235.[2]
M., F. A. Gedanken eines Forstverständigen, über diejen-
igen Unterhaltungsanstalten. 1776. IV. 116.
M., F. W. Rhododendron gloxiniaeflorum. 1893. III.
659.[1]
M., G. Maple with triple samara. 1880. II. 477.[1] .
M., G. E. A plea for protected forests. 1893. IV. 181.[2]
M., G. E. Seeding of Prosopis spicigera. 1888. II. 379.[2]
M., G. G. Taxus adpressa. 1886. III. 288.[1]
M., H. Eenige reizen in de binnenlanden van Borneo. 1838.
III. 276.[1]
M., H. von. Lederkragen als Schutz beim Tragen von Holz.
1896. IV. 390.[1]
M., H. C. Allgemeine praktische Forstnaturgeschichte. See
MOSER, H. C. 1794. IV. 56.[2]
M., I. Een nieuw proces tot extractie van caoutchouc.
1900. III. 232.[2]
M., J. Chêne séculaire. 1842. II. 141.[1]
M., J. Notes from Rewah. 1883. IV. 378.
M., J. Pruning and pollarding trees. 1887. III. 171.

M., J. Les vieux arbres inconnus. 1895. IV. 556.[1]
M., J. The whole art of husbandry. See MORTIMER, John.
1707. III. 108.
M., J. E. d. Houtsoorten van Nederlandsch Indie. 1886.
IV. 400.[1]
M J. G. F.- A note on forest management in Tinnevelly.
1891. IV. 378.
M., J. H. The Common Birch. 1891. IV. 491.[2]
M., J. J. Enfermedad de los Castaños. 1878. IV. 493.[1]
M., L. Promenade à l'Exposition des forêts. 1900. IV.
20.[2]
M., L. A. Arceuthobium shedding its seed. 1872. II. 174.[1]
M., L. B. de. Lettres à Mme. de C. . . . sur la botanique.
See MONTBRISON, L. B. de. 1802. I. 93.
M., L. D. Sketch of the history and sources of Cloves. 1893.
II. 627.[2]
M., M. Beiträge zur Geschichte der Elbflösserei. 1896.
IV. 390.[2]
M., P. Utilisation des aiguilles des Pins. 1900. IV. 463.[1]
M., R. Bambusa nigra. 1885. III. 316.[2]
M., R. Seeding of Strobilanthes on the Nilgiris. 1894. II.
803.[2]
M., R. B. De Kinine-fabriek te Bandoeng. 1899. III. 718.
M., S. Arbres et répartition des essences forestières dans
l'Ouest-Australie. 1897. III. 132.[1]
M., S. The interior of western Australia. 1897. III. 132.[1]
M., T. Bouvardia Humboldtii corymbiflora. 1873. III.
711.[1]
M., T. Chamaedoreas. 1873. III. 321.[2]
M., T. Erica codonodes. 1877. III. 651.[1]
M., T. Hydrangea paniculata grandiflora. 1875. III. 412.[2]
M., T. Hydrangea Thunbergii Sieb. 1870. III. 411.[2]
M., T. Is the Kalmia latifolia poisonous? 1856. III.
652.[2]
M., T. Ligustrum sinense latifolium robustum. 1878. III.
674.[1]
M., T. New Agaves. 1871. III. 340.[2]
M., T. Pelargonium inquinans. 1878. II. 391.[1]
M., T. The stigma of Catalpa. 1883. II. 786.[2] .
M., T. The Weeping Beech. 1870. III. 360.[2]
M., V. Description et culture du Camellia japonica-War-
ratah. 1836. III. 598.[1]
M., V. See also M., B. (Russian alphabet.)
M., V. D. Plantes utiles de la Notasie. 1817. III. 94.[1]
M., V. D. Remarques sur la fève Péchurim. 1816. III.
404.[1]
M., V. D. Thé de Bogota, au Perou. 1817. III. 670.[2]
M., W. Zum Anbaue der Eiche. 1886. IV. 507.
M., W. The Casuarinas. 1874. III. 342.[1]
M., W. Chamaedorea Karwinskiana. 1874. III. 322.[1]
M., W. Chamaerops humilis. 1874. III. 322.[1]
M., W. Cupressus nutkaensis. 1874. III. 301.[1]
M., W. Gordon's Dwarf Fir. 1874. III. 296.[1]
M., W. Peach-leaved Cherry. 1874. III. 439.[1]
M., W. Rosy-flowered Elder. 1874. III. 752.[2]
M., W. Spike-flowered Birch Cherry. 1874. III. 436.[2]
M., W. Tree-clipping in olden times. 1873. III. 202.[2]
M., W. Zur Ueberwinterung der Eicheln. 1887. IV. 507.
M., W. Die Waldbrände in den Karpathenwäldern. 1884.
IV. 184.[1]
., W. J. Culture of Osiers for profit. 1886. III. 349.
., W. T. The Lace bark, or Gauze tree. 1861. III. 628.[1]
., W. T. Renovating specimen Conifers. 1884. III.

M 2.
M9 B. Lewy's expedition to New Grenada. 1852. I. 339.[2]
A M. kir. erdészeti kisérleti állomások működési szabályzata.
1898. IV. 39.[1]
M—. Wälder und Waldverteilung im europäischen Russ-
land. 1891. IV. 346.
M—n. Waldwirthschaft und Wildbachregulirung in Frank-
reich. 1897. IV. 122.[1]
M—r. Die Bestandespflege der Eiche. 1897. IV. 508.
M—r. Der Mineralstoffgehalt in der Fichte. 1875. IV.
459.[2]
M—s. Die Gummibildung im Holze. 1885. I. 181.[1]
M-tcha. See M-ya.
M**. Fruit-tuin Nederlansch Indië. 1857. III. 91.[2]
M**. Jardin fruitier des Indes Néerlandaises. 1857. III.
91.[2]
Ma. Verhalten des neuholländischen Gummibaumes gegen
Kälte. 1878. IV. 532.[2]
Maack, Richard. See also MAACK, P. K.
Maack, Theodor. Der sicherste Schutz gegen die Reblaus.
1885. III. 573.

Maandschrift voor tuinbouw. III. 14.
Maass, G. Mittelform zwischen Crataegus Oxyacantha L. und C. monogynus. 1886. II. 262.²
— Rubus glaucovirens. 1870. II. 307.²
— Rubus sulcatus Vest var. Schulzei Maass. 1884. II. 310.²
Maatschappij ter bevordering van den landbouw te Amsterdam. Verhandelingen. III. 14.
Mabee, T. E. Conifers. 1899. III. 293.
Mabague, V. Les irrigations et le sulfure de carbone. 1879. III. 563.
Mabery, Charles Frederic. On the products of the dry distillation of wood. 1883. I. 155.
Mabille. Vignes préservées de la gelée par la fumée. 1858. III. 549.¹
Mabille, Paul. Catalogue des plantes . . . de Dinan et de Saint-Malo. 1866. I. 413.
— Recherches sur les plantes de la Corse. 1867. I. 419.¹
Mabille, LE ROY-. See LE ROY-MABILLE.
M'Afee, H. H. Instructions for procuring . . . tree seeds and trees. 1876. IV. 111.²
— Report of committee on forestry. 1875. IV. 111.²
Macagno, H. Note relative to the production of tannin in the leaves of Sumac. 1880. III. 526.²
Macagno, Ippolito. Action de la lumière solaire . . . sur la Vigne. 1877. II. 508.¹
— Alcune ricerche sulla funzione fisiologica delle foglie della Vite. 1877. II. 508.²
— Sur une maladie du raisin. 1877. III. 577.
— Recherches sur les fonctions des feuilles de la Vigne. 1877. II. 508.²
— Researches on the physiological function of the Vine-leaves. 1877. II. 508.²
— Sopra talune alterazioni del succo di Limone. 1881. II. 408.¹ III. 502.²
— Transformations subies par le jus de Citron. 1881. III. 502.²
Macaire. La richesse forestière de la Côte d'Ivoire. 1900. IV. 379.¹
Macaire-Prinsep, Isaac François. Mémoire sur la coloration automnale. 1828. I. 185.¹
— Mémoire sur la viscine. 1833. II. 178.³
— Note sur l'action des gaz nuisibles. 1830. III. 185.¹
— & Marcet, François. Extrait d'une note sur une matière grasse produite par le Vateria. 1830. III. 611.³
Macaire-Prinsep, J. Analyse du vernis de la Chine. 1826. III. 526.³
— On the direction assumed by plants. 1848. I. 193.²
Macalister, Alexander & McNab, W. R. Guide to the county of Dublin. 1878. I. 403.
McAlpine, Daniel. Bakterienkrankheit der Maulbeerbäume. 1898. III. 379.²
— Fungus diseases of Citrus trees in Australia. 1899. III. 498.²
— The sooty mould of Citrus trees. 1896. III. 498.²
— & Remfrey, J. R. The transverse sections of petioles of Eucalypts. 1891. II. 623.²
M'Andrew, James. List of the flowering plants of Dumfries-shire. 1882. I. 534.¹
Macar, de. La flore et les cultures du Congo. 189.? I. 492.¹
McArthur, D. On the importance of forestry. 1883. IV. 270.
Macarthur, W. Barked tree stems. 1857. III. 180.¹
Macarthur, William & Moore, Charles. Catalogue des collections de bois indigènes. 1855. IV. 401.³
Macaulay, James. Notes on the physical geography . . . of Madeira. 1840. I. 497.
Macauley, Mary E. See BECKWITH, Florence, MACAULEY, M. E. & FULLER, J. B.
McBride, H. Diervilla candida. 1889. III. 749.¹
McBride, Robert Wesley. Some queries relative to a supposed variety of Solanum Dulcamara. 1894. II. 776.¹
McBride, Thomas Huston. Abstract of a paper on Pear blight. 1891. III. 446.²
— Forestry notes for Dubuque county. 1900. I. 321, IV. 78.²
— Forestry notes for Humboldt county. 1899. I. 321, IV. 78.²
— A key to the . . . plants occurring in the northern United States. 1898. I. 316.
— North American Cycads. 1894. II. 2.¹
— Notes on forest distribution in Iowa. 1896. I. 320, IV. 78.²
— Rhus typhina Linn. 1894. II. 460.¹

McCallum, C. A list of specimens of woods from Australia. 1850. IV. 17.
McCalman, Godfrey. A natural, commercial and medicinal treatise on tea. 1787. III. 606.
M'Cann, Hugh W. Report on the dyes and tans of Bengal. 1883. III. 278.
McCartee, & Fortune, Robert. Chinese white wax. 1857. III. 226.¹
McCartee, D. B. On some wild silkworms of China. 1866. III. 143.¹
MacCartee, Robert. The Long-leaf Pine. 1889. IV. 467.¹
M'Carthy, C. The production of Sandalwood. 1900. IV. 519.³
McCarthy, Gerald. Seed testing. 1894. III. 157.
— See also WOOD, T. F. & McCARTHY, Gerald.
Maccarthy, Robert, comte de. Opinion sur l'aliénation des bois dits de l'état. 1817. IV. 326.
Maccary, Ange. Sur la maladie forficulaire du Mûrier. 1810. III. 373.
Macchiati, Luigi. Sull' accrescimento intercalare della Lonicera. 1883. II. 838.²
— Ancora sugli anestetici delle piante. 1883. I. 211.
— Sulla biologia del Bacillus Baccarinii. 1897. III. 581.
— Caratteri delle principali varietà di Viti. 1888. III. 547.
— Catalogo di pronubi delle piante. 1884. I. 238.
— Sui così detti tubercoli gemini . . . delle Papilionacee. 1897. II. 321.¹
— Esperienze sulla emissione dell' acido carbonico dalle radici. 1879. I. 170.
— Die Farbstoffe der Fichtenzapfen. 1889. IV. 459.³
— I nettarii estraflorali delle Amigdalacee. 1886. II. 271.² III. 482.²
— Nota preventiva di biologia sul fiore del Castagno indiano. 1900. II. 482.²
— Noterelle di biologia fiorale. 1900. II. 834.²
— Osservazioni sui nettarii estranuziali del Prunus Laurocerasus. 1899. II. 274.²
— Prima contribuzione alla flora del Viterbese. 1888. I. 429.
— Ricerche preliminari sulle sostanze coloranti . . . del Castagno indiano. 1890. II. 482.³
— Le sostanze coloranti degli strobili dell' Abies excelsa. 1889. II. 36.²
— Sulle sostanze coloranti gialle e rosse. 1890. I. 185.³
— Studio delle modificazioni che le frutta nelle varie fasi di sviluppo inducono nell' atmosfera. 1879. I. 170.
— Ufficio dei peli . . . dell' Ailanthus. 1899. II. 414.¹
Macchina a doppia azione per la fabbricazione della lana vegetale. 1886. IV. 429.¹
Macchina per sbucciare i vimini. 1890. IV. 434.
McClatchie, Alfred James. Additions to the flora of Los Angeles. 1894. I. 326.
— Eucalypti [in Arizona]. 1899. IV. 530.
— Flora of Pasadena. 1895. I. 326.
M'Clelland, John. Indian turpentine. 1842. IV. 464.²
— A list of the principal trees in the forests of Pegu. 1857. III. 277.
— Papers relating to . . . the cultivation of the Tea plant in India. 1839. III. 602.²
— Report of the Geological survey of India. 1850. I. 472.
— Report on the physical condition of the Assam Tea plant. 1837. III. 602.¹
M'Clue, T. B. Grapes. 1899. III. 551.¹
McCluer, G. W. See BURRILL, T. J. & McCLUER, G. W.
McCormick, J. M. The Big Trees. 1897. II. 46.¹
McCorquodale, D. Are trees injured or benefited by the decomposition of the prunings? 1880. IV. 171.
— Deterioration of Scotch Fir. 1880. IV. 473.
— Forest fires. 1882. IV. 181.²
— To protect trees from rabbits. 1881. IV. 198.¹
— The thinning and pruning. 1882. IV. 172.¹
— See also CHISHOLM, J. & McCORQUODALE, D.
McCorquodale, William. Abies Douglasii. 1880. IV. 483.¹
— On the conversion of coppice land. 1868. IV. 506.
— On the diseases of the Larch. 1863. IV. 450.
— Durability of Silver Fir. 1888. IV. 446.³
— Durability of the Silver Fir as railway sleepers. 1888. IV. 424.¹
— On the education of foresters. 1881. IV. 34.¹
— On judicious pruning. 1884. IV. 172.¹
— The Silver Fir. 1881. IV. 444.³
— Silver Fir for railway sleepers. 1878. IV. 446.³
— Spruce timber. 1878. IV. 459.²
— On successful planting with Scotch Fir. 1863. IV. 472.
— See also McLAREN, John & McCORQUODALE, William.

M'Coy, H. D. What shall we plant? 1900. III. 182.
M'crie, Thomas & others. The Bass Rock. *See* BALFOUR, J. H. 1848. I. 533.
McCulloch, R. W. Coffee-growing. 1893. III. 727.
McDonald, Alexander, (*pseud.*). A complete dictionary of practical gardening. 1807. III. 31.
— Practical agriculture. 1807. III. 109.
McDonald, Charles. Araucaria imbricata. 1873. III. 298.²
Macdonald, George & Allen, James. The botanist's word-book. 1853. I. 71.
Macdonald, George U. *See* BAILEY, Frederick & MACDONALD, G. U.
McDonald, J. E. Encephalartos Moorei. 1881. II. 6.³
Macdonald, John. On three natural productions of Sumatra. 1795. III. 611.¹
MacDonald, W. Forest conservation. 1895. IV. 181.²
— Our timber trees and forest culture. 1894. IV. 380.²
McDonell, J. C. Artificial reproduction of Deodar. 1885. IV. 447.²
— Cones of Pinus longifolia. 1885. IV. 464.¹
— Deodar reproduction. 1887. II. 27.¹
— Experience in the germination of acorns. 1880. IV. 500.²
— Forests in the Telbal Valley, Kashmir. 1896. IV. 378.
— Report on the Bakani slide. 1886. IV. 390.³
— Stick making. 1891. IV. 428.¹
— Table showing periods of ripening seeds of Conifers in the Himalayas. 1886. II. 21.¹
— A tour through Kishtwar. 1896. IV. 378.
— A trip through Chamba. 1882. I. 475.¹
— Weight of Deodar seed. 1882. IV. 447.²
Macdonell, J. C. *See also* BADEN-POWELL, B. H. & MAC-DONELL, J. C.
MacDougal, Daniel Trembly. A contribution to the physiology of tendrils. 1898. II. 356.¹
— Copper in plants. 1899. II. 135.²
— Ueber die Mechanik . . . Krümmungsbewegungen der Ranken. 1896. I. 197.¹
— The mechanism of curvature of tendrils. 1896. I. 197.¹
— The mechanism of movement. 1896. I. 197.²
— The movements of plants. 1897. I. 194.
— The nature and work of plants. 1900. I. 149.¹
— The physiology of tendrils. 1896. I. 197.¹
— Seed dissemination . . . of Razoumofskya. 1899. II. 174.²
— The tendrils of Passiflora coerulea. 1892. II. 578.¹
— Titles of literature concerning the fixation of free nitrogen. 1894. I. 160.
— Transmission of impulses in Biophytum. 1899. II. 392.¹
— *See also* ARTHUR, J. C. & MacDOUGAL, D. T.
MacDougall, Robert Stewart. The bjology . . . of Scolytus. 1899. IV. 205.¹
— The biology of the genus Pissodes. 1899. III. 192.¹
— The genus Pissodes and its importance in forestry. 1898. IV. 208.²
— Insect attacks in 1898–99. 1899. III. 192.¹
— The Pine Geometer moth. 1897. IV. 462.¹
— Report for 1898. 1898. III. 191.
McDowall, A. Cultivation of Kaurie pine. 1882. V. xxxii.³
— & Hooper, E. D. M. Kauri pine plantation. 1885. V. xxxii.³
Macé, Charles. Du Café. 1853. III. 741.³
Macedo, A. de. Notice sur le Palmier Carnauba. 1867. III. 324.³
Macedo, J. T. de. Estudio historico sobre a cultura da La-rangeira. 1855. III. 499.³
Macedo Soares, Antonio Joaquin de. O Mate do Paraná. 1875. III. 531.¹
Maceira, Antonio GARCÍA. *See* GARCÍA MACEIRA, Antonio.
MacElroy, F. C. The reconstruction of our forests. 1857. IV. 155.¹
MacElwee, Alexander. The flora of the Edgehill Ridge. 1900. I. 317.¹
Mac Encroe. *See* LA CROIX, Demetrius de, (*pseud. of* Mac Encroe).
Macer, Aemilius. *See* MACER FLORIDUS.
Macer Floridus, (*pseud.* for ODO. I. 272¹). De herbarum virtutibus. n. d. I. 274.¹
— Macer's Herbal practysyd by Doctor Lynacro. n. d. I. 274.¹
— De materia medica libri V. n. d. I. 274.¹
— A newe herball of Macer. n. d. I. 274.¹
— De viribus herbarum. n. d. I. 274,¹ V. xiv.¹
— De virtutibus herbarum. n. d. I. 274.¹
MacErlean, John. *See* HOGAN, F. E., HOGAN, John & MacERLEAN, John.

Mac Ewan, Peter. Essence de Wintergreen. 1886. III. 652.¹
— Huile de Ruscus ou de Bouleau. 1884. IV. 491.²
M'Ewen, George. The culture of the Peach and Nectarine. 1859. III. 440.²
McEwen, M. C. The comparative anatomy of Corema. 1894. II. 453.²
McEwin, George. On the natural forests of South Australia. 1884. I. 499,³ IV. 89.³
Macfadyen, James. The flora of Jamaica. 1837. I. 335.
— List of plants growing in the plain of Liguanea. 1841. I. 335.
— On the plants . . . for the formation of fences in . . . Jamaica. 1833. III. 214.³
— Some remarks on the species of the genus Citrus. 1830. II. 401.¹
Macfarlan, A. J. Remarks on the applications of photography to botany. 1858. I. 37.¹
McFarland, John Horace. A Japanese success. 1890. III. 502.³
McFarland, N. C. Instructions for making final proof on timber culture entries. 1882. IV. 155,¹ 314.³
Macfarlane, John Muirhead. A comparison of the minute structure of plant hybrids. 1892. I. 100,² 246.¹
— An examination of some Ericas. 1893. II. 664.²
— Hybrid Ribes. 1900. II. 244.³
— Notes on the structure . . . of Cytisus Adami. 1890. II. 368.³
McG., W. *See* MACGILLIVRAY, William.
Mac Gibbon, J. Catalogue of plants in the Botanic garden, Cape Town. 1858. I. 69.¹
McGill, Anthony. Notes on the analysis of coffee. 1887. III. 740.²
Macgillivray, John. Letter from Sidney. 1854. I. 501.
— Narrative of the voyage of H. M. S. Rattlesnake. 1852. I. 536.³
— Some remarks on the Sandal-wood. 1862. IV. 519.¹
Macgillivray, Paul Howard. A catalogue of the flowering plants . . . of Aberdeen. 1853. I. 400.
Macgillivray, Wilham. Description of a . . . Salix found in Braemar. 1830. II. 108.¹
— Essay on the nature and quality of soils. 1829. III. 40.
— A manual of botany. 1840. I. 88.
— The natural history of Dee-Side and Braemar. 1855. I. 400.
— Notice respecting the existence of Fraxinus excelsior. 1830. II. 707.²
— Remarks on Mr. Nicol's Observations on the structure of . . . Coniferae. 1834. II. 16.¹
— Remarks on the phenogamic vegetation of the River Dee. 1832. I. 398.
Macgowan. Note on certain Chinese plants. 1886. III. 273.¹
McGowan, A. T. Tea planting in the outer Himalayah. 1861. III. 603.
Macgowan, Daniel J. Additional information regarding the "Ghú Má." 1850. III. 382.¹
— Der chinesische Talgbaum. 1850. III. 522.¹
— Ueber den Gebrauch von Stillingia sebifera. 1850. III. 522.¹
— Notices regarding the plants yielding . . . grass-cloth. 1848. III. 381.³
— On the Tallow tree 1852. III. 522.³
— On the Tallow tree . . . and the pela. 1864. III. 522.²
— Uses of the Stillingia sebifera. 1850. III. 522.¹
MacGregor, Atholl. Memorandum on the Conolly Teak plantations. 1877. IV. 536.³
Macgregor, James L. Laird. The organization and valuation of forests. 1883. IV. 257.
— Remarks on the new edition of D'Arcy's "Forest working-plans in India." 1896. IV. 250.³
McGregor, John. On the deterioration of the Larch. 1881. IV. 451.
McGrew, James. Cultivation of the Osage Orange. 1855. III. 372.¹
Mach, E. *See* BABO, A., *Freiherr* von & MACH, E.
Mach, Ernst. Zusammenstellung der für den Oenologen wichtigsten Pilzformen. 1875. III. 577.
Machacka, Karl Borromaeus. Conspectus geognostico-botanicus circuli boleslaviensis. 1843. I. 440.
Machado, Carlos Maria Gomes. Catalogo methodico das plantas observadas em Portugal. 1868. I. 421.
Machado, Juan DIAZ. *See* DIAZ MACHADO, Juan.
Machara, Joh. & Tobias, Mich. Schätzung lund Gutachten über den . . . Wald Hlucha. 1865. IV. 335.

Machielse, A. Brief over bestrijding van de Koffiebladziekte. 1880. III. 735.
Machine Ransome pour l'abatage des arbres. *See* RANSOME's patent steam tree-feller. 1878. IV. 383.²
Machray, John. Remarks on the propagating ... by cuttings. 1827. III. 152.
Machtholf, Christian J. F. Specimen ... exhibens ... corticis peruviani ... usum. 1792. III. 720.
Machts, Ferdinand. Der Landwirth als Forstmann. 1877. IV. 111.¹
Macie, James Louis. An account of some chemical experiments on Tabasheer. 1791. II. 59.¹
McIntire, A. L. Manual of forestry prepared for use in the Simla district. 1895. IV. 100.¹
McIntire, Samuel John. Notes on some of the scale insects. 1889. III. 188.¹
McIntosh, Angus. The Ash-bark beetle. 1884. IV. 535.²
— The common Alder. 1881. IV. 489.¹
— On the comparative advantages of pitting. 1880. IV. 152.
— Pruning neglected forest trees. 1879. IV. 171.
— On the selection of plants for general planting. 1881. IV. 152.
McIntosh, Charles. British Oaks, their species. 1849. III. 361.¹
— Flora and pomona. 1829. III. 81.
— The flower-garden. 1838. III. 82.
— The greenhouse, hot house and stove. 1838. III. 82.
— The Larch disease. 1860. IV. 450.
— The new and improved practical gardener. 1828. III. 109.
— The orchard. 1839. III. 142.
— The practical gardener and modern horticulturist. 1828. III. 109.
Mc'Intosh, J. The Misseltoe (Viscum album). 1851. II. 178.¹
MacIntosh, William. The best ... system for the afforestation of waste . . . lands. 1885. IV. 161.¹
M'Intosh, William Carmichael. The boring of marine animals in timber. 1884. IV. 414.³
McIvor, William Graham. Brief hints for the culture in India, of fruit trees. 1854. III. 147.¹
— Notes on the propagation ... of the medicinal Cinchonas. 1863. III. 712.¹
— Observations on the germination . . . of the medicinal Chinchonas. 1867. III. 714.
— Progress of the cultivation of Cinchonas on the Neilgherries. 1863. III. 713.³
— Report on the cultivation of Chinchonas in southern India. 1862. III. 713.³
— Report on the Government . . . gardens, Ootacamund. 1849. I. 66.¹
— Report on the Horticultural garden, Ootacamund. 1849. I. 66.¹
— Report on the vegetable resources ... of Malabar. 1857. III. 278.
— & **Howard,** J. E. Analysis of Cinchona bark. 1864. III. 722.
Mack, R. A. Gamboge of Burma. 1885. III. 609.¹
— Gamboge of Burmah. 1887. III. 609.³
Mackay, George Grant. Plantations on the estate of Glengloy. 1880. IV. 359.¹
MacKay, George Leslie. From far Formosa. 1896. I. 463.¹
Mackay, James Townsend. A brief view of the botany of Ireland. 1838. I. 398.
— Catalogue of plants, Upper Clapton. 1828. I. 54.
— A catalogue of the plants found in Ireland. 1825. I. 397.
— Flora hibernica. 1836. I. 398.
— A systematic catalogue of rare plants found in Ireland. 1806. I. 396.
Mackay, John. Remarks on the oidium. 1863. III. 577.
McKay, Richard & others. Vegetabilia. *See* A CONTRIBUTION ... 1876. I. 402.
M'Kee, Andrew W. The Grape and wine-culture of California. 1859. III. 550.
McKee, J. A. Forest administration in the Central Provinces. 1876. IV. 295.¹
— On the formation of lac preserves. 1876. III. 227.
— On grazing. 1876. IV. 136.¹
McKee, Thos. J. Some facts regarding freshets. 1890. IV. 184.³
M'Ken, M. J. Natal fibres. 1865. III. 234.
Mackenzie. Notice of the produce of the Olive crop. 1858. III. 678.²

Mackenzie, A. Azalea indica. 1882. III. 660.¹
M'Kenzie, Alexander. Boulevard and promenade trees. 1880. III. 209.
— The proposed school of forestry at Epping forest. 1881. IV. 34.¹
— Voyages from Montreal ... through the continent of North America. 1802. I. 309.³
Mackenzie, Colin. Report relative to plantations on the estate of Kilcoy. 1837. IV. 358.²
McKenzie, D. F. On the age at which various timber trees ... may be ... felled. 1878. IV. 384.¹
— On the cheapest ... means of clearing land for planting. 1878. III. 150.³
— Comparative value of timber trees grown in Britain. 1884. IV. 398.²
— On the disease of the Larch. 1878. IV. 450.
— The education of young foresters. 1879. IV. 29.
— Effects of the snowstorms of 1878–9. 1879. IV. 190.
— On establishing an experimental forest area in Scotland. 1898. IV. 38.¹
— The identification of timber. 1900. I. 126, *IV. 63.*¹
— The last Oaks of Birnam. 1878. IV. 515.¹
— Notes on the physiology and structure of trees. 1895. I. 126.
— The plantations on the estates of Murthly. 1881. IV. 59.¹
— On the planting of deer forests. 1881. IV. 136.²
— Preserving timber. 1898. IV. 421.
— Scottish timber and uses. 1884. IV. 398.²
— Sections of woods grown in Britain. 1895. I. 126.
— The timber of exotic Conifers. 1892. IV. 443.¹
— The timber trees of the future. 1878. IV. 396.¹
— On the use of dynamite and tonite in forestry. 1878. III. 50.¹
— The valuation of standing and other timber. 1881. IV. 56.
Mackenzie, George Stewart. Travels in the island of Iceland. 1812. I. 352.
Mackenzie, Keith W. Stewart. Report on plantations on the estate of Fairburn. 1855. IV. 358.²
Mackenzie, Peter. An experiment in planting. 1848. III. 169.³
— Observations on inverted growth. 1851. I. 196.¹
Mackenzie, W. A. The afforestation of large areas. 1893. IV. 161.¹
— The island of Arran as a field for planting. 1893. IV. 59.¹
Mackenzie, William. Report of improvements at Ardross. 1859. IV. 358.²
— Report on the plantations of Muirton. 1841. IV. 358.²
Mackenzie's dendrometer. 1884. IV. 215.
Mackie, J. *See* MACKIE, W. A. & J.
Mackie, J. M. Culture of the Vine. 1839. III. 559.¹
Mackie, W. A. & J. A catalogue of forest trees, fruit trees. 1812. III. 28.¹
Mackinlay, George. Sequoia gigantea. 1897. III. 310.²
Mackintosh, Charles. Old and remarkable trees of Scotland. 1864. I. 296.²
Macklot, H. C. Verslag van het land ... van Nieuw Guinea. 1830. III. 282.¹
McLachlan, Robert. Eucalyptus galls. 1880. IV. 530.²
— Galls on Eucalyptus. 1880. IV. 530.²
— Insect pests of Orange trees. 1884. III. 501.¹
Maclagan. Note. 1860. III. 34.²
Maclagan, Andrew Douglas. On the Bebeeru tree. 1843. III. 407.¹
— Ueber den Bebeerubaum des brittischen Guiana. 1843. II. 227,¹ III. 407.¹
— On "gutta percha." 1845. III. 228.²
— On the medicinal qualities of the Bebeeru bark. 1843. III. 407.¹
— Notice of two cases of poisoning with ... Thevetia. 1857. III. 691.³
— Notice regarding the Bebeeru tree. 1845. III. 407.¹
— Poisoning with the seeds of Thevetia. 1857. III. 691.³
— & **Gamgee,** Arthur. On the alkaloids contained in the wood of Bebeeru. 1869. III. 407.³
— & **Tilley,** T. G. On the constitution of bebeerine. 1845. III. 407.¹
Maclagan, Philip Whiteside. Notice of plants collected in the line of the Rideau canal, Canada west. 1847. I. 310.
Maclagan, Robert C. Two historical fallacies. 1900. III. 649,¹ *IV. 491.*³
McLaren, J. The diseases of the Larch. 1881. IV. 451.

McLaren, John. The Beech. 1881. IV. 495.
— On the Corsican Pine. 1869. IV. 465.²
— Forest and ornamental trees of recent introduction. 1884. III. 78.²
— & **McCorquodale**, William. Has Scotch Fir deteriorated? 1881. IV. 473.
Maclaurin, Archibald. Essay on hedges. 1816. III. 212.¹
Maclay, N. de MIKLOUHO-. See MIKLOUHO-MACLAY, N. de.
Maclean, Evan. The culture of trees on the margin of streams. 1885. IV. 121.
MacLean, James. List and description of Borneo woods. 1886. IV. 400.¹
McLean, John. The collection . . . of forest tree seeds. 1884. IV. 148.
— Natural reproduction of forests. 1887. IV. 140.
Macleay. Oorzaak van de sterfte veler Ijpenboomen. 1837. III. 364.¹
Macleay, William. Observations on an insect injurious to the Vine. 1883. III. 563.
Macleay, William Sharp. Abstract of a report on the state of the Elm trees in St. James's and Hyde parks. 1824. III. 363.²
MacLellan, Alex. Specimen Caryota at Newport. 1900. III. 321.¹
McLendon, S. G. The Georgia Pine. 1890. IV. 467.¹
McLeod, John. On the management of Oak-coppice. 1858. IV. 505.
MacLeod, Julius. Over de bevruchting der bloemen. 1893. I. 239.²
— Sur la fécondation des fleurs. 1893. I. 239.²
— De onderzoekingen van H. Muller. 1885. I. 238.
— Untersuchungen über die Befruchtung. 1885. I. 239.²
— Untersuchungen über die Befruchtung der Blumen. 1887. I. 238.
— De verspreiding der planten. 1887. I. 240.²
McLeran, Benjamin. Louisiana state forest exhibit. 1885. IV. 19.¹
Macloskie, George. Elementary botany. 1883. I. 101.¹
— Stomates on seeds. 1885. I. 131.²
Maclou, Alexander. Du reboisement des parcs et des semis d'arbres. 1870. III. 156.¹
M'Mahon, Bernard. The American gardener's calendar. 1806. III. 99.
— A catalogue of American seeds. 1804. III. 63.¹
MacMahon, Philip. Our botanic gardens. 1897. I. 69.²
— Coffee-leaf disease. 1898. III. 736.
— Sowing Logwood seeds. 1898. III. 478.²
— Spraying tall trees. 1900. III. 198.²
MacMaster, Bryce. On the woods used for sleepers on the Madras railway. 1863. IV. 423.²
MacMillan, Conway. On the formation of circular muskeag. 1896. I. 326.
— The Metaspermae of the Minnesota valley. 1892. I. 316.
— Minnesota plant life. 1899. I. 327.
— Observations on the distribution of plants along shore at Lake of the Woods. 1897. I. 327.
— Some duplicate binomials. 1892. I. 254.¹
Macmillan, H. Holidays in high lands. 1873. I. 436, 535.
Macmillan, H. F. Fruits suitable for the low country. 1899. III. 92.¹
— Selected trees suitable for shade. 1900. III. 92,¹ 129.²
Macmillan, L. J. Cinchona cultivation in Ceylon. 1878. III. 714.
Macmillan's magazine. IV. 539.²
McMinn, J. M. See SAUNDERS, William, COPE, F. J. & McMinn, J. M.
McMullan, C. Epiphyllums. 1890. III. 623.¹
McMurray, John. On the Chinese mode of making green dye. 1857. III. 542.¹
— Treatment of Amherstia nobilis. 1857. III. 466.¹
McMurtrie, R. C. Osage Orange hedges. 1880. III. 372.¹
McMurtrie, William. Report on the culture of Sumac in Sicily. 1880. III. 526.¹
Macnab, James. Account of the rarer plants. 1835. I. 306.
— Arboricultural notes from Perth. 1874. III. 123.¹
— The autumn tints of trees. 1876. III. 207.¹
— Birds and berries. 1878. III. 208.¹
— Climatic changes in Scotland. 1874. III. 123.¹
— On the colour of certain species of Cupressineae. 1873. II. 20.³
— Cotoneaster microphylla. 1873. III. 421.¹
— On cutting large evergreen shrubs. 1867. III. 173.¹
— Deciduous trees in winter. 1875. I. 294.²

— On the discoveries of Mr. John Jeffrey. 1872. II. 14.¹
— Disfiguration of roadside trees. 1873. III. 212.¹
— On the disfigurement of trees along roadsides. 1873. III. 212.¹
— On the economical uses of the roots of coniferous plants. 1859. IV. 443.²
— On the economical uses of the roots of coniferous trees. 1859. IV. 443.²
— Effects of lightning on trees. 1851. IV. 193.³
— On the effects of pruning certain coniferous trees. 1872. III. 295.¹
— On the effects of the late severe winter. 1860. III. 46.²
— On the effects produced by stem pruning the Nidpath Castle Yew. 1873. III. 288.¹
— On the flowering of a variety of Crataegus Oxyacantha. 1859. II. 262.²
— The French Tamarisk tree. 1873. III. 612.¹
— On the growth of the Bamboo-cane. 1859. II. 59.²
— Hardy ericaceous plants. 1874. III. 647.¹
— Holly in flower at Christmas. 1877. II. 463.²
— Ivy-clad trees. 1875. III. 642.²
— Note on the fruiting of Holly. 1877. II. 463.²
— Notes on pruning certain evergreens. 1876. III. 173.¹
— Notes on the "Dogwood" of powder manufacturers. 1870. IV. 528.¹
— Notes on the propagation of the Ipecacuan plant. 1870. III. 747.¹
— Notice of an Ash tree struck by lightning. 1862. IV. 193.³
— Notice of Sabal umbraculifera. 1874. III. 331.¹
— Notice of trees struck by lightning. 1858. IV. 193.²
— Old trees at Hampton court. 1873. I. 297.¹
— Planting to produce landscape effects. 1874. III. 201.
— Plants for railway hedges. 1872. III. 213.
— Propagating Yuccas. 1872. III. 339.²
— Pruning coniferous trees and shrubs. 1872. III. 295.¹
— Pruning Conifers. 1872. III. 295.¹
— On pruning the Redwood. 1875. III. 310.²
— A ramble in Arran. 1873. II. 23.²
— Remarks on some seedling Coniferae. 1866. III. 294.¹
— Remarks on the old trees . . . at Hampton Court. 1873. I. 297.¹
— Remarks on the specimens of Araucaria imbricata. 1862. III. 298.²
— Report on the effects of the late frost. 1861. III. 46.²
— Results obtained from the cutting . . . of a plaited Horn-beam hedge. 1870. III. 213.
— On the re-tubbing of Palms. 1873. III. 317.
— Re-tubbing Palms. 1873. III. 317.
— On stem-pruning certain coniferous trees. 1867. III. 295.¹
— Swollen stemmed Irish Yews. 1873. III. 10.¹
— Thuja occidentalis ericoides. 1868. II. 52.²
— Sur la transplantation des arbustes et arbres vert. 1850. III. 169.¹
— Transplanting deciduous trees in full leaf. 1876. III. 168.²
— Transplanting Hollies. 1875. III. 529.²
— M'Nab's transplanting machine. 1861. III. 167.
— On transplanting moderate sized evergreen shrubs. 1850. III. 169.¹
— Transplanting trees. 1878. III. 167.
— Tree management in and near towns. 1874. III. 209.
— Tree-transplanting. 1861. III. 167.
— Ueber das Verpflanzen immergrüner Sträucher. 1850. III. 169.¹
M'Nab, William. De Capske Erikers Kultur. 1832. III. 649.²
— Ueber die Cultur der capischen Erica-Arten. 1832. III. 649.²
— Hints on the planting . . . of hardy evergreens. 1830. III. 106.²
— Some account of a suspended plant of Ficus australis. 1820. II. 153.¹
— A treatise on the propagation . . . of Cape Heaths. 1832. III. 649.¹
— Winke über das Pflanzen . . . immergrüner Sträucher. 1830. III. 106.¹
McNab, William Ramsay. On the anatomical structure of the leaf . . . of Abies. 1877. II. 21.³
— On the development of leaves. 1866. I. 190,² 191.²
— On the development of the flowers of Welwitschia. 1873. II. 55.³
— On the growth of the roots of Coniferous trees after being felled. 1871. I. 209.²

— Leaf structure of Conifers. 1875. II. 17.[3]
— The movements of fluids in stems. 1878. IV. 416.[1]
— Note on Abies Pattoni Jeffrey mss. 1851. 1882. II. 53.[2]
— Note on the botanical topographical divisions of Ireland. 1885. I. 403.
— Notes on the synonymy . . . of Abies. 1876. II. 21.[3]
— Notice relative to the transmission of foreign-seeds in soil. 1852. III. 154.[2]
— On the parts involved in the process of defoliation. 1866. I. 190,[1] 191.[1]
— On a peculiarity in the structure . . . of Hedera. 1868. II. 649.[2]
— Remarks on the structure of the leaves of certain Coniferae. 1875. II. 17,[1] 53.[1]
— Report on the arctic drift woods. 1882. I. 242.[2]
— A revision of the species of Abies. 1875. II. 21.[3]
— Das Versenden der Samen in Erde. 1852. III. 154.[2]
— See also MACALISTER, A. & McNAB, W. R.
McNeill, James. On dry-rot in Larch and Spruce Fir. 1863. IV. 442.
— On the felling of timber. 1863. IV. 384.[1]
McNeill, N. Report on the cultivation of Cinchona in Java. 1887. III. 716.
M'Nicoll, David Hudson. Dictionary of natural history terms. 1863. I. 71.
Macomber, J. K. The relation of forest to climate. 1876. IV. 53.
Maconet, DUPUITS DE, (jr.). See DUPUITS DE MACONET, (jr.).
Macoun, James Melville. Check list of Canadian plants. 1889. I. 310.
— Contributions from the herbarium of the Geological survey of Canada. 1894. I. 311.[1]
— Contributions to Canadian botany. 1894. I. 311.[1]
— The forest wealth of Canada. 1900. IV. 337.[2]
— List of the plants . . . of the Labrador peninsula. 1896. I. 311.[1]
— A list of the plants of the Pribilof Islands. 1899. I. 312.
— Plants . . . collected by J. W. Tyrrell. 1897. I. 311.[1]
— La richess forestière du Canada. 1900. IV. 337.[2]
— Vaccinium Vitis-Idaea. 1889. III. 664.[1]
Macoun, John. Catalogue of Canadian plants. 1883. I. 310.
— The forests of Canada. 1895. IV. 337.[2]
— The forests of Vancouver Island. 1888. I. 311.[1]
— The mountain forests of Vancouver's Island. 1889. I. 311.[1]
— Notes on Canadian polypetalae. 1883. I. 310.
— Notes on the flora of the Gaspé Peninsula. 1883. I. 310.
— Report on the botanical features . . . from Vancouver Island to Carleton. 1877. I. 311.[1]
— & Gibson, John. The rarer plants of the province of Ontario. 1876. I. 310.
Macoun, William Tyrrell. Report of the Foreman of forestry. 1897. IV. 111.[1]
Macovey, N. C. Ouhlie asupra pădurilor Moldovei. 1892. IV. 375.[1]
Macowan, Peter. Exploitation of the Olive. 1888. III. 679.[1]
— New Cape plants. 1890. I. 495.
— The Olive at the Cape. 1897. III. 679.[2]
— Preum-Besjes. 1891. III. 281.[2]
— Tea substitutes at the Cape. 1891. III. 223.[1]
— & Bolus, Harry. Catalogue of printed books . . . relating to South Africa. 1882. I. 4.[1]
—— Novitates capenses. 1880. I. 495.
Macown, W. T. See SAUNDERS, William & MACOWN, W. T.
Le Macpalxochiquauhitl; ou, Arbre-à-la-main des Mexicains. 1860. II. 532.[2]
Macphall, W. M. & Irving, T. T. Holding power of wood screws. 1900. IV. 409.
McPherson, James. The cultivation of Loranthaceae. 1871. III. 385.[1]
— The Neilgherry Tea planter. 1870. III. 603.
McPherson James (of Trenton). Rosa Wichuriana hybrids. 1898. III. 457.[1]
MacPherson, Peter. Some causes of the decay of the Australian forests. 1886. IV. 210.[3]
Macqret, François Hercule Gaston. Étude sur l'Aloès. 1888. III. 333.[1]
Macquaire, Paul. Contribution à l'étude du Maté. 1896. III. 531.[1]
— Le maté; sa constitution. . . . et ses propriétés physiologiques. 1896. III. 531.[1]
Macquart, Jean. Les arbres et arbrisseaux d'Europe et leurs insectes 1852. III. 189.

Macquer, P. J. Over de caoutchouc . . . van Cayenne. 1773. III. 228.[2]
— Mémoire sur un moyen de dissoudre la résine caoutchouc. 1770. III. 230.
Macquet, G. Le tissu sécréteur des Aloès. 1888. II. 78.[1]
McRae, Alexander. On the rearing of . . . undercover for game. 1898. III. 215.[1]
McRae, T. C. Public forest reservations. 1893. IV. 178.[2]
— 1894. IV. 178.[2] — 1896. IV. 179.[1]
Macreight, Daniel Chambers. Manual of British botany. 1837. I. 398.
Mactier, T. B. & Latter, Thomas. Memoranda respecting . . . Teak plantation at Bancoorah. 1848. IV. 536.[2]
McTurk, Michael. Notes on the forests of British Guiana. 1882. IV. 342.[1]
— Report on Essequebo River district. 1888. IV. 342.[1]
— Woods of British Guiana. 1878. IV. 19.[1]
Macvicar, John Gibson. The beauty of expression. 1878. IV. 55.[2]
— The philosophy of arboriculture. 1868. III. 36.[1]
— The theory of terminal fructification. 1861. I. 114.[2]
— Vegetable morphology. 1860. I. 99.
McWilliam, Robert. An essay on the origin and operation of the dry rot. 1818. IV. 323,[1] 414.[2]
Madagascar. 1900. III. 282.[1]
Madagascar Baobab. 1879. III. 529.[1]
Madagascar ebony. 1888. III. 384,[1] 669.[1]
Madagascar et l'industrie forestière. 1899. IV. 380.[1]
Madagascar magazine. See ANTANANARIVO annual. I. 29.[2]
Madagascar Piassava. 1894. II. 68,[1] III. 324.[2]
Madagascar rubber. 1900. III. 688.[1]
Madariaga, Juan A. de. Datos de las avenidas. 1898. IV. 548.[1]
— Guardería forestal. 1900. IV. 554.[1]
— Repoblación de las cuencas de los pantanos. 1899. IV. 547.[1]
Madariaga, Juan José MUÑOZ DE. See MUÑOZ DE MADARIAGA, J. J.
Madden, Edward. Brief observations on some of the Pines. 1845. II. 15.[2]
— Diary of an excursion to the Shatool. 1846. I. 472.
— Elucidation of some plants . . . of Nepál. 1856. I. 473.
— On Himalayan Coniferae. 1845. II. 15.[2]
— Major Cunningham's Ladak. 1854. I. 473, II. 27.[1]
— Notes of an excursion to the Pindree Glacier. 1847. I. 472.
— Observations on Himalayan Coniferae. 1845. II. 15.[2]
— On the occurrence of Palms and Bambus . . . in the Himalaya. 1853. I. 470,[1] IV. 88.[1]
— Palms and Bambus . . . on the Himalayas. 1853. I. 470,[1] IV. 88.[1]
— Vereintes Vorkommen von Palmen, Bambus . . . in den Himalayen. 1853. I. 470,[1] IV. 88.[1]
Madden, T. A letter . . . giving an account of two women being poisoned by . . . Laurel-leaves. 1733. III. 437.[3]
Madelain, Ez., (jr.). Du genre Croton; ses espèces, sa culture. 1873. III. 515.[2]
— Quelques plantes rares ou nouvelles. 1873. III. 298.[2]
Mader. Ueber die Vorbereitung des Bodens für die Baumschule. 1887. III. 150.[2]
Mader, Carl. Wandtafeln . . . über Zucht . . . der Obstbäume. 1874. III. 146.[1]
— Welche Veredlungsmethoden des Weinstockes haben sich . . . bewährt? 1890. III. 548.[2]
Mader, Fritz. Illustrierter Führer durch die französische Riviera. 1900. I. 419.[1]
La madera de Cedro para la fabricación de lapiceros. 1893. IV. 557.[2]
Maderas de América. 1880. IV. 396.[2]
Maderspach, János. A nyári vágású fák kérdéséhez. 1876. IV. 384.[1]
Madianna, J. B. RICORD-. See RICORD-MADIANNA, J. B.
Madinier, Paul. Algerian products. 1864. III. 487.[2]
— Sur l'introduction en Algérie des plantes économiques. 1888. III. 130.[2]
— Note sur la distribution géographique de quelques plantes économiques de l'Arizona. 1887. I. 325.
— De la nutrition végétale. 1867. I. 159.
Madiot. Buis à feuilles de Romarin. 1830. III. 522.[1]
— De la culture du Mûrier. 1826. III. 374.
— Étude, culture . . . du Mûrier. 1827. III. 374.
— Traité classique et historique des arbres exotiques. 182.? III. 83.[2]
Madon, P. G. Le carbone et la lumière réfléchie. 1881 IV. 67.[2]

Madon, P. G. (*continued*).
— La lumière, le couvert, l'humus dans les taillis sous futaie. 1880. IV. 67.[1]
— The preservation of the forests of the island of Cyprus. 1881. IV. 375.[2]
— The replanting of the island of Cyprus. 1881. IV. 168.[1]
Madras — Department of land records and agriculture. Report. III. 26.[2]
Madras — Department of land records and agriculture. Agricultural branch. Bulletin. III. 26.[2]
Madras forest act. 1882. IV. 332.[1]
Madras journal of literature and science. *See* JOURNAL of literature . . . I. 29.[1]
Madras monthly journal of medical science. *See* MADRAS quarterly journal . . . III. 26.[2]
Madras Presidency. *See* INDIA — MADRAS PRESIDENCY.
Madras quarterly journal of medical science. III. 26.[2]
Madre, Henri. De la mise en rapport des forêts de l'état historique. 1898. IV. 28,[1] 327.[1]
Madrid — **Real academia de ciencias exactas** . . . *See* REAL . . . I. 24.[1]
Madrid — **Real academia medica.** *See* REAL . . . I. 24.[1]
Madrid-Dávila, Alfredo de. *See* JORDANA Y MORERA, José, MADRID-DÁVILA, Alfredo de & ROBLES, Eduardo de.
Madrid y Manrique de la Vega, Matias de la. Memoria sobre los grandes montes y demás riqueza de la Liébana. 1836. IV. 363.[1]
Madriz, F. J. Cultivo del Café. 1869. III. 726.[2]
— Manual para el cultivo del Cafeto. 1890. III. 727.
The **Madroña.** 1890. II. 660.[1]
Madsen, Andreas. Taxen. 1895. II. 10.[1]
Madsen, H. Erica carnea som Stenhøjsplante. 1892. III. 650.[2]
Eine **mächtige** Ceder in Californien. 1853. II. 50.[2]
Mächtige Eiche. 1899. IV. 516.[1]
Maecker, Fr. Gehölze für eingeschlossene Lagen. 1885. III. 42.[1]
Maeder, Daniel. Der Wald in seiner kulturhistorischen . . . Bedeutung. 1886. I. 512, *IV. 44.*
Mädler, (*Dr.*). Das Erwachen der animalischen und vegetabilischen Lebensthätigkeit im Frühlinge. 1837. I. 226.[1]
Mähren. *See* MORAVIA.
Mährisch-schlesische Forst-Schule zu Eulepberg. Berichte. Jahres-Bericht. IV. 15.
Mährisch-schlesische Gesellschaft. *See* K. K. MÄHRISCH-SCHLESISCHE GESELLSCHAFT.
Mährisch-schlesische Gesellschaft für Ackerbau, Natur- und Landeskunde. *See* K. K. MÄHRISCH-SCHLESISCHE . . . III. 25.
Männel. Über die Anheftungsweise der Mistel. 1897. II. 180.[1]
Männel, (*Forstassessor*). Schutz der Nadelhölzer gegen Reh-Verbiss. 1898. IV. 197.[1]
Maenner, Carl. Forstschutz und Jagdschutz. 1895. IV. 319.[1]
Maeno, N. Investigations on the Mulberry tree. 1896. II. 154.[2]
— On the physiological action of amidosulphonic acid. 1896. I. 160.
Märker. Anleitung zur Bindung . . . der Sandschellen. 1826. IV. 145.
Märker, (*Oberförster, Kohlfurt*). In welcher Weise können kleinere Brüche . . . nutzbar gemacht werden? 1897. IV. 434.[1]
Maerker, C. Einiges über die Kernholzbildung der Kiefer. 1885. IV. 481.
— & Borggreve, Bernard. Beobachtungen über den Fang des grossen Kiefern-Rüsselkäfers. 1885. IV. 207.
— & Klopfer, (*Oberförster, Primkenau*). Welcher Grad der Durchforstung . . . der Kiefernbestände? 1893. IV. 474.
Märkischer Forst-Verein. Bericht. IV. 10.
Märtens. Tortrix viridana. 1874. IV. 510.
Märtens. Das Vorkommen und Verhalten der Traubeneiche. 1892. IV. 508.
Märter, Franz Joseph. Ueber das Bedürfniss einer . . . vermehrten Holz-Production. 1810. IV. 123,[2] *268.*
— Characteristik . . . des Mahaleb. 1813. IV. 438.[1]
— Entwurf einer Theorie. über die natürliche Entstehung . . . des Maserholzes. 1815. I. 124, *IV. 421.*
— Fundamenta et termini botanici. 1789. I. 70.
— Die Obstbaumzuchten. 1795. III. 146.[1]
— Verzeichniss aller Bäume, Stauden. 1781. III. 89.[2]
— Verzeichniss der in der grossen systematischen Baumschule zu Hernals bey Wien cultivirten . . . Tafelobst-Sorten. 1805. III. 90.[1]

— Verzeichniss der östreichischen Bäume, Stauden. 1781. III. 89.[2]
— Verzeichniss der östreichischen Bäume und Sträucher. 1781. III. 89.[2]
— Verzeichniss der östreichischen Gewächse. 1780. I. 438.
— Verzeichniss der vegetacion filipina. 1887. I. 464.[1]
Maeso, José Pérez. Aspecto de la vegetacion filipina. 1887. I. 464.[1]
Maestre, I. Las roturaciones. 1878. IV. 283.[1]
Mäule, C. Der Faserverlauf im Wundholz. 1896. I. 207.[2]
Mafat, F. E. Plants capable of yielding tanning materials. 1893. III. 237.[1]
Maffei, Raimondo. Catechismo forestale. 1865. IV. 23.[1]
— Coltivazione artificiale dei tartufi. 1865. IV. 439.
— E conveniente piantare o seminare? 1863. IV. 141.
— Il debbio. 1863. IV. 143.[1]
— Il decreto del 14 agosto 1864. 1864. IV. 277.
— Sugli effetti della libertà forestale. 1864. IV. 277.
— Frammento di dizionario forestale. 1866. IV. 23.[1]
— Influenza delle irrigazioni. 1865. IV. 144.[1]
— Minghetti il guastatore. 1864. IV. 277.
— La Pineta di Ravenna. 1864. IV. 364.
— Proposta per la promulgazione del Codice silvano. 1864. IV. 328.
— Scelta del torno. 1866. IV. 251.[2]
— Selvicoltura in Italia. 1862. IV. 122.[2]
Maffre. De la culture de l'Olivier en Algérie. 1847. III. 675.[2]
Magasin encyclopédique. I. 22.
Magasin pittoresque. III. 20.
Magasijn van vaderlandschen landbouw. III. 14.
Magasijn voor landbouw en kruidkunde. III. 14.
Magasin des Pflanzenreiches. 1793. I, 1, *580.*[1]
Magasin für das Jagd- und Forstwesen. IV. 10.
Magasin für das Neueste aus der Mathematik. IV. 10.
Magasin für die Botanik. I. 26.[2]
Magazine of botany and gardening. I. 18.
Magazine of horticulture. III. 5.
Magazine of natural history. I. 18.
The **Magazine** of natural history and naturalist. *See* The NATURALIST. London. I. 19.
Magazine of zoology and botany. I. 18.
Magazzini, Vitale. Coltivazione toscana. 1625. III. 115.[1]
Magdeburgische Holtz- und Jagt-Ordnung. 1686. IV. 319.[2]
Magee, Thomas. The preservation of our forests. 1892. IV. 178.[2]
Magelssen, W. Slangegranen. 1896. II. 35.[2]
Magenau. Die Eiche im Forstbezirk Heilbronn. 1893. IV. 508.
Magendie, François. Rapport fait . . . à l'occasion de la suppressions du Jardin . . . à Toulon. 1849. I. 58.
Magerle, F. Topographisch-statistische Beschreibung der Herrschaft Grätzer Forste. 1857. IV. 368.
Magerstedt, Adolf Friedrich. Die Bienenzucht. 1863. III. 224.[1]
— Bilder aus der römischen Landwirthschaft. 1858. III. 33.[2]
— Die Obstbaumzucht der Römer. 1861. III. 145.[2]
— Der Weinbau der Römer. 1858. III. 545.[1]
Magerstein, Th. Ueber das Erfrieren der Pflanzen. 1880. I. 212.
Magerstein, Vincent T. Einiges aus der Naturgeschichte der Tannenrindenläuse. 1883. IV. 456.
Maget, G. A. Notice sur les végétaux . . . de l'Archipel japonais. 1878. III. 91.[3]
Magliani. *See* BERTI, P. & MAGLIANI.
Magnah, CROZE-. *See* CROZE-MAGNAN.
Magne, J. H. *See* GILLET, C. G. & MAGNE, J. H.
Magnenus, Johannes Chrysostomus. De manna liber singularis. 1648. III. 220.[2]
Magneville, de. Observations sur l'incision annulaire. 1835. I. 187.
Magnien & Deu. Dictionnaire des productions de la nature et de l'art. 1809. III. 271.[1]
Magnien, Achille. Expériences contre la chlorose des arbres fruitiers. 1899. III. 181.[1]
Magnien, Lucien. *See* SAINT-PIERRE, Camille & MAGNIEN, Lucien.
Magnier, Charles. Catalogue des plantes cultivées au Jardin botanique de la Société . . . à Saint-Quentin. 1878. III. 29.[1]
— Crataegus floribunda Gdgr. 1882. II. 261.[2]
— Fraxinus stenobotrys Gdgr. 1882. II. 709.[1]
— Rhamnus Alaternus var. picenensis. 1885. II. 499.[1]

— Rosa conspicua Bor. 1884. II. 293.[1]
— Rosa genevensis Puget. 1884. II. 294.[1]
— Scrinia florae selectae. See SCRINIA . . . I. 22.
— Spiraea Lindleyana. 1878. III. 459.[1]
Magnin, Antoine. Annotations et additions aux flores du Jura. 1895. I. 418.
— B. Vaivolet. 1887. V. XXII.[1]
— La botanique phytostatique à Lyon. 1880. I. 81.[1]
— Le botaniste lyonnais Claudius Martin. 1899. II. 478.[2]
— Sur la cause de présence des plantes réputées calcifuges. 1886. I. 229.
— Florule adventive des Saules têtards. 1894. I. 234.[2]
— Note sur les monstruosités florales des Saules. 1878. II. 106.[1]
— Notes botaniques. 1897. II. 108.[2]
— Observations sur la flore du Lyonnais. 1881. I. 416.
— Recherches sur la géographie botanique du Lyonnais. 1879. I. 415.
— La végétation de la région lyonnaise. 1886. I. 417.
— Végétation des Alpes françaises. See FALSAN, Albert. 1893. I. 418.
— Végétation des environs de Gap. 1875. I. 414.
— La végétation des monts Jura. 1893. I. 418.
Magnol, Pierre. Botanicum monspeliense. 1676. I. 404.[3]
— Hortus regius monspeliensis. 1697. I. 56.
— Novus caracter plantarum. 1720. I. 290.
— Prodromus historiae generalis plantarum. 1689. I. 288.
— Sur l'usage de la moëlle des plantes. 1711. I. 162.
Magnolias as garden plants. 1895. III. 399.[1]
Magnus, Paul Wilhelm. Ueber A. Weisse's monströse Frucht von Citrus Aurantium. 1900. II. 403.[1]
— Ueber das Auftreten von Einfaltungen der Zellmembran. 1876. II. 59.[1]
— Auftreten zweier Laubblätter unter den Kätzchen von Populus tremula. 1888. II. 98.[2]
— Beobachtungen über Blitzschläge an Bäumen. 1890. IV. 194.
— Ein bei Berlin auf Caragana . . . auftretender Mehlthau. 1899. III. 470.[1]
— Doppelblüthe einer Fuchsia. 1878. II. 643.[2]
— Durchlöcherte Blätter von Fagus sylvatica. 1876. III. 184.[2] IV. 497.
— Einblütige Trauben bei Cytisus Laburnum. 1891. II. 369.[1]
— Einfluss der Unterlage auf das Edelreis. 1871. III. 39.
— Der Einfluss des Pfropfreises auf die Unterlage. 1870. I. 246.[2]
— Einige Beobachtungen über die Heterophyllie von Melaleuca micromera. 1887. II. 630.[1]
— Zur Epheukrankheit. 1895. III. 643.[1]
— Fasciation von Berberis vulgaris. 1876. II. 205.[1]
— F von Amygdalus Persica fol. purpureis. 1893. III. 440rtücht
— Eine interessante monströse Fuchsiablüte. 1893. II. 643.[3]
— Keimpflanzen von Acer platanoides mit verwachsenen Keimblättern. 1876. II. 479.[2]
— Kurze Bemerkung über die Silberweide. 1888. II. 105.[1]
— Kurze Bemerkung zu Herrn Dr. Poselger's Blüthenkalender. 1881. I. 225.
— Kurze Notiz über Hexenbesen. 1886. I. 528.[2]
— Der Mehlthau auf Syringa. 1898. III. 681.[2]
— Melasmia Empetri F. Magn. 1886. III. 523.[1]
— Montröse Ulmenschössinge. 1874. II. 143.[1]
— Natürliches Ankopulieren. 1888. I. 209.[1]
— Die neue Krankheit des Weinstocks. 1883. III. 578.
— Notiz über bemerkenswerthe Vegetationserscheinungen. 1889. I. 225.
— Ueber den Rost der Weymouth-Kiefern. 1891. IV. 470.[1]
— Ueber das spontane Auftreten von Variation an . . . Eichen. 1883. II. 140.[1]
— Ueber einen in Südtirol aufgetretenen Mehlthau des Apfels. 1898. III. 428.[2]
— Transversal neben einander stehende Achselknospen bei Morenia corallina. 1874. II. 71.[2]
— Verwachsungen verschiedener Stämme. 1883. II. 209.[1]
— Das Vorkommen echt dedoublirter Carpelle in Blüthen von Leguminosen. 1876. II. 362.[1]
— Über das Vorkommen von Pinus silvestris L. mit rothen Antheren. 1886. II. 46.[2]
— Weitere Mittheilungen über den Einfluss des Edelreises. 1871. I. 529.[2]
— Wurzelanschwellungen des Rubus Idaeus. 1882. III. 458.[2]
— Wurzeln von Passiflora mit . . . Verdickungen. 1888 III. 615.[2]

— Zwei Fälle im December blühender Sträucher. 1877. II. 244,[1] 655.[3]
— Zwei interessante Fälle jetzt blühender Sträucher. 1877. II. 244.[1]
— Ueber zwei monströse Keimpflanzen von Ricinus. 1876. II. 451.[1]
— Zwei monströse Rosen. 1878. II. 289.[2]
— Zweimaliges Blühen von Aesculus. 1874. I. 225.
— See also ASCHERSON, Paul & MAGNUS, Paul; ROESE & MAGNUS, P. W.
Mágócsy-Dietz, Sándor. Adatok a növények, különösen az Euphorbiaceák tejnedvének ismeretéhez. 1882. II. 434.[1]
— Adatok az Abies excelsa D.C. két fajzatának hazánkban. 1883. II. 34.[2]
— A Cinchona-fa tenyésztése az angolok kelet-indiai birtokán. 1882. III. 714.
— A Forsythia heterostyliája. 1891. II. 706.[2]
— A Gyertyánfa boszorkányseprője. 1900. IV. 492.[1]
— A karos Lucsfenyő és Jegenyenyár. 1900. II. 35,[3] 97.[2]
— Kétszikü fás növények béldiaphragmája. 1899. I. 129.[1]
— A lombosfák védő és gesztfa rétege. 1889. I. 126.
— A magyar állam erdőségei. 1886. IV. 374.[1]
— A német Tülevelü erdők fája. 1886. IV. 443.[1]
— Nyáry- és levélkulcs. 1882. I. 294,[1] 444,[1] IV. 87.[1]
— A vörös virágu erdei Fenyő. 1881. II. 46.[2]
— See also FEKETE, Lajos & MÁGÓCSY-DIETZ, Sándor.
Magretti, Paolo. Di una galla di cinipide. 1885. III. 563.
A magyar birodalomban honos fák szilárdságának kipuhatolása tárgyában. 1873. IV. 410.
Magyar földrajzi társulat. See FÖLDRAJZI közlemények. I. 27.
Magyar gyógyszerkönyv. Pharmacopoea hungarica. 1871. III. 256.[1]
Magyar növénytani lapok. I. 27.
Magyar orvosok és természetvizsgálók nagygyülése. Évkönyve. Munkátok. I. 27.
Magyar természettudományi társulat. See TERMÉSZETTUDOMÁNYI közlöny. I. 28.[1]
Magyar tudományos akadémia. Értesitő. Közlemények. I. 27.
Magyar tudományos akadémia. Évkönyvek. See MAGYAR TUDÓS TÁRSASÁG. I. 520.[1]
Magyar tudós társaság. Évkönyvek. I. 520.[1]
Magyarország földmivelése 1896. 1896. IV. 374.[1]
Mahaleb bain. 1832. III. 438.[1]
Maher, John. On a remarkable property of the Hoya carnosa. 1818. III. 693.[1]
Mahier. De l'action des Amandes amères. 1846. III. 431.[2]
— On the action of bitter Almonds. 1846. III. 431.[2]
Mahieu, J. N. Élémens de phytologie. 1835. I. 87.
Mahler, Julius. Agrikole, zumal forstliche Sprengarbeiten mittelst Dynamit. 1876. IV. 386.
— Die moderne Sprengtechnik. 1873. IV. 386.
— Die Sprengtechnik. 1873. IV. 386.
— Die Sprengtechnik im Dienste der Land- und Forstwirthschaft. 1877. IV. 386.
— Das Stocksprengen. 1878. IV. 386.
Mahlert, Adolf. Beiträge zur Kenntniss der Anatomie der . . . Coniferen. 1885. II. 18.
Mahling, Johannes. Ein Riesen-Tulpenbaum. 1900. III. 398.[2]
Mahogany cultivation in old world. 1888. III. 513.[1]
The Mahonias or Ash Barberries. 1888. III. 395.[1]
Maiden, John Henry. Abnormal colours of native flowers. 1899. II. 510.[2]
— Acrotriche serrulata as a bee-plant. 1893. III. 664.[1]
— Alleged poisonous nature of White Cedar berries. 1893. III. 512.[2]
— Angophora Kino. 1892. II. 620.[1]
— Australian and Tasmanian Sandarach. 1890. III. 299.[1]
— Australian indigenous plants providing human foods. 1889. III. 94.[1]
— Australian Sandarach. 1894. III. 299.[2]
— Beech — "White Beech." 1895. IV. 536.[5]
— A bibliography of Australian economic botany. 1892. III. 1.
— A botanist on Mt. Kosciusko. 1900. I. 505.
— Botany Bay or Eucalyptus kino. 1890. IV. 531.[2]
— Cape Cotton. 1894. III. 693.[1]
— A case of poisoning by Lycium horridum. 1900. III. 701.[1]
— On Cedar gum. 1890. III. 512.[1]
— A chat about Wattles. 1899. II. 323.[1]

Maiden, John Henry (*continued*).
— The chemistry of the Australian indigenous vegetation. 1895. I. 151.[2]
— Coffee leaves as a beverage. 1894. III. 740.[1]
— The Colane. 1893. III. 512.[1]
— Colonial timbers for wine-casks. 1894. IV. 427.[1]
— Concerning Hill Top. 1897. I. 505.
— A contribution towards a flora of Mount Kosciusko. 1898. I. 505.
— Dorrigo forest reserve. 1894. IV. 380.[2]
— The Dorrigo forest reserve. 1894. I. 504.
— Drimys aromatica and D. dipetala. 1891. III..397.[1]
— Durability of colonial timbers. 1894. IV. 413.[2]
— Edible and non-edible Red-gum leaves. 1900. IV. 534.[1]
— Effects on cattle of eating Macrozamia roots. 1900. III. 285.[2]
— The Eucalyptus. 1899. IV. 532.[1]
— Eucalyptus coriacea. 1900. IV. 533.[2]
— The examination of Kinos. 1890. II. 624.[1]
— False Tonquin beans. 1894. III. 287.[1]
— Fibre of Hibiscus heterophyllus. 1894. III. 587.[2]
— Fish-poisons of the Australian aborigines. 1894. III. 283.[1]
— Fruit of Cryptocarya Meissneri. 1894. II. 225.[1]
— A giant Acacia from the Brunswick River. 1896. II. 324.[1]
— On Grass-tree gum. 1891. III. 339.[1]
— On the gum of the Leopard-tree. 1890. II. 407.[1]
— The gum of the Leopard tree. 1891. III. 504.[2]
— Gums, and a resin, produced by Australian Proteaceae. 1889. III. 382.[2]
— Heart-leaf Poison-plant. 1894. III. 477.[1]
— Honey-locust pods for horse and cattle feed. 1897. III. 477.[2]
— Indigenous Australian forage plants. 1889. III. 223.[2]
— Indigenous vegetable drugs. 1899. III. 283.[1]
— Ironbarks. 1893. IV. 531.[1]
— Is Goodia poisonous to stock? 1895. III. 478.[1]
— Kino liquide. 1890. III. 633.[1]
— Les kinos de l'Angophora. 1893. III. 633.[1]
— A large white Honeysuckle. 1899. II. 159.[1]
— Liquid kino. 1890. III. 633.[1]
— A list of plants collected by Mr. R. Helms. 1894. I. 504.
— The Moreton Bay Fig. 1893. III. 371.[2]
— Mount Seaview and the way thither. 1898. I. 505.
— Native food-plants. 1899. III. 283.[1]
— Native plants poisonous to stock. 1895. III. 94.[1]
— A native Senna. 1894. III. 471.[1]
— A native timber suitable for tobacco-pipes. 1894. III. 383.[2]
— New locality for Cryptocarya patentinervis. 1894. III. 225.[1]
— A. New South Wales Bitter Vine. 1894. III. 403.[2]
— Note on the synonymy of Ficus scabra. 1889. II. 153.[1]
— Notes of a trip to the . . . forests of New South Wales. 1895. I. 504.
— Notes on Australian economic botany. 1891. III. 94.[1]
— Notes on colonial timber for carriage-building. 1894. IV. 427.[1]
— Notes on ring-barking. 1894. IV. 385.[1]
— Notes on some indigenous Sago. 1888. III. 282.[1]
— Notes on some vegetable exudations. 1896. III. 228.[1]
— Notes on the commercial timbers of New South Wales. 1895. IV. 401.[2]
— Notes on the exudations . . . of Pittosporum. 1892. II. 248.[3]
— Notes on the geographical distribution of some New South Wales plants. 1890. I. 504.
— Notes on the resins of two Queensland species of Araucaria. 1891. II. 26.[1]
— Observations on the gums . . . of Ceratopetalum. 1890. II. 250.[2]
— Observations on the gums . . . of Ceratopetalum. 1891. III. 415.[2]
— Observations on the vegetation of Lord Howe Island. 1898. I. 508.[2]
— On the occurrence of a gum in Echinocarpus. 1892. III. 584.[2]
— On the oleo-resin of Canarium Muelleri. 1892. III. 510.[1]
— Paddy's Lucerne or Queensland Hemp. 1894. III. 589.[1]
— On Panax gum. 1893. III. 643.[2]
— Pepper-tree oil. 1898. III. 529.[1]
— Plants reputed to be poisonous to stock in Australia. 1898. III. 94.[2]

— Pomaderris apetala. 1898. III. 542.[1]
— A preliminary study of the Prickly-Pears. 1898. III. 624.[1]
— Range of Marlea vitiensis Benth. 1895. II. 615.[1]
— A reputed cough remedy. 1900. III. 384.[1]
— The resin of Myoporum platycarpum. 1889. II. 806.[2]
— Sassafras timber in the Bega district. 1895. IV. 520.[1]
— Some E   s of the New England tableland. 1898. II. 623.[2] ucalypt
— Some native Australian fodder-plants. 1898. III. 223.[2]
— Some N. S. Wales plants worth cultivating. 1896. III. 94.[1]
— Some New South Wales tan-substances. 1888. III. 237.[1]
— Some notes of a trip to the Victorian Alps. 1900. I. 505.
— Some of the pale hardwood timbers of New South Wales. 1892. IV. 531.[1]
— Some plant-foods of the aborigines. 1899. III. 283.[1]
— Some remarks on the sand-drift problem. 1900. IV. 146.[1]
— Some reputed medicinal plants of N. S. Wales. 1889. III. 94.[1]
— Spread of a Cassia this season. 1895. III. 471.[1]
— Sterculia gum. 1889. III. 591.[2]
— Supposed poisoning of sheep. 1899. III. 710.[2]
— Sydney-grown Acacia pycnantha bark. 1894. III. 465.[2]
— Tagosaste, or tree Lucerne. 1900. III. 474.[2]
— The tree Tomato. 1894. III. 699.[2]
— The Turpentine-tree. 1896. IV. 534.[1]
— On two undescribed exudations from the Leguminosae. 1892. III. 462.[2]
— Useful Australian plants. 1893. III. 94.[1]
— The useful native plants of Australia. 1889. III. 94.[1]
— The Valonia Oak. 1900. IV. 502.[2]
— Vegetable exudations. 1892. III. 228.[1]
— Walking-sticks . . . from New South Wales. 1894. IV. 428.[2]
— Wattles and Wattle-barks. 1890. IV. 521.[1]
— The weeds of New South Wales. 1895. III. 132.[1]
— *See also* DRANE, Henry & MAIDEN, J. H.; MUELLER, Ferdinand, *baron* von & MAIDEN, J. H.
— & Baker, R. T. Botanical notes from the Technological museum, Sydney. 1894. I. 504.
— — Description of a new Croton. 1895. II. 439.[2]
— — Description of a new species of Acacia from New South Wales. 1896. II. 327.[2]
— — Description of an apparently new Acacia. 1895. II. 327.[1]
— — Descriptions of some new . . . plants from New South Wales. 1896. I. 505.
— — On a new species of Elaeocarpus. 1896. II. 510.[1]
— & Betche, Ernst. Descriptions of four new . . . New South Wales plants. 1898. I. 505.
— — Descriptions of three new species of Australian plants. 1898. III. 486,[1] 689.[2]
— — On a new Myoporum from South Australia. 1898. II. 806.[2]
— — On a new species of Macadamia. 1896. II. 164.[2]
— — Notes from the Botanic gardens, Sydney. 1898. I. 505.
— — Notes on Sterculia . . . lurida and discolor. 1898. II. 538.[1]
— & Camfield, J. H. Notes on some Port Jackson plants. 1898. II. 159,[1] 690.[2]
— & Campbell, W. S. The flowering plants . . . of New South Wales. 1895. I. 504.
— & De Coque, J. V. Report on turpentine timber. 1895. IV. 534.[1]
— & Smith, H. G. A contribution to the chemistry of Australian myrtaceous kinos. 1895. III. 633.[1]
— — Contributions to a knowledge of Australian vegetable exudations. 1895. I. 181.[2]
— — Sur l'étude chimique des kinos des Myrtacées d'Australie. 1895. III. 633.[1]
— — Preliminary notes on the bark of Carissa. 1895. III. 637.[1]
— Cowdery, G. S. & De Coque, J. V. Report on Spotted Gum. 1897. IV. 533.[2]
The **Maidenhair-tree**. 1882, 1899. III. 287.[1]
Maier, Franz. *See* MAIER, Фрањъ.
Maier, Fritz. Vegetations-Charakter des Nord-Ostens der Vereinigten Staaten. 1855. I. 314.
Maier, Michael. Tractatus de volucri arborea. 1619. I. 517.[1]
Maier, P. J. De bereiding van kamfer in Japan. 1852. III. 404.[2]

— Bereiding van quinium uit afval. 1873. III. 718.
— Eenige grondstoffen en . . . produkten. 1861. III. 274.²
— De Lagamolie van Sumatra. 1852. III. 224.¹
— Nota omtrent het votgehalte der . . . Elais-guianensis-vruchten. 1865. III. 325.¹
— Onderzoek der Karoeingom. 1853. III. 227.
— Scheikundig onderzoek van den sindorbalsem. 1864. I. 181.¹
— Scheikundig onderzoek van . . . Sago-soorten. 1868. III. 327.¹
— Sindor-olie. 1867. III. 487.²
— Over Sindor-olie. 1869. III. 487.²
Maige. Influence de la lumière sur la forme . . . des rameaux de la Vigne. 1898. II. 504.²
Mail. Un nouveau mode de greffage des arbres. 1878. III. 162.
Maillard, L. Notes sur l'Île de la Réunion. 1862. I. 482.
Maillard, Pierre Néhémie. See SAUZÉ, J. C. & MAILLARD, P. N.
Maille, Alphonse. See PUEL, Timothée & MAILLE, Alphonse.
Mailles, Charles. Maladie des Ailantes. 1888. III. 507.¹
Maillet, Benoit de. Description de l'Égypte. 1735. III. 280.¹
Maillot, Éd. Étude comparée du Pignon. 1880. III. 519,¹ 522.¹
Maillot, Eugène. Rapport sur les maladies des Cédratiers en Corse. 1875. III. 502.¹
Main, James. The forest planter. 1839. IV. 108.¹
— Fruit trees: a hand-book. 1841. III. 142.
— Hortus diaetetica. 1845. III. 110.¹
— Illustrations of vegetable physiology. 1833. III. 37.²
— The planter's and pruner's assistant. 1839. IV. 108.¹
— Popular botany. 1836. I. 94.
Main, Thomas. Directions for the transplanting . . . of young Thorn. 1807. III. 212.²
Maine—Forest commissioner. Annual report. IV. 4.
Maine agricultural experiment station. See MAINE STATE COLLEGE . . . III. 5.
Maine state college agricultural experiment station. Annual report. Bulletin. III. 5.
Maine-et-Loire—Comice horticole. See COMICE . . . III. 19.
Maine-et-Loire—Société académique. See SOCIÉTÉ . . . 22.
Maine-et-Loire—Société d'horticulture. See SOCIÉTÉ . . . III. 21.
Maine-et-Loire—Société industrielle d'Angers . . . See SOCIÉTÉ . . . III. 22.
Maine-et-Loire—Société Linnéenne . . . See SOCIÉTÉ . . . I. 23.
Mainetty, Leon P. The Smyrna Fig industry. 1897. III. 369.²
Maingay, Albert Caroll. See MAINGAY, Alexander C.
Maingay, Alexander Caroll. Notes on the silk-worm of the Shantung province. 1865. IV. 501.²
— Notes on the Tapioca plant. 1869. III. 520.²
Maingy, A. See HAMILTON, Francis & MAINGY, A.
Mainwaring, William. Rearing Oak plantations from acorns. 1886. IV. 507.
Maire. Les produits variés des forêts. 1884. III. 271.¹
— See also MUEL, E., NOBL, Arthur & MAIRE.
Maire, E. L'allongement des révolutions de taillis. 1894. IV. 252.
— Boisement à la charrue des terres incultes. 1898. IV. 545.²
— Ce que peut rapporter une jeune sapinière. 1892. IV. 454.
— Extraction de souches à la dynamite. 1882. IV. 387.¹
— Traitement des taillis sous futaie. 1899. IV. 545.¹
— Valeur des bois tendres et fausses. 1899. IV. 259.¹
Maire, Réné. Annotations à la flore de Lorraine de Godron. 1894. I. 418.
— Flore grayloise. 1894. V. XXII.¹
— See also GASSER, Aug. & MAIRE, Réné.
— & Gasser, Aug. Un succédané algérien du Café. 1892. III. 384.¹
Maisch. Sur l'extrait des feuilles de Châtaignier. 1873. III. 360.¹
— Sur le principe vénéneux du Rhus. 1866. III. 528.¹
Maisch, Henry Charles Christian. Illicium floridanum. 1886. III. 398.¹
— Illicium floridanum Ellis; natural order, Magnoliaceae Illicieae. 1885. II. 210.¹
Maisch, J. L'industrie du camphre dans la Floride. 1891. III. 404.¹

Maisch, John Michael. American indigenous plants. 1872. III. 531,² 711.²
— On the balsams of Liquidambar. 1874. III. 417.¹
— The botanical origin of some United States pharmacopœial drugs. 1891. II. 411,¹ *III. 474*,¹ *768*.²
— A manual of organic materia medica. 1882. III. 243.
— A new false Angustura bark. 1874. III. 504.¹
— Notes on a few American drugs. 1878. III. 652.¹
— Notes on some North American medicinal plants. 1891. III. 398,¹ *589*.¹
— On the occurrence of arbutin in ericaceous plants. 1874. III. 647.¹
— Pharmacognostical notes — American indigenous plants. 1872. III. 531,² 711.²
— On the species of Berberis of the Pacific coast. 1878. II. 202.¹
— See also STILLÉ, Alfred & MAISCH, J. M.
Maison, C. Note sur un Frêne remarquable. 1846. II. 708'¹
Maison, E. Consecuencias de la despoblación forestal. 1899. IV. 542.¹
Maison de campagne. III. 20.
Maison rustique du 19e siècle. 184.? III. 113. See also JOURNAL d'agriculture pratique de jardinage. III. 19.
Maisonneuve, Michel Charles DURIEU DE. See DURIEU DE MAISONNEUVE, M. C.
Maisonneuve, Paul. Étude sur la structure . . . du Camphrier de Bornéo. 1875. III. 611.²
Maistre, Jules. Sur les effets des sulfocarbonates. 1877. III. 563.
— Effets des sulfocarbonates dilués sur les Vignes. 1877. III. 563.
— La fièvre ou la malaria. 1899. IV. 55.¹
— De l'influence des forêts. 1867. V. XXIX.¹—1881, IV. 44.
— Influence des forêts sur le climat. 1867. IV. 43, V. XXIX.²
— Moyen de combattre la maladie de la Vigne. 1882. III. 578.
— De l'utilité des reboisements dans le Midi. 1899. IV. 164.²
Maistriau, Ch. See ERRERA, Léo, MAISTRIAU, Ch. & CLAUTRIAU, G.
Maître, A. Vins de dattes et vins de figues. 1894. III. 329,¹ 370.¹
Maître, J. La restauration des pâturages. 1897. IV. 197.²
Maître, Joseph. Écorcement du bois. 1867. IV. 434.
— Die Schälung aller Arten Rinden. 1867. IV. 434.
Maiz, Thomas MORÉNO Y. See MORÉNO Y MAIZ, Thomas.
Majchrowski, W. Opłatwa brodaczkowata. 1889. II. 141.¹
— Plantacye drzew Chinowych. 1899. IV. 55.¹
— Th. Meehem [sic] Szyszki. 1884. II. 45.²
Majer, Carl Eduard. Untersuchungen über die Lenticellen. See MOHL, Hugo von. 1836. I. 132.¹
Majer, Gustavus. Observationes de antherarum excisione. 1830. V. XI.¹
Majer, J. Literatura fizyografii ziemi polskiej. 1862. I. 4.¹
Majetti, Raffaele. Boschi e foreste, inondazione. 1898. IV. 48.¹
Majewski, E. Dictionnaire des noms polonais zoologiques et botaniques. 1894. I. 73.¹
Major, Charles Immanuel FORSYTH-. See STEFANI, Carlo de, MAJOR, C. J. F. & BARBEY, William.
— & Barbey, William. Saria; étude botanique. 1894. I. 809.¹
Major, Richard Henry. Select letters of Christopher Columbus. 1847. III. 266.
The Major Oak. 1890. II. 139.¹
Majus, Heinrich. De plantis et arboribus. 1681. I. 30.
Majus, Johann Heinrich. Dissertatio inauguralis de manna. 1706. III. 221.¹
Mak, Ch. De ziekte der Koffieplanten. 1888. III. 736.
On the making of Chinese paper. 1845. III. 235.¹
Makino, Tomitaro. Bambusaceae japonicae. 1900. II. 58.²
— Botanical notes from the author's private cabinet. 1898. I. 463.²
— Contributions to the study of the flora of Japan. 1899. I. 463.²
— Illustrations of the flora of Japan. 1882. I. 463.¹
— On Lindera umbellata. 1897. II. 226.¹
— Mr. Hisashi Kuroiwa's collections of Liuchoo plants. 1894. I. 463.¹

Makino, Tomitaro (*continued*).
— Notes on Japanese plants. 1892. I. 463.[1]
— Phanerogamae . . . japonicae iconibus illustratae. 1899. I. 463.[2]
— Plantae japonenses novae. 1897. I. 463.[1]
— On Quercus glabra Thunb. 1897. II. 133.[2]
Makovetzki, A. *See* Гурьяновъ, A. & Маковецкій, A.
Makowsky, Alexander. Die Flora des Brünner Kreises. 1863. I. 441.
Makoy, L. Jacob-. *See* Jacob-Makoy, L.
Maksimovitch, Karl Iv. *See* Maximowicz, Carl Johann.
Maksimovitch, M. A. *See* Максимовичъ, M. A.
Malacarne, Clerc Giuseppe. Catalogo delle specie vegetabili . . . nel giardino . . . de liceo del dipartimento della Mella. 1810. I. 61.
Malacca — Forest department. *See* Straits Settlements — Forest department. IV. 16.[2]
Une **maladie** cryptogamique de l'Osier. 1899. IV. 487.[2]
Maladie de l'Épicéa. 1900. IV. 457.
Maladie de la Vigne, combattue avec succès en Algérie. 1855. III. 576.
Maladie de Pin sylvestre; Peridermium. 1899. IV. 479.
Maladie des Peupliers du Canada. 1899. IV. 486.[1]
Maladie du blanc. [Chermès fagi.] 1898. IV. 208.[2]
Maladie du Pin sylvestre. 1900. IV. 480.
La **maladie** du rond. 1895. IV. 559.[1]
Maladie du rond. 1898. IV. 212.
Maladie du rond chez l'Épicéa. 1896. IV. 457.
Une **maladie** épidémique de l'Aune commun. 1900. IV. 489.[1]
Maladie observée sur le Peuplier blanc. 1833. III. 344.[2]
Malafosse, Gaston de. Invasion des vignobles du Narbonnais. 1880. III. 563.
Malafosse, Louis de. L'invasion du Peronospora. 1883. III. 578.
Malagola, G. Agricoltori e selvicoltori; impiantate dei Nocelleti. 1896. IV. 492.[1]
Malaguini. *See* Daccomo, G. & Malaguini.
Malaguti, F. J. Note sur l'absorption des ulmates solubles. 1852. I. 158.
— & **Durocher,** J. Recherches sur la répartition des éléments inorganiques dans les principales familles. 1856. I. 153.
— & **Marteville,** A. Cours de chimie agricole. 1860. III. 37.[1]
Malakhof, M. V. *See* Малаховъ, M. B.
Malangsche vereeniging van Koffieplanters. 1899. III. 731.
Malapert & Alluit. Une reclamation de priorité. 1856. III. 576.
Malaria and the value of the Eucalyptus. 1882. IV. 55.[1]
La **malattia** dei Castagni. 1898. IV. 493.[1]
Malattia del Pino d'Aleppo. 1881. IV. 464.[1]
Una **malattia** della Sughera. 1887. IV. 517.[1]
Malattie dell' Ulivo in territorio di Tivoli. 1897. III. 678.[1]
Malay peninsula — Agricultural bulletin. *See* Agricultural . . . III. 26.[1]
Malayan miscellanies. I. 29.[1]
Malbranche, Alexandre. De l'espèce dans le genre Rubus. 1879. II. 310.[1]
— Essai sur les Rubus normands. 1873. II. 303.[2]
— Note sur le dimorphisme. 1868. I. 99.
— De l'origine des variétés ou espèces d'arbres fruitiers. 1855. I. 247.
— Physiologie végétale. 1853. V. xi.[1]
— *See also* Blanche, H. & Malbranche, Alexandre.
Malcolm, William. A catalogue of hot-house and greenhouse plants, fruit and forest trees. 1771. I. 52.
The **male** Aucuba. 1869. III. 644.[2]
The **male** hardy Palm. 1874. III. 331.
Malegnane, de. Observations relatives à l'opinion . . . sur l'apparition du phylloxera. 1873. III. 565.[2]
Malepeyre, (sr.). Agriculture forestière. 1837. IV. 98.[2]
Ueber die **malerische** Schönheit der Bäume. 1831. V. 132.
Malesherbes, de. Plantes conservant leur saison a fleurir. 1770. I. 220.[1]
Malet & Verlot. Culture pratique des Pelargonium. n. d. III. 491.[1]
Malet, A. Culture du Staphylea colchica. 1880. III. 533.[2]
— Multiplication de l'Exochorda. 1884. III. 424.[1]
Malet, G. Quelques mots sur le Sequoia gigantea. 1858. III. 310.[1]
Malformed Fuchsia. 1884. III. 643.[2]
Malformed Walnut. 1890. II. 114.[1]
Malgin, N. *See* Мальгинъ, H.

Malherbe, Alfred. De l'action du venin du serpent à sonnettes. 1854. I. 211.
— Notice sur quelques espèces de Chênes. 1839. IV. 502.[1]
Malinvaud, Ernest. Un bouquet de Roses. 1890. II. 286.[1]
— Sur un échantillon à pédoncules bractéolés du Tilia grandifolia. 1878. II. 517.[2]
— Excursion botanique . . . Lot et de l'Aveyron. 1874. I. 414.
— Le Palmier nain en Portugal. 1897. III. 322.[1]
— Trois genres critiques de la flore du Limousin. 1891. II. 286,[1] 303.[2]
Maliutin, F. Малютинъ, Ф.
Maliva. Bildung von Weidegenossenschaften. 1895. IV. 309.[2]
— Schutz- und Plänterwald. 1897. IV. 177.[2]
— Ueber die Verbreitung einiger Cynipiden-Artèn. 1898. IV. 210.[1]
— Wald und Weide. 1897. IV. 136.[1]
Maljean. Analyse d'un échantillon de café. 1892. III. 740.[1]
— Quelques dosages de matières tanantes. 1896. III. 237.[2]
Mallada, Lúcas. Causas físicas y naturales de la pobreza de nuestro suelo. 1882. IV. 69.
— La pobreza de nuestro suelo. 1889. IV. 543.[2]
Malle, Adolphe Auguste Jules César Dureau de la. *See* Dureau de la Malle, A. A. J. C.
Malleson, F. A. Vegetable phenomenon. 1846. I. 209.[1]
Mallet. Du taillis composé. 1886. IV. 132.[1]
Mallet, C. Transformation de taillis furetés en futaies. 1878. IV. 128.
— Umwandlung von im Plänterbetrieb stehendem Niederwald in Hochwald. 1878. IV. 128.
Mallet, Ch. Étude de législation forestière; de l'affouage. 1895. IV. 334.[2]
Mallet, John William. On the occurrence in recent Pine-timber of fichtelite. 1872. II. 44.[1]
— Présence de la fichtélite. 1872. II. 44.[1]
Mallet, Quéhen-. *See* Quéhen-Mallet.
Mallet de Chilly. Des hautes futaies et des taillis considérés sous les rapports des produits. 1834. IV. 254, 259.[2]
— Note sur la culture . . . du Chêne à glands doux. 1819. III. 362.[2]
— Note sur la culture et les usages du Pin Laricio. 1820. IV. 465.[1]
— Notes sur les semis du Pin de Riga. 1820. IV. 471.
Mallett, George B. Araucaria imbricata. 1899. III. 299.[1]
— Ornamental economic plants. 1899. III. 78.[2]
Mallèvre, A. *See* Bertrand, Gabriel & Mallèvre, A.
Mally, C. W. On the introduction of insect pests. 1896. III. 187.[1]
— Spraying for orchard insects. 1895. III. 198.[1]
Malmby, Daniel. De origine myrrhae controversa. *See* Afzelius, Adam. 1818. II. 418.[1]
Malme, Gustaf Oscar Anderson. Die Asclepiadaceen des Regnell'schen Herbars. 1900. II. 735.[1]
— Brasilianska akarodomatieförande Rubiaceer. 1900. II. 808.[1]
— Förgreningsförhållandena . . . hos de brasilianska Asclepiadeerna. 1900. II. 735.[2]
— Ex herbario Regnelliano. 1898. I. 344.
Malmgren, A. J. Bihang till Berättelsen om svenska expeditionen till Spetsbergen. 1867. I. 356.
— Öfversigt af Spetsbergens fanerogam-flora. 1862. I. 356.
— & others. Svenska expeditioner till Spetsbergen. *See* Malmgren, A. J. 1867. I. 356.
Malmsten, Olof. De historiae naturalis usu medico. *See* Wallerius, J. G. 1740. III. 238.[1]
Malo, Charles. La corbeille de fruits. 181.? III. 84.[2]
— Histoire des Roses. 1818. III. 447.[2]
Malosse, Th. *See* Battandier, J. A. & Malosse, Th.
Malot, Félix. Exposé pratique de la culture de la Vigne. 1854. III. 440,[2] 555.
— Observations sur la maladie de la cloque. 1841. III. 441.[2]
— Traité succinct de l'éducation du Pêcher. 1841. III. 440.[2]
Malou. Les Noyers d'Amérique. 1867. III. 441.[3]
Malpighi, Marcello. Anatome plantarum. 1675. I. 97.
— Opera omnia. 1675. I. 97.
— Opera posthuma. 1698. I. 97.
Malpighia. I. 25.
Malta, Ignacio José. Eugenia pedunculada, Pitangueira. 1850. II. 627.[2]
— Origem da palavra Marácujá. 1851. II. 577.[1]

Maltass, Sidney H. Notes on some products of Terebinth. 1858. III. 525.[2]
Maltitz, G. A., *Freiherr* von. Briefwechsel aus dem Narrenhause. 1824. IV. 101.
— Humoristische Raupen. 1824. IV. 101.
— Humoristisch-satyrische Plänterhiebe. 1824. IV. 101.
Maltschewsky, P. Sur le dosage du tannin dans le thé. 1890. III. 608.[1]
Maltzan, J. C. E., *Graf* von. Handbuch für Förster. 1805. IV. 96.
— Versuch einer ... Anleitung zur Forstkultur. 1812. IV. 106.
— Versuch einer gründlichen Anleitung zum Bau hölzerner Brücken. 1805. IV. 424.[2]
Malvern naturalists' field club. Transactions. I. 18.
Malý, Carl. Adnotationes ad floram Bosniae. 1895. I. 448.[1]
— Zur Flora von Nordostbosnien. 1894. I. 448.[1]
— Eine monströse Bildung bei der Grauerle. 1893. II. 117.[1]
Maly, Günther Walter. Untersuchungen über Verwachsungen ... von Blumenblättern. 1896. II. 835.[1]
Maly, Joseph Karl. De analogis plantarum affinium viribus. 1823. III. 259.[1]
— Anleitung zur Bestimmung der Gattungen der in Deutschland wildwachsenden ... Pflanzen. 1846. I. 382, 532.[1]
— Botanik für Damen. 1862. I. 95.
— Enumeratio plantarum ... imperii austriaci. 1848. I. 440.
— Flora styriaca. 1838. I. 440.
— Flora von Deutschland. 1860. I. 384.
— Flora von Steiermark. 1838. I. 440.
— Nachträge zur Flora von Steyermark. 1838. I. 440.
— Oekonomisch-technische Pflanzenkunde. 1864. III. 90.[2]
— Systematische Beschreibung der gebräuchlichsten ... Arzneigewächse. 1837. III. 73.
— Systematische Beschreibung der in Oesterreich ... Medizinalpflanzen. 1863. III. 90.[2]
Maly, Richard L. Über Darstellung ... der krystallisirbaren Säure im Harze von Pinus Abies. 1862. II. 36.[2]
Malyuga, I. *See* МАЛЮГА, И.
Malyutin, F. *See* МАЛЮТИНЪ, Ф.
Malzine, Omer de. La flore mexicaine aux environs de Cordova. 1873. I. 331.
Mamayef, S. *See* МАМАЕВЪ, С.
A mammoth Rose bush. 1874. III. 449.
The mammoth trees of California. 1862. II. 50.[2]
Mammutsbaum-Waldungen in Kalifornien. 1895. II. 51.[1]
The "Man Oak" at Elmwood, Conn. 1891. I. 209,[2] IV. 501.[1]
Manceau. Buxus sempervirens L. var. lancifolia. 1868. II. 453.[1]
— Plantes phanérogames du Maine. 1862. I. 412.
Manceau, Émile. Sur le tannin de la galle d'Alep. 1896. III. 237.[1]
Manchester — Literary and philosophical society. *See* LITERARY ... I. 18.
Manchester microscopical society. Transactions. I. 18.
The Manchester quarterly. III. 17.
Mandat, die Wald-Neben-Nutzungen ... betreffend de dato Dresden. 1813. IV. 302.
Mandelik, Dániel. Eszleletek az erdei Fenyő csemeték tűhullatása körül. 1884. IV. 477.
Mandié, M. Grössen-Verhältnisse der gehöften Tüpfel. 1878. II. 323.[2]
Mandirola, F. Agostino. Il giardino de' fiori. 1649. III. 115.[1]
— Italiänischer Blumen- und Pomerantzen-Garten. 1649. III. 115.[1]
— Manuale di giardinieri. 1649. III. 115.[1]
— Manuel du jardinier. 1649. III. 115.[1]
— Der neu-aufgesetzte Blumen-Garten. 1649. III. 115.[1]
Mandon, J. A. Traitement anti-phylloxérique. 1883. III. 761.
Mandruzzato, Salvator. Del facolta febbrifuga ... del Santonico. 1800. III. 754.[1]
Manec. Observation de tétanos traumatique. 1859. III. 683.[1]
— Tétanos traumatique traité sans succès par le curare. 1859. III. 683.[1]
Manès, Henri. Greffe du Caféier. 1894. III. 733.[1]
Manetti, Giuseppe. Catalogus plantarum Caesarei regii horti prope Modiciam. 1842. I. 63.
— Root-grafting. 1840. III. 451.[1]
— Om Rosernes Podning paa Rødder. 1840. III. 451.[2]

Manetti, Saverio. Caroli Linnaei regnum vegetabile. 1756. I. 257.
— Viridarium florentinum. 1751. I. 61.
Manetti, Xaver. *See* MANETTI, Saverio.
The Manetti stock and Roses on the Manetti stock. 1865. III. 455.[1]
Maney, Joseph. On sowing the seeds of forest-trees. 1824. IV. 148.
De Mangabeira. 1885. III. 229.
Die Mangabeira. 1899. III. 688.[2]
Manganotti, Antonio. Cenni di geografia ... Italia settentrionale e Dalmazia. 1854. I. 427.
— Elementi di botanica. 1852. I. 89.
— Della Paulownia imperiale. 1850. III. 703.[1]
Manger, H. L. Vollständige Anleitung zu einer systematischen Pomologie. 1780. III. 70.
— *See also* GERMERSHAUSEN, C. F. & MANGER, H. L.
Manger, H. R. R. Nachricht von den Obstpflanzungen. 1828. III. 211.[1]
Mangin, Arthur. Le cacao et le chocolat. 1860. III. 594.
— Histoire des jardins anciens et modernes. 1888. III. 32.[2]
— Les mémoires d'un Chêne. 1889. IV. 502.[2]
— Les plantes utiles. 1870. III. 53.
Mangin, Louis. Sur l'aération du sol dans les promenades. 1895. III. 211.[2]
— Sur la callose. 1890. I. 138.[2]
— Sur les cellules mucifères ... du Taxus. 1893. II. 10.[2]
— Sur la constitution de la membrane des végétaux. 1888. I. 129.[2]
— Sur la constitution des cystolithes. 1892. I. 139.
— Sur la diffusion des gaz à travers les surfaces cutinisées. 1887. I. 161.
— Sur l'emploi du rouge de ruthénium. 1893. I. 37.[1]
— Études sur la végétation dans ses rapports avec l'aération du sol. 1896. *I. 229,* III. 211.[2]
— Sur l'importance des mycorhizes. 1893. I. 234.[1]
— Die Lebensdauer der Pariser Ulmen. 1900. III. 42.[2]
— Sur le lieu de formation des racines adventives. 1880. I. 103.
— La lutte contre les maladies parasitaires. 1896. III. 197.
— Sur la maladie de la gomme chez le Cacaoyer. 1897. III. 593.[2]
— Sur une maladie des Ailantes. 1894. III. 507.[1]
— Sur la maladie du rouge. 1894. III. 195.[1]
— Sur un nouvel exemple de concrescence des racines. 1885. I. 210.[1]
— Observations sur l'anthracnose maculée. 1892. III. 580.
— Observations sur la membrane cellulosique. 1891. I. 138.[2]
— Observations sur la membrane du grain de pollen. 1889. I. 117.[1]
— Observations sur le développement des fleurs dans les bourgeons. 1888. I. 115.[2]
— Origine et insertion des racines adventives. 1882. I. 104.
— Sur la perméabilité de l'épiderme. 1888. I. 161.
— Sur la présence de thylles gommeuses dans la Vigne. 1894. I I. 581.
— Sur la présence des composés pectiques. 1889. I. 177.
— Sur la production de la gomme chez les Sterculiacées. 1897. III. 589.[2]
— Propriétés ... des composés pectiques. 1892. I. 177.
— Sur les réactifs colorants. 1890. I. 156.[2]
— Recherches sur la pénétration ou la sortie des gaz dans les plantes. 1888. I. 162.
— Recherches sur le pollen. 1886. I. 201.[2]
— Recherches sur les bourgeons. 1886. I. 108,[2] 171.
— Sur le rôle des stomates. 1887. I. 171.
— Sur la structure des mycorrhizes. 1898. I. 234.[1]
— Structure et fonctions des stomates. 1890. I. 131.[2]
— Sur la substance intercellulaire. 1890. I. 138.[2]
— Sur la végétation dans une atmosphère viciée par la respiration. 1896. I. 211.
— *See also* BONNIER, Gaston & MANGIN, Louis.
Mangles, J. H. Hybrid Rhododendron. 1881. III. 658.[2]
— Hybrid Rhododendrons. 1884. III. 655.
— Notes on Rhododendrons. 1884. III. 655.
— Rhododendron Aucklandi. 1881. III. 659.[1]
— Rhododendron grande. 1882. III. 659.[1]
— Rhododendron Metternichii. 1882. II. 682.[1]
— Rhododendrons. 1879. III. 655.
— Varieties of Rhododendron argenteum. 1882. III. 659.[1]
Mangles, James. The floral calendar. 1839. III. 123.[2]
Mango grafting. 1888. III. 524.[1]
Mangold, Chr. Laurus nobilis L., seine Pflege. 1896. III. 406.[1]

Mangold, Johann Kaspar. Praeliminaria de conciliandis methodis Tournefortii, Rivini, Hermanni et Raji. 1716. I. 250.

Mangold, Justus Heinrich. De manna. 1725. III. 221.[1]

Mangoldt, Paul von. Das Forst- und Feldstrafgesetz. 1895. IV. 322.[1]

Mangon, Hervé. *See* HERVÉ-MANGON, C. F.

The **Mangosteen.** 1897. III. 609.[2]

The **Mangosteen,** Garcinia Mangostana. 1855. III. 609.[1]

The **Mangosteen;** Garcinia Mangostana Linn. 1895. III. 609.[3]

The **Mangosteen** of Singapore. 1875. II. 555.[2]

The **Mangosteen,** or Mangostan. 1856. III. 609.[3]

Mangrove bark and extract. 1892. III. 632.[1]

Mangroves. 1895. II. 614,[1] IV. 46.[1]

Manhartsberger Forstverein. Vereinschrift. IV. 15.

The **Manicora** Rubber tree. 1900. III. 520.[3]

Manier in China om de vruchtboomen te vermeerderen. 1806. III. 157.

Della **maniera** di coltivare gli alberi fruttiferi. 1769. III. 145.[1]

La **manière** d'enter et planter. *See* CRESCENZI, Piero de. 1486. III. 98.

Manila Aloe fibre. 1893. III. 341.[1]

Mankowski, H. Ueber die bäuerlichen Wälder in Ostpreussen. 1895. . IV. 119.[1]

Manlius de Bosco, J. J. Luminare maius. 1528. III. 757.[2]

Mann, Benjamin Pickman. The white Coffee-leaf miner. 1872. III. 735.

Mann, Gustav. A descriptive catalogue of the Natal contribution. 1862. III. 281.[2]

— Der Gummibaum. 1873. IV. 519.[1]

— Memorandum on the extraction of crude turpentine from . . . Pinus Khasyana. 1882. III. 307.[3]

— Report on the Caoutchouc plantations in Assam. 1876. III. 371.[1]

— Report on the Caoutchouc tree in . . . Assam. 1869. III. 370.[2]

—& Wendland, Hermann. Des Palmiers de l'Afrique. 1863. II. 62.[1]

— — On the Palms of western tropical Africa. 1863. II. 62.[1]

Mann, Horace. Catalogue of the phænogamous plants of the United States, east of the Mississippi. 1868. I. 307.

— Description of some new species of . . . Schiedea. 1866. II. 194.[1]

— Enumeration of Hawaiian plants. 1866. I. 509.[2]

— Flora of the Hawaiian Islands. 1866. . I. 509.[3]

— Four new genera of Hawaiian plants. 1869. I. 509.[2]

— Notes on Alsinidendron. 1869. I. 509.[2]

— Revision of the Rutaceae of the Hawaiian Islands. 1866. II. 397.[1]

Mann, J. R. Observations on the water supply of Mauritius. 1861. IV. 49.[1]

Mann, James. Australian timber. 1900. IV. 409. ·

Mann, James A. Cocoa; its cultivation. 1860. III. 592,[1] 594.

Mann, Johann Gottlieb. Die ausländischen Arzneipflanzen. 1830. III. 56.

— Deutschlands gefährlichste Giftpflanzen. 1829. III. 73.

Mann, Otto. Die Bambusrohr-Arten. 1885. III. 314.[2]

— Des différentes espèces de Bambous. 1885. III. 314.[2]

Mann, Richard. Ueber Quellungsfähigkeit einiger Baumrinden. 1885. I. 130, 150.[1]

Manna calabrina. 1835. IV. 536.[1]

Mannagetta, Günther, *Ritter* BECK VON. *See* BECK VON MANNAGETTA, Günther, *Ritter* .

Mannaioni, Giovanni · Batista. *See* MICHELI, P. A. & MANNAIONI, G. B.

Manne de l'Hedysarum alhagi. 1836. III. 466.[2]

The **manner** of making coffee, tea. *See* DUFOUR, P. S. 1671. III. 221.[1]

Mannert. Ueber die Schädlichkeit der Dunkelschläge in Kiefern. 1826. IV. 471.

— Ueber die Zweckmässigkeit der Durchforstungen. 1827. IV. 172.[2]

Mannhardt, F. Das Verpflanzen älterer Zierbäume. 1890. III. 168.[1]

— & Deil, F. Die für Strassenpflanzungen . . . passendsten Bäume. 1890. · III. 210.

Mannhardt, Wilhelm. Wald- und Feldkulte. 1875. I. 517.[1]

Mannheimer Verein für Naturkunde. Jahresbericht. I. 520.[1]

Manni, D. M. Della piantagione . . . de' Gelsi. 1767. V. XXVIII.[2]

Mannich, Carl. Chemische Untersuchung der Perubalsamsorten. 1900. III. 482.[1]

Manning, Agnes M. To the Big trees. 1870. II. 51.[1]

Manning, J. H. The preservation of wood with woodcreosote oil. 1889. IV. 421.

— Products of the Pine, II. 1889. IV. 421.

Manning, Jacob Woodward. The Byfield Elm. 1878. II. 143.[2]

— Growing trees on exposed situations. 1886. III. 42.[1]

— What is the best method of .repelling or destroying the insect enemies of fruits? 1883. III. 186.[2]

Manning, Robert. Book of fruits. 1838. III. 61.[1]

— Grafting the Gooseberry on the Missouri Currant. 1879. III. 413.[2]

— The New England fruit book. 1838. III. 61.[1]

Manoncour, Charles Nicolas Sigisbert SONNINI DE. *See* SONNINI DE MANONCOUR, C. S.

Manoury (*of Caen*). *See* DURAND & MANOURY.

Manrique de la Vega, Matias de la MADRID Y. *See* MADRID Y MANRIQUE DE LA VEGA, Matias de la.

Mans — Société royale d'agriculture, sciences et arts. *See* SOCIÉTÉ . . . I. 24.[1]

Mansa, Johan Ludwig. Have-Katekismus. 1787. III. 100.[2]

— Beitrag zur Lehre von der Erziehung der Weisstanne. 1845. IV. 444.[1]

Mansel-Pleydell, John Clavell. Flora of Dorsetshire. 1874. I. 402, 534.[1]

Mansfeld, Josef VON COLLOREDO-. *See* COLLOREDO-MANSFELD, Josef von.

Mansfeld, W. Die Forst-, Jagd- und Fischerei-Strafgesetze des Herzogthums Braunschweig. 1879. IV. 319.[1]

Mansholt, D. R. & H. J. De stikstofvoeding der landbouwcultuurgewassen. 1894. III. 38.[1]

Mansholt, H. J. *See* MANSHOLT, D. R. & H. J.

Mansky, Gottheif Sebastien. Der Feld-, Wiesen- und Gartenbau. 1805. III. 121.[1]

Manso, A. L. P. da Silva. Enumeração das substancias brasileiras que podem promover a Catarze. 1836. III. 269.[1] ·

Manso, Francisco. Aprovechamientos. 1880. IV. 276.[2]

Manson, C. F. Note on the lac industry in the Sonthal Pergunnahs. 1882. III. 232.[2]

— Note on the Mohwa tree. 1886. III. 667.[2]

— Note on the Sal tree in the Sontal Pergunnahs. 1886. III. 611.[2]

— A note on the trees in the Sontal Pergunnahs. 1886. III. 278.

— Phyllanthus reticulatus. 1886. III. 521.[2]

Manson, F. B. Trees as a protection from . . . winds. 1882. III. 215.[1]

— & Haines, H. H. Tables for use with Brandis hypsometer. 1892. · IV. 216.

Manson, James. Essay on raising and managing hedges. 1835. III. 212.[2]

Manson, Marsden. Observations on the denudation of vegetation. 1899. IV. '45.

— *See also* DAVIDSON, George & MANSON, Marsden.

Mansour, Ahmed, (*jr*.). Le Dattier et la datte. 1872. III. 329.[2]

Mantaphounes, A. *See* MANTAΦOΥNHΣ, 'A.

Mantegazza, Paolo. Di alcune piante utili . . . della Repubblica Argentina. 1883. III. 65.[2]

— On the dietetic . . . properties of Erythroxylon. 1860. III. 492.[3]

Mantel. Beitrag zur Pflanzung .mit einjährigen Kiefern. 1886. IV. 473.

Manteuffel, August Wilhelm. Der deutsche Obst- und Fruchtgärtner. 1812. III. 136.

Manteuffel, Hans Ernst, *Freiherr* von. Anweisung zum Hügelpflanzen der Nadelhölzer. 1846. IV. 153.[1]

— L'art de planter . . . plantations en ligne. 1855. IV. 546.[1]

— Auch einige Worte über die Lockerung des Waldbodens. 1859. IV. 68.

— Beleuchtung der Frage: Wann und wo soll man bei der Waldverjüngung . . . den kahlen Abtriebsschlag anwenden? 1860. IV. 453.

— Bemerkungen über Hoch- oder Hügelpflanzungen. 1845. IV. 153.[2]

— Betrachtungen über die für Sachsens Staatswaldungen geeigneten Verjüngungsarten. 1870. IV. 139.[1]
— Die Eiche, deren Ansucht. 1869. IV. 506.
— Einige Worte über das Aufasten der Baume. 1872. IV. 154.[1]
— Einige Worte über Waldstreu-Abgabe. 1869. IV. 437.
— Erfahrungen über Hügelpflanzungen. 1849. IV. 153.[3]
— Gedanken über das allmälige Verschwinden der mit Tannen gemischten Bestände. 1875. IV. 138.[3]
— Gedanken über Durchforstungen. 1869. IV. 173.
— Die Hügelpflanzung. 1855. IV. 153.[2] 546.[1]
— Hügelpflanzung betreffend. 1855. IV. 153.[2]
— Nachträglicher Beitrag . . . die . . . "Hügelpflanzung" betreffend. 1853. IV. 153.[3]
— Plantning af Løv-, Naale- og Frugt-træer . . . med Forhøjninger. 1855. IV. 546.[1]
— Ueber das Verhalten der Hügelpflanzungen. 1861. IV. 153.[2]
Mantovani, V. La condizione del vincolo forestale in Italia. 1897. IV. 277.
— È legale l'accertamento mancando l'avviso. 1897. IV. 277.
— Esame della vigente legge forestale. 1897. IV. 329.
Mantzel, Ernst Johann Frid. De providentia publica circa silvas. 1759. IV. 313.
Manual of arboriculture. 1894. III. 116.[1]
A manual of botany for North America. *See* EATON, Amos. 1817. I. 306.
A manual of botany for the northern and middle states. *See* EATON, Amos. 1817. I. 306.
A manual of botany for the northern states. *See* EATON, Amos. 1817. I. 306, V. xvi.[2]
Manual of forestry prepared for use in the Simla district. *See* McINTIRE, A. L. 1895. IV. 100.[1]
Manual of the common native trees of the northern United States. *See* VASEY, George. 1877. IV. 76.[2]
A manual of the Coniferae. *See* KENT, A. H. 1881. II. 13.[1]
Manual practico de agricultura. 1822. III. 114.[3]
Manuel. Force germinative de la semence de Sapin blanc. 1864. II. 23.[2]
— Keimkraft des Weisstannensamens. 1864. II. 23.[3]
Manuel, Fr. Ueber die Entwicklung des Forstwesens im Kanton Bern. 1869. IV. 366.
Manuel d'arboriculture. 1849. III. 140.[1]
Manuel d'herborisation en Suisse. *See* CLAIRVILLE, J. P. de. 1811. I. 433.
Manuel du jardinier. 1799. III. 112.
Manuel et catalogue officiels de la section de Ceylan. 1900. III. 279.[1]
Manuel théorique et pratique d'horticulture. *See* ANTOINE, (frère). 1883. III. 113.
Manufacture of camphor in Japan. 1884. III. 404.[2]
Manufacture of cutch. 1885. III. 464.[1]
Manufacture of ink. 1862. III. 236.
The **manufacture** of Olive oil in California. 1873. III. 675,[3] 678.[2]
Manufacture of quinine in India. 1888. III. 718. — 1890. III. 718.
Manufacture of Sago. 1839. III. 327.[1]
Manufacture of wood novelties in Maine. 1898. IV. 428.[1]
Manufacturers' gazette. IV. 4.
The **manuring** of Tea estates. 1897. III. 604.[1]
Manuring of tropical plants, Coffee. 1899. III. 734.[1]
Manuring of tropical plants, Oranges and Lemons. 1899. III. 497.[3]
Manwood, John. A treatise and discourse of the lawes of the forrest. 1598. IV. 323.[1]
— A treatise of the lawes of the forest. 1598. IV. 323.[1]
The **Manzanita.** 1891. II. 660.[3]
Manzi, Michelangelo. Sull' allevamento dei bachi dell' Ailanto. 1862. III. 507.[1]
Manzini, J. Cinchovatin. 1842. III. 725.[3]
— Études sur la résine animé. 1841. III. 297,[2] 611.[3]
— Sur un faux quinquina de Loxa. 1840. III. 721.
— Note sur une sorte de quinquina. 1839. III. 724.[3]
Map of lands belonging to the forest preserve situated in the counties of Delaware, Greene. 1899. IV. 339.
The **Maple.** 1842. III. 534.[2]
Maple sugar. 1846. III. 536,[1] 536.[3] — 1860. IV. 527.[1] — 1895. IV. 527.[3]
The **maple** sugar and syrup industry of Canada. 1899. IV. 527.[2]
Maple sugar in New Brunswick. 1864. — IV. 527.[1]

Maple sugar-making. 1836. IV. 527.[1]
Maple-tree. 1835. IV. 527.[1]
The **Maples** of Canada. 1886. IV. 526.[2]
Maplet, John. A greene forest. 1567. I. 394.
Mappus, Marcus. Catalogus plantarum Horti academici argentinensis. 1691. I. 43.
— Dissertationes medicæ tres de receptis. 1691. III. 222.
— Historia plantarum alsaticarum. 1742. I. 373.
— De potu café. 1693. III. 741.[1]
— De potu chocolate. 1695. III. 594.
— De potu Theé. 1691. III. 605.
Maquenne, Léon. L'azote atmosphérique et la végétation. 1891. I. 160.
— Sur les changements de composition qu'éprouvent les graines oléagineuses. 1898. I. 204.
— Sur la composition de la miellée du Tilleul. 1893. II. 516.[1]
— Sur la diffusion de la chaleur par les feuilles. 1878. I. 232.[1]
— Sur l'heptine de la perséite. 1889. III. 407.[3]
— Sur l'hygrométricité des graines. 1899. I. 204.
— Sur le mécanisme de la respiration. 1894. I. 171.
— Sur un nouveau sucre à noyau aromatique. 1889. II. 42.[2]
— Nouvelles recherches sur la respiration des feuilles. 1894. I. 171.
— Sur le poids moléculaire . . . de la perséite. 1888. III. 407.[3]
— Sur le poids moléculaire moyen de la matière soluble. 1897. I. 204.
— Sur la pression osmotique dans les graines germées. 1896. I. 204.
— Sur la détermination des pouvoirs absorbants et diffusifs des feuilles. 1880. I. 186.
— Recherches sur la germination. 1900. I. 204.
— Recherches sur la perséite. 1888. III. 407.[3]
— Recherches sur la respiration des feuilles. 1875. I. 167.
— Sur la synthèse naturelle des hydrocarbures. 1892. I. 177.
— *See also* DEHÉRAIN, P. P. & MAQUENNE, Léon.
Máquina berries for colouring wine. 1890. III. 584.[2]
Máquina eléctrica para cortar árboles. 1889. IV. 384.[1]
Maradjo Lelo, SOETAN. *See* SOETAN MARADJO LELO. 1884. III. 730.
De **Maragogipe-Koffie.** 1884. III. 730.
Marais. Les bois industriels de la Californie. 1900. IV. 398.[1]
Marais, Ambroise VIAUD-GRAND-. *See* VIAUD-GRAND-MARAIS, Ambroise.
Marais, J. H. Note sur l'Aloès de Barbade. 1867. III. 333.[1]
Marangoni, Carlo. Diboscamento e rimboscamento. 1883. IV. 277.
Maranta, Bartholomeo. Methodi cognoscendorum simplicium libri tres. 1559. III. 257.[1]
— Novum herbarium. 1559. III. 257.[1]
Maratti, Giovanni Francesco. Flora romana. 1822. I. 425.
Maravigna, Carmelo. Saggio di una flora medica catanese. 1827. III. 88.[1]
Las **maravillas** y la riqueza de la tierra. *See* M., D. de. 1859. I. 95.
Marburg-Gesellschaft zur Beförderung der gesammten Naturwissenschaften. *See* GESELLSCHAFT . . . I. 12.
Marc. Ueber die Bewaldung . . . mit dem Götterbaume. 1880. IV. 525.
— Die Blumenesche. 1883. IV. 535.[2]
Marc, B. Die schottische Zaunrose. 1883. III. 467.[1]
Marc, Ferenc. Beitrag zur Pflanzengeographie. 1890. I. 301.
— A Bignonia radicans kulturája. 1896. III. 705.
— A Cirbolyafenyő. 1897. III. 307.[1]
— Dendrologische Studien über die Schädigungen durch den verflossenen Winter. 1888. III. 50.[1]
— Eucalyptus globulus. 1876. IV. 533.[1]
— Zur Frage der Verwendbarkeit einiger Heckenbildner. 1889. III. 214.[1]
— A Gránátalma-cserje. 1896. III. 630.[2]
— A Hólabda. 1896. III. 753.[1]
— Die interessantesten Nadelbäume Obercaliforniens. 1887. II. 14.[2]
— A legszebbfelfutó cserjék. 1898. III. 205.[1]
— A Magnoliák családja. 1897. III. 397.[1]
— A nemes Bírsfa válfajtája a mŭvelése. 1899. III. 423.[3]
— Ueber neu eingeführte Zaunsträucher. 1887. III. 214.[1]

Marc, Ferenc (*continued*).
— Der nordische Fieberbaum. 1883. III. 352.[1]
— A Tamariszka. 1898. III. 612.[1]
— A teltvirágú Galagonyákról. 1897. III. 421.[2]
— Unsere zierendsten Herbstflor-Sträucher. 1885. III. 207.[2]
— Die Weide in ihrem Werth. 1882. III. 348.
— Zwei vorzügliche Allee- und Parkbäume. 1890. III. 345,[1] 535.[1]
Marc, François, (*jr.*). Avantages de la greffe par l'emploi de très-longs rameaux. 1862. III. 161.
— Procédé avantageux pour conserver les rameaux destinés à la greffe. 1867. III. 161.
Marcailhou d'Ayméric, Alexandre. Un Arbre à pluie dans l'Ariège. 1893. I. 213.[2]
— *See also* MARCAILHOU D'AYMÉRIC, Hippolyte & Alexandre.
Marcailhou-d'Ayméric, Hippolyte. Aperçus généraux sur la flore du Japon. 1898. III. 91.[2]
— Contribution à la flore de l'Andorre. 1898. V. xxii.[2]
— & Alexandre. Catalogue raisonné des plantes . . . de la haute Ariège. 1898. V. xxii.[1]
Marcano, Vicente. Essais d'agronomie tropicale. 1892. III. 96.[1]
— Observations et expériences sur la circulation de la sève. 1883. I. 165.
— Recherches sur la transpiration des végétaux sous les tropiques. 1884. I. 167.
— Sur le yaraque. 1888. III. 521.[1]
— *See also* MÜNTZ, A. & MARCANO, V.
— & Müntz, A. L'ammoniaque dans l'atmosphère. 1891. I. 160.
Marcatili, Luigi, *conte.* Sui fasci midollari fogliari dei Ficus. 1889. II. 149.[1]
— I vasi laticiferi. 1888. I. 136.[1]
— *See also* PIROTTA, Romualdo & MARCATILI, Luigi.
Marcella, E. Manual of the education of the silkworm. 1846. III. 376.
Marcellus, Avitus. Hortus plantarum patavinus. 1660. I. 60.[1]
Marcellus, Marie Louis Jean André Charles Demartin du Tirac, *comte de.* Opinion sur l'article 2 du titre XI. du projet de loi des finances. 1817. IV. 325.
Marcet, François. De l'action des poisons sur le règne végétal. 1825. I. 210.[3]
— On the action of chloroform on the Sensitive Plant. 1848. II. 372.[1]
— Extrait d'une note sur le changement de couleur qui a lieu dans le bois. 1830. II. 116.[1]
— Note sur l'action du chloroforme sur la Sensitive. 1848. II. 372.[2]
— *See also* MACAIRE-PRINSEP, I. F. & MARCET, François.
Marcet, *Mrs.* Jane. La botanique et la physiologie végétale. 1829. I. 94.
— Conversations on vegetable physiology. 1829. I. 94.
— Conversations sur la physiologie végétale. 1829. I. 94.
— Unterhaltungen über die Physiologie der Pflanzenwelt. 1829. I. 94.
Marcgraf, Georg. Historiae rerum naturalium Brasiliae libri octo. *See* PISO, Willem & MARCGRAF, Georg. 1648. I. 327.
— Tractatus topographicus et meteorologicus Brasiliae. *See* PISO, Willem. 1658. III. 266.
Marchais, A. Les jardins dans la région de l'Oranger. 189.? III. 126.[1]
Marchais, Maxime. Arbustes à floraison estivale. 1895. III. 541.[1]
— Arbustes à floraison tardive. 1898. III. 207.[2]
— Hydrangea paniculata grandiflora. 1894. III. 412.[2]
Marchal, Élie. Araliaceae. 1891. II. 646.[2]
— Diagnoses de deux espèces . . . de Didymopanax. 1889. II. 648.[1]
— Études sur les Hédéracées. 1881. II. 647.[1]
— Hederaceae. 1878. II. 646.[2]
— Notice sur les Hédéracées récoltées par M. de André. 1881. II. 646.[2]
— Notice sur les Hédéracées récoltées par M. Éd. André. 1880. II. 650,[1] 652.[1]
— Révision des Hédéracées américaines. 1879. II. 646.[2]
— & Hardy, Auguste. Catalogue des plantes . . . de la Meuse, de Liège. 1868. II. 285.[1]
Marchal, Em. L'Actinonema du Tilleul. 1899. IV. 528.[1]
— Champignons parasites. 1897. IV. 550.[1]
— Formation et rôle de l'humus dans les forêts. 1897. IV. 543.[2]
— La maladie de l'Érable. 1898. IV. 526.[2]

— La nécrose du Tilleul et du Marronnier d'Inde. 1899. IV. 212.
— & Huberty, Jules. Le noir des feuilles de l'Érable. 1900. III. 534,[1] *IV. 586.[2]*
Marchal, Paul. Sur une nouvelle gomme laque de Madagascar. 1895. III. 228.[1]
Marchand. Emploi de la stadia. 1876. IV. 264.
Marchand, A. Ueber die Entwaldung der Gebirge. 1849. IV. 48.[2]
Marchand, Ernest & Bonjour, S. Sur les fleurs-pièges de l'Araujia sericifera. 1899. II. 728,[1] *736.[1]*
Marchand, L. Mémoire sur le déboisement des montagnes. 1849. IV. 49.[2]
— De radicibus et vasis plantarum. 1830. I. 133.
Marchand, M. L. Uber die Lärche und ihre Harzung. 1870. IV. 449.
Marchand, Nestor Léon. Des classifications et des méthodes en botanique. 1867. I. 252.
— Du Croton Tiglium. 1861. III. 517.[1]
— Énumération des substances fournies . . . par . . . Térébinthacées. 1869. III. 523.[2]
— Histoire de l'ancien groupe des Térébinthacées. 1869. II. 454.[2]
— Mission forestière en Autriche. 1869. IV. 368.
— Monstruosité de Paeonia Moutan. 1880. II. 200.[1]
— Monstruosités végétales. 1862. II. 839.[1]
— Note sur le genre Garuga Roxb. 1866. II. 418.[1]
— Observations sur Prunus Padus. 1866. II. 275.[2]
— Recherches botaniques sur le Croton Tiglium. 1860. II. 440.[1]
— Recherches organographiques . . . sur le Coffea. 1864. II. 814.[1]
— Recherches pour servir à l'histoire des Burséracées. 1866. II. 416.[1]
— Recherches sur l'organisation des Burséracées. 1867. II. 416.[1]
— Recherches sur la fleur femelle du Pistacia Chia. 1867. II. 457.[1]
— Révision du groupe des Anacardiacées. 1869. II. 454.[2]
— Des Térébinthacées. 1869. II. 454.[2]
— Des tiges des phanérogames. 1865. I. 105.
— Les torrents des Alpes et le pâturage. 1872. IV. 185.[2]
Marchand, P. Des Kakis japonais. 1877. III. 669.[1]
Marchand, V. Contre les incendies des forêts en Algérie. 1897. IV. 184.[1]
— Mémoire relatif à un procédé . . . d'ont l'application diminuerait . . . les ravages causés par les incendies. 1897. IV. 183.[2]
— Quelques mots sur l'arboriculture des promenades. 1885. III. 210.
Marchand, X. Aliénation des forêts devant l'opinion publique. 1849. IV. 277.
— Ueber die Entwaldung der Gebirge. 1849. IV. 283.[1]
— Mémoire sur la production . . . des bois dans le canton de Berne. 1852. IV. 365.
— Mémoire sur le déboisement des montagnes. 1849. IV. 283.[1]
— Uber das Verhältniss der Holzproduction zur Holzkonsumation. 1852. IV. 365.
Marchant, Nicolas. Dissertation sur une Rose monstrueuse. 1708. II. 289.[1]
— Observation sur un nouveau phénomène . . . du fruit d'une espèce de Prunier. 1738. II. 271.[2]
— Observations sur la nature des plantes. 1721. II. 839.[1]
Marchese, Giovanni. Provvedimenti contro la mosca olearia. 1899. III. 678.[1]
Marchesetti, Carlo de'. Bibliografia botanica. 1895. I. 448,[1] *519.[1]*
— Botanische Wanderungen in Italien. 1876. I. 428.
— La flora di Parenzo. 1890. V. xxiii.[1]
— Flora di Trieste. 1896. I. 448.[2]
Marchet, Gustav. Forststatistik. 1875. IV. 336.[1]
— & Exner, W. F. Holzhandel und Holzindustrie der Ostsee-Länder. 1876. IV. 403.[2]
Marchet, Julius. Ueber den Einfluss der Wassersättigung auf die Festigkeit des Holzes. 1896. IV. 412.[2]
— England als Holzconsument. 1883. IV. 405.[1]
— Ueber forstliche Arbeiterverhältnisse. 1883. IV. 310.[2]
— Der forstliche Theil der Pariser Weltausstellung. 1889. IV. 20.[2]
— Das forstliche Transportwesen auf der Pariser Weltausstellung. 1890. IV. 59.[1]
— Die Forstwirthschaft in Russland. 1883. IV. 114.
— Ueber Gewichts- und Volumenveränderung am Holze. 1883. IV. 412.[1]

— Ueber Massregeln gegen Hochwasserschäden. 1883. IV. 187.²
— Normalien-hölzerner Brücken. 1891. IV. 267.
— Die Projectierung von Waldwegnetzen. 1893. IV. 267.
— Raumgewicht und Druckfestigkeit des Kiefernholzes. 1897. IV. 482.² — 1898. IV. 482.³
— Studien über Wegtracirung. 1883. IV. 267.
— Technische Untersuchung über Eucalyptus-Hölzer. 1896. IV. 531.¹
— Transportable Stahlbahn. 1883. IV. 391.
— Waldwegebaukunde. 1898. IV. 267.
Marchi, Demetrio. Breve cenno sulle boscaglie della maremma toscana. 1865. IV. 364.
Marchlewski, L. Die Chemie des Chlorophylls. 1895. I. 142.
— See also SCHUNCK, Edward & MARCHLEWSKI, L.
— & **Schunck,** C. A. Otrzymanie chlorofilu w stanie czystym. 1900. I. 142.
Marck, J. L. B. van der. De alkaloide-bepaling in folia Cocae. 1889. III. 493.²
— Over de bereiding van pikrotoxine. 1888. III. 396.²
— Bijdrage tot de bepaling van het alcaloid gehalte in pulvis en extract nucis vomicae. 1889. III. 685.¹
— Bijdrage tot de kennis der . . . Samadera indica. 1900. II. 415.²
— Dosage des alcaloïdes dans les feuilles de Coca. 1889. III. 493.²
— Sur la préparation de la picrotoxine. 1888. III. 396.²
— Sur la préparation de la picrotoxyne. 1888. III. 396.²
— & **Kruijder,** C. A. C. Over de bestanddeelen der Samadera indica. 1890. II. 415.²
Marck, W. von der. Flora Lüdenscheidts. 1851. I. 383.
Marco, E. Skizzen von der Riviera. 1885. III. 125.
Marco, Eugen. Die Gehölz-Verwendung im Landschaftsgarten. 1893. I. 242;¹ III. 44.¹
— Die japanischen Kaki-Arten. 1893. III. 669.³
— Les Kakis du Japon. 1893. III. 669.²
Marco, Gennaro de. Flora di Montecassino. 1886. V. XXII.²
Marcou, Jules. Ueber den Cereus giganteus Englm. 1869. II. 590.¹
— Note sur le Cereus giganteus. 1869. II. 590.¹
Marcq, Adolphe. Les arbustes d'ornement. 189.? III. 106.²
Marquis, Willem. Aloë morbifuga. 1633. III. 333.¹
Marcus. See BOCHEFONTAINE, F. T., FÉRIS, Bazile & MARCUS.
Marcus, A. Recherches expérimentales sur la dessiccation artificielle du bois. 1884. IV. 416.¹
Marcus, Karl Julius. De Coffea. 1837. III. 741.²
Marcus, Samuel. Iconum botanicarum Gesnerio-Camerarianarum minorum nomenclator Linneanus. See HARTMANN, P. E. 1781. I. 78.¹
Marcuse, Adolf. Die Hawaiischen Inseln. 1894. I. 510.¹
Marcy, Oliver. Willows presented to the H. H. Babcock herbarium. 1889. II. 99,⁴ 871.²
Marcy, Randolph Barnes. Exploration of the Red River of Louisiana. See TORREY, John. 1853. I. 318.
— Die geographische Verbreitung des Mesquite-Baumes. 1858. III. 485.¹
Mardigny, de. Mémoire sur les inondations des rivières de l'Ardèche. 1860. IV. 47.¹
Maréchal, Georges. Étude sur les vices des bois. 1882. I. 207.¹ IV. 66.¹
Mareck, B. Der rationelle Weinbau. 1870. III. 553.¹
Mareeuw, W. P. H. van den. See DRIESSEN, W. P. H. van den.
Marek, Josef. Der bosnische Wald. 1886. IV. 374.¹
Marés, Henri Pierre Louis. Sur le danger de l'introduction de certaines Vignes américaines. 1876. III. 556.
— Description des cépages principaux . . . de la France. 1890. III. 547.
— Sur la disparition spontanée du phylloxera. 1877. III. 570.³
— Sur diverses maladies cryptogamiques régnantes de la Vigne. 1885. III. 578.
— Sur l'emploi des sulfocarbonates. 1877. III. 560.
— Sur la maladie de la Vigne. 1873. III. 577.
— Sur la manière dont la fleur de soufre agit contre la maladie de la Vigne. 1855. III. 576.
— Manuel pour le soufrage des Vignes malades. 1856. III. 563.
— Mémoire sur la maladie de la Vigne. 1856. III. 577.
— Des moyens de reconstituer les Vignes . . . détruites par le phylloxera. 1876. III. 556.

— Note concernant l'action du soufre . . . sur l'Oïdium. 1858. III. 577.
— Note sur la maladie de la Vigne caractérisée par le phylloxera. 1873. III. 565.¹
— Phylloxera. 1874. III. 567.²
— Production de galles phylloxériques. 1877. III. 570.³
— Des progrès de la maladie de la Vigne pendant l'hiver. 1874. III. 577.
— De la propagation du phylloxera. 1873. III. 565.²
— Propagation du phylloxera. 1874. III. 567.²
— Sur les résultats des expériences faites par la Commission de la maladie de la Vigne. 1873. III. 577.
— Sur les résultats des expériences faites par la Commission de la maladie de la Vigne en 1874. 1875. III. 577.
— Résultats obtenus dans le traitement des Vignes. 1880. III. 560.
— Résultats obtenus dans le traitement par les sulfocarbonates. 1876. III. 569.¹
— Résultats obtenus sur les Vignes phylloxérées. 1876. III. 569.³
— Du traitement des Vignes phylloxérées. 1880. III. 572.
— Sur le traitement des Vignes phylloxérées. 1881. III. 572.
— Des transformation que subit le soufre en poudre. 1869. III. 563.
— & **Planchon,** J. E. Sur la floraison . . . de la Vigne. 1867. II. 507.¹
Marès, Paul. Aperçu général sur le groupe des îles Baléares. 1865. I. 423.
— Sur les îles Baléares et leur végétation. 1865. I. 423.
— Note sur l'acclimatation . . . d'Eucalyptus en Algérie. 1873. IV. 529.³
— & **Vigineix,** Guillaume. Catalogue raisonné des plantes vasculaires des îles Baléares. 1880. I. 423.
Marescaux, Oscar. Disease in Orange trees. 1887. III. 501.¹
Maresch, J. Auftreten des grauen Lärchenwicklers. 1881. IV. 451.
— Denkschrift über die . . . 1883-1893 ausgeführten Wildbach-Verbauungen in Tirol. 1895. IV. 188.¹
Mareschal, A. A. See LESACHER, E. & MARESCHAL, A. A.
Marest, (jr.). Note sur le Prunus sinensis var. alba flore pleno. 1861. III. 437.¹
Marestang. See GAUCHER, E., COMBEMALE & MARESTANG.
Maret. Nouveau tarif suivant le système décimal, pour le solivage des bois. 1840. IV. 222.
Margat. Extrait d'une notice sur la faculté qu'ont les racines des arbres indigènes de supporter la gelée. 1830. III. 182.
Margency, de. Le Kaki du Japon. 1897. III. 669.²
Margerison, Samuel. British sylviculture. 1900. IV. 121.
— Railway rates. 1895. IV. 285,¹ 403.¹
Marggraf, Johann Gustav. De usu corticis peruviani. See BÜCHNER, J. A. E. 1762. III. 719.
Marggraf, Ω. See Маргграфъ, Ω.
Marggraf, V. See Маргграфъ, В.
Margot, H. & Reuter, F. G. Essai d'une flore de l'île de Zante. 1839. I. 449.
Margottet & Collot. Étude des terrains de la Côte d'Or. 1891. III. 557.¹
Margottin. Sur quelques variations de Rosiers. 1866. III. 39.
Marguerite Delacharlonny, P. Méthode simple de transplantation des gros arbres. 1888. III. 168.¹
Marhula, J. Borkenkäfer in den bosnischen Waldungen. 1894. IV. 204.
— Zur bosnisch-herzegowinischen Karstculturfrage. 1894. IV. 167.²
— Schädliche Insecten. 1894. IV. 210.¹
Mariabrunn — K. k. Forst-Akademie. See K. K. FORST-AKADEMIE . . . IV. 14.
The **Mariana** Plum. 1886. III. 438.³
Mariani, Angelo. Coca and its medicinal application. 1890. III. 493.²
— La Coca et ses applications thérapeutiques. 1890. III. 493.²
Mariani, Domenico. Ancora sull' insegnamento nell' Istituto forestale di Vallombrosa. 1897. IV. 35.²
— Ancora sulla riproduzione agamica del Faggio. 1898. IV. 496.
— Appunti sopra un bruco. 1889. IV. 517.¹
— Osservazioni sulla moltiplicazione agamica del Faggio. 1898. IV. 500.²
Mariano de Rivero & Boussingault, T. B. Memoir on the milk of the Cow-tree. 1825. II. 146.²

Mariboe, Carl. Anvisning til Dyrkning af Frugtbuske. 1890. III. 147.[2]
— Hyld (Sambucus nigra). 1898. III. 752.[1]
— Tjørnehækken. 1898. III. 422.[2]
Marichal. See PONTARLIER & MARICHAL.
Marie. Observations sur une maladie qui attaque les raisins de table. 1850. III. 575.[1]
Marie, François. Moyens de prévenir les inondations. 1862. IV. 185.[2]
Marié, Paul. Recherches sur la structure des Renonculacées. 1885. II. 195.[1]
— Du semen-contra. 1884. III. 754.[2]
Marié de l'Isle, E. B. Manuel complet des marchands de bois. 1835. IV. 402.[2]
Maries, Charles. A branching Date Palm. 1898. II. 73.[1]
— Gum from the Weaver's Beam tree. 1897. III. 680.[1]
— Indian Mangos. 1889. III. 524.[2]
— Remarks on the propagation of Mangoes. 1886. III. 524.[2]
— A visit to Naini Tal, Kumaon. 1898. I. 475.[2]
— Wild Mangos. 1885. III. 524.[2]
Mariez, Louis. Manuel d'arboriculture. 1872. III. 144.
Marilaun, Anton Joseph KERNER VON. See KERNER VON MARILAUN, A. J.
Marillac St. Julien, Th. von. Der ausübende Forstbetrieb. 1863. IV. 243.
Marini, Giovanni Battista FRANCESCHI-. See FRANCESCHI-MARINI, G. B.
Marinucci, Settimio. Sulla respirazione delle piante. 1886. I. 171.
Marinville, baron de. Note sur le Chiranthodendron. 1851. III. 590.[1]
Marion, Antoine Fortuné. Application du sulfure de carbone. 1878. III. 571.
— Sur l'emploi du sulfure de carbone. 1876. III. 568.
— Expériences relatives à la destruction du phylloxera. 1876. III. 569.[1]
— Note sur la floraison du Dracaena Goldieana. 1881. II. 82.[2]
— Note sur le Daphne Mazeli hort. 1881. II. 601.[1]
— Rapport sur les expériences . . . pour combattre le phylloxera. 1876. III. 569.[1]
— Sur la réapparition du phylloxera. 1879. III. 571.
— Sur les résultats obtenus par l'emploi du sulfure de carbone. 1877. III. 570.[2]
— Traitement des Vignes phylloxérées. 1878. III. 571.
— See also SAPORTA, Gaston, comte de & MARION, A. F.
— & **Gastine**, G. Remarques sur l'emploi du sulfure de carbone. 1891. III. 574.
Marion, Fulgence. Les merveilles de la végétation. 1866. I. 95.
Mariotte, Edme. Premier essay de la végétation des plantes. 1679. I. 146.
Marissal, Félix Victor. Catalogue des phanerogames . . . de Tournay. 1846. · I. 392.
Marissen, J. Z. Algemeene plantenteelt. 1898. III. 106.[1]
Mariti, Giovanni. Travels in the island of Cyprus. 1769. I. 536.[1]
— Viaggi per l'isola di Cipro. 1769. I. 451, 536.[1]
Marivault, de. Notions élémentaire de géologie, de physique. 1836. III. 35.
Mariz, Joaquim de. Subsidios para o estudo da flora portugueza. 1884. I. 422.
— Uma excursão botanica em Traz os Montes. 1889. I. 422.
Markee, C. Verzameling van voorscheijden uijtlansche gewasse. 1763. I. 338.[1]
Markendorf, Johann Benjamin. See SCHELLIG, K. F. & MARKENDORF, J. B.
— & **Schellig**, K. J. Erläuterte Forstaufgaben als Entwickelungen . . . zur Abtheilung der Gehölze. 1811. IV. 250.[2]
Markfeldt, Oskar. Ueber das Verhalten der Blattspurstränge immergrüner Pflanzen. 1885. I. 110.
Markgraf. See MARGGRAF.
Markham, Sir Clements Robert. Analysis of Cinchona bark. 1864. III. 718.
— Botanical descriptions of the genus Chinchona. 1862. II. 812.
— Caoutchouc cultivation in British India. 1880. III. 149.
— Chinchona cultivation in Travancore. 1866. III. 714.
— The Chinchona species of New Granada. 1867. II. 812.
— On Cinchona cultivation in Ceylon. 1866. III. 714.
— Cinchona cultivation in India. 1863. III. 713.[2]

— The cultivation of caoutchouc-yielding trees in British India. 1876. III. 518.[2]
— Sur la culture des Cinchonas. 1866. III. 714.
— The introduction of Chinchona cultivation into India. 1866. III. 714.
— On the introduction of the Cinchona plant into India. 1861. III. 713.[3]
— A memoir of the Lady Ana de Osorio. 1874. II. 813.[1]
— Memorandum on Dr. Anderson's report on . . . the introduction of the Chinchona. 1862. III. 713.[2]
— Memorandum on Ipecacuanha. 1870. II.·828.[2]
— Notes on the culture of Cinchonas. 1859. III. 712.[1]
— Peruvian bark. 1880. III. 714.
— Report on Chinchona plantation in Ceylon. 1866. III. 714.
— Travels in Peru and India. 1862. III. 712.[1]
Markham, H. The germination of Palms. 1893. II. 63.[1]
Markham, R. Cocaplanten i Sydamerika. 1885. III. 493.[1]
Markot, R. See МАРКОВЪ, P.
Markovitch, V. V. See МАРКОВИЧЪ, B. B.
Markownikoff. Manne du Turkestan. 1886. III. 466.[2]
Markownikoff, W. Dosage de la théine. 1877. III. 607.
Marks, (Oberförster, Goschütz). Beiträge über das Wald-Ertrags-Vermögen einiger oberschlesischen Forsten. 1849. IV. 260.[1]
— See also FÖLKEL, (Oberförster) & MARKS.
Marks on trees. 1875. I. 210.[2]
Marktanner-Turneretscher, Gottlieb. Ausgewählte Blüthen-Diagramme der europäischen Flora. 1885. I. 115.[1]
— Zur Kenntniss des anatomischen Baues unserer Loranthaceen. 1885. II. 173.[2]
Marlatt, Charles Lester. The Buffalo tree-hopper. 1897. III. 187.
— How to control the San José scale. 1900. III. 197.
— The imported Elm leaf-beetle. 1895. III. 364.[2]
— Insect control in California. 1897. III. 187.
— The Peach-tree borer. 1896. III. 442.[1]
— The Peach twig-borer. 1898. III. 442.[1]
— The Pear slug. 1897. III. 446.[2]
— The Pear-tree Psylla. 1895. III. 446.[2]
— The principal insect enemies of the Grape. 1896. III. 564.[1]
— The Woolly Aphis of the Apple. 1897. III. 428.[2]
— See also HOWARD, L. O. & MARLATT, C. L.
Marle, A. J. van. De gouvernements Koffie-cultuur. 1897. III. 731.
Marle, J. A. van. De landbouw in de bergstreken. 1872. III. 128.
Marler, G. L. The denudation of our forests. 1883. IV. 281.[2]
Marliac, LATOUR-. See LATOUR-MARLIAC.
Marlin. · Culture du Thé vert de Chine au . . . Chiavri. 1887. III. 601.[1]
Marloth, Rudolf. The Acacias of southern Africa. 1888. II. 323.[1]
— Zur Bedeutung der . . . Drüsen der Tamariscineen. 1887. II. 562.[1]
— Leucadendron argenteum R.·Br. 1886. II. 164.[1]
— On the means of the distribution of seeds. 1896. I. 241.[1]
— Über mechanische Schutzmittel der Samen. 1883. · I. 121, 235.[1]
— Die Naros, Acanthosicyos horrida. 1888. II. 844.[1]
— Some adaptions of South African plants. 1890. I. 495.
— Das südöstliche Kalahari-Gebiet. 1887. I. 495.
Marly, H. de. Sparmannia africana. 1899. III. 585.[1]
Marmé, Wilhelm. Sur la taxine. 1876. II. 10.[2]
— See also HUSEMANN, August & MARMÉ, Wilhelm.
Marmocchi, F. G. Prodromo della storia naturale . . . d'Italia. 1844. III. 88.[1]
Marmol, Luis del. Descripción general de Africa. 1573. . I. 482.
Marne — Société d'agriculture, commerce, sciences. See SOCIÉTÉ . . . III. 21.
Marneffe, Émile de. Une question de droits d'usage forestiers. 1898. IV. 334.[1]
— See also CRAHAY, N. I. & MARNEFFE, Émile de.
Marneffe, Gustave de. La fumure des arbres fruitiers. 1894. IV. 545.[2]
— La laine de bois. 1894. IV. 557.[2]
— Le Lupin et la culture forestière. 1894. IV. 545.[1]
— Les plantations des routes. 1894. III. 186.[1]
Marnock, Robert. Cranberries. 1880. III. 663.[2]
— Durability of Elm wood. 1885. IV. 518.[2]

— The Lombard Poplar. 1881. III. 346.[1]
— The plantation, Leighton Buzzard. 1872. I. 55.
— See also DEAKIN, Richard & MARNOCK,·Robert.
Marogna, Nicolò. Commentario ne' trattati . . . dell' Amomo. 1608. I. 284.
— Commentarius in tractatus . . . de Amomo. 1608. I. 284.
Marolda-Petilli, Francesco. Gli Eucalitti. 1879. II. 623.[1]
Maron, (Oberforstmeister, Oppeln). Ueber Pflanzung einjähriger Kiefern. 1847. IV. 472.
Maron, Ch. Les Polygalas frutescents. 1895. III. 514.[1]
— Tecoma Smithii. 1895. III. 707.[2]
Maron, Ernst Wilhelm. Anleitung für Privatwald-Eigenthümer zur . . . Ermittelung des nachhaltigen Material-Ertrages. 1841. IV. 240.
— Forst-Statistik der sämmtlichen Wälder Deutschlands. 1862. IV. 349.[1]
— Der gute Forst-Lehrling und der tüchtige Förster. 1842. IV. 31.
— Die Privat-Forstwirthschaft. 1848. IV. 97.
— Reisebilder aus dem Königreich Polen. 1841. IV. 344.[2]
Maronea. See MAROGNA, Nicolò.
Marosi, Ferenc. Kétféle Csertölgy a lippai uradalomban. 1886. II. 133.[1]
— A lippai m. k. főerdőhivatal kerületéhez tartozó erdők gazdasági viszonyainak leirása. 1890. IV. 374.[1]
Marquand, Ernest David. The flora of Guernsey. 1891. I. 404.[1]
Marquardt, Kurt. Der Kirschbaum in Parkanlagen. 1898. III. 435.[1]
— Ein schöner Zierapfel. 1899. III. 429.[1]
— Die Silberlinde. 1899. III. 586.[1]
— Die strauchartigen Potentillen. 1900. III. 430.[1]
— Wistaria chinensis. 1900. III. 491.[1]
Marquardt, T. L. Neue Methode, die Camellien zu vermehren. 1834. III. 599.[2]
— Ny Methode at formere Camellier paa. 1834. III. 599.[2]
— Verfahrungsart um von der Camellia japonica simplex, bestimmt guten Samen zu erziehen. 1835. III. 599.[2]
Marquart, Louis C. See MARQUART, Ludwig C.
Marquart, Ludwig Clamor. Die Farben der Blüthen. 1835. I. 184.
— Lehrbuch der praktischen und theoretischen Pharmacie. 1841. III. 258.
— Ueber das Studium der Gattung Salix. 1837. II. 99.[1]
— Ueber den Thee. 1838. III. 606.
— See also HENRY, Aimé & MARQUART, Clamor; NEES VON ESENBECK, T. F. L. & MARQUART, L. C.
Marques, Agostinho Sisenando. Os climas . . . das terras de Malange á Lunda. 1889. III. 281.[1]
Marques Loureiro, José. Breve noticia sobre dez arvores florestaes. · 1877. I. 419,[1] IV. 85.[2]
Marquet, François Nicolas. Venimecum de botanique. 1773. III. 55.
Marquis, Alexandre Louis. Sur le Chêne-chapelle d'Allouville. 1822. II. 137.[2]
— Esquisse du règne végétal. 1820. I. 259.
— Essai sur les harmonies . . . du Chêne. 1814. II. 131.[2]
— Fragmens de philosophie botanique. 1821. I. 79.[1]
— Recherches historiques sur le Chêne. 1811. II. 132.[1]
Marquis, F., (jr.). Du Thé. 1820. III. 600.[1]
Marquis, Raoul. Le liège et ses applications. 1888. IV 436,[1] 518.[1]
Marquiset, Armand. Manuel de l'usage dans les bois communaux. 1834. IV. 334.[1]
Marrier de Boisdhyver. Greffage des Pins dans la forêt de Fontainebleau. 1844. III. 160, 806.[2]
— De la prééminence du Chênerouvre sur le Chêne blanc. 1847. IV. 504.
Le marron d'Inde et la fécule de M. Belloc. 1850. III. 538.[1]
Le Marronnier du 20 mars. 1864. II. 482.[1]
Les Marronniers de l'avenue Louise. 1896. III. 181.[2]
Marsais, Georges. Grafting implements. 1880. III. 162.
— Les machines à greffer. 1880. III. 162.
Marschall von Bieberstein, Friedrich August, Freiherr. Beschreibung der Länder zwischen den Flüssen Terek und Kur. 1800. I. 360.
— Centuria plantarum rariorum Rossiae meridionalis. 1810. I. 360.
— Flora taurico-caucasica. 1808. I. 368.[3]
— Sur les genres Salsola, Anabasis. 1806. II. 368.[2]
— Supplementum, continens plantas phanerogamas, per Tauriam atque Caucasum. 1808. · I. 368.[2]
Marschlins, Ulysses von SALIS-. See SALIS-MARSCHLINS, Ulysses von.

Marschner. Ein Prachtexemplar der Rotbuche. 1894. II. 127.[1]
Marsden, William. The history of Sumatra. 1783. III. 275.[1]
— Natürliche . . . Beschreibung der Insel Sumatra. 1783. III. 275.[1]
Marseille — Académie. See ACADÉMIE . . . I. 20.
Marseille — Faculté des sciences. See FACULTÉ . . . I. 21.
Marseille — Institut botanico-géologique colcnial. See INSTITUT COLONIAL DE MARSEILLE. I. 21.
Marseille — Institut colonial. See INSTITUT . . . I. 21.
Marseille — Musée et institut colonial de Marseille. See INSTITUT COLONIAL . . . I. 21.
Marseille — Société de géographie. See SOCIÉTÉ . . . I. 23.
Marseille-médical. I. 22.
Marsh, George Perkins. The earth as modified by human action. 1869. IV. 43.
— Extracts from Man and nature. 1869. IV. 43.
— Man and nature. 1869. IV. 43.
— Le piantagioni nella prateria occidentale degli Stati Uniti. 1880. IV. 155.[1]
— Le reboisement aux États-Unis. 1880. IV. 155.[1]
Marsh, T. W. Measuring the heights of trees. 1872. IV. 215.
Marshall, C. A. The beauties and profit of forestry. 1899. IV. 271.[1]
Marshall, C. F. The evolution of fruits. 1895. I. 120.
— What is the true rank of Salix Sadleri? 1894. II. 109.[2]
— See also HANBURY, F. J. & MARSHALL, E. S.
Marshall, Henry. Beitrag zur Naturgeschichte der Cocos-Palme. 1824. III. 323.[2]
— Of cinnamon as an article of commerce. 1817. III. 406.[1]
— The Cinnamon-tree and its products. 1833. III. 406.[1]
— Contribution to a natural . . . history of the Coco-nut tree. 1824. III. 323.[2]
— Description of the Coco-nut tree. 1833. III. 323.[2]
— A description of the Laurus Cinnamomum. 1817. II. 224.[2]
— Observations on cinnamon. 1840. III. 405.[1]
Marshall, Humphry. Arbustrum americanum. 1785. I. 304, IV. 75.[1]
— Beschreibung der wildwachsenden Bäume und Staudengewächse in den Vereinigten Staaten. 1785. I. 304, IV. 75.[1]
— Catalogue alphabétique des arbres et arbrisseaux . . . dans les États-Unis. 1785. I. 304, IV. 75.[1]
Marshall, J. G. F. Large Simal tree. 1887. II. 529.[2]
Marshall, John & Wood, H. C. Sur l'Hamamelis virginica. 1887. III. 417.[1]
Marshall, Thomas R.· Description of a method of preserving plants. 1857. I. 35.
Marshall, W. G. Through America. 1000. II. 51.[1]
Marshall, William. Planting and ornamental gardening. 1785. III. 81.
— Planting and rural ornament. 1785. III. 81.
— On planting and rural ornament. 1785. III. 81.
Marshall, William, (1815–1890). Botany of the Fenland. 1878. I. 534.[1]
Marsham, Robert. Observations on the growth of trees. 1760. III. 38.[1]
— On the usefulness of washing . . . the stems. 1777. III. 38.[1]
— Watering stems of trees. 1838. III. 38.[1]
Marsham, Thomas. Copy of a letter to the author on the subject of insects destructive to Pines. 1832: IV. 461.[1]
Marsigli, Luigi Ferdinando, conte. Annotazioni intorno alla grana de' tintori. 1711. IV. 502.[2]
— Bevanda asiatica. 1685. III. 738.
— Danubius pannonico-mysicus. 1726. I. 444.
— Description du Danube. 1726. I. 444.
— Notizie di Constantinopoli sopra . . . Caffè. 1703. III. 738.
Marsili, Giovanni. Del Citiso degli antichi. 1809. II. 371.[1]
— Notizie del Pubblico giardino de' semplici di Padova. 1840. I. 63.
Marsillón, Ch. Influencia climatológica de los montes. 1895. IV. 542.[1]
Marsilly, Louis Joseph Auguste de Commines de. Catalogue des plantes . . . en Corse. 1872. I. 419.[1]
Marsson, Theodor Fr. Flora von Neu-Vorpommern. 1869. I. 386.
Marston, Alfred. A guide to the ferns and many of the rarer plants growing round Ludlow. 1870. I. 534.[1]

Marsten, John M. Culture and preparation of Sumach. 1852. III. 524.[1]
Martchenko, A. See Марченко, A.
Martel, Eduard Alfred. Le reboisement des plateaux calcaires. 1897. IV. 164.[1]
— Sulla struttura . . . del frutto dell' Anagyris foetida. 1886. II. 332.[1]
— Sullo sviluppo del frutto del Paliurus. 1888. II. 495.[2]
Martelli, A. Cultivation of the Mulberry. 1866. III. 377.
Martelli, Ugolino, conte. Le Anacardiacee italiane. 1891. II. 454.[2]
— Il black-rot sulle Viti presso Firenze. 1891. III. 580.
— Caso teratologico nella Magnolia anonaefolja. 1889. II. 213.[2]
— Cenni sopra alcune piante utili. 1881. III. 53.
— Sulla Chamaerops humilis var. dactylocarpa. 1889. II. 66.[2]
— Le Cinchone. 1880. III. 718.
— Le Composte raccolte dal Dottor O. Beccari. 1883. II. 849.[2]
— Contribuzione alla flora di Massaua. 1888. I. 489.
— Le Dilleniaceae Malesi e Papuane. 1886. II. 540.[2]
— Dimorfismo fiorale . . . di Aesculus. 1888. II. 481.[1]
— Epoca della formazione del grappolo nelle . . . Vite. 1892. II. 508.[2]
— Florula bogosensis. 1886. I. 489.
— Il Garofano. 1880. III. 635.[2]
— Laurus Camphora Linn. 1880. III.'404.[2]
— Opuntia Ficus indica Mill. 1884. II. 596.[2]
— Sull' origine dei Viburni italiani. 1890. II. 842.[2]
— Sull' origine delle Lonicere italiane. 1891. II. 836.[1]
— Sul Polyporus Gelsorum Fr. 1889. III. 379.[1]
— Sulla Quercus macedonica. 1888. II. 130.[2]
— Webb, Fragmenta florulae aethiopico-aegyptiacae. 1888. I. 489.
Martens. De forskjellige Voxarters naturlige Herkomst. 1844. III. 225.
Martens, (skovforvalter). Nordlandsgranen. 1897. IV. 454.
Martens, Édouard. Histoire ancienne du Pécher.' 1859. II. 276.[2]
— Les plantes alimentaires des anciens. 1858. III. 219,[2] V. x.[1]
— Ueberblick der Flora arctica. 1859. I. 309.[1]
Martens, Friderich. Spitzbergische oder grönländische Reise-Beschreibung. 1675. I. 350.[2]
Martens, Georg von. Erfahrungen . . . über die den Herbarien schädlichen Insekten. .1846. I. 35.
— Die Farben der Pflanzen. 1862. I. 71.
— Italien. 1844. I. 427.
— Missbildung der 'Blätter von Aristolochia Sipho. 1860. II. 182.[2]
— Reise nach Venedig. 1824. I. 426.
— Versuch einer systematischen Aufzählung der venezianischen Pflanzen. 1824. I. 426.
— Über die würtembergische Alp. 1826. I. 377.
— See also Schuebler, Gustav & Martens, Georg von.
— & Kemmler, K. A. Flora von Württemberg und Hohenzollern. 1865. I. 385.
Martens, J. Extractum Oxycocci. 1876. III. 664.[2]
Martens, Martin. Sur les Abelia et le Vesalia. 1847. II. 834.[1]
— Notice sur quelques'. . . plantes indigènes de l'Amérique septentrionale. 1841. II. 277.[2]
— Recherches sur les couleurs des végétaux. 1853. I. 184.
— & Galeotti, H. G. Enumeratio synoptica plantarum . . . ab Henrico Galeotti in regionibus mexicanis collectarum. 1842. I. 331.
— — Notice sur les plantes .'. . des Vacciniées et des Ericacées. 1842. II. 658.[1]
Martersteck, Johann Clemens. Bonnischer Flora erster Theil. 1792. III. 72.
Marteville, A. See Malaguti, F. J. & Marteville, A.
Marthe, François. Catalogue des plantes du Jardin médical de Paris. 1801. I. 57.
Marti, Antonio de. Experimentos y observaciones sobre los sexos. 1791. I. 199.
Marti, F. Die Drahtseilriese. 1892. IV. 392.
Marti, Fr. Der Baumhöhenmassstab Christen. 1893. IV. 216.
— Die Lärchen-Minirmotte. 1880. IV. 451.
— Der Verbau des Bergsturzgebietes der Risbach- und Spreng-'riesete in Lütschenthal. 1894. IV. 187.[2]
— Verbauungen . . . im Hochgebirge. 1882. IV.'187.[1]
— Die Waldungen des Emmenthales. 1885. IV. 367.

Martin, (Colonel). Caprification du Figuier en Kabylie. 1869. III. 369.[2]
Martin, (Dr.). Notice sur la Coca du Pérou. 1841. III. 492.[2]
Martin, (Oberförster). Ueber den Anbau der Eiche. 1890. IV. 508.
— Ueber die Erziehung von Buchen-Starkholz. 1890. IV. 498.
Martin, (sr.). L'horticulture en Algérie. 1897. III. 130.[2]
Martin, Adolf. Die Pflanzennamen der deutschen Flora. 1831. I. 76.[2]
Martin, Benjamin Nicholas. Broussonetia. 1871. II. 147.[1]
Martin, Claude. On the manufacture of indigo. 1792. III. 479.[1]
Martin, Claude. Pflanzengeographisches aus Llanquihue. 1898. I. 347.
Martin, D. E. Victoria. 1888. III. 283.[1]
Martin, E. Étude générale sur la végétation dans le nord de la Chine. 1872. I. 459.
Martin, Émile. Catalogue des plantes . . . de Romorantin. 1875. I. 415.
Martin, F. & Rebau. Historia natural popular. 1873. I. 96.
Martin, Félix. The Eucalyptus and its industrial application. 1877. IV. 531.[1]
— L'Eucalyptus et ses applications industrielles. 1877. IV. 531.[2]
Martin, Franz. Characters of trees. 1817. III. 201.
— Praktische Erfahrungen . . . über . . . Kultur der vorzüglichsten teutschen Holzbestände. 1815. IV. 106.
Martin, Georg. Untersuchung von japanischen Theesorten. 1876. III. 607.
Martin, George Anne. The Undercliff of the Isle of Wight. 1849. I. 400.
— Der höhere forstliche Unterricht. 1897. IV. 33.[2]
Martin, H. A. Notes on quinine. 1900. III. 725.[1]
Martin, H. T. Crataegus Pyracantha. 1900. III. 444.[1]
Martin, Heinrich. Die Forstwirthschaft des isolirten Staates. 1881. IV. 270.
— Theorie und Praxis in der Forstwirthschaft. 1898. IV. 119.[1]
— Wegnets, Eintheilung und Wirthschaftsplan. 1882. IV. 251.[1]
Martin, Joh. Nicolaus. Compendium brevissimum, grosser Potentaten Forst- und Jagd-Gerechtigkeiten. 1720. IV. 313.
— Methodus wie ein grosser Herr das Forst- und Wald-Wesen ' . . . zu bestellen? 1731. IV. 287.
Martin, Joseph. Notice sur la culture des arbres à épiceries. 1802. III.'118.[2]
Martin, Karl Ludwig. Der Wälder Zustand und Holzertrag. 1876. IV. 106, 240.
Martin, Lillie J. A botanical study of the 'mite-gall . . . of Juglans nigra. 1885. III. 354.[2]
Martin, Matthew. The Aurelian's vade mecum. 1785. I. 395, III. 188.[2]
Martin, P. Sur un mode nouveau de culture de la Vigne. 1876. III. 549.[1]
Martin, Paul. Les arbres remarquables en' Lorraine. 1900. V. 85.[2]
— Champignons des bois. 1897. IV. 439.
— Moyen pratique de s'orienter sans boussole. 1897. IV. 266.[1]
Martin, Peregrin Caruana y. See Caruana y Martin, Peregrin.
Martin, Petrus. Catalogus plantarum novarum Joachimi Burseri. 1724. I. 290.
Martin, Robert Montgomery. History of the British colonies. 1834. III. 217.
Martin, Romain. Multiplication du Noyer.' 1866. III. 355.
— Note sur la greffe du Noyer. 1867. III. 355.
— Notice sur le Noyer greffe.' 1865. III. 355.
Martin, Sidney H. C. Report on the action of papain. 1885. III. 617.[2]
— Olives sur branches. 1885. III. 679.[1]
Martin, Stanislaus. Note sur le Timbo. 1877. III. 540.[2]
Martin, W. K. & Thomas, S. B. The autumnal changes in Maple leaves. 1887. II. 477.[1]
Martin, Wilhelm. Ueber die forstliche Bedeutung der Buchenbahnschwelle. 1888. IV. 499.
— Pflanzliche und tierische Schädlinge. 1894. III. 179.

Martin, William, (sr.). A rough sketch ... of training the Grape vine. 1854. III. 550.

Martin de Argenta, Vicente. Album de la flora médico-farmacéutica é industrial. 1862. III. 52.

Martina, G. Sul la composition des gommes solubles. 1894. I. 181.²

Martinand, V. Action de l'air sur le moût de raisin. 1895. III. 583.²

— Influence des rayons solaires sur les levures ... des raisins. 1891. II. 508.²

— Sur la présence de l'invertine ... dans les raisins. 1900. III. 583.²

— & **Rietsch**, M. Des micro-organismes que l'on rencontre sur les raisins. 1891. III. 583.²

Martinati, Pietropaolo. Considerazioni storico-critiche sopra il saggio della legislazione veneta forestale. 1864. IV. 328.

Martindale, Isaac C. On the introduction and disappearance of plants. 1877. II. 41.²

— Notes on the Bartram Oak. 1880. II. 134.¹

— On Opuntia Rafinesquii and O. vulgaris. 1876. II. 596.¹

— Opuntia vulgaris, a New Jersey plant. 1876. II. 597.²

— Sexual variation in Castanea americana. 1881. II. 123.²

Martindale, William. Chian turpentine. 1880. III. 526.¹

— Coca and cocaine. 1886. III. 493.¹

— Coca, cocaine and its salts. 1886. III. 493.¹

— The extra pharmacopœia of unofficial drugs. 1884. III. 255.¹

— Notes on Egyptian opium. 1889. III. 280.²

Martineau, Laurent. Traité sur la taille de la Vigne. 1844. III. 549.¹

Martineit, H. Anleitung zur Waldwertsberechnung. 1892. IV. 253.

— Waldwertsberechnung. 1890. IV. 258.

Martinelli, Amilcare. Il disegno di legge sul rimboschimento. See PACIFICI-MAZZONI, Emidio & others. 1883. IV. 328.

— La giurisprudenza forestale italiana. See PACIFICI-MAZZONI, Emidio & others. 1883. IV. 328.

Martinet. Une exposition forestière en Touraine. 1881. IV. 20.²

Martinet. Organes de sécrétion des végétaux. 1871. I. 134.²

Martinet, A. Die Ausästung der Bäume. 1884. IV. 172.¹

— Considérations et recherches sur l'élagage. 1876. IV. 171.

— Notice sur l'élagage des arbres. 1878. IV. 171.

— Le Pin sylvestre ... en Sologne. 1882. IV. 473.

Martinet, Emile. Note sur la culture de l'Erythroxylon Coca. 1874. III. 492.¹

Martinet, G. Bois et pâturage. 1900. IV. 136.¹

Martinet, H. Bouturage des plantes ligneuses. 1895. III. 158.

— Caesalpinia japonica. 1898. III. 469.¹

— Le Cèdre de l'Atlas et ses variétés. 1896. III. 300.¹

— Chamaedorea formosa. 1893. III. 322.¹

— Le Cocotier dans nos serres. 1895. III. 323.¹

— Deutzia parviflora. 1893. III. 410.¹

— Dracaena Sanderiana. 1893. III. 337.¹

— Les effets de la gelée sur les végétaux. 1895. III. 49.¹

— La fabrication de l'essence de Roses. 1892. III. 454.²

— Le greffage des arbres pleureurs. 1897. III. 204.²

— Le Nicotiana colossea. 1894. III. 701.¹

— Pandanus Baptisii. 1893. III. 313.¹

— Plantes de Chine récemment introduites. 1893. III. 87.

— Les plantes nouvelles [à l'Exposition quinquennale.] 1898. III. 78.¹

Martinet, J. B. Organes de sécrétion des végétaux. I. 112.²

— Sur les organes glanduleux des Rutacées. 1871. II. 397.¹

Martinet, J. B. H. Enumeración de los generos y especies de plantas ... en el Jardin botanico ... de Lima. 1873. III. 64.²

— Note sur le climat ... de Lima. 1874. I. 340.²

Martinet, J. F. Katechismus der Natur. 1780. I. 93.

— Verhandeling over de natuurlijke geschiedenis van ons vaderland. 1795. I. 390.

Martinet, O. Des conditions les plus favorables au semis. 1876. IV. 149.¹

Martinetti, J. B. Les vases à irrigation souterraine. 1897. III. 151.

Martines, Joseph QUER Y. See QUER Y MARTINEZ, Joseph.

Martinez, Leandro. Cultivo y beneficio del Cacaotero. 1894. III. 593.¹

Martinez, Vicente. Apuntes para la ornitologia andaluza. 1898. IV. 544.¹

Martinez Quintanilla, Pedro. La provincia de Gerona. 1865. IV. 363.¹

Martinez y Leache, Miguel. Disputatio de vera et legitima Aloes electione. 1644. III. 333.¹

Martinez Robles, F. A. See LOPEZ, J. A. & MARTINEZ ROBLES, F. A.

Martini. Dissertatio epistolaris de oleo wittnebiano. 1751. III. 636.

Martini, (Pfarrer, Bernkastel). Schnelle Erzielung von Weinstöcken. 1837. III. 548.¹

Ma,rtini, A. de. Sur la coloration de la vue ... par la santonine. 1860. III. 754.²

Martini, J. N. Methode, wie ein grosser Herr das Forst- u. Waldwesen zu bestellen habe. 1731. IV. 94.

Martini van Geffen, A. Dennenteelt. 1852. IV. 472.

Martini van Geffen, Joseph A. Bijdrage ter bevordering van den zijdebouw in Nederland. 1836. III. 375.

— Handleiding ter bevordering van de zijdeteelt in Nederland. 1833. III. 374.

Martinis, Bartholomaeo de. Catalogus plantarum inventarum ... in itinere Montis Baldi. 1707. I. 424.

Martino, Domenico de. Leggi e regolamenti forestali ... di Lavoro. 1898. IV. 305, 329.

Martino, Francisco Garcia. Los montes y el cuerpo de ingenieros. 1871. IV. 293.¹

Martins, Charles Frederic. Accroissement de quelques grands arbres. 1869. III. 38.¹

— Sur l'amélioration des graines de vers à soie. 1857. III. 379.¹

— Anagyris foetida. 1869. III. 467.¹

— Le Châtaignier de Medoux. 1865. II. 124.¹

— Le climat et la végétation des Îles Borromées. 1865. I. 63. — 1866. I. 428.

— De la colonisation végétale des Îles britanniques. 1848. I. 400.

— Coup d'œil sur l'histoire des botanistes ... de Montpellier. 1852. I. 58.

— De la croissance du Bel-Sombra. 1855. III. 388.²

— Croissance du Gingko. 1854. III. 286.²

— De la croissance du Gingko. 1854. III. 286.²

— Cupressus californica. 1875. III. 302.²

— Cyprès de Californie. 1875. III. 302.²

— De la déclination des régions végétales. 1840. I. 349.

— De la distribution des grands végétaux le long des côtes de la Scandinavie. 1842. I. 348, IV. 78.²

— De l'échauffement du sol sur les hautes montagnes. 1859. I. 220.¹

— Des effets de l'hiver de 1853-54. 1854. III. 47.

— Des effets observés pendant l'hiver de 1853-1854. 1854. III. 47.

— Ueber einige merkwürdige Epheu. 1859. III. 642.¹

— Sur l'époque de la floraison de quelques végétaux. 1846. I. 223.¹

— Essai sur la météorologie ... de la France. 1845. I. 410.

— Essai sur la topographie botanique du Mont Ventoux. 1838. I. 409.

— Essai sur la végétation de l'archipel des Féröe. 1843. I. 354.

— Sur l'existence de l'Amyris balsamifera en Egypte. 1834. II. 398.²

— Expériences sur la persistance de la vitalité des graines flottant. 1858. I. 527.

— Floraison en pleine terre du Dasylirion gracile. 1866. III. 336.¹

— De la foliation du Micocoulier. 1857. III. 363.²

— Sur le froid exceptionnel ... de janvier 1855. 1855. III. 47.

— Sur l'hiver de 1868. 1868. III. 48.

— L'hiver de 1870-71. 1871. III. 48.

— Sur l'introduction du Planera crenata. 1862. III. 366.¹

— Le Jardin des plantes de Montpellier. 1854. I. 58.

— Les jardins botaniques d'Angleterre. 1868. I. 38.¹

— Lettre ... sur la germination des graines de plusieurs gousses de Cassia. 1855. I. 241,¹ II. 344.¹

— La métamorphose des plantes. 1843. I. 101.²

— Sur un mode particulier d'excrétion de ... l'Acacia Verek. 1875. III. 466.¹

— Sur un mode particulier d'excrétion de la gomme arabique. 1874. III. 329.¹

— Sur la naturalisation ... du Bambusa mitis. 1871. III. 316.¹

— Note sur la germination ... de Cassia fistula. 1855. II. 344.¹

— Note sur les circonstances qui déterminent la floraison du Bambou. 1833. II. 59.²

— Note sur les végétaux en fleur ... février 1847. 1847. I. 226.²

Martins, Charles Frederic (*continued*).
— Observations sur l'origine glaciaire des tourbières du Jura. 1871. I. 414, 436.
— Sur l'origine paléontologique des arbres . . . du midi de la France. 1876. I. 404,² V. xxi.²
— Sur un pied de Chamaerops humilis. 1862. II. 67.¹
— Les Platanes de Cannosa. 1870. II. 255.¹
— Las poblaciones vegetales. 1873. I. 300,
— Les populations végétales. 1870. I. 241.²
— Promenade botanique le long des côtes de l'Asie-Mineure. 1858. I. 479.
— Sur quelques pieds de Lierre. 1859. III. 642.¹
— Du refroidissement nocturne. 1863. I. 232.¹
— Le Ricin d'Afrique. 1861. III. 521.²
— Du Spitzberg au Sahara. 1866. I. 303.
— Sur la température exceptionnelle de l'hiver de 1846. 1846. I. 226.¹
— De la tératologie végétale. 1851. I. 143.
— Transformation d'un Chamaerops . . . en polygame. 1862. II. 67.¹
— On trees cleft by the direct action of electrical storms. 1849. IV. 193.²
— On the vegetable colonisation of the British Islands. 1848. I. 400.
— La végétation du Spitzberg comparée. 1865. I. 356.
— De la vitalité des graines transportées par des courants marins. 1857. I. 527.
— Voyage botanique le long des côtes septentrionales de la Norvège. 1843. I. 354.
— *See also* BRAVAIS, Auguste & MARTINS, Charles.
— & Bravais, Auguste. Résumé des travaux de Mm. Schimper et Braun. 1837. I. 102.
— & Desor, Édouard. Observations sur le projet de la création d'une mer intérieure dans le Sahara. 1879. I. 489.
Martiny, Eduard. Encyclopädie der medizinisch-pharmaceutischen Naturalien- und Rohwaarenkunde. 1843. III. 243.
Martiny, Julius. Mittheilung über den Cortex Chinae albus. 1838. III. 725.²
Martire, Pietro. Sommario dell' historia dell' Indie Occidentali. 1565. III. 265.²
Martius. Sur le séné sauvage. 1857. III. 708.²
Martius, C. Notice sur le pela . . . et sur la . . . graisse de Stillingia. 1853. III. 522,² 673.²
Martius, Carl. Versuch einer Monographie der Sennesblätter. 1857. III. 470.²
Martius, Ernst Wilhelm. Abdrücke lebendiger Kräuter. 1779. I. 262.
— Die Baumblätter zu sceletiren. 1790. I. 35.
— Gesammelte Nachrichten über den macassarischen Giftbaum. 1792. III. 366.²
Martius, Heinrich von. Prodromus florae mosquensis. 1812. I. 360.
Martius, Karl Friedrich Philipp von. Agaveae. 1855. II. 88.¹
— Amoenitates botanicae monacenses. 1829. I. 46.
— Anonaceae. 1841. II. 215.¹
— Ueber die Architectonik der Blüthen. 1828. I. 114.¹
— Auswahl merkwürdiger Pflanzen des Königl. botanischen Gartens zu München. 1829. I. 46.
— Beiträge zur Kenntniss der Gattung Erythroxylon. 1840. II. 394.¹
— Beitrag zur Kenntniss der . . . Amarantaceen. 1826. II. 189.¹
— Beiträge zur Natur- und Literär-Geschichte der Agaveen. 1855. II. 88.²
— Bemerkungen über den dermaligen Stand der Untersuchung von der Befruchtungsweise. 1842. I. 200.
— Beobachtungen welche . . . über die periodischen Erscheinungen des Pflanzenreiches . . . gemacht worden sind. 1853. I. 224.²
— Beschreibung des ächten Quina-Baumes von Loxa. 1846. II. 813.²
— Beschreibung einiger neuen Nopaleen. 1832. II. 585.¹
— Ueber die botanische Erforschung des Königreichs Bayern. 1850. I. 383.
— On the branching of Palm stems. 1852. II. 62.²
— On certain antediluvian plants. 1825. I. 298.²
— Chamaedorea atrovirens Mart. 1852. II. 66.¹
— Über den Charakter . . . der beiden Pflanzengattungen Labatia. 1861. II. 698.²
— Choix des plantes remarquables du Jardin botanique royal de Munic. 1829. I. 46.
— On Coca and Matico. 1843. III. 492,² 755.¹

— Ueber Coca und Matico. 1843. III. 755.¹
— Conspectus regni vegetabilis. 1835. I. 260.
— Delectus seminum Horti botanici monacensis. 1849. I. 47.
— Sur la disposition géométrique des parties foliacées des Palmiers. 1846. II. 62.²
— Drei neue mexicanische Palmen. 1830. II. 66.¹
— Einige Bemerkungen über Loranthus. 1830. II. 172.¹
— Ueber einige nutzbare Palmen. 1848. III. 319.¹
— Fasciculus plantarum herbarii academici. 1820. I. 266.
— Die Floren-Reiche. 1837. I. 329.
— Fridericia, novum plantarum genus. 1827. II. 788.²
— Ueber die geographischen Verhältnisse der Palmen. 1838. II. 60.²
— Über die gepanzerten Früchte der Palmen. 1846. II. 62.²
— Das Geschlecht . . . der Pflanzen. 1841. I. 199.
— On the growth in length of Bamboo shoots. 1848. II. 59.¹
— On the growth of the stem of Palms. 1845. II. 62.²
— Herbarium florae brasiliensis. 1837. I. 341.
— Historia naturalis Palmarum. 1823. II. 60.²
— Hortus botanicus Regiae academiae monacensis. 1825.
— Imperia florae brasiliensis. 1873. I. 343.
— Kritik des Gattungs-Charakters von Cinchona. 1860. II. 812.
— Ueber das Längenwachsthum . . . des Bambusrohrs. 1848. II. 59.¹
— Liste von Pflanzennamen in der Tupi-Sprache. 1858. I. 72.²
— Zur Literaturgeschichte der Muskatnuss. 1860. II. 221,¹ III. 403.¹
— On Monesia. 1845. III. 668.¹
— Über die Morphologie der Palmen. 1846. II. 62.²
— Mouroucoa Aubl. 1861. II. 746.¹
— The natural history . . . of the aborigines of Brazil. 1844. III. 269.¹
— Das Naturell . . . der Urbewohner Brasiliens. 1844. III. 269.¹
— Ueber den Nelkenzimmtbaum. 1830. II. 225.¹
— Nova genera et species plantarum quas in itinere per Brasiliam . . . collegit. 1823. I. 341.
— Novum plantarum genus. 1822. II. 860.¹
— Observations sur la floraison des plantes. 1842. I. 528.²
— Observations sur la géographie des Cactées au Brésil. 1839. II. 587.²
— On the occurrence . . . of the genuine Cinchona. 1846. II. 812.
— Ordinum plantarum characteres stenographice. 1828. I. 254.²
— Palmarum familia ejusque genera denuo illustrata. 1824. II. 60.²
— Palmetum Orbignianum. 1847. II. 61.¹
— Die Pflanzen und Thiere der tropischen America. 1823. I. 328. — 1831. I. 341.
— Ueber die Pflanzengattung Hornschuchia. 1856. II. 218.¹
— Die Physiognomie des Pflanzenreiches in Brasilien. 1824. I. 341.
— On the physiognomy of the vegetable kingdom in the Brazils. 1824. I. 341.
— Plantae nonnullae Horti academici monacensis. 1814. I. 45. — 1817. II. 390.¹
— Plantarum Horti academici erlangensis enumeratio. 1814. I. 45.
— Plantas aliquot brasilienses. 1841. II. 229,¹ 535.²
— Recherches sur l'accroissement de la tige des Palmiers. 1845. II. 62.²
— Specimen materiae medicae brasiliensis. 1824. III. 65.¹
— Ueber die Stellung der Pflanzengattungen Moutabea. 1856. II. 430,¹ 704.¹
— Syllabus praelectionum de botanica pharmaceutico-medica. 1852. III. 58.
— Systema de materia medica vegetal brasileira. 1843. III. 65.¹
— Systema materiae medicae vegetabilis brasiliensis. 1843. III. 65.¹
— Über die Vegetation der unächten und ächten Parasiten. 1842. I. 233.²
— Die Verbreitung der Palmen in der alten Welt. 1838. II. 60.²
— Versuch eines Commentars über die Pflanzen in den Werken von Marcgrav und Piso. 1853. I. 342.
— Über das Vorkommen . . . der ächten Quina. 1846. II. 812.
— Vorläufige Nachricht über einige Versuche, den Einfluss der verschiedenen farbigen Lichtstrahlen. 1853. I. 229.

— Vorträge über die Florenreiche. 1865. I. 300.
— Über den Wachsthumsprocess der Palmen. 1845. II. 62.[2]
— Wegweiser für die Besucher des K. botanischen Gartens in München. 1852. I. 47.
— *See also* NEES VON ESENBECK, C. G. & MARTIUS, C. F. P. von; SCHRANK, Franz von Paula von & MARTIUS, K. F. P. von; SPIX, J. B. von & MARTIUS, K. F. P. von.
— Eichler, A. W. & Urban, Ignatz. Flora brasiliensis. 1840. I. 342.
— Eschweiler, F. G. & Nees von Esenbeck, C. G. Flora brasiliensis. *See* NEES VON ESENBECK, C. G. 1892. II. 58.[1]
Martius, Theodor Wilhelm Christian. Sur les differentes espèces de camphre. 1853. III. 233.[1]
— Ueber gallae pistacinae. 1837. III. 525.[2]
— Gesammelte Nachrichten über den Campherbaum. 1838. III. 611.[1]
— Grundriss der Pharmakognosie des Pflanzenreichs. 1832. III. 257.[2]
— Die ostindische Rohwaarensammlung. 1853. III. 277.
— On Wai-fa. 1854. III. 488.[1]
Márton, Sándor. A legelőerdők berendezése, kezelése és hasznositása. 1897. IV. 136.[1]
Martorelli, Miguel CUNÍ Y. *See* CUNÍ Y MARTORELLI, Miguel.
Martragny, Eugène de. La Bruyère odorante. 1870. III. 650.[2]
— Le Chêne pyramidal. 1865. III. 362.[2]
— Les Eucalyptus. 1868. IV. 531.[1]
— Le Jasmin de Virginie greffé sur Catalpa. 1870. III. 705.
— Laurier Cerise à larges feuilles. 1870. III. 437.[2]
— Notice historique sur le Palmier de la Chine. 1869. III. 331.[1]
— Les Palmiers rustiques. 1869. III. 317.
— Rhododendrum Blandianum. 1859. III. 657.[2]
— Swainsonia Osbornii Moore. 1862. III. 489.[1]
— De la taille des Magnolia. 1869. III. 399.[1]
Martrès. Expériences sur les Amandes amères. 1819. III. 434.[2]
Martrin-Donos, Victor de. Florule du Tarn. 1864. I. 413.
— & Timbal-Lagrave, Édouard. Observations sur quelques races . . . du Chêne-vert. 1864. II. 134.[1]
Marty, Pierre. L'ascendance de l'Érable plane. 1895. II. 479.[1]
— Feuilles d'Ormeaux bilobées. 1898. II. 143.[1]
— Die Wytweiden des Jura. 1891. IV. 136.[1]
Martyanof, N. *See* МАРТЬЯНОВЪ, Н.
Martyn, John. Abbildung und Beschreibung seltener Gewächse. 1728. I. 290.—1797. I. 264.
— Catalogus Horti botanici cantabrigiensis. 1771. I. 52, 521.[2]
— Historia plantarum rariorum. 1728. I. 290.
— Methodus plantarum circa Cantabrigiam. 1727. I. 294.
— A remark concerning the sex of Holly. 1755. II. 463.[2]
— A short explanation of the technicalywords . . . in botany. 172 . ? I. 69.[2]
— Tabulae synopticae plantarum officinalium. 1726. III. 54.
Martyn, Thomas. Flora rustica. 1792. III. 80.
— Horti botanici cantabrigiensis catalogus. 1794. I. 53.
— Inleiding tot de kruidkunde. 1798. I. 84.
— Introduction à la botanique. 1798. I. 84.
— The language of botany. 1793. I. 70.
— Mantissa plantarum Horti botanici cantabrigiensis. 1772. I. 52, 521.[2]
— Plantae cantabrigienses. 1763. I. 395.
— Thirty-eight plates with explanations. 1788. I. 263, V. XIII.[1]
Martynof, Ivan. *See* МАРТЬЯНОВЪ, Иван.
Marulas, V. A. Utiliter premor; observations . . . relatifs aux forêts. 1863. IV. 217.
Marum, Martin van. Brief aan J. Ingenhousz . . . omtrent de werking van de sapbuizen. 1792. I. 163.
— Catalogue des plantes cultivées . . . dans son jardin à Harlem. 1810. I. 51.[1]
— Dissertatio, qua disquiritur, quo usque motus fluidorum, et caetera . . . functiones consentiunt. 1773. I. 162.
— De motu fluidorum in plantis. 1773. I. 162.
Maruška, V. Srstka nebo Angrešt. 1895. III. 414.[2]
Marvaud, Angel. Étude de physiologie thérapeutique. 1871. III. 222.
A marvellous Date Palm. 1882. II. 73.[1]
Marvin, Arthur Tappan. The Olive, its culture. 1888. III. 676.[1]

Mary. *See* AVRIL, DIDION & MARY.
Maryland — Agricultural college — Maryland agricultural experiment station. Annual report. Bulletin. III. 5.
Maryland academy of science and literature. Transactions. I. 6.
Maryland agricultural experiment station. *See* MARYLAND —AGRICULTURAL COLLEGE . . . III. 5.
Marzari-Pencati, Giuseppe, *conte.* Elenco delle piante . . . nel territorio di Vicenza. 1802. I. 425.
Der Marx'sche Kulturhammer. 1857. IV. 176.[2]
Mas, A. Pomologie générale. 1872. III. 85.
— Le verger. 1865. III. 85.
— & Pulliat, V. Le vignoble. 1874. III. 547.
Mas, Sinibaldo de. Informe sobre el estado de las Islas Filipinas. 1843. IV. 399.[1]
Más sobre el catálogo de montes enajenables. 1897. IV. 552.[1]
Más sobre la roya del Pino sylvestre. *See* Ueber die BEKÄMPFUNG . . . 1900. IV. 559.[2]
Más sobre los ingenieros de montes. 1897. IV. 553.[2]
Masawaih, YŪHANNÁ IBN. *See* YŪHANNÁ IBN MASAWAIH.
Mascall, Leonard. A booke of the arte and maner howe to plant and graffe all sortes of trees. 1572. III. 106.[2]
— The country-mans new art of planting and graffing. 1652. III. 159.[2]
— The country-mans recreation. 1654. III. 107.
Mascaró, J. M. VIDAL Y. *See* VIDAL Y MASCARÓ, J. M.
Maschin, Johann. Dissertatio sistens plantas medicinales Bohemiae. 1843. III. 90.[2]
Maschke, O. Ueber den Bau . . . der Kleberbläschen in Bertholletia. 1859. II. 611.[2]
Masclef. Géographie botanique du nord de la France. 1892. I. 417.
Masclef, Amédée. Catalogue raisonné des plantes . . . du Pas-de-Calais. 1886. V. XXII.[1]
— Les plantes d'Europe. 189.? V. XVIII.[2]
Masella, Massimiliano. La geometria pratica. 1888. IV. 265.
Masferrer y Arquimbau, Ramon. Recuerdos botánicos de Tenerife. 1880. I. 498.
— Recuerdos botánicos de Vich. 1877. I. 421.
Masino, ARCOZZI-. *See* ARCOZZI-MASINO.
Masino, E. A. Sopra un esemplare di Osmanthus aquifolius. 1900. II. 713.[2]
Masius, Georg Heinrich. Tentamen pharmacopoeae pauperum. 1820. III. 72.
Masius, Hermann. Andeutungen zu einer Physiognomik der Bäume. 1849. I. 516.
— Naturstudien. 1852. I. 95.
— Studies from nature. 1852. I. 95.
Maskelyne, Nevil Story. Investigation of the vegetable tallow. 1856. III. 522.[2]
Mason, Francis. Burma, its people and productions. 1850. I. 476.[1]
— Burmah, its people and natural productions. 1850. I. 476.[1]
— Flora burmanica. 1851. I. 476.[1]
— On the gamboge of the Tenasserim Provinces. 1848. III. 609.[1]
— The gum kino of the Tenasserim Provinces. 1848. III. 485.[1]
— The Liquidamber tree of the Tenasserim Provinces. 1848. III. 416.[2]
— The natural productions of Burmah. 1850. I. 476,[1] III. 277.
— Nouvelle sorte de gomme-gutte. 1848. III. 609.[1]
— Tenasserim. 1850. I. 476,[1] III. 277.
Mason, James. Folk-lore of British plants. 1873. I. 518.
Mason, James WOOD-. Report on some insects destructive to the Castor oil plant. 1890. III. 522.[1]
— Report on the Tea-mite and the Tea-bug of Assam. 1884. III. 604.[2]
Mason, Silas Cheever. Five ornamental Oaks. 1896. III. 78.[1]
— Hardy shrubs with ornamental fruit. 1889. III. 208.[1]
— Kansas farmers and Kansas forests. 1890. IV. 340.
— Notes on the distribution of some Kansas trees. 1890. I. 320, IV. 78.[1]
— A preliminary report upon . . . distribution of Kansas trees. 1893. I. 320, IV. 78.[1]
Mason, Thomas. An account of the plants growing at "The Gums," Taita. 1897. I. 69.[2]
— Plants injured by the frost. 1876. III. 50.[1]
Massa, Guillaume. De l'acide sulfureux. 1876. III. 570.

Massachusetts — Agricultural college — Hatch experiment station. Annual report. Bulletin. Special bulletin. III. 5.
Massachusetts — State agricultural experiment station, Amherst. Analyses of . . . fertilizers. Annual report. Bulletin. III. 5.
Massachusetts agricultural college. Annual report. III. 5.
Massachusetts agricultural repository. III. 5.
Massachusetts forestry association. Register. IV. 4.
Massachusetts historical society. Collections. . I. 6.
Massachusetts horticultural society. Catalogue of books in the library. See CATALOGUE . . . 1854. III. 1.
Massachusetts horticultural society. Transactions. III. 5.
Massachusetts medical society. Medical communications. I. 6.
Massachusetts society for promoting agriculture. See MASSACHUSETTS AGRICULTURAL REPOSITORY. III. 5.
Massachusetts society for promoting agriculture. Transactions. III. 5.
Massachusetts state board of agriculture. Annual report. III. 5.
Massalien, O. Missbildungen an Kaiserbirnen. 1844. II. 279.²
Massalongo, Caro. Acarocecidii . . . nella flora italica. 1893. I. 215.²
— Acarocecidii nella flora veronese. 1891. I. 215.²
— Sopra alcune milbogalle. 1894. I. 215.²
— Di alcuni entomocecidii della flora veronese. 1892. I. 215.² III. 488,¹ 564,¹ 678.¹
— Appunti teratologici. 1886. II. 403.²
— Contribuzione all' acarocecidiologia. 1892. I. 215.²
— Contribuzione alla teratologia. 1888. I. 144.¹
— Descrizione di un nuovo entomocecidio. 1895. III. 453.²
— Entomocecidii italici. 1893. I. 215.¹
— Sui fiori mostruosi di Jasminum. 1896. II. 710.¹
— Sulla fitottosi dei fiori dell' Alloro. 1893. III. 406.²
— Sopra le foglie di Nerium Oleander. 1896. III. 689.²
— Intorno alla galla di Pemphigus. 1896. III. 526.¹
— Le galle nell' Anatome plantarum di M. Malpighi. 1898. I. 216.¹
— Miscellanea teratologica. 1894. I. 144.¹
— Mostruosità osservata nei fiori di Jasminum. 1892. II. 710.¹
— Note teratologiche. 1890. I. 144.¹
— Sopra una nuova malattia . . . di Aucuba. 1900. III. 645.¹
— Nuove spigolature teratologiche. 1898. II. 150.²
— Nuovo contributo alla conoscenza dell' entomocecidiologia italica. 1894. I. 215.²
— Intorno ad un nuovo tipo di phytoptocecidio del Juniperus. 1890. III. 303.¹
— Osservazioni intorno ad un rarissimo entomocecidio dell' Hedera. 1893. III. 643.¹
— Sulla scopazzi di Alnus incana. 1892. IV. 489.²
— Sulla scoperta nel Veneto della Taphrina Celtidis. 1895. III. 363.²
— Spigolature teratologiche. 1894. II. 460.¹
— & Ross, Hermann. Ueber sicilianische cecidien. 1898. I. 216.²
Massaloup, J. V. Anleitung zur Anlage . . . von Eichenschälwaldungen. 1851. IV. 504.
— Katechismus der Forstbotanik. 1852. IV. 83.
— Die wichtigsten und interessantesten Forste Deutschlands. 1846. IV. 348.¹
Massalski, V., prince. See Массальскій, В., кназ.
Massara, Giuseppe Filippo. Prodromo della flora valtellinese. 1834. I. 426.
Massara, Luigi. Laine végétale et huile de bois. 1862. IV. 482.¹
Massari, Michele. Alcune foglie mostruose nel Cocculus. 1895. II. 207.²
Massart, Jean. La biologie de la végétation sur le littoral belge. 1893. I. 393.¹
— Un botaniste en Malaisie. 1895. I. 469.¹
— La cicatrisation chez les végétaux. 1898. I. 208.¹
— Le désert. 1898. I. 486.
— Impressions de la nature équatoriale. 1896. I. 219.²
— Sur la morphologie du bourgeon. 1896. I. 109,¹ 236.¹
— Notes javanaises. 1896. V. xxiii.¹
— La récapitulation . . . en embryologie. 1894. I. 123.¹
— Un voyage botanique au Sahara. 1898. I. 486.
Massé. Dictionnaire portatif des eaux et forêts. 1766. IV. 22.¹
— Traité des bois. 1769. IV. 108.¹
Massé, Anatole. Culture et multiplication du Houx. 1859. III. 530.¹
— Hêtre à feuilles panachées. 1850. III. 360,² 474.²
— Nouveautés horticoles. 1853. III. 87.

Masse, E. De l'action de la créosote dans le traitement du sycosis. 1864. IV. 433.²
Massé, H. Sur la chute des feuilles des Orangers. 1899. III. 501.¹
— Le Cormier géant. 1900. III. 460.¹
Massé, ROBIN-. See ROBIN-MASSÉ.
Massee, George. Appearance of American Gooseberry-mildew. 1900. III. 414.².
— A Conifer disease. 1900. III. 295.²
— A Fig disease. 1900. III. 370.¹
— A fungus parasite on Aloe. 1899. III. 333.¹
— A Gooseberry and Currant disease. 1900. III. 414.¹
— Gummosis of Prunus japonica Thunb. 1898. III. 437.²
— A text-book of plant diseases caused by cryptogamic parasites. 1899. IV. 212.
Masseli, Franz. Über das Beschneiden der Pfahl- oder Herzwurzel. 1824. III. 173.¹
Massella, Massimiliano. In risposta al questionario relativo alla riforma della legge forestale. 1897. IV. 329.
— Sempre per le concimazioni degli orti forestali. 1895. IV. 151.²
Masselli, (Erxpriester, Breslau). Erfahrungen hinsichtlich der Reinigung der Obstbäume. 1833. III. 175.¹
Ueber Massenanpflanzung einiger empfehlenswerther Nadelhölzer. 1900. IV. 127.²
Massentaeln zur Bestimmung des Inhaltes der vorzüglichsten teutschen Waldbäume. 1846. IV. 229.
Massey, W. F. Citrus trifoliata as a hedge plant. 1892. III. 503.¹
— The hardiness of the Satsuma Orange. 1892. III. 503.¹
— The northern limit of Sabal Palmetto. 1892. II. 74.²
— Tea-culture in the Carolinas. 1892. III. 600.²
Massias, O. Archontophoenix Cunninghamiana. 1897. III. 319.²
— Ein Beitrag über den Wert der Washingtonia filifera. 1896. III. 332.¹
— Berberis angulisans hort. 1897. III. 394.¹
— Ueber dekorative Gräser. 1899. III. 314.²
— Einige Bemerkungen über die amerikanische Preisselbeere. 1884. III. 663.²
— Hypericum calycinum. 1897. III. 610.¹
— Kanadischer Mondsame. 1897. III. 397.¹
Massicotte, E. Z. Monographies de plantes canadiennes. 1899. I. 311.¹
Massif complet, (pseud.). Grazing in forests. 1887. IV. 136.²
Massink, A. Enkele opmerkingen naar aanleiding van de toekomst der Kinakultuur. 1890. III. 716.
— Houtasch. 1890. III. 151.
Masson, E. Compte rendu d'un voyage horticole fait en Russie. 1849. III. 119.¹
— Note sur un légume nouveau. 1847. III. 469.¹
— Note sur une manière de transplanter des arbres déjà forts. 1845. III. 167.
Masson, Francis. An account of three journeys from the Cape Town. 1776. I. 493.
Masson, Louis. Contribution à l'étude des Cactées. 1890. III. 620.²
Masson-Fouy. Arboretum forestier. 1825. I. 404,² IV. 85.¹
Massot, Aimé. Distribution of plants on Mount Canigou. 1843. I. 409.
— Tableau des limites de végétation . . . du Canigou. 1843. I. 409.
Massow, von, (Forst-Assessor, Königsberg). Entwurf zum Statut für die Holzhauer-Genossenschaften. 1851. IV. 310.¹
— Ueber Fabrikation der Brennspähne. 1847. IV. 428.¹
— Forstliche Bemerkungen. 1851. IV. 146.²
— Kultur durch Absenker. 1847. IV. 149.¹
— Mittheilung über den Frass der Nonne. 1854. IV. 200.
— Promemoria über Holzhauer-Genossenschaften. 1851. IV. 310.¹
— Wachsthums-Verhältnisse der Weisstanne. 1847. IV. 444.¹
— Zusammenstellung im königl. Forstrevier Carlsberg . . . ausgeführten Saaten. 1846. IV. 148.
Massow, von, (Oberforstmeister, Potsdam). Die Försterschule zu Gr. Schönebeck. 1879. IV. 32.
Massoy bark. 1881. III. 407.¹
Massute, Friedrich. Beiträge zur Kenntniss . . . von Quassia amara. 1890. III. 415,¹ III. 508,² 509.⁴ .
— Contribution à l'étude chimique du Quassia. 1890. II. 415,¹ III. 508,² 509.¹

Mast, A. Taille des arbrisseaux. 1883. III. 172.
Masters, G. W.. Observations on the .Assam Tea-plant. 1865. III. 603.
Masters, J. W. The Assam Tea plant. 1844. II. 552.[1]
— Botanical observations in Upper Assam. 1845. I. 476.[1]
— A catalogue of plants growing in the . . . botanic garden, Calcutta. 1844. I. 66.[2]
— A few observations on Tea culture. 1844. III. 602.[2]
— A memoir of some of the natural productions of the Angami Naga Hills. 1848. III. 277.
— A memorandum on the most useful timber trees of Upper Assam. 1844. IV. 400.[2]
— Note on two undescribed species of Melastoma. 1846. II. 639.[1]
— Observations on the flora of the Naga Hills. 1844.' I. 476.[1]
Masters, Maxwell Tylden. Abies amabilis. 1880. II. 22.[1]
— Abies bracteata. 1889. II. 22.[2] — 1890. II. 22.[2]
— Abies concolor. 1880. II. 22.[2] — 1881. II. 22.[2] — 1890. II. 22.[2]
— Abies Fortunei. 1884. II. 32.[2]
— Abies Fraseri. 1890. II. 22.[2]
— Abies grandis. 1885. II. 22.[2]
— Abies lasiocarpa Hooker. 1889. ·II. 22.[2]
— Abies lasiocarpa Hook. and its allies.' 1889. II. 22.[1]
— Abies nobilis. 1885. II. 22.[2]
— Abies (or Picea) grandis. 1881. II. 22.[2]
— Abies (Picea) subalpina. 1881. II. 22.[2]
— Abies Pindrow. 1886. II. 24.[2]
— Abies Pinsapo. 1886. II. 24.[2]
— Abies Webbiana. 1884. II. 25.[1]
— Acalypha Godseffiana. 1898. II. 435.[1]
— Acanthopanax sessiliflorum. 1897. III. 641.[1]
— Acer Van Volxemi.· 1877. II. 478.[1]
— Acer Volxemi. 1891. II. 478.[1]
— Actinidia Kolomikta. 1880. II. 541.[1]
— The Algerian Fir. 1888. III. 296.[2]
— Ampelopsis tricuspidata Siebold et Zuccarini. 1869. II. 504.[2]
— Androgynous cones of Pinus Thunbergii. 1883. II. 48.[2]
— Aphelandra Roezlii. 1867. II. 797.[1]
— Araucaria Bidwillii. 1873. II. 26.[1]
— Ardisia Oliveri. 1877. II. 693.[1]
— Aristolochia Dammeriana. 1895. II. 182.[1]
— Aristolochia Duchartrei sp. n. 1868. II. 182.[1]
— Aristolochiaelegans sp. n. 1885. II. 182.[1]
— Aristolochia floribunda.· 1873. III. 386.[1]
— Aristolochia Goldieana. 1867. II. 182.[1]
— Aristolochia longecaudata. 1890. II. 182.[2]
— Aristolochia promissa. 1879. II. 183.[1]
— Aristolochia salpinx Mast. n. sp. 1886. II. 183.[2]
— Aristolochiaceae. 1875. II. 180.[1]
— Athrotaxis laxifolia. 1885. III. 299.[2]
— Athrotaxis selaginoides. 1888. III. 299.[2]
— Azalea serpyllifolia. 1882. III. 662.[1]
— The Bahn of Gilead Fir. 1895. II. 22.[2]
— Barleria Lichtensteiniana. 1870. II. 798.[1]
— Beiträge zur Geschichte einiger Coniferen-Arten. 1887. II. 13.[2]
— The Bermuda Juniper and its allies. 1899. II. 30.[2]
— The bitter Cola. 1875. II. 555.[1]
— Botany for beginners. 1872. V. x.[2]
— Brachyglottis repanda. 1895. II. 853.[2]
— Bud variation. 1872. I. 244.[2]
— Bud variations or sports. 1891. I. 244.[2]
— The Calabrian Pine. 1888. II. 45.[2]
— Callicarpas. 1871. III. 695.[2]
— Carludovica Drudei Mast. 1877. II. 76.[1]
— The Cedar of Goa. 1894. .II. 29.[2]
— O Cedro de Gôa.· 1894. II. 29.[2]
— Cephalotaxus. 1884. II. 8.[1]
— Die Cephalotaxus-Arten. 1884. II. 8.[1]
— Cephalotaxus drupacea. 1895. II. 8.[2]
— On certain small-fruited Pears. 1876. II. 278.[2]
— A classified synonymic list of . . . Passifloreae. 1874. II. 575.[2]
— On the comparative morphology of Sciadopitys. 1884. II. 49.[2]
— De Coniferis quibusdam sinicis vel japonicis. 1898. II. 16.[1]
— On the Conifers of Japan. 1880. II. 15.[2]
— Contributions to the history . . . of Conifers. 1887. II. 13.[2]
— Contributions to the .'. . Passifloraceae. 1871. II. 575.[2]
— Contributions to vegetable teratology. 1857. II. 676.[2]
— Corokia Cotoneaster, C. buddleioides. 1876. III. 646.[2]
— Corynostylis Hybanthus. 1872. II. 567.[1]
— Cultivated Passion-flowers. 1870. III. 615.[2]
— Cupressus arizonica. 1891. II. 29.[1]
— Cupressus Nabiana. 1891. III. 302.[2]
— Cycas siamensis, Miq. 1878. II. 5.[1]
— On Deidamia Thompsoniana DC. 1875. II. 576.[1]
— Dendropanax argenteus Hort. Bull. 1878. II. 649.[1]
— Disease of Silver Firs. 1882. III. 295.[2]
— Dombeya angulata Cav. 1867. II. 533.[2]
— Doryphora Sassafras. 1895. II. 221.[2]
— Double-flowered Ceanothus. 1889. II. 492.[2]
— Elaeagnus longipes A. Gray. 1873. II. 607.[2]
— Encephalartos acantha. 1878. II. 5.[2]
— Epacris impressa flore pleno. 1865. II. 689.[1]
— Eranthemum Andersoni Mast. 1869. II. 802.[1]
— Eranthemum elegans Mast. 1868. II. 802.[1]
— An erratic Ivy. 1889. II. 649.[2]
— Escallonia macrantha Hook. et Arn. 1873. II. 239.[2]
— Escallonia Philippiana. 1873. II. 240.[1]
— Euadenia eminens. 1882. III. 409.[1]
— The evergreen Beech. 1872. III. 360.[1]
— On the existence of two forms of peloria. 1863. I. 145.[1]
— Ficus stipulata. 1880. II. 152.[2]
— On the flowering plants and ferns of Oxfordshire. 1857. I. 400.
— Flowers of Conifers. 1888. II. 22,[1] 38.[2]
— Flowers of Conifers. 1896. II. 49.[2]
— A friendly lift. 1885. III. 840.[2]
— Fuchsia deformities. 1863. II. 643.[1]
— Fuchsia procumbens. 1874. II. 645.[1]
— Garden varieties of Codiaeum variegatum. 1868. II. 438.[2]
— Garten-Varietäten von Codiaeum variegatum. 1868. II. 438.[2]
— Die Gattung Escallonia und deren Arten. 1873. II. 239.[2]
— A general view of the genus Cupressus. 1896. II. 29.[1]
— The genus Brownea. 1873. II. 337.[2]
— The genus Escallonia. 1873. II. 239.[2]
— On the genus Fremontia. 1869. II. 534.[1]
— Geonoma? Pynaertiana. 1898. II. 68.[2]
— Grafting; its consequences and effects. 1871. I. 246.[1]
— Growth of Conifers. 1887. II. 42.[1]
— The Guadeloupe Cypress. 1895. II. 29.[2]
— Hamamelis arborea. 1874. II. 253.[1]
— The Hungarian Oak. 1876. II. 133.[1]
— On the Hungarian Oak. 1876. III. 362.[1]
— Hybrid Aristolochia. 1897. II. 181.[1]
— Hymenanthera crassifolia. 1875. II. 567.[2]
— Ilex insignis Hook. f. 1880. III. 530.[2]
— The Irish Yew. 1891. II. 10.[1]
— Ivy flowers. 1889. II. 649.[2]
— Japanese Conifers. 1879. II. 15,[1] 22.[1]
— Knight's Cypress. 1894. II. 29.[1]
— The Larches. 1883. III. 304,[2] 309.[1]
— Ledum latifolium. 1878. II. 673.[1]
— Leea amabilis Hort. Veitch. 1882. II. 503.[2]
— Ligustrum Massalongianum. 1881. II. 711.[2]
— List of Conifers and Taxads in cultivation. 1892. II. 13.[2]
— Low's Silver Fir. 1886. II. 22.[2]
— Macadamia ternifolia F. von Müller. 1869. II. 164.[2]
— Macrozamia Mackenzii. 1877. III. 285.[2]
— Macrozamia plumosa. 1873. II. 6.[2]
— The Mexican Silver Fir. 1885. II. 25.[1]
— Monographic sketch of the Durioneae. 1875. II. 528.[2]
— Monographie du Codiaeum variegatum. 1868. II. 438.[2]
— Napoleona. 1886. II. 612.[2]
— Neue hybride Passionsblumen. 1868. II. 579,[1] 579.[2]
— New evergreen Oaks. 1874. II. 131.[1]
— New hybrid Passion-flower. 1870. II. 579.[1]
— New hybrid Passion-flowers. 1868. II. 579,[1] 579.[2]
— New Passifloras. 1883. III. 616.[2]
— New Passifloreae. 1883. II. 575.[2]
— A new Passion-flower. 1888. II. 580.[1]
— New plants at the Ghent exhibition. 1893. III. 78.[1]
— Note on an unusual mode of germination in the Mango. 1862. II. 456.[2]
— Note on the foliation . . . of Buddleia auriculata. 1882. II. 717.[1]
— Note on the genus Byrsanthus. 1873. II. 569.[2]
— Note on the presence of stamens within the ovarium of Baeckea. 1867. II. 620.[1]

Masters, Maxwell Tylden (*continued*).
— Note on the relation between morphology and physiology in the leaves of certain Conifers. 1880. II. 18.
— Note sur le Dombeya angulata Cav. 1867. II. 533.[2]
— Notes on certain Passifloreae. 1885. II. 575.[1]
— Notes on double flowers. 1866. I. 145.[2]
— Notes on root-hairs and root growth. 1879. I. 188.[1]
— Notes on the genera of Taxaceae and Coniferae. 1895. II. 13.[2]
— Concerning Oaks. 1875. III. 361.[1]
— Olearia Haastii Hooker. 1872. II. 862.[1]
— Ophiocaulon cissampeloides. 1871. II. 576.[1]
— Panax Mastersianum Hort. Sand. 1898. II. 651.[1]
— Pandanus Sanderi Hort. 1898. II. 57.[2]
— Passiflora chelidonea Mast. n. sp. 1879. II. 578.[1]
— Passiflora cincinnata Mast. sp. n. 1868. II. 578.[1]
— Passiflora Constance Elliott. 1884. II. 578.[1]
— Passiflora europhylla Mast. sp. nov. 1900. II. 578.[1]
— Passiflora galbana Mast. n. sp. 1896. II. 578.[2]
— Passiflora (§ Granadilla) macrocarpa. 1869. II. 579.[2]
— Passiflora Im Thurnii sp. nov. 1898. II. 579.[1]
— Passiflora Miersii. 1888. III. 616.[1]
— Passiflora organensis Gard. 1869. II. 580.[1]
— Passiflora pruinosa Mast. sp. n. 1897. II. 580.[1]'
— Passiflora sanguinolenta Mast. 1874. II. 580.[2]
— Passiflora sanguinolenta Mast. & Lind. 1868. II. 580.[1]
— Passiflora (sect. astrophea) glauca. 1867. II. 578.[1]
— Passiflora Watsoniana Mast. 1886. II. 581.[1]
— Passifloraceae. . 1872. II. 575.[1]
— On the Passifloreae collected by M. Edouard André. 1884. II. 575.[2]
— Passion-flower, Eynsford Gem. 1889. II. 578.[1]
— Pflanzen-Teratologie. 1869. I. 143.
— Philageria. 1872. II. 84.[1]
— Picea ajanensis. 1880. II. 37.[2] — 1888. III. 305.[2]
— Picea Menziesii. 1886. III. 306.[1]
— Picea Morinda. 1885. III. 306.[2]
— Picea Omorika. 1884. II. 38.[1]
— Picea orientalis. 1886. III. 306.[1]
— Picea pungens. 1891. II. 38.[2]
— Pieris japonica. 1882. III. 654.[1]
— Pinus ayacahuite. 1882. III. 306.[2]
— Pinus Balfouriana var. aristata. 1899. II. 40.[1]
— Pinus Bungeana. 1882. II. 41.[1]
— Pinus canariensis. 1888. II. 41.[1]
— Pinus contorta. 1883. II. 41.[2]
— Pinus Coulteri. 1885. III. 307.[1]
— Pinus Grenvilleae. 1881. II. 43.[1]
— Pinus halepensis. 1888. III. 307.[2]
— Pinus Jeffreyi. 1889. II. 42.[1]
— Pinus (Laricio) Karamana. 1884. II. 43.[2]
— Pinus Laricio var. Pallasiana. 1883. III. 308.[1]
— Pinus monophylla. 1888. II. 42.[2]
— Pinus Montezumae. 1890. II. 43.[1] — 1894. II. 43.[1] — 1899. II. 43.[2]
— Pinus muricata Don. 1884. II. 43.[2]
— Pinus patula. 1885. II. 44.[1]
— Pinus Peuke. 1883. II. 44.[2]
— Pinus ponderosa. 1890. II. 45.[1]
— Pinus Sabiniana. 1888. II. 45.[2]
— Pinus Thunbergii. 1885. II. 48.[2]
— Plagianthus Lampenii. 1884. II. 526.[2]
— Plantae Lehmannianae in Guatemala. 1887. II. 575.[2]
— On polliniferous ovules in a Rose. 1867. II. 289.[2]
— Populus alba var. Bolleana. 1882. III. 345.[1]
— Proliferous cones. 1882. II. 19.
— On prolification in flowers. 1861. I. 145.[1]
— Pseudo-Larix Kaempferi. 1884. II. 49.[1]
— Psychotria jasminiflora. 1879. III. 747.[1]
— Pyrus (§ Cydonia) Maulei. 1874. II. 258.[2]
— Pyrus Maulei. 1874. III. 420.[2]
— Quercus cuspidata. 1879. III. 362.[1]
— Quercus glandulifera Blume. 1880. II. 134.[1]
— Quercus humilis. 1874. II. 134.[1]
— Remarks on the morphology of Rosa berberifolia. 1889. II. 297.[1]
— Remarks on the structure . . . of the genus Aristolochia. 1875. II. 181.[1]
— Review of some points in the comparative morphology . . . of the Coniferae. 1891. II. 16.[2]
— Rhododendron (§ Azaleodendron) Rodigas. 1893. II. 675.[2]
— Rhododendron Oldhami Maximowicz. 1882. II. 682.[2]
— The Rhododendron tribe. 1871. II. 658.[1]

— Rosa berberidifolia. 1889. II. 297.[1]
— Saxe-Gothaea, male flowers of. 1889. II. 10.[1]
— Sciadopitys. 1895. II. 49.[2]
— Skimmias. 1889. II. 411.[1]
— Skimmien. 1889. II. 411.[1]
— Some Cotoneasters. 1879. II. 259.[1]
— Some features of interest in the order of Conifers. 1892. II. 13.[2]
— On some points in the morphology of the Malvales. 1869. II. 519,[2] 581.[1]
— The species of Encephalartos. 1876. II. 5.[2]
— The species of Thuya. 1897. II. 52.[1]
— Strophanthus Bullenianus. 1870. II. 732.[1]
— On the structure of the flower in the genus Napoleona. 1869. II. 612.[2]
— Substitutes for Larch. 1896. IV. 121.
— Succulent seeds. 1895. II. 507.[2]
— Tacsonia Andersoni. 1885. III. 616.[2]
— Tacsonia (§ Bracteogamia) quitensis Benth. 1869. II. 581.[2]
— Tacsonia exoniensis. 1872. II. 581.[2]
— Tacsonia insignis Mast. sp. nov. 1873. II. 581.[2]
— Tacsonia militaris ×. 1899. II. 581.[2]
— Tacsonia Parritae. 1882. II. 581.[2]
— Tacsonia (Bracteogamia) tomentosa Juss. var. speciosa Mast. 1870. II. 581.[2]
— Tacsonias. 1869. II. 581.[1]
— Taxodium and Glyptostrobus. 1900. II. 30.[1]
— Taxodium distichum. 1886. II. 51.[2] — 1893. II. 51.[2]
— Thuia Standishii. 1878. II. 52.[2]
— Thuia (§ Thuiopsis) dolobrata. 1882. III. 312.[1]
— Torreya. 1889. II. 12.[1]
— Torreyas. 1884. II. 12.[1]
— Trees and shrubs for large towns. 1891. III. 42.[2]
— Trochodendron aralioides. 1894. II. 194.[2]
— Tsuga Pattoniana. 1892. II. 53.[2]
— Vegetable morphology. 1882. I. 99.
— Vegetable teratology. 1869. I. 148.
— Veronica Lavaudiana. 1891. III. 704.[2]
— Vitis (Cissus) striata. 1881. III. 544.[2]
— The Welwitschia. 1898. II. 55.[2]
— What is habit? 1883. II. 468.[2]
— Xanthoceras sorbifolia Bunge. 1876. III. 540.[2]
— Zamia? amplifolia. 1878. II. 7.[2]
Masters, W. Hortus duroverni. 1831. III. 28.[2]
Masthoff, E. B. Aanteekeningen omtrent . . . Tabalong en Kloewa. 1888. III. 276.[1]
Mastic. 1893. III. 525.[2]
Masure, Félix. · L'horticulture dans le département du Loiret pendant l'hiver 1879–1880. 1881. III. 48.
— Recherches sur l'évaporation de la terre et de l'eau. 1879. I. 167.
Matani, Antonio. · Delle produzioni naturali del territorio Pistojese. 1762. III. 271.[2]
Matarsch, J. Baummesser. 1849. IV. 231.[1]
Maté, or Paraguayan Tea. 1877. III. 531.[1]
Mateer, S. Remarks on the Tamil popular names of plants. 1873. I. 474.
Mateos, Marcelo RIVAS. See RIVAS MATEOS, Marcelo.
Mater, D. Een Bamboe-praatje. 1877. III. 314.[1]
In materia di Roveri. 1582. IV. 304.[1]
The materia medica of the Pharmacopoeia. 1900. III. 244.
Material-Kontrolle. Trennung von Haupt- und Vornutzung. 1889. IV. 245.
Materialnaya . . . See Материальная . . .
Materialy . . . See Материалы . . .
Matern, A. See Матернъ, A.
Maternus, Georg Christian. De tumore manuum & pedum. 1754. III. 406.[2]
Mathematische und naturwissenschaftliche Berichte aus Ungarn. I. 28.[1]
Mather, G. E. The May-flower. 1884. II. 663.[2]
Mathesius, J. Hedera Helix. 1853. II. 650.[1]
— Iakttagelser öfver några inom Westergöthland förekommande naturalster. 1854. II. 107.[1]
Matheson, Donald. Variation in Ulex europaeus. 1885. II. 387.[2]
Mathews, Ferdinand Schuyler. Familiar trees and their leaves. 1896. I. 305.
— Wayside trees series. 1899. I. 305.
Mathews, William. The flora of Algeria. 1880. I. 485.
— Flora of the Clent and Lickey Hills. 1882. I. 534.
Mathey, Alphonse. Le Chêne de juin. 1898. II. 136.[2]
— Étude sommaire des taillis sous futaie. 1898. IV. 132.[1]

— L'évolution en forêt. Les tourbières. 1898. I. 229, *IV. 74.*²
— L'expérimentation forestière. 1897. IV. 38.²
— Influence de la forêt sur . . . sources. 1898. IV. 52.
— La maladie des Châtaigniers. 1898. III. 359.³
— Le pâturage en forêt. 1900. IV. 135,² *197.*²
— Les Pins en Bourgogne. 1900. IV. 462.²
— Les taillis sous futaie dans le bassin de la Saône. 1898. IV. 131.
— Utilisation industrielle des produits d'une coupe. 1900. IV. 252, 392, 556.²
Mathieu, Carl. Die amerikanische Moosbeere. 1881. III. 663.²
— Die neuen Yucca-Bastarde. 1883. III. 339.²
— Nomenclator pomologicus. 1889. III. 72.
— Populus Eugenii (Populus pyramidalis Meetensis). 1887. III. 345.²
— Der Schnitt der Ziergehölze. 1900. III. 171.
— Der Ursprung der Rosa Manetti. 1883. III. 455.³
— Verzeichnis der im Handel . . . befindlichen Rosen. 188.? III. 449.
Mathieu, Charles. Flore générale de Belgique. 1853. I. 392.
— Supplément à la flore générale de Belgique. 1855. I. 892.
Mathieu, Jean Joseph Auguste. L'Algérie et la commission sénatoriale. 1895. IV. 279.²
— Bibliographie de ses œuvres. *See* BIBLIOGRAPHIE . . . 1892. IV. 2.
— Cours de zoologie forestière. 1859. IV. 90.¹
— Flore forestière. 1858. I. 404,² *IV. 85.*¹
— Les forêts à l'Exposition . . . de Vienne. 1874. IV. 21.¹
— Les forêts de la province d'Oran. 1889. IV. 379.¹
— Les forêts et la vie rurale. 1898. IV. 45.
— Ueber die Gewinnung des Korks. 1883. IV. 517.²
— Invasion des pineraies de la Champagne. 1894. IV. 462.¹
— Météorologie comparée agricole et forestière. 1878. IV. 59.³
— Météorologie forestière. 1866. IV. 59.³
— Note sur le Pinus uncinata. 1879. II. 43.¹
— Note sur les variations de densité des bois de même espèce. 1879. IV. 411.²
— Le projet de loi forestière concernant l'Algérie. 1897. IV. 332.²
— Le reboisement et le regazonnement des Alpes. 1865. IV. 162.
— Le service forestier dans le département d'Oran. 1892. IV. 279.²
— Statistique forestière. 1878. IV. 360.
Mathieu, L. Über die Kultur der Rhododendra. 1824. III. 656.
Mathieu, V. Recherches sur l'accroissement en grosseur. 1856. I. 189.
Mathieu de Dombasle, Christophe Joseph Alexandre. Des forêts considérées relativement à l'existence des sources. *See* DOMBASLE, C. J. A. M. de. 1859. IV. 50.
— Dumode de nutrition des plantes. 1821. I. 157.
Mathsson, Albert. Reisebericht eines Cacteensammlers in Mexiko. 1890. II. 587.²
Mathys, U. Bestimmung der Umtriebszeit. 1886. IV. 252.
Matkovich, Paolo. Cenni generale sulla flora di Fiume. 1877. I. 447.
Maton, George. The natural history . . . of Wilts. 1843. I. 399.
Maton, William George. Some account of the medicinal and other uses of . . . Pinus. 1832. IV. 462.¹
Matoso, Eduardo. Notas sobre plantas utiles escogidas de la flora correntina. 1893. III. 269.²
Matruchot. *See* CONSTANTIN & MATRUCHOT.
Matschke, Wilhelm. Die Vermehrung . . . der Ficus elastica. 189.? III. 370.²
Matsson, Lars Peter Reinhold. Botaniska reseanteckningar från Gotland. 1895. II. 284.¹
— Rosae osilianae. 1900. II. 284.¹
Matsuda, Sadahisa. On the anatomy of Magnoliaceae. 1894. II. 209.¹
Matsumura, Jinzō. Asclepiadaceae formosano-liukiunenses. 1898. II. 735.²
— List of plants found in Nikkō. 1894. I. 463.¹
— Names of plants and their products in English, Japanese and Chinese. 1892.' I. 75.³
— Nippon Shokubutsumeii; or, Nomenclature of Japanese plants. 1884. I. 463.¹
— Notes on Liukiu and Formosan plants. 1898. I. 463.³

— Notes on some Liu-kiu plants. 1897. I. 463.¹
— Notulae ad plantas asiaticas orientales. 1899. I. 463.³
— Oleaceae formosanae. 1898. II. 705.²
— Plantae arborescentes in provincia Hitachi. 1900. I. 461.
— Plantae arborescentes . . . in provinciis Awa et Kazusa. 1900. I. 461.
— Rhamnaceae formosanae liukivensesque. 1898. II. 492.¹
— Shokubutsu Mei-i. 1895. I. 75.²
— *See also* ITO, Tokutarō & MATSUMURA, Jinzō.
Matsuwoka-Gentats'. Bai-hin. 1655. III. 430:¹
— Oo-hin. 1697. III. 431.²
Mattauschek, Wenzel. Der praktische Forstmann. 1865. IV. 99.³
Mattei, Giovanni Ettore. Aggiunte alla flora bolognese. 1886. I. 429.
— Boschi, uccelli e rimboschimento. 1897. IV. 166.¹
— Convolvulacee. 1887. II. 743.²
— I lepidotteri e la dicogamia. 1888. I. 238.
— Noterelle botaniche. 1886. I. 238.
— Relazione che hanno i boschi. 1898. IV. 45.
Mattej, Gustavo, *barone.* Se i corpuscoli rossi di varie Myrsineae. 1897. II. 694.²
In the matter of the inquiry concerning the administration of the laws in relation to the forest preserve. 1891. IV. *178,*¹ 314.³
Matteucci, Carlo. Sur la diffusion des gas. 1863. I. 150.¹
— Quelques expériences sur la respiration des plantes. 1846. I. 170.
Matteucci, E. Contributo allo studio delle placche sugherose. 1897. I. 132.²
Matthaeus Sylvaticus. Liber pandectarum medicine. 1342. I. 275,¹ V. XIV.¹
— Opus pandectarum medicine. 1342. I. 275,¹ V. XIV.¹
Matthei, C. H. De tincturae Sabinae . . . efficacia. 1819. III. 304.¹
Matthew, George Frederic. A forest fire at St. John about 2000 years ago. 1900. IV. 181.²
— On the occurrence of Arctic . . . plants in continental Acadia. 1869. I. 310.
Matthew, Patrick. Ueber den Einfluss der Blitzableiter. 1831. I. 231.¹
— On the infuence of lightning-conductors. 1831. I. 231.¹
— On naval timber and arboriculture. 1831. IV. 120.
Matthews, B. A. Influence of stock on graft. 1887. III. 40.¹
Matthews, Herbert. Curious clipped trees. 1898. III. 202.²
Matthews, John. Reise nach Sierra Leone. 1788. I. 490.
— Voyage à la rivière de Sierra-Leone. 1788. I. 490.
— A voyage to the river Sierra Leone. 1788. I. 490.
Matthias, (*Forstassessor*). Versuche mit dem . . . Nonnenvertilgungs-Apparat. 1898. IV. 202.
Matthiolus, Petrus Andreas. *See* MATTIOLI, P.
Mattioli, Pierandrea, [Pietro Andrea]. Adversus viginti problemata Melchioris Guilandini disputatio. 1562. I. 281.
— Apologia adversus Amathum Lusitanum. 1558. I. 280.
— Commentaires . . . sur les six livres de Pedacius Dioscoride. 1554. V. XV.¹
— Les commentaires sur les six livres des simples de Pedacius Dioscoride Anazarbéen. 1554. I. 279.
— Commentarii in libros sex Pedacii Dioscoridis Anazarbei De medica materia. 1554. I. 279, V. XV.¹
— Compendium de plantis omnibus. 1571. I. 281.
— I discorsi nei sei libri Della materia medicinale di Pedacio Dioscoride. 1554. I. 279.
— I discorsi nei sei libri di Pedacio Dioscoride. 1554.' V. XV.¹
— Disputatio adversus XX. problemata Melchioris Guilandini. 1562. I. 281.
— Epistolarum medicinalium libri quinque. 1561. I. 280.
— Herbář aneb Bylinář. 1561. I. 281.
— Herbars; ginak Bylinarz. 1561. I. 281.
— Kreutterbuch. 1561. I. 280.
— Neu vollkommenes Kräuter-Buch. 1561.' I. 280.
— New Kräuterbuch. 1561. I. 280.
— Opera quae extant omnia. 1598. I. 283.
— Opusculum de simplicium medicamentorum facultatibus.' 1569. I. 281, V. XV.²
— De plantis epitome utilissima. 1586. I. 282.
Mattirolo, Oreste. Sulla influenza che la estirpazione dei fiori esercita sui tuberoli radicali. 1899. II. 322.¹
— Di un nuovo processo di suberificazione . . . nel gen. Tilia. 1885. II. 516.¹

Mattirolo, Oreste (*continued*).
— Sul parassitismo dei tartufi. 1886.   I. 233.²
— Pistacia Lentiscus × Terebinthus.   1893.   II. 457.²
— Reliquiae Morisianae.   1893.   I. 430.
— Skatol e Carbazol.   1885.   I. 36.²
— Sullo sviluppo . . . dei tegumenti seminali nel genere Tilia. 1885.   II. 516.¹
— & **Buscalioni,** Luigi.   Ancora sui bacteroidi delle Leguminose.   1887.   II. 321.²
— — Si contengono bacteri nei tubercoli radicali delle Leguminose?   1887.   II. 321.²
— — Sulla funzione della linea lucida nelle cellule malpighiane.   1890.   I. 121.
— — Osservazioni intorno al lavoro del sig. K. Schips.   1893. II. 321.¹
— — Ricerche anatomofisiologiche sui tegumenti seminali delle Papilionaceae.   1889.   II. 321.¹
— — Sulla struttura degli spazii intercellulari nei tegumenti seminali delle Papilionaceae.   1889.   II. 321.¹
— — Il tegumento seminale delle Papilionacee.   1890.   II. 391.¹
Mattos, J. F. **Pereira de.**   *See* **Pereira de Mattos,** J. F.
Mattos, Vicira de.   Sur la noix d'Acajou.   1831.   III. 523.²
Mattusch, Josef.   Der Flugsand in der Banater Militär-Grenze.   1870.   IV. 145.
Mattuschka, Heinrich Gottfried, *Graf* von.   Enumeratio stirpium in Silesia.   1779.   I. 374.
— Flora silesiaca.   1776.   I. 374.
— Geschlechts- und Namenregister zur Flora silesiaca.   1776. I. 374.
Matuschka, *Graf* von.   Einiges über Melasis buprestoides. 1861.   IV. 492.¹
— Wetterschaden in . . . Schöneiche.   1861.   IV. 189.¹
Matuschka, Balth.   Anweisung zum nützlichen Weinbau. 1802, III. 552.
Matzdorff, C.   Die San José-Schildlaus.   1898.   III. 191.
Matzuno, H.   Kurze Uebersicht der Entwickelung des japanischen Forstwesens.   1900.   IV. 28.²
Mau, Otto.   Ueber Veredlung immergrüner Gehölze.   1870. III. 162.
Mauch, Friedrich, (*jr.*).   Chemische Untersuchung der Co-p-Rinde.   1868.   III. 397,¹ 517.¹ — 1869.   III. 516.¹
Mainin, K.   Chamaecyparis sphaeroidea Andelyensis.   1890. III. 301.²
Mauchart, B. D.   Schönbrunn's botanischer Reichthum. 1805.   I. 65.³
Mauchart, Burchard David.   Butyrum cacao.   1735.   III. 594.
Maude, Thomas.   An account of the Oak at Cowthorp. 1774.   II. 137.¹
Maudet.   De la composition chimique de certains parenchymes.   1873.   I. 153.
Mauduit, Ferdinand.   Semis, plantation et culture du Poirier. n. d.   III. 444.¹
Mauduit, Fernando & **Peluffo,** Vicente.   El jardinero ilustrado.   1886.   III. 100.¹
Mauduyt.   Origine de l'écorce de belaayé.   1830.   III. 726.¹
Mauget.   Notice sur le semis . . . du Rosier.   1844.   III. 452.
Maughan, Henry.   De viribus radicis Sassaparillae antisyphiliticis.   *See* **Boehmer,** G. R.   1803.   III. 338.¹
Maughan, John.   How trees grow.   1890.   IV. 62.¹
— The principles of thinning.   1895.   III. 173.¹
Maugin, Gustave.   Observation de floraison.   1859.   I. 220.¹
— Sur quelques faits de tératologie.   1860.   I. 143.
Maujean.   Note sur une résine nouvelle.   1823.   III. 495.¹
Mauksch, Johann Daniel.   De partibus plantarum.   1776. I. 97.
Maul, Richard.   Ueber Sclerotinienbildung in Alnus-Früchten. 1894.   IV. 489.¹
Maulde, René de.   Étude sur la condition forestière de l'Orléanais.   1881.   IV. 27.¹
Maulny.   Plantes observées aux environs de la ville du Mans. 1786.   I. 406.
Maumené, Albert.   Le Carpenteria californica.   1894.   III. 409.²
— Les Crotons.   1896.   III. 516.²
— Culture des Cycadées.   1896.   III. 284.²
— Le forçage du Mimosa.   1900.   III. 465.¹
— Hypericum Moserianum var. tricolor.   1894.   III. 610.¹
— Les Irésines.   1898.   III. 388.¹
— Les plantes de plein air et leur utilisation.   1898.   III. 203.
— Production des frondes de Cycas.   1897.   III. 285.¹

— Propriétés tinctoriales du Sophora.   1895.   III. 488.¹
— Le Rhus Cotinus.   1894.   III. 524.¹
— Le Rosa rugosa var. calocarpa.   1895.   III. 457.¹
— Spiraea japonica rubra.   1898.   III. 461.²
— & **Tréoignaud,** Claude.   Manuel pratique de jardinage et d'horticulture.   1900.   III. 114.¹
Maumené, E. J.   Absorption de l'eau par les bois.   1878. IV. 412.¹
— Sur l'existence du manganèse.   1884.   I. 154.
— Sur l'œnocyanine.   1882.   III. 583.¹
— Sur la puissance d'absorption de l'eau par les bois.   1878. IV. 412.¹
Maumenet.   Naturalisation de divers végétaux à Nîmes. 1874.   III. 125.
Maund, Benjamin.   The auctarium of the Botanic garden. 1825.   III. 123.³
— The floral register.   1825.   III. 81.
— The fruitist.   1825.   III. 79.
— & **Henslow,** J. S.   Botanist . . . *See* **Botanist.**   1837.   I. 268.
Mauny de Mornay, de.   Livre du forestier.   1838.   IV. 109.¹
— Pratique et législation des irrigations dans l'Italie supérieure.   1844.   III. 150.²
Maupas, Rast-.   *See* **Baudrillart,** J. J. & **Rast-Maupas.**
Maupin.   L'art de la Vigne.   1779.   III. 554.¹
— Nouvelle méthode de cultiver la Vigne.   1763.   III. 554.¹
Maupoil, de.   Manière de multiplier . . . les Pivoines en arbre. 1834.   III. 392.²
— Methode die Paeonia arborea . . . zu vermehren.   1834. III. 392.²
Maupoil, Carlo.   Catalogo generale degli alberi e piante. 1827.   I. 62.
Maur, Dupré de Saint-.   *See* **Dupré de Saint-Maur.**
Maurach, M.   Die practische Forstwirthschaft.   1893.   IV. 104.²
— Praktikaline metsaarjandus.   1893.   IV. 104.²
Maurenbrecher, L.   De Kininemarkt te Batavia.   1899. III. 718.
Maurenbrecher, L. L. A.   Resultaten eener proefneming met hybride Koffie.   1900.   III. 732.¹
Maurer, J. M.   Betrachtungen über . . . in die Forstwissenschaft eingeschlichene irrige Lehrsätze.   1783.   IV. 100.¹
Maurer, Ludwig Heinrich.   Ueber die Ansicht der Rosskastanie.   1871.   III. 537.¹
— Das Beerenobst.   1867.   III. 147.¹
— Das Beerenobst unserer Gärten.   1858.   III. 147.²
— Die Cranberry.   1870.   III. 663.³
— Die erste Cranberry-Pflanzung.   1872.   III. 664.¹
Maurette.   *See* **Braguier,** B. & **Maurette.**
Mauri, Ernesto.   Romanarum plantarum centuria.   1820. I. 425.
— *See also* **Sebastiani,** Antonio & **Mauri,** Ernesto.
— & **Orsini,** Antonio & **Tenore,** Michele.   Enumeratio plantarum . . . per Aprutium.   1830.   I. 426.
Maurice.   *See* **Mauritius.**
Mezurille de Saint Michel, (*père*).   Phytologie sacrée.   1664.
Maurin, Ernest Henri Alfred.   Essai sur la famille des Ménispermées.   1863.   II. 206.¹
Mauritius — Royal society of arts and sciences.   *See* **Royal** . . . I. 29.²
Mauritius — Société d'histoire naturelle . . . *See* **Société** . . . I. 29.²
Mauritius — Société royale des arts et des sciences.   *See* **Royal society of arts and sciences of Mauritius.**   I. 29.²
Mauritius tea.   1892.   III. 604.¹
Maury, D. H., (*jr.*).   Felling timber in the tropics.   1899.   IV. 385.¹
Maury, Louis Ferdinand Alfred.   Les forêts de la France. 1856.   IV. 27.¹
— I es forêts de la Gaule.   1867.   IV. 27.¹
— Des grandes forêts de la Gaule.   1849.   IV. 27.¹
— Histoire des grandes forêts de la Gaule.   1850.   IV. 27.¹
Maury, Paul.   Anatomie comparée de quelques espèces . . . du Sahara algérien.   1888.   I. 100,¹ 486.
— Les Cactées mexicaines.   1889.   II. 587.³
— Les Camoensia.   1887.   III. 469.²
— Le dimorphisme floral . . . du Marronnier d'Inde.   1888. II. 482.²
— Énumération des plantes du Haut-Orénoque.   1889.   I. 338.¹
— Sur un Eranthemum nouveau du Gabon.   1888.   II. 799.²
— Études sur l'organisation . . . des Plombaginacées.   1886. II. 696.¹

— Sur les procédés . . . pour obténir des arbres nains. 1889. III. 175.²
— La Sebastiania Ramirezii. 1897. II. 451.³
— Sur les variations de structure des Vaccinium de France. 1887. II. 685.¹
— *See also* Bois,· Désiré & MAURY, Paul; BONNET, Edmond & MAURY, Paul.
Maury, Pierre. *See* BONNET, Edmond & MAURY, Pierre.
Mauthner, Ödön. Az amerikai Nagyszemü Afonya. 1900. III. 664.¹
— A Clematis. 1897. III. 389.³
— A Clematis Viticella mûvelése. 1898. III. 392.¹
— Az Eukalyptus vagy Mézgafa. 1900. III. 634.¹
— Három jerikói Lonc. 1899. III. 750.¹
Mautt, J. F. De cortice peruviano. 1760. III. 719.
Mauz, E. F. Über den Prozess der Keimung. 1843. I. 202.³
— Versuche, die Pflanzen nach Form und Organisation ihrer Blätter zu demonstriren. 1843. I. 109.³
— Versuche . . . über das Geschlecht der Pflanzen. 1822. I. 199.
Mavor, William. The lady and gentleman's botanical pocket book. 1800. I. 264.
Maw, George. Les forêts du Canada. 1879. IV. 337.¹
— Notes on American forests. 1879. IV. 337.¹
— Notes on the flora of the Pyrenees. 1877. I. 415.
— The Sugar Maple. 1878. IV. 527.¹
Mawe, John. Notes extraites du voyage dans l'intérieur du Brésil. 1815. III. 269.
— Reisen in das Innere von Brasilien. 1815. III. 269.¹
— Travels in the interior of Brazil. 1815. III. 268.¹
— Viaggio nell' interno del Brasile. 1815. III. 269.¹
— Voyages dans l'intérieur du Brésil. 1815. III. 269.¹
Mawe, Thomas. Every man his own gardener. 1769. III. 109.
— & **Abercrombie**, John. The universal gardener and botanist. 1778. III. 81.
Maximowicz, Carl Johann. Abelia B. Br. Synopsis specierum asiaticarum. 1887. II. 834.¹
✓ — Adnotationes de Spiraeaceis. 1879. II. 256.¹
✓ — Das Amurland und dessen Vegetation. 1857. I. 454.³
✓ — Andromeda campanulata. 1873. II. 663.¹
✓ — Ardisia hortorum Maxim. 1865. II. 693.¹
✓ — Sur les collections botaniques de la Mongolie. 1885. I. 460.³
✓ — De Coriaria, Ilice. 1881. II. 454.¹
✓ — Daphne jezoensis Maxim. 1866. II. 601.³
— Diagnoses breves plantarum novarum Japoniae et Mandshuriae. 1866. I. 455.
✓ — Diagnoses plantarum novarum asiaticarum. 1877. I. 456.
— Einfluss fremden Pollens auf die Form der erzeugten Frucht. 1872. I. 201.³
✓ — Enumeratio plantarum hucusque in Mongolia . . . lectarum. 1889. I. 460.³
✓ — Flora tangutica. 1889. I. 460.³
✓ — Ad florae Asiae orientalis cognitionem meliorem fragmenta. 1879. I. 453.¹
— On the influence of foreign pollen on the form of the fruit. 1872. I. 201.³
✓ — A key to the species of Spiraea. 1879. II. 256.¹
✓ — Lonicera Maackii Maxim. 1884. II. 838.¹
— Ein Nachtrag zu meiner Abhandlung. "Rhododendreae Asiae orientalis." 1871. II. 658.¹
✓ — Plantae chinenses Potaninianae. 1889. I. 460.³
✓ — Primitiae florae amurensis. 1859. I. 455.
✓ — Revisio Hydrangeearum Asiae orientalis. 1867. II. 237.³
✓ — Rhamneae orientali-asiaticae. 1866. II. 491.³
✓ — Rhododendreae Asiae orientalis. 1870. II. 658.¹
✓ — Rhododendron macrosepalum Maxim. 1870. II. 681.³
✓ — Spiraea bullata Maxim. 1886. II. 314.³
✓ — Synopsis generis Lespedezae. 1873. II. 369.³
✓ — Ueber die Vegetation von Hakodate. 1861. I. 462.
— Ueber die wichtigeren Bäume und Sträucher des Amurlandes. 1857. I. 454.³
✓ — & **Regel**, Eduard von. Vegetations-Skizzen des Amurlandes. 1857. I. 455.
— & **Ruprecht**, F. J. Die ersten botanischen Nachrichten über das Amurland. 1857. I. 455.
Maximowicz, M. A. *See* МАКСИМОВИЧЪ, M. A.
Maxwell. Observations on the countries of Congo. 1822. III. 281.¹
Maxwell, *Sir* Herbert. London trees. 1894. III. 42.³
— Woodlands. 1891. IV. 357.³
Maxwell, Hugh. Observations on trees as conductors of lightning. 1787. IV. 193.³

Maxwell, John. Dimensions of some trees . . . on the estate of Poloc. 1837. I. 54.
Maxwell, *Mrs*. M. Y. Some old Hampstead trees. 1899. I. 297.¹
Maxwell, T. C. Evergreens, novelties and dwarfs. 1874. III. 290.
— Magnolia glauca. 1877. III. 399.³
Maxwell, W. *See* SCHULZE, E., STEIGER, E. & MAXWELL, W.
May. L'Ajonc ou Jonc marin. 1887. III. 489.³
— Araucaria excelsa var. simplex. 1884. III. 298.³
— Armeniaca lucida. 1875. III. 438.¹
— Des Aucubas à haute tige. 1872. III. 645.¹
— Cerasus pendula rosea. 1876. III. 439.¹
— Chaenomeles japonica umbilicata. 1877. III. 420.¹
— Crataegus Lalandei. 1883. III. 443.³
— Culture de l'Indigofera Dosua sur tige. 1876. III. 479.³
— Culture . . . des Lagerstroemia. 1876. III. 629.³
— Deux Glycines à recommander. 1886. III. 490.³
— Edgworthia [*sic*] chrysantha. 1877. III. 628.¹
— Eleagnus edulis. 1876. III. 628.³
— Evonymus japonica robusta. 1870. III. 532.³
— Genista hispanica. 1884. III. 477.¹
— Hedera macrophylla. 1878. III. 642.³
— Des Ligustrum villosum. 1874. III. 674.¹
— Lonicera Brownii. 1875. III. 750.¹
— Mahonia rotundifolia. 1881. III. 396.¹
— Persica candida plena. 1875. III. 440.¹
— Plantes nouvelles ou pas assez connues. 1878. III. 87.
— Robinia pseudo-acacia monophylla. 1887. III. 487.¹
— Sambucus angustifolia. 1878. III. 751.³
— Sophora japonica. 1870. III. 488.¹
— Spartium junceum. 1870. III. 488.³
— Stranwaesia glaucescens. 1887. III. 462.¹
— Syringa Josikea. 1870. III. 681.¹
— Taille des arbustes d'ornement. 1885. III. 172.
May, H. Daphne Blagayana. 1892. III. 627.¹
May, K. J. Die Entwickelung der Aufastungstechnik. 1888. IV. 172.¹
— Geschichte der Aufastungstechnik und Aufastungslehre. 1889. IV. 24.¹
— Die Lebensdauer der Nadeln bei . . . Nadelhölzern. 1894. II. 21.¹
— Der Universal-Forststock. 1895. IV. 232.
— Zur Verhütung des Aufreissens. 1895. IV. 384.¹
— Versteigerung von Nonnenfrassholz in Bayern. 1892. IV. 388.³
May, Walter. Der Bakonyerwald. 1893. IV. 374.¹
— Entwickelung . . . des Waldwesens in Österreich. 1892. IV. 368.
— "Forste" . . . in der Schweiz. 1893. IV. 367.
— Forstwesen und Holzhandel in Serbien. 1893. IV. 407.¹
— Der Holzhandel der Niederlande. 1892. IV. 404.³
— Holzindustrie und Holzhandel Galiziens. 1898. IV. 407.¹
— Über Wälder und Waldwirtschaft in Schweden und Norwegen. 1895. IV. 342.³
— Über die Waldflora Griechenlands. 1893. IV. 87,³ 89.¹
— Waldwirtschaft etc. in Canada. 1896. IV. 337.³
— Welche Aussichten bieten sich dem deutschen Export in Holz. 1896. IV. 404.³
— Wie ist der Vernichtung der Waldvegetation durch Hüttenrauch . . . abzuhelfen? 1894. IV. 192.³
May, William. Gampholobium polymorphum grandiflorum. 1881. III. 478.¹
May flowering trees and shrubs. 1890. III. 496.¹
Maycock, James Dottin. Catalogue of plants . . . in the British West India colonies. 1837. I. 335.
— Flora barbadensis. 1830. I. 335.
Maycock, Mark M. A class-book of color. 1895. I. 71.
Maydell, T., *Baron*. *See* OETTINGEN, A. J. von & MAYDELL, T., *Baron*.
Mayenberg, Christoph Carl. *See* GÜNZ, J. W. & MAYENBERG, C. C.
Mayenberg, Jos. Aufzählung der um Passau vorkommenden Gefässpflanzen. 1875. I. 387.
Mayer, A. Over de bereiding van cider. 1882. III. 429.¹
— Bijdrage ter beoordeeling van het schillen van akkermaalshout door stoom. 1877. IV. 434.
— Iets over de verschillende wijzen van verdelging der meikevers. 1878. III. 196.
— Kleine bijdrage tot het vraagstuk van de oorzaak der sapbeweging. 1896. I. 166.
— Locistofbepalingen in eikenschors. 1897. IV. 515.³.
— Proefneming met eene boschbemesting. 1895. IV. 144.³
— De voeding der planten. 1878. III. 38.¹ — 1879. I. 159.

Mayer, Adolph. Chemische Technologie des Holzes. 1872.
IV. 408.
— Ueber Sauerstoffabscheidung aus Pflanzentheilen. 1877.
I. 176.
Mayer, Anton. Wederlegging der beschouwingen van H. de
Vries over . . . organische zuren. 1875. I. 180.[1]
— *See also* Майеръ, A.
Mayer, Anton (*of Regensburg*). Einige Salix-Bastarde. 1896.
II. 102.[1]
— Koch'sche Originalweiden. 1898. II. 102.[1]
— Salix ratisbonensis mh. nov. hybr. 1898. II. 109.[1]
Mayer, August. *See* ROHRER, Rudolph & MAYER, August.
— & Wolkoff, A. de. Quelques recherches sur la respiration
des plantes. 1875. I. 170.
Mayer, August Franz Joseph Carl. Supplemente zur Lehre
vom Kreislaufe. 1827. I. 163.
Mayer, C. F. Ein aus sich selbst Nahrung ziehender Baum.
1873. I. 188.[1]
Mayer, E. Abutilon Darwinii. 1873. III. 586.[2]
— Antigonon leptopus und dessen Cultur. 1875. III. 387.[1]
— Das Aufrichten schiefer Stämme. 1890. III. 199.
— Beitrag zur Gartencultur der Cinchonaarten. 1869. III.
712.[1]
— Ein Beitrag zur Kenntniss der Einwirkung des Edelreises.
1878. III. 39.
— Cultur der Lapageria rosea. 1868. III. 337.[2]
— Daphne rupestris Facchini als Zierpflanze. 1875. III.
628.[1]
— Liquidambar Altingiana Blume. 1868. III. 416.[2]
— Multiplication par la greffe-racine. 1878. III. 164.[1]
— Neuer amerikanischer blütenloser Apfel. 1890. II. 267.[1]
— Eine pflanzengeographische Merkwürdigkeit. 1871. III.
45.
— Philesia buxifolia Lam. 1871. III. 337.[2]
— Prunus tomentosa Thunb. 1876. II. 277.[2]
— Tectona grandis L. fil. 1870. III. 697.[2]
— Vermehrung des Brodbaumes. 1867. III. 367.[1]
— Vermehrung durch künstliches Einsetzen von Wurzeln.
1878. III. 164.[1]
— Verwendung des Hibiscus rosa sinensis. 1878. III. 588.[1]
— Winterbedeckung der Coniferen. 1868. III. 183,[1] 292.
Mayer, F. H. Abhandlung von dem Verfall der Waldungen.
1780. IV. 169.[2]
Mayer, Friedrich. Ein verkanntes Cestrum. 1823. II.
770.[1]
Mayer, G. Culture du Frêne. 1856. IV. 535.[1]
— Erfahrungen über die Anzucht der Esche. 1856. IV.
535.[1]
Mayer, G. A. Ueber Berechnung der Kohlenmeiler. 1833.
IV. 222, 594.
Mayer, Johann. Botanische Beobachtungen. 1786. II.
304.[1]
— Pomona franconica. 1776. III. 70.
Mayer, Johann Albrecht. Encyclopädie der Forstwissen-
schaft. 1793. IV. 22.[1]
Mayer, Johann Christophe Andreas. Einheimische Giftge-
wächse. 1798. III. 72.
— Untersuchung der Königschinarinde. 1788. III. 724.[1]
Mayer, Johannes. Experimentum singulare de arboribus ex
folio educatis. *See* TEUMMIG, L. P. 1721. I. 205.
Mayer, Joseph. Uiber ein neues elastisches Harz aus Mada-
gaskar. 1795. III. 281.[2]
Mayer, K. E. Neuestes allgemeines deutsches Gartenbuch.
1827. III. 115.[1]
Mayer, L. T. De Javaan als landbouwer en veefokker.
1898. III. 129.[1]
Mayer, Miklós. Liriodendron Tulipifera. 1898. III. 398.[2]
— Paulownia imperialis. 1899. III. 703.[2]
Mayer, P. J. & Hekmeyer, F. Vergelijkend onderzoek·van
den bast der Cinchona Pahudiana. 1871. III. 722.
Mayer, Paul. Zur Naturgeschichte der Feigeninsecten.
1882. II. 151.[1]
Mayer, Robert. Früchte von Maclura aurantiaca. 1854.
II. 154.[1]
Mayer de Jouhe. De la rusticité de l'Aralia papyrifera.
1872. III. 644.[1]
Mayerhoffer, J. N. *See* STERLER, Alois & MAYERHOFFER, J. N.
Mayersbach, Leopold. Die Bodenkultur auf dem Karste.
1871. IV. 374.[3]
Mayet, Étienne. Ueber die Kultur des Maulbeerbaums.
1790. III. 373.
— Des manufactures de soie. 1810. III. 373.
Mayet, P. Die Ergebnisse der statistatistischen Erhebungen.
1894. IV. 349.[2]

Mayet, Valéry. La cochinilla de las Viñas de Chilé. 1897.
III. 564.[1]
— Les insectes de la Vigne. 1890. III. 564.[1]
— Sur les moyens à employer pour détruire l'œuf d'hiver du
phylloxera. 1881. III. 573.
— Observations sur les pontes du phylloxera ailé. 1879. III.
571.
— Sur l'œuf d'hiver du phylloxera. 1880. III. 572. — 1882.
III. 573.
— Résultats des traitements effectués, en Suisse, en vue de la
destruction du phylloxera. 1882. III. 573.
— *See also* LICHTENSTEIN, Jules & MAYET, Valéry.
— & Viala, Pierre. La maladie rouge de la Vigne. 1893.
III. 581.
Mayevski, P. F. *See* МАЕВСКIЙ, П. Ф.
The Mayflower. III. 5.
Über die **Maykäferlarven** oder Maykäferwürmer. 1789.
III. 188.[2]
Maynard, F. P. & Prain, David. A note on the botany of the
Valuchafghan boundary commission. 1896. I. 475.[3]
Maynard, S. T. Insects and fungi injuring our fruits. 1891.
III. 178.
— Methods of fruit culture and forestry. 1885. III. 133.
Mayoux, A., (*Mlle.*). Recherches sur la production . . . du
tannin chez . . . Pomacées. 1894. II. 257.[1]
— Recherches sur la valeur . . . des appendices superstami-
naux de la fleur des Aristoloches. 1892. II. 181.[1]
Mayr, Georg. Einfluss des Waldes auf Klima und Boden-
beschaffenheit. 1863. IV. 53.
Mayr, Gustav L. Etwas von Eichengallen. 1872. IV. 509.
— Die mitteleuropäischen Eichengallen. 1871. IV. 501.[1]
Mayr, Heinrich. Antrag . . . zur Vornahme von Versuchen
über den Einfluss der Provenienz des Samens. 1900. IV.
147.[2]
— The cultivation of a wood for Tea boxes. 1887. IV. 448.[1]
— Entstehung und Vertheilung der Secretions-Organe der
Fichte und Lärche. 1884. I. 135, II. 18.
— Ergebnisse forstlicher Anbauversuche mit japanischen,
indischen . . . Holzarten in Bayern. 1898. IV. 21.[1]
— Erhebungen betreffend das Verbreitungsgebiet der Haupt-
holzarten. 1900. I. 348,[1] IV. 79.[1]
— Die Erziehungshiebe (Durchforstungen) der neuen Schule.
1899. IV. 175.[3]
— The forests of the United States. 1890. IV. 338.[1]
— Forstliche und floristische Studien in Nordamerika. 1896.
I. 308.
— Ueber den forstlichen Wert der . . . Qualitätsbestimmungen
der Hölzer. 1898. IV. 416.[1]
— Zur Frage der Aufforstungen in Deutsch-Ostafrika. 1899.
IV. 168.[2]
— Die fremdländischen Holzarten im mitteleuropäischen
Walde. 1894. IV. 125.[1]
— Ueber die Güte des . . . Carya-Holzes. 1885. IV. 488.[1]
— Das Harz der deutschen Nadelwaldbäume. 1893. II. 21,[1]
III. 222.[1]
— Das Harz der Nadelhölzer. 1893. II. 21,[1] III. 222.[1]
— Ueber Harzvertheilung im Baume. 1894. I. 181,[1] IV.
437.[1]
— Das Holz der Douglas-Tanne. 1884. II. 49.[1]
— Das Holz der zum Anbau empfohlenen exotischen Laub-
holz-Arten. 1885. IV. 411.[1]
— Ueber die Kiefern des japanischen Reiches. 1894. II.
39.[2]
— Magnolia hypoleuca Honoki. 1898. IV. 520.[1]
— Le Magnolia hypoleuca Honoki. 1898. IV. 520.[1]
— Massenhaftes Auftreten von Chrysomyxa abietis. 1884.
IV. 456.
— Le Mélèze de Sibérie. 1900. IV. 452.[2]
— Monographie der Abietineen des Japanischen Reiches.
1890. II. 16.[1]
— Ein neuer Pflanzenfeind. 1882. IV. 211.[2]
— Ueber den Parasitismus von Nectria cinnabarina. 1882.
IV. 211.[2]
— Polyporus betulinus und Polyporus laevigatus. 1884.
IV. 490.[1]
— Resinosity of the wood of different Conifers. 1888. II.
17.[1]
— Die Unterschiede zwischen der Hondo-Fichte . . . und der
Ajans-Fichte. 1894. II. 37.[2]
— Varietäten . . . der Abietineen Japans. 1891. III. 291.
— Ueber die Vertheilung des Harzes in . . . Coniferen.
1885. II. 21.[1]
— Aus den Waldungen Japan's. 1891. I. 461, IV. 87,[2]
126.[1]

— Die Waldungen von Nordamerika. 1890. I. 305, IV. 76,¹ 337.¹
— The White Pine in Europe. 1888. IV. 469.²
— Zwei Parasiten der Birke. 1884. IV. 490.³
— See also GAYER, Karl & MAYR, Heinrich.
Mayr, Ignaz. Anleitung für Förster und die denselben nöthigen Kenntnisse im Rechnungswesen. 1839. IV. 311.¹
— Das Rechnungswesen für Förster. 1839. IV. 311.²
Mayr, Johann. Deutschlands Flora. 1798. I. 375.
Mayrhofer, Joseph. Flora von Landshut. 1868. I. 386.
Maza, Manuel GÓMEZ DE LA. See GÓMEZ DE LA MAZA, Manuel.
Mazade, M. See HOUDAILLE, F. & MAZADE, M.
Mazade, Marcel. First steps in ampelography. 1900. III. 547.
Mazama. ; I. 6.
Mazaroz, J..P. Conclusion générale sur la destruction du phylloxéra. 1879. III. 760.
— Mémoire sur la destruction du phylloxera. 1879. III. 572, 760.
— Le plus grand péril public du moment. 1879. III. 761.
Mazats, Justin. Étude pratique sur le Prunier d'Ente. 1888. III. 433.¹
Mazé, H. L'assimilation de l'azote nitrique. 1898. I. 160.
— L'assimilation des hydrates de carbone. 1899. I. 160.
— Contribution à la flore de la Guadeloupe. 1892. I. 337.
— Nomenclature des arbres et des arbrisseaux indigènes . . . à la Guadeloupe. 1883. I. 334.
Mazeas, Guillaume, & Miller, Philip. Berigten aangaande den Vernisboom. 1756. III. 526.²
— Two letters concerning Toxicodendron. 1756. III. 526.²
Mazée. Recherches sur la digestion des réserves. 1900. I. 204.
Mazorra, Franca. Tratamiento de la lepra. 1884. III. 614.³
Mazure, J. See COSTER, D. J., HOORN, G. H. & MAZURE, J.
Mazzanti, Elisabetta, contesa, FIORINI-. See FIORINI-MAZZANTI, Elisabetta, contesa.
Mazzarosa, Antonio. Sul modo di concimar gli Ulivi. 1821. III. 675.¹
Mazzetto di fiori per la festa. See PASSERINI, Giovanni. 1855. I. 63.
Mazziari, Domenico. Flora corcirese. 1834. I. 448.²
Mazzoni, Emidio PACIFICI. See PACIFICI-MAZZONI, Emidio.
Mazzucato, Giovanni. Viaggio botanico all' Alpi Giulie. 1811. I. 425.
— Sullo zucchero . . . dei Diospyros. 18 . . ? III. 669.¹
Mead, Enoch. Early history of Iowa horticulture. 1884. III. 118.¹
Mead, H. On the productive resources of Ceylon. 1862. III. 279.¹
Mead, P. B. The Clematis. 1885. III. 389.¹
— An elementary treatise on American Grape culture. 1867. III. 550.
Mead, Theodore Luqueer. Exotic Palms in Florida. 1890. III. 318.¹
Meader, James. The planter's guide. 1779. III. 81.
Meadows, T. T. On the Oak-feeding silkworm of China. 1865. IV. 501.²
Meager, Leonard. The English gardener. 1679. III. 107.
— The mystery of husbandry. 1697. III. 108.
— The new art of gardening. 1697. III. 108.
Méan, A. VAUVERT DE. See VAUVERT DE MÉAN, A.
Meany, Edmond Stephen. Acclimatation d'essences exotiques. 1898. IV. 126.²
Mease, James. Account of a very large tree in Mexico. 1831. II. 52.¹
Measurement of Oaks. 1805. IV. 512.
Measurement of standing timber. 1876. IV. 217.
Measuring log timber, a paradox. 1900. IV. 229.
Meaulle, LEFEUVRE-. See LEFEUVRE-MEAULLE.
Meaume, Édouard. Cantonnement de la forêt de Chiny. 1864. IV. 322.²
— Cantonnement des forêts de Bareilles. 1861. IV. 326.
— Commentaire du code forestier. 1844. IV. 324.
— Des droits d'usage dans les forêts . . . des bois communaux et de l'affouage. 1851. IV. 334.¹
— Étude sur la réorganisation de l'administration des forêts. 1878. IV. 292.
— L'Eucalyptus à la colonie agricole des Trois-Fontaines. 1882. IV. 127,¹ 530.
— Introduction à l'étude de la législation et de la jurisprudence forestières. 1857. IV. 324.
— Introduction générale à l'étude de la législation et de la jurisprudence forestières. 1845. IV. 324

— Du jugement des infractions en matière forestière. 1882. IV. 326.
— Programme du cours élémentaire de législation et de jurisprudence. 1862. IV. 324.
—& La Ménardière, C. de. Mémoire pour les anciens usagers de Plaine. 1868. IV. 334.¹
Meaux — Société d'agriculture, sciences et arts. See SOCIÉTÉ . . . III. 21.
Meaux — Société d'horticulture. See SOCIÉTÉ . . . III. 21.
Mecca balsam and myrrh. 1894. III. 511.¹
Meccanica forestale. — Nuova macchina per spremer l' olio. 1865. III. 224.²
Mechanical tests of Anan wood. 1900. IV. 536.¹
Mechanisch-technisches Laboratorium der K. technischen Hochschule. Mittheilungen. IV. 10.
Méchin. Taille de l'Acacia julibrissin. 1872. III. 466.²
Mechow, L. Die Cultur und Bewirthschaftung der Kiefern-Forsten. 1874. IV. 472.
Mecklenburg — Verein der Freunde der Naturgeschichte. See VEREIN . . . I. 15.
Meddelelser om Grønland. I. 9.¹
Le médecin herboriste. 1802. III. 55.
Mededeeling omtrent de wijze van inzameling . . . van getah pertja. 1866. III. 231.
Mededeelingen omtrent de Kinakultuur op Java. 1884. III. 716.
Mededeelingen over de Koffiecultuur in Brazilie. 1883. III. 728.²
Mededeelingen over Java. 1853. III. 319.¹
Médelsheim, Alphonse CERFBERR. See CERFBERR DE MÉDELSHEIM, Alphonse.
Medén, John Frederic. Horti upsaliensis plantae. See THUNBERG, C. P. 1826. I. 40.
Medical and physical journal. I. 19.
Medical and physical society, [Calcutta]. Quarterly journal. Transactions. I. 29.¹
Medical and physical society of Bombay. Transactions. I. 29.¹
Medical botany; or, History of plants in the Materia medica of the London . . . pharmacopoeias. 1821. III. 56.
Medical facts and observations. See LONDON medical journal. I. 18. .
Medical history of the cortex ruber, or red bark. 1786. III. 720.
Medical observations and inquiries. I. 19.
Medical record. I. 6.
Medical repository. I. 6, III. 5.
Medical society of the state of West Virginia. Transactions. I. 6.
Medical times. See PHILADELPHIA medical times. I. 6.
Medical times and register. See PHILADELPHIA medical times. I. 6.
Medici, Juan Sobre resistencia de materiales de construcción usados en el pais. 1884. IV. 410.
Medici Spada, comte de. Coloration de l'Hortensia. 1856. III. 412.¹
Medicinal plants. 1900. III. 63.¹
Medicinal plants . . . in North Carolina. See HYAMS, C. W. 1898. III. 63.¹
Medicinal properties of the Bay-tree. 1873. III. 406.²
Medicinisch-chirurgische Pharmacopöe. See The NEW medico-chirurgical pharmacopoeia. 1822. III. 758.¹
Medico-botanical society of London. Transactions. I. 19.
Medicus, Friedrich Casimir. Ueber den Akazien-Baum. 1802. IV. 522.²
— Von dem Baue der süsen Pomeranzenstaude. 1776. III. 499.²
— Beiträge zur Kultur exotischer Gewächse. 1806. III. 121.¹
— Beiträge zu schönen Gartenkunst. 1782. III. 121.¹
— Beschreibung der Lagerströmia indica. 1780. II. 609.²
— Beyträge zur Pflanzen-Anatomie. 1799. I. 82.¹
— Botanische Beobachtungen. 1780. I. 262.
— Botanische Beobachtungen des Jahres 1782. 1783. I. 32.
— Ueber einige künstliche Geschlechter aus der Malven-Familie. 1787. II. 518.¹
— Erfahrungen vom Ginko. 1800. III. 286.²
— Ermunterungspreise, den Anbau des unächten Akazien-Baumes betreffend. 1796. IV. 522.¹
— Fassliche Anweisung zum Anbaue . . . der unächten Acacie. 1799. IV. 522.²
— Geschichte der Botanik unserer Zeiten. 1793. I. 251.
— Ueber den gynandrischen Situs. 1790. I. 114.¹
— Index plantarum Horti electoralis manhemiensis. 1771. I. 44.

Medicus, Friedrich Casimir (*continued*).
— Von den mannigfaltigen Umhüllungen der Saamen. 1789. I. 118.²
— Das Mark eines Baumes oder Staude steht unter sich in gar keiner Verbindung. 1790. I. 128.²
— Ueber den merkwürdigen Bau der Zeugungsglieder einiger Geschlechter der Contorten. 1782. I. 117.⁵
— Von der Neigung der Pflanzen sich zu begatten. 1775. I. 236.²
— Ueber nordamerikanische Baume und Sträucher. 1792. III. 120,² IV. 125.¹
— Observationes botanicae. 1775. I. 262.
— Pflanzen-physiologische Abhandlungen. 1803. I. 146.
— Philosophische Botanik. 1789. I. 32.
— Theodora speciosa. 1786. II. 383.²
— Unächter Acacien-Baum; zur Ermunterung des allgemeinen Anbaues. 1796. IV. 522.¹
— Ueber das Vermögen der Pflanzen sich noch durch andere Wege . . . fortzupflanzen. 1790. I. 205
— *See also* LUCAS, Eduard & MEDICUS, Friedrich.
Medicus, G. F. De caffe et chocolatae . . . usu et abusu. *See* MEISNER, L. F. 1720. III. 222.
Medicus, Ludwig Wallrad. Berechnung der Fläche und des Ertrags . . . der Akazienanlage. 1802. IV. 524.¹
— Bericht über die . . . Schläge in der kurfürstlichen Akazienanlage. 1802. IV. 522.²
— Forsthandbuch. 1802. IV. 96.
— Über den Gesichtspunkt, aus welchem der akademische Unterricht in der Landwirthschafts-, Forst- und Bergwerkswissenschaft zu betrachten ist. 1804. IV. 28.²
— Kann der Unterricht einer Special-Forst- und Landwirthschaftsschule durch den Universitätsunterricht . . . surrogiret werden? 1808. IV. 28.²
— *See also* BERGRATH & MEDIKUS, L. W.
Medicus, Wilhelm. Flora von Deutschland. 1893. I. 389.
Medikus. *See* MEDICUS.
Medio de conocer la época del apeo de los árboles. 1884. IV. 384.¹
Mednyánszky, Dionys, *Baron*. Die Dewadaru-Ceder für inländische Forstbestände. 1854. III. 300.¹
Medulla medicinæ universæ. *See* THEOBALD, John. 1749. III. 252.
Medveczky, István. Adatok a Tiszafa termőhelyeihez hazánkban. 1896. II. 11.³
— A Fekete Fenyő maghullatása. 1896. II. 44.¹
Medvyedef, J. S. *See* Медвѣдевъ, Я. С.
Medwedjew. *See* Медвѣдевъ, Я. С.
Meech, William W. Quince culture. 1888. III. 423.¹
Meehan, Joseph. The Climbing Hydrangea. 1896. III. 412.²
— Filling in about trees. 1889. III. 169.²
— Gordonia Altamaha. 1890. III. 596.²
— The hardiness of certain evergreens. 1892. III. 44.¹
— A lesson in transplanting evergreens. 1889. III. 295.¹
— The pruning of shrubs. 1894. III. 173.
— Ripened wood makes hardy trees. 1890. III. 44.¹
Meehan, Thomas. Abies Parsonsiana. 1881. III. 296.¹ .
— Abies pungens. 1886. III. 306.¹
— Absence of bud-scales in Fraxinus quadrangulata. 1871. II. 708.²
— Adaptation in nature. 1883. III. 516.¹
— Aerial roots in Vitis vulpina. 1892. II. 506.²
— On the agency of insects in obstructing evolution. 1872. I. 243.¹
— Alaskan forests. 1891. I. 311.¹
— American Buttonwood. 1886. II. 255.¹
— The American handbook of ornamental trees. 1853. III. 60.
— Amorpha canescens Nutt. 1888. II. 332.¹
— Andromeda arborea. 1878. III. 653.²
— Ueber Andromeda Mariana Lin. 1879. III. 654.¹
— Antigonon insigne. 1881. III. 387.¹
— Aralia elegantissima. 1881. III. 642.¹
— Are insects any material aid to plants in fertilization? 1876. I. 237.
— On the assumption of floral characters . . . in Andromeda Catesbaei. 1889. II. 673.¹
— Autumn color of the Bartram Oak. 1882. II. 134.¹
— On the axial origin of the Pine-needles. 1872. II. 39.²
— Bastard von Apfel und Birne. 1871. II. 267.¹
— Bees and colored flowers. 1884. II. 704.⁵
— On bees and Honey-suckles. 1895. II. 836.¹
— The bluebird and Holly berries. 1877. II. 463.²
— Boring of corollas. 1879. I. 238.

— Botanical notes. 1885. II. 255,¹ 346.² — 1887. II. 314.¹
— On the bract in Tilia. 1888. II. 516.¹
— The brittle branches of Salix sericea. 1882. II. 110.¹
— Bud varieties. 1870. I. 244.²
— Calluna vulgaris in New Jersey. 1878. II. 661.¹
— Calodendron capense. 1884. III. 496.¹
— Catalogue of plants collected . . . in southeastern Alaska. 1885. I. 311.²
— The Cembran Pine. 1887. III. 307.¹
— Cercidiphyllum japonicum. 1886. III. 388.²
— Change by gradual modification not the universal law. 1875. I. 244.²
— On the characters of species in Cacti. 1886. II. 586.²
— Clethra alnifolia. 1887. III. 646.¹
— Clethra alnifolia in relation to its morphology. 1900. II. 657.¹
— Color in autumn leaves. 1882. I. 185.²
— Conservatory of Mr. Henry C. Gibson. 1877. III. 286.¹
— On the consumption of force by plants. 1866. I. 149.¹ʰ
— Continuous growth in fungoidal excrescences. 1874. III. 363.¹
— Contraction of vegetable tissues under frost. 1884. I. 212.
— A contribution to the doctrine of evolution. 1883. I. 243.¹
— Contributions to the life-histories of plants. 1888. I. 218.
— The coronal disk in Spiraea. 1887. II. 314.¹
— Cortical peculiarities in the Plum. 1888. II. 271.²
— Crossandra infundibuliformis. 1884. III. 709.¹
— Croton elegantissimus. 1883. III. 516.¹
— Croton illustris. 1884. III. 516.¹
— Curving towards the north in flower buds. 1871. I. 194.
— Cypress knees. 1888. II. 51.² — 1900. II. 52.¹
— On derivation in Pinus edulis and . . . monophylla. 1885. II. 42,¹ 42.²
— Dichogamy and its significance. 1889. I. 238.
— Differences in the flowers of Bouvardia. 1871. II. 238,² 810.¹
— Dimorphism in a Willow. 1882. II. 103.²
— Dimorphism in Ailantus glandulosa. 1877. II. 413.²
— Dimorphism in Apples. 1874. II. 86.²
— Dimorphism in the leaves of Acer pennsylvanicum. 1874. II. 479.¹
— Dimorphous flowers in Passiflora. 1874. II. 580.¹
— Dioecism in Andromeda Catesbaei. 1881. II. 673.¹
— Direct growth force in roots. 1876. II. 112.¹
— On the direction of the spiral twist in the leaves of the Norway Spruce. 1891. II. 36.¹
— On the disadvantages of deep planting trees. 1849. III. 1⁰9.²
— On disarticulating branches in Ampelopsis. 1881. II. 501.²
— Diurnal opening of the flowers of Magnolia glauca. 1888. II. 212.¹
— Double flowers in Epigaea repens. 1873. II. 663.²
— Double flowers in Gelsemium nitidum. 1885. II. 112,² 597,¹ 718.²
— On the duration of Rubus discolor. 1845. II. 305.²
— Eccentricity of the annual wood circles in Rhus Toxicodendron. 1900. II. 460.¹
— On the effects of girdling. 1872. IV. 385.¹
— Elevation in the fruit of Cactaceae. 1886. II. 588.²
— Elevation of the trunks of trees. 1874. I. 187.
— On the epigynous gland in Diervilla. 1889. III. 834.¹
— Evolution by growth-energy. 1900. I. 243.²
— Euadenia eminens. 1884. III. 409.¹
— Evolution in Walnuts and Hickories. 1900. II. 112.¹
— Evolutionary law as illustrated by abnormal growth in an Apple tree. 1876. II. 267.¹
— Exceptional conditions in the vegetation of forest seed. 1873. IV. 139.²
— On excrescences. 1876. I. 213.²
— Expansive force of root growth. 1879. II. 276.²
— Exudation from flowers. 1884. I. 169.¹
— The fall of the leaf in the Holly. 1895. II. 464.²
— On fasciations. 1870. I. 144.²
— Favorable influence of climate on vegetation in Alaska. 1884. I. 311.¹
— Fertilisation of Yucca filamentosa. 1880. II. 87.²
— On the fertilisation of Yucca. 1878. II. 87.¹ — 1879. II. 87.¹
— A fine Pig-nut Hickory. 1886. II. 112.²
— Flowers of a Fig. 1882. III. 371.¹

— On the flowers of Aralia spinosa. 1870. II. 647,² 649.²
— The flowers of Platanus. 1885. II. 255.¹
— Folial origin of cauline structures. 1898. I. 111.
— The forestry question. 1877. IV. 271.²
— Forests and forestry. 1881. IV. 271.²
— Forests, the results and not the cause of climate. 1874. IV. 53.
— Formation of crow's nest branches in the Cherry tree. 1887. III. 435.²
— On the forms of Lonicera japonica. 1889. II. 838.²
— Fruit of Akebia quinata. 1876. III. 393.²
— On the fruit of Opuntia. 1886. II. 596.²
— Fruiting of double Peaches. 1875. II. 276.²
— Fruiting of Ginko. 1883. II. 7.²
— Fruiting of Robinia hispida. 1895. II. 382.¹
— On the fruiting of Wistaria sinensis. 1888. II. 388.²
— Gelsemium nitidum. 1880. III. 682.¹
— Germination in acorns. 1881. II. 132.¹
— On the gland-bearing leaves in the Peach. 1869. II. 271.²
— On the glands of Cassia and Acacia. 1870. II. 320.²
— Graft hybrids. 1876. I. 246.¹ — 1877. I. 246.³
— Grafting on small roots. 1887. III. 164.¹
— The Great Council tree of the Senecas. 1886. II. 143.²
— On hermaphroditism in Rhus. 1874. II. 458.²
— Historical notes on the Arbor vitae. 1883. II. 52.³
— History of the Weeping Willow. 1881. II. 105.²
— Hybrid Juglans. 1875. II. 113.¹
— Hybrid Oaks. 1882. II. 132,¹ 140.¹
— Hybrids in nature. 1898. I. 246.¹
— Hybrids of Pyrus sinensis. 1875. II. 281.¹
— Improvements in propagating. 1880. III. 159.¹
— Infertile trees and shrubs. 1894. I. 200.
— Influence of the scion on the stock. 1879. III. 39.
— On the interdependence of plants. 1887. I. 218.
— Interpretation of varying forms. 1876. I. 110.
— Investigations in the bark of trees. 1897. I. 131.¹
— The Ixora. 1877. III. 745.¹
— Ixora splendida. 1882. III. 745.³
— Juvenile forms of Coniferae. 1881. II. 18.
— Knaurs and burrs. 1888. I. 213.³
— The Lacquer tree. 1877. III. 528.²
— The law governing sex. 1879. I. 238.
— The law of fasciation. 1871. I. 144.²
— Law of seed germination in swamp plants. 1873. II. 51.²
— On the laws governing the production of seed in Wistaria. 1880. II. 388.¹
— Laws of sex in Juglans nigra. 1873. II. 113.¹
— Leaf plants for room decoration. 1878. III. 285.¹
— On the leaves of Coniferae. 1868. II. 17.¹
— A list of Rubi observed near London. 1848. II. 303.¹
— Longevity of trees. 1883. I. 193.²
— Lonicera coerulea. 1893. II. 837.¹
— On the male . . . flowers of Aesculus. 1891. II. 483.¹
— Medinilla Curtisii. 1885. III. 638.²
— Mr. M. S. Jones' Colorado notes. 1880. II. 270.¹
— The monocotyledon, the universal type of seeds. 1872. I. 120.
— Morphology of carpellary scales in Larix. 1871. II. 32.²
— On the morphology of superimposed stamens. 1887. II. 536.²
— Morphology of the Grape. 1900. II. 506.¹
— Morphology of the Pear. 1876. II. 280.¹
— Morphology of the Pine cones. 1896. II. 20.¹
— Morphology of twin and triune peaches. 1900. II. 276.³
— Motility in plants. 1882. I. 195.²
— Mount Desert. 1892. IV. 46.¹
— On movement in the stigmatic lobes of Catalpa. 1874. II. 786.¹
— Movements in stigmatic lobes. 1873. II. 785.³
— On movements . . . in the leaves of Robinia. 1882. II. 383.¹
— Multiplication of cotyledons . . . in Oak. 1871. II. 131.²
— The native flowers and ferns of the United States. 1878. I. 307.
— Natural hybrids; Quercus heterophylla. 1875. II. 134.¹
— On natural inarching. 1876. I. 209.¹
— The nature of a fasciated branch. 1885. I. 144.²
— On the nature of root fibres. 1876· I. 105.
— A new shade tree. 1854. III. 417.³
— A new weeping tree. 1887. III. 380.³
— Note on a fungoid root parasite. 1873. IV. 456.
— Note on Calycanthus floridus. 1879. II. 242.²

— Note on Chionanthus. 1888. II. 706.¹
— Note on dioicoeus forms of Vitis vinifera. 1866. II. 507.¹
— Note on Opuntia prolifera Eng. 1880. II. 597.¹
— Note on Pinus pungens and its allies. 1890. II. 45.²
— Note on Quercus dentata. 1887. II. 133.³
— Note on Quercus prinoides Willd. 1886. II. 136.¹
— Note on the seed-vessels of Wistaria. 1881. II. 388.¹
— Note on treeless prairies. 1881. I. 308.
— Note on unisexuality. 1891. II. 104.¹
— Notes on Acer rubrum. 1879. II. 480.¹
— Notes on Echinocactus. 1884. II. 591.¹
— Notes on Mistletoes. 1882. II. 174.¹
— Notes on the Sequoia gigantea. 1884. II. 50.³
— Notes on the Virginia Creeper. 1883. II. 504.³
— Number of leaves in Pines. 1871. II. 39.²
— On objections to Darwin's theory of fertilization. 1871. I. 237.
— Observation . . . sur la variabilité du Chêne rouvre. 1882. II. 140.¹
— Observations on Forsythia. 1884. II. 706.³
— Opposite leaves in Salix nigra. 1885. II. 108.²
— Origin and nature of glands in plants. 1898. I. 113.¹
— The origin of coreless apples. 1895. II. 267.¹
— On the origin of the apical cell. 1895. I. 108.²
— On packing trees and plants. 1857. III. 155.
— Panax Victoriae. 1885. III. 644.¹
— On parallel habits in allied species. 1890. II. 467.²
— On parallelism in distinct lines of evolution. 1887. I. 243.¹
— Parthenogenesis. 1900. I. 202.¹
— Pellucid dots in some species of Hypericum. 1898. II. 556.¹
— On the period and ratio of the annual increase in the circumference of trees. 1866. IV. 64.²
— On phyllotaxis. 1870. I. 102.
— Pinus pungens, the Table Mountain Pine. 1879. II. 45.¹
— The plants of Lewis and Clark's expedition. 1899. I. 327.
— Poisonous character of the flowers of Wistaria. 1874. III. 490.²
— Polarity in the leaves of the Compass and other plants. 1898. I. 232.²
— Populus tremuloides, a monoecious case. 1894. II. 98.³
— Pritchardia grandis. 1882. III. 326.²
— On the production of bractea in Larix. 1869. II. 32.³
— The projecting force of the seeds of Hamamelis. 1871. II. 253.¹
— On projection of pollen in the flowers of Indigofera. 1887. II. 365.³
— On purple-leaved plants. 1895. I. 186.
— Rain trees; note on Yucca gloriosa. 1881. II. 88.¹
— Rarer Evergreens. 1867. III. 289.
— The Red-berried Elder. 1889. III. 752.²
— The relation between rhythmic growth and variety in Citrus fruits. 1894. II. 401.³
— On the relation of heat to the sexes of flowers. 1883. I. 200, 232.² — 1883. II. 122.²
— Rhythmic growth in plants. 1898. I. 191.¹
— Rosa rugosa in connection with the evolution of form. 1900. II. 298.²
— Rosemary. 1885. II. 765.²
— Rubus Chamaemorus. 1893. II. 306.²
— Rudimentary Apple flowers. 1873. II. 267.ʳ
— On second inflorescence. 1890. I. 113.³
— Secretion of nectar in Libonia. 1887. II. 800.¹
— On the seed vessels of Forsythia. 1868. II. 706.³
— On self-fertilization and cross-fertilization. 1876. I. 237.
— Self-fertilizing flowers. 1891. I. 238.
— On sex in Castanea americana. 1880. II. 123.³
— Sex in flowers. Corylus rostrata. 1900. II. 122.²
— Sex in Rhus Cotinus. 1873. II. 455.²
— On the sexes of the Holly. 1893. II. 463.¹
— On the sexes of the plants. 1870. I. 199.
— Sexual characters in Cephalotaxus. 1883. II. 8.¹
— On the sexual characters of Rhus. 1893. II. 458.²
— Sexual law in Acer dasycarpum Ehrb. 1868. II. 480.¹
— Sexual law in the Coniferae. 1869. II. 20.³
— Sexual state of Acer rubrum. 1871. II. 480.¹
— Shrubby and tree-like forms of trees. 1872. I. 106.²
— Shrubs with ornamental berries. 1857. III. 203.¹
— Slow or fast growing Oaks. 1886. III. 362.²
— Some facts in regard to the fertilization of flowers. 1873. I. 201.²

Meehan, Thomas (*continued*).
— On some morphological distinctions in . . . Ericaceae. 1893. II. 658.[2]
— Some neglected studies. 1898. I. 112.[1]
— Some new facts in the life history of Yucca. 1889. II. 87.[1]
— Some new facts regarding the fertilization of Yucca. 1882. II. 87.[1]
— Spines in the Citrus family. 1898. II. 401.[2]
— On the stipules of Magnolia. 1870. II. 209.[1]
— On the stipules of Magnolia Frazeri. 1887. II. 211.[2]
— Structure of a trunk of Yucca. 1870. II. 87.[1]
— On the structure of the flowers in Dipteracanthus. 1892. II. 803.[1]
— A study of the Hydrangea in relation to cross-fertilization. 1889. II. 240.[2]
— Sugar in Cladrastis tinctoria. 1885. II. 346.[2]
— Supposed hybrid between Pear and Apple. 1871. II. 278.[1]
— On the timber line of high mountains. 1880. I. 220.[1]
— On the timber line of high mountains. 1881. I. 308.
— On two classes of male flowers in Castanea. 1871. II. 123.[2]
— Ulmus fulva pendula. 1889. III. 365.[1]
— Umbrella Pine. 1887. III. 309.[2]
— On the uniformity of relative characters between . . . European and American trees. 1862. I. 99.
— United twins of Maclura. 1870. II. 154.[1]
— Use of spines in Cactuses. 1885. II. 588.[2]
— Variation in Halesia. 1885. II. 704.[2]
— Variation in Quercus Douglasii. 1872. II. 133.[2]
— Variation in Quercus macrocarpa. 1876. II. 135.[1]
— Variations in Epigaea repens. 1868. II. 663.[2]
— Variations in nature. 1883. I. 244.[2]
— Variations in Taxodium and Pinus. 1868. II. 17.[2]
— Variations in the stipular spines of Robinia Pseud-Acacia. 1875. II. 382.[1]
— Variations in Thuja and Retinospora. 1880. II. 18.
— On the varying character of dichogamy in flowers of Corylus. 1891. II. 122.[1]
— Varying influence of heat. 1882. I. 232.[1]
— Varying phyllotaxis in the Elm. 1898. II. 143.[1]
— The veins of Beech and Hornbeam leaves. 1874. II.: 120,[1] 125.[2]
— Ueber die Veränderlichkeit der Wintereiche. 1882. II. 140.[1]
— Viburnum for lawn planting. 1893. III. 753.[1]
— Viburnum plicatum. 1879. III. 753.[2]
— Virginia Creeper. 1891. II. 504.[1]
— Vitality of serotinous cones. 1880. II. 40.[2]
— Ueber Vitis cordata. 1879. III. 584.[1]
— Vitis heterophylla. 1877. III. 544.[1]
— Watering transplanted trees. 1855. III. 166.
— The Weeping Dogwood. 1881. III. 645.[2]
— West American forest trees. 1884. I. 320, IV. 78.[1]
— The White Fringe tree. 1885. III. 671.[2]
— On a w.-seeded variety of the Honey Locust. 1886. II. 361.[2] hite
— Winter blooming greenhouse plants. 1884. III. 665.[1]
— The wood of Thuja gigantea. 1885. IV. 484.[2]
— The wood of Thuja gigantea and of Cupressus nutkaensis. 1885. IV. 448,[1] 484.[2]
— & Son. The Chinese Quince. 1889. III. 420.[2]
Meehan, William E. A contribution to the flora of Greenland. 1894. I. 309.[1]
Meehans' monthly. III. 5.
Meeker, N. C. Pinus edulis. 1879. III. 307.[1]
Meen, Margaret. Exotic plants from the Royal gardens at Kew. 1790. I. 53.
Meerbeeck, Philippe Jacques van. Recherches . . . sur la vie et les ouvrages de Rembert Dodoens. 1841. I. 523.
Meerburg, Nicolaus. Afbeeldingen van zeldzaame gewassen. 1775. I. 262.
— Over de beplanting der zeeduinen. 1780. IV. 159.
— Naamlyst der boom en heestergewassen. 1782. III. 75.[2]
— Plantae rariores vivis coloribus depićtae. 1789. I. 263.
— Plantarum selectarum icones. 1798. I. 264.
Meersch Bosch, M. van der. Over den Waterwilg. 1812. III. 351.[2]
Meerten, A. van. Tannah pelandjan. 1896. III. 276.[1]
Mees, W. Over de physiologische werking van Eucalyptus-olie. 1873. IV. 531.[1]
Meese, David. Eerste beginselen der planten. 1763. I. 83, 122.
— Flora frisica. 1760. I. 390.
— Plantarum rudimenta. 1763. I. 83, 122.
— Verhandeling over het nut der kruidkunde. 1768. III. 122.[1]

Meeteren, WESTEROÜEN VAN. *See* WESTEROÜEN VAN MEETEREN.
Meetkerke, C. E. The guests of flowers. 1881. V. x.[2]
Megenberg, KONRAD VON. *See* KONRAD VON MEGENBERG.
Megerle von Mühlfeld, Johann Georg. Oestreichs Färbepflanzen. 1813. III. 236.
Megiserus, Hieronymus. Wahrhafftige . . . Beschreibung der . . . Insel Madagascar. 1609. III. 281.[2]
Meguscher, F. S. Il governo de' boschi. 185 . ? IV. 287.
Meguscher, Francesco. Memoria . . . additare la migliore . . . maniera per rimettere i boschi. 1846. IV. 165.
Meguscher, Franz. Ueber die Sandkulturen in der unteren Donaugegend. 1859. IV. 145.
Mehrhundertjährige Eibenbäume. 1896. IV. 440.[2]
Méhu, Adolphe. Les herborisations . . . dans la Campine limbourgeoise. 1873. I. 393.[1]
— Rapport sur les herborisations faites . . . dans la Campine limbourgeoise. 1873. I. 393.[1]
— **Saint-Lager, Jean & Cusin, L.** Herborisations dans les montagnes d'Hauteville. 1876. I. 415.
Méhu, C. Notes sur l'ivoire végétal. 1887. III. 330.[1]
Meidell. Hvilke arbeider til beforring af skovens vekst kan ansees lönnende? 1881. IV. 113.[2]
Meidinger, Freyherr von. Gedanken über das Leuchten . . . des faulen Holzes. 1777. I. 206.[2]
Meier. Comment faut-il opérer les coupes de nettoiement. 1869. IV. 130.
— Wie sind die Weichholzaushiebe . . . auszuführen. 1869. IV. 130.
Meier, A. Ansichten und Erfahrungen über Pflanzenerziehung. 1867. IV. 150.
— Beschädigung an Kiefern durch Hasen. 1855. IV. 475.
— Bestätigung der Wirksamkeit der Beschattung gegen die Schütte. 1866. IV. 476.
— Die Heiden Norddeutschlands. 1874. IV. 158.
— Der nachhaltig höchste Reinertrag der Forsten. 1869. IV. 253.
— Zur Naturgeschichte der Kiefer. 1861. IV. 476.
— Ungewöhnliches Vorkommen von Bostrichus. 1866. IV. 469.[2]
— Warum hält man für die besondere Wirthschafts-Kontrole an einer anderen Material-Berechnung . . . fest? 1868. IV. 243.
Meier, Johann. Beitrag zur Kenntniss der Wirkung des Aspidospermin. 1891. III. 687.[1]
Meier-Girsan. *See* Meitern-Girsan.
Meigen, Friedrich. Biologische Beobachtungen aus der Flora Santiagos in Chile. 1894. I. 347.
— Schutz der Fichte gegen Thiere. 1896. II. 37.[1]
— Skizze der Vegetationsverhältnisse von Santiago in Chile. 1893. I. 346.
Meigen, Johann Wilhelm. Deutschlands Flora. 1836. I. 379.
— Versuch einer Flora der Ufer des Niederrheins. 1823. I. 377.
— & Weniger, H. L. Systematisches Verzeichniss der an den Ufern des Rheins . . . wildwachsenden . . . Pflanzen. 1819. I. 376.
Meigen, Wilhelm. Die deutschen Pflanzennamen. 1898. I. 73.[2]
Meijer, J. Het aanleggen van Dennenbosschen. 1876. IV. 441.
— Is het al of niet voordeelig den grond voor dennenbosch te bewerken? 1889. IV. 473.
Meillet, Alphonse. Lilacine. 1842. II. 716.[1]
Meilleur procédé pour réussir le semis de Saule marsault. 1900. IV. 488.[1]
Mein, A. G. Notes on the occurrence of the Teak borer beetle. 1879. IV. 537.[1]
Meinecke, Johann Ludwig Georg. Der Botaniker ohne Lehrer. 1809. I. 93.
— Ueber den Pflanzenschlaf. 1809. I. 198.
— Ueber das Zahlenverhältniss in den Fruktifikations-Organen. 1809. I. 117.[2]
Meinicke, Carl Eduard. Das Festland Australien. 1837. I. 500.
Meins. Die Flora der Umgegend von Glückstadt. 1862. I. 385.
Meinshausen, Karl Friedrich. Beitrag zur Kakteenkunde. 1858. II. 586.[1]
— Beitrag zur Pflanzengeographie des Süd-Ural-Gebirges. 1860. I. 362.
— Beschreibung einiger neuen Kaktusarten. 1859. II. 594.[2]

— Flora ingrica. 1878. I. 363.
— Mittheilungen über die Flora Ingriens. 1868. I. 362.
— Nachrichten über das Wilni-Gebiet. 1871. I. 456.
— Synopsis plantarum diaphoricarum florae ingricae. 1869. III. 68.[1]
— Zwei neue Mamillarien. 1858. II. 594.[2]
— See also EWALD, W. & MEINSHAUSEN, K. F.
Meintjes, S. J. Remarks on the Vine disease. 1860. III. 577.
Meis, A. Getah pertjah in Palembang. 1851. III. 230.
Meischke, Paul. Über die Arbeitsleistung der Pflanzen bei der geotropischen Krümmung. 1899. I. 196.[1]
Meisel. Forststatistische Uebersicht der Gemeindswälder des Forstinspektions-Bezirkes Zurzach. 1857. IV. 365.
Meisel, X. Der Dynamit als Spreng-Mittel im Walde. 1875. IV. 386.
— La dynamite employée en forêts. 1875. IV. 386.
Meisner, C. H. Handbuch zur Holzersparung. 1801. IV. 280.[2]
Meisner, E. J. Mühlenbeckia varians. 1852. II. 186.[1]
Meisner, Johannes Friedrich. De nectariis florum. See BOEMER, G. R. 1758. I. 118.[1]
Meisner, Karl Friedrich. Bemerkungen zu den Pflanzen des . . . Dr. Behr. 1848. II. 605.[1]
— Contributions toward a flora of South Africa. 1842. I. 494.
— Convolvulaceae. 1869. II. 743.[2]
— Ericaceae. 1863. II. 658.[1]
— Ueber die geographischen Verhältnisse der Lorbeergewächse. 1866. II. 223.[1]
— Hernandiaceae. 1864. II. 228.[1]
— Lauraceae. 1864. II. 223.[1] — 1870. II. 223.[1]
— Lauraceae et Hernandiaceae. 1866. II. 223,[1] 223.[2]
— Leguminosae. 1844. II. 320.[1]
— Leguminosae quaedam australasicae novae. 1855. II. 320.[1]
— A list of the Proteaceae collected in . . . Australia. 1852. II. 158.[2]
— Monographiae generis Polygoni prodromuk. 1826. II. 186.[1]
— New Proteaceae of Australia. 1855. II. 158.[2]
— Note sur les Lauracées. 1864. II. 223.[1]
— Notice sur les Polygonées . . . récoltées . . . dans la haute Asie. 1866. I. 456.
— Ueber die ostindischen Thymeläen. 1841. II. 600.[1]
— Plantae Kegelianae surinamenses. 1848. I. 339.[1]
— Plantae Muellerianae. Thymeleae. 1853. I. 501.
— Plantarum vascularium genera. 1836. I. 260.
— Polygonaceae. 1855. II. 184.[1] — 1857. II. 183.[2]
— Polygonaceae. 1844. II. 185.[1]
— Proteaceae. 1844. II. 158.[2] — 1855. II. 158.[2] — 1857. II. 158.[1]
— On some new species of Chamaelaucieae. 1877. II. 619.[1]
— Synopsis Thymelaearum. 1840. I. 494, II. 600.[1]
— Thymelaeaceae. 1855. II. 600.[1] — 1857. II. 600.[1]
— Ueber die Verwandtschaft der Gattungen Hernandia. 1859. II. 366,[1] 872.[2]
Meisner, Leonhard Ferdinand. De caffe, chocolatae . . . usu et abusu. 1720. III. 222.
— De caffe et chocolatae . . . usu et abusu. 1720. III. 222.
— De camphora. 1737. III. 233.[1]
Meissas, Napoléon. Petite botanique. 1842. I. 88.
— Résumés d'histoire naturelle. 1830. I. 87.
Meisser. Miscellanea botanica. 1838. III. 52.
Meissner. See BUSH & SON & MEISSNER.
Meissner, Carl Leopold. De praecipuis corticis peruviani substitutis. 1810. III. 537.[2]
Meissner, F. C. Anweisung zum rechten Anbau der vorzüglichsten Laub- und Nadelhölzer. 1800. IV. 105.
Meissner, G. Die Werkzeug- und Holzbearbeitungs-Maschinen. 1876. IV. 176.[2]
Meissner, G. E. Can stock be dug and shipped too early? 1890. III. 155.
Meissner, Karl Friedrich. See MEISNER, K. F.
Meissner, Richard. Ueber das mehrjährige Wachsen der Kiefernadeln. 1894. II. 40.[2]
Meister. Eine einfache Imprägnirungs-Anstalt. 1884. IV. 420.
Meister, Georg. Der orientalisch-indianische Kunst- und Lust-Gärtner. 1692. I. 63.
Meister, J. Jusqu'à quel point doit-on préférer la production soignée de plants repiqués. 1864. IV. 152.
— In wie fern ist eine sorgfältige Erziehung von Waldpflänzlingen . . . dem unmittbaren Versetzen von Sämlingen . . . vorzuziehen? 1864. IV. 152.

Meister, Jacob. Flora von Schaffhausen. 1887. I. 437.
Meister, Joh. Ulr. Kurze populäre Anleitung zur Einsammlung . . . des Holzsamens. 1845. IV. 147.[2]
Meister, Ulrich. Betrachtungen über die zürcherische Privatforstwirthschaft. 1875. IV. 309.[2]
— Les plants recépés. 1871. III. 166.
— Qu'y a-t-il à faire pour améliorer l'aménagement des forêts privées fortement morcelées? 1875. IV. 309.[2]
— Die Stadtwaldungen von Zürich. 1883. IV. 367.
— Die Stummelpflanzen. 1871. III. 166.
— Swiss forestry, past and present. 1883. IV. 367.
— Was kann für Hebung der Bewirthschaftung stark parzellirter Privatwaldungen gethan werden? 1875. IV. 309.[2]
— See also BERTHOLET, Charles & MEISTER, U.
— & Bertholet, Charles. Les suites de la sécheresse du commencement de l'été. 1870. IV. 192.[1]
— & others. Die Baumaterialien der Schweiz. See TETMAJER, Lud. 1884. IV. 408.
Meitzen, August. Gutachten über die Bearbeitung der Forststatistik. 1874. IV. 336.[1]
— Die internationale Land- und Forstwirthschaftliche Statistik. 1873. IV. 336.[1]
Meixner, H. Der Wald und seine Bedeutung. 1889. IV. 45.
Mejdell, Th. Om beskaffenheden af de skove. 1859. IV. 343.[2]
— Om foranstaltninger til en mere husholdersk behandling af Norges skove. 1858. IV. 288.[2]
Mejer, Ludwig. Flora von Hannover. 1875. I. 387.
— Die hannoversche Kalkflora. 1879. I. 388.
— Schulbotanik für Hannover. 1886. I. 532.[2]
— Vaccinium uliginosum × Vitis Idaea. 1888. II. 687.[1]
— Die Veränderungen in . . . der hannoverschen Flora. 1867. I. 386.
Mela, Aukusti Juhana. Kasvioppi Suomen koululle. 1892. I. 92.
— Lyhykäinen kasvioppi ja kasvio. 1877. I. 363.
— Pinus Abies viminalis från Birkala, Finland. 1886. II. 35.[1]
— Suomen koulukasvio. 1895. I. 366.
— & Palmen, J. A. Luonnonopillinen kuvasto koulun ja kodon tarpeeksi. 1880. I. 96.
Melandri, Girolamo & Moretti, Giuseppe. Analisi chimica delle radici di Cariofilata. 1805. III. 648.[1]
Melanose in Mandarins. 1900. III. 503.[1]
Mélard, A. Consommation du bois en Angleterre. 1894. IV. 405,[1] 557.[1]
— Deficient production of timber in the world. 1900. IV. 281.[1]
— Un dernier mot sur le Pin Laricio. 1896. IV. 465.[2]
— Les forêts de Hongrie. 1899. IV. 374.[1]
— Les forêts du Canada. 1897. IV. 337.[2]
— Les forêts et le commerce des bois en France. 1891. IV. 405.[1]
— Importations in France des matières ligneuses. 1899. IV. 405.[1]
— Insuffisance de la production des bois d'œuvre. 1900. IV. 281,[1] 552.[1]
— Insuffisance de la production du Chêne en France. 1894. IV. 513.
— Insuficiencia de la producción de madera. 1900. IV. 552.[1]
— Les résineux d'Europe. 1895. IV. 545.[1]
— Le service des aménagements en France. 1898. IV. 249.[1]
— La situation agricole et forestière de l'Irlande. 1895. IV. 556.[1]
— Ueber die Unzulänglichkeit der Nutzholzerzeugung. 1900. IV. 281.[1]
— See also WESMAEL, Alfred & MÉLARD, A.
Melartin, E. G. Ueber die Gewächskunde Finnlands. 1808. I. 80.[1]
Melchar, Anton. Pflanzcultur mittelst Körbchen. 1895. IV. 153.[1]
— Statisticko-topografický popis svěřenských statků hraběte Zdeňka Kolovrata-Krakovského Rychnova n. K. a Černíkovic. 1883. IV. 371.
— Statistisch-topographische Beschreibung der . . . Fideikommiss-Domänen Reichenau und Cernikovic. 1883. IV. 371.
Meldahl, C. V. Nogle Undersøgelser over . . . Naaletræs Styrke. 1893. IV. 410, 443.[2]
Meldola, Aug. Ph. Praktisk Veiledning for Træ- og Brændehandlere. 1865. IV. 214.
— Praktisk Vejledning i Træers Taxation. 1865. IV. 214.

Melero, Marcos de J. 'Goma del Maranon. 1872. III. 524.[1]
— Investigaciones . . . acerca del Anacardo occidental. 1872. III. 524.[1]
Le Mélèze occidental. See The WESTERN Larch. 1896. IV. 558.[2]
Mélèzes et pluies. 1898. IV. 450.
Meli, Domenico. Nuove esperienze . . . di ottenere dal Pepe nero il peperino. 1823. III. 343.[2]
Meliarakes, Spyridon. See MHAIAPAKHE, Σπυρίδων.
Melichar, Alois. Ansichten über den heutigen Bewerthungsmodus. 1891. IV. 258.
— Ein Beitrag zur Lärchenkrankheit. 1883. IV. 451.
— Ein Beitrag zur Pflanzenerziehung. 1888. IV. 147.[1]
— Cizopasné rostling. Studie lesní. 1885. IV. 211.[1]
— Družstva lesní. 1884. IV. 309.[2]
— Durchforstung und Zuwachs. 1889. IV. 176,[1] 197.[1]
— Das modificirte Abstandsverfahren. 1893. IV. 258.
— Semenáčky a přesadníky. 1887. IV. 142.
— Smrk obecný. 1886. IV. 458.
— Stav nynější otázky lesní. 1884. IV. 279,[1] 309.[2]
— Užitek některých lesních stromů a kěrů. 1888. III. 272.[1]
— Význam některých rostlin o lesotvarství. 1886. IV. 55.[2]
— Význam rostlinstva a lesův. 1885. IV. 44.
Melichar, M. Sosna; Dub. 1882. IV. 481, 513.
Melicocq, baron de. See LAFONS, Alexandre de, baron de Melicocq.
Melin, H. M. Novitiae florae 'suecicae. See FRIES, E. M. 1814. I. 352.
Méline. Greffe du Châtaignier sur le Chêne. -1844. III. 359.[1]
Meijoranski, M. See MEJIOPAHCKIЙ, M.
Melius, Peter (Juhász). Herbarium az fáknak. 1578. I. 282.
Mell, Patrick Hues. The flora of Alabama. 1896. V. XVII.[2]
— Woods of Alabama. 1888. IV. 397.
Melleville. Les amours des plantes. 1835. I. 199.
Melliar, A. FOSTER-: Book of the Rose. 1894. III. 451.[1]
Mellichamp, J. H. Ilex opaca with entire leaves. 1887. II. 464.[2]
— Notes from a South Carolina naturalist. 1889. I. 319.
— Pinus Elliottii. 1872. II. 41.[2]
Mellin, A. W., Reichsgraf. Versuch einer Anweisung zur Anlegung . . . der Wildbahnen. .1779. IV. 136.[2]
Melliss, John Charles. St. Helena. 1875. I. 498.[2]
Mellmann, P. Chemisch-technisches Lehrbuch des Beizens. 1899. IV. 422.[2]
Mello, J. de. De l'action de la teinture de fève de Calabar. 1866. III. 483.[2]
Mello, Joaquim C. CORREA DE. See CORREA DE MELLO, J. C.
Mello, Luiz de. Dracaena Draco du Jardin royal du palais d'Ajuda. 1879. II. 82.[2]
Mello Moraes, Alexandre José de. Phytographia ou botanica brasileira applicada. See MORAES, Mello. 1881. III. 65.[2]
Mello-Oliveira. De l'huile d'Anda-assu. 1881. III. 520.[1]
Melloni, Macedonio. Observations sur la cause qui produit la fonte hâtive de la neige autour des plantes. 1838. I. 186.
— Observations upon the cause which produces the speedy melting of snow around plants. 1838. I. 186.
Melnikof, A. See MEJЬHИKOBЪ, A.
Melnikof, N. P. See MEJЬHИKOBЪ, H. П.
Melnikoff, Paul. Untersuchungen über das Vorkommen des kohlensauren Kalkes. 1877. I. 139.
Melsens. Sur la mannite de l'Avocatier. 1840. III. 407.[1]
— Note sur la conservation des bois. 1848. IV. 284.[1]
Melsheimer, Marcellus. Botanische Beobachtungen in . . . Linz. 1876. II. 310.[1]
— Ueber Fasciationen. 1878. I. 94.[2]
— Eine monströse Traube von Vitis vinifera. 1875. II. 507.[1]
— Ueber zwei . . . Früchte von Prunus Armeniaca. 1875. II. 273.[1]
Melter. Nachricht über einige seltene Eichen-Stammie. 1858. II. 138.[1]
Meitzow, August. Über Anpflanzungen . . . mit Frostballen. 1848. III. 167.
Melun — Société horticole et botanique . . . See SOCIÉTÉ . . . III. 22.
Melvill, James Cosmo. The flora of Harrow. 1864. I. 401.
— List of the phanerogams of Key West. 1884. I. 319.
Melville, M. S. Frankincense of Sierra Leone. 1839. III. 227, 280.[2]
Mély, F. de. Strabon et le phylloxera. 1892. III. 574.
— Traitement des Vignes phylloxérées. 1893. III. 574.

Melzer, Hermann. Bienen-Nährpflanzen. 1894. III. 224.[1]
Memminger, Eduard head. Prunus pumila in North Carolina. 1888. II. 277.[1]
Mémoire de la commune de Syam. See GURNAUD, Ad. 1867. IV. 249.[1]
Mémoire instructif sur la manière de rassembler . . . See TURGOT, E. F., marquis de Cousmont. 1758. III. 155.
Mémoire présenté par la Société d'horticulture d'Orléans . . . sur les dégâts 1881. III. 48.
Mémoire soumis . . . par les locataires de forêts . . . victimes des incendies de 1881. 1883. IV. 184.[1]
Mémoire sur l'influence des astres. 1789. V. XII.[2]
Mémoire sur l'utilisation des Bruyères des Landes. n. d. III. 648.[2]
Mémoire sur la carbonisation des bois. See DROMART, Ed. 1876. IV. 394.
Mémoire sur la culture de l'Olivier. 1783. III. 674.[2]
Mémoire sur la culture . . . des oseraies. 1830. III. 347.
Mémoire sur la culture des Pommiers. See RENAULT, P. A. 1795. III. 426.[1]
Mémoire sur la fixation et sur le reboisement des dunes littorales . . . en Russie. See OПИCAHIE . . . 1876. IV. 157.
Mémoire sur les bois communaux de Reauville. 1849. IV. 359.[2]
Mémoire sur quelques insectes qui nuisent à la Vigne. 1841. III. 562.[2]
Mémoires concernant l'histoire . . . des Chinois. See BATTEUX, Charles. 1777. I. 458.
Mémoires pour servir à l'histoire physique et naturelle de la Suisse. I. 520.[1]
Mémoires sur l'agriculture du Boulonnois. See DUMONT DE COURSET, G. L. M. 1784. III. 125.
Memoirs historical and illustrative of the Botanick garden at Chelsea. See FIELD, Henry. 1820. I. 53.
Memoirs of the Rose. 1824. III. 448.
Memoirs relative to Egypt. 1800. III. 630.[1]
A memorable tree. 1884. II. 138.[2]
Memorandum of a scheme for the analysis of the Tea plant. 1890. III. 604.[1]
Memorandum regarding various fibrous materials from Assam. 1848. III. 233.[1]
Memorandum upon the Pauchontee. See CLEGHORN, Hugh. 1858. II. 699.[2]
Memoria acerca de la repoblación de la cuenca del Lozoya. See HERAAS, Luis. 1895. IV. 165.
Memoria-catálogo de la colección de productos forestales. . . . de Filipinas. 1875. IV. 21.[1]
Memoria del Ministerio de fomento. 1883. IV. 363.[2]
Alla memoria di Giuseppe Raddi. 1830. See SAVI, Gaetano. 1830. I. 487.
Memoria i catalogo de las plantas cultivadas en el jardin botánico. See PHILIPPI, Federico. I. 39.
Memoria sobre a Canella do Rio de Janeiro. See GOMES, B. A. 1809. II. 566.[2]
Memoria sobre a cultura da Oliveira. 1827. III. 675.[1]
Memoria sobre los productos de la agricultura española. 1859. III. 271.[2]
Memoria sull' albero Acacia. 1781. IV. 522.[1]
Memoria sulla coltura degli Ulivi. 1781. III. 674.[2]
Memoria sulla coltura delle Viti in Ispagna. 1780. III. 558.[1]
Mémorial alphabétique des matières des eaux et forêts. See NOEL, Michel. 1737. IV. 22.[1]
Memorial and remonstrance to the Congress of the United States . . . against the so-called reciprocity treaty. 1874. IV. 284.[1]
Memorial . . . for the use of the Senate in relation to that part of the Wilson bill which places lumber on the free list. See HALE, Eugene. 1894. IV. 284.[1]
Mémorial forestier; ou, Recueil complet. 1801. IV. 323.[1]
Memorial of the Chamber of commerce . . . of Seattle, relative to forest reserves. 1897. IV. 179.[1]
Memorial urging establishment of national park in southern Appalachian region. 1900. IV. 179.[2]
Memorials, journal . . . of Charles Cardale Babington. 1897. I. 535.[1]
Memorials of Oxford. See DAUBNEY, C. G. B. 1836. I. 54.
Memorie sobre a utilidade dos jardins botanicos. 1770. I. 38.[1]
Memorie van bedenkingen op het Rapport . . . der duincommissie. 1805. IV. 159.
Memson, V. Sur une nouvelle classification des Vignes. See MUNSON, T. V. 1885. III. 547.
Ména, A. Accroissement de la forêt du Clerjus. 1896. IV. 238.

— Détermination du taux d'accroissement des fûts. 1898. IV. 234.
— Étude d'une jeune futaie de Hêtre et Chêne. 1894. IV. 234.
Le ménage des champs et de la ville. 1715. III. 112.
Ménager, Raphael. Herborisations aux environs de Laigle. 1893. II. 564.²
Menalda van Schouwenburg, H. J. De epenspinkever. 1870. IV. 486.²
Menand, L. Autobiography and recollections of incidents connected with horticultural affairs. 1892. III. 117.¹
Menauit, E. La greffe des Châtaigniers. 1895. III. 359.¹
Mencke, (Forstmeister, Wassenheim). Alte und Neues über Fällungszeiten. 1896. IV. 385.¹
— Du vieux et du neuf à propos de la saison où il faut abattre les arbres. 1896. IV. 385.¹
Mendel, Gregor. Versuche über Pflanzen-Hybriden. 1866. I. 245.
Mendell. Le Jacaranda lancifoliata. 1885. III. 706.²
Mendes, A. Lopes. See Lopes Mendes, A.
Mendes, J. C. S. D. Reproduction of Bamboos. 1887. IV. 485.¹
Mendis, Adrian. List of the principal timber trees in Ceylon. 1854. IV. 401.¹
Mendis, Mudaliyar. Timber trees of Ceylon. 1881. IV. 401.¹
Mendoza, Gumesindo & Herrera, Alfonso. El Anacahuite. 1876. III. 695.¹
Mène, Ch. Résultats d'expériences sur l'influence du plâtre. 1850. I. 158.
Mène, Édouard. Le Bambou en Chine et au Japon. 1881. III. 315.¹
— Des productions végétales du Japon. 1880. III. 273.²
— Des produits végétaux de la Chine. 1869. III. 273.¹
— Des usages du Bambou en Chine. 1869. III. 315.¹
— Uses of the Bamboo in China. 1869. III. 315.¹
— The vegetable productions of Japan. 1880. III. 273.²
Meneghini, Giuseppe. Ricerche sulla struttura del caule. 1836. I. 104.
— Intorno alla struttura del tronco. 1843. I. 105.
— Sulla teoria de' meritalli di Gaudichaud. 1844. I. 123.²
— & Savi, Pietro. Sulle appendici apicilari . . . dell' Acacia cornigera. 1844. II. 328.¹
Ménestrel. Taillis sous futaie. 1895. IV. 131.
Menet, André. Cours élémentaire d'arboriculture. 1860. III. 110.²
Ménéville, Félix Édouard Guérin-. See Guérin-Ménéville, F. E.
Menezes, Carlos Azevedo de. Catalogo das phanerogamicas da Madeira. 1894. I. 498.
— Notice sur les phanérogames de Madère. 1899. I. 498.
Menge, Anton. Catalogus plantarum . . . regionis grudentinensis. 1839. I. 380.
Mengen, F. A. Die Landwirthschaft und das Forstwesen im Herzogthume Braunschweig. 1858. IV. 351.²
Meagotti. De l'utilité des bois pour retenir le cours des eaux. 1832. IV. 184.²
Mengotti, Francesco. Dello imboschimento de' monti 1869. IV. 165.
Menier. Emploi de la teinture de Thuja. 1880. III. 311.²
Ménier. See Viaud-Grand-Marais, A. & Ménier.
Ménier, Ch. Note sur le Cosprosma [sic] foliosa. 1891. II. 815.²
Ménigault. Sur l'extraction de l'huile de Laurier. 1835. III. 406.²
Menke, A. E. See Jackson, C. L. & Menke, A. E.
Mennander, Carl Friedrich. De foliis plantarum. 1747. I. 109.¹
— De nutrimento plantarum. 1747. I. 157.
— De radicibus plantarum. 1748. I. 103.
— De seminibus plantarum. 1752. I. 120.
— Om stampe-bark och misse-bröd. 1742. IV. 482.²
— Om swedie ock kytö i Finland. 1742. IV. 273.¹
— De transpiratione plantarum. 1750. I. 166.
Mennesson, Jean Baptiste Augustin Prosper. L'observateur rural de la Marne. 1806. III. 554.²
Mennie, George. Rhamnus Frangula. 1843. III. 543.¹
Menon, V. K. Govinda. See Govinda Menon, V. K.
Menonville, Nicolas Joseph Thiery de. See Thiery de Menonville, N. J.
Mantin, N. Ueber Cultur der China-Bäume. 1884. III. 712.²
Mentz, M. Friderich. De plantis . . ; ad rem magicam. 17 05. I. 517.²

Mentzel. See also Menzel.
Mantzel, Albert & Philipp. Synonyma plantarum. 1618. I. 372, III. 72.
Mentzel, Christian. Centuria plantarum circa nobile Gedanum. 1650. V. xix.¹
— Index nominum plantarum universalis. 1682. I. 72.¹
— Lexicon plantarum polyglotton. 1682. V. ix.¹
— Πίναξ βοτανώνυμος πολύγλωττος καθολικίς. 1682. I. 72,¹ V. ix.¹
Menuzier. Feuilles de Chêne, fourrage pour le bétail. 1894. IV. 438.²
Menuiserie ébénisterie. IV. 12.²
Menze, Otto. Zur Kenntnis der täglichen Assimilation der Kohlehydrate. 1887. I. 174.
Menzel. See also Mentzel.
Menzel. Ueber das Verpflanzen älterer Bäume. 1894. III. 168.₁
Menzel, O. E. Tetratheca pilosa var. floribunda. 1899. III. 513.²
Menzer. Ueber den Waldfeldbau. 1862. IV. 133.
Menzies, James. Sexual states of the Chile Pine. 1890. III. 299.¹
Menzies, William. The history of Windsor great park. 1864. IV. 358.¹
Méplain, Firmin. Du café. 1868. III. 742.¹
Mer, Émile. De l'absorption de l'eau par le limbe des feuilles. 1878. I. 161.
— De l'action physiologique de la gelée. 1870. I. 212.
— L'activité cambiale des arbres; son réveil et son extinction. 1892. I. 190.²
— Le Balai de sorcière du Sapin. 1893. IV. 445.
— Bois de printemps et bois d'automne. 1892. I. 126.
— Le brunissement de la partie terminale des feuilles de Sapin. 1893. IV. 445.
— Causas que producen la excentricidad de la médula. 1888. IV. 543.²
— Des causes de l'étiolement des plantes. 1882. IV. 66.¹
— Sur les causes de variation de la densité des bois. 1892. IV. 411.²
— Des causes diverses de l'étiolement des plantes. 1882. III. 181.¹
— Des causes qui peuvent modifier les effets de l'action directrice de la lumière. 1884. I. 230.
— Des causes qui président à la transformation de l'aubier. 1899. II. 137.²
— Des causes qui produisent l'excentricité de la moëlle dans les Sapins. 1892. II. 22,¹ IV. 543.¹
— Le chaudron du Sapin. 1894. IV. 445.
— De la constitution . . . des feuilles hivernales. 1876. I. 173.
— De la constitution . . . des poils radicaux. 1880. I. 103.
— Culture du Mélèze dans les Vosges. 1885. IV. 449.
— La défoliation des branches basses d'Épicéa. 1892. IV. 457.
— Description d'une maladie nouvelle des rameaux de Sapin. 1890. IV. 445.
— Éclaircie dans les taillis. 1900. IV. 175.²
— Les éclaircies dans les sapinières. 1888. IV. 446.¹
— Sur les effets physiologiques des décortications. 1892. I. 526.¹
— Enseignement forestier supérieur. See Enseignement agricole. 1883. IV. 34.²
— Une excursion forestière dans les Vosges. 1893. IV. 361.
— De la formación de la madera roja. 1887. IV. 414.¹
— Formation du bois parfait. 1890. II. 137.²
— De la formation du bois rouge. 1887. II. 22,¹ 34,¹ IV. 558.²
— De la formation du bois rouge dans le Sapin et l'Épicéa. 1887. II. 17,¹ IV. 558.²
— La glycogénèse. 1873. I. 173.
— Du l'hydrotropisme des racines. 1881. I. 194.
— Influence de l'écorcement sur les propriétés mécaniques du bois. 1893. IV. 409.
— Influence de l'état climatérique sur la croissance des arbres. 1895. I. 219.¹
— Influence de l'état climatérique sur la croissance des Sapins. 1895. II. 24.¹
— Influence de l'exposition sur l'accroissement de l'écorce des Sapins. 1889. I. 190.³
— De l'influence de l'exposition sur le développement des couches annuelles dans les Sapins. 1888. I. 190,³ II. 22.²
— De l'influence de l'ombre et de la lumière sur la structure. . . des aiguilles d'Abies excelsa. 1883. II. 36.²
— Influence de quelques causes internes sur la présence de l'amidou dans les feuilles. 1891. II. 21,¹ IV. 64.¹

Mer, Émile (*continued*).
— Influence des décortications annulaires. 1892. I. 192.²
— De l'influence des éclaircies sur la croissance des Sapins. 1890. IV. 446.²
— De l'influence des éclaircies sur . . . Sapins. 1888. IV. 446.²
— De l'influence des milieux sur la structure des racines. 1879. I. 103.
— De l'influence qu'exerce le milieu. 1882. I. 218.
— Le jardinage appliqué à l'Épicéa. 1886. IV. 458.²
— A kámbium tevékenységének évi felébredése és megszünése. 1892. I. 128.²
— On latent and adventitious buds of trees. 1872. I. 108.¹
— Liste des travaux scientifiques. 1891. IV. 2.
— La lunure du Chêne. 1897. II. 132,¹ 137,¹ IV. 511.
— Du mode de formation des nœuds gris. 1886. IV. 172.¹
— Des modifications de structure et de forme qu'éprouvent les racines. 1880. I. 103.
— Des modifications de structure subies par une feuille de Lierre agée de sept ans. 1886. II. 649.¹
— Des modifications subies par la structure épidermique des feuilles sous diverses influences. 1882. I. 110.
— Moyen d'activer l'allongement des jeunes Sapins. 1890. IV. 444.²
— Moyen de préserver les bois de la vermoulure. 1893. IV. 421.
— Note sur le Betula pubescens. 1881. II. 119.¹
— Note sur le dépérissement des cimes d'Épicéa. 1880. IV. 456.
— Nouvelles recherches sur l'amylogénèse. 1891. I. 177, 179.³
— Nouvelles recherches sur la répartition du tanin dans le bois de Chêne. 1892. IV. 515.²
— Nouvelles recherches sur les conditions de développement des poils radicaux. 1884. I. 188.
— Nouvelles recherches sur un moyen de préserver le bois de Chêne de la vermoulure. 1898. IV. 421, 557.²
— Nuevas investigaciones sobre un medio de preservar de la carcoma la madera de Roble. 1838. IV. 557.²
— Observations sur la répartition des stomates. 1886. I. 131.³
— De l'orientation des feuilles. 1883. I. 195.¹
— De l'origine et du développement des bourgeons dormants. 1872. I. 108.¹
— Particularités de végétation que présentent . . . " Hypoderma." 1890. IV. 442.
— Des phénomènes végétatifs qui précédent . . . le dépérissement et la chute des feuilles. 1876. I. 191.²
— Physiologie végétale; l'activité cambiale des arbres. 1892. I. 128,² IV. 64.¹
— Physiologie végétale. Répartition hivernale de l'amidon. 1892. IV. 64.¹
— De la préparation des baliveaux de Chêne. 1886. IV. 513.
— Préservation du bois de Chêne contre la vermoulure. 1898. IV. 421, 557.²
— Des procédés culturaux à appliquer dans les sapinières. 1887. IV. 444.²
— A propos de la Grapholitha tedella. 1892. IV. 209.¹
— Du ralentissement des fonctions végétatives causé par le froid. 1897. I. 212.
— Rapport de l'accroissement des arbres. 1895. IV. 543.¹
— Recherches expérimentales sur . . . poils radicaux. 1879. I. 100.¹
— Recherches sur la formation du bois parfait. 1888. I. 156.¹
— Recherches sur la formation du bois parfait dans les essences feuillues. 1887. I. 156.¹
— Recherches sur la maladie des branches de Sapin. 1893. IV. 445.
— Recherches sur le mécanisme . . . de la pénétration dans le sol . . . des tiges de Ronce. 1884. I. 306.¹
— Recherches sur le traitement des sapinières vosgiennes. 1889. IV. 454.
— Recherches sur les causes d'excentricité. 1888. I. 106,¹ II. 23.³
— Recherches sur les causes de la structure des feuilles. 1883. I. 110.
— Recherches sur les causes des colorations . . . dans les feuilles en automne et en hiver. 1877. I. 185.²
— Recherches sur les mouvements nyctitropiques. 1884. I. 198.
— De la répartition de l'amidon dans les rameaux. 1879. I. 179.²
— Répartition hivernale de l'amidou. 1891. I. 179.²

— Reveil et extinction de l'activité cambiale dans les arbres. 1892. I. 128.²
— Rôle de la réserve amylacée des arbres. 1890. I. 179.³
— Le roussi des feuilles de Sapin. 1893. IV. 445.
— Sur un Sapin . . . dépourvu de branches. 1885. II. 23.¹
— De la transformation de l'aubier en bois. 1897. II. 132.¹
— De l'utilisation des produits ligneux pour l'alimentation du bétail. 1894. III. 223.²
— Des variations qu'éprouve la réserve amylacée. 1898. I. 180.¹ — 1899. IV. 64.³
— *See also* CORNU, Maxime & MER, Émile.
Mer, René. De l'utilité d'une réorganisation de l'administration des forêts. 1871. IV. 292.
Mérat & Gibert. Sur l'Assocou et son emploi. 1848. III. 519.³
Mérat, François Victor. Destruction des Roses naissantes. 1844. III. 453.¹
— Études des Rosiers. 1849. III. 448.
— Mémoire sur la possibilité de cultiver le Thé . . . en France. 1844. III. 601.¹
— De la mousse des arbres. 1841. III. 175.²
— Note sur la nécessité de cultiver . . . le Grenadier. 1827. III. 630.¹
— Note sur un arbuste qui pourrait fournir les moyens d'avoir des Abricotiers . . . nains. 1839. III. 442.¹
— Note sur un Orme d'une grosseur extraordinaire. 1839. II. 143.²
— Notice sur diverses espèces de Thés. 1841. III. 606.
— Notice sur la culture des Palmiers. 1828. III. 316.²
— Notice sur la destruction des Roses. 1844. III. 453.¹
— Notice sur les essais de culture . . . du Thé en France. 1837. III. 601.¹
— Notice sur les Salix stipularis et lanceolata. 1844. II. 100.¹
— Nouvelle flore des environs de Paris. 1812. I. 407.
— Remarques sur l'ouvrage de Vaillant intitulé: Botanicon parisiense. 1843. I. 78.¹
— Revue de la flore parisienne. 1843. I. 410.
— Synopsis de la nouvelle flore . . . de Paris. 1837. I. 409.
— & LENS, A. J. de. Dictionnaire universel de matière médicale. 1829. III. 242.
Mercadante, Mariano. Sur la formation du sucre dans les fruits. 1876. I. 179.¹
Mercado de tapones de corcho. 1892. IV. 518.¹
Merchant's magazine. III. 5.
Mercier, E. Rubi genevenses. 1861. II. 304.¹
Mercier, Philippe. Choix de plantes exotiques. 1830. II. 450,¹ 534.¹
Mercieul. Nouveau mode d'emploi du soufre contre la maladie de la Vigne. 1860. III. 577.
Merck. *See* HAAXMAN, P. J. & MERCK.
Merck, E. Cocain und seine Salze. 1884. III. 493.¹
Mercklin, Karl Eugen von. Anatomisch-physiologische Notizen. 1851. I. 99.
— Bericht über einige . . . Keimungsversuche. 1853. I. 203.
— Data aus der periodischen Entwickelung der Pflanzen . . . zu St. Petersburg. 1853. I. 223.³
— Zur Entwicklungsgeschichte der Blattgestalten. 1846. I. 109.³
— Monstrositaeten in den maennlichen Kätzchen von Ostrya. 1850. II. 122.³
— Palaeodendrologikon rossicum. 1855. I. 124.
— Über Periderma und Kork. 1864. I. 130, II. 119.¹
— *See also* МЕРКЛИНЪ, КАРЛЪ.
Mercurialis, Hieronymus. Variarum lectionum libri quatuor. 1570. I. 281.
Mercurius. De bestemming der koloniale producten. 1876. III. 274.¹
Meredith, Joseph. Treatise on the Grape vine. 1876. III. 554.¹
Meredith, Mrs. Louisa Anne (Twamley). Some of my bush friends in Tasmania. 1860. I. 505.
Merensky, (*Oberförster, Panthen*). Mittheilungen über den Zustand . . . der k. Oberförsterei Panthen. 1841. IV. 352.
Merensky, A. Beobachtungen über die Wirkung des Eucalyptus globulus. 1882. IV. 533.²
Merget, A. E. Sur les fonctions des feuilles; rôle des stomates. 1878. I. 167.
— Des fonctions des feuilles dans le phénomène des échanges gazeux. 1878. I. 170.
— Sur les fonctions des feuilles dans les phénomènes d'échanges gazeux. 1877. I. 167.
— Recherches sur le rôle des stomates. 1873. I. 170.
Meriale, François. L'ami des jardins d'utilité et d'ornement. 1805. III. 86.

Merian, Maria Sibilla. Dissertatio de generatione et metamorphosibus insectorum surinamensium. 1705. I. 338.[1]
— Histoire des insectes de l'Europe. 1679. I. 348.[1]
— Histoire générale des insectes de Surinam. 1771. I. 338.[2]
— Der Raupen wunderbare Verwandelung. 1679. I. 348.[1]
— Recueil des plantes des Indes. 1768. I. 338.[2]
— Over the voortteeling en wonderbaerlijke veranderingen der Surinaamsche insecten. 1705. I. 338.[1]
Mérice, E. Progrès et développement de la culture de l'Eucalyptus. 1874. IV. 529.[2]
Merino, Manuel, GARCÍA Y. See GARCÍA Y MERINO, Manuel.
Merino y Roman, Baltasar. Contribución á la flora de Galicia. 1897. I. 423.
Merkel, J. See BEHLEN, Stephan & MERKEL, J.
Merkel, L. Practisch geprüfte Methode Gewächse . . . gegen Nachtfröste zu schützen. 1872. III. 183.[1]
Merklein, Fr. Verzeichniss der Gefässpflanzen . . . von Schaffhausen. 1861. I. 435.
Merkus Doornik, J. J. F. H. T. Hortus spaarnbergensis. 1849. I. 51.[2]
— See also ROMBOUTS, J. G. H. & MERKUS DOORNIK, J. J. F. H. T.
Merkwürdige Bäume. 1831. II. 138.[1] — 1834. II. 37.[1]
Merkwürdige Baumexemplare. 1852. II. 10.[2]
Merkwürdige morphologische Verhältnisse der Blutbuche. 1888. II. 127.[2]
Merkwürdiger Rosenstrauch. 1831. II. 290.[1]
Ein merkwürdiger Windbruch. 1849. IV. 189.[1]
Merlet, Jean. L'abrégé des bons fruits, avec la manière de les connoistre et de cultiver les arbres. 1667. III. 142.
Merlet de la Boulaye, Gabriel Eléonor. Herborisations dans le départ. de Maine et Loire. 1809. I. 407.
Merli, Francesco. Il buon uso del the, del caffe. 1769. III. 222.
Merlieux, C. BAILLY DE. See BAILLY DE MERLIEUX, C.
Mernier. Culture des taillis simples. 1898. IV. 132.[2]
Mérode-Westerloo, comte de. Commerce des bourgeons de résineux. 1900. IV. 180.[2]
Merrains du Nord. 1898. IV. 427.[2]
Merrell, Albert. A digest of materia medica. 1883. III. 247.[1]
Merrem, Blasius. Carl von Linné's Vollständiges Pflanzensystem. 1811. I. 259.
— Handbuch der Pflanzenkunde. 1809. I. 255, 259.
— Karl von Linné's Vollständiges Pflanzensystem. See LINNÉ, Carl von. 1774. I. 258.
Merrem, Daniel Karl Theodor. Ueber den Cortex adstringens brasiliensis. 1828. III. 465.[2]
Merrett, Christopher. Observations concerning the uniting of barks of trees cut. 1667. I. 207.[1]
— Pinax rerum naturalium britannicarum. 1666. I. 394.
Merriam, Clinton Hart. Life zones and crop zones of the United States. 1898. I. 308.
— Life zones of Mount Mazama. 1897. I. 327.
— A new Fir from Arizona, Abies arizonica. 1896. II. 22.[1]
— Notes on the distribution of trees . . . of southern California. 1893. I. 320, IV. 78.[1]
— Notes on the geographic and vertical distribution of Cactuses, Yuccas, and Agave. 1893. II. 86,[2] 587.[1]
— Pinus Banksiana. 1883. II. 40.[2]
Merriam, M. H. Influence of the stock upon the graft. 1879. III. 39.
Merrick, J. M. & others. Report of the commission appointed to investigate the matter of wooden pavements. 1873. IV. 425.[2]
Merrifield, Mary Philadelphia. A sketch of the natural history of Brighton. 1860. I. 401.
Merrill, L. H. See WOODS, C. D. & MERRILL, L. H.
Merrill, William E. The relation of forestry to the floods of the Ohio. 188 .? IV. 45.
Mersenne, Marin. L'harmonie universelle. 1636. IV. 428.[1]
Mersey. Les forêts au point de vue militaire. 1891. IV. 45.
Merten. Urwald und Holzbringung in Bosnien. 1900. IV. 374,[3] 391.
Mertens, (Garten-Inspektor). Über die Einwirkung des Gemäuers . . . auf das Reifen der Früchte. 1833. III. 137.
Mertens, (Garten-Meister, Herrenhausen). Über die Behandlung der Orangerie. 1829. III. 156.[1]
Mertens, Alexandre. Question des boisements en Belgique. 1858. IV. 119.[2]
Mertens, É. État de l'arboriculture aux environs de Londres. 1867. III. 123.[1]
Mertens, Karl Heinrich. Notices sur les îles Carolines. 1835. I. 510.[1]

Méry, C. de. Le Cafe, poème. 1837. III. 739.
Mers, Friedrich. Die Aufforstungen . . . im Kanton Tessin. 1900. IV. 187.[2]
— Die Bewirtschaftung der Niederwaldungen im Kanton Tessin. 1895. IV. 131.
— Erfahrungen in den tessinischen Forstgärten. 1894. IV. 151.[1]
— Der Felssturz bei Airolo. 1899. IV. 187.[2]
— Die Köhlerei im Entlebuch. 1885. IV. 395.
— Statistische Notizen über die Land- und Forstwirthschaft des Kantons Tessin. 1892. IV. 367.
— Die Terrainbewegung in Campo. 1899. IV. 187.[2]
— Verbesserung der forstlichen Verhältnisse im Kanton Tessin. 1893. IV. 170.
— Die Versicherung des schweizerischen Forstpersonals. 1900. IV. 311.[2]
— Waldbrände im Kanton Tessin. 1899. IV. 184.[1]
Mes observations sur l'utilité de conserver la juridiction actuelle des eaux & forêts. 18 . . ? IV. 325.
Mesanger. Traité de la charpenterie et des bois. 1753. IV. 220.
Mesch, Anton Hendrik van der BOON. See BOON MESCH, A. H. van der.
Mesch, Hendrik Carel van der BOON. See BOON MESCH, H. C. van der.
Meschayeff, V. Ueber die Anpassungen zum Aufrechthalten der Pflanzen. 1882. I. 167.
Meschiny. See BEUGON, MESCHINY & NOIROT.
Meschwitz, Friedrich Wilhelm. Beitrag zur Lösung der Frage über die Entstehung der Schütte in den Kiefernkulturen. 1884. IV. 477.
— Die Erziehung der Kiefernpflanzen. 1882. IV. 473.
— Die Flugsandbindung. 1882. IV. 145.
— Kiefernblattwespe. 1887. IV. 478.
— Praktische Erfahrungen im Bereiche des . . . Forstverbesserungswesens. 1882. IV. 142.
Mesgrigny, Adrien de. Observations sur la culture des arbres verts. 1823. IV. 121.
Mesnard, Eugène. Sur l'action combinée de la lumière et de l'eau dans le dégagement du parfum des plantes. 1896. I. 182.[2]
— Action de la lumière et de quelques agents extérieurs sur le dégagement des odeurs. 1896. I. 182.[2]
— Appareil nouveau pour la mesure de l'intensité des parfums. 18 8. I. 182.[2]
— Étude critique et expérimentale sur la mesure de l'intensité des parfums des plantes. 1894. I. 182.[2]
— Recherches sur la falsification de l'essence de Santal. 1892. III. 384.[1]
— Recherches sur la formation des huiles grasses. 1893. I. 182,[1] x. [2]
— Recherches sur la localisation des huiles grasses. 1893. I. 204
— Recherches sur la localisation des huiles grasses pendant la formation des graines et des fruits. 1894. I. 179.[1]
— Recherches sur le mode de production du parfum. 1892. I. 182.[2]
Mesquit beans. 1878. III. 485.[1]
The Mesquite. 1878. III. 485.[1]
Méss, H. A. Bijdrage tot de kennis der Menta wei-eilanden. 1870. III. 974.[2]
Message à l'Assemblée fédérale concernant une modification . . . de la loi fédérale du 24 mars 1876. 1880. IV. 331.[1]
Message du conseil fédéral . . . concernant la transformation de l'École forestière. 1869. IV. 36.[1]
Message from the President . . . in relation to the cultivation of timber. 1874. IV. 178,[1] 271.[2]
Message from the President . . . relative to the preservation of forests. 1890. IV. 178,[1] 272.
Messager, Al. Sur la germination. 1880. III. 156.[2]
— Pseudo-greffe et quasi-greffe. 1881. III. 165.
Le Messager agricole. III. 20.
Messdunk, R. SCHULZE-. See SCHULZE-MESSDUNK, R.
Messer, Frederick A. A new and easy method of studying British wild flowers. 1880. I. 403.
Messerschmidt, F. Jærns og Træs Forar' eidelse. 1873. IV. 423.[1]
Messervy, H. Tea planting [in Guiana]. 1896. III. 601.[1]
Il Messico. 1863. IV. 341.[2]
Messrs. Veitch and sons' specialities at Coombe Wood. 1879. III. 301,[2] 614.[1]
Mestre, C. Le jus et le vin d'oranges. 1891. III. 501.[2]
Mestre, P. C. Contribution à l'étude des moyens propres à défendre les vignobles. 1900. III. 502.[1]

Mesue, Giovanni. I libri de i semplici purgativi. 1589. III. 240.
— Opera, quae exstant, omnia. 1561. I. 281.
Mesue, Johannes. *See* MESUE, Giovanni.
Mesures à prendre à l'occasion des incendies de forêts. *See* TESTU. 1866. IV. 184.[1]
Mesures à prendre pour enrayer la propagation des insectes. 1897. IV. 558.[2]
Mészáros, Károly. Az uj erdötörvény. 1857. IV. 331.[2]
Métaxas, Constantin C. Le Figuier en Mésopotamie. 1888. III. 369.[2]
— Fructification d'un Cycas revoluta. 1880. III. 285.[1]
— Le Jujubier de la Mésopotamie. 1889. III. 544.[1]
— Le Grenadier à Bagdad. 1885. III. 630.[2]
— Le Mûrier en Mésopotamie. 1888. III. 378.
— Peuplier de l'Euphrate. 1889. II. 97.[2]
Metch, A. *See* MEVR, A.
Météorologie comparée agricole et forestière. *See* MATHIEU, J. J. A. 1878. IV. 59.[3]
Meteorologie und Pflanzenleben. 1873. IV. 59.[2]
Meth, J. Castanea vesca L. 1884. III. 359.[1]
— Ein jährlich zweimal tragender Birnbaum. 1883. II. 280.[2]
Method of climbing trees. 1874. III. 177.
Method of curing injuries and defects in trees. *See* FORSTER, J. R. 1797. III. 180.[1]
Method of detecting the adulteration of tea. 1830. III. 606.
Method of preserving timber in Japan. *See* PRESERVATION process . . . 1885. IV. 420.
Methven, John. Deciduous trees, with ornamental and coloured foliage. 1890. III. 205.[2]
Mévivier, *vicomte* de. Mémoire sur les chehilles des bois. 1852. IV. 209.[1]
Metlitzký, H. Zur Cultur der Zirbe. 1888. IV. 463.[2]
Metlitzky, Vincenz. Immerwährender Wirthschafts-Kalender. 1877. IV. 98.[1]
Il **metodo**. eclettico nell' assestamento delle fustaie. 1885. IV. 129.
Metodo economico di assiepare un latifondo. *See* GIARDJNA, Giuseppe. 1880. IV. 244.
Método para pulimentar. la madera con carbón. 1890. IV. 422.[1]
Metodo per preservare del danno del verno i giovani oppi. 1866. IV. 191.[1]
Metodo per propagare gli alberi fruttiferi in China. 1863. III. 158.
Metodo semplice di rimboschimento. 1864. IV. 152.
Métral, Joseph. Amélioration de la végétation des arbres d'alignement. 1883. II. 209.
Metsch, Johann-Christian. Darstellung einiger seltneren . . . Varietäten. 1852. II. 125.[2]
— Flora hennebergica. 1845. I. 381.
— Rubi hennebergenses. 1856. II. 301.[2]
Metsopoulos, Konstantinos. *See* MHTΣOΠOYΛOΣ, Κωνσταντῖνος.
Mettenius, Georg Heinrich. Beiträge zur Anatomie der Cycadeen. 1860. II. 3.[1]
— Beiträge zur Botanik. 1850. II. 475.[1]
— Einige Beobachtungen über den Bau der Bignonien. 1847. II. 785.[2]
Mettler, Rudolph. Diplolaena Hügelii. 1846. III. 504.[1]
— Gompholobium polymorphum β latifolium. 1845. III. 478.[1]
— Gompholobium venustum. 1845. III. 478.[1]
— Neue Prachtpflanzen in der Hammer Baumschule. 1845. II. 327.[1] 328.[1]
Metz, Benedict Joseph. Tabellen zur Berechnung des Cubic-Inhalts runder Stämme. 1813. IV. 221.
Metz, Ernst. Über einige Rosen. 1861. III. 452.
— Rosen-Unterlagen. 1863. III. 452.
Metz — **Académie impériale**. *See* SOCIÉTÉ DES LETTRES, SCIENCES, ARTS . . . DE METZ. I. 15.
Metz — **Société d'histoire naturelle**. *See* SOCIÉTÉ D'HISTOIRE NATURELLE . . . DE LA MOSELLE. I. 15.
Metz — Société des lettres, sciences, arts. *See* SOCIÉTÉ . . . I. 15.
Metz-Noblat, Antoine de. Un péril pour l'Algérie; le déboisement. 1878. IV. 283.[2]
— Du projet de loi sur les défrichements. 1851. IV. 326.
Metze, W. Ueber Baumanpflanzungen. 1826. IV. 184.[1]
Metzsen, von, (*Oberförster*). Ist bei den . . . Lobpreisen . . . die neue Anlage von Eichenschälwaldungen . . . zu empfehlen? 1882. IV. 513.
Metzger. Wie können . . . Durchforstungserträge junger Nadelholzbestände . . . verwertet werden? 1900. IV. 175.[2]

Metzger, (*Regierungsrath*). Beobachtungen über den zweiten Trieb der Bäume. 1831. I. 187.
— Über den Einfluss der . . . Feuchtigkeit auf das Reifen der Früchte. 1833. I. 179.[1]
— Über den Einfluss des Schnees auf die Gewächse. 1831. I. 232.[2]
— Frost und Kälte, und deren Wirkung. 1847. III. 182.
— Observations sur la seconde pousse des arbres. 1831. I. 187.
Metzger, A. Die absoluten Schaftformzahlen der Fichte. 1894. IV. 458.
— Bekämpfung der Nonne. 1893. IV. 201.
— Aus meinen Nonnen-Studien. 1894. IV. 201.
— Studien über den Aufbau der Waldbäume. 1894. IV. 63.[2] — 1895. IV. 65.[1]
— Wie können die ersten Durchforstungserträge . . . verwertet werden? 1900. IV. 392.
— Der Wind als . . . Faktor für das Wachsthum der Bäume. 1893. IV. 189.[2]
— & **Müller**, N. J. C. Die Nonnenraupe und ihre Bakterien. 1895. IV. 202.
Metzger, Carl. Die Grundlagen . . . der forstlichen Produktion. 1891. IV. 270.
Metzger, Eduard. Ornamente aus deutschen Gewächsen. 1841. I. 516.
Metzger, Johann. Bemerkungen . . . über die Wirkung der schwarzen und weissen Spalierwände. 1830. III. 136.
— Gartenbuch. 1829. III. 104.
— Die Kernobstsorten des südlichen Deutschlands. 1847. III. 71.
— Der rheinische Weinbau. 1827. III. 552.
— *See also* BABO, Lambert, *Freiherr* von & METZGER, Johann.
Metzner, Reinhold. Botanisch-gärtnerisches Taschenwörterbuch. 1896. I. 71, *III. 30*, V. IX,[1] XXVI.[2]
Meucci, Ferdinando. Diario delle osservazioni sopra le fasi della vegetazione. 1886. I. 226.[2]
Meunier, A. Les téguments séminaux des Cyclospermées. 1890. I. 121.
Meunier, J. *See* VINCENT, Camille & MEUNIER, J.
Meunier, Stanislas. Sur du grès perforé par des racines. 1876. I. 228.[2]
— Perforation d'un grès quartzeux par des racines d'arbres. 1875. I. 188.
— La terre végétale. 1875. III. 37.[1]
Meurer. Beiträge zur Uebersicht der kurhessischen Flora. 1848. I. 382.
Meurer, Noë. Von forstlicher Oberherrligkeit unnd Gerechtigkeit. 1560. IV. 316.
— Jag- und Forstrecht. 1561. IV. 316.
Meuris, F. Les Erica. 1899. III. 650.[2]
Meurisse, G. Étude du genre Santalum. 1892. II. 169.[1]
— Structure . . . de la moelle des Ericacées. 1895. II. 658.[2]
Meuron, de. Notes forestières. 1872. IV. 101.
Meurs, Johann. Arboretum sacrum. 1642. I. 512.
Meurs, F. Berberis Darwini. 1899. III. 394.[2]
Meuse — **Société d'horticulture, d'arboriculture, de viticulture** . . . *See* SOCIÉTÉ . . . III. 21.
The **Mexican** Dagger plant. 1892. II. 87.[2]
Mexican fibre or Istle. 1887. III. 341.[1]
Mexicanarum plantarum imagines. *See* FABER, Johann. 1652. I. 331.
México — Secretaría de fomento. Informes y documentos. 1897. III. 10.[1]
México een toekomstig Koffieproduceerend land. 1891. III. 728.[1]
Mey, J. J. Anweisung zur wilden Baumzucht. 1792. IV. 116.
Meyboom, C. Het snoeien van Theeheesters. 1876. III. 602.[1]
— De ziekte in de Theeheesters. 1873. III. 604.[2]
Meydell, von. Merkwürdige Lärchenpflanzung. 1878. IV. 449.
Meyen, Frans Julius Ferdinand. Anatomisch-physiologische Untersuchungen über den Inhalt der Pflanzenzellen. 1828. I. 136.[1]
— Beiträge zur Bildungsgeschichte verschiedener Pflanzentheile. 1831. II. 149.[2]
— Beiträge zur Botanik. 1843. I. 268.
— Ueber die Bewegung der Säfte. 1839. I. 163.
— Ueber Bewegung der Säfte. 1839. I. 163..
— Comparative remarks on the distribution of vegetation on the greatest heights. 1836. I. 219.[2]
— Einiges über die schönen Cactus-Arten . . . von Südamerika. 1833. II. 587.[1]
— Ueber die Epidermis der Gewächse. 1837. I. 129.[1]

— Erklärung der eigenthümlichen Stellung der Embryonen im Mistel-Saamen. 1840. II. 178.[1]
— Von dem Geruche der Pflanzen. 1838. I. 182.[2]
— Grundriss der Pflanzengeographie. 1836. I. 299, III. 52.
— Ueber die Hochebene im südlichen Peru. 1832. I. 340.[2]
— Matériaux pour servir à l'histoire du développement des diverses parties dans les plantes. 1839. II. 149.[3]
— Mikroskopische Abbildungen. 1830. I. 100.[2]
— Mouvement des sucs dans les végétaux. 1839. I. 163.
— Neues System der Pflanzen-Physiologie. 1837. I. 148.
— Ueber die neuesten Fortschritte der Anatomie und Physiologie der Gewächse. 1836. I. 33.
— Noch einige Worte über den Befruchtungsakt. 1840. I. 200.
— Outlines of the geography of plants. 1836. I. 299, III. 52.
— Pflanzen-Pathologie. 1841. I. 206.[1] See also NEES VON ESENBECK, C. G. 1811. I. 34.
— Phytotomie. 1830. I. 100.[2]
— Reise um die Erde. 1834. I. 303.
— Reise om de aarde. 1834. I. 303.
— Ueber die secretions-Organe der Pflanzen. 1837. I. 112.[2]
— Utkast till växt-geographien. 1836. I. 299.
— Vergleichende Bemerkungen über . . . Vegetation in den grössten Höhen. 1836. I. 219.[2]
Mayen, J. Lettre sur la circulation du latex. 1833. I. 181.[3]
Mayen, J. J. Physikalisch-ökonomische Baumschule. 1791. III. 153.
Mayenberg, Heinrich Julius. Flora einbeccensis. 1712. I. 372.
Meyendorff, Georges de. Reise von Orenburg nach Buchara. 1826. I. 456.
— Voyage d'Orenbourg à Boukhara. 1826. I. 456.
Meyer. Die Behandlung und Benutzung der . . . (öden) Grundflächen Deutschlands. 1852. IV. 118, 274.[1]
Meyer. Volksbibliothek für Länder-, Völker- und Naturkunde. See HÄRING, W. 1854. IV. 46.[1]
Meyer. Bericht über der forstliche Wirksamkeit im Kanton Appenzell. 1864. IV. 366.
— L'économie forestière dans le canton d'Appenzell. 1864. IV. 366.
— Ueber die forstlichen Zustände im Kanton Appenzell. 1864. IV. 366.
Meyer, (Forstmeister). Forstwirtschaft. 1893. IV. 98.[2]
Meyer, (Obe förster, Lindenberg). Beitrag zur Frage über . . . Kiefern-Saatkämpe. 1876. IV. 472.
— Beobachtungen über gemischte Eichen- und Nadelholz-Culturen. 1875. IV. 441, 506.
— Zur Frage des Ueberhaltbetriebes. 1887. IV. 130.
— Raum für die Weichhölzer. 1886. IV. 138.[1]
— Ueber Schütten der Kiefernsaatkämpe. 1889. IV. 478.
— Ueber Theilung und Uebertragung von Servituten. 1871. IV. 777.
Meyer, A. Excursionsflora des Grossherzogthums Oldenburg. 1872. I. 386.
Meyer, A. See MUSCULUS, F. & MEYER, A.
Meyer, Abraham. Observations on the relative growth of virgin forest timber. 1895. IV. 65.[1]
Meyer, Adolf. Anatomische Charakteristik officineller Blätter. 1882. III. 260.[1]
— Ein Beitrag zur Kenntniss des chinesischen Thee's. 1882. III. 607.
— See also PFITZER, Ernst & MEYER, Adolf.
Meyer, Albert. Beiträge zur . . . Anatomie der Ranunculaceen. 1884. II. 196.[1]
— Ranunculaceen. 1885. II. 196.[1]
Meyer, Andreas. Botanicum copiosum dictionarium. 1781. I. 32.
Meyer, Arthur. Beiträge zur Kenntniss pharmaceutisch wichtiger Gewächse. 1881. II. 85,[1] III. 333.[3]
— Bildung der Stärkekörner. 1886. I. 176.
— Das Chlorophyllkorn. 1883. I. 142.
— Ueber die Entwickelung des Wachses der Frucht von Rhus Toxicodendron. 1879. II. 460.[1]
— Sur la formation de l'amidon. 1886. I. 176.
— Ueber den Japantalg. 1879. III. 528.[2]
— Ueber die Methoden zur Nachweisung der Plasmaverbindungen. 1897. I. 137.
— Ueber Smilax China. 1881. II. 85,[2] III. 333.[3]
— Ueber Stärkekörner, welche . . . roth färben. 1886. I. 140.[2]
— Ueber das Suberin des Korkes. 1883. II. 140.[3]
— Untersuchungen ueber die Stärkekörner. 1895. I. 140.[2]

— See also FLÜCKIGER, F. A. & MEYER, Arthur.
— & Sandlund, H. Falsification des leurs de Cousso. 1894. III. 424.[2]
Meyer, Bernhard. See GÄRTNER, P. G., MEYER, Bernhard & SCHERBIUS, Johannes.
Meyer, Carl. See MEYER, Karl.
Meyer, Christian Friedrich. Abhandlung über die Waldhut. 1807. IV. 135.[1]
— Der frühere und dermalige Stand der staatswirthschaftlichen . . . Verhältnisse bei den Waldungen und Jagd.in Deutschland. 1851. IV. 24,[1] 25.
Meyer, E. Mittheilungen über das Gartenwesen von Buenos-Ayres. 1886. III. 119.[1]
Meyer, E. F. Versuch, mehrere Pflanzenarten . . . durch Stecklinge . . . vermehren zu können. 1836. III. 157.
Meyer, Ernst Heinrich Friedrich. Alberta magna, eine neue Pflanzengattung. 1838. II. 808.[2]
— Bericht über das Blühen des gemeinen Bambusrohrs. 1833. III. 316.[3]
— Botanische Erläuterungen zu Strabon's Geographie. 1852. I. 514.[1]
— Commentariorum de plantis Africae. 1835. I. 434.
— Ueber die Coniferen. 1841. II. 12.[2]
— Ueber einige Missbildungen . . . der Linnaea. 1844. II. 35.[2]
— Elenchus plantarum Borussiae. 1835. I. 378.
— Die Entwickelung der Botanik. 1844. I. 79.[2]
— On the geographical distribution . . . in South Africa. 1873. I. 495.
— Geschichte der Botanik. 1854. I. 79.[2]
— Ueber den geselligen Wuchs der Pflanzen. 1834. I. 217
— Ueber den Pflanzenschlaf. 1834. I. 198.
— Plantae Ecklonianae. Leguminosae. 1832. II. 312.[1]
— Plantarum surinamensium. 1824. I. 339.[1]
— De plantis labradoricis libri tres. 1830. I. 311.
— Preussens Pflanzengattungen. 1839. I. 350.
— Das Ueberwallen abgehauener Baumstümpfe. 1834.[1]
— Vergleichende Erklärung eines . . . Pflanzengloss rs. 1837. I. 78.[1]
— Die Vertheilung der Nahrungspflanzen. 1846. I. 299.
— See also PATZE, C., MEYER, Ernst & ELKAN, L.
Meyer, F. Die Eiche zu Pirsch. 1864. II. 138.[2]
— Merkwürdige Bäume in Livland. 1864. II. 138.[2]
Meyer, F. W. Arundinaria nobilis. 1900. III. 315.[2]
— Dacrydium Franklini Hook. 1900. III. 287.[2]
— The dwarfest kinds of shrubs. 1894. III. 205.[1]
— Furcraea longaeva Karw. et Zucc. 1900. III. 341.
— Menabilly. 1899. III. 299,[2] 307.[1]
— Opuntia xanthostema. 1900. III. 625.[1]
— Raphiolepis ovata. 1900. III. 447.[2]
— Rock-gardens. 1899. III. 311.[1]
Meyer, Friedrich. Land- und forstwirthschaftlicher Betriebs-unfall. 1893. IV. 211.[1]
Meyer, Friedrich Albrecht Anton. De cortice Angusturae. 1790. III. 503.[2]
Meyer, Frömmhold. Ueber das Fett der Strychnossamen. 1875. III. 683.[1]
Meyer, G. Ueber Wurzelschnitt der Palmen. 1879. III. 317.
— See also MAYER, G.
Meyer, G. L. A West Indian sugar estate. 1880. I. 338.[1]
Meyer, Georg Friedrich Wilhelm. Chloris hanoverana 1836. I. 379.
— Flora des Königreichs Hannover. 1842. I. 381, V. XIX.[2]
— Flora hanoverana excursoria. 1849. I. 382.
— Primitiae florae essequeboensis. 1818. I. 338.[1]
Meyer, Gottfried. Beiträge zur Anatomie der . . . Cinchonen. 1899. II. 813.[2]
— See also HARTWICH, Carl & MEYER, Gottfried.
Meyer, Gottlob Andreas. De Sycomoro. 1694. I. 512.
Meyer, H. Generalregister zu Dr. Aug. Friedr. Adr. Diel's Systematischer Beschreibung. 1834. III. 71, 444.[1]
Meyer, H. China liquida de Vrij. 1889. III. 723.
— See also HARNACK, E. & MEYER, H.
Meyer, Israel Joseph. De Salicis fragilis usu medico. 1770. III. 352.[1]
Meyer, J. C. Die Doldenkirsche. 1860. III. 438.[1]
— & Schmidt, Friedrich. Flora des Fichtelgebirges. 1854. I. 383.
Meyer, J. G. Der Obstbaumschnitt. 1871. III. 138.
Meyer, J. J. Kurze Anweisung für das Landvolk zu Besorgung der Wälder. 1775. IV. 110.[1]

Meyer, Joh. Akazien-Anbau im Kanton Basel. 1859. IV. 523.[1]
— Cultures d'Acacia dans le canton de Bâle. 1859. IV. 523.[1]
Meyer, Johann Augustus. De Rubo Idaeo officinarum. *See* Schulze, J. H. 1744. III. 458.[2]
Meyer, Johann Christian Friedrich. Formulare zu den Forstinstruktionen. 1810. IV. 287, 299.
— Forstdirektionslehre. 1810. IV. 287.
— Naturgetreue Darstellung der Entwikkelung ... der Pflanzen. 1808. I. 146.
— System einer auf Theorie und Erfahrung gestützten Lehre über die Einwirkung der Naturkräfte. 1806. IV. *61,[2] 63,[1] 68*.
Meyer, Johann Gustav Heinrich. Lehrbuch der schönen Gartenkunst. 1860. III. 203.
— Das Versetzen grosser Bäume. 1864. III. 167.
Meyer, K. A. & others. Anzucht verschiedener Gehölze. 1894. I. 248,[1] *III. 150.[2]*
Meyer, Karl Anton. Bemerkungen über die Gattungen der Daphnaceen. 1843. II. 599.[2]
— Beschreibung einer neuen ... Catalpa. 1837. II. 787.[1]
— Einige Bemerkungen über die Gattung Pimelea. 1845. II. 605.[1]
— Einige Bemerkungen ueber die ... Polygonaceae. 1840. II. 183.[2]
— Einige Bemerkungen über Diervilla, Weigela. 1855. II. 833.[2]
— Über einige Cornus-Arten. 1845. II. 654.[2]
— Einige der schönsten Sorbus-Arten. 1888. III. 459.[1]
— Einige Pflanzenmissbildungen. 1852. I. 143.
— Florula provinciae Tambov. 1844. I. 361.
— Florula provinciae Wiatka. 1848. I. 361.
— Die Gattungen Monolepis Schrad. 1844. II. 188.[2]
— Ideen zur Anpflanzung der Korkeiche. 1856. IV. 516.[2]
— Novae plantarum species. 1829. II. 246.[1]
— Sur quelques espèces de Cornus. 1845. II. 654.[2]
— Reise durch die soongorische Kirgisen-Steppe. 1830. I. 460.[1]
— Remarques sur les genres de Daphnacées. 1843. ¨II. 599.[2]
— Versuch einer Monographie der Gattung Ephedra. 1847. II. 53.[2]
— Verzeichniss der Pflanzen ... im Caucasus und in den Provinzen am westlichen Ufer des Caspischen Meeres gefunden. 1831. I. 368.[2]
— Verzeichniss der von dem Herrn Dr. Kolenati ... gesammelten Pflanzen. 1849. I. 368.[2]
— Über die Zimmtrosen. 1847. II. 282.[1]
— *See also* Bongard, H. G. & Meyer, C. A.; Fischer, F. E. L. & Meyer, K. A.; Trautvetter, E. R. von & Meyer, C. A.
Meyer, Karl Heinrich Gottlieb. Gründliche und treue Anweisung zur Obstbaumzucht. 1826. III. 136.
— Die Obstfrüchte. 1830. III. 70.
Meyer, Lothar. Die Chemie in ihrer Anwendung auf Forstwirthschaft. 1869. IV. 60.[1]
Meyer, W. Ueber den Einfluss von Witterungs- und Bodenverhältnissen. 1899. I. 219.[1]
— & Reiche, von. On the constituents of Canella alba. 1843. III. 613.[2]
— — Ueber einige Bestandtheile der Canella alba. 1843. III. 613.[2]
Meyer, Willy. Die Harzgänge im Blatte der Abietineen. 1883. II. 18.
Meyer-Ahrens. Cd. Die Blüten des Kossobaumes. 1851. III. 280.[2]
Meyer von Knonau. Entwurf, wie die Stadt Zürich mit genugsamen Holze versehen werden könnte. 1765. IV. 123.[1]
Meyer von Knonau, Gerold. Erdkunde der schweizerischen Eidgenossenschaft. *See* Hegetschweiler, Johann. 1838. I. 434.
Meyeringck, von, (*Forstmeister*). Bemerkungen gegen die ... behauptete Unzweckmässigkeit des Köpfens der Weidenbäume. 1833. III. 347.
— Mittheilung über die Obstbaumpflanzungen in den preuss. Elb-Forsten. 1833. III. 136.
Mylink, B. Landbouw-scheikunde. 1855. III. 37.[1]
Meyncke, O. M. The flora of Franklin county. 1885. V. XVII.[1]
Meyners d'Estrey, H. Les bois des Indes. 1890. IV. 538.[1]
— Le camphre. 1895. III. 405.[1]
— Le caoutchouc et ses variétés. 1892. III. 231.
— Des clous dans les arbres. 1893. III. 191.

— Culture du Café aux Philippines. 1893. III. 729.[1]
— Culture du Café dans le Honduras. 1894. III. 728.[1]
— La culture du Gambir. 1892. III. 748.[1]
— Culture du Poivrier au Malabar. 1891. III. 343.[2]
— Sur la destruction des Cocotiers par les scarabées. 1893. III. 323.[2]
— L'écorce du Bouleau. 1888. IV. 491.[2]
— Les espèces de Bambous du Japon. 1894. III. 314.[2]
— Les gommes d'Acacia. 1892. III. 463.[2]
— La maladie des Caféiers au Brésil. 1889. III. 736.
— La maladie du Café aux Indes anglaises. 1891. III. 736.
— Matière colorante du Bixa Orellana. 1890. III. 613.[2]
— La Vigne au Japon. 1892. III. 559.[1]
Meyrac, Albert. La forêt des Ardennes. 1896. IV. 362.
Meyran, Octave. Sur la distribution géographique de quelques plantes alpines. 1898. I. 301.
— Note sur le genre Ulex. 1900. II. 387.[2]
Meyrick, William. The new family herbal. 1790. III. 55.
Mez, Carl Christian. Die amerikanischen Lauraceen. 1888. II. 223.[1]
— Die Arbeit Herrn H. Waldner's. 1884. II. 302.[1]
— Bromeliaceae. 1891. II. 76.[2]
— Broméliacées. 1896. II. 76.[2]
— Über die geographische Anordnung der Lorbeergewächse des tropischen Amerika. 1892. II. 223.[1]
— Geschlechtsänderung einer Weide. 1883. II. 109.[1]
— Lauraceae americanae. 1889. II. 223.[1]
— Morphologische ... Studien über ... Cordieae. 1890. II. 748.[1]
— Morphologische Studien über ... Lauraceae. 1888. II. 223.[2]
— Spicilegium Laureanum. 1892. II. 223.[1]
Mezger, Leo. Zusammenstellung der in Württemberg ... in Forst- und Jagdsachen gegebenen Gesetze. 1834. IV. 322.[2]
Mézières, Nicolas Le Camus de. *See* Le Camus de Mézières, Nicolas.
The **Mezquit-tree**. 1865. III. 485.[1]
Mezzi per conservare il legname. 1861. IV. 418.
Mialaret, Théophile. L'ile des Pins. 1897. III. 132,[2] IV. 402.[1]
Mialhe, Louis. Note pour servir à l'histoire de l'action de la santonine. 1858. III. 754.[2]
Miall, Louis Compton & Carrington, Benjamin. The flora of the West Riding. 1862. I. 401.
— Forest vegetation. 1894. IV. 409.
Mian Moti Singh. Another effect of the influence of climate on forest vegetation. 1894. IV. 409.
— Deodar in Kulu. *See* Singh, M. M. 1882. IV. 448.[1] — 1893. IV. 447.[2]
— The hill forests of Bashahr. 1894. IV. 378.
— Mixed forests of Deodar and Blue Pine. *See* Singh, M. M. 1894. IV. 447.[2]
— Raising Box from seed. 1896. IV. 525.
Miani, Marco Antonio. Relazione letta al Senato della repubblica veneta. 1852. IV. 364.
Mlaskowski, August von. Die Agrar-, Alpen- und Forstverfassung der deutschen Schweiz. 1878. IV. 28.[1]
— Die Verfassung der Land-, Alpen- und Forstwirthschaft der deutschen Schweiz. 1878. IV. 28.[1]
Miasoyedof, A. I. *See* Мисоѣдовъ, А. И.
Micali, Giuseppe. I boschi e l'infiteusi. 1862. IV. 165.
Micard. Gemmage des Pins maritimes du département de la Sarthe. 1844. IV. 467.[2]
Micé, Léopold. Rapport méthodique sur les progrès de la chimie organique. 1869. I. 151.[1]
Miceli, (*ministro di agricoltura*). Intorno alla esecuzione della legge forestale 20 Giugno 1877. 1881. IV. 328.
Michael, von. Grundprincipien für die polygonometrische Messung der geschlossenen Waldungen. 1873. IV. 264.
Michael, J. Forest service in India. 1887. IV. 295.[1]
— Forestry. 1895. IV. 275.
— Report of the Annamullay forests. 1855. IV. 377.[1]
Michael, Paul Oskar. Vergleichende Untersuchungen über den Bau des Holzes der Compositen, Caprifoliaceen. 1885. II. 808,[2] 893,[2] 950.[1]
Michael, Wexionius. De regno vegetabili. 1656. I. 286.
Michaelis, A. Repetitorium und Examinatorium der Botanik. 1851. I. 89.
Michaelis, C. Ueber Anwendung von Probestreifen. 1887. IV. 237.
— Ansucht von Weihnachtsbäumen. 1898. IV. 454.
— Beginn des Lichtungszuwachses in Fichten. 1884. IV. 454.

— Einiges zu unserer Nutzholz-Aushaltúng. 1900. IV. 387.²
— Untersuchungen über den Einfluss des Unterwuchses. 1885. IV. 507.
— Zum Werthzuwachs. 1896. IV. 259.¹
— Der Werthzuwachs der Kiefer. 1887. IV. 481.
— Zuwachsleistung von Kiefern-Ueberhältern. 1887. IV. 481.
— Der "Zuwachsverlust" nach Raupenfrass in Kiefern. 1887. IV. 478.
— & Borggreve, Bernhard. Das mittlere Zuwachs-Procent. 1884. IV. 233.
Michaëlis, Paul. Beiträge zur . . . Anatomie der Gattungen Echinocactus. 1896. II. 588.²
Michalek, Carl. Die Bestandesmassenaufnahme. 1891. IV. 219.
Michalet, Eugène. Notice sur quelques plantes . . . dans le département du Jura. 1854. I. 411.
Michalowsky, Jobaun Jakob. De principio plantarum odoro. 1788. I. 182.¹
Michalus, Sándor. A Syringa Josikaea előjövetéléről. 1887. II. 715.¹
Michaud, Gustave. Achras Sapota. 1891. III. 666.²
— Recherches chimiques sur la sapotine. 1891. III. 666.²
— Sapotine, nouveau glucoside. 1891. III. 666.²
Michaud, Louis. Note sur la végétation de quelques points des Alpes. 1856. I. 435.
— Végétation de la Colline. 1856. I. 435.
Michaux. See VILMORIN & MICHAUX.
Michaux, André. Flora boreali-americana. 1803. I. 305, V. XVI.²
— Geschichte der amerikanischen Eichen. 1801. II. 128.¹
— Histoire des Chênes de l'Amérique. 1801. II. 128.¹
— Mémoire sur la naturalisation des arbres forestiers de l'Amérique septentrionale. 1805. IV. 126.²
— Notice de quelques plantes . . . observées dans l'Amérique septentrionale. 1792. I. 305.
— Portions of the journal . . . written during his travels in the United States. 1889. I. 308.
Michaux, François André. Des Eichen der Vereinigten Staaten. 1812. II. 128.²
— Histoire des arbres forestiers de l'Amérique septentrionale. 1810. I. 304, IV. 75,² V. XVI.²
— Mémoire sur la Zeikoua. 1831. II. 145.¹
— The North American sylva. 1810. I. 304, IV. 75.²
— The North American sylva. 1817. II. 128.²
— Notice sur le Robinia Pseudo-Acacia. 1835. III. 486.¹
— Notice sur les îles Bermudes. 1806. I. 335.
— Oaks of the United States and of Canada. 1812. II. 128.²
— Sur le Pinus australis. 1830. III. 308.¹
— Reise in das Innere der nordamerikanischen Freistaaten. 1804. I. 305.
— Travels to the westward of the Allegany mountains. 1804. I. 305.
— Voyage à l'ouest des monts Alléghanys. 1804. I. 305.
Micheels, Henri. Sur les canaux gommeux chez le Carludovica. 1898. II. 76.²
— Contribution à l'étude anatomique . . . chez Carludovica. 1899. II. 76.²
— De la dénomination des plantes horticoles. 1888. I. 254.¹
— Sur la forme des embryons de Palmiers. 1892. II. 63.¹
— Sur les germinations de Palmiers. 1893. II. 63.¹
— De la présence de raphides dans l'embryon de certains Palmiers. 1891. II. 63.¹
— Recherches . . . sur les axes fructifères des Palmiers. 1893. II. 63.¹
— Recherches sur les jeunes Palmiers. 1889. II. 63.¹
— Remarque au sujet des fruits du Didymosperma. 1892. II. 68.¹
Michel. Considérations sur les plantations dans les villes. 1861. III. 209.
Michel. Projet de loi relatif à la restauration . . . des terrains en montagne. 1880. IV. 163.
Michel & Guinon. Rapport sur le Wei-Hwa. 1847. III. 488.¹
Michel, A. F. Dissolution du lo-kao. 1858. III. 542.¹
— Note sur la substitution du bois de Châtaignier. 1864. IV. 493.¹
— Recherches sur la matière colorante des Nerpruns. 1858. III. 542.¹
Michel, Étienne. Traité du Citronier. 1816. II. 401.¹
Michel, J. P. A. Guide pratique du cultivateur de Mûriers. 1839. III. 375.
Michel, M. Flore de Fraipont. 1877. I. 393.¹
— & Remacle, N. Additions à la flore de Fraipont. 1879. I. 393.¹

Michel, Rudolf Wilhelm. Tentamen botanico-medicum de Artemisiis usitatis. 1834. III. 754.²
Michelazzi, Augustin. Compendium regni vegetabilis. 18 . . ? I. 255.
Michelberger, von. Wahrnehmungen und Erfahrungen über . . . Lebensweise derjenigen Insekten. 1843. IV. 206.
Michelena, Bernabé & Romero Gilsanz, Felipe. Memoria sobre la repoblación . . . de Valladolid. 1882. IV. 165.
Micheletti, Luigi. Circa taluni entomocecidi. 1895. I. 215.²
Micheli. Nuova proprietà della Robinia. 1810. III. 486.²
Micheli, Marc. Contributions à la flore du Paraguay. 1883. I. 345, II. 319.¹
— Deutzia discolor purpurascens. 1895. II. 239.¹
— Erythrina Constantiana. 1896. III. 476.¹
— Greffage du Clianthus Dampieri. 1900. III. 473.¹
— Le jardin du Crest. 1896. I. 65.¹
— Les Légumineuses de l'Ecuador. 1892. II. 319.¹
— Légumineuses. 1883. II. 319.¹
— Légumineuses nouvelles de l'Amérique Centrale. 1894. II. 319.¹
— Leguminosae. 1891. II. 319.¹
— Lupinus arboreus Sims. 1899. III. 481.³
— Marlea begoniifolia. 1898. II. 615.¹
— Note sur les Onagrariées du Brésil. 1874. II. 645.²
— Notes du jardin du Crest. 1899. III. 475.²
— Notes sur quelques plantes nouvelles. 1895. III. 396,¹ 410.¹
— Les nouveaux Opuntia rustiques. 1900. III. 624.¹
— Onagraceae. 1875. II. 642.²
— Principales publications de physiologie végétale. 1877. I. 2.
— Quelques observations sur la matière colorante. 1867. I. 141.
— Quelques travaux récents de physiologie végétale. 1871. I. 147.
— Revue des principales publications de physiologie végétale en 1877. 1878. I. 2.
— Rhododendron Smirnowii. 1899. II. 683.² — 1900. III. 662.²
— On some recent researches in vegetable physiology. 1871. I. 147.
— Spiraea Millefolium. 1900. II. 311.¹
— Vorläufige Mittheilungen neuer Onagrarieen. 1874. II. 645.²
— & André, Édouard. Tamarix hispida. 1894. II. 562.²
Micheli, Pietro Antonio. Catalogus plantarum Horti caesarei florentini. 1748. I. 61.
— Nova plantarum genera. 1729. I. 290.
— & Mannaioni, G. B. Relazione del viaggio . . . stato Senese. 1754. I. 424.
Micheli de Chateauvieux. Über die Naturalisation der Cedern vom Libanon. 1828. III. 300.¹
Michelin. Greffage des Noyers. 1883. III. 355.
— Note sur des arbres fruitiers atteints du blanc des racines. 1876. III. 446.¹
— Note sur un lot d'Olives. 1883. III. 669,³ 676.¹
— Restauration et rajeunissement des arbres. 1880. III. 181.²
Michelini, G. B. Boschi e selve. 1866. IV. 41.¹
Michelis, F. Das Formentwicklungsgesetz im Pflanzenreiche. 1869. I. 261.
Michelson, Henry. Forests in their relation to irrigation. 1899. IV. 52, 542.²
— Les forêts dans leurs rapports avec l'irrigation. 1899. IV. 52.
— Los montes en sus relaciones con los riegos. 1899. IV. 542.²
Michener, Ezra. Notes on the English Walnut. 1884. III. 355.
Michetus, Eugenius. Lexicon botanicum. 1675. I. 287.
Michie, Christopher Young. On the blending and harmonizing of the foliage. 1868. III. 205.¹
— On charcoal-producing plants. 1872. IV. 394.
— On the culture and uses of the common Silver Fir. 1869. IV. 446.¹
— On the diseases most incidental to forest trees. 1868. IV. 195.²
— On diseases of forest trees. 1863. IV. 195.²
— On the economic uses . . . of timber grown in Scotland. 1869. IV. 398.²
— On the effects of dry season of 1868. 1871. III. 183.²
— On the effects of wet as compared with dry seasons. 1874. III. 183.³

Michie, Christopher Young (*continued*).
-- Forestry. 1876. IV. 454.
— On the formation . . . of young plantations. 1865. IV. 120.—1871. IV. 120
— Game covert. 1881. III. 215.¹
— On the general management of plantations. 1872. IV. 120.
— Hedgerow timber. 1882. III. 215.¹
— Hedges. 1882. III. 214.¹
— On home grown timber. 1872. IV. 396.¹
— The Larch. 1882. IV. 449.
— The Larch disease. 1896. IV. 451.
— Ornamental hedges and fences. 1882. III. 214.²
— Planting. 1875. III. 167.
— Della potatura degli alberi forestali. 1881. IV. 172.¹
— The practice of forestry. 1888. IV. 108.²
— Prices of forest produce. 1881. IV. 405.¹
— On the pruning of forest trees. 1869. IV. 171.
— Pruning of forest trees. 1881. IV. 172.¹
. — Report on Larch forests. 1869. IV. 452.¹
— Report on the cultivation of Willows. 1863. III. 347.
— Report on the general management of plantations. 1869. IV. 120.
— Report on the management and sale of timber. 1867. IV. 120.
— Report on the management and value of Poplar. 1869. IV. 485.¹
— Report on trees not liable to be destroyed by rabbits. 1869. III. 186.¹
— The Silver Fir. 1869. IV. 446.¹ — 1884. IV. 444.¹
— On stem and branch pruning of Coniferae. 1873. III. 295.¹
— Surface draining. 1881. IV. 144.¹
— On thinning plantations. 1869. IV. 173.
— Thinning plantations. 1881. IV. 173.
— Thinning Scotch Fir plantations. 1880. IV. 173, 478.
— On the transplanting of forest trees. 1869. III. 167.
— Value of Scotch Fir plantations. 1880. IV. 481.
— On the various kinds of trees . . . suited for planting within the influence of the sea-breeze. 1869. III. 41.¹
Michie, John. A visit to the Thuringian forest. 1895. IV. 356.¹
Michiels, Édouard. Arbres forestiers et d'ornement. 1895. III. 203.
Michiels, Gustave. Le lupin jaune. 1894. IV. 545.²
— Les prairies-vergers. 1888. III. 140.²
Michigan — Agricultural experiment station. See MICHIGAN — STATE AGRICULTURAL COLLEGE . . . III. 5.
Michigan — State agricultural college — Agricultural experiment station. Annual report. Bulletin. Elementary science bulletin. Special bulletin. III. 5.
Michigan — State independent forestry commission. Proceedings. Report. IV. 4.
Michigan academy of science. Report. I. 6.
The Michigan law for tree-planting by the roadsides. 1883. III. 200.²
Michigan state board of agriculture. Annual report. III. 5.
Michigan state horticultural society. Annual report. III. 5.
Michigan state pomological society. Annual report. See MICHIGAN STATE HORTICULTURAL SOCIETY. III. 5.
Michler, Wilhelm. Untersuchungen über die anatomischen Verhältnisse des Chlorophylls. See MOHL, Hugo von. 1837. I. 140.²
Michon, Joseph. See COUANON, Georges, MICHON, Joseph & SALOMON, E.; RIVIÈRE, Charles, COSSON, Ernest & MICHON, Joseph.
Michot, Norbert Louis. Flore du Hainaut. 1845. I. 392.
— De l'instinct des plantes. 1853. I. 193.²
— Tableau botanique de la méthode naturelle. 1842. I. 261.
Miciol. Note sur l'Ulex-Gallii Planch. 1882. II. 387.¹
— Notes sur les Rosiers du Nord-Finistère. 1883. II. 286.¹
Mickey, J. An essay on Osage hedge culture. 1873. III. 372.¹
— Osage Orange hedge. 1879. III. 372.¹
— Osage Orange hedging. 1874. III. 372.¹
Micklitz, Julius. Ueber die Einwirkungen des Waldes. 1877. IV. 50.
— Die forstlichen Vegetations-Verhältnisse des Altvater-Gebirges. 1857. IV. 368.
— Gutachten über den Zustand . . . der . . . Troppau [sic] gehörigen Forste. 1881. IV. 369.
— Ueber Sturmverheerungen. 1852. IV. 189.¹
— See also MICKLITZ, Robert & Julius.
Micklitz, N. Der Femelwald. 1875. IV. 130.

Micklitz, Robert. Die Anwendung der Cameraltaxations-Methode. 1882. IV. 244.
— Beiträge zu der Abhandlung: " Wie weit reicht die Wichtigkeit der Wälder?" 1851. IV. 52.
— Ueber Einigung und Vereinfachung im Taxationswesen. 1860. IV. 243.
— Ueber Forstbetriebseinrichtung. 1894. IV. 246.
— Forstliche Haushaltungskunde. 1859. IV. 287.
— Die forstliche Production. 1874. IV. 118.
— Holz als Papierstoff. 1867. IV. 429.²
— Ueber Holzhauerwerkzeuge. 1860. IV. 383.²
— Der jährliche Nachhaltsbetrieb. 1872. IV. 255.
— Kartirung und Abschätzung der Forste. 1874. IV. 251.¹
— Ueber Massenzuwachs und Nutzungsprocente. 1872. IV. 243.
— Ueber Pottasche-Erzeugung. 1855. IV. 395.
— Die Verordnung für die forstlichen Staatsprüfungen in Oesterreich. 1869. IV. 36.²
— & Julius. Beleuchtung der Grundsätze . . . des Rationellen Waldwirthes von M. R. Pressler. 1861. IV. 243.
— Nachträgliche Beobachtungen über . . . Holzhauerwerkzeuge. 1860. IV. 383.²
— & Lembing, Eduard. Forst-Schematismus für Mähren und Schlesien. 1861. IV. 368.
Micklitz, Th. Die Bewerthung der Schälschäden. 1894. IV. 197.¹
— Versuchsculturen mit Picea sitkaënsis Carrière. 1893. IV. 460.²
La micrographie forestière à l'exposition de 1889. 1890. IV. 37.¹
Microscopic journal. III. 18.
Microscopical society of London. Transactions. I. 19. See also MICROSCOPIC journal. III. 18.
The microscopical theatre of seeds. See PARSONS, James. 1745. I. 120, III. 219.²
Miczyński, Kásmér. Action des gelées sur les tissus du . Poirier. 1889. II. 280.²
— O smaraaniu skanek gruszy. 1890. I. 212, III. 446.²
Een middel tegen sprinkhanen. 1900. III. 737.
Middeldorpf, (*Oberförster*). Drehwüchsige Kiefern. 1873. II. 47.²
— Forstliche Versuche auf vulkanischem Sandboden. 1873. IV. 69.
— Schätzung der Loh-Hecke. 1873. IV. 512.
— Die Vertilgung der Kiefernraupe. 1872. IV. 199,² 476.
— & Bary, Anton de. Beitrag zur Lärchenkrankheit. 1874. IV. 450.
— & Pannewitz, Julius von. Welche Bäume trifft der Blitz nicht? 1866. IV. 194.
Middeldorpf, (*Oberförster, Pütt*). Ueber das Abfangen der Kiefernraupe. 1869. IV. 476.
— Beiträge zur Kenntniss . . . der Schwarzkiefer. 1868. IV. 465.²
— Der Waldpflug. 1867. IV. 143.¹
Middeldorpf, (*Oberförster, Stoberau*). Beiträge zu der Frage: Sind . . . die Oderwälder Schlesiens erheblich vermindert worden. 1863. IV. 353.
— Zum Eichenschälwaldbetrieb. 1854. IV. 512.
— Zum Eichen-Schälwald-Betrieb. 1862. IV. 512.
— Einige Bemerkungen über Erfahrungstafeln. 1860. IV. 236.
— Der Ertrag der schlesischen Weidenwerder. 1859. IV. 487.¹
— Über Ertrag und Gewicht der Waldstreu. 1863. IV. 437.²
— Ertrag und Verwerthung eines . . . Kiefern-Bestandes in k. Forstrevier Stoberau. 1857. IV. 260.²
— Folgen der Ueberschwemmung . . . Stoberau. 1855. IV. 185.¹
— Die Hannemann'sche Keimplatte. 1870. III. 156.¹
— Keimprobe. 1873. III. 156.²
— Kiefern- und Fichtenpflanzung. 1862. IV. 453.
— Massen-Angaben einiger Weissbuchen. 1854. V. XXXI.¹
— Zur Praxis des Holzdiebstahlsesetzes. 1854. IV. 320.
— Rothbuchen im Flussthale. 1862. IV. 494.
— Vermehrung der Holzproduktion. 1864. IV. 141.
— Wie kann bei den Forst-Unterbeamten das Interesse für Kulturen geweckt . . . werden? 1869. IV. 310.²
— Zuwachszang von Kiefern. 1866. IV. 480.
Middeldorpf, F. C. Anleitung zur Waldeintheilung, Schätzung. 1868. IV. 240.
Middelen tegen de Koffiebladziekte. 1899. III. 737.
Middendorff, Alexander Theodor von. Die Gewächse Sibiriens. 1864. I. 454.¹
— Reise in den äussersten Norden und Osten Sibiriens. 1847. I. 455, V. XXIII.¹

Middleton, M. Lyons. Epigaea repens. 1890. II. 663.²
Midland floral magazine. *See* The BIRMINGHAM botanic garden. III. 16.
The **Midland** florist. III. 17.
Midland naturalist. I. 19.
Midloch, Adolf. Dvě odrůdy našich Smrků. 1888. II. 35.¹
— Hra přírody či odruda Sosny? 1884. II. 46.²
— O Jalovcích. 1898. IV. 448.³
— Jehličnaté stromoví v Královské Oboře. 1899. IV. 441. — 1900. II. 16.²
— Larix europaea a varietas pallida. 1896. II. 33.¹
— Mechy našich lesův. 1897. IV. 211.¹
— Neues Dendrometer. 1887. IV. 216.
— O růstu Modřínů na Vlašimsku. 1900. IV. 450.
— Versuche über den Genauigkeitsgrad verschiedener Kubirungs-Methoden. 1886. IV. 228.
Midy, L. L'essence de Santal. 1882. III. 384.²
— Essential oil of Sandal. 1882. III. 384.²
Mieczyński, Adam. Zasady leśnictwa. 1861. IV. 94.
Mieg, Achilles. Specimen miscellaneum anatomico-botanicum. *See* STUPANUS, J. R. 1751. I. 291.
Mieg, Fernando. Breves observaciones sobre la memoria . . . Suelo, clima . . . de Vizcaya. 1858. IV. 363.¹
Miégeville, (*abbé*). Étude des Daphnoidées des Pyrénées. 1888. II. 601.¹
Miehe, A. F. Nonnulla de strychninii applicatione. 1837. III. 682.¹
Mielck, Eduard. Die Riesen der Pflanzenwelt. 1863. I. 295.¹
Mielke, G. Anatomische . . . Beobachtungen an den Blättern einiger Eucalyptus-Arten. 1892. II. 623.²
— De la position qu'occupent les acides tanniques. 1895. I. 180.²
— Ueber die Stellung der Gerbsäuren. 1894. I. 180.²
Mier. *See* BARRIO, Matias & MIER.
Een mier . . . die Sparrenstammen beschadigt. 1871. IV. 445.
Miers, John. On Aextoxicum and Bursinopetalum. 1862. II. 436,¹ 656.²
— On another new species of Lardizabala. 1858. II. 201.³
— On the Apocynaceae of South America. 1878. II. 721.²
— On the Auxemmeae. 1875. II. 747.²
— On the Barringtoniaceae. 1875. II. 611.¹
— On the Canellaceae. 1858. II. 566.¹
— On the comparative carpical structure of the Ehretiaceae. 1869. II. 747.²
— Contributions to botany. 1851. I. 269.
— Contributions to the botany of South America. 1845. II. 768.¹ — 1849. I. 329.
— Descriptions of new species of plants . . . in South Brazil. 1863. I. 343.
— On the development of the vegetable ovule called " anatroplus." 1859. I. 122.
— Un Dichlidanthera. 1859. II. 704.¹
— On the Ehretiaceae. 1860. II. 747.² — 1869. II. 747.²
— On Ephedra. 1862. II. 54.¹
— A few remarks on the Menispermaceae. 1851. II. 205.²
— On the genera Goetzia and Espadea. 1870. II. 771,² 772.¹
— On the genera of the tribe Duboisieae. 1853. II. 768.¹
— On the genus Atamisquea. 1852. II. 229.²
— On the genus Crescentia. 1868. II. 787.²
— On the genus Habrothamnus. 1850. II. 770.¹
— On the genus Lycium. 1854. II. 772.²
— On the genus Symbolanthus. 1869. II. 721.²
— On the genus Villaresia. 1864. II. 476.¹
— On the genus Withania. 1849. II. 778.²
— On Goupia. 1862. II. 469.¹
— On the Hippocrateaceae of South America. 1871. II. 471.²
— On the history of the Maté plant. 1851. II. 462.² — 1861. III. 529.²
— Illustrations of South American plants. 1849. II. 768.¹
— On the Lecythidaceae. 1874. II. 611.¹
— List of species of plants collected by Mr. Weir. 1863. I. 342.
— On Marupa, a genus of the Simarubaceae. 1880. II. 414.²
— On Marupa, a new genus. 1873. II. 414.²
— Menispermaceae. 1864. II. 206.¹
— On the Menispermaceae. 1864. II. 206.¹
— On Napoleona, Omphalocarpum and Asteranthos. 1875. II. 611,¹ 699.³
— On the natural order Styraceae. 1859. II. 704.¹

— On the nature and origin of the external coatings of seeds. 1856. I. 120.
— On a new species of Lardizabala. 1851. II. 201.¹
— Notes on Moquilea. 1880. II. 265.¹
— Observations on some of the Heliotropieae. 1860. II. 747.²
— Observations on some of the Heliotropieae. 1868. II. 747.²
— Observations on the affinities of the Icacinaceae. 1852. II. 474.¹
— Observations on the affinities of the Olacaceae. 1851. II. 170.¹
— Observations on the Bignoniaceae. 1851. II. 784.¹ — 1861. II. 784.¹
— Observations on the Solanaceae. 1853. II. 767.²
— Observations on the structure of the seed . . . in the Clusiaceae. 1855. II. 552.²
— Observations upon several genera hitherto placed in Solanaceae. 1849. II. 767.²
— On the position of Monttea, Reyesia. 1864. II. 781.¹
— Remarks on the nature of the outer fleshy covering of the seed in the Clusiaceae, Magnoliaceae. 1856. I. 120.
— Report on the plants collected by Mr. Weir. 1863. II. 784.²
— On the Schoepfiene and Cervantesieae. 1880. II. 696.²
— On several instances of the anomalous development of the raphe in seeds. 1856. I. 120, *II. 475.*²
— On some genera of the Icacinaceae. 1852. II. 474.¹
— On some genera of the Olacaceae. 1880. II. 170.²
— On some South-American genera. 1880. I. 330.
— On the Symplocaceae. 1880. II. 703.¹
— On three new genera of the Verbenaceae from Chile and its adjacent regions. 1870. II. 760.²
— Travels in Chile and La Plata. 1826. I. 329.
— On the tribe Colletieae. 1860. II. 491.²
— On the Tricuspidarieae. 1860. II. 509.²
— On two genera of plants from Chile. 1853. II. 781.¹
— On Villaresia. 1862. II. 476.¹
— Volksnamen chilesischer Pflanzen. 1862. I. 72.¹
— On the Winteraceae. 1858. II. 208.²
Mierzinski, Stanislaus. Die Gerb- und Farbstoff-Extracte. 1887. III. 236, 237.²
Miessler, Otto. *See* ZIEGLER, H. von, KLIFFHAUSEN & MIESSLER, Otto.
Mietzsch, C. W. Empfehlenswerte Blütensträucher für Einzelpflanzung. 1900. III. 203.
— Prunus serotina pendula. 1882. III. 442.²
Miglinski, A. *See* МИГЛИНСКІЙ, A.
Migliorato, Erminio. Brevi osservazioni sulla natura assile delle spine delle Auranziacee. 1896. II. 401.²
— Elenco di anomalie vegetali. 1896. I. 144.¹
Migneret, S. Traité de l'affouage dans les bois communaux. 1840. IV. 334.¹
Mignerot. Forêts domaniales de Chênes-Liége. 1894. IV. 517.³
Migout, Abel. Additions à la Flore de l'Allier. 1866. I. 535.¹
— Flore du département de l'Allier. 1866. I. 413, 535.¹
— Les Rosa de la flore de l'Allier. 1888. II. 286.¹
Mihálka, Anton. Növénytan. 1856. I. 90.
Mihályffy, Ernő. Az erdő és kögazdasági jelentőségre. 1883. IV. 270.
Mik, Joseph. Flora der Umgebung von Olmütz. 1860. I. 441.
Mikan, J. G. Catalogus plantarum . . . Hortus botanicus pragensis. 1876. I. 66.¹
Mikan, Johann Christian. Delectus florae et faunae brasiliensis. 1820. I. 341.
— Ueber Galläpfel und Knoppern. 1816. IV. 502.¹
— Ueber Zucker-Erzeugung aus Ahorn-Saft. 1811. III. 534.²
Miklos, Alexander SEBEŐK DE SZENT-. *See* SEBEŐK DE SZENT-MIKLOS, Alexander.
Miklosvar, Julius Miklos von. Bietet die Anlage von Weingärten im Sande absoluten Schutz gegen die Reblaus. 1890. III. 574.
Miklouho-Maclay, N. de. List of plants in use by the natives of the Maclay-coast. 1886. III. 93.²
— Note on the " Kéu " of the Maclay-coast. 1886. III. 342.¹
Mikolaschek, Carl. Esperienze sull' elasticità e la resistenza dei principali legnami della Boemia.. 1879. IV. 410.
— Experiencias sobre la elasticidad y la resistencia de las principales maderas de Bohemia. 1879. IV. 410.
— Untersuchungen über die Elasticität und Festigkeit der . . . Nutzhölzer Böhmens. 1879. IV. 410.

Mikosch, Karl. Beiträge zur Anatomie und Morphologie der Knospendecken. 1876. I. 108.[1]
— Ueber die Entstehung der Chlorophyllkörner. 1886. I. 142.
— Ueber die Organe der Ausscheidung der Betulorentinsäure an der Birke. 1876. II. 118.[1]
— Untersuchungen über die Entstehung der Chlorophyll-körner. 1879. I. 141.
— Untersuchungen über die Entstehung und den Bau der Hoftüpfel. 1882. II. 17.[1]
— & Stöhr, Adolf. Untersuchungen über den Einfluss des Lichtes auf die Chlorophyllbildung. 1881. I. 173.
Die mikroskopischen Feinde des Waldes. 1866. IV. 211.[1]
Mikszewicz, Julius. Der Thee. 1852. III. 607.
Milan. Nog eens over zaadkeuze. 1900. III. 733.[2]
Milani, A. Ein Beitrag zur Kenntniss von den Schälbeschädi-gungen. 1895. IV. 197.[1]
Milani, Giovanni Battista. Supplemento alla flora delle Alpi versiliesi. 1885. I. 429.
Milek. *See* TANTON, MILEK & others.
Miller, E. Alnus glutinosa monstrosa. 1879. III. 356.[2]
— Deux nouvelles variétés d'Aulnes. 1879. III. 356.[2]
— Un Palmier de serre froide. 1882. III. 322.[1]
— Le puceron lanigère. 1894. III. 428.[1]
— De wollige bloedluis. 1894. III. 428.[1]
Miles, George Thomas. Darwinia tulipifera. 1879. III. 633.[2]
Miles, S. B. On the neighbourhood of Bunder Marayah. 1872. III. 281.[2]
Milet-Mureau, Louis Marie Antoine Destouff de. Voyage de La Pérouse autour du monde. 1797. I. 302.
Milhau. Dissertation sur le Cacaoyer. 1746. III. 594.
— Dissertation sur le Caffeyer. 1746. III. 741.
Milhe-Poutingon, Albert. Jardins botaniques et Jardins d'essai. 1898. III. 29.[1]
Milius, Josephus. Voltolinas. De hortorum cultura libri tres. 1574. III. 98.
On milk, and its adulterations, in Paris. 1830. III. 434.[2]
Mill, H. R. *See* RATTRAY, John & MILL, H. R.
Mill, J. Abhandlung von der Eichzucht. 1765. IV. 503.[2]
Millardet, Alexis. Sur les altérations que le phylloxera dé-termine. 1878. III. 571.
— Des altérations que produit le Phylloxera. 1880. III. 572.[2]
— Sur l'anatomie ... du corps ligneux dans les genres Yucca et Dracaena. 1865. II. 81,[3] 87.[1]
— Essai sur l'hybridation de la Vigne. 1891. III. 549.[2]
— Essai sur le mildiou. 1882. III. 578.
— Étude des altérations produites par le phylloxéra. 1898. III. 762.
— Étude sur les Vignes d'origine américaine. 1876. III. 570.[1]
— Études sur quelques espèces de Vignes sauvages. 1879. III. 556.
— Histoire des principales variétés ... de Vignes d'origine américaine. 1878. II. 505.[2]
— Sur l'histoire du traitement du mildiou. 1885. III. 579.
— Importance de l'hybridation pour la reconstruction des vignobles. 1894. III. 557.[1]
— Instruction pratique pour le traitement du mildiou. 1889. III. 580.
— Sur le mildew de la Vigne. 1893. III. 581.
— Note sur l'hybridation sans croisement. 1894. I. 246.[1]
— Note sur le cancre du Pommier. 1886. III. 444.[1]
— Note sur les Vignes américaines. 1875. III. 567.[2]
— Note sur quelques hybrides de Vignes américaines. 1880. II. 505.[2]
— Notes sur les Vignes américaines. 1881. III. 556.
— Notice pour servir à l'histoire du développement en épais-seur des parois cellulaires. 1866. I. 138.[1]
— Nouvelles Groot en algemeen kruidkunde de la tension. 1866. II. 373.[1]
— Nouvelles recherches sur la résistance & l'immunité phyl-loxériques. 1892. III. 561.
— Nouvelles recherches sur le développement ... du mil-diou. 1887. III. 561.
— Le pourridié de la Vigne. 1879. III. 578.
— Pourridié et phylloxera. 1882. III. 561.
— La question des Vignes americaines. 1877. III. 556.
— Résistance au phylloxera. 1878. III. 571.
— Théorie nouvelle des altérations que le phylloxera déter-mine. 1878. III. 571.
—Sur le traitement du mildew. 1885. III. 579.
— Traitement du mildiou et du rot. 1886. III. 579.
— *See also* GAYON, Ulysse & MILLARDET, Alexis.
— & Gayon, Ulysse. De l'action du mélange de sulfate de cuivre. 1885. III. 579.
— — De l'action qu'exerce le mélange de chaux. 1885. III. 579.
— — Considérations raisonnées sur les divers procédés de traitement du mildiou. 1887. III. 579.
— — Effets du mildew. 1885. III. 579.
— — Recherche du cuivre sur les ceps de Vignes. 1885. III. 579.
— — Recherches nouvelles sur l'action que les composés cuivreux exercent sur le ... Peronospora. 1887. III. 579.
— — Recherches sur les effets des divers procédés de traite-ment du mildiou. 1887. III. 579.
— & Grasset, Ch. de. Catalogue des hybrides de Vignes. 1894. III. 547.
Millaud. Conifères nouvellement introduits. 1870. III. 290.
— Marsdenia erecta. 1870. III. 694.[1]
— Multiplication de la Glycine blanche. 1872. III. 490.[2]
Mille, Pierre. Notice sur la Côte d'Ivoire. 1900. III. 281.[1]
Miller. Bread from wood. 1878. IV. 433.[2]
— Farine de bois pour fabrication de pain. 1878. IV. 433.[2]
Miller, (colonel). On diseases of the Silver Fir. 1839. IV. 445.
Miller, Adolph W. Mezquite gum. 1876. III. 485.[1]
Miller, Elihu S. Amelanchier canadensis. 1871. II. 257.[2]
— & Young, H. W. Catalogue of the phænogamous ... plants of Suffolk county. 1874. I. 314.
Miller, Ellen & Whiting, M. C. Wild flowers of the north-eastern states. 1895. I. 316.
Miller, Francis. The husbandman's directory. 1770. III. 109.
Miller, G. P. The forestry problem. 1894. IV. 272.[1]
Miller, Heinrich. Phaenologische Beobachtungen. 1895. I. 226.[1]
— Phaenologische Beobachtungen bei Koschmin. 1897. I. 528.[1]
— Starke Eiche bei Ostrowo. 1896. II. 139.[2]
Miller, John. Wooded areas. 1894. V. XVII.[1]
Miller, John (*formerly* Johann Sebastian MUELLER). Illus-tratio systematis sexualis Linnaeani. 1777. I. 258.
— Illustratio systematis sexualis Linnaei. 1777. I. 258.
— An illustration of the sexual system of Linnaeus. 1777. I. 258.
— An illustration of the Termini botanici. 1777. I. 258.
— Tabulae iconum ... ad Illustrationem. 1777. I. 258.
Miller, John (*of Bristol*). Bristol nursery. 1826. I. 54.
Miller, John Frederick. Cimelia physica. 1776. I. 262.
— A curious collection of insects and plants. 1759. I. 261.
— Icones plantarum. 1780. I. 262.
— Various subjects of natural history. 1776. I. 262.
Miller, Joseph. Botanicum officinale. 1722. III. 54.
Miller, K. *See* МИЛЛЕРЪ, К.
Miller, Philip. Abbildungen der nützlichsten, schönsten ... Pflanzen. 1760. III. 81.
— Allgemeines Gärtner-Lexicon. 1731. III. 80.
— Calendrier des jardiniers. 1732. III. 109.
— Catalogus plantarum ... in hortis non procul a Londino. 1730. I. 52.
— Catalogus plantarum officinalium. 1730. I. 52.
— Dictionnaire des jardiniers. 1731. III. 80.
— Das englische Gartenbuch. 1731. III. 80.
— Essai sur les arbres d'ornement. 1778. III. 78.[1]
— Figures of the most beautiful ... plants. 1760. III. 81.
— Gärtnerkalender. 1732. III. 109.
— The gardener's and botanist's dictionary. 1731. III. 80.
— The gardeners and florists dictionary. 1724. III. 30.
— The gardener's dictionary. 1731. III. 80.
— The gardener's dictionary ... abridged. 1735. III. 81.
— The gardeners kalendar. 1732. III. 109.
— Groot en algemeen kruidkundig ... bloemisten-woorden-boek. 1731. III. 80.
— Korte inleiding tot de kruidkunde. 1772. I. 83.
— Maandelijksche tuin oefeningen. 1732. III. 109.
— A method of raising some exotick seeds. 1729. III. 156.[1]
— Remarks upon the letter of Mr. John Ellis. 1758. II. 458.[1]
— Traité complet sur la manière de cultiver la Vigne. 1768. III. 554.[1]
— *See also* MAZEAS, Guillaume & MILLER, Philip.
Miller, Samuel. Grafting the Vine. 1868. III. 548.[1]
— Our native Persimmons. 1894. III. 670.[1]
— Persimmons substituting whisky. 1884. III. 670.[1]
— Timber-tree planting. 1892. IV. 112.

Miller, Samuel· Henry & Skertchly, S. B. J. The Fenland, past and present. *See* MARSHALL, William. 1878. I. 534.[1]
Miller, Thomas. Common wayside flowers. 1860. I. 401, 533.[1]
Miller, Wilhelm. Acalypha. 1900. III. 61.[1]
Miller, Wilhelm von. Untersuchung des amerikanischen Storax. 1882. III. 418.[1]
Miller, Wilham. A dictionary of English names of plants. 1884. I. 74.[1]
— Passiflora macrocarpa. 1870. III. 616.[1]
— Tree measurement. 1887. IV. 216.
Millet. Sur les nouveaux procédés proposés pour la conservation des bois. 1841. IV. 417.
— Nouvelles greffes du Rosier. 1829. III. 160.
Millet d'Aubenton, C. Notice sur la culture des oseraies. 1837. III. 347.
Millet de la Turtaudière, Pierre Aimé. État actuel de l'agriculture dans . . . Maine-et-Loire. 1856. III. 125.
— Indicateur de Maine et Loire. 1864. I. 413.
Milliau, Ernest. Procédé pour reconnaître la pureté des huiles de coprah. 1892. III. 324,[1] 383.[1]
Milligan. The timber of Tasmania. — Blue Gum. 1861. IV. 531.[1]
Milliken, Robert. Those Catalpas again; an inquiry. 1880. III. 705.
Millikin, Daniel. The best practical means of preserving . . . the forests of Ohio. 1871. IV. 178.[1] — 1872. IV. 271.[2]
— The ruin of the hills. 1887. IV. 46.[1]
Millin de Grandmaison, Aubin Louis. Élémens d'histoire naturelle. 1797. I. 93.
— Extrait d'un ouvrage de M. Kurt Sprengel sur l'histoire de la botanique. 1809. I. 79.[1]
Millischer, I. L'évaluation du revenu cadastral des forêts. 1899. IV. 551.[1]
— Exploitation d'une forêt de Pins. 1896. IV. 462,[1] 559.[1]
Millon, E. Mémoire sur la nature des parfums. 1856. I. 182,[2] III. 226.[2]
— Nouvelles propriétés du charbon de bois. 1860. IV. 431.[2]
Millot. Dangers de prendre des greffes sur les arbres malades. 1842. III. 160.
Millot. Histoire pharmaceutique du camphre. 1837. III. 233.[1]
Millot. Rapport sur . . . vignoble phylloxéré dans le midi. 1881. III. 572.
Millot, P. Coup d'œil sur la végétation des environs de Mostaganem. 1880. I. 485.
Mills, Edmund James. On sparteine. 1862. II. 351.[2]
Mills, H. F. Evidences of vorticular motion in the Lawrence tornado. 1892. III. 184.[2]
Mills, Henry. Excrescence on the stem of Cryptomeria. 1885. II. 29.[1]
— Staking trees. 1874. III. 198.[2]
Mills, Jared Warner. The Olive in Chino valley. 1896. III. 676.[2]
Mills, Stephen F. & Co. Catalogue of American trees . . . *See* CATALOGUE . . . 1827. I. 38.[2]
Millspaugh, Charles Frederick. American medicinal plants. 1887. III. 63.[1]
— Contribution to the flora of Yucatan. 1895. I. 333.
— Euphorbiaceae collected by T..S. Brandegee. 1890. II. 444.[1]
— Experiment with Austrian basket Osiers. 1891. III. 340.
— Native trees and shrubs of West Virginia. 1891. I. 517,[2] IV. 77.[2]
— Notes and new species of the genus Euphorbia. · 1898. II. 443.[1]
— Plantae insulae anannasensis. 1900. I. 337.
— Plantae utowanae. · 1900. I. 331.
— Preliminary catalogue of the flora of West Virginia. 1892. I. 319.
— & Nuttall, L. W. Flora of West Virginia. 1896. I. 319.[1]
Milman, Helen. My Roses & how I grew them. 1899. III. 453.[1]
Milne. *See* WHITLEY, BRAMES & MILNE.
Milne, Colin. A botanical dictionary. 1770. I. 32.
— A descriptive catalogue of rare and curious plants. 1773. I. 262.
— Institutes of botany. 1771. I. 257.
— & Gordon, Alexander. Indigenous botany. 1793. I. 396.
Milne, James. On t'e comparative advantages of cutting large timber by the axe or saw. 1872. IV. 383.[2]
Milne, Thomas. The afforesting of waste land. 1885. IV. 161.[1]

Milne, Thomas, (fl. 1795-1837). On the cultivation of the English Cranberry. 1824. III. 664.[1]
Milne, William. Extracts of letters received from . . . Old Calabar. 1864. I. 490.
— On the Palms of the Feejee Islands. 1860. II. 62.[1]
— On some of the plants used for food by the Fiji Islanders. 1859. III. 283.[2]
Milne Edwards, Alphonse. *See* EDWARDS, Alphonse ·MILNE.
Milne Edwards, Henri. *See* EDWARDS, Henri MILNE.
Milroy, Thomas R. S. The rearing . . . of hardwood plantations. 1884. IV. 137.[2]
Miltitz, Friedrich von. Bibliotheca botanica. 1829. I. 2.
— Handbuch der botanischen Literatur. 1829. I. 2.
Milton, Mansfield. Chamaedorea. 1877. III. 321.[2]
— Croton culture. 1876. III. 515.[2]
Milward, Edward. A letter concerning an antidote to the Indian poison. 1744. III. 481.[2]
Milyutin, Sergei N. *See* МИЛЮТИНЪ, С. Н.
Minà-Palumbo, Francesco. Monografia botanica . . . dei Pistacchi. *See* PALUMBO, F. M. 1882. III. 526.[1]
— Notizie sui Frassini di Sicilia. 1847. III. 672.[1]
Minden, Max von. Beiträge zur anatomischen . . . Kenntnis Wasser-secernierender Organe. 1899. I. 169.[2]
Minderer, Raimund. Aloedarium marocostinum. 1616. III. 333.[1]
Une mine d'arbres. 1894. IV. 557.[1]
The Miner Plum. 1882. III. 437.[1]
Der Mineralstoffgehalt der Waldsamen. 1883. IV. 64.[1]
Mines of wood. 1894. I. 459.
Minettus, Hieronymus. Quaestio . . . de Sarzaeparillae . . . viribus. 1593. III. 338,[1] 494.[1]
Mingaud, Galien. La Phyllotoma Aceris. 1900. III. 534.[1]
Mingaud, P. Herbier du basin de Saint-Jean-du-Gard. 1863. I. 412.
Mingaud, Philippe. De l'Arbousier. 1863. III. 647.[1]
— The Arbutus. 1863. III. 647.[1]
Mingioli, Eustachio. Conservazione delle frutta di autunno. 1895. III. 174.[1]
— Criteri . . . degli stabilimenti oleari. 1895. III. 679.[2]
— Monografia sull' analisi immediata delle Olive. 1883. III. 679.[1]
— Gli oli alle ultime esposizioni. 1895. III. 679.[2]
Minguez, Luis PEREZ. *See* PEREZ MINGUEZ, Luis.
A miniature Camellia. 1879. III. 599.[1]
Minichsdorfer, Ignaz. Ueber Aufforstungen mittels dichter Schwarzföhren-Saaten. 1867. IV. 465.[2]
Minière. Nouveau moyen de défense contre le mildiou. 1885. III. 578.
Miniscalchi, Luigi, *conte*. La coltivazione de' Gelsi. 1769. III. 373.
— Mororum libri tres. 1769. III. 373.
Ministère de l'agriculture — Direction des forêts. Bulletin. IV. 12.[2]
Ministère de l'agriculture de Belgique. Bulletin. IV. 15.
Ministerio de fomento. Dirección general de agricultura. 1892. IV. 553.[2]
Ministerio de fomento. Dirección general . . . Montes. 1891. IV. 554.
Ministerio de fomento. — Disposiciones oficiales. 1892. IV. 554.
Ministerio de fomento. — Escalafón general del Cuerpo de ingenieros de montes. 1892. IV. 550.[1]
Ministerio de fomento. Instrucciones para los exámenes de ingreso. 1887. IV. 540.[1]
Ministerio de fomento. Pormenor del presupuesto de gastos. 1892. IV. 553.[2]
Ministerio de ultramar. . . . Real decreto y reglamento para la venta de terrenos . . en Filipinas. 1889. IV. 554.
Del Ministero d'agricoltura . . . e dell' ingerenza dello stato in materia economica. 1864. IV. 286.[2]
Ministero d'agricoltura, industria e commercio. — Decisione di massima. 1864. IV. 305.
Ministerstva . . . *See* МИНИСТЕРСТВА . . .
El Ministro de fomento en la Escuela . . . de montes. 1892. IV. 540.[2]
El Ministro de fomento y la venta de montes. 1894. IV. 552.[1]
Il Ministro dell' agricoltura e la riforma della legge forestale. 1898. IV. 329.
Mink, W. Aufzählung der wilden Phanerogamen um Crefeld. 1839. I. 380.
Minkiewicz, Michael. Beitrag zur Kenntniss der in Urechites suberecta enthaltenen wirksamen Substanzen. 1888. III. 691.[1]

Minneci, (abate). Le Viti americane. 1893. III. 558.[1]

Minnesota — Agricultural experiment station. See MINNESOTA, UNIVERSITY OF . . . III. 5.

Minnesota — Oliea fire warden. Annual report. Forest preservation. IV. 4.

Minnesota — Geological and natural history survey. Botanical series. Bulletin. I. 6.

Minnesota botoni al studies. I. 6.

Minnesota geological and natural history survey. Annual report. I. 519.

Minnesota state horticultural society. Annual report. History. Transactions. III. 5.

Minnesota, University of — Agricultural experiment station. Annual report. Bulletin. III. 5.

Minnikin, G. G. Notes on insect ravages in Pine forests. 1888. IV. 461.[2]

Minoli, P. A. Prima conferenza sulla silvicoltura. 1880. IV. 41.[1]

— Questione importante circa l' arte dell' innestare. 1881. III. 162.

Minor forest products of South Jersey. 1895. IV. 434.

Minto, John. A paper on forestry interests. 1898. IV. 338.[2]

Minuit, Charles. Sur l'hiver 1870-71. 1870. III. 48.

— Quel lues mots sur l'hiver 1869-70. 1870. III. 48.

Miquel, Friedrich Anton Wilhelm. Aanteekening omtrent eenea nieuwen Cycadeen-vorm in Amerika. 1846. II. 5.[1]

— Aanteekeningen over de verdiensten van Rembert Dodoens. 1854. I. 80.[2]

— Adnotationes de Cupuliferis. 1863. II. 123.[1]

— Adnotationes de Ternstroemiaceis. 1868. II. 547.[2]

— Aeschynanthi speciem novam proponit. 1848. II. 793.[2]

— Sur les affinités de la flore du Japon. 1866. I. 462.

— Over de Afrikaansche Vijge-boomen. 1849. II. 149.[1]

— Ampelideae novae. 1863. II. 501.[1]

— Analecta botanica indica. 1850. I. 453,[1] 465.

— Anatomische Bemerkungen über den Bau der Melocacten. 1842. II. 595.[2]

— Animadversiones in herbarium surinamense. 1842. II. 339.[1]

— Animadversiones in nonnullas Bignoniaceas. 1863. II. 784.[2]

— Animadversiones in Piperaceas herbarii Hookeriani. 1845. II. 93.[1]

— Annotationes de Dipterocarpeis. 1867. II. 559.[1]

— Annotationes de Ficus speciebus. 1867. II. 148.[2]

— Annotationes de Phytocrenes speciebus. 1867. II. 475.[1]

— Annotationes in Piperaceas herbarii Arnottiani. 1846. II. 93.[1]

— Anonaceae Archipelagi indici. 1865. II. 215.[2]

— Antidesmeae novae. 1863. II. 437.[1]

— Araliaceae novae. 1863. II. 646.[2]

— Araliacearum indicarum . . . species aliquot novae. 1856. II. 646.[2]

— Artocarpeae. 1867. II. 145.[1]

— Aurantiaceae novae. 1863. II. 397.[1]

— Avicenniese Endl. 1844. II. 753.[2]

— Ueber den Bau eines . . . Stammes von Cycas circinalis. 1844. II. 4.[2]

— Beleuchtung des Geschlechtes Encephalartos. 1838. II. 5.[2]

— Bemerkungen über Schlegelia. 1844. II. 790.[2]

— Bestimmungen einiger . . . in Brasilien gesammelten Pflanzen. 1847. I. 342.

— Beyeria, novum genus Euphorbiacearum. 1844. II. 437.[1]

— Bijdragen tot de flora van Japan, IV. 1870. II. 95.[2]

— Sur les bourgeons des Cycadées. 1839. II. 3.[1]

— Calpicarpum albiflorum. 1864. II. 727.[1]

— Sur le caractère et l'origine de la flore du Japon. 1867. I. 462.

— Casuarineae. 1868. II. 92.[1]

— Casuarineae Mirbel. 1844. II. 92.[1]

— Ueber die Chinakultur auf Java. 1868. III. 715.

— Chloranthaceae et Piperaceae. 1852. II. 93,[1] 95.[1]

— Choix de plantes rares . . . dans le Jardin botanique de Buitenzorg. 1864. I. 68.[1]

— Chrysobalaneae quaedam indicae. 1867. II. 255.[2]

— De Cinchona speciebus quibusdam. 1868. III. 812.

— Cinnamomi generis revisio. 1863. II. 224.[1]

— De Clerodendri quibusdam speciebus. 1867. II. 755.[1]

— Collectanea nova ad Cycadearum cognitionem. 1847. II. 2.[1]

— Combretum arboreum. 1868. II. 616.[1]

— Commentarii phytographici. 1838. I. 268.

— Commentatio de organorum . . . metamorphosi. 1833. I. 101.[2]

— Commentatio de vero Pipere Cubeba. 1839. II. 94.[1]

— Cupressinae Richard. 1844. II. 16.[1]

— Cycadeae quaedam americanae. 1851. II. 2.[1]

— Over de Cycadeen in Nieuw Holland. 1863. II. 2.[2]

— De Cycadeis Loddigesianis. 1842. II. 2.[1]

— Cycadis Rumphii stirps femina. 1852. II. 5.[1]

— Description d'une nouvelle espèce de Zamia. 1842. II. 2.[1]

— Dipterocarpeae novae vel minus cogitae. 1863. II. 559.[2]

— Disquisitio geographico-botanica de plantarum regni Batavi distributione. 1837. I. 391.[1]

— Ebenaceae, Symplocaceae. 1856. II. 700,[2] 703.[1]

— Echinocacti novi descriptio. 1837. II. 585.[1]

— Ecloge Rubiacearum Archipelagi indici. 1868. II. 807.[2]

— Over eenige nieuwe geslachten . . . der Piperaceën. 1842. II. 92.[2]

— Over eenige nieuwe of zeldzame Cycadeen. 1848. II. 2.[1]

— Ueber einige neue oder seltsame Cycadeen in dem Botanischen Garten zu Amsterdam. 1848. II. 2.[1]

— Ueber einige Pflanzen aus Surinam. 1843. I. 339.[1]

— De Encephalarto horrido. 1848. II. 6.[1]

— Enumeratio Piperacearum in Brasilia. 1871. II. 93.[1]

— Epicrisis systematis Cycadearum. 1849. II. 2.[1]

— Sur les Érables du Japon. 1867. II. 476.[2]

— Ericaceae Archipelagi indici. 1863. II. 658.[1]

— Ericaceae japonicae. 1863. II. 658.[1]

— Sur une espèce nouvelle de Zamia. 1851. II. 6.[2]

— Expérience sur l'action des substances vénéneuses. 1837. I. 211.

— Fagraeae species in Archipelago indico . . . detectae. 1865. II. 718.[1]

— Die Familie der Cycadeen. 1870. III. 284.[1]

— Ficuum species nigritianae. 1848. II. 149.[1]

— Flora japonica. 1870. I. 462.

— Flora van Nederlandsch Indië. 1855. I. 463.

— Fragmenta phytographica. 1844. I. 263.

— Genera Cactearum. 1849. II. 585.[2]

— Genera et species Cycadearum viventium. 1843. II. 2.[1]

— Over geographische verspreiding der Ficeae. 1862. II. 148.[2] de

— Heliciae species amboinenses. 1863. II. 163.[1]

— Hippocrateaceae Archipelagi indici. 1868. II. 471.[2]

— Homerische Flora. 1835. I. 514.[1]

— Iets over de literatuur der inlandsche flora. 1834. I. 3.[2]

— Iets over het geslacht Zamia. 1847. II. 6.[2]

— Illigerae species Archipelagi indici. 1863. II. 228.[1]

— Illustrationes Piperacearum. 1846. II. 93.[1]

— Illustrations de la flore de l'Archipel indien. 1871. I. 466.

— Kinakultur in Nederlandsch Indië. 1868. III. 715.

— Leerboek tot de kennis der artsenijgewassen. 1838. III. 57.

— Legnotideae Archipelagi indici. 1865. II. 613.[1]

— Eene lijst der planten . . . in de kolonie Suriname gekweekt. 1843. I. 269. .

— Loranthaceae Don. 1844. II. 173.[1]

— Malvaceae. 1853. I. 465.

— Malvaceae Juss. 1844. II. 519.[2]

— Magnolia stirpium Blanchetianarum. 1849. I. 342.

— Mantissa Piperacearum. 1847. II. 93.[1]

— Mélanges botaniques. 1839. I. 268.

— Melastomaceae a Teysmanno . . . collectae. 1863. II. 635.[1]

— Melocactorum duorum novorum descriptio. 1837. II. 595.[2]

— Monographia Cycadearum. 1842. II. 2.[1]

— Monographia generis Melocacti. 1840. II. 595.[2]

— Monographia Meliacearum Archipelagi indici. 1868. II. 419.[1]

— Myristiceae a Teysmanno et De Vriese collectae. 1863. II. 220.[1]

— Ueber eine neue Cycas aus Siam. 1863. II. 5.[1]

— Nieuwe bijdragen tot de kennis der Cycadeen. 1867. II. 2.[2]

— De Noord-Nederlandsche vegetatie. 1837. I. 391.[1]

— De Noord-Nederlandsche vergiftige gewassen. 1836. III. 76.

— Note additionelle sur autre espèce. 1838. II. 6.[1]

— Note préliminaire sur les genres . . . des Pipéracées. 1839. II. 9.[2]

— Note sur l'Encephalartos lanuginosus. 1839. II. 6.[1]

— Note sur l'Encephalartus horridus. 1838. II. 6.[1]

— Note sur la préfoliation des Cycadées. 1838. II. 3.[1]
— Note sur les Figuiers de la Nouvelle-Hollande. 1861. II. 149.[1]
— Note sur quelques espèces de Cinchona. 1861. II. 812.
— Nouveaux genres indiens de la famille des Apocynées. 1857. II. 722.[1]
— Nouveaux matériaux pour servir à la connaissance des Cycadées. 1867. II. 2.[1]
— Nouvelle espèce de Rhodoleia. 1859. II. 254.[1]
— Nova genera Apocynearum indicarum. 1857. II. 722.[1]
— De novo plantarum genere . . . Araliacearum. 1840. II. 647.[2]
— De Nyctocalo et Radermachera. 1867. II. 784.[2]
— Observatio de generibus Piperacearum. 1841. II. 92.[1]
— Observation sur le canal médullaire . . . de Cecropia. 1838. II. 147.[2]
— Observationes botanicae de quibusdam plantis . . . in colonia surinamensi. 1842. I. 339.[1]
— Observationes botanicae de quibusdam plantis surinamensibus. 1842. I. 339.[1]
— Observationes de . . . Bignoniaceis surinamensibus. 1842. II. 784.[2]
— Observationes de Clusiaceis. 1863. II. 555,[1] 558.[1]
— Observationes de generibus quibusdam indicis. 1867. I. 466.
— Observationes de ovulo . . . Cycadearum. 1845. II. 3.[1]
— Observationes de Piperaceis et Melastomaceis. 1840. II. 92,[1] 634.[2]
— Observationes de quibusdam Piperaceis herbarii Schlechtendaliani. 1844. II. 93.[1]
— Observationes de quibusdam plantis surinamensibus. 1843. I. 339.[1]
— Observationes de Urticeis quibusdam. 1868. II. 156.[1]
— Observationes sur les Cycadées. 1840. II. 2.[1]
— Observationes sur les Cycadées de l'Herbier royal à Leyde. 1838. II. 2.[1]
— Olacineae Mirb. 1844. II. 171.[2]
— Oratio de regno vegetabili. See his De REGNO vegetabili.
— De Orchipeda. 1863. II. 734.[1]
— De Palmis Archipelagi indici. 1868. II. 62.[1]
— Phoenicosperma, Tiliacearum genus. 1865. II. 511.[1]
— Piperaceae. 1863. II. 93.[1]
— Piperaceae Reinwardtianae. 1848. II. 93.[1]
— De Piperaceis Novae Hollandiae. 1866. II. 93.[1]
— Plantae Kegelianae surinamenses. 1849. I. 339.[1]
— Plantae Regnellianae. 1849. I. 342.
— Plantae surinamenses novae. 1844. I. 339.[1]
— Plantarum Cactearum, in Flora fluminensi . . . revisio. 1838. II. 587.[2]
— Plantas Cacteas novas . . . describit. 1838. II. 585.[1]
— Polciiospermum Zippel. genus novum. 1863. II. 157.[2]
— Ueber die Praefoliation der Cycadeen. 1838. II. 3.[1]
— Primulaceae et Myrsineae. 1856. II. 692.[1]
— Prodromus monographiae Ficuum. 1847. II. 148.[2]
— Prodromus systematis Cycadearum. 1861. II. 2.[2]
— Proeven over de prikkelbaarheid der bladen van Mimosa pudica. 1838. II. 372.[2]
— Proeven over de werking van vergiften op planten. 1837. I. 211.
— Prolusio florae japonicae. 1865. I. 462.
— Pterisanthis cissoidis Bl, illustratio. 1844. II. 504.[2]
— Pygei species novae. 1863. II. 278.[1]
— Quelques expériences pour déterminer l'influence de la lumière sur l'exhalaison aqueuse des feuilles. 1838. I. 166. 416,[1] 455.[1]
— De quibusdam Burseraceis et Anacardiaceis. 1868. II. 585.[2]
— De quibusdam Cacteis Horti roterodamensis. 1840. II. 585.[2]
— De quibusdam Cycadeis minus cogniits. 1840. II. 2.[1]
— De quibusdam Rubiaceis, Apocyneis. 1868. II. 722,[1] 755,[1] 807.[2]
— De ramificatione monstrosa. 1853. I. 143.
— Ranunculaceae, Magnoliaceae . . . Archipelagi indici. 1868. I. 466.
— Recherches sur l'irritabilité des feuilles de la Sensitive. 1838. II. 372.[2]
— Recherches sur la structure d'un tronc agé du Cycas circinalis. 1844. II. 4.[2]
— De regno vegetabili in telluris superficie mutanda effi-caci. 1846. I. 217.
— Remarques sur la flore du sud de la Chine. 1861. I. 458.
— Remarques sur la structure . . . des Melocactus. 1842. II. 595.[2]
— Remarques sur le genre Nania. 1861. II. 630.[1]

— Remarques sur les genres Othera et Orixa. 1839. II. 409,[1] 462.[2]
— Responsio ad quaestionem botanicam . . . propositam: Describatur germinatio plantarum. 1832. I. 202.[2]
— Revisio critica Casuarinarum. 1848. II. 92.[1]
— Revue des Palmiers de l'Île de Sumatra. 1861. II. 62.[1]
— Rhodoleiae (Champ.) generis . . . characterem . . . expo-suit. 1857. II. 254.[1]
— Rutacearum quarundam illustratio. 1867. II. 397.[1]
— Salicineae. 1870. II. 95.[2]
— Santalaceae R. Br. 1844. II. 167.[2]
— Sapindaceae Juss. 1844. II. 483.[2]
— Sapoteae. 1863. II. 696.[2]
— Sertum exoticum. 1842. I. 263, II. 207.[1]
— On the sexual organs of the Cycadaceae. 1867. II. 2.[2]
— De soorten van het geslacht Cinchona. 1870. II. 812.
— Species aliquot novas valdivianas . . . proponit. 1852. I. 346.
— Stirpes Novo-Hollandas . . . determinavit. 1859. I. 501.
— Stirpes surinamenses selectae. 1850. I. 339.[1]
— Stirpium novarum sylloge. 1853. I. 269.
— Sumatra, zijne plantenwereld. 1860. I. 467.
— Sylloge plantarum novarum. 1840. I. 268.
— Symbolae ad floram surinamensem. 1844. I. 339.[1]
— Synopsis specierum Casuarinae. 1865. II. 92.[2]
— Systema Piperacearum. 1843. II. 93.[1]
— Over eene tegennatuurlijke ontwikkeling van de bloemen eener Cissus. 1846. III. 544.[2]
— Tentamen florae Homericae. 1835. I. 514.[1]
— Teysmannia Zolling., Palmarum genus. 1868. II. 75.[1]
— Thymelaeacearum genera nova. 1863. II. 600.[1]
— Untersuchungen über die Reizbarkeit der Blätter von Mimosa pudica. 1838. II. 372.[2]
— Urticineae. 1853. II. 156.[1]
— Over de verwantschap der flora van Japan. 1866. I. 462.
— De voedselplanten van den mensch. 1852. III. 219.[2]
— Wormia subsessilis. 1863. II. 543.[2]
— Xanthophylli species. 1863. II. 432.[2]
— Zygophylleae. 1844. II. 395.[1]
— & Groenewegen, J. C. Catalogus Horti botanici am-stelodamensis. 1857. I. 51.[2]
— & others. Plantae Junghuhnianae. 1851. I. 465.
Ueber eine mit unter dem Namen China regia falsa zugekommene Chinarinde. 1833. III. 724.[2]
Mira, G. Método de cortas discontinuas. 1877. IV. 252.
Mira, Jenaro. El Vedad. 1895. IV. 556.[1]
Mirabella, Maria Antonietta. Contribuzioni alla conoscenza dei colleteri. 1897. I. 135.
— Sui laticiferi delle radici aeree di " Ficus." 1897. II. 149.[2]
— I nettari extranusiali . . . di Ficus. 1895. II. 149.[2]
I miracoli dei rimboschimenti. 1881. IV. 163, 165.
Miraglia, Nicola. Introduzione alla raccolta delle leggi forestali. 1866. IV. 328.
Miramon, Severo de AGUIRRE. See AGUIRRE MIRAMON, Severo de.
Mirande, Marcel. Contribution à l'étude du malate neutre de calcium. 1898. I. 178.
Mirandolle, C. De kreosoteering van hout. 1866. IV. 419.
Miraval, LAMBOT. See LAMBOT-MIRAVAL.
Mirbel, Charles François Brisseau de. Anatomische und physiologische Untersuchungen über den Stamm der Dattel-palme. 1843. I. 99.
— Anatomische und physiologische Untersuchungen über einige monokotyledonische Gewächse. 1843. I. 98.
— Considérations sur la graine. 1814. I. 202.[2]
— Coup d'œil sur l'état présent de l'anatomie. 1810. I. 146.
— Description de quelques espèces nouvelles de la famille des Amentacées. 1827. I. 267.
— Développement des ovules. 1812. I. 121.
— Élémens de physiologie végétale. 1815. I. 148.
— Erläuterung und Vertheidigung meiner Theorie des Ge-wächsbaus. 1808. I. 33, 98.
— Essai sur la distribution . . . des Conifères. 1825. II. 12.[2]
— Essai sur la distribution géographique . . . des Chénopo-dées. 1825. II. 186.[2]
— Examen critique d'un passage du mémoire de M. Hugo Mohl sur la structure . . . du grain de pollen. 1831. II. 117.[1]
— Examen de la division des végétaux en endorhizes et ex-orhizes. 1810. I. 120.
— Exposition de la théorie de l'organisation végétale. 1809. I. 98.

Mirbel, Charles François Brisseau de (*continued*).
— Exposition et défense de ma théorie de l'organisation végé-
tale. 1808. I. 33, *98*.
— General obervations on vegetation. 1815. I. 148.
— Histoire naturelle. 1802. I. 33.
— De l'influence de l'histoire naturelle sur la civilisation.
.1801. I. 79.¹
— Mémoire sur l'anatomie . . . des Labiées. 1810. II. 762.²
— Mémoire sur l'anatomie végétale.. 1802. I. 97.
— Mémoire sur l'organisation du péricarpe. 1825. I. 119.
— Mémoire sur l'origine, le développement et l'organisation
du liber et du bois. 1828. I. 124.
— Mémoire sur les fluides contenus dans les végétaux. 1806.
I. 163.
— Methods of transporting exotic plants. 1838. III. 155.
— Note pour servir à l'histoire de la germination. 1812. I.
202.²
— Note sur l'Abies. 1812. II. 22.¹.
— Note sur l'Ephedra. 1812. II. 54.¹
— Note sur l'organisation de la tige d'un . . . Calycanthus.
1828. II. 214.² .
— Note sur le cambium et le liber. 1816. I. 128.¹
— Note sur le Taxus. 1812. II. 10.¹
— Notes pour servir à l'histoire naturelle . . . des Orangers.
1812. II. 396.²
— Nouvelle classification des fruits. 1812. I. 119.
— Nouvelles notes sur le cambium. 1839. I. 98.
— Nouvelles notes sur le cambium, extraites d'un travail sur
la racine du Dattier. 1839. I. 128.¹
— Nouvelles recherches sur la structure et les développements
de l'ovule végétal. 1829. I. 121.
— Observations sur la famille des . . . Conifères. 1810. II.
16.¹
— Observations sur le cambium. 1837. I. 128.¹
— Observations sur un système d'anatomie . . . fondé sur
l'organisation de la fleur. 1809. I. 114.¹
— Précis d'un mémoire . . . Nouvelles recherches sur les car-
actères anatomiques. .1809. I. 98..
—Rapport sur les espèces d'arbres exotiques. 1830.. III.
124.¹
—Recherches anatomiques et physiologiques sur quelques
végétaux monocotylés. 1843. I. 98, II. 80.¹
—Recherches sur la distribution géographique des végétaux.
1827. I. 298.
— Remarques sur la nature et l'origine des couches corticales.
1835. I. 127,¹ *130*.
— Réponse à M. Gaudichaud. 1845. II, 80.¹
— Résumé de différens mémoires sur la graine. 1812. I.
202.²
— Traité d'anatomie et de physiologie végétales. 1802. I.
84.
—*See also* LAMARCK, J. B. A. P. M. de & MIRBEL, C. F.
Brisseau de; SCHOUBERT & MIRBEL, C. F. B. de.
— & Payen, Anselme. Sur la composition du cambium.
1843. I. 128.¹
—— Extrait d'un premier . . . mémoire sur la composition
. . . de plusieurs organismes des plantes. 1846. I. 99.
——Note sur la composition du cambium. 1843. I. 128.¹
——Organographie et physiologie végétale. 1849. I. 34,
99.
— & Spach, Eduard. Note sur l'embryogénie du Taxus.
1844. II. 10.¹
—— Notes pour servir à l'histoire de l'embryogénie. 1839.
I. 121.
—— Notes sur l'embryogénie des Pinus. 1843. II. 18.
— & others. Rapport sur le concours pour . . . Chênes-
Liéges. 1835. IV. 516.²
——Rapport sur un mémoire de M. Gaudichaud, relatif au
développement. 1835. I. 187.
Mirecourt, Sebastien GÉRARDIN DE. *See* GÉRARDIN DE MIRE-
COURT, Sebastien.
Miroir des fleurs. 1900. III. 116.¹
Mirone, Gaetano. Ricerche . . . su di una transudazione
morbosa vegetable. 1829. IV. 509.
Miscellanea di chimica, fisica e storia naturale. I. 25.
**Miscellanea philosophico-mathematica societatis privatae
taurinensis.** I. 25.
Miscellanee medico-chirurgico-farmaceutiche. *See* GIORNALE
toscano di scienze. I. 25.
Miscellaneous observations on planting . . . timber-trees.
See ANDERSON, James. 1777. IV. 120.
Miscellaneous subjects of exhibition. 1848. III. 657.³
Miscellen für Gartenfreunde, Botaniker und Gärtner. *See*
BECKER, W. G. 1802. III. 121.¹

Mischke, Karl. Beobachtungen über das Dickenwachsthum
der Coniferen. 1890. II. 21.¹
Mischler. . . . Wald und Fideicommiss. 1883. IV. 368.
Mise en ferme des forêts de Chênes-liége. 1876. IV. 279.²
Mise en valeur des terrains incultes. 1895. IV. 546.²
Mise en valeur des terres communales incultes. 1899. IV.
161.¹
Misiewicz, M. Lasy w Królestwie Polskiem. 1897. IV. 347.
Misling. Ueber die praktische Verwendung der . . . Flügel-
säge. 1869. IV. 171.
Misonne, Th. Le Pandanus Baptisti. 1893. III. 313.¹
Mispelen. 1843. III. 429.³
**Mississippi — Agricultural college — Mississippi agricul-
tural experiment station.** Annual report. Bulletin. III. 5.
Mississippi agricultural experiment station. *See* MISSIS-
SIPPI AGRICULTURAL COLLEGE . . . III. 5.
Mississippi valley horticultural society. Transactions.
III. 6.
Mississippi valley lumberman. IV. 4.
Missouri — Agricultural college, Columbia. Bulletin. III. 6.
Missouri agricultural experiment station. *See* MISSOURI,
UNIVERSITY OF — COLLEGE OF AGRICULTURE AND MECHANIC
ARTS . . . III. 6.
Missouri botanical garden. Annual report. I. 6.
Missouri state horticultural society. Annual report. III. 6.
**Missouri, University of — College of agriculture and me-
chanic arts — Agricultural experiment station.** Annual re-
port. Bulletin. III. 6.
Die Mistel. 1884. IV. 519.²
Mr. Burbank's work as a hybridiser. 1896. III. 443.²
Mr. Vanderbilt's forest. 1894. IV. 340.
The Mistleto. 1873. II. 178.¹
The Mistletoe. 1859. I. 511.—1872. II. 178.¹
The Mistletoe as a tree pest. 1873. II. 179.¹
The Mistletoe bough. 1892. II. 180.¹
The Mistletoe growing on the Mistletoe. 1874. II. 179.¹
Mistletoe in July. 1886. II. 179.²
Mistra, L. Euphorbiae messanenses. 1873. II. 441.²
Misura per gli alberi. 1861. IV. 215.
Misvär, Hans. Frostrevner i frugtträr. 1895. III. 182.
Misyevitch, V. *See* MICHEEVL, B.
Mita, Oronzio de. Sul progetto di legge forestale pel regno
d' Italia. 1862. IV. 327.
Mitchell, Ann Maria. The White Blackberry. 1899. II.
309.¹
Mitchell, Archibald. Driftwood and insect attacks. 1895.
IV. 208.²
Mitchell, Charles. Alcin. 1876. III. 333.²
— Alcine. 1876. III. 333.²
Mitchell, Cornelius B. Trees in city streets. 1899. III. 208.²
Mitchell, F. Old . . . trees on the estates of Earl Spencer.
1893. I. 297.¹
Mitchell, J. On the export . . . of wattle bark. 1851. III.
463.²
Mitchell, J. B. Russian Apples. 1888. III. 425.²
Mitchell, J. S. An essay on the Arbutus Uva ursi. 1803.
III. 648.¹
Mitchell, John, M. D. (–1772). Dissertatio brevis de prin-
cipiis botanicorum. 1748. I. 305.
— De principiis botanicorum. 1748. I. 305.
Mitchell, John (*of Stanstead, Sussex, 1762–*). Dendrologia.
1827. IV. 120.
Mitchell, Silas Weir. An experimental examination of . . .
sassy-bark. 1860. III. 476.¹
Mitchell, Thomas Livingstone. Three expeditions into the
interior of eastern Australia. 1838. I. 500..
Mitchell, William. On a proximate measurements of the
axial appendages of plants. 1859. I. 254.²
— On trichotomous arrangements of plants. 1860. I. 252.
Mitchill, Samuel L. A discourse . . . account of the writings
which illustrate the botanical history of North and South
America. 1814. I. 80.¹
— An encouragement to the introduction of the Date-bear-
ing Palm into the United States. 1818. II. 328.¹
Mitford, Algernon Bertram FREEMAN-. The Bamboo garden.
1894. II. 58.¹—1896. II. 58.¹
— The Bamboos. 1899. III. 314.²
— On the economic uses of Bamboos. 1896. III. 315.¹
— Hardy Bamboos. 1896. III. 314.²—1898. III. 314.²
Mititzky, Pal. Az Orgona tenyésztése és hajtátásaról. 1899.
III. 680.²
Mitscher, G. *See* SOLFF, F. & MITSCHER, G.
Mitscherlich. Ueber ein geognostisches kolorirtes Relief des
Zobten-Gebirges. 1857. IV. 264.

Mitscherlich, C. G. Lehrbuch der Arzneimittellehre. 1837. III. 258.

Mitscherlich, Gustav Alfred. De cacao. 1857. III. 594.

— Der Cacao und die Chocolade. 1859. III. 594.

Mitscherlich, O. Die Tiefkultur in forstlicher Hinsicht. 186.? IV. 143.¹ — 1871. IV. 143.¹

Mitscherlich, Richard. Extraction de la cellulose du bois. 1883. IV. 432.²

Mitteilungen aus der Staats-Forstverwaltung Bayerns. IV. 539.¹ See also FORSTLICHE Mittheilungen, (Bayern). IV. 8.

Mitteilungen über die Ergebnisse der königlich sächsischen Staatsforstverwaltung im Jahre 1892. 1893. . IV: 261.¹

Mittel, die Hasen von Obstbäumen abzuhalten. 1852. III. 186.¹

Mittel, diejenigen Bäume zu erhalten, welche vom Froste gelitten haben. 1803. III. 182.

Mittel gegen den Harzfrevel. 1862. IV. 436.²

Mittel um anscheinend vertrocknete Bäume zu beleben. 1888. III. 155.

Mittel- und niederrhein — Botanischer Verein. See BOTANISCHER . . . I. 1-1.

Aus dem mittelfränkischen Spannerfrassgebiete. 1897. IV. 208.¹

Mitten, W. & Wallis, A. A sketch of the natural history of Brighton. See MERRIFIELD, M. P. 1860. I. 401.

Mitterpacher, Ludwig. See PILLER, Mathias & MITTERPACHER, Ludwig.

Mittheilungen aus dem Forsthaushalt der Gemeinde St. Gallen. 1838. IV. 365.

Mittheilungen aus dem forstlichen Versuchswesen Oesterreichs. IV. 15.

Mittheilungen aus dem Gesammtgebiete der Botanik. I. 13.

Mittheilungen aus der . . . Geschichte über den Weinbau am Rhein. 1826. III. 552.

Mittheilungen aus Justus Perthes' geographischer Anstalt. I. 13.

Mittheilungen für Obst- und Weinbau. III. 24.¹

Mittheilungen über das Forst- und Jagdwesen in Bayern. See FORSTLICHE Mittheilungen, (Bayern). I. 8.

Mittheilungen über das forstliche Unterrichts- und Prüfungswesen an der Universität München. 188.? IV. 32.

Mittheilungen über die Ergebnisse der königl. sächs. Staatsforstverwaltung im Jahre 1897. 1898. IV: 261.¹

Mittheilungen über die Hölztränkung. 1862. IV. 418.

Mittheilungen über die neuesten Pflanzen. 1869. III. 75.¹

Mittheilungen über die Wirthschaftsergebnisse der herzoglich braunschweigischen Forstverwaltung. 1898. IV. 261.¹

Mittheilungen über Haus-, Land- und Forstwirthschaft für die Schweiz. III. 24,¹ IV. 13.²

Mittheilungen über Obst- und Gartenbau. III. 12.

Mittheilungen von Forschungsreisenden . . . aus dem deutschen Schutzgebieten. III. 13.

Mittler. See ZIMMERMANN, MITTLER & GRUMBACH.

Mittler, Ludwig. Taschenbuch für Cactusliebhaber. 1841. III. 618.²

Mittmann, Robert. Beiträge zur Kenntniss der Anatomie der Pflanzenstacheln. 1889. I. 107,³ 113.¹

Mitzky, C. & Co. Our native Grape. 1893. III. 547.

Mitzky, J. H. De vario coffeae potum parandi modo. See BOEHMER, G. R. 1782. III. 738.

Mitzul. M See MHITYEB, M

Miyabe, Kingo. Ainu names of Hokkaido plants. 1895. I. 75.²

— The flora of the Kurile Islands. 1890. I. 463.¹

— On the starch of ever-green leaves. 1900. I. 140.²

— See also BATCHELOR, John & MIYABE, Kingo; JIMBO, Kotora & MIYABE, Kingo.

Miyachi, T. Can old leaves of plants produce asparagine? 1896. I. 178.

Misauld, Antoine. Alexikepus. 1565. III. 240.

— Artificiosa methodus comparandorum hortensium fructuum. 1565.. III. 240.

— Aratgarten. Von Kreutern. 1565. III. 240.

— Epitome de la Maison rustique. 1576. III. 111.

— Historia hortensium. 1576. III. 111.

— De hortensium arborum insitione opusculum. 1560. III. '59.²

— Nova et mira arteficia comparandorum fructuum. 1565. III. 240.

— Opusculum de Sena. 1573. III. 470.¹

— Secretorum agri enchiridion primum. 1560. III. 124.³

— Traduction des livres de Mizauld. 1576. III. 111.

Mladek, Heinrich. Eine grosse Tanne in Böhmen. 1860. IV. 447.¹

Mlodzianeky, A. K. Acre yield of White Pine in Pennsylvania. 1898. IV. 471.

— Acre-yield of White Pine in the Lake region. 1898. IV. 471.

— Measuring the forest crop. 1898. IV. 219.

— Rate of growth of Loblolly Pine. 1896. IV. 483.¹

— Rate of growth of the Long-leaf Pine. 1896. IV. 467.¹

— Second growth White Pine. 1897. IV. 469.

— Second-growth White Pine in Pennsylvania. 1897. IV. 469.

Mnyenie . . . See Маѣнѣ . . .

Moberg, Adolf. Naturalhistoriska dagboksanteckningar. 1857. I. 223.²

Mobin, B. Essai analytique sur les fruits de l'Aréquier. 1822. III. 320.¹

Mociño, José Mariano. Extracto del discurso . . . en la apertura de las lecciones. 1802. III. 264.²

— See also SESSÉ, Martino & MOCIÑO, J. M.

The Mocker-nut (Carya tomentosa). 1900. III. 353.²

Mode of securing wooden buildings from the effects of fire. 1826. IV. 416.²

Un mode particulier de boisement. 1896. IV. 119.²

Modeer, Adolph. Afhandling om uthus-tak i Calmare höfdingedöme. 1765. IV. 422.³

— Anmärkningar angående det så kallade Manna foliata. 1792. IV. 535.²

Modena — Reale accademia di scienze, lettere ed arti. See REALE . . . I. 25.

Modena — Società dei naturalisti. See SOCIETÀ . . . I. 26.¹

Modera, J. Duurzaamheid der West-Indische houtsoorten. 1858. IV. 398.¹

Modern cemetery. See PARK and cemetery. III. 7.

Modern methods of tree planting. 1900. III. 168.¹

The modern practice of the London hospitals. 1764. III. 252.

Moderne Verfahren der Holzimprägnierung. 1899. IV. 421.

Modification à la loi forestière du canton de Vaud. 1894. IV. 331.¹

Modifications à divers articles du code forestier. 1898. IV. 555.¹

Modin, Bengt Theodor. Afhandling om de wäxter som i Bibelen omtalas. See THUNBERG, C. P. 1828. I. 513.

Modlen, R. Notes on Chian turpentine. 1880. III. 526.¹

Modo de cultivar a Canelleira. See GOMES, B. A. 1809. III. 613.²

Modo di distruggere i bruchi. 1864. IV. 209.¹

Modo di ottenere ottimo filo dal Camerpo. 1864. IV. 485.²

Moe, Elias. Indberetning om reiser i England. 1887. III. 123.²

Moebes, Fraxinus americana, amerikanische Esche. 1897. IV. 535.¹

Möbes, (Revierförster). Ueber Durchforstungen. 1885. IV. 174.

— Grünköpfe oder Harzköpfe. 1889. IV. 66.²

Möbius, D. M. Die mechanischen Scheiden der Secretbehälter. 1884. I. 135.

— Die mechanischen Scheiden der Secretbehälter. 1885. II. 40.¹

— Die mechanischen Scheiden der Secretblätter. 1884. I. 135.

Moebius, Gottfried. Anatomia samphorae. 1660. III. 404.¹

Moebius, Martin. Eine alte Eibe. 1884. II. 11.¹

— Beiträge zur Lehre von der Fortpflanzung. 1897. I. 205.

— Beitrag zur Anatomie der Ficus-Blätter. 1897. II. 149.²

— Ueber Bewegungsorgane an Blattstielen. 1899. I. 112.¹

— Ueber die Blüthen . . . des Papiermaulbeerbaumes. 1900. II. 147.¹

— Ueber ein eigenthümliches Blühen von Bambusa vulgaris. 1898. II. 59.²

— Ueber die Folgen von beständiger geschlechtsloser Vermehrung. 1891. I. 205.

— Ueber den Habitus der Pflanzen. 1894. I. 107.¹

— Der japanische Lackbaum. 1899. II. 460.¹

— Sphärokrystalle von Kalkoxalat bei Cacteen. 1885. II. 588.¹

— Ueber das Vorkommen concentrischer Gefässbündel. 1887. I. 134.¹

— Ueber Wachsausscheidung. 1897. I. 182,¹ II. 458.²

— Welche Umstände befördern und welche hemmen das Blühen der Pflanzen? 1892. I. 200.

Möbius, W. Over de gevolgen van voortdurende vermenigvuldiging . . . langs geslachtelooozen weg. 1890. I. 249.¹

Moeckel, Heinrich August. De Diosma crenata. 1820. III. 495,¹ 517.¹

Der **Mödritschwildbach** in Kärnten. 1888. -IV. 188.[1]
Moegling, Johannes Ludwig. Palingenesia; sive, Resurrectio plantarum. 1683. I. 515.
— Praeludia rei herbariae. 1612. I. 30.
— Προγυμνάσματα βοτανολογικά. 1612. I. 30.
Mögling, Theodor. Anleitung zur Maulbeerpflanzung. 1841. III. 376.
— Das neueste im Gebiete der Land- und Forstwirthschaft. 1845. IV. 40.[2]
Möhl, Heinrich. Hessische Baumriesen. 1890. II. 139.[1]
— Morphologische Untersuchungen über die Eiche. 1861. II. 137.[1]—1862. II. 131.[2]
— Die Pyramidenhainbuche. 1890. III. 357.[2]
— Rinden- und Wurzelbildung im Innern eines Lindenstammes. 1890. I. 188.
— Verwachsene Hainbuchen. 1890. I. 209,[2] II. 121,[1] IV. 492.[1]
Moehring, Paul Heinrich Gerhard. Primae lineae horti privati. 1736. I. 43.
Möllendorff, G. von & **Thunig.** Die Bewirthschaftung des Ackers ohne Waldstreu und Waldweide. 1850. IV. 437.[2]
Moeller, A. Das Forst-Gesetz vom 28. März 1852. 1853. IV. 318.
Möller, Alfred. Ueber die Bedeutung neuerer Pilzforschung. 1897. IV. 212.
— Bekämpfung des Kiefernschüttepilzes. 1900. IV. 480.
— Vom immergrünen südbrasilischen Urwalde zum winterkahlen Laubwald. 1896. I. 330.
— Neue Aufklärungen über den Wurzelschwamm. 1889. IV. 212.
— New-York state college of forestry. 1898. IV. 30.[1]
— Aus dem südbrasilianischen Urwalde. 1891. I. 531.
— Der verbesserte "Waldteufel." 1899. IV. 387.[1]
— Zu welchen forstlichen Massnahmen veranlasst das Vorkommen von Schwammbäumen. 1899. IV. 479.
— Ueber den Wühlspaten. 1900. IV. 153.[2]
Möller, G. F. Beschreibung der besten Kernobstsorten. 1759. III. 70.
Möller, Hans. Forestry in Norway. 1895. IV. 344.[1]
Moeller, Hermann. Utkast till Föreläsningarna öfver Principia botanicae. 1755. I. 83.
Moeller, Hermann. Anatomische Untersuchungen über das Vorkommen der Gerbsäure. 1888. I. 183.
— Ueber Pflanzenathmung. 1884. I. 171.
— Plasmodiophora Alni. 1885. IV. 488.[2]
— Ueber das Vorkommen der Gerbsäure. 1888. I. 183.
Moeller, Johann Anton Arnold. Empfehlung zum Anbau der Akazie. 1796. IV. 522.[1]
Möller, Johann Christopher. De impostura corticis Peruviani. *See* GOELICKE, A. O. 1727. III. 719.
Moeller, Joseph. Aeschynomene aspera Willd. 1879. II. 330.[1]
— Ueber afrikanische Oelsamen. 1880. I. 119, III. 279.[2]
— American drugs. 1884. III. 635.[1]
— Amerikanische Drogen. 1882. III. 262.[2]
— Anatomie der Baumrinden. 1882. I. 130.
— Anatomische Notizen. 1879. II. 251,[1] 784.[1]
— Anpassungserscheinungen in Bau der Rinde. 1882. I. 130.
— Ueber die Bedeckung der Saatkämpe. 1878. IV. 150.
— Beiträge zur Anatomie der Schwarzföhre. 1878. II. 871.[2]
— Beiträge zur vergleichenden Anatomie des Holzes. 1876. I. 125.
— Beitrag zur Kenntniss der Eucalyptus-Blätter. 1874. II. 623.[1]
— Bildung eines eigenthümlichen Holzfaser-Conglomerates in einer kernfaulen Lärche. 1878. IV. 451.
— Cascara sagrada and Frangula barks. 1890. III. 542.[2]
— Ueber Cassiasamen. 1880. II. 343.[1]
— Chaulmoogra seed. 1884, 1885. II. 571,[1] 571,[2] III. 614.[2]
— Ueber Dichtenbestimmungen des Holzes. 1877. IV. 411.[2]
— Über den Einfluss der Bodenbeschaffenheit auf . . . Schwarzföhre. 1878. IV. 465.[2]
— Einige neue Formelemente im Holzkörper. 1876. I. 125.
— Über die Entstehung der Acacien-Gummi. 1875. II. 323.[2]
— Zur Erziehung der Eiche. 1884. IV. 507.
— Die Eucalyptusrinden in der Sammlung. 1875. II. 874.[1]
— Folia Chekan. 1884. III. 635.[1]
— Die forstlichen Acclimatizations-Bestrebungen. 1882. IV. 127.[2]
— Zur Frage der Tüpfelschliessmembran. 1880. I. 125.
— Ueber die freie Kohlensäure im Boden. 1878. IV. 69.
— Lehrbuch der Pharmakognosie. 1889. III. 259.[1]
— Lignum Aloës und Linaloëholz. 1896. II. 600.[1]
— Ueber Muskatnüsse. 1880. II. 221.[1]

— Zur näheren Kenntniss des Storax. 1875. III. 417.[2]
— Ein neues Holz für Xylographen. 1880. III. 416.[1]
— Pflanzen-Rohstoffe. 1879. III. 29.[1]
— Ueber die Pflanzzeit. 1884. IV. 154.[2]—1886. III. 169.[1]
— Pharmakognostischer Atlas. 1892. I. 100,[1] III. 260.[1]
— Ueber Quellung und Keimung der Waldsamen. 1883. I. 528,[1] IV. 65,[2] 148.
— Die Reifezeit der Schwarzföhrensamen. 1886. II. 44.[1]
— Die Rohstoffe auf der Leipziger Ausstellung. 1880. III. 28.[1]
— Die Rohstoffe des Tischler- u. Drechslergewerbes. 1883. III. 218.[2]
— Schwedisches Lilienholz. 1880. IV. 490.[1]
— Versuche mit Schwarzföhrensamen. 1878. IV. 465.[2]
— Waldbauliche Aphorismen. 1884. IV. 154,[2] 507. — 1886. II. 44.[1]
— *See also* REUSS, Hermann, (jr.) & MOELLER, Joseph.
Moeller, L. Flora von Nordwest-Thüringen. 1873. I. 387.
— Die Holzgewächse in Nord- u. Mittel-Deutschland. 1873. I. 371, III. 69, IV. 83.-
— & **Graf,** B. Flora von Thüringen. 1874. I. 387.
Möller, Louis. Gründliche Anleitung zur Vertilgung der schädlichen Raupen. 1883. III. 196.
Möller, Ludwig. Citrus trifoliata. 1900. III. 503.[1]
— Cotoneaster Pyracantha Lalandi. 1888. III. 443.[2]
— Strassen- und Park-Anlagen in Stockholm. 1900. III. 459.[2]
— Unterlagen für Epiphyllum. 1884. III. 623.[1]
Möller, T. Om Treplantning. 1803. III. 165.
Møller-Holst, E. Landbrugs-Ordbog for den praktiske Landmand. 1877. III. 31.
Möller's deutsche Gärtner-Zeitung. III. 13.
Mönch, Konrad. Einige gärtnerische Beobachtungen. 1794. III. 705.
— Enumeratio plantarum indigenarum Hassiae. 1777. I. 374.
— Methodus plantas horti botanici et agri marburgensis. 1794. I. 44.
— Verzeichniss ausländischer Bäume und Stauden des Lustschlosses Weissenstein. 1785. I. 44.
Mönkemeyer, Wilhelm. Der Affenbrodbaum. 1887. III. 589.[1]
— Betrachtungen über das tropische West-Afrika. 1886. III. 131.[1]—1887. I. 492.[1]
— Camoënsia maxima Welw. 1886. II. 341.[1]
— Notice sur la végétation du Bas-Congo. 1885. I. 491..
— Notizen über den Botanischen Garten in Göttingen. 1890. III. 595.[2]
— Rhododendron Forsterianum. 1899. III. 659.[1]
— Vegetationsbilder vom unteren Congo. 1885. I. 491.
— Viburnum tomentosum Thnbg. 1899. III. 753.[2]
Moens, Johann Carel Bernelot. Alkaloidgehalte der zaden van Strychnos tieute. 1865. III. 685.[1]
— Bepaling der alcaloiden in China. 1876. III. 723.
— Bericht nopens de gouvernements-Kinaonderneming. 1876. III. 716.
— Beschrijving van de voor verkoop in Nederland bestemde Java Kinabasten. 1879. III. 718.
— Chemische Untersuchung von Rinden der Cinchona Calisaya. 1869. III. 725.[1]
— De Cinchona Ledgeriana. 1880. III. 813.[2]
— Dammar daging en dammar ambaloe. 1859. III. 227.
— De geschiedenis van 8½ bouw Ledgeriana Kina. 1877. III. 718, 725.[1]
— Getah-melaboeai. 1865. III. 686.[2]
— De Kinacultuur in Azie. 1882. II. 813,[1] III. 713,[2] 716.
— De kinaveiling op 4 Maart 1885. 1885. III. 723.
— De Kina-veiling te Amsterdam. 1873. III. 718.
— Kininegehalte van Cinchona Calisaya Ledgeriana. 1875. III. 725.[2]
— Kleine kinologische mededeelingen. 1885. III. 723.
— Mededeeling over Minjakh-Bengkoe. 1862. III. 224.[2]
— Onderzoek van basten van Cinchona Calisaja. 1869. III. 725.[1]
— Onderzoek van eenige kinabasten van Java. 1869. III. 722.
— Résines. 1859. III. 227.
— Scheikundig onderzoek van den bast van Nauclea. 1859. III. 746.[2]
— Untersuchung einiger Chinarinden von Java. 1869. III. 722.
— Vergelijkend onderzoek van den cortex peruvianus. 1871. III. 722.
— Vergelijkend onderzoek van den cortex peruvianus fuscus. 1870. III. 724.[2]

—Verslag nopens de gouvernements-Kina-onderneming. 1875. III. 716.
— De samenstelling van quinium. 1871. III. 722.
— Zusammensetzung des ... Quinium's. 1871. III. 722.
— See also GORKOM, K. W. van & MOENS, J. C. Bernelot.
— & Scheffer, R. H. C. C. Het "Mossing" systeem bij de Kinacultuur. 1879. III. 716.
Moens, J. G. Bernelot. Topographische schets van het eiland Batjan. 1856.. I. 465.
Moens, J. G. T. B. Opmerking omtrent de al of niet giftige eigenschappen der Boewa Kamirie. 1859. II. 436.[2]
Mørch. Beretning om nogle Forsøg ... med forskjellige Surrogater for Morbærblade. 1841. III. 148.[1]
Mörch, Otto Josias Nicolai. Catalogus plantarum Horti botanici hafniensis. 1839. I. 40.
— Kort Anviisning til paa en let fattelig Maade at ordne Træer. 1838. III. 201.
— En let Maade at overvintre capske ... Planter. 1836. III. 150.[1]
Moerder, W. Astrophytum myriostigma. 1895. III. 622.[1]
— Les Cereus et leur culture. 1895. III. 621.[1]
— Culture des Echinocactus. 1895. II. 591.[2]
— Le greffage des Cactées. 1896. III. 620.[1]
— Les Mammillaires. 1896. III. 623.[2]
— Les monstruosités parmi les Cactées. 1897. II. 588.[1]
— Les Myriostigmées. 1898. III. 622.[1]
— Les Pilocereus et leur culture. 1895. III. 626.[1]
— Pilocereus senilis. 1895. III. 620.[2]
— Les plus belles espèces d'Echinocactus. 1895. III. 622.[1]
— Quelques considérations sur les Cactées. 1895. III. 620.[1]
— Les semis de Cactées. 1896. III. 620.[1]
Mördes. Ueber den Eisdruck im November 1858. 1859. IV. 190.
Moermann, H. D'où vient la "maladie des Platanes"? 1891. III. 418.[2]
— Van waar komt de "ziekte der Platanen"? 1891. III. 418.[2]
— De ziekte der Platanen te Gent. 1892. III. 418.[2]
Mörner, C. T. En form af Betula verrucosa Ehrh. 1889. II. 120.[1]
— Eine Form von Betula verrucosa. 1889. II. 120.[1]
Mörschel. Ein Frass der grossen Kiefernraupe. 1893. IV. 478.
Mørup, E. Om Beskatningen af Skove i Danmark. 1880. IV. 273.[1]
Moesmang, Julius. Verhalten verschiedener Vögel gegenüber der Nonne. 1890. IV. 90,[1] 200.
Mösser, H. A. Gesammelte Beiträge zur Forstwissenschaft. 1805. IV. 100.[2]
Mössler, Johann Christian. Gemeinnütziges Handbuch der Gewächskunde. 1815. I. 376.
— Handbuch der Gewächskunde. 1815. I. 376.
— Taschenbuch der Botanik zur Selbstbelehrung. 1805. I. 4, 631.
Mössmer, J. T. Verwendung der Schlingpflanzen. 1881. III. 204.[2]
— Vorrichtung zum Versetzen grosser Bäume. 1882. III. 168.[1]
Moet men dik, moet men d'un zaaijen. 1869. III. 156.[1]
Moewes, Franz. Ueber Selbstbestäubung bei Cistus-Arten. 1898. II. 564.[1]
Moffett, O. Propagation of Grapes in open air. 1885. III. 548.[2]
Moffit, Edward. Sur le Xanthoxylum fraxineum. 1887. II. 412.[1]
Moggridge, John Traherne. Contributions to the flora of Mentone. 1864. I. 413.
— Pollard Oaks. 1870. I. 188.
Mohammed ben Driz. L'Eucalyptus dans l'oasis de Tuggurth. 1876. IV. 530.
Mohideen Sheriff, khan Bahadur. See SHERIFF, Mohideen.
Mohl, Hugo von. Ueber die Abhängigkeit des Wachsthums der dicotylen Bäume in die Dicke. 1844. I. 189.
— Ueber den Ablösungsprocess saftiger Pflanzenorgane. 1860. I. 192.[1]
— Ueber die anatomischen Veränderungen des Blattgelenkes. 1860. I. 109,[2] 191.[2]
— Ueber den Bau der grossen getüpfelten Röhren von Ephedra. 1831. II. 54.[1]
— Ueber den Bau der porösen Gefässe. 1832. I. 133.
— Ueber den Bau der Ringgefässe. 1839. I. 133.
— Ueber den Bau der vegetabilischen Zellmembran. 1837. I. 137.

— Ueber den Bau des Cycadeen-Stammes. 1832. II. 2.[1]
— Ueber den Bau des Palmenstammes. 1845. II. 62.[2]
— Ueber den Bau und das Winden der Ranken. 1827. I. 236.[1]
— Über den Bau und die Formen der Pollenkörner. 1834. I. 117.[1]
— Beantwortung der Anfrage ... wie sich die Blattorgane ... zur Holz-Massen-Bildung verhalten. 1850. IV. 64.[2]
— Beiträge zur Anatomie und Physiologie der Gewächse. 1834. I. 117.[1]
— Ein Beitrag zur Lehre vom Dickenwachsthum. 1869. I. 190.[1]
— Beobachtungen über die Umwandlung von Antheren in Carpelle. 1845. I. 101.[2]
— Beobachtungen über die Verwandlung von Antheren in Carpelle. 1836. I. 145.[1]
— Ueber die blaue Färbung der Früchte von Viburnum Tinus. 1870. II. 844.[1]
— On the cambium-layer. 1858. I. 128.[2]
— Ueber die Cambiumschicht des Stammes. 1858. I. 128.[2]
— Sur la couche de cambium. 1858. I. 128.[2]
— Ueber die Cuticula der Gewächse. 1842. I. 129.[1]
— Ueber die Cuticula von Viscum. 1849. II. 178.[1]
— Ueber das Eindringen der Cuticula in die Spaltöffnungen. 1845. I. 131.[1]
— Ueber den Einfluss des Bodens auf die Verbreitung der Alpenpflanzen. 1843. I. 228.[1]
— Einige anatomische ... Bemerkungen über das Holz der Baumwurzeln. 1862. I. 125.
— Einige Andeutungen über den Bau des Bastes. 1855. I. 130.
— Einige Bemerkungen über den Bau der getüpfelten Gefässe. 1842. I. 133.
— Einige Bemerkungen über die Baumvegetation in den Alpen. 1843. I. 348.[1]
— Einige Beobachtungen über dimorphe Blüthen. 1863. I. 114.[2]
— Ueber das Erfrieren der Zweigspitzen. 1848. I. 212.
— Erläuterung und Vertheidigung meiner Ansicht von der Structur der Pflanzensubstanz. 1836. I. 123.[2]
— Examen de la question: La cellulose forme-t-elle la base de toutes les membranes? 1847. I. 137.
— Ueber die fibrosen Zellen der Antheren. 1830. I. 116.[1]
— Ueber die Fleckenkrankheit der Maulbeerblätter. 1854. III. 37.[1]
— Ueber die Flora von Württemberg. 1845. I. 381.
— Ueber die Functionen der Blätter. 1836. I. 172.
— Ueber die Gewinnung des venetianischen Terpenthins. 1859. IV. 452.[1]
— On the growth of cell-membrane. 1852. III. 575.[2]
— Grundzüge der Anatomie und Physiologie der vegetabilischen Zelle. 1842. I. 136.[2]
— Ilex Aquifolium als Theepflanze. 1855. III. 530.[1]
— Ilex Aquifolium såsom Thebuske. 1855. III. 530.[1]
— Ueber das Kieselskelett. 1861. I. 134.[2]
— Ueber die männlichen Blüthen der Coniferen. 1837. II. 18.
— Mikrographie. 1846. I. 36.[2]
— Mikroskopische Untersuchung von Hölzern, welche mit holzsauerm Eisen getränkt sind. 1843. IV. 417.
— Ueber den Milchsaft und seine Bewegung. 1843. I. 191.[2]
— Morphologische Betrachtung der Blätter von Sciadopitys. 1871. II. 49.[1]
— Observations sur la structure des vaisseaux ponctués. 1842. I. 133.
— De Palmarum structura. 1823. II. 62,[2] V. xxvi.[1]
— Sur la pénétration de la cuticule dans les stomates. 1845. I. 131.[1]
— On the penetration of the cuticle into the stomata. 1845. I. 131.[1]
— Ueber die Poren des Pflanzen-Zellgewebes. 1828. I. 124, 156.[2]
— On the power of the living plant to restrain the evaporation of the cell-sap. 1847. I. 166.
— Principles of the anatomy and physiology of the vegetable cell. 1842. I. 138.[2]
— Quelles sont les causes qui déterminent la dilatation et le resserrement des stomates? 1856. I. 131.[1]
— Quelques observations sur les fleurs dimorphes. 1863. I. 114.[1]
— Quelques remarques au sujet de la composition du liber. 1855. I. 130.
— Recherches anatomiques sur la chlorophylle. 1837. I. 140.[1]

Mohl, Hugo von (*continued*).
— Recherches sur la coloration hibernale. 1837. I. 185.²
— Recherches sur la cuticule des plantes. 1842. I. 129.¹
— Recherches sur la structure des vaisseaux annulaires. 1839. I. 133.
— Recherches sur le développement du liège. 1836. I. 130.
— Recherches sur le latex et ses mouvements. 1843. I. 181.²
— Recherches sur les relations dans lesquelles l'accroissement . . . des arbres dicotylés se trouve. 1844. I. 189.
— Ueber die Reizbarkeit der Blätter von Robinia. 1832. II. 382.²
— Researches on the mode in which gum-tragacanth is formed. 1857. II. 333.²
— Researches on the structure of annular vessels. 1839. I. 133.
— Sulla simmetria delle piante. 1836. I. 98.
— Sind die Lenticellen als Wurzelknospen zu betrachten? 1832. I. 132.¹
— Some remarks on the structure of dotted vessels. 1842. I. 133.
— Über die Spaltöffnungen . . . der Proteaceen. 1833. II. 158.²
— De la structure de gros tubes ponctués des Ephedra. 1831. II. 54.¹
— Sur la structure et les formes des grains de pollen. 1834. I. 117.¹
— On the supposed existence of cellulose in starch-grains. 1859. I. 140.¹
— Ueber die Symmetrie der Pflanzen. 1836. I. 98.
— Die Traubenkrankheit. 1852. III. 575.²
— Untersuchung der Frage: Welche Autorität soll den Gattungsnamen der Pflanzen beigegeben werden? 1836. I. 253.²
— Untersuchung der Frage, bildet die Cellulose die Grundlage sämmtlicher . . . Membranen? 1847. I. 137.
— Untersuchungen über die anatomischen Verhältnisse des Chlorophylls. 1837. I. 140.²
— Untersuchungen über die Entstehungsweise des Traganthgummi. 1857. II. 333.²
— Untersuchungen über die Entwicklung des Korkes und der Borke. 1836. I. 130.
— Untersuchungen über die Frage: In welchem System des Holzes wird der rohe Nahrungssaft . . . geleitet? 1843. I. 163.
— Untersuchungen über die Lenticellen. 1836. I. 132.¹
— Untersuchungen über die winterliche Färbung. 1837. I. 185.²
— Untersuchungen über die Wurzel-Ausscheidung. 1838. I. 161.
— Die vegetabilische Zelle. 1842. I. 136.²
— Ueber die Verbindung der Pflanzen-Zellen. 1835. I. 123.²
— Vermischte Schriften botanischen Inhalts. 1845. I. 520.¹
— Ueber das Vermögen der lebenden Pflanze die Verdunstung des Zellsaftes zu beschränken. 1847. I. 166.
— Ueber den Vernarbungsprocess bei der Pflanze. 1849. I. 207.¹
— Ueber den vorgeblichen Gehalt der Stärkekörner an Cellulose. 1859. I. 140.¹
— Ueber das Wachsthum der Zellmembran. 1846. I. 137.·
— Welche Ursachen bewirken die Erweiterung und Verengung der Spaltöffnungen? 1856. I. 131.²
— Ueber den Wiederersatz des Korkes bei Quercus Suber. 1848. II. 140.¹

Mohl, Moriz. Einige Beiträge zur Wald-Erhaltungs-Frage. 1879. IV. 180.²

Mohnike, Otto. Blicke auf das Pflanzen- und Thierleben in den niederländischen Malaienländern. 1883. I. 466.

Mohr, Samenbruch bei der Weinbeere. 1872. III. 560.

Mohr, Alfred. Un arbre utile, le Chêne-Liége. 1881. IV. 518.¹
— Les Cycadées. 1876. II. 2.²
— Le Lilas double de Lemoine. 1882. III. 681.¹
— Les Mahonia. 1878. III. 395.¹
— Quelques Macrozamia nouveaux. 1877. III. 285.²
— Les Spirées ligneuses. 1883. III. 460.²

Mohr, C. Über die Anwendung der in den königlich preussischen Provinzen am linken Rheinufer . . . bestehenden französischen Forststrafgesetze. 1834. IV. 320.

Mohr, Charles Theodore. The distribution of some forest-trees in the southern states. 1893. I. 312, *517*,² *IV. 77*.¹
— On the distributions of the . . . trees in the Gulf region. 1882. IV. 77.²
— The Florida Spruce Pine. 1890. II. 41.²
— The forests of Alabama. 1879. IV. 339.

— The forests of the vicinity of Mobile. 188.? I. 317,¹ *IV. 77*.²
— The general features of the vegetation of Louisiana. 1892. I. 319, *III. 264*.¹
— The hardwood forests of the South. 1888. IV. 340.
— Hard-wood timber in the south. 1893. IV. 358.¹
— The last addition to the shrubs of eastern North America. 1889. II. 439.²
— The Long-leaved Pine. 1888. II. 44.¹
— The medicinal plants of Alabama. 1893. III. 63.¹
— Notes on . . . plants of the Alabama flora. 1897. I. 319.
— Notes on some . . . plants of the Alabama flora. 1899. II. 271.¹
— Our remaining hard-wood resources. 1893. IV. 338,¹ 555.²
— The Pecan tree. 1889. III. 354.¹
— Pinus glabra. 1890. II. 42.¹
— Preliminary list of the plants . . . in Alabama. 1880. I. 319.
— Present condition of forests of Longleaf Pine. 1898. II. 44.¹
— Quercus Durandii Buckley. 1883. II. 133.²
— On Quercus Durandii Buckley. 1884. II. 133.²
— Report on the forests of Sand Mountain. 1898. IV. 340.
— Ressources en bois durs des états méridionaux de l'Amérique du Nord. 1893. IV. 555.²
— Rhus cotinoides Nutt. 1883. II. 455.²
— The timber Pines of the southern United States. 1896. *II. 39*,¹ IV. 462.²
— The timber problem in the South. 1893. IV. 340.
— Variation in the leaves of Clematis reticulata. 1892. II. 199.¹

Mohr, Friedrich. Commentar zur Pharmacopoea germanica. 1873. III. 249.
— Commentar zur Preussischen Pharmacopöe. 1847. III. 249.
— The Grape vine. 1864. III. 553.·
— Der Weinbau und die Weinbereitungskunde. 1865. III. -553.¹
— Der Weinstock und der Wein. 1864. III. 553.¹

Mohr, H. Forsög til en Islands Naturhistorie. 1786. I. 352.

Mohr, Karl. Bericht über die . . . Versuche behufs Bekämpfung flanzlicher Schmarotzer. 1900. III. 197.
— Die Insektengifte. 1893. III. 197.
— Über Krankheiten der Pfirsichbäume. 1898. III. 442.¹
— Über die Kupferkalkbrühe als Cryptogamicid. 1899. III. 198.¹
— Mitteilungen über . . . wichtige Produkte des Pflanzenreiches. 1885. III. 218.¹
— Versuche, betreffend die Vertilgung der Cossusraupen. 1894. III. 197.
— Vertilgung der Heckenraupen auf Crataegus. 1894. III. 422.²

Mohr, Karl Friedrich. Erfrieren der Pflanzen. 1872. I. 212.
— *See also* GEIGER, P. L. & MOHR, C. F.
— The Mohwa tree . . . in the Central Provinces. 1880. IV. 554.²

Moichine. Tarif métrique de cubage des bois. 1885. IV. 228.

Moir, E. McA. Cattle-grazing in Deodar forests. 1882. IV. 447.²
— The export works in the Bamsu forest. 1898. IV. 390.¹
— Maps relating to the report on the . . . management of forest reserves in the Jeypore state. 188.? IV. 250.¹
— Remarks on the coppicing powers of certain trees. 1879. IV. 132.¹
— Report of a visit to the torrent regions of the Hautes and Basses Alpes. 1881. IV. *185*,² 360.
— Report on the Deota sledge road. 1886. IV. 389.
— Report on the forests of Ajmere and Merwara. 1883. IV. 378.
— Report on the proposed afforestation of the Hoshiarpur Siwaliks. 1884. IV. 168.¹
— A tour in Japan. 1886. IV. 376.¹
— A tour in the landes. 1896. IV. 362.
— Visit to the Big trees of Mariposa. 1887. II. 51.¹
— Visit to the Culbin Sands. 1894. IV. 359.¹
— & **Fernandez**, E. E. Report on the forests of Ajmere and Merwara. 1882. IV. 377.²

Moiroud, L. Traité élémentaire de matière médicale. 1843. III. 243.

Moissan, Charles Auguste. Flore nantaise. 1839. I. 409.

Moissan, Henri. Sur les volumes d'oxygène absorbé. 1878. I. 170.
— *See also* DEHÉRAIN, P. P. & MOISSAN, Henri.
— & **Landrin**, Ed. Recherches sur la préparation . . . de l'aricine. 1890. III. 726.¹

Moitessier, Albert. Essai sur les propriétés des Solanées. 1856. III. 698.[2]

Moitrier, A. Traité pratique de la culture de l'Osier. 1855. III. 347.

Mojon, J. Sur l'eau-de-vie d'Arbouse. 1814. III. 648.[1]

Mokrý, (*Forstmeister*). Versuche in der Bekämpfung des Nonnenspinners. 1896. IV. 202.

Mokrzhetzki, S. A. *See* Мокржецкій, C. A.

Mola, Alejandro. Cómo se repueblan los montes. 1892. IV. 547.[1]

— Encinares extremeños. 1893. IV. 501.[1]

— El paludismo en la provincia de Cáceres. 1894. IV. 556.[1]

Moldenhauer, F. Ilixanthin und Ilexsäure. 1857. II. 463.[2]

Moldenhawer, J. J. P. Beyträge zur Anatomie der Pflanzen. 1812. I. 98.

— Tentamen in Historiam plantarum Theophrasti. 1791. I. 292, 530.[2]

Moldenhawer, Johann Heinrich Daniel. Dissertatio anatomica de vasis plantarum. 1779. I. 133.

Moldenke, Charles E. Über die in altägyptischen Texten erwähnten Bäume. 1887. I. 514.[2]

Molendo, Ludwig. Beitrag zur Kenntniss der Brombeersträucher Südbayerns. 1857. II. 301.[2]

Molengraaff, Gustaaf Adolf Frederik. *See* HALLIER, H. G. & MOLENGRAAFF, G. A. F.

Molér, Wilhelm. Bidrag till kannedom om vedens byggnad hos Dvergbjörken. 1877. II. 119.[2]

Moleschott, Jakob. Kritische Betrachtung von Liebig's Theorie der Pflanzenernährung.. 1845. I. 157.

— Physiologie des Stoffwechsels. 1851. I. 175.

Molesworth, G. L. Durability of Indian railway sleepers. 1881. IV. 423.[2]

Molina, Giovanni Ignazio. Compendio de la historia geográfica . . . de Chile. 1788. I. 345.

— Compendio della storia geografica, naturale . . . del Chile. 1776. I. 345.

— Essai sur l'histoire naturelle du Chili. 1782. I. 345.

— The geographical, natural and civil history of Chili. 1788. I. 345.

— Saggio sulla storia naturale del Chili. 1782. I. 345.

— Versuch einer Naturgeschichte von Chili. 1782. I. 345.

Molina, Juan Ignacio. *See* MOLINA, G. I.

Molina y Saurín, Alejo. Ensayo aritmético sobre el valor de los plantios. 1856. IV. 254.

Molinariis, Simon de. Ambrosia asiatica. 1672. III. 604.[2]

Molisch, Hans. Ueber das Abfallen der Blätter. 1887. I. 192.[1]

— Über die Ablagerung von kohlensaurem Kalk. 1881. I. 139.

— Über das Ausfliessen des Saftes aus . . . Lianen. 1898. I. 169.[1]

— Das Bewegungsvermögen der Keimpflanze. 1889. I. 194.

— Om Bladenes Affalden. 1887. I. 192.[1]

— Blattgrün und Blumenblau. 1890. I. 185.[1]

— Ueber das Bluten tropischer Holzgewächse. 1898. I. 169.[1]

— Botanische Beobachtungen auf Java. 1898. I. 169,[1] III. 319,[2] 479.[2] — 1899. III. 708.[1]

— Collenchymatische Korke. 1889. II. 769.[2]

— Der Einfluss des Bodens auf die Blüthenfarbe der Hortensien. 1897. II. 241.[1]

— Das Erfrieren von Pflanzen. 1896. I. 212.

— Ueber kalkfreie Crystolithen. 1882. II. 804.[1]

— Zur Kenntniss der Einlagerung von Kalkoxalatkrystallen. 1882. I. 139.

— Zur Kenntniss der Thyllen, nebst Beobachtungen über Wundheilung in der Pflanze. 1889. I. 134.[1]

— Knollenmasern bei Eucalyptus. 1887. II. 623.[2]

— Die Krystallisation . . . des Xanthophylls. 1896. I. 142.

— Ueber das Längenwachsthum geköpfter . . . Wurzeln. 1883. I. 195.[2]

— Ueber Laubfall. 1886. I. 192.[1]

— Ueber merkwürdig geformte Proteinkörper in den Zweigen von Epiphyllum. 1885. II. 594.[1]

— Notiz über das Verhalten von Gingko. 1889. II. 8.[1]

— Zur Physiologie des Pollens. 1893. I. 201.[2]

— Über Pseudoindican. 1899. III. 708.[2]

— Sur les relations entre les sels azotés et la plante. 1888. I. 159.

— Die Secretion des Palmweins. 1898. III. 319.[2]

— Über das sogenannte Indigogährung. 1898. III. 479.[2] I. 212.

— Stirbt die gefrorene Pflanze erst beim Aufthauen? 1897. I. 212.

— Untersuchungen über das Erfrieren der Pflanzen. 1897. I. 212.

— Untersuchungen über den Hydrotropismus. 1884. I. 194.

— Vergleichende Anatomie des Holzes der Ebenaceen. 1879. II. 700.[2]

— Das Vorkommen und der Nachweis des Indicans. 1893. I. 177.

— Ueber das Vorkommen von Indican. 1899. I. 178.

— Über Wurzelausscheidungen. 1888. I. 162.

— *See also* WIESNER, Julius & MOLISCH, Hans.

Molitor, Ágost. Honositásra alkalmas amerikai erdei fák. 1881. IV. 127.[2]

— A kaliforniai Vöröfa. 1877. IV. 484.[1]

Molkenboer, Julian Hendrik & **Kerbert**, C. Flora leidensis. 1840. I. 391.[1]

Moll, Ferdinand. Ansichten . . . über die Dreillingholzverkohlung. 1858. IV. 394.

— Die Hoficer k. k. Militär-Invalidenfonds-Forste. 1862. IV. 250.[1]

— Die Waldwerthschätzung für den Staatsgüterverkauf. 1865. IV. 255.

Moll, Jan Wilhelm. Sur un appareil à sécher les plantes pour l'herbier. 1893. I. 36.[1]

— Over het droppelen . . . van bladeren. 1880. I. 169.[1]

— Handboek der plantbeschrijving. 1900. V. ·IX.[1]

— Invloed van Darwin's afstammingsleer. 1890. I. 243.[1]

— Eene nieuwe microchemische looizuur reactie. 1882. I. 521.[1]

— Quelques observations concernant l'influence de la gelée. 1880. I. 212.

— Recherches sur l'origine du carbone des plantes. 1877. I. 159.

— Een toestel om planten voor het herbarium te drogen. 1893. I. 36.[1]

— Ueber Tropfenausscheidung . . . bei Blättern. 1880. I. 169.[1]

— Untersuchung über Tropfenausscheidung. 1880. I. 169.[1]

— Ueber den Ursprung des Kohlenstoffs der Pflanzen. 1877. I. 159.

Moll, Karl Erenbert, *Freiherr* von. Sammlung der Forstordnungen verschiedener Länder. *See* MÜLLENKAMPF, F. D. F. 1791. IV. 314.[1]

— *See also* SCHRANK, Franz von Paula von & MOLL, K. E., *Ritter* von.

Moll, L. Rapport . . . sur l'agriculture de la Corse. 1837. III. 125.

Molle, Philippe. Recherches de microchimie comparée . . . Solanacées. 1895. II. 768.[2]

Moller, Adolpho F. Der Avocatbaum. 1900. III. 407.[2]

— Einige medizinische Pflanzen von S. Thomé. 1897. III. 93.[2]

— Der Kapokbaum. 1900. III. 589.[2]

— Kautschuk in den portugiesisch-afrikanischen Kolonien. 1897. III. 229.

— Der Obabaum von S. Thomé. 1900. III. 610.[2]

— Observações phaenologicas. 1896. I. 226.[2]

— Pitch Pine. 1895. IV. 559.[1]

— Treculia africana. 1900. III. 381.[1]

Moller, Johann Friedrich. De vera peruviani corticis vi specifica. 1768. III. 111.

Mollet, Claude. Théatre des jardinages. 1660. III. 111.

Molleveaux, Edmondage des betteraves. 1890. IV. 171.

Molliard, Marin. Sur les modifications produites . . . par l'action des Phytoptus. 1899. III. 192.[1]

— Note de pathologie végétale. 1898. III. 670.[1]

Mollier, J. N. De houtsoorten van het Prinsen-eiland. 1863. IV. 399.[2]

Mollin, Joseph. Hortus Academiae aboënsis. *See* HELLENIUS, C. N. 1779. I. 41.

Mollison, J. W. Cultivation of Pepper in the Bombay Presidency. 1900. III. 343.[2]

— Cultivation of the Betel-nut Palm. 1900. III. 320.[1]

Molnár, Istyán. A fatenyésztés különös tekintettel a községi faiskolákra és befásitásokra. 1899. III. 115.[2]

Molnár, Stephan von. Welche Erfahrungen sind . . . mit amerikanischen Rebensorten . . . gemacht worden? 1890. III. 547.

Molon, Girolamo. Le varietà di piante da frutto raccomandabili. 1859. III. 145.[1]

Moloney, Alfred. Sketch of the forestry of west Africa. 1887. IV. 89,[1] 879.[2]

Moltchanof, A. P. *See* Молчановъ, A. П.

Molter, J. B. J. Einschlagen des Blitzes in Rothbuchen. 1828. IV. 496, *548*.[1]

Moly, J. Singular Scotch Fir. 1857. II. 48.³
Molyneux, Edwin. Buddleia globosa. 1889. III. 681.²
— Exochorda grandiflora. 1900. III. 424.¹
— Garden hedges. 1886. III. 214.¹
— Grape growing for amateurs. 1891. III. 554.¹
Monaghan. Beurre de Cocotier. 1890. III. 324.¹
Monahan, F. J. Note on the cultivation of Rhea. 1897. III. 381.²
Monard, Charles, (sr). Monstruosité remarquable d'une poire. 1846. II. 279.²
— Note sur une poire monstrueuse. 1855. II. 279.³
Monardes, Nicolás. Delle cose che vengono portate dall' Indie Occidentali. 1569. III. 265.²
— Description oder Beschreibung des. Holtzes Sassafras. 1613. III. 407.²
— Histoire des simples medicamens apportés de l'Amérique. 1569. III. 265.²
— Della historia de i semplici . . . portate dall' Indie Orientali. 1569. III. 265.²
— Historia medicinal . . . de nuestras Indias Occidentales. 1569. III. 265.²
— Joyfull newes out of the newe founde worlde. 1569. III. 265.³
— Libri tres, magna medicinae secreta. 1551. III. 453.³
— Dos libros, el uno que trata . . . de nuestras Indias Occidentales. 1569. III. 265.²
— Primera y segunda y tercera partes de la historia medicinal. 1569. III. 265.³
— De Rosa et partibus ejus. 1551. III. 453.²
— De simplicibus medicamentis ex occidentali India. 1569. III. 265.³
— Simplicium medicamentorum ex novo orbe. 1569. III. 265.³
Monathliche Beschäftigungen für einen Baum- und Plantagen-Gärtner. See MUENCHHAUSEN, Otto, Freiherr von. III. 101.³
Monatliche Mittheilungen aus dem Gesammtgebiete der Naturwissenschaften. See NATURWISSENSCHAFTLICHER VEREIN DES REGIERUNGSBEZIRKES FRANKFURT.
Monatliche Nachrichten schweizer. Neuheiten. IV. 13.²
Monatsblatt für Gartenbau in Schleswig-Holstein. III. 13.
Monatschrift für das Forst- und Jagdwesen. IV. 10.
Monatsschrift für das württembergische Forstwesen. IV. 10.
Monatsschrift für Kakteenkunde. 1891. II. 586,² III. 13.
Monatsschrift für Obst- und Weinbau. See MITTHEILUNGEN für Obst- und Weinbau. III. 24.¹
Monatsschrift für Pomologie. III. 13.
Monceau, Henri Louis DUHAMEL DU. See DUHAMEL DU MONCEAU, H. L.
Moncel, DELISLE DE. See DELISLE DE MONCEL.
Moncel, Théodore. Conductibilité électrique des arbres. 1877. I. 231.¹
Monchalait. De l'Eucalyptus. 1867. IV. 529.³
Monchanin, Étienne. Traité de palissage. 1856. III. 198.¹
Monck, Sir Charles Miles Lambert. A plan for transplanting large forest trees in parks. 1830. III. 167.
Monckton, E. H. C. On the manufacture of cloth and paper from . . . Müddár. 1850. III. 692.²
Moncrieffe House. 1876. II. 482.²
Die Mondblume (Yucca). 1870. III. 339.²
Le Monde des plantes. I. 22.
Les Mondes. III. 20.
Mondonville, L. F. PERIER-. See PERIER-MONDONVILLE, L. F.
Monecke, (Oberförster). Über den Ertrag der Weidenbäume. 1837. III. 350.²
Monestier, Charles. Sur l'application du sulfure de carbone. 1874. III. 566.¹
— Procédé Ch. Monestier . . . Destruction du phylloxéra par les gaz. 1873. III. 759.
Moneuze-Grand-Jean. Manière de planter les arbres en toutes saisons. 1848. III. 168.²
Money, Edward. The cultivation and manufacture of Tea. 1872. III. 603.
— Essay on the cultivation & manufacture of Tea. 1872. III. 603.
— Prize essay on the cultivation . . . of Tea in India. 1872. III. 603.
— & Watson, J. F. W. Essay on the cultivation . . . of Tea. 1872. III. 603.
— Two prize essays on the cultivation. 1872. III. 603.
Mongenot, C. La joux verte. Production d'une futaie jardinée. 1895. IV. 234
— Note sur l'accroissement. 1892. IV. 258.

— Note sur la production d'une parcelle de aspinière. 1892. IV. 237.
— Note sur les produits des forêts domaniales des Vosges. 1898. IV. 261,¹ 551.¹
— Notice sommaire sur les forêts domaniales du département des Vosges. 1900. IV. 362.
— Les produits des forêts domaniales des Vosges. 1898. IV. 388.²
— Statistique des produits des forêts domaniales des Vosges. 1898. IV. 362.
— Tarifs simplifiés pour le cubage. 1892. IV. 219.
Mongeot, A. DIDIER-. See DIDIER-MONGEOT, A.
Monges, Jules. Étude sur la Rose. 1884. II. 290.²
Monginot, François de. De la guérison des fièvres par le quinquina. 1679. III. 719.
Mongredien, Augustus. The Heatherside manual of hardy trees and shrubs. 1874. III. 78.³
— Trees and shrubs for English plantations. 1870. III. 78.¹
Monhaupt, (Handelsgärtner, Breslau). Behandlung der Pfirsich- und Aprikosenbäume. 1827. III. 430.¹
Monheim, V. See BEY, de, FOERSTER, A. & MONHEIM, V.
Monier, Émile. Mémoire sur la détermination du tannin. 1858. I. 183.
— Note sur la teinture des bois. 1862. I. 521.¹
Moniot, E. Récolte de la faine. 1893. IV. 500.¹
Le Moniteur d'horticulture. III. 20.
Le Moniteur des eaux et forêts. IV. 12.³
Le Moniteur horticole belge. Bruxelles. III. 15.
Le Moniteur horticole belge. Ed. by L. G. Gillekens. III. 15.
Moniteur horticole illustré. See ILLUSTRIRTE Berichte . . . III. 12.
Moniteur officiel du commerce. III. 20.
Le Moniteur scientifique. See REVUE scientifique et industrielle. I. 22.
Monkevitz, A. See MOHKEBHIIE, A.
Monlleó, M. Ruiz. See RUIZ MONLLEÓ, M.
Monnereau, Élie. Le parfait indigotier. 1765. III. 478.²
Monnet, Léon Ernest. De la Kola. 1884. III. 590.²
Monnet, P. & Barbier, Philippe. Sur une nouvelle source de rhodinol. 1893. III. 491.³
Monnier, Denis. Rapport sur le traitement des Vignes phylloxérées. 1878. III. 760.
— & Covelle, E. Le phylloxéra dans le canton de Genève. 1878. III. 760.
Monnot le Roy. Fructification en France . . . du Palmier-dattier. 1877. III. 328.¹
Monnoyer, Baptiste. Livre de toutes sortes de fleurs d'après nature. 169.? I. 516.
Monographie des espèces de Spiraea cultivées. 1858. III. 460.³
Monographie des Noyers et Noisetiers. 1835. III. 354.¹
Monographiya . . . See Монографія . . .
Monro, Sir David. On the leading features of the geographical botany of the provinces of Nelson and Marlborough. 1869. I. 506.²
Monro, Donald. An account of . . . making the otter of Roses, 1790. III. 454.¹
— A treatise on medical and pharmaceutical chymistry. 1788. III. 241.
Monro, James. See MUNRO, James.
Monroe, John. The American botanist. 1824. III. 262.¹
Mons, Jean Baptiste van. Arbres fruitiers. 1835. III. 140.¹
— Bemerkungen über den Rhus radicans. 1803. III. 528.¹
— Catalogue descriptif abrégé. 1823. III. 77.
— Erfahrungen über die heilsame Anwendung des wurzelnden Sumachs. 1801. III. 528.¹
— Essai pomologique. 1819. III. 50.¹
— Sur la fabrication et les usages du vinaigre de bois. 1819. IV. 432.¹
— Incision annulaire. 1831. III. 175.¹
— Pharmacopée usuelle. 1821. III. 250.¹
— Zwei neue Eigenschaften des Zauberringes. 1831. III. 175.¹
A monstrosity of Pilocereus senilis. 1895. II. 591.²
A monstrous form of the Black Spruce. 1895. II. 38.¹
Montagne, Jean François Camille. A brief sketch of the present state of the . . . Vine mildew. 1853. III. 576.
— Coup d'oeil rapide sur l'état actuel de . . . la maladie de la Vigne. 1853. III. 576.
— Sur diverses maladies des Caféiers. 1860. III. 189.
— Rapport de la commission chargée d'examiner les travaux sur la maladie de la Vigne. 1854. III. 576.
— & Decaisne, Joseph. Voyage au Pôle Sud. 1845. I. 509.¹

Montagni, Luigi. Catalogo delle piante coltivate nel Giardino di Bibbiani. 1848. I. 83.
— Le Conifere coltivate a Bibbiani. 1877. I. 64.
— Effetti del gelo del di 12 dicembre 1885. 1886. III. 49.[1]
— L'Eucalyptus populifolia. 1876. III. 634.[3]
— Fruttificazione del Gingko. 1877. II. 8.[1]
— L'Hovenia dulcis Thumb. [sic]. 1876. III. 541.[3]
Montalbani, Ovidio. Arboreae monstrositates. 166.? I. 142.
— Bibliotheca botanica. 1657. I. 1.
— Catalogus alphabeticus plantarum officinalium. 1670. III. 53.
— Geoscopia ampelite. 1635. III. 557.[2]
— Hortus botanographicus. 1660. I. 286.
— Index plantarum omnium. 1624. I. 284.
— Monstrosarum aliquot observationum . . . indicatio. 1660. I. 142.
— Nova antepraeludialis dendranatomes. 1660. I. 97.
Montaña, José GIL Y. See GIL Y MONTAÑA, José.
Montana — Agricultural experiment station. Annual report. Bulletin. III. 6.
Montandon, F. J. & Friche-Joset. See FRICHE-JOSET & MONTANDON, F. J.
Montané. El Jaborandi. 1876. III. 505.[1]
Montanus, Arnoldus. De nieuwe en onbekende weereld. 1671. III. 264.[1]
Montaudry. Traité de cubage des bois. n. d. IV. 220.
Montbéliard — Société d'émulation. See SOCIÉTÉ . . . I. 23.
Montbrison, Louis Bernard de. Lettres à Mme. de C. . . . sur la botanique. 1802. I. 93.
Montbron, comte de. Lettre sur sa collection d'arbres de Clervaut prés Châtellerault. 1831. I. 57.
Monte Pigati, Giovanni Antonio de. Nova . . . universae botanices rudimenta. 1757. I. 83.
Monteath, Robert. The forester's guide. 1820. IV. 108.[1]
— Miscellaneous reports on woods. 1827. IV. 120.
— A new and easy system of draining. 1829. IV. 120.
— Remarks on the culture & utility . . . of home-grown timber. 1832. IV. 120.
Montebello, marquis de & others. Documents relatifs aux concessions des forêts de Chênes-Liége. 1860. IV. 517.[2]
Montefiore, Arthur. Tea-planting in Assam. 1888. III. 604.[1]
Monteiro, Rose. Delagoa Bay. 1891. I. 495.
Monteiro de Nautet, D. G. Germination of Welwitschia. 1882. II. 55.[2]
Montejo, M. A. Breves observaciones sobre la nutricion vegetal. 1884. I. 159.
Montelatici, D. V. A. Progetto nuovo per fare che gli Ulivi . . . non siano danneggiati. 1762. III. 814.[1]
Montell, R. Öfversigt af forstlitteraturen i Finland. 1891. IV. 2.
Montelucci, Ruggero. L' influenza dei fiori sull' organismo umano. 1898. I. 516.
Montemartini, Luigi. Contributo allo studio dell' anatomia . . . delle Opunzie. 1899. II. 596.[1]
— Contribuzione allo studio del passaggio dalla radice al fusto. 1900. I. 106.[1]
— Fisiologia vegetale. 1898. I. 149.[1]
— La Monilia fructigena. 1899. III. 582.[1]
— Un nuovo micromicete della Vite. 1899. III. 592.
— Sopra il parassitismo dell' "Aureobasidium." 1898. III. 582.
— Ricerche intorno all' accrescimento delle piante. 1899. I. 188.
— & **Farneti,** Rodolfo. Intorno alla malattia della Vite nel Caucaso. 1900. III. 582.
Il **Montenegro.** 1865. IV. 374.[2]
Montepío. 1893. IV. 554.[2]
The **Monterey** Cypress. 1874. III. 302.[2]
The **Monterey** Cypress at home. 1886. II. 29.[2]
The **Monterey** Pine. 1896. II. 45.[2]
Montes. Discusión del presupuesto. 1892. IV. 553.[2]
Montes, Paul. Discussion sur la question de savoir s'il y a avantage pour l'état d'exploiter lui-même ses forêts. 1899. IV. 276.[1]
Montes, Victoriano. Dictamen sobre las causas que influyen eu las continuadas sequías . . . de Almería. 1879. IV. 50.
— Medios previsores contra las inundaciones. 1891. IV. 542.[1]
— Principios previsores contra las inundaciones. 1891. IV. 542.[1]
Los **montes** de Bosnia. 1884. IV. 374.[2]
Los **montes** de Dinamarca. 1886. IV. 343.[2]

Montes de Hungria. 1886. IV. 373.
Los **montes** de propios. 1882. IV. 270.
Los **montes** de Rusia. 1884. IV. 346.
Los **montes** en Filipinas. 1875. IV. 376.[2]
Los **montes** . . . en la Exposición universal de Paris. 1900. IV. 540.[1]
Los **montes** en la memoria del Señor Camacho. 1883. IV. 276.[1]
Montes enajenables. 1893. IV. 552.[1]
Los **montes** y la diputación foral de Navarra. 1893. IV. 541.
Los **montes** y los canales según "El Heraldo." 1893. IV. 553.[2]
Montesanto, Giuseppe. Dei libri de Teofrasto Eresio. 1822. I. 292.
Montet. Maladie des Mûriers. 1764. III. 378.
Monteton, Freiherr von. Kurze Nachricht über die Feigen-Bäume zu Priort. 1828. III. 369.[1]
Monteverde, Nicolai. See БАЗАРОВъ, A. & МОНТЕВЕРДЕ, H.
Montevideo — Museo nacional. See MUSEO . . . I. 7.[3]
Montgolfier, J. de. Sur le camphre de Patchouli. 1877. III. 698.[2]
Montgomery. Essay on raising and managing hedges. 1835. III. 212.[2]
Montgomery, W. The 'Agy' tree. 1885. III. 482.[1]
The **Month.** I. 19.
Monthien, Paul. Compte rendu du Congrès pomologique. 1896. III. 85.
The **Monthly** journal of medicine. I. 19.
Monthly journal of natural history for the north of England. See The NATURALIST. Huddersfield. I. 19.
Monthly journal of science. See QUARTERLY journal of science. I. 19.
Monthly microscopical journal. See MICROSCOPICAL SOCIETY OF LONDON. I. 19.
Monti, Antonio. Associazione forestale. 1864. IV. 41.[1]
— Riflessioni sulla decadenza delle foreste. 1864. IV. 293.[2]
Monti, Giuseppe. Exoticorum simplicium medicamentorum varii indices. 1724. III. 54.
— De florum pulchritudini conservanda. 1745. I. 35.
— De gummi quibusdam. 1745. I. 180.[1]
— Indices botanici et materiae medicae. 1724. I. 72.[1]
— Plantarum varii indices. 1724. I. 72,[1] V. IX.[2]
— De plantis venenatis. 1755. III. 59.[2]
— De variis exoticis plantis. 1746. I. 291.
Monti, Lorenzo. Dizionario botanico veronese. 1817. I. 74.[2]
Montif, Lucian. Neu vermehrte Garten-Lust. 1698. III. 102.
— Neue Gartenlust. 1698. III. 102.
Montigny, C. de. Sur le Bambou du nord de la Chine. 1860. III. 814.[1]
Montillot, Louis. Les insectes nuisibles. 1891. III. 191.
Montin, Lars. Anmärkningar vid Flyg-sandens cultiverande. 1768. IV. 158.[1]
— Erica retorta. 1774. II. 669.[1]
— Lyckadt försök, med Askelöfs-saft bota giftiga ormarsbett. 1765. IV. 534.[2]
— Thunbergia, et nytt ört-slägte. 1773. II. 804.[1]
Montmahou, E. de. Manuel médico-légal des poisons. 1824. III. 260.[2]
Montmorency — Société d'horticulture. See SOCIÉTÉ . . . III. 21.
Montoya, Fulgencio. Tabla para hallar la cubicación de los árboles en rollo. 1874. IV. 227.
Montpascal, comte VILLA DE. See VILLA DE MONTPASCAL, comte.
Montpellier, J. A. La sénilisation rapide des bois. 1899. IV. 416.[2]
Montpellier — Académie des sciences et lettres. See ACADÉMIE . . . I. 20.
Montpellier — L'École nationale d'agriculture. See L'ÉCOLE . . . II. 19.
Montpellier médical. I. 22.
Montpéreux, Frédéric DUBOIS DE. See DUBOIS DE MONTPÉREUX, Frédéric.
Montreal — Natural history society. Proceedings. See CANADIAN naturalist and geologist. I. 4.[1]
Montreal agricultural and horticultural society. Report. See MONTREAL HORTICULTURAL SOCIETY. III. 2.
Montreal botanic garden. Annual report. 1886. I. 38.[2]
Montreal horticultural society and fruit growers' association of the province of Quebec. Report. III. 2.
Montréscr, C-te Bourdeille de. Les sources de la flore des provinces . . . de Kieff. 1893. I. 3.[2]
Montresor, V. See МОНТРЕЗОРъ, B.

Montrichard, de (*sous-inspecteur des forêts*). Notice sur la règle à cubage des arbres. 1878. IV. 217.
Montrouzier, Xavier. Flore de l'île Art. 1860. I. 508.[2]
Montsainct, Thomas. Le Jardin senonois. 1604. I. 56.
Montserrat. 1888. III. 267.[1]
Montvalon, *comte* de. Notice sur l'Avaux ou Avaoussé. 1840. III. 758.[1]
— De la reproduction . . . des bois de Pins. 1840. V. xxxii.[2]
Montviel, (*député, Lot-et-Garonne*) VASSAL DE. *See* VASSAL DE MONTVIEL.
Monviliers, Arthur. Deux jolies plantes péruviennes. 1893. III. 338.[2]
Monville, de. Cactées nouvelles. 1839. II. 585.[2]
— Description des fleurs de quelques . . . Mammillaires. 1841. II. 594.[1]
— Note sur l'Euphorbia splendens var. Neumanniana. 1839. III. 518.[2]
Monzini, Antonio. Seminagione delle piante resinose. 1866. IV. 149.[1]
Moodiiar, Ramasawmy. The collection . . . of lac in the Nagpore territory. 1862. III. 540.[1]
Moody, S. The Palm tree. 1864. II. 63.[2]
Moolika sankalitum; or, Mingling of herbs. 1835. III. 277.
Moon, Alexander. A catalogue of the . . . plants growing in Ceylon. 1824. I. 476.[2]
Moon, Samuel C. Clerodendron serotinum. 1890. III. 696.[2]
— The Exochorda grandiflora. 1886. III. 424.[1]
Moon, W. H. Cercis japonica. 1877. III. 472.[1]
Moor, Egon von. Zur Altersschwäche von Obstsorten. 1881. I. 249.[1]
— Crataegus-Hecken als Unterlagen für Birnen. 1881. III. 422.[2]
— Die Forst-Anlagen auf den Steppen Südrusslands. 1885. IV. 157.
Moorcroft, William. Culture des Noyers dans le Cachemire. 1832. III. 354.[1]
— On the fruit trees of Kashmeer. 1838. III. 92.[1]
— Notices of the natural productions . . . of Cashmere. 1832. III. 354.[1]
Moore. *See also* MORE.
Moore. Examen chimique de la cire végétale du Myrica. 1862. II. 111.[1]
Moore. Report on the Prune industry of California. 1892. III. 433.[2]
Moore, Charles. Catalogue of plants in the Government botanic garden, Sydney. 1857. I. 69.[1]
— A census of the plants of New South Wales. 1884. I. 503.
— Description of a new Myrtaceous tree. 1893. II. 627.[1]
— Einige Bemerkungen über. die Gattung Macrozamia . . . 1884. II. 6.[2]
— On the fibre plants of N. S. Wales. 1866. III. 234.
— Handbook of the flora of N. S. Wales. 1893. I. 504.
— Lord Howe's Island. 1869. I. 508.[2]
— Notes on the genus Macrozamia. 1884. II. 6.[2]
— Plants with their habitats, discovered . . . since the publication of the Handbook. 1893. I. 504.
— Remarks on the botany of Lord Howe's Island. 1872. I. 508.[2]
— Vegetation of Lord Howe's Island. 1869. I. 508.[2]
— On the woods of New South-Wales. 1871. IV. 401.[2]
— *See also* MACARTHUR, William & MOORE, Charles.
Moore, Charles van der. Assam-Thee. 1898. II. 661.[2]
Moore, David. Calluna vulgaris in Newfoundland. 1864. II. 661.[2]
— Cultivation of Loranthus europaeus. 1873. III. 385.[1]
— Culture du Loranthus europaeus. 1873. III. 385.[1]
— On the distribution of the Erica mediterranea. 1852. II. 667.[2]
— On a form of Salix arbuscula L. in Ireland. 1870. II. 105.[1]
— On the formation of wood in plants. 1851. I. 189.
— Guide to the Royal botanic gardens, Glasnevin. 1885. III. 28.[1]
— Handbook for the botanic gardens . . . Glasnevin. 1865. I. 55.
— On the loss of a large Screw Pine. 1875. III. 314.[1]
— Note on the occurrence of Salix procumbens. 1857. II. 108.[1]
— Sur quelques plantes d'Irlande. 1867. II. 664.[2]
— Results of farther physiological experiments on the formation of wood. 1860. I. 190.[1]
— Results of physiological experiments on the formation of wood in plants, made in the Royal Dublin society's botanic gardens, Glasnevin, between the years 1839 and 1851. 1851. I. 164.

— On the successful establishment of Loranthus. 1873. III. 385.[1]
— & MORE, A. G. Catalogue of the flowering plants . . . of Dublin. 1878. I. 403.
— — Contributions towards a Cybele hibernica. 1866. I. 402, 534.[1]
Moore, F. W. Effects of the past winter. 1879. III. 46.[2]
— Himalayan Rhododendrons in Ireland. 1893. III. 655.
Moore, Fletcher. The ' re-afforesting ' of Ireland. 1883. IV. 161.[1]
Moore, Francis. Reisen in die inländischen Theile von Africa. 1738. III. 281.[1]
— Travels into the inland parts of Africa. 1738. III. 281.[1]
— A voyage to Georgia. 1744. III. 263.[2]
Moore, Henry F. The destruction of Canadian forests. 1885. IV. 281.[2]
— Forests and railroads. 1882. IV. 423.[2].
— The forests of Europe. 1885. IV. 342.[2]
— Italian forests. 1885. IV. 364.
— The timber trade of Memel. 1885. IV. 404.[2]
Moore, J. G. Creosoting, Bethell process. 1874. IV. 419.
Moore, J. P. Pinus tuberculata and its cones. 1876. II. 48.[2]
Moore, John B. Hybrid perpetual Roses. 1883. III. 450.
— List of the best hardy Roses. 1885. III. 450.
Moore, Spencer Le Marchant. Alabastra diversa. 1877. I. 270.
— The botanical results of a journey into . . . Australia. 1899. I. 505.
— The Camel fodder plants of western Australia. 1897. I. 505.
— Description of some new phanerogamia collected . . . at Kiukiang, China. 1875. I. 459.
— Occurrence of staminal pistillody in an Acanthad. 1877. II. 805.[2]
— The phanerogamic botany of the Mato Grosso expedition. 1895. I. 343.
— On Rosanoff's crystals in . . . Manihot Glaziovii. 1886. II. 447.[2]
— Solanum lasiophyllum Dun. 1897. II. 777.[1].
— Studies in vegetable biology. 1886. II. 447.[2]
— *See also* BAKER, J. G. & MOORE, S. Le M.
Moore, T. B. Notes on the discovery of a new Eucalyptus. 1887. II. 625.[1]
Moore, T. W. Treatise . . . of Orange culture in Florida. 1877. III. 500.[1]
Moore, Thomas. Acer Ginnala. 1881. III. 534.[2]
— Actinidia Kolomikta. 1874. III. 595.[2].
— Agave Victoriae Reginae. 1875. II. 89.[2]
— Allamanda nobilis. 1868. III. 686.[1] — 1869. III. 686.[1]
— Appendiculate Crotons. 1879. III. 516.[1]
— Aralia Chabrieri. 1883. III. 532.[1]
— Aralia filicifolia. 1877. III. 641.[1]
— Aralia Veitchii. 1874. III. 642.[1]
— Araucaria Goldieana. 1877. III. 298.[2]
— Arbutus hybrida. 1879. III. 647.[1]
— Artocarpus Cannoni. 1875. III. 367.[1]
— Aucuba japonica. 1865. III. 644.[2]
— Azalea Rollissoni. 1878. III. 659.[2]
— Azara microphylla. 1874. III. 614.[1]
— The best hardy Clematises. 1879. III. 389.[1]
— The best new plants of 1880. 1881. III. 83.[1]
— The best novelties of 1881. 1882. III. 83.[1]
— The Blue Spruce Fir. 1884. III. 306.[1]
— Boronia elatior. 1877. III. 495.[2]
— Botanical notes on the Rose. 1848. II. 282.[1]
— Bouvardia Vreelandii. 1872. III. 711.[1]
— Bowenia spectabilis revoluta. 1878. III. 284.[2]
— British wild flowers. 1862. I. 401.
— Campsidium filicifolium. 1874. III. 705.
— Chamaerops excelsa. 1875. III. 331.[2]
— Clematis coccinea. 1880. III. 390.[1]
— Clematis Fortunei. 1864. III. 390.[2]
— Clematis Fortuni Moore. 1863. II. 198.[1].
— Clematis Jackmani and its allies. 1867. III. 390.[2]
— Clematis Jackmanni. 1864. III. 390.[2]
— Clematis Jackmanni alba. 1865. III. 391.[1]
— Clematis rubro-violacea. 1865. III. 391.[1]
— Codiaeum (Croton) Weismanni. 1873. III. 515.[2]
— Coffea liberica. 1881. III. 742.[1]
— The common Holly and its varieties. 1874. III. 530.[1]
— Cornus mascula aurea elegantissima. 1877. III. 646.[1]
— Croton Hookeri. 1871. III. 515.[1]
— Croton imperialis. 1876. III. 515.[2]
— Croton Johannis. 1872. III. 515.[1]

— Croton maculatus Katoni. 1879. III. 516.[1]
— Croton majesticus. 1876. III. 515.[2]
— Croton nobilis. 1878. III. 515.[2]
— Croton ovalifolium. 1875. III. 515.[2]
— Croton reginae. 1879. III. 516.[1]
— Croton spirale. 1874. III. 517.[1]
— Croton trilobus and its allies. 1877. III. 515.[1]
— Croton variegatum interruptum. 1872. III. 515.[1]
— Croton variegatum multicolor. 1872. III. 515.[1]
— Croton volutum. 1874. . II. 439.[1]
— Cupressus Lawsoniana erecta viridis. 1870.' III. 301.[1]
— Cupressus Macnabiana. 1874. III. 302.[2]
— Cycas Normanbyana. 1877. III. 285.[1]
— Cydonia Maulei. 1875. III. 420.[2]
— Daphne Blagayana. 1880. III. 627.[1] '
— Deutzia crenata flore pleno. 1864. III. 410.[2]
— Dipladenia amabilis. 1866. III. 687.[1]
— Dipladenia amoena. 1868. III. 687.[2]
— Dipladenia boliviensis. 1869. III. 687.[2]
— Dipladenia carissima. 1879. III. 687.[2]
— Dipladenia insignis. 1872. III. 688.[1]
— Dr. Hogg's classification of Apples. 1876. III. 425.[2]
— The double crimson Chinese Peach. 1852. III. 439.[1]
— Dracaena amabilis. 1874. III. 335. ·
— Dracaena Goldieana. 1877. III. 336.[2]
— Dracaena hybrida. 1876. III. 335.
— Dracaena imperialis. 1873. III. 335.
— Dracaena magnifica. 1871. III. 335.
— Dracaena Mooreana. 1872. III. 437.[1]
— Dracaena regina. 1872. III. 335.
— Dracaena roseo-picta. 1878. III. 335.
— Dracaena Weismanni. 1873. III. 335.
— Dracaenas, Baptistii and Hendersoni. 1875. III. 334.[1]
— The elements of botany. 1865. I. 90.
— Epacris onosmaeflora florepleno. 1876. III. 665.[1]
— Epacris onosmaeflora fl. pl. nivalis. 1878. III. 665.[1]
— The evergreen garden. 1871. II. 206.[1]
— A few choice hardy evergreens. 1879. III. 290.
— A few more Hollies. 1880. III. 530.[1]
— Ficus exsculpta. 1881. III. 371.[1]
— Ficus Parcellii. 1874. III. 371.[1]
— The field botanist's companion. 1862. I. 401.
— Genista virgata. 1875. III. 477.[2]
— The genus Darwinia. 1869. III. 633.[2]
— Geonoma Carderi. 1876. III. 325.[2]
— Geonoma Martiana var. Seemanni. 1873. III. 325.[2]
— Hardy double Azaleas. 1880. III. 655.
— Hibiscus syriacus coelestis. 1879. III. 588.[2]
— Hibiscus syriacus totus albus. 1878. III. 588.[2]
— Hydrangea Otaksa. 1871. · III. 411.[2]
— Idesia polycarpa. 1874. III. 614.[2]
— Ixora Duffii. 1878. III. 745.[1]
— Ixora splendens. 1878. III. 745.[1]
— Jasminum gracillimum. 1881. III. 673.[1]
— Kentia Lindeni. 1884. III. 326.[2]
— Kentia Macarthuri. 1879. III. 326.[1]
— The Kumquat. 1874. III. 502.[1]
— Lasiandra macrantha. 1868. III. 639.[1]
— Ligustrum coriaceum. 1876. III. 673.[2]
— Lisianthus princeps. 1872. III. 685.[2]
— List of Mr. Plant's Natal ferns. 1853. II. 6.[2]
— Lonicera (? sp.) aureo-reticulata. 1863. III. 750.[1]
— Macrozamia Mackenzii. 1878. III. 285.[2]
— Magnolia Lenné. 1865. III. 400.[1]
— Messrs. Jackman's Clematises. 1875. III. 389.[1]
— Mr. Wills' new Dracaenas. 1875. III. 334.[2]
— Neue hybride Dracänen. 1875. III. 334.[2]
— Neue hybride Eriken. 1881. III. 650.[1]
— Neue Varietäten von Clematis Viticella. 1872. III. 392.[1]
— New Bothwell Heaths. 1881. III. 650.[1]
— New Crotons. 1869. III. 515.[1]
— New Crotons or Codiaeums. ·1870. III. 515.[1]
— The new flowers of 1883. 1884. III. 83.
— New garden plants. . 1867. III. 411,[2] 517.[2]
— New Japanese evergreen Oaks. 1875. III. 361.[1]
— New Japanese plants, 1861. 1861. III. 82.
— New plants of 1871. 1872. III. 82.
— The new plants of 1879. 1880. III. 83.[1]
— New varieties of Clematis Viticella. 1872. III. 392.[1]
— New varieties of Hibiscus rosa-sinensis. 1873. .III. 588.[1]
— Notable 'new plants and flowers. 1873. III. 83.[1]
— Note sur la Clématite de Jackmann. 1864. III. 390.[2]
— Notice sur le Deutzia crenata. 1864. III. 410.[2]
— Olearia Haastii. 1874. III. 756.[1]

— Panax plumatum. 1880. III. 643.[1]
— Pandanus Veitchii. 1871. III. 314.[1]
— Parisian tree guards. 1872. III. 198.[2]
— Passiflora alata superba. 1852. III. 615.[2]
— Passiflora cincinnata. 1869. III. 616.[1]
— Passiflora Hahnii. 1883. III. 616.[1]
— Paullinia thalictrifolia. 1873. III. 540.[1]
— Philadelphus primulaeflorus. '1873' III. 413.[1]
— Phoenix rupicola. 1877. III. 330.[1]
— Phyllanthus roseo-pictus. 1878. III. 521.[1]
— Pictures of Palm trees. 1871. III. 317.
— Pultenaea rosea. 1879. III. 486.[1]
— Pyrus Malus floribunda. 1871. III. 429.[1]
— Pyrus Simonii. 1873. III. 447.[1]
— Pyrus spectabilis roseo-plena. 1872 (by error 1852). III. 429,[1] V. xxix.[1]
— Quercus laurifolia. 1873. III. 362.[2]
— Quercus Libani. 1873. III. 362.[2]
— Ransome's tree-feller. 1878. IV. 384.[1]
— Register of novelties. 1882. III. 83.[1]
— Report of the floral committee. 1861. III. 82.
— Report on miscellaneous bedding plants. 1862. III. 640.[2]
— Report on variegated Begonias. 1861. III. 618.[1]
— The Rhododendron as a hardy evergreen. 1872. III. 655.
— Rhododendron balsaminaeflorum. '1883· III. 657.[2]
— Rhododendron Brookeanum flavum. 1873. III. 657.[2]
— Rhododendron Curtisii. 1884. III. 658.[2]
— Rhododendron James Marshall Brooks. 1881. III. 655.
— Rhododendron Lindleyi. 1864. II. 681.[2]
— Rhododendron Lobbii. 1870. III. 661.[1]
— Rhododendron Princess Alice. 1863. III. 658.[1]
— Ridgway's hedge-cutting machine. 1879. III. 213.
— Robinia hispida or Rosa Acacia. 1873. III. 488.[1]
— Robinia Pseud-Acacia pyramidalis. 1874. III. 487.[1]
— Showy Bougainvillaea. 1861. III. 388.[1]
— Skimmia oblata. 1865. III. 505.[2]
— Sophora japonica pendula. 1871. III. 488.[1]
— Staphylea colchica. 1879. III. 533.[2]
— Die Stechpalmen- (Ilex-)Arten und Varietäten. 1874. III. 530.[1]
— Tacsonia Buchanani. 1868. III. 616.[2]
— Tacsonia insignis. 1873. III. 616.[1]
— Tacsonia speciosa. 1871. III. 617.[1]
— Tacsonia Van-Volxemii. 1866. III. 617.[1]
— Taxodium distichum pendulum. 1871. III. 311.[1]
— Tecoma radicans. 1873. III. 705.
— Wallichia caryotoides. 1874. III. 332.[1]
— Waterer's new hardy Azaleas. 1883. III. 655.
— Waterer's variegated Holly. 1872. III. 530.[1]
— Wistaria sinensis flore pleno. 1882. III. 490.[2]
— Young's new Weeping Birch. 1873. III. 357.[1]
— Zamia crassifolia. 1877. III. 286.[1]
— See also LINDLEY, John & MOORE, Thomas.·
& Jackman, George. Die Clematis. 1872. III. 009.[1]
— — The Clematis as a garden flower. 1872. III. 389.[1]
Moore, W. L. The American Blackberry and Dewberry. 1898. III. 457.[2]
Moore's Rural New Yorker. IV. 6.
Moos, Karl von. Ueber Bachverbauung mit Pfählen. 1896. IV. 187.[2]
— De l'emploi des pieux pour la correction des torrents. 1896. IV. 187.[2]
Mooser, W. F. Zustand und Bewirthschaftung der Wälder, mit besonderer Rücksicht auf das Rheinthal. 1831. IV. 365.
Moosmayer, (Forstwalter). Beobachtungen in Fichten-pflanzbeständen. 1888. IV. 454.
Mootooswamy, P. S. Casearia esculenta. 1890. III. 614.[1]
Moquin-Tandon, Christian Horace.Bénédict Alfred. Amaran-taceae. 1849. II. 189.[1]
— Chenopodearum monographica enumeratio. 1840. II. 187.[1]
— Considérations sur les irrégularités de la corolle. 1832. I. 114.[2]
— Conspectus generum Chenopodearum. 1835. II. 187.[1]
— Éléments de botanique médicale. 1861. III. 58.
— Éléments de tératologie végétale. 1841. I. 143.
— Essai sur les dédoublemens. 1826. I. 143.
— Sur les lois de formation des végétaux. 1837. I. 121.[1]
— Mémoires sur la famille des Chénopodées. 1831. II. 186.[2]
— Pflanzen-Teratologie. 1841. I. 143.
— Phytolaccaceae. 1849. II. 192.[2]
— Remarques à l'occasion des communications de MM. Payer et Brongniart. .1859. I. 99.

Moquin-Tandon, Christian Horace Bénédict Alfred (*continued*).
— Salsolaceae. 1849. II. 187.[1]
— *See also* SAINT-HILAIRE, Auguste de & MOQUIN-TANDON, Alfred.
Mora, Mariano del AMO Y. *See* AMO Y MORA, Mariano del.
Moraes, Alexandre Josè de MELLO. *See* MELLO MORAES, A. J. de.
Moraes Soares, R. de. De la sylviculture en Portugal. 1859. IV. 516.[2]
The moral of flowers. *See* HEY, *Mrs.* 1835. V. xxv.[1]
Morales, Sebastian Alfredo de. Flora arboricola de Cuba. 1887. III. 64.[1]
— Monografia de las Ampelideas de Cuba. 1866. II. 501.[1]
Morandi, Giambattista, [Giovanni Battista]. Historia botanica practica. 1744. I. 291, III. 54, V. xvi.[1]
— Osservazioni intorno al sinonimo alfabetico dell' erbe più usuali. 1743. III. 88.[1]
— Risposta alle osservazioni apologetiche fatte d. Cesare Carini. 1743. III. 88.[1]
Morange, Amédée. Le guide de l'élagueur. 1878. IV. 171.
Morans, F. L'Arbre à beurre. 1899. III. 667.[1]
Moravia — Forst-Section für Mähren . . . *See* FORST-SECTION . . . IV. 8.
Morbærtræets Tiltrækning. 1841. III. 376.
Morck, Dietrich. Ueber die Formen der Bakteroiden bei den einzelnen Spezies der Leguminosen. 1891. II. 321.[3]
More. *See also* MOORE.
More, Alexander Goodman. Hippophae rhamnoides in Ireland. 1868. II. 608.[1]
— Recent additions to the flora of Ireland. 1872. I. 402.
— Report . . . Flora of Inish-Bofin. 1876. I. 403.
— A supplement to the 'Flora vectensis.' 1871. I. 402.
— *See also* MOORE, David & MORE, A. G.
More forest-reservations. 1892. IV. 178.[3]
Moreau, Armand. Action du curare. 1860. III. 683.[1]
Moreau, Frédéric. Code du commerce des bois carrés. 1840. IV. 324, 405.[1]
Moreau, P. J. Aperçus théorique et pratique sur l'élagage. 1851. III. 211.[2]
— De la plantation des routes. 1849. III. 209.
Moreau de Jonnès, Alexandre. Carte orographique et botanique du volcan du Piton-du-Carbet. 182 . ? I. 335.
— Histoire physique des Antilles françaises. 1822. I. 335.
— Premier mémoire en réponse à la question . . . Quels sont les changemens que peut occasioner le déboisement. 1825. IV. 42.[2]
— Untersuchungen über die Veränderungen, die durch die Ausrottung der Wälder . . . entstehen. 1825. IV. 42.[3]
Moreillon, Maurice. Les Sapins sans branches de Chaumont. 1896. II. 23.[1]
Moreira, Nicolao Joaquim. Breves considerações sobre . . . Cafeeiro. 1873. III. 728.[2]
— Diccionario de plantas medicinaes brasileiras. 1862. III. 65.[1]
— Historical notes concerning the vegetable fibres. 1876. III. 234.
— Noticia sobre a agricultura do Brasil. 1873. III. 757.[2]
— Vocabulario das arvores brazileiras. 1870. IV. 398.[2]
Morel. Tableau de l'école de botanique du Jardin des plantes de Paris. 1800. I. 56.
Morel, Ch. Le pâturage dans les taillis sous futaie. 1890. IV. 197.[2]
— Principes d'horticulture. 1861. III. 113.
— Propriétés vénéneuses de l'If. 1835. III. 288.[2]
— Rétrogradation de la végétation forestière. 1893. IV. 74.[2]
Morel, Francisque. Arbre ornemental et utile. 1862. III. 355.
— La bouture et la greffe. 1864. III. 39.
— Double floraison d'une variété de Cytisus nigricans. 1891. II. 351.[1]
— Hybride de Clematis Pitcheri et de C. coccinea. 1893. II. 197.[2]
— Hybrids and crosses of Clematis. 1900. III. 389.[2]
— Juniperus chinensis pendula. 1889. III. 303.[1]
— Nouveau mode d'emploi de l'Acacia parasol. 1888. III. 487.[1]
— Observations sur l'emploi de l'Épicéa. 1890. III. 305.[1]
— Paysages et fleurs de France. 1900. II. 286.[3]
— Potatura degli alberi. 1877. III. 170.
— Robinia Pseudo-Acacia angustifolia. 1889. III. 487.[1]
— Tilia dasystyla. 1883. III. 586.[1]
— Variétés de l'Evonymus japonicus. 1883. . III. 532.[2]
Morel, J. F. Nicolas. Catalogue des plantes du Jardin botanique établi à Besançon. 1805. I. 57.

Morel, Jean Marie. Tableau dendrologique. 1800. *I. 293*, III. 83,[3] *IV. 79*.[2]
— Théorie des jardins. 1776. III. 112.
Morel, Julius. The turpentines. 1878. IV. 443.[2]
Morel, Victor VIVIAND-. *See* VIVIAND-MOREL, Victor.
Morelet, Arthur. Le bois de Campêche. 1857. III. 478.[1]
— Description de deux nouvelles espèces de Pins. 1851. II. 39.[1]
— Exploration d'une partie de l'état de Guatimala. 1850. I. 333.
— Nomenclature des différentes espèces de Conifères. 185 . ? II. 12.[2]
— Reisen in Central-Amerika. 1857. · I. 329.
— Travels in Central America. 1857. I. 329.
— Two Central American Pines. 1871. IV. 462.[2]
— Voyage dans l'Amérique centrale. 1857. I. 329.
Morelet, Félix. Le caoutchouc, origines botaniques. 1884. III. 229.
Moreno, Gar. G. Letter . . . relative to the exploration of the volcano of Pichincha. 1858. I. 340.[1]
Moreno, Eduardo PARDO Y. *See* PARDO Y MORENO, Eduardo.
Moréno y Maïs, Thomas. ` Recherches chimiques . . . sur l'Erythroxylum. 1868. III. 492.[2]
Morera, JORDANA Y. *See* JORDANA Y MORERA.
Moret, José VILARDEBÓ Y. *See* VILARDEBÓ Y MORET, José.
Moreton, *3rd earl of. See* DUCIE, H. J. R., *3rd earl of* MORETON.
Moretti, Giuseppe. Sugli Anacardi orientale e occidentale. 1851. II. 454.[2]
— Analyse chimique du quinquina de Ste-Lucie. 1811. III. 744.[1]
— Appendice all' elenco delle piante spontanee del Vicentino. 1813. I. 425.
— Biblioteca agraria. 1826. III. 115.[2]
— Il botanico italiano. 1826. I. 426.
— De Cedro Libani. 1838. II. 28.[1]
— Compendio di nosologia vegetabile. .1839. I. 206,[1] *III. 178*.[3]
— Difesa e illustrazione delle opere botaniche di Pietro Andrea Mattioli. 1844. I. 292.
— De epidermidis plantarum structura. 1823. I. 129.[1]
— Della fecondazione delle piante. 1830. I. 200.
— Intorno alla flora veneta del Sig. Moricaud. 1823. I. 425.
— Guida allo studio della fisiologia vegetabile. 1835. I. 87.
— Lettera all' autore delle Osservazioni intorno all' Viaggio al lago di Garda. 1817. I. 425.
— De nonnullis physiologico-botanicis animadversionibus. 1831. I. 163.
— Notizia sopra diverse piante da aggiungersi alla flora vicentia. 1813. I. 425. ·
— Osservazioni sopra diverse specie di piante indigene dell'. Italia. 1818. I. 425.
— De Pipere nigro. 1826. II. 94.[2]
— De plantarum morphologia. 1838. I. 98.
— Prodromo di una monografia delle specie del genere Morus. 1841. II. 154.[1]
— De radicis vegetabilium officiis. 1837. I. 161.
— De vegetabilium rhachitide. 1839. I. 206.[1]
— *See also* MELANDRI, Girolamo & MORETTI, Giuseppe.
— & **Ghiolini,** Carlo. Sui Gelsi. 1829. III. 374.
— Istruzione nella coltura de' principali alberi. 1834. III. 114.[2]
Morgan. The Carnauba tree. 1876. III. 324.[2]
Morgan, A. C. F. The winged-phylloxera in Portugal. 1886. III. 762.
Morgan, F. A. List of Chinese medicines. 1889. III. 273.[2]
Morgan, Francis P. *See* PRENTISS, D. W. & MORGAN, F. P.
Morgan, H. A. *See* STUBBS, W. C. & MORGAN, H. A.
Morgan, H. R. Forestry in southern India. 1884. IV. 378.
Morgan, J. H. Report on the forests of Canada. 1886. IV. 271.[1]
Morgan, Rhodes. The forests and fauna of British Central Africa. 1896. I. 493.
Morgan, T. O. Flora Cereticae superioris. 1894. I. 400.
Morgan, W. The English Oak. 1881. IV. 507.
— Puriri and Oak trees. 1885. · IV. 501,[1] *533*.[1]
— Wattle Culture. 1882. IV. 520.[3]
Morgana, Mario. Filottassi florale di Tristania conferta. 1899. II. 843.[2]
— Su di un ramo anormale di Viburnum odoratissimum. 1900. II. 843.[2]
Morgenroth. Schütte. 1873. IV. 477.
— Vertilgung der Aspen-Wurzelbrut. 1873. IV. 486.[2]

Morgenthaler, Jakob. Beiträge zur Entwicklungsgeschichte der Quitte. 1897. II. 263.[2]
— Der Wein-, Obst- und Gartenbau auf der Pariser Weltausstellung. 1890. III. 144.
Morgues, Jacques LE MOYNE de. *See* LE MOYNE DE MORGUES, Jacques.
Mori, An on . Contribuzione alla flora del Modenese. 1886. I. 429. t io
— Descrizione istologica del fusto della Periploca. 1876. II. 741.[2]
— Osservazioni sul cistoma del Gasparrini. 1880. I. 131.[2]
— Dei prodotti che si formano nell' atto dell' assimilazione. 1882. I. 176.
— Dei prodotti che si formano nell' atto dell' assimilazione delle piante. 1886. I. 173.
— Saggio monografico sulla struttura . . . delle Crassulacee. 1879. II. 235.[1]
— Sulla struttura del fusto dell' Erythrina Crista-galli. 1878. II. 357.[1]
— Sulla struttura delle foghe delle Ericacee. 1877. II. 658.[2]
— *See also* CARUEL, Teodoro & MORI, Antonio.
Moriarty, Henrietta Maria. Fifty plates of green-house plants. 1803. III. 81.
— Viridarium. 1803. III. 81.
Moricand, Moise Étienne. Flora veneta. 1820. I. 425.
— Plantae americanae rariores. 1830. I. 306.
Moricand, Stefano. Plantes nouvelles d'Amérique. 1833. I. 329.
Morichini, Domenico. Sopra la gomma di Ulivo. 1815. III. 678.[2]
Moride, Édouard. Sur de nouvelles propriétés du charbon de bois. 1855. IV. 431.[2]
— Le preparateur botanique. 1843. I. 35.
Morier, James. A journey through Persia, Armenia. 1812. I. 477.[1]
— A second journey through Persia, Armenia. 1818. I. 477.[1]
Moriére, Jules. Cas de tératologie végétale. 1876. III. 279.[2]
— Cas tératologique offert par . . . Prunier. 1879. II. 272.[1]
— Considerations sur une maladie du Pommier. 1856. III. 27.[1]
— Découverte du Gui sur le Chêne. 1868. II. 179.[1]
— Diamètre de quelques arbres . . . en Normandie. 1873. I. 297.[2]
— Note sur deux cas de tératologie. 1861. I. 143.
Morikouni, OUEKAKI. *See* OUEKAKI-MORIKOUNI.
Morin. Examen chimique des juvias. 1824. III. 631.[1]
Morin. Résistance des matériaux. 1856. IV. 410.
Morin. The silk raiser's manual. 1836. III. 375.
Morin, Arthur Jules. Sur un moyen pratique de préparer du charbon du bois. 1871. IV. 394, 432.[1]
— Note sur les essais d'acclimatation du Quinquina officinal à l'Ile de la Réunion. 1869. III. 725.[2]
— Note sur les progrès de l'acclimatation du Quinquina officinalis à l'Ile de la Réunion. 1871. III. 725.[2]
Morin, B. Recherches analytiques sur l'écorce de Simarouba. 1822. III. 509.[2]
Morin, Édouard. Culture des Cinchona à la Réunion. 1871. III. 717.[1]
— Sur les progrès de l'acclimatation du Cinchona officinalis à l'Ile de la Réunion. 1871. III. 717.[1]
— & Vinson, Auguste. Introduction de l'Arbre à quinquina à l'Ile de la Réunion. 1869. III. 717.[1]
Morin, Georges. Culture du Bougainvillea Sanderiana. 1900. III. 388.[1]
Morin, H. Essence de bois de rose. 1888. III. 406.[1]
— Sur l'essence de licari kanali. 1882. III. 406.[1]
Morin, Louis. Bignonia venusta. 1882. III. 707.[1]
Morin, Pierre. Catalogue de quelques plantes. 1651. I. 56.
— Instruction facile pour connoistre toutes sortes d'Orangers et Citronniers. 1674. III. 496.[2]
— Nouveau traité pour la culture des fleurs. 1682. III. 111.
— Remarques nécessaires pour la culture des fleurs. 1658. III. 124.[2]
Morin, René. Catalogus plantarum horti Renati Morini. 1621. I. 56.
Moringlane, Duponchel, & Bonastre, J. F. Extrait d'un mémoire . . . produits naturels des Térébinthacés et des Conifères. 1822. III. 523.[3] *IV. 443.*[1]
Morini, Fausto. Anatomia del frutto delle Casuarinee. 1890. II. 92.[1]
— Ancora intorno all' area connettiva della guaina fogliare delle Casuarinee. 1895. II. 92.[1]
— Contributo all' anatomia . . . dei nettarli estranuziali. 1886. I. 118.[2]

— Contributo all' anatomia della radice delle Casuarinee. 1896. II. 92.[1]
— Contributo all' anatomia . . . delle Casuarinee. 1894. II. 92.[1]
— Contributo all' anatomia ed alla fisiologia dei nettarii estranuziali. 1886. I. 113.[1]
— Osservazioni intorno ad una mostruosita . . . di Capparis. 1890. II. 232.[1]
Moriniello, Giovanni. Cenno monografico e flora forestale della provincia di Aquila. 1875. I. 423, *IV. 86.*[1]
Moris, Giuseppe Giacinto. Enumeratio plant. novarum. 1846. I. 269.
— Flora sardoa. 1837. I. 426.
— Illustrationes rariorum stirpium horti bot. R. univ. taurin. 1833. I. 63.
— Sovra una nuova . . . specie di pianta Malpighiacea. 1848. II. 427.[1]
— & Notaris, Giuseppe de. Florula Caprariae. 1839. I. 426.
Morison, Giovanni Agostino. Soccinto raguaglio delle stupende e maravigliose virtù . . . dall' erba The. 1720. III. 605.
Morison, Robert. Hallucinationes Caspari Bauhini. 1669. I. 286.
— Hortus regius blesensis. 1635. I. 56.
— Plantarum historiae universalis oxoniensis pars. 1680. I. 287.
— Plantarum umbelliferarum distributio. 1672. I. 287.
Morisset. Ergo Thea chinensium menti confert. 1648. III. 604.[2]
Moritz, Carl. Auszug aus einem Schreiben. 1836. I. 333.
— Bastard-Annona. 1839. II. 215.[3]
Moritz, J. Beobachtungen . . . betreffend die Reblaus. 1893. III. 574.
— Die durch die Phylloxera . . . bewirkte Krankheit der Reben. 1880. III. 572.
— Die Rebenschädlinge. 1880. III. 572.
— Die Wurzellaus des Weinstockes. 1880. III. 572.
— *See also* BLANKENHORN, Adolph & MORITZ, J.
— & Ritter, C. Die Desinfektion von Setzreben. 1894. III. 198,[2] *574.*
— & Seucker, P. Weinbergs-Düngungsversuche. 1887. III. 549.[1]
Moritzi, Alexander. Die Flora der Schweiz. 1844. I. 434.
— Die Pflanzen der Schweiz. 1832. I. 434.
— Die Pflanzen Graubündens. 1839. *I. 434,* V. xxii.[2]
— Réflexions sur l'espèce. 1842. I. 252.
— Systematisches Verzeichnis der von H. Zollinger . . . auf Java gesammelten Pflanzen. 1845. I. 468.
Morkowine, N. Recherches sur l'influence des anesthésiques sur la respiration. 1899. I. 171.
Morland, Samuel. Some new observations upon the parts and use of the flower in plants. 1704. I. 198.
Morlet, Gustave. Les Conifères de petites et grandes dimensions. 1878. III. 290.
— Du degré de rusticité de certains arbres. 1854. III. 47.
— Plantation des Conifères. 1855. III. 294.[2]
— Relevé des végétaux qui ont . . . souffert du froid. 1860. III. 48.
Morley, Henry Forster & Muir, M. M. Pattison. Watts' dictionary of chemistry. *See* WATTS, Henry. 1863. I. 151.[1]
Morlot, E. Observations relatives au Phylloxera. 1874. III. 566.[2]
Mornet, A. Catalogue des plantes . . . du Cher. 1875. I. 414.
Moro, Leopold von. Acides volatils des baies d'Aubier. 1845. III. 753.[2]
— Untersuchung der flüchtigen Säuren in Viburnum Opulus. 1845. III. 753.[2]
Morogues, *baron de* *See* HÉRICART DE THURY, de & MOROGUES, *baron de*.
Morogues, Eudoxe, *baron de*. Le Châtaignier . . . genre rehfermant des espèces. 1879. II. 123.[2]
— Étude sur la pomologie naturelle. 1880. II. 278.[3]
— La maladie du rond. 1877. IV. 467.[1]
— Mémoire. sur la maladie du rond des Pins maritimes. 1876. IV. 467.[1]
— Observations sur la monographie géographique des Pins sylvestres. 1885. II. 46.[3]
— Observations sur les Chênes. 1877. II. 129.[2]
— Observations sur les Pins maritime et sylvestre. 1867. IV. 461.[1]

Morogues, Eudoxe, *baron* de (*continued*).
— Observations sur quelques espèces d'arbres resineux. 1877.
I. 244.²
— Observations sur quelques espèces de Chênes du Loiret.
1877. II. 129.²
— Pins indigènes de la Savoie. 1878. II. 39.²
— De quelques espèces de Conifères. 1877. I. 244.²
— Question concernant les diverses espèces . . . dans le Pin
sylvestre. 1873. II. 46.²
Morong, Thomas. Copernicia cerifera Mart. 1892. III.
324.²
— Jesuits' tea. 1891. III. 531.¹
— Mandioca. 1891. III. 521.¹
— The Smilaceae of North and Central America. 1894. II.
85.¹
— & Britton, N. L. An enumeration of the plants collected
by Dr. Thomas Morong in Paraguay. 1892. I. 345.
Mororum libri tres. *See* MINISCALCHI, Luigi. 1769. III.
373.
Morosov, Dmitri. Le Pin sylvestre est-il calcifuge? 1895.
II. 48.²
Morot, F. S. Recherches sur la coloration des végétaux. 1850.
I. 184.
Morot, Louis. Dobinea et Podoon. 1890. II. 456.¹
— Journal de botanique. *See* JOURNAL . . . I. 21.
— Note sur le liège des feuilles. 1889. I. 111.
— Note sur les affinités . . . du genre Podoon. 1889. I.
456.¹
— Recherches sur le péricycle. 1885. I. 128.²
— Réponse à la note de . . . d'Arbaumont sur le péricycle.
1886. I. 128.²
— *See also* CONSTANTIN, Julien & MOROT, Louis.
Morphy, Juan. *See* JORDANA Y MORERA, Josè & MORPHY,
Juan.
Morren, Charles François Antoine. Abnorme Calceolarien.
1848. II. 779.²
— L'Abricotier Mume du Japon. 1855. III. 438.²
— Acacia squamata Morr. 1847. II. 327.¹
— Aeschinanthus Boschianus De Vriese. 1845. II. 793.¹
— Aeschinanthus speciosus Hook. 1847. II. 793.²
— Allamanda Aubletii Pöhl. 1849. II. 723.¹
— Amherstia nobilis Wallich. 1849. II. 331.²
— Aperçu sur les Palmiers. 1845. III. 316.²
— Les Araucarias bouturés de branches. 1849. III. 297.²
— L'Arbre à fraise ou Benthamia fragifera. 1852. III.
645.²
— Azalea sinensis Lodd. var. Bylsiana. 1845. III. 662.²
— Azaleae Mortierianae var. hortenses. 1847. III. 661.²
— L'Azalée à fleurs crépues de la Chine. 1854. III. 659.¹
— Le Barnadesia rosea de Lindley. 1853. III. 754.²
— Bemerkungen über die Palmen. 1845. III. 316.²
— Biographie d'un Arenga saccharifère. 1846. III. 320.¹
— Biographie des Carnellia. 1845. II. 550.²
— Biographie et culture des Lagerstroemia. 1847. III. 629.²
— Botanique. 1843. I. 34.
— Bouvardia leiantha. 1852. III. 711.²
— Sur le Browallia de Jameson. 1852. III. 698.²
— Burtonia pulchella Meisn. 1848. II. 338.¹
— Camellia japonica Linn. var. centifolia. 1846. III. 598.¹
— Camellia japonica Linn. var. Littae. 1845. III. 598.¹
— Camellia japonica Linn. var. Pirzio. 1845. III. 598.¹
— Camellia japonica var. Rubini. 1846. III. 598.²
— Camellia japonica var. Constantiniana. 1846. III. 598.¹
— Camellia reticulato-japonica. 1845. III. 598.¹
— Cantua bicolor. 1845. II. 746.¹
— Cantua pyrifolia Juss. 1848. II. 746.²
— Ceanothus thyrsiflorus. 1847. II. 493.²
— Le Cèdre argenté de l'Atlas. 1852. III. 299.²
— Les Cèdres Déodora. 1853. III. 300.¹
— Centrostemma multiflorum Dne. 1845. II. 740.¹
— Cérée de Napoléon. 1842. II. 590.²
— Cerise hybride de Laeken. 1847. III. 435.¹
— Sur une charmante Abélie. 1853. III. 748.²
— Le Charme à fruit de houblon. 1853. III. 358.¹
— Le Cheiranthera linearis. 1854. III. 415.¹
— Le Chêne des marais. 1854. III. 362.²
— Le Chêne écarlate, Quercus coccinea. 1854. III. 362.¹
— Le Chêne pyramidal toujours vert. 1854. III. 362.¹
— Clematis indivisa Willd. var. lobata. 1848. III. 390.²
— Clematis violacea. 1845. II. 199.¹
— La Clém 1 e de S. M. la Reine Sophie des Pays-Bas. 1854.
III. 391.² at t
— Clerodendron squamatum Vahl. 1845. II. 756.²
— Clusia; recueil d'observations. 1852. I. 143.

— Le Cognassier ou Poirier du Japon. 1851. III. 420.¹
— Considérations générales sur les déformations. 1852. I.
144.²
— Considérations sur le mouvement de la sève. 1838. I. 163.
— Considérations sur les monstruosités. 1852. I. 143.
— Correa pulchella Lindl. var. 1845. II. 404.²
— Crowea latifolia Lodd. 1848. II. 405.¹
— Culture du Bignonia Lindleyi. 1848. III. 706.²
— Sur la culture . . . du Rosier à feuilles odorantes. 1847.
— Le Cyprès funèbre ou pleureur. 1853. II. 29.¹
— Le Cyprès pleureur. 1852. III. 302.¹
— Sur un Cyprès pyramidal à branches horizontales. 1853.
III. 302.²
— Cyrtanthera catalpaefolia Nees. 1849. II. 800.¹
— Daviesia physodes Cunn. 1846. II. 353.²
— Déplacement . . . d'un Dragonnier. 1849. III. 336.¹
— Le Deutzia gracilis de Zuccarini. 1851. III. 410.¹
— Deutzia staminea. 1847. II. 239.¹
— Sur deux nouvelles Pivoines. 1846. III. 392.²
— Dipladenia nobilis. 1847. II. 725.²
— Dipladenia nobilis Morr. var. rosea. 1848. III. 688.¹
— On the discoid piths of plants. 1840. I. 129.¹
— Dodonaea; ou, Recueil d'observations. 1841. I. 147.
— Dwarfed plants. 1845. III. 175.²
— L'Echinocactus à poils de M. Galeotti. 1854. III. 622.¹
— Effets de l'éclipse du soleil . . . sur la respiration végétale.
. 1836. I. 198.
— Des effets généraux des températures. 1846. III. 182.
— Epacris campanulata Lodd. var. Copelandii. 1847. III.
665.¹
— Erica aristata Linn. var. major. 1847. III. 650.²
— Eriostemon intermedium Hook. 1849. II. 406.¹
— Erythrina erythrostachia Morr. 1849. II. 357.¹
— Escallonia macrantha Hook. et Arn. 1849. II. 239.²
— Études sur l'anatomie du raisin. 1842. II. 507.¹
— Exemple curieux d'un Phoenix dactylifera à sept branches.
1851. II. 72.²
— Expériences . . . sur la gomme des Cycadées. 1839. II. 3,¹
871.¹
— Il ne faut pas condamner . . . le Saule fragile. 1851. III.
352.¹
— Sur le Figuier caoutchouc. 1845. III. 370.²
— Une fleur double de Lilas. 1853. II. 714.²
— D'une fleur double et pleine d'Ajonc épineux. 1852. II.
387.²
— Forsythia viridissima Lindl. 1847. II. 706.²
— Sur la fructification des Fuchsia. 1846. III. 639.²
— Fuchsia; ou, Recueil d'observations. 1847. I. 34.
— Fuchsia macrantha Hook. 1846. II. 644.²
— Le Gastrolobium cuneatum. 1854. III. 477.¹
— Gautiera bracteata. 1845. II. 671.¹
— Le Gincko ou l'Arbre aux quarante écus. 1853. III.
286.²
— Goldfussia isophylla Nees von Esenb. 1848. II. 804.¹
— Greffes de l'Epiphyllum truncatum. 1846. III. 623.¹
— Le Grevillea à feuilles de lavande. 1852. III. 383.¹
— Sur les haies en losange. 1848. III. 213.
— L'Hamamelis de Virginie. 1849. III. 417.¹
— Le Hêtre pleureur ou le Hêtre parasol. 1854. III. 360.²
— Hibiscus grossulariaefolius Miquel. 1848. II. 523.¹
— Histoire littéraire des Browallias. 1855. III. 698.¹
— Histoire naturelle . . . de l'Adamia. 1855. III. 410.²
— Horticulture et philosophie. 1838. III. 35.
— Hoya bella Hook. 1849. II. 739.¹
— Hoya imperialis Lindl. 1848. II. 739.²
— Hoya picta Sieb. 1848. III. 693.²
— Hoya variegata Sieb. 1846. III. 693.¹
— Hydrangea involucrata Zucc. et Sieb. 1846. II. 240.²
— L'Indigotier à fleurs pourpres du Népaul. 1851. II. 365.²
— Sur l'influence des rayons colorés sur la germination. 1832.
I. 202.²
— Ixora javanica Dec. 1848. II. 821.¹
— Ixora odorata Hook. 1848. II. 821.²
— Jasminum nudiflorum Lindl. 1848. II. 710.²
— Der Kastanienbaum mit eingeschnittenen Blättern. 1846.
III. 537.¹
— Lapageria rosea Ruiz et Pav. 1849. II. 84.¹
— Le Lardizabala à feuilles biternées. 1853. III. 393.²
— Leuco pogon Cunninghami. 1846. II. 690.¹
— Le Lierre d'Alger. 1853. III. 642.¹
— Lindleya mespiloides. 1848. II. 265.²
— Le Liquidambar à Styrax. 1853. III. 417.²
— Lobelia; ou, Recueil d'observations. 1851. I. 143.

— Loisirs d'anatomie et de physiologie végétales. 1833. I. 33.
— Macleania punctata Hook. 1849. II. 674.¹
— Le Marronier d'Inde à fleurs doubles. 1854. III. 537.¹
— Sur le Marronnier à feuilles laciniées. 1846. III. 537.¹
— Medinella [sic] speciosa Blume. 1849. II. 638.²
— Mirbelia Meisneri Hook. 1849. II. 373.²
— Mitraria coccinea Cav. 1849. II. 795.¹
— Monographie des espèces de Lippia. 1851. II. 759.¹
— Monographie des Fenstemon. 1851. II. 781.²
— Le Noisetier de Byzance. 1852. III. 358.¹
— Note sur l'effet pernicieux du duvet du Platane. 1837. III. 419.¹
— Note sur l'Orme-Pitteurs. 1848. III. 365.²
— Note sur le Chimonanthus. 1853. III. 401.¹
— Note sur le mouvement des sensitives. 1841. I. 198.
— Note sur le Porphyrocoma lanceolata. 1845. III. 710.¹
— Note sur quelques effets de la compression. 1843. I. 189, 527.
— Notice sur l'autophyllogénie. 1849. II. 640.¹
— Notice sur l'élagage des arbres. 1848. III. 170.
— Notice sur l'Escallonia à grandes fleurs. 1853. III. 410.²
— Notice sur l'Henfreya scandens de Lindley. 1855. III. 709.¹
— Notice sur l'Orme des montagnes. 1848. III. 366.¹
— Notice sur la circulation observée dans l'ovule ... du Figuier. 1838. II. 150.²
— Notice sur la culture ... de quelques Passiflores. 1845. III. 615.²
— Notice sur le Befaria aestuans. 1855. III. 648.²
— Notice sur le Ceanothus floribundus. 1855. III. 541.²
— Notice sur le Chêne des montagnes. 1851. III. 362.²
— Notice sur le Cornouiller sanguin. 1850. III. 646.¹
— Notice sur le Cytisus Adami Poiteau. 1871. II. 368.¹
— Notice sur le Dasylirion longifolium. 1865. II. 84.¹
— Notice sur le Gastrolobium Hugelii. 1853. III. 486.¹
— Notice sur le Métrosidéros. 1855. III. 636.²
— Notice sur le spiralisme tératologique. 1851. I. 144.²
— Notice sur le Stifftia chrysantha. 1853. III. 354.²
— Notice sur le Wang-Shan-Kwei des chinois. 1855. III. 505.²
— Notice sur les anomalies de déplacement. 1851. II. 643.¹
— Notice sur les Lapageria rosea. 1853. III. 337.¹
— Notice sur les Thuyas. 1848. III. 311.¹
— Notice sur trois nouvelles espèces de Céanothus. 1853. II. 492.²
— Notice sur un Chêne vert d'Espagne. 1851. III. 362.¹
— Notice sur un Palmier d'espèce inédite. 1845. II. 67.¹
— Notizen über Thuia. 1848. III. 311.¹
— Nouvelle notice sur deux variétés ... d'Ormes à larges feuilles. 1851. III. 366.¹
— Le Noyer à cavernes. 1853. III. 355.
— Noyer de Pitteurs Morr. 1848. III. 354.²
— Observations anatomiques sur la congélation. 1838. I. 212.
— Observations sur l'anatomie ... de la fleur du Cereus ... grandiflorus. 1838. III. 590.¹
— Observations sur l'épaississement de la membrane ... de l'appareil pileux. 1839. I. 112.²
— Observations sur la formation des huiles. 1839. I. 181.²
— Observations sur la question de savoir si le Hêtre ... ne sont jamais frappés de la foudre. 1849. IV. 193.²
— Observations sur les efflorescences de quelques plantes. 1841. I. 129.¹
— Observations sur les panachures des feuilles. 1841. III. 180,² 806.¹
— Les Ormes de Pitteurs. 1852. III. 366.¹
— Om Overeenstemmelsen imellem Trœernes Blade og almindelige Former. 1855. II. 37.¹
— Palmes et couronnes de l'horticulture de Belgique. 1851. III. 33.¹
— Le Pangang de Java. 1855. III. 641.²
— Passiflora edulis Sims. 1845. II. 578.¹
— Paulownia imperialis Zucc. et Sieb. 1846. II. 781.²
— La pélorisation lagéniforme des Calcéolaires. 1848. II. 779.²
— D'une pélorisation sigmoïde des Calcéolaires. 1851. II. 779.²
— Des phénomènes périodiques de la végétation. 1848. II. 220.²
— La Pilocérée à chevelure d'or. 1853. III. 620.²
— Pimelea Verschaffeltii Morr. 1847. II. 805.²
— Sur les Pivoines en arbre de M. Rodigas. 1846. III. 392.²
— Sur les plantes naines. 1845. III. 175.²

— Le Plaqueminier Pishamin. 1854. III. 670.¹
— Sur le Platane du Nepaul. 1848. III. 419.¹
— Sur le Polygonum vaccinifolium. 1852. III. 387.¹
— Porphyrocoma lanceolata Schwdl. 1846. II. 802.¹
— Prémices (Études) d'anatomie ... végétales. 1841. I. 34.
— Procédé pour transplanter le Cedrus. 1852. III. 300.¹
— Sur le Psidium pyriferum et son fruit. 1846. III. 637.²
— La Pulténée éricoïde. 1852. II. 332.²
— De quelques utilités du Lierre. 1854. III. 642.¹
— Le Quercitron, arbre de forêt et de parc. 1853. III. 363.¹
— Recherches littéraires sur les Fleurs de la passion. 1842. II. 577.¹
— Recherches sur l'ivoire végétal. 1842. II. 73.²
— Recherches sur la synandrie ... dans les Calcéolaires. 1852. II. 779.²
— Recherches sur le mouvement ... des étamines du Sparrmannia. 1841. II. 515.¹
— Recherches sur le mouvement ... du style du Goldfussia. 1839. II. 803.²
— Recherches sur un nouveau genre de monstruosités. 1852. I. 145.¹
— Sur la reproduction des Échinocactus. 1845. III. 618.²
— Sur la reproduction des Rosiers. 1847. III. 452.
— Rhododendron arboreum Sm. var. Boddaertianum. 1845. III. 657.¹
— Rhododendron arboreum Smith var. gandavense. 1847. III. 657.¹
— Rhododendron arboreum var. Tigrinum roseum. 1848. III. 657.¹
— Rhododendron (Azalea) ledifolium DeC. var. versicolor. 1846. III. 661.¹
— Rhododendron (Azalea) ledifolium Ds. var. 1845. III. 661.¹
— Rhododendron campanulatum var. macrantha. 1845. III. 657,¹ 658.¹
— Rhododendron formosum Wall. 1849. II. 679.²
— Rhododendron ponticum DeC. var. azaleoides. 1845. II. 677.²
— Ribes sanguineum Pursh var. flore pleno. 1845. III. 415.²
— Le Sapin de Douglas. 1853. III. 309.²
— Le Saule bleu, Salix caerulea. 1854. III. 351.¹
— Le Saule pleureur du Roi David. 1852. III. 351.²
— Le Serpentin et le Cereus à grandes fleurs. 1847. III. 620.¹
— Siphocampylos nitidus. 1846. II. 846.¹
— Le Sollya de Drummond. 1854. III. 416.¹
— Souvenirs phénologiques de l'hiver 1852–1853. 1853. I. 226.¹
— Spathodea speciosa Brongn. 1849. II. 790.¹
— Spiraea Douglasii Hook. 1845. II. 315.¹
— La Spirée à grandes fleurs. 1855. III. 424.¹
— Stenocarpus Cunninghami Hook. 1847. II. 167.¹
— Sur la structure des Mussaenda. 1849. II. 823.²
— Du Sycomore, de sa nature. 1852. III. 535.²
— Théorie des harmonies entre les feuilles et la forme générale des arbres. 1855. I. 106.¹
— De tuinbouw. 1853. III. 106.¹
— Le Tulipier. 1849. III. 398.³
— Usage du Mahaleb dans la parfumerie. 1851. III. 438.²
— Utilité de l'Epaisvinette. 1850. III. 305.¹
— Sur la variabilité des Fuchsia. 1846. II. 643.¹
— On variegation in plants. 1841. III. 180,² 806.¹
— Sur une variété de Pivoine en arbre. 1846. III. 392.²
— Les Viornes ou Viburnum. 1854. III. 752.²
— Les virescences distinctes des phyllomorphies. 1850. II. 839.¹
— Die Wang-Shan-Kwei der Chinesen. 1855. III. 505.²
— Le Weirela rosea. 1851. III. 749.¹
— Le Wellingtonia gigantea. 1854. II. 50.²
— Whitfieldia lateritia Hook. 1846. II. 805.²
— See also AVOINE, P. J. d' & MORREN, C. F. A.
— & Decaisne, Joseph. Revue des plantes nouvelles ou intéressantes. 1857. III. 77.
— & Decaisne, Joseph. Observations sur quelques plantes du Japon. 1836. I. 461.
Morren, Charles Jacques Édouard. L'acclimatation des plantes. 1865. III. 43.
— L'Azalea vittata var. Beali. 1866. III. 659.²
— Le Cerasus serotina Loisel. 1865. III. 277.¹
— Compte-rendu de l'Exposition du 12 juillet 1864. 1865. III. 43.
— Contagion de la panachure. 1869. III. 181.¹ — 1870. II. 520,¹ III. 59.

Morren, Charles Jacques Édouard (*continued*).
— Courte notice sur l'Ugni. 1860. III. 638.¹
— Le Cyprès chauve. 1856. III. 310.²
— Description du Castanea chrysophylla. 1857. III. 360.¹
— Description du Pavonia Makoyana. 1878. II. 521.²
— Description du Pavonia Wioti. 1875. II. 526.²
— Détermination du nombre des stomates. 1863. I. 131.¹
— Deux notes au sujet de l'évolution spontanée des variétés. 1867. II. 654,¹ *III. 346.²*
— La digestion végétale. 1876. I. 159.
— Dissertation sur les feuilles vertes. 1858. I. 172.
— Duplication des fleurs et panachure . . . chez le Kerria. 1867. I. 145,² *III. 484.²*
— Echeverias. 1874. II. 235.¹
— L'énergie de la végétation. 1873. I. 232.¹
— Esquisse du genre Echeveria. 1874. II. 235.¹
— Hérédité de la panachure. 1865. III. 181.¹
— Histoire et bibliographie de la botanique horticole en Belgique. 1876. III. 1.
— Histoire et description du Mutisia Clematis. 1864. II. 861.¹
— Histoire et description du Quesnelia rufa. 1882. II. 77.¹
— Leuchtembergia [*sic*] principis. 1855. III. 623.¹
— Mémorandum des travaux de botanique . . . de 1772–1871. 1872. I. 2.
— Note sur l'Abutilon Darwini. 1879. III. 586.²
— Note sur l'Abutilon insigne. 1855. III. 586.²
— Note sur l'Abutilon vexillarium. 1864. II. 521.¹
— Note sur l'Aeschynanthus tricolor. 1858. III. 708.¹
— Note sur l'Eugenia Luma. 1858. III. 635.¹
— Note sur l'Escallonia pterocladon. 1855. III. 411.¹
— Note sur l'Opuntia Rafinesqui Engelm. 1874. III. 625.¹
— Note sur le Bigarreau de la caserne. 1866. III. 435.¹
— Note sur le Burtonia à feuilles rudes. 1858. III. 468.¹
— Note sur le Chalef à longue queue. 1883. II. 607.²
— Note sur le Choisya ternata. 1880. III. 496.¹
— Note sur le Grevillea alpestris. 1858. III. 383.¹
— Note sur le Lavatera maritima. 1856. III. 588.²
— Note sur le Lilas double de Lemoine. 1878. III. 681.¹
— Note sur le Passiflora actinia. 1862. III. 615.¹
— Note sur le Pelargonium à grandes fleurs. 1884. III. 491.²
— Note sur le Raphlolepis japonica. 1858. III. 447.²
— Note sur une nouvelle variété d'Amandier. 1858. III. 39.²
— Notice sur l'Aristolochia macroura. 1867. III. 386.²
— Notice sur l'Embothrium coccineum. 1858. III. 383.¹
— Notice sur l'histoire . . . du Cordyline indivisa. 1862. III. 335.
— Notice sur l'Oxycoccos macrocarpa Pers. 1875. II. 686.¹
— Notice sur le Gaultheria discolor. 1858. III. 649.¹
— Notice sur le Lophospore rouge. 1862. III. 703.¹
— Notice sur le Mamillaria senilis Salm Dyck. 1874. II. 505.¹
— Notice sur le Melia Azedarach. 1880. III. 512.²
— Notice sur le Monochaetum ensiferum. 1857. III. 639.¹
— Notice sur le Nicotiana wigandioides. 1873. II. 774.¹
— Notice sur le Pionandra fragrans Miers. 1864. II. 771.¹
— Notice sur le Rhododendron Thomsoni. 1858. III. 662.²
— Notice sur le Seaforthia elegans R. Br. 1858. II. 64.¹
— Notice sur le Spiraea Blumei. 1858. III. 461.¹
— Notice sur le Spiraea callosa. 1858. III. 461.¹
— Notice sur les Bruyères. 1858. III. 650.¹
— Notice sur les Caléolaires ligneuses. 1862. III. 702.²
— Notice sur les changements de couleur. 1858. I. 185.²
— Notice sur les Tacsonia cultivés. 1874. II. 581.¹
— Notice sur un nouveau Pêcher à fleurs de Camellia. 1858. III. 439.²
— Nouvelle variété de l'Arbre aux quarante écus. 1856. III. 286.²
— L'origine des variétés sous l'influence du climat artificiel des jardins. 1867. I. 247.
— Le Pelargonium zonale. 1885. III. 491.²
— Première floraison . . . du Dracaena Goldieana. 1881. III. 336.²
— Quelques considérations sur les organes des plantes. 1857. I. 244.¹
— Quelques considérations sur les variétés des plantes. 1857. I. 244.¹
— De quelques fruits étrangers. 1856. III. 220.¹
— Les relations entre la chaleur et la végétation. 1873. I. 232.¹
— Remarques sur la culture de la Glycine. 1858. III. 490.²
— Sur le rôle des ferments dans la nutrition. 1876. I. 159.

— Saxe-gothaea conspicua. 1856. III. 287.²
— Le Schinus Mulh. 1855. III. 529.¹
— Seconde notice sur la duplication des fleurs et la panachure. 1868. I. 145.²
— De la sensibilité . . . chez les végétaux. 1885. I. 194.
— Spiraea Reevesiana hort. var. flore pleno. 1856. III. 461.¹
— & **Vos**, André de. Index bibliographique de l'hortus belgicus. 1887. I. 271.¹
Morren, F. W. De aaltjesziekte van den Koffieboom. 1898. III. 736.
— Die Arbeiten auf einer Kaffeeplantage. 1900. III. 728.¹
— De boekhouding eener Koffieonderneming. 1896. III. 727.
— Culture . . . du Café de Libéria. 1894. III. 743.¹
— Cultuur, bereiding . . . van Liberia Koffie. 1894. III. 743.¹
— Dr. W. Burck, over de oorzaken van den achteruitgang. van de . . . Koffiecultuur. 1896. III. 731.
— Gouvernements Koffiecultuur. 1897. III. 731.
— Guatemala-Koffie. 1898. III. 728.¹
— Jaarverslag der Soekaboemische landbouwvereeniging. 1897. III. 129.¹
— Kleine landbouwindustrie in Indië. 1894. III. 129.¹
— Koffie in Guatemala. 1898. III. 728.¹
— Koffiebibit in potten. 1898. III. 733.¹
— Koffiecultuur in Guatemala. 1899. III. 728.¹
— Koffiecultuur in Nederlandsch Indië. 1894. III. 730.
— Koffiecultuur op de Hawai-eilanden. 1897. III. 733.¹
— De Koffieteelt in Guatemala. 1899. III. 728.¹
— Kultur, Bereitung und Handel des Liberia-Kaffee. 1894. III. 743.¹
— Eene levenskwestie voor de Koffiecultuur. 1898. III. 731.
— De levenskwestie voor de Koffiecultuur. 1899. III. 731.
— De nematoden der Koffiewortels. 1896. III. 736.
— Proefstations voor Koffiecultuur op Java. 1896. III. 731.
— Werkzaamheden op eene Koffieonderneming. 1896. III. 727.
Morren, P. TROUPIN-. *See* TROUPIN-MORREN, P.
Morrière, Jules. Excursion de la Société Linnéenne à Vire. 1866. I. 443.
Morris, Daniel. Cacao; how to grow. 1882. III. 592.²
— The campaign of 1879 against Coffee leaf disease. 1879. III. 735.
— Cantor lectures on commercial fibres. 1895. III. 235.¹
— A catalogue of the most interesting forest trees. 1879. III. 92.²
— On the characteristics of plants included under Erythroxylon Coca. 1890. II. 394.²
— Chusquea abietifolia. 1886. III. 316.²
— Cinchona growing. 1881. III. 712.¹
— Coffee-leaf disease of Ceylon. 1879. III. 735.
— The Coffee leaf disease of Ceylon. 1880. III. 735.
— The colony of British Honduras. 1883. III. 265.¹
— Cultivation of Cinchona in Jamaica. 1883. III. 713.¹
— Ficus Benjamina. 1887. II. 150.¹
— Grape fruit and Shaddocks. 1896. III. 501.²
— Hassan Jack fruit. 1896. II. 146.¹
— Hydrangeas in the Azores. 1898. III. 412.¹
— Jamaica at the World's exposition. 1885. III. 267.¹
— Native and other fibre plants. 1884. III. 234.
— Note on the structure . . . of Hemileia vastatrix. 1880. III. 735.
— Notes on Liberian Coffee. 1881. III. 743.¹
— Notice sur la végétation de l'Île Ste. Hélène. 1884. I. 498.
— On the phenomena concerned in the production of . . . branched Palms. 1893. II. 63.¹
— Plantes produisant le caoutchouc du commerce. 1898. III. 229.
— Planting enterprise in the West Indies. 1884. III. 118.²
— The plants and gardens of the Canary Islands. 1895. III. 132.¹
— Prosopis juliflora. 1885. III. 485.¹
— Ramie. 1888. III. 382.¹
— Rapporten over proefnemingen betrekkelijk de Koffiebladziekte. 1880. III. 735.
— Report on the economic resources of the West Indies. 1898. III. 64.
— St. Helena. 1884. I. 498.
— On the singular effect produced on certain animals . . . by feeding on . . . wild Tamarind. 1896. III. 481.¹
— Sources of commercial india-rubber. 1898. III. 229.
— Tree Tomato. 1884. III. 699.²
— Tropical fruits. 1896. III. 220.¹
— On the use of certain plants as alexipharmics or snake-bite antidotes. 1887. III. 245.

Morris, G. H. See Brown, H. T. & Morris, G. H.
Morris, J. Sabal umbraculifera. 1882. II. 75.[1]
Morris, James. Ailanthiculture. 1862. III. 506.[2]
Morris, Joseph William. Handbook to Bath. 1888. I. 534.[2]
Morris, O. Der Kaffeebaum und seine Entwickelung. 1899. III. 727.
Morris, Richard. The botanist's manual. 1824. I. 267.
— Flora conspicua. 1826. I. 267.
Morris, Seward. How trees grow and feed. 1893. III. 38.[1]
Morrison, Alex. New Hebrides. 1897. II. 25.[3]
Morrison, Gabriel James. Description of the island of Formosa. 1877. III. 404.[2]
Morrison, John. On the Corsican Fir. 1871. IV. 465.[2]
— On the diseases of the Larch. 1863. IV. 450.
— Report on hedgerow trees. 1869. III. 214.[2]
— Report on the pruning of forest trees. 1869. IV. 171.
Morrison, R. & A. Fernettya ciliaris. 1878. II. 674.[2]
Morsch, (Hofgärtner, Charlottenhof). Auswahl empfehlenswerther Pflanzen. 1855. III. 74.
— Auswahl vorzüglich empfehlenswerther Pflanzen. 1849. III. 74.
Morsch, H. Ailanthus glandulosa, ein vörtreffliches Nutzholz. 1850. IV. 525.
Morse, F. W. The use of gases against scale-insects. 1887. III. 198.[2]
— See also Riley, C. V. & Morse, F. W.
Morse, W. H. Santa Barbara, California, U. S. A. 1900. III. 318.[2]
Morss, Charles Henry. A colony of Alnus glutinosa in eastern Massachusetts. 1900. III. 116.[2]
Mort ou dépérissement de certains arbres dans un parc. 1900. III. 181.[2]
Mortemart de Boisse, baron de. Voyage dans les Landes de Gascogne. 1840. IV. 359.[2]
Mortensen, Hans. Nordostsjællands Flora. 1872. I. 356.
— Tidsvilde Hegn. 1890. I. 357.
Mortensen-Barrit, J. J. Tiden · for Plantning af Enebær. 1891. III. 295.[1]
Morthier, Paul. Flore analytique de la Suisse. 1870. I. 436.
Mortillet, Gabriel de. Le Noyer, sa culture. 1863. III. 355.
Mortillet, H. de. Greffage du Chaenomeles japonica. 1878. III. 420.[1]
— De la greffe du Noyer. 1878. III. 355.
Mortillet, Paul de. Arboriculture fruitière. . . . Le Pêcher. 1865. III. 440.[2]
— Arboriculture fruitière. . . . Le Cerisier. 1866. III. 432.[1]
— Arboriculture fruitière. . . . Le Poirier. 1868. III. 445.[2]
— Greffe du Noyer. Modifications. 1868. III. 355.
— Les meilleurs fruits. 1865. III. 85.
— Quarante poires. 1860. III. 444.[2]
Mortimer, Cromwell. Some experiments concerning the poisonous quality of . . . Laurocerasus. 1732. III. 427.[3]
Mortimer, John Lockhart. The whole art of husbandry. 1707. III. 108.
Morton, J. L. The bark of trees. 1859. IV. 436.[1]
— Hedges, their formation and management. 1855. III. 213.
— The preservation of timber. 1859. IV. 418.
Morton, John. The natural history of Northamptonshire. 1712. I. 094.
Morton, Nathanael. Fixing up a wood lot in Massachusetts. 1898. IV. 469.
Mortzfeldt. Ueber horstweisen Vorverjüngungsbetrieb. 1896. IV. 140.
Morville, G. Beretning om Hedeplantningernes Tilstand. 1869. IV. 343.[1]
— Om Granlusens Optræden. 1870. IV. 455.
— Hvor i Skovene bør man plante Rødgran? 1870. IV. 453.
— Et Par Notitser fra Viborg-Egnen om Oldenborrenes Angreb. 1869. IV. 548.[2]
— Om Træplantning i Hederne. 1866. IV. 156.[1]
Morville, Niels. Mathematisk-statistisk Beregning over Brændsel. 1801. · IV. 412.[2] -
— Udtog af Mathematisk Statistisk Beregning om Brændsel. 1802. IV. 431.[1]
Moscardo, Lodovico, conte. Note overo memorie del museo di Lodovico Moscardo. 1656. I. 60.[1]
Moschettini, Cosimo. Della brusca malattia degli Olivi. 1777. III. 677.[1]
— Lettera della coltivazione degli Ulivi. 1794. III. 677.[1]
Moschkowitz & Siegling. Echinopsis Teṭṭavii. 1855. III. 622.[2]

Moscou — Société impériale des naturalistes. See Société . . . I. 10.
Moscow exhibition. 1882. I. 271.[1]
Moseley, Benjamin. Traité sur les propriétés . . . du café. 1785. III. 741.[2]
— A treatise concerning the properties . . . of coffee. `1785· III. 741.[2]
Moseley, Edwin Lincoln. Sandusky flora. 1899. I. 316.
Moseley, Henry Nottidge. Notes by a naturalist on the "Challenger." 1879. I. 303, V. xvi.[2]
— Notes on plants collected . . . at the Admiralty Islands. 1877. I. 499.[2]
— Notes on the vegetation of Bermuda. 1875. I. 336.
Moselle — Société d'histoire naturelle du département . . . See Société . . . I. 15.
Moselle — Société d'horticulture du département de la . . . See Société . . . III. 22.
Mosén, Carl Wilhelm Hjalmar. · Resebref från Brasilien. 1874. I. 343.
Moser. Ueber die mögliche Verbesserung der Holzköhlerei. 1826. IV. 394.
Moser, Heinrich Christoph. Allgemeine praktische Forstnaturgeschichte. 1794. IV. 56.
— Bemerkungen über kammeralistisch-oekonomisch und technische Gegenstände des Forstwesens. 1799. IV. 100.[1]
— Die Bewirthschaftung einer Wald-Revier. 1794. IV. 239.
— Deutschlands ökonomische Flora. 1796. III. 72.
— Das Forstrecht nach allgemeinen Gründen der Forstwissenschaft. 1806. IV. 320.
— Die praktisch-geometrische Aufnahme der Waldungen. 1797. IV. 263.
— Versuch einer Geschichte der deutschen Forstwirthschaft. 1795. IV. 25.
— Die wesentlichen Kennzeichen der . . . Holzarten. 1794. IV. 81.
Moser, J. Lehrbuch der Chemie für Land- und Forstwirthe. 1870. IV. 60.[1]
Moser, Wilhelm Gottfried von. Grundsäze der Forst-Oeconomie. 1757. IV. 94.
— Von den neuesten Forsteinrichtungen und Forstverbesserungen. 1788. IV. 316.
— Von dem Streumachen in Nadel-Waldungen. 1794. IV. 437.[1]
Mosettig, Johann Ev. Die Riesenplatanen in Cannosa. 1897. IV. 520.[2]
Moshkot, P. S. See Мошковъ, П. С.
Moskalski, P. See Москальскій, П.
Mosley, Sir Oswald. On the Aphis lanigera. 1820. III. 427.[1]
— Over de Aphis lanigera. 1820. III. 427.[1]
— The natural history of Tutbury. See Brown, Edwin. 1863. I. 401.
Moss, John. Structure and development of Pareira stem. 1876. II. 206.[2]
Moss, S. C. Forest treatment in South Tinnevelly. 1891. IV. 378.
— The germination of Teak. 1892. IV. 536.[2]
Mossige, J. Om anlæg og rationel drift af egeskove. 1877. IV. 506.
Mosso. Influence des alcaloïdes sur la germination. 1895. I. 204.
Mosso, Ugolino. Sull' azione fisiologica della cocaina. 1880. III. 493.[1]
The most profitable Willows. 1886. III. 351.[1]
Mostardi-Fioretti, T. Selvicultura chilena. 1866. IV. 342.[1]
Mostra nazionale e concorsi relativi agli spari contro le grandine a Como. 1899. IV. 191.[1]
Motabara-Soosin. Jaku-m'joo-S'jook. 1824. III. 91.[2]
Mote, L. S. Influence du greffon sur le sujet. 1881. III. 39.
Motherby, (Dr. med. of Königsberg). Beobachtungen über einige Taxus-Bäume. 1838. II. 10.[3]
Mothes, Caprand-. See Caprand-Mothes.
Moti Singh, Mian. See Mian Moti Singh.
Motley, James. Castalia purcha of Singapore. 1855. III. 668.[2]
Mott, Frederick Thompson. Flora odorata. 1843. III. 82.
— The fruits of all countries. 1883. III. 220.[1]
— & others. The flora of Leicestershire. 1886. I. 403.
Mott, James. The Pomelo, Shaddock or Grapefruit. 1890. III. 502.[2]
Motta Prego, João da. See Almeida, Verissimo d' & Motta Prego, João da.
Mottareale, G. Contributo alle malattie del Castagno. 1897. III. 359.[2]

Mottareali, Giovanni. Propagation of Camellias. 1896. III. 600.[1]

Mottet, Séraphin Joseph. Les Acacia. 1896. III. 463.[1]
— Les Aralia. · 1894.'' III. 641.[1] ' ·
— L'atavisme et l'hérédité. 1900. I. 248.[2]
— Du bouturage. ·1898. III. 158.
— Caryopteris Mastacanthus. 1894. III. 695.[2]
— Les Clématites. 1900. III. 389.[2]
— Les Clématites à petites fleurs. 1899. III. 389.[3]
— Culture des Clématites. · 1900. III. 389.[2]
— Culture et multiplication des Eucalyptus. 1897.' III. 634.[1]
— Description des plus belles espèces d'Eucalyptus. 1897. III. 634.[1]
— Des effets de la taille sur·un Magnolia. 1900. III. 399.[1]
— Les Eucalyptus. 1897. III. 634.[1]
— Sur la floraison des Cèdres. · 1900. II. 27.[2]
— Guide élémentaire de multiplication des végétaux. 1895. III. 153.
— Hibiscus Manihot. 1900. II. 523.[1]
— De l'influence de la sélection. 1897. III. 153.
— Iochroma tubulosum. 1897. II. 772.[1]
— Kennedya et Hardenbergia. 1896. III. 480.[1]
— Lilacs. 1893. III. 680.[2] ·
— Lonicera Alberti. 1894. II. 839.[2]
— Lupinus arboreus. 1898. III. 481.[2]
— Magnolia macrophylla. ·1899. III. 400.[1]
— Maladie noire des Clématites. 1897. III. 390.[1]
— Multiplication des Clématites. 1900. III. 389.[2]
— Notes sur quelques Chèvrefeuilles.· 1900. II. 836.[1]
— Les Pandanus. 1894. · III. 313.[1]
— Pervenche de Madagascar. 1897. III. 691.[2]
— Petit guide pratique de jardinage. 1897. III. 113.
— Les Phyllocactus. 1895. III. 625.[2]
— Precocious Roses. 1895. III. 456.[1]
— Rosa sericea. 1897. II. 299.[1]
— Rosa Wichuraiana. 1898. II. 300.[1]
— The wild Clematises. 1894. III. 300.[2]
— See also BOUCHER, Georges & MOTTET, D.; COCHET-COCHET & MOTTET, Seraphin.

Mottier, David Myers. On the archegonium . . . in ·-Tsuga . . . and Pinus. 1892. II. 21.[1]
— On the development of the archegonium . . . of Tsuga canadensis and Pinus sylvestris. 1892. II. 19.
— Development of the embryo-sac in Acer rubrum. 1893. II. 477.[1]

Mottraie, AUBRY DE LA. See AUBRY DE LA MOTTRAIE.

Motty, J. B. Leitfaden der Botanik. 1836. I. 87.

Mouat, Frederick John. Correspondence relative to a remarkable variety of caoutchouc. 1843. III. 228.[2]

Mouchelet, E. ·Mémoire sur l'écorcement des bois. 1873; IV. 434.[2]

Les mouches des poires. See ANDRÉ, Édouard. ·1890. III. 446.[2]

Mouchon, Émile. Dictionnaire de bromatologie végétale exotique. 1847. III. 219.[2]
— Monographie des principaux fébrifuges indigènes. 1856. III. 271.[1]
— De la térébenthine. 1858. IV. 443.[2]

Mougeot. De l'opium & du café. 1894. III. 742.[1]

Mougeot, Jean Baptist.' Considérations générales sur la végétation . . . des Vosges. 1845. I. 410.

Mougeot, Joseph Antoine. Le Gui.· 1858. III. 385.[2]

Mougin. Restauration et conservation des terrains en montagne. 1900. IV. 186.[2]

Mouillefert, Pierre, Action du sulfocarbonate de potassium. 1881. III. 572.
— L'Ajone d'Europe. 1892. .III. 489.[2]
— Ajonc, Ulex Lin. 1892. III. 489.[2]
— Application des sulfocarbonates alcalins. 1875. III. 568.
— Application du sulfocarbonate. de potassium. 1879. III. 571.
— Araucaria du Chili. 1890. III. 299.[1]
— Arboretum . . . de Grignon. 1889. I. 59.
— Le Belsombra. 1889. III. 388.[2]
— Le Cap de Bonne-Espérance. 1892. III. 281.[2]
— Le Copalme d'Amérique. 1889. III. 302,[2] 417.[2]
— Culture du Robinier pour échalas. 1898. IV. 523.[2]
— La défense de la Vigne contre le phylloxéra. 1887. III. 574.
— Effets du grand hiver de 1879–1880. 1887. III. 49.[1]
— Effets du sulfocarbonate de potassium. 1874. III. 567.[1]
— Espèces forestières étrangères à propager. 1896. IV. 127.
— État actuel des Vignes soumises au traitement du sulfocarbonate de potassium. · 1876. III. 569.[1]

— Sur l'état des Vignes traitées à Cognac. 1877. III. 570.[2]
— Étude sur les bois de Grignon. .1877. 'IV. 360. ·
— Études de sylviculture. Débit . . . des bois. 1876. IV. 217.
— Expériences faites à la station viticole de Cognac. 1877. III. 570.[2]
— Expériences sur l'emploi des sulfocarbonates alcalins. 1874. III. 566.[2]
— Les merrains et la fabrication des tonneaux. 1896. IV. 427.[2]
— Note sur la présence . . . du phylloxera à Orléans. 1876. III. 569.[1]
— Note sur un nouveau Crataegus. 1890. II. 260,[1] 261.[2]
— Nouvelles expériences avec les sulfocarbonates alcalins. 1874. III. 567.[1]
— Origine du phylloxera à Cognac. 1875. III. 568;
— Le phylloxera. 1876. III. 570.[1]
— Plantes rares de la région de Paris. · 1877. II. 135.[1]
— Les principaux arbres exotiques . . . dans le midi de la France. 1889. III. 84.[1]
— Rapport sur une mission viticole à l'île de Chypre. . 1893. III. 559.[1]
— Reconstitution du vignoble français. .1877. III. 570.[1]
— Remarques, à propos des observations présentées par M. Bouillaud. 1876. III. 569.[2]
— Sur les résultats fournis par le traitement des Vignes phylloxérées. 1879. III. 571.
— Résultats obtenus à Cognac· avec les sulfocarbonates. 1876. III. 569.[2]
— Résultats obtenus à Cognac depuis 1875. 1877. III. 570.[2]
— Résultats obtenus à Cognac sur les Vignes phylloxérées. 1876. III. 569.[2]
— Résumé des expériences faites à la station viticole de Cognac. 1875. III. 568.
— Le Sapin de Douglas. 1897. IV. 484.[1]
— La température des arbres. 1886. I. 186, III. 48.
— Traité des arbres [et] arbrisseaux. 1892. I. 294,[1] III. 84, IV. 85.[2]
— Traitement des Vignes phylloxérées. ·1878· III. 760.
— Traitement des Vignes phylloxérées, en 1882. 1883. III. 573.
— Le Tulipier. 1897. IV. 519.[2]
— Les Vignes japonaises de' M. Degron. 1900. II. 506.[1]

Mouir, Pattison. Sur la gomme-résine Kauri. 1875. III. 297.[2]

Moulin, SCHMITZ DU. See SCHMITZ DU MOULIN.

Mouls, .I. F. Xavier. Les dunes; ou, Sylva maria. 1860. IV. 468.[2]

Moulson, Samuel. Brief instructions for orchard-planting. 1853. III. 133.

Meunier, T. Plantkuilen en greppels bij Koffiecultuur. 1884. III. 730, 734.[1]

Meunier, Th. Ontginningen op Java. 1882. IV. 383.[2]

Mountains, Dydymus. The gardeners labyrinth. 1651. III. 107.

Moura-Brazil. L'ophtalmie purulente factice. 1882. III. 462.[2]

Mourao, Ch. Safrol et isosafrol. 1896.' III. 408.[1]

Mourelo, José RODRIGUEZ. See RODRIGUEZ MOURELO, José.

Moureton, P. Du reboisement des propriétés particulières. 1885. IV. 163.

Mourgeon, L. E. La réserve dans les taillis composés. 1885. IV. 237.

Mourgues, L. E. Sur les matières colorantes du Maqui. 1894. II. 509.[1]

Mourier, Charles. Anvisning til Træplantning. 1806. IV. 113.[1]

Mourier, G. Om Behandling af Egekrat. 1862. IV. 505.

Mourier, O. V. Fuchsiahækker. 1886. III. 640.[1]

Mouriès. Observations sur la maladie de la Vigne. 1853. III. 576.

Moussillac, A. Observations sur la culture . . . de l'Acacia. 1853. IV. 523.[1]

Mouthaan, N. Proeve van een geschiedkundig overzicht der humusachtige lichamen. 1856. III. 38.[1]

Mouton-Fontenille de la Clotte, Jean Philippe. Coup d'œil sur la botanique. 1810. I. 85.
— Dictionnaire des termes techniques de botanique. 1803. I. 70.
— Tableau des systèmes de botanique. 1798. I. 259.
— Tableau de concordance des genres d'un Pinax des plantes européennes. 1814. I. 349, 531.[2]

Le mouton dans les forêts de Californie. See SHEEP-GRAZING in forests. 1899. IV. 197.[2]

Sur les **mouvements** exterieurs des plantes. 1712. I. 193.[2]

Movimento commerciale d' esportazione di prodotti forestali. 1864. IV. 405.²

Movimiento forestal de Inglaterra. 1895. IV. 551.²

Moving large trees. 1883. III. 168.¹—1896. III. 168.¹

Mowat, John Lancaster Gough, (editor). Alphita, a medico-botanical glossary. 1887. I. 292.

Moyen, J. Cours élémentaire de botanique. 1871. V. XVII.¹

Moyen d'obtenir des Pruniers nains. 1840. III. 432.²

Moyen d'obtenir le Datura arborea de très-petite taille. 1862. III. 700.¹

Moyen de faire disparaître la mousse. 1899. IV. 151.²

Moyen de faire mûrir les graines du Coignassier. 1838. III. 420.¹

Sur un **moyen** de preserver les arbres de leur lepre. 1718. III. 193.¹

Moyen de prévenir la pourriture du bois. 1862. IV. 418.

Moyen de produire l'agustie. 1893. . III. 693.¹

Un **moyen** de sauver les graines précieuses. 1892. IV. 196.¹

Moyens à employer pour activer la végétation d'une futaie sur taillis. 1899. IV. 170.

Moyens de combattre l'hylésine. 1900. IV. 480.

Moyens de destruction de l'Hylobius abietis. · 1899. IV. 479.

Moyens de détruire les mauvaises herbes. 1900. IV. 211.¹

Moyens de distinguer le Chêne du Châtaignier. 1857. II. 124.¹

Moyens de préserver·les Peupliers . . . de la dent les rats. 1858. III. 186,¹ 344.¹

Moyens de prévenir les délits de résine. _See_ MITTEL gegen den Harsfrevel. 1862. IV. 436.²

Sur les **moyens** de se délivrer des ravages de la pyrale de la Vigne. 1837. III. 562.²

Moyens pour atténuer les dommages causés en forêt par les locomotives. 1896. IV. 183.²

Moyens préventifs employés contre l'hylobe. 1899. IV. 479.

Moyer, Isaac Shoemaker. _See_ THOMAS, Joseph & MOYER, I. S.

Moynier de Villepoix, R. Recherches sur les canaux sécréteurs du fruit des Ombellifères. 1878. II. 653.¹

Mozard, Jean. Principes pratiques sur l'éducation . . . des arbres fruitiers. 1814. III. 143.

Mozzetti, Ferdinando. Phénomène de végétation. 1840. II. 401.²

Mozziconacci, A. L'exploitation du Chêne vert à Mont-arnaud. 1884. IV. 503.¹

— La furuure du Mûrier. 1900. III. 378.

Mpafu tree of tropical Africa. 1881. III. 510.¹

Mr. Die Lichthöhen normal geschlossener Eichen- und Kiefernbestände. 1898. IV. 474, 509.

Mtz. Lückenhieb oder Besamungsschlag? 1888. IV. 128.

Mucatuso, A. L' erbolaio siciliano. 1863. I. 431.

Mudd, Christopher. The vegetation of New Zealand. 1884. I. 507.

The **Muddar** plant. 1857. III. 692.¹

Mudie, Robert. The botanic annual. 1832. II. 21.²

Mücke, Friedrich. Ueber die Befugnisse der Forst- und Jagd-schutzbeamten in Preussen. 1886. IV. 290.²

— Forstdiebstahl in gemeinschaftlicher Ausübung. 1888. IV. 317.¹

— Forstliche Buch- und Rechnungsführung. 1887. IV. 312.

— Ueber die Frostschütte der Kiefer. 1889. IV. 478.

— Der Kiefernbastkäfer. 1887. IV. 478.

— Pfändung, Beschlagnahme, Durchsuchung. 1892. IV. 317.¹

— Der preussische Forst- und Jagdschutzbeamte. 1884. IV. 290.²

— Das Recht der Privatbeamten. 1900. IV. 309.¹

— Die Rechte und Pflichten der Privatforstbeamten. 1887. IV. 308.¹

— Die rechtliche Stellung der Privatforstbeamten. 1887. IV. 308.¹

— Wald und Wild in der Bibel. 1896. I. 513.

— Wald-Hege und -Pflege. 1885. IV. 107.¹

— Was ist über die Lebensweise des grossen braunen Rüssel-käfers . . . bekannt? 1886. IV. 92.

— _See also_ FEEGER, BALTZ & ·MÜCKE, Fritz.

Mücke, Fritz. _See_ MÜCKE, Friedrich.

Mueggenburg, Stephan. _See_ SCHULZER VON MUEGGENBURG, Stephan.

Mühl, F. The communal forests of the Grand Duchy of Hesse. 1897. IV. 290.¹

Mühlberg, Friedrich. Beschreibung der Weidenarten. 1879. III. 351.¹

— Descriptions des Saules propres à la vannerie. 1879. III. ·351.¹

—Ueber Massnahmen zur Vorbeugung .·. der Phylloxera-Krankheit. 1880. III. 572.

— Die Standorte . . . der Gefässpflanzen des Aargau's. 1880. I. 388, 436.

— & **Kraft**, A. Die Blutlaus. 1885. III. 427.²

—— Le puceron lanigère, sa nature. 1885. III. 427.² ·

Mühle, Vilmos. _See_ MÜHLE, Wilhelm.

Mühle, Wilhelm. Clematis-hybridek. 1888. III. 389.²

—Quercus conferta. 1897. III.·362.¹

Mühlen, Ferdinand, _Freiherr_ von. Anleitung zum rationellen Betriebe der Aussatung. 1873. ¯IV. 171.

— Büschelballenpflanzung und Schütte. 1872. IV. 476.

— Ein neuer Saatrillenzieher. 1871. IV. 149.¹

Mühlen, ZUR. _See_ ZUR MÜHLEN.

Muehlenberg, Gotthilf Heinrich Ernst. Catalogus plantarum Americae septentrionalis. 1813. I. 306.

— Index Florae lancastriensis. 1793. I. 313.

—Kurze Bemerkungen über . . . Gattungen Juglans, Fraxinus und Quercus. 1801. I. 312.

— Über die nordamerikanischen Weiden. 1803. II. 99.¹ ·

— On North American Willows. 1803. II. 99.¹

— Observations of the genera Juglans, Fraxinus and Quercus. 1801. I. 312.

Mühlenberg, Heinrich Ernst. _See_ MÜHLENBERG, G. H. E.

Mühlenpfordt, Eduard. Versuch einer getreuen Schilderung der Republik Mejico. 1844. III. 264.²

Mühlenpfordt, F. Beiträge zur Cacteenkunde. 1847. II. 586.¹

— Bemerkungen über die Blumen einiger Cacteen. 1848. II. 586.¹

— Einige neue Cacteen. 1845. II. 585.¹

— Neue. Cacteen. 1846. II. 585.²

Mühlfeld, Johann Georg MEGERLE VON. _See_ MEGERLE VON MÜHLFELD, J. G.

Mühlhausen, Carl. Das Wegenetz des Lehrforstreviers Gahrenberg. 1876. IV. 266.²

Mühlhausen, F. A. Ueber das Absterben der Kiefern aus Pflanzungen. 1875. IV. 477.

— Ueber forstliche Terrainkarten. 1879. IV. 251.¹

Mührwold. Sur les forêts de Norvège. 1900. IV. 344.¹

Muel, E. La culture . . . des forêts. 1885. IV. 122.¹

— Essai des engrais chimiques. 1881. IV. 144.²

— Les incendies dans les forêts de Pin maritime. 1900.· IV. 183.²

— Notions de sylviculture. 1884. IV. 122.¹

— Reboisement des terrains vagues. 1881. IV. 163.

— Sylviculture . . . dans les Landes. 1896. IV. 122.¹

— **Noel**, Arthur & **Maire**. Conférences forestières. 1885. IV. 41.¹

Mülberger. Ledum palustre am wilden Hornsee. 1885. · II. 673.¹

Müllertz, Johan Carl. Beretning om nogle Forsøg med og Nytten af adskillige norske vilde Bær. 1804. III. 270.¹

Müllenkampf, Franz Damian Friedrich. Anleitung zur Forst-arithmetik. 1789.· IV. 57.

— Von Commun- und Privatwäldern. 1789. IV. 116.

— Einladung zu einer öffentlichen Vorlesung über die Forst-wissenschaft. 1785. • IV. 31.

— Praktische Bemerkungen zur Forstwissenschaft. 1783. IV. 100.¹

— Sammlung der Forstordnungen verschiedener Länder. 1791. IV. 314.¹

— Vermischte Polizei- und Kameralgegenstände. .1791 IV 100.¹

Müller. _See also_ MULLER.

Müller. Cassia alata.· 1858. III. 470.²

Müller. Ueber Clerodendron-Arten. 1853. III. 696.¹

Müller. Iseltwaldkantonnement. 1853. IV. 365.

Müller. Die Streunutzungen in den Hochgebirgswaldungen. 1892. IV. 438.¹

Mueller. Die wichtigsten . . . erzeugten Krankheiten. 1888. IV. 212.

Müller, (_Dr._). Versuch eines Vegetationsgemäldes von Oesel. 1853. I. 361.

Müller, (_Dr. in Emmerich_). Chemische Analyse des Calycan-thus floridus. 1844. II. 214.¹

Müller, (_Dr. med., Genthin_). Ein Beitrag zur Kultur des wilden Rosenstocks. 1839. III. 451.²

Müller, (_Forstamtsassistent_). Auffallende Erscheinungen an Fohrenstämmen. 1899. II. 47.²

Müller, (_Forstmeister_). Ueber Anlage . . . der Eichenschäl-waldungen. 1850. IV. 504.

— Ueber das Aufbewahren der Saat-Eicheln. 1849. IV. 504.

— Erfahrungen . . . über Anlage . . . der Eichenschälwald-ungen. · 1850. IV. 504.

Müller, (Oberförster). Was muss im nordöstlichen Odenwalde geschehen? 1873. IV. 389.
Müller, (Oberforstmeister, Merseburg). Die Entwässerungen. 1884. IV. 144.[1]
— Zur Kiefern-Jährlings-Pflanzung. 1883. IV. 473.
Müller, A. Eine Riesenfichte. 1885. II. 37.[2]
Müller, Adolf. Aphorismen über ... Lärche. 1872. IV. 449.
— Aphorismen über Waldwegbau. 1876. IV. 266.[2]
— Beitrag zur Einführung der gerüsteten und eingemessenen Holzgabe. 1895. IV. 334.[2]
— Die Drahtseilriese im ... Birkenthal. 1898. IV. 392.
— & Karl. Die einheimischen Säugethiere und Vögel. 1873. IV. 90.[1]
Müller, Albert. The gall midge of the Yew. 1873. III. 288.[1]
— Rhododendron excrescences. 1871. III. 657.[1]
— Tree pruning viewed entomologically. 1874. III. 170.
Müller, Albrecht. Die qualitative und quantitative Bestimmung des Holzschliffes im Papier. 1887. IV. 430.
Mueller, Anton. Alphabetisches Wörterbuch synonymer ... Namen der offizinellen Pflanzen. 1866. I. 75.[1]
— Die wichtigsten nützlichen ... Insekten. 1859. IV. 92.
Müller, Arnold. Die gemischten Holzbestände. 1890. IV. 137.[1]
Mueller, Bernhard. De plantarum cognitione medico necessaria. 1626. III. 238.[1]
Müller, C. Beschreibung des Peisterwitzer Oderwaldes. 1853. IV. 352.
Müller, C. Die Verschiedenheit der Südwest- und Südost-Flora Australiens. 1865. I. 502.
Müller, C. Einige Ermittelungen über die Wachsthumsleistung einzeln eingesprengter Kiefern. 1882. IV. 481.
Müller, C. Leitfaden zur Einführung der Lehrlinge in das Forst- und Jagdwesen. 1883. IV. 98.[1]
Müller, C. Abhängigkeit der Holzbeschaffenheit. 1896. IV. 409.
Müller, C. A. Die wichtigsten Rohstoffe des Pflanzenreichs. 1894. III. 218.[2]
Müller, C. F. Das Holzdiebstahls-Gesetz. 1852. IV. 320.
Müller, C. G. Over de drooge destillatie. 1859. IV. 432.[1]
Müller, Carl. See MÜLLER, Karl.
Müller, Daniel. Fraxinus excelsior var. autumnalis. 1857. III. 672.[1]
— Die Veränderung der Pflanzen durch die Kultur. 1855. I. 247.
Müller, Daniel Ernst. Ueber den Afterraupenfrass. 1821. IV. 206.
— Allgemeine Forstkerfkunde. See BECHSTEIN, J. M. 1818. IV. 91.[1]
— Kurze Beschreibung des Forst-Revieres Aschaffenburg. 1824. IV. 350.[2]
— Des Spessart's Holzhandel. 1837. IV. 404.[1]
— Versuch zur Begründung eines allgemeinen Forstpolizeigesetzes. 1825. IV. 268.
Müller, E. G. O. & Pax, Ferdinand. Cucurbitaceae. 1894. II. 844.[2]
Mueller, Elias. Inhalt einer Abhandlung von Fürtrefflichkeit der Gewächse. n. d. III. 269.[1]
Müller, Ernst. Monströse Form von Juglans regia. 1864. II. 113.[2]
Müller, F. Mittheilungen über die Culturgewächse der Colonie Blumenau. 1857. III. 65.[1]
Müller, F. Die Knoppernernte im westlichen Ungarn. 1885. IV. 515.[1]
Mueller, F. A. H. J. Tabellarische Uebersicht des Pflanzenreichs. 1836. I. 260.
Müller, Ferdinand Albrecht Louis. Die Fabrikation des Papiers. 1877. IV. 429.
Mueller, Ferdinand Jacob Heinrich, Baron von. Account of some new Australian plants. 1857. I. 501.
— Account of the Gunyang. 1856. III. 701.[2]
— Additions to the ... flora of South Australia. 1887. I. 503.
— Additions to the lists of the principal timber trees. 1874. III. 132.[1]
— Additions to the Queensland flora. 1886. II. 746.[1]
— Address on the development of rural industries. 1881. IV. 380.[1]
— Sopra alcune piante australiane. 1873. II. 623.[2]
— The Algaroba tree. 1871. III. 758.[2]
— An anti-malarial tree. 1898. III. 636.

— Areca Alicae. 1879. II. 64.[2]
— Australian Cycadeae. 1859. II. 2.[1]
— Australian plants new. 1882. II. 248.[1]
— Australian vegetation. 1867. I. 502, III. 282.[2]
— Auswahl von aussertropischen Pflanzen. 1872. III. 53.
— The Banyan tree of the Staaten River. 1890. II. 152.[2]
— Beobachtungen über die Anwendung der einheimischen Pflanzen. 1854. III. 282.[2]
— Bericht über eine neue Rhododendron-Art. 1884. II. 683.[2]
— Beschreibung einer neuen Grevillea. 1896. II. 161.[2]
— Beschreibung einer neuen papuanischen Bassia. 1885. III. 387.[2]
— Botanical nomenclature. 1883. II. 727.[2]
— Botanical notes from north-west Australia. 1894. II. 529.[1]
— Brief notes on some new Papuan plants. 1893. II. 509.[3]
— Brief record of a new Scaevola. 1885. II. 847.[2]
— Brief remarks on some rare Tasmanian plants. 1892. I. 506.[1]
— Callitris (Frenela) Parlatorei. 1866. II. 27.[1]
— A catalogue of plants collected during Mr. A. Forrest's geographical exploration. 1881. I. 502.
— Catalogue of plants ... in the Melbourne botanic garden. 1858. I. 522.[1]
— Census of the genera of plants ... indigenous to Australia. 1882. I. 503.
— Census of the plants of Tasmania instituted in 1875. 1875. I. 506.[1]
— Census of the plants of Tasmania instituted in 1879. 1880. I. 506.[1]
— A complete census of the flora of Deal Island. 1885. I. 506.[1]
— The conservation of forests. 1872. IV. 396.[1]
— Considerations of phytographic expressions. 1889. I. 254.[2]
— Contributiones ad Acaciarum Australiae cognitionem. 1859. II. 323.[1]
— Contributions to the phytography of Australia. 1885. II. 378.[2]
— Contributions to the phytography of Tasmania. 1869. I. 506.[1] — 1878. I. 506.[1]
— Contributions to the phytography of the New Hebrides. 1870. I. 508.[1]
— Contributions to the phytography of the New Hebrides and Loyalty Islands. 1874. I. 509.[1]
— On the cultivation of the Cinchona in the south of Europe. 1866. III. 713.[2]
— Dacrydium Fitzgeraldi. 1881. II. 9.[1]
— Definitions of rare ... Australian plants. 1855. I. 501.
— Definitions of new Australian plants. 1882. I. 503.
— Dennisonia, Barklya, et Laboucheria. 1859. I. 501.
— Description of a new Chorilaena. 1890. II. 400.[2]
— Description of a new Gompholobium. 1890. II. 362.[1]
— Description of a new Isopogon. 1895. II. 163.[2]
— Description of a new Logania. 1890. II. 719.[1]
— Description of a new Papuan Bassia. 1885. III. 387.[2]
— Description of a new Papuan dilleniaceous plant. 1886. II. 543.[2]
— Description of a new Papuan Ternstroemiaceous plant. 1887. II. 552.[1]
— Description of a new Papuan vacciniaceous plant. 1886. II. 659.[1]
— Description of a new species of Chloanthes. 1889. II. 754.[1]
— Description of a new tiliaceous tree. 1886. II. 510.[1]
— Description of a ... Rhododendron from New Guinea. 1888. II. 678.[1]
— Description of a species of Pycnarrhena. 1887. II. 208.[1]
— Description of an unrecorded Ardisia. 1887. II. 693.[2]
— Description of ... Eucalyptus from New Britain. 1886. II. 625.[1]
— Description of some ... Australian plants. 1888. I. 503.
— Descriptions of hitherto unrecorded Australian plants. 1891. I. 504.
— Descriptions of new Australian plants. 1887. I. 503.
— Descriptions of new West Australian plants. 1889. II. 344.[1]
— Descriptions ... of the myoporinous plants of Australia. 1886. II. 805.[2]
— Descriptions of two new species of Eugenia. 1886. II. 626.[1]
— Descriptions of two ... West Australian plants. 1889. II. 328.[1]

— Descriptive characters of new Alpine plants from . . . Australia. 1855. I. 501.
— Descriptive notes on a new Vaccinium. 1876. II. 687.[2]
— Descriptive notes on Papuan plants. 1875. I. 499.[1]
— Descriptive record of two plants additional to the flora of Australia. 1888. . II. 366.[2]
— Diagnoses of new species of South Australian plants. 1882. II. 536.[1]
— Diagnoses . . . plantarum novarum . . . in Nova Hollandia. 1852. I. 501.
— Diagnostic notes on . . . Australian plants. 1859. I. 501.
— On Duttonia. 1856. II. 807.[1]
— On Dysoxylon Schiffneri. 1883. II. 420.[2]
— Edible fruits from the Maclay-coast. 1886. III. 282.[1]
— On the effects of frost on vegetation. 1870. III. 50.[1]
— Ueber einige nutzbringende . . . Coniferen. 1890. IV. 3.[1]
— Elenco delle piante raccolt . . . nell' Australia centrale. 1873. I. 502.
— Enumeration of plants collected by A. C. Gregory. 1859. V. xxiv.[2]
— Enumeration of the plants collected by Dr. J. Murray. 1863. I. 502.
— Enumeration of the plants collected during Mr. J. Macd. Stuart's expeditions. 1863. I. 502.
— Essay on the plants collected by Mr. E. Fitzalan. 1860. I. 502.
— Eucalyptographia. 1879. II. 623.[1]
— Ueber Eucalyptus für kältere Gegenden. 1879. IV. 530.
— El Eucalyptus globulus. 1873. IV. 533.[1]
— Eucalyptus globulus. 1880. II. 624.[2]
— Eucalyptus of Australia. 1879. IV. 531.[2]
— The Fan-palms of Australia. 1892. II. 70.[1]
— Far southern localities for various plants in New South Wales. 1884. I. 503.
— Flora of King Island. 1888. I. 506.[1]
— The flora of South Australia. 1853. I. 501.
— Forest culture. 1871. IV. 120.
— Forest culture in its relation to industrial pursuits. 1871. IV. 269.
— Fragmenta phytographiae Australiae. 1858. I. 501.
— On a general introduction of useful plants into Victoria. 1858. III. 132.[1]
— First [and second] general report . . . on the vegetation . . . of Victoria. 1854. I. 501, V. xxiv.[2]
— The genus Albizzia. 1872. II. 330.[1]
— On the genus Eremophila. 1859. II. 805.[2]
— A glance on the plants of Tasmania. 1885. I. 506.[1]
— Ueber Härte einiger Cycadeen. 1882. III. 284.[1]
— Hardihood of Cycads. 1882. III. 284.[1]
— On the hybridism of New Zealand plants. 1884. I. 529.
— Iconography of Australian salsolaceous plants. 1889. II. 197.[1]
— Iconography of . Australian species of Acacia. 1887. II. 320.[1]
— Important tanners' plants. 1878. IV. 435.
— Index of the plants described in the Transactions. 1859. . 501.
— Index perfectus ad Caroli Linnaei Species plantarum. 1880. I. 77, 261.
— Indigenous fibres in Australia. 1962. III. 224.
— Indigenous vegetable productions . . . of Victoria. 1862. III. 282.[1]
— Introduction to botanic teachings . . . Victoria. 1877. I. 502.
— Key to the system of Victorian plants. 1885. I. 503.
— A lecture on the flora of Australia. 1882. I. 503.
— Levél a Brassala és Brassaiopsis genusokról. 1879. II. 646.[2]
— List of extra-tropic West Australian plants. 1896. I. 505.
— List of plants collected by Chas. Winnecke. 1886. I. 503.
— List of the plants obtained during Mr. C. Giles's travels. 1877. I. 502.
— Livistona Mariae F. Müll. 1879. II. 70.[2]
— Mémoire sur le boisement de l'Algérie. 1869. IV. 168.[1]
— Monograph of the Eucalypti of tropical Australia. 1859. II. 622.[2]
— Der Murrayscrub; botanisch skizzirt. 1852. I. 501.
— Die Myoporineen Australiens. 1886. II. 805.[2]
— Myoporum insulare. 1886. II. 806.[2]
— The native plants of Victoria. 1879. I. 502.
— The natural capabilities of the colony of Victoria. 1875. III. 132.[1]
— Neuer australischer Pandanus. 1887. II. 57.[2]

— Ein neues Rhododendron von den Papua-Inseln. 1885. II. 683.[2]
— A new fruit tree. 1885. III. 387.[2]
— A new Palm from Queensland. 1882. II. 74.[1]
— New Papuan plants. 1891. I. 499.
— A new tree from the New Hebrides. 1880. II. 509.[2] —
— New Vaccinaceae from New Guinea. 1886. II. 658.[2]
— Note intorno ad alcuni sinonimi nel genere Eucalyptus. 1880. II. 623.[1']
— Note on a hitherto imperfectly known Callistemon. 1883. II. 621.[2]
— Note on Antholoma. 1892. II. 509.[2]
— Note on botanical collections. 1892. I. 499.[1]
— Note on Eucalyptus globulus. 1878. IV. 533.[1]
— Note on the Araucaria of New Guinea. 1888. II. 26.[1]
— Note on the genus Diplanthera. 1867. II. 788.[1]
— Note on the west Australian Fan-Palm. 1893. II. 70.[1]
— Notes made during the recent expedition across . . . Australia. 1857. I. 501.
— Notes on a new species of Eucalyptus. 1890. II. 625.[1]
— Notes on a new species of Hakea. 1883. II. 162.[2]
— Notes on a rare pandanaceous plant. 1891. II. 57.[1]
— Notes on a Thunbergia. 1882. II. 804.[1]
— Notes on an undescribed Acacia from New South Wales. 1893. II. 326.[2]
— Notes on Boronia floribunda Sieber. 1896. II. 400.[1]
— Notes on Dodonaeas. 1892. II. 485.[2]
— Notes on Gastrolobium grandiflorum. 1865. II. 359,[1] III. 477.[1]
— Notes on some salsolaceous plants. 1889. II. 187.[1]
— Notes on the genus Blepharocarya. 1879. II. 455.[2]
— Notes on the plants collected during Mr. J. M. Stuart's recent expedition. 1860. I. 502.
— Notes sur la végétation . . . de l'Australie. 1866. I. 502.
— Notice sur un Cycas indigène aux Iles Fiji. 1883. II. 5.[1]
— Notizen über die Xanthorrhoea-Arten. 1885. III. 339.[1]
— Notulae de quibusdam plantis Australiam incolentibus. 1871. I. 502.
— Notulam de fructu Anodopetali . . . communicat. 1872. II. 250.[1]
— Nova genera et species . . . in plagis Australiae. 1857. I. 501.
— Die nützlichsten Pinus-Arten. 1884. IV. 463.[1]
— Observations on north Australian botany. 1856. I. 501.
— Observations on plants collected during Mr. Joseph Bradshaw's expedition. 1892. I. 504.
— Observations on some Papuan . . . Sterculiaceae. 1886. II. 531.[2]
— Observations on some . . plants from New Zealand. 1861. II. 783.[2] — 1863. II. 782.[2]
— On the occurrence of Nipa fruticans. 1880. II. 71.[2]
— On the Octoclinis Macleayana. 1858. II. 27.[1]
— Plants collected in capricornic western Australia. 1886. I. 503. — 1887. III. 94.[1]
— Plants collected in the vicinity of the Muilligan River. 1887. I. 503.
— The plants indigenous around Sharks Bay. 1883. I. 503.
— The plants indigenous to the colony of Victoria. 1860. I. 502.
— Plants of north-western Australia. 1881. I. 503.
— Plurality of cotyledons in the genus Persoonia. 1882. II. 419.[2]
— Sopra la posizione sistematica del genere Donatia. 1879. II. 239.[1]
— Pozoruhodný Buk. 1896. II. 127.[1]
— The principal timber trees . . . for Victorian industrial culture. 1871. III. 132.[1]
— Record of a new Papuan Rhododendron. 1885. II. 683.[2]
— Record of an undescribed Correa. 1885. II. 404.[1]
— Record of . . . plants from Arnheim's Land. 1890. I. 504.
— A record of the plants collected by Mr. P. Walcott. 1863. I. 502.
— Record of two new Victorian highland Composites. 1890. II. 859.[1]
— Records of observations on . . . plants from New Guinea. 1889. I. 499.[1]
— Remarks on a new Victorian Haloragis. 1888. . II. 863.[2]
— Remarks on the vegetation of King's Island. 1882. I. 506.[1]
— Remarks on the Victorian flora. 1888. I. 504.
— Report of the government botanist. 1874. I. 502.
— Report on a small collection of plants from the Aird-River. 1888. II. 824.[1]

Mueller, Ferdinand Jacob Heinrich, *Baron* von (*continued*).
— Report on the forest resources of western Australia. 1879. II. 623,[1] *IV. 401.*[3]
— Report on the plants collected during Mr. Babbage's expedition. 1858. I. 501.
— Report on vegetable products. 1867. III. 282.[2]
— Rhododendron Lochae sp. n. 1887. II. 681.[2]
— Rhododendron Toverenae. 1884. II. 683.[3]
— Select extra-tropical plants. 1872. III. 53.
— Select plants. 1872. III. 53.
— Select textile plants. 1876. III. 234.
— Some hitherto undescribed plants of New South Wales. 1887. I. 503.
— Some hitherto unknown Australian plants. 1859. I. 501.
— On some new genera of Australian plants. 1857. I. 501.
— Succinct general notes on the flora of British New Guinea. 1892. I. 499.
— Succinct notes on some plants from New Guinea. 1885. I. 499.[1]
— Südaustraliens Flora. 1853. I. 501.
— Suggestions. on the maintenance . . . of forests. 1879. IV. 124.[3]
— Supplement to the enumeration of Victorian plants. 1889. I. 504.
— A systematic arrangement of the plants noticed around the Gulf of Carpentaria. 1862. I. 502.
— Systematic census of Australian plants. 1882. I. 503.
— Systematic index of the plants of Victoria. 1853. I. 501.
— Tea; a lecture. 1876. III. 607. .
— Telopea oreades. 1887. III. 384.[1]
— On two Alpine Eurybiae of the Australian continent. 1859. II. 861.[3]
— The trees of Australia. 185.? I. 499,[2] *IV: 89.*[1]
— Two new . . . plants from New South Wales. 1882. I. 503. ·
— Umbelliferae of Australia. 1862. II. 653.[1]
— An undescribed Casuarina from West Australia. 1867. II. 92.[3]
— Die Vegetation der Gegenden um den Torrens-See.· 1853. I. 501.
— The vegetation of the Chatham-Islands. 1864. I. 506.[2]
— The vegetation of the districts surrounding Lake Torrens. 1853. I. 501.
— Die Vegetation von Victoria. 1861. I. 502.
— Veronica-Arten von baumartigem Wuchs. 1888. II. 783.[1]
— Views on the affinity of Acradenia. 1868. II. 397.[3]
— Wattle bark. 1892. III. 463.[3]
— Die westaustralische Fächer-Palme. 1892. II. 70.[1]
— Die Zucht der Bambusaceen aus Samen. 1894. III. 314.[3]
— *See also* NAUDIN, Charles & MÜLLER, Ferdinand, *Baron* von; TATE, Ralph & MÜLLER, Ferdinand, *Baron* von; WALTER, C. & MUELLER, Ferdinand, *Baron* von.
— & **Hackel,** Eduard. Schizostachyum Copelandi n. sp. 1896. II. 60.[1]
— & **Maiden,** J. H. Description of a new Hakea. 1893. II. 1[0]2.[1]
— — Description of a new species of Acacia. 1894. II. 325.[3]
— & **Tate,** Ralph. Botany . . . of the Elder exploring expedition. 1896. I. 505.
— — Diagnoses of some new plants from South Australia. 1883. II. 176.[1]
— — List of plants collected during Mr. Tietkens' expedition. 1890. I. 504.
— — On a new dilleniaceous plant. 1882. II. 542.[3]
— — On a new rhamnaceous plant from South Australia. 1882. II. 499.[3]
Müller, Frans. Blattlöcherpilz oder Kupferkalkwirkung? 1899. III. 431.[1]
— Die Gebirgs-Bäche. 1857. IV. 185.[1]
Müller, Franz Xaver. Untersuchungen über die Vertheilung der Farben. *See* SCHÜBLER, Gustav. 1831. II. 808.[3]
Müller, Frederico. A correlação das flores versicolores e dos insectos pronubos. 1877. I. 237.
Müller, Friedrich. Hannover'sche Sandkulturen. 1837. IV. 145.
— Merkwürdige Bäume. 1835. II. 10.[3]
Müller, Fritz. Ueber die Befruchtung der Martha. 1866. II. 827.[3]
— Befruchtungsversuche an Cipó alho. 1868. II. 785.[3]
— Bestaubungsversuche [*sic*] an Abutilon-Arten. 1873. II. 520.[1]
— Caprificus und Feigenbaum. 1882. II. 151.[1]

— Ueber eine dimorphe Faramea. 1869. II. 817.[1]
— Feijoa, ein Baum. 1886. II. 632.[1]
— Frucht in Frucht von Carica Papaya. 1890. II. 582.[3]
— Ueber das Haarkissen am Blattstiel der Imbauba. 1876. II. 147.[3]
— Ueber das Holz einiger um Desterro wachsenden Kletterpflanzen. 1866. I. 127.[1]
— Die Imbauba und ihre Beschützer. 1880. II. 147.[3]
— Keimung der Bicuiba. 1887. II. 221.[1]
— Knospenlage der Blumen von Feijoa. 1886. II. 632.[1]
— Mischlinge von Ruellia formosa und silvaccola. 1893. II. 802.[3]
— Nebenspreiten an Blättern einer Begonia. 1887. II. 583.[3]
— Notes on some of the climbing plants. 1867. I. 236.[1]
— Verzeichniss der . . . Bäume und Sträucher in der Umgegend von Blumenau und Desterro. 1891. I. 340,[3] *IV. 78.*[3]
— Zweigklimmer. 1882. I. 236.[1]
Müller, G. Le Vitis tricuspidata. 1892. III. 545.[1]
— Vitis tricuspidata als Ampelpflanze. 1892. III. 545.[1]
Müller, G. L. C. Anleitung zur Kenntniss und Bearbeitung der Potasche. 1830. IV. 395.
Müller, Gustav. Anleitung zur . . . Bestimmung des Gerbstoffes. 1858. I. 183.
— Handbuch bei Erwerbung von Nutzhölzern aller ·Art. 1866. IV. 225.
Mueller, H. A. Trees and shrubs of Hamilton county. 1900. I. 321, *IV. 78.*[3]
Müller, Hans Carl. Ueber die Entstehung von Kalkoxalat-Krystallen. 1890. I. 139.
Müller, Hermann (*of Lippstadt*). Alpenblumen, ihre Befruchtung. 1881. II. 239.[1]
— Über die Anwendung der Darwin'schen Theorie auf Blumen. 1869. I. 237.
— Application of the Darwinian theory to flowers. 1869. I. 237.
— Applicazione della teoria Darwiniana ai fiori. 1869. I. 237.
— Arbeitstheilung bei Staubgefässen. 1883. I. 238.
— Die Befruchtung der Blumen durch Insekten. 1873. I. 237.
— Die Entwickelung der Blumenthätigkeit der Insekten 1881. I. 238.
— Über die Entwickelung der Blumenfarben. 1880. I. 238·
— La fécondation des fleurs par les insectes. 1873. I. 237.
— The fertilisation of flowers. 1873. I. 237.
— On the fertilisation of flowers by insects. 1873. I. 237.
— Geschichte der Erklärungsversuche in Bezug auf . . . Blumenfarben. 1882. I. 236.[1]
— Die Insekten als unbewusste Blumenzüchter. 1878. I. 238.
— Nachtrage und Bemerkungen zu Karsch's Phanerogamenflora der Provinz Westfalen. 1860. I. 384.
— Umbildung von Ovarien in Staubgefässe bei Salix. 1868 II. 103.[3]
— Das Variiren der Grösse gefärbter Blüthenhüllen. 1877. I. 237.
— Weitere Beobachtungen über Befruchtung der Blumen durch Insekten. 1878. I. 238.
Müller, Hermann (*of Thurgau*). Über Bastardirung von Rebensorten. 1882. III. 549.[1]
— Die Edelfäule der Trauben. 1888. II. 508.[3]
— Beitrag zur Erklärung der Ruheperioden. 1885. I. 527.
— Eigentümliche Frostschäden an Obstbäumen. 1900. III. 421.[3]
— Über das Gefrieren und Erfrieren. 1880. I. 212.
— Das Kappen der Reben. 1882. III. 549.[1]
— Über die Ursachen des krankhaften Zustandes unserer Reben. 1890. III. 561.
— Über Wachstum und Bedeutung der Wurzeln. 1875. I. · 188.
Müller, Hugo. *See* GREVILLE-WILLIAMS, J. & MÜLLER, Hugo; LA RUE, Warren de & MÜLLER, Hugo.
Müller, J. (*of Liebenwalde*). Der Scharlachdorn . . . als · Futterpflanze. *See* LIEBENWALDE, J. 1898. III.
Müller, J. B. & Lebl, M. Der Weinstock. 1878. III. 553.[1]
Mueller, J. C. F. Anweisung zur zweckmässigen Behandlung des Obst- und Gemüsegartens. 1796. III. 103.
— Deutschlands Weinbau. 1803. III. 552.
— Der vollständige Monatsgärtner. 1797. III. 103.
— Die wichtigsten Lehren des nützlichen Gartenbaues. 1797. III. 103. ·
Müller, J. F. *See* BARNEVELD, Willem van, & MÜLLER, J. F.
Müller, J. J. Mittheilungen aus dem Gebiete der Waldkultur. 1867. IV. 366.

Mueller, J. P. Flora der Blüthenpflanzen des bergischen Landes. 1876. I. 387.
Müller, Jean (*of Argau*). Apocynaceae. 1860. II. 721.²
— Buxaceae. 1869. II. 452.²
— Daphniphyllaceae. 1869. II. 441.¹
— Euphorbiaceae. 1866. II. 433.² — 1873. II. 434.¹
— Euphorbiaceae. Vorläufige Mittheilungen. 1863. II. 433.²
— Euphorbiaceae novae a cl. Dr. Lorentz . . . lectae. 1874. II. 434.¹
— Euphorbiaceae novae a cl. Dr. Welwitsch . . . lectae. 1864. II. 434.²
— Euphorbiacearum species novae. 1872. II. 433.²
— Genera nova tria Apocynacearum. 1860. II. 721.²
— Monographie de la famille des Résédacées. 1857. II. 234.¹
— Nachschrift zu meiner . . . Arbeit über die Euphorbiaceen. 1866. II. 433.²
— Neue Apocyneen aus Neu-Caledonien. 1870. II. 722.¹
— Neue Euphorbiaceen des Herbarium Hooker. 1864. II. 433.²
— Notice sur deux sortes d'étamines . . . dans les Euphorbiacées. 1864. II. 434.²
— Notice sur l'existence d'anthères triloculaires. 1864. I. 116.¹
— Notice sur la nature des anthères. 1864. II. 446.¹
— Replik auf Dr. Baillon's " Nouvelles observations." 1875. II. 433.²
— Resedaceae. 1868. II. 234.²
— Rubiaceae. Tribus I. Retiniphylleae. 1881. II. 807.²
— Rubiaceae brasilienses novae. 1875. II. 807.²
— Species novae nonnullae americanae ex ordine Apocynearum. 1860. II. 721.²
— System der Euphorbiaceen. 1864. II. 433.²
Mueller, Jean Baptiste. Botanisch prosodisches Wörterbuch. 1840. *I.* 73,² V. IX.¹
— Flora waldeccensis et itterensis. 1841. I. 380.
Müller, Jeremias. De usu et abusu potus Thee in genere. *See* WALDSCHMIEDT, W. U. H. 1692. III. 605.
Müller, Joachim Ludwig. Gedanken, wie dem . . . Mangel des Brennholzes abzuhelfen. 1756. IV. 115.
Müller, Johann. Praktische Anweisung wie dem . . . Klagen über den einreissenden Holzmangel . . . abgeholfen werden kann. 1802. IV. 280.¹
Mueller, Johann Abraham Theodor. De Clematide Vitalba. 1786. III. 391.²
Mueller, Johann Friedrich Theodor. *See* MUELLER, Fritz.
Mueller, Johann Georg. Deliciae hortenses. 1675. III. 102.
— Kurzer Entwurf eines dreifachen Gartenbaues. 1675. III. 102.
Mueller, Johann Gotthilf. Species plantarum secundum vegetationis et fructificationis partes. 1757. I. 261.
Mueller, Johann Heinrich. Catalogus plantarum. 1715. I. 291.
Mueller, Johann Karl August. *See* MÜLLER, K. A. F. W.
Müller, Johann Sebastian. *See* MILLER, John.
Müller, Johann Wolfgang. Ausführliche praktische Anweisung zur . . . Berechnung des cubischen Inhalts der Baumstämme. 1810. IV. 221.
Müller, Johannes. Die Heilmittel der Aerzte im ostindischen Archipel. 1898. III. 2/4.¹
Müller, Johannes. Beiträge zur Anatomie holziger . . . Compositen. 1893. II. 850.²
Müller, Johannes (*of Soest*). Verzeichniss der bis jetzt in dem Regierungsbezirk Arnsberg aufgefundenen Gewächse. 1848. I. 382.
Müller, Johannes Nicolaus. Prodromus historiae naturalis Hassiae. *See* VALENTINI, M. B. 1707. III. 121.¹
Mueller, Joseph. Prodromus der phanerogamischen Flora von Aachen. 1832. I. 532.¹
— Systematisches Verzeichniss der in der Umgegend Aachens wildwachsenden . . . Pflanzen. 1832. I. 378, 532.¹
Müller, Julius. Zur Kenntniss des Runzelschorfes. 1893. III. 195.¹
— Die Rostpilze der Rosa- und Rubus-Arten. 1885. III. 419.¹
— Die Rostpilze der Rosa- und Rubusarten. 1886. III. 453.² 457.²
Müller, K. *See* МЮЛЛЕРЪ, К.
Mueller, Karl, (1817–1870). Anotationes [*sic*] quaedam de familia Elaeocarpeacearum. 1849. II. 509.³
— *See also* WALPERS, W. G. & MUELLER, Karl.
Müller, Karl, (1818–1899). *See* MÜLLER, K. A. F. W.

Müller, Karl (*of Heidelberg?*) · Untersuchung über den Sitz der Alcaloide in der Cinchonarinde. 1866. III. 722.
Müller, Karl, (*Pfarrer*). *See* MÜLLER, Adolf & Karl.
Müller, Karl Alfred Ernst, (1855–1907). Ueber die Balken in den Holzelementen der Coniferen. 1890. II. 17.¹
— Caprifoliaceae, Valerianaceae. 1885. II. 840.²
— Ueber Dammar und Dammar liefernde Pflanzen. 1891. III. 228.¹
— Ueber Dimorphismus der Blüthen von Sambucus australis. 1884. II. 840.²
— Ueber ein fettes Oel aus Lindensamen. 1890. III. 585.²
— Huile de graines de Tilleul. 1890. III. 585.²
— L'huile extraite des graines de Tilleul. 1890. III. 585.²
— Ueber phloëmständige Secretkanäle der Umbelliferen. 1888. II. 647.¹
— Uebersicht der morphologischen Verhältnisse im Aufbau des Sambucus australis. 1884. II. 840.²
Müller, Karl August Friedrich Wilhelm, (1818–1899). Blitzschläge in Beziehung zu Boden. 1898. IV. 195.¹
— Das Buch der Pflanzenwelt. 1857. I. 95.
— Einige Bemerkungen über die harzartigen Ausscheidungen auf den Birken. 1845. II. 118.¹
— Einige Worte über die Bedeutung des Zeilenbaues für die Klassifikation. 1854. I. 252.
— Les merveilles du monde végétal. 1857. I. 95.
— Några ord om betydelsen af cellväfvens byggnad för växternas klassifikation. 1854. I. 252.
— Der Pflanzenstaat. 1861. I. 34.
— De plantenwereld. 1857. I. 95.
— Westindiën in Florida. 1885. I. 319.
Mueller, Klothar Moritz. De Juglandis regiae viribus. 1843. III. 356.¹
Müller, Konrad. Vergleichende Untersuchung . . . der Clusiaceen. 1882. II. 547,² 553.¹
Müller, L. Der praktische Obstbaumzüchter. 1885. III. 139.
Müller, Ludwig. Chemische Untersuchung des Anacahuite-Holzes. 1861. III. 695.¹
Müller, Luise. Grundzüge einer vergleichenden Anatomie der Blumenblätter. 1893. I. 116.¹
Müller, Nikolaus Jakob Karl. Eine allgemeine morphologische Studie. 1869. I. 102.
— Die Anatomie . . . der Spaltöffnungen. 1872. I. 131,² 170.
— Atlas der Holzstructur. 1888. I. 126, *IV. 62.*²
— Beiträge zur Entwicklungsgeschichte der Baumkrone. 1877. I. 102.
— Beziehungen zwischen Verdunstung . . . und Druck. 1872. I. 149.²
— Botanische Untersuchungen. 1872. I. 147.
— Culturresultate an Weidenstecklingen. 1885. I. 209,¹ *III. 349.*
— Ueber die Einwirkung des Lichtes . . . auf das grüne Blatt. 1876. I. 159.
— Handbuch der allgemeinen Botanik. 1880. I. 91.
— Kommen die Röntgenstrahlen im Sonnenstrahl für die Pflanze zur Wirkung? 1896. I. 230.
— Ueber einen kurzen Ausdruck für die Evolution der Baumknospe. 1879. I. 108.¹
— Polarisationserscheinungen. 1885. I. 138.¹
— Polarisationserscheinungen und Molecularstructur. 1886. I. 124.
— Spectralanalyse der Blüthenfarben. 1889. I. 185.¹·
— Untersuchungen über Atmung . . . in der Pflanze. 1909. I. 171.
— Untersuchungen über die Diffusion der atmosphärischen Gase in der Pflanze. 1867. I. 170.
— Untersuchungen über die Krümmungen. 1872. I. 195.¹
— Untersuchungen über die Sauerstoffausscheidung der grünen Pflanzen im Sonnenlicht. 1872. I. 170.
— Untersuchungen über die Vertheilung der Harze. 1866. I. 134.²
— Über die Vertheilung der Molecularkräfte. 1875. I. 165.
— Vorläufige Notiz zu Untersuchungen über die Wachsthumserscheinungen der Wurzel. 1869. I. 188.
— Das Wachsthum des Vegetationspunktes. 1866. I. 132.²
— Die Wachsthumserscheinungen der Wurzel. 1871. I. 188.
— *See also* METZGER, A. & MÜLLER, N. J. C.
Müller, Otto Friedrich. Enumeratio stirpium in Islandia. 1770. I. 351.
— Flora fridrichsdalina. 1767. · I. 351.
Müller, Otto Ladislaus. Beiträge zur Kenntniss der Entwickelungsgeschichte und Verbreitung der Lenticellen. 1877. I. 132.¹
— Untersuchungen über den anatomischen Bau amerikanischer . . . Rebenwurzeln. 1882. II. 505.¹

Müller, Peter Erasmus. Om Ædelgranens Forekomst i nogle franske Skove. 1871. II. 23.[1]
— Bemærkninger i Anledning af Hr. Kammerherre Sehesteds Afhandling. 1899. IV. 273.[1]
— Om Bjergfyrren. 1886. IV. 465.[1]
— Om Blandingsskov. 1872. IV. 138.[2]
— Einige Züge der Naturgeschichte des Waldes. 1879. II.[1] 126.[2]
— Einige Züge der Naturgeschichte des Waldes. 1881. IV. 118.
— Forelaesninger over Skovbrugs-Historie. 1882. IV. 24.[2]
— Forelaesninger over Skovdyrkningslære. 1882. IV. 113.[2]
— The forests of Denmark. 1879. IV. 343.[1]
— Les forêts en Danemark. 1879. IV. 343.[1]
— Grandeaus Theori om Jordbundens Frugtbarhed. 1879. IV. 69.
— Influence des lombrics sur la végétation des plantes à rhizome. 1894. II. 127.[1]
— Nogle Træk af Skovens Naturhistorie. 1879. II. 126.[2]
— Nogle Undersøgelser.af Skovjord. 1878. IV. 69.
— Notice sur les forêts en Danemark. 1879. IV. 343.[1]
— Omrids af en dansk Skovbrugs-Statistik. 1881. IV. 343.[2]
— Omrids en dansk Skovbrugsstatistik. 1879. IV. 343.[1]
— Recherches sur les formes naturelles de l'humus. 1878. IV. 69.
— Om regnormenes Forhold til rhizomplanterne især i Bøgeskove. 1894. II. 127.[1]
— Ueber die sog. Mycorhiza der Buche. 1887. II. 126.[2]
— Studien üb. die natürlichen Humusformen. 1878. IV. 69.
— Studier over Skovjord. 1878. IV. 69.
— Om Træmærkedet. 1872. IV. 404.[1]
— & **Thalbitzer**, S. Optegnelser om vore Skoves mindre Bidrag til Landboernes Fornødenheder. 1881. IV. 343.[2]
Müller, Philipp Jakob.• Beschreibung in der Umgegend von Weissenburg . . . wildwachsenden Arten der Gattung Rubus. 1858. II. 301.[1]
— Description de quelques espèces nouvelles de Rubus. 1855. II. 303.[2]
— Rubologische Ergebnisse einer dreitägigen Excursion.in die granitischen Hoch-Vogesen. 1861. II. 303.[2]
— Versuch einer monographischen Darstellung der gallogermanischen Arten der Gattung Rubus. .1859. .II. 301.[1]
Müller, R. Die Krankheit von Rhododendron. 1881. III. 656.
— Über Behandlung . . . neugepflanzter Coniferen.. 1886.' III. 292.
— Ueber die Behandlung neugepflanzter Koniferenhecken. 1895. III. 295.[1]
— Beschädigungen an Pflanzen durch Rauch. 1899. III. 185.[3]
— Ueber Doppelveredlung. 1883. III. 162.
— Fagus sylvatica atropurpurea pendula. 1884. III. 360.[2]
— Ueber Herbst- und Frühjahrpflanzung. 1887. III. 169.[1]
— Zur Hügelpflanzung bei Koniferen. 1895. III. 295.[1]
— Das Imprägniren des Holzes mit Kupfervitriol. 1879. IV. 420.
— Ist Lycium eine gute Heckenpflanze? 1886. III. 701.[1]
— Ueber Klimmer (Ampelopsis). 1897. III. 545.[1]
— Lonicera (Chamaecerasus) Alberti. 1893. III. 751.[1]
— Noch einmal der schwedische Bocksdorn. 1889. III. 701.
— Notizen über die in den zwei letzten Wintern . . . verursachten Schäden. 1871. III. 45.
— Pirus Malus pendula "Elise Rathke." 1884. III. 425.[2]
— Salix californica hort. 1887. III. 352.[1]
— Ueber das Schneiden und Aufbewahren der Reiser. 1882. III. 162.
— Unsere Spiersträucher. 1898.. III. 460.[2]
— Die Vermehrung der Coniferen durch Stecklinge. 1886. III. 294.[2]
— Weigelia Eva Rathke. 1891. III. 748.[2]
— See also **Wittmack**, Ludwig & **Müller**, R.
— & **Trobchen**, A. Veredlung dér Linden und Blutbuchen. .1898. III. 360,[3] 585.[1]
Müller, R. H. Les Cereus hybridus. 1896. III. 621.[1]
— Schön- und dankbarblühende Phyllokaktus. 1896. III. 621.[1]
— Unsere harten Yucca. 1886. III. 339.[2]
Müller, Rudolf. Ueber Coniferin. 1874. I. 175.
— Zur Gummiflussfrage. 1896. I. 528.[1]
— Die Rinde unserer Laubhölzer. 1875. I. 525, V. xi.[1]
— Die Trauerfichte bei Cadinen. 1899. II. 35.[1]
•**Mueller**, Samuel. Curiöser botanicus. 1687. I. 288.
— Vademecum botanicum. 1687. I. 288.
Müller, Theodor. Der Kiefernprocessionsspinner. 1887. IV. 478.
— La processionnaire du Pin. 1887. IV. 478.

Müller, Udo. Lehrbuch der Holzmesskunde. 1899. IV. 215.
— Über Staatswaldveräusserungen. 1894. IV. 270.
Müller, W. Ein neues Culturgeräth für die Eichelsaat. 1883. IVV507.
— Aus dem slavonischen Walde. 1883. IV. 373.
— & **Pilling**, F. O. Deutsche Schulflora. 1894. I. 532.[2]
Müller, W. C. A few observations on the cultivation . . . of Tea in the Darjeeling district. 1867. III. 603.
Mueller, W. J. Die afrikanische Landschaft Fetu. 1673. I. 385.
Müller, Walther Otto. Flora der reussischen Länder. 1863. I. 385.
— Tafeln zur Bestimmung der in Deutschland . . . wildwach-senden . . . Pflanzen. 1876. I. 387.
Müller, Wilhelm. Flora von Pommern. 1898. I. 532.[2]
Mueller-Beeck, F. George. Verzeichniss der essbaren Pflanzen Japan's. 1886. III. 91.[2]
Müller-Desterro, Fritz. See **Müller**, Fritz.
Müller-Liebenwalde, J. See **Müller**, J. (of Liebenwalde).
Müller-Thurgau, Hermann. See **Müller**, Hermann (of Thurgau).
Müllerklein, B. Morus alba pendula. 1891. III. 380.[2]
Müllner, Michael Ferdinand. Zwei für Niederösterreich neue Eichenhybriden. 1895. II. 136.[2]
Münch, Ch. Mittheilungen über einige Loranthaceen. 1860. II. 173.[1]
München. See **Munich**.
Muenchhausen, Otto, Freiherr von. Bibliotheca botanico-physico-oeconomica. 1765. I. 1.
— Catalogus arborum fruticumque. 1770.' I. 292, III. 68,[2] IV. 81.
— Der Hausvater. 1765. III. 103.
— Das Hausvaters botanische physikalische . . . Bibliothek. 1765. I. 1.
— Monathliche Beschäftigungen für einen Baum- und Plantagen-Gärtner. 1771. III. 101.[2]
— Neues vorläufiges Verzeichniss derer in seinem Garten zu Schwoebbern . . . Bäume, Stauden. 1748. III. 27.[2]
— Verzeichniss aller Bäume und Stauden . . in Deutschland fortkommen. 1770. I. 292, III. 68,[2] IV. 81.
Münden-Forstakademische Bibliothek. Katalog. See **Katalog** . . . 1885. IV. 2.
Mündener forstliche Hefte. IV. 10.
Münderlein, Johannes. Die Rubus-Flora der Umgebung Nürnbergs. 1893. II. 302.[1]
Münscher, K. Über die Erhöhung der Holzpreise. 1839. IV. 274.[1]
Münter, (Forstmeister, Bremervörde). Wall und Knick im Bremenschen. 1865. III. 213.
Muenter, Andreas Heinrich August Julius. See **Muenter**, J. A. H. A. J.
Münter, C. E. Von der Servituten nach dem reinen Sinne der Gesetzgebung. 1806. IV. 332.[2]
— Das Weide-Recht. 1806. IV. 332.[2]
Münter, J. Die Gründung des botanischen Gartens der K. Universität Greifswald. 1864. I. 48.
Münter, Johann Andreas Heinrich August Julius. Über Fichtennadelrost. 1866. IV. 455.
— Über die Keimung bei Eugenia Jambos. 1847. II. 628.[1]
— Ueber Mate (Maté). 1883. II. 462.[2]
— De la naturalisation des Diervilla . . et Xanthorhiza. 1867. II. 800,[2] 835.[1]
— Observations phytophysiologicae. 1841. I. 187.
— Opuntia Rafinesquii. 1870. III. 625.[1]
— Die Rohstoffe und Fabrikate aus Palmen. 1868.' III. 19.[1]
— Ueber das 'Vorkommen zweier amerikanischer . . . Gesträuche. 1867. II. 800,[2] 835.[1]
Münter, Julius. See **Münter**, J. A. H. A. J.
Müntz, Achille. Les arrosages tardifs de la Vigne. 1899. III. 549.[2]
— Emploi des feuilles de la Vigne pour l'alimentation du bétail. 1893. III. 223,[2] 583.[2]
— Études sur la végétation des Vignes. 1894. III. 574.
— Sur l'existence des éléments du sucre de lait. 1886. I.' 176.
— Sur les ferments. 1875. I. 175.
— Sur la fixation du tannin. 1877. 'I. 183.
— De l'influence de l'effeuillage de la Vigne. 1891. II. 508.[2]
— Nouvelles études sur l'utilisation. 1893. III. 583.[1]
— La production du vin. 1895. III. 549.[1]
— Recherches expérimentales sur la culture . . . des Vignes. 1895. III. 557.[1]

— Recherches sur l'effeuillage de la Vigne. 1892. III. 549.²
— Recherches sur les exigences de la Vigne. 1892. III. 549.¹
— Recherches sur les vignobles de la Champagne. 1893. III. 557.¹
— Sur le rôle de l'ammoniaque dans la nutrition. 1889. I. 159.
— Traitement des Vignes phylloxérées. 1887. III. 574.
— Sur le traitement du mildew. 1885. III. 579.
— L'utilisation des marcs de vendange. 1893. III. 583.²
— See also MARCANO, V. & MÜNTZ, A.
— & Alby, Ed. De l'effet des arrosages tardifs sur ... la vendange. 1890. III. 549.¹
— & Marcano, V. Sur la perséite, matière sucrée. 1884. III. 407.²
— & Ramspacher. Dosage du tannin. 1874. I. 183.
— & Rousseaux, E. Recherches sur les vignobles de la champagne. 1893. III. 557.¹
— & Schoen. Étude sur la déperdition en tannin des substances tannantes. 1881. III. 237.²
Muenz, Martin & Raab, Ferdinand. De cortice peruviano. 1812. III. 721.
Müschen, G. B. Der Obstbau in Norddeutschland. 1876. III. 138.
Müttrich, G. Anton. Der Baumhöhenmesser von T. Christen. 1892. IV. 216.
— Beobachtungen der Erdbodentemperatur. 1880. IV. 72.
— Ueber den Einfluss des Waldes auf die Lufttemperatur. 1900. IV. 54.
— Ueber den Einfluss des Waldes auf ... Lufttemperatur. 1890. IV. 54.
— Ueber den Einfluss des Waldes auf ... Niederschläge. 1892. IV. 51, 542.¹
— Ueber die Einrichtung von meteorologischen Stationen. 1900. IV. 54.
— Die zu forstlichen Zwecken im Königreich Preussen ... errichteten meteorologischen Stationen. 1875. IV. 38.¹
— Ueber die auf den forstlich-meteorologischen Stationen in Schweden getroffenen Anordnungen. 1881. IV. 60.¹
— Influencia de los montes sobre la cantidad de lluvia. 1892. IV. 542.¹
— Methode, durch hydrostatische Wägung die Verhältniss-zahl ... von Reisigwellen zu bestimmen. 1876. IV. 227.
— Neue Methode, Baumhöhen ... zu bestimmen. 1878. IV. 215.
— Eine neue schwedische Kluppe. 1896. IV. 232.
— Ein neuer Baumhöhenmesser. 1884. IV. 215.
— Ein neues Dendro-Hypsometer. 1894. IV. 216.
— Ueber phänologische Beobachtungen. 1888. I. 221.
— Das Polarplanimeter von Amsler. 1878. IV. 265.
— Ueber Spät- und Frühfröste. 1898. IV. 192.¹
Mütze, W. E. Chimonanthus praecox. 1898. III. 401.¹
Muhafiz-i-Jangal. Vitality of Teak. 1877. IV. 536.²
Muhammad, BABER. See BABER MUHAMMAD.
Muhl. Aus dem Klefernhochwald. 1875. IV. 472.
Muhl, (Forstmeister, Darmstadt). Zur Ehrenrettung des Kiefern-Jährlings. 1886. IV. 473.
— In welchem Stadium befindet sich die Verjüngung der Holzbestände mittelst Waldfeldbau. 1884. IV. 134.¹
Muhl, (Oberförster, Mönchbruch). Der Waldfeldbau als Kultur-Mittel. 1869. IV. 133.
Muhl, Servatius. Das Pflanzenreich nach natürlichen Familien. 1828. I. 260.
Muhlenberg, Henry. See MÜHLENBERG, G. H. E.
Muhlenbergia. I. 6.
Muir, J. J. Dracaenas. 1875. III. 334.¹
— A new way of growing Poinsettia pulcherrima. 1875. III. 518.¹
Muir, John. The Alaska trip. 1897. I. 312.
— The American forests. 1897. IV. 337.¹
— Botanical notes on Alaska. 1883. I. 311.²
— The coniferous forests of the Sierra Nevada. 1881. II. 14.²
— The forests of Alaska. 1897. I. 312.
— Les forêts de Conifères de la Sierra Nevada. 1881. II. 14.²
— The mountains of California. 1894. I. 326.
— On the post-glacial history of Sequoia gigantea. 1876. II. 50.¹
Muir, Matthew Moncrieff Pattison. See MORLEY, H. Forster & MUIR, M. M. Pattison.
Mukerji, KARUNA NIDHAN. See KARUNA NIDHAN MUKERJI.
Mukharji, Trailokya Nath. Classified list of Indian produce. 1883. III. 278.
— The Eri silk. 1894. III. 522.¹
— A hand-book of Indian products. 1883. III. 278.

Mulack, C. Praktische Winke über Baum- und Beerobst. 1880. III. 138.
The Mulberry tree. 1847. III. 381.¹
The Mulberry-tree with reference to ... silk. 1858. III. 377.
Mulder, Claas. Elenchus plantarum ... prope urbem Leidam. 1818. I. 390.
— Over den invloed van vergiften op planten. 1828. I. 210.²
— Kleverige omwindsels om de stammen tegen opklimmende insecten. 1857. III. 196.
— Kruidkundige aanteekeningen. 1839. I. 143.
Mulder, E. De indigo uit een scheikundig oogpunt beschouwd. 1859. III. 479.¹
Mulder, Gerrit Jan. Amorphe chinine. 1846. III. 722.
— Analyse de l'upas antiar. 1838. III. 366.³
— Over het bederfwerend vermogen van sublimaat voor hout. 1835. IV. 417.
— Over Behen-ohe. 1846. III. 409.¹
— Over blaauwe en gele koffy. 1857. III. 740.¹
— Over coffeine en theine. 1837. I. 175.
— Composition de l'huile de Ben. 1846. III. 409.¹
— Over de condensatie van de stikstof. 1845. I. 157.
— Eiwitgehalte van Eikels, wilde Kastanjes. 1857. I. 175.
— Expériences sur les substances humiques. 1840. I. 155.
— Over looizuur. 1848. I. 183.
— Matières cireuses. 1846. I. 182.¹
— Nog iets over theine. 1836. III. 606.
— Onderzoek naar de kleuren. 1834. I. 185.¹
— Ontleding van eenige plantaardige zelfstandigheden. 1846. I. 152.²
— Over plantaardige proteine-verbindingen. 1848. I. 175.
— Over plantenslijm. 1846. I. 180.²
— Rapport omtrent kaneelvet en Karoein balsem. 1864. II. 559.²; III. 406.¹
— De scheikunde der droogende olien. 1865. I. 182.¹
— Scheikundig onderzoek van Chineesche en Java-Thee. 1835. III. 606.
— Scheikundig onderzoek van de huid der vruchten. 1832. I. 152.¹
— Over stearoptena van Foelie- ... en Bergamot-olie. 1837. I. 181.²
— Theine. 1845. III. 606.
— Over het vergif van den Javaanschen Upasboom. 1837. III. 366.²
— Versuch einer allgemeinen physiologischen Chemie. 1844. I. 152.¹
— Voordeelige bereidingswijze van theine. 1851. III. 607.
— Van waar bekomen de niet bemeste planten haar stikstof? 1855. I. 158.
— Ueber wachsartige Stoffe. 1844. I. 182.¹
— Wasachtige stoffen in planten. 1845. II. 312.¹
— Een woord bij den Catechismus voor landbouwkundige scheikunde. 1847. III. 36.¹
— Over de zamenstelling van Arabische gom. 1838. III. 463.¹
— Over de zamenstelling van eenige etherische olien van Cinnamomum-soorten. 1836. III. 404.¹
— See also VLAANDEREN, C. L. & MULDER, G. J.
Mulder, L. Beplanting der duinen met Pinus Cembra. 1873. IV. 463.²
— De dennenbladwesp. 1875. IV. 477.
— Duinbeplanting. 1865. IV. 501.¹
— Groenbemesting van boomgaarden. 1897. III. 152.
— Hickory-hout. 1877. IV. 488.¹
— Hoe onze kale duinen in Dennenbosschen te veranderen zijn. 1862. IV. 160.¹
— Iepenboomen kwijnende door den iepenspinkever. 1867. IV. 535.¹
— Invloed van lichtgas op de wortels. 1876. III. 185.²
— Kunstmatige vanilline. 1875. IV. 443.¹
— Larf in de dennenbosschen. 1875. IV. 477.
— Leerboek over de mestmakerij. 1854. III. 151.
— Mammouth-boomen. 1867. III. 309.¹
— Nieuwere Coniferen bij ons te lande. 1862. III. 289.
— Een Perenboom te Aalst. 1867. II. 279.²
— De Phylloxera vastatrix. 1871. III. 564.²
— Een praatje over meikevers. 1877. IV. 203.
— Salix acutifolia ... en S. uralensis. 1877. III. 348.
— Schadelijke invloed van lichtgas op boomen. 1862. III. 185.¹
— Wetenschap en landbouw. 1855. III. 36.¹
Mulder, N. J. Verbeterde cultivatie van woeste veen. 1837. IV. 159.¹
Mulder, P. J. Chlorophyllum. 1845. I. 140.²

Mule, Johannes. De Ficu arefacta meditationis. 1739. II. 149.²
Mulford, A. Isabel. A study of the Agaves of the United States. 1896. II. 89.¹
Mulié, Théodore. Le capricorne du Peuplier. 1873. III. 344.²
— Greffe d'été en couronne. 1868. III. 161.
— De vlinder des Populiers. 1872. III. 344.²
Mull, E. Culture du Micocoulier dans le Roussillon. 1869. III. 363.²
Muller. See also MÜLLER.
Muller. Dosage du tannin. 1859. III. 237.¹
Muller, Adam. See VILLEROY, Félix & MULLER, Adam.
Muller, C. Observations en faveur de l'Acacia de Robin. 1801. IV. 522.²
Muller, Eugène. La forêt. 1878. IV. 44, 269.
Muller, Félix. Spicilège de la flore bruxelloise. 1862. I. 392.
— See also PIRÉ, Louis & MULLER, Félix.
Muller, M. J. E. Geneeskundige topographie van Samarang. 1845. III. 275.²
Muller, S. See OORT, P. van & MULLER, S.
Muller, Salomon. Aanteekeningen over de natuurlijke gesteldheid . . . van Sumatra. 1835. I. 467.
Mullet, J. J. CLEMENT-. See CLEMENT-MULLET, J. J.
Mulligan, James H. The Samoan Cocoanut. 1898. III. 324.¹
Mulligan, John. Estimation of tannin. 1861. III. 237.¹
Mullins, J. Multiple cones. 1881. II. 47.²
Mullot, DARLEY. See DARLEY-MULLOT.
Mulnard, E. Sericobonia ignea. 1893. III. 709.²
Mulsant. Ensemencement des glands. 1835. III. 361.²
Multiplication du Daubentonia Tripetiana. 1843. III. 487.³
Munby, Giles. On the botanical productions of . . . Algiers. 1849. I. 484.
— Catalogus plantarum in Algeria. 1859. I. 484.
— Extrait d'une lettre relative au Menziesia coerulea. 1837. II. 675.¹
— Flore de l'Algérie. 1847. I. 484.
— Notice sur les noms arabes des plantes d'Algérie. 1866. I. 76.¹
— Notice sur quelques plantes d'Algérie. 1855. I. 484.
Munch. Proportions d'huile contenue dans diverses semences. 1866. I. 182.¹
Munck af Rosenschöld, E. Underrättelser om resande naturforskare. 1846. III. 530.³
Muncke, Georg Wilhelm. Over het bevorderen van den groei der planten. 1817. III. 38.¹
Muncke, Theodor. Das badische Forstgesetz. 1874. IV. 317.²
Mundella, Aloysius. Epistolae medicinales. 1538. I. 277.
Mundelstrup, Janues Nicolai. De pomis sodomiticis. 1683. I. 512.
Mundt, G. Bereiding van thee. 1886. III. 607.
— Ceylon en Java. 1886. III. 128, 129.²
— De groote cultures van Ceylon-Koffie, Thee. 1887. III. 129.²
— Kinabast. 1899. III. 718.
— Kinine en Kinabast. 1900. III. 719.
— & Eekhout, G. W. De particuliere landbouwnijverheid op Java. 1885. III. 128.
Mundt, H. Om Skovbrugets Bogføring. 1900. IV. 312.
Mundt, O. Katalog der Bibliothek der Königlichen Forstakademie Eberswalde. 1885. IV. 2.
Mundt, Walter. Opuntia clavarioides. 1895. III. 624.²
Munford, George. A list of flowering plants . . . in western Norfolk. 1841. V. xx.²
Munich — Bayerische Gartenbau-Gesellschaft. See BAYERISCHE . . . III. 11.
Munich — Königliche bayerische Akademie der Wissenschaften. See KÖNIGLICHE . . . I. 13.
Municipal affairs. III. 6.
Munier, Jean Baptiste. Quelques observations sur nos forêts de Sapins. 1870. IV. 360.
Munnick, de. Handleiding voor de kultuur . . . der Koffij op Java. 1845. III. 729.¹
Munnick, L. W. H. de. Opmerkingen betreffende den aanleg . . . van Koffietuinen. 1874. III. 726.²
— Proefnemingen met het gebruik van guano. 1874. III. 734.¹
Munniks, J. Nederlands verbeterde land- en akkerbouw. 1780. III. 105.
Muñoz de Madariaga, Juan José. Analisis de la tierra del monte . . . La Herreria. 1883. IV. 69.

— La biblioteca de la Escuela de montes. 1889. IV. 540.²
— Condiciones necesarias al buen éxito de las repoblaciones. 1881. IV. 164.²
— Daños ocasionados á los Robles. 1896. IV. 501.²
— Los deslindes y las repoblaciones. 1881. IV. 164.²
— La doble albura en el Roble. 1877. IV. 514.¹
— Influencia climatológica que ejercen los montes. 1896. IV. 542.¹
— El instituto austriaco de ensayos forestales. 1881. IV. 38.²
— Lecciones de mineralogia ajustadas a los programas de la Escuela. 1896. IV. 542.¹
— Lecciones de petrografia aplicada. 1878. IV. 61.¹
— Lo que hace el Cuerpo de montes. 1899. IV. 554.
— Perjuicios causados en los Robles por el Cynips. 1898. IV. 559.²
— Propiedades tóxicas del Tejo. 1896. IV. 558.¹
— Repoblaciones. 1881. IV. 164.²
— Vos de alarma. 1890. IV. 540.³
Munro. Report on the timber trees of Bengal. 1849. IV. 400.³
Munro, D. R. A description of the . . . trees of New Brunswick. 1862. III. 60.
— The forest trees of New Brunswick. 1862. I. 309.²
Munro, James. Amélioration dans la méthode de transplanter les grands arbres. 1833. III. 167.
— On an improved method of planting large trees. 1833. III. 167.
— On an improved method of transplanting large trees. 1833. III. 167.
Munro, Wilham. Hortus agrensis. 1844. I. 472.
— A monograph of the Bambusaceae. 1868. II. 58.¹
Munroe, Charles E. Analisis del cafe de Costa Rica. 1900. III. 741.¹
Munson, D. O. Evergreen hedges under trees. 1882. III. 215.³
Munson, Thomas Volney. Address on native Grapes of the United States. 1886. III. 545.¹
— American Grapes. 1886. III. 547.
— A classification of American Grapes. 1890. II. 505.³
— Classification . . . of the wild Grapes of North America. 1890. II. 505.²
— Editors' introductory remarks to the classification . . . of American grapes. 1895. II. 505.²
— Forests and forest trees of Texas. 1882, 1883. I. 320, IV. 78.¹
— A good Plum stock. 1881. III. 443.²
— Investigation . . . of American Grapes at the Munson experiment grounds. 1900. III. 547.
— June budding. 1890. III. 164.¹
— The largest Grapevine. 1885. II. 506.²
— A new species of Grape, and the Scuppernong. 1886. II. 506.²
— Sur une nouvelle classification des Vignes. 1885. III. 547.
— Peach and Plum hybrids. 1887. III. 430.²
— Possibilities of our native Grapes. 1891. III. 547.
— Viticultural observations upon . . . American Grapes. 1895. III. 551.¹
— Vitis Baileyana Munson. 1893. II. 506.¹
Munson, Welton Marks. Preliminary notes on the secondary effects of pollination. 1892. I. 201.¹
Munte, Max. Shrubs for the seaside. 1898. III. 42.¹
Munting, Abraham. Aloïdarium. 1680. II. 77.²
— Dissertatio historico-medica de vera herba britannica. 1698. II. 77.²
— Groninger hof-almanach. 1687. III. 105.
— Naauwkeurige beschryving der aardgewassen. 1672. I. 287; III. 105.
— Phytographia curiosa. 1702. I. 289.
— Waare oeffening der planten. 1672. I. 287, III. 105.
Munting, Heinrich. Catalogus plantarum Horti groeningensis. 1653. I. 50.
— Groningae et Omlandiae provincialis botanici hortus. 1646. I. 50.
— Hortus et universae materiae medicae gazophylacium. 1646. I. 285.³
Muntz. See LA LOYÈRE, de & MUNTZ.
Muntz, Achille. See MÜNTZ, Achille.
Muralt, Johann von. Eydgnössischer Lust-Garte. 1710. I. 432.¹
— Physicae specialis pars quarta. Botanologia. 1710. I. 432.²
Muratel, Maurice de BARRAU DE. See BARRAU DE MURATEL, Maurice de.

Muratori, Paulli. Chimica analysis baccarum Rhamn. cathartici. 1842. II. 497.[2]

Muravef. *See* Муравьевъ.

Murbeck, Svante Samuel. Beiträge zur Kenntniss der Flora von Südbosnien. 1891. I. 448.[1]

— Contributions à la connaissance des Plombaginées-Graminées . . . de la Tunisie. 1899. I. 486.

— Contributions à la connaissance des Primulacées-Labiées . . . de la Tunisie. 1898. I. 486.

— Contributions à la connaissance des Renonculacées-Cucurbitacées . . . de la Tunisie. 1897. I. 486.

— Några anteckningar till floran på Norges . . . kust. 1885. I. 357.

— Växtgeografiska· bidrag till Skandinaviens flora. 1886. II. 126.[1]

Murchin, von Homeyer-. *See* Homeyer-Murchin, von.

Murchison, Charles. Notes on the Chaulmoogra seeds. 1856. III. 614.[1]

Murchison, *Sir* Roderick Impey. On a supposed aërolite. 1854. I. 210,[1] III. 850.[1]

Murdleworth, T. H. A new species of Jaborandi. 1894. II. 409.[2]

Murdoch, G. W. Mistletoe and mistle thrush. 1895. II. 179.[2]

Murdoch, J. Historical trees. 1876. II. 138.[2]

Mureau, Louis Marie Antoine Destouff de Milet-. *See* Milet-Mureau, L. M. A. D. de.

Muret, Ernest. Ceylan. 1895. I. 477.[1]

— Encore le contrôle. 1897. IV. 238.

— La estepa rusa. 1898. IV. 555.[2]

— El Instituto forestal finhandés. 1898. IV. 540.[1]

— La méthode du contrôle. 1897. IV. 238.

— À travers la Russie d'Europe. 1898. IV. 347, 555.[2]

Mürier nain, Morus pumila. 1832. III. 380.[1]

Murillo, Adolphe. Plantes medicinales du Chili. 1889. III. 66.[1]

Murion. Essai d'analyse . . . du Cornus sanguinea. 1824. III. 646.[1]

Murith, L. J. Le guide du botaniste . . . dans le Valais. 1810. I. 433.

La Murithienne, Société valaisanne des sciences naturelles. *See* Société Murithienne. I. 27.

Murmann, Otto Alexander. Beiträge zur Pflanzengeographie der Steiermark. 1874. I. 442.

Murner, T. Von der wunderbarlichen Arzney des Holtz Guaiacum. *See* Hutten, Ulrich von. 1519. III. 493.[2]

Muro, L. di. Amenità silvane. 1898. IV. 91.[1]

Murphy, J. J., (*comp.*). Acts, orders and regulations respecting crown lands, etc. in Ontario. 1890. IV. 296.[1]

Murphy, Martin A. Amygdalus communis var. amara. 1882. III. 434.[1]

Murr, Christoph Theophil de. Adnotationes ad bibliothecas Hallerianas. 1805. I. 1.

Murr, Josef. Uber Farbenspielarten. 1898. I. 245, *990*.

— Ueber Farbenspielarten . . . aus Nordtirol. 1887. II. 840.[1]

— Zur Flora von Nordtirol. 1893. II. 108.[3]

— Zur Kenntniss der Kulturgehölze Südtirols. 1900. I. 294,[2] III. 90.[1]

— Die Pflanzenwelt in der griechischen Mythologie. 1890. I. 514.[2]

— Zwei seltene Formen aus Oberösterreich. 1897. II. 680.[1]

Murray, A. On grafting and budding. 1872. III. 162.

Murray, A. S. Tasmanian rivers, lakes and flowers. 1900. I. 536.[2]

Murray, Alexander. Account of the life and writings of James Bruce. *See* Bruce, James. 1808. I. 398.

— The northern flora. 1836. I. 398.

— Thoughts regarding the influence of rocks. 1831. I. 228.[1]

Murray, Andrew. Abies Hookeriana (Abies Williamsonii). 1874. II. 53.[2]

— Account of the insect which infests the seeds of Piceae. 1857. III. 296.[2]

— Botanical expedition to Oregon. 1853. I. 322.

— Catalogue of . . . Botanic garden, Cambridge. 1850. I. 54.

— Cocci of the Orange trees. 1871. III. 500.[2]

— On the course of the sap. 1879. I. 165.

— Cupressus Lawsoniana. 1875. II. 28.[2]

— Description of a new Conifer from Arctic America. 1867. II. 37.[2]

— Description of new coniferous trees·from California. 1855. II. 14.[1]

— On the disguises of nature. 1860. - I. 99.

— Extirpation of injurious insects. 1877. III. 196.

— On the homologies of the . . . flowers of Conifers. 1866. II. 19.

— Libocedrus decurrens. 1872. III. 305.[1]

— Mammoth trees. 1861. II. 50.[2]·

— Monographic sketch of the Conifers of Japan. 1862. II. 15,[2] V. xxv.[1]

— Notes upon Californian trees. 1859. II. 14.[1]

— Phyllotoma aceris. 1876. III. 534.[1]

— Pines and Firs of Japan. 1862. V. xxv.[1]

— Pinus contorta (Dougl.). 1877. II. 41.[2]

— Pinus sylvestris—sub-species haynensis. 1869. II. 46.[1]

— Pinus Tamrac sp. nov. 1869. II. 43.[2]

— Quercus Ravenscroftiana. 1866. II. 136.[1]

— Rare Conifers. 1875. II. 14,[1] 22,[2] 34.[1]

— Rare Conifers. Picea magnifica. 1875. II. 22.[2]

— Rare Conifers; Picea religiosa. 1876. II. 25.[1]

— Rare Conifers, Pinus Balfouriana. 1876. II. 40.[2]

— Rare Conifers; Pinus aristata Engelm. 1874. II. 40.[2]

— Rare Conifers; Pinus deflexa. 1875. II. 42.[1]

— Rare Conifers; Pinus flexilis. 1875. II. 42.[1]

— Remarks on some plants . . . from Old Calabar. 1859. III. 482.[1]

— Remarks on some plants from Old Calabar. 1860. III. 482.[1]

— Report . . . on the forest education on the continent and in England. 1870. IV. 34.[1]

— On the synonymy of various Conifers. 1863. II. 21.[2]

— Tetranychus Taxi. 1875. III. 288.[1]

— What trees are best adapted for . . . the south of Russia. 1870. III. 120.[1·]

Murray, C. A. Persian fruit. 1858. III. 279.[2]

Murray, *Lady* Charlotte. The British garden. 1799. III. 81.

Murray, George. Half-holiday in Grenada. 1888. I. 337.

— A West Indian forest. 1887. I. 336.

Murray, H. Cocoa-nut fibre. 1869. III. 324.[1]

Murray, Hugh. Some German forests. 1882. IV. 350.[2]

Murray, James A. Chaulmugra oil. 1893. III. 614.[2]

— The plants and drugs of Sind. 1881. III. 92.[2]

Murray, Johan Anders. Apparatus medicaminum. 1776. III. 241.

— Commentatio comprehendens observationes in stirpes nonnullas . . . horti botan. 1777. I. 44.

— Commentatio de arboribus Gummi guttae fundentibus. 1789. III. 228.[2]

— Commentatio de Arbuto uva ursi. 1764. III. 648.[1]—

— Commentatio naturam foliorum de arboribus cadentium. 1772. I. 191.[1]

— Descriptiones stirpium aliquot novarum . . . Horti r. botanici. 1785. I. 44.

— Descriptiones stirpium . . . in horto botanico. 1775. II. 771.[1]

— Enumeratio vocabulorum quorundam . . . in re herbaria. 1756. I. 69.[3]

— Illustrationes stirpium . . . Horti R. botan. 1781. II. 557.[1]

— Observationes botanicae. 1778. I. 262.

— Observationes in·plantas aliquot minus cognitas. 1779. I. 262.

— Observationes in stirpes quasdam. 1785. II. 204.[2]

— Observationes super stirpibus aliquot exoticis. 1780. II. 773.[2]

— Opuscula. 1785. I. 520.[2]

— Prodromus designationis stirpium gottingensium. 1770. I. 373.

— De tempore corticis peruviani . . . exhibendi. 1776. III. 720.

— Vindiciae nominum trivialium. 1782. I. 253.[2]

Murray, John, (-1820). Elements of materia medica and pharmacy. 1804. III. 242.

— A system of materia medica and pharmacy. 1804. III. 242.

Murray, John, (-1851). A descriptive account of the Palo de Vaca. 1837. III. 367.[2]

— Experimental researches on the painted corolla of the flower. 1824. I. 184.

— On the physiology of the root. 1822. I. 160.

— Remarks on the phenomena of the fall of the leaf. 1823. I. 191.[2]

Murray, N. F. Black Raspberries. 1899. III. 457.[2]

Murray, Richard Paget. Canarian and Madeiran Crassulaceae. 1899. II. 237.[1]

— The flora of Somerset. 1896. I. 404,[1] V. xxi.[2]

— Further notes on Dorset Rubi. 1893. II. 303.[1]

— A new British Rubus. 1892. II. 307.[1]

— Notes on the botany of the Serra do Gerez. 1887. II. 308.[2]

Murray, Stewart. Companion to the Glasgow botanic garden. 1849. I. 54.
Murray's magazine. III. 17.
Murrell, William. See RINGER, Sydney & MURRELL, William.
Murrill, William Alphonso. The development of the archegonium . . . in the Hemlock Spruce. 1900. II. 53.[1]
— The prevention of Peach leaf-curl. 1900. III. 442.[1]
Murtfeldt, Mary Esther. Shade-tree destroyers. 1875. III. 186.[2]
Murton, H. J. Catalogue of the plants . . . in the Botanical gardens, Singapore. 1879. I. 67.[2]
Musa, Antonio. In hoc opere contenta. See APULEJUS PLATONICUS. 400. I. 274.
Le Muscadier. 1899. III. 403.[1]
Muschitzky, Lucian. Eine in Oesterreich-Ungarn heimische, der Phylloxera widerstehende Weinrebe. 1891. III. 574.
Muschner, (Stoberau). Die königl. Holzflösserei in Schlesien. 1862. IV. 390.[1]
Musculus, Friedrich Alphonse. Sur l'amidou soluble. 1874. I. 140.[1]
— Sur la constitution chimique de la matière amylacée. 1869. I. 140.[1]
— Sur les modifications des propriétés physiques de l'amidon. 1879. I. 140.[1]
— Nouvelle note sur la transformation de l'amidou. 1862. I. 140.[1]
— & Gruber, D. Sur l'amidon. 1878. I. 140.[1]
— & Meyer, A. Sur la transformation de la glucose en dextrine. 1881. I. 176.
Musée botanique de Leide. I. 16.[1]
Musée d'histoire naturelle. Annales. Archives. Bulletin. Mémoires. I. 22, V. VII.[1]
Musés du Congo. Annales. I. 16.[1]
Musés et institut colonial de Marseille. Annales. See INSTITUT COLONIAL . . . I. 21·
Musée forestier. Collections. 1898. IV. 18.[2]
Musée historique lorrain. See SOCIÉTÉ D'ARCHÉOLOGIE LORRAINE. IV. 13.[1]
Musés neuchâtelois. I. 26.[1]
Musée Teyler. Archives. I. 16.[1]
Museo agrario in Roma. Catalogo. 1879. I. 64.
Museo agricola y forestal [instalado en Lisboa]. 1891. IV. 539.[1]
Museo civico di storia naturale di Genova. Annali. I. 25.
Museo de La Plata. Revista. I. 7.[3]
Museo de productos Argentinos. Boletin. I. 7.[3]
Museo di fisica e storia naturale di Firenze. See REALE MUSEO . . . I. 25.
El Museo forestal de Vincennes en Paris. 1892. IV. 539.[2]
Museo nacional; república de Costa Rica. Anales. I. 7.[3]
Museo nacional de Buenos Aires. Anales. Comunicaciones. I. 7.[3]
Museo nacional de Montevideo. Anales. I. 7.[2]
Museo publico de Buenos Aires. See MUSEO NACIONAL . . . I. 7.[3]
Museu botanico do Amazonas. Contribuições. See VELLOSIA. I. 8.[1]
Museu Goeldi. Boletim. See MUSEU PARAENSE DE HISTORIA NATURAL E ETHNOGRAPHIA. I. 7.[3]
Museu nacional do Rio de Janeiro. Archivos. I. 7.[3]
Museu paraense de historia natural e ethnographia. Boletim. I. 7.[3]
Museum botanicum lugduno-batavum. Annales. I. 16.
Muséum d'histoire naturelle de Rouen. Actes. I. 22.
Museum des Neuesten . . . aus dem Gebiete der Naturwissenschaft. See BULLETIN des Neuesten . . . III. 11.
Museum of comparative zoölogy at Harvard college. Bulletin. Memoirs. III. 6.
Museum of foreign literature and science. I. 6.
Museum senckenbergianum. Abhandlungen. See SENCKENBERGISCHE NATURFORSCHENDE GESELLSCHAFT. I. 14.
A museum specimen of Sequoia gigantea. 1892. II. 51.[1]
The music of the leaves. 1874. I. 516.
Muss, (Feldjäger). Einschlagen des Blitzes in die Buche. 1828. IV. 496, 548.[1]
Mussaenda Coffee. 1889. III. 744.[1]
Mussat, E. Les Phylica. 1893. III. 542.[1]
— Sur la structure de quelques bois indigènes. 1876. I. 125.
Mussat, M. E. Rapport sur les fruits et les fruitiers de l'Exposition universelle. 1892. III. 145.[1]
Mussche, Jean Henri. Catalogue des plantes du Jardin botanique . . . de Gand. 1810. I. 49.
— Hortus gandavensis. 1817. I. 49.

Musschenbroek, Samuel Cornelis Jan Willem van. Bepaling van het soortelyk gewicht van eenige Javaansche houtsoorten. 1868. IV. 411.[1]
— Boschproducten. 1883. IV. 400.[1]
— Getah-pertja van Celebes oostkust. 1877. III. 229.
— Mededeelingen omtrent grondstoffen . . . van onzen Indischen Archipel. 1880. III. 274.[2]
— Oost-Indische houtsoorten. 1867. IV. 399.[2]
Musset, Charles. Anomalies par hypergenèse dans . . . l'Érable. 1874. II. 480.[1]
— Sur l'aplatissement des troncs d'arbres. 1869. I. 105.
— Contributions à la statique végétale. 1870. I. 149.[1]
— Enroulement des vrilles de la Grenadille. 1875. II. 577.[2]
— Sur des graines germées d'Érable sycomore. 1869. II. 480.[1]
— Influence présumée de la rotation de la terre sur la forme des troncs d'arbres. 1867. I. 149.[1]
— Sur l'insensibilité spontanée de la Sensitive. 1881. II. 373.[1]
— Note sur la structure d'un stipe de Yucca. 1867.· II. 87.[2]
— Une pluie de sève. 1879. I. 213.[3]
Mussini, Luigi. Scultura in legno. 1873. IV. 427.[2]
Musso, D. J. Comisión de repoblación de la cuenca del Segura. 1896. IV. 547.[1]
Mustel. Arbustes exposés en part au froid et en part au chaleur. 1773. I. 163.
— New observations upon vegetation.· 1773. I. 163.
— Traité théorique et pratique de la végétation. 1781. III. 37.[1]
Mutain, Franciscus Daniel. De natura, usu & abusu caffé, thé. See LE FEVRE, J. F. 1726. III. 222.
Mutel, Auguste. Éléments de botanique. 1820. I. 85. — 1857. I. 90.
— Flore du Dauphiné. 1830. I. 408.
— Flore française. 1834. I. 408, V. xxi.[3]
Muth, Franz. Zur Entwickelungsgeschichte der Skrophulariaceen-Blüte. 1899. II. 779.[1]
Mutilation d'arbres dans les bois des particuliers.· 1897.· IV. 326.
Mutis, José Celestino. Advertencias para el uso del Té de Bogotá. 1802. III. 670.[2]
— El arcano de la quina. 1828. III. 721.
— Batschia, novum plantae genus. 1792. II. 206.[2]
— Instrucción formada por un facultativo . . . relativa de las especies y virtudes de la Quina. 1792. III. 720.
— Monographia de Caryocar almendron. n. d. II. 546.[1]
— Pera arborea. 1784. II. 448.[2]
Mutschler, C., Hornberger, Richard & Hammerbacher, Friedrich. Analysen der Asche der Früchte von Lithospermum. 1875. II. 59.[2]
Der Mutterbaum einer auffallenden Birken-Varietät. 1879. II. 120.[1]
Mussnay, Géza. A romániai öserdőkről. 1899. IV. 375.[2]
Myers, La vulcanización de la madera. 1898. IV. 557.[2]
Myers, J. W. Report on hedging. 1879. III. 213.
Mygind, Frans von. Observationes critico-botanicae. 1897. I. 271.[1]
Myhrvold, A. K. Fremgangsmaaden ved og resultaterne af i andre lande anstillede forsög. 1898. IV. 70.
— Hvilken betydning har skoven. 1898. IV. 45.
Mylius, C. de & Holck, E. Arbejdspriser i Skovene. 1870. IV. 310.[1]
Mylius, Martin. Anmütiger Weissheit Lust Garten. 1597. I. 511.
— Hortus philosophicus. 1597. I. 511.
Myllerus, Conrad. De thermoscopio botanico. See GESSNER, Johann. 1755. I. 529.
Myrin, Claes Gustav. Anmärkningar om Wermlands och Dalslands vegetation. 1831. I. 353.
— Historia rei herbariae in Suecia. 1833. I. 353.
The Myrobalan or Cherry Plum. 1888. III. 436.[1]
Myrrh. 1879. III. 511.[1] — 1881. III. 511.[1]
Myrrh and bdellium. 1896. III. 511.[1]
Mysore. See INDIA — MYSORE.
Mysore Sandalwood. 1876. IV. 519.[1]

— n. Anbauversuche mit fremdländischen Holzarten. 1892. IV. 126.[1]
— n. Einfluss der Wälder auf den Hagelschlag. 1892. IV. 54.
— n. Ueber den Einfluss des Lichtens auf . . . Tanne. 1891. IV. 447.[1]
— n. Die Forstwirthschaft Kroatiens und Slavoniens auf der Budapester Millenniumsausstellung.· 1896. IV. 21.[1]

-n-. Der älteste Baum der Welt. 1900. IV. 484.²
—n—. Pfister's Zuwachsuhr. 1883. IV. 233.
—n—. Ueber Waldbahnanlagen. 1898. IV. 392.
—n—. Waldschutzgesetze in den Alpenländern. 1898. IV. 181.¹
—n—. Die Waldwirtschaft im Granthale. 1900. IV. 374.²
—n—. Die Wichtigkeit der Walderhaltung. 1897. IV. 181.¹
N. The Almonds. 1892. III. 430.²
N. Die Ausbildung der hessischen Forstbeamten. 1896. IV. 290.¹
N. Betrachtungen über die Entwaldung. 1860. IV. 43.
N. The Broom and its allies. 1892. III. 474.¹
N. Cerasus Pseudocerasus. 1890. III. 443.¹
N. The Cornels or Dogwoods. 1893. III. 645.¹
N. Cornus florida L. 1881. III. 645.²
N. Dasylirion. 1880. III. 336.¹
N. Doppel-Aepfel. 1880. II. 267.¹
N. Aus dem Eichen-Schälwald. 1870. IV. 506.
N. Ueber Einrichtung des niederen Forstdienstes. 1885. IV. 287.
N. Evergreen Oaks. 1891. III. 361.¹
N. Der forstliche Unterricht in den Vereinigten Staaten. 1899. IV. 30.¹
N. Die forstlichen Verhältnisse in den Vereinigten Staaten. 1891. IV. 338.¹
N. Die forstlichen Zustände in den Vereinigten Staaten. 1890. IV. 338.¹
N. Forstlich-Organisatorisches aus Hessen. 1900. IV. 290.¹
N. Forstwirtschaftliche Grundtöne. 1898. IV. 349.²
N. The Genistas. 1893. III. 477.¹
N. Die Gordonias. 1889. III. 596.²
N. The Gordonias. 1889. III. 596.²
N. Hardy Azaleas. 1888. II. 675.²
N. Huishoudelijke flora. 1758. III. 76.
N. The Judas tree. 1892. III. 472.²
N. Zum Kapitel der Forstorganisation im Grossherzogtum Hessen. 1893. IV. 290.¹
N. The Magnolias. 1892. III. 399.¹
N. Ueber Missbildungen am Obst. 1880. I. 145.²
N. Organisation des Forstwesens ... Hessen. 1896. IV. 290.¹
N. Papierholz. 1897. IV. 430.
N. Plants for railway hedges. 1887. III. 214.¹
N. Rendement d'une pineraie. 1894. IV. 559.²
N. Retrospectiv-kritische Betrachtungen in besonderem Hinblick auf das Grossherzogtum Hessen. 1879. IV. 290.¹
N. Stellung und Lage der Kommunal-Forstwarte mit besonderer Bezugnahme auf Hessen. 1899. IV. 290.¹
N. Terrains en mouvement. 1897. IV. 187.²
N. Traitement des forêts résineuses en montagne. 1887. IV. 140
N. Die Varietäten der Buche. 1889. III. 360.²
N. Wegenetzlegung ... in Gebirgsforsten. 1884. IV. 267.
N. Weiserprocentloses Wirthschaftliches aus der Nebelregion des Vogelsbergs. 1873. IV. 351.²
N. Die Wiehl'sche Stockkluppe. 1898. IV. 232.
N. Wirtschaftliches aus der Nebelregion des Vogelsberges. 1888. IV. 118.
N. Zusammengefrieren der Baumkronen. 1801. IV. 100.
N., B. The Tamarisk. 1874. II. 562.²
N., B., (jr.). De Lorowedoe-plant ... als middel tegen den gangsir. 1899. III. 737.
N., C. S. Het enten. 1877. III. 162.
N., D. P. R. Memoria histórica y descriptiva de las agallas que cria el Roble comun. 1808. IV. 509.
N., E. Incendies de forêt en 1899. 1900. IV. 183.¹
N., E. Plan tot ontginning van heidegronden. 1869. IV. 160.¹
N., F. Manuel d'agriculture et d'horticulture. 1823. III. 113.
N., F. Schutz der Waldkulturen gegen Feuer. 1895. IV. 181.²
N., G. Cudrania triloba. 1885. III. 368.²
N., G. Eucryphia cordifolia. 1897. III. 596.¹
N., G. Helichrysum rosmarinifolium. 1883. III. 755.²
N., G. Spanish Chestnut grafted on Oak. 1885. III. 359.¹
N., J. The theory and practice of transplanting. 1872. III. 166.
N., J. C. Le Juglans nigra L. en France. 1899. IV. 488.²
N., J. C. Table des inclinaisons des profils. 1896. IV. 390.¹
N., N. Arboreal physiology. 1884. IV. 64.¹

N., N. Decay of fallen leaves. 1884. IV. 71.
N., N. Distribution and arrangement of age classes. 1883. IV. 251.¹
N., Forest ground-rent. 1882. IV. 259.²
N., N. The forest service in Prussia. 1883. IV. 290.²
N., M. A high estimate of revenue from Larch planting. 1883. IV. 452.¹
N., N. Leaf canopy and pruning. 1883. IV. 172.¹
N., N. Memoria storiche sopra l'uso della cioccolata. 1748. III. 594.
N., N. Progress in forestry. 1884. IV. 102.
N., N. Terminology in forestry. 1883. IV. 23.²
N., N. A very old rule. 1883. III. 166.
N., The wind and the woods. 1885. IV. 189.²
N., N. Woods in their earlier stages. 1883. IV. 154.¹
N., N. Een woord op zijn tijd. n. d. III. 372.²
N., R. V. Natuur-kundige verhandeling van de theé. 1701. III. 222.
N., W. Stephanotis floribunda. 1886. III. 694.¹
N. Narayen Rao. The Herikalgudda forest. 1894. IV. 378.
— The Sandalwood tree in Mysore. 1896. IV. 519.²
N***. Quelques mots sur certains Chênes. 1873. III. 361.¹
Naaukeurige versameling der gedenk-waardigste zee en landreysen. 1707. I. 301.
Nabias, B. Les galles et leurs habitants. 1886. I. 214.¹
Nabonnaud. Les Palmiers dans le Midi. 1870. III. 317.
Naccari, Fortunato Luigi. Flora veneta. 1826. I. 426.
Nachricht für diejenigen, welche sich dem ... Forstexamen unterwerfen wollen. See UNDERRETNING ... 1853. IV. 30.²
Nachricht für diejenigen, welche sich dem vollständigen Forst-Examen unterwerfen wollen. See UNDERRETNING ... 1835. IV. 30.²
Nachricht von dem botanischen Garten der Kgl. Universität zu Breslau. 183.? I. 46.
Nachricht von dem Haalholzflössen. 1788. IV. 390.¹
Nachricht von der Einrichtung der Privat-Forst-Lehranstalt in Schwetzingen. See DRAIS, F. H. G., Freiherr von. 1807. IV. 31.
Nachricht von der Verwaltung ... der Warthebrücher. 1787. IV. 143.²
Nachricht von einigen exotischen Arzneigewächsen. 1833. III. 273.²
Nachricht von mehreren Orten allwo Saamen ... von ausländischen Bäumen zu haben sind. 1791. IV. 125.¹
Nachrichten von den kaiserl. österreichischen Naturforschern in Brasilien. 1820. I. 341.
Nachtblühende Cereus. 1892. III. 621.¹
Nachtigal, Gustav. La Coca et la cocaïne. 1886. III. 493.¹
— Sahara et Soudan. 1881. I. 489.
— Sahará und Südân. 1879. I. 485.
Nachtrab, Friedrich Wilhelm von. Anleitung zu dem neuen Waldkultur-Verfahren ... Biermanns. 1846. IV. 117, 152.
Nachweis des Holz- und Geld-Ertrages ... im Lampersdorfer Privatforst. 1867. IV. 261.¹
Nachweisung der ... aufgeführten inländischen Waldbäume von ausgezeichneter Grösse. 1833. I. 296.¹
Nachweisung der Druckformulare der preussischen Forstverwaltung. n. d. IV. 301.
Die Nachwucht der Buchen. 1887. IV. 494.
Nadeaud, Jean. Les Composées arborescentes de Tahiti. 1898. II. 857.²
— Énumération des plantes indigènes de l'île de Tahiti. 1873. I. 510.²
— Le genre Hernandia aux îles de la Société. 1897. II. 228.²
— Note sur quelques plantes ... de Tahiti. 1897. I. 510.²
— Plantes nouvelles des îles de la Société. 1899. I. 510.²
Nadelhölzer durch Steckreiser fortgepflanzt. 1838. IV. 149.²
Die Nadelhölzer in Suchum Kale. 1896. III. 297.¹
Nadelmann, Hugo. Über die Schleimendosperme der Leguminosen. 1890. II. 321.¹
— Ueber die Schleimendosperme der Leguminosensamen. 1889. II. 321.¹
Nadere berigten omtrent het voorkomen ... der getah-pertjah. 1858. III. 229.
Nadji, Abd-Ur-Bahman, Effendi. Empire ottoman. Géographie botanique. 1892. I. 450.
Nadmorski, (Dr.). Wycieczka na półwysęp Hel. 1886. I. 388.
Nägeli, Karl Wilhelm. Ueber die abgeleiteten Pflanzenbastarde. 1866. I. 245.

Nägeli, Karl Wilhelm (*continued*).
— Die Bastardbildung im Pflanzenreiche. 1865. I. 245.
— Ueber die Bedingungen des Vorkommens von Arten und Varietäten. 1865. I. 244.[1]
— Beiträge zur wissenschaftlichen Botanik. 1858. I. 34.
— Bläschenförmige Gebilde im Inhalte der Pflanzenzelle. 1846. I. 136.[3]
— Botanische Mitteilungen. 1863. I. 147.
— Ueber die chemische Zusammensetzung der Stärkekörner. 1863. I. 140.[1]
— Dickenwachsthum des Stengels ... bei den Sapindaceen. 1864. II. 483.[3]
— Ueber den Einfluss äusserer Verhältnisse auf die Varietätenbildung. 1865. I. 244.[1]
— Zur Entwickelungsgeschichte des Pollens. 1842. I. 117.[1]
— Über den Gefässbündelverlauf. 1859. I. 133.
— Das gesellschaftliche Entstehen neuer Spezies. 1872. I. 243.[1]
— Die Individualität in der Natur. 1856. I. 79,[1] 99.
— Ueber den innern Bau der... Zellenmembranen. 1864. I. 138.[1]
— Ueber merismatische Zellenbildung bei der Entwickelung des Pollens. 1846. I. 117.[1]
— On the nuclei, formation and growth of vegetable cells. 1844. I. 136.[3]
— Die Stärkekörner. 1858. I. 140.[1]
— Die Theorie der Bastardbildung. 1866. I. 245.
— On the utricular structures in the contents of cells. 1846. I. 136.[3]
— Verdrängung der Pflanzenformen. 1874. I. 217.
— Ueber die Verdunstung an der durch Korksubstanz geschützten Oberfläche. 1861. I. 166.
— Ueber das Wachsthum ... des Blattes. 1846. I. 190.[3]
— Ueber das Wachsthum der Stärkekörner durch Intussusception. 1881. I. 140.[1]
— Ueber das Wachsthum des Gefässstammes. 1846. I. 105.[1]
— Ueber das Wachsthum des Stammes. 1858. I. 133.
— Wachsthumsgeschichte des Blattes von Aralia spinosa. 1855. II. 647.[2]
— Ueber die Wirkung des Frostes. 1861. I. 212.
— Zellenkerne, Zellenbildung. 1844. I. 136.[1]
— Ueber die Zwischenformen zwischen den Pflanzenarten. 1866. I. 245.
— & **Cramer,** Karl Eduard. Pflanzenphysiologische Untersuchungen. 1855. I. 147.
— & **Leitgeb,** Hubert. Entstehung und Wachsthum der Wurzeln. 1867. I. 188. — 1868. I. 103.
— & **Schwendener,** Simon. Das Mikroskop. 1865. I. 36,[1] V. viii.[1]
Naegeli, Otto. Über die Pflanzengeographie des Thurgau. 1898. I. 438.
Nähere Bestimmungen über die Abgabe und Verwerthung der Forstprodukte ... 1851. IV. 300.[1]
Zur **nähern** Beleuchtung und Verbesserung der est- und lifländdischen Forsten. See **Kriegsheim,** Christoph. 1797. IV. 347.
Nährwerth des Laubfutters. 1877. III. 223.[1]
Naesman, Petrus. Beskrifning öfver Madesiö socken. 1747. IV. 344.[1]
Naets, A. & **Berger,** E. De l'enlèvement des bourgeons de Pin. 1898. IV. 479.
Naszén, Daniel Erik. Index plantarum rariorum ... in urbis Ulricaehamn Vestrogothiae confiniis. 1782. I. 352.
Nagamatsz, Atsusuke. Beiträge zur Kenntniss der Chlorophyllfunktion. 1886. I. 142.
Nagaoka, M. See **Kellner,** O., **Yoshii,** T. & **Nagaoka,** M.
Nagel, A. Quelques mots sur l'Arbre à gomme-élastique. 1861. III. 369.[1]
Nagel, Albrecht Eduard. Die Liebe der Blumen. 1885. I. 238.
Nagel, C. F. Beschreibung der neuesten Fuchsien. 1841. III. 639.[3]
Nagel, Heinrich von. Beitrag zur Beförderung der Landesverschönerung. 1827. III. 34.[1]
— Landesverschönerung und Landesverbesserung. 1831. III. 34.[1]
— Vollständige Uebersicht der monatlichen Verrichtungen im Obst-, Küchen- und Bienengarten. 1823. III. 136.
Nagel, J. De Brem. 1857. III. 474.[3]
Nagelvoort, J. B. Kinine onderzoekingen. 1877. III. 723.
Nagórski, J. J. O chodowaniu jedwabników. 1830. III. 374.
Nagy, Gyula. Háromszékmegye erdészeti leirása. 1885. IV. 373.

— Szabadka.. sz. kir. város erdészeti viszonyainak leirása. 1896. IV. 374.[1]
— A Székelyföld közgazdasági szerepéről és hivatásáról hazánkban. 1884. IV. 279.[1]
Nagy, Károly. A Havasi Fenyő (Pinus Cembra L.) növekvése. 1884. IV. 463.[1]
Nagy, L. von. Abrus precatorius, eine Wetterpflanze. 1888. III. 462.[3]
— Die Aristolochien. 1890. III. 385.[2]
— Drei japanische Pflanzen. 1886. III. 89.[3]
— Die Edelkastanie. 1885. III. 359.[1]
— Einige Bäume und Gesträuche mit gefüllten Blumen. 1880. III. 207.[3]
— Einige Kalthaus-Rhododendron. 1887. III. 655.
— Etwas über Cacteen. 1885. III. 619.
— Die härteste Palme. 1887. III. 327.[3]
— Interessante Wüstensträucher. 1888. III. 387.[1]
— Koelreuteria. 1891. III. 539.[1]
— Koelreuteria paniculata. 1892. III. 539.[1]
— Ligustrum Quihoui, Ibota und vulgare. 1883. III. 673.[3]
— Die Magnolien. 1884. III. 399.[1]
— Myrica. 1884. III. 353.[1]
— Notice sur les Ericas rustiques. 1884. III. 650.[3]
— Rosa rugosa. 1888. III. 456.[3]
— Rosenvermehrung. 1885. III. 452.
— Syringa japonica. 1888. III. 680.[1]
— Syringa vulgaris fol. purp. 1889. III. 456.[3]
— Trauerbäume. 1883. III. 204.[3]
Nahlik, Johann, *Edler* von. Über einige Feinde des Waldes. 1878. IV. 180,[1] 210.[1]
Nahuis, G. H. Schets van Benkoelen. 1825. III. 275.[1]
Nahuys, De Gaspeldoorn. 1852. III. 489.[2]
— Hazelaar als hakhout. 1852. IV. 492.[1]
Nahuys, Alexander Peter. Oratio inauguralis de religiosa plantarum contemplatione. 1775. I. 515.
Over de **Nain-Laurier.** 1772. IV. 87.[3]
Nairne, Alexander Kyd. The flowering plants of western India. 1894. I. 475.[3]
— List of trees, shrubs ... close to Mândeva Bandar. 1878. I. 470.[1]
— Notes on Bombay plants. 1885. I. 475.[1]
Nairne, David. Historical notes on Scottish forestry. 1890. IV. 27.[1]
— Notes on highland woods. 1892. IV. 359.[1]
Naironi, Antonio Fausto. De saluberrima potione cahve. 1671. III. 741.[1]
Nakamura, T. Sur la valeur alimentaire de l'asparagine. 1899. I. 151.[3]
Nakamura, Yaroku. Über den anatomischen Bau des Holzes der wichtigsten japanischen Coniferen. 1882. II. 17.[1]
Nakaz ... See **Наказ** ...
Nalepa, Alfred. Beiträge zur Systematik der Phytopten. 1890. I. 214.[3]
— Katalog der bisher beschriebenen Gallmilben. 1894. I. 214.[3]
— Die Naturgeschichte der Gallmilben. 1894. I. 214.[3]
— Neue Gallmilben. 1891. I. 215.[1]
Nanclér, Samuel. Hortus upsaliensis. See **Linné,** Carl von. 1745. I. 40.
Nancy — Société centrale d'horticulture. See **Société** ... III. 21.
Nancy — Société des sciences. See **Société** ... I. 23.
Nancy — Société royale des sciences et belles-lettres. See **Société** ... I. 24.[1]
Nancy — Station agronomique. Office agricole. See **Station** ... III. 22.
Nanke, Walter. Vergleichend-anatomische Untersuchungen über den Bau von Blüten. 1899. I. 524.[1]
Nan-mu tree of Chinese. 1878. IV. 520.[1]
Nanninga Uitterdyk, J. Over ontginning van woeste gronden. 1899. IV. 160.[3]
Nannizzi, A. Collezioni esistenti nel R. orto botanico di Siena. 1899. I. 64.
— Osservazioni fenologiche. 1898. I. 227.[1]
— Piante grasse coltivate nell' Orto botanico di Siena. 1900. I. 64.
Nanot, Jules. Arrosage des arbres des boulevards. 1891. III. 211.[3]
— Arrosage des arbres sur les boulevards. 1888. III. 211.[3]
— Cultur du Pommier à cidre. 1884. III. 426.[3]
— Destruction des scolytes. 1886. III. 196.
— Échelle double et dendroscope. 1888. III. 171.
— Effet de la gelée sur les plantes. 1891. III. 182.

— Établissement et entretien des plantations d'alignement. 188 .? III. 209.
— Étude sur l'arrosage des arbres des boulevards. 1889. III. 211.[2]
— Étude sur les cultures commerciales de Poiriers et de Pommiers. 1890. .III. 144.
— Guide de l'ingénieur pour l'établissement et l'entretien des plantations d'alignement. 188 .? III. 209.
— L'Orme Dumont et le Robinier monophylle. 1890. III. 364,[1] 487.[1]
— Plantations d'alignement sur les voies publiques. 1888. III. 210.
— Restauration . . . plantés sur les boulevards. 188 .? III. 418.[1]
— La transplantation des gros arbres à Paris. 1886. III. 168.[1]
— Vernieling der schorskevers. 1886. III. 196.
— & Tritschler, L. Traité pratique du séchage des fruits. 1893. III. 174.[1]
— Viala & Ravaz. Greffage de la Vigne. 1893. III. 548.[2]
Nanquette, Henri. Cours d'aménagement des forêts. 1859. IV. 109,[1] £40.
— Cours de technologie forestière, créé à l'École de Nancy. 1859. . IV. 381.
— Exploitation débit et estimation des bois. 1859. IV. 381.
— Mondring der Eiche. 1879. IV. 510.
— Notions pratiques d'exploitation, de débjt. 1858. IV. 217.
Napheys, G. H. Modern medical therapeutics. 1870. III. 243.
— Modern surgical therapeutics. 1870. III. 243.
— Modern therapeutics. 1870. III. 243.
Napier, J. R. Beschreibung eines . . . Verfahrens zum Trocknen des Bauholzes. 1856. IV. 416.[1]
Naples — Accademia delle scienze fisiche . . . See ACCADEMIA . . I. 24.[2]
Naples — Orto botanico della regia università. See ORTO . . . I. 25.
Naples — Reale istituto d'incoraggiamento. See REALE . . . I. 25.
Naples — Reale istituto tecnico e nautico. See REALE . . . III. 23.[2]
Naples — Società di naturalisti. See SOCIETÀ . . . I. 26.[1]
Naples — Zoologische Station. See ZOOLOGISCHE . . . I. 15.
Napoli. See NAPLES.
Napp, Richard. The Argentine Republic. 1876. I. 344.
— Die Argentinische Republik. 1876. I. 344.
— La République Argentine. 1876. I. 344.
Napper, W. The Lucombe Oak. 1891. III. 362.[2]
Nardelli, D. Norme e pratiche sulla conservazione . . . dei boschi. 1870. IV. 122.[2]
Nardo, Luigi. Su alcuni usi ed applicazioni economiche del Pinus maritima. 1831. IV. 468.[1]
— De corticis Pini maritimae analysi chemica. 1831. IV.468.[1]
— Ueber die Rinde von Pinus maritima. 1831. IV. 468.[1]
Nardy, B. Le Dattier. 1900. III. 329.[1]
Nardy, Sébastien, (1830-1909). Les arbres d'avenues autres que les Palmiers. ·1900. III. 210.
— Cépages les plus propres aux cultures méridionales. 1888. III. 547.
— Sous les cieux de l'Oranger. 1897. III. 335.[1]
— Le Cocos australis. 1890. III. 322.[2]
— Les Cordyline sur le littoral méditerranéen 1874 III 334.[1]
— Le Dattier mûrissant ses fruits en Provence. 1897. III. 329.[1]
— De l'emballage des végétaux. 1890. III. 155.
— L'Erythea ou Brahea edulis. 1900. III. 325.[1]
— Les Eucalyptus. 1892. III. 634.[1]
— Les Eucalyptus en Algérie. 1875. IV. 529.[3]
— Les Eucalyptus sur le littoral français. 1874. IV. 529.[3]
— Floraison d'un Agave Consideranti. 1897. III. 325.[1]
— Une floraison du Brahea Roezli. 1900. III. 321.[2]
— Floraison du "Dasylirion longifolium." 1883. III. 337.[2]
— Floraison . . . du Pritchardia filamentosa. 1897. III. 332.[1]
— La fructification à Hyères du Brahea Roezli. 1900. III. 321.[1]
— Les fruits du Diospyros Kaki. 1892. III. 669.[2]
— Les grands Palmiers d'avenues. 1897. III. 318.[1]
— Les jardins en Portugal après l'hiver 1890-91. 1891. III. 49.[1]
— Les Kakis du Japon. 1882. III. 669.[2]
— Les naturalisations végétales dans le midi. 1877. III.125, III. 335.[1]
— Le parc de Madame la Baronne Alice de Rothschild. 1897. III. 335.

— Le Phoenix dactylifera de la place Barrow. 1899. II. 73.[2]
— Quelques mots sur les Dasylirion. 1877. III. 336.[1]
— Un Rosier japonais inédit. 1890. III. 450.
— Un très-remarquable Phoenix dactilifera. 1874. II. 72.[3]
— La végétation en Portugal. 1889. III. 126.[1]
Naredjenje . . . radi dobroga texanja. See TERMINAZIONE . . . per la buona coltura. 1776. IV. 304.[1]
Naredjenje . . . za straxu, nauka i texanje dubravà. See TERMINAZIONE . . . per la custodia . . . 1778. IV. 304.[1]
O narostani . . . See O narostanik . . .
Narushevitch, K. See Нарушевичъ, К.
Nasazhdeniye . . . See Ю., С. Насажденiе . . .
Nash, Alanson. American Hemlock. 1853. III. 312.[1]
— The Sugar Maple or Acer saccharinum. . 1853. IV. 527.[1]
Nash, George Valentine. Notes on some Florida plants. 1895. I. 319.
— Revision of the genus Asimina in North America. 1896. II. 216.[2]
— Viburnum prunifolium var. globosum. 1893. II. 844.[1]
Nasmyth, John Murray. Notes on Pinus austriaca. 1876. IV. 465.[2]
Nassau-Verein für Naturkunde im Herzogthum . . . See VEREIN . . I. 15.
Nassauische zeitschrift für Land- und Forstwirthe.· IV. 10.
Nassauischer Verein für Naturkunde. Jahrbücher. See VEREIN FÜR NATURKUNDE IM HERZOGTHUM NASSAU. I. 15.
Nast, Johann Konrad. · Vollständige Abhandlung des ganzen Weinbaues. 1766. III. 552.
Nastavlenie . . . See Наставленiе . . .
Natal Aloes. 1890. III. 333.[2]
Natal botanic gardens. Report. See DURBAN BOTANIC SOCIETY. I. 29.[2]
Natanson, Józef. Kauczuk i gutaperka. 1882. III. 231.
— Wiek drzew. 1883. I. 193.[2]
Nathan (Oberförster). Waldkulturen . . . mit Getreidenutzung. 1842. IV. 133.
Nathorst, Alfred Gabriel. Om den arktiska vegetationens utbredning öfver Europa. 1873. I. 349.
— Botaniska anteckningar från nordvestra Grönland. 1884. II. 99.[2]
— Sur la distribution de la végétation arctique.en Europe. 1873. I. 349.
— Fortsatta anmärkningar om den grönländska vegetationens historia. 1891. I. 358.
— Kritiska anmärkningar om den grönländska vegetationens historia. 1890. I. 309.[1]
— Nya bidrag till kännedomen om Spetsbergens kärlväxter. 1883. I. 357.
— Studien über die Flora Spitzbergens. 1883. I. 357.
Nathorst, Hjalmar. Om Befrugtning af Pæretræets Blomster. 1895. II. 280.[2]
Nathorst, Theop. Erdm. Flora monspeliensis. See LINNÉ, Carl von. 1756. I. 405.
Nati, Pietro. Florentina phytologica observatio de Malo Limonia citrata-aurantia. 1674. II. 400.[2]
Nation. I. 6.
National academy of sciences. Report. IV. 4.
National-Arboretums zu Zöschen. See DIECK, Georg. 1893, I. 49.
National association of lumbermen. Proceedings. IV. 4.
National builder. See AMERICAN builder. New York. IV. 3.
National convention for the suppression of insect pests. 1897. III. 197.
National convention of fruit growers. Proceedings. See AMERICAN POMOLOGICAL SOCIETY. III. 2.
National coopers' journal. I. 6.
National exposition of railway appliances. 1883. IV. 420.
A national forest-policy. 1892. IV. 272.
The national forest-question. 1891. IV. 272.
National geographic magazine. I. 6.
National institute for the promotion of science, Washington, D. C. Bulletin. Proceedings. I. 6.
The National magazine. III. 6.
National nurseryman. III. 6.
National pharmaceutical convention. Proceedings. See AMERICAN pharmaceutical association. I. 5.
National quarterly review. III. 6.
National review. IV. 539.[2]
National timber preserving company. 1875. IV. 419.
National wholesale lumber dealers' association. Report. IV. 4.
Nationale nederlandsche huishoudelijke maatschappij. Landbouw. I. 16.
The nation's forests. 1889. IV. 178.[1]

Native Fig juices and caoutchouc (India rubber). 1894. III. 229.
Native Forester, (*pseud.*). Effects of forest denudation on the Deccan side. 1882. IV. 49.[1]
— Hirda revenue in the Kolhapur state. 1882. III. 632.[2]
— On the restoration of denuded forests in Kolhapur. 1881. IV. 168.[1]
Native plants for ornamental planting. 1897. III. 202.[1]
Native products of Siam. 1895. III. 609.[3]
The **native** rubbers of the Malay Peninsula. 1900. III. 230.
The **native** White Pine. 1892. III. 309.[1]
Nattermüller, O. Der Obstbau in den zwölf Kalendermonaten. 1887. III. 139.
— Vollständiger Kalender der Obstkultur. 1884. III. 139.
Natton. De la noix de Kola. 1884. III. 590.[2]
Über die **natürliche** Verjüngung der Buche. *See* -CK. 1895. IV. 496.
Die **natürliche** Verjüngung der Kiefer. 1892. IV. 474.
Natürliche Verjüngung im südlichen Buchenhochwalde. 1862. IV. 494.
Ueber das **natürliche** Vorkommen von Cinnamyloocaïn. 1889. III. 493.[1]
De **natuerlijcke** beschrijvingh der boomen. 1663. I. 292.
Natuerlyke historie van de couchenille. *See* RUUSSCHER, Melchior de. 1729. III. 624.[1]
Die **Natur**. III. 13.
Natura. I. 16.
Natural grafting. 1883. I. 209.[1]
The **natural history** club of Philadelphia. Annual report. I. 519.[1]
The **natural** history of chocolate. *See* QUELUS, de. 1719. III. 594.
The **natural** history of coffee, thee, chocolate. 1682. III. 221.[2]
Natural history review. I. 19.
Natural history society of **Northumberland, Durham and Newcastle-upon-Tyne**. Natural history transactions. Transactions. I. 19.
A **natural** non-inflammable wood. 1898. IV. 531.[1]
Natural science. I. 19.
Natural science association of Staten Island. Proceedings. I. 6.
La **Naturaleza**. I. 7.[2]
Ueber die **Naturalisation** der östreichischen Kiefer. 1832. IV. 465.[1]
The **Naturalist**. III. 6.
The **Naturalist**. Huddersfield. I. 19.
The **Naturalist**. London. I. 19.
Il **Naturalista** siciliano. I. 25.
La **Naturaliste**. I. 22.
Naturalization . . . of the larger-fruited Vaccinium. 1826. III. 664.[1]
Naturalizzazione di essenze forestali in Francia. 1863. IV. 127.[1]
Naturally grafted Elm. 1849. I. 209,[1] III. 364.[1]
Nature. I. 19.
La **Nature**. Paris. I. 22.
Nature of hard woods. 1820. I. 154.
Naturen. I. 8.[2]
Naturen og Mennesket. I. 9.[1]
Naturforschende Gesellschaft Graubündens. Jahresbericht. I. 26.[1]
Naturforschende Gesellschaft in Basel. Bericht. Verhandlungen. I. 26.[1]
Naturforschende Gesellschaft in Bern. Mittheilungen. I. 26.[1]
Naturforschende Gesellschaft in Danzig. Neue Sammlung. Neueste Schriften. Schriften. I. 13.
Naturforschende Gesellschaft in Zürich. Abhandlungen. Vierteljahrsschrift. I. 26.[1]
Naturforschende Gesellschaft zu Freiburg i. B.. Berichte. I. 13.
Naturforschende Gesellschaft zu Görlitz. Abhandlungen. I. 13.
Naturforschende Gesellschaft zu Halle. Abhandlungen. Bericht. Festschrift. Neue Schriften. I. 13.
Naturforschende Gesellschaft zu Leipzig. Sitzungsberichte. I. 13.
Naturforschender Verein in Brünn. Verhandlungen. I. 28.[1]
Naturforschender Verein zu Riga. Arbeiten. Correspondenzblatt. Denkschrift. I. 9.[2]
Der **Naturforscher**. I. 13.
Der **Naturforscher**; Wochenblatt. I. 13.
Naturforscher-Gesellschaft zu Dorpat. *See* DORPATER NATURFORSCHER . . . I. 9.[1]

Natur-gemässige Beschreibung der Coffee, Thee. *See* The NATURAL history of coffee, thee, chocolate. 1682. III. 221.[2]
Naturgeschichte der einheimischen . . . nutzbarsten Pflanzen. *See* GLEDITSCH, J. G. 1786. III. 72.
Zur **Naturgeschichte** der italienischen Pappel. 1881. III. 346.[1]
Zur **Naturgeschichte** der Kiefer. 1859. IV. 472.
Zur **Naturgeschichte** der Lärche. 1865. IV. 449, 465,[2] 472.
Naturgeschichte der schädlichen Waldinsekten. 1801. IV. 91.[1]
Zur **Naturgeschichte** der Silberpappel. 1865. II. 96.[1]
Zur **Naturgeschichte** der Stieleiche. 1859. II. 137.[1]
Zur **Naturgeschichte** der Weisstanne. 1861. II. 23.[2]
Naturgeschichte von Guiana. *See* BANCROFT, Edward. 1769. III. 267.[2]
Naturgeschichtliche Beiträge zur Kenntniss . . . von Chur. 1874. I. 436.
Naturgeschichtliche Beschreibung der Nonne. *See* Die NONNE, auch Fichtenspinner. 1890. IV. 200.
Naturhistorie-Selskabet Kjøbenhavn. Skrivter. I. 9.[1]
Naturhistorische Gesellschaft in Colmar. Mittheilungen. *See* SOCIÉTÉ D'HISTOIRE NATURELLE DE COLMAR. I. 15.
Naturhistorische Gesellschaft zu Hannover. Jahresbericht. I. 13.
Naturhistorische Gesellschaft zu Nürnberg. Abhandlungen. Jahresbericht. I. 13.
Naturhistorischer Verein der preussischen Rheinlande (und Westphalens). Verhandlungen. I. 13.
Naturhistorischer Verein in Augsburg. Bericht. V. VII.[1]
Naturhistorischer Verein in Passau. Bericht. I. 13.
Naturhistorischer Verein, "Lotos." *See* LOTOS; Zeitschrift für Naturwissenschaften. I. 27.
Naturhistorischer Verein von Wisconsin. Jahresbericht. I. 6.
Naturhistorischer-medicinischer Verein zu Heidelberg. Verhandlungen. I. 13.
Naturhistorisches Hofmuseum, [Wien]. *See* KAISERLICH-KÖNIGLICHES NATURHISTORISCHES . . . I. 27.
Naturhistorisches Landes-Museum von Kärnten. Jahrbuch. I. 28,[1] V. VII.[1]
Naturhistorisches Noth- und Hülfsbüchlein für deutsche Landmänner, für Forstmänner. 1793. IV. 56.
Naturhistorisk Tidsskrift. I. 9.[1]
Naturhistoriske forening i Kjøbenhavn. Festskrift. Videnskabelige Meddelelser. I. 9.[1]
Naturmerkwürdigkeiten. 1894. IV. 516.[1]
Naturvidenskabelige og mathematiske Afhandlinger. *See* KJØBENHAVNSKE SELSKAB . . . I. 8.[3]
Naturwissenschaftliche Abhandlungen herausgegeben von einer Gesellschaft in Würtemberg. I. 13.
Naturwissenschaftliche Gesellschaft in Winterthur. Mittheilungen. I. 26.[1]
Naturwissenschaftliche Gesellschaft Isis zu Dresden. Denkschriften. Sitzungsberichte. I. 13.
Naturwissenschaftliche Gesellschaft zu Chemnitz. Bericht. I. 13.
Naturwissenschaftliche Rundschau. I. 13.
Naturwissenschaftliche Wochenschrift. III. 13.
Naturwissenschaftlicher Verein an der K. k. technischen Hochschule in Wien. Berichte. I. 28.[1]
Naturwissenschaftlicher Verein an der Universität Wien. Mittheilungen. I. 28.[1]
Naturwissenschaftlicher Verein der Provinz Posen. Zeitschrift. I. 14.
Naturwissenschaftlicher Verein des Harzes in Wernigerode. Schriften. I. 14.
Naturwissenschaftlicher Verein des Regierungsbezirkes Frankfurt. Monatliche Mittheilungen. I. 14.
Naturwissenschaftlicher Verein für das Fürstenthum Lüneburg. Jahresberichte. Jahreshefte. I. 14.
Naturwissenschaftlicher Verein für Schleswig-Holstein. Schriften. I. 14.
Naturwissenschaftlicher Verein für Schwaben und Neuburg. Bericht. *See* NATURHISTORISCHER VEREIN IN AUGSBURG. V. VII.[1]
Naturwissenschaftlicher Verein für Steiermark. Mittheilungen. I. 28.[1]
Naturwissenschaftlicher Verein in Halle. Jahresbericht. I. 14.
Naturwissenschaftlicher Verein in Hamburg. Abhandlungen. Verhandlungen. I. 14.
Naturwissenschaftlicher Verein in Karlsruhe. Verhandlungen. I. 14.
Naturwissenschaftlicher Verein von Neuvorpommern und Rügen in Greifswald. Mittheilungen. I. 14.

Naturwissenschaftlicher Verein zu Bremen. Abhandlungen. I. 14.

Naturwissenschaftlich-medizinischer Verein in Innsbruck. Berichte. I. 28.¹

Natus, Petrus. A phytological observation concerning Orenges and Limons. 1675. II. 401.²

De Natuur. I. 16.

Natuur- en geneeskundig archief voor Neerland's Indië. I. 29.¹

Natuur- en scheikundig archief. I. 16.

Natuurkundige en ophelderende aanmerkingen. 1788. I. 32.

Natuurkundige tijdschrift voor Nederlandsch-Indië. I. 29.¹

Natuurkundige vereeniging in Nederlandsch-Indië. Verbandelingen. I. 29.¹

Natuurkundige Verhandelingen. I. 16.

De natuurlijcke beschrijvingen der boomen. 1663. III. 51.

Natuurlyke historie. See HOUTTUYN, Martin. 1773. I. 258.

Natuurwetenschappelijke genootschap van Ghent. Natura. See NATURA. I. 16.

Nau, Bernhard S. Anleitung zur deutschen Forstwissenschaft. 1790. IV. 95.

— Praktische Anweisung über den Weinbau. 1804. III. 552.

— Vermischte Aufsätze über Land- und Forstwirthschaft. 1804. IV. 100.²

— Vorbereitungslehren zur besseren Erlernung der Forstwissenschaft. 1807. IV. 96.

Naudin, Charles Victor. Les Acacias tannifères d'Australie. 1889. III. 463.²

— Additions à la flore du Brésil méridional. 1844. II. 634.²

— Un arbre dangereux. 1898. III. 528.²

— Arbres gigantesques dans l'île de Van Diemen. 1850. II. 624.¹

— Arrivée de nouvelles espèces de Conifères. 1861. III. 289.

— Le Bambusa Simonii. 1875. III. 315.²

— Berberis Andreana. 1899. II. 204.¹

— Le Brahea filamentosa de Californie. 1876. III. 332.¹

— Les Cactées de plein air. 1869. III. 619.

— Le Caféier de Libéria. 1876. III. 743.¹

— Le Cèdre de l'Himalaya. 1853. II. 27.²

— Le Chamaerops. 1876. III. 322.¹

— Le Chêne Zéen ou de Mirbeck. 1884. IV. 503.²

— The Chinese Persimmon. 1890. III. 669.²

— Chlorocodon Whytei. 1895. III. 737.¹

— Chute d'un Orme en Angleterre. 1861. III. 143.²

— Clematis patens (var. Sophia). 1855. III. 391.²

— Sur le Cocotier des Seychelles. 1864. II. 70.²

— Considérations générales sur l'acclimatation des plantes. 1888. III. 44.¹

— The cultivation of Acacia Farnesiana. 1891. III. 465.¹

— Culture des Azalées. 1848. III. 656.

— De la culture des Palmiers rustiques en France. 1864. III. 317.

— Culture des Passiflores en Angleterre. 1866. III. 615.¹

— Culture du Camellia. 1850. III. 599.²

— Culture du Gardenia Fortunei. 1853. III. 744.²

— Culture du Mangou en Angleterre. 1845. III. 609.²

— Culture en plein air des Rhododendrons. 1864. III. 656.

— Le Dattier à fruits noirs. 1893. III. 329.¹

— Description et emploi des Eucalyptus. 1891. III. 634.¹

— Description et emploi des Eucalyptus introduits en Europe. 1891. III. 634.¹

— Deux nouveaux cas présumés de parthénogénèse. 1864. I. 202.¹

— Diospyros Kaki. 1880. II. 701.²

— Emploi du Maclura aurantiaca. 1854. III. 372.¹

— Emploi du tabac pour combattre le phylloxera. 1874. III. 566,² *IV. 510.*

— Encore un mot sur l'Hortensia bleu. 1847. III. 412.¹

— Études sur la végétation des Solanées. 1842. II. 768.¹

— Les Eucalyptus. 1876. IV. 531.²

— Eucalyptus. 1885. III. 530.

— Eucalyptus Andreana. 1890. II. 624.¹

— Les Eucalyptus de l'île de Van Diemen. 1851. II. 624.¹

— Les Eucalyptus en Provence. 1880. IV. 530.

— Eucalyptus et Cytisus. 1883. III. 474.²

— L'Eucalyptus et l'influenza. 1890. IV. 532.¹

— Eucalyptus globulus. 1856. IV. 532.²

— L'Eucalyptus globulus. 1856. IV. 532.²

— Eucalyptus Mülleri. 1885. III. 634.²

— L'Eucalyptus rostrata. 1882. III. 634.¹

— Un Eucalyptus rouge. 1897. III. 635.¹

— Les Eucalyptus rustiques. 1888. III. 634.¹

— On the European Palm and its varieties. 1876. II. 66.²

— Exemples de formation de racines adventives. 1853. I. 188.

— Expériences tentées dans le but de faire bleuir les fleurs du Viburnum Opulus. 1848. III. 753.¹

— Explosion d'une spathe de Palmier. 1861. II. 64.¹

— Fécondation des Palmiers par les abeilles. 1893. II. 63.²

— Sulla fioritura e fruttificazione della Jubea spectabilis. 1886. III. 326.¹

— Floraison de Cycadées. 1856. III. 284.¹

— Floraison de l'Eucalyptus globulus à Hyères. 1863. III. 634.²

— Floraison du Dammara australis. 1856. III. 297.²

— Forsythia viridissima. 1852. III. 672.¹

— Fructification de l'Aucuba japonica. 1864. III. 644.²

— Fructification du Cocos australis. 1886. III. 322.²

— Fructification du Jubaea spectabilis en France. 1894. III. 326.¹

— Fructification du Pistachier. 1856. III. 526.¹

— Germination of Welwitschia. 1882. II. 55.²

— La gomme d'Australie. 1889. III. 463.²

— Le grand Palmier des Canaries. 1885. II. 72.¹

— On hybridism considered as a cause of variability. 1864. I. 245.

— De l'hybridité considérée comme cause de variabilité. 1864. I. 245.

— Hyères; son territoire, végétaux exotiques. 1852. III. 125.

— Improvement of North American fruits. 1888. I. 248.¹

— Indigofera Dosua. 1849. III. 479.²

— Influence de l'électricité atmosphérique sur la croissance. 1879. I. 231.²

— Introduction de l'Isonandra Gutta. 1856. III. 668.¹

— Les jardins de la Provence et l'hiver de 1859–1860. 1861. III. 48.

— Krankheit der Wellingtonia. 1856. III. 310.¹

— La longévité des graines. 1897. I. 527.

— Maladie du Sequoia. 1856. III. 310.¹

— Maladie de la Vigne, Oïdium. 1850. III. 575.¹

— Le Maniçaba du Brésil. 1898. III. 520.²

— Manihot carthagenense. 1875. III. 520.²

— Melastomacearum . . . descriptionis . . . tentamen. 1849. II. 634.²

— Mémoire sur les Eucalyptus. 1883. III. 623.¹

— Un mot à propos de la culture du Thé. 1861. III. 600.²

— Un mot à propos du Cajan. 1874. III. 469.¹

— Mussaenda frondosa. 1853. III. 746.¹

— Naturalisation de l'Acajou dans l'Inde. 1867. III. 513.¹

— Naturalisation des Rhododendrons. 1852. III. 656.

— De la naturalisation des végétaux. 1854. III. 44,¹ 47.

— A new Date palm. 1893. II. 73.²

— Note on hybridism in vegetables. 1863. I. 245.

— Note sur la floraison . . . du Jubaea spectabilis. 1886. III. 326.¹

— Note sur le Machaerium Tipa. 1899. II. 387.¹

— Note sur le Pinus Bungeana. 1862. II. 41.¹

— Note sur le Pinus Bungeana Zucc. 1862. II. 41.¹

— Notice sur la production de fleurs bleues par les Hydrangéas. 1846. III. 412.¹

— Notice sur les Cucurbitacées. 1860. III. 317,

— Notice sur les Eucalyptus. 1883. II. 623.¹

— Nouveau pot à marcotter. 1855. III. 159.¹

— La nouvelle maladie de la Vigne. 1898. III. 577.

— Nouvelle notice sur le Sequoia. 1855. II. 50.¹

— Une nouvelle plante ornementale. 1895. III. 737.¹

— Nouvelles observations au sujet du Maclura. 1855. III. 372.¹

— Nouvelles recherches sur l'hybridité. 1863. I. 245.

— Nouvelles recherches sur les nodosités . . . des Légumineuses. 1897. III. 322.¹

— Nouvelles recherches sur les tubercules des Légumineuses. 1896. III. 322.¹

— Objections au procédé de l'arrachage des Vignes. 1874. III. 566.¹

— Observations relatives à la fécondation incomplète. 1856. I. 201.¹

— Observations relatives à la formation des graines. 1856. I. 202.¹

— Observations sur l'accroissement de certains ovaires. 1857. I. 119, *145.*²

— Observations sur la rusticité relative de quelques Palmiers. 1870. III. 317.

— L'Orange à trois faces. 1855. II. 402,¹ *III. 164.*²

Naudin, Charles Victor (*continued*).
— L'Oranger du Japon. 1869. III. 502.[1]
— Oranger mandarinier. 1870. III. 502.[2]
— Les Ormeaux de Hyde-Park. 1852. III. 363.[2]
— Sur le Palmier du nord de la Chine. 1861. II. 75.[1]
— Les Palmiers à Collioure. 1875. III. 317.
— Les Palmiers de la Chine en Angleterre. 1855. III. 317.
— Les pavés de bois d'Eucalyptus. 1892. IV. 531.[1]
— Le Pinus Bungeana de la Chine. 1862. II. 41,[1]
— Le Pinus peuce et le Lodoicea sechellarum. 1864. III. 308,[1] 327.[1]
— Les Pitch-pine d'Amérique. 1891. IV. 462.[1]
— Les Pittosporum. 1899. II. 248.[1]
— Plantes d'ornement récemment introduites. 1851. III. 87.
— Plaqueminier de Virginie. 1869. III. 670.[1]
— Préservation des arbres contre le froid. 1862. III. 183.[1]
— Prix Bordin . . . Déterminer expérimentalement les causes de l'inégalité de l'absorption. 1866. I. 161.
— À propos de la mer intérieure du Sahara algérien. 1877. IV. 168.[3]
— Qu'était-ce que le bois de Citrus des anciens? 1858. IV. 447.[3]
— Quelques considérations sur l'espèce et la variété. 1858. I. 252.
— Quelques mots au sujet du Forsythia viridissima. 1852. III. 672.[1]
— Quelques observations sur la fécondation des Palmiers du genre Phoenix. 1893. III. 72.[1]
— Quelques remarques au sujet des Plaqueminiers. 1880. II. 701.[1]
— La question des reboisements , . . en Algérie. 1883. IV. 168.[3]
— Rapport sur la culture du Thé dans l'Himalaya. 1850. III. 602.[3]
— Retour définitif et complet de plantes hybrides. 1862. I. 245.
— Rhododendron Brookeanum. 1855. III. 657.[3]
— Rhododendron Comtesse Ferdinand Visart. 1854. III. 658.[1]
— Rhododendron Hodgsoni. 1855. III. 659.[1]
— Rhododendron javanicum. 1852. III. 660.[2]
— Rhododendron lanatum. 1855. III. 661.[1]
— Riesenbäume auf Van-Diemens-Land. 1850. II. 624.[1]
— Le roi des Conifères. 1853. III. 310.[1]
— Rusticité du Livistona australis. 1870. III. 326.[2]
— Le Sapin de Douglas. 1861. IV. 484.[1]
— Du seringage des arbres et arbustes. 1853. III. 197.
— Serres et orangeries de plein air. 1861. III. 150.[1]
— Le Skimmia à baies rondes. 1865. III. 506.[1]
— Le Sophora secundiflora. 1893. III. 488.[2]
— Le Sumac et le Phylloxéra. 1893. IV. 526.[1]
— Le Tagasate des Canaries. 1875. III. 474.[2]
— Trois nouvelles plantes japonaises. 1862. III. 750.[2]
— Trois Palmiers de Californie. 1890. III. 321.[1]
— Trois Palmiers de Californie. 1891. III. 318.[1]
— Variation désordonée des plantes hybrides. 1875. I. 245.
— Variations climatériques en Europe. 1891. I. 528.[3]
— Végétation de l'Himalaya. 1852. I. 473.
— La Vigne au Brésil. 1898. III. 551.[1]
— Le Wellingtonia gigantea. 1853. III. 310.[1]
— What is Orange peel? 1886. II. 402.[3]
— *See also* DECAISNE, Joseph & NAUDIN, Charles.
— & C . . , Maxime. La greffe du Châtaignier. 1899. III. 359.[1] or U
— & Müller, Ferdinand, *Baron von*. Manuel de l'acclimateur. 1887. III. 53.
Naudin, P. Sur les moyens proposés pour combattre la propagation du phylloxera. 1874. III. 567.[1]
Nathaus, C. Theophilus. Die Verkümmerung der Hochblätter. 1870. I. 111.
Naujoks, W. Hilfstafeln zur Berechnung des Taxwertes von Langnutzhölzern. 1896. IV. 229.
Nauka poznawania i niszczenia owadów leśnych. 1853. IV. 209.[2]
Nauka poznawania i niszczenia owadów w lasach liściowych. 1852. IV. 209.[2]
Nauka stosownego wysadzania krajowych gościńców i dróg owocowem i lesnem drzewem. . n. d. III. 208.[2]
Nauman, Lud. Pomologie. n. d. III. 90.[1]
Naumann, Alexander. Eine Heidelbeere mit grünen Früchten. 1887. II. 680.[2]
Naumann, Arno. Beiträge zur Entwickelungsgeschichte der Palmenblätter. 1887. II. 63.[1]
— Zur Entwickelungsgeschichte der Palmenblätter. 1887. II. 63.[1]

Naumann, Ferdinand Chr. Beitrag zur westlichen Grenzflora des Königreichs Sachsen. 1891. I. 389.
— Rosen-Bastarde. 1896. II. 294.[2]
Naumann, Georg Amadeus Karl Friedrich. *See* NAUMANN, K. F.
Naumann, J. F. Hængeasken. 1840. III. 672.[2]
Naumann, Karl Friedrich. Ueber den Quincunx. 1842. I. 102.
— Ueber den Quincunx . . . vieler Pflanzen. 1845. I. 102.
Naumann, L. F. Gartenbautafeln. 1882. III. 146.[3]
Naumburg, Johann Samuel. Lehrbuch der feinen Botanik. 1798. I. 84.
Nautet, D. G. MONTEIRO DE. *See* MONTEIRO DE NAUTET, D. G. The naval store industry. 1893. IV. 437.[1]
Naval stores review. IV. 4.
Navarette, Martin Fernandez de. Colección de los viajes . . . que hicieron por mar los Españoles. 1825. I. 328.
— Die Reisen des Christof Columbus. 1825. I. 328.
Navarro, Leandro. Una aclaración. 1883. IV. 47.[2]
— Memoria relativa á las enfermedades del Olivo. 1898. III. 678.[1]
Navashin, Serghyei Ghavrilovich. *See* NAWASCHIN, Sergius.
Náves, Andrés. Descripción de la . . . Prosopis Vidaliana. 1877. V. XXVI.[2]
Navi di Sughero. 1896. IV. 518.[1]
Navier, Pierre Touissaint. Observations sur le cacao. 1772. III. 594.
Nawaschin, Sergius. Zur Embryobildung der Birke. 1894. II. 118.[1]
— Zur Entwickelungsgeschichte der Chalazogamen. 1899. II. 122.[1]
— Über die gemeine Birke und die . . . Chalazogamie. 1894. II. 118.[1]
— Kurzer Bericht . . . über die Embryologie der Betulineen. 1894. II. 115.[1]
— Über das Verhalten des Pollenschlauches bei der Ulme. 1898. II. 143.[1]
— *See also* WORONIN, M. & NAWASCHIN, S.; НАВАШИНЪ, С.
Nazari, Vittorio. Esposizione nazionale di olii d'oliva. 1894. III. 679.[3]
Ta nea geoponika. *See* ΤΑ ΝΕΑ γεωπονικά.
Neal, Adam. A catalogue of plants in the garden of John Blackburne. 1780. I. 53.
— A catalogue of the plants in the garden of John Blackburné at Orford. 1779. I. 53.
Neal, J. C. The root-knot disease of the Peach. 1889. III. 187.
Neale, Robert. Transplanting . . . of Grape vines. 1850. III. 550.
Nealley, G. C. Unusual leaf-forms in Platanus. 1886. II. 255.[1]
Neander, Johann. Sassafrasologia. 1627. III. 407.[3]
Neapel. *See* NAPLES.
Nebbien, C. H. Die Kunst des naturgemässen Baumschnitts. 1837. III. 169.[2]
Nebel, Daniel. De balsamo copayba. 1710. III. 473.[1]
— De malo Citreo. 1732. III. 498.[3]
— De plantis incipiente aestate efflorescentibus. 1707. III. 72.
— De plantis verno tempore efflorescentibus. 1706. III. 72.
— De Roremarino. 1710. III. 698.[1]
Nebel, Wilhelm Bernhard. Cortex radicis Pruni sylvestris. 1740. III. 443.[1]
— De corticis peruviani modo operandi. 1740. III. 719.
— Specificum in Paidatrophia. 1740. III. 643.[1]
Nebesky. Beitrag zur Vermehrung der Rhodoraceae. 1871. III. 647.[1]
Nebesky. Die wirthschaftlichen Verhältnisse der Kronforste im russischen Reiche. 1898. IV. 114.
Neblich. Die Buchennutzholzausbeute im Spessart. 1897. IV. 499.[1]
Nebraska — Agricultural experiment station. *See* NEBRASKA, UNIVERSITY OF . . . III. 6.
Nebraska state horticultural society. Annual report. III. 6.
Nebraska, University of — Agricultural experiment station. Annual report. Bulletin. III. 6.
Nebraska — University of — Botanical department. *See* BOTANICAL department . . . I. 5.
Nebraska — University of — Botanical survey. Report. *See* UNIVERSITY . . . I. 7.[1]
Sopra una necessaria riforma dei metodi di determinazione dell' accrescimento. *See* SOPRA una . . . 1882. IV. 233.
De la nécessité de distraire l'administration forestière. 1819. IV. 292.

La nécessité, l'utilité et la nature des mesures relatives à l'aménagement des forêts communales. 1866. IV. 309.[1]
Nechansky, H. Der Controlleimring im Kampfe gegen die Nonne. 1892. IV. 201.
Necker, Natalis Joseph. See NECKER, Noel J.
Necker, Noel Joseph de. Considérations sur le système sexuël des végétaux. 1784. I. 251.
— Corollarium ad Philos. botanicam Linnaei spectans. 1790. I. 97, 251, 254.[2]
— Deliciae gallo-belgicae silvestres. 1768. I. 391,[2] V. xx.[1]
— Elementa botanica. 1790. I. 258.
— Enumeratio stirpium palatinarum. 1770. I. 373.
— Mémoire sur la fécondation. 1784. I. 200.
— Mémoire sur la gradation des formes dans les parties des végétaux. 1790. I. 97.
— Phytozoologie philosophique. 1790. I. 251.
Nectoux, Hipolyte. Voyage dans la haute Égypte. 1808. II. 342.[2]
Nedella, Wilhelm. Die "Breite Föhre" bei Mödling. 1896. IV. 466.[3]
Nederlandsch archief voor genees- en natuurkunde. I. 16.
Nederlandsch Indië. See DUTCH EAST INDIES.
Nederlandsch instituut van wetenschappen, letterkunde . . . te Amsterdam. See KONINKLIJKE NEDERLANDSCH . . . I. 15.
Nederlandsch kruidkundig archief. I. 16.
Nederlandsch tijdschrift voor pharmacie. See TIJDSCHRIFT voor schei- en artsenijbereidkunde. III. 15.
Nederlandsch tijdschrift voòr pharmacie . . . onder redactie van H. Wefers Bettink. See TIJDSCHRIFT voor wetenschappelijke pharmacie. I. 16.
Nederlandsche apotheek. 1826. III. 250.[1]
Nederlandsche entomologische vereeniging. Tijdschrift. III. 14.
Nederlandsche flora en pomona. 1876. III. 77.
Nederlandsche heidemaatschappij. Tijdschrift. IV. 12.[1]
De Nederlandsche hovenier. 1841. III. 105.
Nederlandsche huishoudelijke maatschappij. See NATION-ALE NEDERLANDSCHE . . . I. 16.
Nederlandsche maatschappij ter bevordering van nijverheid. Landbouw. See NATIONALE NEDERLANDSCHE HUISHOUDELIJKE MAATSCHAPPIJ. I. 16.
Nederlandsche maatschappij ter bevordering van nijverheid. Tijdschrift. III. 14.
Nederlandsche maatschappij tot aanmoediging van den tuinbouw. See KONINKLIJKE NEDERLANDSCHE . . . III. 14.
Nederlandsche maatschappij voor tuinbouw en plantkunde. Jaarboekje. III. 14.
Nederlandsche pharmacopee. See NEDERLANDSCHE apotheek. 1826. III. 250.[1]
Nederlandsche tuinkunst. 1837. III. 105.
Nedzelsky, A. Sur les progrès de l'arboriculture fruitière. 1866. III. 76.
Née, Luis. Del buyo. 1803. III. 221.[1]
— Descripcion de varias especies nuevas de Encina. 1801. II. 129.[1]
— Description of several new species of Oak. 1801. II. 129.[1]
Neeb, J. Anweisung zu einer inträglichen Akazienpflanzung. 1829. IV. 522.[2]
Neebauer, G. W. Das Forstwesen in Beziehung auf den Staat. 1805. IV. 268.
Needham, John Tuberville. Account of some new microscopical discoveries. 1745. I. 97.
— Nouvelles découvertes faites avec le microscope. 1745. I. 97.
— Nouvelles observations microscopiques. 1749. I. 198.
— Observations upon the generation . . . of animal and vegetable substances. 1749. I. 198.
The needs of American forestry. 1889. IV. 46.[1]
Neergaard, J. T. Bemaerkninger i Anledning af Hr. Forstcandidat Oldenburgs Nye Bidrag. 1862. IV. 288.[2]
Neergaard, V. Indsamling af Oldenhorner. 1891. IV. 549.[1]
— Skovbruget fremstillet. 1895. IV. 94.
Neerland's Indië. See DUTCH EAST INDIES.
Neerland's plantentuin. III. 14.
Nees von Esenbeck, Christian Gottfried. Acanthaceae. 1847. II. 795,[2] 796.[1]
— Acanthaceae Africae australis. 1841. II. 796.[1]
— Agrostologia brasiliensis. 1829. II. 58.[1]
— Bambuseae brasilienses. 1835. II. 58.[1]
— Über den Bau der Fruchtknotens der Laurinen. 1833. II. 223.[1]
— Berichtigungen zur Disputatio de Cinnamomo. 1831. II. 224.[1]

— Characters or new species of Indian Acanthaceae. 1836. II. 803.[2]
— Chenopodeae Vent. 1844. II. 187.[1]
— Chrysobalaneae R. Br. 1844. II. 316.[1]
— De l'écorce de Cedrela febrifuga. 1825. III. 512.[1]
— Fridericia et Zollernia. 1827. I. 267.
— Ueber die Gattungen Calicanthus. 1823. II. 610.[2]
— Genera et species Astorearum. 1833. II. 848.[1]
— Handbuch der Botanik. 1820. I. 85.
— Handbuch der Pflanzen-Pathologie. 1841. I. 34.
— Horae physicae berolinenses. See HORAE . . . I. 12.
— Hornschuchia. 1822. II. 218.[1]
— De Kamptzia, novo Myrtacearum genere. 1841. II. 633.[1]
— Laurinae. 1848. II. 223.[1]
— Loganiaceae Endl. 1844. II. 719.[1]
— Monograph of the East Indian Solaneae. 1837. II. 768.[1]
— Novum genus arborum Myrtacearum. 1840. II. 633.[1]
— Observationes in Acanthaceas Horti vratislaviensis. 1842. II. 795.[2]
— Plantae javanicae ineditae. 1824. I. 468.
— Plantae Kegelianae surinamenses. 1848. I. 339.[1]
— Plantarum canariensium . . . species quatuor. 1820. I. 497.
— Plantarum Laurinarum . . . expositio. 1833. II. 222.[2]
— Revisio Laurinarum. 1833. II. 223.[1]
— Ueber die Rinde der Cedrela febrifuga. 1825. III. 512.[1]
— Sylloge observationum botanicarum. 1820. II. 774,[1] 775.[1]
— Zur Synonymik der . . . cultivirten Laurinen. 1833. II. 223.[1]
— Systema Laurinarum. 1836. II. 223.[1]
— Systematic view of the plants brought back . . . from . . . [his] tour on the Missouri. 1841. I. 307.
— Systematische Uebersicht der von dieser Reise auf dem Missouri mit zurück gebrachten Pflanzen. 1841. I. 307.
— Verzeichnis der Pflanzen welche der Prinz Maximilian von Wied . . . mit zurückbrachte. 1841. I. 307.
— See also MARTIUS, C. F. P., ESCHWEILER, F. G. & NEES VON ESENBECK, C. G.; WEIHE, K. E. A. & NEES VON ESENBECK, C. G.; WIED-NEUWIED, M. A. P., Fürst von & NEES VON ESENBECK, C. G.
— & T. F. L. De Cinnamomo disputatio. 1823. II. 224.[1]
— & Martius, C. F. P. von. Fraxinellae, plantarum familia naturalis. 1823. I. 341.
— — Goethea. 1823. II. 521.[2]
— & Schauer, J. K. Annotationes botanicae ex Indice seminum Hort. bot. vratislaviensis. 1836. I. 47.
— & Schauer, Sebastian. Enumeratio et descriptiones . . . plantarum in terris mexicanis crescentium. 1847. I. 331.
— & Sinning, Wilhelm. Plantarum in Horto medico bonnensi nutritarum icones selectae. 1824. I. 46.
— Bischof, C. G. & Rothe, H. A. Diê Entwicklung der Pflanzensubstanz. 1819. I. 151.[2]
Nees von Esenbeck, Theodor Friedrich Ludwig. Ueber Artemisia indica. 1832. II. 851.[2]
— Bemerkungen über Chamaedorea elegans. 1834. II. 66.[1]
— Ueber Calycanthus praecox. 1819. II. 214.[2]
— De l'écorce de Cedrela febrifuga. 1825. III. 513.[1]
— Ueber die Gattungen Calycanthus, Meratia. 1823. II. 214.[2]
— Ueber ein neues Arzneimittel: Cortex Alvxiae. 1824. III. 686.[2]
— Sur une nouvelle écorce aromatique. 1824. III. 686.[2]
— Ueber Pinus rotundata. 1834. II. 42.[2]
— & Ebermaier, C. H. Handbuch der medicinisch-pharmaceutischen Botanik. 1830. III. 56.
— & Marquart, L. C. Ueber den Milchsaft der Feigenbäume. 1835. III. 369.[1]
— & Sinning, Wilhelm. Sammlung schönblühender Gewächse. 1831. I. 46.
— & others. Beschreibung officineller Pflanzen. 1828. III. 56.
— — Genera plantarum florae germanicae . . . illustrata. 1835. I. 378.
— — Plantae medicinales. 1828. III. 56.
— — Plantae officinales. 1828. III. 56.
Neese, Nicolaus. Beobachtungen an der Vegetation in Riga. 1854. I. 223.[2]
— Kiew; Vegetations-Periode. 1857. I. 223.[2]
Negami, K. On the physiological action of neutral sodium sulphite. 1897. I. 211.
Negelein, von. Ueber die Flugsandculturen . . . Oldenburg. 1857. IV. 145.
Neger, Franz Wilhelm. Die Araucarienwälder in Chile und Argentinien. 1897. II. 26.[2]

Neger, Franz Wilhelm (*continued*).
— Die Ausbeutung . . . der natürlichen Waldungen in Chile. 1898. IV. 383.[1]
— Zur Biologie der Holzgewächse im südlichen Chile. 1897. I. 347.[1]
— Über einige durch Phytoptus hervorgerufene gallenartige Bildungen. 1895. I. 214.[2]
— Ueber die elementare Zusammensetzung des Eichenholzes. 1894. II. 137.[1]
— Informe sobre las observaciones botánicas. 1899. I. 347.[1]
— Introduccion a la flora de los alrededores de Concepcion. 1897. I. 347.[1]
— Kritische Bemerkungen zu einigen Pflanzen. 1900. II. 476.[1]
— Pflanzengeographisches aus den südlichen Anden und Patagonien. 1900. I. 331.
Neger, Johannes. Excursionsflora Deutschlands. 1871. I. 386, 532.[1]
A neglected British tree. 1882. III. 303.[1]
Nagociado del personal. 1890. IV. 553.[1]
Négrel-Féraud. Culture de l'Azerolier. 1850. III. 421.[2]
Negri, Cristoforo. Idee elementari per una legge in materia di acque. 1865. IV. 328.
— Le leggi forestali. 1864. IV. 313.
Negri, Giovanni de. Analisi dei gas contenuti nei follicoli . . . di Gomphocarpus. 1891. II. 738.[1]
Négrier, G. Die Behandlung der Scrofeln mit Wallnussblättern. 1841. III. 356.[1]
— Sur la traitement . . . 1841. III. 356.[1]
Negro Coffee. 1882. III. 471.[1]
Nehring, A. Aus der älteren Vorzeit des deutschen Waldes. 1892. I. 389.
Nehring, Paul. *See* Beckurts, H. & Nehring, Paul.
Nehring, Henry. Bamboos in Florida. 1897. III. 314.[2]
— Exotic trees and shrubs for Florida gardens. 1894. III. 60.[1]
— Palmen in . . . Vereinigten Staaten. 1887. III. 318.[1]
— Palms at Federal Point, Florida. 1893. III. 318.[1]
Neidhardt. Echo aus dem Eichen-Schälwald. 1888. IV. 507.
— Was bedeutet "Nutzholzwirthschaft"? 1884. IV. 498.
Neidhardt, A. Der Waldwege-Bau. 1852. IV. 266.[2]
Neidigk, Fr. Die Baumzucht um Odessa. 1846. III. 120.[1]
— Die Pinus-Kultur in der Ukraine. 1846. III. 306.[2]
Neigefind, Theod. Gottlieb. De cortice peruviano. 1775. III. 720.
Les neiges et le Pin s lvestre. 1896. IV. 190.
Neil, Samuel. Earlyyplanting in Scotland. 1880. IV. 27.[1]
— Hints towards a science of forestry. 1880. IV. 56.
— On some remarkable trees in Scotland. 1879. I. 297.[1]
— The timber trees of classic times. 1880. I. 514.[2]
Neil, W. E. *See* Katteyer, Morits & Neil, W. E.
Neill, Patrick. Account of the Ayrshire Rose. 1820. II. 292.[1]
— The fruit, flower and kitchen garden. 1838. III. 110.[1]
Neilreich, August. Aufzählung der in Ungarn . . . beobachteten Gefässpflanzen. 1866. I. 445.
— Diagnosen der in Ungarn . . . beobachteten Gefässpflanzen. 1867. I. 445.
— Flora von Nieder-Oesterreich. 1859. I. 441.
— Flora von Wien. 1846. I. 440.
— Über hybride Pflanzen der Wiener Flora. 1852. II. 102.[3]
— Nachträge zu Maly's Enumeratio plantarum. 1861. I. 441.
— Die Vegetationsverhältnisse von Croatien. 1868. I. 447.
Neish, James. The cultivation of the Orange in Jamaica. 1884. III. 500.[1]
— On a new beverage substance, the kola nut. 1887. III. 590.[2]
Nekola, Rudolf. Die Zirbenasucht. 1898. IV. 464.[1]
Nekut, František. Balsamovník. 1875. II. 417.[2]
— Cítlivka stydlivá. 1874. III. 481.[2]
— K dějinám révy vinné. 1875. II. 509.[1]
— Jehličnaté rostliny — Blahočet a Damaroň. 1874. IV. 443.[2]
— Mabagon. 1878. III. 513.[1]
— Mléční rostliny. 1875. III. 218.[2]
Nekut, Josef. Marhaník. 1879. III. 630.[1]
Neligan, J. M. Medicines, their uses and mode of administration. 1844. III. 254.
— Neligan's medicines. 1844. III. 254.
Nélis. Futaie de Chêne. 1897. IV. 559.[2]
— Règlement sur les insectes nuisibles. 1898. IV. 208.[2]

Nelson. Captain Nelson's report of the tracts of country on the Kist-nah. 1866. I. 474.
Nelson, Aven. New plants from Wyoming. 1898. II. 242.[2]
— First report on the flora of Wyoming. 1896. I. 326.
— Some Rocky Mountain Chrysothamni. 1899. II. 853.[1]
— The trees of Wyoming. 1899. I. 321, IV. 78.[2]
— The winter-killing of trees and shrubs. 1893. III. 182.
— Wyoming Junipers. 1898. II. 31.[3]
Nelson, Elias Emmanuel. Some new species of Wyoming plants. 1900. II. 246,[2] 294.[2]
Nelson, John. Pinaceae. 1866. III. 289.
Nelson, Robert. The best evergreen hedge. 1847. III. 305.[1]
Nelson, T. J. The speech of the city solicitor . . . before the Epping forest commissioners. 1876. IV. 180.[2]
Neluski. Galactodendron utile. 1871. III. 367.[2]
Němcová, Božena. Pěstování růžového keře v Bulharsku. 1860. III. 452.
Němec, Bohumil. Ueber die Art der Wahrnehmung des Schwerkraftreizes. 1900. I. 196.[1]
— Neue cytologische Untersuchungen. 1900. I. 137.
Německo-český slovník lesnický. *See* Deutsch-böhmisches. 1883. IV. 23.[2]
Němejc, Jan. Lesy Východní Rumelie. 1892. IV. 375.[1]
Németh, Zoltán. Berberis Darwini. 1900. III: 394.[2]
Nemici della Quercia. 1884. IV. 501.[1]
Nemnich. Die Wälder Java's. 1896. IV. 377,[1] 536.[2]
Nemnich, Philipp Andreas. Allgemeines Polyglotten-Lexicon der Naturgeschichte. 1793. I. 72.[1]
O nemoci vinných hroznů a Rév. 1853. III. 575.[2]
Nencioni, Giuseppe. *See* Cazzuola, Ferdinando & Nencioni, Giuseppe.
Nendtvich, Károli Miksa. Dissertatio, exhibens enumerationem plantarum in territorio Quinque-ecclesiensi. 1836. I. 445.
O neorganitcheskikh . . . *See* O неорганическихъ . . .
Nepp, Josef. Ueber Holztrockenanlagen. 1887. IV. 420.
Nerdrum, Johann G. Forsög med granstiklinger. 1897. III. 305.[1]
— Sammenvoksede Grantræer. 1897. I. 209,[3] III. 305.[2]
Nerlich, (*Oberförster, Turama*). Beitrag: Die Dauer des Holzes zu vermehren. 1854. IV. 417.
— Bericht über die Schütte. 1854. IV. 475.
— Massen-Angaben einiger Kiefern. 1854. IV. 480.
— Verhandlungen . . . "Wie ist . . . der Holzanbau auf flachgrundigem Boden . . . zu bewirken?" 1844. IV. 141.
— Vorschläge: Einen Birkenbestand in einen Fichten- und Tannenbestand zu verwandeln. 1853. IV. 169.[2]
— Unter welchen Verhältnissen empfiehlt es sich, mit der Forstverwaltung einen Brettmühlenbetrieb zu verbinden. 1892. IV. 393.
Nerlinger, Th. & Bach, C. Der landwirtschaftliche Obstbau. 1885. III. 139.
Neronof, I. *See* Heроновъ, И.
Nerrlich, (*Forstmeister, Deutsch-Wartenberg*). Vorkommen . . . der Esche. 1896. IV. 535.[1]
Nesfield, Markham. Remarkable Chestnut tree at Warwick Castle. 1873. II. 124.[2]
Ness, H. *See* Price, R. H. & Ness, H.
Nessler, Julius. Essai de l'eau-de-vie de Cerises. 1882. III. 432.[2]
— Physikalische Wirkung des abgefallenen Laubes. 1861. IV. 71.
— Die Rebwurzellaus. 1875. III. 759.
Nestel's Rosengarten. III. 13.
Nesterof, N. S. *See* Heстеровъ, H. C.
Nestler, A. *See* Villars, Dominique, Lauth, Gustav & Nestler, A.
Nestler, Anton. Die Ausscheidung von Wassertropfen. 1897. I. 169.[2]
— Ein Beitrag zur Anatomie der Cycadeenfiedern. 1895. II. 3.[2]
— Eigenthümlichkeiten im . . . Bau der Laubblätter einiger Ranunculaceen. 1893. II. 196.[2]
— Der Flugapparat der Früchte von Leucadendron. 1893. II. 164.[1]
— Zur Kenntnis der Wasserausscheidung an den Blättern. 1899. II. 156.[2]
— Kritische Untersuchungen über . . . Wasserspalten. 1894. I. 132.[1]
— Die Perldrüsen von Artanthe cordifolia. 1893. II. 94.[1]
— Die Schleimzellen der Laubblätter der Malvaceen. 1898. II. 519.[2]
— Untersuchungen über die Ausscheidung von Wassertropfen. 1896. I. 169.[1]

— Untersuchungen über Fasciationen. 1894. I. 144.[2]
— Ueber das Vorkommen von Pilzen. 1899. III. 303.[2]
— & Schiffner, V. Ein neuer Beitrag zur Erklärung der Zwangsdrehungen. 1892. I. 107.[1]
Nestler, Christian Gottfried. Index plantarum quae in Horto academico argentinensi anno 1871 viguerunt. 1818. I. 45.
— Monographia de Potentilla. 1816. II. 270.[1]
Nestler, J. C. Aushülfe in der Noth um Futter und Dünger. 1836. IV. 437.[2]
Netscher, van der GON. See BLEEKRODE, S. A. & GON NETSCHER, van der.
Netscher, E. Houtsoorten van Riouw. 1852. IV. 399.[2]
Netscher, H. J. Th. Liberia-Koffie. 1893. III. 742.[2]
— De toekomst der gutta-percha. 1899. III. 232.[1]
Nettlau, H. Die schönsten niedrigen Cytisus. 1881. III. 474.[1]
Netto, Ladislau. Addition à la flore brésilienne. 1865. I. 343.
— Additions à la flore brésilienne. 1866. I. 343.
— Aperçu sur la théorie de l'évolution. 1883. I. 243.[1]
— Apontamentos relativos á botanica applicada no Brasil. 1871. III. 65.[1]
— Apontamentos sobre . . . plantas economicas do Brasil. 1866. III. 269.[1]
— Estudos sobre a evolução morphologica dos tecidos nos caules sarmentosos. 1876. I. 127.[1]
— Investigações sobre a Parreira brava. 1871. II. 206.[2]
— Noticia . . . de uma arvore de construcção. 1871. II. 461.[2]
— A Quinicultura no Brazil. 1890. III. 713.[1]
— Rapidas investigações sobre as Quinas Brasileiras. 1871. II. 812.
— Remarques sur la destruction des plantes indigènes au Brésil. 1865. IV. 179.[2]
— Remarques sur les laticifères de plusieurs plantes du Brésil. 1863. I. 135.
— Remarques sur les vaisseaux laticifères de quelques plantes du Brésil. 1865. I. 135.
— Sur la structure anormale des tiges des lianes. 1863. I. 127.[1]
— Trembleya Pradosiana Nett. 1865. II. 642.[2]
Nettscher, H. J. T. See NETSCHER, H. J. T.
Netyksa, M. A. See HETMICA, M. A.
Neu eingeführte Cacteen. 1886. III. 619.
Neu eingeführte Gesträuche für's freie Land. 1882. III. 203.
Neu eröffnete Gärtner-Akademie. See L'ÉCOLE du jardinier. 1764. III. 112.
Neubauer, (Dr.) & Canstein, Freiherr von. Reise-Bericht über den Weinbau an der Haardt. 187 . ? III. 553.[1]
Neubauer, Karl Theodor Ludwig. Ueber das Catechu und seine Säuren. 1855. III. 464,[1] 748.[1]
— Chemische Untersuchungen über das Reifen der Trauben. 1871 II. 508.[1]
— Dosage du tannin dans l'écorce du Chêne. 1872. IV. 515.[1]
— Zusammenstellungen des in Deutschland geltenden Rechts. 1880. IV. 317.[1]
— See also WOHMANN, W., NEUBAUER, C. & LOTICHIUS, C. A.
Neuberger, J. Salix daphnoides-incana mas. 1889. II. 106.[2]
Neubert, Jakob. Der Kaffee. 1838. III. 741.[2]
Neubert, Wilhelm. Abutilon insigne. 1853. III. 586.[2]
— Abutilon vexillarium. 1865. III. 587.[1]
— Allamanda violacea. 1862. III. 686.[1]
— Amygdalus Persica var. camelliaeflora. 1858. III. 439.[2]
— Amygdalus Persica var. sinensis. 1855. III. 439.[2]
— Anleitung . . . Camellien aus Stecklingen zu ziehen. 1839. III. 599.[2]
— Ueber Anpflanzung tropischer . . . Gewächse. 1872. III. 315,[2] 641.[2]
— Ardisia Olivieri. 1879. III. 666.[1]
— Aristolochia galeata. 1857. III. 386.[1]
— Aristolochia picta Karsten. 1850. II. 183.[1]
— Aucuba japonica. 1868. III. 644.[2]
— Baumsägen mit Hackmesser. 1877. III. 177.
— Beaucarnéa recurvata. 1871. III. 337.[1]
— Ueber Begonien. 1855. III. 618.[1]
— Bemerkungen über Befruchtung der Pflanzen. 1859. I. 237.
— Bemerkungen über das Pfropfen auf die Wurzel. 1848. III. 164.[1]
— Berberis aurahuacensis. 1849. II. 203.[1]
— Ueber das Beschneiden der Pflanzen. 1860. III. 170.
— Besonderes Mittel, Stecklingsreiser ausländischer Bäume zu erhalten. 1857. III. 155.

— Betrachtungen der Pflanzen und ihrer einzelnen Theile. 1865. I. 99.
— Blühende Livistonia. 1862. III. 326.[2]
— Blut-Buche und Blut-Eiche. 1876. III. 360,[2] 363.[1]
— Bouvardia Oriana. 1859. III. 711.[2]
— Browallia Jamesoni. 1850. III. 698.[2]
— Eine buntblätterige Weichselkirsche. 1868. III. 436.[1]
— Burtonia pulchella. 1849. II. 338.[1]
— Cacteen-Früchte als Stecklinge. 1871. II. 588.[2]
— Ueber Cactus grandiflorus. 1850. III. 621.[2]
— Camellia auf Prunus Laurocerasus veredelt. 1859. III. 599.[2]
— Cantua dependens. 1852. III. 694.[2]
— Cereus hybridus. 1881. III. 621.[2]
— Cereus pentalophus. 1868. III. 622.[2]
— Cereus Twediei [sic] Hook. 1851. III. 621.[1]
— Chamaecyparis Boursieri filiformis. 1878. III. 301.[1]
— Cobaea penduliflora J. D. Hook. 1870. III. 694.[2]
— Cocos Weddelliana bortul. 1879. III. 324.[2]
— Ueber Crataegus-Arten. 1854. III. 421.[1]
— Cycas revoluta, die Sago-Palme. 1861. III. 285.[1]
— Ueber Cytisus, Bohnenbaum. 1853. III. 474.[1]
— Darstellung des Verfahrens veredelter . . . Pflanzen. 1854. III. 161.
— Deutzia crenata flore pleno. 1864. III. 410.[2]
— Diervilla (Weigelia) amabilis. 1854. III. 749.[1]
— Die Douglas-Fichte. 1878. III. 309.[2]
— Dracaena Guilfoylei. 1871. III. 335.
— Dracaena lineata. 1870. III. 335.
— Dracaena regina. 1868. III. 335.
— Ueber den Einfluss des Edelreises. 1866. III. 39.
— Einladung zur Subscription auf Deutzia gracilis vera. 1851. III. 410.[1]
— Ueber das Erfrieren der Bäume. 1855. III. 182.
— Erythrina Marie Bellanger. 1862. III. 475.[2]
— Eugenia oleoides. 1856. III. 635.[1]
— Ueber die Familie der Rhododendreae. 1848. III. 656.
— Ficus elastica. 1871. III. 370.[2]
— Ficus Suringarii Witte. 1866. III. 371.[2]
— Die forçirte oder Treibveredlung. 1861. III. 161.
— Fortune's double yellow Rose. 1853. III. 455.[1]
— Zur Frage über die Säfte-Circulation. 1876. III. 165.
— Das Früchtetragen der Yucca. 1875. III. 339.[2]
— Ueber Frühlingsfröste. 1848. III. 183.[1]
— Fuchsia corymbiflora alba. 1851. III. 640.[1]
— Fuchsia macrantha Hooker. 1848. III. 640.[2]
— Grischowia hirta Karsten. 1850. II. 640.[2]
— Heidelbeere mit weisser Frucht. 1877. II. 686.[2]
— Heliotropium-Baum. 1859. III. 695.[1]
— Hexacentris mysorensis. 1853. III. 710.[2]
— Hibiscus Cameronii. 1854. III. 587.[2]
— Ein historischer Feigenbaum. 1877. II. 151.[1]
— Hoya bella. 1849. III. 693.[1]
— Hybride strauchartige Calceolaria. 1838. III. 702.[2]
— Jasminum nudiflorum. 1849. III. 673.[1]
— Lapageria rosea et alba. 1864. III. 337.[2]
— Ueber Lechenaultia-Arten. 1849. III. 754.[1]
— Leptodactylum californicum. 1860. III. 695.[1]
— Libonia floribunda. 1863. III. 709.[2]
— Ueber Luculia gratissima. 1854. III. 745.[2]
— Lyperia microphylla. 1852. III. 702.[1]
— Malus floribunda. 1865. III. 429.[1]
— Merkwürdiger Baum. 1861. II. 33.[2]
— Die Modepflanzen unserer Zeit. 1839. III. 598,[1] 618.[2]
— Nachtblühende Cacteen . . . bei Tage zum Aufblühen zu bringen. 1872. II. 590.[1]
— Neue empfehlenswerthe Pflanzen. 1871. III. 75.[1]
— Eine neue Hängetanne. 1857. III. 309.[1]
— Neue und empfehlenswerte Pflanzen. 1879. III. 690.[1]
— Ein neues Hilfsinstrument beim Okuliren. 1880. III. 164.[1]
— Neuheiten des Establissements Froebel & Comp. 1877. I. 65.[1]
— Neuzüchtungen und Einführungen. 1874. III. 429.[1]
— Opuntia Rafinesquii Engln. 1869. III. 625.[1]
— Ueber Opuntia vulgaris. 1867. III. 625.[1]
— Paeonia Moutan oder arborea. 1839. III. 392.[2]
— Ueber Palmen. 1872. II. 63,[1] 1873. III. 317.
— Ueber Panachirung. 1870. III. 181.[1]
— Passiflora amabilis. 1848. III. 615.[2]
— Passiflora Decaisneana. 1854. III. 616.[1]
— Passiflora hybrida. 1853. III. 616.[1]
— Passiflora (hybrida) Philippine. 1851. III. 616.[2]
— Ueber Passionsblumen. 1849. III. 615.[1]

Neubert, Wilhelm *(continued).*
— Ueber Paulownia imperialis. 1849, III. 703.[1]
— Pfirsichbaum mit purpurnen Blättern. 1874. III. 440.[1]
— Die Pfirsich-Mandel. 1868. III. 440.[1]
— Ueber Pflanzenveredlung. 1848. III. 160.
— Phyllocactus crenatus Vogeli. 1881. III. 625.[2]
— Pinus Strobus pendula. 1857. III. 309.[1]
— Ueber Pittosporum. 1855. III. 416.[1]
— Punica Granatum Legrellei. 1861. III. 630.[1]
— Quercus filicifolia. 1855. III. 362.[2]
— Rhododendron Sesterianum. 1872. III. 662.[1]
— Robinia inermis pyramidalis. 1857. III. 486.[2]
— Rosa Brownii. 1849. III. 456.[1]
— Rosa Regeliana. 1872. III. 456.[2]
— Rose jaune de Perse. 1851. III. 455.[2]
— Ueber Rosen. 1850. III. 448.
— Sambucus glauca. 1856. III. 751.[2]
— Schlingpflanzen strauchartig zu ziehen. 1849. III. 204.[2]
— Schutzvorrichtung für junge Bäume. 1869. III. 198.[2]
— Schwerinia superba Karsten. 1850. II. 639.[2]
— Seltene und neue Pflanzen. 1879. III. *336,[2]* 516.[1]
— Steriphoma paradoxum Endlicher. 1850. II. 233.[2]
— Sträucher mit panachirten Blättern. 1866. III. 661,[1] *670.[2]*
— Thunbergia Harrisii. 1859. III. 710.[2]
— Urania speciosa. 1859. III. 341.[2]
— Uraria picta Desv. 1856. III. 490.[1]
— Ueber das Verpflanzen erwachsener Bäume. 1873. III. 167.
— Weigelia amabilis Looymansi aurea. 1877. III. 749.[1]
— Ueber Weigelia rosea. 1852. III. 749.[1]
— Wellingtonia gigantea Lindl. 1855. II. 50.[2]
— Die .Wir^{ku}ng_en der Kälte auf die Pflanzen. 1873. III. 182.
— Ueber die Wirkungen von chemischem Dünger an Cacteen. 1880. III. 619.
— Wisteria (Glycine) macrobotrys Sieb. 1870. III. 490.[2]
— Wisteria oder Glycine sinensis. 1854. III. 490.[1]
— Ueber Yucca, Palmenlilie. 1852. III. 339.[1]
— Zauschneria californica. 1849. III. 641.[1]
— **& Jühlke,** Ferdinand. Zur Cultur der Kranberry. 1874. III. 663.[2]
— **& Tschepe,** Gottlieb. Zur Orangenbaum-Cultur. 1870. III. 499.[2]
Neubrand, Johann Georg. Die Gerbrinde. 1869. IV. 435, *518.*
— Mitteldeutschlands Schälwälder. 1869. IV. 132.[1]
— Ueber das bei Reinigungshieben zu verwendende Arbeiter-personal. 1865. IV. 173.
— Sind reine oder gemischte Eichenschälwaldungen anzu-streben? 1868. IV. 506.
Neubronn, *Freiherr von.* Das badische Gesetz vom 25. Februar 1879. 1879. IV. 317.[2]
Neuburger, Joseph. Die Obstbaumzucht. 1855. III. 137.
Neuchâtel — Société d'histoire du canton. *See* Musée neuchâtelois. I. 26.[1]
Neuchâtel — Société des sciences naturelles. *See* Société . . . I. 27.
Neue allgemeine deutsche Garten- und Blumenzeitung. III. 13.
Eine neue Art von Zwischenbau. 1863. IV. 133.
Neue Blumen-Zeitung. *See* Blumen-Zeitung. III. 11.[2]
Neue buntblätterige Ahorne. 1883. III. 533.[2]
Neue Camellia. 1886. III. 599.[1]
Neue Classification der Pfirsiche. 1897. III. 440.[1]
Eine neue Copulirscheere für Obstbäume. 1849. III. 160.
Eine neue Cycadeen-Art. 1881. III. 285.[1]
Der neue europäische Wachsbaum. 1804. III. 346.[2]
Neue Fuchsien. 1852. III. 640.[1]
Neue Garten-Pflanze. Hoya imperialis. 1847. II. 739.[2]
Eine **n** Geschichte von einem Weintrauben. 1577. II. 507.[2] eue
Eine neue Holzwollemaschine. 1891. IV. 429.
Neue hybride Dracaena. *See* New Dracaenas. 1880. III. 334.[2]
Neue Jahrbücher der Forstkunde. IV. 10.
Neue landesherrliche Verordnungen in Forst- und Jagd-Sachen. 1788. IV. 316.
Neue Malus. 1891. III. 425.[1]
Neue Maschine zum Versetzen der Bäume. 1856. III. 167.
Neue Methode das Bauholz zu verbessern. 179.? IV. 416.[2]
Neue Pflanzen. 1899. III. *309,[2]* 357.[1]
Neue Pflanzen auf den englischen Ausstellungen. 1882. III. 335, *516.[1]*

Neue Pflanzen von den Fijiinseln. 1886. I. 510.[1]
Neue Phyllocactus-Varietäten. 1874. III. 625.[2]
Eine **neue** Rosskastanien-Varietät. 1879. II. 481.[2]
Neue Solanum und ihre Cultur. 1897. III. 701.[2]
Eine **neue** Stockrodemaschine. 1860. IV. 386.
Die neue Tanne Griechenlands. 1860. II. 24.[2]
Neue Untersuchungen über Blitzschläge in Bäume. 1893. IV. 195.[1]
Neue Varietäten des Kastanienbaumes. 1873. III. 359.[1]
Eine neue Veredlungsart. 1898. III. 163.[2]
Die neue Vertikal-, Stamm- und Brettersäge-Einrichtung. 1859. IV. 392.
Eine **neue** Walnuss mit rothem Kerne. 1897. III. 355.
Eine **neue** Weisstannenart; Abies Regia Amalia. 1860. II. 24.[2]
Neue Wiener Hybriden von Abutilon. 1879. III. 587.[1]
Neue Zeitschrift für das Forst- und Jagdwesen in Baiern. *See* Zeitschrift . . . IV. 11.
Neue Zieräpfel. 1896. III. 425.[1]
Neueingeführte Pflanzen. 1862. III. 77.
Die **neuen** Anlagen des K. bot. Gartens zu Berlin. 1890. IV. 18.[2]
Neuer Zaunstrauch. 1878. III. 213.
Neuere und empfehlenswerthe Rhododendron. 1884. III. 655.
Die **neuere** wilde Baumzucht. *See* Ludwig, C. F. 1783. III. 68,[2] *IV. 81.[1]*
Neueres Forstmagazin. *See* (Neueres) Forstmagazin. IV. 8.
Die **neuen** preussischen Taxationsvorschriften in Bezug auf die Kiefernforsten. 1858. IV. 480.
Neues allgemeines Gartenmagazin. *See* Allgemeines teut-sches Garten-Magazin. III. 11.
Neues botanisches Garten-Journal. III. 13.
Ein neues Dendro-Hypsometer. 1893. IV. 216.
Neues Forst-Archiv. *See* Forst-Archiv . . . IV. 7.
Ein **neues** Garten- Baum- und Pelz-büchlein. 1797. III. 103.
Neues hannöverisches Magazin. *See* Hannöverisches . . . IV. 9.
Neues Jahrbuch für Pharmacie. *See* Jahrbuch der praktischen Pharmacie. I. 12.
Neues Journal der Pharmacie. *See* Journal der Pharmacie . . . I. 12.
Neues Magazin für die Botanik. *See* Magazin für die Bo-tanik. I. 26.
Ein **neues** Recept für die Herstellung von Bordeaux-brühe. 1900. IV. 548.[2]
Neues Repertorium für Pharmacie. *See* Repertorium . . . I. 14.
Neues. Taschenbuch für Natur- Forst- und Jagdfreunde. IV. 10.
Neues Verfahren, Stecklinge zu bilden. 1877. III. 158.
Neueste Einführung der Herren Groenewegen & Cie. 1863. I. 51.[1]
Neueste Erfindungen . . . Hooibrenk's Niederbeugungssys-tem. 1863. III. 174.[2]
Neueste Methode des Schnittes . . . der Obstbäume. *See* Du Breuil, Alphonse. 1860. III. 137.
Eine neueste Pottaschenbrennerei. 1863. IV. 395.
Neuester vollständiger Forst- und Jagd-Kalender. 1830. IV. 97.
Neuestes Garten-Jahrbuch. III. 13.
Neuestes vollständiges Gartenbuch. 1838. III. 104.
Ein **neuwes** fast hübsch . . . Pflanzbüchlin. *See* Domitzer, Johan. 1529. III. 135.
Neufchateau, Nicolas Louis, *comte* François de. *See* Fran-çois de Neufchateau, N. L., *comte.*
Neuffer, Wilhelm. Untersuchungen über die Temperatur-veränderungen der Vegetabilien. *See* Schübler, Gustav. 1829. I. 231.[2]
Neufville, J. A. von. *See* Hartig, G. L. & Neufville, J. A. von.
Neugebauer, Benjamin Ehrenfried. De corticis Chinae usu noxio. *See* Goelicke, A. O. 1729. III. 72.[2]
Neugebauer, Ludwig Adolf. De calore plantarum. 1845. I. 186.
Neuhaus, F. W. Het overplanten van den Kinaboom. 1883. III. 135.
Neuheiten aus dem Etablissement des Herrn Späth. 1879. III. 365,[1] *590.[1]*
Neuheiten des Etablissements Froebel & Comp. *See* Neu-bert, Wilhelm. 1877. I. 65.[1]
Neuhof, Wilhelm. Nothsignale praktischer Forstmänner. 1849. IV. 287.

·Ueber die neuholländischen Lasiopetala. 1856. II. 535.²
Neujahrs-Geschenk für Forst- und Jagdliebhaber. IV. 10.
Neukomm, F. Anbauversuche mit ausländischen Holzarten. 1899. IV. 127.²
— Der Schaffhauser-Wald bei Grafenhausen. 1899. IV. 367.
Neuman. See also NEWMAN.
Neuman, Carolo. De camphora. 1726. III. 233.¹
Neuman, Leopold Martin. Anteckningar angående Rubusfloram. 1885. II. 301.¹
— Berättelse om en botanisk resa till Hallands Väderö. 1883. I. 357.
— Bidrag till kännedomen af södra Norrlands flora. 1885. I. 357.
— Bidrag till Medelpads flora. 1889. I. 357.
— Botaniska anteckningar från en resa i Norge. 1896. II. 284.¹
— Botaniska anteckningar från en resa i ... Norrland. 1885. II. 308.¹
— Botaniska anteckningar från norra Tyskland. 1894. I. 389.
— Om Rubus corylifolius Arrh. 1887. II. 301.¹
— Studier öfver Skånes och Hallands flora. 1882. II. 309.¹
— Om tvenne Rubi från mellersta Halland. 1888. II. 301.²
Neumann. Châtaignier de la Nouvelle-Hollande. 1852. III. 471.²
— Deuxième floraison du Castanosperme. 1851. III. 471.¹
— Floraison du Gardénie de Stanley. 1849. III. 747.¹
— Lapageria rosea. 1853. III. 337.²
— Nachricht über eine neue Art, lebende Pflanzen ... auf langen Seereisen zu transportiren. 1837. III. 155.
— Note sur la Passiflora edulis. 1839. III. 616.¹
— Note sur le Dracaena Draco Lin. 1852. III. 336.²
— Nouveau moyen de transporter des plantes vivantes. 1837. III. 155.
— Sur la Rose dite de l'Île Bourbon. 1853. III. 454.²
— Weigelie à fleurs roses, Weigelia rosea. 1849. III. 749.¹
Neumann, (Apotheker). Ueber eine noch unbeschriebene Pinus. 1838. II. 43.¹
Neumann, (Bataillons-Arzt, Erfurt). Syrenernes Kultur. 1842. III. 680.¹
— Syringa, Flieder, Lilac. 1842. III. 680.¹
Neumann, (Oberförster, Grünfelde). Ueber Eichenanbau. 1885. IV. 507.
— Fichten-Enthusiasmus. 1878. IV. 453.
— Das Grünfelder Aufastungseisen. 1885. IV. 172.¹
— Warum misslingen unsere Kulturen? 1883. IV. 287.
— Was ist die Kiefer? 1890. IV. 473.
Neumann, Auguste. Abies taxifolia pendula. 1852. III. 309.²
— Aphelandra fulgens Decaisne. 1847. III. 708.²
— Bignone à grandes fleurs. 1845. III. 705.
— Bignonia Cherere. 1845. III. 707.¹
— Brugmansia candida. 1845. III. 700.¹
— Buddleia Lindleyana. 1846. III. 681.²
— Calotropis géant. 1845. III. 692.¹
— Sur le Cèdre de l'Atlas. 1845. III. 299.²
— Cestrum à fleurs roses. 1845. III. 699.²
— Chalef à rameaux réfléchis. 1843. III. 629.¹
— Chêne phénoménal. 1845. II. 138.¹
— Clérodendron à fleurs éclatantes. 1845. III. 696.²
— Coleonema pulchrum. 1845. III. 503.¹
— Columnea crassifolia. 1845. III. 708.¹
— Culture de l'Aristolochia labiosa. 1839. III. 386.¹
— Culture du Manguier. 1842. III. 524.²
— Culture du Paulownia imperialis. 1843. III. 703.¹
— Culture et multiplication du Stephanotis. 1839. III. 694.¹
— Description du Galphimia hirsuta. 1847. III. 513.²
— Diplolaena speciosa. 1845. III. 504.¹
— Effet singulier d'une greffe de Rosier. 1845. III. 164.²
— Elaeagnus reflexa. 1842. III. 629.¹
— Emploi de la greffe pour guérir les Daphnés Lauréoles malades. 1845. III. 627.²
— Érable à feuilles panachées. 1849. III. 535.¹
— Eugenia brasiliensis. 1845. III. 635.¹
— Fleuraison de branches de Bignonia Catalpa. 1847. II. 787.¹
— Fleuraison du Paulownia. 1842. III. 703.¹
— Floraison à Paris du Charlwoodia australis. 1839. III. 334.²
— Floraison d'un Cactus grandiflorus. 1847. III. 621.²
— Floraison du Livistonia sinensis. 1857. III. 326.²
— Floraison du Paulownia imperialis. 1842. III. 703.¹
— Floraison singulière d'une branche do Bignonia Catalpa. 1847. II. 787.¹

— Fructification du Litchi. 1849. III. 539.²
— Sur le fruit comestible des Passiflora. 1845. III. 616.²
— Fuchsia exoniensis. 1845. III. 640.¹
— Fuchsia serratifolia. 1845. III. 640.²
— Galipea macrophylla. 1845. III. 503.²
— Gerardia furcata. 1845. III. 702.² ·
— Gleditschia pleureur. 1845. III. 477.² ·
— Greffe Dammara. 1842. III. 297.² .
— Habrotamne élégant. 1845. III. 699.²
— Habrothamne fasciculé. 1845. III. 699.²
— Sur l'histoire du Sophora japonica. 1845. III. 488.¹
— How to strike cuttings. 1844. III. 157.
— De l'impossibilité de la naturalisation des végétaux. 1845. III. 43.
— Sur l'introduction du Cedrus Deodora. 1856. III. 300.¹
— Ipomaea Horsfalliae Hook. 1839. II. 745.²
— Jacaranda mimosaefolia. 1845. III. 706.²
— Jasmin nudiflore. 1852. III. 673.¹
— Juanulloa à fleurs orangées. 1845. III. 700.²
— Kunst der Pflanzenvermehrung. 1845. III. 152.
— Die Kunst Stecklinge zu machen. 1844. III. 157.
— Laurencellia rosea. 1845. III. 755.²
— Lemonia remarquable. 1845. III. 505.²
— Lonicera Ledebourii D. S. 1843. III. 750.²
— Manière avantageuse de faire des boutures. 1842. III. 157.
— Marronnier à fleurs doubles. 1845. III. 537.¹
— Morelle à grosses anthères. 1845. III. 702.¹
— Moyen de multiplier le Dammara orientalis. 1841. III. 297.²
— Multiplication du Cycas circinalis. 1838. III. 285.¹
— Multiplication du Tamarix elegans. 1843. III. 612.¹
— Myrica esculenta Ham. 1849. III. 353.²
— Napoléone d'Heudelot. 1852. II. 612.²
— De la naturalisation ... de l'Araucaria imbricata. 1839. III. 298.²
— Neue Pflanzen, welche im Museum zu Paris geblüht haben. 1847. I. 58.
— Note sur de nouvelles Passiflores. 1845. III. 615.²
— Note sur deux Cycadées. 1846. III. 284.¹
— Note sur la fructification du Thé. 1846. III. 600.¹
— Note sur la première floraison du Freycinetia insignis. 1858. III. 313.¹
— Note sur la première fructification du Cryptomeria. 1850. III. 301.²
— Note sur le Celastrus mollis. 1845. III. 531.¹
— Note sur le Tilia argentea. 1853. III. 586.¹
— Note sur les végétaux à l'essai au Muséum. 1845. III. 47.
— Note sur quelques Conifères nouveaux. 1852. III. 289.
— Note sur quelques plantes nouvelles. 1847. I. 58.
— Note sur un Abies taxifolia F. Neumannii. 1852. III. 309.¹
— Note sur un arbre ... regardé comme le Paulownia. 1839. III. 703.¹
— Note sur une nouvelle variété de Fagus. 1852. III. 360.²
— Notice tendant à démontrer que la naturalisation des végétaux est impossible. 1845. III. 43.
— Notions sur l'art de faire les boutures. 1844. III. 157.
— Nouveau Pilocereus, ou Cereus D.C. 1845. II. 598.²
— Nouveau procédé pour opérer les boutures. 1845. III. 158.
— Une nouvelle espèce de Luculia. 1845. III. 745.²
— Nouvelle variété de Hêtre à feuilles blanches. 1852. III. · 360.²
— Oxyanthe à longues fleurs. 1845. III. 746.²
— Palmiers qui ... ont fleuri dans les serres du Muséum. 1852. III. 316.²
— Passiflora alato-coerulea. 1845. III. 615.²
— Passiflora kermesina var. Lemichesiana. 1845. III. 616.¹
— Pavetta australis. 1845. III. 746.¹
— Sur le périsperme et les cotylédons. 1847. I. 202.²
— Pinus silvestris Bujoti. 1853. III. 309.¹
— Plante nouvelle dans nos cultures. 1839. III. 410.²
— Podocarpus macrophylla var. Maki. 1848. III. 287.²
— Polygala de Dalmais. 1845. III. 514.¹
— Porphyrocoma à feuilles lancéolées. 1846. III. 710.¹
— Première floraison, en France, du Stadmane. 1851. III. 539.¹
— Sauge à calice laineux. 1845. III. 698.²
— Saurauja spectabilis. 1845. III. 596.¹
— Stadmannia australis. 1845. III. 539.¹
— Sur la végétation des arbres fruitiers ... en Algérie. 1844. III. 147.¹

Neumann, Auguste (*continued*).
— Végétation extraordinaire de la Glycine de la Chine. 1845. III. 490.[3]
— Vermehrung der Araucaria Cunninghami. 1845. III. 298.[1]
— Véronique éclatante, Veronica speciosa. 1845. III. 704.[2]
— *See also* POITEAU, Antoine & NEUMANN, Auguste.
— & **Poiteau,** Antoine. Notice sur le genre de bouture insolite. 1840. III. 157.
Neumann, Caspar. Lectiones publicæ von vier subjectis diæteticis. 1735. III. 222.
Neumann, F. H. Over schildluizen in Koffieplantsoenen. 1899. III. 737.
— Vijanden der Koffiecultuur. 1897. III. 736.
— Zal de Java-Koffiecultuur door nematoden te gronde gaan. 1899. III. 737.
Neumann, J. Gleditschia triacanthos. 1885. III. 477.[2]
Neumann, Louis. Cladrastis tinctoria. 1885. III. 472.[2]
— Crotalaria arborescens. 1868. III. 473.[1]
— Dragonnier à feuilles zébrées. 1877. III. 336.[2]
— Goodia latifolia. 1864. III. 473.[1]
— Holboellia latifolia. 1877. III. 393.[2]
— Hydrangea Otaksa. 1868. III. 411.[2]
— Leschenaultia splendens. 1864. III. 754.[1]
— Linum trigynum. 1864. III. 492.[1] — 1867. III. 492.[1]
— Monochaetum Naudinianum. 1861. III. 639.[1]
— Note sur l'Holboellia latifolia. 1863. III. 393.[2]
— Note sur la culture . . . des Luculia. 1861. III. 745.[2]
— Nouvelles variétés de Robinia. 1857. III. 486.[2]
— Poinsettia pulcherrima. 1864. III. 518.[1]
— Polymnia pyramidalis. 1867. III. 756.[2]
— Sur le Rhododendron Keysii. 1866. II. 681.[1]
— Solanum sisymbriifolium. 1869. III. 702.[1]
— & **Hérincq,** François. Jasminum nudiflorum. 1852. III. 673.[1]
Neumann, Ludwig. Die Pflanzen- und Tierverbreitung. 1895. I. 350.[1]
— Die Pflanzenwelt Europas. 1895. I. 350.[1]
— *See also* PHILIPPSON, Alfred & NEUMANN, Ludwig.
Neumann, Otto. Anbefalelsesværdige Bouvardier. 1885. III. 711.[1]
— Empfehlenswerthe Bouvardien. 1885. III. 711.[1]
— Ravenea Hildebrandti C. Bouché. 1878. III. 330.[2]
Neumann, R. Der Eibenbaum in Rathmannsdorf. 1900. II. 11.[2]
Neumeister, Max Heinrich August. Altersklassenverhältniss und Umtrieb. 1880. IV. 252.
— Die Bedeutung uhd Bildung der Hiebszüge. 1883. IV. 244.
— Der Drehwuchs der Rosskastanie. 1884. II. 482.[2]
— Forst- und Forstbetriebs-Einrichtung. 1888. IV. 241.
— Die Forsteinrichtung der Zukunft. 1900. IV. 247.[1]
— Forstliches Hilfsbuch für Schule und Praxis. 1888. IV. 241.
— Gebrauchsanweisung zum Pressler-Neumeister'schen Zuwachsbohrer. 1898. IV. 235.[1]
— Mittheilungen über eine Borkenkäferkalamität. 1871. IV. 204.
— Saat und Pflanzung bei der Fichte. 1889. IV. 454.
— Untersuchungen über den Einfluss des Tiefabschnitts bei der Baumrodung. 1884. IV. 218.
— Der verbesserte Pressler'sche Zuwachsbohrer. 1888. IV. 234.
— Die Versicherung der fiskalischen Waldarbeiter in Sachsen. 1888. IV. 311.[1]
— Wichtigkeit des Birkenanflugs. 1885. IV. 490.[1]
— Wie wird man ein Forstwirth? 1887. IV. 29.
Neumeister, R. Sur la présence . . . de ferments pepsiques. 1895. I. 177.
Neuner, Fr. Bemerkungen über die Vermehrung des Calycanthus. 1839. III. 401.[1]
Neunes, Christ. S. A. De cortice peruviano. 1789. III. 720.
Neunheuser, F. de. Sur la cicatrisation des plaies d'arbres. 1850. III. 180.[1]
Neunheuser, F. de. Quelques considérations sur l'Épicéa dans la Fagnenne. 1898. IV. 460.[2]
Neunhof, P. C. *Freiherr* WELSER VON. *See* WELSER VON NEUNHOF, P. C. *Freiherr*.
Neureuter, Ferdinand. Dracaena Draco . . . in Tanger. 1886. II. 82.[2]
Neuseeländische Veronica-Arten. *See* NEW ZEALAND Speedwells. 1885. III. 704.[1]
Neuumschreibung des Kantons in drei Forstkreise. 1879. IV. 306.

Neuvoja metsänkylvössä ja-istutuksessa. 1891. IV. 104.[2]
Neuvorpommern — Naturwissenschaftlicher Verein. *See* NATURWISSENSCHAFTLICHER . . . I. 14.
Neuwied, M. A. P., *Fürst* von WIED-. *See* WIED-NEUWIED, M. A. P., *Fürst* von.
Nevada — Agricultural experiment station. Annual report. Bulletin. III. 6.
Nevada — State university — Agricultural experiment station. *See* NEVADA — AGRICULTURAL EXPERIMENT STATION. III. 6.
Nève, Léon. Du défrichement . . . en Campine. 1900. IV. 161.[1] *274.[2]
Nevianus, Marcus. De plantarum viribus poëmatium. 1563. III. 239.
Neville-Rolfe, E. *See* ROLFE, E. NEVILLE-.
Nevinny, Josef. Additamenta zur Pharmacopœa austriaca. 1900. III. 256.[2]
Nevins, John Birkbeck. The history of the introduction of Peruvian bark trees. 188. ? III. 714.
— On the introduction of . . . Cinchona in India. 1863. III. 713.[2]
— Introduction of the Cinchona plant. 1897. III. 715.
New, William. Catalogue of plants in the Public garden, Bangalore. 1861. I. 67.[1]
— List of plants growing in the Bangalore garden, Mysore. 1861. I. 67.[1]
New Abutilons. 1881. III. 586.[2]
The **new** American dispensatory. 1839. III. 246.
New and rare plants. 1850. III. 82.
New and singular Chinese Peaches. 1847. III. 439.[2]
A **new** Bamboo. 1890. III. 316.[1]
A **new** Brazil wood. 1896. IV. 521.[1]
The **new** British dispensatory. 1781. III. 253.
A **new** budding knife. 1895. III. 164.[2]
New Canadian dye. 1861. III. 305.[1]
The **new** Chinese Weeping Lilac. 1888. III. 681.[1]
New coniferous trees. 1855. II. 38.[2]
New Crotons. 1871. III. 515.[1]
New cyclopaedia of botany. 1868. III. 82.
The **new** Cypress of Nyasaland. 1894. II. 27.[1]
The **new** Dehra Dún forest school rules. 1893. IV. 37.[1]
The **new** dispensatory. *See* LEWIS, William. 1753. III. 252.
A **new** double Poinsettia. 1873. III. 518.[1]
New double Poinsettia. 1876. III. 518.[1]
New Dracaenas. 1880. III. 334.[2]
New dwarf Almonds. 1872. III. 438.[2]
A **new** edible Palm. 1876. III. 322.[1]
New England botanical club. Journal. *See* RHODORA. I. 6.
New England farmer. III. 6.
N w England homestead. *See* AMERICAN agriculturist. III. 2.
New England magazine. *See* BAY STATE monthly. III. 3.
A **new** Euonymus. 1883. III. 533.[1]
New False Acacias. 1876. III. 487.[1]
A **new** febrifuge bark. 1820. III. 704.[1]
A **new** forest law in Russia. 1888. IV. 180.[1]
New forest reservations. 1897. IV. 179.[1]
The **new** forest reserves. 1897. IV. 179.[1]
The **new** forestry law of Massachusetts. 1883. IV. 314.[1]
A **new** fruit. 1889. III. 636.
New fruit at Christmas. 1895. III. 322,[2] *614.[2]
New garden plants. *See* HENFREY, Arthur & others. 1852. III. 82.
New garden plants. 1888. III. 83.
New Hampshire — Agricultural experiment station. *See* NEW HAMPSHIRE — COLLEGE OF AGRICULTURE AND THE MECHANIC ARTS . . . III. 6.
New Hampshire — College of agriculture and the mechanic arts — Agricultural experiment station. Annual report. Bulletin. III. 6.
New Hampshire — Forestry commission. Annual report. Biennial report. . Report. IV. 4.
New Hampshire agriculture. III. 6.
A **new** hardy Papaw. 1887. III. 6.
A **new** hardy shrub. 1875. III. 540.[2]
New hardy shrub. 1880. III. 429.[2]
New homœopathic pharmacopœia & posology. 1850. III.
A **new** hybrid Rose. 1891. III. 456.[1] — 1893. III. 457.[1]
A **new** indiarubber tree. 1893. III. 689.[1]
A **new** industry; a new use for hardwood. 1899. IV. 427.[1]
New Japan Pear. 1875. III. 447.[1]

A new Japanese tree. 1878. III. 670.²
New Jersey — Agricultural college experiment station.
Annual report. III. 6.
New Jersey — Agricultural college experiment station. —
Botanical department. Report. III. 6.
New Jersey — Agricultural experiment station. Bulletin.
Special bulletin. III. 6.
New Jersey — Geological survey. Annual report. Final
report. I. 6, IV. 4.
New Jersey — State agricultural experiment station. An-
nual report. III. 6.
New Jersey agricultural exhibit. List of woods. 1876. IV.
76.²
New Jersey forester. See FORESTER. IV. 4.
New Jersey natural history society. Journal. See TRENTON
NATURAL HISTORY SOCIETY. I. 7.¹
New locality for Prostanthera empetrifolia. 1894. II. 765:¹
New Macrozamias. 1883. III. 285.²
A new Magnolia. 1875. III. 399.¹
A new medicinal, economical and domestic herbal. 1808. III.
80.
The new medico-chirurgical pharmacopoeia. 1822. III.
758.¹
New method of clearing ground of trees. 1874. IV. 383.²
New method of impregnating timber with zinc chloride. 1892.
IV. 421.
A new Mexican Cycad. 1883. II. 5.²
New Mexico — Agricultural experiment station. See NEW
MEXICO — COLLEGE OF AGRICULTURE AND MECHANIC ARTS
. . . III. 6.
New Mexico — College of agriculture and mechanic arts —
Agricultural experiment station. Annual report. Bulletin.
III. 6.
New Mistletoe. 1871. II. 174.¹
New Mountain Aralia. 1886. III. 643.²
A new Oak. 1841. II. 140.¹
New Orleans medical and surgical journal. I. 6.
New ornamental Peach. 1872. III. 436.²
The new pharmacopoeia of the Royal college of physicians.
See PHARMACOPŒIA londinensis. 1618. III. 250.²
New pictorial library. See LEGENDS respecting trees. 1847.
I. 517.¹
New plants. 1850. III. 504.¹
New plants at Mr. Bull's. 1883. III. 643.²
New plants, etc. from the Society's garden. See LINDLEY,
John. 1846. I. 54.
A new poison. 1873. III. 690.¹
A new process for preserving wood. 1866. IV. 419.
New process for recovering loss of gutta percha. 1891. III.
231.
New races of Crotons. 1876. III. 515.¹
New remedies. See AMERICAN druggist . . . I. 4.²
New review. III. 17.
A new Rose (Rosa Pissarti). 1882. III. 456.¹
New rubber industry in Lagos. 1895. III. 688.²
New South Wales — Agricultural gazette. See AGRICUL-
TURAL . . . III. 27.¹
New South Wales — Botanic gardens. Report. 1850. I. 69.¹
New South Wales — Department of agriculture and forests.
Report. See NEW SOUTH WALES — FOREST BRANCH . . . IV.
17.¹
New South Wales — Department of mines and agriculture —
Agriculture and forestry. Report. See NEW SOUTH WALES
— FOREST BRANCH . . . IV. 17.¹
New South Wales — Forest branch — Department of mines.
Annual report. IV. 17.¹
New South Wales — Forest conservancy branch. Report.
See NEW SOUTH WALES — FOREST BRANCH . . . IV. 17.¹
New South Wales — Linnean society. See LINNEAN . . .
I. 29.¹
New South Wales — Philosophical society. See PHILOSO-
PHICAL . . . I. 29.²
New South Wales — Royal society. See PHILOSOPHICAL
SOCIETY OF NEW SOUTH WALES. I. 29.¹
New South Wales — State forest administration. Annual
progress report. See NEW SOUTH WALES — FOREST BRANCH
. . . IV. 17.¹
New species of Eucalyptus. 1899. IV. 532.¹
A new stimulant. 1861. III. 492.²
A new "Tallow tree." 1898. III. 403.¹
New theory of vegetable physiology. 1848. I. 147, 231.¹
A new translation of the Pharmacopoeia of the Royal college
of physicians. See PHARMACOPŒIA londinensis. 1618. III.
250.¹

A new treatise on the art of grafting. 1780. III. 159.¹
A new tree pruner. 1879. III. 170.
A new use for the wood of Herminiera. 1880. III. 466.¹
The new vegetable giant. 1854. II. 50.²
A new view of jardinage. 1889. IV. 131.
A new Walnut. 1888. III. 354.²
A new Wellingtonia gigantea. 1871. II. 51.¹
The new white Hydrangea. 1879. III. 411.²
New York — Agricultural experiment station. Annual re-
port. Bulletin. III. 6.
New York — American institute. Annual report. See
AMERICAN . . . III. 2.
New York — Commissioners of fisheries, game and forests.
Annual report. Preliminary report. IV. 4.
New York — Cornell university — Agricultural experiment
station. Annual report. Bulletin. III. 6.
New York — Forest preserve board. Annual report. IV. 4.
New York — Lyceum of natural history. See LYCEUM . . .
I. 6.
New York — Society instituted in the state for the promotion
of agriculture. See SOCIETY . . . III. 8.
New York academy of sciences. Annals. Transactions. I.
519.¹
New York botanical garden. Bulletin. 1896. I. 39, 519.¹
New York botanical garden. Contributions. Journal.
Memoirs. I. 6.
New York historical society. Collections. I. 6.
New York horticultural society. Monthly report. III. 7.
New York journal of medicine. I. 6.
New York lumber trade journal. IV. 4.
New York medical journal. I. 6.
New York microscopical society. Journal. I. 6.
New York quarterly. I. 6.
New York state agricultural society. Annual report. Trans-
actions. III. 7.
New York state cabinet of natural history. Annual report.
Bulletin. 1848. I. 38.²
New York state college of forestry, Cornell university.
Announcement. Annual report. Bulletin. IV. 4.
New York state forest commission. Annual report. Special
report. IV. 4.
New York state museum. Bulletin. I. 6.
New York state museum of natural history. Annual report.
See NEW YORK STATE CABINET . . . 1848. I. 38.²
New Zealand contributions to Museum. 1894. III. 287.²
New Zealand country journal. III. 27.¹
New Zealand department of agriculture. Leaflets. III. 27.¹
New Zealand institute. Transactions. I. 29.¹
New Zealand journal of science. I. 520.²
New Zealand Speedwells. 1885. III. 704.¹
Newald, Johann. Zur Geschichte der Cameral-Taxations-
Methode. 1881. IV. 257.
— Wer ist der Eigenthümer des Wienerwald-Forstamtes.
1873. IV. 28.¹
— & Grossbauer, Franz. Eine forstliche Studienreise auf
den . . . Domänen Teschen. 1875. IV. 369.
Newberry, John Strong. Botanical report [of the routes in
California and Oregon]. 1857. I. 323.
— Catalogue of the flowering plants . . . of Ohio. 1860. I.
314.
— Descriptions of the forest trees of northern California.
1857. I. 320, IV. 77.²
— Food and fiber plants of the North American Indians.
1887. III. 261.¹
— On the forest trees . . . line of the northern Pacific railroad.
1884. I. 320, IV. 78.¹
— Notes on the geology and botany of . . . Northern Pacific
Railroad. 1883. I. 324.
— Pinus edulis and P. monophylla. 1885. II. 42.¹
— Pinus monophylla and Pinus edulis. 1886. II. 42.²
— The relations of Pinus edulis and P. monophylla. 1885.
II. 42.¹
Newbold, T. J. Description of the valley of Sondur. 1838.
I. 472.
— On the ipoh or upas poison. 1837. III. 366.²
— Political and statistical account of the British settlements
in the Straits of Malacca. 1839. I. 464.²
— Some account . . . of the ceded districts. 1839. I. 472.
Newby, Thomas T. Of the sexes in Chestnut trees. 1885.
II. 123.²
Newcastle-upon-Tyne — Natural history society of North-
umberland . . . See NATURAL . . . I. 19.
Newcombe, Frederick C. Regulatory growth of mechanical
tissue. 1895. I. 134.²

Newe Vorst Ordnung [vom 22. April 1540 vom Herzog Ulrich zu Wirtemberg]. 1540. IV. 322.¹
Newe Vorstordnung des Fürstenthumbs Würtemberg. *See* NEWE Vorst Ordnung vom 22. April 1540. 1540. IV. 322.¹
Newell, Frederick H. The national forest reserves. 1897. IV. 179.¹
Newell, Jane H. The flowers of the Horse Chestnut. 1893. II. 482.¹
— Outlines of lessons in botany. 1889. I. 96.
— A reader in botany. 1889. I. 96.
Newfoundland as a timber country. 1886. IV. 403.¹
Newhall, Charles Stedman. The leaf-collector's hand-book and herbarium. 1891. I. 312.
— The shrubs of northeastern America. 1893. I. 312, *IV.* 77.¹
— The trees of northeastern America. 1890. I. 312, *IV.* 77.¹
— The vines of northeastern America. 1897. I. 316.
Newman. *See also* NEUMAN.
Newman, Edward. Autumnal flowering of trees and shrubs. 1846. I. 220.³
— Occurrence of Erica ciliaris in ... Galway. 1846. II. 665.³
Newman, F. W. Catalogue of plants in the Royal society's gardens, Queen's Park, Hobart Town. 1857. I. 89.¹
Newman, John B. Boudoir botany. 185.? I. 95.
— Flora; or, Outlines of botany. 1848. I. 95.
— Illustrated botany. 1850. I. 95.
Newport, Howard. Coffee culture in Queensland. 1899. III. 733.¹
— Coffee, the poor man's crop. 1900. III. 728.¹
— The root-growth of Coffee plants. 1900. III. 728.¹
— *See also* THOMATIS, D. & NEWPORT, Howard.
Newton. On the thinning and pruning of plantations. 1843. IV. 170.¹
Newton, G. W. A treatise on the growth ... of timber trees. 1859. IV. 120.
Newton, James. A compleat herbal. 1752. I. 291.
— Enchiridion universale plantarum. 1689. I. 288.
Newton, Joseph. Decorative trees and shrubs. 1870. III. 78.³
— Large Tulip tree. 1886. II. 211.¹
Newton, Robert P. On the diseases of the Larch. 1847. IV. 450.
Ney, Carl Eduard. Aus alten Waldordnungen. 1887. IV. 26.
— Ueber den Einfluss des Waldes auf das Klima. 1886. IV. 54.
— L'exploitation systématique des forêts. 1886. IV. 382.¹
— Forst- unndt Waldordnung der Pfaltzgraveschafft bey Rhein. 1884. IV. 317.³
— Forststatistisches aus Elsass-Lothringen. 1886. IV. 349.³
— Die forstwirthschaftlichen Verhältnisse Elsass-Lothringens. 1898. IV. 349.³
— Geschichte des heiligen Forstes bei Hagenau. 1888. IV. 26.
— Die Lehre vom Waldbau. 1885. IV. 107.¹
— Ueber den Preis des Holzes. 1880. IV. 403.¹
— Die Schablonenwirthschaft im Walde. 1886. IV. 124,¹ 130.
— Unholz und unschädlich Holz. 1887. IV. 23.³
— Ueber die verschiedenen Arten der Femelwirthschaft. 1881. IV. 139.³
— Die Versteigerung des Holzes. 1879. IV. 388.¹
— Die Vertilgung des Adlerfarrens. 1880. IV. 210.³
— Der Wald und die Quellen. 1893. IV. 51.
— Ueber den Widerstreit von Einzel- und Gesammtinteresse in der Forstwirthschaft. 1883. IV. 270.
— Die Wirthschaft des höchsten gesammtwirthschaftlichen Bodenerwartungswerthes. 1879. IV. 256.
Ney, Eduard. Ueber die Bedeutung des Waldes. 1870. IV. 44.
— Ueber den Einfluss des Waldes. 1875. IV. 44.
— Die natürliche Bestimmung des Waldes und die Streunutzung. 1869. IV. 71.
Neygenfind, Friedrich Wilhelm. Enchiridium botanicum, continens plantas Silesiae. 1821. I. 376.
— Kalender der schlesischen Flora. 1822. I. 224.³
Neyraut, Jean Edmund. Sur la découverte dans la Gironde de l'Erica Watsoni. 1900. II. 664.³
Ngai Camphor. 1893. III. 754.³
Niaudet, Victor. Des pépinières, semis et plantations. 1839. III. 154.¹
Nibbelink. De berkenbladwesp. 1880. IV. 490.³
— Nog eens de berken-bladwesp. 1881. IV. 490.³
— Wanneer moet men boomen verplanten? 1884. III. 169.¹
— & others. De kaspische Zandwilg. 1883. III. 348.

Niblaeus, Johan Erik. Dissertatio de Brunia. 1804. III. 416.³
Nice — Société centrale d'agriculture, d'horticulture et d'acclimatation. *See* SOCIÉTÉ ... III. 20.
Nicéville, Lionel de. Branching Palms and Tree-Ferns. 1891. II. 63.¹
Nicholls, Frank. An account of the veins ... of leaves. 1731. I. 109.¹
Nicholls, Henry Alfred Alford. On the cultivation of Liberian Coffee. 1881. III. 742.³
— The cultivation of Liberian Coffee. 1884. III. 742.³
— De cultuur van de Liberia-Koffie. 1881. III. 742.³
— Dominica. 1888. III. 267.¹
— An elementary text book of tropical agriculture. 1891. III. 96.¹
— Koffie. 1893. III. 727.
— The Lime industry in Dominica. 1883. III. 502.¹
— Petit traité d'agriculture tropicale. 1891. III. 96.¹
Nicholls, Jasper G. The flowering of Bamboos. 1893. II. 59.³
— The flowering of the Thorny Bamboo. 1896. II. 59.³
— Notes on the flowering of the Katang Bamboo. 1886. II. 59.³
Nichols, E. Physiological effects of severe frost on trees. 1847. III. 182.
Nichols, J. R. The sweet principle of fruits. 1883. I. 176.
Nichols, Susie Percival. *See* ROWLEE, W. W. & NICHOLS, S. P.
Nichols, Thomas. Observations on the propagation ... of Oak trees. 1791. IV. 504.
— *See also* НИКОЛЬСЪ, T.
Nicholson, G. Camoensia maxima. 1881. III. 469.³
Nicholson, George. Aegle sepiaria. 1900. III. 503.¹
— The Ailanto, or Tree of heaven. 1883. III. 507.¹
— Azalea obtusa. 1886. III. 660.¹
— The Barberries. 1889. III. 394.¹
— Berberis Lycium. 1889. III. 395.¹
— The Black Walnut. 1882. IV. 488.¹
— Caesalpinia japonica. 1888. III. 469.¹
— The Catalpas. 1884. III. 705.
— Cistus ladaniferus maculatus. 1886. III. 612.³
— Cladrastis amurensis. 1883. III. 472.³
— Clerodendron trichotomum. 1893. III. 696.³
— Conifers as specimen trees. 1892. III. 291.
— Cook's Araucaria. 1885. II. 26.¹
— Crataegus flava. 1900. II. 261.³
— Development of heat in flowers of Phytelephas. 1881. II. 73.³
— Dictionnaire pratique d'horticulture et de jardinage. 1885. III. 31.
— The double Spanish Broom. 1884. III. 488.³
— Elaeagnus parvifolia. 1892. III. 628.³
— Escallonia Sellowiana. 1883. III. 411.¹
— Flowering trees and shrubs. 1894. III. 207.³
— Gelbe Rosen. 1885. III. 450.
— The genus Cercis. 1884. III. 472.¹
— Giant Arbor-Vitae and White Cedar. 1886. II. 33,³ 52.³
— Hand-list of trees ... grown in Arboretum. *See* HAND-LIST ... 1894. I. 55, *III.* 78.³
— The Holly-leaved Cherry. 1885. III. 437.¹
— The Hop Hornbeams. 1883. III. 358.¹
— The Hornbeams. 1883. III. 357.³
— Horticulture and arboriculture in the United States. 1894. III. 117.¹
— Hydrangea hortensis var. Lindleyana. 1894. III. 411.³
— The illustrated dictionary of gardening. 1885. III. 31.
— The Juneberries. 1892. III. 419.³
— The Kentucky Coffee tree. 1883. III. 478.¹
— The Kew arboretum. 1888. I. 55.
— The Laburnums. 1884. III. 480.¹
— Large-fruited Hawthorns. 1885. III. 421.³
— Magnolia Soulangeana nigra. 1884. III. 400.¹
— The Magnolias. 1883. III. 399.¹ — 1895. III. 399.¹
— The Maples. 1881. III. 533.³
— New hardy evergreen shrub. 1883. III. 680.¹
— New Japanese Oak (Quercus serrata). 1885. III. 363.¹
— A new shrub. 1884. III. 523.¹
— The Oaks. 1882. III. 361.¹
— The origin of the double-flowered Horse-Chestnut. 1889. III. 537.³
— Philadelphus microphyllus Gray. 1887. III. 413.³
— Phillyrea decora. 1888. III. 680.¹
— Pinus aizachuite. 1884. III. 306.¹
— Prunus triloba. 1885. III. 443.³
— Quelques mots sur le Bucklandia populnea. 1880. III. 416.¹

— A rare Mexican-shrub. 1885. III. 425.[1]
— Rhododendron catawbiense at home. 1893. II. 678.[1]
— The Rock Roses. 1884. III. 612.[2]
— Rosa Riparti Déséglise, in Britain. 1886. II. 298.[1]
— The Soap-tree of the Chinese. 1889. III. 478.[1]
— The Sophoras. 1883. III. 487.[2]
— Specimen trees in Kew gardens. 1888. I. 55.
— Spiraea media var. rotundifolia. 1885. III. 461.[1]
— Stuartia Pseudocamellia. 1888. III. 597.[1]
— The Stuartias. 1893. III. 596.[2]
— The Sweet Gums. 1883. III. 417.[2]
— Theophrasta Jussiaei. 1887. III. 665.[2]
— The Turkey Oaks. 1885. III. 362.[1]
— The Umbrella Pine. 1885. III. 309.[2]
— The Whahoo, or Winged Elm. 1896. III. 365.[1]
— The White Birch and its varieties. 1884. III. 357.[1]
— The winter of 1880–81 at Kew. 1881. III. 47.
— Yellow Roses. 1885. III. 450.
— The Yellow Wood. 1883. III. 472.[2]
— The Zelkowas. 1883. III. 366.[1]
— The Zenobias. 1883. III. 664.[2]
Nicholson, Henry. Methodus plantarum. 1712. I. 289.
Nicholson's journal. See JOURNAL of natural philosophy. I. 18.
Nickel, Emil. Bemerkungen über die Farbenreaktion ... des Holzes. 1889. I. 37.[1]
Nickell, J. M. Botanical ready reference. 1881. III. 243.
Nickells, Benjamin. Caoutchouc, or india-rubber. 1861. III. 229.
Nickels, C. Cultur, Benennung ... der Rosen. 1836. III. 448.
Nickels, C. The gardener's note book. 1878. III. 400.[1]
— Note on the propagation of Magnolia grandiflora. 1878. III. 400.[1]
Nickerson, B. R. & others. Preservation of wood. 1871. IV. 419.
Nickerson, M. H. The tree to plant and its care. 1895. III. 166.
Nicklès, Adrien. Le Maté. 1889. III. 531.[1]
Nicklès, Jérôme. Sur la matière colorante du Troëne. 1859. III. 674.[1]
Nicklès, Napoléon. Coup d'œil sur la végétation ... de Schlestadt. 1876. I. 387.
Nico, P. Determinación de la masa leñosa. 1878. IV. 217.
— Sulla determinazione della massa legnosa. 1878. IV. 217.
— Reglas para calcular la edad de los árboles. 1882. IV. 235.[1]
— Regole per calcolare l' età degli alberi. 1882. IV. 235.[1]
— Lo strumento universale di Ertel. 1881. IV. 265.
Nicol, Walter. The forcing, fruit and kitchen gardener. 1797. III. 176.[1]
— Over het planten van woudboomen. 1803. IV. 119.[1]
— The planter's kalendar. 1812. III. 109, IV. 108.[1]
— Practical planter. 1799. IV. 108,[1] 544.[1]
— Der practische Pflanzer. 1799. IV. 544.[1]
— The Scotch forcing gardener. 1797. III. 176.[1]
Nicol, William. Observations on the structure of recent and fossil Coniferae. 1834. II. 16.[1]
— On the structure of the wood ... of Rhamnus. 1836. II. 497.[1]
Nicolai, E. A. De nucis vomicae viribus et usu. 1784. III. 684.[2]
Nicolai, Ernst August, (1800–). Verzeichniss der Pflanzen ... in der Umgebung von Arnstadt. 1836. I. 379.
Nicolai, J. D. Beiträge zur Beantwortung der Frage: Was ist für und wider den Zuckerbau ... zu sagen? 1799. IV. 526.[1]
Nicolai, J. G. Balsamum de Mecca. See LOESCHER, M. G. 1726. III. 510.[2]
Nicolai, Johann Anton Heinrich. Über die Lebensweise ... der Wanderraupe. 1833. IV. 91.[1]
— Die Wander- oder Prozessions-Raupe. 1833. IV. 91.[1]
Nicolai, Johannes. Tractatus de phyllobolia. 1698. I. 515.
Nicolai, Johannes. Actinidia polygama. 1895. III. 595.[2]
— Neue Cereus grandiflorus-Hybriden. 1899. III. 621.[2]
Nicolai, Otto. Eine Bemerkung in Betreff des Wachsthums der Wurzel. 1866. I. 188.
— Das Wachsthum der Wurzel. 1865. I. 188.
Nicolaos Damaskenos. De plantis libri duo. 5 B.C. I. 272.
Nicolas, Cl. See DOMERGUE, A. & NICOLAS, Cl.
Nicolas, J. Les anthonomes. 1895. III. 191.
— Lilas à fleurs doubles. 1895. III. 680.[2]
Nicolas, L. Mémoire sur l'exploitation agricole et forestière d'Arcy-en-Brie. 1879. IV. 380.

Nicolas, M. L. Guide du sylviculteur. 189.? IV. 441.
Nicolas, Pierre. Notices sur l'Indo-Chine, Cochinchine. 1900. III. 276.[2]
Nicoleano, G. N. Introduction à l'ampélographie roumaine. 1900. III. 548.[1]
— La lutte contre le phylloxéra en Roumanie. 1900. III. 762.
— & Brézéano, V. S. État de l'arboriculture en Roumanie. 1900. III. 127.[1]
Nicolet, A. C. Essais physiologiques ... sur les fruits du genre Juniperus. 1831. III. 303.[1]
Nicollet, B. Questions forestières et de défenses contre les inondations. 1892. IV. 186.[1]
Nicollet, Joseph Nicolas. Report intended to illustrate a map of the hydrographical basin of the upper Mississippi River. See TORREY, John. 1843. I. 321.
Nicolson, (père). Essai sur l'histoire naturelle de St. Domingue. 1776. I. 334.
Nicosia, Filippo, Barone di S. Giaime e del Pozzo. Il podere fruttifero. 1735. III. 145.[1]
Le Nicotiana wigandioïdes. 1891. III. 701.[1]
Nicotra, Leopoldo. Addenda ad Floram italicam. 1887. I. 432.[1] — 1893. I. 432.[1]
— Sul calendario di flora. 1897. I. 227.[1]
— Sulla classificazione dei frutti. 1898. I. 120.
— Elementi statistici della flora siciliana. 1884. I. 432.[1]
— Influenza del calcare. 1895. I. 229.
— Introduzione allo studio della flora medica di Messina. 1881. III. 88.[2]
— Dai miei studii sulla letteratura dell' antobiologia. 1896. I. 239.[1]
— Note sopra alcune piante di Sicilia. 1893. I. 432.[1]
— Une nouvelle acquisition pour la flore de Sicile. 1884. II. 518.[1]
— Nuovi studii sulla flora messinese. 1876. I. 431.
— Una pagina storica di biologia della disseminazione. 1898. I. 241.[1]
— Posizione ed ufficii della fitotopografia. 1878. I. 300.
— Prodromus florae messanensis. 1878. I. 431.
— Syllabus florae siculae. 1893. I. 432.[1]
— Tassonomia dei dicotiledoni. 1878. I. 530.[1]
— Ultime note sopra alcune piante di Sardegna. 1896. I. 430.
Nidergefer, E. See Нидерефери, Э.
Niderhöfer, E. See Нидерефери, Э.
Nidwalden. 1894. IV. 38.
Nidwalden. Aufforstungen ... Wildbäche bei Beckenried. 1896. IV. 167.[1]
Nidwalden. Erdrutschung ob Emmetten. 1894. IV. 187.[2]
Nidwalden. Hagelschlag vom 15. August 1894. 1894. IV. 190.
Nidwalden. Die hohe Bedeutung des Bodenüberzuges. 1896. IV. 72.
Nidwalden. Massnahmen zur Erhaltung der Bestockung auf Alpweiden. 1895. IV. 136.[1]
Niebuhr, Carsten. Reisebeschreibung nach Arabien. 1774. I. 480.
— Reisen durch Syrien und Palästina. 1837. I. 478.
— Travels through Arabia. 1774. I. 480.
— Voyage en Arabie. 1774. I. 480.
Nieciengiewicz, Jan. Jedwabnictwo praktycznie i teoretycznie wyłożone. 1865. III. 377.
Niedeken, J. Tuin almanak. 1843. III. 106.[1]
Niedenzu, Franz. Über den anatomischen Bau der Laubblätter der Arbutoideae und Vaccinioideae. 1889. II. 658.[1]
— Blattiaceae. 1893. II. 610.[1]
— Bruniaceae. 1891. II. 251.[2]
— De genere Banisteria. 1900. II. 424.[1]
— De genere Bunchosia. 1898. II. 424.[2]
— De genere Malpighia. 1899. II. 426.[2]
— De genere Stigmatophyllo. 1899. II. 427.[2]
— De genere Tamarice. 1895. II. 562.[2]
— Hamamelidaceae. 1891. II. 252.[1]
— Zur Kenntnis der Gattung Crypteronia. 1893. II. 610.[1]
— Lecythidaceae. 1893. II. 611.[1]
— Malpighiaceae. 1896. II. 423.[2]
— Malpighiaceae africanae. 1892. II. 425.[1]
— Malpighiaceae novae. 1892. II. 423.[2]
— Myrothamnaceae. 1891. II. 251.[1]
— Myrtaceae. 1893. II. 619.[1]
— Ueber eine neue Eintheilung der Malpighiaceae. 1890. II. 423.[2]
— Platanaceae. 1891. II. 254.[1]
— Punicaceae. 1893. II. 610.[2]
— Tamaricaceae. 1895. II. 562.[1]

Niederlein, Gustav. Einige wissenschaftliche Resultate einer argentinischen Expedition nach dem Rio-Negro. 1881. I. 345.
— Herbario "Bettfreund." 1898. V. xviii.[2]
— The republic of Guatemala. 1898. I. 334.
— Resultados botánicos de esploraciones hechas en Misiones. 1890. I. 345.
— La riqueza florestal de la Republica Argentina. 1889. III. 269,[2] V. xxxi.[2]
— *See also* LORENTZ, P. G. & NIEDERLEIN, Gustav.
Niederösterreichischer Forstverein. Mittheilungen. IV. 15.
Niederösterreichischer Gewerbe-Verein. Verhandlungen. Wochenschrift. Zeitschrift. III. 25.
Niederrheinische Gesellschaft für Natur- und Heilkunde zu Bonn. Sitzungsberichte. I. 14.
Niederstadt, (*Oberförster, Grubenhagen*). Ueber das Eingehen der Buchen-Ausschlagstöcke. 1873. IV. 496.
Niederstadt, (*Oberförster, Rotenkirchen*). Die Klemmpflanzung mit dem Sollinger Rodeeisen. 1873. IV. 152.
Niederstadt, Johann Theodor. De efficacia admiranda chinchinae. *See* VATER, Abraham. 1734. III. 719.
Niedman, Vlademir de. Andromedas. 1878. III. 647.[1]
Niedt, (*Dr., of Berlin*). Zur Kacteenkunde, I. 1857. II. 593.[1]
— Zwei neue Echinopsis-Arten. 1857. II. 593.[1]
Nieger, C. V. Le cubage cylindrique du bois d'œuvre. 1881. IV. 228.
— L'exploitabilité relative à la rente la plus élevée. 1878. IV. 252.
— Notice sur un Chêne foudroyé. 1886. IV. 194.
Nieger, G. V. L'estimation des forêts et l'exploitabilité commerciale. 1892. IV. 258.
Niekotoryya ... *See* НѢКОТОРЫЯ ...
Niel, Eugène. Catalogue des plantes ... de l'Eure. 1889. I. 417.
— Note sur les recherches de M. A. Gravis. 188.? II. 279.[1]
Niel, M. Sur un phénomène remarquable de vitalité. 1889. I. 210.[1]
Nielsen. Formering af remonterende Roser. 1868. III. 452.
Nielsen, C. L. Om Pilekulturer. 1891. III. 349.
— Om Skovdyrkning. 1889. IV. 103.[2]
Nielsen, L. Lærebog i Frugttrædyrkning. 1895. III. 134.[2]
Nielsen, P. Dipladenia. 1895. III. 687.[2]
— Tecoma Smithii. 1897. III. 707.[2]
Nielsen, Feder. Hegnsplantning. 1847. III. 213.
Nielsen, Peter. Sydvestsjællands Vegetation. 1873. I. 356.
Niemann, Albert. Sur l'alcaloïde de Coca. 1860. III. 492.[1]
— Ueber eine neue organische Basis in den Cocablättern. 1860. III. 492.[2]
— *See also* WÖHLER; Fr. & NIEMANN, Albert.
Niemann, August. Allgemeine Wälderkunde. 1808. IV. 336.[1]
— Forststatistik der dänischen Staaten. 1809. IV. 342.[1]
— Inbegriff der Forstwissenschaft. 1814. IV. 106.
— Sammlungen für die Forst-Geographie. 1791. I. 298, IV. 336.[1]
— Vaterländische Waldberichte. 1820. IV. 348.[2]
Niemann, K. G. De corticis peruviani virtute. *See* BIRKHOLZ, A. M. 1785. III. 720.
Niemeczky, Daniel. Einleitung in die Pflanzenkur. 1796. I. 33.
Niemetz, W. F. Die Blutwalnuss, Juglans regia rubra. 1898. III. 355.
Niemeyer. Die Gehölze unserer Wälder und Gärten. 1866. III. 270.[2]
Niepce, S. La guerre aux forêts de l'Algérie. 1893. IV. 270.[1]
Niepraschk, J. Die Behandlung und das Gedeihen grosser Palmen. 1884. III. 317.
— Pritchardia filifera. 1876. III. 332.[1]
Nieremberg, Juan Eusebio. Curiosa filosofia y tesoro de marauillas de la naturaleza. 1635. V. xv.[1]
— Filosofia curiosa y tesoro de marauiglias de la naturaleça. 1635. I. 285.[2]
— Historia naturae maxime peregrinae libris XVI. distincta. 1635. I. 285,[2] V. xv.[2]
— Oculta filosofia. 1635. V. xv.[1]
Nierop, J. Over het uitrooijen van hop. 1785. III. 193.[1]
Nieskolko ... *See* НѢСКОЛЬКО ...
Niessing, C. Ueber öffentliche Verschönerung ... von Alleebäumen. 1871. III. 209, 213.

Niessl, Gustav von. Eine Krankheit des Oelbaumes. 1859. III. 677.[2]
Nieter, (*Ober-Landesgerichts-Kassen-Rendant*). Über die Obstbaumpflanzungen. 1831. III. 136.
Nietner, Johannes. Briefliche Mittheilung aus Ceylon. 1852. III. 279.[1]
— The Coffee tree and its enemies. 1861. III. 735.
— Ueber die gesellig wachsenden Pflanzen auf Ceylon. 1854. I. 476.[2]
— Lodoicea Seychellarum Labill. 1853. II. 70.[2]
— Monströse Kokosnussbäume in Ceylon. 1853. II. 67.[2]
— Observations on the enemies of the Coffee tree in Ceylon. 1861. III. 735.
— Observations on the natural history of the enemies of the Coffee-tree in Ceylon. 1861. III. 735.
— Eine Tour an der Koromandel-Küste. 1853. I. 473.
— Eine Wintertour im Delhi-Himalaya. 1853. I. 473.
Nietner, Theodor. Die Rose, ihre Geschichte. 1880. III. 450.
Nietner, Theodor Ed. Beitrag zur Vermehrung der Eriken. 1843. III. 157.
— Beitrag zur Vermehrung der Eriken durch Stecklinge. 1851. III. 650.[1]
— Beitrag zur Wirkung welche die Witterung ... auf die Samenbildung ... ausgeübt hat. 1843. II. 254.[2]
— Crataegus pyracantha. 1838. III. 443.[2]
— Einige Bemerkungen über die Eriken. 1851. III. 650.[1]
— Einiges über das Verpflanzen von bereits starken ... Bäumen. 1836. III. 167.
— Om Formeringen af Ericeerne ved Aflæggere. 1836. III. 649.[2]
— Ueber Schling- oder Rankpflanzen. 1845. III. 204.[2]
— Sicheres ... Mittel gegen den sogenannten Schimmel. 1843. III. 650.[1]
— Ueber Vermehrung der Cydonia japonica. 1837. III. 420.[1]
— Vermehrung der Ericen durch Ableger. 1836. III. 649.[2]
Nieuhof, Jan. L'ambassade de la Compagnie orientale ... vers l'Empereur de la Chine. 1665. I. 457.
— An embassy ... to the Grand Tartar Cham. 1665. I. 458.
— Gedenkweerdige Brasiliaense zee- en lantreize. 1682. III. 268.[2]
— Die Gesandtschaft der Ostindischen Gesellschaft ... an den tartarischen Cham. 1665. I. 457.
— Het gezantschap der Neêrlandtsche Oost-Indische Compagnie, aan den grooten Tartarischen Cham. 1665. I. 457.
— Legatio batavica ad magnum Tartariae Chamum. 1665. I. 458.
Nieuhof, Johann. *See* NIEUHOF, Jan.
Nieuw koortsverdrijvend middel. 1808. III. 516.[2]
Nieuw plaatsvervangend middel voor den Kinabast. 1811. III. 398.[2]
Een nieuw proces van theebereiding in Colombo. 1900. III. 608.[1]
Nieuw tijdschrift voor de pharmacie. *See* TIJDSCHRIFT voor schei- en artsenijbereidkunde. III. 15.
Nieuw tijdschrift voor de pharmacie en Nederland. *See* TIJDSCHRIFT voor wetenschappelijke pharmacie. I. 16.
Een nieuwe caoutchouc-soort. 1884. III. 229.
Nieuwe denkbeelden omtrent de gouvernements Koffiecultuur op Java. 1874. III. 729.[2]
Een nieuwe Gutta-percha boom. 1885. III. 667.[1]
Eene nieuwe Koffiesoort. 1882. III. 590.[1]
Een nieuwe plaag. 1899. III. 737.
Nieuwe soort van Koortsbast. 1805. III. 399.[2]
De nieuwe wijze van landbouw. 1762. III. 105.
Nieuwenhuijs, F. L. A. Verbeterde bereiding van de kina loogzouten. 1823. III. 721.
Nieuwenhuis, A. W. In central Borneo. 1900. III. 276.[1]
De Nieuw-Hollandsche Kastanjeboom. 1855. III. 471.[2]
Nieva, José Maria de. Disertación sobre la necesidad de los bosques. 1822. IV. 268.
Niewerth. Eine botanische Excursion ... von Yedo nach Niko. 1873. I. 462.
Niggl, Max. Das Indol, ein Reagens. 1881. I. 36.[2]
— Ueber die Verholzung der Pflanzenmembranen. 1881. I. 138.[1]
Night-flowering Cereus. 1893. III. 621.[1]
Nigrisoli, Francesco Maria. Febris chinachina expugnata. 1687. III. 719.
Nigst, Fr. Erfahrungen über ... Stacheldrahtzäunen. 1894. IV. 146.[2]

Nihon engei kai zasshi. III. 26.[1]

Nijpels, Paul. Les maladies cryptogamiques. 1896. III. 195.[1]

De nijverheid op Celebes. 1854. III. 274.[1]

Nikandros Kolophonios. Alexipharmaca. 135 B. C. I. 272.
— Alexipharmaca et theriaca. 135 B. C. I. 272, V. XIII.[2]
— Νικάνδρου Θηριακά. 135 B. C. V. XIII.[2]
— Theriaca. 135 B. C. I. 272.
— Theriaca et alexipharmaca. 135 B. C. I. 272.
— Les theriaques et les contrepoisons. 135 B. C. I. 272.

Niklas. Ueber die Anwendung der Pflanzbohrer. 1840. III. 165.

Nikmann, Emil. Die Einwirkung des Frostes auf die Keimfähigkeit. 1886. IV. 66.[2]

Nikodem, Wilhelm. Ueber das Vorkommen und Verhalten der Späteiche. 1897. II. 136.[2]

"Nikolaus," Vintergrønne Beplantninger. 1861. III. 206.[1]

Nikolayef, F. J. See НИКОЛАЕВЪ, Θ. Я.

Nikolić, Emanuel. Phänologische Mittheilungen aus . . . Ragusa's. 1898. I. 227.[3]
— Unterschiede in der Blütezeit einiger Frühlingspflanzen. 1895. I. 227.[2]

Nikols, T. See НИКОЛЬСЪ, T.

Nil Desperandum, (pseud.). The education of young foresters. 1879. IV. 29.

Nilson, Arvid. The timber trees of New South Wales. 1884. IV. 89.[1]

Nilson, Elis. Visit to Larch-woods in Scotland. 1899. IV. 450.

Nilsson, Lars Albert. Assimilationssystemet hos stammen. 1886. I. 106.[1]
— Om barrträdsrötor. 1895. IV. 212.
— Några drag ur de svenska växtsamhällenas utvecklingshistoria. 1899. I. 358.
— Om örtrika barrskogar. 1896. I. 350,[1] IV. 79.[3]

Nilsson, Nils Hjalmar. Myricaria germanica från Skåne. 1885. II. 562.[1]

Nilsson-Ehle, Nils Herman. Iakttagelser öfver de mörka värmestrålarnas i solljuset inflytande. 1897. I. 232.[1]
— Ein für Skandinavien neuer Salix-Bastard. 1894. II. 104.[2]
— En för Skandinavien ny Salixhybrid. 1894. II. 104.[2]

Nîmes — Société d'études des sciences naturelles. See SOCIÉTÉ . . . I. 23.

Nineteenth century. III. 17.

Ningrat, RADEN MAS TOEMENGGOENG HARIO HADIO. See RADEN MAS TOEMENGGOENG HARIO HADIO NINGRAT.

Niobey. See COUTY, LOUIS, GUIMARAES, A. R. & NIOBEY.

Niobey, Domingos Alberto. Papaina sua acção physiologica e therapeutica. 1887. II. 582.[2]

Nipperdey, H. Die Brotfrüchte des Congo-Negers. 1886. III. 281.[1]
— The industrial products . . . of the Congo. 1886. III. 281.[1]

Niquille. Conditions normales de boisement d'une contrée. 1894. IV. 286.[1]

Nisbet, J. Note on the occasional formation of pseudo-autumnal zones of wood. 1894. I. 128.[1]

Nisbet, John. On the advantages of underplanting. 1893. IV. 139.[1]
— The Ash. 1899. IV. 535.[1]
— The black arches, "Nun." 1893. IV. 201, 457.
— British forest trees. 1893. IV. 85.[1]
— British forestry and its future prospects. 1900. IV. 275.
— The climatic and national-economic influence of forests. 1893. IV. 45.
— On the Corsican Fir. 1876. IV. 465.[3]
— The Cutch tree in Upper Burma. 1893. IV. 521.[1]
— The diseases of trees. 1896. IV. 196.[1]
— Concerning the enhancement of increment. 1893. IV. 234.
— Fleischmann's Spiegel-Hypsometer. 1882. IV. 215.
— Forest science; its aim and scope. 1888. IV. 56. ·
— Inspection notes on . . . reserves (Pyinmana division). 1897. IV. 250.[2]
— Measurements of planted Mahogany trees. 1882. III. 513.[1]
— On mixed forests and their advantages. 1893. IV. 137.[3]
— Note on improvement fellings for the benefit of Teak. 1900. IV. 537.[1]
— Note on the Haskin process of vulcanizing timber. 1900. IV. 421.
— Our forests and woodlands. 1900. IV. 120.
— Rate of growth of Teak in the Magayi plantations. 1892. IV. 536.[3]
— Reports on the forests of northern Aracan. 1882. IV. 377.[1]
— On the selection of species of trees for woodland crops. 1893. IV. 121, 142.
— Soil and situation in relation to forest growth. 1893. IV. 70.
— On the soils and subsoils. 1876. III. 41.[1]
— Studies in forestry. 1894. IV. 102.
— Studies in forestry; being a short course of lectures. 1894. IV. 121.
— The Tortrix of the Teak tree. 1892. IV. 537.[1]
— Turpentine from Pinus Khasya. 1896. III. 307.[2]
— Working plan for . . . Earl of Selborne's . . . woods in Hampshire. 1900. IV. 248.[2]

Nisbett, William. The Weeping Willow in New England. 1878. III. 351.[2]

Nissolle, Guillaume. Dissertatio botanica de origine et natura kermes. 1716. IV. 503.[1]
— Dissertation botanique sur . . . kermès. 1716. IV. 503.[1]
— Établissement de quelques nouveaux genres de plantes. 1714. I. 289.

El nitratro sódico. 1893. IV. 545.[2]

Nitsche, Hinrich. Bemerkungen über einige forstschädliche Arten der Gattung Pissodes. 1895. IV. 208.[1]
— Erreichung einer einheitlichen Nomenclatur auf dem Gebiete der Entomologie und der Botanik. 1890. IV. 57.
— Ueber den Frass von Hylesinus crenatus. 1881. IV. 535.[2]
— Ueber den Frass von Lyda hypotrophica. 1888. IV. 456.
— Kleinere Mittheilungen über Forstinsekten. 1896. IV. 208.[1]
— Der neueste Kiefernspannerfrass. 1896. IV. 479.
— Die Nonne. 1892. IV. 201.
— Untersuchungen über den . . . Werth verschiedener Raupenleimsorten. 1893. IV. 200.
— Ueber die von Agrilus bifasciatus Oliv. an Eichenbeständen verursachten Schäden. 1887. IV. 511.
— See also JUDEICH, J. F. & NITSCHE, Hinrich.

Nitschke, Th. Ueber die hybriden Arten der Gattung Rosa. 1856. II. 284.[2]

Nitzsche, W. H. Die bayerische Staatsforst-Verwaltung. 1884. IV. 290.[1]
— Der grosse Nonnenfrass im Voigtlande. 1891. IV. 201.

Nivelet, Constant. Note sur la greffe en fente-écusson. 1858. III. 161.
— Des Poiriers greffés sur Aubépine. 1856. III. 445.[1]

Niven, James C. Jubaea spectabilis hardy at Glasnevin. 1877. III. 326.[1]
— Mühlenbeckia complexa. 1874. III. 387.[1]
— The Pentstemons. 1876. III. 703.[3]
— Stevias. 1875. III. 756.[3]
— The Tree-Heath. 1874. III. 650.[3]

Niven, Ninian. The visitor's companion to the Botanic garden, Glasnevin. 1838. I. 54.

Nivens, J. B. On the phytotype or archetype of the flowering division. 1860. I. 99.

Nivière, Gustave & Loitard, Ernest. Étude sur le Fabiana imbricata. 1887. III. 700.[2]

Nivois. Préparation des traverses par la compagnie de l'Est. 1885. IV. 424.[1]

Nixon, E. S. Poison from Kalmia latifolia. 1881. III. 652.[2]

Niárv, Gyula, báró. A Mahóni és Mahagóni. 1896. III. 513.[1]

Noack, Fritz. De aaltjesziekte van de Koffie. 1898. III. 737.
— Der Einfluss des Klimas auf die Cuticularisation . . . der Nadeln einiger Coniferen. 1887. II. 21.[1]
— Der Eschenkrebs. 1893. IV. 535.[2]
— Die Pfahlwurzelfäule des Kaffees. 1898. III. 737.
— Plakrankheiten der Orangenbäume. 1900. III. 501.[1]
— Rebkrankheiten, in Brasilien. 1899. III. 562.[1]
— Ueber Vergrünung der Knospenschuppen von Rotbuchen. 1895. IV. 497.

Noack, R. Der Obstbau. 1876. III. 138.
— Die verschiedenen Arten der Rose. 1870. V. XXIX.[1]
— Vorschläge zur Hebung des Obstbaues. 1888. III. 139.
— See also ACHENBACH, (Oberconsistorial-Secretair), NOACK, R. & GERNET, (Hofgärtner, Jugenheim).

Noback, A. Neueste Collectaneen des preussischen Forstverwaltungs-Formularwesens. 1871. IV. 302.

Nobbe, Friedrich. Abnorme Zapfenbildungen bei Nadelhölzern. 1879. II. 19.
— Anweisung für die Ausführung von Keimkraftprüfungen. 1890. III. 157, IV. 147.[1]
— Beobachtungen . . . über die Wurzelbildung der Nadelhölzer. 1875. I. 526,[2] II. 20,[2] IV. 64.[3]

Nobbe, Friedrich (*continued*).
— Beschreibung eines Keimapparates. 1870. IV. 147.[1]
— Ueber die Fichtennadelröthe. 1893. IV. 457.
— Ueber den forstlichen Samenhandel. 1899. IV. 148, 545.[2]
— Handbuch der Samenkunde. 1876. III. 156.[2]
— Ueber die Keimungsreife der Fichtensamen. 1874. II. 36.[1] — 1881. II. 36.[2]
— Kleine forstbotanische Mittheilungen. 1890. III. 157, IV. 147,[1] 149.[2]
— Ueber die Mistel. 1884. II. 177.[3]
— Mittheilungen über . . . Hysterium macrosporum. 1892. IV. 457.
— Ueber das numerische Verhältniss der im Saatbeet auflaufenden Kiefern- und Fichtenpflanzen. 1890. IV. 149.[2]
— Ein uralt Kreuterbuch. 1871. I. 80.[2]
— Ueber den . . . Wärmegrad des Keimbetts. 1890. IV. 149.[2]
— Welche fremdländischen Holzarten können . . . Bedeutung gewinnen? 1895. IV. 126.[1]
— Ueber die Wirkungen des Spätfrostes . . . 1876. 1877. IV. 191.[2]
— Ein zweiter Fundort von Loranthus europaeus. 1884. II. 176.[1]
— Ein zweiter Standort der Riemenblume. 1884. II. 872.[1]
— & **Haenlein**, H. De la résistance que les graines opposent aux agents ordinaires de la germination. 1877. I. 203.
— — Ueber die Resistenz von Samen. 1877. I. 203.
— — & **Councler**, Constantin. Beiträge zur Biologie der Schwarzerle. 1880. II. 871.[3]
Nobele, L. de. Les basses températures et les plantes. 1891. III. 182.
— Behandeling der wijngaardziekten. 1888. III. 580.
— De bladluisleeuwen. 1893. III. 191.
— Le bouturage au point de vue biologique. 1891. I. 205.
— La Coca. 1885. III. 493.[1]
— Le Dattier. 1886. III. 329.[2]
— Diagnostic . . . des maladies des arbres fruitiers. 1892. III. 179.
— De druivenziekten. 1887. III. 561.
— Eenvoudige leer der kenteekenen . . . der ziekten der ooftboomen. 1892. III. 179.
— L'épidémie des Platanes à Gand. 1891. III. 418.[3]
— La flore fruitière . . . au temps de Charlemagne. 1899. III. 32.[3]
— L'If commun. 1888. II. 10.[1]
— De koude en de planten. 1891. III. 182.
— Les lions des pucerons. 1893. III. 191.
— La maladie des Platanes à Paris. 1899. III. 418.[2]
— Les maladies parasitaires de la Vigne. 1887. III. 561.
— De ooft- en groentenflora ten tijde van Karel de Groote. 1899. III. 32.[2]
— Le Papayer. 1885. III. 617.[3]
— Pins et Sapins. 1891. III. 306.[2]
— Les Sensitives. 1888. III. 481.[2]
— Traitement des maladies cryptogamiques de la Vigne. 1888. III. 580.
— Ziekte der Platanen te Gent. 1891. III. 418.[1]
— De ziekte der Platanen te Parijs. 1899. III. 418.[2]
Noblat, Antoine de METZ-. *See* METZ-NOBLAT, Antoine de.
Noble. The fruit of the Japan Quince. 1885. III. 420.[1]
— Wistaria sinensis, pods of. 1885. II. 388.[2]
Noble. *See* STANDISH & NOBLE.
Noble, C. S. On the rearing of groves of Nim trees. 1876. IV. 525.
Noble, Charles. Clematis Jackmanni alba. 1888. III. 391.[1]
— Spiraea Nobleana. 1888. III. 461.[2]
Noble, John, (ed.). Illustrated official handbook of the Cape. 1886. I. 495.
— Official handbook . . . of the Cape of Good Hope. 1886. I. 495.
Noble, W. H. The Celastrus scandens. 1878. III. 531.[3]
The **Noble** Diplademe. 1847. III. 688.[1]
A nobleman's flower gardener, (*pseud.*). The Epacris. 1857. III. 665.[1]
— Sur les Epacris. 1857. III. 665.[1]
— The Magnolia. 1857. III. 399.[1]
— Magnolien und ihre Kultur. 1857. III. 399.[1]
Noblet. Eupatorium micranthum. 1872. III. 755.[1]
Nobleville, Louis Daniel ARNAULT DE LA. *See* ARNAULT DE LA NOBLEVILLE, L. D.
Nobody, Fred. Bougainvillea Sand. 189.? III. 388.[4]
Nobre, Augusto. Recherches histologiques sur le Podocarpus Mannii. 1889. II. 9.[2]
Nocca, Domenico. Catalogus Horti botanici mantuani. 1792. I. 61.

— De caussis tantae per multas maxime Insubriae regiones silvarum amputationis. 1795. IV. 283.[1]
— Clavis rem herbariam addiscendi. 1823. I. 426.
— Elementi di botanica. 1801. I. 255.
— Elementi di botanica con varie tavole. 1805. I. 84.
— Flora farmaceutica. 1826. III. 56.
— Historia . . . Horti botanici ticinensis. 1818. I. 62.
— Horti botanici mantuani historia. 1793. I. 61.
— Illustratio usus et nominis plantarum . . . in Julii Caesaris Commentariis. 1812. I. 514.[1]
— Illustrationes nonnularum plantarum Horti botanici mantuani. 1793. II. 193.[2]
— Institutioni di botanica pratica. 1808. III. 37.[1]
— Istituzioni di botanica pratica. 1801. III. 37.[1]
— Nomenclatura stirpium Horti bot. ticinensis. 1807. I. 61.
— Nomina quarundam plantarum italica. 1793. I. 74.[3]
— Observationes botanicae. 1793. I. 264.
— Observationes botanicae. Mimosa speciosa. 1794. II. 331.[1]
— Onomatologia. 1813. I. 62.
— Se Virgilio ha veramente descritto il Limone. 1819. II. 403.[3]
— Sistema sessuale di Linneo. 1801. I. 255.
— Sopra il sonno delle foglie. 1809. I. 198.
— Storia ragionata delle piante nostrati ed esotiche. 1812. III. 51, 220.[3]
— Synonimia plantarum Horti botanici ticinensi. 1804. I. 61.
— Synopsis plantarum Horti botanici ticinensis. 1803. I. 61.
— Ticinensis Horti academici plantae selectae. 1800. I. 61.
— & **Balbis**, G. B. Flora ticinensis. 1816. I. 425.
Un **Noce** fenomenale. 1900. II. 114.[1]
Noch einmal die Heckenzucht. 1857. III. 213.
Noch einmal der Ringelschnitt an Weinreben. 1859. III. 549.[1]
Eine **noch** wenig bekannte Kiefer der Balkanhalbinsel. 1889. IV. 464.[3]
Nochmals die Arve. 1889. IV. 463.[2]
Nocito, Gerardo. Lucidarium medicinae. 1511. I. 276;
Noctua (Trachea) piniperda-perhosen esiintyminen vuosina. 1891. IV. 205.[3]
Nocturnal fragrance of different plants. 1820. II. 602.[2]
Noë, *vicomte* de. Mémoire sur l'Argania. 1853. III. 666.[1]
Noë, Franz. Vegetationsbilder aus Süd-Europa. 1882. I. 452.
Nögen forsök om skogs planteringen och skötsel. 1749. IV. 113.[2]
Noehden, George Henry. Account of the different varieties of the genus Citrus. 1820. III. 496.[3]
Noël, Arthur. Essai sur les repeuplements artificiels. 1882. IV. 142.
— La forêt, œuvre d'art. 1887. IV. 56.
— Les quarts en réserve. 1880. IV. 326.
— La situation des forêts de la France. 1885. IV. 276.[1]
— Statistique des forêts de l'ouest de la France. 1884. IV. 361.
— La sylviculture à l'Exposition d'Anvers. 1885. IV. 19.[2]
— *See also* MUEL, E., NOEL, Arthur & MAIRE.
Noël, Ch. Note sur les essences des Aurantiacées. 1886. IV.
— *See also* GODFRIN, Julien & NOËL, Ch.
Noël, Eugène. Les arbres à cidre et le cidre du pays d'Othe. 1889. III. 426.[2]
Noël, Henri. Historique et florule du Mont-Duplan. 1897. I. 418.
Noel, Michel. Mémorial alphabétique des matières des eaux et forêts. 1737. IV. 2.[1]
Noel, Paul. Quelques maladies du Chêne-Liège. 1896. IV. 517.[1]
— Réflecteur pour la chasse aux insectes. 1896. IV. 200.
Noeldeke, Carl. Flora cellensis. 1871. I. 386.
— Flora der ostfriesischen Inseln. 1872. I. 386.
— Das Vorkommen der Eibe. 1898. II. 11.[3]
Nörager, Christiern. Observationes de potu thee. 1740. III. 805.
Nördlinger. Le rouge des Pins. 1885. IV. 461.[2]
Nördlinger, Hermann. Ueber das Alter der Frostrisse. 1854. IV. 191.[1]
— Anatomische Merkmale der wichtigsten deutschen Wald- und Gartenholzarten. 1881. I. 125.
— Anatomischer Bau unserer Hölzer im hohen Norden. 1879. IV. 543.[1]
— Ankohlen der Hölzer. 1864. IV. 419.
— Die Anpflanzung von Fremdhölzern. 1882. IV. 125.[2]

— Ueber die Anzucht der Weisstanne. 1842. IV. 444.[1]
— Aufästung der Waldbäume. 1861. IV. 170.
— Bedeutung des Winterfrosts. 1860. IV. 66.[2]
— Beschädigung von Fichtengipfeln durch's Eichhorn. 1860. IV. 455.
— Les bois employés dans l'industrie. 1872. I. 37,[2] *IV. 17.*
— Bostrichus domesticus L. in der Birke. 1864. IV. 490.[1]
— Ueber Dauer des Bauholzes im Trocknen. 1866. IV. 499.
— Dauer des Holzes verschiedener Monate. 1878. IV. 413.[2]
— Deutsche Forstbotanik. 1874. IV. 83.
— Druckfestigkeit des Holzes. 1882. IV. 410.
— Eichhorn-Beschädigung an Nadelholzstangen. 1861. IV. 197.[2]
— Eichhornbeschädigungen an Laubholzstangen. 1862. IV. ·197.[2]
— Einbauchungen von Holzringen. 1884. I. 525.
— Einfluss der Harzung auf . . . Schwarzföhre. 1881. IV. 455.[2]
— Einfluss des Lichtstandes auf die Beschaffenheit des Föhrenholzes. 1875. IV. 480.
— Einige Notizen über die beliebte Wellingtonie. 1868. II. 51.[1]
— Fähigkeit des Holzes zu dunsten. 1857. IV. 412.[1]
— Die Federkraft (Elasticität) der Hölzer. 1889. IV. 410.
— Festigkeit der Hölzer zu verschiedenen Jahreszeiten. 1880. IV. 410.
— Die fetten und magern Jahre der Bäume. 1865. I. 127,[2] *IV. 68.[2]*
— Formzahlen und Massetafeln. 1867. IV. 217.
— Die Frühlings- oder Spätfröste. 1860. IV. 191.[1]
— Fünfzig Querschnitte der in Deutschland wachsenden hauptsächlichsten Bau- . . . Hölzer. 1884. I. 38,[1] *IV. 18.[1]*
— Gefährlichkeit des Eibenbaums. 1866. III. 288.[2]
— Die gewerblichen Eigenschaften der Hölzer. 1890. ·IV. 409.
— Gewicht·des Eibenholzes. 1870. II. 10.[1]
— Giebt es Doppeljahresringe? 1861. I. 127,[2] *IV. 68.[1]*.
— Grössere Tragkraft·im Lichtstande erwachsenen Föhrenholzes. 1879. IV.·481.
— Das Gürteln von Bäumen. 1866. IV. 419.
— Herbstliche Färbung und Abfall der Blätter. 1862. I. 191.[2] ·
— Die Hölzertränkungsfrage. 1864. IV. 419.
— Hölzertrocknung durch Hitze. 1879. IV. 416.[1]
— Der Holzring als Grundlage des Baumkörpers. 1871. I. 127,[2] *IV. 64.[1]*
— Hylesinus minor Hrt., und H. piniperda L. ·1868. IV. 455. ·
— Interessante spätausschlagende Eiche. 1856. II. 136.[1]
— Die Kenntniss der wichtigsten· kleinen Feinde der Landwirthschaft. 1871. III. 190.
— Kernholz, reifes Holz, Splint. 1857. I. 124, *IV. 68.[1]*
— Die kleinen Feinde der Landwirthschaft. 1855. III. 189.
— Klimatischer Einfluss der Waldungen. 1862. IV. 53.
— Lebensweise von Forstkerfen. 1848. IV. 92.
— Lehrbuch des Forstschutzes. 1884. IV. 177.[2]
— Leichtere Vermehrung des Eibenbaums. 1864. IV. 440.[1]
— Liegt an schiefen Bäumen das bessere Holz auf der . . . unteren Seite? 1878. IV. 543.[1] ·
— Mémoire sur les essences forestières de la Bretagne. 1845. IV. 122,[1] ·*359.[2]*
— Merkwürdige Holzringbildung in einer jungen Lärche. 1864. IV. 450.
— Ein merkwürdiger Bohnenbaum. 1864. III. 480.[2]
— Der Mond·vermag nichts. 1880. IV. 384.[2]
— Nachträge zu Ratzeburg's Forstinsekten. 1848. IV. 92.
— Nachtrag zu Ratzeburgs Forstinsecten. 1848. IV. 92.
— Natürliche Dauer des Holzes. 1859. IV. 413.[2]
— Natur des Wurzelholzes. 1866. I. 103.
— Der neuentbrannte Waldstreukampf. 1869. IV. 71.
— Ein neuer Reihenkultivator. 1867. IV. 143.[1]
— Noch eine Holzkonservationsmethode. 1866. IV. 419.
— Passt die Tanne auf sehr frische Böden? 1887. IV. 444.[1]
— Die Pflanzenspinne Acarus telarius L. auf der Linde. 1866. IV. 528.[1]
— Querschnitte von elf hundert Holzarten. 1852. I. 37,[2] *IV. 17.*
— Der Regenfall im Walde. 1866. IV. 50. ·
— Die Ringbreite allein noch kein Massstab für die Güte des Holzes. 1866. I. 127.[2]
— Ringelung der Waldbäume. 1866. IV. 198.[1]
— Säulenfestigkeit der Fichte und Lärche. 1877. IV. 410.
— Saftgehalt der Bäume. 1879. IV. 411.[1] ·
— Schaden am Holze durch Wind. 1876. IV. 189.[1]

— Schnee-, Duft- und Eisbruch. 1860. IV. 190.
— Die Schütte der Föhren. 1863. IV. 476.
— Die Schütte junger Föhren. 1878. IV. 477.
— Schwindet das Holz weniger, nachdem es ausgelaugt. 1878. IV. 412.[1]
— Die September-Fröste 1877. 1878. IV. 191.[2]
— Sicheres Mittel, das Blühen der Buche herbeizuführen. 1855. II. 126.[2]
— Spaltbarkeit (fissibilité, fente). 1857. IV. 411.[1]
— Eine starke Esche. 1866. II. 708.[1]
— Die Stümmelpflanzung. 1863. IV. 152.
— Die technischen Eigenschaften der Hölzer. 1860. IV. 408.
— Das Ton- oder Resonanzholz. 1864. IV. 459.[1]
— Traubenförmige Gallen an Eichwurzeln. 1863. IV. 509.
— Trockene Hitze. 1860. IV. 192.[1]
— Trockenrisse . . . an der Fichte. 1878. IV. 456.
— Unterscheidendes Merkmal kranken und gesunden Kernholzes. 1868. I. 207,[1] *IV. 66.[1]*
— Verbesserung des Holzes von Eichen. 1880. . IV. 507.
— Vergleichung des Werthes böhmischen . . . Fichtenholzes. 1878. IV. 459.[2]
— Wachsen die Nadelhölzer anders als die Laubhölzer? 1870. I. 127.[2]
— Ueber den Waldertrag und Werth des Waldbodens. 1862. IV. 255.
— Wann beginnt Bast . . . sich zu lösen? 1879. I. 525.
— Warum taugt die Edelkastanie nicht für unsern Forstbetrieb? 1866. *IV. 492.[2]*
— Was ist Kernholz? 1864. I. 125.
— Was verspricht uns der Hikorybaum? 1870. IV. 488.[1]
— Weitere Betrachtungen über specifisches Grüngewicht. 1880. IV. 411.[1]
— Wiederausschlag abgebrannter Föhrensaaten. 1863. IV. 72.
— Winterkälteschaden an Elsebeer. 1860. III. 460.[1]
— Winterkälteschäden an Waldbäumen. 1863. IV. 191.[1]
— Winterkälteschäden und Sonnenbrand an der Esche. 1863. IV. 535.[1]
— Wirkung des Rindendruckes auf . . . Holzringe. 1880. I. 525.
— Wo erwächst gutes Lärchenholz? 1885. IV. 449.
— Zug-, Druck- und Beugungsfestigkeit der Hölzer. 1887. IV. 410.
— Zug- und Säulenfestigkeit von Weymouthsföhre. 1878. IV. 471.
— Zugfederkraft der Hölzer. 1881. IV. 410.
— Zuwachsbestimmung und Zuwachsprozent. 1866. IV. 232.
— *See also* Нердлингеръ, Г.
— & Fisher, W. R. Descriptive list to accompany collection of sections of Indian woods. 1884. IV. 18.[1]
— & Paulus, (*Topograph.*) ·Reisebericht . . . über die . . . forstliche Excursion. 1847. IV. 356.[1]
Nördlinger, Theodor. Ueber Abrundung der Durchmesser. 1887. IV. 218.
— Die Beobachtungszeiten für die täglichen Aufzeichnungen an den forstlich-meteorologischen Stationen. 1886. IV. 60.[1]
— Ueber die Beziehungen der . . . Baumklassen·zur Mittelstammklasse. 1886. IV. 233.
— Ueber die Beziehungen zwischen Alter und Brusthöhenstärke bei Buchen. 1885. IV. 218.
— Ueber die Beziehungen zwischen Waldluft und Freilandtemperatur. 1886. IV. 54.
— Der Einfluss des Waldes auf die Boden- und Lufttemperatur. 1887. IV. 54.
— Einfluss des Waldes auf die Bodentemperatur. 1886. IV. 54.
— Einfluss des Waldes auf die Luftwärme. 1887. IV. 54.
— Der Einfluss des Waldes auf Luft- und Bodenwärme. 1885. IV. 54.
— Ertragsuntersuchungen in Buchenbeständen. 1886. IV. 498.
— Ueber das Gesetz der Stammbildung. 1886. I. 128.[1]
— Das mittlere·Bestandesalter. 1886. IV. 245.
— Ueber die nothwendige Dauer forstlich-meteorologischer Beobachtungen. 1886. IV. 60.[1]
— Ueber Probestämme. 1887. IV. 218.
— Der Regenfall im Walde. 1887. IV. 51.
— Zuwachs und Zuwachsprozent. 1884. IV. 233.
Noethlichs, J. L. Die Korbweiden-Kultur. 1875. III. 347.
Nœtzli, J. Le Palmier Carnaúba. 1874. III. 324.[2]
Nøvik, Peter. Beretning om en stipendiereise i Sverige. 1886. III. 120.[1]
— Naaletrærnes benævning. 1895. II. 13.[2]
— Dyrkning af frugttrær. 1892. III. 134.[2]

Növik, Zach. Om dansk träskolekultur. 1894. III. 154.²
— Om engelsk träkultur. 1895. III. 123.¹
— Fälde for äble- og päre-snudebillerne. 1898. III. 197.
— Hvorledes kan Roddannelse og Vækst bedst fremmes hos nyplantede Frugttræer? 1898. III. 166.
Nog iets over oude boomen. 1833. II. 713.¹
Nogle Bemærkninger de danske Statsskove vedkommende. See LØVENSKJOLD, E. C. F. 1854. IV. 273.¹ See also L. IV. 343.¹
Nogle Bemærkninger om Podning. See BEMERKUNGEN über das Pfropfen. 1851. III. 163.²
Nogle velmeente Tanker . . . i Anledning af en nødvendig Standsning af den nu trykkende Brændemangel. 1797. IV. 281.²
Nogueira de Gama, M. J. Memoria sobre o Loureiro Cinnamomo. 1797. III. 406.¹
Noirot. De l'aménagement et de l'exploitation des forêts. 1812. IV. 239.
— Considérations sur les forêts. 1819. IV. 275.
— See also BEUGON, MESCHINY & NOIROT.
Noirot. De la culture des forêts. 1856. IV. 122.¹
Noirot, A. L'Algérie agricole, commerciale. 1859. III. 130.¹
Noirot-Bonnet, L. De la capitalisation des droits d'usage dans les forêts. 1846. IV. 334.¹
— Essai sur la théorie de l'aménagement des forêts. 1839. IV. 240.
— Manuel théorique et pratique de l'estimateur des forêts. 1856. IV. 253.
— Théorie de l'aménagement des forêts. 1839. IV. 240.
— Traité de la culture des forêts. 1832. IV. 109.¹
Noisette, Louis Claude. Catalogue des arbres fruitiers. 182.? I. 57.
— Le jardin fruitier. 1821. III. 84.²
— Manuel complet du jardinier. 1825. III. 113.
— Observations sur la Sparmannia. 1813. II. 515.¹
— Traité complet de la greffe. 1852. III. 161.
— Vollständiges Handbuch der Gartenkunst. 1825. III. 113.
— See also POITEAU, Antoine & NOISETTE, L. C.
— Boitard, Pierre. Handbuch der Gemüse und Obstgärtnerei. 1832. III. 176.¹
— — Manuel du jardinier des primeurs. 1832. III. 176.¹
Les noix de Coco de Seychelles. 1895. II. 70.²
Sur la noix de Kola. 1890. III. 590.³
La noix de Kola. 1899. III. 591.¹
Noix muscade; son action narcotique. 1880. III. 403.¹
Nolde, Ferdinand, Baron von. Vorzüge der Plänterwirthschaft vor der Schlagwirthschaft. 1870. IV. 128.
Nolin & Blavet, J. L. Essai sur l'agriculture moderne. 1755. III. 112.
Noll, A. F. Tree-planting in South Australia. 1900. IV. 124.²
— Tree planting in the far north. 1900. IV. 124.².
Noll, Friedrich Carl. Ein Besuch auf dem Montserrat. 1872. I. 421.
— Das Thal von Orotava auf Teneriffa. 1872. I. 498.
— Das Thal von Orotava auf Teneriffa; Schilderung. 1876. I. 498.
— Zwei Abnormitäten an Cactusfrüchten. 1872. II. 596.²
Noll, Fritz. Bemerkung zu Schwendener's Erwiderung. 1886. I. 196.²
— Experimentelle Untersuchungen über das Wachstum der Zellmembran. 1890. I. 138.²
— Ueber frostharte Knospen-Variationen. 1885. I. 244,¹ III. 43.
— Über Geotropismus. 1900. I. 196.¹
— Über die Körperform als Ursache von formativen und Orientierungsreizen. 1900. I. 104.'
— Über die Luftverdünnung in den Wasserleitungsbahnen der höheren Pflanzen. 1897. I. 166.
— Ueber den morphologischen Aufbau der Abietineen-Zapfen. 1894. II. 20.¹
— Über eine neue Eigenschaft des Wurzelsystems. 1894. I. 194.
— Ueber die normale Stellung zygomorpher Blüthen. 1888. I. 115.²
— Die Spannungsfestigung der Wurzelsysteme. 1900. I. 236.²
— Vierundzwanzig Blütendiagramme. 1886. I. 115.¹
— Zwitterblüthe der Larix europaea. 1892. II. 33.¹
Nolte. Ueber Vermehrung der Coniferen. 1872. III. 294.¹
Nolte, E. F. Buchenstamm mit Inschrift. 1847. I. 210,¹ IV. 496.

Nolthenius, G. E. H. TUTEIN. See TUTEIN NOLTHENIUS, G. E. H.
Nomblot, Alfred. Congrès international d'arboriculture et de pomologie. 1900. III. 116.³
Nomenclator botanicus. See OEDER, G. C. 1769. I. 351.
Nomenclator botanicus enumerans plantas omnes. See RÄUSCHEL, E. A. 1772. I. 76.²
Nomenclature of Palms. 1884. II. 61.¹
Nomenclature usuelle de 550 fibres textiles. See BERNADIN, J. 1872. III. 234.
Nomenclaturregeln für die Beamten des K. botanischen Gartens und Museums zu Berlin. 1897. I. 254.¹
Nomi volgari adoperati in Italia a designare le principali p n e di bosco. 1873. I. 74.²
Nomine di commissioni per lo studio dello stato delle foreste. 1861. IV. 41.¹
Nonne, J. P. Flora in territorio erfordensi indigena. 1763. I. 373.
Die Nonne. 1841. IV. 200.
Ueber die Nonne. 1893. IV. 201.
Die Nonne, auch Fichtenspinner. 1890. IV. 200.
Die Nonne im Walde. 1798. IV. 200.
Die Nonne in Bayern. 1891. IV. 200.
Die Nonne (Liparis monacha) in Oberschwaben. 1892. IV. 201.
Die Nonnencalamität in Oesterreich. 1891. IV. 200.
Der Nonnenraupenfrass und die Vögel. 1892. IV. 201.
Noort, Mathieu van. Pomologia batava. 1830. III. 76.
Nooten, Mrs. Bertha Hoola van. Fleurs, fruits et feuillages choisis . . . de Java. 1863. I. 469.¹
Nooten, J. C. C. W. van. Onze Oost en de tuinbouw. 1896. III. 129.¹
Nord — Cercle horticole. See CERCLE . . . III. 19.
Nord — Société royale et centrale d'agriculture, sciences . . . See SOCIÉTÉ . . . III. 22.
Nord de la France — Société Linnéenie. See SOCIÉTÉ . . . I. 23.
Nord-est — Union médicale et scientifique. See UNION . . . I. 24.¹
Nordang, P. Br. Ödeläggelse af frugtträr ved markmus. 1895. III. 186.¹
Nordblad, Ericus And. Instructio peregrinatoris. See LINNÉ, Carl von. 1759. I. 35.
Nordenberg, Anders Johan. Anledning til åtskillige ofelbara närings- och hielpemedel. 1741. III. 270.¹
Nordenflycht, Fresherr von. Wie soll der Landmann seinen Obstbaum behandeln? 1874. III. 138.
Nordenschöld, Carl Fr. Rön om Kärntrådet och ytan i Tall- och Furu-trän. 1758. IV. 443.¹
Nordenskiöld, Nils Adolf Erik. Forests of northern Siberia. 1881. I. 453,¹ IV. 87.²
— "Vega"-expeditionens vetenskapliga iakttagelser. 1881. I. 303.
— Voyage de la Vega autour de l'Asie et de l'Europe. 1881. I. 303.
— The voyage of the Vega round Asia and Europe. 1881. I. 303.
— & Theel, Hjalmar. Redogörelser för de svenska expeditionerna till mynningen af Jenisej. 1876. I. 454.¹
Nordenskjöld, Nils Otto Gustaf. Wissenschaftliche Ergebnisse der schwedischen Expedition nach den Magellanländern. See DUSÉN, Per. 1900. I. 347.
Nordhausen, Max. Zur Kenntnis der Wachstumsvorgänge im Verdickungsringe der Dikotylen. 1897. I. 126, 527.
Nordhoff, C. Tea culture in the United States. 1859. III. 600.³
Nordisk Farmaceutisk Tidskrift. I. 9.¹
Nordisk Have-Tidende. III. 10.³
Nordisk Landvæsens og Landhuusholdnings Magasin. III. 10.²
Nordmann, Alexander von. Vorläufige Diagnosen einiger . . . im westlichen Theile der kaukasischen Provinzen entdeckten . . . Pflanzenspecies. 1837. I. 368.²
Nordmann's Silver Fir. 1885. III. 296.²
Nordstedt, Carl Fredrik Otto. Anmärkningar till Fritsch. 1899. II. 311.²
— En Cycadé under utrotning. 1879. II. 7.¹
— Färgen på frukterna hos Sambucus nigra. 1900. II. 841.¹
— En häg Nyponbuske. 1876. II. 200.²
— Köldens inverkan på frönas grobarhet. 1881. I. 203.
— Kräfta hos Äppleträdet. 1875. III. 427.²
— Medel mot barrens affallande hos pressade Barrträd. 1895. I. 36.¹

— Några iakttagelser öfver årsringarne. 1873. II. 47.[1]
— Några ord om Pinus Abies L. var. virgata. 1877. II. 34.[2]
— Potatisknölar hos Besksötan. 1877. II. 776.[1]
— Rubus Lidforssii Gelert i Skåne. 1891. II. 308.[2]
Nordtirol — Forstverein. See FORSTVEREIN . . . IV. 14.
Nordwestdeutscher Forstverein. Bericht. IV. 10.
Norfolk agricultural society. Transactions. III. 7.
Norfolk and Norwich naturalists' society. Transactions. I. 19.
Norfolk Island Pine. 1872. III. 298.[2]
Norges Landbrugshöiskole. Beretning. III. 10.[2]
Noriega, Thomas. El Ahuehuete. 1879. II. 52.[1]
Norlier, Leone. Le culture forestali artificiali. 1872. IV. 123.[1]
— Der Sumach der österreichischen Südalpen. 1873. III. 524.[3]
Noris, R. Bemestingsleer. 1850. III. 151.
Norman, A. See HOPMAHЪ, A.
Norman, Johannes Musaeus. Florae arcticae norvegiae species. 1893. I. 358.
— Florula tromsöensis. 1893. I. 358.
— Index supplementarius locorum . . . plantarum . . . in provincia arctica Norvegiae. 1864. I. 356. — 1865. I. 356.
— Norges arktiske flora. 1894. I. 358.
— Notationes summatim conceptae observationum florae arcticae. 1881. I. 357.
— Smaaträk af naturens väksthusholdning . . . Granskovhusholdning. 1863. II. 36.[2]
— Specialia loca natalia plantarum . . . in agro arctico Norvegiae. 1868. I. 356.
— Voksesteder for nogle af den norske flora's karplanter söndenfor polarkredsen. 1881. I. 357.
— Yderligere bidrag til kundskaben om karplanternes udbredning. 1883. I. 357.
Normandie — Société d'horticulture du centre de la. See SOCIÉTÉ . . . III. 22.
Normandie — Société Linnéenne. See SOCIÉTÉ LINNÉENNE DU CALVADOS. I. 23.
Normativ für die Betriebs-Regulirung der Domainen-Waldungen. 1819. IV. 299.
Normativ für die Einrichtung der Forstbuchhaltungen. 1819. IV. 299.
Norme e disposizioni stabilite . . . per la coltura ed il taglio dei boschi vincolati. 1896. IV. 305.
Normelli, Emil. Undersökningar om Tallens och Granens tillväxt. 1897. IV. 459,[1] 482.[1]
Normen für den Landtransport der Trifthölzer in der Pfalz. 1876. IV. 389.
Noronha, Fernando. Altingia excelsa malaice et javanice Rasamala. 1790. II. 252.[1]
— Descriptio arboris Ranghas. 1790. II. 454.[2]
— Relatio plantarum javanensium. 1790. I. 467.
Norris, G. P. Grape culture. 1862. III. 550.
Norrin, Johan Petér. Anmarkningsvarda finska kärlväxter. f871. II. 307.[1]
— Arbetsplan för anställande af växtfenologiska observationer i Finland. 1883. I. 223.[1]
— Bidrag till sydöstra Tavastlands flora. 1870. I. 363.
— Flikbladig Alnus incana. 1871. II. 116.[3]
— Flora Kareliae onegensis. 1871. I. 363.
— Kukista ja nüden tarkoituksesta. 1877. I. 237.
— Några för finska floran nya fröväxter. 1871. I. 363.
— En Tallstam. 1876. II. 47.[2]
— Tilia septentrionalis Rupr. i Finland. 1871. II. 518.[1]
Norsk havetidende. III. 10.[3]
De Norske forstforenings aarbog. IV. 5.[2]
Norske forstforenings aarsmøder. Forhandlinger. IV. 5.[2]
Den norske Last-Drager eller Bord-Reduction. See WOLF, E. 1785. IV. 220.
Norske Magasin. I. 8.[3]
Norske universitet. See KONG. NORSKE FREDERIKS UNIVERSITET. I. 8.[3]
Norske videnskabers-selskab. See KONGELIGE NORSKE . . . I. 8.[3]
North, Marianne. Recollections of a happy life. 1892. I. 303, V, XVI.[2]
North American botany. See EATON, Amos. 1817. I. 306.
North American entomologist. III. 7.
North American fauna. See UNITED STATES — DEPARTMENT OF AGRICULTURE — DIVISION OF ORNITHOLOGY AND MAMMALOGY. I. 519.[3]
North American journal of homoeopathy. I. 6.
North American Plums. 1896. III. 433.[1]
North American review. III. 7.

The North American sylva. 1853. I. 516.
North American Thorns. 1894. III. 421.[2]
North Carolina — Agricultural experiment station. Annual report. Bulletin. Special bulletin. Technical bulletin. III. 7.
North China branch of the Royal Asiatic society. See ROYAL ASIATIC SOCIETY . . . I. 28.[3]
North Dakota — Agricultural experiment station. Annual report. Bulletin. Special bulletin. III. 7.
North Dakota — State superintendent of irrigation and forestry. Annual report. IV. 4.
North Louisiana experiment station. See LOUISIANA STATE UNIVERSITY . . . III. 5.
Northeastern lumberman. See MANUFACTURERS' gazette. IV. 4.
Northeim, (Revierförster, Tambach). Die Erziehung der Weisstanne. 1852. IV. 444.[1]
A northern forest. 1895. I. 309.[2]
Northern lumberman. IV. 4.
The Northern Pitch Pine. 1891. II. 45.[2]
Northrop, Birdsey Grant. Arbor day in schools. 1892. IV. 42.[1] V. XXIX.[2]
— Economic tree planting. 1878. IV. 111.[2]
— Forests and floods. 1885. IV. 51.
— How can we promote an interest in forestry? 1885. IV. 51.
— The schools of forestry and industrial schools of Europe. 1878. IV. 30.[2]
— Tree planting, forestry in Europe. 1880. IV. 102.
Northrop, Henry H. Forest changes in Rhode Island. 1889. I. 312, IV. 77.[1]
Northrop, J. I. Pinus rigida Mill. 1889. II. 45.[3]
Northumberland — Natural history society. See NATURAL . . . I. 19.
Northwest horticulturist. III. 7.
Northwestern lumberman. IV. 4.
North-Western provinces and Oudh. See INDIA — NORTH-WESTERN PROVINCES . . .
Nortier, H. KLOETS. See KLOETE NORTIER, H.
Norton, A. On the decadence of Australian forests. 1887. I. 499,[2] IV. 89.[2]
— Notes on a living tree stump. 1887. II. 623.[3]
Norton, James. Fructification of the Bunya. 1882. III. 298.[1]
Norton, John Bitting Smith. A bibliography . . . relating to the effects of wind. 1899. I. 233.[2]
— The effects of wind on trees. 1897. III. 184.[3]
Norwich naturalist's society. See NORFOLK and Norwich naturalists' society. I. 19.
Nos arbres curieux. 1893. IV. 486.[1] — 1894. III. 310,[2] 418,[2] IV. 545,[1] 555,[3] 558,[2] 559,[1] 559.[3] — 1895. II. 97,[1] IV. 516.
Nos arbres curieux. Le Hêtre du Corbeau. 1893. IV. 500.[3]
À nos pépiniéristes. 1894. IV. 545.[1]
Noska, Maximilian. Forstliches aus Ciskaukasien. 1892. IV. 348.[1]
— Wald und Wild in Sibirien. 1893. IV. 370.[1]
Noske, W. C. Vijanden van den tuinbouw en hunne bestrijdingsmiddelen. 1898. III. 197.
Nossek, E. A. See LANGENBACHER, F. L. & NOSSEK, E. A.
Nossek, Emanuel. Ueber die Bedeutung der prädominirenden Stammclasse. 1884. IV. 233.
— Zu Bretschneider's Abstandsverfahren. 1893. IV. 258.
— Ueber den Durchforstungsgrad. 1895. IV. 175.[1]
— Ueber die naturwissenschaftliche Berechtigung der forstlichen Acclimatisationsbestrebungen. 1892. IV. 127.[2]
Nossek, Hugo. Allgemeine Beschreibung des Forstreviers Zabreeg. 1897. IV. 369.
— Beobachtungen über das Verhalten der Raupen der Lithosia-Arten. 1892. IV. 210.[1]
Le nostre principali esportazioni di prodotti agrari e forestali. 1896. IV. 406.[1]
Le nostre principali esportazioni di prodotti . . . e forestali. 1895. IV. 406.[1]
Le nostre principali esportazioni di prodotti . . . silvani. 1895. IV. 406.[1]
Il nostro commercio di importazione di prodotti agrari e forestali negli Stati-Uniti. 1897. IV. 285.[1]
Nota betreffende de behandeling van Kinaplanten. 1877. III. 716.
Nota degli Eucalyptus inviati dal Giardino di Collodi. 1877. III. 633.[1]
Nota van toelichting op het reglement voor het beheer . . . van den lande op Java en Madura. 1876. IV. 376.[2]
Notaris, Giuseppe de. Repertorium florae ligusticae. 1844. I. 427.
— See also MORIS, G. G. & NOTARIS, Giuseppe de.

Notcutt, William Lowndes. A handbook of British plants. 1865. I. 402.
Note,_by_a member, on Col. Bowler's description of the branched Palmyra trees. 1834. II. 65.¹
Note concernant les Lantana. 1868. III. 697.¹
A note from Coorg about forest fires. 1883. IV. 184.¹
Note on a recent case regarding drift timber. 1883. IV. 332.¹
A note on forest management in Tinnevelly. See M., J. G. F.- 1891. IV. 378.
Note on Osmanthus. 1877. II. 713.²
Note on the experimental cultivation of Pithecolobium. 1883. III. 484.²
Note on the Fulwah, Phulwarah, Choree. 1842. III. 667.³
Note on the proposed genus Fitchia. 1855. II. 161.¹
Note on various indigo-giving plants. 1848. III. 236.
Note overo memorie del Museo di Lodovico Moscardo. See MOSCARDO, Lodovico, conte. 1656. I. 60.³
Note rectificative de l'opinion émise par M. Viallanes. 1879. III. 571.
A note regarding certain Indian tanning materials. 1890. IV. 435.
Note sur l'Ampelopsis tricuspidata. 1877. III. 545.¹
Note sur l'arbre ... sous les noms d'Orgueil de la Chine. 1842. III. 512.²
Note sur l'Aristolochia cymbifera. 1869. III. 386.¹
Note sur l'Aristolochia Goldieana Hook. f. 1868. II. 182.²
Note sur l'Echinopsis Zuccarinii Ott. var. Rolandi. 1866. III. 622.²
Note sur l'Epigaea repens. 1859. III. 649.²
Note sur l'Epiphyllum truncatum. 1866. III. 623.¹
Note sur l'Érable plane à feuilles rouges. 1868. III. 535.²
Note sur l'Erica Ingrami. 1857. III. 651.¹
Note sur l'essence de canelle. 1892. III. 406.¹
Note sur l'Idesia polycarpa. 1876. II. 571.²
Note sur l'Opuntia Rafinesqui Engelm. 1876. III. 625.¹
Note sur la cire du Japon. 1859. III. 527.²
Note sur la culture et les usages du Pin Laricio. See MALLET DE CHILLY. 1820. IV. 465.¹
Note sur la forêt de la Joux. 1900. IV. 556.¹
Note sur la greffe Turlure. 1842. III. 160.
Note sur la question du reboisement ... d'Alger. 1884. IV. 168.¹
Note sur le Bignonia speciosa Grab. 1867. III. 706.²
Note sur le Camellia oleifera. 1846. III. 600.¹
Note sur le Cinchona Condaminea. 1869. II. 814.¹
Note sur le Coing de la Chine. 1833. III. 420.²
Note sur le Dendromecon rigidum. 1860. III. 408.²
Note sur le Disemma coccinea. 1865. II. 577.²
Note sur le Dombeya Mastersii. 1870. III. 591.¹
Note sur le Fremontia californica. 1867. III. 591.¹
Note sur le Keteleeria Fortunei Carr. 1872. III. 304.²
Note sur le Lalage ornata Lindl., ou le Lalage paré. 1859. III. 467.²
Note sur le Micocoulier. 1873. III. 363.²
Note sur le Noisetier. See * * * Note sur le Noisetier. 1871. II. 121.²
Note sur le Passiflora fulgens Wallis. 1866. II. 578.¹
Note sur le Paullinia thalictrifolia. 1880. III. 540.¹
Note sur le Pin d'Alep. 1833. II. 45.²
Note sur le Robinier pyramidal. 1864. III. 487.¹
Note sur le Sanchesia nobilis. 1867. III. 710.¹
Note sur le Tacsonia mollissima. 1857. III. 616.²
Note sur le Thyrsacanthus rutilans Pl. 1865. III. 709.²
Note sur les arbres à rameaux pendans. 1831. III. 488.¹
Note sur les Bouvardia hybrides. 1885. III. 711.¹
Note sur les Clématites hybrides. 1877. III. 389.¹
Note sur les pépinières forestières. See GRANDEAU, Louis. 1878. IV. 150.
Note sur les plantations d'arbres exotiques faites par MM. de Thury et ... M. le baron de Morogues. 1832. III. 124.¹
Note sur les semis de bois résineux. See VINGTAIN, Léon. 1869. IV. 441.
Note sur quelques variétés nouvelles. 1857. III. 639.²
Note sur un produit cotonneux. 1848. III. 754.²
Note sur une grappe de raisin. 1822. II. 507.²
Note sur une greffe de Mimosa longifolia. 1835. III. 465.¹
Notemuskaatcultuur. 1885. III. 402.²
Noter, Raphael de. Les Acacias australiens en Algérie. 1883. III. 463.¹
— Arbres fruitiers et plantes officinales. 1883. III. 130.¹
— Les Orangers, Citronniers. 1896. III. 497.²
— Les Palmiers de serre froide. 1895. III. 318.¹
— Sur quelques arbres fruitiers et plantes officinales. 1886. III. 130.²
— La taille des arbres fruitiers. 18?.? III. 172.

Notes and queries on China and Japan. I. 28.²
Notes and queries on the far east. See CHINA review. I. 28.²
Notes and reports on a wax-yielding insect. 1878. III. 226.¹
Notes made ... upon the rate of growth. 1848. I. 191.¹
Notes on arboriculture in the Bombay presidency. 1884. III. 129.²
Notes on Bombay plants. See NAIRNE, A. K. 1885. I. 475.¹
Notes on Coffee from Laborie's Coffee planter. 1895. III. 727.
Notes on Conifers for Kansas planters. 1890. III. 118,¹ 233.
Notes on Egyptian agriculture. 1865. III. 280.²
Notes on Fir timber. 1874. IV. 443.¹
Notes on gutta-percha. 1893. III. 689.¹
Notes on Indian forest produce. 1874. IV. 401.¹
Notes on Kola or Bissy. 1896. III. 590.¹
Notes on Orange-tree plagues in the Azores. 1867. III. 500.³
Notes on plants yielding rubber. 1894. III. 229.
Notes on some new trees and shrubs. 1876. III. 78.²
Notes on some plants ... of south-east Kumaun. 1885. I. 475.¹
Notes on supposed poisonous plants. 1891. III. 479.²
Notes on the art of growing Roses. See FISHER, O. 1867. III. 452.
Notes on the fauna and flora of Round Island. See BARKLY, Sir Henry. 1870. I. 482.
Notes on the forests near Laubach in Oberhesse. See NOTES taken on excursions ... 1900. IV. 351.³
Notes on the International forestry exhibition at Edinburgh. 1885. IV. 21.³
Notes on the Olive. 1878. III. 679.¹
Notes on the Orange. 1896. III. 500.³
Notes on the Orange borer. 1892. III. 498.³
Notes on the Pine trees of lower Virginia. See RUFFIN, Edmund. 1859. II. 39.¹
Notes on the properties of wood. 1867. IV. 408.
Notes on the town forest of Frankfort-on-Main. 1900. IV. 355.¹
Notes on trees suitable for planting in and about towns in the West Indies. 1887. III. 42.³
Notes sur le recrutement du corps forestier. 1884. IV. 54,² 292.
Notes sur les semis du Pin de Riga. See MALLET DE CHILLY. 1820. IV. 471.
Notes sur quelques espèces distribuées. 1874. I. 414.
Notes sur une liane à caoutchouc de l'Indo-Chine. 1900. III. 230.
Notes taken on excursions to forests near Giessen. 1900. IV. 351.³
Notestein, F. N. Mamillaria Notesteinii Britton. 1892. II. 595.¹
Noth- und Hülfstafel zur Vertilgung der schädlichen Wald-raupe. 1797. IV. 200.
Nothnagel, Hermann. Handbuch der Arzneimittellehre. 1870. III. 258.
Nothsignale praktischer Forstmänner. IV. 10.
Nothwendige Kenntnisse und Erläuterungen des Forst- und Jagdwesens in Bajern. 1780. IV. 350.²
Von der nothwendigen Beachtung der Servituten bei den Forsteinrichtungen. 1848. IV. 333.
Notice importante sur deux espèces du genar Callebassier. 1809. II. 787.³
Notice of a species of cannibalism. 1822. III. 611.¹
Notice of Acacia Farnesiana. 1851. III. 465.¹
Notice of various fibrous materials. 1857. III. 234.
Notice sur Félix Louis L'Herminier. See GUIBURT, N. J. B. G. 1834. IV. 358.¹
Notice sur l'Aesculus californica. 1859. III. 536.²
Notice sur l'Andromède du Japon. 1871. III. 656.¹
Notice sur l'emploi du bois dans la construction des chaussées. See SURVILLE. 1840. IV. 425.²
Notice sur l'état des bois et des forêts en France. 1796. IV. 359.³
Notice sur l'Exposition de l'Administration des forêts. 1865. IV. 20.¹
Notice sur la culture de l'Osier en France. See LA BARRE, Gaston de. 19..? III. 349.¹
Notice sur la forêt de Réchicourt. 1881. IV. 360.
Notice sur la laine végétale tirée des feuilles du Pin silvestre. See LAINE végétale ... 1853. IV. 482.²
Notice sur la Nouvelle-Calédonie. 1900. III. 283.²
Notice sur le Baobab. 1859. II. 529.¹
Notice sur le Beloperone plumbaginifolia. 1859. III. 709.¹

Notice sur le Berberidopsis corallina. 1863. III. 614.[1]
Notice sur le Ceanothus Veitchianus. 1860. III. 541.[2]
Notice sur le Chamaebatia foliolosa. 1860. III. 420.[2]
Notice sur le Chêne-chapelle. 1863. II. 138.[1]
Notice sur le Clematis caerulea Lindl. var. Guascoi. 1857. III. 390.[2]
Notice sur le Clerodendron Thomsonae. 1863. III. 696.[2]
Notice sur le Cordyline (Dracaena) metallica. 1872. III. 335.
Notice sur le Cyprès. 1837. III. 302.[2]
Notice sur le dixième arrondissement forestier, Hautes Alpes. See BILLECARD, L. 1889. IV. 361.
Notice sur le Dracaena Massangeana. 1881. III. 336.[2]
Notice sur le Gardenia Stanleyana Hook. 1870. II. 829.[2]
Notice sur le genre Philadelphus. See KOCH, Karl. 1859. III. 413.[1]
Notice sur le Geranium quinquevulnerum. 1859. III. 491.[2]
Notice sur le Jardin botanique de Liège. See LE ROY, Alphonse. 1867. I. 50.
Notice sur le Maackia amurensis. 1870. II. 346.[2]
Notice sur le Rhodotypos kerrioides. 1869. III. 447.[2]
Notice sur le Sapin pleureur de Richard Smith. 1860. III. 305.[1]
Notice sur le Zelkoua. 1831. III. 366.[1]
Notice sur les Érables. 1857. IV. 526.[2]
Notice sur les forêts . . . de Hongrie. 1878. IV. 373.
Notice sur les forêts de l'Algérie. See FILLIAS, Ach. 1878. IV. 379.[1]
Notice sur les forêts de la Tunisie. See LEFEBVRE, Henri. 1889. IV. 379.[1]
Notice sur les forêts des héritiers du Prince Zacharie Jvanovitch Melikoff. See JOURAKOVSKY, V. A. 1897. IV. 348.[1]
Notice sur les modifications que l'administration des forêts a subies depuis 1779. 1849. IV. 292.
Notice sur les Orangers. See HIS, Charles. 1829. II. 401.[2]
Notice sur les Pivoines en arbre. See HIS, Charles. 1842. II. 200.[2]
Notice sur les reboisements du Puy-de-Dôme. See BERTRAND. 1885. IV. 163.
Notice sur Montigny-Leucoup. 1889. II. 28.[1]
Notice sur quelques arbres cultivés dans le territoire de Nice. 1831. III. 84,[1] 184.[1]
Notice sur quelques nouveaux Fuchsias. 1859. III. 640.[2]
Notices of new or remarkable varieties of fruits. 1822. III. 439.[1]
Notices sur l'Exposition de l'École impériale forestière . . . à Paris. 1860. IV. 20.[1]
Notices sur les cartes . . . relatifs aux travaux executés par le service du reboisement. 1875. IV. 162.
Notices sur les forêts du royaume de Roumanie. 1900. IV. 375.[1]
Notices sur quelques espèces rares de bois résineux. See NOTIZEN über einige neue . . . Nadelhölzer. 1875. III. 290.
Noticias forestales de los Estados-Unidos. 1885. IV. 338.[1]
Notions élémentaires de botanique. See DURANDE, J. F. 1781. I. 83.
Notions pratique sur le choix et le classement des bois de marine. See FORCADE, de. 1859. IV. 425.[1]
Notions premières; greffes. 1833. III. 160.
Notions sommaires de sylviculture. 1899. IV. 122.[1]
Notiz über die Maulbeerbäume . . . um Paris. 1834. III. 374.
Notizen aus dem Gebiete der Natur- und Heilkunde. I. 14.
Notizen über Alter . . . einiger Waldbäume im Banater Gebirge. 1860. I. 298.
Notizen über die ärarialische Torfnutzung in Bayern. 1858. IV. 438.[1]
Notizen über einige neue . . . Nadelhölzer. 1875. III. 290.
Notizen und Wegweiser zu den forstlichen Exkursionen . . . zu Olbernhau. 1896. IV. 355.[2]
Notizie delle campagne. 1864. IV. 283.[1]
Notizie entomologiche. 1881. IV. 92.
Notizie intorno ai boschi e terreni soggetti al vincolo forestale. 1886. IV. 293.[1]
Notizie sul regime forestale di diverse contrade. 1863. IV. 111.[1]
Notizie sull' uso dei vasi ad irrigazione sotterranea. See S., M. (Prof.) 1898. III. 151.
Notizie sulla Bosnia. 1866. IV. 374.[2]
Nott, Josiah Clark & Gliddon, G. R. The age of Cypress forests. 1854. II. 51.[2]
Nottberg, P. Experimental-Untersuchungen über die Entstehung der Harzgallen . . . bei unseren Abietineen. 1897. II. 21.[1]

Notting. See SOUPERT & NOTTING.
Notulen der vergadering ter bespreking van de Koffiebladziekte. 1880. III. 735.
Nouel, A. A. Notice sur quelques plantes . . . du Loiret. 1866. I. 413.
Noulet, Jean Baptiste. Flore analytique de Toulouse. 1855. I. 411.
— Flore du bassin sous-Pyrénéen. 1837. I. 409.
— Note sur des semis spontanés de Platane d'orient. 1871. II. 255.[1]
Nourij, Franz Gustav. Historia botanica . . . foliorum Diosmae serratifoliae. 1827. III. 495.[2]
Nourrigat, E. Note relative à la destruction des œufs de phylloxera. 1873. III. 565.[1]
Nourrigat, Émile. Le Mûrier du Japon. ·1873- III. 380.[1]
Sur la nourriture des plantes. 1714. I. 162.
Nourse, Timothy. Campania fœlix. 1700. III. 109.
Nourse, William E. C. On the colours of leaves and petals. 1845. I. 184.
Noury. Bois de Chêne de construction. 1839. IV. 514.[1]
Noury, Raphaël. Tarifs d'après le système métrique pour cuber les bois. 1808. IV. 221.
Un nouveau coin. 1895. IV. 556.[2]
Un nouveau compas forestier. 1878. IV. 231.[2]
Nouveau cours complet d'agriculture. 1809. III. 31.
Nouveau dictionnaire d'histoire naturelle. 1816. III. 31.
Nouveau dictionnaire d'histoire naturelle appliquée. 1803. I. 33.
Nouveau dictionnaire de médecine. 1864. III. 243.
Un nouveau fruit à la Noël. 1899. III. 614.[1]
Le nouveau jardinier illustré. 1897. III. 20.
Nouveau journal asiatique. See JOURNAL . . . I. 21.
Nouveau journal de médecine. See JOURNAL de médecine, chirurgie . . . I. 21.
Un nouveau mode d'arrosage des arbres d'alignement. 1897. III. 211.[2]
Nouveau mode d'arrosage des arbres des boulevards. See Un NOUVEAU mode d'arrosage des arbres d'alignement. 1897. III. 211.[2]
Un nouveau mode de vente des affouages. 1897. IV. 557.[1]
Nouveau Montpellier médical. See MONTPELLIER médical. I. 22.
Nouveau plan de la forêt domaniale de Retz. 1869. IV. 360.
Un nouveau poison. 1849. III. 688.[1]
Nouveau procédé de conservation des fruits. 1895. I. 521.[1]
Nouveau procédé de conservation des plantes. 1880. I. 521.[1]
Un nouveau procédé de gravure sur bois. 1896. IV. 428.[1]
Nouveau système de chaussure économique. 1856. IV. 428,[2] 534.[2]
Un nouveau tannin. 1886. IV. 515.[1]
Nouveau tarif pour le toisé des bois en grume. 1793. IV. 220.
Nouveau Thé. 1833. III. 423.[1]
Sur un nouveau thé du Cap de Bonne-Espérance. 1854. III. 473.[2]
Nouveau traité . . . de l'éducation des vers à soie. 1843. III. 376.
Nouveau traité des Orangers et Citronniers. 1692. III. 496.[2]
Nouveau traité pour la culture des fleurs. See MORIN, Pierre. 1862. III. 111.
Nouveau voyage aux isles de l'Amérique. See LABAT, J. B. 1722. III. 266.
Nouveaux élémens de botanique. See HANIN, L. 1809. I. 85.
Un nouvel alcaloïde. 1887. III. 401.[2]
Un nouvel aménagement de la forêt de Mouterhausen. 1876. IV. 249.[1]
Nouvel arrêté organique du personnel. 1896. IV. 303.[2]
Nouvel Azalée de l'Inde. 1831. III. 659.[1]
Un nouvel emploi de la tourbe. 1896. IV. 144.[2]
Nouvel usage du bois. 1899. IV. 557.[2]
Nouvel usage du Myrte. 1841. III. 637.[1]
Sur une nouvelle classification des Vignes. See MUNSON, T. V. 1885. III. 547.
Une nouvelle écorce tannante. See L'ÉCORCE de Mimosa. 1892. III. 481.[2]
Une nouvelle gomme. 1889. III. 227.
Une nouvelle huile. 1887. III. 583.[1]
Nouvelle instruction facile pour la culture des Figuiers. 1692. III. 369.[1]
La nouvelle maison de campagne. See A., L. E. 1854. III. 113.

Nouvelle méthode pour cultiver toutes sortes d'arbres fruitiers. *See* DU MOULIN. 1763. III. 143.
Nouvelle observation sur la culture de l'Euphorbia jacquiniaeflora. 1840. III. 518.[1]
Nouvelle scie à ruban. 1896. IV. 393.
Une nouvelle société forestière en Allemagne. 1900. IV. 40.[2]
Nouvelle source d'acide citrique. 1869. III. 699.[2]
Une nouvelle source de caoutchouc. 1884. III. 690.[1]
Nouvelle source de théine. 1865. III. 539.[2]
Une nouvelle utilisation du bois. 1895. IV. 558.[1]
Nouvelles annales de la marine. III. 20.
Nouvelles archives des missions scientifiques. III. 20.
Nouvelles observations sur le Cytise-Adam. 1838. II. 368.[2]
Novák, Antonin. Pěstování Vrby košikářské. 1884. III. 348.
— Vrba uralská. 1881. III. 352.[1]
Novák, Theodor. Rašeliny Zdárského pohoři. 1900. I. 444.
Novarum stirpium decades. *See* ENDLICHER, S. L. & FENZL, Eduard. 1839. I. 268.
Novellis, Ettore de. Il male della gomma degli Agrumi. 1879. III. 498.[1]
Novi, Giuseppe. Sur l'emploi des sables volcaniques dans le traitement des Vignes. 1880. III. 572.
— La fillossera devastatrice delle Viti. 1879. III. 572.[.]
Novicki, Constantin von. Die Eisenindustrie in ihrer Beziehung zur Forstwirthschaft in Böhmen. 1867. IV. 278.[2]
— Die fossilen Kohlen und die Forstwirthschaft in Böhmen. 1868. IV. 278.[2]
— Der metallische Bergbau und die Forstwirthschaft in Böhmen. 1866. IV. 278.[2]
Novikof, S. *See* НОВИКОВЪ, С.
Novitzki, Tr. *See* НОВИЦКІЙ, Тр.
Novo-Aleksandriski ... *See* НОВО-АЛЕКСАНДРІЙСКІЙ ...
Novorossiskoye ... *See* НОВОРОССІЙСКОЕ ...
Novotorski, Miksa. Hibiscus subviolaceus. 1900. III. 588.[2]
Nowacki, Anton. Ueber die Gelbsucht der Zwergobstbäume. 1896. III. 181.[1]
— Praktische Bodenkunde. 1899. IV. 70.
— Die Streunoth. 1887. IV. 438.[1]
Nowak, Josef. Ueber den fabrikmässigen Betrieb der trockenen Destillation des Holzes. 1872. IV. 432.[2]
Nowell, John. *See* BAKER, J. G. & NOWELL, John.
Nowicki, Const. von. Ideen über die Aufgabe der Forststatistik in Böhmen. 1883. IV. 371.
— Die Torfmoore Böhmens in klimatischer Beziehung. 1865. IV. 53.
— Die Verkehrsaustalten und der Holzexport in Böhmen. 1867. IV. 406.[2]
Nowicki, Henryk. O naprężeniu tkanek u roślin. 1874. I. 149.[2]
Nowicki, Max. Der Kopaliner Heerwurm. 1868. III. 190.
Nowodworsky, Johann. Elenchus plantarum ... in horto ... Josephi Malabaila de Canal. 1804. I. 65.[2]
Noyer. Forêts vierges de la Guiane française. 1827. IV. 342.[1]
Le Noyer à feuilles laciniées. 1887. III. 355.
Un Noyer de 900 ans. 1895. II. 114.[1]
Le Nûn de Yucatan. 1873. III. 529.[2]
Nürnberg — Naturhistorische Gesellschaft. *See* NATURHISTORISCHE ... I. 13.
Nüssle, Karl. Ueber das Verpflanzen starker Bäume. 1895. III. 168.[1]
Nüsslin, Otto. Die Tannenwurzellaus. 1899. IV. 446.[1]
— Ueber eine Weisstannentrieblaus. 1899. IV. 446.[1]
Nuestro grabado. El Roble de Montoto. 1897. IV. 559.[2]
Nützliches Handwörterbuch für angehende Forst- und Waidmänner. 1796. IV. 22.[1]
Nueva escuela forestal. 1885. IV. 540.[2]
Nueva escuela forestal [en Cooper's Hill]. 1889. IV. 540.[2]
Nueva farmacopea mexicana. 1874. III. 247.[1]
Nueva receta para la preparación del caldo bordelés. *See* Ein NEUES Recept ... 1900. IV. 548.[2]
Nuevas combinaciones. *See* ROSAINZ, Miguel. 1893. I. 337.
Nuevo escalafón. 1889. IV. 553.[1]
Nuevo horno para leñas menudas. 1892. IV. 432.[1]
Nuevos proyectos de ordenación. 1890. IV. 550.[2]
Nul sursis à l'exécution des jugements. 1900. IV. 327.
Number of species of the genus Rosa. 1826. II. 282.[1]
A numerical list of dried specimens of plants. *See* WALLICH, Nathaniel. 1828. I. 471.
Número y cabida de los montes públicos. 1890. IV. 363.[2]
Nunes, Alvaro. Relatione. 1565. III. 265.[2]

Nuñez de Arenas, Bernardino. Cartas sobre la existencia y conservación de los montes. 1854. IV. 363.[1]
Una nuova applicazione del legname d' Abeto rosso. 1883. IV. 429.[1]
Nuova farmacopea germanica. *See* PHARMACOPOEA Germaniae. 1865. III. 249.
Nuova legge forestale della Spagna. 1863. IV. 327.[1]
La nuova legge forestale dinanzi alla Camera. 1898. IV. 329.
Nuova malattia degli Olivi. 1864. III. 677.[2]
Una nuova malattia del Castagno. 1896. IV. 493.[1]
Nuova pianta tessile. 1865. III. 234.
Nuova rivista forestale. IV. 13.[1]
Una nuova scuola forestale. 1888. IV. 34.[1]
D' una nuova sostanza per conservare il legname di Faggio. 1878. IV. 420.
La nuova stazione per l' esame delle sementi. 1896. IV. 147.[1]
Nuove scuole forestali. 1885. IV. 34.[1]
Nuovi annali delle scienze naturali. I. 25.
Nuovo albero ornamentale. 1865. III. 429.[1]
Nuovo baco da seta. 1865. III. 148.[1]
Il nuovo cimento. *See* GIORNALE toscano di scienze. I. 25.
Nuovo dendrometro. 1885. IV. 215.
Un nuovo foraggio. 1895. IV. 485.[1]
Nuovo giornale botanico italiano. *See* GIORNALE ... I. 25.
Nuovo giornale dei letterati. *See* GIORNALE ... I. 520.[1]
Un nuovo modo di trattare i turaccioli di Sughero. 1896. IV. 518.[1]
Un nuovo ramo di piccole industrie forestali in Russia. 1890. IV. 428.[1]
Nuovo regolamento di polizia forestale ... di Sondrio. 1898. IV. 305.
Nuovo surrogato del tannino nella concia delle pelli. *See* LOHEKULǎUR ... 1878. IV. 435.
Un nuovo Thè. 1864. III. 580.[2]
Nurbel, E. Les Aralia. 1898. III. 641.[1]
— Le Cereus giganteus ... du Mexique. 1897. II. 590.[1]
— Les Ixora. 1898. III. 745.[1]
Nussbaumer. Ueber Durchforstungen. 1849. IV. 173, 868.
— Ueber das Vorkommen der Eiche im westlichen Böhmen. 1852. IV. 504.
Nut-bearing trees. 1867. III. 220.[1]
Nut culture in the United States. *See* CORSA, W. P. 1896. III. 62.
Over het nut van den Plataanboom. 1805. III. 418.[2]
Nuthall, W. F. A list of woods indigenous to Arracan. 1845. IV. 400.[2]
Nutius, Michael. Fasciculus, seu elenchus herbarum. 1678. I. 287.
Nutmeg cultivation in Jamaica. 1892. III. 402.[2]
The Nutmeg plantation. 1857. III. 402.[1]
The Nutmeg tree. 1849. III. 402.[2]
Nutmegs. 1888. III. 402.[2]
Nutriamo i bachi da seta con foglia spolverata. 1896. III. 380.[1]
Nuts of commerce. *See* NUTS, old, new, and curious. 1890. III. 220.[1]
Nuts, old, new, and curious. 1890. III. 220.[1]
Nuttall, G. C. The discoloration of cut apples. 1899. II. 267.[2]
— National tree-planting. 1898. IV. 42.[1]
Nuttall, Lawrence William. *See* MILLSPAUGH, C. F. & NUTTALL, L. W.
Nuttall, Thomas. Bizarrerie sur des Pommes. 1830. II. 266.[2]
— Bootan Rhododendrons. 1853. II. 676.[2]
— A catalogue of a collection of plants made in East-Florida. 1822. I. 318:
— A catalogue of new and interesting plants, collected in upper Louisiana. 1813. 1. 318, V. XVII.[2]
— Collections towards a flora of the territory of Arkansas. 1837. I. 318, V. XVII.[2]
— Description and notices of new or rare plants. 1843. I. 307.
— A description of some of the rarer or little known plants indigenous to the United States. 1834. I. 306.
— Descriptions of new species and genera of ... Compositae. 1841. II. 848.[1]
— Descriptions of plants collected by William Gambel. 1848. I. 322.
— Descriptions of ... some species of Rhododendron. 1853. II. 676.[2]
— The genera of North American plants. 1818. I. 306.

— An introduction to . . . botany, 1827. I. 86.
— A journal of travels into the Arkansas Territory. 1821. I. 318, V. XVII.[2]
— The North American sylva. 1842. I. 304, IV. 75,[2] V. XVI.[2]
— Remarques sur les Rhododendron du Bootan. 1853. II. 676.[3]
— Les Rhododendron d'Assam et du Bootan. 1853. II. 676.[3]
— Rhododendron von Assam und von Bootan. 1853. II. 676.[3]
— On Simmondsia. 1844. II. 453.[1]
— Transformed produce of an Apple tree. 1830. II. 266.[3]
— On two new genera of Californian plants. 1838. II. 781.[1]
— See also WYETH, N. B. & NUTTALL, Thomas.
Nuttigheid van het planten der Abeel. 1773. III. 345.[1]
Nutzbarmachung der Früchte des japanischen wilden Quittenbaumes. 1850. III. 420.[1]
Ueber den Nutzen der Eucalyptus. 1880. IV. 530.
Ueber den Nutzen . . . der Zürbelkiefer in Bayern. 1858. IV. 463.[2]
Ueber den Nutzen des Anbaues . . . der . . . Schwarz-Föhre. 1858. IV. 465.[1]
Nutzen und Vortheile der Anzucht von Weiden. 1856. III. 347.
Nutzhorn, Octavius. Forst- og Jagtlov. 1870. IV. 315.[1]
— Skov og Land. 1873. IV. 44, 269.
Nuys, J. van. Over het beplanten van duinen. 1782. IV. 159.
Ny Pharmaceutisk Tidende. See PHARMACEUTISK Tidende. I. 9.[1]
Nya botaniska notiser. See BOTANISKA notiser. I. 8.[1]
Nyáry, Gyula, báró. A Mahóni és Mahagóni. 1896. III. 395.[3]
— A Mandolafa. 1895. III. 434.[1]
— A Som. 1897. III. 646.[1]
Nyberg, Johannes Ulr. Remedia guineensis. See AFZELIUS, Adam. 1813. III. 93,[1] 475.[2]
Nyblaeus, Johan Eric. De Brunia. See THUNBERG, C. P. 1804. II. 251.[1]
Nyctagenea. See ALLEMÃO, F. F. 1845. II. 190.[2]
Nyctère des Amazones. 1833. II. 775.[1]
Nye landoeconomiske Tidender. See LANDOECONOMISKE . . . III. 10.[2]
Nye oeconomiske Annaler. See OECONOMISKE . . . III. 11.
En nye Varietet af Morbærtrœet. 1842. III. 376.
Nyegaard, C. T. Anviisning til Havedyrkning. 1858. III. 100.[3]
— Veiledning til Trœers Opelskning. 1869. III. 100.[1]
Nyeland, Stephan. Alleerne i og omkring Hovedstaden. 1879. III. 209.
— Cydonia Maulii. 1892. III. 420.[3]
— Om Formering ved Stiklinger. 1882. I. 209.[1]
— Frugthavedyrkningen efter den nvere Beskjœringsmaade. 1873. III. 134.[2]
— Kuldens Indflydelse paa Frilands Trœer. 1871. III. 44.[2]
— Mirabellen. 1894. III. 436.[1]
— Rosa carolina. 1891. III. 455.[1]
Nyland, E. Schetsen uit Insulinde. 1892. III. 275.[1]
Nylander, Adolph Abraham. Stirpes cotyledoneae paroeciae Pojo. See ENGSTRÖM, J. M. von. 1844. I. 361.
Nyiander, William. Conspectus florae helsingforsiensis 1850. I. 361.
— Utdrag af ett bref, dat. Kola. 1842. I. 354.
— & Saelan, Thiodolf. Herbarium Musei fennici. 1859. I. 355.
Nylandt, Petrus. De medicyn-winckel. 1679. III. 76.
— De Nederlandtse herbarius. 1670. I. 287, V. XVI.[1]
— Neues medicinalisches Kräuterbuch. 1678. III. 54.
— De nieuwe verstandigen hovenier. 1670. III. 105.
— Den verstandigen hovenier. 1670. III. 105.
Nylund, E. Havupuiden siementen kokoomisesta. 1890. IV. 148.
— Matkamuistoja Ruotsista vuonna 1891. 1892. IV. 344.[2]
— Matkustus Saksassa vuosina 1891-1892. 1893. IV. 349.[2]
Nyman, Carl Fredrik. Acer platanoides med tretalig pistill. 1849. II. 479.[2]
— Bidrag till Gottlands flora. 1840. II. 138.[1]
— Botanikens första grunder. 1849. I. 89.
— Conspectus florae europaeae. 1878. I. 349.
— Maltas vårvegetation. 1845. I. 452.
— Observationes in floram Siculam. 1844. I. 431.
— Öfversigt af vāxt-familjerna. 1843. I. 261.
— Rosa centifolia fl. pleno. 1849. II. 292.[1]

— Om siciliens flora. 1847. I. 431.
— Sylloge florae europaeae. 1854. I. 349.
— Synopsis plantarum Bicornium europæarum. 1851. II. 655.[1]
— Utkast till svenska vāxternas naturhistoria. 1867. I. 356.
Nyman, Eric Olof August. Om några kotteformer af Granen. 1896. II. 35.[3]
Nyman, P. A. Tutkimuksia hongistumisesta Ounasjoen hoitoalueessa kesinä v. 1898 ja 1899. 1900. ·IV. 196.[1]
Nypels, Paul. Les arbres des promenades urbaines. 1898. III. 212.[1]
— Maladies de plantes cultivées. 1898. III. 212.[1]
— Notes pathologiques. 1897. III. 345,[2] IV. 467.[2]
— Les parasites du bois de la Cambre. 1899. IV. 549.[2]
— Le Peridermium du Weymouth. 1900. IV. 470.[1]
Nys, L. C. de. Rapport over de inlandsche nijverheid op het eiland Biliton. 1890. III. 274.[2]
Nyst, P. Catalogue des plantes cultivées dans le Jardin botanique . . . de Bruxelles. 1826. I. 49.
— Catalogue Linnéen des plantes du plateau de St. Pierre. 1821. I. 392.
Nyt Bibliothek. See PHYSIKALSK-OECONOMISK . . . I. 9.[1]
Nyt Magasin for Naturvidenskaberne. I. 8.[3]

—o—. Ist eine Umgestaltung der bisherigen Ausbildungsmethode der Forstschutzbeamten wünschenswert? 1891. IV. 33.[3]
— o —. Parkinsonia als Heckenpflanze. 1882. III. 483.[1]
O. ↓Debe reformarse la Junta consultiva? 1899. IV. 554.
O. Iets over de hybride van Liberia- met Java-Koffie. 1893. III. 742.[3]
O., D. Los montes protectores y las inundaciones. 1893. III. 742.[3]
O., G. W. Élagage des arbres d'avenues. 1895. III. 211.[3]
O., G. W. Poda de los árboles de las calles. 1895. III. 211.[3]
O., G. W. Pruning of.street-trees. 1895. III. 211.[3]
O., H. Ceraeus Spachiana A. Lav. 1879. III. 439.[1]
O., H. Fruchtansatz der Cocos Weddelliana. 1880. III. 324.[2]
O., H. Fuchsia syringaeflora liboniafolia. 1879. III. 640.[1]
O., H. Ueber Nipa fruticans. 1878. III. 327.[2]
O., H. Ptelea trifoliata als Ersatz für Hopfen. 1880. III. 505.[2]
O., J. J. Evergreen Barberries. 1869. III. 393.[2]
O., P. M. La culture du Kapok. 1895. III. 692.[3]
O., P. M. Kapok cultivation. 1895. III. 692.[3]
O., R. Bye-notes on Nile trees. 1872. II. 69.[1]
O., S. Multiplication par boutures du Rhododendrum. 1841. III. 658.[2]
O., S. On the propagation of the·Rhododendron. 1841. III. 658.[2]
O., S. v. d. See S. v. D. O.
O., T. The propagation and culture of Dracaenas. 1885. III. 334.[2]
O., V. v. Iets over duinbeplanting. 1865. IV. 160.[1]
O., W. Bambusa palmata. 1896. III. 316.[1]
O., W. Magnolia Campbelli. 1898. III. 399.[2]
O., W. The Strawberry tree . . . in fruit. 1900. III. 645.[3]
O., W. & Z., G. Corylus algeriensis. 1878. III. 358.[1]
O. S. U. naturalist. See OHIO state university naturalist. I. 6.
O. Y., v. Culture du Pin sylvestre dans les terrains sablonneux. See OUTRYVE D'YDEWALLE, van. 1895. IV. 559.[1]
Oadal, or fibre of Sterculia villosa. 1849. III. 592.[1]
The Oak. 1842. II. 138.[1]
Oak-bark peelers. 1835. IV. 434.
Oak destroyed by lightning. 1884. IV. 194.
Oak-galls and their occupants. 1874. IV. 510.
Of the Oak, its etymology. 1733. III. 361.[1]
The Oak of history and poetry. 1875. II. 132.[1]
Oak of Mamre or Abraham's Oak. 1893. II. 132.[1]
Oak plantations. 1855. IV. 505.
The Oak scale. 1885. IV. 511.
Oak-trees liable to be struck by lightning. 1830. IV. 193.[2]
Oakes, William. Botany of Vermont. 1842. I. 313.
— Notice of some rare plants of New England. 1841. II. 843.[1]
The Oaks of California. 1873. II. 528.[1]
Oates, Frank. Matabele Land and the Victoria Falls. 1881. I. 492.[3]
O'B., T. The propagation of Conifers. 1885. III. 294.[3]
Obach, Eugen Friedrich August. Getah-pertja. 1898. III. 232.[1]
— Die Gutta percha. 1898. III. 232.[1]
— Gutta percha. — Cantor lectures. .1898. III. 232.[1]

Obbarius, K. L. Die Waldhuth- und Waldstreunutzung. 1840. IV. 135.[1]
Oberdieck, Hermann. Etymologie von Obstnamen. 1866. I. 73.[2]
Oberdieck, Johann Georg Conrad. Anleitung zur Kenntniss und Anpflanzung des besten Obstes. 1852. III. 137.
— Aufbewahrung der Edelreiser bis zum Veredeln. 1860. III. 161.
— Beobachtungen über das Erfrieren vieler Gewächse. 1872. III. 182.
— Das beste Mittel, frisch verpflanzte Bäume . . . in Trieb zu bringen. 1878. III. 166.
— Deutschlands beste Obstsorten. 1881. III. 71.
— Erfahrungen über Tauglichkeit . . . der Pflaumen. 1876. III. 432.[2]
— Die Probe- oder Sortenbäume. 1844. III. 71.
— Over de uitwerkselen van felle vorst op boomen. 1828. III. 182.
— Verhandeling ter beantwoording der vrage: Welke zijn de gevolgen van den winter 1822 geweest. 1828. III. 46.[1]
— Wie werden Pfropfreiser . . . vor den Treiben der Augen bewahrt. 1860. III. 161.
— See also JAHN, Fr., LUCAS, Eduard, OBERDIECK, J. G. C.
— & LUCAS, Eduard. Beiträge zur Hebung der Obstcultur. 1857. III. 137.
Oberdörffer. Sur l'essai du baume de Copahu. 1846. III. 473.[1]
Oberhessische Gesellschaft für Natur- und Heilkunde. Bericht. I. 14.
Oberländer, Paul. Recherches sur le baume de Tolu. 1894. III. 482.[2]
— Ueber den Tolubalsam. 1894. III. 482.[2]
Oberlin, Léon. Aperçu systématique des végétaux médicinaux. 1867. III. 58.
— & Schlagdenhauffen, Fr. De l'écorce d'Alstonia. 1880. III. 686.[1]
— — Sur l'écorce d'Alstonia constricta. 1879. III. 686.[2]
— — Écorce de Copalchi. 1878. III. 517.[1]
— — Écorce de Gaïac. 1878. III. 494.[1]
— — Écorce de quinquina bicolore. 1878. III. 724.[1]
— — Sur les écorces dites d'Angusture. 1876. III. 503.[2]
— — Sur l'essence d'Angusture vraie. 1877. III. 503.[1]
— — Étude . . . d'un nouveau succédané de l'écorce d'Angusture. 1874. III. 504.[1]
— — Étude . . . de différentes écorces . . . des Diosmées. 1878. III. 495.[1]
— — Étude histologique . . . de la famille des Diosmées. 1878. III. 724.[2]
Obermann, M. De plantis incipiente aestate efflorescentibus. See NEBEL, Daniel. 1707. III. 72.
Obermüller, Wilhelm. Kleines practisches Gärtner-Lexicon. 1860. I. 76,[2] V. IX.[2]
— Kleines praktisches Blumen-Lexicon. 1860. V. IX.[2]
Oberösterreich. See AUSTRIA.
Oborny, Adolf. Beiträge zur Flora von Mähren. 1877. II. 287.[2]
— Die Flora des Znaimer Kreises. 1879. I. 442.
— Flora von Mähren und Österr. Schlesien. 1885. I. 443.
Obrazy z państwa Flory. 1848. I. 95.
Obreen, H. A. van der SPECK. See SPECK OBREEN, H. A. van der.
O'Brien, James. A group of Bouvardias. 1879. III. 711.[1]
— Phoenix Roebelenii. 1889. III. 330.[1]
Observaciones sobre la influencia de los montes. 1878. IV. 47.[2]
Observation botanique. 1702. I. 213,[1] III. 534.[1]
Observation botanique. 1728. IV. 500.[1]
L'Observation exacte peut seule servir de fondement à une bonne théorie. 1868. I. 117.[2]
Observations ad historiam Theae pertinentes. 1769. III. 605.
Observations climatiques et phénologiques. See PHÄNOLOGISCHE . . . 1870. I. 227.[1]
Observations des phénomènes périodiques. 1841. I. 226.[1]
Observations et mémoires sur la physique. I. 22. See also INTRODUCTION aux observations. V. VII.[2]
Observations impartiales sur l'aménagement des bois du roi. See HENRIQUEZ. 1781. IV. 241.
Observations on . . . articles of Chinese materia medica. 1877. III. 273.[1]
Observations on the influence of the East India company's monopoly on . . . tea. See REPORTS from, and minutes . . . on the affairs of the East India Company. 1831. III. 606.
Observations on the Oheeroo. 1784. II. 60.[1]

Observations relatives aux cultures. See KULTUR-BEOBACHTUNGEN. 1858. IV. 150.
Observations sur l'acclimatation du Cyprès chauve. 1841. II. 51,[2] III. 510.[1]
Observations sur l'aménagement des forêts. See VARENNE de Fenille, P. C. 1791. IV. 241.
Observations sur l'écorce des feuilles. See SAUSSURE, H. B. de. 1762. I. 129.[1]
Observations sur la greffe des Noyers. 1831. III. 355.
Observations sur la physique. See INTRODUCTION aux observations sur la physique. V. VII.[2]
Observations sur la question de l'aliénation des forêts nationales. 1792. IV. 275.
Observations sur le cacao. See NAVIER, P. T. 1772. III. 594.
Observations sur le Mûrier Perrottet. 1833. III. 374.
Observations sur le phylloxera. 1881. III. 560.
Observations sur le système floral. 1820. I. 529.
Observations sur les cultures forestières. See FORST-KULTUR-BEOBACHTUNGEN. 1858. III. 168.[1]
Observations sur les plantes. See BAZIN, G. A. 1741. I. 31.
Observations sur les semis et les plantations des Chênes-verts. 1838. IV. 503.[1]
Observator, (pseud.). On the culture of the Lo-quat. 1842. III. 423.[2]
Observatorio meteorológico del puerto de Malagón. 1891. IV. 542.[2]
Observer, (pseud.). The Liquidambar, or Sweet Gum. 1882. III. 417.[2]
— Liquidambar styraciflua, der Amberbaum. 1882. III. 417.[2]
The Observer. III. 7.
Obshtchestvo . . . See Общество . . .
Obshtcheye . . . See Общее . . .
Obshtchi . . . See Общий . . .
Obstbau auf dem Lande; kurze Anleitung. 1863. III. 145.[2]
Der Obstbaumfreund. III. 13.
Obstbuch für Schleswig, Holstein und Lauenburg. 1859. III. 71.
Der Obstgarten. III. 25.
Die Obstsorten der Königlich württembergischen Obstbaumschule Hohenheim. 1823. III. 70.
Obwalden. Ein bundesgerichtlicher Entscheid. 1898. IV. 331.[1]
Obyasnitelnaya . . . See Объяснительная . . .
Ocean highways. III. 17.
Ochoa y Tapia, Ernesto. Estudio sobre la corteza del Bocconia. 1884. II. 229.[1]
Ochs, Johann Friedrich. De sanguine Draconis. See BAIER, J. J. 1712. III. 336.[2]
Ochsenius, Carl. Ueber Maqui. 1889. II. 509.[2]
— Ueber Mate und Matepflanzen Südamerica's. 1884. III. 222, 529.[2]
O'Connor, J. E. The cultivation of the "Eucalyptus globulus." 1877. IV. 530.
— Lac; production, manufacture and trade. 1874. III. 232.[2]
— Note on lac. 1874. III. 232.[2]
Odart, comte. Ampélographie universelle. 1845. III. 546.
— Exposé des divers modes de culture de la Vigne. 1837. III. 554.[2]
— Manuel du vigneron. 1836. III. 554.[2]
Odendall, Gottfried. Beiträge zur Morphologie der Begoniaceenphyllome. 1874. II. 583.[2]
Odhelius, J. L. Ledi palustris kraft. 1783. III. 653.[1]
— Rön om beskaffenheten . . . af et slags Cinchona. 1792. III. 720.
— Rön om Lepra. 1774. III. 653.[1]
— Rön om Spartium scoparium. 1762. III. 475.[1]
— Ytterligare ron, om kraften af Lendum. 1779. III. 653.[1]
Odier, Louis. See LA ROCHE, Daniel de, ODIER, Louis & DUNANT, C. G.
Odo. See MACER FLORIDUS.
Odonus, Caesar. Theophrasti sparse de plantis sententiae. 1561. I. 281.
Oechsner de Coninck. Action du tannin sur quelques alcaloïdes. 1897. I. 184.
Oechsner de Coninck, W. Contribution à l'étude de la brucine. 1884. III. 683.[2]
Oeconomiske Annaler. III. 11.
Oeder, Georg Christian. Einleitung zu der Kräuterkenntniss. 1764. I. 254.[2]
— Elementa botanicae. 1764. I. 254.[2]

— Enumeratio plantarum florae danicae. 1770. I. 351.
— Nomenclator botanicus. 1769. · I. 351.
— Underretning om Flora danica. 1761. I. 351.
— & others. Icones plantarum . . . Danise. 1761. I. 351.
Oehlgardt, Benno. Eine Auswahl der . . . Ziergehölze für Einzelstellung. 1900. III. 203.
Oehlkers, A. Die Rose, ihre Behandlung. 1877. III. 449.
Oehlschläger, O. & Bernhardt, August. Die preussischen Forst- und Jagdgesetze. 1878. IV. 321.
Oehme, & others. Über die Pflanzung ballenloser Kiefern. 1896. IV. 479.
Oehme, Karl Joseph. Ueber die Reissbarkeit im Pflanzenreich. 1776. I. 197.[1]
Öhngren, E. M. Handbok i trädgårds-skötseln. 1837. III. 100.[1]
Oekonomisch-botanisches Garten-Journal. III. 13.
Ökonomische Fortschritte. III. 13.
Ökonomische Gesellschaft im Königreiche Sachsen. Die Bibliothek. See Die BIBLIOTHEK . . . 1876. III. 1.
— Mittheilungen. Schriften. III. 13.
Oekonomische Handbibliothek. 1836. IV. 1.
Oekonomische Neuigkeiten. IV. 15.
Oelgehalt forstlicher Sämereien. 1866. III. 224.[2]
Oelhafen von Schöllenbach, Karl Christoph. Abbildung der wilden Bäume, Stauden. 1773. I. 370, V. xix.[1]
— Traité des arbres, arbrisseaux. 1773. I. 370. ·
Oelhaßus, Nicolaus. ·Elenchus plantarum circa . . . Dantiscum. 1643. I. 372.
Oelze, Friedrich. Beiträge zur chemischen Kenntniss der Familie der Ericaceen. 1890. III. 647.[1]
Qenologie. See BEGUILLET, E. B. 1770. III. 554.[1]
Önologische und pomologische Lehranstalt in Klosterneuburg. See Die K. k. ÖNOLOGISCHE . . . III. 25.
De oeretplaag in de Koffietuinen. 1899. III. 737.
Ørsted, Anders Sandøe. L'Amérique centrale. 1863. I. 330.
— Zur Beleuchtung der Blumen des brasilianischen Theestrauches. 1866. II. 191,[2] 704.[3] ·
— Til Belysning af Blomsterne hos den brasilianske Thebusk. 1866. II. 191,[2] 704.[1]
— Til Belysning af Slægten Viburnum. 1860. II. 842.[1]
— Om Berberisrust og Graasrust. 1866, III. 394.[1]
— Bidrag til Egeslægtens Systematik. 1866. II. 128.[1]
— Bidrag til Kundskab om Valdnøddplanterne. 1870. II. 111.[2]
— Bidrag til Kundskaben om Egefamilien. 1871. II. 122.[2]
— Bidrag til Naaletræernes Morphologi. 1864. II. 16.[3]
— Et Blik paa Hede- og Klitplantagerne i Jylland. 1869. IV. 156.[2]
— Om Blomstens Bygning hos Mælkeurterne. 1843. II. 429.[2]
— Blomsterplanter uden Blomster. 1861. II. 1.
— Centralamericas Gesneraceer. 1858. II. 792.[2]
— Det centralamerikanske Ambraträe. 1870. II. 253.[2]
— Om det centralamerikanske Balsamträe. 1856. II. 374.[2]
— Central-amerikas Rubiaceae. 1852. II. 807.[2]
— Centralamerikas Rubiaceer. 1852. II. 807.[1]
— Compositae centroamericanae. 1853. II. 848.[1]
— Compte rendu . . . que le Podisoma . . . et le Roestelia . . . sont des générations alternantes. 1865. III. 304.[1]
— Om Dværgtræne. 1862. I. 106.[2]
— Erindringsord til Forelæsninger over de naturlige Familier. 1862. III. 58.
— Études préliminaires sur les Cupulifères. 1871. IV. 123.[1]
— Et Forsøg paa Eristikens Anvendelse. 1868. II. 1.
— Om fremmede Træer, som egne sig til Skovdyning i Danmark. 1864. IV. 125.[1]
— Frilands-Trævæxten i Danmark. 1864. I. 293, III. 66,[1] IV. 79.[2]
— Gesneraceae centro-americanae. 1858. II. 792.[1]
— Guttaperchatræet. 1856. III. 668.[2]
— Iagttagelser over Udviklingen af Hunblomsten af Cryptomeria. 1861. II. 29.[1]
— Et Indlaeg i Hedesagen. 1869. IV. 156,[2] 343.[1]
— Jamaica; en Naturskildring. 1856. I. 335.
— Koglepalmerne eller Cycadeerne. 1860. II. 2.[1]
— Kokospalmen, Piassabapalmen. 1858. III. 319.[1]
— Om den kristtornbladede Eg. 1860. II. 132.[1]
— Malpighiaceae centroamericanae. 1853. II. 423.[2]
— Mexicos og Centralamerikas Acanthaceer. 1854. II. 796.[1]
— Myrsineae centroamericanae et mexicanae. 1861. II. 692.[1]
— Myrtaceae centroamericanae. 1856. II. 619.[1]
— Notis om Pæretræets gitterrust. 1865. III. 446.[1]

— Nyopdagede eller . . . ved deres Anvendelse vigtige Planter. 1856. III. 52.
— Palmae centroamericanae. 1858. II. 61.[2]
— Plantae novae centroamericanae. 1857. I. 329.
— Planterigets Naturhistorie. 1839. III. 52.
— Praecursores florae centroamericanae. 1873. II. 61,[2] 76.[1]
— Recherches sur la classification des Chênes. 1866. II. 128.[1]
— Om en særegen, hidtil ukjendt Udvikling hos visse Snyltesvampe. 1865. III. 446.[1]
— Skildring af Naturen paa Jamaica. 1856. I. 335.
— Om Skovanlæg paa Heder og Klitter i Jylland. 1869. IV. 156.[3]
— De stedsegrønne Bøges Rige. 1861. I. 329, 344.
— Om det sydafrikanske Dværgtræ med to Blade. 1864. II. 55.[2]
— Om sygdomme hos planterne. 1863. III. 194.
— Den tilbageskridende Metamorfose . . . af Gymnospermernes Blomster. 1868. II. 19.
— Viburni generis adumbratio. 1860. II. 842.[1]
— See also BENTHAM, George & ØRSTED, A. S.
— & Weilbach. Anthocercis Labillard. 1842. III. 698.[1]
— Nierembergia Ruiz & Pavon. 1842. III. 701.[1]
Örström, Carl Abraham. Bidrag till kännedomen om . . . Granen. 1874. II. 35.[3]
Oertel, B. Dictionnaire complet . . . de botanique. 1843. I. 71.
Örtenblad, Gustavus Jacob. Remedia guineensia. See AFZELIUS, Adam. 1813. III. 93.[1]
Örtenblad, Veit Thorsten. Om den högnordiska Tallformen Pinus silvestris L. β lapponica. 1888. II. 46.[2]
— Om sammanväxningar hos vedstammar. 1884. I. 209.[1]
— Om Sydgrönlands drifved. 1881. I. 242.[2]
Oeser, C. Untersuchung der ätherischen Oels von Myrtus Pimenta. 1864. III. 637.[1]
Oeser, W. Führer durch Werders Blütenwälder. 187.? III. 138.
Oestberg, Charlotte. Om Odling af Mullbärs-Träd. 1824. III. 374.
— Vägledning for dem som vilja odla Mullbärs-Träd. 1831. III. 374.
Oesterle, Otto. Guttapercha. 1894. III. 231.
— Pharmacologische Studien über Gutta-Percha. 1893. III. 231.
— Studien über die Guttapercha. 1892. III. 231.
Österreich. See AUSTRIA.
Oesterreichische botanische Zeitschrift. See OESTERREICH-ISCHES botanisches Wochenblatt. I. 28.[1]
Oesterreichische Chemiker-Zeitung. See ZEITSCHRIFT für Nahrungsmittel-Untersuchung. III. 25.
Oesterreichische Forst- und Jagd-Zeitung. See OESTER-REICHISCHE Forst-Zeitung. IV. 15.
Der österreichische Forstwirth. IV. 15.
Oesterreichische Forst-Zeitung. IV. 15.
Österr. Handels-Museum. See K. K. ÖSTERR. HANDELS-MUSEUM.
Die österreichische Landes-Pharmakopöe. See PHARMA-COPOEA austriaca. 1818. III. 256.[2]
Oesterreichische Militär-Pharmakopöe. 1859. III. 256.[2]
Oesterreichische Monatschrift für Forstwesen. See OESTER-REICHISCHE Vierteljahresschrift . . . IV. 15.
Oesterreichische Pharmakopöe. See PHARMACOPOEA austriaca. 1818. III. 256.[2]
Oesterreichische Revue. IV. 15.
Oesterreichische Vierteljahresschrift für Forstwesen. IV. 15.
Oesterreichische Zeitschrift für Pharmacie. III. 25.
Die österreichischen Hochgebirgs-Preisaufforstungen. 1868. IV. 167.[1]
Österreichischer Forst-Congress. Verhandlungen. IV. 15.
Oesterreichischer Ingenieur- und Architekten-Verein. Zeitschrift. See OESTERREICHISCHER INGENIEUR-VEREIN. IV. 15.
Oesterreichischer Ingenieur-Verein. Zeitschrift. IV.·15.
Oesterreichischer Touristen-Club. Mittheilungen. I. 28.[1]
Oesterreichisches botanisches Wochenblatt. I. 28.[1]
Österreichs Central-Forst-Organ. IV. 15.
Österreichs Forstwesen 1848–1898. 1898. IV. 28.[1]
Österreich-Ungarns Waren-Ein- und Ausfuhr von Forst-, Jagd- und Fischereiproducten. · 1899. IV. 407.[1]
Östling, Peter Constantin. Horti uppaliensis plantae. See THUNBERG, C. P. 1826. I. 40.
Oestmark, J. P. De Rubo. See THUNBERG, C. P. 1813. II. 300.[1]
Oestreichs Flora. See SCHULTES, J. A. 1794. I. 439.

Oetinger, Ferd. Christoph. Irritabilitatem vegetabilium . . . exploratam . . . proponet. *See* GMELIN, J. F. 1768. I. 197.[1]
Oetoyo. Iets over de Arèn en de petécultuur. 1893. III. 320,[1] *483*.[1]
— Liberiakoffie overal. 1896. III. 743.[1]
— Salammen . . . van volwassen Koffietuinen. 1896. III. 727.
Oettel, Arnold. Systematisches Verzeichniss der in der Oberlausiz wildwachsenden Pflanzen. 1799. I. 375.
Oetteit, Karl Christoph. Abschilderung eines redlichen und geschickten Försters. 1768. IV. 239.
— Etwas über die Harzgeschichte. 1789. IV. 394.
— Practischer Beweis, dass die Mathesis bey dem Forstwesen unentbehrliche Dienste thue. 1764. IV. 57.
Oettingen, Arthur Joachim von. Phänologie der Dorpater Lignosen. 1879. I. 224.[1]
— & Maydell, T., *Baron*. Die Waldgesetze. 1898. IV. 316.
— — Лѣсноые законны. 1898. IV. 316.
Oetzel, Georg. Neue Formeln zur Berechnung des Rauminhaltes. 1892. IV. 219.
Offene Worte der Ruhpoldinger Waldbauern. 189.? IV. 319.[1]
Office forestier. Création d' une annexe pour les recherches botanico-forestières. 1899. IV. 540.[1]
Office forestier de renseignements et de recherches. 1897. IV. 540.[2]
Official catalogue of the Japanese section. 1876. III. 273.[2]
Official guide to the museums of economic botany. 1883. I. 55.
Officieele mededeelingen omtrent de gouvernements Koffiecultuur. 1890. III. 730.
Officieller Katalog der Grossen Rosen-Ausstellung. 1898. III. 451.[1]
Die offizinellen Gewächse in den natürlichen Pflanzenfamilien. *See* STRUMPF, F. L. 1840. III. 57.
[O]Fft vnd vil habe ich bey mir selbest betracht. *See* ORTUS sanitatis. 148.? I. 275.
Ogérien. Histoire naturelle du Jura. *See* MICHALET, Eugène. 1864. I. 413.
Ogilvie, George. Observations on the genetic cycle in organic nature. 1860. I. 199.
— On some peculiarities in the stem of Ivy. 1860. II. 649.[2]
Ogiyevski, Vasili. *See* Оривскхй, Василхй.
Ogle, William. The fertilisation of various flowers by insects. 1870. I. 237.
Oglialoro-Todaro, Agostino. Studî sull' essenza di Pepe Cubebe. 1875. II. 94.[1]
Ogrodnictwo. III. 25.
Ogrodnik doświadczony. 1815. III. 101.[1]
Ogrodnik maly. 1871. III. 101.[1]
Ogrodnik polski. III. 10.[1]
Ohio — Agricultural experiment station. Annual report. Bulletin. Circular. Special bulletin. III. 7.
Ohio lumber journal. IV. 4.
Ohio nurserymen and fruit growers' convention. Transactions. III. 7.
Ohio pomological society. Report. *See* OHIO NURSERYMEN AND FRUIT GROWERS' CONVENTION. III. 7.
Ohio state board of agriculture. Annual report. III. 7.
Ohio state forestry association. Proceedings. IV. 4.
Ohio state forestry bureau. Annual report. IV. 5.[1]
Ohio state horticultural society. Annual report. III. 7.
Ohio state university. University bulletins. I. 519.[1]
Ohio state university naturalist. I. 6.
Ohl, A. E. U. W. Eene waterstudie. 1891. I. 232.[2]
Ohlendorff, J. H. Kultur- und Vermehrungs-Methode . . . durch meinen neuen Zuschnitt der Stecklinge. 1832. III. 157.
— Verzeichniss der im Freien ausdauernden Bäume, Gesträuche . . . im Hamburgischen botanischen Garten. 1834. I. 47.
Ohlert, Bernhard. Beiträge zu einer Kennzeichenlehre der Bäume und Sträucher. 1838. I. 294,[2] *IV. 82*.
— Ueber die Gesetze der Blattstellung. 1854. I. 102.
Ohlert, E. Einige Bemerkungen über die Knospen. 1837. I. 107.[2]
— Ueber die morphologische Stellung der Samen. 1866. I. 120.
Ohlmann, Michel. Retrait de la sève dans les arbres. 1896. I. 517.[2]
Ohlsen, Carlo T. A. Acque e foreste. 1869. IV. 48.[1]
— Della correzione dei torrenti. 1893. IV. 166.[1]
— L' Eucalyptus nell' agro romano. 1877. IV. 530.
— Lı tutela degli uccelli. 1893. IV. 90.[2]

Ohnefalsch-Richter, Max. Eucalyptus auf Cypern. 1884. III. 633.[2]
Ohnesorge, (*Oberförster*). Ueber Anstellung von Nadelholz-Keimproben. 1875. IV. 147.[1]
— Die Esche. 1872. IV. 535.[1]
Ohnesseit. Das Forstwesen in Kur- und Livland. 1900. IV. 348.[1]
Ohnmassgeblicher Vorschlag wie dem . . . Holzmangel . . . abzuhelfen sey. *See* REULING, L. W. 1788. IV. 280.[1]
Ohrdorf, (*Oberförster, Windisch-Marchwitz*). Nachweis des Holz-Ertrages eines jungen Kiefer-Bestandes. 1863. IV. 480.
Ohrt, (*Oberförster*). Zur Kultur des Flugsandes. 1877. IV. 145.
Ohrt, (*Oberförster, Rendsburg*). . Das Ueberwintern der Bucheln. 1884. IV. 495.
Ohster, (*Oberförster zu Guhlau*). Welchen praktischen Erfolg und Einfluss hat das neue Holzdiebstahlgesetz. 1854. IV. 320.
Oijen, A. A. VORSTERMAN VAN. *See* VORSTERMAN VAN OIJEN. A. A.
Oil of Anda-assu. 1882. III. 520.[1]
Oil, paint and drug reporter. III. 7.
The Oil Palm at Loanda. 1888. III. 325.[1]
Oil Palm fibre. 1892. III. 325.[1]
Oil Palm in Labuan. A success and a failure. 1889. III. 325.[1]
The oil-producing plants of Florida. 1894. III. *405*,[1] 522.[2]
Oil-stuffs. 1878. III. 225.
Oil tree, Prioria copaifera Griseb. 1897. III. 485.[1]
Oishi. Sur l'huile de camphre. 1885. III. 404.[2]
Okell, Robert. The shrubby Veronicas of New Zealand. 1893. III. 704.[1]
Oken, Lorenz. Allgemeine Naturgeschichte. 1839. I. 255.
— Entwurf von Oken's philosophischem Pflanzensystem. 1817. I. 251.
— Lehrbuch der Naturgeschichte. 1825. I. 255, V. x.[1]
— Ein natürliches Pflanzensystem. 1825. I. 251.
— Naturgeschichte für Schulen. 1821. I. 255.
Oklahoma — Agricultural experiment station. Annual report. Bulletin. III. 7.
Okubo, Samurō. On the plants of Sulphur Island. 1889. I. 463.[1]
Okuliermesser Schnelläugler. 1895. III. 164.[2]
Okumura, J. On the quantity of wood-gum. 1894. I. 156.[1]
Olafsen, Asbjörn. Nogle iagtagelser paa skovväsenets omraade. 1897. IV. 344.[1]
Olafsen, Eggert & Povelsen, Biarne. Reise durch Island. *See* ZOEGA, Johann. 1772. I. 351.
— — Reise igiennem Island. *See* ZOEGA, Johann. 1772. I. 351.
Olafsen, O. En Barlind i Ullensvang prestegaardhave. 1894. . II. 11.[1]
— Bidrag til havebrugets historie i Sogn. 189.? III. 33.[1]
— Havebrug og frugtavl i Norge i middelalderen. 1898. III. 33.[1]
— Havebrugets og frugtavlens udvikling i Hardanger. 1900. III. 33.[1]
— Eier vort land betingelser for en lönnende frugtavl? 1898. III. 134.[2]
Olafsyn, Olaf. Islendsk urtagards bok. 1770. III. 100.[2]
— Termini botanici. 1772. I. 69.[2]
Olagnier, F. Le guide de l'amateur botaniste. 1826. III. 86.
Olaguibel, Manuel de. Memoria para una bibliografia científica de Mexico. 1889. I. 3.[1]
Olazábal, Domingo. Impresiones forestales de una excursión. 1889. IV. 544.[1]
— Sobre el monte Quintanar. 1889. IV. 363.[1]
Olazábal, Lúcas de. Cuarenta años de propaganda forestal. 1898. IV. 276.[1]
— Sobre la desamortizacion de los montes. 1884. IV. 276.[1]
— Ordenación y valoración de montes. 1883. IV. 241.
— La otra mitad. 1877. IV. 276.[1]
— Pena por premio. 1877. IV. 276.[1]
— Proyecto de ley de montes. 1877. IV. 327.
— Repoblaciones. 1892. IV. 546.[1]
— Suelo, clima, cultivo agrario y forestal de la provincia de Vizcaya. 1857. IV. 363.[1]
— Del usufructo en los montes. 1892. IV. 334.[1]
Olazábal, Santiago de. Alcornocales. 1893. IV. 559.[2]
— Asociación de ingenieros de montes. 1891. IV. 541.
— Crecimientos. 1899. IV..550.[1].

— Redes de caminos forestales. 1892. IV. 389.
— La repoblación de la sierra de España. 1894. IV. 547.¹
— Las turbias del Lozoya. 1899. IV. 547.¹
Olberg, F. A. Hülfs-Tafeln zum Gebrauche bei Reduction von preuss. Klaftern auf Cubikfusse. 1857. IV. 224.
Olbers, Alida. Bidrag till kännedomen om fruktväggens byggnad. 1885. I. 119.
— Om fruktväggens anatomiska byggnad hos Rosaceerna. 1884. II. 256.²
— Om fruktväggens byggnad hos Borragineerna. 1887. II. 748.¹
Olbrich, Stephan. Das Alter und die Stammpflanzen der Blutbuchen. 1894. II. 127.²
— Das Angebot neuer Pflanzen. 1895. III. 641.¹
— Catalpa speciosa. 1891. III. 706.²
— Corylus Colurna als prächtiger Alleebaum. 1891. III. 358.¹
— Dekorations-Blütensträucher. 1900. III. 203.
— Dendrologische Plauderei. 1898. III. 203.
— Hedysarum multijugum Maxim. 1894. III. 478.²
— Die kleinblumigen Clematis-Arten. 1898. III. 389.²
— Durch Kreuzung mit Quitten erzeugte Birnensorten. 1892. III. 445.¹
— Neue Sorten von Cydonia Maulei. 1900. III. 420.²
— Nochmals Pueraria Thunbergiana. 1900. III. 486.¹
— Picea Omorica Panč.· 1887. III. 305.²
— Plauderei über Allee- und Promenadenbäume. 1899. III. 210.
— Rhus copallina. 1897. III. 527.¹
— Rubus phoenicolasius Maxim. 1889. III. 459.¹
— Tecoma (Bignonia) speciosa rubra. 1897. III. 705.
— Die zur Veredelung in Betracht kommenden Unterlagen. 1899. III. 163.²
— Vermehrung und Schnitt der Ziergehölze. 1899. III. 153.
— Das Verpacken und Versenden der Coniferen. 1891. III. 155, 295.¹
— Zur Verwendung der Cydonia japonica. 1887. III. 420.¹
— Wenig verbreitete empfehlenswerte Gehölze. 1899. III. 70.
— Die Widerstandsfähigkeit der Coniferen. 1891. III. 293.
— Winterharte Rosensorten. 1900. III. 451.¹
— Zwei neue . . . Hibiscus syriacus-Sorten. 1896. III. 588.²
Olcese, François Jules Marie. Istruzione sul siroppo e zucchero d' Uva. 1810. III. 220.²
Old and memorial trees. 1887. I. 297.¹
Old and remarkable trees of Scotland. See MACKINTOSH, Charles. 1864. I. 296.²
The old Araucaria imbricata at Kew. 1877. III. 299.¹
An old Banyan in a bowl. 1885. III. 371.²
The old Beech tree at Wentworth Woodhouse. 1895. II. 127.¹
Old city trees. 1886. III. 123.¹
The old Cork Oak at Fulham Palace. 1879. II. 140.¹
Old Forester, (pseud.). On the utilisation of waste produce of forest. 1894. IV. 434.
An old plant of the dwarf Fan Palm. 1872. III. 322.¹
The old topiary work. 1856. III. 202.¹
Old tree in garden-wall at Garnons, Herefordshire. 1876. II. 138.²
Oldberg, Oscar. An unofficial pharmacopœia. 1881. III. 246.
— & Wall, O. A. A companion to the United States pharmacopœia. 1884. III. 247.¹
Olden, E. van. De behandeling van gronden aan den duinkant in Zuid-Holland. 1855. IV. 119,¹ 170.
— Over een middel tegen Champignons in houten vloeren. 1855. IV. 414.²
— Nog iets over Cytisus Laburno-purpureus. 1856. II. 368.²
— Het snoeijen van opgaande boomen. 1860. III. 170.
Oldenbarnevelt, A. C. RAEDT VAN. See RAEDT VAN OLDENBARNEVELT, A. C.
Oldenburg, F. Et nyt Bidrag til Belysning af Statsskovbruget. 1862. IV. 288.²
— Statsskovvæsnet. 1863. IV. 288.²
Oldenhuis Tonckens, L. Boschcultuur-bouwland. 1877. IV. 274.¹
Oldham, Braithwaite. Eenige minder voorkomende drogerijen. 1885. III. 686.²
Oldrieve, W. T. On the best method of maintaining the supply of Teak. 1885. IV. 537.¹
DiepOlearia. 1889. III. 756.¹
Olearius, J. G. Specimen florae hallensis. 1668. I. 43.
Olearius, Johann Christoph. Aloedarium historicum. 1713. III. 333.¹

Olenhusen, Götz von. Ein Wald in der Lüneburger Haide. 1860. IV. 353.
Oleskow, J. Obudowie i sposobie wzrostu pędow drzew owocowych. 1889. III. 38.³
— O odpadaniu liści. 1884. I. 191.²
— Theoretische Grundlagen der Veredlung. 1889. I. 208.³
Oligschläger, F. W. Pflanzengeographische Andeutungen über das Bergische. 1839. I. 380.
Olin, Johan Henrik. De oleo cajuputi. See THUNBERG, C. P. 1797. III. 636.
— Plantae suecanae . . . victui humano inservientes. 1797. III. 270.¹
Oliva, Leonardo. El copal. 1870. III. 233.²
— Flórula del departamento de Jalisco. 1882. I. 332.
Olivan, Alejandro. Utilidad de los árboles. 1861. IV. 122,²
Olive, Marius. Catalogue descriptif des . . . Vignes américaines. 1889. III. 547.
Olive cultivation. 1898. III. 674.² — 1899. III. 676.²
Olive cultivation in Persia. 1897. III. 676.²
Olive culture at Nice. 1873. III. 679.¹
Olive oil. 1844. III. 678.²
The Olive tree. 1851. III. 678.² — 1888. II. 713.²
Olive trees near the Mediterranean. 1875. II. 713.¹
Oliveira, Duarte de, (jr.). Abies Pinsapo. 1880. III. 297.¹
— Un arbre curieux. 1878. III. 165, 672.¹
— Cedrus Deodara. 1880. III. 300.¹
— Cupressus macrocarpa. 1879. III. 302.²
— Diccionario das Peras portuguezas. 1879. III. 445.¹
— Dracaena Draco à Cadix. 1880. II. 82.²
— Wellingtonia gigantea. 1881. III. 310.¹
Oliveira, M. P. de. Relatorio da Commissão de estudo e tratamento das Vinhas do Douro. 1880. III. 761.
Oliveira Carvalho, Carlos de. Le déboisement ·d'un pays. 1894. IV. 233,¹ 542.¹
Oliveira e Silva, A. J. de. Eucalyptus globulus. 1874. III. 634.²
Oliveira Pimentel, Julio Maximo D'. See PIMENTEL, J. M., D' OLIVEIRA.
Der Olivenbau im südlichen Frankreich. 1858. III. 675.²
Oliver, Daniel. The Atlantis hypothesis in its botanical aspect. 1862. I. 300.
— Botany. 1881. I. 492.²
— The botany of the Roraima expedition. 1887. I. 339.¹
— Cardiogyne africana Bureau. 1896. II. 147.¹
— Description of three new genera from West Tropical Africa. 1869. II. 471,² 474,² 553.¹
— Descriptions of three new genera of plants in the Malayan herbarium. 1873. II. 253,³ 392,² 751.²
— Enumeration of the plants collected by Mr. H. H. Johnston. 1887. I. 492.²
— First book of Indian botany. 1869. I. 91.
— On five new genera of west tropical Africa. 1867. I. 490.
— On four new genera of plants of western tropical Africa. 1865. I. 490.
— Guide to the Royal botanic gardens . . . Kew. 1863. I. 55.
— Illustrations of the principal natural orders of the vegetable kingdom. 1874. I. 256.
— Lessons in elementary botany. 1864. I. 90, 523.
— List of the plants collected by Mr. Thomson. 1886. I. 492.²
— Lorantheae mexicanae· et centroamericanae. 1864. II. 173.¹
— Memorandum on the genus Thamnea. 1867. II. 251.²
— The natural order Aurantiaceae. 1861. II. 397.¹
— Note on a collection of North-Celebes plants. 1877. I. 466.
— Note on a fruit from Comassi. 1875. II. 513.¹
— Note on Hamamelis and Loropetalum. 1862. II. 252.¹
— Note on the structure . . . of Pentaclethra. 1864. II. 376.¹
— Note on the structure of the anther. 1862. I. 116.¹
— Notes on the Loranthaceae. 1864. II. 172.³
— Notes upon a few of the plants collected . . . near Nagasaki. 1867. I. 462.
— Observations on the growth in diameter. 1855. I. 189.
— Observations on the structure of the stem . . . Caryophylleae and Plumbagineae. 1859. II. 696.¹
— Official guide to the Kew museums. 1861. I. 55.
— The structure of the stem. 1862. I. 105.
— On Sycopsis. 1860. III. 254.¹
— See also Оливеръ, Д.
— & others. The botany of the Speke and Grant expedition. 1873. I. 488.
— — Flora of tropical Africa. 1868. I. 483.¹

Oliver, F. W. On the effects of urban fog. 1891. IV. 548.¹
— Influencia de la niebla de las grandes ciudades. 1891. IV. 548.¹
— Phenomenon analogous to leaf-fall. 1887. *I. 192,*¹ II. 305.¹
Oliver, George W. The Abelias. 1897. III. 748.¹
— Hybridization. 1899. III. 51.
— The insects most injurious to forest trees. 1887. IV. 208.³
— Late-flowering shrubs. 1896. III. 207.¹
— *See also* SMITH, J. G. & OLIVER, G. W.
Oliver, J. N. Rate of growth of Teak in Burmah. 1883. V. 537.¹
Oliver, Paul. Plantes exotiques. 1881. III. 125.
Oliver, Samuel Pasfield. Barre and the discovery of the Coco-de-mer. 1892. II. 71.¹
— François Leguat and his plants. 1891. I. 482.
— Madagascar. *See* BAKER, J. G. 1881. I. 496.
— The Rofia Palm. 1875. III. 330.²
Oliver, William. A letter concerning the Jesuits bark. 1706. III. 719.
Oliver de Cerres, d' & others. Casa rústica de 1840. 1842. IV. 122.²
Oliveri, V. Étude de l'essence de Citron. 1894. III. 502.²
Olives and oil-making at Sorrento. 1898. III. 676.²
Olivi, Giovanni Battista. De reconditis et praecipuis collectaneis ab Francisco Calceolario in musaeo adservatis. 1584. I. 60.²
Olivier, Ernest. Biskra, souvenirs d'un naturaliste. 1893. I. 486.
— Le Dattier à six têtes de Biskra. 1893. II. 73.¹
— Flore populaire de l'Allier. 1886. I. 74.¹
— Le Gui. 1900. II. 180.¹
— Sur un insecte hyménoptère nuisible à la Vigne. 1890. III. 564.¹
— Un Oranger historique. 1900. II. 403.¹
— Le Peuplier de l'Euphrate. 1899. III. 346.¹
— Les Platanes. 1900. III. 405.²
Olivier, Guillaume Antoine. Sur la cause des récoltes alternes de l'Olivier. 1792. III. 675.¹
— Sur la culture de l'Arbre-à-pain. 1792. III. 118.²
— Voyage dans l'empire Othoman. 1801. I. 302.
— Waarnemingen over de specerij-planten . . . op de Fransche eilanden. 1794. III. 266.
Olivier, Henri. Recherches pour servir à l'histoire naturelle . . . du Hemlock. 1870. III. 312.¹
Olivier, Louis. Sur des combinaisons des cellules. 1885. I. 137.
— Recherches sur l'appareil tégumentaire des racines. 1880. I. 103.
Olivier, Théodore. Traité de botanique élémentaire. 1863. I. 90.
Olliff, Arthur Sidney. Bronzy Orange bug. 1892. III. 501.¹
— The Cherry-tree borer. 1892. III. 432.¹
— The codling moth. 1892. III. 428.¹
— Insect friends and foes. 1891. III. 192.¹
— Insect pests. 1890. III. 192.²
— The introduction of the Fig insect. 1892. II. 151.¹
— A new scale-insect destroying Salt-bush. 1891. III. 387.²
— The Pine case-moth. 1891. IV. 461.¹
— On a species of moth. 1894. III. 192.¹
— Two little-known scale-insects. 1892. III. 192.² ·
— A walking-stick insect destroying Eucalypts. 1891. V. 531.¹
Ollivier, C. P. *See* HENRY, Ossian & OLLIVIER, C. P. ·
Olmedilla y Puig, Joaquín. Sucinta noticia hostórica del Café. 1895. III. 740.¹
L' Olmo succedaneo al Gelso. 1861. III. 148.¹
Olmstead, F. E. A glimpse of forestry in the Himalayas. 1900. IV. 378.
Olmsted, Frederick Law. Foreign plants and American scenery. 1888. III. 202.¹
— The Sycamore blight. 1897. III. 418.³
— Transplanting large trees. 1885. III. 168.¹
— *See also* SARGENT, C. S. & OLMSTED, F. L.
Olney, Stephen Thayer. Catalogue of plants . . . in Rhode Island. 1845. V. XVII.¹
— Rhode Island plants. 1845. V. XVII.¹
Olorinus, Johannes. Centuria arborum mirabilium. 1616. I. 284.
— Centuria herbarum mirabilium. 1616. I. 284.
Olsen. Cubiktabeller til Brug og Lettelse ved Udregning af Trælastladninger. 1842. IV. 223.
Olsen, F. Den forløbne Vinters Virkning paa Frilandsplanter. 1855. III. 44.¹

Olsen-Wiig, O. E. Coniferne i Dropmore Park. 1896. I. 55.
Olshausen, Justus. Gerichtsverfassung und Prozess. 1889. IV. 314.¹
Olsson, Peter. Jemtlands fanerogamer. 1885. V. XIX.¹
Olsson-Seffer, Pehr Hjalmer. Bidrag till kännedomen om floran i Kimito skärgård. 1895. I. 366.
— Svenska växtnamn i sydvästra Finland. 1896. I. 73.¹
Olufsen, Christian. I Anledning af Skovforordningen. 1805. IV. 296.¹
— Om Brændes Værdi og Pris. 1805. IV. 282.¹
— Om Danmarks Brændselsvæsen. 1805. IV. 282.¹
— Danmarks Brændselsvæsen. 1811. IV. 431.¹
— Om en af Hr. Rieffelsen opfunden Maskine til at oprydde Træer. 1806. IV. 385.² · ·
— Lærebog i den danske Landoeconomie. 1805. III. 100.²
— Noget om Skovvæsenet i Engelland. 1805. IV. 357.²
— Om Plantaser til Brændsel og Tømmer. 1797. IV. 113.¹
Omar Khayyam's Rose. 1894. II. 292.²
Ombrometrische Beobachtungen. IV. 15.
Om Omdriften i Statsskovene. *See* PAULSEN, W. 1853. IV. 251.¹
Omeis, Ernst. Untersuchung des Wachsthumsganges . . . eines 110jährigen Kiefernbestandes. 1895. II. 48.²
Omélianski, V. Sur un ferment de la cellulose. 1897. I. 178.
— Sur la fermentation cellulosique. 1897. I. 178.
Ommanney, H. T. A variety of Butea frondosa. 1891. II. 338.¹
Ompteda, Ludwig, *Freiherr* von. Praktische Anleitung zur Pfirsichzucht. 1879. III. 441.¹
— Reinische Gärten von der Mosel bis zum Bodensee. 1886. III. 28.¹
L' on. Niccolini e l' Istituto forestale di Vallombrosa. 1895. IV. 35.²
Ondaatje, Wilham Charles. Cinnamon culture in Ceylon. 1862. III. 279.¹
— Notes on the febrifuge plants of Ceylon. 1862. III. 279.¹
— On the Sack-tree of Ceylon. 1862. III. 366.¹
— On the Samadera wood. 1862.· III. 509.¹
— The starch-producing plants of Ceylon. 1862. III. 279.¹
Onderdonk, G. Additional facts about the Mistletoe. 1886. III. 385.¹
— Yucca gloriosa in Texas. 1879. II. 88.¹
Onderzoek van plantaardige vetten. *See* LOOS, Dirk de. 1884. III. 225.
Onderzoeking naar de geneeskracht van Nauclea. 1860. III. 746.²
One of the world's wonders. 1889. II. 71.¹
O'Neill, E. C. *See* STILLMAN, J. M. & O'NEILL, E. C.
O'Neill, H. E. Report on the fruit candying industry. 1889. III. 220.¹
Ong-Hoe-Hoe. Opmerkingen . . . in den Indischen Archipel. 1852. III. 274.¹
Onimus. Mémoire sur l' aliénation et le défrichement de la forêt . . . de la Harth. 1866· IV. 274.¹
Onnin, P. L. Iets over de getah pertja. 1855. III. 228.²
Onomatologia. *See* NOCCA, Domenico. · 1813. I. 62.
Onomatologia botanica completa. *See* GMELIN, J. F. 1772. I. 32.
Onomatologia forestalis-piscatorio-venatoria. *See* STAHL, J. F. 1772. IV. 22.¹
L' Onore de i Collegi dell' arti della città di Bologna. *See* MONTALBANI, Ovidio. 1670. III. 53.
Gli onorevoli facta e gavazzi contro la vigente legge forestale. 1895. IV. 329.
Ontario — Bureau of forestry. Annual report. Forestry report. IV. 3.
Ontario — Fruit growers' association. *See* FRUIT . . . III. 2.
Ontario — Royal commission on forestry. Report. IV. 3.
Het ontbolsteren van Peper. 1899. III. 343.²
De ontdekking van Koffie. 1884. III. 727.
Ontwouding en de gevolgen daarvan. 1888. IV. 283.²
Oomen, J. H. B. De gouvernementskoffiecultuur} 1890. III. 730.
Oordt, van & others. · Verslag (vijde–zevende en laatste) over den paalworm. 1865. IV. 414.¹
Oort, P. van & Korthals, P. W. Verslag van een tocht van Padang. 1842. I. 467.¹
— & Müller, S. Aanteekeningen gehouden op eene reize over . . . Java. 1835. III. 275.²
Oosten, Henry van. The Dutch gardener. 1700. III. 76.
— Le jardin de Hollande planté & garni de fleurs. 1700. III. 76.

— De nauwkeurige bloemist. 1700. III. 76.
—, De Neederlandsen hof, beplant met bloemen. 1700. III. 76.
— Der niederländische Garten bepflantzet mit Blumen. 1700. III. 76.
—Niederländischer Blumen-, Obst- und Orangeriegarten. 1700. III. 76.
— De nieuwe Nederlandse bloem-hof. 1700. III. 76.
Ooster, Carl von FISCHER-. See FISCHER-OOSTER, Carl von.
Oosterlittens, D. J. KUPERUS VAN. See KUPERUS VAN OOSTERLITTENS, D. J.
Oosterzee, J. J. van. Bijdrage tot de kennis van den Carica Papaya. 1888. III. 617.[1]
— De Kiri boom. 1887. III. 703.[3]
— Reuzen-Papaya. 1887. II. 582.[2]
Oosterzee, J. J. van, (jr.). Vruchtboomen-cultuur. 1890. III. 147.[1]
De **Oost-indische** houtsoorten. 1895. IV. 400.[1]
Opatowski, Heinrich. De Memecyleis. 1838. II. 634.[3]
Opel, F. M. E. Lehrbuch der forstlichen Zoologie. 1869. IV. 90.[1]
Opera agricolationum. See SCRIPTORES rei rusticae. 1470. III. 96.[2]
Opera de medicamentorum. See YŪHANNĀ IBN MĀSAWAIH. 1623. V. XXVIII.[2]
Opinion d'un député du département des Ardennes sur l'affectation de tous les bois de l'état. 1817. IV. 325.
Opiniones de otros periódicos sobre el decreto de 28 de Noviembre. 1883. IV. 276.[1]
Opis niektórych owadów lasom sosnowym najbardziej szkodzących z wyobrażeniem ich postaci. 1827. IV. 475.
Opisaniye . . . See OПИCAHИE . . .
Opiz, Philipp Maximilian. Beiträge zur Naturgeschichte. 1823. I. 267.
— Böheims phänerogamische und cryptogamische Gewächse. 1823. I. 439.
— Zur Gattung Betula. 1855. II. 117.[2]
— Die Gattungen Cornus und Suida. 1853. II. 654.[3]
— Ueber Leonhardia. 1857. II. 387.[1]
— Naturalientausch. 1823. I. 267.
— Die Pelargonien. 1825. II. 390.[1]
— Seznam rostlin květeny České. 1852. I. 440.
— Uebersicht der auf Fagus sylvatica wohnenden Kryptogamen. 1854. IV. 496.
— Erstes Verzeichniss jener Pflanzen . . . zum Tausch oder Kauf . . . vorräthig. 1823. I. 439.
— Auf welchem Wege wäre die Wahrheit das höchste Ziel der reinen Botanik zu erreichen? 1829. I. 79.[1]
— See also BERCHTOLD, Friedrich, Graf von, SEIDL, W. B. & OPITZ, P. M.
— & **Corda**, A. K. J. Chotekia, eine neue Pflanzengattung. 1830. II. 763.[1]
Eenige **opmerkingen** omtrent de planten wereld van Zuid-Afrika. 1889. III. 281.[2]
Opmerkingen omtrent gedane voorstellen tot verbetering der financiën. 1843. III. 128.
Opois. Note sur le jardin de M. Mazel au Golfe Jouan, près Cannes. 1873. I. 59.
Opoix, O. La culture du Poirier. 1896. III. 445.[1]
Oppel, A. Zur Landeskunde von Neu-Guinea. 1893. I. 499.[1]
Oppen, von, (Oberförster). Die Beschädigungen durch Schneebruch. 1892. IV. 190.
— Bewurzelung eines . . . Fichtenzweiges. 1893. II. 37.[1]
— Bruthölzer gegen Hylobius abietis. 1892. IV. 208.[1]
— Ueber Pflanzenerziehungs- und Kulturkosten. 1893. IV. 151.[1]
Oppen, J. F. von. Anfangsgründe der Arithmetik und Geometrie. 1792. IV. 57.
— Arithmetik und Geometrie. 1792. IV. 57.
Oppen, J. F. B. Beskrivelse over et nyt Dendrometer. 1805. IV. 215.
Oppenheim, Alph. Ueber den Menthacampher. 1861. III. 611.[2]
Oppenheimer, Richard. Über Weichselholz-Cultur. 1890. III. 438.[1]
Oppermann. Zur Naturgeschichte der Rothbuche. 1876. II. 127.[1]
Oppermann, Adolf. Aktstykker til Skovenes og Skovbrugets Historie. 1892. IV. 24.[2]
— Om Arvelighed og Racedannelse hos Skovtræer. 1900. I. 248.[2]
— Bidrag til det danske Skovbrugs Historie. 1887. IV. 24.[2]
— C. V. Oppermanns Egeskovsdyrkning. 1886. IV. 507.

— Dalgas Hedesagen Forkæmper. 1895. IV. 156.[3]
— Dalgas og Hedeplantningen. 1894. IV. 156.[3]
— Dansk Kulsvieri. 1889. IV. 395.
— Om "Dansk Skovforening." 1889. IV. 39.[3]
— Driftsplan for Grevskabet Holsteinborg. See — Driftsplan . . . 1896. IV. 247.[1] V. XXXI.[1]
— Forelæsninger over Skovbrugslære. Historie og Statistik. 1896. IV. 336.[3]
— Forelæsninger over Skovbrugslære. Træmaalings- og Tilvækstlære. 1887. IV. 245.
— Forelæsninger over Skovbrugslære: Vare- og Handelslære. 1892. IV. 381.
— Forelæsninger over Taksations- og Tilvækstlære. 1887. IV. 245.
— Forsendelse af Skoveffekter med Statsbanerne. 1894. IV. 284.[1]
— Grundplaner til forstlige Boliger. 1895. IV. 266.[1]
— Kortfattet Vejledning i Skovbrug. 1896. IV. 103.[2]
— Lommetabel for Skovbrugere. 1892. IV. 228.
— Naaletræernes Indvandring i Danmark. 1894. II. 15.[1]
— Parker og Træplantninger i København. 1898. III. 119.[2]
— Et Planlægningsarbejde. 1896. IV. 247.[1]
— Skoven, Skovbruget og det Skønne. 1897. IV. 137.[1]
— Skovene og Skovbruget. 1897. IV. 45, 271.[1]
— Skovplanternes periodiske Livsytringer. 1890. I. 221.
— Et Stebarn i Administrationen. 1894. IV. 288.[2]
— Stormen d. 12te Februar 1894. 1894. IV. 189.[3]
— Tilvirkning af Naaletræ. 1894. IV. 443.[1]
— Undersøgelser over Tilvirkning af Trævarer. 1898. IV. 404.[1]
— Vore Skove i Fortid og Nutid. 1898. IV. 24.[3]
— Vore Skoves Betydning. 1895. IV. 273.[1]
— See also FREDERIKSEN, K. N. & OPPERMANN, A.; HELMS, Joh. & OPPERMANN, A.
— & **Prytz**, C. V. Undersøgelser over Rødgranens Vækst. 1892. IV. 458.
Oppermann, C. A. Mémoire sur la conservation des bois. 1873. IV. 419.
Oppermann, C. V. Egens Kultur og Udbytte. 1860. IV. 505.
— Nogle Bemærkninger om Forholdet mellem Skovens Tilvæxt. 1836. IV. 242.
— Opelskning af Egetræ. 1851. IV. 504.
— Om Rækkeplantning til Opelskning af Naaleskov. 1852. IV. 441.
Oppermann, L. Skovkampen i 1850—55. 1855. IV. 273.[1]
— Svar til mine navngivne Angribere. 1852. IV. 272.[3]
Oppikofer, R. Die Vermehrung der Alpenrosen. 1887. III. 656.
Oppitz, H. Eine seltene Pappel. 1900. IV. 486.[2]
Oppler. Bericht über eine schwarzblühende Rose. 1855. III. 449.
Oppler, Salomon. De strychnini nitrici . . . usu. 1834. III. 682.[3]
Opuntia and its relatives. 1894. II. 596.[1]
Opuntia fruits. 1888. II. 596.[2]
Opuscoli scientifici. I. 25.
Opuscula botanico-physica. See JUNG, Joachim. 1747. I. 31.
Opytni . . . See OПЫTHЫЙ . . .
Orang **Tani**. Eenige fraaie houtsoorten op Java. 1894. IV. 400.[1]
The **Orange**. 1872. III. 501.[3]
Orange culture in Tahiti. 1894. III. 500.[1]
Orange-farming. 1883. III. 500.[1]
The **Orange** groves of Naples. 1896. III. 500.[2]
Orange growing in the Azores. See ORANGES and their growing. 1874. III. 132,[1] 499.[3]
Orange Judd farmer. See AMERICAN agriculturist. III. 2.
Orange-scale in Cyprus. 1891. III. 501.[1]
Orange seedlings. 1887. III. 501.
The **Orange**-tree. 1835. III. 501.[1]
Oranges and their growing. 1874. III. 132,[1] 499.[3]
Orban de Rossius, Ernest. Les fanges de la forêt de Freyr. 1895. IV. 546.[2]
— Rendement des sapinières. 1897. IV. 558.[3]
Orbigny, Alcide d'. Description geográfica . . . de Bolívia. 1845. I. 340.[3]
— Voyage dans l'Amérique méridionale. 1835. I. 329.
Orchard, (pseud.). Arbor day. 1897. IV. 42.[1]
Orchard and garden illustrated. III. 7.
Orchardist's companion. III. 7.
L' **Orchestes** fagi. 1900. IV. 497.

Orcutt, Charles Russell. Bibliography — Cactaceae. 1900. II. 586.²
— The Blue Gum tree. 1890. III. 634.²
— Botany of southern California. 1900. I. 327.
— Cacti at home. 1892. II. 587.¹
— Cactuses of southern California. 1886. II. 587.¹
— California trees and flowers. 1890. I. 325.
— Cereus (Pilocereus) Sargentianus. 1891. II. 598.²
— The Chollas. 1891. II. 596.¹
— Einige Notizen über Echinocactus. 1890. II. 591.²
— Epiphyllum. 1890. III. 623.¹
— Flora of southern and Lower California. 1885. I. 325.
— The forests of Lower California. 1892. I. 320, *IV. 78.²*
— Fouquiera gigantea, new species. 1886. II. 563.¹
— Fruits all the year round. 1892. III. 264.¹
— A lemonade and sugar tree. 1886. III. 527.²
— The Mesquite bean. 1890. III. 485.¹
— New Lower Californian Cactuses. 1886. II. 587.²
— A new species of Cereus. 1889. II. 589.²
— Notes on Cacti in the Gray herbarium. 1898. II. 586.¹
— The Oaks of southern and Lower California. 1886. II. 128.²
— An old-new Opuntia. 1896. II. 597.¹
— The Orange for health. 1890. III. 500.¹
— The Palms of California. 1885. II. 61.¹
— The Rainbow Cactus. 1890. III. 621.¹
— Review of the Cactaceae of the United States. 1897. II. 587.²
— Rosa minutifolia. 1890. II. 296.¹
— A sharp family — the Cactuses. 1885. III. 619.
— Some notes on Echinocactus. 1890. II. 591.²
— Some useful plants of southern California. 1888. III. 437.¹ *523.*¹
— The Strawberry Guava. 1891. III. 637.²
— Trees and shrubs of San Diego county. 1889. I. 320, *IV. 78.*¹
— The Tuna. 1890. III. 624.²
— Washingtonia robusta Wendland. 1885. II. 75.²
Orcutt seed and plant company. California trees and flowers. 1891. III. 60.
Et Ord i Anledning af de otte Rigsdaler en Favn Brænde koster. 1797. IV. 282.¹
Et Ord om Forsarsbeskæring. 1895. III. 171.
Ordinamento dell' Istituto forestale di Vallombrosa. 1880. IV. 2, 35.²
Ordinamento dello Istituto forestale di Vallombrosa. 1886. IV. 35.²
Ordinatziya . . . *See* Ординанія . . .
Ordini regolativi stabiliti dell' . . . Signor Lorenzo Contarini . . . nella materia de boschi. 1754. IV. 304.¹
Ordnung vor die Holzmacher. 1776. IV. 300.¹
Ordnung wie das Burger- und Pension-Holtz im Wald auffgesetzt . . . werden solle. 1733. IV. 305.
Ordnung wie die Holzfuhr-Leut in die oberkeitlich- und bürgerlichen Waldungen fahren . . . sollend. 1736. IV. 305.
Ordnung wie die Waldungen teutschen Lands mehrers geäuffnet . . . werden könne. 1725. IV. 305.
Ordonance du 18 avril 1892 concernant la délimitation des forêts du canton du Valais. *See* VERORDNUNG vom 18. April 1892 . . . 1892. IV. 307.¹
Ordonnance de Louis XIV. 1667. IV. 324.
Ordonnance de Louis XIV. pour les eaux et forêts du royaume. 1821. IV. 326.
Ordonnance de Louis XIV., roy de France et de Navarre, sur le fait des eaux & forêts. 1669. IV. 324.
Ordonnances de la Franche-Comté. 1900. IV. 540.¹
Ordonnances sur l'administration forestière des baillages du Jura. 1824. IV. 306.
Ordoyno, Thomas. Flora nottinghamiensis. 1807. I. 396.
Oré, (*Prof.*). Sur les expériences de M. O. Liebreich. 1872. III. 683.¹
— Des injections intra-veineuses de chloral. 1874. III. 683.¹
Oregon — Fruits and flowers. *See* FRUITS . . . III. 3.
Oregon — Game and forestry warden. Annual report. IV. 5.¹
Oregon — State agricultural college and experiment station. Annual report. Bulletin. III. 7.
Oregon agricultural experiment station. *See* OREGON — STATE AGRICULTURAL COLLEGE . . . III. 7.
Oregon Conifers. 1882. III. 290.
Oregon lumber trade. 1850. IV. 403.¹

Orelli. Waldbrand im Höhragen bei Bülach. 1894. IV. 183.²
Oren. אן Esai. XLIV. 14. 1738. I. 513.
Orenstein & Koppel. Die Anwendung transportabler Stahlbahnen. 1884. IV. 391.
Orfila, Matthieu Joseph Bonaventure. Traité des poisons. 1813. III. 260.²
Organ für die Fortschritte des Eisenbahnwesens. IV. 10.
Organ für die Reformation des Waldbaues. IV. 15.
Organisation, (*pseud.*). Working plans in the Southern circle. 1896. IV. 250.²
Zur Organisation der forstlichen Lehranstalten. 1870. IV. 32.
Die Organisation der königl. bairischen Staats-Forstverwaltung. 1884. IV. 290.¹
Die Organisation der Staatsforst-Verwaltung. 1885. IV. 290.¹
Organisation des écoles spéciales de gardes-forestiers. 1899. IV. 36.²
Über die Organisation des forstlichen Versuchswesens in Bayern. 1887. IV. 541.¹
Über die Organisation der Forstwesens. 1815. IV. 287.
Organisation du personnel employé dans le service des forêts domaniales. 1899. IV. 294.²
Organisation du service des inspections royales des forêts. 1899. IV. 294.²
Die Organisation eines meteorologischen Dienstes. 1879. IV. 59.²
Organization de l'enseignement forestier supérieur. *See* PUTON, Alfred. 1891. IV. 33.¹
Organizzazione del servicio forestale in Ispagna. 1862. IV. 293.¹
Sull' organizzazione e trattamento delle foreste in Francia. 1881. IV. 122.¹
L'orgyie pudibonde. *See* DASYCHIRA pudibunda. 1895. IV. 549.²
Oribasios, Pergamenus. De simplicibus libri quinque. 400. I. 274.
Oriental fruits. 1891. III. 220.²
Oriental Plane trees at Montagnis, France. 1892. III. 419.¹
Origin of Brazil and Sapucaya nuts. 1875. III. 631.²
The origin of rafting timber. 1878. IV. 390.²
Origin of Storax. 1899. III. 417.²
The origin of the Clanbrassil Fir. 1880. II. 36.¹
The origin of the Purple Beech. 1894. II. 127.²
Original habitats of the Rose. 1886. II. 282.¹
Origine botanique de l'encens. 1871. III. 509.²
Origine de l'application du bois d'Acajou à l'ébénisterie. 1851. III. 513.¹
Origine de l'Hortensia. 1890. II. 241.¹
Origine de la gomme Kino. 1845. IV. 522.¹
Origine de la résine caragne. 1830. III. 244,
De l'origine et du progrez du Café. *See* GALLAND, Antoine. 1699. III. 738.
O'Riley, Edward. Note accompanying a few specimens of wood from the Tenasserim coast. 1846. IV. 400.²
— Remarks on Sugar and Coffee culture at Amherst. 1843. III. 732.¹
— The vegetable products of the Tenasserim provinces. 1850. III. 277.
Orillard, Alfred. Des arbres épars en droit romain. 1863. II. 200.²
Orlandini, Orlando. Trattato di boschicultura. 1883. IV. 110.¹
Orlando, Giovanni d'. L'insegnamento nell' Istituto forestale dé Vallombrosa. 1897. IV. 35.²
Orléans — Société d'horticulture. *See* SOCIÉTÉ . . . III. 21.
Orléans — Société des sciences physiques . . . *See* SOCIÉTÉ I. 520.¹
Orléans — Société royale d'agriculture des sciences . . . *See* SOCIÉTÉ ROYALE DES SCIENCES, BELLES-LETTRES . . . D'ORLEANS. I. 24.¹
Orléans — Société royale des sciences, belles-lettres et arts. *See* SOCIÉTÉ . . . I. 24.¹
Orli, P. H. F., BOURGOIN D'. *See* BOURGOIN D'ORLI, P. H. F.
Orlof, Mikhail Mikhailovitch. Les forêts de la Russie. *See* Орловъ, M. M. 1900. IV. 347.
— *See also* Орловъ, M. M.
Orloff, N. A. Ueber eine stickstoffhaltige Substanz aus Fichtensprossen. 1897. II. 37.¹
Orlopp, Rudolf. Los montes de Rumania. 1892. IV. 375.¹
— Situation forestière de la Roumanie. 1892. IV. 375.¹
— Ueber Waldzustände in Rumänien. 1892. IV. 375.¹
Orlová, Marie. Jeřáb jedlý moravský. 1897. III. 460.¹
— Pěstování Fíků pod širým nebem. 1896. III. 369.²

Orlowski, Jan. Ważność lasów oraz sposoby zachowania. 1873. IV. 269.
Ormancey. Observation sur la maladie du raisin. 1851. III. 575.[3]
Un Orme célèbre. 1899. IV. 518.[2]
L'Orme doré de M. Rosseels. 1866. III. 365.[1]
L'Orme Dumont. 1892. III. 364.[1]
Ormerod, Eleanor Anne. Handbook of insects injurious to orchard and bush fruits. 1898. III. 191.
— A manual of injurious insects. 1881. IV. 208.[2]
— Notes . . . of a few new . . . insects of South Africa. 1889. III. 192.[2]
— Notes of observations of injurious insects. 1878. III. 190.
— Report of observations of injurious insects. 1878. III. 190.
— Willow beetle. 1885. IV. 487.[2]
Les Ormes des boulevards bruxellois. 1898. IV. 518.[2]
The ornamental Crabs. 1900. III. 429.[1]
Ornamental evergreen Berberries. 1874. III. 393.[2]
The ornamental flower-garden and shrubbery. See LINDLEY, John. 185.? I. 269.
Ornamental foreign shrubs. 1892. III. 60.
Ornamental planting. 1883. III. 202.[1]
Ornamental shrubs. 1882. III. 203.
Ornamental uses of nuts and seeds. 1891. III. 219.[1]
Ornamental vines. 1882. III. 545.[1]
O'Rorke. On the Kawa. 1856. III. 343.[1]
— Du Kawa-Kawa ou Piper methysticum. 1856. III. 343.[1]
— La manne des Hebreux. 1860. III. 612.[2]
— Note sur le pain de dika du Gabon. 1857. III. 508.[1]
Orosi, Giuseppe. Farmacologia teorica e pratica. 1856. III. 256.[1]
— Formulario farmaceutico officinale. 1853. III. 256.[1]
Orpet, E. O. Actinidia polygama. 1892. III. 595.[2]
Orphal, Wilhelm Christian. Die Jägerschule. 1806. IV. 96.[1]
— Ornithologisches Handbuch. 1805. IV. 90.[2]
— Ein Wort noch zur rechten Zeit über unsere Forst- und Jagdinstitute. 1804. IV. 31.
Orphanides, Theodore Georg. Enumeratio chloridis hellenicae. 1866. I. 449.
— Sur l'état actuel de la flore grecque. 1867. I. 449.
— Des forêts de la Grèce. 1879. IV. 375.[1]
— Sur quelques plantes rares . . . de la Grèce. 1870. II. 712.[2]
— See also 'ΟΡΦΑΝΙΔΗΣ, Θεόδωρος.
Orr, Hector. Premature decay of timber. 1873. IV. 413.[2]
Orsini, Antonio. See MAURI, Ernesto, ORSINI, Antonio & TENORE, Michele.
Országos erdészeti egyesület. Évkönyve. IV. 15.
Ortega, Casimiro Gómes. Aneddoti sopra la chinachina peruana. 1791. III. 720.
— Historia natural de la Malagueta. 1780. II. 632.[1]
— Indice de las plantas . . . en el Real jardin botanico. 1772. I. 60.[1]
— Instrucción sobre el modo . . . de transportar plantas vivas por mar y tierra. 1779. III. 155.
— Novarum aut rariorum plantarum Horti reg. botan. matrit. descriptionum decades. 1797. I. 60.[1]
— Tabulae botanicae. 1773. I. 258.
— & Palau y Verdera, Antonio. Corso elementare teorico di botanica. 1786? I. 92.
— — Curso elemental de botánica. 1785. I. 83.
Ortega, J. SÁNCHEZ. See SÁNCHEZ ORTEGA, J.
Ortel, Felix. Handel mit russischen Hölzern. 1895. IV. 404.[1]
Ortgies, Eduard. Aphelandra aurantiaca Lindl. var. Roezli. 1869. III. 708.[2]
— Beiträge zur Kenntniss der Weisstannen-Arten. 1876. II. 21.[3]
— Bericht über die Reisen und Einführungen des Herrn B. Roezl. 1871. I. 330.
— Eine blühende Rhopala. 1866. II. 166.[3]
— Bouvardia leiantho-longiflora. 1859. III. 711.[2]
— Dalechampia Roezliana β rosea Muell. Arg. 1867. II. 440.[2]
— Dictyanthus stapeliaeflorus. 1857. III. 692.[3]
— Hexacentris mysorensis Wight. 1860. III. 710.[2]
— Importirte Sämereien von B. Roezl. 1875. III. 75.[1]
— Phygelius capensis E. Meyer. 1858. III. 703.[2]
— Rhododendron Edgeworthii. 1856. III. 658.[2]
— Spiraea Reevesiana Lindl. var. fl. pleno. 1859. III. 461.[1]
— Triumphia Harrisii Hook. 1860. III. 710.[2]
— Voyages et découvertes de M. B. Roezl. 1871. I. 330.
Orti, G. Itenerario scientifico. 1807. I. 425.

Ortlob, Johann Friedrich. Analogia nutritionis plantarum et animalium. 1683. I. 157.
Ortmann, Albert. Flora hennebergica. 1887. I. 388.
Ortmann, Anton. Botanische Beobachtungen über einige Pflanzen . . . von Karlsbad. 1835. I. 439.
— Flora carlsbadensis. 1838. I. 440.
— Flora des Elbogner Kreises. 1842. I. 440.
— Flora of Elbogen. 1842. I. 440.
— Flore de Carlsbad. 1831. I. 439.
Orto botanico della regia università di Napoli. Bullettino. I. 25.
L' Orto botanico di Padova. See VISIANI, Roberto de. 1842. I. 63.
Orto botanico di Palermo. See REALE ORTO . . . I. 26.[1]
Ortolani, G. E. & Rafinesque-Schmalz, C. S. Statistica generale di Sicilia. 1810. I. 431.
L' Ortolano. III. 25.
Orton, James. The Andes and the Amazon. 1870. I. 531.
Orton, William Allen. See JONES, L. R. & ORTON, W. A.
Die Ortsgemeinde Bernhardzell . . . hat keine Nutzaniessung am Bernhardzeller-Walde. 1845. IV. 330.
Ortt, F. L. De paalworm. 1887. IV. 414.[3]
Ortus sanitatis. 148.? I. 275,[1] 530,[3] V. XIV.[3]
Ortus sanitatis; translaté de latin en francoys. 148.? I. 275.[3]
Orus, Sobre la enfermedad de los Cocoteros. 1882. III. 323.[1]
The Osage Orange. 1894. III. 372.[1]
Osage Orange hedges. 1858. III. 372.[1]
Osband, Lucy A. An Appletree's freak. 1896. II. 267.[1]
Osbeck, Pehr. Dagbok öfwer en Ostindisk resa. 1757. I. 458.
— Försök at plantera Buxbom af frön. 1764. III. 522.[2]
— Reise nach Ostindien. 1757. I. 458.
— Rön angående svenska Artebusken Spartium. 1765. III. 75.[1]
— A voyage to China and the East Indies. 1757. I. 458.
Osborn, Herbert. Apple worms. 1890. III. 428.[1]
— The Ash-tree borer. 1881. IV. 534.[2]
— The Banded Hickory borer. 1888. III. 353.[1]
— Fighting insect enemies. 1892. III. 187.
— Insects affecting Grapes. 1894. III. 564.[1]
— Notes on Apple pests. 1891. III. 428.[1]
— Some insects which threaten the fruit industry in Iowa. 1898. III. 187.
— Spraying in theory and practice. 1896. III. 198.[1]
Osborn, Robert. A group of hardy Azaleas. 1879. III. 661.[2]
Osborne, Henry S. Plants of the Holy Land. 1860. I. 480, 513.
Osborne, W. Bendthamia fragifera. 1884. III. 645.[2]
Oschatz, Ueber den Anbau . . . des Nadelholzes. 1831. IV. 441.
Osenbrüg, Theodor. Ueber die Entwicklung des Samens der Areca. 1894. II. 64.[2]
Oser, I. Bericht über eine . . . Reise zum Studium der in Frankreich üblichen Hartung der Pinus maritima. 1874. IV. 468.[3]
Oser, Johann. See SCHWACKHÖFER, Franz & OSER, Johann.
— & Schwackhöfer, Franz. Zur Frage der Verwerthung des Rothbuchenholzes. 1885. IV. 499.
Osgood, Francis S. The floral offering. 1847. I. 95.
— Interpretations of flora. 184.? I. 94.
O'Shaughnessy, Sir William Brooke. The Bengal dispensatory and pharmacopoeia. 1841. III. 257.[1]
— On the Gurjun. 1842. III. 611.[1]
— Hemidesmus indicus. 1842. III. 693.[1]
— On the identity of the bark of the Strychnos nux-vomica. 1837. III. 684.[3]
O'Shea, J. Prickly-pear. 1897. III. 624.[2]
— Prickly Pear for stock. 1897. III. 624.[1]
Osiers. 1896. III. 351.[1]
Osiers from Madeira. 1897. III. 352.[1]
Oskamp, Dieterich Leonhard. Afbeeldingen der Artsenygewassen. 1796. III. 55.
— Specimen . . . exhibens nonnulla, plantarum fabricam . . . spectantia. 1789. I. 32.
— Tabulae plantarum terminologicae. 1793. I. 70.
Osler, Edward. Myrtles. 1846. II. 631.[2]
Osmaston, L. S. Attacks of Hyblœa puera on Teak trees. 1900. IV. 537.[1]
Osnovaniye . . . See ОСНОВАНІЕ . . .
Ositius marjain, sienien, puunsiementen ja pihan kokoomiseen. 1868. IV. 439.

Osorio, Nicolas. Estudio sobre las Quinas. 1874. II. 813.[1]

Osservatorii meteorologici forestali. 1878. IV. 59.[3]

Osservazioni di un socio . . . sopra la coltivazione degli Agrumi del territorio pisano. 1767. III. 496.[3]

Osservazioni di un socio . . . sopra la coltivazione degli Agrumi . . . della Riviera, di Genova. 1780. III. 496.[3]

Osservazioni e proposte fatte dalla Commissione degli esperti forestali . . . al fine di restaurare nelle alte regioni della Confederazione, le tre economie. 1864. IV. 278.[1]

Osservazioni fenoscopiche sulle piante. 1887. I. 227.[1]

Osservazioni intorno al principii sui quali debbono essere fondate le leggi forestali. 1853. IV. 313.

Osservazioni sulla flora Virgiliana. See TENORE, Michele. 1826. I. 514.[1]

Osuna y Van der Heede, Manuel de. Noticias sobre la flora . . . de Anaga. 1897. I. 498.

Ost, Jul. Rhododendron-Hybriden. 1900. III. 656.

Ostasien — Deutsche Gesellschaft für Natur- und Völkerkunde. See DEUTSCHE . . . I. 28.[1]

Osten, Heinrich von. See OOSTEN, Heinrich von.

Osten-Sacken, Friedrich, Baron von & Ruprecht, F. J. Sertum tianschanicum. 1869. I. 456.

Ostenfeld, Carl Emil Hansen. See BØRGESEN, F. C. E. & OSTENFELD, C. E. H.

Ostenfeld-Hansen, Carl Emil. See BØRGESEN, F. C. E. & OSTENFELD, C. E. H.

Osterheld, Friedrich. Beschädigungen durch den Kieferspanner. 1881. IV. 477.

— Betrachtungen über den Plänterbetrieb. 1879. IV. 131.

— Die edle Kastanie. 1877. IV. 492.[3]

— Die erfolgreiche Bekämpfung der Kiefernschütte. 1898. IV. 479.

— Die Kastanie in den Vorgebirgswaldungen der Pfalz. 1883. IV. 492.[3]

— Ein Waldpflug. 1900. IV. 143.[3]

Osterholt, Wilhelm Clemens. Beiträge zur Anatomie einiger Aloineenblätter. 1899. II. 88.[3]

Osterhout, George E. A new Atriplex. 1898. II. 187.[3]

— New plants from Colorado. 1900. II. 851.[3]

Osterle, Otto. See TSCHIRCH, Alexander & OSTERLE, Otto.

Ostermeyer, Franz. Beitrag zur Flora der Jonischen Inseln. 1887. I. 450.

— Beitrag zur Flora von Kreta. 1890. I. 452.

Osthoff, L. H. Fragmenten over Sumatra. 1845. III. 128.

Ostinelli, Vincenzo. L' Araucaria Bidwillii. 1893. III. 298.[1]

— Dracaena Draco a foglie variegate. 1893. III. 336.[3]

— Sulla fioritura . . . della Washingtonia filifera. 1895. III. 332.[1]

Ostwald, E. Ueber die Art der Verrechnung der Kulturkosten. 1889. IV. 258.

— Zur Frage der Sicherung des Waldfideicommissvermögens. 1897. IV. 271.[1]

— Inwieweit ist bei dem heutigen Stande der Wirthschaft . . . die Forderung strengster Nachhaltigkeit . . . aufrecht zu erhalten? 1890. IV. 245.

— Zur Theorie und Praxis forstlicher Rentabilitäts-Rechnungen. 1893. IV. 259.[3]

— Ueber die Veranschlagung des Abtriebsertrages. 1890. IV. 237.

— Zur Zuwachsschätzung. 1898. IV. 235.[1]

Ostwald, E. H. Zur Reinertrags-Praxis. 1882. IV. 257.

Oswald. Die Körner-Eichen in Dallwitz. 1897. IV. 516.[1]

Oswald, Felix Leopold. The climatic influence of vegetation. 1877. IV. 53.

— Forest fires. 1893. IV. 182.[1]

— Preservation of forests. 1878. IV. 178.[1]

— Shade trees. 1900. IV. 45.

Oswald, Ferdinand. Beiträge zur Kenntniss . . . des Sternanis. 1889. III. 398.[1]

— Ueber die Bestandtheile . . . des Sternanis. 1889. III. 398.[3]

Oswiecinsky, Theodor Rodowicz-. See RODOWICZ-OSWIECINSKY, Theodor.

Otcherk . . . See Очеркъ . . .

Otevřená dopisy pro zahradnictví. 1878. IV. 25.

Oth, (Forstmeister). Die Seekiefer. 1875. IV. 467.[3]

Othmer, B. Dioon spinulosum Dyer. 1900. III. 285.[1]

— Erica canaliculata Andr. 1900. III. 650.[3]

— Magnolia stellata Maxim. 1900. III. 400.[1]

Ototzki, P. V. Influence des forêts sur les eaux. 1898. IV. 52.

— Influence des forêts sur les eaux souterraines. See ОТОЦКІЙ, II. B. 1896. IV. 46.[3]

— Influence des forêts sur les eaux souterraines. See ОТОЦКІЙ, II. B. 1899. IV. 52.

— See also ОТОЦКІЙ, II. B.

Otra extralimitacion. 1890. IV. 548.[3]

Ott. Propriétés narcotiques du Piscidia erythrina. 1883. III. 484.[1]

Ott, Adolf. Ueber den Anbau . . . des Götterbaumes. 1861. III. 506.[1]

— The Beerizing of timber. 1870. IV. 419.

— Die Fagara-Seidenraupe. 1861. III. 148.[1]

— On various processes for preserving timber. 1869. IV. 419.

Ott, Emma. Beiträge zur Kenntniss der Härte vegetabilischer Zellmembranen. 1900. I. 138.[3]

Ott, Johann. Catalog der Flora Böhmens. 1851. I. 440.

Ott, Johann Jacob. Dendrologia Europae mediae. 1763. IV. 110.[1]

Ottavi, E. La lutte contre le mildiou en Italie. 1886. III. 579.

Ottawa field-naturalists' club. Transactions. I. 4.[3]

The Ottawa naturalist. See OTTAWA FIELD-NATURALISTS' CLUB. I. 4.[3]

Ottchet . . . See Очеть . . .

Otte. Die Elektricität in der Holzindustrie. 1897. IV. 334.[1]

Otte, B. Erica cucullata Tausch. 1887. III. 651.[3]

Otte, Karl. Kurze und möglichst vollständige Belehrung über Besaamung der Forstgründe. 1813. IV. 140.

Ottenhoff, G., (jr.). Eenige wenken voor het snoeien. 1897. III. 171.

— Over de teelt van Druiven. 1897. III. 553.[3]

Otterloo, A. van. De verbreiding van de voornaamste cultuur, boom en heestergewassen in Europa. 1872. I. 242.[1]

Ottleben, Friedrich Bernhard. De potus ex Coffeae seminibus parati noxio effectu. 1780. III. 741.[1]

Ottmann, (Förster). Ueber die Anlage von Erlen-Saatkämpen. 1859. IV. 488.[3]

Otto, (herzogl. Oberförster). Nachtheile der Mittelwaldwirthschaft. 1863. IV. 130.

— Nachtheile des Kahlheirbs. 1864. IV. 129.

— Die Nachtheile des raschen . . . Samenschlagbetriebs. 1870. IV. 139.[1]

Otto, (Oberförster zu Weigelsdorf). Statuten des Vereins schlesischer Privatförster und Jäger. 1854. IV. 40.[3]

Otto, Adolf. Rosenzucht im freien Lande und in Töpfen. 1890. III. 453.[1]

— Der Rosenzüchter. 1858. III. 449.

Otto, B. Beitrag zu der . . . erwähnten constant verbänderten Esche. 1885. II. 36.[1]

Otto, Bernhard Christian. De corticis peruviani usu. See ZEIDLER, C. W. 1804. III. 723.

— De febrifugis in cinchonae . . . passim ipsi praeferendis. See SYDOW, F. W. 1809. III. 721.

Otto, Christoph Friedrich. Die Agave-Arten des K. bot. Gartens. 1842. III. 340.[3]

— Ueber die Anwendung immergrüner Pflanzen. 1852. III. 205.[3]

— Anzeige von einer neuen Magnolia. 1851. III. 400.[1]

— Aufzählung der Pittosporeen der Gärten. 1852. III. 415.[3]

— Ueber ausdauernde Gehölz-Arten. 1854. III. 69.

— Ueber das Aussäen der Samen. 1833. III. 156.[1]

— Die Banksien und Dryandren . . . zu Berlin. 1835. III. 382.[7]

— Eine Bastard-Cactee. 1851. II. 593.[3]

— Beitrag zur Cultur der Clavija ornata. 1837. III. 409,[3] 666.[3]

— Beitrag zur Kultur der Poinciana pulcherrima. 1851. III. 469.[1]

— Beitrag zur Kultur der Poivrea- und Combretum-Arten. 1851. III. 632.[1] .

— Beitrag zur Kultur der Melastomen-Kultur. 1846. III. 638.[1]

— Beitrag zur Pimeleen-Kultur. 1847. III. 628.[1]

— Bemerkungen von Podning . . . af de nyhollandske Acacier. 1841. III. 463.[1]

— Bemerkung zu Echinocactus . . . Eyriesii. 1835. II. 593.[3]

— Bemerkungen über Amicia zygomeres. 1847. III. 466.[3]

— Bemerkungen über Anpflanzung nordamerikanischer Eichen. 1845. III. 361.[3]

— Bemerkungen über Cacteen-Kultur. 1847. III. 618.[3]

— Bemerkungen . . . über Cacteen-Kultur. 1841. III. 618.[3]

— Bemerkungen über Chimonanthus. 1842. III. 401.[1]

— Bemerkungen über das Anpflanzen zarter amerikanischer . . . Pflanzen. 1844. III. 121.[1]

— Bemerkungen über das Aussäen. 1846. III. 156.[1]

— Bemerkungen über das Bedecken der . . . Pflanzen. 1840. III. 183.[1]

— Bemerkungen über das Pfropfen . . . neuholländischer Acacien. 1841. III. 463.[1]
— Bemerkungen über die Chironia-Arten. 1845. III. 685.[2]
— Bemerkungen über die Frühtreiberei. 1850. III. 176.[1]
— Bemerkungen über die kapischen . . . Papilionaceen. 1849. III. 462.[1]
— Bemerkungen über die Kultur der Calotropis. 1844. III. 692.[1]
— Bemerkungen über die Kultur des Brodbaums. 1845. III. 367.[1]
— Bemerkungen über die Kultur einiger Guttiferen. 1848. III. 608.[2]
— Bemerkungen über die südafrikanischen Cycadeen-Arten. 1834. III. 284.[1]
— Bemerkungen über . . . Leguminosen. 1844. III. 462.[1]
— Bemerkungen über . . . Plumeria-Arten. 1849. III. 690.[1]
— Die Benutzung der Lobelien. 1852. III. 754.[1]
— Beobachtungen über die Wirkung des vorjährigen trockenen Sommers. 1843. III. 45.
— Die Berberitzen des K. bot. Gartens. 1842. III. 393.[2]
— Ueber das Beschneiden der Gewächshauspflanzen. 1839. III. 169.[2]
— Beschreibung eines Original-Exemplars von Echinocactus platyacanthus. 1845. II. 592.[2]
— Ueber die Bignoniaceen der Gärten. 1850. III. 704.[2]
— Ueber Brownea Jacq. 1855. III. 468.[1]
— Ueber die Cactus-Pflanzen des hiesigen bot. Gartens. 1833. II. 585.[1]
— Ueber die capischen . . . Rutaceen. 1835. III. 494.[2]
— Die Daphne-Arten in den deutschen Gärten. 1848. III. 626.[2]
— Ueber die Diosma-Arten der Gärten. 1835. III. 504.[1]
— Om Diosma-Arterne. 1835. III. 504.[1]
— Ueber die Diosmeae. 1838. III. 494.[2]
— Ueber einige Arten . . . der Bombaceae. 1854. III. 589.[1]
— Einige Bemerkungen über Anpflanzungen von Nutzbäumen. 1842. III. 120.[2]
— Einige Bemerkungen über . . . Barringtonia und Gustavia. 1851. III. 631,[1] 631.[2]
— Einige Bemerkungen über Coniferen. 1847. III. 291.
— Einige Bemerkungen über die · Mamillarien. 1849. III. 623.[1]
— Einige Bemerkungen über . . . Juglandeen. 1850. III. 353.[2]
— Einige Bemerkungen über . . . Macleania-Arten. 1854. III. 653.[1]
— Ueber in g Phyllanthus-(Xylophylla-)Arten. 1854. III. 521.[2 e 1 e]
— Ueber einige . . . Solanaceen. 1851. III. 698.[2]
— Einiges über Anpflanzung von zarten Ziersträuchern. 1842. III. 69.
— Einiges über die Familie der Acanthaceen. 1850. III. 708.[2]
— Einiges über die Familie der Araliaceen. 1850. III. 641.[1]
— Einiges über die kapischen Diosmeen. 1854. III. 494.[2]
— Einiges über die Kultur der Arbutus-Arten. 1851. III. 647.[2]
— Einiges über die Rhopala-Arten. 1849. III. 383.[2]
— Einiges über neuholländische Papilionaceen. 1854. III. 462.[1]
— Einiges über officinelle Pflanzen. 1840. III. 149.
— Ueber die in den Gärten befindlichen Bruniaceae. 1848. II. 251.[2]
— Ueber die Gattungen Franciscea und Brunfelsia. 1850. III. 698.[2]
— Ueber Gompholobium Smith. 1855. III. 478.[1]
— Die Habrothamnus-Arten. 1850. III. 699.[1]
— Hexacentris mysorensis Wight. 1853. III. 710.[2]
— Historische Nachricht und kurze Beschreibung des . . . Bot. Gartens zu Schöneberg. 1832. I. 47.
— Die Hoya-Arten der Gärten. 1852. III. 693.[1]
— Ueber die Jasmin-Arten. 1851. III. 672.[2]
— Kultur-Bemerkungen über die Nyssa-Arten. 1849. II. 614.[2]
— Kultur-Bemerkungen über einige nordamerikanische Pflanzen. 1849. III. 120.[2]
— Kultur-Bemerkungen über . . . Leguminosen. 1852. III. 462.[1]
— Kultur-Bemerkungen zu den Epacrideen. 1848. III. 664.[2]
— Kultur der Aeschynanthus-Arten. 1851. III. 708.[1]
— Ueber Kultur . . . der Araliaceen. 1856. III. 641.[1]
— Ueber die Kultur der . . . Artocarpeen. 1851. III. 366.[1]
— Ueber die Kultur der Carludovica. 1855. III. 332.[2]
— Kultur der Catesbaea spinosa L. 1849. III. 711.[2]
— Ueber Kultur der Coccoloba-Arten. 1850. III. 387.[1]
— Kultur der Cookia punctata. 1849. III. 503.[1]
— Ueber die Kultur der Echites-Arten. 1850. III. 688.[1]
— Ueber die Kultur der . . . Eriostemon-Arten. 1848. III. 504.[1]
— Kultur der Gardenia. 1852. III. 744.[1]
— Kultur der Gnidia-Arten. 1854. III. 628.[1]
— Kultur der Neptunia oleracea. 1848. III. 482.[2]
— Kultur der nordamerikanischen Magnolien. 1856. III. 399.[1]
— Ueber die Kultur der strauchartigen Sophora- und Edwardsia-Arten. 1839. III. 487.[2]
— Zur Kultur der Thymelaeae. 1838. III. 626.[2]
— Ueber die Kultur einiger . . . Dilleniaceae. 1855. III. 595.[2]
— Kultur einiger Diosmeen. 1849. III. 494.[2]
— Kultur einiger Dipladenia-Arten. 1845. III. 687.[2]
— Kultur einiger Tupa-Arten. 1850. III. 754.[1]
— Kultur einiger Vaccineen und Ericaceen. 1849. III. 646.[2]
— Kultur einiger Vaccineen- und Rhodoraceen-Arten. 1847. III. 646.[2]
— Kultur-Methode des Cereus nycticallus. 1834. III. 621.[2]
— Kurze Bemerkungen über die Kultur einiger Abietinae. 1843. III. 291.
— Kurze Bemerkungen über verschiedene . . . Pflanzen. 1843. III. 74.
— Meddelelser om Dyrkningen af Magnoliaceae. 1838. III. 397.[1]
— Mittheilungen über Kultur der Magnoliaceae. 1838. III. 397.[1]
— Nachricht über den . . . Chamaerops humilis. 1844. II. 67.[1]
— Nachricht . . . von einer blühenden Opuntia microdasys. 1839. II. 597.[1]
— Ueber Nadelholz-Anbau in den Baumschulen. 1841. III. 291.
— Die neuholländischen Eucalyptus-Arten. 1837. III. 633.[2]
— Oversigt over de nyhollandske Myrtaceer. 1835. III. 633.[1]
— Ueber Passifloren. 1851. III. 615.[1]
— Die Philadelphus-Arten der Gärten. 1844. III. 413.[1]
— Ueber Pinus-Kultur. 1848. III. 306.[1]
— Plantae rariores quae in Horto regio berolinensi . . . floruere. 1820. I. 45.
— Die Psoralea-Arten . . . im K. bot. Garten. 1843. III. 485.[1]
— Das Ringeln der Pflanzen. 1833. III. 175.[1]
— Ueber das Samentragen und Keimen der Platane. 1854. II. 254.[2]
— Ueber die Solandra-Arten. 1845. III. 701.[1]
— Tetrathaea ericoides hort. 1855. III. 513.[1]
— Ueber die Thibaudia-Arten. 1851. III. 663.[1]
— Übersicht der neuholländischen Myrtaceen. 1835. III. 633.[1]
— Uebersicht der Spiraea-Arten. 1844. III. 460.[1]
— Versuche über das Keimen alter Samen. 1844. I. 527.
— Wirkung der vorigen Winter-Witterung. 1836. III. 45.
— Wirkung der vorjährigen Winterwitterung. 1838. III. 45.
— Die Wirkung des kalten Winters. 1855. III. 45.
— See also GUIMPEL, Friedrich, OTTO, Friedrich & HAYNE, F. G., etc.; LINK, M. F., KLOTZSCH, J. F. & OTTO, Friedrich.
— & Dietrich, Albert. Ueber die Arten der Gattung Carolinea. 1838. II. 530.[2]
— — Ueber die Arten der Gattung Casuarina. 1841. II. 92.[1]
— — Ueber die Arten der Gattung Hermannia. 1840. II. 535.[1]
— — Aufzählung und Kultur der Lantana-Arten. 1841. II. 758.[1]
— — Ueber die ausländischen nutzbaren Pflanzen. 1846. III. 150.[1]
— — Die Begonien . . . im hiesigen bot. . . . Garten. 1836. II. 583.[2]
— — Begoniernes Beskrivelse og Dyrkning. 1836. II. 583.[2]
— — Bemerkungen über die Degeneration mancher Opuntia-Früchte. 1843. II. 596.[1]
— — Bemerkungen über die strauchartigen Schlingpflanzen. 1844. III. 204.[2]
— — Bemerkungen über ein fruchttragendes Taxodium. 1848. III. 310.[2]
— — Bemerkungen über einige Mamillarien. 1845. II. 594.[2]
— — Bemerkungen zu Zamia Ottonis. 1844. II. 7.[1]

Otto, Christoph Friedrich & Dietrich, Albert (continued).
—— Beschreibung der Begonia lucida. 1848. II. 584.²
—— Beschreibung der Cordyline rubra Hort. 1848. II. 80.²
—— Beschreibung der Juanulloa aurantiaca. 1844. II. 772.²
—— Beschreibung . . . der Mimosa Kermesina. 1835. II. 2.¹
—— Beschreibung . . . der Rhipsalis pentaptera. 1836. II. 37.¹
—— Beschreibung . . . der Uhdea bipinnatifida. 1853. III. 755.¹
—— Beschreibung . . . des Cereus Martianus Zuccar. 1838. III. 621.²
—— Beschreibung des Dasylirion acrotiche. 1848. III. 256.¹
—— Beschreibung . . . des Echinocactus acutissimus. 1835. II. 592.¹
—— Beschreibung des Echinocactus concinnus. 1843. II. 592.¹
—— Beschreibung . . . des Echinocactus hypocrateriformis. 1838. II. 592.²
—— Beschreibung . . . des Echinocactus phyllacanthus. 1836. II. 592.²
—— Beschreibung des Pelargonium Friderici Guilelmi Klier. 1837. II. 390.²
—— Beschreibung einer neuen Cactee. 1841. II. 598.¹
—— Beschreibung einiger neuen . . . Cacteen. 1838. II. 585.¹
—— Beschreibung und Kultur der Clomenocoma montana. 1850. III. 755.¹
—— Die Caragana-Arten . . . in den hiesigen Gärten. 1843. II. 341.²
—— Characteristik einiger . . . nordischer, nicht gewöhnlicher Gehölze. 1838. III. 69.
—— Die Crataegus-Arten der hiesigen Gärten. 1845. III. 421.¹
—— Cultur . . . der Beaufortia splendens. 1834. III. 633.¹
—— Cultur . . . der Calandrinia spectabilis. 1833. II. 194.¹
—— Cultur . . . des Pelargenium [sic] dichotomum. 1835. II. 390.²
—— Cultur . . . des Rhodochiton. 1833. III. 704.¹
—— Einige Betrachtungen über die Begonien. 1843. II. 584.¹
—— Einige Worte über Echeverien. 1844. II. 235.¹
—— Einiges über die Cultur der . . . Genisteae. 1838. II. 351.¹
—— Ueber die Einwirkung der Kälte im letzten Winter. 1845. III. 45.
—— Ueber die Einwirkung der Kälte im letzten Winter auf die immergrünen Pflanzen. 1845. III. 45.
—— Ueber die in den Gärten . . . befindlichen Ribes-Arten. 1842. II. 243.¹
—— Gedanken über Gesnera und Columnea. 1843. III. 708.¹
—— The genus Ribes. 1842. II. 243.¹
—— Die Juniperus- oder Wachholder-Arten. 1845. III. 303.¹
—— Kultur . . . der Kunthia xalapensis. 1833. III. 322.¹
—— Kultur und Beschreibung des Rhodochiton. 1834. II. 782.¹
—— Lantana. 1841. II. 758.¹
—— Ueber die Leptospermum Arten . . . im hiesigen bot. Garten. 1841. II. 628.¹
—— Nachricht von einem zum Erstenmale blühenden Cereus. 1842. II. 591.²
—— Nachricht von einer blühenden Caryota. 1837. II. 65.¹
—— Neue Rhododendron-Varietäten. 1847. II. 677.¹
—— Ueber eine neue Weinart aus Nordamerika. 1842. II. 506.²
—— Die Piperaceae . . . des K. bot. Gartens. 1840. III. 342.¹
—— Ueber die Siphocampylus-Arten . . . in unsern Gärten. 1844. II. 846.¹
—— Stephanotis floribunda Hort. Paris. 1835. III. 742.²
—— Vitis Isabella, en ny Viinart fra Nordamerika. 1842. II. 506.²
—— Zwei neue zierende Spiraea-Arten. 1845. II. 314.¹
— See also GUIMPEL, Friedrich, OTTO, Friedrich & HAYNE, F. G.; KLOTZSCH, J. F. & OTTO, Friedrich; LINK, H. F. & OTTO, Friedrich; PFEIFFER, Ludwig & OTTO, Friedrich.
Otto, Eduard. Abies Nordmanniana Lk. 1866. III..296.²
— Acacia ovoidea. 1855. III. 466.¹

— Acer dasycarpum Wieri laciniatum. 1879. III. 536.¹
— Die ächten Zwergmispeln, Cotoneaster. 1881. III. 420.²
— Ueber Ailanthus glandulosa. 1879. III. 507.¹
— Die amerikanischen . . . Hydrangea-Arten. 1867. III. 411.¹
— Die Ampelideen oder Rebenpflanzen. 1879. III. 544.¹
— Die Arten der Gattung Dipladenia. 1862. III. 687.²
— Auswahl blühender Pflanzen im Botanischen Garten zu Hamburg. 1848. I. 47.
— Eine Auswahl der schönsten Weiss- oder Hagedorn-Arten. 1866. III. 421.²
— Eine Auswahl neuer Pflanzen. 1872. III. 83.¹
— Auszüge . . . über dessen Reise nach Cuba. 1839. I. 335.
— Auszüge . . . über dessen Reise von Cuba nach Nord- und Süd-Amerika. 1840. I. 329.
— Bäume und Sträucher mit hängendem und pyramiden-förmigem Habitus. 1867. III. 204.¹
— Die Bambusrohr-Arten. 1869. III. 314.¹
— Baum- und Straucharten mit bunten Blättern. 1866. III. 206.²
— Beachtenswerthe neue Einführungen. 1879. III. 75.¹
— Begonien . . . in den letzten Jahren . . . eingeführt. 1852. III. 618.¹
— Beiträge zur Kultur der Begonien. 1848. III. 618.¹
— Beiträge zur Cultur der Fuchsien. 1836. III. 639.²
— Bemerkungen über die Gattung Clerodendron. 1848. III. 696.¹
— Bemerkungen über die Kultur der Aeschynanthus Arten. 1848. III. 708.¹
— Die Blasensträucher. 1881. III. 473.¹
— Die Bocksdorn (Lycium)-Arten. 1881. III. 700.²
— Der Brodfruchtbaum. 1882. III. 367.¹
— Brownea grandiceps Jacq., in Blüthe. 1860. III. 468.¹
— Buntblättrige Coniferen. 1873. III. 290.
— Cacteen-Gruppe auf den Bergen Mayquetia. 1844. II. 587.²
— Die Ceanothus- oder Seckelblumen-Arten. 1876. III. 541.¹
— Die Clematis. 1876. III. 389.¹
— Coniferen-Sammlung der Herren P. Smith & Co. 1870. III. 290.
— Die Coniferen-Sammlung der Herren Peter Smith & Co. 1878. III. 290.
— Ueber Crataegus Pyracantha. 1862. III. 443.²
— Croton-Arten und Varietäten. 1879. III. 516.¹
— Cycas revoluta Thunbg. 1852. II. 4.²
— Cydonia (Pyrus) Maulei, ein neuer Zierstrauch. 1875. III. 420.²
— Description . de la fleur de l'Opuntia microdasys, 1839. II. 597.¹
— Ueber Deutzia gracilis. 1851. III. 410.¹
— Drei neue von G. Wallis entdeckte Zamien. 1875. III. 286.¹
— Die Echeverien-Arten. 1873. III. 409.²
— Einfluss des Winters 1870–71 auf die Coniferen. 1871. III. 292.
— Einige Blüthensträucher. 1868. III. 207.¹
— Einige empfehlenswerthe Melastomaceen. 1881. III. 638.¹
— Ueber einige . . . in Handel kommenden Pflanzen. 1864. III. 75.¹
— Einige sich für Schmuckgärten . . . eignende Coniferen. 1879. III. 290.
— Die Elfenbein-Pflanze, Phytelephas. 1873. II. 73.²
— Die Epheu-(Hedera-)Arten. 1881. III. 642.²
— Die Essigbäume, Rhus. 1878. III. 526.¹
— Die Familie der Cycadeen. 1880. III. 284.¹
— Die Familie der Hippocastaneen. 1879. III. 536.²
— Floraison et culture du Brownea grandiceps. 1860. III. 468.¹
— Im Freien aushaltende Coniferen. 1861. III. 292.
— Ueber die im Freien aushaltenden Haidekräuter. 1869. III. 648,² 650.¹
— Fuchsia procumbens. 1876. III. 640.²
— Ueber die in den Gärten aushaltenden Hydrangeen. 1856. III. 411.¹
— Die Gattung Bouvardia. 1854. III. 711.¹
— Die Gattung Cydonia, Quitte. 1883. III. 423.¹
— Die Gattung Deutzia. 1873. III. 410.¹
— Die Gattung Epacris. 1850. III. 665.¹
— Die Gattung Erythrina. 1860. III. 475.²
— Ueber die Gattung Hoya. 1852. III. 693.¹
— Die Gattung Olea. 1878. III. 674.²
— Die Gattung Plumbago. 1858. III. 666.¹

— Der Gewürzstrauch. 1867. III. 401.[1]
— Die Hardenbergien. 1856. III. 480.[1]
— Hardenbergierne. 1856. III. 480.[1]
— Die Heidelbeersträucher. 1881. III. 663.[1]
— Heyderia decurrens C. Koch. 1874. III. 305.[1]
— Die Hollunder-Arten, Sambucus L. 1879. III. 751.[2]
— Om kolde Væxthuusplanters Formering ved Stiklinger. 1836. III. 157.
— Der Kuh- oder Milchbaum. 1873. III. 367.[2]
— Ueber die Kultur der Guajava. 1841. III. 637.[1]
— Zur Kultur der Pimeleen-Arten. 1851. III. 628.[1]
— Ueber Magnoliaceen. 1860. III. 397.[1]
— Der Maulbeerbaum. 1877. III. 378.
— Ueber Mikania odorata Lehm. 1849. III. 755.[2]
— Die in Mittel- und Nord-Europa im Freien aushaltenden Seidelbast-Arten. 1873. III. 626.[2]
— Mittheilung über einen hybriden Cytisus. 1848. III. 480.[2]
— Die Mondblumen oder Yukken. 1875. III. 339.[2]
— Nerium Oleander-Varietäten. 1869. III. 689.[2]
— Neue Croton-Formen. 1877. III. 515.[2]
— Neue Echeveria. 1875. III. 409.[2]
— Neue, in den Handel gegebene Pflanzen. 1881. III. 334,[2] 516.[2]
— Neue in den Handel kommende empfehlenswerthe Pflanzen. 1878. III. 75.[1]
— Die neue Kugel-Rüster. 1879. III. 365.[1]
— Neuheiten von im Freien aushaltenden Stauden. 1870. III. 69.
— Die neuholländischen Akazien. 1883. III. 463.[1]
— Notizen über die Kultur des Kaffees. 1841. III. 726.[2]
— Notizen über Sterculia Balanghas. 1849. III. 591.[2]
— Nouveaux arbres d'ornement. 1879. III. 75.[1]
— Opuntia Rafinesquiana Englm. 1870. III. 625.[1]
— Oreodoxa Regia Kth. 1841. II. 72.[1]
— Die Pappel-, Populus-Arten. 1880. III. 344.[1]
— Die Passionsblumen. 1873. III. 615.[2]
— Paulownia imperialis. 1846. III. 703.[1]
— Ueber Pflanzen mit bunten Blättern. 1833. III. 206.[1]
— Reise nach dem Galactodendron utile. 1841. III. 367.[2]
— Reiseerinnerungen an Cuba. 1838. I. 329.
— Renseignements au sujet de l'Abies Nordmanniana. 1866. III. 296.[2]
— Der Riesenbaum Zamang de Guere. 1841. II. 377.[2]
— Robinia inermis pyramidalis. 1857. III. 486.[2]
— Robinia inermis Rehderi. 1864. III. 487.[1]
— Robinia Pseudacacia pyramidalis. 1874. III. 487.[1]
— Samen- und Pflanzen-Verzeichnisse für 1880. 1880. III. 290.
— Schlingpflanzen. 1853. III. 204.[2]
— Die Seidelbast- oder Daphne-Arten. 1863. III. 626.[2]
— Ueber die sich für unser Klima eignenden Coniferen. 1867. III. 289.
— Ueber Strauchapfelgehölz. 1875. III. 425.[2]
— Tabernaemontana amygdalifolia. 1920. III. 690.[2]
— Der Tupelobaum. 1873. III. 632.[1]
— Uebersicht der in Brasilien vorkommenden Holzarten. 1867. IV. 398.[2]
— Die bei uns aushaltenden Hartriegel-(Cornus-)Arten. 1871. III. 645.[1]
— Ueber die Vermehrung der Proteaceen. 1849. III. 382.[2]
— Vermehrung der zwergartigen Rhododendron. 1851. III. 050.
— Ueber die Vermehrung . . . durch Stecklinge. 1836. III. 157.
— Die verschiedenen Ilex-Arten. 1868. III. 530.[1]
— Verzeichniss einer Auswahl von im Freien ausdauernden Bäumen . . . im Hamburgischen botanischen Garten. 1845. I. 47.
— Wirkung des letzten Winters. 1855. III. 45.
— Die Yucca- oder Mondblumen-Arten. 1882. III. 339.[2]
— Der Zürgelstrauch. 1878. III. 363.[1]
— Der Zürgel-Strauch oder Baum. 1879. III. 363.[2]
— & others. Paa hvilken Maade formere Planter bedst ved Stikkere. 1833. III. 157.
—— Welches ist das beste Verfahren, Pflanzen durch Stecklinge zu vermehren. 1838. III. 157.
Otto, Emanuel. Ratgeber im Obstbau. 1882. III. 139.
Otto, Friedrich. See Otto, C. F.
Otto, G. Aralien des Warmhauses. 1899. III. 641.[1]
Otto, Johann Gottfried. De usu medico Dulcamarae. 1784. III. 701.[2]
Otto, Karl. Der Schlüssel zur Botanik. 1835. I. 378.
— Die vorzüglichsten in Thüringen wildwachsenden Giftpflanzen. 1834. III. 73.

Otto, Richard. Bodenkunde. 1900. IV. 70.
— Die Düngung gärtnerischer Kulturen. 1896. III. 152.
— Ueber den schädlichen Einfluss von . . . Lysollösungen. 1892. III. 197.
— Mit welchen Holzarten sind Ödlandflächen . . . aufzuforsten? 1898. IV. 159.
— See also Frank, B. & Otto, Richard.
Otto of Roses. 1891. III. 453.[1]
Ottolander, J. W. & Son. New Japanese evergreen Oaks. 1874. III. 131.[1]
—— New ornamental Japanese Pears. 1877. III. 447.[1]
Ottolander, K. J. W. Abrikozen en Perziken van zaad. 1877. III. 430.[2]
— De beste Perziken voor Nederland. 1877. III. 441.[1]
— De beste vruchten. 1866. III. 76.
— Eenige van de beste Druiven voor ons klimaat. 1876. III. 547.
— Moerbezie-boomen. 1878. III. 378.
— Nieuwe Dracaena hybriden. 1876. III. 334.[2]
— De nieuwe Engelsche verscheidenheden van Rozen. 1881. III. 450.
— Een paar woorden over de . . . snoeiwijze. 1866. III. 170.
— Pinus sylvestris aurea. 1876. III. 309.[1]
— De praktische ooftkweeker. 1882. III. 140.[1]
— Seringen. 1876. III. 680:[1]
— Over het snoeien der vruchtboomen. 1870. III. 172.
— Vaccinium macrocarpum. 1877. III. 663.[2]
— Zaaibeweging. 1877. I. 247.
— See also Hoff, J. van & Ottolander, K. J. W.
— & T. De Platanen. 1876. III. 418.[1]
Ottolander, T. Beschrijvende lijst der soorten . . . van het geslacht Ilex. 1878. III. 529.[2]
— Eene boomkweekerij op Java. 1879. III. 154.[2]
— Chronologisch-historisch overzicht van . . . Cinchona. 1887. II. 813.[1]
— De Djatti boom. 1880. IV. 536.[2]
— De Eik. 1879. III. 361.[1]
— Het enten van Koffie. 1899. III. 733.[2]
— Het enten van vruchtboomen en heesters. 1884. III. 162.
— Extract uit een Rapport over de Dadap-ziekte. 1892. III. 476.[1]
— Hamamelis arborea. 1876. III. 417.[1]
— Hybridisatie. 1900. III. 733.[2]
— Hybridisatie bij Koffie. 1900. III. 733.[2]
— Hybridisatie door middel van enting. 1877. I. 246.[1]
— Van Java. 1882. III. 276.[1]
— Van Java; een tocht naar den Semeroe. 1883. I. 469.[1]
— Van Java; naar Sendang laya. 1883. III. 128.
— Van Java-Indrukken op reis. 1879. III. 128.
— Op een Koffieland. 1881. III. 727.
— Het Koffieplanten. 1882. III. 727.
— De kultuurtuin te Tjikeumeuh. 1882. III. 128.
— 's Lands plantentuin te Buitenzorg. 1883. I. 68.[1]
— Lezing op het Koffiecongres te Malang. 1899. III. 731.
— Populus canadensis aurea van Geerti. 1876. III. 345.[2]
— Reglement voor de metereologische waarnemingen op Koffielanden. 1899. III. 36.[1]
— Over het snoeien . . . der Koffie. 1899. III. 734.[2]
— Het snoeien van den Koffieboom. 189.? III. 734.[2]
— Het snoeien . . . van Koffieboomen. 1899. III. 734.[2]
— Tentoonstelling van bonte heesters. 1877. III. 206.[2]
— Het snoeien der bosschen. 1881. IV. 376.[2]
— Zaadselectie bij de Koffiecultuur. 1900. III. 733.[2]
Ottow, W. M. Onderzoekingen over den bast van Wistaria. 1886. II. 388.[2]
The Otway forest. 1885. IV. 380.[1]
Oud-Planter, (pseud.). Koffie-varieteiten. 1899. III. 733.[2]
Oude en groote Eikenboom. 1834. II. 138.[1]
Oudemans, A. J. Over eenige Oost-indische vetsoorten. 1868. III. 224.[2]
Oudemans, Anthonie Cornelis. Bijdrage tot de kennis der kinamine. 1878. III. 723.
— Bijdrage tot de kennis der konkinamine. 1879. III. 723.
— Bijdrage tot de kennis van de cuprenine. 1889. III. 723.
— Bijdrage tot de kennis van kinovazuur. 1884. III. 723.
— Caoutchouc en gutta-percha. 1866. III. 230.
— Sur la composition du beurre de Shea. 1863. III. 667.[1]
— Sur le dosage par le polaristrobomètre de la quinine. 1876. III. 723.
— Examen chimique de quelques matières grasses. 1867. I. 182.[1]
— Ueber den Milchsaft von Plumiera. 1876. III. 690.[1]

Oudemans, Anthonie Cornelis (*continued*).
— Over een nieuwe soort van gutta-percha. 1859. III. 668.[1]
— Onderroekingen over het podocarpinezuur. 1874. II. 9.[2]
— Onderzoek naar de vaste vetzuren van de Cocosboter. 1864. III. 324.[1]
— Onderzoek naar de vaste vetzuren van de Kokosolie. 1862. III. 324.[1]
— Onderzoek naar de vetzuren van de Shea-butter. 1863. III. 667.[1]
— Onderzoek naar de vlugtige vetzuren uit de Cocosboter. 1864. III. 324.[1]
— Onderzoek omtrent de bladeren van Dialium. 1878. II. 354.[1]
— Onze flora. 1900. I. 391.[2]
— Sur le pouvoir rotatoire spécifique des principaux alcaloides du quinquina. 1875. III. 723.
— Over de quantitatieve bepaling van kinine. 1876. III. 723.
— Recherches sur l'acide podocarpique. 1873. II. 9.[1]
— Recherches sur la conquinamine. 1879. III. 723.
— Recherches sur la quinamine. 1878. III. 723.
— Over het soortelijk draaiings-vermogen der voornaamste kina-alkaloïden. 1875. III. 723.
— Over wringing van boomstammen. 1897. I. 107.[1]
— Over de zamenstelling van het Palmpittenvet. 1870. III. 325.[1]
— Over de zamenstelling . . . van het Plumierazuur. 1876. III. 690.[1]
— & **Rauwenhoff,** N. W. P. De scheikundige verschijnselen bij de kieming. 1858. I. 203.
Oudemans, Cornelis Antoon Jan Abraham. Aanteekeningen op het systematischen . . . deel der Pharmacopaea neerlandica. 1854. III. 250.
— Alsodeiarum . . . illustrationes et descriptiones. 1867. II. 508.[1]
— Annotationes criticae in Cupuliferas. 1865. II. 131.[1]
— Over de beteekenis der verhevenheden aan de oppervlakte der zaden van Strychnos. 1864. II. 720.[2]
— Bijdrage tot de kennis van de . . . structuur van de vrucht . . . des Kamferbooms. 1855. II. 560.[1]
— Bijdrage tot de kennis van den microscopischen bouw der Kinabasten. 1871. II. 813.[1]
— Over een bijzonere soort van huizen in den Vlierstam. 1872. II. 841.[1]
— Eerste beginselen der plantenkunde. 1868. I. 91.
— Over de eigenschappen der planten met bont blad. 1865. III. 181.[1]
— Encore un mot sur le Cycas inermis. 1868. II. 4.[2]
— Sur une espèce grasse du Sud-existant dans le tronc du Sureau. 1872. II. 841.[1]
— Examen de la matière grasse du pain de dika. 1861. III. 508.[1]
— Ficus Suringarii. 1866. II. 153.[2]
— De flora van Nederland. 1859. I. 391,[1] V. xx.[1]
— Sur un fruit . . . à moitié Citron et à moitié Orange. 1873. II. 401.[2]
— Hälften Citron, hälften Apelsin. 1873. II. 402.[1]
— De Handelsplanten. 1883. III. 53.
— Handleiding tot de pharmacognosie. 1865. III. 258.
— Das Hornprosenchym Wigand's. 1862. I. 125.
— Iets over de kleuren der bloemen. 1865. I. 184.
— Iets over de roest der Granen. 1865. III. 446.[1]
— Leerboek der plantenkunde. 1866. I. 91.
— Lithocarpus scutigera Oud. 1862. II. 133.[1]
— Sur une maladie des Pivoines. 1896. III. 393.[1]
— Mededeeling aangaande een bloeienden Pandanus spurius. 1864. II. 57.[2]
— Mededeeling aangaande eene vrucht . . . half als Citroen en half als Sinaasappel. 1873. II. 401.[2]
— Mededeeling aangaande . . . Encephalartos Altensteinii. 1864. II. 5.[2]
— Mémoire sur la structure . . . du fruit . . . de l'arbre à Camphre. 1855. II. 560.[1]
— Morphologische beschouwingen omtrent de ranken van Vitis. 1851. II. 507.[1]
— Nog een enkel woord over Cycas inermis. 1868. II. 4.[2]
— Nog iets over de roest der granen. 1865. III. 394.[1]
— Note préliminaire sur quelques Cupulifères de Java. 1861. II. 131.[1]
— Note sur . . . Lithocarpus scutigera. 1864. II. 133.[2]
— Notice sur un Pandanus spiralis R. 1862. II. 57.[2]
— Notice sur une plante femelle de Cycas inermis. 1862. III. 285.[1]

— Observations sur la structure microscopique des écorces de Quinquina. 1871. II. 813.[1]
— Onderzoek van vet uit het zoogenaamde dikabrood. 1861. III. 508.[1]
— Over het ontstaan van zwamvlokken aan wortels. 1865. II . 194.
— De ontwikkeling onzer kennis aangaande de flora van Nederland. 1876. I. 80.[2]
— Onze Kinaplantsoenen op Java. 1876. III. 716.
— Poging om Cycas inermis. 1867. II. 4.[2]
— Remarques sur le genre Leptonychia. 1866. II. 536.[1]
— Systematisch overzigt der geneeskrachtige gewassen. 1851. III. 58.
— Tentative pour rétablir au rang d'espèce le Cycas inermis. 1867. II. 4.[2]
— Verklaring van de beteekenis der geslachtsnamen. 1899. I. 76.[2]
— Viburnum plicatum Thunb. var. tomentosum Miq. 1867. III. 753.[2]
— Violaceae. 1867. II. 567.[1]
— Voorloopige mededeeling aangaande . . . eenige Javaansche Cupuliferen. 1861. II. 131.[1]
— De ziekte der Koffieplant. 1877. III. 735.
— & **Stellingwerf,** A. Verslag . . . aangaande den Kina-aanvoer. 1883. III. 718.
— & **Vries,** Hugo de. Leerboek der plantenkunde. 1880. V. x.[2]
Oudh. See INDIA — OUDH; INDIA — NORTH-WESTERN PROVINCES AND OUDE.
De oudste Acacia. 1868. II. 383.[1]
Ouekaki-Morikouni. Yo-san-fi-rok. 1848. III. 376.
Ouest de la France — Société des sciences naturelles. See SOCIÉTÉ . . . I. 23.
Ounous, Léo d'. Sur l'Alisier de Sibérie. 1863. III. 460.[1]
— Amandier pleureur. 1874. III. 434.[1]
— Arbres, arbustes . . . à l'hiver de 1863–64. 1864. III. 48.
— Arbres et arbustes d'ornement. 1861. III. 203.
— Sur les arbres nouveaux acclimatés. 1859. III. 84.[1]
— Deux arbustes à recommander. 1874. III. 421,[1] 682.[1]
— Érable à grandes feuilles. 1879. III. 535.[1]
— Floraison du Cereus monstrosus. 1872. III. 621.[2]
— Les Grenadiers dans le midi. 1869. III. 630.[1]
— Du Mûrier de la Chine. 1868. III. 377.
— Note sur le Pêcher pleureur de Chine. 1876. III. 440.[1]
— Note sur les Féviers. 1877. III. 477.[2]
— Les nouveaux Plaquemıniers du Japon. 1878. III. 669.[2]
— Sur le Noyer à fruits ovales. 1879. III. 354.[2]
— Observations sur diverses plantes . . . après l'hiver . . . 1861. 1861. III. 48.
— Plantes du Sud-Ouest à introduire. 1863. III. 87.
— Le Ragouminier. 1862. III. 442.[2]
— Le Virgilier à bois jaune. 1865. III. 472.[2]
Our annual return of prices of timber etc. See PRICES of forest produce. 1878. IV. 398.[2]
Our forest produce. See PRICES of forest produce. 1878. IV. 398.[2]
Our forest produce table. See PRICES of forest produce. 1878. IV. 398.[2]
Our oil-flasks. 1863. III. 224.[2]
Our tea-table. 1857. III. 601.[2]
Our water-retaining and water-evaporating areas. 1898. IV. 52.
L'ouragan du 1er juillet. 1897. IV. 548.[1]
Ourches, Charles d'. Aperçu général des forêts. 1805. IV. 359.[2]
— Greffe nouvelle. 1820. III. 160.
— Observations et améliorations sur . . . l'agriculture dans les sols sablonneux. 1818. III. 116.
Ournay. La multiplication des Peupliers. 1896. IV. 485.[2]
Out-door flowers in winter. 1900. III. 207.[2]
Out West, (*pseud.*). Osage Orange hedges. 1862. III. 372.[4]
Outhov, Gerard. Exercitatio de manna Israelitarum. 1694. III. 221.[3]
Outryve d'Ydewalle, van. Culture du Pin sylvestre dans les terrains sablonneux. 1895. IV. 559.[2]
— Culture du Pin sylvestre dans les terrains sablonneux des Flandres. 1895. IV. 559.[1]
Ouvray, (*abbé*). La physiologie végétale. 189.[?] I. 147.
Ouvray, E. Les ennemis et les maladies parasitaires. 1899. III. 179.
— Étude des parasites végétaux. 1899. III. 419.[1]
— La gelée en viticulture et en arboriculture. 189.[?] III. 182.
— Manuel d'arboriculture fruitière. 1890. III. 145.[1]
Ouwerkerk, E. The practice of budding fully described. 1899. III. 164.[2]

Ovelgün, R. F. Spiritum vini . . . colore rubello imbuendi modus. 1744. III. 752.[1]
Overbeck, O. C. J. G. L. Handsome flowering Cacti for the garden. 1893. III. 622.[2]
Overbeck, Robert. De plantarum exanthematibus. 1851. III. 40.
Overbeek, A. A. BACKER. See BACKER OVERBEEK, A. A.
Overduyn. Beswaren tegen de gouvernements Koffiecultuur van Liberia Koffie. 1893. III. 730.
Overeijnder, C. G. Acer Lorbergii. 1881. III. 535.[2]
Overin, A. See OBEPИHЪ, A.
Overland monthly. I. 6.
Oversigt over Penge-Udbyttet af Statsskovene i Kongeriget Danmark. See WIMPFEN, F. von. 1860. IV. 260.[1]
Overton, Ernst. Ueber die allgemeinen osmotischen Eigenschaften der Zelle. 1899. I. 150.[2]
— Ueber die osmotischen Eigenschaften der Zelle. 1896. I. 50.[1]
Overzicht van het Museum. 188.? I. 51.[2]
Oversigt der Landbouw-scheikunde voor Nederlanders. 1846. III. 36.[2]
Oversigt van den landbouw . . . in Nederlandsch Oost Indie. 1876. III. 128.
Oviedo y Valdes, Gonzalo Ferdinando de. L'histoire naturelle et générale des Indes. 1535. III. 265.[2]
— Historia general y natural de las Indias. 1535. III. 265.[3]
— Primera parte de la historia . . . de las Indias. 1535. III. 265.[2]
— Sommario della naturale et generale historia dell' Indie Occidentali. 1526. III. 265.[1]
— Sumario de la natural general istoria de las Indias. 1526. III. 265.[1]
Ovington, John. An essay upon the nature and qualities of Tea. 1699. III. 605.
Owek'ia-skee. Koowoki tsikin-s'joo. 1800. I. 461, III. 91.[1]
Owen, D. A. Some strange developments of stomata upon Carya. 1892. III. 353.[2]
Owen, G. B. Melanose [of the Orange]. 1898. III. 501.[1]
Owen, John. Memorandum on the manufacture, &c. of Black Tea. 1843. III. 602.[3]
Owen, Mrs. Maria Louisa. A catalogue of plants . . . in the county of Nantucket, Mass. 1888. I. 315.
Owen, T. C. The Cinchona planter's manual. 1881. III. 712.[2]
— The Tea planter's manual. 1886. III. 763.[2]
Oxamendi, Juan Calixte. De la acción terapeutica del aceite de la nuez del Nogal. 1874. III. 515.[1]
— Aceite de nogal de la India. 1873. III. 515.[1]
— Agua destilada de la Yuca agria. 1870. III. 519.[2]
— Cardol vesicante. 1872. III. 524.[1]
— Cuajani. 1874. III. 431.[1]
— Sur l'huile d'Aleurites triloba. 1876. III. 515.[1]
— Memoria sobre el agua destilada de las hojas del Cuajani. 1874. III. 431.[2]
— Resina de Guaguasi. 1882. III. 614.[2]
— De la resina de Guaguasi. 1882. III. 614.[2]
Oxenstierna, E. G., baron. Försök, at underlätta foderbrist med Granris. 1772. IV. 459.[2]
Oxley, Thomas. Die Banda-Muscatpflanzungen. 1856. III. 402.[1]
— The Banda Nutmeg plantations. 1856. III. 402.[1]
— The botany of Singapore. 1850. I. 476.[1]
— Gutta percha. 1847. III. 228.[2]
— Over de gutta percha. 1848. III. 230.
— Some account of the Nutmeg. 1848. III. 402.[1]
Oye, W. A. SCHIMMELPENNINCK VAN DER. See SCHIMMELPENNINCK VAN DER OYE, W. A.
Oyen, G. A. VORSTERMAN VAN. See VORSTERMAN VAN OYEN, G. A.
Oyster, John Houck. Catalogue of North American plants. 1885. I. 308.
— Catalogue of the phænogamous . . . plants of North America. 1885. I. 308.
Oyuela, Manuel de REVILLA Y. See REVILLA Y OYUELA, Manuel de.
Oyuelos, José DIAZ. See DIAZ OYUELOS, José.
Ozanon, Charles. Rosa alpina-var. 1892. II. 297.[1]
— Rosa belnensis Ozan. 1882. II. 291.[2]
— Rosa caviniacensis Oz. 1892. II. 292.[1]
— Rosa inconspicua Dés. 1888. II. 295.[1]
— Rosa Jundzilliana Bess. 1885. II. 295.[1]
— Rosa lagenarioides Ozanon. 1891. II. 295.[2]
— Rosa Rougeonensis Ozanon. 1891. II. 298.[1]
— Rosa subolida. 1884. II. 299.[1]
— Rosa urbica var. 1892. II. 299.[2]

— Salix cuspidata Sch. 1891. II. 106.[2]
— See also DÉSÉGLISE, Alfred & OZANON, Charles.
— & Crépin, François. Rosa inconspicua Dés. 1892. II. 295.[1]
— & Duffort, Louis. Rosa massilvanensia. 1892. II. 296.[1]
Ozerétskovsky, Nicolaus. De ossibus ligno inclusis. 1802. I. 210.[1]
— De Viburno Opulo. 1806. III. 753.[2]
Ozores, Antonicp de VALENZUELA Y. See VALENZUELA Y OZORES, Antonio de.

P. Abentheur von allerhand Mineralien, Wurtzeln, Kräutern . . . See PLEYER. 1656. III. 272.[2]
P. Die Arnoldsteiner Waldgenossenschaften. 1875. IV. 308.[2]
P. Zur Bewirthschaftung der Kleinwaldbesitzungen. 1886. IV. 245.
P. Ueber die Boden-Entblössung und Auflockerung. 1881. IV. 69.
P. Der breitblättrige Bohnenbaum. 1900. IV. 521.[2]
P. Chênes rouvre et pédonculé. 1897. IV. 559.[2]
P. Clôture des forêts. 1897. IV. 545.[2]
P. La dessiccation des bois. 1898. IV. 421.
P. Die Drachenblutbäume in Orotava. 1889. IV. 485.[2]
P. Italienische Pappel als Kernpflanze. 1879. III. 346.[1]
P. Measuring standing timber. 1879. IV. 217.
P. Eine merkwürdige Lärche in Unterkärnten. 1888. IV. 452.[2]
P. Eine neue Wurzelrodemaschine. 1883. IV. 387.[1]
P. Neuenburg. Sturm- und Schneedruckschaden. 1897. IV. 189.[2]
P. The new double crimson Thorn. 1867. III. 422.[1]
P. Rhododendrons javanais. 1897. III. 655.
P. Rosa rugosa and its hybrids. 1897. III. 457.[1]
P. Schlangentannen und Schlangenkiefern. 1883. IV. 447,[1] 483.[1]
P. Single Roses. 1900. III. 451.[1]
P. De toestand van land, bosch en mijnbouw in Guyana. 1891. IV. 342.[1]
P. Wirthschaftliches von der schwäbischen Alb. 1874. IV. 495.
P., von. Kahnkniee von Kiefern- und Fichtenholz. 1868. IV. 425.[1]
P., A. Eucryphia pinnatifolia. 1891. III. 596.[1]
P., A. Instrucción práctica para las cortas y entresacas de los montes de Pino albar. See PASCUAL, Agustin. 1847. IV. 304.[1]
P., A. Measuring heights of trees. 1885. IV. 215.
P., A. Myrica sapida. 1878. II. 111.[3]
P., A. Note sulle Quercie Sughere. 1885. IV. 517.[2]
P., A. Observations sur la dégénération des variétés. See PLUVIS, A. 184.? I. 248.[2]
P., A. Le parc de Tervueren. 1898. IV. 460.[2]
P., A. Slide-rule timber-measuring. 1887. IV. 218.
P., A. Timber measuring. 1879. IV. 228.
P., A. Timber measuring and slide-rule computation. 1879. IV. 228.
P., A. Yellow Roses. 1898. III. 455.[2]
P., B. Hervorming der grondslagen van de gouvernements-Koffiecultuur. 1899. III. 731.
P., C. D. Mémoire sur l'amélioration des biens communaux. See PALLUEL, C. D. 1790. IV. 161.[2]
P., C. F. Treatment of Conifers. 1866. III. 292.
P., C. J. M. von. Gedanken über verschiedene Gegenstände der Forst-Cameralwissenschaft. 1789. IV. 100.[1]
P., D. Ueber die Alpsrechte. 1891. IV. 335.
P., E. Dauer des Zirbenholzes. 1892. IV. 464.[1]
P., E. Forest and timber trees. 1866. IV. 155.[1]
P., E. Varietäten der Fichte? 1888. IV. 460.[1]
P., E. C. Noisetier gigantesque. 1885. II. 121.[1]
P., F. A. Bestrijding der Koffiebladziekte. 1890. III. 736.
P., F. L. Ivies in winter. 1893. III. 643.[1]
P., F. P. Un mot sur les Cactus, le Cereus Martinii. 1859. III. 621.[2]
P., R. T. Effect of lightning on trees. 1874. IV. 194.
P., G. Cordyline (Dracaena) australis. 1899. III. 335.
P., G. Revue de matière médicale. 1899. III. 283.[1]
P., H. Amerikanische Holzpflasterungen. 1873. IV. 425.[2]
P., H. Ardisia. 1898. III. 666.[1]
P., H. Berry-bearing trees and shrubs. 1888. III. 208.[1]
P., H. Bougainvillea glabra. 1898. III. 388.[1]
P., H. Clerodendron trichotomum. 1892. III. 696.[2]
P., H. Double and single flowered Bouvardias. 1883. III. 711.[1]

P., H. Embothrium coccineum. 1897. III. 383.[1]
P., H. Epiphyllums. 1899. III. 623.[1]
P., H. Fuchsia globosa. 1882. III. 640.[1]
P., H. Fuchsia serratifolia. 1881. III. 640.[2]
P., H. Garden varieties of Abutilon. 1898. III. 586.[2]
P., H. The Genistas. 1881. III. 477.[1]
P., H. Greenhouse Rhododendrons. 1885. III. 655.
P., H. Himalayan Rhododendron. 1889. III. 655.
P., H. Hybrid Java Rhododendrons. 1892. III, 660.[2]
P., H. Eine merkwürdige Weisskiefer. 1873. II. 48.[2]
P., H. Notes on Epacrises. 1889. III. 665.[1]
P., H. Olearia Haasti. 1899. III. 756.[1]
P., H. Ornamental Brambles. 1891. III. 457.[2]
P., H. Ornamental vines. 1886. III. 544.[1]
P., H. Paullinia thalictrifolia. 1897. III. 540.[1]
P., H. Rhododendron Daviesi. 1889. III. 658.[2]
P., H. Rhododendron javanicum. 1888. III. 660.[2]
P., H. Rhododendron Little beauty. 1899. III. 661.[1]
P., H. Rhododendron multicolor hybrids. 1892. III. 661.[2]
P., H. Rhododendron Veitchianum. 1897. III. 662.[2]
P., H. Seaside shrubs. 1882. III. 41.[2]
P., H. Some species of Fuchsia. 1882. III. 640.[1]
P., H. Eine starke Fichte in Unterkärnten. 1891. IV. 460.[2]
P., H. The Thunbergias. 1895. III. 710.[2]
P., H. White-flowered greenhouse Rhododendrons. 1889.
 III. 655.
P., H. Zurückhaltung der Pflanzen-Vegetazion. 1874. III.
 168.[2]
P., H. & **G.**, W. Azalea odorata. 1891. III. 657.[2]
P., H. F. Om Fyrre-Frøets Sæd. 1762. IV. 471.
P., I. Die Harznutzung in den Schwarzkieferforsten. 1865.
 IV. 466.[2]
P., — Bougainvillea spectabilis in India. 1876. III. 388.[2]
P., — Carpologie forestière. 1897. IV. 546.[1]
P., J. Die Culturkosten in der Waldwerthrechnung. 1891.
 IV. 258.
P., J. Des falnées et de leurs produites. 1895. IV. 500.[2]
P., J. Les forêts de Saksouk. 1894. IV. 519.[2]
P., J. Notes sur l'Épicéa. 1896. IV. 454.
P., J. Utilité des coupe-feu. 1900. IV. 181.[2]
P., J. Verdure de la fin d'année. Le Gui. 1897. IV. 519.[2]
P., J. Les voix de la forêt. 1895. IV. 542.[2]
P., M. A. Moyen de suppléer au défaut de paille et de four-
 rage. 1895. III. 223.[2]
P., N. Om de jydske Heder. *See* PETERSEN, N. 1856. IV. 156.[1]
P., R. Im Bákonyer Walde. 1892. IV. 374.[1]
P., R. Die galizischen Flüsse und ihre Beziehungen zur Wald-
 wirthschaft. 1892. IV. 124.[1]
P., R. Aus der hohen Tatra. 1886. IV. 374.[1]
P., R. Holzdraht. 1858. IV. 428.[2]
P., R. The natural history of Oxfordshire. *See* PLOT, Robert.
 1677. V. xx.[2]
P., R. H. Round Maidstone. 1898. II. 125.[1]
P., R. H. Stoneleigh Abbey. 1898. II. 52.[1]
P., S. The history of Rosa devoniensis. 1872. III. 455.[1]
P., S. Olbrzymi Dereń w Olesnycach. 1898. II. 655.[2]
P., V. D. S. de. Le guide du naturaliste. 1792. I. 258.
P., W. Kultura owoców w Austryi. 1900. III. 147.[1]
P., W. Ornamental coverts. 1885. III. 215.[1]
P., W. Zeitgemässe Betrachtungen über die Waldfläche in
 Oesterreich. 1899. IV. 279.[1]
Paar. Bericht ... über die mit der Schuster'schen Rodema-
 schine gemachten Versuche. 1858. IV. 386.
Ein paar weitere Bemerkungen über den Sumach. 1792. III.
 528.[2]
Ein paar Worte über einige Waldübel des bergischen Landes.
 1831. IV. 180.[1]
De **Paardenkastanje.** 1888. III. 537.[1]
Paarmann, P. M. Ligni Quassiae examen. 1772. III. 508.[2]
Paasch, (*Oberförster*). Hochpflanzung ... mit unverschulten
 Pflanzen. 1890. IV. 153.[1]
Paasch, Alexander. Ueber einen Fall frühzeitigen Ergrünens
 der Linde. 1878. III. 516.[2]
Paaw, Peter. Hortus publicus Academiae lugduno-batavae.
 1603. I. 50.
Pabor, William E. Fruit culture in Colorado. 1883. III. 133.
Pabst, (*Gärtner, Zürich*). Ueber die Treiberei der Sträucher
 des freien Landes. 1852. III. 176.[2]
Pabst, C. Die Nutzhölzer in der Colonie Dona Francisca.
 1853. IV. 398.[2]
Pabst, G. Tafeln zur Inhaltsbestimmung runder Hölzer.
 1870. IV. 226.
— Zweistellige Kubik-Tafeln zur Inhaltsbestimmung runder
 Hölzer. 1870. IV. 226.

Pacewicz, Roman. Botanika treściwie zebrana. 1867. I.
 91.
Pacher, Johann. *See* WIESNER, Julius & PACHER, Johann.
Pachorukoff. *See* BIELKIN, W. W., KOBERT & PACHORUKOFF.
Pacific coast wood and iron. *See* WOOD and iron. IV. 5.[2]
Pacific lumber trade journal. IV. 5.[1]
Pacific lumberman. IV. 5.[1]
Pacific monthly. *See* HESPERIAN, San Francisco. I. 5.
Pacific rural press. III. 7.
Pacifici-Mazzoni, Emidio & others. Raccolta delle leggi spe-
 ciali e convenzioni internazionali del regno d' Italia. 1883.
 IV. 328.
Packages. IV. 5.[1]
Packard, Alpheus Spring, (*jr.*). Third annual report on the
 injurious and beneficial effects of insects. 1873. III. 186.[2]
— Third annual report on the injurious and beneficial insects
 of Massachusetts. 1873. III. 186.[2]
— Certain cone-eating insects. 1888. IV. 442.
— Description of the larvae of injurious forest insects. 1883.
 IV. 91.[1]
— Insects injurious to forest and shade trees. 1881. IV.
 205.[1]
— The Labrador coast. 1891. I. 310.
— Report on insects injurious to forest and shade trees. 1881.
 IV. 205.[1]
— Report on the causes of destruction of evergreen forests.
 1883. IV. 205.[1]
Packbusch, Stephan Ludwig. De varia plantarum propaga-
 tione. 1695. I. 204.
Packe, C. Guide to the Pyrenees. 1862. I. 412.
Packing trees. 1889. III. 155.
Packing trees and plants. 1858. III. 155.
Paczoski, Josef von. Stepy kalmuckie. 1891. I. 366.
— Zarys flory okolicy Perejasławia. 1893. I. 443.
Padberg, von. Von der kanadischen Pappel. 1898. IV.
 486.[1]
Paddock, A. S. Report [on public forest reservations]. 1892.
 IV. 178.[2]
Paddock, Wendel. Body blight of Pear trees. 1899. III.446.[2]
Padé, Léon. *See* ARNAUD, Albert & PADÈ, Léon.
Padova — Cesareo-regia accademia di scienze ... *See* CE-
 SAREO-REGIA ... I. 26.[1]
Padova — Reale accademia di scienze, lettere ed arti. *See*
 REALE ... I. 25.
Padova — Società veneto-trentina di scienze ... *See* SOCI-
 ETÀ ... I. 26.[1]
Pässler, Johannes. Ueber Futterwerth und Gerbstoffgehalt
 des Laubes ... der Eiche. 1891. IV. 515.[2]
— Untersuchungen über den Futterwerth der Blätter. 1893.
 IV. 438.[1]
— Wanderung der ... Bestandtheile der Rothbuche. 1893.
 IV. 500.[1]
Paets van Troostwijk, A. Proeve, aanduidende den hoogen
 graad van gevoeligheid ... voor elektrieke ontladingen.
 1818. I. 231.[1]
Paganica, J. C. von C. Praktische Anleitung zur Forstwissen-
 schaft. 1803. IV. 99.[2]
Paganini, Roberto. Timbers of Upper Assam. 1884. IV.
 401.[1]
Page, C. Un emploi du Marron d'Inde. 1898. III. 538.[2]
Page, Henrietta. A method of obtaining Bayberry wax.
 1899. III. 353.[1]
Page, John. The Mistletoe, its propagation. 1882. III. 385.[2]
Page, William Bridgewater. Page's Prodromus. 1817. I. 53.
Une page bien remplie. Forêt du Val. 1898. IV. 238.
Pageisen. Destruction des souris. 1887. IV. 198.[1]
— Zur Mäusevertilgung. 1887. IV. 198.[1]
Pagenstecher. Die Einwirkung der Laubabgabe. 1858. IV.
 71.
Pages, baronne de. L'écussonnage aérien de la Vigne. 18..?
 III. 554.[2]
Pagès, Basile. La Vigne française à racines volantes. 1880.
 III. 761.
Pagès, Hippolyte. *See* ROUX, J. A.; PAGÈS, Hippolyte &
 BÉCHAMP, Antoine.
Paget, Charles J. & *Sir* James. Natural history of Yarmouth.
 1834. I. 398.
Paget, *Sir* James. The gum disease in trees. 1884. I. 528.[1]
— Der Gummifluss bei Bäumen. 1884. I. 528.[1]
— Gumming in fruit trees. 1884. I. 528.[1]
— *See also* PAGET, C. J. & *Sir* James.
Pagnoul, A. Essais relatifs à la transpiration. 1899. I. 168.
— Influence qu'exerce sur la végétation le perchlorate de
 potasse. 1899. I. 160.

Pahl, (*Oberförster, Freudenstadt*). Ueber Kiefernschütte. 1888. IV. 478.
Pahnsch, Gerhard. Beitrag zur Flora Ehstlands. 1881. I. 364.
Pai-cha wood for engraving. 1881. III. 707.²
Paiche, Philippe. Rosa alpestris Rapin. 1895. II. 291.¹
Paich'ha as a substitute for Boxwood. 1879. IV. 526.¹
Pailhade, J. de REY-. *See* REY-PAILHADE, J. de.
Paillet, L., (*jr.*). Greffage des Rhododendrons. 1888. III. 656.¹
— Greffe herbacée de la Clématite. 1888. III. 389.²
— Note sur les arbres . . . à feuillage décoratif. 1890. III. 205.²
Paillieux, Auguste. Culture expérimentale de plantes chinoises. 1883. III. 485.³
— Les Kakis. 1893. III. 669.²
— & **Bois,** Désiré. Les plantes alimentaires spontanées en Grèce. 1890. III. 272.¹
Paillot, Justin. Le baptême d'une fleur. 1867. II. 300.¹
— Excursion à la glacière de la Grâce-Dieu. 1875. I. 414.
— Note sur les Prunus erubescens. 1869. II. 271.¹
— & **Vendrely,** Xavier. Flora Sequaniae exsiccata. 1872. I. 414.
Paine, John Alsop. Catalogue of plants found in Oneida county. 1865. I. 314.
Paine, Martyn. Materia medica and therapeutics. 1848. III. 243.
— A therapeutical arrangement of the materia medica. 1842. III. 243.
Painter, Wilham Hunt. A contribution to the flora of Derbyshire. 1889. I. 404.¹
Pajuistutuksesta. *See* BORENIUS, A. 1890. IV. 487.²
Pala Santo wood. 1861. III. 494.²
Palacký, Johann B. Die alpine Atlasvegetation. 1858. I. 484.
— Über die antarktische Flora Chiles. 1884. I. 347.
— Bruchstück aus der argentinischen Flora. 1862. I. 344.
— Über den Endemismus der Flora von Ceylon. 1889. I. 477.¹
— Über die Entstehung der australischen Flora. 1882. I. 503.
— Zur Flora von Centralasien. 1897. I. 460.¹
— Zur Flora von Domingo-Haiti. 1896. I. 337.
— Über die Flora von Egypten. 1888. I. 489.
— Über die Flora von Hadramaut. 1897. I. 481.¹
— Über die Flora von Neu-Caledonien. 1882. I. 509.¹
— Zur Flora von Palästina. 1859. I. 480.
— Die Flora von St. Helena. 1889. I. 498.
— Die geographische Verbreitung der Coniferen. 1860. II. 13.¹
— Die geographische Verbreitung der Eichen. 1866. II. 122.²
— Über die Gränzen der Mittelmeervegetation in Frankreich. 1887. I. 417.
— Ueber die Gränzen der tropischen Flora in China. 1889. I. 459.
— Zur Hochgebirgsflora der Filippinen. 1896. I. 464.¹
— Zur Homa- (Soma-)Frage. 1887. III. 674.³
— Neue Beiträge zur Flora von Australien. 1882. I. 503.
— Über die Nordgränze der tropischen Vegetation in Mexiko. 1884. I. 332.
— Okřídlení naší vlasti rostlinstem. 1854. III. 127.¹
— Pflanzengeographische Beiträge. 1858. I. 299.
— Pflanzengeographische Studien. 1864. I. 300.
— Die Schimperschen Pflanzen aus Abyssinien. 1860. I. 488.
— Über die südöstliche Gränze der europäischen Flora. 1878. I. 349.
— Uebersicht der von Miquel . . . bestimmten Cumming'schen Philippinen-Pflanzen. 1860. I. 464.¹
— Die Westgrenze unserer Pflanzen. 1883. I. 308.
Palaiologos, Gregorios. *See* ΠΑΛΑΙΟΛΟΓΟΣ, Γρηγόριος.
Palandt, H. W. Der Haselstrauch und seine Kultur. 1881. III. 357.²
— Verzeichnis der Obstsorten . . . für die Provinz Hannover. 1888. III. 71.
Palasso. Essai sur la minéralogie des Monts-Pyrénées. 1781. I. 535.¹
Palau, José REIG Y. *See* REIG Y PALAU, José.
Palau y Verdera, Antonio. *See* ORTEGA, C. G. & PALAU Y VERDERA, Antonio.
Palermo — **Accademia di scienze e lettere.** *See* ACCADEMIA PALERMITANA. I. 24.¹
Palermo — **Reale orto botanico.** *See* REALE . . . I. 26.¹
Palestine exploration fund. Quarterly statement. I. 19.
Palestra scientifica do Rio de Janeiro. Archivos. I. 7.¹

Paley, Frederick Apthorp. List of 400 wild flowering plants . . . of Peterborough. 1860. I. 401.
— Wild flowers of Dover. 1850. I. 400.
Paléieux, Philippe de. Anatomisch-systematische Untersuchung des Blattes der Melastomaceen. 1899. II. 635.²
Paliard, Victor. Recherches thérapeutiques sur la cinchonine. 1875. III. 721.
Palibin, Ivan Vladimirovich. Conspectus florae Koreae. 1898. I. 461.
— Plantae sinico-mongolicae. 1895. I. 460.²
— Revisio generis Enkianthus Lour. 1897. II. 663.¹
Palice, Carlo. Le alberate. 1897. III. 210.
Palimpsestof, I. U. *See* ПАЛИМПСЕСТОВЪ, И. У.
Palin, C. T. The plants and birds of Cutch. 1878. I. 474.
Palisot de Beauvois, Ambroise Marie François Joseph, *baron.* Flore d'Oware et de Benin. 1804. I. 490.
— Mémoire sur les Palmiers. 1809. II. 74.¹
— Mémoires et observations sur l'arrangement et la disposition des feuilles. 1812. I. 102.
— Notice sur une nouvelle expérience relative à l'écorce des arbres. 1811. I. 269, 207.¹
— Omphalocarpum. 1800. II. 699.¹
— Premier (et second) mémoire et observations sur l'arrangement et la disposition des feuilles. 1812. I. 124.
— Premier mémoire . . . sur l'arrangement et la disposition des feuilles. 1812. I. 102.
Palladin, W. Athmung und Wachsthum. 1886. I. 171.
— Bedeutung des Sauerstoffs. 1887. I. 171.
— Bildung der organischen Säuren. 1887. I. 180.¹
— Sur la formation d'acides organiques. 1887. I. 180.²
— Influence de diverses substances . . . sur la formation de la chlorophylle. 1897. I. 142.
— Influence de la lumière sur la formation des substances azotées. 1899. I. 174.
— Influence des changements de température sur la respiration. 1899. I. 171.
— Recherches sur la formation de la chlorophylle. 1897. I. 142.
— Recherches sur la respiration des feuilles. 1893. I. 171, III. 181.¹
— *See also* ПАЛЛАДИНЪ, В.
Palladino, Pietro. Gomma arabica e gomme affini. 1891. III. 228.¹
Palladius, Rutilius Taurus Aemilianus. Das Ackerwerk. 1472. III. 98.
— Agricultur oder Ackerbau. 1472. III. 98.
— Della agricultura. 1472. III. 98.
— The fourteen books of Palladius . . . on agriculture. 1472. III. 98.
— De insitionibus [de re rustica liber XIV.]. 1472. III. 98.
— The middle-English translation of Palladius De re rustica. 1472. III. 98.
— Opus agriculturae. 1472. III. 98.
— Palladius on husbandrie. 1472. III. 98.
— De re rustica libri. 1472. III. 98.
— Scriptores rei rusticae. 1470. III. 96.¹
— La villa di Palladio. 1472. III. 98.
— Volgarizzamento di Palladio. 1472. III. 98.
Pallas, Emmanuel. De l'influence des feuilles dans la fécondation. 1843. I. 200.
Pallas, Peter Simon. Bemerkungen auf einer Reise in die südlichen Statthalterschaften des russischen Reichs. 1799. I. 360.
— Von den besondern Wirkungen eines sibirischen Rhododendron. 1775. III. 658.¹
— Catalogue des espèces de végétaux spontanés observés en Tauride. 1797. I. 360.
— Enumeratio plantarum ordine alphabetico undique collectarum. 1781. I. 41.
— Enumeratio plantarum quae in horto . . . Procopii a Demidof. 1781. I. 41.
— Flora rossica. 1784. I. 359, 453.¹
— Illustrationes plantarum imperfecte . . . cognitarum. 1803. II. 186.²
— Novae species plantarum. 1793. I. 360.
— Physikalisch-topographisches Gemählde von Taurien. 1795. I. 360.
— Plantae novae ex herbario . . . botanici J. Sievers. 1797. I. 360.
— Reise durch verschiedene Provinzen des russischen Reichs. 1771. I. 359.
— Species Astragalorum descriptae. 1800. II. 333.¹
— Tableau physique et topographique de la Tauride. 1795. I. 360.

Pallas, Peter Simon (*continued*).
— Travels through the southern provinces of the Russian Empire. 1799. I. 360.
— Voyages dans plusieurs provinces de l'empire de Russie. 1771. I. 359.
— Voyages en differentes provinces de l'empire de Russie. 1771. I. 359.
— *See also* ПАЛЛАСЪ, П. С.
Pallavicini, Margherita, *marchesa* Misciattelli. Contribuzione allo studio degli acarocecidii. 1895. I. 215.[2]
— Nuova contribuzione all' acarocecidiologia italica. 1899. I. 216.[1]
— Zoocecidii della flora italica. 1894. I. 215.[2]
Pallavicino, Camillo. Cenni sulla legislazione forestale. 1847. IV. 313.
Palliser, John. The journals, detailed reports . . . relative to the exploration of that portion of British North America. 1863. I. 311.[1]
— Papers relative to the exploration of that portion of British North America. 1859. I. 311.[1]
Pallme, Ignatius. Gum Arabic. 1844. III. 463.[2]
Palluel, Cretté D. Mémoire sur l'amélioration des biens communaux. 1790. IV. 161.[2]
Palm, H. Die immergrüne Gartenflora von Görz. 1897. III. 127.[1]
Palm, Ludwig Heinrich. Ueber das Winden der Pflanzen. *See* GMELIN, F. G. von. 1827. I. 196.[1]
Palm, Robert. Beschreibung verschiedener pharmacognostischer Gegenstände. 1870. III. 273.[1]
— Ueber die Gummipflanzen. 1871. III. 227.
The **Palm** and its varieties. 1886. II. 64.[1]
Palm insects. 1891. III. 318.[2]
The **Palm** of Chili. 1864. III. 326.[1]
The **Palm** tribes and their varieties. 1852. III. 316.[2]
Palm weevil in British Honduras. 1893. III. 318.[2]
Palma, Joseph François Charpentier de COSSIGNY DE. *See* COSSIGNY DE PALMA, J. F. C. de.
Palma jagua of the Orinoco. 1855. II. 71.[1]
Palmberg, Johan. Serta florea suecana. 1684. I. 350.[2]
Palmen, Johan Axel. *See* MELA, A. J. & PALMEN, J. A.
Ueber **Palmen** und deren Benutzung. 1857. III. 319.[1]
Die **Palmen-Allee** . . . desCafetal's Angerona. 1844. II.72.[1]
Das **Palmenhaus** in Herrenhausen. 1859. III. 317.
Palmer, Charles W. Demarcating forest reserves. 1883. IV. 251.[1]
Palmer, Edward. Food products of the North American Indians. 1871. III. 261.[2]
— List of plants collected in south-western Chihuahua. 1886. I. 332.
— Opuntia fruit as an article of food. 1889. III. 624.[1]
— On plants used by the natives of North Queensland. 1884. III. 282.[2]
— Die vegetabilischen Nahrungsmittel der Indianer. 1871. III. 261.[2]
Palmer, Frédéric T. Cereus leptacanthus. 1865. III. 622.[2]
— Colletia horrida. 1858. III. 541.[2]
— Culture des Cactées. 1867. III. 619.
— Culture des Cactées en collection. 1864. III. 619.
— Destruction des insectes sur les racines de Cactées. 1861. III. 620.[1]
— Echinocereus Blankii. 1865. III. 622.[2]
— Floraison de l'Echinocactus villosus niger. 1865. III. 622.[2]
— Floraison des Echinopsis amoena et pulchella. 1864. III. 622.[2]
— Sur la greffe des Cactées. 1864. III. 619.
— Lettre sur le développement en rameau de fleurs de Cactées. 1871. II. 589.[1]
— Marche de la sève. 1872. I. 164.
— Origin of the name Horse Chestnut. 1873. II. 482.[2]
— Les Pereskia comme sujets pour greffer. 1860. III. 619.
— Remarques sur la greffe des Cactées. 1861. III. 619.
— Ueber den Saftlauf. 1872. I. 164.
— Végétation des Phyllocactus guyanensis et latifrons. 1864. III. 625.[2]
Palmer, Henry Spencer. The natural capabilities of British Columbia. 1886. I. 311.[2]
Palmer, Johann Ludwig. De plantarum exhalationibus. 1817. I. 169.[2]
Palmgrén, Carl Engelbert. Horti upsaliensis plantae. *See* THUNBERG, C. P. 1826. I. 40.
Un **Palmier** à fruits comestibles; . . . Erythea edulis. 1891. III. 325.[1]
Les **Palmiers** au point de vue pittoresque. 1853. III. 326,[1] 527.[2]

Des **Palmiers** (Phoenicaceae). 1852. III. 316.[2]
The **Palms.** 1876. III. 319.[1]
Palms at home. 1881. II. 61.[2]
Palms for Palm Sunday. 1876. III. 328.[2]
Palms of Lord Howe's Island. 1898. III. 319.[2]
Palmstjerna, Nils. Beskrifning huru Treffle. 1764. III. 357.[1]
Palmstruch, J. W. & Venus, C. W. Svensk botanik. 1802. I. 352.
Palmyra bass fibre. 1892. III. 321.[1]
The **Palmyra** Palm. 1851. III. 321.[1]
Die **Palmyra-Palme.** *See* The PALMYRA Palm. 1851. III. 321.[1]
Palmyra-vezel of Bassine. 18. . ? III. 320.[1]
Paludan, F. Phyllanthus glaucescens. 1895. III. 521.[2]
Palumbo, Francesco MINÀ-. *See* MINÀ-PALUMBO, Francesco.
Palun, Maurice. Catalogue des plantes . . . d'Avignon. 1867. I. 413.
Palustre. Études de botanique. 1840. I. 261.
Pamart, E. Culture du Pêcher dans le nord de la France. n. d. III. 440.[1]
Pammel, Louis Herman. Anatomical characters of the seeds of Leguminosae. 1899. II. 321.[1]
— Botanists and botanical discoveries. 1896. V. x.[1]
— A Cherry disease. 1890. III. 432.[1]
— Climate and its effects on . . . apples. 1893. III. 426.[2]
— Cross and self-fertilization in plants. 1892. I. 238.
— Definite annual growth and its relation to hardiness. 1894. III. 182.
— Diseases of plants at Ames. 1895. III. 193.[2]
— Diseases of the Cherry. 1894. III. 432.[1]
— The effects of cross-fertilization in plants. 1892. I. 238.
— The forest flora of Hardin county. 1900. I. 321, IV. 78.[3]
— Forest vegetation of the upper Mississippi. 1891. I. 312, IV. 77.[1]
— Fungus diseases of the Grape. 1893. III. 581.
— The geographical distribution of plants. 1895. III. 37.[2]
— Leaf spot disease of the Cherry. 1892. III. 432.[1]
— A lecture on pollination of flowers. 1892. I. 238.
— Notes on the flora of Texas. 1893. I. 326.
— Notes on the flora of western Iowa. 1896. I. 326.
— Phenological notes for 1892. 1892. I. 222.[1]
— Pollination of flowers. 1892. I. 238, V. xii.[1]
— Powdery mildew of the Apple. 1900. III. 428.[2]
— Quince fruit with an immense number of seeds. 1900. II. 263.[2]
— On the seed-coats of the genus Euphorbia. 1891. I. 121.
— Some ecological notes on the Muscatine flora. 1899. I. 327.
— Some fungous diseases of fruit trees. 1890. III. 446.[2]
— Some fungus diseases of the orchard. 1891. III. 193.[2]
— Some observations on trees and shrubs in the Rocky Mountains. 1897. V. xvii.[1]
— On the structure of the testa of several leguminous seeds. 1886. II. 320.[2]
— Versuche über die Bekämpfung der Pilzkrankheiten. 1891. III. 197.
— Woody plants of western Wisconsin. 1892. I. 312.
— & Carver, G. W. Fungus diseases of plants at Ames. 1896. III. 193.[2]
— — — Treatment of Currants. 1895. III. 415,[1] 432.[2]
— **Burnip,** J. R. & Thomas, Hannah. Some studies on the seeds . . . of Berberidaceae. 1898. II. 201.[2]
Pampaloni, Luigi. Notizie sul frutto di Aucuba. 1895. II. 654.[2]
Pampaloni, T. La nuova legge forestale italiana. 1878. IV. 328.
Pampaloni, Temistocle. Sunto di un corso elementare di legislazione e giurisprudenza forestale. 1897. IV. 329.
Pamplin, W. & Irvine, Alexander. Botanical tour in . . . Perthshire. 1857. I. 400.
Pamplin, William. A catalogue of the rarer species . . . of Battersea and Clapham. 1827. I. 397.
Pampuch, Albert. Flora tremesnensis. 1840. I. 380.
Pamyatnaya . . . *See* ПАМЯТНЯЯ . . .
The **Panama** hat plant. 1876. III. 332.[2]
Panariou, A. *See* ΠΑΝΑΡΙΟΥ, Α.
Panarolo, Domenico. Iatrologismi. 1643. I. 424.
— Jatrologismorum . . . pentacostae quinque. 1643. I. 424.
— Plantarum amphitheatralium catalogus. 1643. I. 424.
Panasevitch, V. *See* ПАНАСЕВИЧЪ, В.
Pancher. Description de l'Aralia tenuifolia. 1871. II. 648.[1]

Pančić, Josef. Elenchus plantarum . . . in Crna Gora. 1875. I. 449.
— Flora agri belgradensis. 1865. I. 449.
— Aus der Flora von Serbien. 1857. II. 139.²
— Der Kirschlorbeer im Süd-Osten von Serbien. 1887. II. 274.²
— Eine neue Conifere in den östlichen Alpen. 1876. II. 38.¹
— Taxilogia botanica. 1842. I. 268.
— Verzeichniss der in Serbien wildwachsenden Phanerogamen. 1856. I. 449.
— See also Панчић, Јосиф.
Panckow, Thomas. Herbarium. 1654. I. 286.
— Herbarium portabile. 1654. I. 286.
Pandanus furcatus und die Pandanus-Arten. 1878. III. 313.¹
Panek, Johann. Weiden und Weidenbastarde aus . . . Hohenstadt. 1894. II. 103.¹
Paniagua, José Maria. Calendario del selvicultor. 1846. IV. 99.¹
— Manual de la tasación de montes y bosques. 1847. IV. 240.
— Manual del podadór. 1845. III. 169.²
— Selvicultura. 1841. IV. 109.²
Le panier de fruits. See JAUFFRET, L. F. 1807. III. 84.³
Panizzardi. A far durare lungamente i pali delle Vigne. 1865. IV. 419.
— See also ARCOZZI-MASINO & PANIZZARDI.
Panizzi, Francesco. Flora fotografata delle piante . . . di Sanremo. 1870. I. 428.
Panjabi. Jhand coppice. 1881. IV. 522.¹
Pannelier d'Annel. Essai sur l'aménagement des forêts. 1773. IV. 241.
Pannetier. Nature des principes irritants de l'huile de Croton. 1895. III. 517.²
Pannewitz, Guido von. Einige Mittheilungen über die forsthohen Zustände in Russland. 1862. IV. 345.
Pannewitz, Julius von. Ueber Abies reginae Amaliae. 1861. IV. 447.¹
— Abnorme Fichtenzapfen. 1857. IV. 460.¹
— Absatz der Buche zu Nutzholz. 1866. IV. 500.¹
— Abschluss von der Centralkasse des Sterbekassen-Vereins schlesischer Forst-Beamten. 1864. IV. 310.³
— I. Alnus autumnalis. 1866. IV. 488.²
— Der alte Drachenbaum von Orotawa. 1863. IV. 485.²
— Alte schöne Bäume. 1856. IV. 83.
— Vom Anbau der Akazie. 1855. IV. 523.¹
— Der Anbau des Lärchenbaumes. 1855. IV. 423.²
— Angabe über Holzmassen-Vorräthe . . . Peisterwitz. 1859. IV. 236.
— Ueber die Anlage von Hecken. 1862. IV. 146.¹
— Anleitung zu Versuchen über . . . Durchforstung. 1864. IV. 173.
— Anleitung zum Anbau der Sandflächen. 1832. IV. 154.² 158.
— Anleitung zur Anlage lebendiger Hecken. 1842. III. 212.²
— Anleitung zur zweckmässigen Bepflanzung der Strassen. 1840. III. 209.
— Anwendung der Elektrizität für den Waldbau. 1859. IV. 67.¹
— Ueber Anzucht der süssen Kastanie. 1866. IV. 492.²
— Aphoristische Mittheilungen über verschiedene Forstkultur-Gegenstände. 1841. IV. 141.
— Aufmaass-Ergebniss von zwei Flächen . . . Reinerz. 1854. IV. 235.²
— Beantwortung der Frage: "Ob der Samen von kraukhaften [sic] Stämmen einen . . . Einfluss . . . hat?" 1867. IV. 74.²
— Beantwortung der Frage: Ob Fichtenbüschel-Pflanzungen . . . erfolgreicher sind. 1844. IV. 452.²
— Beantwortung der Frage: Welche Dauerfähigkeit haben die Laubholzstöcke. 1844. IV. 132.¹
— Beantwortung der Frage: Wie ist der die Schwarzkiefer, welche im Sommer zwar trocken . . . anzubauen? 1852. IV. 141.
— Das Bedürfniss der Holz-Erziehung in den schlesischen Forsten. 1855. IV. 274.¹
— Beitrag zu Preussens und namentlich Schlesiens Forst-Statistik. 1857. IV. 352.
— Die Benutzung der Sprengschraube. 1843. IV. 385.²
— Der Bericht über den Böhmischen Forst-Verein. 1864. IV. 370.
— Bericht über die Reise zur Versammlung deutscher Land- und Forstwirthe. 1862. IV. 349.¹
— Ueber das Beschneiden . . . der Pflanzhejster. 1866. IV. 506.

— Beschreibung einer merkwürdigen abnormen Fichtenbildung. 1861. IV. 460.¹
— Beschreibung eines merkwürdigen Lindenstammes. 1852. IV. 528.¹
— Die Bewaldung der Berge in Frankreich. 1865. IV. 162.
— Ueber das Biermanns'sche Kulturverfahren. 1846. IV. 148.
— Ueber die Birkensucht. 1843. IV. 491.¹
— Ueber Chrysomela pini. 1852. IV. 475.
— Darstellung einer merkwürdigen . . . Erscheinung an einer Fichte. 1863. IV. 455.
— Ueber die Dauer der Hölzer. 1867. IV. 419.
— Drainage im Walde. 1856. IV. 143.² — 1866. IV. 144.¹
— Die Eberesche. 1851. IV. 520.¹
— Eichel-Ernte in den königlichen Forsten. 1863. IV. 505.
— Ueber eigenthümliche Servituten. 1863. IV. 333.³
— Der Einfluss der Wälder auf Klima. 1859. IV. 43.
— Einige Bemerkungen über . . . Bewirthschaftung von Niederwaldungen. 1846. IV. 132.¹
— Einige Bemerkungen über die giftige Eigenschaft des Taxus. 1862. IV. 440.¹
— Einige Bemerkungen über Nadelholz-Samen-Darren. 1857. IV. 147.²
— Einige Worte über die Schwarz-Kiefer. 1864. IV. 465.²
— Einige Worte über die Verhältnisse der Lampersdorfer Privat-Forst. 1862. IV. 353.
— Einige Worte über Durchforstungen. 1861. IV. 173.
— Ueber die Entstehung des Honigthaues. 1852. IV. 65.²
— Erfahrungs-Tafeln über den Massengehalt der Kiefern- . . . Birkenbestände. 1854. IV. 235.³
— Ueber die Erziehung . . . der süssen Kastanie. 1855. IV. 492.²
— Ueber Fichtenpflanzungen im Gebirge. 1854. IV. 453.
— Zur Forstarbeiter-Frage. 1858. IV. 310.¹
— Forst-Grund-Steuer. 1865. IV. 284.¹
— Ein forstlicher Besuch in dem v. Jagow'schen Forst-Revier Garbe. 1862. IV. 353.
— Forstliches Cotta-Album. 1844. IV. 101.
— Ueber Forstservituten-Ablösungs-Verhältnisse. 1862. IV. 333.
— Forst-statistische Mittheilungen über Schlesiens Staats- und Privatforsten. 1856. IV. 352.
— Das Forstwesen von West-Preussen. 1829. IV. 352.
— Ein ganz ungewöhnlich starker . . . Aprikosen-Baum. 1866. III. 434.³
— Gedrängte Darstellung der Verhältnisse des königlichen Forst-Reviers Katholisch Hammer. 1847. IV. 352.
— Das Gewicht der Eichen-Spiegelrinde. 1851. IV. 514.³ · ·
— Grundzüge eines forstlichen Stiftungs-Statuts. 1865. IV. 32.
— Holz-Ertrag aus dem . . . Forstrevier Auersberg. 1863. IV. 260.²
— Holzmassen-Nachweis [von Weymouths-Kiefern.] 1855. IV. 470.¹
— Ueber Holzverkohlung im Walde. 1851. IV. 394.
— Kiefer 12 Jahre alt mit 350 Zapfen. 1857. IV. 483.¹
— Die Kork-Eiche. 1864. IV. 516.³
— Kurze Anleitung zum künstlichen Holzanbau. 1845. IV. 141.
— Kurze Beantwortung der Frage: Wie findet die Benutzung holzleerer Flächen . . . statt? 1853. IV. 141.
— Kurze forstliche Notizen. 1860. IV. 141.
— Kurzer Umtrieb nach Pressler's Theorie. 1865. IV. 251.²
— Ueber Lohrinden-Gewinnung und Benutzung. 1843. IV. 514.²
— Der Maikäfer-Schaden. 1864. IV. 202.
— Merkwürdige Wurzelbildungen bei der Fichte. 1861. IV. 460.¹
— Mittheilung über die Schlangenfichte. 1863. IV. 460.¹
— Mittheilung über die Verwendung von Fichtensaamen zur Oelbereitung. 1851. IV. 459.³
— Mittheilungen über den Anbau . . . der Lärche. 1855. IV. 449.
— Nachweis alter, starker . . . Bäume. 1863. IV. 83.
— Nachweis des Kubikinhalts mehrerer Stämme im k. Forst-revier Scheidelwitz. 1858. IV. 260.³
— Nachweis hoher Material-Erträge im Stadtwald bei Ohlau. 1846. IV. 260.¹
— Nachweisung der Flächen-Grössen . . . in den schlesischen Staatsforsten des Regierungs-Bezirkes Oppeln. 1863. IV. 353.
— Nachweisung der . . . in den k. Forsten des Regierungsbezirks Breslau ausgeführten Kulturen. 1861. IV. 141.

Pannewitz, Julius von (*continued*).
— Nachweisung des Material-Holz-Ertrages von einem . . . Kiefern-Bestande. 1867. IV. 260.[2]
— Nachweisung über die . . . Erträge aus den königl. Forsten des Regierungs-Bezirkes Breslau. 1863. IV. 353.
— Nachweisung von den Natural- und Gelderträgen der k. Forsten in der Provinz Schlesien. 1853. IV. 260.[1]
— Nauka o zakładaniu i pielęgnowaniu żywych płotów. 1842. III. 213.
— Nauka o zakładaniu żywych płotów. 1842. III. 212.[2]
— Ueber eine neue Stock-Rodemaschine. 1861. IV. 386.
— Eine Notiz über die Ausnutzung des Kiefern-Stabholzes. 1860. IV. 480.
— Notiz über einige waldverderbende Raupen. 1855. IV. 206.
— Nutzholz-Absatz für die Rothbuche. 1865. IV. 499.
— Ueber Prüfung der Forstlehrlinge. 1851. IV. 32.
— Der Riesenbaum von Kalifornien. 1857. IV. 484.[2]
— Schlussworte über die Besprechung der Vertilgung des Kiefernspinners. 1862. IV. 476.
— Die Schütte der Kiefern betreffend. 1858. IV. 475.
— Ueber das Schütten der Kiefer. 1853. IV. 475.
— Schutz der Fichten-Pflanzungen. 1865. IV. 453.
— Schutz der Pflanzungen gegen Wildschaden. 1865. IV. 196.[2]
— Den Schutz gegen Hochwildschaden betreffend. 1866. IV. 196.[2]
— Ueber Sphinx pinastri L. 1855. IV. 206.
— Statistische Notizen aus den k. hannoverschen Forsten. 1865. IV. 353.
— Statut für den Sterbe-Kassen-Verein der schlesischen Forstbeamten. 1857. IV. 310.[1]
— Ueber Stockholz-Verwerthung. 1866. IV. 387.[2]
— Die Surrogate für die zum Gerben verwendete Eichen- etc. Rinde betreffend. 1846. IV. 435.
— Uebersicht über den Beitritt von Mitgliedern zum Sterbe-Kassen-Verein. 1860. IV. 310.[2]
— Die Urwälder Krummauus. 1856. IV. 370.
— Ueber Verkauf der Eichenrinde. 1866. IV. 512.
— Verpachtung der Wälder. 1865. IV. 269.
— Die Vertilgung des Kiefernspinners. 1861. IV. 476.
— Verwachsung zweier Kiefern. 1861. IV. 476.
— Ueber die Verwendung des Gerber-Sumachs. 1861. IV. 525.[1]
— Das Wachsthum der Bäume in die Dicke. 1859. IV. 64.[3]
— Die Wälder Frankreichs, 1863. 1864. IV. 360.
— Ueber Wald-Erträge im Vergleich zu landwirthschaftlichen Erträgen. 1867. IV. 259.[3]
— Ueber die Waldwolle aus den Nadeln der Kiefer. 1842. IV. 482.[2]
— Ueber das Wasserglas. 1860. IV. 418.
— Weiss-Erlen-Ertrag. 1857. IV. 489.[2]
— Zusammenstellung der Flächen und Holzarten der k. Forsten im Reg.- Bez. Liegnitz. 1863. IV. 353.
— Zusammenstellung der in den Hochwaldungen . . . Breslau . . . erfolgten Abnutzung an Derbholz. 1862. IV. 248.[1]
— *See also* BELING, Theodor & PANNEWITZ, Julius von; BLANK-ENBURG & PANNEWITZ, von; HAASS & PANNEWITZ, Julius von; MIDDELDORFF, & PANNEWITZ, Julius von; SCHMIEDL, Johann & PANNEWITZ, Julius von; ULBRICH & PANNEWITZ, Julius von.
— & GÖPPERT, H. R. Wald-Protokoll über die Ueberwallung der Weisstannen-Stöcke. 1843. IV. 66.[2]
— & others. Ueber das von Alemann'sche Pflanzverfahren. 1850. IV. 152.
— — Kommissionsverhandlung, die Gründung einer Waldbauschule in Schlesien betreffend. 1854. IV. 32.
— — Ueber die Mischung von Kiefer- und Fichtenbeständen. 1858. IV. 441.
— — Mittheilungen von Holz-Massen und Forstgeld-Erträgen. 1860. IV. 260.[2]
— — Die Ueberwallung abgeschnittener Nadelholz-Stöcke. 1862. IV. 66.[2]
Pannilini, Augusto, *conte* de GORI. *See* GORI PANNILINI, Augusto, *conte* de.
Panphyton siculum. *See* CUPANI, Francesco. 1713. I. 431.
Pansch, Adolf. Klima und Pflanzenleben auf Ostgrönland. 1874. I. 309.[1]
Panzner, Lorenz von. Erster Versuch einer systematischen Anordnung der Stachelbeersorten. 1846. III. 414.[2]
— Versuch einer Monographie der Stachelbeeren. 1852. III. 414.[2]
Pantocsek, Josef. Adnotationes ad floram et faunam Hercegovinae. 1874. I. 447.

— Beiträge zur Flora und Fauna der Hercegovina. 1874. I. 447.
— Plantae novae quas . . . per Hercegovinam et Montenegro collexit. 1873. I. 449.
Panzer, Georg Wolfgang Franz. Beitrag zur Geschichte des ostindischen Brotbaums. 1783. II. 146.[1]
Panzer, R. *See* HOLDHAUS, C. & PANZER, R.
Panzer, V. M. von. *See* ПАНЦЕРЪ, В. М. ФОНЪ.
Paoletti, Giulio. Contribuzione alla flora del bacino di Primiero. 1892. I. 430.
— Sui movimenti delle foglie nella Porlieria. 1892. II. 396.[1]
— Nota preliminare sui movimenti delle foglie nella Porlieria. 1890. II. 396.[1]
— *See also* FIORI, Adriano & PAOLETTI, Giulio.
Paoli, Domenico. Sulla gomma di Ulivo. 1815. III. 678.[2]
— Mémoire sur la gomme d'Olivier. 1815. III. 678.[2]
Paolillo, Bartolomeo. Sugli Ulivi coltivati nei circondarii di Cerreto. 1870. III. 675.[2]
Paolino da San Bartolomeo. *See* WESDIN, J. P.
Paolucci, Luigi. Flora marchigiana. 1890. I. 429.
— : . Piante . . . dei Monti Sibillini. 1879. I. 428.
Papadopoli, N. C. Historia Gymnasii patavini. *See* PONTEDERA, Giulio. 1726. I. 61.
Papain. 1897. III. 618.[1]
Paparelli, Louis. Étude chimique de l'Olivier. 1888. III. 679.[1]
— Proper fertilization for Olive trees. 1891. III. 676.[1]
Papasogli, G. P. Sulle gemme del Platanus vulgaris. 1882. II. 254.[2]
— La solfolina liquido. 1900. III. 198.[1]
— Studi genetici . . . sopra l' Ulivo. 1878. II. 713.[1]
The Papaw. 1885. III. 617.[1]
Papaw bark. 1879. III. 401.[2]
The Papaw tree. 1880. III. 617.[2]—1893. III. 617.[2]
Pape, L. P. A. Das Schälen des Rothwildes. 1858. IV. 196.[2]
Pape, W. Epiphyllum Russelianum . . . als Kronenstamm. 1890. III. 625.[2]
Paper in foreign countries. 1900. IV. 430.
Paper-materials. 1877. IV. 429.
Paper mill and wood pulp news. 1874. IV. 5.[1]
Paper of Daphne Laurel. 1852. III. 627.[3]
Papers regarding the forests and iron mines in Kumaon. 1855. IV. 377.[1]
Papers regarding the Tea industry in Bengal. 1873. III. 603.
Papers relating to state forests. 1874. IV. 295.[2]
Papers relating to . . . the cultivation of the Tea plant in India. *See* MACCLELLAND, John. 1839. III. 602.[2]
Papers respecting the Phylloxera. 1873. III. 759.
Papi, Ciro. Alcune ricerche sulla struttura del fusto . . . di Juniperus drupacea. 1900. II. 31.[1]
Papier de bois et de paille. 1883. IV. 429.[2]
Papier de Lauréole. *See* PAPER of Daphne Laurel. 1852. III. 627.[2]
Le **Papier** [provenant de pâte de bois] en France. 1898. IV. 558.[2]
Aus den **Papieren** des alten Forstmannes. *See* Ueber WALDAUSREUTUNGEN. 1853. IV. 43.
Aus den **Papieren** eines alten Forstmannes. *See* Die BIRKE . . . 1853. IV. 490[1]; Das VERHALTEN der Arve. 1853. IV. 452.[1]
Papierfabrication in China. 1856. III. 315.[1]
Papillon, F. *See* RABUTEAU, A. & PAPILLON, F.
Papius, K. Die Beschreibung der natürlichen Verhältnisse einer Holzwirthschaft. 1822. IV. 117.
— Beyträge zu der Lehre von der Wald-Werth-Berechnung. 1827. IV. 254.-
— Ueber die Bildung des Forstmannes. 1823. IV. 29.
— Büschelpflanzung. 1846. IV. 452.[2]
— Durchforstungen. 1838. IV. 173.
— Ueber Forstpolizei. 1824. IV. 268.
— Gedanken über Waldfeldbau. 1837. IV. 133.
— Die Grundsteuer von der Holzwirthschaft. 1842. IV. 254.
— Die Holznoth. 1839. IV. 281.[1]
— Die Holznoth und die Staatsforste. 1840. IV. 281.[1]
— Die Holzwirthschaft. 1827. IV. 106.
— Der Holzwuchs in der Natur. 1826. IV. 106.
— Die Ordnung der Holzwirthschaft. 1829. IV. 240, 237.
— Die verschiedenen Betriebsarten der Holzwirthschaft. 1820. IV. 128.
Pappe, Karl Wilhelm Ludwig. Cape gum. 1851. III. 465.[2]
— Cape mastic. 1861. III. 755.[1]
— Contributions to the Cape oeconomic flora. 1856. III. 93.[2]

— Enumerationis plantarum phaenogamarum lipsiensium specimen. 1827. I. 377, V. XIX.[1]
— Florae capensis medicae prodromus. 1850. III. 93.[2]
— Die Kap'sche Wachsbeeren-Pflanze. 1854. III. 353.[2]
— A list of South African indigenous plants. 1847. III. 93.[2]
— Myrica cordifolia. 1854. III. 353.[2]
— Silva capensis. 1854. III. 93.[2]
— Südafrika's Waldbäume. 1854. III, 93.[2]
— Synopsis plantarum . . . agro lipsiensi indigenarum. 1828. I. 378.
Pappenheim, Karl. Zur Frage der Verschlussfähigkeit der Hoftüpfel. 1889. II. 17.[1]
— Eine Methode zur Bestimmung der Gasspannung. 1892. I. 150.[1]
Papstein-Lapa, A. Maté aus Brasilien. 1900. III. 531.[2]
Papworth, H. Washingtonia filifera. 1893. III. 332.[1]
Papworth, Wyatt. Notes on the assumed use of Chestnut timber. 1858. IV. 493.[1]
Paque, Egide, (abbé). De vlaamsche volksnamen der planten. 1896. I. 73.[2]
Paquet, Victor. Lettre . . . sur la greffe par copulation. 1837. III. 160.
— Moyen peu usité d'emballer . . . les plantes. 1843. III. 155.
— Multiplication des arbres verts résineux. 1845. III. 294.[1]
— Note on a fungus disease of Rose-bushes. 1846. III. 453.[2]
— Note sur un Mûrier. 1843. III. 376.
— Note sur une maladie causée par un champignon. 1846. III. 445.[2]
— Traité de la conservation des fruits. 1844. III. 143, 220.[1]
— Traité de la culture des plantes de terre de bruyère. 1844. III. 110.[1]
The Para and Ceara rubbers. 1879. III. 473,[1] 514.[1]
Para rubber. 1898. III. 519.[1]
Para rubber in Ceylon. 1893. III. 519.[1]
Para rubber notes. 1898. III. 519.[1]
Parabilium medicamentorum scriptores antiqui. See APULE-JUS PLATONICUS. 400. I. 274.
Paracelsus. See BOMBAST VON HOHENHEIM, A. P. T.
Parada y Barreto, Adolfo. Claves dicotómicas para le determinacion. 1878. IV. 75.[2]
— Enfermedad de los Castaños. 1878. IV. 493.[1]
— Sobre la enfermedad de los Castaños. 1878. IV. 493.[1]
— La filoxera vastatrix. 1880. III. 572.
— Los insectos de la Vid. 1878. III. 563.
Parade, A. Reboisement des montagnes. 1862. IV. 162.
The paradisus londinensis. See SALISBURY, R. A. 1805. I. 53.
Paraguay indigo. 1892. III. 755.[1]
Paraguay Jaborandi. 1891. III. 505.[1]
Paraguay Tea. 1898. III. 531.[1]
Paraguay Tea or Yerba Maté. 1899. III. 531.[1]
Sur la parallelisme de la touffe des arbres avec le sol qu'elles ombragent. 1702. I. 106.[1]
Los páramos de la Brújula. 1892. IV. 546.[2]
Parandier. Dissertation sommaire . . . sur le reboisement. 1866. IV. 162.
Parandier, A. N. Note sur la mise en valeur . . . des communaux incultes. 1897. IV. 546.[2]
Parasites du Chêne. 1900. IV. 511.
Parasitismus und Epiphytismus. See Is Mistletoe injurious? 1853. II. 174.[1]
The Parasol Pine. 1888. III. 309.[2]
Paratore, Emanuele. Ricerche istologiche sui tubercoli . . . delle Leguminose. 1899. II. 322.[1]
Paravey, Ch. de. Sur l'emploi fait . . . de la gomme des vieux Mélèzes. 1855. IV. 452.[1]
— Sur l'histoire du papier. 1858. III. 235.[1]
— Lettre sur les arbres qui donnent du sucre. 1851. III. 227.
— Note on a wax collected by the Chinese. 1850. III. 673.[2]
— Note sur une galle employée . . . pour la teinture. 1850. III. 236.
— Recherches relatives à une plante inconnue de la Chine. 1847. III. 273.[1]
Parc. Amélioration de taillis clairiérés. 1899. IV. 170.
Le parc de Lovenjoul. 1894. III. 28.[2]
The parcellaire system of grazing in Nellore. 1900. IV. 136.[2]
Parco, Gottfried. Oeconomia in nuce. 1719. IV. 115.
IV. 324.
Pardé, Léon Gabriel Charles. Cours de droit forestier. 1900. IV. 324.
— Notice sur les végétaux ligneux exotiques. 1900. III. 84.[2]
— Les principaux végétaux ligneux exotiques. 1900. IV. 127,[1] 545.[1]

Pardeller, C. Über die erste Anpflanzung der Pinie in Tirol. 1898. III. 308.[2]
Pardo, Eduardo. Congreso contra las inundaciones. 1885. IV. 47.[2]
Pardo de Tavera, Trinidad Herménégilde. Plantas medicinales de Filipinas. 1892. III. 91.[2]
Pardo y Moreno, Eduardo. El Esparto, importancia y utilidad. 1888. IV. 439.
Pardo y Sastrón, José. See LOSCOS Y BERNÁL, Francisco & PARDO Y SASTRÓN, José.
Parent. Experiences pour connoître la résistance des bois de Chêne & de Sapin. 1708. IV. 446,[2] 513.
Parenti, Luigi. Intorno la sfrenata liberta della recisione degli alberi. 1845. IV. 285.[2]
Le parfait vigneron; almanach du moniteur vinicole. 1870. III. 555.
Parfenow, Ilja. Chemisch-pharmacognostische Untersuchung der braunen amerikanischen Chinarinden. 1885. III. 725.[1]
Parigi non ama la Quercia. 1863. IV. 505.
Paris, Charles. Colonies indigènes de plantes erraticas. 1892. I. 437.
— A propos d'un Marronnier. 1892. III. 210.
— Quelques raretés botaniques. 1892. I. 437.
Paris, John Ayrton. Pharmacologia. 1812. III. 257.[2]
Paris — Académie royale des sciences. See ACADÉMIE . . . I. 20.
Paris — Congrès de botanique . . . 1889. See CONGRÈS . . . I. 21.
Paris — Congrès international de botanique. See CONGRÈS . . . I. 21.
Paris — Congrès international de botanique et d'horticulture. See CONGRÈS . . . I. 520.[1]
Paris — Gazette médicale. See GAZETTE . . . I. 21.
Paris — Musée d'histoire naturelle. See MUSÉE . . . I. 22.
Paris — Société d'encouragement pour l'industrie nationale. See SOCIÉTÉ . . . III. 21.
Paris — Société d'histoire naturelle. See SOCIÉTÉ . . . I. 23.
Paris — Société Linnéenne. See SOCIÉTÉ . . . I. 23.
Paris — Société philomatique. See SOCIÉTÉ . . . I. 23.
Paris — Société royale d'horticulture. See SOCIÉTÉ . . . III. 22.
Paris — Société royale et centrale d'agriculture. See SOCIÉTÉ . . . III. 22.
Parisel. Sur l'emploi d'un produit . . . pour combattre . . . la maladie de la Vigne. 1853. III. 576.
Parisel, Émile. Conservation . . . du domaine forestier de l'état. 1894. IV. 551.[2]
— Considérations sur la production et le traitement des plants. 1884. IV. 150.
— Cubage & estimation en matière. 1886. IV. 218.
— Organisation d'une bonne station expérimentale forestière. 1895. IV. 541.[1]
— Les pinières de la Campine et le lophyre. 1876. IV. 477.
— Récolte des graines d'arbres forestiers. 1898. IV. 148.
— Vulgarisation de la sylviculture. 1896. IV. 40.[1]
Parisel, Joseph. Les insectes ravageurs des forêts. 1894. IV. 549.[2]
Parish, C. S. P. Pwai-Ngyet. 1867. III. 227.
Parish, Charles. The Amherstia. 1885. III. 331.[2]
— Botanical notes made during a month's tour from Moulmein to the three Pagodas. 1859. I. 476.[1]
— Notes of a trip up the Salween. 1865. I. 476.[1]
Parish, Samuel Bonsall. The arborescent Yuccas of California. 1891. II. 86.[2]
— Californian Palms. 1890. III. 318.[1]
— Contributions to southern California botany. 1900. I. 327.
— Distribution of southern California trees. 1893. I. 320, IV. 78.[1]
— Morphological notes; nature of the petiolar glands in Armeniaca. 1893. II. 273.[1]
— New Californian plants. 1892. II. 596.[2]
— New or little-known plants of southern California. 1898. I. 327.
— The Palms of the southern California border. 1890. II. 75.[2]
Parish, W. F. Yucca Whipplei. 1890. II. 88.[1]
Parish, W. H. On the influence of forests on climate. 1850. IV. 52.
Parisius. Anlage . . . von Obstbaumpflanzungen. 1883. III. 139.
Parisot, Léon. Notice sur la flore des environs de Belfort. 1858. I. 411.
Park, Samuel. Seedling and budded Peaches. 1897. III. 441.[1]

Park and cemetery. III. 7.
Parke. Culture du Cinchona dans le Kangra. 1870. III. 714.
Parke, Davis & Co. Cascara sagrada. 188. ? III. 543.²
— — Collective investigation of drugs. 1884. III. 260.¹
— — Manaca (Franciscea uniflora). 1884. III. 699.¹
— — Organic materia medica. 1890. III. 244.
— — Reports on . . . hydrochlorate of cocaine. 1885. III. 493.¹
— — Saw Palmetto. 1884. III. 331.¹
— — The therapeutic properties of Saw Palmetto. 1898. III. 331.¹
— — Tonga; a compound fluid. 1884. III. 697.¹
— — Working bulletin for the collective investigation of Jamaica Dogwood. 1888. III. 484.²
— — Working bulletin for the scientific investigation of the newer materia medica. 1883. III. 260.¹
Parker. Note sur les plantes médicinales de Madagascar. 1884. III. 93.²
Parker, E. H. Canton plants. 1887. I. 75.²
— Sz Ch'uan plants. 1883. I. 75.²
— & Ford, Charles. The flora of Hainan. 1893. I. 75.²
Parker, F. H. Reports of tests on the strength of structural material. 1883. IV. 410.
Parker, George William. A Malagasy materia medica. 1881. III. 282.¹
Parker, Richard. Berberis Darwini. 1898. III. 394.²
Parker, S. D. Culture of Grapes in graperies. 1861. III. 550.
Parker, S. J. Salt on trees. 1873. III. 186.¹
Parkin, J. Caoutchouc or Indiarubber. 1899. III. 230.
— Notes on India rubber. 1899. III. 230.
— Observations on latex and its functions. 1900. I. 181.³
— Some observations bearing on the function of latex. 1899. I. 181.²
Parkinson, C. F. D. Bunya-Bunya. 1856. II. 26.¹
Parkinson, John. Paradisi in sole Paradisus terrestris. 1629. I. 285,¹ 530.²
— Theatrum botanicum. 1640. I. 285.³
Parkinson, Richard. A tour in America. 1805. IV. 396.¹
Parkinson, Sydney. A journal of a voyage to the South Seas. 1773. III. 283.²
— Die Pflanzen der Insel Outahitée. 1777. III. 94.²
Parkman, Francis. The book of Roses. 1866. III. 449.
— The forests of the White Mountains. 1888. IV. 339.
— The garden classification of the Rose. 1862. III. 449.
Parks, La Fayette I. Successful Tea growing in America. 1898. III. 601.¹
Parlamento italiano. Camera dei deputati. — Progetto di legge . . . sulla legge forestale. 1863. IV. 327.
Parlamento italiano. Camera dei deputati . . . Sunto della discussione sul bilancio passivo per l' esercizio 1863 [1862] del Ministero d' agricol-industria e commercio per la parte che riguarda il ramo forestale. 1863. IV. 293.²
Parlamento italiano . . . Discussione del progetto di legge per vendita dei beni demaniali. 1863. IV. 277.
Parlamento italiano . . . Interpellanza sulla condizione economica della Sardegna. 1863. IV. 277.
Parlamento nazionale. — Progetto di legge . . . per promulgazione . . . della legge forestale 21 Agosto 1826. 1865. IV. 328.
Parlasca, Simone. Il fiore della Granadiglia. 1609. II. 577.¹
Parlatore, Filippo. Les collections botaniques du Musée . . . de Florence. 1874. I. 64.
— On the composition of the cone of the Coniferae. 1861. II. 19.
— Coniferae. 1868. II. 13.¹
— Coniferas novas nonnullas descripsit. 1863. II. 13.¹
— Considérations sur la méthode naturelle en botanique. 1863. I. 34.
— Description de trois espèces nouvelles de Cyprès. 1860. II. 29.¹
— Études sur la géographie botanique de l'Italie. 1878. I. 428.
— Flora palermitana. 1844. I. 431.
— Flora panormitana. 1847. I. 426.
— Gnetaceae. 1868. II. 53.²
— Sul kamala. 1848. III. 520.¹
— Lezionidi botanica comparata. 1843. I. 100.²
— Note sur l'Araucaria. 1861. II. 25.²
— Note sur la composition du cône des Conifères. 1861. II. 19.
— Note sur une monstruosité des cônes de l'Abies Brunoniana. 1862. II. 53.³

— Notizia sulla Pachira alba. 1843. II. 530.²
— Le specie dei Cotoni. 1866. II. 522.¹
— Studi organografici sui fiori e sui frutti delle Conifere. 1864. II. 19.
— Viaggio alla catena del Monte Bianco. 1850. I. 434.
— & Caruel, Teodoro. Flora italiana. 1848. I. 427.
— & Webb, P. B. Florula aethiopico-aegyptiaca. 1849. I. 453.
Parlos, Maria. A talk about preserving fruit. 1892. III. 174.¹
Parmentier. Tanker over Frugttræernes Beskjæring. 1803. III. 174.²
Parmentier, Antoine Augustin. Aperçu des résultats obtenus de la fabrication des sirops. 1812. III. 582.
— Instruction sur les moyens de suppléer le sucre. 1808. III. 582.
— Mémoire qui a remporté le prix de l'Académie de Besançon. 1772. III. 219.¹
— Recherches sur les végétaux nourissans. 1781. III. 219.¹
— Traité de la châtaigne. 1780. III. 360.¹
— Traité sur l'art de fabriquer les sirops. 1808. III. 582.
Parmentier, Joseph. Catalogue des plantes cultivées dans le jardin de Mr. Joseph Parmentier. 1812. I. 49.
— Plant. Abiétinées du département du Doubs. 1895. III. 291, IV. 441.
— La botanique systématique et les théories de M. Vesque. 1894. I. 253.¹
— Les classifications établies depuis les grands embranchements jusqu'aux simples espèces. 1896. I. 253.¹
— Contribution à l'étude de la famille des Dilléniacées. 1896. II. 540,¹
— Contribution à l'étude des Magnoliacées. 1895. II. 209.¹
— L'espèce végétale en classification naturelle. 1897. I. 253.¹
— Flore nouvelle de la chaîne jurassique. 1895. I. 418.
— Sur le genre Euclea. 1891. II. 702.²
— Sur le genre Royena. 1891. II. 703.¹
— Histoire des Magnoliacées. 1895. II. 209.¹
— Histologie comparée des Ébénacées. 1892. II. 700.²
— À propos de Roses. 1898. II. 283.¹
— Recherches anatomiques . . . sur le Rosa berberifolia. 1897. II. 297.¹
— Recherches anatomiques . . . sur les Onothéracées. 1897. II. 643.¹
— Recherches anatomiques . . . sur les Rosiers. 1897. II. 289.¹
— Recherches sur les glandes pétiolaires de . . . Amygdalées. 1900. II. 271.²
— Du rôle de l'anatomie pour la distinction des espèces. 1896. I. 253.¹
Parodi, Domingo. Algunas observaciones sobre . . . Amarantáceas. 1880. II. 189.¹
— Apuntes sobre la familia de las Nictagíneas. 1882. II. 190.²
— La Bombonasa; Carludovica palmata .R. et Pav. 1877. III. 332.²
— Contribuciones á la flora del Paraguay. 1877. I. 344.
— Dos nuevas especies pertenecientes á . . . las Euforbiáceas. 1881. III. 434.¹
— Ensayo de botánica médica argentina. 1881. III. 65.²
— Ensayo sistemático para la distribucion de las Mirteas. 1879. II. 619.¹
— Notas sobre algunas plantas usuales del Paraguay. 1877. III. 65.²
— Nuevo alcaloide hallado en "el Naranjillo." 1880. II. 412.²
— Tayua. 1880. III. 753.²
Parquet, L. Les forêts de la Suède septentrionale. 1889. IV. 344.²
— Influence des forêts sur le régime des eaux. 1889. IV. 51.
— The influence of forests on water supply. 1889. IV. 51.
— Oliviers et Chênes-lièges en Algérie. 1888. IV. 279.²
— Le reboisement en Algérie. 1883. IV. 379.¹
Parra, Antonio. Discurso sobre los medios de connaturalizar . . . los Cedros de la Havana. 1799. III. 49.¹
Parrish. Olneya Tesota. 1882. III. 482.²
Parrot, Friedrich. Reise zum Ararat. 1834. I. 478.
— See also ENGELHARDT, Mortiz von & PARROT, Friedrich.
Parry, Charles Christopher. Botanical observations in western Wyoming. 1874. I. 323.
— Botany of the region along the route of the Kansas Pacific railway. 1869. I. 323.
— Californian Manzanitas. 1887. II. 660.²
— Ceanothus L., a synoptical list. 1889. II. 492.²

— Historical notice of Pinus Torreyana. 1884. II. 48.[1]
— Introduction [to the botany of the United States.] 1859. I. 307.
— List of plants collected . . . Wyoming expedition. 1875. I. 324.
— New genus of Euphorbiaceaé. 1884. II. 452.[1]
— The Pacific coast Alders. 1887. II. 115.[2]
— The Rocky Mountain Alpine region. 1870. I. 323.
— & Engelmann, George. Coniferae of Dr. Parry's collection. 1862. II. 14.[1]
— A new North American Rose. 1882. II. 296.[1]
Parry, Mrs. Charles Christopher. See PARRY, Mrs. E. R.
Parry, Mrs. E. R. Catalogue of the herbarium of the late Dr. Charles C. Parry. 1891. I. 308.
Parry, Ernest. J. The chemistry of essential oils. 1899. I. 182.[1]
— Note on Eucalyptus oil. 1898. IV. 534.[1]
Parry, J. R. Nuts for profit. 1897. III. 134.[1]
Parry, William. Fifty years among small fruits. 1884. III. 147.[2]
Parry, William Edward. Narrative of an attempt to reach the north pole. See HOOKER, Sir W. J. 1828. I. 308.
Parshad, GUNGA. See GUNGA PARSHAD.
Parskius, Fr. Rosa aurea omnique aevo sacra. 1728. II. 290.[2]
Parsons, Charles-William. Forests.' 1878. IV. 44.
Parsons, George H. The climate of Colorado. 1888. I. 320, IV. 78.[1]
— Colorado Conifers for eastern planting. 1891. III. 293.
— The White River forest reservation. 1891. IV. 178.[2]
Parsons, J. P. Conifers for gardens. 1875. III. 290.
— An impervious hedge. 1875. III. 443.[2]
Parsons, James. The microscopical theatre of seeds. 1745. I. 120, III. 219.[2]
Parsons, Mary Elizabeth. The wild flowers of California. 1897. I. 327.
Parsons, Samuel, (jr.). The comparative hardiness of . . . Ligustrums. 1880. III. 673.[1]
— Landscape gardening. 1891. III. 202.[1]
— The most promising . . . trees and shrubs. 1881. III. 60.
— Ornamental climbing vines. 1880. III. 204.[2]
Parsons, Samuel B. Abies canadensis macrophylla. 1879. III. 312.[1]
— Broad-leaved evergreens. 1875. III. 206.[1]
— Broad-leaved Hemlock Spruce. 1878. III. 312.[1]
— Chinese Cypress. 1877. III. 311.[1]
— Color and form in trees. 1886. III. 205.[2]
— Culture . . . of the Zante Currant Grape. 1859. III. 550.
— Grafting. 1890. III. 163.[1]
— The hardy Catalpa on the lawn. 1880. III. 706.[1]
— Hardy Rhododendrons. 1888. III. 656.
— Japanese Persimmons. 1879. III. 669.[2]
— Magnolia glauca. 1877. III. 399.[1]
— Magnolias. 1885. III. 399.[1]
— A new hardy Magnolia. 1876. III. 400.[2]
— A new late flowering Magnolia. 1877. III. 400.[1]
— A new Magnolia. 1881. III. 400.[1]
— A new method of propagating Exochorda. 1877. III. 424.[1]
— Parsons on the Rose. 1847. III. 448.
— Paulownia imperialis. 1847. III. 703.[1]
— Picea Parsoniana. 1875. III. 296.[1]
— Picturesque hedges. 1880. III. 214.[1]
— On the productions of the Ionian Islands. 1860. III. 272.[1]
— Rare lawn-trees. 1880. III. 60.
— The Rose, its history. 1847. III. 448.
— & sons. New hardy trees and shrubs. 1879. III. 60.
Parsons, Theophilus & Sprague, C. J. Involuted growth of the bark of an Elm tree. 1859. I. 127,[1] II. 143.[1]
Parsons & Co. Japanese trees. 1862. III. 60.
Part of a letter to Dr. Sloane wherein is an account of a double pear. 1702. II. 279.[1]
Partage de l'affouage par tête. 1898. IV. 555.[1]
Partanski, N. P. See Партанскій, Н. П.
Parte ufficiale. Decisioni del ministero d' agricoltura . . . Uniforme dei guardia generali forestali. 1864. IV. 304.[1]
A partial list of the native flora of Waltham, Mass. 1883. I. 315.
La participation des femmes à la solution de la question forestière. See The ACTION of the New Jersey state federation . . . 1896. IV. 39.[1]
Partie de pineraie de 15 ans, incendiée. 1900. IV. 170.
Partington, Charles Frederick. Introduction to botany. 1836. I. 87.

Partsch, Paul. Bericht über das Detonationsphänomen. 1826. I. 447.
Parville, de. L'humidité des arbres. 1899. I. 168.
Parville, Henri de. La lune et la coupe des arbres. 1900. IV. 557.[1]
— & Bruyn, Léon de. La protection des oiseaux insectivores. 1897. IV. 544.[1]
Parvy, Ludwig von. Beitrag zur rationellen Kubirung der Hölzer. 1857. IV. 217.
Pas, D. Over kakao en chocolade. 1863. III. 594.
— Over Piper Cubeba van den handel. 1861. III. 342.[2]
Pas vignobles atteints par le phylloxera. See DUCLAUX, Emile. 1876. III. 570.[1]
Pascal. Elenchus plantarum Horti . . . parmensis. 1802.' I. 61.
Pascal, A. Mémoire sur la maladie de la Vigne. 1853. III. 576.
Pascal, Noël. De l'alcoolé de guaco. 1863. III. 755.[2]
— & others. Du Guaco et de ses effets. 1863. III. 524.[1]
Pascalis, Félix. Practical instructions . . . for Silkworm nurseries. 1829. III. 374.
Paschen, F. Ueber die Anwendung von Fanggräben. 1882. IV. 199.[2]
— Curculio (Strophosomus) obesus. 1886. IV. 207.
Paschke, F. Verpflanzen grosser Palmen. 1900. III. 318.[1]
Paschkis, Heinrich. Contributions to a closer knowledge of. some little known leaves. 1881.' III. 630.[1] — 1882. III. 652.[2]
— Henna leaves and powder. 1881. III. 630.[1]
— Kalmia latifolia leaves. 1882. III. 652.[2]
Paschwitz, J. Rudolph von. Der Zuckerahorn. 1837. IV. 526.[2]
Pascoe, J. F. South Australia. 1888. III. 283.[1]
Pascual, Agustin. Estudios forestales. 1852. IV. 287.
— Instrucción práctica para las cortas y entresacas de los montes de Pino albár. 1847. IV. 304.[1]
— Recuerdos de Rusia. 1873. IV. 345.
Pasewaldt, (Obergärtner, Berlin). Über einige Ziersträucher der Gewächshäuser. 1855. III. 69.
— See KOCH, Karl & PASEWALDT.
The Pashiuba Palm. 1872. II. 69.[2]
Pashkevitch, V. See Пашкевичъ, В.
Pasini, Antonio. Annotazioni ed emendazioni nella traddotizione di P. A. Matthioli. 1592. I. 283.
Pasqua, Ignazio. La Terebentina di Scio. 1881. III. 526.[1]
Pasquale, Fortun. Atlante di piante medicinali. 1880. III. 59.[1]
— Bibliografia botanica. 1894. I. 4.[1]
— Su di una nuova teoria carpellare. 1892. I. 119.
— Sulla pioggerella avvenuta sotto alcuni alberi di Tiglio. 1893. II. 516.[2]
— Quelques mots sur la géographie botanique . . . de Naples. 1878. I. 428.
— Rapporto . . . sul legname di Pioppo attaccato. 1891. III. 344.[1]
— Sulla varietà pompeiana del Laurus nobilis. 1891. II. 225.[1]
Pasquale, Giuseppe Antonio. Su di una anomalia della foglia del Carubo. 1874. II. 346,[1] III. 471.[1]
— L' Anona Cherimolia. 1878. III. 401.[1]
— Catalogo del Real orto botanico di Napoli. 1867. I. 63.
— Cenni sulla flora di Assab. 1885. I. 489.
— Sui corpuscoli oleosi delle Olive. 1873. II. 713.[1]
— Sulla eterofillia. 1867. I. 110.
— Della eterofillia nel Cupressus funebris. 1872. II. 29.[2]
— Flora vesuviana. 1869. I. 428.
— Su d' una forma involuta della cupola della Quercus Ilex. 1869. II. 134.[1]
— Su di una importante varietà d'Ulivo. 1873. II. 712.[2]
— Manuale di arboricoltura. 1876. III. 114.[1]
— Nota su di un raro fatto di fecondità d' un Mandarino. 1876. II. 402.[2]
— Nota sulla Pachira glabra. 1869. II. 530.[2]
— Nota sulla Tetranthera caustica. 1869. II. 228.[1]
— Notizia sui canali resiniferi . . . del Taxodium. 1862. II. 52.[1]
— Notizie botaniche relative alla provincia di Napoli. 1876. I. 428.
— Notizie botaniche relative alle provincie meridionali d'Italia. 1881. I. 429.
— Notizie botaniche relative alle provincie meridionali d'Italia pel 1878. 1878. I. 428.
— Su di una nuova specie di Lonicera. 1875. II. 839.[2]
— Osservazioni sui canali resiniferi . . . dei Coniferi. 1863. II. 19.

Pasquale, Giuseppe Antonio (*continued*).
— Su di un ramo mostruoso della Opuntia fulvispina. 1871. II. 597.[1]
— Intorno la sede dell' odore della Serissa. 1867. II. 831.[2]
— Studî botanici . . . sull' Ulivo. 1873. II 713.[1]
— Su di una varietà di Fico d' India. 1872. II.·596.[2]
— & Fortunato. Elementi di botanica ordinati. 1884. I. 271.[1]
— *See also* TENORE, Vincenzo & PASQUALE, G. A.
— & Avellino, Giulio. Flora medica della provincia di Napoli. 1841. III. 88.[1]
— & Licopoli, Gaetano. Di un viaggio botanico al Gargano. 1873. I. 428.
Pasquier, Antoine. De l'Eucalyptus. 1873. IV. 531.[1]
Passa, F. JAUBERT DE. *See* JAUBERT DE PASSA, F.
Passaeus, *See* DU PAS, Crispinus.
Passaglia, Quirino. La spiaggia di Chiavari. 1881. IV. 48.[1]
Passau-Naturhistorischer Verein. *See* NATURHISTORISCHER . . . I. 13.
Passavant, Claude. Theses anatomico-botanicae. 1733. I. 290.
Passeratus, Johannes. De Oliva carmen. 1588. III. 678.[1]
Passerini, Carlo. Alcune notizie sopra . . . Thrips dannoso agli Ulivi. 1834. III. 677.[1]
— Sopra due specie d' insetti nocivi. 1830. III. 562.[2]
— Notizie relative ad alcuni insetti . . . del Fico. ·1851. III. 369.[2]
— Notizie sopra due specie d' insetti nocivi agli alberi. 1849. III. 189.
— Osservazioni sopra alcune larve e tignole dell' Ulivo. 1832. III. 677.[1]
— Osservazioni sul baco danneggiatore delle Ulive. 1829. III. 677.[1]
— Sul punteruolo dell' Ulivo. 1827. III. 677.[1]
Passerini, Giovanni. · Flora dei contorni di Parma. 1852. I. 427.
— Flora Italiae superioris. 1844. I. 427.
— Mazzetto di fiori per la festa. 1855. I. 63.
— *See also* CESATI, Vincenzo, *barone*, PASSERINI, Giovanni & GIBELLI, Giuseppe.
Passerini, Jean. Effets de l'été dernier sur . . . quelques Conifères. 1862. III. 292.
— Wirkungen des Sommers 1861 auf den Wuchs einiger Nadelhölzer. 1862. III. 292.
Passerini, Napoleone. Azione dell' acqua calda . . . sul germogliamento dei semi di Olivo. 1898. II. 713.[1]
— Il baco dell' Uva. 1894. III. 561.
— Manuale pratico di viticultura. 1885.· III. 558.[1]
— Sulla presenza di fermenti zimici ossidanti. 1899. I. 178.
— Su di una sostanza gommosa contenuta nelle galle dell' Olmo. 1898. III. 365.[2]
Passerini, Valentino. Sogno . . . nella licenza, ch' ei prende da Monte Baldo. 1684. I. 424.
Les Passiflores. 1899. III. 615.[2]
Passion-flower coming on a tendril. 1898. II. 577.[1]
Die Passionsblumen. 1871. III. 615.[2]
Passow. Die Pflanze und die Luft. 1861. I. 170.
Passy, Antoine François. Effets produits par la foudre sur un Peuplier. 1871. IV. 194.
— *See also* DEKIN, A. & PASSY, A. F.
Passy, Jacques. Sur la diffusion des parfums. 1895. I. 182.[2]
— Sur un nouveau mode d'obtention du parfum des fleurs. 1897. III. 227.
Passy, Pierre. Un ennemi du Poirier. 1897. III. 446.[2]
— Les Groseilliers. 1899. III. 414.[1]
— Les maladies du Poirier et du Pommier. 1899. III. 444.[2]
— À . . . s de la greffe coulée sous l'écorce. 1900. III. 3. propos
— Traité d'arboriculture fruitière. 1897. III. 145.[1]
La pasta di carta. 1864. IV. 429.
Pasta de madera. 1885. IV. 430.
Pasteur, Louis. Observations verbales. 1880. III. 560.
— Recherches sur les alcaloïdes des quinquinas. 1853. III. 722.
— Remarque au sujet de la note communiquée par M. van Tieghem. 1863. I. 521.[1]
— Réponse à M. Blanchard. 1880. III. 560.
— *See also* BIOT, J. B. & PASTEUR, Louis.
Pastre, J. Observations relatives aux accidents survenus dans les Vignes traitées. 1881. III. 560.
Pasture in hill forests. 1885. IV. 136.[1]
Paszlavszky, József. A bazai fenyvek magyar nevei. 1886. I. 75,[1] IV. 87.[1]

Patchoski, I. K. *See* Пачоскій, I. К.
La pâte de bois. 1896. IV. 430.
Pateck, Johann. Die Giftpflanzen. 1866. III. 59.[2]
Patein. Note sur l'Abrus precatorius. 1884. III. 462.[2]
Patel. De l'aménagement des forêts résineuses dans les montagnes des Monts-Jura. 1866. IV. 122.[1]
Patent die neue Organisation des Forstwesens . . . im Herzogthum Gotha betreffend. 1829. IV. 303.[1]
Paternò, Emanuele. Investigaciones sobre el acido . . . del Lapacho. 1882. II. 791.[2]
— & Briosi, Giovanni. Ueber Hesperidin. 1876. III. 499.[1]
— — Sur l'hespéridine. ·1876. III. 499.[1]
Paterson, Andrew. On the construction of roads. 1865. IV. 389.
— Report on trees and shrubs . . . transplanted . . . by McGlashen's transplanting apparatus. 1805. III. 166.
Paterson, Wilham. A narrative of four journeys into the country of the Hottentots. 1789. I. 494.
— Quatre voyages chez les Hottentots. 1789. I. 494.
— Reisen in das Land der Hottentotten. 1789. I. 494.
Pathak, Sunder Lall. Re-afforestation of the Mahasu-Fagu Ridge. 1896. IV. 168.[1]
Pathault, Louis. Du bromure de camphre. 1877. III. 404.[2]
Patin, Charles. Sur les avantages que le Jatropha curcas présenté. 1900. III. 519.[2]
— Propriétés vulnéraires du Peuplier baumier. 1872. III. 345.[2]
Paton, James. Oriental spices. 1871. III. 403,[1] 404,[1] 635.[1]
Patouillard, Narcisse. Note sur quelques plantes des environs de Paris. 1880. II. 517.[2]
Patout, Marie Rose. Abrégé des plantes médicinales. 1864. III. 86.
Patrick, G. E. A chemical study of Apple twigs. 1889. II. 267.[2]
Patrick, William. A popular description of . . . plants of Lanarkshire. *See* PATRIK, William. 1831. V. xx.[2]
Patrigeon, Gabriel. Sur un insecte qui attaque le jeune raisin. 1884. III. 563.
— Le mildiou. 1887. III. 579.
Patrin, Eugène Louis Melchior. Relation d'un voyage aux monts d'Altaï. 1783. I. 453.[1]
Patriotischer Unterricht von . . . Anpflanzung lebendiger Zäune. 1775. III. 212.[2]
Patris, J. B. Essai sur l'histoire naturelle . . . du Cassie. 1777. III. 470.[1]
Patruban, von. Ueber die Fabrikazion von Eichenfässern. 1870. IV. 515.[1]
Patschke, Wolfgang. Catalogus stirpium in sylvis saxonicis. 1699. I. 372.
Patten, C. G. Apple stocks for the North. 1877. III. 425.[1]
— Experience in experimental fruit growing. 1897. III. 134.[1]
— The progress of Plum culture in the Northwest. 1899. III. 433.[1]
— Relation of forest trees to climate. 1887. IV. 54.
— Tests of hardiness. 1893. III. 182.
— Top-grafting the Apple. 1879. III. 426.[2]
— Twenty-six years experience with Apple seedlings. 1895. III. 425.[2]
Patten, J. C. Black Walnut and forest planting. 1882. III. 354.[2]
Patterson, D. B. Care of native trees on lawn or street. 1900. III. 208.[2]
Patterson, Mrs. Flora Wambaugh. An Exoascus upon Alnus leaves. 1896. IV. 489.[1]
Patterson, G. *See* WRIGHT, Alder & PATTERSON, G.
Patterson, Harry Norton. Catalogue of the . . . plants of Illinois. 1876. I. 314.
— A list of plants collected in the vicinity of Oquawka. 1874. I. 314.
— Patterson's numbered check-list of North American plants. 1892. I. 308.
Patterson, J. S. Forests and fruit-growing. 1873. IV.·53.
Patton, George. Measurement of certain coniferous trees. 1859. III. 292.
Patton's Spruce. 1897. II. 53.[2]
Pâturage dans les bois. 1894. IV. 545.[1]
Patureau, (Francœur). Culture de la Vigne. 1861. III. 559.[1]
Patze. Weidenbastarde. 1861. II. 108.[1]
Patze, C., Meyer, Ernst & Elkan, L. Flora der Provinz Preussen. 1848. I. 383.
Patzelt, Joseph Eduard. Wildwachsende Thalamifloren der Umgebungen Wiens. 1842. I. 440.

Patzig, O. I. *See* ПАТЦИГЪ, О. И.
Pau, Carlos. Broussonet, Cavanilles y J. Ball. 1897. I. 486.
— Consideráciones sobre algunas curiosas plantas. 1896. I. 423.
— Especies europeas propias también de la flora española. 1897. II. 314.²
— Notas botanicas a la flora española. 1887. I. 422.
— Notas sobre unas formas criticas de plantas españolas. 1898. II. 30.²
— Plantas recogidas por Don Juan Benedicto. 1895. I. 423.
— Salix incana var. longebracteata. 1892. II. 107.² .
Pau, Joanne Benedicto. *See* DOMENECH, Bernardo & PAU, J. B.
Pauchon, A. De l'influence de la lumière sur la respiration des semences. 1880. I. 203.
— Recherches sur le rôle de la lumière dans la germination. 1880. I. 203, *230.*
Paugam, L. & Blanchard, J. L'hiver 1879–80 et le Camellia en Basse-Bretagne. 1884. III. 599.²
Paul, Benjamin H. The Annatto bush. 1888. III. 613.¹
— The Argan tree. 1879. III. 666.²
— Boldo. 1875. III. 403.²
— Brazil nuts. 1875. II. 611.²
— Cacao cultivation in Colombia. 1889. III. 592.²
— Camphor. 1896. III. 233.²
— The cancer of Cinchona. 1889. III. 717.²
— Canellae radix. 1897. III. 613.²
— Cascarilla. 1898. III. 516.²
— Ceylon gamboge. 1884. III. 609.¹
— Chemical composition of woody tissues. 1884. I. 155.
— Die Chinarindenkultur in Columbia. 1889. III. 713.¹
— Cinchona cultivation in Bengal. 1872. III. 714.
— Cinchona cultivation . . . in Bengal. 1885. III. 715, *718.*
— Cinchona cultivation in Ceylon. 1882. III. 714.
— Cinchona cultivation in Columbia. 1889. III. 713.¹
— Cinchona cultivation in India. 1871. III. 714. — 1873. III. 714.
— Cinchona cultivation in Java. 1871. III. 715.
— Cinchona cultivation in Mauritius. 1876. III. 717.¹
— Cinchona cultivation in New Caledonia. 1876. III. 717.²
— Cinchona cultivation in private plantations. 1876. III. 712.²
— Cinchona in Jamaica. 1872. III. 713.¹
— Cinchona in Madeira. 1875. III. 717.²
— Cinchona plantations in British Sikkim. 1872. III. 714.
— Cinchona robusta. 1884. III. 726.¹
— Cinchonae rubrae cortex. 1898. III. 726.²
— Cinnamon and cassia barks. 1894. III. 404.¹
— The Coca plants in cultivation. 1892. III. 492.¹
— Coconut Palm and weevils. 1893. III. 323.²
— The Coffee-leaf disease. 1881. III. 735.
— The cultivation of Cinchona in Ceylon. 1882. III. 714.
— Cultivation of Cinchonas. 1883. III. 712.²
— The cultivation of Cinchonas in India. 1875. III. 714.
— The culture of Cinchonas in Java. 1878. III. 716.
— Eucalyptus; ses produits. 1886. IV. 531.²
— Eucalyptus globulus. 1872. IV. 533.¹
— Eucalyptus products. 1886. IV. 531.¹
— Failure of the Cinchona cultivation in St. Helena. 1884. III. 717.²
— The genus Eucalyptus. 1873. IV. 529.²
— The growth of Cinchonas. 1874. III. 712.¹
— The Guava. 1871. III. 637.²
— Hints and suggestions for raising Cinchona plants. 1882. III. 712.²
— Hybridization of Cinchona. 1871. II. 812.
— Die Kakaokultur in Columbia. 1889. III. 592.²
— A milk-yielding tree. 1871. III. 668.¹
— The month. 1878. III. 456,² III. 438,¹ 648.¹ .
— The movement of water in plants. 1875. II. 274.²
— Olive cultivation in Syria. 1873. III. 675.²
— Periodic motions of leaves and petals. 1874. I. 197.²
— Piscidia erythrina, Jamaica Dogwood. 1886. III. 484.²
— Review of " Government report on Cinchona in Sikkim." 1878. III. 714.
— Review of " The cultivation of the Cinchonas . . . in Java." 1871. III. 715.
— The true Gamboge plant. 1875. II. 555.¹
— & **Cownley,** A. J. Dosages de la caféine dans les cafés. 1887. III. 740.³
— — Sur l'homoquinine et les alcaloïdes de l'écorce dite cuprea. 1885. III. 747.¹
— — Influence de la torréfaction sur . . . caféine. 1887. III. 740.²

— — The new alkaloids of Cuprea bark. 1885. III. 747.¹
— — Note chimique sur le thé. 1888. III. 607.
— — Sur la quantité de caféine contenue dans le café. 1887. III. 740.²
Paul, George. The Copper Austrian Brier. 1890. III. 455.²
— Flowering shrubs. 1894. III. 207.²
— Fuchsia tree at Ballme House. 1886. II. 644.²
— Single Roses. 1900. III. 451.¹
— & **Klein.** Über die Anbauwürdigkeit von Quercus rubra. 1899. IV. 516.³
Paul, M. de. Sobre un Phytoptus. 1898. III. 678.¹
Paul, William. American plants. 1858. III. 82.
— Bouquet of Moss Roses. 1880. III. 455.¹
— The Camellia as a seaside plant. 1898. III. 600.¹
— Camellias and Camellia culture. 1879. III. 599.¹
— On colour in the tree scenery. 1870. III. 205.²
— Contributions to horticultural literature. 1892. III. 124.¹
— Der Epheu und dessen Varietäten. 1867. III. 642.²
— Ueber die Farbe in der Baum-Scenerie. 1870. III. 205.²
— Ueber die Farbenschattirungen der Gehölzparthien. 1870. III. 205.²
— On form in tree scenery. 1872. I. 516.
— Die Formen des Epheu's. 1870. III. 642.²
— The future of Epping forest. 1880. IV. 358.¹
— The garden Ivies. 1870. III. 642.²
— On the grouping of the garden varieties of Roses. 1889. III. 450.
— Hardy pictorial trees. 1866. III. 203.
— The Ivy. 1867. III. 642.²
— Om Mangel paa Farverigdom i Træplantningerne. 1870. III. 201.
— Notes on the varieties of common Yew. 1861. III. 288.¹
— Notes on the varieties of English Holly. 1863. III. 530.¹
— Ornamental planting. 1864. III. 205.¹
— Planting ornamental trees for their colors. 1871. III. 205.²
— Rose annual. *See* ROSE annual. III. 18.
— The Rose garden in two divisions. 1848. III. 448.
— Rosengartneren. 1848. III. 448.
— Roses and Rose-culture. 1874. III. 449.
— Transplanting evergreens. 1880. III. 169.¹
— On trees and shrubs in large towns. 1891. III. 42.²
— Varieties of the common Yew. 1861. III. 288.¹
— & **Courtin,** Albert. Die Kultur der Rosen in Töpfen. 1854. III. 452.
— — Observaciones sobre . . . Rosales en macetas. 1854. III. 452.
— — Observations on the cultivation of Roses in pots. 1854. III. 452.
— — Observations sur la culture des Rosiers en pots. 1854. III. 452.
— & **Son.** Catalogue of Roses. 1924. III. 450.
Paul Friedrich Wilhelm, *Herzog* von Württemberg. Erste Reise nach den nördlichen Amerika. 1835. I. 306.
Paulet, Jean Jacques. Examen d'un ouvrage . . . " Illustrationes Theophrasti." 1816. I. 292.
— Examen de la partie botanique de l'essai d'une histoire . . . de la médecine par Kurt Sprengel. 1815. I. 79.¹
— Flore et faune de Virgile. 1824. I. 514.¹
Paulet, Maxime. Chimie agricole. 1840. III. 151.
— Sur la décomposition et la conservation des bois. 1875. IV. 419.
— Sur quelques procédés indiqués par Florentinus. 1876. III. 560.
— Traité de la conservation des bois. 1874. IV. 419.
Paulitschke, Josef. Eine forstliche Excursion in den mährischen Karpathen. 1884. IV. 369.
Paulitschke, Philipp. Harar. *See* BECK VON MANNAGETTA, Günther, *Ritter* von. 1888. I. 489.
Paulli, Johan. Dansk oeconomisk urte-bog. 1761. III. 66.¹
Paulli, Simon. Commentarius de abusu tabaci. 1665. III. 604.²
— Flora danica. 1648. I. 350.²
— Quadripartitum botanicum. 1639. I. 285,² V. xv.²
— A treatise on Tobacco, Tea, Coffee. 1665. III. 604.²
— Viridaria varia. 1653. I, 38.¹
Paullini, Christian Franz. Sacra herba, sive nobilis Salvia. 1688. III. 740.²
Paullinus, C. F. Μοσχοκαρυογραφία; . . . Nucis moschatae curiosa descriptio. 1704. III. 402.³
Paulownia imperialis in der Herbstblüthe. 1859. II. 781.¹

Paulsen. Bemærkninger over sjældne Droguer. 1841. III. 244.
Paulsen, H. C. Echte berichten van den akkerbouw der Oostersche volkeren. 1762. III. 33.²
Paulsen, J. C. Erfahrungstafeln über den Ertrag der Rothbuchen-... Kiefern-Hochwaldbestände. ·1847. IV. 235.²
— Kurze praktische Anweisung zum Forstwesen. 1795. IV. 239.
Paulsen, Ove. *See* Børgesen, Frederik & Paulsen, Ove.
Paulsen, W. Om Omdriften i Statsskovene. 1853. IV. 251.¹
Paulucci, Marianna. Gli alberi lungo le pubbliche strade. 1886. III. 210.
— Il parco di Sanmezzano e le sue piante. 1889. I. 64. ·
Paulus, (*Oberförster*). Ueber Anstellung von Keimproben. 1886. III. 157.
Paulus, (*Topograph*). *See* Nördlinger, Hermann & Paulus.
Paulus Ægineta. Pharmaca simplicia. 1531. III. 239.
Pauly, A. Die Nonne in den bayerischen Waldungen. 1891. IV. 201.
Pauly, J. H. Anweisung zur Benutzung grösserer und kleinerer Flächen und Waldungen. 1815. IV. 117.
— Hülfsbuch für Gutsbesitzer ... zum Anbau der nutzbarsten Laub- und Nadelhölzer. 1805. IV. 105.
Pauquy, Charles Louis Constant. Statistique botanique; ... de la Somme. 1831. I. 408.
Pausa, G. Der Holzkohlungsbetrieb bei der Tergover Eisenhüttengewerkschaft. 1883. IV. 395.
— Die Rollbahn des Bešlinacer Berg- und Hüttenwerkes. 1883. IV. 391.
— Die Schätzungspraxis für Eichenholzverkäufe in Kroatien. 1884. IV. 513.
Pausch, (*Forstmeister, Weiden*). Sur une chute maladive des aiguilles du Pin sylvestre. 1864. IV. 476.
— Die Schütte der Föhre. 1864. IV. 476.
— Ueber Wiederaufforstung tiefgründigen Keupersandbodens. 1866. IV. 472.
Pausch, (*Oberförster*). Eine Windhose am 8. Juli 1875. 1875. IV. 189.¹
Pausey, P. P. N. Henrion de. *See* Henrion de Pausey, P. P. N.
Pausinger, Josef. A Tölgyekről. 1877. · IV. 500.²
— A Vörösfenyő (Larix europea) tenyészetéről és erdőgazdasági kezeléséről. 1876. IV. 449.
Pauwert, M. J. van den. Een eh ander omtrent vruchtenteelt. 1900. III. 147.¹
Du pavage en bois. 1895. IV. 426.¹
Le pavage en bois. 1890. IV. 426.¹
Pavani, Eugenio. Sull' imboscamento del Carso. 1865. IV. 167.¹
Paver, J. B. De l'importance de l'organogénie. 1859. I. 99.
Les pavés en bois. 1894. IV. 557.²
Pavette, O. Notions élémentaires ... d'agriculture, d'horticulture. 1889. III. 113.
Pavia. Nouveau succédané de la quinine. 1869. III. 523.¹
Pavia—Istituto botanico dell' Università. *See* Istituto, ... I. 25.
Pavia—Laboratorio di botanica crittogamica presso la R. università. *See* Laboratorio ... III. 23.⁵
Pavia macrostachya at Coombe Wood. 1894. II.·483.¹
Pavillon, A. Huet du. *See* Huet du Pavillon, A.
Le pavillon des forêts à l'Exposition ... de Rouen. 1896. IV. 20.²
Pavimentazione in legno. 1898. IV. 426.¹
Pavimento de corcho. 1892. IV. 426.¹
Pavimento de las calles. 1886. IV. 426.¹
Pavlovitch, B. E. *See* Павлович, В. Э.
Pavlovitch, P. E. *See* Павлович, П. Э.
Pavon, José. Disertacion botánica sobre los generos Tovaria. 1791. I. 264.
— Disertacion botánica sobre los generos Tovaria ... con la reunion de algunos ... distintos. 1797. I. 340.¹
— *See also* Ruiz Lopez, Hipólito & Pavon, José.
Paweach, H. Eichhörnchenschäden im Murthale. 1882. IV. 198.¹
Pawlikowski, Gwalbert. *See* Błażek, Józef & Pawlikowski, Gwalbert.
The Pawpaw. 1867. III. 401.²
Pax, Ferdinand. Acer Heldreichii Orph. 1885. II. 478.¹
— Aceraceae. 1896. II. 476.¹
— Aizoaceae. 1889. II. 193.²
— Allgemeine Morphologie der Pflanzen. 1890. I. 101.¹
— Amaryllidaceae. 1888. II. 88.²

— Die Anatomie der Euphorbiaceen. 1884. II. 433.²
— Beiträge zur Kenntnis der Capparidaceen. 1888. II. 229.¹
— Buxaceae. 1896. II. 452.²
— Capparidaceae. 1891. II. 229.¹
— Capparidaceae africanae. 1892. II. 229.²
— Caryophyllaceae. 1889. II. 194.¹ ·
— Cleomodendron. 1891. II. 232.²
— Dioscoreaceae. 1888. II. 90.²
— Dréi neue Euphorbiaceen-Gattungen aus Afrika. 1900. II. 434.²
— Empetraceae. 1896. II. 453.²
— Euphorbiaceae. 1896. II. 433.²
— Euphorbiaceae africanae. 1893. II. 434.²
— Euphorbiaceae somalenses. 1897. II. 434.²
— Az európai erdei fák eredetéről. 1886. I. 348.¹
— Ueber die Gliederung der Karpathenflora. 1897. I. 446. 1898. I. 447.
— Hippocastanaceae. 1896. II. 480.²
— Ueber einen interessanten ... Ahorn, A. nikoënse. 1892. II. 479.¹
— Lauraceae. 1891. II. 223.¹
— Monimiaceae. 1891. II. 221.²
— Monographie der Gattung Acer. 1885. II. 476.¹
— Moringaceae. 1891. II. 234.²
— Myrsinaceae. 1891. II. 692.²
— Myrsinaceae, subfam. Theophrastoideae. 1889. II. 691.²
— Ord. Euphorbiaceae. 1900. II. 434.¹
— Pittosporaceae. 1891. II. 247.¹
— Plantae Lehmannianae ... Euphorbiaceae. 1899. II. 434.²
— Plumbaginaceae. 1891. II. 696.¹
— Portulacaceae. 1889. II. 194.¹
— Primulaceae. 1889. II. 695.¹
— O roślinności karpackiej. 1897. I. 447.
— Salicaceae. 1889. II. 95.²
— Staphyleaceae. 1896. II. 473.¹
— Über Strophanthus. 1893. II. 732.¹
— Über die systematischen ... Verhältnisse der Gattung Acer. 1886. II. 476.²
— Ueber den Ursprung der europäischen Waldbäume. 1886. I. 348.¹
— Velloziaceae. 1888. II. 90.¹
— Velloziaceae africanae. 1893. II. 90.¹
— *See also* Müller, E. G. O. & Pax, Ferdinand.
Paxton, George. The Ash. 1896. II. 707.¹
— The Beech. 1896. II. 127.¹
— The Birch. 1896. II. 117.³ ·
— The Lime. 1896. II. 517.¹
Paxton, Joseph. On acclimatising greenhouse plants. 1848. III. 43.
— The Almug oder Algumbaum. 1848. IV. 519,¹ *522,*¹ *525.*
— The Almug or Algum tree of the ancients. 1848. IV. 519,¹ *522,*¹ *525.*
— On arranging and planting hardy ornamental trees and shrubs. 1839. III. 201.
— The Azalea. 1840. III. 654.²
— The Balm or Balsam of Gilead. 1849. III. 511.¹
— Bemerkungen über die Cultur etc. des Genus Isopogon. 1848. III. 383.²
— On the Bombax Ceiba. 1849. III. 589.¹
— Budding. 1846. III. 164.¹
— On the Camphire ... of the ancients. · 1849. III. 404.²
— On the cassia of the ancients. 1849. III. 404.¹
— Conifers and Taxads. 1847. III. 289.
— On the cultivation of ... Ixora. 1848. III. 745.¹
— On the cultivation of the Avocado. 1849. III. 407.¹
— On the cultivation of the Cherimoyer. 1848. III. 401.¹
— Cultivation ... of the genus Clerodendron. 1847. III. 696.¹
— On the cultivation of the Lee-chee. 1848. III. 539.¹
— On the cultivation of the Mangosteen. 1849. III. 609.
— On the cultivation of the Sapota. 1849. III. 666.²
— Ueber die Cultur des Cherimoyer. 1848. III. 401.
— Cultur des Genus Lagerstroemia. 1848. III. 629.¹
— Ueber die Cultur des Li-chi. 1848. III. 539.²
— Cultur des Mango. 1848. III. 524.¹
— Sur la culture ... des Clerodendrum. 1847. III. 696.¹
— Culture of Andromeda. 1834. III. 647.²
— Culture of Pomegranates. 1834. III. 630.¹
— Culture of the Akee tree. 1838. III. 539.¹
— Culture of the Arbutus or Strawberry tree. 1834. III. 647.²

— Culture of the Bengal Quince. 1849. III. 495.[1]
— Culture of the Carambola and Blimbing. 1849. III. 491.[2]
— Culture of the Durion. 1849. III. 589.[3]
— Culture of the genus Citrus. 1834. III. 497.[1]
— Culture of the genus Edwardsia. 1837. III. 487.[2]
— Culture of the genus Erica. 1834. III. 649.[2]
— Culture of the genus Gaultheria. 1834. III. 652.[1]
— Culture of the genus Lagerstroemia. 1848. III. 629.[2]
— Culture of the Jambosade. 1849. III. 635.[1]
— On the culture of the Mamey or Mammee Apple. 1849. III. 610.[1]
— Culture of the Mango. 1848. III. 524.[2]
— On the culture of the Mombin. 1849. III. 529.[2]
— Culture of the Rabbit-berry. 1838. III. 629.[1]
— On the culture of the Ramontchi. 1849. III. 614.[1]
— Culture of the Wampee tree. 1849. III. 503.[1]
— Culture of the West Indian Honey-berries. 1849. III. 539.[2]
— On the culture of various species of Star-apple. 1849. III. 667.[1]
— Different methods of treating Passion flowers. 1846. III. 615.[1]
— Dwarf evergreens. 1841. III. 205.[2]
— A few remarks on . . . Ericea. 1836. III. 646.[2]
— A few remarks on the propagation of Cunninghamia. 1836. III. 293.
— The frankincense of the ancients. 1848. III. 227.
— The Fuchsia as a standard. 1847. III. 639.[2]
— Gaines' seedling Corraeas. 1846. III. 503.[1]
— General treatment of the genus Pinus. 1840. III. 306.[2]
— The genus Glycosmis. 1848. III. 504.[2]
— Of the genus Thunbergia. 1837. III. 710.[1]
— Gopher wood of the ancients. 1849. III. 630,[1] IV. 448.[1]
— On grafting Cacti. 1838. III. 618.[3]
— On grafting Leschenaultias. 1846. III. 754.[1]
— On grouping ornamental plants. 1842. III. 201.
— On growing climbers. 1844. III. 172.
— Growing the Lanseh and Caraunda as table-fruit. 1849. III. 512,[2] 637.[1]
— Hints for promoting the fertility of climbers. 1846. III. 204.[1]
— Hints on the genus Thibaudia. 1838. III. 663.[1]
— Improvements in grafting Cacti. 1843. III. 618.[2]
— Die Jasmine. 1848. III. 710.[2]
— On the Jujube as a fruit tree. 1849. III. 544.[1]
— Ketmie de Caméron, Hibiscus Cameronii. 1849. III. 522.[2]
— Kultur der Carambola und des Blimbing. 1849. III. 491.[2]
— Ueber die Kultur . . . der Gattung Ixora. 1848. III. 745.[1]
— Ueber die Kultur der Mangostin. 1849. III. 609.[3]
— Kultur der westindischen Honigbeeren. 1849. III. 539.[1]
— Kultur des Wampee-Baumes. 1849. III. 503.[1]
— Ueber die Kultur des Mammey- oder Mammee-Apfels. 1849. III. 610.[1]
— Ueber die Kultur des Ramontschi. 1849. III. 614.[1]
— The Lign Aloes, Lignum Aloes. 1849. III. 626.[2]
— The Lote or Lotos of the ancients. 1849. II. 500,[2] 701.[1]
— Der Loto oder Lotos der Alten. 1849. II. 500,[2] 701.[2]
— Mahogany. 1838. IV. 525.[2]
— Management of a few species of Bignonia. 1842. III. 201.
— On Manettia bicolor and cordifolia. 1846. III. 746.[1]
— The Mustard tree. 1848. II. 473.[1]
— Les Myrtes. 1849. III. 637.[1]
— The Myrtle. 1849. III. 637.[1]
— Natural mode of training climbers. 1844. III. 204.[2]
— Notice sur la culture de . . . Ixora. 1848. III. 745.[1]
— Observations on the culture etc. of the genus Isopogon. 1848. III. 383.[2]
— The Oleander. 1846. III. 689.[2]
— Sur les Passiflores à cultiver. 1847. III. 615.[1]
— On planting isolated trees. 1841. III. 201.
— On planting showy shrubs in masses. 1844. III. 201.
— On planting shrubs in beds. 1842. III. 201.
— A pocket botanical dictionary. 1840. I. 34.
— Pruning and training. 1847. III. 170.
— On pruning . . . plants to form standards. 1844. III. 204.[1]
— The Purple Beech tree. 1838. III. 360.[3]
— Remarks on a few select flowering shrubs. 1849. III. 207.[1]
— Remarks on arboretums. 1841. I. 38.[1]
— Remarks on the Astrapaea. 1837. III. 591.[1]
— Remarks on the culture of . . . shrubs. 1836. III. 123.[1]

— On removing and supporting detached trees. 1834. III. 165.
— Schlingpflanzen . . . als buschige und zwerzige zu ziehen. 1844. III. 172.
— Seedling Fuchsias. 1844. III. 639.[2]
— Selection of stove climbers. 1836. III. 204.[2]
— Shrubs fitted for planting in beds. 1842. III. 201.
— A singular fact connected with an Oak tree. 1838. I. 188.
— Standard Portugal Laurels. 1841. III. 204.[1]
— Standish's seedling Fuchsias. 1844. III. 639.[2]
— The Sweet Calamus. 1849. III. 321.[1]
— Les Tabernaemontana. 1854. II. 732.[2]
— Thunbergie à fleurs orangées. Thunbergia aurantiaca. 1839. II. 804.[2]
— On training Honeysuckles. 1843. III. 749.[2]
— On the treatment of Hovea Celsii. 1843. III. 478.[1]
— Treatment of Leycesteria formosa. 1841. III. 749.[2]
— Treatment of Tecoma grandiflora. 1841. III. 705.
— Twéedie à fleurs bleu de ciel. 1839. II. 741.[1]
— Der Weihrauch der Alten. 1848. III. 227.
— Die Wistaria sinensis. 1844. III. 490.[1]
— The Wistaria sinensis. 1844. III. 490.[1]
— See also LINDLEY, John & PAXTON, Joseph.
Paxton's flower garden. I. 19.
Paxton's magazine of botany. I. 19, III. 17.
Payen, Anselme. Amidon des fruits verts. 1861. I. 179.[1]
— Amidon et cellulose. 1859. I. 175.
— Analyse de la partie corticale de la racine du Vernis du Japon. 1824. II. 413.[2]
— Le cacao et le chocolat. 1859. III. 594.
— Le Café, sa culture. 1859. III. 739.
— Sur les caractères distinctifs entre le bois de Chêne et le bois de Châtaignier. 1856. II. 124,[1] 131,[2] 137.[1]
— Sur le carbonate de chaux . . . dans les plantes. 1854. I. 152.[2]
— Sur une collection de mémoires sur les developpements des végétaux. 1844. I. 525.
— Complément d'un mémoire sur la composition chimique du tissu. 1840. I. 152.[2]
— Composition . . . de deux espèces de gousses. 1866. III. 475,[2] 477.[2] .
— Composition de l'enveloppe des plantes. 1859. I. 155.
— Composition élémentaire de l'amidou. 1836. I. 139.
— Composition et produits du Manioc. 1857. III. 521.[1]
— Conservation des bois. 1861. IV. 418.
— Développement des végétaux. 1871. I. 151.[1]
— Dextrine et glucose. 1861. I. 175.
— Différents états de la cellulose. 1859. I. 138.[1]
— Documents à l'appui des recherches sur la composition des végétaux. 1846. I. 152.[1]
— Sur l'état actuel des cultures de la Vigne. 1855. III. 576.
— Extrait d'un mémoire sur la gutta-percha. 1852. III. 230.
— Extrait d'un mémoire sur les ligneux. 1839. I. 155.
— Kaffe og dens Bestanddele. 1846. III. 740.[1]
— Leçons sur la conservation des bois. 1861. IV. 418.
— Maladies des plantes cultivées. 1853. III. 575.[1]
— Mémoire sur l'amidon. 1838. I. 139.
— Mémoire sur l'amidon, la dextrine. 1843. I. 175.
— Mémoire sur la composition chimique de tous les organes des végétaux. 1837. I. 152.[1]
— Mémoire sur la composition chimique des racines. 1835. III. 186.[1]
— Mémoire sur la composition chimique des végétaux. 1842. I. 152.[2]
— Mémoire sur la composition du tissu. 1838. I. 155.
— Mémoire sur la conservation des bois. 1861. IV. 418.
— Mémoire sur le Café. 1846. III. 740.[1]
— Mémoire sur le caoutchouc et la guttapercha. 1852. III. 230.
— Mémoire sur les applications . . . des propriétés du tissu. 1839. I. 150.[1]
— Mémoire sur les développements des végétaux; états différents d'aggrégation du tissu des plantes. 1842. I. 123,[2] 150,[1] 152.[2]
— Note sur des composés à bases minérales. 1842. I. 152.[2]
— Note sur la composition immédiate de l'épiderme. 1856. I. 153.
— Note sur le bois d'une roue. 1864. IV. 425.[2]
— Nouveaux faits relatifs aux développement des plantes. 1841. I. 150.[1]
— Observations sur les tissus végétaux. 1859. I. 175.

Payen, Anselme (*continued*).
— De la potasse et de la soude. 1869. I. 159.
— Précis . . . des substances alimentaires. 1865. III. 308.[2]
— Propriétés distinctives entre les membranes végétales et les enveloppes des insectes. 1843. I. 151.[1]
— Rapport . . . relative à la fibrilia. 1861. III. 234.
— Rapport sur les moyens . . . pour distinguer les fibres textiles. 1849. III. 233.[2]
— Rapport sur les travaux de M. Hardy. 1844. III. 130.[1]
— Recherches sur la matière incrustante des bois. 1839. I. 155.
— Recherches sur le Café. 1846. III. 740.[1]
— Relevé des plantes qui ont résisté à la gelée. 1860. III. 48.
— Structure et constitution des fibres ligneuses. 1867. III. 234.
— Sucres extraits du lait de la noix de Coco. 1839. III. 323.[1]
— Sucs acides, neutres et alcalins. 1848. I. 180.[1]
— Suite des observations sur les tissus végétaux. 1859. I. 151.[1]
— Le thé, son rôle hygiénique. 1860. III. 607.
— Tissu ou trame de cellulose. 1868. III. 621.[2]
— *See also* BERLÈSE, Laurent & PAYEN, Anselme; MIRBEL, C. F. B. de & PAYEN, Anselme.
— & Chevalier, A. Note sur la matière colorante des fruits du Bois de Sainte-Lucie. 1822. III. 438.[2]
— & Richard, Achille. Précis d'agriculture. 1851. III. 113.
Payen, Édouard. Le caoutchouc et la gutta-percha. 1897. III. 232.[1]
Payen, J. F. *See* DEROSNE, Bernard, HENRY, Ossian & PAYEN, J. F.
Payens. Sucres extraits du lait de la noix de Coco. 1839. III. 624.[2]
Payer, Jean Baptiste. Addition au mémoire touchant l'action de la lumière sur les végétaux. 1844. I. 194.
— Des classifications et des méthodes en histoire naturelle. 1844. I. 252.
— Considérations générales sur la nature . . . des diverses parties qui constituent le pistil. 1854. I. 117.[2]
— Éléments de botanique. 1857. I. 90.
— Essai sur la nervation des feuilles. 1840. I. 109.[3]
— Études . . . sur les inflorescences dites anomales. 1842. I. 113.[1]
— Famille des Ficoïdes. 1851. II. 193,[3] 583.[1]
— De la famille des Malvacées. 1852. II. 519.[1]
— Famille des Nitrariées. 1851. II. 145.[2]
— Familles des Cucurbitacées. 1853. II. 583,[1] 872.[2]
— Familles des Hypéricinées. 1853. II. 552.[2]
— Familles des Polygonées. 1853. II. 547.[2]
— Importance de l'organogénie. 1859. I. 99.
— Leçons sur les familles naturelles des plantes. 1860. I. 256.
— Mémoire sur la tendance des racines à fuir la lumière. 1843. I. 194.
— Mémoire sur la tendance des racines à s'enfoncer dans la terre. 1844. I. 195.[2]
— Mémoire sur la tendance des tiges vers la lumière. 1842. I. 194.
— Observations sur les fleurs males du Bouleau. 1858. II. 118.[1]
— Organogénie de la classe des Cactoidées. 1852. II. 201,[2] 588,[1] 872.[2]
— Organogénie de la classe des Polygalinées. 1851. II. 429.[1]
— Organogénie de la famille des Capparidées. 1852. II. 29.[1]
— Organogénie de la famille des Myrtacées. 1853. II. 619.[2]
— Organogénie des familles des Berbéridées. 1852. II. 201.[2]
— Organogénie des familles des Myrtacées. 1853. II. 287,[2] 619.[2]
— Organogénie des familles des Orchidées. 1854. II. 90.[2]
— Organogénie des familles des Tamariscinées. 1851. II. 561,[2] 563.[2]
— Organogénie des Limnanthées. 1853. I. 116.[1]
— Organogénie des Punicées. 1852. II. 610.[2]
— Organogénie des Tiliacées. 1852. II. 512,[1] 519.[2]
— Rapport . . . sur un mémoire de M. Baillon intitulé : Recherches organogéniques. 1860. II. 19.
— Remarques à l'occasion du mémoire de M. Frémy (Recherches chimiques). 1859. I. 153.
— Traité d'organogénie végétale comparée de la fleur. 1857. I. 114.[1]
— Sur les trois genres Pelletiera, Meliosma et Batis. 1858. II. 114,[2] 490.[2]

Payo Vicente, Celedonio Rojo. Arte de cultivar el Olivo. 1840. III. 675.[1]
Payot, Venance. Florule du Mont-Blanc. 1882. I. 437.
— Roses de la vallée de Chamonix. 1895. II. 287.[1]
— Sur une transformation du Rosa alpina. 1883. II. 297.[1]
Payr, Heinrich von. Früchte von Syringa vulgaris. 1856. II. 716.[1]
Payrau, Vincent. Recherches sur les Strophanthus. 1900. III. 690.[2]
Pays de la couronne de Hongrie. Catalogue special " Forêts." 1900. IV. 21.[2]
Paysan des Landes, (*pseud.*). Vérités sur les Landes de la Gascogne. 1841. IV. 359.[2]
Peach and Nectarine on the same branch. 1877. III. 440.[1]
Peaches. 1885. III. 440.[1]
Peaches and nectarines on the same tree. 1874. II. 276.[1]
Peaches and plums; their cultivation. 1885. III. 430.[2]
Peacock, George. Fibre from the Malva Lavatera arborea. 1874. III. 588.[3]
Peacock, R. W. Our western lands. 1900. III. 224.[1]
— Some edible trees and shrubs of the West Bogan. 1900. III. 224.[1]
Peal, S. E. Bamboo forking. 1886. II. 59.[1]
— Bamboo spathes. 1882. II. 59.[1]
— Growth of Bombax malabaricum. 1884. II. 529.[2]
— Maiphak as a substitute for Teak. 1884. II. 407,[1] IV. 524.[2]
— The recent nature of mixed forest in Assam. 1883. IV. 378.
— The Tea-bug of Assam. 1874. III. 604.[2]
— Timbers for Tea boxes. 1884. IV. 538.[2]
Pear blossoms. 1878. III. 445.[1] — 1880. II. 279.[1]
Pear insects. 1850. III. 445.[3]
About Pear-trees. *See* ABOUT Pear-trees. 1856. III. 447.[1]
Pearce, George M. Notes on the forests of British Guiana. 1882. IV. 342.[1]
Pearless, *Mrs. See* PRATT, Anne.
Pears and Junipers. 1885. III. 422.[2]
Pearson, A. W. Grafting. 1892. III. 163.[1]
Pearson, George. Observations . . . on a wax-like substance. 1794. III. 225.
Pearson, George Falconer. Forest management. Natural and artificial causes. 1882. IV. 244.
— Forestry. 1882. IV. 102.
— Forestry in France. 1882. IV. 249.[1]
— On the possibility of adopting the cubic foot . . . as the unit of measurement in the case of Bamboos. 1880. IV. 485.[1]
— The recent attack on the French forest service. 1885. IV. 292.
— Report on forest management in France. 1873. IV. 122.[1]
— Report on the Deodar forests at the head of the Jumna. 1869. IV. 448.[1]
— Report on the Deodar forests of Jaunsar-Bawar. 1869. IV. 448.[1]
— Report on the forests of Kumaon. 1869. IV. 377.[2]
— Teaching of forestry. 1882. IV. 29.
Pearson, H. H. W. Anatomy of the seedling of Bowenia. 1898. II. 3.[1]
— The botany of the Ceylon Patanas. 1899. I. 477.[1]
Pearson, Henry Clemens. Crude rubber. 1899. III. 232.[1]
Pearson, John. Canker in fruit trees. 1857. III. 193.[1]
— On the varieties of the common Oak. 1864. III. 362.[2]
Pearson, Richard. A practical synopsis of the materia alimentaria. 1808. III. 242.
Pease, F. E. Shrubs. 1898. III. 118.[1]
Peaslee, John Bradley. Arbor-day and tree planting. 1886. IV. 41.[2]
— Arbor-day celebrations. 1884. IV. 41.[2]
— Trees and tree-planting. 1884. IV. 41[1]; *see also* HOUGH, F. B. & PEASLEE, J. B. 1885. IV. 41.[2]
— *See also* HOUGH, F. B. & PEASLEE, J. B.
Péch, Dezső. Külföldi facsemeték termelése a Görgényszentimrei m. kir. erdőőri szakiskolánál. 1900. IV. 151.[2]
— A nemes Fűsek leirása, azok tenyésztése és a kosárfonóipar fejlesztése. 1892. III. 349.
— A Szabédi kosérleti telep. 1899. IV. 39.[1]
Pech, F. Catalogue of the United States plants. 1867. V. XVI.[1]
Pech, R. Die frühere Harzgewinnung in Thüringen. 1897. IV. 437.[1]
Pechey, John. The compleat herbal of physical plants. 1694. I. 288, III. 54.
Pechlin, Johann Nicolaus. Theophilus bibaculus. 1684. III. 605.

Pécholier, G. Recherches expérimentales sur le traitement de la fièvre typhoïde par la créosote. 1869. IV. 433.²
— **& Saintpierre,** C. Expériences sur les propriétés toxiques du boundou. 1866. III. 684.¹
Pechtold, F. Zur forstlichen Bedeutung des Tannenhehers. 1879. IV. 463.²
Pechuël-Loesche, Eduard. Die Vegetation am Kongo. 1886. I. 492.¹
— *See also* GÜSSFELDT, Paul, FALKENSTEIN, Julius & PECHUËL-LOESCHE, Eduard.
Pecirka, I. Die Giftgewächse des österreichischen Kaiser-thums. 1859. III. 90.²
Peck, Charles Horton. The Black Spruce. 1876. II. 38,¹ IV. 460.²
— Opuntia Rafinesquii Engelm. 1871. II. 597.¹
— Plants of North Elba, Essex county. 1899. I. 316.
— Plants of the summit of Mt. Marcy. 1880. I. 314.— 1899. I. 316.
— The Spruces of the Adirondacks. 1897. II. 34.¹
Peck, Ellen Brainerd. The founder of Arbor-day. 1900. IV. 42.¹
Peck, F. Die Flora der Umgegend von Schweidnitz. 1871. I. 386.
Peck, William Dandridge. A catalogue of American and for-eign plants . . . in the Botanic garden, Cambridge, Massa-chusetts. 1818. I. 38.²
Peckinpah, L. A. R. Bolander's Bladder Nut in Madera county. 1898. II. 473.²
Peckolt, Gustav. *See* PECKOLT, Theodor & Gustav.
Peckolt, Theodor. Analyses de materia medica brasileira. 1868. III. 65.¹
— Die brasilianischen Nutz-und Heilpflanzen. 1891. III. 65.²
— Carica Papaya and papayotin. 1879. III. 617.²
— Sur le Carica Papaya et la papayotine. 1879. III. 617.²
— Carica Papaya Linné und Papayotinum. 1879. III. 617.²
— Catalog der pharmacognostischen . . . Sammlung aus der brasilianischen Flora. 1868. III. 27.²
— On the culture of Bixa Orellana. 1868. III. 610.¹
— Cynco Folhas und Sparattospermlnum. 1878. III. 707.²
— Guaraná oder Uaraná. 1867. III. 539.²
— Heil- und Nutzpflanzen Brasiliens. Bombacaceae. 1900. III. 589.¹
— Heil- und Nutzpflanzen Brasiliens. Gentianaceae. 1899. III. 685.²
— Heil- und Nutzpflanzen Brasiliens. Malvaceae. 1900. III. 586.¹
— Heil- und Nutzpflanzen Brasiliens. Rutaceae. 1899. III. 495.¹
— Heil- und Nutzpflanzen Brasiliens. Sterculiaceae. 1900. III. 589.²
— Heil- und Nutzpflanzen Brasiliens. Tiliaceae. 1898. III. 584.²
— Heil- und Nutzpflanzen Brasiliens . . . Anacardiaceae. 1898. III. 523.²
— Heil- und Nutzpflanzen Brasiliens aus . . . Simarubaceae und Burseraceae. 1898. III. 506,² 509.²
— Heil- und Nutzpflanzen Brasiliens . . . der Anonaceae. 1897. III. 401.¹
— Heilpflanzen Brasiliens aus der Familie der Violaceae. 1897. III. 613.²
— Historia das plantas alimentares . . . do Brasil. 1871. III. 65.¹
— L'Ipé-tabaco. 1874. III. 707.²
— Maté, or Paraguay Tea. 1882. III. 531.¹
— Maté, Paraguay-Thee. 1882. III. 531.¹
— Monesia and its congeners. 1888. II. 698.²
— Monographia do Café. 1884. III. 740.¹
— Monographia do Milho e da Mandioca. 1878. III. 520.²
— Myroxylon peruiferum. 1881. III. 482.²
— Plantas adstringentes brasileiras. 1881. III. 65.¹
— Sicopira, Bowdichia major Mart. 1877. III. 467.²
— La Sparattospermine. 1878. III. 707.²
— Volksbenennungen der brasilianischen Pflanzen. 1898. I. 73.¹
— & Gustav: Historia das plantas medicinaes e uteis do Brasil. 1888. III. 65.²
Pecktold, Anton. Das Territorium von Igels. 1846. I. 460.
Pecori, Raffaello. La culture dell' Olivo in Italia. 1891. III. 676.¹
Pecquet. Loix forestières de France. 1753. IV. 323.²
Pector, D. La question du Café du Nicaragua. 1900. III. 728.²
Pedersen, Chr. Araucaria imbricata. 1877. III. 299.¹

— Beplantning af Jærnbaneskraaninger og Pileplantning. 1893. III. 349.
— Kortfattet Anvisning til Plantning og Røgt af Frugttræer. 1880. III. 134.²
— Nogle Bemærkninger om . . . Rubus-Arter. 1895. III. 457.²
— Om Vurdering af Frugttræer. 1878. III. 200.¹
Pedersen, G. Beiträge zur Kenntniss der Aloe. 1898. III. 333.²
— Contribution à l'étude de l'Aloès. 1898. III. 333.²
Pedersen, P. Vaarens Komme. 1854. I. 223.¹
Pedersen, Rasmus. Berberisbusken. 1877. III. 394.¹
— Sur le développement du cyathium de l'Euphorbe. 1873. II. 442.¹
— Haben Temperaturschwankungen . . . einen ungünstigen Einfluss auf das Wachsthum? 1874. I. 232.¹
— Hvilken Rolle spiller Væxtspidsens Kløvning ved Forgre-ningen. 1873. I. 106.²
— Koppens Udvikling hos Vortemaelken. 1873. II. 442.¹
— Quel rôle joue la partition du cône végétatif dans la rami-fication. 1873. I. 106.²
Pedicino, N. A. Studii sulla struttura . . . di alcuni fusti. 1876. I. 105.
Pée-Laby, E. Sur quelques éléments de soutien de la feuille. 1891. I. 111.
— Recherches sur l'anatomie comparée des cotylédons et des feuilles des cotylédonées. 1892. I. 111.
Peebles, Andrew. On the present state and prospects of arboriculture in Hampshire. 1878. IV. 358.¹
— Report on the woods and plantations of Highclere. 1872. IV. 358.¹
Peek, W. H. An exploration of the Pilot Range. 1886. IV. 339. — 1887. I. 315.
Peelen, H. J. E. Eenige opmerkingen omtrent de Koffieblad-ziekte. 1888. III. 736.
Peglion, Vittorio. Diagnosi di funghi parassiti nuovi. 1894. III. 195.¹
— La distruzione degli insetti noci. 1892. III. 197.¹
— Le malattie crittogamiche. 1899. III. 195.²
— Osservazioni critiche . . . sopra l' efficacia dei compósti cuprici. 1894. III. 446.²
— Sulla preparazione di concimi per gli Olivi. 1898. III. 676.²
— Ricerche anatomiche sopra i tumori . . . di Pero. 1893. III. 446.²
— Il seccume del Cotogno. 1893. III. 423.²
— Il seccume del Frassino. 1893. IV. 535.²
— La ticchiolatura del Pero. 1892. III. 446.³—1899. III. 446.²
— Sopra i trattamenti antiperonosporici. 1896. III. 581.
— I zoocecidii della flora avellinese. 1894. I. 215.²
Pehersdorfer, Anna. Beitrag zur Rosenflora im Gebiete des Mittallaufes der Enns. 1897. II. 283.²
— Botanische Terminologie. 1897. I. 71.
Peicker, C. R. Anleitung zum Baumsatz. 1872. III. 138.
Peicker, G. Wenig bekannte und seltene . . . immergrüne Laubhölzer. 1900. III. 206.¹
Peignon. Nouveau système de cloture économique. 1891. IV. 146.²
Peikert, G. Zur Kultur der Schwarzkiefer. 1884. IV. 465.²
Peine, Elias. Der Bosensche Garten. 1690. I. 43.
— Hortus Bosianus. 1690. I. 43.
— Vocabularium hortulanorum usui dicatum. 1713. III. 29.¹
Peinemann, Karl. Beiträge zur pharmazeutischen . . . Kennt-nis der Cubeben. 1896. III. 342.¹
Peintner, Rigsbaron Carl v. Hügels Plantesamling. 1841. I. 66.¹
Peirce, B. Mathematical investigation of the fractions .. in phyllotaxis. 1850. I. 102.
Peirce, George James. Variation in leaf arrangement in a Maple. 1897. II. 477.¹
Peitzer, Ernst. Der botanische Garten der Universität Heidelberg. 1880. I. 48.
Peixoto, R. dos G. Dissertation inaugurale sur les médicamens brésiliens. 1830. III. 269.¹
Peixoto, Benjamin F. Report . . . on the ravages of the phyl-loxera in France. 1882. III. 761.
Pejoux, C. Le balivage des taillis sous futaie. 1891. IV. 237.
Pekarek. Zur Lebensweise . . . des schwarzen Fichtenbast-käfers. 1887. IV. 456.
Pélagand, E. L'Eucalyptus, sa culture forestière. 1880. IV. 530.

Pelagus. Om Pile og andre bløde Træers. 1757. III. 343.³
Pelée de Saint-Maurice. L'art de cultiver les Peupliers d'Italie. 1762. III. 346.¹
— Die Kunst italienische Pappelbäume aufzuziehen. 1762. III. 346.¹
The **Pelican** flower. 1890. II. 182.²
Peligot, Eugène Melchior. De l'action que l'acide borique et les borates exercent. 1876. I. 180.¹
— De l'action que l'acide borique et les borates exercent. 1877. I. 159.
— Études chimiques . . . sur les vers à soie. 1851. III. 379.³
— Note sur le sulfure de carbone. 1884. III. 573.
— Observations sur une note de M. Cloëz, relative à la composition du salin. 1869. I. 175.
— Sur un procédé propre à déterminer . . . la quantité d'azote. 1847. I. 156.²
— Recherches sur la composition chimique du thé. 1843. III. 606.
— Sur la répartition de la potasse. 1867. I. 153.
Pélikan, Eugène. Notice sur les propriétés physiologo-toxicologiques du curare. 1857. III. 682.¹
— Sur un nouveau poison . . . l'Inée ou Onage. 1865. III. 690.³
— Nouvelles recherches sur le poison du Nerium. 1866. III. 689.¹
— *See also* DYBKOWSKY, W. & PELIKAN, Eugène; KÖLLIKER, A. & PÉLIKAN, Eugène.
Pell, Robert L. On the culture of the Apple. 1844. III. 426.¹
— Forest trees of America and their uses. 1853. III. 60.
Pellegrini, F. *See* ROSSE, H. & PELLEGRINI, F.
Peller, Joseph. De chocolata. 1835. III. 594.
Pellerin. Réflexions sur la phyllotaxie. 1899. I. 103.
Pellerin, F. A. Analyse des bourgeons du Peuplier noir. 1822. III. 346.²
Pellet, H. Études nouvelles sur la composition des végétaux. 1879. I. 153.
— De l'existence de l'ammoniaque dans les végétaux. 1880. I. 153.
Pelletan, Gabriel. *See* CHEVALLIER, Alphonse & PELLETAN, Gabriel.
Pelletan, J. Le microscope. 1876. I. 36.²
Pelletier, Auguste. *See* PELLETIER, Eugène & Auguste.
Pelletier, Eugène & Auguste. Le thé et le chocolat. 1861. III. 594, 607.
Pelletier, J. J. Sur la résine de Gayac. 1841. III. 494.²
— & **Deville,** H. Mémoire sur la résine de Gayac. 1844. III. 494.²
Pelletier, Ludovic. Les premiers pas dans l'arboriculture. 1886. III. 110.²
Pelletier, Pierre Joseph. Essai sur la nature des substances connues sous le nom de gommes résines. 1812. I. 180.²
— Essai sur le rôle que les terres jouent. 1838. I. 228.¹
— Mémoire sur la gomme d'Olivier. 1816. III. 678.³
— *See also* FRANÇOIS, CAVENTOU, J. B. & PELLETIER, Joseph.
— & **Caventou,** J. B. Sur l'analyse de la fève de Saint-Ignace. 1818. III. 682.³
—— Analyse des quinquina. 1821. III. 722.
—— Essai analytique . . . du Médicinier cathartique. 1818. III. 519.³
—— Essai chimique sur le quinquina de Sainte-Lucie. 1821. III. 744.¹
—— Examen chimique de l'écorce . . . kina-nova. 1821. III. 722.
—— Examen chimique du Quinquina Carthagène. 1821. III. 743.²
—— M m é oire sur un nouvel alcali végétal. 1819. III. 682.³
—— Notes pour faire suite aux mémoires sur les quinquinas. 1821. III. 722.
—— Notes sur la composition chimique des écorces de Saule et de Marronier d'Inde. 1821. III. 351,² 587.²
—— Notice sur la matière verte des feuilles. 1817. I. 140.²
—— Recherches chimiques sur les quinquinas. 1820. III. 722.
Pelletier de Frépillon. Essai sur la taille des arbres fruitiers. 1773. III. 171.¹
Pelletier-Sautelet. Description et figure du Patchouly. 1843. II. 765.¹
La pelletierina, alcaloide . . . del Granado. 1878. III. 630.²
Pelouze, T. Jules. Fester und flüssiger Borneo-Champhor. 1841. III. 611.¹
— Mémoire sur la saponification des huiles. 1855. I. 182.¹

— Memoire sur la sorbine. 1852. II. 312.¹
— Note sur la celluloze. 1859. I. 138.¹
— Sur une nouvelle matière sucrée extraite . . . de Sorbier. 1852. II. 312.¹
— & **Bernard,** Claude. Recherches sur le curare. 1850. III. 682.²
— & **Boudet,** Félix. Recherches sur les corps gras. 1838. II. 63.²
Peltzer. Bemerkungen über Cacteen-Kultur. 1843. III. 618.²
Peluffo, Vicente. *See* MAUDUIT, Fernando & PELUFFO, Vicente.
Pena, Pierre & **Lobel,** Mathias de. Dilucidae simplicium medicamentorum explicationes. 1570. I. 281.
—— Nova stirpium adversaria. 1570. I. 281.
—— Stirpium adversaria nova perfacilis vestigatio. 1570. I. 281.
Penang — Forest department. *See* STRAITS SETTLEMENTS — FOREST DEPARTMENT. IV. 16.²
Pencati, Giuseppe, *conte* MARZARI-. *See* MARZARI-PENCATI, Giuseppe, *conte*.
Pendulous trees. 1900. III. 204.²
Péneau, T. Études chimiques sur la Vigne. 1877. III. 583.¹
Penetrazione dell' acqua a grandi profondità. 1866. IV. 412.¹
Penevert, Louis Hubert, (*sr.*). Instruction sur l'exploitation des bois de Chêne. 1828. IV. 512.
Penfold, Jane Wallas. Madeira flowers, fruits, and ferns. 1845. I. 497.
— A selection of Madeira flowers, fruits and ferns. 1845. I. 497.
Penford, C. Berberis Darwini. 1878. III. 394.²
Pengelly, Alfred. The French imperial school of forestry. 1870. IV. 34.²
— The means of obtaining length of stem for timber. 1876. IV. 171.
Penhallow, David Pearce. Botanic gardens. 1885. I. 38.²
— The Cercidiphyllum. 1879. III. 388.²
— Distribution of the reserve material of plants in relation to disease. 1885. I. 179.³
— On the establishment of a botanic garden . . . in Montreal. 1885. I. 38.³
— Fertilization of Kalmia. 1882. II. 672.¹
— The food of plants. 1889. I. 159.
— The generic characters of the North American Taxaceae and Coniferae. 1896. II. 17.¹
— Hardy trees. 1888. III. 60.
— Mechanism of movement in Cucurbita. 1886. I. 194.
— Normal condition . . . and Peach yellows. 1883. III. 441.²
— Note on a peculiar growth in Black Walnut. 1891. I. 207,¹ *III. 564.²*
— Notes on Shepherdia canadensis. 1889. III. 629.²
— Notes on the flora of Cacouna. 1891. I. 310.
— Notes on the flora of St. Helen's Island. 1891. I. 310.
— Notes on the trees and shrubs of northern Japan. 1884. I. 461.
— Observations upon some structural variations in certain Canadian Coniferae. 1895. II. 16.²
— Peach yellows. 1883. III. 441.²
— Phenomena of growth in plants. 1882. I. 194.
— The relation of annual rings of exogens to age. 1885. I. 128.¹
— The relation of climate to vegetation. 1889. I. 218.
— A review of Canadian botany from 1800. 1897. I. 80.¹
— A review of Canadian botany from the first settlement. 1888. I. 80.¹
— Rhus poisoning. 1895. III. 528.¹
— Snowberry jelly. 1888. III. 649.¹
— Temperature of trees. 1883. I. 186.
— Teratological notes. 1896. II. 290,¹ *643.²*
— Variation of water in trees. 1887. I. 149.¹
— Yellows in Peach trees. 1882. III. 441.²
— & **Stone,** W. E. Experiment orchard and Peach yellows. 1883? III. 441.¹
Penido, Miguel COLMEIRO Y. *See* COLMEIRO Y PENIDO, Miguel.
Penilleau, A. Étude sur le café. 1864. III. 742.¹
Peninsula horticultural society. Transactions. III. 7.
The **Penn** monthly magazine. III. 7.
Penn treaty Elm. 1892. III. 168.¹
Pennant, Thomas. Flora indica. 1800. I. 536.¹
— The view of the Malayan Isles. 1800. III. 274.¹
Pennetier, Georges. Le Café. 1878. III. 739.

Penninck, Charles. Les Gardenia. 1900. III. 744.[1]
Pennsylvania — Agricultural experiment station. *See* PENNSYLVANIA — STATE COLLEGE . . . III. 7.
Pennsylvania — Botanical society. *See* BOTANICAL . . . I. 5.
Pennsylvania — Commissioner of forestry. Preliminary report. Report. IV. 5.[1]
Pennsylvania — Department of agriculture. Annual report. *See* PENNSYLVANIA BOARD OF AGRICULTURE. III. 7.
Pennsylvania — Department of agriculture. Bulletin. III. 7.
Pennsylvania — Franklin institute. *See* FRANKLIN . . . III. 3.
Pennsylvania board of agriculture. Annual report. III. 7.
Pennsylvania college — Linnaean association. *See* LINNAEAN . . . I. 6.
Pennsylvania forestry association. Forest leaves. *See* FOREST . . . IV. 4.
Pennsylvania forestry association. Primer series. IV. 5.[1]
Pennsylvania fruit growers society. Report. III. 7.
Pennsylvania, State college — Agricultural experiment station. Annual report. Bulletin. III. 7.
Pennsylvania state horticultural society. Report. *See* PENNSYLVANIA FRUIT GROWERS SOCIETY. III. 7.
Pennsylvania, University of. Contributions from the botanical laboratory. *See* UNIVERSITY . . . I. 7.[1]
Penny, Frederick. On the valuation of indigo. 1853. III. 479.[1]
Penny cyclopaedia. 1833. I. 33.
Penny magazine. III. 18.
Penzal, (*Oberförster*). Zum zweihiebigen Hochwaldsystem. 1881. IV. 129.
Pentz, Carol. Joh. De Diosma. *See* THUNBERG, C. P. 1797. II. 405.[1]
Penzance, (*lord*). Modern Roses and hybridisation. 1889. III. 450.
— Rose conference. 1889. III. 450.
Penzig, Alberto Giulio Ottone. Anatomia e morfologia della Vite. 1881. II. 507.[1]
— Appunti sulla struttura simpodiale della Vite. 1883. II. 507.[2]
— La bizzarria. 1887. I. 246.[2]
— I cristalli del Rosanoff nelle Celastracee. 1880. II. 465.[2]
— Die Dornen von Arduina ferox. 1879. II. 724.[1]
— Ueber einige . . . Gärten der westlichen Riviera. 1883. I. 59.
— Flora popolare ligure. 1897. I. 74.[2]
— Florae ligusticae synopsis. 1897. I. 430.
— Il freddo del gennaio 1893. 1893. III. 49.[2]
— Funghi agrumicoli. 1882. III. 498.[1]
— Il giardino del Palazzo Orengo. 1883. I. 64.
— Il giardino Ricasoli. 1885. I. 64.
— Zu H. Dingler's Aufsatz Der Aufbau des Weinstockes. 1885. II. 507.[2]
— L 'Istituto botanico Hanbury. 1892. V. VIII.[2]
— Die Krankheit der Edelkastanien. 1906. III. 350.[2]
— Miscellanea teratologica. 1884. I. 144.[1]
— Il Monte Generoso. 1879. . I. 436.
— Note di biologia vegetale. 1894. II. 791,[1] 830.[2]
— Sopra una nuova pianta formicaria d' Africa. 1894. II. 791.[1]
— Sopra una nuova specie di Prosopis. 1898. II. 379.[1]
— Sopra un nuovo caso d' imitazione di polline. 1894. II. 830.[1]
— Un nuovo flagello degli Agrumi. 1883. III. 498.[2]
— O. Beccari's neuere Arbeitren über die myrmekophilen Pflanzen. 1886. I. 235.[1]
— Ueber die Perldrüsen des Weinstockes. 1893. I. 113.[1]
— Pflanzen-Teratologie. 1890. I. 144.[1]
— Piante nuove o rare trovate in Liguria. 1889. I. 429.
— Piante raccolte in un viaggio botanico fra i Bogos ed i Mensa. 1893. I. 489.
— I prodotti vegetali del mercato di Buitenzorg. 1898. III. 276.[1]
— Studi botanici sugli Agrumi. 1887. II. 397.[2]
— *See also* CAMUS, Giulio & PENZIG, Ottone.
Penzoldt, FRANTZ-. *See* FRANTZ-PENZOLDT.
Pepe, Marcello. Della coltivazione degli alberi da frutta in Italia. 1886. III. 145.[2]
Pepe, Raffaele. Dello stato e conservazione de' boschi della provincia di Molise. 1811. IV. 363.[2]
Pepe, Vincenzo & Cupido, Gaetano. Analisi del frutto del Platano orientale. 1837. III. 418.[2]
De **Peperkultuur**. 1876. III. 343.[1]
Pépin, Pierre Denis. Acacie, arbre de soie. 1841. III. 466.[1]
— Amandier glanduleux. 1845. III. 437.[1]

— Amandiers. 1846. III. 434.[1]
— Arbres exotiques . . . dans l'Anjou. 1863. I. 58.
— Arbres exotiques . . . de Nantes. 1863. I. 58.
— Sur des arbres obtenus de semis. 1860. III. 84.[1]
— Arbustes nouveaux propres à la décoration. 1864. III. 203.
— De l'avantage . . . de greffer le Glycine sinensis. 1841. III. 490,[1] 490.[2]
— Le Bambou noir. 1859. III. 316.[2]
— Sur les Bambous nigra et metake. 1869. III. 314.[1]
— Bentham fragifère ou Porte-fraise. 1845. III. 645.[2]
— Benthamia fragifera. 1845. III. 645.[2]
— Boutures de Ginkgo. 1861. III. 286.[2]
— Boutures de racines du Paulownia. 1845. III. 703.[1]
— Casse hybride, Cassia hybrida. 1845. III. 471.[1]
— Sur le Catalpa Bungei. 1856. III. 706.[1]
— Chalef brunâtre. 1844. III. 628.[1]
— Chamaerops excelsa. 1865. III. 331.[2]
— Sur le Chêne à feuilles glabres. 1859. III. 362.[1]
— Chèvre-feuille ou Chamécerisier de Tartarie. 1845. III. 751.[1]
— Sur le Chèvrefeuille semper des fleuristes. 1855. III. 750.[1]
— Chrysanthème frutescent à fleurs jaunes. 1845. III. 755.[1]
— Sur une collection d'arbres exotiques. 1861. I. 58.
— Sur des Cryptomeria japonica . . . de boutures. 1861. III. 302.[1]
— Cryptomeria japonica . . . de boutures. 1866. III. 302.[1]
— Culture . . . du Tecoma grandiflora. 1839. III. 705.
— Destruction d'arbres par la sécheresse. 1862. III. 183.[2]
— Deutzia gracilis Sieb. et Zucc. 1851. III. 410.[1]
— Développement . . . d'un Cereus speciosissimus. 1841. III. 621.[2]
— Dimensions extraordinaires d'un individu de Cereus speciosissimus. 1844. III. 621.[2]
— Sur le Diospyros calycina. 1850. III. 669.[1]
— Le Dragonnier parasol. 1859. III. 337.[1]
— Sur la durée des propriétes germinatives. 1855. I. 193.[1]
— Effets de la gelée sur quelques arbres pendant l'hiver 1854–55. 1856. III. 47.
— Encore un mot sur l'Épine-vinette. 1847. II. 205.[2]
— Sur l'Escallonia macrantha. 1859. III. 410.[2]
— De la faculté germinative . . . du Baobab. 1847. III. 589.[1]
— Fleur monstrueuse de Fuchsia. 1848. II. 643.[1]
— Fleuraison abondante du Crataegus glabra. 1847. III. 30.[1]
— Floraison du Cereus monstruosus. 1864. III. 621.[1]
— Floraison . . . du Styphnolobium. 1864. III. 488.[1]
— Om Fordelen . . . at pode Glycine sinensis. 1841. III. 490.[1]
— Fructification de l'Abies Pinsapo. 1860. III. 297.[1]
— Fructification du Dammara australis. 1863. III. 297.[2]
— Frustification du Pinus cembro. 1842. III. 307.[1]
— Sur la fructification du Robinier faux Acacia pyramidal. 1859. III. 486.[1]
— Fructification du Sequoia gigantea. 1865. III. 310.[1]
— Genista sibirica fl. pleno. 1853. III. 477.[1]
— Over den geschiksten tijd voor hets tekken van boomen en heesters. 1846. III. 158.
— Greffe digénère. 1851. I. 209.[1]
— Greffe du Cocoloba pubescens. 1846. III. 887.[1]
— De la greffe du Glycine sinensis. 1852. III. 490.[1]
— Greffes d'arbres sur des sujets appartenant à des genres différents. 1845. III. 164.[2]
— Halesia tetraptera rosea. 1845. III. 670.[2]
— Halésie à deux ailes. 1844. III. 670.[2] — 1845. III. 670.[2]
— Hedera Regnoriana. 1862. III. 642.[2]
— Le Hêtre tortueux. 1861. III. 360.[2]
— Hybrides des Abutilon striatum et venosum. 1849. III. 586.[2]
— De l'influence du sujet sur les greffes d'arbres fruitiers. 1848. III. 39.
— Sur l'instant des Lilas. 1861. III. 680.[2]
— Sur l'introduction en France des arbres verts résineux. 1860. III. 289.
— Sur l'introduction en France du Pinus Laricio. 1863. III. 307.[2]
— Sur le Juglans olivaeformis. 1869. III. 354.[1]
— Ligustrum ovalifolium. 1853. III. 674.[1]
— Lilas des monts Emodi. 1846. III. 680.[2]
— Malus floribunda. 1865. III. 429.[1]
— Mémoire sur des espèces d'arbres resineux . . . d'Harcourt. 1858. I. 58.

Pépin, Pierre Denis (*continued*).
— Mortalité des arbres . . . où des espèces malfaisants avaient vécu. 1845. III. 193.[1]
— Moyen facile de faire germer les graines du Cèdre. 1845. III. 300.[2]
— Moyens de convertir les plantes annuelles en plantes vivaces. 1836. I. 247.
— Multiplication des arbres de bouture. 1853. III. 158.
— Sur la multiplication . . . du Sequoia gigantea. 1861. III. 310.[1]
— Multiplication par greffe d'une variété d'Ajonc. 1850. III. 489.[2]
— Myrtus tenuifolia Smith. 1846. III. 637.[1]
— Nerium multiflorum phoeniceum. 1846. III. 689.[2]
— Note sur de nouvelles plantes. 1849. III. 615.[2]
— Note sur de nouvelles variétés d'arbres. 1849. III. 439.[1]
— Note sur des coléoptères qui attaquent . . . les jeunes rameaux. 1851. III. 189.
— Note sur des cônes de Cèdre du Liban. 1844. II. 28.[1]
— Note sur des fruits . . . de semis provenant du Ribes palmatum. 1847. III. 414.[1]
— Note sur des greffes faites sur des sujets appartenant à d'autres genres. 1844. III. 164.[2]
— Note sur des Groseilliers d'ornement. 1849. III. 413.[2]
— Note sur des Pins d'Europe. 1846. II. 39.[2] — 1847. III. 306.[2]
— Note sur des plantes nouvellement introduites. 1852. III. 87.
— Note sur des Ribes d'ornement. 1849. III. 413.[2]
— Note sur des variétés d'arbres. 1853. III. 392.[1]
— Note sur l'effet de la gelée survenue du 15 au 26 mai. 1839. III. 47.
— Note sur l'Erythrina crista-galli var. 1846. III. 476.[1]
— Note sur l'étêtage des arbres. 1860. III. 173.[1]
— Note sur l'Eutassa excelsa. 1854. III. 298.[1]
— Note sur la culture . . . de l'Urtica nivea. 184.? III. 382.[1]
— Note sur la culture . . . du Bignonia grandiflora. 1839. III. 705.
— Note sur la durée des fleurs d'Azalea lateritia. 1851. III. 659.[2]
— Note sur la fécondation d'un Salix babylonica. 1845. III. 351.[2]
— Note sur la maladie qui a sévi sur des Poiriers. 1847. III. 445.[2]
— Note sur la mortalité des arbres. 1845. III. 185.[1]
— Note sur la persistance au froid des greffes . . . de Prunus Lauro-Cerasus. 1843. III. 437.[2]
— Note sur la séve . . . du Virgilia lutea. 1847. II. 346.[2]
— Note sur le Chèvrefeuille semper. 1845. III. 750.[1]
— Note sur le Gaultheria procumbens. 1871. III. 652.[1]
— Note sur le gonflement ou bourrelet . . . à l'insertion de la greffe. 1853. I. 208.[1]
— Note sur le Gracillaria syringella. 1862. III. 680.[2]
— Note sur le Gymnocladus canadensis. 1858. III. 478.[1]
— Note sur le Juglans praeparturiens. 1840. III. 355.
— Note sur le Lonicera pallida Host. 1846. III. 750.[1]
— Note sur le moyen de reformer la tige des Cèdres. 1854. III. 299.[2]
— Note sur le Mûrier Lou. 1853. III. 376.
— Note sur le Nerprun purgatif. 1861. III. 497.[2]
— Note sur le Poirier du Mont Sinat. 1838. III. 447.[1]
— Note sur le Rhizoctonia Mali DC. 1851. III. 427.[1]
— Note sur le Robinia pseudo-acacia Uterhartii. 1845. III. 486.[2]
— Note sur le Sophora du Japon. 1844. III. 488.[1]
— Note sur le Sophora japonica. 1859. III. 488.[1]
— Note sur les arbres plantés dans la propriété de M. Féret. 1849. I. 58.
— Note sur les boutures de racines du Paulownia. 1845. III. 703.[1]
— Note sur les dards épineux des Poiriers. 18.? III. 445.[1]
— Note sur les dimensions extraordinaires . . . d'un pied de Cactus speciosissimus. 1843. III. 621.[2]
— Note sur les variétés d'Acacia. 1844. III. 322.[2]
— Note sur quelques arbres . . . introduits à Paris. 1853. I. 58.
— Note sur quelques nouveaux arbres à rameaux pendants. 1853. III. 204.[1]
— Note sur un empoisonnement de chèvres. 1845. III. 57.[1]
— Note sur un Prunus Lauro-cerasus chlorosé. 1853. III. 437.[1]
— Note sur un Rhus cotinus Linn. 1845. II. 455.[2]
— Note sur un semis de Fagus purpurea. 1853. III. 360.[2]
— Note sur un semis naturel de Pinus Strobus sur le Salix. 1863. I. 234.[2]
— Note sur une floraison particulière . . . de Paulownia. 1858. II. 781.[2]
— Notice sur des arbustes nouveaux . . . de M. Bertin. 1840. III. 473.[2]
— Notice sur la taille du Ribes sanguineum. 1839. III. 415.[2]
— Notice sur les effets de la gelée survenue du 15 au 26 mai. 1839. III. 47.
— Une nouvelle variété de Troëne. 1861. III. 674.[1]
— Noyer commun à feuilles variables. 1845. III. 355.
— Observations faites à Harcourt . . . sur les arbres qui ont souffert. 1861. III. 48.
— Observations sur la faculté . . . de conserver longtemps leur puissance végétative. 1841. I. 192.[2]
— Observations sur la susceptibilité à la gelée des racines de l'Orme. 1843. III. 365.[2]
— Das Pfropfen der Wistaria chinensis. 1852. III. 490.[1]
— Sur le Pinus muricata. 1868. III. 307.[2]
— Pinus sylvestris Bujotii. 1856. III. 309.[1]
— Plantes nouvelles . . . de M. Chauvière. 1846. III. 415.[1]
— Sur le premier Robinia importé en France. 1845. II. 383.[1]
— Prunus Cocomilia Tenore. 1843. III. 436.[2]
— Prunus Lauro-Cerasus chlorosé. 1853. III. 437.[1]
— Quillaya saponaria Molina. 1853. III. 447.[1]
— Rapport fait . . . sur la culture du Prunier d'Agen. 1864. III. 432.[2]
— Rapport fait . . . sur les services que M. de Montigny a rendus à l'agriculture. 1855. III. 125.
— Rapport . . . sur l'écorcement des Rosiers tiges. 1850. III. 452.
— Revue rétrospective sur les effets produits par les gelées . . . pendant l'hiver 1854–55. 1856. III. 48.
— Rhododendron dahuricum. 1860. III. 658.[2]
— Robinier pyram dal. 1845. III. 488.[2]
— Rusticité de plusieurs espèces d'arbres résineux. 1854. III. 291.
— Rusticité de quelques Cactées. 1855. III. 619.
— Salix japonica Thunb. 1846. III. 352.[1]
— Sambucus nigra L. var. heterophylla. 1842. III. 751.[2]
— Saule blanc. 1866. III. 351.[1]
— Second rapport sur les expériences de M. Eusèbe Gris sur les sels de fer. 1847. III. 181.[1]
— Un semis naturel de Pinus Strobus sur un Salix. 1861. I. 234.[2]
— Le Sequoia gigantea. 1861. III. 310.[1]
— Soins à prendre pour la plantation des Magnolia grandiflora. 1850. III. 399.[2]
— Sur les Spiraea Fortunei et Douglasii. 1862. III. 460.[2]
— Stranvaesia glaucescens. 1847. III. 462.[1]
— De la taille et des soins à donner aux arbres plantés en lignes. 1863. III. 209.
— Tamarix tetrandra Pallas. 1845. III. 612.[2]
— Thuya d'Orient, filiforme. 1844. III. 311.[2]
— Thuya orientalis flagelliformis. 1860. III. 311.[2]
— Ulmus campestris virgata. 1860. III. 365.[1]
— Variétés de Cytisus Adami. 1854. III. 480.[2]
— Sur un Yucca du Mexique. 1860. III. 339.[2]
— *See also* CAMUZET, J. B. & PÉPIN.
Pépinières. Fumure. 1898. IV. 151.[2]
Pépinières. Pralinage [au minium] des graines. 1898. IV. 149.[2]
Les **pépinières** André Leroy à Angers. *See* GERMAIN DE SAINT-PIERRE, Ernest. 1875. I. 59.
The **Pepper-tree.** 1895. III. 529.[1]
Peppercorne, F. S. Influence of forests on climate and rainfall. 1880. IV. 44.
Pepys, W. H. On the respiration of the leaves. 1843. I. 170.
Pequeño, D. Alcohol de Madroños. 1890. IV. 534.[1]
Pequeño, Diego. Arboricultura. Ligera idea de los progresos . . . por medio del cultivo del Pino maritimo. 1867. IV. 467.[1]
Peragallo, Alexandre. Études d'entomologie appliquée. 1884. III. 757.[1]
— Études sur les insects nuisibles. 1885. III. 190.
— L' Olivier. 1882. III. 675.[2]
Peralta, Ricardo BEAUMONT DE MIRAS. *See* BEAUMONT DE MIRAS PERALTA, RICARDO.
Pérard, Alexandre. Catalogue raisonné des plantes . . . de Montluçon. 1869. I. 414.

Pérard, H. Les lapins. 1893. IV. 198.[2]
Perassi, Giuseppe. Club alpino italiano. . . . Commissione d'imboschimento alpino. 1880. IV. 165.
Pérau, E. Excursion forestière en 1897. 1897. IV. 540.[1]
Perceval, Westby Brook. New Zealand timber. 189.? IV. 402.[1]
Percie du Sert, FLEURY. *See* ROSTAING, Léon & Marcel & FLEURY PERCIE DU SERT.
Percival, Exley. Wild flowers of Georgetown. 1889. I. 339.[2]
Percival, Robert. An account of the island of Ceylon. 1803. III. 279.[1]
— Cinnamon, the staple commodity of Ceylon. 1803. III. 406.[1]
Percival, Thomas. An account of a . . . method of preparing pot-ash. 1781. IV. 395.
— Also hätten die Pflanzen Vorstellungen. 1785. I. 197.[1]
— Betrachtungen über das Empfindungsvermögen der Pflanzen. 1785. I. 197.[1]
— Essays medical . . . On the Columbo root. 1773. III. 397.[1]
— Speculations on the perceptive power of vegetables. 1785. I. 197.[1]
Perdrigeat, C. A. Anatomie comparée des Polygonées. 1900. II. 184.[1]
Perdrizet, A. L'aménagement des forêts communales . . . de Montbard. 1890. IV. 249.[1]
— Buffon et la forêt communale de Montbard. 1888. IV. 27.[2]
— La crise des bois de feu. 1895. IV. 276.[1]
— Reboisement des terres incultes. 1896. IV. 164.[1]
— Les révolutions de Plombières. 1895. IV. 129.
Pereboom, Cornelis. Systema characterum plantarum. 1788. I. 854.[2] 522.[2]
Pereboom, Nicolaas Ervoud. Materia vegetabilis. 1787. I. 70.
Pereira, Jonathan. On Alcornoque bark. 1847. IV. 518.[1]
— Dr. Pereira's Elements of materia medica and therapeutics. 1839. III. 242.
— The elements of materia medica. 1839. III. 242.
— On the flower buds of Calysaccion. 1851. III. 610.[1]
— Handbuch der Heilmittellehre. 1839. III. 242.
— Introductory lecture on materia medica. 1842. III. 243.
— On kokum butter. 1852. III. 609.[1]
— The Kosso or Brayera anthelmintica. 1851. III. 424.[1]
— Manual of materia medica and therapeutics. 1839. III. 242.
— Om Myrospermum fra Sonsonate. 1851. III. 482.[1]
— On the Myrospermum of Sonsonate. 1851. III. 482.[1]
— On Myrospermum pubescens. 1851. III. 482.[2]
— Notice of Nag-Kassar. 1851. III. 610.[2]
— Observations on the Chinese gall. 1844. III. 525.[1]
— On some vegetable . . . products of New Zealand. 1846. III. 283.[1]
Pereira-Arnstein, Adolf, *Freiherr* von. Volkswirthschaftliche Bedeutung der Obstweinerzeugung. 1890. III. 174.[1]
Pereira da Fonseca, A. A. M. V. A. Estudo comparativo da estructura do peciolo . . . de Quercus. 1896. II. 131.[1]
Pereira de Mattos, José Franco. Algumas palavras sobre a cultura do Alfarrobeira. 1900. III. 471.[1]
Periskratof, K. *See* Перекрестовъ, К.
Perels, Emil. Hodgson's Drathseilbahn. 1872. IV. 391.
Perelygin, P. *See* Перелыгинъ, П.
Perotchen . . . . *See* Перечень, . . .
Peretti, A. Greffe en fente du Noyer. 1865. III. 355.
Peretti, Pietro. Osservazioni sulla preparazione della chinina. 1823. III. 721.
Pereyra, Emanuele de SYLVA. *See* SYLVA PEREYRA, Emanuele de.
Perez, Gaspar. De balsamo. 1530. III. 510.[1]
Perez, Giuseppe. Le alluvioni di Messina. 1864. IV. 48.[1]
Pérez, J. M. ESCRIBANO Y. *See* ESCRIBANO Y PÉREZ, J. M.
Pérez, Jean. Instruction élémentaire sur le phylloxéra. 1874. III. 759.
Perez, José ALVAREZ. *See* ALVAREZ PEREZ, José.
Perez, Juan Zoilo FERNANDEZ Y. *See* FERNANDEZ Y PEREZ, J. Z.
Perez, Lorenzo. De medicamentorum . . . delectu. 1599. I. 283.
Perez, Victor. El Tagasaste. 1879. III. 474.[1]
— & Sagot, Paul. Le Tagasaste. 1892. III. 474.[2]
— — De la végétation aux îles Canaries. 1867. III. 131.[2]
Perez de la Sala, Pedro. Estudios sobre las inundaciones. 1871. IV. 50.

Perez Lara, José Maria. Florula gaditana. 1886. I: 422.
Perez Minguez, Luis. El Haya. El Roble. 1866. IV. 494, 506.
— Manual del agricultor asturiano. 1864. IV. 109.[1]
Perfect, Grosvenor. *See* PERFECT, John & Grosvenor.
Perfect, John & Grosvenor. A catalogue of forest-trees, fruit-trees, evergreen and flowering-shrubs. 1787. I. 53.
Perfect, Thomas. The practice of gardening. 1759. III. 757.[2]
Perfume of the Rose. 1890. III. 454.[1]
Perfume plants in Australia. 1892. III. 226.[2]
Pergande, Theodore. The Plum plant-louse. 1897. III. 433.[2]
— *See also* HUBBARD, H. G. & PERGANDE, Theodore.
Pergaut, C. Osservazioni sul bruco. 1863. IV. 210.[3]
Perger, Anton, *Ritter* von. Der deutsche Mythos und unsere Pflanzen. 1872. I. 518.
— Deutsche Pflanzensagen. 1864. I. 517.[2]
— Die Flora William Shakespeare's. 1870. I. 514.[2]
— Ueber den Gebrauch unserer heimischen Pflanzen. 1861. I. 515.
— Pflanzenaberglaube. 1870. I. 518.
— Studien über die deutschen Namen der . . . Pflanzen. 1858. I. 73.[2]
Pericolosa concorrenza alle traversine di legno per ferrovie. 1881. IV. 423.[1]
Perier, (*Doctor*). Las inundaciones en el Mediodia. 1888. IV. 547.[2]
Perier-Mondonville, L. F. De l'exploitation du Chêne. 1798. IV. 511.
Perilepsis hodegiai peri ekteleseōs tou BXMB nomou. *See* ΠΕΡΙΑΗΨΙΣ ὁδηγίαι περὶ ἐκτελέσεως τοῦ BXMB' νόμου.
Périmètre de restauration. — Droits de passage. 1900. IV. 327.
Périnet, Ovide. *See* GODARD, L. E. & PÉRINET, Ovide.
Peringuey, L. Insects injurious to forest trees in South Africa. 1887. IV. 210.[2]
— A note on the Phylloxera vastatrix at the Cape. 1887. III. 574.
Perini, Agostino. *See* PERINI, Carlo & Agostino.
Perini, Carlo & Agostino. Flora dell' Italia settentrionale. 1854. I. 427.
— Osservazioni sulle zone di vegetazione del Trentino. 18 .? I. 424.
Perint, Charles. Nouveau plan de la forêt de Compiègne. n. d. IV. 359.[1]
Peritara, E. L. Rubber; the handmaid of civilization. 1899. III. 232.[1]
Perkin, Arthur G. The colouring matters of various tanning materials [*sic*]. 1899. I. 184.
— Some constituents of the leaves of Rhus Metopium. 1900. II. 363,[1] 459.[1]
— *See also* HUMMEL, J. J. & PERKIN, A. G.
— & Allen, G. Y. Colouring matter of Sicilian Sumach. 1896. II. 458.[3]
— & Cope, Frank. The constituents of Artocarpus integri-folia. 1896. III. 367.[1]
— & Gunnell, Oswald. The colouring matter of Quebracho colorado. 1896. III. 687.[1]
— & Hummel, J. J. The colouring matters . . . in various British plants. 1896. II. 262.[2]
Perkins, *Mrs.* E. E. The elements of floristy. 1837. I. 87.
Perkins, *Mrs.* Elizabeth Steele. *See* PERKINS, *Mrs.* E. E.
Perkins, Frederick B. *See* GUILD, W. H., (*jr.*) & PERKINS, F. B.
Perkins, George Henry. Catalogue of the flora of Vermont. 1882. I. 315.
— Catalogue of the flowering plants of Vermont. 1872. V. XVII.[1]
— Flora of Vermont. 1882. I. 315.
— A general catalogue of the flora of Vermont. 1882. I. 315.
— Insects injurious to the Elm. 1890. III. 364.[2]
Perkins, Janet Russell. Beiträge zur Kenntnis der Monimiaceae. 1898. II. 221.[3]
— Monographie der Gattung Mollinedia. 1900. II. 222.[1]
Perkins, Mary L. S. The American Dogwood. 1897. III. 646.[1]
Perkins, Nevill. Report on Formosa. *See* HENRY, Augustine. 1896. I. 463.[3]
Perla, Francesco. De orientali opobalsamo. 1641. III. 510.[2]
Perleb, Karl Julius. Clavis classium, ordinum et familiarum. 1838. I. 260.
— De Horto botanico friburgensi. 1829. I. 46.
— Lehrbuch der Naturgeschichte des Pflanzenreichs. 1826. I. 86.

Die **Pernettien.** 1888. III. 653.¹
Pernetty, Antoine Joseph, (abbé). Histoire d'un voyage aux isles Malouines. 1769. I. 347.
— The history of a voyage to the Malouine. 1769. I. 347.
— Journal historique d'un voyage fait aux Îles Malouines. 1769. I. 347.
Pernettyas. 1882. III. 653.²
Pernhoffer, Gustav. Versuch einer Darstellung der pflanzengeographischen Verhältnisse der Umgebungen des Curortes Wildbad-Gastein. 1856. I. 441.
— Verzeichniss der in der Umgebung von Seckau . . . wachsenden Phanerogamen. 1896. I. 444.
Pernitzsch, Heinrich. Anleitung zur Einrichtung . . . der Forste. 1836. IV. 240.
— Anweisung zur Waldwerthberechnung. 1820. IV. 252.
— Die Arithmetik und Algebra. 1823. IV. 58.
— Flora von Deutschlands Wäldern. 1825. I. 377.
— Riesenhafte Weisstannen. 1826. II. 24.¹
Pernitzsch, Heinrich Gottlieb. Beobachtungen und Erfahrungen beim Anbaue . . . der Fichtenbestände. 1847. IV. 453.
— Einige Worte über die Gewinnung der Fichtenrinde. 1851. IV. 458.
— Ueber Holzmangel und Forstfrevel. 1850. IV. 281.¹
— Praktische Anweisung zur Anstellung von Versuchen . . . für forstwissenschaftliche Zwekke. 1842. IV. 37.¹
— Untersuchungen über Zuwachs, Bewirthschaftung. 1842. IV. 254.
Péron, François. Observations sur la dysenterie des pays chauds. 1804. III. 342.¹
— Voyage de découvertes aux Terres Australes. See LESCHENAULT DE LA TOUR, L. T. 1816. I. 500.
Peron, Tomás. Estudio sobre la corteza de Quebracho blanco. 1878. III. 686.²
Perona, Vittorio. Sull' afrancasione delle servitù boschive. 1880. IV. 353. — 1878. IV. 334.¹
— Di alcuni metodi per determinare la ripresa dei boschi. 1895. IV. 238.
— Ancora sulla riproduzione agamica del Faggio. 1898. IV. 496.
— Nel bosco e fuori. 1895. IV. 70.
— La colonizzazione del Montello. 1896. IV. 329.
— Sulla coltivazione dei Salici da vimini. 1896. IV. 487.²
— La coltura dei Salici di vimini. 1883. III. 348, IV. 487.¹
— Le concimazioni nei vivai forestali. 1895. IV. 151.²
— Sulle condizioni forestali in Germania. 1886. IV. 349.²
— Sulla cultura del Sommacco. 1881. IV. 526.¹
— Sulla cultura della Sughera. 1879. IV. 516.²
— Economia forestale. 1892. IV. 99,¹ 110.¹
— L' insegnamento forestale. 1895. IV. 35.²
— Ueber die Kultur des Gerber-Sumachs. 1879. IV. 526.¹
— Sul legno e sul frutto di alcune Quercie. 1895. IV. 502.¹
— Le matricine migliori. 1895. IV. 140.
— Maturità boschiva e turno. 1896. IV. 252. — 1897. IV. 252.
— La mia ultima parola sulle matricine migliori ecc. 1895. IV. 140.
— Nota süll' articolo " Insetti che danneggiano i boschi di Migliarino." 1889. IV. 209.²
— Le piante legnose italiane. 1894. IV. 86.¹
— Le piccole industrie forestali all' estero. 1885. IV. 403,¹ 428.
— La politica forestale. 1895. IV. 270.
— A proposito di una critica. 1896. IV. 487.¹
— Sulla rendita dei boschi inalienabili. 1894. IV. 238.
— Trattato di selvicoltura. 1880. IV. 110.¹
— Vallombrosa o Perugia? 1898. IV. 35.¹
Pérot. Plantes nouvelles cultivées chez M. Linden à Bruxelles. 1851. I. 50.
Pérot, F. Les bois de Sapin. 1892. IV. 446.²
— Les vieux arbres du Bourbonnais. 1898. I. 297.²
Perottet. Notes regarding two species of silk-yielding worms. 1861. III. 148.¹
Perotti, Carlo. Delle cagioni fisiche e politiche della grande estirpazione de' boschi in Piemonte. 1811. IV. 276.²
— Fisiologia delle piante. 1810. I. 148.
— Observations physiques sur les inconvénients de planter des arbres fruitiers dans les prairies. 1812. III. 145.¹
Perpeet, C. H. Der Bordholz-Berechner. 1840. IV. 222.
— Der Klotzholz-Berechner. 1840. IV. 222.
Perpignan — Société philomatique. See SOCIÉTÉ . . . I. 24.¹
Perraud, Joseph. Sur les époques de développement du black rot. 1897. III. 582.
— Sur les époques de traitement du black rot. 1898. III. 582.
— Sur les formes de conservation . . . du black rot. 1899. III. 582.
— Sur une nouvelle bouillie cuprique. 1898. III. 582.
— Recherches sur quelques moyens permettant d'augmenter l'adhérence des bouillies cupriques. 1898. III. 582.
Perrault, A. De l'écorçage du Chêne. 1856. IV. 512.
Perrault, Claude. De la circulation de la sève. 1721. I. 162.
— Observations sur les fruits. 1721. II. 279.³
— Œuvres diverses de physique. 1721. I. 31.
— **Charras,** Moyse & **Dodart,** Dionys. Des Herren Perrault, Charras und Dodarts Abhandlungen zur Naturgeschichte. 1757. I. 291.
Perrédès, Pierre Élie Félix. A contribution to the pharmacognosy of official Strophanthus seed. 1900. II. 732,¹ III. 690.²
Perrée, W. F. Notes on destructive insects in the Goalpara division. 1900. IV. 528.²
Perrens, Jean Jules. Étude sur les Quinquinas de culture. 1887. III. 722.¹
Perret. Culture et préparation du Manioc. 1898. III. 521.¹
Perrey, Ad. Sur la destruction du mildew. 1885. III. 579.
— Sur l'emploi du sulfate de cuivre pour la destruction du mildew. 1884. III. 578.
— Sur l'origine des matières sucrées. 1882. I. 176.
Perreymond. Plantes phanérogames . . . de Fréjus. 1833. I. 408.
Perrier, Alfred. Note sur une prolification fructipare. 1865. II. 403.¹
Perrier, Ch. De la maladie de la Vigne. 1853. III. 576.
Perrier, E. See SONGEON, André & PERRIER, E.
— & **Songeon,** André. Indication de quelques plantes . . . en Savoie. 1855. I. 411.
Perrin. See RENARD, PERRIN et Cie.
Perrin. Reise durch Hindostan. 1811. III. 277.
Perrin, G. S. The Eucalypts and decorative woods of Tasmania. 1886. IV. 402.¹
— Forests of Tasmania. 1898. IV. 380.²
— Report on Macquarie Harbour Pine. 1886. IV. 402.¹
— Some notes upon . . . Tasmanian Eucalypts. 1890. II. 623.¹
Perring, W. Lexikon für Gartenbau und Blumenzucht. 1882. III. 31.
Perrins, J. D. Sur la présence de la berbérine. 1853. III. 396.³
Perris, Édouard. Histoire des insectes du Pin maritime. 1852. IV. 467.²
— Quelques considérations sur les insectes nuisibles. 1851. III. 189.
— Quelques mots au sujet de l'Ailante. 1860. III. 506.²
— Traité de la culture du Mûrier. 1846. III. 376.
— Le Vernis du Japon. 1860. III. 506.²
Perron. Le guide du consommateur de chocolat et de thé. 1845. III. 222.
Perroncito, Edoardo. Studi preliminari per combattere la fillossera. 1893. III. 762.
Perrot, Charles. Le Manihot Glaziovii dans l'Afrique. 1899. III. 520.²
— Manihot Glaziovii in Deutsch-Ostafrika. 1899. III. 520.²
Perrot, Émile. Anatomie comparée des Gentianacées. 1898. II. 721.¹
— Contribution à l'étude histologique des Lauracées. 1891. II. 223.²
— Sur le mode de formation des îlots libériens intraligneux des Strychnos. 1895. II. 720.¹
— Sur l'origine de l'anneau scléreux des Cannelles. 1890. II. 224.¹
— Sur le tissu conducteur surnuméraire. 1897. I. 134.¹
— Le tissu criblé. 1899. I. 134.²
Perrottet, George Samuel. Catalogue des plantes du Jardin botanique . . . à Pondichéry. 1867. I. 67.¹
— Catalogue raisonné des plantes introduites. 1825. III. 148.
— Sur la culture du Mûrier. 1840. III. 376.
— Extrait d'une lettre . . . à M. Benjamin Delessert. 1837. I. 472.
— Mémoire sur la culture des Indigofères. 1832. III. 479.¹
— Sur sa mission dans l'Inde . . . concernant l'industrie sérigène. 1842. III. 376.
— Note concernant l'arbre qui produit la résine copal. 1842. III. 489,² 611.³
— Sur la culture . . . du Mûrier. 1829. III. 380.²
— Notice sur la fécondation artificielle du Dattier. 1854. II. 3.¹

— Observations sur le Morus intermedia. 1840. II. 154.[1]
— Observations sur le Morus multicaulis. 1833. II. 154.[1]
— Observations sur les essais de culture tentés au Sénégal. 1831. III. 131.[1]
— Phénomène observé sur une espèce de Bauhinia. 1825. II. 335.[1]
— Rapport sur les manuscrits de météorologie et de botanique . . . dans l'Inde. 1841. I. 472.
— *See also* GUÉRIN-MÉNEVILLE, F. E. & PERROTET, G. S.; GUILLEMIN, J. B., PERROTTET, Samuel & RICHARD, Achille.
Perroud, Louis. Herborisations dans la Grande Kabylie. 1882. I. 485.
— Série d'herborisations dans les Alpes françaises. 1877. I. 415.
Perry. *See* KNIGHT, Joseph & PERRY.
Perry, G. W. A treatise on turpentine farming. 1859. IV. 436.[1]
Perry, Matthew Calbraith. Narrative of the expedition . . . to the China seas and Japan. *See* GRAY, Asa. 1856. I. 462.
Perry, W. A treatise on the identity of Herne's Oak. 1867. II. 138.[2]
Perry, W. G. Plantae varvicenses selectae. 1820. I. 397.
Persian Olives. 1896. III. 674.[2]
The Persimmon. 1895. II. 702.[1]
El personal del Cuerpo de ingenieros de montes. 1897. IV. 553.[2]
Personnat, Camille. Sur les Chênes dont se nourrit le ver-à-soie du Chênes. 1867. IV. 502.[1]
— Le ver à soie du Chêne. 1866. IV. 502.[1]
Personne, J. (*jr.*). Sur un nouvel alcool retiré de la gu du Houx. 1884. II. 464.[1]
Personne, Jacques. Emploi de l'essence de térébenthine. 1869. IV. 443.[2]
— Sur l'iodure d'amidon. 1872. I. 140.[1]
— Recherches pour servir à l'histoire de l'essence de térébenthine. 1856. IV. 443.[2]
Person, Christian Hendrik. An account of a remarkable variety of the Beech. 1800. II. 125.[2]
— Species plantarum; seu, Enchiridium botanicum. 1805. I. 259.
— Synopsis plantarum. 1805. I. 259.
Persoz, Jean François. Étude des propriétés . . . du vert de Chine. 1858. III. 542.[1]
— Sur une matière colorante verte qui vient de Chine. 1852. III. 542.[1]
— Note sur la teinture en jaune avec le Hoangtchi. 1858. III. 744.[1]
— Nouveau procédé pour la culture de la Vigne. 1848. III. 555.
— Observations sur quelques faits relatifs à la végétation. 1847. III. 151, 555.
Persson, Johan. Quercus sessiliflora var. subintegrifolia. 1885. II. 140.[1]
Perthuis, de. Mémoires tirés du traité de la conservation et de l'aménagement des forêts. 1800. IV. 292.
— Traité de l'aménagement . . . des bois et forêts. 1803. IV. 109.[1]
Pertuis & Sager. L'art de fabriquer le salin et la potasse. 1779. IV. 395.
Pertusati, Francesco, *comte.* Dell' acclimamento dei vegetali. 1857. III. 43.
— Note sur le Ginkgo. 1870. III. 287.[1]
Perty, Max. Eine in Weingeist aufbewahrte Birne. 1853. II. 279.[2]
Peruvian Bark-tree. 1857. III. 712.[1]
Peruvian Walnut. 1894. II. 112.[2]
Perzikpittenolie. 1883. III. 442.[2]
Pesch, F. J. van. Beknopte handleiding tot de kennis van den Nederlandschen landbouw. 1880. III. 106.[1]
Peschier, C. G. Lettre sur la salicine. 1830. III. 350.[2]
Peschier, Jacques.· Analyse des feuilles du Redoul. 1828. II. 454.[1]
— De l'influence du gypse. 1830. I. 228.[1]
— & Jacquemin. Analyse de plusieurs parties de l'Anagyre fétide. 1830. II. 332,[1] 369.[1]
Peschier, Jean. De irritabilitate animalium et vegetabilium. 1797. I. 197.[1]
Peschke, J. N. Zur Bewirthschaftung der Hochgebirgsforste. 1874. IV. 129.
— Ueber Düngungsmittel in . . . Pflanzkämpen. 1873. IV. 144.[2]
Peschke, Julius. Ueber die Aufstellung finanzieller Ertragstafeln. 1889. IV. 258.
— Die "Königseiche." 1895. IV. 516.[1]

Peschl, A. J. Ueber die Verkohlung des Holzes. 1885. IV. 433.[2]
Pesneau, J. B. Catalogue des plantes . . . de la Loire inférieure. 1837. I. 409.
Pesotzki, N. A. *See* Пecoцĸiй, H. A.
Pessard. Sur le reboisement des montagnes. 1874. IV. 162.
— Des semis de Frêne. 1868. III. 672.[1]
Pestalozzi, Anton. Die Gattung Boscia Lam. 1898. II. 230.[1]
Petagna, L., Terrone, G. & Tenore, Michele. Catalogo degli alberi ed arbusti . . . nelle provincie di Terra di Lavoro. 1827. I. 423.
—$\frac{}{26.}$— Viaggio in alcuni luoghi della Basilicata. 1827. I.
Petagna, Vincenzo. Delle facultà delle piante trattato. 1796. I. 259.
— Institutiones botanicae. 1785. I. 258.
Petel, Prosper. De la culture . . . des Rhododendron. 1858. III. 656.
Peter, Adolf. Hydrophyllaceae. 1892. II. 747.[1]
— Polemoniaceae. 1897. II. 746.[2]
Peter, Albert. Ein braun austreibender Ahorn. 1874. II. 479.[1]
— Convolvulaceae. 1897. II. 743.[2]
— Ueber Gefässe und gefässartige Gebilde im Holze. 1874. I. 125.
— Die Pflanzenwelt Norwegens. 1888. I. 357.
— Populus tremula mit zerrissenem Stamm. 1874. II. 98.[2]
Peter, Max. Schaal'sches Setzeisen. 1889. IV. 153.[1]
— Wie verfährt man bei der Einsaat eines Kiefernsaatkampes. 1889. IV. 473.
— Zwei Baumriesen. 1891. IV. 447,[1] 516.[1]
Petermann. La nocuité du nitrate de soude perchloraté. 1900. IV. 145.
Petermann, Arthur. Analyse de la Bruyère. 1883. II. 360,[1] III. 849.[1]
— Recherches sur les graines originaires des hautes latitudes. 1878. I. 217, IV. 147.[1]
Petermann, Guilielmus Ludovicus. *See* PETERMANN, W. L.
Petermann, Wilhelm Ludwig. Analytischer Pflanzenschlüssel für . . . Leipzig. 1846. I. 381.
— Beiträge zur deutschen Flora. Salix. 1844. II. 101.[1]
— In codicem botanicum Linnaeanum index. 1840. I. 77.
— Deutschlands Flora mit Abbildungen. 1849. I. 382.
— Flora des Bienitz. 1841. I. 380.
— Flora lipsiensis excursoria. 1838. I. 379.
— Handbuch der Gewächskunde. 1836. I. 255.
— Das Pflanzenreich in vollständigen Beschreibungen aller · wichtigen Gewächse. 1838. III. 52.
— Schlüssel zu den Gattungen der in Nord- und Mittel-Deutschland vorkommenden Pflanzen. 1879. I. 388.
— Taschenbuch der Botanik. 1842? 1 380.
Petermann's Mittheilungen aus Justus Perthes' geographischer Anstalt. *See* MITTHEILUNGEN aus Justus . . . I. 13.
Peters. Waldbrände in der K. Oberförsterei Bederkesa. 1900. IV. 182.[2]
— Die Aristolochien. 1887. III. 385.[2]
— Eine Auswahl der schönsten Solanum-Arten. 1878. III. 701.[1]
— Das Beerenobst. 1879. III. 147.[2]
— Brombeeren als Zierpflanzen. 1884. III. 457.[2]
— Die Brotfrucht. 1881. III. 367.[1]
— Cactusarten als Kletterpflanzen. 1887. III. 619.
— Die Cassien. 1880. III. 470.[1]
— Columnea L. 1883. III. 708.[1]
— Daphne. 1888. III. 626.[2]
— Der Jasmin. 1879. III. 672.[2]
— Kadsura. 1883. III. 398.[2]
— Kleines Taschen-Lexikon für Gärtner. 1870. III. 29.[3]
— Die Klimmen (Cissus). 1882. III. 544.[2]
— Leichtblühende Bignonien. 1886. III. 705.[1]
— Die Menispermen. 1883. III. 397.[1]
— Die Schönrebe. 1883. III. 706.[2]
— Sparmannia africana. 1881. III. 585.[1]
— Wachspflanzen. 1877. III. 226.[1]
Peters, J. P. *See* BUEK, J. N. & PETERS, J. P.
Peters, John E. Baccharis halimifolia in Atlantic county. 1892. III. 852.[2]
Peters, Wilhelm. Die Heidflächen Norddeutschlands. 1862. IV. 118.
Peters, Wilhelm Carl Hartwig. Naturwissenschaftliche Reise nach Mossambique. 1862. I. 492.[1]

Petersen, Andreas. Bidrag til Kundskab om Sandeltræerne. 1886. II. 169.[1]
— Contribution to the knowledge of sandal wood. 1885. III. 225.
— Contribution to the knowledge of Sandal woods. 1886. II. 169.[1]
Petersen, Christian & Schödler, F. Ueber den absoluten Werth der gebrauchlichsten Holzarten als Brennmaterial. 1836. IV. 431.[1]
— — Sur la valeur absolue des espèces de bois les plus employées comme combustible. 1836. IV. 431.[1]
Petersen, Clairant. Ueber den Einfluss der Waldungen. 1846. IV. 52.
Petersen, F. Den lille Skovdyrker. 1886. IV. 103.[2]
Petersen, Johann Christian Petrus. De cortice peruviano. 1763. III. 719.
— De cortice peruviano pars prior. See LINNÉ, Carl von. 1758. III. 719.
Petersen, N. Om de jydske Heder. 1856. IV. 156.[1]
— Spørgsmaal til den offentlige Mening. 1862. IV. 156.[1]
Petersen, Otto Georg. Aaringsstudier. 1899. I. 128.[1]
— Anatomie de la tige chez l'Eggersia buxifolia. 1888. II. 191.[1]
— Über das Auftreten bicollateraler Gefässbündel. 1882. I. 134.[1]
— Bicollaterale Karbundter. 1882. I. 134.[1]
— Bidrag til Nyctagine-Stængelens Histiologi. 1880. II. 190.[1]
— En Bøg med en fastvexet hængende Gren. 1897. I. 209,[1] IV. 497.
— En ejendommelig Grenfordobling hos en Pil. 1897. II. 104.[1]
— Études sur les phénomènes vitaux des racines des arbres. 1898. I. 162.
— Forstbotanik. 1896. IV. 79.[2]
— Halorrhagidaceae. 1893. II. 646.[1]
— Lille Vildmose og dens Vegetation. 1896. I. 358.
— Músaceae. 1889. II. 90.[2]
— Musaceae, Zinziberaceae, Cannaceae, Marantaceae. 1890. II. 90.[2]
— Nogle Bemærkninger om abnorme Løvforholds Indflydelse paa Aarringsdannelsen. 1896. I. 128.[1]
— Nogle Undersøgelser over Træernes Rodliv. 1898. I. 162.
— Quelques remarques sur l'influence exercée par un feuillage anormal sur le développement de la couche annuelle. 1896. I. 128.[1]
— Ueber Quernetæe in Gefässen. 1888. II. 191.[1]
— Stængelbygningen hos Eggersia buxifolia. 1888. II. 191.[1]
— Stivelsen hos vore Løvtræer under Vinterhvilen. 1896. I. 179.[1]
— Sur la structure . . . de la tige chez les Nyctaginées. 1880. II. 190.[1]
— Trigoniaceae. 1896. II. 428.[1]
— Vochysiaceae. 1896. II. 428.[2]
Petersen, P. Die Borkenkäfer. 1888. IV. 204.
— Zur forstlichen Bedeutung der Spechte. 1889. IV. 90.[2]
Petershagen, C. G. T. Vollständige Anweisung zur Kultur des Weinstocks. 1843. III. 552.
Peterson. Gegen die einjährige Kiefernpflanzung. 1884. IV. 473.
Peterson, (Forstmeister, Friedrichsmoor) & . others. In Sachen des Bruchbodens. 1874. IV. 489.[1]
Peterstein, Johann. Bemerkung über Aesculus Hippocastanum. 1852. II. 482.[1]
Peteut. La cueillette des graines forestières. 1869. IV. 148.
Pethybridge, George H. Beiträge zur Kenntniss der Einwirkung der anorganischen Salze. 1899. I. 229.
Petif, C. Enumeratio plantarum in ditione florae palatinatus. 1830. I. 378, 532.[1]
Petilli, Francesco MAROLDA-. See MAROLDA-PETILLI, Francesco.
Petion, E. O konserwacyi drzewa. 1875. IV. 419.
Petit, A. De l'acide chrysophanique. 1885. III. 467.[1]
— Sur l'alcaloide du pituri. 1879. III. 700.[1]
— The alkaloid of pituri. 1879. III. 700.[1]
— De la disparition des acides du raisin. 1869. III. 583.[1]
— Note relative à l'emploi du qoaltar. 1871. III. 566.[1]
— En plantegeografisk Skizze af Monte Generoso. 1889. I. 429.
— Sur quelques matières propres à la destruction du phylloxera. 1873. III. 565.[2]
— Sur le sucre contenu dans les feuilles de Vigne. 1873. III. 583.[1]

— & Polonovski, M. Contribution à l'étude de la pilocarpine. 1897. III. 505.[1]
— — Sur deux nouveaux alcaloïdes. 1897. III. 505.[1]
— — Étude sur l'éserine. 1894. III. 484.[1]
— & Terrat, P. Sur le dosage de la caféine dans le thé. 1896. III. 608.[1]
Petit, BALTET-. See BALTET-PETIT.
Petit, Charles Paul Michel. Thèse sur le Ricin. 1860. III. 522.[1]
Petit, Eugène. L'exploitation du caoutchouc. 1893. III. 149.
— Plantefysiognomiske Studier fra Corsica. 1884. I. 419.[1]
Petit, Julien. La culture de l'Osier en Allemagne. 1889. III. 349.
— La culture des Rosiers en Turquie. 1891. III. 450.
— Fleurs exotiques comestibles. 1890. III. 219.[2]
— Industrie des Oranges et des Citrons. 1891. III. 497.[2]
Petit, Louis. Sur la disposition . . . des faisceaux dans le pétiole. 1887. I. 112.[1]
— De la distribution des stomates foliaires. 1893. I. 131.[2]
— Emploi de la chaux des épurateurs à gaz. 1874. III. 566.[2]
— Sur l'importance taxonomique du pétiole. 1886. I. 253.[1]
— Note complémentaire sur l'anatomie du pétiole des dicotylédones. 1888. I. 112.[1]
— Nouvelles recherches sur le pétiole. 1889. I. 112.[1]
— Sur le parcours des faisceaux dans le pétiole. 1886. I. 112.[1]
— Sur le parcours des faisceaux libéro-ligneux dans le pétiole. 1887. I. 112.[1]
— Le pétiole des dicotylédones. 1887. I. 112.[1]
— Le phylloxéra. 1874. III. 759.
Petit, Othon. Des emplois chimiques du bois. 1888. IV. 433.
— Études calorimétriques sur la combustion des bois. 1886. IV. 413.[1]
Petit, Pierre. Thea. 1685. III. 605.
Petit-Coq, P. P. Calendrier du rosiériste. 1895. III. 453.[1]
Petit de La Saussaye, Sauveur. Réfutation—(à propos d'un article de M. Du Mortier). 18 . . ? III. 84.[2]
Petit guide du Jardin botanique de Bruxelles. 1877. I. 50.
Le Petit jardin illustré-hebdomadaire. III. 20.
Petit-Lafitte, Augustin. Renseignemens . . . sur la culture de la Vigne. 1842. III. 554.[1]
— La Vigne dans le Bordelais. 1868. III. 555.
Petit-Radel, Philippe. De amoribus Pancharitis et Zoroae. 1798. I. 199.
— Le mariage des plantes. 1798. I. 199.
Petitcollot. See THIÉRY, E. & PETITCOLLOT.
Petitmengin, Marcel. Sur l'adaptation aux sols calcaires de plantes silicicoles. 1900. II. 662.[1]
Petiver, Jacob. A catalogue of plants . . . about Geneva. 1702. I. 432.[2]
Petiver, James. An account of divers rare plants. 1712. I. 52.
— An account of some Indian plants. 1699. I. 470.[2]
— Botanicum anglicum. 1713. I. 394.
— Botanicum londinense. 1709. I. 394.
— A catalogue of Mr. Ray's English herbal. 1713. I. 394. — 1715. I. 280.
— Catalogue of 600 plants. 1713. I. 394.
— A catalogue of some Guinea-plants. 1698. III. 93.[1]
— Catalogue of the more rare plants . . . physick garden at Leyden. 1711. I. 50.
— Catalogus classicus & topicus. 1709. I. 52.
— A classical and topical catalogue. 1706. I. 52.
— English herbal occidental. 1713. I. 394.
— Gazophylacii naturae & artis. 1702. I. 52.
— Herbarij britannici clariss. D. Raij catalogus. 1713. I. 394.
— Herbarium capense. 1709. I. 493.
— Hortus peruvianus medicinalis. 1715. III. 64.[2]
— Hórtus siccus chirurgicus. 1767. III. 54.
— Hortus siccus pharmaceuticus. 1767. III. 54.
— J. P. his book, for a collection of . . . trees, shrubs, herbs. 1690. I. 35.
— The manner of making Styrax liquida. 1710. III. 417.[1]
— Mr. Ray's method of English plants. 1711. I. 394.
— Monspelii desideratarum plantarum catalogus. 1716. I. 405.
— Musei Petiveriani centuria. 1695. I. 52.
— Opera historiam naturalem spectantia. 1764. I. 291.
— Petiveriana. 1716. I. 52.
— Plantae silesiacae rariores. 1717. I. 372.
— Plantarum aegyptiacarum rariorum icones. 1717. I. 486.

— Plantarum Etruriae rariorum catalogus. 1715. I. 424.
— Rudiments of botany. 1764. I. 83.
— Some attempts made to prove that herbs of the same make
 . . . have the like vertue. 1700. III. 259.[1]
Petö, Lajos. A Coniferák dugványozás utján való szaporítá-
sáról. 1884. III. 294.[2]
Petraschek, Carl. Der bewegliche Rechen mit fixirter Basis.
 1883. IV. 390.[1]
— Le développement de la sylviculture en Bosnie et en Herzé-
govine. 18 . . ? IV. 374.[2]
— Ueber die Erfordernisse einer guten Bundgattersäge. 1895.
 IV. 393.
— Forstliches Vademecum. 1883. IV. 228.
— Die Fremdlinge unter den deutschen Gehölzen. 1869.
 IV. 127.[2]
— Das Gefälle der Holzriesen. 1878. IV. 390.[2]
Petrelli, Eugenio. Vera narratio fruticis . . . in occidentalibus
Indiis nascentium. 1610. II. 577.[1]
Petri, August. Vom Anbau . . . des unächten Akazien-
baumes. 1796. IV. 522.[1]
— Auf Erfahrung gegründete Anleitung nützliche Waldungen
 . . . anzupflanzen. 1793. IV. 105.
Petri, Bernhard. Ueber Pflanzen-Ernährungsgrundsätze.
 1839. III. 40.
Petri, Cornelis. Annotatiunculae aliquot in quatuor libros
Dioscoridis. 1533. I. 276, V. xiv.[2]
Petri, F. Über Brongniart's Verwerfung der Apetalae. 1865.
 I. 252.
Petrich, Georg von. Der gründliche Obstgärtner. 1820.
 III. 146.[1]
Petrie, Donald. Description of a new species of Carmichaelia.
 1885. II. 342.[1]
— Description of a new species of Coprosma. 1879. II.
 815.[2]
— Description of a . . . species of Coprosma. 1898. II. 815.[1]
— Description of new species of native plants. 1885. II.
 815.[2]
— Descriptions of new native plants. 1891. II. 861.[2]
— Descriptions of new native plants. 1894. II. 815.[1]
— List of the flowering plants indigenous to Otago. 1896.
 I. 508.[1]
— New species of New Zealand plants. 1884. II. 342.[1]
— Notice of Olearia Hectori. 1884. II. 862.[1]
— A visit to Stewart Island. 1881. I. 507.
Petrograd. See St. Petersburg.
Petrović, Sava. Description de quelques espèces de Serbie.
 1889. II. 360.[2]
— Flora agri nyssani. See Петровић, Сава. 1882. I. 449.
— See also Петровић, Сава.
Petrovski, F. See Петровскій, Ѳ.
Petros, H. & **Robinet.** Examen chimique de l'écorce du Ca-
rapa. 1821. III. 511.[2]
— Examen chimique des fruits du Lilas. 1824. II. 716.[1]
Petrucci, Gino Bargagli-. See Bargagli-Petrucci, Gino.
Petsche, Albert. Le bois et ses applications au pavage. 1896.
 IV. 426.[1]
— Erfahrungen mit Holzpflaster. 1896. IV. 426.[1]
— Le pavage en bois. 1896. IV. 426.[1]
Pettenkofer, Max von. On the hygienic value of plants.
 1878. IV. 55.[1]
— Ueber Mikania Guaco. 1844. II. 860.[2]
— Ueber die wichtigsten Grundsätze der Bereitung . . . des
Holzleuchtgases. 1857. IV. 433.[1]
Petter, Franz. Botanischer Wegweiser in der Gegend von
Spalato. 1832. I. 447.
Petter, Karl. Bericht über die auf einer Reise nach den Quar-
nerischen Inseln gesammelten Samenpflanzen. 1862. I. 447.
Pettersen, O. Om aarsagerne til vegetationsperiodens tid-
ligere. 1899. I. 222.[1]
Petterson, A. M. Beretning om stipendiereise . . . paa Vest-
landet. 1890. III. 119.[2]
— Havebrug for den miðre jordbruger. 189 . ? III. 100.[2]
Pettigrew, W. The habitat and peculiarities of some of our
timbers. 1878. III. 282.[2]
Petunnikof, Alexis. Note sur la cuticule. 1867. I. 129.[1]
— Note sur la formation de la manne. 1867. II. 707.[1]
— Sur quelques organes sécréteurs des plantes. 1867. I.
 118.[2]
— Recherches sur la cuticule. 1866. I. 129.[2]
— Verzeichniss der im Gouvernement Tambow wildwachsen-
den Pflanzen. 1865. I. 362.
— Ueber den Wert anatomischer Merkmale zur Unterschei-
dung der Abies-Arten. 1900. II. 22.[1]
— See also Петунниковъ, А.

Petzold. Ueberwindung einer Störung im Dickenwachsthum.
 1900. I. 208.[1]
Petzold, Carl Julius. Die Rose, deren Geschichte. 1875.
 III. 449.
Petzold, Eduard Carl Adolf. Die Anpflanzung . . . von Allee-
bäumen. 1878. III. 209.
— The best Oaks. 1878. III. 361.[1]
— Die besten Eichen. 1878. III. 361.[1]
— Die Mutter unserer Pyramiden-Eiche. 1876. II. 136,[2]
 IV. 516.[1]
— Ueber die Wirkungen der Pflanzen. 1844. III. 201.
— & **Kirchner**, G. Arboretum muscaviense. 1864. I. 48,
 III. 69.
Petzold, Wilhelm. Ueber die Vertheilung des Gerbstoffs.
 1876. I. 183.
— Volkstümliche Pflanzennamen. 1890. I. 73.[2]
Peupion, Auguste. Le corps des forestiers. 1882. IV. 292.
— Traité pratique de pisciculture. 1898. IV. 122.[2]
Peuplement de Pin sylvestre très clairiéré. 1900. IV. 474.
Peuplements d'Épicéas. Attaques d'insectes. 1899. IV.
 457.
Peuplements résineux. Exploitation. 1900. IV. 252.
Peuplier blanc, dit Eucalyptus. 1898. IV. 486.[1]
Peuplier d'Italie femelle. 1894. IV. 486.[1]
Le Peuplier dit régénéré. 1897. IV. 486.[1]
Un Peuplier phénoménal. 1885. II. 98.[1]
Peuplier picard. 1899. IV. 486.[1]
Peuplier picard et Peuplier blanc de Hollande. 1899. IV.
 485.[2]
Peupliers attaqués par la saperde. 1899. IV. 485.[2]
Peut-on planter le Douglas . . . où le gibier est abondant?
 1900. IV. 483.[2]
Peverell. Trees and shrubs on chalk. 1872. III. 41.[1]
Peyer, J. J. De cortice peruviano. 1745. III. 719.
Peyer, Johann. Pentas quaestionum de plantis. 1623. I.
 284.
Peyerimhoff, Henri de. Le ver de la Vigne. 1870. III. 563.
Peyl, Josef. Die landwirthschaftliche Pilzkunde. 1863.
 III. 194.
Peyotes de la familia de las Cactáceas. 1900. III. 620.[3]
Peyre, A. See Rabuteau, A. & Peyre, A.
Peyre, B. L. Méthode analytique-comparative de botanique.
 1823. I. 407.
Peyreleau, Eugène Édouard Boyer-. See Boyer-Peyre-
leau, Eugène Édouard.
Peyrer, Karl. Massregeln der Gesetzgebung . . . zur Hebung
der Forstkultur. 1870. IV. 278.[3]
— Die Zusammenlegung der Grundstücke. 1873. IV. 333.
Peyritsch, Johann. Beiträge zur Flora Mexico's. 1860. I.
 331.
— Beitrag zur Flora von Tirol und Vorarlberg. 1891. I.
 443.
— Erythroxylaceae. 1878. II. 394.[1]
— Hippocrateaceae. 1070. II. 471.[1]
— Ueber künstliche Erzeugung von gefüllten Blüthen. 1889.
 I. 145.[3]
— Eine neue Gattung der Hippocastaneen. 1858. II. 483.[1]
— Ueber Pelorienbildungen. 1872. I. 145.[1]
— Über Placentarsprosse. 1879. I. 118.[1]
— Zur Synonymie einiger Hippocrates-Arten. 1874. II.
 471.[2]
— Zur Teratologie der Ovula. 1876. I. 143.
— Untersuchungen über die Aetiologie pelorischer Blüthen-
bildungen. 1878. I. 145.[1]
— See also Kotschy, Theodor & Peyritsch, Johann; Wawra
von Fernsee, Heinrich, Ritter & Peyritsch, Johann.
Peyron, J. Sur l'atmosphère interne des insectes comparée à
celle des feuilles. 1886. I. 154.
— Sur les variations que présente la composition des gaz dans
les feuilles aériennes. 1885. I. 151.[2]
— See also Grétrant, N. & Peyron, J.
Peyssonnel, John Andrew. Singular observations upon the
Manchenille apple. 1759. III. 519.[1]
Peyton, (colonel). The collection of . . . myrobalams. 1880.
 III. 632.[2]
Pezeyre, J. The husks of the Vinegrapes. 1868. III. 583.[1]
Pezold, Christian Philipp. Mittel der . . . Raupen zu ver-
nichten. 1794. IV. 205.[2]
Pezzo. (Pinus picea Linn.) 1883. IV. 444.[2]
Pfaeffin, Paul. Untersuchungen über Entwicklungsge-
schichte . . . der Nabelspalte . . . wichtiger Papilionaceen-
Samen. 1897. II. 321.[1]
Pfälzische Garten-Zeitung. III. 13.
Pfälzischer Forst-Verein. Bericht. Verhandlungen. IV. 10.

Pfaff, Chr. H. De corticum peruvianorum diversae speciei partibus. 1813. III. 721.

Pfaff, Franz. On the active principle of Rhus. 1897. III. 528.[2]

— Ueber den Betrag der Verdunstung einer Eiche. 1870. I. 167.

— Ueber die giftigen Bestandteile des Timbós. 1891. III. 540.[2]

— Ueber Oleo de Tamacoaré. 1893. III. 608.[2]

— Sur le principe vésicant du Rhus. 1896. III. 528.[1]

— Sur les principes du Timbo. 1891. III. 540.[2]

Pfaff, Friedrich.. See FROMMEL, W. & PFAFF, Friedrich.

Pfaler, Eric Johan von. Strödde anmärkningar rörande fruktträns skötsel i Finland. See HELLENIUS, C. N. 1789. III. 134.[2]

Pfalz — Naturwissenschaftlicher Verein. See POLLICHIA. I. 14.

Pfalzneuburgische Forstordnung. 1800. IV. 299.

Pfannenschmidt, August. Die Conservation des Holzes. 1848. IV. 417.

Pfau, G. Der schwarze Brenner. 1879. III. 578.

Pfau, Philipp. Beitrag zur Cultur der Azaleen. 1835. III. 656.

— Beitrag zur Cultur der Rhododendron. 1835. III. 656.

— Cultur der Yucca gloriosa. 1834. III. 339.[1]

— Die Kultur der Rosen. 1846. III. 452.

Pfaundler, Leopold. Über die Wärmecapacität verschiedener Bodenarten. 1866. I. 228.[1]

— See also HLASIWETZ, H. & PFAUNDLER, Leopold.

Pfeffer, Georg Konrad. De Pipere. See HEISTER, Lorenz. 1740. V. XXVI.[1]

Pfeffer, Wilhelm. Ueber die Beziehung des Lichts zur Regeneration von Eiweissstoffen. 1874. I. 203.

— Zur Blüthenentwicklung der Primulaceen. 1872. II. 501.[2]

— Druck- und Arbeitsleistung durch wachsende Pflanzen. 1893. I. 149.[1]

— Über die Fortpflanzung des Reizes bei Mimosa. 1873. II. 373.[1]

— De l'influence de la lumière sur la régénération des matières albuminoïdes. 1874. I. 203.

— Zur Kenntnis der Kontaktreize. 1885. I. 196.[2]

— Über periodische Bewegungen der Blätter. 1874. I. 197.[2]

— Die periodischen Bewegungen der Blattorgane. 1875. I. 198.

— Pflanzenphysiologie. 1897. I. 149.[1]

— Pflanzenphysiologie, ein Handbuch. 1881. I. 148.

— The physiology of plants. 1881. I. 148.

— Studien zur Energetik der Pflanze. 1893. I. 149.[1]

— Untersuchungen über die Proteinkörner. 1872. I. 203.

— Die Wanderung der organischen Baustoffe. 1876. I. 179.[1]

— Die Wirkung farbigen Lichtes auf die Zersetzung der Kohlensäure in Pflanzen. 1874. I. 173.

Pfefferkorn, R. Gelände-Erwerbungen des grossh. badischen Domänenärars. 1900. IV. 274.[2]

Die **Pfeifensträucher** (Philadelphus). 1859. II. 241.[2]

Pfeifer, Otto. Ein interessanter Baum. 1895. IV. 527.[2]

Pfeifer von Forstheim, Johann, Ritter. Beitrag zur Streufrage. 1861. IV. 437.[2]

— Bericht über die Aufforstung öder Hochgebirgsflächen. 1869. IV. 167.[1]

— Die Domaine Freudenthal. 1858. IV. 368.

— Forstgeschichte der... Domäne Freudenthal. 1891. IV. 28.[1]

— Nachtrag zur Streufrage. 1862. IV. 437.[2]

— Resultat einer Ansaatung... aus einem Fichtenpflanzwalde. 1883. IV. 458.

Pfeiffer. Le Peuplier du Canada en Belgique. 1896. IV. 488.[1]

Pfeiffer, von. Grundris der Forstwissenschaft. 1781. IV. 95.

Pfeiffer, (Forstmeister in Freudenthal). Forstliche Notizen. 1861. IV. 138.[1]

— Ueber die Umtriebszeit der Tanne. 1860. IV. 446.[1]

Pfeiffer, A. Die Arillargebilde der Pflanzensamen. 1891. I. 121.

Pfeiffer, Karl. Daphne altaica Pall. 1898. III. 627.[1]

— See also FERRANT, Adolf, PFEIFFER, Karl & PODOLL, Adolf; JANORSCHKE, O., PFEIFFER, Karl & REEDER, Alfred.

Pfeiffer, Ludwig. Bemerkungen über die Frage: Welche Autorität soll den Gattungsnamen... beigegeben werden? 1838. II. 585.[1]

— Bemerkungen über die Nomenklatur mehrerer Cactus-Arten. 1835. II. 585.[1]

— Beschreibung eines blühenden Echinocactus leucanthus. 1835. II. 593.[2]

— Beschreibung einiger neuen Cacteen. 1835. II. 585.[1]

— Beschreibung und Synonymik der... Cacteen. 1837. II. 585.[1]

— Ueber die Bestimmungsmethode zweifelhafter Cacteen. 1837. II. 585.[1]

— Description de quelques nouveaux Cactus. 1835. II. 585.[1]

— Einige Bemerkungen über den Cereus peruvianus. 1839. II. 589.[1]

— Ueber einige neue Cacteen. 1838. II. 585.[1]

— Ueber einige Samenvarietäten der Cacteen. 1836. II. 585.[1]

— Ueber einige sehr verbreitete Irrthümer in der Nomenklatur der Cactusarten. 1835. II. 585.[1]

— Einiges über die Cultur der Cactus. 1835. III. 618.[1]

— Enumeratio diagnostica Cactearum. 1837. II. 585.[1]

— Flora von Niederhessen und Münden. 1847. I. 382.

— Ueber die Gattungen Lepismium und Rhipsalis. 1836. III. 618.[2]

— Ueber die Kultur der Cacteen. 1838. III. 618.[2]

— Ueber Lemaire's Beschreibung einiger neuen Cacteen. 1838. II. 585.[1]

— Ueber die Mammillaria Lehmanni. 1838. II. 594.[1]

— Neuere Erfahrungen über mehrere Cacteen. 1839. II. 585.[2]

— Nomenclator botanicus. 1873. I. 77.

— Synonymia botanica locupletissima generum. 1870. I. 77.

— Übersicht der bisher in Kurhessen beobachteten... Pflanzen. 1844. I. 381.

— Vorschlag zu einer neuen... Anordnung der Cacteen. 1835. II. 585.[1]

— & Otto, Friedrich. Abbildung... blühender Cacteen. 1843. II. 585.[2]

Pfeiffer, Otto. Chemische Untersuchungen über das Reifen des Kernobstes. 1875. I. 179.[1]

Pfeil, (Regierungs- und Forstassessor). Die Siegener Haubergswirthschaft. 1842. IV. 133.

Pfeil, Gr. Klöstzer-Marqueur. 1846. IV. 387.[1]

Pfeil, J. F. Tabellen zur Berechnung des Kubikinhalts runder Hölzer. 1845. IV. 223.

Pfeil, Theodor. Chemische Beiträge zur Pomologie. 1880. II. 267.[2]

Pfeil, Wilhelm. Anleitung zur Ablösung der Waldservitute. 1828. IV. 333.

— Anleitung zur Feststellung der vom Forstgrunde zu erhebenden Grundsteuer. 1835. IV. 284.[1]

— Ueber Auswahl und Bearbeitung des Bodens zu Pflanzkämpen. 1842. IV. 149.[2]

— Die Bauernforsten in den östlichen Provinzen Preussens. 1841. IV. 308.[1]

— Ueber die Bedeutung und Wichtigkeit der wissenschaftlichen Ausbildung des Forstmannes. 1822. IV. 29.

— Ueber Befreiung der Wälder von Servituten. 1821. IV. 333.

— Die Behandlung und Schätzung des Mittelwaldes. 1824. IV. 130.

— Beispiele einer nothwendig verschiedenartigen Behandlung des Mittelwaldes. 1847. IV. 130.

— Beiträge zur Kenntniss des Verhaltens der Kiefer. 1826. IV. 471.

— Beitrag zur Bodenkunde. 1876. IV. 68.

— Bemerkungen über die Arrondirung der Betriebs- und Altersklassen. 1836. IV. 251.[2]

— Bemerkungen zu den von der General-Kommission in Schlesien... aufgestellten Preisaufgaben. 1846. IV. 333.

— Ueber die Berechnung des nachhaltigen Ertrages im Mittelwalde. 1836. IV. 235.[1]

— Die Birke, Betula alba. 1858. IV. 490.[1]

— Die Buche. 1855. IV. 494.

— Die deutsche Holzzucht. 1860. IV. 107.[1]

— Ueber dichte und dünne Saat. 1827. IV. 148.

— Die Düngerlehre für den Forstwirth. 1845. IV. 144.[1]

— Der Einfluss der verschiedenen Temperaturgrade. 1841. IV. 72.

— Einige Bemerkungen über die Durchforstung des Buchenhochwaldes. 1848. IV. 173.

— Einiges über die Krankheiten... der Waldbäume. 1842. IV. 195.[2]

— Erfahrungen und Bemerkungen zur bessern Cultur der Waldungen. 1816. IV. 117.

— Erfahrungen und Bemerkungen zur bessern Kultur der Waldungen. 1825. IV. 117.

— Ueber Erfahrungstafeln in Kiefern. 1837. IV. 480.
— Die Erlen. 1859. IV. 488.[2]
— Von der Ermittlung des Verkaufspreises. 1823. IV. 253.
— Erörterung einiger zweifelhaften Gegenstände bei der Waldwerthberechnung. 1838. IV. 254.
— Erziehung der Weisstanne. 1842. IV. 444.[1]
— Die Erziehung des Baumholzes. 1846. IV. 138.[2]
— Die Fichte. 1859. IV. 453.
— De la formation de l'écorce. 1854. I. 130.
— Forstbenutzung und Forsttechnologie. 1831. IV. 381.
— Die Forstgeschichte Preussens. 1839. IV. 25.
— Die Forstkultur im 16. bis zur Mitte des 17. Jahrhunderts. 1825. IV. 23.[2]
— Forstliche Bodenkunde. 1842. IV. 68.
— Forstliche Bodenkunde. . . . [Die Birke.] 1850. IV. 490.[1]
— Forstliche Bodenkunde. . . . [Die Buche.] 1849. IV. 494.
— Forstliche Bodenkunde. . . . [Die Eiche.] 1847. IV. 504.
— Die forstliche Statik. 1848. IV. 254.
— Das forstliche Verhalten der deutschen Waldbäume. 1829. IV. 82.
— Die Forstpolizeigesetze Deutschlands und Frankreichs. 1834. IV. 268, 314.[1]
— Die Forsttaxation. 1833. IV. 240.
— Forsttchutz und Forstpolizeilehre. 1831. IV. 180.[1]
— Die Forstwirthschaft. 1831. IV. 97.
— Ueber forstwissenschaftliche Bildung. 1820. IV. 29.
— Zur Geschichte der Lerchenanbaues. 1830. IV. 449.
— Gewährt der kürzere Umtrieb dadurch einen Gewinn für die Volkswirthschaft. 1849. IV. 254.
— Grundsätze der Forstwirthschaft. 1822. IV. 287.
— Die Hainbuche. 1858. IV. 491.[2]
— Holzwirthschaft der Perser, Griechen und Römer. 1824. IV. 23.[2]
— Ueber Insectenschaden in den Wäldern. 1827. IV. 206.
— Die Kiefer . . . und ihre Erziehung. 1856. IV. 472.
— Kiefernsaat und Kiefernpflanzung. 1834. IV. 471.
— Kiefern-Samenschläge. 1849. IV. 472.
— Kritisches Repertorium der Forstwissenschaft. 1830. IV. 1.
— Der kurze Umtrieb. 1830. IV. 251.[2]
— Ueber kurzen Umtrieb. 1834. IV. 254.
— Die Lärche. 1858. IV. 449.
— Die Lehre von der Forstbenutzung. 1823. IV. 382.[1]
— Noch etwas über den normalen Zustand und den normalen Vorrath. 1847. IV. 254.[2]
— O owadnach lasom szkodliwych. 1836. IV. 91.[2]
— Die periodische Ausgleichung. 1834. IV. 235.[2]
— Pflanzenphysiologische Aphorismen. 1844. IV. 63.[1] — 1854. I. 130.
— Revision der Theorie der Wirthschaftsführung im Mittelwalde. 1848. IV. 130.
— Die Rindenbildung der Waldbäume. 1854. I. 130.
— Rührt der niedrige Wasserstand der Flüsse . . . von der Verminderung der Wälder her? 1837. IV. 48.[1]
— Die sogenannte Harzbildung in den Stöcken der Kiefer. 1847. II. 47.[2]
— Specielle Erörterung einiger Gegenstände der Wirthschaftseinrichtung. 1852. IV. 242.
— Specielle Holzkenntniss; die Eiche. 1853. IV. 504.
— Von dem Unterschiede des idealen, normalen und realen Ertrages der einzelnen Holzgattungen. 1834. IV. 235.[1]
— Über die Ursachen des schlechten Zustandes der Forsten. 1816. IV. 282.[2]
— Ueber die Verbindung des praktischen mit dem theoretischen Unterrichte. 1840. IV. 29.
— Das Verhalten der oesterreichischen Schwarzkiefer im Meeresboden. 1850. IV. 465.[1]
— Verschiedener Gang des Zuwachses. 1857. IV. 232.
— Verzeichniss der im K. Forst-Garten zu Neustadt-Eberswalde . . . Holzgewächse. 1835. I. 47, IV. 18.[1]
— Vollständige Anleitung zur Behandlung . . . der Forsten. 1820. IV. 97.
— Welche Holzgattungen können zusammen . . . erzogen werden. 1837. IV. 137.[1]
— Welche Vortheile muss sich der Waldbesitzer anrechnen lassen, um danach die Entschädigung zu anrechnen. 1852. IV. 333.
— Werthberechnung des Forstgrundes. 1841. IV. 254.
— Wie weit geht die Berechtigung . . . des Staats in Beaufsichtigung . . . der Privat-Holzgrundstücke? 1844. IV. 285.[2]
— Die Witterungsverhältnisse der Forstmann. 1841. IV. 72.
— Worin ist das berichtigte Fachwerk noch von einer Schätzung . . . verschieden?. 1839. IV. 235.[2]
— Zwei Kapitel aus einem Lehrbuche der Holzzucht. 1853. IV. 67.[1]

Pfennigwerth, H. Schädliche Forstinsecten. 1897. IV. 205.[2]
Pfifferling, G. L. Ueber das Verfahren bei der natürlichen Verjüngung der Rothbuche. 1844. IV. 494.
Pfister. Microscopie du miel. 1896. I. 524.[2]
Pfister, F. A. Deutzia corymbiflora. 1899. III. 410.[2]
— Deutzia Lemoinei. 1895. III. 410.[1]
— Deutzia parviflora. 1894. III. 410.[1]
— Polygonum baldschuanicum. 1897. III. 387.[1]
— Ueber strauchartige Begonien. 1892. III. 618.[1]
Pfister, F. J. Ueber Aralia papyrifera. 1862. III. 644.[1]
Pfister, J., SCHOBINGER-. See SCHOBINGER-PFISTER, J.
Pfister, J. A. Die verbesserte Zuwachsuhr. 1883. IV. 233.
Pfister, Rudolf. Beitrag zur vergleichenden Anatomie der Sabaleenblätter. 1892. II. 63.[1]
— Zur Kenntniss der Zimmtrinden. 1893. III. 404.[1]
— Zur Kenntniss des . . . Sternanis. 1892. II. 210.[1]
Pfitzer, Ernst Hugo Heinrich. Beiträge zur Kenntniss der Hautgewebe. 1869. I. 129.[2]
— Beobachtung über Pfropfhybriden. 1869. I. 246.[1]
— Ueber die Einlagerung von Kalkoxalat-Krystallen. 1872. I. 139.
— Ueber Früchte . . . einiger Palmen. 1885. II. 63.[1]
— Ueber die Geschwindigkeit der Wasserbewegung. 1877. I. 165.
— Ueber die Geschwindigkeit der Wasserströmung. 1878. I. 165.
— Immergrüne Laubhölzer im Heidelberger Schlossgarten. 1898. I. 49.
— Magnolia hypoleuca. 1898. III. 400.[1] — 1899. III. 400.[1]
— Über die mehrfache Epidermis. 1869. I. 129.[2]
— Eine an einer Rose des Bonner botanischen Gartens gemachte Beobachtung. 1869. III. 39.
— Untersuchungen über die Entwicklung des Embryo's der Coniferen. 1871. II. 19.
— & Meyer, Adolf. Zur Anatomie . . . von Artocarpus integrifolia L. 1896. II. 471.
Pfizenmayer, (Forstrat of Blaubeuren). Die Bergföhre auf der Alb. 1900. II. 43.[1]
Pfizenmayer, Fr. Antheeren der Nadelholztriebe gegen Wildverbiss. 1881. IV. 196.[2]
— Ueber Einfriedigungen von Hochwild-Thiergärten. 1861. IV. 146.[1]
Pfizenmayer, W. Giftigkeit des Taxus. 1896. III. 288.[2]
— Ein neuer Keimapparat. 1893. III. 157.
— Schutz gegen Schäden durch Mäuse. 1878. IV. 198.[1]
Pfizenmayer, E. F. Versuche und Erfahrungen eines Försters von der Holzpflanzung. 1798. IV. 117.
Pfizmaier, August. Denkwürdigkeiten von den Bäumen China's. 1875. I. 517.[1]
Die Pflanzen und Thiere des tropischen America. See MARTIUS, K. F. P. von. 1831. I. 341.
Pflanzen, welche zur Nahrung des Menschen dienen. 1837. III. 219.[2] ᚠ ⟨...⟩
Pflanzenarten mit gefüllten Blumen. 1865. I. 145.[2]
Pflanzengeographie, mit besonderer Rücksicht auf . . . Forstgewächse. 1853. IV. 75.[1]
Pflanzenkunde [von Baden]. See DÖLL, J. C. 1884. I. 388.
Das Pflanzenreich, in tabellarischer Uebersicht. 1837. I. 260.
Das Pflanzenreich in vollständigen Beschreibungen aller wichtigen Gewächse. See PETERMANN, W. L. 1838. III. 52.
Die pflanzlichen Wurzelparasiten. 1888. IV. 211.[2]
Die Pflanzung der Kiefern mit entblösster Wurzel. 1851. IV. 472.
Die Pflanzung mit dem Buttlar-Eisen. 1859. IV. 152.
Ueber Pflanzung mit künstlichen Ballen. 1856. IV. 152.
Die Pflanzung mit und ohne Erdballen. 1856. IV. 152.
Pflaum. Ueber die Nachzucht der Kiefer. 1857. IV. 472.
Pflaum, Fritz. Anatomisch-systematische Untersuchung des Blattes der Melastomaceen. 1897. II. 635.[2]
Ueber die Pflege der in Buchenbestände eingesprengten Eichen. 1887. IV. 507.
Pflug, August. Der tausendjährige Rosenstock. 1893. II. 290.[1]
— Die wirtschaftliche Erschliessung öder . . . Liegenschaften. 1892. IV. 155.[1]
Pfost. Beschreibung der im Fürstlich-Hohenzollern'schen Revier Thiergarten . . . ausgeführten Pflanzungen. 1858. IV. 118.
— Ueber Pflanzen-Erziehung. 1858. IV. 146.[2]
Pfotenhauer, Carl Friedrich. Systema plantarum sexuale. See TITTUS, J. D. 1767. I. 257.

Pfrenger, Max. Les phénols du goudron du bois de Bouleau. 1891. IV. 491.²
Pfrimmer, Charles. Les arbres fruitiers exotiques en Algérie. 1884. III. 147.¹
— De quelques arbres fruitiers . . . en Algérie. 1896. III. 147.¹
Ueber das Pfropfen der Baum-Päonie. See GREFFE de la Pivoine . . . 1834. III. 392.²
Propfstecklinge oder Stecklingsveredlung. 1889. III. 163.¹
Pfuel, von. Ausschlagfähigkeit der Kiefer. 1873. II. 48.¹
Pfuhl, Fritz. Baumriesen in der Provinz [Posen]. 1895. I. 296.²
— Floristische Skizze der Umgegend von Kozanowo. 1898. I. 390.
— Verfärbung und Fall des Laubes. 1896. I. 192,¹ 226.¹
— Der Wald bei Czerniejewo. 1899. I. 390.
— Der Wald von Krummfliess. 1899. I. 390.
— Die Wirkung des diesjährigen heissen . . . Sommers. 1900. III. 184.¹
Pfund. Botanische Reisebr. aus Kordofan und Darfur. 1878. I. 488.
Pfungen, Otto von. Notizen über amerikanische Holz-Debitage. 1878. IV. 403.²
Pfurtscheller, Paul. Zur Anatomie der Coniferenhölzer. 1885. IV. 62,² V. xxv.¹
— Beiträge zur Anatomie der Coniferenhölzer. 1885. II. 17,¹ IV. 62,² V. xxv.¹
Phänologische Beobachtungen . . . im Kanton Bern. 1870. I. 227.¹
Phal. Rapport présenté à la Commission des améliorations agricoles et forestières. 1897. IV. 276.¹
Phalänen zur Unterhaltung für Forst und Weidmänner. IV. 10.
Phalamirus. See FALIMIERZ, Stefanek.
Pharmaceutical archives. I. 6.
Pharmaceutical journal and transactions. I. 19.
Pharmaceutical record. I. 6.
Pharmaceutical review. See PHARMACEUTISCHE Rundschau. I. 6, III. 7.
Pharmaceutische Centralhalle. I. 14.
Pharmaceutische Gesellschaft. Berichte. See DEUTSCHE PHARMACEUTISCHE . . . I. 11.
Pharmaceutische Monatsblätter. See ARCHIV des Apothekervereins. I. 10.
Pharmaceutische Post. I. 28.¹
Pharmaceutische Rundschau. I. 6, III. 7.
Pharmaceutische Zeitschrift für Russland. I. 9,² 519.²
Pharmaceutische Zeitung. I. 14.
Pharmaceutisches Central-Blatt. I. 14, III. 13.
Pharmaceutisches Handelsblatt. See PHARMACEUTISCHE Centralhalle. I. 14.
Pharmaceutisk Tidende. I. 9.¹
Pharmacology of the newer materia medica. I. 6.
Pharmacopea lusitana augmentada. See PHARMACOPEA lusitana reformada. 1711. III. 256.¹
Pharmacopea lusitana reformada. 1711. III. 256.¹
Pharmacopea portuense. 1766. III. 256.¹
Pharmacopéa portuguea. 1876. III. 256.¹
Pharmacopée à l'usage des hospices civils. 1806. III. 248.
Pharmacopée belge. See PHARMACOPŒA belgica. 1823. III. 250.¹
Pharmacopée belgique. See PHARMACOPŒA belgica. 1823. III. 250.¹
Pharmacopée du College royal des médecins de Londres. See PHARMACOPŒA londinensis. 1618. III. 250.²
Pharmacopée française. See CODEX medicamentarius. 1638. III. 255.²
Pharmacopoea ad pauperes curandos accommodata. 1829. III. 249.
Pharmacopoea ad usum Nosocomii phthisicorum. 1848. III. 254.
Pharmacopoea amstelædamensis. See PHARMACOPŒA amstelredamensis. 1660. III. 249.
Pharmacopœa amstelodamensis nova. See PHARMACOPŒA amstelredamensis. 1690. III. 249.
Pharmacopoea amstelredamensis. 1660. III. 249.
Pharmacopoea austriaca. 1818. III. 256.²
Pharmacopoea austriaco-castrensis. 1795. III. 256.²
Pharmacopoea austriaco-provincialis. 1774. III. 256.²
Pharmacopoea badensis. 1841. III. 249.
Pharmacopoea batava. 1805. III. 250.¹
Pharmacopoea bavarica jussu regio edita. 1822. III. 248.
Pharmacopoea belgica. 1823. III. 250.¹
Pharmacopoea belgica; or, The Dutch dispensatory. 1659. III. 250.¹

Pharmacopoea borussica. 1799. III. 248.
Pharmacopœa borussica; oder, Preussische Pharmacopöe. See PHARMACOPŒA borussica. 1799. III. 248.
Pharmacopoea bruxellensis. 1702. III. 250.¹
Pharmacopoea Collegii regii medicorum dublinensis. 1818. III. 254.
Pharmacopoea danica. 1772. III. 247.¹
Pharmacopoea edinburgensis. See PHARMACOPŒIA Collegii regii medicorum edinburgensis. 1722. III. 252.
Pharmacopoea fennica. 1819. III. 247.¹
Pharmacopoea Germaniae. 1865. III. 249.
Pharmacopoea germanica. See PHARMACOPŒA Germaniae. 1865. III. 249.
Pharmacopoea hagana. 1738. III. 249.
Pharmacopoea hagiensis. 1659. III. 249.
Pharmacopoea hannoverana. 1819. III. 248.
Pharmacopoea helvetica. 1771. III. 256.¹
Pharmacopoea helvetica. 1872. III. 256.²
Pharmacopoea Hessiae electoralis. 1827. III. 249.
Pharmacopoea hispana. 1803. III. 255.²
Pharmacopoea in usum officinarum reipublicae bremensis. 1792. III. 248.
Pharmacopoea japonica. Editio latina. 1886. III. 256.²
Pharmacopoea leidensis. 1718. III. 249.
Pharmacopoea londinensis. 1618. III. 250.¹
Pharmacopoea militaris borussica. 1868. III. 249.
De pharmacopœa nederlandica en pharmacopœa belgica onderling vergeleken. 1853. III. 250.¹
Pharmacopoea neerlandica. See NEDERLANDSCHE apotheek. 1826. III. 250.¹
Pharmacopoea norvegica. 1854. III. 247.²
Pharmacopoea Nosocomiorum civilium argentinensium. 1830. III. 249.
Pharmacopoea oldenburgica. 1801. III. 248.
Pharmacopoea pauperum. 1855. III. 249.
Pharmacopoea rossica. 1782. III. 247.²
Pharmacopœa rossica et fennica. 1825. III. 247.²
Pharmacopoea saxonica. 1820. III. 248.
Pharmacopoea servica. 1881. III. 256.²
Pharmacopoea slesvico-holsatica. 1831. III. 249.
Pharmacopoea suecica. 1775. III. 247.¹
Pharmacopoea taurinensis. 1833. III. 256.²
Pharmacopoea wirtenbergica. 1741. III. 248.
Pharmacopœa bernensis tentamen. 1852. III. 256.¹
Pharmacopoeae würtembergicae novae pars altera. 1845. III. 249.
Pharmacopœia argentoratensis. 1725. III. 248.
Pharmacopœia augustana. See PHARMACOPŒA seu medicamentarium . . . 1574. III. 247.¹
Pharmacopœia chirurgica. 1794. III. 253.
Pharmacopœia Collegii regii londinensis. See PHARMACOPŒA londinensis. 1618. III. 250.¹
Pharmacopœia Collegii regii medicorum et reginæ in Hibernia. See PHARMACOPŒA Collegii regii medicorum dublinensis. 1818. III. 254.
Pharmacopœia Collegii regalis Londini. 1618. See PHARMACOPŒA londinensis. 1618. III. 250.¹
Pharmacopœia Collegii regalis medicorum londinensis. See PHARMACOPŒA londinensis. 1618. III. 250.¹
Pharmacopœia Collegii regii medicorum edinburgensis. 1722. III. 252.
Pharmacopœia, edinburgensis. See PHARMACOPŒIA Collegii regii medicorum edinburgensis. 1722. III. 252.
Pharmacopœia edinburgensis pauperum. See PHARMACOPŒIA pauperum in usum Nosocomii regii edinburgensis. 1746. III. 252.
Pharmacopœia hermetica. 1719. III. 251.
Pharmacopœia in usum nosocomii dicti the London hospital. 1842. III. 254.
Pharmacopœia in usum Nosocomii londinensis Sancti Thomae. 1772. III. 253.
Pharmacopœia in usum Nosocomii regii edinburgensis. See PHARMACOPŒIA Nosocomii regii edinburgensis. 1795. III. 253.
Pharmacopœia Lemeriana contracta. 1700. III. 251.
Pharmacopœia londinensis collegarum. See PHARMACOPŒA londinensis. 1618. III. 250.¹
Pharmacopœia manualis . . . utriusque Nethæ. 1812. III. 250.¹
Pharmacopœia Meadiana. 1756. III. 252.
Pharmacopœia nosocomii neo-eboracensis. 1816. III. 246.
Pharmacopœia Nosocomii regalis Sancti Thomae. See PHARMACOPŒIA in usum Nosocomii londinensis Sancti Thomae. 1772. III. 253.

Pharmacopoeia Nosocomii regii edinburgensis. 1795. III. 253.

Pharmacopoeia of St. Thomas's hospital. *See* PHARMACOPŒIA in usum Nosocomii londinensis Sancti Thomae. 1772. III. 253.

Pharmacopoeia of the American institute of homœopathy. 1897. III. 247.[1]

The **pharmacopoeia** of the London hospital. *See* PHARMACO-PŒIA in usum nosocomii dicti the London hospital. 1842. III. 254.

The **pharmacopoeia** of the Massachusetts medical society. 1808. III. 246.

The **pharmacopoeia** of the Royal college of physicians. *See* PHARMACOPŒA londinensja. 1618. III. 250.[2]

The **pharmacopoeia** of the Royal college of physicians at Edinburgh. *See* PHARMACOPŒA Collegii regii medicorum edinburgensis. 1722. III. 252.

The **pharmacopoeia** of the United States of America. 1820. III. 246.

Pharmacopœia pauperum in usum Nosocomii regii edinburgensis. 1746. III. 252.

Pharmacopoeia Radcliffeana. 1716. III. 251.

Pharmacopœia reformata. 1744. III. 252.

Pharmacopœia regni Poloniæ. 1821. III. 248.

Pharmacopœia seu medicamentarium pro Rep. augustana. 1574. III. 247.[2]

Pharmacy and allied sciences. 1899. III. 495.[1]

Pharmakoffsky, N. Sur le goudron de l'écorce de Populus tremula. 1894. IV. 487.[1]

Pharmakopöe der Vereinigten Staaten. *See* The PHARMACO-PŒIA of the United States of America. 1820. III. 246.

Pharmakopöe für das Königreich Bayern. *See* PHARMACOPŒA bavarica jussu regio edita. 1822. III. 248.

Pharmakopöe für das Königreich Hannover. *See* PHARMACO-PŒA hannoverana. 1819. III. 248.

Pharmakopöe für das Königreich Württemberg. *See* PHAR-MACOPŒA wirtenbergica. 1741. III. 248; *see also* PHARMA-COPŒAE würtembergicae. 1845. III. 249.

Pharmakopöe für Schleswig und Holstein. *See* PHARMACOPŒA slesvicoholsatica. 1831. III. 249.

Pharmatzevtitcheski . . . *See* Фармацевтическiй . . . III. 319.[1]

Phayre, A. P. & others. Production of Palm sugar. 1859. III. 311.[1]

Philippe-Beaulieux. Mémoire sur les arbres d'ornement. 1847. III. 124.[1]

Phelps, Mrs. Almira Hart LINCOLN. Familiar lectures on botany. 1829. I. 86, V. x.[1]

Phelps, Lyman. Direct influence of pollen on the Orange. 1889. II. 403.[1]

Phelps, R. H. Cultivation of Grapes in New England. 1859. III. 550.

Phelps, William. Calendarium botanicum. 1810. I. 396.

Phelsum, Murk van. Explicatio partis IV. Phytographiae Leonhardi Phuc'neti. 1769. I. 292.

Phenè, John Samuel. Sparta, the Kermes Oak. 1877. II. 133.[1]

Phi. Mons. Robert's patent for renovating diseased Elms. 1863. III. 180.[2]

Philadelphia, (pseud.). Laurus Sassafras. 1877. II. 228.[1] . . . I. 4.[1]

Philadelphia — Academy of natural sciences. *See* ACADEMY . . . I. 4.[1]

Philadelphia — American philosophical society. *See* AMERICAN . . . I. 5.

Philadelphia — Engineers' club. *See* ENGINEERS' . . . IV. 3.

Philadelphia — Natural history club. *See* NATURAL . . . I. 519.[1]

Philadelphia college of pharmacy. Journal. *See* AMERICAN journal of pharmacy . . . I. 4.[2]

Philadelphia florist. *See* The FLORIST and horticultural journal. III. 3.

Philadelphia medical times. I. 6.

Philadelphia society for promoting agriculture. Memoirs. III. 7.

Philaretos, Petros. *See* ΦΙΛΑΡΕΤΟΣ, Πέτρος.

Philbert, J. Du choix des espèces . . . fruitières à planter sur les routes. 1897. III. 211.[1]
— Dispositions générales des plantations sur les routes. 1897. III. 211.[2]

Philbert, J. C. Dictionnaire abrégé de botanique. 1803. I. 70.
— Dictionnaire universel de botanique. 1804. I. 33.
— Exercices de botanique. 1801. I. 84.
— Introduction à l'étude de la botanique. 1799. I. 84.
— Notions élémentaires de botanique. 1802. I. 84.

Philip, Robert. On hedgerow timber trees. 1865. III. 214.[2]
— On planting. 1858. IV. 152.
— Preparation of waste land for planting. 1863. III. 150.[2]
— On pruning forest trees. 1858. IV. 170. — 1863. IV. 170.
— On thinning plantations. 1858. IV. 173.

Philipp, Karl. Deutsch-englisches und englisch-deutsches. 1900. IV. 23.[3]
— Dictionary of German and English forest-terms. 1900. IV. 23.[3]
— Hülfstabellen für Forst-Taxatoren. 1893. IV. 231.[1]
— Irregular woods in the Black Forest. 1897. IV. 131.
— Peuplements jardinés dans la Forêt Noire. 1897. IV. 131.
— The woods of the Bauland. 1897. IV. 119.[1]

Philipp, Robert. Ueber die Anwendung der Eichenrinde zur Reinigung des Rübensaftes. 1854. IV. 514.[3]

Philippar, François Haken. Catalogue des végétaux . . . dans le jardin d'étude de l'Institution royale agronomique de Grignon. 1837. I. 57.
— Catalogue méthodique des végétaux cultivés dans le Jardin de Versailles. 1843. I. 58.
— Études silvicoles. 1842. IV. 121.
— Extrait des observations sur . . . Cyprès de la Louisiane. 1836. III. 310.[2]
— Notice sur la coupe des taillis. 1834. IV. 382.[1]
— Rapport sur l'état de l'horticulture . . . de Seine-et-Oise. 183 .? III. 125.

Philippe, Matthieu. Sur l'Eucalyptus globulus. 1862. II. 624.[1]
— Sur l'Eucalyptus globulus et l'Hovenia dulcis. 1864. III. 541,[3] 634.[2]
— Extrait d'une lettre sur quelques végétaux . . . dans les jardins de M. Denis. 1849. I. 58.
— Notice sur les Araucaria imbricata de M. Kersauson. 1846. III. 298.[2]
— Sur le Schinus Molle. 1862. III. 529.[1]
— Tableau indiquant la nomenclature . . . dans le Jardin botanique de la marine, à Toulon. 1849. I. 58.

Philippe, Xavier. Flore des Pyrénées. 1859. I. 412.

Philippe de la très-saincte Trinité. Voyage d'Orient. 1669. III. 277.

Philippeau. La déstruction du phylloxéra. 1900. III. 575.[1]

Philippi, Federico. Algunas plantas forrajeras. 1880. III. 223.[1]
— El árbol de Sándalo de la isla de Juan Fernandez. 1892. II. 169.[2]
— Botanische Reise nach der Provinz Atacama. 1887. I. 346.
— Catalogus plantarum vascularium chilensium. 1881. I. 346.
— Catalogus praevius plantarum in itinere ad Tarapaca . . . lectarum. 1891. I. 346.
— Disease of the Vines in Talca. 1905. III. 562.[1]
— Excursion botanica . . . a la provincia de Atacama. 1886. I. 346.
— La flora de las islas San Ambrosio. 1875. I. 346.
— Ilustraciones de la terminolojía botánica. 1879. I. 71.
— Informe sobre las enfermedades de los Viñedos. 1895. III. 562.[1]
— Jardines botánicos. 1877. I. 38.[1]
— Memoria i catalogo de las plantas cultivadas en el jardin botánico. 1882. I. 39.
— Der Sandelholzbaum der Insel Juan Fernandes. 1892. II. 169.[2]
— Verzeichniss der . . . auf der Hochebene der Provinzen Antofagasta und Tarapacá gesammelten Pflanzen. 1891. I. 346.
— Verzeichniss der von D. Francisco Vidal Gormaz . . . gesammelten Gefässpflanzen. 1890. I. 346.
— A visit to the northernmost forest of Chile. 1884. I. 346.
— Von Yerbas Buenas nach Matanzas. 1895. I. 347.
— & R. A. Botanische Abhandlungen. *See* PHILIPPI, Federico. 1892. II. 169.[2]

Philippi, Rudolf Amandus. Ueber Adenostemum nitidum Pers. 1868. III. 221.[2]
— Analogien zwischen der chilenischen und europäischen Flora. 1893. I. 346.
— Anfrage, Fuchsia macrostemma . . . betreffend. 1876. II. 644.[1]
— Bemerkungen über Alona rostrata Lindl. 1884. II. 767.[3]
— Bemerkungen über die chilenischen Arten von Edwardsia. 1873. II. 384.[1]
— Bemerkungen über die chilenischen Myrtaceen. 1857. II. 619.[1]

Philippi, Rudolf Amandus (continued).
— Bemerkungen über die Flora bei den Bädern von Chillan. 1892. I. 346.
— Bemerkungen über die Flora der Insel Juan Fernandez. 1856. 'I. 510.[3]
— Bemerkungen über die Flora der Wüste Atacama. 1857. I. 346.
— Beschreibung einiger neuer Cactus. 1872. II. 592,[3] 596.[3]
— Botanische Excursion in das Araukanerland. 1896. I. 347.
— Botanische Excursion in die Provinz Aconcagua. 1861. I. 346.
— Eine botanische Exkursion in die Provinz Aconcagua. 1883. I. 346.
— Botanische Mittheilungen, I. 1868. II. 596.[1]
— Botanische Reise nach der Provinz Valdivia. 1858. I. 346.
— Catalogo de las plantas cultivadas ... Santiago. 1882. I. 39.[1]
— Ueber die chilenische Palme. 1859. II. 69.[3]
— Clasificacion de varias plantas del desierto de Atacama. 1878. I. 346.
— Commentar zu den von Molina beschriebenen chilenischen Pflanzen. 1864. I. 346.
— Comparacion de las floras i faunas de las repúblicas de Chile i Arjentina. 1893. I. 330.
— Descripcion de algunas plantas nuevas chilenas. 1863. I. 346.
— Descripcion de algunas plantas nuevas chilenas. 1884. I. 346.
— Descripcion de las plantas nuevas. 1872. I. 330.
— Descripcion de unas plantas nuevas, recojidas ... en la provincia del Maule. 1862. I. 346.
— Echinocactus senilis Ph. 1886. II. 593.[1]
— Ueber einige chilenische Pflanzengattungen. 1889. II. 247.[1]
— Escursion al cajon de los Cipreses. 1875. I. 346.
— Sobre los especies chilenas del jenero Polyachyrus. 1886. II. 863.[3]
— Excursion botánica en Valdivia. 1865. I. 346.
— Une excursion botanique dans la province d'Aconcagua. 1883. I. 346.
— Sobre la flora de la Nueva Zelanda. 1872. I. 507.
— Ueber die Flora Siciliens. 1836. I. 431.
— Florula atacamensis. 1860. I. 346.
— Latua Ph., ein neues Genus der Solanaceen. 1858. II. 772.[1]
— Merkwürdige Monstruosität einer Cactus-Blume. 1868. II. 596.[1]
— Merkwürdige Nekrosis des Holzkörpers. 1875: I. 207.[3] — 1876. I. 207.[1]
— Necrosis del sistema leñoso. 1875. I. 207.[3]
— Neue Pflanzen Chili's. 1884. II. 861.[1]
— Noch ein Wort über Betula odorata. 1846. II. 117.[3]
— Opuntia Poeppigi Otto und O. Segethi. 1883. II. 594,[1] 597.[1]
— Sobre la Opuntia Segethi. 1879. II. 597.[1]
— Osteocarpus rostratus Philippi. 1884. II. 767.[3]
— Phoenix dactylifera, Jubaea spectabilis. 1879. II. 69,[2] 691,[1] III. 323.[3]
— Plantarum novarum chilensium centuria. 1856. I. 346.
— Sobre las plantas descritas por el padre Feuillée. 1867. I. 346.
— Plantas nuevas chilenas de las familias Cruciferas, Bixáceas. 1893. I. 346.
— Sobre las plantas que Chile posee en comun con Europa. 1875. I. 346.
— Reise durch die Wüste Atacama. 1860. I. 346.
— Remarques sur la flore de l'Ile de Juan Fernandez. 1856. I. 510.[3]
— Ribes integrifolium Philippi. 1881. II. 245.[1]
— El Sándalo de la isla de Juan Fernandez. 1876. II. 169.[2]
— Ueber den Sandelholzbaum der Insel Juan Fernandez. 1876. II. 169.[3]
— Sertum mendocinum. 1862. I. 346.
— Statistik der chilenischen Flora. 1860. I. 346.
— Über die Vegetation am Ätna. 1832. I. 431.
— On the vegetation of Etna. 1832. I. 431.
— Zwei neue Gattungen der Taxineen. 1860. II. 8.[1]
— Ueber zwei neue Pflanzen-Gattungen. 1865. II. 215.[1]
— See also RENJIFO, Cárlos & PHILIPPI, R. A.
Philippson, Alfred. Der Peloponnes. 1891. I. 450.
— & Neumann, Ludwig. Europa, eine allgemeine Landeskunde. See NEUMANN, Ludwig. 1895. I. 350.[1]

Philippo, James Cecil. On the cultivation of the Rami. 1884. III. 381.[1]
Phillips, Charles D. F. Materia medica and therapeutics. 1879. III. 243.
Phillips, Henry. The companion for the orchard. 1831. III. 79.
— Flora domestica. 1823. I. 511, III. 81.
— Flora historica. 1824. III. 33.[1]
— Floral emblems. 1825. I. 515.
— History of cultivated vegetables. 1822. III. 32.[3]
— Pomarium britannicum. 1820. III. 220.[1] — 1821.' III. 79.
— Sylva florifera. 1823. III. 78.[1]
Phillips, J. & others. Process of grafting Mangoes. 1882. III. 524.[3]
Phillips, J. L. See ALWOOD, W. B. & PHILLIPS, J. L.
Phillips, James & Battle, K. P. & R. H. Dates of the flowering. 1884. I. 222.[1]
Phillips, John. On the ancient ... forests of Holderness. 1834. I. 393.[3]
Phillips, Reginald Wilham. See DARWIN, Francis & PHILLIPS, R. W.
Phillips, Richard. An experimental examination of ... Pharmacopoeia londinensis. 1811. III. 253.
Phillips, William. Guide to the botany ... of Shrewsbury. 1878. I. 403.
— The Shelton (Glendower's) Oak. 1879. II. 138.[3]
Phillips, William B. Turpentine and rosin. 1889. IV. 463.[1]
Das Phillyrin. 1837. III. 680.[1]
Philodasike henosis. See ΦΙΛΟΔΑΣΙΚΗ ΕΝΩΣΙΣ.
Philomel, (pseud.). Banksian Roses. 1900. III. 454.[3]
— Hybrid and other Roses at Kew. 1900. III. 451.[1]
— Rosa rugosa and its best varieties. 1900. III. 457.[1]
Philoparchus, Germanus, (pseud.). [Der] kluge Forst- und Jagdbeamte. 1774. IV. 94.[3]
Philosophical institute of Victoria. Transactions. See PHILOSOPHICAL SOCIETY ... I. 30.
Philosophical magazine. I. 19.
Philosophical society of Adelaide. Transactions. I. 29.[3]
Philosophical society of Glasgow. Proceedings. I. 19.
Philosophical society of Great Britain. See VICTORIA INSTITUTE. I. 20.
Philosophical society of New South Wales. Transactions. I. 29.[1]
Philosophical society of Victoria. Transactions. I. 30.
Philosophical transactions. See ROYAL SOCIETY OF LONDON. I. 20.
Philo-Sylva, (pseud.). The management of forest trees. 1841. IV. 120.
Philpot, Mrs. J. H. The sacred tree. 1897. I. 517.[3]
Phin, John. Open air Grape culture. 1862. III. 550.
Phinney, A. J. Catalogue of the flora of central-eastern Indiana. 1883. V. XVII.[1]
Phinney, H. B. Cultivation of the Pitch Pine on the seacoast. 1865. IV. 468.[3]
Phippen, G. D. Impressions of the flora of Texas. 1879. I. 324.
Phipps, Ramsay Weston. Report on the necessity of preserving ... forests. 1883. IV. 177,[3] 271,[1] 337.[1]
Phipson, T. L. Action de la santonine sur la vue. 1859. III. 754.[3]
— Sur les couleurs des feuilles. 1858. I. 185.[3]
— Identité de la cascarine avec la rhamnoxanthine. 1892. III. 542.[3]
— Irritability in Robinia. 1880. II. 383.[1]
— Note sur quelques substances extraites du fruit du Juglans. 1869. II. 114.[1]
— Note sur une matière colorante extraite du Rhamnus Frangula. 1858. III. 543.[1]
— Sur un phénomène de sensibilité observé dans l'Acacia. 1880. II. 383.[1]
— Réginaine. 1875. III. 356.[1]
Phisalix, C. See DYBOWSKI, Jean, BERTRAND, Gabriel & PHISALIX, C.
Phoebus, Philip. De la culture des Quinquinas. 1866. III. 712.[1]
— Die Delondre-Bouchardatschen China-Rinden. 1864. II. 813.[1]
Phoenix, F. K. Root grafting. 1846. III. 164.[1]
— Seedlings vs. grafts. 1853. III. 161.
Photographs of cutch-boilers' camp. 1900. III. 464.[3]
Phraas, N. K. See ΦΡΑΑΣ, N. K.
Le phylloxéra. 1877? III. 760.
Phylloxéra. Commission départementale de l'Hérault. 1877. III. 760.

Phylloxera and other diseases of the Grapevine. 1891. III. 762.

Le **phylloxéra** dans le canton de Genève. 1889. III. 762.

Le **phylloxéra** dans le canton de Neuchâtel. 1878. III. 760.

Le **phylloxéra** en Suisse. 1881. III. 761.

Phylloxéra; rapport du Département de l'agriculture. 1887. III. 762.

Die **Phylloxera** (Reblaus), ihr Wesen. 1880. III. 572.

Le **phylloxéra**; submersion des Vignes. 1874. III. 759.

Phylloxera vastatrix; enquête de l'Academie. 1879. III. 571.

The **Physic** garden at Chelsea. 1886. *II. 28,*[1] III. 609.[2] — 1890. II. 28.[2]

Physicalische Belustigungen. I. 14.

Physician, (*pseud.*). *See* PARIS, J. A.

Physics of timber. 1898. IV. 411.[1]

Physikalisch-medicinische Gesellschaft, Würsburg. Sitzungsberichte. Verhandlungen. Würsburger naturwissenschaftliche Zeitschrift. I. 14.

Physikalisch-medicinische Societät zu Erlangen. Sitzungsberichte. I. 14.

Physikalisch-ökonomische Baumschule. 1792. III. 135.

Physikalisch-ökonomische Bemerkungen über die sich so sehr verbreitende Trockniss. *See* TRZEBITZKY, F. X. 1798. IV. 203.

Physikalisch-ökonomische Gesellschaft zu Königsberg. *See* KÖNIGLICH PHYSIKALISCH . . . I. 13.

Physikalsk-oeconomisk . . . Bibliothek for Danmar kog Norge. I. 9.[1]

Physiographiska sällskapet. Tidskrift. I. 8.[1]

Physiological society. Proceedings. *See* JOURNAL of physiology. I. 18.

Physiologie végétale; mémoire sur le Noyer. 1845. III. 356.[1]

Physiologisches Laboratorium der landwirthschaftlichen Lehranstalt. Botanische Untersuchungen. III. 13.

Physique et physiologie végétale applicable aux arbres gelés. 1839. III. 182.

Phytographische Blätter. I. 14.

Phytolacca elettrica. 1882. IV. 519.[2]

Phytologia britannica. *See* HOW, William. 1650. I. 394.

The **Phytologist.** I. 19.

Piaget, Éd. Sur l'épiderme des plantes. 1896. I. 130.

Piallatrice universale per scorniciare ed incanalare. 1886. IV. 422.[1]

Pianigiani, U. I boschi di Castagno. 1895. III. 359,[1] *IV. 422.*[2]

— La foresta di Migliarino. 1887. IV. 364.

— Sulla pensione delle guardie forestali provinciali. 1899. IV. 311.[2]

— Sulla scomparsa del Faggio. 1899. IV. 500.[2]

Piano e terminazione . . . in proposito dei boschi di Rovere della Trevisana. 1792. IV. 304.[1]

Piano formato . . . in proposito dei boschi di Roveri delle due provincie Padovana e Vicentina. 1792. IV. 304.[1]

Delle piantagioni in città. 1866. IV. 55.[1]

Delle piante industriali. *See* GORINI, Gemello. 1878. III. 53.

Piante silvane allignanti. 1884. IV. 75.[2]

Piassaba fibre. 1880. III. 320.[1]

Pistnitzki, A. P. *See* ПЯТНИЦКИЙ, А. П.

Piaz, Antonio, Die Waldungen Siciliens. 1890. IV. 364.

— Waldungen und Maquis in Griechenland. 1891. IV. 375.[2]

Piazza, G. A. Tariffa dei legnami in magazzino. 1845. IV. 405.[2]

Picaglia, Luigi. Bibliografia botanica . . . di Modena. 1892. I. 4.[1]

Picard, Edmond & **Hoffschmidt,** Joseph. Le code forestier belge. 1884. IV. 323.[1]

Picard, Étienne. Le cahier de doléances . . . de la maitrise . . . d'Autun. 1887. IV. 27.[2]

— Le commerce du bois de chauffage. 1896. IV. 405.[1]

— Des délits et des peines en matière forestière. 1891. IV. 326.

— Les forêts de l'abbaye de Citeaux. 188.? IV. 27.[2]

— Les forêts du Charollais. 1876. IV. 27.[2]

— Les forêts du département de l'Yonne. 1889. IV. 361.

— Histoire d'une forêt communale. 1898. IV. 362.

— Les réformes forestières en Bourgogne. 1876. IV. 27.[2]

Picardi, Gaetano. Del caffè, racconto storico-medico. 1845. III. 741.[2]

Picardie — Société d'horticulture. *See* SOCIÉTÉ . . . III. 22.

Picatoste y Rodriguez, Felipe. Apuntes para una biblioteca científica española del siglo XVI. 1891. I. 3.[2]

Piccaluga, Giuseppe. Arboricoltura. 1862. III. 114.[2]

Piccard, Jules. Sur les bourgeons de Peuplier. 1874. II. 96.[2]

Piccardo, Angelo. Breve . . . relatione del viaggio nel regno di Congo. 1692. III. 281.[1]

Piccardt, R. A. S. De geschiedenis van het cultuurstelsel in Nederlandsch Indië. 1873. III. 128.

Piccioli, Antonio. L'antotrofia. 1834. III. 88.[2]

— Catalogo delle piante del giardino botanico . . . di Firenze. 1841. I. 63.

— Catalogus plantarum Horti botanici florentini. 1829. I. 62.

— Nuovo metodo per la riproduzione delle piante per margotto. 1829. III. 159.[1]

— Pomona toscana. 1820. III. 88.[1]

Piccioli, Francesco. Sopra alcune norme per regolare e facilitare la riuscita dei rimboscamenti. 1878. IV. 165.

— Anfangsgründe der endlichen Differenzen. 1878. IV. 59.[1]

— Una breve excursione degli alunni . . . a Moncioni. 1885. I. 64; *see also* Una BREVE escursione. 1885. IV. 364.

— Elementi di calcolo alle differenze finite. 1878. IV. 59.[1]

— Elementi di tassazione ed assestamento forestale. 1876. IV. 241.

— Elementos de tasación forestal. 1876. IV. 241.

— Escursione nelle foreste di Camaldoli. 1878. IV. 364.

— Note alle lezioni di stima e statica forestale. 187.? IV. 255.

— Sui rimboschimenti eseguiti in Francia. 1887. IV. 163.

— La Scuola forestale di Barres. 1879. IV. 34.[2]

— Seghe forestale. 1887. IV. 393.

— Sul tannino. 1880. IV. 435.

— Trabajos de repoblación practicados en Francia. 1887. IV. 163.

Piccioli, Giuseppe. Catalogus plantarum horti botanici . . . florentini. 1818. I. 62.

Piccioli, Lodovico. Alcuni casi d'albinismo. 1887. IV. 90.[1]

— Sopra alcuni Viscum. 1887. IV. 519.[2]

— La coltura dei Salici. 1896. III. 349.

— Un' escursione degli alunni dell' Istituto forestale di Vallombrosa. 1888. IV. 364.

— Guida alle escursioni botaniche nei dintorni di Vallombrosa. 1888. I. 429, IV. 35.[2]

— Importanza forestale dei millepiedi. 1887. IV. 92.

— Il legno delle più importanti piante. 1889. IV. 409.

— Metodo per curare le cicatrici degli alberi. 1887. IV. 66.[1]

— Le piante legnose italiane. 1890. I. 423,[2] *IV. 86.*[1]

— Raccolta di vocaboli botanici e forestali italiani e tedeschi. 1890. I. 71, *IV. 23.*[2]

— Rapporti biologici fra le piante e le lumache. 1892. I. 235.[2]

— Salis [*sic*] peloritana Prest. 1894. IV. 488.[1]

— Lo scoiattolo (Sciurus vulgaris L.). 1888. IV. 90.[2]

— Lo sviluppo del Sughero. 1894. IV. 517.[2]

Piccioli, Antoine. Rapport sur les plantes . . . des Hespéridées. 1864. III. 497.[1]

Picciuoli, Giuseppe. Hortus Panciaticus. 1783. I. 61.

Le **piccole** industrie forestali in Italia. 1883. IV, 405.[3]

Piccone, Antonio. Di alcune piante liguri disseminate da uccelli carpofagi. 1886. I. 240.[2]

— Instruzione scientifiche per viaggiatori. 1874. I. 35.

— Sulla malattia del falchetto nei Gelsi. 1879. III. 379.[1]

— Primi studii per una monografia . . . d'Ulivo coltivate nella zona ligure. 1879. II. 713.[1]

Picconi, Giammaria. Saggi sull' economia olearia. 1808. III. 678.[2]

De Piceae Pinique silvestris resina. *See* ROBERG, Lars. 1714. IV. 443.[1]

Pichard, P. Sur un acarien destructeur du phylloxera gallicole. 1880. III. 572.

— Action de quelques substances antiparasitaires. 1885. III. 579.

— Assimilabilité plus grande de l'azote nitrique. 1893. I. 160.

— Contribution à la recherche . . . des conditions sous lesquelles le chlore du sol pénètre. 1899. I. 160.

— Contribution à la recherche du manganèse. 1898. I. 157.

— Dosage rapide de l'azote nitrique. 1895. I. 156.[2]

— Quelques reactions colorées de la brucine. 1896. III. 684.[1]

— Recherche et dosage rapides du manganèse. 1898. I. 157.

Pichi, P. Alcuni esperimenti fisiopatologici sulla Vite. 1891. III. 580.

— Sulla fitoptosi della Vite. 1888. III. 564.[1]

Pichi, P., (continued).
— Sulla infezione peronosporica. 1890. III. 580.
— Una nuova forma di Peronospora. 1890. III. 580.
— Osservazioni istologiche sull' . . . Vite. 1888. II. 506.[1]
— Poche parole sull' infezione peronosporica. 1888. III. 580.
— Risposta alla critica del Prof. A. N. Berlese. 1893. III. 581.
Pichi des Péruviens. 1886. III. 700.[2]
Pichler, Ch. Exposé über . . . Staatsforste des k. k. Salzkammergutes. 1873. IV. 369.
Pichlmayr, M. F. See HINTERHUBER, Julius & PICHLMAYR, M. F.
Pichon & Broca. Catalogue raisonné . . . à l'École de botanique de Brest. 1811. I. 57.
Pick, Heinrich. Ueber die Bedeutung des rothen Farbstoffes. 1883. I. 173.
— Beiträge zur Kenntniss des assimilirenden Gewebes armläubiger Pflanzen. 1881. I. 123.[2]
Pickel, G. Die diessjährigen Wetterbeobachtungen. 1804. III. 552.
— Die Witterung des Jahres 1805. 1806. III. 552.
Pickel, Ignaz. Praktischer Unterricht, wie man sich bey der Ausmessung . . . grosser Wälder zu verhalten habe. 1785. IV. 216.
Pickell, J. M. Ashes as a fertilizer. 1891. I. 156.[1]
Pickering, Charles. Chronological history of plants. 1879. I. 72,[1] 79.[2]
— The geographical distribution of animals and plants. 1863. I. 300.
— On the geographical distribution of plants. 1830. I. 299.
— History of the introduction of domestic animals and plants. 1863. I. 242,[1] 300.
— Plants in their wild state. 1863. I. 300.
Pickering, Spencer U. See BEDFORD, duke of & PICKERING, S. U.
Pickering, Timothy. The felling of trees for timber. 1822. IV. 384.[2]
— On the Locust tree. 1821. IV. 523.[2]
Picoré, J. J. Culture . . . de la Vigne du vignoble lorrain. 1891. III. 557.[1]
— Les grands maîtres de l'arboriculture. 1890. III. 557.[2]
Picot, Charles. Culture de la Vigne. 1878. III. 556.
Picot, J. B. C. Nouveau procédé de taille de la Vigne. 1875. III. 556.
Picquenard, Charles Armand. Catalogue des plantes vasculaires . . . d'Ille-et-Vilaine. 1897. I. 418.
Piotet, Raoul. Sur la fabrication de la pâte de bois. 1884. IV. 430.
Pictorius, Johann Baptist. Der in Blumen-Küchen-Arzeney-und Baumgarten gründlich instruirte Gärtner. 1729. III. 103.
Picture of vegetation on the surface of the globe. 1826. I. 94.
Piddington, Henry. An English index to the plants of India. 1832. I. 75.[2]
— On the soil suitable for Cotton, Tobacco. 1836. III. 602.[1]
— A tabular view of the generic characters in Roxburgh's Flora indica. 1836. I. 472.
Piderit, Philippe Jacobi. Additamenta ad Dispensatorium electorale hassiacum. 1816. III. 248.
— Pharmacia rationalis. 1782. III. 248.
— Versuch einer Darstellung der ausländischen Arzneymittel. 1810. III. 242.
Il pidocchio di San José scale e la "Pro Montibus." 1899. III. 192.[1]
Piednagel. Note sur un moyen préventif de la fièvre puerpérale. 1856. III. 585.[2]
Piekarski, F. B. Ekonom kolegom kraju nowowcielonego sposoby. 1810. III. 146.[1]
Pielmann, A. Vertilgung des Kiefernspinners. 1889. IV. 478.
Pielmann, R. Des Försters Nummerbuch. 1886. IV. 387.[2]
Piepenbring, George Heinrich. Lehrbuch der Fundamental-Botanik. 1805. I. 84.
— Teutscher Caffee und Thee. 1798. III. 458.[2]
Pieper, Philipp Anton. Das wechselnde Farben-Verhaltniss. 1834. I. 185.[1]
Pieper, Reinh. Die japanischen Hortensien. 1869. III. 411.[1]
Piepers. Over de vernieling van Theebladen. 1886. III. 604.[2]
Piepers, M. C. Over schade door rupsen aan Klapperboomen toegebracht. 1893. III. 323.[2]
Piérard. Instruction sur la plantation . . . des arbres. 1829. III. 124.[1]
— Mémoire sur la culture des arbres à cidre. 1821. III. 426,[1] 445.[1]

Pierce, C. H. Examinations of drugs, medicines. 1852. III. 258.
Pierce, J. W. The cultivation and marketing of Apples. 1879. III. 426.[2]
— Ripening and marking pears. 1878. III. 445.[2]
Pierce, L. B. Good lawn trees. 1884. III. 204.[1]
— Half a dozen good shrubs. 1884. III. 203.
Pierce, Newton B. The California Vine disease. 1892. III. 580.
— Grape diseases on the Pacific coast. 1895. III. 562.[1]
— Olive culture in the United States. 1897. III. 676.[2]
— Peach leaf curl. 1900. III. 442.[2]
Pieri, Michele Trivoli. Della corcirese flora centuria. 1808. I. 448.[2]
— Florae corcirensis centuriae. 1824. I. 448.[2]
Pierot, J. Specimen medicum inaugurale de Mudar. 1839. III. 692.[1]
Pierpont, J. de. Traité des arbres et arbustes rustiques. 1865. III. 77.
Pierquin de Gembloux, Claude Charles. Réflexions sur le sommeil des plantes. 1839. I. 198.
Pierre. La botanique par le capitaine Pierre. 1845. I. 94.
Pierre, (abbé). Une galle du Saule. 1896. III. 350.[2]
Pierre, Camille SAINT-. See SAINT-PIERRE, Camille & MAGNIEN, Lucien.
Pierre, E. Sur deux espèces d'Epicharis. 1881. II. 420.[2]
— Sur le genre Pteronema des Simarubacées. 1897. II. 415.[1]
— De quelques produits du genre Garcinia. 1882. III. 609.[1]
Pierre, Édouard. L'oxyde de fer et le phylloxéra. 1880. III. 761.
Pierre, Jacques Henri BERNARDIN DE SAINT-. See SAINT-PIERRE, J. H. B. de.
Pierre, Joachim Isidore. Chimie agricole. 1890. III. 37.[1]
— Sur l'épuisement du sol par les Pommiers. 1875. II. 280.[1]
— Fragment d'études sur les époques d'assimilation. 1869. I. 159.
— Sur la matière colorante des fruits du Mahonia. 1875. III. 395.[1]
— Note sur l'emploi, comme fourrage, des feuilles. 1856. III. 223.[1]
— Note sur l'épuisement du sol par les Pommiers. 1875. II. 267.[2]
— The nutrition of plants. 1869. I. 159.
— Sur la présence de la potasse. 1869. I. 153.
Pierre, Louis. Sur l'Ancylobothrys pyriformis. 1899. II. 727.[2]
— Les arbres d'abri pour les plantations de Caféiers. 1900. III. 734.[2]
— Caractères du fruit de l'Acrosepalum. 1899. II. 512.[2]
— Diploknema sebifera. 1883. II. 698.[1]
— Flore forestière de la Cochinchine. 1880. I. 469,[2] IV. 83.[1]
— Sur le genre Allexis des Violacées. 1898. II. 567.[1]
— Sur le genre Amalocalyx des Echitidées. 1898. II. 724.[1]
— Sur le genre Antrocaryon. 1898. II. 455.[1]
— Sur le genre Chloromyrtus. 1898. II. 625.[2]
— Sur le genre Crioceras . . . des Apocynacées. 1897. II. 725.[1]
— Sur le genre Helictonema. 1898. II. 472.[1]
— Sur le genre Lirayea. 1896. II. 797.[1]
— Sur le genre Melientha. 1888. II. 170.[2]
— Sur le genre Microchonea. 1898. II. 728.[1]
— Sur le genre Nouettea des Echitidées. 1898. II. 729.[1]
— Sur le genre Ongokea. 1897. II. 171.[2]
— Sur le genre Paravallaris. 1898. II. 730.[1]
— Sur le genre Peripeplus des Psychotriées. 1898. II. 826.[2]
— Sur le genre Perithryx des Périplocées. 1898. II. 736.[1]
— Sur le genre Plagiostyles. 1897. II. 450.[1]
— Sur le genre Stixis. 1887. II. 233.[2]
— Sur le genre Suringaria. 1888. II. 611.[2]
— Sur le genre Telotia. 1888. II. 208.[1]
— Sur le genre Tirania. 1887. II. 233.[2]
— Sur le genre Xylinabaria des Echitidées. 1898. II. 734.[1]
— Sur le genre Zollingeria. 1886. II. 490.[2]
— Sur les genres Allanblackia et Pentadesma. 1898. II. 553,[1] 558.[2]
— Sur les genres Oricia et Diphasia. 1898. II. 405,[2] 409.[1]
— Sur l'Harmandia. 1889. II. 171.[1]
— Sur la laque de Cochinchine. 1898. II. 457.[1]
— Sur le Monotes glandulosa sp. nov. 1897. II. 560.[2]
— Sur le N'Dyembo ou Landolphia Klainii. 1898. II. 727.[2]
— Notes botaniques. Sapotacées. 1890. II. 696.[2]
— Observations sur quelques Bixacées. 1899. II. 565.[2]
— Observations sur quelques Landolphiées. 1898. II. 721.[2]

— Observations sur quelques Ménispermacées africaines. 1898. II. 206.¹
— Sur l'Omphalocarpum Radlkoferi. 1886. II. 699.²
— Plantes à Gutta-percha. 1885. II. 699,¹ 699.²
— Plantes du Gabon. 1896. I. 491.
— À propos d'une Macarisiée du Gabon. 1898. II. 613.²
— Sur quelques Olacacées de Gabon. 1898. II. 172.¹
— Sur quelques Olacacées du Gabon. 1897. II. 170.²
— Sur quelques·Phytocrénacées. 1897. II. 474.¹
— Sur quelques Rhaphiostyles. 1897. II. 475.²
Pierre, Simon. De l'utilité de l'écorce de l'Adansonia. 1850. III. 589.¹
Pierret, Valentin. Invasion de chenilles. 1894. IV. 549.²
— L'Orgyie pudibonde. 1894. IV. 549.²
Pierron. Nouveau mode de contention des greffes. 1888. III. 163.¹
Pierson, Nikolaas Gerard. Het kultuurstelsel; zes voorlezingen. 1868. III. 128.
Piesse, Charles Henry. See WRIGHT, C. R. A. & PIESSE, C. H.
—, & Wright, Alder. Sur l'essence de Citron. 1877. III. 502.³
— — Note on otto of Limes. 1877. III. 502.³
Piesse, George William Septimus. The art of perfumery. 1855. III. 226.²
— Lecture on perfumes. 1865. III. 226.¹
— Des odeurs, des perfums et cosmétiques. 1855. III. 226.²
— Scent-yielding plants. 1877. III. 226.²
Pieszczek, E. Chemische Untersuchung der Rinde von Nerium. 1890. III. 689.¹
— Étude chimique de l'écorce de Laurier-rose. 1890. III. 689.²
Pieters, Adrian John. The influence of fruit-bearing on the development of mechanical tissue. 1896. I. 113,² III. 39.
— The plants of Lake St. Clair. 1894. V. XVII.¹
— Seed selling, seed growing. 1900. III. 157.
— Testing seeds at home. 1896. III. 157.
Pietsch, Johann Gottbold. Abhandlung von Anziehung ... der Kastanienbäume. 1776. III. 358.¹
— Versuch eines Entwurfs der Grundsätze des Forst- und Jagd-Rechts. 1779. IV. 313.
Piette, Ed. Études d'ethnographie préhistorique. 1896. I. 523.
Pigati, Giovanni Antonio de MONTE. See MONTE PIGATI, G. A. de.
Pigeaux, (dr.). Ce que doivent faire ceux qui ne veulent pas être obligés de tailler les arbres à fruits. 18 .. ? III. 171.
— Note sur l'Abricotier à amande douce. 1867. III. 434.²
— Note sur le Maté. 1864. III. 530.²
— Notice sur l'Abricotier à amande douce. 1867. III. 434.²
— Usage de la Coca en Europe. 1865. III. 492.²
Pignède, Th. Sur un mode de traitement des Vignes phylloxérées. 1876. III. 569.¹
Pignal, Armand. Système économique de défrichement et de culture dans les Palmiers-nains. 1851. III. 322.¹
Pigot, J. L. The production of Sandal-wood. 1900. IV. 519.²
— Report on the manufacture of spirit of turpentine. 1897. III. 228.¹
Pigott, B. A. F. Flowers and ferns of Cromer. 1885. I. 534.³
Piguet, Léopold. Betula nana L. 1896. II. 119.²
Pijnaert, Charles. See PYNAERT, Charles.
Pike, J. W. Forestry in northern Ohio. 1890. IV. 339.
Pike, Nicolas. A visit to Round Island. 1870. I. 482.
Pilkington, James. Derbyshire. 1789. I. 533.
Piller, Mathias & Mitterpacher; Ludwig. Iter per Poseganam Slavoniae provinciam. 1783. I. 444.
Pillet, L. See CHARABOT, Eugène, DUPONT, J. & PILLET, L.
Pilleterius, Caspar. Plantarum . . . in Walachria . . . nascentium synonymia. 1610. I. 390.
Pillichody, Albert. Un Genévrier arborescent. 1900. II. 31.¹
— Sapins et Épicéas de formes extraordinaires. 1900. II. 23,¹ 35.²
— Ein stattlicher Wachholder. 1900. II. 31.²
Pillichody, C. Combien? Où? Quand? Et comment? 1854. IV. 242.
— Facteurs de conversion. 1853. IV. 387.¹
— Neuer Baumhöhenmesser. 1854. IV. 215.
— Nouveau dendromètre. 1854. IV. 215.
Pilling, F. O. See MÜLLER, W. & PILLING, F. O.
Pilotti, G. B. Ancora a proposito . . . delle sabbie mobili. 1899. IV. 146.¹
Pilz. Die festliegenden Waldbahnen. 1900. IV. 392.

Pilz, (Oberförster). Zur Frage über die Bedeutung der forstlichen Reinerträge. 1876. IV. 256.
— Hiebszugs- oder Bestandeswirthschaft. 1883. IV. 244.
Pim, Bedford & Seemann, Berthold. Dottings on the roadside in Panama. 1869. I. 333.
Pim, Greenwood. A contribution to the natural history of the hairs of the andrœcium. 1885. I. 116.²
— Note on an abnormal development of Picea Pinsapo. 1885. III. 297.¹
Pimentel, C. A. de SOUSA. See SOUSA PIMENTEL, C. A. de.
Pimentel, Julio Maximo d' OLIVEIRA. See also BOUIS, Jules & PIMENTEL, J. M. D'OLIVEIRA.
— & Bouis, Jules. Nouvelle production d'acide palmitique. See OLIVEIRA PIMENTEL D' & BOUIS, J. 1855. I. 182.¹
Pimento. 1866. III. 637.¹
Pimento and its insect foes. 1895. III. 637.²
Pin, C. Flore élémentaire. 1873. I.·414.
Un Pin colossal. See Een REUSACHTIGE Dennenboom. 1894. III. 307.¹
Le Pin de Bank. 1896. IV. 463.¹
Pin Laricio d'Autriche et de Corse. 1898. IV. 465.²
Le Pin Laricio de Salzmann. 1899. II. 44.¹
Le Pin sylvestre dans les taillis. 1899. IV. 479.
Le Pin Weymouth. 1896. IV. 470.²
Pin Weymouth et Pin Cembro. 1898. IV. 461.¹
Pinaceae. See NELSON, John. 1866. III. 289.
Pinaeus, Anton. See Du PINET, Antoine.
Pince, Robert T. Tacsonia Van Volxemi Funck. 1866. III. 617.¹
Pinchot, Gifford. The Adirondack Spruce. 1898. IV. 339.
— Biltmore forest. 1893. IV. 340.
— Forest-policy abroad. 1891. IV. 270.
— Forest reserves of the United States. 1900. IV. 179.²
— The forests of Lake Ne-Ha-Sa-Ne Park in northern New York. 1893. IV. 339.
— Government forestry abroad. 1891. IV. 270; 288,¹
— Mining and the forest reserves. 1898. IV. 179.¹
— Notes on some forest problems. 1899. IV. 338.²
— Notes on the forests of New Jersey. 1896. IV. 339.
— Notes on the history of forest policy. 1892. IV. 270.
— Practical assistance to farmers. 1898. IV. 113,¹ 308.¹
— Practical assistance to tree planters. 1899. IV. 153.¹
— A primer of forestry. 1899. IV. 57.
— Progress of forestry in the United States. 1900. IV. 338.²
— The relation of forests and forest fires. 1899. IV. 182.¹
— Report on examination of the forest reserves. 1898. IV. 179.¹
— The Sihlwald. 1890. IV. 367.
— A study of forest fires. 1899. IV. 182.¹
— The sustained yield of Spruce lands. 1898. IV. 460.²
— Three New Jersey Pines. 1897. II. 40.²
— Work of the division of forestry for the farmer. 1899. IV. 288.¹
— & Ashe, W. W. Timber trees and forests of North Carolina. 1897. I. 317,¹ IV. 77.³
— & Graves, H. S. The White Pine. 1896. IV. 470.²
Pinckert, Friedrich August. Het boerenboekje. 1854. III. 106.¹
— Die Korbweide. 1862. III. 347.
Pinder, (Oberlandesgerichtsrath). Über das Ausroden und Urbarmachen der Wälder. 1899. IV. 42.
Pinder, R. Der Ahornzucker in Nordamerika. 1894. IV. 527.²
— Aufforstung von Heide- und Moorland in Dänemark. 1893. IV. 156.²
— Beobachtungen über die Erziehung von Nadelholzpflanzen. 1886. IV. 69.
— Forstliches aus Nordamerika. 1892. IV. 337.¹
— Die Holzproduction der Vereinigten Staaten. 1888. IV. 420. — 1889. IV. 403.²
— Die Waldschutzbewegung in den Vereinigten Staaten. 1893. IV. 178.²
Pine lands and Pine timber on Red Lake reservation. 1897. IV. 341.¹
Pine-leaf fibre of Silesia. 1854. III. 307,¹ IV. 482.²
Pine supplies of America. 1883. IV. 470.²
The Pine weevil, Hylobius abietis. 1885. IV. 208.⁴
Pineau, J. Recherches sur la formation de l'embryon chez les Conifères. 1849. II. 18.
Pinège, W. Aanplant van Notemuskaat. 1888. III. 402.²
Pineraie dépérissante. 1900. IV. 193.¹
Pineraies. Dégâts de rongeurs. 1899. IV. 479.
Pineraies. Dommages causés par les fumées d'usines. 1898. IV. 193.¹

Pineraies mal venantes en sol sablonneux. 1899. IV. 482.¹
Pines and their uses. 1878. IV. 443.¹
On the Pines of Mammoth-tree-vale. 1857. II. 50.²
The Pinetum at Wellesley. 1892. I. 39. — 1894. I. 39.
The pinetum britannicum. *See* RAVENSCROFT, Edward. II. 13,¹ V. XXV.¹
Pinetum woburnense. *See* FORBES, James. 1839. II. 12.²
Pinguet-Guindon. Nouvelle greffe anglaise de la Vigne. 1892. III. 548.²
Pinguia, HILDEGARDIS DE. *See* HILDEGARDIS DE PINGUIA.
Les pinières de la Campine et le lophyre. *See* PARISEL, Émile. 1876. IV. 477.
Pink, James. The first blue Hydrangea. 1875. III. 412.²
Pinkwart, Hermann. Rosa glauca Vill. × graveolens. 1899. II. 297.²
— Rubus pedemontanus mh. 1898. II. 309.²
Pinney, George. An essay upon the culture . . . of forest trees. 1869. IV. 103.¹
Pinnock. Catechism of botany. 1822. I. 94.
Il Pino pei-go-song. 1864. IV. 463.¹
Pino Pinastro, (*pseud.*). Esami di concorso nell' amministrazione forestale. 1899. IV. 294.¹
Pinon Real. 1857. III. 476.¹
Pins géants. 1893. II. 40.³
Pins sylvestres et rongeurs. 1895. IV. 548.³
Pinus del Doctor. 1891. II. 44.¹
Pinus Deodara en zijn stam of timmerhout. 1853. IV. 448.¹
Pinus Gloucesterensis, (*pseud.*). Variations among Conifers. 1852. II. 39.²
— Des variations chez les Conifères. 1852. II. 39.²
Pinzger, Paul. Kritischer Vergleich der im Gouvernement Moskau wildwachsenden Pflanzen. 1868. I. 362.
Pio di Savoja. Il commercio dei legnami a Trieste. 1888. IV. 405.²
Piolet, J. B. Le caoutchouc à Madagascar. 1897. III. 231.
— De l'exploitation et de la culture du caoutchouc à Madagascar. 1898. III. 149.
Pion, Petrus. Phytologia. 1598. I. 283.
Piotrovski, V. *See* ПІОТРОВСКІЙ, B.
Plovan, G. Sulla causa delle rotte dei fiumi. 1882. IV. 48.¹
— Il grido generale del giorno. 1882. IV. 166.¹
Piper, A. Single Roses. 1897. III. 451.¹
Piper, Charles Vancouver. Conifers on Mount Ranier. 1891. II. 14,² 53.²
— New and noteworthy northwestern plants. 1899. II. 314.² — 1900. I. 327.
— An undescribed Blackcap Raspberry. 1897. II. 307.²
Piper, Richard Upton. The trees of America. 1855. I. 304.
Piper, W. G. The Mistletoe. 1884. II. 180.¹
Piper, Wilhelm. Taschenbuch der norddeutschen Flora. 1846. I. 382.
Piquet. Examen des avantages résultant de l'emploi de la scie, au lieu de la hache. 1809. IV. 392.
Pirck, Johann Lorenz. De camphora. 1767. III. 404.²
Piré, Louis. Analyse des familles et des genres de la flore bruxelloise. 1880. I. 393.¹
— Considérations sur la flore de l'Hindoustan. 1876. I. 81.²
— Les forêts. 1872. I. 217.
— Le Jardin botanique de Bruxelles. 1876. I. 521.²
— Les vieux arbres de la Suisse. 1881. I. 297.²
— & Muller, Félix. Flore analytique du centre de la Belgique. 1866. I. 392.
Pirès, Thomé. Carta escripta de Cochin. 1838. III. 276.¹
Piret, A. J. Poinciana Gillietii [*sic*] Hook. 1898. III. 469.¹
Piret, Léandre. L'Abies Pinsapo Bois. 1898. III. 297.¹
— Les Solanum grimpants. 1894. III. 701.¹
Piria, Raffaele. Ueber das Populin. 1852. IV. 487.¹
— Sur la populine. 1852. IV. 487.¹
— Sur quelques propriétés de l'asparagine. 1845. I. 175.
Pirolle. L'horticulteur français. 1824. III. 113.
— Le jardinier amateur. 1824. III. 113.
Pirona, G. J. Vocabulario friulano. 1871. I. 74.²
Pirona, Giulio Andrea. Florae forojuliensis syllabus. 1855. I. 427.
Pirotta, Alessandro. Bambusa quadrangularis. 1893. III. 316.¹
— Fruttificazione della Jubaea spectabilis. 1900. III. 326.¹
— Gli Illicium. 1893. III. 398.¹
Pirotta, Romualdo. Intorno all' amido . . . di certi Rhamnus. 1889. III. 542.²
— Ancora sul mildew. 1880. III. 578.
— Sur l'apparition du mildew. 1879. III. 578.
— Sopra un carattere delle Gelsominee. 1892. II. 705.²
— Sulla comparsa del mildew. 1879. III. 578.

— Contribuzione all' anatomia comparata della foglia. 1885. II. 705.²
— Contribuzioni alla conoscenza della flora dell' Africa orientale. 1894. I. 489.
— Sul dimorfismo fiorale del Jasminum revolutum. 1885. II. 710.³
— Sull' endosperma delle Gelsominee. 1887. II. 705.²
— Sul genere Keteleria di Carrière. 1887. II. 32.¹
— Sulla germinazione . . . della Keteleeria Fortunei. 1897. II. 32.²
— Sulla malattia dei grappoli. 1887. III. 579.
— Oleacee. 1885. II. 705.²
— La Peronospora viticola. 1881. III. 578.
— Primi studii sul mal nero. 1882. III. 578.
— Pseudolarix Kaempferi Gordon. 1887. II. 49.¹
— Intorno ad una Sensitiva dell' Argentina. 1888. II. 373.²
— Sugli sferocristalli del Pithecoctenium clematideum. 1886. II. 790.¹
— Per la storia dei batteroidi delle Leguminose. 1888. II. 21.²
— Sulla struttura del seme nelle Oleacee. 1883. II. 705.² — 1885. II. 705.²
— Sulla struttura . . . della Keteleeria Fortunei. 1891. II. 32.²
— Sulla struttura delle foglie dei Dasylirion. 1888. II. 81.¹
— *See also* GIBELLI, Giuseppe & PIROTTA, Romualdo.
— & Chiovenda, Emilio. Flora romana. 1900. I. 430.
— & Marcatili, Luigi. Sui rapporti tra i vasi laticiferi ed il sistema assimilatore. 1885. I. 136.¹
Pirrault, J. X. Systematic timber-cutting in Quebec. 1890. IV. 382.²
Pirrie, Alexander. On the early management of plantations. 1858. IV. 169.¹
Pirum, (*pseud.*). A monster tree. 1879. II. 280.²
Pisa — Istituto botanico della R. Università. *See* ISTITUTO . . . I. 25.
Pisa — Società toscana di scienze naturali . . . *See* SOCIETÀ . . . I. 26.¹
Pisani Ciancio, A. B. Catalogo delle piante che si coltivano nel botanico giardino del Signor D. A. B. P. C. in Catania. 1816. I. 62.
Piscicelli, Francesco de VITO. *See* VITO PISCICELLI, Francesco de.
Piskaref, N. *See* ПИСКАРЕВЪ, H.
Piso, Willem. Historia medica Brasiliae. 1817. III. 65.¹
— Historiae naturalis et medicae Indiae Occidentalis libri V. 1658. III. 266.
— De Indiae utriusque re naturali . . . libri. 1658. III. 266.
— Mantissa aromatica. 1658. III. 266.
— De medicina brasiliensi. 1648. III. 65.¹
— De medicina brasiliensi libri quatuor. *See* PISO, Willem & MARCGRAF, Georg. 1648. I. 327.
— & Marcgraf, Georg. Historia naturalis Brasiliae. 1648. I. 327.
Pison-du-Galland, A. F. Rapport . . . sur le nombre . . . des agens de l'administration forestière. 1817. IV. 325.
Pissis, Aimé. Geografía física de la república de Chile. 1875. I. 346.
Pissot. Sur une anomalie végétale remarquée sur un Hêtre. 1856. II. 126.²
— Description de cinq Robiniers. 1857. III. 486.²
— Examen des nouveaux appareils pour l'écorcement des bois. 1876. IV. 434.
— Instructions sur les plantations en général. 1860. III. 166.
— Note sur le Châtaignier. 1854. IV. 493.¹
— Note sur le Gleditschia triacanthos inermis. 1862. III. 477.³
— Quelques remarques sur les arbres. 1862. III. 124.¹
— Rapport sur . . . l'adjonction de la bouture à la greffe. 1858. III. 161.
— Rapport . . . sur le procédé de M. Borniche. 1861. III. 180.¹
Pissot, A. Les chenilles au bois de Boulogne. 1865. III. 189.
— À propos des défrichements et des inondations. 18 . . ? IV. 49.³
— Rapport sur les graines et les plantes d'essences forestières. 1881. IV. 85.³
Pistachio cultivation in Cyprus. 1890. III. 526.¹
Pistone, Antonio. Di alcune etsti tannifere. 1895. I. 184.
— Le liane del genere Solandra Sw. 1894. II. 774.¹
Pistorius, A. W. P. VERKERK. *See* VERKERK PISTORIUS, A. W. P.

Pistorius, Philipp Heinrich. De pilis cum ovulis . . . in Ceraso. 1747. III. 436.²
Pistorius, Thomas. Korte . . . beschryvinge . . . van Zuriname. 1763. III. 267.²
Pisulewski, Szymon. Botaniką krótko zebrana. 1841. I. 88.
— Botanika popularna. 1845. III. 68.²
— Gromady przyrodzone królestwa roślin. 1841. I. 261.
Pitacco, Luigi. La restaurazione delle montagne. 1890. IV. 166.¹
Pitard, C. J. Sur la polystélic chez les Sterculiacées. 1900. II. 532.¹
Pitard, J. Dénivellements tardifs du parenchyme péricyclique. 1900. I. 128.²
— Étirement et aplatissement du péricycle. 1900. I. 128.²
— De l'évolution des parenchymes corticaux. 1898. I. 131.¹
— De l'évolution des péricycles hétérogènes. 1899. I. 128.²
— Nivellement et dénivellement de la zone péricyclique hétéromère. 1900. I. 128.²
— Recherches sur l'anatomie . . . des pédicelles. 1898. I. 114.¹
— La région péricyclique. 1900. I. 128.²
— Relations entre l'accroissement du péricycle et des tissus corticaux. 1900. I. 128.¹
— Variations anatomiques et morphologiques des axes floraux groupés en ombelles. 1893. I. 113.³
Pitasch, Josef. Betrachtungen über die Buchenwirthschaft. 1864. IV. 494.
— Einiges über die Lawinen des vorigen Winters. 1878. IV. 183.³
— Keimungsversuche. 1865. IV. 465.²
— Ein neues und doch altes Pflanzeisen. 1872. IV. 152.·
— Pinus Pinaster. 1875. IV. 468.¹
— Soll man dicht säen? 1866. IV. 149.¹
Pitcaithley, Alexander. Arboriculture in the counties of Dumfries. 1893. IV. 359.¹
— On the plantations and trees on the estate of Brahan. 1887. IV. 359.¹
Le Pitchpin. 1894. IV. 462.¹
Le Pitch-Pine. 1888. IV. 466.²
Pithecolobium Saman; précis of reports. 1886. III. 484.³
Pitorius, P g n s. Opobalsami Romani censura. 1642. III. 510.³ ere⁴ı⁴u
Pitot, Édouard. Arbres de l'île Maurice. 18 . . ? I. 481.²
Pitra, Adolph. Ueber die Anheftungsweise einiger phanerogamen Parasiten. 1861. II. 178.²
— Ueber das Verhaeltniss der Milchsaftgefaesse zu den Bastzellen. 1860. I. 135.
— Versuche über die Druckkraft der Stammorgane. 1878. I. 168.
Pitsch, O. & Ritzema Bos, J. Meikevers. 1875. IV. 203.
Pitschel, Friedrich Lebegott. See LANGGUTH, M. G. A. & PITSCHEL, F. L.
Pitt, Edmund. Extract of a letter . . . concerning Sorbus pyriformis. 1678. II. 312.²
Pittier, Henri. See DURAND, Théophile & PITTIER, Henri.
Pittius, Hermann. Die Kenntniss der wichtigsten Waldbäume. 1882. IV. 107.¹
Pittonia. I. 6.
Pitury, an Australian rival of coca. 1877. III. 700.¹
Il più vecchio albero del mondo. 1000. I. 205.²
Il piviere minore. 1866. IV. 90.¹
Pizarro. Sur le Maté. 1874. III. 531.¹
Pizarro, João Joaquim. Solanaceas brasileiras. 1872. II. 768.¹
Pjetschka, F. Bosniens Waldschätze und Holzhandel. 1883. IV. 406.³
— Der Karst. 1889. IV. 167.²
Plá, Eduardo; SERRANO y. See SERRANO y PLÁ, Eduardo.
Plá y Rave, Eugenio. Maderas de construcción naval. 1874. IV. 425.¹
— Manual de cultivo de árboles forestales. 1880. IV. 109.²·¹
— Manual de cultivo de árboles frutales. 1880. III. 114.¹
— Manual del maderero. 1882. IV. 228, 381.
— Marcos de maderas. 1879. IV. 228.
— Marcos de maderas para la construcion. 1880. IV. 405.²
— Tratado de maderas de construcción. 1880. IV. 423.²
En se plaçant au point de vue de la propagation des insectes nuisibles, quelle est la meilleure époque pour l'exploitation. 1899. IV. 208.²
Place, Franz. De usu corticis radicis Granati. 1825. III. 630.²
Der Plänterwald und dessen Behandlung. 1878. IV. 131.
Plaga de orugas en los alcornocales. 1889.· IV. 550.¹

Plan . . . See Плань . . .
Plan du Jardin botanique [de Buitenzorg]. 1898. I. 68.²
Plan du Jardin d'essais [de Buitenzorg]. 1898. I. 68.²
Plan for de Forststuderendes Undervisning og Examen ved den Kgl. Veterinair- og Landbohøiskole. 1864. IV. 30.²
A plan to save the forests. 1894. IV. 178.²
Plan und Gesetze für die Herzoglich Coburg-Meiningische . . . Lehranstalt der Forst- und Jagdkunde. 1801. IV. 31.
Planche, Louis Antoine. Considérations sur l'existence et l'état du soufre. 1822. I. 152.¹
— Description des Angustures du commerce. 1816. III. 503.²
— Einige Thatsachen zur pharmakologischen Geschichte der Quassia. 1837. III. 508.²
— Note sur l'huile fixe extraite de la noix Pacane. 1839. III. 54.¹
— Quelques faits pour servir à l'histoire pharmacologique du Quassia. 1837. III. 508.²
— Recherches pour servir à l'histoire du sagou. 1837. III. 220.²
— Untersuchung einiger Sagosorten. 1837. III. 220.²
— Untersuchungen zur Geschichte der Sago's. 1837. III. 220.²
Planchenault, N. Notice historique . . . sur la culture de la Vigne. 1866. III. 555.
Planchon, François Gustave. Sur les caractères de structure des écorces . . . des Strychnos. 1880. III. 720.¹
— Les caractères des drogues simples. 1868. III. 243.
— Considérations générales sur la distribution géographique des médicaments simples. 1876. I. 300.
— Du curare de l'Orénoque. 1880. II. 720.¹
— Curare de la Guyane anglaise. 1880. III. 685.¹
— Curare de la Guyane française. 1880. III. 684.¹
— Curare de la Haute-Amazone. 1880. III. 684.¹
— Distribution géographique des médicamentes simples. 1891. I. 301.
— Des diverses sortes de Pareira brava. 1875. III. 396.²
— Sur l'écorce de Hoang-nan. 1877. III. 684.²
— Ecorce de Palo mabi. 1879. III. 541.²
— L'enseignement de l'histoire naturelle. 1896. III. 238.²
— Sur le genre Remijia. 1884. II. 830.¹
— Sur l'introduction des Vignes américaines. 1878. III. 556.
— Le Jardin des apothicaires. 1894. III. 59.²
— Le Jardin des apothicaires de Paris. 1895. I. 59.
— Le kermès du Chêne. 1864. IV. 502.¹
— Matériaux pour la flore médicale de Montpellier. 1868. III. 86.
— Matières premières tirées des végétaux et des animaux. 1881. III. 243.
— Des modifications de la flore de Montpellier. 1864. I. 413.
— Note sur l'état des vignobles. 1886. III. 561.
— Note sur l'Exposition des Quinquinas. 1877. III. 718.
— Note sur la structure des écorces . . . de Cannelles. 1873. II. 224.¹
— Note sur le Poivre. 1885. II. 94,² 713,¹ III. 679,¹ 753.¹
— Note sur la quinquina à cinchonamine. 1882. III. 718.
— Note sur le thé vert. 1879. III. 607.
— Note sur les échantillons de baume de la Mecque. 1896. III. 611.¹
— Note sur les écorces de Remijia. 1882. II. 830.¹
— Note sur les Styrax. 1876. III. 417.²
— Notes sur la matière médicale des États-Unis. 1880. III. 262.²
— Notes sur le Cédron et le Valdivia. 1881. III. 415,¹ 415.²
— Sur un nouveau medicament du Bresil. 1875. III. 505.¹
— Nouvelles notes sur les Strychnos. 1882. III. 683.²
— Peruvian barks. 1864. II. 812.·
— Sur les plantations de Quinquinas . . . à l'Île de la Réunion. 1880. III. 717.¹
— Sur les plantes médicinales des Indes néerlandaises. 1900. III. 92.¹
— Plantes qui entrent dans la composition du curare. 1880. III. 683.²
— Plantes qui fournissent le curare. 1880. III. 683.²
— Sur les plantes qui servent de base aux divers curares. 1880. III. 720.¹
— Les principes de la méthode naturelle. 1860. I. 252.
— Sur quelques monstruosités du Melianthus comosus. 1857. II. 491.²
— Des Quinquinas. 1864. II. 812.
— Sur les Quinquinas de Java. 1880. III. 718.
— Sur la reconstitution des vignobles. 1883. III. 556.

Planchon, François Gustave (*continued*).
— Revue de matière médicale. 1886. III. 244.
— Sur la structure des écorces . . . de Strychnos. 1879. II. 720.[1]
— Studies of the genus Strychnos. 1881. II. 719.[2]
— Traité pratique de la détermination des drogues simples. 1875. III. 258.
— & Collin, Eugène. Les drogues simples d'origine végétale. 1895. III. 244, 259.[1]
— *See also* PLANCHON, J. E. & G.
Planchon, Jules Émile. Abies jezoensis. 1853. II. 32.[2]
— Sur les affinités de l'Ophiocaryon. 1849. II. 491.[1]
— Sur les affinités des genres Henslowia. 1845. II. 610.[1]
— Affinités et synonymie de quelques genres nouveaux. 1854. I. 269.
— La botanique à Montpellier. 1884. I. 81.[1]
— Botanique pittoresque. 1850. II. 29.[1]
— Caligula (Klotzsch) macrantha. 1852. III. 647.[2]
— Calycanthus occidentalis. . 1854. III. 401.[1]
— Sur les caractères . . . du Jaborandi. 1875. II. 409.[2]
— Sur une chenille qui attaque le Pinus excelsa. 1870. IV. 464.[1]
— Les Cistes de Montpellier. 1862. III. 612.[2]
— Conseils sur le traitement des Vignes atteintes du phylloxéra. 1871. III. 759.
— Le Crataegus Aronia. 1872. II. 261.[1]
— Une curieuse monstruosité des fruits du Cognassier. 1866. II. 263.[2]
— Cydonia (Chaenomeles) japonica var. umbilicata. 1849. III. 420.[1]
— Le Cyprès funéraire des Chinois. 1850. II. 29.[1]
— La défense contre le phylloxéra. 1875. III. 568.
— Description de deux genres . . . des Euphorbiacées. 1845. II. 437,[2] 452.[1]
— Description de quelques espèces . . . de Centropogon. 1850. II. 846.[1]
— Description d'un genre nouveau, voisin du Cliftonia. 1846. II. 462.[1]
— Description d'un nouveau genre . . . des Diosmées." 1845. II. 408.[1]
— Sur deux plantes . . . sous le nom de Pistacia narbonensis. 1864. II. 457.[2]
— Développements et caractères des vrais et des faux arilles. 1844. I. 120.
— Sur la distribution géographique des Ulmidées. 1872. II. 141.[1]
— Encore les Vignes du Soudan. 1881. II. 501.[1]
— Essai monographique d'une nouvelle famille . . . Ancistrocladées. 1850. II. 584.[2]
— Essais préliminaires sur la destruction du phylloxéra. 1870. III. 758.[2]
— L'Eucalyptus globulus. 1875. IV. 533.[1]
— The Eucalyptus globulus. 1875. IV. 533.[1]
— Sur l'extension actuelle du phylloxera. 1872. III. 565.[1]
— Sur la famille des Linées. 1847. II. 392.[1]
— Sur la famille des Salvadoracées. 1848. II. 472.[1]
— Sur des fleurs anomales de la Vigne. 1866. II. 507.[2]
— Floraison du Monochaetum umbellatum. 1852. III. 639.[1]
— Sur le genre Godoya. 1846. II. 544,[1] 544.[2]
— Sur l'histoire botanique . . . des . . . Azalées de l'Inde. 1853. II. 675.[2]
— Histoire des ovules de quelques Véroniques. 1844. II. 753.[2]
— Hortus donatensis. 1854. I. 63.
— Krankheit der Kastanienbäume in den Cevennen. 1878. III. 359.[1]
— Des limites de la concordance entre les formes . . . des plantes et leurs propriétés médicinales. 1851. III. 259.[2]
— La maladie des Châtaigniers. 1878. III. 359.[2]
— On Meliantheae. 1851. II. 491.[1]
— Mémoire sur la famille des Simaroubées. 1847. II. 413.[1]
— Mémoire sur les développements et les caractères des vrais et des faux arilles. 1844. I. 120.
— Le mildew, ou faux oïdium. 1879. III. 578.
— Des modes d'invasion des vignobles par le phylloxéra. 1869. III. 758.[2]
— Les mœurs du phylloxéra. 1877. III. 760.
— Monographie des Ampélidées vraies. 1887. II. 501.[1]
— Note sur le Correa cardinalis Mucll. 1856. II. 404.[2]
— Note sur le faux arille de la Noix Muscade. 1855. II. 221.[1]
— Note sur une collection de plantes récoltées au Labrador. 1864. I. 310.

— Notice sur le Meyenia erecta. 1857. III. 710.[1]
— Nouveaux détails sur la synonymie . . . de Dracaena et de Cordyline. 1850. II. 79,[2] 81.[1]
— Sur une nouvelle espèce de Cissus. 1881. II. 503.[1]
— Sur la nouvelle famille des Cochlospermées. 1847. II. 566.[1]
— Nouvelles observations sur le Puceron de la Vigne. 1868. III. 564.[2]
— Observations on the genus Ulex. 1849. II. 387.[1]
— Observations sur l'Amoreuxia DC. 1847. II. 183.[2]
— Observations sur les Cistinées. 1862. II. 563.[2]
— Observations sur les Ulex. 1849. II. 387.[1]
— Sur l'origine du phylloxera. 1878. III. 571.
— Sur l'orme épineux des Chinois. 1872. II. 142.[1]
— On the parasitism of Osyris. 1858. II. 169.[1]
— Sur le parasitisme de l'Osyris. 1858. II. 169.[1]
— Passiflora Decaisneana. 1855. III. 616.[1]
— Passiflora forma hortensis Decaisneana. 1852. III. 616.[2]
— La phthiriose ou pédiculaire de la Vigne. 1870. III. 563.
— Le phylloxéra en Europe et en Amérique. 1874. III. 567.[2]
— Le phylloxéra et les Vignes américaines. 1874. III. 759.[2]
— Le phylloxéra et les Vignes américaines à Roquemaure. 1874. III. 566.[1]
— Sulla Phylloxera vastatrix. 1876. III. 570.[1]
— Prodromus monographiae ordinis Connaracearum. 1850. II. 316.[2]
— Sur quelques espèces d'Ulex. 1849. II. 387.[2]
— Quelques mots sur l'origine du styrax calamite. 1857. III. 671.[2]
— Quelques mots sur les inflorescences épiphylles. 1853. II. 406.[2]
— Quelques mots sur les Quisqualis. 1850. III. 632.[2]
— Quelques mots sur les Yucca. 1851. II. 81.[1]
— La question phylloxérique. 1877. III. 760.
— Rapport . . . au sujet du Congrès phylloxérique. 1877. III. 760.
— Rapport de la Commission départementale de l'Hérault. 1876. III. 570.[1]
— Rapport sur la maladie du phylloxera. 1870. III. 758.[2]
— Recherches sur les caractères et les développements des vrais et des faux arilles. 1844. I. 120.
— Remarks on the European species of Ulmus. 1848. II. 143.[1]
— Revue de la famille des Simaroubées. 1846. II. 413.[1]
— Rhododendron Maddeni. 1855. III. 661.[1]
— Rhododendron Thomsoni. 1855. III. 683.[2]
— Roellia ciliata. 1854. III. 754.[1]
— Rondelet, et ses disciples. 1866. I. 81.[1]
— Rosier bengale à fleurs vertes. 1856. II. 292.[2]
— Thyrsacanthus rutilans Planch. et Lind. 1852. III. 709.[2]
— Traitement au moyen de l'acide phénique. 1871. III. 564.[2]
— Ulmaceae. 1873. II. 141.[1]
— Sur les Ulmacées. 1848. II. 141.[1]
— La végétation de Montpellier. 1879. I. 415.
— Sur la végétation des terrain siliceux . . . du Gard. 1854. I. 222,[2] 411.
— Les Vignes américaines. 1875. III. 556.
— Les vignes des tropiques du genre Ampelocissus. 1884. II. 501.[1]
— Les Vignes du Soudan. 1880. II. 501.[1]
— Les Vignes du Soudan de feu Th. Lécard. 1881. II. 501.[1]
— Les Vignes japonaises de M. H. Degron. 1884. III. 547.
— Les Vignes sauvages des États-Unis de l'Amérique du Nord. 1874. II. 505.[1]
— Le Vitis Berlandieri. 1880. II. 506.[1]
— Le Vitis monticola Buckley. 1881. II. 505.[2]
— Le Vitis palmata. 1884. II. 505.[2]
— Les Xanthorrhoea. 1849. II. 86.[1]
— *See also* BAZILLE, Gaston, PLANCHON, J. E. & SAHUT, Félix; DECAISNE, Joseph & PLANCHON, J. E.; LINDEN, Jean & PLANCHON, J. E.; MARÈS, Henri & PLANCHON, J. E.; TRIANA, José & PLANCHON, J. E.
— & G. Les Citronniers et les Orangers de Roquebrun. 1865. III. 497.[1]
— & Houtte, Louis van. Lapageria rosea. 1850. III. 337.[1]
— & Lichtenstein, Jules. De l'identité spécifique du phylloxera. 1870. III. 564.[2]
— — Maladie de la Vigne. 1870. III. 564.[2]
— — Maladie de la Vigne; le phylloxéra. 1870. III. 758.[2]
— — De la marche . . . du phylloxera. 1873. III. 565.[2]
— — Le phylloxera. 1872. III. 565.[1]
— — Le phylloxéra. 1873. III. 759.

— — Le phylloxera de la Vigne en Angleterre. 1871. III. 564.²
— — Le phylloxera et son action. 1871. III. 564.²
— & Lin n, J. Praeludia florae colombianae. 1853. I. 339.², de
— & Saintpierre. Premières expériences sur la destruction du puceron de la Vigne. 1868. III. 564.²
— & Triana, José. Sur les bractées des Marcgraviées. . 1863. II. 546.¹
— — Études sur la famille des Guttifères. 1860. II. 552.²
— — Sur la famille des Guttifères. 1880. II. 552.²
— — Mémoire sur la famille des Guttifères. 1860. II. 552.²
— — Réponse aux critiques de M. le professeur Grisebach. 1861. II. 557,² 553.²
Planchon, Louis. Accidents causés par le contact du Rhus. 1887. III. 528.¹
— Les Aristoloches. 1891. III. 386.¹
— Le commerce actuel de l'herboristerie . . . du Languedoc. 1826. III. 271.¹
— Étude sur les produits de la famille des Sapotées. 1888. III. 666.²
— Produits fournis à la matière médicale par . . . Apocynées. 1894. III. 685.²
— See also SCHLAGDENHAUFFEN, Fr. & PLANCHON, Louis.
Planchud. Quelques mots sur l'huile d'Olive. 1880. III. 679.¹
Plane trees. 1896. II. 254.²
Planellas Giralt, José. Ensayo de una flora fanerogámica Gallega. 1852. I. 421.
Planer, Johan Jacob. Index plantarum . . . in agro erfurtensi. 1788. I. 374.
— Versuch einer teutschen Nomenclatur der Linneischen Gattungen. 1771. I. 73.¹
Planer til Brug ved Underviisningen i Have- og Skovbrugstegning ved den . . . Landbohøiskole. 1868. IV. 30 ²; see also HOFF, E. 1868. IV. 264.
Plank. Grundriss der Veterinärbotanik. 1840. III. 57.
Plank, E. N. A botanical journey in Texas. 1896. I. 326.
— A botanical journey through New Mexico. 1896. I. 326.
— Botanical notes from Texas. 1892. I. 326.
— Kansas forests and forestry. 1881. IV. 585.²
— Shrubs with ornamental berries. 1858. III. 208.¹
Planken, Joseph van der & Ranwez, F. Falsification des noix de muscade. 1900. III. 403.¹
— — Verfälschung von Muskatnüssen. 1900. III. 403.¹
Plant, Moriz. Die neuentdeckten Wellingtonia-Wälder. 1879. II. 51.¹
Plant industries of Lagos. 1893. III. 281.¹
Plant, T. L. The weather and public health. 1868. I. 226.¹
Plant life in Australia. 1880. II. 624.¹
Plant lore. 1885. I. 518.
Plant world. I. 6.
Planta, A. von. Sur la bébéerine. 1851. III. 407.²
— Ueber die chemische Zusammensetzung des Blüthenstaubes der gemeinen Kiefer. 1886. II. 48.¹
— Ueber die chemische Zusammensetzung des Blüthenstaubes der Haselstaude. 1885. II. 122.¹
— Sur la composition de quelques espèces de nectars. 1886. V. XI.²
— On the constitution of bebeerine. 1851. III. 407.²
— Ueber die Zusammensetzung einiger Nektararten. 1886. V. XI.²
Planta, A. D. von. Die Alpwirthschaft. 1860. IV. 102, 607.
— Waldbüchlein. 1848. IV. 365.
Planta, P. C. von. Libretto dei boschi. 1848. IV. 365.
Planta-Reichenau, A. von. Kultur und Schnitt von Spalierbirnen. 1874. III. 145.²
Plantaardig ivoor. 1878. III. 330.¹
Plantae Horti botanici pesthiensis. See KITAIBEL, Paul. 1809. I. 65.²
Plantae horti botanici Regiae universitatis hung. See KITAIBEL, Paul. 1812. I. 65.²
Plantae in ordine simplici vocabulis propriis delineatae. 1777. I. 77.
Plantae vapincenses. See CHAIX, Dominique. 1786. I. 406.
Plantae woodfordienses. See WARNER, Richard. 1771. I. 395.
Plantage Voorburg en de Liberia-Koffiecultuur. 1894. III. 742.²
Plantarum index. 1661. I. 286.
Plantarum indigenarum et exoticarum icones. 1788. I. 263.
Plantarum minus cognitarum decuria. See WEBER, G. H. 1784. I. 263.
Plantarum seu stirpium icones. See LOBEL, Matthias de. 1581. I. 282.

Plantation d'arbres fruitiers sur routes. 1897. III. 211.¹
Plantation d'Épicéas. Emploi de la raupenleim. 1900. IV. 457.
Plantation d'Épicéas. Moyens à employer pour activer la végétation. 1899. IV. 454.
Plantation de Bouleau dans les taillis ruinés. 1899. IV. 490.²
Plantation de Pin noir d'Autriche. 1899. IV. 466.¹
La plantation du Café en Nouvelle-Calédonie. See CAMOUILLY. 1899. III. 733.¹
Plantation en bordure d'un terrain sablonneux. 1899. IV. 153.¹
Plantation et entretien des haies vives de clôture. 1898. III. 214.¹
The plantation, Leighton Buzzard. See MARNOCK, Robert. 1872. I. 55.
Plantation superficielle. 1892. IV. 153.¹
Les plantations au Tonkin et en Annam. See JUNG & GANTER. 1899. III. 129.¹
Sur les plantations d'Eucalyptus dans les colonies françaises. 1873. IV. 529.²
Les plantations dans les cimetières. 1896. III. 34,² IV. 55.¹
Plantations de Chêne en Campine et en Hesbaye. 1899. IV. 509.
Plantations de Résineux en Ardenne. 1899. IV. 357.¹
Les plantations des routes. 1897. III. 210.
Les plantations des routes. 1899. III. 210.
Les plantations des routes dans le grand-duché de Luxembourg. 1897. III. 210.
Les plantations des routes . . . de Namur. 1895. III. 211.¹
La plante à encre. 1887. III. 523.²
Plante fébrifuge. 1820. III. 704.¹
Plante nouvelle pour la flore française, Arceuthobium. 1843. II. 174.²
Plantele indigene din Românica. See GRECESCU, Demetrius. 1899. V. XXIII.¹
Planten, H. O. W. & Wertheim, C. J. M. Verslagen van de wetenschappelijke opnemingen . . . op de Keyeilanden. 1893. I. 466.
A planter, (pseud.). Indian Tea. 1882. III. 603.
Planters' monthly. II. 27.²
Plantes dont l'horticulture s'est enrichie en 1892. See NEW garden plants. 1888. III. 83.
Plantes et arbustes d'agrément. See CLAIRVILLE, J. P. de. 1791. I. 264.
Plantes nouvelles. 1844. III. 707.¹
Plantes nouvelles . . . de M. M. Groenewegen & Comp. 1862. I. 51.²
Plantes nouvelles et d'agrément. 1836. III. 696.¹
Plantes nouvelles introduites du Japon. 1862. III. 77.¹
Plantes nouvelles ou rares introduites. 1859. II. 252.²
Plantes phanérogames . . . de Fréjus. See PERREYMOND. 1833. I. 408.
Plantes phanérogames, qui croissent naturellement aux environs de Toulon. See ROBERT. 1838. I. 409.
Plantes tinctoriales de l'Annam et du Tonkin. 1898. III. 237.¹
Les plantes vénéneuses. See GODET, Charles. 1845. III. 89.²
Planting. 1884. III. 169.¹
Planting and ornamental gardening. See MARSHALL, Wilham. 1785. III. 81.
Planting for autumn effect. 1888. III. 207.¹
Planting near the sea. 1890. III. 600.¹
The planting of shrubberies. 1897. III. 202.¹
Planting opinion. III. 26.²
Planting out Saltbush. 1900. III. 387.²
Planting trees in school grounds. See HOUGH, F. B. & PEASLEE, J. B. 1885. IV. 41.²
Plants in the Crimea. 1854. I. 369.
Plants of Kumaon. See WATSON, J. F. 1874. I. 474.
1855. I. 95.
Plants yielding tea. 1861. II. 552.¹
Plantsman, (pseud.). Genetyllis tulipifera. 1891. III. 633.²
— Hybrid and other Rhododendrons for pot culture. 1891. III. 655.
— Luculias. 1892. III. 745.²
Plappart, Joachim Friedrich. De Juglande nigra. 1777. II. 113.¹
— & Jacquin, N. J., Baron von. Juglans nigra . . . aucta Juglande cinerea. 1778. II. 112.²
Die Platanen. 1875. III. 419.¹
Ueber den Platanen-Husten. 1888. III. 419.¹
Platania, Salvadore. Sopra una essudazione spontanea della Quercia. 1825. IV. 509.

Plateau, Félix. Comment les fleurs attirent les insectes. 1895. I. 239.[1]
Plato, Karl Gottlieb. Deutschlands Giftpflanzen. 1829. III. 73.
Platon. Das Kastanienholz zur Gerberei. 1868. IV. 493.[2]
Platt, Sir Hugh. Floraes Paradise, beautified. 1608. III. 80.
— The garden of Eden. 1608. III. 80.
Platt, R. H. Toyon berries in the North Coast Ranges. 1899. II. 269.[2]
Platzmann, Julius. Aus der Bai von Paranaguá. 1872. I. 343.
— La Baie de Paranagua. 1872. I. 343.
Platzpflanzung . . . bei der Kultur der Fichte. 1872. IV. 453.
Plawsiego, Alexandra. Słownik wyrazów botanicznych. 1830. I. 70.
Playfair, Sir R. Lambert. Culture of Eucalyptus. 1877. IV. 530.
— Eucalyptus in Algeria. 1877. IV. 530.
— Report on the progress of Tunis. 1888. III. 676.[1]
— Supplementary report on the culture of Eucalyptus in Algeria. 1877. IV. 530.
Plaz, Anton Wilhelm. Caulis plantarum explicatus. 1745. I. 104.
— De flore plantarum. 1749. I. 114.[1]
— Foliorum in plantis historia. 1740. I. 109.[1]
— Historiam radicum exponit. 1733. I. 103.
— De motu humorum in plantis. 1764. I. 162.
— Organicarum in plantis partium historia. 1751. I. 146.
— De plantarum seminibus. 1736. I. 120.
— De plantarum virtutibus ex ipsarum charactere haudquaquam addiscendis. 1762. III. 259.[1]
— De potus cafe abusu. 1744. III. 741.[1]
Plaza, G. Montes y canales. 1893. IV. 553.[2]
Plebst, G. See STOLZ, C. & PLEBST, G.
Plée, Auguste. Le jeune botaniste. 1812. I. 94.
— & François. Herborisations artificielles aux environs de Paris. 1811. I. 407, V. xxi.[1]
Plée, François. Glossologie botanique. 1854. I. 74.[1]
— Types de chaque famille et des principaux genres des plantes . . . en France. 1844. I. 410.
— See also PLÉE, Auguste & François.
Pleibel, A. Tabellen zur Bestimmung des kubischen Inhalts runder und vierkantiger Stämme. 1871. IV. 226.
Pleijte, W. Bloemen en planten uit oud Egypte. 1883. I. 81.[2]
Pleischl, Adolph. Der Thee (Thea) in chemischer . . . Beziehung. 1844. III. 606.
Een pleitrede voor de boomen. 1874. IV. 180.[2]
Plenck, Joseph Jakob von. Abbildungen der Medicinalpflanzen. 1788. III. 55.
— Anfangsgründe der botanischen Terminologie. 1798. I. 255.
— Elementa terminologiae botanicae. 1796. I. 70.
— Elementos de la nomenclatura botanica. 1798. I. 255.
— Fisiologia e patologia delle piante. 1794. I. 148.
— Icones plantarum medicinalium. 1788. III. 55.
— Physiologia et pathologia plantarum. 1794. I. 148.
— Physiologie et pathologie des plantes. 1794. I. 148.
— Physiologie und Pathologie der Pflanzen. 1794. I. 148.
— Tossicologia. 1785. III. 260.[2]
— Toxicologia. 1785. III. 260.[2]
Pleniger, Andreas. Ueber Pflanzenphysiologie. 1841. I. 147.
Die Plenterdurchforstung als Hauptgrundlage für die Bewirthschaftung. 1889. IV. 174.
Ples, D. Over den aanleg . . . van gouvernements -Koffietuinen. 1879. III. 729.[1]
— Bijdrage tot de kennis der kajapoeti-olie. 1858. III. 636.
— Koffiecultuur. 1875. III. 734.[2]
— Nog iets over het op stomp kappen van Koffieboomen. 1875. III. 734.[2]
— Nota over het stronk kappen van Koffieboomen. 1873. III. 734.[2]
— Nota's over het op stomp kappen van oude Koffijboomen. 1871. III. 734.[2]
— Note sur l'huile de Cajouputi. 1858. III. 636.
— Onderzoek naar de zamenstelling eener witte stof . . . Djatikapos. 1858. III. 697.[1]
— See also GORKOM, K. W. van, PLES, D. & HOLLE, K. F.
Plesch, Josef Wilhelm. Beitrag zur Kenntniss der Wirkung des Arecolin. 1895. III. 320.[1]
Plessis, E. HUARD DU, (jr.). See HUARD DU PLESSIS, E., (jr.).

Pletenie . . . See Плетеніе . . .
Pley, George. Précis of Geo. Pley's letter about " yearly destruction " in Newfoundland. 1893. IV. 271.[1]
Pleydell, J. C. MANSEL-. See MANSEL-PLEYDELL, J. C.
Pleyer. Abentheur von allerhand Mineralien, Wurtzeln. 1656. III. 272.[2]
Plieninger, Th. Gemeinfassliche Belehrung über den Maikäfer. 1834. IV. 202.
— Monographie der Maikäfer. 1834. IV. 202.
Pliester, A. C. Heide-ontginning. 1888. IV. 119.[2]
Plinguet, Jean Baptiste. Examen analytique des causes du dépérissement des bois. 1806. IV. 282.[2]
— Manuel de l'ingénieur-forestier. 1831. IV. 98.[1]
— Traité sur les réformations et les aménagemens des forêts. 1789. IV. 248,[1] 359.[1]
Plinius Secundus, Cajus. I due primi libri della storia naturale. 79. I. 274.
— Histoire naturelle de Pline. 79. I. 274.
— Historia mundi naturalis. 79. I. 273.[1]
— Historia natural. 79. I. 273.[1]
— Historia naturalis. 79. I. 273.[1]
— Historiae naturalis libri XXXVII. 79. I. 273,[2] 530,[2] V. xIV.[1]
— The historie of the world. 79. V. xiV.[1]
— Index in C. Plinii Nat. Hist. libros. 79. V. xiV.[1]
— Naturalis historiae libri. 79. I. 273,[2] V. xiV.[1]
— Naturgeschichte. 79. I. 274.
Plitt, Carl. Beiträge zur . . . Anatomie des Blattstiels. 1886. I. 112.[1]
Pliushtch. See Плющъ.
Pliwa, Ernst. Fachkalender mit Vormerkblättern für Holzverarbeitung. 1894. IV. 403.[1]
— Die industrielle Verwertung des Rothbuchenholzes. 1884. IV. 499.
Plock. Der Anbau der Robinie. 1843. IV. 523.[1]
Ploeg, B. J. De oxalzure kalk in de planten. 1879. I. 139.
Ploem, J. C. Eenige middelen tegen schadelijke insecten. 1881. III. 196. — 1882. III. 192.[2]
Ploner, Eduard. Erfolg der Zirbenpfropfung. 1865. IV. 463.[2]
— Erfolg der Zirbenpfropfung in den ungarischen Karpathen. 1865. III. 307.[1]
— Greffe de l'Arôle. 1865. III. 307.[1]
— Die Schwarzföhre auf dem Löss. 1873. IV. 465.[2]
Plosel, J. Deutzia gracilis in Baumform. 1876. III. 410.[1]
Plot, Robert. A discourse concerning the most seasonable time of felling of timber. 1691. IV. 384.[1]
— The natural history of Oxfordshire. 1677. I. 394, V. xx.[2]
— The natural history of Strafford-Shire. 1686. I. 394.
Plotti, Alessandro. Questioni forestali nella Svizzera. 1896. IV. 286.[2]
Ploucquet, W. G. Ueber den Holzmangel. 1780. IV. 280.[1]
Plowman, Sydney. The chemistry of Ngai camphor. 1874. III. 754.[2]
Plowright, Charles B. Abies pectinata. 1891. IV. 445.
— Canker in Apple trees. 1888. III. 427.[2]
— Destructive fungi. 1899. III. 195.[2]
— Diseases of plants. 1891. III. 194.
— Einige Impfversuche mit Rostpilzen. 1891. III. 194.
— Oak tree broken by rime. 1889. III. 185.[1]
— Podisoma juniperi and Roestelia lacerata. 1882. III. 422.[2]
Plowright, Walter B. Infection of the Juniper. 1886. III. 303.[1]
Pluchard. Reclamation de priorité sur Prevet. 1864. III. 472.[1]
Plucker, Théodore. Aperçu de la flore de l'Amour. 1872. I. 456.
— Aperçu de la végétation des provinces de l'Amour. 1872. I. 456.
Plues, Margaret. Rambles in search of wild flowers. 1863. I. 401.
Plüss, Benjamin. Unsere Bäume und Sträucher. 1884. I. 371, V. xIx.[1]
Plugge, P. C. Alcaloïden van Sophora tomentosa L. 1891. III. 488.[1]
— Das Alkaloid von Sophora tomentosa. 1891. III. 488.[1]
— Ueber Andromedotoxin. 1882. III. 654.[1]
— Ueber Andromedotoxine. 1882. III. 654.[1]
— Andromedotoxine-houdende Ericaceen. 1891. III. 647.[1]
— Andromedotoxinhaltige Ericaceen. 1891. III. 647.[1]
— Bijdrage tot de kennis der Cerberine. 1893. III. 687.[1]
— Eenige opmerkingen naar aanleiding van het onderzoek van den heer J. F. Eijkman. 1882. III. 654.[1]

— Fortgesetzte Untersuchungen ueber die Verbreitung des Andromedotoxins. 1885. III. 647.[1]
— Giftige honig van Rhododendron ponticum. 1891. III. 662.[1]
— Giftiger Honig von Rhododendron ponticum. 1891. III. 662.[1]
— Over de identiteit van sophorine. 1894. III. 488.[2]
— J. van der Moer's onderzoek over cytisine. 1891. II. 321.[2]
— Onderzoekingen over het voorkomen van andromedotoxine. 1885. III. 647.[1]
— Over het voorkomen van andromedotoxine. 1883. III. 647.[2]
— & Rauwerda, A. Voortgezette onderzoekingen over het ... cytisine. 1896. II. 322.[1]
Plukenet, Leonard. Opera omnia botanica. 1691. I. 288.
Plum blossoms. 1878. III. 432.[2]
Plumandon, J. R. Influence des forêts ... sur les orages à grêle. 1893. IV. 54.
Plumb, C. S. The American Persimmon. 1896. III. 670.[1]
— The quality of modern process maple-sugar. 1894. IV. 527.[2]
Plumer, M. M. Dissemination of seeds. 1881. I. 240.[2]
Plumier, Charles. Catalogus plantarum americanarum. 1703. I. 334.
— Description des plantes de l'Amérique. 1693. I. 334.
— Plantarum americanarum fasc. 1755. I. 334.
Plummer, A. B. As to the planting of trees in streets. 1884. III. 210.
Plummer, F. G. Mount Rainier forest reserve. 1900. IV. 341.[2]
Plummer, J The Vine in Australia. 1899. III. 559.[2]
A plumose Cycad. 1875. III. 286.[1]
Plums and Plum culture. 1899. III. 433.[1]
The plunder of the Adirondack reservation. 1896. IV. 178.[2]
Plunkett, Robert. On the manufacture of hemp ... from the Lavatera. 1859. III. 588.[2]
Plunkett, Wilham. Determination of the specific gravity ... of wood from British Guiana. 1864. IV. 411.[1]
Pluquet, Fréderic. Extrait des observations sur l'origine ... de quelques plantes du Bessin. 1824. III. 271.[1]
La plus grande forêt du globe. 1895. IV. 555.[1]
Le plus vieux Rosier du monde. 1894. II. 290.[1]
Plusieurs cultivateurs et propriétaires du Mâconnais. 1837. III. 562.[2]
Pluskal, F. S. Beiträge zur Teratologie und Pathologie der Vegetation. 1854. II. 482.[1]
— Das Blattstielblatt an Aesculus. 1854. II. 482.[1]
— Ueber meinen Corylus Sérényiana. 1852. II. 121.[2]
— Neue Methode.die Pflanzen ... für das Herbar zu trocknen. 1849. I. 35.
Pluszczewski, Émile. Étude de la famille des Pipéracées. 1885. II. 93.[2]
Pluvial trees. 1826. I. 213.[1]
Pluygers. Egyptische en Senegalgom. 1888. III. 466.[1]
Pobéguin, H. Notes sur la Côte d'Ivoire. 1896. I. 491.
Pochhammer, von. Erfolg des Aufrufes an alle Pomologen. 1855. III. 137.
Pocklington, Henry. Eucalyptus globulus. 1873. II. 624.[2]
— The microscope in pharmacy. 1875. III. 259.[2]
— Mr. Darby on the colouring matter of leaves. 1874. I. 185.[2]
Pococke, Richard. A description of the East and some other countries. 1743. I. 301.
Podagra, Septimo, (pseud.). Der profitable Apotheker-Tod. 1721. III. 605.
Om Podequistens Indvirkning paa Stammen. See On the INFLUENCE ... 1841. III. 39.
Podestà, Giovanni. Il bosco Umbra-Jacotenente. 1895. IV. 364.
— La coltivazione del Sommacco nelle Pughe. 1886. IV. 526.[1]
— La lava delle Murge Baresi. 1886. IV. 186.[2]
— Il legname del Faggio nelle costruzioni navali. 1886. IV. 425.[1]
— Il Melacero del bosco Umbra-Jacotenente. 1886. IV. 526.[2]
— Un nuovo bosco demaniale inalienabile. 1886. IV. 28.[1]
— Le piccole industrie forestali nel Gargano. 1887. IV. 405.[2]
— La Querce fragna. 1894. IV. 503.[2]
— Un tronco di Quercia gigantesco. 1887. IV. 502.[2]
Podewils, Graf von. Über den Ertrag der Zucker, Caffee und Baumwollen-Pflanzungen in Surinam. 1803. III. 729.[1]

Podhorsky, J. Das Schmarotzen von Fichte auf Tanne. 1898. IV. 74.[1]
Podhradtzky, Endre. Valami a tölgyculturákról. 1864. IV. 505.
Om Podning. 1857. III. 161.
Podoli, Adolf. See FERRANT, Adolf, PFEIFFER, Karl & PODOLL, Adolf.
La Podredumbre seca. 1885. IV. 415.[1]
Podwissotzki, Valerian. Lippia mexicana. 1882. III. 697.[1]
Pöch, Joseph. Bemerkung zur Spiraea decumbens. 1844. II. 315.[1]
— Enumeratio plantarum ... Cypri. 1842. I. 452.
Poederle, Eugène Joseph Charles Gilain Hubert d'Obnen, baron de. Manuel de l'arboriste. 1772. III. 106.[1]
Poedeste, de. Manuel de l'arboriste et du forestier. 1774. IV. 108.[2]
Pöey, Andrés. Influence de la lumière violette sur la croissance de la Vigne. 1871. II. 508.[1]
Pöehl, Alexander. Ueber die Alkaloïde der Calabarbohne. 1878. III. 484.[1]
— Chemische ... Untersuchung der Eucalyptusblätter. 1877. II. 623.[2]
— Untersuchung der Blätter von Pilocarpus officinalis. 1880. II. 409.[2]
Poehlmann, Fritz. Ein Schutzbrief für den Wald. 187.? IV. 43.
— Zu unserer Rentenfrage. 1882. IV. 257.
— Zur Waldrentabilitätsfrage. 1873. IV. 256.
Pöhlmann, Robert & Reiche, Karl. Beiträge zur Kenntnis der Flora der Flussthäler Camarones und Vitor. 1900. I. 347.
Poenicke, Ed. Veredlungsbänder von Papier. 1881. III. 162.
Pöpel, H. F. Die Altersklassen-Zerreissung. 1882. IV. 244.
— Ueber Saatkampvermachungen. 1881. IV. 146.[2]
— Der Stichlitz. 1890. IV. 153.[1]
Pöppel. Zur Ansicht der Wellingtonia gigantea. 1870. IV. 454.[1]
— Zur Naturgeschichte der Buche. 1863. IV. 494.
Poeppig, Eduard Friedrich. Account of the Araucaria imbricata. 1835. II. 26.[2]
— Ueber die Araucaria. 1835. II. 26.[2]
— The Araucaria imbricata. 1835. II. 26.[2]
— On the Cascarillas of Cuchero and Huanuco. 1835. III. 717.[2]
— Die Cultur.der Verbrauch ... der Coca. 1835. III. 492.[1]
— Die Fieberrinden von Cuchero. 1836. III. 721.
— Fragmentum synopseos plantarum ... in Chile lectarum. 1833. II. 316.[1]
— Notes on the Cinchona trees of Huanuco. 1861. III. 713.[1]
— Ueber Pourretia coarctata Ruiz et Pav. 1835. II. 77.[1]
— Reise in Chile, Peru. 1835. I. 329.
— Some account of the uses ... of Coca. 1835. III. 492.[1]
— & Endlicher, S. L. Nova genera ac species plantarum. 1835. I. 329.
Pösel, Joseph. Gründlich und vollständiger Unterricht, sowohl für die Wald- als Gartenbienenzucht. 1784. IV. 438.[2]
Pössl, Wilhelm. Fichte mit abnormen Habitus. 1888. IV. 460.[1]
— Holz-Kubirungs-Tafeln nach Metermass. 1876. IV. 227.
— Tafeln zur sicheren Schätzung des Holzgehaltes stehender Waldbäume. 1874. IV. 217.
Poetry of trees. 1854. I. 511.
Poets and their favourite trees. 1878. I. 511.
Poeverlein, Hermann. Über das Vorkommen von Vaccinium intermedium. 1897. II. 686.[1]
Pogankov, I. See ПОГАНКОВЪ, И.
Poggenburg, J. F. See BRITTON, N. L., STERNS, E. E. & POGGENBURG, J. F.
Poggi, Augusto. I disoscamenti in rapporto all' economia. 1881. IV. 44.
Poggi, J. J. Manuel pour extraire le sucre du raisin. 1808. III. 582.
Poggio, Carlo di. Memoria sul taglio delle macchie di Viareggio. 1823. IV. 47.[2]
Poggio — Accademia valdarnese ... See ACCADEMIA ... I. 24.[1]
Pogson, J. F. The Bael tree. 1859. III. 495.[1]
— Note regarding Gossypium arboreum. 1882. III. 587.[2]
— Remarks on the wild medicinal Bael. 1872. III. 495.[1]
Pohl, Johann Baptist Emmanuel. Des Freiherrn von Hochberg botanischer Garten zu Hlubosch. 1811. I. 65.[3]
— Neue brasilianische Gewächse. 1827. I. 341.
— Plantarum Brasiliae icones. 1827. I. 341.
— Reise im Innern von Brasilien. 1832. I. 341.
— Tentamen florae Bohemiae. 1810. I. 439.

Pohl, Johann Ehrenfried. Animadversiones in structuram ac figuram foliorum. 1771. I. 109.[1]
— De soli differentia in cultura plantarum. 1773. III. 40.
Pohlens, Edward. Leśnictwo praktyczne. 1875. IV. 94.
Pohndorf, F. A memoir on Olive growing. 1884. III. 676.[1]
Pohnert, Victor. De plantis medicinalibus. 1841. III. 238.[1]
Poids des écorces de Chêne. 1898. IV. 515.[2]
Poids du mètre cube de bois. 1896. IV. 411.[2]
Poincaré. Rapport sur le rôle joué dans les forêts par la tourterelle et le moineau. 1899. IV. 91.[1]
Poincaré, Émile Leon. Sur les effets des inhalations d'essence de térébenthine. 1879. IV. 443.[2]
Poinsot. L'ami des jardiniers. 1803. III. 112.
Poirault, G. See BERTRAND, Gabriel & POIRAULT, G.
Poirault, J. Catalogue des plantes . . . de la Vienne. 1875. I. 414.
Poiret. Résultats des expériences faites en vue d'accentuer le coloris. 1893. III. 152.
Poiret, Jean Louis Marie. Histoire philosophique . . . des plantes de l'Europe. 1825. I. 349.
— Leçons de flore. 1819. I. 85.
— Leçons de flore. Cours de botanique. 1823. I. 85.
— Reise in die Barbarey. 1789. I. 483.[2]
— Voyage en Barbarie. 1789. I. 483.[2]
— See also CHAUMETON, F. P., CHAMBERET & POIRET, J. L. M.; LAMARCK, J. B. A. P. M. Chevalier de & POIRET, J. L. M.
Poirot. Sur les effets produits par la culture de l'absinthe. 1880. III. 572.
Poirson, A. De la culture du Chêne. 1845. IV. 504.
— Mouvement de la sève. 1846. I. 164.
— Notice sur le Chêne de Saint-Jean. 1842. II. 138.[1]
— Observations sur le choix . . . des arbres d'ornement dans les promenades. 1849. III. 209.
The Poison Ivy and an antidote. 1899. III. 528.[2]
The Poison of the Yew. 1892. III. 288.[2]
Poisoned by Virginia Creeper. 1877. III. 545.[1]
Poisoning by milk. 1863. III. 514.[1]
Poisoning by Rhododendron. 1885. III. 657.[1]
Poisoning from Turnsole in Persia. 1889. III. 515.[1]
Poisonous Legumes. 1878. III. 462.[1]
Poisonous leguminous plant. 1892. III. 488.[2]
The poisonous plants of the Malay peninsula. 1898. III. 92.[1]
The poisonous principle of the Yew. 1878. III. 288.[2]
Poisson, Jules. Sur l'Aratacio du Brésil. 1900. III. 522.[1]
— Boisement des dunes. 1899. IV. 164.[2]
— Consolidation des talus par la végétation. 1896. III. 214,[1] IV. 186.[1]
— Du dégagement de chaleur . . . inflorescences mâles de Dioon. 1878. II. 5.[1]
— Sur une espèce nouvelle de Castilloa. 1900. II. 147.[2]
— Étude sur le nouveau genre Hennecartia. 1885. II. 222.[1]
— Sur l'exploitation et la production du caoutchouc. 1900. III. 230.
— Sur la fixation des dunes dans l'ouest. 1900. IV. 164.[2]
— Sur le genre nouveau Hennecartia. 1885. II. 222.[1]
— Le Gingko ou Arbre aux quarante écus. 1894. III. 287.[1]
— Sur le Linaloe. 1884. II. 416.[1]
— Note sur le caoutchouc de la Nouvelle-Calédonie. 1900. III. 230.
— Note sur le développement des épines de l'Idria. 1895. II. 563.[1]
— Note sur le genre Casuarina. 1872. II. 92.[1]
— Note sur les produits industriels fournis par les Bassia. 1881. III. 667.[1]
— Un nouveau fourrage pour l'Algérie. 1895. III. 485.[2]
— Sur un nouveau genre de Celtidées. 1888. II. 142.[1]
— Les propriétés de l'Aristotelia maqui. 1886. III. 584.[2]
— Sur quelques plantes remarquables de Basse-Californie. 1895. I. 332.
— Recherches sur les Casuarina. 1874. II. 92.[1]
— Du siége des matières colorées dans la graine. 1877. I. 120.
— Sterculia rupestris. 1878. II. 538.[2]
— Toxicophlaea spectabilis. 1879. III. 686.[1]
Poisson, M. J. Palm-trees and their uses. 1889. III. 319.[2]
— Les Palmiers. 1889. III. 319.[2]
Poiteau, Antoine. Amandier d'Ispahan à fleurs doubles. 1832. III. 434.[1]
— Analyse d'une lettre de M. Rantonnet. 1842. III. 47.
— Andromède à feuilles de Buis. 1833. III. 647.[1]
— Application de l'incision annulaire. 1835. III. 175.[1]
— Azalées de l'Inde. 1829. II. 675.[2]

— Buginvillaea spectabilis. 1836. III. 388.[1]
— Cajanus indicus. 1846. III. 469.[1]
— Camellia Sophiana Poit. 1835. III. 597.[2]
— Caractères génériques du Garrya. 1842. II. 110.[2]
— Cèdre Deodora. 1837. III. 300.[1]
— Cereus nycticalus Link. 1838. II. 591.[1]
— Clematis montana Ham. 1841. III. 391.[1]
— Des Conifères. 1845. III. 289.
— Cours d'horticulture. 1845. III. 113.
— Daubentonia Benth. 1840. II. 383.[1]
— Daubentonia Tripetiana. 1841. II. 383.[2]—1842. III. 487.[2]
— Description abrégée de deux Euphorbes. 1838. III. 517.[2]
— Description de deux nouvelles variétés de Pivoines. 1842. III. 392.[2]
— Description du Philippodendrum. 1837. II. 526.[2]
— Destruction des punaises . . . des Orangers. 1832. III. 500.[1]
— Sur les différens essais tentés pour obtenir de bons fruits comestibles par semis. 1832. I. 246.[1]
— De l'emploi du Mûrier multicaule. 1835. III. 380.[2]
— Des engluements propres à recouvrir les plaies des arbres. 1844. III. 180.[1]
— Épine féroce. 1836. III. 422.[1]
— Erica Wilmoriana. 1842. III. 651.[2]
— Établissement d'une nouvelle famille de plantes . . . les Cyclanthées. 1822. II. 76.[1]
— Exposition plus exacte des caractères du . . . Ludovia. 1822. II. 76.[1]
— Extrait d'une notice de M. His. 1843. II. 200.[1]
— Extrait d'une tournée horticole. 1833. III. 125.
— Fuchsie à longues fleurs. 1842. III. 640.[1]
— Exposition [sic] des caractères de deux genres. 1815. II. 574.[1]
— Garrya. 1842. II. 110.[2]
— Gay-Lussac à fleurs rouges. 1845. III. 652.[2]
— Sur le genre Ludovia. 1822. II. 76.[1]
— Germination du Cocotier. 1829. II. 67.[2]
— Germination du Zamia pumila. 1829. II. 7.[2]
— De la greffe avec des parties herbacées. 1851. III. 163.[2]
— De la greffe du Cèdre Deodara. 1838. III. 300.[1]
— Greffe du Pin Laricio. 1833. III. 307.[1]
— La greffe Faucheux. 1833. III. 497.[1]
— Greffe podocéphale. 1833. III. 160.
— Groseillier sanguin à fleurs pleines. 1845. III. 415.[1]
— Histoire des Palmiers de la Guiane. 1822. II. 61.[1]
— Sur l'hypothèse de la transformation des feuilles . . . des plantes Conifères. 1810. II. 17.[2]
— Sur l'impossibilité de la naturalisation des végétaux. 1842. III. 43.
— Sur les incommodités que peut causer le duvet des feuilles du Platane. 1838. III. 419.[1]
— Le jardin botanique de l'École de médecine de Paris. 1816. I. 57.
— Luculie parfumée, Luculia gratissima. 1837. III. 745.[1]
— Maclura aurantiaca Nut. 1838. III. 372.[1]
— Marronnier à fleurs doubles. 1844. III. 537.[1]
— Mémoire sur la culture de l'Oranger. 1830. III. 499.[2]
— Mémoire sur le genre Drypetes. 1815. II. 441.[1]
— Mémoire sur le Thouinia. 1804. II. 489.[2]
— Mémoire sur les Lécythidées. 1825. II. 611.[1]
— Mémoire tendant à faire admettre . . . la théorie de Lahire sur l'origine et la direction des fibres ligneuses. 1831. I. 128.[1]
— Moyen d'accélérer la croissance de l'Hybiscus. 1846. III. 588.[1]
— Napoléone d'Heudelot, Napoleona Heudelotii. 1845. II. 612.[2]
— De la nécessité d'établir une classification parmi les Camellia. 1835. III. 598.[1]
— Nerium Hacvilli Hortul. 1832. III. 689.[2]
— Note sur cinq espèces de Sauges. 1833. III. 698.[1]
— Note sur deux variétés de Robinia. 1842. III. 486.[2]
— Note sur l'art de forcer le Lilas de Marly. 1834. III. 680.[1]
— Note sur l'influence de la greffe sur le sujet. 1836. III. 39.
— Note sur l'origine du Cereus monstruosus. 1841. II. 590.[2]
— Note sur la greffe Kew, Thouin. 1838. III. 160.
— Note sur la multiplication des Pivoines ligneuses. 1835. III. 392.[2]
— Note sur le Cembro. 1837. IV. 464.[1]
— Note sur le Figuier rampant. 1831. III. 371.[1]

— Note sur le Ginkgo femelle. 1836. III. 286.²
— Note sur le grossissement de deux arbres. 1842. III. 38.¹
— Note sur le Maclura aurantiaca. 1835. III. 372.¹
— Note sur le Marronnier royal du jardin des Tuileries. 1842. II. 482.¹
— Note sur le Mûrier multicaule. 1835. III. 380.²
— Note sur une seconde fructification de deux Poiriers. 1835. II. 279.¹
— Notice historique sur la théorie van Mons. 1834. III. 50.¹
— Notice physiologique sur le Cytise-Adam. 1832. II. 368.²
— Notice ... que le voisinage de l'Épine-vinette ... soit nuisible au Blé. 1831. III. 395.¹
— Notice sur la culture des Nopals. 1834. III. 623.²
— Notice sur la manière de traiter les boutures des Abies. 1828. III. 293.
— Notice sur la manière dont eu pu se former les orangers appellés bizarrerie. 1832. III. 497.¹
— Notice sur le Pin du Lord Weymouth. 1835. III. 308.²
— Notice tendant à fixer le sens des mots " naturaliser " et " acclimater " les végétaux. 1837. III. 43.
— Notions de physiologie végétale. 1838. I. 147.
— Nouveau procédé pour multiplier le Mûrier multicaule. 1838. III. 380.¹
— Nouvelle explication des directions que prennent la racine. 1829. I. 195.²
— Nouvelle explication sur la greffe en fente. 1841. III. 39.
— Nouvelles observations sur la multiplication des Bruyères. 1835. III. 649.¹
— Nouvelles recherches sur ... la cloque. 1842. III. 431.¹
— Observation sur ... Azalée de la Chine. 1832. III. 662.²
— Observation sur trois espèces d'Aunes. 1832. III. 356.²
— Observations botaniques faites à Saint-Domingue. 1842. I. 335.
— Observations nouvelles sur l'Erythrina. 1832. III. 475.²
— Observations sur le Pedilanthe. 1812. II. 448.²
— Paeonia Moutan napoleoniana. 1840. III. 392.²
— Paeonia reginae His. 1846. III. 392.²
— Passiflora carmisina. 1830. II. 579.¹
— Paulownia imperialis. 1844. III. 703.¹
— Plantefysiologiske Bemerkninger. 1838. I. 147.
— Plantes d'agrément. 1835. III. 86.
— Plantes intéressantes. 1829. III. 454,² 455.¹
— Pomologie française. 1838. III. 84.¹
— Première fleuraison de la Paulownia. 1842. III. 703.¹
— Pronay élégant, Pronaya elegans. 1845. III. 416.¹
— Rapport d'une commission ... pour examiner ... les deux Daubentonia. 1843. III. 487.¹
— Rapport ... sur une notice de M. Duval. 1836. III. 363.²
— Recherches sur le moyen d'obtenir le Gingo. 1834. III. 286.²
— Remède contre les ulcères des Ormes. 1830. III. 364.¹
— Réponse à la notice de M. Turpin sur les usurpations végétales. 1834. II. 377.¹
— Retrait de la sève dans les arbres. 1833. I. 517.¹
— Revue des Pivoines ligneuses. 1839. III. 392.¹
— Rhipsalis grandiflorus. 1832. III. 626.¹
— Seconde note sur le Paulownia. 1841. III. 703.¹
— Stevensia. 1804. III. 832.¹
— Sucre de Châtaignes. 1838. IV. 493.¹
— Sur la théorie et la pratique des marcottes. 1830. III. 159.¹
— Théorie van Mons. 1834. I. 247, III. 50.¹
— Die Theorie van Mons. 1834. I. 247.
— Van Mons Theorie. 1834. III. 50.¹
— See also NEUMANN, Auguste & POITEAU, Antoine; RISSO, J. A. & POITEAU, Antoine.
— & Neumann, Auguste. Mendevilla. 1845. III. 689.¹
— & Noisette, L. C. Greffe par copulation. 1835. III. 160.
— & Turpin, P. J. F. Flora parisiensis. .1808. I. 407.
— Notice sur les arbres verts. 1835. II. 45.¹
Poitiers — Société académique d'agriculture, belles-lettres, sciences ... See SOCIÉTÉ ... III. 20.
Poitou, J. Étude pratique sur la reconstitution du vignoble. 1889. III. 557.¹
Pojero, Michele LOJACONO. See LOJACONO POJERO, Michele.
Pokorny, Alois. Blättermasse österreichischer Holzpflanzen. 1877. I. 110.
— Ueber die Blattform von Ficus elastica. 1877. III. 151.²
— Blumen und Insecten. 1879. I. 238.
— Ueber den Dickezuwachs ... der Bäume. 1866. I. 193,¹ IV. 64.²
— Einige Notizen über Paulownia. 1851. III. 703.¹

— Die Erde als Wohnplatz der Pflanzen. 1881. I. 218.
— Ueber Grösse und Alter österreichischer Holzpflanzen. 1865. I. 193.¹
— Ueber Kletterpflanzen. 1878. I. 236.¹
— Nachrichten über den Laibacher Morast. 1858. I. 441.
— Ueber die Nervation der Pflanzenblätter. 1858. I. 109.²
— De l'origine des plantes alpines. 1868. I. 220.¹
— Ueber Pflanzenphaenologie. 1864. I. 221.
— Über phyllometrische Werthe. 1875. I. 110.
— Plantae lignosae imperii austriaci. 1864. I. 438, IV. 86.²
— Untersuchungen über die Torfmoore Ungarns. 1861. I. 445.
— Ueber den Ursprung der Alpenpflanzen. 1868. I. 220.¹
— Ueber die Vegetation der Moore. 1858. I. 228.²
— Die Vegetationsformen des ungarischen Tieflandes. 1860. I. 445.
— Die Vegetationsverhältnisse von Iglau. 1852. I. 440.
— Ueber das Wandern der Pflanzen. 1863. I. 241.²
— See also ETTINGSHAUSEN, Constantin, Freiherr von & POKORNY, Alois.
Pokorný, Emanuel. O tvrdých Palmách. 1899. III. 318.²
Pol, L. Das Pflanzenreich im Unterengadin. 1804. I. 433.
Polacios, G. D. Contribución al estudio del Cafe en Venezuela. 1895. III. 729.¹
Polack, Moses. De nucis vomicae viribus. 1840. III. 684.²
Polak, Johann Maria. Untersuchungen über die Staminodien der Scrophulariaceen. 1900. II. 779.¹
Polák, Karel. Dvousliják. 1890. III. 539.²
— O Lejnicích. 1884. III. 591.²
— O rostlinách slézovitých. 1890. III. 586.¹
— O sázení trnovníku obecného " Akát " zvaného. 1877. IV. 523.¹
— O vonných dřevech. 1896. IV. 396.²
Polák, Karl. Recensio plantarum phanerogamarum in com. Castriferrei Hungariae. 1839. I. 445.
Polakowsky, Hellmuth. Beitrag zur Kenntniss der Flora von Costa-Rica. 1877. I. 333.
— La flora de Costa Rica. 1879. I. 333.
— Die Pflanzenwelt von Costa-Rica. 1879. I. 333.
— Plantas costaricenses anno 1875 lectas enumerat. 1877. III. 315.²
Polder, Léon van de. De cultuur der Bamboe in Japan. 1894. III. 315.²
— Paulownia imperialis in Japan. 1891. III. 703.²
Poleck, Theodor. Analysen der Samen von Pinus. 1844. II. 40.¹
— Illicium religiosum Sieb. und anisatum. 1881. III. 397.²
Polenske, Ed. & Busse, Walter. Beiträge zur Kenntniss der Mate-Sorten. 1899. III. 529.²
Polesini, Giampaolo. Della preservazione degli Olivi. 1795. III. 675.¹
Poletayef, I. See ПОЛЕТАЕВЪ, И.
Poletavef, Q. See ПОЛЕТАЕВЪ, О.
Poli, Aser. Contribuzioni alla istologia vegetale. 1884. I. 139.
— I cristalli di ossalato calcico nelle piante. 1882. I. 139.
— Peronospora dei grappoli. 1888. III. 580.
La police forestière en Autriche. 1900. IV. 294.²
Polier. The process of making attar ... of Roses. 1788. III. 453.²
Poling in Agave plants. 1893. III. 341.¹
Politinà, Gothofredus Samuele. Myrrhologia. 1688. III. 509.²
Poll, Nicolaus. De cura morbi gallici. 1535. III. 494.¹
Pollacci, Egidio. Sur les matières colorantes des peaux de raisin. 1878. III. 583.¹
Pollacci, Gino. Appunti di patologia vegetale. 1899. III. 195.²
— Intorno all' assimilazione clorofilliana. 1899. I. 174.
— Sulla distribuzione del fosforo nei tessuti. 1894. I. 154.
— Sulla ricerca microchimica del fosforo. 1895. I. 157.
Pollak, Franz. Die Birke im Auwalde. 1894. IV. 490.²
— Das Forst- und Jagdwesen Ungarns. 1897. IV. 374.¹— 1898. IV. 374.¹
— Die Holzverluste bei der Aufarbeitung der Schläge. 1896. IV. 387.²
— Processionsspinner. 1889. IV. 199.²
— Rentirt sich die Akazie im Walde? 1891. IV. 524.¹
— Unsere Donau-Auen und ihre Bewirthschaftung. 1889. IV. 124.¹
Pollard, Charles Louis. The genus Cassia in North America. 1894. II. 342.²
— The genus Zenobia. 1895. II. 687.²
— Studies in the flora of the central Gulf region. 1897. I. 319.
— A visit to the home of Neviusia. 1900. II. 268.²

Pollen, John Hungerford.- Ancient and modern furniture. 1875. IV. 426.²

Pollender, Aloys. Ueber das Entstehen . . . der kreisrunden Oeffnungen in der äusseren Haut des Blütenstaubes. 1867. I. 524.²
— Neue Untersuchungen über das Entstehen . . . des Blütenstaubes. 1868. I. 524.²
— Wem gebührt die Priorität . . . dem Grew oder dem Malpighi? 1867. I. 79.²

Pollet, Julien. Excursion forestière de juin 1899. 1900. IV. 357.¹

Polli, Jean. Expériences sur l'action du curare. 1861. III. 683.¹

Pollich, Johann Adam. Historia plantarum in Palatinatu electorali. 1776. I. 374.

Pollichia, ein naturwissenschaftlicher Verein der bayerischen Pfalz. Jahresbericht. Mittheilungen. I. 14.

Pollini, Carlo. Sopra una curiosa deformazione di un grappolo d' Uva. 1889. III. 561.

Pollini, Ciro. Sopra alcune malattie degli Ulivi. 1818. III. 677.¹
— Catalogo delle piante dell' Orto botanico veronese. 1814. I. 62.
— Catalogus plantarum Horti botanici veronensis. 1812. I. 62.
— Discorso istorico sulla botanica. 1812. I. 79.¹
— Elementi di botanica compilati. 1810. I. 85.
— Flora veronensis. 1822. I. 425.
— Horti et provinciae veronensis plantae novae. 1816. I. 62, 266.
— Osservazioni intorno al Viaggio al lago di Garda, e al Monte Baldo. 1817. I. 425.
— Saggio di osservazioni . . . sulla vegetazione degli alberi. 1815. I. 146, 187.
— Synonymia botanica moderna. 1804. I. 77.
— Sopra la teoria della riproduzione vegetale. 1818. I. 205.
— Viaggio al lago di Garda e al Monte Baldo. 1816. I. 425.

Pollmer, F. Crataegus oxyacantha fl. pl. rubra. 1878. II. 262.¹

Pollock, Allan. A botanical index to all the medicinal plants. 1872. I. 72.²

Poloneau, A. R. Considérations générales sur les causes des ravages produits par les rivières à pentes rapides. 1844. IV. 185.¹

Polonovsky, M. See PETIT, A. & POLONOVSKY, M.

Polonski, F. See Полонскій, Ф.

Polozheniye . . . See Положеніе . . .

Polsterer, Albert Johann. Hyères in der Provence. 1834. I. 408.

Polstorff, K. & Schirmer, P. Sur la conessine. 1887. III. 688.²

Polstorff, L. See WIEGMANN, A. F. & POLSTORFF, L.

Połujański, Alexander. Botanika leśna. 1861. IV. 80.
— Leśnictwo polskie. 1861. IV. 94.
— Opisanie lasów Królestwa Polskiego. 1854. IV. 345.
— Wykład popularny nauki gospodarowania w lasach. 1860. IV. 240.

Polwka, František. Názorná květena zemí koruny české. 1900. I. 444.

Polyakov, I. S. See Поляковъ, И. С.

Polybiblion. I. 520.¹

Polytechnisches Centralblatt. IV. 539.¹

Polytechnisches Journal. III. 13.

Polzeniusz, F. See GODLEWSKI, Emil & POLZENIUSZ, F.

Pomarius, Alfred. Siebenbürgisch-sächsische Forstverhältnisse. 1895. IV. 374.¹

Pomata y Gisbert, Eladio. Catálogo de plantas . . . de Toledo. 1882. I. 422.

Pomel, Auguste. Matériaux pour la flore atlantique. 1860. I. 484.
— Note sur le périsperme du Prunier. 1877. II. 271.²
— Notice sur le pays des Beni-bou-Saïd. 1855. I. 484.
— Nouveaux matériaux pour la flore atlantique. 1874. I. 485.

Pomerana, C. Über das Phenol des Sassafrasöls. 1891. III. 408.¹

Pomeroy, N. Experience with the English Walnut. 1900. III. 355.

Pomet, Pierre. Aufrichtiger Materialist und Spezereyhändler. 1694. III. 240.
— A compleat history of druggs. 1694. III. 240.
— Droguier curieux. 1695. III. 240.
— Histoire générale des drogues. 1694. III. 240, 257.¹
— Le marchand sincère; ou, Traité général des drogues. 1694. III. 240.

Pomier. Abhandlung von den Maulbeerbäumen. 1754. III. 372.²
— L'art de cultiver les Mûriers-Blancs. 1754. III. 372.²
— Traité sur la culture des Mûriers Blancs. 1763. III. 373.

Pommaret, E. de. Note sur la floraison du Ruscus. 1858. II. 84.²

Pommerehne, H. Beiträge zur Kenntnis der Alkaloide von Berberis Aquifolium. 1895. III. 395.²

Pommerol, F. La chenille du Pommier. 1900. III. 428.²

Pommerscher Forstverein. Bericht. Verhandlungen. IV. 10.

Pommier, A. Arbres et plantes d'ornement. 188.? III. 87.

Pommier vert hybride. 1832. III. 425.¹

Pomologia. See ZINCK, Christoph. 1766. III. 70.

Pomologia. See LINDLEY, John. 1828. III. 79.

La Pomologie agricole. III. 20.

Pomologie de la France. 1863. III. 85.

La Pomologie française. III. 20.

Pomologische Monatshefte. See MONATSSCHRIFT für Pomologie. III. 13.

Pomologische vereeniging te Boskoop. Verslag. III. 14.

The pomologist. See WESTERN pomologist. III. 9.

Pomona, (pseud.). Cerasus multicarpa. 1875. III. 436.²

Pomona. See EVELYN, John. 1664. III. 141.

Pomona; allgemeine deutsche zeitschrift. III. 13.

Pompe, (Forstmeister). Die Königstanne. 1859. IV. 447.¹

Pompe, (Waldmeister). Ueber die Erhaltung der Bodenkraft des Waldes. 1855. IV. 68.

Pompe, Anton. Zwei Tage im Böhmerwalde. 1875. IV. 207.

Pompe, Karl. Einige Worte über Waldfeldbau. 1864. IV. 133.
— Die Excursion durch die Wälder der Domäne Friedland. 1868. IV. 371.
— Die Excursion durch die Wälder der Domaine Dobřisch. 1864. IV. 370.
— Die Excursion durch die Wälder der Domaine Pürglitz. 1869. IV. 371.

Pompe, Ludwig. Die Excursion . . . des Böhmischen Forst-Vereins zu Wittingau. 1863. IV. 370.
— Die Excursion . . . des Böhmischen Forst-Vereins zu Jičin. 1863. IV. 370.

Pomrencke, Werner. Vergleichende Untersuchungen über den Bau des Holzes einiger sympetaler Familien. 1892. I. 126.

Pomum, (pseud.). Spring growth of trees. 1892. I. 188.

Pona, Francesco. Il paradiso de fiori. 1622. I. 424.

Pona, Giovanni. Monte Baldo descritto. 1595. I. 424.
— Plantae seu simplicia . . . in Baldo Monte. 1595. I. 424.
— Del vero balsamo. 1623. III. 510.¹

Ponce, J. Traité d'agriculture et d'économie rurale. 1869. III. 113.

Poncelet, A. Mittheilung über die Versuche . . . in Bezug auf die Erhaltung des Holzes . . . angestellt. 1852. IV. 417.
— Rapport sur un mémoire de M. M. Eug. Chevandier et Wertheim. 1847. IV. 408.

Poncelet, Léon. Excursion forestière . . . La Nederlandsche Heidemaatschappij. 1898. IV. 357.¹
— Le Pin Laricio de Corse. 1900. IV. 466,¹ 466.²
— Le taillis simple. 1897. IV. 545.¹

Pondaven, L. Du greffage des Azalées de l'Inde. 1900. III. 657.¹

Poneropoulos, Eustathios. See ΠΟΝΗΡΟΠΟΥΛΟΣ, Εὐστάθιος.

Poneta, Karl. Anfangsgründe des forstlichen Wissens. 1881. IV. 100.¹

Pons, Giovanni. Primo [e secondo] contributo alla flora popolare valdese. 1900. III. 88.¹

Pons, Jacques. In Historiam generalem plantarum Rovillii . . . annotationes et animadversiones. 1600. I. 283.

Pons, Simon. Catalogue des Roses. 1893. II. 286.¹
— Étude comparative des Rosa micrantha. 1900. II. 286.²
— Étude critique des Roses des Pyrénées-Orientales. 1893. II. 286.¹
— Recherches rhodologiques dans les Pyrénées-Orientales. 1900. II. 286.²

Ponse, H. Leerboek over den landbouw. 1810. III. 105.

Ponson. De l'arboriculture. 1870. III. 145.²

Ponsot, Mme Francis. De la reconstitution et du greffage des Vignes. 1880. III. 556.

Pontanus, J. J. Horti hesperidum libri duo. 1514. II. 402.¹
— De hortis Esperidum. 1505. III. 494.¹

Pontarlier & Marichal. Catalogue des plantes . . . de la Vendée. 1794. V. XXII.¹
— Catalogue des plantes vasculaires . . . de la Vendée. 1894. I. 418.

Pontedera, Giulio. *See* PONTEDERA, Julius.
Pontedera, Julius. Anthologia. 1720. I. 31.
— Compendium tabularum botanicarum. 1718. I. 424, V. XXII.²
— Epistolae ac dissertationes. 1791. I. 292.
— Epistolae duae de Horto patavino. 1726. I. 61.
Pontén, Johan Pehr. Dissertatio philosophico-botanica de serie vegetabilium. 1800. I. 33.
Pontey, William. The forest pruner. 1805. IV. 170.
— The profitable planter. 1800. IV. 108.¹
— The rural improver. 1822. III. 109.
Pontifex, S. R. *See* WONFOX, W. J. & PONTIFEX, S. R.
Pontin, David Davidis. Arboretum suecicum. *See* LINNÉ, Carl von. 1759. I. 350,¹ *III. 66*,¹ 119.¹
Pontoppidan, Erich. Det förste Forsög paa Norges naturlige Historie. 1752. I. 351, III. 270.¹
— Kürzgefasste Nachrichten, die Naturhistorie in Dännemark betreffend. 1765. III. 270.¹
— The natural history of Norway. 1752. I. 351.
— Versuch einer natürlichen Historie von Norwegen. 1752. I. 351.
Pontoppidan, Johannes.' De manna Israelitarum. 1756. III. 221.¹
Ponselin, J. von. Grundsatze über Hervorbringung vollständigerer Verbrennung des Heitzmaterials. 1841. IV. 412.²
Poock, Daniel. Theoretisch-praktische Anweisung zur Erziehung... der Privatforsten. 1842. IV. 97.
Pool, J. E. Nekoc, een indiaansch vischvergift. 1898. III. 481.²
Pool, J. F. Balsamum Copaivae surinamensis. 1897. III. 473.¹
The Poor Salai, (*pseud.*). An apology for Salai. 1881. IV. 525.¹
Pope, Marion Manville. Where the Teak wood grows. 1894. IV. 538.¹
Popert, E. P. Note on Casuarina planting. 1895. III. 342,¹ IV. 485.¹
Popis exkurse Českou jednotou lesnickou dne 3. srpna 1885 do lesů královského města Plzně konané. *See* BESCHREIBUNG der Exkursion des Böhmischen Forstvereines... 1885. IV. 371.
Popis reviru libhavského přislušného k panství lanškrounskému. *See* BESCHREIBUNG des zur Fürst Johann... 1900.. IV. 373.
Popis vycházky do lesů panství Hořovického. *See* BESCHREIBUNG der Exkursionstour des Böhm. Forstvereines... 1892. IV. 372.
Popis vycházky České lesnické jednoty do lesů svěřenského statku rychnovského hraběte Zdeňka z Kolovrat. *See* BESCHREIBUNG der Excursionstour... 1883. IV. 371.
Popis vycházky konané Českou lesnickou jednotou do hvozdů panství Rožmitálského. *See* BESCHREIBUNG der Excursionstour. 1891. IV. 372.
Popis vycházky pořádané Českou lesnickou jednotou dne 4. srpna 1890 do lesů panství Vorlického. *See* BESCHREIBUNG der Exkursion veranstaltet vom Böhm. Forstvereine... in die Forste der Herrschaft Worlik. 1890. IV. 372.
Poplars and Elms in Tumut district. 1897. III. 344,² 364.¹
Popof, N. *See* ПОПОВЪ, N.
Popof-Vedenski, V. N. *See* ПОПОВЪ-ВЕДЕНСКIЙ, B. H.
Popowitsch, Johann Siegmund Valentin. Versuch einer Vereinigung der Mundarten von Teutschland. 1700. I. 70.¹
Popp, P. B. Flora von Sobeyern. 1887. I. 388.
Poppe, Johann. Kräuterbuch. 1625. I. 285.¹
Poppey, R. C. Destruction of trees in cities. 1881. III. 212.¹
Poppo, F. V. C. Auf 30jährige Erfahrung... gegründete Anweisung, den Weinstock... zu behandeln. 1825. III. 552.
Populäre Vorträge aus allen Fächern der Naturwissenschaft. *See* VEREIN ZUR VERBREITUNG NATURWISSENSCHAFTLICHER KENNTNISSE IN WIEN. I. 15.
Populäres Verfahren bei Regulirung der Wälder. 1847. IV. 242.
Populaire Gebrauchsanweisung zum Zuwachsbohrer. *See* PRESSLER, M. R. 1869. IV. 232.
Popular cyclopaedia of natural science. *See* CARPENTER, W. B. 1841. I. 94.
Popular evergreen trees. 1867. III. 289.
Popular gardening and fruit growing. III. 7.
Popular gardening for town and country. *See* POPULAR gardening and fruit growing. III. 7.
Popular geography of plants. *See* C., E. M. 1855. I. 95.
Popular science monthly. I. 6.

Popular science review. I. 19.
Populus tremula, (*pseud.*). Bitte einer Verkannten. 1865. IV. 486.²
Por qué carecen de árboles las praderas de América? 1892. IV. 544.¹
Porcelli, Vincenzo. Contribuzione allo studio delle ipertrofie prodotte dalla Roestelia. 1897. III. 422.²
Porcher, Félix. Étude sur la dégénérescence. 1871. I. 248.²
— Le Fuchsia. 1848. III. 639.²
— Fuchsia; nouvelles espèces et variétés. 1851. III. 639.²
— Du Fuchsia; observations générales. 1854. III. 639.²
— Du Fuchsia... Résumé du mode de culture. 1854. III. 639.²
— Fuchsia; tableau dressé. 1867. III. 639.²
— Histoire et culture du Fuchsia. 1848. III. 639.²
— Des Pelargonium. 1870. III. 491.²
— Pelargonium heteranthum. 1848. III. 491.²
— Remarques sur la culture et la nomenclature des Fuchsias. 1848. III. 639.²
Porcher, Francis Peyre. A medico-botanical catalogue of the plants and ferns of St. John's. 1847. I. 318.
— Report on the indigenous medicinal plants of South Carolina. 1849. III. 62.
— Resources of the southern fields and forests. 1863. III. 62.
Porchet, F. *See* CHUARD, E. & PORCHET, F.
Porcius, Florian. Diagnosele plantelorü... in Transilvania. 1893. V. XXIII.¹
— Enumeratio plantarum... districtus quondam naszódiensis. 1878. I. 446.
— Flora din fostulü districtü romănescü alü năsăuduluï in Transilvania. 1885. I. 446.
Porro, Girolamo.' L'Horto dei semplici. *See* CORTUSO, J. A. (*by error*). 1591. I. 60,² V. VIII.²
Port, Arnold DODEL. *See* DODEL-PORT, Arnold & Carolina.
Port, Carolina DODEL. *See* DODEL-PORT, Arnold & Carolina.
Porta, Giovanni Battista. Phytognomonica octo libris contenta. 1588. I. 282.
— Suae villae pomarium. 1583. III. 88.¹
— Villae libri XII. 1592. III. 115.¹
Porta, Pietro. Stirpium in insulis Balearium... enumeratio. 1887. I. 423.
— Viaggio botanico... in Calabria. 1879. I. 428.
Portal, Salvator. Catalogus plantarum Horti botanici Salvatoris Portae Albaevillae. 1826. I. 62.
Porte, A. Contributions à l'étude du Cassia alata. 1879. III. 470.²
Porte, Marius. Ein Blick in die Familie der Palmen. 1859. III. 319.¹
— Note sur quelques produits... de Palmiers. 1859. III. 319.¹
— Notice sur les usages... de quelques Palmiers. 1859. III. 319.¹
Portefeuille des horticulteurs. III. 20.
Porter, George Richardson. De landbouw tusschen de keerkringen. 1833. III. 96.¹
— The tropical agriculturist. 1833. III. 96.¹
Porter, H. J. Failure of natural reproduction in the Teak forests. 1894. IV. 536.²
— The management of forests containing Teak. 1896. IV. 537.²
Porter, J. C. Thuber measurer. 1871. IV. 220.
Porter, Thomas Conrad. Additions to our native flora. 1889. II. 672.¹
— Audibertia Vaseyi n. sp. 1881. II. 765.¹
— Catalogue of plants [collected at the headwaters of the Yellowstone River.] 1872. I. 323.
— Magnolia glauca. 1894. II. 212.¹
— A new variety of Azalea nudiflora L. 1900. II. 682.²
— Notes on two Rhododendrons. 1889. II. 678.¹
— Prunus alleghaniensis. 1877. II. 272.¹
— Prunus alleghaniensis. 1890. II. 272.¹
— Rare plants of southeastern Pennsylvania. 1900. I. 317.¹
— The Table Mountain Pine (Pinus pungens). 1893. II. 45.²
— The Twin-flower... in Pennsylvania. 1900. III. 835.¹
— & Coulter, J. M. Synopsis of the flora of Colorado. 1874. I. 323.
Porterfield, D. A. Shelter belts. 1894. III. 215.²
Portes & Ruyssen. La Vigne en Crimée. 1891. III. 551.²
Portes, Lud. De l'asparagine des Aruygdalées. 1877. II. 257.¹
— Sur l'existence de l'asparagine dans les Amandes. 1876. II. 272.²—1877. III. 434.²
— Origine de la Vigne. 1884. II. 505.¹

Portes, Lud. (*continued*).
— Sur les ravages produits dans les Vignes. 1877. III. 577.
— Recherches sur les Amandes amères. 1877. III. 434.[2]
— Sur le traitement de l'anthracnose. 1879. III. 578.
— Sur le traitement de l'anthracnose de la Vigne. 1878. III. 578.
Le porteur universel. 1877. IV. 391.
Portici — Reale scuola superiore d'agricoltura. *See* REALE ... III. 23.[2]
Portier. Semaille du Tabac dans les vignobles. 1874. III. 566.[1]
The Portland catalogue of Maine plants. *See* GOODALE, G. L. & BLAKE, Joseph. 1868. I. 314.
Portland society of natural history. Proceedings. I. 519.[1]
Porto-Alegre, Paulo. Monographia do Café. 1879. III. 726.[2]
Portugal — Commissão central anti-phylloxerica. 1883. III. 761.
Portugal — Direcção geral da agricultura. Annuario. III. 23,[1] V. XXIX.[1]
Portugal — Real sociedade nacional de horticultura. *See* REAL SOCIEDADE ... III. 23.[1]
Porubszky, Gyula. A magyar Tölgy ismertetéséhez. 1886. II. 133.[1]
— A Tölgykorcsok gyakorlati jelentősége. 1889. IV. 508.
Poryadok upravleniya. *See* Порядокъ управленія.
Porządek leśnictwa i myśliwstwa, uchwalony dla Zachodnich Prus. 1805. IV. 320.
Posada-Arango, André. L'Arbre à pluie. 1892. I. 213.[2]
— Note sur le Bejugo de Agua. 1871. III. 707.[2]
— Note sur quelques Palmiers de la Colombie. 1878. II. 64,[1] 71.[1]
— Note sur quelques plantes féculentes. 1871. I. 140.[1]
— Note sur un nouvel arbre à Caoutchouc. 1880. III. 444.[1]
— Nouvelles espèces de plantes de la Colombie. 1871. II. 165,[1] 344.[1]
Poscharsky, Gustav Adolf. Beiträge zur Flora von Croatien. 1896. I. 448.[2]
Poselger, H. Beitrag zur Blüthezeit der Gewächse. 1881. I. 225.
— Beitrag zur Kakteenkunde. 1853. II. 586.[1]
— Beschreibung einiger neuer Cacteen-Arten. 1855. II. 586.[1]
Posen — Naturwissenschaftlicher Verein. *See* NATURWISSENSCHAFTLICHER ... I. 14.
Posizione ed uffici della fitotopografia. *See* NICOTRA, Leopoldo. 1878. I. 300.
Posnikof, A. V. *See* Посниковъ, А. В.
Posodka derevev ... *See* Посодка деревьевъ ...
Pospíchal, Eduard. Flora des Flussgebietes der Cidlina. 1881. V. XXIII.[1]
— Flora des oesterreichischen Küstenlandes. 1897. I. 448.[2]
Posse, Adolph. Mass- und Gewichts-Tafeln zur Vergleichung der ... Holz- und Frucht-Masse. 1841. IV. 229.
Post, George Edward. The botanical geography of Syria and Palestine. 1888. I. 480.
— Diagnoses plantarum novarum orientalium. 1888. I. 480.
— Flora of Syria, Palestine. 1883. I. 480.
— List of plants collected ... principally in Moab, Gilead and Haurân. 1888. I. 480.
— Narrative of a scientific expedition in the Trans-Jordanic region. 1888. I. 480.
— Notes on the behavior of Fig trees. 1880. II. 151.[1]
— Plantae Postianae. 1890. I. 480.
— & Autran, E. Plantae Postianae. 1890. I. 480.
Post, Hampus Adolf von. Försök till systematisk uppställning af vextställena i mellersta Sverige. 1862. I. 356.
— Om Grauens kvist-toppfällning. 1874. II. 36.[1]
— Om Ljungens och Mjölonrisets bortdöende. 1858. I. 206.[1]
— Om vextgeografiska skildringar. 1851. I. 217.
— Westra Målarstrandens cotyledoner. 1844. I. 354.
Post, Tom von. *See* KUNTZE, Otto & POST, Tom von.
Postal microscopical society. Journal. *See* JOURNAL of microscopy ... I. 18.
Postel, Emil. Der Führer in die Pflanzenwelt. 1856. I. 532,[1] V. XIX.[2]
— Vademecum für Freunde der Pflanzenwelt. 1860. I. 95.
— *See also* Постель, Э.
Posthumus, Ludovicus. De ademhaling der planten. 1880. I. 171.
— Anatomisch onderzoek van Japansche houtsoorten. 1874. I. 125.
— Iets over sommige "noten." 1879. III. 220.[1]
— Over den invloed ... der zwammen. 1876. III. 194.

Pot, D. *See* POT, J. & D. van der.
Pot, J. & D. van der. Bedenkingen tegen het kyaniseeren van hout opgeheven. 1884. IV. 420.
The Potato and Buttonwood diseases. 1851. III. 418.[2]
Potebnya, A. *See* Потебня, А.
Potel, H. Sobre o Phylloxera vastatrix no Brazil. 1894. III. 574.
Von den Potenzen als Hülfsmittel für Zins- und Zinseszins-Berechnungen. 1855. IV. 254.
Potiez-Defroom, J. L. F. Catalogue des plantes cultivées dans les jardins de la Société ... d'agriculture ... du département de Nord. 1835. I. 57.
Potomac-side naturalists' club. Bulletin. *See* FIELD and forest. I. 5.
Potonié, Henry. Ueber die Bedeutung der Steinkörper ... der Birnen. 1880. II. 256.[2]
— Die Entwickelung der Pflanzenwelt Norddeutschlands. 1886. I. 388.
— Ueber den Ersatz erfrorener Frühlingstriebe. 1881. I. 108.[1]
— Illustrierte Flora von Nord- und Mittel-Deutschland. 1885. I. 388, 532.[2]
— Der K. botanische Garten und das K. botanische Museum in Berlin. 1882. I. 48.
— Ueber eine Linden-Varietät. 1880. II. 517.[2]
— Die Morphogenie des ... Blattes und Stengels. 1897. I. 101.[2]
— Die pflanzengeographische Anlage. 1890. V. VIII.[2]
— Das Skelet der Pflanzen. 1881. I. 134.[2]
— Steinkörperchen der Birne. 1881. II. 278.[2]
— Znaczenie utworów kamienistych w miąsiwie Gruszek. 1880. II. 256.[2]
Potrat, Camille. Du bouturage du Rosier. 1897. III. 453.[1]
— Le Catalpa, son emploi. 1895. III. 705.
— Picea excelsa var. nana. 1893. III. 305.[1]
— Les plantes fleuries en culture forcée. 1897. III. 533.[2]
Pott, Carl Wilhelm. De camphorae circumspecto usu medico. *See* ALBERTI, Michael. 1722. III. 404.[2]
Potter, Michael Cressé. Observations on the protection of buds in the tropics. 1891. I. 108,[2] 819.[2]
— & Gardiner, Walter. On the thickening of the stem in ... Thunbergia. 1889. I. 805.[1]
Potter, P. Les Cèdres du Liban. 1886. II. 28.[2]
Potter, Richard. Gaultheria nummularioides. 1884. III. 652.[1]
— Hypericum Coris. 1884. III. 610.[1]
Potter, Samuel O. L. Handbook of materia medica. 1887. III. 244.
Potter, Thomas Rossell. The history and antiquities of Charnwood forest. 1842. I. 399.
Potter's American monthly. III. 7.
Pottevin, Henri. La tannese. 1900. I. 178.
Pottier. Procédés économiques pour dépouiller de son principe amer la pulpe du marron d'Inde. 1849. III. 538.[1]
Pottier. Fructification de l'Araucaria Bidwilli. 1897. III. 298.[1]
Pottier, André Ariodant. *See* BRIERRE DE BOISMONT, A. J. F. & POTTIER, A. A.
Pottier, Arsène. Les Aucuba du Japon. 1879. III. 645.[1]
— Hibiscus rosa sinensis miniatus semiplenus. 1879. III. 588.[1]
Pottinger, E. & Prain, David. A note on the botany of the Kachiu Hills. 1898. I. 475.[2]
Potts, Thomas Henry. Through a young plantation. 1878. IV. 124.[2]
— & Gray, William. On the cultivation of some species of native trees. 1871. III. 132.[2]
Le pou de San-José. 1899. III. 192.[1]
Le pou laineux du Hêtre. 1896. IV. 497.
Pouchet, Felix Archimede. Considérations sur le Jardin botanique de Rouen. 1832. I. 57.
— Essai sur l'histoire naturelle ... des Solanées. 1827. III. 698.[2]
— Flore; ou, Statistique botanique de la Seine-inférieure. 1834. I. 408.
— Histoire naturelle ... des Solanées. 1829. III. 698.[2]
— Traité élémentaire de botanique appliquée. 1835. I. 255.
Poucin. Culture du Chêne-Liège. 1882. IV. 517.[1]
— Exploitation des Lièges. 1883. IV. 517.
Poucin, Théodore. Mémoire sur les procédés de boisement ... en Sologne. 1866. IV. 162.
— Du repeuplement des forêts. 1859. IV. 141.
De la poudre de vieux bois. 1859. IV. 432.[1]
Pouget, Louis. Note sur le développement extraordinaire d'un Juniperus communis L. 1892. II. 31.[1]

Poughkeepsie society of natural science. Proceedings. I. 6.

Pougnet, P. F. Armand. Étude sur le Noyer commun. 1875. III. 356.[1]

Pouillon-Boblaye. Sur l'aspect des campagnes dans quelques parties de l'Algérie. 1838. I. 484.

Foulet, V. Recherches sur les principes de la digestion végétale. 1896. I. 160.

Poulin, Marcel. De la possibilité de provoquer des anomalies végétales. 1888. I. 144.[1]

Poullain-Grandprey, & others. Projet de code forestier. 1799. IV. 325.

Pouloux, François. Contribution à l'histoire médicale du Laurier-Rose. 1888. III. 689.[2]

Poulsen, Christian Marinus. Om den Brandfare Landets Skove. 1875. IV. 182.[1]

— Om Foranstaltninger til Forebyggelse af Skovbrand. 1876. IV. 182.[2]

— Om nogle i vort Skovbrug anvendelige Naaletræer. 1879. IV. 125,[1] 441, 433.[1]

Poulsen, D. T. Nogle Iagttagelser over Frostens Virkninger paa forskjellige Planter. 1875. III. 44.[2]

Poulsen, Viggo Albert. Om den abnorme Rodbygning hos en Art af Slægten Myristica. 1895. II. 220.[3]

— Botanische Mikrochemie. 1880. I. 156.[1]

— Botaniskt mikrokemi. 1880. I. 156.[2]

— Om Forekomsten af de Rosanoffske Krystalgrupper hos Rosa. 1874. II. 289.[1]

— Nogle extraflorale Nektarier. 1897. I. 135.

Poumarède, J. A. & Figuier, Louis. Mémoire sur le ligneux. 1846. I. 155.

Pouméroulie, Charles. Un mode de greffage peu connu. 1887. III. 162.

Pound, Roscoe. Bibliography of the flora of Nebraska. 1894. I. 326.

— See also SMITH, J. G. & POUND, ROSCOE.

— & Clements, F. E. The phytogeography of Nebraska. 1900. I. 327.

Pouppé-Desportes, J. B. R. Catalogue des plantes de S. Domingue. 1770. I. 334.

— Traité . . . des plantes usuelles de S. Domingue. 1770. III. 64.[1]

Pouriau, (Prof., Grignon). Culture des plantes à parfums. 1876. III. 226.[2]

Pourret, P. A. Projet d'une histoire générale . . . des Cistes. 1875. II. 564.[1]

Pourret, Pierre André. Extrait de la Chloris narbonnensis. 1788. I. 406.

Pourriture de l'Épicéa. 1896. IV. 457.

La pourriture de l'Épicéa.' 1897. IV. 559.[1]

Pourtales, Louis François. Hints of the origin of the flora . . . of the Florida keys. 1877. I. 319.

Poussat, J. See DUGAST, J. & POUSSAT, J.

Poutingon, Albert MILKE-. See MILKE-POTTINGON, Albert.

Pouvoir calorifique du bois. 1898. IV. 413.[1]

Pouzolz, Pierre Charles Marie de. Catalogue des plantes . . . dans le Gard. 1842. I. 409.

— Flore du département du Gard. 1856. I. 411.

Povalo-Shvyikovski, J. See ПОВАЛО-ШВЫЙКОВСКIЙ, Я.

Povelsen, Biarne. See OLAFSEN, Eggert & POVELSEN, Biarne.

Powell, B. H. BADEN-. See BADEN-POWELL, B. H.

Powell, David. On a method of securing the scion. 1824. III. 160.

Powell, Edward Payson. Country houses and winter shrubs. 1893. III. 208.[1]

— A desirable tree. 1894. III. 478.[1]

— The gift of tongues in trees. 1892. I. 516.

— Hedges, windbreaks. 1900. III. 214,[1] 215.[2]

— A plea for more street trees. 1892. III. 208.[2]

— Trees in winter. 1892. III. 208.[1]

Powell, F. M. The Grape; its medicinal value. 1896. III. 583.[2]

Powell, G. S. Memorial to the Congress of the United States from the Appalachian national park association. 1900. IV. 179.[1]

Powell, George Harold. Bud variations. 1897. I. 245.

— The Cherry in Delaware. 1897. III. 432.[1]

— The European and Japanese Chestnuts. 1898. III. 358.[2]

— Improving varieties. 1897. I. 245.

— Plant breeding. 1897. I. 245.

— Some climatic . . . troubles of the Chestnut. 1899. III. 358.[2]

— See also BAILEY, L. H. & POWELL, G. H.

Powell, I. L. Best effects with Rhododendrons. 1892. III. 656.

Powell, J. New fruit-bearing shrub, Eugenia Ugni. 1856. III. 638.[1]

Powell, John Wesley. Report on the lands of the arid region of the United States. 1878. IV. 340.

Powell, Thomas. On the nature and mode of use of the vegetable poisons. 1878. III. 260.[2]

— On various Samoan plants. 1868. I. 510.[1]

Power, Frederick Belding. Sur l'essence de Bouleau. 1891. III. 426.[1]

— & Weimar, Henry. On the constituents of Wild Cherry bark. 1888. II. 277.[1]

— & Werbke, N. C. On the constituents of Wintergreen leaves. 1889. III. 652.[1]

Power, Georges. Traité de la culture du Pommier. 1890. III. 426.[2] ·

Power, J. Calendar of flora at Market Bosworth. 1807. I. 396.

Power, J. B. Sur l'essence de Bouleau. 1891. IV. 491.[2]

Power, Thomas. The botanist's guide for the county of Cork. 1845. I. 399.

Powers, Stephen. Aboriginal botany. 1875. III. 62.

Powerscourt, viscount. The re-afforesting of Ireland. 1883. IV. 161.[1]

Poyvre, Pierre. Voyages d'un philosophe. 1768. III. 116.[2]

Pozdnyakof, N. See ПОЗДНЯКОВЪ, Н.

Pozemelno- . . . liesnoi . . . See ПОЗЕМЕЛЬНО- . . . ЛѢСНОЙ . . .

Pozos Dulces, conde de. Sobre la variabilidad de las especies. 1868. I. 244.[1]

Pozsony szab. kir. város erdészete. 1899. IV. 374.[1]

Pozzetti, Pompilio. Sopra alcune Rose particolari. 1804. II. 290.[2]

Prachien, J. S. KOZAK A. See KOZAK A PRACHIEN, J. S.

On the practicability of the Tea-culture in the United States. 1858. III. 600.[1]

Practical engineer. III. 18.

Practical hints on the culture of the Mulberry tree. 1839. III. 375.

The practical husbandman and planter. 1733. III. 109.

Practical lessons from Jutland. 1884. IV. 156.[2]

Practical magazine. IV. 539.[2]

Practical pharmacography. 1898. III. 636.[1]

Practical pharmacography. Amygdalae. 1897. II. 272.[2]

Practical pharmacography; Anisi fructus. 1897. III. 398.[1]

Practical pharmacography; Belae fructus. 1897. III. 398.[1]

Practical pharmacography. Cocae folia. 1899. III. 493.[1]

Practical planter, (pseud.). Fast growing shade trees. 1859. III. 208.[2]

A practical treatise on planting. See HAYES, S. 1794. IV. 108.[1]

Practisch beschreven naamlijst der voornaamste groepen Azaleas. 1896. III. 655.

Practische beschrijvende lijst van het geslacht Clematis. 1890. III. 389.[2]

Pradas, L. De la culture du Prunier. 1889. III. 433.[1]

Pradel, Colomb. See GUÉNOT, L. & PRADEL, Colomb.

Pradel, Paul. Étude sur le Gelsemium sempervirens. 1884. III. 682.[1]

Praedium rusticum. See ESTIENNE, Charles. 1554. IV. 121.

Praël, Edmund. Vergleichende Untersuchungen über Schutz- und Kernholz. 1887. I. 126.

Praeger, Robert Loyd. Open-air studies in botany. 1897. I. 535.

Præparater til Belysning af Tilvæxtgangen. See LÜTKEN, Christian. 1872. IV. 233.

Praetorius, George Otto. Cultivation of the Chestnut. 1889. III. 358.[2]

— The Hickory in Germany. 1887. III. 353.[2]

Praetorius, Johannes. De plantis. 1677. I. 30.

Prahl, Johann Friedrich. Index plantarum . . . circa Gustroviam. 1837. I. 379, V. XIX.[2]

Prain, David. An additional species of Ellipanth[i]us. 1891. II. 317.[1]

— The botanical sources of Padauk. 1900. IV. 522.[1]

— Botany of the Laccadives. 1892. I. 481.[2].

— On a botanical visit to Little Andaman. 1892. I. 481.[2]

— On the flora of Narcondam and Barren Island. 1893. I. 481.[2]

— A list of Diamond Island plants. 1891. I. 481.[2]

— A list of the Asiatic species of Ormosia. 1900. II. 375.[1]

— Memoirs and memoranda, chiefly botanical. 1894. I. 475.[2]

— A new Burmese timber-tree. 1900. III. 376.[1]

— The non-indigenous species of the Andaman flora. 1891. I. 481.[2]

Prain, David (*continued*).
— Note added to [A.] Barclay's paper. 1890. III. 465.[1]
— Note on lo-kao. 1888. III. 542.[2]
— Noviciae indicae. 1891. II. 317,[1] 762.[2] — 1893. II. 371.[1] — 1897. II. 774.[2] — 1898. II. 319.[1]
— Report on the Indian species of Pterocarpus. 1900. II. 380.[1]
— Sisal Hemp. 1900. III. 341.[1]
— Some additional Leguminosae. 1898. II. 319.[1]
— Some additional Solanaceae. 1897. II. 774.[2]
— Some additional species of Convolvulaceae. 1894. II. 744.[1]
— Some additional species of Labiatae. 1891. II. 762.[2]
— Two additional species of Glyptopetalum. 1892. II. 469.[1]
— An undescribed Mezoneuron. 1893. II. 371.[1]
— The vegetation of the Coco group. 1892. I. 481.[2]
— *See also* KING, Sir George & PRAIN, David; MAYNARD, F. P. & PRAIN, David; POTTINGER, E. & PRAIN, David.
Prairie marécageuse. Boisement. 1898. IV. 489.[1]
Praktische Anleitung zur Bereitung des Zuckers aus Ahorn. 1812. IV. 526.[1]
Die praktische, auf Erfahrung gegründete Holzzucht. *See* KUPFER, K. A. 1821. IV. 106.
Die praktische Ausbildung des Forstverwaltungspersonals in der Schweiz. 1897. IV. 36.[1]
Praktische Baumbefestigung. 1882. III. 199.
Praktische Bedeutung des Lichtungszuwachses. 1866. IV. 236.
Praktische Bemerkungen zur Forstwissenschaft. *See* MÜLLENKAMPF, F. D. F. von. 1783. IV. 100.[1]
Praktische Blätter für Pflanzenschutz. III. 13.
Der praktische Forstwirth für die Schweiz. IV. 13.[2]
Der praktische Gartenfreund. III. 24.[1]
Die praktische Messkunst. *See* LEGELER, W. 1877. III. 200.[1]
Der praktische Obstbaumgärtner. 1813. III. 136.
Praktische volksalmanak. III. 14.
Praktische Vorschläge und Bemerkungen . . . über verschiedene Gegenstände aus der Forstwirthschaft. 1797. IV. 268.
Praktischer Führer im Obstbau. 1881. III. 138.
Praktisches Handbuch über . . . Kultur des Maulbeerbaumes. *See* ZOLLINGER, C. von. 1843. V. XXVIII.[2]
Praktisk Haandbog for Trælasthandlere. 1875. IV. 402.[2]
Prangé. Note sur la maladie de la Vigne. 1851. III. 575.[1]
Prantl. *See* FÜRST, Hermann & PRANTL.
Prantl, Karl. Eine amerikanische Cuscuta als Feind der Weiden. 1878. III. 350.[1].
— Anonaceae. 1891. II. 215.[1]
— Beiträge zur Kenntniss der Cupuliferen. 1887. II. 123.[1]
— Beiträge zur Morphologie . . . der Ranunculaceen. 1888. II. 195.[2]
— Bemerkungen über einige Pflanzen des hiesigen Gartens. 1873. I. 48.
— Berberidaceae. 1891. II. 201.[2]
— Betulaceae. 1889. II. 115.[1]
— Calycanthaceae. 1891. II. 214.[1]
— Cruciferae. 1891. II. 233.[2]
— Cuscuta, ein Feind der Weiden. 1878. III. 350.[1]
— Ueber den Einfluss des Lichts auf das Wachsthum der Blätter. 1874. I. 190,[2] 230.
— An elementary text-book of botany. 1874. I. 91.
— Fagaceae. 1889. II. 123.[1]
— Hysterium Pinastri. 1877. IV. 461,[1] 477.
— Lardizabalaceae. 1891. II. 201.[1]
— Lehrbuch der Botanik. 1874. I. 91.
— Magnoliaceae. 1891. II. 208.[2]
— Manuale di botanica. 1874. I. 91.
— Menispermaceae. 1891. II. 206.[1]
— Myristicaceae. 1891. II. 220.[1]
— Notiz über einen neuen Blüthenfarbstoff. 1871. II. 323.[2]
— Ranunculaceae. 1891. II. 195.[1]
— Studien über Wachsthum, Verzweigung und Nervatur der Laubblätter. 1883. I. 110.
— Trochodendraceae. 1891. II. 194.[2]
— Die Ursache der Kiefernschütte. 1877. IV. 477.
— Verzeichniss der im botanischen Garten der Kgl. Forstlehranstalt Aschaffenburg cultivirten Pflanzen. 1879. I. 48, *IV. 13*.[2]
— Weitere Beobachtungen über die Kiefernschütte. 1880. IV. 442.
— *See also* ENGLER, Adolf & PRANTL, Karl.
— & **Kündig**, Jakob. Papaveraceae. 1891. II. 229.[1]

Praschil, Wenceslaus Wilhelm. Plantae venenatae in territorio vindobonensi. 1840. III. 90.[2]
Prasse, (*Revierförster*). Erfahrung über den Ertrag eines Lerchen-Bestandes. 1851. IV. 452.[1]
Pratesi. Tavole di botanica elementare disegnate ed incise. 1801. I. 97.
Pratt, (*consul*). Clove cultivation in Zanzibar. 1890. III. 635.[2]
— Culture du Girofle à Zanzibar. 1890. III. 635.[2]
Pratt, Anne. The flowering plants and ferns of Great Britain. 1855. I. 400, 533.
— Flowers and their associations. 1846. I. 94.
— Haunts of the wild flowers. 1863. I. 401.
— Wild flowers. 1852. I. 400, 533.
— Wild flowers of the year. 1851. I. 400.
Pratten, M. A. My hundred Swiss flowers. 1887. I. 437.
Pratz, LE PAGE DU. *See* LE PAGE DU PRATZ.
Pravila . . . *See* ПРАВИЛА . . .
Praxa, A. Zwei neue Säemaschinen. 1883. IV. 149.[1]
Préaubert, Ernest & **Bouvet**, Georges. Observations sur quelques plantes critiques de l'ouest. 1899. II. 286.[2]
— Roses hybrides des environs d'Angers. 1899. II. 286.[2]
Prebble, J. G. The Pisa tree and the Indian Willow. 1894. II. 110,[2] 223.[2]
— Some notes on economic botany. 1894. III. 53.
Précautions à prendre pour les boisements en Pin Laricio. 1900. IV. 466.[1]
Prechtl. Eau-de-vie d'Arbousier. 1820. III. 648.[1]
Précis de Geo. Pley's letter about "yearly destruction" in Newfoundland. *See* PLEY, George. 1893. IV. 271.[1]
Précis of reports on . . . the Cow-tree seed. 1883. III. 367.[2]
Préclaire, J. L. Traité théorique et pratique d'arboriculture. 1864. III. 144.
Preda, Agilulfo. Alcune osservazioni su di . . . Dasylirion glaucum Zucc. 1896. II. 81.[1]
— Sopra alcuni frutti di Pirus Malus var. Appina. 1894. II. 266.[2]
— Indoppimento . . . di un fiore di Rubus discolor. 1895. II. 307.[1]
Prédaval. *See* GÉRARD & PRÉDAVAL.
Prediger, E. Zum Artikel "Forstliche Buch- und Rechnungsführung." 1887. IV. 312.
— Zur Aufforstung verödeter Kalkberge. 1887. IV. 158.
— Axt und Keil. 1887. IV. 384.[1]
— Betrachtungen der beim Holzhauereibetriebe gebräuchlichen Sägen. 1886. IV. 393.
— Die Birke in sanitärer Beziehung. 1888. IV. 490.[2]
— Empfiehlt es sich . . . die Erziehung von Starkholz im gruppenweisen Bestande anzustreben? 1887. IV. 128.
— Sind in Nord-Deutschland Versuche mit dem Anbau der Schwarzkiefer gemacht. 1888. IV. 466.[3]
— Was kann der Forstmann zur Verschönerung der Waldungen thun? 1887. IV. 137.[1]
— Welche Ansichten herrschen heute über die Durchforstungen? 1886. IV. 174.
— Welche Bedeutung haben die Laufkäfer für den Wald. 1888. IV. 93.
— Welche Sägelängen haben sich . . . als die bestgeeigneten . . . herausgestellt. 1891. IV. 393.
— Welche Vorteile gewährt die Waldweide. 1888. IV. 135.[1]
— Wie ist die Waldköhlerei . . . zu betreiben? 1887. IV. 395.
Prefontaine, M. Maison rustique à l'usage des habitans de Cayenne. 1763. III. 99.
Preijer, Axel. De caoutchouc-cultuur . . . in Java. 1900. III. 149.
— Over caoutchouc-cultuur en bereiding. 1900. III. 149.
— Die Kautschukkultur . . . in Java. 1900. III. 149.
Preis auf die Anpflanzung des Papier-Maulbeerbaumes. 1831. III. 367.[2]
Der Preis der Arbeit im Staatsforstdiens. 1893. IV. 311.[1]
Preisser, F. Dissertation sur l'origine et la nature des matières colorantes. 1843. I. 184.
— *See also* GIRARDIN, J. & PREISSER, F.
Preissler, J. Ueber eine neue Gattung . . . der Loranctheen. 1828. II. 672.[1]
Preissmann, Ernest. Beiträge zur Flora von Steiermark. 1896. I. 444.
Preis-Tabellen für runde Hölzer nach Metermass. 1875. IV. 402.[2]
Prejevalski, N. M. *See* PRZHEVALSKI, N. M.
Preliminary list of the plants . . . in Alabama. *See* MOHR, C. T. 1880. I. 319.
Prell. Ueber Pflege von Waldungen im Privatbesitze. 1900. IV. 309.[1]

Premi proposti dalla Società degli agricoltori della Francia. 1882. IV. 41.¹
Premiazione. 1888. IV. 18.¹
Premier code de la ville de Berne. Chapitre des forêts. See ERSTE Gerichtssatzung . . . 1864. IV. 330.
Première floraison du Bois d'arc. 1832. III. 372.¹
La première forêt. 1898. IV. 547.¹
Premio proposto dalla Società . . . d' agricoltura di Francia per la determinazione . . . del tessuto legnoso. 1865. IV. 82.¹
Přemysl. III. 25.
Prenleloup, L. A. Remarques sur quelques Zamias. 1871. III. 286.¹
La prensa y los montes. 1890. IV. 547.²
Prentice, Charles. French locality for Ulex australis. 1856. II. 387.¹
Prentiss, Albert Nelson. The Hemlock. 1890. IV. 484.²
— The Hemlock in its forestal aspects. 1890. IV. 484.¹
— Hygroscopic movements in the cone-scales. 1889. II. 21.¹
— On the mode of the natural distribution of plants. 1872. I. 240.²
Prentiss, D. W. & Morgan, F. P. Mescal buttons. 1896. III. 620.²
— — Therapeutic uses of Mescal buttons. 1896. III. 620.²
La préparation de l'eau de fleurs d'Oranger. 1887. III. 501.²
Préparation du charbon. 1850. IV. 394.
Préparation du Sagou à l'Ile d'Amboine. 1858. III. 327.³
The preparation of vegetable tallow in China. 1891. III. 522.²
Preparing and cooking bread fruit. 1861. III. 367.¹
Presas, Joseph de. Instrucción para el cultivo de la planta Nopal. 1825. III. 623.²
Presburg—Verein für Naturkunde. See VEREIN . . . I. 28.¹
Prescott, Albert Benjamin. The chemistry of coffee and tea. 1882. III. 607, 740.²
Prescott, William H. History of the conquest of Mexico. 1843. III. 624.¹
Prescrizioni di massima per la coltura e taglio dei boschi. 1879. IV. 249,² 328.
Prescrizioni di massima per la coltura silvana . . . di Cuneo. 1900. IV. 305.
Prescrizioni di massima per la coltura silvàna . . . di Lucca. 1894. IV. 305.
Prescrizioni di massima per la coltura silvana . . . di Novara. 1896. IV. 305.
Prescrizioni di massima per la coltura silvana e pel taglio dei boschi sottoposti al vincolo forestale. 1899. IV. 305.
Prescrizioni di massima stabilite dal comitato forestale di reggio Calabria. 1881. IV. 305.
The present prospectus of the forest service branch of Cooper's Hill college. 1891. IV. 34.²
Preser, Carl. Ueber den Einfluss entwaldeter Höhen. 1884. IV. 44.
Préservation des piquets de clôture. 1898. IV. 146.⁴
Préservation des plantes contre les gelées. 1896. IV. 191.²
Préservation des substances végétales par le sublimé corrosif. 1837. IV. 417.
Préservation du bois contre l'humidité. 1890. IV. 421.
Préservation of fruit-trees from hares. 1831. III. 186.¹
The preservation of Scotch Fir timber. 1881. IV. 420.
Preservation of the forests in the N. W. P. of India. 1848. IV. 181.¹
The preservation of timber. 1844. IV. 417.
Preservation of timber. 1858. IV. 418.
Preservation of timber. 1890. IV. 421.
The preservation of timber; report. 1885. IV. 420.
On the preservation of timber by creosote. 1852. IV. 417.
The preservation of timber by hot-air drying. 1892. IV. 421.
Preservation of timber from damp. 1893. IV. 421.
Preservation of wood. See NICKERSON, B. R. & others. 1871. IV. 419.
Preservation of wood and lumber from mould. 1869. IV. 419.
The preservation of wood by coal-tar. 1869. IV. 419.
Preservation of woods and forests. 1855. IV. 178.¹
Preservation process applied to timber store. 1865. IV. 420.
La preservazione dei legname di Pino di Scozia. See The PRESERVATION of Scotch Fir . . . 1881. IV. 420.
Preservazione del legno. 1864. IV. 419.
On preserving and propagating trees. 1799. IV. 111.³
Preserving timber by salts of copper. 1875. IV. 419.
Presgrave, D. On grafting and budding. 1838. III. 160.
Presidencia del Consejo de ministros: real decreto. 1887. IV. 553.¹

Presl, Jan Swatopluk. Všeobecný rostlinopis. 1846. III. 52.
— See also BERCHTOLD, Friedrich, Graf zu & PRESL, J. S.
— & K. B. Deliciae pragenses. 1822. I. 266.
— — Flora čechica. 1819. I. 439.
— — Mantisse I. ad Floram čechicam. 1822. I. 439.
Presl, Karel Boriwog. Beschreibung einer neuen böhmischen Ulmenart. 1841. II. 872.¹
— Botanische Bemerkungen. 1844. I. 269.
— Epimeliae botanicae. 1849. I. 269.
— Epistola de Symphysia. 1827. II. 672.¹
— Erwiederung auf den Nachtrag des Herrn Fiskaladjunkten Preissler. 1828. II. 672.¹
— Flora of Carlsbad. 1835. I. 439.
— Flora sicula. 1826. I. 431.
— Metamorphose der Carpelle an Prunus Padus. 183.? II. 275.²
— Plantarum rariorum Siciliae . . . diagnoses. 1822. I. 431.
— Prodromus monographiae Lobeliacearum. 1836. II. 845.¹
— Reliquiae Haenkeanae. 1825. I. 267.
— Repertorium botanicae systematicae. 1834. I. 268.
— Symbolae botanicae. 1830. I. 268, V. XIII.²
— Theilweise Füllung der Blumen an Robinia. 183.? II. 382.³
Press, A. See Пресс, А.
Pressler, Max Robert. Allgemeine Multiplications- u. Divisionstafel. 1875. IV. 230.
— Anweisung zur Wald- und Waldboden-Werthschätzung. 1861. IV. 255.
— Aufforderung an die Schweizer-Forstleute in Sachen der Holzmesskunst. 1857. IV. 217.
— Aufforderung und Erfahrungen bezugs der . . . neuen Stammschätzungsmethode. 1857. IV. 217.
— Zur Baum- und Waldmassenschätzung. 1877. IV. 236.
— Die bayerischen Massentafeln. 1865. IV. 230.
— Die beiden Weiserprocente als Grundlage. 1881. IV. 257.
— Die beiden Weiserprocente als Grundlage . . . wie der product ivsten Bestandswirthschaft überhaupt. 1885. IV. 257.
— Beiträge zur Forst- und Landwirthschafts-Mathematik, II. 1853. IV. 216.
— Beiträge zur Forst-Mathematik. 1855. IV. 215, 216.
— Bestands-Erwartungswerth und Weiserprocent. 1874. IV. 256.
— Der compendiöse Forsttaxator. 1868. IV. 230.
— Compendiöser Forsttaxator. 1868. IV. 230.
— Compendiöser Holzcubirer für's Liegende u. Stehende. 1874. IV. 227.
— Der compendiös-practische Forsttaxator. 1868. IV. 230.
— Einfaches Verfahren, die Höhe der Bäume ohne Standlinie zu messen. 1855. IV. 215.
— Ergänzung zu den . . . 1871 amtlich eingeführten metrischen Cubirungs-Tafeln. 1877. IV. 217, 227.
— Ueber die Fehler bei der Stärkemessung. 1853. IV. 216.
— Forst- und bauwirthschaftliche Supplementstafeln. 1869. IV. 230.
— Zur Forstbetriebseinrichtung. 1868. IV. 243.
— Zur Forsteinrichtung mit Bezug auf einen . . . rationellen Waldbau höchsten Reinertrags. 1868. IV. 243.
— Zur Forstfinanzrechnung. 1886. IV. 253.
— Forstliche Cubirungstafeln nach metrischem Maas. 1871. IV. 226.
— Die forstliche Ertrags- und Bonitirungs-Tafeln. 1870. IV. 236.
— Die forstliche Finanzrechnung. 1859. IV. 243.
— Forstliche Tafeln und Regeln für Waldbau. 1867. IV. 225.
— Forstliche Zuwachs-, Ertrags- und Bonitirungs-Tafeln. 1870. IV. 236.
— Der forstliche Zuwachsbohrer. 1866. IV. 232.
— Forstliches Hülfsbuch für Schule und Praxis. 1857. IV. 213.
— Forstliches Messknechts-Practicum. 1883. IV. 231.¹
— Die Forstwirthschaft der sieben Thesen. 1865. IV. 269.
— Zur Forstzuwachskunde. 1868. IV. 232.
— Zur Forstzuwachskunde mit besonderer Beziehung auf den Zuwachsbohrer. 1868. IV. 232.
— Fundamente und Regeln einer rationellen Stammkubirung. 1854. IV. 216.
— Das Gesetz der Stammbildung. 1864. IV. 232.
— Die Hauptlehren des Forstbetriebs. 1871. IV. 241.
— Der Hochwaldbetrieb der höchsten Bodenkraft. 1865. IV. 243.

Pressler, Max Robert (*continued*).
— Das Hochwaldsideal der höchsten Wald- bei höchster Boden-Rente. 1872. IV. 243.
— Høiskovsdriften som Industri. 1865. IV. 243.
— Zur Holzmesskunst. 1860. IV. 214.
— Holzwirthschaftliche Tafeln. 1872. IV. 230.
— Hülfstafeln zur Baum- und Wald-Massenschätzung. 1876. IV. 230.
— Der Ingenieur-Messknecht. 1876. IV. 230.
— Zur Klärung in Sachen des Reinertragswaldbau's. 1876. IV. 236.
— Korrespondenz. An meine grünen Freunde in der Schweiz. 1855. IV. 215.
— Kritik und Schule. 1847. IV. 101.
— Zur Kunst, den laufenden Zuwachs am Stehenden zu ermitteln. 1871. IV. 232.
— Zur Lehre vom forstlichen Nutzeffecte. 1880. IV. 236.
— Zur Lehre vom Reinertragswaldbau. 1879. IV. 236.
— Zur Lehre von den Erleichterungen bei Berechnung der Zuwachsprocente. 1878. IV. 233.
— Eine lehrreiche Zuwachsveränderung. 1872. IV. 233.
— Zur Lichtungszuwachs-. . . frage im Fichtenwalde. 1878. IV. 458.
— Das mathematische Aschenbrödel. 1866. IV. 214.
— Der Messknecht. 1852. IV. 229.
— Metrologischer Anhang: Preussische u. allgemeine Reductionstafeln. 1871. IV. 226.
— Neue holzwirthschaftliche Tafeln. 1857. IV. 213, 224.
— Neue Stammschätzungsmethode. 1855. IV. 216.
— Die neuere Opposition gegen Einführung eines . . . correcten Reinertragswaldbau. 1880. IV. 244.
— Die Normalertragstafel, ihre Bedeutung. 1878. IV. 458.
— Populaire Gebrauchsanweisung zum Zuwachsbohrer. 1869. IV. 232.
— Der practische Holzcubirer. 1866. IV. 225.
— Die Praxis der Forstfinanzrechnung. 1871. IV. 255.
— Om det Presslerske Tilvæxtbor. 1868. IV. 232.
— Die Richtigkeit der Wagener'schen Einwürfe. 1877. IV. 236.
— Sächsische Reductionstafeln zur Maas-, Gewichts- und Preis-Übersetzung. 1872. IV. 230.
— Selbständige Supplemente zu Pressler's Forstlichem Hülfsbuch. 1867. IV. 214.
— Der umfassend-practische Holzcubirer für's Liegende und Stehende. 1866. IV. 225.
— Vier Streitfragen aus der land- und forstwirthschaftlichen Pädagogik. 1846. IV. 29.
— Ueber die wahre wissenschaftliche und wirthschaftliche Auffassung . . . der Formzahlen der Bäume. 1853. IV. 216.
— Der Waldbau des Nationalökonomen. 1865. IV. 243.
— Des Waldbau's Zustände und Zwecke. 1858. IV. 269.
— Zum Weiserprocent. 1869. IV. 255.
— Zum Zuwachsbohrer. 1883. IV. 233.
— *See also* Преслеръ, M. P.
— **& Kunze,** Max. Die Holzmesskunst in ihrem ganzen Umfange. 1872. IV. 214.
Presta, Giovanni. Degli Ulivi. 1794. III. 678.[2]
Prestandrea, Antonio. Su di un proposto problema di fillotassi. 1843. I. 102.
— Su di una . . . ramificazione della Yucca. 1845. II. 87.[1]
— Om en sällsynt och märkvärdig förgrening hos Yucca. 1845. II. 87.[1]
Prestele, Joseph. Die wichtigsten Giftpflanzen Deutschlands. 1843. III. 73.
Prestinari, J. N. Handbuch der Cameralchemie. 1826. IV. 60.[2]
Prestoe, Henry. Catalogue of plants cultivated in . . . Trinidad. 1870. I. 39.
— Palms of Trinidad. 1873. II. 61.[2]
— Report on the Coffee cultivation in Dominica. 1875. III. 728.[2]
Preston, Carleton Estey. Nonsexual propagation of Opuntia. 1900. II. 596.[2]
— Observations on the root system of certain Cactaceae. 1900. II. 588.[2]
Preston, Georg. Catalogus omnium plantarum . . . in seminario medicinae. 1716. I. 52.
Preston, Scott-. *See* Scott-Preston.
Preston, Thomas Arthur. Flora of Marlborough. 1863. I. 401.
— The flowering plants of Wilts. 1888. I. 404.[1]
Preston's log measure. 1897. IV. 232.
El presupuesto. 1898. IV. 554.
El presupuesto de fomento. 1900. IV. 554.

El presupuesto de montes. 1895. IV. 553.[2]
El presupuesto de montes en Francia. 1888. IV. 553.[1]
El presupuesto del Ramo de montes. 1893. IV. 553.[2]
El presupuesto del Ramo de montes para el año económico de 1890 á 1891. 1890. IV. 553.[1]
Presupuesto forestal de Prusia. 1893. IV. 552.[2]
Presupuesto general del estado para. 1893. IV. 553.[2]
Presupuestos de 1896–97. 1896. IV. 553.[2]
De la **prétendue** h bridation par la greffe. 1868. I. 246.[1]
Preuschen, Alfredy Die Spaltpflanzung. 1866. IV. 152.
— Die Sprengschraube. 1862. IV. 385.
Preusker, (*Revierförster, Kleinkmehlen*). Einiges von der Schuster'schen Stockrodemaschine. 1857. IV. 385.[1]
Preuss, Paul. Über das Auffinden der echten . . . Kickxia africana. 1899. III. 688.[2]
— Über Ausnutzung , . . von Kautschukpflanzen in Kamerun. 1899. III. 149.
— Bericht . . . über eine botanische Exkursion . . . auf den Kamerun-Pic. 1892. I. 491.
— Bericht über Kultur- und Nutzpflanzen im Kamerungebiet. 1892. III. 93.[1]
— Die Beziehungen zwischen dem anatomischen Bau und der physiologischen Funktion der Blattstiele. 1885. I. 112.[1]
— Culture de la fève Tonka. 1900. III. 475.[3]
— Über Kautschukpflanzen und Kickxia africana. 1898. III. 688.[2]
— Der Perubalsam in Centralamerika. 1900. III. 482.[2]
— Schattenbäume in Victoria. 1898. III. 211.[1]
— Ueber die Standortsverhältnisse der Kickxia africana. 1895. II. 727.[1]
— Ueber westafrikanische Kickxia-Arten. 1897. II. 727.[1]
— Over het winnen van Balata. 1899. III. 118.[2]
— Wirtschaftliches über Surinam. 1899. III. 595,[1] 668.[1]
— Über die Zimmetpflanze . . . in Victoria. 1897. III. 405.[3]
Preussens landwirthschaftliche Verwaltung. IV. 10.
Preussische Akademie der Wissenschaften zu Berlin. *See* Königliche Akademie der Wissenschaften zu Berlin. I. 13.
Das **preussische** Gemeinheits- und Forsten-Teilungs-Verfahren. 1882. IV. 308.[2]
Preussische Jahrbücher. I. 14.
Preussische Pharmacopöe. *See* Pharmacopoea borussica. 1799. III. 246.
Die preussischen Forst-, Jagd- und Fischereigesetze. 1884. IV. 321.
Aus der **preussischen** Staatsforstverwaltung: 1892. IV. 291.[1]
Preussischer botanischer Verein. Bericht. *See* Königlich physikalisch-ökonomische Gesellschaft zu Königsberg. I. 13.
Preussischer Forstverein . . Versammlung. IV. 10.
Prevention of dry rot in timber. *See* Dry rot . . . 1884. IV. 420.
Prevet. Note sur un boisson préparé des graines du Caroubier. 1864. III. 472.[1]
Le previsioni sul raccolto delle ulive. 1894. III. 679.[3]
Prévost. Description comparée du faux Deutzia corymbosa. 1845. III. 413.[2]
— De l'emploi de l'essence de térébenthine. 1854. III. 189.
— Moyen simple pour préserver l'écorce . . . de la dent des lapins. 1848. III. 186.[1]
— Note sur le Garry à feuilles elliptiques. 1849. II. 110,[2] III. 352.[2]
— Note sur plusieurs espèces de bois exotiques. 1850. IV. 396.[1]
— Note sur quelques arbres. 1848. I. 297.[2]
— Note sur un Maclura aurantiaca femelle. 1848. III. 372.[1]
— Observations · sur les genres Deutzia et Philadelphus. 1845. III. 410,[1] 413.[1]
Prévost. Traité pratique de l'éducation . . . du Pommier. 1852. III. 426.[1]
Prévost, (*jr.*). Catalogue descriptif . . . du genre Rosier. 1829. III. 448.
— Essai sur l'éducation . . . des arbres fruitiers pyramidaux. 1825. III. 171.
— Note sur le Noisetier à feuilles laciniées. 1831. III. 358.[1]
— Note sur un Cytise nouveau. 1830. II. 168.[1]
Prevost, G. F. Inspection of the forest operations in the Andamans. 1897. IV. 250.[2]
Prevost, J. L. & Binet, Paul. Recherches expérimentales, relatives à . . . Cytisus Laburnum. 1887. III. 481.[1]
Prevost, Jean. Catalogue des plantes . . . en Bearn, Navarre et Begorre. 1655. I. 404.[3]

Prevost, Jean Louis. Collection des fleurs et des fruits. 1805. I. 265.

Prevost, Louis. California silk grower's manual. 1867. III. 377.

Prevost, Pierre. De l'influence que la dépression du sol peut avoir sur la gelée. 1826. I. 211.

Preyer, Axel. Der Milchsaft von Ficus elastica. 1900. III. 371.[1]

— Wiederholte Anzapfung von Ficus elastica. 1900. III. 370.[2]

Preyer, William Thiery. Sur le principe actif du curare. 1865. III. 683.[1]

Prezzi correnti di prodotti forestali. 1865. IV. 405.[2]

Prezzo generale di prodotti forestali. 1865. IV. 405.[1]

Prianischnikow, D. Ueber die Ausnutzung der Phosphorsäure. 1900. I. 160.

Pribyl, Leo & others. Das goldene Buch der Land- und Forstwirthschaft in Österreich-Ungarn. 1890. IV. 368.

Price, Eli Kirk. Michaux trees. 1876. IV. 76.[2]

— Sylviculture. 1878. IV. 111.[2]

— Zelkova crenata. 1877. III. 366.[1]

Price, Ferris W. Tree names. 1896. II. 21.[2]

Price, R. H. Classification of varieties of Peaches. 1897. II. 276.[1]

— & Ness, H. The Grape. 1898. III. 551.[1]

Price, Sarah Frances. Abnormal leaves and flowers. 1900. II. 481.[1]

— Flora of Warren county, Kentucky. 1893. I. 319.

— Trees and shrubs of Kentucky. 1898. I. 317,[1] IV. 77.[2]

Price, T. S. Aesculus californica. 1881. III. 536.[2]

Price, Thomas D. On Magnolia glauca. 1802. III. 399.[2]

Price, William W. Description of a new grove of Sequoia gigantea. 1893. II. 50.[2]

— Discovery of a new grove of Sequoia gigantea. 1892. II. 50.[1]

Prices of forest produce. 1878. IV. 398.[2]

Prichard, A. W. Case of poisoning by Rhus venenata. 1891. III. 528.[1]

Prickly Pear in Mexico. 1892. III. 624.[2]

Prickly Pear in South Africa. 1888. III. 624.[2]

Prickly Pear in South Africa. 1890. III. 624.[1]

The **Prickly** Pear pest. 1900. III. 624.[2]

Pride, W. H. Delamere forest and its management. 1898. IV. 358.[2]

The **Pride** of China tree. 1894. II. 421.[1]

Priem, M. Aufzählung der Gefässpflanzen ... im Vilsthale. 1869. I. 386.

Priemer, Franz. Die anatomischen Verhältnisse der Laubblätter der Ulmaceen. 1893. II. 141.[1]

Priester, F. Ueber die natürliche Verjüngung der Buche. 1891. IV. 495.

Prieto, José. De los resultados obtenidos con las nuevas miras. 1887. IV. 265.

Prillieux, Édouard Ernest. De l'action de la gelée sur les plantes. 1881. IV. 66,[2] 191.[2]

— Sur l'altération des grains de raisin par le mildew. 1882. III. 578.

— Une altération des Olives. 1882. III. 677.[2]

— Altérations produites dans les plantes par la culture dans un sol surchauffé. 1880. I. 213.[2]

— Anciennes observations sur les tubercules des racines des Légumineuses. 1890. II. 321.[1]

— Sur l'anthracnose. 1880. III. 578.

— L'anthracnose de la Vigne. 1879. III. 578.

— Apparition du black rot aux environs d'Agen. 1887. III. 579.

— Le bois de Pin maritime gelé. 1880. IV. 468.[1]

— Cause du rot des raisins, en Amérique. 1882. III. 578.

— Sur les causes qui ont amené l'invasion du phylloxera dans le Vendômois. 1877. III. 570.[2]

— Sur la cloque du Pêcher. 1872. III. 441.[2]

— Sur la coloration en vert du bois mort. 1877. I. 207.[1]

— Considérations sur la nature des vrilles de la Vigne. 1856. II. 507.[1]

— Effectos de la helada. 1881. IV. 66.[2]

— Effet de la gelée sur les fruits. 1869. I. 212.

— Des effets de la gelée sur la production de la térébenthine du Pin maritime. 1881. IV. 468.[2]

— Das Entstehen von Gummi bei Obstbäumen. 1874. I. 213.[1]

— Étude sur la formation de la gomme. 1874. I. 213.[1] — 1875. I. 181,[1] II. 272.[2]

— Étude sur la formation ... de quelques galles. 1876. I. 214.[1]

— Étude sur les courbures. 1868. I. 194.

— Expériences sur la fanaison des plantes. 1870. I. 149.[2]

— Sur la formation de glaçons. 1869. I. 212.

— Fruits momifiés des Cognassiers de l'Aveyron. 1892. III. 423.[2]

— Hairs in Oleaceae and Jasminaceae. 1855. II. 705.[2]

— Hypertrophie et multiplication des noyaux. 1881. I. 137.

— De l'influence de la congélation sur le poids. 1872. I. 212.

— De l'influence de la lumière artificielle sur la réduction de l'acide carbonique par les plantes. 1869. I. 172.

— Influence de la lumière bleue sur la production de l'amidon dans la chlorophylle. 1870. I. 172.

— La madera del Pino maritimo helada. 1880. IV. 468.[1]

— Une maladie de la Barbe de capucin. 1893. III. 580.

— Sur une maladie du Cognassier. 1892. III. 423.[2]

— Sur la maladie du Pêcher. 1872. III. 441.[2]

— Sur la maladie de la Vigne en 1877. 1887. III. 561.

— Les maladies de la Vigne en 1877. 1887. III. 561.

— Maladies des plantes ... causées par des parasites végétaux. 1895. IV. 212.

— Medio de conocer la época del apeo de los árboles. 1875. IV. 384.[2]

— Sur les mouvements des graines de chlorophylle. 1870. I. 141.

— Movements of chlorophyll under influence of light. 1870. I. 141.

— Sur un moyen de reconnaître l'époque d'abatage des bois. 1875. IV. 384.[2]

— Sur la nature ... des tubercules ... des Légumineuses. 1879. II. 321.[2]

— On a new test for ascertaining the season at which timber has been felled. 1875. IV. 384.[2]

— Note sur des fleurs monstrueuses de Fuchsia. 1861. II. 647.[2]

— Note sur l'introduction de la culture du Thé à Java. 1874. III. 602.[2]

— Observations sur la matière colorante des raisins noirs. 1866. III. 583.[1]

— Sur le parasitisme du Coniothyrium. 1887. III. 579.

— Le pourridié des Vignes de la Haute-Marne. 1881. III. 578.

— La production de la gomme. 1874. I. 213.[1]

— Sur les productions ... des possessions hollandaises des Indes orientales. 1874. IV. 400.[1]

— Sur les propriétés endosmotiques des cellules gelées. 1869. I. 212.

— Quelques mots sur le rot des Vignes. 1880. III. 578.

— Raisins malades dans les Vignes de la Vendée. 1886. III. 579.

— Le Roesleria hypogaea. 1881. III. 578.

— Sur les spores d'hiver du Peronospora viticola. 1891. III. 578.

— De la structure des poils des Oléacées. 1855. II. 705.[2]

— Sur les taches nécrosées des rameaux de Pêcher. 1886. III. 442.[2]

— Sur les tavelures ... des poires. 1877. III. 446.[1]

— Traitement efficace du black rot. 1888. III. 580.

— Les tumeurs à bacilles de l'Olivier comparées à celles du Pin d'Alep. 1909. IV. 404.[1]

— Les tumeurs à bacilles des branches de l'Olivier et du Pin d'Alep. 1889. III. 677,[2] IV. 464.[1]

— Tumeurs ligneuses ou broussins des Vignes. 1888. III. 561.

— Tumeurs produites sur le bois des Pommiers. 1875. III. 427.[2]

— Sur le verdissement des plantes étiolées. 1869. III. 181.[1]

— & **Delacroix**, Georges. La brûlure des feuilles de la Vigne. 1894. III. 581.

— Le champignon parasite de la larve du hanneton. 1891. III. 196.

— — La gommose bacillaire des Vignes. 1894. III. 581.

— — Maladie bacillaire des Vignes du Var. 1894. III. 581.

— — Maladie des branches des Mûriers. 1897. III. 379.[2]

— — Sur la maladie des Pruniers. 1899. III. 433.[2]

— — Sur une maladie des raisins des Vignes du Caucase. 1900. III. 582.

— — Maladies bacillaires de divers végétaux. 1894. III. 49.[2]

— — Maladies des Mûriers. 1893. III. 379.[1]

— — Les maladies des Noyers en France. 1898. III. 356.[1]

— — Rapport sur les maladies du Mûrier. 1893. III. 379.[1]

Prime notizie intorno alla fillossera delle Viti. 1888. III. 762.
Primer concurso científico mexicano. I. 7.²
Primitive forests of the equator. 1871. I. 219.²
Primo, Francisco BALAGUER Y. See BALAGUER Y PRIMO, Francisco.
Il primo " Arbor's day." 1899. IV. 42.¹
Il primo congresso forestale italiano. 1897. IV. 41.¹
Prince, William. Prince's annual catalogue. 1822. I. 38.²
— Annual catalogue of fruit and ornamental trees. 1822. V. VIII.¹
— Catalogue of American indigenous trees, plants and seeds. 1820. I. 38.²
— Catalogue of fruit and ornamental trees and plants. 1822. I. 38.³ V. VIII.¹
— A short treatise on horticulture. 1828. III. 99.
— A treatise on fruit and ornamental trees and plants. 1820. I. 38.²
— See also PRINCE, W.·R. & William.
Prince, William Robert.' Prince's manual of Roses. 1846. III. 448.
— & William. The pomological manual. 1831. III. 61.¹
— — A treatise on the Vine. 1830. III. 549.²
The prince of Lisianths. 1849. III. 685.¹
The prince of Palms.' See TRELOAR, Thomas. 1852. III. 323.²
Le principali foreste d' Italia. 1885. IV. 364.
Principes actifs·et emploi thérapeutique du Cytise. 1862. III. 480.²
Principes de botanique. See SUFFREN, de. 1802. I. 425.
Principes élémentaires de botanique. 1796. I. 259.
Principia botanica. 1787. I. 254²; see also DARWIN, R. W. 1787. I. 83.
Principii di amministrazione e direzione boschive. 1882. IV. 277; see also BÉRENGER, Adolfo di. 1883. IV. 287.
Principios elementales de la botánica. See CAVANILLES, A. J. 1802. I. 84.
Principj elementari di botanica. See CAVANILLES, A. J. 1802. I. 84.
Principles of forest economy. 1899. IV. 271.¹
Principles of silviculture. 1899. IV. 113.¹
Pringle, C. R. Annual address at the second session of the Southern forestry congress. 1887. IV. 178,¹ 272.
Pringle, Cyrus Guernsey. Dimorpho-dichogamy in Juglans cinerea. 1879. II. 113.¹
— The forest vegetation of northern Mexico. 1888. I. 331, IV. 78.²
— The forest vegetation of the lower Rio Grande valley. 1889. I. 320, IV. 78.¹
— The Mexican Ash. 1894. III. 672.¹
— Notes of Mexican travel. 1893. I. 332.
— Notes on new species of Mexican trees. 1893. III. 204.¹
— Notes on the ligneous vegetation of the Sierra Madre of Nuevo Leon. 1890. I. 331, IV. 78.²
— Sargentia Greggii. 1890. II. 410.²
Pringle, W. H. Mode of rearing the Tussur silk worm. 1861. III. 633.¹
Pringsheim, Nathanaël. Über die Abhängigkeit der Assimilation. 1887. I. 174.
— Ueber die Absorptionsspectra der Chlorophyllfarbstoffe. 1874. I. 141.
— Della azione primaria della luce. 1882. IV. 67.²
— Ueber die chemischen Theorien der Chlorophyllfunction. 1886. I. 173.
— De forma et incremento stratorum crassiorum in plantarum cellula. 1848. I. 136.²
— Gesammelte Abhandlungen. 1895. I. 34.
— Ueber das Hypochlorin. 1879. I. 142.
— Ueber Inanition der grünen Zelle. 1887. I. 174.
— Zur Kritik der bisherigen Grundlagen der Assimilationstheorie. 1881. I. 173.
— Ueber Lichtwirkung und Chlorophyll-Function. 1879. I. 141.
— Über Lichtwirkung und Chlorophyllfunktion. 1879. I. 173.
— Ueber' natürliche Chlorophyllmodificationen. 1876. I. 141.
— Recherches sur le rôle de la chlorophylle. 1881. I. 142.
— Remarques sur la chlorophylle. 1879. I. 142.
— Untersuchungen über das Chlorophyll. 1874. I. 141.
— Untersuchungen über den Bau . . . der Pflanzenzelle. 1854. I. 136.²
— Untersuchungen über Lichtwirkung und Chlorophyllfunction. 1881. I. 173.

Prins, A. H. J. BLOYS VAN TRESLONG. See BLOYS VAN TRESLONG PRINS, A. H. J.
Prins, H. J. Gouvernements-Koffiecultuur ter Sumatra's westkust. 1894. III. 730.
— Handleiding voor de Koffiekultuur. 1878. III. 729.²
— De oeret-plaag in de Koffie . . . Suikerriettuinen. 1892. III. 192.²
— De oeret-plaag in de Koffietuinen op Java. 1885. III. 735.
Prinsep, H. C. Autumn tints. 1897. III. 207.¹
Prinsep, I. F. MACAIRE-. See MACAIRE-PRINSEP, I. F.
Printz, Eduard. Die Bau- und Nutzhölzer. 1884. IV. 396.²
Printz, Han Christian. Beretning om en . . . botanisk reise i Valders. 1865. I. 356.
Printz, Jacob. Plantae rariores africanae. See LINNÉ, Carl von. 1760. I. 493.
Prinz, W. Les variations de la température à l'intérieur d'un arbre. 1893. I. 187.
Prior, Richard Chandler Alexander. Plant preserving. 1878. I. 36.¹
— On the popular names of British plants. 1863. I. 74.¹
Prior, W. D. Hardy shrubs. 1881. III. 78.²
— Rose growing for amateurs. 187.? III. 449.
— Roses and their culture. 187.? III. 449.
Příspěvky ku statistice lesů v Cechách. 1885. IV. 371.
Pritchard, Stephen F. An alphabetical list of . . . plants . . . of St. Helena. 1836. I. 498.
Prittwitz, von, (Oberförster, Nimkau). Starke Eichen . . . Nimkau. 1859. IV. 515.²
Pritzel, Ernst. Der systematische Wert der Samenanatomie. 1897. I. 121.
Pritzel, George August. Iconum botanicarum index locupletissimus. 1855. I. 77.
— Specimen bibliographiae botanicae. 1845. I. 511.
— Thesaurus literaturae botanicae. 1851. I. 2.
— & Jessen, C. Die deutschen Volksnamen der Pflanzen. 1882. I. 73.²
Pritzkow, Wilhelm. Denuce vomica. 1831. III. 684.²
Die Privatforste Ungarns und Siebenbürgens. 1890. IV. 374.¹
The Privet. 1887. III. 673.²
Privilegirte Meilerkohlung Boutin, Poinsot et Comp. 1862. IV. 394.
Prix des bois dans quelques forêts de l'état de Vaud. 1854. IV. 406.¹
Prix des bois dans quelques-unes des forêts de l'état de Vaud. 1854. IV. 406.¹
Pro-Montibus; association·italienne. 1900. IV. 41.¹
Pro Montibus. Associazione italiana per la protezione delle piante. 1898? IV. 166.²
La " Pro-Montibus italicis." 1898. IV. 42.¹
Probable effects of vegetation on climate. 1851. IV. 52.
El problema forestal en Rusia. See The FOREST question. 1883. IV. 273.²
Probst, Johann Ernst. Verzeichniss der in- und ausländischen Bäume, Stauden . . . des Kaspar Bosischen Gartens. 1738. I. 43.
— Wörterbuch, worinnen deren Kräuter Nahmen. 1741. I. 73.¹
Probst, Josst. Zur Kenntnis der in Oberschwaben wild wachsenden Rosen. 1887. II. 284.²
Probst, M. Ueber den Werth der Periodenbildung. 1872. IV. 251.²
Procédé de cubage des arbres debout. 1898. IV. 219.
Procédés de conservation & de coloration des bois. See BOUCHERIE, Auguste. 1852. IV. 417.
Procedimento per render plastico il legno. 1866. IV. 422.²
Processo di torrefazione del legno. 1864. IV. 394.
Proclama degl' . . . provveditori alle legne e boschi. 1760. IV. 304.¹
Proclama ·degli . . . deputati dall' eccelso consiglio di 10 sopra la valle di Montona. 1780. IV. 304.¹
Proclama degli provveditori e patroni al arsenal. 1700. IV. 304.¹
Proclama degli provveditori sopra il bosco del Montello. 1721. IV. 304.¹
Proclama del . . . Capitano di Raspo . . . nella materia de boschi. 1764. IV. 304.¹
Proclama del provveditor generale nella patria del Friuli. 1743. IV. 304.¹
Proclama del provveditor sopra boschi della Trevisana bassa. 1734. IV. 304.¹
Procter, Henry Richardson. A text-book of tanning. 1885. III. 237.³

Procter, John Robert. Report on the resources of the region adjacent to the Kentucky union railway company. 1881. IV. 397.
— Resources of the North Cumberland valley. 1880. IV. 397.
Procter, William, (jr.). On Erythrophleum judiciale. 1852. III. 476.[2]
— An essay on Sassafras. 1866. III. 408.[1]
— Observations on the sassy bark. 1851. III. 476.[1]
Proctor, Barnard Simpson. Substitutes for wax. 1864. III. 226.[1]
Proctor, Stephen. Analyse der Rinde von Prunus virginiana. 1835. II. 277.[3]
Prodotti forestali importati ed esportati. 1865. IV. 405.[2]
Prodromus florae argentoratensis. See SPIELMANN, J. R. 1766. I. 373.
Prodromus Florae batavae. 1851. I. 391.[1] V. xx.[1]
The **produce** of the Cherry. 1844. III. 432.[2]
Production and preparation of Malaga raisins. 1882. III. 558.[1]
La **production** de l'indigo au Soudan. 1899. III. 479.[1]
Production de la pâte de bois au Canada. 1896. IV. 284.[1]
Production des forêts des Landes. 1885. IV. 276.[1]
Production des peuplements d'Épicéas. 1900. IV. 261.[2].
La **production** du Café. 1899. III. 740.[1]
Production et commerce des bois de construction en Californie. 1899. IV. 403.[2]
The **production** of illuminating gas from wood. 1898. IV. 433.[2]
The **production** of Kauri gum in New Zealand. 1893. III. 297.[2]
The **production** of Sandalwood. 1900. IV. 519.[2]
Los **productos** forestales . . . de España. 1895. IV. 557.[1]
Los **productos** forestales en el comercio exterior de España. 1895. IV. 557.[1]
Products of the Vacoa. 1866. III. 314.[1]
Produit d'une exploitation de Liége en Algérie. 1863. IV. 517.[1]
Sur le **produit** des fruits à baies. See WALDBEERENERTRAG. 1865. IV. 439.
Les **produits** des forêts domaniales du Jura. See ROUX, E. & BOUVET, Maurice. 1899. IV. 261.[3]
Produits secondaires des forêts. 1894. IV. 558.[1]
Produkten van den landbouw in de residentie Kediri. 1865. III. 275.[2]
La **produzione** annua di traversine in Italia. 1894. IV. 424.[1]
La **produzione** . . . degli olii d' oliva. 1894. III. 679.[2]
Della **produzione** . . . del legname nella Calabria. See SIMONETTI, Michele. 1872. IV. 405.[2]
La **produzione** . . . delle olive in Spagna. 1899. III. 679.[2]
La **produzione** ed il commercio dei semi forestali in Darmstadt. 1890. IV. 438.[1]
Produzione forestale del Salernitano. 1865. IV. 364[1]
De **proefaanplantingen** van caoutchouc- en getah-pertja leverende houtsoorten te Tjipetir. 1900. III. 149.
Professional, (pseud.). Broad-leaved evergreens. 1862. III. 183.[1]
Professor Willkomm's Forschungen über die Rothfäule. 1866. IV. 211.[1]
Proff, Karl, Freiherr von. Beyträge zur Beförderung . . . der Land- und Forst-Kultur. 1802. IV. 268.
Profitable hedges. 1874. III. 213.
Profits of growing locust timber. 1846. V. xxxii.[2]
Profumo della gaggia. 1866. IV. 521.[1]
Progel, Augustus. Flora des Amtsbezirkes Waldmünchen. 1882. I. 388.
— Gentianaceae. 1865. II. 721.[1]
— Loganiaceae. 1868. II. 716.[1]
— Oxalideae. 1877. III. 392.[1]
Progetto del codice forestale. 1869. IV. 328.
Progetto di legge. Progetto . . . tendente ad estendere . . . l' applicazione della legge forestale. 1865. IV. 328.
Progetto di legge forestale. 1863. IV. 327. —1873. IV. 328.
Progetto di legge intorno al bonificamento delle regioni di malaria in Italia. 1882. IV. 328.
Progetto di legge presento dal ministro . . . legge forestale. 1862. IV. 327.
Progetto di legge sull ordinamento forestale. 1868. IV. 328.
Progetto di vendita delle foreste di Francia. 1865. IV. 275.
Progetto nuovo per fare che gli Ulivi . . . non siano danneggiati. See MONTELATICI, D. V. A. 1762. III. 674.[2]
Programas para los exámenes de ingreso en la Escuela especial de ingenieros de montes. 1893. IV. 540.[3]

Programm der K. k. Forst-Akademie . . . in Mariabrunn. 1873. IV. 36.[1]
Programm der K. preuss. Forstakademie Eberswalde. 186.[?] IV. 32.
Programm und Satzungen für die Candidaten der K. bayer. Central-Forstlehranstalt zu Aschaffenburg. 1865. IV. 32.
Programm und Satzungen für die kgl. bayerischen Waldbauschulen. 1888. IV. 33.[1]
Programma . . . See ПРОГРАММА . . .
Programma der Tentoonstelling van geneeskrachtige en nuttige planten. 1895. III. 28.[2]
Programme d'un concours pour la culture des Mûriers. 1831. III. 374.
Programme d'un prix pour le reboisement des montagnes. See HÉRICART DE THURY, L. E. F., vicomte. 1840. IV. 161.[2]
Programme de l'enseignement de l'École nationale forestière. 1876. IV. 34.[2]
Programme des études d'aménagement de futaie. 1849. IV. 242.
Programme général du reboisement. 1884. IV. 168.[2]
Programme of the forest classes at the College of science, Poona. n. d. IV. 37.[1]
Le **Progrès** agricole. III. 20.
Le **Progrès** agricole et viticole. III. 20.
Progress, Paul. Culture of the genus Chorozema. 1850. III. 472.[2]
Progress in timber physics. See ROTH, Filibert. 1898. IV. 409.
Prohaska, Karl. Der Embryosack . . . in der Gattung Daphne. 1883. II. 601.[1]
— Zur Frage der Endospermbildung bei Daphne. 1884. II. 601.[1]
Prohibition against introduction of shrubs and trees into Tasmania. 1900. III. 200.[2]
Projet de code forestier pour l'Algérie. 1897. IV. 332.[2]
Projet de créer un Jardin d'acclimatation . . . à Liége. 1863. III. 28.[1]
Projet de loi concernant le code rural et forestier. 1893. IV. 323.[1]
Projet de loi concernant les échangistes. 1818. IV. 326.
Projet de loi portant modification des articles 31 et 103. 1897. IV. 327.
Le **projet** de loi sur l'affouage. 1900. IV. 555.[1]
Un **projet** de loi sur les aliénations de Chênes-liège. 1896. IV. 332.[2]
Projet de loi tendant à abroger l'article 153. 1897. IV. 327.
Projet de reforme et plan d'une nouvelle administration des forêts & bois du roi. 1789. IV. 291.[3]
Proklamation der Verwaltungs-Kammer des Kantons Luzern zum Schutze des . . . Forstwesens. 1798. IV. 306.
Das **Proletariat** und die Waldungen. 1851. IV. 196.[2]
Proliferous buds of Pinus sylvestris. 1899. II. 47.[2]
Proliferous Oranges. 1891. II. 404.[1]
Proliferous Raspberry. 1889. II. 305.[2]
Prolification in Sciadopitys. 1884. II. 49.[2]
Prolongo, Pablo. Ampeloidia, del Oidium Tuckeri. 1853. III. 576.
Prolusioni lette alle tre scuole forestali. 1865. IV. 101.
Promenade dans le Musée commercial. 1893. III. 28.[2]
Les **promenades** et boulevards bruxellois. 1898. III. 212.[1]
Prometheus. See ПРОМИѲЕУѮ.
Promnitz, (Oberförster, Chrzelitz). Kurze Darstellung der Verhältnisse des k. Forstreviers Chrzelitz. 1851. IV. 352.
Promnitz, J. Der Holzbau (der praktische Zimmermann). 1868. IV. 423.[1]
— Der praktische Zimmermann. 1868. IV. 423.[1]
Prompt treatment of the gypsy-moth. 1892. III. 187.
Per **promuovere** l'innesto degli Olivastri. 1896. III. 676.[2]
Per **promuovere** la olivicoltura in Sardegna. 1896. III. 676.[2]
Pronville, Auguste de. Nomenclature des espèces, variétés . . . du genre Rosier. 1814. II. 281.[2]
— Nomenclature raisonnée des espèces, variétés . . . du genre Rosier. 1814. II. 281.[3]
— Du Rosier . . . comme arbrisseau d'ornement. 18 . . ? III. 447.[2]
— Sommaire d'une monographie du genre Rosier. 1822. II. 282.[1]
Prony, de. Instruction sur l'ouvrage de M. de Sept-Fontaines et sur la cubature des bois. 1815. IV. 213.
Prooyen, A. van. Verhandeling over de houtteelt. 1794. IV. 119.[1]
On the **propagation** and culture of ornamental shrubs. 1871. III. 153, 158.

The **propagation** of Cycads from cuttings. 1896. III. 284.²
On the **proper** management of forest trees. 1842. IV. 120.
The **properties** of the kola nut. 1895. III. 590.²
Proportion d'huile contenue dans quelques semences forestières. *See* OELGEHALT forstlicher Sämereien. 1866. III. 224.²
Proportion of bark to wood in Kikar. 1900. IV. 521,¹ *529*,¹ *529*.¹
À **propos** d'élagage. 1899. IV. 172.²
À **propos** de l'aménagement des forêts dans les cantons de hautes montagnes. *See* WALDWIRTHSCHAFT. 1858. IV. 123.¹
À **propos** de l'élagage. 1894. IV. 547.¹
À **propos** de l'origine des graines. 1895. IV. 545.²
À **propos** du Dimorphoteca Eckloni. 1899. III. 749.²
A **proposal** for improving and adorning the island of Great Britain. *See* WADE, Edward. 1755. IV. 120.
Proposed amendment to the constitution of the state of New York, to preserve its forests. 1894. IV. 314.²
A **proposito** delle ultime promozioni nel personale 'dell' amministrazione forestale. 1898. IV. 293.¹
Proposta per una statistica forestale della regione settentrionale d' Italia. 1863. IV. 364.
Le **proposte** della Commissione della camera circa le riforme alle legge forestale. 1897. IV. 329.
Le **proposte** della commissione incaricata di studiare le modificazioni da introdurre al disegno di legge forestale. 1897. IV. 329.
Proprietà dell' Acacia e del Gelso della China. 1865. IV. 429.
Proprietà tecniche dell' Ailanto. 1886. IV. 525.
La **proprietà** di Planchiment. 1897. IV. 556.¹
Proprietà des bois de la principauté de Chimay. 1881. IV. 323.¹
Propriété forestière. Améliorations. 1898. IV. 129.
Sur **propriétés** toxiques de l'Ailante. *See* TOXICITÉ des feuilles d'Ailante. 1885. III. 507.²
Propriétés vénéneuses de l'Aesculus Pavia. 1874. III. 539.¹
O **prorastani** . . . *See* O прорастанiи . . . .
Proschowsky, A. R. Branched Cocos etc. 1900. II. 63.²
— Palms, their age when planting. 1900. III. 318.¹
Proskowetz, Max, *Ritter* von. Berlcbt über die Verbandlungen . . . des Internationalen land- und forstwirthschaftlichen Congresses Wien. 1890. IV. 39.²
Prospectus of the forest branch of the Royal Indian engineering college, Cooper's Hill. 1888. IV. 34.¹
Prospetto della flora euganea. *See* TREVISAN, Vittore, *conte.* 1842. I. 427.
Prospetto delle importazioni ed esportazioni dei prodotti forestali . . . della Francia. 1862. IV. 405.¹
La **prossima** abrogazione della legge forestale. 1896. IV. 329.
Prost. Note sur la sensibilité des feuilles du Catalpa. 1839. II. 786.¹
Prost, Att. Sur les plantations d'Arbres à Thé. 1842. III. 405.¹ *604*.¹
Proteaux, A. Practical guide for the manufacture of paper. 1866. IV. 429.
Protección al arbolado. 1882. IV. 165.
Protect the forests. 1890. IV. 182.¹
Protecting trees from cattle. 1857. III. 186.¹
Protection contre les dégâts du gibier. 1899. IV. 197.¹
Protection des arbres. 1899. III. 197.
La **protection** des arbres et des forêts. 1897. IV. 541.¹ — 1898. IV. 177.²
Protection des bois nationaux. 1897. IV. 552.²
La **protection** des oiseaux insectivores. 1898. IV. 91.¹
Protection des richesses forestières du Congo. 1899. IV. 279.²
Protection des Sapins contre les attaques du gibier. 1895. IV. 548.²
Protection et reboisement des forêts. 1898. IV. 177.²
Protection of the Yellowstone Park. 1890. IV. 178.¹
Una **protesta** de la " Revista de montes." 1890. IV. 553.¹
Protič, Georg. Zur Kenntniss der Flora der Umgebung von Vareš. 1900. I. 448.²
Protin, J. B. Culture de l'Althea commun. 1879. III. 588.²
Protits, Georg. Vergleichend-anatomische Untersuchungen über . . . Kerrieen. 1891. II. 257.¹
Protokoli . . . *See* Протоколы . . .
Protokoll, die Ausscheidung . . . der Eichenreserv-Horste . . . im Neuburger-Walde betreffend. 1886. IV. 300.¹
Protokoll über die akademische Forstreise [der Akademie Tharand] in den Harz. 1864. IV. 353.
Protokoll über die Verhandlungen . . . zur Besprechung über . . . Förderung der Obstbaumzucht. 1865. III. 145.²

Prou, Juan. Administración de los montes públicos por el estado. 1886. IV. 293.¹
— La Administración forestal ¿cumple bien su misión? 1890. IV. 553.¹
— Amojonamiento de los montes públicos. 1885. IV. 233.
— Cambio de especies arbóreo-forestales. 1888. IV. 543.²
— El Cuerpo de montes. 1887. IV. 553.¹
— La cuestion social y los montes comunales. 1886. IV. 276.²
— Ordenación rápida de los montes públicos. 1885. IV. 293.¹
— Organización del servicio forestal. 1890. IV. 553.¹
— Planes decenales de aprovechamiento. 1885. IV. 237.
Proudlock, Robert L. On growing American India-rubber trees in South India. 1899. III. 149.
Prouvé. Outillage pour semis et plantations. 1877. IV. 150.
— Outils pour semis et plantations. 1877. IV. 150.
Prouvé, Charles. Régénération artificielle des coupes de futaie. 1897. IV. 142, 545.²
— Régénération par plantation des coupes de futaie. 1898. IV. 142.
— Les repeuplements artificiels. 1884. IV. 142.
Prouvé, G. Délimitations générales amiables. 1893. IV. 309.¹
Una **prova** dell' influenza dell' Eucalyptus. 1882. IV. 55.¹
Provancher, Léon. Les arbres d'ornement et forestiers. 1874. III. 166.
— Une excursion aux climats tropicaux. 1890. V. XVIII.¹
— Flore canadienne. 1862. I. 310.
— Les oiseaux insectivores. 1874. IV. 544.¹
— Traité élémentaire de botanique. 1858. V. X.²
— Le verger canadien. 1862. III. 132.²
— Le verger, le potager. 1874. III. 99.²
Prove di fatto che le piene dei fiumi crescono. 1880. IV. 50.
Provence — **Union médical.** *See* MARSEILLE-MÉDICAL. I. 22.
La **Provence** agricole et horticole. III. 20.
To **provide** for the appointment of a commission to investigate . . . the establishment of . . . Appalachian national park. 1900. IV. 170.²
Provinciaal Utrechtsch genootschap van kunsten en wetenschappen. Nieuwe verhandelingen. Verhandelingen. III. 14.
Provisorische Bestätigung der alten Forstordnungen. 1798. IV. 306.
Provisorisches Regulativ für das Domanial-Forstrechnungswesen im Grossherzogthum Hessen. 1831. IV. 301.
Provvedimenti a favore della Sardegna. 1898. IV. 41.¹
Proyecto de corrección de barrancos en la sierra de España. 1894. IV. 548.¹
Sobre el **proyecto** de ley de repoblación de montes. 1877. IV. 164.²
El **proyecto** de ordenación. 1890. IV. 550.²
Proyecto de ordenación del Monte Irisasi. 1893. IV. 550.²
Proyekt . . . *See* Проектъ . . .
Prschewalski, N. M. *See* PRZHEWALSKI, N. M.
Prudhomme, Henri. De la réforme du code forestier. 1892. IV. 314.¹
Prüfung der Bemerkungen eines badischen Forstmannes über die Forstschule in Karlsruhe. 1834. IV. 31.
Prugneaux, Étienne. Tarif pour cuber les bois. n. d. IV. 220.
Prunet, Adolphe. Sur les bourgeons dormants. 1890. I. 108.¹
— Caractères extérieurs de la chytridiose. 1894. III. 581.
— Sur une chytridinée parasite de la Vigne. 1894. III. 581.
— Contribution à l'étude des réserves d'eau des plantes. 1891. I. 168.
— Les époques favorables dans le traitement du black rot. 1897. III. 582.
— Sur l'évolution du black rot. 1897. III. 582.
— Sur les faisceaux foliaires. 1889. I. 111.
— Les formes de conservation . . . du parasite du black-rot. 1896. III. 581.
— Sur les invasions de black rot. 1897. III. 582.
— La maladie du Mûrier. 1895. III. 379.²
— Sur le mécanisme de la dissolution de l'amidon. 1892. I. 140.²
— Sur les modifications de l'absorption . . . dans les plantes atteintes par la gelée. 1892. I. 212.
— Sur un nouveau mode de propagation du pourridié. 1894. III. 581.
— Sur la propagation du pourridié de la Vigne par les boutures et les greffes-boutures mises en stratification dans le sable. 1893. III. 581.

— Rapport sur le black-rot. 1899. III. 582.
— Sur les rapports biologiques du Cladochytrium. 1894. III. 581.
— Recherches anatomiques . . . sur les nœuds. 1891. I. 06.¹
— Recherches sur le black rot de la Vigne. 1898. III. 582.
— Recherches sur les nœuds. 1891. I. 106.¹
— Sur la structure comparée des nœuds. 1890. I. 106.¹
Prunier, Léon. Sur quelques propriétés physiques de la quercite. 1877. IV. 515.¹
— Quinquinas. 1881. III. 721.
— Les quinquinas; histoire naturelle. 1881. III. 721.
— Recherches sur la quercite. 1876. IV. 515.¹
Pruning evergreens. 1857. III. 173.¹
Pruning of Oaks. 1857. III. 361.²
Pruning shrubs. 1891. III. 173.¹ — 1896. III. 173.¹
Pruning trees and shrubs. 1898. III. 171.
Pruns, *marquis* d'**APCHIER DE.** *See* **APCHIER DE PRUNS,** *marquis* d'.
Prussia; Finanz-Ministerium. *See* ANLEITUNG über das Verfahren beim Schneideln der Eiche; ANLEITUNG zur Ausführung der Taxations-Revisionen; ANLEITUNG zur Führung des Flächenregisters; ANLEITUNG zur Führung des Taxations-Notizenbuchs; ANWEISUNG zur Anlegung und Führung des Controlbuchs.
Prussia; Kön. Ministerial-Forstbureau. *See* ANLEITUNG zur Waldwerthberechnung.
Pruys van der Hoeven, A. De Peperkultuur in Benkoelen. 1872. III. 343.¹
Pryor, Reginald Alfred. On the botanical work of the past season. 1876. V. XXI.²
— A flora of Hertfordshire. 1887. I. 403.
— Notes on a proposed re-issue of the Flora of Hertfordshire. 1875. V. XXI.¹
— Notes on the herbarium of Abbot. 1881. II. 144.¹
Prytz, Carl Vilhelm. Om Forstlig Læsning. 1893. IV. 30.²
— Den Internationale Skovbrugsudstilling i Edinburg. 1884. IV. 20.¹
— Nouvelle méthode de cubage. 1891. IV. 219.
— Et Par Ord om Skovbrugernes practiske Uddannelse. 1885. IV. 30.²
— Piledyrkning i Danmark. 1899. III. 349.
— Piledyrkning i vore Skove. 1900. IV. 487.²
— Skov-Administration. 1897. IV. 288.²
— Skovbrugets Driftslære. 1893. IV. 241.
— Skovens Vedforraad. 1891. IV. 258.
— *See also* OPPERMANN, A. & PRYTZ, C. V.
Prytz, Laurentius Johannes. Florae fennicae breviarium. 1819. I. 360.
— Florae fennicae breviarium; ex schedulis auctoris. 1869. I. 363.
— De Styrace. *See* THUNBERG, C. P. 1813. II. 704.²
Przhevalski, Nikolai Mikhailovich. Mongolia, the Tangut country. 1876. I. 460.¹
— Reisen in Tibet. 1884. I. 460,² 536.¹
— *See also* Пржевальскій, Н. М.
Przibislawsky, Franz. Die forstlichen Verhältnisse des Gutes M.-Trübau. 1866. IV. 369.
Przybytek, *See* FAMINTZIN, André & PRZYBYTEK, D. S.
Przynda i przemysl. III. 10.¹
Psani otevřene pro zahradnictví. III. 25.
Pseudo-gutta-perchas. 1885. III. 229.
Pt., V. Hortensias à fleurs bleues. 1844. III. 412.¹
Sur le **Ptelea** trifolié. 1814. III. 505.²
Pteris, (*pseud.*). The Abies nobilis at Thorpe Perrow. 1888. III. 296.²
Pù ërh tea. 1889. III. 607.
Puaux. *See* ROESER & PUAUX.
Public forest reservations. *See* McRAE, T. C. 1893. IV. 178.² — 1894. IV. 178.² — 1896. IV. 179.¹
Til **Publikum.** *See* LINSTOW, C. H. von. 1791. IV. 288.¹
Public timber bands. *See* BOWERS, E. A. 1888. IV. 272.
Pucci, Angiolo. L'Abelia triflora R. Brown. 1894. III. 748.²
— Acacia celastrifolia Benth. 1897. III. 464.²
— Gli alberi vecchi. 1894. III. 181.²
— Allamanda Williamsii. 1893. III. 686.¹
— Amsonia punicea. 1897. III. 695.²
— Aristolochia arborea. 1895. III. 386.¹
— Aristolochia gigas. 1891. III. 386.¹
— Dei Bambù. 1899. III. 314.¹
— Dei Berberis. 1879. III. 394.¹
— Bignonia purpurea. 1899. III. 706.²

— Cleyera Fortunei Hook. 1895. III. 596.²
— Cocos australis Mart. 1895. III. 322.²
— Le Conifere di Moncioni. 1882. I. 64.
— Le Conifere per i piccoli giardini. 1898. III. 291.
— I Cotoneaster. 1900. III. 420.²
— Croton Président Demole. 1897. III. 516.²
— Croton Torrigianianum. 1884. III. 516.¹
— Datura sanguinea. 1889. III. 700.¹
— Deutzia corymbiflora. 1898. III. 410.²
— Il Diospyros Kaki. 1890. III. 669.²
— Diplacus glutinosus Nutt. 1892. III. 703.¹
— Dracæna Sanderiana. 1897. III. 337.¹
— Drimys Winteri. 1896. III. 397.²
— Erica verticillata Forsk. 1894. III. 651.²
— Frutti minori. 1895. III. 148.¹
— Giardino della Casa Bianca. 1895. III. 49.¹
— Graptophyllum picturatum. 1896. III. 709.¹
— Insetti e insetticidi. 1899. III. 192.¹
— Le Jochroma. 1891. III. 700.²
— Lonicere cespugliose. 1899. III. 750.¹
— Maclura aurantiaca inermis. 1896. III. 372.¹
— Macrozamia spiralis. 1893. III. 286.¹
— L' Oliva bianca Ascolana. 1887. III. 676.¹
— Gli Ontani. 1900. III. 356.²
— Passiflora princeps Lodd. 1897. III. 616.²
— Pittosporum flavum Hook. 1892. III. 416.¹
— La potatura degli alberi. 1895. III. 171.
— Prunus lusitanica var. myrtifolia. 1897. III. 438.¹
— Prunus Myrabolana var. rosea plena. 1898. III. 436.¹
— Pyrus angustifolia. 1893. III. 425.¹
— Relazione sugli esperimenti di acclimazione alla Casa Bianca. 1894. III. 49.²
— Rhodochiton volubile. 1893. III. 704.¹
— Scelta di alberi. 1899. III. 41.¹
— Templetonia retusa. 1892. III. 489.¹
— Thunbergia laurifolia Lindl. 1896. III. 710.²
— Trapiantamento degli alberi. 1896. III. 168.¹
— Xanthoceras sorbifolia Bunge. 1897. III. 540.²
Puccinelli, Benedetto. Catalogo dell' Orto botanico di Lucca. 1843. I. 63.
— Synopsis plantarum in agro lucensi. 1841. I. 426.
Puchner, W. A. An odd Fuchsia. 1888. II. 643.²
Puchot, Éd. Observations sur l'iode réactif de l'amidou. 1876. I. 140.¹
Pucich, Josef. Die Karstbewaldung im . . . Küstenlande. 1900. IV. 168.¹
Pudelewicz, Br. Wycieczka do śląskich lasów. 1899. IV. 370.
Pückler-Muskau, Hermann Ludwig Heinrich, *Furst* von. Die grosse Cypresse von Mistra. 1881. II. 30.¹
Puel, Timothée. Catalogue des plantes qui croissent dans le département du Lot. 1845. I. 410.
— Études sur les divisions géographiques de la flore française. 1858. I. 411.
— Revue critique de la flore du département du Lot. 1860. I. 412.
— & **Maille**, Alphonse. Catalogue de l'herbier de Syrie publié par I. Blanche et C. Gaillardot. 1854. I. 480.
Fuenieux, A. Contribution à l'étude du reboisement de la plaine du Rhône. 1897. IV. 167.¹
— Des coupes rases dans les forêts des régions élevées. 1900. IV. 130.
— Des coupes rases dans les hautes régions. 1900. IV. 130.
— Épicéa à verrues. 1900. II. 37.¹
— L'Épicéa et l'Arôle. 1899. II. 35,² 41.²
— Le flottage des bois dans le canton de Vaud. 1895. IV. 390.²
— La forêt cantonale du Risoud. 1896. IV. 334.²
— Une journée de course dans les Alpes. 1897. IV. 65.¹
— Mélèzes en dépérissement. 1900. IV. 451.
— Des pâturages boisés. 1890. IV. 136.¹
Ein **Pürschgang** auf dem Gebiete der Forstwirtschaft. 1892. IV. 24.¹
Puerta, Gabriel de la. Botanica descriptiva . . . de las plantas . . . en España. 1876. III. 89.¹ — 1891. I. 422.
— Influencia de las plantas. 1880. IV. 55.¹
— Tratado práctico de determinación de las plantas . . . de uso medicinal. 1876. III. 89.¹
Püschel, Alfred. Die Baummessung und Inhaltsberechnung. 1871. IV. 214, 217.
— Die Forst-Einrichtung. 1869. IV. 240.
— Kurzgefasste Forst-Encyklopaedie. 1860. IV. 22.²
— Taschenbuch für Forstwirthe und Holzhändler. 1863. IV. 214.

Puget. See LAGGER & PUGET.
Puget, (abbé). Botanique. Plantes des environs d'Annecy. 1855. I. 435.
— Coup d'œil sur la dispersion des plantes. 1856. I. 435.
— Sur la végétation du Salève. 1866. I. 435.
Puget Sound lumberman. IV. 5.[1]
Pugh, Evan. See LAWES, J. B., GILBERT, J. H., & PUGH, Evan.
Puibusque, A. de. Sur l'Érable à sucre. 1860. IV. 527.[1]
Puig, Joaquin OLMEDILLA Y. See OLMEDILLA Y PUIG, Joaquín.
Puig y Valls, Rafael. La asociación y la cooperación en el campo. 1898. IV. 552.[1]
— Breves consideraciones sobre la importancia industrial ... de la alta cuenca del Llobregat. 1881. IV. 363.[2]
— Causas de la humedad existente en las dunas de Torroella de Montgri. 1897. IV. 556.[2]
— Dictamen sobre repoblación de montes. 1887. IV. 546.[2]
— La electricidad en la Escuela de ingenieros de montes. 1899. IV. 541.[1]
— Los ingenieros de montes en la Exposición. 1889. IV. 540.[1]
— El Llobregat. Aguas y montes. 1890. IV. 542.[1]
— La patria y el árbol. 1898. III. 34.[1]
Puiggener. Piña prolifera del Pinus Pinea. 1890. II. 45.[1]
Puihn, Johann Georg. Materia venenaria regni vegetabilis. 1785. III. 260.[2]
Puissant, A. Genista Andreana. 1886. III. 474.[2]
Pujade. Reboisement des terrains en pente. 1851. IV. 162.
Pujade, J. V. J. Dissertation sur l'utilité de la botanique. 1805. III. 238.[1]
Pujoulx, Jean Baptiste. La botanique des jeunes gens. 1810. I. 93.
— Promenades au marché aux fleurs. 1811. I. 93.
Pullein, Samuel. The culture of silk. 1758. III. 372.[2]
Pulliat, V. Manuel du greffeur de Vignes. 1884. III. 548.[2]
— Mille variétés de Vignes. 1888. III. 547.
— Vitis Thunbergii. 1882. III. 584.[1]
— See also MAS, A. & PULLIAT, V.
Puligny, vicomte de. Rapport sur les Conifères cultivés au Chesnay-sur-Écos. 1875. III. 292.
La pulpe de bois du Canada. 1900. IV. 430.
Pulping Liberian Coffee. 1893. III. 743.[1]
Puls, Jacques Charles. De bladluis en de Perzikboom. 1880. III. 441.[2]
— Un ennemi de nos arbres d'alignement. 1887. III. 212.[1]
— Feuilles de Vignes attaquées par le "Phytoptus vitis." 1886. III. 563.
— Le Groseillier épineux. 1882. III. 414.[2]
— Le "Lecanium aesculi." 1882. III. 536.[2]
— De "Lecanium aesculi." 1882. III. 536.[2]
— De Olmen der openbare plaatsen. 1885. III. 364.[2]
— De Olmen en hunne verwoesters. 1887. III. 364.[2]
— Les Ormes des places publiques. 1885. III. 364.[2]
— Les Ormes des places publiques et leur plus fatal ennemi. 1886. III. 364.[2]
— Les Ormes et leur destructeurs. 1887. III. 364.[2]
— Le puceron et le Pêcher sous abri vitré. 1880. III. 441.[1]
— De Stekelbeziestruik. 1882. III. 414.[2]
— La Vigne et l'Otiorynchus sulcatus. 1881. III. 563.
— La Vigne et le Pulvinaria Vitis. 1881. III. 578.
— Een vijand der boomen onzer wandelingen. 1887. III. 212.[1]
— De wijngaard en de Otiorynchus. 1881. III. 563.
— De wijngaard en de Pulvinaria Vitis. 1881. III. 578.
— Wijngaardbladeren aangetast door de "Phytoptus vitis." 1886. III. 563.
Pulteney, Richard. An account of some ... plants observed in Leicestershire. 1757. I. 804.
— Catalogue of rare plants ... of Leicester. 1790. I. 395.
— Catalogues of ... rare plants of Dorsetshire. 1799. I. 396.
— De Cinchona officinali Linnaei. 1764. III. 720.
— Esquisses historiques et biographiques des progrès de la botanique en Angleterre. 1790. I. 81.[1]
— A general view of the writings of Linnaeus. 1781. I. 520.[2]
— Geschichte der Botanik. 1790. I. 80.[2]
— Historical and biographical sketches of the progress of botany in England. 1790. I. 80.[2]
— Revue générale des écrits de Linné. 1781. I. 520.[2]
— Some observations upon the sleep of plants. 1759. I. 198.

Punjab. See INDIA — PUNJAB.
Puporef, K. See Пупоревъ, К.
Purchas, Samuel. Purchas his pilgrimes, in five bookes. 1625. I. 301.
Purchas, William Henry. Flora of Herefordshire. 1867. I. 402, V. xxi.[1]
— Rubus rubicundus. 1894. II. 310.[1]
— On some peculiarities in the growth of the Hawthorn-tree. 1865. II. 262.[2]
— & Ley, Augustin. A flora of Herefordshire. 1889. I. 404.[1]
Purdie, William. Cedron. 1851. III. 509.[1]
— Die Elfenbein-Palm-Nuss. 1845. III. 330.[1]
— The Ivory-Palm nut. 1845. III. 330.[1]
— Journal of a botanical mission to the West Indies. 1844. I. 335.
— Sur la noix d'ivoire. 1845. III. 330.[1]
Purdy, Carl. The Chemise world. 1897. I. 327.
— Cupressus Macnabiana at home. 1896. II. 29.[2]
— The flora of the California coast range. 1896. I. 326.
— The flora of the Ukiah valley. 1897. I. 327.
— The Madroña at Ukiah. 1897. II. 660.[1]
— Pinus muricata. 1896. II. 43.[2]
— Quercus lobata at Ukiah, California. 1897. II. 135.[1]
— The Redwood forest. 1890. II. 49.[2]
— Redwood timber. 1891. IV. 484.[1]
Puriewitsch, K. Physiologische Untersuchungen über die Entleerung der Reservestoffbehälter. 1898. I. 180.[1]
— Ueber die selbstthätige Entleerung der Reservestoffbehälter. 1896. I. 179.[2]
Puring, N. I. See Пурингъ. H. И.
Purkinje, Johannes Evangelista. Beobachtungen über den Bau des Narbenkanals. 1832. I. 117.[2]
— De cellulis antherarum fibrosis. 1830. I. 117.[1]
Purkyně, Emanuel von. Das vom Böhmischen Forstvereine ... errichtete ombrometrische Netz. 1879. IV. 59.[2]
— Etwas über die Waldfrage. 1875. IV. 53.
— Zur Geschichte und Diagnose der Catalpa speciosa. 1882. II. 787.[1]
— Ueber die histiologischen Unterschiede der Pinusspecies. 1876. II. 40.[1]
— Humus a raseliny. 1866. IV. 68.
— Lesy. 1853. I. 217.
— Ueber neuerdings durch Verheidung entstandene Ortsteinbildung. 1879. IV, 69.
— Eine ostasiatische Conifere in den Balkanländern. 1877. II. 38.[1]
— Die roth- und grünzapfigen Fichten. 1880. II. 34.[2]
— O rozšíření českých lupenatých stromů v Evropě. 1860. I. 348,[1] IV. 80.
— Rozšířenost českých sosnovitých rostlin v evropském rusku. 1859. II. 15.[1]
— Šumava a její rostlinstvo. 1859. I. 441.
— Die Verbreitung der böhmischen Forstgewächse. 1859. IV. 80.
— Ueber zwei in Mitteleuropa wachsende Fichtenformen. 1877. II. 34.[2]
Purkyně, Jan Evangelista. See PURKINJE, J. E.
The Purple Beech. 1889. III. 360.[2]
The purple Beech and Filbert. 1873. III. 205.[2]
The Purple Beech, Broomhouse, Fulham. 1898. II. 127.[2]
The Purple Myrobalan. 1899. III. 436.[1]
Purpus, A. Acer carpinifolium. 1899. III. 534.[2]
— Acer diabolicum. 1896. III. 534.[2]
— Aussaatenbericht. 1895. I. 49.
— Besuch der Baumschulen von H. A. Hesse in Weener a. Ems. 1897. I. 49.
— Buntblätterige ... Gartenformen des gemeinen Ligusters. 1898. III. 674.[1]
— Dracaena arborea Lk. 1889. III. 336.[1]
— Einige neue oder seltene ... Pentstemon. 1896. III. 703.[2]
— Empfehlenswerte, wenig verbreitete Blütensträucher. 1896. III. 413,[1] 483,[1] 758.[2]
— Halesia tetraptera. 1900. III. 670.[2]
— Juglans mandschurica. 1899. III. 354.[2]
— Lonicera Maacki Maxim. 1900. III. 750.[2]
— Neue und seltene Gehölze. 1893. III. 534.[2]
— Neue winterharte Kakteen. 1900. III. 620.[1]
— Robinia Pseudacacia. 1898. III. 486.[1]
— Sambucus nigra L. var. fol. luteis. 1898. III. 752.[1]
— Verschiedene Mittheilungen. 1900. III. 70.
— Wenig verbreitete, frühblühende Sträucher. 1897. III. 416,[2] 417.[1]

Purpus, C. A. Bericht über meine diesjährige Sammeltour. 1896. I. 321.
— Bericht über meine Tour in die La Sol Mountains. 1899. T. 321.
— Bericht über meine Tour in die südliche Sierra Nevada. 1897. I. 321.
— Bericht . . . über seine Tour in . . . Nevada. 1898. I. 321.
— Die Chapparalregion . . . von Kalifornien. 1897. I. 321.
— Neuheiten in der L. Späthschen Baumschule Rixdorf-Berlin. 1893. I. 49.
— Picea pungens Engelm. 1893. II. 38.²
— Pinus Balfouriana Jeffr. 1897. II. 40.²
— Pinus Murrayana. 1897. II. 43.²
— Seltene oder neue Gehölze aus der Sierra Nevada. 1896. I. 321.
— Sequoia gigantea Torr. 1896. II. 50.¹
Purpus, C. A., und seine Einführungen. *See* C. A. PURPUS und seine Einführungen.
Pursch, Friedrich Traugott. *See* PURSH, Frederick.
Pursh, Frederick. Flora Americae septentrionalis. 1814. I. 306.
— Hortus orloviensis. 1815. I. 41.
— Journal of a botanical excursion in the northeastern parts . . . of Pennsylvania and New York during the year 1807. 1869. I. 314.
— Verzeichnis der im Plauischen Grunde . . . wildwachsenden Pflanzen. 1799. I. 375.
Purton, Thomas. A botanical description of British plants. 1817. I. 397.
Puszcza Bialowieska. n. d. IV. 344.²
Puteo, Zacharias de. Historia de gumma indica. 1628. III. 244.
Putevoditel . . . *See* ПУТЕВОДИТЕЛЬ . . .
Putnam, Bessie L. A day-blooming Cereus grandiflorus. 1895. II. 590.¹
— Fertilization of the Crimson Thread-flower. 1897. II. 339.¹
— The White Blackberry. 1900. II. 309.¹
Putnam, H. C. Forest fires. 1882. IV. 182.¹
— The forests of Europe as seen by an American lumberman. 1888. IV. 342.²
— The forests of the United States. 1888. IV. 338.¹
Putnam, Joseph Duncan. Report on bark-lice. 1880. III. 186.²
— Report on Maple bark louse. 1878. III. 536.²
Putnam, Lucy A. Adam's Peak, Ceylon. 1893. I. 477.¹
— The crater of Mt. Misery, St. Kitts. 1888. I. 337.
Putnam's magazine. *See* PUTNAM's monthly magazine. III. 8.
Putnam's monthly magazine. III. 8.
Puton, Alfred. Accertamento della rendita annuale. 1893. IV. 238.
— L'aménagement des forêts. 1867. IV. 240.
— Code de la législation forestière. 1883. IV. 324.
— Détermination du revenu annuel des forêts. 1878. IV. 236.
— Détermination du revenu des futaies jardinées. 1879. IV. 236.
— Estimations concernant la propriété forestière. 1886. IV. 253.
— Les forêts communales en 1877. 1878. IV. 309.¹
— Les forêts et le crédit agricole. 1883. IV. 326.
— Les forêts et le projet de code rural. 1870. IV. 326.
— Die Forsteinrichtung im Nieder- und Hochwaldbetriebe. 1867. IV. 240.
— L'impôt foncier des forêts. 1882. IV. 257.
— Incendies dans les forêts. 1877. IV. 183.¹
— Manuel de législation forestière. 1876. IV. 324.
— Notice sur l'École forestière en 1883. *See* ENSEIGNEMENT agricole. 1889. IV. 34.
— Organization de l'enseignement forestier supérieur dans l'empire d'Allemagne. 1885. IV. 33.¹
— Quel est . . . en matière forestière, le point de départ des délais de prescription de la peine. 1877. IV. 326.
— Une question d'administration concernant des forêts sectionales. 1882. IV. 292.
— Questions de droit forestier. 1876. IV. 326.
— Questions sur le droit d'occupation des concessionnaires de mines dans les forêts. 187. ? IV. 326.
— Du régime des forêts communales. 1863. IV. 309.¹
— Du régime des forêts communales de nouvelle origine. 1864. IV. 309.¹
— Du régime des forêts communales possédées par les sections de communes. 1865. IV. 292.
— La révision du titre 6 du Code forestier. 1879. IV. 326.
— Le Sapin des Vosges. 1887. IV. 446.¹
— Service administratif des chefs de cantonnement. 1870. IV. 292.
— Le tarif des douanes et les produits forestiers. 1887. IV. 285.¹
— Traité d'économie forestière. 1888. IV. 241.
Putterlick, Aloys. Pittosporeae. 1844. II. 247.¹
— Synopsis Pittosporearum. 1839. II. 247.¹
Putzeys, Félix & **Romiée**, H. Mémoire sur l'action physiologique de la Gelsémine. 1878. III. 682.¹
Puvilland. Plantes nouvelles d'introduction anglaise. 1879. III. 87.
Puvis, Marc Antoine. De l'art séricicole. 1840. III. 376.
— De la dégénération et de l'extinction des variétés. 1837. T. 192.²
— De l'effet des gelées de printemps. 1843. III. 47.
— De l'importance et de la nécessité des semis pour l'amélioration . . . des variétés. 1848. I. 247.
— Mise à fruit des arbres par la greffe Luiset. 1849. III. 160.
— Multiplication des végétaux. 1841. III. 152.
— Notice sur l'hiver de 1838 et ses effets. 1838. III. 47.
— Observations sur la dégénération des variétés. 184. ? I. 248.²
— Plantation des terrains en pente. 1839. IV. 161.²
— Sujets divers d'horticulture. 1844. III. 125.
— De la taille des arbres fruitiers. 1861. III. 172.
Puy-de-Dôme — Société d'horticulture du. *See* SOCIÉTÉ . . . III. 22.
Puydt, P. E. de. Les arbustes de serre froide. 1860. III. 84.¹
— Guide de l'amateur de fleurs. 1886. III. 84.¹
— L'Oranger à feuilles de Myrte. 1878. III. 500.¹
— Les Palmiers et les grandes plantes ornementales de serre froide. 1863. III. 317.
— Les plantes de serre. 1866. III. 150.¹
— Traité . . . de la culture des plantes de serre froide. 1873. III. 150.¹
Puymaurin, de, (jr.). Recherches sur le ver blanc. 1788. III. 188.²
Puyvallée, C. A. de BENGY-. *See* BENGY-PUYVALLÉE, C. A. de.
Py. Cacao et chocolat. 1895. III. 595.¹
Py. Die Photogrammetrie oder Bildmesskunst. 1891. IV. 265.
Pychowska, *Mrs.* Lucia D. Botanical notes made . . . at Randolph, N. H. 1883. I. 315.
— Loon Pond Mountain. 1881. I. 315.
Pye, Walter. *See* BRUNTON, T. L. & PYE, Walter.
Le Pyengadow ou bois de fer. 1868. IV. 401.¹
Pyinkado. 1900. IV. 524.¹
Le Pyinkado de Birmanie. 1894. IV. 524.²
Pylaie, August Jean Marie, BACHELOT DE LA, *See* BACHELOT DE LA PYLAIE, A. J. M.
Pynaert. Farbenvarietäten von Ulmen. 1879. II. 144.¹
Pynaert, Charles. Allamanda Williamsii. 1893. III. 686.¹
— Les Lapageria. 1892. III. 337.²
Pynaert, Édouard. Abutilon Thompsoni flore pleno. 1885. III. 587.¹
— Acer colchicum tricolor hort. 1886. III. 534.²
— Acer rufinerve albo limbatum. 1878. III. 536.¹
— Aeschynanthus tricolor. 1884. III. 708.¹
— De afstand tusschen de boomen der wandeldreven. 1894. III. 211.²
— Les Althées ou Ketmies des jardins. 1877. III. 588.¹
— Amygdalopsis Lindleyi. 1892. III. 443.²
— Andromeda (Pieris) japonica. 1885. III. 654.¹
— Aralia Chabrieri. 1887. III. 532.¹
— L'Araucaria excelsa. 1878. III. 298.¹
— Araucaria imbricata. 1872. III. 298.²
— Un arbre qui boude. 1895. III. 181.²
— Les arbres pleureurs. 1873. III. 204.¹
— Aristolochia elegans. 1886. III. 386.¹
— Aristolochia tricaudata. 1894. III. 386.²
— Le Biota filiformis erecta hort. 1875. III. 311.²
— Een boom die pruilt. 1895. III. 181.²
— Camoensia maxima. 1886. III. 469.²
— Causerie sur les grands froids. 1881. III. 46.²
— De Cederboom van den Himalaya. 1872. III. 300.¹
— Le Cèdre de l'Himalaya. 1872. III. 300.¹
— Les Cestrum L. 1900. III. 699.¹
— De Chamaecyparis Boursieri. 1872. III. 301.¹
— Le Chamaecyparis Boursieri. 1872. III. 301.¹

Pynaert, Édouard (*continued*).
— Chamaecyparis Boursieri pyramidalis alba nana. 1878. III. 301.¹
— Choisia ternata. 1879. III. 496.¹
— Clerodendron squamatum Vahl. 1896. III. 696.²
— Clethra arborea Ait. à feuilles panachées. 1893. III. 646.²
— Cocos sp. (Weddeliana?) minima glauca hort. 1891. III. 324.²
— The common Walnut. 1896. III. 356.¹
— Crataegus Oxyacantha punicea fl. pl. 1898. III. 422.¹
— Croton Reginae. 1879. III. 516.¹
— Cyrtoceras reflexum Bennet. 1886. III. 693.²
— Les Deutzia Thunb. 1876. III. 410.²
— Les Dipladenia. 1891. III. 687.²
— Des distances à conserver entre les arbres d'alignement. 1894. III. 211.²
— Drie nieuwe soorten van Olmen. 1879. III. 363.²
— Epiphyllum Makoyanum hort. 1889. III. 625.²
— Étude pour servir à l'histoire de la pomologie. 186.? III. 77.
— Études historiques sur les progrès de l'arboriculture fruitière. 1865. III. 32.²
— Fagus sylvatica atropurpurea tricolor. 1886. III. 360.¹
— Faut-il rajeunir les Conifères atteintes par la gelée? 1861. III. 295.¹
— Franciscea calycina. 1893. III. 699.¹
— Le fruit de la Passiflore. 1894. III. 615.²
— Of de fruitboomen ontaarden? 1865. I. 248.¹
— Les Gardenia. 1897. III. 744.²
— De gegroefde otiorhynk. 1870. III. 563.
— Geonoma acaulis Mart. 1893. III. 325.²
— Geschiedkundige schets van den vooruitgang der fruitboomteelt. 1865. III. 32.¹
— Grevillea alpestris Meissn. 1897. III. 383.¹
— Een groote boom. 1882. II. 97.¹
— Hibiscus rosa sinensis. 1879. III. 588.¹
— Iets over de groote koude. 1881. III. 46.²
— Iets over den Gingko biloba L. 1874. III. 287.¹
— De l'influence de la lumière sur la coloration des feuilles. 1880. I. 185.³ — 1881. I. 185.²
— Ixora Pilgrimi. 1885. III. 745.¹
— Le Juania australis Drude. 1896. III. 326.¹
— Le Kentia (Grisebachia) Balmoreana. 1884. III. 325.²
— Korte snoeijing der wortels. 1867. III. 173.²
— Lapageria rosea Ruiz et Pav. 1882. III. 337.²
— Lea amabilis. 1883. III. 544.²
— Magnolia stellata. 1880. III. 400.²
— Le Mahonia Bealii. 1875. III. 396.¹
— Maladie des Tilleuls provoquée par le Tetranychus. 1863. III. 585.¹
— Manuel de l'amateur de fruits. 1866. III. 140.¹
— Manuel . . . de la culture forcée des arbres fruitiers. 1861. III. 176.²
— Le Marronnier d'Inde. 1890. III. 537.¹
— De Mespelaar met groote vruchten. 1877. III. 429.²
— Metrosideros florida. 1886. III. 637.¹
— Moyens d'améliorer les races fruitières. 1866. I. 247.
— Mûrier noir. 1890. III. 381.¹
— Myoporum parvifolium R. Br. 1899. III. 710.²
— De la nécessité de recourir à la reproduction par voie de semis. 1865. I. 248.² — 1866. I. 192.¹
— Le Néflier à gros fruits. 1877. III. 429.²
— Een nieuwe rangschikking der Appels. 1885. III. 425.²
— Een nieuwe vijand der Sparreboomen. 1870. IV. 442.
— Note sur l'Arbre aux quarante écus. 1874. III. 287.¹
— Un nouvel arbre fruitier. 1899. III. 637.¹
— Un nouvel arbuste rustique à feuillage pourpre. 1883. III. 435.²
— Une nouvelle classification des Pommes. 1885. III. 425.²
— L'otiorhynque sillonné. 1870. III. 563.
— Pandanus microcarpus. 1881. III. 313.²
— Passiflora coerulea var. Constance Elliott. 1898. III. 16.¹
— Pavonia Wioti Ed. Mn. 1879. III. 588.²
— Le Pentas carnea Benth. 1895. III. 746.²
— Pernettia lilacina. 1886. III. 653.²
— Le Phygelius capensis E. Meyer. 1899. III. 703.²
— Le Picea Morinda. 1873. III. 306.¹
— De Picea Morinda. 1873. III. 306.¹
— Plantations d'alignement; distances à observer. 1894. III. 211.²
— Principes généraux de la taille. 1866. III. 170.
— À propos d'Epiphyllum. 1896. III. 623.¹

— Prunus Pissardi. 1883. III. 435.²
— Le Prunus Pissardi. 1883. III. 435.²
— Psychotria cyanococca. 1882. III. 747.¹
— Reinwardtia tetragyna. 1888. III. 492.¹
— Le Retinospora leptoclada Zucc. 1876. III. 301.²
— Rhododendron javanicum var. Maiden's Blush. 1888. III. 660.²
— Ribes alpinum pumilum aureum. 1878. III. 414.¹
— Over de richting der boomen volgens de windrichting. 1869. I. 233.¹
— Le Sapin parasol. 1876. III. 309.²
— Les serres-vergers. 1861. III. 176.²
— Les Skimmia. 1885. III. 505.²
— Sollya heterophylla Lindl. 1895. III. 416.¹
— Staphylea colchica Steud. 1884. III. 533.²
— Stephanotis floribunda. 1883. III. 694.¹
— La teigne de la Vigne. 1894. III. 564.¹
— La terre de bruyère. 1864. III. 41.¹
— Thuia gigantea. 1872. III. 311.²
— Le Toxicophlaea spectabilis. 1876. III. 685.²
— De treurboomen. 1873. III. 204.¹
— Trois nouvelles variétés d'Ormes. 1879. III. 363.²
— Variétés nouvelles de Crassula hybrides. 1890. III. 409.¹
— Veronica Traversi hort. Veitch. 1883. III. 704.²
— Wellingtonia gigantea. 1872. III. 310.¹
— Wellingtonia gigantea pendula. 1878. III. 310.¹
— De wijngaardmot. 1894. III. 564.¹
— Winterenting voor fruitboomen. 1866. III. 161.
— De zomer-verplantingen. 1867. III. 168.²
— De Zwarte Moerbezieboom. 1890. III. 381.¹
— *See also* KERCHOVE DE DENTERGHEM, Oswald, *comte* de & PYNAERT, Édouard.
— & **André**, Édouard. Epiphyllum truncatum var. 1887. III. 660.²
— & **Geert**, Auguste van. Azalea mollis × sinensis. 1894. III. 660.²
— Azalea mollis × sinensis Jas. H. Laing. 1891. III. 660.²

Pynaert, Léon. Les Arundinaria Michx. 1898. III. 315.²
— Les Bambous rustiques. 1897. III. 314.²
— Greffage de plantes grasses. 1898. III. 620.¹
The **Pyracantha** for hedges. 1857. III. 443.²
Pyrale attaquant les aiguilles d'Épicéa. 1899. IV. 457.
La **pyrale** des pousses. 1898. IV. 479.
Pyrénées-Orientales — Société agricole, scientifique et littéraire. *See* SOCIÉTÉ PHILOMATIQUE DE PERPIGNAN. I. 24.¹
On **pyrogallic** acid. 1843. III. 237.¹
Pyrros, Aristeides. *See* ΠΎΡΡΟΣ, Ἀριστείδης.
Pyrros, Dionysios. *See* ΠΎΡΡΟΣ, Διονύσιος.

The best sweet-scented indoor shrub. 1875. III. 745.²
. The Caramanian Podocytisus. 1876. III. 480.²
. Cissus Davidiana. 1875. III. 545.²
. The Conifer for chalky soils. 1888. III. 297.¹
. Seaforthia elegans. 1874. III. 319.²
. The Screw Pines. 1877. III. 313.²
. Tan for hedge-growing. 1874. III. 213.
. Trees for autumn effect. 1886. III. 207.¹
., P. Assainissement du Bas-Congo. 1895. IV. 542.²
Q., P. La dernière gelée en Ardenne. 1894. IV. 548.¹
Q., P. Le Pinus rigida. 1895. IV. 559.¹
Q., P. T. Trees girdled by field-mice. 1869. III. 180.²
Quadro comparativo dei prodotti forestali importati nel porto di Genova. 1862. IV. 405.²
Quadro dei ripartimenti forestali e del personale. 1864. IV. 293.²
Quadro delle importazioni di prodotti forestali. 1863. IV. 405.²
Quadro delle importazioni e delle esportazioni di prodotti forestali. 1865. IV. 405.²
Quaedvlieg, Louis. La flore de la République Argentine. 1875. I. 344.
Quaet-Faslem, (*Oberförster zu Hannover*). Zur Dampfpflugkultur. 1877. IV. 143.¹
Quaet-Faslem, G. Ueber die Aufforstung der Haideflächen in Hannover. 1882. IV. 158.
— Ueber die Aufforstungs-Bestrebungen der Hannoverschen Provinzial-Verwaltung. 1882. IV. 158.
— Die Aufforstungsbestrebungen der hannoverschen Provinzialverwaltung. 1896. IV. 159.
— Die Bepflanzung von Chausseen. 1889. III. 210.
— Der Forstkulturbetrieb auf den Heidflächen bei Niebeck. 1875. IV. 158.

Quali sono le prerogative del Gelso primitivo. 1896. III. 378.
La qualité des cuirs australiens. 1898. IV. 521.[1]
Des qualités et de l'usage des bois. 1853. IV. 396.[1]
Quality of Deodar timber. 1853. IV. 448.[1]
Quanta foglia di Gelso occorra per nutrire i bachi. 1896. III. 380.[1]
Quantin, H. Sur l'emploi du sulfure de carbone. 1891. III. 197.[2]
Quantité de tannin contenue dans différentes substances. 1865. I. 183.
Quaranta, Raffaele. Delle acque termo-minerali. 1874. IV. 48.[1]
Quarizius, C. G. Die verschiedenen Brennstoffe. 1848. IV. 281.[1]
Quarles van Ufford, J. De Indigo-teelt op Java. 1860. III. 479.[1]
Quarles van Ufford, J. K. W. Cultures op Java en Ceylon. 1898. III. 731.
— Kaspische Zandwilg. 1886. IV. 160.[1]
— De Liberia-Koffj. 1877. III. 742.[1]
The Quarterly journal of agriculture. III. 18.
Quarterly journal of microscopical science. See MICROSCOPIC journal. III. 18.
Quarterly journal of science. I. 19.
Quarterly journal of science, literature and the arts. See ROYAL INSTITUTION OF GREAT BRITAIN. III. 18.
Quassia as an insecticide. 1894. III. 508.[2]
The Quassia tree. 1875. III. 509.[2]
Quassiaholz als Hopfen-Surrogat. 1884. III. 508.[3]
Sur le quassol. 1895. III. 509.[1]
Quatember. I. 10.
Quatre traictez utiles et délectables de l'agriculture. 1560. III. 110.[2]
Quatrefages de Bréau, Jean Louis Armand de. Élevage des vers à soie. 1864. III. 380.[1]
— Mémoire sur la culture et l'importance du Mûrier. 1836. III. 375.
— Mémoire sur la destruction des termites. 1853. IV. 417.
— Mémoire sur les injections gazeuses appliquées à la destruction des termites. 1853. IV. 417.
— Nouvelle maladie des feuilles de Mûrier. 1857. III. 379.[1]
— Observations sur la méthode de Jussieu. 1857. I. 252.
— Questions sur l'étisie. 1857. III. 379.[3]
— Remarques . . . à l'occasion de Dufour, B. J. Sur la culture du Mûrier sauvageon. 1860. III. 377.
Le quatrième livre du Rustican. See CRESCENZI, Piero de. 1864. III. 555.
Quazarius, C. G. Pharmaceutische Rohwaarenkunde. 1858. III. 258.
Que planter en sol calcaire. 1899. IV. 70.
Quéan-Quincy. Sur le Palmier . . . cocos des Maldives. 1807. II. 70.[1]
Quebec — Fruit growers' association. See MONTREAL HORTICULTURAL SOCIETY. III. 2.
Quebec — Literary and historical society. See LITERARY . . . I. 4.[2]
The queen of Fuchsias. 1848. III. 640.[1]
Queensland — Department of agriculture. Bulletin. Botany bulletin. III. 27.[1]
Queensland — Royal society. See ROYAL. I. 30.
Queensland agricultural journal. III. 27.[1]
The Queensland court . . . Timber. 1879. IV. 22.[1]
Quéhen-Mallet. Boisement et reboisement des terrains pauvres. 1888. IV. 163.
— Les haies. 1884. III. 214.[1]
— Note sur la marcotte herbacée. 1862. III. 159.[1]
— La Vigne et le Phylloxera vastatrix. 1884. III. 573.
Quejas. 1892. IV. 553.[2]
Quekett, E. J. On the regular arrangement of crystals. 1846. I. 138.[2]
Quekett, John. Lectures on histology. 1852. I. 123.[2]
Quekett microscopical club. Journal. I. 19.
A quel âge recèpe-t-on les plantations? 1899. IV. 169.[2]
Quelch, J. J. A journey to the summit of Roraima. 1895. I. 339.[2]
— The materials of the urali poison. 1895. III. 685.[2]
À quelle distance doit-on planter le Pin sylvestre? 1899. IV. 474.
À quelle distance doit-on planter les Peupliers? 1899. IV. 485.[2]
Quelle est la saison la meilleure pour le recepage de l'Aune? 1900. IV. 488.[2]
Das Quellen der Samen. 1865. IV. 147.[2]

Quelmaltz, Samuel Theodor. De infuso foliorum Theae. 1747. III. 605.
— De oleo Palmae. 1750. III. 318.[2]
— De pane succedaneo, corticeque Tiliae. 1757. III. 585.[2]
Quelques arbres remarquables de la vallée du lac Léman. 1851. I. 297.[2]
Quelques Conifères exotiques. 1890. III. 291.
Quelques considerations sur l'organisation de l'administration des forêts. 1886. IV. 292.
Quelques considérations sur les excès du déboisement. See HUMBERT, Joseph. 1847. IV. 282.[2]
Quelques détails sur la culture des Pistachiers. 1847. III. 526.[1]
Quelques détails sur le Sequoia (Wellingtonia). 1859. II. 50.[2]
Quelques expériences de pépinière. 1900. IV. 151.[1]
Quelques expériences en pépinière. 1899. IV. 151.[2]
Quelques mots sur l'histoire du Camellia. See The CAMELLIA. 1860. III. 598.[2]
Quelques mots sur les causes de dégradence [sic] des forêts . . . de la Gruyère. 1852. IV. 365.
Sur quelques nouvelles graisses. 1886. III. 225.
Quelques nouvelles remarques sur la variation du Cereus speciosissimus. 1832. II. 591.[1]
De quelques plantes nouvelles annoncées. 1865. III. 77.
Quelques sous-produits forestiers. 1898. IV. 434.
Quélus, de. Histoire naturelle du cacao. 1719. III. 594.
— The natural history of chocolate. 1719. III. 594.
Quensell, C. G. L. Lebendige Hecken. 1888. III. 214.[1]
— Rathgeber bei Anpflanzung nutsbarer Bäume. 1889. III. 70.
Quer, Joseph. Flora española. 1762. I. 419.[2]
Quer y Martinez, Joseph. Dissertación physico-botanica sobre la passión nephritica. 1763. III. 648.[1]
Quercetanus Du Chesne, Joseph. La pharmacopée des dogmatiques. 1607. III. 245.
— Pharmacopoea dogmaticorum restituta. 1607. III. 245.
— Le ricchezze della riformata farmacopea. 1607. III. 245.
Quercu, Leodegarius à. See DUCHESNE, Léger.
Quercus, (pseud.). Resuscitation of the stems of aged Yews. 1868. III. 288.[1]
Quesiti svolti agli esami di promozione per merito dagli ufficiali forestali. 1896. IV. 35.[2]
Un quesito di stima forestale. 1897. IV. 259.[1]
Del quesito intorno all' alzamento del letto dei fiumi. 1881. IV. 186.[2]
La question des forêts en Algérie. See WACHI, G. 1885. IV. 279.[2]
La question des forêts en Russie. See The FOREST question . . . 1883. IV. 273.[2]
La question de montagnes. 1893. IV. 276.[1]
La question du Café. See SANTA-ANNA NERY, F. J., baron de. 1883. III. 739.
La question forestière en Angleterre. 1885. IV. 357.[2]
Questions allouagères: juridiction administrative. 1897. IV. 327.[1]
Quetelet, Adolphe. Différence des temps entre Bruxelles et Vienne. 1862. I. 222.[2]
— Influence de la température sur . . . la floraison. 1852. I. 231.[2]
— De l'influence des températures. 1855. I. 232.[1]
— Sur les moyens de faire donner aux plantes leurs feuilles. 1852. III. 176.[1]
— Les phénomènes périodiques de la végétation. 1870. I. 226.[1]
— Sur la relation entre les températures et la durée de la végétation. 1855. I. 232.[1]
— Second floraison du Lilas. 1854. II. 714.[2]
— Sur la température et l'état de la végétation. 1853. I. 226.[1]
— Linster, Ch. & Fritsch, Karl. Sur les époques comparées de la feuillaison. 1865. I. 222.[2]
Quétier. Bouturage des Rosiers. 1867. III. 452.
— Note sur la fécondation du Yucca. 1865. III. 339.[2]
— Thuya meldensis. 1855. III. 311.[3]
Queva, Charles. Caractères anatomiques de la tige des Dioscoreés. 1893. II. 90.[2]
Quick growth in trees. 1891. III. 309.[1]
Quiescenae, aspettative e destitutzioni. 1863. IV. 293.[2]
Quihou, Antoine. Catalogue des Vignes . . . au Jardin zoologique. 1876. III. 547.
— Effets de l'hiver 1854–55. 1855. III. 47.
— Extrait d'une lettre sur les suites du froid à Fromont. 1855. III. 47.
— Note sur quelques plantes . . . au Jardin d'acclimatation. 1869. I. 58.
— Rapport sur les cultures faites. 1865. III. 125.

Quin, Charles W.   City trees.   1879.   III. 42.[2]
— Dye plants.   1878.   III. 236.
— Fruit trees from an ornamental point of view.   1878.   III. 201.
— The horticultural comprachicos of Japan.   1878.   III. 175.[2]
— Juglans longirostris.   1878.   III. 354.[2]
Quin, F. F.   Pharmacopœia homœopathica.   1834.   III. 254.
Quin, John J.   The lacquer industry of Japan.   1881.   III. 232.[2]
— Report on the lacquer industry of Japan.   1882.   III. 528.[2]
Quinche, S.   Le Sapin rouge . . . au point de vue du climat.   1872.   II. 36.[2]
Quincey, John.   Pharmacopœia officinalis & extemporanea.   1718.   III. 251.
Quincy, QUÉAU-.   *See* QUÉAU-QUINCY.
Quindos y **Baena**, J. A. ALVAREZ DE.   *See* ALVAREZ DE QUINDOS Y BAENA, J. A.
Quinn, P. T.   Pear culture for profit.   1869.   III. 445.[2]
Quinn, William.   Rapport sur le commerce des bois.   1861.   IV. 402.[2]
Quinquaud, Charles Eugene.   Sur certains points de l'action physiologique du tanguin.   1885.   III. 691.[1]
Les Quinquinas à Java.   1880.   III. 716.
Les Quinquinas dans l'Inde.   1868.   III. 714.
Quintanilla, Pedro MARTINEZ.   *See* MARTINEZ QUINTANILLA, Pedro.
Quintino, Mastro.   Serre o briglie.   1896.   IV. 186.[2]
Quinto, Agustin de.   Curso de agricultura practica.   1818.   III. 114.[1]
Quiqueran, Pierre.   Nouvelle agriculture.   1551.   III. 110.[2]
— Primaria relatensium de laudibus provinciae.   1551.   III. 110.[2]
Quiquerez, Alb.   Culture du Chêne.   1872.   IV. 506.
— Histoire d'un Chêne dans le Jura.   1881.   II. 138.[2]
— Notice historique et statistique sur les mines, les forêts . . . de Bâle.   187.?   IV. 366.
— Notice sur le déboisement des Franches-Montagnes.   1862.   IV. 283.[1]
Quiroga.   Sur l'arginine.   1896.   I. 178.
Quiroga y **Rodriguez**, Francisco.   Les Dragos de Tenerife.   1892.   II. 82.[2]
Quito—**Universidad**.   *See* UNIVERSIDAD . . . I. 8.[1]
Qvade, C. A.   Anlægsomkostninger og Udbytte af en Naaletræes Kultur.   1873.   IV. 442.[2]
— Bidrag til Oplysning om vore Skovprodukters Prisbevægelser.   1876.   IV. 404.[1]
Qvenzel.   Rechtskunde für Forstbeamte im Königreiche Sachsen.   1869.   IV. 322.[1]
Qvenzel, (*Landgerichtsrath*).   Die Forstverwaltung im Königreich Sachsen.   1888.   IV. 291,[1] 303.[1]

— **r**.   Die Holzproduction und der Holzhandel Kroatien-Slavoniens.   1888.   IV. 420.
— **r**.   Morcheln- und Champignonzucht.   1895.   IV. 439.
r.   Rasenhügel-Culturen.   1867.   IV. 153.[2]
r.   Die Verbindung der Obstbaumzucht mit der Mittel- und Niederwaldwirthschaft.   1849.   IV. 134.[2]
R.   Annals of nature.   *See* RAFINESQUE-SCHMALTZ, C. S.   1820.   I. 306.
R.   Bredasche.hovenierderijen.   1853.   III. 122.[1]
R.   Chamaebatia foliosa.   1873.   III. 420.[2]
R.   Early flowering Magnolias.   1900.   II. 213.[1]
R.   Fortschritte auf dem Gebiete der Forstvermessung.   1890.   IV. 265.
R.   Gelées tardives.   1900.   IV. 192.[1]
R.   Der Goldafter-Spinner.   1870.   IV. 509.
R.   Hardy Heaths.   1899.   III. 650.[2]
R.   Instruktion für Aufastung.   1899.   IV. 172.[2]
R.   Neuchâtel.   Le régime de l'Areuse.   1895.   IV. 187.[2]
R.   Ueber den Nutzen des Bohnenbaums.   1828.   III. 480.[2]
R.   Le Pin de Corse.   1899.   IV. 466.[1]
R.   Repoblaciones en la cuenca del Segura.   1891.   IV. 546.[2]
R.   Rosa macrantha.   1900.   II. 296.[1]
R.   St. Gallen.   Ein Waldbrand.   1898.   IV. 183.[2]
R.   Sandalwood.   1843.   IV. 519.[1]
R.   Sapins et Hêtres.   1888.   IV. 74.[1]
R.   Spätfröste und Laubholznachzucht.   1871.   IV. 137.[2]
R.   S d n über die rationelle Waldbehandlung.   1860.   IV. 236.tu ie
R.   Untersuchungen über den Feuchtigkeitsgehalt . . . des Waldes und des Freilandes.   1891.   IV. 54.
R.   Variegated Yews.   1868.   III. 288.[1]
R.   Vente des 10 août et 12 novembre 1900 au Mans.   1900.   IV. 388.[2]

R., van.   Kunstmatig bereide Reukstoffen.   1897.   III. 227.
R., A. D.   Estudios sobre la pérdida del tanino en las cortezas curtientes.   1881.   IV. 435.
R., A. D.   Servicio de montes en las Islas Filipinas.   1885.   IV. 294.[2]
R., A. D.   Sistemas de descorche.   1880.   IV. 516.[1]
R., B.   Die Nutzholzproduktion als Ziel der Waldwirtschaft.   1900.   IV. 271.[1]
R., B.   La production du bois d'œuvre comme but de la sylviculture.   1900.   IV. 271.[1]
R., B.   Vom Weihnachtsbaum-Markt.   1898.   IV. 434.
R., C.   Salix annularis, Lockenweide.   1900.   III. 351.[2]
R., C. von.   Bemerkungen über den Heuwurm.   1855.   III. 563.
R., E.   Compas forestier enregistreur.   1888.   IV. 231.[2]
R., E.   L'exploitabilité commerciale et les traditions françaises.   1892.   IV. 27.[2]
R., E. A.   The Carterets.   1862.   I. 531.[1]
R., E. A. von.   Ueber die Ausartung der Fruchtbäume.   *See* REGEL, E. A. von.   1858.   I. 248.[2]
R., E. P.   De l'emploi du Rosier Banks.   1882.   III. 454.[2]
R., F.   Epiphyllums and their propagation.   1890.   III. 623.[1]
R., F.   The incense or frankincense of Scripture.   1846.   II. 416.[1]
R., F.   Leycesteria formosa.   1889.   III. 749.[1]
R., F.   Mode of transmitting cuttings from England to India.   1846.   III. 155.
R., F.   Palms.   1890.   III. 318.[1]
R., F.   Rubus odoratus.   1889.   III. 458.[2]
R., G.   Des coupes par volume.   1877.   IV. 236.
R., G. M.   Calotropis procera.   1898.   III. 692.[2]
R., H.   Thinning forests.   1894.   IV. 174.
R., H. N.   Cytisus Adami.   1884.   II. 368.[2]
R., H. S.   Cedrone seed.   1851.   III. 509.[1]
R., J.   Fir timber.   1873.   IV. 462.[2]
R., J.   Hardy Heaths.   1870.   III. 650.[1]
R., J.   Nützliche Forstinsekten.   1886.   IV. 92.
R., J.   Pistacia and their uses.   1877.   III. 525.[1]
R., J.   The Tonquin bean.   1877.   III. 475.[1]
R., J.   Auf welche Weise prüft man die Keimfähigkeit der Waldsämereien?   1886.   IV. 147.[1]
R., J. T.   Hickory, Black Hickory.   1897.   II. 112.[1]
R., J. T.   Tree form and tree photography.   1897.   I. 37.[2] .
R., L. B.   Le charbon de bois destiné à la fabrication de la poudre noire.   1896.   IV. 432.[1]
R., M.   *See also* P., M.   (Russian alphabet.)
R., M.   Forest demarcation in South Arcot.   1896.   IV. 251.[2]
R., M.   Note on experiments on charcoal.   1894.   IV. 395.
R., M.   The Rain tree for avenues.   1896.   III. 484.[2]
R., M.   Voyages to the Madeira.   *See* RIDDELL, Maria.   1792.   III. 266.
R., M. G. V.   *See* VAN RENSSELAER, Mariana Griswold.
R., N.   *See* P., H.   (Russian alphabet.)
R., P. W.   Un ennemi de l'Oranger.   1876.   III. 500.[2]
R., P. W.   Een vijand des Oranjebooms.   1876.   III. 500.[2]
R., R.   Habrothamnus fasciculatus.   1881.   III. 699.[2]
R., R.   Welchen Wert hat die Verwendung von künstlichen Dungstoffen.   1889.   IV. 144.[2]
R., T.   Brazilian fruits.   1861.   III. 269.[1]
R., T.   The Cedarwood of the ancients.   1854.   II. 30.[1]
R., T.   Establishing plantations on the seacoast.   1885.   III. 41.[2]
R., T.   Sumak woskowy.   1888.   III. 527.[2]
R., W.   Cedars of Lebanon in England.   1890.   II. 28.[2]
R., W.   Climbers and their artistic use.   1896.   III. 205.[1]
R., W.   English gardens abroad.   1897.   III. 464.[2]
R., W.   A fine clipped Yew.   1873.   III. 288.[1]
R., W.   Girdling trees.   1895.   IV. 385.[1]
R., W.   Hardy Cacti.   1872.   III. 619.
R., W.   Notes on ancient British forests.   1879.   IV. 27.[1]
R., W.   Oak timber.   1873.   IV. 514.[1]
R., W.   The philosophy of clipping trees.   1893.   III. 202.[1]
R., W.   Professor Owen's garden, Sheen Lodge.   1872.   III. 477.[2]
R., W.   Superstitions and facts connected with trees.   1878.   I. 517.[1]
R., W.   Timber.   1873.   IV. 396.[1]
R., W.   Time and planting.   1900.   III. 167.
R., W.   The Weeping Oak at King's Acre.   1874.   III. 363.[1]
R., W.   Whichwood forest.   1878.   IV. 358.[1]
R., W. W.   Advantage of home nurseries to proprietors.   1878.   IV. 150.
R., W. W.   Education of foresters.   1879.   IV. 29.

R., W. W. How many timber varieties of Pinus sylvestris are cultivated in Britain? 1879. IV. 473.
R. . . . Die schottische Zaunrose. 1887. IV. 520.[2]
R—r. Über den Anbau von fremdländischen Holzarten in den österreichischen Staats- und Fondsforsten. 1893. IV. 127.[2]
Raab. Ueber ein neues Solanum [S. littorale]. 1819. II. 776.[1]
Raab, Ferdinand. See MUENZ, Martin & RAAB, Ferdinand.
Raab, R. Bijdrage tot de geschiedenis . . . van de bereiding van papier. 1886. III. 235.[2]
Raatz. Mittheilungen über das Auftreten . . . des Maikäfers. 1891. IV. 203.
Raatz, Wilhelm. Die Stabbildungen im secundären Holzkörper. 1892. I. 126.
— Ueber Thyllenbildungen in den Tracheïden der Coniferenhölzer. 1892. II. 17.[1]
Rabaté, Ed. Essai industriel des gemmes. 1900. IV. 437.[1]
— Répartition des canaux sécréteurs de résine dans le Pin maritime. 1900. II. 871.[2]
Rabbeno, Aronne. Le foreste in Italia; leggi attuali. 1877. IV. 328.
— Legge forestale. 1883. IV. 328; see also PACIFICI-MAZZONI, Emidio & others. 1883. IV. 328.
Rabé. Notice sur les larves qui dévorent les pousses . . . de Pins sylvestres. 1887. IV. 478.
Raben, Friedrich. Beskrifning om löfmasken på Vildapel, Bok och Törne. 1749. III. 188.[1]
Rabenau, Hugo von. Die Gefässkryptogamen, Gymnospermen . . . der . . . Ober-Lausitz. 1874. I. 387.
— Vegetationsskizzen vom unteren Laufe des Hudson. 1887. I. 315.
Rabenhorst, Ludwig. Flora des Königreichs Sachsen. 1859. I. 384.
— Flora lusatica. 1839. I. 380.
— Zur Kenntniss der Krankheit der Maulbeerblätter. 1853. III. 379.[1]
— Populär praktische Botanik. 1843. I. 381.
— Ueber Septoria Mori Léveillé. 1853. III. 379.[1]
Rabot, Charles. Les limites d'altitude des cultures et des essences forestières dans la Scandinavie. 1896. I. 350,[2] IV. 79.[2]
Rabourdin. Lutte contre le phylloxera. 1894. III. 574.
Rabourdin, H. De l'essai des poivres du commerce. 1884. III. 679,[1] 758.[1]
Rabuteau, Antoine Pierre Athanase. De l'influence du café et du cacao. 1870. III. 222, 694, 739.
— Des variations de l'urée sous l'influence de la caféine. 1873. III. 742.[1]
— & Papillon, F. Observations touchant l'action de certaines substances toxiques. 1873. III. 683.[1]
— & Peyre. Recherches sur les effets toxiques du m'boundou. 1870. III. 230,[2] 684.[1]
Raccolta delle circolare dell' azienda generale dell' interno sull' amministrazione de' boschi e selve. 1845. IV. 304.[2]
Raccolta delle leggi forestali. 1866. IV. 328.
Il raccolto delle Arancie nella Florida. 1896. III. 497.[2]
Il raccolto delle carrube a Creta. 1899. III. 472.[1]
Il raccolto delle Castagne. 1894. III. 493.[2] — 1898. IV. 493.[2]
Il raccolto delle olive nella campagna. 1897. III. 679.[2]
Il raccolto delle olive in Italia. 1896. III. 679.[1]
Il raccolto delle sementi forestali in Germania. 1898. IV. 148.
Il raccolto delle ulive nel 1894–95. 1895. III. 679.[1]
Rach, Louis. Die Ericaceen der Thunbergischen Sammlung. 1853. II. 657.[1]
Rach, Ludwig. See REGEL, Eduard von, RACH, Ludwig & HERDER, Ferdinand von.
Rachat de droits d'usage. 1899. IV. 334.[1]
Raciborski, Maryjan. Ueber das Absterben der Djowarbäume. 1898. III. 471.[1]
— Beiträge zur Biologie des Blattes. 1900. I. 233.[1]
— Ueber die Chromatophilie der Embryosackkerne. 1893. I. 137.
— Ein Inhaltskörper des Leptoms. 1898. I. 178.
— Klony polskie. 1889. II. 476.[2]
— O Modrzewiach w Polsce. 1890. II. 32.[2]
— Morphogenetische Versuche. 1900. I. 100.[2]
— Ueber myrmecophile Pflanzen. 1900. II. 55,[1] 537.[1]
— O nieznanym gatunku sosny krajowej. 1891. II. 43.[1]
— Osobliwe formy Modrzewia i Bagna. 1888. II. 32.[2]
— Ueber die Verzweigung. 1900. I. 107.[1]
— Ueber die Vorläuferspitze. 1900. I. 233.[1]
— Weitere Mittheilungen über das Leptonim. 1898. I. 178.
— Zmiany zaszle we florze okolic Krakowa. 1884. I. 443.

Racine. Lettre de Bolivie. 1895. III. 119.[1]
Rackow, H. Die Land- und Forstwirtschaft in unseren Kolonien. 1897. IV. 379.[2]
— Das Schneiden der Kakaobäume. 1898. III. 593.[1]
Raczynski, S. Notice sur la distribution de la salicine. 1866. II. 104.[1]
Rad jugoslavenske akademije. Znanosti. I. 28.[1]
Radais, Maxime. Sur un appareil conducteur dans les graines de quelques Conifères. 1895. II. 20.[1]
— Contribution à l'anatomie comparée du fruit des Conifères. 1894. II. 20.[1]
— Contribution à l'étude de l'anatomie comparée du fruit des Conifères. 1894. II. 20.[1]
— La fleur femelle des Conifères. 1894. II. 20.[1]
Radcliffe, E. A. T. The Bamboo forests . . . of the Jummoo and Kashmere states. 1900. IV. 485.[1]
Dr. Radcliffe's practical dispensatory. See PHARMACOPOEIA Radcliffeana. 1716. III. 251.
Radde, Gustav Johannes. Berichte über die . . . Untersuchungen in den Kaukasusländern. 1866. I. 369.
— Berichte über Reisen im Süden von Ost-Sibirien. 1861. I. 455.
— Grundzüge der Pflanzenverbreitung in den Kaukasusländern. 1899. I. 370.
— Reisen und Forschungen im Kaukasus. 1868. I. 369.
— Versuch einer Pflanzen-Physiognomik Tauriens. 1854. I. 361.
— & others. Die Fauna und Flora des südwestlichen Caspi-Gebietes. 1886. I. 457.
Raddi, Giuseppe. Agrostographia brasiliensis. 1823. II. 58.[1]
— Di alcune specie di Pero indiano. 1821. II. 632.[2]
— Dell' Araucaria del Brasile. 1827. II. 26.[1]
— Catalogo di piante egiziane. 1837. I. 487.
— Enumerazione delle specie di Piper. 182.? II. 93.[2]
— Melastome brasiliane. 1828. II. 634.[2]
— Quaranta piante nuove del Brasile. 1820. I. 341.
Raddin, Charles S. See HIGLEY, W. K. & RADDIN, C. S.
Radeck, (Stadt-Oberförster in Lauban). Beitrag zur Beantwortung der . . . Frage: "Welchen Vortheil hat man von der Entwässerung . . . zu erwarten?" 1844. IV. 143.[2]
Radel, Philippe PETIT-. See PETIT-RADEL, Philippe.
Raden Mas Toemenggoeng Hario Hadio Ningrat. Blimbingcultuur in Demak. 1892. III. 491.[2]
Radermacher, Jakob Cornelis Matthaeus. Beschrijving van het eiland Borneo. 1784. III. 276.[1]
— Beschrijving van het eiland Sumatra. 1787. III. 275.[1]
— Korte beschrijving van het eiland Celebes. 1786. III. 274.[1]
— Naamlyst der planten . . . op het eiland Java. 1780. I. 467.[1]
— & Hogendorp, S. W. C., comte de. Korte schets van de bezittingen der Nederlandsche Oostindische maatschappij, 1781. III. 274.[1]
Radhakant, Deb. On the Bair or Beer tree. 1838. III. 544.[1]
Radiation from trees. 1830. I. 186.
Radics, P. von. Die Entwickelung des Forstwesens in Görz. 1891. IV. 369.
— "Ueber die Fortpflanzung der Wälder." 1888. IV. 142.
— Der Lorbeerhain von Abbazia. 1890. IV. 520.[1]
Rading, Hermann von. Beschreibung . . . des Weinhaues . . . Russlands. 1791. III. 551.[2]
Radisson. Culture . . . de la Badiane. 1899. III. 398.[1]
Radius, Justus. Dissertatio de Pyrola et Chimophila. 1821. II. 657.[2]
Radl, Florian. Dankbar blühende Aristolochien. 1892. III. 385.[2]
— Neue Aloe-Hybriden des Abts Beguin. 1896. III. 333.[1]
— Phyllokakteen. 1896. III. 625.[2]
— & Rosen, Andreas von. Die Vermehrung der Kakteen. 1891. III. 619.
Radlkofer, Ludwig. Sur l'accroissement anormal . . . dans les Ménispermées. 1858. II. 206.[1]
— Anhang zur Monographie der Gattung Serjania. 1874.
— Ueber das anomale Wachsthum . . . bei Menispermeen. 1858. II. 206.[1]
— Sopra un arillo speciale di una Sapindacea. 1878. II. 488.[1]
— Die Befruchtung der Phanerogamen. 1856. I. 201.[1]
— Der Befruchtungsprozess im Pflanzenreiche. 1857. I. 201.[1]
— Ein Beitrag zur africanischen Flora. 1883. I. 483.[1]
— Conspectus . . . generis Serjaniae. 1874. II. 489.[1]

Radlkofer, Ludwig (*continued*).
— Ueber Cupania. 1879. II. 483.[2]
— Ueber das Dickenwachsthum. 1859. I. 190.[1]
— Drei neue Serjania-Arten. 1893. II. 489.[1]
— Drei Pflanzen aus Central-Madagascar. 1884. I. 496.
— Ueber die durchsichtigen Punkte . . . der Connaraceen. 1887. II. 316.[2]
— Ueber einige Capparis-Arten. 1885. II. 230.[2]
— Ueber einige Sapotaceen. 1885. II. 696.[2]
— Ueber die Entstehung der secundären Holzkörper . . . gewisser Sapindaceen. 1877. II. 483.[2]
— Ueber fischvergiftende Pflanzen. 1887. III. 59.[2]
— Sur la fleur des Sapindacées. 1867. II. 483.[2]
— Sopra il fusto anomalo della Serjania piscatoria. 1892. II. 489.[2]
— Ueber die Gliederung der Familie der Sapindaceen. 1890. II. 483.[2]
— Ueber eine von Grisebach unter den Sapotaceen aufgeführte Daphnoideae. 1885. II. 602.[2]
— Zur Klärung von Theophrasta. 1889. II. 691.[1]
— Ueber eine Leptospermee der Sammlung von Sieber. 1884. II. 620.[2]
— Ueber die Methoden in der botanischen Systematik. 1883. I. 252.
— Monographiae generis Serjaniae supplementum. 1875. II. 489.[1]
— Neue Beobachtungen über Pflanzen mit durchsichtig punktirten Blättern. 1887. I. 111.
— New species of Sapindaceae from South America. 1898. II. 483.[1]
— Ueber Nothochilus. 1889. II. 547.[1]
— Paullinia Sapindacearum genus. 1895. II. 488.[1]
— Ueber Pausandra. 1870. II. 448.[2]
— Sapindaceae. 1892. II. 483.[2] — 1896. II. 483.[1] .
— Über die Sapindaceen Hollandisch-Indiens. 1879. II. 483.[1]
— Ueber Sapindus. 1878. II. 483.[1]
— Serjania Sapindacearum genus. 1875. II. 489.[1]
— Ueber den systematischen Werth der Pollenbeschaffenheit bei den Acanthaceen. 1883. II. 796.[1]
— Ueber den systematischen Werth symmetrischen Blüthenbaues bei den Sapindaceen. 1877. II. 483.[1]
— Three new species of Sapindaceae. 1895. II. 489.[1]
— On true parthenogenesis in plants. 1887. I. 202.[1]
— Sopra i varii tipi delle anomalie . . . nelle Sapindaceae. 1875. II. 483.[2]
— Vegetationsverhältnisse [des ostbayerischen Grenzgebietes]. 1863. I. 385.
— Ueber das Verhältniss der Parthenogenesis zu den anderen Fortpflanzungsarten. 1858. I. 202.[1]
— Sur la véritable parthénogénèse des plantes. 1857. I. 202,[1] II. 436.[1]
— Ueber die Versetzung der Gattung Dobinea. 1889. II. 456.[1]
— Ueber wahre Parthenogenesis bei Pflanzen. 1857. I. 202,[1] II. 436.[1]
— Ueber die Zurückführung von Forchhammeria. 1884. II. 233.[1]
— Ueber die Zurückführung von Omphalocarpum. 1882. II. 699.[2]
— Ueber zwei Buddleieen des Herbarium Willdenow. 1884. II. 716.[2]
Radloff, Fredrik Wilhelm. De Myristica moschata. *See* THUNBERG, C. P. 1788. II. 221.[1]
Radošević, M. M. Die Stammpflege. 1895. IV. 169.[2]
Radtke, Richard. Handbuch für den preussischen Förster. 1894. IV. 321.
Radzibor, Karl Wladimir. De nuce vomica. 1837. III. 682.[2]
Rae, Samuel & Co. Prima arborum. 1887. III. 679.[1]
Rääf, Leonard Fredrik. Uppgifter om stora träd och buskar. 1871. I. 296.[1]
Ráde, Károly. A Cissus discolor. 1898. III. 544.[2]
— Diospyros Kaki. 1900. III. 670.[1]
— Der Epheu als Hochstamm. 1899. III. 643.[1]
Raedt van Oldenbarnevelt, A. C. Die Köffiecultuur op Java. 1898. III. 731.
Räthel, J. N. Kurze Darstellung nebst einer vollständigen Tabelle, zur . . . Bestimmung der Geld-Preise. 1802. IV. 221.
Raes, Jean. Culture de l'Oranger. 1898. III. 500.[2]
Raesfeldt, *Freiherr* von. Ein Besuch in Vallombrosa. 1880. IV. 364.
— Ein Fichtenzapfenfrass. 1889. IV. 456.

— Eine forstliche Reise im südöstlichen Frankreich. 1884. IV. 361.
— Forstwirthschaftliche Benützung des Bodens. *See* Die LANDWIRTHSCHAFT im Regierungsbezirk Oberbayern. 1885. IV. 351.[1]
— Der Wald in den Alpen. 1878. IV. 367, 369.
— Der Wald in Niederbayern. 1894. IV. 351.[1]
— Ueber die Waldstreufrage. 1879. IV. 438.[1]
— Über Waldtheilung und Waldgenossenschaften. 1880. IV. 307.[2]
— Wie weit soll sich der Einfluss des Staates auf die Bewirthschaftung der Privatwaldungen erstrecken? 1879. IV. 285.[2]
Raess, Hubert Josef. Zur richtigen Berechnung und Anwendung des Zuwachsprozentes. 1893. IV. 234.
— Die Waldertragsregelung. 1890. IV. 241.
— Waldwegenetz und Waldeintheilung im Gebirge. 1880. IV. 266.[2]
Räuschel, Ernst Adolph. Nomenclator botanicus. 1772. I. 76.[1]
Räs, (*Forstdirektor*). Klimatologische und phaenologische Beobachtungen im Kanton Bern. 1883. I. 227.[1]
— Observations climatologiques et phénologiques. 1883. I. 227.[1]
Rafarin. Araliacées nouvelles. 1876. III. 641.[1]
— Berberidopsis corallina. 1867. III. 614.[1]
— Coloration des feuilles à l'automne. 1873. I. 185.[2]
— Dracaena Goldieana. 1878. III. 336.[2]
— Revue de quelques plantes nouvelles. 1877. III. 87.
— Verschaffeltia splendida. 1869. III. 332.[1]
Raff- und Leseholz- wie auch Waldstreu-Ordnung ' für . . . Schwarzburg-Sondershausen. 1841. IV. 322.[1]
Raffeneau-Delile, Alire. *See* DELILE, Alire Raffeneau.
Raffles. Nachrichten von dem Upas-Baum. 1832. III. 366.[2]
Rafia from West Africa. 1895. III. 330.[1]
Rafinesque-Schmaltz, Constantine Samuel. Account of 32 n. sp. of plants from Florida. 1832. I. 318.
— Alsographia americana. 1838. I. 304.
— American manual of the Grape vines. 1830. II. 505.[1]
— American manual of the Mulberry trees. 1839. II. 154,[1] III. 375.
— Analyse de la nature. 1815. I. 259.
— Annals of nature. 1820. I. 306.
— Autikon botanikon. 1840. I. 307.
— Botany of Kentucky. 1824. I. 318.
— Catalogo delle piante particolari alla Sicilia. *See* ORTOLANI, G. E. & RAFINESQUE-SCHMALZ, C. S. 1810. I. 431.
— Chloris aetnensis. 1813. I. 431.
— Confirmation of the important discovery of the property of sulphur . . . to destroy all insects. 1832. III. 196.
— On the Custard-apples. 1832. II. 216.[2]
— Definizioni delle nuove classi naturali di vegetabili. 1814. I. 259.
— Definizioni di due nuove specie . .'. del genere Brassica. 1814. II. 234.[1]
— Description des plantes trouvées dans les États-Unis d'Amérique. 1808. I. 305.
— Description of a new Cherry tree. 1832. II. 277.[1]
— Description of the Ioxylon pomiferum. 1817. II. 153.[2]
— Descriptions of two new shrubs from Kentucky. 1819. II. 120,[1] 655.[2]
— Sopra due nuovi alberi del Monte Etna. 1814. I. 430.
— An essay on the exotic plants. 1811. I. 306.
— Essential . . . characters of some new genusses. 1808. I. 305.
— Extrait d'une lettre adressée à M. le professeur De Candolle. 1830. I. 306.
— First catalogue . . . of the Botanical garden of Transsylvania university. 1824. I. 38.[2]
— Flora telluriana. 1836. I. 260.
— Florula ludoviciana. 1817. I. 318.
— Florula of the White Mountain. 1817. I. 313.
— Florula texensis. 1832. I. 321.
— The good book and amenities of nature. 1840. I. 307.
— Herbarium Rafinesquianum. 1833. I. 306.
— Index of the Florula mandanensis. 1833. I. 321.
— On the introduction . . . of the Tea-plant. 1818. III. 600.[2]
— Letter on the Date-tree or Palm. 1818. III. 328.[1]
— Medical flora. 1828. III. 62.
— Neogénito esotico. 1814. I. 266.
— Neogenyton. 1825. I. 306.
— Neogenytum Siculum. 1817. II. 102.[2]

— New flora of North America. 1836. I. 306.
— New plants from Bartram's botanic garden. 1832. II. 548.[2]
— New sylva of North America. 1836. I. 304.
— On a new tree of Kentucky. 1824. II. 346.[2]
— Nomenclature synandrique. 1820. I. 116.[1]
— Orospodias corymbosa. 1832. II. 277.[1]
— Pleuradena coccinea. 1832. II. 443.[1]
— Précis [de ses] . . . découvertes et travaux somiologiques. 1814. I. 266.
— Prodrome d'une monographie des Rosiers: 1820. II. 283.[1]
— Prospectus of . . . [his] two intended works on North-American botany. 1808. I. 305.
— Prospectus relatif à deux ouvrages sur la botanique du nord de l'Amérique. 1808. I. 305.
— Remarques botaniques sur quelques plantes de l'Amérique septentrionale. 1833. I. 306.
— Remarques sur les Convolvulacées. 1821. II. 743.[2]
— Remarques sur les rapports naturels des genres Viscum, Samolus et Viburnum. 1820. II. 177,[2] 848.[1]
— Review of Flora Americae septentrionalis. 1817. I. 306.
— Review of The genera of North-American plants. 1818. I. 306.
— Salix or Willows. 1838. II. 99.[1]
— The school of flora. 1827. V. xiii.[2]
— Selection of twenty-four . . . new species of plants. 1832. II. 843.[2]
— On 17 new species of plants from upper Canada. 1832. I. 310.
— Six new Firs of Oregon. 1832. II. 14.[1]
— On some new genera of American plants. 1818. II. 458,[1] 465.[1]
— Specchio delle scienze. See SPECCHIO . . . I. 26.[1]
— Sylva telluriana. 1838. I. 293.[1]
— Tableau analytique des ordres naturels. 1820. I. 259.
— Three decades of undescribed American plants. 1817. I. 306.
— Twenty new genera of plants from the Oregon mountains. 1832. I. 321.
— See also ORTOLANI, G. E. & RAFINESQUE-SCHMALZ, C. S.
Rafn, Carl Gottlob. Danmarks og Holsteens Flora. 1796. I. 352.
— Efterretning om Taxtraet. 1800. II. 10.[3]
— Entwurf einer Pflanzenphysiologie. 1796. I. 148.
— Förtjenster om Skandinaviens flora. See C. G. RAFNS förtjenster om Skandinaviens flora. 1841. II. 100.[1]
— Udkast til en Plantephysiologie. 1796. I. 148.
— Utkast til en växt-physiologie. 1796. I. 148.
Rafn, Johannes. Arter, Varieteter og Kulturformer. 1897. I. 253.[1]
— Etwas über Samenuntersuchungen. 1900. IV. 545.[2]
— Notes on the importance of tree seed-testing. 1900. IV. 147,[2] 545.[2]
Rafter, George W. Data of stream flow in relation to forests. 1899. IV. 52.
Ragionieri, Attilio. La Heterospathe elata Scheff. 1882. III. 325.[2]
Ragský, Frans. Beitrag zur chemischen Untersuchung der Maulbeerblätter. 1849. II. 154.[2]
Rahn, J. H. & others. Bemerkungen von der Würkung der Fieberrinde. 1761. III. 719.
Rahn, L. Ueber phänologische Inversionen. 1882. I. 221.
Raihand L'Ange, Henri. L'Olivier, sa culture. 1861. III. 675.[2]
Railway fuel in the Punjab. 1867. IV. 377.[2]
Raimann, Rudolf. Ueber einige Krankheits-Erscheinungen der Nadelhölzer. 1889. IV. 442.
— Mittheilungen über Fichtenformen. 1888. II. 35.[1]
— Onagraceae. 1893. II. 642.[2]
— Über unverholzte Elemente in der . . . Xylemzone. 1889. I. 126.
— Ueber verschiedene Ausbildungsweisen dicotyler Stämme. 1889. I. 126.
Raine, Thomas. Notice in regard to Macquarie Island. 1824. I. 506.[1]
Rainey, George. An experimental inquiry into the cause of the ascent and descent of the sap. 1847. I. 164.
Rainey, Phinehas. On the dry rot. 1838. IV. 414.[2]
Rainier, Peter. On the removal of the Banyan tree. 1824. III. 371.[1]
Die **Rainweiden** oder Ligustrum-Arten. 1877. III. 673.[1]
Raison, Th. Vente à l'unité de produits. 1886. IV. 326.
Raleigh, Sir Walter. The discoverie of . . . Guiana. 1596. III. 267.[2]
— The discovery of . . . Guiana. 1596. III. 267.[2]

Ralfs, John. The British phænogamous plants. 1839. I. 399, V. xx.[2]
Ralph, Thomas Shearman. On the Coccus affecting the Orange. 1865. III. 500.[2]
— Descriptio itineris plantarum investigationis ergo suscepti in agrum cantianum. See JOHNSON, Thomas. 1632. I. 394.
— Icones carpologicae. 1849. II. 320.[1]
Ram, DAULAT, (Babu). See DAULAT RAM, (Babu).
Ram Bimbhat, DAULAT. See DAULAT RAM BIMBHAT.
Rama Rao, A. R. Gum kino. 1900. III. 485.[2]
Ramage, James L. Trees suitable for various soils. 1884. III. 41.[1]
Ramaley, Francis. Comparative anatomy of hypocotyl and epicotyl. 1899. I. 123.[1]
— Seedlings of certain woody plants. 1899. I. 123.[1]
— On the stem anatomy of certain Onagraceae. 1896. II. 643.[1]
The **Ramanas** Rose. 1876. III. 456.[2]
Ramann, Emil. Der Aschengehalt des Fichtenpollen. 1898. II. 37.[1]
— Der Aschengehalt erfrorener Baumblätter. 1881. I. 155.
— Beschädigung von Kiefern durch Meilerrauch. 1888. IV. 192.[2]
— Ueber Bildung und Kultur des Ortsteins. 1886. IV. 69.
— Chemisch-physikalische Untersuchungen über Waldfeldbau. 1890. IV. 134.[1]
— Effets de la fumée sur les feuilles du Pin. 1888. IV. 192.[2]
— Der Einfluss verschiedener Bodendecken. 1898. IV. 70.
— Die Einwirkung der Streuentnahme auf Sandboden. 1883. IV. 71.
— Die Einwirkung von Wasser auf Buchen- und Eichenstreu. 1888. IV. 72.
— Die Ernährungsverhältnisse vorherrschender, mitherrschender und beherrschter Stämme. 1892. IV. 70, 474.
— Les feuilles comme nourriture de plantes avant leur chute. 1898. I. 180.[1]
— Forstliche Bodenkunde und Standortslehre. 1893. IV. 70.
— Forstliche Standortslehre. 1888. IV. 67.[1]
— Der Harzgehalt des Kiefernholzes. 1894. II. 48.[2]
— Holzwolle und ihre Anwendung für Streuzwecke. 1890. IV. 429.
— Mineralstoff-Bedarf . . . zur Holzerzeugung. 1887. IV. 63.[2]
— Movements of plant-food before the fall of the leaf. 1898. I. 180.[1]
— Ueber den Nachweis von Rauchschäden. 1894. IV. 193.[1]
— Neue Versuche über Verwendung der Holzwolle. 1890. IV. 429.
— Ueber Rauchbeschädigungen. 1896. IV. 193.[1]
— Untersuchung streuberechter Böden. 1898. IV. 72.
— Untersuchungen über den Mineralstoffbedarf der Waldbäume. 1883. IV. 63.[2]
— Die Verwesung der Fichtennadeln. 1894. II. 37.[1]
— Wald und Moor in den russischen Ostseeprovinzen. 1895. IV. 114.
— Die Waldstreu. 1890. IV. 72.
— Waldbeschädigungen durch Flusssäure. 1893. IV. 192.[2]
— Wandern die Nährstoffe beim Absterben der Blätter? 1898. I. 180.[1]
— Der Wassergehalt der Waldböden. 1895. IV. 73.[2]
— Der Wassergehalt streuberechter Flächen. 1890. IV. 72.
— Die Wirkung der Streuentnahme auf Sandboden. 1887. IV. 71.
— Die Zeit des Abfalles der Fichtenstreu. 1888. II. 36.[2]
— See also SCHAUER, Paul & RAMANN, Emil.
— von. Holzfütterung und Reisigfütterung. 1890. III. 223.[2]
— & JENA-CÖTHEN, von. Holzfütterung und Reisigfütterung. 1890. III. 223.[2]
— & KALITSCH, von. Die Anwendung der Holzwolle als Streumaterial. 1889. IV. 429.
— & WILL, Heinrich. Beiträge zur Statik des Waldbaues. 1881. I. 155, IV. 60,[2] 63.[2]
— & others. Anzahl und Bedeutung der niederen Organismen in Wald- und Moorböden. 1899. IV. 70.
Ramann, G. Das Herbarium. 1871. I. 35.
Rambaldi, Angelo. Ambrosia arabica. 1691. III. 738.
Rambert, Eugène. Les Alpes suisses. 1866. I. 435.
Rambosson, Jean Pierre. Histoire et légendes des plantes. 1868. I. 95.
Rambousek, K. Pěstování Vrby košíkářské. 1883. III. 348.
Ramdohr, Ludwig. Feuerungskunde. 1887. IV. 413.[1]

Ramé, A. Les insectes nuisibles aux arbres fruitiers. 1890. III. 191.
— Les insectes utiles et . . . nuisibles. 1888. III. 190.
— Les Lithocolletis. 1889. III. 191.
— Note sur des ennemis du Buxus. 1890. III. 523.[1]
Le Rameau de Sapin. IV. 13.[2]
Rameaux, J. F. Des températures végétales. 1843. I. 186.
De Rameh. 1883. III. 382.[1]
Ramel, Prosper. Des Eucalyptus. 1864. IV. 531.[1]
— Les Eucalyptus en Australie. 1875. IV. 529.[1]
— L'Eucalyptus Globulus. 1862. II. 624.[2]
— L'Eucalyptus Globulus de Tasmanie. 1861. II. 624.[2] — 1862. III. 634.[2]
Ramey, J. C. Manuel d'horticulture et d'agriculture. 1849. III. 113.
— Traité élémentaire de la taille des arbres. 1846. III. 172.
Ramie as food for silkworms. 1890. III. 382.[1]
Ramie or Rhea. 1888. III. 382.[1]
Ramie Rhea, China grass. 1894. III. 382.[2]
Ramires, Ad. Baptista. O parasitismo das grandes plantas lenhosas. 1899. III. 179.
— O parasitismo no sobreiro. 1899. III. 179.
Ramirez, José. Sobre algunas excursiones á las Montañas del Ajusco. 1895. I. 332.
— Datos para el estudio de los Cuajiotes. 1896. II. 416.[2]
— Una especie nueva de Erythroxylon. 1897. II. 394.[2]
— Una especie nueva de Pterostemon. 1894. II. 243.[1]
— Una especie nueva de Stirax de México. 1899. II. 705.[1]
— Lista de las plantas recogidas . . . à las Mixtecas. 1893. I. 332.
— La Mocinna heterophylla. 1894. II. 582.[1]
— Una nueva especie de Casimiroa. 1896. II. 400.[2]
— Otros datos para la historia de las " semillas brincadoras." 1897. II. 451.[2]
— Tres monstruosidades en ovarios inferos. 1897. II. 588.[2]
— La vegetación de México. 1899. I. 333.
— See also Altamirano, Fernando & Ramirez, José.
— & others. Datos para la materia médica mexicana. 1894. III. 265.[1]
Ramirez, José Antonio de Alzate y. See Alzate y Ramirez, José Antonio de.
Ramirez, Ricardo. Legislación acerca de los bosques. 1897. IV. 315.[1]
Ramm, S. Ueber die Frage der Anwendbarkeit von Düngung im forstlichen Betriebe. 1893. IV. 144.[2]
Ramme, Gustav. Die wichtigsten Schutzeinrichtungen der Vegetationsorgane der Pflanzen. 1895. I. 235.[2]
Rammelsberg, D. C. On the inorganic substances in . . . plants. 1847. I. 152.[2]
— Ueber die Vertheilung der unorganischen Stoffe in . . . -Pflanzen. 1847. I. 152.[2]
Rammlow, J. C. Etwas über den Lhou-Maulbeerbaum. 1853. III. 376.
— Seidenzucht und Maulbeerbaum. 1840. III. 376.
Ramon de la Sagra. See Sagra, Ramon de la.
Ramond, baron. See Ramond de Carbonnières, L. F. E., baron.
Ramond, A. Sur une floraison estivale du Lilas. 1877. II. 716.[1]
Ramond de Carbonnières, Louis François Elisabeth, baron. État de la végétation au sommet du Pic du Midi. 1825. I. 407.
— Mémoire sur . . . la végétation au sommet du Pic du Midi. 1827. II. 109.[2]
— Observations faites dans les Pyrénées. 1789. I. 406.
— Plantes in édites des Hautes-Pyrénées. 1800. II. 606.[2]
— De la végétation sur les montagnes. 1804. I. 219.[2]
— Voyages au Mont-Perdu. 1801. I. 406.
Ramos, Emilio. Indices de las disposiciones contenidas en la legislación de montes. 1887. IV. 327.
— Legislación de montes. 1887. IV. 327.
Ramos, José Édouard. Apuntes botanicos sobre . . . " Cola." 1882. III. 590.[1]
— Historia del Uredo cocivoro. 1882. III. 323.[1]
— Importancia del estudio de la botánica médica. 1867. III. 238.[1]
— Informe sobre la enfermedad de los Cocoteros. 1890. III. 323.[2]
— Necesidad de un plan para estudiar . . . la flora medica é industrial. 1889. III. 84.[1]
— Patalogia vegetal. [La enfermedad de las Palmeras.] 1887. III. 318.[1]
— Teratalogia vegetal. 1894. II. 292.[2]
Rampon, Calixte. Les ennemis de l'agriculture. 1898. III. 191.
Rampon, Eugène. Note sur une nouvelle espèce de Tacsonia. 1855. II. 581.[1]
Ramsay, James. On the vascular flora of the west of Scotland. 1876. I. 403.
Ramsay, R. B. Wardlaw. On an Ivy tree blown down. 1883. III. 642.[1]
Ramsay, W. Het trekken van Guttapercha. 1898. II. 699.[2]
Ramsay, William. On the antiseptic power of pyroligneous acid. 1820. IV. 432.[1]
Ramspacher. See Müntz, A. & Ramspacher.
Ramspeck, Jakob Christoph. Selectarum observationum . . . specimen. 1751. I. 291.
Ramstedt. See Pahnsteen.
Ramus. Sur la greffe des Cactées. 1869. III. 619.
Ramus, Jonas. Norriges Beskrivelse. 1715. I. 351.
Ramusio, Giovanni Battista. Delle navigationi et viaggi. 1563. I. 301, 531.[1]
Rand, Edward Lothrop. Pinus Banksiana on Mt. Desert Island. 1899. II. 41.[1]
— Pinus Banksiana on the coast of Maine. 1889. II. 40.[2]
— Pinus Banksiana on the Maine coast. 1889. II. 40.[1]
— Salix balsamifera. 1893. II. 105.[2]
— & Redfield, J. H. Flora of Mount Desert Island. 1894. I. 316.
Rand, Edward Sprague, (jr). Calluna vulgaris, a native of the United States. 1862. II. 661.[2]
— Fruits of the Amazon. 1885. III. 269.[1]
— Garden flowers, how to cultivate them. 1866. III. 63.[1]
— A garden in Para. 1884. III. 119.[1]
— The Rhododendron and American plants. 1871. III. 206,[1] 655.
— Rhododendron experience. 1869. III. 656.
Rand, Isaac. A catalogue of fifty plants from Chelsea garden. 1726. I. 52.
— Horti medici chelseiani, index. 1739. I. 52.
— Index plantarum officinalium. 1730. I. 52.
Random notes on natural history. I. 6.
Randrup, A. S. Nogle Inden . . . Iagttagelser, Forstvæsenet-angaaende. 1803. IV. 100.[2]
Ranfft, Frans Anton. Catalogus horti botanici in Universitate salisburgensi. 178 . ? I. 65.[2]
Ueber die Rangordnung der Buche, Weisstanne. 1858. IV. 139.[1]
Ranieri, Pini. Delle condizioni . . . alle colture forzate delle frutta. 1887. III. 145.[2]
Rank, Albert. Beitrag zum Bau der Solanaceen-Blätter. 1883. II. 574.[2]
Ranke, Wilhelm. Der Geldwerth der Forstbereehtigungen. 1855. IV. 333.
Ranouw, W. van. Kabinet der natuurlijke historien. 1721. I. 290.
Ransom, Arthur. On the office of trees in the economy of nature. 1884. IV. 44, 270.
Ransom, Leander. Marks on a blazed tree. 1863. I. 210.[1]
Ransome, Allen. Timber. 1887. IV. 396.[2]
Ransome, James Stafford. How to select wood-working machinery. 189 .? IV. 422.[1]
Ransome, L. H. The conversion of timber. 1887. IV. 403.[1]
Ransome's patent steam tree-feller. 1878. IV. 383.[2]
Ransonnet-Villez, Eugen von. Ceylon; Skizzen . . . des Pflanzenlebens. 1868. I. 476.[2]
— Sketches of the . . . vegetation . . . of Ceylon. 1868. I. 476.[2]
Rantaniemi, P. A. Anmärkningsvärda växter från Kemi. 1900. II. 101.[1]
Rantonnet. Acacia longissima glauca pendula. 1866. III. 465.[2]
— Coronilla pentaphylla. 1867. III. 473.[2]
— Euphorbia dendroides. 1869. III. 517.[2]
— Polygala cordata atropurpurea. 1867. III. 514.[1]
— Solanum acanthocarpum. 1867. III. 701.[2]
— Solanum anthropophagum. 1867. III. 702.[1]
— Solanum reclinatum. 1867. III. 701.[2]
Rantonnet, Victor. Note et liste de divers végétaux . . . acclimatés à Hyères. 1829. I. 57.
Ranwez, F. Falsification de la poudre de muscade. 1900. III. 403.[1]
— See also Planken, Joseph van der & Ranwez, F.
Rao, N. Narayen. See N. Narayen Rao.
Raoul, (abbé). Manuel pratique d'arboriculture. 1863. III. 144.
Raoul, Édouard F. A. Choix de plantes de la Nouvelle-Zélande. 1844. I. 506.[2]
— Culture du Caféier. 1894. III. 727.
— Les gages nécessaires. 1885. III. 91.[2]

Rapin, Daniel. Deux nouvelles espèces de Rose. 1875. II. 287.[1]
— Le guide du botaniste . . . Vaud. 1842. I. 434.
— Note sur les Rosiers du bassin du Léman. 1856. II. 286.[3]
Rapin, René. Of gardens. 1665. III. 99.
— Hortorum libri IV. 1665. III. 98.
— Les jardins. 1665. III. 99.
Rapp, A. Flora der Umgebung Lemsals und Laudohns. 1895· I. 366.
Rapport à Monsieur le gouverneur général sur les études de botanique agricole. 1893. III. 130.[2]
Rapport adressé à M. le Ministre de l'agriculture . . . l'étude de la nouvelle maladie de la Vigne. 1871. III. 564.[3]
Rapport annuel de l'administration forestière de la ville royale de Pisek. 1899. IV. 373.
Rapport au Président . . . décret chargeant l'Administration des forêts de l'étude des projets . . . des travaux d'utilisation agricole. 1897. IV. 293.[1]
Rapport au Président . . . et décret relatif aux fonctionnaires admis à faire valoir leurs droits à la retraite. 1897. IV. 293.[1]
Rapport au Président . . . relatif à la protection des forêts autour de Brazzaville. 1900. IV. 295.[2]
Rapport betreffende het onderzoek van verdacht Steranijs. 1880. III. 397.[2]
Rapport d'experts sur demandes en dommages contre Henry Merle & Cie. See Roux, J. A., Pagès, Hippolyte & Béchamp, Antoine. 1872. IV. 192.[1]
Rapport de la commission chargée de rechercher les meilleurs moyens d'arrêter les ravages . . . dans les pineraies de la Campine. 1891. IV. 461.[3]
Rapport de la commission d'inspection forestière. 1884. IV. 291.[2]
Rapport de la commission instituée pour l'expérimentation du procédé d'écorçage des bois par la chaleur. See Durand, Léon. 1878. IV. 434.
Rapport der Staatscommissie voor de gouvernements Koffie-cultuur. 1890. III. 730.
Rapport fait . . . concernant le service des forêts. 1835. IV. 261.[3]
Rapport omtrent de werkzaamheden verricht aan het botanisch laboratorium der Kina onderneming. 1896. III. 724.[1]
Rapport . . . omtrent . . . woeste gronden in Drenthe. 1900. IV. 70.
Rapport over het Haagsche bosch. 1878. IV. 356.[3]
Rapport . . . 1°. L'état et le succès de diverses plantations. See Beugon, Meschiny & Noirot. 1808. IV. 121.
Rapport présenté à l'Association bretonne sur l'établissement d'un jardin fruitier. See Arnoult, Georges. 1875. I. 59.
Rapport présenté au Conseil général de la Dordogne. . 1878. III. 760.
Rapport sur l'écorçage par la vapeur. 1877. IV. 434.
Rapport sur l'état du Jardin botanique de Buitenzorg. See Scheffer, R. H. C. C. 1879. I. 68.[1]
Rapport sur la culture d'Arbres à gutta-percha . . . à Tjipetir. 1899. III. 149.
Rapport sur le phylloxera en Hongrie. 1881. III. 572.
Rapport sur le reboisement . . . . de la Corse. See Suzzoni & others. 1860. V ꭓꭓꭓ¹
Rapport sur le reboisement des montagnes. See Legrand, Victor. 1848. IV. 161.[2]
Rapport sur les cultures fruitières et . . . de l'Olivier. See Bourde, Paul. 1893. III. 676.[2]
Rapport sur les forêts de l'état. 1860. IV. 292; see also Forcade, de. 1860. IV. 360.
Rapport sur les procédés de guérison appliqués au mas de Las Sorres. 1874. III. 769.
Rapport sur les quinquinas employés en pharmacie. 1880. III. 721.
Rapport sur un mémoire de M. Devèze de Chabriol, relatif au repeuplement. See Bosc, L. A. G. 1842. IV. 161.[2]
Rapport van den directeur van Binnenlandsch bestuur over de gouvernements Koffiecultuur. 1892. III. 730.
Rapport van den Gouverneur generaal over de gouvernements Koffiecultuur. 1892. III. 730.
Rapport van het departementaal bestuur . . . wegens de duinen. 1805. IV. 159.
Rapporten over Koffie, op Java uit Mokkazaad geteeld. 1873. III. 729.[1]
Rapporto al Consiglio federale sulla economia forestale nella Svizzera. See Bericht an den Bundesrath über das Forstwesen in der Schweiz. 1856. IV. 365.

Il rapporto dell' ufficio centrale del Senato intorno alla legge della malaria. 1882. IV. 328.·
Rapporto della Commissione per studiare la malattia degli Agrumi di Sicilia. 1868. III. 498.[1]
Rapporto sulla situazione dell' Impero francese. 1865. IV. 360.
Rapports sur les productions agricoles des États-Unis. 1889. III. 262.[3]
Rare or interesting plants now in bloom at Kew. 1866. III. 82.
Rasch, Gustav & Köhler, K. Forst- und Jagdbuch. 1858. IV, 98.[1]
Ueber rasches Wachstum der Fichte. 1855. IV. 453.
Raschig, C. G. Der Fruchtgarten. 1833· III. 71.
Raschig, M. Obstbaumzucht im Kleinen und Grossen. 1827. III. 136.
Rasciotti, Donato. Copia del fiore a frutto che nasce nelle Indie orientali. 1609. I. 470.[2]
Raseau, de. See Beauvais. See Beauvais Raseau, de.
Rashefski, P. I. See Рашевскій, П. И.
Rasmussen, J. Om Beplantning af Jyllands Heder. 1862. IV. 156.[1]
Rasmussen, P. V. Clematis indivisa lobata. 1893. III. 390.[3]
— Formering af Blodbøgen ved Frø. 1892. III. 360.[2]
— & Helweg, L. Findes de flere Sorter af Taxus hibernica? 1896. III. 288.[1]
Rasmussen-Søkilde, N. Mere om Plantning af Baandpil. 1875. III. 347.
— Et par Ord om Hegn. 1873. III. 213.
Raspail, François Vincent. Mémoire concernant l'ouverture que Grew a décrite le premier sur le test des graines. 1827. I. 120.
— Nouveau système de chimie organique. 1833· I. 151.[3]
— Nouveau système de physiologie végétale. 1837. I. 87.
— Nouvelles observations sur les cristaux calcaires. 1828. II. 57.[1]
— Observations . . . à démontrer que les granules . . . du grain de pollen . . . ne sont pas des membres des corps organisés. 1828. I. 201.[1]
— Recherches chimiques et physiologiques. 1827. I. 146.
Raspail, Xavier. Observations complémentaires sur . . hanneton. 1896. IV. 203.
— La protection des oiseaux utiles. 1894. IV. 90.[2]
A Raspberry-Blackberry. 1897. III. 458.[1]
Rasper, Eugen. Caryopteris Mastacanthus Schauer. 1899. III. 695.[2]
Rassl, Gustav. Ueber die Anwendung der Körbchencultur. 1897. IV. 153.[1]
— Zur Bewaldung Südtirols. 1897. IV. 369.
— Ueber Forstcultur im Hochgebirge. 1893. IV. 142.
— Ueber Pflanzenverschulung. 1897. IV. 151.[2]
Rassmann, C. Einige Worte über das forstliche Ausästen. 1845. IV. 170.
— Lohrinde vom Saalweiden. 1826. III. 351.[2]
Rassmann, W. C. C. Bemerkungen und Erfahrungen im praktischen Forstwesen. 1830. IV. 171.
— Grundriss der Vorbereitungs-Wissenschaften für das Forstwesen. 1827. IV. 56.
— Tabellarische Übersicht . . . aller inländischen Holzpflanzen. 1827. IV. 82.
Rast-Maupas, See Baudrillart, J. J. & Rast-Maupas.
Rasteiro, Joaquim. Um insecto das Oliveiras. 1900. III. 678.[1]
Rastoin, Édouard. Lettre d'un frère à sa sœur sur la botanique. 1829. I. 86.
Raszl, Gustav. Zirbensaat im Saatbeete. 1888. IV. 463.[2]
Ratchinski, A. See Рачинскій, А.
Ratchinsky, S. Notice sur quelques mouvements. 1857. I. 195.[1]
— See also Рачинскій, С.
Rate of growth of indigenous forest trees. 1897. IV. 65.[1]
Rath, von. Das Verhalten der Koniferen meiner Sammlung nach dem bösen Winter 1879/80. 1880. III. 46.[1]
Ráthay, Emerich. Ueber das Auftreten von Gummi in der Rebe. 1896. III. 562.[1]
— Die Blattgallen der Rebe. 1889. III. 564.[1]
— Die californische Rebenkrankheit. 1893. III. 581.
— Über die von Exoascus-Arten hervorgerufene Degeneration. 1878. III. 431.[1]
— Über den "Frass" von Helix hortensis auf Baumrinden. 1898. III. 191.
— Die Gabler- oder Zwiewipflerreben. 1882. II. 507,[1] III. 561.

Ráthay, Emerich (*continued*).
— Ueber die Geschlechtsverhältnisse der Reben. 1887. II. 507.[1]
— Über die Hexenbesen der Kirschbäume. 1881. III. 435.[1]
— Über eine merkwürdige, durch den Blitz an Vitis vinifera hervorgerufene Erscheinung. 1891. III. 561.
— Ueber myrmecophile Eichengallen. 1891. I. 235.[2]
— Ueber die in Nieder-Oesterreich als Gabler . . . bekannten Reben. 1883. III. 558.[2]
— Die Peronospora-Krankheit der Weinrebe. 1887. III. 579.
— Vorläufige Mittheilung über die Hexenbesen der Kirschbäume. 1880. III. 435.[1]
Rathke, Jens. Enumeratio plantarum horti botanici Universitatis . . , christianiensis. 1823. I. 40.
Rathlef, E. L. Akridotheologie. 1748. III. 188.[1]
Rathoff, (*Stadtförster*). In welcher Weise sorgt der junge Forstmann der niederen Laufbahn am besten für seine Fortbildung? 1890. IV. 33.[2]
Rathouis, C. Étude sur le Coccus pé-la. 1880. III. 226.[1]
Rathvon, S. S. Entomology. 1862. III. 186.[2]
Rational forest policy for the forested lands of the United States. 1896. IV. 272.
Ratkof, A. P. *See* PATKOFF, A. II.
Rattan, Volney. A popular California flora. 1879. I. 324.
— A popular flora. 1879. I. 324.
Ratti, Annibale. Monografia del Gelso. 1848. III. 376.
Rattke, Wilhelm. Die Verbreitung der Pflanzen. 1884. I. 388.
Rattray, James. A botanical chart. 1835. I. 255.
Rattray, John & Mill, H. R. Forestry and forest products. 1885. IV. 102.
Ratzeburg, Julius Theodor Christian. Abfälle an Kiefern. 1871. IV. 461.[1]
— Anfrage ob Ueberwallung abgehauener Tannen . . . nur an verwachsenen vorkommt. 1860. I. 209.[2]
— Aufforderung zur ferneren Beobachtung der überwallten Stöcke. 1860. IV. 66.[1]
— Aufforderungen, die Naturgeschichte des Knieholzes . . . zu verfolgen. 1843. IV. 464.[2]
— Betrachtungen über den Gang des Todes an absterbenden Bäumen. 1871. I. 206.[2]
— Eichen-Beschädigung durch Schildläuse. 1870. IV. 509.
— Das Ergrünen der Rothbuche. 1871. II. 126.[2]
— Ueber die Esche und den Eschenborken-Käfer. 1870. IV. 535.[1]
— Ein Fall von ungewöhnlicher Verbreitung des Rüstern-Borkenkäfers. 1871. III. 364.[1]
— Die Fichten-Stockverwallung. 1871. I. 209.[2]
— Die Forst-Insecten. 1839. IV. 91.[2]
— Forstinsekten. 1853. IV. 206.
— Das forstliche Verhalten der Kiefer nach dem Eulenfrass. 1863. IV. 476.
— Forstnaturwissenschaftliche Reisen. 1842. IV. 348.[2]
— Forstwissenschaftliches Schriftsteller-Lexikon. 1872. IV.1.
— Ueber Frost und Insektenfrass. 1866. IV. 195.[2]
— Ueber geographische Verbreitung . . . der Maikäfer. 1843. IV. 202.
— Die Ichneumonen der Forstinsekten. 1844. IV. 92.
— Kiefern-Keimlinge des Jahres 1868. 1870. IV. 476.
— Ueber Leben und Bedeutung der Ichneumonen. 1846. IV. 92.
— Die Linden am Schlossberge bei Freienwalde. 1869. II. 516.[2]
— Mittheilungen über verschiedene forstnaturwissenschaftliche Gegenstände. 1843. IV. 202, 464.[2]
— Die Nachkrankheiten und die Reproduction der Kiefer nach dem Frass der Forleule. 1862. II. 373.[1]
— Neue Beobachtungen über den Frass der Nonne. 1870. IV. 200.
— Neue Beobachtungen über Doppelringe. 1869. I. 127.[2]
— Neue, die Forleule . . . betreffende Erfahrungen. 1870. IV. 207.
— Observationes ad peloriarum indolem definiendam. 1825. II. 764.[2]
— Eine Pflanzenschule für Forstinsecten. 1871. IV. 476.
— Zur Reproduction der Esche. 1873. IV. 535.[1]
— Reproduktion junger, vom Feuer zerstörter Kiefern. 1857. IV. 475.
— Reproduktions-Erscheinungen an unsern Waldbäumen. 1869. IV. 65.[2]
— Rinden- und Holzkrankheiten von Esche. 1871. IV. 535.[1]

— Ueber die Saftbewegung in der Hainbuche. 1861. I. 164, *II. 181.*[1].
— Die Schlangenkiefer (Pinus silvestris var. tortuosa). 1864. II. 46.[2]
— Ueber die Schmarotzer, welche sich in Ostpreussen bei der Beendigung des Borkenkäferfrasses betheiligten. 1860. IV. 204.
— Sind die Beispiele von geringelten Bäumen, welche auffallend viele Früchte ansetzen, häufig? 1866. IV. 65.[2]
— Die Standortsgewächse und Unkräuter Deutschlands. 1859. I. 384.
— Untersuchungen über Formen und Zahlenverhältnisse der Naturkörper. 1829. I. 98.
— Ueber Verdoppelung des Jahrringes. 1871. I. 127,[2] *IV. 68.*[2]
— Die verschiedenen Arten der Rüster. 1844. II. 142.[2]
— Die Waldverderber und ihre Feinde. 1841. IV. 91.[2]
— Die Waldverderber und ihre Feinde; ein Handbuch für Forstmänner. 1841. IV. 92.
— Die Waldverderbniss. 1866. IV. 195.[2]
— Wirkung von Spätfrösten auf Acer platanoides. 1871. II. 479.[1]
— *See also* BRANDT, J. F. & RATZEBURG, J. T. C.; WEINSCHENK, J. M. & RATZEBURG, J. T. C.
— & Karsten, Hermann. Weitere Nachrichten über die Breitnadeltriebe oder Rosetten der Kiefer. 1865. II. 47.[2]
Ratzell, (*Amtsgerichtsrath*). Die Änderung des bisherigen Rechtszustandes durch das Forstdiebstahlsgesetz. 1880. IV. 321.
Ratzka, Vitus. Das Ausästen der Waldbäume. 1874. IV. 171.
— Das Schneideln als Baumcultur. 1859. IV. 172.[2]
Ratzlow, C. L. Kurze Anweisung den Cubikinhalt runder Baumstämme zu berechnen. 1856. IV. 223.
Rau, Ambrosius. Enumeratio Rosarum circa Wirceburgum. 1816. II. 284.[1]
Rauch, F. A. Régénération de la nature végétale. 1818. IV. 42.[2]
Rauch, Julius. Holzstöckel-Pflaster. 1878. IV. 425.[2]
Rauchfuss, Johann Karl Friedrich. De Ledi palustris natura. *See* GRUNER, C. G. 1793. III. 653.[1]
Zur **Rauchschadenfrage**. 1899. IV. 193.[1]
Raudot. De la liberté des défrichements. 1852. IV. 275.
Rauhut & Witte. Untersuchungen über den Zuwachs mit Fichten unterbauter Eichen. 1884. IV. 507.
Raulin. *See* CROLAS & RAULIN.
Raulin, Jules. Études chimiques sur la végétation. 1872. I. 159.
— De l'influence de la nature des terrains. 1891. I. 229.
Raulin, Victor. Description physique de l'ile de Crète. 1858. I. 452.
— Essai d'une division de la France en régions naturelles et botaniques. 1852. I. 411.
Rauner, St. *See* PAYHEPЪ, CT.
Raunkiær, Christen. Cellekjaernekrystalloider hos Stylidium. 1888. IV. 792.[2]
— Dansk Exkursions-Flora. 1890. I. 357.
— Vesterhavets Øst- og Sydkysta Vegetation. 1889. I. 357.
Rausch, Julius. Aufgelassene Fichtensaatkämpe. 1888. IV. 151.[1]
— Die Bewirthschaftung des Schutzwaldes am Rennsteige. 1883. IV. 355.[2]
— Die forstgerechte Eintheilung des Wintersteiner Forstes. 1891. IV. 26.
— Hilfstafeln zur Ermittlung des Massengehaltes von Blochen. 1875. IV. 227.
— Der Ursprung des Massenfachwerks. 1889. IV. 24,[1] *131.*
Rauschenberg, A. S. The action of certain drugs on the Sensitive plant. 1884. II. 373.[1]
Rauscher, Haselfichte. 1854. II. 34.[1]
Rauscher, Paul. Beschreibung des Holzverkohlungs-Betriebes. 1873. IV. 394.
Rauser Zdenêk, Josef. Lesnictví v Srbsku. 1890. IV. 375.[1]
— Lesy poloostrova Athonského. 1890. IV. 375.[1]
Rautenbach, (*Soest*). Beobachtungen und Erfahrungen bei der Blumenkultur. 1832. III. 412.[1]
— Blaue Hortensien. 1832. III. 412.[1]
— Gekrönte Beantwortung der Preisfrage: Lassen sich Abänderungen in der Farbe der Blumen dadurch hervorbringen. 1832. I. 245.
Rauter, Joseph. Zur Entwicklungsgeschichte einiger Trichomgebilde. 1871. I. 112.[2]
Rauwenhoff, N. W. P. De anatomische zamenstelling der schors van Robinia. 1860. II. 382.[2]

— De beschouwingen van Dr. H. de Vries over de rol van melksap. 1879. I. 147.
— Bijdrage tot de kennis van Dracaena Draco. 1863. II. 82.[1]
— De bosschen en hun invloed. 1858. IV. 43.
— Sur les causes des formes anormales des plantes qui croissent dans l'obscurité. 1877. III. 181.[1]
— Eenige opmerkingen over zickten van planten. 1882. III. 179.
— Het melksap der planten. 1859. · I. 135.
— Observations sur les caractères . . . du liège. 1869. I. 130.
— Onderzoek naar de betrekking der groene plantendeelene tot de zuurstof. 1853. I. 172.
— Over de oorzaken der abnormale vormen van in het donker groeiende planten. 1877. III. 181.[1]
— Phyto-physiologische bijdragen. 1868. I. 164.
— Twee domein-bosschen in Nederland. 1861. IV. 356.[2]
— Het verband tusschen de verdamping en de opneming van water. 1869. I. 167.
— Het vermogen van het hout om vocht door te laten. 1869. I. 164.
— De wortles der planten. 1863. I. 161.
— See also OUDEMANS, A. C. & RAUWENHOFF, N. W. P.
— & others. De natuurkundige grondslagen van den landbouw. 1856. III. 36.[1]
Rauwerda, A. Bijdrage tot nadere kennis van cytisine. 1900. II. 322.[1]
— Voortgezette onderzoekingen over het . . . cytisine. 1897. II. 322.[2]
— See also PLUGGE, P. C. & RAUWERDA, A.
Rauwolf, Leonhart. Aigentliche beschreibung der Raiss . . . gegen Auffgang inn die Morgenländer. 1582. I. 477.[1]
— Seer aenmerkelyke reysen na en door Syrien. 1582. I.478.
— Travels into the eastern countries. 1582. I. 478.
Ravages des insectes; coupe des bois en sève. See INSEKTENFRASS und Saft-Hieb. 1858. IV. 384.[2]
The ravages of Liparis Monacha. 1891. IV. 200.
Ravanel. Note sur les acariens du Poirier. 1886. III. 446.[1]
Ravaud, (abbé). L'herborisation à la Moucherolle. 1875. I. 414.
• Ravaz. See NANOT, J., VIALA & RAVAZ.
Ravaz, L. Sur une maladie de la Vigne. 1894. III. 581.
— Recherches sur le bouturage de la Vigne. 1890. III. 548.[2]
— See also FOËX, Gustave & RAVAZ, L.; VIALA, Pierre & RAVAZ, L.
— & Bonnet, A. Sur le parasitisme du Phoma reniformis. 1900. III. 582.
— & Gouirand, G. Action de quelques substances sur la germination des spores du black-rot. 1896. III. 581.
Rave, Antonio. Influencia de la luz sobre la vegetacion. 1879. IV. 67.[2]
Rave, Eugenio PLÁ Y. See PLÁ Y RAVE, Eugenio.
Ravenel, Henry William. A catalogue of the natural orders of plants . . . of the Santee Canal, S. C. 1850. I. 318.
— Gordonia pubescens. 1881. II. 548.[2]
— Large Grape-vines. 1882. II. 506.[1]
— A list of the . . . plants of South Carolina. 1883. I. 319.
— Native locality for Robinia viscosa. 1886. II. 383.[1]
— Notice of some new . . . plants. 1856. II. 42.[1]
— Paper on Grapes. 1859. III. 546.
— Peach culture. 1867. III. 441.[1]
— Yellow pine. 1877. IV. 467.[1]
Ravenscroft, B. C. Town gardening. 1883. III. 42.[2]
Ravenscroft, Edward. The pinetum britannicum. 1884. II. 13,[1] V. xxv.[1]
Ravenshaw, Thomas Fitzarthur Torin. A new list of the flowering plants . . . of Devon. 1860. I. 401, V. xxi.[1]
Raveret-Wattel, Casimir. Conséquences du déboisement. 1875. IV. 48.[2]
— L'Eucalyptus. 1871. IV. 529.[2]
— Nota sobre a vegetação, producto . . . d'alguns Eucalyptos. 1877. IV. 531.[2]
— Note sur la végétation, les produits . . . de quelques Eucalyptus. 1877. IV. 531.[2]
— De quelques végétaux australiens. 1873. III. 130.[1]
Ravin, Eugène. Catalogue méthodique et raisonné des plantes. . . . de l'Yonne. 1860. I. 412.
— Découvertes botaniques dans l'Yonne. 1899. I. 418.
— Flore de l'Yonne. 1860. I. 412.
Ravius, Christian. De Dudaim Rubenis. 1656. I. 512.
Ravn, Frederik Kölpin. Om Anatomien af Viscum articulatum. 1897. II. 180.[1]
— Sur l'existence de " cystolithes rudimentaires." 1897. II. 173.[2]

Rawle, Edwin John. Annals of the ancient royal forest of Exmoor. 1893. IV. 27.[1]
Raws, (Dr.). The Tallow tree. 1848. III. 522.[1]
Rawson-Walker, E. H. See WALKER, E. H. RAWSON-.
Ray, John. Catalogus plantarum Angliae. 1670. I. 394.
— Catalogus plantarum circa Cantabrigam. 1660. I. 394.
— Catalogus stirpium in exteris regionibus. 1673. I. 348.[1]
— A collection of curious travels and voyages. 1653. I. 301.
— Fasciculus stirpium britannicarum. 1688. I. 394.
— Historia plantarum. 1686. I. 288.
— Index plantarum agri cantabrigiensis. 1660. I. 394.
— Methodus plantarum. 1682. I. 287.
— Observations topographical . . . made in a journey through part of the low-countries. 1673. I. 348.[1]
— Philosophical letters. 1718. I. 31.
— Select remains. 1760. I. 520.[2]
— Stirpium europaearum extra Britannias nascentium sylloge. 1694. I. 348.[1]
— Stirpium orientalium rariorum catalogi tres. 1738. I. 478.
— Synopsis methodica stirpium britannicarum. 1690. I. 394.
— Travels through the low countries. 1673. I. 348.[1]
— De variis plantarum methodis. 1696. I. 250.
— The wisdom of God. 1691. V. IX.[2]
Ray society. Botanical . . . memoirs. Reports. I. 19.
Raybaud. Observations sur les huiles essentielles. 1834. III. 224.[1]
Raybaud-Lange. Sur la maladie des morts-flats. 1869. IV. 433.[2]
Rayet, G. Sur les incendies des landes de la Gironde. 1893. IV. 183.[1]
Rayevski, Nicolaus. See РАЕВСКІЙ, Н.
Raymond, Charles. Notice sur le Quillay. 1857. III. 447.[1]
Raymond, Emmeline. L'esprit des fleurs. 1884. I. 536.[1]
Raymondi, A. Sur la Coca. 1862. III. 492.[2]
Raynal, A. L. Du refoulement progressif du phylloxéra. 1879. III. 761.
Zur Razionalisirung unseres Gerbrinden-Gewerbes. 1881. IV. 435.
Razoumowski, Grégoire, comte de. Voyage aux environs de Vevay. 1784. I. 433.
O razvedeni . . . See О разведеніи . . .
Razvedeniye . . . See Разведеніе . . .
—re—. Waldbeschädigungen durch den Fichtennestwickler. 1892. IV. 457.
Re, Filippo. Sopra alcune di quelle produzioni . . . Rose di Quercia. 1815. V. 509.
— Elementi di agricoltura. 1802. III. 35.
— Florae atestinae prodromus. 1816. I. 425.
— Il giardiniere avviato. 1812. III. 88.[1]
— L'ortolano dirozzato. 1811. III. 31.
— Osservazioni sopra quegli alberi . . . di frutta senza semi. 1809. I. 145.[2]
— Saggio di bibliografia georgica. 1802. III. 1.
— Saggio di nosologia vegetabile. 1805. I. 206.[1] — 1807. III. 178.
— Saggio teorico-pratico sulle malattie delle piante. 1807. III. 178.
Re, Giovanni Francesco. Flora segusiensis. 1805. I. 425.
— La flora segusina. 1881. I. 429.
— Flora torinese. 1825. I. 426.
— Ad floram pedemontanam appendix. 1821. I. 425.
De re hortensi libellus. See ESTIENNE, Charles. 1535. I. 277, V. xiv.[2]
De re rustica. See SCRIPTORES rei rusticae. 1470. III. 96.[1]
De re rustica selectorum libri XX. See CASSIANUS BASSUS. 1538. III. 98.
Rea, John. Flora; seu, De florum cultura. 1665. III. 80.
Réactions de l'Aloès. 1883. III. 333.[2]
Read, Matthew C. Hints from nature on forest culture. 1884. IV. 112.
— What shall we do with . . . swamp lands in Ohio? 1884. IV. 178.[1]
Read, Quintin. The Box avenue at Beckford Hall. 1894. II. 453.[1]
Reade, A. De Thee en het gebruik van thee. · 1884. III. 607.
Reade, Joseph Bancroft. On the existence of spiral vessels in the roots. 1838. I. 103.
Reade, Oswald A. Cinchona cultivation in St. Helena. 1873. III. 717.[1]
— Culture du Cinchona à Sainte-Hélène. 1873. III. 717.[2]
— Plants of the Bermudas or Somers' Islands. 1883. I. 336.
Reader, F. M. Contributions to the flora of Victoria. 1897. I. 505.

The ready method of transplanting. 1881. III. 170.
Re-afforesting Ireland. 1884. IV. 161.[1]
Real academia de ciencias exactas ... de Madrid. Memorias. I. 24.[1]
Real academia de ciencias médicas, físicas y naturales de la Habana. Anales. I. 7.[3]
Real academia medica de Madrid. Memorias. I. 24.[1]
Real decreto e regolamento per l' amministrazione e custodia de' boschi di Serra. 1859. IV. 304.[3]
El real decreto sobre repoblación ictícola. 1895. IV. 547.[1]
Real-Index und Auszug der hochfürstlich-württembergischen Forst-Ordnung. See NEWE Vorst Ordnung ... 1540. IV. 322.[3]
Real sociedade nacional de horticultura de Portugal. Boletim. III. 23.[1]
Real società economica di Firenze ossia de' georgofili. See REALE ACCADEMIA ECONOMICO-AGRARIA DEI GEORGOFILI ... III. 23.[3]
Reale accademia de' fisiocritici. See REALE ACCADEMIA DELLE SCIENZE DETTA DE' FISIOCRITICI. I. 25.
Reale accademia dei georgofili. Catalogo della biblioteca. See BIGAZZI, Pietro. 1863. I. 2.
Reale accademia dei lincei. Atti. Memorie. Rendiconti. Transunti. I. 25.
Reale accademia delle scienze detta de' fisiocritici. Atti. I. 25.
Reale accademia delle scienze di Torino. Atti. Memorie. See MISCELLANEA philosophico-mathematica ... I. 25.
Reale accademia delle scienze, sezione della Società reale borbonica. Atti. Memorie. Rendiconti. I. 25.
Reale accademia di scienze, lettere ed arti di Modena. Memorie. I. 25.
Reale accademia di scienze, lettere ed arti in Padova. Atti. I. 25.
Reale accademia economico-agraria dei georgofili di Firenze. Atti. III. 23.[3]
Reale accademia lucchese di scienze. Atti. I. 25.
Reale istituto botanico di Roma. Annuario. I. 25.
Reale istituto d' incoraggiamento di agricoltura ... in Sicilia. Effemeridi. Giornale. III. 23.[3]
Reale istituto d' incoraggiamento ... di Napoli. Atti. I. 25.
Reale istituto lombardo di scienze e lettere. Giornale. Memorie. Rendiconti. I. 25, V. VII.[3]
Reale istituto tecnico di Bari. Annuario. III. 23.[3]
Reale istituto tecnico e nautico di Napoli. Annali. III. 23.[3]
Reale museo di fisica e storia naturale di Firenze. Annali. I. 25.
Reale orto botanico di Palermo. Bolletino. I. 26.[1]
Reale scuola superiore d'agricoltura in Portici. Annali. Annuario. III. 23.[3]
R. società toscana d'orticultura. Catalogo speciale della collezione di alberi fruttiferi. See CATALOGO ... 1862. III. 29.[1]
Reale società toscana di orticultura. Bullettino. III. 23.[3]
Reale università degli studi di Siena. Bulletino. I. 26.[1]
Reale università di Genova. Atti. I. 26.[1]
Rasii, Agostino. Gli alberi e gli arbusti del territorio Camerte. 1871. III. 88.[1]
R. decreti sulle indennità di missione ... estesi all' amministrazione forestale delle provincie venete. 1867. IV. 305.
Reasoner, E. N. Another new Palm. 1889. II. 75.[1]
Reasoner, P. W. The Loquat. 1888. III. 424.[1]
— Native Florida Cactuses. 1890. II. 587.[1]
— Our native Palms of the southeastern U. S. 1887. II. 61.[1]
— Palms in central Florida. 1888. III. 318.[1]
— See also VAN DEMAN, H. E., REASONER, P. W. & KLEE, W. G.
Reassumirung der Erläuterungen, Vereinfachungen. 1830. IV. 299.
Réaumont. L'aménagement des forêts en Saxe. 1888. IV. 248.[1]
— L'exploitation ... en Allemagne. 1893. IV. 383.[1]
— Le jardinage qualifié. 1895. IV. 131.
Reaumur, de. Réflexions sur l'état des bois du royaume. 1723. IV. 359.[1]
Rebattu. Le régime forestier de l'Algérie. 1900. IV. 295.[3]
Rebau. See MARTIN, F. & REBAU.
Rébecque, J. C. de. Essay de la Pharmacopée des Suisses. 1709. III. 271.[3]
Rebel, Karl. Einiges über das Forsteinrichtungswesen in Sachsen. 1892. IV. 248.[1]
— Qualitative Untersuchungen im Fichten-Buchen-Mischwald. 1891. IV. 409.
— Die wirtschaftliche Erschliessung der Lüneburger Heide. 1892. IV. 159.

Von den Rebenstichern. 1767. III. 562.[1] — 1771. III. 562.[1]
Rebenstorff, J. Ampelopsis radicantissima. 1887. III. 545.[1]
Rebentisch, Johann Friedrich. Index plantarum circa Berolinum. 1805. I. 375.
— Prodromus florae Neomarchiae. 1804. I. 375, V. XIX.[1]
Reber, B. Le genre Strophantus. 1887. III. 690.[1]
Reber, Peter. Grundsätze der Wald-Taxation. 1827. IV. 240.
— Handbuch der Arithmetik, Geometrie. 1841, IV. 58.
— Handbuch der Wald-Taxation. 1827. IV. 240.
— Handbuch des Waldbaues. 1831. IV. 106.
— Der Waldschutz und die Forstdirektion. 1842. IV. 177,[1] 287.
— See also BEHLEN, Stephan & REBER, Peter.
Reblaus-Gesetze. Sammlung der im Königreich Preussen geltenden ... Vorschriften. 1890. III. 762.
Rebmann, (Oberförster, Barr). Bedeutung und Ausführung der Reinigungshiebe. 1881. IV. 173.
Rebmann, E. Eine merkwürdige Umbildung von Fuchsiablüthen. 1888. II. 643.[3]
Reboisement de terrains incultes. 1865. IV. 162.
Reboisement de terrains sablonneux épuisés. 1898. IV. 170.
Reboisement de terres vagues ou cultivées. 1899. IV. 161.[1]
Le reboisement des montagnes. 1898. IV. 164.[1]
Reboisement des montagnes; rapport. 1876. IV. 162.
Le reboisement des pineraies. 1897. IV. 559.[1]
Reboisement des terrains communaux incultes dans la Côte-d'Or. 1899. IV. 546.[1]
Reboisement des terres ruinées. See KIRWAN, Charles de. 1874. IV. 162.
Le reboisement en Emyrne. 1898. IV. 547.[1]
Le reboisement en Espagne. 1899. IV. 165.
Reboisement en France. 1878. IV. 163.
Le reboisement en Grèce. 1900. IV. 168.[1]
Le reboisement en Italie. 1888. IV. 166.[1]
Reboisement et aménagement des eaux. See CAUTEGRIL, (Conservateur des fôrets). 1884. IV. 51.
Reboisement (et gazonnement) des montagnes. 1862. IV. 162.
Reboisement et gazonnement des montagnes. 1875. IV. 162.
Reboisement et gazonnement des montagnes. 1878. IV. 163.
Du reboisement ou de la plantation des Pins. See ST. DENIS. 1855. IV. 460.[1]
Reboisements de Baume-les-Dames. 1897. IV. 546.[1]
Reboisements presentant des difficultés. 1890. IV. 168.[1]
Rebouças, André & José. Ensaio de indice geral das madeiras do Brazil. 1877. IV. 398.[3]
Rebouças, José. See REBOUÇAS, André & José.
Reboud, Victor. Note sur l'ancienne forêt de Bièvre. 1860. IV. 27.[1]
— Note sur le Djedari. 1867. III. 526.[3]
Reboul & Bénéguet. Concessions de forêts de Chênes-liége de l'Algérie. 1887. IV. 279.[3]
Rebsch, B. A. The commutation of privileges in Bahraich. 1893. IV. 335.
Recensement des bois et des terrains incultes. 1900. IV. 357.[1]
Recensio plantarum hucusque in Repositorio botanicorum depictarum. See KER, J. B. 1801. I. 265.
Recension der Beiträge zur Kenntniss des russischen Reiches. See BULMERINCQ, M. E. von. 1857. IV. 345.
A recent fire in the Sierra Madres. 1900. IV. 182.[1]
Recepage d'une plantation d'Aunes. 1900. IV. 489.[1]
Recepage de taillis en terrains submergés. 1900. IV. 132.[3]
Le recepage des brins de Chêne dans les taillis. 1895. IV. 545.[1]
Recepage des plantations. 1900. IV. 153.[3]
Le recepage des plantations d'essences feuillues. 1895. IV. 547.[1]
Recept wider den Baumkrebs. 1799. III. 180.[1]
The recess committee and forestry. 1896. IV. 357.[3]
Reche, E. F. Th. De Amyridis speciebus officinalibus. 1801. III. 495.[1]
Recherches sur la fumure des arbres fruitiers. See ERFAHRUNGEN über Obstbaumdüngung. 1897. III. 152.[1]
Recherches sur le Quinquina pitaya. 1835. III. 726.[1]
Rechinger, Karl. Ballota Wettsteinii sp. n. 1898. II. 763.[1]
— Ueber den Polymorphismus ... bei Populus canescens. 1899. II. 97.[1]
— Vergleichende Untersuchungen über die Trichome der Gesneraceen. 1899. II. 792.[3]

Rechnenschieber zum Kubieren von Rundholz. 1899. IV. 229.

The reciprocal action of scion and stock. 1898. III. 40.

Recisione di alberi col mezzo del vapore. 1882. IV. 384.[1]

Reck, *Freiherr* von der. Aphorismen über die preussische Staats-Forstverwaltung. 1882. IV. 290.[2]

— Betrachtungen eines alten Praktikers. 1887. IV. 130.

— Entwurf einer kurzen Anleitung zur Waldwerth-Berechnung. 1877. IV. 256.

— Ueber die Erziehung der Eiche im Eichenhochwalde. 1875. IV. 506.

— Ueber die Erziehung der Eiche im Hochwalde. 1875. IV. 506.

— Nochmals über Haupt- und Vornutzung. 1883. IV. 237.

Reckendorfer, Ferdinand. Einige Ratschläge für die Weinbauer. 1896. III. 558.[2]

Recknagel. Ueber Spätfröste und Schutzmittel gegen dieselben. 1879. III. 182.

Reclaiming the barren Province lands. 1897. IV. 155.[2]

Reclus, Élisée. Étude sur les dunes. 1865. IV. 145.

Recluz, C. A. Note sur les fruits du Genévrier. 1827. III. 303.[2]

— Des sucs végétaux aqueux. 1828. I. 150.[3]

Récolte de la gomme gutte. 1874. III. 609.[1]

Récolte des graines d'arbres forestiers. 1898. IV. 148.

Récolte des graines de Charme. 1900. IV. 491.[2]

Récolte du caoutchouc au Brésil. 1883. III. 519.[1]

Récolte du caoutchouc au Brésil. 1884. III. 231.

Récolte du mastic à Chios. 1860. III. 525.[1]

Recreative science. I. 19.

Recrutement des gardes forestiers et de pêche. 1896. IV. 303.[2]

Recueil d'arrests et règlements, concernants la jurisdiction des eaues & forests. *See* EDICTS ... 1588. IV. 323.[1]

Recueil de lois et ordonnances forestières pour le Jura bernois. *See* SAMMLUNG der Gesetze ... 1874. IV. 330.

Recueil de mémoires de médicine. *See* JOURNAL de médecine, de chirurgie ... I. 21.

Recueil de travaux relatifs à la philologie.... egyptiennes. I. 22.

Recueil méthodique des lois, règlements, décisions, et de la jurisprudence en matière forestière. 1840. IV. 324.

Recul de la végétation arborescente. 1892. IV. 75.[2]

Recum, *Freiherr* von. Kann ... ein ausgerottetes Weinbergsfeld ... wieder mit Weinreben angepflanzt werden? 1828. III. 552.

Recum, A. VAN-. *See* VAN-RECUM, A.

Recupero, Giuseppe. Storia naturale e generale dell' Etna. 1815. I. 431.

The Red Astrachan Apple. 1847. III. 425.[2]

The Red Cedar. 1895. II. 32.[1] — 1897. II. 32.[1]

The Red-gum forests of New South Wales. 1900. IV. 531.[1]

The Red Mulberry-tree. 1894. II. 155.[1]

The Red Oak. 1891. II. 199.[2]

Reddall, Frederic. Royal forests of England. 1899. IV. 358.[2]

Reddelien, Johann Christian Ludwig. De Taxo baccata Linn. *See* LODER, J. C. 1794. III. 288.[1]

Redfield, John Howard. Corema Conradi and its localities. 1884. II. 453.[2]

— On the flora of Martha's Vineyard and Nantucket. 1886. I. 313.

— Note on Pinus Banksiana. 1890. II. 41.[1]

— Pinus Banksiana with Corema Conradi. 1889. II. 40.[1]

— *See also* RAND, E. L. & REDFIELD, J. H.

Redhead, J. F. A. Trinidad. 1888. III. 267.[2]

Redhead, Richard Milne. Notes on the flora of the desert of Sinai. 1867. I. 480.[3]

Redi, Francesco. Esperienze intorno a diverse cose naturali. 1686. V. XVI.[1]

— Notizie intorno alla natura delle Palme. 1863. II. 871.[2]

— Remarks concerning factitious salts. 1699. I. 150.[3]

Redl, H. Ueber Eichenrinden-Gewinnung. 1852. IV. 512.

Redmond, D. The Myrtle Orange. 1889. III. 500.[1]

— Pomological resources of the South. 1859. III. 133.

Redouté, Pierre Joseph. Le bouquet royale. 1843. III. 448.

— Catalogue de 486 Liliacées et de 168 Roses. 1829. III. 448.

— Choix des plus belles fleurs. 1827. III. 86.

— Les Liliacées. 1802. II. 77.[1]

— *See also* THORY, C. A. & REDOUTÉ, P. J.

Redowsky, D. Enumeratio plantarum quae in horto comitis Alexii a Razumowsky. 1804. I. 41.

Redtenbacher, Jos. Acide contenu dans le fruit du Caroubier. 1846. III. 472.[1]

— Ueber die Säure des Johannisbrodes. 1846. III. 472.[1]

Reducing too tall plants. 1899. III. 159.[1]

Reduction of all the genera of plants contained in the Catalogus ... of the late Dr. Muhlenberg. *See* CORREA, (*abbé*). 1815. I. 306.

Reduction of the duty on Teak timber. 1882. IV. 285.[2]

Redwood, Boverton. *See* DEERING, W. H. & REDWOOD, Boverton.

Redwood, Theophilus. Aloes wood, Woorari. 1844. III. 472.[1]

— Gray's supplement to the pharmacopoeia. 1847. III. 254.

— Notices of specimens in the museum of the Pharmaceutical society. 1844. III. 472,[1] 626,[2] 885.[1]

— A supplement to the pharmacopoeia. 1847. III. 254.

— Bentley, Robert & Barnard, John. Cinchona cultivation in India. 1864. III. 714.

— — — Cinchona cultivation in Jamaica. 1864. III. 712.[2]

— — — Growth of Balsam of Peru tree. 1865. III. 482.[2]

— — — Growth of Cinchona in Jamaica and Himalaya. 1865. III. 712.[2]

— — — Introduction of Cinchona into India. 1864. III. 714.

— — On the introduction of Cinchona trees into India. 1861. III. 713.[2]

— — The introduction of the Cinchona into ... Jamaica. 1869. III. 713.[1]

The Redwood. 1874. II. 49.[2] — 1890. II. 49.[2]

Redwood and lumbering in California forests. *See* CHERRY, Edgar & Co. 1884. IV. 484.[1]

The Redwood, the woodpeckers. 1890. I. 210,[3] II. 49,[3] III. 310.[3]

The Redwoods. A suggestion. 1897. IV. 179.[1]

The Redwoods of northern California. 1886. IV. 484.[1]

Reece. A practical dictionary of domestic medicine. 1808. III. 242.

Reed, Edwyn Carlos. Compendio de historia natural de Chile. 1892. III. 66.[1]

Reed, Richard. Some communications about an early swarm of bees. 1671. I. 162, *III. 168.*[3]

Reemelin, Charles. The vine-dresser's manual. 1858. III. 550.

Rees, Abraham & others. The cyclopaedia. 1819. I. 33.

Rees, Jonathan. A living tree alphabet. 1897. I. 517.[1]

Rees, P. van. Beredeneerde catalogus van houtsoorten op Java. 1861. IV. 399.[2]

Reese, D. Meredith. Rudiments of vegetable physiology. 1846. I. 148.

Reess, Maximilian. Der Botanische Garten zu Erlangen. 1878. I. 48.

— Chrysomyxa Abietis Unger. 1865. IV. 455.

— Ueber Elaphomyces. 1885. I. 233.[2]

— Zur Kritik der Böhm'schen Ansicht über die Entwickelungsgeschichte und Function der Thyllen. 1868. I. 125.

— Lehrbuch der Botanik. 1896. I. 92.

— Pflanzenreste aus den Todtenbäumen von Oberfacht. 1874. I. 80.[2]

— Ueber die Pflege der Botanik in Franken. 1884. I. 80.[2]

— Die Rostpilzformen der deutschen Coniferen. 1869. IV. 449.

— Weitere Mittheilungen über Elaphomyces. 1885. I. 233.[2]

Reeve, James Knapp. Cocoanut-growing in Florida. 1892. III. 323.[1]

Reeves, Eimer M. Blackberries. 1889. III. 457.[2]

— Forest planting. 1899. IV. 113.[1]

— Forestry belts for protection. 1885. III. 215.[1]

— Native Plums. 1893. III. 433.[1]

— The Sand Cherry. 1895. III. 435.[2]

— Timber planting from the standpoints of orchard shelters. 1895. III. 215.[1]

Reeves, James A. Sap; does it rise from the roots? 1890. I. 166.

Reeves, N. A. Timber growing in Floyd county. 1882. IV. 112.

Reeves, W. de G. New Zealand. 1888. III. 283.[2]

— Referat des böhmischen Forstvereines über die deutschen Holzzölle. 1886. IV. 284.[2]

Reflectionen über die Sprossbildung innerhalb der Samenhüllen von Coelebogyne. 1857. II. 436.[1]

Reflexions sur les différents systèmes de botanique. 1804. I. 251.

Reforms en la Escuela forestal de Nancy. 1889. IV. 540.²
Refugium botanicum. I. 19.
Réfutation à propos d'un article de M. Du Mortier. *See* PETIT DE LA SAUSSAYE, Sauveur. 18..? III. 84.²
Regal, José. Asociación de ingenieros de montes. 1892. IV. 541.
Regarnissage des vides dans les plantations d'Épicéas. 1899. IV. 454.
Regel, Albert. Die einheimischen ... Kulturpflanzen des oberen Amudaria. 1884. III. 127.²
— Aus Kuldscha. 1878. I. 457.
— Mulberries. — The fruits of Turkestan. 1887. III. 378.
— Reiseberichte. 1880. I. 457.
— Reisebriefe. 1876. I. 454.¹
Regel, Eduard August von. Abies balsamea Ait. im Park zu Ropscha. 1884. II. 22.¹
— Abies Nordmanniana Lk. 1871. II. 23.¹
— Ueber das Absterben von Tannen- und andern Bäumen. 1860. IV. 205.¹
— Abutilon Darwini Hook. β trinerve. 1874. II. 520.¹
— Abutilon megapotamicum A. St. Hil. 1870. II. 520.²
— Acacia Ausfeldi Rgl. 1867. II. 324.¹
— Acacia marginata R. Br. var. brevifolia. 1853. III. 465.¹
— Acacia pentaëdra Rgl. 1852. II. 325,¹ *III. 485.*¹
— Acacia viscidula A. Cunningh. 1883. II. 329.¹
— Die ächten Vitis-Arten Nordamerikas. 1873. II. 505.¹
— Aeschynanthus Horsfieldii Brown. 1860. II. 793.¹
— Die äusseren Einflüsse auf das Pflanzenleben. 1847. III. 40.
— Die Agave-Arten des Kais. bot. Gartens. 1858. III. 340.²
— Agave Maximowicziana Rgl. 1889. II. 89.¹
— Akklimatisation von Pflanzen. 1860. III. 43.
— Almeidea rubra St. Hilaire. 1866. II. 398.¹
— Amelanchier Botryapium als Heckenpflanze. 1866. III. 419.²
— Ampelopsis serjaniaefolia Bunge. 1867. II. 501.¹
— Animadversiones de plantis vivis nonnullis Horti botanici imperialis petropolitani. 1871. I. 42.
— Anopterus glandulosus Labill. 1868. II. 237.²
— Die Arten der Gattung Dracaena. 1871. II. 81.¹
— Die Arten der Gattungen Dracaena und Cordyline. 1859. II. 79.²
— Atragene alpina L. 1870. II. 196.¹
— Atragene macropetala Ledb. 1870. II. 198.²
— Aucuba japonica Thbrg. var. concolor. 1876. III. 645.¹
— Aufzählung der im St. Petersburger Klima noch ausdauernden Bäume. 1872. III. 67.¹
— Aufzaehlung der von Radde in Baikalien, Dahurien ... gesammelten Pflanzen. 1861. I. 455.
— Aufzählung der Yucca-Arten. 1859. III. 339.²
— Ueber die Ausartung der Fruchtbäume. 1858. I. 248.²
— Die ausdauernden schlingenden Loniceren. 1853. III. 749.²
— Die Ausstellung zu Gent vom 29 März. 1868. III. 77.
— Baeckea parvula DC. 1876. II. 620.²
— Bäume und Sträucher ... in den Gärten in und bei St. Petersburg hart. 1859. III. 67.²
— Bambusa agrosto-striata Rgl. 1865. II. 59.²
— Bambusa aureostriata Rgl. 1865. II. 59.²
— Bambusen-Gruppe ... zu Syon-house. 1884. III. 316.¹
— Bauhinia forficata Lk. et Otto. 1861. II. 335.¹
— Bemerkungen über die Gattungen Betula und Alnus, nebst Beschreibung einiger neuer Arten. 1865. II. 115.¹
— Bemerkungen ... über ... Larix. 1871. II. 32.²
— Bemerkungen über neue Pflanzen. 1852. I. 65.¹
— Bemerkungen über neue und seltene Zierpflanzen des Petersburger Gartens. 1856. I. 42.
— Bemerkungen über Pflanzen des Petersburger Gartens. 1857. I. 42.
— Bemerkungen über zwei Aeschynanthus unserer Gärten. 1889. II. 793.¹
— Bemerkungen zu Mittheilungen über die Einwirkung des Winters. 1871. III. 44.¹
— Berberis vulgaris L. var. atropurpurea. 1860. III. 395.¹
— Ueber das Beschneiden der oberirdischen Theile. 1859. III. 170.
— Over het besnoeien by het verplanten. 1859. III. 170.
— Besprechung einiger neuer Pflanzen. 1866. III. 696.¹
— Betula Medwediewi Rgl. und B. Raddeana. 1887. II. 119,² *180.*¹
— Betula tortuosa Ledb. β Kusmischeffii Rgl. 1860. II. 118.²
— Betulaceae. 1868. II. 115.¹

— Ueber Betulaceen. 1862. II. 117.²
— Billbergia Quesneliana. 1875. II. 76.²
— Blühende Palmen. 1862. III. 317.
— Blüthe der Paullownia. 1853. III. 703.²
— Blutbirke. 1876. III. 357.¹
— Die Blutbuche. 1855. II. 127.²
— Boronia fastigiata Lindl. 1861. II. 400.¹
— Brassaiopsis glomerulata Blume. 1863. II. 648.¹
— Bredia hirsuta Blume. 1870. II. 636.²
— Buntblätterige Pflanzen Japans. 1864. III. 91,² *206.*²
— Calophaca grandiflora Rgl. 1886. II. 340.²
— Calophaca Hoveni Schrenk. 1860. II. 340.²
— Calyptrostigma Middendorfiana. 1857. III. 749.²
— Capparis cynophallophora L. var. laetevirens. 1862. II. 231.²
— Caragana frutescens L. 1861. II. 341.²
— Caragana jubata Poir. 1861. II. 341.²
— Caragana microphylla Lam. var. intermedia Rgl. 1861. II. 342.¹
— Cardiandra alternifolia Sieb. et Zucc. 1865. II. 238.¹
— Carludovica Drudel Masters. 1881. III. 332.²
— Carludovica Wallisi Rgl. . 1879. III. 332.²
— Cassia laevigata. 1854. III. 471.¹
— Catalogus plantarum quae in Horto aksakoviano coluntur. 1860. I. 42.
— Celastrus crispulus Rgl., Celastrus punctatus. 1860. II. 466.¹
— Ceratozamia Küsteriana. 1876. II. 4.¹
— Cereus Engelmanni Engelm. 1884. II. 593.¹
— Cereus hypogaeus Weber. 1882. II. 590.¹
— Cereus Landbecki Philippi. 1875. II. 589.²
— Cereus pectinatus Engelm. 1874. II. 593.¹
— Cereus Philippi. 1882. II. 590.²
— Cereus serpentinus Lagasca. 1882. II. 591.¹
— Cheiranthera linearis. 1852. III. 415.¹
— Chinesische Kultur der Sophora japonica pendula. 1879. III. 351,² *488.*¹
— Chionanthus virginica Linné β maritima. 1867. II. 706.¹
— Choisya grandiflora Rgl. 1876. II. 400.¹
— Citrus japonica Thbrg. 1882. III. 502.¹
— Clavija Riedeliana Rgl. 1870. II. 691.¹
— Clavija umbrosa Rgl. 1869. II. 691.²
— Clematis fusca Turcz. var. mandschurica. 1864. II. 198.¹
— Clerodendron Kaempferi Fisch. 1856. III. 696.²
— Clerodendron Lindleyi Dne. 1862. II. 755.²
— Clethra barbinervis Sieb. et Zucc. 1870. II. 657.¹
— Colea undulata Rgl. 1870. II. 787.²
— Colletia cruciata Gill. et Hook. 1867. II. 493.²
— Conspectus specierum generis Vitis. 1873. II. 505.¹
— Cookia punctata Retz. 1860. II. 404.¹
— Coprosma Baueriana Endl. var. aureo-marginata. 1893. III. 743.²
— Cordyline australis Endl. 1864. II. 80,¹
— Cordyline Haageana. 1871. II. 80.¹
— Ueber Cordyline indivisa Kunth. 1860. II. 80.¹
— Cordyline rubra Hügel. 1864. II. 80.²
— Corokia buddleioides A. Cunn. 1871. II. 656.¹
— Crataegus pinnatifida Bnge. 1862. II. 263.¹
— Die cultivirten Arten der Gattung Panax. 1859. II. 646.¹
— Die Cultur der Erythrinen. 1862. III. 476.¹
— Cultur der Pflanzen unserer höheren Gebirge. 1856. III. 121.²
— Cultur der Poinciana Gilliesii. 1859. III. 469.¹
— Ueber die Cultur einiger seltenen Alpenpflanzen. 1875. III. 662.²
— Cycadearum generum specierumque revisio. 1876. II. 2.²
— Die Cycadeen. 1876. II. 2.²
— Die Cycadeen des Botanischen Gartens in Petersburg. 1857. II. 2.¹
— Cycas Riuminiana. 1863. II. 5.¹
— Damnacanthus major S. u. Z. 1868. II. 816.¹
— Daphne altaica Pall. 1863. II. 601.¹
— Daphne Blagayana Freyer. 1880. III. 627.¹
— Daphne Genkwa Sieb. et Zucc. 1866. II. 601.²
— Descriptiones plantarum ... a cl. Olga Fedtschenko in Turkestania ... lectarum. 1882. I. 457.
— Descriptiones plantarum nonnullarum Horti imperialis botanici. 1887. I. 42.
— Descriptiones plantarum novarum. 1873. I. 270.
— Deutzia parviflora Bnge. β amurensis Rgl. 1862. II. 239.¹
— Dibrachion peltatum Rgl. 1866. II. 445.¹
— Dillwynia Drummondi. 1863. II. 354.²

— Dispositio specierum . . . generis Cotoneaster. 1873. II. 259.[1]
— Dracaena concinna H. Berol. 1864. II. 82.[1]
— Dracaena ensifolia Wall. 1864. II. 82.[3]
— Dracaena ensifolia Wall. β Greigi. 1871. II. 82.[2]
— Dracaena latifolia Rgl. var. Schmidtiana. 1880. III. 336.[3]
— Dracaena Saposchnikowi Rgl. 1871. II. 83.[1]
— Drei neue Pflanzen. 1851. II. 770.[1]
— Echinocactus centeterius Lehm. 1882. II. 592.[1]
— Echinocactus cylindraceus Engelm. 1877. II. 592.[1]
— Echinocactus texensis Hopfer. 1888. II. 593.[1]
— Echinopsis valida Monv. var. densa. 1852. III. 622.[3]
— Der Einfluss des Standortes auf Ueberwinterung der Holzgewächse. 1871. III. 43.
— Einfluss des Wildlings auf das Edelreis. 1871. III. 39.
— Einfluss des Wildlings auf den Edelstamm. 1874. III. 39.
— Einige neue Pflanzen des botanischen Gartens in Zürich. 1853. II. 766.[3]
— Einige neue Pflanzenarten des botanischen Gartens zu Zürich. 1852. I. 65.[1]
— Eleutherococcus senticosus Maxim. 1863. II. 647.[1]
— Encephalartos cycadifolius Lehm. var. Friderici Guilelmi. 1880. II. 5.[3]
— Encephalartos Lehmanni. 1865. II. 6.[1]
— Encephalartos Verschaffelti Rgl. 1875. II. 2.[2]
— Eparis impressa Lab. var. ardens. 1871. III. 665.[1]
— Epiphyllum Russelianum Hook. var. Gärtneri. 1884. III. 625.[3]
— Er det rigtigt at beskære Træer samtidigt med at vi omplante dem? 1859. III. 170.
— Erica cyathiformis Salsb. var. 1853. III. 651,[1] 651.[2]
— Erythrina insignis Todaro. 1879. II. 357.[3]
— Erythroxylon mexicanum. 1869. II. 394.[2]
— Des espèces de Dracaena. 1871. II. 81.[2]
— Eucalyptus globulus Labill. 1882. III. 634.[2]
— Eugenia compactiflora Spring. 1859. III. 635.[1]
— Euonymus japonicus and its varieties. 1866. II. 468.[2]
— Eupatorium omphaliaefolium. 1853. III. 755.[1]
— Eupatorium riparium Hort. 1866. II. 857.[1]
— Eupatorium Weinmannianum. 1867. II. 857.[1]
— Eurybia lirata Sims β quercifolia. 1876. II. 862.[2]
— Eurybia nitida Hook. fil. β dentata. 1865. II. 862.[1]
— Evonymus japonicus Thbrg. und dessen Abarten. 1866. II. 468.[2]
— Die Familie der Coniferen. 1859. II. 16.[1]
— Von Fatsia japonica . . . Samen zu erziehen. 1872. III. 642.[1]
— Fatsia japonica Thbrg. 1863. II. 648.[2]
— Feronia elephantum Corea [sic]. 1885. II. 407.[1]
— Ficus Carica L. im Grimston-Park. 1883. II. 151.[1]
— Ficus Porteana Rgl. 1882. II. 152.[2]
— Om Formering af Rhododendrer. 1859. III. 158.
— Franciscea calycina Benth. 1866. II. 769.[2]
— Froebelia fasciculiflora Rgl. 1852. II. 688.[1]
— Om Frostens skadelige Indvirkning. 1872. III. 182.
— Früchte ohne Embryo. 1858. I. 202,[1] II. 3.[1]
— Gardenia Maruba Sieb. 1866. II. 818.[1]
— Ueber Garten-Instrumente. 1855. III. 177.
— Die Gattung Oerstedannia und ihre Arten. 1876. II. 4.[1]
— Gaultheria glabra D. C. β caracasana. 1873. II. 671.[1]
— Generis Encephalarti conspectus specierum adhuc cognitarum. 1875. II. 5.[2]
— Generis Evononymi species. 1876. II. 467.[2]
— The genus Encephalartos. 1875. II. 5.[2]
— Die grosse Ulme unweit Eriwan. 1881. II. 144.[2]
— Hagebutten für kalte Klimate. 1876. II. 523.[1]
— Die Hauptmomente der Gärtnerei durch Physiologie begründet. 1840. III. 35.
— Hedera Helix var. colchica C. Koch. 1862. II. 649.[1]
— Heliotropium submolle Kl. 1853. II. 751.[1]
— Heterocentron subtriplinervium. 1862. II. 637.[3]
— Hibbertia perfoliata Hügel var. fl. pleno. 1873. III. 596.[1]
— Hibiscus insignis Mart. 1876. II. 523.[1]
— Die Himbeere und Erdbeere. 1881. III. 458.[1]
— Hippomane Mancinella. 1866. III. 519.[1]
— Hoya imperialis Lindl. var. Rauschii. 1855. III. 693.[3]
— Hydrangea japonica Sieb. et Zucc. δ macrosepala. 1866. II. 241.[1]
— Hydrangea paniculata Sieb. var. floribunda. 1867. II. 241.[1]
— Hydrangea stellata Sieb. et Zucc. var. prolifera. 1866. II. 241.[1]

— Hypericum patulum Thbrg. 1866. II. 557.[1]
— Index seminum quae Hortus botanicus . . . petropolitanus . . . offert. 1855. I. 42.
— Ixora alba L. 1881. III. 745.[1]
— Ixora crocata Lindl. var. Prince of Orange. 1880. III. 745.[1]
— Jacquinia mexicana H. Petrop. 1866. II. 691.[1]
— Jambosa Korthalsi Blume. 1872. II. 627.[3]
— Jasminum Sambac Ait. δ trifoliatum. 1862. II. 711.[1]
— Jochroma Warscewiczii. 1855. II. 772.[1]
— Jubaea spectabilis Humb. et Knth. 1884. II. 69.[2]
— Kennedya arenaria Bnth. 1853. II. 367.[2]
— Die kleinen sibirischen Aepfel. 1862. II. 266.[1]
— Die Kultur der Eriken. 1842. III. 650.[1]
— Die Kultur und Aufzählung der . . . Eriken. 1842. III. 650.[1]
— Kurze systematische Uebersicht der russischen Aepfelsorten. 186.? III. 425.[2]
— Lagerstroemia indica. 1857. III. 629.[3]
— Landrosen im rauhen Klima. 1874. III. 452.
— Lantana nivea Vent. et var. 1865. III. 697.[1]
— Laubhölzer im Sommer . . . zuverpflanzen. 1862. III. 168.[3]
— Laubwerfende Bäume, welche im Herbste die Blätter halten. 1881. III. 182.
— Lepidozamia Denisoni Rgl. 1876. II. 6.[3]
— Lepidozamia Peroffskyána. 1870. II. 6.[2]
— Lespedeza bicolor Turcz. 1860. II. 369.[3]
— Lhotakya hirta Rgl. 1863. II. 629.[1]
— Das Licht und dessen Einwirkung auf die Pflanzenwelt. 1852. I. 229.
— Ligustrina amurensis Rupr. 1863. II. 714.[3]
— Lonicera Alberti Rgl. 1881. II. 839.[3]
— Lonicera hispida Pall. 1882. II. 838.[1]
— Lonicera Kesselringi Rgl. 1891. II. 838.[2]
— Lonicera Ledebouri Eschsch. 1853. III. 750.[3]
— Lonicera Maximowiczii Rupr. 1868. II. 838.[2]
— Lonicera orientalis Lam. 1862. II. 838.[3]
— Lonicera Ruprechtiana Rgl. 1870. II. 839.[2]
— Lonicera tatarica L. und Abarten. 1869. III. 751.[1]
— Luma Cheken Asa Gray β apiculata. 1877. II. 631.[1]
— Macrozamia Miq. 1876. II. 6.[1]
— Malpighia Loddigesii Rgl. 1859. II. 426.[2]
— Malpighia urens L. oblonga. 1858. III. 513.[2]
— Malva Creeano-miniata. 1852. III. 589.[1]
— Mamillaria Schelhasii Pfr. β sericata Salm. 1857. III. 623.[2]
— Mammillaria barbata Engelm. 1885. II. 594.[1]
— Mammillaria echinata DC. 1885. II. 594.[3]
— Mammillaria sanguinea. 1883. II. 595.[1]
— Martinezia disticha, Acanthorhiza Wallisi. 1879. II 64.[1] 66.[1] 71.[1]
— Maximowiczia chinensis. 1862. II. 213.[2]
— Miconia Teysmanniana. 1867. II. 640.[1]
— Monographia Betulacearum. 1861. II. 115.[1]
— Monographie des Dracaena vrais. 1871. II. 81.[3]
— Monographische Bearbeitung der Betulaceen. 1861. II. 115.[1]
— Monopanax Ghiesbreghti Rgl. 1869. II. 651.[1]
— Neue oder empfehlenswerthe Zierpflanzen. 1873. III. 75.[1]
— Neue oder seltenere Pflanzen . . . in Petersburg. 1856. III. 301.[1]
— Die neuen strauchigen Calceolarien. 1855. III. 702.[3]
— Noch einmal Betula alba L. 1862. II. 118.[3]
— Notice sur l'acclimatation des plantes. 1860. III. 43.
— Notice sur les espèces des genres Dracaena et Cordyline. 1859. II. 79.[2]
— Observations sur les espèces du genre Larix. 1871. II. 32.[3]
— Der Obstbau des Kantons Zürich. 1855. III. 89.[1]
— Olearia ramulosa Benth. 1882. II. 862.[1]
— Oreopanax Brownii Witte. 1863. II. 649.[1]
— Oreopanax peltatum Linden. 1862. II. 651.[1]
— Oxycoccos macrocarpa Pers. 1871. II. 686.[1]
— Pachira stenopetala Cav. 1860. II. 531.[1]
— Palmen Amerika's. 1876. II. 64,[1] 68,[1] 71.[1]
— Palmen von Wallis im tropischen Amerika entdeckt. 1880. II. 64,[2] 68,[1] 74.[2]
— Panax sessiliflorum Rupr. et Maxim. 1862. II. 647.[1]
— Papaya gracilis. 1879. II. 582.[1]
— On parthenogenesis. 1858. I. 202.[1]
— Zur Parthenogenesis. 1858. I. 202.[1]
— Die Parthenogenesis im Pflanzenreiche. 1859. I. 202.[1]

Regel, Eduard August von (*continued*).
— Ueber Parthenogenesis und Pflanzen-Bastarde. 1857. I. 202.[1]
— Passiflora alba-nigra Parp. 1852. III. 615.[2]
— Passiflora truncata Rgl. 1859. II. 581.[1]
— Die Pflanze und ihr Leben. 1855. III. 37.[2]
— Phoenix cycadifolia h. Athen. 1879. III. 328.[1]
— Phyllocactus crenato × grandiflorus. 1884. III. 625.[2]
— Phyllocactus crenatus Salm. var. roseus grandiflorus. 1862. III. 625.[2]
— Phyllocactus crenatus Salm. var. splendens Rgl. 1861. III. 625.[2]
— Phyllocactus speciosissimo-crenatus Paxt. var. Franzi. 1881. III. 626.[1]
— Picea Parryana Rgl. et Hort. 1886. II. 13.[2]
— Pinus Abies L. var. fennica. 1863. II. 34.[2]
— Pittosporum discolor H. Berol. 1852. II. 248.[2]
— Pittosporum Enderi Rgl. 1868. II. 248.[1]
— Pittosporum revolutum Ait. 1867. II. 249.[1]
— Plantae regiones turkestanicas incolentes. 1877. I. 457.
— Platycrater arguta Sieb. et Zucc. 1866. II. 243.[1]
— Plectranthus fruticosus L'Hér. 1864. II. 764.[2]
— Polygala myrtifolia L. var. Dalmaisiana. 1856. III. 514.[1]
— Pomologia rossica. 1868. III. 68.[1]
— Populus diversifolia Schrenck. 1858. III. 346.[1]
— Potentilla fruticosa L. var. floribunda. 1863. III. 430.[1]
— Potentilla glabra Lodd. 1860. II. 270.[1]
— Proposition de construire de cartes de la distribution géographiques . . . de plantes ligneuses. 1885. I. 300.
— Psychotria jasminiflora. 1881. III. 747.[2]
— Pultenaea Ausfeldi Rgl. 1865. II. 381.[1]
— Pultenaea Gunni Benth. 1884. II. 381.[1]
— Puya chilensis Molina. 1858. III. 333.[1]
— Pyrus thianschanica Ruprecht. 1891. II. 313.[2]
— Pyrus ussuriensis Maxim. 1861. II. 281.[1]
— Revisio specierum Crataegorum. 1871. I. 270.
— Revisio specierum generis Crataegi. 1871. II. 260.[2]
— Revisio specierum generis Dracaenae. 1871. II. 81.[2]
— Revisio specierum generis Laricis. 1871. II. 32.[2]
— Revisio specierum sectionis "Azalea." 1871. II. 675.[2]
— A revision of the genus Dracaena. 1871. II. 81.[2]
— Rhamni species imperium rossicum incolentes. 1876. II. 496.[2]
— Rhododendron-Arten der europäischen Alpen. 1874. II. 675.[2]
— Rhododendron Aucklandi Hook. fil. 1866. II. 679.[2]
— Rhododendron (Azalea) rhombicum. 1868. II. 683.[1]
— Rhododendron calophyllum Nutt. β longifolium. 1868. II. 682.[1]
— Rhododendron calophyllum Nutt. flore roseo. 1865. II. 682.[1]
— Rhododendron camelliaeflorum Hook. 1865. II. 678.[1]
— Rhododendron caucasicum Pall. β flavidum. 1867. II. 678.[2]
— Rhododendron caucasicum var. luteum. 1875. II. 678.[2]
— Rhododendron ciliatum Hook. β roseo-album. 1867. II. 678.[2]
— Rhododendron Falconeri. 1870. II. 679.[1]
— Rhododendron hirsutum L., R. ferrugineum L., R. Chamaecistus L. 1864. II. 676.[1]
— Rhododendron Hookeri Nutt. 1863. II. 680.[1]
— Rhododendron Jenkinsii Nutt. 1860. II. 681.[1]
— Rhododendron kamtschaticum. 1887. III. 660.[2]
— Rhododendron Keysii Nutt. 1863. II. 681.[1]
— Rhododendron longifolium Nutt. 1862. II. 679.[2]
— Rhododendron niveum Hook. fil. 1871. II. 682.[2]
— Rhododendron parvifolium Adams. 1877. II. 683.[1]
— Rhododendron semibarbatum Maxim. 1870. II. 683.[2]
— Rhododendron yēdoēnse Maxim. 1886. II. 681.[2]
— Rhopala heterophylla Pohl. var. pinnata Meisn. 1863. II. 166.[2]
— Rhopala macrophylla Schott. 1863. II. 166.[2]
— Rhynchospermum jasminoides Lindl. 1859. III. 691.[2]
— Rhytiglossa cristata Rgl. 1852. II. 800.[2]
— Ribes rubrum L. und nigrum. 1867. III. 413.[2]
— Roezlia granadensis. 1871. II. 640.[2]
— Rogiera gratissima. 1865. III. 747.[2]
— Rosa laxa und Fröbels Wildling. 1890. III. 455.[2]
— Rosa pimpinellifolia L. 1862. III. 457.[1]
— Rosa rugosa Thbrg. a typica. 1881. II. 298.[1]
— Rosa rugosa Thbrg. var. purpurea plena. 1875. II. 298.[1]
— Rubus crataegifolius Bnge. 1868. II. 306.[2] — 1878. II. 306.[1]

— Rubus leucodermis var. Golden cap. 1870. III. 458.[2]
— Rubus Roezli Rgl. 1875. II. 309.[2]
— Salix purpurea L. var. pendula Rgl. 1860. III. 352.[1]
— Ueber die Schädigung unserer cultivirten Bäume. 1872. III. 182.
— Schmarotzergewächse. 1854. III. 193.[2]
— Sebastiana brasiliensis Sprgl. 1859. II. 451.[2]
— Senecio Ghiesbreghtii H. Hal. 1860. II. 865.[1]
— Sollya Drummondi Morr. 1859. III. 416.[1]
— Spiraea amurensis Maxim. 1865. II. 269.[2]
— Spiraea Pallasii Rgl. et Tiling. 1860. II. 311.[1]
— Stangeria Katzeri. 1874. II. 6.[2]
— Staphylea colchica Steven. 1875. II. 473.[2]
— Stellera (Wickströmia) Alberti Rgl. 1887. II. 606.[1]
— Styrax japonicum Sieb. et Zucc. 1868. II. 705.[1]
— Synopsis Berberidis. 1873. II. 202.[1]
— Tabernaemontana laeta Mart. 1861. II. 733.[1]
— Tentamen florae ussuriensis. 1861. I. 455.
— Tentamen Rosarum monographiae. 1877. II. 282.[2]
— Tetratheca ericifolia Sm. 1871. II. 429.[1]
— Theophrasta imperialis Linden. 1864. II. 696.[2]
— Thibaudia Hendersoni Rgl. 1875. II. 684.[2]
— Thomasia glutinosa Lindl. var. latifolia. 1885. II. 539.[1]
— Thunbergia laurifolia Lindl. 1865. III. 710.[2]
— Thyrsacanthus lilacinus Lindl. 1881. III. 709.[2]
— Tilia euchlora C. Koch. 1881. III. 586.[1]
— Toxicophlaea Thunbergi Harv. 1878. II. 722.[2]
— Tragopyrum lanceolatum M. Bieb. var. latifolia. 1891. II. 184.
— Trevesia sundaica Miq. 1864. II. 653.[1]
— Tripterygium Hook. 1869. II. 471.[1]
— Uebersicht und Beschreibung der Arten der Gattung Berberis. 1873. II. 202.[1]
— Urostigma bibracteatum Rgl. 1859. II. 150.[1]
— Urostigma magnificum Rgl. 1859. III. 368.[2]
— Die Vegetationsverhältnisse des Winters 1852. 1853. I. 227.[1]
— Zur Verbreitung von Rhododendron ponticum. 1881. II. 683.[2]
— Veredlungen mit krautartigen jungen Aesten. 1867. III. 163.[2]
— Vermehrung der Rhododendron. 1859. III. 158.
— Vermehrung der Rhopalen. 1874. III. 383.[2] *665.[2]
— Vermehrung der Sikkim-Rhododendron. 1859. III. 656.
— Verpflanzung grosser Palmen. 1860. III. 317.
— Verwachsungen bei Tannen. 1859. I. 209,[1] *IV. 445.
— Viburnum orientale Pall. 1868. II. 843.[2]
— Viburnum Thunb. var. lucidum. 1856. III. 753.[2]
— Villaresia grandiflora Fisch. 1857. II. 476.[1]
— Vitis Thunbergii Sieb. et Zucc. 1864. II. 506.[1]
— Vitis vinifera L. var. amurensis. 1861. II. 506.[1]
— Wallisia princeps. 1875. II. 721.[1]
— Ueber Wellingtonia gigantea. 1859. III. 310.[1]
— Westringia lucifolia R. Br. 1878. II. 767.[2]
— Winterschnitt bei unseren Bäumen. 1870. III. 170.
— Wolkensteinia Theophrasta. 1865. II. 545.[2]
— Xerophyta retinervis Baker. 1877. II. 90.[1]
— Sur les Yucca et leur culture. 1859. III. 339.[1]
— Zwei neue Cycadeen. 1857. II. 1.[2]
— Zwei neue Rhododendron des Kaukasus. 1885. II. 683.[2]
— Zwei neue Rhododendron vom Kaukasus. 1886. II. 683.[2]
— Zwei Rubus aus Asien. 1892. III. 459.[1]
— Zwei Rubus in Asien. 1892. II. 305.[1]
— *See also* HEER, Oswald & REGEL, Eduard; MAXIMOWICZ, C. J. & REGEL, Eduard von; SCHMITZ, J. J. & REGEL, Eduard von; PERAZN, E. Л.
— & Haage & Schmidt. Mammillaria barbata. 1894. III. 623.[2]
— & Herder, F. von. Enumeratio plantarum in regionibus cis- et transiliensibus a cl. Semenovio anno 1857 collectarum. 1864. I. 454.[1]
— Plantae Severzovianae et Borszcovianae. 1864. I. 454.[1]
— & Körnicke. Strelitzia Nicolai Rgl. et Körn. 1858. II. 91.[2]
— & Tiling, Heinrich. Florula ajanensis. 1858. I. 455.
— Rach, Ludwig & Herder, Ferdinand von. Verzeichniss der . . . zwischen Jakutsk und Ajan gesammelten Pflanzen. 1859. I. 455.
Regel, Fritz. Der Thüringer Wald. 1892. IV. 355.[2]
— Die Vermehrung der Begoniaceen. 1876. III. 583.[2]
Regel, Robert. Einige Beobachtungen über den Geruch der Blüthen. 1892. I. 182.[2]

Regelsperger, Gustave. La protection des arbres, le reboisement. 1897. IV. 47,[1] 181.[1]
— The protection of forests. 1897. IV. 47,[1] 181.[1]
Regener, Emilius. Erfahrungen über den Nahrungsverbrauch . . . der grossen Kiefern-Raupe. 1865. IV. 476.
The regeneration of alpine forest land. 1872. IV. 166.[2]
Regensburg — Königlich baierische botanische Gesellschaft. See KÖNIGLICH . . . I. 13.
Regensburg — Kgl. botanische Gesellschaft. Katalog der Bibliothek. See VOLLMANN, Franz. 1895. I. 3.[1]
Regensburg — Königl. botanische Gesellschaft. Literaturblätter. See LITERATURBLÄTTER . . . 1828. I. 1.
Regenstein. Zur Mäusevertilgung. 1900. IV. 198.[2]
Regenval en reboisatie in Deli. 1898. IV. 168.[2]
Reghini, Carlo COSTA. See COSTA-BEGHINI, Carlo.
Régi. Note sur l'Acacia Moringa. 1882. II. 234.[2]
Regia scuola superiore di agricoltura in Portici. See REALE SCUOLA . . . IN PORTICI. III. 23.[2]
Regia societas physiographica lundensis. Acta. See LUNDS UNIVERSITETS. I. 519.[2]
Regia societas scientiarum upsaliensis. Acta. I. 8.[1]
Régimbeau. Examen analytique des sèves-de Vignes. 1832. III. 582.
Regimbeau, M. Le bupreste du Chêne vert. 1876. IV. 503.[1]
— Le Chêne yeuse ou Chêne vert dans le Gard. 1879. IV. 503.[1]
— Des coupes de régénération dans les futaies. 1878. IV. 159,[2] 461.[1]
— Destruction du Balaninus. 1878. IV. 510.
— Études sur les forêts. 1860. IV. 50.
— Fertilité du Chêne-yeuse. 1880. IV. 503.[1]
— On methods of cutting to secure natural reproduction in Pine forests. 1878. IV. 461.[1]
— Nouvelles observations sur le bupreste du Chêne vert. 1877. IV. 503.[1]
— Des rapports entre les racines et les branches des arbres. 1873. III. 43.
Régime forestier du Sénégal. 1900. IV. 307.[2]
Le regime forestier en Italie. 1897. IV. 329.
Regio, GREGORIUS DE. See GREGORIUS DE REGIO.
Regio decreto col quale si sopprime la segreteria del Consiglio forestale. 1866. IV. 293.[2]
Région du Chêne-Liége en Europe. See COMBE, Ad. 1889. IV. 517.[1]
Regisseur, (pseud.). Caractères différentiels des arbres de Belgique. 18. . ? I. 391,[2] IV. 84.[2]
Register der geslagten van de drie rijken der natuur. 1781. I. 72.[1]
Registre matricule revisé des meilleures sortes de fruits à pepins pour le canton de Berne. See REVIDIRTES Stammregister . . . 1886. III. 88.[1]
Reglus hortus botanicus tauricnsis. Enumeratio seminum. 1820. I. 62.
Reglamento para el régimen interior de la Junta consultiva de montes. 1896. IV. 554.
Reglamento para el régimen interior de la Junta facultativa de montes. 1892. IV. 554.
Reglamento para la ejecución de la ley de 9 de Julio. 1878. IV. 555.[1]
Reglamento para la ejecución del real decreto de esta fecha reorganizando la Asociación general de ganaderos. 1892. IV. 554.
Reglamento para la Escuela especial de ingenieros de montes. 1883. IV. 35.[1]
Reglamento para la Escuela especial de ingenieros de montes. 1887. IV. 540.[2]
Reglamento para la Escuela especial de ingenieros de montes. 1894. IV. 541.
Règlement d'exécution pour la loi fédérale concernant la haute surveillance . . . que la police des forêts. 1876. IV. 330.
Du règlement des exploitations dans une petite sapinière. See BROILLIARD, Charles. 18. . ? IV. 446.[1]
Règlement des forêts. 1870. IV. 307.[1]
Règlement fait par messieurs les commissaires . . . pour la réformation des eaux & forêts . . . de Bar. 1691. IV. 291.[2]
Règlement fait par messieurs les commissaires . . . pour la réformation des eaux & forêts . . . de Lorraine & de Barrois. 1686. IV. 291.[2]
Reglement für den Oberforstmeister des Kantons Zürich. 1839. IV. 306.
Reglement für die Bannwarte. 1836. IV. 306.
Reglement für die Forstmeister des Kantons Zürich. 1838. IV. 306.

Reglement für die Forstvermessungen in dem Fürstenthume Leiningen. 1805. IV. 299.
Reglement für die Gemeinds- und Genossenschaftsförster. 1841. IV. 306.
Reglement für die im preussischen Staate öffentlich anzustellenden Feldmesser. 1872. IV. 302.
Reglement, nach welchem die ständige Zehrungen in Forst- und Jagd-Sachen . . . passieren-sollen. 1776. IV. 300.[2]
Règlement pour la vente et la distribution du bois d'affouage dans les forêts de la Bourgoisie. 1849. IV. 306.
Règlement pour le service des gardes de la forêt du Risoud. 1866. IV. 306.
Règlement pour les examens forestiers. 1873. IV. 36.[1]
Reglement über den Verkauf der Waldprodukte in den Staatswaldungen. 1861. IV. 306.
Reglement über die Anwendung des metrischen Masses . . Hessen. 1870. IV. 301.
Reglement über die Ausführung der Holzverkäufe in den Staatswaldungen. 1839. IV. 306.
Reglement über die Holzpreise . . . in den Domanial-Waldungen des Grossherzogthums Hessen. 1870. IV. 301.
Reglement über die vertheilten offenen Korporationsgemeindelandgüter . . . Münster. 1841. IV. 306.
Reglement wegen Führung des Haues . . . in den königl. preussischen Forsten. 1796. IV. 301.
Règlements de l'École nationale forestière. 1876. IV. 34.[2]
Règlements et programmes d'enseignement de l'École nationale forestière. 1887. IV. 34.[2]
Regler, der indtil videre blive at iagttage ved Udarbeidelsen af de i Loven af 25/2 1851 § 3. 1855. IV. 296.[1]
Regnard, P. De l'action de la chlorophylle. 1885. I. 142.
Régnaud, C. Note sur les propriétés vermifuges . . . du Quisqualis. 1860. III. 632.[2]
— Report . . . of the water supply commission. 1871. IV. 49.[1]
Régnault, Charles. Histoire naturelle . . . du Cocotier. 1856. II. 67.[1]
Regnauld, Jules & Villejean, E. Analyse des graines oléagineuses du Symphonia. 1884. III. 610.[2]
— — Note sur un échantillon de " Cinchona succirubra." 1883. III. 726.[1]
— — Sur la purification de l'alcool méthylique. 1884. IV. 433.[1]
Regnault. L'arbre inconnu des Chinois. 178 . ? II. 384.[2]
Regnault. Note sur une méthode de prévenir la maladie de la Vigne. 1852. III. 575.[2]
Regnault, Félix. Déboisement et décadence. 1896. IV. 45.
Régnault, François. La botanique mise à la portée de tout le monde. 1774. III. 51.
Regnault, Gustave. Recherches sur les affinités de structure . . . des Cyclospermées. 1860. I. 105.
Régné, comte de VASSELOT DE. See VASSELOT DE RÉGNÉ, comte de.
Regneault, F. F. Cours de stéréométrie appliqué spécialement au cubage des bois. 1847. IV. 223.
— De l'interpolation appliquée à l'expression de la marche de la végétation. 1839. IV. 232.
— Traité de topographie et de géodésie. 1844. IV. 264.
Régnier. Mussaenda theifera Pierre. 1883. III. 746.[1]
Régnier, Ch. Les Medinilla en haut culture. 1896. III. 638.[2]
Regnier, L. On the country where the Apricot tree grows wild. 1890. II. 273.[2]
Regnier, Louis. Liste de plantes découvertes en Suisse. 1788. I. 433.
Regnum florae. See GMELIN, P. F. & BÖHMER, G. R. 1788. I. 292.
Regolamenti forestali della provincia di Verona. 1899. IV. 305.
Regolamenti organico e disciplinare degli agenti forestali . . . di Aquila degli Abruzzi. 1899. IV. 305.
Regolamento concernente le modificazioni di alcuni articoli da osservarsi in . . . Castellammare. 1846. IV. 304.
Regolamento contenente le norme e prescrizioni di massima pel taglio e coltura dei boschi . . . di Arezzo. 1894. IV. 305.
Regolamento contenente le prescrizioni di massima per la coltura . . . di Bergamo. 1899. IV. 305.
Regolamento di polizia forestale. 1885. IV. 305.
Regolamento di polizia forestale nei boschi. 1893. IV. 305.
Regolamento di polizia forestale prescritto dell'art. 24. . 1881. IV. 305.
Regolamento di servizio per le guardie forestali. 1867. IV. 305.
Regolamento intorno alla coltura silvana . . . di Messina. 1896. IV. 305.

Regolamento organico delle guardie forestali . . . di Parma. 1894. IV. 305.
Regolamento organico di disciplina e di servizio per gli agenti forestali della provincio di Salerno. 1899. IV. 305.
Regolamento organico e disciplinare del corpo delle guardie forestali provinciali. 1900. IV. 305.
Regolamento organico e disciplinare per le guardie forestali della provincia di Alessandria. 1880. IV. 305.
Regolamento per l' ammissione e disciplina delle guardie forestali della provincia di Molise. 1886. IV. 305.
Regolamento per l' ammissione e disciplina delle guardie forestali per la provincia di Bergamo. 1898. IV. 305.
Regolamento per l'ammissione e la disciplina degli agenti forestali provinciali. 1900. IV. 305.
Regolamento per l' esercizio dei diritti d' uso nei boschi. 1863. IV. 334.[2]
Regolamento per l' impianto di un istituto forestale nelle fattorie di Paterno e Vallombrosa. 1869. IV. 35.[1]
Regolamento per l' ispettorato generale dei boschi delle provincie venete. 1831. IV. 304.[3]
Regolamento per la coltura silvana . . . di Napoli. 1880. IV. 305, 323.
Regolamento per la custodia ed amministrazione dei boschi. 1811. IV. 304.[3]
Regolamento per le guardie forestali . . . di Cuneo. 1880. IV. 305.
Regolamento per le guardie forestali . . . di Torino. 1895. IV. 305.
Regolativo forestale del Vicerè Eugenio Napoleone. 1805. IV. 304.[2]
La regolazione delle acque del Jura svizzero. 1881. IV. 187.[1]
Réguis, Marius. Nomenclature franco-provençale de plantes. 1877. I. 74.[1]
Regulation no. 1 of 1892 [for Ajmere and Marwara]. 1892. IV. 307.[3]
Regulativ, betreffend die bauliche Unterhaltung der Dienstetablissements der Staats-Forstverwaltung. 1882. IV. 302.
Regulativ betreffend die Krankenfürsorge für die in den Betrieben der k:. b. Staatsforstverwaltung beschäftigten Arbeiter. 1899. IV. 311.[1]
Regulativ das Harz-Scharren und Theer-Schwehlen in den Waldungen. 1811. IV. 303.[1]
Regulativ für die k. Commission zu den Prüfungen für den höheren Staatsforstdienst. 1884. IV. 33.[1]
Regulativ für die K. höhere Forstlehranstalt zu Neustadt-Eberswalde. 1864. IV. 32.
Regulativ über Ausbildung, Prüfung und Anstellung für die unteren Stellen des Forstdienstes. 1879. IV. 32.
Regulativ über Ausbildung und Prüfung für die unteren Stellen des Forstdienstes. 1872. IV. 32.
Reh, L. Untersuchungen an amerikanischen Obst-Schildläusen. 1899. III. 188.[1]
— Zucht-Ergebnisse mit Aspidiotus. 1900. III. 192.[1]
Réhabilitation horticole des plantes dites grasses. 1851. III. 333.[1]
Rehdantz, C. Die Rhododendron javanicum. 1888. III. 660.[2]
Rehder, Alfred. Abelia. 1900. III. 61.[1]
— Acanthopanax ricinifolium. 1897. III. 641.[1]
— Actinidia. 1900. III. 595.[3]
— Aesculus parviflora. 1897. III. 538.[2]
— Aralia chinensis L. 1897. III. 641.[1]
— Aristolochia macrophylla Lam. 1898. III. 386.[2]
— Das Arnold-Arboretum. 1898. I. 39.
— Die Arten der Gattung Andromeda. 1898. III. 647.[1]
— Ein Ausflug nach Nord-Carolina. 1900. I. 320.
— Azalea pontica und A. sinensis. 1898. III. 655.
— Azalea Vaseyi. 1899. III. 662.[2]
— Beiträge zur Flora des Muldenthals. 1886. V. xx.[1]
— Berberis Thunbergi. 1898. III. 395.[1]
— Betula Maximowiczi Rgl. 1897. III. 357.[1]
— The Canadian Elder. 1899. III. 751.[3]
— Cassinia fulvida Hook. fil. 1896. III. 755.[1]
— Ceanothus Fendleri Gray. 1897. III. 541.[1]
— Cercis canadensis. 1899. III. 472.[1]
— Chionanthus virginica. 1899. III. 671.[3]
— Cladrastis lutea. 1899. III. 472.[2]
— Clematis montana Hamilt. 1896. III. 391.[1]
— Clematis paniculata Thbg. 1898. III. 391.[1]
— Cornus candidissima und verwandte Arten. 1900. III. 645.[1]
— Cornus florida L. 1898. III. 646.[1]
— Cornus Kousa. 1899. III. 646.[1]

— Corylopsis pauciflora und C. spicata. 1897. III. 416.[3]
— Culture du Cassinia fulvida. 1897. III. 755.[1]
— Daphne Cneorum. 1900. III. 627.[1]
— Ueber Deutzia Lemoinei. 1896. II. 239.[1]
— Ueber Dimorphismus bei Forsythia. 1891. II. 706.[2]
— Drei empfehlenswerte weissblühende Ziersträucher. 1899. III. 411,[1] 413,[1] 671.[1]
— Einige empfehlenswerte winterharte Schlingpflanzen. 1898. III. 205.[1]
— Einige empfehlenswerte zierfrüchtige Gehölze. 1899. III. 208.[1]
— Einige frühblühende winterharte Ericaceen. 1898. III. 647.[1]
— Einige neue oder weniger bekannte Gehölze. 1894. I. 294,[1] III. 70.
— Einige zierliche Ahornarten. 1889. III. 534.[1]
— Empfehlenswerte Amelanchier-Arten. 1900. III. 419.[1]
— Empfehlenswerte Liguster-Arten. 1899. III. 673.[1]
— Empfehlenswerte Stuartien. 1900. III. 596.[3]
— Empfehlenswerte Treibsträucher. 1896. III. 177.
— Empfehlenswerte Zieräpfel. 1899. III. 425.[1]
— Epheu in Baumform und Quercus Ilex. 1898. III. 362,[2] 643.[1]
— Escallonia Philippiana Mast. 1896. III. 411.[1]
— Evonymus obovata. 1898. III. 533.[1]
— Fendlera rupicola. 1897. III. 411.[1]
— Forsythia suspensa. 1896. II. 706.[2]
— Forsythien-Hecken. 1896. III. 672.[1]
— Aus den Gärten Newports. 1899. III. 398.[3]
— Die Gattung Deutzia. 1895. III. 410.[1]
— Die Gattung Enkianthus. 1900. III. 649.[1]
— Die Gattung Syringa. 1899. II. 714,[3] III. 680.[3]
— Gordonia pubescens L'Hérit. 1899. III. 596.[1]
— Die härtesten unserer Tannenarten. 1897. III. 295.[1]
— Halesia und Pterostyrax. 1899. III. 670.[2]
— Hedera Helix digitata. 1897. III. 643.[1]
— Hibiscus syriacus. 1897. III. 588.[3]
— Hydrangea petiolaris. 1897. III. 412.[3]
— Die japanischen Pflaumen. 1899. III. 443.[3]
— Die kanadische Felsenbirne. 1896. III. 419.[2]
— Die Kirschpflaume. 1896. III. 436.[1]
— Kreuzungen der Clematis coccinea. 1898. III. 390.[1]
— Die Kreuzungen der Gattung Lonicera. 1893. II. 836.[1]
— Le Lierre grimpant et ses variétés. 1897. III. 643.[1]
— Lonicera Caprifolium in Hochstammform. 1896. III. 750.[1]
— Lonicera nervosa. 1896. III. 750.[2]
— Die Loniceren unserer Gärten. 1895. III. 750.[1]
— Magnolia stellata Maxim. 1895. III. 400.[3]
— Der Missbrauch mit buntlaubigen Pflanzen. 1898. III. 207.[1]
— Neue Gehölze. 1896. III. 70.
— Neue winterharte Rhododendron. 1896. III. 662.[3]
— Paeonia arborea als Einzelpflanze. 1896. III. 392.[3]
— Paeonia lutea. 1897. III. 392.[1]
— Parrotia persica. 1897. III. 418.[1]
— Philadelphus Lemoinei. 1896. III. 413.[2]
— Phillyrea Vilmoriniana Boiss. 1898. III. 680.[1]
— Picea Breweriana Wats. 1896. III. 305.[3]
— Picea sitchensis. 1896. III. 306.[1]
— Plantes grimpantes rustiques. 1898. III. 205.[1]
— Polygonum baldschuanicum. 1896. III. 387.[1]
— Prunus pendula. 1900. III. 439.[1]
— Pueraria Thunbergiana Benth. 1897. III. 485.[1]
— Quelques Ericacées rustiques à floraison précoce. 1898. III. 647.[1]
— Quelques Stuartia. 1900. III. 596.[3]
— Rhododendron Metternichi. 1897. III. 661.[3]
— Rhododendron und andere Gehölze auf dem Ohrberg bei Hameln. 1897. I. 49.
— Rhus Cotinus. 1896. III. 524.[1]
— Rhus semialata. 1899. III. 527.[3]
— Rhus typhina laciniata. 1900. III. 528.[3]
— Rosa hybrida, Anemonen-Rose. 1896. III. 455.[3]
— Rosa multiflora. 1896. III. 456.[1]
— Rosa setigera. 1900. III. 457.[1]
— Rosa Wichuraiana Crép. 1898. III. 457.[1]
— Rubus sorbifolius. 1898. III. 458.[1]
— Salix alba vitellina pendula. 1896. III. 351.[1]
— Sambucus canadensis Linn. 1899. III. 751.[3]
— Les Saules pleureurs. 1898. III. 349.
— Die Schlingpflanze Actinidia Kolomikta. 1896. III. 595.[3]
— Der schwedische Bocksdorn. 1896. III. 701.[1]
— Selbstklimmender wilder Wein. 1895. III. 544.[3]

— Sophora japonica und verwandte Arten. 1898. III. 487.²
— Der Speierling, Sorbus domestica. 1897. III. 460.¹
— Stephanandra Tanakae. 1897. III. 462.¹
— Strassenbäume in östlichen Nord-Amerika. 1900. III. 208.²
— Strassen-Bepflanzungen in nordamerikanischen Städten. 1900. III. 208.²
— Styrax Obassia. 1898. III. 671.¹
— Styrax Obassia und verwandte Arten. 1898. III. 671.¹
— Syringa japonica und Syringe pekinensis. 1899. III. 680.²
— Trauer-Caraganen. 1897. III. 469.²
— Trauerweiden. 1898. III. 349.
— Tsuga canadensis var. pendula. 1900. III. 312.¹
— Ulmus campestris umbraculifera. 1889. III. 365.²
— Die Vermehrung der Coniferen durch Wurzelstecklinge. 1896. III. 294.²
— Viburnum dilatatum. 1899. III. 753.¹
— Viburnum Tinus als Hochstamm. 1896. III. 753.¹
— Viburnum tomentosum. 1898. III. 753.²
— Viburnum tomentosum et V. plicatum. 1898. III. 753.²
— Vitis Coignetiae Pull. 1897. III. 584.¹
— Weeping Willows. 1898. III. 349.
— Winterharte immergrüne Gehölze. 1897. III. 206.¹
— Winterharte Kakteen. 1897. III. 624.¹
— Winterharte Magnolien. 1896. III. 399.¹
— Wistarien in Hochstammform. 1898. III. 490.²
— Wörlitz. 1896. I. 49.
— Xanthoceras sorbifolia. 1900. III. 540.²
— Yucca filamentosa L. 1896. III. 339.²
— Zierfrüchtige Gehölze. 1897. III. 208.¹
— Zw empfehlenswerte frühblühende de Spiraeen. 1900. III. 460.²
— Zwei empfehlenswerte Pyramidenbäume. 1898. III. 366,¹ 586.¹
— See also JANORSCHKE, O., PFEIFFER, Karl & REHDER, Alfred.
— & Weigelt, C. Elaeagnus longipes = Elaeagnus edulis. 1892. III. 629.¹
— & others. The propagation of Xanthoceras sorbifolia. 1895. III. 540.²
——— Vermehrung von Xanthoceras sorbifolia. 1895. III. 540.²
Rehder, Jakob Heinrich. Bericht über eine neue . . . Art von Robinia inermis. 1847. III. 486.¹
— Etwas über die entstehenden Lücken in den Pflanzungen. 1847. III. 201.
Rehfelt, Abraham. Hodegus botanicus menstruus. 1717. I. 289.
Rehling, H. Remarks on the propagation of plants by leaves. 1848. III. 159.¹
Rehm, J. See HUBER, J. C. & REHM, J.
Rehmann. See BRUNNER, Friedrich & REHMANN.
Rehmann, Anton. Einige Notizen über die Vegetation . . . des Schwarzen Meeres. 1872. I. 369.
— O formacyach roślinnych w Galicyi; (a.) obwód żółkiewski. 1870. I. 442.
— O formacyach roślinnych w Galicyi; (b.) obwód złoczowski. 1871. I. 442.
— Geobotaniczne stosunki południowej Afryki. 1880. I. 495.
— Jezioro Switeź i Kołdyczewskie. Skład lasów. 1891. I. 366.
— Materyały do flory wschodnich Karpat. 1873. I. 446.
— O początkach współczesnych okręgów roślinnych. 1880. I. 300.
— Przegląd roślin zebranych w obwodach Tarnopolskim i Czortkowskim. 1873. I. 442.
— O roślinności Bieskidów zachodnich. 1865. I. 445.
— Sprawozdanie z wycieczki botanicznej w zachodnią część Galicyi. 1868. I. 442.
— O utworach żywicznych roślin. 1869. V. XI.²
— Ueber die Vegetations-Formationen der taurischen Halbinsel. 1875. I. 369.
— Zapisek botaniczny z nad brzegów Popradu. 1869. I. 442.
Rehmann, Joseph. Beschreibung einer thibetanischen Handapotheke. 1811. III. 272.²
— Sur les briques de Thé des Mongoles. 1809. III. 606.
Rehnelt, F. Abrus precatorius L., eine häufig verwechselte Pflanze. 1896. III. 462.²
— Dombeya Wallichii Benth. 1897. III. 591.¹
— Fabiana imbricata R. et P. 1898. III. 700.²
— Genista radiata Scop. 1896. III. 477.¹

— Idesia polycarpa Maxim. 1896. III. 614.²
— Lespedeza Sieboldi Miq. var. alba. 1896. III. 481.¹
— Mackaya bella Harv. 1897. III. 469,¹ 709.²
— Mimosa Spegazzini. 1898. III. 482.²
— Ochna multiflora DC. 1898. III. 596.¹
— Ruscus racemosus L. 1898. III. 336.¹
— Winterharte Kakteen. 1897. III. 620.¹
— Zwei seltene Koniferen. 1899. III. 304,² 809.¹
Ueber den Rehschaden durch Verbeissen. 1898. IV. 197.¹
Rei rusticae scriptores. See SCRIPTORES rei rusticae. 1470. III. 96.²
Reiber, Ferd. Les insectes de la promenade Lenôtre. 1874. III. 190.
— Notice sur le phylloxera en Alsace-Lorraine. 1885. III. 574.
Reich, Eduard. Die Nahrungs- und Genussmittelkunde. 1860. III. 219.²
Reich, Heinrich, BÖHNKE-. See BÖHNKE-REICH, Heinrich.
Reich, Louis. Les Tamarix et leurs applications. 1891. IV. 529.¹
Reichard, Arthur. Phyllocactus crenatus Salm. 1891. III. 625.²
Reichard, Frans von. Beitrag zur deutschen forstlichen Bibliographie. 1875. IV. 2.
Reichard, Johann Jakob. Animadversiones quaedam botanicae. 1778. I. 114.¹
— Botanische Bemerkungen. 1780. I. 262.
— Enumeratio stirpium Horti botanici Senkenbergiani. 1782. I. 44.
— Flora moeno-francofurtana. 1772. I. 373.
— Sylloge opusculorum botanicorum. 1782. I. 263.
Reichardt, (Oberförster, Tillowitz). Besprechung der transportabeln Waldeisenbahnen. 1886. IV. 392.
Reichardt, Eduard. Ueber die chemischen Bestandtheile der Chinarinden. 1855. III. 722.
— De plantarum partibus anorganicis. 1856. I. 153.
Reichardt, Heinrich Wilhelm. Eine alte Linde im Hofe des Schlosses zu Buchheim. 1874. II. 516.²
— Flora der Insel Jan Mayen. 1886. V. XIX.¹
— Hypericaceae. 1878. II. 552.²
— Kleinere Mittheilungen aus dem botanischen Laboratorium. 1877. II. 43.²
— Ueber eine Missbildung der gemeinen Föhre. 1866. II. 47.²
— Ein neuer Brandpilz. 1867. III. 370.¹
— Uebersicht der Pflanzen des alten Aegypten. 1859. I. 483.
— Vier neue Pflanzenarten aus Brasilien. 1884. I. 343.
— Das Vorkommen verzweigter männlicher Kätzchen bei Populus tremula. 1868. II. 98.¹
— Ueber das Vorkommen von Exobasidium Vaccinii. 1872. III. 664.²
— Ueber das Vorkommen von Vaccinium Myrtillus. 1867. II. 680.¹
— Die in den Werken von Clusius enthaltenen Nachrichten über Gallen. 1866. I. 214.²
Reichart, Christian. Abhandlungen von allerhand Saamenwerke. 1751. III. 121.¹
— Von der Baumzucht. 1753. III. 101.²
— Deutschlands Gartenschatz. 1751. III. 121.¹
— Land- und Gartenschatz. 1751. III. 121.¹
Reiche, von. See MEYER, W. & REICHE, von.
Reiche, Karl. Über anatomische Veränderungen, welche in den Perianthkreisen . . . vor sich gehen. 1885. I. 115.¹
— Beiträge zur Anatomie der Inflorescenzaxen. 1887. I. 113.²
— Beiträge zur Kenntnis der chilenischen Buchen. 1897. II. 127.²
— Beiträge zur Kenntnis der Gattung Azara. 1896. II. 569.¹
— Die botanischen Ergebnisse meiner-Reise in die Cordilleren. 1897. I. 330.
— Cistaceae. 1895. II. 563.²
— Elementos de la morfolojía i sistemática botanica. 1896. I. 256.
— Erythroxylaceae. 1896. II. 394.¹
— Estudios críticos sobre la flora de Chile. 1899. I. 347.
— Flora de Chile. 1896. I. 347.
— Die Flora von Leipzig. 1887. I. 388.
— Geflügelte Stengel und herablaufende Blätter. 1888. I. 106.¹
— Geraniaceae. 1896. II. 389.¹
— Humiriaceae. 1896. II. 393.²
— Kenntnis der chilenischen . . . Oxalis. 1894. II. 392.²

Reiche, Karl (*continued*).
— Zur Kenntniss der Lebensthätigkeit einiger chilenischer Holzgewächse. 1897. I. 148, *347*.
— Zur Kenntniss von Gomortega nitida. 1896. II. 221.²
— Linaceae. 1896. II. 392.²
— Litteratur zur Flora des Königsreichs Sachsen. 1889. I. 3.²
— Oxalidaceae. 1896. II. 392.¹
— Über polster- und deckenförmigwachsende Pflanzen. 1893. I. 107.¹
— Die Vegetationsverhältnisse am . . . Rio Maule. 1896. I. 347.
— Die Verbreitungsverhältnisse der chilenischen Coniferen. 1900. II. 15.¹
— *See also* HARMS, Hermann & REICHE, C.; PÖHLMANN, Robert & REICHE, Karl.
— & Taubert, Paul. Violaceae. 1895. II. 567.¹
Reichel, Abraham Gottlieb. De veris herbae Thee proprietatibus. *See* STAHL, I. J. 1734. III. 605.
Reichel, C. F. Ueber China-Rinden. 1856. III. 722.
Reichel, Friedrich Daniel. Standorte der seltneren . . . Pflanzen in der Umgegend von Dresden. 1837. I. 379.
Reichel, Georg Christian. De vasis plantarum spiralibus. 1758. I. 133.
Reichelt, (*Oberförster in Szyglowitz bei Tost*). Ueber Einfassung der jungen Nadelholzbestände. 1867. IV. 141.
Reichelt, Karl. Geschichte der Veredlungsarten. 1882. III. 162.
Reichenau, von, (*nassauischer Oberförster*). Anbau der Weiss-Erle. 1855. IV. 489.²
— Ueber die landwirthschaftliche Zwischennutzung des Waldbodens. 1850. IV. 133.
Reichenau, A. von PLANTA-. *See* PLANTA-REICHENAU, A. von.
Reichenau, W. Die Bepflanzung der Strassen mit Obstbäumen. 1887. II. 211.¹
Reichenbach, von (*Landrath*). Fortschritte der neuen köstlichen Obstbaumsorten. 1827. III. 70.
— Neueste Obstkörbe. 1830. III. 70.
— Obstkörbe. 1822. III. 70.
Reichenbach, Graf von. Bemerkungen gegen die . . . behauptete Unzweckmässigkeit des Köpfens der Weidenbäume. 1833. III. 347.
Reichenbach, Anton Benedict. Handbuch des natürlichen Pflanzensystems. 1837. I. 260.
— Der Kaffeebaum. 1867. III. 739.
— Naturgeschichte des Pflanzenreichs. 1837. I. 260.
— Naturgeschichte des Pflanzenreichs für Gymnasien. 1840. I. 255.
Reichenbach, E. Sur la composition des feuilles de Mûrier. 1867. II. 154.²
— Ueber Seidenraupenzucht. 1867. III. 377.
— Untersuchungen über die Zusammensetzung der Maulbeerblätter. 1867. II. 154.²
Reichenbach, Heinrich Gottlieb Ludwig. Aufstellung dreier neuen Pflanzengattungen. 1824. II. 827.¹
— Botanik für Damen, Künstler. 1828. I. 94.
— Conspectus regni vegetabilis. 1828. I. 260.
— Flora exotica. 1834. III. 74.
— Flora germanica excursoria. 1830. I. 378.
— Flora lipsiensis pharmaceutica. 1817. III. 72.
— Flora saxonica. 1842. I. 381.
— Die Flora von Deutschland nach ihren Gattungen. 1833. I. 378.
— Florae germanicae clavis synonymica. 1833. I. 378.
— Florae lipsiensis pharmaceuticae specimen. 1817. III. 72.
— Gäa von Sachsen. 1843. I. 381.
— Icones et descriptiones plantarum. 1842. I. 266.
— Iconographia botanica. 1823. I. 377.
— Iconographia botanica exotica. 1827. I. 267.
— Index in herbarium florae germanicae. 183.? V. XIX.³
— Kupfersammlung ausländischer Gewächse. 1827. III. 59.²
— Kupfersammlung zum praktischen deutschen Botanisirbuche. 1836. I. 379.
— Magazin der aesthetischen Botanik. 1822. I. 266.
— Das Pflanzenreich. 1834. I. 255.
— Repertorium herbarii. 1841. I. 77.
— Taschenbuch für Gartenfreunde. 1827. III. 74.
— Verzeichniss . . . neuer Pflanzen aus der Flora lusitanomaderensis. 1830. I. 497.
— & H. G. Deutschlands Flora, mit . . . Abbildungen. 1834. I. 378.
— — Icones florae germanicae et helveticae. 1834. I. 378.

Reichenbach, Heinrich Gustav. Botanische Notizen. 1872. II. 179.¹
— Ueber den Cundurango. 1872. II. 740.³
— Cycadeen-Bastarde. 1883. III. 284.¹
— Eine neue Conifere in den östlichen Alpen. 1877. II. 38.¹
— *See also* REICHENBACH, H. G. L. & G. H.
Reichenbach, Karl, *Freiherr* von. Die Pflanzenwelt in ihren Beziehungen zur Sensitivität. 1858. I. 147.
Reichert, Carl Bogislaus. Über die Saftströmung. 1867. I. 149.²
— On the sap-currents. 1867. I. 149.³
Reichert, Johann Friedrich. Hortus Reichertianus. 1804. I. 45.
Reicholdt, Christoph & Reider, J. E. von. Die pharmacéutische Waarenkunde. 1844. III. 258.
Reichsgerichtliche Erkenntnisse in Forst- und Jagd-Sachen. 1790. IV. 316.
Reichsgräflich Schaffgotsch'sche Oberförsterei Petersdorf. 1884. IV. 354.
Reichsstadt-ulmische Forstordnung. 1802. IV. 318.
Der Reichswald. 1856. IV. 352.
Reid, Clement. The origin of the British flora. 1899. I. 404.¹
Reid, H. F. Studies of Muir glacier, Alaska. 1893. I. 311.³
Reid, Hugo. Outlines of medical botany. 1832. III. 57.
Reid, John. The Scots gard'ner. 1683. III. 107.
Reid, John. Transplanting machine. 1865. III. 167.
— Transplanting machines. 1871. III. 167.
Reid, T. Anderson. Preparation of wood-pulp. 1885. IV. 430.
Reider, Jakob Ernst von. Abbildung von fünfundzwanzig . . . Pelargonien. 1829. III. 491.¹
— Anleitung für Landleute über die Anlegung . . . der Obstbäume. 1847. III. 145.³
— Beschreibung aller bekannten Pelargonien. 1829. III. 491.¹
— Beschreibung der neuesten . . . Ziergewächse. 1828. III. 74.
— Die Beschreibung und Kultur der Azaleen. 1834. III. 74.
— Bloemkundige, beschrijving van meer dan 500 gewassen. 1830. I. 268.
— Das einzig richtige Prinzip der Forstwirthschaft. 1840. IV. 268.
— Das Ganze der Obstbaumzucht. 1830. III. 136.
— Das Ganze der Rosenkultur. 1829. III. 451.³
— Das Ganze des Weinbaues. 1835. III. 552.
— De rosenteelt. 1829. III. 451.³
— Der schnell unterscheidende Botaniker. 1835. III. 74.
— *See also* REICHOLDT, Christoph & REIDER, J. E. von.
Reiffenstein, Edmund von. Der umsichtige Forst- und Weidmann. 1842. IV. 97.
Reifferscheid-Dyck, Joseph, *Fürst und Altgraf* von SALM-. *See* SALM-REIFFERSCHEID-DYCK, *Fürst und Altgraf* von.
Reig y Palau, José. El valle de Arañ. 1896. IV. 363.
Reig, Johann Christian. De Cassiae speciebus officinalibus. 1801. III. 470.¹
Reilingh, W. De cultures van Nederlandsch Oost Indie. 1897. III. 129.¹
Reimann, C. Schlüssel zur Bestimmung von Weiden. 1868. II. 101.²
Reimann, G. Gomme savakine. 1881. III. 466.¹
Reimenschneider, F. E. Die officinellen . . . Pflanzen des Botanischen Gartens der Veterinär-Schule zu Dorpat. 1861. I. 42.
Reimer, Ernst. Bericht über . . . in die Hauptfrassgebiete der Nonne unternommenen Studien-Reisen. 1896. IV. 202.
Reimers, M. N. Les Quinquinas de culture. 1900. II. 813.²
Reimers, Martin. Respirationis plantarum explicatio. 1839. I. 169.²
Reims—Académie nationale. *See* ACADÉMIE . . . I. 2D.
Rein, Johannes Justus. Di alcuni alberi ed arbusti del Giappone. 1877. I. 461.
— Ueber Anbauversuche mit dem japanischen Lackbaum. 1893. III. 528.²
— Beobachtungen aus dem Botanischen Garten zu Valencia. 1889. I. 297.³
— Camellias. 1889. II. 550.²
— Ueber einige bemerkenswerthe Gewächse aus . . . Mogador. 1873. I. 485.
— The industries of Japan. 1889. III. 273.³
— Japan nach Reisen und Studien. 1881. IV. 376.¹

— Über japanische Gehölze. 1877. I. 461.
— Magnolias. 1889. II. 212.[1]
— Naturwissenschaftliche Reisestudien in Japan. 1873. I. 462.
— Note sur les arbres et arbustes japonais. 1877. I. 461.
— Notes on Japanese trees and shrubs. 1877. I. 461.
— Observaciones sobre la Sierra Nevada. 1896. IV. 556.[2]
— Ueber die Vegetations-Verhältnisse der Bermudas-Inseln. 1873. I. 336.
— Vorkommen und Nutzen der Camellia in ... Japan. 1885. III. 600.[1]
— Zier- und Obstbäume der Bermuda-Inseln. 1896. III. 118.[2]

Reinaud de Fonvert, Am. Note sur l'Arceuthobium Oxycedri. 1846. II. 174.[2]
Reinboth, J. E. De Agallocho. 1732. III. 626.[2]
Reinders, G. L'alios de nos bruyères. 1889. IV. 543.[2]
— Handboek voor den Nederlandschen landbouw. 1875. III. 106.[1]
— De oerbanken onter heidevelden. 1889. IV. 69, 543.[2]
— Onderzoek naar de voedings en mest waarde van koeken uit kapokpitten. 1869. III. 587.[2]
Reinders, H. C. Bijdrage tot de houtteelt. 1834. IV. 119.[1]
Reineccius, C. A. De חשיל הצצבצה; sive, Rosa saronitica. *See* ROSENFELD, Daniel. 1715. I. 512.
Reinecke, Franz. Die Flora der Samoa-Inseln. 1898. I. 510.[1]
— Über die Knospenlage der Laubblätter. 1893. I. 108,[2] 111.
— Die Nutzpflanzen Samoas. 1896. III. 283.[2]
Reinecke, Julius. Ueber die Anzucht der Epacris-Arten. 1844. III. 664.[2]
— Beitrag zur Kultur der Euphorbia pulcherrima. 1844. III. 518.[1]
— Beitrag zur Kultur der Kokos-Palme. 1854. III. 322.[2]
— Bemerkungen über das fehlerhafte Tiefpflanzen. 1844. III. 169.[2]
— Bemerkungen über die eigenthümliche Keimung ... der ... Palmen. 1874. II. 63.[1]
— Beobachtungen über Ceroxylon Klopstockia. 1860. II. 66.[1]
— Der heilige und braunblüthige Anisstrauch. 1857. III. 397.[2]
— Ueber das Keimen sehr alter Acacien-Samen. 1844. III. 463.[1]
— Ueber die Kultur der Befaria. 1848. III. 648.[2]
— Mittheilung von einer blühenden Paulownia. 1851. III. 703.[2]
— Mittheilungen über die Anzucht der Palmen. 1855. III. 317.
— Mittheilungen über die Anzucht der Palmen und Cycadeen. 1849. III. 316.[2]
— Über Palmensaaten. 1853. III. 316.[2]
— Verfahren bei der Kultur der Stelzenpalme Iriartea. 1856. III. 326.[1]
— *See also* KOCH, Karl & REINECKE.

Reinecken, Rudolph. Interessante Beobachtung ungewöhnlicher Knospenbildung einer Kiefer. 1880. II. 40.[1]
— Om Plantning af store Træer. 1876. III. 167.
— Das Verpflanzen grosser Bäume. 1876. III. 167.
Reinemer. Rindenbeschädigungen durch Tiere. 1897. IV. 196.[1]
— Welchen Gefahren sind die Kiefer ... ausgesetzt? 1895. IV. 457, 479.
Reiner, Joseph & Hohenwarth, S. von. Botanische Reisen nach einigen Oberkärntnerischén ... Alpen. 1792. I. 439.
Reinhard, H. Das Microscop. 1864. I. 36.[1]
Reinhard, J. J. Tractatus de iure forestali Germanorum. 1738. IV. 316.
Reinhard, Ludvig Vasilevitch. *See* PeЙнгарДъ, Л. B.
Reinhard, Ludwig. Die Untersuchung und Aburtheilung der Forstfrevel. 1854. IV. 318.
Reinhardt, Johannes Theodor. Brasiliens Urskov. 1863. I. 342.
— Nogle Bemærkninger om den Indflydelse de idelige Markbrande ... de brasilianske Campos. 1863. I. 342.
Reinhardt, Max Otto. Das leitende Gewebe einiger anorma gebauten Monocotylenwurzeln. 1884. I. 104.
Reinhart. Ueber die Ausbildung der Förster. 1885. IV. 29.
Reinholt, A. Zur Bewegung des Wassers in der Pflanze. 1878. I. 165.

Reinhold, C. L. Beschreibung eines Erdmikrometers. 1780. IV. 57.
Reinholm, H. A. Suomalaisia kasvu-nimejä. 1850. I. 73.[1]
Reinick, H. A. Beiträge zur Waldschutz- und Aufforstungs-Frage. 1881. IV. 274.[1]
Reinicke, Friedrich. Beiträge zur neueren Mikroskopie. 1858. I. 36.[1] V. VIII.[1]
Reinige, (*Apotheker in Lippstadt*). Ein weissblühendes Sarothamnus. 1851. II. 351.[2]
Reinitzer, Friedrich. Bemerkungen zur Physiologie des Gerbstoffs. 1889. I. 183.
— Der Gerbstoffbegriff. 1891. I. 183.
— Über die physiologische Bedeutung der Transpiration. 1881. I. 167.
— Untersuchungen über den Zusammenhang zwischen Wärmeleitung und Struktur der Hölzer. 1878. IV. 412.[2]
— *See also* GINTL, W. F. & REINITZER, Friedrich.
Reinke, Johannes. Andeutungen über den Bau der Wurzel von Pinus Pinea. 1872. II. 45.[1]
— Die Assimilationsorgane der Asparageen. 1898. II. 77.[2]
— Beiträge zur Anatomie der an den Laubblättern ... vorkommenden Secretionsorgane. 1876. I. 110, *135*.
— Ueber die Function der Blattzähne. 1874. I. 110.
— Zur Geschichte unserer Kenntnisse vom Bau der Wurzelspitze. 1872. I. 103.
— Zur Kenntnis der Oxydationsvorgänge. 1887. I. 171.
— Lehrbuch der allgemeinen Botanik. 1880. I. 91.
— Morphologische Abhandlungen. 1873. II. 16.[2]
— Notiz über die Abhängigkeit der Blattenwicklung von der Bewurzelung. 1884. II. 21.[1]
— Die optischen Eigenschaften der grünen Gewebe. 1883. I. 173.
— Photometrische Untersuchungen über die Absorption. 1886. I. 173.
— Der Process der Kohlenstoffassimilation. 1881. I. 173.
— Protoplasma-Probleme. 1881. I. 151.[2]
— Untersuchungen über die Assimilationsorgane der Leguminosen. 1897. II. 321.[1]
— Untersuchungen über die relative Geschwindigkeit des Längenwachsthums. 1872. I. 187.
— Untersuchungen über Wachsthumsgeschichte ... der Phanerogamen-Wurzel. 1871. I. 188.
— & **Braunmüller**, E. Untersuchungen über den Einfluss des Lichtes auf den Gehalt ... an Aldehyd. 1899. I. 174.
— & **Krätzschmar**, L. Ueber das Vorkommen und die Verbreitung flüchtiger reducirender Substanzen. 1883. I. 173.
Reinsch. Préparation de l'acide malique au moyen du Sumac. 1866. III. 527.[1]
Reinsch, Adolf. Über die anatomischen Verhältnisse der Hamamelidaceae. 1889. II. 252.[1]
Reinsch, H. Scheikundige onderzoeking van ... Sassafras. 1845. III. 408.[1]
— Taschenbuch der Flora von Deutschland. 1855 [1854] I. 383, 532.
Reinsch, Paul Friedrich. Die Alpenflora des mittleren Theiles von Franken. 1866. I. 385.
— Beiträge zur chemischen Kenntniss der weissen Mistel. 1860. II. 178.[2]
— Ueber eine eigenthümliche morphologische Umbildung der männlichen Blüthe von Salix cinerea. 1858. II. 106.[1]
— Zur Kenntniss der chemischen Bestandtheile der weissen Mistel. 1862. II. 178.[2]
— Das Mikroskop. 1867. I. 36.[2]
— Ueber das Vorkommen von drei Kotyledonen bei Fagus. 1860. II. 126.[2]
Reinwardt, Caspar Georg Carl. Account of Professor Reinwardt's journey through the Preanger regencies of Java. 1819. I. 468.
— Berigt over een reis door de Preanger-regentschappen. 1819. I. 468.
— Over den boom van Boerhaave. 1845. II. 708.[2]
— Brief bevattende een nader berigt van zijne tweede reize over den vulkaan Goenoeng Goentoer. 1819. I. 468.
— Ueber den Character der Vegetation ... des Indischen Archipels. 1828. I. 465.
— Über den Charakter ... der Gewächse auf Magelhaensland. 1849. I. 347.
— Over het eigenaardige ... der gewassen in de Magellaansche landen. 1849. I. 347.
— Over de hoogte en verdere natuurlijke gesteldheid van eenige bergen in de Preanger regentschappen. 1823. I. 468.
— Nova plantarum indicarum genera. 1825. I. 468.
— Observatio de Mangiferae semine polyembryoneo. 1824. II. 456.[2]

Reinwardt, Caspar Georg Carl (*continued*).
— Onderzoek van Indie. 1823. I. 464.[1]
— Reis naar het oostelijk gedeelte van den Indischen Archipel. 1858. I. 465.
— Végétation dans l'Archipel Indien. 1828. I. 465.
— The vegetation of the Indian Archipelago. 1828. I. 465.
— *See also* ELJS, J. N. van & REINWARDT, C. G. C.
Reischauer, C. *See* VOGEL, August & REISCHAUER, C.
Reiset, Jules. Mémoire sur les dommages causés à l'agriculture par le hanneton. 1867. III. 190, *IV. 202.*
Reisigl, F. A. Von Ueberwerfung [Ableitung] der Salzahe. 1791. IV. 143.[2]
— Unpartheyische Gedanken über die Forstwirthschaft im Fürstenthume Salzburg. 1791. IV. 278.[2]
Reisinger, Joseph. Kurze Anleitung zu . . . Anpflanzung des Philippinischen Maulbeerbaums. 1843. III. 376.
Reiss, A. Zur Frage des Lichtungszuwachses. 1899. IV. 474.
— Die fürstlich Isenburg-Birstein'schen Waldungen. 1891. IV. 354.
— Der Lichtungsbetrieb mit Unterbau bei Kiefernbeständen. 1885. IV. 473.
— Mischbestände von Kiefer, Fichte und Lärche. 1900. IV. 138.[1]
— Zur Naturverjüngung der Kiefer. 1898. IV. 474.
Reiss, R. Ueber die Natur der Reservecellulose. 1889. I. 204.
Reissek, Siegfried. Die Befruchtung und Keimbildung. 1862. I. 201.[1]
— Celastrineae, Ilicineae et Rhamneae. 1861. II. 462,[1]
...[1]
—[?]Die Farbenwandlung der Blüthen. 1870. I. 184.
— Monographische Erläuterung der Gattung Pennantia. 1842. II. 475.[1]
— Die Palmen. 1861. II. 63.[2]
— Plantae Muellerianae. Celastrineae. 1858. II. 465.[2]
— Rhamneae . . . Synopsis specierum Novae Hollandiae. 1846. II. 492.[1]
— Über die selbstständige Entwickelung der Pollenzelle. 1845. I. 200.
— Die Vegetation von Südasien. 1864. I. 453.[1]
— Ueber die wilde Vegetation der Rebe im Wiener Becken. 1856. II. 505.[2]
Reissig. Die Lerchenmotte. 1869. IV. 450.
Reissig, W. Handbuch für Holz- und Torfgas-Beleuchtung. 1863. IV. 433.[2]
Reiter. *See* LAMBERT & REITER.
Reitsma, A. T. De oorspronkelijke wouden van het Amazonegebied. 1868. I. 330.
Reitter, Johann Daniel. Nachricht von der Herzoglich-Württembergischen Jäger-Garde. 1788. IV. 31.
— & **Abel**, G. F. Abbildung der hundert deutschen wilden Holz-Arten. 1790. I. 370, *IV. 81.*
— — Beschreibung und Abbildung der in Deutschland seltener wildwachsenden . . . Holzarten. 1790. I. 370, *IV. 81.*
Reitz, F. W. Timmerhoutsoorten uit den Oranje-Vrystaat. 1891. IV. 401.[1]
Reitzenstein, A. *Freiherr* von. Betrachtungen über die Rentabilität der Waldungen. 1894. IV. 259.[2]
Reivas dell' Ibis. I miti e i simboli delle piante presso i Greci ed i Romani. 1857. I. 517,[2] V. xxv.[2]
Reizen en onderzoekingen in den Indischen Archipel. *See* VERHANDELINGEN . . . 1839. I. 465.
Rejou, R. Note concernant l'emploi des feuilles de tabac. 1873. III. 565.[2]
Rejuvenescence of old trees. 1888. III. 181.[2]
The rejuvenescence of old trees. 1897. III. 181.[2]
Rektorys, Johann. *See* HAAS, Friedrich & REKTORYS, Joh.
— & **Haas**, Friedrich. Akklimatisation fremder Holzarten. 1876. IV. 125.[1]
— — Aufforstungen von Gemeindehutweiden. 1875. IV. 167.[1]
— — Forstlehranstalten. 1876. IV. 30.[2]
Relação das plantas cultivadas no Jardim da Commissão. 1896. I. 40.
Relatorio acêrca da arborisação geral do paiz. 1868. IV. 164.[2]
Relatorio da administração geral das matas. 1881. IV. 363.[1]
Relatorio da commissão nomeada para estudar a influencia da resinagem no Pinhal de Leiria. 1881. IV. 462.[1]
Relazione all' onorevole municipio di Gargnano sul censo stabile dei boschi. *See* SAMUELLI, Tommaso. n. d. IV. 363.[2]
Relazione della commissione tecnica per verifica dei rimboscamenti nella provincia di Aquila. 1889. IV. 166.[1]

Relazione della giunta composta dei deputati Bonfadini . . . sul progetto di legge presentato dal Ministro. 1871. IV. 328.
Relazione di alcuni argomenti trattati dalla Congregazione provinciale di Belluno. 1865. IV. 122.[2]
Relazione . . . di ricercare quale fra i diversi metodi d'injezione dei legnami. 1860. IV. 418.
Relazione ed atti della commissione parlamentare. 1884. III. 573.
Relazione intorno all' amministrazione dei boschi demaniali dichiarati inalienabili. 1881. IV. 293.[2]
Relazione intorno alla esecuzione della legge forestale 20 Giugno 1877. 1881. IV. 328.
Relazione sui provvedimenti contro la fillossera. 1884. III. 761.
Relhan, Richard. Flora cantabrigiensis. 1785. I. 395.
Religion emblemed in flowers. 1869. I. 515.
Reling, H. & **Bohnhorst**, J. Unsere Pflanzen nach ihren . . . Volksnamen. 1882. I. 511.
Relph, John. An inquiry into the medical efficacy of a new species of Peruvian bark. 1794. III. 720.
Remacle, N. *See* MICHEL, M. & REMACLE, N.
A remarkable admeasurement of a Walnut-tree. 1733. II. 871.[2]
A remarkable Beech tree. 1874. II. 127.[1]
A remarkable collection of trees and shrubs. 1875. I. 59.
Remarkable Fig-tree. 1821. II. 151.[1]
Remarkable internal combustion of the trunks of Scots-Fir trees. 1821. IV. 475.
Remarkable Mexican tree. 1847. III. 341.[2]
Remarkable whirlwind. 1824. III. 184.[1]
Remarks from the Secretary to the Chief Commissioner on the forest report for the Central Provinces. 1871. IV. 294.[2]
Remarks on Mr. McIntosh's work on the disease of the Larch. 1863. IV. 450.
Remarks on the impolicy of restrictions on commerce. 1821. IV. 404.[2]
Remarks on the importance of woods and forests in influencing rain. *See* How the woods . . . 1856. IV. 49.[2]
Remarks on the manufacturing of maple sugar. 1790. IV. 527.[1]
Remarks on the . . . productions of Tasmania. *See* BACKHOUSE, James. 1842. III. 283.[1]
Remarks regarding Sterculia foetida. 1854. III. 591.[2]
Une remarque sur les éclaircies dans les pineraies. 1896. IV. 175.[1]
Remarques sur les propriétés des végétaux en général. 1820. III. 259.[2]
Remèdes à employer contre les attaques de l'hylobe. 1900. IV. 208.[2]
Remedial action of the Ailanthus. 1874. III. 507.[2]
Remfrey, J. R. *See* McALPINE, Daniel & REMFREY, J. R.
Remilly. *See* THIBIERGE, Adolphe & REMILLY.
Remington, J. P. Ditain. 1878. III. 686.[2]
Rémont. Note sur le Sequoia gigantea. 1853. III. 310.[2]
Rémont. Note sur quelques Noyers d'Amérique. 1842. III. 353.[2]
Rémont, A. *See* RICHE, Alfred & RÉMONT, A.
Removal of large Screw Pines. 1895. III. 313.[1]
Remplacer. Tafel van de hoeveelheid der oplosbare bestanddeelen. 1790. I. 152.[1]
Remus, Petre S. ANTONESCU-. *See* ANTONESCU-REMUS, Petre S.
Rémusat, Abel. Addition à la note sur les noms des thés. 1824. III. 606.
Remy, E. Jules. Analecta boliviana. 1846. I. 340.[2]
— Les arbres monstrueux du comté de Calaveras. 1856. II. 50.[2]
— Compuestas [de Chile]. 1847. II. 848.[1]
— Observations inédites sur les Composées . . . du Chili. 1849. II. 848.[2]
— Voyage au pays des Mormons. 1860. I. 531.
Remy, Esprit Alexandre. Flore de la Champagne. 1858. I. 411.
Renard, Adolphe. Sur le goudron de Pin. 1894. II. 40,[1] 44.[1]
— Recherche et dosage de l'huile d'Arachide. 1871. III. 678.[2]
— The resin industry in the Landes department. 1884. IV. 461.[1]
Renard, Éd. Bambou à tiges carrées. 1875. III. 316.[1]
— Note sur une nouvelle espèce de Bambou. 1875. III. 315.[1]
Renard, Ernest & **Lacour**, Eymard. De la manne du désert. 1880. III. 221.[2]

Renard, Joseph Claudius. Die inländischen Surrogate der Chinarinde. 1809. III. 269.²
Renard, Perrin et Cⁱᵉ. Note sur la couleur et la conservation des bois. 1848. IV. 417.
Renau, Victor. Forêts de l'Algérie. 1842. IV. 379.¹
Renaudet, Georges. Les principes chimiques des plantes de la flore de France. 1900. I. 154, *III. 271.²*
Renauld, Ferdinand. Aperçu phytostatique . . . de la Haute-Saône. 1873. I. 414.
— *See also* DELAMORE, E., RENAULD, F. & CARDOT, J.
— & others. Contribution à la flore de la Haute-Saône. 1883. I. 416.
Renault, (*pépiniériste*). Des arbres résineux. 186 .? IV. 441.
Renault, Albert. Conditions du développement du rougeot. 1894. III. 581.
— Sur les exigences de la Vigne. 1893. III. 549.¹
Renault, B. Note sur les tourbes. 1899. IV. 491.¹
Renault, Bernard. *See also* BERTRAND, C. E. & RENAULT, Bernard.
— & **Sagot**, Paul. Note sur la matière colorante de l'ébène verte. 1872. III. 707.²
Renault, Léon. Conditions forestières du bassin de la Romanche. 1893. IV. 361.
Renault, P. A. Flore du département de l'Orne. 1804. I. 406.
— Mémoire sur la culture des Pommiers. 1795. III. 426.¹
Renaut, Bertin & Boschi. La Ramie, Ortie de Chine. 1883. III. 381.¹
Renaux, A. Note concernant un moyen de combattre le phylloxera. 1874. III. 566.²
Rendella, Prospero. Tractatus de Vinea, vindemia. 1629. III. 557.²
Rendement d'une pineraie de 65 ares. 1895. IV. 559.²
Rendement de la récolte des graines forestières en Allemagne. 1894. IV. 546.¹
Rendements de l'Épicéa. 1900. IV. 459.¹
Per rendere il legno incombustibile. 1897. IV. 421.
Rendle, Alfred Barton. A British Palm. 1894. II. 61.¹
— A contribution to the flora of eastern tropical Africa. 1895. I. 493.
— Dr. Donaldson Smith's Acanthaceae. 1896. II. 796.²
— New African Convolvulaceae. 1896. II. 745.¹
— New African plants. 1896. I. 493.
— New and interesting Acanthaceae. 1897. II. 796.²
— A new group of flowering plants. 1892. II. 92.¹
— New Philippine plants. 1896. I. 464.¹
— New plants from Somaliland. 1898. I. 490.
— Note on Plectocomia Griffithii. 1877. II. 74.¹
— Tropical African Screw Pines. 1894. II. 57.¹
— *See also* BAKER, E. G. & RENDLE, A. B.; BRITTEN, James & RENDLE, A. B.; HIERN, W. P. & RENDLE, A. B.; SCHLECHTER, Rudolf & RENDLE, A. B.
Rendu. Essai relatif à l'influence du sujet sur la greffe. 1833. III. 39.
— Note sur les effets de la sécheresse de 1835. 1836. III. 506.²
— Note sur une greffe en fente. 1845. III. 164.²
— Notice sur . . . la fixation des greffes. 1842. III. 160.
— Observation sur l'effet désastreux produit sur des Orangers. 1836. III. 500.²
— Observations sur un Vernis du Japon . . . foudroyé. 1838. IV. 193.²
Rendu, Alphonse. De la culture du Thé dans la province de Saint-Paul. 1848. III. 601.¹
— Études topographiques, médicales . . . sur le Brésil. 1848. III. 65.¹
— Note sur le Café. 1848. III. 728.¹
Rendu, Victor. Ampélographie française. 1854. III. 546.
— Botanique. 1838. I. 87.
— Les insectes nuisibles. 1876. IV. 209.¹
— De la maladie de la Vigne dans le midi. 1853. III. 576.
— Rapport-au nom de la Commission . . . pour la destruction du ver blanc. 1836. IV. 202.
— *See also* LEBLOND, Charles & RENDU, Victor.
René, C. Eine neue Methode der Präparation trockenen Holzes. 1885. IV. 420.
Reneaulme, Paul de. Pauli Renealmi . . . specimen historiae plantarum. 1611. I. 284.
Reneaume. Observations sur le suc nourricier. 1708. I. 150.²
Renforçons la production de nos forêts. 1900. IV. 40.²
Rengas-hout van Sumatra. 1885. IV. 526.¹
Rengger, Johann Rudolf. Reise nach Paraguay. 1835. III. 269.²

Renjifo, Cárlos & **Philippi**, R. A. Descripcion de algunas plantas. 1884. II. 861.¹
Rennard, Eduard. Ueber Gelsemium sempervirens. 1875. III. 682.¹
— Ueber Jaborandi. 1875. III. 504.²
Renne. Eichenwickler-Kalamität. 1890. IV. 511.
Rennes, de. Les merveilles et miracles. 1622. I. 517.²
Rennie & Goyder, G. Note on the alkaloids of Strychnos psilosperma. 1892. III. 685.¹
Rennie, Eduard Henry. On the acids of the native Currant. 1881. II. 168.²
— Fluorescence of Bursaria spinosa. 1890. II. 247.²
— Glycyphylline. 1887. III. 338.²
— Sur la gomme Kauri. 1881. III. 297.²
— On the New Zealand Kauri gum. 1881. III. 297.²
— Notes on the sweet principle of Smilax glycyphylla. 1887. III. 338.²
— Preliminary note on the coloring matter of Lomatia. 1893. II. 164.²
— *See also* WRIGHT, Alder & RENNIE, E. H.
— & **Turner**, E. F. On the occurrence of aesculin in Bursaria spinosa. 1890. II. 247.²
— — On the poisonous constituents of Stephania. 1893. II. 208.²
— Some notes on . . . Stephania hernandiaefolia. 1895. III. 397.¹
Rennie, George, (*jr.*). Account of experiments made on the strength of materials. 1818. IV. 409.
Rennie, James. Aloe arborescens. 1833. III. 334.¹
— Alphabet of medical botany. 1833. III. 57.
— Botany for the use of beginners. 1833. I. 86.
— Chorizema nanum. 1834. III. 472.²
— Daphne Cneorum. 1834. III. 627.¹
— Handbook of plain botany. 1834. I. 87.
— A new supplement to the pharmacopoeias of London, Edinburgh. 1826. III. 254.
— Remarks showing the comparative difference and dispositions of trees. 1837. I. 516.
— Rosa berberifolia. 1833. III. 456.²
Renodaeus. *See* RENOU, Jean de.
Renoir, Edmond. Protection des forêts . . . par la protection des oiseaux. 1894. IV. 196.¹
Renou. Sur une galle de Chêne. 1857. IV. 509.
Renou. Sur le choix des arbres à planter dans les avenues. 1884. III. 209.
Renou, E. Sur les froids de mai et de juin 1871. 1871. III. 48.
— Sur l'hiver de 1877 à Paris. 1877. III. 48.
Renou, F. *See* HARDOUIN, L., RENOU, F. & LECLERC, E.
Renou, Jean de. Dispensatorium medicum. 1645. III. 245.
— A medicinal dispensatory. 1645. III. 245.
Renou, Victor. Notice sur les forêts de Cèdres de l'Algérie. 1845. II. 27.¹
Renouard, Alfred, (*jr.*). Les plantes textiles. 1883. III. 234.
— Les plantes textiles de l'Algérie. 1882. III. 322.¹
— Sur les produits naturels du Dattier. 1884. III. 329.²
Renovirte und verbesserte Holtz-, Mast- und Jagd-Ordnung . . . in der Mittel, Alte, Neue und Ucker-Mark. 1720. IV. 301.
Renovirte und verbesserte Holtz-, Mast- und Jagd-Ordnung vor das Herzogthum Magdeburg. 1743. IV. 319.²
Renos, Charles. De la culture du Café au Mexique. 1894. III. 728.¹
Renseignemens . . . sur la culture de la Vigne. *See* PETIT-LAFITTE, Augustin. 1842. III. 554.²
Renseignements statistiques sur les coupes . . . dans la Franche-Comté. 1898. IV. 556.¹
Renseignements sur le Pin sylvestre d'Écosse. 1899. IV. 474.
Renselaar, A. van. Aanmerkingen wegens de cultuur der heidegronden. 1802. IV. 159.
Renton, James. The causes of Larch disease. 1880. IV. 451.
Rentzsch, Heinrich Hermann. Die Nachtheile aus der Verwüstung der Privatwaldungen. 1859. IV. 307.²
— Ueber die Verwüstung der Privatwaldungen. 1859. IV. 307.²
— Der Wald im Haushalt der Natur. 1859. IV. 307.²
Renz, C. *See* SCHÜBLER, Gustav & RENZ, C.
Renz, Carl Friedrich. Untersuchungen über das specifische Gewicht der Samen. *See* SCHÜBLER, Gustav. 1826. I. 120.
Die **Reorganisation** der bayerischen Staatsforstverwaltung. 1884. IV. 290.¹

Reorganización de la Escuela forestal de Nancy. 1886. IV. 540.[1]
Répertoire de chimie appliquée. I. 22.
Répertoire de chimie pure. I. 22.
Répertoire de pharmacie. I. 22.
Repertorio di agricoltura. III. 23.[1]
Repertorio fisico-natural de la Isla de Cuba. I. 7.[2]
Repertorio médico-farmacéutico. III. 10.[1]
Repertorium annuum literaturae botanicae periodicae. 1873. I. 2.
Repertorium der Pharmacie. See APOTHEKER-ZEITUNG, I. 10.
Repertorium für die Pharmacie. I. 14.
Repertorium zum Forstgesetz vom 28. März 1852. 1862. IV. 318.
Repetere Juvad. 1882. IV. 277.
Repiquage des Épicéas en pépinière. 1899. IV. 151.[2]
Replanting in Hong Kong. 1880. IV. 168.[1]
A reply to the observations of a British merchant on the report ... relative to the timber trade. 1821. IV. 404.[2]
Repoblación de las montañas y del litoral. 1887. IV. 546.[1]
La repoblación de los montes en España. 1886. IV. 165.
Repoblación de los terrenos pobres con Acacias. 1892. IV. 546.[1]
La repoblación forestal en la provincia de Burgos. 1892. IV. 547.[1]
Repoblación importante. 1885. IV. 546.[1]
Repoblaciones en el monte Quintanar. 1886. IV. 165.
Report from the Select committee on forest conservancy. 1875. V. XXXI.[1]
Report from the Select committee on the vine diseases bill. 1886. III. 762.
Report ... Mysore government garden at Bangalore. 1864. I. 67.[1]
Report of Chinchona commission. 1870. III. 721.
Report of progress. See VERMEULE, C. C. & GIFFORD, John. 1895. IV. 333.[2]
Report of the commission appointed to investigate the matter of wooden pavements. See MERRICK, J. M. & others. 1873. IV. 425.[2]
Report of the commission of inquiry to Santo Domingo. 1871. I. 336.
Report of the committee appointed for the reorganisation of the forest department in the state of Travancore. 1884. IV. 295.[1]
Report of the Crown surveyor on forests in British Guiana. 1881. IV. 342.[1]
Report of the cultivation of Cinchonae at Darjeeling. See ANDERSON, Thomas. 1866. III. 714.
Report of the Forestry commission appointed by the comptroller. 1885. IV. 339.
Report of the New Hampshire forestry commission. 1893. IV. 288.[1] 339.
Report of the select committee ... on forestry. 1887. IV. 34.[1]
Report of the special committee ... as to what lands should be acquired within the forest preserve. 1897. IV. 179.[1]
Report of the State forestry association to the governor of Minnesota. 1877. IV. 39.[1]
Report on arboriculture in the Hyderabad Assigned districts. 1886. III. 129.[2]
Report on Cassia lignea. See FORD, Charles. 1882. III. 405.[1]
Report on forests. 1900. IV. 339.
Report on Kansas forestry. See KANSAS horticultural report ... IV. 4.
Report on Macwarrieballi. See JENMAN, G. S. 1888. III. 688.[1]
Report on public forest reservations. See PADDOCK, A. S. 1892. IV. 178.[1]
Report on roadside arboriculture in the Central Provinces. 1892. III. 129.[2]
Report on some of the india-rubber ... trees of British Guiana. See JENMAN, G. S. 1883. III. 231.
Report on the canal plantations. 1887. III. 129.[2]
Report on the examination of some Indian substitutes. 1898. III. 228.[1]
Report on the existence of Teak trees on the banks of the Thaddé stream. 1845. II. 761.[1]
Report on the exotic trees in the fuel plantations of the Nundidroog division. 1878. III. 129.[2]
Report on the expedition to procure seeds of C. Condaminea. See CROSS, Robert. 1862. III. 712.[1]
Report on the experiments ... in the treatment of the downy mildew. 1889. III. 580.

Report on the forest conditions of the Rocky Mountains. 1888. IV. 340.[1]
Report on the forest wealth of Canada. See JOHNSON, George. 1895. IV. 337.[1]
Report on the Government Cinchona plantations in Java. 1875. III. 716.
Report on the Hon'ble company's botanic gardens, Calcutta. See GRIFFITH, William. 1843. I. 66.[2]
A report on the insects of Massachusetts. See HARRIS, T. W. 1841. III. 186.[2]
Report on the manufacture of spirits of turpentine. See PIGOT, J. L. 1897. III. 228.[1]
Report on the relation of railroads to forest supplies. See FERNOW, B. E. 1887. IV. 424.[1]
Report on the scientific results of the voyage of H. M. S. Challenger. See HEMSLEY, W. B. 1885. I. 303.
Report on the trees and shrubs ... of Massachusetts. See EMERSON, G. B. 1846. I. 312, IV. 76.[2]
Report upon the Nelambur Teak plantations. See BEDDOME, R. H. 1878. IV. 536.[2]
Report upon the present condition ... of Tea cultivation in the North-west provinces. See JAMESON, Wilham. 1857. III. 603.
Report upon the Tea plantations in the North Western provinces. See FORTUNE, Robert. 1851. III. 602.[2]
Reports and letters ... on the proper season for cutting timber. See ROBERTS, A. S. 1850. IV. 384.[2]
Reports, etc. on Dr. Boucherie's patent for preserving timber from decay. 1856. IV. 418.
Reports from, and minutes ... on the affairs of the East India Company. 1831. III. 606.
Reports of explorations and surveys, to ascertain the ... route for a railroad ... to the Pacific Ocean. I. 519.[1]
Reports of state fruit committees. 1853. III. 133.
Reports of tests on the strength of structural material. See PARKER, F. H. 1883. IV. 410.
Reports on the arboricultural operations. 1893. III. 129.[2]
Reports on the cultivation of the Spanish Chestnut. See BIRDWOOD, Sir George & others. 1892. III. 359.[1]
Reports on the durability of New Zealand timber. 1875. IV. 413.[2]
Reports on the forests of Canada. 1885. IV. 337.[2]
Reports on the forests of the Straits Settlements. See CANTLEY, N. 1883. IV. 378.
Reports on the production of Tea in Japan. 1873. III. 601.[2]
Reports on the Royal botanic garden, Peradenia. 1844. I. 66.[2]
Reports on the tea and tobacco industries in India. 1874. III. 607.
Reports regarding fruit trees imported ... in ice. 1850. III. 155.
Reports respecting the production and consumption of timber in foreign countries. 1875. IV. 402.[2]
Reppert, Ferdinand. Forest trees and shrubs of Muscatine county. 1899. I. 321, IV. 78.[2]
Représentation des bois, des arbres & arbrisseaux tant du pays qu' étrangers. See HOUTTUYN, Martin. 1773. I. 124.
A representation of inland and foreign wood. See HOUTTUYN, Martin. 1773. I. 124.
Sur la reproduction des Pins par bouture. 1850. III. 306.[2]
Repsold, G. J. Die Weinzucht unter Glas. 1878. III. 553.[1]
Repton, Humphrey. Observations on the supposed effects of Ivy upon trees. 1815. III. 642.[1]
Repulles y Vargas, E. M. De las inundaciones en España. 1877. IV. 47.[1]
Request to educators for coöperaton. See FERNOW, B. E. 1886. IV. 30.[1]
Requien, Esprit. Catalogue des végétaux ligneux ... en Corse. 1852. I. 419.[1]
— Note adressée d'Avignon. 1836. III. 635.[1]
— Observations sur quelques plantes ... de la flore française. 1825. II. 115.[1]
Rérat. See SERRÈS & RÉRAT.
Rérolle, Louis. Notes sur la flore des régions de la Plata. 1881. I. 345.
— Une série d'excursions botaniques ... entre Lyon et les Alpes. 1883. I. 416.
Resa, Fr. Untersuchungen über die Periode der Wurzelbildung. 1878. I. 526,[2] IV. 64.[1]
Resch, F. A. Der Bohnenbaum. 1800. III. 480.[2]
Resch, Ludwig, (jr.). Die Kultur der Band- und Flechtweiden. 1884. III. 348.
Von den Reserven. 1840. IV. 235.[2]
Des réserves dans les taillis. 1896. IV. 131.

Reserves for timber and state forests. 1885. V. xxx.²
Réserves forestières des États-Unis. 1897. IV. 338.¹
Resinación en los montes de Arévalo. · 1890. IV. 436.²
Résineux (pseud.). Époque d'abatage. 1899. IV. 385.¹
— Époque de la plantation. Élagage. 1898. IV. 441.
The resins, gums, and gum-resins of Victoria. 1865. III. 227.
Résistance des boisages dans les mines. 1899. IV. 425.²
Resoconto di alcuni argomenti pertrattati nelle ultime sedute della congregazione provinciale di Belluno. 1865. IV. 165.
Resoluciones de la Dirección de agricultura. — Montes. 1892. IV. 554.²
Resolution on the forest policy . . . of India. 1894. IV. 279.²
Resolutiones wegen Abstellung derer in Forst- und Holtz-Sachen eingerissenen Missbräuche. 1698. IV. 321.
Respinger, Johann Heinrich. Theses anatomico-botanicae. · 1733. I. 97.
Responsabilité du garde-vente. 1898. IV. 327.
Ressel, Joseph. Anleitung zur schnellen und richtigen Flächen-Inhalts-Berechnung. 1817. IV. 263.
Ressons, de. Manière de greffer les arbres. 1718. III. 159.²
— A method of changing the fruit of a whole garden. 1727. III. 141.
— A method to preserve trees from moss. 1727. III. 175.¹
La restauration des montagnes. See COURTON, P. de. 1888. IV. 163.
Restauration . . . des Platanes. 1889. III. 418²; see also NANOT, Jules. 188.? III. 418.¹
De la restauration du sol épuisé des pineraies. 1894. IV. 559.¹
Restauration et conservation des terrains en montagne. 1882. IV. 185.²
Restauration et conservation des terrains en montagne; compte rendu sommaire. 1900. IV. 186.¹
Restituzione dei diritti d' importazione del legname . . . nel Belgio. 1865. IV. 284.²
— See also DUJARDIN-BEAUMETZ & RESTREPO, A. E.
Restrepo, Alejandro Eduardo. Étude du Cédron, du Valdivia. 1881. III. 508,² 509.¹
Result of trials with certain manures on Tea gardens. 1882. III. 603.
Resultate der Forstverwaltung . . . Wiesbaden. IV. 10.
Resultate über die durch Kalkwasser beförderte Keimkraft des Kiefer-Samens. 1860. IV. 472.
Résultats des divers procédés de guérison . . . pour combattre la nouvelle maladie de la Vigne. 1873. III. 759.
Résultats des diverses expériences faites . . . sur l'Acajou de Honduras. 1858. IV. 525; see also LANG, D. & others. 1858. IV. 408.
Résultats des ventes des coupes domaniales . . . 1894. 1894. IV. 551.¹
Résultats des ventes des coupes domaniales . . . 1896. 1895. IV. 551.¹
Résultats sommaires des adjudications de coupes de l'automne 1897 en Franche-Comté. 1897. IV. 551.¹
Résultats sommaires des adjudications de coupes de l'automne 1898 en Franche-Comté. 1898. IV. 551.¹
Résultats sommaires des adjudications de coupes de l'automne 1899 en Franche-Comté. 1899. IV. 551.¹
Results of examination of . . . Sisal Hemp fibre. 1896. III. 341.¹
Results of the trial at the hill station of Mussooree of the North American fruit trees. 1854. III. 147.¹
Résumé du catalogue de la section brésilienne. 1873. III. 269.¹
Résumé historique de l'économie et de la législation forestières de la Suède. 1880. IV. 315.¹
Résumé of a report . . . on the production of coffee in Brazil. 1899. III. 729.¹
Rethoré. Carte forestière de Chantilly. 1861. IV. 360.
Retinosporas — Japanese Cypress. 1879. III. 300.²
The retir'd gardener. See GENTIL, François. 1704. III. 111.
Les retraites des forestiers communaux. 1895. IV. 311.²
Rettig, (Regierungsdirector). Noch ein Wort über das Ausroden . . . der Wälder. 1899. IV. 43.
Rettig, Ernst. · Actinidia Kolomikta Maxim. 1899. III. 595.²
— Dischidia Rafflesiana. 1895. III. 744.²
— Habituelle Unterschiede der Geschlechter bei Ginkgo. 1894. II. 7.³
— Leuchtenbergia principis Fisch. 1900. III. 623.¹
— Rubus illecebrosus Focke. 1900. III. 458.²
— Zamia Katzerjana. 1896. II. 7.¹

Rettstadt. · Soll der · Forstmann forsttechnische · Gewerbe leiten. 1862. IV. 392.
Rettstadt, G. Beiträge zur Frage der Bodenlockerung. 1868. IV. 143.¹
— Eine Durchforstung . . . im Buchenhochwalde. 1840. IV. 494.
— Ueber den Einfluss der Senkung von Seespiegeln. 1876. IV. 73.²
— Der Kiefernkrebs. 1870. IV. 476.
— Miscellanea aus dem grünen Walde. 1889. IV. 102.
— Ueber die Moosdecke in den Nadelholzbeständen. 1868. IV. 68.
Rettungsmittel bey Obst- und Waldbäumen . . . den Gefahren des Erfrierens ausgesetzt. 1793. IV. 191.¹
Returns of prices of timber. 1858. IV. 261.²
Retzius, Anders Johan. Anmärkningar rörande Cinchona Cattukambar. 1814. II. 832.²
— Anmærkninger over Phaseolus nanus. 1802. II. 266.¹
— Berättelse om de försök som blifvit gjorda med åtskilliga utländska träd och buskarter. 1798. III. 119.²
— Botanico-oeconomisk afhandling om Berberis buskens nytta och skada. 1807. II. 202,¹ III. 594.¹
— Dissertatio botanica, sistens methodum Tournefortianum. 1805. I. 351.
— Dissertatio, sistens Supplementum . . . in editionem secundam Prodromi Florae Scandinaviae. 1779. I. 352.
— Einleitung in die Lehre von den Arzneien des Pflanzenreichs. 1786. III. 257.²
— Fasciculus observationum botanicarum. 1774. I. 262.
— Flora Virgiliana. 1808. I. 514.¹
— Florae Scandinaviae prodromus. 1779. I. 352.
— Försök til en Flora oeconomica Sueciae. · 1806. III. 67.¹
— Forsøg med udenlandske Træer og Buske. 1798. III. 119.²
— Observationes botanicae. 1779. I. 262.
— Observationum botanicarum pugillus. 1810. II. 832.²
— Observationum in Criticam botanicam Caroli a Linné specimen. 1811. I. 265, 529.²
— Pentapetes suberosa. 1794. II. 537.²
— De plantis cibariis romanorum. 1808. III. 88.¹
— Tankar om natural-historiens nytta och värde. 1811. I. 79.¹
— Tvänne nya species af Dianthera. 1775. II. 800.¹
Reubel, Johann. Entwurf eines Systems der Pflanzenphysiologie. 1804. · I. 148.
— De novo gummi purgante epistola. 1625. III. 244.
Reul, Adolphe. Le gland du Chêne. 1892. IV. 515.²
Reuleaux. Some American Conifers at home. 1894. IV. 338.²
— Waldbilder aus den Vereinigten Staaten. 1894. IV. 338.²
Reuling, L. W. Ohnmassgeblicher Vorschlag, wie dem . . . Holzmangel . . . abzuhelfen sey. 1788. IV. 280.¹
Reum, Johann Adam. Anwendung der Raumgrössen-Lehre. 1836. IV. 263.
— Bemerkungen om Trævæxters Opelskning. 1835. III. 119.²
— Einige Ergebnisse über Zucht . . . der Holzpflanzen. 1829. III. 120.³
— Einige Erscheinungen beim Wachsen . . . der Holzpflanzen. 1831. I. 157.
— Grundlehren der Mathematik. 1823. IV. 58.
— Grundriss der deutschen Forstbotanik. 1814. IV. 82. ··
— Pflanzen-Physiologie. 1835. IV. 63.¹
— Uebersicht des Forstwesens. 1828. IV. 101.
— Verzeichnis der im K. S. Forstgarten zu Tharandt befindlichen Baum- und Strauchgattungen. 183.? I. 46, IV. 18.¹
Reumert, E. Grip Skov. Et Stykke dansk Natur. 1897. I. 358.
Reuning, (Dr.). Beiträge zur der Frage über die . . . Grundprincipien des Waldbaues. 1871. IV. 269.
Réunion — Société d'acclimation et d'histoire naturelle . . . 1836. IV. 268.²
— de la Société géologique de France à Porrentruy. See THURMANN, Jules. 1838. · I. 434.
Réunions publiques organisées par la Société centrale d'agriculture de l'Hérault. 1881. III. 556.
Een reusachtige Dennenboom. 1894. III. 307.¹
Reusch, (Prof.). Ueber eine eigenthümliche Knickung, welche das Holz. 1869. IV. 410.
Reuss. Exploitation du Liège en régie par l'état. 1896. IV. 295.²
Reuss. Zur Frage über die Anbauwürdigkeit ausländischer Holzarten. 1885. IV. 126.¹

Reuss. Die Klaubholznutzung. 1884. IV. 438.[1]

Reuss. Vergleichende Untersuchung über die Widerstandsfähigkeit der ... Fichtenbestände. 1888. IV. 454.

Reuss, (*Forstamtsassistant*). Beiträge zur württembergischen Flora. 1888. I. 389.

Reuss, (*Forstassessor*). Einige Notizen über die Erträge der Hasel. 1851. IV. 492.[1]

— Lerchen-Erträge. 1851. IV. 452.[1]

Reuss, Carl. Gutachten über Rauchbeschädigung in ... Miechowitz-Rokittnitz. 1893. IV. 192.[2]

— Haben sich die aus Einzelpflanzung ... hervorgegangen Bestände ... widerstandsfähiger gezeigt? 1887. IV. 190.

— Hüttenrauchschaden in den Waldungen des Oberharzes. 1881. IV. 192.[2]

— Nachtrag zu dem Werke: Rauchbeschädigung in ... Myslowitz-Kattowitz. 1893. IV. 192.[2]

— Rauchbeschädigung in ... Myslowitz-Kattowitz. 1893. IV. 192.[2]

— *See also* SCHROEDER, Julius von & REUSS, Carl.

Reuss, Christian Friedrich. Compendium botanices ... selectiora plantarum Germaniac indigenarum ... genera. 1774. I. 374.

— Dictionarium botanicum. 1781. I. 32.

— Kenntniss derjenigen Pflanzen ... Färbern zum Nutzen. 1776. III. 235.[3]

— Physisch-ökonomische Beobachtungen, Vorschläge und Erfahrungen über den Gebrauch des Holzes. 1802. IV. 426.[1]

Reuss, E. Les écoles primaires de sylviculture en Bavière. 1889. IV. 33.[3]

Reuss, Eduard. Aperçu de la situation forestière des pays ..., représentés. 1886. IV. 362.

— Notice sommaire sur la forêt de Fontainebleau. 1900. IV. 362.

— *See also* BOPPE, Lucien & REUSS, Eduard.

— & **Bartet,** E. Étude sur l'expérimentation forestière. 1884. IV. 37.[3]

Reuss, Friedrich Anton. Die ersten botanischen und Kunstgärten Bayerns. 1862. I. 48.

— De libris physicis S. Hildegardis commentatio. 1835. I. 292.

Reuss, Georg Christian. Pflanzenblätter in Naturdruck. 1862. I. 71.

Reuss, Hermann. Aufforderung ... zur Bekämpfung der Nonne. 1892. IV. 201.

— Die Aufgaben des forstlichen Versuchswesens. 1886. IV. 37.[3]

— Die Baummesskluppe. 1882. IV. 231.[1]

— Beiträge zur Wachsthumsthätigkeit des Baumes. 1893. II. 518.[1] IV. 65.[1]

— Ueber die Bewehrung von Windrissen. 1881. IV. 189.[3]

— Die " Coulissendurchforstung." 1896. IV. 175.[1]

— Einige Versuche mit Fichtensamen. 1884. II. 36.[3]

— Forstliche Mittheilungen aus dem Himalaya. 1883. IV. 378.

— Zur Illustration der Folgenachtheile der Schälbeschädigung. 1900. IV. 457.

— Influence désavarageuse produite sur l'avenir des peuplements. 1900. IV. 454.

— Der Lichtwuchsbetrieb und die Praxis. 1885. IV. 175.[3]

— Participation à l'étude sur les conséquences fâcheuses de la décortication. 1900. IV. 197.[1] 457.

— Die Schälbeschädigung durch Hochwild. 1888. IV. 196.[2]

— Die Stellung der Durchforstungspraxis zur Mischwuchsfrage. 1897. IV. 175.[1]

— Versuch zur Minderung der Schälschäden. 1889. IV. 197.[1]

— Ueber Waldarrondierung. 1899. IV. 308.[1]

— Die waldbaulich-wirthschaftliche Bedeutung der Bestandesgründung durch Pflanzung. 1890. IV. 142.

— Der Waldfeldbau. 1889. IV. 134.[1]

— Die Zuchtwahl in der Forstwirthschaft. 1890. I. 529, IV. 75.[1]

— & **Moeller,** Joseph. Mittheilungen aus einem Versuchspflanzkamp. 1879. IV. 453.

Reuss, Jeremias. David. Repertorium commentationum. 1801. I. 1.

Reuss, Karl. Die Harzer schneebrüche. 1884. IV. 190.

Reuss, L. Entgegnung auf den Artikel des Herrn Forstdirectors Jäger. 1870. IV. 118.

— Ueber die Entwässerung der Gebirgswaldungen. 1874. IV. 144.[1]

— Die Lärchenkrankheit. 1870. IV. 450.

Reuss, Leopold. Flora des Unter-Donaukreises. 1831. I. 378.

— Flora von Passau. 1838. I. 379.

Reuter. Die Staatswaldungen sind im Interesse der Völker zu bewirthschaften. 1839. IV. 268, 552.[3]

— Wie lassen sich die Schwierigkeiten des Anbaues von Waldblössen ... erklären. 1829. IV. 154.[3]

Reuter. Ueber Vermehrung der Thuja-Arten. 1857. III. 311.[1]

Reuter. *See* DAHS, REUTER & Co.

Reuter, (*Dr.*). Der Boden und die atmosphärische Luft. 1833. IV. 67.[1]

— Der Ludwigskanal. 1837. IV. 46.[2]

Reuter, (*Hofgärtner, Pfaueninsel*). Eine grosse Paulownia. 1888. III. 703.[3]

— Die Resultate der Samenvermehrung bei verschiedenen Gehölzvarietäten. 1878. I. 248,[3] III. 156.[1]

— Die Resultate verschiedener Veredlungsarten. 1870. III. 165.

Reuter, (*Revierverwalter in der Garbe*). Beschreibung der Lage ... des Forstreviers in der Garbe. 1854. IV. 169.[2]

— Nachweis des Ertrages eines Eichenschäl-Waldes. 1855. IV. 512.

Reuter, A. Resultate der Samenvermehrung. 1896. III. 156.[3]

— Verschiedene Resultate bei dem Pfropfen. 1896. III. 165.

Reuter, A. P. Der Boden und die atmosphärische Luft. 1833. I. 157.

Reuter, Enzio Raphaël. Coccider på blåbärs- och lingonris. 1896. III. 663.[1]

— Coleophora laricella härjande Lärkträd. 1895. IV. 451.

— Entomologiska och växttopografiska notiser från Finland. 1891. II. 31.[1]

— Rostsvamp på Balsampopplar. 1895. III. 345.[2]

— Tallkottgyttring från Åbo. 1893. II. 47.[3] [*]

Reuter, Fr. Die Kultur der Eiche und der Weide. 1860. IV. 133, 505.

— Mittheilung über das Kulturverfahren in ... der Garbe. 1860. IV. 141.

— Pilekultur i Skovdistriktet Garben. 1876. III. 348.

Reuter, George François. Aspect de la végétation de l'Algérie. 1852. I. 484.

— Catalogue détaillé des plantes ... de Genève. 1832. I. 434.

— Essai sur la végétation de la Nouvelle Castille. 1843. I. 420.

— Quelques notes sur la végétation de l'Algérie. 1852. I. 484.

— *See also* BOISSIER, Edmond & REUTER, G. F.; MARGOT, H. & REUTER, F. G.

Reuter, Ludwig. Zur Geschichte des Eucalyptus-Honigs. 1889. IV. 531.[1]

Reuter, Odo Morannal. Chionaspis salicis L., en coccid på Sorbus. 1883. III. 459.[3]

— Chionaspis sorbi, en ny coccid på Sorbus. 1893. III. 459.[3]

— En ny Capsid på Rhamnus Frangula. 1886. III. 543.[1]

— Schizoneura Ulmi L., en bladlus. 1883. III. 364.[3]

Reuther, A. M. Experimental regeneration fellings in the Beech forests. 1894. IV. 496.

— Forest management in the grand duchy of Baden. 1896. IV. 248.[3]

— Reboisement of landslip ... areas. 1894. IV. 166.[3]

— State forests of the Spessart in Bavaria. 1896. IV. 351.[1]

— The town-forest of Frankfort. 1894. IV. 354.

— Wire-rope slide in the Brückwald. 1894. IV. 392.

Reutovitch. *See* PEYTOREVS.

Reutter. Die Brennmaterialien ausser dem Holze. 1838. IV. 280.[3]

Reutty, X. Der Kork als Verschlussmaterial. 1900. IV. 435.

Revell, Pierre Oscar. De l'action des poisons. 1866. I. 211.

— Application de la dialyse à la recherche des poisons végétaux. 1864. I. 156.[2]

— De la dialyse et de son application à la recherche des substances toxiques. 1865. I. 156.[3]

— Note sur les feuilles de Caroba. 1856. III. 789.[1]

— Note sur les feuilles de Caroba et sur quelques produits du Paraguay. 1856. III. 269,[3] 706.[3]

— Note sur les Résiniers des Landes. 1865. III. ? III. 308.[1]

— Du Pin maritime. 1865. IV. 467.[1]

— Procédé de conservation des plantes. 1856. I. 35.

— *See also* DUPUIS, Aristide & RÉVEIL, Oscar; DUPUIS, Aristide, GERARD, Frédéric, REVEIL, Oscar & HÉRINCQ, François.

Revel, Joseph. Essai de la flora du sud-ouest de la France. 1885. I. 417.
— Recherches botaniques faites dans le sud-ouest de la France. 1865. I. 413.
Reventlow, Christian Ditlev Frederik, *Graf af.* Formeentlige Resultater . . . angaaende Indflydelsen af Træernes giensidige Afstand. 1818. III. 169.[1]
— Forslag til en forbedret Skovdrift. 1879. IV. 241, 343.
Reventlow-Farve, Ernst **& Warnstedt,** H. A. von. Beiträge sur land- und forstwirthschaftlichen Statistik der Herzogthümer Schleswig und Holstein. 1847. IV. 352.
Reverchon, Julien. Botanische Exkursion in Texas. 1886. I. 325.
— Botanizing in Texas. 1886. I. 325.
— A few Texas shrubs. 1892. III. 60.
— Notes on some Texas trees. 1893. III. 60.
— Notes sur quelques arbres du Texas. 1893. III. 60.
Reverchon, P. Catalogue raisonné des plantes . . . de la Mayenne. 1891. I. 417.
Revidirte allgemeine Grundregeln bezüglich des . . . Kulturbetriebes in den Staats-Waldungen der Oberpfalz. 1867. IV. 118.
Revidirte elev- und märkische wie auch geldern- und meursische Jagd- und Wald-Ordnung. 1822. IV. 320.
Revidirte Flossordnung für den fränkischen Wald. 1876. IV. 300.[1]
Das **revidirte** Forstgesets für die Landestheile rechts des Rheins. 1880. IV. 318.
Revidirte Forstordnung der Stadt Winterthur. 1833. IV. 306.
Revidirte Trift- und Floss-Ordnung für den Regen. 1868. IV. 300.[1]
Revidirtes Forststrafgesetz der Pfalz. 1879. IV. 318.
Revidirtes Stammregister vorzüglicher Kernobstsorten des Kantons Bern. 1886. III. 89.[1]
Review of Mr. Lambert's Description of the genus Pinus. 1805. II. 38.[2]
Review of reviews. London. III. 18.
Review of reviews. New York. III. 8.
Review of the Cactaceae of the United States. *See* ORCUTT, C. R. 1897. II. 587.[2]
A **review** of the genus Jasminum. 1823. II. 709.[1]
Review of the recent correspondence on the Letpet tea. *See* WATT, George. 1896. III. 763.[2]
A **review** of the references to the Hortus malabaricus. *See* DILLWYN, L. W. 1839. I. 78.[1]
Revigin, Carolus. De generatione ac nutritione arborum. *See* TROZEL, C. B. 1768. I. 146.
Révigtio, Maurizio. Osservazioni teorico-pratiche sulla . . . Chinachina. 1837. III. 338.[2]
Révil, J. & **Déresse,** Antoine. Guide du jeune botaniste aux environs de Villefranche. 1875. I. 414.
Revilla y Oymels, Manuel de. Instrucción sobre el cultivo de algunas semillas. 1865. IV. 149.[1]
Revised catalogue of fruits recommended for cultivation in . . . the United States. 1899. III. 62.
Revised list of fruit trees. 1894. III. 94.[1]
Revised regulations, Department of crown lands. 1888. IV. 295.[1]
Revision cadastrale des propriétés non bâties. 1899. IV. 285.[1]
Revision des évaluations cadastrales. 1899. IV. 205.[1]
Revista botanica. 1879. I. 4.[1]
Revista científica mexicana. I. 7.[1]
Revista corcho-taponera. 1892. IV. 539,[1] 559.[2]
Revista de agricultura práctica. III. 23.[1]
Revista de horticultura. III. 10.[1]
Revista de la facultad de agronomia y veterinaria, La Plata. Publicación. I. 8.[1]
Revista de los progresos de las ciencias exactas. I. 24.[1]
Revista de montes. Anuario. IV. 13.[1]
Revista de montes. IV. 13.[1]
Revista forestal. IV. 539.[1]
Revista forestal. IV. 13.[1]
Revista horticola andaluza. III. 23.[1]
Revista padurilor. III. 26.[1]
Révoil, Georges. Faune et flore des pays çomalis. 1882. I. 489.
La **Revue** agricole. III. 20.
Revue agricole et forestière de Provence. III. 20.
Revue agricole . . . Maurice. III. 26.[2]
Revue algérienne et des colonies. *See* REVUE coloniale. III. 20.
Revue archéologique. I. 520.[1]
Revue botanique; recueil mensuel. 1845. . I. 2.

Revue coloniale. III. 20.
Revue de botanique. I. 22.
Revue de géographie. I. 520.[1]
Revue de l'horticulture. III. 20.
Revue de l'horticulture belge. III. 15.
Revue de l'Orient. I. 520.[1]
Revue de viticulture. III. 20.
Revue des cours scientifiques. I. 22.
Revue des cultures coloniales. III. 20.
Revue des deux mondes. III. 20.
Revue des eaux et forêts; annales. IV. 12.[2]
Revue des eaux et forêts; répertoire de législation. IV. 12.[2]
Revue des questions scientifiques. *See* SOCIÉTÉ SCIENTIFIQUE DE BRUXELLES. I. 17.
Revue des sciences naturelles. I. 22.
Revue des sciences naturelles appliquées. *See* SOCIÉTÉ IMPERIALE ZOOLOGIQUE D'ACCLIMATATION. III. 22.
Revue des sciences naturelles de l'Ouest. I. 22.
Revue des Vignes, hybrides franco-américaines. III. 20.
Revue encyclopédique. *See* MAGASIN encyclopédique. I. 22.
Revue et magasin de zoologie. *See* REVUE zoologique. III. 20.
Revue générale de botanique. I. 22.
Revue générale des sciences pures et appliquées. I. 22.
Revue horticole. III. 20.
Revue horticole de l'Algérie. III. 27.[1]
Revue horticole de la Côte-d'Or. III. 20.
Revue horticole . . . de la Suisse romande. III. 24.[1]
Revue horticole des Bouches-du-Rhône. III. 20.
Revue maritime et coloniale. *See* REVUE coloniale. III. 20.
Revue progressive d'agriculture. *See* L'AGRICULTEUR praticien. III. 18.
Revue régionale agricole et horticole. *See* ASSOCIATION HAUT-MARNAISE . . . III. 19.
Revue scientifique. *See* REVUE des cours scientifiques. I. 22.
Revue scientifique du Bourbonnais. I. 22.
Revue scientifique et industrielle. I. 22.
Revue scientifique et industrielle de l'année. III. 20.
Revue viticole, agricole et horticole. III. 20.
Revue zoologique. III. 20.
Rexès, F. G. Le phylloxéra détruit. 1876. III. 760.
Rexford, E. E. Some good native vines. 1885. III. 204.[2]
Rey, J. B. Marius. Sur l'origine d'echantillons de bois de Cèdre. 1837. II. 27.[1]
Rey, Louis. L'administration des forêts. 1895. IV. 288.[1]
Rey, Ph. *See* BOCHEFONTAINE & REY, Ph.
Rey-Pailhade, J. de. Rôles respectifs du philothion. 1895. I. 204.
Reybert, D. M. Mémoire sur la maladie de la Vigne. 1853. III. 576.
Reyers, O. *See* BYLL, A. de, TIMMER, W. & REYERS, O.
Reyes, A. W. Sobre las propi edades de la "Carica Papaya." 1880. III. 617.[1]
Reyes, E. de los. Pantanos y repoblaciones. 1900. IV. 547.[1]
Reyes, Manuel Ortega. El gigante de la flora mexicana. [1884], 1883. *II. 58.*[1] IV. 484,[2] *V. xxv.*[2]
— Ein Riesenbaum. 1883. IV. 484,[2] *V. xxv.*[2]
Reyffert, Mark Hendrik. De nuce vomica. 1836. III. 684.[2]
Reyger, Gottfried. Die um Danzig wildwachsende Pflanzen. 1700. I. 973.
— Tentamen florae gedanensis. 1764. I. 373.
Reyher, C. Die grosse Kiefernraupe. 1872. IV. 476.
Reymond, Lucien. Ueber die Biermann'schen Pflanzungen. 1860. IV. 152.
— Einige Worte über die Erhaltung des grössten Holzkapitals in den Gebirgen. 1863. IV. 135.[2]
— Quelques mots sur la marche à suivre pour obtenir sur les montagnes le plus grand capital forestier. 1863. IV. 135.[2]
— Remarques sur les plantations dans la forêt du Risoud. 1860. IV. 152.
Reymond, M. L. A. Flore utile de la France. 1854. III. 86.
Reynal *See* CHEVALLIER, L., DUCHESNE, Émile & REYNAL.
Reynal, BERRY. *See* BERRY-REYNAL.
Reynard. Le cubage des bois. 1886. IV. 214.
— Du cubage mental des Sapins. 1900. IV. 446.[2]
— Le cubage parabolique. 1890. IV. 218.
— De la forme de la tige des arbres. 1884. IV. 218.
Reynard, Joseph. La question forestière en Algérie. 1882. IV. 279.[2]
— Restauration des forêts . . . du sud de l'Algérie. 1880. IV. 168.[2]
— & **Dianous.** Les dayats du sud de Laghouat. 1885. IV. 379.[1]

Reynaud, F. Le Pommier à cidre dans les Hautes-Alpes. 1892. III. 426.²
Reynaud, Joseph. De l'Olivier. 1862. III. 678.²
Reynaud-Ducreux. Considérations relatives aux futaies de Sapins du Jura. 1861. IV. 446.¹
Reynès. El cancer y el cundurango. 1872. III. 693.²
Reynier. Notice sur l'Olivier de Crimée. 1855. III. 675.²
Reynier, Louis. Considérations générales sur l'agriculture de l'Egypte. 1802. III. 328.¹
— De la culture de la Vigne chez les anciens Grecs. 1822. III. 545.¹
— Description de quelques espèces . . . de Rosiers. 1784. II. 286.²
— De l'économie publique et rurale des Arabes. 1820. III. 33.²
— De l'économie publique et rurale des Celtes. 1818. III. 33.¹
— De l'économie publique et rurale des Égyptiens. 1823. III. 33.¹
— De l'économie publique et rurale des Grecs. 1825. III. 33.²
— De l'économie publique et rurale des Perses. 1819. III. 33.²
— De l'influence du climat. 1792. I. 217.
Reynolds, Cuyler. Forest preservation in the state of New York. 1898. IV. 179.¹
Reynolds, James Emerson. Wood spirit and its detection. 1866. IV. 432.²
Reynolds, W. H. See WACE, E. G. & REYNOLDS, W. H.
Reynoso, Alvaro. Apuntes acerca de varios cultivos cubanos. 1867. III. 118.²
— Étude sur l'agriculture dans les pays chauds. 1864. III. 116.²
— Expériences pour servir à l'histoire de l'empoisonnement par le curare. 1854. III. 682.²
Reyntkens, J. B. Den sorghvuldighen hovenier. 1676. III. 106.¹
Řezáč, J. K. Praktický štěpař. 1889. III. 115.²
Rhagor, Daniel. Erneuerter Pflantz-Garten. 1639. III. 102.
— Pflanz-Gart. 1639. III. 102.
Rhamnine. 1852. III. 543.¹
The Rhapis Palms. 1892. III. 331.¹
Rhea and Conocephalus niveus. 1890. II. 156,² 157.¹
Rhea or China-grass. 1898. III. 381.¹
Rhea (Rîha) or China-grass. 1900. III. 382.²
Rheede tot Draakestein, H. A. van. Horti malabarici pars prima. 1678. I. 470.²
— Hortus indicus malabaricus. 1678. I. 470.³
— Malabaarse kruidhof. 1678. I. 470.²
Rhein, G. F. Beiträge zur Anatomie der Caesalpiniaceen. 1888. II. 347.¹
Rheinhard. Forstliche Aufgaben . . . auf dem Gebiete der Wasserwirthschaft. 1886. IV. 73.²
Rheinische Gartenschrift. III. 13.
Rheinischer Forst-Verein. Verhandlungen. IV. 10.
Rheinischer Gartenfreund. See RHEINISCHE Gartenschrift. III. 13.
Rheinisches Jahrbuch für Gartenkunde. See JAHRBUCH . . . III. 12.
Rheinisches Magazin zur Erweiterung der Naturkunde. I. 14.
Rheinpfalz — Naturwissenschaftlicher Verein. See POLLICHIA. I. 14.
Rhind, William. A catechism of botany. 1833. I. 86.
— A history of the vegetable kingdom. 1857. I. 95.
Rhiner, Joseph. Abrisse (Esquisses complémentaires) zur zweiten tabellarischen Flora der Schweizerkantone. 1892. I. 437.
— Abrisse zur tabellarischen Flora der Schweizer-Kantone. 1868. I. 435.
— Die Gefässpflanzen der Urkantone. 1893. I. 437.
— Nachtrag zu dem 1866 zu Schwyz erschienenen Volkstümlichen Pflanzennamen. 1895. I. 75.¹
— Prodrom der Waldstätter Gefässpflanzen. 1870. I. 436.
— Tabellarische Flora der Schweizer Kantone. 1869. I. 435.
Rhipsalis: its mode of growth etc. 1876. II. 508.²
Rhode Island — Agricultural experiment station. See RHODE ISLAND — STATE AGRICULTURAL SCHOOL . . . III. 8.
Rhode Island — State agricultural school — State agricultural experiment station. Annual report. Bulletin. III. 8.
Rhode Island state board of agriculture. Annual report. III. 8.

Rhodes, Jean Baptiste. L'epigéonosie. 1854. III. 559.²
Rhodion, Eucharius. See ROSSLIN, Eucharius.
Die Rhododendren . . . Indiens. See Les RHODODENDRON. 1849. II. 676.¹
Rhododendren vom Himalaya. 1889. III. 655.
Rhododendron dahuricum, Chimonanthus fragrans. 1890. III. 207.²
Les Rhododendron de l'Inde. 1849. II. 676.¹
Rhododendron grafting. 1898. III. 657.¹
Rhododendron occidentalis and Pickeringia montana. 1878. III. 484.¹.
Rhododendron Schlippenbachii. 1894. III. 662.¹—1896. III. 662.¹
Rhododendrons in a natural wood. 1895. III. 655.
Rhodora. I. 6.
Rhodotypus kerrioides Sieb. et Zucc. 1866. II. 281.²
Rhône — Société d'horticulture pratique . . . See SOCIÉTÉ . . . III. 22.
Le rhum de Laurier. 1892. III. 637.¹
Rhumelius, Janus Chunradus. Theologia vegetabilis. 1626. II. 508.²
Rhus Toxicodendron; Poison Ivy. See The POISON IVY and an antidote. 1899. III. 528.¹
Rhyne, Wilhelm ten. Excerpta ex observationibus suis. . . . de frutice Thee. 1678. III. 604.²
— Fasciculus rariorum plantarum in Promontorio Bonae Spei. 1678. I. 493.
Riant, A. Le café, le chocolat, le thé. 1875. III. 222.
Riassunto delle tre cause da noi dedotte. 1880. IV. 48.¹
Ribadieu, (Dr.). Essai d'acclimatation de l'Arbre à quinquina en Algérie. 1864. III. 717.¹
Riban, Joseph. Sur la coriamyrtine et ses dérivés. 1866. II. 454.¹
— Sur le principe toxique du Coriaria. 1863. III. 523.²
— Recherches expérimentales sur le principe toxique . . . 1863. III. 523.²
— Recherches expérimentales sur le . . . Redoul. 1863. III. 523.²
— Sur la transformation du camphre des Laurinées. 1875. III. 403.²
Ribbe, Charles de. Le déboisement et le reboisement. 1858. IV. 275.
— Des incendies de forêts dans la région des Maures. 1866. IV. 183.¹
— La province au point de vue des bois. 1857. IV. 359.¹
— Rapport . . . pour examiner les mémoires présentés sur la question forestière. 1861. IV. 275.
— Le reboisement des montagnes. 1860. IV. 162.
Ribbentrop, Berthold. Forest fires and their effects on the reproduction of Teak. 1899. IV. 537.¹
— Forest policy in Bombay. 1894. IV. 279.²
— Forestry in British India. 1900. IV. 378.
— Forestry in India. 1884. IV. 378.
— The forests of Victoria. 1896. IV. 380.²
— Hints on arboriculture in the Panjab. 1873. IV. 124.¹
— Impregnation of Indian timbers. 1899. IV. 421.
— Inspection note on the Abbaspur Babul tree. 1900. IV. 521.¹
— Note on an inspection of the forests in Assam. 1889. IV. 250.²
— Note on an inspection of the forests in Oudh. 1886. IV. 250.¹
— Note on the fructification of Deodar. 1899. II. 27.³
— Note on the injury done . . . by sheep. 1889. IV. 197.².
— Note on the inspection of the forests in the Central Provinces. 1886. IV. 250.²
— Note on the question of the admission of natives into the Indian forest service. 1887. IV. 295.¹
— Notes on the Deodar. 1899. IV. 448.¹
— Notes on the Kulu forest division, Punjab. 1884. IV. 153.¹
— The reorganisation of the provincial and subordinate services. 1892. IV. 295.¹
— Report on the Box-wood supply in the Punjab. 1885. IV. 525.
— Reproduction of Teak. 1899. IV. 537.¹
— Woods used in India for the construction of beer-barrels. 1894. IV. 427.²
— & Dunstan, W. R. Tannin extracts from Pterocarpus. 1900. III. 485.²
Ribbius. Rapport over een proef-aanplant van Liberia Koffie. 1895. III. 743.¹
Ribes odoriferum C. Koch. 1859. II. 245.¹
Ribon, C. Martinez. Metodo para el cultivo del árbol del Cacao. 1890. III. 592.²

Riboud. Opinion . . . sur le projet de loi relatif aux finances. 1814. IV. 275.

Riboud, Thomas. Mémoire sur les différentes espèces de haies. 1810. III. 212.[2]

Ricardou, J. M. Contribution à l'étude des Asclépiadacées. 1893. II. 735.[2]

Ricasoli-Firidolfi, Giovanni. Alcune notizie sul rimboscamento di Pratomagno. 1883. IV. 166.[1]

Ricasoli, Vincenzo. Catalogo delle collezioni di piante. 1874. I. 64.

— Il freddo dell' inverno 1879–80. 1880. III. 49.[2]

— Monographie der Beaucarnea-Arten. 1881. II. 84.[1]

— Otto anni di esperimento di piante al Monte Argentario. 1876. III. 49.[2]

— Le Phoenix tenuis e Phoenix reclinata. 1890. III. 328.[1]

— Il Pistacchio di Brolio. 1878. III. 526.[1]

— Il Pittosporum phillyraeoides. 1888. III. 416.[1]

— Rivista dei Dasilyrion. 1882. II. 81.[1]

— Rivista delle Beaucarnee. 1881. II. 84.[1]

— Rivista delle Yucche. 1881. II. 86.[2]

— Della utilità dei giardini d' acclimazione. 1888. I. 64.

— Una visita all' Orto botanico di Genova. 1879. I. 64.

Ricaud, J. Remèdes contre la tavelure des poires. 1887. III. 446.[2]

— Traitement du mildiou. 1887. III. 579.

Ricca, Luigi. Alcune osservazioni relative alla dicogamia. 1870. II. 679.[1]

— Catalogo delle piante . . di Diano Marina. 1870. I. 428.

— Contribuzioni alla teoria dicogamica. 1871. I. 239.[2]

Ricca-Rosellini, Giuseppe. Il R. istituto forestale di Valle-Ombrosa. 1869. IV. 35.[1]

Ricchi, Teobaldo. L'Eucalyptus nell' Italia meridionale. 1881. IV. 530.

Ricci, A. M. L' orologio di flora. 1827. I. 220.[2]

Ricciardi, Leonardo. Sulla composizione delle ceneri . . . dell' Arancio. 1880. II. 402.[1]

— Ricerche sulla diffusione dell' allumina nei vegetali. 1889. I. 154.

Riccius, Christian Gottlieb. Zuverlässiger Entwurf von der in Teutschland üblichen Jagtgerechtigkeit. 1736. IV. 316.

Riccobono, Vincenzo. Monografia delle specie e varietà di Agrumi. 1899. II. 401.[2]

— Le specie e le varietà di Agrumi. 1898. II. 401.[2]

Rice, R. C. Our native trees and shrubs. 1898. III. 61.[1]

Rich, O. W. Three good forest trees for the country home. 1890. III. 118.[1]

Rich, Obadiah. A synopsis of the genera of American plants. 1814. I. 306, V. xvi.[2]

Rich, Oliver O. See RICH, Obadiah.

Rich, W. P. The five best ornamental shrubs. 1896. III. 61.[1]

Richard. Action de la cocaïne sur les invertébrés. 1885. III. 493.[1]

Richard. Manual du forestier. 1801. IV. 92.[1]

Richard, (Jardinier botaniste). Catalogue des végétaux cultivés au Jardin du gouvernement à l'Île de la Réunion. 1856. I. 68.[2]

Richard, A. Sur la culture des Palmiers dans des terrains imprégnés de sel marin. 1883. III. 328.[2]

Richard, Achille. Botanique médicale. 1823. III. 56.

— Élémens d'histoire naturelle médicale. 1831. III. 57.

— Elements of botany. 1819. I. 85.

— Essai d'une flore de la Nouvelle-Zélande. 1832. I. 506.[1]

— Flora cubana. 1845. I. 335.

— Flore de la Nouvelle-Zélande. 1832. I. 302.

— Histoire physique . . . de l'Ile Cuba . . . de Botanique. 1845. I. 335.

— Medizinische Botanik. 1823. III. 56.

— Mémoire sur la famille des Rubiacées. 1829. II. 807.[1]

— Monographie de la famille des Elaeagnées. 1823. III. 607.[1]

— Ueber die Mutterpflanze des Bdelliums. 1833. III. 511.[1]

— Neuer Grundriss der Botanik. 1819. I. 85, V. x.[1]

— Nieuwe beginselen der kruidkunde. 1819. I. 85.

— Note sur l'existence du canal médullaire dans l'intérieur des racines. 1823. I. 103.

— Note sur la plante qui fournit le bdellium. 1833. III. 511.[1]

— Note sur les plantes dites Conifères. 1810. II. 12.[2]

— Nouveaux élémens de botanique. 1819. I. 85, 523, V. x.[1]

— Nuevos elementos de botanica y de fisiologia vegetal. 1819. I. 523.

— Observations sur le genre Couma. 1824. II. 725.[1]

— Observations sur le genre Couratari. 1824. II. 612.[1]

— Observations sur le genre Quartinia. 1841. II. 380.[2]

— Observations sur les familles des Jasminées. 1826. II. 705.[2]

— Observations sur les genres Toluifera et Myroxylum. 1824. II. 374.[1]

— Plantes nouvelles d'Abyssinie. 1840. I. 487.

— Précis de botanique et de physiologie végétale. 1852. I. 9.

— Rapport sur un mémoire de M. Tréoul . . . Observations relatives à l'accroissement en diamètre. 1852. I. 189.

— Sertum Astrolabianum. 1832. I. 302.

— Tentamen florae abyssinicae. 1847. I. 487.

— Voyage de découvertes de l'Astrolabe. 1832. I. 302.

— See also BRONGNIART, Adolphe, RICHARD, Achille & JUSSIEU, Adrien; CHEVALLIER, J. B. A., RICHARD, Achille & GUILLE-MIN, J. A.; GUILLEMIN, J. B., PERROTTET, Samuel & RICHARD, Achille; PAYEN, Anselme & RICHARD, Achille; РИШАРЬ, А.

Richard, Emilien. Nomenclature des principales essences forestières de Cochinchine. 1898. IV. 88.[1]

Richard, Jules. De la culture . . . des plantes indigènes de la Vendée. 1881. III. 271.[1]

— Excursions botaniques en Espagne. 1891. I. 422.

— Tableau explicatif du système sexuel. 18 . . ? I. 259.

Richard, L. Catalogus plantarum . . . e Cayenna missarum. 1792. I. 338.[2]

Richard, Louis Claude Marie. Analyse botanique des embryons endorhizes. 1811. I. 120, 121.

— Commentatio botanica de Conifereis et Cycadeis. 1826. II. 2.

— Démonstrations botaniques; ou, Analyse du fruit. 1808. I. 119.

— Mémoire sur l'introduction de diverses plantes. 1799. I. 241.[2]

— Mémoire sur une famille . . . les Calycérées. 1820. II. 847.[2]

— Note sur une variété monstrueuse de l'Erica Tetralix. 1817. II. 669.[2]

— Observations on the structure of fruits and seeds. 1808. I. 119.

— Plantae novum . . . genus constituentis illustratio. 1815. II. 424.[1]

Richard, O. J. Florule des clochers et des toitures des églises de Poitiers. 1888. I. 417.

— Notice sur la culture de la Ramie. 1891. III. 381.[1]

Richardot, Nicolas DOUETTE-. See DOUETTE-RICHARDOT, Nicolas.

Richards, Herbert Maule. The evolution of heat by wounded plants. 1897. I. 208.[1]

— The respiration of wounded plants. 1896. I. 171, 208.[1]

Richards, R. W. Wood pavements in Sydney. 1894. IV. 426.[1]

Richardson, (Dr.). On the scarcity of wood suitable for railway sleepers in India. 1870. IV. 423.[1]

Richardson, A. D. On Ribes subvestitum Hook. & Arnott. 1896. I. 245.[1]

— Stem-ringing experiments. 1896. I. 166, IV. 385.[1]

— On the twisting of the leaves . . . of the flat-leaved Spruces. 1900. II. 18.

— On variation in the leaves of the White Beam tree. 1896. II. 312.[1]

Richardson, David Lester. Flowers and flower-gardens. 1855. III. 92.[2]

Richardson, James. Evergreen trees. — The American Holly. 1854. III. 530.[2]

— Evergreens. 1852. III. 205.[2]

— A note concerning the varieties of Date-palm. 1851. III. 328.[1]

— Note on the dates of Fezzan. 1850. III. 328.[1]

Richardson, Sir John. Arctic searching expedition. 1851. I. 310.

— Botanical appendix. 1823. I. 306.

— Remarks on the climate . . . of the Hudson's Bay countries. 1825. I. 306, 310.

Richardson, Richard. Extracts from the literary and scientific correspondence. 1835. I. 81.[1]

Richardson, W. The practical timber merchant. 1876. IV. 227.

Riche. Falsification du thé en Chine. 1890. III. 608.[1]

Riche, Alfred. See LACAZE-DUTHIERS, F. G. H. & RICHE, Alfred.

— & Rémont, A. Note sur le Bassia longifolia. 1880. III. 667.[1]

Riche, Claude Antoine Gaspard. De chemia vegetabilium. 1786. I. 150.[2]

— Considérations sur la chimie des végétaux. 1787. I. 150.[2]

Richen, Gottfried. Die botanische Durchforschung von Vorarlberg. 1897. I. 444.
Richesse du givre en combinaisons azotées. 1895. IV. 64.[1]
Richesses forestières de l'est de la Cochinchine. 1900. IV. 377.[1]
Richet, Ch. De l'action de la strychnine. 1880. III. 683.[2]
— D'un mode particulier d'asphyxie . . . par la strychnine. 1880. III. 683.[2]
— See also LANGLOIS, P. & RICHET, Ch.
Richir, Octave. Altomètre Franck. 1898. IV. 216.
— La pépinière de la C$_{roix}$-Noire. 1899. IV. 151.[2]
— Les plantations d'Epicéas dans la forêt de Hertogenwald. 1898. IV. 119.[2]
— Principaux tenthredinides de l'Hertogenwald. 1900. IV. 208.[2]
Richmann, E. S. Fruits and forest, shade and ornamental trees. 1893. III. 118.[1]
— Notes on forest and fruit trees . . . of the Agricultural college experiment station. 1892. III. 118.[1]
Richmond, J. T. Rise and fall of the Orange industry. 1895. III. 500.[2]
Richon. Bière de glands. 1860. IV. 514.[2]
Richoux, Ch. & others. Procédé . . . pour la conservation des bois. 1859. IV. 418.
Richter (Forstrat, Breslau). Baumanpflanzungen in den Strassen. 1896. III. 210.
— See also TÄGER & RICHTER.
— & Riebel, Paul. Welche Umtriebszeiten sind . . . für die Staatsforsten die geeignetsten? 1895. IV. 252.
Richter, (Hofgärtner, Dessau). Beobachtung über . . . Heimia myrtifolia. 1833. III. 629.[2]
— Briefliche Mittheilung über das Keimen des Anacardium. 1847. III. 523.[2]
— Mittheilung über eine blühende Paulownia. 1848. III. 703.[1]
— Ueber das Schneiden der Stecklinge. 1834. III. 157.
— Ueber Veredlung der Cytisus-Arten. 1833. III. 473.[2]
Richter, Aladár. Anatomiai és rendszertani vizsgálatok az Artocarpeák köréből. 1895. II. 145.[2]
— Ueber die Blattstructur der Gattung Cecropia. 1898. II. 147.[1]
— Gömör megye Rosaceái. 1889. II. 256.[1]
— Rubus Fabryi Alad. Richt. 1889. II. 299,[1] 307.[1]
— A tropikus flora három vitás génusa. 1895. II. 145.[1]
— Vergleichende anatomische Untersuchungen über Antiaris und Artocarpus. 1897. II. 145,[2] 146.[2] —
Richter, August Gottfried. De Junipero Sabina. See VOGT, T. K. A. 1803. III. 304.[1]
Richter, Daniel. Die Entlaubung eines Waldes durch Heuschrecken. 1866. IV. 496.
Richter, E. Bemerkungen über einige Solaneen. 1854. III. 702.[1]
Richter, E. H. Abriss der Terminologie der phanerogamischen Gewächse. 1837. I. 70.
Richter, Ed. Abgebrochener Liquidambar styraciflua in Wörlitz. 1899. II. 253.[2]
— Ueber Anzucht von Abies Nordmanniana. 1887. III. 296.[2]
Richter, Edv. Bemærkninger om de vilde Rosers Formering. 1839. III. 451.[2]
Richter, F. Greffage à la mousse. 1898. III. 548.[2]
— Vignes américaines; greffage à la mousse. 1898. III. 548.[2]
Richter, G. M. Dissertatio medica sistens observationes botanicas. See HOFFMANN, G. F. 1787. I. 263.
Richter, Gustav. Eisenbahntarife für Holz. 1882. · III. 284.[1]
— Ueber die Kaffeekultur in Ostindien. 1876. III. 732.[2]
— Leitfaden für die Vorlesungen über allgemeine Wirthschaftslehre. 1877. IV. 269.
— Der Stand der Holzzoll-Bewegung. 1883. IV. 284.[1]
— Unterlagen . . . Eisenbahntarife für Holz betreffend. 1878. IV. 284.[2]
Richter, Heinrich. Augsburger Blüthenkalender. 1863. I. 385.
Richter, Hermann Eberhard Friedrich. See KLETT, G. T. & RICHTER;, H. E. F.
Richter, J. Die Pflanzhaue. 1900. IV. 153.[2]
Richter, J. A. See BONNET, Edmond & RICHTER, J. A.
Richter, Karl. Beiträge zur genaueren Kenntniss der Cystolithen. 1878. I. 18.
— Die botanische Systematik. 1885. I. 253.[1]
— Neue und interessante Pflanzen. 1891. II. 100.[1]
— Notizen zur Flora Niederösterreichs. 1887. I. 443.
— Plantae europaeae. 1890. I. 350.[1]

— Untersuchungen über den Einfluss der Beleuchtung auf . . . Keimwurzeln. 1880. I. 195.[2]
— Was ist Atragene Wenderothii? 1886. II. 200.[1]
Richter, Ludwig. Beiträge zu einer Flora von Presburg. 1863. II. 106.[1]
Richter, Max OHNEFALSCH-. See OHNEFALSCH-RICHTER, Max.
Richter, Oswald. Ein neues Macerationsmittel. 1900. I. 37.[1]
Richter, Reinhard. Die Flora von Saalfeld. 1846. I. 381.
Richters, Ferd. Ueber die Wechselbeziehungen zwischen Blumen und Insekten. 1884. I. 238.
Von **richtiger** Anlegung der Gehaue. 1794. IV. 250.[2]
Richtsteig, (Oberförster, Camens i. Schl.). See TÄGER & RICHTSTEIG.
Ricinus-olie. 1883. III. 522.[1]
Rickmann. Ueber die Blüthezeit von Ulex europaeus L. 1870. II. 387.[2]
Rico y Sinobas, Manuel. Memoria sobre las causas meteorológico-físicas que producen las constantes sequías de Murcia. 1851. IV. 47.[2]
Ricome, Hilaire. Sur le développement des plantes étiolées. 1900. III. 181.[1]
— Influence de la pesanteur . . . sur l'organisation dorsiventrale des rameaux dans les inflorescences. 1898. I. 113.[2]
— Sur le polymorphisme des rameaux dans les inflorescences. 1897. I. 113.[2]
— Recherches . . . sur la symétrie des rameaux floraux. 1898. I. 114.[1]
Ricord-Madianna, J. B. Analyse chimique des gousses de l'Acacie odorante. 1830. II. 325.[1]
— Analyse des fleurs de Poincillade. 1833. II. 339.[1]
— Ueber die Blüthen von Poinciana pulcherrima L. 1833. II. 339.[2]
— Histoire naturelle . . . de l'Asclépias géant. 1830. III. 692.[2] ²
— Histoire naturelle . . . de la Barbadine. 1831. III. 616.[1]
— Histoire naturelle . . . du Lilas des Antilles. 1833. III. 512.[2]
— Histoire naturelle . . . du suc laiteux du Pantouflier. 1832. III. 518.[1]
— Ueber Melia sempervirens. 1833. III. 512.[2]
— Mémoire sur l'histoire naturelle et chimique de l'Avocatier. 1829. III. 407.[2]
— Naturgeschichte und . . . Versuche mit dem Milchsafte · des Pantoffelbaums. 1832. III. 518.[1]
— Observations . . . on the seeds of the Cerbera Thevetia. See MADIANNA, J. B. R. 1824. III. 691.[1]
— Recherches et expériences sur les poisons d'Amérique. 1826. III. 260.[2] ·
— Recherches sur la quantité de fécule amylacée. 1830. III. 266, 267.[1]
— Researches . . . . on some species of the genus Passiflora. See MADIANNA, J. B. R. 1824. III. 615.[2]
I **ricordi** di Nane Castaldo. See BELLATI, Giambattista. 1884. III. 558.[1]
Riddell, John Leonard. Catalogus florae ludovicianae. 1852. I. 318.
— Monograph of the ligneous plants . . . Ohio. 1838. I. 312.
— New and hitherto unpublished plants of the South West. 1853. V. XVII.[2]
— A supplementary catalogue of Ohio plants. 1836. I. 313.
— A synopsis of the flora of the western states. 1835. I. 306.
Riddell, L. S. Calluna vulgaris in Nantucket. 1880. II. 662.[1]
Riddell, Maria. Voyages to the Madeira and Leeward Caribbean Isles. 1792. III. 266.
Riddell, R. Notice regarding Müddär Gutta percha. 1854. III. 692.[2]
— Notice regarding the oil . . . of Juglans Camirium. 1854. III. 514.[2]
— Result of experiments on . . . Madar. 1852. III. 692.[2]
Riddermarck, Anders. De Ulmo. 1692. II. 142.[1]
Rideal, S. Notes on some Indian gum samples. 1892. III. 228.[1]
Rideau, L. Notes sur la culture . . . du Cocotier. 1900. III. 323.[1]
Ridgway, Robert. Additions and corrections to the list of native trees of the lower Wabash. 1883. I. 312, IV. 77.[1]
— Fine forest growth in the Wabash Valley. 1873. I. 312, IV. 76.[1]
— The forests of the Wabash valley. 1883. I. 312, IV. 77.[1]

— Grosse Bäume. 1876. I. 295.[1]
— Have we two native species of Trumpet-flower? 1896. II. 786.[3]
— The little Cypress swamp of Indiana. 1876. II. 51.[2]
— On the local segregation of trees. 1893. I. 305.
— A nomenclature of colors. 1886. I. 71.
— A northern station for Quercus lyrata. 1890. II. 135.[1]
— Notes on the Catalpa. 1876. II. 786.[3]
— Notes on the native trees of the lower Wabash. 1883. *I. 318*, IV. 76.[3]
— Notes on the vegetation of the lower Wabash Valley. 1872. I. 312, *IV. 76*.[3]
— Transplanting the Trailing Arbutus. 1892. III. 649.[3]
— The Tulip tree. 1876. II. 210.[3]
— The woods and prairies of the upland portions. 1873. IV. 76.[3]
Ridler, Charles E. The flora of Willoughby Notch. 1884. I. 315.
— List of plants found on Owl's Head. 1884. I. 310.
Ridley, Heury Nicholas. Cyrtandreae malayenses. 1896. II. 792.[3]
— Descriptions and notes on . . . plants from Madagascar. 1884. II. 90.[1]
— Dispersal of seeds by birds. 1896. I. 241.[1]
— On the dispersal of seeds by mammals. 1894. I. 241.[1]
— The Dracaenas of the Malay Peninsula. 1896. II. 81.[2]
— The flora of Singapore. 1900. I. 464.[3]
— On the flora of the eastern coast of the Malay Peninsula. 1893. I. 464.[3]
— Gambir. 1892. III. 748.[1]
— Golden flowers. 1899. I. 518.
— Linospadix Micholitzii. 1895. II. 70.[1]
— Livistona Woodfordi n. sp. 1898. II. 70.[2]
— Malay materia medica. 1897. III. 275.[1]
— On the monocotyledonous plants of New Guinea. 1886. I. 499.[1]
— New species of Entada. 1898. II. 355.[3]
— Notes on the botany of Fernando Noronha. 1891. I. 498.
— Report on diseases of the Nutmeg. 1896. III. 402,[3] *635.*[3]
— Report on the destruction of Coco-nut Palms by beetles. 1889. III. 323.[1]
Ridolfi, C. Catalogo delle piante coltivate a Bibbiani. 1843. I. 63, *III. 297*,[1] *541*,[1] *639*.[3]
— Del Nespolo del Giappone. 1827. III. 423.[3]
Ridolo. Sur la maladie de la Vigne. 1856. III. 576.
Riebe, E. Ist der schwedische Bocksdorn als Heckenpflanze zu gebrauchen? 1898. III. 701.[1]
— Ueber das Veredeln der Blutbuchen. 1900. III. 360.[3]
Riebel. Forstliche Mittheilungen aus Finnland. 1879. IV. 114.
Riebel, Fr. Ueber die Ermittelung des Waldbodenwerthes. 1895. IV. 258.
Riebel, Paul. Sind bei dem . . . Abschluss neuer Handelsverträge Aenderungen an den . . . Zolltarifen für Holz . . . anzustreben. 1900. IV. 284.[1]
— Unter welchen Verhältnissen ist in Schlesien die Verbindung holzverarbeitenber Industrie-Anlagen mit dem Forstbetriebe gerechtfertigt. 1897. IV. 274.[3]
— *See also* RICHTER, (*Forstrath, Breslau*) & RIEBEL, Paul.
Riechelmann, R. *See* FORSTER, A. & RIECHELMANN, R.
Rieohers, F. A. (*jr.*) Azalia nymphaeifolia. 1898. III. 643.[3]
Riecke, A. Die gefüllte Rosskastanie. 1856. III. 537.[1]
— Philesia buxifolia. 1856. III. 337.[3]
Riecke, F. J. P. Die Lehre von den Kegelschnitten. 1841. IV. 58.
Riecke, Friedrich. Ueber die Berechnung des Geldwerths der Waldungen. 1837. IV. 254.
— Ueber die Berechnung des Geldwerths der Waldungen; Einladungs-Programm. 1829. IV. 254.
— Ueber die Berechnung des körperlichen Inhalts unbeschlagener Baumstämme. 1849. IV. 223.
Riecke, V. A. *See* BERGE, Fr. & RIECKE, V. A.
Rieckher. Dosage de l'amygdaline dans les Amandes amères. 1866. III. 434.[3]
Riedel. Maclura aurantiaca Nutt. 1849. III. 372.[1]
Riedel, von (*Dr.*). Denkschrift, den Vollzug der Reorganisation der bayerischen Staatsforstverwaltung betreffend. 1886. IV. 290.[1]
Riedel, A. Friedrich der Grosse und der Wald. 1891. IV. 26.
— Samenmenge für Saatbeete . . . von Kiefern-Jährlingen. 1879. IV. 472.
— Ueber die Waldverhältnisse der Vereinigten Staaten. 1881. IV. 337.[3]

Riedel, A. F. Die Domainen und Forsten . . . des preussischen Staates. 1849. IV. 352.
Riedel, J. G. F. De sluik en kroesharige rassen. 1886. III. 274.[3]
Riedel, L. *See* TAUNAY, C. A. & RIEDEL, L.
Riedel, Ludwig. Tableau synonymique des plantes les plus usitées . . . Brésil. 1839. I. 342.
Riedel, Rudolph. Zur Verbesserung der Wandbekleidung mit wildem Wein. 1881. III. 545.[1]
Riedel, Y. C. Kurzgefasstes Garten-Lexikon. 1751. III. 30.
Riedheim, C. T., *Freiherr* von. Naturhistorische Beschreibung des hessen-darmstädtischen Odenwaldes. 1843. I. 381.
Riedl, A. Euealyptusholz, Greenheart. 1881. IV. 532.[3]
Rieffelsen, P. Beschreibung . . . der . . . Kraft- oder Hebe-Maschine. 1810. III. 167.
Riegel. Die Fichtenschildlaus. 1857. IV. 455.
— Ueber die forstwirthschaftlichen Verhältnisse des Ellwanger Waldes. 1860. IV. 356.[1]
Riegel, E. Sur l'essai des quinquinas. 1852. III. 722.
Riegels. Til Træplantningens Fremme. 1848. IV. 156.[1]
Riegels, C. & F. V. Om Træplantning. 1862. III. 166.
Riegels, F. V. *See* RIEGELS, C. & F. V.
Riegels, F. V. Hvorledes bør de jydske Heder cultiveres. 1856. IV. 156.[2]
Riegels, H. C. Brudstykker fra en Udflugt over Hannover. 1846. III. 121.[1]
— Hvad og hvorledes bør man plante. 1856. IV. 152.
— Spessarten og dens Skove. 1855. IV. 351.[1]
Rieger, J. C. *See* ZEYHER & RIEGER, J. C.
Rieger, Rudolf. Zur Etatsermittlung im Planterwalde. 1896. IV. 131.
Riegler, Wahrmund. Zur Anatomie der Schwarzföhre. 1878. II. 871.[3]
— Beiträge zur Lehre von den Moosdecken. 1879. IV. 71.
— Beobachtungen über die Abfuhr meteorischen Wassers. 1879. IV. 73.[3]
— Beobachtungen über die Bodenfeuchtigkeit. 1883. IV. 69.
— Gedanken über die Herbstknospe. 1899. I. 109,[1] *222*.[3]
Riemsdijk, H. M. D. van. Anatomisch onderzoek van het bont van . . . Rubiaceen. 1875. II. 808.[1]
— Beginselen der kruidkunde. 1870. I. 391.[3]
Riepenhausen-Crangen, Karl von. Stechginster. 1889. III. 490.[1]
Riese, H. Die Carludovica-Arten als Zimmerpflanzen. 1885. III. 332.[3]
Riések. Les Bambous sont-ils monocarpiques? 1866. II. 59.[3]
Riesenbaum. 1884. II. 52.[1]
Ein **Riesenbaum.** 1883. *See* REYES, M. O. 1884. V. xxv.[3]
Riesenbeck, Carl Friedrich Christian. D. inaug. . . . de eximiae chinae regiae virtute. 1797. III. 720.
Rieseneiche. 1878. II. 138.[3]
Eine **Rieseneiche.** 1894. II. 139.[1] — 1899. IV. 516.[1]
Rieseneiche in Frankreich. 1889. IV. 515.[3]
Riesenfichte. 1887. IV. 460.[1]
Riesenkampff, Alexander von. Bemerkungen über einige . . . Anomalien in der Form und Farbe der Gewächse. 1882. I. 454.[1]
Ein **Riesenkastanienbaum.** 1884. II. 482.[3]
Die **Riesenkiefer** . . . Pinus Lambertiana. 1877. II. 42.[1]
Die **Riesenkiefer** von Japan. 1892. II. 40.[3]
Eine **Riesenpappel.** 1883. II. 98.[1]
Riesentanne. 1886. IV. 447.[1]
Eine **Riesentanne.** 1887. IV. 447.[1]
Riesenthal, O. von. Bilder aus der Tuchler Haide. 1874. IV. 102.
— Wald und Jagd. 1890. IV. 119.[1]
Eine riesige Aristolochie. 1887. III. 386.[3]
Riesige Epheustämme. 1890. IV. 534.[1]
Die "Riesige Linde" bei Turbet nächst Travnik. 1900. IV. 528.[1]
Rieth, von BÜLOW-. *See* BÜLOW-RIETH, von.
Rietler, N. Scheikundig onderzoek van de hars der Garcinia Mangostana. 1860. III. 609.[3]
Rietmann, M. Bemerkungen über das Vorwaldsystem. 1847. IV. 128.
— Von den Eigenschaften der Weisstanne und Rothtanne. 1852. IV. 444,[1] *453*.
— Der geeignetste Standort der Lärche. 1847. IV. 451.
— Mittheilungen zur Beförderung einer volksthümlichen Holz-Erziehung. 1829. IV. 41.[1]
— Musterung einiger Waldwirthschafts- und Kulturmethoden. 1852. IV. 123.[1]

Rietmann, M. (*continued*).
— Offene Erklärung. 1842. IV. 330.
— Ueber das Verfahren beim Baum- und Stockroden. 1827. IV. 385.[2]
Rietmann, Othmar. Notizen über die Flora der Umgebung von Sydney. 1862. I. 502.
— Die Nutzpflanzen von Neu-Südwales. 1865. III. 94.[1]
Rietner, J. Een togt langs de kust van Coromandel. 1853. III. 129.[2]
Rietsch, M. *See* MARTINAND, V. & RIETSCH, M.
Rietz, Rud. Ein weiterer Beitrag zur Florula der Kopfweiden. 1894. I. 234.[2]
Rifaud, J. J. Voyage en Égypte, en Nubie. 1830. I. 487.
Riffaud, P. Note sur les jardins de feu Camille Dognin. 1889. I. 59.
La riforma della legge forestale. 1897. IV. 329.
Riga — **Naturforschender Verein.** *See* NATURFORSCHENDER . . I. 9.[2]
Rigassi, Clément. Un chemin d'utilité forestière. 1891. IV. 389.
Rigaud, A. Traité pratique de la culture du Café dans . . . Madagascar. 1896. III. 732.[2]
Rigaud, L. Ueber das Quercitrin. 1854. II. 140.[2]
Rigaudie, CHILHAUD DE LA. *See* CHILHAUD DE LA RIGAUDIE.
Rigaux. Sevrage des marcottes. 1892. III. 159.[1]
Rigaux, E. Chlorophylle et chlorose. 1897. III. 181.[1]
— Les rongeurs nuisibles à l'agriculture. 1897. III. 186.[2]
Rigg, Robert. On the evolution of nitrogen. 1838. I. 157.
Righini, Giovanni. Punicine. 1844. III. 630.[2]
The right to top a neighbour's trees. 1894. III. 34,[2] 200.[2]
Rights and privileges. 1891. IV. 335.
Rigo, Gregorio. Relazione botanica del viaggio . . . nelle provincie meridionali d' Italia. 1877. I. 428.
Rigoley. L'art du charbonnier. 1775. IV. 394.
Riis, C. P. Veiledning i havedyrkning. 1861. III. 100.[2]
Riis, J. Fragt-Lyng, Daboëcia polifolia. 1899. III. 649.[1]
Riise, A. H. Om nogle i Vestindien almindeligt brugte Droguer. 1861. III. 267.[2]
— Pharmacognostiske Notitser. 1853. III. 64.[1]
Rijckevorsel, Alphons van. Boschwezen en Heide-maatschappij. 1897. IV. 160.[2]
— Over het dunnen der bosschen. 1889. IV. 174.
— De houtteelt. 1895. IV. 107.[1]
— Staats-boschkultuur en particulier initiatief. 1890. IV. 270.
Rijk, F. de. L'âge des végétaux dans les pays tropicaux. 1892. I. 193.[2]
— L'Arbre à savon. 1883. III. 540.[1]
— Le Cocotier. 1881. III. 322.[2]
— Hemileia vastatrix. 1880. III. 735.
— Koffiecultuur. 1883. III. 730.
Rijn, J. J. L. van. Ueber das Carpaïn. 1893. III. 617.[2]
— Carpaïne, het alkaloïd. 1893. III. 617.[2]
Rijn van Alkemade, J. van. Stelselmatig oversigt der voornaamste artsenij en vergiftplanten. 1860. III. 58.
Rikli, Martin. Die mitteleuropäischen Arten der Gattung Ulex. 1898. II. 387.[1]
— Ueber die Vielgestaltigkeit der Fichte. 1898. II. 35.[2]
— Windformen der Bäume. 1899. I. 233.[2]
— *See also* SCHRÖTER, Carl & RIKLI, Martin.
Riley, Charles Valentine. Annual report on the noxious . . . insects of the state of Missouri . . . 1869. III. 186.[2]
— Concerning black rot. 1890. III. 431.[1]
— On the cause of deterioration in . . . Grape-vines. 1872. III. 550.
— Les espèces américaines du genre Phylloxera. 1874. III. 567.[2]
— Sulla fecondazione delle Yucche. 1873. II. 87.[1]
— The fertilization of the Fig. 1892. II. 151.[1]
— Fig-insects. 1883. II. 151.[1]
— Further notes on Yucca insects. 1893. II. 87.[1]
— Further remarks on Pronuba yuccasella. 1878. II. 87.[1]
— The imported Elm leaf-beetle. 1885. III. 364.[2]
— Insectes nuisibles à la Vigne. 1871. III. 759.
— Insecticides. 1890. III. 363.[2]
— Insects affecting the Hackberry. 1890. III. 363.[2]
— Insects injurious to the Grape-vine. 1874. III. 567.[2]
— Insects injurious to the Hackberry. 1890. III. 363.[2]
— Late experience in dealing with insects injurious to fruits. 1892. III. 187.
— Mexican jumping beans. 1891. II. 451.[2]
— The Mulberry silk-worm. 1879. III. 378.
— On a new genus in the lepidopterous family Tineidae. 1873. II. 87.[1]

— Notes on the natural history of the Grape phylloxera. 1875. III. 759.
— Observations on the fertilization of Yucca. 1883. II. 87.[1]
— Our shade trees and their insect defoliators. 1887. III. 187.
— Recherches de M. G. Foëx sur le mildew. 1884. III. 578.
— Remarks on the insect defoliators of our shade trees. 1887. IV. 205.[1]
— The scale-insects of the Orange. 1887. III. 501.[1]
— The silkworm. 1879. III. 378.
— Some interrelations of plants and insects. 1892. II. 87.[1]
— Ueber dem Weinstock schädliche Insekten. 1874. III. 567.[2]
— The Yucca moth and Yucca pollination. 1892. II. 87.[1]
— & Howard, L. O. The Plum Curculio. 1889. III. 433.[2]
— & Morse, F. W. The icerya or fluted scale. 1887. III. 187.
Rimbach, A. Beiträge zur Physiologie der Wurzeln. 1899. I. 162.
— Ueber die Ursache der Zellhautwellung in der Exodermis der Wurzeln. 1893. I. 104.
— Ueber die Ursache der Zellhautwellung in der Endodermis der Zellen. 1893. I. 104.
— Durch Wanzen verursachte Schädigung des Cacao. 1895. III. 593.[2]
Rimboschimenti. 1897. IV. 166.[1]
I rimboschimenti eseguiti nel Carso. 1894. IV. 167.[2]
Per il rimboschimento. 1899. IV. 166.[2]
Rimboschimento di letti de fiumi. 1881. IV. 165.
Rimedi contro la malattia degli Agrumi. 1864. III. 498.[1]
Rimmel, Eugene. The book of perfumes. 1866. III. 226.[2]
— The commercial uses of flowers and plants. 1865. III. 226.[2]
— Notes on the permanent exhibition of Algerian . . . products. 1861. III. 280.[1]
— On the odorous substances. 1863. III. 226.[2]
— The perfumery trade. 1863. III. 226.[2]
Rimmer, Franz. Über die Nutationen . . . der Keimpflanzen. 1884. I. 194.
Rimscha, Robert von. Chemische Untersuchung einer falschen Chinarinde. 1891. III. 745.[2]
Rinaldi, Giovanni de'. Il mostruosissimo mostro. 1584. I. 515, V. xxv.[2]
Rindengehalt eines Kiefern-Altholzes. 1889. IV. 481.
Rindenverluste beim Nadelholz. 1853. IV. 387.[1] — 1855. IV. 387.[1]
Ring. Soll Tilia grandifolia nur Varietät seyn? 1807. II. 517.[1]
Ring-barking in Australia. 1888. IV. 385.[1]
Ringel, Friedrich. De natura et viribus herbae Ledi. 1824. III. 653.[1]
Ringer, Sydney & Murrell, William. On Pituri. 1878. III. 700.[1]
Ringier, Victor Abraham. De distributione geographica plantarum Helvetiae. 1823. I. 433.
— & Schübler, Gustav. Ueber die Vegetationsverhältnisse der Schweiz. 1824. I. 433.
Ringing of Walnut-trees. 1823. III. 354.[1]
Ringius, Gustaf Erland. Vegetationen på Vermlands hyperitomräden. 1888. I. 357.
Ringius, J. E. Novitiae florae suecicae. *See* FRIES, E. M. 1814. I. 352.
Ringstrand, (*Magister*). Nya växtfynd af lärjungar vid Strengnäs gymnasium. 1845. I. 354.
— Sällsynta växter, funna i Södermanland. 1844. II. 100.[1]
Riniker, Hans. Ueber Baumform und Bestandesmasse. 1873. IV. 217.
— Die Berufsbildung des Forstmannes. 1877. IV. 36.[1]
— Die Ergebnisse der ersten Probe-Flächen-Aufnahmen im Aargau. 1875. IV. 217.
— Das Forstwesen des Kantons Aargau. 1878. IV. 367.
— Das Forstwesen des Kantons Thurgau. 1878. IV. 367.
— Die Hagelschläge. 1881. IV. 48.[2]
— Eine Krankheit der Pyramidenpappel. 1879. III. 346.[1]
— Maladie des végétaux. 1879. IV. 442.
— Ueber Pflanzenkrankheiten. 1879. IV. 442.
— Que doivent faire les forestiers en présence de la hausse du bois de Tremble? 1874. IV. 486.[2]
— Résultats obtenus par le dénombrement des premières surfaces d'essai, dans le canton d'Argovie. 1875. IV. 217.
— Was hat die Forstwirthschaft gegenüber der gesteigerten Nachfrage nach Aspenholz zu thun? 1874. IV. 486.[2]
— Welchen Einfluss üben die Waldungen auf . . . den Verlauf der Hagelwetter. 1884. IV. 48.[1]
— Der Zuwachsgang in Fichten- und Buchenbeständen. 1887. IV. 175,[2] 234.

Riniker, Jean. *See* RINIKER, Hans.

Rink, H. Die Nikobarischen Inseln. 1847. I. 481.[1]

Rinnovellamento . . . dei boschi alpini. 1882. IV. 128.

Rinz, J. *See* RINZ, S. & J.

Rinz, Jacob. Azalea pontica L. var. Graf von Meran. 1854. III. 661.[1]

— Bidrag til Ericernes Cultur. 1837. III. 646.[2]

— Briefliche Mittheilung über . . . Camellia japonica francofurtensis. 1834. III. 597.[2]

— Familien Rhodoraceae og dens Cultur. 1837. III. 646.[2]

— Die im Freien überwinternden Magnolien. 1853. III. 399.[1]

— Zur Geschichte . . . des Agnostus sinuatus. 1858. III. 384.[1]

— Magnolia Yulan Desf. var. grandis. 1856. III. 400.[1]

— Neue Varietäten von Rhododendron. 1855. III. 654.[2]

— Notizen über Telopea speciosissima. 1838. III. 384.[1]

— Die wichtigsten immergrünen Bäume. 1857. III. 289.

Rinz, S. & J. Einige Abarten von Robinia Pseudacacia. 1898. III. 487.[1]

— Evonymus radicans fol. albo var. 1897. III. 533.[1]

Rio, José del. Landas de Gascuña. 1893. IV. 544.[2]

Rio de Janeiro — Museu nacional. *See* MUSEU . . . I. 7.[2]

Rio de Janeiro — Palestra scientifica. *See* PALESTRA SCIENTIFICA . . . I. 7.[2]

Rio de la Loza, L. & Craveri, E. Opusculo sobre los pozos artesianos. 1854. V. XVIII.[1]

Rio de la Loza y Miranda, Francisco. Estudio sobre la Cascara amarga. 1893. III. 743.[2]

Riomet, Louis Bienaimé. Géographie botanique du canton de Marle. 1899. I. 418.

Rion, Joseph Alphonse. Guide du botaniste en Valais. 1872. I. 436.

Riondet, Alexis. L'Olivier. 187.? III. 675.[2]

— *See also* PIÔNAE, 'Αλέξι.

Riordinamento del servizio forestale. 1864. IV. 293.[2]

Ripa, Ludovicus a. Historiae universalis plantarum scribendae propositum. 1718. I. 289.

Riparo all' espansione dei fiumi dall' Enza al Panaro. 1865. IV. 186.[2]

Ripart, E. Classification des Roses européennes. 1890. II. 283.[2]

Ripley, Catharine F. The trees of the wood. 1890. I. 394.

Ripley, F. W. Notice regarding certain descriptions of . . . rat-tans. 1854. III. 233.[2]

Rippa, Giovanni. I nettarii fiorali dell' Idesia. 1899. II. 572.[1]

Rippel, Hans. Die Ameisenpflanzen. 1889. I. 235.[1]

Rippel, József. A Hibiscus Manihot. 1898. III. 587.[2]

Rippert, de. Extrait de la lettre sur l'effet de la gelée du 27 au 28 décembre. 1854. III. 47.

Riqueza agrícola [y forestal] de España. 1892. IV. 363.[2]

La riqueza forestal de Rusia. 1887. IV. 346.

Rigitier. Mémoire sur la culture du Mûrier. 1826. III. 375.

Riseis, Panfilo de. Raccoglitore di Ulive, Fronde ed altri frutti. 1844. III. 145.[1]

Risler, Eugène. Sur l'évaporation du sol. 1869. I. 167.

— Végétation de la Vigne à Calèves. 1883. II. 508.[2]

Risler, Jacob. Descriptio Cacti triangularis Linn. 1762. II. 591.[2]

Risler, Josua. Catalogus Malorum aurantiorum. 1747. III. 496.[2]

— Serenissimi Marchionis . . . Hortus carlsruhanus. 1747. 44.

Rispettate gli uccelli! 1865. IV. 90.[2]

Rissi, Domenico. Memoria sopra un nuovo metodo di propagare i Gelsi. 1837. III. 375.

Risso, J. Antoine. Citrus Rissoa. 1839. II. 403.[2]

— Essai sur l'histoire naturelle des Orangers. 1813. II. 401.[1]

— Flore de Nice. 1844. I. 410.

— Histoire naturelle des principales productions de l'Europe méridionale. 1826. III. 84.[2]

— Mémoire sur l'histoire naturelle des Orangers. 1818. II. 401.[1]

— Mémoire sur les êtres organisés nuisibles aux Oliviers. 18 . . ? III. 677.[1]

— Oranger de Gordon. 1839. II. 403.[1].

— & Poiteau, Antoine. Histoire et culture des Orangers. 1818. II. 401.[1]

— — Histoire naturelle des Orangers. 1818. II. 401.[1]

Riston, Victor. Les dunes mouvantes d'Aïn-Séfra. 1890. IV. 146.[1]

Risueño, Emiliano, RODRIGUEZ. *See* RODRIGUEZ RISUEÑO, Emiliano.

Il risveglio della frutticoltura in Ungheria. 1899. III. 147.[1]

Ritgen, Ferdinand August von. Andeutungen zu einer natürlichen Gruppirung der Pflanzenwelt. 1831. I. 260.

— *See also* WILDBRAND, J. B. & RITGEN, F. A.

Ritgiörd um birkiskóga vidurhald. *See* EINARSSON, B. 1827. IV. 490.[1]

Ritschel, Franz. Ueber das Pfropfen ganzer Zweige. 1851. III. 161.

Ritschkow, Peter. Versuch vom Birkenwasser. 1774. IV. 491.[1]

— Von vorsichtigerm Gebrauche und Vermehrung der Wälder. 1775. IV. 273.[1]

Ritschl, Georg. Flora des Grossherzogthums Posen. 1850. I. 383.

Rittenhouse, David. On the expansion of wood by heat. 1799. IV. 411.[2]

Ritter. Ueber Magnolia und deren Kultur. 1854. III. 399.[1]

Ritter, Charles. Influence des forêts sur les nappes liquides. 1880. IV. 50.

Ritter, Christian Wilhelm Jonathan. Versuch einer Beschreibung der in den Herzogthümern Schleswig und Holstein . . . wildwachsenden Pflanzen. 1816. I. 376.

Ritter, Jobann Albert. Allgemeines deutsches Gartenbuch. 1832. III. 104.

Ritter, Johannes Jacob. Animadversiones in floram Riedeseliam. 1752. I. 373.

— Meletemata ad historiam naturalem suidnicensem. 1783. I. 374.

— Tentamen historiae naturalis ditionis Riedeselio-auimontanae. 1754. I. 373.

Ritter, J. W. Elektrische Versuche an der Mimosa pudica. 1811. II. 372.[2] .

Ritter, Karl. Die Ceder am Libanon. 1854. II. 28.[1]

— Die Cedern auf dem Libanon. 1854. II. 28.[1]

— Die Entwicklungsgeschichte der Reblaus. 1893. III. 574.

— Die Erdkunde im Verhältniss zur Natur und zur Geschichte des Menschen. 1854. II. 28.[1]

— Der indische Feigenbaum, Asvattha. 183.? II. 148.[2]

— Naturhistorische Reise nach der westindischen Insel Hayti. 1836. I. 335.

— Ueber Rhizophora Mangle. 1833. II. 614.[1]

— Die Verbreitung der Dattel- und Kokospalme in Indien. 184.? II. 62.[1]

— Die Verbreitung der Pfefferrebe, Banane . 184.? II. 456.

— Die Verbreitung der Pfefferrebe . . . in Indien. 184.? II. 94,[2] 456.[2]

— Verbreitung der Theecultur. 1833. III. 606.

— *See also* MORITZ, J. & RITTER, C.

— & Rübsaamen, E. H. Die Reblaus und ihre Lebensweise. 1900. III. 575.[1]

Ritter, W. L. Korte Aanteekeningen over het rijk van Atjin. 1879. III. 275.[1]

Rittershausen, Paul. Anatomisch-systematische Untersuchung . . . der Acalypheen. 1892. II. 435.[1]

Rittinghaus, Peter. Einige Beobachtungen über das Eindringen der Pollenschläuche. 1886. I. 201.[1]

— Ueber die Widerstandsfähigkeit des Pollens. 1886. I. 201.[2]

Rittmeyer, Robert. Bannwald und Schutzwald. 1896. IV. 177.[2]

— Aus der Bodenkunde. 1889. IV. 61.[2]

— Eine deutsche Muster-Forstwirtschaft in Rumänien. 1892. IV. 375.[1]

— Ueber Durchmessermessungen an Hängen. 1898. IV. 219.

— Een en ander over de bosch en water kwestie. 1893. IV. 51.

— Einiges über Wald- und Wasserfrage. 1893. IV. 51.

— Die forstliche Reserve. 1889. IV. 245.

— Der forstliche Teil der . . . Ausstellung in Wien. 1890. IV. 21.[1]

— Aus dem Gebiete der forstlichen Zuchtwahl. 1899. IV. 75.[1]

— Gegen Gastropacha pini. 1889. IV. 208.[1]

— Zur Geschichte der Fichtenkultur. 1887. IV. 454.

— Zur Geschichte der Holzconservierung. 1897. IV. 421.

— Ueber Holzmassenaufnahme. 1889. IV. 218.

— Die Nonne. 1891. IV. 201.

— Sind die Nebennutzungen . . . mit in Anrechnung zu bringen. 1888. IV. 257.

— Ueber die Stammform der Nadelhölzer. 1898. I. 524.[2]

— Die Veranschlagung der Durchforstungserträge. 1887. IV. 237.

Rittmeyer, Robert (*continued*).
— Verschiedene Ansichten über die Ursache der Schütte. 1888.   IV. 478.
— Zur Vertheidigung des Mittelwaldes.   1890.   IV. 131.
— Wertberechnung eines Eichenschutzmantels.   1890.   IV. 258.
— Die Wertsermittlung beim Verkaufe auf dem Stocke.   1888.   IV. 257.
— Die Wirthschaftsform der Schutzwaldungen.   1896.   IV. 177.[3]
— Der Zuckerahorn.   1896.   IV. 526.[3]
Ritzema Bos, Jan.   Aanteekeningen betreffende . . . de schadelijkheid der Cetonia's.   1899.   III. 192.[1]
— Het afsterven der uiteinden van den penwortel . . . bij de Dennen.   1898.   IV. 479.
— Agaricus melleus.   1897.   III. 195.[3]
— L'anguillule de la tige.   1892.   III. 191.
— De Appelbloesemkever.   1897. · III. 428.[3]
— Een bacterienziekte der Syringen.   1899.   III. 680.[3]
— Bestrijding van de dennenbastaardrupsen.   1895.   IV. 479, 559.[3]
— Bestrijding van plantenziekten.   1891.   III. 196.
— De Beukengalmug.   1895.   IV. 497.
— De bladwesp der Pruimeboomen.   1878.   III. 433.[3]
— Een bladziekte van den Moerbeiboom.   1896.   III. 379.[3]
— Botrytis Douglasii v. Tub.   1897.   IV. 479.
— De dennebladwesp.   1878.   IV. 477.
— De dennescheerder.   1879.   IV. 477.
— De eikenaardvloo.   1878.   IV. 510.
— Het gesloten blijven der Rozenknoppen.   1896.   III. 453.[3]
— Een gevaarlijke vijand der ooftboomen.   1899.   III. 195.[3]
— De glasvleugelige vlinders.   1897.   III. 191.
— Insnoeringsziekten.   1898.   III. 195.[3]
— De kleine in een kokertje levende rups.   1875.   III. 444.[1]
— De kleine sparrebladwesp.   1878.   IV. 456.
— De krulloten der Cacaoboomen.   1900.   III. 593.[3]
— Over krulloten . . . in de Cacaoboomen.   1900.   III. 593.[3]
— Landbouwdierkunde.   1877.   III: 95.
— Le lophyre du Pin.   1895.   IV. 559.[3]
— Een merkwaardige ophooping van Dennen kegels.   1900.   II. 44.[3]
— Die Minierende Ahornafterraupe.   1892.   III. 534.[1]
— Mittel sur Bekämpfung der Lophyrus-Arten.   1895.   IV. 208.[3]
— Nouveaux moyens employés pour combattre les différentes espèces de lophyre.   1895.   IV. 208.[3]
— Nuttige en schadelijke zoogdieren.   1885.   III. 95.
— Een prachtige Conifeer.   1895.   III. 296.[1]
— De roest van den Weijmouthspijn.   1897.   IV. 470.[1]
— Rupsen in de Populieren.   1889.   III. 344.[3]
— De San-José schildluis.   1899.   III. 192.[1]
— Schadelijkheid der Meidoornheggen.   1900.   II. 263.[1] — III. 423.[1]
— Door spechten veroorzaakte " ringboomen."   1898.   IV. 199.[1]
— De " Spruitvreter " der bessenstruiken.   1897.   III. 191.
— De stryd van den dentelaer tegen zijn vijanden.   1882.   III. 196.
— Tierische Schädlinge und Nützlinge.   1891.   III. 95.
— Verslag omtrent . . . de San José-schildluis.   1898.   III. 191.
— Over de voeding van sommige boomen door schimmels.   1886.   I. 233.[3]
— Waarnemingen aangaande inlandsche schorskevers.   1876.   IV. 549.[1]
— De Wilgenspinner.   1897.   III. 350.[3]
— De " worm " in de wormstekige Appelen.   1896.   III. 428.[3]
— De " wormen " in de wormstekige Appelen.   1875.   III. 427.[3]
— Ziekte der vruchten en twijgen van den Perzikboom.   1898.   III. 442.[1]
— Ziekte in de Morellenboomen.   1896.   III. 436.[3]
— Ziekten en beschadigingen der kultuurgewassen.   1897.   III. 179.
— De ziektenleer der planten.   1895.   III. 40.
— *See also* **Lovink**, H. J. & **Ritzema** Bos, J.; **Pitsch**, O. & **Ritzema** Bos, J.; **Tutein Nolthenius**, G. E. H. & **Ritzema** Bos, Jan.
— & **Lovink**, H. J.   Schadelijkheid van de dennenlotrups.   1894.   IV. 478.
Riunione degli scienziati italiani.   Atti.   I. 520.[1]
La riunione degli ufficiali forestali a Roma.   1895.   IV. 277.
Rivas Mateos, Marcelo.   Estudios preliminares para la flora . . . de Cáceres.   1897.   I. 423.

Rivendicazione della Pineta di Ravenna.   1864.   IV. 277.
Rivera, Alejandro **Tapia y.**   *See* **Tapia y Rivera**, Alejandro.
Rivera, Francisco **Suarez de.**   *See* **Suarez de Rivera**, Francisco.
Rivero, R. L. del, **Brefiosa**, Rafael & **Castellarnau**, J. de.   Memoria de ordenación de las reales matas de Valsain.   1886.   IV. 249.[1]
— — Ordenación de las matas de Roble de Valsain.   1886.   IV. 249.[1]
Rivers, John James.   The Oaks of Berkeley.   1887.   IV. 501.[1]
Rivers, T. Francis.   The Bijou Lemon.   1884.   III. 502.[1]
— The Mount Atlas Nut.   1878.   III. 358.[1]
— Root-pruning.   1880.   III. 173.[3]
— The Tangierine Orange.   1877.   III. 502.[3]
Rivers, Thomas.   The London Plane trees.   1860.   II. 255.[1]
— The miniature fruit garden.   1840.   III. 142.
— Die Obstbaumsucht in Töpfen und in Kübeln.   1851.   III. 176.[3]
— The orchard house.   1851. ·III. 176.[1]
— Platanus acerifolia.   1860.   II. 255.[1]
— On raising Peaches, Nectarines.   1866.   III. 441.[1]
— The Rose amateur's guide.   1837.   III. 448.
— Weeping Elms.   1869.   III. 363.[3]
Rivet.   Note sur l'influence des engrais iodurés.   1853.   III. 576.
Rivet.   Notice sur l'Alisier, du Cerisier-Merisier.   1878.   IV. 85.[3]
Rivet.   Le traitement des bois en France.   1878.   IV. 122.[1]
Rivet, Gabriel.   Influence de plantations d'Epine-vinette sur . . . la rouille.   1871.   III. 394.[1]
— *See also* **Groenland**, J., **Cornu**, Maurice & **Rivet**, Gabriel.
Riviera, (*pseud.*)   Araujia sericifera and moth.   1896.   II. 736.[1]
— The effect of soil on Palms.   1896.   III. 318.[1]
— Hybridization of the Acacia.   1893.   II. 322.[1]
— Nolina longifolia.   1894.   III. 337.[1]
— The species of Phoenix.   1893.   III. 328.[1]
— Washingtonias (Pritchardia).   1893.   III. 332.[1]
Rivière, Auguste.   Effeuillement des arbres des promenades.   1875.   III. 212.[1]
— L'Eriodendron phœsanthum.   1870.   II. 530.[1]
— L'Eucalyptus globulus.   1875.   II. 623.[1]
— Hebeclynium macrophyllum.   1866.   III. 755.[1]
— Le Jardin du Hamma.   1872.   I. 522.[1]
— Lettre [sur des Cereus grimpants].   1869.   III. 621.[1]
— Lettre [sur quelques végétaux cultivés au Hamma].   1872.   I. 68.[3]
— Lettre sur un insecte qui attaque les Poiriers.   1874.   III. 446.[1]
— Multiplication de la Vigne par bouturage.   1872.   III. 548.[1]
— Multiplication du Figuier commun.   1865.   III. 369.[3]
— Note sur certains végétaux cultivés au Jardin d'essai du Hamma.   1869.   I. 68.[3]
— Note sur l'Eriodendron phaeosanthum.   1870.   III. 589.[3]
— Note sur la germination du Quinquina.   1870.   III. 712.[1]
— Rapport sur une nouvelle variété du Pandanus utilis.   1866.   III. 313.[3]
— Une visite à la ferme Barrot à Planchamp.   1871.   III. 130.[1]
— & Charles.   Les Bambous. ·1878.   III. 314.[3]
Rivière, **Boursier de la.**   *See* **Boursier de la Rivière.**
Rivière, Charles.   Sur l'acclimatation des Dattiers en Australie.   1896.   III. 329.[1]
— Algérie; horticulture générale.   1889.   III. 130.[3]
— Contribution à la bibliographie du Brucea antidysenterica.   1900.   II. 414.[1]
— La culture industrielle . . . en Algérie.   1896.   III. 130.[3]
— Diffusion des Dattiers algériens.   1898.   III. 329.[1]
— Emballage des sarments de Vignes.   1899.   III. 549.[3]
— Les Ficus à Caoutchouc dans l'Afrique.   1899.   III. 369.[1]
— Le latex du Ficus rubiginosa en Algérie.   1900.   III. 371.[3]
— Le Manioc en Algérie.   1899.   III. 369.[1]
— Le Niaouli.   1882.   III. 636.[1]
— L'Opuntia inerme.   1899.   III. 624.[3]
— Sterculia nobilis.   1898.   III. 591.[3]
— **Cosson**, Ernest & **Michon**, Joseph.   Essais d'une végétation assainissante au Gabon.   1885.   III. 314,[3] IV. 580.
Rivière, F.   La Vigne en Algerie.   1873.   III. 559.[1]
Rivière, Gustave.   Essai sur la nature des vrilles.   1879.   II. 507.[1]
— Résumé de conférences agricoles.   1899.   III. 557.[1]
— & **Bailhache**, G.   Contribution à la physiologie de la greffe.   1897.   I. 246.[3]

Riville, GODEHEU DE. *See* GODEHEU DE RIVILLE.
Rivinius, L. *See* DAFERT, F. W. & RIVINIUS, L.
Rivinus, August Quirinus. Icones plantarum : . . flore irregulari hexapetalo. 1690. I. 288.
— Introductio generalis in rem herbariam. 1690. I. 288.
— De methodo plantarum. 1696. I. 529.
— Ordo plantarum . . . flore irregulari monopetalo. 1690. I. 288.
— Ordo plantarum . . . flore irregulari ˙pentapetalo. 1690. I. 288.
— Ordo plantarum . . . flore irregulari tetrapetalo. 1690. I. 288.
— Quaestio phytologica, an plantarum vires ex figura . . . cognosci possint? *See* RIVINUS, Q. S. F. 1670. III. 259.[1]
Rivinus, Quintus Septimus Florenz. Quaestio phytologica, an plantarum vires ex figura . . . cognosci possint? 1670. III. 259.[1]
Rivista di patologia vegetale. I. 26.[1]
Rivista di viticoltura. III. 23.[2]
Rivista forestale. IV. 13.[1]
Rivoiron, Em. Steptanotis floribunda. 1885. III. 694.[1]
Rivois, G. Les Caryota. 1897. III. 321.[2]
— Les Tethratheca. 1900. III. 513.[2]
Rivoli, J. Ueber den Einfluss der Wälder auf die Temperatur. 1869. IV. 53.
— Die Serra da Estrella. 1880. IV. 363.[1]
— O wpływie lasów na temperaturę najniższych warstw powietrza. 1869. IV. 53.
Rixon, Theodore F. *See* DODWELL, Arthur & RIXON, T. F.
Rispoloshinski, R. *See* РИЗПОЛОЖИНСКІЙ, P.
Rizzetti, Carlo. Come il governo dovrebbe per ora incoraggiare i rimboschimenti. 1898. III. 380.[1]
Rizzi, Domenico. Alcune parole ancora sul Gelso delle Filippine. 1839. III. 380.[1]
— Sulle cause principali del disboscamento . . . nelle Venete provincie. 1868. IV. 277.
— Trattato sulla coltivazione della Robinia Falsacacia. 1847. IV. 523.[1]
Rizzi, P. Arte forestale primitiva. 1895. IV. 56.
— Sulle industrie del legname. 1894. IV. 405.[2]
— Intorno alla coltivazione della Sughera. 1894. IV. 517.[1]
— Il legname adoperato per traversine da ferrovie. 1894. IV. 424.[1]
— Le opinioni predominanti intorno alla coltura boschiva. 1895. IV. 56.
— Tecnologia forestale. 1897. IV. 381.
Rob. Minjak Tengkawang. 1888. III. 611.[3]
Robb, Charles. Descriptive list of . . . Canadian timber trees. 1861. I. 309,[3] *IV. 76.*[1]
Robb, James. Remarks on an anomalous form of the Plum. 1841. II. 271.[2]
Robb, Wilham. The true and false in arboriculture. 1883. IV. 170.[1]
Robbe. Catalogue des plantes usuelles du Jardin botanique d'Amiens. 1867. III. 29.[1]
Robbins, C. Sur quelques principes du Jasmin sauvage. 1877. III. 682.[1]
Robbins, Mary C. A corner in Pines. 1892. IV..469.
— A remarkable group of Pines. 1895. II. 46.[1]
— The rescue of an old place. 1892. III. 117.[1]
— A tree museum, Arnold Arboretum. 1893. III. 27.[2]
— What can be done in nine years. 1897. III. 38.[1]
Roberg, Lars. Grundvahl til plantekjaenningen. 1730. I. 31.
— De Piceae Pinique silvestris resina. 1714. IV. 443.[1]
— Plantarum generatio leviter adumbrata. 1738. I. 198.
— De succedaneis Acaciae aegyptiacae. 1737. III. 244.
Robert. Extrait d'une lettre . . . sur quelques plantes. 1831. I. 57.
— Influence desséchante du Cupressus disticha. 1832. III. 310.[2]
— Sur le Mimosa latifolia. 1828. III. 484.[2]
— Plantes phanérogames, qui croissent naturellement aux environs de Toulon. 1838. I. 409.
— Résultats du froid de l'hiver 1829–30. 1831. III. 47.
Robert. Distique sur les sépales de la Rose. 1884. II. 290.[2]
Robert, Eugène. Sur les bourgeons terminaux. 1850. I. 107.[2]
— Les destructeurs des arbres d'alignement. 1867. III. 212.[1]
— Expédition scientifique d'Islande. 1836. I. 353.
— Instructions pratiques . . . pour la destruction des insectes. 1861. III. 212.[1]
— Instructions pratiques sur les mœurs et les ravages des Scolytes. 1859. III. 364.[1]

— Sur l'intervention d'une espèce d'Aphis. 1868. III. 563.
— Lettre concernant l'emploi du cuivre contre le Phylloxera. 1872. III. 565.
— Lettre sur les moyens de destruction des hylésines piniperdes. 1852. IV. 461.[1]
— Mémoire sur les ravages des scolytes. 1847. III. 189.
— Note sur un procédé destiné à mettre les Ormes et les Pommiers à l'abri des insectes. 1846. III. 196.
— Note sur un procédé destiné: 1° à mettre les Ormes . . . à l'abri des insectes. 1849. III. 38,[1] *IV. 208.*[2]
— Procédés de décortication des Ormes. 1851. III. 364.[1]
— Les ravageurs des plantations d'alignement. 1876. III. 212.[1]
— Réclamation de priorité. 1852. IV. 209.[1]
— Relation entre la famille des Oléinées et les Morilles. 1865. II. 705.[2]
— Voyage en Islande et au Groenland. *See* VAHL, J. L. M. 1841. I. 354.
— *See also* LA BLANCHÈRE, Henri de & ROBERT, Eugène.
Robert, J. B. Le Papayer et la papaïne. 1884. III. 617.[2]
Robert, L. F. Le Rhododendron du Creux-du-Van. 1891. II. 679.[2]
Robert, Nicolas. Variæ ac multiformes florum species. 1665. V. XVI.[1]
Robert, Victor RUPRICH-. *See* RUPRICH-ROBERT, Victor.
Roberts, Algernon S. Reports and letters . . . on the proper season for cutting timber. 1850. IV. 384.[2]
Roberts, Arkew & Woodall, Edward. The gossiping guide to Wales. 1893. I. 534.[2]
Roberts, Edward P. A manual, containing directions for . . . raising of the Mulberry tree. 1835. III. 375.
Roberts, Isaac Phillips & Atwood, G. G. Soil depletion in respect to the care of fruit trees. 1895. III. 41.[1]
Roberts, J. Passiflora edulis. 1896. III. 616.[1]
Roberts, Mary. Ruins and old trees. 18. . ? I. 296.[2]
— Voices from the woodlands. 1850. I. 393.[2]
Roberts, O. W. Size and value of mahogany. ˙1828. IV. 525.[2]
Roberts, Thomas P. Is the destruction of forests a cause for the increase in the frequency and heights of floods? 1884. IV. 51.
Roberts, W. Dwarfed Japanese trees. 1899. III. 176.[1]
— Heligan, Cornwall. 1896. I. 55.
— Orange growing in California. 1900. III. 500.[2]
Robertson. Tea cultivation in Japan. 1876. III. 601.[2]
Robertson, A. M. Note on the vegetation of western Australia. 1885. IV. 401.[2]
Robertson, Archibald. Colloquia de rebus praecipuis physiologiae vegetabilium. 1822. I. 146.
Robertson, Charles. Flowers and insects. 1889. I. 238. — 1892. I. 238.
Robertson, J. A. Edible scrub on the Narran and Culgoa. 1900. III. 234.[1]
Robertson, John. On planting Cape Ericas. 1834. III. 649.[2]
Robertson, Lida B. The Rain tree. 1897. I. 213.[2]
Robertson, P. S. On the flowering and fruiting of Aucuba. 1870. II. 654.[1]
— Notice of poisoning of goats. 1868. III. 657.[1]
Robertson, R. A. On contact negatives for the comparative study of woods. 1900. I. 97.[2]
— On the photomicrography of opaque stem sections. 1900. I. 37.[2]
— Preliminary note on some witches' brooms. 1900. I. 528.[2]
Robertson, W. T. The cultivation . . . of Tea. 1891. III. 604.[1]
Roberval. *See* CARTIER, Jacques, ROBERVAL, & ALPHONSE, Jean.
Robiano, *comte* de. Observations sur les plantations des routes. 1850. III. 209.
Robiati, Ambrosio. Atlante elementare di botanica. 1847. III. 209.
Robidé van der Aa, Christian Pieter E. De aankweeking der Acacia in Nederland. 1843. IV. 523.[1]
Robie, Thomas. An account of a large quantity of alcalious salt. 1723. IV. 502.[2]
Robillard. L'Oranger, sa maladie. 1875. III. 500.[1]
Robillard. Transformation du système foliaire du Pelargonium capitatum. 1867. II. 390.[2]
Robillard, Félix. Floraison du Parkinsonia. 1849. III. 483.[1]
Robillard, J. Les semis du Robinia Decaisneana. 1890. III. 487.[1]

Robillard D'Argentelle, Louis Marc Antoine. Catalogue des fruits et des plantes (de l'Inde). 1827? I. 57.
Robilliar, (*sr.*). Sur le Corypha umbraculifera. 1848. III. 324.[1]
— Sur quelques espèces d'Illicium. 1848. III. 397.[2]
Robin. Les forêts de Chênes-Lièges en Algérie. 1884. IV. 517.[2]
Robin, Albert. Mémoire [sur le Jaborandi]. 1875. III. 505.[1]
Robin, C. Traité du microscope. 1877. I. 36.[2]
Robin, Charles. Mémoire sur l'existence d'un œuf ou ovule. 1848. I. 199.
Robin, Claude C. Voyages dans l'intérieur de la Louisiane. 1807. I. 318.
Robin, Édouard. Rapport que les végétaux comme les animaux présentent entre la quantité de vie. 1851. I. 147.
— Respiration des plantes. 1851. I. 170.
— Rôle de l'oxygène dans la respiration. 1851. I. 170.
— Rôle de l'oxygène dans la vie des végétaux. 1851. I. 170.
Robin, Jean. Catalogus stirpium . . . quae Lutetiae coluntur. 1601. I. 56.
— Enchiridion isagogicum. 1624. I. 56.
— Exoticae quaedam plantae. 1603? I. 56.
— Histoire des plantes nouvellement trouvées à l'isle Virgine. 1620. I. 56[1]
Robin, Jules. De l'avenir des forêts en Alsace et en Algérie. 1872. IV. 275, *279.*[2]
Robin Hood, (*pseud.*). Deodar sowings in the Punjab Hills. 1880. IV. 447.[2]
— Valuation or counting of the forest. 1878. IV. 217.
Robin-Massé. Expériences relatives à l'action de l'iode. 1844. I. 211.
Robineau-Desvoidy, André Jean Baptiste. Mémoire sur la maladie de la Vigne. 1851. III. 575.[2]
— Mémoire sur les gallinsectes. 1852. I. 214,[1] *III. 498,*[1] *677,*[2] *689.*[1]
Robinet. Note sur l'alcool de figues. 1855. III. 370.[1]
Robinet. Un nouveau procédé pour la transplantation des vieux arbres. 1859. III. 167.
— Procédé pour la transplantation des arbres. 1859. III. 167.
Robinet, Gabriel. Recherches sur le Niaouli. 1874. II. 630.[1]
Robinet, H. Effet de l'immersion . . . sur quelques plantes. 1875. III. 185.[1]
Robinet, Stéphane. Manuel de l'éducateur de vers à soie. 1848. III. 379.[2]
— Memoire [I.–II.] sur le Mûrier. 1840. III. 379.[2]
— Observations sur la Salsepareille. 1825. III. 338.[1]
— *See also* PETROZ, H. & ROBINET, Stephan.
La Robinia. 1890. IV. 523.[2]
The **Robinia** at Fulham palace. 1879. II. 383.[1]
Robinia hispida Linn. in fruit. 1893. III. 382.[1]
Robinia Pseudacacia Decaisneiana. 1865. IV. 524.[2]
Die **Robinien.** 1879. III. 486.[1]
Robinson, A. Sur l'utilisation, pour la culture de la Vigne, des terrains sablonneux. 1883. III. 556.
Robinson, Armand. Bois et forêts. 1879. IV. 396.[2]
Robinson, Benjamin Lincoln. Beiträge zur . . . Stammanatomie von Phytocrene. 1889. II. 475.[2]
— A blue-fruited Huckleberry. 1900. II. 672.[1]
— Descriptions of new plants . . . collected in Mexico. 1891. I. 332.
— Miscellaneous notes and new species. 1894. II. 353.[1]
— New phanerogams . . . from Mexico and Central America. 1900. I. 331.
— New plants collected . . . in western Mexico. 1891. I. 332.
— Revision of the North American . . . Mimosa. 1898. II. 371.[1]
— On the stem-structure of Iodes. 1890. II. 474.[1]
— Synopses of the genera Jaegeria and Russelia. 1900. II. 782.[1]
— Three new Choripetalae from North America. 1899. II. 371.[1]
— Two undescribed species of Apodanthes. 1891. III. 193.[1]
— Variations of Ilex verticillata. 1900. II. 465.[1]
— *See also* DEANE, Walter & ROBINSON, B. L.
— & Fernald, M. L. New plants collected by Messrs. C. V. Hartman and C. E. Lloyd . . . Mexico. 1895. I. 333.
— & Greenman, J. M. Descriptions of new or little known phanerogams, chiefly from Oaxaca. 1897. I. 333.
— — Further new . . . plants collected in Mexico. 1894. I. 332.
— — A new genus of Sterculiaceae. 1896. II. 537.[1]
— — A provisional key to . . . Porophyllum. 1897. II. 863.[2]

— — Revision of the genera Montanoa, Perymenium. 1899. II. 856,[1] *863,*[1] *868.*[2]
— — Revision of the genus Gymnolomia. 1899. II. 858.[1]
— — Revision of the Mexican . . . Calea. 1897. II. 854.[1]
— — Synopsis of the genus Verbesina. 1899. II. 867.[2]
— — Synopsis of the Mexican . . . Mikania. 1897. II. 860.[2]
— & Schrenk, H. von. Notes upon the flora of Newfoundland. 1897. I. 311.[1]
— & Seaton, H. E. Additions to the phaenogamic flora of Mexico. 1893. I. 332.
Robinson, C. J. The Mulberry-tree. 1870. III. 377.
Robinson, Charles Knowles. On the Mango and Peach trees. 1838. III. 524.[2]
Robinson, E. Kay. How India has saved her forests. 1898. IV. 279.[1]
Robinson, Edward. On the Apples of Sodom. 1842. III. 692.[2]
Robinson, H. The evils of grafting. 1890. III. 165.
— *See also* THORPE, T. E., ROBINSON, H. & WILLER, A. K.
Robinson, H. G. R. Notes on the vegetation of the island of St. Kitt's. 1897. I. 336.
Robinson, J. A British school of forestry. 1883. IV. 34.[1]
Robinson, J. F. A curious tree. 1873. II. 262.[1]
— On the pruning of hardwood trees. 1890. IV. 172.[1]
Robinson, John. Date of flowering of trees. 1881. I. 222.[1]
— Essay on ornamental arboriculture. 1882. III. 60.
— The flora of Essex county. 1880. I. 315.
— Forestry . . . in Massachusetts. 1888. IV. 112.
— The life of a Pine tree. 1878. II. 40.[1]
— Notes on the flora of Essex County. 1881. I. 80.[1]
— Notes on the . . . woody plants of Essex county. 1879. I. 312.
— Ornamental trees. 1881. III. 60.
— Our trees. 1891. I. 312.
— Our trees in winter. 1882. I. 294,[2] *IV. 76.*[2]
— Report of the committee on forest trees. 1884. IV. 112.
Robinson, Joseph. On preserving timber from decay. 1857. IV. 418.
Robinson, R. E. Old time sugar making. 1896. IV. 527.[2]
Robinson, Ralph. The Kauri gum industry. 1889. III. 297.[2]
Robinson, Robert. On English timber. 1890. IV. 398.[2]
— The felling . . . of British timber. 1895. IV. 384.[1]
Robinson, S. H. The Date tree. 1853. III. 328.[2]
— On the manufacture of date sugar. 1861. III. 329.[2]
— A practical treatise on general or partial debility . . . and the Round-leaf Cornel. 1829. III. 646.[1]
Robinson, Samuel. A course of fifteen lectures on medical botany. 1832. III. 242.
Robinson, William (*of Gowhatti Government Seminary*). A descriptive account of Asam. 1841. III. 602.[2]
Robinson, William (*F. L. S.*). Bahamas fibre. 1891. III. 341.[1]
— Among the big trees in California. 1872. I. 320, *II. 51.*[1]
— The English flower garden. 1883. III. 83.[1]
— A holiday in the South. 1874. IV. 183.[2]
— The subtropical garden. 1871. III. 82.
— Trees for city parks. 1868. III. 42.[2]
Robiquet, Edmund. Note sur l'application du gutta-percha. 1857. III. 668.[1]
Robiquet, Pierre Jean. Ueber die Aloë. 1846. III. 333.[1]
— Rapport sur un extrait sec de bois de Campêche. 1838. III. 363.[1]
— Rapport sur un mémoire de M. Jaume Saint Hilaire. 1838. III. 236.
— Rapport sur un procédé de M. Besseyre pour l'extraction des matières colorantes. 1839. III. 236.
— & Boutron-Charlard. Notice historique . . . sur les Amandes amères. 1837. III. 434.[2]
— — Notice sur le Café. 1837. III. 739.
Robison, J. & Tredgold, Thomas. A rudimentary treatise on the principles of construction in carpentry. 1859. IV. 423.[4]
Roble notable [en el monte "La Torre"]. 1886. IV. 502.[2]
Robles, Eduardo de. *See* JORDANA Y MORERA, José, MADRID-DAVILA, Alfredo de & ROBLES, Eduardo de.
Robles, F. A. MARTINEZ. *See* LOPEZ, J. A. & MARTINEZ ROBLES, F. A.
Robles, J. M. VILA Y. *See* VILA Y ROBLES, J. M.
Robley, Augusta J. A selection of Madeira flowers. 1845. I. 269.
Robottom, Arthur. Rattans and their uses. 1861. III. 321.[1]
Robotiam, A. Considérations sur quelques faits . . . à élucider . . . la maladie spéciale de plusieurs végétaux. 1851. III. 40.

— Exposé succinct d'observations . . . de guérir les Vignes de la maladie spéciale. 1853. III. 575.²
— Sur la maladie de la Vigne. 1854. III. 576.
— Moyen simple . . . de préserver la Vigne de la maladie spéciale. 1852. III. 575.²
— Thérapeutique de la maladie spéciale des végétaux. 1851. III. 196.
Robsahm, Olof Abrahm. Dissertatio geographiam plantarum adumbrans. See THUNBERG, C. P. 1813. I. 241.²
Robson, E. R. Report on senilisation of wood. 1900. IV. 416.¹
Robson, Edward. Description of the Ribes spicatum. 1797. II. 246.²
Robson, J. Old Cork Tree at Linton Park. 1873. III. 363.¹
Robson, J. E. Botanical labels for labelling herbaria. 1873. I. 402.
Robson, J. W. The experimental planting of trees. 1884. III. 123.¹
Robson, John. Fruit-bearing Conifers at Lintons. 1871. III. 290.
Robson, Stephen. The British flora. 1777. I. 395.
Rocafull, Aurelio DIAZ. See DIAZ ROCAFULL, Aurelio.
Rocamora, José. El Eucalyptus globulus. 1877. IV. 533.¹
— Del Eucalyptus globulus. 1881. IV. 533.²
Rocard. L'exploitation des bois à Madagascar. 1891. IV. 401.²
Rocardus, Claudius. De plantis absinthii tractatus. 1589. III. 754.¹
Roch, (Forstconducteur). An den Ausschuss zu Berathung der Aenderungen in der [kgl. sächs.] Forstverwaltung. 1849. IV. 291.¹
Roch, Emil. Ueber die Entwickelung des Forstkulturwesens in Sachsen. 1866. IV. 25.
Roch, H. Referat über den Verlauf des Raupenfrasses im Gohrischer Forstrevier. 1880. IV. 207.
Roché, Marie Edme Étienne Henri. De l'action de quelques composées du règne minéral. 1862. I. 211.
Rochebrune, Alphonse TRÉMEAU DE. Sur la fabrication des papiers chinois. See TRÉMEAU DE ROCHEBRUNE, Alphonse. 1865. III. 235.²
— Observations sur le Ruscus aculeatus. 1861. II. 84.¹
— Recherches d'ethnographie botanique . . . d'Ancon. 1879. I. 80.¹
— Recherches physiologiques . . . sur les Didierea. 1895. II. 485.²
— Toxicologie africaine. 1897. III. 93.¹
— & Arnaud, A. L. Recherches . . . sur le ouabaïo. 1882. III. 685.²
— & Savatier, Alexandre. Catalogue raisonné des plantes . . . de la Charente. 1860. I. 412.
Rochefort, César de. Histoire naturelle des îles Antilles. 1639. III. 63.¹
Histoire naturelle et morale des îles Antilles. 1639. III. 63.²
— Historische Beschreibung der Antillen-Inseln. 1639. III. 63.²
— The history of the Caribby-Islands. 1639. III. 63.²
— Naturlyke en zedelyke historie van d'eylanden, de voor-eylanden van Amerika. 1639. III. 63.²
Rochel, Anton. Botanische Reise in das Banat. 1838. I. 445.
— Naturhistorische Miscellen über den nordwestlichen Karpath. 1821. I. 445.
— Plantae Banatus rariores. 1828. I. 445.
Rochel, L. See POXEXH, Л.
Rocher, E. Mine de bois au Tonkin. 1894. IV. 400.³
Rocher, G. Un nouveau Jaborandi des Antilles françaises. 1898. III. 505.¹
Rochester academy of science. Proceedings. I. 6.
Rochet d'Héricourt, C. F. X. Note sur les résultats scientifiques d'un voyage dans le royaume de Choa. 1845. I. 487.
— Observations faites . . . dans le pays d'Adel. 1841. I. 487.
— Second voyage sur les deux rives de la Mer Rouge. 1841. I. 487.
— Voyage sur la côte orientale de la Mer Rouge. 1841. I. 487.
Rochleder, Friedrich. Über Aesculus Hippocastanum. 1867. III. 538.²
— Anleitung zur Analyse von Pflanzen. 1858. I. 156.²
— Beiträge zur Phytochemie. 1847. I. 151.¹
— Über die Blätter von Aesculus Hippocastanum. 1868. III. 538.²

— Ueber der Boheasäure . . . von Thea bohea. 1847. III. 606.
— Über das Caffein. 1849. III. 740.¹
— Über die Calluna vulgaris. 1852. III. 648.²
— Chemisk Undersøgelse af Kaffebønner. 1846. III. 740.¹
— Über die chinesischen Gelbschoten. 1855. II. 818.¹
— Sur l'écorce de la racine de Pommier. 1866. II. 267.¹
— Über einige Bestandtheile der Blätter . . . von Cerasus acida. 1869. II. 273.³
— Über einige Bestandtheile der Früchte von Cerasus acida. 1870. II. 273.³
— Examen des semences de Café. 1844. III. 740.¹
— Examination of Coffee seeds. 1844. III. 740.¹
— Sur la famille des Rubiacées. 1852. III. 710.¹
— Sur les fleurs mâles du Noyer. 1867. II. 113.¹
— Über den Gerbstoff der Rosskastanie. 1867. III. 538.²
— Über die Kaffeegerbsäure. 1848. III. 740.¹
— Über die Kapseln der Rosskastanienfrüchte. 1868. III. 538.²
— Über die krystallisirten Bestandtheile der Rosskastanie. 1863. III. 538.²
— Über die Nadeln von Abies. 1868. II. 23.²
— Über die natürliche Familie der Ericineae. 1852. III. 647.¹
— Ueber die natürliche Familie der Rubiaceae. 1852. III. 710.²
— Notiz über die Bestandtheile der Wurzelrinde des Apfelbaumes. 1866. II. 267.¹
— Notiz über die Blätter von Epacris. 1866. II. 688.²
— Notiz über die männlichen Blüthen von Juglans. 1867. II. 114.¹
— Ueber die Pflanzen der Familie der Ericineae. 1852. III. 647.¹
— Phytochemie. 1854. I. 152.¹
— Présence de la fraxine. 1860. III. 538.¹
— Présence du quercitrin dans . . . Marronnier d'Inde. 1859. III. 538.¹
— Sur les principes constituants de l'écorce du Maronnier d'Inde. 1866. III. 538.¹
— Sur les principes immédiats . . . de Ericinées. 1853. III. 647.¹
— Über Quercitrin. 1867. I. 175.
— Recherches sur le Café. 1848. III. 740.¹
— Recherches sur le thé. 1847. III. 606.
— Über die Säure des Blätter von Ilex paraguayensis. 1848. III. 530.²
— Über die Stammrinde von Pyrus Malus. 1867. II. 267,¹ III. 538.²
— Untersuchung der Kaffeebohnen. 1846. III. 740.¹
— Untersuchung der reifen Samen der Rosskastanie. 1862. III. 538.¹
— Untersuchung von Calluna vulgaris. 1852. III. 648.²
— Über das Vorkommen des Fraxin. 1860. III. 538.¹
— Über das Vorkommen des Quercitrin als Blüthenfarbestoff. 1859. I. 164.
— Über das Vorkommen von Mannit. 1870. III. 521.¹
— Über das Vorkommen von Quercetin in Calluna. 1866. III. 648.²
— Vorläufige Notiz über den Gerbstoff von Aesculus. 1865. III. 538.²
— & Hlasiwetz, Heinrich. Examen chimiques des câpres. 1851. III. 408.¹
— — Untersuchung der Blüthenknospen von Capparis. 1851. III. 408.²
— Ueber die Wurzel der Chiococca racemosa. 1850. III. 744.¹
Rochlitz, Michaëlis BAPST VON. See BAPST VON ROCHLITZ, Michaëlis.
Rochon, Alexis Marie. A voyage to Madagascar. 1793. I. 496.
— Voyages à Madagascar. 1793. I. 496.
Rochussen, Jan Jacob. Sur la culture du Quinquina à Java. 1863. III. 715.
— Culture et fécondation artificielle des céréales et des arbres fruitiers. 1864. III. 38.²
— Daniel Hooibrenk's künstliche Behandlung . . . der Körnerfrüchte und Bäume. 1864. III. 38.³
— Daniel Hooibrenk's kunstmatige bewerking . . . van granen en boomen. 1864. III. 38.²
Rock, Thomas A. Monkey bread nuts. 1861. III. 589.¹
Rock, Thomas D. On Balsam seeds. 1862. III. 482.²
— A visit to the great exhibition. 1862. III. 28.³
The Rock Oak (Quercus Prinus L.). 1895. II. 136.¹
Rockhill, William Woodville. The land of the lamas. 1891. I. 298.

Rockwell, Alfred Perkins. Roads and pavements in France. 1896. IV. 426.¹
Rocky caves covered with Ivy. 1877. III. 642.²
The Rocky Mountain Bramble. 1875. III. 458.¹
Rocquigny-Adanson, G. de. L'Araucaria imbricata de Lon-guerne. .1896. III. 299.¹
— Les arbres nourriciers du Gui. 1894. II. 179.²
— Le Citrus triptera. 1892. III. 503.¹
— Le genre Adansonia. 1898. II. 528.³
— Le Gui et les arbres exotiques. 1895. II. 179.²
— Le Juglans nigra L. 1900. III. 354.¹
— Reproduction spontanée du Cèdre en France. 1899. III. 300.²
— Taxodium distichum Rich. 1900. II. 52.¹
Roczniki gospodarstwa krajowego. III. 10.¹
Roda, Guiseppe. See Roda, Marcellino & Guiseppe.
Roda, Marcellino & Guiseppe. Nozioni principali sulla arbo-ricoltura. 1869. III. 114.²
Rodati, Aloysio. Linnaei de plantarum ordine brevis inter-pretatio. 1785. I. 258.
Rodati, Luigi. Catalogue des plantes cultivées dans le jardin de Mr. de Spin. 1804. I. 61.
— Index plantarum quae extant in Horto publico Bononiae. 1802. I. 61.
Rodatz, Hans. Eine neue Pflanzmethode des Kaffees. 1900. III. 734.²
Rodegher, Emilio & Venanzi, Giuseppe. Prospetto della flora della provincia di Bergamo. 1894. I. 430.
Rodenberger, Jóhann Friedrich. De corticis peruviani praes-tantia. 1763. III. 719.
Roder, Karl. Die polare Waldgrenze. 1895. I. 301.
Rodericus, Joannes, de Castello Albo. See Amatus Lusi-TANUS.
Rodet, Henri Jean Antoine. Botanique agricole et médicale. 1857. III. 217.
— Cours de botanique élémentaire. 1847. I. 89.
— Leçons de botanique élémentaire. 1847. I. 89.— 1857. III. 217.
— Note sur l'anatomie et sur la physiologie d'un cône de Pin. 1861. II. 39.²
Rodewald, H. Quantitative Untersuchungen über die Wärme-und Kohlensäure-Abgabe. 1887. I. 171.
— Untersuchungen über den Stoff- und Kraft-Umsatz im Athmungsprocess. 1888. I. 171.
Rodewald, Heinrich Ludwig. De opportuno corticis peru-viani in febribus . . . usu. 1793. III. 720.
Rodger, James. Description and sketches of lever appliance. 1900. IV. 176.³
— The formation of plantations. 1895. IV. 142.
Rodham, Olivia. Zur Kenntniss der Gefässzertnetze. 1890. I. 134.¹
Rodiczky, Jenő. Az Ailanthus-fák ügyéhez. 1871. III. 507.¹
— A Fekete Bodza. 1898. III. 752.¹
Rodie, H. On beberine from the Greenheart tree. 1863. III. 407.²
— Remarks on the Bebeeru. 1845. III. 407.¹
Rodigas, Émile. L'Abies Douglasi de Dropmore. 1883. III. 309.²
— Action du froid sur les végétaux. 1894. III. 182.
— Aralia monstrosa. 1884. III. 641.¹
— Araucaria Mülleri. 1882. II. 26.²
— L'arboriculture au Congrès agricole. 1883. III. 121.²
— Arbres forestiers de Belgique. 1898. IV. 84.²
— Les arbres fruitiers dans les jardins. 1889. III. 202,¹
— Azaleodendron Rod. 1893. III. 655.
— Bastaardsoortén van kloeke Azalea's. 1893. III. 681.¹.
— Une belle collection de Cycadées. 1890. III. 284.¹
— Bemesting der oofthoomen. 1884. III. 152.
— Berberis stenophylla hort. 1880. III. 395.¹
— De boomteelt in het Landbouwcongres. 1883. III. 121.²
— Boronia elatior, B. heterophylla. 1890. III. 495.²
— De bruinziekte der wiingaarden. 1893. III. 564.¹
— Bruinsure, maladie de la Vigne. 1893. III. 564,¹
— Cactées rustiques. 1900. III. 624.²
— Le Carya olivaeformis. 1886. III. 354.¹
— De Clematis. 1897. III. 389.³
— Les Clématites. 1897. III. 389.²
— Cloque du Pêcher. 1896. III. 442.¹
— Les Conifères de Dropmore. 1882. II. 26.³
— Cornus variegata Sailleri. 1900. III. 645.²
— Cri d'alarme. 1897. III.191.
— Culture des Cycadées. 1889. III. 284.³
— Cycadées de choix. 1889. III. 284.³
— Dégâts de l'hiver 1890-1891. 1891. III. 46.³

— De dènnebosschen van de Kempen. 1891. IV. 549.²
— Een driehonderdjarige Linde. 1899. II. 517.¹
— Enkyanthus sinensis. 1900. III. 649.¹
— Ennemi du Pommier. 1897. III. 425.²
— Les Erica. 1896. III. 650.²
— Les Eucalyptus. 1879. III. 633.²
— Fécondation artificielle des fleurs de Poirier. 1897. III. 175.¹
— Fêtes florales à Gand. 1893. III. 28.²
— Fumure des arbres fruitiers. 1894. III. 152.
— Een groote Kastanjeboom. 1898. II. 125.¹
— Groseillier à maquereau sans épines. 1897. III. 414.²
— Hybried van Berberis. 1898. II. 204.²
— Invloed der koude op de gewassen. 1894. III. 182.
— Invloed der wouden op het grondwater. 1898. IV. 52.
— Kermès de San José. 1898. III. 191.
— Koelreuteria bipinnata. 1900. III. 539.¹
— Kruisbezien zonder stekels. 1897. III. 414.²
— Krulziekte der Persikboomen. 1896. III. 442.¹
— Kunstmatige bevruchting der ooftbloemen. 1897. III. 175.¹
— De kwestie van de phylloxera. 1880. III. 572.
— Le Licuala grandis Wendl. 1882. III. 326.¹
— Ligustrum ovalifolium fol. var. 1895. III. 674.¹
— De Lindeboom van Kadier-en-Keer. 1890. II. 517.¹
— De merkwaardigste Cipresboomen. 1891. II. 30.¹
— Miconia velutina. 1894. III. 639.¹
— Middelen tegen de schildluizen. 1898. III. 191.
— Nectarinen. 1893. III. 440.¹
— Nectarines. 1893. III. 440.¹
— Noodkreet. 1897. III. 191.
— Notice sur les ascidies tératologiques d'un Caragana. 1866. II. 341.²
— Nouveaux Croton. 1878. III. 515.²
— Nouveaux hybrides, Azaleodendron. 1892. III. 655.
— Het wat der Robinia Pseudo-Acacia. 1884. IV. 523.¹
— Opuntia pseudotuna. 1900. III. 625.¹
— L'Orme gras à larges feuilles. 1868. III. 366.¹
— Een overgroote Kastanjeboom. 1890. II. 125.¹
— Parthenocissus Engelmanni. 1900. III. 545.¹
— Le phylloxera de la Vigne. 1880. III. 572.
— Plantations publiques dans les grandes villes. 1891. III. 42.³
— Une plante à déclasser. 1896. III. 415.²
— Prunus Pissardi Carr. 1893. III. 436.¹
— À quel moment peut-on transplanter les arbres toujours verts? 1894. III. 295.²
— La question du phylloxera. 1880. III. 572.
— Remèdes contre les kermès. 1898. III. 191.
— Een reuzen Camellia. 1892. II. 551.¹
— De reuzenboomen van Vlaanderen. 1887. I. 296.²
— Reuzengewassen. 1893. II. 104,² 181.²
— De Reuzenkastanjeboom van St. Antoine. 1887. II. 125.¹
— Rhododendron Forsterianum. 1900. III. 659.¹
— De Robinia. 1879. III. 486.¹
— Les Robinia. 1879. III. 486.¹
— Le Robinier du Jardin des plantes. 1898. IV. 524.²
— Le Roupellia grata. 1899. III. 690.²
— Der Saft circulirt nicht. 1872. I. 164.
— Schade door den winter 1890-91 veroorzaakt. 1891. III. 46.³
— Sehildluis van San José. 1898. III. 191.
— Een schoone Olm. 1890. II. 143.²
— La sève ne circule pas. 1872. I. 164.
— Statistiek der wouden. 1891. III. 644.¹
— Tentoonstelling van bloemen te Gent. 1893. III. 28.²
— Trevesia eminens. 1884. III. 644.¹
— Les trois plus belles plantes nouvelles. 1894. III. 338.²
— Twee merkwaardige boomen te Brussel. 1891. I. 296.⁵
— Twee reuzenboomen. 1889. I. 295.¹
— Utilité du Robinia Pseudo-Acacia. 1884. IV. 523.¹
— Véroniques néo-zélandaises. 1896. III. 704.¹
— Vignobles aux Pays-Bas. 1891. III. 553.¹
— Vijand van den Appelboom. 1897. III. 428.²
— Wijnbergen in Nederland. 1891. III. 553.²
— De woekerluis des wijngaards. 1880. III. 572.
— De Ypenboom van Somma. 1895. II. 11.²
— See also Linden, Lucien & Rodigas, Émile.
Rodin, Hippolyte. Esquisse de la végétation . . . de l'Oise. 1864. I. 413.
— Les plantes médicinales et usuelles. 1872. III. 86.
Rodino, Giuseppe. La legge forestale del 20 Giugno 1877. 1879. IV. 328.

Rodon y Bell, Martin. Breve discurso de la botanica. 1788. I. 32.

Rodowicz-Oswiecinsky, Theodor. Tropische Gewächse . . . in den deutschen Colonie Dona Francisca. 1853. III. 65.[1]

Rodrigue, Alice. Contribution à l'étude des mouvements spontanés . . . des feuilles. 1894. I. 197,[2] *II. 322*.[1]

— Recherches sur la structure du tégument séminal des Polygalacées. 1893. II. 430.[1]

— *See also* CHODAT, Robert & RODRIGUE, Alice.

Rodrigues, João BARBOSA. Attalea oleifera. 1881. II. 65.[1]

— Bactris Constanciae (Nob.). 1876. II. 65.[1]

— O calor das flores masculinas da Guilielma. 1898. I. 187, *II. 65*.[1]

— Eclogae plantarum novarum. 1888. I. 343.

— Enumeratio Palmarum novarum. 1875. II. 61.[2]

— Enumeratio plantarum in Horto botanico fluminensi culturum. 1893. I. 40.

— Esterhazya superba. 1885. II. 780.[1]

— O genero Osmidrophora. 1896. II. 789.[2]

— As Heaveas ou Seringueiras. 1900. III. 518.[2]

— Hortus fluminensis. 1894. I. 40.

— Hymenaea Correana, H. chapadensis. 1898. II. 364.[2]

— Notas a Luccok sobre a flora e fauna do Brazil. 1882. I. 343.

— Palmae amazonenses novae. 1888. II. 61.[2]

— Palmae Hasslerianae novae. 1900. II. 61.[1]

— Palmae mattogrossenses. 1898. II. 61.[2]

— Palmae novae paraguayenses. 1899. II. 61.[2]

— Les Palmiers. 1882. II. 61.[2]

— Passifloraceae Meisner; Tetrastylis. 1882. II. 580.[1]

— Plantae mattogrossenses. 1898. I. 344.

— Plantas novas cultivadas no Jardim botanico do Rio de Janeiro. 1891. I. 40.

— Protesto-appendice ao Enumeratio Palmarum novarum. 1875. II. 61.[2]

— Relatorio sobre trabalhos do Jardim botanico. 1893. V. VIII.[1]

— Rutaceae Juss.; Esembeckia [*sic*] fasciculata. 1883. II. 406.[2]

— O Tamakoaré. 1887. II. 553.[2]

Rodríguez, F. A. Climatología. 1892. IV. 543.[2] Felipe.

Rodriguez, Felipe PICATOSTE Y. *See* PICATOSTE Y RODRIGUEZ, Felipe.

Rodriguez, Francisco QUIROGA Y. *See* QUIROGA Y RODRIGUEZ, Francisco.

Rodriguez, João, DE CASTELLO BRANCO. *See* AMATUS LUSITANUS, (*pseud*).

Rodríguez, Joseph. *See* LAGASCA, Mariano & RODRIGUEZ, Joseph.

Rodríguez, Juan Joaquin. *See* RODRIGUEZ Y FEMENIAS, Juan Joaquin.

Rodriguez-Ferrer, Miguel. Naturaleza. 1876. I. 336, IV. 341.[1]

Rodriguez Mourelo, José. Aprovechamiento del Pino en España. 1900. IV. 462.[2]

Rodriguez Risueño, Emiliano. Estudio micrográfico de los Aloes. 1889. II. 78.[1]

Rodriguez y Femenías, Juan Joaquin. Additions à la flore de Minorque. 1878. II. 360.[1]

— Catálogo razonado de las plantas vasculares de Menorca. 1895. I. 423.

— Excursion botánica al Puig de Torella. 1879. I. 422.

— Herborización en Panticosa. 1890. I. 422.

Rodtwitt, L. G. Patriotiske Tanker angaaende Fyrreskov. 1763. IV. 342.[1]

Rodway, James. Death in the forest. 1892. I. 243.[1]

— The fibre yielding plants of British Guiana. 1886. III. 234.[1]

— In the Guiana forest. 1894. I. 339.[1]

— On some of the domestic medicines used in Guiana. 1885. III. 268.[1]

— The struggle for life in the forest. 1891. I. 219.[2]

— The struggle for life in the swamp. 1892. I. 219.[2]

Rodway, Leonard. Botanical notes. 1900. I. 506.[1]

— Forestry for Tasmania. 1900. IV. 380.[2]

Roe, E. P. A manual on the culture of small fruits. 1876. III. 147.[2]

— Success with small fruits. 1880. III. 147.[1]

Röber, D. F. A. Versuch einer rationellen Anleitung zum Weinbaue. 1825. III. 552.

Roeber, Franz Eduard. Explicatio systematis plantarum naturalis pharmacodynamica. 1841. III. 244.

Röder, von. Die Fichten-Büschelpflanzung. 1830. IV. 452.[2]

Roeder Marck Ordnungen. 1788. IV. 25.

Rödiger, Fr. Häage und Zäune in der . . . Alpenwirthschaft. 1881. III. 214.[1]

Röhling, Johann Christoph. Deutschlands Flora. 1796. I. 375.

Röhrig, G. Lophyrenfrass am Knieholze. 1895. IV. 465.[1]

Roelants, I. M. A. De specifieke werking der nux vomica. 1843. III. 684.[2]

Roell, J. J. Iets over de Fourcroya gigantea. 1888. III. 341.[2]

Roelofs, H. Verhandeling over de houtteelt. 1794. IV.119.[1]

— Welke meest en min bekende soorten van . . . houtgewassen kunnen in onze republiek geplant worden? 1791. IV. 119.[1]

Roelsius, Tobias. [De . . . plantis] epistola ad Carolum Clusium. 1601. III. 63.[2]

Roemer, E. van de. Djaticultuur. 1893. IV. 536.[2]

Roemer, Ferdinand. Texas; mit besonderer Rücksicht auf deutsche Auswanderung. *See* SCHEELE, Adolph. 1849. I. 322.

Roemer, Georg Chr. *See* ZEYHER, J. M. & ROEMER, G. C.

Römer, Heinrich. Flora der Schweiz. 1843. I. 434.

Roemer, Hermann. Alter des Hildesheimer Rosenstocks. 1882. II. 290.[1]

— Der tausendjährige Rosenstock. 1892. II. 290.[r]

Roemer, Johann Jakob. Catalogus horti botanici Societatis physicae turicensis. 1802. I. 65.[1]

— Collectanea ad omnem rem botanicam. 1809. I. 33.

— Encyklopädie für Gärtner. 1797. III. 30.

— Flora europaea inchoata. 1797. I. 348.[2]

— Scriptores de plantis hispanicis. 1796. I. 341.

— Versuch eines . . . Wörterbuchs der botanischen Terminologie. 1816. I. 70.

— & Usteri, Paul. Myristica. 1789. II. 220.[1]

— — Observationum botanicarum sylloge. 1787. I. 263.

— — Philadelphus floribundus. 1790. II. 628.[2]

— — Sophora tetraptera Linn. und Sophora hirsuta. 1790. II. 378,[1] *384*.[2]

Römer, Julius. Die Alpenrose. 1887. II. 676.[1]

— Ueber das Vorkommen der " Königsblume." 1894. II. 601.[1]

Roemer, M. J. Familiarum naturalium regni vegetabilis synopses monographicae. 1846. I. 261.

— Geographie und Geschichte der Pflanzen. 1840. I. 299.

— Handbuch der allgemeinen Botanik. 1835. I. 87.

Rönne, Ludwig von. Das Domainen-, Forst- und Jagdwesen des preussischen Staates. 1854. IV. 320.

Röntgen, C., (*jr.*) Over de Maqui-bessen. 1890. III. 584.[2]

Röper, Johannes August Christian. Bemerkungen über die Araliaceen. 1848. II. 649.[1]

— Normales und Abnormes. 1852. II. 658.[2]

— Observations sur la nature des fleurs. 1826. I. 113.[1]

— De organis plantarum. 1828. I. 98.

Röepstorff, C. S. de. Forstlig Stat. 1881. IV. 288.[2]

— Meddelelser om danske Forstkandidater. 1881. IV. 288.[2]

Rörig, Adolph. Die gemischten Holzbestände. 1867. IV. 137.[2]

Rörig, G. Die Krähen Deutschlands. 1900. IV. 199.[1]

— Magenuntersuchungen . . . wichtiger Vögel. 1900. IV. 100.[1]

— Ein neues Verfahren zur Bekämpfung des Schwammspinners. 1900. III. 197.

Rösch, J. G. Aufzählung der in Bünden bisher entdeckten Bergpflanzen. 1807. I. 433.

— Bemerkungen über die Vegetation einiger Kalkgebirge in Bünden. 1806. I. 433.

Roese & Magnus, P. W. Hexenbesen an einer Birke. 1894. IV. 491.[1]

Röse, Aug. Ueber die Absprünge der Bäume. 1865. I. 192.[1]

— Ueber die . . . Absprünge der Bäume. 1866. IV. 196.[1]

— Der Burgberg bei Waltershausen. 1868. II. 313.[1]

— Die Fichtennadelbräune. 1867. IV. 455.

— Ueber die Fichtennadelkrankheit. 1866. IV. 455.

— Taxus baccata L. in Thüringen. 1864. II. 11.[1]

— Ueber Taxus und sein Aussterben. 1865. IV. 440.[1]

— Ein zweiter Buchenausschlag im Herbste. 1866. I. 221.

Roese, H. & Pellegrini, F. Anlage . . . dichter Weissdornhecken. 1890. III. 422.[2]

Röseler, P. Das Dickenwachsthum . . . bei den baumartigen Lilien. 1889. II. 77.[2]

Roeser & Puaux. Analyse de la gomme du Grevillea robusta. 1899. III. 383.[1]

Rösler, Gottfried. Forstmathematische Aphorismen. 1869. IV. 58.
Roesler, Leonhard. Analysen von Föhren- und Fichtenholz. 1863. II. 20.[1]
— Istruzione popolare sulla Phylloxera. 1875. III. 759.
— Mitteilungen aus der K. k. chemisch-physiologischen Versuchsstation für Wein- und Obstbau. 1878. III. 138.
— Die Phylloxera vastatrix. 1875. III. 759.
Rösler, Max. Verwendung des Buchenholzes zu Bauzwecken. 1885. IV. 499.
Rösling, C. L. Über Potasch- und Salpetersiederei. 1806. IV. 395.
Roessig, Karl Gottlob. Handbuch für Liebhaber englischer Pflanzungen. 1796. III. 74.
— Oekonomisch-botanische Beschreibung der . . . Rosen. 1799. II. 281.[2]
— Die Rosen. 1801. II. 281.[2]
— Les Roses. 1801. II. 281.[2]
Rössing, A. von. Die forstlichen Verhältnisse des Herzogthums Anhalt. 1882. IV. 350.[1]
— Das Forstrevier Ertinghausen. 1863. IV. 353.
Rössler, Mathias. Pomona bohemica; oder Tabellarisches Verzeichniss . . . Obstsorten. 1795. III. 90.[1]
— Sistematisches Verzeichnis aller in . . . der podiebrader Dechantey kultivirten Obstsorten. 1798. III. 90.[1]
Rössler, O. Distinction chimique du succin et du copal. 1900. I. 181.[2]
Rösslin, Eucharius. Herbarum, arborum, fruticum . . . imagines. 1533. I. 277.
— Kreutterbuch von allem Erdtgewächs. 1533. I. 276.
— Kreutterbuch vonn aller Kreuter, Bäum. 1533. I. 276.
Röthe, C. F. Analyse der Asche von Erica carnea. 1853. II. 664.[1]
Röthel, H. Beobachtungen über das Auftreten des grünköpfigen Kiefernspanners. 1875. IV. 477.
Roettel, F. I. De Vitis cultura. 1770. III. 552.
Roezl, Benedict. Catalogue des graines de Coniferes mexicains. 1857. II. 14.[1]
— Catalogue et description de Pins du Mexique. 1862. II. 14.[1]
— Die Coniferen Mexico's. 1857. II. 14.[3]
— De los jardines botanicos. 1872. I. 39.
— Mexican Conifers.— Pinus Popocatepetli Lindl. 1884. II. 40.[1]
— Mon dernier voyage à la côte occidentale du Mexique. 1882. I. 332.
— Notes sur les découvertes botaniques . . . faites en Amérique. 1883. I. 332.
— Reiseberichte aus Mexico. 1860. I. 331.
Die Rösl'schen Koniferen. 1858. IV. 14.[1]
Rogalski. Analyses de chlorophylle. 1880. I. 142.
Rogalski, A. Wykaz roślin . . . zebranych w Spiskich Tatrach. 1881. I. 446.
Roger, (abbé). See SCHABOL, Jean.
Roger-Desgenettes, C. Le Camellia . . . sous le climat de Paris. 1864. III. 599.[1]
Rogers, Charles Gilbert. A Burmese timber cart. 1896. IV. 390.[1]
— Flowering of Bamboos in the Darjeeling district. 1900. II. 58.[1]
— Journal of the Hill tour. 1892. IV. 378.
— A large Banyan tree. 1896. II. 150.[1]-
— Life history of Melasoma populi. 1896. III. 344.[3]
— A ma a of forest engineering for India. 1900. IV. 100.[1] nu [1]
— Sissu and Mulberry at Changa Manga. 1899. IV. 521.[3]
Rogers, Henry. Count de Cars' book. 1886. IV. 172.[1]
— Report on the effects of the cutting down of forests. 1873. IV. 49.[1]
— On treatment of plantations. 1880. IV. 169.[1]
Rogers, J. Notice of the Pines introduced. 1847. III. 291.
Rogers, John. The fruit cultivator. 1834. III. 79, 142.[1]
Rogers, Patrick Kerr. An investigation of the properties of the Liriodendron. 1802. III. 398.[3]
Rogers, William Moyle. An essay at a key to British Rubi. 1892. II. 303.[1]
— Handbook of British Rubi. 1900. II. 303.[2]
— Radnorshire and Breconshire Rubi. 1899. II. 303.[1]
— On the Rubi list in " London catalogue." 1895. II. 303.[1]
— Rubi notes. 1894. II. 303.[1]
— On some Scottish Rubi. 1897. II. 303.[1]
— Two new Brambles from Ireland. 1896. II. 303.[1].
Roget, Peter Mark. Animal and vegetable physiology. 1834. I. 146.

Rogg, J. Anfangsgründe der Naturwissenschaft für Forstmänner. 1828. IV. 56.
— Lehrbuch der Forstwirthschaft. 1826. IV. 56.
— Sammlung mathematischer Aufgaben. 1827. IV. 58.
Roggenbau, F. A. W. Anviisning til Opelskning af Skov. 1864. IV. 156.[1]
Roggeri, G. G. Catalogo delle piante native del suolo romano. 1677. I. 424.
Rogovitch, A. See POPORITZ, A.
Rogron. Codes forestier, rural, de la chasse. 1841. IV. 322.[2]
Rogron, J. A. Codes forestier. 1836. IV. 324.
Rohan, Henrique, visconde de BEAUREPAIRE-. See BEAUREPAIRE-ROHAN, Henrique, visconde de.
Rohart, F. Action sur la Vigne du sulfure de carbone. 1879. III. 560.
Rohart, F. F. Destruction pratique du phylloxéra. 1875. III. 759.
— État de la question phylloxera. 1875. III. 568.
Rohart, P. Lettre concernant l'action exercée par les terres sur les gaz insecticides. 1874. III. 563.
Rohde, Michael. Monographiae Cinchonae generis tentamen. 1804. II. 312[2] III. 720.
Rohlfs, Gerhard. Drei Monate in der libyschen Wüste. 1875. I. 485.
Rohr, von, (Lieut.). Plante-Slægter. 1792. I. 264.
Rohr, J. V. von. Historia naturalis arborum. 1732. IV. 81.
Rohr, Julius Bernard von. Physicalisch-oeconomischer Tractat von den Nutzen der Gewächse. 1736. III. 217.
— Phytotheologia. 1740. I. 515.
Rohrbach, Carl. Beiträge zur Frage der Wasserleitungsfähigkeit des Kernholzes. 1884. I. 165.
— Ueber die Wasserleitungsfähigkeit des Kernholzes. 1885. I. 165.
Rohrbach, Paul. Beiträge zur Morphologie der Leguminosen. 1870. II. 320.[3]
Rohrer, Rudolph & Mayer, August. Vorarbeiten zu einer Flora der mährischen Gouvernements. 1835. I. 439.
Roibon, Enrique. Plantas indigenas medicinales . . . de Corrientes. 1875. III. 65.[3]
Roithner, M. F. Die Unfallversicherung der forst- und landwirtschaftlichen Arbeiter. 1899. IV. 310.[1]
Rojnovsky, St. de. Société moscovite d'économie forestière. 1899. IV. 114.
Roland (de Fourtou). Lettre du Bostangi-Bachi de Fourtou . . . contenant les instructions nécessaires pour former . . . les pépinières. 1804. III. 153.
— Seconde lettre du Bostangi-Bachi . . . sur l'utilité de la racine pivotante. 1805. III. 173.[1]
Roland, Arthur. Tree-planting. 1879. III. 123.[1]
— Tree-planting. 1892. III. 106.[2]
Roland-Gosselin, Robert. Acacias calcicoles et Acacias calcifuges. 1897. III. 463.[1]
— Cactées en pleine terre. 1895. III. 620.[1]
— Documents nouveaux sur les qualités ignifuges des Opuntia. 1900. III. 624.[3]
— Sur l'emploi des Opuntia pour arrêter les incendies forestiers. 1899. III. 624.[3]
— Les Rhipsalidées. 1898. III. 626.[1]
Rolander, Daniel. Doliocarpus, en ört af nytt genus från Ameria. 1756. II. 541.[3]
Rolfe, Allen. Botany. 1889. I. 492.[3]
Rolfe, Eustace NEVILLE-. Carob or Locust-bean tree. 1897. III. 471.[3]
— Carob tree. 1897. III. 471.[3]
— Report on the cultivation of the Carob tree. 1897. III. 471.[3]
— Report on the cultivation of the Olive in Italy. 1897. III. 676.[3]
Rolfe, Robert Allen. Acorn galls. 1886. IV. 511.
— Athrotaxis in Britain. 1887. II. 27.[1]
— Cytisus racemosus and its allies. 1888. I. 351.[3]
— On the flora of the Philippine Islands. 1886. I. 464.[1]
— Hybridisation between the standpoint of systematic botany. 1900. I. 246.[1]
— New Formosan plants. 1882. I. 463.[3]
— Notes on Carruthersia and Voacanga. 1883. II. 722.[1]
— On the Selaginese. 1884. II. 778.[3]
— Supplementary list of Philippine plants. 1885. I. 464.[1]
— Veronica cupressoides. 1887. III. 704.[1]
— See also SCHUMANN, Karl, BAKER, J. G., ROLFE, R. A. & COGNIAUX, Alfred.
Rolfink, Werner. Liber de purgantibus vegetabilibus. 1667. III. 240.
— De vegetabilibus, plantis. 1670. I. 30.

Rolfs, G. Drei Monate in der libyschen Wüste. 1875. I. 488.
Rolfs, Peter Henry. Downy mildew of the Grape. 1892. III. 580.
— Plants hurt by a late frost. 1893. III. 44.[1]
— The seed coats of Malvaceae. 1892. II. 519.[2]
— Variation from the normal. 1900. I. 144.[1]
Rolin, G. Théorie des régles en usage pour le cubage des bois. 1821. IV. 213.
Roll. Ratschläge zur Hebung der Obstkultur. 1877. III. 138.
Rolland. Réponse à M. Brongniart, sur la substitution de Datura Stramonium pour tabac. 1874. III. 566.[1]
Rolland, Eugène. Flore populaire. 1896. I. 74,[2] 513.
Rolland, Georges. Sur l'hiver 1879–1880 au Sahara. 1881. II. 457.[2]
— Les oasis sahariennes et le Palmierdattier. 1888. III. 329.[1]
— Les progrès récents de l'agriculture au Sahara. 1898. III. 130.[2]
— Régime du bassin artésien de l'Oued Pu'r'. 1898. III. 151.
Rollet, Émile. Le bois Béhague. 1889. IV. 249.[1]
Rollier, Louis. Le sol des forêts dans le Jura bernois. 1890. IV. 61.[2]
Rollof, A. K. See РОЛЛОВЪ, А. X.
Rolloff, Ad. Cuscuta monogyna auf Reben. 1897. III. 562.[1]
Rolnik; organ Hospodáŕsko-lesnické. III. 25.
Rolnik czasopismo dla gospodarzy wiejskich. III. 25.
Roloff, C. L. Index plantarum ... Berolini in Horto celebri Krausiano. 1746. I. 485.
Rom, von. See KOCH, Karl & ROM, von.
Rom, N. C. Vejledning til Piledyrkning og Kurvefletning. 1874. III. 347.
Roma — Corrispondenza scientifica. See CORRISPONDENZA ... I. 25.
Roma — Reale istituto botanico. See REALE ... I. 25.
Romagnési, C. F. VERGNAUD-. See VERGNAUD-ROMAGNÉSI, C. F.
Romains, R. Sur certains produits rétirés du bois de Teck. 1888. III. 697.[2]
Roman, Baltasar MERINO Y. See MERINO Y ROMAN, Baltasar.
Roman, J. G. Catalogus plantarum usualium ... in Horto academico groningano. 1802. I. 51.[1]
Romanet du Caillaud, Frédéric. Des deux Vignes chinoises. 1882. III. 545.[1]
— Présentation du graines de deux espèces de Vignes chinoises. 1881. III. 545.[2]
— A propos des Vignes chinoises. 1888. II. 505.[2]
— Spinovitis Davidi et Vitis Romaneti. 1883. III. 584.[1]
— Les Vignes américaines aux 16e et 17e siècles. 1886. III. 553.[1]
— Vignes chinoises. 1881. II. 505.[2]
— Des Vignes chinoises. 1885. II. 505.[1]
Romaní, Rafael ESCRIVÁ DE. See ESCRIVÁ DE ROMANÍ, Rafael.
Romanis, R. Report on ash of wood. 1886. I. 155, IV. 64.[1]
Romano, Antonio. Plantae officinales in Europa. 1837. III. 66.[1]
Romano, Girolamo. Catalogus plantarum italicarum. 1820. I. 425.
— Le piante fanerogame Euganee. 1828. I. 426.
Romanovski, M. See РОМАНОВСКІЙ, M.
Romans, Bernard. A concise natural history of East and West-Florida. 1776. I. 317.[1]
Rombouts, E. J. De microphotographie. 1873. I. 37.[1]
Rombouts, J. G. H. & Merkus Doornik, J. J. F. H. T. Flora amstelaedamensis. 1852. I. 391.[1]
Romburgh, Pieter van. Aanteekeningen over de in den Cultuurtuin te Tjikeumeuh gekweekte gewassen. 1892. I. 68.[1]
— Bemesten van Koffietuinen. 1898. III. 734.[1]
— Over bemesting van Theetuinen. 1899. III. 602.[1]
— Bemestingsproeven in Theetuinen. 1899. III. 602.[1]
— Caoutchouc en getah-pertja in Nederlandsch-Indië. 1900. III. 232.[2]
— Over caoutchouc-leverende boomen. 1899. III. 230.
— Over Caoutchouc-leverende planten. 1900. III. 687.[2]
— Divi-divi. 1891. III. 468.[2]
— Eenige aanteekeningen over Albizzia moluccana. 1898. III. 466.[2]
— Gekweekte gewassen in den Kultuurtuin te Tjikeumeh. 1892. I. 68.[1]

— Getah pertja. 1897. III. 232.[1]
— Iets over Djoeloetoeng en Djongkang. 1900. III. 669,[1] 686.[2]
— Iets over kaneel. 1895. III. 406.[1]
— De Kemiri. 1892. III. 514.[2]
— Koffieschillen als mest in Koffietuinen. 1897. III. 734.[1]
— Im Kulturgarten zu Tjikeumeuh gezogene Gewächse. 1892. I. 68.[1]
— Notices phytochimiques. 1899. I. 151.[2]
— Opwekking tot het nemen van bemestingsproeven bij de Theecultuur. 1899. III. 602.[2]
— Plantes renfermant de l'éther méthyl-salycylique. 1899. I. 154.
— Sur la présence du salicylate de methyle. 1899. I. 154.
— Het vermenigvuldigen van Ficus Ribes. 1899. III. 371.[2]
— Over het voorkomen van eenige vluchtige producten. 1897. III. 225.
— Eene waarschuwing voor planters van Ficus elastica. 1900. III. 371.[1]
— Een te weinig gebruikte schaduwboom. 1900. III. 483.[1]
— Een woord ter opwekking tot het nemen van bemestingsproeven bij de Theekultuur. 1900. III. 602.[1]
— & Lohmann, C. J. E. Verslag over de onderzoekingen betreffende op Java gecultiveerde Theeën. 1894. III. 608.[1]
— & Wigman, H. J. Over de Liberia-Koffiecultuur. 1897. III. 743.[1]
Romegialli, E. A. La carta [derivata del legno]. 1894. IV. 430.
— I derivati del legno. 1894. IV. 433.[1]
Romein, M. De Balata-cultuur in Suriname. 1885. III. 668.[1]
— De balata-industrie in Suriname. 1885. III. 668.[1]
Romeral, Manuel. Tratado de las plantas tintoreas. 1844. III. 236.
Romero, Agustin. Orientación. 1878. IV. 265.
Romero, Ismael José. Manual completo sobre la historia ... del caucho. 1899. III. 149.
Romero, Matias. Coffee and India-rubber culture in Mexico. 1898. III. 368,[2] 728.[1]
— Cultivo del Café en ... Chiapas. 1874. III. 728.[1]
Romero Fernandez de Landa, Joseph. Reglamento de maderas necesarias para la fábrica de los baxeles del Rey. 1784. IV. 424.[2]
Romero y Gilsanz, Felipe. Los amojonamientos como complemento de la rectificación de montes. 1882. IV. 265.
— Los años forestal y económico. 1891. IV. 553.[2]
— El articulo 32 del reglamento para la aplicacion de la ley de expropiación forzosa. 1881. IV. 327.
— Aspiraciones y realidades. 1897. IV. 553.[2]
— Ayudantes de montes y capataces de cultivos. 1892. IV. 540.[2]
— El Cnethocampa pythiocampa. 1877. IV. 209.[1]
— Cria, cultivo ... del Pino piñonero. 1886. IV. 468.[2]
— El cuerpo de ingenieros de montes. 1888. IV. 553.[1]
— Desaparición de montes públicos. 1895. IV. 552.[1]
— Descuajes en los montes. 1886. IV. 283.[1]
— El distrito forestal de Valladolid. 1898. IV. 556.[2]
— Guardería forestal. 1891. IV. 553.[1]
— Indemnizaciones del servicio ordinario. 1898. IV. 554.
— Inundaciones y repoblación de montes. 1891. IV. 542.[1]
— Lluvias torrenciales. 1900. IV. 540.[1]
— Mejoras realizadas en los montes públicos de la provincia de Valladolid. 1890. IV. 541.
— Misión del ingeniero de montes. 1881. IV. 293.[1]
— Modificación del caso dudoso sobre competencia administrativa. 1896. IV. 555.[1]
— Los montes en los planes del Señor Camacho. 1883. IV. 276.[1]
— De los pinares ... de Valladolid. 1884. IV. 462.[1]
— El Pino piñonero en la provincia de Valladolid. 1886. IV. 468.[2]
— Propiedad pública forestal. 1892. IV. 551.[2]
— ¿Qué métodos son los más adecuados para el aprovechamiento científico? 1896. IV. 550.[2]
— Rectificación del catálogo. 1894. IV. 552.[1]
— Rectificaciones y amojonamientos. 1895. IV. 251.[1]
— Revisión decenal del abetal de Vallombrosa. 1889. IV. 249.[2]
— Roturaciones arbitrarias en los montes públicos. 1878. IV. 283.[1]
— Sobre la supresión de las Secciones de fomento. 1893. IV. 553.[2]
— El título de los ingenieros. 1889. IV. 553.[1]
— See also MICHELENA, Bernabé & ROMERO GILSANZ, Felipe.

Romershausen. Spiegeldiopter und Längenmesser. 1845. IV. 264.

Romiée, H. *See* PUTREYS, Félix & ROMIÉE, H.

Romieu. Vertoog over eene nieuwelings ontdekte takschieting van de Kamfer. 1762. III. 233.[1]

Rommel, R. Ein kleiner Beitrag zur Aufastungsfrage. 1873. IV. 171.

Rommerdt, Johann Christian Carl. Handbuch der Land- und Wasserbaukunst. 1827. IV. 266.[1]

Rommerdt, K. C. Taschenbuch für Forst- u. Feldgeometer. 1811. IV. 263.

Rommeswinkel, (*Förster*). Was ist von der Aufastung . . . älterer Eichen zu halten? 1886. IV. 507.

Rommier, Alphonse. Sur la dissociation du sulfo-carbonate de potassium. 1875. III. 560.

— Sur l'emploi de la solution aqueuse de sulfure de carbone. 1884. III. 573.

— Sur l'emploi des alcalis du goudron. 1874. III. 566.[1]

— Sur l'emploi du sulfure de carbone. 1891. III. 574.

— Expériences faites à Montpellier sur des Vignes phylloxérées. 1874. III. 566.[2]

— Expériences relatives au traitement des Vignes phylloxérées. 1876. III. 569.[2]

— Sur l'influence toxique que le mycélium des racines de la Vigne exerce sur le phylloxera. 1880. III. 572.

— Mémoires et notes divers sur le phylloxéra. 1877. III. 760.

— Note sur la tache phylloxérée de Mancey. 1876. III. 569.[1]

— Note sur le traitement des Vignes phylloxérées. 1875. III. 568.

— Sur les nouveaux points attaqués par le phylloxera dans le Beaujolais. 1874. III. 566.[3]

— Sur une nouvelle matière colorante. 1868. IV. 432.[2]

— Nouvelles expériences à tenter pour combattre le phylloxera. 1877. III. 570.[1]

— Nouvelles notes sur le phylloxéra. 1879. III. 761.

— Observations relatives au Phylloxera. 1874. III. 566.[2]

— Recherches sur les matières colorantes vertes. 1860. III. 542.[1]

Romondt, E. A. van. Aanteekeningen op Liberiakoffie. 1889. III. 742.[2]

— Liberia-Koffiecultuur in de West. 1888. III. 742.[3]

Romunde, R. van. Bericht omtrent de gouvernements-Kina-onderneming. 1884. III. 716.

— Beschouwingen over schaduwboomen in Koffietuinen. 1875. III. 734.[2]

— Chinaplfanzung auf Java. 1889. III. 716.

— Koffiebladziekte en Koffie-kultuur. 1892. III. 736.

— Koffie-zaadbeddingen onder Dadap. 1874. III. 733.[1]

— Nog iets over ontwonding. 1879. IV. 283.[3]

— Het uitdunnen van Kina-plantsoenen. 1879. III. 716.

— Verslag omtrent de gouvernements Kinaonderneming in de Preanger Regentschappen. 1890. III. 716.

— Verslag over de gouvernements-Kinaonderneming. 1885. III. 716.

Ronalds, Hugh. Pyrus Malus brentfordiensis. 1831. III. 425.[2]

Ronalds, Nathanael. Chatsworth . . . Catalogue of plants. 1874. I. 69.[1]

Roncajoli, Giuseppe. Manuale . . . di economia forestale. 1874. IV. 99.[1]

— Sunto di cenni agricoli-forestali. 1871. III. 115.[3]

Roncati, M. 'ichele'. La divisa degli ufficiali forestali. 1896. IV. 293.[2]

— Elenchi di vincolo forestale. 1897. IV. 277.

— Legge e vincolo forestale. 1897. IV. 277.

— Per una nuova legge forestale. 1896. IV. 329.

— Un nuovo progetto di legge . . . veramente forestale. 1897. IV. 329.

— Rimboscamenti . . . sulla carta. 1896. IV. 166.[1]

Ronces voagienses. *See* BOULAY, J. N. 1864. V. XXVI.[2]

Ronconi, Agostino. Osservazioni su la Flora napolitana. 1811. I. 425.

Ronconi, Ignazio. Dizionario d'agricoltura. 1771. III. 30.

Rondonneau, L. Code rural et forestier. 1810. IV. 323.[2]

— Manuel rural et forestier. 1819. IV. 323.[2]

Rondot, Natalis. Het Chinesche groen lo-kao. 1858. III. 542.[1]

— Sur diverses plantes tinctoriales de Chine. 1858. III. 536.

— The green dye of China. 1858. III. 542.[2]

— Note sur les propriétés tinctoriales . . . du Sophora. 1858. III. 488.[1]

— Notice du vert de Chine. 1858. III. 236, 542.[2]

Rongger, Niklaus. Über die Bestandteile der Samen von Picea excelsa. 1898. II. 37.[1]

— *See also* SCHULZE, E. & RONGGER, Niklaus.

Ronicke, F. Pfropfen und Veredeln. 1889. III. 40.

— Wirkung des einschlagenden Blitzstrahles. 1892. IV. 195.[1]

Ronna, A. Il Gelso e i filugelli negli Abruzzi. 1899. III. 380.[1]

Ronnberg, A. Over het aankweeken der fruitboomen. 1854. III. 139.

— Traité de la culture du Mûrier. 1853. III. 377.

— Verhandeling over de kweeking der Moerbezienboomen. 1853. III. 377.

Ronsmans, P. J. De bladluizen des Perzikbooms. 1876. III. 441.[2]

— Les pucerons du Pêcher. 1876. III. 441.[2]

Ronte, Heinrich. Beiträge zur Kenntniss der Blüthengestaltung. 1891. II. 76.[1]

Roo-Kwa-Tei. Kitsu-Hin (Kippin) id est Bladhia genus Thunb. 1797. II. 692.[2]

Roo van Westmaas, E. A. de. Abricosen en Perziken van zaad. *See* DE ROO VAN WESTMAAS. 1877. III. 430.[2]

— De Japansche Zijderups. 1864. IV. 501.[2]

— Perziken van zaad. 1876. III. 441.[1]

— Première éducation du ver à soie du Chêne. 1864. IV. 501.[2]

— Zaaien van Abrikozen en Perziken. *See* DE ROO VAN WESTMAAS. 1876. III. 430.[2]

— De zijderups van de Ailanthus. 1863. III. 507.[2] — 1865. III. 507.[2]

Rooke, Hayman. A description of the great Oak in Salcey. 1797. II. 137.[2]

— Descriptions . . . of some remarkable Oaks. 1790. II. 137.[2]

Roos, L. & **Thomas,** Ernest. Contribution à l'étude de la végétation de la Vigne. 1892. II. 508.[2]

— — Sur la végétation de la Vigne. 1892. III. 583.[2]

Root fusion. 1884. I. 210.[2]

Rooth, Jöran. De Betula Alno. *See* LIDBECK, E. G. 1779. II. 116.[1]

Roots. 1856. III. 166.

On the roots . . . of Van Diemens Land. *See* BACKHOUSE, James. 1833. III. 283.[1]

Rootsey, Samuel. A general dispensatory. 1815. III. 253.

— Observations upon some of the medical plants mentioned by Shakspeare. 1834. I. 514.[2]

— Syllabus of a course of botanical lectures. 1818. I. 85.

Rooy, de. De Koffiecultuur ter Sumatra's westkust. 1890. III. 730.

Roper, Freeman Clark Samuel. On the additions to the flora of the Cuckmere district. 1890. I. 404.[1]

— Flora of Eastbourne. 1875. I. 402.

— Supplement to the Flora of Eastbourne. 1873. I. 402.

Roque, L. de BELFORT DE LA. *See* BELFORT DE LA ROQUE, L. de.

Roques, F. La production du camphre à Formose. 1893. III. 405.[1]

Roques, Joseph. Nouveau traité des plantes usuelles. 1837. III. 57.

— Phytographie médicale. 1821. III. 56.

— Plantes usuelles. 1807. III. 55.

Roquet. Observations botaniques faites aux environs du Lude. 1885. I. 417.

Rosa, Gabriele. L' agricoltura, gl' insetti. 1866. IV. 209.[2]

— Le condizioni de' boschi . . . di Bergamo. 1862. IV. 48.[1]

— Le selve ed i boschi nella Lombardia. 1865. IV. 364.

Rosa, Gumersindo de la. Generalidades sobre la patología de la Vid. 1880. III. 560.

La **Rosa** e sua istoria. *See* INNAMORATI, Giuseppe. 1821. II. 290.[2]

Rosa inter flores. *See* JOURNAL des roses. 1877. III. 20.

Rosa micrantha in Scotland. 1877. II. 296.[1]

Rosa polyantha als Unterlage. 1887. III. 456.[1]

Rosainz, Miguel. Nuevas combinaciones de nombres para les especies. 1893. I. 337.

Rosanoff, S. Ueber den Bau der Schwimmorgane von Desmanthus. 1871. II. 374.[2]

— Zur Kenntniss des Baues . . . des Pollens der Mimoseae. 1865. II. 320.[1]

— Ueber Kieselsäureablagerungen. 1871. I. 180.[1]

— Ueber die Krystalldrusen im Marke von Kerria. 1865. II. 265.[1]

— Morphologisch-embryologische Studien. 1866. I. 122.

Rosarian's year-book. III. 18.
Rosarium. III. 15.
Rosbach, (*Dr.*). Fagus sylvatica L. forma umbraculifera. 1875. II. 126.[1]
— Mittheilung über Rosa gallica. 1877. II. 294.[1]
Rosbach, Conrad. Paradeissgärtlein. 1588. I. 283, 515.
Rosbach, Heinrich. Flora von Trier. 1880. I. 388.
Rosca, Xavier. Liste des plantes ... du midi de la France et de la Corse. 1841. I. 409.
Rosch, (*Oberförster, Klodnitz*). Beschreibung des k. Forst-Reviers Kosel. 1855. IV. 352.
— & **Wilaki,** (*Oberförster*). Bericht über die ... Waldex-kursion in die zur freien Standesherrschaft Kynast gehören-den Forst-Reviere. 1858. IV. 353.
Roscher, Wilhelm. Nationalökonomik des Ackerbaues. 1860. IV. 269.
— Ein nationalökonomisches Hauptprincip der Forstwissen-schaft. 1854. IV. 269.
Roschmann, Anton. Regnum animale, vegetabile ... tyro-leuse. 1738. I. 438.
Roscoe, William. A catalogue of plants in the Botanic garden at Liverpool. 1808. I. 53.
Rose, Frank. Note on the Feronia elephantum. 1886. IV. 524.[1]
— Uses of the flower of Pandanus odoratissimus. 1886. III. 313.[1]
Rose, Hermann. Statistische Mittheilungen über das Her-zogthum Sachsen-Coburg. 1857. IV. 355.[1]
Rose, Hugh. The elements of botany. 1775. I. 83, 250.
Rose, John. The English vineyard vindicated. 1675. III. 553.[1]
Rose, Joseph Nelson. Agave angustissima. 1893. II. 89.[1]
— Agave attenuata. 1897. II. 89.[1]
— Agave expatriata and other Agaves. 1899. II. 89.[1]
— Agave washingtonensis and other Agaves. 1898. II. 89.[1]
— Descriptions of plants, mostly new, from Mexico. 1895. I. 333.
— List of plants collected ... in Arizona. 1891. I. 325.
— List of plants collected ... in western Mexico-and Arizona. 1891. I. 332.
— List of plants collected ... on Carmen Island. 1892. I. 334.
— A new Tabebuia from Mexico. 1892. II. 791.[1]
— Notes on useful plants of Mexico. 1899. II. 527.[1]
— Notes upon Corylus rostrata and C. Californica. 1895. II. 122.[1]
— Plants from the Big Horn Mountains. 1896. I. 326.
— Report on a collection of plants made in the states of Sonora and Colima. 1895. .I. 333.
— Some notes on tree Ipomoeas of Mexico. 1894. II. 745.[1]
— Studies of Mexican and central American plants. 1897. I. 330.
— Tabebuia Donnell-Smithii n. sp. 1892. II. 791.[1]
— *See also* COULTER, J. M. & ROSE, J. N.; VASEY, George & ROSE, J. N.
— & **Baker,** E. G. Robinsonella. 1897. II. 527.[1]
Rose, L. J. Grape culture in California. 1882. III. 550.
Rose, N. J. The Coral-trees. 1895. III. 476.[1]
— Juniperus communis. 1896. II. 31.[1]
Die **Rose.** *See* BENEMANN, J. C. 1742. II. 290.[1]
The **Rose** and its history. 1856. II. 290.[1]
Rose annual for 1858–81. 111. 18.
Rose-Belford's Canadian monthly and national review. *See* CANADIAN ... III. 2.
The **Rose-bush** of Hildesheim. 1891. II. 290.[1]
Rose Crimson rambler. 1897. III. 456.[1]
Rose farming as a colonial industry. 1880. III. 452.
Rose-growing and pressing in Saxony. 1893. III. 454.[1]
Rose legends. 1889. II. 290.[1]
The **Rose** of Hildesheim. 1884. II. 290.[1]
Rose Pink Roamer. 1900. III. 457.[1]
Roselli, Enrico. Le Viti tuberose. 1883. III. 547.
Rosellini, Giuseppe RICCA-. *See* RICCA-ROSELLINI, Giuseppe.
Rosen, Andreas von. *See* RADL, Fl. & ROSEN, Andreas von.
Rosén, Eberhard. De cortice peruviano. 1744. III. 719.
— Observationes botanicae circa plantas quasdam Scaniae. 1749. I. 351.
Rosen, H. C. Om Plantning af Rødgran. 1874. IV. 453.
Rosen, Walter, *Baron* von. Über den Einfluss der Wärme-menge ... auf die Blütenentfaltung. 1883. I. 221.
Rosen; Sammlung der neuesten u. schönsten. 1836. III. 448.
Die **Rosen** und ihre neuesten Sorten. 1858. III. 449.
Rosenbach. *See* ROSBACH, Conrad.

Rosenberg, von, (*auf Puditsch*). Ueber den Nutzen der Weisserle. 1842. IV. 489.[2]
Rosenberg, *Baron* von. Beilage zur Zeichnung des Kiefer-baumes. 1849. IV. 483.[1]
— Nachweis über die hohe Ausnutzung zweier starker Eichen. 1844. IV. 512.
— *See also* WAGNER, (*Forstmeister, Konradshammer*), BLANK-ENBURG, & ROSENBERG, *Baron* von.
Rosenberg, H. von. Beschrijving eener reis naar de zuidwest-kust ... van Nieuw Guinea. 1859. I. 499.[1]
— Verhaal eener reis naar de eilanden Misool. 1862. I. 466.
Rosenberg, Johann Carl. Rhodologia. 1628. II. 281.[2]
Rosenberger, F. Die Bestandespflege im Nadelholzhoch-walde. 1895. IV. 169.[2]
— Die Durchforstung im Nadelholzhochwalde. 1895. IV. 175.[1]
— Die Durchreiserung im Nadelholzhochwalde. 1895. IV. 175.[1]
— Der Reinigungshieb im Nadelholzhochwalde. 1895. IV. 175.[1]
— Die Verjüngung der Fichte auf natürlichem Wege. 1896. IV. 454.
Rosenberger, Otto Friedrich. Anleitung, die Fruchtbäume ... zu veredeln. 1808. III. 159.[2]
Rosendahl, Henrik Viktor. Några lappländska växtformer. 1892. II. 687.[2]
Rosenfeld, Daniel. De חבצלת השרן; sive, Rosa saronitica. 1715. I. 512.
Rosenhain, C. M. Die Holz-Cellulose. 1878. IV. 430.
Rosenmüller, Ernst Friedrich. Karl. Biblische Naturge-schichte. 1830. I. 513.
— The mineralogy and botany of the Bible. 1830. I. 513.
Rosenschöld, E. MUNCK AF. *See* MUNCK AF ROSENSCHÖLD, E.
Rosensten, Anders. Gründeliga underwisning om skogars skötsel. 1752. IV. 103.[2]
Rosenstiehl, A. De la solubilité de la matière colorante rouge du raisin. 1897. III. 583.[2]
Rosenthal. Über Giftpflanzen ... der Leguminosen. 1865. III. 462.[2]
Rosenthal, A. C. Aesculus Hippocastanum Schirnhoferi. 1882. III. 537.[1]
— Aesculus parviflora. 1886. III. 538.[2]
— Biota orientalis laxenburgensis. 1888. III. 311.[2]
— Chamaecyparis Lawsonianum Rosenthalii. 1885. III. 301.[1]
— Einige vorzügliche und interessante Haselsträucher. 1883. III. 357.[2]
— Fünf vorzügliche Eibischsträucher. 1885. III. 588.[1]
— Picea pungens argentea. 1887. II. 38.[2]
— Pomologisches Handbuch für Nieder-Oesterreich. 1893. III. 90.[1]
— Ueber das sachgemässe Verpacken lebender Pflanzen. 1885. III. 155.
— Die Sinuous-Pflaume. 1882. III. 443.[1]
— Spiraea Van Houttei Hort. 1884. III. 462.[1]
— Unsere besten Wallnüsse. 1886. III. 355.
Rosenthal, Christian Fr. Flora belgica. *See* LINNÉ, Carl von. 1760. I. 391.[2]
Rosenthal, David August. Synopsis plantarum diaphorica-rum. 1862. III. 58.
Rosenthal, Gottfried Erich. Geometrische Abhandlung von der Bestimmung der Grösse ... einer Holzbaumes. 1771. IV. 357.[1]
— Versuche die zum Wachsthum der Pflanzen benöthigte Wärme zu bestimmen. 1784. I. 231.[2]
Rosenthal, I. Alkaloid der Rinde der Rabelaisia philippi-nensis. 1896. II. 408.[1]
— Über ein Herzgift aus Manila. 1895. III. 504.[2]
Rosenthal, J. Sur un phénomène observé dans l'empoisonne-ment par la strychnine. 1867. III. 683.[1]
Rosenthal, Konrad. Dendrologisches. 1871. II. 368,[1] *III,* 535.[1]
Rosenvinge, L. Kolderup. Anatomisk Undersøgelse af ... Salvadora. 1880. II. 473.[1]
— Andet Tillæg til Grønlands Fanerogamer. 1892. I. 309.[1]
— Nye Bidrag til Vest-Grønlands Flora. 1896. I. 309.[1]
— Recherche anatomique sur ... Salvadora. 1880. II. 473.[1]
— Det saftigste Grønlands Vegetation. 1896. I. 309.[2]
— Om Vegetationen i en sydgrønlandsk Fjord. 1889. I. 309.[1]
Rosen-Zeitung. III. 13.
Roseraie de l'Haÿ. *See* GRAVEREAUX, Jules. 1899. V. xxix[1]; 1900. III. 451.[1]

Roses et Rosiers par des horticulteurs. 187.? III. 449.
Rosetti, Emilio. Propiedades físicas de las maderas de la República Argentina. 1879. IV. 408. — 1885. IV. 408.
Rosnati, Bartolommeo. Nozioni più interessanti sul Caffè. 1834. III. 739.
Rosny, Léon de. Botanique du Nippon. 1872. I. 4.[1]
— Notice sur le Thuya de Barbarie (Callitris quadrivalvis). 1856. II. 27.[1]
— L'Opuntia ou Cactus raquette d'Algérie. 1857. II. 596.[1]
Rosnyôi, László. Rosa rugosa calocarpa. 1895. III. 457.[1]
Rosoleno. 1887. IV. 436.[2]
Rosoll, Alexander. Beiträge zur Histochemie der Pflanze. 1884. I. 151.[2]
— Über den Sitz . . . des Strychnin. 1884. III. 683.[2]
Ross, A. J. The felling and barking of Oak. 1898. IV. 435.[1]
Ross, Alexander Milton. The forest trees of Canada. 1875. I. 309.[2]
Ross, B. R. An account of the . . . products useful to the Chipewyan tribes. 1862. III. 262.[1]
Ross, David. Account of botanical excursions around the environs of Paris. 1862. I. 412.
— Account of botanical rambles in the Pyrenees. 1863. I. 412.
— Botanical tour . . . in . . . Auvergne. 1861. I. 412.
Ross, Hermann. Sugli acarodomazii di alcune Ampelidee. 1893. II. 501.[2]
— Der Ahorn-Runzelschorf. 1899. III. 534.[1]
— Beiträge zur Anatomie abnormer Monocotylenwurzeln. 1883. I. 104.
— Beiträge zur Entwickelung des Korkes. 1886. I. 130.
— Beiträge zur Flora von Sicilien. 1899. I. 432.[1]
— Beiträge zur Kenntnis des Assimilationsgewebes. 1887. I. 124.
— Contribuzioni alla conoscenza del periderma. 1889. I. 131.[1]
— Contribuzioni alla conoscenza del tessuto assimilatore. 1889. I. 129,[2] 174.
— Icones et descriptiones plantarum . . . Horti botanici panormitani. 1896. II. 80.[1]
— Die rote und weisse Holzraupe. 1899. III. 192.[1]
— Sulla struttura fiorale della Calate. 1893. II. 338.[2]
— See also MASSALONGO, Caro & Ross, Hermann.
Ross, James. Hobart Town almanack for 1834. See BACK-HOUSE, James. 1833. III. 283.[1]
— Hobart Town almanack for 1835. 1834. I. 505.[2]
Ross, Sir James Clark. A voyage of discovery . . . in the southern and antarctic regions. 1847. I. 510.[2]
Ross, John. A voyage of discovery made . . . for the purpose of exploring Baffin's Bay. See BROWN, Robert. 1819. I. 309.[3]
Ross, L. S. On the structure and development of the Lemon. 1890. II. 403.[2]
Ross, Leonard W. The exploitation of the sand dunes of Cape Cod. 1897. IV. 155.[2]
Ross, Robert. On the best mode of propagating plants in India. 1843. III. 157.
— On the peeling . . . of native barks. 1881. IV. 434.
Ross, S. Measurement of trees at Highclere. 1880. III. 123.[1]
Ross, W. J. Clunies. Notes on the flora of Bathurst. 1898. I. 505.
Rossel, D. J. Is het voordeel om boomen oud te laten worden? 1855. IV. 512.
Rossi, de. Aus dem Wupperthal. 1886. IV. 442.
Rossi, Giovanni Battista de. Piante iconografichi e prospettiche di Roma. 1879. I. 81.[1]
Rossi, Johannes. Catalogus plantarum Horti regii modocetiensis. 1826. I. 62.
Rossi, L. Hrvatsko primorje z bilinskog gledišta. 1877. I. 448.[1]
Rossi, Pietro. Istoria di ciò che è stato pensato intorno alla fecondazione delle piante. 1794. I. 199.
— De nonnullis plantis quae pro venenatis habentur. 1762. III. 527.[2]
Rossi, Stefano. Studi sulla flora ossolana. 1883. I. 429.
Rossignol, Louis. Notice historique sur le Jardin des plantes d'Orléans. 1874. I. 59.
Rossignol de Vallouise, Jean Joseph. Botanique élémentaire. 1790. I. 83.
Rossignon, Jules. Sur une cause de mortalité des tiges. 1843. I. 206.[1]
— Deuxième mémoire sur la cellulogénésie. 1842. I. 137.
— Sur l'état naturel du sucre. 1842. I. 175.
— Manual del jardinero y arbolista. 1859. III. 100.[1]

— Sur un nouveau principe volatil, cyanoïle. 1841. I. 175.
— Rapport sur les Hortensias à fleurs bleues. 1843. III. 412.[1]
Rossiskaya . . . See POCCIЙCKAЯ . . .
Rossius, Ernest ORBAN DE. See ORBAN DE ROSSIUS, Ernest.
Rossmaessler, Emil Adolph. Charakterbilder deutscher Waldbäume. 1863. I. 371.
— Flora im Winterkleide. 1854. I. 95.
— Forstinsekten. 1834. IV. 91.[2]
— Rhamnus und Frangula generisch verschieden. 1846. II. 496.[2]
— Systematische Uebersicht des Thierreichs. 1833. IV. 89.[2]
— Versuch einer anatomischen Charakteristik des Holzkörpers. 1847. I. 524,[2] IV. 62.[1]
— Der Wald. 1863. I. 82,[2] IV. 55.[2]
— Das Wichtigste vom innern Bau . . . der Gewächse. 1843. I. 88.
— See also AUERSWALD, Bernard & ROSSMÄSSLER, E. A.; BREHM, A. E. & ROSSMÄSSLER, E. A.; DIETRICH, Heinrich & ROSSMÄSSLER, E. A.; Россмесслеръ, Э. А.
Rossmann, G. W. Julius. Der Aufbau der Kiefern. 1864. II. 47.[1]
— Ueber den Bau des Holzes der . . . Bäume und Sträucher. 1862. I. 125, IV. 68.[1] — 1865. I. 371, IV. 83.
— Ueber den Bau des Holzes der wichtigsten . . . Bäume. 1862. I. 125.
— Beiträge zur Kenntnis der Phyllomorphose. 1857. I. 109.[2]
— Pilzfäden in sog. ersticktem Kiefernholze. 1864. IV. 476.
Rossmarin-Büchlein. 1685. III. 698.[1]
Rosso, Emanuele Taranto & Gerbino, Xaverio. Catalogus plantarum in agro Calato-Hieronensi collectarum. 1845. I. 431.
Rost, (Forstobergeometer). Tabellen zur Bestimmung des körperlichen Inhaltes der Baumstämme. 1854. IV. 216.
Rost, B. Anleitung zur Anlage allerhand Einfriedigungen. 1873. III. 213.
Rost van Tonningen, D. W. Berigt over eenige hars eri getahsoorten. 1861. III. 227.
— Iets over den teleöen en soerenbast. 1851. III. 512,[1] 632.[2]
— Iets over de kaoetsjoek en getaperja. 1856. III. 228.[2]
— Over de op Java aangekweekte Sarsaparilla. 1858. II. 86.[1]
— Over de nieuwste vorderingen der landbouwscheikunde. 1860. III. 594.
— Onderzoek van de gomhars van Garcinia Mangostana. 1851. III. 609.[2]
— Onderzoek van de gomhars van Hymenaea. 1851. III. 489.[2]
— Rapport over de aanwezigheid van grondstoffen . . . tot bereiding van papier. 1859. III. 235.[2]
— Samaderine. 1859. III: 509.[1]
— Samaderine, een nieuw ligchaam. 1857. II. 415.[2]
— Over het scheikundig onderzoek van Javaansche planten. 1852. III. 722.
— Scheikundige analysen van den bast, de bladeren . . . van den Kakaoboom. 1859. III. 594.
— See also TEYSMANN, J. E. & ROST VAN TONNINGEN, D. W.
Rostafiński, Josef. Cynamony. 1891. III. 406.[1]
— Dwie prelekcye o Palmach. 1888. III. 319.[2]
— Florae polonicae prodromus. 1872. I. 363.
— Kananga. 1891. III. 401.[2]
— De plantis quae in Capitulari de villis . . . Caroli Magni commemorantur. 1885. I. 80.[1]
— Śmocokrzew. 1891. III. 321,[1] 336.[2]
— Średniowięczana historya naturalna w Polsce. 1900. III. 239.
— Symbola ad historiam naturalem medii aevi. 1900. III. 239.
Rostaing, Léon & Marcel & Fleury Percie du Sert. Précis historique . . . des végétaux propres à la fabrication de la cellulose. 1899. III. 235,[2] IV. 430.
Rostaing, Marcel. See ROSTAING, Léon & Marcel, & DU SERT, F. P.
Rostkovius, Friedrich Wilhelm Gottlieb & Schmidt, W. L. E. Flora sedinensis. 1824. I. 377.
Rostovtchef, S. I. See Ростовцевъ, С. Н.
Rostovtzef, P. V. See Ростовцевъ, П. В.
Rostrup, Emil. Afbildning og Beskrivelse af de farligste Snyltesvampe. 1889. III. 194, IV. 212.
— Beretning . . . om en . . . foretagen Rejse for at undersøge de der forefundne Svampeangreb. 1888. IV. 212.
— Beretning om en i de jydske Statsskove . . . i Oktober 1881 foretagen Rejse. 1881. IV. 461.[2]

— Beretning om en i nogle af de nordsjællandske Skove ... foretagen Rejse. 1879. IV. 211.²
— Beretning ... om en ... Rejse for at undersøge Angreb af Snyltesvampe. 1887. IV. 211.²
— Beretning ... om en . . Rejse for at undersøge de der forefundne Svampeangreb. 1893. IV. 212.
— Beretning ... om en ... Rejse for at undersøge en i Rødgranbevoxningerne optrædende Sygdøn. 1889. IV. 205.¹
— Beretninger om Undersøgelser ... angaaende Snyltesvampeangreb. 1885. IV. 211.²
— Coryneum Beyerinckii. 1896. III. 442.¹
— Færøernes Flora. 1870. I. 356.
— Til Finantsministeriet. 1881. IV. 550.¹
— Forsøg ... for at faa Klarhed over Plantesygdommenes Aarsag. 1888. III. 179.
— Den forsvundne Fyrreskov paa Læsø. 1898. II. 47.¹
— Fortsatte Undersøgelser over Snyltesvampes Angreb. 1883. IV. 211.²
— Insektangreb i en Pinsapogran. 1892. III. 297.¹
— Katalog over en plantepathologisk Samling. 1888. III. 194.
— Lollands Vegetations Forhold. 1864. I. 356.
— Misdannelser hos Planterne. 1892. I. 144.¹
— Om nogle af Snyltesvampe foraarsagede Misdannelser. 1884. III. 194.
— En ny Sygdom hos Lindetræer. 1899. III. 585.²
— Plantepatologi. 1900. III. 180.¹
— Plantesygdomme. 1886. III. 179.
— Plantesygdomme i Haverne. 1892. III. 179.
— Pyramidepoppelens Undergang. 1886. III. 346.²
— Sur quelques déformations des phanérogames. 1884. III. 194.
— Rosens Bladskimmel. 1894. III. 453.²
— Rosens Sygdomme. 1886. III. 453.²
— Rust og Berberis. 1884. III. 394.¹
— Slimskimmel paa Kimplanter af Bjergfyr. 1895. IV. 465.¹
— En Svampesygdom hos Fersken. 1888. III. 442.¹
— En Sygdom hos Pære-Vildlinger. 1886. III. 446.¹
— En Sygdom hos Viburnum Tinus. 1890. III. 753.²
— En Sygdom i Vindruer. 1890. III. 561.
— Uddrag af en Beretning ... angaaende Snyltesvampe-Angreb. 1883. IV. 211.²
— Der Untergang der Pyramidenpappeln. 1884. III. 346.²
— Om Vegetationen i den udtørrede "Lersøe." 1859. I. 355.
— Vejledning i den danske Flora. 1860. I. 355.
— & Weismann, C. Hussvampen. 1898. IV. 415.²
Rostrup, F. G. E. Danmarks Plantverden i Fortid og Nutid. 1898. I. 358.
Rostrup, O. Die Sclerotienkrankheit der Erlen-Früchte. 1897. IV. 489.¹
Rostrup, Sofie. Danske Zoocecidier. 1896. I. 215.¹
— Grønlandske Phytoptider. 1900. I. 214,² III. 350,² 583,¹ IV. 491.¹
Ross, Hermann. Milbengallen an den Blütenständen der Esche. 1898. IV. 535.²
Roszkowski, E. Przyczynek do flory Lubelskiego. 1899. I. 367.
Rot von Schreckenstein, Friedrich, Freiherr & Engelberg, J. M. von. Flora der Gegend um den Ursprung der Donau und des Neckars. 1804. I. 375.
Rota, Lorenzo. Enumerazione delle piante ... della provincia Bergamasca. 1843. I. 427.
— Nova Ulmi species. 1855. II. 144.²
— Prospetto della flora della provincia di Bergamo. 1853. I. 427.
Rotering, F. Gesetz betreffend den Forstdiebstahl. 1895. IV. 321.
Roters. Ein Waldbrand in der K. Oberförsterei Segeberg. 1894. IV. 182.²
Roth, (Oberförster.) Anwendung der Deckgitter. 1872. IV. 150.¹
— Ueber die Anwendung des Waldteufels. 1858. IV. 386.
— Beiträge zur Rentabilitätsfrage der · Waldungen. 1877. IV. 256.
— Ueber die Benutzung der Nadelholzstangen. 1867. IV. 387.²
— Ueber die Berechnung des normalen Holzvorrathes der Hochwaldungen. 1858. IV. 236.
— Bericht über eine forstliche Reise durch den Thüringer- und Fränkischen Wald. 1868. IV. 355.²
— Bessere Benutzung der Hainbuche. 1862. IV. 492.¹
— Ueber die Bewirthschaftung der Fehmelwaldungen im obern Kinzigthale. 1859. IV. 130.

— Durchführung eines praktischen Beispiels der Abtretung von Waldgelände. 1878. IV. 256.
— Ueber Eichenschälrindenutzung. 1866. IV. 434.—1867. IV. 434, 506.
— Aus dem Eichenschälwalde. 1868. IV. 506.
— Ueber die Fertigung von Eisenbahnschwellen. 1874. IV. 423.²
— Die Forstgesetzgebung des Kantons Zürich. 1869. IV. 330.
— Ueber Holzzurichtung. 1870. IV. 387.¹
— Die national-ökonomische Seite der Zahlungsfrist bei Holzverkäufen. 1882. IV. 388.¹
— Ein neuer Holztransportkarren. 1877. IV. 389.
— Notices sur l'administration ... des forêts jardinées ... de la Kinzig. 1859. IV. 130.
— Nutzung aus Haseln. 1868. IV. 492.¹
— Ueber Reisig- und Wellenzurichtung. 1875. IV. 387.²
— Ein Rindenschäler für Nadelholz. 1875. IV. 434.
— Zur Rothfäule der Fichte. 1870. IV. 455.
— Sprengung von Stöcken mit Dynamit. 1873. IV. 386.
— Stand und Bewirthschaftung der Eichenschälwaldungen. 1860. IV. 505.
— Starke Weisstanne. 1876. II. 24.¹
— Starke Weisstannen. 1872. II. 24.¹
— Ein starker Ahorn. 1861. II. 477.²
— Die Waldräumung. 1865. IV. 388.²
— Ueber Wellen- und Kohlholzzurichtung. 1873. IV. 387.²
— Ueber Zahlungsfristen und Skontiren beim Holzverkaufe. 1878. IV. 388.¹
— Ueber die Zurichtung von Telegraphenstangen. 1837. IV. 387.²
Roth, (Rechnungsrat). Die fürstlich fürstenbergischen Waldungen bei Rippoldsau im Schwarzwald. 1880. IV. 350.²
— Ueber Hochwaldverjüngungs-Richtung an Bergwänden. 1885. IV. 129.
— Ueber Holzaustrocknung. 1888. IV. 412.¹
— Die Reinertragstheorie. 1880. IV. 256.
— Sonnenbrand. 1893. IV. 192.¹
— Unterschied zwischen Bodenreinertrag und Waldreinertrag. 1889. IV. 258.
— Das Verhanfen gegen Rehschaden. 1894. IV. 197.¹
Roth, Albrecht Wilhelm. Anweisung für Anfänger Pflanzen ... zu sammeln. 1778. I. 262.
— Anweisung, Pflanzen zum Nutzen und Vergnügen zu sammeln. 1803. I. 375.
— Beantwortung der ... Preisfrage: Was sind Varietäten im Pflanzenreiche. 1811. I. 251.
— Beyträge zur Botanik. 1782. I. 263.
— Botanische Abhandlungen und Beobachtungen. 1787. I. 263.
— Botanische Bemerkungen und Berichtigungen. 1807. I. 265.
— Catalecta botanica. 1797 † 264
— Enumeratio plantarum phaenogamarum in Germania. 1827. I. 377.
— Erinnerungen und Beiträge zu der neuen Ausgabe der Specierum plantarum. 1802. I. 265.
— Manuale botanicum. 1830. I. 378.
— Neue Beyträge zur Botanik. 1802. I. 265.
— Novae plantarum species praesertim Indiae orientalis. 1921. I. 471.
— Observationes plantarum. 1783. I. 263.
— Observationes plantarum quarundam. 1787. I. 263.
— Observationes quaedam botanicae. 1794. I. 375.
— Tentamen florae germanicae. 1788. I. 374.
— Verzeichniss derjenigen Pflanzen, welche ... nicht in den gehörigen Klassen ... des Linnéischen Systemes stehen. 1781. I. 262.
— Verzeichniss verschiedener Pflanzen ... im Herzogthum Oldenburg. 1782. I. 374.
Roth, Emil. Profits of forest culture. 1884. IV. 260.¹
Roth, Ernst. Additamenta ad Conspectum florae europaeae. 1886. I. 349.
— Beiträge zu C. F. Nymanns Conspectus florae europaeae. 1886. I. 349.
— Ueber blüthentragende Schmarotzerpflanzen. 1899. II. 174.¹
— Ueber einige Schutzeinrichtungen der Pflanzen gegen übermässige Verdunstung. 1895. I. 168.
— Ueber die Pflanzen, welche den atlantischen Ocean auf der Westküste Europas begleiten. 1883. I. 349.
— Schutzmittel der Pflanzen gegen Thierfrass. 1900. I. 235.²
— Die Verbreitungsmittel der Pflanzen. 1896. I. 241.¹

Roth, F. R. De indico, medicamine. 1834. III. 479.[1]
Roth, Filibert. Le bois du Cyprès chauve. 1898. IV. 409.
— Forest conditions of Wisconsin. 1898. IV. 339.
— Forestry conditions and interests of Wisconsin. 1898. IV. 339.
— On the forestry conditions of northern Wisconsin. 1898. IV. 339.
— How can we prolong the supply of White Pine? 1898. IV. 471.
— Notes on the structure of the wood of the five southern Pines. 1896. II. 40.[1]
— Progress in timber physics; Bald Cypress. 1898. IV. 409.
— Timber. 1895. IV. 397, *409.*
— The uses of wood. 1897. IV. 396.[2]
— Ueber das Verhalten der verholzten Zellwand während des Schwindens. 1894. IV. 412.[1]
— The wood of the White Cedar. 1895. II. 28.[2]
— Woods fit for paper pulp. 1898. IV. 430.
— The work in timber physics. 1899. IV. 416.[1]
Roth, Friedrich Karl. Ueber die Bedeutung des normalen Holzvorrathes. 1863. IV. 255.
— Handbuch des Forstrechts. 1863. IV. 318.
— Ueber das Prozentverhältniss des Waldertrags. 1863. IV. 255.
— Theorie der Forstgesetzgebung. 1841. IV. 268, *313.*
Roth, G. Beiträge zur Rentabilitätsfrage der Waldungen. 1873. IV. 256.
Roth, Karl. Ueber Abtrieb und Verjüngung des Waldes. 1880. IV. 24.[1]
— Einiges über die Rechtsverhältnisse in den alten Bann-forsten. 1869. IV. 26, *317.*[1]
— Ueber die fortschreitende Ausbildung der Taxation und Betriebsregulirung. 1879. IV. 24,[1] *244.*
— Zur Geschichte der Gerichtsbarkeit in Forst- und Jagd-sachen. 1872. IV. 26.
— Zur Geschichte der . . . Waldungen in Deutschland. 1878. IV. 26.
— Geschichte des Forst- und Jagdwesens in Deutschland. 1879. IV. 26.
— Ueber Grundeigenthumserwerb durch Waldrodung. 1869. IV. 274.[1]
— Ueber Grundrente und Waldrente. 1873. IV. 256.
— Ueber Wald und Waldbenutzung. 1880. IV. 382.[1]
— Weissenburg und Seligenstadt. 1867. IV. 25.
Roth, L. Tabelle über den Kubikinhalt der Bäume. 1873. IV. 227.
Rothamsted. 1875. III. 585.[1]
Rothdauscher, Heinrich. Ueber die anatomischen Verhält-nisse . . . der Phyllantheen. 1896. II. 435.[1]
Rothe, C. *See* LORENZ VON LIBURNAU, J. R. *Ritter* & ROTHE, C.
Rothe, Chr. Om de jydske Heder. 1847. IV. 156.[1]
Rothe, H. H. Der grosse braune Rüsselkäfer. 1900. IV. 208.[1]
Rothe, Heinrich August. *See* NEES VON ESENBECK, C. G., BISCHOF, C. G. & ROTHE, H. A.
Rothe, Rudolph. Om de almindeligste danske Skovtræers Anvendelse i Havesanlæg. 1843. III. 119.[2]
— Bemærkninger om Frugttraeernes knopper. 1849. I. 107.[2]
— Om Frugttræers Beskjæring. 1841. III. 172.
— Landskabsgartneriske Betragtninger over Danmark. 1853. III. 119.[2]
— Nogle Bemærkninger over Stedforholdene i Almindelighed ved Haver i Danmark. 1841. III. 120.[1]
— Oculation mit Spitzentrieben. 1881. III. 162.
Rothe, T. I. Anledning af de jydske Heeders Bebyggelse. 1760. IV. 155.[2]
Rothe, Tyge. Afplukning af almindelig Opbevaring af træ-frugt i Haverne. 1880. III. 173.[2]
— Anweisung zum Pflanzen-Treiben. 1885. III. 176.[2]
— Et bidrag til oplysning om seiglivethed hos Vinstokken. 1870. II. 508.[2]
— Febergummitræet. 1878. IV. 533.[1]
— Frugttræ-Beskjæring i Danmark. 1883. III. 172. — 1884. III. 134.[2]
— Grundlag for Vejledning i Plante-Drivning. 1885. III. 100.[2]
— Lysaky Plantekulturer. 1881. III. 100.[2]
— Das Slechthum der Pyramiden-Pappeln. 1884. III. 346.[2]
— *See also* JACOBSON, J. C. & ROTHE, Tyge.
Rothe Lamberts-Nuss. 1886. III. 357.[2]
Rohenbach. Einfluss des Waldes auf . . . Quellen. 1898. IV. 52.

Rother, A. Die Urheimath des weissen Maulbeerbaumes. 1863. II. 154.[2]
Rotheram, John. The sexes of plants vindicated. 1790. I. 199.
Rotheray, Lister. Flora of Skipton and district. 1900. I. 535.
Rotherham, Johannes. Medicamenta purgantia. *See* LINNÉ, Carl von. 1775. III. 241.
Rothert, Wladislaw. Ueber den Bau der Membran der pflanzlichen Gefässe. 1898. I. 134.[1]
— O budowie blony naczyń roślinnych. 1898. I. 134.[1]
— Einige Bemerkungen zu Arthur Meyer's "Untersuchungen ueber die Stärkekörner." 1897. I. 140.[2]
— Ueber Heliotropismus. 1894. I. 195.[1]
— Ueber parenchymatische Tracheïden . . . von Cephalotaxus-Arten. 1899. II. 8.[1]
— *See also* POPEPTB, B.[¹]
— & **Zalenski**, W. Ueber eine besondere Kategorie von Krystallbehältern. 1899. I. 139.
Rothfelser, Ernst Abraham DEHN-. *See* DEHN-ROTHFELSER, E. A.
Die **Rothholzwälder** an der pacifischen Küste. 1893. IV. 484.[1]
Rothkögel, Philipp. Anleitung zur Kenntniss der Forst-wissenschaft. 1854. IV. 99.[2]
Rothmaler, Otto. Ueber die Wirkungskraft von Strychnin. 1893. III. 684.[1]
Rothof, Lorens Wolt. Anmärkningar öfver kärr eller måssar, hvarutur träd-rötter årligen upflyta. 1767. I. 350.[1]
— Försök gjorde vid mossars upodling. 1761. III. 346.[2]
Rothrock, Joseph Trimble. American forestry. 1883. IV. 397.
— The American Linden. 1896. II. 517.[1]
— The American, or White Elm. 1894. II. 143.[2]
— The Beech (Fagus ferruginea Ait.). 1895. II. 125.[2]
— Big White Oaks. 1899. II. 132.[2]
— A bit of primeval forest. 1900. I. 313, *IV.* 77.[1]
— The Bitter Nut Hickory. 1895. II. 112.[2]
— The Black Spruce. 1899. II. 38.[1]
— The Black Walnut. 1893. II. 113.[2]
— The Butternut, or White Walnut. 1899. II. 113.[1]
— The Buttonwood. 1895. II. 255.[1]
— California collection. 1878. I. 324.
— Century of American lumbering. 1894. IV. 382.[2]
— A century of American lumbering. 1895. IV. 281.[2]
— The Chestnut tree. 1889. II. 123.[2]
— Along the coast northward. 1889. I. 315.
— Cottonwood, Carolina Poplar. 1900. II. 97.[1]
— Diplopappus ericoïdes T. & G. 1877. II. 852.[1]
— Dogwood. Flowering Dogwood. 1900. II. 655.[1]
— Fire and flood. 1895. IV. 178.[2]
— Forest protection in Canada. 1896. IV. 178.[1]
— Forests of Pennsylvania. 1894. IV. 339.
— On the growth of the forestry idea in Pennsylvania. 1894. IV. 272.
— The Hemlock. 1894. II. 53.[1]
— Honey Locust. 1898. II. 362.[1]
— The internal cambium ring in Gelsemium. 1886. II. 718.[2]
— The Locust tree. 1895. II. 382.[2]
— Magnolia, Swamp Magnolia. 1899. II. 212.[1]
— The Manchineal tree. 1898. III. 519.[2]
— Mangroves. 1890. II. 614,[1] *753.*[2]
— Notes on Colorado. 1878. I. 324.
— Notes on economic botany. 1878. III. 62.
— Notes on New Mexico. 1878. I. 324.
— Notes on the economic botany of western United States. 1880. III. 62.
— Nyssa sylvatica, Gum tree. 1897. II. 614.[2]
— The Old-Field or Loblolly Pine (Pinus Taeda). 1890. II. 48.[1]
— Our Pennsylvania forests. 1895. IV. 339.
— Concerning our Sassafras trees. 1889. II. 228.[1]
— Our Shell-bark Hickory. 1893. II. 112.[2]
— The Over-cup Oak. 1893. II. 135.[2]
— A Pennsylvania Sequoia. 1899. III. 310.[2]
— The Persimmon—Diospyros virginiana. 1893. II. 702.[1]
— Pin Oak, Spanish Oak. 1898. II. 136.[1]
— Pinus rigida on the dunes at Cape Henlopen. 1889. II. 45.[1]
— Poisonous properties of the Leguminosae. 1877. III. 488.[1]
— Post Oak, Iron Oak, Barrens White Oak. 1900. II. 140.[1]
— The Poverty Pine. 1894. II. 45.[2]
— Poverty Pine. 1900. II. 45.[2]

— Preliminary report on the botany of central Colorado. 1874. I. 323.
— Red Cedar Savin. 1890. II. 32.¹
— Red Maple, Swamp Maple. 1898. II. 480.¹
— Red Oak (Quercus rubra). 1899. II. 139.²
— Red Pine. Norway Pine. (Pinus resinosa.) 1896. II. 45.²
— The Red Spruce. 1898. II. 38.²
— Remove the tax from timber land. 188.? IV. 284.¹
— River Birch (Betula nigra L.). 1894. II. 119.²
— Rock Oak, Rock Chestnut Oak. 1897. II. 136.¹
— The Row Farm Walnut tree. 1890. II. 113.²
— The sand-dunes of Lewes, Del. 1890. I. 319.
— Sanitary relations of our highlands to the state. 1898. IV. 46.¹
— Silver Maple. White Maple. 1896. II. 480.²
— Sketch of the flora of Alaska. 1868. I. 311.²
— Some aspects of the present forestry agitation. 1890. IV. 272.
— Some big trees of our region. 1888. I. 295.²
— Some microscopic distinctions between good and bad timber. 1883. IV. 413.²
— The Sugar Maple. 1895. II. 480.²
— The Swamp White Oak. 1896. II. 132.²
— Tree growth as determined by location. 1889. II. 132.²
— The Tulip Poplar, or Poplar tree. 1891. II. 210.²
— A Walnut freak. 1897. II. 113.¹
— Wasted resources. 188.? IV. 281.²
— The White Ash. 1894. II. 707.¹
— White Birch, American White Birch. 1899. II. 120.¹
— White Pine. 1894. IV. 469.
— Willows along the banks of our rivers. 1895. IV. 184.²
— Wood structure in its relation to mechanical purposes. 1893. IV. 409.
— Woodlands and floods. 1894. IV. 184.²
— Yellow Birch, Gray Birch. 1898. II. 119.²
— & others. Catalogue of plants collected in Nevada, Utah. 1878. I. 324.
— — Reports upon the botanical collections made in portions of Nevada, Utah. 1878. I. 324.
Rothschild, Jules. L'aliénation des forêts de l'état. 1865. IV. 275.
— Flore pittoresque de la France. 1885. I. 417.
Rothstein, E. E. von. ·Försök öfver träcts tilltagande i vigt genom insugning af vatten. 1860. IV. 411.¹
Rothtannen-Rinde-Verkauf als Gerberlohe. 1857. IV. 458. Les rotins de l'Indo-Chine. 1898. III. 235.¹
Rotrou, de. Lettre sur la destruction du tigre du Pêcher. 1850. III. 441.²
Rottböll, Christian Friis. Anmærkninger . . . til M. P. Cato de re rustica. 1790. III. 99.
— Beskrivelse over nogle Planter fra de malebariske Kyster. 1782. I. 471.
— Botanikens Udstrakte nytte foredraget i et Indbydelses Skrift. 1771. I. 79.¹
— Descriptiones plantarum quarundam surinamensium. 1776. I. 338.²
— Descriptiones rariorum plantarum . . . e terra surinamensi fragmentum. 1776. I. 338.²
— Plantas horti universitatis. 1773. I. 40.
Rottenbach, Heinrich. Zur Flora Thüringens. 1880. I. 388.
— Die Verbreitung der Rosa pimpinellifolia. 1896. II. 299.¹
Rottenberg, Baron von. Die Ausschlagsfähigkeit der gepflanzten Birken. 1842. IV. 490.¹
— Bericht . . . über . . . forstwissenschaftliche Reise. 1844. IV. 348.²
— Beschreibung eines in einer haubaren Fichte . . . gefundenen Schwammes. 1841. IV. 455.
— Den kahlen Abtrieb, Dunkelschlag · . . betreffend. 1842. IV. 247.²
— Saat und Pflanzenkämpe betreffend. 1844. IV. 149.²
— & **Fuchs**, von, (Oberförster, Krascheow). Die Waldstreu betreffend. 1843. IV. 437.²
Rottenheusser, H. Ein Beitrag zur Frage der Umkehrversuche. 1895. I. 196.¹
— Taxodium distichum Rich. 1891. II. 51.²
Rotter, Franz. Beschreibung der Exkursion . . . in die Wälder der königl. Leibgedingstadt Königgrätz. 1886. IV. 371.
— Popis exkurse Českou jednotou lesnickou dne 2. srpna 1886 do lesů král věnného mesta Hradce Králové konané. 1886. IV. 371.
Rotterdam-Bataafsch genootschap der proefondervindelijke wijsbegeerte. See BATAAFSCH . . . I. 15.

Rottier, D. Recherches sur la conservation du bois. 1863. IV. 419.
— Recherches sur la conservation du bois au moyen des sels de cuivre. 1874. IV. 419.
Rottler, Johann Peter. Botanische Bemerkungen auf der Hin- und Rückreise von Trankenbar nach Madras. 1803. I. 401.
Rôtulos para viveros. 1892. IV. 546.¹
Sobre las **roturaciones** indebidas. · 1890· IV. 551.² ·
1898. III. 559.¹
Rouanet, Jules. La vinification et la viniculture en Algérie. 1898. III. 559.¹
Rouard. See DENIS & ROUARD.
Rouba, W. Wspomnienia z wycieczki po Krajn odbytej w miesiącu Lipcu r. b. 1886. I. 365.
Roubíček, Emil. Die " Coulissendurchforstung." 1896. IV. 175.²
— Gefällmesser zur Tracierung von Waldwegen. 1897. IV. 267.
Roubiczek, Ludwig. Ueber Durchforstungen. 1896. IV. 175.¹
Roubieu, G. J. Opuscules d'anatomie. 1816. II. 836.¹
Roucel, François Antoine. Flore du nord de la France. 1803. I. 406.
— Traité des plantes . . . des villes de Gand, d'Alost. 1792. I. 392.
Roucher. Sur l'industrie de la soie en Algérie. 1859. III. 507.¹
Rouchy, (abbé). Le jordanisme et l'anti-jordanisme. 1879. I. 252.
— Sur quelques espèces dites Jordaniques. 1878. II. 271.¹
Rouen-Académie des sciences, belles-lettres et arts. See ACADÉMIE . . . I. 20.
Rouen-Musée d'histoire naturelle. See MUSÉUM . . . I. 22.
Rouen-Société libre d'émulation. See SOCIÉTÉ . . . I. 23.
Rouffia, Côme. Ampélographie du Roussillon. 1866. III. 546.
Rouffiandis. Procédé expéditif et rationnel de cubage des bois ronds. 1867. IV. 226.
Rouffiandis, J. Expériences physiologiques sur les Vignes. 1887. III. 561.
Rouffignon, Fernand. Une visite du parc du domaine de la guerre, à Beverloo. 1899. IV. 357.²
Rouge. Empoisonnement par les fleurs de Cytise. 1868. III. 481.¹
Rougemont, Philippe Albert de. Deux plantes curieuses du jardin du Cercle du musée. 1879. II. 504.¹
Rouget. Hygiène forestière. 1861. IV. 310.¹ ·
Rouget, Charles. Les vignobles du Jura. 1897. III. 547.
Rougier de la Bergerie, Jean Baptiste, baron. Les forêts de la France. 1817. IV. 47.¹
— Mémoire au roi . . . sur la destruction des bois. 1831. IV. 180.²
— Opinion . . . sur l'aliénation . . . des forêts nationales 181.? IV. 275.
— Réflexions sur une maladie du seigle et la funeste destruction des arbres. 1804. IV. 282.²
Rouillard. Des Bambous; culture et multiplication. 1866. III. 314.¹
— Note sur les Pivoines de la Chine. 1863. III. 392.²
— Note sur quelques Conifères récemment introduites. 1863. III. 289.
La rouille vésiculeuse du Pin Weymouth. 1899. IV. 470.¹
Rouillé-Courbe. L'Aylantus glandulosa, ou le Vernis du Japon. 1860. III. 507.¹
— Rapport général sur la sériciculture . . . d'Indre-et-Loire. 1860. III. 125.
— Le soufrage de la Vigne en Touraine. 1863. III. 577.
Rouis, E. La gestion des forêts . . . du Gard. 1897. IV. 170.
— Notice sur le developpement & la gestion des forêts. . . du Gard. 1896. IV. 249.¹
Roujou, A. Le Buis sur le feu. 1900. II. 542.²
Roulet, Charles. Recherches sur l'anatomie comparée du genre Thunbergia. 1894. II. 804.²
— Résumé d'un travail d'anatomie . . . du genre Thunbergia. 1893. II. 804.²
— See also CHODAT, Robert & ROULET, Charles.
Roulet, J. A. Recueil de mémoires sur la culture de la Vigne. 1808. III. 558.¹
Roulet, James. Encore la question du cubage. 1899. IV. 215.
— Nouvelle loi forestière du canton de Neuchâtel. 1898. IV. 331,¹ 555.¹

Roulleau. Caractères distinctifs des glands de Chêne. 1892. II. 137,[1] 372.[1]

Roulleau, R. Le élésimètre Goulier. 1887. IV. 216.

— Expériences sur la destruction des vers blancs. 1889. IV. 203.

— Les impositions des forêts de l'État. 1891. IV. 285.[1]

— *See also* BROILLIARD, Charles & ROULLEAU, R.

Roumeguère, Casimir. Note sur une espèce nouvelle de Mamillaria. 1855. II. 594.[3]

— Nouveaux documents sur l'histoire des plantes . . . des Pyrénées. ·1876· I. 415.

— Réfutation des inconvénients attribués au Platane. 1874. III. 419.[1]

— Statistique botanique . . . de la Haute-Garonne. 1876. I. 415.

Round, O. S. Talk about trees. 1860. I. 82.[1]

The Round-leaved Prostanther. 1848. III. 698.[1]

Roupell, Arabella E. Specimens of the flora of South Africa. 1849. I. 494.

Rousse, A. Maladie de la Vigne, sa cause. 1853. III. 576.

Rousseau. Emploi, contre le phylloxera des résidus d'enfer. 1874. III. 566.[1]

— Invasion de l'Oecidium pini. 1885. IV. 478.

— Météorologie. 1877. IV. 50.

— Nouvelle maladie des Pins d'Alep. 1878. IV. 464.[1]

Rousseau, Em. Emploi de la créosote. 1861. IV. 432.[1]

Rousseau, J. Notice sur la viticulture en Égypte. 1873. III. 559.[1]

Rousseau, Jean Jacques. Botanik für Frauenzimmer. 1771. I. 93.

— La botanique. 1771. I. 93.

— Essais élémentaires sur la botanique: 1771. I. 93.

— Letters·on the elements of botany. 1771. I. 93.

— *See also* Руссо, Ж. Я.

Rousseau, L. F. Emmanuel. De l'efficacité des· fetuilles du Houx. 1831. III. 530.[1]

— An essay on the use of Holly. 1834. III. 529.[2]

Rousseau, Louis & Lemonnier, C. Promenades au Jardin des plantes. 1837. I. 58.

Rousseau, Philéas. Catalogue des plantes vasculaires spontanées de l'île de Ré. 1899. I. 419.[1]

Rousseau, Théodore. Greffe en écusson de printemps. 1872. III. 164.[1]

— Guide pratique de reboisement. 1886. IV. 163.

— Monographie du Chêne vert. 1876. IV. 503.[1]

— Notice forestière sur . . . l'Aude. 1890. IV. 361.

— Le régime des cours d'eau dans . . . l'Aude. 1877. IV. 47.[1]

— Les Vignes américaines dans l'Aude. 1887. III. 556.

Rousseaux, E. *See* MÜNTZ, A. & ROUSSEAUX, E, 1893. ·III. 557.[1]

Roussel, Ch. Les incendies de forêts en Algérie. 1874. IV. 184.[1]

— Waldbrände in·Algerien. 1874. IV. 184.[1]

Roussel, Henri François Anne de. Flore du Calvados. 1796. I. 406.

— Tableau des plantes usuelles. 1792. III. 55.

Roussel, Joseph. Avantages de la taille tardive pour prévenir la maladie de la Vigne. 1852. III. 575.[1]

Roussel, Lucien. Enseignement du droit forestier. 1895.· IV. 35.[1]

— Le thermomètre avertisseur de la sécherie de Haguenau. 1877. IV. 148.

— *See also* BARRÉ, Henri & ROUSSEL, Lucien.

Rousselier, J. Traitement des Vignes phylloxérées. 1876. III. 569.[2]

— Traitement des Vignes phylloxérées à Aimargues. 1876. III. 569.[1]

Rousselon. Sur le cryptogame qui attaque·le Vigne. 1850. III. 575.[1]

— Note sur quelques végétaux . . . dans l'établissement d'horticulture de M. Rantonnet. 1848. I. 58.

— Thoka des Birmans. 1848. ·III. 466.[1]

— & others. Sur l'hybridation. 1852. I. 245.

— — Sur la maladie de la Vigne. 1854. III. 576.

Roussen, León de. El injerto por la médula. 1894. III. 163.[1]

Rousset. Formation ligneuse anormale. 1898. IV. 66.[3]

Rousset, Antonin. De l'âge des arbres d'après leurs couches ligneuses. 1885. I. 193.[2]

— Culture . . . du Chêne-Liége. 185.? IV. 517.[1]

— Culture et exploitation des arbres. 1882. IV. 57.

— Dictionnaire général des forêts. 1871. IV. 292, 324.

— Les études de Maître Pierre. 1864. IV. 43.

— De l'exploitation . . . des forêts de Chênes-Liéges. 1858. IV. 517.[1]

— The forest waters the farm. 1864. IV. 43.

— Le jardinage et la possibilité par pieds d'arbres. 1885. IV. 237.

— Observations sur une formation ligneuse. 1898. I. 207.[1]

— Le pâturage sur les terrains gazonnés et boisés. 1878. IV. 135.[1]

— De la possibilité par pieds d'arbres. 1883. IV. 237

— La possibilité par pieds d'arbres. 1884. IV. 237.

— Recherches expérimentales sur les écorces à tan du Chêne yeuse. 1878. IV. 503.[1]

Roussille, Albert. Recherches relatives à la maturation des Olives. 1878. II. 713,[1] III. 679.[1]

Roussin, Alfred. *See* RUINET DU TAILLIS & ROUSSIN, Alfred. Les routes fruitières. 1896. III. 211.[1]

Routledge, Thomas. Bamboo en ampas . . . voor papierbereiding. 1875. III. 315.[1]

— Bamboo and its treatment. 1879. III. 314.[3]

— Bamboo considered as a paper-making material. 1875. III. 315.[1]

Rouvier, E. G. De la fixation de l'iode par l'amidou. 1892. I. 140.[2]

Roux. Traité de la culture . . . des arbres. 1750. IV. 108.[2]

Roux, E. Étude sur la carbonisation des bois. 1870. IV. 419.

— Les produits des forêts domaniales du Jura. 1899. IV. 238. — 1900. IV. 399.[1]

— Des variations dans la quantité d'urée . . . sous l'influence du thé et du café. 1873. III. 607, 742.[1]

— & Bouvet, Maurice. Les produits des forêts domaniales du Jura. 1899. IV. 261,[2] 551.[1]

Roux, Fréd. Observations sur quelques maladies de la Vigne. 1879. III. 560.

Roux, Gabriel. Coloration des feuilles de Vigne. 1890. III. 561.

Roux, Honoré. Catalogue des plantes de Provence. 1881. I. 416.

Roux, J. A. Claudius. La chlorose ou flavescence des végétaux fruitiers. 1900. III. 181.[1]

— Traité historique . . . des plantes. 1900. III. 181.[1]

— Végétation défectueuse et chlorose. 1900.· I. 229.

Roux, Jacques André, Pagès, Hippolyte & Béchamp, Antoine. Rapport d'experts sur demandes en dommages contre Henry Merle & Cie. de Salindres. 1872. IV. 192.[1]

Roux, Joseph. Essai d'analyse chimique de la fleur de Tilleul. 1825. III. 586.[1]

Rouy, Georges. Sur l'aire géographique de l'Abies Pinsapo. 1885. II. 24.[3]

— Description de cinq espèces françaises nouvelles du genre Rosa. 1875. II. 285.[2]

— Diagnoses d'espèces nouvelles pour la flore de la péninsule ibérique. 1887. I. 422.

— Diagnoses de plantes nouvelles pour la flore européenne. 1890. II. 340.[1]

— Espèces nouvelles pour la·flore·française. 1891. II. 662.[1]

— Excursions botaniques en Espagne. 1881. I. 422.

— Herborisations à Lus la Croix-Haute. 1882. II. 286.[1]

— Icones plantarum Galliae rariorum. 1897. I. 418.

— Matériaux pour servir à la révision de la flore portugaise. .1882. I. 422.·

— Observations sur quelques Malvacées. 1897. II. 525.[1]

— Plantes de Gibraltar et d'Algeciras. 1887. I. 422.

— Les Rosiers hybrides européens de l'herbier Rouy. 1900. II. 283.[2]

— Salix Reuteri Moritzi. 1885. II. 109.[3]

— Sorbus erubescens Kerner. 1889. II. 312.[3].

— Suites à la " Flore de France " de Grenier et Godron. 1882. I. 416.

— & Foucaud, Julien. Flore de France. 1893. I. 418.

Rovasenda, Joseph, *comte* de. Essai d'une ampélographei universelle. 1887. I. 547.

Rovelli, Achille. L'inverno 1879–1880. 1880. III. 49.[3]

Rovers, J. L. Aanteekeningen betreffende de particuliere Kinakultuur. 1878. III. 716.

— De bemesting van Koffielanden. 1871. III. 734.[1]

— Iets over eene ziekte der Theeplant. 1875. III. 604.[2]

Rovira. La corteza del Tolco. 1878. III. 267.[1]

Roviroso, José N. Bosquejo de la flora tabasqueña. 1897. I. 333.

— Calendario botánico de San Juan Bautista. 1897. I. 222.[1]

— Productos vegetales en las palizadas del Grijalva. 1891. I. 332.

Rowan, *Mrs.* Ellis. A flower-hunter in Queensland. 1898. I. 505.
Rowan, John J. Forest trees of Canada. 1876. IV. 337.[1]
— The forests of Canada. 1876. IV. 337.[1]
Rowe, Samuel. A perambulation of the antient [*sic*] and royal forest of Dartmoor. 1848. IV. 357.[2]
Rowe, T. W. Observations on the development of the flower of Coriaria ruscifolia. 1887. II. 454.[1]
Rowland, Róbert. Erdészeti köbözési táblák. 1876. IV. 227.
Rowland, Vilmos. A Czirbolya-Fenyő. 1882. IV. 463.[1]
Rowland, William. Beitrag zur Würdigung des Werthes forstlicher Nebennutzungen. 1878. IV. 439.
— Der Götterbaum als Waldbaum. 1883. IV. 525.
— Statistisch-topographische Beschreibung der Composses-sorat-Herrschaft Arva. 1877. IV. 373.
— Die Tanninfabrication. 1883. IV. 435.
Rowlee, Willard Winfield. Descriptions of two Willows from central Mexico. 1899. II. 100.[1]
— Historic trees of North America. 1899. I. 295.[2]
— List of plants collected near Muir glacier. *See* REID, H. F. 1893. I. 311.[2]
— North American Willows. 1900. II. 99.[2]
— & Hastings, G. T. The seeds and seedlings of some Amentiferae. 1898. II. 112,[1] *183*.[2]
— & Nichols, S. P. The taxonomic value of the staminate flowers of . . . Oaks. 1900. II. 129.[1]
— & Wiegand, K. M. Salix candida Willd. and its hybrids. 1896. II. 105.[2]
Rowney, Thomas. *See* HOW, Henry & ROWNEY, Thomas.
Roxas Clemente y Rubio, Simon de. *See* CLEMENTE Y RUBIO, Simon DE ROXAS.
Roxburgh, Wilham. An alphabetical list of plants . . . of St. Helena. 1816. I. 498.
— Beschreibung der Jonesie. 1795. II. 383.[1]
— Beschreibung der Prosopis aculeata. 1795. II. 379.[1]
— A botanical . . . account of Bassia Butyracea. 1805. II. 698.[1]
— A botanical description of a new species of Swietenia. 1793. III. 513.[1]
— A botanical description of Urecola. 1798. II. 734.[1]
— Botany of St. Helena. 1842. I. 498.
— A description of the Jonesia. 1795. II. 383.[1]
— A description of the plant Butea. 1792. II. 338.[1]
— Flora indica. 1820. I. 471.
— On the genus Aquilaria. 1854. II. 600.[1]
— Hortus bengalensis. 1814. III. 29.[2]
— On the lacsha, or lac insect. 1790. III. 232.[2]
— Plants of the coast of Coromandel. 1795. I. 471.
— Prosopis aculeata Kœnig. 1795. II. 379.[1]
— & Colebrooke, H. T. On the specific differences existing between Melaleuca Cajuputi and M. Leucadendron. 1828. II. 630.[1]
Roy, E. F. R. Sur l'essence d'écorce de Massoy. 1890. III. 407.[1]
Roy, Henricus van. Hortus academicus ultrajectinus. 1650. I. 50.
Roy-Chevrier, J. Ampélographie rétrospective. 1900. III. 548.[1]
— Le Houx. — Les plantes fastes. 1899. II. 463.[2]
— Nouveau mode de culture appliqué à la Vigne. 1886. III. 556.
Roy van Buldewyn, L. de. De bestijding der gewone Koffie-schildluis. 1900. III. 737.
Royal agricultural & commercial society of British Guiana. Journal. *See* TIMEHRI. I. 8.[1]
Royal agricultural society of England. Journal. III. 18.
Royal Asiatic society, Bombay branch. Journal. I. 29.[1]
Royal Asiatic society, Ceylon branch. Journal I. 29.[1]
Royal Asiatic society, North China branch. Journal. I. 28.[2]
Royal Asiatic society of Great Britain and Ireland. Journal. I. 19.
Royal Asiatic society, Straits branch. Journal. III. 26.[2]
Royal botanic garden, Calcutta. Annals. I. 29.[1]
Royal botanic garden, Edinburgh. 1900. I. 55.
Royal botanic gardens, Ceylon. Circular. 1897. I. 29,[1] 67.[1]
Royal botanic gardens, Trinidad. Annual report. 1881. I. 521.[1]
Royal botanic gardens, Trinidad. Bulletin. 1888. I. 40.
Royal botanic institution of Glasgow. 1881. I. 55.
Royal botanic society's June exhibition. 1850. III. 410,[2] 688,[1] 690.[2]
Royal Caledonian horticultural society. Memoirs. III. 18.
Royal colonial institute. Catalogue of the library. *See* CAT-ALOGUE . . . 1895. III. 1.

Royal colonial institute. Proceedings. III. 18.
Royal commission on forestry in Ontario. 1898. IV. 271.[2]
Royal Dublin society. Journal. Scientific proceedings. Scientific transactions. I. 19.
The Royal gardens at Kew. 1879. III. 123.[2]
Royal gardens at Kew. Report. 1856. I. 54.
Royal gardens, Kew. Official guide to the museums of economic botany. 1886. I. 38,[1] *IV. 13*.[1]
Royal geographical society of Australasia. Transactions. I. 30.
Royal geographical society of London. Journal. Proceedings. Supplementary papers. I. 19.
Royal horticultural society of London. Journal. Proceedings. *See* HORTICULTURAL SOCIETY OF LONDON. III. 17.
Royal Indian engineering college. Forest branch. *See* Prospectus of the forest branch. 1888. IV. 34.[1]
Royal institution of Great Britain. Journal. Journal of science. Proceedings. III. 18.
Royal institution of South Wales. Annual report. I. 20.
Royal Irish academy. Proceedings. Transactions. I. 20.
Royal microscopical society. Journal. Transactions. *See* MICROSCOPICAL SOCIETY OF LONDON. I. 19.
The Royal Palm. 1900. III. 328.[1]
(Royal) Scottish arboricultural society. · 1879. IV. 359.[1]
Royal Scottish arboricultural [society]. 1893. II. 139.[1]
Royal Scottish arboricultural society. *See also* SCOTTISH . . . IV. 12.[1]
Royal Scottish society of arts. Transactions. III. 18.
Royal society of arts and sciences of Mauritius. Transactions. I. 29.[2]
Royal society of Canada. Proceedings. I. 4.[2]
Royal society of Edinburgh. Proceedings. Transactions. I. 20.
Royal society of London. Philosophical transactions. Proceedings. I. 20.
Royal society of New South Wales. Journal. Transactions. *See* PHILOSOPHICAL SOCIETY OF NEW SOUTH WALES. I. 29.[2]
Royal society of Queensland. Proceedings. I. 30.
Royal society of South Australia. Transactions. *See* PHILOSOPHICAL SOCIETY OF ADELAIDE. I. 29.[2]
Royal society of Tasmania. Papers. *See* ROYAL SOCIETY OF VAN DIEMEN'S LAND. I. 30.
Royal society of Van Diemen's Land. Papers. I. 30.
Royal society of Victoria. Proceedings. Transactions. *See* PHILOSOPHICAL SOCIETY . . . I. 30.
Royal statistical society. *See* STATISTICAL . . . III. 18.
Royce, R. The propagation of shrubs. 1881. III. 153.
Royen, Adrian van. Carmen elegiacum de amoribus et connubiis plantarum. 1732. I. 198.
— Ericetum africanum. 17 . . ? II. 664.[2]
— Florae leydensis prodromus. 1740. I. 50.
Royer. Catalogue des plantes. 1760. I. 56.
Royer, Charles. Sur des anomalies de Néflies et de Poire. 1865. II. 968,[2] 970.[2]
— Anomalies du Salix cinerea. 1882. II. 106.[1]
— Essai sur le sommeil des plantes. 1868. I. 198.
— Faut-il greffer à basse tige ou à haute tige? 1866. III. 161.
— Flore de la Côte-d'Or. 1881. I. 416.
— Greffe et surgreffe nuisent. 1869. III. 165.
— Note relative au bourrelet des Poiriers greffés sur Cognassier. 1868 I. 208,[1] *III. 446*.[2]
— Note au l'écoulement annulaire. 1860. III. 175.[1]
— Note sur la taille des arbustes à fleurs. 1863. III. 172.
— Note sur une bande d'écorce engagée entre les couches ligneuses. 1866. I. 127,[2] 207.[2]
— Sur le sommeil des fleurs. 1860. I. 198.
— Les Sorbus scandica Fries, fallacina. 1883. II. 311.[2]
Royer, Johann. Beschreibung des ganzen Fürstlich Braunschweigischen Gartens zu Hessen. 1648. I. 43.
Royle, John Forbes. Abstract of a paper on the kino of Butea. 1846. III. 468.[1]
— On Benthamia fragifera. 1834. II. 655.[1]
— On the cultivation of Tea in . . . India. 1834. III. 602.[1]
— On East Indian kino. 1846. III. 485.[2]
— An essay on the antiquity of Hindoo medicine. 1837. III. 277.
— Essay on the productive resources of India. 1840. III. 277.
— The fibrous plants of India fitted for cordage. 1855. III. 233.[2]
— On the Hyssop of Scripture. 1844. II. 232.[1]
— On the identification of the Mustard tree. 1846. II. 473.[1]
— On the identification of the Mustard tree and the Hyssop of Scripture. 1844. II. 232.[1]

Royle, John Forbes (*continued*).
— Illustrations of the botany . . . of the Himalayan Mountains. 1839. I. 472.
— On Indian fibres fit for textile fabrics. 1854. III. 233.[1]
— Ueber das Lycium des Dioscorides. 1835. III. 394.[2]
— On the Lycium of Dioscorides. 1837. II. 201.[2]
— A manual of materia medica. 1847. III. 243.
— Materia medica and therapeutics. 1847. III. 243.
— Observations on the vegetation . . . of Afghanistan. 1842. I. 472, 477.[1]
— Report on the progress of the culture of the China Tea plant. 1849. III. 602.[2]
— On the tree yielding African olibanum. 1846. II. 416,[1] III. 509.[2]
— On the useful properties of the Deodar. 1853. IV. 448.[1]
— & Gordon, George. Official papers on the basts of Arracan. 1857. III. 234.
Roys, *marquis* de. Lettre [sur les effets du froid au] Château de Saint-Ange. 1872. III. 48.
Roze, Ernest. Aperçu historique sur le Laurier-cerise. 1899. II. 274.[2]
— Étude des parasites végétaux. 1898. III. 419.[1]
— La flore d'Étampes en 1747. 1889. I. 417.
— Le Jardin des plantes en 1636. 1888. I. 59.
— La maladie de la brunissure. 1897. III. 195.[2]
— Sur la maladie des châtaignes. 1897. III. 359.[1]
— Le Marronnier et sa seconde floraison. 1897. II. 482.[2]
— Notes et souvenirs extraits de l'Histoire des plantes rares de Charles de l'Escluze. 1899. II. 52.[2]
— Les plantes observées au XVIe siècle. 1900. III. 33.[2]
— Sur la propagation au Pseudocommis. 1897. III. 195.[2]
— Sur le Pseudocommia Vitis Debray. 1897. III. 581.
— Résultats de quelques expériences mycologiques. 1870. III. 194.
— Le retard de la fleuraison des plantes printanières. 1895. I. 226.[2]
— Sur le rôle que joue le Pseudocommis Vitis. 1897. III. 582.
Rozen, G. G. *See* Розенъ, Г. Г.
Rozet. Voyage dans la régence d'Alger. 1833. III. 280.[1]
Rozier, François. Cours complet d'agriculture. 1781. III. 30.
— Curso completo ó diccionario universal de agricultura. 1781. III. 30.
— Mémoire sur la culture du Noyer. 1789. III. 354.[2]
Rozin, A. Herbier portatif des plantes . . . de Liège. 1791. I. 406.
Rozmara, Josef. O Cedru. 1898. IV. 447.[2]
Rozsicská, Josef. Engerlingfrass an Pappeln. 1863. III. 344.[2]
—тт—. Ueber den Ursprung der europäischen Waldbäume. 1886. IV. 79.[1]
Rubattel, Ch. Beobachtungen über die . . . Forstkulturen. 1855. IV. 150.
— Insectes dangereux. 1855. IV. 209.[2]
— Observations sur les cultures forestières. 1855. IV. 150.
— Schädliche Forstinsekten. 1855. IV. 209.[2]
Rubber. 1897. III. 149.
Rubber and Coffee in Lagos. 1897. III. 688.[2]
Rubber culture in Ecuador. 1898. III. 149.
The Rubber forests of the Hukong Valley. 1898. II. 151.[2]
Rubber in Guatemala. 1899. III. 368.[2]
Rubber planting. 1900. III. 149.
Rubbia, Conrad. Der Lorbeer als Waldbaum. 1888. IV. 520.[1]
Rubens, Ferdinand. Immerwährender Obstbau-Kalender. 1848. III. 137.
— Leichtfassliche Anleitung zur Erziehung . . . des Weinstockes. 1844. III. 552.
— Der Obstbaumfreund. 1846. III. 137.
— Schädliche Insekten für Obst- und Weinbau. 1872. III. 190.
— Traité des maladies des arbres fruitiers. 1848. III. 178.
— Vollständige Anleitung zur Obstbaumzucht. 1843. III. 137.
Rubens, Johann Ferdinand. Das Winzerbuch. 1858. III. 553.[1]
Rubio, Simon DE ROXAS CLEMENTE Y. *See* CLEMENTE Y RUBIO, Simon de Roxas.
Rubisson, John. Sur le Mango. 1834. III. 524.[2]
Ruchinger, Giuseppe. Flora dei lidi veneti. 1818. I. 425.
Ruchinger, Giuseppe Maria. Cenni intorno all' orto bot. del Liceo convitto di Venezia. 1842. I. 63.
— Cenni storici dell' Imp. regio orto bot. in Venezia e catalogo delle piante in esso coltivate. 1847. I. 63.
— Della coltivazione degli Ilex. 1877. III. 529.[2]

Ruda, Joseph. Phytotoxicologiae cechicae tentamen. 1834. III. 392.[1]
Rudbeck, Olof. Catalogus plantarum, quibus Hortum . . . ubsaliensem . . . instruxit. 1658. I. 40.
— Deliciae Vallis Jacobaeae. 1666. I. 40.
— Hortus botanicus. 1685. I. 40.
— Hortus upsaliensis academiae. 1666. I. 40.
— Nora Samolad. 1701. III. 270.[1]
— Reliquiae Rudbeckianae. 1789. I. 292.
Rudbeck, Olaf, (*jr.*) Disputatio . . . de fundamentali plantarum notitia. 1690. I. 78,[2] 250.
— Dissertatio de fundamentali plantarum notitia. 1690. I. 78,[2] 250.
— Dudaim Rubenis.. 1733. I. 512.
— De Hedera. 1707. III. 643.[1]
— Index plantarum . . . in itinere laponico. 1720. I. 351.
— Propagatio plantarum botanico-physica. 1686. I. 204, III. 152.
Rudberg, August. Några spridda botaniska iakttagelser. 1897. II. 117.[1]
Rudder, Augustus. Forest wealth of Gloucester. 1895. IV. 380.[2]
— The waste of our timber. 1897. IV. 283.[2]
— *See also* BROWN, G. R. & RUDDER, Augustus.
Rudeloff, Max. Bericht über die . . . ausgeführten Holzuntersuchungen. 1889. IV. 409.
— Untersuchungen über den Einfluss des Blauwerdens auf . . . Kiefernholz. 1897. IV. 482.[2]
Rudenschöld, Ulrich. Rön om Furuträdens ålder uti Finnland. 1746. II. 47.[2]
Rudge, Edward. Description of . . . new species of plants from New Holland. 1807. I. 500.
— Description of a new species of Dimorpha. 1808. II. 356.[1]
— Plantarum Guianae rariorum icones. 1805. I. 338.[2]
Rudio, Franz. Uebersicht der Phanerogamen und Gefässcryptogamen von Nassau. 1851. I. 383.
— Large trees near New York City. 1880. I. 123.[2]
— Large trees near New York City. 1880. I. 295.[2]
Rudnick, H. Beitrag zur Waldwerthberechnung. 1889. IV. 192,[2] 255.
— Berechnung des Werthes der Waldbestände. 1864. IV. 255.
— Der französische Baumhöhen-Messer. 1876. IV. 215.
— Kleiner Beitrag zur Massenschätzung. 1876. IV. 256.
— Zur Lehre vom Reinertrags-Waldbau. 1885. IV. 245.
— Der Zinsfuss in der Waldwerthsberechnung. 1862. IV. 255.
Rudolph, (*Rathsforster*). Vortrag über die Pilzkrankheit Septoria parasitica. 1898. IV. 457.
Rudolph, E. F. L. Bruchstücke aus dem praktischen Forst- und Cameralwesen. ·1794. IV. 100.[1]
Rudolph, F. C. Tabernaemontana coronaria fl. pl. 1893. III. 690.[2]
Rudolph, Johann Friedrich. Erfahrungen und Vorschläge über den Anbau einheimischer Gewerb- und Fabrikhölzer. 1846. IV. 117.
Rudolph, Johann Stephan. Christo-Poma. *See* FIKENSCHER, D. J. 1674. II. 267.[2]
Rudolph, Jules. Aralia nymphaefolia. 1898. III. 643.[2]
— Bowenia spectabilis serrulata. 1900. III. 284.[2]
— Le Coccoloba pubescens. 1891. III. 387.[1]
— Les Crotons et leur culture. 1897. III. 516.[2]
— Dracaena umbraculifera. 1900. III. 337.[1]
— Quelques plantes utiles exotiques. 1897. III. 87.
— Le Rhodora canadensis. 1892. III. 658.[1]
— Rusticité du Camellia. 1894. III. 600.[1]
— Les semis de. Cactées. 1892. III. 620.[1]
— Tamarindus indica. 1892. III. 489.[1]
Rudolph, Ludwig. Atlas der Pflanzengeographie. 1852. I. 299.
— Ueber die Bedeutung der Pflanzengeographie. 1855. I. 299.
— De myrteagtige Planter. 1859. II. 619.[1]
— Die Pflanzendecke der Erde. 1853. I. 299.
— La végétation sous la zone équatoriale. 1862. I. 219.[2]
— *See also* Рудольфъ, Л.
Rudolphi, Fridericus Carolus Ludovicus. Systema orbis vegetabilium. 1830. I. 260.
Rudolphi, Karl Asmund. Anatomie der Pflanzen. 1807. I. 100.[1]
— Bemerkungen aus dem Gebiet der Naturgeschichte. 1804. III. 269.[2]
— Einige botanische Beobachtungen. 1799. II. 667,[1] 669.[1]

Rudorf, (*Oberforstmeister*). Aus der Praxis der Vorverjüngung. 1873. IV. 139.[2]
— Ueber Sortimentsbildung. 1875. IV. 387.[2]
Rudorf, August Gottlieb. Tafeln zur Bestimmung des Inhalts der runden Hölzer. 1825. IV. 222.
Rudow, Ferdinand. Einige Missbildungen an Pflanzen. 1891. I. 144.[1]
— Die Pflanzengallen Norddeutschlands. 1875. I. 215,[1] *III. 344,*[2] *350.*[1]
— Uebersicht der Gallenbildungen. 1875. I. 215,[1] *III. 344,*[2] *350,*[1] *585.*[2]
Rudzski, A. *See* Рудзкій, А.; Береха, П. & Рудзкій, А.
Rübner, Hermann Ernst Ludwig. De acido pyrolignoso. 1824. IV. 432.[1]
Rübsaamen, Ewald H. Beschreibung neuer Gallmücken. 1889. III. 475.[1]
— Die Gallmücken. 1890. I. 215.[1]
— Mittheilungen über . . . Gallmücken. 1892. I. 215.[2]
— Über russische Zoocecidien. 1896. I. 215.[1]
— *See also* RITTER, C. & RÜBSAAMEN, E. H.
Das **Rücken** der Brennhölzer mittelst Handschlitten. 1876. IV. 389.
Rücker, (*Oberförster, Grüssau*). Ueber das Baumroden. 1857. IV. 385.[2]
Ruecker, Otto Georg. De camphorae virtute medica. 1835. III. 233.[1]
Rückert. "Die Strassburger Tanne." 1889. IV. 447.[1]
Rückert, (*Oberförster in Üllersdorf*). Wie kann dem Windbruche in den Wäldern Einhalt gethan werden? 1842. IV. 189.[1]
Rückert, Ernst Ferdinand. Flora von Sachsen. 1840. I. 380.
Rückert, G. C. A. Chemisch-ökonomische Abhandlung über . . . Akazie. 1800. IV. 522.[2]
Rüdel, C. Beiträge zur Kenntnis der Alkaloide von Berberis. 1891. III. 394.[2]
Rüdenburg, Viktor. Die alpinen Daphne-Arten. 1889. III. 626.[2]
— Xanthoceras sorbifolia. 1895.* III. 540.[2]
— A Xanthoceras sorbifolia szaporitása. 1897. III. 540.[2]
Rüdiger, Max. Beiträge zur Baum- und Strauchvegetation. 1890. I. 372.
— Beiträge zur Kenntniss der Baum- und Strauch-Gewächse . . . von Frankfurt a. O. 1889. I. 371.
— Eine neue einheimische Pappel. 1890. II. 98.[2]
— Populus Viadri n. sp. 1890. II. 98.[2]
— Weitere Mittheilungen über Regenschutz. 1894. I. 233.[1]
— Wie wird Regen und Thau an den Bäumen abgeleitet? 1892. I. 233.[1]
Rüedi. Die Einmessung des Nutzholzes. 1895. IV. 229.
Rüedi, (jr.). Naturgesetzliche Grundlage des Waldbaues. 1898. IV. 57.
Rüedi, J. Die Wasserverheerungen vom Herbste 1868. 1869. IV. 187.[1]
— *See also* BOURGEOIS, Conrad & RÜEDI, J.
Rügen — **Naturwissenschaftlicher Verein von Neuvorpommern** . . . *See* NATURWISSENSCHAFTLICHER . . . I. 14.
Rüger, Georg. Beiträge zur Kenntniss der Gattung Carica. 1887. II. 582.[1]
Rühl, Fritz. Eine Seuche unter den Afterraupen der Kiefernblattwespe. 1887. IV. 478.
Rühling, Wilhelm. Ueber die Wurzelnutzung der Nadelhölzer. 1845. IV. 385.[2]
Rühm, (*Revierförster, Paulinzelle*). Ueber Durchforstung . . . Fichten-Wüchse. 1851. IV. 453.
Ruel, Jean. De natura stirpium libri tres. 1536. I. 277, V. XIV.[1]
Rüling, (*Forstinspector*). Einige Worte über die von Buttlar'sche Pflanzweise. 1861. IV. 152.
— Die finanzielle Bedeutung . . . der Buche. 1864. IV. 494.
Rüling, (*Oberforstmeister*). Streunutzung. 1868. IV. 71.
Rüling, Johann Philipp. Commentatio botanica de ordinibus naturalibus. 1766. I. 250, 267.
— Ordines naturales plantarum. 1774. I. 258.
— Physikalisch-medizinisch-ökonomisch Beschreibung der . . . Stadt Nordheim. 1779. I. 374.
— Verzeichniss der an und auf dem Harz wildwachsenden Bäume. 1786. I. 374.
Ruellius, Joannes. *See* RUEL, Jean.
Rümke, C. L. Over de werking van carpaïne op het hart. 1892. III. 617.[1]
Rümpler, Theodor. Illustriertes Gartenbau-Lexikon. 1890. III. 31.

— Die Sukkulenten. 1892. III. 75,[2] *620.*[1]
— *See also* BABO, A., *Freiherr* von & RÜMPLER, Theodor; HARTWIG, J. & RÜMPLER, Theodor.
Rueneuve, ANGRAN DE. *See* ANGRAN DE RUENEUVE.
Rueppell, Eduard. Reise in Nubien. 1829. I. 487.
Rüppell, Julius. Doppelbenennung von Coniferen. 1895. III. 311.[1]
— Nomenklatur der Koniferen. 1887. III. 290.
Ruer, Herz Israel. De vi corticis peruviani antispasmodica. 1779. III. 720.
Rüsch, G. Ueber appenzellisches Forstwesen. 1846. IV. 365.
Der **Rüsselkäfer** (Curculio pini). 1856. IV. 209.[2]
Rüst, W. A. Die Holzbearbeitungen. 1838. IV. 422.[1]
Ruete, Benno. Ueber die Calabar-Bohne. 1865. III. 483.[2]
Ruf eines Einwohners im Stuttgarter Thal über die enorme Holztheurung. 1797. IV. 282.[1]
Ruffin, Edmund. Notes on the Pine trees of lower Virginia. 1859. II. 39.[1]
Rufz de Lavison. Sur le ver à soie du Chêne Yama-maï. 1863. IV. 501.[2]
Ruginelli, Julius Caesar. De arboribus controversis resolutionum. 1688. V. XXXI.[1]
— Resolutiones de arboribus controversis. 1688. IV. 313, V. XXXI.[1]
The **Rugosa** type of Roses. 1892. III. 456.[2]
Rug-Verordnung [des Fürstenthums Aschaffenburg.] 1803. IV. 299.
Rohemann & **Steinner**. Sur l'acide anacardique. 1887. II. 455.[1]
Ruhland, Reinhold Ludwig. Fragmenta de nutritione plantarum. 1809. I. 157.
Ruhmer, Gustav. Die in Thüringen bisher wild beobachteten . . . Pflanzenbastarde. 1881. I. 271.[2]
Ruijs, Johannes Marinus. De verspreiding van planten door dieren. 1893. I. 241.[1]
Ruinet du Taillis à Brandon, Alfred. Naturalisation de végétaux exotiques en Bretagne. 1890. III. 126.[1]
Ruiz, Sebastian Joseph Lopez. Defensa y demostración del verdadero descubridor de las quinas del reyno de Santa Fé. 1802. III. 720.
Ruiz Amado, Hilarion. Correspondencia. 1890. IV. 553.[1]
— Dibujo dasográfico-matemático. 1890. IV. 551.[1]
— Estudios forestales. *See* AMADO, H. R. 1870. IV. 44.
— A los ingenieros de montes. 1890. IV. 550.[2]
— El llano del Llobregat. 1893. IV. 548.[1]
— El negociado de montes. 1891. IV. 553.[2]
— No se venderán los montes. 1883. IV. 276.[2]
Ruiz Casaviella, Juan. Catálogo metódico de las plantas observadas como espontáneas en Navarra. 1880. I. 422.
Ruiz Lopez, Hipólito. Della China e delle altre sue specie. 1792. II. 811.[1]
— Description of the tree known . . . under the name of Quin quino. 1821. III. 482.[2]
— Memoir on the virtues and uses of . . . the Star-reed. 1805. III. 386.[1]
— Memoir on the virtues . . . of the root . . . called Yallhoy. 1821. III. 513.[2]
— Memoria sobre la Ratanhia. 1797. III. 480.[1]
— Memoria sobre las virtudes y usos de . . . Bejuco de la estrella. 1805. III. 386.[1]
— Memoria sobre las virtudes y usos de la raiz de Purhampuy. 1821. III. 338.[2]
— Von dem offizinellen Fieberrindenbaum. 1792. II. 811.[2]
— Quinologia. 1792. II. 811.[2]
— Sobre la raiz de China. 1797. II. 85.[2]
— Respuesta para desengaño del público á la impugnacion . . . contra el Pródromo de la flora del Perú. 1796. I. 340.[1]
— & Pavon, José. Beauharmonia. 1808. II. 558.[2]
— — Flora peruviana et chilensis. 1798. I. 340.[1]
— — Florae peruvianae et chilensis prodromus. 1794. I. 340.[1]
— — Responsa ad dubia . . . Jussiei. 1801. I. 340.[1]
— — Supplemento a la Quinologia. 1801. I. 340,[1] *II. 812.*
— — Systema vegetabilium florae peruvianae et chilensis. 1798. I. 340.[1]
Ruiz Moulleó, M. Nuevo procedimiento para la inyección de creosota en las traviesas. 1898. IV. 557.[2]
Rukovodstvo . . . *See* Руководство . . .
Ruland, Joseph. Ueber das botanische System des Rivinus. 1832. I. 260.
Rules and regulations governing forest reserves. 1897. IV. 179.[1]
Rules for the administration of forests and waste lands in . . . Mysore. 1878. IV. 307.[2]

Rules for the administration of forests in British Burma. 1875. IV. 307.²

Rules made under the forest act (Act VII. of 1878) for the forest of the lower provinces. 1882. IV. 332.¹

Rules of inspection of the Chicago lumberman's board of trade. 1874. IV. 403.²

Rulf, Paul. Ueber das Verhalten der Gerbsäure. 1884. I. 204.

Rullmann, A. Die Giftpflanzen und Giftschwämme Deutschlands. 1837. III. 73.

Die rumänischen Staatsforste. 1900. IV. 375.²

Rumetius, Ludwig. Sacrorum Bibliorum arboretum morale. 1606. I. 512.

— Scripturae Saerae viridarium. 1626. I. 512.

Rumford, comte de. Recherches sur les bois et le charbon. 1812. IV. 407.²

Rumm, C. Zur Frage nach der Wirkung der Kupfer-Kalksalze. 1893. III. 581.

— Ueber die Wirkung der Kupferpräparate. 1893. III. 581.

Rumpel, A. Glycine (Wistaria) sinensis als Hochstamm. 1891. III. 491.¹

Rumpelt, A. Unfall- und Krankenversicherung für Land- und Forstwirthschaft im Königreich Sachsen. 1888. IV. 311.¹

— Unfall- und Krankenversicherung für Land und Forstwirthschaft im Königreich Sachsen; Ausführungsbestimmungen. 1888. IV. 311.¹

Rumpf, Georg Eberhard. Herbarium amboinense. ' 1741. I. 464.²

Rumpf, H. F. Kurzer Inbegriff der reinen Mathematik. 1825. IV. 58.

Rumphius, Georgius Everhardus. See RUMPF, G. E.

Runacher, Ant. Utilité de l'introduction du Sapin et de l'Épicéa dans les taillis. 1899. IV. 558.²

Runde, W. Araucarien. 1898. III. 298.¹

Rundgang durch den Königlich botanischen Garten zu Berlin. 1892. III. 28.¹

Rundspaden. Der modificirte Buchen-Hochwald. 1867. IV. 494.

Runeberg, Edward Fr. Försök at med electricitetens tilhjälp drifva växter. 1757. III. 176.¹

— Proefnemingen om door middel van het elektrizeeren, den groey . . . te bevorderen. 1765. I. 230.

Runeberg, Ephraim Otto. Beskrifning öfver Lajhela socken. 1758. IV. 347.

Runge, Carl. Zwei neue Cacteen. 1889. II. 592,¹ 595.¹

Runge, Friedlieb Ferdinand. Effets remarquables de l'huile de térébenthine sur . . . Mimosa pudica. 1833. II. 372.²

— Das Kupferoxydhydrat als Reagens. 1830. I. 156.¹

— Merkwürdige Wirkung des Terpentinöls auf . . . Mimosa. 1833. II. 372.²

— Resultate chemischer Untersuchungen. 1830. II. 63.²

Runnebaum, Adolf. Das Absterben . . . der Kiefer im Stangenholzalter. 1892. IV. 478.

— Die Befestigung der Fahrbahn durch Holzknüppel. 1885. IV. 389.

— Besenpfrieme und Waldfeldbau. 1890. IV. 134,¹ 581.²

— Der Entwurf . . . von Waldwegenetzen. 1884. IV. 389.

— Forstliche Reiseeindrücke aus Nord-Amerika. 1895. IV. 338.²

— Die Kiefern im Buchen-Unterwuchse. 1885. IV. 473.

— Der Kiefernbaumschwamm. 1891. IV. 478.

— Die transportablen Wald-Eisenbahnen. 1884. IV. 391.

— Die Vermessungen im Walde. 188 . ? IV. 265.

— Verminderung der Transportkosten. 1883. IV. 274.²

— Die Waldeisenbahnen. 1886. IV. 392.

— Waldvermessung und Waldeintheilung. 1890. IV. 251.¹

— Der Weidengerbetrieb . . . Eberswalde. 1885. III. 349.

— Welche Gesichtspunkte sind bei der Forstvermessung . . . zu berücksicht? 1880. IV. 251,¹ 265.

Runzler, H. Sorten und Werthe im Vergleich zu andern Ländern. 1892. III. 89.¹

Ruotte, J. See GRIMAUX, E. & RUOTTE, J.

Rupe, Hans. Die Chemie der natürlichen Farbstoffe. 1900. V. XII.¹

Ruppius, Heinrich Bernhard. Flora jenensis. 1718. I. 372.

Rupprecht, (K. k. Bücher-Censor, Wien). Über die Vermehrung des Weinstocks. 1839. III. 548.¹

Ruprecht, Franz Joseph. Bambuseae. 1839. II. 58.¹

— Barometrische Höhenbestimmungen im Caucasus. 1863. I. 369.

— Ein Beitrag zur Frage über die Parthenogenesis. 1858. I. 202.¹

— Bericht über das Werk des Herrn C. J. Maximowicz. Primitiae florae amurensis. 1859. I. 455.

— Bericht über eine botanische Reise im Gouvernement St. Petersburg. 1854. I. 361.

— Chupp-tatt, ein neues . . . Bambusrohr. 1850. II. 58.²

— Decas plantarum amurensium. 1859. I. 455.

— Die Edeltanne von Pawlowsk. 1859. I. 209,¹ II. 22,¹ IV. 445.

— Ueber einige neue brasilianische Bambusrohre. 1841. II. 58.¹

— Einige Worte über die Gattung Calyptrostigma. 1856. II. 834.²

— Die ersten botanischen Nachrichten über das Amurland. 1857. I. 454.²

— Flora boreali-uralensis. 1854. I. 361.

— Flora Caucasi. 1869. I. 369.

— Flora ingrica. 1860. I. 362.

— Flores Samojedorum cisuralensium. 1845. I. 361.

— Hatte die diesjährige Sonnenfinsterniss . . . Einfluss auf die täglichen periodischen Erscheinungen im Pflanzenreiche? 1851. I. 198.

— In historiam stirpium florae petropolitanae diatribae. 1845. I. 361.

— Neuere geo-botanische Untersuchungen über den Tschornosjom. 1866. I. 362.

— Parthenogenesis bei Pflanzen. 1858. I. 202.¹

— Symbolae ad historiam . . . plantarum rossicarum. 1846. I. 361.

— Ueber die Verbreitung der Pflanzen im nördlichen Ural. 1848. I. 361.

— Vorläufiger Bericht über meine Reise nach dem Caucasus. 1863. I. 369.

— Über die wissenschaftliche Bedeutung des Tschornosjom. 1864. I. 362.

— See also MAXIMOWICZ, C. J. & RUPRECHT, F. J.; OSTEN-SACKEN, Friedrich, Baron von & RUPRECHT, F. J.

Ruprich-Robert, Victor. Flore ornementale. 1865. I. 516.

Tegen de rups in de Haagdoorns. See TEGEN . . . 1876. III. 422.²

Rural affairs. III. 8.

Rural cemeteries. 1856. III. 201.

Rural New Yorker. See MOORE'S Rural New Yorker. III. 6.

Rural recreations; or, The gardener's instructor. 1802. III. 109.

Rusby, Henry Hurd. The affinities of Dendrobangia Rusby. 1897. II. 474.²

— Blüten von Mutisia viciaefolia. 1889. III. 755.²

— Bocconia, a new medicinal genus. 1891. III. 408.¹

— The botanical origin of . Coca leaves. 1900. II. 394.²

— Carica Papaya L.; Papaw. 1889. III. 617.²

— Cascara sagrada and its allies. 1890. III. 542.²

— On the collections of Mr. Miguel Bang in Bolivia. 1892. I. 340.²

— Cross-fertilization in Cereus phoeniceus. 1881. II. 593.¹

— The cultivated Cinchonas of Bolivia. 1888. II. 813.¹

— The cultivation of Cinchona in Bolivia. 1887. III. 713.¹

— An enumeration of the plants collected . . . in South America. 1898. I. 331.

— Floral features of the Amazon valley. 1889. I. 343.

— General floral features of the San Francisco and Mogollon Mts. of Arizona. 1888. I. 325.

— The lateral lines in the leaf of Erythroxylon Coca. 1887. II. 394.¹

— New genera of plants from Bolivia. 1893. I. 340.²

— Notes on the trees of the South-west. 1882. I. 320.

— Ueber Phoradendron flavescens. 1889. III. 385.¹

— Two new genera of plants from Bolivia. 1894. II. 860.¹

— See also BRITTON, N. L. & RUSBY, H. H.

— & Jelliffe, S. E. Essentials of vegetable pharmacognosy. 1895. I. 101,¹ III. 758.¹

— — Morphology and histology of plants. 1899. I. 92.

Rusch, (Oberförster, Grudschütz). Beobachtungen über den Rüsselkäfer. 1842. IV. 206.

— Reichlicher Zapfen-Träger. 1866. IV. 483,¹ 506.

Rusch, Heinrich. Kubik-Tabellen zur Bestimmung des Inhalts runder . . . Hölzer. 1873. IV. 227.

Ruschenberger, William Samuel Waithman. Elements of natural history. 1850. I. 89.

— A report on the origin . . . of cundurango. 1873. III. 693.²

Rush, Benjamin. An account of the Sugar Maple-tree. 1791. IV. 527.¹

— Berigt van den Suiker-ahorn. 1791. IV. 527.¹

— Nachricht von dem Zucker-Ahorn. 1791. IV. 527.¹

Rush, Richard. Growth and manufacture of silk. 1828. III. 374.

Rush, W. B. Orange flowers. 1879. III. 501.²
Rushforth, James. The forests of Russia. 1878. IV. 345.
Ruskin, John. The Pine. 1872. III. 306.²
Rusegger, Joseph. Reisen in Europa, Asien . . . See FENZL, Eduard. 1841. I. 480.
Russell, Alexander. Naauwkeurige en natuurlyke beschrijving van de Stad Aleppo. 1756. I. 479.
— The natural history of Aleppo. 1756. I. 479.
— Naturgeschichte von Aleppo. 1756. I. 479.
Russell, Mrs. Anna Worsley. Catalogue of plants. 1839. I. 399, V. xx.²
Russell, Charles E. M. Some account of the Eria silkworm. 1884. III. 522.¹
Russell, Gordon W. A fine specimen of Amelanchier canadensis. 1885. II. 257.²
— Large Sassafras trees. 1886. II. 228.¹
— Large trees of Connecticut. 1879. II. 143.²
— A remarkable Sassafras tree. 1877. II. 228.¹
Russell, Harry Luman. Observations on the temperature of trees. 1889. I. 186.
Russell, Henry Chamberlaine. Notes on the rate of growth of some Australian trees. 1891. III. 132,¹ IV. 65.¹
Russell, J. Spiral ringing of branches. 1852. I. 164, III. 175.¹
Russell, J. E. Horticulture in Mexico and Central America. 1882. III. 118.¹
Russell, J. L. Artificial planting of trees. 1857. III. 117.¹
— Notes on some species of Oak indigenous to California. 1868. III. 361.¹
— Some notes on the Coniferae of California. 1868. III. 290.
Russell, Levi W. Native trees. 1891. I. 312, V. xvii.¹
— The native trees of Rhode Island. 1885. I. 312. — 1900. I. 313, IV. 77.¹
— The propagation, planting . . . of native trees. 1887. III. 117.¹
— Rare trees of Rhode Island. 1889. I. 312, IV. 77.¹
Russell, Patrick. An account of the tabasheer. 1791. III. 315.¹
Russell, Robert. Old and remarkable trees in Scotland. 1863. I. 296.²
Russell, V. F. The Olive and its oil in California. 1872. III. 678.²
Russell, William. The Cocoa-Nut Palm. 1876. III. 324.¹
— Contributions à l'étude de l'influence du climat sur la structure des feuilles. 1895. I. 219.¹
— Sur les faisceaux corticaux de quelques Genista. 1890. II. 359.²
— Influence de l'adaptation sur la structure de quelques plantes méditerranéennes. 1896. I. 219.²
— Influence du climat méditerranéen. 1895. I. 219.²
— Notes on the forests of British Guiana. 1882. IV. 342.¹
— Nouvelle note sur les pelotes marines. 1893. I. 242.¹
— Observations sur . . . l'inflorescence mâle du Noyer. 1892. II. 113.²
— Observations sur quelques cas de fasciation. 1894. I. 144.²
— Recherches sur la vrille des Passiflores. 1890. II. 576.¹
— Recherches sur le développement . . . des cladodes du Petit-Houx. 1890. II. 84.²
— Recherches sur les bourgeons multiples. 1890. I. 105.¹— 1892. I. 108.²
— Sur la structure du tissu assimilateur des tiges. 1892. I. 124.
— Transformation des cônes de Pins. 1892. I. 242.²
Russia — Société d'économie rurale de la Russie méridionale. See SOCIÉTÉ . . . III. 10.¹
The Russian Apricot. 1886. III. 443.¹
The Russian Apricot; opinions and experiences. 1890. III. 443.¹
A Russian visitor, (pseud.). Floriculture in Palermo. 1878. III. 307.¹
Aus dem russischen Norden. 1899. IV. 376.¹
Russkoye . . . See Русское . . .
Aus Russland. 1893. IV. 346.
Aus Russland. Aspenholz. 1894. IV. 487.¹
Russow, Edmund August Friedrich. Über den anatomischen Bau . . . der Coriarieen. 1881. II. 454.¹
— Über die Auskleidung der Intercellularen. 1886. I. 137.
— Über den Bau der . . . Siebröhren. 1882. I. 134.¹
— Betrachtungen über das Leitbündel- und Grundgewebe. 1875. I. 123.²
— Ueber die Boden- und Vegetationsverhältnisse . . . an der Nordküste Estlands. 1886. I. 365.

— Über die Entwickelung des Hoftüpfels. 1881. II. 17.¹
— Flora der Umgebung Revals. 1862. I. 362.
— Gegenbemerkungen zu den Bemerkungen Dr. C. Sanio's. 1882. II. 17.¹
— Über den Inhalt der parenchymatischen Elemente der Rinde. 1884. I. 179.²
— Zur Kenntniss des Holzes. 1883. II. 17,¹ V. xxv.¹
— Über die Perforation der Zellwand. 1884. I. 138.²
— Über das Schwinden . . . der Stärke in der Rinde. 1884. I. 179,² V. xi.²
— Sur la structure . . . des tubes cribreux. 1882. I. 134.¹
— Ueber die Verbreitung der Callusplatten. 1884. I. 134.¹
— Ueber Wurzelbildung im Innern hohler Birkenstämme. 1881. I. 188.¹
Russworm. See GLEICHEN, W. F., Freiherr von.
Rust, A. Der Holzberechner. 18 . . ? IV. 220.
— Praktische Anleitung zum Ausroden der Stubben in den Forsten. 1847. IV. 385.²
Rust, J. Beschreibung des Baumhöhenmessers. 1850. IV. 215.
— Massengehalt einer 80 Jahr alten Kiefer. 1855. IV. 480.
— Notizen über den Holzgehalt einer Fichte. 1853. IV. 458.
— Notizen über die Durchforstungs-Erträge im Patschkauer Stadtwalde. 1862. IV. 260.²
— Notizen über Forstkulturen. 1853. IV. 148.
Rust, J. F. Ueber die Ablösung der Servitute. 1835. IV. 333.
Rustici latini volgarizzati. See SCRIPTORES rei rusticae. 1470. III. 97.
Rustico. Accrescimento delle proprietà germogliative. 1865. IV. 149.¹
Ruthe, Johann Friedrich. Flora der Mark Brandenburg. 1827. I. 377.
Rutherford, Daniel. Characteres generum plantarum. 1793. I. 258.
Rutherford, H. K. & others. Tea, Cardamoms and Areca cultivation. 1885. III. 320,¹ 603.
Rutherford, J. On drainage. 1858. III. 150.²
— On thinning. 1858. IV. 173.
— Will it pay to plant arable land? 1880. IV. 134.¹
Rutilius, TAURUS AEMILIANUS PALLADIUS. See PALLADIUS RUTILIUS TAURUS AEMILIANUS.
Rutland, James. The timber of Nesodaphne Tawa. 1884. IV. 520.¹
Rutland, Joshua. The fall of the leaf. 1889. I. 192.¹
Rutter, John. The culture and diseases of the Peach. 1880. III. 441.¹
Rutter, John & Carter, Daniel. Modern Eden. 1769. III. 109.
Rutty, John. Observations on the London and Edinburgh dispensatories. 1776. III. 253.
Rutty, W. The natural history of cochineal. 1731. III. 624.¹
Ruusscher, Melchior de. Natuurlyke historie van de couchenille. 1729. III. 624.¹
Ruys, J. Mar. De verspreiding der phanerogamen in arktisch Europa. 1884. I. 349.
Ruyssen. See PORTES & RUYSSEN.
Ryan, G. M. The spread of Loranthus in the Konkan. 1900. II. 175.¹
— Trade in Terminalia bellerica nuts. 1900. III. 632.²
Ryan, J. Catalogus herbarii J. Ryani. 1809. I. 40.
Ryan, T. Pittosporums. 1899. III. 416.¹
Rybak, K. Die Seuche der Entwaldung. 1885. IV. 281.¹
Rybářské listy. See HÁJ. IV. 14.
Rychner, A. Forstliche Verhältnisse im untern Misox. 1883. IV. 367.
Ryckevorsel, van. Tegen ontwouding. 1885. IV. 279.¹
Ryckevorsel, A. van. Staats-boschcultuur en partikulier initiatief. 1890. IV. 309.¹
Ryckevorsel, T. C. van. Berigt aan de Hollandsche huishoudelijke maatschappij te Haarlem wegens den staat zijner Dennebosschen. 1806. IV. 356.¹
— Overhet aanleggen van 20 morgen onbebouwde grond tot Dennen. 1806. IV. 159.
Rydberg, Per Axel. On the American Black Cottonwood. 1893. II. 96.¹
— Catalogue of the flora of Montana. 1900. I. 327.
— Cespitose Willows of Arctic America. 1896. II. 99.²
— Composition of the Rocky Mountain flora. 1900. I. 327.
— Flora of the Black Hills of South Dakota. 1896. I. 326.
— Flora of the sand hills of Nebraska. 1895. I. 326.

Rydberg, Per-Axel (*continued*).
— New species from the western United States. 1899. II. 841.[3]
— Notes on two western plants. 1897. II. 837.[2]
— Rarities from Montana. 1897. I. 327.
— A revision of the nomenclature of the Nebraska Polypetalae. 1894. II. 332.[1]
— Studies on the Rocky Mountain flora. 1900. II. 848.[2]
— What is Prunus insititia? 1899. II. 274.[2]
Rydelius, Anders. Dissertatio de Palma. 1720. II. 63.[1]
Ryder. The hypertrophied hairs on Ampelopsis. 1890. II. 504.[3]
Ryder, John Adam. Honey glands on Catalpa leaves. 1880. II. 787.[1]
Ryet, de. Multiplication des Cycadées. 1892. III. 284.[2]
Ryff, Gualther Hermann. *See* RYFF, Walter Hermann.
Ryff, Walter Hermann. Der ander Theyl der kleynern teütschen Apoteck. 1552. III. 239.
— Confectbuch unnd Haus-Apoteck. 1571. III. 240.
— Der erst Theyl der kleinen Apoteck. 1552. III. 239.
— Kurtzer Auszug und summarischer Bericht . . . der Wurtzel China. 1548. III. 338.[1]
— New erfundne, heylsame . . . Arstney . . . Würckung des indianischen Holtz Guaicum. 1541. III. 494.[1]
— Newe aussgerüste deutsche Apoteck. 1573. III. 53.
— Reformierte deütsche Apoteck. 1573. III. 53.
Ryhiner, J. H. Analysis chemica seminum Coffeae. 1762. III. 740.[1]
Rykens, R. H. Kina-veredelingen. 1885. III. 716.
Ryn van Alkemade, J. van. Handleiding der algemeene plantenkunde. 1855. I. 89.
Rynkler. L'arpentage des forêts est-il nécessaire. 1872. IV. 243.
— Ist die Vermessung der Waldungen . . . nothwendig? 1872. IV. 243.
Ryshkof, V. *See* РЫШКОВЪ, B.
Ryssel, Carl Heinrich. Schraube zum Sprengen von Baumstöcken. 1880. IV. 387.[1]
Rysselberghe, Fr. van. Réaction osmotique des cellules. 1898. I. 150.[5]
Rywosch, Solom. Einiges über ein in den grünen Zellen vorkommendes Oel. 1897. I. 186.
— Ueber Harzgänge im Centralcylinder zweiblättriger Pinus-Arten. 1895. II. 40.[1]
— Ueber das Vorkommen von Lacunen bei den Gymnospermen. 1895. II. 1.
Rzacynski, Gabriel. Auctuarium historiae naturalis curiosae regni Poloniae. 1721. I. 359.
— Historia naturalis curiosa Poloniae. 1721. I. 359, 531.[2]
Rzecz o Modrzewiach. *See* B., M. 1851. IV. 452.[1]
Rzehak, A. Die Ahorne und ihre Verbreitung auf der Erdoberfläche. 1887. IV. 526.[2]
— Eine aussterbende europäische Fichte. 1892. IV. 460.[2]
— Die geognostischen Verhältnisse Mährens. 1885. IV. 87.[1]
— Die Vertheilung des Waldes in Europa. 1886. IV. 342.[1]
— Der Wald in Australien. 1890. IV. 380.[1]
— Die Waldverhältnisse Nordamerikas. 1887. IV. 337.[1]
Rzehak, J. Die Drathriese. 1863. IV. 391.
— Zur Vorverjüngung. 1875. IV. 139.[2]

— **s.** Over Clerodendron R. Br. 1853. III. 696.[1]
— **S.** Waldschutz und Schutzwald. 1874. IV. 181.[1]
S. Anfertigung von Reliefkarten. 1890. IV. 265.
S. Angabe einer uralten Fichte. 1843. II. 37.[1]
S. Aralia spinosa. 1888. II. 648.[1]
S. Beispiele alter Linden. 1843. II. 516.
S. Bern. Grosse Waldbäume. 1897. II. 24.[2]
S. British forestry; thinning. 1893. IV. 174.
S. Le budget des forêts. 1887. IV. 292.
S. Californische Reuzen-pijn. 1854. II. 50.[2]
S. La catastrofe de Saint-Gervais. 1892. IV. 547.[2]
S. Choisya ternata. 1877. III. 496.[1]
S. Conflicting forestry schools. 1894. IV. 102.
S. Croton Prince of Wales. 1878. III. 515.[2]
S. Ueber die Dauer des Eichen- und Lärchenholzes. 1860. IV. 452,[1] 514.[1]
S. Aus dem Eichenschälwalde. 1895. IV. 513.
S. Over de enting van Glycine sinensis. 1853. III. 490.[1]
S. Die Erkennung der Laubhölzer. 1891. IV. 84.[1]
S. De Eucalyptus globulus. 1875. III. 634.[2]
S. L'évolution en forêt, l'Épicéa pleureur et l'Épicéa de Sibérie. 1895. II. 34,[1] IV. 452.[2]
S. Die Excursion in die Forste von Eger. 1851. IV. 350,[2] 370.

S. Die Forstgrenzen. 1890. IV. 287.
S. Haben Waldabtrieb . . . Einfluss auf Gewitter- und Windzüge? 1854. IV. 52.
S. Holzpreise in Baselland. 1854. IV. 406.[1]
S. Iets over den aanplant van Koffie boomen. 1889. III. 734.[3]
S. Iets over het afleggen van Eikenloten. 1852. IV. 504.
S. Imprägnier-Anstalten. 1891. IV. 421.
S. Zur Kultur der Weiss-Tanne. 1831. IV. 444.[1]
S. The Locust tree. 1878. IV. 524.[1]
S. Zur Naturgeschichte der Buche. 1864. II. 127.[1]
S. Notes from the Pinetum. 1858. III. 289.
S. The Pinetum at West Chester. 1893. I. 39.[1]
S. Polygala Chamaebusus purpurea. 1878. III. 514.[1]
S. Rechtzeitige Holzabfuhr. 1890. IV. 388.[2]
S. Schizophragma hydrangeoides. 1888. III. 415.[2]
S. Silhouettes alpestres. 1894. IV. 129.—1895. IV. 170.
S. Eine starke Eiche. 1862. II. 138.[1]
S. De la stratification des greffes. 1892. III. 163.[1]
S. Substitutes for Boxwood. 1879. IV. 427.[1]
S. The Sumachs. 1889. III. 526.[1]
S. Uralter Taxusbaum. 1843. II. 10.[2]
S. Variétés de l'Épicéa commun. 1895. IV. 452.[2]
S. Die weissrindige Kiefer. 1892. IV. 464.[2]
S. Der Wildstand in den thüringischen Staaten. 1898. IV. 136.[2]
S. Willow Oak. 1878. II. 136.[1]
S. Die winterharten Eriken. 1899. III. 650.[2]
S., (*Oberförster*). Behandlung von Windwurf-, Brand- und Raupenfrassflächen. 1891. IV. 382.[1]
S., (*Oberförster*). Die Entwickelung der Durchforstungslehre in neuerer Zeit. 1891. IV. 174.
S., (*Oberförster*). Welche Form empfiehlt sich für die Anlegung des Kontrollbuches? 1890. IV. 245.
S., A. Cedry prawdziwe i tak zwane cedry. 1889. III. 291.
S., A. Encore les tarifs. 1895. IV. 219.
S., A. Estaciones de experimentos forestales. 1885. IV. 541.[1]
S., A. Estaciones forestales. 1884. IV. 37.[2]
S., A. Flowering of Strobolanthes [*sic*] in Jaunsar. 1896. II. 803.[2]
S., A. Influencia de la composicion química del suelo en la vegetation del Castaño. 1884. IV. 492.[1]
S., A. Inundaciones? 1885. IV. 186.[1]
S., A. O owocach wyrastających z pnia. 1889. II. 349.[2]
S., A. Temperatura del árbol. 1885. IV. 73.[1]
S., B. Transplanting without balls of earth. 1878. III. 166.
S., C. Fuchsia splendens. 1879. III. 640.[2]
S., C. B. Seaside planting. 1881. III. 41.[2]
S., C. F. W. Bemerkungen über verschiedene Gegenstände der praktischen Forstwissenschaft. 1792. IV. 100,[1] 116.
S., C. S. *See* SARGENT, C. S.
S., D. De l'utilité de la Ronce. 1848. III. 457.[1]
S., E. -Abelias. 1898. III. 748.[1]
S., E. The Common Beech and its varieties. 1899. III. 360.[2]
S., E. The Crataegus (Thorns). 1898. III. 423.[1]
S., E. Cupressus macrocarpa lutea. 1897. III. 302.[2]
S., E. The Elaeagnus. 1899. III. 628.[1]
S., E. Forsythias. 1899. III. 671.[2]
S., E. Genista sagittalis. 1900. III. 477.[1]
S., E. Lycium afrum. 1899. III. 700.[2]
S., E. Pernettyas. 1900. III. 653.[2]
S., E. Varieties of Cedrus Deodara. 1898. III. 300.[1]
S., F. De oorzaken van den verkorten levensduur onzer vruchtboomen. 1876. I. 248.[2]
S., F. van. Den verstandighen hovenier. *See* STERBEECK, Francis van. 1667. III. 106.[1]
S., F. I. Osservazioni sullo schema di legge forestale. *See* STECCHETTI, F. I. 1869. IV. 328.
S., G. Les forêts de la Corse. 1882. IV. 361.
S., H. Proeftuinen met groene bemesting. 1900. III. 734.[1]
S., H. System of manuring and settling timber in Siam. 1896. IV. 229.
S., H. Too much fire-protection in Burma. 1896. IV. 184.[1]
S., H. Zickte in de Cacao. 1899. III. 593.[2]
S., H. W. Vegetabilium omnium generum icones. 1736. V. XIII.[1]
S., I. F. Catechismo forestale. 1879. IV. 109.[2]
S., J. Der Ankauf der Herrschaft Nadwórna in Galizien. 1891. IV. 369.

S., J. La commission de réorganisation de l'École forestière. 1886. IV. 34.²
S., J. Early-flowering shrubs. 1884. III. 207.³
S., J. Evergreens; transplanting and propagating. 1884. III. 169.¹
S., J. Garrya elliptica. 1877. III. 352.³
S., J. The Himala an Spruce Fir. 1864. III. 306.¹
S., J. How shouldywe top trees? 1874. III. 173.¹
S., J. Kurzer Beytrag zu einer jüngst herausgekommenen ... Forsthaushaltung. 1785. IV. 95.
S., J. Luculia gratissima. 1873. · III. 745.²
S., J. Oesterreichische Forst-, Jagd- und Torf-Statistik. 1897. IV. 368.
S., J. Open situations best for Conifers. 1877. III. 292.
S., J. The Pine tree region in Britain. 1900. IV. 121.
S., J. Pyrus floribunda. 1882. III. 429.¹
S., J. Rami czyli Pokrzywa chińska. 1890. III. 381.²
S., J. Sturmschaden durch eine Windhose. 1882. IV. 189.²
S., J. C. & Carleson, Edvard. Om bevarande af Citroner från förruttnelse. 1748. III. 502.²
S., J. C. von. Ökonomisches Bedenken von dem Nachtheile der Gehaue in ... schwarzen Hölzern. See SCHÜTZ, J. C. von. 1757. IV. 116.
S., J. L. Analyse du suc de Manioc amer. 1871. III. 521.¹
S., J. L. Empoisonnement par les semences de Laburnum. 1869. III. 481.¹
S., J. M. Z borów jodłowych (na podgórzu Karpat). 1899. IV. 370.
S., L. Gomme arabique dans le Soudan. 1871. III. 463.¹
S., L. G. F. Beyträge zur Geschichte der Wurmtrockniss. See SCHUSTER, L. G. F. 1787. IV. 203.
S., M. (Prof.). Notizie sull' uso dei vasi ad irrigazione sotterranea. 1898. III. 151.
S., P. Corrispondenza [concernente . . . disboscamento]. 1882. IV. 48.¹
S., P. See also C., H.
S., P. L. The Caper bush. 1884. III. 409.¹
S., P. L. West Indian medicinal plants. 1871. III. 755.¹
S., R. Acclimatisation. 1861. III. 43.
S., R. Die Kampferwaldungen auf den Hochgebirgen von Formosa. 1899. IV. 528.²
S., R. Reflexions sur l'acclimatation. 1861. III. 43.
S., R. The Sugar Maple in flower. 1891. III. 536.²
S., R. Wood wax: 1894. II. 361.¹
S., T. Cordyline (Dracaena) australis in Devonshire. 1876. III. 334.²
S., T. A. On transplanting evergreens. 1848. III. 294.²
S., T. K. Anbau der natürlichen Ordnung Ericeae. 1833. III. 646.²
S., T. K. Culture of the natural order Ericeae. 1833. III. 646.²
S., T. W. Notice respecting an Oak tree struck by lightning. 1829. · IV. 193.²
S., W. The Crack Willow. 1885. III. 359.¹
S., W. Leichte Vermehrung von Clematis azurea. 1853. III. 390.²
S., W. Mangroves at the Royal botanic society's garden. 1884. III. 695.²
S., W. Propagation of plants by cuttings. 1860. III. 158.
S., W. A ramble with our poets amongst forest trees. 1879. I. 511.
S., W. G. Ancient resuscitated Yew. 1877. II. 11.¹
S., W. G. Cwm Hir Abbey, Radnorshire. 1895. I. 526.²
S., W. G. Destruction of the Holt Elm. 1885. II. 143.²
S., W. G. A disease of ornamental Conifers. 1899. III. 295.²
S., W. G. Diseased Palm roots. 1875. III. 318.¹
S., Z. Bambus. 1897. III. 315.²
S., Z. Palma daktylowa o czarnych owocaeb. 1897. II. 73.²
S., Z. Palma morska a dziworzesznia seszelska. 1895. II. 71.¹
S., Z. Walka o byt pośród drzew dzikich. 1895. I. 243.²
S. E. Salandra e la "festa degli alberi." 1899. IV. 423.²
Til S. T. Magistraten, angaaende den dyre Tid paa Brændet. 1797. IV. 282.¹
S. v. d. O. Iets over het uitrooijen van akkermaalsbosschen. 1854. IV. 505.
S—n. Aufforstungen in Hannover. 1891. IV. 159.
S—n. Die Baum- und Stockrode-Riesenmaschine. 1891. IV. 387.¹
S-r. Om Hegnplanter og Hegnplantning. 1844. III. 213.
Saage, Martin Joseph. Catalogus plantarum phanerogamarum circa Brunsbergam. 1846. I. 381.

Saalborn, (Oberförster). Aphoristische Bemerkungen über die Kultur . . . der Eiche. 1878. IV. 507.
— Die Aufforstung der Oedländereien. 1877. IV. 155.¹
— Bericht über die Leistungen und Fortschritte im Waldbau für . . . 1879–88. 1889. IV. 2.
— Ueber einige Kulturmethoden. 1859. IV. 141.
— Ueber die Ermittelung der forstwirthschaftlichen Bodenbenutzung. 1879. IV. 256.
— Wie weit soll sich der Einfluss des Staates auf die Bewirthschaftung der Privatwaldungen erstrecken? 1879. IV. 286.¹
Saárossy-Kapeller, Ferencz. Az erdőtörvény (1879. évi XXXI. t. cz.) magyarázata. 1883. IV. 331.²
Saat der Ulme. 1833. IV. 518.³
Die Saat gekeimter und ungekeimter Eicheln. 1853. IV. 504.
Saat oder Pflanzung. 1854. IV. 141.
Saat oder Pflanzung.—Aus den Papieren eines alten Forstmannes. 1853. IV. 141.
Sabarthez, Henri. Étude physiologique du café. 1870. III. 742.¹
Sabaté, J. Destruction du phylloxéra. 1877. III. 760.
— Sur la destruction du phylloxera. 1876. III. 569.¹
— Résultats obtenus par la décortication des ceps. 1876. III. 569.²
— Traitement des Vignes phylloxérées. 1882. III. 761.
· Sabatier, E. See DIRICQ, Jules & SABATIER, E.
Sabatier, J. See BELLOT DES MINIÈRES & SABATIER, J.
Sabbati, Liberato. Collectio plantarum, quae in solo romano. 1745. I. 424.
— Synopsis plantarum quae in solo romano. 1745. I. 424.
Sabicù wood. 1887. IV. 521.²
Sabin, A. C. Raspberries and Blackberries. 1889. III. 457.²
Sabin, Henry. Ornamentation . . . of school grounds. 1897. III. 32.¹
La Sabina si sveglia ed agisce. 1896. IV. 448.²
Sabine, Joseph. Account of a newly produced hybrid Passiflora. 1822. II. 577.³
— Account of some remarkable Holly hedges. 1830. II. 463.²
— Account of the Rosa Banksiae. 1822. III. 454.²
— An account of two varieties of the Mango. 1826. III. 524.²
— On the Ayrshire Rose. 1822. II. 298.²
— Description . . . of the varieties of double Scotch Roses. 1822. III. 457.¹
— On Glycine sinensis. 1826. III. 490.²
— Notes on . . . Magnolia glauca. 1820. III. 399.²
— Notice respecting a native British Rose. 1837. II. 293.¹
— Observations on . . . ringing the bark. 1822. III. 174.²
— On the Paeonia Moutan. 1826. III. 392.¹
— Some account of the edible fruits of Sierra Leone. 1824. III. 290.²
— Some account of the purple-fruited Passion flower. 1820. III. 615.¹
Sabine, Lorenzo. Forest lands and timber trade of Maine. 1844. · IV. 403.¹
Sabini, Caterino. Trattato generale sui boschi. 1844. IV. 253.
Sablon, Mathieu LECLERC DU. See LECLERC DU SABLON, Mathieu.
Sabonadière, William A. Coffee. 1887. III. 728.²
— The Coffee planter of Ceylon. 1866. III. 732.¹
— O fazendeiro de Café em Ceilão. 1866. III. 732.¹
Le sabotier ardennais. 1896. IV. 428.²
Sabransky, Heinrich. Zur Batographie Niederösterreichs. 1887. II. 304.¹
— Batographische Miscellaneen. 1889. II. 300.¹
— Beiträge zur Brombeerenflora der Kleinen Karpathen. 1886. II. 304.²
— Ein Beitrag zur Kenntniss der mährischen Brombeerenflora. 1889. II. 304.²
— Zur Kenntniss des Rubus Pseudoradula. 1886. II. 309.¹
— Eine neue Brombeere der kleinen Karpathen. 1886. II. 309.²
— Ueber eine neue Brombeere der kleinen Karpathen. 1887. II. 307.¹
— Pozsony környékének Rózsái. 1886. II. 288.¹
— Ueber Rubus nigroviridis. 1891. II. 309.¹
— Zur Rubusflora Bosniens. 1887. II. 304.¹
— Weitere Beiträge zur Brombeerenflora der Kleinen Karpathen. 1891. II. 304.¹
— Zwei westungarische Brombeeren. 1886. II. 304.²

Sacc. Note sur un hybride des Cereus. 1847. ·III. 620.²
— Rhipsalis Swarzii portant des rudiments floraux. 1846. II. 599.¹
Sacc. El Árbol del sebo. 1888. III. 353.¹
— Le Cereus lumbricoides. 1865. III. 626.¹
Sacc. Chimie du sol. 1894. III. 37.¹
Sacc, (*Dr., Wesserling*). Culture et usage de l'Oranger du Japan. 1859. III. 502.¹
— De la gomme adragante. 1857. III. 467.²
Sacc, Frédéric. Sur la composition de la graine du Cotonnier en arbre. 1884. III. 587.²
— Étude chimique de divers produits de l'Uruguay. 1882. III. 371,¹ *404.²*
— Des fonctions de l'acide pectique. 1846. I. 180.¹ .
— Sur un nouveau principe immédiat extrait du cachou. 1861. III. 464.¹
— Sur les résines. 1870. III. 227.
Saccardo, Andrea. Il Montello. 1894. IV. 277.
— Le strade in costruzione nell' ex bosco del Montello. 1895. IV. 389.
Saccardo, Pietro Andrea (Pierandrea). La botanica in Italia. 1895. I. 4.\
— Chromotaxia. 1891. I. 71.
— Sulla introduzione dell' Ailantus. 1890. III. 507.¹
— L' Orto botanico di Padova. 1895. I. 64.
— Prospetto della flora trevigiana. 1864. I. 427.
— Sopra un ragguardevole individuo di Sterculia. 1886. II. 538.²
— Della storia ... della flora venata sommario. 1869. I. 428.
— Il Viscum laxum B. & R. in Italia. 1879. II. 180.²
— *See also* VISIANI, Roberto de & SACCARDO, P. A.
Sacchéro, Giacomo. Importanza di taluni Eucalyptus. 1868. IV. 529.²
— Utilità dell' Eucalyptus globulus. 1868. IV. 532.²
Sacconi, Agostino. Ristretto delle piante. 1697. I. ·288.
Sach, Johann Heinrich Karl. Deutschlands wilde Gewächse. 1804. I. 375.
Sacher, Josef. Der Eichelsaatstecher. 1885. IV. 511.
Sachs, Carl. Aus den Llanos. 1879. I. 338.¹ -·.
Sachs, Ferdinand Gustav Julius von. Sur l'activité de l'assimilation dans les feuilles. 1884. I. 176.
— Apparition et dissolution de l'amidou. 1884. I. 176.
— Ein Beitrag zur Kenntniss der Ernährungsthätigkeit der Blätter. 1884. I. 176. — 1888. I. 174.
— Ein Beitrag zur Kenntniss des aufsteigenden Saftstroms. 1882. I. 165.
— Beobachtungen . . . über den absteigenden Saft. 1862. I. 164.
— Sur la chlorophylle incolore. 1859. I. 141.
— Über die Durchleuchtung der Pflanzentheile. 1861. I. 229.
— Ueber den Einfluss der Lufttemperatur ... auf die ... Aenderungen des Längenwachsthums. 1874. I. 191.¹
— Erfahrungen über die Behandlung chlorotischer Gartenpflanzen. 1888. III. 181.¹
— Gesammelte Abhandlungen über Pflanzen-Physiologie. 1892. I. 147.
— Geschichte der Botanik. 1875. I. 79,² V. x.¹
— Über die gesetzmässige Stellung der Nebenwurzeln. 1858. I. 103.
— Grundzüge der Pflanzen-Physiologie. ; 1873. I. 148.
— Handbuch der Experimental-Physiologie. 1865· I. 148, 525; *see also* HOFMEISTER, Wilhelm. 1865. I. 90.
— Histoire de la botanique. 1875. V. x.¹
— History of botany. 1875. I. 79.³
— Zur Keimungsgeschichte der Dattel. 1862. II. 73.¹·
— Längenwachsthum der Ober- und Unterseite ... sich aufwärts krümmender Sprosse. 1874. I. 194.
— Lectures on the physiology of plants. 1882. I. 148.
— Lehrbuch der Botanik. 1868. I. 91.
— Sur la limite supérieure de la température. 1864. I. 232.¹
— O nemoci Vinných kеřů. 1855. III. 576.
— Notiz über Schlingpflanzen. 1882. I. 196.²
— Ueber die obere Temperatur-Gränze der Vegetation. 1864. I. 232.¹
— Ueber orthotrope und plagiotrope Pflanzentheile. 1882. I. 194.
— Palmy. 1855. II. 60.³
— Physiologie végétale. 1865. I. 148.
— Physiologische Mittheilungen verschiedenen Inhaltes, V. 1860. IV. 412.¹
— Physiologische Untersuchungen über die Abhängigkeit der Keimung von der Temperatur. 1860. I. 203.

—.Ueber die Porosität des Holzes. 1877· I. 125.
— Ueber die Porosität des Holzes. 1882. IV. 412.¹
— Quellungserscheinungen an Hölzern. 1860. IV. 412.¹
— Sosny. 1854. II. 15.¹
— Stoff und Form der Pflanzenorgane. 1882. I. 100,¹ *194.*
— Studien über das Längenwachsthum der Wurzeln. 1872. I. 188.
— Text-book of botany. 1868. I. 91.
— Traité de botanique. 1868. I. 91.
— Über das Vergeilen. 1862. III. 181.¹
— Ueber das Vorhandensein eines farblosen Chlorophyll-Chromogens. 1859. I. 141.
— Vorlesungen über Pflanzen-Physiologie. 1882. I. 148.
— Ueber das Wachsthum der Haupt- und Nebenwurzeln. 1874. I. 188.
— Ueber die Wasserbewegung im Holz. 1888. I. 166, *IV. 412.*
— Ueber Zellenanordnung und Wachsthum. 1882. I. 125, *190.¹*
— O zrůstu stromových kmenů. 1854. I. 124.
— *See also* САХС, Ю. Д.
Sachs, J. Oesterreichisch-ungarischer Fassdaubenverkehr. 1897. IV. 427.³
— Oesterreichs Auslandsverkehr in Walderzeugnissen. 1897. IV. 407.³
— Oesterreich-Ungarns Auslandsverkehr in Walderzeugnissen. 1897. IV. 407.¹ — 1898. IV. 407.¹
— Oesterreich-Ungarns Holzhandel. 1897. IV. 407.¹
— Ungarns Auslandsverkehr in Wild und Walderzeugnissen. 1897. IV. 407.¹
— Ungarns Holzhandel. 1897. IV. 407.¹
Sachs von Lewenheimb, Philipp Jakob. Ἀμπελογραφία; sive, Vitis viniferae . . . consideratio. 1661. II. 508.²
Sachse. Draht-Spriegelzäune. 1879. IV. 146.²
Sachse, Karl Traugott. Beobachtungen über die . . . Vegetationsverhältnisse des Dresdner Elbthales. 1853. I. 224.²
— Zur Pflanzengeographie des Erzgebirges. 1855. I. 383.
Sachsen. *See* SAXONY.
Sachsens Forstorganisation. 1865. IV. 291.¹
Sachsse, R. Ueber die Proteïnkrystalloïde von Bertholletia. 1876. III. 631.³
— Ueber das **Xanthophyll.** 1876. I. 141.
Sachtleben, Johann Heinrich. L'art d'économiser le bois. 1792. IV. 280.¹
Sack. Die alten . . . Bäume in Braunschweig. 1866. I. 296.¹
Sack, Albert, *Baron* von. Beschreibung einer Reise nach Surinam. 1821. III. 268.¹
Sacken, Friedrich OSTEN-, *Baron* von. *See* OSTEN-SACKEN, Friedrich, *Baron* von & RUPRECHT, F. J.
Sackl, Joseph Anton. Praktische Anleitung, dem Weinstock den höchsten Ertrag abzugewinnen. 1839. III. 558.¹
Sacleux, Ch. Essai de catalogue des plantes de Zanzibar. 18 . . ? I. 536.¹
Sacleux, R. P. Note sur un Arduina à fleurs tétramères. 1893. II. 724.³
Sacramento, Fr. Leandro do. Memoria economica sobre a plantação . . . do Chá. 1825. III. 601.¹
Sacramento, P. L. de. Nova plantarum genera e Brasilia. 1821. I. 341.
The **sacred** Olive-tree of Blidah. 1890. II. 713.³
Sacred tree of Kum-Bum. 1896. II. 715.³
Sada, A. Flore médicale. 1891. III. 92.¹
— Liste des principales plantes dont on se sert généralement dans l'Inde. 1892. III. 92.¹
— Melia Azadirach. 1892. III. 512.²
— Melia Azadirachta. 1892. III. 513.¹
— Pandanus odoratissimus. 1892. III. 313.²
— Tinospora cordifolia. 1893. III. 397.¹
Sadebeck, Richard Emil Benjamin. Ueber das Auftreten und die Verbreitung einiger Pflanzenkrankheiten. 1895. IV. 212.
— Einige bisher weniger bekannte Rohstoffe. 1886. III. 281.¹
— Ueber die in den europäischen Handel gelangenden Ebenhölzer. 1887. IV. 396,³ *584.²*
— Zur Frage über Nag-Kassar von Mesua ferrea. 1889. II. 557.²
— Die Heterotrophie der Cupuliferen. 1885. IV. 73.³
— Kritische Untersuchungen über die durch Taphrina-Arten hervorgebrachten Baumkrankheiten. 1891. III. 194.
— Die Kulturgewächse der deutschen Kolonien. 1899. III. 53.
— De montium intra Vistritium et Nissam . . . flora. 1864. I. 385.

— Morphologisches Verhalten gefüllter Kirschblüthen. 1876. II. 272.[1]
— Neutre Untersuchungen über einige Krankheitsformen von Alnus. 1888. IV. 488.[2]
— Ostafrikanischen Nutzpflanzen und Colonialproducte. 1889. III. 281.[3]
— Die parasitischen Exoasceen. 1893. III. 195.[1]
— Ueber die durch Pilzangriffe hervorgebrachten maserähnlichen Zeichnungen. 1889. I. 126.
— Über die Samen von Raphia vinifera. 1886. III. 330.[2]
— Über die Seehöhen der Pflanzen im schlesischen Riesenbirge. 1865. I. 385.
— Die tropischen Nutzpflanzen Ostafrikas. 1891. III. 131.[2]
— Untersuchungen über die Pilzgattung Exoascus. 1884. III. 194.
— Die wichtigeren Nutzpflanzen. 1897. III. 53.
— Ueber wohlriechende Antheren der Clusiaceen. 1888. III. 610.[1]
Sadhu Singh, Bhai. See Bhai Sadhu Singh.
Sadler, John. Botanical trip to Ben Nevis. 1877. I. 403.
— On the flowering of Yucca gloriosa. 1883. III. 340.[2]
— Narrative of a ramble . . . on the Moffat Hills. 1857. I. 533.
— Notes on the healing of wounds in Acer. 1873. I. 207,[2] III. 536.[1]
— Notice of a new Alpine Willow. 1874. II. 109.[2]
— Notice of Salix Sadleri. 1874. II. 109.[1]
— On a peculiarly branching Silver Fir. 1883. II. 23.[1]
— Remarks on the bursting of the spathe of Palms. 1863. II. 64.
— I. Report on temperatures and open-air vegetation. 1882. III. 47.
— Report on temperatures during the winter of 1880–81. 1882. III. 47.
— Silver Fir at Conishead Priory. 1883. II. 24.[1]
— See also Balfour, J. H. & Sadler, John.
— & Bell, William. Notes in reference to the bursting of the spathe of Seaforthia. 1862. II. 64.[1] — 1863. II. 63.[2]
Sadler, Joseph. Flora comitatus pestinensis. 1825. I. 445.
— Verzeichniss der um Pesth und Ofen wildwachsenden . . . Gewächse. 1818. I. 445.
Sadler, Michael. Specimen inaugurale sistens synopsin Salicum Hungariae. 1831. II. 102.[2]
Sadler, Samuel C. On the Palm trees of Old Calabar. 1868. III. 319.[1]
Sadovostva . . . See Садоводства . . .
Sächsische Akademie für Forst- und Landwirthe zu Tharandt. See Königlich sächsische . . . I. 13.
Sächsische Gesellschaft der Wissenschaften. See Königlich sächsische . . . I. 13.
Sächsische Obstbau-Zeitung. III. 13.
Sächsische Pharmakopöe. See Pharmacopoea saxonica. 1820. III. 248.
Die sächsische Staatsforstverwaltung im Jahre 1884. 1885. IV. 261.[1]
Ueber den sächsischen Forstdienst. 1863. IV. 291.[1]
Sächsischer Forst . . . Kalender. See Zwickauer Forst . . . IV. 12.[1]
Sächsischer Forstverein. Bericht. IV. 10. — Festgabe. IV. 11.
Sägespäne als Brennmaterial. 1806. IV. 431.[1]
Saelan, Theodor. Öfversigt af Finlands botaniska litteratur. 1867. I. 3.[2]
Saelan, Thiodolf. En bastard mellan Betula verrucosa och B. nana. 1886. II. 120.[1]
— Betula verrucosa × nana i Finland. 1886. II. 120.[1]
— En Ekstam funnen i Karislojo socken. 1891. II. 136.[1]
— Om en i Finland förekommande . . . Tilia. 1880. II. 5[1]5.
— För Finland nya barlast- och ruderatväxter. 1888. II. 387.[1]
— Fruktbärande blodbok vid Fagervik. 1896. II. 127.[2]
— Om ett fynd af Picea Pichta (Loud.) i Finland. 1876. II. 25.[1]
— Hybrider emellan Salix phylicifolia och S. nigricans. 1881. II. 109.[1]
— Om kottarna af Larix sibirica. 1878. II. 33.[3]
— Kultur af Juglans regia i Finland. 1881. III. 355.
— Märkvärdiga Salix-former från Finland. 1893. II. 101.[1]
— Mellanform mellan Picea excelsa f. viminalis och f. virgata. 1891. II. 35.[1]
— Monströsa Salixformer. 1871. II. 103.[3]
— Om odling af Juglans cinerea i Finland. 1879. III. 354.[1]
— Pinus Pichta i Mäntsälä, Finland. 1878. II. 25.[1]

— Salix phylicifolia × nigricans i Finland. 1881. II. 109.[1]
— Den sannolikt nordligaste lokalen för Ek. 1871. II. 136.[1]
— Om det sibiriska Lärkträdet. 1880. II. 33.[1]
— Sjukdom hos Granen. 1871. IV. 455.
— Skillnaden mellan Larix sibirica och Larix europaea. 1881. II. 32.[2]
— Svampsjukdom på Gran i Finland. 1872. IV. 456.
— En i toppen barrbärande Grankotte. 1871. II. 36.[1]
— Vinterns 1879–1880 inverkan på Koniferer. 1881. III. 44.[2]
— See also Nylander, Wilhelm & Saelan, Thiodolf.
— **Kihlman, A. O. & Hjelt, H.** Plantae vasculares. See Nylander, Wilhelm & Saelan, Thiodolf. 1859. I. 355.
Sällskapet pro fauna et flora fennica. Notiser. I. 10.
Saenz, Nicolás. Memoria sobre el cultivo del Cafeto. 1895. III. 729.[1]
Særlige Bestemmelser for Trærhateriale. 1895. IV. 425.[2]
Säulenförmige Kiefern. 1886. II. 46.[1]
Säve, Carl. Synopsis florae gothlandicae. See Wahlenberg, Göran. 1837. I. 253.
Ueber die Saft-Circulation in den Holzpflanzen. 1841. I. 163.
Sagard, F. G. Le grand voyage du pays des Hurons. 1632. III. 261.[1]
Sage, C. Edward. Analyse de cinq échantillons de Thé du Natal. 1898. III. 604.[1]
Sage, J. R. Influence of forests on rainfall. 1897. IV. 52.
— Shelter belts from the standpoint of lessened evaporation. 1895. III. 215.[2]
Sager. See Pertuis & Sager.
Sager, Arthur. Eine Wasserriese. 1895. IV. 390.[2]
Sageret, Augustin. Discussion sur l'existence des deux sèves. 1818. I. 163.
— Des fécondations étrangères. 182.? III. 50.[1]
— Moyen de restauration d'un mauvais bois. 1810. IV. 169.[2]
— Notice pomologique. 1830. III. 37,[2] 143.
— Notice sur quelques greffes présumées nouvelles. 1837. III. 160.
— Pomologie physiologique. 1830. III. 37,[2] 143.
— Questions: Y a-t-il possibilité d'exercer quelque influence sur la couleur et l'odeur les fleurs. 182.? I. 246.[2]
— Remarques sur la reprise des boutures. 1834. III. 157.
Saggio dei semi forestali. 1865. IV. 147.[1]
Saggio di una flora dell' agra urbinate. See Federici, Antonio & Serpieri, A. 187.? I. 226.[2]
Saggio sul Castagno d' India. See Canzoneri, Francesco. 1823. III. 537.[1]
Saggio sulla coltivazione de' Gelsi. 1840. III. 375.
Saggio sulla maniera d' impedire la confusione. See Viviani, Domenico. 1800. I. 253.[2]
Sághy, István. Japáni télálló Citromfa. 1900. III. 498.[1]
Sagnier, Henry. Cours d'horticulture fruitière et potagère. 1887. III. 144.
— Rapport sur la suite . . . relativement à la protection des oiseaux. 1895. IV. 544.[1]
— See also Barral, J. A. & Sagnier, Henry.
Sago. 1895. III. 327.[3]
Sago cultivation in North Borneo. 1894. III. 327.[2]
The Sago Palm. [Japan.] Scientific notes. 1864. III. 285.[1]
Sagorski, Ernst. Berichtigungen zur Flora von Thüringen. 1889. II. 179.[2]
— Einige Bemerkungen zur Bearbeitung der genera Hieracium. 1887. II. 284,[3] 302.[1]
— Einige neue Rubusformen aus Thüringen. 1887. II. 302.[1]
— Ergänzungen zu den Rosen von Thüringen. 1886. II. 284.[2]
— Floristische Mittheilungen. 1893. II. 291.[2]
— Neue Rosenformen aus Thüringen. 1885. II. 284.[1]
— Ein neuer Weiden-Bastard. 1897. II. 110.[1]
— Plantae criticae Thuringiae. 1888. I. 389.
— Ueber Rosa obovata und graveolens. 1886. II. 296.[1]
— Die Rosen der Flora von Naumburg a. / S. 1885. II. 284.[2]
— Die Rosen der Hohen Tatra. 1889. II. 288.[1]
— Zwei neue Rubusformen. 1894. II. 302.[1]
— & Schneider, Gustav. Flora der Central-karpathen. 1891. I. 446.
Sagot, Paul. Agriculture de la Guyane française. 1873. III. 118.[2]
— De l'Arbre à pain. 1872. III. 367.[1]
— Catalogue des plantes . . . de la Guyane française. 1880. I. 339.[2]
— De l'état sauvage et des résultats de la culture. 1865. I. 247.

Sagot, Paul (*continued*).
— Études sur la végétation des plantes potagères. 1860. III. 36.[1]
— Exploitation des forêts à la Guyane française. 1869. IV. 382.[2]
— Fruits comestibles de l'Afrique. 187.? III. 279.[2]
— Généralités sur la Guyane. 1873. I. 339.[3]
— Du Manioc. 1871. III. 521.[1]
— Manuel pratique des cultures tropicales. 1893. III. 96.[1]
— Note sur la variation . . . des graines dans les genres Mucuna et Dioclea. 1875. II. 355,[2] *373.[2]*
— Note sur le dimorphisme du fruit du Jubelina. 1879. II. 426.[2]
— Note sur un Clusia mâle. 1877. II. 554.[1]
— Observations sur les îles Canaries. 1865. III. 131.[2]
— Quelques souvenirs d'herborisation. 1871. I. 414.
— Remarques générales sur les plantes . . . à la Guyane. 1873. III. 118.[2]
— Remarques sur le Mélastomacées de la Guyane. 1883. II. 635.[1]
— Des végétaux fruitiers cultivés à la Guyane. 1872. III. 118.[2]
— Sur une Vigne sauvage à fleurs polygames. 1878. II. 505.[2]
— *See also* PÉREZ, Victor & SAGOT, Paul; RENAULT, Bernard & SAGOT, Paul.
Sagra, Ramón de la. Historia fisica, politica y natural de la isla de Cuba. 1842. IV. 341.[2]
— Icones plantarum in flora cubana. 1863. I. 336.
— Informe sobre el estado actual del jardin y de la catedra de botanica . . . de la Habana. 1825. I. 39.
— Investigaciones para enriquecer las fincas. 1841. III. 126.[1]
— Lettre relative à une exposition faite à Madrid des produits. 1866. I. 60.[1]
— Memorias para servir de introducción á la horticultura cubana. 1827. III. 99.
— Notice sur l'Ortie de la Chine. 1869. III. 382.[1]
— Nouvel acide extrait d'une plante mexicaine. 1856. III. 756.[1]
— Sur un Palmier présentant une subdivision remarquable au haut de sa tige. 1870. II. 72.[1]
— Principios fundamentales. 1824. V. x.[1]
— El problema de los bosques. 1854. IV. 276.[1]
— Le problème des forêts. 185.? IV. 43.
Sahlberg, J. R. Ett klot af tallbarr. 1893. I. 242.[2]
Sahlberg, John. Cecidomyia Strobi. 1890. IV. 457.
— Det förhärjande uppträdandet af Rhodites centifoliae. 1881. III. 453.[2]
— Gallbildningar på Ek. 1881. IV. 510.
— Notis om Salix myrtilloides. 1873. II. 108.[2]
— Rubus Idaeus med hvitgula frukter. 1888. II. 308.[1]
Sahlén, Anders Johan. Wenersborgs flora. 1854. I. 355.
Sahlin, Lars Eric. Afhandling om de wäxter som i Bibelen omtalas. *See* THUNBERG, C. P. 1828. I. 513.
Sahune, *baron* de. Du libre défrichement des bois. 1856. IV. 282.[2]
Sahut, F. G. Erythrina crista-galli L. 1856. III. 476.[1]
— Les Glycines. 1858. III. 490.[1]
Sahut, Félix. De l'acclimatation par sélection. 1898. III. 44.[4]
— De l'adaptation au sol dans la question des Vignes américaines. 1886. III. 556.
— De l'affinité spécifique entre le sujet et le greffon. 1885. I. 208.[2]
— Die amerikanischen Reben. 1885. III. 556.
— L'arboriculture et la viticulture aux États-Unis. 1897. III. 134.[1]
— Arbustes nouveaux pour 1873. 1873. III. 302,[2] *629,[2] 705.*
— La Bretagne et sa végétation arborescente. 1898. I. 404,[1] *III. 184.[2]*
— Le centenaire de la découverte des Eucalyptus. 1889. II. 623.[1]
— La circulation de la sève dans les plantes greffées. 1885. I. 208.[2]
— Compte rendu du Congrès viticole . . . à Bordeaux. 1896.
— Les conifères pluviomètres. 1900. IV. 73.[2]
— Considérations générales sur le greffage. 1885. . III. 165.
— La crise viticole. 1894. III. 557.[1]
— La culture fruitière aux États-Unis. 1893. I. 295,[2] *III. 134,[1] V. xvi.[1]*
— La défense du vin et la découverte du phylloxéra. 1900. III. 575.[1]
— L'École nationale d'horticulture de Versailles. 1897. III. 2.[1]

— Les effets du greffage. 1885. III. 165.
— Un épisode rétrospectif à propos de la découverte du phylloxera. 1899. III. 575.[1]
— Essai de destruction du puceron lanigère. 1865. III. 427.[2]
— Les Eucalyptus. 1888. IV. 530.
— Le greffage de la Vigne. 1890. III. 548.[2]
— Le greffage des Eucalyptus. 1894. III. 634.[1]
— Des greffes hétéroclites. 1885. III. 165.
— L'hiver à Montpellier. 1889. III. 49.[1]
— Influence des gelées tardives. 1894. III. 182.
— De l'influence directe du sujet sur le greffon. 1885. III. 40.
— Influence réflexe dù greffon sur le sujet. 1885. III. 40.
— Le lac Majeur et les îles Borromées. 1883. I. 429.
— Limites de la possibilité du greffage. 1885. III. 165.
— Liste des variétés de fruits . . . à cultiver dans la region de Montpellier. 1896. III. 85.
— La Normandie et sa végétation arborescente. 1897. III. 124.[2]
— Notes relatives à la reconstitution des vignobles. 1891. III. 557.[1]
— Poinciana Gilliesii Hooker. 1856. III. 469.[1]
— La pomologie aux États-Unis. 1899. III. 62.
— À propos du greffage des Eucalyptus. 1893. III. 634.[1]
— Quelles sont les méthodes de greffage de la Vigne. 1890. III. 548.[2]
— Quelques mots sur la conservation et la reconstitution des vignobles. 1887. III. 556.
— Rapport sur un ouvrage de M. Charles Naudin. 1885. III. 634.[1]
— Der rückwirkende Einfluss des Edelreises. 1885. III. 40.
— La taille de la Vigne dans le nœud. 1891. III. 549.[1]
— La taille herbacée des Vignes gelées. 1898. III. 549.[1]
— Traitement des Vignes gelées. 1891. III. 549.[2]
— Traitement des Vignes grêlées. 1893. III. 549.[2]
— La végétation dans le Limousin. 1892. III. 124.[2]
— La végétation en Australie. 1888. I. 504.
— Les végétaux considérés comme des thermomètres enregistreurs. 1891. III. 49.[1]
— *See also* BAZILLE, Gaston, PLANCHON, J. E. & SAHUT, Félix; ÉPRÉMESNIL, *comte* d' & SAHUT, Félix.
Sailer, Franz Seraphin. Flora der Linzergegend. 1844. I. 440.
— Die Flora Oberöstreichs. 1841. I. 440.
Saillard, D. Floraison du Cereus Napoleonis. 1852. III. 621.[1]
Sailly, de. Les conséquences d'une adjudication forestière à long terme. 1897. IV. 27.[2]
— Fors et coutumes du Béarn. 1897. IV. 27.[2]
— Onomastique forestière des Pyrénées. 1895. IV. 23.[2]
— Le périmètre du Rialsesse. 1896. IV. 164.[1]
Sailly, Paulus Franciscus de. Dissertatio inauguralis de manna. 1740. III. 221.[1]
Sainctelette. Note sur la maladie de la Vigne. 1854. III. 576.
Sainctyon, de. Les edicts et ordonnances des roys . . . jugemens notables des eaues et forets. 1610. IV. 323.[2]
Saint-Aignan, *comte* de. Nécessité de la conservation des forêts. 1867. IV. 275.
Saint-Amans, Jean Florimond Boudon de. Le bouquet du département de Lot-et-Garonne. 1821. I. 407.
— Flore agenaise. 1821. I. 407.
— Fragmens d'un voyage sentimental et pittoresque dans les Pyrénées. 1789. I. 406.
— Recherches sur la cause . . . de la maladie, qui détruit les arbres des promenades. 1789. III. 212.[1]
Saint André, Édouard. Recherches sur les causes qui permettent à la Vigne de résister aux attaques du phylloxera. 1881. III. 572.
St.-Ange, G. M. On Monesia. 1844. III. 667.[2]
Saint-Ange, Legros. De l'aliénation projetée des forêts de l'état. 1848. IV. 275.
— *See also* SÉGURET, S. & SAINT-ANGE, Legros.
Saint-Arroman, A. De l'action du café. 1845. III. 222.
— Coffee, tea and chocolate. 1845. III. 222.
Saint-Briac, J. de. L'arbre fruitier des jardins. 1884. III. 144.
Saint-Brody, Gustavus. The flora of Weston and its immediate neighbourhood. 1856. I. 400.
St. Christopher. 1888. III. 267.[1]
Saint-Claire Deville, Henri. Études sur l'essence de térébenthine. 1839. IV. 443.[1]

— Note sur les produits . . . de la résine galac. 1843. III. 494.²
— Note sur les propriétés d'élemi. 1841. I. 180.²
— Nouvelles recherches sur l'essence de térébenthine. 1841. IV. 443.¹
— Recherches sur la créosote. 1844. IV. 432.¹
— See also PELLETIER, J. J. & DEVILLE, H.
St. Denis. Du reboisement ou de la plantation des Pins. 1855. IV. 460.¹
Saint-Denys, Leon *Marquis* d'HERVEY. *See* HERVEY SAINT-DENYS, Leon *Marquis* d'.
Saint-Estienne, Claude. Nouvelle instruction pour connoistre les bons fruits. 1660. III. 142.
Saint Èvre, Édouard. Recherches chimiques sur les acides du beurre de coco. 1847. III. 594.
— Recherches sur l'huile essentielle de Sassafras. 1844. III. 408.¹ — 1846. III. 408.¹
— Untersuchung des Sassafrasöls. 1844. III. 408.¹
St.-Felix, A. J. M. de. Instruction pratique sur la culture forestière. 1840. IV. 109.¹
Saint-Gal. Le bouturage du Pommier. 1888. III. 426.²
Saint-Gal, Joseph. Flore des environs de Grand-Jouan. 1874. I. 414.
St. Gallen. Ueber die Lärchenminiermotte. 1889. IV. 451.
— Schaden durch Rehwild. 1900. IV. 197.¹
— Verheerungen des Trübbaches. 1896. IV. 187.²
Saint-Geniez, CLAVEL DE. *See* CLAVEL DE SAINT-GENIEZ.
St. Germain, J. J. de. Manuel des végétaux. 1784. I. 258.
Saint-Germain-en-Laye — Société d'horticulture. III. 22.
Saint-Hilaire, Augustin François César PROUVENSAL de, *called* August de. Account of a case of poisoning, caused by the honey of the Lecheguana wasp. 1824. III. 269.¹
— Aperçu d'un voyage dans l'intérieur du Brésil. 1822. I. 341.
— Botanical climatology. 1841. I. 222.²
— Caractères du genre Sida. 1826. II. 527.¹
— Comparaison de la végétation d'un pays en partie extratropical. 1850. I. 217, 342.
— Comparaison des genres Buttneria. 1825. II. 532,¹ 533.¹
— Conspectus Polygalaearum Brasiliae meridionalis. 1828. II. 429.²
— Description des principales espèces nouvelles de la flore du Brésil. 1823. I. 341.
— Description des principaux genres nouveaux . . . de la flore du Brésil. 1823. I. 341.
— Description du Metrodorea. 1825. II. 408.²
— Sur les fleurs de quelques genres de Sapindacées. 1828. II. 483.²
— Genres nouveaux de la flore du Brésil. 1824. II. 215.¹
— Histoire de l'indigo. 1837. III. 479.¹
— Histoire des plantes les plus remarquables du Brésil. 1824. I. 341.
Indication abrégée des plantes de la flore du Brésil. 1924. I. 341.
— Indication des plantes de la famille des Ménispermées. 1824. II. 206.²
— Sur un insecte qui ravage les Vignes du Bas-Langue-doc. 1837. . III. 562.²
— Leçons de botanique. 1840. I. 98.
— Lettre au sujet d'une notice lue à la Société royale. 1846. III. 43.
— Mémoire sur la nouvelle famille de Vochisiées. 1820. II. 428.²
— Mémoire sur la série linéaire des plantes polypétales. 1827. I. 251.
— Mémoire sur les Cucurbitacées et les Passiflorées. 1819. II. 575.²
— Mémoire sur les Cucurbitacées, les Passiflorées. 1823. II. 575.²
— Mémoire sur les Myrsinées, les Sapotées. 1836. II. 483,² 692.¹
— Mémoire sur les plantes auxquelles on attribue un placenta central libre. 1815. I. 117.²
— Note comparative des époques de la végétation. 1841. I. 222.²
— Note des principales espèces de Sida. 1826. II. 527.¹
— Note sur l'herbe du Paraguay. 1833. II. 464.²
— Note sur l'inflorescence extraaxillaire. 1825. II. 536.²
— Note sur l'origine du Manioc. 1833. III. 521.¹
— Note sur la patrie de l'Anona squamosa. 1825. II. 216.²
— Note sur le calice du genre Drymis. 1824. II. 209.¹
— Note sur le genre Malachra. 1826. II. 525.²
— Notice sur 70 espèces et quelques variétés de plantes . . . du Loiret. 1810. I. 407.

— Du nouveau genre Anaxagorea. 1825. II. 215.¹
— Observations sur l'inégalité des cotyledons dans le Sorocea. 1821. II. 155.²
— Observations sur la famille des Amaranthacées. 1833. II. 189.¹
— Observations sur la famille des Rutacées. 1823. II. 397.¹
— Observations sur le genre Anacardium. 1831. II. 455.¹
— Observations sur le genre Cuphea. 1833. II. 608.²
— Observations sur le genre Escallonia. 1833. II. 239.²
— Observations sur le Sauvagesia. 1817. II. 545.¹
— Observations sur les caractères du genre Melochia. 1825. II. 536.²
— Observations sur plusieurs genres . . . des Salicariées. 1834. II. 608.¹
— Ueber den Paraguaythee. 1833. III. 530.²
— Plantes usuelles des Brasiliens. 1824. III. 65.¹
— Premier . . . mémoire sur la structure . . . des Résédacées. 1833. II. 234.²
— Premier mémoire sur le gynobase. 1823. I. 117.²
— Relation d'un empoisonnement causé par le miel de la guêpe Lecheguana. 1824. III. 269.¹
— Tableau de la végétation . . . de Minas Geraes. 1831. I. 341.
— Tableau général d'un pays aurifère. 1847. I. 342.
— Tableau monographique des plantes de la flore du Brésil méridional. 1824. I. 341.
— Voyage dans l'intérieur du Brésil. 1850. I. 342.
— Voyage dans le district des Diamans. 1833. I. 341.
— Voyage dans les provinces de Rio de Janeiro. 1830. I. 341.
— Voyage dans les provinces de Saint-Paul. 1551. I. 342.
— **Jussieu,** Adrien de & **Cambessèdes,** Jacques. Flora Brasiliae meridionalis. 1825. I. 341.
— & **Moquin-Tandon,** Alfred. Mémoire sur la symétrie des Capparidées. 1830. II. 229.²
— — Premier [– deuxième] mémoire sur la famille des Polygalées. 1828. II. 429.²
— & **Tulasne,** L. R. Revue de la flore du Brésil méridional. 1842. I. 342.
Saint-Hilaire, Isidore GEOFFROY. Notions historiques sur les règnes de la nature. 1854. I. 79.¹
Saint-Hilaire, Jean Henri JAUME. *See* JAUME SAINT-HILAIRE, J. H.
St. Hubertus. IV. 11.
St. John, *Sir* Spenser B. Life in the forests of the Far East. 1862. I. 469,¹ III. 276.¹
— Notes on Borneo woods. 1863. IV. 39.²
St. Julien, Th. von MARILLAC. *See* MARILLAC ST. JULIEN, Th. von.
Saint-Lager, Jean. L'appétence chimique des plantes et la concurrence vitale. 1895. I. 229.
— Catalogues des plantes vasculaires de la flore du bassin du Rhône. 1883. I. 416.
— Un chapitre de grammaire à l'usage des botanistes. 1892. I. 254.¹
— Distribution géographique de l'Adenocarpos. 1884. II. 329.²
— Étude de l'influence chimique exercée par le sol. 1877. I. 228.¹
— Histoire des herbiers. 1885. I. 80.¹
— Notice sur la végétation de la forêt d'Arvières. 1876. I. 415.
— Les nouvelles flores de France. 1894. I. 3.²
— Nouvelles remarques sur la nomenclature botanique. 1881. I. 253.²
— La perfidie des homonymes. 188 . ? I. 253.²
— Plantes calcicoles et silicicoles. 1894. I. 229, 418.
— Priorité de l'Acer trilobatum. 1894. II. 478.²
— La priorité des noms de plantes. 1889. I. 254.¹
— Le procès de la nomenclature. 1886. I. 254.¹
— Quel est l'inventeur de la nomenclature binaire. 1883. I. 254,¹ V. xii.²
— Recherches historiques sur les mots " plante mâle et plante femelle." 1884. I. 529, V. xii.²
— Recherches sur les anciens herbaria. 1886. I. 80.¹
— Réforme de la nomenclature botanique. 1880. I. 253.²
— Rémarques historiques sur les mots plantes mâles et plantes femelles. 1884 V. xii.²
— La Vigne du Mont Ida et le Vaccinium. 1895. II. 509,¹ 685.¹
— *See also* CARIOT, Antoine & SAINT-LAGER, Jean; CONVERT & SAINT-LAGER, Jean; MÉHU, Adolphe, SAINT-LAGER, Jean & CUSIN, L.
St. Lazare, Pierre BERTHOLON DE. *See* BERTHOLON DE ST. LAZARE, Pierre.

Saint-Léger, L. Azalées de l'Inde. 1891. III. 656.
— Taille des arbustes à fleurs. 1892. III. 173.¹
— *See also* BELLAIR, Georges & SAINT-LÉGER, L.
St. Louis — Academy of science. *See* ACADEMY . . . I. 4.²
St. Louis lumberman. IV. 5.¹
Saint-Loup, Rémy. Expériences de M. Millardet sur l'hybridation. 1895. III. 51.
Saint Lucia — Botanical garden. *See* BOTANICAL . . . 1897. I. 39.
Saint-Marsal, GUIRAUD DE, *baron*. *See* GUIRAUD DE SAINT-MARSAL, *baron*.
St. Martin, Jacques Joseph JUGE DE. *See* JUGE DE ST. MARTIN, J. J.
Saint Martin, L. de. Recherches sur la santonine. 1872. III. 754.²
Saint-Maur, DUPRÉ DE. *See* DUPRÉ DE SAINT-MAUR.
Saint-Maurice, PELÉE DE. *See* PELÉE DE SAINT-MAURICE.
Saint Michel, MAURILLE DE. *See* MAURILLE DE SAINT MICHEL.
St. Moulin, Vincent Joseph de. Commentatio botanico-oeconomica de quibusdam arboribus. 1827. I. 293,¹ *III. 77, IV. 84.²*
— Monographia Quercus Roboris. 1828. II. 136.¹
St. Paul-Illaire, Ulrich, *Baron* von. Abies amabilis. 1881. II. 22.¹
— Befruchtung der Coniferenblüten. 1897. III. 294.²
— Berberis Thunbergii. 1899. II. 205.¹
— Bewurzelung von Zweigen. 1900. III. 297.¹
— Disanthus cercidifolia Maximowicz. 1900. II. 252.²
— Eine gelbbunte Pinus Laricio. 1900. III. 308.¹
— Neuere oder wenig verbreitete . . . Gehölze. 1895. III. 70.¹
— Die nordamerikanischen Eichen. 1900. III. 361.¹
— Notizen über einige . . . Gehölze. 1893. III. 70.
— Picea Breweriana Wats. 1895. III. 305.¹
— Pinus pyrenaica Lapeyrouse. 1897. III. 308.¹
— Rhododendron mucronulatum. 1898. II. 682.¹
— Schöne Herbstfärbungen. 1897. III. 207,¹ *207.³*
— Vergleichung der Temperatur-Verhältnisse von Europa und Nord-Amerika. 1880. IV. 483,¹ 538.³
— Zapfen von Pinus Jeffreyi. 1898. III. 307.³
St. Petersburg — Academia scientiarum imperialis petropolitana. *See* ACADEMIA . . . I. 9.¹
St. Petersburg — Académie impériale des sciences. *See* ACADEMIA SCIENTIARUM IMPERIALIS PETROPOLITANA. I. 9.¹
St. Petersburg — Congrès botanique et d'horticulture. *See* CONGRÈS . . . I. 9.²
St. Petersburg — Congrès international de botanique et d'horticulture. *See* CONGRÈS . . . I. 9.²
St. Petersburg — Freye oekonomische Gesellschaft. *See* FREYE . . . III. 10.¹
St.-Petersburg — Jardin impérial de botanique. Catalogue alphabétique et méthodique de dessins de plantes. *See* BERG, Ernst von. Catalogue . . . 1857. I. 2.
St. Petersburg — Kaiserliche freie ökonomische Gesellschaft. *See* KAISERLICHE . . . III. 10.¹
St.-Petersburger Kalender für das Jahr 1872. *See* HERDER, F. G. von. 1871. I. 222.³
S.-Peterburgskaya . . . *See* С.-Петербургская . . .
S.-Peterburgskii . . . *See* С.-Петербургскій . . .
S.-Peterburgskoye . . . *See* С.-Петербургское . . .
Saintpierre. *See* PLANCHON, J. E. & SAINTPIERRE.
Saintpierre, C. *See* PÉCHOLIER, G. & SAINTPIERRE, C.
Saint-Pierre, Camille & Magnien, Lucien. Recherches expérimentales sur la maturation du raisin. 1878. II. 508.²
— — Recherches sur les gaz . . . du Baguenaudier. 1876. II. 347.¹
Saint Pierre, E. Note relative à la présence du phylloxera. 1872. III. 565.¹
Saint-Pierre, Ernest GERMAIN DE. *See* GERMAIN DE SAINT-PIERRE, Ernest.
Saint Pierre, Jacques Henri Bernardin de. Botanical harmony delineated. 1797. I. 524.¹
— Voyage à l'Isle de France, à l'Isle de Bourbon. 1773. III. 279.¹
Saint-Pol, *vicomte* de. Enquête sur les cépages américains. 1891. III. 547.
Saint Preuve. Sur la conservation des bois. 1848. IV. 417.
— Note sur la conservation des bois par l'imbibition. 1845. IV. 417.
Saint Quentin. Sur le meilleur mode d'application du soufre. 1855. III. 576.
Saint-Quentin, A. de. Utilisation de l'Ailante. 1899. IV. 525.
Saint-Venan, J. de. Forêt de Boulogne. 1879. IV. 249.¹

Saint-Victor. Abbildung und Beschreibung einer ökonomischen Maschine. 1803. IV. 385.²
Saint-Victor, Gabriel de. Le Jardin botanique de Coïmbra. 1890. I. 60.³
— Parcs et forêts du Portugal. 1892. IV. 363.¹
— Portugal. 1892. III. 126.¹
— Rapport sur la culture des bois dans les montagnes du Forez. 1870. IV. 360.
— Rapport sur la culture forestière. 1876. IV. 360.
St. Vincent, Jean Baptiste George Marcellin BORY DE. *See* BORY DE ST. VINCENT, J. B. G. M.
Sainte Claire Deville, Charles Joseph. Sur les froids du 18 mai et des premiers jours de juin. 1871. III. 48.
Sainte-Fare, A. de. Conservation des glands. 1875. III. 361.²
— Un procédé économique de conservation des glands. 1875. III. 361.²
— Le régime forestier en Alsace-Lorraine. 1879. IV. 289.²
Sainte-Gertrude, G. GÉNEAU DE. *See* GÉNEAU DE SAINTE-GERTRUDE, G.
Saintini, E. N. La plante dans l'antiquité, légendes. 1897. I. 512.
Sainz de Andino, Eduardo ABELA Y. *See* ABELA Y SAINZ DE ANDINO, Eduardo.
Sainz de Baranda, José. La legislación de montes en Suiza. 1877. IV. 330.
— Memoria sobre la producción de los montes públicos de Filipinas. 1887. IV. 376.²
Sainz Gutierrez, Pedro. Memoria sobre la utilidad de los montes. 1862. IV. 43.
Sainz y Gutierrez, Luis. Compendio de arboricultura. 1871. II. 114.¹
Sairas, Hippolyte. Opinion sur l'article 1er du titre XI. de la loi sur les finances. 1817. IV. 325.
Saitz, A. Beschreibung der . . . Domäne Krumau. 1898. IV. 373.
— Popsáni velkostatku "Krumlova." 1898. IV. 373.
Saitz, August. Die landwirthschaftliche Benützung des Waldbodens. 1877. IV. 133.
Sajó, Karl. Die Akazien-Schildlaus. 1896. IV. 523.²
— Der Catalpabaum. 1896. IV. 538.¹
— Ueber Insektenfeinde von Pinus. 1895. IV. 462.¹
— Ueber Parkanlagen auf Flugsand. 1896. III. 41.²
— A Tisszafáról. 1899. IV. 440.²
— Valgus hemipterus L. im lebenden Akazienbaum. 1895. IV. 523.²
Sakellarios, Athanasios. *See* ΣΑΚΕΛΛΑΡΙΟΣ, Ἀθανάσιος.
Sakharof, v. *See* САХАРОВЪ, B.
Sakünlünski, Adolph SCHLAGINTWEIT-. *See* SCHLAGINTWEIT-SAKÜNLÜNSKI, Adolph.
Sakünlünski, Hermann von SCHLAGINTWEIT-. *See* SCHLAGINTWEIT-SAKÜNLÜNSKI, Hermann von.
Sal bark as a tanning material. 1889. III. 611.²
Sal timber in the Garo Hills. 1886. IV. 529.¹
Sala, Pedro PEREZ DE LA. *See* PEREZ DE LA SALA, Pedro.
Salaberry, Charles Marie d'Irumberry, *comte* de. Opinion sur l'aliénation des bois de l'état. 1817. IV. 325.
Saleroux, A. Nouveaux élémens d'histoire naturelle. 1835. I. 87.
Salamech Ben Cand Gadi (sectá) al Zalecchi. Hortus rerum mirabilium terrae et regionum. 1585. I. 282.
Salazar, Antonio. Proyecto de un taquímetro auto-reductor. 1898. IV. 551.²
— El taquímetro auto-reductor. 1898. IV. 551.²
Salberg, Johan Julius. Sätt at förwara, hwarjehanda träbyggnader från röta. 1742. IV. 416.³
Salberg, Johannes. Fructus esculenti. *See* LINNÉ, Carl von. 1763. III. 219.³
Saldanha, Luis de. Notas de viagem . . . ao Estreito de Magalhães. 1887. I. 347.
Saldanha da Gama, José de. Catalogue of the products of the Brazilian forests. 1876. IV. 19.¹
— Classement botanique des plantes alimentaires du Brésil. 1867. III. 269.¹
— Configuração e descripção . . . das principaes madeiras . . . da provincia do Rio de Janeiro. 1865. I. 343.
— Configuração e estudo botanico dos vegetaes seculares da provincia do Rio de Janeiro. 1865 (1872). I. 343. *III. 65.¹*
— Discours prononcé au Congrès international des économes forestiers à Vienne. 1874. IV. 342.¹
— Notes sur quelques arbres employés dans l'industrie brésilienne. 1874. IV. 78.³
— Notice sur quelques plantes utiles du Brésil. 1873. II. 791.¹

— Sur une nouvelle espèce d'Euphorbiacée. 1867. II. 435.²
— Quelques mots sur les bois du Brésil. 1867. IV. 19.¹
— Synonymia de diversos vegetaes do Brasil. 1868. I. 72.²
— Tableau résumé des richesses de l'empire du Brésil. 1887. III. 269.²
— Travaux au sujet des produits du Brésil . . . à l'Exposition universelle de Paris. 1867. III. 269,¹ IV. 19.¹
— & Cogniaux, Alfred. Bouquet de Mélastomacées brésiliennes. 1887. II. 635.¹
Salfeld, A. De ontginning der Nederlandsche heiden. 1890. IV. 119.²
Salictum woburnense. See FORBES, James. 1829. II. 98.²
De Salicum rosis fictis. See ALBRECHT, J. S. 1748. I. 517,¹ II. 104.²
Salies, d'ANOUILH DE. See ANOUILH DE SALIES, d'.
Salini, Luigi. Osservazioni teorico-pratiche sulla vendita de' tagli in piedi. 1864. IV. 388.¹
— Il Pino domestico. 1867. III. 308.²
Salis, Adolf von. De l'aménagement des eaux en Suisse. 1883. IV. 187.¹
— Das schweizerische Wasserbauwesen. 1883. IV. 187.¹
— Die Wildbachverbauung in der Schweiz. 1890. IV. 187.¹
Salis-Marschlins, Ulysses von. Aufzählung der in Korsika . . . bemerkten Cotyledonarpflanzen. 1833. I. 419.¹
Salisbury, Richard Anton. The characters of several genera in . . . Coniferae. 1807. II. 12.¹
— On the coniferous plants of Kaempfer. 1817. II. 15.²
— Description of a new genus . . . Rudgea. 1807. II. 830.²
— Description of Bauera rubiaefolia. 1805. II. 238.¹
— The generic characters in the English botany. 1806. I. 396.
— Icones stirpium rariorum. 1791. I. 264.
— An illustration of the genus Solandra. 1802. II. 774.²
— Observations on the perigynous insertion of the stamina of plants. 1807. I. 116.¹
— The paradisus londinensis. 1805. I. 53.
— Prodromus stirpium in horto ad Chapel Allerton. 1796. I. 53.
— A short account of nectarines and peaches. 1812. II. 276.¹
— Some account of the Chiogenes. 1818. III. 649.¹
— Some account of the Melidora pellucida. 1818. III. 649.¹
— Some remarks on the plants now referred to Sophora. 1808. II. 384.¹
— Species of Erica. 1802. II. 664.¹
Salisbury, William. The botanist's companion. 1816. I. 396.
— A catalogue of the Brompton botanic garden. 1803. I. 53.
— A catalogue of the London botanic garden. 1809. III. 28.²
— Hints addressed to proprietors of orchards. 1816. III. 142, 486.¹
— Hortus paddingtonensis. 1797. I. 53, 521.²
Salisch, Heinrich von. Ueber Anlegung von Waldwiesen. 1878. IV. 137.¹
— Beiträge zur Forstästhetik. 1881. IV. 55.²
— Die Beziehungen zwischen dem Schönen und dem Nützlichen im Forstwesen. 1892. IV. 55.²
— Einige Beiträge zur Forst-Aesthetik. 1876. IV. 55.²
— Erste Durchforstung eines Kiefernbestandes. 1898. IV. 474.
— Farbenlehre der Landschaft. 1881. IV. 55.²
— Forstästhetik. 1885. IV. 55.²
— Forstästhetische Reise-Ergebnisse. 1879. IV. 55.²
— Forstästhetische Tagesfragen. 1898. IV. 55.²
— Die Holzarten in ihrer forstästhetischen Bedeutung. 1881. IV. 55.²
— Die Kiefer in ihrer forstästhetischen Bedeutung. 1883. III. 309,¹ IV. 55,² 483.¹
— La première éclaircie dans une pineraie. 1899. IV. 55.²
— Das Siechthum der Pyramiden-Pappeln. 1884. III. 346.¹
— Verpflanzen von Kiefern ohne Ballen. 1889. IV. 473.
— Was kann der Staat zur Sicherung eines nachhaltigen Wirthschaftsbetriebes unserer Privatforsten thun? 1891. IV. 286.²
— Weitere Beiträge zur Forst-Aesthetik. 1879. IV. 55.²
— Weitere Beiträge zur Forstästhetik. 1900. IV. 55.²
— Welche Bedeutung haben die Coulissenschläge? 1891. IV. 128.
— See also CUSIG, Alfred, (Oberförster, Kuhbrück) & SALISCH, Heinrich von; KAYSER, (Forstmeister, Breslau) & SALISCH, Heinrich.
— & Kayser. Unter welchen Verhältnissen ist . . . Pflanzung von Eichenheistern noch zulässig? 1893. IV. 508.

Salkind, Joseph. Ein Beitrag zur Kenntniss der Benzoeharze. 1893. III. 671.¹
Sallač, Karl. Die Cultur und Bearbeitung der Weiden. 1886. III. 349.
— Nauka o rationelním pěstování a zužitkování Vrby. 1886. III. 349.
Sallier, J., (jr.). Boronia heterophylla. 1889. III. 495.²
— Crataegus Pyracantha et Jasminum nudiflorum. 1884. III. 443,² 673.¹
— Les Epiphyllum. 1884. III. 623.¹
Salm-Horstmar, Wilhelm Friedrich Carl August, Fürst zu. Recherches sur la nature des substances minérales nécessaires au développement d'un végétal. 1849. I. 152.²
— Versuche . . . über die Nahrung der Pflanzen. 1856. I. 158.
— Versuche über die nothwendigen Aschenbestandtheile einer Pflanzenspecies. 1849. I. 152.²
Salm-Reifferscheid-Dyck, Joseph, Fürst. Beitrag zur Cacteen-Kunde. 1850. II. 586.¹
— Bemerkungen über . . . Agave und Fourcroya. 1859. II. 88.²
— Bemerkungen über . . . Agaveen. 1861. II. 88.²
— Bemerkungen über die Gattung Echinopsis. 1855. II. 593.¹
— Beschreibung einer neuen mexikanischen Pflanze. 1854. II. 235.¹
— Beschreibung eines neuen ausgezeichneten Cactus. 1842. II. 594.²
— Beschreibung eines neuen Melocacti. 1836. II. 595.²
— Beschreibung einiger neuen Cacteen. 1845. II. 585.²
— Beschreibung zweier neuen Cacteen. 1840. II. 585.²
— Cacteae in Horto Dyckensis cultae. 1845. II. 585.²
— Catalogue raisonné des espèces et variétés d'Aloès. 1817. II. 77.²
— Ueber die Familie der Cacteen. 1839. II. 585.²
— Sur la famille des Cactées. 1839. II. 585.²
— Hortus Dyckensis. 1834. I. 47.
— Index plantarum succulentarum. 1822. I. 46.
— Index plantarum succulentarum anno 1829. 1829. I. 46.
— Index plantarum succulentarum anno 1843. 1843. III. 613.²
— Monographia generum Aloes et Mesembryanthemi. 1836. II. 77,² 123.²
— Nachträge zu meinen Cacteae in Horto Dyckensi. 1854. II. 586.¹
— Observationes botanicae in Horto Dickensi. 1822. V. XIII.²
— Observations botanicae in Horto Dickensi. 1822. V. XIII.²
— Observations sur la famille des Agavées. 1861. II. 88.¹
— Plantae succulentae horti Dyckensis. 1821. III. 121.¹
— Verzeichnis der verschiedenen Arten . . . Aloë. 1817. II. 77.²
Salmasius, Claudius. See SAUMAISE, Claude.
Salmen, E. T. Havaintoja metsänhoidosta sotilasvirkataloissa. 1889. IV. 114.
Salmon, Gordon. Bud transference and its effects on fruit. 1897. III. 40.
Salmon, John Drew. On the division of the county of Surrey into botanical districts. 1852. I. 400, V. XXI.¹
— A flora of Surrey. 1852. V. XXI.¹
Salmon, William. Botanologia, the English herbal. 1710. I. 289, V. XVI.¹
— Doron medicum. 1683. III. 251.
— Pharmacopoeia londinensis. 1676. III. 251.
— Seplasium, the compleat English physician. 1693. III. 240.
Salmoniceps, (pseud.). Avenues. 1877. III. 346.¹
— Dendrophilia. 1876. III. 166.
— Instrument for measuring the height of trees. 1879. IV. 231.²
— Value of Pinus Pinaster for seaside planting. 1874. IV. 467.²
Salomon, de. Culture du Châtaignier en Alsace. 1844. III. 359.¹
— Traité de l'aménagement des forêts. 1837. IV. 240.
Salomon, Carl. Die Arten der Gattung Pirus und Sorbus. 1874. II. 378.²
— Beitrag zur Dendrologie. 1882. II. 498.¹
— Bemerkungen über verschiedene . . . Freilandgehölze. 1879. III. 69.
— Biota orientalis var. pendula Endl. 1871. II. 52.²
— Ein Blick auf die Familie der Euphorbiaceen. 1872. III. 514.¹
— Coronilla emeroides Boiss. et Sprunn. 1875. II. 348.¹
— Cupressus Lawsoniana hort. 1868. III. 301.¹

Salomon, Carl (*continued*).
— Deutschlands winterharte Bäume und Sträucher. 1884. III. 68.
— Einige Notizen über verschiedene . . . Gehölze . . . im Botanischen Garten zu Würzburg. 1869. I. 48.
— Die Familie der Anacardiaceen. 1874. III. 523.²
— Ueber die Familie der Sapotaceen. 1881. III. 666.²
— Handbuch der höheren Pflanzenkultur. 1880. III. 75.¹
— Kultur und Vermehrung der Protraceen. 1879. III. 382.²
— Die Magnolien als Standbäume. 1877. III. 399.¹
— Notizen über einige interessante Pflanzen. 1887. III. 637.¹
— Die Palmen. 1887. III. 318.¹
— Die Palmen des temperirten Gewächshauses. 1884. III. 317.
— Pomaderris phillyraeoides. 1874. II. 496.²
— Spyridium globulosum Benth. et Hook. 1874. II. 499.².
— Die Stellung der Thymelaeaceen. 1881. III. 626.¹
— Das Verhalten der Fruchtbäume . . . unter den Temperaturverhältnissen des Winters 1879–80. 1881. III. 46.¹
— Ueber das Verhalten . . . einer Anzahl von Gehölzen. 1876. III. 69.
— Ueber das Verhalten verschiedener Gehölze . . . im Winter 1870–71. 1872. III. 45.
— Verzeichniss der botanischen Autoren. 1870. I. 79.¹
— Die wertvollsten . . . Melastomaceen. 1898. III. 638.¹
— Wirkung des Winters 1863–64. 1865. III. 45.
— Wörterbuch der botanischen Gattungsnamen. 1887. I. 77.
— Wörterbuch der botanischen Kunstsprache. 1880. I. 522.² III. 30.
— Wörterbuch der deutschen Pflanzen-Namen. 1881. V. ix.²
— Zierbäume und Ziersträucher für Parkanlagen. 1893. III. 203.
Salomon, Étienne. *See* COUANON, Georges & SALOMON, Étienne; COUANON, Georges, HENNEGUY, Félix & SALOMON, E.; COUANON, Georges, MICHON, Joseph & SALOMON, E.
Salomon, René. Greffe herbacée de la Vigne. 1892. III. 548.¹
Salse. Sucinta descripción de los arboles mas propios para los paseos. 1854. III. 126.¹
Salt, Henry. Neue Reise nach Abyssinien. 1814. I. 487.
— Voyage en Abyssinie. 1814. I. 487.
— A voyage to Abyssinia. 1814. I. 487.
Salter, J. H. Zur näheren Kenntniss der Stärkekörner. 1898. I. 140.³
Salter, James. On planting on chalk soils. 1875. III. 41.¹
— Salix Basfordiana. 1882. II. 105.³
Salter, Josiah.. The Clematis. 1885. III. 389.¹
Salter, S. James A. On a sexual monstrosity . . . of Passiflora. 1863. II. 577.¹
Salter, Thomas Bell. Appendix, illustrative of the botany of Poole. 1839. I. 399.
— Critical notes on British Brambles. 1850. II. 303.¹
— Description of three new species of Rubus. 1845. II. 302.¹
— A descriptive table of British Brambles. 1850. II. 303.¹
— Observations on the genus Rubus. 1845. II. 302.²
— Remarks on Rubus diversifolius. 1845. II. 307.¹
— Remarks on some forms of Rubus. 1845. II. 302.²
— Short account of the botany of Poole. 1839. I. 399.
Saltus, (*pseud*.). *See* KIRWAN, Charles de.
Salzmann, Johan Rudolph. De Rosa. 1670. II. 290.³
Salvadori, Ferdinando. L' agraria nelle scuole elementari e la selvicoltura? 1899. IV. 36.¹
— Ancora sulle matricine migliori. 1895. IV. 140.
— Due leggi forestali e qualcos' altro. 1899. IV. 329.
— Farnia, Rovere ed i querceti italiani allo sterminio. 1896. IV. 283.¹ 501.¹
— Leggi forestali. 1897. IV. 329.
— Le matricine migliori. 1895. IV. 140.
— Perugia, Vallombrosa od altro posto? 1898. IV. 35.¹
— Sempre sulle concimazioni degli orti forestali. 1895. IV. 151.¹
Salvadori, Otto von. Massentafel für Klötzer. 1880. IV. 230.
Salvagnini, Enrico & GAZETTI, Francesco. Programma per l' istituzione . . . di una società d' imboschimento. 1865. IV. 41.¹
— — Programma per l' istituzione d' una società di imboschimento. 1865. IV. 41.¹
Salvarezza, G. Cenni teorico-pratici sulla utilità della coltura boschiva. 1833. IV. 122.³

Salvat, J. Le Pin maritime. 1891. IV. 467.²
Salvator Ellis, J. De Cacao-cultuur in Suriname. 1887. III. 592.²
Salvi, E. Riordinamento del servizio forestale. 1863. IV. 293.³
Salviati, Bardo CORSI-. *See* CORSI-SALVIATI, Bardo.
Salvini? Tabella di cubazione pei legni rotondi. 1844. IV. 223.
Salwey, Thomas. A list of certain plants . . . of Barmouth, Dolgelley. 1863. I. 401.
Salzburg — Forst-Verein. *See* FORST-VEREIN FÜR ÖSTERREICH . . . IV. 14.
Die salzburgische Forstverfassung. 1860. IV. 294.²
Die salzburgischen Forst-Ordnungen. 1796. IV. 331.¹
Salze. Fructification du Palmier-Dattier à Marseille. 1854. III. 328.²
Salzmann, (*Ober-Forstrath, Gotha*). Material für den Entwurf eines Gesetzes zum Schutze der . . . Vögel. 1858. IV. 199.¹
Salzmann, F. Z. Pomologia oder Fruchtlehre. 1774. III. 70.
— Pomologie. 1774. III. 70.
Salzmann, J. G. Allgemeines deutsches Gartenbuch. 1817. III. 103.
Šámal, Arnošt. Hodnota sadů a stromů ovocných. 1886. III. 146.²
Samanos, Éloi. Traité de la culture du Pin maritime. 1864. IV. 468.¹
Sambin. Destruction de la pyrale de la Vigne. 1838. III. 562.²
Sambuc, (*Professor at Algiers*). Similitude des flores d'Amérique et d'Afrique du sud. 1892. I. 301.
Sambuc, Camille. Contribution à l'étude de la flore . . . médicale de la Sénégambie. 1887. III. 93.¹
Samec, Johann Wladimir. Die rationellen Forsttaxations-Methoden. 1864. IV. 243.
Das **Samenjahr** 1856. 1856. IV. 147.²
Samios, Konstantinos. *See* ΣΑΜΙΟΣ, Κωνσταντῖνος.
Sammlung der Gesetze und Verordnungen über das Forstwesen für den bernischen Jura. 1874. IV. 330.
Sammlung der hochfürstlich speierischen Jagd- und Forstverordnungen. 1789. IV. 318.
Sammlung der Akaziensamens. 1839. IV. 523.¹
Sammlung gemeinverständlicher wissenschaftlicher Vorträge. I. 14.
Sammlung nach der Natur gemalter Abbildungen in- und ausländischer Pflanzen. 1788. III. 59.³
Sammlung naturwissenschaftlicher Vorträge. I. 14.
Sammlung neuerer königlich württembergischer Gesetze und Verordnungen in Forst- und Jagdsachen. 1841. IV. 322.²
Sammlung oeconomischer Nachrichten. 1762. IV. 116.
Sammlung verschiedenartiger Pflanzenabbildungen. 1845. I. 269.
Sammlung von 50 in Kupfer gestochenen Abdrücken der . . . Laubhölzer. 1797. IV. 81, 490.¹
Sammlungen zur Physik und Naturgeschichte. I. 14.
Sampayo, Diego CARBALLO Y. *See* CARBALLO Y SAMPAYO, Diego.
Sampson, (*Dr.*). Die Koka-Pflanze. 1867. III. 492.² — 1874. III. 493.¹
Sampson, George Vaughan. Memoir explanatory of chart . . . of Londonderry. 1814. I. 533.
Samson, J. J. Krameria triandra. 1817. III. 480.¹
Samtale Imellem en Bonde og en Urtegaardsmand om en Hauges Indretning med Frugt-Træer. 1781. III. 134.²
Samuelli, Tommaso. Relazione all' onorevole municipio di Gargnano sul censo stabile dei boschi. n. d. IV. 363.²
Samzelius, Abraham. Blomster-krants af the allmännaste . . . uti Neriket befintliga växter. 1760. I. 351.
Samzelius, Hugo. Vegetationsiakttagelser inom Pajala socken. 1890. I. 357.
Sanabria, Diego de CORTAVILLA Y. *See* CORTAVILLA Y SANABRIA, Diego de.
Sánchez Ortega, J. Integración de la propiedad de los perímetros de masa cortese. 1900. IV. 547.¹
— Ventajas del servicio forestal graduado. 1899. IV. 554.
Sánchez y Lozano, Eusebio. Nuevos aparatos auxiliares de cálculo. 1894. IV. 551.¹
Sanchez y Sanchez, Domingo. Une maladie des Caféiers aux Philippines. 1900. III. 737.
Sanchez y Sanchez, José. Formulario de los formularios de medicina. 1871. III. 255.¹
Sandahl, O. Ramuli et folia Eucalypti globuli. 1870. IV. 532.¹

Sandahl, Oskar Theodor. Om barken af Prunus virginiana. 1861. III. 443.²
— Om frukten af Aegle Marmelos. 1861. III. 495.¹
— Några farmakologiska meddelanden. 1861. III. 259.²
The **Sandal-wood** of Juan Fernandez. 1894. II. 169.¹
The **sandalwood** trade and traders of Polynesia. *See* GORDON, J. D. 1862. III. 384.¹
Sandbinding plants in India. 1884. IV. 146.¹
Sandbindung in der . . . Militär-Grenze. 1869. IV. 145. ·
Sandblast. 1878. III. 184.²
Sandéen, Peter Frédrik. Morphologiska iakttagelser öfver Bladknopparne hos några Polygoneae. 1865. II. 184.¹
Sandelholzbaum. 1833. III. 384,² *485.²*
Sander, F. La germination des graines de Kentia. 1897. III. 326.¹
Sander, G. Beitrag zur Kenntnis der Strychnosdrogen. 1896. III. 684.¹
— Sur la composition des semences de strychnées. 1896. III. 684.¹
Sanders, John. A practical treatise on the culture of the Vine. 1851. III. 553.²
Sanders, T. W. The Black Walnut. 1886. II. 113.²
— An encyclopaedia of gardening. 1897. III. 31.
— The Snowy Mespilus. 1886. III. 419.²
Sanders van Loo, D. J. Indische houtsoorten en houtbereiding. 1875. IV. 400.¹
— Minjak Tangkawang. 1886. III. 225.
Sanderson, E. Dwight. Cock's-comb Elm gall. 1899. III. 365.¹
— The Grape-leaf trumpet-gall. 1899. III. 564.²
— New woolly louse on Maples. 1899. III. 536.²
Sanderson, George P. Pack gear for elephants. 1883. IV. 389.
Sanderson, John Scott Burdon. Note on the supposed Antheridia of Rhamnus. 1854. II. 497.¹
Sandersson, John & **Armitage**, Edward. Botanical appendix. 1858. I. 494.
Sandhagen, Jodoeus Edmund. De nominum plantarum mutatione utili ac noxia. *See* HEISTER, Lorenz. 1741. I. 253.²
Sandhof, Carl August. Anweisung zur sichern Holzersparnis. 1792. IV. 280.¹
— Unterricht über den Anbau der nützlichsten . . . Laub- und Nadelhölzer. 1798. IV. 105.
Sandi, Alessandro Francesco. Enumeratio stirpium . . . agri belluensis. 1837. I. 426.
Sandick, R. A. van. L'avenir du commerce de la gutta-percha. 1899. III. 232.¹
— De toekomst van den getah-pertjahandel. 1899. III. 232.¹
Sandiford, G. Elenchus plantarum . . . *See* BRUGMANS, S. J. 1818. I. 51.¹
Sandifort, Edvard. Rön om Quassiae-trädets verkan emot gikt. 1770. III. 508.²
— Thesaurus dissertationum . . . ad omnem medicinae ambitum pertinentium. ' 1768. III. 238.¹
Sandlund, H. *See* MEYER, Arthur & SANDLUND, H.
Sandmark, C. G. Flora jamaicensis. *See* LINNÉ, Carl von. 1759. I. 334.
Sandri, Giulio. Sul falchetto del Gelso. 1861. III. 379.¹
— Nota alla memoria sulle macchie nella foglia de' Gelsi. 1844. III. 379.¹
Sandwith, Thomas B. The Cork tree in the forests of Tunis. 1888. IV. 518.¹
— Report on the forests of Tunis. 1887. IV. 379.¹
— Tunesische Wälder. 1887. IV. 379.¹
— Die Wälder von Tunis. 1887. IV. 379.¹
Sandys, John. An essay on pruning. 1842. III. 169.¹
San Giorgio, Contessa di. Catalogo poliglotto delle piante. 1870. I. 72.²
Sangiorgio, Paolo. Elementi di botanica. 1808. I. 85.
— Istoria delle piante medicate. 1809. III. 55.
Sangüesa, Mariano. Exposición y proyecto sobre plantales. 1856. III. 154.¹
Sanguinetti, Petro. Centuriae tres prodromo florae romanae addendae. 1837. I. 426.
— Florae romanae prodromus. 1864. I. 427.
Sangwin, William. Choisya ternata. 1896. III. 496.¹
— Garrya elliptica in Devon. 1897. III. 352.²
Sanio, Karl Gustav. Anatomie der gemeinen Kiefer (Pinus sylvestris). .1873. II. 47.¹
— Einige Bemerkungen in Betreff meiner über Gefässbündelbildung geäusserten Ansichten. 1865. I. 133.
— Einige Bemerkungen über den Bau des Holzes. 1860. I. 125.
— Einige Bemerkungen über den Gerbstoff. 1863. I. 183.
— Ueber endogene Gefässbündelbildung. 1864. I. 133.
— Florula lyceensis. 1858. I. 384.
— Gegenbemerkung zu den Bemerkungen des Herrn Prof. Dr. Leopold Dippel. 1874. II. 47.¹
— Über die Grösse der Holzzellen bei . . . Pinus silvestris. 1872. II. 47.¹
— Ueber Monoecie bei Taxus. 1883. II. 10.¹
— Notiz über Verdickung des Holzkörpers . . . bei Tecoma. 1864. II. 786.²
— Notiz zu Schübeler's Viridárium norvegicum. 1887. II. 98,¹ *181.²*
— Ueber die in der Rinde . . . vorkommenden krystallinischen Niederschläge. 1857. I. 138.²
— Untersuchungen über die im Winter Stärke führenden Zellen des Holzkörpers. 1858. I. 179.²
— Untersuchungen über diejenigen Zellen . . . welche . . . im Winter assimilirte Stoffe führen. 1858. I. 179.²
— Ueber die Varietäten von Juniperus communis. 1883. II. 31.¹
— Vergleichende Untersuchungen über den Bau und die Entwickelung des Korkes. 1860. I. 130.
— Vergleichende Untersuchungen über die Elementarorgane des Holzkörpers. 1863. I. 125.
— Vergleichende Untersuchungen über die Zusammensetzung des Holzkörpers. .1863. I. 125.
— Zahlenverhältnisse der Flora Preussens. 1882. I. 388.
Sanitzki, P. P. *See* САНИЦКИЙ, П. П.
Sankt Gallische naturwissenschaftliche Gesellschaft. Bericht. I. 26.²
Sankt-Peterburg. *See* S[ain]t PETERSBURG.
Sankt-Peterburgskaya . . . *See* С.-Петербургская . . .
San Martin y Burgos, Antonio de. El labrador vascongado. 1791. III. 114,¹ *IV. 122.²*
San Martino, Giambatista da. Memoria sopra la nebbia dei vegetabili. 1785. III. 178.
Sanna Solaro, Giammaria. La malattia dell' Uva. 1853. III. 576.
Sannier, A., (*sr.*). De la culture des Poiriers. 1874. III. 444.¹
— Sur les moyens de hâter la mise à fruit. 1874. III. 444.¹
Sannier, Arsène. Note sur la destruction des chenilles. 1891. III. 196.
Sanson, A., **Flückiger**, F. A. & **Spadaro**. Sur la térébenthine de Chio. 1881. III. 526.¹
Sansovino, Francesco. Della materia medicinale libri IV. 1561. *I. 881,* III. 239, V. xv.¹
Santa-Anna Nery, Frederico José, *baron* de. La question du Café. 1883. III. 739.
Santa Barbara society of natural history. Bulletin. I. 6.
Santa Hildegardis. *See* HILDEGARDIS DE PINGUIA.
Santa Maria, Fernando de. Manual de medicinas caseras. 1815. III. 56.
Santagata, Antonio. De Hippophae ramnoidis veneno. 1844. II. 278,¹ *III. 689.¹*
— De Hypophae ramnoide. 1842. III. 629.¹
— De nonnullis plantarum fructibus. 1839. I. 145.¹
Le **Santal** de Juan Fernandez. *See* The SANDAL-WOOD. 1894. II. 169.¹
Santé, P. Middelen om Klapperboomen aan 't dragen te krijgen. 1872. III. 322.²
Santesson, Carl Gustaf. Notis über " Douradinha." 1894. III. 746.²
— *See also* SANTESSON, H. & C. G.
Santesson, H. & C. G. Ueber das Pfeilgift der wilden Stämme von Maláka. 1893. III. 684.¹
— — Sur le poison des flèches des tribus sauvages de Malacca. 1893. III. 684.¹
Santheuvel, van den. Duinbeplanting. 1862. IV. 160.¹
Santi, D. C. Sulle crete senesi. 1865. IV. 68.
Santi, Giorgio. Naturhistorische Reise durch einen Theil von Toscana. 1795. I. 424.
— Viaggio al Montamiata. 1795. I. 424, V. xxii.²
— Viaggio primo per la Toscana. 1795. V. xxii.²
— Viaggio secondo per le due provincie Senesi. 1795. V. xxii.²
— Voyage au Montamiata. 1795. I. 424.
Santiago — Deutscher wissenschaftlicher Verein. *See* DEUTSCHER . . . I. 7.²
Santilli, Agostino. Selvicoltura. 1891. IV. 110.¹
Santoni. Le Pin Laricio de Corse. 1894. IV. 466.²
Sanz, José, GARCÍA. *See* GARCÍA SANZ, José.
São Paulo — Instituto agronomico. *See* ESTAÇÃO AGRONOMICA DE CAMPINAS. III. 10.¹
São Paulo (estado de), Brazil. — Commissão geographica e geologica. Boletim. I. 8.¹

Saône-et-Loire — Société des sciences naturelles. *See*
Société . . . I. 23.
Le saoria, nouveau ténifuge importé d'Abyssinie. 1854. III.
666.[1]
La saperde. 1900. IV. 208.[2]
Sapetza, Josef. Die Flora von Neutitschein. 1864. I. 441.
— Verzeichniss der Pflanzen Karlstadts. 1867. I. 441.
Der Saphn-Baum. *See* ENGLER, Adolf. 1891. III. 510.[1]
Le Sapin argenté. 1899. IV. 444.[1]
Le Sapin de Williamson. 1860. III. 312.[2]
Sapin géant. 1876. II. 24.[1]
Sapins morts de soif. 1896. IV. 445.
Saporta, Ch. de.   Lettre [sur la résistance de quelques plantes
au froid]. 1876. III. 48.
Saporta, Louis Charles Joseph Gaston, *marquis* de.   Discours
. . . [sur la flore de Provence]. 1879. I. 415.
— Effets de l'hiver de 1870–71. 1870. III. 48.
— Étude des Chênes européens. 1877. II. 129.[2]
— Naturalisation de Conifères exotiques. 1854. III. 291.
— Observations sur l'effet du froid en Provence. 1861. III.
48.
— The origin of forest-groupings. 1889. I. 218.
— Origine paléontologique des arbres cultivés. 1888. I.
529.
— Sur l'ornementation des fibres ligneuses . . . de Conifères.
1875. II. 16.[1]
— Préliminaires d'une étude des Chênes européens. 1877.
II. 129.[2]
— Prodrome d'une étude comparative des Chênes. 1880.
II. 130.[1]
— Sur quelques hybrides. 1889. I. 417.
— Sur les retards de la frondaison. 1890. I. 226.[2]
— Sur des semis naturels et spontanés d'espèces frutescentes
. . . en Provence. 1893. I. 242.[1]
— & Marion, A. F.   Observations sur un hybride spontané
du Térébinthe et du Lentisque. 1871. II. 457.[2]
Saposchnikoff, W.   Beitrag zur Kenntniss der Grenzen der
Anhäufung von Kohlenhydraten. 1893. I. 174.
— Bildung und Wanderung der Kohlenhydrate. 1890. I.
177.
— Ueber die Grenzen der Anhäufung der Kohlenhydrate.
1891. I. 174.
— Die Stärkebildung aus Zucker. 1889. I. 177.
Sapper, Carl.   Ueber die geologische Bedeutung der tropi-
schen Vegetationsformationen in Mittelamerica. 1900. I.
331.
— Über Kautschukproduktion in Mittelamerika. 1899. III.
230.
Sarakomenos, D.   *See* ΣΑΡΑΚΩΜΕΝΟΣ, Δ.
Sarauw, G.   Anviisning for Bonden i den skovløse Egn til
vilde Træers Opelskning. 1829. IV. 119.[2]
— Beytrag zur Bewirthschaftung buchener Hochwaldungen.
1801. IV. 493.[2]
— Beytrag zur Bewirthschaftung buchener Holzwaldungen.
1801. IV. 493.[2]
— Ueber die Eichensaat. 1802. IV. 504.
— Forstlige Vink med særligt Hensyn til private Skovejere.
1839. IV. 342.[1]
Sarauw, George F. L.   Askefrøets Spiring. 1894. IV. 535.[1]
— Cromerskovlaget i Frihavnen. 1897. I. 350,[2] *IV. 79.*[2]
— Ret og vrang paa Blade og Grene. 1894. I. 100.[1]
— Rødsymbiose og Mykorrhizer. 1892. I. 234.[1]
— Vore Skovtræers Mykorrhizer. 1892. I. 234.[1]
Sarcé, C.   Assèchement des marais. 1894. IV. 546.[2]
— Création de pineraies dans la Sarthe. 1895. IV. 559.[1]
— Essai de réhabilitation des crampons. 1897. IV. 547.[2]
— Essai de réhabilitation du pic vert. 1899. IV. 91.[1]
— Le Genêt, moyen infaillible de le détruire. 1896. III.
475,[1] *IV. 211.*[1]
— Inondations. Boisement. 1898. IV. 551.[2]
— La mésange à tête bleue et les chenilles. 1898. IV. 91.[1]
— Petit manuel du propriétaire s..lviculteur. 18 . . ? IV. 121,
— Le Peuplier suisse blanc. 1895. III. 345.[1]
— La sylviculture dans la Flandre orientale. 1894. IV. 555.[1]
— Une visite aux pépinières de l'état à Lanklaer. 1895. IV.
546.[1]
Sardagna, M.   La flora alpina del Trentino. 1885. I. 429.
Sargent, Charles Sprague.   Abies. 1900. III. 295.[2]
— Ueber Abies Douglasii, A. Menziesii und A. Engelmanni.
1877. II. 14.[1]
— Abies Fraseri. 1889. II. 22.[2]
— An addition to the trees of Florida. 1889. II. 626.[2]
— Aesculus Parryi. 1890. II. 483.[1]
— Alberi dell' America del Nord. 1899. I. 305.

— Alnus maritima. 1891. II. 117.[1]
— Alnus tinctoria. 1897. II. 117.[1]
— American forestry. 1879. IV. 271.[2]
— The American Rock or Western Rock Elm. 1879. IV.
519.[1]
— The American White Birches. 1895. II. 120.[1]
— The American Wild Black Cherry. 1880. IV. 520.[2]
— Amount of tannin in the bark of some of the trees of the
United States. 1883. IV. 435.
— Arbutus arizonica. 1891. II. 660.[1]
— Asarum Crux-Andrae [sic]. 1892. II. 553.[2]
— Berberis heteropoda. 1895. II. 203.[2]
— Berberis Sieboldii. 1890. II. 204.[2]
— Berberis Thunbergii. 1889. II. 205.[1]
— Buckleya distichophylla. 1890. II. 168.[1]
— The Bur Oak. 1889. II. 135.[2]
— The Carolina Hemlock. 1889. II. 53.[1]
— Carpinus cordata. 1895. II. 121.[1]
— A catalogue of the forest trees of North America. 1880.
I. 304, *IV. 76.*[1]
— The Catalpa. 1879. II. 786.[2]
— Catalpa speciosa. 1881. II. 787.[1]
— Catalpa wood. 1878. IV. 538.[2]
— Celastrus articulata. 1890. II. 466.[2]
— Cercidiphyllum japonicum. 1894. II. 195.[1]
— Cereus Pringlei. 1889. II. 590.[2]
— A Chinese Peach. 1892. II. 276.[1]
— Cladothamnus pyroliflorus. 1897. II. 662.[2]
— Clematis brevicaudata. 1892. II. 197.[1]
— Clematis connata. 1891. II. 197.[2]
— Clematis paniculata. 1890. II. 199.[1]
— Clethra alnifolia var. tomentosa. 1891. II. 657.[1]
— The climbing Hydrangea. 1879. III. 415.[2]
— The Colorado Spruces. 1877. II. 14.[1]
— The confused Catalpas. 1880. II. 787.[1]
— Coriaria japonica. 1897. II. 454.[1]
— A curious form of Kalmia. 1890. II. 672.[2]
— Darbya umbellata. 1894. II. 168.[2]
— Dendrological notes. 1886. I. 317.[2]
— Deutzia parviflora. 1888. II. 239.[1]
— Deux arbres japonais. 1898. IV. 491.[2]
— Diervilla japonica. 1896. II. 835.[1]
— The double-flowered Chinese Crab Apple. 1888. III.
429.[2]
— Elaeagnus longipes. 1888. II. 607.[2]
— Elliottia racemosa. 1894. II. 663.[1]
— Fendlera rupicola. 1889. II. 240.[1]
— A few suggestions on tree planting. 1876. III. 117.[1]
— The first account of some western trees. 1897. I. 321.
— Forest fires. 1883. IV. 182.[1]
— Forest flora of Japan. 1893. I. 461, *IV. 87.*[2]
— Le foreste della Nevada centrale. 1879. IV. 340.
— The forests of California. 1881. IV. 340.
— The forests of central Nevada. 1879. IV. 340.
— The forests of Oregon. 1882. IV. 340.
— The forests of Washington territory. 1882. IV. 340.
— The forests of West Virginia. 1883. IV. 340.[1]
— Les forêts du Nevada central. 1879. IV. 340.
— Fothergilla Gardeni. 1895. II. 253.[1]
— Fraxinus Bungeana. 1894. II. 707.[2]
— Fraxinus rhyncophylla. 1893. II. 709.[1]
— Im Frühling blühende Magnolien. 1889. II. 211.[1]
— The fruit of Akebia quinata. 1891. II. 201.[1]
— The fruit of Sequoia gigantea. 1897. II. 50.[1]
— Fuel value of some of the more important woods of the
United States. 1882. IV. 431.[2]
— Halesia tetraptera Meehani. 1892. III. 670.[2]
— The height of the Redwood. 1897. II. 49.[2]
— A hybrid Catalpa. 1889. II. 787.[1]
— A hybrid Walnut tree. 1894. II. 113.[1]
— Hydrangea vestita var. pubescens. 1890. II. 240.[2]
— Hypericum aureum. 1889. II. 556.[1]
— Hypericum Buckleyi. 1891. II. 556.[2]
— Hypericum opacum. 1892. II. 556.[1]
— Ilex Amelanchier. 1889. II. 463.[1]
— Importance of the Catalpa tree. 1878. IV. 538.[2]
— Japanese Apples. 1888. III. 429.[1]
— The Japanese Hamamelis. 1891. II. 253.[1]
— The Japanese Photinia. 1891. II. 269.[1]
— Kalmia cuneata. 1895. II. 672.[1]
— The Kentucky Coffee-tree. 1889. II. 363.[1]
— Koelreuteria bipinnata. 1888. II. 487.[1]
— The Larches of western North America. 1886. II. 32.[2]
— Larix Lyalli. 1893. II. 33.[2]

— Lettre au sujet du bois rouge de la côte. 1900. IV. 484.[1]
— The Lindens of western Europe. 1889. II. 515.[2]
— The Liquidambar. 1889. II. 253.[2]
— List of Coniferae, hardy. 1882.- III. 292.
— Litsea geniculata. 1895. II. 226.[2]
— The Live Oak. 1888. II. 141.[1]
— Lycium pallidum. 1888. II. 773.[2]
— Magnolia hypoleuca. 1888. II. 212.[1]
— Magnolia Thompsoniana. 1888. II. 212,[2] III. 400.[2]
— A Manchurian Bird Cherry. 1888. III. 439.[1]
— The names of some North American tree Willows. 1895. II. 99.[2]
— The native woods of Essex county. 1885. IV. 77.[1]
— The Nettle tree. 1890. II. 141.[1]
— A new Californian Spruce. 1886. II. 37.[3]
— The new fastigiate Poplar. 1879. III. 345.[1]
— A New Jersey Pine forest. 1888. II. 45.[3]
— New or little known North American trees. 1899. I. 305.
— A new Palm. 1888. II. 74.[1]
— Notes from the Arnold Arboretum. 1889. II. 211.[1]
— Notes on cultivated Conifers. 1897. III. 291.
— Notes on North American Oaks. 1895. II. 129.[1]
— Notes on North American trees. — Description of the wood of certain species. 1890. IV. 409.
— Notes on some of the new Conifers. 1875. III. 292.
— Notes on the forest flora of Japan. 1893. I. 461, IV. 87.[3]
— Notes on trees and tree-planting. 1878. III. 117.[1]
— Notes on trees in the arboretum of Humphrey Marshall. 1880. I. 39.
— Notes upon Lilacs. 1888. II. 714.[2]
— Notes upon some North American trees. 1889. I. 304.
— Ornamental trees for Massachusetts plantations. 1882. III. 203.
— Partial estimate of the consumption of forest products as fuel in the United States. 1883. IV. 431.[2]
— Philadelphus Falconeri. 1895. II. 242.[1]
— Photinia villosa. 1888. II. 269.[2]
— Picea Breweriana. 1890. II. 37.[2]
— Pine supply of Texas. 1881. II. 14,[2] IV. 397.
— Pinus latifolia. 1889. II. 42.[2]
— Populus monticola. 1891. II. 97.[2]
— Prunus orthosepala. 1894. II. 275.[2]
— Prunus pendula. 1888. II. 275.[2]
— Prunus Pseudo-cerasus. 1897. II. 277.[1]
— Prunus Watsoni. 1894. II. 277.[2]
— Pseudophoenix Sargenti. 1888. II. 74.[1] — 1889. II. 74.[1]
— Pseudotsuga macrocarpa. 1897. II. 49.[1]
— Ptelea aptera. 1890. II. 410.[1]
— Pyrus arbutifolia. 1890. II. 312.[1]
— Pyrus betulifolia. 1894. II. 278.[2]
— Pyrus Miyabei. 1894. II. 311.[2]
— Pyrus occidentalis. 1897. II. 313.[2]
— Pyrus Tschonoskii. 1894. II. 264.[1]
— Quercus texana. 1894. II. 140.[2]
— Report of the director of the Arnold Arboretum. 1874. I. 39.
— Report on the forests of North America. 1884. I. 304, IV. 397.[1]
— Rhamnus crenata. 1896. II. 498.[1]
— Rhamnus occidentalis. 1897. II. 498.[2]
— Rhododendron (Azalea) arborescens. 1888. II. 677.[1]
— Rhododendron (Azalea)-Vaseyi. 1888. II. 684.[1]
— Rhododendron brachycarpum. 1888. III. 657.[2]
— Rhododendron mucronulatum. 1896. III. 661.[2]
— Rhus Michauxii. 1895. II. 459.[1]
— Rhus trichocarpa. 1897. II. 460.[1]
— The River Birch. 1889. II. 119.[2]
— Rosa multiflora. 1890. II. 296.[2]
— Rosa Watsoniana. 1890. II. 300.[1]
— Rosa Wichuraiana. 1891. II. 300.[1]
— Salix balsamifera. 1893. II. 105.[2]
— Sambucus melanocarpa. 1897. II. 841.[1]
— Schools of forestry. 1881. IV. 30.[1]
— The silva of North America. 1891. I. 305, IV. 76.[1]
— Smilax Pseudo-China. 1892. II. 86.[1]
— Some additions to the Sylva of North America. 1886.. I. 304.
— Some Japanese trees in New England. 1889. III. 60.
— A Sonora hillside. 1888. I. 320.
— Southern Pine. 1882. IV. 403.[2]
— Die spätblühende amerikanische Traubenkirsche. 1880. IV. 520.[2]
— Specific gravity and ash of the woods of the United States. 1882. IV. 411.[2]

— Spiraea arbuscula. 1897. II. 315.[2]
— Spiraea bracteata. 1894. II. 314.[2]
— Spiraea longigemmis. 1894. II. 315.[1]
— Spiraea Millefolium. 1889. II. 311.[1]
— Spiraea pubescens. 1888. II. 315.[2]
— Staphylea Bolanderi. 1889. II. 473.[2]
— Statistics of the lumbering industry of the United States. 1882. IV. 403.[2]
— Symphoricarpus occidentalis. 1890. II. 841.[2]
— Syringa amurensis. 1889. III. 680.[2]
— Syringa pekinensis. 1890. II. 715.[2]
— Syringa pubescens. 1888. II. 715.[2]
— Syringa villosa. 1888. II. 715.[2]
— Thrinax in Florida. 1896. II. 75.[1]
— Der Trompetenbaum, Catalpa bignonioides. 1878. IV. 538.[2]
— Tsuga caroliniana. 1886. II. 53.[1]
— Two American Honeysuckles. 1890. II. 837,[2] 839.[2]
— Two American St. Johnsworts. 1890. II. 556,[2] 557.[1]
— Vaccinium hirsutum. 1889. II. 685.[2]
— Viburnum cotinifolium. 1892. II. 843.[1]
— Viburnum dilatatum. 1891. II. 843.[1]
— Viburnum erosum. 1896. II. 843.[1]
— Viburnum lantanoides. 1889. II. 843.[1]
— Viburnum molle. 1891. II. 844.[1]
— Viburnum pubescens. 1890. II. 844.[1]
— Viburnum Sieboldi. 1889. II. 844.[1]
— Viburnum tomentosum. 1891. II. 844.[1]
— Vitality of the seeds of Pinus contorta. 1880. II. 41.[2]
— Vitis palmata. 1889. II. 506.[2]
— Die Wälder von Nordamerika. 1884. IV. 337.[1]
— The Wax Myrtles of the sea-coast. 1894. II. 111.[1]
— The Weeping Pinus ponderosa. 1888. III. 308.[2]
— The White Mountain forests. 1892. IV. 339.
— The wild Fig-tree of Florida. 1888.. II. 150.[1]
— On the wood of Quercus lobata. 1884. IV. 503.[2]
— The woods of the United States. 1885. I. 38,[1] IV. 18,[1] 397.
— The Yellow-wood. 1888. II. 346.[2]
— Yucca angustifolia. 1888. II. 87.[2]
— Yucca elata. 1889. II. 87.[2]
— Yucca elifera. 1888. II. 87.[2]
— Yucca Treculiana. 1888. III. 340.[2]
— & Olmsted, F. L. Letter to C. H. Dalton. 1880. III. 208.[2]
— & others. Forest policy for the forested lands of the United States. 1897. IV. 272.
— — Report of the commission . . . upon a forest policy for the forested lands of the United States. 1897. IV. 272.
— — Report [of the forestry commission]. 1885. IV. 338.[1]
Sargent, Frederick Le Roy. Barberries. 1894. II. 202.[2]
— An economical Linden. 1881. I. 188.[3]
— The national flower movement. 1899. I. 516.
Sargent, Henry Winthrop. Effects of the severe winter on rare evergreens. 1852. III. 291.
— Evergreen shrubs. 1855. III. 205.[2]
— Evergreens in the spring of 1857. 1857. III. 291.
— A fine Kentucky Coffee tree. 1878. III. 478.[1]
— The new Coniferae. 1854. III. 291.
— Pinus ponderosa pendula. 1878. III. 308.[2]
— Select lists of trees and shrubs, I. 1881. III. 60.
— A third winter on the new evergreens. 1856. III. 291.
— The winter of 1860–61 on evergreens. 1861. III. 292.
Sargent, Winthrop. List of forest and other trees northwest of the river Ohio. 1787. I. 304.
Sarnthein, Ludwig, Graf von. See DALLA TORRE, K. W. von & SARNTHEIN, Ludwig, Graf von.
Sarradin, Stanislas Eugène. Étude chimico-physiologique sur les cendres des végétaux. 1855. I. 153.
Sarrasin frutescent, Polygonum frutescens Lin. 1836. III. 387.[1]
Sarrazin. L'Érable à sucre. 1732. IV. 527.[1]
Sarrazin, de. Notice sur la greffe du Noyer. 1850. III. 355.
Sarrazin, F. Invasion inquiétante du peridermium du Pin. 1885. IV. 461.[3]
Sarrazin, H. Sur l'origine . ., du caoutchouc au Soudan. 1899. II. 869.[1]
Sarsaparilla of the Mundrucus. 1862. III. 339.[1]
Sartelsen, H. Medinilla magnifica. 1861. III. 638.[2]
Sarthe — Société d'agriculture, sciences et arts. See SOCIÉTÉ ROYALE D'AGRICULTURE, SCIENCES . . . DU MANS. I. 24.[1]
Sarthe — Société d'horticulture de la. See SOCIÉTÉ . . . III. 21.

Sartiaux, A. *See* Fautrat, L. & Sartiaux, A.
Sartorelli, Giovanni Battista. Degli alberi . . . dell' Italia superiore. 1816. I. 423, *IV. 86.*[1]
— Mezzi di conservare i boschi. 1826. IV. 181,[1] V. xxx.[2]
— Osservazioni sopra i mezzi di conservare i boschi. 1826. IV. 242, V. xxx.[2]
Sartori, Franz. Specimen nomenclatoris plantarum . . . in Styria. 1808. I. 439, V. xxiii.[1]
Sartorius, Josef. *See* Bouros, Johann, Landerer, Xaver & Sartorios, Josef; *also* Βοῦρος, Ἰωάννης, Λάνδερερ, Ξαυέριος & Σαρτόριος, Ἰωσήφ.
Sarwey, T. H. De Rubo Idaeo. *See* Camerarius, R. J. 1721. III. 458.[2]
Sarzeau. Sur la présence du cuivre dans les végétaux. 1830. I. 152.[1]
Sas, J. 't. Gouvernements Koffiecultuur op Sumatra's westkust. 1895. III. 731.
Sasaki, C. On the scale insect of Mulberry trees. 1894. III. 379.[1]
Sass, Arthur, *Baron* von. Beitrag zur Flora der Insel Runoe. 1860. I. 362.
— Die Phanerogamen-Flora Oesells. 1860. I. 362.
The Sassafras. 1894. II. 228.[1]
Sassafras oil. 1871. III. 408.[1]
Sasse, (*Legationsrath*). Ueber die Kultur feinerer Gehölze. 1855. III, 45, 120.[1]
Sasse, O. Über die Wasser-Abnahme. 1880. IV. 47.[1]
Sastrón, José Pardo y. *See* Loscos y Bernál, Francisco & Pardo y Sastrón, José.
Satin wood, Fagara flava Kr. & Urb. 1897. IV. 524.[2]
Satorras, Luis. Comunicado. 1897. IV. 553.[2]
Satow, *Sir* Ernest. The cultivation of Bamboos in Japan. 1899. III. 314.[2]
— *See also* Dickins, F. V, & Satow, *Sir* Ernest.
The Saturday review of politics. III. 18.
Satzungen der K. bayer. forstlichen Hochschule Aschaffenburg. 1899. IV. 33.[2]
Satzungen und Geschäfts-Anweisung der Sterbe-Kasse für das deutsche Forstpersonal. 1892. IV. 311.[1]
De Sau-boom in de Theetuinen. 1885. III. 466.[2]
Sauce. L'Exposition forestière de Bruxelles. 1898. IV. 19.[2]
Saucerotte, Constant. Élémens d'histoire naturelle. 1834. I. 87.
Sauer. Bemerkungen über die Kulture der Pandaneae. 1841. III. 313.[1]
— Cultur der Palmen im K. bot. Garten zu Berlin. 1834. III. 316.[1]
— Expériences sur l'incision annulaire. 1833. III. 175.[1]
— Ueber Verknorpelung bei den Stecklingen. 1834. III. 157.
Sauer, Fritz. Catalogus plantarum in canariensibus insulis. 1880. I. 498.
Sauerbrunn, K. G. H. Forst-Rügen. 1798. IV. 273.[2]
Sauerwein, Johann. Des Försters Rechenknecht. 1872. IV. 59.[1]
Saul, Andrew. The American Arbor Vitae for screens. 1846. III. 311.[1]
— On propagating trees and shrubs by . . . roots. 1847. III. 158.
Saul, John. On the acclimatation of plants. 1850. III. 43.
— Asiatic Conifers. 1853. III. 289.
— Cedrela sinensis. 1893. III. 512.[1]
— On coniferous stocks. 1851. III. 294.[1]
— How to cut Willows. 1855. III. 347.
— On Magnolia grandiflora. 1853. III. 399.[2]
— Rhododendrons. 1857. III. 656.
— Some hints on budding Roses. 1850. III. 164.[1]
— On Spiraea prunifolia flore pleno. 1852. III. 461,[2] 672.[1]
Saul, M. On Conifers. 1867. III. 292.
— On the culture of Erythrinas. 1866. III. 476.[1]
— A few remarks on pruning Conifers. 1867. III. 295.[1]
— The forcing of hardy shrubs. 1865. III. 176.[1]
— Monstrous pear. 1832. II. 279.[2]
— Poire-Jargonelle monstrueuse. 1832. II. 279.[2]
Saulcy, E. de. Éducations de vers à soie de races diverses. 1868. III. 148.[1]
Saulcy, Félicien de. Voyage autour de la Mer Morte. *See* Cosson, Ernest & Kralik, Louis. 1854. I. 480.
Un Saule blanc remarquable. 1896. IV. 487.[2]
Saulget, Grisard du. *See* Grisard du Saulget.
Saumaise, Claude (Salmasius, Claudius). Exercitationes de homonymis hyles iatricae. 1689. V. xvi.[1]
— De Hyssopo in cruce Christi epistolae tres. 1646. II. 763.[1]

— De manna commentarius. 1689. III. 221.[1]
— Plinianae exercitationes. 1689. I. 288, V. xvi.[1]
— Responsio in quaestionem Reveroviici de Hyssopo Evangelii. 1654. II. 764.[1]
Saundby, Robert. Note on the digestive action of Carica. 1881. III. 617.[2]
Saunders, C. F. New Jersey Pine barrens in July. 1900. I. 317.[1]
— Smilax glauca in winter. 1897. III. 338.[2]
Saunders, De Alton. Ferns and flowering plants of South Dakota. 1899. I. 327.
Saunders, James. British parasitic flowering plants. 1899. I. 529.[1]
Saunders, M. T. The flora of colonial days. 1897. I. 80.[1]
Saunders, Robert. Some account of the . . . productions of Boutan. 1789. III. 277.
— Some account of the vegetable . . . productions of Bootan and Tibet. 1800. I. 460.[1]
Saunders, Samuel. A short and easy introduction to . . . botany. 1792. I. 83.
Saunders, *Sir* Sidney Smith. On the Cynips caricae. 1883. II. 149.[2]
Saunders, William, (1743–1819). Observationes quibus praestantiores vires corticis peruviani rubri . . . stabiliuntur. 1782. III. 720.
— Observations on the superior efficacy of the red Peruvian bark. 1782. III. 720.
Saunders, William, (1822–1900). Catalogue of economic plants. 1891. I. 39.
— Cranberry culture. 1894. III. 664.[1]
— Descriptive catalogue of plants. 1872. I. 39.
— Evergreen shrubs. 1855. III. 205.[2]
— An experiment in Tea culture. 1897. III. 601.[1]
— A new hedge-plant. 1859. III. 753.[1]
— Observations on the soils and products of Florida. 1883. III. 117.[2]
— Pruning of trees and other plants. 1899. III. 171.
— Remarks on Grape culture. 1862. III. 577.
— Shade trees. 1869. III. 208.[2]
— Tea-culture as a probable American industry. 1879. III. 600.[2]
— Transplanting Kalmias and Rhododendrons. 1854. III. 656.
— When and how to plant trees. 1855. III. 166.
— Cope, F. J. & McMinn, J. M. Both sides of the Grape question. 1860. III. 550.
Saunders, William, (1835–1914). Canadian fruits. 1887. III. 262.[1]
— Horticulture in Canada. 1898. III. 116.[2]
— On the importance of economizing . . . our forests. 1883. IV. 177.[2]
— On the influence of sex on hybrids among fruits. 1883. I. 246.[1]
— Insects injurious to fruits. 1883. III. 187.
— Ornamental trees and shrubs . . . hardy at Ottawa. 1895. III. 44.[1]
— Past experiences . . . of fruit-growing in the Canadian northwest. 1896. III. 132.[2]
— Pine-tree insects. 1880. IV. 461.[2]
— Results of experiments in tree-planting. 1895. III. 116.[2]
— & Macoun, W. T. Catalogue of the trees and shrubs in the arboretum . . . Ottawa. 1899. I. 38.[2]
— & Sharpe, T. A. Catalogue of fruit trees under test . . . at Agassiz. 1900. III. 62.
— & others. Colonial fruit. 1887. III. 220.[1]
Saunders, William Wilson. Note on a disease in the Ash. 1879. IV. 535.[1]
— Notes on a diseased Acacia. 1879. IV. 523.[2]
— Notes on some wild Pear-trees. 1877. II. 279.[1]
Saupe, A. Der anatomische Bau des Holzes der Leguminosen. 1887. II. 320.[2]
Saurin, Alejo Molina y. *See* Molina y Saurin, Alejo.
Saussay. Traité des jardins. 1732. III. 112.
Saussaye, Sauveur Petit de La. *See* Petit de La Saussaye, Sauveur.
Sassine, G. La culture du Colatier. 1898. III. 590.[1]
Saussure, Henry de. De la vegetacion sobre las altas montañas de México. 1877. I. 332.
Saussure, Horace Bénedict de. Observations sur l'écorce des feuilles. 1762. I. 233.[1]
— Reisen durch die Alpen. 1779. I. 433.
— Voyages dans les Alpes. 1779. I. 433.
Saussure, Nicolas Théodore de. De l'altération de l'air par la germination. 1834. I. 233.[1]

— Chemische Untersuchungen über die Vegetation. 1804. I. 150.²
— De l'influence des fruits verts sur l'air. 1821. I. 169.²
— Sur la nutrition des végétaux. 1842. I. 157.
— Observations on oily substances. 1820. III. 224.¹
— Recherches chimiques sur la végétation. 1804. I. 150.²
Sautelet, Pelletier-. *See* Pelletier-Sautelet.
Sauter, Anton Eleutherius. Blüthen von Prunus Padus in Büscheln. 1878. II. 275.²
— Flora der Gefässpflanzen des Herzogthums Salzburg. 1866. I. 441.
— Flora des Herzogthums Salzburg. 1866. I. 441.
— Mathias Mielichhofer. Nekrolog. 1849. II. 108.¹
— Die Vegetationsverhältnisse des Pinzgaus. 1863. I. 441.
— Versuch einer geographisch-botanischen Schilderung der Umgebungen Wiens. 1826. I. 439.
Sauvage. Mémoire sur la fabrication en forêt du bois torréfié. 1840. IV. 394.
Sauvageau, Camille. Le bouturage du Vitis Berlandieri. 1893. III. 583.²
— Le pourridié de la Vigne. 1892. III. 195.¹
— Sur la présence de diaphragmes dans des canaux aérifères de la racine. 1888. I. 104.
— À propos d'une note de William Russell. 1893. I. 242.²
— À propos d'une Nouvelle note sur les pelotes marines. 1893. I. 242.²
— *See also* Viala, Pierre & Sauvageau, C.
Sauvages, Boissier de la Croix de. *See* Boissier de la Croix de Sauvages.
Sauvaigo, Émile. Les cultures sur le littoral de la Méditerranée. 1894. III. 87.
— Flora mediterranea exotica. 1899. I. 271,¹ III. 88,¹ V. xxviii.¹
— Note sur les Figuiers ... dans les environs de Nice. 1889. III. 369.¹
— Les Phoenix cultivés dans les jardins de Nice. 1894. II. 72,¹ III. 329.²
— Les plantes exotiques ... le dernier coin de France. 1892. I. 59.
— Les plantes exotiques ... villa Hutner à San Remo. 1891. I. 59.
— La villa de Cessole à Nice. 1894. I. 59.
Sauvalle, F. A. Clasificacion botánica de algunas plantas indígenas. 1868. I. 336.
— Cundurango. 1872. III. 693.²
— Del "Eucalyptus." 1881. IV. 533.²
— Flora cubana; enumeratio nova. 1868. I. 336.
— La flora médica de Cuba. 1867. III. 64.¹
— Notas sobre algunas plantas venenosas ... de Cuba. 1867. III. 64.¹
— Nueva especie de planta de la isla de Cuba. 1868. III. 7.¹
— Peso específico de algunas maderas de la isla de Cuba. 1866. IV. 411.¹
— Revisio catalogi Grisebachiani. 1868. I. 336.
Sauvan, L. Localisation des principes actifs. 1896. I. 151.²
— Sur le mode de formation des îlots libériens intra-ligneux du Strychnos. 1895. II. 720.¹
— Recherches sur la localisation de la brucine. 1895. III. 684.¹
— Recherches sur la localisation de la daphnine. 1896. III. 627.¹
Sauzé, J. Charles, Exploration botanique ... de Bressuire. 1867. I. 413.
— & Maillard, P. N. Catalogue des plantes ... des Deux Sèvres. 1864. I. 413, 535.¹
—— Flore du département des Deux-Sèvres. 1872. I. 414.
Sava, R. Lucubrazioni sulla flora e fauna dell' Etna. 1844. I. 431.
Savaresi, A. M. T. Memorie ed opuscoli ... sull' Egitto. 1808. I. 487.
Savastano, Francesco Eulalio. Botanicorum seu institutionum rei herbariae libri IV. 1712. I. 289.
— I quattro libri delle cose botaniche. 1749. I. 291.
Savastano, Luigi. Adattamento della specie alla practica. 1897. I. 248.¹
— Di alcune colture arboree della provincia di Napoli. 1885. III. 126.²
— Di alcune varietà di Agrumi. 1882. II. 401,¹ III. 497.¹
— Il batterio del marciume dell' Uva. 1887. III. 579.
— Le condizioni agrumarie. 1898. III. 499.¹
— Conferenze arboree. 1900. IV. 36.¹
— Della cura della gommosi e carie degli Agrumi. 1887. III. 498.²
— Esperimenti di inoculazioni del batterio della tubercolosi dell' Olivo. 1887. III. 677.²

— Esperimenti sui rapporti tra i fatti traumatici. 1887. I. 528.¹
— I fatti traumatici nella gommosi degli Agrumi. 1885. III. 180.²
— Le forme teratologiche ... degli Agrumi. 1884. II. 402.¹
— Gommose caulinaire et radicale. 1884. I. 213,¹ III. 370,¹ 431,¹ 498,¹ 677.²
— Hypertrophie des cônes à bourgeons ... du Caroubier. 1885. III. 471.²
— Innesti eterogeni. 1897. I. 208.²
— Innesto o selezione. 1886. I. 208.²
— Il mal dello spacco nei frutti delle Auranziacee. 1889. III. 494.²
— Les maladies de l'Olivier. 1886. III. 677.²
— Les maladies de l'Olivier; hyperplasies et tumeurs. 1886. III. 677.²
— Malattie dell' Olivo. 1886. III. 677.²
— Il marciume del Fico. 1884. III. 370.¹
— Note di patologia arborea. 1897. III. 179.
— Note preliminari per un' arboricoltura comparata. 1897. I. 248.¹
— Nuovi tempi e nuovi agrumicoltori. 1900. III. 498.¹
— Parallelo tra la vegetazione vesuviana e la sorrentina. 1897. I. 430.
— La patalogia vegetale dei Greci. 1890. I. 206.¹
— Contro la peronospora. 1896. III. 581.
— Le piante apistiche del Napoletano. 1883. I. 239.²
— Il rimboschimento dello Appennino. 1893. IV. 166.¹
— Tuberodlosi ... dell' Olivo. 1887. III. 677.²
— Tumori nei coni gemmarii del Carrubo. 1888. III. 471.²
— La vajolatura degli Agrumi. 1887. III. 498.²
— Le varietà di Agrumi del Napoletano. 1883. III. 497.¹
— La varietà in arboricoltura. 1899. I. 248.¹
— *See also* Jatta, G. & Savastano, L.
Savatier, Alexandre. Étude sur les Pyrus, Malus et Prunus. 1883. II. 256.¹
— Note sur les Vitis sauvages de la Charente-inférieure. 1883. II. 505.¹
— *See also* Rochebrune, A. T. de & Savatier, Alexandre.
Savatier, Ludovic. On the increase of the flora of Japan. 1874. I. 462.
— *See also* Franchet, Adrien & Savatier, Ludovic.
Save the Adirondack forests. 1883. IV. 178.¹
Savi, G. B. A. Spiegazione etimologica de' nomi generici delle piante. 1815. I. 76.¹
Savi, Gaetano. Sopra alcune Acacie egiziane. 1830. II. 323.¹
— Botanicon etruscum. 1808. I. 425.
— Catalogo di piante egiziane. 1836. I. 487, II. 323.¹
— Sul Cedro del Libano. 1818. II. 28.¹
— Sul Ciliegio pendulo. 1832. II. 273.¹
— Sul Citrus Hystrix. 1837. II. 401.¹
— Della coltivazione di alcune piante esotiche. 1830. III. 421,² 669.¹
— Sulla Cornucchiola fragiformis. 1836. II. 733.¹
— Cose botaniche. 1832. II. 328.²
— Descrizione d' una specie d' Elaeagnus. 1836. II. 607.²
— Due centurie di piante appartenenti alla flora etrusca. 1804. I. 425.
— Enumeratio stirpium in Horto pisano. 1804. I. 61.
— Flora italiana. 1817. I. 266.
— Flora pisana. 1798. I. 424.
— Istituzioni botaniche. 1805. I. 86.
— Sul legname d'Abeto. 18 ..? IV. 446.²
— Lezioni di botanica. 1811. I. 85.
— Magnolia grandiflora. 1809. II. 212.¹
— Sulla Magnolia grandiflora. 1819. II. 211.¹
— Materia medica vegetabile toscana. 1805. III. 88.¹
— Sulla Mimosa bimucronata. 1836. II. 373.¹
— Sulla naturalisazione delle piante. 1822. III. 43.
— Notizie per servire alla storia del giardino ... di Pisa. 1828. I. 62.
— Notizie sul Tè della China. 1836. III. 606.
— Nuovi elementi di botanica. 1820. I. 85.
— Observationes botanicae. 1797. I. 264.
— Osservazioni sopra diverse piante. 1816. I. 266.
— Pugillo di piante da aggiungersi al Botanicon etruscum. 1808. I. 425.
— Rapporto sulla collezione di piante raccolte in Egitto. 1830. I. 487.
— Scelta di generi di piante. 1826. I. 259.
— Sullo stabilimento d' alcuni nuovi generi di piante. 1799. II. 212.¹
— Trattato degli alberi della Toscana. 1801. III. 88.¹
— Sul Viscum album ed il Loranthus. 1823. II. 173.¹

Savi, P. G. Ragionamento sui boschi. 1827. IV. 276.[2]
Savi, Pietro. Sull' acrescimento dei cauli delle Palme. 1859. II. 63.[2]
— Alcune osservazioni . . . sopra un fenomeno fisico, presentato dalle fronde dello Schinus Molle. 1837. II. 460.[2]
— Sull' Araucaria Ridolfiana. 1842. II. 26.[2]
— Sul Biophytum sensitivum. 1861. II. 392.[1]
— Sopra la circolazione dei liquidi. 1831. I. 163.
— Considerazioni morfologiche sulla fronda dell' Arduina bispinosa. 1844. II. 724.[2]
— Descrizione di una nuova specie d' Araucaria. 1846. II. 26.[1]
— Florula gorgonica. 1844. I. 427.
— Sopra la microscopica composizione degli strobili di alcune conifere. 1841. II. 18.
— Nota sulla morfologia. . . . delle Cicadacee. 1860. II. 3.[1]
— Observations sur le phénomène physique qu'offrent les feuilles du Schinus Molle. 1837. II. 460.[3]
— Osservazioni botaniche sul fungo microscopico. 1851. III. 575.[3]
— Osservazioni sulla struttura . . . degli stomi. 1840. I. 131.[1]
— Sul valore tassonomico delle stipole. 1840. I. 111.
— See also MENEGHINI, Giuseppe & SAVI, Pietro.
Savignon, F. de. Le phylloxera en Californie. 1881. III. 572.
— Les Vignes sauvages de Californie. 1881. II. 505.[3]
Savitzki, P. See САВИЦКІЙ, П.
Savoia, PIO DI. See PIO DI SAVOIA.
Savoureux. Considérations sur l'époque . . . pour la plantation des arbres verts résineux. 1845. III. 294.[2]
— Note sur un Pin Mugho. 1846. II. 43.[1]
— & others. Rapport de la commission chargée d'examiner une Vigne remarquable. 1846. II. 509.[1]
Saw-mill gazette. IV. 5.[1]
Sawer, John Charles. Allspice or Pimento. 1896. III. 637.[3]
— Rhodologia; a discourse on Roses. 1894. III. 454.[2]
Sawyer, A. M. Disease of Cocoanut trees in Travancore. 1894. III. 323.[2]
— System of tapping the Caryota urens. 1896. III. 321.[2]
— See also GUNNING, E. H., THOMSON, Robert & SAWYER, A. M.
Sawyer, J. C. Odorographia. 1892. III. 226.[2]
Sawyer, James. Growing gold. 1835. III. 362.[2]
Sawyer, Lemuel. The Vine of North Carolina. 1850. III. 584.[1]
Sax, Frans. Vollständige Anleitung zur Holzsparkunst. 1804. IV. 280.[2]
Sax, Julius. Forst- und Jagdwesen im Hochstift Eichstätt. 1889. IV. 26.
Saxon names of plants collected. 1864. I. 74.[1]
Saxony — Ökonomische Gesellschaft . . . See ÖKONOMISCHE . . . III. 13.
Saxton, C. M. The American Rose culturist. 1852. III. 448.
Sayers, E. A treatise on the culture of · the Dahlia and Cactus. 1839. III. 618.[2]
Sayers, J. H. P. Beknopte geschiedenis van de landbouwwetenschap. 1896. III. 38.[1]
Sayre, Lucius E. Alexandria and India Senna. 1897. III. 470.[2]
— Essai des Sénés de l'Inde et d'Alexandrie. 1897. III. 470.[2]
— Senna. 1896. III. 470.[2]
Sbornik . . . See СБОРНИКЪ . . .
Scaeffer, J. D. De corticis chinae efficacia. See DETHARDING, G. C. 1746. III. 719.
Das Scalenrädchen. 1866. IV. 264.
Scalia, Giuseppe. See BACCARINI, Pasquale & SCALIA, Giuseppe.
Scaliger, Julius Caesar. Commentarii et animadversiones in sex libros de causis plantarum Theophrasti. 1566. I. 281.
— Exotericarum exercitationum liber quintus decimus de subtilitate. 1557. I. 280.
— In libros de plantis Aristoteli inscriptos commentarii. 1556. I. 280.
— In libros duos . . . de plantis, Aristotele autore, libri duo. 1556. I. 280.
Scaling, William. The cultivation of the Willow or Osier. 1868. III. 347.
— On the growth and cultivation of Willows in Scotland. 1879. III. 348.
— Rules for Willow planters. 1877. III. 348.

— The Salix or Willow. 1868. III. 347.
— The Willow; its history and uses. 1881. III. 348.
— Willows. 1873. III. 347.
Scannagatta, Josue. Appendix specierum plantarum. 1805. V. XXVIII.[1]
— Synopsis plantarum Horti regii bot. bononiensis. 1813. I. 62.
— Systema vegetabilium. See LINNÉ, Carl von. 1774. I. 530.
The Scarlet Clematis. 1881. III. 390.[1]
Scarsez de Locqueneuille. Les arbres calomniés. 1896. IV. 119.[2]
— Le Pin Laricio. 1896. IV. 465.[2]
— Résistance des résineux à la gelée. 1896. IV. 66.[2]
— Le rond et la rouille dans les pineraies. 1898. IV. 479.
Scato Trip, H. Kort berigt wegens den aard der onbebouwde Dallen. 1810. III. 150.[1]
Scazzola, Giovanni Antonio. Filosofia dei fiori. 1836. I. 34.
Della scelta degl' alberi e delle piante. 1781. III. 201.
Scented tea. Extracted by Robert Fortune. 1855. III. 607.
Scepin, Constantinus. De acido vegetabili. 1758. I. 180.[1]
— sch. Der Weinheimer Coniferen-Wald. 1898. I. 49.
Sch. Bem. Schneedruckschaden. 1896. IV. 191.[1]
Sch. Expériences relatives aux effets extraordinaires du charbon de bois. 1845. III. 151.
Sch. Kiefernballen aus Lehmguss. 1900. IV. 153.[2]
Sch. Eine Kiefern-Fichte. 1867. II. 34.[2]
Sch. Los montes en Grecia. 1885. IV. 375.[2]
Sch. Die Nadeln und die Verzweigung der Gemeinen Kiefer. 1892. IV. 483.[1]
Sch. Die Nadeln und die Verzweigung der Lärche. 1892. IV. 452.[3]
Sch. Die Trocknung der Eichenlohrinde. 1891. IV. 508.
Sch. Die Waldverhältnisse Griechenlands. 1885. IV. 375.[3]
Sch., A. Les nouvelles théories des éclaircies. 1888. IV. 174.
Sch., C. Polygonum baldschuanicum. 1900. III. 387.[1]
Sch., H. Ficus stipulata Thunb. 1875. III. 371.[1]
Sch—ld, von. Einige Bemerkungen über den schädlichen Einfluss des Berberitzenstrauchs. 1805. III. 394.[1]
Schaafthausen, Herman Joseph. Ein Pinienzapfen zwischen römischen Alterthümern. 1876. II. 45.[1]
Schaak, Frank Milton. Analysis of the bark of Populus alba. 1892. III. 345.[1]
Schaal, A. F. Aufastungsziel und Aufasten. 1874. IV. 171.
— Ueber das Bedecken der Fichtensaatkämpe mit Saatgittern. 1880. IV. 453.
— Eine Buchenkrankheit. 1867. IV. 496.
— Ueber Kubirung stehender Stämme. 1865. IV. 217.
— Die Kulturerde. 1895. IV. 153.[1]
— Das Numerieren der Nutzhölzer. 1874. IV. 387.[2]
— Die 250 bis 500 Jahre alten Tannen. 1873. II. 24.[1]
Schaap (Butin). Enten van Java of Maragogipe op Liberia-Koffie. 1899. III. 733.[2]
Schaar, Ferdinand. Die Reservestoffbehälter der Knospen von Fraxinus. 1891. II. 708.[1]
Schaar, J. M. Anvüsning til Saadning af sand Nytte af de forskjellige Have- og Skovväxter. n. d. III. 394.[1]
Schaarschmidt, Gyula. Az Euphorbiaceák, Rutaceák . . . szerves sphaerokrystalljai. 1882. I. 525.[2]
— A protoplastok összeköttetéséről és a sejtközi plasmáról. 1884. I. 137.
Schabel, A. Flora von Ellwangen. 1837. I. 379.
Schabol, Jean. Dictionnaire pour la théorie et la pratique du jardinage. 1767. III. 30.
— La pratique du jardinage. 1770. III. 112.
— Theoretische und praktische Abhandlung vom Gartenbau. 1775. III. 103.
— La théorie du jardinage. 1771. III. 35.
Schach, von, (Oberförster). Seltene Stärke der . . . Besenpfrieme. 1888. II. 352.[1]
— Seltene Stärke der Stechpalme. 1888. II. 463.[2]
Schacht, Hermann. Über anormes Wachsthum des Stammes der Dikotyledonen-Gewächse. 1861. I. 127.[1]
— Les arbres. 1853. I. 82.[1]
— Über den Bau einiger Pollenkörner. 1860. I. 117.[1]
— Der Baum. 1853. I. 82. V. x.[1]
— Über die Befruchtung bei den Gymnospermen. 1864. II. 1.
— Beiträge zur Anatomie und Physiologie der Gewächse. 1854. I. 34.
— Beitrag zur Entwicklungsgeschichte flächenartiger Stammorgane. 1853. I. 105.

— Die Blüthe und die Befruchtung von Santalum. 1865. II. 169.¹

— Ueber eigenthümliche . . . Erscheinungen in den Verdickungsschichten gewisser Holzzellen. 1850. I. 124.

— Entwickelungs-Geschichte der Blüthe . . . von Manglesia. 1853. II. 872.¹

— Entwicklungsgeschichte des Pflanzenembryon. 1850. I. 122.

— Ueber die gestielten Traubenkörper . . . vieler Urticeen. 1854. II. 156,¹ 796.²

— Grundriss der Anatomie und Physiologie der Gewächse. 1859. I. 90.

— Zur Kenntniss der Visnea Mocanera. 1859. II. 552,¹ 657.¹

— Les laticifères du Carica Papaya. 1856. II. 582.²

— Lehrbuch der Anatomie und Physiologie der Gewächse. 1852. I. 89.

— De maculis in plantarum vasis. 1860. I. 125.

— Madeira und Tenerife. 1859. I. 497.

— Le microscope et son application. 1851. I. 36.²

— The microscope in its special application. 1851. I. 521.¹

— Das Mikroskop und seine Anwendung. 1851. I. 36,¹ 521.¹

— Die Milchsaftgefässe der Carica Papaya. 1856. II. 582.²

— Sur l'origine de l'embryon végétal. 1855. I. 200.

— Über Pflanzen-Befruchtung. 1858. I. 201.¹

— Physiologische Botanik. 1852. I. 89.

— Planternes anatomi og physiologi i grundtraek. 1859. I. 90.

— Die Prüfung der im Handel vorkommenden Gewebe. 1853. I. 36.²

— Die sogenannten Milchsaft-Gefässe der Euphorbiaceen. 1851. I. 135.

— Ueber den Stamm . . . der Araucaria brasiliensis. 1862. II. 26.¹

— Ueber die Tüpfel der Gefäss- und Holzzellen. 1859. I. 124.

— Ueber die Zucht der Cochenille. 1857. III. 624.¹

— See also ШАХТЪ, F.

Schacht, J. E. Præparata chemica . . . in Pharmacopoeæ borussicæ editionem septimam non recepta. 1863. III. 249.

Schade. Ueber die Verjüngung der zum Austrocknen . . . geneigten Bodenpartien. 1890. IV. 142.

Schadeberg, J. Holztabellen. n. d. IV. 220.

Schaden der Stürme von Januar 1899. 1899. IV. 189.²

Schaden durch Auerhähne. 1899. IV. 199.¹

Schaden durch Duftanhang. 1897. IV. 191.¹

Schaden durch Eichhörnchen. 1850. IV. 475.

Schaden durch Mäuse. 1840. IV. 496.

Schadt, E. Ueber den Eisbruch in . . . Birkenfeld. 1861. IV. 190.

Schaeck, de. Empoisonnement des faisans par les feuilles de l'If. 1890. III. 200.²

— Huile de Palme africaine. 1892. III. 325.¹

— De l'influence du froid sur les plantes. 1894. III. 182.

— Résistance des bois de l'Inde. 1895. IV. 401.¹

— Le tanin des Myrica. 1895. III. 353.¹

— Les trois arbres sacrés de la création. 1894. I. 517.²

— Utilité de deux Palmiers américains. 1893. III. 319.¹

Schäde, J. Charakteristik der Bäume. 1853. I. 516.

— Die Zeit des Baumschnitts. 1852. III. 170.

Schädelin, W. Von der Eiche und Buche im Spessart. 1898. IV. 129.

Schaedler, Carl. Die Technologie der Fette und Oele. 1883. III. 225.

Ueber schädliche Nagethiere und ihre Vertilger. 1854. IV. 197.¹

Schaedtler, Georg. Abelia rupestris, ein blütenreicher Zierstrauch. 1887. III. 748.²

— Mémoire sur les Palmiers. 1875. III. 317.

— Die Palmen . . . zu Herrenhausen. 1875. III. 317.

— Les Palmiers . . . de Herrenhausen. 1875. III. 317.

— Die Pandaneen, Cyclantheen. 1875. III. 284,¹ 313.¹

Schäfer, G. L. Bestimmung von Aloïn in Aloë. 1897. III. 333.¹

— Dosage de l'aloïne dans l'Aloës. 1897. III. 333.²

Schaefer, H. Vegetationsverhältniss von Neuvorpommern. 1872. I. 386.

Schäfer, M. Triersche Flora. 1826. I. 377.

Schaefer, R. Über den Einfluss des Turgors der Epidermiszellen. 1888. I. 171.

Schäffer. Bemerkungen über die Kultur der Aristolochia Sipho. 1855. III. 386.¹

Schaeffer. Ständige oder Wanderkämpe. 1874. IV. 150.

Schaeffer, (Fürstlicher Kammer-Assessor). Extract aus dem Jahres-Bericht . . . über dessen Kopulations-Methode. 1834. III. 160.

Schaeffer, (Kammer-Assessor). Extrakt aus einem Schreiben . . . über die Vertilgung der grünen Apfel-Blattlaus]. 1833. III. 427.¹

Schäffer, (Kammer-Rath, Pless in Ober-Schlesien). Noch etwas über die Vertilgung der grünen Apfel-Blattlaus. 1839. III. 196.

Schaeffer, A. Aménagement des taillis dans le canton de Genève. 1898. IV. 513.

— Une conversion de taillis à écorce. 1899. IV. 129.

— Conversion rapide d'un taillis simple en futaie. 1898. IV. 545.¹

— Enseignement forestier supérieur en Allemagne. 1898. IV. 33.¹

— Estimation du Sapin. 1891. IV. 237, 446.²

— Une forêt traitée par la méthode du contrôle. 1890. IV. 249.¹

— Forêts du domaine Kammer Teschen. 1899. IV. 140.

— Le Hêtre en taillis sous futaie. 1899. IV. 499.

— Inventaire des massifs sur pied. 1899. IV. 219.

— Maïkäfer oder Kiefer! 1889. IV. 549.¹

— Méthode d'exploitation de Worlück. 1900. IV. 247.¹

— Du nettoiement dans les bois. 1897. IV. 175,¹ 547.²

— Opportunité de créer un sous-étage. 1898. IV. 130.

— De la périodicité des éclaircies. 1891. IV. 174.

— Les pierres et la fertilité du sol. 1900. IV. 70.

— Les Plainbois. 1894. IV. 362.

— Quelques conseils aux sylviculteurs du Chablais. 1894. IV. 362.

— La question du sous-étage en Allemagne. 1898. IV. 132.²

— Du respect des gros arbres. 1899. IV. 547.¹

— La sapinière idéale. 189.? IV. 446.²

— Un type de futaie jardinée. 1900. IV. 545.¹

— Das Verhalten der Eiche in verschiedenen . . . Bodenarten. 1884. IV. 507.

— Une vieille revue forestière. 1897. IV. 24.²

Schäffer, Cäsar. Über die Variabilität der Hainbuche. 1895. II. 120.²

Schaeffer, Jacob Christian. Botanica expeditior. 1760. I. 257.

— Epistola de studii botanici . . . methodo. 1758. I. 78.²

— Erleichterte Arzneykräuterwissenschaft. 1759. III. 54.

— Isagoge in botanicam expeditiorem. 1759. I. 97.

— Lettre . . . contenant la manière de rendre l'étude de la botanique plus facile. 1758. I. 78.²

— Neue Versuche . . . zum Papiermachen. 1765. III. 235.¹

Schaeffer, Karl. Deliciae botanicae hallenses. 1662. I. 372.

Schäffer, Martin Gottlieb. Afhandling om Skoves Opelskning. 1811. IV. 272.

— Anvisning til Skovdyrkningen. 1799. IV. 103.¹

— Bemærkninger over Veirliget og dets Indflydelse paa Trævegetationen. 1904. I. 322.¹

— Bemærkninger over Veirliget og dets Virkning paa Trævegetationen. 1804. I. 350,¹ IV. 79.¹

Schaer, Ed. Ueber Cortex Quebracho. 1881. III. 687.¹

— Sur l'emploi de l'hydrate de chloral. 1900. I. 157.

— Sur l'emploi de la résine de Gayac. 1895. III. 494.²

— Ueber Fouquiera splendens. 1898. III. 612.²

— Zur Geschichte des Berberins. 1893. I. 177.

— Historisch-geographische Mittheilungen über den chinesischen Zimmt. 1883. III. 404.¹

— Neue Ergebnisse aus Java über die Verbreitung der Alkaloide in der Cinchona-Pflanze. 1897. III. 724.¹

— Ueber die Verbreitung chemischer Verbindungen. 1888. I. 154.

— & others. Sur le siège des alcaloides des Quinquina. 1879. III. 723.

Schätzung und Erträge. 1858. IV. 248.¹

Schaffer, J. M. Reports on fruit-growing in the different counties in Iowa. 1872. III. 133.

Schaffer, Karl. Die trockene Destillation des Holzes. 1891. IV. 433.¹

Schaffhausen. Eine ansehnliche Fichte. 1898. II. 37.²

Schaffner, John Henry. General methods in botanical microtechnique. 1899. V. VIII.¹

— Origin of timber belts. 1899. I. 305.

Schaffranek, A. Floral almanac. 1888. I. 319.

Schagerström, Johann August. De antheris plantarum. 1848. I. 116.¹

— Conspectus vegetationis Uplandiae. 1845. I. 354.

— Lärobok i Skandinaviens växt-familjes. 1846. I. 355.

— & Söderbaum, A. G. Plantae cotyledoneae paroeciae Roslagiae Bro. 1839. I. 354.

Schalin, Z. Alnus glutinosa var. laciniata i Finland. 1876. II. 116.[1]

Schamal, Johann. Andeutungen zur Zucht der Obstbäume. 1858. III. 137.

— Das Entblättern der zeitlich im Herbste zu verpflanzenden Bäume. 1858. III. 168.[2]

— Etwas über die Rosenzucht. 1855. III. 449.

— Obstbäume und Sträucher. 1858. III. 146.[2]

— Tidig Afbladning af Træer. 1858. III. 168.[2]

— Vertilgung der Engerlinge. 1858. III. 196.

— Vortheile der Zimmerkopulation. 1858. III. 161.

— Die Wasserkur gegen den Gummifluss. 1856. I. 213.[1]

Schambach. Ueber Salix longifolia Host. und dasyclados. 1884. II. 106.[2]

Schams, Franz. Betrachtungen über Ungarns Weinbau. 1830. III. 558.[1]

— Der Weinbau des Oesterreichischen Kaiser-Staates. 1832. III. 558.[2]

Schandorff, T. L. Toxicophlea. 1888. III. 685.[2]

Schanz, Georg. Im Königreich Bayern zu Recht bestehende Gesetze und Verordnungen. 1891. IV. 319.[1]

Scharfenberg, Georg Ludwig. *See* BECHSTEIN, J. M. & SCHARFENBERG, G. L.

Scharff, A. Kinakultuur. 1880. III. 716.

Scharff, Alois. Ueber Holzbearbeitungs-Maschinen. 1868. IV. 393.

Scharff, Benjamin. Σὺν τῷ θεῷ ἀρκευθολογία. 1679. III. 303.[1]

— Juniperi descriptio curiosa. 1679. III. 303.[2]

Scharlatanerieen der neuern Forstwirthschaftskunde. IV. 11, 100.[2]

Scharling, E. A. Beiträge zur Beleuchtung derjenigen chemischen Verhältnisse ... bei ... Balsamen. 1856. III. 482.[2]

Scharmer, Christian Carl. Einige in der Erfahrung gegründete Gedanken über die Conservation der ... Höltzungen. 1739. IV. 115.

Scharnaggl, Simon. Der Celtis australis. 1875. III. 363.[2]

— Die Forstwirthschaft im österreichischen Küstenlande. 1873. IV. 374.[2]

Scharrer & Keiss. Standorte einiger Pflanzen im Anschlusse an Sendtners " Vegetationsverhältnisse." 1869. I. 386.

Scharrer, H. Der Dselkwa-Baum. 1887. III. 366.[1]

— Einfluss des letzten Winters in Tiflis. 1883. III. 45.

— Die Erscheinung der ersten Blüthe. 1882. I. 224.[1]

— Ficus Carica in Transkaukasien. 1883. II. 150.[1]

— Nochmals Abies Eichleri. 1890. III. 297.[1]

— Notizen über die Wirkungen des Frostwetters im Februar. 1874. III. 44.[2]

Scharrer, W. Prunus armeniaca L. var. schirassica. 1864. III. 434.[1]

Scharschmidt, S. T. Note on Ceara rubber. 1898. III. 520.[2]

Schaschetzy, Anton. Abnorme Stammbildung an einer Fichte. 1885. II. 36.[1]

Schatel, G. D. J. Letterkundige bijdragen tot de geschiedenis van den Tabak, de Koffij en de Thee. 1848. III. 739.

De **schatten** der oppervlakte en de schatten der waters. 1879. III. 122.[2]

Schattenmann. Lettre à M. Dumas sur le rôle que l'ammoniaque joue dans la végétation. 1842. I. 157.

— Mémoire sur la culture de la Vigne dans ... Haut et du Bas-Rhine. 1863. III. 555.

Schatz, Joseph Anton. Über die angebliche Salix glabra. 1895. II. 107.[1]

— Die badischen Formen der Salix supertriandra × viminalis. 1895. II. 108.[1]

— Geschichtliche ... Bemerkungen über Salix livida. 1887. II. 100.[1]

— Revision der Salix multiformis. 1894. II. 108.[1]

— Salix aurita-viminalis Wimmer. 1855. II. 105.[1]

— Salix babylonica × fragilis. 1891. II. 105.[2]

— Salix Caprea × grandifolia var. heterogama. 1891. II. 106.[1]

— Salix Caprea × purpurea mas. 1890. II. 106.[1]

— Salix incana × viminalis ♂ bei Hüfingen. 1893. II. 107.[2]

— Salix pentandra-alba mas Ritschl. 1887. II. 108.[2]

— Zum Verständnis der Salix mollissima. 1895. II. 108.[1]

— Winke für angehende Salicologen. 1892. II. 99.[1]

Schatz, N. *See* KONDAKOW, Iwan & SCHATZ, N.

Schatz, Wilhelm. Flora halberstadensis excursoria. 1839. I. 380.

— Flora von Halberstadt. 1854. I. 383.

Schau. Rosers Dækning. 1893. III. 453.[1]

Schaub, Johannes. Dissertatio sistens Lauro Cerasi qualitates medicas. 1792. III. 438.[1]

Schauenburg, *Freiherr* von. Der Holzhandel des badischen Schwarzwaldes. 1899. IV. 388.[2]

Schauer. Die Winter 1837-38 und die Wirkungen der Kälte. 1838. III. 45.

Schauer, C. Ueber das Pfropfen der Cactus-Arten. 1833. III. 618.[1]

Schauer, Johann Konrad. Über die australischen Myrtaceen. 1836. II. 619.[1]

— Chamaelaucieae. 1841. II. 618.[2]

— Dissertatio phytographica de Regelia, Beaufortia. 1843. II. 618.[3]

— Ueber die von Dr. L. Preiss ... gesammelten Myrtaceae. 1843. I. 501.

— Einige neue ... Zierpflanzen des K. botanischen Gartens zu Breslau. 1833. I. 47.

— Genera Chamaelauciearum nova quaedam. 1836. II. 619.[1]

— Genera Myrtacearum nova vel denuo recognita. 1843. II. 618.[2]

— Der Königliche botanische Garten zu Breslau. 1843. I. 47.

— Die Melaleucen der deutschen Gärten. 1835. II. 629.[1]

— Monographia Myrtacearum xerocarpicarum. 1841. II. 618.[2]

— Myrtaceae R. Br. 1844. II. 619.[2]

— Plantae Kegelianae surinamenses. 1848. I. 339.[1]

— Plantae Regnellianae. 1849. I. 342.

— De Regelia, Beaufortia et Calothamno. 1843. II. 618.[2]

— Ueber die Sumpfkiefer, Pinus uliginosa Neumann. 1840. II. 43.[1]

— Verbenaceae. 1847. II. 752.[2]

— Verbenaceae. — *In* KLOTZSCH, J. F. 1847. II. 752.[2]

— *See also* NEES VON ESENBECK, Christian Gottfried & SCHAUER, J. K.

Schauer, Sebastian. Beitrag zur Cultur der Camellien. 1833. III. 599.[1]

— Ueber die Gattungen und Arten der Pomaceen. 1848. III. 419.[1]

— Kritische Revision der ... Arten der Gattung Leptospermum. 1841. II. 628.[2]

— *See also* NEES VON ESENBECK, C. G. & SCHAUER, Sebastian.

Schaumburg, C. Einige Mittheilungen über das Kappen der Bäume. 1839. III. 173.[1]

Schedae ad herbarium florae rossicae. 1898. I. 367.

Scheden, von, (*Oberförster*). Mittheilung über die Folgen der Streunutzung. 1854. IV. 71.

Scheden, Adolph. Rationell practische Anleitung zur Conservirung des Holzes. 1859. IV. 418.

Scheden, J. *oder* E. A. Der preussische Staats-Forstbeamte. 1844. IV. 35? 290.[1]

Scheden, Julius. Die wesentlichsten Mängel der preussischen Staats-Forstverwaltung. 1848. IV. 290.[2]

Schedlbauer, J. R. Dissertatio circa phytotoxicologiam cechicam. 1834. III. 90.[1]

Schedler, Ulr. Der Holzhandel des alten Landes Schwyz. 1898. IV. 406.[1]

Scheel, H. von. Die Waldschutzfrage. 1876. IV. 269.

Scheele, Adolf. Beiträge zur deutschen und schweizerischen Flora. 1843. I. 381.

— Beiträge zur Flora von Texas. 1848. I. 322.

— Beiträge zur Kenntniss der Euphorbiaceen. 1852. II. 433.[1]

— Beiträge zur Kenntniss der Pflanzenwelt. 1844. II. 856.[1]

— Beiträge zur Kenntniss des Pflanzenreiches. 1848. I. 269.

— Botanische Beiträge. 1843. I. 269.

— Verzeichniss der von Ferdinand Roemer aus Texas mitgebrachten Pflanzen. 1849. I. 322.

Scheele, Carl Wilhelm. Anmärkning om Citron-saft. 1784. II. 402.[1]

— Om frukt- och bär-syran. 1785. I. 152.[1]

— Om Rhabarberjordens närvaro uti flera vegetabilier. 1785. I. 174.

— Om sal essentiale gallarum. 1786. IV. 514.[1]

Scheen, J. Om bihugster i skov. 1896. IV. 382.[2]

— Om törskovdannelsen og midlerne til at forebygge samme. 1897. III. 119.[2]

Scheer, Frederick. A brief description of a new species of Mammillaria. 1845. II. 595.[1]

— Kew and its gardens. 1840. I. 54.

Scheffelaar, P. D. Handboek voor den timmerman. 1867. IV. 423.[1]

Scheffler. Een ziekte van den Koffieboom. 1878. III. 735.

Scheffer, C. F., *Friherre.* Berättelse om Mulbärs-träds planteringen. 1753. III. 372.²
Scheffer, Henrie Theophil. Anmärkningar öfver Herr Nicolai Seländers svar på trenne ... förestälde frågor. 1750. III. 235.²
Scheffer, J. Waarachtige en aenmerkenswaardige historie van Lapland. 1682. I. 350.²
Scheffer, R. Een woord over de Eucalyptus globulus. 1877. IV. 532.²
Scheffer, Rudolph Hermann Christian Carl. Bijdragen ... tot de kennis der flora van den Indischen Archipel. 1874. I. 466.
— Commentatio de Myrsinaceis archipelagi indici. 1867. II. 692.¹
— Sur deux espèces du genre Gonocaryum Miq. 1876. II. 474.²
— Ueber einige Palmen ... der Arecineae. 1871. II. 62.¹
— Énumération des plantes de la Nouvelle-Guinée. 1876. I. 499.¹
— Het geslacht Diplanthera. 1869. II. 788.¹
— Inlandsche plantennamen. 1879. I. 76.¹
— Liberia-Koffie. 1880. III. 742.²
— Limacia sumatrana. 1873. II. 208.²
— Observationes de ... Euphorbiaceis Archipelagi indici. 1868. II. 434.¹
— Observationes phytographicae. 1869. I. 466.
— Sur quelques Palmiers du groupe des Arécinées. 1871. II. 62.¹ — 1876. II. 60.²
— Sur quelques plantes ... de l'Archipel Indien. 1885. II. 215.²
— Rapport sur l'état du Jardin botanique de Buitenzorg. 1879. I. 68.¹
— On Sundanese vernacular names. 1871. I. 76.¹
— Verhaal van een paar dienstreizen in de adsistent residentie Buitenzorg. 1873. I. 469.¹
— Verslag omtrent de staat van 's Lands plantentuin. 1875. III. 128.
— Verslag omtrent den staat van 's Lands plantentuin. 1879. III. 128.
— *See also* MOENS, J. C. Bernelot & SCHEFFER, R. H. C. C.
— & **Holle**, K. F. Een Sagoboom op Java. 1873. III. 327.²
Schefold. Rechte und Pflichten des Privatwaldbesitzers. 1880. IV. 321.
Scheidecker, P. Zur Kultur der Bouvardia-Arten. 1881. III. 711.¹
Scheidemantel, (*Oberförster*). Ueber die Berechnung der Erträge aus der Berechtigung auf Raff- und Leseholz. 1855. IV. 438.¹
— Ueber Verjüngung der Buchen auf Sandboden. 1855. IV. 494.
Scheidnagel, Leopoldo. Apuntes sobre los sistemas más en uso en Francia para la conservación y preparación de las maderas. 1858. IV. 418.
— Apuntes y noticias sobre los sistemas conocidos para la conservación de las maderas. 1858. IV. 418.
Scheidweiler, J. Beschreibung einiger neuen Pflanzen-Gattungen. 1842. II. 440.²
— Notice sur quelques nouveaux genres ... de plantes. 1842. II. 406,¹ 440.¹
— Oonthos chimamonoides. 1937. II. 227.¹
Scheidweiler, Michel Joseph. Ariocarpus retusus. 1838. II. 589.¹
— Aristolochia glandulosa. 1837. II. 182.¹
— Beschreibung einer ... wenig bekannten Kirsche. 1844. II. 273.¹
— Beschreibung einiger neuen Cacteen. 1841. II. 585.²
— Beschreibung einiger neuen Cactus aus Mexiko. 1840. II. 587.²
— Beschreibung einiger neuen Pflanzen. 1842. I. 268. — 1847. I. 269.
— Chênes du Mexique. 1837. II. 129.¹
— Ein Dasylirion und zwei Agaven. 1841. II. 81.¹
— Descriptio diagnostica nonnullarum Cactearum. 1838. II. 585.²
— Description d'une nouvelle espèce de Cereus du Mexique. 1837. II. 589.²
— Description d'une nouvelle espèce de Mammillaria. 1837. II. 594.²
— Description de quelques nouveaux Cactus du Mexique. 1837. II. 594.²
— Francisque à fleurs d'Hortensia. 1848. III. 699.¹
— Mamellaria candida. 1838. II. 594.²
— Mammillaria conopsea. 1838. II. 594.²

— Mammillaria echinops. 1838. II. 594.²
— Mammillaria rosea. 1838. II. 595.¹
— Neue Varietät von Rhododendrum arboreum. 1841. II. 677.¹
— Les Pincenectia. 1859. II. 84.¹
— Pincenectia der Gärten. 1859. II. 84.¹
Scheiffele, (*Pfarrer*). Volkstümliche Pflanzennamen. 1890. I. 73.²
Scheiger, Josef, *Edler* von. Von dem Einflusse der Pflanzen auf die Zerstörung der Ruinen. 1857. III. 34.²
De **echeikunde** in hare toepassing op den landbouw. *See* B., C. W. 1856. III. 37.¹
Scheikundige aanteekeningen. *See* SCHEIKUNDIGE onderzoekingen. III. 15.
Scheikundige onderzoekingen. III. 15.
Scheikundige verhandelingen. *See* SCHEIKUNDIGE onderzoekingen. III. 15.
Scheit, Max. Beantwortung der Frage nach dem Luftgehalt des wasserleitenden Holzes. 1885. I. 165.
— Beitrag zur Widerlegung der "Imbibitionstheorie." 1886. I. 165.
— Die Tracheidensäume der Blattbündel der Coniferen. 1883. II. 18.
— Die Wasserbewegung im Holze. 1886. I. 165.
— Die Wasserbewegung im Holze. Vorläufige Mittheilung. 1884. I. 165.
Schelhammer, Günther Christoph. Catalogus plantarum ... in hortulo domestico. 1683. I. 43.
— De nova plantas cognoscendi methodo disquisitio. 1691. I. 250.
— De nova plantas in classes digerendi ratione. 1695. I. 250.
— Viae regiae ad artem stadium primum. 1705. I. 78.²
Schelhas. Beschreibung der Alpenpflanzen-Anlagen ... des Dr. Wild in Kassel. 1829. I. 46.
— Beschreibung einer blühenden Zamia horrida. 1829. II. 6.¹
Schelhase, August. Cultur der Rosa Banksiae. 1835. III. 454.²
— Über Paeonia arborea. 1837. III. 393.¹
— Verzeichnis von Topfgewächsen. 1825. III. 28.¹
Scheliessnig, J. Ueber Saatkämpe in Hochlagen. 1896. IV. 151.²
Schelinguer. De la greffe Luizet. 1855. III. 161.
Schell, Julius. *See* ШЕЛЛЬ, Ю. К.
Schelle, E. Aufruf, betreffend die Winterschäden an Gehölzen. 1895. III. 46.¹
— Empfehlenswerte Schlinggewächse. 1900. III. 205.¹
— Erfahrungen aus den letzten Wintern. 1895. III. 46.¹
— Monodora Myristica Dun. 1900. III. 402.¹
— Monströse Buchenblätter. 1892. II. 126.¹
— Rhus semialata Murray var. Osbecki. 1897. III. 527.²
— Winterharte Cacteen. 1894. III. 624.¹
— Winterharte Nadelhölzer. 1898. III. 202.
Schellenberg, Hans Conrad. Zur Entwickelungsgeschichte des Stammes von Aristolochia Sipho. 1899. II. 183.¹
— Ueber die Sklerotienkrankheit der Quitte. 1899. III. 423.²
Schellig, K. J. *See* MARKENDORF, J. B. & SCHELLIG, K. J.
— & **Markendorf**, J. B. Forst-Fragen als Entwickelungen ... zur Abtheilung der Gehölze. 1799. IV. 250.²
Schelver, Frans Joseph. *See* SCHELVER, Friedrich Joseph.
Schelver, Friedrich Joseph. Kritik der Lehre von den Geschlechtern der Pflanze. 1812. I. 199.
— Lebens- und Formgeschichte der Pflanzenwelt. 1822. I. 33.
Schember. Zur Geschichte der Mittelwaldwirtschaft in Hessen. 1887. IV. 26.
Schember, (*Revierförster, Sandberg*). Geschichte der Lehre von der Bestandsmischung. 1867. IV. 137.²
Schember, C. Das Auftreten der Schütte. 1858. IV. 476.
— Ueber die Pflanzweite. 1858. IV. 154.¹
Schembera, Josef. Der unpartheyische Forstmann. 1807. IV. 100.²
Schemmann, Wilhelm. Beiträge zur Flora der Kreise Bochum. 1884. I. 388.
— Beiträge zur Phanerogamen- und Gefässkryptogamen-Flora Westfalens. 1889. I. 389.
Schemmnigg, Joh. Werkzeuge für Hügel-Pflanzungen. 1881. IV. 153.²
Schenardi, Andrea. Monografia del distretto forestale di Bonorva. 1867. IV. 364.
Schenck. *See also* SCHENK.
Schenck, A. Beiträge zur Kenntniss der nassauischen Cynipiden. 1862. I. 215.¹

Schenck, August. Anleitung zur Bestimmung der im Herzogthum Nassau ... wildwachsenden Pflanzengattungen. 1846. I. 381.
Schenck, C. H. Afforestation of abandoned fields. 1898. IV. 155.²
Schenck, Carl Albert. Dissertatio ... sistens gummi-kino usum. 1794. III. 485.²
Schenck, Carl Alwin. The capitalist and economic forestry. 1899. IV. 271.¹
— Forestry as applied to reservations used as parks. 1898. IV. 137.¹
— Forestry at Biltmore. 1896. IV. 340.
— Our Yellow Poplar. 189.? IV. 519.²
— Private forestry and state forestry. 1897. IV. 286.¹
— Die Rentabilität des deutschen Eichenschälwalds. 1896. IV. 513.
— Some remarks on forestry as a business. 1900. IV. 259.²
Schenck, J. Observationum medicarum rariorum libri. VII. 1643. III. 240.
Schenck, Johann Heinrich Rudolf. Ueber das Aërenchym. 1889. I. 131.¹
— Ueber die Auskleidung der Intercellulargänge. 1885. I. 124.
— Beiträge zur Biologie und Anatomie der Lianen. 1892. I. 127,¹ 236.²
— Ueber brasilianische Lianenhölzer. 1894. I. 127.¹
— Ueber den Einfluss von Torsionen ... auf das Dickenwachsthum. 1893. I. 190.²
— Über Jugendformen ... speciell von Larix europaea. 1893. II. 33.¹
— Ueber die Luftwurzeln von Avicennia. 1889. II. 617,¹ 753.²
— Untersuchungen über die Bildung von centrifugalen Wandverdickungen an Pflanzenhaaren. 1884. I. 113,¹ 189.²
— Über die Zerklüftungsvorgänge in anomalen Lianenstämmen. 1895. I. 127.¹
Schenck, Johann Theodor. Catalogus plantarum Horti medici jenensis. 1659. I. 43.
— De cinnamomo. 1670. III. 405.²
— Historia plantarum generalis. 1656. I. 30; III. 58, (by error 1856).
Schenck, Karl Friedrich. Die Folgen der freien Privat-Waldwirthschaft. 1831. IV. 308.¹
— Handbuch über Forstrecht und Forstpolizei. 1825. IV. 268, 313.
Schenck, Rudolf. Botanisch-pharmacognostische Untersuchungen der Qumacai cipó. 1894. III. 540.¹
Schenck von Grafenberg, Johann Georg. Horust patavinus. 1600. I. 60.²
Schenckbecher, Johann George. Bericht von den heilsamen Wirkungen der Kinkina. 1769. III. 720.
Schenckel, J. Das Pflanzenreich. 1847. I. 95.
Schenk. See also SCHENCK.
Schenk, C. Einige Bemerkungen über die Bepflanzungen von Alleen. 1846. III. 209.
Schenk, Ernst. See SCHLECHTENDAL, D. F. L. von, LANGETHAL, C. E. & SCHENK, Ernst.
Schenk, Georg, Edler von. Der lebende Weissdorn Spalier Zaun. 1834. III. 422.²
Schenk, J. Die Obstbäume ohne Pfähle zu ziehen. 1838. III. 134.²
Schenk, Johann Theodor. See SCHENCK, J. T.
Schenk, Joseph August. Der botanische Garten der Universität zu Würzburg. 1860. I. 48.
— Ueber die chinesischen Galläpfel. 1850. III. 527.¹
— On the ciliary motion of pollen grains. 1850. I. 117.¹
— Ueber die Flimmerbewegung der Pollenkörner. 1850. I. 17.¹
— Flora der Umgebung von Würzburg. 1848. I. 382.
— Handbuch der Botanik. 1879. I. 91.
— Zur Kenntniss des Baues der Früchte der Compositen. 1877. II. 850.¹
— Ueber Parthenogenesis im Pflanzenreiche. 1860. I. 202.¹
— Plantarum species quas in itinere per Aegyptum. 1840. I. 478.
— Umwandlung von Blatt in Blüthensprosse. 1860. II. 17.²
— Wurzelbildung an Zweigen bei Coniferen. 1860. II. 20.¹
— See also GRISEBACH, August & SCHENK, August.
Schenkel, L. Over het vermoedelijk ontstaan ... van den boomkanker. 1859. I. 206.²
Scheppach, G. A. Karakteristisches Verzeichniss der vorzüglichsten ... Holzarten. 1791. III. 68,² IV. 81.
Scheppler, Karl. Das Nivelliren und der Waldwegbau. 1863. IV. 266.²
— Der Waldwegbau und das Nivelliren. 1863. IV. 266.²

Scherbius, Johannes. See GÄRTNER, P. G., MEYER, Bernhard & SCHERBIUS, Johannes.
Scherel, (Oberförster). Das Wasser, ein Mittel die Bodenkraft zu heben. 1863. IV. 73.¹
Scherel, (Oberforstmeister). Mittheilungen aus dem Gebiete der Unfallversicherung. 1890. IV. 311.¹
Scherer & Wasmer. Abschätzungs- und Einrichtungs-Operat des Gemeindewaldes von Ebringen. 1846. IV. 247.²
Scherer, Johann Andreas. Ueber Gerbsäure. 1804. I. 182.²
Scherfel, Aurel W. Der älteste botanische Schriftsteller Zipsens. 1895. I. 446.
Schering. Theodolith oder Bussole im Walde? 1900. IV. 266.¹
Scherk, Carl, (jr.). Anleitung zur Bestimmung des wirksamen Gerbstoffgehaltes in den Naturgerbstoffen. 1891. I. 183, IV. 435.
Schermbeek, A. J. van. Eene bijdrage tot de kennis van den boschgrond. 1892. IV. 70.
— Le boisement des bruyères de la Campine. 1898. IV. 161.¹
— Het bosch. 1898. IV. 107,² 119.²
— Het bosch in het huishouden van den staat. 1893. IV. 270.
— Het boschbedrijf. 1889. IV. 356.²
— Boschexploitatie van staatswege. 1885. IV. 376.²
— Het boschwezen in Nederlandsch Indië. 1894. IV. 377.¹
— De exploitatie van's lands bosschen op Java. 1881. IV. 383.²
— Herbossching van Java's bergen. 1880. IV. 168.¹
— Inrichting van het Liesbosch onder Prinsenhage. 1892. IV. 356.¹
— Over de mogelijkheid om de Koffiebladziekte. 1879. III. 735.
— Een woord over het boschbouwvak en de opleiding daarvoor. 1892. IV. 33.²
— & others. Inrichting van het Mastbosch. 1900. IV. 357.¹
Schertel, Arnulf. See SCHROEDER, Julius von & SCHERTEL, A.
Scherzer, Carl. See WAGNER, Moritz & SCHERZER, Carl.
Schets van het eiland Nossakambangan. 1838. III. 274.¹
Scheuch, Fred H. The Cork tree and the cork industry. 1890. IV. 517.²
Scheuchzer, Johannes Jakob. Bibliotheca scriptorum historiae naturali ... inservientium. 1716. I. 1.
— Helvetiae historia naturalis. 1716. I. 432.²
— Historiae helveticae naturalis prolegomena. 1700. I. 432.²
— Itinera alpina. See his Οὐρεσιφοίτης helvetiens. 1708. I. 432.²
— Itinera per Helvetiae alpinas regiones. See Οὐρεσιφοίτης helveticus. 1708. I. 432.²
— Οὐρεσιφοίτης helvetiens. 1708. I. 432.²
— Physica sacra iconibus illustrata. 1732. I. 512.
— Physique sacrée. 1732. I. 512.
— Plantae rarae in Alpibus rhaeticis. 1775. I. 433.
Scheuerle, Joseph. Botanische Funde und Fundorte. 1887. II. 101.²
— Die frühblütigen Weiden. 1889. II. 101.²
— Schleichers 86 Arten der Salix nigricans. 1889. II. 108.²
— Ein südlicher Standort der Salix livida. 1888. II. 108.¹
— Die Weiden-Arten Württembergs. 1888. II. 101.²
— Zwanzig neue Weidenbastarde. 1887. II. 101.²
Scheuerlein, Fedor. See GOLLMANN, O., KRAUSE, Rudolf & SCHEUERLEIN, Fedor.
Scheuing. Aus dem fränkischen Mittelwaldgebiete. 1884. IV. 351.¹
Scheurer-Kestner, Auguste. Nouvelles recherches sur la ... préparation de la soude. 1867. IV. 396.¹
— Pouvoir calorifique des combustibles. 1896. IV. 413.¹
Scheurl, G. C. W. von. Forsthandbuch. 1803. IV. 96.
Scheurl, J. C. W. von. Kurze Darstellung des Wichtigsten von Forstwesen. 1802. IV. 105.
Scheutz, Nils Johan Wilhelm. Berättelse om en botanisk resa i Bohuslän. 1880. II. 284.¹
— Bidrag till kännedomen om slägtet Rosa. 1873. II. 284.²
— Bidrag till Ölands flora. 1881. II. 298.¹
— Conspectus florae smolandicae. 1887. I. 355.
— De duabus Rosis britannicis. 1888. II. 285.¹
— Herbarium Rosarum Scandinavica. 1880. II. 284.¹
— Några ord till herr J. A. Leffler. 1873. II. 284.¹
— Nya växtlokaler. 1873. II. 301.¹
— Öfversigt af Sverges och Norges Rosa-arter. 1877. II. 284.¹

— Plantae vasculares jeniseenses. 1888. I. 454.[1]
— Ueber Rosa Brotheri n. sp. 1880. II. 291.[2]
— Rosa sclerophylla funnen i Danmark. 1877. II. 298.[2]
— De Rosis nonnullis caucasicis. 1879. II. 284.[1]
— Smålands flora. 1864. I. 356.
— Spridda växtgeografiska bidrag. 1878. I. 357. — 1881. II. 299.[2]
— Studier öfver de skandinaviska arterna af slägtet Rosa. 1872. II. 283.[2]
— Two varieties of Roses new to Scotland. 1888. II. 285.[1]
Schexel, (Oberforstmeister, Moritzburg). De la réserve lors des coupes définitives. 1896. IV. 130.
Schg. Die partielle Vorverjüngung. 1869. IV. 139.[1]
Schibler, Wilhelm. Beiträge zu einer . . . Anatomie . . . der Boragineen. 1887· II. 748.[1]
Schickendantz, Federico. Noticia preliminar sobre Berberis flexuosa. 1879. II. 203.[2]
Schickler, C. Robinia inermis pyramidalis. 1857. III. 486.[2]
Schiebler, H. Die Coniferen. 1881. II. 13.[1]
— Japanesische Pflanzen und Gärten. 1877. III. 127.[2]
Schiebler, J. L. & Sohn. Ueber Anlage von Weissdorn-Hecken. 1879. III. 214.[1]
Schiebler, Sohn & J. L. See SCHIEBLER, J. L. & Sohn.
Schiede, Christian Julius Wilhelm. Botanische Berichte aus Mexico. 1829. I. 331.
— Sur la nature de la végétation . . . du Mexique. 1829. I. 331.
— De plantis hybridis sponte natis. 1825. I. 271.[2]
Schiedermayer, Karl. Ein zweites Blühen von Prunus Cerasus. 1864. II. 273.[2]
Schiefferdecker, W. Die Cocapflanze. 1861. III. 492.[2]
Schiel, Heinrich. Grundzüge der Pflanzenkunde. 1838. I. 87.
Schier, A. Zur Rentabilität des Mittelwaldes. 1875. IV. 130.
— Die Weymouthskiefer. 1873. IV. 470.[1]
Schier, R. Der Fichtenrindenwickler. 1874. IV. 456.
— Ueber die finanzielle Bedeutung der Birke. 1892. IV. 490.[2]
— Die Lehre von den gemischten Beständen. 1874. IV. 137.[2]
Schier, W. Zur Entwickelung . . . der Borkenkäfer. 1898. IV. 96.
— Die Kohlenrauchschäden im Chemnitzer Stadtwalde. 1893. IV. 192.[2]
— Waldbeschädigung durch den Harzrüsselkäfer. 1892. IV. 208.[1]
Schiera, Giovanni Maria. Dissertationes duae, quarum una de plantarum sexu. 1750. I. 195,[1] 198.
Schierbeck. Beretning om nogle forsög i plantekultur paa Island. 1886. III. 120.[1]
Schierl, Adalbert. See LAUS, Heinrich & SCHIERL, Adalbert.
Schiermann, V. Ueber die Bewirthschaftung der Bauern-wälder. 1883. IV. 123.[2]
Schiewek, Ottokar. Ueber Pflanzen-Verbänderung. 1867. I. 144.[2]
Schiff, F. See HERZIG, J. & SCHIFF, F.
Schiff, Hugo. Sur la constitution de l'amygdaline. 1869. I. 175.
— Recherches sur la quinoline. 1863. III. 722.
Schiff, Julius. Das ätherische Oel von Sassafras. 1884. III. 408.[1]
Schiffel, Adalbert. Altersklassenverhältniss und Umtrieb. 1881. IV. 252.
— Ueber Bestandeshöhen und Bestandesformzahlen. 1900. IV. 219.
— Ueber Bestandsmassenaufnahmen. 1897. IV. 219.
— Betriebseinrichtung und Plänterwald. 1889. IV. 245.
— Form und Inhalt der Fichte. 1899. IV. 459.[1]
— Ueber forstliche Ertragstafeln. 1897. IV. 238.
— Zur forstlichen Ertragsregelung. 1884. IV. 244.
— Kritische Betrachtungen über die Holzmassenermittlung. 1898. IV. 219.
— Das normale Altersclassenverhältniss im Femelschlag-betriebe. 1890. IV. 245.
— Untersuchungen über den Genauigkeitsgrad einiger Dendrometer. 1898. IV. 216, 232.
Schiffner, Victor. See NESTLER, A. & SCHIFFNER, V.
Schilbersky, Karl. Beobachtungen über unregelmässige Blüthezeiten. 1886. I. 227.[1]
— Corylus Avellana nova var. Pilisiensis. 1891. II. 121.[2]
— Kihalófélben levő növények. 1891. I. 219.[1]
— A lőcsei szomorú Luczfenyő. 1892. II. 35.[1]

— Monographie de la horticulture en Hongrie. 1900. III. 127.[1]
— Némely tülevelü fáról. 1887. III. 290.
— A Szomorúfüz hazája és bevándorlásának ideje. 1886. II. 105.[2]
Schilcher, F. S. Ueber die zweckmässigste Methode den Ertrag der Waldungen zu bestimmen. 1796. IV. 235.[1]
Schild, Hermann. Über die Bestimmung der absoluten Feuchtigkeit des Holzes. 1886. IV. 412.[1]
Schildbach, Karl. Beschreibung einer Holz-Bibliothek. 1788. I. 37,[2] IV. 17.
Schildknecht, J. Führer durch die Flora von Freiburg. 1863. I. 385.
— Nachtrag zu Spenners Flora friburgensis. 1862. V. XIX.[2]
Schillbach, C. Beiträge zur Kenntniss des Berberins. 1886. I. 176, III. 394.[2]
Schillen van akkermaalshout door stoom. 1875. IV. 434.
Schiller. Durchforstungs-Ertrag eines Eichen-Mischbestandes. 1876. IV. 175.[2]
Schiller, August. Der chinesische Thee. 1881. III. 607.
Schiller, Eduard. Grundzüge der Cacteenkunde. 1886. III. 619.
Schiller, J. C. Die Baumzucht im Grossen. 1795. III. 153.
Schiller, Karl. Zum Thier- und Kräuterbuche des mecklenburgischen Volkes. 1861. I. 517.[2]
Schiller-Tietz: Die Ueberwinterung der Holzgewächse. 1900. IV. 385.[1]
Schilling, August Jakob. Der Einfluss von Bewegungshemmungen auf die Arbeitsleistungen der Blattgelenke von Mimosa. 1895. II. 373.[1]
Schilling, Ernst Morits. Forst- und jagdrechtliche Erörterungen, als erster Nachtrag zu dem Handbuche des im Königr. Sachsen giltigen Forst- und Jagd-Rechts. 1827. IV. 321.
— Handbuch des im Königreiche Sachsen giltigen Forst- und Jagd-Rechts. 1827. IV. 321.
— Lehrbuch des gemeinen in Deutschland giltigen Forst- und Jagd-Rechts. 1822. IV. 316.
— Ueber das Roden der Stöcke. 1823. IV. 385.[2]
— Tabellarische Uebersicht der deutschen Forstbotanik. 1828. IV. 82.
— Der Waldschutz; oder Vollständige Forstpoliceilehre. 1826. IV. 177.[1]
Schilling, Heinrich, Freiherr von. Die Schädlinge des Obst-und Weinbaues. 1893. III. 191.
Schilling, Johann Jakobs. Phytologiae; seu, Physices plantarum specimen I.— [III]. 1752. I. 31.
Schilling, L. Das Abstecken der Waldwege. 1891. IV. 267.
— Betriebs- und Ertragsregelung eines ca. 1500 ha grossen Privatwaldes. 1891. IV. 241, 246.
— Die Betriebs- und Ertragsregelung im Hoch- und Niederwalde. 1091. IV. 241.
— Ertragsregelung im Hoch- und Niederwalde. 1891. IV. 246.
— Geschichte des Bunzlauer Stadtforstes. 1895. IV. 354.
— Geschichte des Bunzlauer Stadtforstes 1594–1894. 1894. IV. 26.
— & Elias, (Oberförster, Kotzenau). Ist die Versicherung gegen Waldbrandschaden im Vereinsgebiete zu empfehlen? 1897. IV. 2/4.[1]
— & Euen, (Forstrath, Oppeln). Welchen Einfluss haben die in jüngster Zeit abgeschlossenen Handelsverträge auf den Holzabsatz. 1896. IV. 404.[2]
Schilling, Samuel. Gemeinnütziges Handbuch der Botanik. 1840. I. 255.
Schilling von Cannstadt, Carl, Freiherr. Mistel, Wald und Misteldrossel. 1882. III. 385.[1]
— Verwendung und Eigenschaften in- und ausländischer Nutzhölzer. 1875. IV. 408.
Schilthuis, G. Berigt omtrent de Djati-rups. 1861. IV. 537.[1]
— De bewerking der berekeningen en het vervoer van hout in de bosschen van Z. Duitschland. 1857. IV. 404.[1]
— Opgave van eenige geschikte houtsoorten . . . in de residentie Rembang. 1861. IV. 399.[2]
Schilthuis, U. G., (jr.). Verhouding van den landbouw. 1853. III. 122.[1]
Schimák, Jos. Dienstinstruction für Wirthschafts- und Forstbeamte. 1883. IV. 309.[2]
Schimert, Johann Peter. De systemate sexuali. 1776. I. 258.
Schimmel. Sur l'huile de camphre. 1888. III. 404.[2]

Schimmel, F. W. De Koffie-cultuur op Java. 1899. III. 731.
Schimmelfennig, Rudolf. Bericht über Forstwirthschaft und Jagd. 1874. IV. 19.[1]
— Der Dampfpflug. 1873. IV. 143.[1]
— Die forstliche Ausstellung . . . zu Bremen 1874. 1874. IV. 19.[1]
— Samenschläge in Fichten. 1888. IV. 454.
— Volk, Wald und Jagd in Ostfriesland. 1879. IV. 118.
Schimmelpenninck van der Oye, A. J. See BARTELINK, E. J. & SCHIMMELPENNINCK VAN DER OYE, A. J.
Schimmelpenninck van der Oye, W. A. Iets over Populieren. 1858. III. 345.[2]
— Ontginnen van heide. 1856. IV. 159.
Schimper, Andreas Franz Wilhelm. Sur l'amidon et les leucites. 1887. I. 177.
— Ueber Bau und Lebensweise der Epiphyten Westindiens. 1884. I. 234.[2]
— Bilder aus der Pflanzenwelt des australischen Continentes. 1900. I. 505.
— Die epiphytische Vegetation Amerikas. 1888. I. 234.[2]
— Die Gebirgswälder Java's. 1893. I. 467, IV. 88.[1]
— The hili forests of Java. 1893. I. 467, IV. 88.[1]
— Die indo-malayische Strandflora. 1891. I. 466.
— Ueber Kalkoxalatbildung. 1888. I. 139.
— Pflanzen-Geographie. 1898. I. 219.[1]
— Researches on the growth of starch grains. 1881. I. 140.[3]
— Rhizophoraceae. 1893. II. 613.[1]
— Über Schutzmittel des Laubes gegen Transpiration. 1890. I. 168.
— Untersuchungen über das Wachsthum der Stärkekörner. 1881. I. 140.[2]
— Untersuchungen über die Chlorophyllkörner. 1885. I. 142.
— Untersuchungen über die Proteinkrystalloide. 1878. I. 139.
— Die Wechselbeziehungen zwischen Pflanzen und Ameisen. 1888. I. 235.[1]
Schimper, Karl Friedrich. Description du Symphytum Zeyheri. 1830. I. 102.
— Geometrische Anordnung der um eine Axe peripherischen Blattgebilde. 1836. I. 102.
Schimper, Wilhelm. Médicaments employés en Abyssinie. 1848. III. 280.[2]
— Reise nach Algier. 1834. I. 484.
Schimpfky, Richard. Deutschlands wichtigste Giftgewächse. 1893. III. 74.
— Unsere Heilpflanzen in Bild und Wort. 1893. III. 74.
Schimpke, Josef. Die Bedeutung der Schneissennetzes für Hochgebirgsforste. 1893. IV. 251.[1]
— Die Bestandeswirthschaft in Hochgebirgsforsten. 1891. IV. 246.
— Gegen den Femelschlagbetrieb im Hochgebirge. 1884. IV. 131.
— Ueber das Schneideln der Waldbäume. 1885. IV. 172,[1] 172.[2]
— Der Siebenschläfer im Dienste der Forstwirthschaft. 1888. IV. 90.[2]
— Unsere Waldameisen. 1884. IV. 92.
Schinabeck, J. Ausländische Coniferen und deren Kultur. 1881. III. 292.
— Fixierung der Baumformen. 1883. I. 106,[1] III. 209.
— Die Spiraeaceen und ihre Kultur. 1882. III. 460.[3]
Schindler, A. Die Wildbach- und Fluss-Verbauung. 1888. IV. 187.[1]
Schindler, C. E. Das österreichische Holz- und Weiderechet-Ablösungsgesetz. 1854. IV. 334.[2]
Schindler, Karl. Allgemeiner Forstkulturkosten-Tarif. 186.7 IV. 243.
— Die Forst- und Jagdgesetze der österreichischen Monarchie. 1866. IV. 331.[2]
— Die Forste der . . . Staats- und Fondsgüter. 1864. IV. ³⁄₆₈.
— Die K. k. Forstlehranstalt zu Mariabrunn. 1863. IV. 36.[2]
— Krankheiten und Feinde der Ulme. 1861. IV. 518.[2]
— Lesy v Čecháeh. 1883. IV. 371.
— Mathematische Aufgaben nebst ihren Lösungen. 1865. IV. 58.
— Notiz über die Dauer der Eiche und Lärche. 1861. IV. 449, 505.
— Oesterreich's Bauholzverbrauch. 1858. IV. 418.
— Portefeuille für Forstwirthe, Ingenieure. 1872. IV. 230.
— Schematismus und Statistik der Staatsforste. 1864. IV. 367.
— Veškeré nauky lesnické. 1865. IV. 99.[2]
— Zwei Lärchbäume. 1857. IV. 452.[1]

Schinne, J. E. C. van. Catalogus plantarum . . . in Hórto medico rotterodamensi. 1809. I. 51.[1]
Schinz, Christoph Salomon. Praktischer Commentar zu Johann Gessners phytographischen Tafeln. 1800. I. 264.
Schinz, Hans. Amarantaceae. 1893. II. 189.[1]
— Beiträge zur Kenntnis der afrikanischen Flora. 1893. I. 483.[3]—1899. II. 744.[2]
— Beiträge zur Kenntniss der Flora von Deutsch-Südwest-Afrika. 1888. I. 495.
— Beitrag zur Kenntniss afrikanischer Passifloraceae. 1893. II. 576.[1]
— Ueber Cladostigma hildebrandtioides. 1899. II. 744.[2]
— Die deutsche Interessensphäre in Südwest-Afrika. 1890. I. 495.
— Deutsch-Südwest-Afrika. 1891. I. 495.
— Diagnoses plantarum Africanum novarum. 1900. II. 423.[2]
— Zur Kenntnis der Flora der Aldabra-Inseln. 1897. I. 482.
— Observations sur une collection de plantes du Transvaal. 1891. I. 495.
— Die Pflanzenwelt Deutsch-Südwest-Afrikas. 1896. I. 495.
— Seebälle. 1893. I. 242.[2]
— Die Seebälle des Silsersees. 1884. I. 242.[2]
— Untersuchungen über den Mechanismus des Aufspringens der Sporangien und Pollensäcke. 1883. I. 117.[1]
— See also DURAND, Théophile & SCHINZ, Hans.
— & AUTRAN, Eugène. Des genres Achatocarpus Triana et Bosia. 1893. II. 189.[1]
— & Junod, Henri. Zur Kenntnis der Pflanzenwelt der Delagoa-Bay. 1899. I. 495.
— & Keller, Robert. Flora der Schweiz. 1900. I. 438.
Schinz, R. Beschreibung der in der welschen Schweiz üblichen Holzgeleiten. 1784. IV. 390.[1]
Schinz, Salomon. Anleitung zu der Pflanzenkenntniss. 1774. III. 55.
— Beschreibung einiger . . . Seltenheiten. 1761. I. 143.
— Dissertationis physicae de itineribus per Helvetiam. 1781. III. 271.[2]
— Primae linae botanicae. 1775. I. 32.
— Registerü über die Historia stirpium Leonh. Fuchsii. 1778. I. 255.[3]
Schiødte, Jørgen Matthias Christian. Om Angreb af Insecter paa Naåleskovene. 1857. IV. 442.
— Beretning om Angreb af Insekter. 1855. IV. 442.
— Et Par Bemærkninger om Angreb af Insecter paa vore Naaletræ-Plantager. 1857. IV. 442.
Schiötz, Er jordbrugets förbrug af skovprodukter for ödselt. 1883. IV. 282.[1]
Schiötz, Joha. Nogle iagtagelser paa skovväsenets omraade. 1897. IV. 344.[1]
Schiötz, Johannes. Om skovforholdene i Romsdals amt. 1858. IV. 343.[2]
Schiötz, Th. Beretning om en botanisk Reise. 1860. I. 355.
Schipper, W. W. Stapelplaatsen van boomen als oorzaak van besmetting met splintkevers. 1895. IV. 204.
Schips, K. Ueber die Cuticula . . . in den Samenschalen der Papilionaceen. 1893. II. 321.[1]
Schirach, Adam Gottlieb. Waldbienenzucht. 1774. IV. 438.[2]
Schirmer, H. Auf dem Vogesensandstein der Pfalz gedeihen Eichen. 1887. IV. 118.
Schirmer, P. See POLSTORFF, K. & SCHIRMER, P.
Schirnhofer, Gerhard. Praktisches Handbuch zur Obstbaumzucht. 1875. III. 146.[1]
Schirnhofer, P. Gerhard. Ueber Wellingtonia gigantea. 1878. III. 310.[1]
Schirò, Giorgio. Attuale condizione forestale di quattro provincie Siciliane. 1862. IV. 364.
— Attuale condizione forestale e solforifera di Sicilia. 1860. IV. 364.
— Osservazioni e aspirazioni sul progetto di legge forestale. 1864. IV. 328.
Schittel, Adalbert. Zur forstlichen Ertragsregelung. 1884. IV. 237.
Schiweck, Die Festlegung . . . der Wanderdünen. 1894. IV. 146.[1]
Schkuhr, Christian. Botanisches Handbuch der . . . in Deutschland . . . ausdauernden Gewächse. 1791. I. 375.
— Einige botanische Bemerkungen. 1794. I. 264.
— Enchiridion botanicum. 1805. I. 348.[2]
Schl. Zur Hebung des Schälwaldbetriebes. 1893. IV. 515.[3]
Schlaberndorf, von & others. Instruction für den Rathmann Morath zur Vermessung der k. ohlauschen Amts-Forsten. 1850. IV. 301.

Schläfli, Alexander & **Wolf,** Rudolf. Verzeichniss der Dattel-varietäten der Provinz Irak. 1862. II. 72.[2]

Schläpfer, Johann Georg. Versuch einer naturhistorischen Beschreibung des Cantons Appenzell. 1829. I. 433.

Schlagdenhauffen, Frédéric. Étude chimique du Spermolepis. 1892. III. 637.[3]

— *See also* HECKEL, Édouard & SCHLAGDENHAUFFEN, Fr.; OBERLIN, Léon & SCHLAGDENHAUFFEN, Fr.

— & **Planchon,** Louis. Sur un Strophanthus du Congo fran-çais. 1898. III. 690.[3]

Schlagintweit, Robert von. Der Charakter der Vegetation im Himalaya. 1866. I. 474.

Schlagintweit-Sakünlünski, Adolph. Beiträge zur Kenntniss der Vegetationsverhältnisse oberhalb der Schneelinie. 1854. I. 219.[3]

— Contributions to a knowledge of the vegetation above the snow line. 1854. I. 220.[1]

— Pflanzengeographische Untersuchungen. 1850. I. 220.[3]

— Recherches sur les phénomènes périodiques. 1850. I. 220.[3]

— Untersuchungen über die Grenzen der Vegetation . . . der Alpen. 1851. I. 434.

— *See also* SCHLAGINTWEIT-SAKÜNLÜNSKI, Hermann & Adolph.

Schlagintweit-Sakünlünski, Hermann von. Anlage des Her-bariums während der Reisen. 1877. I. 36.[1]

— Sur la distribution de la température . . . dans l'Inde. 1863. I. 473.

— Ueber das Genus Rosa in Hochasien. 1874. III. 454.[1]

— Klimatischer Charakter der pflanzengeographischen Regio-nen Hochasiens. 1876. I. 457, 460.[1]

— Die neuen Compositen des Herbarium Schlagintweit. 1878. II. 849.[3]

— Reisen in Indien und Hochasien. 1869. I. 453.[1]

— & Adolph. Untersuchungen über die physicalische Geogra-phie der Alpen. *See* SCHLAGINTWEIT-SAKÜNLÜNSKI, Adolph. 1850. I. 220.[3]

Schlaiher. Hoher Geldertrag eines Kiefernbestandes in Bel-gien. 1857. IV. 480.

Schlatter, Theodor. Die Bewaldung des Kantons St. Gallen. 1893. IV. 28.[1]

— Die Einführung der Kulturpflanzen. 1893. IV. 28.[1]

— Die Einführung der Kulturpflanzen in den Kantonen St. Gallen. 1893. III. 127.[1]

— Ueber die Verbreitung der Alpenflora. 1874. I. 436.

— *See also* WARTMANN, Bernhard & SCHLATTER, Theodor.

Schlechtendal, Diedrich Franz Leonhard von. Abbildung und Beschreibung aller in der Pharmacopoea borussica aufge-führten Gewaechse. 1830. III. 56.

— Abnorm entwickelter Pflanzen. 1856. II. 103,[2] 714.[3]

— Abnorme Bildung an einer Pinie. 1866. II. 45.[1]

— Abnorme Bildungen. 1855. I. 143.

— Abnorme Fruchtbildungen. 1862. II. 31,[1] 268.[3]

— Abnormitäten au Pinus-Zapfen. 1059. II. 90.[3]

— Ueber Acacia retinodes Schldl. 1853. II. 328.[1]

— De Anonaceis brasiliensibus. 1835. II. 215.[1]

— Ueber die Auswüchse der Terebinthe. 1836. II. 457.[3]

— Beiträge zur Kenntniss der Coniferen. 1865. II. 13.[1]

— Ein Beitrag zur Flora der Inseln des grünen Vorgebirges. 1851. I. 497.

— Bemerkungen über die amerikanischen Kirschen-Arten. 1839. II. 270.[1]

— Bemerkungen über die Gattung Frenela. 1866. II. 27.[1]

— Bemerkungen über einige mexikanische Pflanzen. 1838. II. 41.[3]

— Bemerkungen über einige Ribes-Arten. 1862. II. 243.[3]

— Bemerkungen über zweimal blühende Holzgewächse. 1849. I. 220.[3]

— Bemerkungen zu den Coniferen. 1860. II. 170.[1]

— Beobachtungen über die Cactus-Pflanzen. 1832. III. 618.[1]

— Ueber Beschorneria yuccoides. 1864. II. 89.[3]

— Bestimmung . . . der von Dr. Behr . . . gesammelten Pflanzen. 1847. I. 501.

— Betrachtungen über die Zwergmandeln. 1854. II. 270.[3]

— Zur Birkenfrage. 1846. II. 117.[3]

— Blüthen der Rosskastanie. 1863. II. 482.[1]

— Über eine im botanischen Garten gezogene Eichenart. 1863. III. 362.[1]

— Ueber die Buchen und ihre Verbreitung. 1858. II. 125,[3] IV. 79.[1]

— Ueber die chinesischen Galläpfel. 1850. III. 527.[3]

— Cocculus laurifolius D. C. 1852. II. 207.[1]

— Coniferae mexicanae. 1858. II. 14.[3]

— Corollarium observationum in plantas hortenses Halae Saxonum. 1851. I. 47.

— Dodonaeae confertae descriptio. 1852. II. 486.[1]

— Eichenfragen. 1857. II. 129.[3]

— Einige abnorme Blattbildungen. 1855. II. 144,[1] 289.[3]

— Ueber einige Blattmissbildungen. 1844. I. 144.[3]

— Ueber einige mexicanische Arzeneimittel. 1859. III. 264.[3]

— Elaeagnaceae. 1857. II. 607.[1]

— Elaeagnacearum in Candollei Prodromo (vol. xiv.) exposi-tarum adumbratio. 1860. II. 607.[1]

— Über die europäischen Eichenarten. 1860. II. 129.[3]

— Ueber die Flor von Labrador. 1836. I. 310.

— Flora berolinensis. 1823. I. 377.

— Zur Flora Croatiens. *See* KLINGGRÄFF, Hugo von. 1862. I. 447.

— Florula insulae Sti. Thomae. 1828. I. 335.

— Die Gattung Bouvardia. 1853. II. 810.[1]

— Ueber die Gattung Pisonia Plum. 1848. II. 191.[3]

— Über die geographische Verbreitung der Buche. 1860. II. 125.[1]

— Hortorum botanicorum plantae novae et adnotationes. 1844. I. 269.

— Hortus halensis. 1841. I. 47.

— Index seminum Horti academici halensis. 1849. I. 47.

— Zur Kenntniss der Gattung Beschorneria. 1863. II. 89.[3]

— Ueber Lonicera Xylosteum und deren Abänderungen. 1862. II. 840.[1]

— Lycium barbarum. 1835. II. 773.[1]

— Ueber Magnolia mexicana. 1864. II. 211.[1]

— De Meyna Roxburghii. 1829. II. 833.[1]

— Miscellanea botanica. 1853. I. 269.

— Eine neue Baechea aus Sumatra. 1846. II. 620.[3]

— Ueber eine neue Mahonia. 1854. II. 202.[1]

— Eine neue Saurauja aus Guatemala. 1853. II. 542.[3]

— Observationes botanicae. 1840. I. 268.

— Observationes quaedam in . . . Solanacearum genera. 1832. II. 767.[3]

— Pflanzen-Missbildungen. 1833. II. 293.[3]

— Pflanzen-Missbildungen. 1835. II. 773.[1]

— Pflanzen-Missbildungen. Amorpha. 1833. II. 332.[1]

— Plantae Ecklonianae. Bruniaceae. 1831. I. 494.

— Plantae Lechlerianae. 1856. I. 329.

— Plantae Leiboldianae. 1844. I. 331.

— Plantae phanerogamae . . . agri berolinensis. 1823. I. 377.

— Plantae Wagenerianae columbicae. 1853. I. 339.[3]

— Plantarum capensium descriptio. 1826. II. 230.[1]

— Plantarum novarum . . . adumbrationes. 1837. II. 848.[1]

— De plantis mexicanis. 1832. I. 331.

— De plantis variis mexicanis. 1853. I. 331.

— Wegen Pyrus Pollveria. 1846. II. 313.[3]

— Ueber den Quebracho der argentinischen Staaten. 1861. II. 794.[1]

— Sur le retranchement du pivot des arbres. 1827. III. 173.[1]

— Revision der . . . Verhandlungen über das Beschneiden der Pfahlwurzel. 1827. III. 173.[1]

— Ribes-Arten aus dem botanischen Garten. 1863. II. 243.[3]

— Ribes spicatum. 1863. III. 415.[3]

— Schubertia Keforsteinii. 1852. II. 742.[3]

— De Sterilis nonnullis mexicanae. 1040. II. 866.[3]

— On twice-flowering trees. 1849. I. 220.[1]

— Ueber das Vorkommen des Eibenbaums. 1847. II. 10.[3]

— Vorläufige Nachricht über die mexicanischen Coniferen. 1838. II. 14.[3]

— Widdringtonia. 1865. II. 27.[1]

— Ein Wort über Pisonia aculeata. 1854. II. 191.[3]

— Ueber die Zwergmandeln. 1865. II. 271.[1]

— *See also* CHAMISSO, Adalbert von, SCHLECHTENDAL, D. F. L. von & others.

— & **Chamisso,** Adalbert von. Plantarum mexicanarum . . . recensio brevis. 1830. I. 331.

— **Langethal,** C. E. & **Schenk,** Ernst. Flora von Deutsch-land. 1841. I. 380.

— & others. Collectio plantarum bahiensium. 1840. I. 342.

Schlechtendal, Dietrich H. R. von. Beiträge zur Kenntniss der Phytoptocecidien. 1886. I. 215.[1]

— Beiträge zur Kenntniss der Phytoptocecidien. 1887. I. 215.[1]

— Bemerkungen zu der Arbeit über . . . Phytoptocecidien von J. J. Kieffer. 1885. I. 215.[1]

— Bemerkungen zu Dr. Eckstein's "Pflanzengallen." 1893. I. 215.[3]

Schlechtendal, Dietrich H. R. von (*continued*).
— Beobachtungen über Blüthenmissbildungen an Salix. 1876. II. 106.[1]
— Beobachtungen über das Bräunen der Blätter. 1895. III. 191.
— Über Cecidien. 1884. I. 215.[1]
— Über einige zum Theil neue Phytoptocecidien. 1883. I. 215.[1]
— Die Gallbildungen. 1891. I. 215.[1]
— Kleine Beiträge zur Kenntniss der Verbreitung der Milben-gallen. 1880. I. 215.[1]
— Pflanzenabnormitäten. 1875. I. 143.
— Pflanzenmissbildungen. 1874. I. 143.
— Teratologische Aufzeichnungen. 1890. I. 144.[1]
— Uebersicht der ... mitteleuropäischen Phytoptocecidien. 1882. I. 215.[1]
— Verzeichniss der Pflanzen-Abnormitäten. 1877. I. 143.
Schlechter, Rudolf. Asclepiadaceae Kuntzeanae. 1895. II. 735.[2]
— Asclepiadeae Elliotianae. 1895. II. 735.[2]
— Beiträge zur Kenntnis der Orchidaceen und Asclepiadaceen Süd-Afrikas. 1894. II. 737.[1]
— Beiträge zur Kenntnis südafrikanischer Asclepiadaceen. 1894. II. 735.[2]
— Contributions to South African Asclepiadology. 1894. II. 735.[2]
— Decades plantarum novarum austro-africanarum. 1896. I. 495.
— Kautschuk-Expedition nach Westafrika. 1900. III. 230.
— Kautschuk im Congostaate. 1900. III. 230.
— Plantae Schlechterianae. 1898. I. 495.
— Revision of extra-tropical South African Asclepiadeae. 1896. II. 735.[2]
— La transplantation des Kickxia de Lagos. 1899. III. 688.[2]
— Two new genera of Asclepiadeae. 1895. II. 743.[1]
— Die Überführung der Kickxia von Lagos nach Kamerun. 1899. III. 688.[2]
— Westafrikanische Kautschuk-Expedition. 1900. *I. 491,* III. 230.
— & Rendle, A. B. New African Asclepiads. 1896. II. 735.[2]
Schleese, M. R. Die ungarische Schälmethode. 1893. IV. 434.
Schleicher. The American resin industry. 1896. IV. 437.[1]
— Harz-Industrie. 1896. IV. 437.[1]
— Minor forest products. American naval stores. 1896. IV. 437.[1]
Schleicher, J. C. Catalogus hucusque absolutus omnium plantarum in Helvetia. 1800. I. 433.
— Catalogus plantarum in Helvetiae. 1800. I. 433.
— Catalogus Salicum Helvetiae. 1807. II. 102.[2]
Schleicher, Wilhelm. Mittheilungen über die der Land- und Forstwirthschaft nützlichen Thiere. 1869. IV. 90.[1]
Schleichert, Franz. Das diastatische Ferment. 1893. I. 177.
Schleiden, Matthias Jakob. Andeutungen über die anato-misch-physiologischen Verschiedenheiten der Stengelgebilde. 1839. I. 105.
— Ueber Bastarderzeugung und Sexualität. 1839. I. 200.
— Ueber den Bau des Eichens bei den Ericeen. 1839. I. 121.
— Für Baum und Wald. 1870. IV. 44.
— Beiträge zur Anatomie der Cacteen. 1839. II. 587.[2]
— Beiträge zur Botanik. 1844. I. 34.
— Beiträge zur Kenntniss der Sassaparille. 1847. III. 338.[2]
— Bemerkungen über Spiralbildungen. 1839. I. 136.[2]
— Über Bildung des Eichens. 1839. I. 121.
— Ueber die Blüthe der Loranthaceen. 1839. II. 173.[1]
— Die Botanik als inductive Wissenschaft. 1842. I. 88.
— Botanische Notizen. 1839. I. 117,[1] 121, 200, II. 173,[1] 223,[1] 607,[1] 614.[1]
— Ueber einige eigenthümliche Bastzellen. 1839. II. 614.[1]
— Ueber Ernährung der Pflanzen. 1846. I. 164.
— Ueber den Familiencharacter der Elaeagneae. 1839. II. 607.[1]
— Sur la formation de l'ovule. 1839. I. 121.
— Grundriss der Botanik. 1846. I. 88.
— Grundzüge der wissenschaftlichen Botanik. 1842. I. 88.
— Handbuch der medizinisch-pharmaceutischen Botanik. 1852. III. 58.
— Hints on the anatomico-physiological differences in the organization of stems. 1839. I. 105.
— Ueber die morphologische Bedeutung der Placenta. 1839. I. 117.[2]

— Die neuern Einwürfe gegen meine Lehre von der Befruch-tung. 1844. I. 200.
— Observations on spiral formations. 1839. I. 136.[2]
— Die Pflanze und ihr Leben. 1847. I. 95, 524.[1]
— Die Physiologie der Pflanzen und Thiere. 1851. I. 148.
— The plant. 1847. I. 95.
— La plante et sa vie. 1847. I. 95.
— Poetry of the vegetable world. 1847. I. 95.
— Populaire voorlezingen over de plant en har leven. 1847. I. 95.
— Principles of scientific botany. 1842. I. 88.
— Die Rose. 1873. II. 290.[1]
— Sur la signification morphologique du placentaire. 1839. I. 117.[2]
— Ueber die Spiralzellenschicht in der Frucht der Laurineen. 1839. II. 223.[1]
— On the structure of the ovule in plants. 1839. I. 121.
— Studien. Populäre Vorträge. 1855. I. 95.
— *See also* Шлейденъ, M. H.
— & Vogel, J. R. Theodor. Über das Albumen, insbesondere der Leguminosen. 1842. II. 320.[1]
— — Beiträge zur Entwickelungsgeschichte der Blüthen-theile bei den Leguminosen. 1839. II. 320.[1]
Schleif, William. Le principe cristallin de l'écorce de Dios-pyrus. 1890. III. 670.[1]
Schleifentag, Gabriel. De plantis. 1625. I. 30.
Schleinitz, *Baron* von. Bericht über die ... Excursion in die Liegnitzer Stadtforst. 1867. IV. 353.
Schlenkert, Friedrich Christian. Ansichten der höheren Forstwissenschaft. 1818. IV. 56.
— Das Hochfest der 50jährigen Regierung ... insbesonders Ansichten der höheren Forstwissenschaft. 1818. IV. 101.
— *See also* Cotta, Heinrich & Schlenkert, F. C.
Schlepegrell, Gustav von. Beiträge zur vergleichenden Ana-tomie der Tubifloren. 1892. I. 124.
Schlesien. *See* Silesia.
Schlesinger, J. Forstliche Vermessungs-Arbeiten. 1874. IV. 264.
— Holz-Cubirungs-Tabellen. 1900. IV. 231.[1]
Schlesische Gesellschaft für vaterländische Cultur. Ab-handlungen. Denkschrift. Jahresbericht. Uebersicht der Arbeiten. I. 14.
Schlesischer Forstverein. Jahrbuch. Statuten. Verband-lungen. IV. 11.
Schleswig-Holstein — Haide-Cultur-Verein. See Haide ... IV. 9.
Schleswig-Holstein — Naturwissenschaftlicher Verein. *See* Naturwissenschaftlicher ... I. 14.
Schleswig-holsteinische Zeitschrift für Obst- und Gartenbau. *See* Monatsblatt für Gartenbau ... III. 13.
Schlich, William. Afforestation in Great Britain. 1886. IV. 161.[1]
— L'approvisionnement de l'Empire britannique en bois d'œuvre. 1898. IV. 405.[1]
— Het boschwezen in Britsch-Indie. 1890. IV. 378.
— British forestry. 1900. IV. 121.
— The Douglas Fir in Scotland. 1888. IV. 484.[1]
— Forestry education. 1898. IV. 29.
— Forestry in the colonies and in India. 1890. IV. 378.
— The Larch bug. 1890. IV. 451.
— A manual of forestry. 1889. IV. 98.[1]
— Remarks on the Sunderbuns. 1876. IV. 377.[2]
— Report on forest administration in the Chota Nagpore di-vision of Bengal. 1885. IV. 295.[1]
— Report on the Pyinkadoh forests of Arakan. 1870. IV. 524.[2]
— Suggestions regarding forest administration in the Central Provinces. 1883. IV. 295.[1]
— Suggestions regarding forest administration in the Hyder-abad assigned districts. 1883. IV. 295.[1]
— Suggestions regarding the demarcation ... of the forests in Kulu. 1882. IV. 250.[2]
— Les Sunderbuns (Ilots du delta du Gange). 1876. IV. 377.[2]
— The timber supply of the British Empire. 1898. IV. 405.[1]
— Treatment of tap-roots. 1874. III. 173,[2] IV. 536.[2]
— The utility of forests. 1890. IV. 270.
— Vana paripalana Nili. 1893. IV. 100.[1]
— On working plans. 1878. IV. 244.
— Yield tables for the Scotch Pine. 1888. IV. 481.
Schlicht, A. Beitrag zur Kenntniss der Verbreitung ... der Mykorhizen. 1889.. I. 234.[1]
Schlichtkrull, Olof Nicolai Christopher. De officinelle Planter. 1832. III. 57.

Schlickum, J. Ueber die chemischen Vorgänge beim Reifen der Weintraube. 1861. II. 508.[1]
— Zweiter Nachtrag über die chemischen Vorgänge beim Reifen der Weintraube. 1866. II. 508.[1]
Schlickum, O. Botanisches Taschenwörterbuch. 1863. I. 71.
— Exkursionsflora für Deutschland. 1881. I. 532.[2]
Schlieben, W. E. A.· Der selbstlehrende Feldmesser. 1811. IV. 263.
— Vollständiges Hand- und Lehrbuch der gesammten Feldmesskunst. 1857. IV. 264.
Schlieckmann, E. Die Anwendbarkeit der Kiefern-Sägemachine. 1882. IV. 473.
— Die Gewinnung des Kiefernsamens. 1885. IV. 473.
— Handbuch der Staatsforstverwaltung in Preussen. 1883. IV. 290.[2]
— Ueber Kiefernbestandsbegründung. 1889. IV. 481.
Schlieper, R. Die Dattelpalme in Egypten. 1890. III. 829.[1]
Schlimmer, J. W. Aanteekeningen betreffende getah-pertja. 1883. III. 229.
Schlimpert, Alfred Moritz. Rosenformen der Umgebung von . Meissen. 1900. II. 285.[1]
Schlippe, Thom. Untersuchung des Crotonöles. 1858. III. 517.[1]
Schloesing, Théophile. Sur l'absorption de l'ammoniaque. 1874. . I. 159.
— Comparaison entre les deux états d'une terre en partie boisée, en partie défrichée. 1871. I. 228.[2]
Schloesing, Théophile, (jr.) Dosage de l'acide phosphorique. 1868. I. 175.
— Sur les échanges d'acide carbonique. 1892. I. 171.
— Sur les échanges gazeux entre les plantes entières et l'atmosphère. 1900. I. 172.
— Sur les pertes d'azote. 1895. I. 229.
— Utilisation, par les plantes, de l'acide phosphorique. 1898. I. 160.
— Utilisation, par les plantes, de la potasse. 1900. I. 160.
— Végétation avec et sans argon. 1897. I. 160.
— & **Laurent**, Émile. Sur la fixation de l'azote libre. 1892. I. 160.
Schloesing frères et C[le]. Les maladies de la Vigne. 1900. III. 582.
Schlossberger, Julius Eugen. Sur la fibre ligneuse dénuée de structure. 1861. I. 125.
— Lehrbuch der organischen Chemie. 1852. V. XI.[2]
Schlosser-Klekovski, Joseph Calosanz. Bilinar. Flora excursoria Croatiae.· 1876. I. 447.
— De Papilionaceis in Germania sponte crescentibus. 1836. II. 319.[1]
— & **Vukotinović**, L. F. Flora croatica. 1869. I. 447.
— Syllabus florae croaticae. 1867. I. 447.
Schlotheim, *Freiherr* von. General-Repertorium forstlich wichtiger Gesetze. 1880. IV. 321.
Schlotterbec, Phil. Jac. Kruidkundige waarnemingen over de wanschepselen der planten. 1773. I. 271.[2]
— Schediasma botanicum de monstris. 1755. I. 142.
Schlotterbeck, B. Cubik-Tabellen zur Bestimmung des Inhalts von kantigen Hölzern. 1871. IV. 226.
— Cubik-Tabellen zur Bestimmung des Inhalts von Rundhölzern. 1871. IV. 226.
Schlotterbeck, Julius Otto. Beiträge zur Entwicklungsgeschichte pharmakognotisch wichtiger Samen. 1896. I. 121, II. 440.[1]
Schlotthauber, August Friedrich. Agave (yucćaefolia Willdenow?). 1870. III. 341.[2]
┬ Ausgezeichnete einheimische Pflanzen-Individuen. 1860. . 296.[1]
— Bildung von Luftwurzeln holziger einheimischer Gewächse. 1860. I. 188.
— Dasylirium acrotrichum. 1871. III. 336.[1]
— Physiologische und systematische Beiträge. 1860. I. 164, 188, 207,[2] 210,[1] 296.[1]
— Steigen des Saftes im Kernholze. 1860. I. 164.
— Ueberwachsen der Einschnitte in Baumrinde. 1860. I. 207,[2] 210.[1]
Schlottmann. Ueber die Anbauwürdigkeit der amerikanischen Roteiche. 1897. IV. 126,[1] 516.[2]
Schluch, P. G., **Barn**et **Lyon**, G. H. & **Gongryp**, J. R. C. Verslag der commissie . . de voor de kultuur meest aanbevelenswaardige cacaosoorten. 1887. III. 592.[2]
Schlütimbach, Friedrich Alexander von. Abbildung der hauptsächlichsten . . . Nadelbäume. 1810. III. 289.

Schluep. Die Aufstellung provisorischer Wirthschaftspläne in Gebirgsgegenden. 1878. IV. 249.[2]
— De l'établissement de plans d'aménagement provisoires. 1878. IV. 249.[2]
Schlüssel zum Bestimmen der wichtigsten bei Elbing vorkommenden Pflanzengattungen. 1867. I. 386.
Schlumberger, F. Cereus Olfersii. 1885. III. 621.[1]
Schlumberger, Henri. Ueber die Indigprobe. 1842. III. 479.[1]
— On the testing . . . of the indigo of commerce. 1842. III. 479.[1]
Schlumberger, M. Floraison anormale du Lilas. 1890. II. 714.[2]
Schlumberger, P. Cereus splendens et Echinopsis Kuotti. 1854. III. 621,[1] 622.[2]
— Floraison de Cactées nouvelles. 1855. III. 619.
— Floraison de quelques espèces de Cactées. 1856. III. 619.
— Floraison du Mamillaria senilis. 1853. III. 623.[2]
— Sur quelques espèces de Cactées. 1857. III. 619.
Schlup. Kann durch eine veränderte Aufbereitung der Entwertung des Reisigs . . . vorgebeugt werden? 1883. IV. 387.[2]
— & **Berthelot**, Charles. Quels moyens peut-on admettre . . . pour conserver . . . la faculté germinatrice? 1864. IV. 147.[1]
— Welche Mittel sind zulässig . . um die ungeschwächte Keimfähigkeit . . . zu erhalten? 1864. IV. 147.[1]
Schlupp, M. Rapport sur là nécessité d'établir des chemins. 1871. IV. 389.
Schmalhausen, Johannes. Aufzählung der im Gouvernement von St. Petersburg vorkommenden Bastard- und Zwischenformen. 1875. II. 100.[2]
— Beiträge zur Kenntniss der Milchsaftbehälter. 1877. I. ´ 136.[1]
— Vaccinium macrocarpum Ait. 1883. II. 686.[1]
— *See* Шмальгаузенъ, И. Ѳ.
Schmaltz, Constantine Samuel RAFINESQUE. *See* RAFINESQUE-SCHMALTZ, C. S.
Schmals, E. U. W. Hand- und Hülfs-Lexikon. 1825. IV. 23.[1]
Schmalz, Eduard. Dispositio . . . plantarum circa Dresdam. 1822. I. 377.
Schmalz, Friedrich. Auch der Waldbau darf nicht vernachlässigt werden. 1836. IV. 268.
— Theorie des Pflanzenbaues. 1840. III. 35.
Schmalz, T. Handleiding voor land, bosch en tuinbouwers. 1842. III. 36.[1]
— Theorie der plantenteelt. 1842. III. 169.[2]
Schmaus, Leonardi. De morbo gallico tractatus. 1728. III. 494.[1]
Schmeiss, O. Phoenix canariensis . . . bei Lindau. 1890. III. 929.[1]
Schmelzing, Julius. Repertorium der . . . Gesetze und Verordnungen über das Forst- und Jagdwesen. 1818. IV. 318.
Schmid, Alfred. Die Anpflanzung . . . der Korb- und Bandweiden. 1883. III. 348.
Schmid, Bernhard. Ueber die Lage des Phanerogamen-Embryo. 1894. I. 122.
Schmid, C. Beschreibung der Bauhölzer. 1853. IV. 398.[2]
Schmid, G. V. Handbuch aller seit 1560 bis auf die neueste Zeit erschienenen Forst- und Jagd-Gesetze des Königreichs Sachsen. 1839. IV. 321.
Schmid, J. A. Quand faut-il semer les faines? 1870. IV. 495.
— Wann soll man Bucheln säen? 1870. IV. 495.
Schmid, J. C. E. Geprüfte Anweisung zu der Erziehung . . . der hochstämmigen und Zwerg-Fruchtbäume. 1776. III. 135.
Schmid, Ludwig. Beschreibung· der Exkursions-Tour . . . in den Forsten der Herrschaft Starkenbach. 1879. IV. 371.
— Mitteilungen über Vorkommen . . . des Knieholzes. 1884. IV. 464.[2]
— Statistisch-topografische Beschreibung der . . . 'Domaine Starkenbach. 1879. IV. 371.
Schmid, Stefan. Eine forstliche Lehrreise nach Steiermark. 1898. IV. 370.
Schmid, W. Ueber das Mangostin. 1855. III. 609.[2]
— Sur la mangoustine. 1855. III. 609.[2]
Schmid, Walther. Die Weidenblattwespe. 1892. III. 350.[2]
Schmidberger, Joseph. Beiträge zur Obstbaumzucht. 1827. III. 136.
— Leichtfasslicher Unterricht über Erziehung . . . der Obstbäume. 1837. III. 146.[2]

Schmidberger, Joseph (*continued*).
— Leichtfasslicher Unterricht von der Erziehung der Obst-bäume. 1824. III. 146.[1]
— Leichtfasslicher Unterricht von der Erziehung der Zwerg-bäume. 1821. III. 136.
Schmidel, Casimir Christoph. Descriptio itineris per Helve-tiam, Galliam et Germaniac partem. 1794. I. 348.[2]
— Icones plantarum. 1747. I. 291.
— De medulla radicis ad florem pertingente. 1783. . I. 123.[2]
— De medulla radicis ad florem pertingente epistola. 1759. I. 128.[2]
Schmidely, Auguste. Annotationsau Catalogue des plantes . . . de Genève de G. F. Reuter. 1884. . I. 437.
— Catalogue raisonné des Ronces . . . de Genève. 1888. II. 304.[1]
— Description de quatre Rosiers nouveaux. 1880. II. 287.[r]
— Note sur le Rubus rigidus. 1884. II. 309.[2]
— Note sur le Salix Rapini. 1884. II. 109.[1]
— Notes floristiques. 1899. II. 287.[2]
— Une nouvelle Rose hybride. 1894. II. 291.[1]
— Quatre nouvelles formes de Rosiers. 1879. II. 287.[1] .
— Rosa rubrifolia Vill. . . . forma diminuta. 1897. II. 298.[1]
Schmider, S. Dé Balsamo peruviano nigro. *See* LEHMANN, J. G. C. 1797. III. 482.[1]
Schmidl, Ludwig. Zur Kultur der Korbweide. 1872. III. 347.
— Die Waldstreu. 1861. IV. 71.
Schmidl, Maximilian. On the constitution of oil of Cajeput. 1859. III. 636.
Schmidlin. Gartenbuch. 1875. III. 104.
Schmidlin, Eduard. Anleitung zum Botanisiren. 1846. I. 35.
— Die Blumensprache. 1839. I. 380.
— Flora von Stuttgart. 1832. I. 378.
— Populäre Botanik. 1857. I. 95.
Schmidlin, Johann Gottlieb. Handbuch der württemberg-ischen Forst-Gesetzgebung. 1822. IV. 322.[2]
Schmidlin, W. Antwort auf des Hrn. Forstmeisters Karl Kritische Beleuchtung meiner Beiträge. 1840. IV. 268.
— Beiträge zur Lösung einiger volkswirthschaftlichen Wider-sprüche in der Forstwirthschaft. 1837. IV. 266.
Schmidt. *See* HAAGE & SCHMIDT; REGEL; Eduard von & HAAGE & SCHMIDT.
Schmidt. Die Einwirkung des Blitzschlages. 1889. IV. 194.
— Die Erziehung der hochstämmigen Bäume. 1881. III. 204.[1]
— Kiefern-Fichten-Mischwald. 1895. IV. 138.[1]
— Das Schneiden der Hochstämme. 1881. III. 170.
Schmidt, (*Förster zu Blumberg bei Schwedt*). Auszug aus des Herrn . . . v. Flotow Bemerkungen über die Theorie des Herrn van Mons. 1839. I. 247.
Schmidt, (*Forstmeister*). Die Domänenforste im Herzog-thum Sachsen-Meiningen. 1894. IV. 355.[2]
— Ueber den Einfluss starker Durchforstungen in Fichten-beständen. 1895. IV. 458.
— Wie sind die . . . durch die Nonne . . . kahlgefressenen Nadelholzbestände . . . zu behandeln? 1896. IV. 202.
Schmidt, (*herzogl. Hofgärtner, Georgengarten bei Dessau*). Die Orangerien. 1861. III. 499.[3]
Schmidt (*Hofgärtner*). Motive der Baumerziehung in Baum-schulen. 1881. III. 154.[1]
Schmidt, (*Kunstgärtner, Gross-Strelitz*). Beschreibung einer Weinbergs-Anlage. 1837. III. 552.
Schmidt, (*Oberförster*). Systematisches Verzeichnis einer Sammlung Obstsorten. 1841. III. 28.[1]
Schmidt, (*Oberförster, Grasegrund*). Allgemeine Revierbe-schreibung vom Bunzlauer Stadtforst. 1861. IV. 253.
Schmidt, (*Oberförster in Panten*). Bericht über die prak-tische Anwendbarkeit des Hartig'schen Waldstockes. 1850. IV. 231.[1]
Schmidt, (*Plantagen-Direktor, Ludwigslust*). Die beste Art den Weissdorn . . . zu Hecken aus Samen zu ziehen. 1844. III. 422.[1]
— Picea vulgaris . . . mit gutem Erfolg zu verpflanzen. 1844. III. 294.[2]
Schmidt, Alexander. Die Bekämpfung der Nonne. 1893. IV. 201.
— Einiges über die Kultur der Birke. 1887. IV. 190.[1]
— Einiges über die Verwendung der Sägespäne. 1888. IV. 393.
— Die Nonne, Liparis monacha. 1893. IV. 201.
— Radfelgen aus einem Stück. 1886. IV. 427.[1]
— Die Verwendung der Weisstanne zu Stallpflasterungen. 1889. IV. 446.[2]

Schmidt, Antoni. Katechizm hodowania drzew owocowych. 1878. III. 146.[2]
Schmidt, C. A. Handbuch der medizinischen und Farbe-kräuter. 1832. III. 73.
— Wilhelms Wanderungen in das Gebiet der Giftpflanzen. 1838. III. 73.
Schmidt, C. F. Afhandling om Indhegninger. 1800. III. 212.[2]
— Alvorlige Betragtninger over Træmangelen. 1799. IV. 282.[1]
— Forslag til nogle Forbedringer i Hauge- og Træefrugt-Dyrk-ningen. 1793. III. 100,[2] 119.[2]
— Forsøg til en Opdagelse af nærværende Træ- og Brænde-mangels Aarsager. 1783. IV. 113.[1]
— Kort Anviisning til Vilde Træers Opelskning. 1790. IV. 113.[1] .
— Vollständiger und gründlicher Garten-Unterricht. 1798. III. 103.
— Der wohlerfahrene Baum- und Küchengärtner. 1798. III. 103.
— *See also* BERG, Otto & SCHMIDT, C. F.
Schmidt, C. P. Neue Methode, die phanerogamischen Pflan-zen zu trocknen. 1831. I. 35.
Schmidt, David. Taschenbuch der pharmaceutisch-vege-tabilischen Rohwaarenkunde. 1847. III. 258.
Schmidt, Emil. Ein Beitrag zur Kenntnis der Hochblätter. 1889. I. 112.[1]
Schmidt, Erich. Ein Beitrag zur Kenntniss der secundären Markstrahlen. 1889. I. 126.
Schmidt, Ernst. Ueber das Aloin der Barbados-Aloë. 1875. III. 333.
— Sur l'aloine de l'Aloës des Barbades. 1875. III. 333.[1] .
— Ueber einige Bestandtheile der Cubeben. 1877. II. 94.[2] .
— Mélange, alternance. 1888. IV. 138.[1]
— & **Berendes**, J. Zur Kenntnis . . . des Crotonöls. 1878. III. 517.[1]
Schmidt, F. Beiträge . . zur Cultur neuerer . . . . Coniferen. 1877. III. 290.
— Citrus dimorpha. 1873. III. 499.[2]
— Interessante Veredlung. 1883. III. 290.
— Krautartige Veredlung der Eichen. 1882. III. 361.[2]
— Die Veredlung des Clianthus. 1882. III. 472.[2]
— Zwei sehr werthvolle Linden. 1883. III. 585.[1]
Schmidt, F. A. A. J. Anweisung zur Forsthaushaltungs-Wissenschaft. 1776. IV. 95.
Schmidt, Franz. Anleitung zur sicheren Erziehung . . . Ahornarten. 1812. III. 533.[2]
— Oesterreichs allgemeine Baumzucht. 1792. I. 293, III. 89,[3] IV. 86.[2]
Schmidt, Franz. Abies Fortunei. 1884. III. 304.[3]
Schmidt, Franz Wilibald. Flora boëmica. 1793. I. 439.
— Neue und seltene Pflanzen. 1793. I. 264.
— Sammlung physikalisch-ökonomischer Aufsätze. 1795. I. 32.
— Versuch einer Topographie der Stadt Plan. 1789. I. 438.
— Verzeichniss der um Wosetschau . . . wildwachsenden seltneren Pflanzen. 1791. I. 439.
Schmidt, Friedrich. Botanische Nachrichten über Sachalin. 1863. I. 455.
— Flora der Insel Moon. 1854. I. 361.
— Flora des silurischen Bodens von Ehstland. 1855. I. 362.
— Reisen im Amur-Lande. 1868. I. 455.
— Wissenschaftliche Resultate der . . . an den unteren Jenissei ausgesandten Expedition. 1872. I. 454.[1]
— *See also* MEYER, J. C. & SCHMIDT, Friedrich; ШМИДТ, Ф. В.
Schmidt, Georg. Aenderungen im Waldbesitze Ober-Steier-marks. 1895. IV. 279.[1]
— Die Forstwirthschaft in Obersteiermark. 1900. IV. 285.[2]
Schmidt, H. C. Treatise on forestry in Texas. 1882. IV. 340.
Schmidt, Hermann. Schutz der Waldungen bei Eisenbahn-bauten. 1848. IV. 180.[1]
Schmidt, J. *See* SEEMANN, Berthold & SCHMIDT, J.
Schmidt, J. C. Lebenszähigkeit von Cycadeen. 1886. II. 3.[2]
— Die Rose, ihre Erziehung und Pflege. n. d. III. 447.[1]
Schmidt, J. H. Kininebepäling in basten. 1891. III. 724.[c]
— Ueber die zweckmässigste Cultur der einheimischen Bau- und Nutzhölzer. 1849. IV. 117.
Schmidt, Johann Anton. Anleitung zur Kenntniss der natür-lichen Familien der Phanerogamen. 1865. I. 256.
— Beiträge zur Flora der Cap Verdischen Inseln. 1852. I. 497.
— Beobachtungen über die Verbreitung . . . phanerogam-ischer Pflanzen Deutschlands. 1850. I. 383.

— Flora von Heidelberg. 1857. I. 384.
— Pflanzenarten welche auf den Cap Verdischen Inseln ... als Nahrungsmittel dienen. 1852. III. 93.³
— Phytolaccaceae et Nyctagineae. 1872. II. 190,² 198.²
— Scrophularinae. 1862. II. 778.²
Schmidt, Johann August Friedrich. Handledning i trädgårds-skötseln. 1841. III. 100.¹
Schmidt, Johann Joachim. Aeusserungen über ein System in der Pflanzenkunde. 1797. I. 251.
— Botanisches Jahrbuch für Jedermann. 1799. I. 255.
— Gründliche Anleitung zum Anbau ... des unächten Accacienbaums. 1797. IV. 522.²
Schmidt, Johann Karl. Allgemeine ökonomisch-technische Flora. 1827. III. 52.
Schmidt, Karl Eduard Franz. Beziehungen zwischen Blitz-spur und Saftstrom. 1893. IV. 195.¹
Schmidt, M. Beitrag zur Cultur der Haselnüsse. 1863. III. 357.²
Schmidt, Oscar. Das Zustandekommen der fixen Lichtlage. 1883. I. 230.
Schmidt, Otto. See JESSEN, W. & SCHMIDT, Otto.
Schmidt, Paul. Die Holzwolle. 1887. IV. 429.
— Ueber einige Wirkung des Lichtes. 1870. I. 230.
Schmidt, Paul Wilhelm. De praestantia majorum Citriorum in medicina. 1715. III. 498.¹
Schmidt, R. Antheeren von Kieferntrieben. 1879. IV. 477.
— Über Bildungsabweichungen an Blättern der Feldrüster. 1899. II. 144.¹
Schmidt, Richard. Die Einführung des sogenannten doppel-wüchsigen Buchenhochwaldbetriebes. 1881. IV. 495.
— Ueber die Schüttekrankheit der Kiefer. 1886. IV. 478.
— Unsere schlingenden Tecoma. 1880. III. 705.
Schmidt, Robert. Flora von Gera. 1857. I. 384.
— Die Maschinen zur Bearbeitung des Holzes. 1861. IV. 422.¹
Schmidt, T. A. Enumeration of the Labiatae and Scrophu-larineae, collected ... in High Asia. 1868. I. 460.¹
Schmidt, Vinzenz. Worin liegt der Grund des allmäligen Ver-schwindens der Eichenwaldungen? 1895. IV. 508.
Schmidt, W. J. L. Over land en tuinbouw in Nederlandsch Indie. 1882. III. 128.
Schmidt, Walther. Die Waldverwüstungen in den Roches d'Orvin. 1889. IV. 209.²
Schmidt, Wilhelm. Das Beizen, Schleifen und Poliren des Holzes. 1871. IV. 422.¹
Schmidt, Wilhelm Ludwig Ewald. Botanischer Wegweiser. 1837. I. 87.
— Flora von Pommern und Rügen. 1840. I. 380.
— Getreue ... Beschreibung der officinellen Pflanzen. 1831. III. 57.
— See also ROSTKOVIUS, F. W. G. & SCHMIDT, W. L. E.
Schmidt-Deines. Einiges über die Vermehrung der Aralia Sieboldii. 1860. III. 642.¹
Schmidt-Göbel, Hermann Max. Der Rebenstecher. 1862. III. 563.
— Die schädlichen und nützlichen Insecten. 1881. IV. 92, 207, 549.²
Schmidt von Bergenhold, Johann Ferdinand. Vier Vorträge über Maulbeerbaumpflege. 1866. III. 377.
Schmidtbauer, M. Das Seitenpfropfen. 1881. III. 162.
Schmidtmeyer, Peter. Travels into Chile over the Andes. 1824. I. 328.
Schmiedeberg, Oswald. Grundriss der Arzneimittellehre. 1883. III. 259.¹
Schmiedel, T. Kurze topographisch-statistische Forst-be-schreibung der Herrschaft Wlaschim. 1849. IV. 370.
Schmieden, Theophil. Ueber die Bedeutung der Gerbstoffe. 1868. I. 183.
Schmieder, C. C. Ueber die blasenziehende Schärfe. 1880. I. 176.
— Ueber die Natur der narkotischen Pflanzengifte. 1880. I. 176.
Schmiedl, J. Nachweis von Durchforstungs-Erträgen. 1862. IV. 260.²
Schmiedl, Johann. Die Waldservitut-Verhältnisse in ... Krain. 1862. IV. 335.
— & Pannewitz, Julius von. Einige Worte über den Zuwachs des Lärchenbaumes. 1867. IV. 449, 469.
Schmiedlein, Gottfried Benedikt. Beyträge zu der Natur-geschichte der schädlichen Waldraupen. 1797. IV. 91.¹
— Handwörterbuch der Naturgeschichte. 1800. I. 33.
Schmitt. Ist es zweckmässig, im Eichenschälwald Oberholz zu erziehen? 1880. IV. 507.

Schmitt, Adolf. Anlage und Pflege der Fichten-Pflanzschu-len. 1875. IV. 150, 453.
Schmitt, Franz. Die Gewinnung der Eichenlohe. 1873. IV. 512.
Schmitt, Georg. Beitrag zur ... Frage: "Wie soll künftig für die Bewirthschaftung der Gemeindewaldungen gesorgt werden?" 1849. IV. 308.¹
Schmitt, J. R. Nachlese zu Schönbrunns botanischem Reich-tum. 1808. I. 65.²
Schmitt, Johann Anton. Anleitung zur Erziehung der Wal-dungen. 1821. IV. 110.²
— Grundsätze zum Entwurf einer zweckmässigen Schlagord-nung. 1810. IV. 251.²
— Die Lehre der künstlichen Holzzucht. 1808. IV. 140.
— Theoretisch-practische Anleitung zur Forstgehaubestim-mung. 1819. IV. 239.
Schmitz, Friedrich. Beobachtungen über die Entwicklung der Sprossspitze. 1874. I. 132.²
— Die Blüthen-Entwicklung der Piperaceen. 1872. II. 93.²
— Das Fibrovasalsystem im Blüthenkolben der Piperaceen. 1871. II. 93.²
Schmitz, J. Joseph & Regel, Eduard von. Flora bonnensis. 1841. I. 380.
Schmitz, Joseph. Amélioration et aménagement du domaine forestier communal. 1898. IV. 357.¹
— Assainissement des fanges du Luxembourg. 1898. IV. 160.²
— La forêt de Freyr. 1894. IV. 555.²
— Mise en valeur des terrains incultes. 1894. IV. 546.²
Schmitz-Dumont, W. Besoins du Pin sylvestre en éléments nutritifs. 1894. IV. 482.¹
— Ueber den Futterwerth einiger Wald-pflanzen. 1894. IV. 438.²
— Ueber den Nährstoffbedarf der ... Kiefern. 1894. IV. 482.¹
— See also SCHROEDER, Julius von & SCHMITZ-DUMONT, W.
Schmitz du Moulin. De strijd over Palembang als Kofhe land. 1895. III. 731.
Schmolz, C. Die Wendelinus-Eiche bei Geisfeld. 1897. IV. 516.¹
Schmuckermair, Bartholomäus. Dauerhaftigkeit des Holzes. 1871. IV. 413.³
Schmuttermayer, F. Erläuterte Grundsätze der praktischen Forst-Wirthschaft. 1820. IV. 110.²
Schnaase. Ueber die Grundsätze der hypothekarischen Be-leihung der Privatforsten. 1896. IV. 270.
Schnaase, E. Ueber das Anpflanzen von Viscum. 1851. III. 285.¹
— Bemerkungen zu J. F. Schouw's Beobachtungen über die Mistel. 1851. II. 178.¹
— Einige Bemerkungen zu Dr. H. Schacht's Beobachtungen über die Mistel. 1855. II. 178.¹
— Einiges über die Mistel. 1855. II. 178.¹
— Vergleichende Zusammenstellung der Früchte ... von Loranthus. 1854. II. 173.¹
— Ueber die Wucherung der Mistel. 1854. II. 178.¹
Schneck, Jacob. Blighted Hickory-nuts. 1883. II. 112.²
— Cross fertilization of the Chestnut tree. 1881. II. 123.²
— Notes on Phoradendron flavescens. 1884. II. 177.¹
— Notes on some Illinois Grapes. 1888. II. 505.²
— Red calyx in Sambucus canadensis. 1880. II. 840.¹
— Second blooming of Catalpa. 1885. II. 797.¹
— Two Oaks grown together. 1883. I. 209,¹ IV. 508.²
Schnee. Ceylon-Früchte. 1900. III. 279.²
Schneeberger, Anton. Catalogus medicamentorum simpli-cium. 1561. I. 281.
— Catalogus stirpium. 1557. I. 280.
Ueber Schneebruchbeschädigungen in den Waldungen. 1878. IV. 190.
Die Schneebruchkalamität im Harz. 1894. IV. 190.
Schneedruckbeschädigung. 1884. IV. 190.
Schneegans, (Dr.). Sur le principe odorant des semences de Cynorrhodon. 1890. III. 455.¹
Schneegans, August & Gerock, J. E. Ueber Gaultherin. 1895. IV. 491.²
— — Sur la gaulthérine. 1895. IV. 491.²
Schneer, Alexander. Ueber Wald-Dünger. 1855. IV. 144.¹
Schneevoogt, G. Voorhelm. Brief over uitwas op de bladen van Pereboomen. 1814. III. 445.²
— Icones plantarum rariorum. 1793. I. 264.
Schnehen, Rudolf, Freiherr von. Die Hazel. 1897. IV. 492.²
— Le Noisetier. 1897. IV. 492.¹
Schneideln und Aufasten. 1872. IV. 172.²

Das **Schneiden** der Ziergehölze. 1898. III. 171.

Schneider. Über den Blattwespenfrass am Knieholze. 1883. IV. 464.[2]

Schneider. Die Waldflora der Voreifel. 1894. IV. 84.[1]

Schneider, (*Oberförster, Buchwald*). Beitrag zur Frage über das Verhalten der Lärche. 1868. IV. 449.

Schneider, (*Oberförster, Hoh-Gieradorf*). Führer zur Excursion . . . durch die Schweidnitzer Stadtforst. 1895. IV. 355.[1]

Schneider, A. Die vorzüglichsten Giftpflanzen Deutschlands. 1846. III. 73.

Schneider, Albert. Beitrag zur Kenntniss der Rhizobien. 1894. I. 234.[1]

— Mutualistic symbiosis of algae . . . with Cycas. 1894. II. 4.[1]

— The phenomena of symbiosis. 1897. I. 234.[1]

Schneider, Camillo Karl. Ueber die Aussaat der Gehölze. 1899. III. 156.[2]

— Pirus arbutifolia L. fil. 1897. III. 419.[2]

Schneider, E. *See* Шнейдеръ, Э.

Schneider, F. Voorstel van maatregelen ter wering . . . der Koffiebladziekte. 1879. III. 735.

Schneider, Felix. Untersuchungen über den Zuwachsgang . . . der Esche. 1896. II. 708.[1]

Schneider, Ferdinand. Taschenbuch der Flora von Basel. 1880. I. 436.

Schneider, Friedrich. Cryptomeria japonica. 1857. III. 302.[1]

Schneider, Friedrich (II.). Liste des Rosiers les plus recommandables. 1879. III. 449.

— Rangliste der edelsten Rosen. 1879. III. 449.

— Rosenjahrbuch. 1883. III. 450.

— Select list of the most beautiful Roses. 1879. III. 449.

Schneider, Friedrich Wilhelm. Anweisung zum Gebrauch eines Flächenmaassstabes. 1844. IV. 264.

— Anweisung zum Gebrauch eines Rechenstabes. 1825. IV. 58.

— Bibliothek der Forst- und Jagd-Literatur. 1856. IV. 1.

— Erfahrungs- Tafeln über Massengehalt der . . . Holzarten in verschiedenem Alter. 1843. IV. 229.

— Rechenstab für Forstmänner. 1825. IV. 58.

— Taschenbuch der Maass- und Gewichts-kunde. 1839. IV. 229.

Schneider, G. Le Luculia gratissima. 1887. III. 745.[2]

— Quelques Chênes remarquables en Angleterre. 1896. II. 139.[2]

Schneider, Gustav. *See* Sagorski, Ernst & Schneider Gustav.

Schneider, H. K. De landbouw. 1860. III. 106.[1]

Schneider, Johann Gottlob. Libri de historia et de causis plantarum. *See* Theophrastos Eresios. 286. I. 272.

Schneider, Josef. Untersuchungen einiger Treibhölzer. 1886. I. 242.[2]

Schneider, Karl Friedrich Robért. Flora von Bunzlau. 1837. I. 532.[1]

— Die Vertheilung und Verbreitung der schlesischen Pflanzen. 1838. I. 379.

Schneider, Ludwig. Ueber Ableitung . . . des Wortes "Forst." 1889. IV. 23.[2]

— Die Bedeutung des Windmantels. 1891. IV. 154.[2]

— Beschreibung der Gefässpflanzen des Florengebiets von Magdeburg. 1877. I. 387.

— Ueber die Beseitigung der Einfuhr ausländischer Gerbrinde. 1888. IV. 284.[1]

— Bodenpflege und Naturbesamung im Buchenhochwald. 1888. IV. 495.

— Der Eichenlichtungsbetrieb mit Buchenunterbau. 1891. IV. 138.[2]

— Ueber die Erhöhung der Keimfähigkeit des Lärchensamens. 1889. IV. 450.

— Zur Erhöhung der Keimfähigkeit des Lärchensamens. 1890. IV. 450.

— Erörterungen über die Frage: "Reiner oder gemischter Hochwald?" 1889. IV. 137.[2]

— Das forstliche Verhalten der Schlaggewächse. 1889. IV. 211.[1]

— Der Frass der grossen Fichtenbastkäfers. 1897. IV. 457.

— Über den Frass des Strophosomus. 1897. IV. 208.[1]

— Ein interessantes über Über-führung des Eichenschälwaldes zum Hochwalde. 1894. IV. 508.

— Ist es zweckmässig . . . Juglans regia, im Forste zu kultivieren? 1890. IV. 488.[1]

— Die Krankheitserscheinungen an der Lärche. 1895. IV. 51.

— Merkwürdige Bäume. 1889. IV. 66.[2]

— Die Mischung der Buche mit der Eiche. 1888. IV. 138.[2]

— Die Mischung der Buche mit der Kiefer. 1888. IV. 138.[2]

— Die Nachhaltigkeit der reinen Eichenhochwaldwirtschaft. 1890. IV. 508.

— Der Pflanzenwuchs als Miterzeuger des Bodens. 1891. IV. 69.

— Starke Eichen. 1891. IV. 516.[1]

— Die Steinbuche. 1889. IV. 500.[2]

— Die Trauben- und Stieleiche . . . Trier-Saarbrücken. 1898. IV. 509.

— Das Verhalten der forstlich schädlichen Gräser. 1890. IV. 211.[1]

— Die Verwendung der Hagebutte. 1890. III. 454.[1]

— Wachstum und Begünstigung der Eiche. 1889. IV. 508.

— Wann muss der Forstmann seine Durchforstungen auszeichnen? 1890. IV. 174.

— Wertberechnung eines Eichenschutzmantels. 1890. IV. 258.

Schneider, Numa. Du choix des arbres et des sujets de greffage. 1895. III. 40.

— Le Jardin de la Chaire. 1891. I. 55.

Schneider, Oscar. Ueber die Flora der Wüste von Ramleh. 1872. I. 488.

Schneider, R. Gespräche über die Ueberschwemmung im Seelande. 1835. IV. 187.[1]

Schneider, W. von. Ueber Pollen und Wachsbildung. 1872. I. 527.[2]

Schneider, Zygmunt. Las Kutkowiecki. 1894. IV. 346.

Schneidt, A. Buchen-Eisenbahnschwellen. 1896. IV. 424.[1] — 1897. IV. 499.

— Die Verwendung buchener Eisenbahnschwellen. 1896. IV. 499. — 1898. IV. 424.[1]

Ueber die **Schneitelstreu** in den Alpen. 1859.. IV. 172.[2]

Schnekker, Johann Daniel. Idea generalis ordinis plantarum verticillatarum. 1777. I. 251.

Schnell, Joannes. Historia veneni upas antiar. 1815. III. 366.[1]

Schnepp, B. De la Yerba Maté. 1864. III. 530.[2]

Schnetzler, Jean B. De l'action du curare. 1865. I. 211.

— Action du sulfure de carbone. . 1876. I. 36.[1]

— Sur une cause de développement anormal des raisins. 1885. III. 561.

— Colonie de Rhododendron hirsutum à fleurs blanches. 1868. II. 680.[1]

— Contributions à l'étude des matières colorantes. 1880. I. 185.[1]

— Lettre concernant la maladie de la Vigne. 1874. III. 577.

— Notice sur le pollen d'Ephedra helvetica. 1874. II. 54.[2]

— Notice sur une excroissance trouvée sur un Sapin rouge. 1868. IV. 455.

— Observations de Vignes américaines. 1876. III. 569.[1]

— Observations faites sur une maladie de la Vigne. 1877. III. 577.

— Observations sur la diffusion des matières colorantes. 1877. I. 185.[1]

— Observations sur la maladie de la Vigne. 1879. III. 578.

— Observations . . . sur les mouvements des étamines de l'Épine vinette. 1868. II. 205.[2]

— Sur la présence du tannin dans les cellules végétales. 1879. I. 183.

— Quelques mots sur l'histoire naturelle du Phylloxera. 1874. III. 567.[2]

— De quelques phénomenes de diffusion. 1878. I. 151.[2]

— Ueber den rothen Farbstoff der Blätter von Ampelopsis. 1880. II. 504.[2]

— Ueber den Wurzelpilz des Weinstockes. 1886. III. 579.

Schneyder, Johann. Ueber den Wein- und Obstbau der alten Römer. 1846. III. 33.[1]

Schnider, Th. Alte und seltene Bäume. 1894. II. 480.[2]

Vom **Schnitt** der Kugelakazien. 1890. III. 487.[1]

Die zur **Schnittblumencultur** geeigneten Blüthensträucher. 1899. III. 207.[2]

Schnittspahn, (*Oberförster*). Das Aussortiren von Kiefern-Pfahlholz. 1883. IV. 432.[1]

— Ueber die Berechnung des Schadenersatzes. 1886. IV. 257.

— Ueber erste Durchforstungen. 1884. IV. 173.

— Zur Frage der Umtriebszeit. 1882. IV. 252.

— Die Katastrirung und Besteuerung der Waldungen im Grossherzogthum Hessen. 1884. IV. 261.[1]

— Kopuliren der Nadelhölzer. 1885. I. 208,[2] IV. 444.[1]

— Die Methode der Tauschwerte. 1892. IV. 246.

— Nochmals zur Frage der Umtriebszeit. 1888. IV. 252.

— Ueber Unternehmergewinn und Bodenwert. 1893. IV. 258.

— Das Verpflanzen der Eiche. 1883. IV. 507.

Schnittspahn, Georg Friedrich. Flora der Gefässe-Pflanzen des Grossherzogthums Hessen. 1839. I. 380.
— Flora der . . . Gewächse des Grossherzogthums Hessen. 1839. I. 380.
Schnitzer, Fr. Chemische Untersuchung der Lopezwurzel. 1862. III. 506.[1]
Schnizlein, Adalbert. Abbildungen der natürlichen Familien des Gewächsreiches. 1843. I. 261.
— Analysen zu den natürlichen Ordnungen der Gewächse. 1858. I. 266, 349.
— Auswahl von fremden Pflanzen. 1865. I. 270.
— Botanik, als Gegenstand der allgemeinen Bildung. 1868. I. 78.[2]
— Botanische Beobachtungen. 1861. II. 244.[1]
— Die Flora von Bayern. 1847. I. 382.
— Flore exotique. 1865. I. 270.
— Gespaltene Staubfäden und einfächerige Beutel. 1852. I. 116.[1]
— Iconographia familiarum . . . regni vegetabilis. 1843. I. 261.
— Kurze Beschreibung des Botanischen Gartens der Universität Erlangen. 1857. I. 47.
— Lacistemaceae. 1857. II. 95.[2]
— Morphologische Miscellen. 1850. I. 145.[1]
— Der Pflanzenwuchs Mittelfrankens. 1865. I.[2] 385.
— Uebersichten zum Studium der . . . Botanik. 1860. III. 58.
— Untersuchung über die . . . Stacheln bei der Section Grossularia. 1861. II. 244.[1]
— Die Vegetationsverhältnisse des Keuper- und bunten Sandsteins. 1865. I. 385.
— Vegetationsverhältnisse von Oberfranken. 1865. I. 385.
— & **Frickhinger,** Albert. Die Vegetationsverhältnisse der Jura- und Keuperformation in den Flussgebieten der Wörnitz. 1848. I. 382.
Schnücke, R. Der Lyda-Frass in . . . Wennigsen. 1898. IV. 457.
— Eine verbesserte Holz-Mess-Kluppe. 1898. IV. 232.
Schnürch, Alfons. Schäden infolge von Leimungen der Tanne. 1898. IV. 445.
Schnyder. Quels principes faut-il admettre pour l'établissement de l'aménagement des forêts. 1877. IV. 136.[1]
— Welche Grundsätze sind bei der Aufstellung von Wirthschaftsplänen . . . zu beachten? 1877. IV. 136.[1]
Schnyder, Otto. Apuntes sobre la flora argentina. 1877. II. 327.[2]
— Contributions à la connaissance de la flore Argentine. 1877. I. 344.
— Enumeracion de las Leguminosas halladas en la República Argentina. 1877. II. 318.[2]
Schober, Alfred. Ueber eine doppelte Secretion bei Xanthorrhoea. 1893. II. 86.[2]
— Ein Versuch mit Röntgen'schen Strahlen. 1896. I. 230.
— Ueber das Wachstum der Pflanzenhaare. 1885. I. 113.[1]
— Das Xanthorrhoeaharz. 1892. II. 86.[1]
Schober, Hugo. Zur Geschichte der Akademie für Forst- und Landwirthe zu Tharand. 1866. IV. 32.
Schober, J. De toestand en de toekomst der heidevelden. 1879. IV. 119.[2]
Schober, J. H. Afval van boschen 1881. IV. 434.
— Over Coniferen geskikt voor ons klimaat. 1878. III. 292.
— Houtteelt in Nederland. 1892. IV. 119.[2]
— Mededeeling over Coniferen. 1894. IV. 441.
— Pinetum Schoberianum. 1892. III. 292.
— Proefnemingen omtrent . . . buitenlandsche Coniferen. 1886. III. 292.
— Staat ter vergelijking van den groei . . . van eenige Dennensoorten. 1892. III. 293.
— Statistieke opgaaf van den groei . . . van verschillende Dennensoorten. 1892. III. 293.
— Statistische Uebersicht über das Wachstum . . . Koniferen zu Schovenhorst. 1900. I. 51,[2] III. 293.
— Waarnemingen over Coniferen. 1881. III. 292.
— Welke ondervinding is hier te lande opgedaan met . . . Coniferen. 1890. III. 294,[2] IV. 136.[2]
Schobinger-Pfister, J. Taschenbuch für reisende Botaniker im Kanton Luzern. 1866. I. 435.
Schoch, (Revierförster). Den Maikäfer betreffend. 1865. IV. 202.
Schoch, G. A. Manual of instructions for raising Mulberry trees. 1886. III. 378.
Schoch, Gottlieb. Der Garten zu Wörlitz. 1896. I. 49.

— Verzeichniss der Gehölze in den öffentlichen Gärten und Parkanlagen Magdeburgs. 1900. I. 49.
— Der Park zu Wörlitz. 1896. I. 49.
Schoch, Gustav. Naturgeschichte der Phylloxera. 1880. III. 572.
— & **Winter,** G. Ueber die Kirschbaumkrankheit. 1883. III. 432.[1]
Schoch, Ludwig, (sr.). Auszug aus der Abhandlung . . . das Geschichtliche des Wörlitzer Gartens. 1829. I. 48.
— Bericht über den vom grossen Sturmwind . . . verursachten Schaden. 1835. III. 184.[1]
— Erfahrungen über den Schutz der Holzgewächse. 1834. III. 183.[1]
— Nordamerikanische Blattbäume. 1829. III. 69.
— Nordamerikanische Laub- und Nadelholz-Bäume. 1829. III. 69.
— Nordamerikanische Nadelhölzer. 1829. III. 289.
— Über zwei nordamerikanische Eichen. 1828. III. 361.[1]
— Ueber zwei nordamerikanische Nadelholzbäume. 1828. III. 289.
Schoder, G. F. H. Die Erdarten im Gebiete der Pflanzenvegetation. 1825. I. 228.[1]
Schoebel, Philipp. Beitrag zur Kenntnis der Wirkung des Piperidin. 1893. III. 343.[3]
Schödler, F. See PETERSEN, Christian & SCHÖDLER, F.
Schoedler, Fryderyk. Księga przyrody. 1866. I. 95.
Schoedtler, Georg. Die Pandaneen, Cyclantheen. 1875. III. 332.[3]
Schöler, N. P. Berberissens skadelige Indflydelse. 1813. III. 394.[1]
Schöllenbach, Karl Christoph, OELHAFEN VON. See OELHAFEN VON SCHÖLLENBACH, K. C.
Schoen. See MÜNTZ, A. & SCHOEN.
Schoen, M. J. Les Cycas, leur culture. 1892. III. 284.[2]
Schönach, Hugo. Beiträge zur Flora von Tirol. 1892. V. XXIII.[1]
Schoenbein, Christian Friedrich. Présence des azotites . . . dans le règne végétal. 1862. I. 153.
— Ueber das Vorkommen salpetrig- und salpetersaurer Salze. 1862. I. 153.
Schönberg, O. von. Holz als Pflastermaterial. 1879. IV. 426.[1]
Schönberger. Ueber das Durchforsten der Holzbestände. 1830. IV. 172.[2]
Schöne. Veredelte Stecklinge von Nadelhölzern. 1877. III. 294.[1]
Die "Schöne Eiche" bei Ubetz. 1900. IV. 516.[1]
Schöne Rothtannen im Toggenburg. 1864. II. 37.[1]
Schönebeck, Constantin von. Vollständige Anleitung zur Vermehrung . . . der Obstbäume. 1806. III. 136.
Schoenefeld, W. de. Sur les floraisons automnales. 1859. I. 220.[3]
Schönemann, Ueber den Anbau fremdländischer Holzarten. 1866. IV. 125.[2]
— Les beaux arbres de la Suisse. 1898. I. 298.
Schönenberger, F. Die Baumriesen der Schweiz. 1898. I. 298.
Schönfeld. Das preussische Forstdiebstahlsgesetz. 1884. IV. 321.
Schöngarth, (Forstverwalter in Celle). Gutachten über . . . Feststellung der Normalpreise. 1850. IV. 333.
Schönheit, Friedrich Christian Heinrich. Einige Bemerkungen über thüringische Pflanzen. 1832. II. 313.[1]
— Ergänzender . . . Nachtrag zu dem Taschenbuche der Flora von Thüringen. 1850. I. 383.
— Der sich selbst belehrende Forstbotaniker. 1851. I. 371, IV. 82.
— Taschenbuch der Flora Thüringens. 1850. I. 383.
Schönhuth, Arthur. Die forstliche Bedeutung der Vögel. 1890. IV. 90.[1]
Schoenichen, Walther. Blütenbiologische Schemabilder. 1900. I. 239.[1]
Schönland, Selmar. Campanulaceae. 1894. II. 845.[1]
— Contributions to the morphology of the Mistletoe. 1888. II. 178.[1]
— Crassulaceae. 1891. II. 235.[1]
— Über die Entwicklung der Blüten . . . bei den Platanen. 1893. II. 254.[2]
— Goodeniaceae. 1894. II. 846.[2]
— & **Baker,** E. G. New species of Crassula. 1898. II. 236.[1]
Schönrock, E. I. See ШЕНРОКЪ, Э. И.
Die schönsten Ahornarten. 1885. III. 534.[1]
Schönwald. Die Schütte. 1894. IV. 478.

Schoepf, Johann David. Materia medica americana. 1787. III. 261.²
— Reise durch einige der mittlern und südlichen vereinigten nordamerikanischen Staaten. 1788. I. 305.
— Über die Temperatur der Pflanzen. 1788. I. 186.
Schoepf, M. Kurze Regeln zur Erziehung . . . von Privatwaldungen. 1899. IV. 107,¹ *119.*¹
Schoepfer. *See* HEROLD.
Schöpfer, Franz Xaver. Flora oenipontana. 1805. I. 439.
Schöyen, Wilhelm Maribo. Bärbuskenes skadeinsekter. 1888. III. 190.
— Bærbuskenes skadelige Insekter. 1888. III. 190.
— Berberisbusken og kornrusten. 1897. III. 394.²
— Beskyttelse af frugttrærne mod frostmaalerne. 1890. III. 191.
— Bringebärenes skadeinsekter. 1889. III. 458.²
— Einige Bemerkungen zu A. B. Frank: Die tierparasitären Krankheiten. 1898. III. 186.¹
— Ueber einige Insektenschädlinge . . . in Norwegen. 1893. IV. 549.²
— Frugttrærnes skadeinsekter. 1888. III. 190.
— Hindbærrets skadelige Insekter. 1889. III. 458.²
— Les insectes nuisibles du Rosier. 1887. III. 453.²
— Larvehärjinger paa birkeskoven i Tromsö amt. 1894. IV. 549.²
— Om løv mod Berberis. 1895. III. 200.²
— Petrolmischungen etc. gegen Raupen. 1895. III. 198.¹
— Rosens skadeinsekter. 1887. III. 453.²
— Rosens skadelige Insekter. 1887. III. 453.²
Schollaert, P. La protection des oiseaux insectivores. 1898. IV. 91.¹
Schollenberg und Reutha, J. T., *Freiherr* zu. Anmerkungen über das bairische Mandat . . . in Betreff der Wildschützen und Landskultur. 1778. IV. 318.
Scholler, Friedrich Adam. Flora barbiensis. 1775. I. 374.
Schollmayer, (*Oberförster, Masun*). Waldbeschädigungen durch Schlafmäuse. 1898. IV. 198.²
Schollmayer, Ethbin & Heinrich. Der bäuerliche Kleinwaldbesitz. 1900. IV. 100,¹ *309.*²
Schollmayer, F. Die Aufforstung einer alten Blösse. 1877. IV. 465.²
Schollmayer, Heinrich. *See* SCHOLLMAYER, Ethbin & Heinrich.
Schollmayer, K. Beitrag zur Kenntniss der Eichenschildläuse. 1888. IV. 511.
Schollmayr, Fr. Rumäniens Holzhandel. 1883. IV. 407.¹
Scholtz, Heinrich. Flora der Umgegend von Breslau. 1843. I. 381.
Scholtz, J. C. H. Ueber einen neuen Birkenfeind. 1859. IV. 490.²
Scholtz, Max. Die Nutation der Blüthenstiele. 1892. II. 504.²
— Die Orientirungsbewegungen des Blüthenstieles von Cobaea. 1893. II. 747.¹
Scholtz, Mortimer. Ueber eigenthümliche Gerüche des Holzes. 1895. I. 156.¹
— Ueber Evonymus japonicus. 1874. III. 532.²
— Die Kriechel als eingelegte Frucht. 1886. III. 437.¹
— Sambucus nigra als Topfpflanze. 1879. III. 751.¹
— Ueber Symphoricarpus racemosus Mchx. 1894. III. 752.²
Scholz. Zur Pflanzen-Ueberwinterung in Kellern. 1876. III. 183.¹
Scholz, Ad. Allgemeine Übersicht über . . . Gartenkultur im Umkreise von Marienwerder. 1849. III. 121.¹
Scholz, Eduard. Ein neuer Feind der Weymouthskiefer. 1898. IV. 470.¹
— Rhizoctònia Strobi. 1897. IV. 470.¹
Scholz, Josef. Blütendüfte als Anlockungsmittel für Insekten. 1900. III. 227.
Scholz, Lorenz. Catalogus arborum, fruticum . . . horti medici D. L. Scholzii. 1594. I. 42.
— Hortus Vratislaviae. 1587. III. 27.²
Schomburgk, Moritz Richard. Botanical reminiscences in British Guiana. 1876. I. 339.²
— Botanische Reise-Skizze. 1845. I. 339.¹
— Catalogue of the plants under cultivation in the Government botanic garden, Adelaide. 1871. I. 69.¹
— Le climat et les jardins de l'Australie méridionale. 1878. III. 132.¹
— Cultures diverses en Australie méridionale. 1891. III. 132.¹
— Economic botany of . . . Victoria. 1873. III. 282.²
— Einfluss der Walder auf das Klima. 1882. IV. 53.
— The flora of South Australia. 1875. I. 502.
— La flore de la Guyane anglaise. 1871. I. 339.¹

— Flüchtige Skizze über Guianas Kulturpflanzen. 1847. III. 268.¹
— Forest reserves and planting trees on . . . roads. 1873. IV. 180.²
— Forest tree planting and its influences on climate. 1878. IV. 53.
— Influence of forests on climate. 1873. IV. 53. — 1882. IV. 53.
— Influence of trees on climate. 1882. IV. 53.
— On the naturalised and other plants in S. Australia. 1879. III. 94.¹
— Ueber den ökonomischen Werth der verschiedenen Eucalyptus-Arten. 1878. IV. 531.²
— Papers read before the Philosophical society. 1873. I. 34.
— Poisonous plants. 1873. III. 59.²
— Report relative to the economical value of . . . ' Eucalypts.'' 1878. IV. 531.² ⁴
— Some account of the Curata. 1841. II. 59.¹
— Some notes on introduced plants. 1890. III. 132.¹
— South Australian Eucalypts. 1878. IV. 531.² ⁴
— Souvenirs d'une exploration en Guyane. 1883. II. 721.²
— Ueber das tödtliche Pfeilgift Urari. 1873. III. 685.¹
— On the urari. 1873. III. 685.¹
— The uses and properties of plants. 1873. III. 218.¹
— Versuch einer Fauna und Flora von Britisch-Guiana. 1848. I. 339.¹
— Wattle farming. 1884. III. 463.¹
Schomburgk, *Sir* Robert Hermann. On the Aeta Palm. 1886. III. 327.¹
— On the Ant tree of Guiana. 1838. II. 186.²
— Die Barbacenia Alexandrinae und . . . Imperatricis. 1845. II. *90,*¹ 331.²
— Beschreibung dreier neuen Pflanzen. 1847. II. *340,*² 428,¹ 866.²
— Caractères de deux plantes nouvelles. 1845. II. *90,*¹ 331.²
— Characters of two new plants discovered in British Guiana. 1845. II. *90,*¹ 331.²
— Description of a new species of Calycophyllum. 1841. II. *10.*²
— A description of British Guiana. 1840. III. 268.¹
— Description of Calycophyllum Stanleyanum. 1841. II. *10.*²
— A description of Ophiocaryon paradoxum. 1845. II. 490. ²description
— Description of the Mora tree. 1841. II. 355.¹
— Description of the Snake-nut tree of Guiana. 1840. I. 338.²
— On the forest-trees of British Guiana. 1853. IV. 398.¹
— Geographisch-statistische Beschreibung von Brittisch-Guiana. 1840. III. 268.¹
— Ueber die giftigen Wirkungen des Manschinell-Baums. 1838. III. 519.¹
— The history of Barbados. 1848. I. 335.
— Over den invloed van het keerkrings klimaat. 1853. I. 231.³
— Nachrichten über die Verhältnisse der Gartenkultur in Nordamerika. 1830. III. 116.²
— The Paper-tree of Siam. 1864. III. 381.¹
— Reisen in Guiana und am Orinoko. 1841. I. 329.
— Remarks on Anegada. 1832. I. 335.
— Siamese products. 1862. III. 276.²
— On two new species of . . . Laurineae. 1844. II. 223,² 227.¹
— On the urari. 1841. II. 720.²
— The vegetable products of Siam. 1861. III. 276.²
— Visit to the valley of Constanza. 1852. I. 335.
— West Indian fruits and esculents. 1847. III. 267.¹
— Westindische Früchte und Nahrungsmittel. 1847. III. 267.¹
Schomerus, Johannes. Akebia quinata. 1900. III. 393.²
— Laburnum Adamii. 1899. III. 489,² *537.*²
— Rosskastanien und Ulex. 1898. III. 489,² *537.*²
— Zwei wenig verbreitete immergrüne Gehölze. 1900. III. 543,¹ *651.*¹
Schondorf. Arbres et arbrisseaux cultivés en pleine terre dans le Jardin royal d'Oliva. 1859. III. 45.
— Gehölze, die im K. Garten zu Oliva . . . kultivirt werden. 1859. III. 45.
— Der Königl. Garten zu Oliva. 1877. I. 48.
Schondorff, Johannes Balthasar. Disputatio inauguralis medica de china china modo operandi. *See* HOFFMANN, Friedrich. 1704. III. 719.

Schonger, J. B. Beitrag zur Kenntnis der . . . cultivirten amerikanischen Crataegus-Arten. 1882. II. 260.²
— Notizen über Sorbus L. 1882. II. 311.¹
— Ueber Salix livida Wahlenb. 1871. II. 108.¹
Schoningh, Lüppo. Ueber die Wirkung des Strychnin. 1892. III. 684.¹
Schoon, Theodor. Waare oeffening . . . der planten. 1692. I. 30.
Schoor, W. K. J. De plantennamen Thehuy, Uan. 1892. I. 82.¹
Schoopf, Fr. J. Die Forstverfassung . . . in den Provinzen Niederösterreich, Oberösterreich. 1835. IV. 294,¹ 331.¹
— Handbuch der Forstverfassung . . . für die Kronländer Ungarn, Croatien. 1858. IV. 294,² 331.¹
— Die österreichische Forstverfassung. 1835. IV. 294,¹ 331.²
— Pflanzet Holz! 1854. IV. 167.¹
— Die Waldordnung des Landes Steyermark. 1843. IV. 331.²
Schörler, Bernhard. Die Flora der oberen Saale. 1895. I. 389.
— Untersuchungen über die Zellkerne in den stärkeführenden Zellen der Hölzer. 1883. I. 125, 137.
Schorss, (Forstassessor, Breslau). Nach welchen Grundsätzen ist die Entschädigung zu ermitteln, welche den Besitzern der an der Oder gelegenen Waldungen . . . zu gewähren sein wird? 1894. IV. 274.²
Schot, J. G. Nog iets over Minjak Tangkawang. 1881. III. 611.³
Schotel, G. D. J. Letterkundige bijdragen tot de geschiedenis van den tabak, de koffij en de thee. 1848. III. 222, 606.
Schott, (Oberförster). Die Begründung der Normal-Ertragsansätze. 1845. IV. 235.¹
Schott, Anton. Beiträge zur Flora des Böhmerwaldes. 1897. II. 302.¹
— Über Pflanzen-Volksnamen im Böhmerwalde. 1895. I. 75.¹
— Verzeichniss der im Böhmerwalde beobachteten Pflanzen-arten. 1893. I. 443.
Schott, Georg Friderich. Diplomatische Nachricht von der Winterhauch. 1790. IV. 25.
Schott, Heinrich. Tagebücher . . . von dessen Reisen in die Campos am Paraiba. 1822. IV. 25.
Schott, Heinrich Wilhelm. Ein neues europäisches Rhododendron. 1851. II. 681.¹
— Rutaceae, fragmenta botanica. 1834. II. 396.²
— Urostigma catalpaefolium Miquel. 1854. II. 153.²
Schott, J. H. L. Anweisung zur Messung der Bäume. 1807. IV. 216.
Schott, Peter Carl. Der anatomische Bau der Blätter der Gattung Quercus. 1900. II. 131.²
Schott, Wilhelm. Der naturgeschichtlichen Leistungen der Chinesen. 1843. I. 4.¹
— Über die naturgeschichtlichen Leistungen der Chinesen. 1842. I. 81.²
— Skizze zu einer Topographie der Producte des chinesischen Reichs. 1842. III. 273.¹
Schott von Schottenstein, H. W. Einige Worte über Auflockerung des Waldbodens. 1862. IV. 143.¹
— Ergebnis einer Heisterpflanzung. 1887. IV. 138.¹
— Forststatistik des Gebiets der freien Stadt Frankfurt. 1861. IV. 353.
— Forststatistische Beschreibung des Frankfurter Stadtwaldes. 1884. IV. 354.
— Mittheilung von Ergebnissen des Waldfeldbetriebs. 1857. IV. 133.
— Ueber den Samen-Ertrag der Weymouthskiefer. 1886. IV. 469.
— Ueber die Verbindung des Feldbaues mit dem Waldbau. 1840. IV. 133.
Schotte, (Oberförster, Katholisch-Hammer). Ansicht über die Ermittelung des Ertrages der Waldstreu. 1844. IV. 437.²
— Uebersicht des Material-Abnutzes vom Holzschlage im rothen Sande. 1846. IV. 260.¹
— Vortrag . . . über die Werth-Berechnung der Waldstreu-Nutzung. 1841. IV. 254.
Schottische Zaunrosen. 1887. III. 456.²
Schottländer, G. A. E. Die vorzüglichsten . . . Giftpflanzen. 1837. III. 73.
Schotzka, P. P. "American forests." 1887. IV. 337.¹
Sch . . . , C. A. S. Om Udbredelse af Poppelplantning. 1856. II. 244.¹
Schoubert, & **Mirbel,** C. F. B. de. Notes sur le Thuya, le Juniperus. 1812. II. 12.²
Schouppé, Anton von. Bewaldungsfrage Böhmens. 1878. IV. 278.¹

— Zur Cultur der Korbweiden. 1880. III. 348.
— Einiges über Korbweidenzucht. 1879. IV. 487.¹
— Welche sind mit besonderer Rücksichtnahme auf die Verhältnisse Böhmens die geeigneten Mittel, um . . . die Aufforstung . . . zu fördern? 1878. IV. 167,¹ 278.¹
Schousboe, Peder Kafad Anker. Beobachtungen über das Gewächsreich in Marokko. 1800. I. 483.²
— Iagttagelser over Vextriget i Marokko. 1800. I. 483.²
— Observations sur le règne végétal au Maroc. 1800. I. 484.
— On the real origin . . . of sandarac. 1799. III. 464.¹
— Sur la véritable origine de la résine . . . sandarac. 1799. III. 299,² 464.¹
Schouw, Joakim Frederik. Bemærkninger over en Samling af Blomstertegninger. 1849. I. 40.
— Caffetræets Historie. 1834. III. 739.
— Les Conifères d'Italie. 1842. II. 15.¹
— The Conifers of Italy. 1842. II. 15.¹
— Cycas circinalis i Blomst. 1846. III. 285.¹
— Dissertatio de sedibus plantarum originariis. 1816. I. 298.
— Ege- og Birke-Familiens geographiske og historiske Forhold i Italien. 1847. II. 115,¹ 123.¹
— Die Erde, die Pflanzen und der Mensch. 1837. I. 299.
— Erindringsord til en Forelæsning over de vigtigste . . . Planter. 1844. III. 52.
— Erindringsord til en Forelæsning over Lægeplanterne. 1844. III. 57.
— Esquisse d'un cours sur la géographie des plantes. 1833. I. 299.
— Essai sur la géographie botanique. 1824. I. 298.
— Foreløbig Fortegnelse over den Kjøbenhavnske botaniske Haves Planter. 1847. I. 40, 521.²
— On the geographic distribution of the Gramineae. 1825. II. 57.²
— On the geographical distribution of Palms. 1826. II. 60.²
— On the geographical distribution of the Vine. 1824. II. 506.¹
— Om de geographiske og historiske Forhold af de i Italien voxende Træer . . . Egefamilien. 1846. II. 123.¹
— De geographiske og historiske Forhold, som de italienske Træer af Egefamilien frembyde. 1846. II. 123.¹
— De geographiske og historiske Forhold, som de italienske Træer . . . til Birkefamilien frembyde. 1847. II. 115.¹
— Om de geographiske og historiske Forholde, som Birkefamilien frembyde i Italien. 1847. II. 115.¹
— Grundtræk til en almindelig Plantegeographie. 1822. I. 298.
— Grundzüge einer allgemeinen Pflanzengeographie. 1822. I. 298.
— Italiens Nadelhölzer. 1842. II. 15.¹
— De italienske Naaletræers. 1842. II. 15.¹
— Momente zu einer Vorlesung über die pflanzengeographischen Reiche. 1833. I. 299.
— Naturen i Nordafrika. 1837. I. 484.
— Naturen paa Sydhave-Øerne. 1835. I. 509.¹
— Naturschilderungen. 1837. I. 299.
— Natur-Skildringer. 1837. I. 299.
— Oversigt over de geographiske og historiske Forhold, som de italienske Lyngvæxter frembyde. 1843. II. 658.¹
— Pflanzengeographischer Atlas. 1822. I. 298.
— Plantarum species novae in Indice seminum Horti hauniensis. 1848. I. 40.
— Plantegeographisk Atlas. 1822. I. 298.
— De plantenwereld van Nieuw-Holland. 1855. I. 501.
— Om Planteverdenens Veteraner. 1832. I. 295.¹
— Populaire schetsen uit het gebied der plantengeographie. 1837. I. 299.
— Tableau du climat . . . de l'Italie. 1839. I. 426.
— Vlinrankens Historie. 1836. III. 509.¹
Schouwenburg, H. J., **Menalda van,** See **Menalda van Schouwenburg,** H. J.
Schovelin, A. Mærkelige gamle danske Træer. 1881. I. 296.¹
Schow, Peter. Observatione de potu thee. See **Nörager,** Christiern. 1740. III. 605.
Schr. Erzehung der Pflanzlinge. 1858. IV. 146.²
Schrader, Note sur Rosa gallica. 1893. III. 284.²
Schrader, (jr.). Der peruanische Zauberbaum. 1857. III. 694.³
Schrader, (Oberförster, Pless). Ueber das zur Verminderung . . . des Kieferspinners . . . angewandte Verfahren. 1856. IV. 475.

Schrader, C. Rosa gallica × repens Christ. 1887. II. 294.[1]
Schrader, Christian Friedrich. Genera plantarum selecta. 1780. I. 254.[2]
— Index plantarum Horti botanici Paedagogii regii glauchensis. 1772. I. 44.
Schrader, F. Verdickungen an Retinospora. 1888. III. 300.[1]
Schrader, Heinrich Adolf. Annotationes botanicae ex Indice seminum Horti academici gottingensis. 1836. I. 47.
— Catalogus Horti goettingensis. 1806. I. 45.
— Einige neue und seltene Gewächse ... im Botanischen Garten zu Göttingen. 1810. I. 45.
— Flora germanica. 1806. I. 376.
— Genera nonnulla plantarum. 1808. I. 265.
— De Halophytis Pallasii. 1810. II. 186.[2]
— Hortus gottingensis. 1809. I. 45.
— Reliquiae Schraderianae. 1838. II. 201,[2] 241.[2]
— Sertum hannoveranum. 1795. I. 44.
— Spicilegium florae germanicae. 1794. I. 375.
— Verzeichniss der Treib- und Glashauspflanzen ... aus dem Botanischen Garten zu Göttingen. 1810. I. 45.
Schrader, H. L. Ueber gallenbildende Insekten in Australien. 1863. IV. 530.
Schrader, Johann Christian Karl. Die norddeutschen Arzneipflanzen. 1792. III. 72.
Schrader, Johann Eduard Julius. De monocotyledonearum et dicotyledonearum circa gemmarum explicationem differentia. 1834. I. 107.[2]
Schrader, Otto. Thier- und Pflanzengeographie im Lichte der Sprachforschung. 1883. I. 300.
Schrader, W. Kurze Anleitung zum Anbau der Fuhre und Taune. 1859. IV. 441[·]
Schraeder, Wilhelm. Die Thüringer Flora. 1852. I. 383.
Schraff, C. D. Lehrbuch der Pharmacologie. 1862. III. 258[·]
Schrámek, Alois. Buntblätterige Birne. 1876. III. 445.[1]
Schramm, (*Forstinspector*). Einiges über Wald-Entwässerung. 1852. IV. 143.[1]
Schramm, (*Oekonomie-Commissionsrath*). Zur Flora der Mark Brandenburg. 1858. II. 301.[2]
— Flora von Brandenburg. 1857. I. 384.
Schramm, J. D. De hortis veterum Hebraeorum. *See* SCHROEDER, J. J. 1722. III. 33.[2]
Schramm, Johannes Augustin. Die seltneren Pflanzen der schlesischen Flora. 1840. I. 380.
Schrank, Frans von Paula von. De Acacia penuriam ligni resarciente. 1793. IV. 522.[1]
— Anfangsgründe der Botanik. 1785. I. 83.
— Animadversiones in quaedam loca Promptuarii Turicensis. 1790. I. 32.
— Aufzählung einiger Pflanzen aus Labrador. 1818. I. 309.[2]
— Baiersche Flora. 1789. I. 374.
— Baiersche Reise. 1786. I. 374.
— Bemerkungen über einige seltnere Pflanzen. 1822. I. 46.
— Botanische Bemerkungen. 1803. II. 786.[1] — 1808. II. 386,[2] 390.[2]
— Botanische Beobachtungen. 1807. I. 265. — 1814. I. 266. — 1815. II. 389.[2] — 1824. I. 267.
— Catalogus plantarum Horti academici landishutani. 1805. I. 45.
— Eine Centurie botanischer Anmerkungen. 1781. I. 263.
— Commentatio de rarioribus quibusdam ... plantis. 1820. I. 266.
— Einige seltene Pflanzen Sicilien's. 1819. I. 431.
— Ueber einige Ziergewächse. 1806. III. 650.[2]
— Flora monacensis. 1811. I. 376.
— Grundriss einer Naturgeschichte der Pflanzen. 1803. I. 84.
— De Juglande nigra penuriam ligni resarciente. 1793. III. 54.[3]
— Maximiliana regia. 1819. II. 71.[1]
— Naturhistorische ... Briefe über das Donaumoor. 1795. IV. 143.[2]
— Von den Nebengefässen der Pflanzen. 1794. I. 112.[2]
— Observationes in P. Leandri ... Nova genera. 1821. II. 612.[1]
— Observationum in fasciculos Promtuarii botanici Turicensis. 1790. I. 32.
— Vom Pflanzenschlafe. 1792. I. 198.[1]
— Plantae novae aut minus cognitae. 1824. I. 267.
— Plantae rariores Horti academici monacensis. 1819. I. 45.
— Plantae Virgilianae. 1793. I. 78,[1] 514.[1]
— De plantis Gnaphaloideis. 1824. II. 849.[2]

— De plantarum methodis. 1793. I. 251.
— De plantis quibusdam africanis commentariolus. 1824. I. 494.
— Primitiae florae salisburgensis. 1792. I. 439.
— Quatuor nova genera plantarum. 1824. II. 526,[1] 763.[2]
— Ueber die Sparsamkeit der Formen im Pflanzenreiche. 1811. I. 98.
— Vier neue Pflanzen, IV. 1819. II. 71.[1]
— Zwey neue Pflanzengattungen. 1809. II. 755.[2]
— **& Martius,** K. F. P. von. Hortus regius monacensis. 1829. I. 46.
— **& Moll,** K. E., *Ritter* von. Naturhistorische Briefe über Oestreich. 1785. I. 438.
Schranks Baiersche Flora. 1793. I. 375.
Schravendyk, J. C. van. Eenige opmerkingen omtrent de herbosschng ... in Frankryk. 1897. IV. 164.[1]
Schreber, Johann Christian Daniel. Icones et descriptiones plantarum. 1766. I. 262.
— Mantissa editioni quartae Materiae medicae Equitis a Linné adjecta. 1782. III. 55.
— Über das Pfeilgift der Amerikaner. 1783. III. 64.[2]
— Plantae verticillatae unilabiatae. 1773. I. 262.
— Plantarum verticillatarum unilabiatarum genera et species. 1773. I. 262.
— Programma de Persea aegyptiorum. 1788. II. 748.[2]
— Spicilegia observationum de Cacto hexagono. 1791. II. 590.[1]
— Spicilegium florae Lipsiae. 1771. I. 373.
— Stirpium obscurarum ... decuria I.-II. 1767. I. 262.
Schreck, F. A. Die selbstthätig Bewässerungsanlagen für Strassenbäume. 1886. III. 211.[2]
Schreckenstein, Friedrich, *Freiherr* ROT VON. *See* ROT VON SCHRECKENSTEIN, Friedrich, *Freiherr*.
Schreder, Josef. Ueber die Oxydationsproducte des Colophoniums. 1874. I. 181.[1]
Schreder, R. I. *See* ШРЕДЕРЪ, Р. И.
Schrefeld, Otto. Das Ausmauern hohler Bäume. 1886. III. 181.[1]
Schreger, Bernhard Nathaniel Gottlob. De corticis Fraxini excelsioris natura. 1791. IV. 535.[2]
Schreiben an Hrn. Ostermann mit Beantwortung seiner ... Aufgabe, auf was Art dem Holzmangel abzuhelfen. 1766. IV. 123.[1]
Schreiber. Die Ausbesserung lückenhaft gewordener Mittelwaldschläge. 1861. IV. 130.
— Erziehung ... der Eichenpflänzlinge. 1860. IV. 505.
— Die Hainbuchensaaten. 1862. IV. 491.[2]
— Das rinnenweise Einlegen der Nadelholzsamen. 1860. IV. 148.
Schreiber, Franz. Das Dickenwachsthum. 1865. I. 190.[1]
— Entwickelungsgeschichte der Siebröhren. 1864. I. 133.
— Fasciculi vasorum. 1864. I. 133.
Schreiber, H. Abies concolor. 1893. III. 296.[1]
— Abies Nordmanniana ... zu Steglitz. 1893. III. 296.[2]
— Chamaecyparis Lawsoniana Parl. 1893. III. 301.[1]
— Pinus Laricio Poir. var. austriaca. 1893. III. 308.[1]
Schreiber, J. C. Kurze ... Anweisung, zum Beschneiden der Fruchtbäume. 1890. III. 171.
Schreiber, J. F. Vernünftige und bescheidene Gegenantwort auf die Antwort ... Tobias Conrad Hoppens. 1748. II. 103.[2]
Schreiber, Paul. Die Einwirkung des Waldes auf Klima. 1899. IV. 54. — 1900. IV. 54.
Schreiner. Ueber das Vorkommen zweier gefährlicher Buprestiden. 1882. IV. 477.
Schreiner. Welche Bedeutung hat der Anbau von Stickstoffsammlern für die Waldcultur? 1896. IV. 143.[2]
Schrenk, Alexander Gustav. Enumeratio plantarum species ... in Songaria. 1842. I. 460.[1]
— Plantae novae ... quas ... ad fluvium Tschu versus legit. 1844. I. 456.
Schrenk, Hermann von. A disease of Taxodium distichum. 1900. III. 311,[1] IV. 452.[2]
— Notes on Arceuthobium pusillum. 1900. II. 174.[2]
— Notes on some diseases of southern Pines. 1898. IV. 462.[1]
— Oedema in roots of Salix nigra. 1897. III. 352.[1]
— Some diseases of New England Conifers. 1900. IV. 44.[2]
— The trees of St. Louis as influenced by the tornado. 1898. III. 184.[1]
— Two diseases of Juniperus. 1898. III. 303.[1]
— Two diseases of Red Cedar. 1900. III. 304.[1]
— *See also* ROBINSON, B. L. & SCHRENK, H. von.

Schrenk, Joseph. The eccentricity of the pith in Rhus Toxicodendron. 1878. II. 460.[1]
— Sassafras officinale. 1880. II. 228.[1]
Schréter, G. A. De constructione herbarii. 1826. I. 35.
Schreyer, Max. Führer durch die Zittauer Gebirgsreviere. n. d. IV. 355.[1]
Schribaux. Quelles sont les meilleures graines? 1893. IV. 147.[1]
Schriften aus dem ganzen Gebiete der Botanik. I. 10.
Schrocka. Prunus avium fructu nigricante. 1801. III. 435.[2]
Schrodt, Jul. Beiträge zur Oeffnungsmechanik der Cycadeen-Antheren. 1888. II. 3.[1]
Schroeck, Luca. De catechu. 1678. III. 464.[1]
Schroeder. Ueber das Auftreten . . . der Eiche. 1883. IV. 507.
Schrøder, C. H. Om Regler for Gjennemhugning og Bestandspleje. 1882. IV. 173.
Schröder, E. Ueber eine eigenthümliche Wirkung der Veredlung. 1888. I. 246.[2]
Schrøder, F. Kaurigum og Gumgraverne. 1892. III. 297.[2]
Schröder, G. Über die Austrocknungsfähigkeit der Pflanzen. 1886. I. 232.[1]
Schroeder, Henry. Emploi de l'acide oxalique. 1896. I. 36.[1]
— German Prunes. 1899. III. 433.[1]
Schroeder, J. J. De hortis veterum Hebraeorum. 1722. III. 33.[2]
Schröder, J. R. Eine Auswahl von 25 Sorten . . . Weidenarten. 1863. III. 347.
— Beobachtungen über die im Forstinstitut zu St. Petersburg cultivirten Bäume und Sträucher. 1862. III. 44.[2]
— See also Шредеръ, Н. Р.
Schröder, Johann. The compleat chymical dispensatory. 1649. III. 245.
— Pharmacopeia medico-chymica. 1649. III. 245.
— Pharmacopœia universalis. 1649. III. 245.
— Vollständige und nutzreiche Apotheke. 1649. III. 245.
Schroeder, Julius. Beiträge zur Chemie des Holzes. 1874. IV. 63.[2]
— Beiträge zur Kenntniss des Mineralstoffgehaltes der Streumaterialien. 1875. IV. 482.[2]
— Beitrag zur Kenntniss der Frühjahrsperiode am Ahorn. 1869. II. 479.[2]
— Über die Beschädigung der Vegetation durch Rauch. 1895. IV. 193.[1]
— Ueber die Düngung der Saatkämpe. 1893. IV. 144.[1]
— Ueber eine einfache Methode . . . Abbildungen des Holzzuwachses. 1884. IV. 233.
— Einfache Methode zur Bewerthung der Fichtenrinden. 1890. IV. 458.
— Eine einfache Methode zur Untersuchung . . . der Eichenrinden. 1890. IV. 513.
— Ueber den Einfluss des Streurechens auf . . . Zuwachs des Rothbuchenhölzes. 1876. IV. 498.
— Einige Versuche über den Einfluss der Witterung auf den Gerbstoffgehalt der Fichtenrinde. 1888. IV. 459.[2]
— Die Einwirkung der schwefligen Säure. 1872. III. 185,[1] IV. 192.[2]
— Étude sur la méthode de Löwenthal. 1885. I. 183.
— Die Feldpflanzen und Waldbäume in ihren Ansprüchen. 1877. IV. 69.
— Forstchemische und pflanzenphysiologische Untersuchungen. 1878. I. 151,[1] IV. 64,[1] 446.[2]
— Das Holz der Coniferen. 1872. II. 16,[2] IV. 543.[1]
— Zur Kenntniss des Mineralstoffgehaltes der Birke. 1878. IV. 491.[1]
— Zur Kenntniss des Mineralstoffgehaltes der Fichte. 1874. IV. 459.[2]
— Zur Kenntniss des Mineralstoffgehaltes der Tanne. 1878. IV. 446.[2]
— Migration de l'azote. 1878. I. 176.
— Studien über die Löwenthal'sche Gerbstoffbestimmungsmethode. 1885. I. 183.
— Untersuchung der chemischen Constitution des Frühjahrssaftes der Birke. 1865. II. 118.[1]
— Untersuchung erfrorenen Buchenlaubes. 1878. II. 126.[2]
— Untersuchung über den Nährstoffbedarf . . . des Eichenschälwaldes. 1890. IV. 515.[2]
— Untersuchungen über den Einfluss der Fällungszeit. 1874. IV. 384.[2]
— Untersuchungen über den Stickstoffgehalt des Holzes. 1878. IV. 64.[1]
— Untersuchungen über Quebrachoholz. 1889. III. 529.[1]
— Wanderung des Stickstoffs. 1878. I. 176, II. 479.[2]

— Zusammenstellung einiger in Tharand ausgeführter Untersuchungen. 1873. IV. 192.[2]
— See also STÖCKHARDT, Adolph & SCHRÖDER, Julius von.
— & Reuss, Carl. Die Beschädigung der Vegetation durch Rauch. 1883. IV. 192.[2]
— & Schertel, A. Die Rauchschäden . . . bei Freiberg. 1884. IV. 192.[2]
— & Schmitz-Dumont, W. Neue Beiträge zur Rauchfrage. 1896. IV. 193.[1]
Schrøder, L. Det danske Hedeselskab. 1892. IV. 39.[2]
Schröder, R. Daphne Sophiae. 1895. III. 628.[1]
— Index plantarum quae in horta dendrologica Instituti ruralis mosquensis. See Шредеръ, Р. Указатель растеній дендрологическаго сада. 1899. I. 42.
— Zur Richtigstellung der Namen einiger . . . Wildrosen. 1895. III. 451.[1]
— See also Шредеръ, Р. И.
Schröder, Romeo. Kurze Beschreibung der forstlich-statistischen Verhältnisse der Domaine Rothenhaus. 1860. IV. 370.
Schröder, Samuel. Förhärjande af Granskogen i Braunschweig. 1752. IV. 205.[2]
Schröder, Wilhelm. Cormus domestica Spach. 1897. III. 460.[1]
— Erfahrungen bei Strassenpflanzungen in Städten. 1900. III. 210.
— Picea pungens argentea. 1898. III. 306.[1]
— Rhus Osbecki. 1897. III. 527.[2]
Schroedter, (Oberförster, Georgenthal). Bemerkungen . . . über die . . . gelungene Methode . . . Nadelhölzer durch Stecklinge zu vermehren. 1835. III. 293.
Schröfl, M. J. Allgemeine Forstordnung. 1807. IV. 331.[1]
— Entwurf einer allgemeinen Forstordnung. 1807. IV. 331.[1]
Schroepfer. See HEROLD.
Schroer, J. C. Curiöse Beschreibung des Eschenbaumes. 1700. IV. 535.[2]
Schroeter. See DEITZ, TRIMBLE & SCHROETER.
Schröter, C. Ueber Hemmungsbildungen an Fichtenzapfen. 1900. IV. 460.[2]
Schröter, Carl. Über abnorme Beerenzapfen von Juniperus communis. 1897. II. 31.[1]
— Der Bambus und seine Bedeutung. 1885. III. 315.[2]
— Beitrag zur Kenntniss des Malvaceen-Androeceums. 1883. II. 519.[2]
— Le Châtaignier comme plante mellifère. 1894. III. 360.[1]
— Description sommaire des formes suisses du Pinus silvestris et du P. montana. 1895. II. 39.[2]
— Juniperus communis var. thyiocarpos. 1899. II. 31.[1]
— Das St. Antönierthal im Prättigau. 1895. I. 438.
— Über die Seychellen-Nuss. 1880. II. 70.[2]
— Ueber die Vielgestaltigkeit der Fichte (Picea excelsa Link.). 1898. II. 35.[2]
— Die Wetallenstäbe. 1896. I. 242.[2]
— See also SCHRÖTER, Ludwig & Carl; STEBLER, F. G. & SCHRÖTER, Carl.
— & Rikli, Martin. Seebälle aus dem Silsersee. 1899. I. 242.[2]
Schroeter, H. Sur l'hydrangine. 1890. III. 411.[1]
Schroeter, J. Ueber die Stammfäule der Pandaneen. 1875. III. 313.[1]
Schröter, Johann Samuel. Die Aesthetik der Blumen. 1902. I. 516, III. 34.[2]
— Erfahrungen in meinem Blumen-, Obst- und Gemüsegarten. 1802. III. 34.[1]
Schröter, Ludwig. Anleitung zur Pflege . . . der Cacteen. 1871. III. 619.
— Die Nadelhölzer und immergrünen Sträucher. 1867. III. 101,[2] 206.[1]
— & Carl. Coloured vade-mecum to the Alpine flora. 1889. I. 437.
— — Flore coloriée portative du touriste dans les Alpes. 1889. I. 437.
— — Taschenflora des Alpen-Wanderers. 1889. I. 437.
Schrötter von Kristelli, Hermann, Ritter. Über den Farbstoff des Arillus von Afzelia. 1893. II. 91,[2] 532.[2]
Schroff, Carl Damian von. Ueber die . . . mitgebrachten chilenischen Droguen. 1862. III. 269.[1]
Schroka, D. G. Von Verbesserung der Forsten. 1791. IV. 116.
Schroven, B. H. Insulinde. 1888. III. 128.
— Schetsen van Nederlandsch Indie. 1887. III. 128.
Schubarth, E. O. Die Feldeisenbahnen. 1884. IV. 391.
— Über Holzpflaster. 1891. IV. 426.[1]

Schube, Theodor. Beiträge zur Kenntniss der Anatomie blattarmer Pflanzen. 1885. I. 100,[1] II. 320.[2]
— Schlesiens Kulturpflanzen. 1896. III. 33.[1]
— See also FIEK, E. & SCHUBE, Th.
Schuberg, (Bezirksförster, Heidelberg). Ueber Stutzerpflanzungen. 1857. IV. 154.[1]
Schuberg, Karl. Ueber die Aufstellung, Prüfung und Anwendung von Baum-Massentafeln. 1893. IV. 231.[1]
— Baum- und Derbformzahlen der Eiche. 1898. IV. 513.
— Zur Betriebsstatik im Mittelwalde. 1898. IV. 131.
— Ein einfaches Verfahren zur Veranschlagung von Wegebaukosten. 1879. IV. 266.[1]
— Der Einfluss der Hochlage auf die Bestandsentwickelung. 1891. IV. 237.
— Die Einführung der Schienenwege in den forstlichen Betriebsdienst. 1886. IV. 392.
— Die Einführung der Waldbahnen. 1889. IV. 392.
— Einiges über Harznutzung. 1870. IV. 436.[2]
— Ueber die Einrichtung des forstlichen Versuchswesens. 1870. IV. 38.[1]
— Erfahrungen über strengere Methoden der Untersuchung des Waldertrags. 1888. IV. 237.
— Ertragsuntersuchungen im Eichenschälwalde. 1892. IV. 513.
— Der Femelbetrieb in Schule und Wald. 1876. IV. 130. .
— Formzahlen und Massentafeln für die Weisstanne. 1891. IV. 446.[1]
— Die Forschungsaufgaben im Walde. 1889. IV. 37.[2]
— Forstbenutzung: Transportwesen. 1887. IV. 389.
— Forstwirtschaft [des Grossherzogtums Baden]. 1884. IV. 350.[2]
— Das Gesetz der Stammzahl. 1880. IV. 236.
— Die Gewichtsabnahme des Brennholzes durch Aufspalten. 1870. IV. 387.[2]
— Die Grösse des Normalvorrats. 1889. IV. 237.
— Der Holzvorrath in einfachen und im combinirten Wirthschaftsbetriebe. 1878. IV. 236.
— Die K. Heyersche Waldertragsregelung. 1893. IV. 258. 233.
— Ueber die Kulminationszeit des Zuwachses. 1884. IV. 233.
— Der Kulturaufwand im Bereiche der natürlichen Verjüngung. 1896. IV. 140.
— Der Massengehalt . . . der Weisstanne. 1878. IV. 446.[3]
— Massentafeln für Nadelholzstangen. 1898. IV. 443.[1]
— Die Nutzholzwirtschaft im Femelschlag- und Femelbetrieb. 1896. IV..131.
— Der Raum- und der Derbmeter. 1871. IV. 226.
— Die Rothbuche im . . . Hochwalde. 1894. IV. 499.
— Schlaglichter zur Streitfrage; schlagweiser Hochwald- oder Femelbetrieb? 1886. IV. 128.
— Der Sturmschaden des 26. Oktobers 1870. 1871. IV. 189.[1]
— Untersuchungen über das Verhalten der Bestandsfactoren. 1882. IV. 237.
— Untersuchungen über den Wuchs der Esche im Mittelwalde. 1888. IV. 535.[2]
— Untersuchungen über die Erträge des Eichenschälwaldes. 1879. IV. 513.
— Untersuchungen über Eichenschälwald-Erträge. 1875. IV. 512.
— Vergleichende Untersuchungen über den Festgehalt der Weisstannen-, . . . holzstangen. 1885. IV. 442.
— Die Verschiedenheit der . . . Ertragstafeln für Weisstanne. 1897. IV. 446.[2]
— Versuche mit Stocksprengungen. 1878. IV. 386.
— Die Waldstreufrage. 1869. IV. 71. .
— Der Waldwegebau und seine Vorarbeiten. . 1873. . IV. 266.[2]
— Weisstanne. 1898. IV. 446.[3] .
— Die Weisstanne . . . in geschlossenen Beständen. 1888. IV. 446.[1]
— Der wirthschaftliche Charakter des Holzvorrathscapitals. 1877. IV. 256.
— Der Wuchs . . . der Eiche im Mischbestand. 1891. IV. 508.[1]
— Die Wuchsverhältnisse der gemischten Hochwaldbestände. 1892. IV. 234.
— See. also BÜHMERLE, Karl, KUNZE, M. F. & SCHUBERG, Karl; GRUNDNER, Fritz; SCHUBERG, Karl & SCHWAPPACH, Adam.
Schubert. Zur Berechnung des Zuwachses. 1889. IV. 234.
— Zur Berechnung des Zuwachsprozentes. 1889. IV. 234.
Schubert, A. Pflanzenkunde. 1888. V. x.[5]
Schubert, Bruno. Ueber die Parenchymscheiden in den Blättern. 1897. I. 111.

Schubert, Carl. "Abbazia," der Wintergarten am Quarnero. 1883. I. 66.[1]
— Acclimatisations-Versuche . . . im Garten . . . des Erzherzogs Josef zu Fiume. 1885. I. 66.[1]
— Der Park von Abbatia. 1894. V. ix.[1]
— Der Park von Abbazia. 1894. III. 29.[2]
Schubert, F. C. Das landwirthschaftliche Rechenwesen. 1858. IV. 58.
— Landwirthschaftlicher Wege- und Brückenbau. 1878. IV. 266.[2]
— Mathematisches Vademecum. 1858. IV. 58.
Schubert, Ferdinand. Handbuch der Forstchemie. 1848. IV. 60.[1]
Schubert, Franz. Versuch zur sichern Auswinterung der guten Pfirsichen. 1831. III. 430.[1]
Schubert, Gotthilf Heinrich von. Die Geschichte der Erde. 1836. I. 87.
— Lehrbuch der Naturgeschichte. 1823. I. 85.
— Welche Arten von Bäumen wachsen in Labrador? 1841. I. 309.[2]
Schubert, H. Die Pressler'sche Reinertragslehre. 1873. IV. 244.
Schubert, Johannes. Bodentemperatur im Freien und im Buchenwalde. 1888. IV. 54.
— Ueber den Einfluss der schlesischen Kiefernwaldungen. 1897. IV. 47.[1]
— Der Einfluss der Wälder auf das Klima. 1900. IV. 54.
— Einfluss der Windstärke. 1890. IV. 73.[1]
— Ueber die Ermittelung der Temperatur- und Feuchtigkeitsunterschiede zwischen Wald und Feld. 1893. IV. 54.
— Influence du couvert sur la température du sol à diverses profondeurs. 1888. IV. 54.
— Die jährlichen Temperaturextreme. 1893. IV. 73.[1]
— Klimatische Schutzwirkung des Waldes in Nordamerika. 1894. IV. 46.[1]
— Mathematisches Repetitorium. 1890. IV. 59.[1]
— Monats- und Jahresmittel der Bodentemperatur. 1888. IV. 54.
— Temperatur und Feuchtigkeit der Luft. 1895. IV. 54.
— Temperatur und Feuchtigkeit der Luft. 1897. IV. 73.[1]
— Die Weber'sche Hypothese über das Höhenwachsthum. 1895. IV. 234.
Schubert, Max. Die Cellulosefabrikation. 1892. IV. 430.[2]
Schubert, Michael. Catalogue des plantes du Jardin botanique de l'université de Varsovie. 1820. I. 41.
— Opisanie drzew i krzewów leśnych Królestwa Polskiego. 1827. IV. 79.[2]
— Spis roślin ogrodu botanicznego królewsko-warszawskiego uniwersytetu. 1820. I. 41.
— Spis roślin treibhauzowych : . . w Ogrodzie botanicznym. 1827. I. 42.
— Spis roślin treibhauzowych . . . w Ogrodzie botanicznym warszawskim. 1824. I. 41.
Schubert, W. Verzeichniss der Gefässpflanzen . . . in der Umgegend Oberschützens. 1858. I. 384.
Schuch, F. W. Die Cultur der Rose. 1880. III. 452.
Schuch, Josef. Ist der Epheu die einzige Pflanze, welche bei uns Luftwurzeln bildet? 1876. I. 66.[1]
— Mikor képződik a fákhan tömöttebb farész, ősssel-e vagy tavasszal? 1875. I. 190.[1]
Schuchardt, Theodor. Beiträge zur Entwickelungsgeschichte der Saamenknospe der Gattung Tetratheca. 1854. II. 429.[1]
— Synopsis Tremandrearum. 1853. II. 429.[1]
Schüderoff, J. Landesverschönerung. 1825. III. 34.[2]
Schübeler, Frederik Christian. Araucaria imbricata Pav. 1886. II. 26.[2]
— Barkbröd. 1885. IV. 436.[1]
— Carte géographique des végétaux du royaume de Norvège. 1873. I. 357.
— Die Culturpflanzen Norwegens. 1862. I. 356, III. 67,[1] V. xviii.[2]
— Om frøavl . . . af frøkontrolstationer. 1880. III. 156.[2]
— Über die geographische Verbreitung der Obstbäume . . . in Norwegen. 1887. I. 350.[3]
— Hängegramen. 1877. III. 34.[2]
— Har havebrug nogen betydning som binäring ved det norske landbrug? 1879. III. 120.[1]
— Hasselbusken. 1877. II. 121.[2]
— Hasselen, Corylus Avellana. 1887. III. 358.[1]
— Hedera Helix L. 1887. II. 649.[2]
— L'horticulture en Norwège. 1882. III. 67,[1] V. xviii.[2]
— Hylletroet. 1860. III. 752.[2]
← Ilex aquifolium L. 1888. II. 463.[2]
— Ueber den Juniperus communis. 1876. II. 31.[1]

— Kjämpeträet i Californien. 1877. II. 51.[1]
— Levende gjärder i Norge. 1890. III. 214.[1]
— Magnolia acuminata L. 1887. II. 211.[2]
— Mandelträet (Amygdalus communis L.). 1888. II. 272.[2]
— En merkelig forplantelsesmaade hos Granen. 1878. II. 36.[2]
— Ueber die nördlich-geographische Verbreitung der Obstbäume. 1857. I. 299, 350.[1]
— Nogle af de sødringer . . . ved at dyrkes paa en höi nordlig breddegrad. 1879. I. 218.
— Oljeträet (Olea). 1880. II. 713.[1]
— Ornäs-birken, Betula verrucosa γ laciniata. 1886. II. 120.[1]
— Pflanzengeographische Karte über das Königreich Norwegen. 1873. I. 357.
— Die Pflanzenwelt Deutschlands. 1873. I. 357.
— Die Pflanzenwelt Norwegens; die Birke. 1876. II. 118.[2]
— Die Polargrenze unserer Bäume. 1873. I. 348,[1] IV. 79.[1]
— Rosmarinus officinalis L. 1886. II. 765.[3]
— Slangegranen. 1891. II. 35.[1]
— Studier over klimaets indflydelse paa plantelivet. 1879. I. 218.
— Sukkerlön. 1888. IV. 527.[1]
— Synopsis of the vegetable products of Norway. 1862. III. 67,[1] V. xviii.[2]
— Syrenen. 1859. II. 714.[1]
— Tillæg til Viridarium norvegicum. 1885. I. 357.
— Träforädling. 1866. III. 50.[2]
— Träplantning. 1865. III. 166.
— Uebersicht der vegetabilischen Produkte Norwegens. 1862. III. 67,[1] V. xviii.[2]
— Växtlivet i Norge. 1879. I. 357.
— Viridarium norvegicum. 1885. I. 357.
— Wellingtonia gigantea Lindl. 1886. II. 50.[1]
Schuebler, Gustav. Beiträge zur Naturkunde . . . Oberschwabens. 1832. I. 378.
— Beobachtungen über die Temperatur der Vegetabilien. 1826. I. 231.[2]
— Beobachtungen über jährlich periodisch wiederkehrende Erscheinungen im . . . Pflanzenreich. 1831. I. 224.[2]
— Beobachtungen und Versuche über die Beziehung der Nectarien. 1833. I. 237.
— Dissertatio. sistens observationes quasdam botanico-physiologicas. 1833. I. 145.[3]
— Etwas über blaue Hortensien. 1833. III. 412.[1]
— Grundsätze der Agricultur-Chemie. 1830. IV. 60.[3]
— Recherches sur les couleurs des fleurs. 1825. I. 184.
— Systematisches Verzeichniss der . . . Pflanzen um Tübingen. 1822. I. 377.
— Over den Temperatur, som forskjellige Træer og Buskarter ere istand til at udholde i Tydsklands Clima. 1829. III. 45.
— Über die Temperatur, welche Baum- und Strauacharten im Clima Deutschlands zu ertragen im Stande sind. 1830. III. 45.
— Untersuchungen über das specifische Gewicht der Samen. 1826. I. 120.
— Untersuchungen über die Bedeutung der Nektarien. 1832. I. 237.
— Untersuchungen über die Einwirkung verschiedener Stoffe . . . auf das Leben der Pflanzen. 1826. I. 206.[1]
— Untersuchungen über die Farben der Blüthen. 1833. I. 184.
— Untersuchungen über die Farbenveränderungen der Blüthen. 1833. I. 184.
— Untersuchungen über die Farbenverhältnisse in den Blüten der Flora Deutschlands. 1833. I. 236.[3]
— Untersuchungen über die Farbenverhältnisse in den Blüten der Flora Frankreichs. 1833. I. 236.[3]
— Untersuchungen über die mittlere Zeit der Blüthenentwicklung. 1831. I. 224.[3]
— Untersuchungen über die pflanzengeographischen Verhältnisse Deutschlands. 1827. I. 377.
— Untersuchungen über die Temperaturveränderungen der Vegetabilien. 1829. I. 186, 231.[1]
— Untersuchungen über die Vertheilung der Farben. 1831. I. 182,[3] 184.
— Untersuchungen über die Vertheilung der Farben . . . der Rubiaceen. 1831. II. 808.[2]
— Untersuchungen über die Vertheilung der Farben . . . in den Familien der Asperifolien, Primulaceen. 1831. II. 196,[2] 257.[1]
— Untersuchungen über Obst- und Weintrauben-Arten Würtembergs. 1827. III. 546.
— See also RINGIER, V. A. & SCHÜBLER, Gustav.

— & **Martens,** George von. Flora von Würtemberg. 1834. I. 378.
— & **Renz,** C. Pesanteur spécifique des graines. 1827. I. 149.[1]
— — Untersuchungen über das Eigengewicht der Saamen. 1827. I. 149.[1]
Schübler, Val. Die Holznoth und die Mittel zu ihrer Beseitigung. 1861. IV. 281.[1]
Schüle. Ueber die Castanea vesca. 1873. III. 359.[1]
Schünemann. Die Sommer-Pflanzung. 1867. IV. 154.[2]
Schünemann, H. Die Pflanzenvergiftungen. 1891. III. 260.[2]
Schürch, B. Neue Methoden zum Entfernen . . . der . . . Baumraupen. 1863. III. 196.
Schürlen, G. Untersuchungen über die Frage: In welchem System des Holzes wird der rohe Nahrungssaft . . . geleitet? See MOHL, Hugo von. 1843. I. 163.
Schüssler (*Seminarlehrer*). Was uns Baum und Wald erzählt. 1882. I. 296.[1]
Schuette, Jachim Heinrich. Contribution on wild and cultivated Roses. 1898. II. 283.[1]
— Wald und Marsch um Greenbay. 1890. I. 315.
Schütte, R. Die Tucheler Haide. 1893. IV. 26.
— Die Tucheler Haide. 1889. IV. 354.
Schütz, Ad. von. Die Pflege der Eiche. 1870. IV. 506.
Schütz, Cosmas. Welche Erfahrungen liegen über die Ersatzmittel des Streustrohes und der Waldstreu vor? 1890. IV. 438.[1]
Schütz, J. C. von. Ökonomisches Bedenken von dem Nachtheile der Gehaue in . . . schwarzen Hölzern. 1757. IV. 116.
Schnetz, Karl Emil. De Taxo baccata ejusque veneno. 1840. III. 288.[2]
Schütze, C. Untersuchungen an Wurzeln der gemeinen Fichte. 1892. II. 871.[1]
Schütze, W. Ueber den Aschengehalt einjähriger Kiefern. 1879. II. 48.[1]
— Ueber den Aschengehalt . . . von Pinus sylvestris. 1876. II. 48.[1]
— Die Aufgabe der chemisch-physikalischen Abtheilung der forstlichen Versuchs-Stationen. 1874. IV. 37.[1]
— Beziehungen zwischen chemischer Zusammensetzung und Ertragsfähigkeit des Waldbodens. 1869. IV. 69.
— Die Gerbung mit Eisenoxydsalz. 1879. IV. 435.
— Ueber die Menge und den Aschengehalt der . . . Nadeln in Kiefernbeständen. 1879. II. 48.[1]
— Ueber die Nothwendigkeit der Düngung. 1872. IV. 144.[2]
— Untersuchung von Boden und Holz . . . durch Sturmfluthen der Ostsee beschädigt. 1876. IV. 185.[1]
— Untersuchungen über den Gerbstoffgehalt der Eichenrinde. 1879. IV. 515.[1]
Schützenberger, Paul. Sur les matières colorantes de la graine de Perse. 1868. III. 542.[3]
— Note sur deux nouveaux dérivés de la quinine. 1859. III. 721.
— Untersuchungen über Pflanzenbasen. 1858. I. 175.
Schütz, (*Forstassessor*). Wachsthum um Ertrag der Rothbuche. 1897. IV. 499.
Schuez, Georg Emil Carl Christoph. Flora des nördlichen Schwarzwaldes. 1858. I. 384.
Schuhmacher, W. Sur l'évaporation à travers les membranes. 1905. I. 107.
Schuiling, R. Nederland tusschen de tropen. 1889. III. 128.
Schuitemaker, L. F. TUYL. See TUYL SCHUITEMAKER, L. F.
Schuld, F. W. Nog iets over de schadelijkheid van den Iepenboom. 1849. II. 143.[2]
— De uspbeweging in de planten. 1876. III. 170.
Schuldt, U. Ph. Ein blühendes Dasylirion glaucophyllum. 1875. III. 336.[1]
Schulemann. Beitrag zur Abwendung des Rüsselkäferfrasses. 1878. IV. 207.
Schulemann, (*Oberförster, Carlsberg*). Abbildung eines Fichtenstocks. 1853. IV. 458.
— Nachweisung der Material-Abnutzung eines . . . Kiefernbestandes. 1857. IV. 260.[2]
— Spezielle Bestandsaufnahme . . . im kgl. Forstrevier Karlsberg. 1853. IV. 352.
— Spezielles Massen-Ergebniss der auf einem Morgen . . . des k. Forstreviers Carlsberg eingeschlagenen Holzmasse. 1854. IV. 260.[1]
— See also WAGNER, A. & SCHULEMANN.
Schulenburg, Freiherr von der. Anweisung wie bey Eintheilung der . . . Reviere zu verfahren. 1789. IV. 241.
— Anweisung wie der Lärchen-Baum-Saamen auszusäen. 1788. IV. 448.[3]

Schulenburg, *Freiherr* von der (*continued*).
— Anweisung wie reiner Kienen-Saamen ohne Flügel gesäet. 1788. IV. 471.
— Anweisung zum Anbau der Weiss- oder Edel-Tanne. 1790. IV. 444.[1]
— Anweisung zum Anlegen der Eichel-Kämpe. 1790. IV. 504.
— Anweisung zum Pappeln- und Weidenpflanzen. 1790. IV. 151.[2]
— Anweisung zum Sammeln und Aussäen des Birken-saamen. 1788. IV. 490.[1]
— Anweisung zum Verbessern der Erlen. 1790. IV. 488.[2]
— Anweisung, zur Vermehrung der Rüstern. 1790. IV. 518.[2]
— Circulair-Verordnung . . . wornach sie die Kienäpfel nicht zu früh einsammlen. 1788. IV. 471.
Schulenburg, Willibald von. Die Königserle. 1881. II. 116.[2]
— Die Obstbäume des Spreewaldes. 1881. III. 138.
Schulman, O. K. Kasvilajien tieteel listen nimien selityksiä. 1891. I. 76.[3]
Schulte, A. Fermenteering van cacao. 1900. III. 595.[2]
Schultens, Albert. Dissertatio de Palma ardente. 1725. II. 63.[2]
Schultes, G. von. Anleitung zur landwirthschaftlichen Holzzucht. 1841. IV. 106.
— Der neue Sylvan. 1832. IV. 268.
— Der Streuwald. 1849. IV. 71.
Schultes, Joseph August. Ausflüge nach dem Schneeberge. 1802. I. 439.
— Baierns Flora. 1811. I. 376.
— Catalogus Horti regii botanici Landishuti Bojorum. 1810. I. 45.
— Catalogus plantarum horti botanici C. r. universit. Cracoviae. 1806. I. 65.[2]
— Flora austriaca. 1794. I. 439.
— Grundriss einer Geschichte und Literatur der Botanik. 1817. I. 79.[1]
— Observationes botanicae. 1809. I. 265.
— Österreichs Flora; ein Handbuch. 1794. I. 439.
— Oestreichs Flora. 1794. I. 439.
— Reise auf den Glockner. 1824. I. 439.
— Reisen durch Oberöstreich. 1809. I. 439.
Schultes, Julius Herman. Beiträge zur Nomenclatur der Flora Japans. 1855. I. 75.[2]
— *See also* HOFFMANN, Johann. & SCHULTES, J. H.
Schultheis. Rosa gigantea. 1890. III. 455.[2]
— Rosa polyantha grandiflora. 1887. III. 456.[1]
Schultheis, (*Gebrüder*). Deutsches Rosen-Buch. 1889. III. 450.
Schultheiss, Ch. Die Waldbedeckung des Grossherzogthums Baden. 1892. IV. 350.[2]
Schultheiss, Friedrich. Beobachtungs-Daten der phänologischen Station Nürnberg. 1892. I. 225.
— Phänologischer Bericht. 1891. I. 225.
— Die Thätigkeit der phänologischen Station Nürnberg. 1891. I. 225.
Schultness, A. *See* TSCHUDI, Friedrich von & SCHULTHESS, A.
Schultz. Der Nonnen- und Käferfrass in Ostpreussen. 1873. IV. 200.
Schultz, (*Forstmeister, Gumbinnen*). Der Frass der Nonnenraupe in . . . Litthauen. 1856. IV. 200.
— Der Frass der Nonnenraupe . . . in . . . Litthauen. 1858. IV. 200.
— Holz-Ertrag zweier Flächen . . . auf Revier Poppelau. 1867. IV. 261.[1]
— Den Insektenfrass im . . . Gumbinnen betreffend. 1863. IV. 207.
— Der Insektenfrass im Regierungs-Bezirk Gumbinnen. 1860. IV. 207.
— Der Insektenfrass im Regierungsbezirk Gumbinnen. 1861. IV. 207.
— Ueber den weitern Verfolg des Frasses der Nonnenraupe in . . . Litthauen. 1857. IV. 200.
Schultz, (*Oberförster, 'Poppelau*). Ueber den Einfluss der Witterung auf Raupen. 1842. IV. 206.
— Ueber den summarischen Holz- und Geld-Ertrag des k. Forst-Reviers Poppelau. 1843. IV. 260.[1]
Schultz, A. Einige Erfahrungen über die Veredlung der Blutbuche. 1884. III. 360.[3]
— Wie beschneidet man Bäume. 1885. III. 171.
Schultz, A. N. Kultur durch Steklinge. 1875. IV, 506.
— Die Sprengtechnik im Forsthaushalte. 1886. IV. 387.[1]
— Zuwachsverhältnisse der Edelkastanie. 1888. 1889. IV. 493.[1]

Schultz, Adam Gottfried. Commentatio ad quaestionem . . . Quaenam est ad antheras pollinis formatio ejusque evolutio? 1822. I. 200.
— Quaenam est ad antheras pollinis formatio ejusque evolutio. 1822. I. 116.[2]
Schultz, F. J. Abbildung der in- und ausländischen Bäume . . . in Oesterreich. 1792. I. 293, III. 89,[2] IV. 86.[2]
Schultz, Friedrich Wilhelm. Flora der Pfalz. 1846. I. 382.
— Grundzüge zur Phytostatik der Pfalz. 1863. I. 385.
— Liste des plantes contenues dans cet Herbarium normale. 1854. I. 349.
— Vegetationsverhältnisse [der Rheinpfalz]. 1867. I. 386.
— Zusätze . . . zur Phytostatik der Pfals. 1863. I. 385.
Schultz, Friedrich Wilhelm Ferdinand. Pharmacopöe zum Gebrauch für die Armenpraxis. 1805. III. 248.
Schultz, Imre. A növénytan teljes kézikönyve. 1878. I. 91.
Schultz, J. A. Der Holzessig. 1844. IV. 432.[1]
— Neues, wohlfeiles und bewährtes Verfahren, das Holz zu conserviren. 1844. IV. 417.
Schultz, Karl Friedrich. Prodromus florae stargardiensis. 1806. I. 376.
— Rosa viscida. 1825. II. 300.[1]
Schultz, Karl Heinrich (*Bipont*). Adnotationes in Cassiniaceas Wrightianas. 1863. II. 849.[1]
— Beitrag zum Systeme der Cichoriaceen. 1866. II. 848.[1]
— Cassiniaceae uniflorae. 1861. II. 848.[1]
— Ueber die Cassiniaceen unter den . . . Nilgherry-Pflanzen. 1852. I. 473.
— Compositae. 1847. II. 848.[3]
— Enumeratio Cassiniacearum a cl. G. Mandon . . . lectarum. 1866. II. 849.[1]
— Enumeratio Compositarum a cl. Dr. Krauss . . . lectarum. 1844. I. 494.
— Ueber die Gattung Zaluzania. 1861. II. 868.[2]
— Ueber Loricaria thyoides. 1860. II. 867.[1]
— Lychnophora Martius. 1863. II. 848.[1]
— Plantae Karstenianae. Cassiniaceae. 1860. I. 340.[1]
— Plantae Regnellianae. 1849. I. 342.
— Verzeichniss der Cassiniaceen, welche Herr Edelstan Jardin . . . gesammelt hat. 1856. II. 850.[1]
— Ueber die von W. Lechler . . . gesammelten . . . Cassiniaceen. 1855. II. 848.[3]
— Zollingeria, eine neue Gattung der Artemisieen. 1854. II. 864.[3]
Schultz-Schultzenstein, Karl Heinrich. Die Anaphytose oder Verjüngung der Pflanzen. 1843. III. 37.[2]
— Anaphytose und Phytodomie des Baums. 1854. I. 82.[1]
— Ueber den Baumwuchs in der Mark. 1861. I. 190.[1]
— Ueber die Bedeutung der Verzweigung. 1861. I. 106.[2]
— Sur la circulation des fluides. 1831. I. 163.
— Die Cyklose des Lebensaftes. 1841. I. 163.
— De la différence qui existe entre la théorie de l'anaphytose . . . et la théorie de la métamorphose. 1867. I. 101.[1]
— Die Entdeckung der wahren Pflanzennahrung. 1844. I. 157.
— Ueber die Entstehungsgeschichte der Lebensaftgefässe. 1861. I. 133.
— Ueber die Formenconstanz der Brombeeren. 1866. II. 301.[3]
— Ueber die Klassification der Pflanzen. 1864. I. 252.
— Ueber einen Koniferen-Steckling. 1856. II. 36.[1]
— Über die Krankheit der Orangenbäume. 1861. III. 500.[1]
— Über den Kreislauf des Saftes. 1824. I. 163.
— Mémoire . . . Les organes . . . désignés sous le nom de vaisseaux du latex. 1833. I. 135.
— Mémoire sur la circulation et sur les vaisseaux laticifères. 1839. I. 135.
— Mémoire sur les vaisseaux du latex. 1837. I. 135.
— Memoria sopra la circolazione del sugo. 1831. I. 163.
— Die morphologischen Gesetze der Blumenbildung. 1863. I. 114.[2]
— Das natürliche System der Morphologie der Früchte. 1864. I. 119.
— Natürliches System des Pflanzenreichs. 1832. I. 260.
— Die Natur der lebendigen Pflanze. 1823. I. 146.
— Neue Beobachtungen über den Holzsaft. 1842. I. 175.
— Neues System der Morphologie der Pflanzen. 1847. I. 100.[1]
— Nouvelles observations sur la circulation dans les plantes. 1838. I. 163.
— Nouvelles observations sur les vaisseaux laticifères. 1857. I. 135.
— Sur l'origine de l'oxygène exhalé par les plantes. 1844. I. 172.

— Ueber Pflanzenernährung. 1864. I. 158.
— Rapports des vaisseaux laticifères. 1867. I. 136.[1]
— Sur les rapports des vaisseaux laticifères avec le bois. 1867. I. 136.[1]
— Ueber die Saamenträger bei Passiflora quadrangularis. 1870. II. 580.[1]
— Schreiben . . . an Herrn Flourens. 1847. I. 158.
— Ueber die tödtende Wirkung des Frostes. 1862. I. 212.
— Ueber die Umbildung von Holzsaft in Lebenssaft. 1866. I. 175.
— Ueber den Unterschied von Veredelung und Pfropfung. 1870. III. 165.
— Ueber den Unterschied zwischen Metamorphose und Anaphytose. 1866. I. 145.[2]
— Ueber den Ursprung und die Natur des Cambiums. 1831. I. 128.[1]
— Die Verjüngung im Pflanzenreich. 1851. I. 187.
— Ueber die Verpflanzung der Chinabäume. 1856. III. 715.
— Welchen Nutzen können wir aus der Kenntniss des Cambiums . . . ziehen? 1832. III. 37.[2]
— See also Шультцъ, K. Г.
Schultze. Mededeelingen omtrent de karet. 1863. III. 685.[2]
Schultze, A. G. R. Compendium der officinellen Gewächse. 1840. III. 57.
Schultze, A. N. Due Ausnützung der Rothbuche. 1885. IV. 498.
— Waldverhältnisse und Forstwirthschaft in Bosnien. 1885. IV. 374.[2]
Schultze, J. C. L. Die Aestung der Waldbäume. 1835. IV. 170.
— Beiträge zur Würdigung der Vorzüge der künstlichen Verjüngung der Buche. 1840. IV. 493.[1]
— Ueber die Durchforstung. 1835. IV. 173.
— Die Eiche und ihre Anziehung. 1835. IV. 504.
— Die Forstbenutzung. 1852. IV. 381.
— Ueber Forst-Culturen. 1836. IV. 141.
— Lehrbuch der Forstwissenschaft. 1841. IV. 97.
— Ueber den lichten oder dunkeln Stand der Buchen-Besamungs- und Licht-Schläge. 1834. IV. 493.[1]
— Ueber die natürliche Verjüngung der Buche. 1835. IV. 493.[2]
— Der Schluss der deutschen Waldbäume. 1837. IV. 173.
— Verwaltungs- und Geschäftskunde im Forst- und Jagdwesen. 1849. IV. 287.
— Die Wald-Erziehung. 1839. IV. 106.
Schultze, J. F. Om Ærendselsbesparelse ved Opvarmning af vore Værelser. 1859. IV. 281.[1]
Schultze, Nicolaus. De nuce moschata. See Vallan, Jacobus. 1709. III. 402.[2]
Schultzenstein, K. H. Schultz-. See Schultz-Schultzenstein, K. H.

Schulz, (Königlicher Ober-Baurath, Sanssouci). Gutachten über vorstehende Abhandlung. 1824. III. 70.
Schulz, Alexander Nikolaus. Etwas von der Weimuthskiefer. 1873. IV. 470.[1]
— Mittheilungen über die Phal. tortrix histrionana. 1862. IV. 445.
— Raupenfrass in Kompagnie. 1872. IV. 509.
— Zuwachs-Berechnung von Pinus strobus. 1873. IV. 470.[2]
Schulz, August. Beiträge zu Morphologie und Biologie der Blüthen. 1892. I. 115.[1]
— Beiträge zur Kenntniss der Bestäubungs-einrichtungen. 1888. I. 238.
— Bemerkungen zu dem Berichte über die Organisation eines meteorologischen Dienstes. 1879. IV. 60.[1]
— Über die Entwicklungsgeschichte der . . . Flora und Pflanzendecke der skandinavischen Halbinsel. 1900. I. 358.
— Entwicklungsgeschichte der phanerogamen Pflanzendecke Mitteleuropas. 1899. I. 350.[1]
— Grundzüge einer Entwicklungsgeschichte der Pflanzenwelt Mitteleuropas. 1894. I. 350.[1]
Schulz, C. F. Gründliche Anleitung für Maulbeerbaumzucht. 1854. V. xxviii.[1]
Schulz, Ernst. Ueber Reservestoffe in den immergrünen Blättern. 1888. I. 179.[2]
Schulz, Franz. Botanischer Kalender für Nord-Deutschland. 1869. I. 386.
— Deutschlands Wälder und Haine. 1868. I. 371. — 1874. I. 294.[1] III. 69, IV. 83.
Schulz, Hugo. Das Eucalyptus-Oil. 1881. IV. 531.[2]
— Excerpts from [his] treatise on Eucalyptus oil. 1881. IV. 531.[2]
— On the therapeutic value of Eucalyptus oil. 1881. IV. 531.[2]

Schulz, J. H. Grundriss der Zoologie und Botanik. 1846. I. 88.
Schulz, O. Die Vertilgung der Maikäfer. 1887. IV. 203.
Schulz, Paul. Anatomische Studien über . . . Bignonia aequinoctialis. 1884. II. 788.[1]
— Das Markstrahlengewebe. 1882. I. 125.
Schulz, Th. Om botaniske haver. 1895. III. 31.
Schulz, Witold von. Ein Beitrag zur Kenntniss der Sarsaparille. 1892. III. 339.[1]
— Ueber ein Glycosid aus Chionanthus virginica. 1893. II. 706.[1]
— Prüfung des Rosskastanienextractes. 1894. III. 538.[2]
Schulze, (Forstingenieur). Zur Ermittelung des Massenzuwachsprocentes. 1877. IV. 236.
— Mittheilungen aus der Praxis der forstlichen Reinertragstheorie. 1875. IV. 256.
Schulze, (Oberförster). Fichten-Dammsaat. 1887. IV. 454.
Schulze, Carl. Die Benutzung des Obstes. 1881. III. 174.[1]
— Die Rose. 1879. III. 452.
— Grundriss im Feldmessen, Nivellieren. 1882. III. 200.[1]
Schulze, Ernst August. Über die Bildungsweise des Asparagins. 1888. I. 177.
— Sur la composition chimique de la membrane cellulaire. 1893. I. 138.[2]
— Über den Eiweissumsatz im Pflanzenorganismus. 1880. I. 176.
— Sur la formation . . . de bases organiques azotées. 1893. I. 177.
— Zur Kenntnis der chemischen Zusammensetzung der Pflanzenzellmembranen. 1889. I. 154.
— Ueber die stickstofffreien Reservestoffe einiger Leguminosensamen. 1889. II. 321.[1]
— & Barbieri, J. Présence de l'allantoïne. 1882. I. 176.
— — Ueber das Vorkommen von Allantoin. 1882. I. 176.
— & Frankfurt, S. Sur la présence du sucre de canne. 1894. I. 177.
— & Rongger, Niklaus. Über die Bestandteile der Samen von Pinus Cembra. 1899. II. 41.[2]
— Steiger, E. & Maxwell, W. Sur la composition chimique de la membrane cellulaire. 1890. I. 154.
Schulze, Ferd. Forst- und jagdgeschichtliche Fragmente von den . . . obererzgebirgischen Waldungen. 1863. IV. 25.
Schulze, Franz. Beitrag zur Kenntniss des Lignins. 1856. I. 175.
Schulze, Friedrich Gottlob. Nationalökonomie. 1856. IV. 269.
— Über volkswirthschaftliche Begründung der Gewerbswissenschaften. 1826. IV. 268.
— Über Wesen und Studium der Wirthschafts- oder Cameral-Wissenschaften. 1826. IV. 268.
Schulze, Gustav Albrecht Ewald. Ueber die Grössenverhältnisse der Holzzellen. 1882. I. 125.
Schulze, Heinrich. Bäume und Sträucher für salzhaltigen Boden. 1900. III. 41.[2]
Schulze, Hilmar. Beiträge zur Anatomie des Blattes bei den Chloranthaceen. 1900. II. 95.[1]
Schulze, Johann Ernst Ferdinand. Toxicologia veterum. 1788. III. 260.[2]
Schulze, Johann Heinrich. De Aloe. 1723. III. 333.[1]
— De granorum kermes. See Berthold, J. C. F. 1743. III. 362.[1]
— Nonnulla ad camphoram spectantia. 1745. III. 404.[2]
— De oleo Olivarum. 1740. III. 678.[1]
— De Rubo Idaeo officinarum. 1744. III. 458.[2]
Schulze, K. F. Anleitung zur wohlfeilen Kultur der Waldblössen. 1857. IV. 141.
Schulze, Max. Ueber aus der Flora von Jena. 1888. II. 275.[2]
— Jenas wilde Rosen. 1886. II. 284.[2]
— Rosa canina × trachyphylla, R. Naumannii. 1896. II. 296.[2]
— Rosa jenensis. 1885. II. 295.[1]
Schulze, Richard. Durchforstungsergebnisse auf Steinbacher Revier. 1881. IV. 173.
— Die Ernte der Weidenculturen. 1884. III. 348.
— Die Hegerwirthschaft. 1884. III. 348.
— Die Korbweide, ihre Kultur. 1885. III. 349.
— Die Kultur der kaspischen Weide. 1873. III. 351.[1]
— Die Kultur der Korbweide. 1874. III. 347.
— Die rationelle Weidencultur. 1884. III. 348.
— Die Schädlinge der Korbweide. 1883. III. 350.[1]
— Zur Weidenzucht. 1874. III. 352.[1] IV. 488.[1]
— Die wirthschaftliche Behandlung der Weidenculturen. 1884. III. 348.

Schulze, Wilhelm. Gärtnerische Samenkunde. 1883. III. 156.[1]

Schulze-Messdunk, R. Die Bedeutung der Korbweidenwirthschaft für die österreichischen Kronländer. 1883. IV. 487.[2]
— Die Culturweiden. 1883. IV. 488.[1]

Schulzen, Franz Matthias. Forstwesen, Waldkultur und Feldschutz in Preussen. 1881. IV. 321.
— Korbweiden-Kultur. 1882. III. 348.

Schulzer von Müggenburg, Stefan. Pilze an Quittenästen. 1871. III. 423.[2]

— Kanitz, August & Knapp, J. A. Die bisher bekannten Pflanzen Slavoniens. 1866. I. 447.

Schumacher, Christian Friedrich. Beskrivelse af guineiske Planter. 1827. I. 490.
— Enumeratio plantarum in partibus Saellandiae. 1801. I. 352.
— Den kjøbenhavnske Flora. 1804. I. 352.
— Medicinsk Plantelære. 1825. III. 56.
— Om Slægten Paullinia Linn. 1794. II. 487,[2] 488.[2]
— & Herholdt, J. D. De officinelle Lægemidler af Planteriget. 1808. III. 67.[1]

Schumacher, Heinrich Christian Friedrich. See SCHUMACHER, C. F.

Schumacher, Hubert. Beiträge zur Förderung der Buchenverwerthungsfrage. 1889. IV. 500.[1]
— Die Buchennutzholz-Verwertung in Preussen. 1888. IV. 499.
— Ein einfaches Verfahren zur Ermittelung des Massenzuwachsprocentes. 1891. IV. 234.
— Der Einfluss der Mast auf die Holzproduktion. 1890. IV. 495.
— Ueber die forstliche Bedeutung der Buchenbahnschwelle. 1887. IV. 500.[1]
— Der technische Werth des Lichtungszuwachses der Buche. 1888. IV. 500.[1]
— Der Werthzuwachs der Buche. 1889. IV. 498.
— Das Wildgatter. 1890. IV. 146.[2]
— Zuwachsleistung unterdrückter . . . Buchen. 1887. IV. 498.

Schumacher, Wilhelm. Die Diffusion in ihren Beziehungen zur Pflanze. 1861. I. 153, 164.
— Die Physik in ihrer Anwendung auf Agricultur. 1864. IV. 57.[1]

Schumann, (Forstassessor). Auf welche Weise prüft man am zuverlässigsten den Samen? 1888. IV. 147.[1]

Schumann, C. R. G. Anatomische Studien über die Knospenschuppen. 1889. I. 108.[1]

Schumann, Karl Moritz. Die Aestivation der Blüthen. 1886. I. 115.[1]
— Ueber afrikanische Ameisenpflanzen. 1891. I. 235.[2]
— Über die afrikanischen Kautschukpflanzen. 1893. II. 727.[3]
— Die Ameisenpflanzen. 1889. I. 235.[1]
— Apocynaceae. 1895. II. 721.[2]
— Apocynaceae africanae. 1897. II. 722.[1]
— Asclepiadaceae. 1895. II. 735.[1]
— Asclepiadaceae africanae. 1893. II. 735.[2]
— Aufbau blühender Pandanus-Zweige. 1896. II. 57.[1]
— Basiloxylon. 1886. II. 532.[1]
— Beiträge zur Kenntniss der Etymologie . . . der Gewürznelke. 1884. II. 627.[2]
— Beiträge zur vergleichenden Blüthenmorphologie. 1887. I. 115.[2]
— Bignoniaceae. 1895. II. 784.[1]
— Blühende Kakteen. 1900. II. 586.[2]
— Blüthenmorphologische Studien. 1889. I. 115.[2]
— Bombacaceae. 1895. II. 528.[2]
— Bombacaceae. 1886. II. 528.[1]
— Cactaceae. 1886. II. 586.[2]
— Die Cactaceae der Republik Paraguay. 1899. II. 587.[2]
— Die Centrifugation der Kautschuksäfte. 1897. III. 232.[1]
— Chlaenaceae. 1895. II. 511.[1]
— Cornaceae. 1894. II. 556.[1]
— Dickenwachsthum und Cambium. 1873. I. 190.[1]
— Echidnopsis Virchowii. 1893. II. 737.[2]
— Einige Bemerkungen über . . . Ariocarpus. 1900. II. 589.[2]
— Ueber einige interessante Kakteen des K. bot. Gartens. 1895. II. 586.[2]
— Einige neue Ameisenpflanzen. 1888. I. 235.[1]
— Ueber einige verkannte . . . Rubiaceen Südamerikas. 1888. II. 807.[2]
— Einige weitere Ameisenpflanzen. 1890. I. 235.[1]
— Elaeocarpaceae. 1895. II. 509.[2]

— Die epiphytischen Kakteen. 1899. II. 589.[1]
— Euphorbia canariensis L. 1898. II. 442.[1]
— Euphorbia cereiformis L. 1898. II. 442.[2]
— Die Flora des deutschen ost-asiatischen Schutzgebietes. 1887. I. 499.[1]
— Die Gattung Ariocarpus. 1898. II. 589.[1]
— Gesamtbeschreibung der Kakteen. 1899. II. 586.[2]
— Die Gliederung der Gattungen Phyllocactus. 1898. II. 597.[1]
— Der Ibo-Kaffee. 1895. III. 732.[3]
— Kickxia africana Benth. 1895. II. 727.[1]
— Ueber Kolanüsse und ihre Stammpflanzen. 1900. II. 533.[1]
— Die Kolanuss. 1900. II. 533.[1]
— Kritische Untersuchungen über die Zimtländer. 1883. III. 404.[1]
— Die Kultur der Kautschukpflanzen. 1898. III. 149.
— Lehrbuch der systematischen Botanik. 1894. I. 256.
— Malvaceae. 1895. II. 519.[1]
— Malvaceae, I. 1891. II. 519.[1]
— Musaceae. 1900. II. 91.[1]
— Die Mutterpflanze der echten Kola. 1900. II. 533.[1]
— Eine neue Familie der Malvales. 1900. II. 539.[1]
— Neue Untersuchungen über den Blüthenanschluss. 1890. I. 115.[2]
— Les noix de Kola et les arbres à Kola. 1900. II. 533.[1]
— Oreobambos, eine neue Gattung. 1895. II. 60.[1]
— Pilocereus Houlletii Lem. 1893. II. 598.[1]
— Plantae Bammlerianae. 1895. I. 499.[1]
— Plantae Dahlianae aus Neupommern. 1895. I. 499.[2]
— Rubiaceae. 1891. II. 807.[1] — 1892. II. 808.[1]
— Rubiaceae africanae. 1897. II. 808.[1]
— Rubiaceae ins. St. Thomae et Principis. 1892. II. 808.[1]
— Rubiaceae Tribus VII. Paederieae. 1888. II. 807.[2]
— Ueber das Sammeln von Kakteen. 1897. I. 521,[1] II. 588.[2]
— Über die Stammpflanzen des Kolanuss. 1900. II. 533.[1]
— Sterculiaceae. 1886. II. 531.[2] — 1895. II. 531.[1]
— Sterculiaceae africanae. 1893. II. 531.[2] — 1900. II. 531.[1]
— Sterculiaceae Beccarianae. 1898. II. 531.[2]
— Tiliaceae. 1886. II. 512.[1] — 1895. II. 512.[1]
— Tiliaceae africanae. 1893. II. 512.[1]
— Tiliaceae, Sterculiaceae . . . in Harar et in Somalia . . . lectae. 1897. I. 489.
— Der Togo-Kautschuk. 1900. III. 689.[1]
— Triuridaceae . . . Batidaceae, Goodenoughiaceae, Cornaceae. 1894. II. 114,[2] 846.[2]
— Untersuchungen über das Borragoid. 1889. I. 113.[2]
— Die Verbreitung der Cactaceae. 1899. II. 586.[2]
— Ueber die Verbreitung der Mascarenhasia elastica. 1900. II. 728.[2]
— Vergleichende Blüthenmorphologie der cucullaten Sterculiaceen. 1886. II. 531.[2]
— Verzeichniss der . . . in den Kulturen befindlichen Kakteen. 1897. II. 586.[2]
— Die Verzweigung der Pandanaceen. 1897. II. 56.[1]
— Ein Wort für die Phyllocacteen. 1900. III. 625.[2]
— Zwei neue Arten der Gattung Kickxia. 1900. II. 727.[1]
— See also BUREAU, Édouard & SCHUMANN, Karl.
— & Hollrung, Max. Die Flora von Kaiser Wilhelms Land. 1889. I. 499.[1]
— & Lauterbach, Karl. Die Flora der deutschen Schutzgebiete in der Südsee. 1900. I. 499.[1]
— Baker, J. G., Rolfe, R. A. & Cogniaux, Alfred. Plantae africanae novae. 1893. I. 492.[2]
— & others. Die Flora von Neu-Pommern. 1897. I. 499.[2]

Schumann, Paul. Beiträge zur Kenntniss der Grenzen der Variation. 1891. I. 100,[1] 844.[2]

Schunck, C. A. Sur un pigment jaune des feuilles. 1900. I. 186.
— See also MARCHLEWSKI, L. & SCHUNCK, C. A.

Schunck, Edward. The chemistry of chlorophyll. 1889. I. 142.
— & Marchlewski, L. Sur la chlorophylle. 1894. I. 142.
— Phlorose. 1893. I. 177.

Schupp, Abies Pichta. 1886. III. 297.[1]

Schupp, Roderich. Das Einrichtungsverfahren in den Forsten der Stadt Lemberg. 1895. IV. 250.[1]
— Die vorzüglichsten Taxations-Methoden. 1865. IV. 243.

Schuppan, Paul. Beiträge zur Kenntniss des Holzkörpers der Coniferen. 1889. II. 17.[1]

Schuppli, M. Die Linnaea borealis am Engstligenfall. 1878. II. 855.[2]

Schur, Philipp Johann Ferdinand. Beiträge zur Flora von Wien. 1861. II. 350,[1] 837.[1]
— Beiträge zur Flora von Wien. 1863. II. 104.[2]
— Beiträge zur Kenntniss der siebenbürgischen Eichen. 1857. II. 129.[2]
— Beiträge zur Kenntniss des Florengebietes Siebenbürgen. 1856. I. 445.
— Botanische Rundreise durch Siebenbürgen. 1859. I. 445.
— Enumeratio plantarum Transsilvaniae. 1866. I. 445.
— Phytographische Mittheilungen . . . aus verschiedenen Florengebieten des oesterreichischen Kaiserstaates. 1877. I. 442.
— Phytographische Mittheilungen . . . aus verschiedenen Florengebieten der oesterreichisch-ungarischen Monarchie. 1895. I. 444.
— Sertum florae Transsilvaniae. 1853. I. 445.
— Der südliche Hochgebirgs-Zug Siebenbürgens. 1858. I. 445.
Schurz, Carl. The need of rational forest policy. 1889. IV. 272.
Schuschny, Henrik. Az Eucalyptus globulus hatása a légkörre. 1879. IV. 533.[2]
Schuster, Adolph. Durchforstung. 1863. IV. 173.
— Ueberblick des gegenwärtigen Culturverfahrens bei der Fichte. 1863. IV. 453.
Schuster, Gottwald. De Rosa monstrosa. 1742. II. 289.[1]
Schuster, H. Aristolochia elegans. 1886. III. 386.[1]
Schuster, Heinrich Adolph. Anweisung zum wohlfeilsten und gründlichen Baum- und Stockroden. 1859. IV. 386.
— Die Ausrede, oder besser die Baum- und Stockrode-Maschine. 1857. IV. 385.[2]
— Einige Worte über Waldrodung. 1856. IV. 385.[2]
— Die Hauptlehren der rationellen Forstwissenschaft. 1869. IV. 241.
Schuster, Johann Christian. Terminologia botanica. 1808. I. 70.
Schuster, L. G. F. Beyträge zur Geschichte der Wurmtrockniss. 1787. IV. 203.
Schuster, M. J. Die Baumkultur im Haushalte der Natur. 1886. IV. 44.
Schut, J. Berigt eener zeldzaame spelinge der natuur. 1758. I. 142.
Ueber den Schutz gegen Spätfröste. 1851. IV. 191.[1]
Schutzenberger, Paul. Recherches sur la strychnine. 1858. III. 682.[2]
— Recherches sur les alcaloïdes de la noix vomique. 1858. III. 685.[1]
Schutzwer, Nachum. Das Caffein. 1882. III. 742.[1]
Schuuringa, H. P. J. & Kassel, E. Over Koffie in Palembang. 1894. III. 730.
Schuurman, H. E. Over den Koffiepluk in vrijheid. 1899. III. 727.
Schuurmans Stekhoven, H. Kruidkundig handboek. 1815. I. 390, V. xx.[1]
Schuyl, Florentinus. Catalogus plantarum Horti academici Lugduni batavi. 1668. I. 50.
Schw. Anbauversuche mit Ulmus laciniata (Mayr). 1895. IV. 519.[1]
Schwab, C. G. Die Conflicte zwischen der Flösserei auf öffentlichen Flüssen und den Mühlenberechtigten. 1844. IV. 316.
Schwab, G. Ueber Düngung ständiger Forstgärten. 1896. IV. 144.[2]
Schwab, Wilhelm. Die Obstbaumzucht in Töpfen. 1879. III. 138.
— Zur Verbreitung der Obstcultur. 1874. III. 138.
Schwabach, E. Bemerkungen zu den Angaben von A. Tschirch über die Harzabscheidungen in Coniferennadeln. 1900. II. 18.
— Zur Kenntniss der Harzabscheidungen in Coniferennadeln. 1899. II. 18.
— Ueber die Vorgänge bei der Sprengung des mechanischen Ringes bei einigen Lianen. 1898. I. 190.[2]
Schwabe, (Kunstgärtner). Bemerkung über Anwendung von grüner Düngung. 1837. III. 151.
— Bemerkungen über die hiesige Baumzucht. 1830. III. 185.[1]
— Ein Nachtrag zu den Bemerkungen über die Baumzucht. 1837. III. 185.[1]
— Om Nedkrogningen af . . . Noisetteroser. 1838. III. 451.[1]
— Niederhaken der . . . Noisette-Rosen. 1838. III. 451.[1]
Schwabe, A. Etwas über Aufsatzungen. 1889. IV. 172.[1]
Schwabe, G. A. Ueber einige, bei der Ausführung einer Forsteinrichtung wesentlich zu berücksichtigenden Momente. 1836. IV. 242.

— Noch einiges über die natürliche Verjüngung der Buchen-Hochwaldungen. 1846. IV. 494.
— Rosen auf Orangen-Bäumchen zu richten. 1838. III. 164.[2]
— Ueber Wesen und Zweck der Durchforstungen. 1833. IV. 173.
Schwabe, Johann Stephan. Vorschläge zur Holz-Vermehrung. 1769. IV. 105.
Schwabe, L. Vorrichtungen zum Fangen schädlicher Insekten. 1890. IV. 199.[2]
Schwabe, Paul. Über die chemischen Bestandteile von Cortex Frangulae. 1888. III. 542.[2]
— Sur les principes actifs des écorces de Bourdaine. 1888. III. 542.[2]
Schwabe, Samuel Heinrich. Flora anhaltina. 1838. I. 379.
— Flora von Anhalt. 1838. I. 379.
Schwabe, Willmar. Pharmacopœa homœopathica polyglottica. 1872. III. 245.
Schwachheim, Johann Moritz Ludewig. Abhandlung von der Baumzucht. 1772. III. 101.[2]
Schwacke, Wilhelm. Bereitung des Curare-Pfeilgiftes. 1884. III. 684.[1]
— Celastrineae, Myristicaceae. 1886. II. 220,[2] 470.[1]
— Eine neue Olacinee. 1889. II. 172.[1]
— Plantas novas mineiras. 1898. I. 344.
— Skizze der Flora von Manáos. 1884. I. 343.
Schwackhöfer, Franz. Die Forstbenutzung. 1887. IV. 382.[1]
— Tecnología química forestal. 1887. IV. 382.[1]
— Volum-Hygrometer. 1878. IV. 59.[2]
— See also OSER, Johann & SCHWACKHÖFER, Franz.
— & Oser, Johann. Versuche über die Imprägnirung des Rothbuchenholzes. 1886. IV. 499.
Schwaegrichen, Christian Friedrich. Anleitung zum Studium der Botanik. See HEYNE, F. A. 1804. I. 375.
— Topographiae botanicae . . . lipsiensis specimen. 1799. I. 375.
Schwaiger, Ludwig. Bestimmung der bairischen Weiden-arten. 1877. II. 101,[2] V. xxvi.[1]
— Bestimmung der Weiden-Arten nach den Blättern. 1877. V. xxvi.[1]
— Tabelle zur Bestimmung der Weidenarten. 1886. II. 100.[1]
Schwalbe, Christian George. De China officinarum. 1715. III. 338.[1]
Schwandner, L. Gesetz über die Ausübung und Ablösung der Weiderechte. 1873. IV. 334.[1]
Schwaner, C. A. L. M. Borneo. 1853. I. 469.[1]
Schwappach, Adam. Absterben der Fichte im norddeutschen Küstengebiete. 1889. IV. 456.
— Ueber den Anbau der Carya- und Juglans-Arten. 1888. IV. 488.[1]
— Der Anbau fremdländischer Holzarten. 1900. IV. 126.[1]
— Die Aufforstung der Dünen. 1899. IV. 146.[1]
— Ueber die Aufstellung von Ertragstafeln 1888. IV. 257.
— Die Bedeutung des Waldes für das Volkswohl. 1889. IV. 45.
— Beiträge zur Kenntniss der Qualität das Kiefernholzes. 1892. II. 48.[1]
— Beiträge zur Kenntniss der Qualität des Rothbuchenholzes. 1894. IV. 499.
— Beiträge zur Kenntniss der Wachsthumsleistung von Weymouthskiefernbeständen. 1890. IV.[1]470.[3]
— Beiträge zur Kenntniss der Wachsthumsleistungen von Weymouthskiefernbeständen. 1896. IV. 470.[3]
— Ein Beitrag zur Kenntniss der Kiefern-Schütte. 1877. IV. 477.
— Denkschrift betreffend die Ergebnisse der . . . Anbauversuche mit fremdländischen Holzarten. 1891. IV. 126.[1]
— Die Druck-Registrir-Kluppe von Eck. 1888. IV. 231.[3]
— Ueber den Einfluss des Blauwerdens . . . auf die Güte des Kiefernholzes. 1900. IV. 482.[2]
— Ueber den Einfluss des Lichtstandes auf die Qualität des Kiefernholzes. 1892. II. 48.[1]
— Ueber den Einfluss des Streurechens. 1887. IV. 71.
— Ueber den Einfluss des Streurechens auf . . . Buchenbestände. 1900. IV. 496.
— Ueber den Einfluss des Unterbaues auf den Zuwachs der Oberstandes. 1887. IV. 496.
— Ueber den Einfluss verschiedener Durchforstungs- und Lichtungsgrade auf . . . Buchenbestände. 1899. IV. 176.[1]
— Ueber den Einfluss verschiedener Durchforstungs- und Lichtungsgrade auf . . . Kiefernbestände. 1897. IV. 176.[1]
— Ueber den Einfluss verschiedener Durchforstungsgrade auf das Holzwachsthum. 1888. IV. 174.

Schwappach, Adam (*continued*).
— Die Entwickelung der Forstwirtschaft in Preussen. 1897. IV. 26.
— Ergebniss der Holzsamen-Ernte. *See* ERGEBNISS ... 1875. IV. 438.[1]
— Ergebnisse der Anbauversuche mit japanischen und ... amerikanischen Holzarten. 1896. IV. 126.[1]
— Erörterung über die Beteiligung des Internationalen Verbandes forstlicher Versuchsanstalten an den Untersuchungen der technischen Eigenschaften des Holzes. 1900. IV. 416.[1]
— Formzahlen und Massentafeln für die Kiefer. 1890. IV. 481.
— Die forst- und jagdgeschichtliche Bedeutung der deutschen Volksrechte. 1883. IV. 26, 317.[1]
— Forstgeschichte. 1888. IV. 26.
— Die forstgeschichtliche Bedeutung der lex salica. 1882. IV. 317.[1]
— Eine forstliche Studienreise nach Schottland. 1896. IV. 359.[1]
— Forstpolitik, Jagd- und Fischereipolitik. 1894. IV. 270.
— Forstverwaltung. 1887. IV. 287.
— Forstwissenschaft. 1899. IV. 98.[2]
— Zur Frage der Erziehung von Eichenheistern. 1887. IV. 507.[1]
— Le Frêne blanc d'Amérique. 1896. IV. 535.[1]
— Ueber den gegenwärtigen Zustand der forstlichen Verhältnisse Nordamerikas. 1880. IV. 337.[1]
— Die Geschichte des Eberswalder Stadtforstes. 1888. IV. 26.
— Griechische Forstgesetzgebung. 1888. IV. 332.[1]
— Grundriss der Forst- und Jagdgeschichte Deutschlands. 1883. IV. 26.
— Handbuch der Forst- und Jagdgeschichte Deutschlands. 1886. IV. 26.
— Handbuch der Forstverwaltungskunde. 1884. IV. 287.
— Das Holz unserer Waldbäume. 1872. I. 125, IV. 452.[2]
— Das Holz von Taxodium distichum. 1899. IV. 484.[2]
— The importance of density. 1898. IV. 154,[2] 175.[1]
— Ueber die Intensität einiger forstlicher Betriebssysteme. 1881. IV. 128.
— Die Juni-Eiche. 1895. IV. 508.
— Kiefer. 1898. IV. 482.[1]
— Leitfaden der Holzmesskunde. 1889. IV. 214.
— Ueber Lichtstandszuwachs in Kiefernschirmschlägen. 1890. IV. 234. — 1893. IV. 482.[1]
— Ueber Lichtungszuwachs in Kiefernschirmschlägen. 1887. IV. 473.
— Loi forestière de la Grèce. 1888. IV. 332.[1]
— Le Mélèze du Japon. 1896. IV. 452.[2]
— Zur Methode der Massenermittelung. 1891. IV. 219.
— Ueber Mineraldüngung in Forstgärten. 1891. IV. 151.[1]
— Neuere Untersuchungen über Wachsthum ... normaler Kiefernbestände. 1896. IV. 482.[1]
— Die neuesten Lehren der Nationalökonomie. 1878. IV. 269.
— Phellodendron amurense. 1893. III. 504.[2]
— Zur Praxis der Wertsberechnung von Kiefernböden. 1899. IV. 482.[2]
— Zu Pressler's Theorie der Waldwirthschaft. 1874. IV. 256.
— Die Produktionsmittel der Forstwirtschaft. 1889. IV. 270.
— Le Prunus serotina. 1896. IV. 520.[2]
— De quelle manière faudrait-il completer l'organisation. 1890. IV. 37.[1]
— Report on a visit to the forests of Scotland. 1896. IV. 359.[1]
— Die Revision des italienischen Forstschutzgesetzes. 1898. IV. 329.
— Die Samenproduktion ... in Preussen. 1895. IV. 148.
— Die süsse Eberesche. 1891. III. 459.[2]
— Zur Theorie der Kiefernschütte. 1879. IV. 477.
— Untersuchungen über die Festigkeit von Grubenhölzern. 1899. IV. 425.[2]
— Untersuchungen über die technischen Eigenschaften der Hölzer. 1893. IV. 416.[1]
— Untersuchungen über Raumgewicht und Druckfestigkeit des Holzes. 1897. IV. 409.
— Die Verbauung der Wildbäche. 1898. IV. 186.[1]
— Versuche über die Verwendbarkeit des Rothbuchenholzes zu Eisenbahnschwellen. 1898. IV. 424,[2] 499.
— Ueber die Verwendung von Pinus rigida zu Oedlandkulturen. 1891. IV. 468.[2]
— Das Wachsthum der wichtigsten Waldbäume in Ostpreussen. 1889. IV. 118.

— Wachsthum ... normaler Kiefernbestände. 1889. IV. 481.
— Wachsthum und Ertrag der Kiefer ... Hessen. 1886. IV. 481.
— Wachsthumsleistung der Lärchenbestände. 1893. IV. 483.[2]
— Wachsthumsleistung von Pseudotsuga Douglasii. 1896. IV. 98.[2]
— Wachsthumsleistungen von Pseudotsuga ... und Picea sitchensis. 1892. IV. 460,[2] 483.[2]
— Wachstum ... normaler Fichtenbestände. 1890. IV. 458.
— Wachstum ... normaler Rothbuchenbestände. 1893. IV. 498.
— In welcher Weise wäre die bisherige Organisation des forstwirthschaftlichen Versuchswesens zu ergänzen. 1890. IV. 37.[1]
— Die Weymouthskiefer in Nordamerika. 1900. IV. 469.
— Ueber Zuwachsprozente. 1888. IV. 234.
— *See also* GRUNDNER, Fritz, SCHUBERG, Karl & SCHWAPPACH, Adam; ШВАППАХЪ, АДАМЪ.
— & others. Neudammer Försterlehrbuch. 1899. IV. 98.[2]
— Repetitorium zum Neudammer Försterlehrbuch. 1900. IV. 98.[2]
Schwappach, Adolph. Der Borkenkäfer im bayrischen Walde. 1875. IV. 204.
Schwartz, E. Leitfaden zur Handhabung des Unfallversicherungsgesetzes. 1889. IV. 311.[1]
Schwartze, August Jakob. Observationes de virtute corticis Geoffraeae. 1792. III. 467.[1]
Schwarz. Ein Beitrag zur Buchenwirthschaft. 1870. IV. 495.
— Ueber Mischung von Buche und Fichte. 1869. IV. 495.
— Schutz der jungen Heegen gegen Wildverbiss. 1883. IV. 196.[2]
Schwarz. Welche Betriebsformen empfehlen sich für die Taunuswaldungen. 1890. IV. 119.[1]
Schwarz, (*Eisenbahnbaumeister*). Bericht über Konservirung von Eisenbahnschwellen. 1853. IV. 423.[2]
Schwarz, (*Revier-Verwalter*). Abschätzung des 10jährigen Kiefernbestandes. 1855. IV. 480.
Schwarz, A. de. Du partage des affectations ... dans les aménagements de futaie. 1864. IV. 243.
Schwarz, August. Die Forstberechtigungen in den ... Departementen des linken Rheinufers. 1864. IV. 333.
Schwarz, August Friedrich. Phanerogamen- und Gefässkryptogamen-Flora der Umgegend von Nürnberg-Erlangen. 1892. I. 389.
Schwarz, C. & **Wehsarg**, K. Die Form der Stigmata. 1884. I. 118.[1]
Schwarz, F. Ueber Mischung von Buche und Fichte. 1869. IV. 453.
Schwarz, F. J. Die Forstwissenschaft. 1852. IV. 99.[2]
Schwarz, Frank. Ueber den Einfluss des Wasser- und Nährstoffgehaltes des Sandbodens auf ... Pinus silvestris. 1892. II. 48.[1]
— Die Erkrankung der Kiefern durch Cenangium. 1895. IV. 479.
— Forstliche Botanik. 1892. IV. 84.[1]
— Physiologische Untersuchungen über Dickenwachsthum ... von Pinus silvestris. 1899. II. 48,[2] IV. 482.[2]
— Ueber eine Pilzepidemie an Pinus silvestris. 1892. IV. 478.
— Die Wurzelhaare der Pflanzen. 1883. I. 188.
Schwarz, George Frederick. To protect the beauty of the woods. 1896. IV. 137.[1]
— The way to estimate cordwood. 1900. IV. 229.
Schwarz, H. Sur l'acide contenue dans les raisins verts. 1852. III. 583.[1]
— Analysen von Rasen-Aschen. 1852. IV. 68.
— Ueber die Säure in unreifen Weintrauben. 1852. III. 583.[1]
Schwarz, Robert. Sur la composition de l'écorce de Quinquina royal. 1851. III. 725.[2]
— Untersuchung der Blätter des Rhododendron ferrugineum. 1852. II. 679.[1]
— Untersuchung der China regia. 1851. III. 725.[2]
— Untersuchung der Königs-Chinarinde. 1851. III. 725.[2]
Die schwarze Birke in Amerika. 1885. IV. 491.[2]
Schwartzenbach, (*Dr.*) & **Henkel**, (*Dr.*). Commentar zur Pharmakopoe für das Königreich Bayern. 1858. III. 249.
Schwarzer, Guido von. Biographien zur Gallerie berühmter und verdienter Forstmänner. 1870. IV. 1.
— & **Langenbacher**, Ferdinand. Dr. Remelé und das Lehrbuch der forstlichen Chemie. 1896. IV. 60.[2]
— Lehrbuch der forstlichen Chemie. 1868. IV. 60.[2]

Schwarzkopf, S. A. Der Kaffee in naturhistorischer . . . Hinsicht. 1881. III. 739.
— Lehrbuch der Droguenwaarenkunde. 1855. III. 258.
Schwarzrock. Alleen und Alleebäume. 1880. III. 209.
Der Schwarzwald in forstwirthschaftlicher Beziehung. 1833. IV. 348.[2]
Schwediaur, F. X. Pharmacologia. 1803. III. 257.[2]
Schwedische Akademie der Wissenschaften. See KONGL. (SVENSKA) VETENSKAPS AKADEMIEN. 1822. I. 1.
Schwedische Pharmakopöe 1845. See PHARMACOPOEA suecica. 1775. III. 247.[1]
Schwedler, (Hofgärtner, Fulda). Erfahrungen eines Gärtners. 1834. III. 451.[2]
— Etwas über das Veredeln der Passifloren. 1844. III. 615.[1]
Schweickhardt. Ueber den Weisstannenkrebs im Schwarzwald. 1885. IV. 445.
Schweigger, August Friedrich. Enumeratio plantarum Horti botanici regiomontani. 1812. I. 45.
— Nachrichten über den Botanischen Garten zu Königsberg. 1819. I. 45.
— De plantarum classificatione naturali. 1820. I. 251.
— Specimen florae erlangensis. 1804. I. 375.
— & Körte, Franz. Flora erlangensis. 1811. I. 376.
Schweinfurth, Georg August. Abyssinische Pflanzennamen. 1893. I. 76.[1]
— Aegyptens auswärtige Beziehungen hinsichtlich der Culturgewächse. 1891. I. 82.[1]
— Ueber den afrikanischen Ursprung aegyptischer Kulturpflanzen. 1873. I. 488.
— Allgemeine Betrachtungen über die Flora von Socotra. 1884. I. 489.
— Aufzählung . . . der Acacienarten des Nilgebietes. 1863. II. 323.[1]
— Ausflüge um Kosser. 1865. I. 488.
— Über Balsam und Myrrhe. 1893. III. 511.[1]
— Barbeya Schwf. gen. nov. Urticacearum. 1891. II. 141.[1]
— Beitrag zur Flora Aethiopieas. 1867. I. 488.
— Bericht über die botanischen Ergebnisse der ersten Niam-Niam-Reise. 1871. I. 488.
— Ein Besuch auf Socotra. 1884. I. 489.
— Sur certains rapports entre l'Arabie heureuse. 1890. I. 489.
— Ueber Crossopterix aus Abyssinien. 1867. III. 743.[2]
— Sur les dernières trouvailles botaniques dans les tombeaux de l'ancienne Égypte. 1887. I. 82.[1]
— Ueber den Einfluss der Nordwinde auf die Vegetations-Verhältnisse des Rothen Meeres. 1867. I. 480.
— Flora des Soturba an der nubischen Küste. 1865. I. 488.
— Sur la flore des anciens jardins arabes. 1888. III. 131.[1]
— De la flore pharaonique. 1883. I. 81.[2]
— Über die Florengemeinschaft von Südarabien. 1891. I. 489.
— The heart of Africa. 1874. V. XXIV.[1]
— Herbariumexemplar eines präparirten Zweiges von Ficus Sycomorus. 1888. III. 153.[2]
— Neue Beiträge zur Flora des alten Aegyptens. 1883. I. 81.[2]
— Notice sur les restes de végétaux de l'ancienne Égypte. 1884. I. 81.[1]
— Novae species aethiopicae. 1868. I. 488.
— Pflanzengeographische Skizze des Nil-Gebietes. 1868. I. 488.
— Ueber Pflanzenreste aus altaegyptischen Gräbern. 1884. I. 81.[1]
— Phanerogamen. 1892. I. 492.[3]
— Le piante utili dell' Eritrea. 1891. III. 93.[1]
— Plantae quaedam niloticae. 1862. I. 488.
— Récolte et conservation des plantes. 1889. I. 36.[1]
— Reise an der Küste des Rothen Meeres. 1865. I. 488.
— Reise in das Depressionsgebiet im Umkreise des Fajum. 1886. I. 489.
— Reliquiae Kotschyanae. 1868. I. 488.
— Restes de végétaux de l'ancienne Égypte. 1885. I. 81.[2]
— Sammlung arabisch-aethiopischer Pflanzen. 1894. I. 481.[1]
— Eine sechsästige Dattelpalme. 1874. III. 73.[1]
— Vegetationsskizzen aus dem südnubischen Küstengebirge. 1868. I. 488.
— Vegetations-Skizzen vom Bachr-el-Gâsâl. 1870. I. 488.
— Végétaux cultivés en Egypte. 1873. I. 488.
— Versuch einer Vegetationsskizze der Umgegend von Straussberg. 1861. I. 385.
— Une visite au port de Tobrouk. 1884. I. 489.
— Vorläufige Aufzählung der während der Expedition gesammelten Pflanzen. 1892. I. 492.[2]

— Wahrnehmungen auf einer Fahrt von Chartûm. 1870. I. 488.
— See also ASCHERSON, Paul & SCHWEINFURTH, Georg.
— & Ascherson, Paul. Primitiae florae marmaricae. 1893. I. 486.
— & Volkens, Georg. Liste des plantes recoltées par les princes Démètre et Nicolas Ghika-Comanesti. 1897. I. 489.
Schweinitz, H. L. von. Über die Dattelpalme. 1878. III. 329.[2]
Schweinitz, Ludwig David von. Narrative of an expedition to the source of St. Peter's River. 1825. I. 310.
Schweitzer, Adolph. Ueber Conservirung des Holzes. 1852. IV. 417.
— Ueber Conservirung von Holz gegen Fäulniss. 1852. IV. 417.
Schweitzer, Lorenz Wilhelm. Zur Geschichte des Forstwesens in . . . S. Weimar-Eisenach. 1836. IV. 25.
Schweizer, Eduard. Over de aetherische olie der Thuja. 1843. III. 311.[1]
— Sur l'huile de Thuja. 1843. III. 311.[1]
— Ueber das Thujaöl. 1843. III. 311.[1]
Schweizer, J. J. Das Faulhorn im Grindelwald. 1832. See GUTHNICK, K. 1832. I. 434.
Schweizer Alpenclub. Jahrbuch. I. 26.[2]
Schweizer Alpen-Zeitung. I. 26.[2]
Zur schweiz. Forststatistik. 1853. IV. 365.
Der Schweizer Kräutersammler. 1879. I. 436.
Schweizer Monatschronik. See MONATLICHE Nachrichten schweizer. Neuheiten. IV. 13.
Schweizerische Alpenwirthschaft. IV. 13.[3]
Schweizerische botanische Gesellschaft. Berichte. I. 26.[1]
Schweizerische Centralanstalt für das forstliche Versuchswesen. Mittheilungen. IV. 13.[2]
Der schweizerische Gartenbau. See Der PRAKTISCHE Gartenfreund. III. 24.[1]
Schweizerische Gesellschaft für die gesammten Naturwissenschaften. See ALLGEMEINE SCHWEIZERISCHE . . . I. 26.[1]
Schweizerische naturforschende Gesellschaft. See ALLGEMEINE SCHWEIZERISCHE GESELLSCHAFT . . . I. 26.[1]
Der schweizerische Obstbauer. III. 24.[1]
Schweizerische Obstsorten. 1863. III. 89.[1]
Schweizerische Wochenschrift für Chemie. See SCHWEIZERISCHE Zeitschrift für Pharmacie. I. 26.[2]
Schweizerische Wochenschrift für Pharmacie. See SCHWEIZERISCHE Zeitschrift . . . I. 26.[2]
Schweizerische Zeitschrift für das Forstwesen. See SCHWEIZERISCHES Forst-Journal. IV. 13.[2]
Schweizerische Zeitschrift für Gartenbau. See SCHWEIZERISCHE Zeitschrift für Land- und Gartenbau. III. 24.[1]
Schweizerische Zeitschrift für Land- und Gartenbau. III. 24.[1]
Schweizerische Zeitschrift für Obst- und Weinbau. See MITTHEILUNGEN für Obst- und Weinbau. III. 24.[1]
Schweizerische Zeitschrift für Pharmacie. I. 26.[2]
Schweizerischer Forstverein. Versammlung. See VERSAMMLUNG SCHWEIZERISCHER FORSTWIRTHE. IV. 13.[2]
Schweizerisches Forst-Journal. IV. 13.[2]
Schwencke, Martin Wilhelm. Kruidkundige Beschrijving der . . . gewassen, welke . . . in gebruik zijn. 1766. III. 54.
— Novae plantae Schwenckia . . . brevis descriptio. 1766. II. 774.[1]
— Officinalium plantarum catalogus, quae in Horto medico, qui Hagae Comitum est. 1752. I. 51.[1]
Schwenckfelt, Caspar. Stirpium & fossilium Silesiae catalogus. 1600. I. 531.
Schwendener, Simon. L'accroissement terminal de la racine. 1881. I. 104.
— Ueber Bau und Mechanik der Spaltöffnungen. 1882. I. 131.[1]
— Einige Beobachtungen an Milchsaftgefässen. 1885. I. 136.[1]
— Die Gelenkpolster von Mimosa pudica. 1897. II. 372.[2]
— Zur Kenntniss der Blattstellungen. 1894. I. 103.
— Zur Kenntniss der Schraubenwindungen. 1882. I. 196.[2]
— Zur Kritik der neuesten Untersuchungen über das Saftsteigen. 1892. I. 166.
— Das mechanische Princip im anatomischen Bau der Monocotylen. 1874. I. 134,[1] 149.[1]
— Mechanische Theorie der Blattstellungen. 1878. I. 102.
— Nochmals über die optisch anomale Reaction des Traganth- und Kirschgummis. 1890. I. 181.[1]
— Über den Öffnungsmechanismus der Antheren. 1899. I. 116.[2]

Schwendener, Simon (*continued*).
— Die periodischen Erscheinungen der Natur. 1856. I. 227.[1]
— Ueber das Scheitelwachsthum der Phanerogamen-Wurzeln. 1881. I. 104.
— Über Scheitelwachsthum und Blattstellungen. 1885. I. 102.
— Die Schumann'schen Einwände gegen meine Theorie der Blattstellungen. 1899. I. 103.
— Die Schutzscheiden. 1882. I. 134.[3]
— Ueber die Stellungsänderungen seitlicher Organe . . . bei den Coniferen. 1877. II. 17.[2]
— Die Theorie der Blattstellungen. 1879. I. 102.
— Zur Theorie der Blattstellungen. 1883. I. 102.
— Untersuchungen über das Saftsteigen. 1886. I. 165.
— Ueber die " Verschiebungen " der Bastfasern. 1894. I. 131.[1]
— Ueber das Winden der Pflanzen. 1882. I. 196.[2]
— Zur Wortmann'schen Theorie des Windens. 1886. I. 196.[2]
— *See also* NAEGELI, Karl & SCHWENDENER, Simon.
— & **Krabbe**, Gustav. Über die Beziehungen zwischen . . . Turgordehnung und . . . Längenzunahme. 1893. I. 150.[1]
— — Untersuchungen über die Orientirungstorsionen. 1892. I. 194.
Schwerdt, H. Der beste Schutz für junge Baumpflanzungen. 1881. III. 198.[3]
Schwerdtfeger, (*Oberförster*). Resultat der Abschätzung eines Probemorgens . . . Rybnik. 1846. IV. 260.[1]
Schwerin, Fritz, *Graf* von. Ueber Einführung . . . ausländischer Ahorn-Arten. 1900. III. 534.[1]
— Ueber einige zum Teil neue Ahorn-Arten. 1894. II. 476.[2]
— Erster [bis fünfter] Beitrag zur Gattung Acer. 1893. II. 476.[3]
— Der persische Ahorn. 1898. II. 478.[1]
— Ueber Variation beim Ahorn. 1896. II. 476.[2]
— Die Varietäten der Gattung Acer. 1893. II. 476.[2]
— Zwei pontische Ahorne. 1898. II. 477.[1]
Schwerin, Johann David. Nahmregister derjenigen . . . Bäume, Pflantzen . . . im Horn vor der Stadt Hamburg belegenen Garten. 1710. I. 43.
Schwertschlager, Joseph. Der botanische Garten der Fürstbischöfe von Eichstätt. 1890. III. 28.[1]
— Die Rosenflorula von Eichstätt. 1896. II. 285.[1]
Schwestka, A. P. Theoretisch-praktisches Forsthandbuch. 1820. IV. 99.[2]
Schweyckert, J. M. Catalogus plantarum Horti botanici carolsruhani. 1791. I. 44.
Schwickert, Joseph. Cubictafeln zur Berechnung des Schnittmateriales. 1875. IV. 227.
— Walzentafeln zur Berechnung des cubischen Inhaltes der Rundhölzer. 1875. IV. 227.
Schwikkard, Ludewig Heinrich. Entwurf zur Anlage einer Holzarten-Sammlung. 1800. I. 37,[2] IV. 17.
Schwilgué, Charles Joseph Antoine. Traité de matière médicale. 1805. III. 242.
Schwind, Franz, *Ritter* von. Der Wärmeverbrauch des Pflanzenlebens. 1871. I. 186.
Schwyter, Anton. Bericht über den gegenwärtigen Zustand der Gemeindsgenossen-Waldungen der March. 1869. IV. 366.
— Correspondance de Thurgovie. 1864. IV. 406.[1]
— Von der Kiefer im Thurgau. 1899. IV. 482.[1]
— Korrespondenz aus dem Thurgau. 1864. IV. 406.[1]
Schwytter. Ist das Bau-, Säg- und Nutzholz mit oder ohne Rinde gemessen zum Verkauf zu bringen? 1885. IV. 227.
Schwytz. Sapin géant. 1872. II. 24.[1]
Schwytzer, (*Ingr.*). Beschreibung über . . . am Bürgenberg eingerichtete Draht-Seil-Riese. 1862. IV. 391.
— Description du lançoir construit en cable de fils de fer . . . au Bürgenberg. 1862. IV. 391.
Schwyz. Die Holzabfuhr am Rossberg. 1898. IV. 390.[1]
Schychowsky, Iwan. De fructus plantarum phanerogamarum natura. 1832. I. 119.
Scidmore, Eliza Ruhamah. Our national forest reserves. 1893. IV. 178.[3]
Scie à vapeur transportable. 1877. IV. 393.
Science. I. 7.[1]
Science progress, I. 20.
Scientific American. I. 7.[1]
Scientific memoirs by medical officers . . . of India. I. 29.[1]
La scienza forestale in Francia. 1864. IV. 56.
The Scilly Islands. 1887. II. 80.[1]
Scion, (*pseud.*). The Eucalyptus, the soil and the graft. 1899. III. 634.[1]
— & others. Is grafting wrong? 1889. III. 165.

La sciure de bois en horticulture. 1898. IV. 431.[1]
Sckell, Armin. Beitrag zur Kultur der Orangen. 1870. III. 499.[2]
— Empfehlenswerthe Einrichtungen zum Schutze der Bäume. 1864. III. 198.[2]
Sckell, Julius. Die Baumschule. 1864. III. 154.[1]
Sckell, O. Beitrag zur Kultur der Hydrangea Hortensia. 1883. III. 411.[1]
Scoffern, John. Outlines of botany. 1857. I. 90.
Scofield, D. C. Profit and method of forest raising. 1871. IV. 111.[2]
— Scotch Larch. 1868. IV. 449.
— Transplanting large . . . trees. 1868. III. 167.
Scolari, Filippo. Delle relazioni accademiche . . . intorno al saggio sull' antica storia e giurisprudenza forestale. 1860. IV. 327.
Sconce, A. & **Teil**, John. Notices regarding the valuable tanning properties of the pod of a tree. 1848. III. 468.[1]
Scoperta d' una foresta sotterranea. 1863. IV. 61.[1]
Scopoli, Johann Anton. Abhandlung von Kohlenbrennen. 1773. IV. 393.
— Annus I.–V. historico-naturalis. 1769. I. 262.
— De cultura Mori albae. 1770. III. 373.
— Deliciae florae et faunae insubricae. 1786. I. 263.
— Dubia botanica. 1770. I. 250.
— Examen de quelques espèces de bois de Pins. 1788. II. 20.[1]
— Flora carniolica. 1760. I. 438.
— Florescentia plantarum. 1770. I. 226.[2]
— Fundamenta botanica. 1783. I. 83.
— Introductio ad historiam naturalem. 1777. I. 262.
— De lue epidemica Mori albae. 1770. III. 378.
— Methodus plantarum. 1754. I. 257.
— De propagatione sylvarum. 1770. IV. 122.[2]
— Specimen botanicum de Astragalo. 1788. II. 333.[2]
— Specimen botanicum de Celti australi. 1786. II. 141.[2]
— De vario robore Abietini ligni. 1770. IV. 446.[2]
Per scoprire le frodi nella vendita del Sommacco di Sicilia. 1897. IV. 524.[1]
Scops bengalensis, (*pseud.*). Indian forests. 1869. IV. 377.[2]
Scoresby, William, (*jr.*). Experiments on the effect of pressure of the sea at great depths. 1819. IV. 411.[1]
— Journal of a voyage to the northern whale-fishery. 1823. I. 308.
— Observations on the impregnation of wood with sea-water. 1822. IV. 411.[3]
Le scorie Thomas. 1896. IV. 144.[2]
Scortecciamento a vapore. 1865. IV. 434.
Scortechini, B. Contribution to a South Queensland flora. 1882. I. 503.
— Sul genere Pellacalyx Korth. 1885. II. 614.[1]
— Half century of plants new to South Queensland. 1883. I. 503.
— A new genus of Myrtaceae. 1885. II. 625.[3]
Scot, David. Contributiones ad historiam naturalem biblicam. 1830. I. 513.
— On the Mustard plant. 1832. II. 473.[1]
Scotch Fir, (*pseud.*). Natural versus artificial reproduction. 1882. IV. 142.
The Scotch Golden-edged Holly. 1877. III. 530.[1]
The Scotch Pine. 1884. II. 47.[1]
Scotland—Highland society. *See* HIGHLAND . . . III. 17.
The Scots gardiners director. *See* JUSTICE, *Sir* James. 1754. III. 109.
Scott. Grouping of Palms on lawns. 1878. III. 317.
Scott, A. Mode of cultivating the Mango in England. 1846. III. 524.[2]
Scott, A. E. A visit to Mitchell and Roan Mountains. 1884. I. 319.
Scott, David. Manures for Passion-fruit vines. 1900. III. 615.[1]
Scott, Dunkinfield Henry. The anatomical characters presented by the peduncle of Cycadaceae. 1897. II. 3.[2]
— The distribution of laticiferous tissue. 1889. I. 136.[1]
— Zur Entwickelungsgeschichte der gegliederten Milchröhren. 1881, 1882. I. 136.[1]
— An introduction to structural botany. 1894. I. 92.
— On the occurrence of articulated laticiferous vessels in Hevea. 1886. II. 445.[1]
— & **Brebner**, George. On the anatomy and histogeny of Strychnos. 1889. II. 720.[1]
— — On internal phloëm. 1890. I. 131.[1]
— — On the secondary tissues in certain monocotyledons. 1893. II. 77.[1]

Scott, D. S. Landscape forestry. 1879. IV. 137.[1]
— The Larch disease, heart-rot. 1879. IV. 451.
— Our Indian forest department. 1882. IV. 295.[1]
— Protecting river sides. 1878. IV. 185.[1]
— Storms. 1883. IV. 189.[2]
— Surface drainage. 1881. IV. 144.[1]
— The timber supply of North America. 1878. IV. 403.[1]
— Training of young foresters for India. 1879. IV. 29.
Scott, Frank Jesup. The art of beautifying suburban home grounds. 1870. III. 60.
Scott, J. Ivy on evergreen trees. 1875. III. 642.[2]
Scott, Joannes. Dissertatio inauguralis de plantis medicinalibus in insula Ceylona. 1819. III. 92.[1]
Scott, John. Branching Palms. 1873. II. 63.[1]
— Indian Loranths. 1871. II. 174.[1]
— Loranthaceae, the Mistleto order. 1871. II. 174.[1] V. XXVI.[1]
— Note sur la stérilité . . . de quelques . . . Passiflora. 1864. II. 576.[1]
— Notes on horticulture in Bengal. 1871. II. 174.[1]
— Notes on sterility and hybridization . . . of Passiflora. 1864. II. 576.[1]
— Untersuchungen über einige indische Loranthusarten. 1871. II. 174.[1] — 1874. II. 169.[1]
Scott, John (of Crewkerne). The orchardist. 1868. III. 79.
Scott, John (of Iowa). Report on hedging. 1877. III. 213.
Scott, John (of Weymouth). The Tree-Medick (Medicago arborea). 1874. III. 41.[1]
Scott, K. M. On the treatment of the Peach. 1848. III. 440.[2]
Scott, Robert. Remarks on the growth of Bambusa. 1849. II. 59.[1]
Scott, Wentworth LASCELLES-. See LASCELLES-SCOTT, Wentworth.
Scott, William. The Japanese Ampelopsis. 1897. III. 545.[1]
Scott-Elliot, G. F. See ELLIOT, G. F. SCOTT-.
Scott-Preston. Der Kiefern-Anbau auf Pflugwällen. 1888. IV. 473.
Scotti, A. G. Manuale popolare forestale. 1881. IV. 110.[1]
Scotti, Giberto. Flora medica della provincia di Como. 1872. III. 88.[1]
(Royal) Scottish arboricultural society. Transactions. IV. 12.[1]
The Scottish gardener. III. 18.
Scottish geographical magazine. I. 20.
The Scottish naturalist. I. 20.
Scottish society of arts. See ROYAL SCOTTISH . . . III. 18.
Scott's orchardist. See SCOTT, John. 1868. III. 79.
Scotus, (pseud.). The Mistletoe. 1879. II. 179.[1]
The screw bean . . . in the Punjab. 1880. III. 485.[1]
Scriba, (Revierförster, Fechenheim). Das Baum- und Stockroden. 1859. IV. 386.
Scriba, J. See DOSCH, Ludwig & SCRIBA, J.
Scribe, Francis. Memoire sur la résine Icica. 1844. III. 511.[3]
— Note sur la résine icica. 1844. III. 511.[3]
Scribner, Frank LAMSON-. Fungus diseases of the Grape and other plants. 1890. III. 193.[2]
— Notes on the Orange leaf scab. 1886. III. 501.[1]
— Orange leaf scab. 1886. III. 501.[1]
— The ornamental and useful plants of Maine. 1875. III. 2.
— Report on the experiments . . . in the treatment of the downy mildew. 1888. III. 580.
— Report on the fungus diseases of the Grape vine. 1886. III. 579.
— & Viala, Pierre. Black rot. 1888. III. 580.
— — Le Greeneria fuliginea. 1887. III. 579.
Scribner, J. M. Scribner's enlarged lumber and log book. 1895. IV. 229.
Scribner's magazine. III. 8.
Scribner's monthly. III. 8.
Scribonius Largus. De compositione medicamentorum liber. 40. I. 272.
— Compositiones mediae. 40. I. 272.
— De compositionibus medicamentorum liber. 40. I. 272, V. XIV.[1]
Scrinia florae selectae. I. 22.
Scriptores agriculturae seu rusticae rei. See SCRIPTORES rei rusticae. 1470. III. 96.[1]
Scriptores rei rusticae. 1470. III. 96.[1]
Scrobischewsky. See SKROBISHEVSKI, L.

Scrobischowsky, W. See SKROBISHEVSKI, V. J.
Scrofani, Xavier. Voyage en Grèce. 1801. I. 448.[1]
Scudder, Samuel Hubbard. The Pine moth of Nantucket. 1883. IV. 461.[2]
Scuderi, Salvatore. Trattato dei boschi dell' Etna. 1825. I. 430, IV. 86.[1]
Scultetus, K. W. Gedichte von Hancke und Wachtel auf seinen Orangeriegarten. 1731. III. 496.[2]
La scuola di selvicoltura in Cittaducale. 1899. IV. 36.[1]
La scuola e l' amministrazione forestale in Spagna. 1882. IV. 293.[1]
Scuola forestale . . . della Croazia. 1863. IV. 36.[1]
Scuola forestale di Costantinopoli. 1862. IV. 37.[1]
Scuola forestale liberista. 1882. IV. 56.
Scuola forestale regolamentaria. 1882. IV. 56.
Scuola superiore d'agricoltura in Portici. See REALE SCUOLA . . . III. 23.[2]
Scuole forestali. 1864. IV. 35.[1]
The Sea Buckthorn. 1888. III. 629.[1]
Seabra Silva Telles, Vicente, COELHO DE. See COELHO DE SEABRA SILVA TELLES, Vicente.
Seamos prácticos. 1892. IV. 552.[1]
Sears, F. C. Conifers . . . of the Kansas agricultural college. 1896. III. 293.
— Some Utah shade trees. 1897. III. 61.[1]
Sears, F. S. Vitis Doaniana. 1896. III. 584.[1]
Sears, John Henry. Buds and the ramification of branches. 1883. I. 106.[1]
— Notes on the forest trees of Essex. 1882. I. 312, IV. 76.[2]
Seaside planting. 1898. III. 42.[1] — 1899. III. 42.[1]
Seasoning Oak wood. 1890. IV. 514.[1]
Seaton, H. E. See ROBINSON, B. L. & SEATON, H. E.
Seaton, William John & Hill, H. C. Forestry in British Burma. 1884. IV. 378.
Seba, Albert. Historia exotiquorum corundam medicamentorum simpliclum. 1737. III. 244.
— Locupletissimi rerum naturalium thesauri accurata descriptio. 1734. I. 290.
Sebastiani, Antonio. Esposizione del sistema di Linneo. 1819. I. 62.
— & Mauri, Ernesto. Florae romanae prodromus. 1818. I. 425.
Sebeók de Szent-Miklos, Alexander. Dissertatio medico-botanica de Tataria hungarica. 1779 III. 90.[2]
Sebert, Hippolyte. Notice sur les bois de la Nouvelle Calédonie. 1874. I. 508,[2] IV. 89,[3] 402.[1]
Sébille, A. de. La cétoine dorée (Cetonia aurata). 1897. IV. 549.[2]
— Les forêts du Canada. 1900. IV. 337.[2]
Sebille-Auger, L. Notice sur la culture du Mûrier. 1839. III. 375.
Sébire, A. Les plantes utiles du Sénégal. 1899. III. 93.[2]
— Les plantes utiles du Sénégal, plantes indigènes. 1899. III. 93.[2]
Sebland, Carl. Weitere Notizen über den Frostschaden des strengen Winters von 1879–80. 1882. III. 46.[1]
Secall, José. Apuntes, noticias y datos de una excursión forestal. 1888. IV. 363.[2] — 1889. IV. 363.[2]
— Un caso monstruoso . . . en un Pino piñonero. 1891. IV. 468.[2]
— Catálogo metódico de las plantas leñosas . . . en San Lorenzo del Escorial. 1888. I. 419,[3] IV. 86,[1] 644,[1] V. XXII.[1]
— Las ciencias naturales en la Escuela general preparatoria. 1890. IV. 540.[2]
— Clave analítica para . . . las principales especies leñosas. 1893. I. 419,[2] IV. 86.[1]
— De conversación. 1899. IV. 554.
— Dos dias herborizando. 1886. IV. 544.[1]
— Dimorfismo notable. 1895. IV. 558.[2]
— La Escuela de ingenieros de montes. 1891. IV. 540.[1]
— Del ingreso en las escuelas especiales. 1900. IV. 541.[1]
— La ley de protección á las aves útiles. 1896. IV. 544.[1]
— El " Merulius lacrymans " Fr. 1897. IV. 557.[1]
— El personal subalterno de montes. 1897. IV. 553.[2]
— El Pinus insignis Dougl. 1896. IV. 559.[1]
— Plantas vasculares de San Lorenzo del Escorial. 1889. I. 422.
— Repoblaciones y torrentes. 1891. IV. 185.[2]
Secall é Inda, J. Notas sobre la influencia de los montes. 1883. IV. 47.[2]
Le sécateur-recépeur de Pons. 1894. IV. 547.[1]
Die Sechellen-Nuss (Lodoicea Sechellarum). 1877. II. 70.[2]

Seckendorf, Christian Adolph, *Freiherr* von. Ueber die bessere Behandlung der Kopfweide. 1800. III. 347.
— Forst-Rügen. 1799. IV. 100.[2]
— Ueber die höchste Benutzung der Birke. 1800. IV. 490.[1]
— Vorschläge wider den Holzdiebstahl. 1800. IV. 196.[2]
Seckendorff, Arthur, *Freiherr* von. *See* SECKENDORFF-GU-DENT, Arthur, *Freiherr* von.
Seckendorff, Robert, *Freiherr* von.   Russlands Wälder. 1892. IV. 346.
Seckendorff-Gudent, Arthur, *Freiherr* von.   Beiträge zur Kenntniss der Schwarzföhre. 1881. IV. 466.[1]
— Beiträge zur Waldwerthrechnung. 1867. IV. 255.
— Sulle condizioni forestali della Francia. 1879. IV. 122.[1]
— Conferenza . . . intorno alla influenza delle foreste sulle strade ferrate. 1881. IV. 44.
— Das forstliche System der Wildbach-Verbauung. 1886. IV. 188.[1]
— Das forstliche Unterrichtswesen. 1874. IV. 29.
— Ueber forstliche Verhältnisse Frankreichs. 1879. IV. 122.[1]
— Das forstliche Versuchswesen. 1874. IV. 37.[1] — 1881. IV. 37.[1]
— Die forstlichen Verhältnisse Frankreichs. 1879. IV. 360.
— Zur Geschichte der Wildbach-Verbauung. 1886. IV. 188.[1]
— Inwieweit vermag der Forstmann auf die Sicherheit und Rentabilität des Bahnbetriebes einzuwirken? 1881. IV. 44, 541.[1]
— Kreisflächentafeln für Metermaass. 1870. IV. 230.
— Le reboisement dans les Alpes. Visite du comte de Falkenhayn. 1883. IV. 163.
— Relaciones que existen entre el servicio facultativo forestal y el caminos. 1881. IV. 541.[1]
— Special-Catalog der Ausstellung der K. k. Staats- und Fondsforstverwaltung. 1873.ˑ IV. 21.[1]
— Studienreise . . . des Herrn Ackerbauministers Grafen Julius Falkenhayn. 1883. IV. 163.
— Untersuchungen über den Festgehalt . . . des Holzes. 1877. IV. 411.[1]
— Verbauung der Wildbäche, Aufforstung. 1884. IV. 187.[2]
— Ueber die Verbreitung der Schwarzföhre. 1882. .-II. 43.[2]
— Ueber Wildbach- und Lawinenverbauung. 1881. IV. 184.[2]
— Die Wildbäche, ihr Wesen. 1886.- IV. 188.[1]
— Über die wirthschaftliche Bedeutung der Wildbachverbauung. 1883. IV. 187.[2]
Le second livre . . . contenant le vray discours . . . du voyage fait . . . sous la conduite de l'Admiral Jaques Cornille Nec. 1609. I. 464.[3]
Secondat, Jean Baptiste, *baron de*. Branche d'un Poirier bon Chrétien. 1785. II. 279.[3]
— Description de la fleur du Cierge du Pérou. 1785. III. 590.[3]
— Mémoire sur la culture des Vignes. 1785. III. 554.[3]
— Mémoires sur l'histoire naturelle du Chêne. 1785. III. 128.[1]
— Observations sur quelques arbres forestiers de la Guienne. 1785. IV. 398.[2]
Seconde lettre du Bostangi-Bachi.   *See* ROLAND, (*de Fourtou*). 1805. III. 173.[1]
Secor, Eugene.   Forestry for shelter and profit. 1887. IV. 112.
— Relation of forests to climate. 1887. IV. 54.
Sections of native wood. 1886. I. 38,[1] IV. 18.[1]
Securius, Thomas.   Diss. X. de plantis. 1625. I. 30.
Sedding, J. D. Garden-craft, old and new. 1892. III. 124.[1]
Sedgwick, William Thompson. Ancient and modern theories of disease. 1899. III. 193.[2]
Sedláček, W.   Der Waldfeldbau auf . . . Drhowle. 1889. IV. 134.[1]
Sedlaczek, E.   Wälder im Kaukasus. 1894. IV. 348.[1]
Sedy, Catalogue alphabétique des plantes. 1810.· I. 57.
Sée, Germain. Un programme d'observations de météorologie forestière. 1878. IV. 59.[2]
— Sur les quantités d'eau absorbées par le bois. 1877. IV. 412.[1]
— & Bochefontaine. Sur les effets physiologiques de l'érythrophléine. 1880. III. 476.[2]
Seebach, C. von. Betrachtungen über die Verjüngung des Buchen-Hochwaldes. 1846. IV. 494.
— Ertrags-Untersuchungen im Buchen-Hochwalde. 1846. IV. 497.
— Ueber die Formzahlen der Buchen. 1846. IV. 497.
— Gedanken über die Anwendbarkeit des . . . Buchenhochwaldbetriebes. 1867. IV. 494.
— Zur Holzmesskunst. 1861. IV. 214. . .
— Ueber den Lichtungshieb. 1863. IV. 494.

— Der modificirte Buchen-Hochwalds-Betrieb. 1845. IV. 494.
— Der modificirte Buchen-Hochwaldbetrieb. 1858. IV. 494.
Seeber, Johann Ludwig. De spinis plantarum. *See* KÜCHEL-BECKER, G. G. 1756. I. 107.[1]
Seebohm, Henry. Forest trees of the Yenesay. 1883. I. 453,[1] IV. 87.[3]
Seedling Epacrises. 1851. III. 665.[1]
A seedling Palm in flower. 1873. II. 63.[2]
Seeger, (*Missionar*). Kaffeeschädlinge im Togogebiet. 1896. III. 63.[1]
Seeger, (*Oberförster*). Forststatische Untersuchungen über Gewinnung der Eichen-Lohrinden. 1870. IV. 512.
— Gruppenweiser Hochwald-Femel-Betrieb. 1870. IV. 128.
— Ueber Stockholzgewinnung. 1868. IV. 386.
— Ueber Waldbewässerung. 1870. IV. 144.[1]
Seeger, V. Tisvilde. 1896. IV. 343.[3]
Seehaus, C. Ist die Eibe ein norddeutscher Baum? 1862. II. 11.[1]
Seehaus, P. Höhe, Dicke und Alter der Bäume. 1896. I. 295.[3]
Seeland, Max. Untersuchung eines am Pasterzengletscher gefundenen Holzstrunkes. 1873. II. 41.[1]
Seelbach, C. Landwirthschaftliche Waldfragen der Gegenwart. 1865. IV. 71, 317.[1]
Seeli. Der Wildheuet in den Waldungen. 1895. IV. 136.[1]
Seelig, Wilhelm. Koniferen im Winter 1870–71. 1871. III. 292.
— Wallnuss-Blüten. 1895. II. 114.[1]
Seligmann, (*publisher*). Abbildung inn- und ausländischer Hölzer. 1773. IV. 17.
Seeligmann, Th., Lamy-Torrilhon, G. & Falconnet, H. Le caoutchouc et la gutta-percha. 1896. III. 231.
Seeligmüller, E. R. Dombeya Wallichii Bentham. 1898. III. 591.[1]
— Styrax japonica. 1899. III. 661.[1]
— Triphasia trifoliata. 1886. III. 503.[1]
Seemann, Berthold. On Anacahuite wood. 1862. II. 748,[3] III. 695.[1]
— On the antâ or vegetable ivory. 1852. III. 330.[1]
— Antiaris Bennettii. 1862. II. 145.[3]
— On Antiaris Bennettii. 1862. II. 145.[3]
— Antigonon leptopus. 1868. II. 184.[1]
— Application of Pine trees. 1853. IV. 482.[2]
— Astianthus viminalis. 1862. II. 785.[3]
— Auswahl der seltensten und ausgezeichnetsten Blumen. 1844. V. XIII.[2]
— Beitrag zur Kenntniss der Natur der Cacteen. 1846. III. 618.[3]
— Bignonia peruviana Linn. = Vitis bipinnata. 1859. II. 502.[3]
— Bignoniacearum a cl. Fr. Welwitsch . . . collectarum descriptio. 1865. III. 784.[2]
— A bipinnate Cycadea from N. E. Australia. 1863. II. 3.[2]
— The botany of the voyage of H. M. S. Herald. 1852. I. 269.
— On Camellia japonica var. variegata. 1866. III. 599.[1]
— Ueber Camellia spectabilis Champ. 1858. II. 550.[3]
— Campsidium chinense. 1862. II. 786.[1]
— Campsidium Reiss. et Seem. 1870. II. 786.[1]
— Catalpa Pottsii Seem. 1851. II. 787.[1]
— Die Cocos Palme. 1857. III. 322.[1]
— Das Cohune-Oel. 1857. III. 322.[3]
— Ueber die Compositen-Gattung Fitchia. 1862. II. 857.[2]
— Condazzia Krstn. et Trian. = Delostoma. 1859. II. 788.[1]
— Contributions to the Annals and magazine of natural history. 1862. I. 270.
— Die Crescentiaceen unserer Gärten. 1856. II. 784.[1]
— On the cultivation of the Nutmeg. 1852. III. 402.[1]
— Cultur der Palmen. 1856. III. 317.
— Cyrtandra Pritchardii. 1861. II. 794.[1]
— Delostoma Lobbii. 1862. II. 788.[1]
— Description of two new species of Vitis. 1869. II. 501.[1]
— Endlicher's Paradisus vindobonensis. 1852. III. 322.[2]
— Epacris impressa Labill. fl. pleno. 1865. .II. 689.[1]
— Die in Europa eingeführten Acacien. 1852. II. 322.[2]
— On Faradaya. 1865. II. 757.[1]
— Ferdinandoa magnifica. 1870. II. 788.[2]
— Flora and fauna of the Isthmus of Panama. 1853. I. 333.
— Flora of north-western Mexico. 1852. I. 331.[3]
— Flora of the island of Hongkong. 1852. I. 460.[3]

— Flora of the Isthmus of Panama. 1852. I. 333.
— Flora of western Eskimauxland. 1852. I. 311.[2]
— Flora vitiensis. 1865. I. 510.[1]
— Die Flora von Oahu. 1853. III. 94.[2]
— Fortune's Yellow Camellia. 1859. II. 551.[2]
— Die Gattung Attalea. 1857. III. 320.[2]
— Die Gattung Borassus. 1856. III. 321.[1]
— Die Gattung Cocos Linné. 1857. III. 322.[1]
— Die Gattungen Camellia und Thea. 1880. II. 550.[2]
— Gefüllte Blumen. 1861. II. 821.[1]
— On the genus Ceodes of Forster. 1863. II. 191.[2]
— Het geslacht Arenga. 1858. III. 320.[1]
— Het geslacht Attalea. 1857. III. 320.[2]
— Het geslacht Borassus. 1856. III. 321.[1]
— Het geslacht Chamaerops. 1859. III. 322.[1]
— Het geslacht Cocos. 1857. III. 322.[1]
— Over het geslacht Elaeis. 1858. III. 325.[1]
— Het geslacht Metroxylon. 1858. III. 327.[2]
— Die giftigen Pflanzen der Viti- oder Fiji Inseln. 1861. III. 94.[1]
— Gutta Taban. 1853. III. 668.[2]
— On gutta tuban. 1852. III. 668.[2]
— Hannoversche Sitten und Gebräuche in ihrer Beziehung zur Pflanzenwelt. 1859. I. 517.[2]
— On Hedera Canariensis as an Irish plant. 1865. II. 649.[1]
— Hederaceae novae. 1865. II. 648.[1]
— Die Heetoo-Rinde Abyssiniens. 1853. III. 543.[2]
— Histoire naturelle du genre Borassus. 1863. II. 65.[1]
— The island of Hongkong. 1853. I. 460.[1]
— Ueber Kellettia und Prockia. 1862. II. 573.[1]
— Knallendes Aufspringen einer Palmenscheide. 1861. II. 63.[2]
— Der Lichterbaum in Panama. 1852. III. 707.[1]
— Lindenia vitiensis. 1862. II. 822.[2]
— Loureiro's Cathetus fasciculata. 1859. II. 449,[1] 549.[1]
— On Mammillaria Scheerii Mühlenpf. 1863. II. 595.[1]
— Der Mammoth-Baum Ober-Californicus. 1858. II. 50.[1]
— On the Mammoth-tree of upper California. 1858. II. 50.[1]
— The Mistleto and the Appletree. 1869. II. 179.[1]
— On Nag-kassar. 1853. III. 610.[2]
— Ueber Nag-Kassar. 1856. II. 558.[1]
— Narrative of the voyage of H. M. S. Herald. 1853. I. 303.
— On the native country of Tecoma capensis. 1860. II. 792.[1]
— The natural history of the Cedron. 1853. III. 509.[1]
— Neue Phyllarthron-Art von Madagascar. 1859. II. 790.[1]
— Ueber neue und verkannte Clerodendron-Arten. 1862. II. 755.[1]
— The new Arcadian Fir. 1861. II. 24.[2]
— A new genus of Celastrineae. 1870. II. 470.[2]
— A new pitcher-plant. 1870. II. 546.[2]
— New South Sea Island plants. 1864. I. 509.[2]
— A new species of Oreopanax. 1869. II. 651.[1]
— On the Newfoundland Heather. 1866. II. 661.[1]
— Note on the genera Cupheanthus and Punica. 1866. II. 622.[1]
— Note on the genera Streptostigma. 1854. II. 486.[2]
— Note on the spines of Cactuses. 1852. II. 588.[1]
— Notes on the Sandwich Islands. 1852. I. 509.[2]
— Notiz über Habrothamnus Endl. 1859. II. 770.[1]
— Notizen über Südsee-Pflanzen. 1862. I. 509.[2]
— On the occurrence of Calluna vulgaris in America. 1864. II. 661.[1]
— Oil of Calophyllum indophyllum. 1865. III. 608.[1]
— Opening of a Palm-spathe with an audible report. 1861. II. 63.[2]
— On the Palm of Timbuctoo. 1857. II. 65.[1]
— Die Palme von Timbuktu. 1857. II. 65.[1]
— Die Palmen. 1858. II. 60.[2]
— De Palmen. 1858. III. 319.[1]
— Die Palmen im nördlichen Europa. 1856. III. 317.
— Palms. 1870. II. 60.[2]
— Die Palmyra. 1856. III. 321.[1]
— On the Palo de Velas or Candle tree. 1852. III. 707.[1]
— Paper. 1862. III. 368.[1]
— Paradisus vindobonensis. 1844. V. xiii.[2]
— Peruvian-bark trees and their transplantation. 1863. III. 712,[1] 718.
— Pflanzen-Elfenbein. 1852. II. 73.[2]
— The Piassaba fibre of commerce. 1862. III. 320.[2]
— Pimia rhamnoides und Disemma caerulescens. 1862. II. 537,[1] 576.[2]

— Plantae vitienses. 1861. I. 510.[1]
— Les plantes à fleurs doubles. 1864. I. 145.[2]
— On plants producing double flowers. 1864. I. 145.[2]
— Podocarpus? dulcamara. 1861. II. 9.[2]
— Podocarpus dulcamara. 1862. II. 9.[2]
— Podocarpus vitiensis. 1863. II. 10,[1] III. 287.[2]
— Poisonous plants of the Viti or Fiji Islands. 1861. III. 94.[2]
— Popular history of the Palms. 1856. II. 60.[2]
— The popular nomenclature of the American flora. 1851. I. 72.[2]
— Pritchardia pacifica. 1862. II. 74.[1]
— On the properties . . . of Crescentiaceae. 1857. III. '04.[2]
— Reise um die Welt. 1853. I. 303.
— Remarks on Guaco-plants. 1853. II. 860.[2]
— Remarks on Passifloraceae and Turneraceae. 1854. II. 574,[2] 575.[2]
— Remarks on Sarsaparilla. 1856. III. 339.[1]
— Remarks on the natural order Bignoniaceae. 1862, 1863. II. 784.[1]
— Revision der Crescentiaceen-Gattung Tanaecium. 1856. II. 791.[2]
— Revision of the genera Crescentia, Parmentiera. 1854. II. 787,[2] 789,[1] 789.[2]
— Revision of the genus Tanaecium. 1856. II. 791.[2]
— Revision of the natural order Bignoniaceae. 1862. II. 784.[1] — 1863. II. 784.[1]
— Revision of the natural order Hederaceae. 1864. II. 646.[2]
— On Sapranthus. 1866. II. 218.[2]
— On the Simaba cedron. 1852. III. 509.[1]
— Ueber den Simaba Cedron. 1872. III. 509.[1]
— Sketch of the vegetation of the Isthmus of Panama. 1851. I. 333.
— Smythea pacifica. 1862. II. 499.[2]
— The Solana of tropical Polynesia. 1863. II. 775.[1]
— Solanum anthropophagorum. 1862. II. 778.[1]
— On some genera with one-celled ovary. 1864. II. 654.[1]
— Spathodea ilicifolia. 1859. II. 791.[1]
— Storckiella vitiensis. 1861. II. 385.[2]
— On the synonymy of some acanthaceous plants. 1864. II. 796.[1]
— Synopsis Crescentiacearum. 1860. II. 784.[1]
— Synopsis of the genera Camellia and Thea. 1859. II. 550.[2]
— Synopsis plantarum vitiensium. 1861. I. 510.[1]
— Tecoma . . . capensis; eine brasilianische Pflanze. 1860. II. 792.[1]
— The Thief Palm. 1865. II. 72.[1]
— On two new genera of Smilacineae. 1868. II. 85.[1]
— Two new species of Citriosma. 1864. II. 222.[2]
— Ueber das Vaterland der Bignonia capensis. 1860. II. 792.[1]
— Vegetable ivory plant. 1856. II. 73.[2]
— Verzeichniss derjenigen Pflanzenarten . . . mit gefüllten Blumen. 1864. I. 145.[2]
— Viti. 1862. III. 283.[2]
— Die Volksnamen der amerikanischen Pflanzen. 1851. I. 72.[2]
— Was the Cocoanut known to the ancient Egyptians? 1863. II. 67.[1]

See also PIM, Bedford & SEEMANN, Berthold.
— & Schmidt, J. Descriptiones plantarum. 1844. I. 269.
— Buchenöl. 1855. IV. 500.[1]
Seemann, Wilhelm E. G. On Beech oil. 1855. IV. 500.[1]
— Buchenöl. 1855. IV. 500.[1]
Seemen, Otto von. Abnorme Blütenbildung bei einer Salix fragilis. 1895. II. 107.[1]
— Eine Bemerkung über die Diagnose für Salix triandra. 1896. II. 105.[1]
— 13 neue Arten Fagaceen. 1897. II. 123.[1]
— Einiges über abnorme Blütenbildungen bei den Weiden. 1887. II. 103.[1]
— Einiges über die Cupuliferen des Malayischen Archipels. 1900. II. 131.[1]
— (Fünf) neue Weidenarten. 1896. II. 99.[1]
— Eine mächtige Eiche. 1877. II. 138.[2]
— Salix Aschersoniana von Seemen. 1895. II. 105.[1]
— Salix purpurea × fragilis. 1889. II. 108.[1]
— Verzeichnis . . . bei Berlin beobachteten Weiden. 1892. II. 101.[2]
— Zwei neue Salices aus der Sammlung: "Plants of southern Colorado." 1900. II. 99.[2]
— Zwei neue Weiden, Salix Straehleri. 1889. II. 101.[2]
— Zwei neue Weidenarten aus Süd-Afrika. 1900. II. 103.[1]

Seenus, Joseph, *Freiherr* von. Beschreibung einer Reise nach Istrien. 1805. I. 447.
Seetzen, Ulrich Jasper. Systematum generaliorum de morbis plantarum. 1789. I. 206.[1]
— Voorslag om de heivelden tot bosschen aan te leggen. 1814. IV. 159.
Seezen, E. L. Verzeichniss . . . der in Esth-, Liv- und Curland . . . Giftgewächse. 1883. III. 68.[2]
Seffer, P. H. OLSSON-. *See* OLSSON-SEFFER, P. H.
Sega speciale da potersi usare a mano od a vapore. 1886. IV. 393.
Segala, Giuseppe. A proposito del trattato di rimboscamento . . . del Sig. P. Demontzey. 1883. IV. 166.[1]
Segerdahl, G. Erinringar uti skogstaxationsläran. 1861. IV. 243.
— Forstliga jakttagelser under en resa i Danmark. 1861. IV. 343,[1] 349.[1]
— Lärokurs uti skogshushållningen. 1852. IV. 240.
— Om svenska skogshushållningens statsekonomiska betydenhet. 1854. IV. 273.[1]
Segerdahl, H. F. Skogsbruks-praktika. 1866. IV. 94.
Segerstedt, A. J. De pharmacis indigenis. 1787. III. 270.[1]
Segerstedt, Frider. De Galipea Cusparia. *See* THUNBERG, C. P. 1825. III. 504.[1]
Segerstedt, Per. Studier öfver buskartade stammars skyddsväfnader. 1894. I. 106,[1]
Segesser, A. von. Ueber die Staatswaldungen. 1850. IV. 365.
Seghers, N. Amasonia punicea Vahl. 1894. III. 695.[2]
— Le Chorozema × Lowii hort. 1894. III. 472.[2]
— Les Eriostemon linifolium et densiflorum. 1894. III. 504.[1]
— Heterocentron mexicanum fl. alba. 1894. III. 638.[2]
— Swainsonia coronillaefolia Salisb. 1892. III. 489.[1]
Segnitz, Gottfried von. *See* EMMERT, Friedrich & SEGNITZ, Gottfried von.
Segondat. Hilfstabellen zur leichtern Berechnung des viereckigen und runden Holzes. 1782. IV. 220.
— Holztabellen zu leichter Berechnung des viereckigen und runden Holzes. 1782. IV. 220.
— Holztabellen zur leichten Berechnung des Cubikinhalts vierkantiger und runder Hölzer. 1782. IV. 220.
— Traité des mesures des bois. 1782. IV. 220.
Seguier, Jean François. Bibliotheca botanica. 1740. I. 1.
— Catalogus plantarum quae in agro veronensi. 1745. I. 424.
— Icones plantarum. 1721. I. 290.
— Plantae veronenses. 1745. I. 424.
— Plantarum quae in agro veronensi . . . supplementum. 1745. I. 424.
Séguinard, H. Conversion des taillis en futaie pleine. 1884. IV. 128.
— De la régénération des montagnes. 1886. IV. 163.
— Régénération des montagnes des Alpes. 1885. IV. 185.[2]
— Traitement des futaies de Chênes. 1885. IV. 513.
Segundo catalogo del Museo de productos argentinos. 1890. III. 269.[3]
Segura, José C. Insrucciones [*sic*] sobre el cultivo del Cacaotero. 1889. III. 592.[2]
— & Cordero, M. D. Reseña sobre el cultivo de algunas plantas industriales. 1884. III. 118.[1]
Segura, Mariano LAGASCA Y. *See* LAGASCA Y SEGURA, Mariano.
Segura Sempere, Fernando. El mejor de los árboles [el Eucalipto]. 1891. IV. 532.[1]
Séguret, S. & Saint-Ange, Legros. Du déboisement du sol forestier. 1846. IV. 282.[2]
— — Question du déboisement et du reboisement des montagnes. 1846. IV. 282.[2]
Segvelt, Edm. van. Grafting vines. 1865. III. 39, 548.[1]
— De l'influence du sujet sur la greffe. 1865. III. 39, 548.[1]
Ein sehenswerter Baum. 1879. II. 516.[2]
Sehenswürdigkeiten im . . . Garten zu St. Petersburg. 1900. II. 98.[1]
Seherr-Thoss, *Graf* von. Ueber das Vorkommen des Taxus. 1862. IV. 440.[1]
Sehested, F. I Anledning af Spørgsmaalet om Skovtvangens Afskaffelse. 1867. IV. 273.[1]
— Der er for lidt Skov i Landet. 1867. IV. 343.[1]
— Nu skal altsaa Danmark miste sit pragtfuldeste Smykke! 1866. IV. 343.[1]
Sehested, K. Bør man vedblivende lade de private Skove passe sig selv? 1899. IV. 273.[1]
Von einem sehr alten . . . Akazienbaume zu Burg-Friedberg. 1803. II. 383.[1]

Seibt, (*Forstassessor, Heissenstein*). The forests of Java and their management. 1900. IV. 377.[1-]
— Die Wälder Javas und ihre Bewirtschaftung. 1900. IV. 377.[1]
Seide, Michael. Uiber [*sic*] den Holzzuwachs im Hochwalde. 1837. IV. 235.[1]
Seidel, A. Beiträge zur Kenntnis des Urwaldes. 1848. IV. 235.[2]
Seidel, C. A. Ausführliche Anweisung zur richtigen Pflege . . . grosser Orangerieen. 1842. III. 499.[2]
Seidel, C. F. Die mächtigste Rüster Deutschlands. 1879. II. 144.[3]
— Eine Skizze des Tatragebirges. 1867. I. 445.
— Starke Ahornbäume. 1880. II. 477.[2]
— Ueber Verwachsungen von Stämmen. 1880. I. 209.[1]
Seidel, G. F. Orangetreets Behandling. 1840. III. 499.[2]
Seidel, H. F. Dyrkningen af Rhododendron. 1837. III. 656.
Seidel, J. H. Synonymisches Verzeichniss aller im Kurfürstlichen Orangengarten zu Dresden befindlichen Gewächse. 1794. I. 44.
— Verzeichniss der Glas- und Treibhauspflanzen, ingleichen der Bäume. 1794. I. 44.
Seidel, Jakob. Theses de causis . . . plantarum. 1610. I. 30.
Seidel, Jakob Friedrich. Ueber die Kultur der Camellien. 1830. III. 599.[1]
Seidel, Karl August. Orangerie-Pflege. 1863. III. 499.[2]
Seidel, O. M. Excursionsflora für Anfänger im Pflanzenbestimmen. 1880. I. 388.
Seidel, Traugott Jakob. Anleitung zur Kultur . . . der Camellien. 1837. III. 599.[2]
— Die Camellien. 1830. III. 599.[1]
— Neue Rhododendron-Hybriden. 1899. III. 657.[3]
— Die Rhododendreae. 1843. III. 646.[2]
— Die Rhodoraceae oder Rhododendreae. 1843. III. 646.[2]
Seidelin, K. H. En fordelagtig Benyttelse af knastede og krumvoxne Egetræer. 1802. IV. 513.
Seidemann, G. E. Ausmessung fester Körper und Hohlräume. 1840. IV. 222.
Seidensticker, August. Die alte Linde bei Coppenbrügge. 1846. II. 516.[2]
— Ueber Bodenbearbeitung . . . in den Buchen-Verjüngungsschlägen. 1863. IV. 494.
— Die Czarenfichte im Garten zu Schwöbber. 1869. IV. 460.[1]
— Rechts- und Wirthschafts-Geschichte norddeutscher Forsten. 1896. IV. 26.
— Seltenes Wachsthum eines Weymouths-Kiefernbestandes. 1844. IV. 469.
— Waldgeschichte des Alterthums. 1886. IV. 24.[1]
— Wald-Metamorphosen. 1858. IV. 74.[1]
— Wie verhalten sich Licht und Schatten in unseren Waldungen? 1849. IV. 67.[2]
Seidensticker, H. A. Ueber den geschichtlichen Ursprung . . . der hannöverschen Interessentenforsten. 1853. IV. 25.
— Ein mönströser [*sic*] Kiefernzweig. 1850. II. 47.[1]
Seidl, A. Beiträge zur Kenntnis des Urwaldes. 1849. IV. 216.
Seidl, Heinrich. Das Verschulen mittelst Maschine. 1885. IV. 151.[1]
Seidl, W. B. *See* BERCHTOLD, Friedrich, *Graf* von, SEIDL, W. B. & OPITZ, P. M.
Seidlitz, Nikolai von. Ueber die Anpflanzung des Theebaumes im Kaukasus. 1884. III. 601.[1]
— Botanische Ergebnisse einer Reise durch das östliche Transkaukasien. 1857. I. 369.
Seifert, Ede. Chinai Sail. 1888. III. 365.[2]
— Ligustrum lucidum. 1888. III. 674.[1]
Seifert, L. Abnormitäten an Fichte und Eiche. 1884. II. 36,[1] 157.[1]
Seifferth, (*Oberförster*). Einfluss der Harzung der Schwarzkiefer. 1879. II. 44.[1]
Seine — Société d'horticulture de la. *See* SOCIÉTÉ . . . III. 21.
Seine — Société nationale et centrale d'agriculture du département . . . *See* SOCIÉTÉ ROYALE ET CENTRALE D'AGRICULTURE DE PARIS. III. 22.
Seine-et-Oise. — Société d'agriculture du département. *See* SOCIÉTÉ . . . III. 21.
Seine-et-Oise — Société des sciences naturelles. *See* SOCIÉTÉ . . . I. 23.
Seine-Inférieure — Cercle pratique d'horticulture et de botanique. *See* CERCLE . . . III. 19.

Seine-Inférieure — Société centrale d'agriculture ... See
Société ... III. 20.
Seine-Inférieure — Société impériale et centrale d'horticul-
ture. See Société ... III. 22.
Seits, T. A. Allgemeine ökonomische Samen- und Früchte-
lehre. 1822. I. 119.
Seits, Tobias. Die Rosen nach ihren Früchten. 1825. II.
282.[1]
Seitz, (Hofgärtner). Anzeige einiger neuen Gewächse. 1834.
I. 47.
— Bemerkungen über Herbst- und Frühlings-Pflanzungen.
1840. III. 168.[2]
— Eine verbesserte Art von Mooskratzer. 1835. III. 175.[2]
Seitz, Adalbert. Ueber Frassschäden. 1892. IV. 208.[1]
— Injury by insects. 1892. IV. 208.[1]
Seitz, C. Betrachtung der zwei Hauptveredlungsarten. 1837.
III. 160.
— Nachricht über Cassia rostrata. 1827. II. 343.[2]
— Nachricht über den Weinbau in Tyrol. 1832. III. 558.[1]
Seitz, C. L. Kurze Anleitung über die Erziehung ... des
weissen Maulbeerbaumes. 1825. III. 374.
Seitz, Franz. Nachrichten über Griechenland's Feld- und
Gartenbau. 1836. III. 127.[1]
Seitz, Georg Friedrich. Über Forst- und Jagd-Frevel. 1817.
IV. 318.
Seitz, Karl Ludwig. Katechismus der Obstbaumzucht. 1828.
III. 136.
Seitz, L. C. Der Winter 1837–38 um München. 1838. III.
45.
Séjour, Dionis-du-. See Dionis-du-Séjour.
Sekreta ogrodnikom potrzebne i innym zdatne. 1817. III.
127.[1]
Sekyrka, Ferdinand. Nauka o pěstování lesů. 1892. IV.
111.[1]
Der Selam des Orients. See Symanski, J. D. 1841. I. 515.
Selberg, Eduard. Reis naar Java en bezoek op ... Madura.
1846. III. 275.[2]
Selbstherr, Carl. Die Rosen. 1832. II. 282.[1]
Selby, Augustine Dawson. The flora of Franklin county,
Ohio. 1898. I. 316.
Selby, Prideaux John. A history of British forest-trees. 1842.
I. 393.[2]
Selby, W. C. Underwoods. 1853. IV. 132.[1]
Selections from the records of the Bengal gov't. III. 26.[1]
Séligman-Lui. Rapport à Monsieur le Ministre des postes et
des télégraphes sur les origines de la gutta-percha. 1883.
III. 149.
Seligmann, Franz Romeo. Ueber drei höchst seltne Persische
Handschriften. 1833. III. 238.[1]
— Liber fundamentorum pharmacologiae. 1830. III. 257.[1]
— Prolegomena in codicem vindobonensem. 1859. III.
238.[2]
Salivanowski, I. See Селиванновскiй, И.
Selkirk, James. Recollections of Ceylon. 1844. III. 92.[1]
Sell. Die Eichenheisterbestände. 1890. IV. 508.
Sell, Eduard. Ueber Calpicarpum Roxburghii. 1858. II.
727.[1]
— Die Kautschukgewinnung in Costa-Rica. 1862. III. 368.[1]
Seller, (Dr.). Osseous legumen of Hymenaea Courbaril.
1853. II. 364.[2]
Seller, William. Examination of the views adopted by Liebig
on the nutrition of plants. 1845. I. 157.
Sellheim, (Forstmeister). Die Eiche im Buchengrundbestande.
1895. IV. 508.
Sello, Emil. Ueber das Reinigen der ... Cactus-Pflanzen.
1840. III. 618.[3]
—.Die Wellingtonia ... der Kronprinzessin. 1877. III.
310.[1]
Selmar, C. Beiträge zur Kultur der Rhododendron. 1888.
III. 655.
A Selmeczi m. k. bányász- és erdészakadémia évszázados fen-
nállásának emlékkönyve. 1871. IV. 36.[2]
Selmer, M. M. Les forêts de la Norvège. 1889. IV. 344.[1]
— Hvilken betydning kan the tillægges kunstig opelskning af
skov i vort land? 1879. IV. 344.[1]
Selow, O. van. Nieuwe plantwijze voor Koffieboomen. 1894.
III. 734.[2]
Selskabet for Norges Vel. Beretning. III. 11.
Selskoye ... See Сельское ...
Seltene Rosenspecies. 1892. III. 456.[1]
La Selvicoltura all' Esposizione di Arezzo. 1895. IV. 20.[2]
Selys-Longchamps, Michel Edmond de. Les arbres à Long-
champs-sur-Geer. 1880. III. 46.[1]
— Les corbeaux. 1895. IV. 199,[1] 544.[1]

— Destruction des insectes nuisibles. 1895. IV. 199.[1]
— Les gelées du printemps. 1897. IV. 548.[1]
— Les gelées printanières. 1894. IV. 548.[1]
— Note sur une variété pyramidale du Populus virginiana.
1864. II. 97.[1]
— Oiseaux que l'on peut considérer comme utiles. 1895. IV.
544.[1]
— Le parc de Longchamps sur Geer. 1894. III. 28.[2]
— Le Peuplier de Virginie pyramidal. 1864. II. 97.[1]
La Semaine horticole. See L'Illustration horticole. III.
15.
Semanario de agricultura y artes. III. 23.[1]
Semenof, P. See Семеновъ, П.
Semenof, V. See Семеновъ, В.
Semenow, A. M. Beiträge zur Pharmacognosie der Kawa-
Kawa-Wurzel. 1890. III. 343.[1]
— Histologisch-pharmakognostische Untersuchung ... der
Pernambuco-Jaborandi. 1889. III. 505.[1]
Semi-tropic California. See Southern California horticul-
turist. III. 8.
Semi-tropical. III. 8.
Semichon, L. See Bouffard, A. & Semichon, L.
Semillas forestales. 1892. IV. 546.[1]
Seminarium et plantarium. See Estienne, Charles. 1540.
III. 110.[1]
Seminarium sive plantarium. See Estienne, Charles. 1537.
I. 292.
Semis de Douglas. Installation d'un peuplement de cette
essence. 1900. IV. 441, 433.[2]
Semis de graines d'Aubépine. 1900. III. 422.[2]
Semis de Pin sylvestre. 1900. IV. 474.
Semis de Saule marsault. 1895. IV. 488.[1]
Du semis du Mûrier. 1840. III. 375.
Les semis en pépinière. 1900. IV. 151.[2]
Semis, en pépinière et en place. 1899. IV. 149.[2]
Semis et plantations d'arbres forestiers. See Clément,
Eugène. 184.? IV. 121.
Semler, H. Die Hebung der Obstverwertung. 1883. III.
149.
Semler, Heinrich. Ueber einige nützliche Wüstenpflanzen.
1889. III. 42.[1]
— Die gesamte Obstverwertung. 1883. III. 174.[1]
— Die Hebung der Obst-Verwertung. 1883. III. 174.[1]
— Die tropische Agrikultur. 1886. III. 96.[1]
— Tropische und nordamerikanische Waldwirtschaft. 1888.
IV. 111,[1] 596.[2]
Semmedo, João Curvo. See Curvo Semmedo, João.
Semmola, Vincenzo. Del baco dell' Uva. 1851. III. 559.[2]
— Esperienze delle caprificazione. 1845. II. 150.[2]
— Su la natura e genesi del moschetino del Caprifico. 1847.
II. 150.[2]
— Delle varietà de' Vitigni del Vesuvio. 1855. III. 546.
Semon, Julius. De olei Juniperi aetherei vi. 1844. III,
303.[2]
Semper Indagator, (pseud.). Sølvpoppelen. 1869. III. 345.[1]
— Det usagte Acacie-Træ. 1869. III. 487.[1]
Sempere, Fernando Segura. See Segura Sempere, Fer-
nando.
Sempers, Frank W. Injurious insects and the use of insecti-
cides. 1894. III. 187.
Sempervivens. III. 13.
Semple, Robert Hunter. Catalogue of the plants in the So-
ciety of apothecaries' garden at Chelsea. 1878. I. 55.
Sempolowski, A. Zur Vertilgung der Mäuse. 1895. III.
186.[2]
Sempre intorno alla crisi agrumaria. 1897. IV. 285.[1]
Senckenbergische naturforschende Gesellschaft. Abhand-
lungen. Bericht. I. 14.
Sendschreiben an die Herrn Redakteren der forstlichen Zeit-
schrift für Baden. See Klauprecht, J. L. 1838. IV. 350.[1]
Sendtner, Otto. Bemerkungen über die Methode die pe-
riodischen Erscheinungen an den Pflanzen zu beobachten.
1851. I. 220.[2]
— Beschreibung einer neuen Gattung. 1846. II. 778.[1]
— Zur Kenntnis der bayerischen Brombeersträucher. 1856.
II. 301.[2]
— Monographia Cyphomandrae. 1845. II. 771.[1]
— Solanaceae et Cestrineae. 1846. II. 768.[1]
— Vegetationsverhältnisse des bayrischen Süddonau-Ge-
bietes. 1860. I. 384.
— Die Vegetations-Verhältnisse des bayerischen Waldes.
1860. I. 384.
— Die Vegetations-Verhältnisse Südbayerns. 1854. I. 383.
— See also Johnson, H. S. & Sendtner, O.

Senebier, Jean. Dissertatio de Polygamia. 1765. I. 236.[2]
— Mémoire sur la grande probabilité qu'il y a que l'air fixe est décomposé par les plantes. 1793. I. 172.
— Mémoires physico-chimiques sur l'influence de la lumière solaire. 1782. I. 172.
— Physikalisch-chemische Abhandlungen über den Einfluss des Sonnenlichts. 1782. I. 172.
— Physiologie végétale. 1791. I. 146.
— Physiologie végétale . . . une description des organes des plantes. 1800. I. 148.
— Rapports de l'air avec les êtres organisés. 1807. I. 172.
— Recherches sur l'influence de la lumière solaire. 1783. I. 172.
— Théorie de l'évolution des boutons. 1793. I. 107.[2]
— Waarnemingen op dieren en planten ter voorspellinge van het weder. 1793. I. 220.[1]
— *See also* HUBER, François & SENEBIER, Jean.
Seneci, D. Rapporti forestale; provincia di Brescia. 1870. IV. 364.
Sénéclause, Adrien. Sur le Cèdre de l'Atlas. 1845. III. 299.[2]
— Les Conifères. 1867. III. 289.
— Essai sur la taille . . . du Mûrier. 1840. III. 376.
Sénégal-Soudan; agriculture. 1900. III. 281.[1]
Senftnský, Jan. Původ (stáff) rostlin. 1895. IV. 87.[1]
Senff, M. Ueber die trockene Destillation des Holzes. 1885. IV. 433.[1]
Senft, von. Einiges über die Waldstreu-Beschränkung. 1886. IV. 438.[1]
Senft, Christian Carl Friedrich Ferdinand. Fels und Erdboden. 1876. IV. 61.[1]
— Die Humus-, Marsch-, Torf- und Limonitbildungen. 1862. IV. 61.[1]
— Lehrbuch der forstlichen Botanik. 1857. IV. 83.
— Lehrbuch der forstlichen Geognosie. 1857. IV. 61.[1]
— Lehrbuch der forstlichen Zoologie. 1857. IV. 89.[2]
— Lehrbuch der Gebirgs- und Bodenkunde. 1847. IV. 61.[1]
— Lehrbuch der Gesteins- und Bodenkunde. 1867. IV. 61.[1]
— Der Steinschutt und Erdboden. 1867. IV. 61.[1]
— Systematische Bestimmungstafeln von Deutschlands . . . Holzgewächsen. 1868. I. 371, *IV. 83.*
— Die Vegetationsverhältnisse der Umgegend Eisenachs. 1865. I. 385.
Senft, D. Betrachtung des humushaltigen oder Culturbodens. 1875. IV. 69.
Senguerd, Wolferd. Camphorae historia. 1715. III. 404.[2]
— Disputatio . . . de China officinarum. 1715. III. 338.[1]
Senier, Harold. The colouring matter in the petals of Rosa. 1877. II. 294.[1]
— Sur l'huile de Croton tiglium. 1884. III. 517.[1]
Senilis. Pinaceae. *See* NELSON, John. 1866. III. 289.
Senlis = Société d'horticulture et d'apiculture . . . *See* SOCIÉTÉ . . . III. 22.
Senn van Basel, W. H. Cinchona cultuur. 1884. III. 716.
— De onbebouwde gronden op Borneo's westkust. 1880. III. 128.
Senna Alexandrina. 1866. III. 470.[2]
Senner, Johann Konrad. De Senna. *See* BAIER, J. J. 1733. III. 470.[1]
Senoner, Adolf. Acacia Farnesiana. 1860. III. 465.[1]
— Akklimatisationsversuche am Como-See. 1871. III. 49.[1]
— Coltivazione del Prunus Mahaleb. 1884. III. 438.[2]
— Cultur der Cacteen. 1857. III. 619.
— Cultur der Capparis spinosa. 1874. III. 408.[2]
— Die Feinde der Pomeranzen- und Limonienbäume. 1883. III. 498.[1]
— Krankheit des Kastanienbaums. 1871. III. 537.[1]
Sentei, Adolf. A Magyartölgy. 1880. II. 133.[1]
Sentenze ultronee di un professore di agraria e forestale coltura. 1871. IV. 255.
Sentimental objections to felling trees. 1888. III. 202.[1],
Sentimentalism and tree-felling. 1893. III. 202.[2]
Senus, A. H. C. van. Bijdrage tot de kennis der cellulose gisting. 18 . . ? I. 137.
Sepp, Clemens. Die Rothstreifigkeit des Bau- und Blochholzes. 1889. IV. 415.[1]
Sepp, Jan Christiaan. Houtkunde. 1773. IV. 17.
Sept-Fontaines, Louis Marie Blanquart de. L'art de toiser les bois. 1815. IV. 216.
— Forêts et bois. 1791. IV. 22.[1]
Sequeira, Eduardo. Algumas variedades de Oliveiras de valor. 1897. III. 676.[2]
— La culture des Rosiers en Portugal. 1897. III. 453.[1]
— De Rozenkweek in Portugal. 1897. III. 453.[1]

Sequeira, Joaquim Pedro Fragoso de. Memoria ácerca da cultura . . . dos Castanheiros. 1790. III. 358.[2]
— Memoria sobre as azinheiras. 1790. III. 361.[2]
La Sequoia gigantea. 1863. IV. 484.[1]
La Sequoia gigantea a Tremezzo. 1863. IV. 484.[2]
The Sequoia reservation. 1892. IV. 178.[2]
Les Sequoias. *See* LES SEQUOIAS. 1896. IV. 484.[2]
Serab, EBN. *See* EBN SERAB.
Serafini, Lor. Lettera . . . intorno all' uso della cioccolata. 1728. III. 594.
Serapion. Insignium medicorum Joan. Serapionis Arabis de simplicibus medicinis opus. 1200. I. 274.
— Liber Serapionis aggregatus in medicinis simplicibus. 1200. I. 274.
— De simplicium medicamentorum historia libri VII. 1200. I. 274.
Seras. Noticias sobre el cultivo del Eucaliptus. 1889. IV. 530.
Die serbischen Forste. 1886. IV. 375.[1]
Sereix, Rafael ALVAREZ. *See* ALVAREZ SEREIX, Rafael.
Sererhard, N. Einfalte Delineation aller Gemeinden gemeiner freien Bünden beschrieben im Jahr 1742. 1872. IV. 367.
Sergent, E. Resistance des bois à la flexion et à la compression. 1887. IV. 410.
Sericulture and silk reeling. 1899. III. 355.
Serière, G. de. Bijdrage tot de kennis van den tegenwoordigen toestand der Molukkos. 1851. III. 635.[2]
Seringe, Nicolas Charles. Amygdaleae. 1825. II. 255.[2]
— Bemerkungen über Hortensia. 1844. II. 241.[1]
— Chilopsis linéaire. 1847. III. 706.[2]
— Critique des Roses desséchées. 1818. II. 282.[1]
— Description, culture et taille des Mûriers. 1855. II. 154.[1]
— Description de la Rosa rubrifolia. 1818. II. 298.[1]
— Description . . . des Mûriers. 1855. III. 377.
— Élémens de botanique. 1841. I. 88.
— Essai d'une monographie des Saules de la Suisse. 1815. II. 102.[2]
— Flore des jardins et des grandes cultures. 1845. III. 86.
— Flore du pharmacien. 1852. III. 86.
— Flore et pomone lyonnaises. 1847. III. 87.
— Hydrangea. 1830. II. 240.[2]
— Mélanges botaniques. 1818. I. 266.
— Mélèze européen pyramidal. 1847. III. 304.[2]
— Mémoire sur la famille des Mélastomacées. 1828. II. 634.[2]
— Musée helvétique d'histoire-naturelle. 1818. I. 266.
— Notice sur le Maclure orangé. 1837. II. 154.[1]
— Nouvelle disposition des familles végétales. 1856. I. 252.
— Observations générales sur les Roses. 1818. II. 282.[1]
— Pommier monstreux de St.-Vallery. 1830. II. 266.[1]
— Remarques sur les Roses de Mr. Redouté. 1818. II. 282.[1]
— Viorne Tin à grandes fleurs. 1847. III. 753.[2]
— Weinmannia. 1830. II. 250.[2]
— & Guillard, Achille. Essai de formules botaniques. 1836. I. 254.[2]
Seringueira or Latex. 1900. III. 519.[1]
Serna, Fernando de la. Disertación sobre la prática y métodos de ingertár. 1817. III. 160.
Sernander, Johan Rutger. Ett bidrag till kännedomen om Sveriges Ekflora. 1886. I. 357.
— Einige Beiträge zur Kalktuff-Flora Norrlands. 1886. I. 357.
— Die Einwanderung der Fichte in Skandinavien. 1893. II. 35.[2]
— Några bidrag till den norrländska kalktuff-floran. 1890. I. 357.
— Studien über den Sprossbau bei Linnaea. 1891. II. 835.[2]
— Studier öfver de sydnerikiska Barrskogarnes utvecklingshistoria. 1900. II. 15.[1]
— Studier öfver den gotländska vegetationens utvecklingshistoria. 1894. I. 358.
— Studier öfver skottbyggnaden hos Linnæa. 1891. II. 835.[2]
— Studier öfver vegetationen i mellersta Skandinaviens fjälltrakter. 1899. I. 358.
— Om undraformationer i svenska fjälltrakter. 1898. I. 358.
— Om de upländska torfmossarnes byggnad. 1892. II. 130.[2]
La Serpentaire Barbanson. 1864. III. 621.[1]
Serpetro, Nicolò. Il mercato delle maraviglie della natura. 1653. I. 286.
Serpieri, A. *See* FEDERICI, Antonio & SERPIERI, A.
Serra, José Francisco CORREA DE. *See* CORREA DE SERRA, J. F.

Serrano y Plá, Eduardo. Importancia y necesidad del conocimiento de " Las variedades de la Vid." 1880. III. 547.
Serrant, Émile. Les Quinquinas en Algérie. 1878. III. 717.³
Serre. De l'emploi de l'huile de cade. 1846. III. 303.²
Serre, Paul. Le Diplosis Pini insignis. 1899. IV. 462.¹
— Note sur la chenille du Chêne. 1899. IV. 501.³
Serres. Note on Vancouver Island timber. 1862. IV. 484.¹
Serrès & Rérat. Note relative à l'emploi du Colza. 1877. III. 549.¹
Serres, Hector. Notice sur la culture du Pin maritime. 1837. IV. 467.¹
Serres, Jean Joseph. Flore abrégée de Toulouse. 1836. I. 409.
Serres, Marcel de. Des animaux et des végétaux figurés sur les monuments de l'antiquité. 1846. I. 79.³
— Mémoire sur la distribution primitive des végétaux. 1850. I. 299.
Serres, Olivier de, *Seigneur du Pradel.* The perfect use of silkwormes. 1607. III. 372.²
— The preparation of the barke of the White Mulberrie. 1603. III. 379.²
— La seconde richesse du Meurier blanc. 1603. III. 379.²
— Le théâtre d'agriculture. 1600. III. 111.
Serret, de. Catalogue des arbres . . . cultivés à Beernem. 1839. I. 49.
Serrurier, J. J. F. De beste tijd om boomen te hakken. 1824. IV. 384.³
— Chineesch middel om slechte boomen te krijgen. 1824. III. 181.²
— Fruitkundig woordenboek. 1805. III. 139.
— Het gieten van bloeijende vruchtboomen. 1820. III. 139.
— Ontdekking van ongedierte aan gezaaide Dennen. 1824. IV. 441.
— Over de ontginning van woeste gronden. 1820. III. 150.¹
— Raad om de sneeuw van de leidboomen te stoffen. 1824. III. 184.²
— Verhandeling over den landbouw. 1816. III. 105.
Serrurier, L. De pionier. 1891. I. 36.¹
Sertorius, Adolf. Beiträge zur Kenntnis der Anatomie der Cornaceae. 1893. II. 654.¹
Sértum botanicum. *See* GEEL, P. C. van. 1828. I. 267.
Sérullas. La gutta-percha à Singapore. 1890. III. 668.²
— Sur l'Isonandra percha. 1890. III. 668.³
— Rediscovery of Gutta percha tree at Singapore. 1890. III. 668.²
Servais, Gaspard Joseph de. Korte verhandeling van de boomen. 1789. III. 75,³ *IV. 84.*¹
Servais, Max. Effets de la gelée sur les arbres fruitiers. 1880. III. 182.
— Uitwerksel der vorst op de fruitboomen. 1880. III. 182.
Serval. L'enseignement forestier en Bavière. 1883. IV. 33.¹
Serval, G. Le Chêne des partisans. 1863. II. 138.¹
— *See also* BROILLIARD, H. & SERVAL, G.
Le **service** de recherches . . . en matière forestière. 1896. IV. 38.¹
Le **service** forestier de l'Algérie. 1876. IV. 295.¹
Service spécial de recherches . . . en matière forestière. 1896. IV. 38.¹
Servicio de ordenaciones de los montes públicos. *See* JORDANA Y MORERA, José. 1891. IV. 304.¹
Servier, Jean. Influence des Conifères sur les phénomènes hydrologiques. 1900. IV. 52.
— Observation de phénomènes hydrologiques. 1900. IV. 52.
Servizio forestale. 1864. IV. 293.²
Servizio forestale nel Messico. 1864. IV. 288.²
Servizio forestale nella Svizzera durante il 1881. 1882. IV. 294.¹
60 **mila** lire per un rimedio contro "la mosca olearia." 1899. III. 678.¹
Sessé, Martino & Mociño, J. M. Flora mexicana. 1887. I. 332.
— — Plantae Novae His aniae. 1887. I. 332.
Sessevalu, de. Examen de l'essai sur l'amenagement des forêts de Mr. Pannelier. 1779. IV. 248.³
Sessions, Kate O. Notes on planting. 1890. III. 118.¹
Sestini, Domenico. Lettere scritte dalla Sicilia e dalla Turchia. 1779. I. 262.
— Opuscoli. 1785. III. 127.¹
Sestini, Fausto. Azione del vapore di diverse sostanze sopra i semi. 1879. I. 203.
— Il Caffè. 1867. III. 739.

La seta in Italia. 1899. III. 380.¹
Seta vegetale. 1866. III. 234.
Settegast, H. Holzungen und Wald. 1875. IV. 44, 133.
Settegast, O. Kan door de Berberis (B. vulgaris) aan nabijstaande Rogge de roest worden meegedeeld? 1868. II. 202,² *III. 394.*¹
Setterblad, Andreas Erik. Horti upsaliensis plantae. *See* THUNBERG, C. P. 1826. I. 40.
Ueber das Setzen von Baumpfählen. 1886. III. 199.
Seubert, A. Ueber den Anbau des Djati-Baumes. 1897. IV. 537.¹
— The cultivation of Teak in the Dutch Netherlands. 1897. IV. 537.²
Seubert, Karl. Die chemische Untersuchung des Krebses. 1894. IV. 445.
Seubert, Moritz. Amarantaceae. 1875. II. 189.¹
— Excursionsflora für das Grossherzogthum Baden. 1863. I. 385.
— Excursionsflora für das südwestliche Deutschland. 1868. I. 386, 532.¹
— Excursionsflora für Mittel- und Norddeutschland. 1869. I. 386.
— Excursionsflora für Süddeutschland. 1868. I. 532.¹
— Flora azorica. 1844. I. 497.
— Grundriss der Botanik. 1868. I. 91.
— Hypoxideae . . . Vellosieae . . . Liliáceae, Amaryllideae. 1847. II. 77.¹
— Lehrbuch der gesammten Pflanzenkunde. 1849. I. 89.—1853. I. 89.
— Die Pflanzenkunde. 1849. I. 89.
— De plantenkunde. 1849. I. 89.
— Ueber Sarcobatus Maximiliani Nees. 1844. II. 188.¹
— Styraceae. 1868. II. 704.¹
— & Hochstetter, Carl. Übersicht der Flora der azorischen Inseln. 1843. I. 497.
Sencker, P. *See* MORITZ, J. & SEUCKER, P.
Seuffert, J. M. Die Flora des japanischen Insel-Reichs. 1870. III. 91.³
— Vegetation und Landeskultur in Norwegen. 1879. I. 357.
— Ueber die Zirbel-Kiefer, Pinus Cembra. 1878. II. 41.¹
Seuffert, N. Höhenbewaldung. 1886. IV. 158.
Seunik, J. & Delić, Stephan. Daphne Blagayana Freier. 1893. II. 601.¹
Seurat, Léon Gaston. La flore des régions arides . . . de Mexico. 1898. I. 333.
— Note sur la pollination des Cactées. 1898. II. 589.¹
— Observations biologiques sur les parasites des Chênes. 1900. IV. 501.³
Seurrat de la Boulaye, J. Mémoire sur la maladie ronde des Pins. 1878. IV. 461.³
— Observations sur la maladie ronde. 1880. IV. 461.²
Seurre, H. L. Les forêts de Sapin du Haut-Beaujolais. 1897. IV. 382.
Seutter, A. L. von. Die Forst-Polizei-Straf-Gesetzgebung. 1831. IV. 313.
Seutter, Arnold von. Draht- und Drahtseil-Riesen. 1897. IV. 392.
— Kastanien-Selven. 1895. III. 359.¹
— Zum schweizerischen Forstgesetz. 1900. IV. 331.¹
Seutter, J. G. von Abriss der gegenwärtigen Forst-Verfassung Württembergs. 1820. IV. 291.¹
— Allgemeine Ansicht der Forstwirthschaft. 1808. IV. 117.
— Anleitung zu Anlage . . . der Saam- und Baumschulen. 1807. IV. 149.³
— Bemerkungen über den Vortrag des Herrn Vice-Präsidenten Zahn. 1820. IV. 291.¹
— Ueber den Bestand und die Behauptung des Forst-Regales. 1824. IV. 285,² *913.*
— Ueber die Einführung der Hack-Wald-Wirthschaft. 1820. IV. 132.²
— Entwurf der Grundsätze, nach welchen der Bestand sämtlicher Waldungen der Reichs-Stadt Ulmischen Herrschaft aufgenommen . . . werden kann. 1797. IV. 247.²
— Forstbotanik. 1810. IV. 82.
— Grundsätze der Werths-Bestimmung der Waldungen, 1814. IV. 253.
— Versuch einer Darstellung der allgemeinen Grundsäze der Forstwirthschaft. 1804. IV. 96.
— Vollständiges Handbuch der Forstwirthschaft. 1880. IV. 61.³
— Ueber Wachsthum . . . der Buch-Waldungen. 1799. IV. 493.²

Seutter, Matthaeus. Disputatio botanico-medica inaugu-ralis de nuce vomica. 1691. III. 682.[1]
The seven sisters at Kew. 1883. II. 144.[2]
Sevenhoven, J. J. van. Beschrijving van de hoofdplaats van Palembang. 1823. III. 275.[3]
Sevenhuyzen, J. Iets over oleum cajeputi. 1851. III. 636.[2]
Severi, N. Le Phoenix dactylifera. 1900. II. 72.[3]
— Des plantations d'arbres d'alignement. 1900. III. 211.[1]
Severin, A. Ueber Akklimatisirung zarterer Sträucher. 1863. III. 43.
— Wie gelangen die Pandanen . . . zu einem . . . gesunden Wachsthume? 1860. III. 313.[1]
Séverin, G. Règlement sur les insectes nuisibles. 1898. IV. 323.[1]
— See also BERGER, C. & SEVERIN, G.
Severing, W. R. Onderzoek van den bast des Tapaloebooms. 1853. III. 233.[3]
Sevětinský, Jan. Dějiny lesů v Čechách. 1895. IV. 28.[2]
Seward, Albert Charles & Gowan, J. The Maidenhair tree. 1900. II. 8.[1]
Seweloh, Carl. Gränzrevision und Gränzregulirung. 1808. IV. 263, 313.
The sexes of the Willow. 1879. II. 103.[2]
Sexton, A. H. The chemistry of materials of engineering. 1899. IV. 409.
Sexton, J. Nursery propagation. 1885. III. 153.
Seybold, Karl. Die Arbeiterversicherungs-Gesetzgebung. 1892. IV. 311.[1]
— Gehört die Holzabfuhr zum forstwirtschaftlichen Betrieb. 1893. IV. 311.[1]
— Die land- und forstwirthschaftliche Unfallversicherung, zum Gebrauch in Elsass-Lothringen. 1892. IV. 311.[1]
Seydler, Fr. Verzeichnis der in Baden Braunsberg . . . wildwachsenden Phanerogamen. 1891. I. 389.
— Vorkommen . . . Taxus baccata in Ostpreussen. 1892. IV. 440.[3]
Seyffarth, F. C. Theoretisch-praktisches Examinatorium über die gesammte Forstwissenschaft. 1816. IV. 96.
Seyfferth, Emanuel. Zuwachs an geharzten Schwarzföhren. 1882. IV. 466.[1]
Seyler, Andreas. Vom Anbau der unächten Acazie und des Bohnenbaums. 1798. IV. 521,[2] 522.[2]
— Empfehlung des Bohnenbaums (Cytisus Laburnum Linn.). 1799. IV. 521.[2]
— Unpartheyische Prüfung des Beweises, dass durch . . . Anzucht der weissblühenden Acacie . . . Brennholzmangel nicht abgeholfen werden kann. 1799. IV. 522.[2]
Seymour, Arthur Bliss. Orchard rusts. 1886. III. 446.[2]
— Rose rusta. 1890. III. 453.[3]
— See also FARLOW, W. G. & SEYMOUR, A. B.
Seymour, John F. Agricultural address. 1868. IV. 43.
— On the preservation of forests. 1868.. IV. 43.
Seynes, Jules de. De la germination. 1863. I. 203.
— La maladie des Châtaigniers. 1879. III. 359.[1]
— Le parasite de la maladie du Châtaignier. 1880. III. 359.[2]
Sèze, comte de. Opinion sur le projet de loi concernant les échangistes. 1818. IV. 326.
Sgarzi, Gaetano. Della Chibaca salutaris. 1854. II. 224.[1]
— Studii analitici . . . intorno al Mavi dei Caffri. 1851. III. 476.[2]
Shaddock, S. G. On the fall of branchlets in the Aspen. 1883. II. 98.[3]
Shade trees. 1898. III. 211.[1]
Shade trees in cities. 1852. III. 506.[2]
Shade trees in our large cities. 1875. III. 208.[2]
Shafranof, Nicolai S. See Шафрановъ, H. C.
Shaler, Nathaniel Southgate. American swamp Cypress. 1883. II. 51.[3]
— Forests of North America. 1887. I. 304.
— The knees of the Bald Cypress. 1890. II. 51.[3]
— Notes on the Taxodium distichium or Bald Cypress. 1887. II. 51.[3]
— On the possible effects of the gypsy moth. 1900. IV. 205.[1]
— & Crandall, A. R. Report on the forests of Greenup. 1875. IV. 397.
Shamba; journal of agriculture for Zanzibar. III. 27.[1]
Shand, John Loudoun. The tea industry in Ceylon. 1888. III. 604.[1]
Shanghai literary and scientific society. Journal. See ROYAL ASIATIC SOCIETY, NORTH CHINA BRANCH. I. 28.[2]
Shannon, William Pollock. The Buckeye canoe of 1840. 1895. II. 483.[1]
— The range of the Blue Ash. 1895. II. 708.[1]

Shapiro, S. See Шапиро, С.
Sharon Cactus guide. III. 8.
Sharp, A. P. On oil of Sassafras. 1862. III. 408.[1]
Sharp, D. See HEMSLEY, W. B. & SHARP, D.
Sharp, J. B. Tropical vegetable fibres. 1857. III. 234.
Sharp, T. H. How to gather Logwood seed. 1897. III. 478.[3]
Sharpe, Thomas A. See SAUNDERS, William & SHARPE, T. A.
Sharples, Stephen Paschall. Experiments on American woods. 1883. I. 155.
— The forests of West Virginia. 1884. IV. 340.
— The specific gravity . . . of the wood of certain shrubs and exotic trees. 1884. IV. 411.[3]
Sharrock, Robert. The history of the propagation. 1660. III. 107.
Shatilof, I. N. See Шатиловъ, И. Н.
Shattock, Samuel G. On the scars . . . on the stem of Dammara robusta. 1888. II. 25.[3]
Shavrof, N. N. See Шавровъ, H. H.
Shaw, J. S. See FREEMAN, Strickland & SHAW, J. S.
Shaw, John. On the changes going on in the vegetation of South Africa. 1874. I. 495.
— Die Veränderungen der Vegetation von Süd-Afrika. 1874. I. 495.
Shaw, S. History and antiquities of Staffordshire. 1798. I. 533.
Shaw, Thomas. Catalogus plantarum . . . in variis Africae & Asiae partibus. 1738. I. 478.
— Reisen . . . Barbarei und Levante betreffend. 1738. I. 483.[2]
— Travels . . . relating to several parts of Barbary. 1738. I. 483.[2]
— Voyage dans la Barbarie et le Levant. 1738. I. 483.[2]
Shaw, Walter Robert. Contributions to the life history of Sequoia sempervirens. 1896. II. 49.[3]
Shaw school of botany. Contributions. I. 7.[1]
Shaw-Lefevre, G. See LEFEVRE, G. SHAW-.
The Shea butter of Africa. 1861. III. 667.[1]
Shecut, John Louis Edward William. Flora caroliniaensis. 1806. III. 62.
Sheep-bushes and Salt-bushes. 1896. III. 387.[3]
Sheep-grazing in forests. 1899. IV. 197.[2]
Sheidnagel, Leopoldo. See SCHEIDNAGEL, Leopoldo.
Sheldon, Asa Goodell. Life. See LIFE of Asa G. Sheldon.
Sheldon, William. Sur l'application faite en Amérique du bois de Chataignier. 1818. IV. 492.[2]
— Application of Chestnut wood. 1818. IV. 492.[2]
Sheldrake, Timothy. Botanicum medicinale. 1764. III. 80.
Shelford, R. S. A trip to Mt. Penrissen, Sarawak. 1900. I. 469.[3]
Shelgunof, N. V. See Шелгуновъ, H. B.
The Shell-bark Hickory. 1889. II. 112.[3]
Shelton, E. M. Preserving Mangoes. 1894. III. 525.[1]
— Tree-planting for shade and ornament. 1892. III. 132.[1]
Shen, Ram Comol. On the native drug called gulancha. 1827. III. 397.[1]
Shenderovitch, Z. See Шендеровичъ, З.
Shenshin, N. S. See Шеншинъ, H. C.
Shepard, Charles Upham. Special report on Tea-raising in South Carolina. 1893. III. 600.[3]
— Tea culture. 1899. III. 601.[1]
— Tea-culture in North America. 1893. III. 600.[3]
Shepard, Harvey N. Statutes of the Commonwealth of Massachusetts relating to trees. 1900. IV. 314.[2]
Shepherd, David. The cultivation of the Olive. 1864. III. 675.[3]
Shepherd, Theodosia B. The tree Tomato. 1896. III. 699.[1]
Sheppard, John. Pinus insignis and other trees. 1880. III. 308.[3]
— Transplanting evergreens. 1875. III. 169.[1]
— On trees, their uses and biography. 1848. I. 82.[1]
Sheppard, William. On the geographical distribution of the Coniferae in Canada. 1861. II. 14.[1]
Sherard, William. The cultivation of the Olive. 1864. III. 527.[2]
Sherard, William. A farther account of the [Poyson]-tree. 1723. III. 527.[2]
Sheridan, Philip Henry. Report of an exploration of parts of Wyoming, Idaho and Montana. See FORWOOD, W. H. 1882. I. 324.[1]
Sheriff, Mohideen, khan Bahadur. Materia medica of Madras. 1891. III. 279.[1]
Sherman, E. M. Tree agents laws. 1890. III. 200.[2]
Sherwood forest. 1878. IV. 27.[1]
Shesterikof, P. See Шестериковъ, П.

Shestidesyatilyetni . . . See Шестидесятилѣтнiй . . .
Shevyref, Ivan. See Шевыревъ, Ив.
Shibata, K. Beiträge zur Wachstumsgeschichte der Bambusgewächse. 1900. II. 58.[2]
Shiells, James. A catalogue of evergreen and deciduous trees. 1773. I. 521.[2]
Shier, John. Report on the starch-producing plants of . . . Guiana. 1847. I. 140.[1]
Shiercliff, E. Bristol and Hotwell guide. 1793. I. 396.
Shilof, D. See Шиловъ, Д.
Shimek, Bohumil. The distribution of forest trees in Iowa. 1900. I. 321, IV. 78.[2]
— Perfect flowers of Salix amygdaloides. 1896. II. 105.[1]
Shimoyama, Y. Beiträge zur Kenntnis der Bukublätter. 1888. III. 495.[2]
Shingles, Thomas. Castanea chrysophylla. 1882. III. 360.[1]
Shinia in Cyprus. 1897. III. 525.[2]
The "Shinia" leaves of Cyprus. 1899. III. 406,[2] 525.[2]
Shinn, Charles Howard. The African Date Palm. 1893. III. 329.[1]
— In the Amador second-growth forests. 1893. IV. 340.
— Australian salt-bushes. 1899. III. 223,[2] 397.[2]
— California forests and irrigation. 1890. IV. 46.[1]
— The California university gardens. 1890. III. 60.
— The Californian Azalea at home. 1889. II. 682.[2]
— The Californian Wild Grape. 1889. III. 583.[2]
— A few magnificent single trees of California. 1879. I. 295.[2]
— The Great Sequoia. 1889. II. 50.[1]
— Growth of trees . . . on alkali soils. 1896. II. 41.[2]
— The Japanese Oranges. 1890. III. 497.[2]
— The new Eucalyptus grove. 1898. IV. 530.
— Observations in California forests. 1895. IV. 340.
— The Olive in California. 1890. III. 676.[1]
— The Olive in California; a marvelous fruit industry. 1892. III. 676.[2]
— Pomegranates and Oleanders in California villages. 1897. III. 61.[1]
— Seedling Almonds in California. 1891. III. 434.[1]
— Seeds and seed planting. 1878. III. 156.[2]
— Among the Siskiyou forests. 1889. IV. 340.
— Some trees at Rancho Chico. 1894. I. 39.
— Timber and shade trees. 1898. III. 118.[1]
— Tree planting on Mount Hamilton. 1893. IV. 112.
— Trees and shrubs. 1898. III. 118.[1]
— The Visalia Oaks. 1897. II. 135.[1]
— Willows at Chico forestry station. 1897. III. 349.
— Work of the [forestry] stations of Santa Monica. 1894. IV. 112.
Shipp, H. A. Prize essay on the cultivation . . . of Tea in Cachar. 1867. III. 603.
Shipton, Johanne. De usu corticis peruviani. 1733. III. 710.
Shirai, Mitsutarō. Contributions to the knowledge of the forest flora of Japan. 1898. I. 461, IV. 87.[2]
— Über den genetischen Zusammenhang zwischen Roestelia koreaensis. 1900. III. 195.[2]
— Japanese species of Betula. 1894. II. 118.[1]
— A new Japanese species of Villebrunea. 1895. II. 158.[1]
Shirasawa, Homi. Die Gattung Tilia in Japan. 1900. II. 510.[1]
— Iconographie des essences forestières du Japon. 1899. I. 461, IV. 87.[2]
— Die japanischen Laubhölzer im Winterzustande. 1895. I. 294,[2] IV. 87.[2]
— Eine neue Coniferenart in Japan. 1895. V. xxv.[2]
Shirley, J. F. The native Grape vines of America. 1892. III. 551,[1] 559.[2]
Shirley, John. Peculiarities of the flowers of the order Proteaceae. 1898. II. 159.[1]
Shita-boku shiriyaku Dai Nihon. See DAI NIHON ju-moku shiryaku.
Shoemaker, R. M. Report of the committee on the drug market. 1873. III. 227.
Shokubutsu hyohin mokuroku. See CATALOGUE of plants . . . 1886. I. 66,[1] 463.[1]
Shontz, B. Summer pruning of Grapes. 1900. III. 549.[1]
Shore, Robert. Hydrangea Otaksa, a Japanese gem. 1890. III. 411.[2]
Short, Charles Wilkins. Instructions for the gathering and preservation of plants. 1833. I. 35.
— Progress of botany. See his A sketch of the progress of botany.
— Observations on the botany of Illinois. 1845. I. 314.
— A sketch of the progress of botany in western America. 1836. I. 80,[1] 321.
Short, F. W. See DUNSTAN, Wyndham & SHORT, F. W.
Short, Thomas. Discourses on tea, sugar, milk. 1750. III. 605.
— A dissertation upon Tea. 1730. III. 605.
— Medicina britannica. 1746. III. 80.
A short account of the Big trees. 1900. II. 51,[1] IV. 484.[2]
A short account of the late donation of a botanic garden to the University of Cambridge. 1763. I. 52.
A short attempt to recommend the study of botanical analogy. 1784. III. 259.[2]
A short explanation of the technical words . . . in botany. See MARTYN, John. 172.? I. 69.[2]
A short treatise on forest-trees. See HAMILTON, Thomas. 1765. III. 123.[2]
Shortt, John. On branched Palms in southern India. 1871. II. 63.[1]
— List of wild plants . . . used as food. 1878. III. 278.
— A monograph on the Cocoanut Palm. 1888. III. 324.[1]
Shortt, T. K. On certain species . . . Crataegus and Pyrus. 1866. III. 421,[1] 444.[1]
Shrigley, E. A. Historic trees of Philadelphia. 1899. I. 295.[2]
Shriver, Howard. Flora of Cumberland, Maryland. 18..? I. 318.
Shrubbery beneath trees. 1898. III. 216.
The shrubbery in winter. 1896. III. 208.[2]
Shrubs and trees with golden foliage. 1885. III. 206.[2]
Shrubs native and foreign. 1896. III. 61.[1]
Shrubs on lawns. 1899. III. 123.[1]
Shrubs which succeed beneath trees. See SHRUBBERY beneath trees. 1898. III. 216.
Shrubs with ornamental berries. 1882. III. 208.[1]
Shtcheglof, N. See Щегловъ, Н.
Shtchekotof, I. P. See Щекотовъ, I. П.
Shtchepkin, S. See Щепкинъ, С.
Shtchurovski, G. E. See Щуровскiй, Г. Е.
Shulgin, N. See Шульгинъ, Н.
Shull, George Harrison. Accessory buds. 1896. I. 109.[1]
— Disguises in bud arrangement. 1897. I. 109.[1]
Shuttleworth, Robert James. Account of a botanical excursion in the Alps. 1838. I. 434.
Shvykovski, J. Povalo-. See Повало-Швыйковскiй, Я.
Siam benzoin. 1895. III. 228.[1]
Siam gamboge. 1895. III. 609.[1]
Siarczyński, Franciszek. Sztuka ogrodnicza. 1802. III. 115.[2]
Sias, A. W. The wild Crab for the northwest. 1890. III. 429.[1]
Sibbald, A. T. Malayan fruit. 1880. III. 274.[2]
Sibbald, Sir Robert. Nuncius scoto-britannicus. 1684. I. 394.
— Scotia illustrata. 1684. I. 394.
The Siberian Larch. 1900. IV. 452.[2]
Sibree, James. The great African island. 1880. I. 496.
— Madagascar wild flowers. 1888. I. 496.
— Malagasy folk-lore. 1880. I. 518.
— Mr. Alfred R. Wallace on the fauna and flora of Madagascar. 1881. I. 496.
— Notes on the Traveller's tree. 1877. III. 341.[2]
Sibru. Iets over meïkevers. 1874. IV. 203.
Sibson, A. Beginselen der landbouw-scheikunde. 1859. III. 37.[1]
Sibthorp, Johannes. Flora graeca. 1806. I. 448.[2]
— Flora oxoniensis. 1794. I. 396.
— Florae graecae prodromus. 1806. I. 448.[2]
Siburgh, G. Pepercultuur in de Tamiangsche landschappen. 1888. III. 343.[1]
Sicard, Adrien. Études sur l'huile antiphylloxérique Alexis-Roux. 1883. III. 573.
— Études sur l'introduction de l'Eucalyptus globulus. 1868. IV. 532.[2]
Sicherer, Johann Conrad Ludwig. Over santaline. 1878. III. 485.[2]
Sicily — Annali civili del regno delle due Sicilie. See ANNALI . . . I. 24.[2]
Sicily — Reale istituto d' incoraggiamento di agricoltura. See REALE . . . III. 23.[2]
Sicily — Società di acclimazione e di agricoltura. See SOCIETÀ . . . III. 23.[2]
Sick. Om Plantning og Saaning af Fyr i Campinen. 185.? IV. 472.

Sickenberger, Ernest. Les plantes égyptiennes d'Jbn el Bei-thar. 1890. I. 489.
Sickesz, C. J. In zake de Veluwsche bosschen. 1883. IV. 356.[2]
Sickler, Friedrich Karl Ludwig. Allgemeine Geschichte der Obstkultur. 1802. III. 32.[2]
Sickler, Johann Volkmar. Om Bladenes Afplukning. 1803. III. 183.[1]
— Der deutsche Obstgärtner. 1794. III. 70.
— Gartenhandlexikon für Unerfahrne. 1811. III. 31.
— Des Kurfürsten August von Sachsen Künstliches Obstgar-tenbüchlein. 1802. III. 136.
— Der vollkommene Orangerie-Gärtner. 1815. II. 401,[1] III. 496.[2]
Sickmann, Johann Rudolf. Enumeratio stirpium ... circa Hamburgum. 1836. I. 379.
Sidka ... See Сидка ...
Sidorof, M. Der gemeine Lerchenbaum als Baumaterial. See Сидоровъ, M. 1871. IV. 452.[1]
— See also Сидоровъ, M.
Sidorof, V. See Сидоровъ, B.
Sie-Ance. Een reisje van Salatiga naar Tebing-Tinggi. 1893. III. 276.[1]
Siebdrat, G. A. See HELD, G. F. & SIEBDRAT, G. A.
Siebeck, Rudolf. Die Verwendung der Blumen und Ge-sträuche. 1860. III. 201.
Siebenbürgischer Karpathen-Verein. Jahrbuch. I. 28.[1]
Siebenbürgischer Verein für Naturwissenschaften. Ver-handlungen. I. 28.[1]
Sieber, Franz Wilhelm. Herbarium florae aegyptiacae. 1820. I. 487.
— Herbarium florae creticae. 1820. I. 451.
— Neue und seltene Gewächse. 1822. II. 376.[2]
— Reise nach der Insel Kreta. 1823. I. 451.
— Reise von Cairo nach Jerusalem. 1823. I. 513.
Siebert, August. Ueber Caryota maxima. 1893. III. 321.[1]
— Herrliche Medinilla. 1897. III. 638.[2]
— Der japanische Lackbaum. 1897. III. 528.[2]
— Laportea gigas Wedd. 1900. III. 382.[1]
— Der Palmengarten zu Frankfurt a/M. 1895. III. 28.[1]
— See also VOSS, Andreas & SIEBERT, A.
Siebod, Carl Theodore von. Ueber Cecidomyia saliciperda. 1853. IV. 487.[2]
Siebold, Philipp Franz von. Aardrijks- en volkenkundige toelichtingen tot de ontdekkingen van M. G. Vries. 1858. I. 462.
— Anbau und Bereitung des Thees auf Japan. 1832. III. 601.[2]
— Beschrijving van ... nieuw ingevoerde heesters. 1845. I. 293.
— Catalogue raisonné. 1863. III. 28.[1]
— Coloration des plantes. 1864. I. 185.[2]
— Einige Worte über den Zustand der Botanik auf Japan. 1829. I. 81,[2] II. 240.[2]
— Erwiederung auf W. H. de Vriese's Abhandlung: Het gezag van Kaempfer. 1837. II. 209.[2]
— Sur l'état de l'horticulture au Japon. 1863. III. 127.[2]
— Flora japonica. 1826. I. 461, V. xxIII.[2]
— Kruidkundige naamlijst van ... Japansche en Chineeschè planten. 1844. I. 51.[1]
— Nippon. 1832. III. 601.[2]
— Plaat-verklaring. 1846. III. 703.[1]
— Synopsis Hydrangeae generis specierum japonicarum. 1829. II. 240.[2]
— Synopsis plantarum oeconomicarum universi-regni japonici. 1830. III. 91.[2]
— Tabulae synopticae usus plantarum. 1827. III. 56.
— & Vriese, W. H. de. Chaenomeles japonica var. umbili-cata. 1848. II. 258.[2]
— & Zuccarini, J. G. Florae japonicae familiae naturales. 1843. I. 462, V. xxIII.[1]
— — Icones et descriptiones Hydrangearum. 1835. II. 240.[2]
— — Plantarum quas in Japonia collegit Dr. Ph. Fr. de Sie-bold, genera nova. 1843. I. 462.
— & Co. Naamlijst van Oost-Indische en bepaaldelijk Ja-vaansche gewassen. 1844. I. 51.[1]
— — Eene nieuwe Japansche Abrikoos. 1853. III. 438.[2]
— — Prijslijst voor 1845. 1844. I. 51.[2]
— — Verslag vanwege de kweekerij van von Siebold & Comp. 1844. I. 51.[2]
Sieboldia. III. 15.
Sieck, Willy. Die schizolysigenen Secretbehälter. 1895. I. 135, V. xI.[1]
— Die schizolysigenen Sekretbehälter, vornehmlich tropischer Heilpflanzen. 1894. I. 135.

Siedhof, Carl. Allmäliges Entarten einiger Baumfrüchte. 1878. I. 249.[1]
— Die baumartige Heidelbeere. 1877. III. 663.[1]
— Ueber das Beschneiden der gefüllt blühenden Mandel- und Pfirsichbäume. 1880. III. 430.[2]
— Ein Birnbaum ... der viermal in einem Sommer blühte. 1879. II. 280.[1]
— Cercis japonica. 1877. III. 472.[1]
— Coverings for wounds of trees. 1875. III. 180.[2]
— Lagerströmia indica. 1879. III. 629.[2]
— Ein Malus spectabilis, welcher um Weihnachten ... blühte. 1879. II. 268.[1]
— Vermehrung der Exochorda. 1876. III. 424,[1] 496.[1]
Siedler, (Dr.). Die Kultur des Kampherbaums. 1898. III. 404.[1]
Siedler, Paul. Ueber den radialen Saftstrom in den Wurzeln. 1892. I. 166.
— & Waage, Th. Proportion de cendres fournies par le kamala. 1891. III. 520.[2]
Siefvert, Johannes Victor. De esculentorum e regno vege-tabili. 1762. III. 219.[1]
Siegert. Beiträge zur schlesischen Flora. 1850. II. 101.[2]
Siegert, Hugo. Bemerkungen über die Anlage von Fichten-saatbeeten. 1862. IV. 150.
Siegesbeck, Johann Georg. Botanosophiae verioris brevis sciagraphia. 1737. I. 250.
— Primitiae florae petropolitanae. 1736. I. 41.
— Vaniloquentiae botanicae specimen. 1741. I. 250.
Siegfried, J. J. Die Pflanzen in ihrer Anwendung auf Forst-und Landwirthschaft. 1840. III. 52.
— Der schweizerische Jura. 1851. I. 434.
Siegler von Eberswald. Naphtha als Schutzmittel gegen das Verbeissen. 1882. IV. 196.[2]
Siegling. See KOCH, Karl & SIEGLING; MOSCHKOWITZ & SIEGLING.
Siehe, Walter. Grewia parviflora Bge. 1889. III. 585.[1]
— Die Nadelhölzer des Cilicischen Taurus. 1897. II. 16.[1]
— Shepherdia argentea Nutt. 1889. III. 629.[1]
— Der Weinstock im Hausgarten. 1896. III. 553.[1]
Siehr, Robert. De cortice radicis Granati. 1829. III. 630.[2]
Siélain, R. Atlas de poche des plantes des champs. 1894. I. 535.
Siemens, W. Aplicaciones de la electricidad á la horticul-tura. 1882. IV. 67.[1]
Siemers, C. L. Trädgårdsskötsel i ekonomiskt afseende. 1844. III. 119.[2]
Siemiątkowski, Piotr. Ogrodnictwo, porządkiem alfabetu ułożone. 1821. III. 31.
Siemiradzki, Józef. Puszcza Bialowieska. 1885. I. 364.
— ... z wycieczki w Góry S-to Krzyskie. 1887. I. 365.
Siemoni, Giovanni Carlo. Dei boschi nella provincia di Roma. See Della INFLUENZA ... 1884. IV. 48.[1]
— Die Eukalyptus-Kultur in Italien. 1879. IV. 532.[2]
— La legge forestale ed i suoi oppositori. 1872. IV. 44.
— Manuale teorico-pratico d'arte forestale. 1864. IV. 109.[2]
— Relazione sul boschi ed i loro prodotti ... all' Esposi-zione di Vienna. 1873. IV. 21.[2]
— Relazione sulla silvicoltura. 1868. IV. 20.[1]
— & Devincenzi. I prodotti forestali all' Esposizione uni-versale di Parigi. 1866. IV. 20.[1]
Siemssen, Adolph Christian. Naturgeschichte der grossen Tannenraupe. 1794. IV. 475.
— Naturgeschichte des Hausschwammes. 1809. IV. 414.[2]
— Über die sicherste Befestigung ... der Dünen zu Warne-münde. 1805. IV. 145.
Siena — Laboratorio botanico della R. Università. See LABORATORIO : .. I. 25.
Siena — Reale università degli studi ... See REALE ... I. 26.[1]
Sienikasvit metsän vihollisina. 1893. IV. 212.
Siennicki, K. See DZIARKOWSKI, H. A. & SIENNICKI, K.
Siennik, Marcin. Herbarz. 1568. I. 281.
Sierakowski, v. Skizzirte forstliche Beschreibung der ... Pless'schen Forst-Reviere. 1856. IV. 352.
— & Linz, T. Ueber Mäusefrass an Lärchen. 1858. IV. 197.[2]
Sierra club. Bulletin. I. 7.[1]
En la sierra de España. 1892. IV. 547.[1]
Sierstorpff, Caspar Heinrich von. Die Beschreibung der Fichte. 1813. IV. 457.
— Die Eiche. 1796. IV. 504.
— Einige Bemerkungen über die in dem Winter 1788 und 1789 verfrorenen Bäume. 1790. IV. 191.[1]

— Ueber einige Insektenarten . . . den Fichten vorzüglich schädlich. ·1794· IV. 455.
— Ueber forstmässige Erziehung . . . der vorzüglichsten inländischen Holzarten. 1796. IV. 105.
Siesmayer, Josef. Araucaria imbricata. 1898. III. 299.[1]
— Cassia floribunda. 1899. III. 471.[1]
— Sequoia (Wellingtonia) gigantea. 1898. III. 310.[2]
Siesmayer, Joseph A. Die japanischen Ahorn-Arten. 1888. III. 535.[2]
Sieule. Wijze om de boomen . . . te snoeijen. 1813. III. 440.[1]
Sieulle. Fait de physiologie végétale. 1828. I. 207,[1] III. 535.[1]
Sieurin, J. Berättelse öfver en botanisk resa i Norra Halland. 1844. I. 354.
— & Thedenius, K. F. Handbibliothek i trädgårds-skötseln. 1842. III. 100.[2]
Sieuve, Lazare. Mémoire et journal d'observations . . . de garantir les Olives de la piqûre des insectes. 1769. III. 674.[2]
— Osservazioni ed esperienze sulle maniere di preservare le Ulive dal guasto dei vermi. 1769. III. 674.[1]
Sieveking, Albert Forbes. Gardens ancient and modern. 1899. III. 32.[2]
Sievers, Johann. Briefe aus Sibirien. 1796. I. 453.[1]
Sievers, T. Virkeligt Udbytte af et med Naaletræ tilcultiveret. 1848. IV. 442.
Siewert. Unempfindlichkeit der Ahornwurzeln gegen Gas. 1891. III. 185.[3]
Siewert, M. Zur Kenntniss der Korksubstanz. 1867. II. 140.[3]
Siewert, Max. Tanning materials of South America. 1878. III. 237.[2]
Siezd . . . See Съѣздъ . . .
Siezd (VII.-VIII.) Russkich estestvoispitatelei. See Съѣздъ (VII.-VIII.) Русскихъ естествоиспытателей. I. 519.[2]
Sigaud. Note sur deux espèces de cire végétale du Brésil. 1844. III. 225, 321.[1]
Sigel. Ueber Buchenballenpflanzung. 1879. IV. 495.
— Die Verjüngung der Buchen-Hochwaldungen. 1878. IV. 495.
Sigismund, Reinhold. Die Aromata in ihrer Bedeutung für Religion. 1884. I. 511.
Sigmond, George Gabriel. On the bark of the Ulmus campestris. 1838. III. 365.[2]
— Tea, its effects, medicinal and moral. 1839. III. 606.
Signoret, Victor. Essai sur les cochenilles. 1868. I. 214.[1]
— Observations sur les points . . . au sujet des espèces connues du genre Phylloxera. 1874. III. 567,[1] IV. 610.
— Du phylloxera et de son évolution. 1873. III. 565.[2]
— Phylloxera vastatrix. 1869. III. 564.[2]
— Quelques observations à propos des espèces du genre Phylloxera. 1874. III. 567.[2]
Signorini, Carlo. Ricordi intorno ai boschi . . . di Arezzo. 1888. IV. 364;
Siguier, L. Un árbol indicador de la lluvia. 1890. IV. 520.[2]
Sigwart, Georg Friedrich. Dissertatio . . . sistens historiam corticis peruv. See UHLAND, G. I. J. 1782. III. 720.
— De insectis coleopteris, nec non de plantis. See KOELREUTER, J. G. 1755. II. 460,[1] 703.[1]
Sihiwald near Zürich. 1900. IV. 367.
Sihoo, Kitasawa. Yama-mayu kai-foo hiden. 1864. IV. 501.[3]
Sijp, J. van der. Cocaine, oorsprong, geschiedenis. 1885. III. 493.[1]
Sijpesteijn, C. A. van. Gebruik van West-Indische houtsoorten. 1858. IV. 524.[2]
— Over het Mambarklakhout. 1858. IV. 529.[1]
Silander, Johan. Beskrifning på Caffe-trädet i Suriname. 1757. II. 814,[1] III. 729.[1]
Silantef, Anatoli A. See Силантьевъ, А. А.
Silber, P. See CIAMICIAN & SILBER, P.
Der Silberbaum des Orientes und Occidentes. 1857. III. 628,[2] 629.[1]
Silbermann, Maximilian Joseph Anton von. Praktische Verfassung einiger Forsttabellen. 1785. IV. 95.
Silberschlag, Joseph Esaias. Klosterbergische Versuche in der Naturlehre. 1768. IV. 385.[1]
— Lettre à Mr. M.*** sur les expériences faites à Schöneiche sur un tronc d'arbre. 1773. IV. 385.[1]
— Nachricht von einigen zu . Schöneiche angestellten Versuchen. 1773. IV. 385.[1]
Siler, A. L. Beautiful shrubs of s[outhern] Utah. 1876. III. 629.[1]
— Culture of Cactuses. 1885. III. 619.

Silesia—Forst-Section für Mähren und. Schlesien. See FORST-SECTION . . . IV. 8.
Silfverstråhle, Gustaf. Bestämning af blad och knoppars divergence. 1838. I. 102.
— Om blads . . . ställning å växters yta. 1839. I. 102.
Silhol, Félix. Funestes effets du déboisement. 1891. IV. 47.[1]
— Les Orangers . . . dans l'Hérault. 1886. III. 500.[1]
Silipranti, Giovanni. Contribuzione alla flora dei dintorni di Noto. 1887. I. 429.
Silk. 1881. III. 148.[3]
The Silk Cotton-tree. 1890. II. 530.[1]
The Silk culturist and farmer's manual. III. 8.
Silk farming. See LONG, E. C. 1884. III. 378.
The Silk grower and farmer's manual. III. 8.
Silkworm culture. 1865. IV. 501.[2]
Silkworm Thorn. 1888. III. 368.[2]
Sillén, Nicolaus Jacobus. Flora paroeciae Bränkyrka. 1827. I. 353.
Sillevoldt, H. E. T. van. Derrid en pacchyrhizid. 1899. III. 475,[1] 483.[1]
Silliman, Benjamin & others. American journal of science and arts. See AMERICAN . . . I. 4.[3]
Sitemann, Johann Rudolph. De cortico Winterano. 1711. III. 397.[2]
Silva, A. J. de OLIVEIRA E. See OLIVEIRA E SILVA, A. J. de.
Silva, Ercole, conte. Dell' arte dei giardini inglesi. 1801. III. 201.
Silva, Francisco Manuel BARROSA DA. See BARROSA DA SILVA, F. M.
Silva, João José CERNEIRO DA. Estudos agricolas. 1872. III. 757.[2]
Silva, Johannes Baptista. An senibus Thé? 1712. III. 605.
Silva, S. J. FERREIRA DA. See FERREIRA DA SILVA, S. J.
Silva Coutinho. Note sur un nouveau médicament . . . le Jaborandi. 1874. III. 505.[1]
Silva-Coutinho, João Martino da. Ueber die Uarauá. 1869. III. 539.[2]
Silva Lisboa, Balthazar da. Riqueza do Brasil em madeiras. 1823. IV. 398.[1]
Silva Telles, Vicente, COELHO DE SEABRA. See COELHO DE SEABRA SILVA TELLES, Vicente.
Silvano. L' industria forestale all' Esposizione . . . di Torino. 1899. IV. 20.[2]
Silver, Alexander. Outlines of elementary botany. 1865. I. 90.
The Silver Fir. 1884. II. 24.[1]
The Silver Fir at Roseneath. 1887. II. 24.[1]
The Silver Maple. 1891. II. 480.[3]
Silvester. Mahoniecultuur. 1885. III. 513.[1]
Silvestre, Armand. Le bois sacré. 1897. IV. 547.[2]
Silvestre, de. Rapport fait . . . sur l'état . . . du domaine royale et rural de Grignon. 1827. IV. 359.[3]
Silvestri, Orazio & Tornabene, Francesco. Malattia degli Agrumi. 1874. III. 498.[1]
Silvicola, (pseud.). Eenige beschouwingen omtrent het boschwezen in Nederlandsch-Indië. 1879. IV. 376.[3]
— Nog iets over de vraag of . . . een exploitatie der Djatibosschen door den staat. 1880. IV. 537.[1]
Silvio. Accroissement des Chênes de taillis sous futaie. 1891. IV. 140.
— Alternance, mélange et substitution des essences. 1890. IV. 140.
— Une cause de détérioration des arbres de réserve. 1889. IV. 192.[1]
— Le Coignassier. 1898. III. 423.[1]
— L'évolution en forêt. 1893. IV. 67.[2]
— Forest soil. 1894. IV. 70.
— Gelées printanières. 1898. IV. 54.
— La grêle et les forêts. 1898. IV. 54.
— Une invasion de Chrysomyxa abietis. 1896· IV. 457.
— Une nouvelle maladie cryptogamique du Sapin. 1897. IV. 445.
— Le Pin de Salzmann. 1899. IV. 466.[2]
— La terre sous bois. 1894. IV. 70, 543.[3]
— De l'utilisation des pineraies en Bourgogne. 1892. IV. 192.[1]
Silvius. Des matières tannantes. 1863. IV. 435.
— De la production des gommes et résines. 1863. III. 227.
Sim, J. D. Cinchona cultivation in the Madras presidency. 1867. III. 714.
Sim, John. Botany of Scotston Moor. 1868. I. 402.
Sim, Thomas Robertson. Sketch and check-list of the flora of Kaffraria. 1894. I. 495.

Šimáček, Josef. České vinařství. 1880. III. 558.²
— O vinařství Českém po 16 tileté zkušenosti. 1886. III. 558.²

Simbald. Bois des colonies françaises. 1862. IV. 19.²
— Essences forestières de la Norwége. 1863. IV. 79.¹
— Exploitation du Liége en Algérie. 1862. IV. 517.²
— Exploitation du Liége en Gascogne. 1863. IV. 517.²
— Exposition universelle de 1862 à Londres, produits forestiers. 1863. IV. 19.²

Šimek, František. Křovité rostliny vedené do stromečků. 1889. III. 204.¹

Simi, Emilio. Flora Alpium versiliensium. 1851. I. 427.

Simirenko, Léon. Chaenomeles japonica var. Simirenkiana. 1888. III. 420.¹
— Jardinage et commerce des fruits en Crimée. 1893. III. 135.
— *See also* Симиренко, Л. П.

Simkovics, (*afterwards* Simonkai). *See* SIMONKAI, Lajos.

Simla naturalist's society. Journal. I. 29.¹

Simler, J. Jacob. Dissertationes physicae de itineribus per Helvetiam. *See* SCHINZ, Salomon. 1781. III. 271.²

Simler, Josias. Vallesiae descriptio libri duo. 1574. I. 432.²

Simler, Rudolph Theodor. Botanischer Taschenbegleiter des Alpenclubisten. 1871. I. 436, 535.³

Simmen, Johann Friedrich. Der rationelle Obstbau in Garten und Feld. 1866. III. 145.³

Simmer, W. Trauer-Lärche. 1829. II. 33.¹

Simmonds, Edward J. L. West African woods. 1866. IV. 401.¹

Simmonds, Peter Lund. L'Aloès: 1873. III. 333.²
— The Betel-nut of commerce. 1862. III. 320.¹
— Botany Bay, or Grass tree gum. 1866. III. 339.¹
— Cedrela odorata. 1874. IV. 525.²
— Coffee and Chicory, their culture. 1864. III. 739.
— The colonial exhibition; the Cocoanut Palm. 1886. III. 324.¹
— The commercial products of the vegetable kingdom. 1854. III. 217.
— Conservations du Cocotier de mer. 1880. II. 71.ᵇ.
— The culture and trade of Sumach. 1864. III. 526.¹
— The economic use of barks. 1889. IV. 436.¹
— The economic uses of leaves. 1863. III. 218.² — 1891. III. 219.¹
— Edible Cacti. 1875, 1884. III. 620.²
— Essbare Cacteen. 1884. III. 620.²
— The fibres of commerce. 1865. III. 234.
— Fragrant woods. 1872. III. 226.²
— The furniture woods of commerce. 1863. IV. 426.²
— The hard woods of commerce. 1864. IV. 396.¹
— On Indian fibres suited for the paper maker. 1864. III. 235.²
— On Japanese paper. 1864. III. 367.²
— Das Jarrahholz. 1886. IV. 534.¹
— The medicinal plants of Australia. 1854. III. 282.²
— On the Myrica. 1854. III. 353.¹
— The myrobalans of commerce. 1862. III. 632.²
— Notes on Kittool fibre. 1862. III. 234, 321.³
— On nuts, their produce and uses. 1872. III. 220.¹
— Oils and fats shown at the International exhibition. 1863. III. 224.²
— Past, present and future sources of the timber supplies of Great Britain. 1885. IV. 405.¹
— Produits médicinaux de l'Australie. 1873. III. 636.
— Report on the products of forest cultivation. 1867. IV. 20.¹
— Sandal wood. 1892. III. 384.²
— Sandal wood and oil. 1895. III. 384.¹
— Saponaceous plants. 1871. III. 540.¹
— Science and commerce. 1871. III. 218.²
— Some economic uses of nuts. 1864. III. 220.¹
— The supply of turpentine and resin. 1865. IV. 463.¹.
— The Teak forests of India. 1885. IV. 537,³ 538.¹
— On the trade in Cork bark. 1864. IV. 518.¹
— The trade in logwood. 1864. IV. 521.²
— The trade in nuts. 1863. III. 220.¹.
— Tropical agriculture. 1877. III. 96.¹
— Turpentine & rosin. 1862. IV. 462.²
— Varieties of sugar. 1861. III. 220.²
— Vegetable wax from the Candleberry myrtle. 1854. III. 353.¹
— Wohlriechende Hölzer. 1872. III. 226.²
— Wood-pulp for paper. 1866. IV. 420.

Simmons, Herman Gustaf. Några botaniska iakttagelser från östra Schleswig-Holstein. 1894. I. 389.

Simmons, W. J. A contribution to the study of the Mango weevil. 1890. III. 525.¹

Simon, Charles. Multiplication . . . des Phyllocactus. 1900. III. 625.²

Simon, Eduard. Ueber die Blätter des Kirschlorbeerbaumes. 1839. III. 431.¹
— Sur le principe actif de l'écorce de la racine de Sureau. 1839. III. 752.¹
— Ueber den wirksamen Bestandtheil der Wurzelrinde des Flieders. 1839. III. 752.¹

Simon, Eugène. Sur les conditions de végétation du Gui. 1890. II. 180.¹
— Sur un envoi d'animaux et de végétaux du Japon. 1862. III. 273.²
— *See also* FOUCAUD, Julien & SIMON, Eugène.

Simon, Friedrich. Beiträge zur . . . Anatomie der Epacridaceae und Ericaceae. 1890. II. 658,² 688.¹

Simon, G. Beiträge zur Geschichte des deutschen Jagd- und Forstwesens im Mittelalter. 1865. IV. 25.
— Die Forst- und Waldordnungen des 16., 17. und 18. Jahrhunderts in Deutschland. 1867. IV. 25, 298.²
— Zur Geschichte des deutschen Jagd- und Forstwesens im Mittelalter. 1863. IV. 25.

Simon, G. Eugène. Ueber Bannforste. 1861. IV. 180.¹
— Le Pin Pei-go-song de Chine. 1863. II. 39.²

Simon, Heinrich. Das Forst- und Jagd-Recht von Schlesien. 1848. IV. 320.

Simon, Johann Eduard. Ueber den flüssigen Storax. 1839. III. 417.²
— Sur le Styrax liquide. 1839. III. 417.²

Simon, Léon. L'Abricot-Pêche de Nancy. 1890. III. 441.¹
— Nomenclature de tous les noms de Roses. 1899. III. 451.¹

Simon-Favier. Note sur les Tilleuls de l'avenue Serpenoise. 1874. III. 585.¹
— Notice sur la culture des arbres d'avenue. 1862. III. 209.

Simon Januensis. Incipit Clavis sanationis per . . . Simonem Jahuensem. 1300. I. 275,¹ III. 239.
— Simonis Januensis opusculum cui nomen Clavis sanationis. 1300. I. 275,¹ III. 239.
—— . . . Synonyma medicinae. 1300. I. 275,¹ III. 239.

Simon-Louis, frères. Les Aucuba. 1870. III. 645.¹
— Crataego-mespilus. 1899. III. 421.¹
— Crataego-mespilus Dardari. 1899. III. 421.¹
— Guide pratique de l'amateur de fruits. 1876. III. 144. — 1895. III. 72.

Simonde, Jean Charles Léonard. Gemälde der toskanischen Landwirthschaft. 1801. III. 126.²
— Tableau de l'agriculture toscane. 1801. III. 126.²

Simonds, A. B. & others. Catalogue of the . . . plants of Fitchburg. 1885. I. 315.
—— "Flora of Fitchburg and vicinity." 1885. I. 315.

Simonds, Ossian C. The Pepperidge tree, or Nyssa. 1893. III. 632.¹
— The use of Poplars in landscape work. 1893. III. 344.²

Simonet. Notice sur les principaux bois des colonies françaises. ·1893. IV. 19.¹

Simonett. Drahtseilriese über die Viamala. 1899. IV. 392.

Simonetti, Michele. Dello intervento governativo in materia di boschi. 1866. IV. 285.²
— Della produzione . . . del legname nella Calabria. 1872. IV. 405.²

Simonetti, Tommaso. The Carob. 1879. III. 471.²
— La Carruba. 1879. III. 471.²
— Le Carrube. 1879. III. 471.²
— Ceratonia Siliqua, the Carob tree. 1879. III. 471.²

Simonin, L. Les Cèdres géants de la Californie. 1861. II. 50.³

Simonis, Ludwig. Žur Hügelpflanzung. 1878. III. 166.

Simonkai, Lajos. Az Abies génusznak és fajainak magyar nevei. 1888. II. 21.³
— Aradmegye és Aradváros növényvilága. 1893. I. 446.
— Aradmegye három érdekessége. 1887. II. 134,² 463.³
— Bánsági és hunyadmegyei utazásom. 1878. I. 446.
— Bemerkungen zur Flora von Ungarn. 1888. I. 446.
— Enumeratio florae transsilvanicae vesculosae [sic] critica. 1886. I. 446.
— Erdély edényes flórájának helyesbitett foglalata. 1886. I. 446.
— Hazánk és a földkerekség Hársfajainak biráló átnézete. 1888. II. 515.¹
— Hazánk Tölgyfajai és Tölgyerdei. 1890. II. 130.²
— Jurányi Hársfa. 1888. II. 517.²
— A magyar erdők Hársai. 1888. II. 515.²

— Magyarország és környékének zanótjai. Cytisi Hungariae. 1888. II. 349.²
— Nagyváradnak és vidékének növényvilága. 1890. I. 446.
— Néhány középmagyarországi növényről. 1878. I. 446.
— Oshonos és termesztett Szilfáink fajai. 1898. II. 143.¹
— Quercus Haynaldiana. 1883. II. 130.¹
— Revisio Tiliarum hungaricarum. 1888. II. 515.¹
— Ueber Rosa reversa W. K. 1883. II. 298.¹
— Tilia Braunii n. sp. 1886. II. 517.¹
— Tilia Haynaldiana Simk. és tizszirmu Hársfáink. 1887. II. 515.²
— Tölgyfáink alapos ösmeretének gyakorlati fontossága. 1891. IV. 501.¹
— Uj alakok hazai Tölgyfajaink közt. 1887. II. 130.²
— Uj növények leirásai. 1877. I. 446.
— Ujdonságok hazánk flórájából. 1889. I. 446.
Simons, Elizabeth A. Comparative studies on the rate of circumnutation. 1898. I. 196.²
Simonsen, CEDERFELT DE. See CEDERFELT DE SIMONSEN.
Simony, Friedrich. Beitrag zur Kunde der obersten . . . Baumgrenze in Westtirol. 1870. I. 442.
— Fragmente zur Pflanzengeographie des österreichischen Alpengebietes. 1853. I. 440.
— Das Pflanzenleben der afrikanischen Wüsten. 1881. I. 495.
— Schutz dem Walde! 1877. IV. 177.¹
— Die Vegetationszonen der Alpen. 1876. I. 436.
Simony, Oscar. Analytische Untersuchungen über den Zusammenhang . . . Stammformen mit ihren Formzahlen. 1877. IV. 217.
— Ueber einige allgemeine für die Holzmesskunde belangreiche Cubirungsformeln. 1876. IV. 217.
— Ueber das Problem der Stammcubirung. 1879. IV. 217.
Simounet, P. Importation de la cochenille à Alger. 1843. III. 624.¹
A simple tree-measurer. 1889. IV. 216.
Simpson, James H. Report of explorations across the Great Basin of the territory of Utah. See ENGELMANN, George. 1876. I. 324.
Simpson, John. The Deodar as a forest tree. 1897. IV. 448.¹
— English and Scotch woods. 1900. IV. 121.
— German woods — German forestry. 1897. IV. 119.¹
— Height growth in plantations. 1899. IV. 65.¹
— Planting forest trees; density. 1900. IV. 154.²
— Quick fruit culture. 1900. III. 142.
— Rotation in forestry. 1900. IV. 74.²
— Second crop of Oak. 1897. IV. 508.
— The treatment of game preserves. 1900. IV. 136.²
— The utilisation of land . . . by planting with forest trees. 1895. IV. 161.¹
Simpson, John M. Osier culture. 1898. III. 349.
Sims, John, (ed.). See BOTANICAL magazine. I. 17.
Simson, Augustus. Notes on a species of Zieria new to Tasmania. 1882. II. 413.¹
— On recent additions to the flora of Tasmania. 1880. I. 506.¹
Sin nombre. 1892. IV. 553.²
Sinä, IBN-. See IBN-SINÄ.
Sinai, Friedrich. Die Clematis als Treibsträucher. 1891. III. 389.²
Sinclair, George. Hortus ericaeus woburnensis. 1825. II. 664.¹ See also FORBES, James. 1825. III. 649.²
— Useful and ornamental planting. 1832. III. 106.³
Sinclair, Mrs. Isabella. Indigenous flowers of the Hawaiian Islands. 1885. I. 509.²
Sinclair, Sir John. L'agriculture pratique et raisonnée. 1817. III. 35.
— The code of agriculture. 1817. III. 35.
— Grundgesetze des Ackerbaues. 1817. III. 35.
— Kodeks rolnictwa i zarazem uwagi dotyczące ogrodów. 1817. III. 35.
Sinclair, W. F. A branching Areca-nut Palm. 1889. II. 64.²
— Nux-vomica. 1894. III. 720.²
Sind die Eiben in der Mark noch wild? 1899. II. 11.²
Sind wechselnde Saatkämpe . . . vorzuziehen? 1854. IV. 150.
Sing-tsao-yo-sing-lu-yao. n. d. III. 237.²
Singapore — Forest department. See STRAITS SETTLEMENTS — FOREST DEPARTMENT. IV. 16.²
Singer, Carl. Bericht über die Gewinnung . . . des Schwarzföhrenharzes. 1873. IV. 466.²

Singer, J. Flora ratisbonensis. 1865. I. 385.
Singer, John W. Cactaceous plants. 1894. III. 620.¹
Singer, Max. Beiträge zur näheren Kenntnis der Holzsubstanz. 1882. I. 155.
Singer, Max (of Tournai). Dictionnaire des Roses. 1885. III. 450.
Singers, Rev. William. Barberry bushes in hedgerows. 1839. III. 395.¹
— Essay on converting to economical uses trees usually treated as brushwood. 1829. IV. 382.¹
Singh, BHAI SADHU. See BHAI SADHU SINGH.
Singh, MIAN MOTT. See MIAN MOTI SINGH.
Single, Christian. Abbildungen der . . . Traubensorten Württembergs. 1860. III. 546.
The single Kerria. 1877. III. 424.²
Single Roses. 1898. III. 457.¹
On a singular luminous property of wood. 1820. I. 154.
Sinning, Wilhelm. Ueber Cytisus Adami. 1858. II. 368.¹
— Mittheilungen über die Gipfelfäule der Pandanus. 1836.
— Waarneming eener merkwaardige bastaardvorming van een' gouden regen. 1860. II. 368.¹
— See also NEES VON ESENBECK, T. F. L. & SINNING, Wilhelm.
Sinobas, Manuel RICO Y. See RICO Y SINOBAS, Manuel.
Sinossi della condizione economica di alcune province d' Italia. 1863. IV. 277.
Sintenis, F. Forstinsecten der Ostseeprovinzen. 1900. IV. 205.²
Sintenis, Paul. Cypern und seine Flora. 1881. I. 452.
Sintzel, Joseph. Bemerkungen auf einer Forst-Reise durch Böhmen und Sachsen. 1835. IV. 355.¹ 370.
— Ueber das Durchforsten. 1852. IV. 173.
— Ueber das Ernähren . . . der Pflanzen. 1856. IV. 63.¹
— Etwas über den weissen Maulbeerbaum. 1828. IV. 519.¹
— Ueber den Holzzuwachs. 1833. IV. 232.
— Noch etwas über den Zustand der Kiefernwaldungen. 1836. IV. 471.
— Praktische Anleitung zum rationellen Holzbau. 1863. IV. 107.¹
— Ueber die Stockholznutzung. 1833. IV. 385.²
— Taschenbuch für Forstwirthe und Forsttaxatoren. 1828. IV. 216.
Sipière, Louis. Du mildew. 1895. III. 581.
Sir Henry Steuart's theory of transplantation. 1828. III. 122.²
Sira-kawa. Traité de l'éducation du vers à soie au Japon. 1868. III. 377.
Siragusa, Francesco Paolo Camillo. L' anestesia nel regno vegetale. 1879. I. 211.
— La clorofilla. 1879. I. 141.
— Sulle funzioni delle radici. 1874. I. 161.
Sirand, A. De l'oïdium dans le département de l'Ain. 1854. III. 576.
Siraux, A. De la disposition des feuilles de Pandanus. 1875. II. 57.¹
Sire, Eugène. Les Chênes du Jura. 1889. II. 130.²
— Le Groseiller des roches. 1867. II. 246.¹
— Présence au-dessus de Neuchâtel du Sorbus Aria × torminalis. 1892. II. 313.¹
— Rosier de Godet. Rosa Godeti. 1888. II. 294.¹
— Le Sorbier hybride. 1874. II. 313.¹
Sirodot, E. Maladies des arbres fruitiers. 1894. III. 179.
Sirrine, F. A. Notes on methods of cross-pollination. 1891. III. 50.¹
Sirvent, Melitón, ATIENZA Y. See ATIENZA Y SIRVENT, Melitón.
Sisal Hemp. 1892. III. 341.¹ — 1897. III. 341.¹
— Sisal Hemp in the Bahamas. 1894. III. 341.¹
— Sisal Hemp industry in Yucatan. 1892. III. 341.¹
Sisley, Jean. Camellias in Japan. 1878. III. 551.²
— Rusticité des Conifères. 1872. III. 292.
Sissû planting in the Gorakhpur forests. 1887. IV. 521.²
Sistema der natuurlyke historie. 1765. V. XIII.¹
Sistema historiae naturalis. See SISTEMA der natuurlyke historie. 1765. V. XIII.¹
Systematitcheski . . . See Систематическій . . .
Système d'histoire naturelle. See SISTEMA der natuurlyke historie. 1765. V. XIII.¹
Sur les systèmes de botanique. 1719. I. 250.
Sitenský, Franz. Phytopathologické poznámky. 1897. III. 40.²
Sitgreaves, L. Report of an expedition down the Zuñi and Colorado Rivers. See TORREY, John. 1853. I. 322.

Sitovski, N. See Оверинъ, A. & Ситовскій, H.
Situation forestière du canton de Lucerne. See FORSTLICHE Situation im Kanton Luzern. 1863. IV. 366.
Siuzef. See Сюзевъ.
Sivén, Albert. Grundsätze zur Berechnung des Höhenwachstums der Nadelhölzer. 1896. IV. 216.
Sivers, A. von. Dendrologische Mittheilungen über die Folgen des strengen Winters. 1889. III. 45.
Sivers, Jegor von. Drei merkwürdige Riesenbäume in Livland. 1864. I. 296.[1]
— Merkwürdige Bäume in Livland. 1865. I. 358.
Sivers, Max von. Ueber Naturalisation fremdländischer Holzarten. 1898. IV. 125.[1]
— Die pflanzengeographische Anlage in Roemershof. 1900. I. 521.[2]
— Ueber die Vererbung von Wuchsfehlern bei Pinus sylvestris L. 1895. IV. 474. — 1896. II. 48.[2]
— Versuch einer Anleitung zur Naturalisation von Forst- und Parkbäumen in Livland. 1889. III. 45.
— Verzeichniss der in Livland anbauwürdigen Gehölze. 1892. III. 68.[1]
Sjöborg, Harald. Novitiae florae suecicae. See FRIES, E. M. 1814. I. 352.
Sjögreen, C. M. Anteckningar under en resa i Tysklands. 1859. IV. 348.[2]
Sjögren, Gustaf. See LAGERHEIM, Carl & SJÖGREN, Gustaf.
Sjöstrand, Magnus Gustaf. Calmar Läns och Ölands flora. 1863. I. 356.
SK. Das Verschwinden der Weisstanne. 1866. IV. 444.[1]
Om **skadelige** Forstinsekter. See EIDE, F. C. 1857. IV. 205.[1] 442.
Skalitzky, Dan. J. W. De oleo Crotonis Tiglii. 1838. III. 517.[1]
Skal'kowski, A. A. Historische Uebersicht der Entwickelung des Gartenbaues. 1853. III. 33.[1]
Skalozubof, N. L. See Скалозубовъ, H. Л.
Skandinaviska halföns fanerogamer. See HARTMAN, Carl. 1864. I. 531.[1]
Skandinaviske Naturforskeres Møde. Forhandlinger. I. 9.[1]
Skårman, Johan Albert Otto. Om Alnus incana (L.) Willd. f. arcuata. 1889. II. 116.[2]
— Beiträge zur Entwicklungsgeschichte der Salixformationen. 1887. II. 100.[2]
— Bidrag till Salixformationernas utvecklingshistoria. 1887. II. 100.[2]
— Eine monströse Salix depressa × repens Brunner. 1888. II. 104.[1]
— En Salix depressa × repens. 1888. II. 106.[2]
— Om Salix hastata × repens. 1890. II. 107.[2]
— Ueber Salix hastata × repens. 1890. II. 107.[2]
— Ueber die Salixflora an den Ufern des Klarelfs. 1886. II. 100.[2]
— Om Salixfloran på Klarelfvens stränder. 1886. II. 100.[2]
— Om Salixvegetationen i Klarelfvens floddal. 1892. II. 100.[2]
Skeels, F. E. Present condition of Michigan forests. 1898. IV. 339.
Skeete, Thomas. Experiments . . . on quilled and red Peruvian bark. 1786. III. 720.
Skeleton leaves. 1862. I. 35.
Skell, Friedrich. Entwurf zu einer Verordnung . . . die Bepflanzung der Chausseen mit Bäumen betreffend. 1803. III. 209.
Skelton, C. Coffee-growing. 1898. III. 727.
Skepper, Edmund. See HENSLOW, J. S. & SKEPPER, Edmund.
Skertchly, S. B. J. See MILLER, S. H. & SKERTCHLY, S. B. J. A sketch of the vegetation of the Swan River colony. See LINDLEY, John. 1839. I. 500.
Sketches, civil and military. See STOCKDALE, J. J. 1811. III. 275.[2]
Skhedion nomou peri dasōn. See ΣΧΕΔΙΟΝ νόμου περὶ δασῶν.
Skimmias. 1886. III. 505.[2]
Skinner, Charles Rufus. Arbor day manual. 1890. IV. 42.[1]
Skinner, Stephen. Etymologicon botanicum. 1671. I. 73.[2]
Skinner, T. W. Description and strength of some of the Indian and Burman timbers. 1862. IV. 401.[1]
Skizze der Forstgeschichte des Preussischen Staats. 1833. IV. 25.
Skizze der Natur. 1800. I. 93.
Skizze einer vollkommnen Bewirthschaftung der Waldungen. 1801. IV. 117.
Skogs-styrelsens underdåniga berättelse. IV. 539.[1]

Skogsstyrelsens underdåniga memorial. 1877. IV. 344.[2]
Skokan, Josef. Zerstörung eines Erlenwaldes. 1853. IV. 489.[1]
Skórkowski, Kazimierz & Bielski, Władysł. Zdanie sprawy z Wystawy rolniczej krakowskiej; płody leśne. 1860. IV. 21.[1]
Skou-Forordning i Danmarck. 1680? IV. 296.[1]
Skov-Forordning udi Danmarck. 1687? IV. 296.[1] — 1710. IV. 315.[1] — 1733. IV. 296.[1]
Om **Skovreguleringens** rare Skat. See WINGE, P. 1889. IV. 245.
Skrobishevski, L. Recherches sur l'embryogénie des Papilionacées. 1885. II. 320.[2]
Skrobishevski, V. J. Ueber das Glasigwerden der Früchte. See Скробишевскій, В. Я. 1883. I. 528.[1]
— Ueber den Ursprung des Fadenapparates bei Viscum. See Скробишевскій, В. Я. 1883. II. 178.[1]
— See also Скробишевскій, В. Я.
Skurdal, Hans O. Beretning om stipendiereise i Danmark. 1892. III. 120.[1]
— Indberetning om en stipendiereise i Tyskland. 1894. III. 121.[2]
Slack, Henry James. A fungus in Teak. 1868. III. 697.[2]
— The Juniper fungus. 1871. III. 303.[1]
Slade, Avery P. . Forest tree planting. 1885. IV. 112.
Slade, H. Manufacture of cutch in Burma. 1886. III. 464.[1]
— Notes on girdling in Tharrawaddy. 1896. IV. 537.[2]
Slater, Andrew. Appliances used in forestry. 1880. IV. 176.[2]
— On the best size of plants, and methods of planting. 1884. IV. 153.[2]
— Hedges; as they are. 1883. III. 214.[1]
— Note on a wood damaged by gases. 1875. IV. 192.[2]
— Noxious gases versus vegetation. 1878. IV. 192.[2]
— The protection of river banks. 1882. IV. 185.[1]
— The rearing . . . of hardwood plantations. 1884. IV. 137.[2]
— On the tools used in forestry. 1881. IV. 176.[2]
— On the various modes of enclosing plantations. 1881. IV. 146.[2]
A **slaughtered giant.** 1890. II. 51.[1]
Slavíček, Fr. Josef. Beitrag zur Flora von Mähren. 1897. I. 444.
— Bestimmungstabellen zum ersten Studium der Weiden. 1892. II. 103.[1]
— Zur Kenntnis der Keimlinge zumeist fremdländischer Coniferen. 1899. IV. 444.[1]
— Die in Mitteleuropa cultivierten . . . Pinus-Arten. 1894. II. 38.[2]
— Morphologische Aphorismen über einige Coniferen-Zapfen. 1896. II. 20.[1]
— Tabel tot het determineeren der Pinus soorten. 1894. II. 38.[2]
— Tabellen zum ersten Studium der Weiden Böhmens. 1892. II. 103.[1]
Slavonia — Forst-Section der Landwirthschafts-Gesellschaft. See FORST-SECTION . . . IV. 8.
Sleeman, W. H. On the lac insect. 1839. III. 232.[2]
Sleen, N. van der. De anorg. bestanddeelen van kinabast. 1887. III. 723.
— Dubbel-alkaloiden (?) van kinine. 1887. III. 723.
— Kleine kinologische mededeelingen. 1887. III. 723.
Sleepers for Ceylon railways. 1896. IV. 424.[1]
Siendziński, A. Przyczynek do flory obwodów Tarnopolskiego. 1874. I. 442.
— Przyczynek do flory obwodu Kołomyjskiego. 1875. I. 442.
— Rośliny między rzecza Zbruczu i Seretu. 1878. I. 442.
— Rośliny z okolic Podola. 1877. I. 442.
— Wykaz roślin zebranych . . . Kołomyja. 1876. I. 442.
Slevogt, Johann Hadrian. Balsamum verum quod vulgo opobalsamum dicitur. 1705. III. 510.[2]
— De cinnamomo. 1707. III. 405.[2]
— De cortice Culilavan. 1705. III. 244.
— De opobalsamo. 1717. III. 510.[2]
— De Theá romaná et hungaricá. 1709. III. 605.
Slevogt, Karl. Beiträge zur Geschichte der Eichenkultur. 1804. IV. 504.
— Beiträge zur nähern Kenntniss der Natur des Thonbodens. 1807. IV. 68.
— Beiträge zur Naturgeschichte des Lerchenbaums. 1804. IV. 448,[2] 490.[1]
— Beleuchtung einiger Modeartikel aus der Physiologie. 1805. I. 146.

— Bemerkungen . . . über den Anbau . . . der italiänischen Pappel. 1807. IV. 486.[1]
— Bemerkungen über die in Zweifel gezogene Festigkeit unserer . . . Bauhölzer. 1804. IV. 409.
— Beobachtungen bei der Zergliederung einer Menge Baumwurzeln. 1804. I. 103.
— Beobachtungen . . . über abgeworfene grüne Zweige alter Eichen. 1804. IV. 509.
— Beobachtungen über den Fehler unserer Forstbäume. 1804. I. 107,[1] IV. 62,[1] 414.[1]
— Beobachtungen über den Graswuchs in Wäldern. 1804. IV. 438.[2]
— Beobachtungen über den Wurzelaustrieb verschiedener Baumzweige. 1804. IV. 65.[2]
— Beobachtungen über den Zustand der Esche . . . nach äussern Beschädigungen. 1804. IV. 535.[1]
— Beobachtungen . . . über die . . . abgetrennten jungen Zweigspitzen der Fichte. 1804. IV. 455.
— Beobachtungen über die Weissfäule. 1804. IV. 211.[1]
— Beobachtungen über Schlagholzanlagen. 1804. IV. 140.
— Betrachtungen . . . über Waldkulturanstalten. 1804. IV. 117.
— Erfahrungen . . . über den Anbau der Kiefer. 1804. IV. 471.
— Erfahrungen . . . über die . . . Heidereviere. 1804. IV. 65.
— Fragmentarische Bemerkungen über den Wachsthums-Prozess der jungen Buchen. 1807. IV. 493.[2]
— Fragmentarische Notizen aus dem Böhmer-Walde. 1804. IV. 370.
— Kleine Reisebemerkungen . . . Kulturgeschichte des Lerchenbaums. 1804. IV. 448.[2]
— Korbweiden-Kulturmethode. 1804. IV. 487.[1]
— Kurze Beschreibung der Reichsfreiherrlich von Marschalkischen Waldungen. 1804. IV. 370.
— Litterarische Nachweisung, die sogenannten Spiegelfasern . . . betreffend. 1804. IV. 62.[1]
— Nachricht von einigen Eichenpflanzungen des Herzogs von Portland. 1804. IV. 504.
— Nachtrag zu den Beobachtungen über die Drehsucht. 1804. IV. 62.[1]
— Notamina aus der Forstplantage zu Schwarzenberg. 1805. IV. 125.[1]
— Probe eines extrahirten Reise-Journals. 1804. IV. 368.
— Sammlung neuer Entdeckungen und Beobachtungen. 1804. IV. 61,[2] 63.[1]
— Tabella. Ueber den Zuwachs von zwölf Bäumen. 1804. IV. 64.[1]
— Ueber das Vermögen alter Baumstöcke . . . fort zu vegetiren. 1804. I. 192,[2] IV. 64,[1] 66.[1]
Sleskin, P. R. See Слескинъ, П. Р.
Slieptzof, Mrs. M. See Слѣпцова, М.
Slingerland, Mark Vernon. The Cherry fruit-fly. 1899. III. 433.[1]
— The cigar-case-bearer. 1895. III. 187.
— The codling-moth. 1898. III. 444.[2]
— The Currant-stem girdler. 1897. III. 415,[1] 457.[2]
— Emergency report on tent caterpillars. 1899. III. 188.[1]
— The Grape root-worm. 1900. III. 564.[2]
— The Grape-vine flea-beetle. 1898. III. 564.[1]
— Green fruit worms. 1896. III. 444.[2]
— The Peach-tree borer. 1899. III. 442.[1]
— The Pear Psylla. 1896. III. 433.[1]
— The pistol-case-bearer in western New York. 1897. III. 428.[2]
— A Plum scale in western New York. 1894. III. 433.[2]
— The Quince Curculio. 1898. III. 423.[2]
— Some new notions about some old insects. 1899. III. 188.[1]
— Wireworms and the bud moth. 1896. III. 428.[2]
Śliwka, Jan. Historya naturalna. 1865. I. 95.
Sloane, Hans. An account of a . . . feather of the bird cuntur and of the Coffee-shrub. 1695. II. 814.[2]
— An account of the true cortex Winteranus. 1693. III. 397.[2]
— An account of two plants . . . from the Cape of Good-Hope. 1693. I. 493.
— Catalogus plantarum . . . in insula Jamaica. 1696. I. 334.[1]
— A description of the Pimienta. 1691. I. 334.[1]
— Some observations . . . concerning some wonderful contrivances of nature in . . . plants in Jamaica. 1700. II. 173.[2]
— A . . . ag to the islands of Madera, Barbados. 1707. I. 334. voy e
— Wild Cinamon-tree. 1688. III. 613.[2]

Sloboda, Daniel. Rostlinníctivi. 1852. I. 269.
Sloet, L. A. J. W., baron. De planten in het Germaansche volksgeloof. 1890. I. 518.
Słósarski, Antoni. Mechanizm ruchów wywolywanych w pręcikach Berberysu. 1894. II. 202.[2]
— Palmy woskowe. 1890. III. 819.[2]
Slot, W. S. Uitroeijen van schadelijke insecten. 1856. III. 196.
Slowe, John. Mejicanische Pinus. 1844. II. 39.[1]
— Mexican Pines. 1844. II. 39.[1]
Sluiter, Carel Philip. Over eenige nieuwe . . . gevallen van aanpassing . . . van sommige dieren en planten. 1887. I. 235.[1]
Sluyter, H. F. G. Beiträge zur Kenntniss des antomischen Baues einiger Gnetum-Arten. 1899. II. 55.[1]
Sluyter, Hermann Alfred Arnold Friedrich. Untersuchungen über den Wassergehalt in den Laubblättern. 1900. I. 168.
Slym, M. J. Memorandum on jungle fires. 1877. IV. 184.[1]
Sm. Ein Beispiel von hohem Alter der Birke. 1844. II. 118.[2]
Smalian, H. L. Allgemeine Holzertrag-Tafeln. 1837. IV. 235.[1]
— Anleitung zur Untersuchung . . . des Waldzustandes. 1840. IV. 240.
— Baumhöhenmesser. 1840. IV. 213.
— Beiträge zur Forstwissenschaft. 1842. IV. 101.
— Beitrag für Untersuchung des Holzwachsthumganges. 1841. IV. 480.
— Beitrag zur Holzmesskunst. 1837. IV. 213.
— Buchenhochwaldbetrieb. 1846. IV. 497.
— Walzentafel zur Erleichterung der Holzmassenberechnung. 1846. IV. 213.
Small, Henry Beaumont. Canadian forests. 1884. IV. 337.[2]
— Vegetation in the Bermudas. 1898. I. 337.
Small, John Kunkel. An apparently undescribed species of Prunus. 1896. II. 274.[1]
— The genus Bumelia in North America. 1900. II. 697.[1]
— The genus Gaylussacia in the southern states. 1897. II. 671.[2]
— Morphological notes on the genus Brunnichia. 1894. II. 184.[1]
— Shrubs and trees of the southern states. 1897. I. 317,[2] IV. 77.[2]
— Some new hybrid Oaks from the southern states. 1895. I. 129.[1]
— Studies in North American Polygonaceae. 1898. II. 185.[1]
— Studies in the botany of the southeastern United States. 1894. I. 319.
— Undescribed species from the southern United States. 1896. I. 319.
— & Heller, A. A. On the flora of western North Carolina. 1897. I. 319.
Smallenburg, F. van Catz. See Catz Smallenburg, F. van.
Smart, Joseph. Valuations of timber a century ago. 1890. IV. 261.[2]
Smedt, Is. de. De la transplantation des arbres. 1890. III. 166.
— Over het verplanten der fruitboomen. 1869. III. 166.
Smedt, J. F. de. Beknopte handleiding . . . tot het aanleggen en onderhouden van boschen. 1878. IV. 119.[2]
Smedt, M. de. Beplanting der Belgische Kempen. 1881. IV. 160.[2]
Smee, Alfred. A brief sketch of the best varieties of fruits. 1876. III. 79.
— My garden. 1872. I. 55.
Smelovsky, T. Descriptiones plantarum rariorum horti imp. Academiae scientiarum petropolitanae. 1813. II. 78.[2]
Smet, J. M. de. Faut-il élaguer les grands arbres qu'on transplante? 1879. III. 170.
— Moet men de groote boomen snoeien. 1879. III. 170.
Smets, Gérard. La culture du Pin sylvestre. 1892. V. xxxii.[2]
— La fertilisation des sols forestiers. 1894. IV. 543.[2]
— Recherches sur les besoins nutritifs du Salix viminalis. 1895. III. 352.[2]
Smid, H. Johann. Handboek voor de kultuur . . . der Koffie. 1876. III. 726.[2]
— De landbouw in de bergstreken. 1872. III. 128.
— Liberia en andere Afrikaansche Koffie producten. 1882. III. 732.[2]
— Thurbers nieuw werk over Koffie. 1882. III. 727.
— Wat deert onze Koffieboomen? 1883. III. 735.

Smidth, Jens Hansen. Arboretum scandinavicum. 1831. I. 293,¹ 350,¹ *III. 66*,¹ *IV. 79*.¹
— Noget om Climatisering af fremmede Landes Planter. 1839. III. 43.
— Om den Skade . . . af Frosten. 1835. III. 182:
Smielovsky, Timotheus. Hortus petropolitanus. 1806. II. 804,¹ *869*.¹
Smieta . . . *See* Смѣта . . .
Smilax, Linnaeus, (*pseud*.). Sarsaparilla. 1854. III. 338.²
Smirnof, N. *See* Смирновъ, Н.
Smirnof, S. D. *See* Смирновъ, С. Д.
Smirnoff, Alexander. Handbok i finsk pomologi. 1894. III. 68.¹
— Fuuhedelmien viljelemisestä Suomessa sekä käytännöllisiä neuvoja vasta alkaville. 1893. III. 135.
— Suomen pomologuan käsikirja kirjoittanut. 1864. III. 68.¹
Smirnov, Mikhail. Deux essences caractéristiques pour la limite supérieure de la végétation arborescente. 1883. I. 368,¹ *IV. 80*.
— Enumération des espèces de plantes vasculaires du Caucase. 1884. I. 369.
— De corticum peruvianorum diversae speciei partibus. *See* PFAFF, C. H. 1813. III. 721.
Smissen, Hermanu v. d. De corticum peruvianorum diversae speciei partibus. *See* PFAFF, C. H. 1813. III. 721.
Smissen, J. van der. De zwarte vliegen. 1852. III. 189.
Smissen, J. P. J. van der. Pflanzen-Oratorium. 1834. I. 268.
Smit, J. De bastaardrups in de Bessen. 1879. III. 414.¹
Smith. Vegetable ivory, or Taqua plant. 1843. III. 330.¹
Smith. Sur l'Yaupon ou Thé de la Caroline. 1875. III. 531.²
Smith. *See* LUKER & SMITH.
Smith, A. T. Oil from the nut of the Terminalia. 1843. III. 632.²
Smith, Adolphe. The garden of Hyères. 1882. III. 125.
Smith, Alexander. On Aberdeenshire woods. 1874. IV. 358.²
— Notes on the principal plants employed in India. 1862. III. 92.³
— Opening of Palm spathes with an audible report. 1863. II. 63.²
— On the preparation of sugar . . . from Palms. 1856. III. 319.¹
Smith, Andrew. A contribution to South African materia medica. 1888. III. 281.²
Smith, Anna Maria. Flora von Fiume. 1878. I. 448.¹
Smith, Aubrey H. A new materia for Corema Conradii. 1883. II. 453.²
Smith, C. G. Timber in marine works. 1879. IV. 420.
Smith, C. Michie. The absorption spectra. 1890. I. 185.¹
Smith, Charles Roach. On the scarcity of home-grown fruits in Great Britain. 1863. III. 123.²
Smith, Christian. Dagbog paa en Reise til Kongo. 1819. I. 491.
Smith, Clinton D. Forestry legislation. 1898. IV. 314.²
Smith, Edw. Kaffee ist wirklich Gift. 1845. III. 741.²
Smith, Edwin. Tecoma Smithii. 1894. III. 707.²
Smith, Elias. The medical pocket-book. 1822. III. 242.
Smith, Elisha. Botanic physician. 1830. III. 238.¹
Smith, Emily A. The Maple-tree bark-louse. 1878. III. 534.¹
Smith, Ernest C. A trip to Mount Rainier. 1894. I. 326.
Smith, Erwin Frink. Additional evidence on . . . Peach yellows. 1891. III. 442.¹
— The chemistry of Peach yellows. 1889. III. 442.¹
— Crataegus tomentosa var. punctata. 1880. II. 263.¹
— A Date-palm fungus. 1888. III. 329.¹
— Experiments with fertilizers for . . . Peach yellows. 1893. III. 442.¹
— Peach growing for market. 1895. III. 441.¹
— Peach rot and Peach blight. 1889. III. 442.¹
— Peach yellows. 1892. III. 442.¹
— Peach yellows; a preliminary report. 1888. III. 442.¹
— Peach yellows and Peach rosette. 1894. III. 442.¹
— The spread of plant diseases. .1898. III. 178.
— On the value of superphosphates . . . in the treatment of Peach yellows. 1892. III. 442.¹
— On the value of wood ashes in . . . . Peach yellows. 1892. III. 442.¹
— *See also* WHEELER, C. F. & SMITH, E. F.
Smith, Eugene Allen. The Cotton belt. 1885. I. 317,¹ *IV. 77*.²
Smith, Frederick Porter. Contributions towards the materia medica . . . of China. 1871. III. 273.¹

Smith, G. B. The Catalpa timber for posts. 1845. IV. 538.¹
Smith, Gerard Edwards. A catalogue of . . . plants collected in South Kent. 1829. I. 397.
Smith, H. D. Transverse strength . . . of Yellow Pine timber. 1897. IV. 410.
Smith, Henrick. Een skön loestig ny urtegaardt. 1546. I. 278.
Smith, Henry. Flora sarisburiensis. 1817. I. 396.
Smith, Henry George. On the amyl ester of eudesmic acid. 1900. IV. 532.¹
— On the aromadendrin. 1897. IV. 532.¹
— On the constituent of peppermint odour . . . in many Eucalyptus oils. 1900. II. 624.¹
— On the constituents of thé sap of the "Silky Oak." 1897. III. 383.¹
— On the crystalline camphor or Eucalyptus oil. 1899. IV. 532.¹
— L'eudesmol. 1900. IV. 532.¹
— On a new aromatic aldehyde. 1900. IV. 532.¹
— Notes on myrticolorin. 1897. IV. 533.²
— On the pinenes of the oils of the genus Eucalyptus. 1898. IV. 532.¹
— On the saccharine . . . exudations of the "Grey Gum." 1897. IV. 533.²
— *See also* BAKER, R. T. & SMITH, H. G.; MAIDEN, J. H. & SMITH, H. G.
Smith, J. Culture of the Hedaromas. 1865. III. 633.²
— Emploi de la dynamite pour l'extraction des racines. 1880. IV. 387.¹
— Extraction of tree roots by dynamite. 1880. IV. 387.¹
— The Great Fan Palm. 1867. III. 324,² *351*.¹
— Remarks upon Araucaria Rulei. 1863. III. 299.²
— Theophrasta Jussiaei. 1888. III. 665.²
Smith, J. J., (*jr.*). Beplanting van wegen. 1899. III. 211.¹
— Gazonplanten. 1897. III. 203.
— Lijst der families en geslachten van niet kruidachtige gewassen in den Botanischen tuin. 1892. I. 68.¹
— Een nieuwe Koffie-plantwijze. 1897. III. 734.²
— Een paar nieuwe Acalypha's. 1899. III. 514.¹
— Siervruchten. 1895. III. 208.¹
— Een tocht naar de Koraaleilanden. 1900. I. 467.
— Vermenigvuldiging van planten. 1895. III. 153.
— Verzeichniss der Familien und Gattungen der nicht-krautartigen Gewächse in dem Botanischen Garten. 1892. I. 68.¹
Smith, James. Essay on the Apple. 1875. III. 426.¹
Smith, James, (*fl.* 1880). Account of the growth of some Cedars of Lebanon. 1826. III. 300.¹
— Dry rot. 1832. IV. 414.²
— On the Hya-hya or Milk-tree of Demerara. 1830. III. 691.¹
— On the prevention of dry rot. 1832. IV. 414.²
Smith, *Sir* James Edward. An account of several plants presented to the Linnean society. 1791. II. 326,² *528*.²
— An account of two new genera of plants. 1794. II. 378,¹ *846*.²
— Anleitung zum Studium der physiologischen und systematischen Botanik. 1807. I. 85.
— Beschreibung einiger neuen Pflanzengattungen aus Georgien. 1797. I. 318.
— Botanical characters of four New-Holland . . . Myrti. 1802. II. 619.¹
— Botanical characters'of some . . . Myrti. 1797. II. 619.¹
— Botanical characters of Neu-Holland. 1793. I. 500.
— Botanische Grammatik. 1821. I. 255.
— Caratteri di un nuovo genere . . . Salisburia. 1797. II. 7.²
— Characters of a new genus . . . Salisburia. 1797. II. 7.²
— Characters of Platylobium, Bossiaea. 1808. II. 336,¹ *378*,¹ *378*.²
— Characters of three new species of Boronia. 1807. II. 399.²
— The characters of twenty new genera of plants. 1798. I. 500.
— Charaktere von zwanzig neuen Pflanzengattungen. 1798. I. 500.
— Compendium florae britannicae. 1800. I. 396.
— A compendium of the English flora. 1829. I. 397.
— Descriptio novi plantarum generis Boroniae. 1798. II. 399.²
— Descriptio novi plantarum generis, Sprengelia. 1794. II. 690.¹
— Descriptio novi plantarum generis Westringiae. 1797. II. 767.¹

— Description of a new genus . . . Boronia. 1798. II. 399.²
— Description of a new genus . . . Sprengelia. 1794. II. 690.¹
— Description of a new genus . . . Westringia. 1797. II. 767.¹
— Description of the fruit of Cycas revoluta. 1802. II. 4.²
— Éclaircissements sur le bois de Rhodes.. 1818. II. 255,² III. 417.²
— Einige Bemerkungen über die Reitzbarkeit der Pflanzen. 1788. II. 205.²
— The English flora. 1824. I. 397.
— Exotic botany. 1804. I. 265.
— Flora britannica. 1800. I. 396.
— A grammar of botany. 1821. I. 255.
— Histoire naturelle des lépidoptères . . . de Georgie. 1797. I. 318.
— Icones pictae plantarum rariorum. 1790. I. 263.
— An inquiry into the genus . . . Abelicea cretica. 1808. II. 145.¹
— An inquiry into the structure of seeds. 1808. I. 120.
— An introduction to physiological and systematical botany. 1807. I. 84.
— An introduction to the study of botany. 1807. I. 84.
— The natural history of the .. . . insects of Georgia. 1797. I. 318.
— Plantarum icones hactenus ineditae. 1789. I. 263.
— Plants of New Holland. 1790. I. 500.
— Ueber die Reitzbarkeit der Staubfäden des Sauerdorns. 1788. II. 205.²
— Remarks on some British species of Salix. 1802. II. 102.¹
— Remarks on the generic characters of the decandrous papilionaceous plants of New Holland. 1805. II. 319.²
— A sketch of a tour on the continent. 1793. V. XVIII.²
— Some information respecting the Lignum rhodium. 1818. II. 255,¹ III. 417.²
— Some observations on the irritability of vegetables. 1788. I. 197,¹ II. 205.²
— Some remarks on the synonyms . . . of Hypericum ealyeinum. 1811. II. 556.²
— Specific characters of the decandrous papilionaceous plants of New Holland. 1808. II. 319.²
— A specimen of the botany of New Holland. 1793. I. 500.
— Spicilegium botanicum. 1791. I. 264.
— Sprengelia et nytt Örteslägte. 1794. II. 690.¹
— Syllabus of a course of lectures on botany. 1795. I. 32.
— Tracts relating to natural history. 1798. I. 33.
— Westringia et nytt örteslägte. 1797. II. 767.¹
Smith, James Henry. Forest culture in Hesse. 1888. IV. 351.²
Smith, Jared Gage. Fodder and forage plants. 1900. III. 224.¹
— & Oliver, G. W. Acanthophoenix. 1900. III. 318.²
— & Pound, Roscoe. Flora of the Sand Hill region of Sheridan. 1893. I. 326.
Smith, Joel W. Some ill effects of trees. 1894. III. 34.²
Smith, John. A treatise on the growth of the Peach. 1843. III. 440.²
Smith, Capt. John, (1579–1631). The generall historie of Virginia. 1624. III. 261.¹
— The true travels . . . in Europe, Asia. 1630. III. 266.
Smith, John, (1798–1888). The Araucaria Bidwilli at Kew. 1873. III. 298.¹
— Bible plants. 1877. I. 513.
— The Coco-nut Palm at Syon. 1862. III. 322.²
— A dictionary of popular names of the plants. 1882. III. 31, 53.
— Domestic botany. 1871. III. 53. — 1883. III. 53.
— Die grosse Fächer-Palme. 1872. III. 331.¹
— History of the introduction of Palms. 1885. III. 318.¹
— Notice of a plant which produces perfect seeds without . . . pollen. 1841. III. 436.¹
— Observations on a remarkable Cycadaceous plant. 1854. II. 6.²
— See also LINDLEY, John & SMITH, John.
Smith, John, (of Glasgow?). Treatise on the management . . . of forest trees. 187.? IV. 108.²
Smith, John, (of Kilwinning, Ayrshire). Botany of Ayrshire. 1896. I. 535.
Smith, John, (of London?). England's improvement reviv'd. 1670. III. 107.
Smith, John, (of Romsey, Hampshire). On British Oaks. 1893. III. 361.¹
— Copse-wood in Hampshire. 1882. IV. 132.¹
— The hygienic effects of plants and trees. 1883. IV. 55.¹

— The ligneous plants of Hampshire. 1890. I. 394.
— On the present state . . . of arboriculture in Hampshire. 1887. III. 123.¹
— Quercus rubra and Cedrus libani. 1883. III. 123.¹
Smith, John Alexander. On certain New Zealand and Australian barks. 1879. IV. 435.
— On the effects of lightning on an Ash-tree. 1860. IV. 193.²
— Measurements of trees at Dryburgh Abbey. 1862. III. 35.¹
Smith, John Bernhard. Cranberry culture in New Jersey. 1890. III. 663.²
— The flat-head Pear-borer. 1894. III. 446.²
— The Gingko tree. 1897. II. 7.²
— Is the woodpecker useful? 1893. IV. 90.¹
— A new enemy to Willows. 1890. III. 350.²
— The Oak-pruners. 1892. IV. 501.¹
— An Oak scale. 1891. IV. 501.¹
— The rôle of insects in the forest. 1900. IV. 205.¹
— Some insects injurious to shade trees. 1894. III. 187.
— The White Pine weevil. 1889. IV. 470.¹
— Why certain Hickories died. 1895. III. 353.²
Smith, John Donnell. Another station for Rhododendron Vaseyi. 1888. II. 684.¹
— Enumeratio plantarum guatemalensium. 1889. I. 334. 1898. I. 330.
— An enumeration of the plants collected in Central America. 1898. I. 334.
— Polypetalae, pars [& gamopetalae]. 1898. I. 334.
— Undescribed plants from Guatemala. 1887. I. 333.
Smith, John Jay. Address to the senate on the new botanic garden. 1846. I. 38.²
— The Buckwheat-tree. 1857. III. 529.²
— The growth of the Cork tree. 1876. IV. 516.²
— flints respecting plants which will grow in the shade. 1846. III. 42.¹
— Planting trees. 1855. IV. 155.¹
— Topiary work. 1860. III. 202.¹
Smith, Junius. Cultivation of the Tea-plant in the United States. 1850. III. 600.²
— Culture of Tea in South Carolina. 1850. III. 600.²
— Golden Grove Tea plantation. 1851. III. 600.¹
Smith, Lucio C. See CONZATTI, Cassiano & SMITH, L. C.
Smith, Peter. The Indian doctor's dispensatory. 1813. III. 261.²
— & Co. Die Handelsgärtnerei der Herren P. Smith & Co. 1866. III. 289.
— — Die Zwergformen der verschiedenen Coniferen-Arten. 1867. III. 289.
Smith, R. G. The nodule organism of the Leguminosae. 1900. III. 462.¹
Smith, Ralph E. The soft spot of Oranges. 1897. III. 501.¹
Smith, Ralph Sidney & others. The Redwood reserve. 189.? IV. 178.¹
Smith, Richard & Co. Plants of the Fir tribe. 187.? III. 290.
Smith, Robert. Report of planting on the estate of Balgowan. 1857. IV. 358.²
— Smith's improved method of grafting. 1897. III. 163.²
Smith, Robert Henry. Experiments upon the strength of Japanese woods. 1876. IV. 410.
Smith, S. Percy. Note on a branched Nikau tree. 1878. II. 60.²
Smith, Samuel. The history of the colony of Nova-Caesaria. 1765. III. 263.¹
Smith, Stephen. Vegetation, a remedy for the summer heat of cities. 1899. III. 34.²
Smith, T. Autumn tints. 1879. III. 207.¹
— Berberidopsis corallina. 1879. III. 614.¹
— Berry-bearing trees and shrubs. 1882. III. 208.¹
— The Hillsborough Pernettyas. 1884. III. 653.²
Smith, Thomas. Traité d'agriculture et d'horticulture. 1825. III. 113.
Smith, W. Baxter. On planting arable lands. 1880. IV. 134.¹
— Planting unprofitable land. 1882. IV. 142.
Smith, W. W. Cordyline australis and C. indivisa. 1900. III. 334.²
Smith, Watson. Produits de la distillation de bois. 1874. IV. 432.²
Smith, Wilfred. A curious pollard Ash-tree and Beach-tree. 1745. I. 296.²
— A natural history of Nevis. 1745. III. 63.²
Smith, Wilham George. A dangerous disease of the Weymouth Pine. 1898. IV. 470.¹

Smith, William George *(continued).*
— Ricerche morfo-anatomiche sulle deformazioni prodotte dalle Exoascaceae. 1894. IV. 212.
— Shelter belts at Coteau farm. 1900. III. 215.[2]
— Untersuchungen der Morphologie . . . der durch Exoasceen verursachten . . . Deformationen. 1894. IV. 212.
Smith, William Robertson. Old testament notes. 1885. II. 267.[2]
— Rambling notes on trees in the streets. 1899. III. 208.[2]
Smith, Wilson. The big trees of Indiana. 1880. I. 295.[2]
Smith, Worthington George. Acacia disease. 1881. III. 463.[1]
— Antiquités végétales. 1873. II. 138.[2]
— Camellia japonica. 1875. IV. 528.[2]
— Cleyera japonica. 1875. IV. 528.[2]
— Croton spirale. 1874. III. 517.[1]
— Disease of Larch and Pine seedlings. 1886. III. 295.[2]
— Disease of Rhododendron roots. 1885. III. 657.[1]
— Disease of Yew. 1884. III. 288.[1]
— The Eve Oak. 1873. II. 138.[2]
— Gigantic Fig tree at Roscoff. 1889. II. 151.[1]
— Gooseberry disease. 1881. III. 414.[2]
— Guaiacum officinale. 1875. IV. 524.[2]
— A holiday in Shropshire. 1881. I. 209,[1] II. 114,[1] *IV. 510.*
— Oaks at Moccas Court. 1874. II. 138.[2]
— Pyrus Maulei. 1875. III. 420.[2]
— Ternstroemia japonica. 1875. IV. 528.[2]
— Trees at Holm Lacy. 1873. I. 297.[1]
— A vegetable horse. 1874. II. 144.[2]
— Willow disease. 1881. III. 350.[1]
— Woods suitable for wood engraving. 1875. IV. 427.[2]
— *See also* FITCH, W. H. & SMITH, W. G.
Smithers, George F. Chinese Oil tree. 1898. III. 514.[2]
Smithson, James. On a substance from the Elm tree. 1813. II. 143.[1]
Smithsonian contributions to knowledge. I. 7.[1]
Smithsonian institution. Annual report. I. 7.[1]
Smithsonian miscellaneous collections. I. 7.[1]
Smitt, J. Nogle ord om vore skove. 1895. IV. 344.[1]
Smolář, Gustav. Lipa širolistá s listy kápovitými. 1891. II. 518.[1]
Smoler, Franz Xaver. Historische Blicke auf das Forst- und Jagdwesen. 1847. IV. 23.[2]
Smoler, Moriz. Der Wald in seinen Beziehungen. 1863. IV. 43.
— Die Wirkung des Blitzes auf Bäume. 1860. IV. 193.[2]
Smooth-leaved Bumelia, or Iron-wood. 1858. III. 667.[1]
Smucker, Isaac. Tree culture on prairies. 1884. IV. 39.[1]
Smyrna Fig harvest. 1890. III. 370.[1]
Smyth, Bernard Bryan. Check list of the plants of Kansas. 1892. I. 326, V. XVIII.[1]
Smyth, Charles Piazzi. On the manner of growth of Dracaena Draco. 1859. II. 82.[1]
Smyth, John B. On the comparative return from capital invested in cropping, grazing, or planting land. 1878. IV. 259.[2]
— Pruning in relation to the production of timber. 1878. IV. 171.
Smythe, William. Cupressus Lawsoniana var. erecta viridis. 1891. III. 301.[1]
— Notes. 1900. III. 617.[1]
Smythies, A. Canson's hydraulic motor. 1877. IV. 393.
— The Chir forests. 1879. IV. 377.[2]
— Examination of the annual rings of Chir. 1881. IV. 464.[2]
— Forest terminology with especial reference to the more important terms. 1876. IV. 23.[2]
— Fruit culture in the north-west Himalaya. 1895. III. 147.[1]
— Improvement fellings in the Dehra Dún Sál forests. 1888. IV. 528.[2]
— Journal of the Hill tour. 1888. IV. 378.
— Note on the artificial cultivation of Cedrus Deodara. 1881. IV. 447.[2]
— Notes on Changa Manga. 1896. IV. 519,[1] 521.[2]
— Notes on French forests. 1883. IV. 361.
— Report on the preparation of Bamboo fibre for paper making. 1878. III. 315.[1]
— Ripening of Deodar seed. 1882. II. 27.[2]
— A tour in Jaunsar. 1893. IV. 378.
— Wood pavements. 1883. IV. 426.[1]
— The working of the Dehra Dún Sál forests. 1893. IV. 528.[2]
— *See also* FISHER, C. P. & SMYTHIES, A.
Smythies, A. & Dansey, E. Report at Dehra Dun. *See* FOREST conference. IV. 16.
— & Fordyce, C. Note on the use of Simul wood for tea boxes. 1894. IV. 528.[1]

Smyttère, Philippe Joseph Emmanuel de. Phytologie pharmaceutique et médicale. 1829. III. 56.
— Précis élémentaire de botanique médicale. 1837. III. 57.
— Tableaux synoptiques d'histoire naturelle médicale. 1829. III. 56.
Snabilié, C. Nieuwe bronnen. 1886. III. 225.
Snackey. *See* HAS & SNACKEY.
Sneath, R. G. Wine, brandy and olive oil. 1889. III. 679.[1]
Snell, F. H. Ueber den Einfluss des Heerrauchs. 1858. III. 182, *185.*[1]
Snell, J. The Cowthorpe Oak, Yorkshire. 1895. II. 139.[1]
Snellen van Vollenhoven, Samuel Constant. Description d'un lépidoptère. 1862. III. 148.[1]
— Description d'un lépidoptère nouveau. 1862. III. 148.[1]
— De insecten welke den landbouwer schaden. 1852. III. 189.
— Nouveaux vers à soie. 1862. III. 148.[1]
— De schadelijke insecten in tuinen. 1843. III. 189.
— De wurm in het hout. 1875. IV. 414.[1]
Snellman, W. Egendomligt utbildad Tallgren. 1871. II. 47.[2]
Snijders, A. J. C. De beteekenis der boschcultuur. 1894. IV. 45.
Snippendal, Johannes. Catalogus plantarum Horti amstelodamensis. 1646. I. 50.
Snöberg, G. P. Stirpes agri femsionensis. *See* FRIES, E. M. 1825. I. 353.
Over het **snoeien** der sierboomen. 1864. III. 172.
Het **snoeien** der Theestruiken. 1884. III. 602.[1]
Snoeijen der boschboomen. 1867. IV. 171.
Snooke, W. D. Flora vectiana. 1823. I. 397.
A **Snowdrop,** *(pseud.)*. The berries and heaths of Rannoch. 1881. V. XXI.[2]
Soares, Antoine Joaquin DE MACEDO. *See* MACEDO SOARES, A. J. de.
Soares, R. de MORAES. *See* MORAES SOARES, R. de.
Soave, Marco. Sulla funzione fisiologica dell'acido cianidrico. 1899. II. 272.[1]
— *See also* GIACOSA, P. & SOAVE, M.
Sobernheim, J. F. Handboek tot de practische leer der geneesmiddelen. 1836. III. 258.
— Handbuch der praktischen Arzneimittellehre. 1836. III. 258.
— Handbuch der speciellen praktischen Arzneimittellehre. 1836. III. 258.
Sobieszczański, F. M. Ogrody w Warszawie i jej okolicach. 184. I. 42.
Sobitschewski, Vasili T. *See* Собичевскій, B. T.
Sobitschewski. Les forêts de la famille impériale de Russie. 1898. IV. 347.
— Die Forsten der kaiserlichen Familiengüter in Russland. 1898. IV. 347.
Sobó, Jenő. Erdészeti építéstan. 1898. IV. 266.[1]
Sobolef, Alexei N. *See* Соболевъ, Алексѣй Н.
Sobolevski, Gregor. Flora petropolitana. 1799. I. 360.
— *See also* Соболевскій, F.
Sobotka, Primus. Lipa. 1878. IV. 526.[1]
Sobrero, Ascanio. Sur l'acide pyrogaïque . . . de Gaïac. 1843. III. 494.[2]
— Examen de la résine d'Olivier. 1845. III. 678.[2]
— Ueber das Hars des Olivenbaums. 1845. III. 678.[2]
— Note sur l'huile essentielle de Bouleau. 1842. IV. 491.[1]
Sociedad científica argentina. Anales. I. 8.[1]
Sociedad científica de Chile. Actas. *See* SOCIÉTÉ SCIENTIFIQUE DU CHILI. I. 8.[1]
Sociedad de ciencias físicas y naturales de Caracas. Boletin. I. 8.[1]
Sociedad española de historia natural. Anales. I. 24.[2]
Una **sociedad** forestal. 1892. IV. 541, *551.*[1]
Sociedad mexicana de historia natural. *See* LA NATURALEZA. I. 7.[2]
Sociedad nacional de agricultura. Boletin. III. 10.[1]
Sociedade Broteriana. Boletim. I. 24.[1]
Sociedade nacional de agricultura. Boletim. III. 757.[1]
Sociedade nacional de horticultura de Portugal. *See* REAL SOCIEDADE . . . III. 23.[1]
Sociedade vellosiana. Trabalhos. I. 8.[1]
Società adriatica di scienze naturali in Trieste. Bollettino. I. 28.[1]
Società agraria della provincia di Bologna. Annali. Memorie. III. 23.[2]
Società agricola-forestale valmaggese. Almanacco. III. 24.[1]

Società agricole-forestale del cantone ticino. *See* L' AGRI-
COLTORE ticinese. III. 24.[1]
Società Ailantina d' imboschimento. 1865. IV. 525.
Società botanica italiana. Bullettino. I. 26.[1]
Società cantonale d'agricoltura e silvicoltura. *See* L' AGRI-
COLTORE ticinese. III. 24.[1]
La Società degli amici degli alberi. 1894. IV. 41.[1]
Società dei naturalisti in Modena. Atti. Annuario. I.
26.[1]
Società di acclimazione e di agricoltura in Sicilia. Atti.
Giornale. III. 23.[2]
Società di naturalisti in Napoli. Bollettino. I. 26.[1]
Società elvetica delle scienze naturali. *See* ALLGEMEINE
SCHWEIZERISCHE GESELLSCHAFT . . . I. 26.[1]
Società entomologica italiana. Bullettino. III. 23.[2]
Società geografica italiana. Bollettino. Memorie. I. 26.[1]
Società geologica. Atti. *See* SOCIETÀ ITALIANA DI SCIENZE
NATURALI. I. 26.[1]
Società italiana delle scienze. Memorie. I. 26.[1]
Società italiana di scienze naturali. Atti. I. 26.[1]
Società ligustica di scienze naturali e geografiche. Atti.
I. 26.[1]
Società reale Borbonica. *See* REALE ACCADEMIA DELLE
SCIENZE, SEZIONE DELLA SOCIETÀ . . . I. 25.
Società toscana di orticultura. *See* REALE SOCIETÀ . . . III.
23.[2]
Società toscana di scienze naturali residente in Pisa. Atti.
I. 26.[1]
Società triennale . . . della selvicoltura in Italia. 1880. IV.
41.[1]
Società triennale . . . della silvicoltura in Italia. Bollettino.
IV. 13.[1]
Società veneto-trentina di scienze . . . Padova. Atti. I.
26.[1]
Societas physico-medica basiliensis. Acta helvetica. I. 27.
Societas pro fauna et flora fennica. Meddelanden.
See SÄLLSKAPET PRO FAUNA ET FLORA FENNICA. I. 10.
Societas regia scientiarum gottingensis. Commentarii. Novi
commentarii. Commentationes. Commentationum . . .
Sylloge. I. 14.
Societas scientiarum fennicae. Acta. I. 10.
Societas . . . scientiarum gottingensis. *See* SOCIETAS REGIA
. . . I. 14.
Societas scientiarum Indo-neerlandica. Acta. *See* NATUUR-
KUNDIGE VEREENIGING . . . I. 29.[1]
Société académique d'agriculture, belles-lettres, sciences . . .
de Poitiers. Bulletin. III. 20.
Société académique d'agriculture des sciences, arts . . . de
l'Aube. Mémoires. *See* SOCIÉTÉ D'AGRICULTURE, SCIENCES
ET ARTS . . . DE L'AUBE. I. 22.
Société académique de Cherbourg. *See* SOCIÉTÉ NATIONALE
ACADÉMIQUE . . . I. 23.
Société académique de Maine-et-Loire. Mémoires. I. 22.
Société agricole, scientifique et littéraire des Pyrénées-
Orientales. Bulletin. *See* SOCIÉTÉ PHILOMATIQUE DE PER-
PIGNAN. I. 24.[1]
Société algérienne de climatologie, sciences physiques &
naturelles. *See* SOCIÉTÉ DE CLIMATOLOGIE . . . I. 29.[2]
Société archéologique, historique et scientifique. Bulletin.
I. 520.[1]
Société archéologique, scientifique et littéraire de Ven-
dômois. Bulletin. I. 520.[1]
Société belge de microscopie. Annales. Bulletin. I. 17.
Société botanique de Copenhague. Journal de botanique.
See BOTANISK Tidsskrift. I. 8.[2]
Société botanique de France. Bulletin. I. 22.
Société botanique de Genève. Bulletin. I. 27.
Société botanique de Lyon. Annales. Bulletin. I. 22.
Société botanique des Deux-Sèvres. Bulletin. I. 22.
Société botanique du grand-duché de Luxembourg. Recueil.
I. 16.
Société botanique rochelaise. Comptes-rendus des excursions
botaniques. I. 520.[1]
Société botanique suisse. Bulletin. *See* SCHWEIZERISCHE
BOTANISCHE GESELLSCHAFT. I. 26.[2]
Société centrale d'agriculture, d'horticulture et d'acclimata-
tion de Nice . . . Bulletin-journal. III. 20.
Société centrale d'agriculture, d'horticulture et d'acclimata-
tion des Alpes-Maritimes. *See* SOCIÉTÉ CENTRALE D'AGRI-
CULTURE . . . DE NICE . . . III. 20.
Société centrale d'agriculture de Belgique. Journal. III.
15.
Société centrale d'agriculture de France. *See* SOCIÉTÉ ROY-
ALE ET CENTRALE D'AGRICULTURE DE PARIS. III. 22.

Société centrale d'agriculture de Meurthe-et-Moselle. An-
nales. *See* Le BON cultivateur. III. 19.
Société centrale d'agriculture de Paris. *See* SOCIÉTÉ ROYALE
ET CENTRALE D'AGRICULTURE DE PARIS. III. 22.
Société centrale d'agriculture du département de la Haute
Saône. Recueil agronomique. III. 20.
Société centrale d'agriculture du département de la Seine-
Inférieure. Extraits des travaux. Mémorial. III. 20.
Société centrale d'agriculture et des comices agricoles . . .
de l'Hérault. *See* SOCIÉTÉ D'AGRICULTURE DU DÉPARTEMENT
DE L'HÉRAULT. III. 21.
Société centrale d'agriculture, sciences . . . du département
du Nord. *See* SOCIÉTÉ ROYALE ET CENTRALE . . . III. 22.
Société centrale d'apiculture & d'insectologie. *See* BULLETIN
D'INSECTOLOGIE. III. 19.
Société centrale d'arboriculture en Belgique. Bulletin. *See*
ANNALES de l'horticulture en Belgique. III. 15.
Société centrale d'horticulture de France. *See* SOCIÉTÉ ROY-
ALE D'HORTICULTURE DE PARIS. III. 22.
Société centrale d'horticulture de la Seine-Inférieure. Cata-
logue des fruits moulés . . . *See* CATALOGUE . . . 1894. III.
29.[1]
Société centrale d'horticulture de Nancy. Bulletin. III. 21.
Société centrale d'horticulture du département de la Seine-
Inférieure. *See* SOCIÉTÉ IMPÉRIALE ET CENTRALE . . . III.
22.
Société centrale d'horticulture du Nord. Journal. *See*
CERCLE HORTICOLE DU NORD. III. 19.
Société centrale forestière de Belgique. Bulletin. IV. 12.[1]
Société chimique. Bulletin. I. 22.
Société cultivatrice des landes de Danemark. *See* DALGAS, E.
1893. IV. 39.[2]
Société d'acclimatation. Bulletin. *See* SOCIÉTÉ IMPÉRIALE
ZOOLOGIQUE D'ACCLIMATATION. III. 22.
Société d'acclimatation et d'histoire naturelle de l'île de la
Réunion. Bulletin. III. 26.[2]
Société d'agriculture . . . *See also* SOCIÉTÉ ROYALE D'AGRICUL-
TURE . . .
Société d'agriculture, commerce, sciences . . . du départe-
ment de la Marne. Compte annuel. Séance publique.
Mémoires. III. 21.
Société d'agriculture, d'horticulture et d'acclimatation du
Var. Bulletin. III. 21.
Société d'agriculture de l'Aude. Journal. III. 21.
Société d'agriculture, des sciences . . . de l'arrondissement
de Valenciennes. Mémoires. III. 21.
Société d'agriculture, des sciences . . . du département de la
Haute-Saône. Bulletin. Mémoires. III. 21.
Société d'agriculture du département de l'Hérault. Bulletin.
Recueil. Réunions viticoles. III. 21.
Société d'agriculture du département de la Gironde. An-
nales. III. 21.
Société d'agriculture du département de Loir-et-Cher.
Bulletin. Séances générales. III. 21.
Société d'agriculture du département de Seine-et-Oise.
Mémoires. III. 21.
Société d'agriculture du département du Cher. Bulletin.
III. 21.
Société d'agriculture et d'horticulture de Vaucluse. Bulletin.
III. 21.
Société d'agriculture et d'horticulture du Gers. Bulletin.
III. 21.
Société d'agriculture et de botanique de Gand. *See* SOCIÉTÉ
ROYALE D'AGRICULTURE . . . I. 17.
Société d'agriculture et de commerce de Caen. *See* SOCIÉTÉ
ROYALE D'AGRICULTURE . . . III. 22.
Société d'agriculture, industrie, sciences . . . du département
de la Loire. Annales. III. 21.
Société d'agriculture, industrie, sciences . . . du département
de la Lozère. Bulletin. III. 21.
Société d'agriculture, sciences, arts . . . du département
d'Indre-et-Loire. Annales. III. 21.
Société d'agriculture, sciences et arts d'Angers. Bulletin.
III. 21.
Société d'agriculture, sciences et arts de la Sarthe. Bulletin.
See SOCIÉTÉ ROYALE D'AGRICULTURE, SCIENCES . . . DU
MANS. I. 24.[1]
Société d'agriculture, sciences et arts de Meaux. Publica-
tions (bulletin). III. 21.
Société d'agriculture, sciences et arts du département de
l'Aube. Annuaire. Mémoires. I. 22.
Société d'agriculture, sciences et arts du département de
l'Eure. Bulletin. Journal d'agriculture. III. 21.
Société d'agronomie pratique. Journal. III. 21.

Société d'amateurs des sciences, de l'agriculture et des arts à Lille. Mémoires. Recueil. I. 22.
Société d'archéologie lorraine. Bulletin. Mémoires. IV. 13.[1]
Société d.Arcueil. Mémoires. I. 23.
Société d'économie rurale de la Russie méridionale. Bulletins. Mémoires. III. 10.[1]
Société d'émulation d'Abbeville. Mémoires. I. 23.
Société d'émulation de Montbéliard. Compte-rendu. Mémoires. I. 23.
Société d'émulation du département des Vosges. Annales. I. 23.
Société d'émulation du département du Doubs. Mémoires. I. 23.
Société d'encouragement pour l'industrie nationale (Paris). Bulletin. III. 21.
Société d'étude des sciences naturelles de Béziers. Bulletin. I. 23.
Société d'études des Hautes-Alpes. Bulletin. I. 23.
Société d'études des sciences naturelles de Nîmes. Bulletin. I. 23.
Société d'études scientifiques d'Angers. Bulletin. I. 23.
Société d'études scientifiques . . . de Draguignan. Bulletin. I. 23.
Société d'études scientifiques du Finistère. Bulletin. I.'23.
Société d'histoire du canton de Neuchâtel. See MUSÉE NEUCHÂTELOIS. I. 26.[1]
Société d'histoire naturelle de Colmar. Bulletin. I. 15.
Société d'histoire naturelle d'Autun. Bulletin. I. 23.
Société d'histoire naturelle de l'Ile Maurice. Rapport. I. 29.[1]
Société d'histoire naturelle de Metz. Bulletin. See SOCIÉTÉ D'HISTOIRE NATURELLE . . . DE LA MOSELLE. I. 15.
Société d'histoire naturelle de Paris. Actes. Mémoires. I. 23.
Société d'histoire naturelle de Strasbourg. Mémoires. I. 15.
Société d'histoire naturelle de Toulouse. Bulletin. I. 23.
Société d'histoire naturelle du département de la Moselle. Bulletin. I. 15.
Société d'horticulture, d'agriculture et de botanique de Montmorency. See SOCIÉTÉ D'HORTICULTURE DE MONTMORENCY. III. 21.
Société d'horticulture, d'agriculture et de viticulture de Vichy-Cusset. Bulletin-journal. III. 21.
Société d'horticulture d'Alger. Bulletin. See REVUE horticole de l'Algérie. III. 27.[1]
Société d'horticulture d'Angers et du département de Maine-et-Loire. See SOCIÉTÉ D'HORTICULTURE DE MAINE-ET-LOIRE. III. 21.
Société d'horticulture, d'arboriculture, de viticulture . . . de la Meuse. Bulletin. III. 21.
Société d'horticulture, d'arboriculture et de viticulture du canton d'Argenteuil (Seine-et-Oise). Bulletin. III. 21.
Société d'horticulture d'Eure-et-Loire. Bulletin. III. 21.
Société d'horticulture d'Orléans. Bulletin. III. 21.
Société d'horticulture de Cherbourg. Bulletin. III. 21.
Société d'horticulture de Dôle. Bulletin. III. 21.
Société d'horticulture de Gand. Journal. III. 15.
Société d'horticulture de Genève. Bulletin. III. 24.[1]
Société d'horticulture de l'arrondissement de Bayonne. Bulletin. III. 21.
Société d'horticulture de l'arrondissement de Dieppe. Bulletin. III. 21.
Société d'horticulture de l'Aube. Bulletins. 'III. 21.
Société d'horticulture de l'Auvergne. Bulletin. III. 21.
Société d'horticulture de la Charente. Bulletin. III. 21.
Société d'horticulture de la Gironde. Annales. III. 21.
Société d'horticulture de la Haute-Garonne. Annales. III. 21.
Société d'horticulture de la Sarthe. Bulletin. III. 21.
Société d'horticulture de la Seine. Bulletin. III. 21.
Société d'horticulture de Maine-et-Loire. Annales. III. 21.
Société d'horticulture de Meaux. Annales. Bulletin. III. 21.
Société d'horticulture de Montmorency. Bulletin. III. 21.
Société d'horticulture de Paris. See SOCIÉTÉ ROYALE D'HORTICULTURE DE PARIS. III. 22.
Société d'horticulture de Picardie. Bulletin. III. 22.
Société d'horticulture de Rouen. Bulletin. See SOCIÉTÉ IMPÉRIALE ET CENTRALE D'HORTICULTURE DU DÉPARTEMENT DE LA SEINE-INFÉRIEURE. III. 22.
Société d'horticulture de Saint-Germain-en-Laye. Bulletin. III. 22.
Société d'horticulture de Tunisie. Bulletin. III. 27.[1]

Société d'horticulture de Vosges. Bulletin. III. 22.
Société d'horticulture du canton de Vaud. Journal. III. 24.[r]
Société d'horticulture du centre de la Normandie. Bulletin. III. 22.
Société d'horticulture du département de la Moselle. Bulletin. Journal. III. 22.
Société d'horticulture du Doubs. Bulletin. III. 22.
Société d'horticulture du Japon. Journal. See NIHON engei kai zasshi. III. 26.[1]
Société d'horticulture du Puy-de-Dôme. Bulletin. III. 22.
Société d'horticulture et d'acclimatation de la Dordogne. Bulletin. III. 22.
Société d'horticulture et d'acclimatation du Var. See SOCIÉTÉ d'agriculture, d'horticulture . . . III. 21.
Société d'horticulture et d'agriculture d'Hyères. Bulletin. III. 22.
Société d'horticulture et d'apiculture de l'arrondissement de Senlis. Bulletin. III. 22.
Société d'horticulture et d'arboriculture des Deux-Sèvres. Bulletin. III. 22.
Société d'horticulture et d'arboriculture du Doubs. Journal. III. 22.
Société d'horticulture et d'histoire naturelle de l'Hérault. Annales. See SOCIÉTÉ D'HORTICULTURE ET DE BOTANIQUE DE L'HÉRAULT. I. 23.
Société d'horticulture et de botanique de Beauvais. Bulletin. III. 22.
Société d'horticulture et de botanique de l'Hérault. Bulletin. I. 23.
Société d'horticulture et de botanique des Bouches-du-Rhône. See REVUE horticole des Bouches-du-Rhône. III. 20.
Société d'horticulture et de botanique du centre de la Normandie. See SOCIÉTÉ D'HORTICULTURE DU CENTRE DE LA NORMANDIE. III. 22.
Société d'horticulture et de botanique . . . du Havre. Bulletin. See CERCLE PRATIQUE D'HORTICULTURE . . . DU HAVRE. III. 19.
Société d'horticulture et de viticulture d'Épernay. Bulletin. III. 22.
Société d'horticulture et de viticulture d'Eure-et-Loire. See SOCIÉTÉ D'HORTICULTURE D'EURE-ET-LOIRE. III. 21.
Société d'horticulture et de viticulture de Dôle. See SOCIÉTÉ D'HORTICULTURE DE DÔLE. III. 21.
Société d'horticulture et de viticulture de Vosges. See SOCIÉTÉ D'HORTICULTURE DE VOSGES. III. 22.
Société d'horticulture et de viticulture des Basses-Pyrénées. Bulletin. III. 22.
Société d'horticulture et de viticulture du Puy-de-Dôme. See SOCIÉTÉ D'HORTICULTURE DU PUY-DE-DÔME. III. 22.
Société d'horticulture pratique de l'Ain. See CHRONIQUE horticole. III. 19.
Société d'horticulture pratique du département du Rhône. Bulletin. Journal. III. 22.
Société dauphinoise pour l'échange des plantes. Bulletin. I. 23.
Société de biologie. Comptes rendus. I. 23.
Société de botanique de Belgique. See SOCIÉTÉ ROYALE DE BOTANIQUE . . . I. 17.
Société de climatologie, sciences physiques & naturelles de l'Algérie. Bulletin. I. 29.[2]
Société de géographie. Bulletin. Recueil. I. 23.
Société de géographie commerciale de Bordeaux. Bulletin. III. 22.
Société de géographie d'Anvers. See SOCIÉTÉ ROYALE DE GÉOGRAPHIE . . . III. 15.
Société de géographie de Marseille. Bulletin. I. 23.
Société de pharmacie d'Anvers. Journal de pharmacie. See JOURNAL . . . I. 16.
Société de physique et d'histoire naturelle de Genève. Mémoires. I. 27.
Société de pomologie et d'arboriculture de Chauny. Bulletin. III. 22.
Société de secours mutuels des préposés forestiers . . . des Hautes-Alpes. Annuaire. IV. 13.[1]
Société de statistique, des sciences naturelles . . . de l'Isère. Bulletin. I. 23.
Société de statistique, sciences . . . Deux-Sèvres. Mémoires. I. 23.
Société des agriculteurs de France. Annuaire. III. 22.
Société des amis des sciences, des lettres, de l'agriculture et des arts à Aix. Recueil de mémoires. I. 520.[1]
Société des amis des sciences naturelles. Bulletin. I. 23.

Société des antiquaires de France. Mémoires. IV. 13.[1]
Société des arts de Genève. Bulletin. Table des matières. III. 24.[2]
Société des arts et des sciences de Maurice. *See* ROYAL SOCIETY OF ARTS AND SCIENCES OF MAURITIUS. I. 29.[3]
Société des lettres, sciences, arts et d'agriculture de Metz. Mémoires. Séance générale. I. 15.
Société des naturalistes à l'Université impériale de Kazan. Travaux. *See* Общество естествоиспытателей. I. 519.[3]
Société des naturalistes à l'Université impériale de Kharkov. Travaux. *See* Общество испытателей природы. I. 519.[3]
Société des naturalistes de Kiev. Mémoires. *See* Киевское общество естествоиспытателей. I. 519.[3]
Société des naturalistes de l'Université impériale de Moscou. *See* SOCIÉTÉ IMPÉRIALE DES NATURALISTES DE Moscou. I. 10.
Société des naturalistes de la Nouvelle-Russie. Mémoires. *See* Новороссийское общество естествоиспытателей. I. 519.[3]
Société des naturalistes de Moscou. Journal. *See* SOCIÉTÉ IMPÉRIALE DES NATURALISTES DE Moscou. I. 10.
Société des naturalistes de St. Pétersbourg. Travaux. *See* С.-Петербургское общество Естествоиспытателей. I. 519.[3]
Société des Pyrénées-Orientales ... Bulletin. *See* SOCIÉTÉ PHILOMATIQUE DE PERPIGNAN. I. 24.[1]
Société des sciences ... *See also* SOCIÉTÉ ROYALE DES SCIENCES ...
Société des sciences, agriculture et arts de la Basse-Alsace. Bulletin. I. 15.
Société des sciences, agriculture et arts du Bas-Rhin. *See* SOCIÉTÉ DES SCIENCES ... DE LA BASSE-ALSACE. I. 15.
Société des sciences, de l'agriculture et des arts à Lille. *See* SOCIÉTÉ D'AMATEURS DES SCIENCES .. I. 22.
Société des sciences de Liège. *See* SOCIÉTÉ ROYALE DES SCIENCES ... I. 17.
Société des sciences de Nancy. Bulletin. I. 23.
Société des sciences, des arts et des lettres du Hainaut. Mémoires. I. 17.
Société des sciences historiques et naturelles de l'Yonne. Bulletin. I. 23.
Société des sciences médicales et naturelles. *See* SOCIÉTÉ ROYALE DES SCIENCES ... I. 17.
Société des sciences naturelles ... de Cherbourg. *See* SOCIÉTÉ IMPÉRIALE DES SCIENCES ... I. 23.
Société des sciences naturelles de l'Ouest de la France. Bulletin. I. 23.
Société des sciences naturelles de Neuchâtel. Bulletin. Mémoires. I. 27.
Société des sciences naturelles de Saône-et-Loire. Bulletin. I. 23.
Société des sciences naturelles de Seine-et-Oise. Mémoires. I. 23.
Société des sciences naturelles de Strasbourg. *See* SOCIÉTÉ D'HISTOIRE NATURELLE DE STRASBOURG. I. 15.
Société des sciences naturelles de Strasbourg. Bulletin. *See* SOCIÉTÉ DES SCIENCES DE NANCY. I. 23.
Société des sciences naturelles du grand-duché de Luxembourg. [Publications.] I. 16.
Société des sciences physiques ... de l'Algérie. *See* SOCIÉTÉ DE CLIMATOLOGIE, SCIENCES PHYSIQUES ... I. 29.[2]
Société des sciences physiques de Lausanne. Bulletin. I. 520.[1]
Société des sciences physiques de médecine et d'agriculture d'Orléans. Bulletin. I. 520.[1]
Société des sciences physiques et naturelles. [Toulouse.] Bulletin. I. 23.
Société des sciences physiques et naturelles de Bordeaux. Mémoires. I. 23.
Société des sciences physiques et naturelles du departement d'Ille-et-Vilaine. Mémoires. I. 23.
Société des viticulteurs de France. Bulletin. III. 22.
Société du muséum d'histoire naturelle de Strasbourg. *See* SOCIÉTÉ D'HISTOIRE NATURELLE DE STRASBOURG. I. 15.
Société éduenne des lettres, sciences et arts. Mémoires. I. 23.
Société éduenne (des lettres, sciences et arts). Mémoires d'histoire naturelle. I. 520.[1]
Société entomologique de France. Annales. Bulletin. III. 22.
Société forestière. Bulletin. IV. 13.[1]
Société forestière de France. Bulletin. IV. 13.[1]
Société forestière de Franche-Comté & Belfort. Bulletin. IV. 13.[1]
Société forestière française des amis des arbres. Bulletin. *See* SOCIÉTÉ FRANÇAISE ... IV. 13.[1]

Société française d'horticulture de Londres. Bulletin. III. 22.
Société française de botanique. Bulletin. *See* REVUE de botanique. I. 22.
Société française des amis des arbres. Bulletin. IV. 13.[1]
See also SOCIÉTÉ CENTRALE D'AGRICULTURE, D'HORTICULTURE DE NICE ... III. 20.
Société française des amis des arbres.
Société fribourgeoise des sciences naturelles. Bulletin. I. 27.
Société Hallérienne. Bulletin. I. 27.
Société helvétique d'horticulture de Genève. *See* Le JARDINIER suisse. III. 24.[1]
Société helvétique des sciences naturelles. Actes. Compte rendu. *See* ALLGEMEINE SCHWEIZERISCHE GESELLSCHAFT ... I. 26.[1]
Société hollandaise des sciences. *See* HOLLANDSCHE MAATSCHAPPIJ DER WETENSCHAPPEN TE HAARLEM. I. 15.
Société hollandaise des sciences à Harlem. Archives néerlandaises. *See* ARCHIVES néerlandaises. I. 15.
Société horticole et botanique de l'arrondissement de Melun. Bulletin. III. 22.
Société horticole, vigneronne et forestière à Troyes. *See* Société horticole ... de l'Aube. III. 22.
Société horticole, vigneronne et forestière de l'Aube. Annale. III. 22.
Société horticole, viticole et forestière de la Haute-Marne. Annales. III. 22.
Société impériale des naturalistes de Moscou. Bulletin. Mémoires. I. 10.
Société impériale des sciences naturelles ... de Cherbourg. Mémoires. I. 23.
Société impériale et centrale d'agriculture de France. *See* SOCIÉTÉ ROYALE ET CENTRALE D'AGRICULTURE DE PARIS. III.
Société impériale et centrale d'horticulture de France. Journal. *See* SOCIÉTÉ ROYALE D'HORTICULTURE DE PARIS. III. 22.
Société impériale et centrale d'horticulture du département de la Seine-Inférieure. Bulletin. III. 22.
Société impériale zoologique d'acclimatation. Annuaire. Bulletin. III. 22.
Société industrielle d'Angers et du département de Maine-et-Loire. Bulletin. III. 22.
Société jurassienne d'émulation. Actes. Coup d'œil. I. 27.
Société libre d'agriculture, sciences, arts ... du département de l'Eure. Recueil. *See* SOCIÉTÉ D'AGRICULTURE, SCIENCES ... III. 21.
Société libre d'émulation de Rouen. Séance. Bulletin. I. 23.
Société libre des sciences et belles-lettres. [Montpellier.] Recueil des sciences. I. 520.[1]
Société Linnéenne de Bordeaux. Actes. Bulletin. I. 23.
Société Linnéenne de Bruxelles. *See* SOCIÉTÉ ROYALE LINNÉENNE ... I. 17.
Société Linnéenne de Lyon. Annales. I. 23.
Société Linnéenne de Normandie. Bulletin. Mémoires. *See* SOCIÉTÉ LINNÉENNE DU CALVADOS. I. 23.
Société Linnéenne de Paris. Bulletin. Mémoires. I. 23.
Société Linnéenne du Calvados. Mémoires. I. 23.
Société Linnéenne du département de Maine-et-Loire. Annales. I. 23.
Société Linnéenne du nord de la France. Mémoires. I. 23.
Société malacologique de Belgique. Annales. I. 17.
Société Murithienne. Bulletins. I. 27.
Société nantaise d'horticulture. Annales. Résumé. Séance. III. 22.
Société nationale académique de Cherbourg. Mémoires. I. 23.
Société nationale d'acclimatation de France. Bulletin. *See* SOCIÉTÉ IMPÉRIALE ZOOLOGIQUE D'ACCLIMATATION. III. 22.
Société nationale d'agriculture de France. *See* SOCIÉTÉ ROYALE ET CENTRALE D'AGRICULTURE DE PARIS. III. 22.
Société nationale d'horticulture de France. Catalogue de la bibliothèque. *See* GIRAULT, Georges. Catalogue ... 1900. III. 2.
Société nationale d'horticulture de France. Journal. *See* SOCIÉTÉ ROYALE D'HORTICULTURE DE PARIS. III. 22.
Société nationale et centrale d'agriculture du département de la Seine. *See* SOCIÉTÉ ROYALE ET CENTRALE D'AGRICULTURE DE PARIS. III. 22.
Société neuchateloise des sciences naturelles. *See* SOCIÉTÉ DES SCIENCES NATURELLES DE NEUCHÂTEL. I. 27.

Société ouralienne d'amateurs des sciences naturelles. Bulletin. See Уральское общество. I. 519.²
Société philomatique de Paris. Bulletin. Nouveau bulletin. I. 23.
Société philomatique de Perpignan. Bulletin. I. 24.¹
Société phytologique d'Anvers. Annales. I. 17.
Société pomologique de France. See La Pomologie française. III. 20.
Société pour l'étude de la flore frauco-helvétique. 1900. I. 419.¹
Société pour la propagation des connaissances scientifiques et industrielles. Bulletin. See Bulletin des sciences naturelles. 1824. I. 1.
Société régionale d'horticulture du nord de la France. Journal. III. 22.
Société royale d'agriculture des sciences . . . d'Orléans. Mémoires. See Société royale des sciences, belles-lettres . . . d'Orléans. I. 24.¹
Société royale d'agriculture et de botanique de Gand. Journal d'horticulture. I. 17.
Société royale d'agriculture et de commerce de Caen. Mémoires. III. 22.
Société royale d'agriculture, histoire naturelle . . . de Lyon. Annales. Mémoires. I. 24.
Société royale d'agriculture, sciences et arts du Mans. Bulletin. I. 24.¹
Société royale d'horticulture des Pays-Bas. Annuaire. See Koninklijke Nederlandsche maatschappij tot aanmoediging van den tuinbouw. Jaarboek. III. 14.
Société royale de botanique de Belgique. Bulletin. I. 17.
Société royale de géographie d'Anvers. Bulletin. III. 15.
Société royale de Turin. Mélanges. See Miscellanea philosophico-mathematica . . . I. 25.
Société royale des arts et des sciences de Maurice. Transactions. See Royal society of arts and sciences of Mauritius. I. 29.¹
Société royale des sciences, belles-lettres et arts d'Orléans. Annales. Mémoires. I. 24.¹
Société royale des sciences, de l'agriculture . . . de Lille. Mémoires. See Société d'amateurs des sciences . . . I. 22.
Société royale des sciences de Liège. Mémoires. I. 17. .
Société royale des sciences et belles-lettres de Nancy. Mémoires. Précis. I. 24.¹
Société royale des sciences médicales et naturelles. Annales. I. 17.
Société royale du Canada. See Royal society of Canada. I. 4.²
Société royale et centrale d'agriculture de Paris. · Bulletin. Mémoires. Recueil. III. 22.
Société royale et centrale d'agriculture, sciences . . . du département du Nord. Mémoires. III. 22.
Société (royale) Linéenne de Bruxelles. Bulletin. I. 17.
Société scientifique de Bruxelles. Annales. I. 17.
Société scientifique du Chili. Actes. I. 8.¹
Société scolaire forestière de Dortan. 1900. IV. 541.
Société séricicole . . . en France. Annales. III. 8.
Société suisse des sciences naturelles. See Allgemeine schweizerische Gesellschaft . . . I. 26.¹
Société vaudoise d'agriculture et de viticulture. Bulletin. III. 24.²
Société vaudoise des sciences naturelles. Bulletin. I. 27.
Société vigneronne de l'arrondissement de Beaune. Bulletin. III. 22.
Société zoologique d'acclimatation. See Société impériale zoologique . . . III. 22.
Société zoologique de France. Bulletin. Mémoires. III. 22.
Sociétés sœurs. 1900. IV. 541.²
Society for the promotion of useful arts. Transactions. See Society instituted in the state of New York . . . III. 8.
Society instituted at Bath for the encouragement of agriculture. Letters. III. 18.
Society instituted at London for the encouragement of arts. Journal. Transactions. III. 18.
Society instituted in the state of New York for the promotion of agriculture. Transactions. III. 8.
Society of arts, London. See Society instituted at London . . . III. 18.
Society of biblical archæology. Proceedings. I. 44.
Socotra Aloes. 1881. III. 334.¹
Soden, Hugo von. Ueber die Bestandteile des ostindischen Sandelholzöles. 1900. III. 384.¹
Soderini, Giovanvittorio. Trattato degli arbori. 1817. III. 114.²

— & Davanzati Bostichi, Bernardo. Coltivazione toscana delle Viti. 1600. III. 557.²
— — Trattato della coltivazione delle Viti. 1600. III. 557.²
— — Trattato della coltivazione delle Viti e del frutto. 1600. III. 557.²
Sodiro, Aloysius. Compositae aequatorianae. 189. ? II. 849.¹
— Plantae ecuadorenses. 1898. I. 340.¹
Sodiro, R. P. Luis. Contribuciones al conocimiento de la flora ecuatoriana. 1900. II. 93.¹
— Observaciones sobre la enfermedad del Cacao. 1891. III. 593.²
Sodomka, F. Calycanthus L. a Chionanthus L. 1899. III. 401.¹
Sodomka, J. Některé plně kvetoucí příbuzné druhy stromů ovocných. 1897. III. 68.¹
Soeckeland, B. Einige Andeutungen über den Unterricht in der Naturbeschreibung. 1832. I. 78.²
Söderbaum, A. G. See Schagerström, J. A. & Söderbaum, A. G.
Söderberg, Christian. Examen classis dioeciae. See Thunberg, C. P. 1825. I. 251.
Söderberg, W. Frederiksminde Lyst-Anlæg ved Aalborg. 1839. IV. 343.¹
Soederstedt, Johann Gustav. De oleo cajuputi. See Thunberg, C. P. 1797. III. 636.²
Söderström, A. Anteckningar om vårens utvekling.. 1844. I. 223.¹
Söderström, B. A. Iakttagelser öfver växternas blomningstid. 1869. I. 223.¹
Söhrens, F. Le Jubaea spectabilis dans sa patrie. 1888. II. 69.²
Söhrens, Johannes. Ein Ausflug in die Kordillera von Santiago. 1892. I. 346.
— Zwei chilenische Loranthus-Arten. 1890. III. 385.¹
Soekaboemische landbouwvereeniging. Jaarbericht. See Jaarbericht . . . 1900. III. 129.¹
— Jaarverslag. See Morren, F. W. 1897. III. 129,¹ and Jaarbericht . . . 1900. III. 129.¹
Soekaboemische landbouwvereeniging. Rapport. 1896. III. 129.¹
Søkilde, N., Rasmussen-. See Rasmussen-Søkilde, N.
Soemmerring, Samuel Thomas von. Ueber eine neue Art Wein zu veredlen. 1817. III. 548.¹
Soennerberg, Jacob. Dijudicatio emendationum systematis sexualis. 1798. I. 251.
Sörensen, Henrik Lauritz. Beretning om en botanisk reise i omegnen af Fæmunsjøen. 1867. I. 356.
— Norsk flora for skoler. 1885. I. 357.
Sörensen, V. Tabeller til Udregning af Trælastfacturær. 1898. IV. 404.¹
Sörensen, William. Fra et Ophold i en sydamerikansk Obraje. 1883. I. 345.
Soest, Gerard Hubert van. Het boschwezen op Java. 1869. IV. 376.²
— Geschiedenis van het kultuurstelsel. 1869. III. 128.
— De Koffiecultuur op Java. 1871. III. 729.²
Soetan Madjo Lelo. De denkbeelden van den heer K. F. Holle over rationeele kultuur. 1892. IV. 279.¹
Soetens, C. De bron; onmisbaar handboek voor alle standen. 1841. III. 105.
Soeterwoude, M. E. T. Elout. See Elout van Soeterwoude, M. E. T.
So gar in Böhmen säet man Holz. See So gar in Böhmen. 1788. IV. 145.
Ueber sogenannte Neuholländer. 1859. II. 384.¹
Die sogenannte Parthenogenesis der Coelebogyne. 1857. II. 436.¹
Die sogenannte Wundertanne bei Rotweil. 1832. II. 24.¹
Sohrt, A. Cultur des Epiphyllum truncatum. 1869. III. 623.¹
— Ueber die Vermehrung einiger Pflanzen. 1868. III. 153.
Soignie, Jules de. Plantations le long des voies de communication. 1894. III. 210.
— Les plantations routières. 1896. III. 210.
Soils for the Larch. 1885. III. 304.¹
Sokolof, N. V. See Соколовъ, N. V.
Sokolowa, C. Naissance del 'endosperme . . . de quelques gymnospermes. 1891. II. 1.
Soland, Aimé de. Catalogue des plantes du Jardin de botanique d'Angers. 1853. I. 58.
— Étude sur les Chênes de Maine-et-Loire. 1862. II. 129.²
— Mélanges d'histoire naturelle. 1867. II. 296,¹ III. 316.¹
— Note sur le Bambusa mitis Poir. 1867. III. 316.¹
— Note sur le Rosa macrantha. 1867. II. 296.¹
— Note sur une variété de l'Hedera Helix. 1869. II. 649.²

Soland, E. Transformation des Lilas. 1896. III. 680.[2].
Solander, Daniel. See BANKS, Sir Joseph & SOLANDER, Daniel.
Solander, Daniel Carl. An account of the Gardenia. 1763. II. 817.[1]
Solaro, Giammaria, SANNA. See SANNA -SOLARO, Giammaria.
Soldin, A. & S. Danske Flora. 1807. I. 352.
Soldin, S. See SOLDIN, A. & S.
Sołdraczyński, Ignacy. Gospodarstwo rolnicze w górach Ziemi Sanockiej. 1866. III. 127.[1]
Solereder, Hans. Zur Anatomie und Systematik der Combretaceen. 1885. II. 615.[1]
— Aristolochiaceae. 1889. II. 180.[2]
— Beiträge zur ... Anatomie der Aristolochiaceen. 1889. II. 180,[1] 288.[2]
— Ein Beitrag zur anatomischen Charakteristik . . . der Rubiaceen. 1893. II. 808.[1]
— Buddleia Geisseana. 1898. II. 759.[1]
— Ueber einige Fälle anomaler Zweigstructur. 1890. II. 800.[1]
— Loganiaceae. 1895. II. 716.[2]
— Loganiaceae africanae. 1893. II. 716.[2]
— Zur Morphologie ... der Gattung Cercidiphyllum. 1899. II. 195.[1]
— Ueber eine neue Oleacee. 1891. II. 712.[1]
— Ueber eine aus den Samen von Swietenia humilis Zucc. bestehende Droge. 1891. III. 513.[1]
— Ueber die Staphyleaceengattung Tapiscia. 1892. II. 473.[2]
— Studien über die Tribus der Gaertnereen. 1890. II. 716.[2]
— Systematische Anatomie der Dicotyledonen. 1898. I. 101.[1]
— Ueber die systematische Stellung . . . Hymenocnemis. 1891. II. 820.[2]
— Ueber den systematischen und phylogenetischen Werth der Gefässdurchbrechungen. 1888. I. 124.
— Ueber den systematischen Wert der Holzstructur. 1885. I. 125, 853.[1]
— Uebe die Versetzung der Gattung Melananthus. 1891. II. 773.[2]
— Ueber die Zugehörigkeit der Gattung Platymitium. 1896. II. 473.[1]
— Ueber die Zugehörigkeit des von Masters als Bragantia . . . beschriebenen anomalen Stammstückes. 1894. II. 55,[1] 181.[2]
— Zwei Beiträge zur Systematik der Solanaceen. 1898. II. 768.[1]
Solf. Ueber die forstlichen Verhältnisse des Elsass-Lothringens. 1880. IV. 349.[1]
— Massregeln gegen die Maikäfer. 1865. IV. 202.
Solff, F. & Mitscher, G. Die in Elsass-Lothringen geltenden Forst- und Jagdgesetze. 1876. IV. 317.[1]
Solger, Zucht und Pflege der Aprikosen- und Pfirsich- und Reineklauden-Bäume. 1813. III. 430.[1]
On solid vegetable oils. 1845. III. 224.[1]
Solignac, C. L'Eucalyptus dans le midi de la France. 1890. IV. 530.
— Le Mimosa dealbata dans le Midi. 1889. III. 464.[1]
— Les Palmiers . . . dans le midi de la France. 1891. III. 124.[2]
The solitary or Carthusian gard'ner. See GENTIL, François. 1704. III. 111.
Soliva, Salvador. Dissertación sobre el Sen de España. 1774. III. 470.[1]
Solla, Rüdiger Felix. Sopra alcune speciali cellule nel Carrubo. 1893. II. 345.[1]
— Alcuni saggi teratologici della flora di Vallombrosa. 1896. I. 144.[1]
— Beiträge zur näheren Kenntniss . . . der Intercellularsubstanz. 1879. I. 138.[1]
— Caratteri propri della flora di Vallombrosa. 1893. I. 430.
— Caso di poliembrionia nel Carrubo. 1893. II. 345.[1]
— Cenni sulle Rose di Vallombrosa. 1896. III. 286.[2]
— Contribuzioni allo studio della flora della Campagna romana. 1883. I. 429.
— Sui cristalli di silice . . . nelle Palme. 1884. II. 63.[1]
— Enumerazione di casi patologici osservati nella foresta di Vallombrosa. 1896. IV. 209.[1]
— Die Hölzer auf der Oesterr.-ungar. Industrie- . . . Ausstellung in Triest. 1883. IV. 399.[1]
— Note di fitopatologia. 1888. IV. 209.[2]
— Notizie botaniche dell' Italia centrale. 1892. I. 430.[1]
— Zwei neue Eichengallen. 1892. IV. 511.

Sollers, Basil. Check-list of plants . . . Baltimore. 1888. I. 315.
Sollewyn Gelpke, J. H. F. Hemileia vastatrix. 1879. III. 735. — 1880. III. 735.
— De vruchtenteelt op de erven der inlanders. 1880. III. 147.[1]
Solly, Edward. Experiments on the Dhak Gond. 1844. III. 468.[1]
— De l'influence de l'électricité. 1846. I. 231.[1]
— On the influence of electricity. 1846. I. 231.[1]
— On the yellow colour of the Barberry. 1843. III. 394.[2]
Solms. Forstdiebstahls-Gesetz vom 15. April 1878. 1882. IV. 321.
Solms-Laubach, Herman, Graf zu. Über den Bau und die Entwicklung der Ernährungsorgane parasitischer Phanerogamen. 1867. I. 233.[2]
— Ueber den Bau von Blüthe . . . der Pandanaceae. 1878. II. 56.[1]
— Über die von Beccari . . . Neu-Guinea gesammelten Pandanaceae. 1883. II. 56.[1]
— Ueber die Beobachtungen . . . an den Smyrnafeigen. 1893. II. 151.[1]
— Caricaceae. 1889. II. 582.[1] — 1894. II. 582.[1]
— Chloranthaceae. 1869. II. 95.[1]
— Ueber einige geformte Vorkommnisse oxalsauren Kalkes. 1871. I. 139, II. 17.[2]
— Die Geschlechterdifferenzirung bei den Feigenbäumen. 1885. II. 150.[2]
— Das Haustorium der Loranthaceen. 1875. II. 173.[2]
— Die Heimath . . . des cultivirten Melonenbaumes. 1889. II. 582.[2]
— Die Herkunft . . . des gewöhnlichen Feigenbaums. 1882. II. 150.[1]
— Monographia Pandanacearum. 1879. II. 56.[1]
— Pandanaceae. 1889. II. 56.[1]
— Die Sprossfolge der Stangeria. 1890. II. 3.[1]
Solomons, T. S. Mt. Goddard and its vicinity. 1896. II. 41.[2]
Solon, Martin. Emploi du suc de la racine de Sureau. 1832. III. 752.[1]
Solórzano, Justino. Instrucciones sobre el cultivo del Naranjo. 1889. III. 500.[1]
Soltsien, P. Zur Kenntniss einiger Citrusöle. 1886. III. 499.[1]
Soltwedel, F. Koffiezdekten in Brazilië. 1889. III. 736.
Sóitz, Gyula & Fekete, Lajos. Az erdőbecsléstan kézikönyve. 1882. IV. 214.
Sombart, Werner. Der Holz-Zoll. 1883. IV. 284.[2]
Some account of the Cacao tree. 1834. III. 594.
Some account of the Napoleona imperialis. 1844. II. 612.[2]
Some account of the Paraguay Tea. 1842. III. 530.[1]
Some celebrated Yews. 1885. II. 11.[1]
Some facts regarding the production of resins . . . in India. 1888. IV. 463.[1]
Some foreign trees for the southern states. See JONES, J. D. & others. 1895. IV. 124.[1]
Some hortulan communications about the curious engrafting of Orenges and Lemons. 1667. III. 496.[1]
Some Indian food plants. 1889. III. 629.[1]
Some natural enemies of the fluted scale. 1890. III. 192.[1]
Some new Indian insect pests. 1892. III. 192.[1]
Some notes on the genus Eucalyptus. 1890. IV. 530.
Some notices of the Sorb trees of Wyre forest. 1855. II. 312.[2]
Some of the pale hardwood timbers of New South Wales. See MAIDEN, J. H. 1892. IV. 531.[1]
Some phenomena connected with the cambium-layer. 1882. I. 210.[2]
Some popular English plant names. 1889. I. 74.[1]
Some remarks on forest concessions in Oudh. 1900. IV. 335.
Some sacred trees. 1884. I. 295.[1]
On some species of Acokanthera. 1894. II. 722.[2]
Some timely lessons from the forests of India. — Forest fires. 1896. IV. 295,[2] 554.
On some woods . . . in Japan. 1880. IV. 399.[1]
Someren, G. J. van. Forests. 1886. IV. 378.
— Germination of Babul seeds. 1887. II. 377.[1]
— List of forest trees in Mysore and Coorg. 1879. I. 470.[1]
— List of trees in the Melghát forests. 1887. I. 470,[2] IV. 88.[2]
— Notes on . . . the Carob tree. 1880. III. 471.[1]
Somers, Fred M. Forests of the California coast range. 1889. I. 320, IV. 78.[1]

Somerville, W. D. The Pine beetle. 1891. IV. 461.[2]
Somerville, William. The distribution of trees in a wood. 1890. IV. 154.[1]
— Experiments with tree seeds. 1898. III. 156.[2]
— The growth of trees. 1890. III. 38.[2]
— How to combat the attack of injurious forest insects. 1893. IV. 200.
— Influences affecting British forestry. 1890. IV. 357.[2]
— Larix europaea as a breeding-place for Hylesinus. 1890. IV. 451.
— The natural regeneration of woods. 1893. IV. 140.
— A new enemy of the Larch. 1895. IV. 451.
— The quality of coniferous timber. 1892. IV. 443.[1]
— Recent investigations in Prussia in regard to the quality of timber. 1898. IV. 409.
— Report on the effects of frost. 1895. III. 47.
— Report on the inquiry . . . into the disease of the Larch. 1890. IV. 451.
— The science of forestry. 1889. IV. 34.[2]
— A short account of the state forests of Prussia. 1895. IV. 355.[1]
Sommer, Fr. Kurze Beschreibung des Reviers Polnisch-Ostrau. 1900. IV. 370.
Sommer, Gustav. Die Bäume und Sträucher der Grossh. Schlossgartenanlagen zu Karlsruhe. 1886. I. 48.
— Führer durch den Grossh. Botanischen Garten zu Karlsruhe. 1888. I. 48.
Sommer, Johann. *See* OLORINUS, Johannes.
Sommerfeldt, Christian. Afhandling om nyttige Have-Vexters Dyrkning. 1780. III. 100.[2]
— Forsøg om de vigtigste Natur-Produkter . . . i Norge. 1776. III. 270.[1]
Sommerfelt, Sören Christian. Physisk-oeconomisk beskrivelse over Saltdalen. 1824. I. 353.
— Supplementum Florae lapponicae. 1826. I. 353.
Sommermeyer. Ueber die Vermehrung nicht ganz winterharter Gehölze. 1887. III. 153.
Sommier, F. *See* HUTEAU, H. & SOMMIER, F.
Sommier, Stefano. Aggiunte alla florula di Capraia. 1898. I. 430.
— Ancora delle fioriture anormali. 1897. I. 227.[1]
— Cenno sui resultati botanici di un viaggio nel Caucaso. 1892. I. 369.
— Una cima vergine nelle Alpi Apuane. 1894. II. 498.[1]
— Il Cistus laurifolius. 1899. II. 564.[2]
— Un' estate in Siberia fra Ostiacchi. 1885. V. xxiii.[1]
— Flora dell' Ob inferiore. 1892. I. 454.[2]
— L' isola del Giglio e la sua flora. 1900. I. 430.
— Della presenza di stipole nella Lonicera. 1890. II. 836.[2]
— Risultati botanici di un viaggio all' Ob inferiore. 1892. I. 454.[2]
— *See also* LEVIER, Émile & SOMMIER, Stefano.
— & Levier, Émile. Decas plantarum novarum Caucasi. 1892. II. 843.[2]
— — Enumeratio plantarum . . . in Caucaso lectarum. 1900. I. 370.
Sonck, J. G., **Timgren**, G. O. & **Hannikainen**, P. W. Ruotsalais-suomalainen metsänhoitosanasto. 1893. IV. 23.[2]
Sonder, Otto Wilhelm. Beiträge zur Flora von Südafrika. 1850. I. 494.
— Beschreibung der Spathodea Jenischii. 1848. II. 790.[2]
— Enumeratio Santalacearum in Africa australi. 1857. II. 167.[2]
— Epacrideae R. Brown. 1844. II. 687.[2]
— Flora hamburgensis. 1851. I. 383.
— Plantae Muellerianae. . . . Compositae. 1852. I. 501.
— Plantae Muellerianae. Epacrideae. 1853. I. 501.
— Plantae Regnellianae. 1849. I. 342.
— *See also* HARVEY, W. H. & SONDER, O. W.
Sondriò, Pietro, CAIMI DA. *See* CAIMI DA SONDRIÒ, Pietro.
Songeon, André. *See* PERRIER, E. & SONGEON, André.
— & Chabert, Alfred. Herborisations aux environs de Chambéry. 1896. I. 418.
— & Perrier, E. Notes sur des plantes rares . . . de la Savoie. 1859. I. 435.
Sonnenburg, Albert. Arithmonomia naturalis. 1838. I. 98.
Sonnenschein, Le Gelsemium sempervirens. 1877. III. 682.[1]
Sonnerat, Pierre. Reise nach Ostindien und China. 1782. I. 302.
— Voyage à la Nouvelle Guinée. 1776. I. 499.[1]
— Voyage aux Indes Orientales. 1782. I. 302.
Sonneville, G. de. Conférence de M. F. Vassillière. 1898. III. 582.

Sonnini, **Veillard** & **Chevalier**. Vocabulaire portatif d'agriculture. 1810. III. 29.[2]
Sonnini de Manoncour, Charles Sigisbert. Travels in Greece and Turkey. 1801. I. 448.[2]
— Travels in upper and lower Egypt. 1799. III. 280.[2]
— Voyage dans la haute et basse Egypte. 1799. III. 280.[2]
— Voyage en Grèce et en Turquie. 1801. I. 448,[2] V. xxiii.[1]
Sonntag, C. O. A pocket flora of Edinburgh. 1894. I. 535.
Sonntag, Christoph. Paralipomena quibus ligna Sittim explicata. 1710. I. 512.
Sonntag, Cl. Garrya elliptica. 1889. III. 352.[2]
Sonntag, Paul. Über Dauer des Scheitelwachsthums. 1887. I. 191.[1]
Sontagh, Nikolausz von. A növényzeti viszonyokról. 1873. I. 446.
Soobrazheniya . . . *See* Соображенія . . .
Soosin, MOTABARA. *See* MOTABARA-SOOSIN.
Sur la sophistication du thé. *See* Die VERFÄLSCHUNG des Thee's. 1853. III. 607.
Die Sophora-Arten. 1884. III. 487.[2]
The old Sophoras at Kew. 1886. III. 488.[1]
Sorauer, Paul. Ueber das Abwerfen der Blätter. 1888. I. 192.[1]
— Arbeiten der pflanzenphysiologischen Versuchsstation. 1876. III. 40.
— Das Begiessen der Linden bei Strassenpflanzungen. 1895. III. 585.[1]
— Die Beschädigungen der Vegetation durch Asphaltdämpfe. 1897. III. 185.[2]
— Düngungsversuche bei Obstbäumen. 1880. III. 151.
— Der Einfluss der Luftfeuchtigkeit. 1878. I. 232.[2]
— Einige Bemerkungen zu den von . . . Magnus gegebenen Mitteilungen. 1895. III. 643.[1]
— Die Entstehung der Rostflecken auf Aepfeln. 1875. III. 444.[1]
— Erkrankungsfälle durch Monilia. 1899. III. 195.[2]
— Die Fleckenkrankheit . . . der Birnen. 1878. III. 446.[1]
— Ueber Frostbeschädigungen. 1882. I. 212.
— Ueber Frostschorf an Apfel- und Birnenstämmen. 1891. III. 444.[2]
— Handbuch der Pflanzenkrankheiten. 1874. III. 179.
— Ueber Intumescenzen. 1899. I. 213.[2]
— Ueber die Keimungsarbeit der Fichtensamen. 1875. II. 36.[2]
— Ueber die Knotensucht des Gummibaumes. 1890. III. 370.[2]
— Krebs an Ribes nigrum. 1891. III. 415.[1]
— Ueber den Krebs der Apfelbäume. 1877. III. 427.[2]
— Die Kunst des Giessens. 1899. III. 151.
— Die Lohkrankheit an Kirschen. 1889. III. 435.[2]
— Die " Lohkrankheit " der Bäume. 1899. III. 180.[1]
— Mittheilungen aus dem Gebiete der Phytopathologie. 1890. I. 213.[2]
— Zur Monilia-Krankheit. 1899. III. 195.[2]
— Nachweis der Verweichlichung der Zweige unserer Obstbäume. 1892. III. 444.[2]
— Die Obstbaumkrankheiten. 1879. III. 179.
— Ein Pilsbrand bei Ulmus Pitteursi. 1895. III. 364.[2]
— Populäre Pflanzenphysiologie. 1891. I. 149.[1]
— A popular treatise on the physiology of plants. 1891. I. 149.[1]
— Ringelungsversuch an Kirschen. 1872. V. xi,[2] xii.[1]
— Die Rostkrankheiten der forstlichen Kulturpflanzen. 1890. IV. 212.
— Ueber die Rotfärbung der Spaltöffnungen bei Picea. 1897. III. 185,[2] IV. 457.
— Schaden Asphaltdämpfe den Berliner Gärten? 1897. III. 185.[2]
— Die Schäden der einheimischen Kulturpflanzen. 1888. III. 179.
— Schutz der Obstbäume gegen Krankheiten. 1900. III. 180.[1]
— Studien ueber die Ernährung der Obstbäume. 1877. I. 159.
— Studien über Frostbeschädigungen. 1891. I. 167.
— Die symptomatische Bedeutung der Intumescenzen. 1890. I. 213.[2]
— Die in der Umgegend Berlins . . . aushaltenden Nadelhölzer. 1863. III. 289.
— Ein Versuch mit Botrytis tenella. 1894. III. 197.
— Die Versuchs-Stationen für Gartenbau. 1878. III. 32.[1]
— Vorläufige Notiz über Veredlung. 1875. I. 208.[1]
— Die Wassersucht bei Ribes aureum. 1880. III. 414.[1]

— Welche Massnahmen sind . . . eingeleitet worden, um die Erforschung der . . . Pflanzenkrankheiten zu befördern. 1890. III. 179.
— Wirkungen künstlicher Fröste. 1885. I. 212.
— Der Wurzelkropf bei Kernobstbäumen. 1885. I. 213,² *III. 444.*¹
— *See also* FRANK, A. B. & SORAUER, Paul.
— & **Ramann**, Emil. Sogenannte unsichtbare Rauchbeschädigungen. 1899. III. 185.²
Soravia, Pietro. Descrizione delle risine e palorci. 1885. IV. 389.
— Tecnologia botanico-forestale. 1877. IV. 86.¹.
Soravia, Roberto. Il Cansiglio, foresta demaniale inalienabile. 1879. IV. 28.¹
Sordelli, Ferdinando. Fruttificazione anomala . . . nel Pino di Corsica. 1880. II. 44.¹
Sorgenfrei. *See* Зоренфрей.
Soria, R. F. de. Proposición de ley, determinando las condiciones y forma en que pueden convalidarse los derechos del colonato. 1887. IV. 327.
Sornander, Rutger. Ueber das Vorkommen von subfossilen Strünken. 1891. I. 350,² *IV. 79.*²
Sorokine, Nikolai Vasilevitch. Courte description d'un voyage dans l'Asie centrale. 1884. II. 188.¹
— *See also* СОРОКИНЪ, Н. В.
Sorolla, Ildefonse. Épitome medices. 1642. I. 285.¹
Sospizio, C. Le foreste in Italia. 1866. IV. 122.²
Šostarić, Max. Anatomische Untersuchungen über . . . Salicineen. 1898. II. 96.¹
Sostegni, L. *See* BERLESE, A. N. & SOSTEGNI, L.
Sostoyaniye . . . *See* Состояние . . .
Soto, Ferdinando de. The discovery and conquest of Terra Florida. 1609. III. 263.²
— A narrative of the expedition . . . into Florida. 1609. III. 263.²
— Virginia, richly valued. 1609. III. 263.¹
— The worthye and famous history of the travailes . . . of Terra Florida. 1609. III. 263.¹
Soto, Manuel. Cultivo del Pino maritimo. 1889. IV. 467.²
Soubeiran, Eugène. Analyse chimique de l'humus. 1850. III. 151.
— De l'état de la pectine dans les fruits. 1847. I. 179.¹
— Expériences sur la racine de Manioc. 1828. III. 519.²
— Over de geneeskrachtige eigenschappen der planten. 1829. III. 268.¹
— Sur la gutta percha. 1847. III. 668.¹
— Mémoire sur les semences de quelques Euphorbiacées. 1829. III. 514.¹
— Note sur les propriétés médicales du Séné du Sénégal. 1828. III. 471.¹
— Sur la racine de l'Arbousier. 1853. III. 648.¹
Soubeiran, J. Léon. Des applications de la botanique à la pharmacie. 1854. III. 238.¹
— Une ascension à la Maladetta. 1863. I. 421.
— Culture des Cinchona à la Jamaïque. 1870. III. 713,¹ *717.*¹
— Culture des Cinchona à Sainte-Hélène. 1869. III. 717.²
— Culture du Cinchona . . . à la Jamaïque. 1877. III. 713.¹
— Culture du Cinchona aux Indes anglaises. 1877. III. 714.
— Description de deux espèces de galles . . . sur le Quercus. 1859. IV. 509.
— De l'écorce du Cailcédra. 1856. III. 512.²
— Études micrographiques sur quelques fécules. 1853. I. 140.¹
— Études sur les Badianes. 1886. III. 397.²
— Des gommes du Sénégal. 1856. III. 227, 463.²
— Histoire des gommes du Sénégal. 1856. III. 463.²
— Sur un Irvingia (Irvingia Oliveri) de Cochinchine. 1886. III. 508.¹
— Mode de préparation du cachou. 1871. III. 464.¹
— Note on the manna of the Alhagi. 1861. III. 466.²
— Note sur de la gomme de Sonora. 1855. III. 477,¹ *481.*²
— Note sur la récolte de la gomme adraganthe. 1857. III. 467.²
— Note sur le Bassia latifolia. 1881. III. 667.²
— Note sur le Palo-Mabi. 1887. III. 541.²
— Note sur le Bassia de l'Inde. 1870. III. 667.¹
— Note sur les huiles de bois. 1884. III. 610.²
— Note sur quelques produits de la Nouvelle Calédonie. 1870. III. 283.²
— Note sur une Loranthacée toxique. 1861. III. 385,¹ *385.*²
— Nouveau dictionnaire des falsifications . . . des aliments. 1874. III. 218.²

— Des plantes à sucre. 1862. III. 220.²
— Récolte du mastic à Chio. 1870. III. 525.²
— Le Sagou à Bornéo. 1889. III. 327.²
— Some particulars respecting the gums from Senegal. 1856. III. 463.²
— Du sucre de jagre ou de Palmier. 1857. III. 319.¹
— & **Darby de Thiersant**, Philibert. Études sur la matière médicale des Chinois. 1873. III. 273.¹
— — La matière médicale chez les Chinois. 1874. III. 273.¹
— & **Delondre**, Augustin. De l'acclimatation des Cinchonas dans les Indes. 1867. III. 713.²
— — De l'introduction . . . des Cinchonas dans les Indes. 1867. III. 713.²
— — Note sur la culture des Cinchonas. 1867. III. 714.
— — Produits végétaux du Portugal. 1867. III. 271.²
Soucha, Wilhelm. Beschreibung der Excursionstour . . . in die . . . Forste der Domaine Tetschen-Bodenbach. 1880. IV. 371.
— Beschreibung der Exkursion . . . in die . . . Forste der Domäne Tachau. 1872. IV. 371.
— Exkursion . . . in die Forste der . . . Domaine Worlik. 1878. IV. 371.
— *See also* DITTRICH, Gustav & SOUCHA, Wilhelm.
Souché, Baptiste. Flore du Haut Poitou. 1894. I. 418.
— Flore populaire des environs de Pamproux. 1892. III. 86.
Soudés, Louis. Étude synthétique sur le Coca. 1874. III. 493.¹
Souheur, Jean. Instruction pratique pour le traitement du mildiou. 1892. III. 196.
— Praktische handleiding der behandeling van den valschen meeldauw. 1892. III. 196.
Soukup. Der Vogel-Kirschbaum. 1863. III. 435.²
Soulange-Bodin, Étienne. Ueber Ailanthus glandulosa. 1834. IV. 525.
— Azalea nudiflora var. thyrsiflora. 1832. III. 661.²
— Beau phénomène de fructification, Magnolia. 1831. III. 398.²
— Sur les boutures. 1829. III. 157.
— Cactus (Epiphyllum) Ackermanni. 1832. III. 625.²
— Camellia mutabilis. 1831. III. 597.²
— Comparaison d'emploi des feuilles du Mûrier. 1832. III. 374.
— Conseil général de l'agriculture; rapport . . . sur le reboisement des montagnes. 1842. IV. 161.²
— De la culture des plantes dites de terre de bruyère. 1828. III. 40, 181.¹
— Description du Magnolia Soulangiana. 1828. II. 212.²
— Greffe du Mûrier multicaule. 1834. III. 380.²
— De la greffe herbacée. 1829. III. 163.²
— Vom krautartigen Pfropfen. 1829. III. 163.²
— Liquidambar styraciflua Lin. 1835. III. 253.²
— Liriodendron Tulipifera. 1834. IV. 519.²
— Mémoire sur l'introduction des arbres forestiers exotiques. 1833. IV. 126.²
— Moyen facile de propager rapidement les Bruyères. 1832. III. 649.²
— Notice sur l'élagage. 1829. III. 169.¹
— Notice sur le Maclura aurantiaca. 1827. III. 372.¹
— Notice sur les soins à donner aux Camellias. 1827. III. 599,¹ V. XXIX.²
— Notice sur une nouvelle espèce de Magnolia. 1826. *II, 212,*¹ III. 400.¹
— Nouvelle espèce de Pin d'Écosse. 1832. IV. 471.
— Nouvelles variétés de Magnolia Soulangiana. 1834. III. 400.¹
— Observations sur la culture du Pinus australis. 1830. III. 308.¹
— Ueber die Pflege der Camellien. 1827. III. 599.¹
— Plantes cultivées à Fromont. 1831. III. 415.¹
— Plantes nouvelles. 1832. III. 455,¹ *659.*²
— Propagation des Camellia doubles. 1832. III. 599.¹
— Qualités du Vernis du Japon. 1834. IV. 525.
— Quelques observations sur les greffes. 1832. III. 160. — 1833. I. 208.¹
— Revue forestière américaine. 1832. IV. 7.5.²
— Robinier jaune. 1831. III. 486.²
Soulavie, J. L. GIRAUD-. *See* GIRAUD-SOULAVIE, J. L.
Soulié. Note sur une méthode employée de combattre les maladies de la Vigne. 1853. III. 559.²
Soulié, J. *See* COSTE, Hippolyte & SOULIÉ, J.
Soupert & Notting. Traité sur la culture des Rosiers. 1894. III. 453.¹
Sourbets, G. Le Pin maritime. 1870. IV. 468.¹
The sources of manna. 1861. III. 221.¹

The sources of musk. 1861. III. *512*,[1] 513.[1]
The sources of rubber. *See* JOHNSON, Thomas. 1899. III. 230.[1]
Sources of rubber supply. 1892. III. 229, *231*.
Sourdeval, Ch. de. Sur quelques curiosités végétales. 1860. I. 234.[2]
Sousa Pimentel, Carlos Augusto de. Algunas observaciones sobre la formacion del duramen. 1884. IV. 64.[2]
— Les arbres géants du Portugal. 1894: I. 297.[2]
— Arvores giganteas de Portugal. 1894. I. 297.[2]
— Carvalhos. 1878. IV. 500.[2]
— O Castanheiro. 1877. III. 360.[1]
— Ciprés de Bussaco. 1886. IV. 448.[1]
— Creação e exploração dos Pinhaes. 1878. IV. 462.[1]
— Duas arvores para matta. *See* PIMENTEL, C. A. de S. 1877. IV. 122,[2] 127.[1]
— Estudos florestaes. 1894. IV. 363.[1]
— Eucalypto globulus. 1876. IV. 532.[2]
— Eucalyptos. 1878. IV. 530.
— The giant trees of Portugal. 1894. I. 297.[2]
— Pinhaes, soutos e montados, cultura. 1882. IV. 109.[3]
— O Taxodium distichum. 1877. III. 311.[1]
Sousa Tellos, J. J. de. Visitas ao horto-botanico da Eschola medico-chirurgica de Lisboa. 1846. I. 60.[1]
South African agriculturists' year book. III. 27.[1]
South African Bamboo. 1879. III. 315.[2]
South African industrial exhibition, Cape Town. 1885. IV. 401.[1]
South African philosophical society. Transactions. I. 29.[2]
South Australia — Botanic garden & government plantations. Report. 1879. I. 69,[1] V. IX.[1]
South Australia — Forest board. Annual report. IV. 17.[1]
South Australia — Journal of agriculture ... *See* JOURNAL ... III. 27.[1]
South Australia — Royal society. *See* PHILOSOPHICAL SO-CIETY OF ADELAIDE. I. 29.[2]
South Australia — Woods and forests department. Annual progress report. *See* SOUTH AUSTRALIA — FOREST BOARD. IV. 17.[1]
South Carolina — Agricultural experiment station. *See* SOUTH CAROLINA — CLEMSON AGRICULTURAL COLLEGE ... III. 8.
South Carolina — Clemson agricultural college — Experiment station. Annual report. Bulletin. III. 8.
South Carolina; resources. *See* HAMMOND, Harry. 1883. III. 264.[1]
South Dakota — Agricultural college — Agricultural experiment station. Annual report. Bulletin. III. 8.
South Dakota — Agricultural experiment station. *See* SOUTH DAKOTA — AGRICULTURAL COLLEGE. III. 8.
South Wales — Royal institution. *See* ROYAL ... I. 20.
Southall, H. & Watkins, B. M. Earliest dates of flowering. 1861. I. 226.[1]
In the southern Alleghenies. 1899. IV. 179.[2]
Southern bivouac. III. 8.
Southern botanic journal. I. 7.[1]
Southern California acclimatizing association. General catalogue. 1900. I. 521;[1] *see also* FRANCESCHI, Francesco. 1900. V. XXVII.[2]
A southern California canyon. 1892. I. 326.
Southern California horticulturist. III. 8.
Southern florist and gardener. III. 8.
Southern horticulturist. III. 8.
Southern industrial and lumber review. IV. 5.[1]
The Southern literary messenger. III. 8.
Southern lumber journal. IV. 5.[1]
Southern lumberman. IV. 5.[1]
Southern milling and lumber journal. IV. 539.[1]
The southern science record. I. 520.[2]
Southron, (*pseud.*). The Aphelandras. 1895. III. 708.[2]
— The Granadilla. 1897. III. 616.[2]
— The Stove Aristolochias. 1896. III. 386.[1]
Southwestern iron and lumber record. IV. 5.[1]
Southwick, Edmund B. Economic entomology in relation to trees. 1896. III. 187.
Le soutrage et la multiplication des insectes. 1896. IV. 72.
Soutter, Wilham: Questions concerning the temperature of plants. 1898. I. 187.
— Rhea (Boehmeria nivea), Ramie or China grass. 1899. III. 382.[2]
Sowerby, Charles Edward. An illustrated catalogue of British plants. 1841. I. 399.
Sowerby, James. Account of the difference of structure in the flowers of six species of Passiflora. 1794. II. 577.[1]

— Botanical drawing-book. 1788. I. 37.[1]
— Botanisches Zeichenbuch. 1788. I. 37.[1]
— An easy introduction to drawing flowers. 1788. I. 37.[1]
— English botany. *See* SOWERBY, James & SMITH, J. E. 1790. I. 395.
— Introduction to the art of drawing flowers. 1788. I. 37.[1]
— & Smith, J. E. English botany. 1790. I. 395.
Sowerby, John Edward. An illustrated key to ... British wild flowers. 1865. I. 402.
Sowerby, William. Note on the cultivation of the Mangrove tree. 1870. III. 632.[1]
Soyaux, Herman. Aus West-Afrika. 1879. I. 491.
Soyer-Willemet, Hubert Felix. Sur les Erica multiflora et E. vagans. 1833. II. 664.[1]
— Mémoire sur le nectaire. 1826. I. 118.[2]
— Observations sur le mémoire de M. Braconnot. 1845. I. 158.
— Observations sur quelques plantes de France. 1828. I. 408.
Sp., R. Die Umwandlung von Wald in Weideland. 1883. II. 708.[2]
Spaan, A. J. *See* LITH, P. A. van der, SPAAN, A. J. & POKKENS, F.
Spach, Eduard. Bemerkungen über die Platanen. 1841. II. 254.[2]
— Conspectus monographiae Cistacearum. 1836. II. 563.[2]
— Conspectus monographiae Hypericacearum. 1836. II. 552.[2]
— Description of some new Cistaceae. 1836. II. 565.[2]
— Generum et specierum Hippocastanearum revisio. 1834. II. 480.[2]
— Histoire naturelle des végétaux. 1834. I. 260.
— Hypericacearum monographiae fragmenta. 1836. II. 552.[2]
— Monographia generis Amygdalus. 1843. II. 270.[2]
— Monographia generis Acerum. 1843. II. 385.[1]
— Monographia Onagrearum. 1835. II. 642.[2]
— Note sur les Carpinus. 1841. II. 120.[2]
— Note sur les Ostrya. 1841. II. 122.[2]
— Note sur les Planera. 1841. II. 142,[2] *145*.[1]
— Note sur les Platanes. 1841. II. 254.[2]
— Note sur les Ulmacées. 1841. II. 141.[1]
— Notes on the genus Corylus. 1841. II. 121.[1]
— Notes sur les Corylus. 1841. II. 121.[1]
— Onagrearum novarum ... descriptiones. 1835. II. 642.[2]
— Organographie des Cistacées. 1836. II. 563.[2]
— Revisio Betulacearum. 1841. II. 115.[1]
— Revisio Celticum genuinarum. 1841. II. 141.[2]
— Revisio generis Acerum. 1834. II. 476.[1]
— Revisio generis Genista. 1844. II. 359.[1]
— Revisio generis Tiliarum. 1834. II. 515.[1]
— Revisio Grossulariearum. 1835. II. 243.[1]
— Revisio Populorum. 1841. II. 96.[1]
— Revisio Tiliarum. 1842. II. 515.[2]
— Revisio Ulmorum. 1841. II. 142.[2]
— Révision des Juniperus. 1841. II. 30.[1]
— Synopsis monographiae Onagrearum. 1835. II. 642.[2]
— *See also* JAUBERT, H. F. comte de & SPACH, Eduard; MIR-BEL, C. F. B. de & SPACH, Eduard.
Spada, *comte de* MEDICI. *See* MEDICI SPADA, *comte de*.
Spadaro. *See* SANSON, A., FLÜCKIGER, F. A. & SPADARO.
Spadoni, Paolo. Lettera dissertatoria relativa à due Rose profifiche. 1790. III. 289.[1]
— Pellegrinazione alle gessaje di S. Angelo. 1813. I. 425.
— Delle siepi vive di Spino bianco. 1790. III. 422.[1]
— Xilologia picena applicata alle arti. 1826. III. 88.[1]
Spae, D. Asalea indica var. setosa, barbata hort. 1848. III. 659.[2]
— Azalea ledifolia DeC. var. lacteola striata. 1848. III. 661.[1]
— Azalea Mortieriana var. 1846. III. 661.[2]
— Azalea sinensis var. macrantha. 1847. III. 662.[2]
— Camellia fulgens plenissima. 1849. III. 598.[2]
— Camellia japonica Linn. var. Alcina rosea. 1847. III. 598.[2]
— Camellia japonica Linn. var. americana. 1847. III. 598.[2]
— Camellia japonica Linn. var. Augustina. 1847. III. 598.[2]
— Camellia japonica Linn. var. Mathotiana. 1847. III. 598.[2]
— Camellia japonica Linn. var. Verschaffeltiana. 1847. III. 598.[2]
— Crataegus Oxyacantha Linn. var. punicea. 1847. III. 422.[1]

— Fuchsia macrostemma. 1847. III. 640.[1]
— Gompholobium virgatum Sieber. 1846. II. 362.[2]
— Lonicera hirsuta Eaton. 1849. II. 838.[1]
— Rhododendron (Azalea) ledifolium DeC. var. Ambrosil. 1847. III. 661.[1]
— Rhododendron hybridum var. amoenum. 1848. III. 659.[1]
— Spiraea amoena Nob. 1846. II. 314.[2]
— Spiraea decumbens Koch. 1849. II. 315.[1]
— Wisteria brachybotrys. 1847. II. 388.[1]
Spaendonck, Gerard van. Fleurs dessinées d'après nature. 182.? I. 266.
— Souvenirs de Van Spaendonck. 1825. I. 267.
Spätfröste im Frühjahr 1882. 1882. IV. 191.[1]
Die Spätfröste im Jahre 1857. 1858. IV. 191.[1]
Spätfröste und Laubholznachzucht. 1871. IV. 191.[1]
Späth, Johann Leonhard. Abhandlung über den forstlichen Zuwachs. 1798. IV. 242. — 1799. IV. 232.
— Abhandlung über die periodischen Durchforstungen. 1802. IV. 172.[2]
— Anleitung die Mathematik . . . auf das Forstwesen . . . nützlich anzuwenden. 1797. IV. 57.
— Berichtserstattung wegen Devastation einer Waldung. 1798. IV. 253.
— Beschreibung und . . . weisung eines . . . Taxationsinstrumentes. 1802. IV. 231.[1]
— Handbuch der Forstwissenschaft. 1801. IV. 96.
— Inhaltsanzeige der Privat-Vorlesungen . . . über das Forstwesen. 1797. IV. 31.
— Ueber die örtliche progressive Wachsthumszunahme der Waldbäume. 1796. IV. 232.
— Praktische Abhandlung über das Verkohlen des Holzes. 1800. IV. 394.
— Taxation der Hut- . . . und eigenherrlichen Rechte. 1824. IV. 254.
Späth, Ludwig. Abelia rupestris hort. 1892. III. 748.[2]
— Acer carpinifolium. 1892. III. 534.[2]
— Acer palmatum Thbg. var. Aokii. 1892. III. 535.[2]
— Acer rubrum L. var. Drummondii. 1892. III. 536.[1]
— Catalpa hybrida Hrt. 1898. III. 706.[1]
— Einige neue und seltene Gehölze der Späth'schen Baumschule. 1896. I. 49.
— Exochorda grandiflora Lindl. 1898. III. 424.[1]
— Die Frucht der Actinidia polygama. 1895. III. 595.[2]
— Gehölz- und Kakteen-Neuheiten. 1900. I. 49.
— Gehölz-Neuheiten. 1883. III. 69.
— Ein interessanter geschichtlicher Baum. 1896. II. 144.[1]
— Neue und sehr wenig verbreitete Ziergehölze. 1889. I. 48.
— Neuheiten von harten Gehölzarten. 1883. III. 536.[1]
— Neuzüchtigungen und Neueinführungen der Späth'schen Baumschule. 1890. I. 49.
— New trees and shrubs. 1896. III. 70.
— About Opuntias. 1900. III. 624.[2]
— Prunus Lauro-Cerasus Schipkaënsis. 1892. III. 437.
— Pyrus Malus aurea Späth. 1896. III. 684.[1]
— Pyrus (Malus) floribunda. 1898. III. 429.[1]
— Stephanandra Tanakae. 1900. III. 432.[1]
— Syringa amurensis Rupr. 1896. III. 680.[2]
— & Wittmack, Ludwig. Rubus deliciosus Torrey. 1898. III. 458.[1]
— Corylopsis pauciflora. 1899. II. 252.[2]
Spätherbst oder Frühfröste. 1860. IV. 191.[1]
Spalding, Thomas. Culture of Indigo. 1846. III. 479.[1]
Spalding, Volney Morgan. The dunes of Lake Michigan. 1882. IV. 145.
— Forestry in Michigan. 1882. IV. 338.[1]
— Guide to the study of common plants. 1893. I. 37.[1]
— Progress in forestry under state control. 1900. IV. 338.[2]
— The traumatropic curvature of roots. 1894. I. 194.
— The White Pine. 1899. IV. 471.
Spalding, William A. The Orange. 1885. III. 497.[1]
Spalikowski, Edmond. Sur la croissance du Gui en Normandie. 1900. II. 180.[1]
— Remarques sur la croissance du Gui dans la Seine-Inférieure. 1896. II. 179.[2]
Spalkhover. Beaucarnea longifolia Baker, in Blüthe. 1874. III. 337.[2]
Spall, P. W. A. van. Verslag over de Koffij- en Kaneelkultuur op . . . Ceylon. 1863. III. 405.[2] 733.[1]
Spallanzani, Lazaro, (abbé). Expériences pour servir à l'histoire de la génération. 1785. I. 199.
— Versuche über die Erzeugung der Thiere und Pflanzen. 1785. I. 199.

Spamer, A. Untersuchungen über Holzreife. 1882. I. 232,[2] IV. 72.
Spampani, Giuseppe. Alcune osservazioni sulla formazione dell' olio nell' Oliva. 1899. II. 713.[1]
Spandet, W. Om Græsning i Skove. 1858. IV. 134.[2]
Spangenberg, (Forstmeister, Creusburgerhütte). Ist die horstweise Einmischung der Eiche . . . vortheilhaft? 1895. IV. 138.[2]
— Umfang und Bedeutung der Waldstreu-Nutzung. 1886. IV. 438.[1]
— & Cusig, Alfred. Welche Grundsätze sind für die Mischung der Kiefer mit der Fichte . . . als massgebend anzusehen? 1892. IV. 138.[1]
— & Cusig, Paul. Unter welchen Verhältnissen ist . . . Pflanzung von Eichenheistern noch zulässig. 1894. IV. 508. (by error Cusig, [Alfred]).
Spangenberg, Ernst. Beitrag zur Kenntnis der Wirkung des Cytisin. 1891. III. 481.[1]
Spangenberg, H. G. von. Einige Vermuthungen über die Wechselfälle denen unsere deutschen Wälder . . . ausgesetzt sein möchten. 1842. IV. 274.[1]
— Ueber die frühere Forst-Barbarei. 1841. IV. 281.[1]
— Ueber die nothwendig zunehmende Erniedrigung der Productionskraft des Bodens. 1842. IV. 68.
Die Spanische Weisstanne. 1870. III. 297.[1]
Spanischer Ginster. 1828. III. 488.[2]
The Spanish Broom as a fibre plant. 1892. III. 488.[2]
The Spanish Broom as a textile plant. 1875. III. 488.[2]
The Spanish Chestnut. 1885. III. 359.[1]
Spanitz, Johann Nepomak. Eine forstfinanzielle Studie. 1877. IV. 256.
Spanjer, Otto. Untersuchungen über die Wasserapparate. 1898. I. 169.[2]
Spankeren, von. Bestands-Beschreibung und Angabe des Material-Ertrages . . . in dem k. Forstreviere Peisterwitz. 1859. IV. 260.[2]
Spanmuth. Epiphyllum truncatum. 1867. III. 623.[1]
Spanmuth, Fr. Das Hochpflanzen der Gehölze. 1872. III. 169.[2]
Spanoghe, J. B. Brief aan C. L. Blume uit Koepang op Timor. 1832. I. 465.
— Prodromus florae timorensis. 1836. I. 465.
Gli spari contro la grandine. 1899. IV. 191.[1]
Sparling, G. Deodar planting. 1885. IV. 447.[1]
Sparrman, Andreas. Beskrifning på en ny växt, en species af Protea. 1777. II. 165.[1]
— Iter in Chinam. See Linné, Carl von. 1452.
— Et nytt genus . . . Ekebergia. 1779. II. 420.[2]
— Reise nach dem Vorgebirge der Guten Hoffnung. 1783. I. 493.
— Resa till Goda-Hopps Udden. 1783. I. 493, V. xxiv.[2]
— Voyage au Cap de Bonne-Espérance. 1783. I. 493, V. xxiv.[2]
— Voyage to the Cape of Good Hope. 1783. I. 493.
Sparschuch, Heinrich. Potus coffeae. See Linné, Carl von. 1761. III. 741.[1]
Spasski, V. See Cnacckiй, B.
Spausta, Wladyslaw. [Cis.] Taxus baccata. 1893. IV. 440.[2]
— Jemioła. 1895. II. 179.[2]
— Limba. 189.? IV. 463.[2]
Specchio delle scienze. I. 26.[1]
Specht, C. Ueber die Bestandtheile der Cacaobutter. 1854. III. 594.
— Sur les principes constituants du beurre de cacao. 1854. III. 594.
Special-Arbeitsplan für Kulturversuche. 1888. IV. 142.
Special-Katalog der Collectiv-Ausstellung von Producten der Holzzucht. 1882. III. 272.[1]
Special-Katalog der Graf Erwin Schönborn Buchheim'schen Herrschaften Munkács. 1890. IV. 374.[1]
Special-Katalog der Prinz August von Sachsen Coburg-Gotha'schen Collectiv-Ausstellung. 1873. IV. 19.[2]
Special-Katalog, zugleich Forstbeschreibung der . . . Domäne Goldenstein. 1890. IV. 369.
Special report on legislation. 1888. IV. 314.[2]
Species of Cotoneaster. 1882. III. 420.[2] ·
The species of Forsythia. 1878. III. 671.[2]
Specimen approuvé par décision ministérielle . . . délimitation général de la forêt domaniale de la Joux. 1867. IV. 360.
Specimen florae; or, British botany exemplified. 1847. I. 399.
Specimen florae hallensis. See Olearius, J. G. 1668. I. 43.
Specimens of the flora of South Africa. See Roupell, A. E. 1849. I. 494.

Speck Obreen, H. A. van der. Beschryving van de timmerhoutsoorten die in Europeesch Guiana wassen. 1864. IV. 398.[1]
Spectacular effect of trees. 1873. III. 201.
The Spectator. III. 18.
Speechly, William. A treatise on the culture of the Vine. 1790. III. 553.[2]
Speede, G. T. Frederic Barlow. Indian hand-book of gardening. 1840. I. 75,[2] III. 116.[1]
— The new Indian gardener. 1848. III. 116.[1]
Speer, R. P. Causes of blight, mildew, rust, etc. 1880. III. 193.[1]
— Causes of injuries to fruit trees. 1874. III. 178.
— Characteristics of hardy and tender fruit trees. 1889. III. 182.
— The effect of different soils upon fruit trees. 1871. III. 41.[1]
— How are fruit trees affected by our climate? 1892. III. 41.[1]
— My last shot at American Apples. 1888. III. 182.
— Orchard sites, varieties of the tree fruits. 1894. III. 134.[1]
— Propagation of hardy fruit trees from seeds. 1887. III. 50.[2]
Spegazzini, Carlos. Cecidiodomacios de las Villaresias. 1900. II. 476.[1]
— Contribución al estudio de la flora de la Sierra de la Ventana. 1896. I. 345.
— Las enfermedades del Cafeto en Costa Rica. 1896. III. 736.
— Irritabilidad de los estambres en las Cacteas. 1900. II. 589.[1]
— Néctar narcótico y venenoso. 1900. III. 622.[1]
— Nectarios extraflorales. 1900. II. 188,[1] 597.[1]
— Notas botánicas. 1900. II. 186,[1] 597.[1]
— Nova addenda ad floram patagonicam. 1899. I. 345.
— Una planta nueva de la flora uruguaya. 1899. II. 569.[1]
— Plantae argentinae novae vel criticae. 1880. I. 344.
— Plantae novae nonnullae Americae australis. 1883. I. 330.—1898. I. 345.
— Plantae Patagoniae australis. 1897. I. 345,
— Plantae per Fuegiam anno 1882 collectae. 1896. I. 347.
— Las plantas dioicas. 1900. I. 239.[1]
— Primitiae florae chubutensis. 1897. I. 345.
— Relazione preliminare sulle collezioni botaniche fatte in Patagonia. 1883. I. 347.
Spehr, Paul. Sur l'éphèdrine de l' "Ephedra monostachia." 1890. II. 54,[1] III. 312.[2]
— Pharmacognostisch-chemische Untersuchung der Ephedra monostachia. 1890. II. 54,[1] III. 312.[1]
Speidel, Emil. Ertrags-Untersuchungen in Forchenbeständen. 1886. IV. 481.
— Das Forst-Schutz- und Hilfs-Personal in Württemberg. 1878. IV. 291.[1]
— Langsamwüchsigkeit und Ausdauer der Fichte. 1887. IV. 458.
— Die Untersuchung der Wuchsverhältnisse von Fichten-, Tannen- und Buchenbeständen. 1893. IV. 234.
— Waldbauliche Forschungen in württembergischen Fichtenbeständen. 1889. IV. 454.
— Wie soll das Nadelholzstammholz gemessen werden? 1886. IV. 228.
Speke, John Hanning. Journal of the discovery of the source of the Nile. 1863. I. 488.
Spelter, P. Das Wandern der Pflanzen. 1895. I. 241.[2]
Spencer, Baldwin & French, Charles. Trip to Croajingolong. 1890. I. 504.
Spencer, Guilford L. & Ewell, E. E. Food and food adulterants. Pt. VII. Tea, coffee and cocoa preparations. 1892. III. 223.[1]
Spencer, Herbert. On circulation and the formation of wood. 1866. I. 164.
Spencer, W. Baldwin. A trip to Queensland. 1893. I. 504.
Spéneux. See LETELLIER, Augustin & SPÉNEUX.
Spengler. Tabellen ten gebruike bij de houtmeetkunde. 1890. IV. 228.
Spengler, F. Iets over twee soorten van amerikaansche Pijnboomen. 1858. IV. 462.[2]
Spengler, F. R. Karakterkunde der boomen. 1862. I. 217.
— Het verfraaijen onzer landgoederen. 1853. III. 202.[2]
— Over den Viscum album. 1862. II. 178.[1]
— Vluchtige opmerkingen omtrent eenige . . . groenblijvende boomen. 1858. III. 289.
Spengler, G. C. Eenige opmerkingen over de boschbeplanting der duinen. 1890. IV. 160.[2]

— Handleiding voor boschcultuur. 1894. IV. 107.[1]
— Konijnenschade. 1890. IV. 198.[1]
— De Larix. 1890. IV. 452.[1]
— Twee groote vijanden onzer dennenbosschen. 1889. IV. 478.
— Het vastleggen en opbosschen van duinen. 1891. IV. 160.[2]
— Welke houtsoorten moeten op heidegrond gepoot worden. 1889. IV. 160.[1]
— Welke rol speelt hout tegenwoordig als grondstof bij de papierfabricage. 1890. IV. 430.
Spenner, Fridolin Carl Leopold. Flora friburgensis. 1825. I. 377.
— Handbuch der angewandten Botanik. 1834. I. 378.
— Teutschlands phanerogamische Pflanzengattungen. 1836. I. 379.
Speranza, Carlo. Teofrasto primo botanico. 1861. I. 292.
Sperk, Gustav. Die Lehre von der Gymnospermie. 1869. I. 118.[1] II. 1.
Sperl, Wenzel. Der Sturm und der Baumwuchs. 1863. IV. 189.[1]
Sperling, Johannes. Carpologia physica posthuma. 1661. I. 118.[2]
— Exercitatio de traductione formarum in plantis. 1648. I. 97.
Sperling, Otto. Catalogus plantarum Horti regii hafniensis. 1642. I. 40.
— Hortus Christianaeus. 1642. I. 40.
Sperling, Paul. Die Erzfeinde des Waldes. 1878. IV. 195.[2]
Speschneff, N. Zur Frage der Abwärtskrümmung von Wurzeln. 1870. I. 195.[2]
Speschnew, N. von. Über Parasitismus von Phoma reniformis. 1899. III. 582.
Der Spessart und seine forstliche Bewirthschaftung. 1847. IV. 350.[1]
Sphetsos, Georgios. See ΣΦΗΤΣΟΣ, Γεώργιος.
Spica. Sur le Buchu, Barosma crenata. 1886. III. 495.[2]
Spica, Matteo. Falsification du Sumac. 1898. III. 526.[2]
Spicer, William Webb. A handbook of the plants of Tasmania. 1878. I. 506.[1]
Spiegazione etimologica de' nomi generici delle piante. See SAVI, G. B. A. 1815. I. 76.[1]
Spiegel, von (Dammer). Die Schütte der Kiefer. 1855. IV. 475.
Spiegel, Freiherr von. Forstfiskalische Erwerbungen und Aufforstungen. 1900. IV. 159.
Spiegel, Adrian. Isagoges in rem herbariam libri duo. 1606. I. 82.[2]
Spiegel, S. A Thea-növény. 1888. III. 600.[2]
Spieker, Th. Vegetationscharacter der Insel Sylt. 1859. I. 384.
Spiekerkoetter, C. G. H. Anleitung zur Kenntniss der . . . Giftpflanzen. 1844. III. 73.
— Die Giftpflanzen Deutschlands. 1844. III. 73.
Spieler, Alexander Julius Theodor. De plantis venenatis Silesiae. 1841. III. 73.
Spielmann, Jakob Reinhold. Acaciae officinalis historia. 1768. III. 443.[1]
— Anleitung zur Kenntniss der Arzneimittel. 1774. III. 241.
— Institutiones materiae medicae. 1774. III. 241.
— Pharmacopoea generalis. 1783. III. 248.
— Prodromus florae argentoratensis. 1766. I. 373.
— De vegetabilibus venenatis Alsatiae. 1766. III. 72.
— Vegetatio. 1773. I. 32.
— De viticultura richovillana. See FAUDEL, F. W. 1780. III. 552.
Spiering, Andreas. Notizen über Neuseeland. 1877. I. 507.
Spies, Johann Karl. Rosmarini coronarii historia medica. 1718. III. 698.[2]
Spiessenhoff, Karl Eugen Luchini von. Solanum caule inermi, flexuoso. 1742. III. 701.[2]
Spin, marquis de. Catalogue des plantes cultivées dans le jardin de Mr. de Spin. See RODATI, Luigi. 1804. I. 61.
— Le jardin de St. Sébastien. 1809. I. 61, 522.[1]
Spindle tree. 1897. III. 532.[1]
A spineless Gooseberry. 1895. III. 414.[2]
Spines and prickles; a batch of cactaceous pointers. 1890. III. 619.
Spiraeas. 1879. III. 460,[2] 461.[1]
Spirées gardant le plus longtemps leur feuillage. See WELCHE Spiräen-Arten. 1885. II. 314.[1]
The spirit of the woods. 1837. I. 511.

Spirituous liquors derived from trees. 1825. III. 667.²
Spis celniejszych roślin w ogrodzie Niedźwiedzkim. 1825. I. 65.²
Spis ogólny strojnych roślin ogrodu Niedźwiedzkiego. 1838. I. 66.¹
Spisok ... See Списокъ ...
Spittal, Robert. Repetition of M. Dutrochet's experiments on the Mimosa. 1830. II. 372.²
Spitz, Anselm Christoph. Erziehung guter, auch neuer Obst- und Spielarten auf Kernstämmen. 1798. III. 135.
— Kurze Beschreibung des Ulmenbaums. 1796. IV. 518.²
— Pátriotische Vorschläge zur Aussaat und Anpflanzung solcher Holzarten. 1791. IV. 116.
— Der Rathgeber in der Holzzucht. 1805. IV. 105.
Spitz, Félix. De jurisdictione forestali. 1756. IV. 313.
Spitzenberg, G. K. Die Spitzenberg'schen Kulturgeräthe. 1898. IV. 176.²
Spitzner, Václav. Ostružiny vysočiny Drahavské. 1893. II. 304.¹
Spix, Johann Baptist von & **Martius,** Karl Friedrich Philipp von. Reise in Brasilien. 1823. I. 341.
— — Travels in Brazil. 1823. I. 341.¹
Splitgerber, Friedrich Ludwig. Description du genre Urania non Schreb. 1843. II. 870.²
— Observationes de Bignoniaceis surinamensibus. 1842. II. 784.²
— De plantis novis surinamensibus. 1842. I. 339.¹
Spokesman of the carriage and associate trade. IV. 5.¹
Spolkový časopis pro lesnictví. See **Vereinsschrift** für Forst ... und Naturkunde. IV. 15.
Spon, Edward & F. N. Encyclopaedia of the industrial arts. 1882. III. 31.
Spon, Jacob. Bevanda asiatica. 1705. III. 741.¹
Sponek, Carl F., *Graf* von. Ueber den Anbau und Behandlung des wein- und spitzblättrigen Ahorns. 1811. IV. 526.¹
— Ueber die Anlegung ... der Holzgärten. 1816. IV. 388.¹
— Anleitung zu Einsammlung ... des Saamens. 1803. IV. 147.²
— Ueber die Beschaffenheit ... und Cultivirung der Sümpfe. 1806, 1807. IV. 117, 143.²
— Ueber die Einrichtung und Behandlung der sogenannten Harz-Waldungen. 1802. IV. 436.¹
— Forstliche Aufsätze und Bemerkungen. 1810. IV. 100.²
— Forstwissenschaftliche und botanische Abhandlungen. 1807. IV. 117.
— Handbuch des Flosswesens. 1825. IV. 390.¹
— Ueber den Holzdiebstahl. 1823. IV. 196.²
— Die italiänische Fichte, Pinus Pinaster. 1810. IV. 467.¹
— Praktische Bemerkungen über ... Nadelhölzer. 1816. IV. 440.²
— Praktischer Beweis ... dass die Nadelholzsaamen ... lange Jahre ihre Keimungskraft behalten. 1825. I. 193,¹ IV. 65.¹
— Über den Schwarzwald. 1817. IV. 348.¹
— Ueber die Umformung der Wälder. 1812. IV. 140.
— Ueber die Veräusserung von Staatswaldflächen. 1823. IV. 268.
— Ueber vermischte Wälder. 1825. IV. 137.¹
— Ueber den Zustand ... des Neuenbürger Oberforstes. 1806. IV. 356.¹
— Ueber den Zustand ... desjenigen Theils ... welcher den Neuenbürger Oberforst ausmacht. 1806. IV. 356.¹
Sponi. Note sur le Châtaignier. 1854. IV. 493.¹
Spony. De la commission du Châtaignier. 1856. IV. 493.¹
Spoof, A. R. Gummibildning på Körsbärsträd. 1893. III. 435.²
Spooner, Alden. The cultivation of American Grape vines. 1846. III. 549.²
Spooner, E. A. & others. Analyses of the ashes of certain commercial teas. 1851. III. 607.
Spooner, William H. Hybrid Roses. 1888. III. 450.
— Sonic experience in hardy Rose culture. 1881. III. 452.
Spoor, W. C. Gids voor tuinbouw en bloementeelt. 1856. III. 106.¹
— Is het noodig dat de boomen ... gesnoeid worden? 1863. III. 170.
— De Rozenteelt. 1858. III. 449.
— Over den schadelijken invloed der gassen. 1861. III. 185.¹
— Het verplanten van oude boomen. 1861. III. 167.
Sports. 1900. II. 121.²
Sposov ... See Спосовъ ...
Spottswood. A catalogue of plants ... of: Tangier. 1696. I. 483.²

Sprague, Charles J. Apple tree with apetalous flowers. 1866. II. 267.¹
— Is the Heath indigenous to the United States? 1865. II. 661.²
— *See also* Parsons, Theophilus & Sprague, C. J.
Sprague, T. B. Fibre Balls. 1898. I. 242.²
Spratt, George. Flora medica. 1829. III. 56.
— The medico-botanical pocket-book. 1836. III. 57.
Spratt, Thomas Abel Brennage & **Forbes,** Edward. Travels in Lycia, Milyas. 1847. I. 478.
Sprawozdanie komisyi fizyograficznéj. I. 28.¹
Sprawozdanie sekcyi leśnej. C. k. towarzystwa gospodarstwa rolniczego krakowskiego. 1871. IV. 369.
Sprawozdanie Zarządu spółki jedwabniczej za czas od 1 maja 1858 do 1 maja 1859 roku. 1860. III. 377:
Spraying. 1896. III. 108.¹
Spraying fruits for insect pests. See Willits, Edwin. 1892. III. 198.¹
Spreckelsen, Theodor von. Epiphyllum truncatum und seine Varietäten. 1854. III. 623.¹
— Die Gattung Cantua. 1854. III. 694.²
— Ländliche Zierden an Wohnhäusern. 1857. III. 203.
— Ueber Lebensbäume. 1858. III. 311.¹
— Die Manetti-Rose. 1862. III. 455.²
— Neues Verfahren die Wein- und Rosenkrankheit ... zu vernichten. 1858. III. 196.
Spreeuwenberg, A. F. van. Een blik op de Minahassa. 1845. I. 465.
Der **Spreewald.** 1828. IV. 352.
Spreitzenhofer, G. C. Beitrag zur Flora der Jonischen Inseln. 1878. I. 449.
Sprengel, (*Oberförster, Proskau*). Der Holzverkauf auf dem Stamme. 1876. IV. 388.¹
Sprengel, Anton. Anleitung zur Kenntniss aller in der Umgegend von Halle wildwachsender ... Gewächse. 1848. I. 382.
— Tentamen supplementi ad Systematis vegetabilium Linnaeani editionem decimam sextam. 1828. I. 267; see also Linné, Carl von. 1774. I. 258.
Sprengel, Carl. Ueber die Benutzung des Baumlaubes als Viehfutter. 1830. IV. 438.²
— Chemie für Landwirthe, Forstmänner. 1831. IV. 60.²
— Ueber die feuerfesten Bestandtheile des Splintes. 1834. I. 154.
— Die Lehre von den Urbarmachungen. 1838. IV. 155.¹
— Meine Erfahrungen im Gebiete der ... Pflanzenkultur. 1847. III. 104.
— Die Widerstandsfähigkeit von Pinus rigida gegen Waldbrand. 1896. IV. 469.
Sprengel, Christian Konrad. Das entdeckte Geheimniss der Natur. 1793. I. 236.²
— Die Nützlichkeit der Bienen. 1811. I. 236.²
Sprengel, Franz. Eine forstliche Studienreise durch Moor und Heide. 1879. IV. 349,¹ 356.²
Sprengel, Kurt. Anleitung zur Kenntniss der Gewächse. 1802. I. 84.
— Antiquitatum botanicarum specimen primum. 1798. I. 514.¹
— Von dem Bau und der Natur der Gewächse. 1812. I. 85.
— Der botanische Garten der Universität zu Halle. 1800. I. 45.
— Buchanania Lanzan, eine neue Gattung. 1801. III. 455.²
— Curtii Sprengelii Opuscula academica. 1844. I. 34.
— Description de deux genres nouveaux. 1823. II. 192.¹
— Epitome Florae indicae. 1820. I. 471.
— Florae halensis tentamen novum. 1806. I. 376.
— Geschichte der Botanik. 1817. I. 79.²
— Geschichte der Medicin im Alterthume. 1792. III. 238.²
— Histoire de la médecine. 1792. III. 238.²
— Historia rei herbariae. 1807. I. 79.¹
— Index plantarum ... in Horto botanico halensi. 1807. I. 45.
— Mantissa prima Florae halensis. 1806. I. 376.
— Neue Entdeckungen im ganzen Umfang der Pflanzenkunde. 1820. I. 33.
— Neue Pflanzenarten ... im botanischen Garten zu Halle. 1801. II. 387.¹
— Novi proventus Hortorum academicorum halensis et berolinensis. 1819. I. 266.
— Plantarum minus cognitarum pugillus. 1813. I. 266.
— Species plantarum minus cognitae. 1820. I. 266.
— Storia prammatica della medicina. 1792. III. 238.²
— Urceola elastica, Ostindischer Kaoutchouk. 1801. II. 734.¹

Sprengel, Kurt (*continued*).
— Om växternas byggnad och natur. 1812. I. 85.
— Versuch einer pragmatischen Geschichte der Arzneikunde. 1792. III. 238.²
— Wikströmia novum plantae genus. 1821. II. 856.²
— *See also* CANDOLLE, A. P. de & SPRENGEL, Kurt.
Sprenger, Carl. Acacia Farnesiana Willd. 1895. III. 465.¹
— Acer palmatum und seine Formen. 1889. III. 535.² .
— Dell' Aesculus Hippocastanum. 1888. III. 536.²
— Aloe abyssinica Lam. 1896. III. 333.²
— Aloe vulgaris Bauhin. 1896. III. 334.¹
— Gegen den Anbau der Eucalyptus-Arten. 1884. IV. 530.
— Ansucht der Melocactus aus Samen. 1892. III. 623.²
— Aristotelia. 1893. III. 584.¹
— Ausdauernde Daphne und ihre Cultur. 1894. III. 626.²
— Bignonia venusta Kerr. 1888. III. 707.²
— Die Bodenkunde. 1837. IV. 61.¹
— Der botanische Garten in Padua. 1898. I. 64.
— Calanchoe Pers. . . . marmorata. 1896. III. 409.²
— Cappernsträucher. 1900. III. 408.²
— Caryopteris Mastacanthus. 1896. III. 695.²
— Aus Castellamare (Sicilien), Sumach. 1900. III. 527.¹
— Les Citrus. 1899. III. 497.²
— Clematis della Nuova Zelanda. 1892. III. 389.²
— Die Coniferen im Seengebiete. 1897. III. 291.
— Cotyledon quitense. 1893. III. 409.²
— Der Dezemberfrost in Neapel. 1886. III. 49.²
— Gegen die Eucalyptus. 1884. IV. 530.
— Euphorbia heterophylla Lin. 1890. III. 518.¹
— Exochorda Alberti Rgl. 1892. III. 424.¹
— Die Gärten Venedigs. 1898. III. 126.²
— Zur Geschichte der Cryptomeria elegans. 1884. III. 302.¹
— I giardini più belli dell' Italia meridionale. 1884. I. 64.
— Gomphocarpus arborescens. 1890. III. 692.²
— Gossypium Comesii. 1889. II. 522.¹
— Hibiscus vitifolius. 1893. III. 588.²
— Insektenfänger (Arauja albens). 1892. II. 736.¹
— Die japanische Mispel. 1891. III. 424.¹
— Der Johannisbrotbaum. 1883. III. 472.¹
— Ligustrum japonicum. 1896. III. 673.²
— Magnolia grandiflora. 1899. III. 400.¹
— Magnolia grandiflora var. Pravertiana. 1897. II. 212.¹
— Melocactus aus Samen. 1895. III. 623.²
— Melocactus humilis Sur. 1897. III. 623.²
— Di una metamorfosi nel fiore della Sparmannia. 1888. II. 515.¹
— Notizen über Rosen. 1896. III. 451.¹
— Opuntien in Calabrien. 1900. II. 596.¹
— Orniamo con Palme i nostri giardini. 1889. III. 318.¹
— Palmenfülien. 1897. III. 359.²
— Peschi di Nagasaki. 1892. III. 438.²
— Pinus calabrica Del. 1885. III. 308.¹
— Poinsettia pulcherrima. 1889. III. 518.¹
— Quercus Robur L. var. apennina aurea. 1886. III. 363.¹
— Rosa berberidifolia. 1892. III. 456.¹
— Rosa centifolia muscosa var. Salernitana. 1895. III. 455.¹
— Die schönsten Gärten Süd-Italiens. 1884. I. 64.
— Solanum Dammannianum. 1891. III. 701.²
— Solanum muticum N. E. Brown. 1894. III. 702.¹
— Solanum Seaforthianum. 1895. III. 702.¹
— Tannen und Kiefern Japans. 1885. III. 290.
— Washingtonia robusta. 1886. II. 75.² — 1889. III. 332.²
— Der Weinstock im heutigen Italien. 1891. III. 558.¹
— Wilde Rosen. 1887. III. 450.
— Ein wilder oder verwildeter Apfel. 1900. II. 266.²
— Die Zirbelkiefern Ost-Asiens. 1885. IV. 461.¹
Sprenger, Philipp Stephan. Horti medici catalogus. 1597. I. 42.
Sprenger van Eyck, (*ministre des finances*). Boisement par l'état de terrains incultes. 1897. IV. 546.²
Sprewitz, A. von. Tabellarische Uebersicht: 1) Der Naturgeschichte derjenigen Raupenarten. 1831. IV. 91.²
Spribille, Franz. Die bisher in der Provinz Posen beobachteten Rubi. 1897. II. 302.²
— Einige Bemerkungen über die Rubi und Rosae. 1899. II. 285.¹ 302.²
— Floristische Beobachtungen aus Schlesien. 1900. II. 302.²
— Neue Standorte für Posener Rubi. 1898. II. 302.²
Spring, Anton Fr. Ueber die naturhistorischen Begriffe von Gattung. 1838. I. 244.¹
Spring, Eduard. Ermittelung des Massengehaltes stehender Bestände. 1888. IV. 218.
— Ist die Einmischung der Birke . . . vortheilhaft? 1886. IV. 490.²

— Gehört die Akazie zu den forstlich wichtigen Waldbäumen. 1886. IV. 523.²
— Die Laufkäfer. 1888. IV. 93.
— Mein Forstgarten. 1888. IV. 151.¹
— Ueber Pflanzung ballenloser Kiefern. 1887. IV. 473.
— Die Pilze im forstlichen Haushalte. 1888. IV. 212.
— Prüfung des Laubholzsamens. 1889. IV. 147.¹
— Welches ist die zweckmässigste Art der Holzverwertung in Privatforsten. 1887. IV. 388.²
Spring-flowering Rhododendrons. 1878. III. 655. — 1882. III. 658.² 662.¹
Spring-flowering shrubs. 1878. III. 646.¹
Springenfeldt, Moritz. Beitrag zur Geschichte des Seidelbastes. 1890. III. 627.²
Springer, J. S. Forest life and forest trees. 1851. IV. 382.²
Springer, Leonard A. Ampelopsis Graebneri. Dr. C. Bolle. 1900. II. 504.¹
— Aucuba's. 1898. III. 645.¹
— Boomkweekerijen en dendrologie. 1899. III. 75.²
— Coniferen op 't Loo. 1897. I. 51.²
— Dendrologische Plaudereien. 1889. III. 70.
— Dendrologische schetsen. 1896. I. 294,² III. 75.² — 1898. II. 706.²
— Enkele groenblijvende struiken. 1900. III. 206.¹
— Het geslacht Cotoneaster. 1898. III. 420.²
— De Grove Den . . . als zierboom. 1896. III. 309.¹
— De Haarlemmerhout van 1583–1896. 1896. IV. 356.²
— Ist Ampelopsis Graebneri (Bolle) eine neue Species. 1899. II. 504.¹
— Magnolia Soulangeana. 1897. III. 400.¹
— Sambucus racemosa plumosa foliis aurels. 1896. III. 752.²
— De tuinkunst. 1897. III. 106.¹
— Een te weinig bekende proef van duin ontginning. 1899. IV. 160.²
— Een wonderlijk vergroeide Spar. 1896. II. 36.¹
— Xanthorrhiza apiifolia Spr. 1897. II. 200.²
Spruce, Richard. Berigten over oliegevende planten in Venezuela. 1855. III. 64,¹ 224.²
— Botanical objects . . . from the Amazon River. 1850. III. 65.¹
— Edible fruits of the Rio Negro. 1853. III. 269.¹
— Extract of a letter, relating to vegetable oils. 1854. III. 269.¹
— On five new plants from eastern Peru. 1859. I. 340.²
— Journal of a voyage up the Amazon and Rio Negro. 1851. I. 342.
— Leopoldinia Piassaba. 1855. II. 70.¹
— On the mode of branching of some Amazon trees. 1861. I. 106.²
— Note on Clusiaceae. 1855. II. 552.²
— A note on Palms. 1870. II. 60.³
— Note on the India rubber of the Amazon. 1855· III. 518.²
— Note sur le caoutchouc de la rivière des Amazons. 1855. III. 518.²
— Notes of a visit to the Cinchona forests. 1860. III. 718.
— Notes on the indigenous vegetation of northern Peru. 1865. I. 340.²
— Palmae amazonicae. 1871. II. 61.²
— Regelmässiger Wechsel in der Entwickelung diclinischer Bluthen. 1899. I. 199.
— Report on the expedition to procure . . . Cinchona succirubra. 1861. III. 726.¹
— On the separation of the sexes. 1869. I. 199.
— On the Siphonia. 1852. III. 519.¹
— Two letters on Cinchona seed collection. 1863. III. 713.²
— *See also* CORRÉA DE MELLO, Joaquim & SPRUCE, Richard.
The Spruce-gall aphis. 1881. IV. 456.
The Spruce-trees of eastern North America. 1896. II. 34.¹
Spruces and Firs on the Maine coast. 1892. I. 312.
Spry, Henry Harpur. Suggestions received . . . for extending the cultivation . . . of useful . . . plants. 1841. III. 129.²
Sprygin, I. *See* CHRPATHEB, H.
Spurious St. Ignatius beans. 1898. III. 485.²
Spychiger, Arnold. Ueber Imprägnierung des Holzes. 1895. IV. 421.
Squarcialupus, Marcellus. De Amygdalarum amararum in ebrietatem vi. 1568. III. 434.¹
A square-stemmed Bamboo. 1875. III. 316.¹
Square-stemmed Bamboo. 1876. III. 316.¹
Squibb, Edward R. Pharmacy of the Cinchonas. 1867. III. 721.

Squier, Ephraim George. Tropical fibres. 1863. III. 234.
— Tropical fibres; their production. 1861. III. 234.
Squire. On some preparations of Roses. 1842. III. 454.[1]
Squire, Peter. A companion to the British pharmacopoeia. 1864. III. 255.[1]
— Companion to the last edition of British pharmacopoeia. 1864. III. 255.[1]
— The pharmacopoeias of seventeen of the London hospitals. 1863. III. 254.
— The pharmacopoeias of thirteen of the London hospitals. 1863. III. 254.
— The pharmacopoeias of thirty of the London hospitals. 1863. III. 254.
— The pharmacopoeias of twenty-five of the London hospitals. 1863. III. 254.
— The pharmacopoeias of twenty-nine of the London hospitals. 1863. III. 254.
— The pharmacopoeias of twenty-two of the London hospitals. 1863. III. 254.
Squire, W. S. On the Daphne tribe of plants. 1842. III. 627.[1]
Srb, Josef. Pěstování a zužitkování Vrby košíkářské. 1885. III. 349.
Srb, Karel. Palmy na vých. břehu Afriky. 1896. II. 62.[1]
Sredinski, N. K. See Срединскій, Н. К.
Srogl, Karl. Einfluss des Lichtes auf . . . Hochwaldbestände. 1885. IV. 67.[2] 129.
— Der forstliche Zinsfuss und Bodenwert. 1899. IV. 259.[1]
— st. Ueber Theuerung der Sämereien. 1858. IV. 147.[2]
St. Bismarckia nobilis Hildebr. et Wendl. 1891. III. 320.[2]
St. Das Eiben-Schwesternpaar . . . zu Fahrafeld. 1896. IV. 440.[2]
St. Licuala grandis Wendland. 1891. III. 326.[2]
St. See K. & St.
St., R. Ueber Beförsterung der Körperschafts-Waldungen. 1851. IV. 309.[2]
St., R. Der japanesische Mispelbaum. 1878. III. 423.[2]
St., R. Die räumliche Eintheilung der Hochgebirgsforste. 1891. IV. 251.[1]
St. . . . l. Ueber den Anbau des Zuckerahorns. 1798. IV. 526.[2]
Die staatliche Forstaufsicht in Oesterreich. See LA POLICE . . . 1900. IV. 294.[2]
Staats, G. Ueber den gelben Blattfarbstoff. 1896. I. 186.
Staats, W. Einige Mittheilungen über die geographischen . . . Verhältnisse Charkows. 1885. III. 120.[1]
Die Staats- und Fondsforste Oesterreichs. 1893. IV. 368.
Die Staats- und Fondsforste Oesterreichs; ein Leitfaden. 1900. IV. 21.[2]
Die Staatsforste Finlands. 1893. IV. 348.[1]
Stables, William Gordon. Tea, the drink of pleasure. 1882. III. 607.
Staby, Ludwig. Ueber Quellung des Holzes. 1888. IV. 412.[1]
— Ueber den Verschluss der Blattnarben. 1886. I. 192.[1]
Stace, E. V. Report on the Aloe fibre industry. 1892. III. 333.[2]
Stache, Guido Carl Heinrich. De Casuarinis. 1855. II. 92.[1]
Stackhouse, John. Extracts from Bruce's Travel in Abyssinia. 1815. II 417.[2]
— Illustrationes Theophrasti. 1811. I. 514.[1]
— De Libanoto, Smyrna & Balsamo Theophrasti. 1814. I. 514.[1]
Stade, Hermann. Die geographische Verbreitung des Theestrauches. 1890. II. 552.[1]
Stadelmeyer, Ernst. Echites novae species brasilienses. 1840. II. 726.[1]
Stadler, A. Ueber Holzconservirung. 1877. IV. 420.
Stadler, S. Beiträge zur Kenntniss der Nectarien. 1886. I. 115,[1] 233.
Stadt, H. van de. Jaarringen en jaargetijden. 1878. I. 127.[1]
Staedeler, G. Sur les principes contenus dans la noix d'Acajou. 1848. II. 455.[1]
Die städtischen Baumpflanzungen in Wien. 1880. III. 209.
Stähelin, Christoph & Hofstetter, Joh. Chemische Untersuchung einiger Rinden. 1844. I. 155.
Staehelin, J. R. Specimen observationum anatomicarum et botanicarum. 1751. I. 97.
Die ständische Beratung des Etat der kgl. württemb. Forstverwaltung. 1895. IV. 291.[2]
Die stärkste Eiche in Deutschland. 1889. IV. 515.[2]
Die stärkste Tanne gans Thüringens. 1887. II. 24.[1]

Staes, Gustave. De cryptogamische ziekten. 1896. III. 195.[1]
— De echte meeldauw. 1896. III. 581.
— Over het gebruik van Bordeaux'sche pap. 1895. III. 98.[1]
— Het gebruik van steenkoolteerolie. 1895. III. 197.
— De Gele Kruis of Stekelbesbladwesp. 1895. III. 414.[2]
— Korstmossen op boomstammen. 1895. III. 193.[1]
— De krulziekte der Perzikbladen. 1896. III. 442.[1]
— De krulziekte van den Perzik. 1900. III. 442.[2]
— Over Mistel. 1900. II. 180.[1]
— Een praktische en eenvoudige insectenband. 1898. III. 197.
— Over de roode rotting van de Spar. 1899. IV. 457.
— De roode spin of spinnende mijt. 1898. III. 191.
— De San José-schildluis. 1898. III. 191.
— Het " schurft " van de takken. 1895. III. 195.[2]
— De vernieling van rupsen. 1895. III. 197.
— Verslag over plantenziekten . . . in Belgie. 1895. III. 179.
— Het Wilgenhaantje. 1896. III. 350.[2]
— Een ziekte van de Populieren. 1897. III. 344.[1]
Staffel, E. Asche der Rosskastanie. 1850. II. 114,[1] III. 533.[2]
Stafford, B. L. Stafford's Pine log, Cypress and timber reckoner. 1890. IV. 228.
Stagemeier, Axel. Tre-former. 1885. I. 218.
Stahel, Heinrich. Populäre Forstverwaltung. 1853. IV. 287.
Stahl, (Oberförster zu Rüdersdorf). Beiträge zur Holzertragskunde. 1865. IV. 243.
— Formzahlen in Tausendtheilen. 1855. IV. 235.[2]
— Kahnkniee von Kiefernholz. 1867. IV. 482.[2]
— Zuwachsberechnung an stehenden Bäumen. 1852. IV. 232.
Stahl, Agustin. Estudios sobre la flora de Puerto-Rico. 1883. I. 336.
— El Tortugo Amarillo de Puerto-Rico. 1875. II. 698.[2]
Stahl, Ernst. Ueber die Bedeutung des Pflanzenschlafs. 1895. I. 198.
— Ueber die biologische Bedeutung der Rhaphiden. 1886. I. 139, 235.[1]
— Ueber bunte Laubblätter. 1896. I. 236.[2]
— Ueber den Einfluss des sonnigen oder schattigen Standortes. 1883. I. 230.
— Einige Versuche über Transpiration. 1894. I. 168.
— Entwickelungsgeschichte . . . der Lenticellen. 1873. I. 132.[1]
— Pflanzen und Schnecken. 1888. I. 235.[2]
— Ueber den Pflanzenschlaf. 1897. I. 198.
— Regenfall und Blattgestalt. 1893. I. 111, 233.[1]
— Der Sinn der Mycorhizenbildung. 1900. I. 234.[1]
Stahl, Gustav. Beiträge zur Holzertragskunde. 1865. IV. 214.
— Handbuch der Forstwissenschaft. 1858. IV. 235.[1]
— Kubiktabelle für runde Hölzer. 1847. IV. 223.
— Kubiktabelle nebst vollständiger Preistabelle und Schlagerlohns-Tabelle. 1871. IV. 226, 402.[2]
— Kubiktabelle für runde Hölzer. 1847. IV. 223.
— Massentafeln zur Bestimmung des Holzgehaltes stehender Bäume. 1852. IV. 229.
— Die Stellung und Verhältnisse der preussischen Förster und Jäger. 1847. IV. 290.[1]
Stahl, Ivo Johannes. De veris herbae Thee proprietatibus. 1734. III. 605.
Stahl, Johann Friedrich. Onomatologia forestalls-piscatoriovenatoria. 1772. IV. 22.[1]
Stahl, John M. The Ash-leaved Maple. 1885. III. 535.[1]
— Ornamental hedges. 1886. III. 214.[1]
— Tree guard. 1893. III. 199.
Stahl, L. O. R. Rathgeber des Königl. preussischen Försters in Forst-Rechnungssachen. 1874. IV. 59.[1]
Stahl, R. Anflugkiefern in Altholzbeständen. 1878. IV. 472.
— Die sogenannte Hartseitigkeit des Holzes. 1880. II. 16.[2]
Stahl und Eisen. IV. 11.
Stahlmann. Abteilung oder Unterabteilung als Einheit des Betriebsplanes? 1897. IV. 246.
Stahlschmidt, Johann Karl Fr. Ueber Paraguaythee. 1861. III. 530.[2]
— Sur le Thé de Paraguay. 1861. III. 530.[2]
Staining wood black. 1895. IV. 422.[2]
Stakel. Papper af löf och sågspån. 1751. III. 235.[1]

Stakman, M. C. E. De afdeeling Toelang-Bawang. 1885. III. 275.²
— De afdeelingen Lintau en Boea. 1885. III. 275.³
Stålhammar, C. L. Försök, at af Lönn- och Björk-lake koka sirup. 1773. III. 534,¹ *IV. 491.*¹
Stalkarts, J. Nog iets over de ziekte der Theeplant. 1878. III. 604.²
Stalker, Donald. The formation . . . of plantations. 1885. IV. 121.
— Natural and transplanted Larch. 1881. IV. 449.
— Plantations on the estates of Benmore. 1883. IV. 359.¹
Stalsberg, Th. Lidt af skogindustrien. 1870. IV. 382.¹
Stam, G. Iets over de Hollandsche houtzagerij. 1873. IV. 393.
Stam, G. J. Het hout. 1888. I. 126, *IV. 409.*
Stamatiades, S. *See* ΣΤΑΜΑΤΙΑΔΗΣ, Σ.
Stamațian, Grigorie. Domeniul nostru agricol și forestier. 1887. IV. 375.¹
Stamm, Alois. Die Rechnungslegung für Förster. 1882. IV. 312.
Stamm, Fernand. Verhältnisse der Volks-, Lands- und Forstwirthschaft des Königreichs Böhmen. 1856. IV. 370.
Stammler, Georg Christian Carl. Dissertatio inauguralis medica sistens Aquae Lauro-Cerasi vires. 1796. III. 438.¹
Stammregister vorzüglicher Kernobstsorten. 1865. III. 89.¹
Stanchfield, Daniel. History of lumbering in Minnesota. 1900. IV. 24,¹ 382.²
Stand der Forstkultur im Kanton Zürich. 1829. IV. 365.
Standfest, Franz. Ein Beitrag zur Phylogenie der Gattung Liquidambar. 1889. II. 253.²
Standfuss, M. Bemerkungen über Steganoptycha. 1894. IV. 209.²
Standish, Arthur. New directions of experience . . . for the planting of timber. 1613. IV. 120, V. xxx.²
Standish, John. Evergreens for towns. 1867. III. 42.²
— Grafting Rhododendrons. 1871. III. 656.
— Observations on hybridising and hybrid Rhododendrons. 1858. III. 654.²
—& **Noble**, Charles. A chapter in the history of hybrid Rhododendrons. 1850. III. 654.²
— — Greffe des Rhododendrons. 1855. III. 656.
— — Practical hints on planting ornamental trees. 1852. III. 78.¹
— — Reminiscences of the effects of the winter of 1852–53. 1853. III. 46.²
—·— Rhododendrons; grafted or not grafted. 1855. III. 656.
— — Seedling Rhododendrons. 1855. III. 656.
— — Suggestions for employing evergreens. 1855. III. 206.¹ 40.
Stange, F. Über die Anwendung des Lehms. 1853. III. 40.
Stange, F. F. Zweimaliges Blühen von Bäumen. 1858. I. 220.²
Stange, Johann Karl Thomas. Index plantarum . . . in agro francofurtano. 1839. I. 380.
Stangeland, G. E. Om skovplantning paa myr. 1899. IV. 156.²
Stanley, J. On the antiseptic power of the pyroligneous acid. 1821. IV. 432.¹
Stansbury, Howard. Exploration and survey of the valley of the Great Salt Lake of Utah. *See* TORREY, John. 1852. I. 322.
Stanton, E. W. The economic side of the forestry problem. 1889. IV. 272.
Stanton, G. H. Das Holz als Pflasterungsmaterial. 1884. IV. 426.¹
Stanton, W. J. The Newland Oak. 1892. II. 139.¹
— The Tortworth Chestnut tree. 1892. II. 125.¹
Stanzel, Vitus. Wichtiges über Obstbau und Obstverwertung. 1898. III. 174.¹
Stapf, Otto. Artemisia pallens. 1898. III. 754.²
— Die Arten der Gattung Ephedra. 1889. II. 54.¹
— Beiträge zur Flora von Lycien. 1885. I. 479.
— Die botanischen Ergebnisse der Polak'schen Expedition. 1885. I. 477.²
— Dicellandra Hook. f. and Phaeoneuron. 1900. II. 641.¹
— On the flora of Mount Kinabalu. 1894. I. 469.²
— Die Gärten Persiens. 1887. III. 130.¹
— Der Landschaftscharakter der persischen Steppen. 1888. V. xxiv.¹
— Lonicera Korolkowii. 1894. II. 838.¹
— Pedaliaceae. 1895. II. 792.¹
— Persische Culturbäume. 1887. III. 130.¹
— R c   botanical exploration in southern Perisa. 1895. I. 477ª ent

— On the structure of the female flower . . . of Sararanga sinuosa. 1896. II. 57.²
— Vegetationsbilder aus . . . Persien. 1886. I. 477.²
— *See also* CLARKE, C. B. & STAPF, Otto.
Stappaert, de. Les Cerisiers. 1899. III. 431.¹
— Les Dracaena. 1881. III. 335.
— Le Genista Andreana hort. 1893. III. 475.¹
— Le Marronnier et sa seconde floraison. 1891. II. 482.²
— Le Panax Victoriae. 1883. III. 643.²
— Le Pavonia Makoyana Ed. Morr. 1881. III. 587.¹
— Quelques Aralia intéressants. 1882. III. 641.¹
— Rhododendrum Dalhousiae var. Victorianum. 1887. III. 658.²
The **Star-apple** or Caimite [sic]. 1890. III. 667.¹
Starcke, Johann Georg Wilhelm. Gyros Convolvulorum . . . evolvere tentabit. *See* WAGNER, C. R. 1705. I. 196.¹
Staring, A. C. W. Memorie betreffende de gewinning van hars. 1815. IV. 436.¹
— Een woord over het aanplanten van Amerikaansche Populieren. 1834. I. 488.¹
Staring, W. C. H. Aanleggen van dennenbosschen in de duinen. 1869. IV. 160.¹
— De bodem van Nederland. 1856. I. 391.¹
— Dennen poten zonder kluit. 1855. IV. 472.
— Dennenteelt. 1868. IV. 441.
— Duinbeplanting. 1865. IV. 160.¹
— Duinontginningen. 1857. IV. 160.¹
— Hoe onze kale duinen in Dennenbosschen te veranderen zijn. 1862. IV. 160.¹
— Houtteelt in Nederland. 1872. IV. 119.²
— Huisboek voor den landman in Nederland. 1860. III. 106.¹
— Landbouw lessen in 1862 te Londen verzameld. 1863. III. 122.²
— Landbouw-statistiek. 1876. III. 122.²
— Landbouwverbeteringen in Nederland. 1857. III. 122.¹
— Over de Nederlandsche bosschen. 1865. IV. 356.²
— Nieuwe houtsoorten. 1560. IV. 126.²
— Overzigt over den Nederlandschen landbouw. 1849. III. 122.¹
— Stoomschillen van Eikenhakhout. 1875. IV. 434.
— Ober den toestand der houtteelt in Nederland. 1856. IV. 356.²
— Het verplanten van boomen. 1846. III. 166.
— Verslag over de pogingen tot het veranderen van kale duinen in bosschen. 1867. IV. 160.¹
— Verslag van den landbouw. 1862. III. 122.¹
— Windvormingen 1861. IV. 145.
— De wortelbladluis der wijngaarden. 1874. III. 563.
— & **Kinder de Camarecq**. Kunstmatige bevruchting van granen. 1864. III. 175.¹
Stark, James. Notice of the copalchi bark. 1850. III. 244.
— On the shedding of branches. 1876. I. 192.¹
Eine **starke** Kiefer. 1899. IV. 483.¹
Eine **starke** Silberpappel. 1868. II. 97.¹
Starke Tannen in Frankreich. 1889. II. 24.²
Eine **starke** Zierbelkiefer. 1890. IV. 463.²
Starker Ahorn im Toggenburg. 1864. II. 477.²
Starnes, Hugh N. Imperfect pollination. 1895. II. 506.¹
Starr, Frederick, (jr.). American forests. 1866. IV. 271.²
Starý, Karel. Lipa. 1861. II. 517.¹
The **state** and the forest. 1892. IV. 46.¹
State forestry for Scotland. 1898. IV. 275.
The **state** of the crown forests. 1853. IV. 357.²
Staten Island — **Natural** science association. *See* NATURAL . . . I. 6.
Statescu, George. Influența și importanța padurilor in Romania. 1884. IV. 279.¹
Statham, S. Hortus arnoldiensis. 1906. I. 53.
Station agronomique de Nancy. Office agricole. Bulletin. III. 22.
La **station** forestière de Giessen. 1882. IV. 33.¹
La **statique** chimique des forêts. *See* EBERMAYER, Ernst. 1878. IV. 71.
La **statistica** dei boschi del regno e la logica. 1863. IV. 364.
Statistica dei boschi e dei beni incolti in Italia. 1862. IV. 364.
Della **statistica** forestale. 1865. IV. 364.
Statistica forestale; parte prima. 1870. IV. 364.
Statistica forestale dell' Annover. 1866. IV. 353.
Statistica forestale della Francia. 1862, 1865. IV. 360.
A **statistical** account of the towns and parishes . . . of Connecticut. *See* DWIGHT, Timothy. 1811. I. 313.

Statistical society of London. Journal. III. 18.
Statisticko-topografický popis . . . panství Hořovic. *See* STATISTISCH-TOPOGRAFISCHE Beschreibung der . . . Domäne Hořowitz. 1892. IV. 372.
Statisticko-topografický popis panství Poděbrady. *See* STATISTISCH-TOPOGRAFISCHE Beschreibung der Herrschaft Poděbrad . . . 1806. IV. 372.
Statistics of forestry. 1876. IV. 337.[2]
The statistics of Nutmegs. 1849. III. 402.[2]
Statistik der Forstpolizei- und Gemeindeforstverwaltung des Grossherzogthums Baden. 1856. IV. 350.[1]
Statistique comparée des vignobles. 1893. III. 557.[1]
Statistique des chemins de fer de l'État belge. 1900. IV. 285.[1]
Statistique des forêts de l'état . . . en Autriche. *See* Die STAATS- und Fondsforste Oesterreichs. 1893. IV. 368.
Statistique des forêts de l'état roumain. 1900. IV. 375.[2]
Statistique des forêts de la France. 1894. IV. 556.[1]
Statistique du département de l'Eure. *See* CHESNON, C. G. 1846. I. 410.
Statistique du phylloxera. 1888. III. 574.
Statistique forestière. *See* MATHIEU, Auguste. 1878. IV. 360.
Statistique forestière de la province d'Oran. *See* CHERRIER, H. de. 1856. IV. 379.[1]
Statistique forestière du département de l'Allier. *See* DU GUINY. 1885. IV. 361.
Statistiques des forêts soumises au régime forestier. 1894. IV. 362.
Statistische Beschreibung der . . . Domäne Gross-Zdikau. 1873. IV. 371.
Statistische Daten aus den ungarischen Staatsforsten. 1873. IV. 373.
Statistische Daten über die Domaine Grosskaler Forste. 1867. IV. 371.
Statistische Nachweisungen aus der Forstverwaltung. IV. 11.
Statistische Tabellen über die Forstverwaltung der . . . Fideikommiss-Domäne Tetschen. 1883. IV. 371.
Statistische Übersicht für die Domanialforsten von Schwarzburg-Rudolstadt. 1889. IV. 355.[1]
Statistische Zusammenstellungen betreffend die Stadt- und Spitalwaldungen Schaffhausens. 1889. IV. 367.
Statistischer Ausweis über die im Jahre 1885 in Oesterreich vorgekommenen Waldbrände. 1888. IV. 184.[1]
Statistischer Versuch über das Fürstenthum Neuenburg. 1818. IV. 365.
Statistisches über die Staatsforste in Dänemark. 1889. IV. 343.[2]
Statistisch-topografische Beschreibung der . . . Domäne Hořowitz. 1892. IV. 372.
Statistisch-topographische Beschreibung der . . . Domänen Eisgrub, Feldsberg. 1886. IV. 369.
Statistisch-topographische Beschreibung der . . . Fideicommiss-Herrschaft Gratzen . . . *See* WAGNER, Theodor. 1895. IV. 372.
Statistisch-topografische Beschreibung der Franz J. Fürst von Auersperg'schen Herrschaft Žleb. 1897. IV. 372.
Statistisch-topographische Beschreibung der Herrschaft Poděbrad. 1896. IV. 372.
Statistiske Oplysninger om Statsskovene i Danmark. 1888. IV. 342.[1]
Statkovski, B. I. *See* СТАТКОВСКІЙ, B. H.
Statut des Ehstländischen Forst-Vereins. 1883. IV. 40.[1]
Statut des Vereins Baltischer Forstwirthe. 1890. IV. 40.[1]
Statut für freiwillige Bewaldung unfruchtbarer Ländereien. 188. ? IV. 158.
Statuten für die Studirenden der Königlichen Forst-Akademien zu Eberswalde und Münden. 1884. IV. 33.[1]
Statuts de la Société centrale forestière de Belgique. 1900. IV. 40.[2]
Staub, Moriz. Beitrag zur Lehre von den constanten Wärmesummen. 1882. I. 221.
— Fiume és legközelebbi környékének floristikus viszonyai. 1877. I. 448.[1]
— A Magyarországon tett phyto- és zoophenologiai észleletek összeállítása. 1870. I. 227.[2]
— A szelid Gesztenye talajáról. 1879. II. 124.[1]
— Ültetett növény[1]e nálunk a szelid Gesztenye? 1879. II. 124.[1]
— Zwei phänologische Erscheinungen. 1875. I. 221.
Staubsand. Beobachtungen . . . beim Schneideln junger Eichen. 1879. IV. 507.
— Zur Vorverjüngung. 1878. IV. 139.[2]

Staudigl, Karl. Tabelle zur Berechnung von Tagelöhnen. 1890. IV. 59.[1]
Staudtmeister. Om Træplantning. 1803. IV. 151.[2]
Stauffer, J. European Larch. 1879. IV. 449.
Stauffer, Ottmar. Untersuchungen über spezifisches Trockengewicht . . . des Holzes der Birke. 1892. II. 118.[1]
Staunton, *Sir* George. An authentic account of an embassy . . . to the Emperor of China. 1797. I. 458.
Stavanger Museum. Aarsberetning. Aarheft. I. 8.[2]
The stave trade in foreign countries. 1900. IV. 427.[2]
Staverman, H. Vruchten van den Djokoboom. 1864. III. 633.[1]
Staverman, H. J. Verslag betreffende het vraagstuk van bemesting der Koffietuinen. 1869. III. 734.[1]
La stazione federale per il controllo delle sementi. · 1896. IV. 147.[1]
Le stazioni sperimentali agrarie italiane. III. 23.[2]
Le stazioni sperimentali in Germania ed in Austria. 1886. IV. 37.[2]
Stearns, A. T., Lumber Co. Cypress lumber and its uses. 1895. IV. 484.[2]
Stearns, Robert Edwards Carter. Araujia albens as a mothtrap. 1887. II. 736.[1]
— On the economic value of certain Australian forest trees. 1873. IV. 529.[2]
— Forest tree culture in California. 1882. IV. 112. — 1883. IV. 112.
— On the growth of certain California forest trees. 1882. IV. 64.[2]
Stearns, Samuel. The American herbal. 1801. III. 261.[2]
Stebbing, Edward Percy. An injurious insect in Jodhpur. 1896. III. 525.[1]
— Injurious insects of Indian forests. 1899. IV. 210.[2]
— The monorail portable railway. 1900. IV. 392.
— A note on Ceroplastes ceriferus. 1896. III. 226.[1]
— Note on the Myauktaung Teak plantation. 1900. IV. 537.[1]
Stebler, Friedrich Gottlieb. Untersuchungen über das Blattwachsthum. 1878. I. 190.[2]
— & Schröter, Carl. Arve im Avers. 1892. II. 41.[1]
— & Thielé, Eugène. Rapport technique de la Station fédérale d'essais de semences. 1893. III. 157.
Steechetti, F. I. Osservazioni sullo schema di legge forestale. 1869. IV. 328.
Stechmann, J. P. De Artemisiis. 1775. II. 851.[1]
Steck, Abraham. De Sagu. 1757. III. 327.[2]
Steck, F. G. Nominative staat van houtsoorten in de Lampongsche districten. 1856. IV. 399.[2]
Stecklingsvermehrung unterm Glassturze. 1863. III. 158.
Stedman, John Gabriel. Narrative of a five years expedition against the revolted negroes of Surinam. 1796. I. 338.[2]
— Voyage à Surinam et à l'intérieur de la Guiane. 1796. I. 338.[2]
Steeb, C. A. Fassliche Anleitung zum Weinbau. 1831. III. 552.
Steeb, Johann Heinrich. Ueber Holzmangel, Theurung, Wucher und Cultur. 1798. IV. 280.[2]
Steedman, A. H. Monograph on the cultivation of Coffee. 1880. III. 727.
Steeger, (*Forstinspector, Chemnitz*). Beschreibung der . . . zur Ausführung der Plätzesaaten angewandten Instrumente. 1864. IV 149.[1]
Steeger, J. A. Ansichten aus dem Pflanzenreiche. 1822. I. 94.
Steele, Andrew. The natural . . . history of peat-moss. 1826. III. 40.
Steele, Edward S. Can perfumery farming succeed in the United States? 1899. III. 227.
Steele, James G. The Pines of California. 1889. II. 39.[1]
Steele, Richard. An essay upon gardening. 1793. III. 81.
Steele, W. C. Cactus growing in Florida. 1890. III. 619.
— The Japanese Persimmon. 1887. III. 669.[1]
Steele, William Edward. Handbook of field botany. ·1847· I. 400, 533.
Steen, A. Om Plantagerne paa Bornholm. 1896. IV. 343.[2]
Steen, Adolf. Bidrag til Kundskab om Bøgens Væxtforhold. 1886. IV. 498.
Steenbergen, J. T. F. Gomelastiek en getah-pertja. 1885. III. 229.
Steenfeld, J. E. von KOCH-. *See* KOCH-STEENFELD, J. E. von.
Steenstrup, Johannes Japetus Smith. Geognostisk-geologisk Undersøgelse af Skovmoserne Vidnesdam- og Lillemose. 1842. I. 354.

Steenstrup, K. J. V. Om Klitternes Vandring. 1894. IV. 146.[1]
Steer, Franz. Analyse der Früchte von Juniperus communis. 1856. II. 31.[1]
Steetz, Joachim. Brownea Jacq. 1860. II. 337.[3]
— Büttneriaceae R. Br. 1846. II. 531.[2]
— Compositae. 1852. II. 848.[2]
— Compositae Vaill. 1844. II. 850.[1]
— Duhaldea chinensis. 1857. II. 859.[2]
— Enumeration of the Compositae of . . . Panama. 1852. II. 848.[2]
— Die Familie der Tremandreen. 1853. II. 429.[1]
— Genus novum a cl. Steudelio . . . recensitum. 1846. II. 527.[1]
— Monographie du genre Brownea. 1860. II. 337.[2]
— Revisio generis Comesperma. 1847. II. 430,[1] 531.[2]
— Tremandreae R. Br. 1844. II. 429.[1]
Steeven, H. Cedron seeds. 1885. III. 509.[1]
Stefani, A. Contribuzione alla flora di Pirano. 1884. I. 429.
Stefani, Carlo de, **Major,** C. J. F. & **Barbey,** William. Karpathos. 1895. I. 479.
— — Samos. 1891. I. 479.
Stefani, Stefano de. Cenni storici . . . sopra la nuova malattia del Ricino. 1866. III. 522.[1]
— Sopra una nuova malattia che attacca il Ricino. 1864. III. 521.[2]
— Storia della coltivazione del Ricino. 1858. III. 521.[1]
Stefani, Teodosio de. Zoocecidii dell' Orto botanico di Palermo. 1897. I. 216.[1]
Stefánsson, Stefán. Fra Islands Væxtrige. 1890. I. 357.
Steffan, Domenico. Sopra alcune varietà di Castagne. 1893. III. 359.[1]
Steffani, Giacomo. Della necessità . . . conservare e migliorare i boschi dei monti. 1852. IV. 122.[2]
— Della necessità . . . d'imboschire i monti. 1842. IV. 165.
Steffanoni, Luigi. Osservazioni generali sui boschi. 1863. IV. 122.[2]
Steffeck, (*Dr., Berlin*). Mittel zur Verhütung des Aufsteigens der Raupen. . 1834. III. 196.
Steffens, von (*Oberforstmeister*). Historisches Bild der Waldungen in der Rheinprovinz. 1851. IV. 352.
— Instruktion über die Verbesserung der Nieder- und Mittelwaldungen. 1863. IV. 130, 132.[1]
Steger, Victor. Ursprung der schlesischen Gebirgsflora. 1884. I. 388.
Steggall, John. The pupil's introduction to botany. 1829. I. 86.
— A text-book of materia medica. 1837. III. 254.
Steiermärkische Landesobst- und Weinbauschule bei Marburg. Berichte. Programm. III. 25.
Steiermärkische Landwirtschafts-Gesellschaft. *See* K. K. STEIERMÄRKISCHE . . . III. 25.
Steiermärkischer Forstverein. Zeitschrift. IV. 15.
Steiermärkischer Gartenbau-Verein. *See* K. K. STEIERMÄRKISCHER . . . III. 25.
Steiermark — K. k. Gartenbau-Gesellschaft. *See* K. K. STEIERMÄRKISCHER GARTENBAU-VEREIN. III. 25.
Steiermark — Naturwissenschaftlicher Verein. *See* NATURWISSENSCHAFTLICHER . . . I. 28.[1]
Steige, Joachim. Beschreibung des Lindenbaums. 1657. II. 517.[1]
Ueber das Steigen der Holzpreise. 1857. IV. 402.[2]
Steiger, (*Pastor*). Über die Behandlung der Weiden. 1834. III. 347.
Steiger, E. *See* SCHULZE, E., STEIGER, E. & MAXWELL, W.
Steiger, Jakob Robert. Die Flora des Kantons Luzern. 1860. I. 435.
Steiger, W. Ein merkwürdiger Baum. 1866. II. 125.[1]
Steigertahl, J. G. Description of the Cereus which flowered at Norimberg. 1731. II. 589.[1]
Steigerwalt, W. F. Raspberry and Blackberry culture. 1898. III. 457.[1]
Stein, (*Forstmeister*). Die slavonische Fassdauben-Industrie. 1863. IV. 427.[1]
Stein, *Freiherr* von. Über die Anzucht verschiedener amerikanischer Holzarten. 1828. IV. 524.[1]
— Einige Bemerkungen über . . . Anbau Nordamerikanischer Holzarten. 1831. IV. 125.[2]
Stein, Berthold. Alnus japonica Tbbg. 1886. III. 357.[1]
— Ein altes Bild. 1886. II. 267.[1]
— Bambusa quadrangularis Fenzi. 1885. III. 316.[1]
— Beitrag zur Rosenflora Schlesiens. 1876. II. 284.[2]
— Einige neue Rhododendron. 1886. II. 676.[2]

— Leptospermum (Glaphyria) Annae Stein. 1885. II. 628.[2]
— Die Omorika. 1898. III. 305.[2]
— Picea alpestris Brügger. 1887. II. 35.[1]
— Picea Omorica Panč. 1887. II. 38.[1]
— Des Reichskanzlers Palme; Bismarckia. 1886. II. 65.[1]
— Rhododendron Apoanum Stein. 1885. II. 677.[1]
— Rhododendron Kochii Stein. 1885. II. 681.[1]
— Strophanthus Ledieni. 1887. II. 732.[2]
— Tristania conferta R. Br. 1885. II. 633.[2]
— Verwachsungen und Ueberwallungen. 1886. I. 209.[1]
— Vitis pterophora Baker. 1888. II. 503.[1]
— Zwei neue Rhododendron von den Philippinen. 1885. II. 677,[1] 681.[1] .
Stein, Friedrich. Beiträge zur Forstinsectenkunde. 1852. IV. 455.
— Ueber einige Borkenkäferarten. 1854. IV. 475.
— Grundriss der organischen Naturgeschichte. 1845. I. 100.[2]
— Über die Schütte. 1852. IV. 475.
— Ueber zwei Schmarotzerpilze. 1853. IV. 211.[1]
Stein, G. A. De fabo St. Ignatii. 1793. III. 682.[2]
Stein, Johann Heinrich. Versuche . . . über Angewöhnung ausländischer Pflanzen. 1787. III. 45, IV. 125.[1]
Stein, W. Ueber die Farbstoffe des Pflanzenreiches. 1863. I. 184.
— Sur les matières colorantes des fleurs. 1863. I. 184. .
— Ueber das Pflanzengelb. 1862. I. 184.
Steinbeis, Ferdinand. Die Holzbringung im bayerischen Hochgebirge. 1897. IV. 390.[1]
Steinbrinck, Carl. Ueber die Abhängigkeit der Richtung hygroskopischer Spannkräfte von der Zellwandstruktur. 1888. I. 138.[2]
— Ueber ein Bauprincip der aufspringenden Trockenfrüchte. 1884. I. 119.
— Ueber elastische Schwellung von Geweben. 1899. I. 150.[1]
— Zur Frage der elastischen Schwellung von Pflanzengeweben. 1900. I. 150.[1]
— Ueber die Grenzen des Schrumpfelns. 1900. I. 138.[3]
— Grondbeginselen van de openingsmechaniek van stuifmeel en eenige sporehouders. 1895. I. 116.[3]
— Ueber den hygroskopischen Mechanismus. 1899. I. 197,[2] 233.[2]
— Ist die Luftdurchlässigkeit einer Zellmembran ein Hinderniss für ihre Schrumpfelung? 1900. I. 138.[2]
— Ueber den Oeffnungsmechanismus der Hülsen. 1883. I. 119.
— Ueber die Steighöhe einer capillaren Luft-Wasserkette. 1894. I. 166. '
— Zur Terminologie der Volumänderungen pflanzlicher Gewebe. 1900. I. 150.[1]
— Zur Theorie der hygroskopischen Flächenquellung. 1890. I. 137.
— Untersuchungen über die anatomischen Ursachen des Aufspringens der Früchte. 1873. II. 714.[3]
Steinbrügg, C. H. Note sur un procédé . . . de faire disparaître les pucerons de la Vigne. 1891. III. 574.
Steinegger, C. Die süddeutsche Klassifikation als Grundlage für . . . Holzpreise. 1894. IV. 403.
Steiner. Verjüngung der Hochgebirgswaldungen. 1885. IV. 139.[2]
Steiner, Friedrich. Ueber das Fallgesetz der Riese. 1878. IV. 390.[2]
— Ueber die Riese constanter Fallgeschwindigkeit. 1878. IV. 390.[3]
Steiner, Johann Friedrich Rudolph. Praktische Anleitung zur Berechnung der Bau- und Nutzhölzer. 1803. IV. 221.
— Versuche über die Herkunft des Borken-Käfers. 1785. IV. 549.[1]
Steinheil, Adolf. Altérations dans la forme des feuilles du Lonicera Periclymenum. 1840. II. 839.[1]
— Considérations sur l'usage que l'on peut faire des rapports de position qui existent entre la bractée et les parties de chaque verticille floral. 1839. I. 114.[2]
— De l'individualité considérée dans le règne végétal. 1835. I. 98.
— Observations sur la végétation des dunes à Calais. 1835. I. 409.
— Observations sur le mode d'accroissement des feuilles. 1837. I. 150.[3]
— Qu'entend-on par endosmose et exosmose? 1838. I. 163.
— Quelques observations relatives à la théorie de la phyllotaxis. 1835. I. 102.
Steininger, Jean. Bemerkungen . . . über das Klima . . . der Rheinländer. 1827. I. 377.

Steinkauler, Th. *See* LUNGE, G. & STEINKAULER, Th.

Steinlein, O. & Kampffmeyer, Wilhelm. Bericht über die gegenwärtige Lage der Schälwaldfrage. 1857. IV. 505.

Steinmetz, C. P. C. Handleiding voor de gouvernements Koffijkultuur. 1865. III. 729.[2]

Steinner. *See* RUHEMANN & STEINNER.

Steinvorth, Heinrich. "Een Boom as he in'n Book steit." 1865. I. 296.[1]

— Der Buchen-Krüppelbestand im Süntel. 1870. II. 126.[1]

— Die Eichen des Fürstentums Lüneburg. 1865. II. 129.[2]

— Kleine Mitteilungen und Bemerkungen. 1890. II. 685,[2] 835.[2]

— Linnaea borealis. 1890. II. 835.[2]

— Merkwürdige Föhrenbildung der Haide. 1878. II. 48.[2]

— Phanerogamenflora des Fürstenthums Lüneburg. 1849. I. 382.

— Die schmucke Eiche. 1870. II. 138.[1]

— Vaccinium intermedium Ruthe. 1890. II. 685.[3]

— Eine Vergiftung mit Rhus Toxicodendron. 1865. III. 528.[1]

— Die Zaubereiche bei Priorsgehäge. 1878. II. 138.[2]

Der steierische Landbote. *See* K. K. STEIERMÄRKISCHE LANDWIRTSCHAFTS-GESELLSCHAFT. III. 25.

Steitz. Ulex europaeus L. in der Flora von Frankfurt. 1887. II. 387.[1]

Stekhoven, H., SCHUURMANS. *See* SCHUURMANS STEKHOVEN, H.

Stell, W. W. Mulberry notes. 1893. III. 378.

Stella, A. Rimboschiamo le nostre Prealpi. 1895. IV. 166.[1]

Stellati, Vincente. Istituzione botanica. 1809. I. 85.

— Istituzioni di filosofia botanica. 1809. I. 85.

Steller, Georg Wilhelm. Beschreibung von dem Lande Kamtschatka. 1774. I. 454.[2]

Stelling, Ed. Ein Wort über Aussaàt der Nadelhölzer. 1876. III. 294.[1]

Stellingwerf, A. *See* OUDEMANS, C. A. J. A. & STELLINGWERF, A.

Die Stellung der Weisstannennadeln. 1895. II. 24.[1]

Die Stellung des Forstschutzpersonals. 1858. IV. 289.[1]

Stellwagen, A. W. De beteekenis der wouden voor 't klimaat. 1875. IV. 53.

Stelmasiewicz, A. K. Ogrodnictwo dla użytku wieśniaków polskich. 1866. III. 135.

Stelzner, A. Cordyline indivisa vera. 1864. III. 135.

— Cupressus Lawsoniana fol. aur. var. 1865. III. 301.[1]

— Einige empfehlenswerthe . . . Coniferen. 1866. III. 289.

— Einige Worte über die Verwendung der Rhododendron hybridum. 1862. III. 654.[3]

— Einige Worte über werthvolle neue Coniferen. 1865. III. 289.

— Ein gärtnerisches Urtheil über die neuesten Einführungen panachirter Pflanzen Japans. 1867. III. 520.[1]

— *See also* LORENTZ, P. G. & STELZNER, A.

Stemler, Johann Gottlieb. Specimen parallelismi inter systema Linneanum et Jussieuanum. 1810. I. 251.

Sten, A. Betula nana × verrucosa från Ylivieska. 1900. II. 119.[3]

Stengel, Karl. Hortensius et dea flora cum pomona. 1647. III. 121.[1]

— Hortorum, florum, et arborum historia. 1650. I. 286.

— Paralipomena . . . de arboribus fructiferis in India. 1650. III. 277.

Stengel, Karl, *Freiherr* von. Rechtsencyclopädie zum Gebrauche für Forstmänner. 1900. IV. 314.[1]

Stengel, Stephan, *Freiherr* von. Die Austrocknung des Donau-Mooses. 1791. IV. 143.[3]

Stenhouse, John. On the action of nitric acid on various vegetables. 1851. I. 158.

— Ueber Aloïn. 1851. III. 333.[1]

— Bestimmung des Theingehalts des Guarana. 1857. III. 539.[2]

— Determination of the amount of théine in Guarana. 1857. III. 539.[2]

— On the dried Coffee-leaf of Sumatra. 1854. III. 739.

— Sur l'essence de feuilles de Cannelle. 1855. III. 406.[1]

— Examination of . . . products from India. 1856. III. 277.

— Des feuilles du Caféier comme succédané du thé. 1854. III. 739.

— Ueber die getrockneten Kaffeeblätter von Sumatra. 1854. III. 739.

— On larixinic acid. 1862. II. 33.[1]

— Ueber Larixinsäure. 1862. II. 33.[1]

— Note on Morindone. 1864. III. 746.[1]

— Notis über Morindon. 1864. III. 746.[1]

— On the resin of Xanthorrhoea. 1846. III. 339.[1]

— Résine de Xanthorrhoea. 1846. III. 339.[1]

— Ueber das sogenannte Fraxinin. 1854. II. 708.[1]

— On some varieties of tannin. 1862. I. 183.

— On xanthoxyline. 1854. II. 412.[1]

— Sur la xanthoxyline. 1854. II. 412.[2]

— *See also* GRAHAM, Thomas, STENHOUSE, John & CAMPBELL, Dugald.

— & Groves, C. E. Sur l'encens ou gomme hyawa. 1876. III. 511.[3]

— — On gardenin. 1879. III. 744.[2]

— — Ueber das Gardenin. 1879. III. 744.[2]

— — Sur la gardénine. 1877. III. 744.[2]

— — Note on gardenin. 1877. III. 744.[2]

— — Note on incense resin. 1876. III. 511.[2]

— — Ueber das Weihrauchharz. 1876. III. 511.[2]

Stenhouse, W. *See* BRANDIS, *Sir* Dietrich, BADEN-POWELL, B. H. & STENHOUSE, W.

Stennekes, L. De Hooglandskoffie van Sierra-Leone. 1898. III. 743.[3]

— Eene levenskwestie voor de Koffiecultuur. 1898. III. 731.

Stenrooå, (*afterwards* KIWIRIKKO) K. E. Kärlväxter från Nurmijärvi. 1893. II. 35.[3]

— Nurmijärven pitäjän . . . kasvisto. 1894. V. XIX.[1]

Stenström, K. O. E. Ueber das Vorkommen derselben Arten in verschiedenen Klimaten. 1895. I. 219.[1]

Stentzel, C. G. De Ruta medicamento ac veneno. *See* STERNBERG, J. C. 1735. III. 505.[3]

— De Salvia in infuso adhibenda. 1723. III. 698.[1]

Stenzel, Georg. Anatomie der Laubblätter . . . der Celastraceae und Hippocrateaceae. 188 . ? II. 465.[3]

Stenzel, Karl Gustav Wilhelm. Beobachtungen an durchwachsenen Fichtenzapfen. 1876. II. 19.

— Über Bildungsabweichungen an der . . . Eichel. 1885. II. 137.[1]

— Blütenbildungen beim Schneeglöckchen. 1890. II. 137.[1]

— Über Carpinus Betulus quercifolia. 1880. II. 120.[3]

— Früchte des Bergahorns. 1890. II. 480.[1]

— Über die Keimung der Eichel. 1864. II. 131.[2]

— Ueber eine merkwürdige Rindenbildung bei der Edeltanne. 1862. II. 23,[3] IV. 445.

— Das Riesengebirge als Vegetationsgrenze. 1872. I. 387.

— Ueber die Ueberwallung abgestorbener Aeste. 1859. IV. 65.[3]

— Über das Vorkommen des Knieholzes im Isergebirge. 1877. II. 43.[1]

— Zwei keimlose Dattelkerne. 1892. II. 73.[1]

— Über Zweigabsprünge bei der Schwarzpappel. 1882. II. 98.[1]

— Zweige einer Edeltanne. 1881. II. 23.[2]

Step, Edward. Wayside and woodland blossoms. 1895. I. 535.[1]

— & Watson, William. Favourite flowers of garden and greenhouse. 1896. III. 83.[2]

Stephan. Die Reihen-Dreieckspflanzung. 1877. IV. 154.[1]

Stephan, Friedrich. Enumeratio stirpium agri mosquensis. 1792. I. 360.

— Icones plantarum mosquensium. 1797. I. 360.

— Nomina plantarum quas alit ager mosquensis. 1804. I. 41.

— Plantae novae Sibiriae. 1809. II. 270.[1]

Stephan, Karl. *See* WALBAUM, Heinrich & STEPHAN, Karl.

Stephanos, I. *See* ΣΤΈΦΑΝΟΣ, Ί.

Stephanotis fruit. 1885. III. 694.[1]

Stephens, A. B. Ficus elastica. 1898. III. 370.[3]

Stephens, E. F. Tree planting in Nebraska. 1898. IV. 113.[1]

Stephens, George. The practical irrigator and drainer. 1834. III. 150.[2]

Stephens, Henri. Élagage en crochet. 1854. III. 170.

— Mémoire sur les moyens d'utiliser les terrains incultes. 18 . . ? IV. 160.[2]

Stephens, Thomas. Method and plain process for making potash. 1755. IV. 395.

Stephens, Thomas. Notes on a species of Eucalyptus. 1882. II. 624.[1]

Stephenson, John & Churchill, J. M. Medical botany. 1831. III. 57.

Steppuhn, Hermann. Beiträge zur vergleichenden Anatomie der Gelsemiaceen. 1895. III. 540.[2]

Sterbeeck, Francis van. Citricultura. 1682. III. 121,[2] 496.[2]

— Den verstandighen hovenier. 1667. III. 106.[3]

Sterckx, R. Contribution à l'anatomie des Renonculacées. 1897. II. 196.[2]
— Recherches anatomiques sur l'embryon . . . des Renonculacées. 1900. II. 195.[1]
Sterk, Konrad. Corylus glandulosa Schuttl. 1889. II. 121.[2]
Sterler, Alois. Hortus nymphenburgensis. 1821. I. 46, *III. 22.*[1]
— **& Mayerhoffer**, J. N. Europas medicinische Flora. 1820. III. 66.[1]
Sterler, Wilhelm. Einige Winke zur Kultur der Ericeen. 1883. III. 650.[2]
Stern, Siegmund. Die mechanische Holz-Verkleinerung. 1878. IV. 392, *431.*[2]
Sternberg, Charles H. The flora of the Dakota group. 1884. I. 325.
Sternberg, Franz, *Baron* UNGERN-. *See* UNGERN-STERNBERG, Franz, *Baron.*
Sternberg, J. C. De Ruta medicamento ac veneno. 1735. III. 505.[2]
Sternberg, Kaspar, *Graf* von. Abhandlung über die Pflanzenkunde in Böhmen. 1817 (1818). I. 81,[1] *459*, 523.
— Botanische Wanderung in den Böhmer Wald. 1806. I. 376.
— Bruchstücke . . . einer naturhistorischen Reise von Prag nach Istrien. 1826. I. 439, II. 287.[2]
— Catalogus plantarum ad septem varias editiones Commentariorum Mathioli. 1821. I. 78.[1]
— Ueber einige Eigenthümlichkeiten der böhmischen Flora. 1829. I. 439.
— Historisch-chronologische Entwickelung der Fortschritte der Pflanzenkunde in Böhmen. 1818. I. 439, 523.[1]
— Kritische Beurtheilung der in Böhmen erschienenen Werke, die von Pflanzen handeln. 1818. I. 439, 523.[1]
— Ueber die östreichische Schwarzkiefer. 1821. II. 43.[3]
— Reise in die Rhetischen Alpen. 1806. I. 433.
— Reise durch Tirol. 1806. I. 447.
Sterndale, H. B. On the uses of Pandanus. 1886. III. 313.[1]
Sternegg, K. T. von, INAMA-. *See* INAMA-STERNEGG, K. T. von.
Sternheim, Karl von. Uebersicht der Flora Siebenbürgens. 1846. I. 445.
Sternitzky, *(Feldmesser, Chrzelitz).* Den pro 1845 u. 1846 . . . stattgefundenen Raupenfrass betreffend. 1846. IV. 206.
— Ertrag einer Wald-Torf-Fläche. 1847. IV. 438.[1]
— Die Humusbildung durch den Wurzelbau. 1846. IV. 68.
— Resultate und Ereignisse aus dem Forstreviere Chrzelitz. 1847. IV. 352.
— Streu-Erträge. 1847. IV. 437.[2]
— Die Werthschätzung der Weymuthskiefer. 1846. IV. 470.[1]
Sternitzky, *(Forst-Inspector, Chrzelitz).* Beantwortung der Frage: Warum sind bei gleichem Frass der Nonne auf Fichten . . . erstere mehr dem . . . Absterben ausgesetzt? 1842. IV. 200.
Sterns, E. E. The fruit of Calycanthus L. 1888. II. 214.[1]
— Note on the inflorescence of Camellia. 1887. II. 551.[1]
— Notes on Smilax pumila. 1888. II. 86.[1]
— Some peculiarities in the seed of Smilax. 1888. II. 85.[1]
— *See also* BRITTON, N. L., STERNS, E. E. & POGGENBURG, J. F.
Stetkiewicz, Stefan. O wpływie lasów na klimat Australii. 1888. IV. 49.[2]
Stettler, L. Bericht . . . über die Frage: Ist es rathsam, dass . . . der Handel mit Holz . . . beschränkt werde? 1839. IV. 406.[1]
Stettner, J. Observations on Manna. 1849. III. 672.[1]
— On the production of manna. 1850. IV. 536.[1]
Steuart, *Sir* Henry (*bart.*). Le guide du planteur. 1829. III. 167.
— The planter's guide. 1828. III. 122.[2]
Steube, J. H. Neues theoretisch-praktisches Lehrbuch der gesammten Gartenkunst. 1822. III. 104.
Steuchius, Elavus. Dissertatio de nutritione · arborum. 1722. I. 157.
Steudel, E. T. Büttneriaceae Brown. 1844. II. 531.[2]
— Dilleniaceae De Cand. 1844. II. 540.[2]
— Ranunculaceae Juss. 1844. II. 196.[1]
— Rhamneae Brown. 1844. II. 492.[1]
— Volksnamen chilesischer, abyssinischer und arabischer Pflanzen. 1855. I. 72,[2] 76.[1]
Steudel, Ernst Gottlieb. Bemerkungen über Kap-Pflanzen. 1830. I. 494.
— Einige Beiträge zu der chilesischen und peruanischen Flora. 1856. I. *340*,[2] 346.

— Ueber einige surinamische Pflanzen. 1843. I. 339.[1]
— Nomenclator botanicus. 1821. I. 77.
— Urticeae nondum descriptae. 1850. II. 157.[2]
— & Hochstetter, C. F. Enumeratio plantarum Germaniae. 1826. I. 377.
Steudener, Arnold. Das Symbol des Zweiges. 1857. I. 515.
Steusloff, A. Zwei " schmarotzende " Buchen. 1900. II. 121.[1]
— Eine zweibeinige Buche. 1900. II. 127.[1]
Steven, Christian von. Annotationes botanicae. 1848. II. 473.[2]
— Beschreibung des Kaiserlichen Gartens zu Nikita. 1829. I. 42.
— Decas plantarum nondum descriptarum Iberiae et Rossiae. 1809. I. 368.[2]
— Nouvelles espèces de Pins. 1838. II. 39.[1]
— Observationes in plantas rossicas. 1817. I. 360.
— Über den Obstbau in der Krymm. 1839. III. 134.[2]
— De Pinubus taurico-caucasicis. 1838. II. 39.[1]
— Verzeichniss der auf der taurischen Halbinsel wildwachsenden Pflanzen. 1856. I. 362.
— Von den zwei Feinden des Weinstocks. 1862. III. 563.
Stevens, Frank Lincoln. Vegetable pathology. 1897. I. 206.[2]
Stevens, Kaerle & Libaut, Jan. De veltbouw ofte lantwinninghe. 1588. III. 104.
Stevenson, David. On the building materials of the United States. 1841. IV. 422.[2]
— Notice of the ravages of the Limnoria. 1862. IV. 418.
— Notice relative to Long's American frame-bridge. 1841. IV. 424.[2]
— De vernieling van met kreosoot behandeld hout, door Limnoria terebrans. 1862. IV. 418.
Stevenson, H. The gentleman gardener instructed. 1716. III. 108.
— The young gard'ner's director. 1716. III. 108.
Stevenson, Robert Louis. On the thermal influence of forests. 1873. IV. 53.
Stevenson, W. Fleming. The Palm-tree. 1882. II. 63.[3]
Stevenson, William. Chapters on timber. 1877. IV. 396.[1]
— Nomenclature of timber. 1876. IV. 23.[1]
— Timber nomenclature. 1876. IV. 23.[1]
— The trees of commerce. 1876. IV. 396.[3]
Stevius, J. Sur le sucre de Palmier d'Inde. 1846. III. 320.[1]
Stewardson. Remarks on the Ailanthus silkworm. 1862. III. 507.[2]
Stewart, (*baronet*). The planters guide. 1828. III. 109.
Stewart, F. E. An illustrated monograph on Kola. 1894. III. 590.[2]
Stewart, Fred Carlton. Origin of cultivated fruits. 1892. III. 50.[2]
— The stomata and palisade cells. 1893. I. 131.[2]
— Witches' brooms on Cherry-trees. 1895. III. 435.[2]
Stewart, Henry. Forests and climate. 1872. IV. 53.
— Irrigation for the farm. [1]1877. III. 150.[2]
Stewart, J. H. M. On timber in the neighbourhood of Cuddapah. 1860. IV. 400.[1]
Stewart, James. On mottled Kauri. 1875. IV. 447.[1]
Stewart, Jane A. The Tea industry in the South. 1899. III. 601.[1]
Stewart, John Lindsay. Journal of a botanizing tour in Huzara. 1867. I. 474.
— List of the principal trees . . . of northern India. 1876. I. 470.[1]
— Memoranda on the Peshawur valley, chiefly regarding its flora. 1863. I. 473.
— Notes of a tour in the Punjab Salt Range. 1869. I. 474.
— Note on the flora of the country passed through by the . . . force under Brig. Chamberlain. 1862. I. 473.
— Proceedings of a conference of Punjab forest officers at Lahore. *See* FOREST de nutritione · arborum.
— Punjab plants. 1869. III. 92.[2]
— Report on the food of the inhabitants . . . of Bijnour. 1865. III. 278.
— Sketch of the flora of the country passed through by the . . . force under Brig. Chamberlain. 1862. I. 473.
— The Sub-Siwalik tract. 1863. IV. 377.[2]—1865. III. 278.
— The timber trees . . . of the Bijnour forest. 1866. III. 278.
— *See also* BRANDIS, *Sir* Dietrich, STEWART, J. L. & WOOD, E.
Stewart, J. T. Shade trees, indigenous shrubs. 1877. I. 312.

Stewart, R. B. Outlines of botany. 1835. I. 87.
Stewart, Robert. Handbook of the Torquay flora. 1860. I. 533.
— On the progress of Tea cultivation in Cachar. 1859. III. 603.
— The Torquay flora. 1860. I. 401, 533.
Stewart, Samuel Alexander & Corry, Thomas Hughes. A flora of the north-east of Ireland. 1888. I. 404.[1]
Stewart, W. North Devon handbook. 186.? I. 533.
Stubbe, L. Koffie-bereiding . . . ter Sumatra's westkust. 1895. III. 731.
Sticke, (Förster). Erfahrungen über forstliche Ausnutzungen und Erträge. 1853. IV. 254.
Stickel, Carl. Aetherisches Oel einiger . . . Melaleuca-Arten. 1836. III. 636.[1]
— Huile volatile de quelques espèces du Melaleuca. 1836. III. 636.[1]
Stickmann, Olavus. Herbarium amboinense. See LINNÉ, Carl von. 1754. I. 464.[2]
Stickney, J. L. Evergreens for hedges. 1868. III. 214.[2]
Stickney, J. S. What shall we plant for hedges. 1869. III. 213.
Stieben. Écorce de bois de Santal du Mexique. 1885. III. 384.[2]
Stieber, Ferdinand. Erfahrungen über die sogenannten Taschen der Pflaumen. 1847. III. 433.[2]
— Die Vertilgung der Raupen und Maikäfer. 1847. III. 196.
Stieff, Johann Ernst. De vita nuptiisque plantarum. 1741. I. 146.
Stieglitz, Christian Ludwig. Geschichtliche Darstellung der Eigenthumsverhältnisse an Wald und Jagd in Deutschland. 1832. IV. 25.
Stiehler, Bernhard. Einige Bemerkungen über künstliche Rosenbefruchtung. 1827. III. 451.[1]
— Über Rosen-Vermehrung. 1829. III. 451.[2]
Stiemer. Torfmaschine zur Massenproduction. 1883. IV. 438.[2]
— Vier Fragen die Privat-Forsten in den baltischen Provinzen betreffend. 1880. IV. 273,[2] 308.[1]
Stiemer, (Steuerinspector). Über Gespinnstfaser liefernde Pflanzen. 1874. III. 234.
Stiemer, J. G. F. Schutzmittel . . . Plantagen gegen . . . Baumweisslingsraupe zu sichern. 1831. III. 196.
Stierlin-Hauser, R. Aufforstungen auf Rigi-Scheidegg. 1897. IV. 167.[1]
Stika, Otto. Kurze Uebersicht der Phanerogamen . . . der Stadt Brüx. 1857. I. 441.
Stiles, M. H. The staining of wood sections. 1876. I. 36.[2]
Stillé, Alfred & Maisch, J. M. The national dispensatory. 1879. III. 246.
Stiller, & others. Nachweis des . . . im Ohlauer Stadtwalde stattgehabten Holz-Ertrages. 1840. IV. 260.[1]
Stillesen, Morten. Om Pingveolum Aesculi Hippocastani. 1861. III. 538.[1]
Stillingfleet, Benjamin & Berger, A. M. The calendar of flora. 1775. I. 222.[1]
Stillingia sebifera or Tallow-tree. 1875. III. 522.[2]
Stillman, Abel. Preparation of timber with salt. 1845. IV. 417.
Stillmann, John Maxson. Sur l'essence d'Oreodaphne. 1881. III. 408.[1]
— & O'Neill, E. C. On the occurrence of a new fat acid in . . . the California Bay tree. 1882. III. 408.[1]
Stimpson, William. On botanical and zoological nomenclature. 1860. I. 253.[2]
Stimulating the germination of Teak seed. 1900. IV. 537.[1]
Stirling, Mrs. On an easy and effective style of nature-printing. 1863. I. 37.[1]
Stirling, J. B. Remarks on culture . . . of Roses. 1871. III. 449.
Stirling, James. Notes on the flora of Mount Hotham. 1888. I. 504.
— Notes on the Rutaceae of the Australian Alps. 1887. II. 397.[1]
— The phanerogamia of the Mitta Mitta source basin. 1883. I. 503.
— The Proteaceae of the Victorian Alps. 1883. II. 158.[1]
Stirpium orientalium rariorum catalogi tres. See RAY, John. 1738. I. 478.
Stirum, comte de LIMBURG-. See LIMBURG-STIRUM, comte de.
Stisser, Friederich Ulrich. Forst- und Jagd-Histoire der Teutschen. 1737. IV. 25.

Stisser, Johann Andreas. Botanica curiosa. 1697. I. 288.
— Horti medici helmstadiensis catalogus. 1699. I. 43.
Stivanello, Luigi Carlo. Il Montello. 1874. IV. 364.
Stizenberger, Ernst. Kriegsbereitschaft im Reiche Flora's. 1875. I. 235.[2]
Stobbe. Studien auf dem Gebiete der Korbweiden-Kultur. 1895. III. 349.
Stobbe. Taxus baccata als Waldbaum in Ostpreussen. 1899. II. 11.[2]
Stock, van der. De invloed van het bosch op het klimaat. 1891. IV. 54.
Stock, Andr. De eo, quod iustum est circa arbores. 1691. IV. 313.
Stock, Georg. Ein Beitrag zur Kenntniss der Proteinkrystalle. 1892. I. 139.
Stockbridge, Levi. Fertilizers. 1877. III. 151.
Stockdale, John Joseph. Sketches, civil and military, of the island of Java. 1811. III. 275.[2]
Ueber die Stockfäule in Fichtenwaldungen. 1852. IV. 455.
Stockhausen, von. Beiträge zur Forst-, Jagd- und Fischerei-Statistik des Grossherzogthums Hessen. 1859. IV. 351.[2]
Stockman, Ralph. Arrow poisons. 1898. III. 367,[1] 685.[2]
Stockmann. Sur le principe actif du Séné. 1886. III. 470.[2]
Stocks, John Ellerton. On the Balsam trees producing myrrh and bdellium. 1849. II. 417.[2]
— Ueber die Balsambäume, welche Myrrhe und Bdellium erseugen. 1849. II. 417.[2]
— Botany, (chiefly economic) of Scinde. 1848. III. 92.[1]
— Notes on Beloochistan plants. 1852. I. 477.[2]
— Notes on the botany of Scinde. 1846. I. 472.
— On two Balsam trees . . . from Scinde. 1849. II. 417.[2]
1850. III. 511.[1]
Stodder, Charles. Disease of Sycamore trees. 1856. III. 418.[2]
Stöckel, H. F. A. Bau-, Kunst- und Möbelschreiner. 1826. IV. 426.[2]
— Neues praktisches Handbuch der Tischlerkunst. 1826. IV. 426.[2]
— Die Tischlerkunst in ihrem ganzen Umfange. 1826. IV. 426.[2]
Stöckert, H. Auslese schöner Ziergehölze für Rasenschmuck. 1900. III. 203.
Stöckhardt. Futterwerth des Laubes. 1869. III. 223.[1]
Stöckhardt, Adolph & Schröder, Julius von. Waldschäden durch schweflige Säure. 1878. IV. 192.[2]
Stöckhardt, J. A. Algemeene landbouwscheikunde. 1854. III. 36.[2]
— Forstwirthschaftlich-chemische Untersuchungen. 1851. IV. 60.[2]
— Plantenvoedsel en plantenvoeding. 1860. I. 158.
— Rückblick auf die . . . forstlich- und physiologisch-chemischen Untersuchungen. 1866. IV. 60.[1]
— Untersuchung junger Fichten. 1853. IV. 60.[2]
— Untersuchungen über die schädliche Einwirkung des Hütten- und Steinkohlenrauches. 1871. IV. 192.[2]
Stoeckli, J. Aperçu sur les forêts du canton de Fribourg. 1871. IV. 367.
Stoeder, W. Alcaloïdbepalingen van Granaatbast. 1887. III. 631.[1]
— Over Alcaloïdenbepalingen. 1875. III. 723.
— Alsaloïden bepalingen van de Bolivia-kina. 1878. III. 723.
— Alcaloïdenbepalingen van Java-kina. 1874. III. 723.
— De alkaloïdenbepaling voor cortex Granati. 1894. III. 631.[1]
— Alkaloïdgehalte van indische Granaat-wortelbasten. 1890. III. 631.[1]
— Arbutine. 1887. III. 648.[2]
— Bereiding en onderzoek van extractum chinae liquidum. 1889. III. 723.
— Een merkwaardige Java-kina. 1873. III. 723.
— Over roode Java-kina. 1876. III. 726.[1]
Stöger, Paul. Zur Berechnung des Stockzinses der Fichtenrinde. 1897. IV. 459.[1]
— Der Eichenschälwald. 1898. IV. 509.
Stöger, Wilhelm. Die Feinde der Schwarzföhre. 1874. IV. 466.[1]
— Ueber die Harzung der österreichischen Schwarzföhre. 1881. IV. 465.[2]
— Neues über die Schwarzföhre. 1881. IV. 466.[2]
— Die Schwarzföhre in Mischung. 1889. IV. 466.[2]
Stöhr, Adolf. Über Vorkommen von Chlorophyll in der Epidermis. 1879. I. 129.[2]
— See also MIKOSCH, Karl & STÖHR, Adolf.

Stoeklin, J. Boiséments dans les Grands-Marais. 1873. IV. 154.¹
— Versuch über Aufforstung im grossen Moos. 1872. IV. 166.¹
— Waldanpflanzung im Grossen Moos. 1873. IV. 154.²
Stoekzl. Conservation des couleurs naturelles des plantes. 1880. I. 36.¹
Stoerck, Anton. Instituta Facultatis medicae vindobonensis. 1775. I. 65.²
Störig, J. E. J. Lehrbuch des gesamten Obstbaues. 1823. III. 136.
Stoessner. Flora der nächsten Umgebung von Annaberg. 186.? I. 384.
Stötzer, Hermann. Ueber die Bestimmung der ... Abtriebszeiten. 1900. IV. 252.
— Die Eisenacher Forste. 1900. IV. 356.¹
— Die Ermittelung des laufenden Massenzuwachses. 1880. IV. 233.
— Die finanzielle Seite der Mittelwaldwirthschaft. 1890. IV. 258.
— Die Forstbenutzung. 1887. IV. 382.¹
— Die Forsteinrichtung. 1898. IV. 241.
— Zur Frage der Rätlichkeit des Fichtenanbaues. 1887. IV. 454.
— Frühzeitiges Absterben von Schwarzkiefern. 1889. IV. 466.¹
— Höchster Durchschnittsertrag. 1890. IV. 258.
— Nochmals höchster Durchschnittsertrag. 1891. IV. 258.
— Der Streit um den Reinertrag. 1896. IV. 259.¹
— Waldwegebaukunde. 1877. IV. 266.³
— Waldwertrechnung und forstliche Statik. 1894. IV. 253.
— Weitere Nachrichten über den Ursprung des Massenfachwerks. 1897. IV. 26, 131.
— See also Oreuperz, Г.
Stoffel, Bernard. Over het afsterven van jonge Dennen aanplantingen. 1899. IV. 479.
— Een causerie over de waarde van eene woudboomen. 1899. IV. 119.¹
— Les conifères de la Hollande. 1900. IV. 119.² -.
— De Nederlandsche Dennenbosschen. 1898. IV. 357.¹
— Over wringing van boomstammen. 1897. I. 107.¹
Stoffel, Michel. Rapport sur la maladie de la Vigne. 1873. III. 759.
Stohmann, F. Ueber einige Bedingungen der Vegetation. 1862. I. 158.
Stoizner, Ladislaus, Reichsedler von. Abhandlungen vom Seiden-, Flachs- und Hanfbau. 1788. III. 373.
— Praktisch-ökonomische Abhandlungen von Wald- und Fruchtbäumen. 1789. IV. 116.
— Zufällige Gedanken von dem Holzmangel. 1788. IV. 280.¹
Stojković, Aleksa. See Crojković, Алекса.
Stok, van der. Eucalyptus globulus. 1876. IV. 533.¹
Stoker, T. G. Notes on the management of the Tea plant. 1874. III. 603.
Stokes, J. Lort. Discoveries in Australia. See BYNOE. 1846. II. 623.²
Stokes, Jonathan. Botanical commentaries. 1830. I. 260.
— A botanical materia medica. 1812. III. 55.
Stoklasa, Jules. Fonction physiologique du fer. 1898. I. 151.²
— Über die Verbreitung ... des Lecithins. 1896. I. 178.
Stolberg, Graf zu. Notizen über die Messungs- und Holz-Resultate der Königsfichte. 1852. IV. 460.¹
Stoll, Gustav. Obstbaulehre. 1882. III. 139.
— Sollen die Wurzeln der Bäume beim Pflanzen ... geschnitten werden? 1878. III. 173.²
— Das Veredeln von Birnen auf Aepfel. 1876. III. 445.³
Stoll, Rudolf. Ueber Aepfel und Birnen des Wiener Marktes. 1889. III. 444.¹
— Die amerikanischen Frühpfirsiche. 1889. III. 441.¹.
— Ueber die Bildung des Kallus. 1874. I. 208.²
— Forandring af Vævene paa Stiklingernes Snitflade. 1874. I. 209.¹
— Ueber den Krebs der Apfelbäume. 1875. III. 427.²
— Oesterreichisch-Ungarische Pomologie. 1883. III. 90.¹
— Ueber Ringelungen. 1876. III. 175.¹
— Die Veränderungen der Gewebe an ... Stecklingen. 1874. I. 209.¹
— Wurzelschnitt. 1878. IV. 154.¹
Stollenhaus, Georg. Betrachtungen zur Frage: "Reiner oder gemischter Hochwald?" 1888. IV. 137.¹
— Ueber Unfallverhütung bei Waldarbeiten. 1889. IV. 310.¹
— Ueber die Verwendung der Fichtennadeln. 1889. IV. 459.¹

Stoltenberg, N. Beiträge zur Kenntniss der Flora Tonderns. 1877. I. 387. .
Stoltz, J. L. Ampélographie rhénane. 1852. III. 546.
— Manuel élémentaire du cultivateur alsacien. 1842. III. 104.
Stolyetiye ... See Столѣтіе ...
Stolz, C. & Plebst, G. Five hundred Indian plants. 1881. III. 92.¹
Stolz, Johann Christian. Flore des plantes ... du Haut et Bas-Rhin. 1802. I. 375.
Stone. Berigt wegens het genezen van afgaande koortsen door middel van den bast van willige boomen. 1772. III. 351.¹
Stone, Alfred. Government timber-tests. 1897. IV. 416.¹
Stone, George Edward. Autumnal coloration of leaves. 1900. I. 186.
Stone, Herbert. Ceylon timbers. 1900. IV. 401.¹
Stone, I. N. Dewberry culture. 1895. III. 457.²
Stone, William H. The flora of Mt. Monadnock. 1885. I. 315.
— The Royal Pine of New Hampshire. 1896. IV. 24.²
Stone, Winthrop Ellsworth. Autumn foliage. 1883. I. 222.¹
— The chemical composition of the nectar of Poinsettia. 1892. II. 443.¹
— Fasciation in Rubus. 1883. II. 305.²
— The growth of trees. 1885. I. 221.
— See also PENHALLOW, D. P. & STONE, W. E.
The Stone Pine. 1885. III. 308.²
A stoneless Plum, Prunus tenerrima. 1874. III. 443.¹
Stonhill, W. John. Paper pulp from wood. 1885. IV. 430.
Stooling of gutta percha. 1897. III. 668.¹
Stoppeiaar, A. de. Enten van Java op Liberiakoffie. 1898. III. 733.²
Storch, Franz. Skizzen zu einer naturhistorischen Topographie des Herzogthumes Salzburg. 1857. I. 441.
Storch, Johann Wilhelm. Geschichte des Forst- und Jagdwesens in dem Grossh. S. eisenachischen Kreise. 1841. IV. 25.
Storch, Josef. Forst-Statistik des mähr. Bezirkes Gaya. 1868. IV. 369.
Storck, Jacob. Plantae vitienses. 1862. I. 510.¹
Storck, Jacob P. The Coffee-leaf disease. 1882. III. 735.
— De Koffiebladziekte. 1882. III. 735.
Storer, Francis Humphreys. On the agricultural value of spent dye-woods and tan. 1877. IV. 432.²
— Analysis of a sample of ashes left on burning the Bamboo baskets. 1898. II. 59.²
— Cold dilute alkaline solutions dissolve very little wood-gum. 1898. II. 21.¹
— Doty Birch wood yields little wood-gum. 1898. II. 118.²
— Estimations of cellulose ... in Peach-stones. 1898. II. 276.²
— Observations on ... substances in the trunks of trees. 1897. I. 156.¹
— On the results of a search for other sugars than xylose. 1900. I. 156.¹
Storey, T. H. Thunbergia grandiflora. 1891. III. 710.¹
Storia delle piante forestiere. See CASTIGLIONI, Luigi, conte.
Stork, William. An account of East Florida. 1767. I. 317.²
— A description of East-Florida. 1767. I. 317.²
Storm, V. Notitsœr til Trondhjems omegns flora. 1885. I. 357.
— Veiledning i Throndhjems omegns flora. 1869. I. 356.
Storm, William. A list of specimens of 14 kinds of woods from Jamaica. 1850. IV. 17.
A storm-tossed veteran. 1898. II. 41.¹
Stormonth, J. Manual of scientific terms. 1879. I. 71.
Storp, Ferdinand. Beiträge zur Erklärung der ... Schädigungen des Baumwuchses. 1891. IV. 189.²
— Über den Einfluss von kochsalz- und zinksulfathaltigem Wasser. 1883. I. 211.
— Locale Untersuchungen über das Umtriebsalter ... für die Buche. 1887. IV. 498.
— Untersuchung über Lichtzuswachs in Kiefern. 1887. IV. 481.
— Versuch einer Umtriebsbestimmung für die Kiefernbestände. 1887. IV. 481.
Storrie, John. Flora of Cardiff. 1886. I. 534.²
Storrs school agricultural experiment station. See CONNECTICUT — STORRS SCHOOL ... III. 3.
Story, W. H. Ericas. 1851. III. 650.¹
Story of the old Elm on Boston Common. See WATERSTON, R. C. 1876. II. 143.²

Stosch, H. von. Antwort an Herrn Oberforstrath von Berg. 1867. IV. 274.[1]

Stotter, Michael & **Heufler,** Ludwig, *Ritter* von. Geognostisch-botanische Bemerkungen auf einer Reise durch Oetzthal. 1840. I. 440.

Stowell, H. Tree-life; blizzards. 1900. III. 184.[2]

Stowell, H. A. Dates of the foliation of trees and shrubs. 1855. I. 226.[1]

Strabo, WALAFRIDUS. *See* WALAFRIDUS STRABO.

Strachan. Observations made in the island of Ceilan. 1704. III. 405.[2]

— Some observations on coral. 1704. II. 152.[1]

Strachey, *Sir* Richard. Narrative of a journey to the lakes Rakas-Tal. 1900. I. 460.[2]

Strachey, William. The historie of travaile into Virginia Britannia. 1849. III. 263.[1]

Strada ferrata economica per il trasporto dei legnami. 1886. IV. 391.

Straehler, Adolph. Ein Beitrag zu Rosenflora von Schlesien. 1895. II. 285.[1]

— Eine neue schlesische Rose. 1896. II. 298.[2]

— Rhodologisches. 1894. II. 285.[1]

— Salicologisches. 1890. II. 106.[1] — 1896. II. 102.[1]

— Salix marchiaca mihi. 1895. II. 108.[1]

— Salix repens L. var. Rieseana. 1877. II. 109.[2]

— Salix silesiaca Willd. 1897. II. 110.[1]

— Die Weiden Sprembergs. 1878. II. 101.[2]

— Zwei neue Weiden-Tripelbastarde. 1895. II. 102.[1]

— Zweiter Nachtrag zur Phanerogamen- und Gefässcryptogamen-Flora von Goerbersdorf. 1877. II. 284.[2]

Strahl, J. Eigenthümliche Pfropfungen. 1875. III. 294.[1]

— Eine gelbbunte Acacie. 1872. III. 487.[1]

— Wirkung des künstlichen Lichtes. 1877. I. 230.

Straits branch of the Royal Asiatic society. *See* ROYAL ASIATIC ... III. 26.[2]

Straits Settlements. 1888. III. 274.[2]

Straits Settlements — Botanic gardens. Annual report. 1883. I. 67.[1]

Straits Settlements — Botanic gardens and forest department. Annual report. 1883. I. 67[1]; *see also* STRAITS SETTLEMENTS — FOREST DEPARTMENT. IV. 16.[1]

Straits Settlements — Forest department. Annual report. IV. 16.[2]

Straits Settlements — Gardens and forest department. Agricultural bulletin. *See* AGRICULTURAL ... III. 26.[2]

Strakhof, P. *See* Страховъ, П.

Strampffer, Georg Wilhelm. Vom Hutrechte. 1798. IV. 332.[2]

Strand, Benedictus Joh. Flora palaestina. *See* LINNÉ, Carl von. 1756. I. 479.

Strand, George W. Deciduous tree-seeds. 1899. III. 156.[2]

Strand magazine. III. 18.

Strandman, Petrus. Purgantia indigena. *See* LINNÉ, Carl von. 1766. III. 270.[1]

Strandmark, P. W. Blomställningen hos Empetrum nigrum. 1880. II. 454.[1]

Strangways, Mary Fox-, *Countess* of Ilchester. *See* Fox-STRANGWAYS, Mary.

Strantz, M. von. Die Blumen in Sage und Geschichte. 1875. V. xxv.[2]

— Unsere Gemüse. 1877. III. 219.[2]

Strasburg — Société d'Histoire naturelle. *See* Société ... I. 15.

Strasburg — Société des sciences naturelles. *See* SOCIÉTÉ D'HISTOIRE NATURELLE DE STRASBOURG. I. 15. *See also* SOCIÉTÉ DES SCIENCES DE NANCY. I. 23.

Strasburg — Société du muséum d'histoire naturelle. *See* SOCIÉTÉ D'HISTOIRE NATURELLE DE STRASBOURG. I. 15.

Strasburger, Eduard. Die Angiospermen und die Gymnospermen. 1879. I. 122.

— Ueber den Bau ... der Leitungsbahnen in den Pflanzen. 1888. I. 124.

— Ueber die Bedeutung phylogenetischer Methoden. 1874. I. 249.[1]

— Die Befruchtung bei den Coniferen. 1869. II. 20.[2]

— Ueber Befruchtung und Zelltheilung. 1877. I. 201.[1]

— Ein Beitrag zur Entwicklungsgeschichte der Spaltöffnungen. 1866. I. 131.[1]

— Die Bestäubung der Gymnospermen. 1871. II. 1.

— Das botanische Praktikum. 1884. I. 36.[2]

— Die Coniferen und die Gnetaceen. 1872. II. 16,[2] 53.[2]

— Die Endospermbildung bei Daphne. 1884. II. 601.[1]

— Ueber fremdartige Bestäubung. 1886. I. 201.[1]

— Handbook of practical botany. 1884. I. 36.[2]

— Histologische Beiträge. 1888. I. 124.

— Karyokinetische Probleme. 1895. I. 137.

— Zur Kenntniss der Archispermenwurzel. 1872. I. 103.

— Über Kern- und Zelltheilung. 1888. I. 124.

— Das kleine Prakticum für Anfänger. 1884. I. 36.[2]

— Microscopic botany. 1884. I. 36.[2]

— Ueber Polyembryonie. 1878. I. 122.

— Zu Santalum und Daphne. 1885. II. 169,[1] 601.[1]

— Ueber Sciadopitys und Phyllocladus. 1873. II. 9,[1] 49.[2]

— "Sind die Coniferen Gymnospermen oder nicht?" 1873. II. 19.

— Ueber das Verhalten des Pollens. 1888. I. 124.

— Ueber das Verhalten des Pollens ... bei den Gymnospermen. 1892. II. 1.

— Die Vertreterinnen der Geleitzellen. 1890. II. 1.

— Ueber Verwachsungen und deren Folgen. 1885. I. 208.[2]

— Über das Wachsthum vegetabilischer Zellhäute. 1888. I. 124.

— Ueber Zellbildung und Zelltheilung. 1875. I. 136.[2]

— *See also* Страсбургеръ, Э.

— & others. Lehrbuch der Botanik. 1894. I. 92, 523.[2]

— — A text-book of botany. 1894. I. 92.

— — Trattato di botanica. 1894. I. 92.

Straschiler, Franz. Der Bau des Geschlachtenwald-Riesweges. 1899. IV. 391.

— Ueber räumliche Stellung der Waldpflanzen. 1886. IV. 154.[1]

Strassberger, M. Nachschlagewerk für alle Holzinteressenten. 1883. IV. 368, 406.[1]

Strassburger, E. Góry mauretańskie i Dąb korkowy. 1896. II. 140.[1]

— Z Riviery. 1896. III. 126.[1]

Strassenstaub gegen die Traubenkrankheit. 1861. III. 577.

Strassheim, C. R. Rosenabstimmung. 1889. III. 450.

Stratingh, E. S. Berigt omtrent eenige inlandsche siropen. 1811. III. 220.[2]

Stratingh, G. A. De cinchonio. 1828. III. 722.

Stratingh, S. Scheikundige verhandeling over de cinchonine. 1822. III. 722.

Straton, C. R. Alternating generations. *See* ADLER, Hermann. 1881. IV. 510.

Stratton, Frederic. Wild flowers of the Isle of Wight. 1900. I. 535.[1]

Stratton, James & others. Extracts from letters to Mr. McNab. 1861. III. 46.[1]

Straub, Johann Caspar. Characteristice et descriptiones ... plantarum Horti academici tubingensis. *See* KIELMEYER, C. F. 1814. I. 266.

Strauch, von, (*Forstcandidat*). Anlegung ... der Eichensaat und Pflanzkämpe. 1848. IV. 504.

— Notizen über die Erträge der Eichenpflanzwaldungen. 1848. IV. 512.

Strauss, Anselm Franz. Chemie und Physik als Hülfsmittel bei dem Studium der Forstwissenschaft. 1821. IV. 60.[2]

— Chemisch-physikalische Abhandlung. 1821. IV. 60.[2]

— Grundlehren der allgemeinen Chemie. 1824. IV. 60.[2]

— Wiedererneuerung ... der K. baierischen National-Forstlehr-Anstalt. 1820. IV. 31.

Strauss, Emil G. Ueber einige Bestandtheile des Copaivabalsams. 1868. III. 473.[2]

Strauss, Heinrich. Die Cacteensammlung des Herrn ... Gruson. 1885. III. 610.

Strauss, Lorenz. Encomium Rosae. 1662. II. 290.[1]

— De potu coffi. 1686. III. 741.[1]

Strauwald, Bruno. Ueber Baumbinder. 1889. III. 199.

— Beitrag zur Hebung der Unfruchtbarkeit unserer Obstbäume. 1882. III. 174.[2]

— Heckenumfriedigungen. 1878. III. 213.

— Die Heckenumfriedigungen. 1878. III. 213.

— Die Pflanzung des Chaussee- oder Strassenbaumes. 1885. III. 210.

— Ueber seine beim Veredeln ... zu beobachtende Manipulation. 1876. III. 162.

— Ueber Verwendung der Caraganen. 1877. III. 469.[2]

Stray leaves from Indian forests. *See* INDIAN forester. IV. 16.[2]

Strecha, Alois. Ein transleithanischer Baumriese. 1897. IV. 486.[1]

Strecker, Adolph. Ueber das Arbutin. 1858. III. 660.[1]

— Études sur les transformations de la théobromine, de la caféine. 1861. I. 175.

— Recherches sur l'acide tannique de la noix de galle. 1855. IV. 514.[2]

— Untersuchungen über die Constitution des Chinins. 1854. III. 722.

Street, John. On acclimatising plants at Biel. 1830. III. 123.²
Street planting. 1895. III. 210.
Street trees. 1888. III. 208.²—1890. III. 208.²—1895. III. 208.²
Strehle, Max. Paliurus australis. 1900. III. 542.¹
Strehler, L. F. Mittheilungen aus meinem Tagebuche. 1832. III. 275.¹
— Uebersicht der um Ingolstadt wildwachsenden . . . Pflanzen. 1841. I. 380.
Strength of timber. 1895. IV. 410.
Strength of timbers. 1896. IV. 410.
Strettell, George W. The Ficus elastica in Burma. 1876. III. 371.¹
— Note on Caoutchouc obtained from the Chavannesia. 1874. III. 691.²
— See also COGSWELL, W. H. & STRETTELL, G. W.
Streu, Eduard. Der Rosenfreund. 1842. III. 451.²
Streu als Hauptnutzung. 1864. IV. 71.
Streubel. Die Vermehrung der Sträucher. 1876. III. 158.
Stricht, Édouard van der. Le Peuplier noir. 1890. III. 346.¹
Strickland, Agnes. Floral sketches, fables. 1836. I. 511.
Strictures on Sir Henry Steuart's Planter's guide. 1830. III. 123.¹
Striking a light. 1885. III. 315.²
Stringer. Report . . . on the trade of Chiengmai. 1892. IV. 538.¹
Stringfellow, H. M. Hybridism by grafting and budding. 1896. I. 246.²
— The new horticulture. 1896. III. 99.
Strobel, B. B. An experimental enquiry into . . . Aralia spinosa. 1826. III. 641.²
Strobelberger, Johann Stephen. Mastichológia. 1628. III. 525.²
— Recens nec antea sic visa Galliae politico-medica descriptio. 1620. I. 404.²
Strobl, Gabriel Carl. Der Etna und seine Vegetation. 1880. I. 432.¹
— Flora der Nebroden. 1878. I. 431.
— Flora des Etna. 1880. I. 432.¹
— Aus der Frühlings-Flora und Fauna Illyriens. 1872. I. 447.
Strobl, Josef. Die Betriebseinrichtung in den Forsten der Oesterreichischen alpinen Montangesellschaft. 1889. IV. 250.¹
Ströbele, Maximilian. Ueber die Functionen der Blätter. 1867. IV. 133.
See MOHL, Hugo von. 1836. I. 172.
Ström, Isr. Vägledning; skogshushållningen. 1860. IV. 273.¹
Strömer, Mårten. Tankar om orsaken, hwarföre trän uti stark winter frysa bort. 1739. I. 211.
Strömfelt, Harald Fredrik George. Islands kärlväxter. 1884. I. 357.
Strohecker, Jonas Rudolph. Die Hackwaldwirthschaft. 1883. IV. 133.
— Die molecularen Ursachen der Pflanzengestalten. 1878. I. 100.¹
— Systematische Anleitung zu botanischen Excursionen in Mitteleuropa. 1869. I. 386.
Stroink, J. H. H. Bereiding van tannas chinini. 1892. III. 724.¹
Stromberg, T. See Штромберг, Ч.
Stromeyer, August Adolf Ludwig. De radice Columbo. 1829. III. 397.¹
Stromeyer, Friederich. Historiae vegetabilium geographicae specimen. 1800. I. 298.
Stromeyer, Johann Friedrich. Dissertatio . . . sistens plantarum Solanacearum ordinem. 1772. III. 698.²
Strong, A. B. The American flora. 1846. III. 58.
Strong, William C. Color in Conifers. 1891. III. 291.
— Crooked Norway Maples. 1889. III. 535.²
— Culture of the Grape. 1866. III. 550.
— Evergreen trees. 1891. III. 206.¹
— The forest interests of Massachusetts. 1886. IV. 339.
— New and useful shrubs. 1883. III. 153.
— Ornamental shrubs. 1887. III. 60.
— Planting Conifers in August. 1890. III. 295.¹
— Protecting trees from canker worms. 1890. III. 186.²
— Roses. 1879. III. 452.
— Select lists of trees and shrubs, III. 1881. III. 60.
— Transplanting Conifers in August. 1889. III. 295.¹
Strong, Woodbridge. Universal side cleft grafting. 1882. III. 162.

Strunge, Francis. De cultuur van Koffie in Mexico. 1896. III. 728.¹
— Report on the cultivation of Coffee in Mexico. 1896. III. 728.¹
Le Strophosomus Coryli. 1896. IV. 208.²
Strother, David H. The Ailanthus. 1869. III. 507.¹
Strott, G. K. Über Heizmaterialien. 1876. IV. 413.¹
— Das Wichtigste über die Eigenschaften der im Bauwesen am häufigsten zur Verwendung kommenden Baumaterialien. 1878. IV. 423.¹
Stroud, T. B. Elements of botany. 1821. I. 85.
Strout, A. S. Camellias in Alabama. 1883. III. 599.²
O stroyeni . . . See О строенiи . . .
Strube, J. M. Kurze Anleitung zur Forstwissenschaft. 1791. IV. 95.
Strube, Wilhelm. Exanthemata phytoparasitica. 1863. III. 194.
Struck, Carl. Blühender Ulex im Januar. 1890. II. 387.²
— Starke Stämme von Hedera Helix. 1882. II. 650.¹
— Starke Stämme von Hedera Helix L. in den Wäldern Mecklenburgs. 1890. II. 650.¹
— Starker Epheustamm. 1875. II. 650.¹
Strübing, Otto. Die Vertheilung der Spaltöffnungen bei den Coniferen. 1888. II. 18.
Strugnell, W. B. See WITCHELL, C. A. & STRUGNELL, W. B.
Strumiłło, Józef. Ogrody północne. 1820. III. 101.¹
— Rocznik ogrodniczy powszechny. 1844. III. 101.¹
Strumpf, E. Zur Histologie der Kiefer. 1898. II. 47.¹
— Z hrzyrodzoł Sosny. 1899. II. 40.¹
— Las jako typ biologiczny. 1897. I. 528.²
— Mechanika w państwie roślinnem. 1898. I. 149.²
— Rośliny żyworodzące. 1898. I. 205.
— Technika lotu u roślin. 1899. I. 241.¹
Strumpf, Ferdinand Ludwig. Allgemeine Pharmakopöe. 1859. III. 249.
— Die offizinellen Gewächse in den natürlichen Pflanzenfamilien. 1840. III. 57.
Strumpff, L. F. De vorderingen der scheikunde in hare toepassingen op den landbouw. 1854. III. 36.²
Strutt, Jacob George. Deliciae sylvarum. 1829. I. 516.
— The principal forest trees of Europe. 1829. I. 348.¹
— Sylva britannica. 1822. I. 296.².
Struve, Jacob Bernhard. De Erica. See THUNBERG, C. P. 1785. II. 664.¹
Struve, Karl Friedrich. Von inländischen Gewürzen. 1801. III. 221.²
Struven, Georg Adam. De jure sylvarum et arborum. 1735. IV. 313.
Struvius, Ernst Gotthold. De corticum Ulmi in hydrope virtute. 1747. III. 365.¹
— De corticum Ulmi pariter ac Alni efficacia. 1752. IV. 489.¹
Strzelecki, Heinrich. Beitrag zur Berechnung des Normalvorrathes. 1885. IV. 237.
— Eine einfache Ermittlungsweise der Schaftformzahlen. 1883. IV. 218.
— Ueber den Genauigkeitsgrad bei Berechnung des Normalvorrathes. 1883. IV. 218.—1884. IV. 257.
— Klucz do rospoznawania drewna. 1881. I. 125, IV. 68.²
— Klucz do rospoznawania drzew i krzewów leśnych i ogrodowych, zestawił. 1881. III. 67.²
— Las w stanie natury. 1874. IV. 57.
— O lasach mieszanych u nas. 1900. IV. 137.²
— Nouvelle manière simple de mesurer le volume d'une tige. 1883. IV. 218.
— O przyrodzonem rozsiedleniu drzew leśnych w Galicyi. 1894. I. 433, IV. 87.¹
— Uszkodzenie jodłowego drewna przez Jemiołę. 1879. IV. 445.
— Verhältniss zwischen dem nach dem Haubarkeits-Durchschnittszuwachse berechneten und dem wahren Vorrathe. 1884. IV. 257.
— Weitere Beiträge zur Formzahlenermittlung. 1891. IV. 214.
— Wykłady na kursie leśniczym . . . Cięcie lasu. 1874. IV. 382.¹
Strzelecki, P. E. de. Physical description of New South Wales. 1845. I. 501.
Strzemcha, Karl. Allgemeine Forstbeschreibung der . . . Domaine-Kammer Teschen. 1873. IV. 369.
— Der Eis- und Schneebruch in . . . schlesischen Beskiden. 1890. IV. 190.
— Wald und Forstwirtschaft in Schlesien. 1897. IV. 369.
Stschégléew, Serge. Descriptio Epacridearum novarum. 1859. II. 688.¹

— Enumeratio plantarum in regionibus altaicis . . . collectarum. 1854. I. 453.[2]
— Nouveau supplément à la Flore altaïque. 1854. I. 453.[2]
Stuart, A. J. Forests and rain-fall in Madras. 1882. IV. 49.[1]
Stuart Pecan Company. The Pecan. 1893. IH. 354.[1]
Stubbe, Fr. Alcaloïdes du Berberis Aquifolium. 1890. III. 395.[2]
Stubbe, Henry. The Indian nectar. 1662. III. 593.[2]
Stubbs, William Carter. Ramie. 1895. III. 382.[1]
— & Morgan, H. A. The Orange and other Citrus fruits. 1893. III. 497.[2]
Stubenrauch, Franz Anton Edler von. Anfangsgründe der Forstwissenschaft. 1771. IV. 94.
— Kurzer Bericht von Knoppern und Eichenlohe in Baiern. 1775. IV. 511.
— Recht und Billigkeit in Forst- und Jagdsachen. 1779. IV. 313, 318.
Stuckert, Teodoro. Una Leguminosa nueva de la flora argentina. 1899. II. 379.[1]
— Observaciones al capitulo: La flora argentina. 1899. I. 345.
— El Vinalillo. 1900. II. 379.[2]
Student and intellectual observer of science. See RECREATIVE science. I. 19.
Studi della Commissione idrometrica della Svizzera. 1866. IV. 50.
Studien für eine nachhaltige Bewirtschaftung schweizerischer Korporations-Wälder. 1856. IV. 249.[2]
Ueber das Studium der Botanik als eine der nützlichsten . . . Beschäftigungen. 18.. ? I. 79.[1]
Studnička, F. J. Über die Bedeutung der sogenannten Wärmesumme. 1896. I. 221.
Study of timber physics. 1895. IV. 416.[1]
Stünkel, Carl. Ueber das Daphnetin. 1879. III. 627.[1]
— Sur la daphnétine. 1879. III. 627.[1]
Stürcke, H. Ueber die chemischen Bestandtheile des Carnaubawachses. 1884. II. 68.[1]
Stürler, F. A. von. Palmen en Bamboes. n. d. III. 315,[1] 313.[2]
Die Stürme von 20. Februar . . . 1879. See COAZ, Johann. 1880. IV. 189.[1]
Stuers, A. de. De Gemoetoe-boom der Molukko's. 1846. III. 274.[1]
— Losse aanteekeningen over de Nagel-kultuur. 1842. III. 635.[1]
— De Sago-boom der Molukko's. 1846. III. 327.[1]
Stützer, Friedrich. Die grössten . . . Bäume Bayerns. 1900. I. 296.[1]
Stuhlmann, Franz. Botanische Notizen über die . . . Reise nach Uluguru. 1896. I. 493.
Stuhr, A. F. Über die Abfindung der Hutungsberechtigten. 1834. IV. 333.
Stummer, Roman. Nachhaltigkeit und Rentabilität. 1899. IV. 247.[1]
Stumpf, Carl. Anleitung zum Waldbau. 1849. IV. 106.
Stumpf, J. G. De Robiniae Pseudoacaciae praestantia et cultu. 1796. IV. 522.[1]
Stumpff. Die Schütte und ihre Bekämpfung. 1900. IV. 480.
Stumph, Georg. Die nordamerikanischen Bäume in der böhmischen Landwirthschaft. 1791. I. 65.[1]
Stupanus, Johannes Rudolph. Specimen miscellaneum spetomico-botanicum. 1751. I. 291.
Stupper, C. L. Medizinisch-pharmazeutische Botanik. 1841. III. 57.
Stur, Dionys Rudolf Josef. Aufzählung der phanerogamen Nutzpflanzen Oesterreichs. 1857. III. 90.[2]
— Über den Einfluss des Bodens auf die Vertheilung der Pflanzen. 1856. I. 441.
— A Gesztenyefa előjövetelére vonatkozó adatok. 1879. II. 124.[1]
Sturge, E. A. The Betel tree. 1881. III. 320.[1]
Sturgis, William Codman. Fungi. 1894. III. 193.[1]
— Literature of plant-diseases. 1900. III. 193.[2]
Sturing, J. Botanie in den winter. 1897. I. 295.[1]
Stürler, Willem Louis de. Algemeene opmerkingen betrekkelijk de teelt . . . der Koffij. 1860. III. 729.[1]
— Beschrijving der houtsoorten, voorkomende in Nederlandsch Oost-Indie. 1866. IV. 399.[2]
— Catalogue descriptif des espèces de bois de l'Archipel des Indes Orientales. 1866. IV. 399.[2]
— Handboek voor den landbouw in Nederlandsch Oost-Indië. 1863. III. 116.[1]
— Korte beschouwing van . . . voortbrengselen van den Indischen bodem. 1848. III. 274.[1]

Sturm, Benjamin Christian Gottlieb. Visci quercini descriptio botanica. 1796. III. 385.[1]
Sturm, F. W. C. On the beneficial raising of trees. 1879. III. 132.[2]
Sturm, Jakob. Deutschlands Flora. 1798. I. 375.
Sturm, Roland. Febrifugi peruviani vindiciarum pars. 1659. III. 719.
Sturmfeder, Freiherr von. Ertrag einer ausgestockten Fläche. 1861. IV. 260.[2]
— Die Färbereiche. 1860. IV. 518.[2]
— Ueber die Kultur der zahmen Kastanie. 1864. IV. 492.[2]
— Zur Naturgeschichte der Buche. 1863. IV. 494.
— Ueber Reinigungshiebe und Durchforstungen. 1863. IV. 173.
— Eine starke Weide. 1861. II. 105.[1]
— Tenthredo pini betreffend. 1861. IV. 207.
— Das Verhalten der Fichte auf aufgeforsteten Feldern. 1863. IV. 453.
Der Sturmschaden vom 6./7. Dezember 1895. 1896. IV. 189.[2]
Sturmschäden. 1898. IV. 189.[2]
Sturrock, Archibald. Report on the agriculture of Ayrshire. 1867. IV. 358.[2]
Sturt, Charles. Narrative of an expedition into central Australia. See BROWN, Robert. 1849. I. 501.
Sturtevant, E. Lewis. Cow trees. 1890. III. 223.[1]
— Huckleberries and Blueberries. 1890. II. 671,[2] 685.[1]
— Influence of the stock on the scion. 1881. III. 39.
— Notes on edible plants. 1883. III. 219.[2]
— Poison Ivy. 1889. III. 528.[1]
— Seedless fruits. 1881. I. 145.[2] — 1889. I. 119.
— Variation and human interference. 1884. I. 248.[1]
Stutzer. See EWING, T. J. & STUTZER.
Stutzer, F. Die Waldservitute. 1877. IV. 333.
Suard. Catalogue des plantes vasculaires du dép. de la Meurthe. 1843. I. 409.
— Plantes vasculaires . . . de la Meurthe. 1843. I. 409.
Suardus, Paulus. Thesaurus aromatariorum. 1504. III. 239.
Suarez de Rivera, Francisco. Clave botanica, o medicina botanica. 1738. III. 54.
Sobre as substancias mineraes do Cafeeiro. See SOBRE . . . 1893. III. 740.[2]
Substitutes for gutta-percha. 1866. III. 668.[1]
Les subventions pour l'entretien des chemins vicinaux. 1890. IV. 326.
Un succédané de la gutta-percha. 1891. III. 231.
De succedaneis Acaciae aegyptiacae. See ROBERG, Lars. 1737. III. 244.
Successful cultivation of the Sissoo tree. 1846. III. 475.[1]
Succession possible de deux récoltes de résineux en terrain ardennais. 1900. IV. 74.[2]
Succinum. Commentatio physica de lucis effectibus chemicis. 1823. I. 172.
Succulents. 1892. III. 622.[1]
Suchánek, Fr. Z délného severu. Upomínky z lesní výzkumné cesty po Skandinavii a Rusku. 1892. IV. 342,[2] 346.
Suchaux, F. Des éclaircies dans les futaies. 1889. IV. 174.
— Une page d'histoire forestière. 1888. IV. 27.[2]
Suckering plants. 1886. III. 34.[2]
Suckow, F. W. L. Flora mannheimensis. 1822. I. 377.
Suckow, Georg Adolph. Anfangsgründe der theoretischen und angewandten Botanik. 1786. III. 37.[1]
— Diagnose der Pflanzen-Gattungen. 1792. I. 258.
— Oekonomische Botanik. 1777. III. 51.
— Versuche über die Wirkungen verschiedener Luftarten auf die Vegetation. 1782. I. 189.[2]
— See also CYKNOEB, T. A.
Suckow, Laurenz Johann Daniel. Bezeichnung der vornehmsten Pflanzen. 1794. III. 51.
— Einleitung in die Forstwissenschaft. 1776. IV. 95..
Suckow, Sigismund. Ueber Pflanzenstacheln. 1873. I. 112.[2]
Suden, W. Die Akazienrindenlaus. 1887. IV. 523.[1]
— Zur Besteuerung des Waldes. 1888. IV. 284.[1]
— Aus der Praxis der Forsttriangulation. 1889. IV. 265.
Sudre, Henri. Excursions batologiques dans les Pyrénées. 1898. III. 341.[2]
Sudworth, George Bishop. Battlement Mesa forest reserve. 1900. IV. 341.[3]
— Check list of the forest trees of the United States. 1898. I. 305, IV. 76.[1]

Sudworth, George Bishop (*continued*).
— Forest flora of the Rocky Mountain region. 1888. IV. 78.[1]
— The forest nursery. 1900. IV. 151.[2]
— Forest trees and forest conditions of eastern and middle Tennessee. 1897. IV. 340.
— Forests of Allegany county. 1900. IV. 340.
— On legitimate authorship of certain binomials. 1893. I. 254.[1]
— On the name of the American Chestnut. 1892. II. 123.[2]
— On the names of some North American trees. 1891. II. 227,[2] 693.[1]
— On the names of two species of Rhus. 1892. II. 458.[1]
— Nomenclature of the arborescent flora of the United States. 1897. I. 305, *IV. 76.*[1]
— Note on nomenclature. 1893. II. 693.[1]
— Notes on nomenclature. 1892. II. 129.[1]
— Prunus ilicifolia var. occidentalis. 1891. II. 275.[1]
— Report on an examination of the street and park trees of Savannah. 1897. III. 117.[2]
— Serotinous Pines. 1892. II. 41.[2]
— Stanislaus and Lake Tahoe forest reserves. 1900. IV. 341.[2]
— Trees important in forestry. 1898. IV. 76,[1] 544.[1]
— Trees of the United States important in forestry. 1898. IV. 76.[1]
— Trees of Washington, D.C. 1891. I. 39.
— White River Plateau timber land reserve. 1900. IV. 341.[2]
Die **südböhmische** Resonanzholzfabrication. 1896. IV. 428.[1]
Sündermann, Anton. Die Rinden-Umkleidung als Schutz ..., gegen die Schälschäden. 1891. IV. 197.[1]
— & **Haschke**, Josef. Statisticko-topografický popis knížecího arcibiskupského panství Rožmitálského. 1891. IV. 372.
— — Statistisch-topografische Beschreibung der ... Domaine Rožmital. 1891. IV. 372.
Suermondt, G. & **Hope Loudon**, H. West-Java-Koffij-cultuur-maatschappij. 1866. III. 729.[2]
— — West-Java-Koffij-cultuur-maatschappij; toegelicht:.1865. III. 729.[1]
— — West-Java-Koffij-cultuur-maatschappij verdedigd tegen de aanvallen van Volksblad, en Arnhemsche courant. 1865. III. 729.[2]
Süss, P. Sur le dosage de la theobromine. 1893. III. 595.[1]
Die **süsse** Eberesche. 1890. III. 459.[2]
Süssenbach, (*Forstmeister*). Instruction zur Holtzung im Gehauen, vor dem Forst-Amt Brieg. 1850. IV. 301.
Süzef, A. *See* Сюзевъ, A.
Suffren, de. Principes de botanique. 1802. I. 425.
Sugar from the Arenga palm. 1865. III. 320.[2]
The Sugar Maple. 1891. III. 536.[2]
The Sugar Pine. 1887. III. 307.[2]
Suire, E. Floraison de l'Echinocactus gibbosus celsianus. 1866. III. 622.[1]
Suis, A. *See* BROENER, L. & SUIS, A.
La **Suisse** universitaire; revue mensuelle. I. 520.[1]
Au sujet des ouvriers forestiers. *See* WALD-ARBEITER-VER-HÄLTNISSE. 1860. IV. 311.[2]
Le sujet et la greffe. 1866. III. 19.
Sukatchef, V. *See* Сукачевъ, B.
Sukker-Ahorn. 1893. III. 536.[2]
Suksdorf, William Nikolaus. Washingtonische Pflanzen. 1898. I. 327.
— & **Howell**, Thomas. The flora of Mount Adams. 1896. I. 326.
Sullivan, D. A complete census of the flora of the Grampians. 1890. I. 504.
— The Epacrideae of the Grampians. 1882. II. 688.[1]
— Native plants of the Grampians. 1882. I. 503.
— Victorian Leguminosae. 1882. II. 320.[1]
Sullivan, William K. On the influence which the physical geography ... productions exert upon the languages. 1858. I. 516.
— Sur la présence de l'ammoniaque ... dans la séve. 1858. I. 526.[1]
— On the presence of ammonia ... in the sap. 1858. I. 526.[1]
Sullivant, William Starling. A catalogue of plants ... in the vicinity of Columbus, Ohio. 1840. I. 313.
Sulzberger, Robert. La Rose, histoire, botanique. 188.? II. 282.[2]
Le Sumac, ses propriétés. 1870. III. 526.[2]
Sumach. 1895. III. 527.[1]
Der **Sumach**. 1873. IV. 525.

Der **Sumachstrauch** im Occupationsgebiete. 1894. IV. 526.[1]
Summa vegetabilium Scandinaviae. *See* SWARTZ, Olof. 1814. I. 352.
Summers, H. E. The San José scale. 1899. III. 188.[1]
Sumner, Charles. Vegetable products [of Russian America]. 1868. III. 262.[1]
Sumner, George. A compendium of physiological and systematic botany. 1820. I. 85.
Sumner, John. A popular treatise on tea. 1863. III. 607.
Sundberg, Arvid. Synopsis florae gothlandicae. *See* WAHLENBERG, Göran. 1837. I. 353.
Sundberg, Carl Magn. Afhandling om de wäxter som i Bibelen omtalas. *See* THUNBERG, C. P. 1828. I. 513.
Sunder Lal Pathak. The propagation of the common male Bamboo. 1900. III. 316.[2]
Sundermann, Fr. Verirrte Meerstrandskiefern. 1873. IV. 467.[2]
Sundevall, H. Bok (Fagus sylvatica), längt i Norr. 1849. II. 125.[2]
— Samtidiga (fenologiska) observationer. 1848. I. 223.[1]
Sundvik, Ernst Edvard. Om En-harts. 1895. II. 31.[1]
— Om förekomsten af en ... Crataegus-art ... i Karislojo. 1900. II. 262.[1]
Sunn-hemp fibe. 1896. III. 473.[1]
Sunto di risoluzioni proposte al Ministero delle finanze. 1865. IV. 305.
Sunto fatto dalla classe di fisica e di storia naturale. 18.? II. 150.[2]
Suomen kansalainen, (*pseud.*). Lyhykäinen osoitus metsän-hoitoon. 1860. IV. 104.[1]
— Maanviljelyskirjasto. 186.? IV. 104.[1]
— Meidän metsät. 1877. IV. 347.
Suomen Metsänhoitolehti. IV. 6.
Suomen suoviljelysyhdistyksen vuosikirja. III. 10.[2]
Suomi. I. 10.
Superficie boschiva dei diversi stati europei. 1882. IV. 342.[2]
Superficie boschiva soggetta a vincolo forestale. 1882. IV. 364.
Supplement to Report on forest management. *See* BRANDIS, Sir Dietrich. 1873. IV. 113.[1]
A supplement to the description of the Coffee-tree. 1727. III. 738.
Supplementum in secundum librum. *See* YŪḤANNĀ IBN MĀSAWAIH. 1623. V. XXVIII.[2]
Supplementum Pharmacopoeae borussicae hamburgense 1868. III. 249.
Supplementum pharmacopoeae danicae. 1850. III. 247.[1]
The supply of resin. 1866. III. 19.
The supposed influence of the moon. 1833. I. 233.[1]
On the supposed influence of the Papaw. 1862. III. 617.[1]
Supposed poisonous plants. 1893. II. 413.[1]
Supprian, Karl. Beiträge zur Kenntnis der Thymelaeaceae. 1894. II. 599.[1]
Sur, JOGESWAR. *See* JOGESWAR SUR.
Surauer, Alois. Ueber Pflanzen-Erziehung. 1897. IV. 151.[2]
— Die Pflanzen-Erziehung. 1900. IV. 147.[1]
— Ueber Pflanzenerziehung ... bei der Fichte. 1894. IV. 454.
— Die Pflanzen-Erziehung und deren Kosten. 1900. IV. 142.
A sure method of improving estates. *See* LANGLEY, Batty. 1728. IV. 120.
Surell, Alexandre. Étude sur les torrents des Hautes-Alpes. 1841. IV. 185.[1]
Surian, Joseph Donat. Catalogus plantarum. 1698. I. 334.
Surie, J. S. De aetherische olie van Piper peltatum. 1899. II. 95.[1]
— Het melksap van de Hura crepitans. 1900. III. 519.[2]
— De werkzame bestanddeelen in de bladeren der Bixa. 1898. III. 613.[2]
Suringar, Gerhard Konrad Bernhard. Commentatio ... : Quaeritur concinna expositio eorum, quae de foliorum plantarum ortu ... innotuerunt. 1820. I. 109.[1]
Suringar, Willem Frederik Reinier. De beteekenis der plantengeographie. 1857. I. 299.
— Botanische excursie naar Nederlandsch West-Indië. 1886. I. 336.
— Handleiding tot het bepalen van de in Nederland wildgroeiende planten. 1870. I. 391.[2]
— Illustrations du genre Melocactus. 1897. III. 595.[2]
— De kruidkunde in Nederland. 1889. I. 80.[2]
— Het leven der natuur. 1857. I. 217.

— Melocacti novi ex insula Aruba. 1889. II. 595,³ 873.²
— Melocacti novi ex insulis Archipelagi indici. 1885. II. 595.²
— Musée botanique de Leide. *See* Musée . . . I. 16.
— Nederlandsch West-Indische expeditie. 1886. I. 336. .
— Nieuwe bijdragen tot de kennis der Melocacti. 1889. II. 873,² 874.¹
— Plantarum species . . . ex insula Java . . . introductae. 1863. I. 469.¹
— Het plantenrijk. 1895. V. xiii.²
— Quelques observations de monstruosités végétales. 1873. II. 144.¹
— Over de verwantschapsbetrekkingen in het plantenrijk. 1895. I. 261.
— Vierde bijdrage tot de kennis der Melocacti. 1896. II. 595.²
— Waarnemingen van eenige plantaardige monstruositeiten. 1873. II. 144.¹
— Zakflora. Handleiding. 1870. I. 391.²
Surmont. Recherches chimiques . . . sur la toxicité de genièvre. 1896. III. 303.¹
Surozh, O. I. *See* Сурожъ, О. И.
Over surrogaten van kina. 1849. III. 724.²
Survey of forest reserves. 1897. IV. 179.¹
Surveyor and engineer. IV. 5.¹
Surveyors' institution. *See* Institution of surveyors. IV. 12.¹
Surveys of forest reserves. 1898. IV. 179.¹
Surville. Notice sur l'emploi du bois dans la construction des chaussées. 1840. IV. 425.²
Suscettibilità di alcune specie legnose nel condurre il calorico. 1882. IV. 412.²
Suárutas. Áyurvédas. Id est medicinae systema. 1844. III. 238.²
Sutchkof, Vl. *See* Сучковъ, Вл.
Suter, Johann Rudolf. Flora helvetica. 1802. I. 433.
Sutherland, James. On the medicinal properties of the Red Gum. 1863. IV. 534.¹
Sutherland, James, (*fl.* 1684—1703). Hortus medicus edinburgensis. 1683. I. 52.
Sutherland, Wilham. On pruning. 1885. III. 171, *IV. 172.¹*
Sutter. Ueber die Düngung der Obstbäume. 1896. III. 152.
— Ueber Pflanzung . . . von Obst- und Schattenbäumen. 1884. III. 210.
— Vorschläge zur zweckmässigen Bepflanzung unserer Strassen. 1893. III. 210.
Suttner, A. G. *Freiherr* von. Die Bewaldungs- und Jagdverhältnisse des Kaukasus. 1885. IV. 348.¹
Suttor, A. Bruce-. Clearing Prickly-pear. 1893. III. 625.¹
Suttor, George. The culture of the Grape-vine . . . in Australia. 1843. III, 559.²
Suzuki, Umetaro. On the behaviour of active albumin. 1897. I. 180.¹
— Can strontium and barium replace calcium? 1900. I. 160.
— A contribution to the knowledge of arginin. 1900. I. 178.
— On the formation of arginin in coniferous plants. 1900. II. 21.²
— On the formation of asparagine. 1896. I. 178.
— On the formation of proteids. 1897. I. 178.
— On an important function of leaves. 1897. I. 174.
— Report of investigations on the Mulberry-dwarf troubles. 1900. III. 379.¹
Suzzoni & others. Rapport sur le reboisement . . . de la Corse. 1860. V. xxx.²
Sv. Zur Anpflansung der Haselnuss. 1867. IV. 492.¹
Svanlund, Johan Fredrik Eberhard. Anteckningar till Blekinges flora. 1886. I. 357. — 1859. II. 111.¹
Svatoš, Albert. Statisticko-topografické popsání . . . panstvi Březnice. 1891. IV. 372.
— Statistisch-topografische Beschreibung der . . . Herrschaft Březnic. 1891. IV. 372.
Svensk botanik. 1801. I. 352.
Svenska blomsterspråket. 1645. I. 515.
Den svenska farmakopeen. *See* Pharmacopoea suecica. 1775. III. 247.¹
Svenska landtbruks-academiens. *See* Kongl-svenska . . . III. 10.²
Svenska cert-slagen. *See* Liljeblad, Samuel. 1792. I. 352.
Svenska trädgårdsföreningen. Tidskrift. III. 11·

Svenska vetenskaps academien. *See* Kongl. svenska . . . I. 8.¹
Svenska Vetenskaps akademien. *See* Kongl. (svenska) Vetenskaps . . . 1822. I. 1.
Svensson, Nikolaus A. Om den fanerogama . . . vegetationen kring Kaitumsjöarne. 1895. I. 358.
Svida, A. *See* Свида, А.
Sviedyeniya . . . *See* Свѣдѣнія . . .
Sviluppo dell' industria serica negli Stati Uniti. 1894. III. 148.¹
Svoboda, M. Rozmnožování Aralie papyrifery. 1880. III. 644.¹
Sw. The Forest school at Dehra Dún. 1882. IV. 37.¹
Swaab, S. L. Fibrous substances. 1864. III. 234.
Swagerman, E. P. Verhandeling over dat soort van vaten in de planten. 1782. I. 133.
— Verhandeling over een soort van Appelboomen. 1779. II. 266.²
Swainson, William. Botanical report [on Victoria]. 1853. I. 501.
— Botanical report, principally relating to the Eucalypti. 1854. II. 92,¹ 622.²
— Naturalist's guide for collecting. 1822. I. 35.
— Sketch of a journey through Brazil. 1819. I. 341.
Swallow, G. C. Grape culture in Missouri. 1858. III. 550.
The **Swamp** or Pin Oak. 1887. III. 362.²
The **Swamp** White Oak. 1891. II. 132.²
Swan, W. Magnolia salicifolia and M. stellata. 1898. III. 399.²
— Passiflora alata. 1897. III. 615.²
Swan River; sketch of the vegetation. *See* Lindley, John. 1839. I. 500.
Swar på frågan, om ekar och andra loefträd kunna. 1763. IV. 113.²
Swartz, Ernest. Examen classis diandriae. *See* Thunberg, C. P. 1824. I. 251.
Swartz, Olof. Adnotationes botanicae. 1829. I. 267.
— Beskrifning på nio slags Nässlor. 1785. II. 156.¹
— The botanical history of the Canella alba. 1791. II. 566.²
— Botanische Geschichte der weissen Canelle. 1791. II. 566.²
— Botaniske anmärkningar om Bomullsslagen. 1790. II. 521.¹
— Chloranthus, a new genus of plants. 1787. II. 95.²
— Cinchona angustifolia. 1787. II. 816.²
— Fischera, nouveau genre . . . des Rosages. 1817. II. 673.¹
— Flora Indiae occidentalis. 1797. I. 335.
— Icones plantarum . . . in India occidentali. 1794. I. 335.
— Nova genera et species plantarum. 1788. I. 334.
— Observationes botanicae . . . Indiae occidentalis. 1791. I. 334.
— Observations on some species of Menziesia. 1811. II. 674.¹
— Ochroma, nytt örteslägte. 1792. II. 530.¹
— Quassia excelsa, ny växt. 1788. II. 415.³
— Solandra, et nytt ört-slägte. 1787. II. 774.¹
— Stylosanthes, et nytt örteslägte. 1789. II. 385.²
— Summa vegetabilium Scandinaviae. 1814. I. 352.
— Tolf nya slag af Urticae slägte, från Vest-Indien. 1787. II. 156.¹
Swasey's southern gardener. *See* Southern horticulturist. III. 8.
Swayne, George. On the fertilization of the female blossoms of Filberts. 1824. III. 357.²
— On the management of the Fig tree. 1822. III. 369.¹
Swederus, Magnus Bernhard. Botaniska trädgården i Upsala. 1877. I. 40.
Swediaur, François Xavier. Pharmacopoeia medici practici universalis. 1803. III. 245.
Sweert, Emanuel. Florilegium. 1612. I. 284, V. xv.²
— Florilegium amplissimum et selectissimum. 1612. I. 284.
Sweet, Robert. The botanical cultivator. 1821. III. 81.
— The British flower garden. 1823. I. 267.
— Cistineae. 1825. II. 563.²
— Flora australasica. 1827. I. 498.
— The florist's guide and cultivator's directory. 1827. III. 81.
— Geraniaceae. 1820. II. 389,¹ *III. 491.¹*
— Hortus britannicus. 1826. I. 267, III. 81.
— Hortus suburbanus londinensis. 1818. I. 53.

Sweet, Robert (*continued*).
— The hot-house and green-house manual. 1821. III. 81.
— & **Don**, David. Ornamental flower garden and shrubbery. 1852. III. 82.
— & Weddell, H. British botany. 1834. I. 397.
Swete, Edward Horace. Flora bristoliensis. 1854. I. 400.
Swezey, Goodwin Deloss. Nebraska localities for flowering plants. 1891. I. 325.
Swieten, H. J. Iets over schadelijk gedierte. 1867. III. 186.¹
— De invoering . . . van het Koffijstelsel. 1863. III. 729.¹
— Korte beschrijving van 43 Indische vezelplanten. 1880. III. 234.
— De snuitkever in de Koffie en de Lagoepdie. 1881. III. 735.²
— De zoete Cassave. 1875. III. 520.²
Swinburne, P. Aanteekeningen over Thee. 1885. III. 602.¹
Swingle, Walter Tennyson. Bordeaux mixture. 1896. III. 198.¹
— Danger of introducing a . . . Coffee disease into Hawaii. 1898. III. 736.
— The dioecism of the Fig. 1899. III. 369.²
— *See also* Kellerman, W. A. & Swingle.
— & Webber, H. J. Hybrids and their utilization. 1898. I. 248,¹ III. 51.
— — The principal diseases of Citrus fruits. 1896. III. 498.²
Swinhoe, Robert. List of plants from the island of Formosa. 1860. I. 463.²
— Products of the island of Hainan. 1871. III. 273.¹
Switzer, Stephen. A dissertation on the true Cythisus. 1731. II. 350.¹
— Ichnographia rustica. 1715. III. 108.
— The nobleman, gentleman and gardener's recreation. 1715. III. 108.
— The practical fruit-gardener. 1724. III. 141.
Swoboda, Ed. Die grössherzogl. Toscana'sche Domaine Brandeis. 1864. IV. 250.¹
— Der Kiefernspinner. 1869. IV. 210.¹
Swoboda, Wenzel. Soll man dicht säen oder licht pflanzen? 1867. IV. 453.
Swygenhaven, Ch. van. La gutta-percha. 1848. III. 230.
Sycamore at Grimston Park. 1881. II. 480.¹
Sychrovský, (*Ingenieur*). Ueber den Bau von Forsthäusern. 1897. IV. 266.¹
Sychrowský. Ueber den Nutzeffect der Waldbahnen. 1887. IV. 392.
Sydenham, John. The history of the town and county of Poole. *See* Salter, T. B. 1839. I. 399.
Sydney magazine of science and art. III. 27.¹
Sydow, Friedrich Wilhelm. De febrifugis in cinchonae passim ipsi praeferendis. 1809. III. 721.
Sygietyński, Edmund. Podniesienie ogrodnictwa krajowego. 186.? III. 32.¹
Sykes, William Henry. Remarks on the origin of the popular belief in the Upas. 183.? II. 145.²
The **Swiss** Stone Pine at home. 1885. II. 41.¹
Sykyta, Wenzel. Das Holz. 1882. IV. 413.²
Sylloge plantarum novarum. I. 15.
Sylva, (*pseud.*). Crataegus alnifolia. 1875. III. 421.²
Sylva. Frutetum. Collis. *See* Estienne, Charles. 1538. I. 277.
Sylva Pereyra, Emanuele de. Metodo sicuro d' ordinare la china china. 1709. III. 719.
Sylvan. *See* Neujahrs-Geschenk . . . IV. 10.
Sylvan, C. De plantis cibariis romanorum. *See* Retzius, A. J. 1808. III. 88.¹
Sylvaneion. IV. 11.
Sylvaticus, Matthaeus. *See* Matthaeus Sylvaticus.
Sylvestre. Bois australiens. 1900. IV. 402.¹
— Le gaz de bois. 1896. IV. 433.²
Sylvestris, (*pseud.*). Les bourgeons de résineux. 1899. IV. 479.
La **sylviculture** à l'Exposition d'Anvers. 1894. IV. 540.¹
La **sylviculture** en Belgique. 1896. IV. 119.²
Sylvio. De l'étiolement des arbres en forêt. 1892. IV. 66.¹
Sylvius, Johannes. Oratio de Rosis. 1601. II. 290.¹
Sylwan. Lwowie. IV. 15.
Sylwan. Warszawa. IV. 6.
Symanski, Johann Daniel. Der Selam des Orients. 1841. I. 515.
Syme, George. Abies concolor. 1880. II. 22.²
— Abies nobilis. 1886. II. 23.¹

— Abies polita. 1878. III. 306.¹
— American Firs. 1878. II. 22.²
— Aucuba berries. 1879. III. 645.¹
— Entada scandens. 1881. II. 356.¹
— Golden-leaved Chestnut. 1879. III. 360.¹
— How to graft Larix Kaempferi. 1878. III. 309.¹
— Japanese Conifers. 1879. II. 22.¹
— The Long-thatch palm of Jamaica. 1880. III. 325.²
— New Conifers and their synonyms. 1875. III. 305.¹
— Notes on rare Conifers. 1875. II. 34.¹
— Notes on Retinosporas. 1876. III. 300.²
— Pinus excelsa. 1878. III. 307.¹
— Pinus insignis and its timber. 1878. IV. 464.²
— Pinus parviflora. 1878. III. 308.¹
— The Redwood (Sequoia sempervirens). 1877. II. 49.²
— Retinospora ericoides. 1888. III. 311.¹
— Retinospora juniperoides. 1877. III. 311.²
— The Retinosporas. 1882. II. 28.²
— Robinia Pseudacacia aurea. 1878. III. 487.¹
— Thuja gigantea. 1879. II. 52.¹
— Tsuga Pattoniana. 1880. II. 53.²
— Yews, English and Japanese. 1877. III. 287.²
Syme, John Thomas Boswell. On Salix Sadleri Syme. 1875. II. 109.²
Syme, Patrick. Werner's nomenclature of colours. 1821. I. 70.
Symes, Michael. An account of an embassy to the kingdom of Ava. 1800. I. 475.²
Symonds, W. A. The Palmyra Palm. 1892. III. 321.¹
Symons, Jelinger. Synopsis plantarum insulis britannicis indigenarum. 1798. I. 396.
Symons, W. H. *See* Gerrard, A. W. & Symons, W. H.
Symphoria und Lycium. 1859. III. 700,¹ 752.³
Syndicat central des agriculteurs de France. Bulletin. IV. 23.¹
Synonyma plantarum. *See* Mentzel, Albert & Philipp. 1618. I. 372, III. 72.
A **synopsis** of the genera of American plants. *See* Rich, O. O. 1814. I. 306.
Synopsis Opuntiarum Horti botanici aquisgranensis. 1883. II. 586.²
Synopsis plantarum horti bot. Musei regii florentini. *See* Zuccagni, Attilio. 1782. I. 61.
Synopsis plantarum Horti botanici ticinensis. *See* Nocca, Domenico. 1803. I. 61.
Syon House. 1882. II. 52.¹
Sypesteyn, C. A. van. Het Surinaamsche hout. 1851. IV. 398.¹
— Over Surinaamsche houtsoorten. 1855. IV. 398.¹
Syrenius, Szymon. Viridarium. Herbarium. 1613. I. 284.
— Zielnik. Herbarzem. 1613. I. 284.
Syrénski. *See* Syreniusz, Szymon.
Syringa chinensis Willd. 1859. II. 714.²
Syruczek, Eugen. Anhang über sämmtliche in den k. k. . . . regionen . . . bestehenden Forstgesetze. 1846. IV. 331.²
— Das Forstgesetz vom 3. Dezember 1852. 1853. IV. 331.²
— Kurzer Abriss der allgemeinen Forstbotanik. 1846. IV. 86.³
Syrutschek, Julius. Ueber das bäuerliche Aufforstungswesen. 1895. IV. 167.²
— Ueber den geodätischen Vorgang bei der Festlegung gebrochener Forsteintheilungslinien. 1886. IV. 265.
— Eine Heuschreckenart als Waldschädling. 1892. IV. 210.¹
— Die "Lergét" Gewinnung. 1885. IV. 452.¹
— Untersuchungen über den Wachsthumsgang vom Weidevieh verbissener Fichten. 1880. IV. 456.
The **system** of forest management in Switzerland. 1887. IV. 367.
System of natural history. *See* Sistema der natuurlyke historie. 1765. V. XIII.¹
Systematic catalogue of green and hothouse plants. *See* Catalogue of plants. 1800. I. 53.
Systematische Uebersicht aller . . . Kernobstsorten. *See* Ahrenthal, J. L., *Freiherr von*. 1833. III. 71.
Systematisches Verzeichniss derjenigen ausländischen . . . Bäume . . . in dem amerikanischen Garten zu Hohenheim. 1785. IV. 18.¹
Systematisk förteckning på de i Blekinge vildtwäxande slägten af fanerogamer. *See* Gosselmann, C. A. 1861. I. 356.
Système de culture des arbres à fruits. 1869. III. 144.
Systems of tissue; leaves. 1895. III. 260.¹

Systems of tissue; stem wood. 1894. III. 260.[1]
Szabó, Adolf. Az alföldi ákáczosok fordaidejének kérdéséhez. 1877. IV. 524.[1]
Szabó, Ferenc. A Vadfüge és a jóféle Füge. 1883. II. 150.[1]
Szabó, Frans. See KLEIN, Julius & SZABÓ, Franz.
Szabo, Jos. See CZIHAK, Jakob von & SZABO, Jos.
Szakmáry, François. Mesures de defense contre le "Liparis moine." 1900. IV. 202.
Széchenyi, Béla, Gróf. Die wissenschaftlichen Ergebnisse der Reise des Grafen Béla Széchenyi in Ostasien. See KANITZ, August. 1891. I. 459.
Szechenyi, Paul, Graf. Mittheilungen über Holzsprengungen mittelst Dynamit. 1878. IV. 386.
Szécsi, Zsigmond. As erdőhasználattan kézikönyve. 1884. IV. 381.
— A Selmeczi m. k. erdészeti akadémia értesítője. 1885. IV. 36.[2]
Székely, Irén. A Narancsról. 1897. III. 500.[2]
Székely, Mihály. A Jegenyefenyő és a Nyárfa vegyiszerkezetéről. 1875. II. 96,[2] III. 295.[1]
Szent-Miklos, Alexander SEBEŐK DE. See SEBEŐK DE SZENT-MIKLOS, Alexander.
Szilágyi, János. A hási Berkenye. 1897. III. 460.[1]
Szilágyi, Ottilia. A japán Naszpolya. 1899. III. 424.[1]
Szinnyei, József & Dr. József. Bibliotheca hungarica historiae naturalis et matheseos. 1878. I. 4.[1]
Szinnyei, Dr. József. See SZINNYEI, József & Dr. József.
Szokalski, W. Acacia lophanta. Mimosa pudica. 1889. I. 197.[2]
— O Czulku. 1886. II. 373.[1]
Szontagh, Miklós. Melyik a legnagyobb fa? 1880. I. 295.[1]
Szontagh, Nikolaus von. Enumeratio plantarum . . . comitatus arvensis in Hungaria. 1863. I. 445.
— Enumeratio plantarum . . . territorii soproniensis. 1864. I. 445.
Sztolcman, J. Rośliny użyteczne Peru i Ekwadoru. 1888. III. 64.[2]
Szubert, Michał. See SCHUBERT, Michael.
Szyszyłowicz, Ignaz, Ritter von. Caryocaraceae (Rhizoboleae). 1895. II. 546.[1]
— Une excursion botanique au Monténégro. 1889. I. 450.
— Lipowate, monografia rodzajów. 1886. II. 512.[1]
— Marcgraviaceae. 1895. II. 546.[2]
— Pugillus plantarum novarum Americae. 1894. I. 330.
— Zur Systematik der Tiliaceen. 1885. II. 512.[1]
— Theaceae. 1895. II. 547.[2]
— Wskazówki dla uczączych się botaniki. 1880. I. 91.
— Zwei neue Weinmannien aus Südamerika. 1890. II. 251.[1]
— See also BECK VON MANNAGETTA, Günther, Ritter & SZYSZYŁOWICZ, Ignaz von.

— t. Der Alex. Ritterv. Lenzendorf'sche Waldbesitz Tragöss. 1898. IV. 370.
— t. Aus den Bukowinaer Urwäldern. 1897. IV. 369.
— t. Die Kreuz- oder Bildföhre. 1895. IV. 466.[2]
— t. Seltene Waldbäume in Norddeutschland. 1899. IV. 460.[2]
— t. Aus den Urwäldern der Bukowina. 1897. IV. 369.
— t.—, Ueber den Einfluss des Waldes auf . . . Lufttemperatur. 1892. IV. 54.
T, Anbau der Kiefer in der Main-Rheinebene. 1898. IV. 474.
T. Beaumontia grandiflora. 1896. III. 687.[1]
T. The best hardy Heath. 1884. III. 650.[2]
T. Brugmansia chlorantha. 1896. III. 700.[1]
T. Caesalpinia japonica. 1891. III. 469.[1]
T. Die Catalkilforste. 1888. IV. 339.
T. Chimonanthus fragrans. 1892. III. 401.[1]
T. Citrus triptera. 1884. III. 503.[1]
T. The Cork Oak. 1890. III. 363.[1]
T. Crataegus Oxyacantha semperflorens. 1886. III. 422.[1]
T. The Daphnes. 1886. III. 626.[2]
T. Die Eichen der alten Griechen. 1890. IV. 502.[2]
T. Evergreen wall shrubs. 1896. III. 205,[1] 806.[1]
T. Exkursion in die Waldungen der Domäne Pürglitz. 1857. IV. 370.
T. Eine Forstordnung aus der Zeit des Herzogs Heinrich des Jüngeren von Braunschweig. 1897. IV. 26, 300.[1]
T. Garden varieties of Clematis. 1894. III. 389.[1]
T. Garrya elliptica. 1891. III. 352.[2]
T. Greenhouse Rhododendrons from cuttings. 1884. III. 656.[1]
T. Hybrid shrubs. 1893. III. 395.[1]
T. Ilex crenata. 1887. III. 530.[2]

T. The Incense Cedars. 1886. III. 305.[1]
T. Kalmia myrtifolia. 1886. III. 652.[2]
T. Malayan Rhododendrons and their hybrids. 1899. III. 656.[1]
T. The Mock Oranges. 1891. III. 413.[1]
T. Ein neuer Treibstrauch, Deutzia parviflora. 1894. III. 410.[1]
T. Pernettyas. 1890. III. 653.[2]
T. The Pink Broom of New Zealand. 1893. III. 482.[2]
T. Rhododendron ciliatum. 1890. III. 658.[1]
T. The smaller-flowered Camellias. 1893. III. 599.[1]
T. Small-flowered Azaleas. 1892. III. 660.[1]
T. Starke Fichten im Harze. 1897. IV. 460.[2]
T. Timber forming. 1861. IV. 170.
T. Trees and shrubs certificated 1893–1899. 1894. III. 78.[2]
T. Trees and shrubs for towns. 1889. III. 42.[2]
T. Two winter-flowering shrubs. 1889. III. 420,[1] 627.[2]
T. Die Ueberwinterung der Fichten- und Lärchenalns. 1887. IV. 210.[1]
T. Varieties of Laurel. 1885. III. 437.[2]
T. The Witch Hazels. 1891. III. 417.[1]
T., A. Le dendromètre Bayard. 1885. IV. 215.
T., A. Some weeping Conifers. 1885. III. 290.
T., A. L. La physique des bois d'œuvre. 1892. IV. 409.
T., Ch. The Paris exhibition. 1883. III. 330,[1] 615.[1]
T., D. Influence du sujet sur le fruit de la greffe. 1835. III. 39.
T., D. The Vine as a hardy ornamental plant. 1872. III. 584.[1]
T., E. Unusual form of a Scotch fir. 1862. II. 42.[1]
T., E. L. Quelques observations sur le livre de M. Vallés. 1866. IV. 275.
T., F. von. Die Platane des Hippokrates. 1884. II. 254.[2]
T., F. W. On the culture of Chorozemas. 1856. III. 472.[2]
T., G. On the cultivation of Pleroma elegans. 1849. III. 639.[1]
T., H. Bericht über die . . . Excursion in die herzogl. Saganer Haide. 1854. IV. 352.
T., J. The Scottish Pine. 1775. IV. 472.
T., J. A self-adjusting tree-measurer. 1873. IV. 215.
T., J. A table of the scantlings of beams of Teak. 1835. IV. 409.
T., J. F. Arboricultura y floricultura cubana. 1893. III. 64.[1]
T., K. Kuusen ja Männyn käpyjen kokoomisesta. 1895. IV. 148.
T., L. Eenige mispassen van eerstbeginnenden in ontginningszaken. 1892. IV. 160.[2]
T., L. Enten — zaaien. 1878. I. 247.
T., L. Het verouderen van vruchtboomen. 1878. I. 249.[1]
T., M. Il Pineto di Sorbar presso Momiano. 185.? II. 46.[1]
T., R. Bougainvillaea spectabilis. 1860. III. 388.[1]
T., R. Konserwacya drzewa w wodzie. 1898. IV. 421.
T., R. T. W. Historical remarks on the Moutan Paeony. 1857. III. 392.[2]
T., R. T. W. Remarques historiques sur la Pivoine en arbre. 1857. III. 392.[2]
T., S. Common-good. See TAYLOR, Silvanus. 1652. IV. 274.[2]
T., W. Calculating the height of a tree. 1879. IV. 215.
T., W. The Monterey Cypress as a hedge plant. 1872. III. 302.[2]
T., W. Snowy Mespilus. 1900. III. 419.[2]
T., W. C. Dimensions of a Larch tree. 1831. II. 33.[1]
T., W. T. A hardy Protead. 1876. II. 162.[1]
Tabella di cubazione per legni rotondi. See SALVINI. 1844. IV. 223.
Tabella di cubazione per li legni rotondi. n. d. IV. 219.
Tabellarische Beschreibung aller schädlichen Waldinsekten. 1798. IV. 91.[1]
Tabellarische Uebersicht der . . . Holzkonservirungsmethoden. 1852. IV. 417.
Tabellarische Uebersicht der Naturgeschichte der hundert deutschen wilden Holzarten. 1822. IV. 82.
Tabelle di cubazione pei legnami quadrati. 1852. IV. 223.
Tabelle per la cubazione del legname. 1861. IV. 224.
Tabelle zu Bestimmung des kubischen Innhalts der Baumstämme. 1812. IV. 221.
Tabellen über den körperlichen Inhalt der Stamm- und Nutzhölzer. 1797. IV. 220.
Tabellen, worinnen der cubische Inhalt eines jeden Stammes . . . richtig ausgerechnet zu finden. 1771. IV. 220.
Tabellen zur Berechnung des Kubikinhalts liegender Baumstämme. 1899. IV. 229.

Tabellen zur Bestimmung des körperlichen Inhaltes der Baumstämme. *See* Rost. 1854. IV. 216.

Tabellen zur Umwandlung des bayerischen Längen- und Flächenmasses in metrisches Mass. 1878. IV. 230.

Tabellen zur Werthbestimmung der Stammhölzer. 1871. IV. 255.

Taber, G. L. The Satsuma Orange again. 1890. III. 502.[3]

Tabernaemontanus, Jacob Theodor. Eicones plantarum. 1590. I. 283.

— Neu vollkommen Kräuter-Buch. 1588. I. 283.

— Neuw Kreuterbuch. 1588. I. 283, V. xv.[3]

— Neuw und volkommenlich Kreuterbuch. 1588. I. 283.

— New vollkommenlich Kräuter-Buch. 1588. I. 283.

Tablada, José de Hidalgo. *See* Hidalgo Tablada, José de.

Table of contents of descriptive catalogue of Iona Vines. *See* General remarks on the Grape-vine. 1862. III. 546.

Table oils from Beech and Linden. 1884. III. 586,[1] IV. 500.[1]

Tableau de l'école de botanique du Jardin des plantes de Paris. *See* Morel. 1800. I. 56.

Tableau des plantes cultivées dans les serres de M. Leprince-Clairsigny. 1806. I. 57.

Tableau du travail annuel de toutes les académies de l'Europe. *See* Introduction aux observations sur la physique. V. vii.[2]

Tableau pour la plantation . . . du jardin de botanique . . . de Strasbourg. *See* Villars, Dominique. 1806. I. 45.

Tableaux de la vie forestière. 1898. IV. 122,[1] 124.[1]

Tables de cubage des bois donnant, en mesures décimales, le volume en grume des bois. 1891. IV. 228.

Tables de cubage pour l'évaluation des bois. 1876. IV. 227.

Tables showing the cubical contents of logs in Hindi. n. d. IV. 219.

Tabley, *Lord* de. *See* Warren, J. B. L., *Lord de Tabley.*

Tablitza . . . *See* Таблица . . .

Tablitzij . . . *See* Таблицы . . .

Tabula locum et tempus. *See* Kentmann, Theophilus. 1659. V. xvi.[1]

Tabulae Panphytonis siculi. *See* Cupani, Francesco. 1713. I. 431.

Tabulae synopticae plantarum officinalium. *See* Martyn, John. 1726. III. 54.

Tacchetti, Carlo. Sull' allevamento dei bachi della Quercia. 1872. IV. 502.[1]

Tachard, Guy. Second voyage du Père Tachard. 1689. I. 469.[2]

— Voyage de Siam des pères jesuites. 1687. III. 276.[1]

Taché, J. C. Collection des produits des eaux et forêts du Bas-Canada. 1862. IV. 19.[1]

Tacke. Die Bewirthschaftung der . . . Hochmoore. 1900. IV. 155.[1]

Taddei, Gioacchino. Elementi di farmacologia. 1837. III. 258.

— Repertorio dei veleni et contravveleni. 1835. III. 260.[2]

Täger, Arthur. Zum zweihiebigen Kiefernhochwald-Betrieb. 1885. IV. 473. — 1887. IV. 473.

— & **Helwig,** (*Regierungs- u. Forstrath*). Unter welchen Verhältnissen empfiehlt es sich . . . den Kahlschlagbetrieb im Hochwalde anzugeben? 1893. IV. 130.

— & **Richter,** (*Forstmeister, Breslau*). Welche Mittel giebt uns der Waldbau an die Hand, zur Erziehung werthvollen Starkholzes? 1890. IV. 128.

— & **Richtsteig,** (*Oberförster, Camenz i. Schl.*). Bedingen die neueren Fortschritte . . . Aenderungen des . . . Betriebs-Regulirungs-Verfahrens? 1894. IV. 246.

Tätzner, L. Ueber Vermehrung der Coniferen. 1868. III. 294.[1]

Tafel § zu Heinrich Cotta's Tafeln zur Bestimmung des Inhaltes der runden Hölzer. *See* Cotta, Heinrich. 1841. IV. 222.

Tafeln zum Cubiren der Rundhölzer. 1870. IV. 226.

Tafeln zur Berechnung für den Kubikinhalt walzen- und kegelförmiger . . . Hölzer. *See* Jahn, G. A. 1843. IV. 223.

Tafeln zur Bestimmung des Inhaltes und Zuwachses der . . . Holzarten. *See* Cotta, Heinrich. 1819. IV. 216.

Tafeln zur Bestimmung des Inhalts und des Preises runder unbeschlagener Stämme. 1815. IV. 221.

Tafeln zur Bestimmung der körperlichen Inhalts runder . . . Baumstämme. 1823. IV. 222.

Tafeln zur Ermittelung des körperlichen Inhalts der Baumstämme. 1872. IV. 227.

Tafeln zur Statistik der Land- und Forstwirthschaft des Königreiches Böhmen. 1861. IV. 370.

Tafeln zur Umrechnung des Wiener Masses in metrisches Mass. 1876. IV. 227.

Tagányi, Károly. Magyar erdészeti oklevéltár. 1896. IV. 28.[2]

Tagasaste. 1891. III. 474.[2]

Tagault, Jean. Tractatus de purgantibus medicamentis simplicibus. 1537. III. 244.

Tagliabue, Giuseppe. Storia e descrizione della Littaea geminiflora. 1816. II. 89.[1]

Tagliabue, José. Breves apuntes sobre el cultivo de la Morera. 1900. III. 378.

Taglini, Carlo. Se l' Aglio . . . possa conferire alla Rosa una maggior fragranza. 1747. II. 290.[1]

Del taglio degli alberi col mezzo di macchine. 1879. IV. 284.[1]

Taglio del Cerro e del Leccio nei cedui. 1865. IV. 251.[2]

Taiani, Domenico. Memoria sulla estrazione della corteccia dei boschi cedui di Quercia. 1864. IV. 434.

— Rilievi . . . sulla relazione dell' onor cav. Dorotea. 1864. IV. 434.

Taillasson, René de. Invasion des chenilles Lasiocampa. 1894. IV. 209.[1]

— Notice sur les reboisements . . . de l'Aube. 1877. IV. 163.

— Les plantations forestières dans . . . l'Aube. 1878. IV. 163, 360.

— Les plantations résineuses de la Champagne. 1894. IV. 362, 468,[1] 550.[1]

— Travaux de consolidation du Péguère. 1892. IV. 164.[1]

Taillet, Paul. Forêts de l'île de Rhodes. 1894. IV. 556.[2].

Taillis, Marcel, (*pseud.*). Agitation. 1885. IV. 34.[1]

— M. Viette et le budget des forêts. 1885? IV. 261.[3]

Taillis de Pin. 1894. IV. 559.[1]

Taillis et sapinières. 1899. IV. 169.[2]

Taillon. Sur le développement des Mûriers. 1869. III. 377.

Taillotte, Auguste. De l'Eucalyptus globulus. 1872. IV. 533.[2]

Tailor, C. B. *See* Taylor, C. B.

Tairof, Vasili. *See* Таиров, Василій.

Tait, Andrew. On the management of hedges. 1863. III. 213.

— On a new method of planting hedges. 1861. III. 213.

Tait, David. The best mode of selling timber. 1879. IV. 388.[1]

— On the comparative value of the different timber trees. 1890. IV. 261.[1]

— Drainage in connection with planting. 1884. III. 150.[1]

— Hedges and hedging. 1878. III. 213.

— Management of hardwood plantations. 1881. IV. 137.[1]

— Peeling Oak standing. 1885. IV. 515.[1]

— Planting undrained clay land. 1880. IV. 142.

— The rearing . . . of hardwood plantations. 1881. IV. 137.[1]

— A word about planting. 1880. IV. 152.

Tait, P. G. On phyllotaxis. 1871. I. 102.

Tait, W. C. Cultura das Acacias. 1885. III. 463.[1]

Tajani, Domenico. Memoria sulla condizione forestale della . . . Citra. 1864. IV. 122.[3]

Takabayashi, S. On the poisonous action of ammonium salts. 1897. I. 211.

Takasima. Le ver a soie du Châtaignier. 1886. III. 148.[1]

Taksa . . . *See* Такса . . .

Taksy . . . *See* Таксы . . .

Talamini, Natale. Appendice alla memoria sui boschi del Cadore. 1867. IV. 364.

— I boschi del Cadore. 1867. IV. 364.

Talaväsek, F. Acacia platyptera. 1899. III. 463.[1]

Talbot, Josiah W. Influence of the stock upon the graft. 1879. III. 89.

— New varieties of Pears. 1882. III. 445.[1]

— Sports physiologically considered. 1883. I. 244.[1]

Talbot, William Alexander. New species of western peninsular plants. 1897. I. 475.[3]

— Systematic list of the trees . . . of the Bombay presidency. 1894. I. 470,[1] IV. 89.[1]

— Value of 'Pynkado' for sleepers. 1894. IV. 524.[1]

Talegon, Juan Gualberto. Flora biblico-poética. 1871. I. 513.

Tales about plants. *See* Goodrich, S. G. 1839. I. 517.[1]

Taliew, W. I. Ueber die russischen myrmecophilen Pflanzen. 1900. II. 708.[1]

— *See also* Таліевъ, B. H.

A talk on Clematis. 1898. III. 389.[1]

The tall trees of Victoria. 1890, II. 624.[1]

Tallack, J. C. The Medlar. 1897. III. 429.²
Tallavignes, Charles. En forêt; rimes forestières. 1881. IV. 102.
Taller mecánico para el aserrado de maderas. 1884. IV. 393.
The tallest trees in the world. 1895. II. 624.¹
Tallotte. Amenagement des forêts. 1879. IV. 241.
Talou, A. de. Arbres et arbustes nouveaux. 1859. III. ·84.¹
— Une avenue de Catalpa. 1859. III. 706.¹
— Le Bambusa gracilis. 1858. III. 316.¹
— Les Casses, Cassia floribunda. 1861. III. 471.¹
— Cerasus caucasica. 1865. III. 437.²
— Chamaebatia foliolosa Benth. 1861. III. 420.²
— Cuphea jorulensis De Coud. 1861. III. 629.²
— Decumaria barbara. 1863. III. 410.¹
— Les Hydrangea. 1861. III. 411.²
— Lonicera flava. 1863. III. 750.²
— Les Saules de la route de Trente à Roveredo. 1859. III. 351.²
— De la transplantation des gros arbres. 1862. III. 167.
— Vitis elegans. 1866. III. 544.¹
Tam o' Shanta, (pseud.). South Australia; its forest at Wirrabara. 1880. IV. 380.¹
— South Australia and its forests. 1880. IV. 380.¹
Tamarinds. 1898. III. 489.¹
Tamaro, Domenico. Gelsicoltura. 1894. III. 378.
Tamayo, (Dr.). Investigationes sobre los parásitos de las Palmeras. 1890· III. 318.²
Tambon, J. Des Illicium en général. 1886. III. 398.¹
Tamkatra bark. 1884. III. 287.²
Tamlander, Z. See JUSTANDER, J. G. & TAMLANDER, Z.
Tammes, Tine. Uber den Einfluss der Sonnenstrahlen auf die Keimungsfähigkeit von Samen. 1900. I. 204.
— Pomum in pomo. 1900. II. 267.¹
Tan Eng Tjoen. Mangga's onder bescherming van mieren. 1897. II. 457.¹
Tanaka & Yekoussima. Notices sur le Daphné papyrifère. 1867. III. 628.¹
Tanaka, T. Notes regarding the cultivation . . . of the Paper Mulberry. 1882. III. 368.¹
Tanaka, Yoshio. Useful plants of Japan. 1888. III. 91.²
— Yūyō shokubutsu zusetsu. 1888. III. 91.¹
Tanara, Vincenzo. L' economia del cittadino in villa. 1644. III. 115.¹
Tanberg, E. Garvesyremængden i endel inden- og udenlandske barksorter. 1884. I. 183, IV. 455.
— Garvesyremängden i vore indenlandske barksorter. 1885. I. 183.
Tancred, Thomas. Notes on the natural history . . . of Canterbury. 1856. I. 506.¹
Tandon, Christian Horace Bénédict Alfred MOQUIN-. See MOQUIN TANDON, C. H. B. A.; ST.-HILAIRE, Auguste de & MOQUIN-TANDON, C. H. B. A.
Tanfani, Enrico. Cenno sulla distribuzione altimetrica dell' Olivo. 1888. II. 713.¹
— Sulla Chamaedorea Verschaffeltii. 1888. II. 66.²
— Sul Dasylirion quadrangulatum. 1884. II. 81.¹
— Sulla Dolichandra cynanchoides. 1891. III. 707.²
— Florula di Giannutri. 1890. I. 429.
— Una gita nelle Alpi Cadoriche. 1800. I. 420.
— Sull' Hakea laurina. 1888. II. 162.²
— Loniceraceae. 1887. II. 833.²
— Nuova specie di Bignoniacea. 1887. II. 789.²
— Sul Pandanus utilis. 1886. II. 57.²
— Viscum album e Viscum laxum. 1889. II. 177.²
Tanfiljef, G. Ueber subfossile Strünke auf dem Boden von Seen. 1891. I. 301.
— See also ТАНФИЛЬЕВЪ, Г. И.
Tangl, Eduard. Beitrag zur Kenntniss der Perforationen an Pflanzengefässen. 1871. I. 233.
— Zur Lehre von der Continuität des Protoplasmas. 1885. I. 137.
— Über offene Communicationen zwischen den Zellen des Endosperms einiger Samen. 1879. I. 120.
— Vorläufige Mittheilung. Coniferin. 1874. I. 175.
Tangl, Frans. Bakteriologischer Beitrag zur Nonnenraupenfrage. 1893. IV. 201.
Tanker i Anledning af S. T. Hr. Overforstmester C. H. Linstows Skrift. 179 .? IV. 342.²
Tannin contenu dans l'écorce de Chêne. See GERBSTOFFGEHALT . . . 1865. IV. 514.²
Tannin extracts. 1900. IV. 435.
Tanno di Castagno. 1866. IV. 493.¹

Tanret, Charles. Sur les alcalis du Grenadier. 1879. III. 631.¹
— Sur deux sucres nouveaux retirés du Québracho. 1889. III. 687.¹
— Sur l'ergotinine. 1879. III. 631.¹
— Sur les modifications moléculaires du glucose. 1895. I. 177.
— Sur la pelletiérine. 1878. III. 630.²
— Peptones et alcaloïdes. 1881. I. 176.
— Sur la picéine. 1894. II. 37,¹ IV. 459.²
— Sur quelques principes immédiats de l'écorce d'Orange amère. 1886. III. 501.²
— De la waldivine. 1880. III. 508.²
— & Georges. Sur le rhamninose. 1899. III. 543.¹
— & Villiers, A. Sur une matière sucrée retirée des feuilles de Noyer. 1877. II. 113.¹
Tanret, Georges. See TANRET, Charles & Georges.
Tanton, Milek & others. Alte Bäume. 1884. IV. 65.¹
Tapering trees. 1872. III. 204.¹
Tapia, Ernesto, OCHOA Y. See OCHOA Y TAPIA, Ernesto.
Tapia, F. F. Huile de Caparrapi. 1897. III. 407.¹
Tapia y Rivera, Alejandro. Biblioteca historica de Puerto Rico. 1854. I. 335.
Tapisserie de bois. 1898. IV. 430.
Taplin, J. S. Some handsome flowering trees. 1893. III. 207.²
Tarade, Alfred de. Culture des Rosiers . . . sur Églantiers. 1828. III. 451.²
Taratchkoff, Al. Observations sur le développement des plantes . . . d'Orel. 1854. I. 223.²
— See also ТАРАЧКОВЪ, А.
Tardent, Charles. Essai sur l'histoire naturelle de la Bessarabie. 1841. I. 361.
Tardieu, Ambrose. Mémoire sur l'empoisonnement par la coralline. 1869. III. 517.¹
Tardy. See BOUCHARDAT, G. & TARDY.
Tardy, Frédéric. Les Chênes mariés. 1895. I. 209,² IV. 511.
Tarelli, Camillo. Ricordo d' agricoltura. 1577. III. 114.²
Targioni-Tozzetti, Adolfo. Sopra alcune specie di cocciniglie. 1888. III. 190.
— Di alcuni rapporti delle coltivazioni cogli insetti. 1885. III. 358,¹ 677.²
— Bibliographia botanica Targioniana. 1874. I. 2.
— La fillossera a Valmadrera. 1879. III. 572.
— La fillossera e le malattie delle Viti. 1883. III. 761.
— Fillossera o pidocchio della Vite. 1878. III. 571.
— Della malattia del pidocchio. 1875. III. 568.
— Sulla malattia delle Uve. 1856. III. 576.
— Notizie e indicazioni sulla malattia del pidocchio. 1875. III. 568. — 1879. III. 761.
— Sull organo femmineo del genere Citrus. 1843. II. 401.²
— Delle più recenti infezioni fillosseriche della Germania. 1886. III. 762.
— Sur les propositions de M. Balbiani pour combattre le phylloxera. 1883. III. 573.
— Relazione sopra la seta moogha delle Indie. 1866. III. 148.¹
— Saggio di studi intorno al guscio dei semi. 1854. I. 120.
— & Guercio, Giacomo del. Catalogo della mostra di animali diversi. 1898. III. 191.
Targioni-Tozzetti, Antonio. Catalogo delle piante che si coltivano nel giardino del March. Cav. Pietro Torrigiani. 1841. I. 63.
— Catalogo delle piante coltivate nell' Orto botanico-agrario detto dei semplici in Firenze. 1841. I. 63.
— Cenni storici sulla introduzione di varie piante. 1853. I. 241.¹
— Corso di botanica medico-farmaceutica. 1847. III. 58.
— Historical notes on fruit trees. 1853. I. 241.¹
— Historical notes on the introduction of various plants. 1853. I. 241.¹
— Historische Notizen über unsere Fruchtbäume. 1853. I. 241.¹
— Nota sopra la gutta-percha. 185 .? III. 230.
— Raccolto di fiori, frutti ed agrumi. 1825. I. 267.
— Scelta di piante officinali. 1824. III. 58.¹
— Sommario di botanica medico-farmaceutica. 1828. III. 56.
Targioni-Tozzetti, Giovanni. Olja ur Boknötter. 1769. IV. 500.¹
— De praestantia et usu plantarum. 1734. III. 217.
— Relazioni d' alcuni viaggi . . . Toscana. 1751. I. 424.

Targioni-Tozzetti, Ottaviano. Catalogus plantarum medicinalium in Etruria. 1829. III. 88.[1]
— Catalogus seminum collectorum in Horto botanico-agrario florentino. 1818. I. 62.
— Delle cognizioni botaniche di Dante. 1828. I. 514.[2]
— Disionario botanico italiano. 1809. I. 74.[3]
— Sopra una falsa specie di china. 1804. III. 724.[1]
— Instituzioni botaniche. 1794. I. 54.
— Lettera contenente l'istoria d'una malattia prodotta dal Rhus Vernix. 1817. III. 528.[2]
— Della necessità di osservare le parti della fruttificazione avanti e dopo la fiorescenza. 1823. I. 114.[1] — 1825. I. 117.[2]
— Observatiónum botanicarum. Decas. 1808. I. 265.
— Osservazioni botaniche. 1829. I. 267.
Targonski, V. A. *See* Таргонскій, B. A.
Tarif C. G. no. 1 pour les bois en grumes. *See* GRANDGEORGE, n. d. IV. 219.
Tarif C. G. No. 6 spécial pour le cubage des bois de mines. *See* GRANGE, n. d. IV. 219.
Tarif de cubage des bois en grume. 18..? IV. 229.
Tarif officiel pour la recette et la classement des bois de construction. *See* HAMELIN. 1859. IV. 425.[1]
Tarif pour le bois en grume. *See* TABELLEN. 1899. IV. 229.
Tariff zu Preiss-Bestimmung der Bau- und Werkholzstämme. 1806. IV. 402.[2]
Tarifs de douanes. 1891. IV. 285.[1]
Tarnow, J. M. Ueber die zur Lohe tauglichen meklenburgischen Gewächse. 1794. III. 237.[1]
Tartaglini, Lione. Erbolario. 1558. I. 280.
Tartarinov, Alexander. Catalogus medicamentorum sinensium. 1856. III. 273.[1]
Taschenberg, E. L. Deutschlands Pflanzengattungen. 1845. I. 381.
— Entomologie für Gärtner und Gartenfreunde. 1871. III. 190.
— Forstwirthschaftliche Insekten-Kunde. 1874. IV. 92.
— Handbuch der botanischen Kunstsprache. 1843. I. 71.
— Die Insekten nach ihrem Schaden und Nutzen. 1882. III. 95.
— Schutz der Obstbäume. 1874. III. 190.
— Wandtafel zur Darstellung der Reblaus. 1878. III. 190.
— Was sind Holzwürmer? 1883. IV. 414.[1]
— Die dem Wein- und Obstbau schädlichen Insekten. 1872. III. 190.
— *See also* BURMEISTER, Hermann & TASCHENBERG, E. L.
Taschenbuch des verständigen Gärtners. 1824. III. 104.
Taschen-Buch für angehende Forstmänner. 1821. IV. 392.
Taschenbuch für Forst- und Jagdfreunde. *See* NEUJAHRS-GESCHENK... IV. 10.
Taschenbuch für Forst- und Jagdmänner. IV. 11.
Taschenbuch für Gartenfreunde. Ed. by W. G. Becker. III. 13.
Taschenbuch für Gartenfreunde. Ed. by C. C. L. Hirschfeld. III. 13.
Taschenbuch für Natur- und Gartenfreunde. III. 13.
Taschenbuch für Pomologen. III. 13.
Taschenbuch zum Nutzen... für Wald- und Jagdfreunde. *See* NEUJAHRS-GESCHENK... IV. 10.
Taschenbuch zur Belehrung... für Wald- und Jagdfreunde. *See* NEUJAHRS-GESCHENK... IV. 10.
Taschen-Kalender für Pflanzen-Sammler. 1878. I. 387.
Tasmania-Conservator of forests. Report. IV. 17.[1]
Tasmania — Crown land office. Annual report. IV. 17.[1]
Tasmania — Royal society. *See* ROYAL SOCIETY OF VAN DIEMEN'S LAND. I. 30.
Tasmania — Woods and forests. Report of the Conservator of forests. *See* TASMANIA — CONSERVATOR OF FORESTS. IV. 17.[1]
Tasmanian Beech. 1899. IV. 499.
Tasmanian journal of natural science. I. 30.
Tasmanian woods. 1889. IV. 402.[1]
Tassa sul taglio dei boschi in Lombardia. 1863. IV. 285.[1]
Tassart. Note sur un Daphné hybride. 1828. II. 601.[3]
Tassazione della foresta inalienabile di Vallombrosa. 1878. IV. 249.[2]
Tassel, (pseud.). The Oak. 1853. IV. 504.
— Robinia Pseud-acacia. 1855. III. 486.[2]
— Sparmannia africana. 1845. III. 585.[1]
Tassi, Attilio. Cenno sulla botanica agraria. 1865. III. 88.[2]
— Sulla flora della provincia senese. 1862. I. 427.
— Della fruttificazione dell' Hoya carnosa. 1856. II. 739.[2]
— Sulla irritabilità delli stami. 1843. I. 197.[3]

— Del modo di compilare i cataloghi di semi. 1856. I. 38.[1]
— Dello svolgimento di calore ne' fiori della Magnolia. 1856. II. 212.[1]
Tassi, Flaminio. Dell' anestesia. 1887. I. 211.
— Anomalie vegetali. 1898. I. 144.[1]
— Degli effetti anestesici nei fiori. 1885. I. 211.
— La linea lucida nelle cellule Malpighiane... dell' Hippophaë. 1897. II. 608.[1]
— Il parco sperimentali di Conifere nella Villa Moncioni. 1898. I. 64.
— Le Proteaceae in specie dello Stenocarpus. 1898. II. 158.[2]
— Ricerche anatomo-biologiche sull' Hoya. 1898. II. 739.[2]
— Dello sviluppo dell' ovulo... nella Tibouchinia. 1897. II. 642.[1]
— Sulla variegatura. 1885. I. 185.[2]
— Un viaggio in Oriente. 1885. I. 475.[1]
Tassilly, E. Sur le dosage de la caféine dans le café. 1897. III. 740.[2]
Tassinari, G. Composizione de la gomme gutte. 1897. III. 609.[1]
Tassy, Louis. État des forêts en France. 1887. IV. 361.
— État des forêts envisagées dans leur ensemble. 1887. IV. 361.
— Études sur l'aménagement des forêts. 1858. IV. 240.
— Note sur le défrichement des bois. 1854. IV. 275.
— Réorganisation du service forestier. 1879. IV. 292.
— La restauration des montagnes. 1877. IV. 162.
— Restauration et conservation des terrains en montagne. 1883. IV. 185.[3]
— Service forestier de l'Algérie. Rapport. 1872. IV. 295.[2]
— Les taillis et les futaies. 1880. IV. 236.
Tassy, Victor. Notes sur l'extinction des torrents. 1874. IV. 185.[2]
— Notes sur le Pin Cembro. • 1873. IV. 463.[3]
Tatar, M. Persica vulgaris var. semiplena. • 1889. III. 440.[1]
Tatar, Mathias. Pirus Bollwylleriana De C. var. 1878. III. 460.[1]
Tate, George Ralph. The geology, botany and zoology... of Alnwick. 1869. I. 402.
— *See also* BAKER, J. G. & TATE, G. R.
Tate, Nahum. Panacea; a poem upon Tea. 1700. III. 605.
Tate, Ralph. Additions to the flora of... South Australia. 1885. I. 503.
— Additions to the flora of... South Australia, including descriptions. 1886. II. 176.[1]
— Additions to the flora of South Australia. 1882. I. 503.
— Additions to the flora of the Port Lincoln. 1889. I. 504.
— The botany of Kangaroo Island. 1883. I. 503.
— Botany of the Horn expedition. 1896. I. 505.
— A census of the... plants and ferns of extra-tropical South Australia. 1880. I. 502.
— A census of the... plants... of extra-tropical South Australia. 1889. I. 504.
— Definitions of four new species of Australian plants. 1889. II. 494.[2]
— Descriptions of new species of South Australian plants. 1885. I. 503.
— Flora belfastiensis. The plants around Belfast. 1863. I. 401.
— On the geographic relations of the floras of Norfolk and Lord Howe Islands. 1893. I. 508.[2]
— On the geological... features of Southern Yorke-Peninsula. 1890. I. 504.
— A handbook of the flora of extratropical South Australia. 1890. I. 504.
— The host plants of the Australian Loranthaceae. 1898. II. 174.[1]
— A list of plants collected by the Calvert expedition. 1897. I. 505.
— List of plants unrecorded for Southern Eyre peninsula. 1883. I. 503.
— List of some plants... of the Lake Torrens basin. 1883. I. 503.
— A list of unrecorded plants... of this colony. 1883. I. 503.
— The natural history... of the Great Australian Bight. 1879. I. 502.
— A new variety of Andromeda polifolia. 1866. II. 659.[3]
— Note on the presence of tannin in the Polygonum. 1883. III. 186.[1]
— Plants of the Lake Eyre basin. 1889. I. 504.
— A review of the characters available for the classification of the Eucalypts. 1898. II. 623.[3]
— A revision of the flora of Kangaroo Island. 1889. I. 504.

— On some new . . . South Australian plants. 1898. II. 327.[1]
— See also MUELLER, Ferdinand, Baron VON & TATE, Ralph.
Tatem, James G. Some particulars on the fact of two horses dying shortly after eating of . . . branches of the Yew tree. 1835. III. 288.[2]
Tatin, A. Principes raisonnés . . . de la culture des arbres fruitiers. 1811. III. 110.[1]
Tatnall, Edward. Catalogue of the phænogamous . . . of Newcastle county. 1860. I. 319.
Tatter, W. Anleitung zur Obsttreiberei. 1879. III. 176.[1]
— Das Wichtigste aus der Obsttreiberei. 1879. III. 176.[2]
Tatti, Giovanni. Della agricoltura libri cinque. 1560. III. 114.[1]
Tatum, Lawrie. Experience in planting forest trees. 1884. IV. 112.
Taube, Johann. Beiträge zur Naturkunde des Herzogthums Zelle. 1766. I. 373.
Taubert, Paul. Beiträge zur Kenntnis der Flora des central-brasilianischen Staates Goyaz. 1896. I. 343.
— Eminia, genus novum Papilionacearum. 1891. II. 355.[2]
— Die Gattung Phyllostylon. 1890. II. 142.[2]
— Zur Kenntniss einiger Leguminosengattungen. 1892. II. 318.[1]
— Leguminosae. 1894. II. 318.[2]
— Leguminosae africanae. 1897. II. 319.[2]
— Leguminosae novae . . . austro-americanae. 1859. II. 319.[1]
— Zur Nomenclatur einiger Genera . . . der Leguminosen. 1891. II. 318.[2]
— Plantae Glazaiovianae. 1890. I. 330.
— Revision der Gattung Griselinia. 1893. II. 656.[1]
— Ueber das Vorkommen der Gattung Physostigma. 1894. II. 376.[2]
— See also REICHE, Karl & TAUBERT, Paul.
Tauche, F. Die Buntlaubigkeit. 1894. III. 206.[2]
Taunay, C. A. & Riedel, L. Manual do agricultor brazileiro. 1839. III. 100.[1]
La taupe. 1895. IV. 58.[2]
Taupenot, J. M. Recherches sur l'organisation des Synanthérées. 1851. II. 850.[1]
Taurus AEMILIANUS, PALLADIUS RUTILIUS. See PALLADIUS RUTILIUS TAURUS AEMILIANUS.
Tausch, _g az Friedrich. Bemerkungen über Acer. 1829. II. 476.[2][3]
— Bemerkungen über das Willdenowische Herbar. 1832. II. 98.[2]
— Bemerkungen über Erica. 1834. II. 664.[1]
— Bemerkungen über Lavatera. 1829. II. 525.[1]
— Beobachtung einer neuen Pflanzen um Prag. 1819. II. 287.[2]
— Beobachtungen über einige Salices. 1837. II. 101.[1]
— Botanische Bemerkungen. 1829. I. 267.
— Botanische Beobachtungen. 1829. I. 268.
— Botanische Notizen. 1842. I. 268.
— Ueber die in . . . Dendrotheca exotica bohemica ausgegebenen neuen Arten. 1838. I. 268.
— Ueber einige neue . . . Arten der Gattung Erica. 1839. II. 664.[1]
— Ueber Erica purpurascens. 1839. II. 667.[2]
Hortus saaalius. 1822. I. 65.[1]
— Index plantarum . . . in horto . . . Josephi Malabaila de Canal. 1821. I. 65.[2]
— Nachricht über zwei bereits im J. 1828 censurirte Handschriften. 1851. I. 269.
— Observations sur plusieurs espèces d'Erica. 1834. II. 664.[1]
— Ueber Pyrus sudetica Tausch. 1834. II. 313.[1]
— Das System der Compositen. 1852. II. 848.[1]
— Ueber das System der Gattung Erica. 1837. II. 664.[1]
— Ueber zwei bisher unbeschriebene . . . Alpenpflanzen. 1836. II. 681.[1]
Tau-tha, (pseud.?). Three months' privilege leave to New Zealand. 1886. IV. 380.[2]
Tau-tha-ma, (pseud.). The cultivation of Para Rubber. 1900. III. 519.[1]
Tavanti, Giuseppe. Trattato teorico-pratico completo sull. Ulivo. 1819. III. 675.[1]
Tavel, A. von. Ueber das Wesen der Wälder. 1834. IV. 277.
Tavera, Trinidad Herménégilde, PARDO DE. See PARDO DE TAVERA, T. H.
Taverna, comte. Sur la rusticité des arbres verts. 1862. III. 292.

Taverner, J. W. Report on phylloxera. 1899. III. 762.
Tavi, Gusztáv. See BUND, Károly, TAVI, Gusztáv & VADAS, Jenő.
Tavola per desumere la rendita media annua di un bosco ceduo. n. d. IV. 241.
Il Tavoliere di Puglia. 1863. IV. 54.
Die Taxation des Niederwaldes. 1850. IV. 242.
Taxodium dictichum in Zerbst. 1896. II. 52.[1]
Der Taxus und seine Eigenthümlichkeiten. 1858. IV. 440.[1]
Ein Taxusbestand. 1846. II. 10.[2]
Tayler, A. J., WALLIS-. See WALLIS-TAYLER, A. J.
Tayler, William. Thaumato-dendra. 1877. I. 517.[1]
Taylor, A. G. The Mammoth tree. 1856. II. 50.[2]
Taylor, A. H. De Anti-lepra heester. 1900. III. 520.[1]
Taylor, C. B. Application of Mowah oil. 1846. III. 667.[2]
— Remarks on a few kinds of edible oils. 1845. III. 224.[1]
— Remarks on the applicability of the Nerium . . . tinctorium. 1845. III. 692.[1]
Taylor, C. P. A short campaign against the white borer . . . in the Coffee districts. 1868. III. 735.
Taylor, Ellen M. Madeira. 1882. V. xxiv.[2]
Taylor, George. Hybrid greenhouse Rhododendrons. 1879. III. 660.[2]
— Notice of some remarkable specimens of Cycas revoluta. 1850. II. 4.[2]
Taylor, Isaac. The ethnological significance of the Beech. 1890. II. 127.[1]
Taylor, J. Berberis Darwini. 1872. III. 394.[2]
Taylor, J. E. Flowers, their origin. 1878. I. 115,[1] 147.
— The sagacity & morality of plants. 1884. I. 96.
Taylor, James. Notice of flowering plants and ferns. 1862. I. 310.
Taylor, James W. Forest and fruit culture in Manitoba. 1882. IV. 111.[1]
Taylor, Jefferys. The forest. 1831. I. 393.[1]
Taylor, Joseph. Arbores mirabiles. 1812. I. 82.[1]
— The wonders of trees, plants. 1823. V. x.[2]
Taylor, Meadows. On the juice of the Múddár. 1854. III. 692.[2]
Taylor, Samuel. On different modes of securing newly planted trees. 1839. III. 198.[2]
— Des différentes manières de protéger contre les grands vents. 1839. III. 198.[2]
Taylor, Silvanus. Common-good. 1652. IV. 274.[2]
Taylor, William. Les Vignes de Longleat. 1883. III. 553.[1]
Taylor, William Alton. The fruit industry. 1898. III. 62.
— Small-fruit culture for market. 1896. III. 148.[1]
Taylor, Yardley. How wood is formed. 1859. I. 190.[1]
Tchebyshef, V. L. See Чебышевъ, В. Л.
Tchernigoff. Le commerce du thé entre la Chine et la Russie. 1893. III. 608.[1]
Tchernof, K. See Черновъ, К.
Tchernyayef, V. M. See Черняевъ, В. М.
Tchernyshef, N. E. See Чернышевъ, Н. Е.
Tchernyshef, S. A. See Чернышевъ, С. А.
Tchihatchef, Pierre de. See TCHIHATCHEF, P. A.
Tchihatchef, Piotr Aleksandrovitch. Asie Mineure; description physique. 1866. I. 479.
— Le Bosphore et Constantinople. 1864. I. 479.
— Conifères de l'Asie Mineure. 1854. II. 31.[1]
— Discours sur la géographie botanique de l'Asie-Mineure. 1857. I. 479.
— Espagne, Algérie et Tunisie. 1880. I. 485.
— Études climatologiques sur l'Asie Mineure. 1856. I. 479, IV. 49.[1]
— Études sur la végétation des hautes montagnes de l'Asie-Mineure. 1857. I. 479.
— Note sur la végétation du mont Argée. 1854. I. 479.
— Observations faites pendant un voyage dans l'Asie Mineure. 1853. I. 479.
— Sur la végétation. 1857. I. 479.
— Verslag van de wetenschappelijke reize over den oostelijken Altai. 1845. I. 453.[2]
— Voyage scientifique dans l'Altai. 1845. I. 453.[2]
Tchistiakoff, Ivan Dorofeevich. Beiträge zur Entwickelungsgeschichte der Cuticula. 1869. I, 129.[2]
— Beiträge zur Physiologie der Pflanzenzelle. 1875. II. 19.
— Observations sur le . . . pollen des Conifères. 1875. II. 19.
— Pollen. 1875. II. 19.
— See also Чистяковъ, Д.
Tchouproff, Olga. Étude sur les causes qui déterminent le fractionnement du bois axial chez Mendoncia. 1897. II. 801.[2]
— Quelques notes sur l'anatomie . . . des Acanthacées. 1895. II. 796.[2]

El **Té**, su historia, cultivo y elaboración. 1877. III. 607.
Tea and coffee substitutes. 1878. III. 222.
Tea blights. 1898. III. 604.²
Tea cultivation. 1861. III. 603.
Tea cultivation in Ceylon. 1894. III. 604.¹
Tea cultivation in India. 1865. III. 603.
Tea cultivation in southern India & Ceylon. 1880. III. 603.
Tea cultivation (India). 1839. III. 602.²
The **Tea** cyclopaedia; articles on Tea. 1881. III. 600.³
Tea oil and cake. 1888. III. 600.¹
On the **Tea-plantations** in India. 1841. III. 602.²
The **Tea** plantations in the N.-W. Provinces of India. 1848. III. 602.²
The **Tea** planter's vade mecum. 1885. III. 603.
Tea-planting in Assam. 1880. III. 603.
Tea-planting in India and the Lewshai tribes. 1872. III. 603.
Tea planting in the outer Himalayah. *See* McGOWAN, A. T. 1861. III. 603.
The **Tea** purchaser's guide. 1785. III. 605.
The **Tea** Rose Crab. 1888. III. 429.¹
Teak. 1882. IV. 536.¹
Teak; the produce of India, Siam and Burmah. 1896. IV. 538.¹
Teak en Djatihout. 1884. III. 697.³
The **Teak** forests of Burma. 1896. IV. 378.
A **Teak** tree with alternate leaves. 1880. II. 761.¹
Teak uit Engelsch of Djati uit Nederlandsch Indie. 1885. IV. 538.¹
Das **Teakholz**. 1884. IV. 538.¹
Teas, John C. A month among the Catalpa trees. 1880. IV. 538.²
Teasdale, Washington. Culture of parasites. 1873. III. 385.¹
— The Mango and its varieties. 1873. III. 524.¹ 525.¹
Teatino, Paolo CULTRERA. *See* CULTRERA TEATINO, Paolo.
Technische Vorschriften für die Samenprüfungen. 189.? III. 157.
Technische Vorschriften und Instruktion für den Bau ... der ... Waldstrassen. 1861. IV. 389.
De **technologie** van vetten en olien. 1882. III. 225.
Technologisches Gewerbe-Museum. Mittheilungen. IV. 15.
Technologisches Gewerbe-Museum, Wien. Mittheilungen. III. 25.
Technologist. III. 18.
Le **Technologiste**. III. 23.¹
Techow, H. Fussböden aus Rotbuchenholz. 1894. IV. 499.
El **Teck**. 1887. IV. 538.¹
Tedin, Hans. Om den primära barken. 1886. I. 130.
— Ueber die primäre Rinde. 1889. I. 131.¹
Teenstra, M. D. De landbouw in de kolonie Suriname. 1835. III. 118.²
— Verslag wegens de meest bekende ... houtsoorten ... in de kolonie Suriname. 1831. I. 338.²
Teenstra, U. D. *See* UILKENS, T. F. & TEENSTRA, U. D.
Teerlink, C. C. J. De bepaling van de anorganische bestanddeelen der planten. 1888. I. *163*, 156.²
Teesdale, Robert. Plantae eboracenses. 1794. I. 396.
Tegenwoordige toestand der Java-Koffiecultuur. 1899. III. 737.
Téglás, Gábor. Erdővédelem. 1887. IV. 177.²
Téglás, Károly. Erdővédelemtan. 1893. IV. 177.³
Teichert, Oskar. Beobachtungen an der Färbung des Laubes. 1856. III. 207.¹
— Gärtnerische Veredlungskunst. 1869. III. 162.
— Der Garten zu Klein-Watkowitz. 1861. I. 48.
— Geschichte der Fuchsia. 1866. III. 639.²
— Geschichte der Ziergärten ... in Deutschland. 1865. III. 33.¹
— Histoire du Fuchsia. 1866. III. 639.²
— Die Veredlungskunst. 1893. III. 162.
— Veredelungskunst im siebzehnten Jahrhundert. 1900. III.
Teichmann, Friedrich. Die den Obstbäumen schädlichsten Raupenarten. 1829. III. 188.²
Teichmeyer, Hermann Friedrich. Institutiones botanicae. 1731. I. 82.¹
— Programma II. de Caapeba. 1730. III. 396.²
Teijsmann, Johannes Elias. *See* TEYSMANN, Johannes Elias.
Teil, John. Report of further tanning experiments with ... "Teree." 1848. III. 468.¹
— *See also* SCONCE, A. & TEIL, John.

Teil, Thomas. Report on the tanning properties of ... "Dhak." 1854. III. 468.¹
Teilman, Christian. Anviisning til Norske Frugttræsköler. 1797. III. 134.²
Teintzer, Johann. Praktische Anleitung zur ... Vermessung und Berechnung aller ... Rundhölzer. 1842. IV. 223.
Teirlinck, I. De folklore van den Eik. 1891. II. 132.¹
— Een kruidboek van 1514. 1890. I. 78.²
Teisserenc de Bort, Léon. Sur l'orage du 18 août. 1890. III. 184.²
Teissonnier, P. La Guinée française. 1899. III. 268.¹
Teixeira, Carlos. O café do Brazil. 1883. III. 740.¹
— Der Kaffee von Brasilien. 1883. III. 740.²
Teixidor, Primitivo ARTIGAS Y. *See* ARTIGAS Y TEIXIDOR, Primitivo.
Tejada, Casimiro de, BONA Y GARCIA DE. *See* BONA Y GARCIA DE TEJADA, Casimiro de.
Le **Tek**. 1888. IV. 536.²
Telégrafo óptico con aplicación á los anuncios de incendios. 1879. IV. 183.²
Teleki, János. A Fojtós Berkenyefáról. 1898. III. 430.¹
Telles, J. J. de SOUSA. *See* SOUSA TELLES, J. J. de.
Telles, Vicente, COELHO DE SEABRA SILVA. *See* COELHO DE SEABRA SILVA, TELLES, Vicente.
Tellès d'Acosta. Instruction sur les bois de marine. 1782. IV. 424.² *511*.
Tellier, A. L. De l'influence des forêts au point de vue du climat. 1895. IV. 54.
Tellière, Louis, (jr.). Grevillea robusta. 1868. III. 383.¹
— Solanum betaceum. 1869. III. 699.²
Tellier, J. Conseils pratiques sur l'arboriculture. 1885. III. 124.¹
Telopea speciosissima R. Br. 1834. III. 384.¹
El **tema** sobre "Canales." 1889. IV. 390.²
Temi di legislazione e giurisprudenza forestale. 1872. IV. 328.
Temme, F. Über die Pilzkröpfe der Holzpflanzen. 1887. IV. 194.
— Über Schutz- und Kernholz. 1885. I. 125, *207*.²
Die **Temperatur-** und Feuchtigkeitsverhältnisse der Streudecke. 1888. IV. 71.
Temperature of plants. 1828. I. 186.
Tempest, Ernest, BORDE DE. *See* BORDE DE TEMPEST, Ernest.
La **tempête** de la nuit du 12 au 13 novembre. 1894. IV. 548.¹
Il **tempio** della fedeltà la cioccolata. 1774. III. 222.
Temple, C. L. Report on the state of Amazonas. 1900. III. *473*,¹ 519.¹
— The rubber industry in the Amazonas state. 1900. III. 519.¹
Temple, F. L. The Halesias. 1893. III. 670.²
— New species of Lilacs. 1887. III. 680.¹
— Notes on European nurseries. 1890. III. 119.¹
— Pyrus spectabilis, Parkmani. 1887. III. 425,¹ *681*.²
— Transplanting large Rhododendrons. 1889. III. 656.
Temple, M. Garrya elliptica. 1899. III. 352.²
Temple, Sir Richard. Forest conservancy in Bombay. 1880. IV. 181.²
— Forest conservancy in India. 1881. IV. 279.¹
— Forests of India. 1884. IV. 378.
— Instruction in forestry. 1884. IV. 56.
The **Temple** show. 1897. III. 83.²
Templin, L. J. Experiments in timber raising in Kansas. 1877. IV. 111.²
— Lightning & Beech trees. 1878. IV. 194.
— A Rocky Mountain Oak. 1887. III. 363.¹
— The Upas tree. 1886. III. 366.²
Tench, Watkin. Compleat account of the settlement of Port Jackson. 1788. I. 500.
— Reise nach der Botany-Bay. 1794. I. 500.
Tengah bark. 1887. III. 632.¹
Tengkawang-vet of plantaardige talk. 1884. III. 225. — 1885. III. 225.
Tengmalm, Petro Gust. Pan suecicus. *See* LINNÉ, Carl von. 1749. III. 223.¹
Tengström, Johannes Magnus von. In distributionem vegetationis per Ostrobothniam. 1846. I. 361.
— De fructus in phanerophytis evolutione. 1841. I. 119.
— Naturhistoriens studium: Finland för Linnés tid. 1843. I. 80,² 361.¹
— Stirpes cotyledoneae paroeciae Pojo. 1844. I. 361.
Tenison-Woods, Julian Edmund. *See* WOODS, J. E. TENISON-.
Tennent, Sir James Emerson. Ceylon. 1859. I. 476.²
— Ceylons Naturforhold. 1864. I. 476.²
— Mustard-tree of Scripture. 1859. II. 473.¹
— Notes on the botany of Ceylon. 1861. III. 279.¹

Tennessee —Agricultural experiment station. See TEN-
NESSEE, UNIVERSITY OF — AGRICULTURAL ... III. 8.
Tennessee, University of —Agricultural experiment station.
Annual report. Bulletin. Special bulletin. III. 8.
Tennessee, University of. Report of the experimental ...
work. III. 8.
Tennyson's knowledge of trees. 1873. I. 515.[1]
Tenore, Michele. Sopra alcune specie di Cipressi. 1853. II.
30.[1]
— Su di alcune specie di Opunzie. 1843. II. 596.[2]
— Intorno all' Amygdalus pumila. 1847. II. 270,[2] V. XXVI.[2]
— Annotazioni alla florâ Grecâ. 1842. II. 44.[2]
— Sull' Arancio Mandarino. 1825. II. 402.[2]
— Botanique. 1825. II. 129.[1]
— Della Candidea. 1839. II. 868.[2]
— Catalogo degli alberi ed arbusti ... del Real orto botanico
di Napoli. 1836. I. 63.
— Catalogo della collezione agraria del Real giardino delle
piante. 1815. I. 62.
— Catalogo delle piante del giardino botanico del Signor
Principe de Bisignano. 1809. I. 61.
— Catalogo delle piante del Real giardino botanico di Napoli.
1807. I. 61.
— Catalogo ... nel R. orto botanico di Napoli. 1845. I.
63.
— Catalogus plantarum Horti regii neapolitani. 1812. I.
62.
— Catalogus seminum Horti regii neapolitani. 1850. I.
63.
— Cenno sulla geografia ... di Napoli. 1827. I. 426.
— Corso delle botaniche lezioni. 1806. I. 84.
— Descrizione di due alberi ... del genere Ficus. 1840.
II. 148.[2]
— Sopra i due nuovi generi di piante Syncarpia. 1840. II.
441,[1] 633.[1]
— Sopra due piante leguminose. 1842. II. 335,[2] 351.[2]
— Essai sur la géographie ... de Naples. 1827. I. 426.
— Flora medica universale. 1823. I. 426, III. 56.
— Flora napolitana. 1811. I. 425.
— Florae neapolitanae prodromi. 1823. I. 426.[1]
— Ad Florae neapolitanae prodromum. 1823. I. 426.[1]
— Sulla Hypocyrta perianthomega. 1847. II. 828.[1]
— Index seminum in Horto botanico neapolitano 1839 col-
lectorum. 1840. I. 63.
— Della Maeria. 1847. II. 749.[2]
— Memoria sopra due piante esotiche. 1832. II. 52,[2] 81.[2]
— M m a su di una nuova specie di Acero. 1819. II.
479.b ori
— Memoria sul Pruno Cocumiglia. 1828. II. 273.[2]
— Memoria sull' Acero di Lobel. 1832. II. 478.[2]
— Memoria sull' Ontano a foglie cordate. 1825. II. 116.[1]
— Memoria sulle peregrinazioni botaniche ... nella provincia
di Napoli. 1832. I. 426.
— Nota su di una nuova specie di Aristolochia. 1842. I.
344.
— Intorno ad una nuova specie di Pogostemon. 1847. II.
765.[1]
— Osservazioni sulla flora di Teocrito. 1836. I. 514.[1]
— Osservazioni sulla flora Virgiliana. 1826. I. 514.[1]
— Su di una pianta Conifera del genere Taxodium. 1853.
II. 52.[1]
— Proposta di una descrizione sistematica generale de' Vitigni.
1847. III. 546.
— Raccolta di viaggi fisico-botanici effettuati nel regno di
Napoli. 1812. I. 425.
— Relazione del viaggio ... Abruzzo citeriore. 1832. I.
426.
— Ricerche intorno ad alcune specie di Aceri. 1846. II. 476.[2]
— Ricerche sull' Arancio fetifero. 1843. II. 403.[1]
— Ricerche sulla classificazione de' Platani. 1856. II.
254.[2]
— Ricerche sulla geografia botanica ... dell' Italia. 1836.
I. 426.
— Saggio sulla botanica italiana. 1832. I. 426.
— Saggio sulle qualità medicinali delle piante della flora
napolitana. 1808. III. 271.[2]
— Succinta relazione del viaggio fatto in Abruzzo. 1830.
I. 426.
— Sylloge plantarum vascularium florae neapolitanae. 1831.
I. 426.
— Synopsis novarum plantarum quae in Prodromo florae nea-
politanae anno 1811–13 edito describuntur. 1819. I. 425.
— Trattato di fitognosia. 1833. I. 86.
— Viaggio per diverse parti d' Italia. 1828. I. 349.

— Una visita all' isola d' Ischia. 1842. I. 427.
— Della Zurlos nuovo genere. 1840. II. 420.[1]
— See also GUSSONE, Giovanni & TENORE, Michele; MAURI,
Ernesto & ORSINI, Antonio & TENORE, Michele; PETAGNA,
L.; TERRONE, G. & TENORE, Michele.
— & Gussone, Giovanni. Osservazioni botaniche raccolte in
un, viaggio ... terra di Lavoro e di Abruzzo. 1843. I.
427.
Tenore, Vincenzo & Pasquale, G. A. Atlante di botanica popo-
lare. 1872. I. 270.
— — Compendio di botanica. 1847. I. 89.
Circa il tenore del progretto di legge forestale. See CIRCA il
tenore ... 1896. IV. 329.
Tensi, W. Johannis- und Stachelbeerwein. 1892. III. 174.[1]
Tentamen pharmacopoeae pauperum. See MARIUS, G. H.
1820. III. 72.
Teny, H. A. Best Plums and Cherries for the farmers' orchard.
1891. III. 430.[2]
Tenzel, Franz Bernhard Richard. Beschreibung einer be-
sondern Pflanzenkrankheit. 1819. III. 178.
— Nomenclator systematicus in Leonardi Plukenetii phyto-
graphiam. 1820. I. 78.[1]
Teodoresco, Emanuel C. Action indirecte de la lumière sur la
tige et les feuilles. 1899. I. 230.
— Influence de l'acide carbonique sur la forme. 1899. I. 219.[1]
— Influence des différentes radiations lumineuses. 1899. I.
230.
— & Coupin, Henri. Influence des anesthésiques sur la for-
mation de la chlorophylle. 1898. I. 142.
Teodorovits, Ferenc. Növénytenyészeti megfigyelések a kirá-
lyhalmi között erdészeti kisérleti állomáson 1899-ben. 1900.
I. 227,[2] IV. 67.[2]
Tepelmann, R. Rosennamen-Dolmetscher. 1890. III. 450.
Teplouchof, Theodor. Ein Beitrag zur Kenntniss der sibi-
rischen Fichte. 1890. II. 38.[1]
— Beobachtungen eines Forstmannes am Uralgebirge. 1849.
IV. 345.
— See also ТЕПЛОУХОВЪ, Θ.
Teploukhof, A. See ТЕПЛОУХОВЪ, A.
Tepper, J. Gottlieb O. Additions to the flora of Kangaroo
Island. 1887. I. 503.
— Bemerkungen über die Kangaroo-Insel. 1888. I. 504.
— On the characteristics ... of the ... plants about Ardros-
san. 1880. I. 502.
— Descriptions of South Australian brachyscelid galls. 1893.
IV. 531.[1]
— Discovery of Tasmanian plants near Adelaide. 1884.
I. 503.
— The flora of Roebuck Bay. 1893. I. 504.
— Die Flora von Clarendon. 1895. I. 504.
— Influence of vegetation on climate and the rainfall. 1898.
IV. 54.
— Notes on ... the flora of Kangaroo Island. 1888. I. 504.
— Plants of Kangaroo Island. 1885. I. 503.
— Probable curative properties of Melaleuca uncinata.
1880. III. 636.
— Remarkable malformation of the leaves of Beyera. 1884.
II. 437.[2]
— Trees and their rôle in nature. 1897. IV. 49.[2]
Téran, V. Chlorose des arbres fruitiers. 1896. III. 181.[1]
— Culture de l'Airelle. 1894. III. 664.[1]
— Geelriekte der oothbomen. 1896. III. 181.[1]
— De roode schimmel der Epicea. 1899. IV. 457.
— Sucre dans les fruits. 1894. III. 220.[2]
— Suiker in de vruchten. 1894. III. 220.[2]
— Teelt der roode Boschbezie. 1894. III. 664.[1]
— Vaccinium macrocarpum. 1894. III. 664.[1]
Terdonck, Charles DU TRIEU DE. See DU TRIEU DE TER-
DONCK, Charles.
Természetrajzi füzetek. I. 28.[1]
Természettudományi füzetek. I. 28.[1]
Természettudományi közlöny. I. 28.[1]
Terminazione del magistrato ... e provveditori alle legne e
boschi. 1734. IV. 304.[1]
— Terminazione ... in proposito dei boschi dei Roveri della
terza classe. 1794. IV. 304.[2]
— Terminazione ... in proposito dei boschi di Rovere della
Trevisana. 1792. IV. 304.[2]
— Terminazione ... in proposito dei boschi pubblici. 1792.
IV. 304.[2]
— Terminazione ... per la buona coltura, custodia e sussistenza
de boschi dell' Isola di Veglia. 1776. IV. 304.[1]
— Terminazione ... per la custodia, disciplina e coltura dei
boschi della provincia dell' Istria. 1778. IV. 304.[1]

Terminazione, regolazioni e ordini stabiliti per l' importante custodia e tutela de boschi e Roveri della Terraferma. 1767. IV. 304.[1]

Terminazione, regolazioni et ordini per gl' appalti de publici legni di Belluno. 1743. IV. 304.[1]

Terminazioni degl' . . . provveditori e patroni all' arsenal in materia de licenze de Roveri. 1746. IV. 304.[1]

Terminazioni, regolazioni et ordini per l' importante custodia e tutela de' boschi e Roveri. 1703. IV. 304.[1]

Termini botanici; in usum . . . Academicae edinensis. 1767. I. 522.[2]

Terminologie botanique. See COPPENS, Bernard. 1797. I. 70.

Termo, M. B. Schlüssel zur Botanik. 1837. I. 255.

Terneden, J. L. Over het vermeerderen der duurzaamheid van hout. 1872. IV. 419.

Ternisien, A. de. Culture de quelques Rhododendrons. 1864. III. 656.

— Sur l' élagage des Conifères. 1865. III. 295.[1]

— Embothrium coccineum. 1868. III. 383.[1]

— Floraison à Cherbourg . . . de trois Rhododendron de l'Himalaya. 1867. III. 654.[2]

— Floraison à l'air libre du Chamaerops excelsa. 1867. III. 331.[2]

— Floraison à l'air libre . . . du Rhododendron argenteum. 1867. III. 659.[1]

— Ne taillez pas les Azalées. 1866. III. 656.

— Plantes exotiques qui ont résisté. 1867. III. 48.

— Rhododendrons de l'Himalaya. 1867. III. 654.[2]

Ternisien, T. de. Effets de l'hiver 1870–71 à Cherbourg. 1870. III. 48.

— Notice sur quelques végétaux exotiques . . . à Cherbourg. 1860. III. 125.

Terpentingange. 1861. IV. 452.[1]

Terquem. Rapport sur la coloration des bois. 1842. IV. 417.

Terracciano, Achille. Le Agave . . . descritte nell' ultimo decennio. 1897. II. 89.[1]

— Aloineae et Agaveae novae. 1897. II. 78.[1]

— La biologia e la struttura fiorale della Jacaranda. 1897. II. 789.[1]

— Coltura ed usi dell' Agave Sisalana. 1898. III. 341.[1]

— Conspectus specierum generis Doryanthes. 1898. II. 89.[2]

— Contributo alla storia del genere Lycium. 1890. II. 72.[2]

— Contribuzione alla flora del paese del Somali. 1892. I. 489.

— Contribuzione alla flora romana. 1891. I. 430.

— Escursioni botaniche nelle terre . . . della Colonia Eritrea. 1892. I. 489.

— La flora delle isole Tremiti. 1890. I. 429.

— Florula di Anfilah. 1894. I. 489.

— I nettarii estranuziali nelle Bombacee. 1897. II. 528.[2]

— Note anatomo-biologiche sulla " Aeschynomene indica L." 1897. II. 330.[1]

— Notizie preliminari sulla flora delle Isole Palmarie. 1884. I. 429.

— Osservazioni fenologiche. 1897. I. 227.[1]

— Le Palme coltivate nel R. orto botanico di Palermo. 1897. II. 61.[1]

— Le piante nuove o rare . . . nei Delectus seminum e nell' Hortus panormitanus. 1898. I. 64.

— Primo contributo ad una monografia delle Agave. 1885. II. 89.[1]

— Le specie del genere Brachychiton. 1897. II. 532.[1]

Terracciano, Nicola. Ancora intorno agli effetti del freddo. 1870. I. 212.

— Intorno a certe piante da serra. 1864. III. 49.[1]

— La Chorisia speciosa. 1894. III. 530.[1]

— Die Cultur der Eucalyptus. 1881. III. 633.[1]

— Descrizione di una nuova specie di Pruno. 1888. II. 273.[1]

— Enumeratio plantarum vascularium in agro murensis. 1873. I. 428.

— Florae Vulturis synopsis. 1869. I. 428.

— I legnami della terra di Lavoro. 1880. IV. 399.[1]

— Nota su di alcune piante . . . del Volturno. 1867. I. 428.

— Notizie intorno a certe piante . . . a Castelporziano. 1885. II. 197,[2] 278.[2]

— Notizie intorno all' Ailanthus. 1869. III. 507.[1]

— Osservazioni sulla vegetazione dei dintorni di Caserta . . . 1867–71. 1872. I. 428.

— Osservazioni sulla vegetazione dei dintorni di Caserta . . . 1878. 1879. III. 49.[2]

— Osservazioni sulla vegetazione dei dintorni di Caserta . . . 1879. 1881. I. 429, III. 49.[2]

— Osservazioni termometriche e di fenomeni periodici. 1867. I. 226.[2]

— La Peronospora viticola de Bary. 1881. III. 578.

— Produzione di radici avventizie nel cavo di un Cipresso. 1886. I. 188.

— Relazione 4a intorno alle peregrinazioni botaniche . . . Lavoro. 1878. I. 428.

— Synopsis plantarum vascularium Montis Pollini. 1890. I. 429.

— Intorno alla trasformazione degli stami in carpelli nel Capsicum. 1878. II. 769.[2]

— Wink über den botanischen Garten . . . zu Caserta. 1878. I. 64.

— Die Wirkungen der Kälte im Winter 1879–80. 1881. III. 49,[2] V. XXII.[2]

Terras, de. Trois mémoires sur la chaleur. 1849. I. 231.[2]

Terras, James Adam. Note on the occurrence of tannin in Dacrydium. 1893. II. 8.[2]

— The relation between the lenticels and adventitious roots of Solanum Dulcamara. 1900. I. 132,[2] II. 776.[1]

Terrassen-aanleg bij de Koffiecultuur. 1893. III. 727.

Terrat, P. See PETIT, A. & TERRAT, P.

Terrats, F. de. Reboisement par les Pins maritimes. 1881. IV. 467.[2]

Le terre coltivate in Germania. 1895. IV. 349.[2]

Le terre incolte del regno. 1899 IV. 364.

Terreil, A. De l'acide phytolaccique. 1880. III. 388.[2]

— Nouvel appareil pour doser les tannins. 1874. I. 183.

— See also FRÉMY, Edmond & TERREIL, A.

Terrone, G. See PETAGNA, L., TERRONE, G. & TENORE, Michele.

Terroux, Paul. Sylviculture. 18 . . ? IV. 110.[1]

Terry, H. A. Cherries. 1898. III. 436.[2]

— Crab apples and hybrids. 1889. III. 426.[2]

— Cultivation and varieties of Currants. 1899. III. 415.[1]

— Currants and Gooseberries. 1898. III. 414.[1]

— Fall planting the Plum. 1900. III. 433.[1]

— Native Plums. 1890. III. 433.[1]

— Not well known shrubs, trees and Conifers. 1886. III. 60.

Terry, Hubert L. Resinous constituents of caoutchouc. 1889. III. 231.

Tertrin, Paul. Le Bombyx du Pin. 1895. IV. 549.[1]

Tesauro di Evonomo Filatro. See GESNER, Conrad. 1558. III. 239.[1]

Teschemacher, James Englebert. Analysis of the forms of pears. 1847. III. 444.[2]

— Note on Melocactus viridescens Nutt. 1845. II. 593.[1]

— Ueber das Wachs von Chamaerops. 1846. II. 66.[2]

Tesnière, T. J. Essai sur la poisons végétaux . . . en France. 1809. III. 271.[1]

Tessier, (abbé). Mémoire sur . . . Cupressus disticha. 1788. III. 310.[2]

— Observation sur une substance ramassée aux pieds de jeunes Peupliers d'Italie. 1787. I. 213,[1] III. 346.[2]

Tessier, F. Le versant méridional du massif du Ventoux. 1900. IV. 282.[2]

Tessier, Henri Alexander. Mémoire sur l'importation et les progrès des arbres à épicerie. 1794. III. 221.[2]

— Observation sur une substance ramassée aux pieds de jeunes Peupliers d'Italie. 1787. II. 97.[2]

Tessier, T. La disette de fourrage et les forêts. 1894. III. 223.[2]

— Die Verwerthung der Futtermittel des Waldes. 1894. III. 223.[2]

Tessin. Gerbereiindustrie. 1896. IV. 493.[2]

Tessin, Wilhelm, Freiherr von. Ueber den Anbau des Nadelholzes durch Stecklinge. 1840. IV. 149.[2]

— Anleitung zur praktischen Geometrie. 1818. IV. 263.

— Beiträge zu der Lehre von der Ausmittelung des Holzertrages. 1839. IV. 216.

— Ueber Durchforstungen. 1834. IV. 173.

— Forststatistik von Württemberg. 1823. IV. 356.[1]

— Ueber die Gewinnung des Stock- und Wurzelholzes in den Wäldern. 1836. IV. 385.[2]

— Ueber den Holzzuwachs. 1838. IV. 232.

— Eine merkwürdige Eiche. 1831. II. 138.[1]

— Ueber die Niederwald-Wirthschaft. 1834. IV. 132.[1]

— Ueber den Waldbau im Allgemeinen. 1838. IV. 129.

Tessmann, (Oberförster in Rossla). Der Wald in Skandinavien. 1879. IV. 342.[2]

Testimony taken before the Assembly committee on public lands and forestry. 1891. IV. 339.

Testrup, Søren. Om Skoves Opelskning med Hensyn til den danske Flaades Skibsbyggerie. 1811. IV. 424.[2]

Tests. 1899. IV. 411.[1]
Tests of timber. 1894. IV. 416.[1]
Tests of western Australian timbers. 1898. IV. 409.
Testu. Mesures à prendre à l'occasion des incendies de forêts. 1866. IV. 184.[1]
Tetmajer, Lud. Holz. 1884. IV. 408.
— Methoden und Resultate der Prüfung der schweiz. Bauhölzer. 1884. IV. 415.[1]
Tétreau, A. Commentaire de la loi du 4 avril 1882. 1883. IV. 185.[2]
Tettelbach, Moritz. Hülfsblätter zum Studium der Botanik. 1821. I. 85.
Tetzlaff, Gotthard. Die Holzreste von Leubingen. 1881. IV. 62.[2]
Tetzner, Walter VOIGTLANDER-. See VOIGTLANDER-TETZNER, Walter.
Teulère, Joseph. Observations sur les montagnes. 1809. IV. 185.[1]
Teusscher, R. Een voor Indie aanbevelenswaardige Appel. 1899. III. 426.[2]
Der **Teutsche** Fruchtgarten. III. 13.
Der **Teutsche** Obstgärtner. III. 13.
Die mit **teutschen** Saiten überzogene heilige Kron-Harffe. See HOHBERG, W. H., Freiherr von. 1680. V. xxv.[3]
Teuwsen, Eugen. Die Erhöhung der Nutzholzausbeute. 1889. IV. 245.
— Oberholz-Erziehung im Mittelwalde. 1889. IV. 131.
Texas — Agricultural and mechanical college — Agricultural experiment stations. Annual report. Bulletin. III. 8.
Texas — Agricultural experiment stations. See TEXAS — AGRICULTURAL AND MECHANICAL COLLEGE ... III. 8.
Texas; her resources and capabilities. 1881. III. 264.[1]
Texas state medical association. Transactions. I. 7.[1]
Texidor y Cos, Juan. Apuntes para la flora de España. 1869. I. 421.
— & **Casasa,** Antonio. Farmacopea general. 1875. III. 256.[1]
Texte de la première ordonnance forestière ... Zurich. See HOCH-OBERKEITLICHES Mandat ... 1715. IV. 305.
Textile American and manufacturers' gazette. See MANUFACTURERS' gazette. IV. 4.
Textile plants. 1856. III. 233.[2]
Textor, Benedict. Stirpium differentiae ex Dioscoride. 1534. I. 277.
Textor, F. Prijsvraag ... over B. te Gempt. Verhandeling over het aanleggen van bosschen. 1831. IV. 140.
— Voorgesteld onderzoek over het geen eene doelmatige behandeling van bosschen. 1831. IV. 47.[1]
Teyler's tweede genootschap. Verhandelingen. I. 16.
Teysmann, Johannes Elias. Aanteekeningen uit het dagboek mijner reis over Bangka. 1873. I. 466.
— Aanteekeningen van inlandsche plantennamen van Bangka. 1864. I. 76.[1]
— Over den Arênboom. 1853. III. 320.[2]
— Bamboe-ringkod en tembelang. 1865. II. 59.[1]
— Bekort verslag eener botanische dienstreis naar de Molukken. 1877. I. 466.
— Bekort verslag eener dienstreis naar Billiton. 1875. I. 469.[2]
— Bepaling der planten Toembaran en Saloewai. 1868. II. 146.[1] 153.[2]
— Bijdrage tot de geschiedenis der Kinakultuur. 1863. III. 715.
— Botanische reis over Banka. 1857. I. 467.
— Botanische Reise durch das westliche Sumatra. 1857. I. 467.
— Botanische Reise über Banka. 1857. I. 467.
— Dagverhaal eener botanische reis over de westkust van Sumatra. 1857. I. 467.
— Eenige aanteekeningen omtrent de Cycas circinalis. 1851. II. 4.[2]
— Enumération des plantes envoyées de Java. 1859. I. 68.[1]
— Extrait du récit d'un voyage à la Nouvelle-Guinée. 1876. I. 499.[1]
— De Gambier-kultuur. 1874. III. 748.[1]
— Getah pertja. 1875. III. 668.[3]
— Getah pertjah en andere getahsoorten. 1851. III. 228.[2]
— Handleiding voor de Katoen kultuur. 1862. III. 587.[1]
— Iets over de Widjojo Koesoemo. 1855. III. 388.[3]
— Over de Kajoe-Bengkoe. 1862. III. 274.[3]
— Over kamferbereiding in Japan. 1865. III. 404.[2]
— De Kamferboom in den Liengga-Archipel. 1875. III. 611.[3]
— Over de Kroeing boomen. 1862. III. 610.[3]

— Kruidkundige waarnetuingen ... Buitenzorg. 1850. I. 67.[3]
— 's Lands plantentuin te Buitenzorg in 1850. 1851. I. 67.[1]
— De Lodoicea sechellarum. 1870. III. 327.[1]
— Mienjak krowreng. 1875. III. 610.[2]
— Nog iets over de Nagelteelt. 1843. III. 635.[3]
— Notes recueillies pendant un voyage dans les Moluques. 1861. I. 465.
— Peperkultuur en bereiding. 1875. III. 343.[1]
— Over de Petier- en Bengkoe-boomen. 1867. III. 483,[1] 669.[1]
— Over de plant Kelajangan. 1868. II. 471.[2]
— Reise nach den Molukken. 1861. I. 466.
— Sagoe kultuur en bereiding. 1875. III. 327.[2]
— De Tangkalak of Malehboom. 1873. III. 407.[1]
— Taroentoem. 1875. IV. 529.[1]
— Uittreksel uit een dagverhaal eener reis door Midden-Java. 1855. I. 469.[1]
— Uittreksel uit het dagverhaal eener reis door Oost-Java. 1856. I. 469.[1]
— Over eene verhoogde temperatuur, bij den mannelijken bloei van Cycas circinalis. 1851. II. 4.[2]
— Verslag eener botanische reis naar Banka. 1874. I. 466.
— Verslag eener botanische reis naar Borneo's Westkust. 1875. I. 469.[2]
— Verslag eener botanische reis over Timor. 1874. I. 466.
— Verslag eener reis naar Nieuw-Guinea. 1881. I. 499.[1]
— Verslag eener reis naar Siam. 1863. I. 469.[2]
— Verslag over de . . reis in de Molukken. 1861. I. 466.
— Over di ziekte van den Kakaoboom. 1862. III. 593.[2]
— Over eene zijdelingsche bloem-ontwikkeling aan den stam van Fourcroya tuberosa. 1851. II. 89.[2]
— See also BINNENDIJK, Simon & TEYSMANN, J. E.; VRIESE, W. H. de & TEYSMANN, J. E.
— & **Binnendijk,** Simon. Bijdrage tot de kennis van het echte Ijzerhout. 1863. II. 225.[1]
— — Catalogus plantarum ... in Horto botanico bogoriensi. 1866. I. 68.[1]
— — Over eenige planten ... welke gezegd worden getah op te leveren. 1854. III. 230. — 1855. III. 228.[3]
— — Ueber Kaju Garu. 1862. II. 512.[1]
— — Over een nieuw plantengeslacht ... Capellenia. 1866. II. 441.[1]
— — Nieuwe plantensoorten in 's Lands plantentuin te Buitenzorg. 1851. I. 465.
— — Plantae novae Horti bogoriensis. 1855. I. 465.
— — Plantae novae Horti bogoriensis ... quas ... adjunctas ... communicat G. H. De Vriese. 1854. I. 67.[2]
— — Plantae novae ... in Horto bogoriensi. 1862. I. 68.[1]
— — Plantae novae in Horto bogoriensi. 1862. I. 68.[1]
— — Sur quelques plantes nouvelles de la flore indienne. 1861. I. 465.
— & **Rost van Tonningen,** D. W. Berigt aangaande eenige plantendeelen. 1861. III. 275.[1]
Teysmannia. III. 26.[1]
Teyssedre. Barème métrique pour le cubage des bois. 1849. IV. 223.
Teza, E. Che nomi abbia nell' India la pianta detta Cachi da N. de Conti. 1898. II. 146.[3]
Teza, Emilio. Dei nomi dell' Olivo. 1878. II. 713.[2]
Th., V. Die Korkeiche in Spanien. 1891. IV. 517.[2]
Thaarup, Frederik. Den danske Stats Forst- og Jagt-Statistik. 1842. IV. 343.[1]
— Fragmenter om hvad hidtil hos os er foretaget i Henseende til Brændebesparelse. 1796. IV. 281.[3]
— Om Norges Skovvæsen. 1792. IV. 343.[3]
Thacher, Mrs. G. W. Alpine flowers of Colorado. 1889. I. 325.
Thacher, James. The American new dispensatory. 1810. III. 246.
— The American orchardist. 1822. III. 132.[2]
Thackeray, W. M. Pruning forest trees. 1844. IV. 170.
Thaer, (Dr.). Unter welchen Voraussetzungen ist es gerathen, landwirthschaftlich benutzten Boden aufzuforsten. 1890. IV. 155.[1]
Thaer, A. D. Grondbeginselen van den wetenschappelijken landbouw. 1842. III. 36.[1]
Thakur Das, LALA. See LALA THAKUR DAS.
Thal, Richard. Erneute Untersuchungen über Zusammensetzung ... des Ericolins. 1883. III. 647.[1]
Thalacker, J. F. F. De gummi et ligni Guajaci virtutibus. 1800. III. 494.[1]
Thalbitzer, S. Skovtræernes Saaning og Plantning. 1876. IV. 103.[2]
— See also MÜLLER, P. E. & THALBITZER, S.

Thaler. Beitrag zur Durchforstungsfrage. 1897. IV. 175.[1]
Thalius, Joannes. ·Sylva Hercynia. 1588. I. 372.
Thaon, L. Aménagements des forêts d'Utelle. 1880. IV. 360.
Tharander forstliches Jahrbuch. *See* FORSTWIRTHSCHAFT-LICHES Jahrbuch. IV. 8.
Tharandt — Königl. Forstakademie. Katalog der Bibliothek. *See* BECK, Richard. 1900. IV. 2.
Thate, Alexander. Über die Wasserverteilung in heliotropisch gekrümmten Pflanzenteilen. 1882. I. 167.
Thayer, Emma Homan. Wild flowers of the Pacific Coast. 1887. I. 325.
Thays, Charles. Le Chêne gigantesque de la Balme. 1886. II. 139.[1]
— Les Eucalyptus en Angleterre. 1883. III. 633.[2]
— Nouveau collier pour arbres. 1889. III. 199.
— Utilisation des écorces d'oranges. 1885. III. 501.[2]
Sur le thé. 1848. III. 606.
Le Thé comme feuille à fumer. 1895. III. 608.[1]
Le Thé de l'Europe. *See* ANDRY DE BOISREGARD, Nicolas. 1712. III. 605.
Le Thé de la Caroline. 1874. III. 531.[2]
Thea cultivation in the Caucasus. 1895. III. 601.[1]
Theatrum florae. 1622. I. 284.
Thébat-Larché. Les Conifères nouveaux employés dans la grande culture. 1858. III. 291.
— L'Érable à sucre. 1858. IV. 527.[1]
— Multiplication du Pistachier. 1858. III. 526.[1]
— Naturalisation d'arbres résineux. 1858. III. 291.
— Le Sapin Épicea. 1857. III. 305.[1]
Thedenius, Knut Frederik. Anmärkningar om Herjedalens vegetation. 1838. I. 354.
— Beredning af stärkelse ... ur frukterna af Aesculus. 1854. III. 538.[1]
— Beskrifning på Ulmus montana With. var. coriifolia. 1890. II. 144.[1]
— Botaniska Exkursioner i Stockholmstrakten. 1859. I. 355.
— Konung Fredrik den Stores Lind. 1852. II. 516.[1]
— Märkvärdiga träd i Sachsen. 1856. I. 296.[1]
— Mångfaldigt begagnande af den vanliga Tallen. 1852. IV. 482.[2]
— Ötoba. 1855. III. 402.[1]
— Ovanligt blomningssätt. 1851. I. 237.
— Säckträdet. 1853. III. 366.[1]
— Sjuhundradeåriga Orangeriträd. 1851. II. 402.[1]
— Skandinaviska florans novitier. 1853. II. 517.[2]
— Stockholmstraktens phanerogamer. 1850. I. 355.
— Svensk skol-botanik. 1861. I. 356.
— *See also* ANDERSSON, N. J. & THEDENIUS, K. F.; SIEURIN, J. & THEDENIUS, K. F.
Theecultuur in Britsch Indië en op Java. 1838. III. 602.[1]
Theecultuur op Ceylon. 1900. III. 604.[1]
Theel, Hjalmar. *See* NORDENSKIÖLD, A. E. & THEEL, Hjalmar.
De Theeplant. Is zij uit China afkomstig? 1880. II. 552.[1]
De Theeplant, haar vaderland en de legende van Djarma. 1885. II. 552.[1]
Theile, Friedrich.· De viribus Daphnes Mezerei nonnulla. 1838. III. 627.[2]
Theile, R. Ueber Legumin.· 1868. I. 175.
Theilemann, (*Oberforster, Oberherold*). Bericht über den Erfolg und die Kosten des Leimens. 1897. IV. 202.
Theilkuhl, Friedrich. Land- und forstwirthschaftliche Verhältnisse. 1852. IV. 68.
Théis, Alexandre de. Glossaire de botanique. 1810. I. 76.[2]
Thelaus, V. M. Om skogarne och skogsväsendet. 1865. IV. 101.
Thelning, Carolus August. Rémedia guineensia. *See* AFZELIUS, Adam. 1813. III. 93.[1]
Thélu. Forestry at the Paris exhibition. 1879. IV. 185.[1]
— Notice sur les étais de mines en France. 1878. IV. 425.[2]
— La sylviculture à l'Exposition universelle. 1878. IV. 163.
Thénard, Arnold Paul Edmond. Note sur la manière dont les phosphates passent dans les plantes. 1858. I. 161.
— Recherches sur la destruction de l'eumolpe. 1854. III. 563.
— Réponse aux questions de M. Fremy. 1879. III. 571.
— Ueber die Vertilgung des Weinstock-Fallkäfers. 1854. III. 563.
Thenius, Georg. Die Theise und ihre Producte. 1879. III. 227.
— Das Holz und seine Destillations-Producte. 1880. IV. 432.[2]
— Die Meiler- und Retorten-Verkohlung. 1885. IV. 395.

Theobald, G. L. *See* CASSEBEER, J. H. & THEOBALD, G. L.
Theobald, John. Medulla medicinae universae. 1749. III. 252.
Le Theobroma Cacao. 1897. III. 595.[1]
Theolander, David. Novitiae florae suecicae. *See* FRIES, E. M. ·1814. I. 352.
Theophrastos Eresios. Dell' historia delle piante. 286 B. C. I. 272.
┬ De historia plantarum et de cansis plantarum. 286 B. C. . 271.[2]
— De historia plantarum libri. 286 B. C. I. 271.[2]
—L   de historia et de causis plantarum. 286 B. C. I. 272ibri
— La storia delle piante. 286 B. C. V. XIII.[2]
— Theophrasti de causis plantarum. 286 B. C. I. 272.
— Theophrasti de historia et causis plantarum libri quindecim. 286 B. C. I. 271,[1] V. XIII.[2]
— Theophrasti de historia et de causis plantarum, 286 B. C. I. 271,[2] 530.[1]
— Theophrasti de historia plantarum lib. IX. 286 B. C. I. 530,[1] V. XIII.[2]
— Theophrasti de suffruticibus, herbisque. 286 B. C. I. 272.
— Theophrasti Eresii graece et latine Opera omnia. 286 B. C. I. 272.
— Theophrasti Eresii Historia plantarum. 286 B. C. I. 272.
— Theophrasti Eresii Opera. 286 B. C. I. 272, 530.[2]
— Theophrasti Eresii quae supersunt Opera. 286 B. C. I. 272.
— Theophrasti Opera. 286 B. C. I. 272.
— Theophrasti Περὶ φυτῶν ἱστορίας καὶ περὶ φυτῶν αἰτιῶν. 286 B. C. I. 271.[1]
— Theophrast's Naturgeschichte der Gewächse. 286 B. C. I. 272.
Theoretisch-praktische Anleitung zur neueren Forstwissenschaft. *See* BENECKENDORF, von. 1783. IV. 95.
Theorie en praktijk bij de Koffie-cultuur. 1899. III. 727.
La théorie et la pratique du jardinage. *See* DEZALLIER D'ARGENVILLE, A. J. 1711. III. 105.
Theorie und Praxis der Forstpolitik. 1872. IV. 269.
Les théories passent, les faits restent. 1868. I. 117.[1]
Theorin, G. R. A. Om växternas hår och yttre glandler. 1868. I. 112.[1]
— Växtgeografisk skildring af södra Halland.. 1865. I. 356.
Theorin, Per Gustaf Emanuel. Om bladtandsglandlerna hos en del Salices. 1881. II. 103.[2]
— Några växtmikrokemiska anteckningar. 1885. I. 176.
— Utvecklingen ... hos några växters taggar och borst. 1880. I. 112.[2]
— Om de värmemängder, som synas vara nödvändiga för ... växters första lifsyttringar. 1868. I. 232.[1]
— Växtmikrokemiska studier. 1884. I. 176.
— Växt-triehomernas benägenhet till formförändringar. 1876. I. 112.[2]
Therapeutic gasette. I. 7.[1]
The therapeutic properties of Saw Palmetto. *See* PARKE, Davis & Co. 1898. III. 331.[1]
Thériot. Quelques faits de tératologie végétale. 1887. II. 103.[2]
Thesaurus aromatariorum. *See* SUARDUS, Paulus. 1504.[2] III. 239.
Thesaurus Evonymi Philiatri de remediis secretis. *See* GESNER, Conrad. 1558. III. 239.
Thesaurus rei herbariae hortensisque. *See* GMELIN, P. F. & BÖHMER, G. R. 1788. I. 292.
Thesleff, Arthur. Hvitbladig lönn. 1895. II. 479.[2]
— Svampvegetationen i Raivola Lärkträdsskog. 1893. III. 304.[2]
Thessmann. Die Presslersche Reinertragstheorie. 1877. IV. 256.
Theulier, Henri, (*jr.*). Les Antigonons. 1895. III. 386.[1]
— Les Aralias et leur culture. 1899. III. 641.[1]
— De la chlorophylle. 1894. I. 142.
— Culture du Daubentonia Tripetiana. 1897. III. 487.[2]
— L'Eucalyptus à Madagascar. 1896. III. 634.[1]
— La greffe par approche. 1899. III. 163.[2]
— Les Kennedya. 1899. III. 480.[1]
— Multiplication des arbres verts résineux. 1896. III. 294.[2]
— Multiplication et culture du Tamarix. 1896. III. 612.[1]
— Du rôle de la chlorophylle. 1895. III. 181.[1]
— Le Spartium hispanicum. 1899. III. 477.[1]
Theunen, August. Guide à l'usage des amateurs de Roses. 1893. III. 450, V. XXIX.[1]
— Handleiding voor rozenliefhebbers. 1891. V. XXIX.[1]

Theunis, G. Oreopanax Sanderianum. 1893. III. 643.²
Theurer, (*Director*). Die Verwendung von Rosskastanien. 1891. III. 538.²
Theuriet, André. L'épeichette, la sittelle, le grimpereau. 1899. IV. 91.¹
Theuss, Theodor. Allgemeines Blumen-Lexicon. 1811. III. 74.
— Handbuch des gesammten Gartenbaues. 1804. III. 103.
— Die Obstbaumzucht. 1804. III. 136.
Thevenot. Catalogue des plantes . . . de Lons-le-Saunier. 1879. I. 415.
Thévenot, Arsène. Le Bombyx du Pin. 187.? IV. 461.¹
Thevenot, Jean de. Relation d'un voyage fait au Levant. 1664. I. 478.
— Relation de l'Indostan. 1684. I. 470.²
Thevenot, Melchisedec. Relation de divers voayges [*sic*]. 1683. V. xvi.²
— Relations de divers voyages curieux. 1663. III. 217.
Thevet, André. Les singularites de la France antarctique. 1558. I. 327, 347.
Thézard, Arthur. Les engrais chimiques. 1898. IV. 145.
— Du reboisement et de la fertilisation des forêts. 1897. IV. 155.¹
— Les scories ou phosphate basique. 1897. IV. 545.²
Thiac, Eug. de. Discours concernant la sylviculture. 1882. IV. 122.¹
Thibault, Paul. Note sur l'évonymine. 1883. III. 532.¹
Thibault, R. Des incendies de forêts en Algérie. 1866. V. xxx.¹
Thibault de Chanvalon, J. B. *See* CHANVALON, J. B. T. de.
Thibaut. Culture des Pelargonium. 1835. III. 491.¹
Thibaut. Anopterus glandulosa. 1868. III. 409.²
— Clematis Fortunei. 1867. III. 390.²
— Clematis Jackmannii. 1868. III. 390.²
— Deutzia crenata flore pleno. 1867. III. 410.²
— Fuchsia erecta superba. 1868. III. 640.¹
Thibierge, Adolphe. Note sur l'acide du Sureau à grappes. 1847. III. 752.²
— & Remilly. De l'amidou du marron d'Inde. 1857. III. 538.¹
Thibout, E. Recherches sur l'appareil mâle des gymnospermes. 1896. II. 1.
Thickened branch of Laburnum. 1868. III. 480.²
Thicknesse, Ralph. A treatise on foreign vegetables. 1749. III. 54, 441.
Thiébaut, L. Additions au catalogue de M. de Lambertye des plantes . . . de la Marne. 1881. I. 416.
Thiébaut, Victor. Le phylloxéra en France. 1900. III. 575.¹
Thiébaut de Berneaud, Arsenne. Coup d'œil historique . . . sur le Monte Circello. 1814. I. 425.
— Exposition de la doctrine botanique. 1822. I. 79.²
— Du Genêt. 1810. III. 474.¹ 477.¹ 488.²
— Manuel . . . du vigneron français. 1824. III. 554.²
— Mémoire sur le Cactus Opuntia. 1813. III. 623.²
— Mémoire sur le Cirier ou Arbre à cire. 1810. III. 352.²
— Mémoire sur les époques historiques de l'Orme en France. 1825. II. 142.²
— Monographie de l'Orme. 1811. II. 142.²
— Recherches sur les époques historiques de l'Orme. 1814. II. 142.¹
— Recherches sur les plantes connues des anciens sous le nom de Cytise. 1814. II. 350.¹
— Traité élémentaire de botanique. 1837. I. 87.
— The vine-dresser's . . . manual. 1824. III. 554.²
— Voyage à Ermenonville. 1826. I. 408.
Thiede, C. G. Das Ganze des Seidenbaues. 1845. III. 376.
Thiel. Sur un nouveau taenicide; le Moussena. 1889. III. 466.¹
Thielau, Friedrich von. Ueber die Abtriebserträge der Fichte. 1853. IV. 458.
— Beschreibung eines reinen Ahornbestandes. 1850. IV. 526.²
— Einíge neuere Beobachtungen aus Prof. Dr. Schübeler's jüngstem Werk. 1876. III. 67.¹
— Ertrags-Resultat aus dem Abnutz . . . im Niederforst des Lampersdorfer Vorbergs-Reviers. 1855. IV. 260.²
— Ueber die Folgen äusserer Verletzungen der Bäume. 1874. III. 180.³
— Forstbeschreibung von Lampersdorf. 1852. IV. 352.
— Holzanbau mit Rasenasche. 1849. IV. 152.
— Nachweis der Verwerthung von . . . Eschen-Nutzholz. 1859. IV. 535.²

— Nachweis des Holz- und Geld-Ertrages von einem Morgen Wald zu Lampersdorf. 1857. IV. 260.²
— Schöne Waldbäume . . . Lampersdorf. 1863. I. 296.¹
— Die Wälder, das Luftmeer und das Wasser. 1855. IV. 43.
Thiele, Eugène. *See* STEBLER, F. G. & THIELÉ, Eugène.
Thiele, J. P. Disputatio juridica de jure seminis. 1693. IV. 313.
Thiele, Rudolf. Casi di danneggiamenti . . . causati dal Morimus asper. 1899. III. 192.¹
— Frühlingsfarben der Gehölzarten. 1893. III. 205.²
— Über eine Krankheit der Lindenblüten. 1896. III. 585.²
— Neues aus dem Leben der Blutlaus. 1899. III. 192.¹
Thiele, Wilhelm. Tafeln zur Inhaltsbestimmung der Rundhölzer. 1871. IV. 226.
Thielens, Armand. Acquisitions de la flore belge. 1870. I. 392.
— Compte-rendu de la onzième herborisation générale de la Société de botanique de Belgique. 1872. I. 386.
— Flore médicale belge. 1862. III. 77.²
— Nouvelles annotations à la flore . . . 1868. II. 350.²
— Voyage botanique et paléontologique en Eifel. 1872. I. 386.
— & Wesmael, Alfred. Annotations à la flore . . . du Brabant. 1862. I. 392.
Thiem, (*Oberförster, Seitenberg*). Aphoristische Bemerkung über Fichtenvollsaat. 1849. IV. 453.
— Beleuchtung der Abhandlung Heft 1853, p. 259 ff. 1854. IV. 190.
— Bericht über die . . . Wald-Exkursionen in das k. Forst-Revier Klodnitz. 1855. IV. 352.
— Beschreibung des k. prinzlichen Forstreviers Seitenberg. 1846. IV. 352.
— Beschreibung einer seltenen Tanne. 1856. IV. 447.¹
— Nachricht über einen noch unbekannten Insektenfrass. 1849. IV. 455.
— Notizen über Durchforstungen in Gebirgs-Revieren. 1846. IV. 173.
— Notizen über Schneedruck. 1850. IV. 189.¹
— Statuten für die Holzhauer-Genossenschaft im Forstrevier Seitenberg. 1852. IV. 310.¹
— Ueber verdämmende . . . Forstunkräuter. 1849. IV. 210.³
— Wie ist die Kultur der Fichte . . . zu bewirken? 1852. IV. 453.²
— Wie ist die Nachzucht der Rothbuche . . . zu erzielen? 1851. IV. 494.
— Wie stellen sich die Abtriebs-Erträge der Fichte. 1853. IV. 458.
— Ueber Windbruch im Gebirge. 1847. IV. 189.¹
— Zusammenstellung der Einnahmen und Ausgaben der Holzhauer-Genossenschafts-Kasse. 1856. IV. 310.¹
— *See also* KLINGNER & THIEM.
Thienaeus, Antonius Maria. Series plantarum . . . in horto botanico . . . Antonii Mariae Thienaei. 1802. I. 61.
Thienemann, Fr. August Ludwig & Guenther, G. B. Reise im Norden Europas. 1824. I. 353.
Thienemann, R. Bericht über eine Reise nach Mauritius. 1898. I. 482.
Thiercelin, L. Action des sels solubles de strychnine. 1866. III. 683.¹
— Note sur l'emploi du curare. 1860. III. 683.¹
Thieren, Alexander. Anleitung zur Forstwirthschaft. 1878. IV. 104.¹
Thieriot, Albert. Cawford's Stockrode- und Hebe-Apparat. 1872. IV. 386.
— Zur Forstarbeiter-Frage. 1859. IV. 310.¹
— Der Forstwirthschaftsbetrieb in den küstenländischen Staatsforsten. 1873. IV. 374.²
— Die Nothwendigkeit wissenschaftlicher Ausbildung für den Forstmann. 1829. IV. 29.
— Poradnik dla dziedziców i gospodarzy lasów. 1845. IV. 101.
— Techuologia leśna. 1856. IV. 381.
Thierriat. Observations sur la culture des arbres à hôte tige. 1753. III. 143, *IV. 121.*
— Osservazioni sopra la cultura degli alberi di alto fusto. 1753. III. 143, *IV. 121.*
Thierry, A. J. Un ennemi du Cacaoyer. 1900. III. 593.²
— Het enten van den Koffie-, den Cacao- en den Notemuskaatboom. 1899. III. 163.²
— Notes sur la greffage du Caféier. 1899. III. 733.²
Thierry, H. Een vijand van den Koffieboom. 1900. III. 737.

Thiersant, Philibert DABRY DE. *See* DABRY DE THIERSANT, Philibert.

Thiersch, E. L. Die Forstkäfer. 1830. IV. 91.[2]

Thiersch, Ernst. Bemerkungen und Notizen über die Cultur ... der Buche. 1848. IV. 494.

— Ueber die Dauerhaftigkeit der Samen. 1845. I. 527,[1] *IV. 147.*[1]

— Eine merkwürdige Abnormität von einer Fichte. 1844. II. 37.[1]

— Ueber den Waldbau. 1823. IV. 117.

Thiéry, E. Dendromètre Raoult. 1886. IV. 215.

— Étude sur les petits chemins de fer forestiers. 1897. IV. 392.

— Une nouvelle lame de soie. 1885. IV. 393.

— Le tachéomètre Sanguet. 1897. IV. 265.

— Traité sur les sciéries. 188.? IV. 393.

— Les transports par cables aériens. 1897. IV. 392.

— & **Demonet**, **Ch.** Les transports par cables aériens. 1896. IV. 392.

— & **Petitcollot.** Rapport ... sur la résistance des bois résineux. 1896. IV. 410.

Thiery de Menonville, Nicolas Joseph. Traité de la culture du Nopal. 1787. III. 623.[2]

Thil, André. Achat, récolte ... des graines résineuses. 1884. IV. 148.

— Constitution anatomique du bois. 1900. *I. 126,* IV. 63.[1]

— Description des sections transversales de 100 espèces de bois indigènes. 1895. I. 38,[1] *IV. 18.*[1]

— Étude sur les fractures des bois. 1900. IV. 411.[1]

— La sylviculture à l'Exposition universelle. 1879. IV. 336.[1]

— & **Thouroude.** Sur une étude micrographique du tissu ligneux. 1889. I. 126, *IV. 63.*[2]

Thile, Johann. De usu et abusu potus calidi cum herba Thee. 1690. III. 605.

Thilenius, H. C. De aquae Laurocerasi medico usu. 1795. III. 438.[1]

Thilmany, Waldemar. American wood preserving company. 1875. IV. 419.

Thinard, G. Crotons et Dracaenas, leur multiplication. 1896. III. 158.

Thinning a plantation of Abies Douglasi. 1887. IV. 483.[2]

Thirault, C. J. Encore quelques mots sur la maladie de la Vigne. 185.? III. 575.[1]

— Nouveau mode d'emploi du soufre dans le traitement de la maladie de la Vigne. 1855. III. 576.

— Traitement de la maladie de la Vigne. 1856. III. 576.

Thiriart, T. F. Catalogue des plantes et arbustes cultivés au jardin botanique de Cologne. 1806. I. 485.

Thiriat, X. Notes sur quelques plantes ... des Vosges. 1878. I. 415.

Thiriaux, Jean Baptiste Joseph. Essai sur la topographie ... de Saint-Antoine de Guagno. 1829. I. 419.[1]

Thiselton-Dyer. *See* DYER, THISELTON-.

Thode, Justus. Die botanischen Höhenregionen Natals. 1894. I. 495.

— Die Küstenvegetation von Britisch-Kaffrarien. 1890. I. 495.

Tholen, N. G. De Abeelboom. 1855. III. 345.[1]

— Het gommen der Kersenboomen. 1856. III. 435.[1]

— Handleiding voor boomkweekers. 1855. III. 104, IV. 107.[1]

— Over de Laurierkers van Carolina. 1855. III. 435.[2]

Tholór, E. T. Examen classis gynandriae. *See* THUNBERG, C. P. 1824. I. 251.

Thomae, C. Alphabetisches Verzeichniss der in der Umgegend von Wiesbaden wildwachsenden Pflanzen. 1841. I. 380.

Thomann, A. Synopsis der in der Umgebung von Krems wildwachsenden Phanerogamen. 1859. I. 441.

Thomas. Histoire naturelle de quelques plantes médicinales du Mexique. 1867. III. 58.

— Sur le Sericographis Mohitli. 1866. III. 709.[1]

Thomas, D. Du classement des meilleures variétés de Rosiers. 1896. III. 451.[1]

Thomas, David. On the Locust tree. 1817. II. 382.[1]

— Travels through the western country. 1819. I. 313.

Thomas, Emanuel. Catalogue des plantes de Sardaigne. 1841. I. 426, V. XXII.[3]

Thomas, Ernest. *See* ROOS, L. & THOMAS, Ernest.

Thomas, F. W. L. On the geological age of the pagan monuments of the Outer Hebrides. 1862. I. 401.

Thomas, Friedrich August Wilhelm. Aeltere und neue Beobachtungen über Phytopto-Cecidien. 1877. I. 214.[1]

— Die Ansiedelung der ... Moosbeere (Cranberry). 1895. III. 664.[1]

— Beiträge zur Kenntnis der in den Alpen vorkommenden Phytoptocecidien. 1886. I. 216.[1]

— Beiträge zur Kenntniss der Milbengallen. 1873. I. 215.[1]

— Beitrag zur Kenntniss alpiner Phytoptocecidien. 1885. I. 216.[1]

— Eine Bemerkung zu Julius Sachs' physiologischen Notizen. 1898. I. 214.[2]

— Bemerkungen über die Holzkröpfe. 1888. *I. 213,*[2] *III. 544,*[1] IV. 486,[2] *490.*[2]

— Beschreibung neuer ... Acarocecidien. 1876. I. 215.[1]

— Dauerfaltungen der Rothbuchenblätter. 1894. IV. 497.

— Die dicke Tanne bei Elgersburg. 1898. II. 24.[3]

— Diervilla canadensis Willd. im Thüringer Wald. 1883. II. 835.[1]

— Die Eiben am Veronikaberg bei Martinroda. 1899. II. 11.[3]

— Ueber einige neue deutsche Cecidien. 1882. III. 414.[1]

— Ueber einige neue exotische Cecidien. 1889. I. 214.[3]

— Eintheilung der Phytoptocecidien. 1877. I. 214.[1]

— Entwicklungsgeschichte zweier Phytoptus-Gallen an Prunus. 1872. III. 431.[1]

— Ueber ein ... Exemplar einer vielgipfigen Fichte. 1883. II. 37.[1]

— Die Fenstergalle des Bergahorns. 1895. III. 536.[1]

— De foliorum ... Coniferarum structura anatomica. 1863. II. 17.[2]

— Ueber die ... Gallen der Birnbäume. 1880. III. 446.[1]

— Ueber die von Grapholita Zebeana Rtzb. verursachten Lärchenastknoten. 1881. IV. 451.

— Der Holzkropf von Populus tremula. 1874. IV. 486.[3]

— Kurze Anleitung zur Zimmerkultur der Kakteen. 1896. III. 158.

— Larve und Lebensweise der Cecidomyia Pseudococcus. 1890. III. 351.[2]

— Über die Lebensweise der Stachelbeermilbe. 1896. III. 414.[2]

— Ueber die Mückenblattgalle von Vitis vinifera. 1886. III. 563.

— Ein neuer Stachelbeerfeind. 1877. III. 414.[2]

— Phänologische Beobachtungen aus ... Sachsen-Gotha. 1884.? I. 225.

— Phaenologische Beobachtungen zu Ohrdruf. 1888. I. 225.

— Ueber Phytoptus Duj. 1869. I. 214.[1]

— Schweizerische Milbengallen. 1872. I. 216.[1]

— Ein sechstes Phytoptocecidium von Acer. 1879. III. 534.[1]

— Suldener Phytoptocecidien. 1886. I. 216.[2]

— Ueber das durch eine Tenthredinide erzeugte Myelocecidium von Lonicera. 1888. III. 750.[1]

— Teratologisches von Engstlenalp. 1886. II. 290,[1] *679.*[1]

— Zur vergleichenden Anatomie der Coniferen-Laubblätter. 1865. II. 17.[2]

— Vielgipflige Fichten und Tannen. 1897. I. 296.[3]

— Ueber 42 neue ... Cecidien. 1878. I. 214.[3]

Thomas, Gaëtan. Les réformes forestières sous Colbert. 1880. IV. 27.[1]

Thomas, H. S. Prickly-Pear as a protection for saplings. 1883. III. 624.[3]

Thomas, Hannah. *See* PAMMEL, L. H., BURNIP, J. R. & THOMAS, Hannah.

Thomas, J. K. Patriotischer Vorschlag zur Umschaffung aller öden ... Waldreviere in nutzbarem Holzbestand. 1802. IV. 169.[2]

Thomas, Jean Bazile. Des coupes sombres. 1853. IV. 382.[1]

— Inondations et reboisement. 1846. IV. 49.[3]

— Lettre du bucheron de la Nièvre. 1842. IV. 101.

— Traité général de statistique ... des bois. 1840. IV. 359.[1]

Thomas, John J. The American fruit culturist. 1846. III. 133.

— Circle culture of fruit trees. 1859. III. 133.

— Fruit culture. 1851. III. 133.

— Hedge plants and hedges. 1884. III. 214.[1]

Thomas, Joseph & **Moyer**, I. S. The plants, birds and mammals of Bucks county. 1876. I. 314.

Thomas, K. Die Kultur der Myrthe communis. n. d. III. 637.[1]

Thomas, Mason B. An apparatus for determining ... root pressure. 1892. I. 169.[1]

— The sab of trees. 1894. I. 156.[1]

— Periodicity of root pressure. 1897. I. 169.[1]

Thomas, O. Guide pratique de l'amateur de fruits. 1876. III. 85.

Thomas, Otto. Pflanzengeographisches Bild des Seoberges. 1876. I. 387.

— Wie steht es mit dem Saftlauf? 1873. III. 39.

Thomas, S. B. *See* MARTIN, W. K. & THOMAS, S. B.
Thomatis, D. & **Newport,** Howard. Peaberries and male Coffee plants. 1899. III. 733.[2]
Thomayer, František. České ovoce. I. Jablka. 1894. III. 426.[1]
— Heliotropium peruvianum à haute tige. 1892. III. 695.[1]
— Prunus Šimoni. 1887. III. 443.[1]
— Vysazování rostinových skupin. 1886. III. 166.
— Zvláštní umělé tvary ovocných stromů. 1886. III. 146.[2]
Thomé. Mémoire sur la culture du Mûrier blanc. 1763. III. 373.
— Mémoires sur la culture du Mûrier blanc. 1763. III. 373.
— Mémoires sur la manière d'élever les vers à soie. 1763. III. 373.
Thomé, Otto Wilhelm. Flora von Deutschland Oesterreich. 1886. I. 388.
— Das Gesetz der vermiedenen Selbstbefruchtung. 1870. I. 237.
— Lehrbuch der Botanik. 1874. I. 91, V. x.[2]
— Pflanzenbau und Pflanzenleben. 1874. I. 96.
— Text-book of structural and physiological botany. 1874. I. 91.
— Thier- und Pflanzengeographie. 1875. I. 300.
— Ueber das Vorkommen des Amygdalins. 1865. II. 272.[2]
Thomé, P. La cannelle d'Annam. 1893. IV. 520.[1]
— Les forêts de l'Annam et du Tonkin. 1890. IV. 377.[1]
— Les forêts de l'Indo-Chine. 1891. IV. 377.[1]
Thompson, A. On pruning forest trees. 1844. IV. 170.
Thompson, Caroline B. The structure . . . of internal phloem in Gelsemium. 1898. II. 718.[2]
Thompson, Charles Henry. The species of Cacti . . . under . . . Anhalonium. 1898. II. 589.[1]
Thompson, David D. Influence of forests on water courses. 1882. IV. 51.
Thompson, Eduard T. The wild Plums of Kansas. 1874. III. 432.[2]
Thompson, G. M. Botanical evolution. 1885. I. 529.[1]
Thompson, H. M. Plan of forest planting for the great plains of North America. 1883. IV. 155.[2]
Thompson, J. L. Olive culture. 1891. III. 676.[1]
Thompson, J. S. B. Trees, structure and growth. 1891. III. 37.[2]
Thompson, James. A complete treatise on the mensuration of timber. 1805. IV. 221.
Thompson, John. Botany displayed. 1798. I. 255.
Thompson, John Vaughan. A catalogue of plants . . . of Berwick. 1807. I. 396.
Thompson, *Lady* Mary. On the new Chinese silkworm. 1865. III. 507.[1]
Thompson, Phillips. Forestry, a neglected industry. 1897. IV. 271.[2]
Thompson, R. Report on insects destructive to woods. 1868. IV. 210.[2]
— Report on the forests of Mauritius. 1881. IV. 379.[1]
Thompson, R. S. On shelter-trees. 1900. III. 215.[2]
Thompson, Robert. Englische Stachelbeersorten. 1846. III. 414.[3]
Thompson, T. L. Brazil and its miraculous Palm tree. 1898. III. 324.[1]
— Brazil, its commerce and resources. 1898. III. 324.[1]
— A miraculous Palm tree. 1898. III. 324.[2]
Thompson, Thomas. Cedars and Deodars. 1850. II. 27.[1]
— Die Ceder und die Deodara. 1853. II. 27.[1]
Thompson, William. Comparison of the periods of flowering of certain plants. 1846 (1847). I. 222,[2] 226.[1]
— The English flower garden. 1855. III. 82.
Thompson, William J. Notes on Grape vines. 1894. III. 551.[1]
Thoms, George. Über die weisse Ablagerung im Teakholz. 1880. III. 697.[2]
— Ueber die Zusammensetzung einer weissen Ablagerung im Teak-Holz. 1877. III. 697.[2]
Thoms, Hermann. Ueber afrikanische Gummiproben. 1897. III. 466,[1] 468,[1] 473.[1]
— Analyse de fruits de l'arbre Mkomavi. 1900. III. 511.[3]
— Analyse der Früchte des Mkomavibaumes. 1900. III. 511.[3]
— Sur le baume de Pérou. 1898. III. 482.[1]
— Chemische Untersuchung des Pfeilgiftes . . . Enaeé. 1900. III. 690.[2]
— Ueber ein deutsch-ostafrikanisches Gummi. 1897. III. 463.[1]
— Ueber das Kautschukharz einer Euphorbie. 1897. III. 517.[2]

— Ueber ein ostafrikanisches kino aus Kilossa. 1897. II. 380.[1]
— Ueber Perubalsam. 1898. III. 482.[1]
— Rinde von Acacia Ferrotii/Warb. 1897. II. 327.[2]
— Semences de Paullinia. 1893. III. 540.[1]
— Ueber Telfairia-Oel. 1900. III. 754.[1]
— Untersuchung von Pflanzenteilen der Strychnos Dekindtiana. 1897. II. 720.[1]
Thoms, J. H. F. Anleitung zur Behandlung der Obstbäume. 1835. III. 137.
Thomsen, C. Roskilde-Egnens Flora. 1874. I. 357, V. XVIII.[2]
— Sams-Øgruppens Plantevækst. 1875. I. 357.
Thomsen, Th. Chemiske Undersøgelser over Sammensætningen af Træernes Ved. 1878. I. 155.
— Recherches chimiques sur la composition du bois des arbres. 187-. I. 155.
Thomson. Cultivation of Cacao, Bananas, and Indiarubber. 1894. III. 118.[2]
Thomson, A. On the injurious effects of Uroceras. 1857. IV. 445.
Thomson, Alexander. Observations on recent plantations. 1839. III. 123.[1]
Thomson, Anthony Todd. A conspectus of the pharmacopœias of the London, Edinburgh. 1825. III. 254.
— Elements of materia medica. 1832. III. 242.
— Lectures on the elements of botany. 1822. I. 100.[2]
— The London dispensatory. 1811. III. 253.
— Thomson's conspectus adapted to the British pharmacopœia of 1825. 1825. III. 254.
— Vereinigte Pharmacopoeen der Londoner, Edinburgher and Dubliner Medicinal-Collegien. 1825. III. 254.
Thomson, David. Handy book of fruit culture under glass. 1873. III. 142.
Thomson, Georg. Short method of discovering the virtues of plants. 1734. III. 259.[1]
Thomson, George. Quickset hedges. 1879. III. 422.[2]
Thomson, George M. On the fertilization etc., of New Zealand flowering plants. 1881. I. 240.[1]
— The flowering plants of New Zealand. 1883. I. 240.[1]
— Note on the cleistogamic flowers of Melicope. 1892. II. 408.[2]
— Notes on some Otago plants. 1877. I. 507.
Thomson, J. G. The expediency of establishing home nurseries. 1868. III. 154.[1]
Thomson, J. P. British New Guinea. *See* MUELLER, Ferdinand, *Baron* von. 1892. I. 499.
Thomson, *Mrs.* J. S. R. A beautiful southern native vine. 1886. III. 396.[2]
— A native Hydrangea. 1886. III. 412.[2]
Thomson, J. T. General report on the residency of Singapore. 1850. III. 129.[1]
Thomson, John. Planting on moss land. 1858. III. 150.[2]
— On the reclamation of neglected plantations. 1858. IV. 169.[2]
Thomson, R. Wodrow. The amateur's rosarium. 1862. III. 449.
Thomson, Robert. The Tapioca plant. 1900. III. 521.[1]
— *See also* GUNNING, E. H., THOMSON, Robert & SAWYER, A. M.
Thomson, Robert D. On tea oil. 1845. III. 606.
— Untersuchung des Harzes von Dammara australis. 1842. III. 297.[1]
Thomson, Samuel. New guide to health. 1822. III. 242.
— The Thomsonian materia medica. 1822. III. 242.
Thomson, Spencer. Wanderings among the wild flowers. 1854. I. 400.
— Wayside weeds. 1864. I. 401.
Thomson, Thomas. Chemistry of organic bodies. 1838. I. 151.[2]
— Einige Worte über das Klima und die Vegetation des Himalaya. 1851. I. 473.
— A list of timbers at the Port Blair settlement. 1861. IV. 400.[2]
— Note on the genus Hemigymnia. 1858. II. 748.[1]
— Notes on the herbarium of the Calcutta botanic garden. 1857. I. 67.[1]
— Report on the Hon'ble company's botanic garden. 1857. I. 67.[1]
— Sketch of the climate and vegetation of the Himalaya. 1851. I. 473.
— Some experiments on the milk of the Cow-tree. 1831. III. 367.[2]
— On the structure of seeds of Barringtonia. 1858. II. 611.[1]

Thomson, Thomas (*continued*).
— On two new genera of Compositae Mutisiaceae. 1867. II. 854.[1]
— Western Himalaya and Tibet. 1852. I. 473.
— *See also* HOOKER, *Sir* J. D. & THOMSON, Thomas.
Thomson, William. Oak bark. 1858. IV. 512.
— On plantation fences. 1858. IV. 146.[1]
— On planting. 1858. IV. 152.
— Practical arboriculture. 1872. III. 123.[1]
— A practical treatise on the cultivation of the Grape vine. 1862. III. 554.[1]
— On the reclamation of neglected plantations. 1872. IV. 169.[2]
— On thinning. 1858. IV. 173.
— Vinstokkens Dyrkning under Glas. 1862. III. 554.[1]
Thomson, *Sir* William. Sur les antécédents mécaniques du mouvement, de la chaleur et de la lumière. 1855. I. 229, *232*.[1]
Thon, C. F. G. Holzbeizkunst. 1822. IV. 422.[2]
Thon, Friedrich. Nützliches Handwörterbuch für angehende Forst- und Waidmänner. 1808. IV. 22.[2]
Thon, Theodor. Die Botanik in ihrer practischen Anwendung. 1828. III. 52.
Thonner, Frans. Im afrikanischen Urwald. 1898. I. 492.[1]
— Analytical key to the natural orders. 1895. I. 261.
— Clave para a determinação das familias das plantas. 1895. I. 261.
Thoorn, N. A. M. von der & **Alberts**, G. Over groenhart-hout. 1883. IV. 520.[1]
Thore, Jean. Essai d'une chloris ... des Landes. 1803. I. 406.
Thoreau, Henry David. Succession of forest trees. 1861. IV. 74.[1]
Thorel, Clovis. Notes médicales du voyage d'exploration du Mékong et de Cochinchine. 1870. I. 469.[3]
Thormählen, C. Ueber die verschiedenen Waldbodenarten. 1887. IV. 69.
— Was kann der Forstmann zur Verschönerung der Waldungen thun? 1887. IV. 137.[1]
— Welche Vorteile gewährt die Waldweide. 1887. IV. 135.[1]
— Wie soll die Verjüngung zurückgegangener Buchenorte am zweckmässigsten erfolgen. 1887. IV. 495.
Thorn embedded in a Hornbeam. 1890. II. 262.[2]
Thorne, C. E. Profitable forest-tree culture. 1883. IV. 112.
Thornton, C. G. *See* WYATT, W. & THORNTON, C. G.
Thornton, Conway. Report on the Swiss forest laws. 1887. IV. 331.[1]
— Swiss forest laws. 1887. IV. 331.[1]
Thornton, Robert John. Botanical extracts. 1810. *I. 202,*[2] III. 43.
— The British flora. 1812. I. 396.
— An easy introduction to the science of botany. 1823. I. 94.
— Elementary botanical plates. 1810. I. 85.
— Elements of botany. 1812. I. 255.
— A family herbal. 1810. III. 55.
— A grammar of botany. 1818. I. 522.[2]
— Juvenile botany. 1818. I. 94.
— A new family herbal. 1810. III. 55.
— New illustration of the sexual system. 1807. I. 265.
— The new London pharmacopoeia. 1815. III. 253.
— Select plants. 1799. I. 264.
— Temple of flora. 1812. I. 265.
Thornton, W. T. Forest denudation and famines. 1878. IV. 49.[1]
— Irrigation regarded as a preventive of Indian famines. 1878. IV. 49.[1]
Thorpe, Francis Newton. The Rose, the Lily and the Vine in history. 1888. I. 512.
Thorpe, Thomas Eduard. Aschenbestandtheile eines kranken Orangenbaumes. 1869. III. 501.[1]
— A dictionary of applied chemistry. 1890. III. 31.
— Sur l'essence de Pinus Sabiniana. 1879. II. 45,[2] *III. 308.*[2]
— Ueber Heptan von Pinus Sabiniana. 1879. II. 45,[2] *III. 308.*[2]
— **Robinson**, H. & **Willer**, A. K. La franguline. 1893. III. 543.[1]
Thorsen. Insekt- og sopskade i 1887 i skovanläggene paa Jäderen. 1888. IV. 549.[1]
Thorsen, S. Granens formering ved stiklinger. 1898. III. 305.[3]
Thory, Claude Antoine. Examen critique du Rosa Candolleana elegans. 1823. II. 292.[1]
— Monographie ... du genre Groseillier. 1829. II. 243,[1] *III. 413.*[1]

— Prodrome de la monographie ... du genre Rosier. 1820. II. 282.[1]
— Rosa Candolleana. 1819. II. 292.[1]
— Rosa Candolleana; seu, Descriptio novae. 1819. II. 292.[1]
— Rosa Redutea. 1817. II. 297.[2]
— & **Redouté**, P. J. Les Roses. 1817. II. 282.[1]
Thoss, *Graf* von SEHERR-. *See* SEHERR-THOSS, *Graf* von.
Thouars, Du PETIT-. *See* DU PETIT-THOUARS.
Thouin, André. Anleitung zur Anlegung ... einer Pflanzenschule. 1821. III. 153.
— Annonce d'un envoi de végétaux étrangers. 1803. IV. 536.[2]
— Cours de culture. 1845. III. 113.
— Cours de culture et de naturalisation des végétaux. 1827. III. 113.
— On the cultivation of the Jamrosade. 1802. III. 636.[1]
— Description d'une nouvelle espèce ... du genre Pêcher. 1806. II. 276.[1]
— Description d'une nouvelle sorte de greffe, nommée greffe Vilmorin. 1815. III. 159.[1]
— Description de la greffe Daubenton. 1823. III. 160.
— Description de la greffe Juge. 1815. III. 159.[3]
— Description de la greffe Palissy. 1817. III. 160.
— Description de la greffe Sainclair. 1815. III. 159.[2]
— Description du Jardin des semis du Muséum. 1804. III. 53.
— Greffe. 1822. III. 160.
— Histoire d'une nouvelle espèce d'arbre fruitier. 1812. II. 258.[2]
— Histoire ... d'une nouvelle espèce de Poirier. 1815. II. 281.[1]
— Instruction sur l'établissement des pépinières. 1821. . III. 153.
— Mémoire sur l'usage du terreau de bruyère. 182. ? III. 40.
— Mémoire sur la culture des Bruyères. 1803. III. 649.[3]
— Mémoire sur la greffe Banks. 1815. III. 159.[2]
— Mémoire sur la greffe Risso. 1815. III. 160.
— Mémoire sur la prétendue greffe Columelle. 1822. III. 160.
— Mémoire sur une nouvelle sorte de greffe. 1808. III. 159.[3]
— Mémoire sur une nouvelle sorte de greffe, nommée greffe en arc. 1809. III. 159.[2]
— Mémoire sur une nouvelle sorte de greffe par approche. 1809. III. 159.[2]
— Mémoire sur une plantation à travers des arbres. 1824. III. 160.
— Monographie des greffes. 1821. III. 160.
— Monographie des Pfropfens. 1821. III. 160.
— Note sur la culture ... du Pin Laricio de Corse. 1818. III. 160.
— Note sur les effets ... de la plaie annulaire. 1805. III. 74.[2]
— Notes sur la fructification d'un Jamrosade. 1802. III. 636.
— Notice sur l'introduction des Bruyères en Europe. 1804. III. 649.[2]
— Observations sur l'effet des gelées précoces. 1806. III. 47.
Thouin, Oscar LECLERC-. *See* LECLERC-THOUIN, Oscar.
Thoureau, J. DUCHESNE-. *See* DUCHESNE-THOUREAU, J.
Thouroude. *See* THIL, André & THOUROUDE.
Thouvenel. Eine neue Art zu pfropfen. 1830. III. 160.
Thouvenin, François Maurice. Note sur la structure des Myristicacées. 1887. II. 220.[2]
— Recherches sur la structure des Saxifragacées. 1890. II. 237.[2]
— Remarques sur l'origine des Bois d'Aloès. 1893. III. 26.[2]
— Sur la structure des Aquilaria. 1892. II. 600.[1]
— Sur la structure des Rhamnacées. 1889. II. 492.[1]
Thozet, A. The Cocoa-nut in Australia. 1869. II. 67.[2]
— Notes on some of the roots ... of North Queensland. 1866. III. 262.[2]
— Notes sur l'habitat, l'utilité ... de quelques plantes subtropicales de l'Australie. 1872. III. 94.[1]
— Quelques détails sur l'Australie. 1872. III. 282.[2]
Thränhardt, Adolph. Der Weinbau bei Naumburg. 1845. III. 552.
Thran, Christian. Index plantarum Horti carolsruhani tripartitus. 1733. I. 43.
Three Aloes. 1877. III. 340.[2]
Threlfall, Richard. Note on some products from the fruit of Pittosporum. 1895. II. 249,[2] *460.*[2]
Threlkeld, Caleb. Synopsis stirpium hibernicarum. 1727. I. 394.

Thresh, John Clough. Capsicin. 1876. III. 699.[1]

Thryllitius, Valentin Hermann. Plantarum historia fabularis. 1713. I. 511.

Thudichum, John Louis William & **Dupré**, August. A treatise on the origin ... of wine. 1872. III. 550.

Thüer, L. Ueber Altersschwäche und Lebensmüdigkeit. 1894. I. 249.[1]

Thümen, Felix, *Baron* von. Der Ahornrunzelschorf. 1889. IV. 526.[2]

— Altrömische Forstbotanik. 1885. IV. 28.[1]

— Die amerikanische Esche als Entsumpfungsbaum. 1884. IV. 535.[1]

— Der Apfelbaum-Mehlthau. 1888. III. 428.[1]

— Ueber die Aschenkrankheit. 1878. III. 758.[2]

— Der Baumwuchs auf den österreichischen Laguneninseln. 1888. IV. 167.[2]

— Die Beeinflussung der Qualität des Rothbuchenholzes. 1887. IV. 499.

— Die Behandlung von Obstbruchwunden. 1885. III. 180.[2]

— Beiträge zur Kenntniss der auf der Schwarzföhre ... vorkommenden Pilze. 1883. IV. 466.[1]

— Die Bekämpfung der Pilzkrankheiten. 1886. III. 194.

— Die Berghaiden unserer südöstlichen Kalkalpen. 1883. IV. 369.

— Die Beziehungen zwischen Bodenbeschaffenheit und Vegetation. 1883. IV. 69.

— Birnen-Missbildungen. 1886. II. 280.[1]

— Ein bisher nicht beachteter Weidenschädling. 1887. IV. 487.[2]

— Die Blasenrostkrankheit der Weymouthskiefer. 1889. IV. 470.[1]

— Die Blasenrost-Pilze der Coniferen. 1881. IV. 442.

— Ueber den "Blattbrand" der Aepfelbäume. 1886. III. 428.[1]

— Blüthenabnormitäten bei Waldbäumen. 1886. IV. 63.[1]

— Die Blumenesche. 1887. IV. 536.[1]

— Californien's Wälder und das Aufforstungsgesetz. 1883. IV. 340.

— Die Cedern des Libanon. 1885. IV. 448.[1]

— Die Dammara- und Kaurifichten. 1886. IV. 447.[1]

— Der Dattelpalmenrost. 1886. III. 328.[1]

— Ueber einige Krankheiten der Gartenrosen. 1885. III. 453.[2]

— Ueber einige, lebende Aspenblätter bewohnende Pilze. 1883. IV. 486.[2]

— Ueber einige lebende Blätter bewohnende Pilze. 1883. IV. 211.[2]

— Ueber einige merkwürdige Bäume. 1886. IV. 87.[1]

— Ueber einige Pilze auf Birkenblättern. 1885. IV. 490.[2]

— Ueber einige Pilzkrankheiten unserer ... Palmen. 1887. III. 318.[1]

— Die Erinosis unserer Holzgewächse. 1886. IV. 210.[1]

— Eriobotrya japonica. 1885. III. 424.[1]

— Die Farnkräuter. 1887. III. 194.

— Fungi pomicoli. 1879. III. 194.

— Das Gähren lebender Bäume. 1886. IV. 66.[1]

— Die Gährung des Holzes. 1884. IV. 415.[1]

— Die Gelbfleckensucht der Mandelbäume. 1886. III. 434.[1]

— Die geographische Verbreitung der Nadelhölzer. 1886. IV. 80.

— Zur Geschichte der Einbürgerung fremdländischer Holzgewächse. 1884. IV. 125.[2]

— Die Gewinnung des Kiefernterpentins. 1885. IV. 436.[1]

— Die grossen Baumschwämme. 1885. III. 194.

— Die Grün- und die Blaufäule des Holzes. 1884. IV. 415.[1]

— Die Hemlockstanne und ihre Rinde. 1885. IV. 484.[1]

— Die Hexenbesen der Rothbuche. 1886. IV. 497.

— Das Holz der westaustralischen Eucalyptus-Bäume. 1887. IV. 531.[1]

— Das Holzgeschäft in Canada. 1885. IV. 403.[1]

— Die immergrüne Eiche, Quercus Ilex Lin. 1887. IV. 503.[1]

— Japans zwei werthvollste Bäume. 1884. III. 526.[2]

— Zur Kenntniss der Waldvegetation Nordamerika's. 1884. IV. 76.[1]

— Kiefern als Nahrungspflanzen. 1887. IV. 463.[1]

— Krankheit der edlen Kastanie. 1878. III. 359.[2]

— Die Krankheit der Keimlingspflänzchen. 1884. IV. 146.[1]

— Eine Krankheit der Robinien. 1888. IV. 523.[2]

— Der Krebs der Laubbäume. 1888. IV. 212.

— Il mal di cenere. 1888. III. 758.[2]

— Melampsora salicina, der Weidenrost. 1879. IV. 487.[3]

— Merkwürdige alte Pflanzen im Pilnitzer Schlossgarten. 1886. II. 241,[1] 551.[1]

— Ein merkwürdiger Tannenparasit. 1887. IV. 445.

— Ein merkwürdiges Beispiel der Copulation zweier Bäume. 1886. IV. 66.[3]

— Eine monströse Kiefer. 1885. IV. 483.[1]

— Ueber Moosbrüche. 1885. IV. 155.[1]

— Der nadelbewohnende Kiefernblasenrost. 1886. IV. 478.

— Neue Beiträge zur Kenntniss der ... Rostpilze. 1884. IV. 211.[3]

— Neue Beobachtungen über Mykorhiza. 1890. IV. 74.[1]

— Eine neue Fichtenart der Alpen. 1887. IV. 460.[1]

— Die neue Krankheit der Pappeln. 1884. IV. 485.[2]

— Eine neue Lindenart. 1887. IV. 528,[1] V. xxvii.[1]

— Eine neue österreichische Tilia. 1877. II. 518.[1]

— Eine neue Pilzkrankheit der Weisstanne. 1885. IV. 445.

— Eine neue und schöne Eichenvarietät. 1886. IV. 516,[1] V. xxvi.[1]

— Ein neuer Bürger unserer Waldflora. 1884. IV. 536.[1]

— Ein neuer Ulmenschädling. 1883. IV. 518.[2]

— Ein neuer Wundparasit der Eichen. 1888. IV. 511.

— Neues über den Verursacher der "Weisspfeifigkeit" des Holzes. 1885. IV. 415.[1]

— Nordamerika's wichtigste ... Laubholzbäume. 1888. IV. 76.[1]

— Nordamerika's wichtigste ... Nadelhölzer. 1888. IV. 76.[1]

— Una nuova specie di Tiglio. 1887. V. xxvii.[1]

— Una nuova varietà di Querce. 1886. V. xxvi.[1]

— Die Nusskiefer. 1887. IV. 464.[1]

— Ueber die orientalischen Coniferen. 1885. IV. 444.[1]

— Die Paulownia als Forstgewächs. 1889. IV. 538.[1]

— Die Pflanze als Zaubermittel. 1881. I. 518.

— Die Phoma-Krankheit der Weinreben. 1886. III. 579.

— Die Pilze der Birken. 1887. IV. 490.[2]

— Die Pilze der Erlen. 1887. IV. 488.[2]

— Die Pilze der Esche. 1886. IV. 534.[2]

— Die Pilze der Hainbuche. 1887. IV. 492.[1]

— Die Pilze der Obstgewächse. 1887. III. 194.

— Die Pilze der Pappeln. 1889. IV. 485.[2]

— Die Pilze der Rothbuche. 1888. IV. 497.

— Die Pilze der Schwarzföhre. 1884. IV. 466.[1]

— Die Pilze der Ulmen. 1886. IV. 518.[2]

— Die Pilze des Weinstockes. 1878. III. 578.

— Die Pilze und Pocken auf Wein und Obst. 1885. III. 194.

— Die Pilzkrankheit der Ahornkeimlingspflanzen. 1880. III. 536.[1]

— Die Pilzkröpfe der Aspen. 1887. IV. 486.[2]

— Die Pilzkröpfe der Korbweide. 1887. IV. 487.[2]

— Die pilzlichen Krankheiten der Weiden. 1884. III. 350.[1]

— Le Pin à noix. 1887. IV. 464.[1]

— Die "Pineries" am Lake Superior. 1883. IV. 338.[2]

— Die Pocken des Weinstockes. 1880. III. 578.

— Polyporus Schweinitzii als Nadelbaumtödter. 1884. IV. 211.[2]

— Rigonfiamenti delle radici. 1886. IV. 74.[1]

— Rothe Kiefernblüthen. 1883. IV. 483.[1]

— Der Russthau unserer Forstgewächse. 1885. IV. 211.[2]

— Die im St. Petersburger Klima winterharten Tannen und Fichten. 1886. IV. 125.[1]

— Samentragende Douglasfichten. 1887. IV. 484.[1]

— Schildläuse als Zerstörer der Schwarzpappeln. 1887. IV. 486.[1]

— Schlangenfichte und Hängefichte. 1889. IV. 460.[2]

— Der Schleimfluss an Birken und Hainbuchen. 1891. IV. 212.

— Die schnelle Ausbreitung der Lärchenkrebskrankheit. 1887. IV. 451.

— Die Terpentin liefernden Nadelhölzer Nordamerika's. 1886. IV. 436.[3]

— Die Traubenwurzeln der Erlen. 1884. IV. 489.[1]

— Die auf unsern Waldbäumen lebenden Pilze. 1884. IV. 211.[3]

— Die Verletzung der Bäume durch Blitzschläge. 1885. IV. 194.

— Das verschiedenartige Vorkommen der Schwämme. 1887. IV. 211.[2]

— Ueber die Verwachsung von Bäumen. 1884. IV. 66.[2]

— Verzeichniss der ... Pilze auf dem Weinstock. 1876. III. 194.

— Der vorzeitige Laubfall beim Ahorn. 1884. III. 534.[1]

— Die Wälder der Insel Formosa. 1885. IV. 376.[1]

— Die Wälder des australischen Festlandes. 1886. IV. 380.[1]

— Die Wälder des Staates Indiana. 1886. IV. 339.

— Die Wälder des Staates Pennsylvanien. 1885. IV. 339.

Thümen, Felix, *Baron* von (*continued*).
— Die Wälder . . . in Bulgarien. 1884. IV. 375.[1]
— Der Wald auf den Balearischen Inseln. 1884. IV. 363.[2]
— Der Wald in Alaska. 1885. IV. 340.
— Der Wald in Lappmarken. 1885. IV. 347.
— Wald und Waldbäume in den nord-amerikanischen Süd-staaten. 1883. IV. 340.
— Die Waldbäume Nordamerika's und ihre geographische Vertheilung. 1884. IV. 76.[1]
— Die Waldbäume Russlands. 1883. IV. 80.
— Die Waldvegetation auf der kurischen Halbinsel. 1885. IV. 347.
— Die Weinreben im dendrologisch-hortikulturistischen Sinne. 1884. III. 545.[2]
— Zur weiteren Kenntniss der Kieferndrehkrankheit. 1884. IV. 477.
— Eine wenig gekannte Krankheit der Kirschen. 1885. III. 432.[1]
— Ein wenig gekannter Apfelbaum-Schädling. 1891. III. 428.[1]
— Das Wesen und die Ursachen der Verkarstung. 1883. IV. 283.[2]
— Wie heisst der den "Lärchenkrebs" verursachende Pilz? 1888. IV. 451.
— Der Wundkrebs unserer Laubgehölze. 1886. III. 194.
— Die Wurzelanschwellungen bei Forstgewächsen. 1886. IV. 74.[1] *211.*[2]
— Der Zürgelbaum. 1887. IV. 518.[1]
— Zwei gemeinsame Fichtenschädlinge. 1883. IV. 456.
— Zwei Krankheiten der Edelkastanie. 1889. IV. 493.[1]
— Zwei werthvolle Unterhölzer der südösterreichischen Wälder. 1885. IV. 485.[2] *526.*[1]
Thümen, Nikolaus, *Freiherr* von. Verbesserte Methode, die Champinsche Veredelung auszuführen. 1889. III. 163.[1]
Thuemmig, Ludwig Philipp. De arborum inversione. 1723. I. 527.
— Von den Bäumen . . . aus Blättern auferzogen. 1723. III. 159.[1]
— De circulis annuis. 1723. I. 127.[1]
— Experimentum singulare de arboribus ex folio educatis. 1721. I. 205.
— De succo arborum per frigus manante. 1723. I. 168.
— Versuch einer gründlichen Erläuterung der merkwürdigsten Begebenheiten in der Natur. 1723. I. 31.
— Von Verwahrung der Blumen etliche Jahr über. 1723. I. 35.
Thürig, X. Forstwesen in Malters. 1870. IV. 367.
Thüringen — Botanischer Verein. Abhandlungen. *See* Ir-mischia, I. 12.
Thüringen — Geographische Gesellschaft. *See* Geogra-phische . . . I. 12.
Thüringen — Versammlung der Forstwirthe. *See* Versamm-lung . . . IV. 11.
Thüringischer botanischer Verein. Mittheilungen. I. 15.
Thürmer, C. Die Baum- und Stockrodemaschine von Schus-ter. 1859. IV. 386.
— Einige Worte über Forstculturen. 1860. IV. 114.
— Erziehung der Holzpflanzen in Rasenaschenbeeten. 1859. IV. 150.
— Ueber die Nothwendigkeit der Forstculturen in Russland. 1863. IV. 273.[3]
— Semis de végétaux ligneux dans de la cendre de gazon. 1859. IV. 150.
— *See also* Тюрмеръ, К. Ф.
Thuilier. Observation sur les effets dangereux du Fustet. 1813. III. 524.[1]
Thuillier, Jean Louis. La flore des environs de Paris. 1790. I. 406.
Thum, (*Oberförster, Laubach*). Zur Geschichte des Femel-schlagbetriebs. 1880. IV. 24,[1] *131.*
Thuma, Al. Nejlepší druhy Lístkových Oříšků. 1893. III. 357.[1]
Thunberg, Carl Peter. Aanmerkingen over de Kaneel op Ceylon. 1786. II. 224.[1]
— De Acere. 1793. II. 476.[1]
— Afhandling om de växter som i Bibelen omtalas. 1828. I. 513.
— Afhandling . . . over nogle . . . Arter af Rohria. 1793. II. 853.[1]
— De Aloe. 1785. II. 77.[3]
— Anmärkningar vid canelen gjorde på Ceylon. 1780. III. 405.[2]
— Anvisning till de svenska pharmaceutiska växternas igen-kännede. 1826. III. 67.[1]

— Arbor toxicaria macassariensis. 1788. II. 145.[2]
— De Aspalatho. 1802. II. 333.[1]
— De Benzoe. 1793. III. 671.[1]
— Beschrijving van twee nieuwe soorten van palmboom-achtige gewassen. 1782. II. 2.
— Beskrifning på ett nytt örte-genus. 1776. II. 146.[1]
— Beskrifning på et . . . örte-genus . . . Fagraea ceilanica. 1782. II. 718.[2]
— Beskrifning på Weigela japonica. 1780. II. 835.[1]
— Beskrivelse over en . . . Plante-Slægt Dahlia. 1792. II. 254.[1]
— Beskrivelse over set Arter af Slægten Rohria. 1799. II. 853.[1]
— Betula. 1807. II. 117.[1]
— De Blaeria. 1802. II. 661.[2]
— The botanical history of the genus Dillenia. 1791. II. 541.[1]
— Botanical observations on the Flora japonica. 1794. I. 461.
— Botanische Geschichte der Gattung Dillenie. 1791. II. 541.[1]
— Botanisk beskrifning på tvänne species äkta Muskot. 1782. II. 220.[1]
— De Brunia. 1804. II. 251.[2]
— Cajoputi oljans nytta och bruk i medicine. 1782. III. 636.
— De Caryophyllis aromaticis. 1788. III. 635.[2]
— Celastri plures species. 1805. II. 466.[1]
— De Cinchona. 1811. II. 812.
— De cortice Angosturae. 1793. II. 405,[1] III. 503.[2]
— Crassulae generis 28 novas species. 1778. II. 236.[1]
— Descriptiones nonnullarum specierum plantarum in . . . Promontorio Bonae Spei. 1804. II. 405.[1]
— De Diosma. 1797. II. 405.[1]
— Dissertatio botanica de Borbonia. 1811. II. 336.[1]
— Dissertatio geographiam plantarum adumbrans. 1813. I. 241.[2]
— Dissertationes academicae Upsaliae habitae. 1799. I. 264.
— De Dracaena. 1808. II. 81.[1]
— De Erica. 1785. II. 664.[1]
— Examen classis diandriae. 1824. I. 251.
— Examen classis dioeciae. 1825. I. 251.
— Examen classis gynandriae. 1824. I. 251.
— Examen classis monoeciae. 1825. I. 251.
— Examen classis polygamiae. 1825. I. 251.
— Ficus genus. 1786. II. 143.[1]
— Flora capensis. 1807. I. 494.
— Flora japonica. 1784. I. 461.
— Flora strengnesensis. 1791. I. 352.
— Florula javanica. 1825. I. 476.[2]
— Florula javanica. 1825. I. 468.
— Fructificationis partium varietates. 1800. I. 118.[2]
— Om fyndet af en Granstubbe. 1764. I. 351.
— De Galipea Cusparia. 1825. III. 504.[1]
— De Gardenia. 1780. II. 817.[1]
— In genus Echitis observationes. 1819. II. 726.[1]
— Gift-trädet på Goda Hopps Udden, Toxicodendrum. 1796. II. 452.[1]
— De Hermannia. 1794. II. 535.[1]
— Horti upsaliensis plantae. 1826. I. 40.
— Horti upsaliensis plantae cultae. 1803. I. 40.
— Icones plantarum japonicarum. 1794. I. 461.
— An illustration . . . of Lycium . . . at the Cape of Good Hope. 1808. II. 773.[1]
— Om inhemske träd och buskar. 1821. I. 350.[1]
— De Krameria dissertatio botanico-medica. 1822. III. 480.[1]
— Licuala, et nytt Palm-slägte. 1782. II. 70.[1]
— De medicina Africanorum. 1785. III. 281.[2]
— Monographie af Urteslægten Gorteria. 1798. II. 853.[1]
— De moxae atque ignis . . . usu. 1788. III. 754.[1]
— Museum naturalium Academiae upsaliensis. 1787. I. 40.
— De Myristica. 1788. II. 220.[1]
— De Myristica moschata. 1788. II. 221.[1]
— Nipa, et nytt genus. 1782. II. 71.[2]
— Nova genera plantarum. 1781. I. 263.
— Nova plantarum genera. 1799. I. 264.
— Novae species plantarum capensium. 1803. I. 494.
— De nutritione plantarum. 1819. I. 157.
— Et nytt species af Muscot. 1799. II. 220.[2]
— Oedmannia, et nytt ört-slägte. 1800. II. 381.[2]
— De oleo cajuputi. Pars 1. 1797. III. 636.
— De oleo cajuputi. Pars 2. 1797. III. 636.

— De Palmís. 1825. II. 60.[2]
— De Phylica. 1804. II. 495.[2]
— Piper nigrum. 1827. III. 343.[2]
— De Pipere Cubeba. See LIEDBECK, P. J. 1827. III. 342.[2]
— Plantae Contortae. 1805. II. 722,[1] 735.[2]
— Plantarum brasiliensium decas. 1817. I. 341.
— Plantarum japonicarum novae species. 1824. I. 461.
— De plantis venenatis. 1822. III. 59.[2]
— Prodromus plantarum capensium. 1794. I. 494.
— De Protea. 1781. II. 165.[2]
— Proteae, plantae generis, species novae. 1806. II. 165.[2]
— Reise durch einen Theil von Europa, Afrika und Asien. 1788. I. 302.
— Reisen in Afrika und Asien. 1788. I. 302.
— Resa uti Europa, Africa, Asia. 1788. I. 302.
— Rhamni capenses. 1817. II. 497.[1]
— Rothmannia et nytt örte-genus. 1776. II. 818.[2]
— De Rubo. 1813. II. 300.[1]
— Solana capensia. 1817. II. 775.[1]
— De Styrace. 1813. II. 704.[2]
— Tractatio anatomica. See WAHLENBERG, Georg. 1806. I. 98.
— Travels in Europe, Africa and Asia. 1788. I. 302.
— Om utländske träd, buskar och blomsterväxter. 1820. I. 266.
— Voyage en Afrique et en Asie. 1788. I. 302.
— Voyages . . . au Japon. 1796. I. 461, 494.
Thunig. See MÖLLENDORFF, G. von & THUNIG.
Thunn, M. I boschi. 1882. IV. 166.[1]
Thurant, Johann Baptist. An morbis chronicis caffé potus? See COSNIER, L. H. 1751. III. 741.[1]
Thurber. Californian manna. 1877. IV. 443.[2]
Thurber, Francis Beatty. Coffee from plantation to cup. 1881. III. 739.
Thurber, George. An Orange within an Orange. 1877. II. 403.[1]
Thurén, A. See ASPELIN, E. F. & THURÉN, A.
Thuret, Gustave. Expériences sur des graines de diverses espèces plongées dans de l'eau de mer. 1873. I. 240,[2] 588.[1]
Thurgau, Hermann, MÜLLER-. See MÜLLER-THURGAU, Hermann.
Thurgauische naturforschende Gesellschaft. Mittheilungen. See THURGAUISCHER NATURFORSCHENDER VEREIN. I. 27.
Thurgauischer naturforschender Verein. Mittheilungen. I. 27.
Thurmann, Jules. Enumération des plantes . . . de Porrentruy. 1848. I. 434.
— Essai de phytostatique appliqué à la chaine du Jura. 1849. I. 434.
— De la marche à suivre dans l'étude de la dispersion des espèces végétales. 1853. I. 228.[1]
— Réunion de la Société géologique de France à Porrentruy. 1838. I. 434.
Thurn, Everard Ferdinand IM. See IM THURN, E. F.
Thurneisser zum Thurn, Leonhard. Historia sive descriptio plantarum omnium. 1578. I. 282.
— Historia und Beschreibung influentischer . . . Wirckungen aller . . . Erdgewechsen. 1578. I. 282.
Thurston, Charles Orion. See DUDLEY, W. R. & THURSTON, C. O.
Thurston, Edgar. Adhatoda vasica. 1892. III. 709.[2]
— Al (Morinda) dye and dyeing. 1899. III. 746.[1]
— Blackwood or Rosewood. 1893. IV. 521.[2]
— Castor oil. 1893. III. 522.[1]
— Cutch. 1892. III. 464.[1]
— East Indian Walnut. 1893. IV. 521.[1]
— Fibres used for brush-making. 1892. III. 235.[1]
— Index [to Watt's] Dictionary. 1896. I. 75.[2]
— Indian woods for tea-boxes. 1892. IV. 427.[1]
— India-rubber from Ficus elastica. 1893. III. 371.[1]
— Kaméla dye. 1893. III. 520.[2]
— Note on a tour in Mysore. 1894. I. 475.[2]
— Padauk wood. 1892. IV. 522.[1]
— The Palmyra Palm. 1894. III. 321.[1]
— Resin and turpentine from Indian Pines. 1892. IV. 463.[1]
— Tans of southern India. 1893. IV. 435.
Thurston, John Bates. Catalogue of trees, shrubs and foliage plants, at . . . Taviuni, Fiji. 1886. I. 69.[1]
Thurston, Robert Henry. On the effect of prolonged stress upon . . . Pine timber. 1881. IV. 462.[2]
— On Flint's investigation of the Nicaraguan woods. 1887. IV. 409.
— The relative strength of metals and timber. 1894. IV. 410.
— On the strength of American timber. 1879. IV. 410.

Thury. On the law of the production of the sexes. 1863. I. 199.
— Mémoire sur la loi de production des sexes. 1863. I. 199.
— Remarques sur quelques objections élevées contre la loi de production des sexes. 1864. I. 199.
— le comte HÉRICART DE. See HÉRICART DE THURY, vicomte.
Thury, C. F. CASSINI DE. See CASSINI DE THURY, C. F.
Thury, Jean Marc Antoine. Mémoire sur le plan . . . d'une nouvelle flore de la Suisse. 1856. I. 435.
— Observations sur la morphologie . . . des Passiflores. 1896. II. 577.[1]
Le Thuya occidentalis convient-il pour le boisement des terres tourbeuses et humides? 1899. IV. 484.[2]
Thwaites, George Henry Kendrick. The Ceylon Coffee fungus. 1878. III. 735.
— Cinchona cultivation in Ceylon. 1864. III. 714.
— Description of some new genera and species of Ceylon plants. 1854. I. 476.[2]
— Description of some new . . . Pangiaceae. 1855. II. 571,[2] 574.[1]
— Note on the genus Ancistrocladus. 1854. II. 584.[2]
— Note on the genus Prosorus. 1856. II. 449.[1]
— Observations on the cell-membrane. 1846. I. 137.
— Reports on the Royal botanic garden, Paradenia. 1856. I. 67.[2]
— On Sphragidia and Eccremanthus. 1855. II. 440,[2] 445,[1] 488.[1]
— On Tetracrypta and Kokoona. 1853. II. 469.[2]
— On two new plants, Epicarpurus . . . and Doona. 1851. II. 155.[2]
— On Urandra. 1855. II. 170.[2]
— See also WILSON, Nathaniel & THWAITES, G. H. K.
— & Hooker, Sir J. D. Enumeratio plantarum Zeylaniae. 1858. I. 476.[2]
Thygeson, T. G. C. F. de. Træplantning i de jydske Klitter. 1868. IV. 156.[2]
Thym, Johann Friedrich. Die Nutzbarkeit, fremde Thiere, Bäume . . . einzuführen. 1775. III. 43.
— Die Practic des Seidenbaues. 1777. III. 373.
Thys, I. Memorie of vertoog over het uijtgeven . . . der vage en inculte gronden. 1792. IV. 159.
Thysse, Jac. P. De Hazelaar (Corylus Avellana). 1897. II. 122.[1]
Tiburtius. Beskrifning öfver Vreta Closters socken. 1755. IV. 344.[1]
Tice, C. V. Ailanthus. 1888. III. 507.[2]
Tice, Hardin. Pruning trees to secure long life. 1899. III. 171.
— Timber growing for profit. 1891. IV. 112.
— Wind-breaks. 1890. III. 215.[2]
Tichebourne, Ch. Sur l'extraction et la conservation des principes aromatiques. 1865. III. 226.[2]
Tichomirow, Wladimir Andreewitsch. See TIKHOMIROF, Vladimir Andreevitch.
Tichy, Anton. Eigene Gedanken über Organisation des forstlichen Versuchswesens. 1892. IV. 38.[2]
— Die Forsteinrichtung in Eigenregie. 1884. IV. 244.
— Neues Dendrometer-Konstruksionsprinzip. 1879. IV. 231.[2]
— Der qualificirte Plenterbetrieb. 1891. IV. 131.
Tidal, A. J. R. Index plantarum in Horto botanico conimbricensi. 1850. III. 29.[1]
Tideman, B. Deodora Ceder. 1853. III. 300.[1]
Tiedemann, Johann Rudolph. Historia Sambuci vulgaris. 1733. III. 752.[1]
Tidicaeus, Franz. Phytologia generalis. 1582. I. 282.
Tidmarsh, E. Tacsonia militaris ×. 1900. III. 616.[2]
Tidning för Trägårds-Skötsel och ellmän Växt-Kultur. III. 11.
Tidskrift för skogshushållning. Ed. by C. L. Obbarius. IV. 539.[1]
Tidskrift för skogshushållning. Ed. by Cnattingius. IV. 539.[1]
Tidskrift for det norske landbrug. III. 11.
Tidsskrift for Frugttrædyrkere. III. 11.
Tidsskrift for Havevæsen. III. 11.
Tidsskrift for Landoekonomi. See LANDOECONOMISKE Tidender. III. 10.[2]
Tidsskrift for Naturvidenskaberne. I. 9.[1]
Tidsskrift for populære Fremstillinger af Naturvidenskaben. I. 9.[1]
Tidskrift for Skovbrug. IV. 5[1]; see also Den NORSKE forstforenings aarbog. IV. 5.[2]
Tidsskrift for Skovvaesen. IV. 5.[2]

Tiefdüngung der Obstbäume mit Sutter's Locheisen. 1896. III. 152.

Tiefenthal, Oskar. Pirus angustifolia. 1892. III. 425.[1]

Tieghem, Philippe Édouard Léon van. Abnormes Wachsthum der Zweige bei der Seestrandskiefer. 1886. IV. 467.[2]

— Aciella, genre nouveau. 1894. II. 174.[2]

— Acrogamie et basigamie. 1895. I. 118.[2]

— Anatomie comparée de la fleur femelle et du fruit des Cycadées. 1869. II. 1.

— Anatomie de la fleur des Santalacées. 1869. II. 168.[1]

— Anatomie de la fleur femelle et du fruit du Noyer. 1869. II. 113.[2]

— Anatomie des fleurs et du fruit du Gui. 1869. II. 178.[1]

— Sur une anomalie des branches du Pin maritime. 1884. II. 44.[2]

— Avicenniacées et Symphorémacées, place de ces deux nouvelles familles dans la classification. 1898. II. 752.[2]

— Sur les Bixacées, les Cochlospermacées. 1900. II. 565,[2] 566.[1]

— Sur les Buxacées. 1897. II. 452.[2]

— Sur les canaux à gomme des Sterculiacées. 1885. II. 531.[2]

— Sur les canaux oléo-résineux des Ombellifères. 1872. II. 647.[1]

— Sur les canaux sécréteurs des Liquidambarées. 1884. II. 252,[1] 413.[2]

— Sur les canaux sécréteurs . . . des Ombellifères. 1884. II. 647.[1]

— Sur les canaux sécréteurs . . . des Pittosporées. 1884. II. 247.[1]

— Sur les Canellacées. 1899. II. 566.[2]

— Sur les caractères et les affinités des Grubbiacées. 1897. II. 170.[1]

— Classification anatomique des Mélastomacées. 1891. II. 634.[2]

— Sur la classification des Loranthacées. 1894. II. 172.[1]

— Classification nouvelle des phanérogames. 1897. I. 253.[1]

— Sur les Cnéoracées. 1898. II. 396.[2]

— Sur une coloration rose. 1863. I. 521.

— Sur les Coulacées. 1899. II. 170.[2]

— Deformed Fir branch. 1884. II. 44.[2]

— Deux genres nouveaux pour la famille des Coulacées. 1899. II. 170.[2]

— Sur deux Loranthacées . . . de Basse-Californie. 1895. II. 173.[1]

— Sur les dicotylédones du groupe des Homoxylées. 1900. II. 195,[1] 209.[1]

— Sur la digestion de l'albumens. 1877. I. 203.

— Sur la disposition des canaux sécréteurs. 1884. I. 135.

— Sur les divers modes de nervation de l'ovule. 1871. I. 120.

— Eléments de botanique. 1886. I. 92.

— Sur l'élongation des nœuds. 1897. I. 188.

— Sur l'existence de feuilles sans méristèles dans la fleur. 1896. II. 173.[2]

— Sur les feuilles assimilatrices . . . des Danae. 1884. II. 80.[2]

— Sur la formation quadrisériée des radicelles. 1887. I. 104.

— Sur les formations libéro-ligneuses secondaires des feuilles. 1879. I. 110.

— Sur les Fouquiériacées. 1899. II. 563.[1]

— Sur le genre Arceuthobium. 1895. II. 174.[1]

— Sur le genre Erythrosperme. 1900. II. 570.[2]

— Sur le genre Simmondsie. 1898. II. 453.[2]

— Sur les genres Actinidie et Sauravie. 1899. II. 540.[1]

— Sur les genres Basi-icarpus. 1895. II. 172.[2]

— Sur les genres méconnus . . . des Thyméléacées. 1893. II. 600.[1]

— Sur les genres Pentaphylace et Corynocarpe. 1900. II. 462.[1]

— Sur le groupement des espèces . . . dans la tribu des Élytranthées. 1895. II. 172.[2]

— Sur le groupement des espèces . . . dans la tribu des Gaiadendrées. 1895. II. 172.[2]

— Sur le groupement des espèces . . . dans la tribu des Psittacanthées. 1895. II. 172.[2]

— Sur le groupement des espèces . . . dans les Ginalloées. 1896. II. 172.[2]

— Sur le groupement des espèces . . . dans les Loranthacées. 1894. II. 172.[2]

— Sur le groupement des espèces . . . dans les Loranthées ou Dendrophthoées. 1895. II. 172.[2]

— Sur le groupement des espèces . . . dans les Loranthées . . . ou Struthanthées. 1895. II. 172.[2]

— Sur les Inséminées à nucelle nu. 1897. II. 168.[1]

— Sur les inséminées à nucelle pourvu d'un seul tégument. 1897. I. 253,[1] II. 474.[1]

— Sur les inséminées à nucelle pourvu de deux téguments. 1897. I. 253.[1]

— Sur les inséminées à ovules sans nucelle. 1897. I. 253,[1] II. 672.[1]

— Sur les Inséminées sans ovules. 1897. II. 172.[2]

— Korthalsella, genre nouveau. 1896. II. 174.[2]

— Légèreté spécifique . . . de l'embryon de quelques Légumineuses. 1874. II. 320.[2]

— Sur la limite de la tige et de la racine. 1891. I. 106.[1]

— Sur les Loranthoïdées d'Australie. 1895. II. 173.[1]

— Sur les Loranthoïdées de la Nouvelle-Zélande. 1895. II. 173.[1]

— Loxania et Ptychostylus. 1895. II. 172.[2]

— Sur les Loxanthera, Amylotheca et Treubella. 1894. II. 172.[2]

— Sur une maladie des Pommiers. 1879. III. 427.[2]

— Sur une manière de dénommer les diverses directions de courbure des plantes. 1884. I. 118.[1]

— Mémoire sur les canaux sécréteurs des plantes. 1872. I. 135.

— Nec contentum exteriori naturae conspectu . . . introspicere. 1868. I. 117.[2]

— Note sur les colorations developpées par les acides. 1863. I. 184.

— Un nouvel exemple de tissu plissé. 1891. I. 104, II. 18.[2]

— Sur une nouvelle sorte de basigamie. 1897. II. 6.[2]

— Nouvelles remarques sur la disposition des canaux sécréteurs. 1891. I. 135.

— Observations sur la légèreté spécifique . . . de l'embryon de quelques Légumineuses. 1875. II. 320.[2]

— Observations sur la structure . . . des anthères des Loranthacées. 1895. II. 173.[2]

— Origine . . . des tubercules radicaux des Légumineuses. 1888. II. 320.[2]

— Origine exodermique des poils post-staminaux des sépales chez les Santalacées. 1897. II. 168.[1]

— Sur les phanérogames à ovule sans nucelle. 1896. II. 168.[1]

— Sur les phanérogames sans graines. 1897. I. 253,[1] 271.[1]

— Quelques compléments à l'étude des Loranthées . . . ou Phénicanthémées. 1894. II. 172.[2]

— Quelques conclusions d'un travail sur les Loranthinées. 1896. II. 172.[2]

— Sur quelques exemples nouveaux de basigamie. 1896. I. 118.[1]

— Quelques genres nouveaux . . . des Loranthées. 1894. II. 172.[2]

— Sur quelques plantes rapportées du Congo. 1895. I. 492.[1]

— Sur les racines doubles. 1887. I. 104.

— Recherches physiologiques sur la germination. 1873. I. 203.

— Recherches physiologiques sur la végétation libre du pollen et de l'ovule. 1869. I. 201.[1]

— Recherches sur la disposition des radicelles. 1887. I. 104.

— Recherches sur la structure . . . des Thyméléacées. 1893. II. 599.[1]

— Recherches sur la structure du pistil. 1868. I. 117.[2]

— Recherches sur la structure du pistil et sur l'anatomie. 1871. I. 118.[1] — 1875. I. 115.[1]

— Recherches sur la symétrie de structure de l'ovule. 1869. I. 122.

— Recherches sur la symétrie . . . des plantes vasculaires. 1870. I. 100.[1]

— Recherches sur la symétrie . . . des végétaux. 1869. I. 100.[1]

— Remarque au sujet d'un mémoire de Dutrochet. 1872. II. 776.[1]

— Sur le réseau sus-endodermique de la racine. 1888. II. 320,[2] 658.[2]

— Sur le réseau sus-endodermique de la racine des Caprifoliacées. 1887. II. 833.[2]

— Sur le réseau sus-endodermique de la racine des Rosacées. 1887. II. 256.[2]

— Sur le second bois primaire de la racine. 1887. I. 104.

— Sur les Stachyuracées et les Koeberliniacées. 1900. II. 566,[1] 574.[2]

— Sur la structure de l'ovule . . . des Salicacées. 1900. II. 96.[1]

— Sur la structure de la fleur des Nuytsia. 1893. II. 173.[2]

— Structure de la racine dans les Loranthacées parasites. 1894. II. 173.[2]

— Structure de quelques ovules. 1898. I. 118.[1]
— Sur la structure des Aquilariées. 1892. II. 600.[1]
— Sur la structure des feuilles des monocotylédones. 1869. I. 110.
— Structure du fruit . . . de la Nuytsie. 1898. II. 177.[1]
— Structure du pistil des Primulacées. 1869. II. 691.[2]
— Structure et affinités des Abies. 1891. II. 16.[2]
— Structure et affinités des Cephalotaxus. 1891. II. 8.[1]
— Structure et affinités des Mastixia. 1884. II. 656.[3]
— Structure et affinités des Stachycarpus. 1891. II. 9.[1]
— Sur la structure et les affinités des Mémécylées. 1891. II. 635.[3]
— Sur la structure et les affinités des . . . Nallogia et Triarthron. 1894. II. 172.[3]
— Sur la structure et les affinités des Pittosporées. 1884. II. 247.[1]
— Sur la structure et les affinités des Tupeia, Ginalloa. 1895. II. 172.[3]
— Sur la structure et les affinités du Nuytsia. 1893. II. 173.[3]
— Sur la structure primaire et les affinités des Pins. 1891. I. 16.[3]
— Thylles chez les Clusiacées. 1887. II. 557,[3] 559.[3]
— Traité de botanique. 1884. I. 92.
— Trithecanthera, Lysiana et Alepis. 1894. II. 172.[3]
— Sur trois Loranthus de l'herbier de Desvaux. 1896. II. 172.[3]
— Sur les tubes criblés extralibériens. 1891. I. 134.[1]
— Valeur morphologique des cellules annelées . . . des Cactées. 1885. II. 588.[1]
— & Douliot, H. Origine des radicelles . . . chez les Légumineuses. 1886. II. 320.[3]
— — Origine des radicelles . . . dans les Rubiacées. 1887. I. 104.
— — Sur les plantes qui forment leurs radicelles sans poche. 1888. I. 104.
— — Recherches comparatives sur l'origine des membres endogènes. 1888. I. 104.
— & Guignard, Léon. Observations sur le mécanisme de la chute des feuilles. 1882. I. 191.[1]
— & Lecomte, Henri. Structure et affinités du Leitneria. 1886. II. 111.[1]
Tiemann, Ferdinand & Haarmann, Wilhelm. Ueber das Coniferin. 1874. II. 20.[3]
— — On coniferine. 1874. II. 20.[1]
— — Recherches sur la coniférine. 1874. II. 20.[1]
Tietkens, W. H. The hitherto unexplored West Central Australia. 1890. I. 504.
Tietoja Suomenmaan puiden kasvattamisesta. 1861. IV. 114.
Tietz, (Oberförster). Der Reichswald bei Cleve. 1855. IV. 352.
Tietz, A. O. Q. Über die Keimung einiger Coniferen und Laubhölzer. 1876. I. 203.
Tietz, Schiller-. See Schiller-Tietz.
Tieze, (Forstmeister). Jugendliche Fichtensaamen-Erzengung. 1861. IV. 460.[1]
Tiflisski . . . See Тифлисскій . . .
Il Tiglio di Nostra Signora del Buon Soccorso. 1863. IV. 528.[1]
Le tignuole delle Viti. 1897. III. 564.[1]
Tigri. Du Mûrier et du ver à soie. 1870. III. 377.
Tijdschrift over boomteeltkunde. See Leeraarkaring tot volmaaktere . . . III. 15.[2]
Tijdschrift van algemeene kunsten en wetenschappen. I. 16.
Tijdschrift van het binnenlandsch bestuur. III. 26.[1]
Tijdschrift van het Indisch landbouw-genootschap. III. 26,[1] 757.[1]
Tijdschrift voor de wis- en natuurkundige wetenschappen. I. 16.
Tijdschrift voor Indische taal-, land- en volkenkunde. I. 29.[3]
Tijdschrift voor land- en tuinbouw en boschkultuur in Nederlandsch Oost-Indië. III. 26.[3]
Tijdschrift voor natuurlijke geschiedenisen physiologie. I. 16.[1]
Tijdschrift voor Neerland's Indië. I. 29.[3]
Tijdschrift voor nijverheid en landbouw in Nederlandsch Indië. See Tijdschrift voor nijverheid in Nederlandsch Indië. III. 26.[3]
Tijdschrift voor nijverheid in Nederlandsch Indië. III. 26.[3]
Tijdschrift voor plantenziekten. III. 15.[1]
Tijdschrift voor schei- en artsenijbereidkunde, . III. 15.[1]
Tijdschrift voor tuinbouw. III. 15.[1]
Tijdschrift voor wetenschappelijken landbouw. III. 15.[1]

Tijdschrift voor wetenschappelijke pharmacie. I. 16. See also Tijdschrift voor schei- en artsenijbereidkunde. III. 15.[1]
Tijdstip voor het vellen van boomen. 1900. IV. 385.[1]
Tijl. Rapport nopens de voornaamste rotanstruiken. 1874. III. 229, 234.
Tijssen, Jan. Nog eens de sapbeweging. 1876. III. 170.
Tikhanof, Leo. See Тихановъ, Левъ.
Tikhomirof, Vladimir Andreevitch. Die Cinchonencultur . . . auf Java und Ceylon. 1894. III. 713.[3]
— Zur Frage über die Expertise von gefälschtem . . . Thee. 1890. III. 608.[1]
— Sur les inclusions intracellulaires du parenchyme charnu de la Datte. 1885. II. 73.[1]
— Java-Skizzen; die Cinchonencultur. 1894. III. 713.[3]
— Die Kultur . . . des Thees auf Ceylon, Java und in China. 1892. III. 601.[3]
— Ueber die mikrochemischen Eigenschaften . . . der Samen von Abrus. 1883. II. 322.[3]
— Morphologie . . . der Blüte von Pilocarpus pinnatifolius. 1883. II. 409.[3]
— Zur Morphologie des Melonenbaumes. 1888. II. 582.[3]
— Die Paternoster-Bohnen. 1884. II. 321.[3]
— See also Тихомировъ, В. А.
Tikhonof, V. See Тихоновъ, В.
Tilden, W. C. See Craig, B. F. & Tilden, W. C.
Tilden, William Augustus. Sur l'aloïne. 1872. III. 333.[1]
— Essence de Laurier-cerise. 1878. III. 438.[1]
Tilemann. Beschreibung der königlich hannover'schen Forstreviere Siedenholz und Schafstall. 1862. IV. 353.
Tilemann, C. Ueber den abnormen Wuchs der Buchen. 1844. IV. 496.
— Ueber das Keimen des Samens. 1838. I. 202.[3]
— Die Nachzucht der Eiche. 1838. IV. 504.
Tilesius, Wilhelm Gottlieb. Cheirostemon platanoides. 1815. II. 532.[2]
Tiling, Heinrich. See Regel, Eduard von & Tiling, Heinrich.
Tilintekoja maanviljelystaloudellisista kokeista. IV. 6.
Tillaeus, Petrus C. Potus Theae. See Linné, Carl von. 1765. III. 605.
Til-Landz, Elias. Catalogus plantarum . . . prope Aboam. 1673. I. 359.
— Icones novae in usum selectae. 1683. I. 359.
Tillery, William. Crossing Azalea mollis and indica. 1875. III. 655.
— On the cultivation of the Guava. 1849. III. 637.[1]
— Roots of trees filling up the tiles in deep drains. 1849. III. 34.[1]
— Thuja Lobbii as a bedge plant. 1889. III. 311.[1]
— Transplanting large . . . trees. 1859. III. 167.
Tillet. Le Gui du Chêne. 1879. II. 179.[1]
Tillet, P. Les Grands et les Petits Goulets. 1883. I. 416.
Le Tilleul. 1896. IV. 528.[1]
Tilleuls. 1898. IV. 528.[1]
Tilley, Thomas G. See Maclagan, Douglas & Tilley, T. G.
Tilli, Giovanni Lorenzo. Enumeratio stirpium in Horto academico pisano. 1806. I. 51.
Tilli, Michael Angelo. Catalogus plantarum Horti pisani. 1723. I. 60.[1]
Tille, Joseph. See Fraser, T. R. & Tille, Joseph.
Tilmann, Adolf. Forststatistik. 1876. IV. 354.
Tilschkert. Ueber die Prüfung des Baumöles. 1896. IV. 415.[3]
Tilt, Edward John. Trees in the Dolomite district of the Tyrol. 1884. III. 127.[1]
Tilton's journal of horticulture. See American journal of horticulture.
Timbal-Lagrave, Édouard. Catalogue des plantes . . . de la Haute-Garonne. 1859. I. 412.
— Étude sur quelques Cistes de Narbonne. 1861. II. 564.[1]
— Étude sur quelques Sideritis de la flore française. 1872. II. 766.[3]
— Une excursion botanique à Cascastel. 1874. I. 414.
— Une excursion botanique de Bagnères-du-Luchon à Castanèse. 1864. I. 421.
— Excursion botanique . . . St. Paul-de-Fenouillet. 1875. I. 414.
— Florule des Corbières orientales. 1892. I. 417.
— Note sur le Pinus pyrenaica. 1888. II. 45.[3]
— Observations botaniques sur quelques plantes de la Peña blanca. 1862. I. 421.
— Observations critiques . . . sur l'herbier Chaix. 1856. I. 411.
— Précis des herborisations. 1871. I. 414.

Timbal-Lagrave, Édouard (*continued*).
— Quelques synonymes du Chloris narbonnensis. 1868. II. 564.[1]
— Rapport sur l'herborisation faite à Esquierry. 1864. I. 413.
— Rapport sur la course faite . . . à Font-Romeu. 1872. II. 299.[2]
— Reliquiae Pourretianae. 1875. I. 270.
— Rhamnus Alaternus s.-v. obovata. 1885. II. 497.[2]
— *See also* BAILLET, C., JEANBERNAT, Ernest & TIMBAL-LAGRAVE, Édouard; FILHOL, E. J. E., JEANBERNAT, Ernest & TIMBAL-LAGRAVE, Édouard; JEANBERNAT, Ernest & TIMBAL-LAGRAVE, Édouard; MARTRIN-DONOS, Victor de & TIMBAL-LAGRAVE, Édouard.
— & **Jeanbernat**, Ernest. Rapport sur l'herborisation . . . au bois de Larramet. 1864. I. 413.
— & **Loret**, Henri. L'herbier de Marchand et Lapeyrouse. 1860. I. 412.
Timbaran tree of N. E. Borneo. 1894. III. 367.[1]
Timber and construction. 1870. IV. 423.[1]
Timber-bending. 1856. IV. 422.[1]
Timber bridges and viaducts. 1894. IV. 424.[2]
Timber culture for profit. 1871. IV. 111.[2]
Timber, &c. on Frazer's Island. *See* HILL, Walter. 1879. V. XXXI.[2]
Timber for tea boxes in China. 1884. IV. 427.[1]
Timber in Texas. 1884. IV. 397.
Timber news. IV. 12.[1]
Timber of the English colonies. 1886. IV. 396.[2]
The **timber** of Washington. 1900. IV. 341.[1]
Timber of Yoruba-land. 1891. IV. 401.[1]
Timberman. IV. 5.[1]
Timber-preserving. 1883. IV. 420.
The **timber-supply** of the United States. 1893. IV. 178.[2]
Timber-testing. 1883. IV. 415.[2]
Timber trade terms. 1876. IV. 402.[2]
Timber trades journal. IV. 12.[1]
The "**Timber** trades journal" list of shipping marks. 1895. IV. 403.[2]
Timber trees of Straits Settlements. 1890. IV. 400.[1]
Timber versus metal sleepers. 1888. IV. 424.[1]
Timber's hidden enemies. 1888. IV. 414.[1]
Timbers of Victoria. 1877. IV. 401.[2]
Timbo, its properties and composition. 1877. III. 540.[2]
In the time of Yuccas. 1874. III. 339.[1]
Timehri. I. 8.[1]
Times and register. *See* PHILADELPHIA medical times. I. 6.
Timgren, G. O. *See* SONCK, J. G., TIMGREN, G. O. & Hannikainen, F. W.
Timiriazeff, C. La chlorophylle et la réduction de l'acide carbonique. 1886. I. 173.
— Sur la décomposition de l'acide carbonique. 1878.[1] I. 173.
— La distribution de l'énergie dans le spectre solaire. 1883. I. 142.
— Effet chimique et effet physiologique de la lumière sur la chlorophylle. 1885. I. 142.
— Enregistrement photographique de la fonction chlorophyllienne. 1890. I. 174.
— L'état actuel de nos connaissances sur la fonction chlorophyllienne. 1885. I. 142.
— La protophylline. 1889. I. 177.
— La protophylline naturelle. 1895. I. 178.
— Sur le rapport entre l'intensité des radiations solaires et la décomposition de l'acide carbonique. 1889.[1] I. 174.
Timm, Jachim Christian. Florae megapolitanae prodromus. 1788. I. 374.
Timmer, W. *See* BYLL, A. de, TIMMER, W. & REYERS, O.
Timmerhout voor waterwerken in Suriname. 1894. IV. 398.[1]
Timmerhoutsoorten en reuzenboomen in Polynesien. 1853. IV. 402.[1]
Timpe, Heinrich. Beiträge zur Kenntnis der Panachierung. 1900. I. 111, *III. 181.[2]*
Tinant, François Auguste. Flore luxembourgeoise. 1836. I. 392.
Tincher, George W. The Catalpa in Kansas. 1893. IV. 538.[2]
Tinelli, Carlo. Sull' allevamento del baco dell' Ailanto. 1863. III. 507.[2]
Tinelli, Giovanni. Dizionario elementare di botanica. 1809. I. 33.
Tinelli, L. W. Culture of the Olive. 1850. III. 675.[2]
Tinelli, Luigi. Hints on the cultivation of the Mulberry. 1837. III. 375.

Tineo, Giuseppe. Index plantarum horti bot. Academiae regiae panormitanae. 1790. I. 61.
— Synopsis plantarum Horti academici panormitani. 1802. I. 61.
Tineo, Vincenzo. Catalogus plantarum Horti regii panormitani. 1827. I. 62.
— Plantarum rariorum Siciliae . . . fasc. 1846. I. 431.
— Plantarum rariorum Siciliae . . . pugillus. 1817. I. 431.
Tinti, Carl, *Baron*. Blühen von Paulownia imperialis. 1863. II. 781.[2]
Tintura in Palissandro. 1865. IV. 422.[2]
Tippenhauer, L. G. Die Insel Haiti. 1893. I. 337.
Tiralineas de puntas múltiples. 1890. IV. 551.[1]
Tiran. Rapport sur la maladie des Orangers. 1865. III. 500.[2]
Tirant, Gilbert. Les bois odoriférants de la Cochinchine. 1886. IV. 400.[2]
Tirol — **Consiglio** provinciale d'agricoltura . . . *See* CONSIGLIO . . . III. 24.[2]
Tirol — **Ferdinandeum**. *See* FERDINANDEUM . . . I. 27.
Tirol — **Forstverein**. *See* FORSTVEREIN FÜR NORDTIROL. IV. 14.
Tisandier, Ch. El corcho y sus aplicaciones industriales. 1882. IV. 435.[2]
Tischauer, A. S. Qver salicine. 1833. III. 345.[1]
Tischbein, P. Beobachtungen über eine der Lärche sehr nachtheilige Blattwespenlarve. 1840. IV. 450.
Tischler. Neue Heckenpflanze. 1889. III. 641.[1]
Tischmayer, L. Eichel- und Kastanienmehl. 1855. III. 538,[1] *IV. 514.[2]*
Tisdale, William M. The forest reservations of southern California. 1897. IV. 179.[1]
— Lemons in California. 1896. III. 502.[1]
— The Olive and the Lemon in southern California. 1895. III. 502,[1] *676.[2]*
Tisdall, Henry Thomas. Under eastern Baw Baw. 1897. I. 505.
Tishtchenko, V. *See* TИЩЕНКО, B.
Tison, Adrien. Sur la chute des feuilles. 1899. I. 192.[1]
— Sur la cicatrisation du système fasciculaire. 1899. I. 192.[1]
— Recherches sur la chute des feuilles. 1899. I. 192,[1] V. XII.[1]
Tison, Édouard. Sur l'androcée du Muscadier. 1874. II. 220.[2]
— Description d'un nouveau Metrosideros. 1877. II. 630.[2]
— Histoire de la fève de Calabar. 1873. III. 484.[1]
— Les prétendus phyllodes des Eucalyptus. 1878. II. 623.[2]
— Recherches sur les caractères de la placentation . . . dans les Myrtacées. 1876. II. 619.[2]
— Structure de l'écorce d'Alstonia constricta. 1879. II. 723.[2]
— Sur la valeur que présente . . . dans les Myrtacées, le manque plus ou moins grand d'adhérence entre l'ovaire et le réceptacle. 1876. II. 619.[2]
— Sur la valeur que présente la forme des placentas . . . dans les Myrtacées. 1876. II. 619.[2]
Tissandier, Albert. Forêts de la province de Washington. 1894. IV. 555.[2]
Tisserand Eugène. Rapport sur les travaux administratifs entrepris contre le phylloxera. 1881. III. 573. — 1886. III. 762.
Tissier, Ch. Sur les travaux de feu M. Soubeiran, concernant le rôle de l'azote. 1859. I. 158.
Tissière, P. G. Guide du botaniste sur le Gd. St. Bernard. 1868. I. 435.
Tita, Antonio. Catalogus plantarum quibus consitus est Patavii amaenissimus hortus. 1713. I. 60.[2]
Titan. *See* HOGG's weekly instructor. III. 17.
Titford, Wilham Jowit. Sketches towards a hortus botanicus americanus. 1811. III. 362.
Titius, Georg Christian. De cinnamomo. *See* WEDEL, G. W. 1707. III. 405.[2]
Titius, Johann Daniel. Anmerkungen über die Eintheilung der Pflanzen. 1768. I. 250.
— Gemeinnützige Abhandlungen zur Beförderung der Erkenntniss . . . natürlicher Dinge. 1768. III. 51.
— Systema plantarum sexuale. 1767. I. 257.
Titius, Michael. Catalogus plantarum Horti electoralis regiomontani. 1654. I. 43.
Titius, Salomon Constantin. De acido vegetabilium elementari. 1788. I. 180.[1]
— De aere in Coluteae leguminibus contento. 1800. II. 347.[1]
Titof, A. *See* ТИТОВЪ, A.

Titot. Ficus elastica in Blüthe. 1847. III. 370.²

Tittmann, (*Forstconducteur*). Zur Durchforstungsfrage. 1869. IV. 480.

Tittmann, (*Oberförster*). Duft-, Eis-, Schnee- und Windbruch auf dem . . . Hermsdorfer Staatsforstreviere. 1874. IV. 190.

Tittmann, H. Beobachtungen über Bildung und Regeneration des Periderms. 1897. I. 130.

— Physiologische Untersuchungen über Callusbildung an Stecklingen. 1895. I. 209.¹

Tittmann, Johann August. Botanisch-karpologische Bemerkungen. 1819. II. 39,² 243.³

— Darstellung der in Sachsen wild wachsenden Medicinal-Pflanzen. 1810. III. 72.

— Ueber den Embryo des Saamenkorns. 1817. I. 121.

— Die Keimung der Pflanzen. 1821. I. 123.¹

Tivendale, William. On the most certain method of getting rid of beetles. 1875. III. 295.³

— Report on the Houston pinetum. 1875. I. 55.

Tixon. Détermination de substances . . . de Haïti 1857. III. 267.¹

Tjoen, TAN ENG. *See* TAN ENG TJOEN.

Tkany, F. Vegetations-Verhältnisse der Stadt Olmütz. 1879. I. 442.

Toase, W. K. A series of botanical tables. 1835. III. 57.

Tobago. 1888. III. 267.¹

Tobi, E. Reboiseeringen in 't gebergte van Bagelen. 1894. IV. 168.¹

— Eine Wald-Excursion in Java. 1884. IV. 124.¹

Tobias, Mich. Messkreuz zur Holzmassen-Aufnahme. 1865. IV. 231.²

— *See also* MACHARA, Joh. & TOBIAS, Mich.

Tobler, L. Ueber "Wunn und Weid," 1864. IV. 330.

Tocl, Karel. Pámelník. 1898. III. 752.³

— Severni hranice stromovl v Sibiři. 1899. I. 453,¹ *IV*. 87.²

Tocquaine, Adolphe. Note relative au développement d'un jeune Sapin. 1868. II. 23.³

Toda y Güell, Eduart. La agricultura en Xina. 1884. III. 127.²

Todaro, Agostino. Hortus botanicus panormitanus. 1876. I. 64.

— Sopra una nuova specie di Fourcroya. 1879. II. 90.¹

— Nuovi generi e nuove specie . . . nel Real orto botanico di Palermo. 1858. I. 63.

— Osservazioni su talune specie di Cotone. 1863. II. 522.¹

— Plantae novae Horti regii botanici panormitani. 1858. I. 63.

— Prodromus monographiae generis Gossypii. 1878. II. 522.¹

— Relazione sui Cotoni coltivati al R. orto botanico. 1864. II. 522.¹

— Relazione sui Cotoni coltivati nel R. orto botanico di Palermo. 1877. II. 522.¹

— Relazione sulla cultura dei Cotoni in Italia. 1877. II. 522.¹

— Se le Querce conosciute in commercio coi nomi di Farnia e di Rovere nascono in Sicilia. 1878. II. 130.¹

Todaro, Agostino OGLIALORO-. *See* OGLIALORO-TODARO, Agostino.

Todd, A. S. Report of the committee on the medical botany of . . . West Virginia. 1871. III. 02.

Todd, James Edward. Notes on the distribution of timber in southwestern Iowa. 1878. *I. 380,* IV. 78,¹ 544.¹

— The relation of forests to rainfall. 1879. IV. 50.

Todd, Sereno Edwards. The Apple culturist. 1871. III. 426.¹

Todd, William. The North-west prospect of Whinfield forest. 17 . .? II. 137.²

Tögersen, Th. Praktisk havebog. 1873. III. 100.²

Toekamp Lammers, G. De Azalea indica. 1878. III. 660.¹

— Van Batavia naar Bandong. 1882. III. 128.

— Iets over de vergroening van Kina-Plantage Tji-Njiroean. 1883. III. 716.

— De Rhododendrons en hare kweekwijze. 1878. III. 656.

— Het vermenigvuldigen van de Ficus elastica. 1881. III. 370.²

De **toekomst** der Kina. 1899. III. 718.

De **toekomst** der Kinacultuur op Java. 1899. III. 717.¹

Toensen, A. C. E. De analysi . . . Smilacis Sassaparillae. 1826. III. 338.¹

Töpfer, H. Phänologische Beobachtungen in Erfurt. 1882. I. 225.

— Phänologische Beobachtungen in Sondershausen. 1882. I. 225.

— Phänologische Beobachtungen in Thüringen. 1882. I. 225.

Toepffer, Gust. Ad. Kurze Anleitung zur Cultur des Maulbeerbaumes. 1860. III. 377.

Török, János. A német mezőgazdák és erdőszök Boroszlón tartott 9. gyűlésének rövid vázolata. 1845. IV. 40.¹

Over den **toestand** van het houtgewas . . . bij 's Gravenhage.' 1852. III. 121.²

Toggenburg. *See* TOGGENBURG. 1878. II. 24.¹

Toggenburg. 1878. II. 24.¹

Togni, Michele. Raccolta delle singolari qualità del caffè. 1675. III. 741.¹

Tognini, Filippo. Anatomia vegetale. 1897. I. 101.¹

— Caso teratologico nella germinazione d' una Castagna. 1895. II. 124.²

— Contribuzione allo studio . . . degli stomi. 1897. I. 132,¹

— Ricerche di morfologia . . . sul fiore femminile . . . del Castagno. 1894. II. 124.²

Togno, Joseph. North Carolina Grapes. 1852. III. 584.¹

The toilet of flora. *See* BUCHOZ, P. J. 1771. III. 218.²

Toilette de flore. *See* BUCHOZ, P. J. 1771. III. 218.²

Le toise et le tarif général des bois. 1696. IV. 220.

Toker, E. J. Our forests in danger. 1893. IV. 178.¹

Tőkés, Lajos. A lomblevelek biológiája. 1900. I. 219.²

Tokmakof, I. *See* TOKMAKOBЪ, И.

Tokubuchi, Eijiro. On some species of Salix of Hokkaido. 1896. II. 103.¹

Tokyo —Botanical magazine. *See* BOTANICAL . . . I. 28.³

Tokyo botanical society. Botanical magazine. *See* BOTANICAL . . . I. 28.³

Toldt, Carl. Zur Waldfrage in den österreichischen Alpengebieen. 1883. IV. 181.¹

Tollard, Henri. Manuel de l'herboriste. 1828. III. 52.

— *See also* JULIA DE FONTENELLE, J. S. E. & TOLLARD, Henri.

Tollat von Vochenberg, Johann. Ain meisterlichs büchlein der artzney. 1497. I. 276.

Tollens. *See* KOCH, WHEELER & TOLLENS.

Tollens, L. J. A. Handboek voor handel . . . in Nederlandsch Indie. 1860. III. 274.¹

Tollet, C. Agua que absorben los materiales de construcción. 1891. IV. 412.¹

Tolomei, Giulio. Azione del magnetismo sulla germinazione. 1893. I. 204.

Tolvinski, A. A. *See* TOЛЬВИНСКІЙ, А. А.

Tomaschek, Anton. Zur Abhandlung des Dr. Kreuz. 1881. III. 545.¹

— Bemerkungen zur Flora . . . des Winters. 1881. I. 227.²

— Das Bewegungsvermögen der Pollenschläuche. 1882. I. 201.³

— Über Binnenzellen . . . des Pollenkorns einiger Coniferen. 1878. II. 19.

— Ueber die Entwicklungsfähigkeit der Blüthenkätzchen von Corylus. 1859. II. 122.¹

— Zur Flora der Umgebung Lembergs. 1859. I. 441.

— Ueber ein merkwürdiges Accommodations-Vermögen der Kätzchen von Corylus. 1876. II. 122.¹

— Mittel-Temperaturen als thermische Vegetations-Constauten. 1876. I. 221.

— Ueber pathogene Emergenzen auf Ampelopsis. 1879. III. 545.¹

— Phänologische Beobachtungen. 1855. I. 227.¹

— Phaenologische Rückblicke. 1890. I. 227.¹

— Studien über das Wärmebedürfniss der Pflanzen. 1873. I. 232.¹ —1874. II. 122.¹

— Thermische Konstanten. 1863. I. 227.²

— Thermo-physiologische Untersuchungen über die Entwicklung der Blüthenkätzchen von Corylus. 1874. II. 122.¹

— Uebersicht der . . . angestellten phänologischen Beobachtungen. 1868. I. 227.²

Tomaschek, Eduard. Berechnungsschlüssel und Forstverwaltungslehre. 1846. IV. 287.

Tomcsányi, Gusztav. A Douglas Fenyő fájáról. 1884. IV. 484.¹

— Erdei facsemeték nevelése. 1889. IV. 147.¹

— A Havasi Fenyő . . . telepítéséről. 1883. IV. 463.¹

— A Jegenyefenyő és a Bükk tenyésztése. 1882. IV. 441.

— Légfütött berendezett magpergető. 1885. IV. 148.

— Tölgymakk telelő kunyhó. 1886. IV. 507.

Tomcsányi, Gyula. Az alátelepítésről. 1887. III. 216.

— A garamménti kincstári erdőkben alkalmazott szállítási rendszer ismértetése. 1895. IV. 389.

— Szolgálati utasítás a beszterczebányai m. k. erdőigazgatósági kerület részére. 1897. IV. 307.¹

Tomek, Antonín. Něco o Araucaria excelsa. 1897. III. 298.²
— Pěstění Rhododendronů či pěniánků. 1897. III. 657.¹
— Pěstování Azalea indica. 1897. III. 657.¹
Tominz, Raimondo. Piante officinali e della flora del litorale Austro-Ungarico. 1881. I. 66.¹
Tommaselli, Giuseppe. Analisi dei vegetabili. 1794. I. 254.²
— Compendio di fisiologia vegetale. 1800. I. 148.
Tommasini, Muzio de. Der Berg Slavnik im Küstenlande. 1839. I. 447.
— Die Vegetation der Sandinsel Sansego. 1862. I. 452.
— Sulle vegetazione dell' isola di Veglia. 1875. I. 447.
Tommesen, Jens Lassen. Bidrag til Berberissens Forsvar. 1814. III. 394.¹
Tonckens, L. OLDENHUIS. *See* OLDENHUIS TONCKENS, L.
Tondeur, Charles. Almanach de la Vigne et du vin. 1869. III. 555.
Tonduz, Adolphe. Exploraciones botánicas . . . de Costa Rica. 1893. I. 334.
— Exploraciones botánicas en Talamanca. 1895. I. 334.
— Flora de Costa Rica. 1897. I. 334.
— La fumagina del Cafeto. 1897. III. 736.
— Herborisations au Costa-Rica. 1895. I. 334.
— Informe sobre una enfermedad del Cacaotero. 1895. III. 593.²
Toneles de Pino. 1887. IV. 427.¹
Tonge, Ezerel. A continuation of the answers to the queries about vegetation. 1669. I. 162.
— A letter . . . about the retarding the ascent of sap. 1670. I. 162.
— Some further inquiries concerning the running of sap in trees. 1670. I. 162, III. 159.¹
— Some inquiries relating particularly to the bleeding of Walnuts. 1670. I. 168.
— *See also* BEALE, F. & TONGE, Ezerel.
— & **Willoughby,** Francis. Some observations . . . concerning the motion of sap in trees. 1670. I. 162.
Toni, Giovanni Battista de. Intorno ad alcuni alberi . . . nei giardini di Padova. 1887. I. 64.
— Intorno all' epoca di fondazione dell' Orto botanico parmense. 1893. I. 522.¹
— Sull' esistenza . . . del Cistus laurifolius. 1894. II. 564.²
Tonini, L. Ancora della riproduzione agamica del Faggio. 1898. IV. 496.
— Il governo del Faggio. 1899. IV. 500.²
— Sulla moltiplicazione agamica del Faggio. 1898. IV. 500.²
La **tonite,** nouvelle poudre brisante. 1878. IV. 386.
Tonkof, R. N. *See* TOHROFF, P. H.
Tonkoff, W. Ueber die Blattstielanschwellungen bei Atragene. 1894. II. 196.²
Les **tonneaux** en bois de Hêtre et comprimés. 1896. IV. 427.²
Tonnerre, Tillette de CLERMONT-. *See* CLERMONT-TONNERRE, Tillette de.
Tonning, Henrik. Norsk medicinsk och oekonomisk Flora. 1773. III. 67.¹
— Rariora Norvegiae. *See* LINNÉ, Carl von. 1768. I. 351.
Tonningen, D. W. ROST VAN. *See* ROST VAN TONNINGEN, D. W.
A tool for transplanting buds. 1900. III. 164.¹
Toonu or Tunu. 1898. II. 147.²
Toorn, J. van-der. Invloed van het entrijs op den wild stam. 1880. III. 39.¹
Top, W. G. *See* BONDAM, R. & TOP, W. G.
Topf, Alfred. Picea excelsa var. Hagemanniana. 1857. III. 305.¹
Topham, John. Wood formed by the descending sap. 1857. I. 189.
Topiary gardening in Japan. 1889. III. 202.²
Topitz, Anton. Neue oberösterreichische Formen der Gattung Rubus. 1892. II. 304.²
Topographisch-statistische Beschreibung des Kantons Aargau. 1816. IV. 365.
Topp, C. A. Botanical . . . notes on a visit to New South Wales. 1889. I. 504.
Tops, (pseud.?). Light grazing in forests. 1886. IV. 136.²
Torchon, Henri. Précis sur les arbres verts. 1833. IV. 441.
Toree, Olof. · Reise nach Surate und China. 1772. III. 272.²
Torell, O. Frukt af Entada gigalobium. 1862. I. 242.¹ II. 356. tto
Torelli. Proposta del governo della provincia di Sondrio. 1861. IV. 186.¹

Torelli, Luigi. Assainissement des régions fiévreuses par les plantations d'Eucalyptus. 1880. IV. 530.
— Il bonificamento delle regioni di malaria. 1880. IV. 48,¹ 530.
— L'Eucalyptus e l'agro romano. 1878. IV. 531.²
— L'Eucalyptus e Roma; memoria. 1879. IV. 530.
Torevel. The Stephanotis; its culture. 1895. III. 694.¹
Torgoblya . . . *See* TOPROBLE . . .
Torino — **Reale accademia delle scienze.** *See* MISCELLANEA philosophico-mathematica . . . I. 25.
Torka, Valentin. Verfärbung und Fall des Laubes . . . von Paradies-Jordan-Schwiebus. 1900. I. 528.²
Tornabene, Francesco. Sopra alcuni fatti di anatomia . . . vegetable. 1838. I. 34.
— Considerazioni sulle anomalie florali. 1841. I. 114.²
— Descrizione d'un individuo teratologico . . . dell' Opuntia. 1844. II. 596.¹
— Flora Aetnea. 1889. I. 432.¹
— Flora sicula viva et exsiccata. 1887. I. 432.¹
— Hortus botanicus Regiae universitatis studiorum Catinae. 1887. I. 64.
— Notizia d' una carta topografico-botanica per la Sicilia. 1846. I. 431.
— Sopra un nuovo albero . . . del genere Celtis. 1855. II. 142.¹
— Osservazioni sopra gli endogeni. 1840. I. 98.
— Quadro storico della botanica in Sicilia. 1847. I. 81.¹
— Ricerche bibliografiche sulle opere botaniche. 1840. I. 2.
— Saggio di geografia botanica per la Sicilia. 1845. I. 431.
— *See also* SILVESTRI, Orazio & TORNABENE, Francesco.
Torner, Ericus. *See* JUSLENIUS, A. D. & TORNER, Ericus.
Torner, Jorge. El Cuerpo forestal francés. 1898. IV. 553.¹
Tornos, Lucas de. Nueva clasificación de las tierras de labor. 1862. I. 155.
Toro, Cayetano del. El cundurango. 1872. III. 693.³
Toronto — **Canadian** Institute. *See* CANADIAN . . . I. 4.¹
Torraca, Gaetano. Specimen experimentorum . . . corticis peruviani vis. 1765. III. 720.
Torralbas, José Ildefonso. Los insectes y la seleccion natural. 1891. I. 243.²
Torre, dalla. *See also* DALLA TORRE.
Torre, Giorgio dalla. (Turre, Georgius a.) Catalogus plantarum Horti, patavini. 1660. I. 60.²
— Dryadum Amadryadum, Cloridisqz triumphus. 1685. I. 287.
Torre y Huerta, Carlos de la. Enfermedad de los Cocoteros. 1890. III. 323.²
— Observaciones al trabajo del Dr. Tamayo. 1890. III. 318.²
Torrenté, Ant. de. Les forêts et les avalanches. 1888. IV. 188.²
Pei **torrenti** e pel rimboschimento in Calabria. *See* PEI torrenti. 1897. IV. 187.¹
Torrey, John. An account of several new genera and species. 1848. II. 453.²
— [Botanical] appendix. *In* EMORY, W. H. 1848. I. 322.
— Botanical report of routes in California. 1856. I. 323.
— Botany of the [United States and Mexican] boundary. 1859. I. 323.
— Botany[of the Zuñi and Colorado Rivers]. 1853. I. 322.
— Catalogue of North-American genera of plants. 1831. I. 306.
— Catalogue of plants collected . . . between the Mississippi and Missouri Rivers. 1843. I. 321.
— Catalogue of plants collected by Lieutenant Frémont. 1845. I. 321.
— Catalogue of plants collected . . . valley of the Great Salt Lake. 1852. I. 322.
— A catalogue of plants growing spontaneously within thirty miles of the city of New York. 1819. I. 313.
— A compendium of the flora of the northern and middle states. 1826. I. 313.
— On the Darlingtonia californica. 1853. V. XXVII.²
— Description of the general botanical collections . . . by Lieut. A. W. Whipple. 1856. I. 323.
— Description of the plants collected during the expedition [to the Red River of Louisiana]. 1853. I. 318.
— Descriptions of plants collected . . . by W. P. Blake. 1857. I. 323.
— A flora of the northern and middle sections of the United States. 1824. I. 313.
— A flora of the state of New York. 1843. I. 313.
— Icones ineditae ad Floram philadelphiae illustrandam destinatae. 183. ? I. 313.

— Notice of . . . plants suitable for hedges. 1858. III. 213.
— Notice of the California Nutmeg. 1855. III. 288.[2]
— Observations on the Batis maritima. 1853. II. 114.[3]
— Phanerogamia of Pacific North America. 1874. I. 323.
— Plantae Frémontianae. 1854. I. 322, V. XVII.[2]
— Plants collected by F. Crenzfeld in the Kansas. 1854. I. 322.
— Some account of a collection of plants made . . . by Edwin P. James. 1828. I. 321.
— On some new plants discovered by Col. Frémont. 1851. I. 322.
— & Frémont, J. C. Descriptions of some new genera and species of plants, collected in . . . expedition to Oregon. 1845. I. 321.
— & Gray, Asa. A flora of North America. 1838. I. 306.
— — Report on the botany of the expedition. Route near the thirty-second parallel. 1855. I. 322.
— — Report on the botany of the expedition. Route on the forty-first parallel. 1855. I. 322.
— — A revision of the Eriogoneae. 1870. II. 185.[2]
Torrey botanical club. Bulletin. Memoirs. I. 7.[1]
Torrigiani, Pietro. Catalogo delle piante che si trovano nel giardino del Marchese Pietro Torregiani. 1822. I. 62.
Torrilhon, G., LAMY-. See LAMY-TORRILHON, G.
Tortosa y Cerdá, Vicente. Memoria sobre los árboles de monte ó bosque. 1859. IV. 122.[2]
Tosquinet, Jules. Les ichneumons. 1895. IV. 544.[2]
Tostrup, Tho. Le commerce des bois de Norvège. 1889. IV. 404.[1]
— See also GELMER & TOSTRUP, Tho.
Touchard, F. De la greffe du bourgeon anticipé. 1861. III. 161.
— Greffe par approche du bourgeon anticipé. 1860. III. 163.[2]
Tougard. Tableau alphabétique . . . des variétés de Poires. 1852. III. 444.[3]
Toujours les inondations. 1896. IV. 51.
Toula, Franz. Über Wildbach-Verheerungen. 1892. IV. 188.[1]
Toulmouche A. Mémoire concernant l'action des plantes contenant du tannin. 1835. I. 182.[2]
Toulouse— Académie royale des sciences, inscriptions et belles-lettres. See ACADÉMIE . . . I. 20.
Toulouse— Société d'histoire naturelle. See SOCIÉTÉ . . . I. 23.
Toulouse— Société des sciences physiques et naturelles. See SOCIÉTÉ . . . I. 23.
Toumey, James Wilham. Agave Palmeri. 1897. II. 89.[2]
— The Date Palm. 1898. III. 329.[1]
— Echinocactus Wislizeni. 1895. II. 593.[1]
— An inquiry into the cause . . . of crowngall. 1900. III. 193.[2]
— Natural reforestation in the Southwest. 1899. IV. 341.[1]
— A new Mamillaria. 1896. II. 595.[1]
— Notes on scale insects in Arizona. 1895. III. 187.
— Notes on the Pine forests of . . . Arizona. 1897. II. 39.[1]
— Notes on the tree flora of the Chiricahua Mountains. 1895. I. 320, IV. 78.[1]
— Opuntia arborescens in the South-west. 1896. II. 597.[1]
— Opuntia fulgida. 1896. II. 806.[2]
— Practical tree planting in operation. 1900. IV. 113,[1] 155.[2]
— Progress in tree planting in the United States. 1900. IV. 155.[2]
— Sensitive stamens in the genus Opuntia. 1899. II. 596.[2]
— The tree Opuntias of the United States. 1898. II. 596.[1]
— Vegetal dissemination in the genus Opuntia. 1895. II. 596.[2]
Tour, Jean Baptiste Louis Claude Théodore LESCHENAULT DE LA. See LESCHENAULT DE LA TOUR, J. B. L. C. T.
Le Tour du monde. III. 23.[1]
La tourbe des forêts de Hertogenwald et de Freyr. 1898. IV. 438.[2]
Tournefort, Joseph Pitton de. Abrégé des élémens de botanique. 1749. I. 254.[2]
— Beschreibung einer . . . Reise nach der Levante. 1718. I. 478.
— Beschrijving van eene reize naar de Levant. 1718. I. 478.
— The compleat herbal. 1719. I. 289.
— Corollarium institutionum rei herbariae. 1703. I. 478.
— Description de deux espèces de Chamaerhododendros. 1706. II. 676.[2]
— Élémens de botanique. 1694. I. 288.

— Élémens de botanique . . . édition augmentée. 1797. I. 259.
— Établissement de quelques nouveaux genres de plantes. 1706. I. 289.
— Explorações botanicas em Hespanha. 1898. I. 423.
— Histoire des plantes . . . de Paris, avec leur usage dans la médecine. 1698. I. 405.
— Histoire des Tamarins. 1702. III. 489.[1]
— History of plants growing about Paris. 1698. I. 405.
— Institutiones rei herbariae. 1700. I. 289.
— Materia medica. 1708. III. 241.
— Observations sur les maladies des plantes. 1706. I. 206.[1]
— De optima methodo instituenda in re herbaria. 1697. I. 250.
— Plantae novae . . . observatae in orientalibus regionibus. 1703. I. 478.
— Relation d'un voyage du Levant. 1718. I. 478.
— Traité de la matière médicale. 1708. III. 241.
— A voyage into the Levant. 1718. I. 478.
Tourney, E. Note sur les forêts. 1846. IV. 180.[2]— 1847. IV. 359.[2]
— Nouvelle méthode d'aménagement. 1832. IV. 242.
— Nouvelle méthode de semis . . . des bois. 1828. IV. 109.[1]
Tournon, Dominique Jerome. Flore de Toulouse. 1811. I. 407.
Tourres. Bouture herbacée. 1831. III. 157.
— Sur la culture du Magnolia grandiflora. 1830. III. 399.[2]
— Sur la culture du Prunier Robe-Sergent. 1832. III. 432.[2]
Tourrès, P. Essai sur la culture . . . du Camelia. 1836. III. 599.[2]
Toursky. La forêt de l'Academie agricole de Petrowsky près de Moscou. 1893. See Турскій, M. K. IV. 346.
Toussaint, Anatole & Hoschedé, Jean Pierre. Flore de Vernon et de la Roche-Guyon. 1898. I. 535.
Toussaint, Friedrich Wilhelm. Der Einfluss des Waldes auf Quellenbildung. 1884. IV. 51.
— Die landwirthschaftliche Wasserfrage. 1878. IV. 144.[1]
— Die ökonomische Vertheilung und Benutzung von Boden und Wasser. 1882. IV. 270.
Toussaint, O. Forêts et forges. 1898. IV. 28.[1]
Towarzystwo ogrodnicze w Krakowie. Biblioteka i zbiory. See BIBLIOTEKA . . . 1900. III. 2.
Towers, John. The course of the sap in plants. 1850. I. 164.
— On excretions from the roots of plants. 1834. I. 160.
— On the excretory powers of plants. 1834. I. 160.
Town, F. E. Bighorn forest reserve. 1899. IV. 341.[1]
Town forest of Bamberg, Bavaria. 1900. IV. 351.[2]
Town trees. 1889. III. 42.[2]
Townley, John. On the season for transplanting. 1841. III. 168.[1]
Townley, Walter. Report on the cultivation of Olives. 1891. III. 676.[1]
Townsend, C. H. T. On an apparently microlepidopterous leaf-miner of the Vine. 1892. III. 564.[1]
— An account of San Francisco Mountain. 1893. I. 326.
— Insects frequenting Yucca blooms. 1892. II. 87.[1]
— On a leaf-miner of Populus Fremonti. 1892. III. 346.[1]
— The Peach and Apricot borer. 1892. III. 431.[1]
— Some larvae on Scrub Oak. 1893. IV. 501.[1]
— Chittenden, F. H., Cockerell, T. D. A. & Oraw, Alexander. Some Mexican and Japanese injurious insects. 1896. IV. 187.
Townsend, Charles Orrin. The correlation of growth under the influence of injuries. 1897. I. 208.[1]
Townsend, Frederick. Flora of Hampshire. 1883. I. 534.[1]
— Notes on the flora of Hampshire. 1879. I. 403.
Townsend, Joseph. A journey through Spain. 1791. I. 420.
— Reise durch Spanien. 1791. I. 420.
— Voyage en Espagne. 1791. I. 420.
Townsen, Robert. Travels in Hungary. 1797. I. 444.
— Voyage en Hongrie. 1797. I. 444.
Tozzetti, TARGIONI-. See TARGIONI-TOZZETTI.
Tr. Magnolien in dem Norden der Vereinigten Staaten. 1894. III. 399.[1]
Trabajos de repoblación en Portugal. 1889. IV. 546.[2]
Trabajos de restauración de montañas en Francia. 1892. IV. 546.[2]
Trabajos del Dr. Brown. 1886. IV. 540.[1]
Trabaud, P. Du Palmier bleu et de sa récente floraison. 1897. III. 325.[1]
Trabut, Louis. L'Abies numidica. 1889. II. 23.[1]
— Dattiers précoces. 1895. III. 329.[1]

Trabut, Louis (*continued*).
— Sur la déhiscence des capsules dans le genre Eucalyptus. 1892. II. 623.¹
— Détermination du Sapindus cultivé en Algérie. 1895. II. 488.¹
— Deux ennemis des Orangers. 1898. III. 501.¹
— Développement des carpelles chez un Dattier mâle. 1892. II. 73.¹
— De Djidjelli aux Babors. 1889. I. 486.
— Enriquecimiento de la tierra por las raices de las Acacias. 1890. IV. 543.²
— L'essence du Cèdre de l'Atlas. 1900. IV. 447.¹
— État de l'horticulture en Algérie. 1900. III. 130.²
— Eucalyptus hybrids in the Mediterranean region. 1900. II. 623.³
— Feuilles d'arbres comme fourrage. 1894. IV. 438.¹
— Germination du Cocos nucifera. 1892. II. 67.²
— Un hybride dans le genre Eucalyptus. 1892. II. 625.²
— Les hybrides du Quercus Suber. 1889. II. 140.¹
— Le Karri Eucalyptus diversicolor ou colossea. 1898. III. 634.²
— La mélancse des Mandarines. 1898. III. 503.¹
— L'Olivier en Algérie. 1900. III. 677,¹ 679.²
— D'Oran à Mécheria. 1887. I. 485.
— Précis de botanique médicale. 1891. III. 59.¹
— Rapport sur la culture du Dattier dans le Chélif. 1897. III. 329.¹
— Le Sapindus Savonnier. 1895. III. 540.¹
— Sapindus utilis. 1895. III. 540.¹
— Le Savonnier. 1895. III. 540.¹
— Le Sumac des corroyeurs. 1900. III. 527.¹
— Sur les variations du Quercus Mirbeckii. 1892. II. 135.¹
— Les zones botaniques de l'Algérie. 1888. I. 486.
— *See also* BATTANDIER, J. A. & TRABUT, Louis.
Trachenberger Fürstenthumsforsten. 1886. IV. 354.
Tracts on practical agriculture and gardening. *See* WESTON, Richard. 1769. III. 109.
Tracts relative to botany. *See* KONIG, Charles. 1805. I. 265.
Tracy, Cyrus Mason. Studies of the Essex flora. 1858. I. 314.
Tracy, Samuel Mills. Catalogue of the . . . plants of Missouri. 1886. I. 319, V. XVIII.¹
— Grape growing in the South. 1900. III. 551.¹
Tracy, W. W. A venerable top-worked Cherry tree. 1893. II. 273.¹
The **trade** in Siamese Teak. 1896. IV. 538.¹
Tradescant, John. Musaeum Tradescantianum. 1656. I. 52.
Tradescant, L. G. Remarks on the euphorbiaceous plants. 1837. II. 433.¹
Traduction d'anciens ouvrages latins relatifs à l'agriculture. *See* SCRIPTORES rei rusticae. 1470. III. 97.
Trælasttolden og Skovbruget. *See* FREDERIKSEN, K. N. & OPPERMANN, A. 1890. IV. 284.¹
Trafvenfelt, Erik Carl. Anmärkningar om natural-historiens lärande. 1818. I. 78.¹
Tragus. *See* BOCK, Hieronymus.
Traicté nouveau de l'agriculture. 1551. III. 110.¹
Trail, James William Helenus. Description of a new species of Bactris. 1876. II. 65.¹
— Descriptions of new species and varieties of Palms. 1876. II. 61.¹
— The gall-making Diptera of Scotland. 1887. I. 215.²
— Scottish galls. 1871. I. 215.²
— Scottish Oak galls. 1885. IV. 511.
— Some remarks on the synonymy of Palms of the Amazon valley. 1877. II. 61.¹
Trailing Arbutus. 1882. III. 649.²
Traill. Tests of strychnine and brucine. 1857. III. 682.¹
Traill, Mrs. Catherine Parr (STRICKLAND). Canadian wild flowers. 1869. I. 310.
— Our forest trees. 1878. I. 309.¹
— Studies of plant life in Canada. 1885. I. 310.
Traill, D. M. Paper and paper making. 1891. III. 235.²
Traill, James. Accounts . . . of the several plants belonging to the genus Hoya. 1830. II. 739.¹
Traill, Thomas Stewart. On the detection of strychnine. 1856. III. 682.¹
Traill, William. Notes on horticultural experience at Russelconda. 1861. III. 129.¹
— On submarine forests. 1867. I. 393.¹
Trainer, Wilhelm Adolph Bartholomaeus. Examen chemicum mannae. 1793. III. 221.¹

Training for the forest service in Prussia. *See* ZUSAMMENSTELLUNG . . . 1882. IV. 33.¹
Training of forest officers. 1878. IV. 37.¹
Training of Indian forest officers at Cooper's Hill. 1886. IV. 37.¹
Traité abregé de la culture des arbres fruitiers. 1784. III. 145.²
Traité complet de la culture des Orangers. 1782. III. 496.²
Traité de l'éducation des vers à soie au Japon. *See* SIRAKAWA. 1868. III. 377.
Traité de l'Olivier. *See* AMOREUX, P. J. 1784. III. 674.²
Traité des arbres fruitiers. 1768. III. 145.²
Traité des bois. *See* MASSÉ. 1769. IV. 108.²
Traité des jardins. *See* LE BERRYAIS, L. R. 1775. III. 112.²
Traité du Café, contenant l'histoire. 1798. III. 738.
Traité ou abrégé curieux et très utile . . . *See* B***, M. 1706. III. 143.
Traité usuel du chocolat. *See* BUC'HOZ, P. J. 1812. III. 592.¹
Traitement des bois d'un domaine en Campine. 1899. IV. 119.²
Traitement des sapinières. 1899. IV. 169,² 444.²
Traitement du taenia par l'écorce . . . de Grenadier. 1885. III. 631.¹
Traitement et produit des oseraies. 1864. III. 347.
Traitement préventif des Vignes péronosporées. 1895. III. 581.
Traitté de la culture des Orangers, Citroniers. 1676. III. 143.
Tralles, Alexander von. Original-Text und Übersetzung. 1878. III. 239.
Tramblay, L. Manuel du marchand de bois. 1799. IV. 220.
Tramnitz. Über Forstzuwachskunde. 1872. IV. 233.
Tramnitz, (*Forstinspektor, Breslau*). Bericht über eine forstliche Reise. 1859. IV. 348.¹
Tramnitz, Adolf. Die Forstwirthschaft [in Schlesien]. 1869. IV. 353.
— Die Oder und die Waldungen ihres Stromgebietes. 1884. IV. 354.
— Schlesiens Forsten. 1869. IV. 353.
Tramnitz, Robert. Die westfälischen Wälder. 1861. IV. 353.
Trampusch, Fr. Thatbestand . . . der Bisthumsfonds-Domaine Freywaldau. 1850. IV. 368.
La transformation des fanges de Freyr. 1896. IV. 160.²
Transformation of woody fibre into sugar. 1859. I. 175.
Transformed pears. 1856. II. 279.²
La transmisión por cables. 1890. IV. 392.
Transplantation d'arbres. Soins. 1899. IV. 153.¹
Transplantation d'un grand Abies Pinsapo. 1861. III. 297.¹
Transplanted Hollies. 1889. III. 530.¹
Transplanting, B. C. 1600. 1892. III. 168.¹
Transplanting evergreens. 1874. III. 169.¹
Transplanting large Mango trees. 1900. III. 525.¹
Transplanting of evergreens. 1849. III. 169.¹
Transplanting Palms at Santa Barbara, Cal. 1896. III. 318.¹
Transplanting trees. 1883. III. 168.¹— 1894. III. 168.¹
Transplanting trees in August. 1875. III. 168.²
Transsylvania university — Botanical garden. First catalogues. *See* RAFINESQUE-SCHMALTZ, C. S. 1824. I. 38.¹
Transylvania journal of medicine. 1. 7.¹
Trapp, Julius. Ueber das ätherische Oel des Porst. 1868. III. 653.¹
— Ueber das ätherische Oel des Sumpfporst. 1874. III. 653.¹
— Sur l'huile essentielle du Ledum. 1874. III. 653.¹
— Oleum aethereum Ledi. 1895. III. 653.¹
Trapp, M. Rosmarin-Kultur und Kultus. 1879. III. 698.¹
Trappen, Jan Everhard van der. Bijdrage tot de kennis van Neerland's flora. 1852. I. 391.¹
— Over de druiventeelt in het westland. 1859. III. 577.
— Herbarium vivum. 1839. III. 76.
— Specimen historico-medicum de coffea. 1843. III. 741.²
— *See also* KOPS, Jan & TRAPPEN J. E. van der.
Trask, Blanche. Field notes from Santa Catalina Island. 1899. I. 327.
Tratman, Eduard Ernest Russell. Economy in the consumption of timber for railway purposes. 1890. IV. 424.¹
— Metal ties for railways. 1899. IV. 424.²
— Preliminary report on the use of metal track on railways. 1889. IV. 424.¹
— Report on the substitution of metal for wood in railroad ties. 1890. IV. 424.¹
— Report on the use of metal railroad ties. 1894. IV. 424.¹

Trattato della coltura de' Persici e degli albèri da frutto. 1792. III. 145.[1]
Trattato di fitognosia. *See* TENORE, Michele. 1833. I. 86.
Trattinnick, Leopold. Archiv der Gewächskunde. 1812. I. 265.
— Ausgemahlte Tafeln aus dem Archiv der Gewächskunde. 1812. I. 265.
— Auswahl vorzüglich schöner . . . Gartenpflanzen. 1821. I. 266.
— Botanisches Album. 182 . ? V. XIII.[2]
— Botanisches Taschenbuch. *See* BOTANISCHES Taschenbuch. 1821. I. 1.
— Calliope und Flora. 1819. I. 94.
— Flora des österreichischen Kaiserthumes. 1816. I. 439.
— Genera nova plantarum . . . illustrata. 1825. I. 267.
— Genera plantarum. 1802. I. 259.
— Der Kaiserkrans zum 12. Febr. 1829. 1829. II. 769.[1]
— Neue Arten von Pelargonien deutschen Ursprunges. 1825. II. 390.[1]
— Observationes botanicae. 1811. I. 265.
— Oestreichscher Blumenkrans. 1819. I. 94.
— Rosacearum monographia. 1823. II. 255.[2]
— Die Schule der blühende Natur. 1843. I. 94.
— Synodus botanica. 1823. II. 255.[2]
— Thesaurus botanicus. 1805. I. 265.
Trauer-Nadelhölzer. 1879. III. 290.
Traumüller. Der Teakbaum und seine Verbreitung. 1884. II. 761.[1]
Traun, Heinrich. Versuch einer Monographie des Kautschuks. 1859. III. 231.
Traunsteiner, Joseph. Monographie der Weiden von Tirol. 1842. II. 102.[2]
Traustedt, M. Beretning om Herlufsholms Pinetum for 1891. 1891. I. 41.
Trautfettert. Collection d'échantillons de bois. 1867. I. 37,[1] *IV. 17.*
Trautmann, G. Die kleinen Feinde und Freunde der Land- und Forstwirthschaft. 1865. III. 189.
Trautschold, H. Bemerkungen und Versuche zur Frage über den Einfluss des Bodens. 1858. I. 228.[2]
— Polarland und Tropenflora. 1897. I. 219.[1]
— Ueber die Winterflora von Nizza. 1896. I. 226.[2]
Trautvetter, Ernst Christian von. Das Laubwerk. 1842. I. 101.[2]
— De novo systemate botanico. 1841. I. 252.
Trautvetter, Ernst Rudolph von. Ueber Betula divurica [sic] Fall. 1857. II. 119.[2]
— Catalogus plantarum . . . in Mongolia orientali lectarum. 1871. I. 456.
— Conspectus florae insularum Nowaja-Semlja. 1871. I. 363.
— Contributio ad floram Turcomaniae. 1886. I. 457.
— Contributionem ad floram Dagestanicam. 1897. I. 269, 531.
— Elenchus stirpium . . . isthmo caucasico lectarum. 1881. I. 369.
— Enumeratio plantarum . . . in Armenia rossica. 1873. I. 369.
— Enumeratio plantarum songoricarum. 1860. I. 460.[1]
— Flora riparia kolymensis. 1878. I. 456.
— Flora terrae Tschuktschorum. 1879. I. 430.
— Florae rossicae fontes. 1880. I. 3.[1]
— Florula boganidensis phaenogama. 1856. I. 455.
— Florula taimyrensis phaenogama. 1856. I. 455.
— Grundriss einer Geschichte der Botanik in Bezug auf Russland. 1837. I. 80.[2]
— Incrementa florae phaenogamae rossicae. 1883. I. 364.
— Ueber die Krzemieniecer botanischen Garten. 1844. I. 42.
— Ueber die Nebenblätter. 1830. I. 111.
— Observations in plantas a Dre. G. Radde . . . in Turcomania et Transcaucasia lectas. 1871. I. 456.[2]
— De Pentastemone genere commentatio. 1839. I. 781.[1]
— Die pflanzengeographischen Verhältnisse des europäischen Russlands. 1849. I. 361.
— Phaenogame Pflanzen aus dein Hochnorden. 1856. I. 454.[1]
— Phaenogame Pflanzen aus dem Hochnorden. *In* MIDDENDORFF, A. T. von., 1856. I. 455, V. XXIII.[2]
— Pinus Cembra var. arborea. 1883. II. 41.[1]
— Plantae a Capit. Maloma . . . in Turcomania collectae. 1871. I. 457.
— Plantae jenisseenses. 1856. I. 455.

— Plantarum imagines et descriptiones. 1844· I. 361.
— Plantarum messes . . . in Armenia. 1875. I. 369.
— Plantas a Dre. G. Radde . . . lectas. 1876. I. 369.
— Plantas caspio-caucasicas . . . dilucidavit. 1877. I. 369.
— Plantas quasdam in insulis praefectoriis nuper lectas lustravit. 1886. I. 456.
— Plantas Sibiriae borealis . . . enumeravit. 1877. I. 454.[1]
— Rhododendrorum novorum par descripsit. 1885. II. 676.[1]
— Rossiae arcticae plantas . . . enumeravit. 1880. I. 454.[1]
— Salicetum. 1836. II. 98.[1]
— De Salicibus frigidis Kochii. 1832. II. 98.[2]
— De Salicibus livonicis. 1832. II. 100.[2]
— Stirpium sibiricarum collectiunculas binas commentatus est. 1882. I. 454.[1]
— Syllabus plantarum Sibiriae borealiorientalis. 1888. I. 456.
— Ueber die Ulmen des Kiew'schen Gouvernements. 1857. II. 143.[1]
— Ueber die Weiden des Hortus Hostianus. 1836. II. 102.[2]
— *See also* Траутфеттеръ, Р. Э.
— & Meyer, C. A. Florula ochotensis phaenogama. 1856. I. 455, V. XXIII.[2]
— & others. Einleitung, Klimatologie, Geognosie, Botanik. 1856. I. 455, V. XXIII.[2]
Trautwein, (*Oberförster, Eichelsdorf*). Eichenkultur und Aufmunterungsbetrieb. 1897. IV. 508.
Trautzschen, von (*Hauptmann*). Die bürgerliche Baukunst. 1823. IV. 266.[1]
Trauzl, Isidor. Die Dynamite. 1876. IV. 386.
Travani, G. B. Manuale pratico per coltivare il Gelso. 1835. III. 375.
Travaux chimiques sur les plantes. 1814. III. 627.[1]
Travaux d'automne. Plantations. 1899. IV. 154.[2]
Travaux militaires dans les forêts de la Lorraine. 1898. IV. 390.[1]
A **Traveller**, (*pseud.*). The Oak. 1881. II. 138.[2]
— The Scotch Fir. 1883. IV. 481.
The **Travellers'** tree. 1874. II. 91.[2]
The **Traveller's** tree of Madagascar. 1872. II. 91.[1]
Travers, William Thomas Locke. On the changes effected in the natural features . . . by the introduction of civilized races. 1870. I. 300.
— On hybridization. 1869. I. 245.
— On the spread of Cassinia leptophylla. 1874. II. 854.[1]
Des **traverses** de Pin et de Peuplier. 1851. IV. 423.[2]
Traverso, G. B. Intorno all'influenza della luce sullo sviluppo degli stomi nei cotiledoni. 1900. I. 172.
Travis, William. Catalogus plantarum circa Scarborough. 1800. I. 396. (*By error* 167 .? *I. 394.*)
Le **Tre** Fontane e la malaria. 1883. IV. 55.[1]
Le **Tre** Fontane presso Roma. 1881. IV. 530.
Tre trattati riguardanti l' agricoltura. 1840. III. 126.[2]
The **treasure** of Evonymus. *See* GESNER, Conrad. 1558. III 239.[2]
Treat, Mary. Autumn fruits in the Pines. 1867. III. 208.[1]
— Climbing plants in the Pines. 1892. III. 205.[1]
— Evergreens in the New Jersey Pine region. 1890. III. 206.[1]
— Ornamental fruit in the Pines. 1890. III. 208.[1]
— In the Pines. 1882. I. 315.
A **treatise** on some of the insects injurious to vegetation. *See* HARRIS, T. W. 1841. III. 186.[2]
A **treatise** on some of the insects of New England. *See* HARRIS, T. W. 1841. III. 186.[2]
A **treatise** on the Coco-nut tree. 1831. III. 323.[1]
A **treatise** on the cultivation of the Grape. *See* BUCHANAN, Robert. 1850. III. 549.[2]
A **treatise** on the manner of raising forest trees. 1761. IV. 107.[2]
A **treatise** on the origin . . . of the silk manufacture. 1831. III. 374.
Treatment of the downy mildew and black-rot. 1887. III. 579.
Treatment of the Hemlock. 1855. III. 312.[2]
The **treatment** of trees in drought. 1890. III. 211.[2]
Treatment of winter-injured trees. 1899. III. 183.[2]
Trebeljahr, W. Ein Beitrag zur Behandlung des Buchenwaldes. 1898. IV. 496.
— Die Rentabilität der Forstwirthschaft. 1897. IV. 259.[1]
Trébignaud, Claude. *See* MAUMENÉ, Albert & TRÉBIGNAUD Claude.
Trebra, von, (*Vice-Berghauptmann*). Nachrichten vom schwarzen Wurm. 1783. IV. 454.
Trécul, Auguste Adolphe Lucien. De l'accroissement de l'amidon. 1859. I. 140.[1]

Trécul, Auguste Adolphe Lucien (*continued*).
— Accroissement des végétaux dicotylédonés ligneux. 1852.
I. 207.¹
— Sur les cellules qui existent à l'intérieur des canaux . . .
du Brucea. 1887. II. 414.¹
— Changement de couleur de la chlorophylle. 1877. I. 141.
— De la chlorophylle cristallisé. 1879. I. 141.
— De la circulation dans les plantes. 1857. I. 164.
— De la cuticule à l'intérieur des végétaux. 1856. I. 130.
— Des divers états de la substance amylacée. 1858. I. 175.
— Extrait d'une mémoire intitulé: Recherche sur l'origine
des racines. 1846. I. 103.
— Sur la formation de glaçons. 1870. I. 212.
— Formation des feuilles. 1853. I. 109.²
— Formation des feuilles chez les Palmiers. 1853. II. 62.²
— De la formation des feuilles des Aesculus. 1891. II. 481.¹
— Formation des vaisseaux au-dessous des bourgeons. 1853.
I. 108,¹ *153*.
— Sur les formations secondaires dans les cellules végétales.
1854. I. 137.
— Formations spirales . . . des Cactées. 1854. II. 588.¹
— Sur les formations spirales . . . des Cactées. 1854. II.
588.¹
— Des formations vésiculaires. 1858. I. 136,² *184*.
— Fragment d'histoire concernant l'accroissement en dia-
mètre. 1867. I. 190.¹
— De la gomme et du tannin dans le Conocephalus. 1868.
II. 148.¹
— Des inflorescences centrifuges du Figuier. 1854. II.
145.²
— De l'influence des décortications annulaires. 1855. I. 207.
— Lacunes à gomme dans des Quiinées. 1866. II. 547.¹ —
1867. II. 547.¹
— Des laticifères dans les Cichoracées. 1865. II. 850.¹
— Sur les laticifères . . . dans les Euphorbes. 1865. II. 434.
— Des laticifères dans les Papavéracées. 1865. II. 229.¹
— Laticifères des Campanulacées. 1865. II. 845.¹
— Laticifères et liber des Apocynées et des Asclépiadées.
1865. II. 722.¹
— Maladie de la gomme chez les Cerisiers. 1860. III. 431.¹
— Matière amylacée . . . de plusieurs Apocynées. 1865. II.
722.²
— Mémoire sur l'origine . . . de la cuticule. 1856. I. 129.¹
— Mémoire sur la famille des Artocarpées. 1847. II. 145.¹
— Mémoire sur le développement des loupes. 1853. I. 213,²
523.²
— Mémoire sur les formations secondaires dans les cellules
végétales. 1854. I. 123.²
— Mémoire sur les formations spirales. 1854. II. 588.¹
— Mémoire sur les inflorescences centrifuges. 1854. I. 113.¹
— Des mucilages chez les Malvacées. 1866. II. 516,¹ *519*,²
531.²
— Naissance de l'amidon granuleux. 1858. I. 140.¹
— Nécessité de la réunion des canaux sécréteurs aux vaisseaux
du latex. 1887. I. 136.¹
— Note sur des cristaux organisés. 1858. I. 139.
— Note sur la formation des feuilles. 1853. I. 109.²
— Note sur les biforines. 1856. I. 138.³
— Nouvelles observations relatives à l'accroissement en dia-
mètre. 1853. I. 189.
— Du nucléus ou vésicule nucléaire. 1858. I. 136.²
— Observations relatives à l'accroissement en diamètre. 1852.
I. 189.
— Observations sur la nature des diverses parties de la fleur.
1872. I. 115,¹ II. 845.¹
— Observations sur les laticifères des Convolvulacées. 1865.
II. 744.¹
— Observations sur quelques assertions de M. Gaudichaud,
concernant l'accroissement. 1852. I. 189.
— De l'ordre d'apparition des premiers vaisseaux. 1877. II.
320.³
— De l'ordre d'apparition des premiers vaisseaux dans les
bourgeons de Lysimachia et de Ruta. 1877. II. 410.²
— Origine des grains d'amidon composés. 1859. I. 140.¹
— Origine et composition des fibres ligneuses. 1852. I. 124.
— Origine et développement des fibres ligneuses. 1853. I.
189.
— Origine et développement des loupes. 1852. I. 528.²
— De la présence du latex dans les vaisseaux. 1857. I. 135,
II. *582*.²
— On the presence of latex in the . . . vessels of plants. 1857.
I. 135.
— Production de plantules amylifères. 1865. I. 140.¹
— Production du bois par l'écorce. 1853. I. 127,¹ *189*, 207.³

— Des propriétés nutritives du latex . . . des Calophyllum.
1887. II. 553.²
— Sur quelques phénomènes de végétation dans des conditions
anormales. 1855. I. 207.²
— Quelques remarques sur l'anatomie comparée. 1869. I.
100.¹
— La ramification . . . est-elle partout et toujours acropète?
1881. I. 106.³
— Rapport des laticifères avec le système fibro-vasculaire.
1860. I. 135..
— Des rapports des laticifères avec le système fibrovasculaire.
1887. I. 136.¹
— Rapports des vaisseaux du latex avec le système fibro-
vasculaire. 1865. I. 135.¹
— Recherches sur l'origine des bourgeons adventifs. 1847.
I. 107.²
— Recherches sur l'origine des racines adventives. 1846.
I. 103.
— Réflexions sur la formation de l'amidou. 1877. I. 159.
— Remarques sur l'origine des lenticelles. 1871. I. 132.¹
— Réponse à une lettre de M. Schultz concernant les vais-
seaux du latex. 1867. I. 136.¹
— Réponse aus deux questions, concernant la chlorophylle.
1879. I. 141.
— Reproduction du bois et de l'écorce. 1852. I. 207.¹
— Résumé d'observations sur les vaisseaux. 1866. I. 136.¹
— Structure anomale dans quelques végétaux. 1866. II.
207,² *647*.²
— On the structure of the leaves of Palms. 1853. II. 62.²
— Du suc propre dans les feuilles des Aloès. 1871. III.
. 333.²
— Sur les sucs propres des Apocynées. 1862. I. 526.²
— Du tannin dans les Légumineuses. 1865. II. 321.²
— Du tannin dans les Rosacées. 1865. II. 257.¹
— De la théorie carpellaire d'après les Amygdalées. 1873.
II. 256.²
— De la théorie carpellaire d'après des Hippocastanées. 1874.
II. 480.³
— De la théorie carpellaire d'après des Liliacées. 1874. II.
87.¹
— De la théorie carpellaire d'après des Renonculacées. 1873.
II. 195.¹
— De la théorie carpellaire d'après des Tiliacées. 1875. II.
512.²
— De la théorie carpellaire d'après le Passiflora Loudoni.
1873. II. *579*.³
— Théorie de la greffe. 1853. III. 161.
— Des vaisseaux . . . dans les Musacées. 1867. II. 90.³
— Des vaisseaux propres dans les Araliacées. 1867. II. 647.¹
— Des vaisseaux propres dans les Clusiacées. 1866. II.
553.¹
— Des vaisseaux propres dans les Ombellifères. 1866. II.
653.¹
— Des vaisseaux propres dans les Térébenthinées. 1867.
II. 455.¹
— Des vaisseaux propres en général. 1862. I. 525.
— Des vésicules colorées ou chromulifères. 1858. I. 136.²
— Des vésicules fausses vacuoles, ou vacuoles. 1858. I.
136.²
Tredgold, Thomas. Elementary principles of carpentry. 1820.
IV. 408.
— On the nature and properties of timber. 1820. IV. 408.
— A report on a process for seasoning timber. 1828. IV.
416.¹
— *See also* ROBISON, J. & TREDGOLD, Thomas.
Tree and shrub planting in towns. 1890. III. 42.²
Tree-felling and philosophy. 1896. III. 202.³
A **tree** for bee-keepers. 1892. III. 408.²
Tree growing in the Transvaal. 1900. III. 131.²
Tree land. 1882. I. 320, *IV*. 78.¹
A **tree** land. 1882. III. 167.
Tree lifter. 1872. III. 167.
Tree lopping at midnight in Epping forest. 1873. IV. 323.¹
Tree-mover. 1860. III. 167.
The **tree** of Solomon. 1852. II. 71.¹
The "**tree** of the Janissaries." 1891. II. 255.¹
The **tree** Palms of the United States. 1896. II. 61.¹
Tree planting. 1883. III. 150.²
Tree-planting. 1888. III. 166. — 1889. III. 166.
Tree planting. Dotting and grouping. 1883. III. 202.¹
Tree planting abroad. 1886. IV. 49.¹
Tree planting and fountain society of Brooklyn, N.Y. Annual
report. Bulletin. Circular. III. 8.
Tree planting, Hongkong. 1880. III. 127.³
Tree-planting in Australia. 1882. IV. 124,² *169*.¹

Tree planting in Ireland. 1883. IV. 120.
Tree planting in Mexico. 1883. IV. 155.²
Tree-planting in towns. 1890. III. 42.³
Tree-pruning. 1861. III. 170.
Tree pruning. 1897. III. 171, *181*.²
Tree roots and buildings. 1886. III. 34.²
The tree Rose. *See* B., A. H. 1845. III. 452.
Tree sculpture. 1876. III. 202.²
Tree superstitions. 1889. I. 517.¹
Tree surgery. 1875. III. 180.²
Tree Tomato. 1887. II. 771.¹
The tree Tomato. 1887. III. 699.²
Tree which produces the caoutchouc, or elastic gum. 1821. III. 228.²
On the tree which yields the gutta percha. 1847. III. 668.²
The tree Yuccas in the United States. 1895. II. 87.¹
Trees. 1848. I. 516.
About trees. *See* ABOUT trees. 1855. I. 516.
Trees and lightning. 1883. IV. 194.
Trees and shrubs at Fota. 1896. I. 55.
Trees and their uses. 1862. I. 82.¹
Trees for planting in America. 1888. III. 203.
Trees for rural cemeteries. 1854. III. 201.
Trees for seaside plantations. 1886. III. 41.²
Trees for streets and avenues. 1853. III. 208.²
Trees, fruits and flowers of Minnesota. *See* MINNESOTA STATE HORTICULTURAL SOCIETY. III. 5.
Trees in a hygienic point of view. 1865. IV. 55.¹
Trees in assemblances. 1874. III. 201.
Trees in October. 1892. III. 207.¹
Trees in their spring attire. 1890. III. 203.
Trees in Washington. 1888. III. 208.²
Trees of the United States. 1885. I. 88,¹ *IV. 18.*¹
Trees on which Mistletoe is found. 1877. II. 179.¹
Trees, plants and flowers. *See* BAILEY, W. L. 1870. I. 95.
Trego, Charles B. A geography of Pennsylvania. 1843. I. 313.
Trégomain, Arthur de. Le Haut-perche. 1893. IV. 361.
— Les insectes du Chêne vert. 1876. IV. 503.¹
— Le Polygonum cuspidatum. 1894. IV. 146.¹
Treiber, Karl. Ueber den anatomischen Bau des Stammes der Asclepiadeen. 1891. II. 735.³
Treichel, Alexander. Ueber Blitzschläge an Bäumen. 1886. IV. 194.
— Botanische Notizen. 1886. II. 182.²— 1888. I. 209,¹ 296,¹ II. 104,¹ *IV. 497.*
— Fortwachsen einer Weide trotz Feuerzerstörung. 1888. II. 104.¹
— Mehrfache Verwachsung zweier Kiefern. 1876. II. 47.²
— Monstrosität am Blatte von Aristolochia Sipho. 1886. II. 182.²
— Polnisch westpreussische Vulgärnamen von Pflanzen. 1881. I. 73.³
— Starke oder benannte Bäume. 1888. I. 296.¹
— Verwachsene Rothbuchen. 1888. I. 209,¹ *IV. 497.*
— Volksthümliches aus der Pflanzenwelt. 1881. I. 518.
Treillaud, E. Azaleas grafted on Rhododendrons. 1897. III. 657.¹
— Les Azalées greffées sur Rhododendrons. 1897. III. 657.¹
Treise, Friedrich August. De Sambuco. *See* WEBEL, G. W. 1720. III. 752.¹
Trelease, Wilham. Botanical observations on the Azores. 1897. I. 498.
— The classification of botanical publications. 1899. I. 3.¹
— The cork-wings on the Sweet Gum. 1888. II. 253.²
— Cotyledon orbiculata L. 1894. II. 235.²
— Crassula quadrifida Baker. 1894. II. 236.¹
— Detail illustrations of Yucca. 1892. II. 86.²
— On the fertilization of Euphorbia . . . pulcherrima. 1879. II. 443.²
— The foliar nectar glands of Populus. 1881. II. 96.²
— Further studies of Yuccas. 1893. II. 86.²
— Ilex longipes. 1890. II. 462.²
— Juglandaceae of the United States. 1896. II. 112.¹
— Leitneria floridana. 1894. II. 111.¹
— Miscellaneous observations on Yucca. 1898. II. 86.²
— Nectar, its nature, occurrence and uses. 1879. I. 238.
— Nectar, what it is. 1879. I. 238.
— The nectary of Yucca. 1888. II. 87.¹
— North American Rhamnaceae. 1889. II. 491.²
— Pachira sp. 1894. II. 530.²
— Revision of North American Ilicineae and Celastraceae. 1889. II. 462.¹
— On the structures which favor cross-fertilization. 1883. I. 238.
— The Sugar Maples. 1894. II. 476.²
— The swamps of south-eastern Missouri. 1897. I. 327.
— Synoptical list of North American species of Ceanothus. 1889. II. 492.²
— Yucca guatemalensis Baker. 1894. II. 88.¹
— & Gray, Asa. The botanical works of the late George Engelmann. 1887. I. 308.
Trelissick, near Truro. 1894. I. 55.
Treloar, Thomas. The prince of Palms. 1852. III. 323.²
Treloar, William Purdie. The prince of Palms. 1884. III. 324.¹
Tremblay, D. J. Nouveau manuel métrique du marchand de bois. 1839. IV. 222.
Trémeau de Rochebrune, Alphonse. *See* ROCHEBRUNE, Alphonse TREMEAU DE.
Tremel, Johannes Bartholomaeus. Meditationes circa febrem. 1764. III. 720.
Trenkle, J. B. Der Korker Waldbrief von 1476. 1880. IV. 26.
Trentepohl, J. F. Oldenburgische Flora. 1839. I. 380.
Trenton natural history society. Journal. I. 7.¹
Tretzel, A. G. De insigni . . . usu corticis peruviani. 1761. III. 719.
Treub, Melchior. Der botanischer Garten . . . zu Buitenzorg. 1892. I. 68.¹
— Les bourgeons floraux du Spathodea. 1889. II. 790.²
— Sur les Casuarinées. 1891. II. 92.¹
— Driemaandelijksch botanisch literatuuroverzicht. 1874. I. 2.
— Eenige woorden over knop-bedekking in de tropen. 1890. I. 108.¹
— L'embryon du Barringtonia Vriesei. 1884. II. 611.²
— 's Lands plantentuin te Buitenzorg. 1892. I. 68.¹
— Het leven der planten. 1809. I. 148.
— Sur la localisation . . . de l'acide cyanhydrique dans le Pangium. 1892. II. 572.³
— In de lucifers-fabriek der firma Noothout & Co. 1897. IV. 429.
— Le meristème primitif de la racine. 1875. I. 103.
— Sur le Myrmecodia echinata Gaudich. 1883. II. 824.³
— Eene nieuwe categorie van klimplanten. 1882. I. 236.¹
— Notes sur l'embryon. 1883. I. 122.— 1884. II. 611.²
— Notice sur l'amidon dans les laticifères des Euphorbes. 1883. II. 435.¹
— Notice sur la nouvelle flore de Krakatau. 1888. I. 466.
— Sur une nouvelle catégorie de plantes grimpantes. 1882. I. 236.¹
— Nouvelles recherches sur le Myrmecodia de Java. 1888. II. 824.³
— Observations sur le sklérenchyme. 1877. II. 63.¹
— Observations sur les Loranthacées. 1881. II. 178.²
— Observations sur les plantes grimpantes. 1883. I. 236.¹
— Sur la pluralité des noyaux. 1879. I. 137.
— Recherches sur les Cycadées. 1881. II. 3.²
— De rol der bastvezels. 1876. I. 130.
— Over de urnen van Dischidia. 1882. II. 737.²
— Voordracht op het Koffiekongres. 1899. III. 727.
Treumann, Carl. Beiträge zur Kenntnis der Aloe. 1880. III. 333.³
De Treur-cypres, Cypressus funebris Endl. in Sikkim-Himalaya. 1856. II. 29.¹
Treutler, Paul. Fünfzehn Jahre in Süd-Amerika. 1882. I. 346.
Trevelyan, Walter Calverley. Outline of the Tamil system of natural history. 1850. I. 252.
— Remarks on a peculiar colouring matter in decayed wood. 1838. I. 206.²
— On the vegetation . . . of the Faroe Islands. 1835. I. 353.
— Yew and Laburnum. 1844. III. 288,² *480.*²
Treviranus, Gottfried Reinhold & Ludolf Christian. Vermischte Schriften. 1821. I. 33.
Treviranus, Ludolf Christian. Die Anwendung des Holzschnitts. 1855. I. 37.¹
— Ueber Bau und Entwicklung der Eychen . . . der Mistel. 1853. II. 178.¹
— Beiträge zur Pflanzenphysiologie. 1841. I. 147.
— Bemerkungen über die Führung von botanischen Gärten. 1848. I. 38.¹
— Comparatio florae wratislaviensis et bonnensis. *See* SCHIMTZ, J. J. & REGEL, Eduard von. 1841. I. 380.

Treviranus, Ludolf Christian (*continued*).
— De compositione fructus in Cactearum . . . ordinibus. 1851. II. 588.[1]
— Ueber einige Arten anomalischer Holzbildung. 1847. I. 126.
— Einige Bemerkungen über die Gattung Artemisia. 1839. II. 851.[1]
— Einige Betrachtungen über . . . Cytisus Adami. 1858. II. 368.[1]
— Ueber einige Stellen in des jüngeren Plinius Naturgeschichte der Gewächse. 1859. II. 72.[1]
— Über die Entwickelung der Früchte . . . der Mistel. 1843. II. 178.[1]
— Von der Entwicklung des Embryo. 1815. I. 121.
— Etwas den Ueberzug von Schuppen . . . betreffende. 1857. I. 112.[2]
— Etwas über die süssen Ausschwitzungen der Blätter. 1821. I. 213.[1]
— Flora bonnensis. *See* SCHMITZ, J. J. & REGEL, Eduard von. 1841. I. 380.
— Ueber Frucht- und Saamenbau der Mistel. 1859. II. 178.[1]
— Ueber die Frucht von Chimonanthus. 1880. II. 214.[2]
— Ueber die Frucht . . . von Magnolia. 1858. II. 211.[3]
— Ueber die Gattung Porteria. 1853. II. 844.[3]
— Horti botanici vratislaviensis plantarum . . . manipulus. 1826. I. 46.
— In Hyperici genus ejusque species animadversiones. 1861. II. 556.[1]
— Ueber das Insect welches die wilden Feigen in Oberitalien bewohnt. 1827. II. 150.[2]
— Vom inwendigen Bau der Gewächse. 1806. I. 100,[2] 163.
— Über ein den Kieferpflanzungen schädliches Insekt. 1829. IV. 461.[1]
— Die Lehre vom Geschlechte der Pflanzen. 1822. I. 199.
— Über die Oberhaut der Gewächse. 1821. I. 129.[1]
— Observationes botanicae. 1812. II. 101.[1]
— Observationum carpologicarum specimen. 1831. J. 119.
— De ovo vegetabili. 1828. I. 121.
— Physiologie der Gewächse. 1835. I. 148.
— De plantis Orientis unde pharmaca . . . colliguntur. 1825. III. 272.[1]
— Symbolarum phytologicarum . . . facsiculus I. 1831. I. 268.
— Ueber die taschenförmige Bildung der Pflaumen. 1846. III. 433.[3]
— Weitere Bemerkungen über monströse Blätter von Aristolochia macrophylla. 1860. II. 182.[2]
— Welwitschia mirabilis Jos. Hook. 1863. II. 55.[1]
— Wie entsteht die sogenannte Oberhaut der Saamenschale? 1863. I. 120.
— Wie lässt sich bei Gewächsen eine unächte . . . Befruchtung denken? 1862. I. 143.
— Ueber zwei Pflanzen-Missbildungen. 1859. II. *182,*[2] 258.[1]
— *See also* KOCH, W. D. J. & TREVIRANUS, C. L.
Treviranus, L. B. Nachtrag zu den "Betrachtungen über Cytisus Adami." 1859. II. 368.[1]
Trevisan, Vittore, *conte.* Prospetto della flora euganea. 1842. I. 427.
Trew, Christoph Jakob. Apologia et mantissa observationis de Cedro Libani. 1767. II. 12.[1]
— Brevis historia . . . Cerei serpentis. 1752. II. 589.[1]
— Brevis historia naturalis arboris Sassafras. 1759. II. 228.[1]
— Cedri montis Libani characteres. 1757. II. 27.[2]
— Cedrorum Libani historia. 1757. II. 27.[3]
— De Cerei plantae charactere generico. 1752. II. 589.[1]
— Cerei triangularis flos denuo examinatus. 1754. II. 591.[2]
— De femellae per marem foecundatione in plantis. 1757. I. 200.
— Hortus nitidissimis. 1750. I. 291.
— Librorum botanicorum catalogi duo. 1752. I. 1.
— Die Nahrungs-Gefässe in den Blättern. 1748. I. 109.[1]
— Plantae rariores. 1763. I. 261.
— Plantae selectae. 1750. I. 291.
— Uitgezochte planten. 1750. I. 291.
— Waarnemingen omtrent den Sassaphrasboom. 1759. II. 228.[1]
Triana, José. The botanical source of Cinchona cuprea. 1882. II. 830.[1]
— Choix de plantes de la Nouvelle-Grenade. 1858. I. 340.[1]
— Les Condurangos. 1873. II. 740.[3]
— Dispositio Melastomatacearum. 1866. II. 634.[2]
— Eleagia [*sic*] utilis Wedel. 1863. III. 743.[3]

— Enumeracion de las Melastomaceas de Chontales. 1867. II. 635.[1]
— Sur le Gonolobus cundurango. 1872. III. 693.[2]
— Nouvelles études sur les Quinquinas. 1870. II. 812.
— Nuevos jéneros e especies de plantas para la Flora neogranadina. 1854. I. 339.[3]
— Plantas usuelles de la Nouvelle-Grenade. 1858. III. 64.[3]
— Le Quinquina cuprea. 1882. III. 747.[1]
— *See also* PLANCHON, J. E. & TRIANA, José.
— & **Planchon,** J. E. Prodromus florae novogranatensis. 1862. I. 340.[1]
Tridan. Du copahu et du styrax. 1863. III. 473,[1] 671.[3]
Trie, A. L. de. Recherches sur l'écorce de racine de Grenadier. 1831. III. 630.[2]
Triebel, R. Ueber Oelbehälter in Wurzeln von Compositen. 1885. II. 850.[1]
Trientl, Adolf. Die Waldstreu. 1873. IV. 71.
— Die Waldwirthschaft in den Alpenländern. 1893. IV. 124.[1]
Trier. Beskrivelse af nogle nye Droguer. 1841. III. 244.
Trieste — Società adriatica di scienze naturali. *See* SOCIETÀ . . . I. 28.[1]
Trieux calcaires. 1900. IV. 70.
Triewald, Mårten. Rön och försök angående möjeligheten at Svea Rike kunde ega egit rådt silke. 1745. III. 372.[2]
Trifet, (*Dr.*). Histoire et physiologie du café. 1846. III. 741.[2]
Trilety, Josef. Die Obstbaumpflanzungen auf den Strassen in Niederösterreich. 1895. III. 146,[2] 211.[1]
Trillat, A. Recherche et dosage de la gélatine. 1898. I. 178.
— *See also* ADRIAN & TRILLAT, A.
Triller, Daniel William. De corticis peruviani usu. 1758. III. 719.
Trillich, H. & **Göckel,** H. Sur les propriétés et le dosage de la caféine. 1897. III. 740.[3]
Trimble. *See* DEITZ, TRIMBLE & SCHROETER.
Trimble, Henry. Die beiden Catechuhandelssorten. 1889. III. 464.[1]
— Chestnut-bark tannin. 1892. IV. 492.[2]
— Chestnut-wood tannin. 1891. IV. 492.[2]
— Mangrove tannin. 1892. III. 632.[1]
— Oil of Birch. 1895. IV. 491.[2]
— Purshia tridentata. 1892. III. 443.[2]
— Report on tannin from . . . Pterocarpus Draco. 1895. III. 485.[1]
— A robust Pin Oak. 1894. III. 362.[2]
— Salt and sugar in Washingtonia. 1896. II. 75.[2]
— The source of abietene. 1897. IV. 463.[1]
— The tannin value of some North American trees. 1896. IV. 435, 443.[2]
— The Tannins. 1892. III. 237.[2]
— The tannins of the Palmettos. 1896. III. 331.[1]
— *See also* BASTIN, E. S. & TRIMBLE, Henry.
Trimble, Isaac P. A treatise on the insect enemies of fruit and fruit trees. 1865. III. 186.[2]
Trimen, Henry. The botany of Cinchona Ledgeriana. 1884. II. 813.[2]
— Camoensia maxima. 1894. III. 469.[2]
— Ceylon. 1888. III. 279.[1]
— Ceylon's Flora. 1885. I. 476.[2]
— Cinchona Ledgeriana. 1883. II. 813.[2]
— Cinchona Ledgeriana a distinct species. 1881. II. 813.[2]
— Economic plants in Ceylon. 1891. III. 279.
— The effect of altitude on the alkaloids of Red bark. 1883. III. 718.
— Effets de l'altitude sur les alcaloïdes des écorces des Quinquinas rouges. 1883. III. 718.
— On the flora of Ceylon. 1886. I. 477.[1]
— The Giant Bamboo in Ceylon. 1881. II. 60.[1]
— A hand-book to the flora of Ceylon. 1893. I. 477.[1]
— Hermann's Ceylon herbarium. 1888. I. 477.[1]
— Hortus zeylanicus. 1888. I. 67.[1]
— Note on the genus Oudneya. 1880. II. 234.[1]
— Notes on some trees yielding india-rubber. 1882. III. 149.
— Notes on the flora of Ceylon. 1885. I. 476.[2]
— On the plant affording Ceará India-rubber. 1880. II. 447.[1]
— The plants affording myrrh. 1879. II. 417.[3]
— Remarks on the composition . . . of the Ceylon flora. 1885. I. 476.[1]
— Salix Pontederana. 1872. III. 109.[1]
— A systematic catalogue of the flowering plants . . . in Ceylon. 1885. I. 476.[2]

— Trees yielding india-rubber. 1882. III. 229.
— *See also* BENTLEY, Robert & TRIMEN, Henry.
— & Dyer, W. T. THISELTON-. Flora of Middlesex. 1868. I. 402.
Trimmer, J. On Gorse, as a winter food for horses. 1844. III. 490.[1]
Trimmer, Kirby. Flora of Norfolk. 1866. I. 402.
Trimoulet, A. Henri. Mémoire sur la maladie de la Vigne. 1872. III. 565.[1]
— Mémoire sur la maladie de la Vigne, le phylloxéra. 1872. III. 565.[1]
Trinchinetti, Augusto. Sulla facoltà assorbente delle radici. 1843. I. 161.
— Su gli odori dei fiori. 1841. I. 182.[2]
Trinci, Cosimo. L' agricoltore sperimentato. 1738. III. 115.[1]
Trinidad — Jardines real botanicos. *See* ROYAL BOTANIC GARDENS, TRINIDAD. 1888. I. 40.
Trinidad — Royal botanic gardens. *See* ROYAL . . . 1888. I. 40.
Trinidad Coffee. 1888. III. 740.[1]
Trinidad Ipecacuanha. 1888. III. 747.[1]
Trinité, PHILIPPE DE LA TRÈS-SAINCTE. *See* PHILIPPE DE LA TRÈS-SAINCTE TRINITÉ.
Trinius, Carl Bernhard. Bambusaceas quasdam novas describit. 1835. II. 58.[1]
— Genera plantarum ad familias suas redacta. 1835. I. 77.
— *See also* LEDEBOUR, Joseph & TRINIUS, Karl; Триниусъ, К. & Лэдэбуръ, O.
Trinobomie. Dr. W. Burck en de gouvernements Koffiecultuur. 1897. III. 731.
Trionfetti, Giovanni Battista. Observationes de ortu ac vegetatione plantarum. 1685. I. 30, 530.[2]
— Praelusio ad publicas herbarum ostensiones. 1700. II. 775.[1]
— Syllabus plantarum horto medico Romanae sapientiae. 1688. I. 60.[1]
— Vindiciarum veritatis a castigationibus quarundam propositionum. 1703. I. 30.
Trip, H. SCATO. *See* SCATO TRIP, H.
Tripaldi, Andrea Canonico. Su taluni insetti che fanno disseccare i rami degli Ulivi. 1822. III. 677.[1]
Tripet, Fritz. L'Argousier Faux Nerprun. 1900. II. 608.[1]
— Découverte de l'Argoussier Faux-Nerprun. 1880. II. 608.[1]
— Localités et plantes nouvelles pour la flora du Jura. 1893. II. 287.[1]
— Nouvelle station du Genista Halleri. 1894. II. 350.[2]
— Rhododendron hirsutum. 1879. II. 680.[1]
Tripet-Leblanc. Lettre sur la multiplication du Paulownia. 1842. III. 703.[1]
Triquet, R. Instructions pour les arbres fruictiers. 1653. III. 142.
Triska, Éándor. Nehány szó Gránátfáink érlekéhen. 1900. III. 630.[2]
Tristan, *comte de*. Exposé sommaire de l'opinion . . . sur les organes que les plantes emploient pour absorber. 1843. I. 161.
Tristan, *marquis de*. La maladie des pineraies, dite " du Rond." 1892. IV. 461.[2]
Tristan, A. de. Harmonie des organes végétaux. 1838. I. 98.
— Histoire du Pin maritime. 1851. IV. 467.[1]
— Note sur la production de la résine. 1864. IV. 436.[2]
— Note sur les échantillons de bois de Pin maritime. 1851. IV. 468.[1]
Tristan, Jean, *comte de*. Rapport . . . d'une nouvelle méthode de greffer. 1830. III. 160.
Tristan, Jules Marie Claude, *marquis de*. Études phytologiques. 1840. I. 123.[1]
— Mémoire sur la situation botanique de l'Orléanais. 1810. I. 407.
— Mémoire sur le genre Linné. 1810. II. 38,[2] 39.[3]
— Mémoire sur les développements des bourgeons. 1813. I. 524.[2]
— Note sur la germination du Bertholletia. 1833. II. 611.[2]
— Note sur une monstruosité du Saule Marceau. 1811. II. 106.[1]
— Notice sur une maladie du Pin maritime. 1811. IV. 467.[1]
— Observations sur la foliation des Pins. 1812. IV. 467.[3]
— Recherches sur l'importance de quelques . . . caractères spécifiques dans . . . Pinus et Quercus. 1851. II. 38,[2] 123.[1]
— Tableau des époques de la végétation. 1818. I. 226.[3]
Tristram, Henry Baker. The natural history of the Bible. 1867. I. 513.
— The survey of western Palestine. 1888. I. 480, V. XXIV.[1]

Tritschler, L. *See* NANOT, J. & TRITSCHLER, L.
Trobchen, A. *See* MÜLLER, R. & TROBCHEN, A.
Troceon, Paulus. Note sur la maladie de la Vigne. 1852. III. 575.[2]
Trochu, J. L. Création de la ferme et des bois de Bruté. 1846. III. 125.
— Du défrichement . . . des landes et bruyères. 1820. IV. 161.[2]
Die **Trocknung** des Holzes. 1889. IV. 416.[2]
Troeger, J. *See* BECKURTS, H. & TROEGER, J.
Trsyel, Frans Wilhelm. Forsøg til Besvarelse . . . Afhandling om de vigtigste Sorter af Popler og Pile. 1800. III. 344.[1]
Trog, Hans. Studien über den Perubalsam. 1894. III. 482.[1]
Troilius, A. M. Om Westerästrakten i botanisk afseende. 1860. I. 355.
Trois jolies plantes de Nouvelle-Hollande. 1900. III. 464,[3] 474,[3] 623.[1]
Troisvilles, *chevalier*, GOUFFÉ DE. *See* GOUFFÉ DE TROISVILLES, *chevalier*.
Trojan, Johannes. Eibenbäume in Deutschland. 1894. II. 11.[2]
Trojanowsky, Piers. Chemische Untersuchung der Zimmt- und Cassiarinden. 1874. II. 224.[1]
Trojel, F. W. Fuldstaendig Afhandling om alle Slags Indhegninger. 1784. III. 212.[2]
Trolard, Dr. La colonisation et la question forestière. 1891. IV. 279.[2]
— La colonisation et les forêts en Algérie. 1890. IV. 279.[3]
Trolard, P. Bréviaire du ligueur. 1893. IV. 168.[1]
— La forêt; conseils aux indigènes. 1883. IV. 168.[1]
— La question du reboisement en Algérie. 1886. IV. 168.[2]
— La question forestière algérienne devant le sénat. 1893. IV. 168.[1]
Trolle, Vilhelm. Er der nogen Fare ved Skovtvangens Ophævelse? 1867. IV. 273.[1]
Trolliet. Plantation de boutures. 1835. III. 157.
Trombellus, J. C. Ad F. M. Zanottum . . . epistola . . . filum ex Genista ad telas contexendas. 1783. III. 488.[2]
— De tela ex Genistarum corticibus. 1757. III. 488.[2]
Trommer, C. Die Bodenkunde. 1857. IV. 68.
Trommsdorff, Johann Bartholomaeus. Analyse chimique du suc . . . du Cocotier. 1816. II. 67.[2]
— Analyse des girofles. 1814. III. 635.[2]
— Chemische Untersuchung der Gewürznelken. 1814. III. 635.[2]
— Einige Bemerkungen über den Paraguay-Thee. 1836. III. 530.[2]
— Ueber die salzigen Bestandtheile . . . des Gerbersumachs. 1834. II. 453,[2] III. 527.[1]
— Sur les substances salines . . . du Sumach des corroyeurs. 1834. III. 527.[1]
Tromp. Over de Rotan en Getah-pertjah cultuur . . . van Borneo. 1874. III. 149, III. 234.
Tromsdorff, Johann Samuel. Ros mellis, non ros. 1699. I. 213.[1]
Tromsø museum. Aarshefter. I. 8.[2]
Trone, G. Expériences sur l'emploi du tabac pour combattre le phylloxéra. 1874. III. 566.[2]
Troop, James. Close root-pruning in trees. 1897. III. 173.[2]
— Cultivating the Persimmon. 1895. III. 670.[1]
— & Hadley, O. M. The American Persimmon. 1896. III. 670.[1]
Troost, J. Genaue Beschreibung von 250 häufig vorkommenden . . . Pflanzen. 1884. V. XIX.[2]
Troostwijk, A. PAETS VAN. *See* PAETS VAN TROOSTWIJK, A.; DEIMAN, J. R. & TROOSTWIJK, A. P. van.
Der **Tropenpflanzer**. 1897. II. — Beihefte. III. 14.
Tropical agriculturist. III. 26.[3]
Tropical fruits for Christmas. 1900. III. 220.[2]
Troschel, Franz Ernst Innocenz. Untersuchungen über das Mestom. 1879. I. 125.
Trost, C. Abnorme Zapfenproduktion. 1900. II. 47.[2]
— Ein Beitrag zur Kenntnis der Lebensweise des kleinen braunen Kiefernrüsselkäfers. 1890. IV. 478.
— Der Festgehalt von Durchforstungs-Langhaufen. 1900. IV. 229.
— Aus der Praxis . . . gegen die Nonne. 1892. IV. 201.
— Untersuchungen über den Festgehalt und das Gewicht der Brennholz-Langhaufen. 1889. IV. 228.
— Untersuchungen über den Festgehalt und das Gewicht des Brennreisigs. 1889. IV. 228.
Trott, H. W. *See* CUMMING, L. & TROTT, H. W.

Trotter, Alessandro. Comunicazione intorno a vari acaro-cecidi. 1900. I. 216.[1]
— Communicazione intorno alle galle. 1899. I. 216.[1]
— Contributo alla conoscenza degli entomocecidi italiani. 1899. I. 216.[1]
— Intorno alla Phillyrea media. 1900. II. 714.[4]
— Ricerche intorno agli entomocecidi. 1900. I. 216.[1]
— Zoocecidi della flora mantovana. 1895. I. 215.[2]
— Zoocecidi della flora modenese. 1898. I. 216.[1]
Trotter, Spencer. The relation of birds to the distribution of forests. 1895. I. 241.[1]
Trotti, Lodovico. Relazione sull' imboschimento . . . dei monti di Bellagio. 1881. IV. 166.[1]
Trottier. Boisement dans le désert et colonisation. 1869. IV. 168.[2]
— Boisement et colonisation. 1876. IV. 49.[1]
— L'Eucalyptus. 1871. IV. 529.[2]
— Taillis d'Acacia leiophylla. 1876. III. 466,[2] IV. 521.[1]
Trotzky, Petrus Kornuch. De plantarum phanerogamarum germinatione. 1832. I. 202.[2]
Troubetskoy, Pierre, prince. Sulla coltura dell' Eucalyptus sul Lago Maggiore. 1879. IV. 530.
— Culture de l'Eucalyptus au Lac Majeur. 1879. IV. 530.
— Les Eucalyptus en Italie. 1867. IV. 530.
— Sull' utilità degli Eucalyptus. 1878. IV. 531.[2]
Trouchaud. Sur la présence du phylloxera dans les Vignes sub-mergées. 1876. III. 568.
Trouessart, Édouard Louis. L'origine de la faune et de la flore de la Nouvelle-Zélande. 1885. I. 507.
Trouette, Édouard. De l'introduction . . . des Quinquinas à l'Île de la Réunion. 1879. III. 717.[1]
Trouette, Émile. Acclimatation des Arbres à caoutchouc à la Réunion. 1875. III. 149.
— See also LÉPERVANCHE, Paul & TROUETTE, Émile.
Trouillet, Éloi. Culture de la Vigne. 1856. III. 555.
— Notions préliminaires d'arboriculture. 1859. III. 144.
— Nouvelle culture de la Vigne. 1856. III. 555.
— Régénération de la Vigne. 1858. III. 555.
Troup, R. S. Abnormal growth of Spruce at high altitudes. 1900. II. 37.[1]
— A destructive fungus on Xylia. 1900. III. 491.[1]
Troupin-Morren, P. Situation de la pomologie agricole. 1878. III. 142.[2]
Trouvelot, L. Upon the tendency of trees to bend toward the east. 1871. I. 233.[1]
Trowbridge, F. Cranberries. 1873. III. 663.[2]
— Cranberry culture. 1858. III. 663.[2] — 1861. III. 663.[2]
— Kultur der Cranberry; uebersetzt von H. Maurer. 1861. III. 663.[2]
Trowell, Samuel. The farmer's instructor. 1739. III. 109.
— Neue Abhandlung vom Ackerbau, der Gärtnerei. 1739. III. 109.
— A new treatise of husbandry. 1739. III. 109.
Trowsdale, Thomas B. The largest Oak in Britain. 1880. II. 138,[2] IV. 514.[1]
— The largest Oak in Great Britain. 1880. II. 138.[2]
Troy, Paul. Étude sur les moyens de faciliter l'exécution de la loi . . . sur le reboisement. 1861. IV. 162.
Troyel, F. W. See TROJEL, F. W.
Trozelius, Clas Blechert. De generatione ac nutritione ar-borum. 1768. I. 146.
— Landtmannas genväg til fruktträn. 1780. III. 134.[1]
— Physico-oeconomisk beskrifning öfver Mistelåhs. socken. 1766. I. 351.
— Tankar om Såcker och Sirup af inhemska växter. 1771. III. 270.[1]
— Om trän och buskar i allmänhet. 1781. I. 531.
Trubrig, J. Die Beschreibung und Schätzung der Tiroler Amtswälder vom Jahre 1555. 1897. IV. 28.[2]
— Die Waldwirthschaft der Römer. 1887. IV. 28.[1]
Truchot. Sur l'état des Vignes phylloxérées dans . . . Mezel. 1878. III. 571.
Truchot, Pierre. Le Kirsch d'Auvergne. 1875. III. 435.[2]
Trudy . . . See Труды . . .
True, C. H. Native Plums. 1889. III. 433.[1]
— Seven principles in Grape growing. 1897. III. 551.[1]
True, Rodney Howard. On the influence of sudden changes of turgor. 1895. I. 188.
— See also CHENEY, L. S. & TRUE, R. H.
A true account of the Aloe americana. See BRADLEY, Richard. 1729. III. 620.[3]
True and Wild Service trees. 1886. III. 460.[1]
A true lover of plants, (pseud.). Rhododendrons javanais. 1892. III. 655.

Trübswetter, Adam. Bedeutung des Vorwuchses. 1885. IV. 138.[2]
— Zur Frage der Kiefernschütte. 1900. IV. 480.
Truelle, A. L'art de reconnaître les fruits des pressoirs. 1893. III. 426,[1] 446.[1]
— Atlas des meilleures variétés de fruits à cidre. 1896. III. 85.
— L'enseignement de la pomiculture. 1900. III. 31.
— Étude d'une variété de Pomme à cidre. 1893. III. 426.
— Guide pratique des meilleurs fruits. 1895. III. 85.
— Note sur l'utilité de l'analyse chimique. 1877. III. 444.[2]
— Note sur les fruits de pressoir allemands. 1899. III. 72.
— Des poires et des pommes. 1878. III. 444.[2]
Trümbach, E. Das " Drehscheibenquadrat." 1898. IV. 266.[1]
— Studien . . . im Kärnthner Wildbachgebiet. 1889. IV. 188.[1]
Truesdell, Burgess. A plea for the Sumach. 1867. III. 528.[2]
Truffaut, Georges. Andromeda floribunda. 1869. III. 654.[1]
— Les Aralias de serre chaude. 1891. III. 641.[1]
— L'Araucaria excelsa; sa multiplication. 1892. III. 298.[2]
— Sur le Bambusa gracilis. 1867. III. 316.[1]
— Brachysema acuminata. 1866. III. 468.[1]
— Étude sur la culture . . . de l'Azalea indica. 1893. III. 660.[1]
— Des formes sous lesquelles l'azote est le mieux absorbé. 1899. III. 152.
— Hot-house Aralias. 1891. III. 641.[1]
— Les Kentia. 1889. III. 326.[1]
— Le Rhododendron indico-javanicum. 1889. III. 659.[1]
— Rhododendron virgatum album. 1866. III. 662.[2]
— Usages des Palmiers. 1890. III. 319.[2]
— Yucca acutifolia. 1869. III. 340.[1]
— Yucca gloriosa minor. 1869. III. 340.[1]
— See also HÉBERT, Alexandre & TRUFFAUT, Georges.
Truguet, Gustave de. Petite notice sur quelques arbres du territoire de Bevaix. 1869. I. 297.[2]
Trümmer, Frans. Systematische Classification . . . der im Herzogthume Steiermark . . . Rebensorten. 1841. III. 546.
Trumpy, J. R. On pruning coniferous trees. 1884. III. 295.[1]
Trunk, J. B. Das bayerische Gesetz über die Vermarkung der Grundstücke. 1879. IV. 318.
Trunk, Johann Jakob. Neuer Plan der allgemeinen Revo-lution in der bisherigen Forstökonomie-Verwaltung. 1802. IV. 287.
— Neues vollständiges Forstlehrbuch. 1788. IV. 95.
— Praktische Forsttabellen. 1789. IV. 95.
— Relation und Gutachten des . . . Oberforstmeisters über de . . . Zustand . . . des Wald- und Forstwesens. 1793. IVn 116.
— Systematisch-praktischer Forst-Katechismus. 1799. IV. 96.
— Die vortheilhafteste Art die Laubwaldungen zu behandeln. 1802. IV. 117.
Truss, Szymon. Przyczynek do flory Galicyi. 1882. I. 443.
— Przyczynek do flory Galicyi, a względnie Buczacza i okolicy. 1884. I. 443.
— Wycieczki botaniczne w okolice Złoczowa. 1884. I. 443.
Trutat. La forêt de Cèdres de Teniet-el-Haâd. 1881. I. 485.
— La photographie appliquée à l'histoire naturelle. 189.? IV. 541.[1]
Trutat, Eugène. Les Pyrénées. 1894. I. 418.
Truxa, Robert & Karl, Kraus. Die Reise durch die Urwälder des Böhmerwaldes. 1849. IV. 370.
Trymalium daphnoides Reiss. und Gomphocarpus. 1859. III. 543,[2] 698.[2]
Tryon, Henry. The disease affecting the Orange orchards. 1894. III. 501.[1]
— Pernicious or San José scale. 1898. III. 191.
— See also BENSON, A. H. & TRYON, Henry.
Tryon, J. H. A practical treatise on Grape culture. 1887. III. 551.[1]
Tryon, Thomas. The way to health. 1691. V. XXVIII.[2]
Trzebiński, J. Flora lasów garwolinskich i sąsiednich okolic. 1900. I. 368.[1]
Trzebitsky, F. X. Physikalisch-ökonomische Bemerkungen über die sich so sehr verbreitende Trockniss. 1798. IV. 203.
Tschaplowitz, F. Ueber den Einfluss der Blattflächen . . . auf die Verdunstung. 1877. I. 167.
— Gibt es ein Transpirations-Optimum? 1883. I. 167.

— Ueber das Grösserwerden der Blätter im Norden. 1887. I. 218.

— Vermag die Pflanze . . . Wasser mittelst ihrer Laubblätter aus der Luft aufzunehmen? 1878. I. 161.

Tscharner, Niklaus Emanuel. Anleitung zum Forstbau. 1768. IV. 86.[3]

Tschek, Carl. Ueber eine neue Galle auf Eichen. 1869. IV. 503.[3]

Tschepe, Gottlieb. See NEUBERT, Wilhelm & TSCHEPE, Gottlieb.

Tschepke, Julius. Beschreibung der Görlitzer Haide. 1885. IV. 354.

Tschermak, Erich. Über die Bahnen von Farbstoff- und Salzlösungen. 1896. I. 166.

Tscherning. Ueber Pinus silvestris L. f. Baenitsii. 1899. II. 47.[1]

Tscherning, Friedrich August. Beiträge zur Forstgeschichte Württembergs. 1854. IV. 25.

— Untersuchungen über die Entwicklung einiger Embryonen. 1872. II. 10.[1]

— Zusammenstellung der in Würtemberg . . . in Forst- und Jagdsachen gegebenen Gesetze. 1842. IV. 322.[3]

Tscherning, J. Fra Universitetets botaniske Have. 1882. I. 40.

— Medinilla magnifica. 1887. III. 638.[1]

Tschierske, Paul. Beiträge zur vergleichenden Anatomie . . . einiger Dryadeenfrüchte. 1886. II. 305.[3]

Tschiffeli, Daniel. L'école des jardiniers. 1696. III. 115.[2]

Tschirch, Wilhelm Oswald Alexander. Der anatomische Bau des Blattes von Kingia. 1882. II. 84.[1]

— Angewandte Pflanzenanatomie. 1889. I. 101.[1]

— Ueber durch Astegopteryx. 1890. III. 671.[1]

— Beiträge zur Kenntniss der Harzbildung. 1899. I. 135.

— Beiträge zur Kenntniss der Wurzelknöllchen. 1887. II. 321.[3]

— Beiträge zur Kenntniss des mechanischen Gewebesystems. 1885. I. 134.[3]

— Beiträge zur vergleichenden Anatomie des Spaltöffnungsapparates. 1881. I. 131.[1]

— Über die Bildung von Harzen. 1893. I. 181,[1] 182.[1]

— Chinarinden und Cinchona. 1887. III. 725.[1]

— Ueber Durchbrechungen der mechanischen Ringe. 1884. I. 134.[3]

— Ueber einige Beziehungen des anatomischen Baues der Assimilationsorgane. 1881. I. 131,[3] 213.

— Ueber die Entwicklungsgeschichte einiger Sekretbehälter. 1888. I. 135.

— Sur la formation des résines. 1893. I. 132.[1]

— Généralités sur la constitution des résines. 1899. I. 181.[2]

— Grundlagen der Pharmacognosie. See FLÜCKIGER, F. A. 1873. III. 258.

— Grundriss der Anatomie. 1889. I. 101.[1]

— Die Harze und die Harzbehälter. 1900. I. 135, III. 228.[1]

— Den Harzfluss und die Harzgallen bei den Coniferen. 1899. II. 21.[3]

— Indische Fragmente. 1890. II. 720.[3]

— Indische Heil- und Nutzpflanzen. 1892. III. 92,[2] 130.[1]

— Ueber die Inhaltsstoffe der Zellen des Arillus von Myristica. 1888. II. 221.[1]

— Der javanische Urwald. 1894. I. 467, IV. 88.[1]

— Die Keimungsgeschichte von Myristica. 1894. II. 221.[1]

— Zur Morphologie der Chlorophyllkörner. 1883. I. 142.

— Nouvelles recherches sur les résines des Conifères. 1898. II. 21.[3]

— Ueber den Ort der Oel-, bezw. Harzbildung bei den schizogenen Secretbehältern. 1893. I. 135.

— Physiologische Studien über die Samen. 1891. I. 121, 204.

— Der Quarzspektrograph. 1896. I. 185.[1]

— Über die Rolle des Chlorophyllfarbstoffes. 1885. I. 173.

— Ueber Secrete. 1894. V. XI.[1]

— Strychnos nux vomica. 1890. II. 720.[3]

— Untersuchungen über das Chlorophyll. 1883. I. 142.

— Untersuchungen über die harzführenden Sekretbehälter. 1889. I. 135.

— & Brüning, Eduard. Ueber den Harzbalsam. 1900. III. 295.[2]

— — Ueber den Harzbalsam von Picea vulgaris Link. 1900. IV. 460.[1]

— — Ueber den Harzbalsam von Pinus Pinaster. 1900. IV. 468.[3]

— & Oesterle, Otto. Anatomischer Atlas der Pharmakognosie. 1900. III. 259.[1]

— & Weigel, George. Ueber den Harzbalsam von Abies pectinata. 1900. IV. 447.[1]

— — Ueber den Harzbalsam von Larix decidua. 1900. IV. 452.[1]

Tschistiakoff, J. See TCHISTIAKOFF, I. D.

Tschudi, JENNI-. See JENNI-TSCHUDI.

Tschudi, Friedrich von & Schulthess, A. Der Obstbaum und seine Pflege. 1873. III. 145.[3]

Tschudi, Jean Baptiste Louis Théodore, baron de. Traité des arbres résineux. 1768. III. 289.

Tschudi, Johann Jakob von. The Chirimoya. 1847. III. 401.[1]

— On Coca. 1847. III. 492.[3]

— Die Kokkelskörner. 1847. III. 396.[1]

— Récolte du quinquina. 1847. III. 717.[2]

— Reisen durch Südamerika. 1866. I. 330.

— Travels in Peru. 1847. III. 268.[2].

Tschudy, baron de. De la transplantation. 1778. III. 43.

Tschudy, J. J. C. R. baron de. Essai sur la greffe de l'herbe. 1819. III. 163.[3]

Tschuppik, Friedrich. Beiträge über die Anwendbarkeit der Theorie zur Ermittlung der Umtriebszeiten. 1868. IV. 251.[3]

— Die Betriebseinrichtungsvorschrift für die österreichischen Staatsforste. 1857. IV. 249.[3] .

— Der Wiener-Wald. 1870. IV. 369.

— Der Wiener Wald. Ein Beitrag. 1871. IV. 28.[1]

Tserofski. Village forests. 1892. IV. 335.

Tsevett, M. Sur la chlorophylline bleue. 1900. I. 142.

Tsiology. See A TEA DEALER. 1826. III. 606.

Tsounemassa, Iwasaki. Phonzo Zoufn. 1828. I. 461.

Tsvett, Michael Semenovitch. Sur la constitution de la matière colorante des feuilles. 1899. I. 186.

— Sur quelques cas tératologiques dans l'anatomie de Lycium. 1894. II. 773.[1]

— Ueber die Verknüpfung des . . . Leptoms der Solanaceen. 1899. III. 768.[1]

tt. Über den Stand der Forstbetriebseinrichtung in der österreichischen Staats- und Fondsforstverwaltung. 1894. IV. 250.[1]

Tuberous branches. 1890. II. 369,[1] 841.[3]

Tubeuf, Karl, Freiherr von. Ueber Anatomie . . . des Samenflügels der Abietineen. 1892. II. 20.[1]

— Ueber die Anpassungs-Erscheinung auf der Galle auf Thujopsis. 1895. III. 312.[1]

— Ueber Aschenanalysen von Viscum. 1890. II. 179.[2]

— Beiträge zur Kenntnis der Baumkrankheiten. 1888. IV. 195.[3]

— Beitrag zur Kenntnis der Morphologie . . . des Samenflügels bei den Abietineen. 1892. II. 20.[1]

— Beitrag zur Kenntnis der Morphologie . . . des Samenflügels bei den Abietineen. 1893. I. 121.

— Bekämpfung der Kiefernschütte. 1898. IV. 479.

— Die Blutlaus. 1898. III. 428.[2]

— Die Buchenkeimlinge vom Sommer 1889. 1890. II. 126.[3]

— Diseases of plants induced by cryptogamic parasites. 1895. IV. 212.

— Einführung der Kupfermittel. 1898. IV. 212.

— Emploi de la bouillie bordelaise en sylviculture. 1898. IV. 212.

— E   z   g lebender Fichtenäste durch den Blitz. 1892. IV.108.[1]

— Erica carnea . . . durch . . Hypoderma Ericae befallen. 1895. III. 651.[1]

— Ueber Formen von Viscum album. 1889. II. 177.[2]

— Die Haarbildungen der Coniferen. 1896. II. 17,[3] 18.

— Hexenbesen an Pinus montana Mill. 1892. IV. 465.[1]

— Hexenbesen der Laerche. 1893. IV. 451.

— Hexenbesen der Rothbuche. 1892. IV. 497.

— Insektenbeschädigung an Fichtenbecken. 1896. IV. 457.

— Die kleinen Parasiten . . . unserer Obstbäume. 1898. III. 192.[1]

— Kranke Weisserlen. 1893. IV. 489.[3]

— Lärchenzweige, deren Kurztriebe . . . krank waren. 1895. IV. 451.

— Die Mistel, Viscum album. 1898. II. 180.[1]

— Mittheilungen über einige Pflanzenkrankheiten. 1893. III. 195.[1]

— Die Nadelhölzer. 1897. II. 14.[1]

— Eine neue Krankheit der Douglastanne. 1888. IV. 483.[3]

— Ueber eine neue Krankheit der Weisstanne. 1890. IV. 445.

— Eine neue Spritze zum Gebrauche im . . . Pflanzenschutz. 1899. III. 198.[1]

Tubeuf, Karl, *Freiherr* von (*continued*).
— Neuere Beobachtungen über die Cecidomyien-Galle der Lärchenkurztriebe. 1897. IV. 451.
— Ueber normale und pathogene Kernbildung. 1889. I. 207.[2] *IV. 66*.[1]
— Pflanzenkrankheiten durch kryptogame Parasiten. 1895. IV. 212.
— Phytoptus Laricis n. sp. 1897. IV. 451.
— Eine Pilzkrankheit der Douglastanne. 1888. IV. 483.[2]
— Pilzkrankheiten der Pflanzen. 1894. IV. 212.
— Pinus Strobus forma nova monophylla. 1898. II. 46.[1]
— Ueber die praktische Bedeutung der Kirschenhexenbesen. 1898. III. 435.[2]
— Pseudotsuga japonica Shirasawa. 1898. IV. 483.[1]
— Le Pseudotsuga japonica Shirasawa. 1898. IV. 483.[1]
— Der Rindenblasenrost der Weymouthskiefer. 1898. IV. 470.[1]
— Der Rosenrost und seine Bekämpfung. 1898. III. 453.[2]
— Samen, Früchte und Keimlinge. 1891. I. 119.
— Die San José-Laus. 1900. III. 192.[2]
— Ueber das Schmarotzen von Loranthaceen auf den eigenen Aesten. 1890. II. 174.[1]
— Vegetationsbilder aus dem böhmischen Urwalde. 1890. IV. 372.
— Ueber den Verschluss der Coniferenzapfen. 1896. II. 20.[1]
— Viscum album auf der deutschen Eiche. 1890. II. 179.[2]
— Ueber den Wachholder-Rost. 1891. III. 303.[1]
— Über wichtige Baumkrankheiten. 1900. IV. 195.[2]
— Wie vertilgt man die Feldmäuse? 1898. III. 186.[2]
— Ueber die Wurzelbildung einiger Loranthaceen. 1888. II. 173.[2]
— Zwei Feinde der Alpenerle. 1892. IV. 489.[2]
— *See also* Тюбефъ, К.
Tubilla, Tomás Andrés y. *See* Lázaro é Ibiza, Blas & Andrés y Tubilla, Tomás.
Tuchen. Composition du cacao. 1860. III. 594.
Tucker, Arabella Hannah. Trees of Worcester. 1894. I. 312.
Tucker, *Mrs.* F. H. *See* Tucker, *Mrs.* Mary (Lathrop).
Tucker, *Mrs.* Mary (Lathrop). Forestry in Massachusetts. 1900. IV. 339.
— Roadside treatment. 1899. III. 208.[2]
Tuckerman, Edward. On Oakesia. 1842. II. 453.[2]
Tuckerman, Edward & Frost, C. C. A catalogue of plants ... of Amherst. 1875. I. 314.
Tuckey, James Hingston. An account of a voyage to establish a colony at Port Philip. 1805. V. xxiv.[2]
— Narrative of an expedition to explore the river Zaire. *See* Brown, Robert. 1818. I. 491.
Tuckey, James Kingston. *See* Tuckey, J. H.
Tuckwell, W. Tongues in trees. 1889. I. 74.[1]
Tudor, J. R. The Orkneys and Shetland. 1883. I. 534.[2]
Tübingen — Botanisches Institut. Untersuchungen. *See* Untersuchungen ... I. 15.
Türckhiem, von. Die Laubstreu. 1877. IV. 71.
Türk, Wilhelm von. Anleitung zur Pflege ... der Maulbeerbäume. 1841. III. 376.
— Bemerkungen über die verderblichen Wirkungen des Winters von 1837/38. 1839. III. 45.
— Über die Kultur des Maulbeerbaums. 1833. III. 374.
— Über den Maulbeerbaum. 1828. III. 374.
— Über den Morus multicaulis. 1839. III. 380.[2]
— Über die Wirkung der Fröste ... auf ... Arten des Maulbeerbaumes. 1838. III. 379.[1]
Türke, F. F. Versuch einer Beantwortung der ... Frage: "Wodurch kann die Waldstreu ... entbehrlich gemacht werden?" 1842. IV. 437.[2]
Tuinbouw-Courant. III. 15.
Tuinen, H. K. van. Nederlandsche planten. 1874. III. 76.
Tuinen, K. Bisschof van. *See* Bisschop van Tuinen, K.
Tuke. Notice of some of the woods used ... in New Zealand. 1863. III. 283.[1]
Tulasne, Louis René. Antidesmata et Stilaginellas. 1851. II. 433.[1]
— Antidesmeae. [Hieronymus.] 1861. II. 445.[2]
— De Aubletianis generibus, Quiina et Poraqueiba. 1849. II. 475.[2] *547*.[1]
— Diagnoses ... e Monimiacearum recensione. 1855. II. 221.[2]
— Embryogénie des végétaux. 1855. I. 122.
— Études d'embryogénie végétale. 1847. I. 122, 202.[2] — 1849. I. 200.
— Florae madagascariensis fragmenta. 1856. I. 496.

— Flore de la Colombie. 1846. I. 339.[2]
— Gnetaceae. 1863. II. 53.[2]
— Gnetaceae Americae australis. 1858. II. 53.[2]
— Légumineuses arborescentes de l'Amérique du Sud. 1844. II. 318.[2]
— Monimiaceae. 1857. II. 221.[2]
— Monographia Monimiacearum primum tentata. 1855. II. 221.[2]
— New researches in vegetable embryogeny. 1855. I. 122.
— Note sur le champignon qui cause la maladie de la Vigne. 1853. III. 575.[2]
— Nouvelles études d'embryogénie végétale. 1855. I. 122, *800*.
— Nova quaedam proponit genera in Leguminosarum classe. 1843. II. 318.[2]
— Prix Bordin. ... Déterminer par des recherches anatomiques s'il existe dans la structure des tiges. 1863. I. 252.
— Rapport sur les travaux de M. P. Duchartre, relatifs aux ... Aristolochiées. 1854. II. 180.[2]
— *See also* Saint-Hilaire, Auguste de & Tulasne, L. R.
Tulinof, A. *See* Тулиновъ, А.
The **Tulip** tree. 1874. III. 398.[2] — 1890. III. 398.[2]
Tully, William. Materia medica. 1857. III. 243.
Tulpe, Nicolaus. Observationes medicae. 1639. III. 604.[2]
Tuma, Ed. & Ém. Ueber den Cyanwasserstoffgehalt ... von Prunus Padus. 1892. III. 439.[1]
— — Sur la proportion d'acide cyanhydrique dans ... "Prunus Padus." 1892. III. 439.[1]
Tuma, Ém. *See* Tuma, Ed. & Ém.
Tuma, K. I. *See* Тумскій, К. И.
Tundermann, Karl. Meletemata de Sennae foliis. 1856. III. 470.[2]
Tunis, Theophilus. Some comments on Senate document no. 40 ... relating to "timber supply." 1897. IV. 403.[2]
Tunis — Bulletin agricole .... *See* Bulletin ... III. 27.[1]
Tunis — Société d'horticulture. *See* Société ... III. 27.[1]
La **Tunisie**; histoire et description. 1896. I. 486.
Tunmann, Otto. Über die Sekretdrüsen. 1900. I. 135.
The **Tupelo**, Nyssa sylvatica. 1894. II. 614.[2]
The **Tupelo** tree. Nyssa aquatica. 1890. II. 614.[1]
Tupper, J. P. An essay on the probability of sensation in vegetables. 1811. I. 146, *197*.[1]
Turczaninow, Nicolaus. Animadversiones ad primam ... partem herbarii Turczaninowiani. 1854. I. 269.
— Appendix prima ad primam partem Catalogi plantarum. 1857. I. 270.
— Asclepiadeae aliquae indescriptae. 1848. II. 735.[1]
— Catalogus plantarum herbarii Universitatis ... Charkoviensis. 1855. I. 42.
— Catalogus plantarum in regionibus baicalensibus. 1838. I. 455.
— Decades quatuor plantarum ... Sibiriae. 1840. I. 455.
— Decades tres plantarum ... Chinae boreali ... inoolarum. 1832. I. 458.
— Decas [1]-8 generum plantarum. 1843. I. 269.
— Description des Elaeocarpées. 1841. II. 509.[1]
— Enumeratio plantarum ... in China boreali. 1837. I. 458.
— Flora baicalensi-dahurica. 1842. I. 455.
— Myrtaceae xerocarpicae. 1862. II. 619.[2]
— Papilionaceae, Podalyrieae et Loteae australasicae. 1853. II. 320.[1]
— Quelques observations sur ... Clethra. 1863. II. 657.[1]
— Synanthereae quaedam hucusque indescriptae. 1851. II. 848.[1]
— Verbenaceae et Myoporaceae. 1863. II. 752.[2] 805.[1]
Turczyński, Emeryk. Dodatek do flory okolic Drohobycza. 1869. I. 442.
— Notatki botaniczne z wycieczki na Sywulę i Wysoką. 1882. I. 443.
— Spis roślin około Przemyśla dziko rosnących. 1872. I. 442.
— Spis roślin w okolicy Stanisławowa. 1875. I. 442.
— Zapiski botaniczne ze wschodniej Galicyi. 1878. I. 442.
Turgan. Les grandes usines de France. 1868. III. 124.[1]
Turgot, Étienne François, *Marquis de Cousmont*. Essai sur les arbres d'environ. 1778. III. 83.[2]
— Mémoire instructif sur la manière de rassembler ... curiosités d'histoire naturelle. 1758. III. 155.
— Mémoire sur les arbres résineux. 1786. III. 291.
Turin — Académie royale des sciences. *See* Miscellanea philosophico-mathematica ... I. 25.
Turin — Société royale. *See* Miscellanea philosophico-mathematica ... I. 25.

Turio, Bernardino. Specimen plantarum . . . in agro clava-riensi aliisque dipartimenti Appenninorum locis. 1806. I. 425.

Turkey-Oak in South Africa. 1894. III. 362.[1]

Turley. Schwedens Forstwesen im Jahre 1892. 1894. IV. 344.[1]

Turlure. Extrait . . . sur les avantages d'une greffe de côté. 1837. III. 160.

Turnbull, Robert. The diameter-increment of the wood of coniferous trees at Braemar. 1900. II. 21,[2] *III. 38.*[2]

— Index of British plants. 1889. I. 534.[1]

— & **Waite**, P. C. Measurement of the girth of coniferous trees. 1900. II. 21,[2] *III. 38.*[2]

Turnbull, W. S. Spines on Holly leaves. 1893. II. 463.[2]

Turner, Dawson & **Dillwyn**, L. W. The botanist's guide through England and Wales. 1805. I. 396.

Turner, E. F. *See* RENNIE, E. H. & TURNER, E. F.

Turner, Edward & **Christison**, Robert. Over de uitwerkselen van vergiftige gazsoorten op gewassen. 1828. I. 210.[2]

Turner, Frederick. On budding. 1891. III. 164.[1]

— The cultivation of the Black or Green Wattle. 1891. III. 465.[1]

— The forage plants of Australia. · 1891. III. 223.[2]

— The India-rubber tree. 1891. III. 149.

— A list of exotic trees . . . affected by Australian Loranths. 1895. II. 174.[1]

— New commercial crops for N. S. W. 1891. III. 132.[1]

— The supposed poisonous plants of N. S. Wales. 1891. III. 94.[1]

— The Zamia Palm. 1893. III. 286.[1]

Turner, John Henry Tudsbury. Japanese timber. 1887. IV. 399.[1]

— Notes upon useful Japanese timber. 1887. IV. 399.[1]

Turner, Lucien M. Contributions to the natural history of Alaska. 1886. I. 311.[2]

Turner, Robert. Βοτανολογία, the Brittish physician. 1687. III. 79.[2]

— The Brittish physician. 1687. III. 79.[2]

Turner, Samuel. An account of an embassy to the court of the Teshoo Lama in Tibet. 1800. I. 460.[1]

— Ambassade au Tibet et au Boutan. 1880. I. 460.[1]·

Turner, Wilhelm. Beiträge zur vergleichenden Anatomie der Bixaceen. 1885. II. 565.[2]

Turner, William. The first and seconde partes of the Herbal. 1551. I. 278.

— Gulielmus Turnerus, anglus, historiam de naturis-herbarum . . . edidit. 1544. I. 278.

— Libellus de re herbaria novus. 1538. I. 277.

— The names of herbes in Greke, Latin, Englishe, Duche & Frenche. 1548. I. 71.

— A new herball. 1551. I. 278.

— The thirde parte of William Turners Herball. 1551. I. 278.

Turneretscher, Gottlieb MARKTANNER-. *See* MARKTANNER-TURNERETSCHER, Gottlieb.

Turot, Paul. Les forêts, les finances et l'agriculture. 1866. IV. 275.

— La question des forêts. 1872. IV. 275.

The turpentine forests. 1872. IV. 467.[1]

Turpin, François René. Histoire civile et naturelle . . . de Siam. 1771. III. 276.[1]

Turpin, Pierre Jean François. Analyse microscopique . . . du Cereus peruvianus. 1830. II. 590.[2]

— Bemerkungen über die Familie der Cactus-Pflanzen. 1830. II. 585.[1]

— Castela, Polygamie monoecie Lin. 1806. II. 414.[1]

— Cristaux d'oxalate . . . du tronc du Cierge du Pérou. 1830. II. 590.[2]

— Description d'une nouvelle espèce de Thouinia. 1804. II. 490.[1]

— Essai d'une iconographie elémentaire . . . des végétaux. 1820. I. 266.

— Examen d'une chloranthie . . . du Saule Marceau. 1833. II. 106.[1]

— Flore usuelle. 1834. III. 52.

— Iconographie végétale. 1820. I. 266. — 1841. I. 34, 98.

— Lettre à M. le Baron de Beauvois. 1817. II. 72.[2]

— Mémoire de nosologie végétale. 1833. I. 206,[1] III. *441.*[2] 585.[1]

— Mémoire sur l'organe par lequel le fluide fécondant peut s'introduire. 1806. I. 200.

— Mémoire sur la différence qu'offrent les tissus cellulaires de la Pomme et de la Poire. 1838. II. 256.[2] — 1840. III. 278.[2]

— Mémoire sur la greffe. 1831. I. 208.[1]

— Note relative à la production de tiges nouvelles par les feuilles. 1839. I. 205.

— Notice sur les usurpations végétales. 1834. I. 104.

— Notice sur une maladie . . . des Mûriers. 1838. III. 379.[1]

— Observations générales sur l'organogénie. 1835. I. 33.

— Observations générales sur l'organogénie . . . considérés. 1838. I. 147.

— Observations sur la famille des Cactées. 1830. II. 585.[1]

— Observations sur les Rhus aromaticum et suaveolens. 1804. II. 458.[1]

— Organographie végétale. 1829. I. 98.

— Organographie végétale; observations sur l'origine . . . de tous les corps propagateurs. 1828. I. 121.

— *See also* POITEAU, Antoine & TURPIN, P. J. F.

Turra, Antonio. Della febbrifuga facoltà dell' Ippocastano. 1780. III. 537.[2]

— Florae italicae prodromus. 1780. I. 424.

Turre, Georgius a. *See* TORRE, Giorgio dalla.

Turrel, L. Cladrastis tinctoria. 1849. III. 469,[1] *472.*[2]

— Les Conifères exotiques. 185.? IV. 441.

— Étude sur quelques végétaux économiques. 1876. III. 408,[1] *IV. 518.*[2]

— Les maladies de la Vigne. 1874. III. 560.

— Dei mezzi più efficaci per prevenire la distruzione degli uccelli di passaggio. 1866. IV. 90,[2] 544.[1]

— Des moyens . . . pour prévenir la destruction des oiseaux. 1866. IV. 544.[1]

— Un Mûrier nain. 1875. III. 380.[1]

— Note sur le Câprier sans épines. 1864. II. 232.[1] — 1865. III. 409.[1]

— Notes sur l'acclimatation de quelques végétaux. 1866. III. 125.

— Un nouveau Nérium. 1874. III. 689.[1]

— Oranger Chamouti. 1869. III. 499.[1]

— La protection des oiseaux insectivores. 1866. IV. 544.[1]

— Les reboisements du Faron. 1869. IV. 162.

— Les semis du Câprier inerme. 1879. III. 408.[2]

— Ein Zwerg-Maulbeerbaum. 1875. III. 380.[1]

Tursén, Erland. Sätt at lättast plantera Ekar. 1750. IV. 503.[2]

Turski, Mitrofan Kuzmitch. Russische Beobachtungen über die Schütte. 1882. IV. 477.

— Die Schütte der Kiefern. 1881. IV. 477.

— *See also* Турскiй, M. K.

Turtaudière, Pierre Aimé MILLET DE LA. *See* MILLET DE LA TURTAUDIÈRE, P. A.

Turton, William & **Kingston**, J. F. The natural history of the district [Teignmouth]. 1828. I. 533.

Tuscan, (*pseud.*). Forest administration in the Central Provinces. 1892. IV. 295.[2]

The Tuscan olive oil industry. 1896. III. 679.[2]

Tusch, JENSSEN-. *See* JENSSEN-TUSCH.

Tussac, F. R. de. Brosimum Alicastrum. 1808. II. 146.[2]

— De la culture du Séné. 1808. III. 470.[1]

— Flora Antillarum. 1808. I. 335.

— Flore des Antilles. 1808. I. 335.

— Histoire du Brosimum Alicastrum. 1808. II. 146.[2]

— Notice sur différens végétaux qui produisent le caoutchouc. 1808. III. 228.[2]

— Notice sur l'Aristoloche à grandes fleurs. 1813. II. 182.[2]

— Notice sur le Manguier de l'Inde. 1813. III. 525.[1]

— Observations botaniques . . . sur le Mancenillier. 1813. III. 519.[1]

Tutcher, W. J. Lagerstroemia Pordi. 1900. II. 609.[2]

— Magnolia fuscata. 1900. III. 400.[2]

— Randia densiflora. 1900. II. 829.[2]

— On some species of plants at Hong-kong. 1893. III. 91.[1] III. 157.

Tutein Nolthenius, G. E. H. Een drijvende kiemschijf. 1889. III. 157.

— Eenige opmerkingen over het schillen van akkermaalshout. 1893. IV. 435.[1]

— Eenige opmerkingen naar aanleiding van de beschouwingen . . . van den heer van Schermbeck. 1889. IV. 356.[2]

— Handleiding vóór het aanleggen . . . van grove-dennen-bosschen. 1891. IV. 474.

— De invloed van den zaaitijd op . . . Grove Dennen. 1889. IV. 454, V. xxxvi.[2]

— & **Ritzema Bos**, Jan. Over de beschadiging, door rupsen teweeggebracht, in eenige bosschen van Grove Dennen. 1889. IV. 442, 549.[2]

Tutela . . . forestale. 1898. IV. 277.

Tuttle, A. G. Causes of the injury to the south side of bodies of fruit trees. 1868. III. 184.[1]

Tutzevitch, V. K. See Туцевичъ, В. К.
Tuxen, Chr. Fr. A. Nogle kemiske og fysiske Undersøgelser af Jordbunden. 1884. IV. 69.
— Nogle kemiske Undersøgelser af Jordbunden i Bøgeskove. 1879. II. 125.²
Tuyl Schuitemaker, L. F. Beknopte landbouw-natuurkunde. 1882. III. 36.¹
Tuyssuzian, O. · Note sur l'Olivier de Crimée. 1857. III. 675.²
Tuzson, János. Anatomiai és physiologiai vizsgálatok a vörösfenyő fáján. 1899. II. 32,¹ 33.¹
— A fák anatomiai szerkezetéről. 1898. I. 126.
— A Fenyőcsemeték Botrytis-betegségéről. 1900. IV. 442.
— A Vörösfenyő (Larix europaea DC.) tenyésztése az alsóbb vidékeken. 1897. IV. 450.
Tvende Foredrag, holdte under Forhandlingerne om Hedesagen. 1866. IV. 156.¹
Twamley, Louise Anne. Flora's gems. 1837. I. 511.
— Our wild flowers. 1838. I. 398.
— The romance of nature.. 1836. I. 94.
Twardowska, M. Notatka o kilku rzadszych roślinach flory litewskiej. 1891. I. 443.
— Odmiany roślin rozmnażające się tylko przez gałęzie. 1899. I. 245.
Tweedy, Frank. Flora of the Yellowstone National Park. 1886. I. 325.
— The forests of the Yellowstone National Park. 1888. III. 320, IV. 340.²
— Notes on the Coniferae of Washington Territory. 1883. II. 14.²
— Salix and Rubus. 1880. II. 305.²
Twelve tree planting pointers. 1888. III. 166.
Twemlow, George. On the properties of the "Dowree" plant. 1842. III. 510,¹ 630.¹
Twent, A. P. Proeve of eenige aanteekeningen wegens het planten op duinen van Raaphorst. 1800. IV. 159.
Twining, Elizabeth. Illustrations of the natural orders of plants. 1849. I. 269.
Twining, Richard. An answer to the second report of the East India directors. 1785. III. 605.
— Observations on the tea. 1784. III. 605.
— Remarks on the report of the East-India directors, respecting ... tea. 1784. III. 605.
Two African Holarrhenas. 1896. III. 688.²
Two hardy shrubs. 1880. III. 395,¹ 628.¹
Two historic trees. 1896. I. 295.²
On two kinds of timber trees peculiar to new Zealand. 1825. IV. 402.¹
Two large British Columbian Conifers. 1900. IV. 484.²
Two late-flowering Privets. 1900. III. 673.²
Two new Podocarpus. 1892. III. 287.¹
On two South African genera of ... Passifloreae. 1839. II. 575.²
Two spring-flowering shrubs. 1896. III. 429,² 651.¹
Ty. S w s Forstwesen im Jahre 1889. 1891. IV. 344.² ch eden
Ty. Ueber die schwedische Holzstoffindustrie. 1891. IV. 430.
Ty. Ueber das Vordringen der Tanne im Norden. 1891. IV. 447.¹
Tyas, Robert. Favourite field flowers described. 1848. I. 400.
— Flowers from the Holy Land. 1851. I. 513.
— The Rose, its propagation. 1844. III. 452.
— Wild flowers of England. 1859. I. 401.
— Woodland gleanings. 1837. I. 393.²
Tydelski, V. I. See Тыдельскій, В. И.
Tyler, Ansel Augustus. An examination of the pubescence of the styles ... of Lonicera. 1894. II. 836.²
— The nature and origin of stipules. 1897. I. 112.¹
Tyneside naturalists' field club. Transactions. I. 20.
Tyniecki, Władysław. Leśnictwa ... na Wystawie krajowej. 1894. IV. 21.¹
— O obecnej roślinności piaskowej góry kolo Lwowa. 1880. I. 442.
— Z ogrodu botanicznego Krajowej szkoly gospodarstwa lasowego we Lwowie. 1896. I. 66.¹
— Plantacja Wierzb koszykarskich w Messadunk. 1878. III. 348.
— O przedwczesnem owocowaniu u Sosny. 1894. II. 48.¹
— Sprawozdanie ... w celu zbadania uprawy Wierzb koszykarskich. 1879. III. 348.
— O Wiązach galicyjskich. 1885. II. 143.¹
— Wpływ lasu na źródła. 1899. IV. 52.

— Wyciecska na Podole. 1877. I. 442.
— Wyniki dotychczasowych prób aklimatyzacyi obcych drzew w Europie. 1891. IV. 125.¹
Tz., P. Les ramilles utilisées comme fourrage. 1895. III. 223.²
Tzabel, N. E. See Пабель, Н. Е.
Tzeil, M. A. See Цейль, М. А.
Tzigra, Ivan. See Цигра, Ив.
Tzin, K. See Цинъ, К.
Tzinger, V. J. See Цингеръ, В. Я.
Tziundzevitzki, V. See Цюндзевицкій, В.
O trvietoizmyeneni ... See О цвѣтоизмѣненіи ...

—u—. Die Holzhandelsverhältnisse in Mittelböhmen. 1884. IV. 406.²
U. Een woord over de afschaffing der gouvernements Koffiecultuur. 1883. III. 730.
U., W. van. Landbouw in Suriname. 1886. III. 118.²
Ubaldini, Giuseppe. See Luca, S. de & Ubaldini, G.
Učík, L. Pěstění Růží ze semena. 1896. III. 453.¹
Ucria, Bernardino da. Hortus regius panhormitanus. 1789. I. 61.
Udal, J. S. Old Oak. 1883. IV. 514.¹
Uddrag af Rosens Historie. 1885. II. 290.²
Udintzef, S. A. See Удинцевъ, С. А.
Udkast til Lov om Statsskovenes Bestyrelse. 1851. IV. 315.¹
Ueber, C. A. Remedy for the Poison Rhus. 1887. III. 528.¹
Überblick der K. k. Staatsforste im Wienerwalde. 1868. IV. 369.
Ueberführung des Mittelwaldes in Hochwaldwirtschaft. 1887. IV. 128.
Uebersicht der durch Schönheit ... merkwürdigen Bäume der sächsischen Staatswälder. 1853. I. 531.¹
Uebersicht der Fackeldisteln des bot. ... Gartens in Aachen. See Synopsis Opuntiarum. 1833. II. 586.²
Uebersicht über die Hauptergebnisse der Untersuchungen über den Holzwachsthumsgang. 184.? IV. 235.²
Uebersicht über die Holz-Ein und Ausfuhr ... in der Schweiz. 1860. IV. 406.¹
Uebersicht über die Organisation, die Zwecke ... der K. württemb. land- und forstwirthschaftlichen Akademie Hohenheim. 1873. IV. 32.
Uebersicht über die zweckmässigste Reihenfoge des Ausbildungsganges für den k. Forstverwaltungsdienst. 188.? IV. 32.
Uebersichtliche Zusammenstellung der ... aufgestellten Ertragstafeln. See Weber, Rudolf. 188.? IV. 236.
Übersichts-Karte von den Waldungen Preussens. 1887. IV. 354.
Uebersichts-Karte von sämmtlichen in Elsass-Lothringen vorhandenen Waldungen. 1877. IV. 349.²
Uechtritz, Rudolf von. Beiträge zur Flora von Schlesien. 1864. I. 385.
— Die bemerkenswerthesten Ergebnisse der Durchforschung der schlesischen Phanerogamenflora. 1873. I. 387.
— Nachträge zur Flora von Schlesien. 1861. II. 275.²
— Ueber Rosa umbelliflora. 1880. II. 283.²
Uexküll-Gyllenband, Graf von. Ueber den Einfluss der Lage auf das Gedeihen der Holzarten im württemb. Schwarzwald. 1877. IV. 119.
Uffelmann & Börner. Composition chimique de la noix de Kola. 1895. III. 590.²
Ufford, J. K. W. Quarles van. See Quarles van Ufford, J. K. W.
Ugaldezublaur, Santiago. Memoria descriptive de la provincia de Manila. 1880. I. 484,¹ IV. 376.²
— Reseña de la flora del Archipiélago filipino. 1883. I. 464.¹
Ugeskrift for Landmænd. III. 11.
Ugla, Peter. Γάμος φυτῶν; sive, Nuptiae arborum. See Wallin, Georg. 1729. I. 517.¹
— De praefectura Naesgardensis Dalekarliae. 1734. I. 351.
Ugolini, Guglielmo. Acacia dealbata. 1898. III. 464.²
— Dell' Acero. 1891. III. 534.¹

Over het **uitrooijen** van de hop uit de houtlanden. 1794. III. 193.[1]

Uitterdyk, J. NANNINGA. *See* NANNINGA UITTERDYK, J.

Egy uj Tölgyfaj s összes hazai Tölgyeink. 1883. II. 130.[1]

Ulbrich, (*Forstmeister, Bernstadt*). Ueber die Benutzung des Farrenkrautes als Bettfüllung. 1853. IV. 438.[2]

— Mittheilung in Bezug auf den . . . von Massowschen Vorschlag zur Bildung von Holzhauer-Genossenschaften. 1852. IV. 310.[1]

— & **Pannewitz**, Julius von. Waldstreu zur Düngerbereitung ist fast gleich nachtheilig für Wald und Feld. 1862. IV. 437.[2]

Ulbricht, R. Untersuchungen über den Einfluss der Fällungszeit. 1869. IV. 384.[2]

Uldall, F. P. & **Børgesen**, F. Vore vestindiske Øer. 1898. I. 337.

Uldall, J. Prydplanter og Nytteplanter. 1886. III. 120.[1]

Ule, Ernst. Ueber Blütheneinrichtungen einiger Aristolochien. 1898. II. 181.[2]

— Ueber die Blütheneinrichtungen von Dipladenia. 1896. II. 725.[2]

— Blumenblätter als Lockspeise. 1900. II. 631.[2]

— Dipladenia atro-violacae. 1897. II. 725.[2]

— Ueber einen experimentell erzeugten Aristolochienbastard. 1899. II. 181.[2]

— **Extraflorale** Schauapparate als Anlockungsmittel. 1900. I. 241.[1]

— Fledermäuse als Verbreiter von Samen. 1900. I. 241.[1]

— Massenhafter Besuch von Insecten. 1900. I. 239.[1]

— Relatorio de uma excursão botanica feita na Serra do Itatiaia. 1896. I. 343.

— Schutzameisen der Cecropia. 1900. II. 147.[2]

— Die Vegetation von Cabo Frio. 1900. I. 344.

— Verschiedenes über den Einfluss der Thiere auf das Pflanzenleben. 1900. I. 235.[1]

— Weiteres zur Blütheneinrichtung von Purpurella. 1896. II. 641.[2]

Ulex, Georg Ludwig. Ueber den Einfluss des Kohlenwasserstoffgases. 1852. III. 185.[1]

— On the influence of coal gas. 1852. III. 185.[1]

Uline, E. B. Epidermis and spines of Cactaceae. 1893. II. 588.[2]

— & **Bray**, W. L. Synopsis of North American Amaranthaceae. 1894. II. 189.[1]

Ulisch, H. Ueber das künstlerische Verständniss der symmetrischen . . . Baumformen. 1864. I. 516.

Ulitzsch, Karl August. Botanische Schattenrisse. 1796. I. 255.

Dell' **Ulivo** e sua coltivazione. 1840. III. 675.[1]

Ullgren, Olof Mathias & **Hallberg**, Carl. De plantis tinctoriis suecanis. 1815. III. 236.

Ullmark, Hinricus & **Ferber**, Johannes Jacobus. De prolepsi plantarum. *See* LINNÉ, Carl von. 1760. I. 97.

Ulloa, Antonio de. Memoires philosophiques . . . concernant la découverté de l'Amérique. 1772. III. 261.[1]

— Noticias americanas. 1772. III. 261.[1]

— Physikalische . . . Nachrichten vom südlichen und nordöstlichen America. 1772. III. 261.[1]

— Relacion historica del viage à la America meridional. 1748. I. 328.

Voyage historique de l'Amérique méridionale. 1748. I. 328.

— A voyage to South America. 1748. I. 328.

— *See also* JUAN, George & ULLOA, Antoine de.

Ullyett, Henry. The neighbourhood of Folkestone. 1870. I. 402.

— Rambles of a naturalist round Folkestone. 1880. I. 534.[1]

Die **Ulme** als Heckenpflanze. 1882. III. 365.[1]

Ulmenstein, Rudolf, *Freiherr* von. Bericht über die 49. General-Versammlung des Schlesischen Forstvereines. 1891. IV. 354.

— Statistisch-topografische Beschreibung der . . . Herrschaft Nachod. 1878. IV. 371.

Ulmgrehn, Harald. De Ulmo. *See* RIDDERMARCK, Anders. 1692. II. 142.[2]

Ulmine from wood. 1820. I. 174.

Uloth, Wilhelm. Bildungsabweichungen an Rosen. 1878. II. 289.[2]

— Birne mit Kelch. 1878. II. 280.[1]

— Botanische Mittheilungen. 1878. I. 106,[2] II. 280,[1] 289.[2]

— Ueber die Verzweigungsweise der Bäume mit hängenden Aesten. 1878. I. 106.[2]

Ulrich, A. Ueber die Anzucht der Coniferen. 1878. III. 294.[1]

Ulrich, Aug.　Beiträge zur bündnerischen Volksbotanik. 1896. I. 75.[1]
Ulrich, Emanuel.　Forst-Beschreibung der . . . Domaine Wiesenberg in Mähren. 1852. IV. 368.
Ulrich, F. W.　Praktische Anweisung zur Obstbaumzucht. 1851. III. 137.
— Praktyczna nauka hodowania. 1851. III. 137.
Ulrich, P.　Dänische und deutsche Buchenhochwaldwirthschaft. 1897. IV. 499.[1]
Ulrich, S.　Den fordelagtigste Behandlingsmaade af smaa Skovhaver. 1858. IV. 113.[2]
Ulrich, Wilhelm.　Dictionnaire international des plantes. 1872. I. 72.[3]
— Internationales Wörterbuch der Pflanzennamen. 1872. I. 72.[3]
Ulrici.　Beobachtungen über das Auftreten des Hylesinus. 1873. IV. 204.
Ulrici, (Oberförster zu Kottwitz).　Die Nachzucht des Oberbaumes. 1881. IV. 128.
Ulrici, (Oberforstmeister).　Die wissenschaftliche Reinertragslehre. 1867. IV. 255.
Ulricksen, F.　Kirsebærblommetræet. 1890. III. 436.[1]
Ulrika, LOVISA.　See LOVISA ULRIKA.
Ulriksen, F.　Populus alba L. var. pyramidalis. 1891. III. 345.[1]
— Yderligere Bemærkninger om . . . Rubus-Arter. 1895. III. 457.[2]
Ulsamer, J. A.　Unsere deutschen Obst- und Waldbäume. 1893. I. 372.
The Umbrella Pine. 1890. III. 309.[2]
Umney, John C.　African copaiba. 1894. III. 473.[1]
— Report on . . . dried juice of Carica. 1896. III. 618.[1]
Die Umpflanzung der Ränder der . . . Wirthschaftsfiguren. 1853. IV. 138.[1]
Umrisse zur Geographie . . . des Kantons Bern. 1819. IV. 365.
Umständliche Beschreibung derer Raupen. 1731. III. 188.[1]
Umwandlung der Zweige junger Erlen in Wurzeln. 1837. IV. 488.[3]
Umwandlung von Aesten einer Weisstanne in Hauptstämme. 1869. II. 24.[1]
Umwandlung von Niederwald in Hochwald. 1856. IV. 128.
Un Alpinista.　See ALPINISTA, Un, (pseud.).　Un saggio di rimboscamento in Mugello. 1886. IV. 166.[1]
Un ami des forêts, (pseud.).　Enlèvement des feuilles mortes. 1894. IV. 543.[2]
Un Ancien, (pseud.).　Les ourdons ou virées de balivage dans les taillis sous futaie. 1897. IV. 556.[2]
Un ancien forestier, (pseud.).　Hêtres et Sapins. 1888. IV. 74.[2]
Un Anglo-Américain, (pseud.).　De l'emploi des arbres d'ornement dans l'Amérique du Nord. 1834. III. 202.[2]
Un ayudante, (pseud.).　Contraste. 1898. IV. 554.
— Más contrastes. 1898. IV. 554.
Un botánico de afición, (pseud.).　El Árbol del Paraíso. 1887. III. 512.[2]
Un forestal, (pseud.).　El ramo de montes. 1890. IV. 542.[1]
— Reformas y observaciones acerca del reglamento de la Junta consultiva de montes. 1899. IV. 554.
Un homme du Sud, (pseud.).　La culture du Dattier dans le sud Constantinois. 1898. III. 329.[1]
Un ingeniero de montes, (pseud.).　Algo que sea servicio forestal. 1898. IV. 554.
Un Ingeniero Ordenador, (pseud.).　Informe abierto. 1895. IV. 550.[2]
Un Jurassien, (pseud.).　Quelques réflexions sur l'accroissement futur. 1876. IV. 233.
Un Vandale, (pseud.).　La réserve de la forêt de Fontainebleau. 1877. IV. 180.[1]
Un vieux forestier, (pseud.).　Le polypore du Bouleau. 1882. IV. 439.
— The Red Birch polyporus. 1882. IV. 439.
Unanue, Jose Hipolito.　Disertacion sobre el aspecto . . . de la famosa planta . . . Coca. 1794. II. 394.
Underdånig berättelse angående förvaltningen af kronoskogarne i Finland. 1877. IV. 289.[1]
Underdånigt betänkande och förslag. 1871. IV. 288.[2]
Underdånigt betänkande och förslag angående åtgärder för befrämjande af en förbättrad skogshushållning. 1856. IV. 344.[1]
Underrättelse om wilda träds och buskars plantering. 1764. III. 119.[1]
Underretning for dem, som agte at underkaste sig den fuldstaendige Forst-Examen. 1835. IV. 30.[3]
Underretning for dem, som ville underkaste sig den . . . Forstexamen. 1853. IV. 30.[3]
Underretning, om hvorledes Traeer . . . See DU HAMEL DU MONCEAU, H. L. 1753. III. 154.[2]
Underwood, John.　A catalogue of plants . . . in the botanic garden . . . at Glasnevin. 1804. I. 53.
Der unfehlbare Raupenvertilger. 1827. IV. 206.
Ungarische Rosen-Zeitung. III. 25.
Ungarischer Forstverein. Jahresschrift. Mittheilungen. IV. 15.
Ungarn.　See HUNGARY.
Ungarns Ausfuhr an Forstproducten. 1893. IV. 407.[1]
Ungebauer, Johann Andreas.　De cultura plantarum. 1741. III. 103.
Unger, von, (Forstmeister).　Durchpflanzung der Fichtenculturen mit Lärchen. 1861. IV. 138.[1]
— Ueber Eichenzucht. 1868. IV. 506.
— Ueber Fichtenpflanzungen. 1863. IV. 453.
— Gemischte Buchen- und Fichtenpflanzungen. 1861. IV. 138.[1]
— Ueber das Gewicht des Fichtenholzes. 1837. IV. 459.[1]
Unger, Alfred.　Japanische Bambus. 1891. III. 314.[2]
— Japanische Coniferen. 189.? II. 15.[2]
— Japanische Gebirgs-Flora. 1897. I. 463.[1]
— Japanische Zier-Ahorn. 1890. III. 535.[2]
— Juniperus Sanderi, eine weitere Berichtigung. 1900. II. 28.[2] III. 301.[2]
— Mitteilungen aus Japan. 1890. III. 273,[2] 535.[2] — 1891. III. 314.[2]
— Myrica rubra Sieb. et Zucc. 1889. III. 353.[2]
— Das Obst der Japaner. 1890. III. 273.[2]
— Pueraria Thunbergiana Benth. 1899. III. 485.[2]
Unger, Ephraim Salomon.　Anleitung zu dem Feldmessen. 1828. IV. 263.
— Uebungen aus der angewandten Mathematik. 1835. IV. 58.
— Uchungen aus der reinen und angewandten Stereometrie. 1830. IV. 263.
— Uebungen aus der Statik und Mechanik der festen Körper. 1835. IV. 58.
Unger, Franz.　Der Amber oder das Storax-Harz. 1865. III. 417.[2]
— Anatomie und Physiologie der Pflanzen. 1855. I. 89.
— Aphorismen zur Anatomie und Physiologie. 1838. I. 147.
— Ueber den Bau und das Wachsthum des Dicotyledonen-Stammes. 1840. I. 105.
— Ueber die Bedeutung der Lenticellen. 1836. I. 132.[1]
— Beiträge zur Anatomie . . . der Pflanzen. 1867. I. 34. — 1869. I. 34.
— Beiträge zur Anatomie . . . der Pflanzen. 1862. I. 164, 165, 166.
— Beiträge zur Kenntniss der parasitischen Pflanzen. 1840. I. 232.[2] V. XII.[1]
— Beiträge zur Physiologie der Pflanzen. 1854. I. 158.
— Beiträge zur vergleichenden Pathologie. 1840. I. 206.[1]
— Botanical letters to a friend. 1852. I. 95.
— Botanische Beobachtungen. 1847. I. 127, IV. 442. — 1849. I. 440.
— Botanische Briefe, 1852. I. 95.
— Botanische Streifzüge auf dem Gebiete der Culturgeschichte. 1857. III. 219,[2] 221,[2] V. XXV.[1] — 1859. I. 517.[2] — 1860. I. 81.[2] — 1862. I. 81.[2] — 1865. I. 447, IV. 87.[1] — 1867. I. 81,[2] III. 698.[1]
— Chrysomyxa abietis. 1840. IV. 455.
— Ueber den Einfluss des Bodens auf die Vertheilung der Gewächse. 1836. I. 228,[1] 440.
— Einiges über das Wachsthum des Stammes. 1858. I. 189.
— Die Exantheme der Pflanzen. 1833. III. 193.[2]
— Upon the formation of crystals in the cells of plants. 1838. I. 138.[2]
— Genesis der Spiralgefässe. 1841. I. 193.
— Geologie der europäischen Waldbäume. 1869. I. 348,[1] IV. 79.[1]
— Ueber einen in grosser Verbreitung an Nadelhölzern beobachteten Fadenpilz. 1847. IV. 144.
— Ueber den Grund der Bildung der Jahreslagen. 1847. I. 27.[1]
— Grundlinien der Anatomie und Physiologie der Pflanzen. 1866. I. 90.
— Grundzüge der Anatomie und Physiologie der Pflanzen. 1846. I. 88.
— Inhalt eines alten ägyptischen Ziegels. 1862. I. 81.[2]

— Die Interocllularsubstanz. 1847. I. 137.
— Über Krystallbildungen in den Pflanzenzellen. 1838. I. 138,[2] V. xi.[1]
— Das Ladanum-Harz. 1865. III. 612.[2]
— Das Mastix-Harz. 1865. III. 525.[1]
— Mémoire sur l'origine des vaisseaux spiraux. 1841. I. 133.
— Über merismatische Zellbildung bei der Entwicklung des Pollens. 1844. I. 117.[1]
— Die Nahrungspflanzen des Menschen. 1857. III. 219.[2]
— Die Natur der Lenticellen. 1840. I. 132.[1]
— Nehmen die Blätter der Pflanzen dunstförmiges Wasser aus der Atmosphäre auf? 1852. I. 161.
— Neue Untersuchungen über die Transspiration. 1862. I. 166.
— Noch einige alte Bäume. 1856. I. 295.[1]
— Die organischen Einschlüsse eines Ziegels. 1867. I. 81.[2]
— Die Pflanze als Erregungs- und Betäubungsmittel. 1857. III. 221.[2]
— Die Pflanze als Todtenschmuck. 1867. I. 515.
— Die Pflanze als Zaubermittel. 1859. I. 517.[2]
— Die Pflanzen des alten Ägyptens. 1860. I. 81.[2]
— Pflanzengeschichtliche Bemerkungen über den Kaiserwald. 1849. I. 440.
— Die Pflanzenwelt der Jetztzeit. 1852. I. 249.[1]
— Recherches sur la formation des couches ligneuses annuelles. 1847. I. 127.[1]
— Der Rosmarin und seine Verwendung. 1867. III. 698.[1]
— Studien zur Kenntniss des Saftlaufes. 1865. I. 164.
— Versuche über Luftausscheidung lebender Pflanzen. 1853. I. 170.
— Der Waldstand Dalmatiens. 1865. I. 447, IV. 87.[1]
— Weitere Untersuchungen über die Bewegung des Pflanzensaftes. 1868. I. 164.
— Wissenschaftliche Ergebnisse einer Reise in Griechenland. 1862. I. 449.
— See also ENDLICHER, Stephan & UNGER, Franz.
— & Hruschauer, Franz. Beiträge zur Lehre von der Bodenstetigkeit. 1850. I. 228.[1]
— & Kotschy, Theodor. Die Insel Cypern. 1865. I. 452.
Unger, Michael. Animadversiones circa Jussieui methodum plantarum naturalem. 1806. I. 251.
Ungern-Sternberg, Franz, Baron. Salicorniearum synopsis. 1876. II. 187.[1]
— Versuch einer Systematik der Salicornieen. 1866. II. 187.[1]
Eine ungewöhnlich grosse Weymouthskiefer. 1878. II. 46.[1]
Ungewöhnlicher Eichenwuchs auf Sandboden. 1856. II. 138.[1]
Ungius, Nicolaus Thomas. Encomion historiae plantarum. 1636. I. 79.[1]
Unificación de las notaciones usadas en las fórmulas de cubicación. 1899. IV. 530.[1]
Uniforme des agents et préposés. 1896. IV. 303.[2]
Uniform-Reglement für die königlich preussischen Forstbeamten. 1896. IV. 302.
Union médical de la Provence. See MARSEILLE-MÉDICAL. I. 22.
Union médicale du Nord-est. See UNION MÉDICALE ET SCIENTIFIQUE DU NORD-EST. I. 24.[1]
Union médicale et scientifique du Nord-est. I. 24.[1]
United gardeners' and land-stewards' journal. III. 18.
United States — Commissioner of agriculture. Report. See UNITED STATES — COMMISSIONER OF PATENTS. III. 8.
United States — Commissioner of patents. Report. III. 8.
United States — Department of agriculture. Annual report. See UNITED STATES — COMMISSIONER OF PATENTS. III. 8.
United States — Department of agriculture — Botanical division. Bulletin. III. 9, 757.[1]
United States — Department of agriculture — Botanical division — Section of vegetable pathology. Bulletin. See UNITED STATES — DEPARTMENT OF AGRICULTURE — BOTANICAL DIVISION. Bulletin. III. 9.
United States — Department of agriculture — Botanical division — Section of vegetable pathology. Circular. III. 9.
United States — Department of agriculture — Chemical division. Bulletin. III. 9.
United States — Department of agriculture — Division of biological survey. Bulletin. See UNITED STATES — DEPARTMENT OF AGRICULTURE — DIVISION OF ORNITHOLOGY AND MAMMALOGY. I. 519.[2]
United States — Department of agriculture — Division of botany. Inventory. III. 9.
United States — Department of agriculture — Division of entomology. Bulletin. Circular. Report. Special reports III. 9.
United States — Department of agriculture — Division of forestry. Annual reports. Bulletin. Circular. IV. 5.[1]
United States — Department of agriculture — Division of gardens and grounds. Circular. III. 9.
United States — Department of agriculture — Division of ornithology and mammalogy. Bulletin. North American fauna. I. 519.[2]
United States — Department of agriculture — Division of pomology. Bulletin. Circular. Report. III. 9.
United States — Department of agriculture — Division of vegetable pathology. Bulletin. Circular. III. 9.
United States — Department of agriculture — Division of vegetable physiology and pathology. See UNITED STATES — DEPARTMENT OF AGRICULTURE — DIVISION OF VEGETABLE PATHOLOGY. III. 9.
United States — Department of agriculture. Experiment station record. Farmers' bulletin. Reports. Special reports. III. 8. — Special reports; miscellaneous. III. 9. — Yearbook. III. 9.
United States — Department of agriculture — Fibre investigations. Reports. III. 9.
United States — Department of agriculture. Monthly weather review. IV. 5.[1]
United States — Secretary of agriculture. Report. See UNITED STATES — COMMISSIONER OF PATENTS. III. 8.
United States consular reports. III. 8.
United States entomological commission. Bulletin. Report. III. 9.
United States exploring expedition during the years 1838–42. See TORREY, John. 1874. I. 323.
United States geological and geographical survey of the territories. Bulletin. I. 7.[1]
United States geological survey. Annual report. I. 7,[1] IV. 541.[1]
United States national herbarium. Contributions. I. 7.[1]
United States national museum. Bulletin. Proceedings. I. 7.[1]
The United States of Venezuela. 1893. III. 267.[2]
United States special consular reports. III. 8.
United States tenth census. Forestry bulletin. IV. 5.[2]
Universidad central de Venezuela. Revista. I. 8.[1]
Universidad de agricultura de Viena. 1892. IV. 541.[1]
Universidad de Chile. Anales. I. 8.[1]
Universidad de Quito. Anales. I. 8.[1]
Università degli studi di Siena. See REALE UNIVERSITÀ ... I. 26.[1]
Università di Genova. See REALE UNIVERSITÀ ... I. 26.[1]
Universitas hafniensis. Acta. I. 9.[1]
Universitas imperialis jurjevensis. Acta. I. 10.
Universitas lundensis. Acta. See LUNDS UNIVERSITETS. I. 510.[2]
Université de Lyon. Annales. Sciences. I. 24.[1]
University of Nebraska. Botanical survey. Report. I. 7.[1]
University of Pennsylvania. Contributions from the botanical laboratory. I. 7.[1]
Unmassgebliche Vorschläge, wie die Fichten- und Kiefernsaaten ... unternommen werden können. See COTTA, Heinrich. 1800. IV. 111.
Uonius, Olof. Disputio physica de plantis. 1647. I. 30.
Der unparthenysche Forstmann. See SCHEMBERA, Josef. 1807. IV. 100.[2]
Unser Fassholzgewerbe. 1873. IV. 427.[1]
Unser Kastanienwald. 1874. IV. 492.[2]
Unsere Arve auf dem Aussterbeetat. 1889. IV. 463.[2]
Unsere Flieder oder Lilaksträucher. 1869. III. 680.[1]
Unsere Industrie ... mit eichenen Fasshölzern. 1869. IV. 427.[1]
Unsere jüngsten Wasserverheerungen. 1880. IV. 73.[2]
Unsere österr.-ungarischen Eichenarten. 1881. II. 130.[1]
Unsere Weichselrohrsucht. 1875. III. 438.[2]
Unterhaltungen aus der Naturgeschichte. See WILHELM, G. T.. 1810. I. 93.
Unterhaltungen des Lehrers Erich ... im Walde. 1831. IV. 123.[2]
Unterhaltungen über die Physiologie der Pflanzenwelt. See UNTERHALTUNGEN DES LEHRERS ERICH ...
Unterhuber, Alois. Ueber die Stellung der Schuppen der Frucht von Ceratozamia mexicana. 1870. II. 4.[1]
Unterricht in der Zucht ... der nützlichsten Waldbäume. 1851. IV. 123.[2]

Unterricht über die Pflanzung der Wasserweiden. 1796. III. 347.

Unterricht von der wilden Baumzucht. 1754. IV. 149.²

Unterricht, wie in Kärnthen die lebendige Zäune zu pflanzen. 1767. III. 212.²

Unterricht zum Holzanbau für Heidereuter. 1791. IV. 105.

Untersuchungen aus dem Botanischen Institut zu Tübingen. I. 15.

Untersuchungen aus dem botanischen Laboratorium der Universität Göttingen. I. 15.

Untersuchungen über die Festigkeit der Hölzer. See JENNY, Karl. 1873. IV. 410.

Untersuchungen über die Pitaya-China. See RECHERCHES sur le Quinquina pitaya. 1835. III. 726.¹

Unverricht, Karl. Anleitung zur Pflanzenkenntniss. 1842. I. 380.

Unwin, W. C. Comparison of the strength of Ceylon timbers. 1900. IV. 411.¹

— Mechanical tests of Pyinma wood. 1899. II. 609.²

— Report on the results of mechanical tests applied to a series of logs . . . from . . . Ceylon. 1900. IV. 409.

— A revision of the dictionary article on Lagerstroemia Flosreginae. 1897. III. 629.²

Unzer, (Forstschreiber zu Ilsenburg). See Ueber das in HAMBURG übliche Kappen der Bäume. 1793. III. 173.¹

Unzer, (Forst-Secretarius). Betrachtung über die mehrten Holzungen. 1789. IV. 138.¹

— Schreiben . . . über des Hrn. Prof. Gleditsch Abhandlung. 1788. IV. 455.

— Ueber die Verkohlung des Stockholzes. 1790. IV. 394.

Unzer, C. F. Om Skoves Opelzkning med Hensyn til den danske Flaades Skibsbyggerie. 1811. IV. 425.¹

Unzer, Johann August. Betrachtungen über einige Besonderheiten. 1766. I. 31.

— Vom Gefühle der Pflanzen. 1766. I. 31.

— Sammlung kleiner Schriften. 1766. I. 31.

— Untersuchung, wie die Bäume . . . zu bewahren sind. 1766. I. 31.

De Upas of Giftboom op Java. 1853. III. 366.²

The Upas tree. 1895. III. 366.² ·

Upendranath Kanjilal (Babu). The Bhalkua Bans . . . of Bengal. 1891. IV. 485.¹

— The Date sugar industry of Bengal. 1892. III. 330.¹

— See also BIRBAL & UPENDRANATH KANJILAL.

Upham, Warren. Catalogue of the flora of Minnesota. 1884. I. 315, V. XVII.²

— Geographic limits of species of plants in the basin of the Red River. 1892. I. 316.

— Supplement to the flora of Minnesota. 1884. V. XVII.²

Ob upotrebleni . . . See Объ употребленіи . . .

Upper Burma. See INDIA — UPPER BURMA.

The Upper Burma forest regulation VI. of 1887. 1895. IV. 307.²

An uprooted Araucaria imbricata. 1897. III, 299.¹

Uproshtchennyya . . . See Упрощенныя . . .

Upsala — Regia societas scientiarum upsaliensis. See REGIA . . . I. 8.¹

Upton, H. T. Woodlands in Sussex.· 1878. IV. 358.¹

Uralskoye . . . See Уральское . . .

Eine uralte Linde zu Bisenz. 1875. II. 516.²

Uralte Waldreste im Elbeflusse. 1894. IV. 84.¹

Urbain, V. Conférence sur les différents principes qui constituent les tissus. 1883. I. 154.

— Le déboisement et la consommation du papier. 1897. IV. 558.¹

— See also FRÉMY, Edmond & URBAIN, V.

Urban, Ignatz. Additamenta ad cognitionem florae Indiae occidentalis. 1892. I. 337.

— Ueber die Bestäubungseinrichtungen bei . . . Ruiingia. 1883. II. 537.²

— Zur Biologie der einseitswendigen Blüthenstände. 1885. I. 113,¹ 238.

— Zur Biologie und Morphologie der Rutaceen. 1883. II. 397.¹

— Ueber den Blüthenstand von Dalechampia. 1883. II. 440.¹

— Damiana.· 1882. II. 575.¹

— Dasylirion longifolium Zucc. 1884. II. 84.¹

— Ueber einige Rubiaceen-Gattungen. 1897. II. 807.²

— Ueber einige Ternstroemiaceen-Gattungen. 1896. II. 547.²

— Ueber einige tropisch-amerikanische Bauhinia-Arten. 1886. II. 334.²

— Enumeratio specierum, varietatum . . . in catalogis seminum. 1881. I. 77.

— Ueber die Familie der Turneraceen. 1883. II. 574.²

— Zur Flora Südamerikas. 1882. I. 343.

— Ueber die Früchte von Dacryodes. 1886. II. 418.²

— Führer durch den botanischen Garten zu Berlin. 1887. III. 28,₁

— Führer durch den K. botanischen Garten zu Berlin. 1887. I. 48.

— Ueber die Gattung Trematosperma. 1884. II. 475.¹

— Humiriaceae et Lineae. 1877. II. 393,¹ 593.²

— Kleinere Mittheilungen über Pflanzen des Berliner botan. Gartens und Museums. 1884. II. 475.² — 1886. II. 334,² 415,² 418,² 546.²

— Der Königl. botanische Garten und das Botanische Museum zu Berlin. 1891. I. 521.²

— Krugia, eine neue Myrtaceengattung. 1893. II. 628.¹

— Ueber die Loranthaceen-Gattung Dendrophthora. 1896. II. 174.²

— Über mexikanische Turneraceen. 1900. II. 574.²

— Monographia Loasacearum. 1900. II. 583.¹

— Monographie der Familie der Turneraceen. 1883. II. 574.²

— Moringaceae. 1889. II. 284.²

— Morphologie der Gattung Bauhinia. 1885. II. 334.¹

— Ueber die morphologische Bedeutung der Stacheln bei den Aurantieen. 1883. II. 397.²

— Eine neue Marcgravia-Art Puerto-Rico's. 1886. II. 546.²

— Eine neue Simaruba-Art Puerto-Rico's. 1886. II. 415.²

— Papayaceae africanae. 1893. II. 583.¹

— Patascoya, eine neue Ternstroemiaceen-Gattung. 1896. II. 549.¹

— Plantae novae americanae imprimis Glaziovianae. 1897. I. 330.

— Ueber die Sabiaceengattung Meliosma. 1895. II. 490.²

— Simaruba Tulae Urb. 1889. II. 416.¹

— Symbolae antillanae. 1898. I. 337.

— Trematosperma, novum genus Somalense. 1883. II. 475.²

— Turneraceae. 1883. II. 574.²

— Turneraceae somalenses. 1896. II. 574.²

— Umbelliferae. 1879. II. 653.¹

— See also MARTIUS, K. F. P. von, EICHLER, A. W. & URBAN, Ignatz.

Urban, Josef. Beschreibung der k. k. Reichsdomäne Pardubitz.· 1852.· IV. 370.

— Beschreibung der Reichsdomäne Brandeis. 1856. IV. 370.

— Die Reichsdomäne Brandeis. 1855. IV. 370.

Urbano de Castro, Arthur. O Café. 1899. III. 727.

Urbina, Manuel. Catálogo de plantas mexicanas. 1897. I. 333.

— La Chia y sus aplicaciones. 1891. III. 698.²

— Una Papaya prolifica.· 1900. II. 583.¹

Ure, Alexander. On the Malambo. 1844. II. 440.¹

Urera fibre. 1888. III. 382.¹

Urff, (Oberförster). Die Verjüngung gemischter Kiefernbestände. 1885. IV. 481.

— Wie verfährt man bei der Verjüngung von Buchenbeständen. 1888. IV. 495.

Urff, C. Ueber Forstkulturen. 1885. IV. 118.

— Forstkulturen und Behandlung von Forstbeständen. 1885. IV. 118.

— Führer zu forstlichen Excursionen in die Oberförsterei Neuhaus. 1892. IV. 354.

Uri. Waldbrände. 1895. IV. 183.²

Urich. Ueber Probestamm-Systeme. 1881. IV. 213.

— Das Schwanken der Holzpreise. 1884. IV. 403.¹

Urich, Karl. Ueber Ablösung von Forstservituten. 1877. IV. 333.

— Ablösung von Waldgerechtsamen. 1885. IV. 334.¹

— Die Auswahl von Probestämmen. 1878. IV. 236.

— Die Berechnung des Holzbodenwertes. 1889. IV. 258.

— Die Bodenreinertragslehre. 1891. IV. 246.

— Die deutsche Holzzollgesetzgebung. 1888. IV. 284.²

— Das Eindringen von Nutzholzarten in Buchengrundbestand. 1888. IV. 495.

— Ein einfaches Probestamm-System. 1884. IV. 218.

— Einhaltung der Haupt- und Zwischennutzungs-Etats. 1873. IV. 256.

— Ueber Ertragstafeln für schlagweise bewirtschaftete Hochwaldbestände. 1890. IV. 237.

— Die Festsetzung der Fällungs-Etats. 1887. IV. 237.

— Freunde und Gegner der Forstfinanzwirtschaft. 1888. IV. 257.

— Die Gewinnung des Stockholzes. 1869. IV. 386.

— Holzart und Umtriebszeit. 1881. IV. 252.
— Das Holzmasse-Ermittelungsverfahren. 1871. IV. 217.
— Holzverwerthung und Holzverwerthungs-Conjuncturen im Buchenhochwald. 1882. IV. 498.
— Ist es, um der vermehrten Nachfrage nach Nutzholz ... nothwendig, die Buchenhochwaldwirthschaft zu verlassen. 1880. IV. 498.
— Juglans regia unter Schirmbestand. 1881. IV. 488.²
— Kann die deutsche Waldwirthschaft bei Aufrechthaltung des Freihandelssystems bestehen? 1879. IV. 274.¹
— Ueber die Lichtseiten des forstlichen Universitäts-Unterrichts. See HESS, Richards & URICH, Carl. 1882. IV. 29.
— Lichtwuchsbetrieb im Buchenhochwald. 1888. IV. 495.
— Die Modifikationen der Draudt'schen und der Kreisflächen-Methode. 1867. IV. 214.
— Die Sprengschraube. 1860. IV. 386.
— Ueber Stockholzgewinnung. 1867. IV. 386.
— Unterbau von Lichtholzarten. 1884. IV. 139.¹
— Verwendbarkeit des Buchenholzes zu Bauzwecken. 1887. IV. 499.
— Waldreinertrag und Walderwartungswert. 1887. IV. 257.
— Auf welchem Standpunkt befindet sich dermalen die Frage der natürlichen Verjüngung. 1885. IV. 139.²
— Die Weymouthskiefer. 1884. IV. 469.
— Die Zündnadel-Sprengmaschine. 1876. IV. 386.
— Die Zündnadel-Sprengschraube. 1876. IV. 386.
— Die Zwangs-Ablösung der Servituten. 1874. IV. 333.
— See also HESS, Richard & URICH, Carl.
Urich, P. Bestandsmassenermittelung. 1896. IV. 219.
— Die Besteuerung der Waldungen im Grossherzogtum Hessen. 1900. IV. 284.²
— Die Bewertung des landwirtschaftlich und des forstwirtschaftlich benutzten Bodens. 1899. IV. 259.¹
— Bodenerwartungswert und Rentabilität. 1896. IV. 259.¹
— Die Ermittelung der Holzmasse. 1900. IV. 219.
— Das forstliche Verzinsungsprozent. 1898. IV. 259.¹
— Land- und forstwirtschaftlicher Ertrag. 1892. IV. 258.
— Lichtwuchsbetrieb und Rentabilität. 1897. IV. 259.¹
— Lichtwuchskulissenbetrieb. 1894. IV. 130.
— Nutzholzzucht im Vogelsberg. 1893. IV. 119.¹
— Die bei der preussischen Hauptstation ... in Anwendung kommende Holzmassenermittelungs-Methode. 1897. IV. 219.
— Die Regelung des Walderstrags in den ... Waldungen des Grossherzogtums Hessen. 1899. IV. 248.²
— Eine Vereinfachung des Urich'schen Holzmassenaufnahme-Verfahrens. 1900. IV. 219.
— Verschiedene Methoden der Holzmasseermittelung. 1895. IV. 219.
— Wald- und Boden-Reinertrag. 1890. IV. 258.
— Wald- und Boden-Reinertragswirtschaft. 1893. IV. 258.
— Die Zündnadel-Sprengschraube. 1894. IV. 387.¹
Uricoechea, Ezequiel. La botánica desde 1810 hasta 1859. 1860. I. 80.¹
— On the cinchona barks of New Granada. 1854. III. 724.²
— Sur le corps gras du Myristica Otoba. 1854. III. 402.¹
— La espedicion botánica. 1860. I. 80.¹
— Ueber das Fett der Myristica Otoba. 1854. III. 402.¹
Urk, D. R. van. Koffiecultuur in Transvaal. 1899. III. 732.²
Urkundliche Beleuchtung des Prozesses der Ortsgemeinde Altstädten. 1846. IV. 330.
Urkundliche Darstellung der Rechte und Ansprachen des Klosters Pfäffers. 1832. IV. 329.
Urkundlich rechtliche Beleuchtung der Streitfrage: Ist der Bernhardzeller-Wald Eigenthum der Ortsgemeinde. 1843. IV. 330.
Urlander, Harald. Rön at färga castor-svart kläde. 1753. III. 648.¹
Urlandt, Edwin. Vermehrung, Kultur ... der Clematis. 1887. III. 389.²
Urquhart, A. T. On the natural spread of the Eucalyptus. 1884. II. 623.²
— Notes on Epacris microphylla. 1882. II. 689.¹
Urquijo de Irabien, Francisco. Bases establecidas por la diputación ... para precaver los daños ... en los montes. 1845. IV. 181.¹
— Medidas adoptadas ... sobre plantación de árboles. 1845. IV. 41.¹
Ueber die Ursache der häufigen Absterbens der Lärche. 1865. IV. 450.
Ueber die Ursache der Holztheuerung. 1846. IV. 281.¹
Ueber die Ursachen der Vermagerung der Waldböden. 1866. IV. 68.

Urseren. 1863. IV. 181.¹
Ursinus, Fulvius. Notæ ad M. Catonem, M. Varronem. 1587. III. 98.
Ursinus, Johannes Heinrich. Arboreti biblici continuatio. 1665. I. 512.
— Arboretum biblicum. 1663. I. 512.
— Continuatio historiae plantarum biblicae. 1665. I. 512.
Ursprung, Alfred. Beiträge zur Anatomie und Jahresbildung tropischer Holzarten. 1900. I. 128.¹
Urumoff, J. K. Zur Flora von Bulgarien. 1899. I. 451.
Urville, Jules Sébastien César DUMONT D'. See DUMONT D'URVILLE, J. S. C.
Urzȩdow, Marcin. Herbarz polski. 1595. I. 283.
De l'usage du caphé, du thé. See DUFOUR, P. S. 1671. III. 221.²
Usagers et impôts. 1900. IV. 327.
Usages locaux du département de la Vendée. 1859. IV. 383.¹
The use of compressed timber. 1893. IV. 422.²
The use of forests. 1876. IV. 44.
Use of Semal wood for packing cases. 1887. IV. 528.¹
The use of trees ... with leaves of abnormal colors. 1897. III. 205.²
The use of wood-pulp. 1893. IV. 430.
Use of woods in the household of nature. 1862. IV. 43.
Useful and ornamental planting. See SINCLAIR, George. 1832. III. 106.²
Useful applications of the Ash-tree. 1843. IV. 534.²
Useful applications of the Beech-tree. 1843. IV. 500.¹
Useful applications of the Lime-tree. 1843. III. 585.²
The useful family herbal. See HILL, John. 1754. III. 80.
Useful plants of Japan. See TANAKA, Yoshio. 1888. III. 91.²
Useful plants of New Zealand. 1865. III. 283.¹
On the uses of Hornbeam wood. 1880. IV. 492.¹
Uses of the Chestnut-tree. 1843. III. 360.¹
Uses of the Elm-tree. 1844. III. 365.¹
Uses of the Hazel. 1844. III. 358.¹
Uses of the Horse Chestnut. 1865. III. 538.²
Uses of the Walnut-tree. 1843. III. 356.¹
Ushba. 1890. I. 369.
Uslar, B. von. Der Weinstock am Spalier. 1882. III. 553.¹
Uslar, Johann Julius von. Chemico-physiological observations on plants. 1794. I. 146.
— Ueber den Einfluss der Verkoppelungen in Nord-Deutschland. 1806. IV. 282.¹
— Forstwirthschaftliche Bemerkungen auf einer Reise gesamlet. 1792. IV. 348.³
— Fragmente neuerer Pflanzenkunde. 1794. I. 146.
— Ist es vortheilhafter gemischte Buchwaldungen als Baum- oder Schlagholz zu bewirthschaften? 1794. IV. 493.²
— Pyralis hercyniana. 1798. IV. 206.
— Schreiben naturgeschichtlichen Inhalts. 1810. IV. 206.
Uso dei Mogano per bastimenti. 1801. IV. 423.¹
Uspenski, P. P. Ueber die Vermehrung der Picea pungens glauca. See УСПЕНСКИЙ, П. П. 1891. III. 306.¹
— See also УСПЕНСКИЙ, П. П.
Ussèle, L. Un reboisement dans les Indes anglaises. 1891. IV. 168.¹
— La sylviculture au Japon. 1890. IV. 376.¹
— À travers le Japon. 1891. IV. 376.¹
Ustav ... See УСТАВЪ.
Usteri, Alfred. Beiträge zu einer Monographie der Gattung Berberis. 1900. II. 202.¹
— Beiträge zur Kenntnis der Platanen. 1900. II. 254.¹
— Berberis Fremonti Torr. 1900. II. 203.¹
— Berberis japonica R. Brown. 1900. II. 204.¹
— Berberis nepalensis Spreng. 1900. III. 396.¹.
— Berberis nervosa Pursh. 1900. III. 396.¹
— Das Geschlecht der Berberitzen. 1899. II. 202.¹
— Die Strassenpflanzungen in Zürich. 1899. III. 210.
— Torreya und Cephalotaxus. 1899. II. 8,³ 12.¹
— Zusammenstellung der Forschungen über die Reizerscheinungen an den Staubfäden von Berberis. 1900. II. 202.²
Usteri, Leonhard. Anleitung für die Landleute in Absicht auf die Pflanzung der Wälder. 1766. IV. 110.¹
Usteri, Paul. Delectus opusculorum botanicorum. 1790. I. 263.
— See also RÖMER, J. J. & USTERI, Paul.
Ustyanowicz, Mikolaj. Praktyczna nauka o hodowaniu Wynnoi lozy. 1879. III. 558.²
Utah — Agricultural college — Experiment station. Annual report. Bulletin. III. 9.

Utah — **Agricultural experiment station**. *See* UTAH — AGRI-
CULTURAL COLLEGE. III. 9.
Uteg. Zur Schüttekrankheit der Kiefern in Saatkämpen.
1889. IV. 478.
Uterhart. Note sur un nouvel Acacia. 1843. III. 486.²
Uth, (*Forstmeister*). Die Holzkonservirung. 1892. IV. 421.
— Zur Rettung der Buchenbahnschwelle. 1892. IV. 499.
Uth, (*Oberförster*). Preis-Differenzen bei der Verwerthung
gleichalteriger haubarer Kiefernbestände. 1886. IV. 481.
Utilidad del Eucalipto. 1887. IV. 531.²
Utilisation d'Érables indigènes et exotiques. 1900. IV. 526.²
L'utilisation de la sciure de bois pour le chauffage. 1900.
IV. 431.¹
Utilisation des eaux d'égout. 1898. IV. 145.
Utilisation des sciures et déchets dans les scieries. 1898. IV.
431.¹
Utilisation des sciures et déchets de bois. 1898. IV. 431.¹
Utilisation du bois pour la fabrication du sucre. 1898. IV.
558.¹
L'utilisation du Marron d'Inde. 1896. III. 538.²
Utilisation du terreau. 1899. IV. 143.²
Utilita del Gelso selvatico. 1864. III. 148.¹
Utilita delle foglie di Salcio. 1865. IV. 487.²
Utilité de l'écorce du Tilleul. 1854. III. 585.²
Utilization of saw-dust. 1890. IV. 431.¹
Utmutatás a filloxerás szőlőknek szénkéneggel való gyéritő
kezelésére. 1890. III. 762.
Utrecht — **Academia Rheno-Traiectina**. *See* ACADEMIA . . .
I. 15.
Utsch, Jacob. Diagnosen neuer Brombeer-Bastarde. 1896.
II. 300.²
— Erwiderung. 1898. II. 302.²
— Hybriden im Genus Rubus. 1894. II. 302.¹
— Rubus kuenicus Schott. 1898. II. 308.¹
— Ueber Rubus tomentosus Borkh. 1893. II. 310.²
Uxküll-Gyllenband, Kuno Otto, *Graf* von. Einige Worte über
die Anlegung von Saat- und Pflanzenschulen. 1896. IV.
149.²
— Kurze Beschreibung der oestreichischen Schwarzkiefer.
1845. IV. 466.¹
Uzielli, Gustavo. Sopra alcune osservazioni botaniche di
Leonardo da Vinci. 1869. I. 81.¹

V. Beitrag zur Lehre über die Buchenzucht. 1861. IV.
494.
V. Over het bemesten van Koffie. 1896. III. 734.¹
V. Eenige beschouwingen over de gouvernementskoffiecul-
tuur op Java. 1890. III. 730.
V. Eenige opmerkingen over Koffiehybriden. 1897. III.
733.²
V. Het enten van Koffie-hybriden. 1897. III. 733.¹
V., Forststatistik, Kanton Zürich. 1860. IV. 365.
V. Iets over het al of niet toppen van Koffieboomen. 1897.
734.²
V. De invloed van het toppen op de productie der Koffie-
boomen. 1895. III. 734.²
V. Kew notes. 1894. III. 390.¹
V. Over kweekbedden voor Koffie. 1896. III. 733.¹
V. Lawson's Holly. 1877. III. 530.¹
V. Le Lupin et les plantations. 1897. IV. 545.¹
V. Opstellen uit de practijk der Koffiecultuur. 1896. III.
733.¹ 734.¹
V. Penjerrick. 1899. III. 287.¹ 316.²
V. Pinanga Veitchi. 1880. III. 330.²
V. Procedimientos heliográficos. 1889. IV. 265.
V. Statistique forestière, canton de Zurich. 1860. IV. 365.
V. Zum Ueberfluss noch etwas über das Buttlar'sche Pflanz-
verfahren. 1862. IV. 152.
V., A. Note sur la destruction des larves du Cossus ligniperda.
1894. IV. 549.² .
V., A. Noyers et Caryers. 1894. IV. 488.¹
V., A. Ombre et lumière. 1896. IV. 67.²
V., A. Utilité et emploi des bois en Amérique. 1895. IV.
397.
V., D. Nouvelles de botanique médicale. 1814. III. 509.¹
V., H. Le vin de Sureau. 1890. III. 752.¹
V., H. de. Le Cormier à fruits comestibles. 1889. III. 460.¹
V., J. C. Nürnbergische Hesperides. *See* VOLCKAMER, J. C.
1708. II. 400.²
— , M. Nog iets over Koffiebladziekte. 1881. III. 735.
— , M. Vandalismo. 1864. IV. 283.¹
— , N. *See* B., H. (Russian index.)
V., R. P. La Exposición universal. España. 1888. IV.
540.¹

V., S. Het systeem Ples bij de gouvernements Koffiecultuur.
1888. III. 730.
V., S. C. Over eenige merkwaardige boomen in Mexico.
1831. I. 295.²
V., T. Strophanthus dichotomus Dec. 1858. III. 690.²
V., Th. Gevolgen van de bladziekte. 1894. III. 736.
V., V. de. De gouvernements Koffiekultuur. 1890. III. 730.
V., V. F. y L. El Ciprés. 1863. IV. 448.¹
V.-B., M. *See* VANDEN-BERGHE, Maximilien.
Vaccari, Lino. La continuità della flora delle Alpi Graie.
1900. I. 438.
Vaccinium Arctostaphylos as a tea substitute. 1895. III.
663.¹
Vacher, Marcel. Les haies. 1899. IV. 134.² 545.¹
— Los setos; utilidad, plantación, poda. 1899. IV. 545.¹
Vadas, Eugène. *See* VADAS, Jenő.
Vadas, Jenő. Az árvédelmi Füzesek telepitése és müvelése.
1898. IV. 487.²
— Erdőmüveléstan. 1898. IV. 124.¹
— A hazai fenyvek magyar nevei. 1888. II. 21.³
— Histoire de l'École forestière supérieure de Selmeczbánya.
1896. IV. 36.²
— Kisérletek nemes Füzek tenyésztésével. 1900. III. 349.
— A nagy városi utczák fáinak tenyészeti viszonyairól.
1900. III. 42.³
— Plantation . . . des Saules contre les inondations. 1899.
III. 349, *IV. 188.*¹
— A Selmeczbányai m. k. erdőakadémia története és ismerte-
tője. 1896. IV. 36.²
— Szervezzük a magyar erdészeti kisérletügyet! 1896. IV.
38.³
— A Tölgycsemeték neveléséről. 1888. IV. 508.
— *See also* BUND, Károly, TAVI, Gusztáv & VADAS, Jenő.
Le **vade-mecum** du botaniste voyageur aux environs de Paris.
See DESHAYES, G. P. 1803. I. 406.
Vademecum für die Wald-Excursionen des Schweizerischen
Forstvereins. 1864. IV. 366.
Vagner, Karel. Wigandia caracasana. 1897. III. 695.¹
Vagrant (*pseud.*). A high forest of Quercus dilatata. 1887.
IV. 503.¹
— Located fellings. 1893. IV. 295.²
Vahl, Jens Lorenz Muestre. Observations sur la végétation en
Islande. 1841. I. 354.
Vahl, Martin. Bemerkungen aus einer Reise durch Norwegen.
1792. I. 352.
— Beskrivelse over nye Planteslægter. 1810. I. 265.
— Eclogae americanae. 1796. I. 328.
— Enumeratio plantarum. 1805. I. 259.
— Icones illustrationi plantarum americanarum in Eclogis
descriptarum inservientes. 1798. I. 328.
— Nogle Iagttagelser ved en Reise gjennem Norge. 1792.
I. 352.
— Om Perdicium og . . . Rohria. 1790. II. 853.¹
— Om Slægten Cinchona og dens Arter. 1790. II. 811.²
— Symbolae botanicae. 1790. I. 264.
— Tillæg til Afhandlingen om Slægten Cinchona. 1810. II.
812.
— Tillæg til Beskrivelsen over Slægten Garcia. 1802. II. 444.³
— Om Voxtræet fra Puertorico. Laurus cerifera. 1810. II.
227.¹
Vail, Anna Murray. Notes on Covillea and Fagonia. 1899.
II. 395.²
— Notes on Parosela. 1897. II. 352.¹
— Notes on the spring flora of southwestern Virginia. 1890.
I. 319.
Vaillant, Maréchal. Des forêts et leur influence sur les
sources. 1866. IV. 50.
— Gémissement des Chênes-lièges. 1866. I. 168.
Vaillant, Sebastien. Botanicon parisiense. 1727. I. 405.
— Botanicon parisiense; operis majoris prodituri prodromus.
1723. I. 405.
— Discours sur la structure des fleurs. 1727. I. 114.
— Établissement de nouveaux caractères . . . Araliastrum. 1718.
II. 651.¹
— Établissement de nouveaux caractères de trois familles.
1719. I. 290.
— Sermo de structura florum. 1718. I. 289. — 1727. I.
114.¹
— Suite de l'éclaircissement de nouveaux caractères de plantes.
1724. I. 290.
Val de Lièvre, Anton. Beiträge zur Flora von Innsbruck.
1858. I. 441.
— Beiträge zur Kenntniss der Ranunculaceen. 1871. II.
195.³

Le valanghe. 1863. IV. 188.[2]
Valbreuse, de. Lettre sur les Glycines de la Chine. 1853. III. 490. [1]
La Valcamonica. 1864. IV. 364.
Valcarenghi, Paolo. In Ebenbitar tractatum de Malis Limoniis commentaria. 1758. II. 402.[1]
Valcourt, de. L'hiver de 1870-71 à Paris. 1871. III. 48.
Valder, George. Forage plants at Wagga Wagga. 1897. III. 474.[2]
Valdes, Gonzalo Ferdinando de OVIEDO Y. See OVIEDO Y VALDES, G. F. de.
Valdes, Nicolas. Descripción y resistencia de las maderas . . . de las Islas Filipinas. 1858. IV. 410.
— Maderas de las islas de Cuba y Santo Domingo. 1866. IV. 398.[1]
Valdrome, CHEVANDIER DE. See CHEVANDIER DE VALDROME.
Vale of Sharon. 1848. III. 328.[1]
Valenciennes, Achille. Observations sur les animaux marins qui s'attachent aux vaisseaux. 1864. IV. 414.[1]
— Rapport sur les collections faites dans la Nouvelle-Grenade. 1851. I. 339.[2]
— Rapport sur les travaux . . . par M. Morelet pendant son voyage dans l'Amérique centrale. 1850. I. 329.
Valenciennes — Société d'agriculture, des sciences . . . See SOCIÉTÉ . . . III. 21.
Valenta, Eduard. Beitrag zur Kenntniss des Harzes von Doona. 1891. II. 560.[1]
— Sur la matière grasse contenue dans . . . Bassia longifolia. 1886. III. 667.[2]
— Ucuhubafett. 1889. III. 403.[1]
Valente, Antonio. Recensio plantarum . . . horto . . . Francisci Caetani. 1803. I. 61.
Valentin, G. Die Untersuchung der Pflanzen- und der Thiergewebe in polarisirtem Lichte. 1861. I. 123.[2]
Valentin, Johann Christoph. De plantarum succis. 1795. I. 150.[2]
Valentine, C. S. The delights of a New Jersey Oak barren. 1891. I. 316.
Valentini, Christoph Bernhard. Tournefortius contractus. 1715. I. 289.
Valentini, Michael Bernhard. Aurifodina medica e triplici naturae regno. 1716. I. 289.
— De Cassia cinnamomea. See DEXBACH, J. G. 1700. III. 404.[1]
— De china chinae. 1695. III. 719.
— Historia simplicium reformata. 1716. I. 289, V. XVI.[1]
— India literata; seu, Dissertationes. 1716. I. 471.
— Museum museorum. 1704. I. 289.
— Ost-indianisch Send-Schreiben. 1704. I. 471.
— Prodromus historiae naturalis Hassiae. 1707. III. 121.[1]
— Viridarium reformatum. 1719. I. 289.
Valentyn, François. Beschryving van Amboina. 1724. I. 452.
— Beschryving van Groot Djava. 1724. I. 452.
— Beschryvinge van de Kaap der Goede Hoope. 1726. I. 493.
— Keurlyke beschryving van Choromandel. 1724. I. 452.
— Omstandig verhaal van de geschiedenissen . . . den Godsdienst betreffende. 1724. I. 452.
— Oud en nieuw Oost-Indiën. 1724. I. 452.
— Uitlandse boomen en gewassen in den thuin der E. Maatschappy. 1726. I. 69.[1]
Valenzuela y Ozores, Antonio de. Memoria geognóstico-agrícola sobre . . . Pontevedra. 1856. III. 126.[1]
Valet, F. Uebersicht der in der Umgegend von Ulm wildwachsenden . . . Pflanzen. 1847. I. 382.
Valeton, Theodoric. Aglaia eximia Miq. 1897. II. 419.[1]
— De anatomische methode in de classificatie. 1888. I. 253.[1]
— Les Cerbera du Jardin botanique de Buitenzorg. 1895. II. 725.[1]
— Critisch overzicht der Olacineae. 1886. II. 170.[2]
— Description d'un nouveau genre . . . des Apocynacées. 1895. II. 727.[2]
— Dysoxylon acutangulum Miq. 1897. II. 420.[2]
— Les Ochrosia du Jardin botanique de Buitenzorg. 1895. II. 729.[1]
— De verspreiding van vruchten door dieren. 1893. I. 241.[1]
— See also KOORDERS, S. H. & VALETON, Theodoric.
Valeur agricole de la litière des forêts. 1898. IV. 438.[1]
Valeur du Pin sylvestre et de l'Épicéa. 1899. IV. 252.
Valin, Pierre. Floraison anormale de l'Adhatoda vasica. 1866. III. 709.[2]
— Les nuages artificiels. 1873. III. 183.[1]

Valk, W. W. The Wistaria sinensis. 1848. III. 490.[2]
Valkenhoff, T. A. C. Srie-olie van Nieuw-Guinea. 1873. III. 224.[2]
Valla, Georgius. De simplicium natura liber unus. 1528. III. 257.[1]
Vallan, Jacobus. De nuce moschata. 1709. III. 402.[2]
Valle, Manuel del. Apuntes sobre el servicio del ramo de montes. 1859. IV. 293.[1]
Vallée, Auguste. Culture de l'Eucalyptus aux Trois-Fontaines. 1882. IV. 530.
Vallée, George. See BERTIN, Jules & VALLÉE, George.
Vallée, L. L. & E. Du boisement nouveau ou renouvelé. 1860. IV. 53.
Vallemont, Pierre Lorrain de. Curiosidades de la naturaleza y del arte. 1705. III. 124.[2]
— Curiositez de la nature et de l'art. 1705. III. 124.[1]
— Curiosities of nature and art. 1705. III. 124.[3]
— Merckwürdigkeiten der Natur und Kunst. 1705. III. 124.[1]
Vallerand, Eugène. Constatation des dégats de l'hiver 1879-1880. 1880. III. 48.
— Effet des inondations sur les arbres fruitiers. 1883. III. 185.[1]
— Recépage des Sequoia sempervirens. 1888. III. 310.[2]
— Rusticité de l'Aralia Sieboldi. 1887. III. 642.[1]
Vallerius, Georg. Descriptio saxi in Quercu. 1739. I. 210,[1] IV. 509.
Valles, Francisco. De iis, quae scripta sunt physice in Libris Sacris. 1588. I. 512.
— De sacra philosophia. 1588. I. 512.
Vallès, François. De l'aliénation des forêts. 1865. IV. 275.
— Études sur les inondations. 1857. IV. 49.[2]
— The influence of forests upon rainfall. 1857. IV. 49.[2]
— Mémoire sur les inondations. 1860. IV. 185.[2]
— Nouvelles études sur les inondations. 1860. IV. 185.[2]
Vallier, G. Dracaena Eeckhautei. 1899. III. 335.
— Dracaena Victoria. 1899. III. 337.[1]
— Ficus radicans variegata. 1898. III. 371.[2]
— Jasminum nitidum. 1899. III. 673.[1]
— Prunier Mirobolan Louis Asselin. 1899. III. 436.[1]
Vallisneri, Antonio VALLISNIERI DE. See VALLISNIERI DE VALLISNERA, Antonio.
Vallisnieri de Vallisnera, Antonio. Abbogliamenti medicinali sopra gli effetti della chinachina. 1697. III. 719.
— De chinae chinae in febribus utilitate. 1699. III. 719.
— Index plantarum . . . juxta Liburnum. 1710. I. 424.
— Indice delle piante che sono attorno Livorno. 1733. I. 424.
— Opere fisiche-mediche stampate e manoscritte. 1733. I. 520.[2]
— Prima raccolta d'osservazioni. 1710. I. 289.
— Raccolta di varj trattati. 1715. I. 31.
— Saggio di' istoria medica e naturale. 1733. I. 31.
— Note sur le tenthredo de la Vigne. 1844. III. 562.[2]
Valiot. On the galls of the Terebinth. 1830. III. 595.[2]
Vallot, Antoine. Hortus regius. 1665. I. 56.
Vallot, Jean Nicolas. Sur deux espèces de fausses galles. 1836. III. 751.[1]
— Histoire de la botanique en Bourgogne. 1828. I. 81.[1]
— Des insectes qui se volent sur la Vigne. 1822. III. 562.[2]
Vallot, Joseph. Les arbres nains du Japon. 1889. III. 175.[2]
— Causes physiologiques qui produisent le rabougrissement des arbres. 1889. III. 176.[2]
— Essais d'acclimatation de plantes exotiques. 1888. III. 49.[1]
— Études sur la flore du Sénégal. 1882. I. 490.
— Excursion au mail Henri IV. 1881. I. 416.
— Le Juniperus phoenicea à forme spiculaire. 1888. II. 32.[1]
— Persistance de la vie chez un Sapin. 1891. I. 210.[1]
— Rapport sur la course au mail Henri IV. 1881. I. 416.
— Recherches physico-chimiques sur la terre végétale. 1883. I. 229, 300.
— Le Sapin et ses déformations. 1887. II. 23.[2]
Vallouise, Jean Joseph ROSSIGNOL DE. See ROSSIGNOL DE VALLOUISE, J. J.
Valls, Rafael PUIG Y. See PUIG Y VALLS, Rafael.
Valmont-Bomare, J. C. Dictionnaire raisonné universel d'histoire naturelle. 1764. I. 31.
Valois, Julius von. Über die forstpoliceiliche Beaufsichtigung der bürgerlichen Privatwaldungen in Württemberg. 1842. IV. 286.[1]
Valonia in Cyprus. 1888. IV. 502.[2]
Valori e provenienze dei legnami . . , importati a Genova. 1863. IV. 405.[2]

Valpian, A. Médication sudorifique — Du Jaborandi. 1880. III. 505.[1]

Valsaín y el Real Patrimonio. 1890. IV. 550.[2]

Valserres, Jacques. La restauration des Alpes françaises. 1877. IV. 162.

A valuable new tree. 1877. III. 614.[3]

Value of the Sycamore. 1891. IV. 526.[3]

Value of underwood. 1886. IV. 405.[1]

Value of wood pulp. 1896. IV. 430.

Vana paripalana Nül. See SCHLICH, William. 1893. IV. 100.[1]

Van Brunt, Cornelius. The wild flowers of the Canadian Rockies. 1899. I. 311.[2]

Vance, John. Poisoning by Laburnum seeds. 1877. III. 481.[1]

Vance, L. J. The future of the Long-leaf Pine belt. 1895. IV. 487.[1]

Vandamme, Henri. Flore complète. 1864. I. 392.

— Flore de l'arrondissement d'Hazebrouck. 1850. I. 410.

Vandas, K. Beiträge zur Kenntniss der Flora Bulgariens. 1889. I. 450.

— Beiträge zur Kenntniss der Flora von Süd-Hercegovina. 1888. I. 448.[1]

Vandelli, Domingos. De arbore Draconis. 1796. III. 336.[2]

— Diccionario dos termos technicos de historia natural. 1788. I. 70.

— Dissertatio de arbore Draconis. 1768. II. 81.[1]

— Fasciculus plantarum. 1771. I. 262. — 1796. I. 264.

— Florae et faunae lusitanicae specimen. 1787. I. 419.[2]

— Florae lusitanicae et brasiliensis specimen. 1788. I. 341.[1] [19.]

— Memoria sobre a ferrugem das Oliveiras. 1789. III. 677.[1]

— Memoria sobre algumas producções naturaes. 1789. III. 268.[2]

— Memoria sobre algumas producções naturaes deste reino. 1789. III. 271.[2]

— Memoria sobre as producções naturaes do reino. 1789. III. 271.[2]

— Viridarium Grisley lusitanicum. 1789. I. 419.[2]

Van Deman, H. C. Dwarf June Berry again. 1878. III. 419.[2]

Van Deman, H. E. The Cocoanut at Lake Worth. 1890. III. 323.[1]

— The fruit industry in the United States. 1891. III. 262.[2]

— How to treat winter killed trees. 1899. III. 183.[2]

— The relative merit of various stocks upon which to bud Oranges. 1892. III. 497.[2]

— Report of the pomologist. 1887. III. 433.[1]

— The work of the Pomological division. 1891. III. 133.

— **Reasoner**, P. W. & **Klee**, W. G. Report on the condition of tropical and semi-tropical fruits. 1888. III. 61.[2]

Vanden-Berghe, Maximilien. L'Acacia dealbata. 1889. III. 464.[2]

— Les Anones et leurs fruits. 1891. III. 401.[1]

— L'Arbousier des Pyrénées. 1890. III. 648.[1]

— L'Arbre à baume de Tolu. 1891. III. 482.[2]

— L'Arbre à pain. 1890. III. 367.[1]

— L'Arganier ou Arbre à huile du Maroc. 1889. III. 666.[2]

— L'Astragale et sa gomme. 1889. III. 467.[2]

— L'Aune. 1890. III. 357.[1]

— Le baume du Copayer officinal. 1894. III. 473.[1]

— Le Ben ailé. 1894. III. 409.[1]

— Le beurre de cây-cây en Cochinchine. 1892. III. 508.[1]

— Le Chêne et ses applications. 1889. IV. 515.[2]

— La cire végétale du Japon. 1894. III. 527.[2]

— Le Cirier de la Louisiane. 1892. III. 353.[1]

— Composition chimique des bois de Santal rouge. 1894. III. 384,[1] 478.[1]

— L'écorce du Mançone. 1894. III. 476.[2]

— Les écorces d'Andira. 1894. III. 467.[4]

— Emploi médical de l'écorce de Barbasco. 1894. III. 484.[1]

— Le Genêt d'Espagne et sa toile. 1891. III. 488.[1]

— La gomme éléphantine. 1892. III. 504.[2]

— La gomme laque. 1893. III. 369.[1]

— Les graines jaunes. 1893. III. 542.[2]

— Le Hêtre. 1890. IV. 500.[1]

— L'Hovenia dulcis. 1893. III. 542.[1]

— Huile et résine de Calaba. 1891. III. 608.[2]

— Les huiles de bois. 1891. III. 485.[2]

— Le mastic et la térébenthine de Chio. 1893. III. 525.[1]

— Le Mudar. 1895. III. 692.[1]

— La noix de Kola. 1890. III. 590.[2]

— Le Noyer. 1890. III. 356.[1]

— Produits commerciaux du Tilleul. 1891. III. 586.[1]

— Les produits de l'Acajou à fruit. 1893. III. 524.[1]

— Propriétés tinctoriales du Sophora. 1893. III. 488.[1]

— Propriétés vénéneuses du Cytise. 1894. III. 474.[1]

— Résine et fruit du Courbaril. 1894. III. 478.[2]

— Le Sola de l'Inde. 1890. III. 466.[1]

— L'Upas-Antiar ou Arbrepoison de Java. 1891. III. 366.[2]

— L'Upas tieute des Javanais. 1891. III. 685.[1]

— Usage des baies de Sapindus. 1893. III. 540.[1]

— Le Vomiquier, noix vomique. 1891. III. 685.[1]

— See also GRISARD, Jules & VANDEN-BERGHE, Maximilien.

Vandercolme, Édouard. Histoire botanique . . . des Salsepareilles. 1870. II. 85,[1] III. 558.[2]

— Observations botaniques sur les Smilax. 1871. II. 85.[1]

Van der Heede, Manuel de OSSUNA Y. See OSSUNA Y VAN DER HEEDE, Manuel de.

Vandevelde, A. J. J. Bijdrage tot de physiologie der gallen. 1896. I. 214.[2]

— Bijdrage tot de scheikundige physiologie van den stam der boomen. 1897. I. 156.[1]

— Sur l'influence de la grandeur des graines sur la germination. 1898. I. 204.

— Over den invloed van de grootte der zaden op de kieming. 1898. I. 204.

— De kieming der zaadplanten. 1896. I. 204.

Vandevoorde, P. Les Azalea rustica à fleurs doubles. 1893. III. 655.

Van Diemen's Land — Royal society. See ROYAL . . . I. 30.

Van-Dik, (pseud.). La sorte dei boschi. 1899. IV. 329.

Van Dollen. See ФАНЪ ДОЛЛЕНЪ.

Van Dyk. See also DYK, van.

Van Houten, George. Evergreens. 1893. III. 293.

— Propagating nursery stock. 1887. III. 154.[3]

— Propagating the Cherry. 1887. III. 432.[1]

— Propagation and uses of the Conifers. 1887. III. 294.[2]

— Pruning. 1884. III. 170.

— Wind-breaks. 1890. III. 215.[2]

Van Hulle, H. J. Levensduur van sommige planten. 1897. IV. 543.[1]

— Longévité de quelques arbres. 1897. IV. 543.[1]

— Longévité de quelques plantes. 1897. IV. 543.[1]

Vanière, Jacques de. Economie rurale. 1706. III. 112.

— Praedium rusticum. 1706. III. 112.

— Vollständiger Mayerhof. 1706. III. 112.

La vanilline. 1896. IV. 433.[1]

Vannuccini, V. Esperimenti sulla rogna dell' Olivo. 1895. III. 678.[1]

Van-Recum, A. Observations sur la necessité d'établir, en France, des écoles forestières. 1807. IV. 34.[2]

Van Rensselaer, Mariana Griswold. The choice of a "national flower." 1889. II. 672.[2]

— The Mountain Maple. See R., M. G. V. 1893. III. 536.[2]

— Some questions of color. 1897. III. 207.[1]

— The Woodcock Oak. 1892. II. 132.[2]

Sui **vantaggi** dei boschi. See HARMANT, Antonio d'. 1883. IV. 44.

Vantaggi dell' imboschimento. 1866. IV. 255.

Vanutberghe, H. Exploitation commerciale des forêts. 1900. IV. 381.

— Exploitation technique des forêts. 1900. IV. 381.

Van Volxem, Jean. Acer velutinum? 1882. II. 478.[1]

— Hybrid Pawpaws. 1883. III. 617.[1]

— Phillyrea decora. 1882. III. 680.[1]

— Robinia hispida. 1881. III. 486.[1]

Var — Société d'agriculture, d'horticulture et d'acclimatation. See SOCIÉTÉ . . . III. 21.

Varangot, Victor. Bouture automnale . . . pour multiplier les Rosiers. 1861. III. 452.

— De l'influence réciproque du sujet et de la greffe. 1862. III. 39.

Varangot, Victor, (sr.). Reflexions sur la nécessité . . . de détruire les hannetons. 1879. IV. 202.

Vard, Edmond. Influence du greffon sur le sujet. 1891. III. 40.

Varecka, W. Phanerogamenflora der Umgebung von Neusohl. 1857. I. 445.

Varendorff, von, (Forstmeister). Ueber Aufforstungen auf dem Schleswig'schen Mittelrücken. 1880. IV. 158.

— Ueber Bestreichen von Holzpflanzen zum Schutze gegen das Verbeissen. 1880. IV. 196.[3]

— Ueber Erziehung von Eichenheisterpflanzen. 1881. IV. 507.

— Ueber die Kiefernschütte. 1890. IV. 478.
— Zur Verminderung der Feuersgefahr in den Forsten. 1893. IV. 182.²
— Ueber Vertilgung des Kiefernspanners. 1886. IV. 199.²
Varenius, Gustaf. Afhandling om de wäxter som i Bibelen omtalas. *See* THUNBERG, C. P. 1828. I. 513.
Varenna. La economia forestale nel cantone Ticino. 1873. IV. 278.³
Varenne de Fenille, Philibert Charles. Essai sur les qualités individuelles et comparées des bois indigènes. 1807. IV. 407.²
— Mémoire sur l'aménagement des bois. 1791. IV. 359.¹
— Mémoires sur l'administration forestière. 1792. IV. 241, 399.¹
— Observations sur l'aménagement des forêts. 1791. IV. 241.
Varennes, C. de. Quelle différence y a-t-il entre le Camellia Normanii. 1852. III. 598.²
Varennes, DUGAS DES, (*député, Loire*). *See* DUGAS DES VARENNES.
Vargas, E. M. REPULLES Y. *See* REPULLES Y VARGAS, E. M.
Vargas de Bedemař, E. A. *Graf*. Forst-Ertrags- und Zuwachsuntersuchungen im Gouvernement St. Petersburg. 1849. IV. 235.²
— Forst-Ertrags- und Zuwachsuntersuchungen im Gouvernement Tula. 1847. IV. 235.²
— *See also* Варгасъ-де-Бедемаръ.
Vargasia. *See* SOCIEDAD DE CIENCIAS FÍSICAS Y NATURALES DE CARACAS. Boletín. I. 8.¹
Varia; Rhododendron occidentale et Pickeringia montana. *See* RHODODENDRON occidentalis. 1878. III. 484,¹ 661.³
Variaciones de "El Imparcial." 1886. IV. 276.³
Variation. 1895. II. 29,¹ 276.³
Variation in sex in the Ailanthus. 1873. II. 413.²
Variations produced by grafting. 1900. I. 246.²
Variegated Sugar Maple. 1881. III. 535.¹
Ueber eine **Varietät** der Stieleiche. 1892. IV. 508.
Die **Varietäten** der Dracaena ferrea. *See* NOTICE sur le Cordyline … 1872. III. 335.
Variété. *See* FORSTBENUTZUNG. 1859. IV. 498.
Variétés horticoles de Cactées. 1854. III. 618.¹
Varignon. Lignes suivant lesquelles des arbres doivent être plantés. 1719. III. 201.
Varngud, A. Alcune osservazioni di un vecchio taglialegna. 1863. IV. 383.³
Varnish trees at Frankfurt. 1891. III. 528.²
Varro, Marcus Terentius. De re rustica libri tres. 1472. III. 98.
— Rerum rusticarum, libri tres. 1472. III. 98.
— Scriptores rei rustica. 1470. III. 96.¹
— The three books of M. T. Varro concerning agriculture. 1472. III. 98.
— Tres de agricultura libri. 1472. III. 98.
Varvaro, Simone Biveo. Monografia sul Fico d'India in Sicilia. 1895. III. 625.¹
Vasey, George. Abies macrocarpa. 1876. II. 49.¹
— Additions to and corrections of the Catalogue of forest trees of the United States. 1876. I. 304, *IV. 76, 397.*
— Cactus landscapes. 1890. II. 587.¹
— Catálogo de las especies forestales de los Estados Unidos. 1876. I. 304, *IV. 397.*
— A catalogue of the forest trees of the United States. 1876. I. 304, *IV. 76,¹ 397.*
— Characteristic vegetation of the North American desert. 1888. I. 325.
— The Coniferae of the United States and Canada. 1882. IV. 443.²
— The distribution of North American forest trees. 1884. I. 304, *IV. 76.¹*
— Exotic trees in Washington. 1875. III. 60.
— Fasciation in Sophora secundiflora. 1887. II. 384.³
— Forest trees of the United States centennial collection. 1876. I. 304, *IV. 76,¹ 397.*
— Manual of the common native trees of the northern United States. 1877. IV. 76.² ·
— The origin of the cultivated Apple. 1877. II. 266.¹
— Rare and noteworthy trees in Washington. 1875. III. 60.
— On three hybrid Oaks near Washington. 1883. II. 128.²
— Trees of southern Florida. 1876. I. 317,¹ *IV. 77.*¹
— & Rose, J. N. List of plants collected … in Lower California. 1890. I. 325.
— — List of plants collected … in Lower California (and western Mexico). 1890. I. 332.
— — Plants from southern California. 1890. I. 325.

Vasilef, J. K. *See* Васильевъ, Я. К.
Vasilescu, Mihail. Die forstwirtschaftlichen Verhältnisse Rumäniens. 1894. IV. 375.³
Vasnyevski, Yu. N. *See* Васнѣвскій, Ю. H.
Vassal, de. Le Chêne de l'Évangile. 1843. II. 138.¹
Vassal de Montviel, (*député, Lot-et-Garonne*). Opinion sur la loi de finance, contre la vente des forêts de l'état. 1817. IV. 325.
Vassalli, Antonmaria. Spiegazione delle esperienze recate contro l'influsso dell'elettricità. 1788. I. 231.¹
Vassard, G. Production et commerce des fruits au Cap. 1894. III. 131.²
Vasselot de Régné, *comte* de. Le Cap de Bonne-Espérance [à l'Exposition … d'Edimbourg]. 1884. IV. 21.²
— The Cape forests. 1882. IV. 379.³
— Les forêts de la colonie du Cap. 1882. IV. 379.²
— Forêts domaniales de Chênes-Liége. 1894. IV. 517.¹
— Notice sur les dunes de la Coubre. 1878. IV. 145.
— Selection and seasoning of wood. 1885. IV. 416,¹ 420.
— Le service forestier au Cap de Bonne-Espérance. 1882. IV. 379.³
Vasseur, Ursin. Taille des arbres en espalier. 1852. III. 172.¹
Vaste plantaardige vetten. 1884. III. 225.
Vas Visser, G. De Kaspische Zandwilg. 1876. III. 351.¹
Vatebender, G. C. C. Mengelingen etc. bevattende verhandelingen over de cultuur der duinen. 1802. IV. 159.
Vater, Abraham. Anatome trunci Ulmi. 1741. I. 210,¹ *III. 364.¹*
— Balsami de Mecca naturam … exponit. 1720. III. 510.³
— Catalogus plantarum … Horti academici wittenbergensis. 1721. I. 43, V. VIII.²
— Catalogus variorum exoticorum … in museo suo. 1726. I. 43.
— Cornu cervi monstrosum a trunco arboris Fagi. 1744. I. 210,¹ *III. 560.¹*
— De efficacia admiranda chinchinae. 1734. III. 719.
— De Laurocerasi indole venenata. 1737. III. 438.¹
— Supplementum Catalogi plantarum. 1721. I. 43.
— Syllabus plantarum … in horto medico Academiae wittenbergensis. 1738. I. 43.
Vater, Christian. Rei herbariae aestimatoribus et cultoribus … ad solennes plantarum in agris … wittebergensibus lustrationes … invitat. 1692. I. 372.
Vater, Heinrich. Der Nachweis von Rauchschäden. 1897. IV. 193.¹
Das **Vaterland** der Rosskastanie. 1880. I. 242.¹
Vatke, Wilhelm. Adnotationes criticae. 1875. I. 48.
— Ueber drei … Eupatoria der Gärten. 1873. II. 856.²
— Ueber die Gattung Abelia R. Br. 1872. II. 834.¹
— Leguminosae Hildebrandtianae madagascarienses. 1882. I. 496.
— Notulas de stirpibus quibusdam novis … proposuit. 1872. I. 270,¹
— Plantae abyssinicae … Schimperianae. 1873. I. 488.
— Plantas … ab J. M. Hildebrandt collectas determinare pergit. 1882. I. 492.³
— Plantas … ab J. M. Hildebrandt collectas determinat. 1875. I. 492.³
Vattemare. Sur une nouvelle matière, le fibrilia. 1861. III. 234.
Vattier, Charles. *See* LEGRAND, Charles & VATTIER, Charles.
Vaucher, Edmond. Culture des arbres fruitiers. 1888. III. 146.¹
— Culture du Pêcher. 1866. III. 441.¹
— Le jardin fruitier. 1887. III. 146.¹
Vaucher, J. P. E. Histoire physiologique des plantes d'Europe. 1830. I. 148, 525.²
— Mémoir on the fall of leaves. 1821. I. 191.²
— Mémoire sur la chute des feuilles. 1821. I. 191.²
— Mémoire sur la sève d'août. 1811. I. 163.
— Mémoire sur la sève d'août et sur les divers modes de développement des arbres. 1821. I. 163.
Vaucluse — Société d'agriculture et d'horticulture. *See* SOCIÉTÉ … II. 21.
Vaucourt. Tables donnant le cube des bois. n. d. IV. 220.
Vaud — Société d'horticulture du canton. *See* SOCIÉTÉ … III. 24.³
Vaudin, L. Sur la migration du phosphate de chaux. 1895. I. 160, 178.
Vaughan, James. On a bark called Heetoo. 1853. III. 280.¹
— Droguen … zu Aden in Arabien im Handel vorkommen. 1853. III. 279.³
— Notes upon the drugs observed at Aden. 1853. III. 279.²

Vaulot, Georges. De l'estimation des forêts . . . par inventaire. 1882. IV. 257.
— De l'estimation des forêts . . . recherche raisonnée. 1883. IV. 257.
— Le jardinage. 187 . ? IV. 130.
— Nouvelle méthode d'exploitation des futaies. 1876. IV. 244.
— Petit manual forestier. 1882. IV. 99.[1]
— Principes d'économie forestière. 1887. IV. 245.
— Principes généraux d'économie forestière. 187 . ? IV. 255.
— Tarifs homogènes pour le cubage des bois. 1876. IV. 230.
Vaultrin, H. Cubage des bois d'œuvre. 1886. IV. 228.
— Observations sur une manière simple de cuber le volume d'une tige. 1884. IV. 218.
Vaulx, Charles de, & **Foelix,** Jacques. Code forestier annoté. 1827. IV. 324.
Vaupell, Christian. Bemærkninger over nogle danske Træarters Forekomst. 1846. I. 350.[1]
— Bøgens Indvandring i de Danske Skove. 1857. II. 125.[2]
— De danske Skove. 1863. I. 350,[2] IV. 79,[1] 343.[1]
— Erläuternde Bemerkungen zum Referat in der Botanischen Zeitung. 1859. I. 350,[2] IV. 79.[1]
— Om de Forandringer, som det danske Skovlands Udstrækning. 1862. I. 350,[2] IV. 79.[1]
— De l'invasion du Hêtre. 1857. I. 350,[2] II. 125,[2] IV. 79,[1] 500.[2]
— Om Lysets og Skyggens Indflydelse paa Skovtræernes Form og Tilværelse. 1861. IV. 67.[1]
— Nissas Vinterflora. 1858. I. 226.[2]
— De nordsjaellandske Skovmoser. 1851. IV. 68.
— Oliventræet i Provence. 1858. III. 675,[2] 678.[2]
— Om Opelskning af Frugttræser ved Frø. 1859. III. 134.[2]
— Parfumekulturen i Provence. 1863. III. 226.[2]
— Om Planteindivdet. 1855. I. 99.
— Planterigets Naturhistoire. 1854. I. 256.
— Om Skovtræernes Selvsaaning. 1861. I. 240,[1] IV. 74.[1]
— Om Træernes Forgrening. 1855. I. 106.[2]
— Om Træernes Formøring ved Grene eller Knopper. -1859. I. 208.[2]
— De vildtvoxende Træers Udbredning i Danmark. 1860. I. 350,[2] IV. 79.[1]
— Vinstokkens Dyrkning i Frankrig. 1863. III. 555.
— Om Vinsygdommen i Frankrig. 1858. III. 577.
Vauquelin, Louis Nicolas. Analyse d'une gomme-résine . . . de Madagascar. 1809. III. 282.[1]
— Analyse d'une matière colorante végétale. 1815. III. 236.
— Analyse de l'écorce de Malambo. 1815. III. 516.[2]
— Analyse de l'écorce du Solanum pseudoquina. 1825. III. 702.[1]
— Analyse des feuilles aromatiques du Raven-tsara. 1809. II. 228.[1]
— Analyse du fruit du Baobab. 1822. III. 589.[1]
— Sur le beurre de Galam. 1830. III. 667.[1]
— Examen chimique de l'écorce du Strychnos pseudoquina. 1823. III. 685.[1]
— Examen chimique de quelques substances végétales. 1809. II. 228,[1] III. 282.[1]
— Examen chimique des Cubèbes. 1820. II. 94.[1]
— Examen d'une excroissance végétale de Madagascar. 1809. III. 282.[1]
— Expériences sur la substance visceuse . . . du Robinia viscosa. 1804. II. 383.[1]
— Expériences sur le Daphne alpina. 1812. III. 627.[1]
— Expériences sur les sèves des végétaux. 1799. · I. 163.
— Expériences sur . . . Marronier d'Inde. 1811. III. 537.[2]
— Observations sur la préparation de l'acide acétique retiré du bois. 1815. I. 154.
— Observations sur une maladie des arbres. 1799. III. 365.[2]
— Quelques expériences sur le Daphné alpina. 1824. III. 627.[1]
— Recherches chimiques sur la couleur verte. 1806. IV. 413.[2]
— Sur le Robinia viscosa. 1799. II. 383.[1]
— Sur le suc de Papayer. 1802. III. 617.[1]
See also FOURCROY, A. F. & VAUQUELIN, N. L.
Vautherin, François Auguste. De la glande de Croton Tiglium. 1864. III. 517,[1] 519.[2]
Vauvel, L. Eriobotrya japonica. 1870. III. 423.[2]
— Evonymus japonica. 1869. III. 532.[2]
— Des Lycium au point de vue de l'ornement. 1869. III. 700.[2]

— Nouveau traitement du Pêcher. 1880. III. 441.[1]
— Passiflora cœrulea. 1869. III. 616.[1]
— Le Virgilia lutea. 1870. III. 472.[2]
Vauvert de Méan, A. Culture des Eucalyptus en Californie. 1883. IV. 530.
Vaux, Antoine Alexis CADET DE. See CADET DE VAUX, A. A.
Vavasseur, P. See EDWARDS, H. M. & VAVASSEUR, P.
— Cottereau, P. L. & Gillet de Grandmont, A. Dictionnaire universel de botanique agricole. 1836. III. 86.
Vavin, Eugène. Du Citron et des avantages. 1884. III. 502.[2]
— Coup d'œil sur le Jardin botanique de Brest. 1871. I. 59.
— Note sur les cultures faites en 1870 et 1871. 1872. III. 72.[1]
— Rapport au nom de la Commission du reboisement des montagnes par l'Ailante. 1879. IV. 525.[1]
Vayreda y Vila, Estanislao. Catálech de la flora de la vall de Nuria. 1882. I. 422.
— Nuevos apuntes para la flora catalána. 1882. I. 422.
— Plantas notables por su utilidad . . . en Cataluña. 1879. I. 422.
Vayssière, A. Étude sur le Chionaspis evonymi. 1886. III. 532.[1]
Veatch, J. A. About Cerros Island. 1860. I. 323.
— Lent's Sumac. 1859. II. 459.[1]
— & Kellogg, Albert. Rhus Veatchiana Kellogg. 1860. II. 461.[1]
Večeř, Ant. Ot. Frt. Měřictví výkonné. 1893. IV. 265.
Vedenski, V. N. POPOF-. See POPOF-VEDENSKI, V. N.
Vedrof, S. V. See ВЕДРОВЪ, С. В.
Vés, Amédée. Recherches . . . sur la fève du Calabar. 1865. III. 483.[3]
Veeljarige waarnemingen . . . van een Liberia-Koffie planter. See FELLE, Wilhelm 1894. III. 742.[2]
Veen, H. Aanteekeningen omtrent de Koffiebereiding. 1886. III. 740.[1]
— Lijst van insecten . . . schadelijk . . . voor de Koffiecultuur. 1897. III. 736.
— Schadelijke insecten van de Kina. 1897. III. 717.[2]
Veesenmeyer, Gustav. Ueber die Vegetationsverhältnisse an der mittlern Wolga. 1854. I. 361.
Vega, Eduardo de la. Las ordenaciones de montes. 1896. IV. 550.[2]
Vega, Garcia Lasso de la. See GARCILASSO DE LA VEGA, Inca.
Vega, J. M. L. de la. Cantidad de tanino en las cortezas de Paraca. 1879. IV. 435.
— & Loza, Manuel Rio de la. Analisis de la corteza de la Quina Calisaya. 1876. III. 725.[2]
Vega, Matias de la MADRID Y MANRIQUE DE LA. See MADRID Y MANRIQUE DE LA VEGA, M. de la.
Vegetable food. 1866. III. 219.[2]
Vegetable ivory. 1893. III. 330.[1]
The vegetable ivory of commerce. 1864. III. 330.[1]
Vegetable-ivory substitutes. 1879. III. 319.[1]
Vegetable oils in the Amazon and Rio Negro districts. 1855. III. 224.[1]
Vegetable poisons and insecticides. 1878. III. 260.[2]
Vegetable products in New Guinea. 1891. III. 282.[1]
Vegetable resources of India. 1894. III. 279.[1]
Vegetable substances; materials of manufactures. 1833. III. 217.
Vegetable substances used for the food of man. 1832. III. 219.[1]
Vegetable substances used in the arts. 1830. IV. 396.[1]
Vegetable wax in Japan. 1871. III. 526.[2]
Vegetatio. See SPIELMANN, J. R. 1773. I. 32.
Die Vegetation der Mosquitolandes. 1845. I. 329.
Vegetationen og Havevæsenet paa Christiansø. 1841. III. 120.[1]
Die **Vegetationsperioden** der wichtigsten . . . Holzarten. 1836. IV. 87.[1]
Veiledning ved Træplantning i Hedegne. 1871. IV. 103.[1]
See also DALGAS, Enrico. 1871. IV. 156.[2]
Veillard, CHEVALIER. See SONNINI, VEILLARD & CHEVALIER.
Veitch, Harry James. Autumnal tints. 1893. III. 207.[1]
— The Coniferæ of Japan. 1892. II. 16.[1]
— Rhododendron javanicum Hook. var. 1887. III. 660.[2]
Veitch, James & son. Hoya bella and Mitraria coccinea. 1851. III. 693,[1] 708.[2]
Veitch, James & sons. Amasonia pennosa. 1885. III. 695.[2]
— — A double greenhouse Rhododendron. 1887. III. 657.[2]
— — Hymenanthera crassifolia. 1877. III. 614.[1]
— — Jasminum gracillimum. 1882. III. 673.[1]
— — Leea amabilis. 1883. III. 544.[1]

Veitch, James Herbert. Deciduous trees and shrubs of Japan. 1894. I. 461.
— A traveller's notes. 1893. II. 59.[1]
— A traveller's notes; or, Notes of a tour through India. 1896. I. 304.
Veitch, John Gould. Extracts from Mr. J. G. Veitch's letters. 1860. I. 462.
— Extraits de la correspondance de M. J. G. Veitch. 1860. I. 462.
— A list of the principal timber trees . . . Japan. 1862. IV. 399.[1]
— Notes on the agriculture, trees and flora of Japan. 1863. I. 462.
— Notes on the coniferous plants of Japan. 1862. II. 15.[2]
— Notes on the vegetation of Japan. 1860. I. 462.
— La végétation du Japon. 1860. I. 462.
— Verzeichniss der vorzüglichsten Nutzbäume in der Nähe von Kanagawa und Yeddo. 1862. IV. 399.[1]
Veitch collection of Japanese vegetable products. 1894. III. 273.[1]
Veith, Emanuel. Abriss der Kräuterkunde für Thierärzte. 1813. III. 90.[2]
— Systematische Beschreibung der . . . in Oestreich . . . gewöhnlichen Arzneigewächse. 1813. III. 90.[2]
Vejledning til Piledyrkning. See ROM, N. C. 1874. III. 347.
Velasco, Ildefonso. Purgantes del reino vegetal. 1887. III. 245.
Velasco, José M. Estudio sobre la familia de las Cacteas de México. 1870. II. 591.[1]
— Flora mexicana. 1870. I. 331.
Velaz, José Maria FIVALLER DE. See FIVALLER DE VELAZ, J. M. de.
Velenovský, Josef. Die Achselknospen der Hainbuche. 1900. II. 121.[1]
— Ueber die Achselsprosse einiger Smilax-Arten. 1885. II. 85.[1]
— Beiträge zur Kenntniss der bulgarischen Flora. 1886. I. 450.
— Ein B   ag zur Kenntniss der böhmischen Rosen. 1884. II. 288.[1]eitr
— Botanické náčrtky z okolí Lounského. 1885. I. 443.
— Zur Deutung der Fruchtschuppe der Abietineen. 1888. II. 19.
— Flora bulgarica. 1891. I. 450.
— Na horách Osogovských. 1888. I. 450.
— O nejpamátnějších rostlinách Evropy. 1897. I. 350.[1]
— O nepravidelném abnormnim vývoji druhých květů u vlasského Ořechu. 1888. II. 113.[1]
— O nervatuře listů rostlin dvouděložných. 1879. I. 110.
— Neue Beiträge zur Kenntniss der Flora von Ost-Rumelien und Bulgarien. 1888. I. 450.
— Neue Nachträge zur Flora von Bulgarien. 1892. I. 450.
— Plantae novae bulgaricae. 1890. I. 450.
— Resultate der zweiten botanischen Reise nach Bulgarien. 1889. I. 450.
— Sequoia sempervirens. 1889. II. 49.[1]
— O serialnich pupenech. 1885. I. 108.[1]
— Taxodium distichum. 1889. II. 51.[1]
— Zajímavé stromy a keře v královské Oboře. 1897. III. 90.[1]
— O zvláštní přeměně tyčinek ve květech Vrby popelavé. 1884. II. 103.[1]
Vella, L. De l'antagonisme qui existe entre la strychnine et le curare. 1860. III. 683.[1]
— Emploi de curare. 1859. III. 683.[1]
Vellosia. I. 8.[1]
Velloso da Conceição, José Marianno. Alographia dos alkalis fixos vegetal ou potassa. 1798. I. 174.
— Florae fluminensis. 1825. I. 341.
— Florae fluminensis icones. 1825. I. 341.
— Memorias, e extractos sobre a Pipereira negra. 1798. III. 343.[1]
— Quinografia portugueza. 1799. II. 812.
Velten, Wilhelm. Ueber die Entwickelung des Cambium. 1875. I. 128.[1]
— Über die Folgen der Einwirkung der Temperatur auf die Keimfähigkeit. 1876. I. 203, IV. 453.
— Die physikalische Beschaffenheit des pflanzlichen Protoplasma. 1876. I. 137.
— Vitis vinifera. 1873. V. XXVII.[1]
— Ein zweckmässiger Thermostat. 1877. IV. 37.[1]
Veltheim, Graf von. Notizen über den Zustand . . . der Lustwälder und Plantagen . . . zu Harbke. 1828. I. 46.

De Veluwsche gemeenteheiden. 1891. IV. 160.[2]
Ven, A. J. van der. L'acide cyanhydrique chez les Prunacées. 1898. III. 419.[2]
— Over het cyaanwaterstof in Prunaceae. 1898. III. 419.[2]
Venable, Francis Preston. Analysis of the leaves of Ilex Cassine. 1885. III. 531.[2]
— Ueber einige Derivate des Heptans aus Pinus Sabiniana. 1881. II. 45,[2] III. 308.[2]
— A partial chemical examination of . . . Ilex. 1888. II. 463.[1]
— Some notes on plant transpiration. 1885. I. 167.
Venanzi, Giuseppe. See RODEGHER, Emilio & VENANZI, Giuseppe.
Vendel, Q. B. Veredlung des Epheu. 1894. III. 643.[1]
Venditti, N. Benemerenza forestale. 1899. IV. 277.
— questione del rimboschimenti in Italia. 1898. IV. 166.[1]
Vendôme — Société archéologique, scientifique et littéraire. See SOCIÉTÉ . . . I. 520.[1]
Vendrell, Adolf. Notes on a disease that has attacked the Coffee plant. 1890. III. 736.
Vendrely, Xavier. See PAILLOT, Justin & VENDRELY, Xavier.
Venegas, Miguel. Histoire naturelle et civile de la Californie. 1757. III. 264.[1]
— Natural and civil history of California. 1757. III. 264.[1]
— Noticia de la California. 1757. III. 264.[1]
Venel, Henri de. Forêts. 1891. IV. 102.
— La gestion des forêts au Ministère des finances. 1884. IV. 292.
Venetian Sumach. 1900. III. 524.[1]
Venette, Nicolas. L'art de tailler les arbres fruitiers. 1683. III. 171.[1]
— The art of pruning fruit-trees. 1685. III. 171.[1]
Venetz, Ignace. Catalogus plantarum in Valesia. 1817. I. 433.
Venezuela — Universidad central. See UNIVERSIDAD . . . I. 8.[1]
O Vengerskom Dubye. See О Венгерскомъ Дубѣ.
Venice — Accademia d'agricoltura, arti . . . dello stato veneto. See ACCADEMIA . . . I. 24.[1]
Venice — Imperiale reale istituto veneto di scienze. See IMPERIALE . . . I. 25.
Venier, J. Ansichten über den Einfluss der Waldwirthschaft. 1856. IV. 68.
— Quecksilberhältige Tanne. 1851. IV. 447.[1]
Venta de los montes. 1883. IV. 276.[2]
La venta de los montes enajenables. 1897. IV. 552.[1]
Vente du bois de service. See BAUHOLZ-VERKAUF. 1860. IV. 388.[1]
Ventenat, Étienne Pierre. Anfangsgründe der Botanik. 1795. I. 84.
— Catalogue des livres de la bibliothèque. 1808. I. 519.[1]
— Choix de plantes . . . dans le jardin de Cels. 1803. I. 57.
— Decas generum novorum. 1800. I. 205.
— Description des plantes nouvelles . . . dans le jardin de J. M. Cels. 1800. I. 57.
— Dissertation sur le genre Dalea. 1799. II. 352.[1]
— Sur l'Epigea repens L. 1797. II. 663.[2]
— Extrait d'une monographie du genre Tilleul. 1800. II. 515.[1]
— Jardin de la Malmaison. 1803. I. 57.
— Mémoire contenant la déscription de . . . Robinia viscosa. 1804. II. 383.[1]
— Monografia del género Tilo. 1800. II. 515.[1]
— A monograph of the genus Tilia. 1800. II. 515.[1]
— Monographie du genre Tilleul. 1800. II. 515.[1]
— Note descriptive sur les lianes du Chili. 1797. II. 201.[1]
— Notice sur les plantes . . . de l'ouvrage intitulé: Choix de plantes. 1807. II. 663.[1]
— Nouveau genre Fourcraea. 1793. II. 89.[2]
— Observations sur l'Epigaea repens L. 1797. II. 663.[2]
— Observations sur la famille à laquelle il faut rapporter . . . Samyda et Casearia. 1808. II. 568.[2]
— Principes de botanique. 1795. I. 84.
— Tableau du règne végétal. 1799. I. 259.
Il venticinquesimo anniversario dell' Istituto forestale di Vallombrosa. 1894. IV. 35.[2]
Venturi, Antonio. Plantae in horto Antonii Venturi . . . collectae. 1835. I. 63.
Venukoff. Sur les rapports qui existent entre les caractères géologiques . . . du sol et la végétation . . . dans la Russie centrale. 1886. I. 365.
Venus, C. W. See PALMSTRUCH, J. W. & VENUS, C. W.
Vera, Francisco de Asis. See ASIS VERA, Francisco de.

Ueber verbesserte Anlegung von Baumgärten. 1817. III. 121,[1] *IV. 117.*

Verbesserte Forst- und Holz-Ordnung der Grafschaft Hanau-Münzenberg. 1779. IV. 301.

Verbeteringen en aanvullingen van Veth's Java. 1887. III. 276.[1]

Verbindung des Feldbaues mit dem Waldbau. 1844. IV. 133.

Die **Verbreitung** der Dattel- und Kokospalme in Indien. *See* RITTER, Karl. 184.? II. 62.[1]

Ueber die **Verbreitung** der Fichte. 1834. II,.34.[1]

Die Verbreitung der Pfefferrebe, Banane. *See* RITTER, Karl. 184.? II. 94,[2] 456.[2]

Verbrugge, P. Les Palmiers cultivés en touffes. 1899. III. 318.[2]

Verbrugge, W. A. VIRULY. *See* VIRULY VERBRUGGE, W. A.

Ueber die **Verbuchung** der zufälligen Ergebnisse. 1888. IV. 237.

Verdeil, F. Recherches sur la matière colorante verte. 1851. I. 140.[2]

Verdera, Antonio PALAU Y. *See* PALAU Y VERDERA, Antonio.

Verdier, Eugène, (*jr.*). Culture des Pivoines arborescentes ou ligneuses. 1855. III. 393.[1]
— Spiræa Reevesianá var. flore pleno. 1855. III. 461.[1]

Verdier, Eugène, (*sr.*). Note sur la culture des Rosiers. 1860. III. 452.
— Sur la rusticité de quelques arbustes.- 1851. III. 47.

Verdier-Latour, E. Études sur le Bambou. 1854. III. 315.[1]

Verdries, Johann Melchior. De succi nutritii in plantis circuitu. 1707. I. 162.

Veredeling van vruchten. 1878. III. 162.

Ueber die **Veredlung** auf die Wurzel. 1830. III. 164.[1]

Verein Baltischer Forstwirthe. Protokolle. IV. 6.

Verein bölmischer Forstwirthe.. Vereinsschrift für Forst... und Naturkunde. *See* VEREINSSCHRIFT... IV. 15.

Verein der Freunde der Naturgeschichte in Mecklenburg. Archiv. I. 15.

Verein deutscher Forstleute in Böhmen. Organ. IV. 15.

Verein deutscher forstlicher Versuchsanstalten. Versammlung. IV. 11.

Verein deutscher Gerber. Bericht. III. 14.

Verein deutscher Ingenieure. Zeitschrift. IV. 11.

Verein für Erdkunde zu Dresden. Jahresberichte. I. 15.

Verein für forstwissenschaftliche Ausbildung. Abhandlungen. IV. 11.

Verein für Land- und Forstwirthschaft ... Braunschweig. Mittheilungen. *See* LAND- UND FORSTWIRTHSCHAFTLICHER VEREIN... IV. 10.

Verein für Natur- und Heilkunde zu Presburg. Verbandlungen. *See* VEREIN FÜR NATURKUNDE ZU PRESBURG. I. 28,[1]

Verein für Naturkunde im Herzogthum Nassau. Jahrbücher. I. 15.

Verein für Naturkunde zu Cassel. Bericht. I. 15.

Verein für Naturkunde zu Presburg. Verhandlungen. I. 28.[1]

Verein für Naturkunde zu Zwickau. Jahresbericht. I. 15.

Verein für Naturwissenschaft zu Braunschweig. Jahresbericht. I. 15.

Verein für vaterländische **Naturkunde in Württemberg**. Jahreshefte. I. 15.

Verein für Volkskunde. Zeitschrift. III. 14.

Verein mecklenburgischer **Forstwirthe**. Bericht. IV. 11.

Verein nassauischer Land- und Forstwirthe. Forstliche Beilage. IV. 11.

Verein nassauischer Land- und Forstwirthe. Wochenblatt. *See* NASSAUISCHE Zeitschrift... IV. 10.

Verein zum Schutze des österreichischen Weinbaues. Mitteilungen. III. 25.

Verein **zur Beförderung des Gartenbaues in den königl.** preussischen Staaten. Katalog der Bibliothek. *See* KATALOG... 1897. III. 1.

Verein **zur Beförderung des Gartenbaues in den königlich** preussischen Staaten. Monatsschrift, Verhandlungen. Wochenschrift. III. 14.

Verein **zur Verbreitung naturwissenschaftlicher Kenntnisse** in Wien. Schriften. I. 15.

Vereinbarungen des internationalen Verbandes forstlicher Versuchsanstalten betreffs ... Formelschreibung. 1897. IV. 215.

Vereinigte Frauendorfer Blätter. *See* ALLGEMEINE deutsche Garten-Zeitung. III. 11.

Vereinigte Staaten Amerikas. Forstl. Lehranstalt des Staates New-York. 1898. IV. 30.[1]

Vereinsblatt des Land- und forstwirthschaftlichen Hauptvereins Hannovers. IV. 11.

Vereinsschrift für Forst-, Jagd- und Naturkunde. IV. 15.

Verekha, Petr Nikolaevitch. *See* WEREKHA, P. N.

Die **Verfälschung** des Thee's. 1853. III. 607.

Verfahren bei Gewinnung des Maulbeersamens. 1857. IV. 519.[1]

Verfassung, Gesetze u. Einrichtungen d. Königl. Forstlehranstalt zu Kiel. 181.? IV. 31.

Verfügung betreffend die Abänderung ... der Instruction für die Einrichtung ... der Staatsforste in Württemberg. 1862. IV. 303.[1]

Verfügung [vom 16. April 1808 zur Rug-Verordnung.] 1808. IV. 299.

Vergara, Mariano. Bibliografia de la Rosa. 1892. II. 283,[1] *III. 450.*
— Cultivo de los Rosales en macetas. 1889. III. 450.

Vergé, Charles. *See* DALLOZ, Édouard, (*jr.*) & VERGÉ, Charles.

Verger. III. 23.[1]

Vergiftung durch Taxbaumblätter. 1861. III. 288.[1]

Vergnaud-Romagnési, C. F. Mémoire sur le Maronnier d'Inde. 1825. III. 537.[2]

Vergne, de la. *See* LA VERGNE, de.

Verhaal van de opkomst en vordering der tuinierkonst te Montreuil. 1761. III. 33.[1]

Die **Verhältnisse** der königl. sächsischen Staatsforste. 1884. IV. 355.[2]

Das **Verhalten** der Arve und Lerche. 1853. IV. 452,[1] *463.*[2]

Verhalten der Fichte auf Brandfeldern. 1855. IV. 453.

Verhandelingen over de natuurlijke geschiedenis der Nederlandsche overzeesche bezittingen. 1839. I. 465.

Verhandlungen der Weinbau-Enquête in Wien 1873. 1873. III. 558.[1]

Verheggen, A. Des plantations en résineux. 1895. IV. 239.[2]

Verhoeff, Carl W. Biologische Beobachtungen auf der ... Insel Norderney. 1891. II. 662.[1]
— Blumen und Insekten der Insel Norderney. 1893. I. 239.[2]

Ver-Huell, Quirijn Maurits Rudolph. Iets over het eiland Diégo Garçia. 1823. I. 481.[1]
— De ravijn Calhaboca. 1856. III. 402.[1]

La **vérité** sur la visite faite au jardin du grand-séminaire d'Autun. 1884. III. 174.[2]

Vérités sur les Landes de la Gascogne. 1841. IV. 121, *460.*[2]

Die **Verjüngung** der Fichte. 1864. IV. 453.

Ueber die **Verkaufsverhältnisse** ... der alten Eichenrinde. 1854. IV. 512.

Verkerk Pistorius, A. W. P. Oberzigt van den landbouw op Java gouvernements-kultures. 1863. III. 128.
— De particuliere Koffie-aanplantingen. 1863. III. 729.[1]

Verloren, H. Waarnemingen over de buitengewone vermenigvuldiging der Noctua piniperda. 1846. IV. 441.
— Waarnemingen over Noctua piniperda. 1847. IV. 442.

Verlot. *See* MALET & VERLOT.

Verlot, Bernard. Adenocalymna nitidum. 1869. III. 704.[2]
— L'Araucaria excelsa. 1855. III. 298.[1]
— Bignoniacées brésiliennes nouvelles. 1868. III. 704.[2]
— Carludovica humilis. 1869. III. 332.[2]
— La Carludovique palmée. 1861. III. 332.[2]
— Chamaedorea Karwinskiana. 1869. III. 322.[1]
— Le Chamaerops de Griffith. 1870. III. 331.[2]
— Cyclanthus bipartitus. 1869. III. 332.[1]
— Des effets de la gelée pendant l'hiver de 1851–52. 1853. III. 47.
— Sur l'Encephalartos pungens. 1854. III. 285.[2]
— Enumération des Agavées cultivées au Muséum. 1873. III. 340.[2]
— Fleur monstrueuse de Fuchsia globosa. 1873. II. 644.[1]
— La flore au point de vue horticole en France. 1885. III. 113.
— Franciscea calycina. 1868. III. 699.[1]
— Une greffe exceptionelle. 1867. III. 165.
— Le guide du botaniste herborisant. 1865. I. 413.
— Lopezia hirsuta. 1877. III. 640.[2]
— Mémoire sur la production ... des variétés. 1864. I. 247.
— Multiplication du Cheirostemon. 1855. III. 590.[1]
— Note sur quelques arbres remarquables ... du Loiret. 1861. I. 58.
— Nuttallia cerasiformis. 1876. III. 429.[2]
— Opuntia vulgaris. 1869. III. 625.[1]
— Passiflora coerulaea var. Neumanni. 1869. III. 616.[1]
— Les plantes alpines. 1873. III. 87.

— Le premier Robinier introduit en Europe. 1873. II. 383.[1]
— Pyrostegia ignea. 1873. III. 707.[1]
— Sur quelques arbres remarquables du Loiret. 1855. I. 297.[2]
— Rapport de . . . collections dendrologiques de Segrais. 1875. I. 59.
— Rapport sur la culture du Clethra arborea. 1869. III. 646.[2]
— Robinías. 1873. II. 383.[1]
— Seaforthia elegans. 1873. III. 319.[2]
— Thibaudia cordifolia. 1866. III. 663.[1]
— La Vigne à fleurs monstrueuses. 1867. II. 507.[2]
—& Lebas, E. Plantes nouvelles, rares ou peu connues. 1866. III. 87.
— & Lecoq-Dumesnil. Rapport sur les Dracaena. 1876. III. 334.[2]
Verlot, Jean Baptiste. De l'action du froid pendant l'hiver de 1857–58. 1858. III. 48.
— Anomalie présentée par un Poirier. 1876. II. 280.[1]
— Catalogue des plantes cultivées au Jardin botanique de la ville de Grenoble. 1857. I. 58.
— Catalogue raisonné des plantes vasculaires du Dauphiné. 1872. I. 414.
— Historique des Cerisiers à fruits comestibles. 1868. III. 432.[1]
— Liste des plantes du Chili. 1875. III. 66.[1]
— Note sur l'existence du Genista delphinensis. 1876. II. 360.[1]
— Du Noyer et de ses produits dans les cantons de Tullins. 1864. III. 355.
— Sur une variété du Wisteria frutescens. 1876. III. 490.[2]
— Yucca argospatha. 1868. III. 340.[1]
Verman, E. See Верманъ, Э.
Die Vermehrung der Nadelhölzer durch Stecklinge. 1834. IV. 149.[2]
Ueber Vermehrung der Pflanzen. 1859. III. 158.
Die Vermehrung der Pflanzen durch Stecklinge. 1898. III. 158.
Ueber Vermehrung und Erhaltung einiger Pflanzen. 1853. III. 153.
Vermeule, Cornelius Clarkson The forests of New Jersey. 1900. IV. 339.
— Report on forestry in . . . New Jersey. 1895. IV. 339.
— & Gifford, John. Forestry. Report of progress. 1895. IV. 338.[2]
Vermeulen, Th. De invloed van het toppen op de productie der Koffieboomen. 1895. III. 734.[2]
— Nog cens het toppen van Koffieboomen. 1896. III. 734.[2]
Zur Verminderung der in der Gegend des Voigtlandes die Wälder verwüstenden Waldraupen. 1798. IV. 205.[2]
Vermischte freye Gedanken eines Forstliebhabers bey den Klagen über Holzmangel. See BOECKLIN. IV. 280.[1]
Vermont — Commissioners on forestry. Report. IV. 5.[2]
Vermont — (State) agricultural experiment station. Annual report. Bulletin. III. 9.
Vermont — University of — Botanical department. Contributions. See CONTRIBUTIONS to the botany . . . I. 5.
Vermont maple sugar and syrup. 1894. IV. 527.[2]
Vermont maple sugar makers' association. Annual meeting. 1900. IV. 527,[2] 559.[1]
Vermont medical society. Transactions. I. 7.[1]
Vermont state board of agriculture. Report. III. 9.
Vermorel, V. See BENDER, E. & VERMOREL, V.; CROLAS, (Dr.) & VERMOREL, V.
Vernatti, Sir Phil. Answers to some of the queries . . . recommended by Sir R. Moray. 1669. III. 274.[1]
Vernau, Constantin de. Rudimentum physiographiae Moldaviae. 1836. I. 440.
Verne, Claude. Étude sur le Boldo. 1873. II. 222.[1] — 1883. III. 403.[2]
— See also BOURGOIN, Edme & VERNE, Claude; DUJARDIN-BEAUMETZ & VERNE, Claude.
Vernet, L. Sur un glycooside extrait du Lierre. 1881. III. 643.[1]
Verneuerte Instruktion . . . vermög welcher die holzgerechten Jäger . . . geprüfet werden sollen. 1799. IV. 36.[1]
Verneuil, Auguste Victor. See ARNAUD, A. & VERNEUIL, A.
Vernière, P. Le sulfure de calcium, remède . . . contre le phylloxéra. 1874. III. 759.
Vernieuwing der vruchtsoorten door zaaijing. 1850. I. 247.
Vernon, J. J. Newer varieties of American Plums. 1900. III. 433.[1]
Verona — Accademia d'agricoltura. See ACCADEMIA . . . I. 24.[2]

Veronica, (pseud.). Hypericum reptans. 1883. III. 610.[1]
Verordnung betreffend das Hagen, Lorchen und Marken. 1860. IV. 306.
Verordnung betreffend die Versicherung (der Holzhauer im Staatswalde). 1888. IV. 307.[1]
Verordnung der Direktion des Innern . . . betreffend die Abwehr des drohenden Borkenkäferfrasses. 1858. IV. 306.
Verordnung des hohen Landrathes betreffend den Geisstrieb. 1876. IV. 306.
Verordnung des Kleinen Raths Zürich wegen des Borkenkäfers. 1803. IV. 203.
Verordnung des Regierungsstatthalters P. C. Pfenninger gegen die Räubereyen in den Nationalwaldungen. 1799. IV. 306.
Verordnung des Regierungsstatthalters Ulrich betreffend die Holzfrevel. 1799. IV. 306.
Verordnung M. Gned. H. H. betreffend die Steigerung des Holzpreises für die Stadt Zürich. 1796. IV. 306.
Verordnung über amtliche Besichtigung bei Holzverkäufen zu Niederschlägen. 1875. IV. 306.
Verordnung über das Trattrecht in Waldungen. 1865. IV. 306.
Verordnung über die Benutzung und Oeffnung der Winterfahrrechte. 1859. IV. 306.
Verordnung über die Bewirthschaftung der Amts- und Korporationswaldungen im Kanton Appenzell. 1872. IV. 306.
Verordnung über die Forst-Organisation im Grossherzogthum Hessen. 1811. IV. 300.[2]
Verordnung über die Pflege und Benutzung der Gemeinds-Genossen-Waldungen des Bezirkes March . . . vom 15. April 1852. 1855. IV. 306.
Verordnung über die Pflege und Benutzung der Gemeinds-Genossen-Waldungen des Bezirkes March . . . vom 2. Mai 1870. 1870. IV. 306.
Verordnung und Anweisung für Forstinspektoren . . . des Kantons Aargau. 1803. IV. 306.
Verordnung vom 18. April 1892, betreffend die Vermarkung der Waldungen des Kantons Wallis. 1892. IV. 307.[1]
Verordnung wegen der Verwaltung der Privatwaldungen in Russland. 1847. IV. 315.[1]
Verordnung zu Verhütung vom Feuersgefahr in und bei Waldungen. 1835. IV. 183.[2]
Vérot, Félix. L'arboriculture forestière. 1882. IV. 124.[2]
Die Verpflanzung der Ceder vom Libanon. See GESCHICHTE der Verpflanzung zweier Coniferen. 1865. IV. 300.[2]
Die Verpflanzung der Zuckertanne nach Europa. See GESCHICHTE der Verpflanzung . . . 1865. III. 307.[2]
Verplanting van boomen. 1852. III. 166.
Verri, Charles, comte. L'art de cultiver les Mûriers. 1826. III. 374.
— Die Kunst der Maulbeerbaumzucht. 1826. III. 374.
Verrier. Effets produits par l'action de la chaleur et du froid. . 1860. III. 48.
— Nouvelle forme à donner aux arbres fruitiers palissés. 1859. III. 170.
Verryst, A. Aanmerkingen over het nuttig gebruik van den cortex peruvianus. 1784. III. 720.
Versailles — Association des anciens élèves de l'École nationale d'horticulture. See ASSOCIATION . . . III. 19.
Versammlung der Forstwirthe aus Thüringen. Protocoll. IV. 11.
Versammlung deutscher Forstmänner. Bericht. See VERSAMMLUNG DEUTSCHER LAND- UND FORSTWIRTHE. IV. 11.
Versammlung deutscher Land und Forstwirthe. Amtlicher Bericht. IV. 11.
Versammlung hessischer Forstwirthe. Protocoll. IV. 11.
Versammlung schweizerischer Forstwirthe. Verhandlungen. IV. 13.[2]
Versammlung süddeutscher Forstwirthe. Protokolle. Verhandlungen. IV. 11.
Versammlung thüringischer Forstwirthe. See VERSAMMLUNG DER FORSTWIRTHE . . . IV. 11.
Verschaffelt, Ambroise. Nouvelle iconographie des Camellias. 1848. III. 598.[2]
— Plantes nouvelles. 1863. I. 50, III. 77.
Verschaffelt, Ed. Galton's "Regression to mediocrity." 1899. I. 249.[1]
— Ueber graduelle Variabilität von pflanzlichen Eigenschaften. 1894. I. 244.[2]
Verschaffelt's Palmen in Gent. 1858. III. 317.
Verschiedene Durchforstung. 1850. IV. 173.
Der verschiedene Gang des Holzwuchses. 1836. IV. 67.[1]
Verschiedene Konstruktionen des Waldpfluges. 1853. IV. 143.[1]
Von verschiedenen Arten des Kohl-Holzes. 1796. IV. 394.

Die verschiedenen Güteklassen des Bodens für Kiefern. 1854. IV. 480.

Verschiedenes, Forstinsekten . . . betreffend. 1832. IV. 206.

Verschiedenheit der Feuersgefahr bei jungen Kiefern- und Fichtenbeständen. 1853. IV. 182.[1]

Verschiedenheit des Windbruchs in Kiefern und Fichten. 1843. IV. 189.[1]

Verschoor, J. Proefondervindelijk vertoog over het beste middel om . . . hop . . . te overwinnen. 1785. III. 193.[1]

Das Verschwinden der Eiche. 1856. IV. 505.

Der versicherungsrechtliche Charakter der Holzabfuhr. 1898. IV. 311.[1]

Verslag der Maatschappij voor boschcultuur te Zuidwolde. 1888. IV. 40.[2]

Verslag nopens de cultuur van getahpertjah . . . te Tjipetir. 1898. III. 149.

Verslag omtrent de Koffie-cultuur op Java. 1899. III. 731.

Verslag omtrent de Thee-cultuur door de Soekaboemi'sche landbouw-vereeniging. 1899. III. 602.[1]

Verslag over de cultuur . . . van kaneel op Ceylon. 1863. III. 405.[2]

Verslag over de dennenrups. 1847. IV. 549.[2]

Verslag over de gom-elastiek . . . uit de residentie Cheribon. 1866. III. 231.

Verslag over ontginningen van heidegronden. 1871. IV. 160.[1]

Verslag van de gedeputeerde staten aan de staten der provincie Overyssel. 1877. IV. 356.[1]

Verslag van de proefnemingen op het gebied van den tuinbouw. 1898. III. 140.[1]

Verslag van de werkzaamheden der Commissie wegens de duinen. 1804. IV. 159.

Verslag van een duitsch boomkweeker. 1822. IV. 174.[3]

Verslag van het beheer en den staat der Nederlandsche bezittingen. 1857. III. 118,[2] 188, IV. 124.[1]

Verslag van het onderzoek omtrent . . . Koffij op het eiland Ceylon. 1863. III. 732.[1]

Verslagen over de onderzoekingen betreffende op Java gecultiveerde Theeen. 1894. III. 602.[1]

Varsteeg, W. F. De ontdekkingstocht naar Djambi en Korintji. 1875. I. 466.

— Overzigt van den landbouw . . . in Nederlandsch Oost-Indie. 1873. III. 128.

— De wetenschappelijke expeditie naar Midden-Sumatra. 1876. III. 275.[1]

Versteegh, A. J. De Kaspische Zandwilg . . 1876. III. 351.[1]

— Proeven met den Kaspischen Zandwilg. 1878. III. 351.[1]

Versteegh, C. A. Over het maken van luchtgaten in Kofhetuinen. 1899. III. 727.

Varstege, Ch. Opmerkingen omtrent sommige voortbrengselen van Biliton. 1874. III. 274.[1]

Varsteigerungs-Protokoll von Eichen-Spiegel-Rinde. 1867. IV. 512.

Verster, A. H. Salix acutifolia of S. pruinosa. 1877. III. 348.

Verstolk, A. J. Neemt een regel boomen op de kanten der zaai . . . te veel zon en plaats weg? 1783. III. 214.[3]

Versuch einer Anweisung zur Anlegung. See MELLIN, A. W. Reichsgraf.

Versuch einer Beschreibung der grossen Schwemmanstalt auf der Herrschaft Krummau. 1831. IV. 390.[1]

Versuch einer Flora der Ufer des Niederrheins. See MEIGEN, J. W. 1823. I. 377.

Versuch einer geregelten Forstwirtschaft in den Vereinigten Staaten. 1897. IV. 272.

Versuch einer teutschen Nomenclatur der Linneischen Gattungen. See PLANER, J. J. von. 1771. I. 73.[1]

Versuch einer Widerlegung der irrigen Meynung . . . dass die Forst-Wissenschaft auf keinen . . . Hauptstücken beruhe. 1790. IV. 56.

Ueber Versuche beim Anbau der Fichte. 1863. IV. 453.

Versuche mit Vertilgungsmassregeln gegen die Nonne. 1894. IV. 201.

Versuche über das Austrocknen von Bauhölzern. 1888. IV. 420.

Versuche zur Hervorbringung der blauen Farbe bei den Hortensien. 1831. III. 412.[1]

Verteuil, L. A. A. de. Trinidad, its geography. See CRÜGER, Herman. 1858. I. 338.[1]

Die Vertheilung der Bürger-Holzabgaben. 1857. IV. 334.[2]

Das Vertriften der Brennhölzer. 1857. IV. 390.[1]

Verwachsene Bäume. 1880. I. 209.[1]

Verwaltung der Gemeindeforsten in der Rheinprovinz und Westfalen. 1888. IV. 308.[1]

Verwaltungsbericht des ständigen Komités des Schweizerischen Forstvereins. 1866. IV. 366.

Die Verwaltungsordnung der Communalwaldungen im Grossherzogthum Hessen. 1837. IV. 319.[1]

Ueber die Verwechslung des Betriebsalters mit dem Umtriebsalter. 1833. IV. 251.[2]

Verwendung des Buchenholzes zu Eisenbahnschwellen. 1884. IV. 499.

Die Verwendung von Buchen-Eisenbahnschwellen. 1897. IV. 499.

Verwerthung der Früchte des Rosskastanienbaumes. 1877. III. 538.[1]

Zur Verwerthung der Rothbuche. 1888. IV. 499.

Verwolden, A. P. R. C. van der BORCH VAN. See BORCH VAN VERWOLDEN, A. P. R. C. van der.

Verwolden, P. A. van der BORCH TOT. See BORCH TOT VERWOLDEN, P. A. van der.

Verwüstung der Wälder Böhmens . . . 1868. 1870. IV. 190.

Verwüstung des Knieholzes. 1883. IV. 464.[2]

Verzeichnis der auf den Friedländischen Gütern kultivierten Gewächse. See WILLDENOW. 1815. III. 27.[2]

Verzeichnis der im K. S. Forstgarten zu Tharandt befindlichen Baum- und Strauchgattungen. See REUM, J. A. 183.? I. 46, IV. 18.[1]

Verzeichnis der Zierbäume und Sträucher zu Wilhelmshöhe. 1851. III. 28.[1]

Verzeichnis einer systematisch geordneten Sammlung von Weinreben-Sorten. 1843. III. 546.

Verzeichnis von Bäumen und Sträuchern in Althaldensleben. 1825. III. 28.[1]

Verzeichniss aller in Spanien . . . befindlichen Baumarten. 1866. IV. 85.[2]

Verzeichniss der auf den Friedländischen Gütern cultivirten Gewächse. See WALTER, F. 1815. I. 45.

Verzeichniss der Ausstellungsgegenstände des Schweizerischen Forstvereins. 1873. IV. 20.[2]

Verzeichniss der Bäume, Sträucher und Halbsträucher . . . K. Baumschule bei Potsdam. 1851. I. 47.

Verzeichniss der Bäume und Sträucher . . . auf der Kön. Plantage zu Herrenhausen. 1787. I. 44.

Verzeichniss der Birnen, welche auf dem 3. pomologischen Kongress . . . besprochen wurden. 1858. III. 444.[2]

Verzeichniss der exotischen Kalt- und Warmhauspflanzen . . . in dem von Rothschild'schen Garten. 1823. I. 46.

Verzeichniss der Gewächse im Grossh. Pr. Garten zu Ludwigslust. 1855. I. 47.

Verzeichniss der Glas- und Treibhauspflanzen . . . auf dem Königl. Berggarten zu Herrenhausen. 1787. I. 44; see also WENDLAND, J. C. 1797. I. 44.

Verzeichniss der Holzgewächse in der Königl. Forstbaumschule bei Kiel. 1822. I. 46, IV. 18.[1]

Verzeichniss der im Freien ausdauernden Bäume, Gesträuche . . . im Hamburg'schen botanischen Garten. 1830. I. 46; see also OHLENDORFF, J. H. 1834. I. 47.

Verzeichniss der in der grossen systematischen Baumschule zu Herrnals bey Wien cultivirten . . . Tafelobst-Sorten. See MÄRTER, F. J. 1805. III. 90.[1]

Verzeichniss der Pflanzen des botanischen Gartens der . . . Universität zu Dorpat. See GERMANN, G. A. 1807. I. 41.

Verzeichniss der Pflanzen . . . in dem Garten der K. k. Gartenbau-Gesellschaft in Wien. 1839. I. 66.[1]

Verzeichniss der Pflanzen und Sämereien . . . aus dem botanischen Garten zu Göttingen. 1803. I. 45.

Verzeichniss der verschiedenen Arten . . . Aloe. See SALM-REIFFERSCHEID-DYCK, Joseph, Fürst & Altgraf. 1817. II. 77.[2]

Verzeichniss der Vorlesungen . . . aus den Gebieten der Forstwissenschaft . . . [der Universität Giessen]. 1881. IV. 33.[1]

Verzeichniss derjenigen Obstsorten. See AEHRENTHAL, J. L., Freiherr von. 1840. III. 90.[1]

Verzeichniss einer auserlesener Sammlung botanischer Werke. 1818. IV. 1.

Verzeichniss einer Auswahl von im Freien ausdauernden Bäumen . . . im Hamburgischen botanischen Garten. See OTTO, Eduard. 1845. I. 47.

Verzeichniss einer Handbibliothek der vorzüglichsten ökonomischen und forstwissenschaftlichen Werke. 1819. IV. 1.

Verzeichniss einiger ausländischen . . . Bäume und Sträucher welche . . . zu Belvedere . . . geblühet haben. See DIETRICH, F. G. 1795. I. 44.

Verzeichniss einiger ausländischen Pflanzen welche . . . zu Weimar . . . geblühet haben. See DIETRICH, F. G. 1795. I. 44.

Verzeichniss sichtbar blühender Gewächse . . . um den Ursprung der Donau. 1799. I. 375.

Verzeichniss und kurze Beschreibung der . . . Bäume und Sträucher . . . in dem botanischen Garten der K. Akademie der Wissenschaften. 1773. I. 44.

Verzeichniss von Gewaechshauspflanzen . . . zu St. Petersburg auf der Apotheker-Insel. *See* LÜDICKE, Herrmann. 1845. I. 42.

Verzeichniss von in- und ausländischen Pflanzen des Grossh. Orangengartens Belvedere. 1816. I. 45.

Verzeichniss von in- und ausländischen Pflanzen . . . im Grossherzogl. Residenzgarten in Würzburg. *See* KRAUSS, Gregor. 1812. I. 45.

Das **Verzwergen** der Pflanzen. 1888. III. 175.[3]

Vesalius, Andreas, (1514–1564). De radice Chinae. 1728. III. 338.[1]

— Radicis Chynae usus. 1547. III. 338.[1]

Veselý, J. Ein Ausflug in die Krivošćije und auf den Orjen. . 1890. I. 448.[1]

Veselý, Wilhelm. Die Namen unserer Waldbäume. 1880. I. 75.[1]

— Nomenclatur der Forstinsekten. 1878. IV. 92.

Vesling, Johannes. Catalogus. 1642. I. 60.[1]

— Catalogus plantarum horti Gymnasii patavini. 1642. . I. 60.[1]

— Opobalsami veteribus cogniti vindiciae. 1644. III. 510.[1]

— Paraeneses ad rem herbariam. 1644. I. 511.

— De plantis Aegyptiis observationes. 1638. III. 280.[1]

Vesmír. III. 25.

Vesque, Julien. L'absorption comparée . . . à la transpiration. 1878. I. 161.

— De l'absorption de l'eau par les racines. 1876. I. 161, 167.

— Amassez plus de matériaux. 1874. I. 130.

— De l'anatomie des tissus appliquée à la classification des plantes. 1881. I. 100.[1]

— Sur l'appareil aquifère des Calophyllum. 1886. II. 553.[3]

— Sur les canaux sécréteurs . . . des Calophyllum. 1887. II. 553.[3]

— Sur les caractères anatomiques de la feuille . . . des Vismiées. 1885. II. 553.[1]

— Caractères des principales familles gamopétales tirés de l'anatomie de la feuille. 1885. I. 110.

— Catalogue de la bibliothèque de . . . Joseph Decaisne. 1883. I. 2.

— Sur les causes et sur les limites des variations. 1883. I. 244.[3]

— Sur la classification et l'histoire des Clusia. 1891. II. 554.[1]

— Sur les Clusia de la section Anandrogyne. 1891. II. 554.[1]

— De la concomitance des caractères anatomiques et organographiques des plantes. 1883. I. 100.[1]

— Contributions à l'histologie systématique de la feuille des Caryophyllinées. 1883. I. 110.

— Développement du sac embryonnaire. 1878. I. 122.

— De l'emploi des caractères anatomiques. 1889. I. 253.[1]

— Epharmosis. 1888. I. 100.[1]

— L'épiderme simple considéré comme réservoir d'eau. 1886. I. 168.

— Espèces nouvelles du genre Dipterocarpus. 1874. II. 559.[3]

— Essai d'une monographie anatomique . . . des Capparées. 1882. II. 229.[3]

— Études microphysiologiques sur les réservoirs d'eau des plantes. 1886. I. 166.

— Expériences sur la grande période et les oscillations de la transpiration. 1884. I. 167.

— Folia Capparearum. 1888. II. 229.[1]

— Genitalia foliacae Clusiearum. 1892. II. 553.[1]

— Genitalia foliacae Garciniearum. 1889. II. 553.[1]

— Sur le genre Eurya. 1895. II. 548.[1]

— Les genres de la tribu Clusiées. 1891. II. 552.[1]

— Les groupes nodaux . . . dans le genre Clusia. 1891. II. 554.[1]

— Guttiferae. 1893. II. 552.[3]

— L'histoire des Garcinia du sous-genre Rheediopsis. 1892. II. 555.[1]

— Histoire des Garcinia du sous-genre Xanthochymus. 1892. II. 555.[1]

— De l'influence de la pression extérieure sur l'absorption de l'eau par les racines. 1883. I. 161.

— De l'influence de la température du sol sur l'absorption de l'eau par les racines. 1878. I. 161.

— De l'influence des matières salines sur l'absorption de l'eau par les racines. 1879. I. 161.

— Sur l'interprétation d'une expérience de Hales. 1883. I. 165.

— Mémoire sur l'anatomie comparée de l'écorce. 1875. I. 130.

— Note sur l'anatomie du Goodenia. 1876. II. 847.[1]

— Note sur les appareils laticifères de l'Hartighsea. 1873. II. 420.[3]

— Nouvelles recherches sur le développement du sac embryonaire. 1878. I. 122.

— Observation directe du mouvement de l'eau. 1883. I. 165.

— Observation directe du mouvement de l'eau . . . des plantes. 1882. I. 165.

— Observations sur les cristaux d'oxalate de chaux. 1874. I. 139.

— Sur l'organisation mécanique du grain de pollen. 1883. I. 117.[1]

— Die Pflanzenanatomie im Dienste des Gärtners. 1883. I. 244.[3]

— Sur le prétendu rôle des tissus vivants dans l'ascension de la sève. 1885. I. 165.

— Recherches anatomiques et physiologiques sur la structure .du bois. 1876. I. 125.

— Recherches sur le mouvement · de la sève ascendante. 1884. I. 165.

— Remarques critiques sur les travaux récents concernant le mouvement de l'eau. 1883. I. 165.

— Revision du genre Eurya Thunb. 1895. II. 548.[1]

— Sur le rôle des tissus morts dans l'ascension de la sève. 1885. I. 165.

— Du rôle des vaisseaux ligneux. 1883. I. 165.

— Sur le rôle physiologique des ondulations des parois latérales de l'épiderme. 1883. I. 129.[3]

— La sève ascendante. 1891. I. 166.

— Traité de botanique agricole et industrielle. 1885. III. 53.

— La tribu des Clusiées. 1891. II. 553.[1]

— *See also* ARBOIS DE JUBAINVILLE, A. d' & VESQUE, Julien; DEHÉRAIN, P. P. & VESQUE, Julien.

— & Viet, Charles. De l'influence du milieu. 1881. I. 218.

Véssey, Ferenc. Egy óriási Nyárfa. 1882. II. 96.[3]

Vessiot, Paul. Des aménagements de futaie. 1895. IV. 246, 550.[3]

— Sobre las ordenaciones de monte alto. 1895. IV. 550.[3]

— Futaies jardinées. Accroissement. 1899. IV. 238.

— Règle à calcul pour déduire les angles. 1897. IV. 265.

Vest, Lorenz Chrysanth von. Anleitung zum gründlichen Studium der Botanik. 1818. I. 255.

— Cytisus virgatus. 1824. II. 351.[1]

— Manuale botanicum . . . sistens stirpes totius Germaniae phaenogamas. 1805. I. 376.

— Plantarum quorundam novarum . . . descriptiones. .1820. II. 855.[3]

— Rubi nonnulli Styriae. 1824. II. 304.[1]

— Versuch einer systematischen Zusammenstellung der in Steyermark cultivirten Weinreben. 1826. III. 546. II. 272.[1]

Vestal, George & Garcia, Fabian. Report upon Plums. 1898. II. 272.[1]

Om **Vesterjyllands** Opdyrkning. 1847. IV. 156.[1]

Vesterlund, Otto. Växtnamn på folkspråket. 1893. I. 73.[1]

Vetenskaps academien. *See* KONGL. SVENSKA VETENSKAPS . . . I. 8.[1]

Veterinarian, (*pseud.*). Yew poisoning. 1875. III. 288.[3]

Veth, Pieter Johannes. Aanteekeningen op het eerste deel van "Java." 1875. III. 276.[1]

— Balische planten en plantennamen. 1870. I. 76.[1]

— Borneo's wester afdeeling. 1854. III. 276.[1]

— Feestbundel van taal-, letter . . . aardrijkskundige bijdragen. *See* FEESTBUNDEL . . . I. 520.[3]

— Java. 1875. III. 276.[1]

— De Koffie. 1861. III. 726.[3]

— De Sago. 1866. III. 327.[3]

— Wilde planten uit Europa naar Java overgebracht. 1869. III. 91.[3]

Vétillart, L. De la culture des Pins dans le département de la Sarthe. 1860. IV. 460.[3]

Vétillart, Marcel. Étude sur les filaments végétaux. 1870. III. 234.

— Études sur les fibres végétales textiles. 1876. III. 234.

— Note sur une nouvelle manière d'élaguer. 1829. III. 169.[3]

— Observations pratiques sur la culture du Pin maritime. 1835. IV. 467.[1]

Vetter. Beitrag zur Cultur der Protaceen. 1879. III. 382.[3]

Vetter, J. J. Die Tabulae rhodologicae von Gandoger. 1883. II. 282.[1]

Vetters, K. Botanische Betrachtungen über das Vorkommen der flüchtigen Oele. 1891. I. 182.[1]
Vetters, Karl Ludwig. Die Blattstiele der Cycadeen. 1884. II. 3.[1]
Vettori, Pietro, (the elder). Petri Victorii explicationes suarum in Catonem. 1542. III. 98.
— Lodi e coltivazione degli Ulivi. 1569. III. 674.[2]
— Delle lodi e della coltivazione degli Ulivi. 1569. III. 674.[2]
— Trattato delle lodi ... de gl' Ulivi. 1569. III. 674.[2]
De vessel der Palmboomen. 1885. III. 319.[2]
Vezérfonal a filloxerás szőlőknek szénkéneggel való gyérítő kezelésére. 1891. III. 762.
Viaggio alle Indie Orientali. See WESDIN, J. P. 1796. III. 277.
Viaggio in alcuni luoghi della Basilicata. See PETAGNA, L., TERRONE, G. & TENORE, Michele. 1827. I. 426.
Viaggio nell' Arabia Felice. See LA ROQUE, Jean de. 1716. III. 738.
Vial, Augustin. Lectures sur le gazonnement ... des montagnes. 1865. IV. 162.
Vial, E. La Ramie et son traitement. 1888. III. 381.[2]
Viala, Pierre. Sur le développement du black rot. 1896. III. 581.
— Sur le développement du pourridié. 1890. III. 580.
— Sur le développement du rot blanc. 1897. III. 581.
— L'état actuel de la viticulture en France. 1893. III. 557.[1]
— Les hybrides-Bouschet. 1886. III. 547.
— Une maladie des greffes-boutures. 1891. III. 561.
— Les maladies de la Vigne. 1889. III. 561.
— Les maladies de la Vigne: Péronospora, Oïdium. 1885. III. 579.
— Une mission viticole en Amérique. 1889. III. 557.[1]
— Monographie du pourridié. 1891. III. 194.
— Monographie du pourridié des Vignes. 1891. III. 194.
— Sur les périthèces de l'oïdium de la Vigne. 1894. III. 581.
— La resistance de la Vigne au phylloxera. 1893. III. 574.
— Les Vignes sauvages et les Vignes cultivées. 1889. II. 505.[2]
— Le white rot ou rot blanc. 1887. III. 579.
— See also DEGRULLY, Léon & VIALA, Pierre; FOËX, Gustave & VIALA, Pierre; MAYET, Valery & VIALA, Pierre; NANOT, J., VIALA & RAVAZ; SCRIBNER, F. L. & VIALA, Pierre.
— & BOYER, G. Sur l'Aureobasidium Vitis. 1894. III. 581.
— — Sur un basidiomycète inférieur. 1891. III. 580.
— — Une nouvelle maladie des raisins. 1891. III. 580.
— & FERROUILLAT, Paul. Traitement du mildiou. 1887. III. 579.
— & RAVAZ, L. Le black rot américain. 1885. III. 578.
— — Sur le brunissement des boutures de la Vigne. 1896. III. 581.
— — Sur la mélanose, maladie de la Vigne. 1886. III. 579.
— — Mission viticole pour la reconstitution des vignobles. 1891. III. 557.[1]
— — Sur les périthèces du rot blanc. 1894. III. 581.
— — Recherches expérimentales sur les maladies de la Vigne. 1888. III. 580.
— & SAUVAGEAU, C. Sur la brunissure. 1892. III. 580.
— — La brunissure et la maladie de Californie. 1892. III. 580.
— — Nouvelles observations sur la brunissure. 1893. III. 581.
Viale, Benedetto & Latini, Vincenzo. Sulla natura degli aromi nelle piante. 1855. I. 182.[2]
— — Sur la nature des aromes dans les plantes. 1855. I. 182.[2]
Viali, Felix. Plantae satae in seminario Horti patavini. 1686. I. 60.[2]
Vialla, Louis. Des Cépages américains. 1880. III. 556.
— Le phylloxéra. 1869. III. 758.[2]
— Programme des leçons pratiques sur le greffage des Vignes américaines. 1880. III. 548.[3]
Viallanes, Alfred & Arbaumont, Jules d'. Flore de la Côte-d'Or. 1889. I. 417.
Viallanes, Henri. Sur le phylloxera dans la Côte-d'Or. 1879. III. 571.
Viansson, L. Notes sur le phylloxera. 1874. III. 567.[1]
Viard, Émile. Traité général de la Vigne. 1892. III. 557.[1]
Viardin, L. L'estimation des Sapins. 1887. IV. 237, 446.[1]
Vias, A. Culture de la Vigne en chaintres. 1875. III. 556.
Viator, J. Casuarina sumatrana. 1874. III. 342.[1]
Viaud-Grand-Marais, Ambroise. Catalogue des plantes vasculaires de l'île de Noirmoutier. 1892. I. 417.

— Note sur la gemmation surnuméraire du Carpinus Betulus 1880. II. 120.[2]
— & MÉNIER. Excursion botanique à l'île d'Yeu. 1878. I. 415.
Vibert. Des anomalies du Rosier. 1865. II. 289.[3]
Vibert, J. P. Culture exclusive du Rosier. 1836. III. 448.
— Essai sur les Roses. 1824. III. 448.
— Influence de l'hiver de 1845 sur les cultures de Camellias. 1845. III. 599.[2]
— De la nécessité d'en appeler aux semis de la Vigne. 1842. III. 548.
— Note sur l'acclimatation. 1837. III. 43.
— Note sur la fécondation artificielle des Roses. 1831. III. 451.[2]
— Observations relatives à l'influence qu'exerce la greffe sur le sujet. 1863. III. 39.
— Observations sur la nomenclature ... des Roses. 1824. III. 448.
— Réponse ... aux assertions de M. Pirolle. 1827. III. 451.[2]
Viborg, Erik Nissen. Beschreibung der Sandgewächse und ihrer Anwendung. 1788. IV. 155.[3]
— Botanisk Bestemmelse af de i danske Lov omtalte Sandvexter. 1795. IV. 156.[1]
— Botanisk-oekonomisk Beskrivelse over de ... vigtigste Aspe- og Piilearter. 1800. II. 98,[2] III. 344.[1]
— Efterretning om Sandvexterne. 1788. IV. 155.[2]
— Om Pilevaands-Afharkning og Plantning. 1821. III. 347.
Vibraye, P., marquis de. Note sur l'acclimatation du Sequoia gigantea. 1863. III. 310.[1]
— Rapport ... sur le reboisement des montagnes. 1861. IV. 162.
— Rapport sur les travaux ... sylvicoles de la terre de Cheverny. 1844. IV. 121.
Vicaire. Projet de rapport ... pour rechercher les causes des inondations. 1878. ? IV. 185.[1]
Vicaire, H. Wiederbewaldung der Gebirge in Frankreich. 1864. IV. 162.
Vicary, N. Some notes on the botany of Sinde. 1848. I. 472.
Vicat, Philipp Rudolf. Histoire des plantes vénéneuses de la Suisse. 1776. III. 89.[2]
Vicente, Celedonio Rojo, PAYO. See PAYO VICENTE, C. R.
Vichy-Cusset — Société d'horticulture, d'agriculture et de viticulture. See VICHY... III. 21.
Vick's illustrated monthly magazine. See VICK's monthly ... III. 9.
Vick's monthly magazine. III. 9.
Vicq, Léon Bonaventure Éloy de. De la végétation sur le littoral ... de la Somme. 1876. I. 415.
— & BRUTELETTE, Blondin de. Catalogue raisonné des plantes ... de la Somme. 1865. I. 413.
Victoria — Acclimatisation society. See ACCLIMATISATION ... III. 27.[1]
Victoria — Field naturalists' club. See VICTORIAN naturalist. I. 30.
Victoria — Philosophical institute. See PHILOSOPHICAL SOCIETY ... I. 30.
Victoria — Philosophical society. See PHILOSOPHICAL ... I. 30.
Victoria — Royal society. See PHILOSOPHICAL SOCIETY ... I. 30.
Victoria — Zoological and acclimatisation society. See ACCLIMATISATION SOCIETY ... III. 27.[1]
Victoria, Australia — Botanic garden. Annual report of the government botanist and director. See BOTANIC GARDEN, MELBOURNE. I. 69.
Victoria institute. Journal. I. 20.
Victorian branch of the Royal geographical society of Australasia. See ROYAL GEOGRAPHICAL SOCIETY OF AUSTRALASIA. I. 30.
Victorian naturalist. I. 30.
Vida de los árboles. 1886. IV. 233.
Vidal. The useful plants of Japan. 1876. III. 91.[2]
Vidal, A. Considérations sur les principales conditions ... pour l'acclimatation des espèces végétales. 1879. III. 43.
Vidal, A. J. R., Index. 1850. I. 60.[1]
— Index plantarum in Horto botanico academico. 1850. I. 60.[1]
— Index seminario Horti ... conimbricensis. 1871. I. 60.[1]
Vidal, Émile. Mémoire sur la nécessité de modifier la loi forestière du 6 juillet 1870. 1881. IV. 183,[1] 326.
— Sur le traitement du Peronospora Vitis. 1885. III. 578.[1]

idal, J. Note sur les usages du Bambou. 1874. III. 315.[1]
idal, Louis. Note sur un Genévrier des environs de Grenoble. 1897. II. 32.[1]
— Recherches sur le sommet de l'axe dans la flore. 1900. I. 524.[3]
idál y Mascaró, J. M. El triunfo de la savia de los árboles. 1839. IV. 425.[1]
idal y Soler, Domingo. Manual del maderero en Filipinas. 1877. IV. 100.[1]
idal y Soler, Sebastián. Botánica y productos forestales. 1887. IV. 21.[2]
— Breve descripción de algunas de las maderas . . . de las Islas Filipinas. 1874. IV. 399.[2]
— Catálogo metódico de las plantas leñosas . . . de Manila. 1880. I. 483,[2] IV. 87.[2]
— Memoria sobre el ramo de montes en las Islas filipinas. 1874. I. 464.[1]
— Phanerogamae Cumingianae Philippinarum. 1885. I. 464.[1]
— Revision de plantas vasculares filipinas. 1886. I. 464.[1]
— Sinopsis de . . . plantas leñosas de Filipinas. 1883. I. 464,[1] IV. 88.[1]
— See also JORDANA Y MORERA, José & VIDAL Y SOLER, Sebastian.
Vidau, A. Considérations sur la destruction du phylloxera. 1875. III. 568.
Videnskabernes Selskab. Skrifter. See KJØBENHAVNSKE SELSKAB . . . I. 8.[3]
Videnskabs-Selskabet i Christiania. Forhandlinger. I. 8.[2]
Der Viehbiss im Jungholze. 1874. IV. 197.[1]
Eine vielgipfelige Fichte. 1884. IV. 460.[1]
Vieillard, Eugène. Étude sur les Palmiers de la Nouvelle-Calédonie. 1872. II. 62.[1]
— Études sur les genres Oxera et Deplanches. 1862. II. 759,[2] 788.[1]
— Notes sur quelques plantes . . . de la Nouvelle-Calédonie. 1866. I. 508.[1]
— Sur l'Omphalocarpum procerum. 1882. II. 699.[2]
— Plantes de la Nouvelle-Calédonie. 1865. I. 508.[3]
— Plantes utiles de la Nouvelle-Calédonie. 1862. III. 94.[2]
— Production de chaleur. 1872. II. 7.[1]
— & Deplanche, Émile. Essais sur la Nouvelle-Calédonie. 1862. I. 508.[2]
Der vielstengliche Maulbeerbaum. 1834. III. 380.[2]
Vienna — Gartenbau-Gesellschaft. See GARTENBAU . . . III 24.[3]
Vienna — Handels-Museum. See HANDELS-MUSEUM. III. 24.[2]
Vienna — Kaiserlich-königliche geographische Gesellschaft. See KAISERLICH-KÖNIGLICHE . . . I. 27.
Vienna — Kaiserlich-königliches naturhistorisches Hofmuseum. See KAISERLICH-KÖNIGLICHES . . . I. 27.
Vienna — K. k. technische Hochschule-Naturwissenschaftlicher Verein. See NATURWISSENSCHAFTLICHER VEREIN . . . I. 28.[1]
Vienna — Kaiserlich königl. technologisches Gewerbe-Museum. See TECHNOLOGISCHES . . . IV. 15.
Vienna — Kaiserlich-königliche zoologisch-botanische Gesellschaft. See KAISERLICH-KÖNIGLICHE . . . I. 27.
Vienna — Kaiserliche Akademie der Wissenschaften. See KAISERLICHE . . . I. 27.
Vienna — Technologisches Gewerbe-Museum. See TECHNOLOGISCHES . . . III. 25.
Vienna — Universität — Naturwissenschaftlicher Verein. See NATURWISSENSCHAFTLICHER VEREIN . . . I. 28.[1]
Vienna — Verein zur Verbreitung naturwissenschaftlicher Kenntnisse. See VEREIN . . . I. 15.
Vienne, Émile. Notice sur Moyotte et les Comores. 1900. III. 282.[1]
Viennot, T. De l'introduction . . . du Mûrier en France. 1869. III. 377.
Viera y Clavijo, José de. Diccionario de historia natural de las islas Canarias. 1866. I. 498.
Vierenklee, Johann Ehrenfried. Anfangsgründe der theoretisch-praktischen Arithmetik und Geometrie. 1767. IV. 57.
— Mathematische Anfangsgründe der Arithmetik. 1767. IV. 57.
Vierne, Henri. Les Tamarissières de la Méditerranée. 1864. III. 612.[1]
Viernheim state forest, Hesse-Darmstadt. 1900. IV. 351.[2]
Vierteljahresschrift für praktische Pharmacie. I. 15.
Vierteljahrshefte zur Statistik des deutschen Reichs. IV. 11.
Vieshtchitzki, A. F. See ВѢШИЦКІЙ, А. Ф.
Viet, Charles. See VESQUE, Julien & VIET, Charles.

Vietinghoff-Scheel, Baron. Le dendromètre. 1889. IV. 231.[2]
Vietz, Ferdinand Bernhard. Icones plantarum medico-oeconomico-technologicarum. 1800. III. 51.
Vieux arbres. 1899. IV. 86.[1]
Vieux Chênes. 1898. IV. 559.[2]
Un vieux forestier, (pseud.). Les traverses métalliques. 1898. IV. 424.[2]
Un Vieux praticien, (pseud.), Places d'expérimentation dans les futaies. 1886. IV. 38.[2]
Viéville, G. BAGUENAULT DE. See BAGUENAULT DE VIÉVILLE, G.
A view in Mr. Arderne's garden, Cape Town. 1898. III. 634.[1]
Vigener, A. Über Perezia-Arten aus Mexico. 1884. III. 756.[2]
Vigier, Ferdinand. Analyse des feuilles et écorces de Quinquinas. 1871. III. 722.
— Des huiles ou essences de Bouleau. 1892. IV. 491.[2]
Vigier, Joaon. Historia das plantas da Europa. 1718. III. 51.-
Vigilate sui boschi. 1865. IV. 183.[2]
Vigineix, Guillaume. See MARÈS, Paul & VIGINEIX, Guillaume.
Viglietta, Giuseppe. Notizie statistiche sul patrimonio boschivo dell' Umbria. 1872. IV. 364.
Vigna, Dominico. Animadversiones . . . in libros de historia et de causis plantarum Theophrasti. 1625. I. 285.[1]
Vigne, G. T. Travels in Kashmir. 1842. I. 472.
La Vigne américaine. III. 23.[1]
Vignéras, Sylvain. Notice sur la Côte française des Somalis. 1900. III. 281.[2]
Vigneron, C. Mauvais effets d'une taille trop courte. 1872. III. 170.
— Mauvais effets d'une taille trop courte sur des arbres vigoureux. 1869. III. 170.
Les Vignes américaines et la situation phylloxérique. See DUPOUR, Jean. 1899. III. 575.[1]
Les Vignes géantes. 1889. II. 509.[1]
Vigneux, A. Flore pittoresque des environs de Paris. 1812. I. 407.
Le vignoble de l'Hérault en 1900. 1900. III. 557.[2]
Vignon, Léo. Dosage du tannin. 1898. I. 184.
— & Barillot. Dosage du cuivre et du mercure dans les raisins. 1899. III. 562.[1]
De Vijgeboom. 1853. III. 369.[1]
Vila, Estanislao VAYREDA Y. See VAYREDA Y VILA, Estanislao.
Vila y Robles, J. M. Elementos de agricultura general. 1865. III. 114.[3]
Vilardebó y Moret, José. El tabaco y el café. 1888. III. 742.[1]
Vilaró Diaz, Juan. Elementos de botanica. 1892. I. 92.
— Insecto dañoso. 1880. III. 418.[2]
— Nota acerca de un insecto destructor de los Platanales. 1880. III. 418.[2]
Vilbouchevitch, Jean. Considérations sur le caractère halophyte du Cocotier. 1900. II. 67.[2]
— Encore un Salt-bush. 1898. III. 387.[2]
— L'étude géo-botanique des terrains salants. 1892. I. 229.
— Le Nitraria Schoberi. 1891. III. 494.[2]
— Le Peuplier de l'Euphrate. 1891. III. 346.[1]
— La question des "Salt-bushes." 1893. III. 007.[7]
— La question des Salt-bushes, l'Atriplex nummularia. 1894. III. 387.[2]
— Renseignements sur des plantes de terrains salants. 1893. III. 387.[2]
— Le Tamarix articulé. 1892. III. 612.[1]
— Les Tamarix et leurs applications. 1890. IV. 529.[1]
— See also GRISARD, Jules & VILBOUCHEVITCH, Jean; ВѢЛЬбушевитъ, Н. О.
Vilbuschewicz, Eugen. See WILBUSCHEWICZ, Eugen.
Vilbushevitch, I. O. See VILBOUCHEVITCH, Jean.
Vilbuszewitcz, V. See WILBUSZEWITCZ, V.
Vilcocq, Albert. Les maladies des arbres. Les broussins. 1899. I. 213.[2]
Villa, Antonio & G. B. I boschi nella Lombardia. 1873. IV. 364.
— — Necessità dei boschi nella Lombardia. 1886. IV. 276.[2]
— — Utilità dei boschi montani nella Lombardia. 1847. IV. 47.[2]
Villa, Calliste. Flora delle Alpi. 1883. I. 437.
Villa, Estevan de. Libro de simples incognitos en la medicina. 1643. III. 240.
— Ramillete de plantas. 1637. I. 285.[1] — 1646. III. 53.

Villa, G. B. *See* VILLA, Antonio & G. B.
Villa de Montpascal, *comte*. Sur l'utilité du Mûrier des Philippines. 1838. III. 380.[2]
Villa-Franca, *baron* de. Note sur les plantes utiles du Brésil. 1879. III. 65.[3]
Villa Nova, ARNOLDUS DE. *See* ARNOLDUS DE VILLA NOVA.
Villada, Manuel M. El Árbol del hule. 1876. III. 368.[1]
— La Casimiroa pubescens J. Ram. 1897. II. 400.[2]
— El Erythroxylon ellipticum. 1898. II. 394.[2]
— Estudios relativos á la Bocconia. 1897. II. 229.[1]
— Estudios sobre la flora de Pachuca. 1865. I. 531.
— La goma laca de México. 1897. III. 463,[2] 494.[2]
— Noticia . . . de una variedad de la Breweria mexicana. 1897. II. 744.[2]
— *See also* HERRERA, Alfonso & VILLADA, M. M.
— & **Armendaris**, Eduardo. Necesidad de la conservación de los bosques. 1897. IV. 272.
Village forests. 1882. IV. 181.[1]
Villagómez, I. O. Vegetacion espontánea . . . de Verácruz. 1884. I. 332, 531.
Villain, F. P. Observations sur la manière d'opérer pour l'arpentage des bois. 1800. IV. 213.
Villanueva, Maximo LAGUNA Y. *See* LAGUNA Y VILLANUEVA, Maximo.
Villard, DEREGHAT DE. *See* DEREGHAT DE VILLARD.
Villard, Th. Les fleurs à travers les âges. 1900. III. 32,[2] 88.[1]
Villareal de Berriz, P. Bernardo. Maquinas hidraúlicas de molinos y herrerías. 1736. IV. 392.
Villari, E. Ricerche sperimentali intorno ad alcune proprietà fisiche del legno. 1866. IV. 408.
Villars, Dominique. Catalogue des substances végétales, qui peuvent servir à la nourriture. 1793. III. 271.[1]—1794. III. 219.[1]
— Catalogue méthodique des plantes du jardin de l'École de médecine de Strasbourg. 1807. I. 45.
— Flora delphinalis. 1779. I. 405.
— Histoire des plantes de Dauphiné. 1786. I. 406.
— Mémoire sur les moyens d'accélérer les progrès de la botanique. 1801. I. 78.[1]
— Prospectus de l'histoire des plantes de Dauphiné. 1779. I. 405.
— Tableau pour la plantation . . . du jardin de botanique . . . de Strasbourg. 1806. I. 45.
— **Lauth**, Gustav & Nestler, A. Précis d'un voyage botanique, fait en Suisse. 1812. I. 433.
Villé, Georges. Absorption de l'azote de l'air. 1854. I. 161.
— Sur l'assimilation du gaz azote. 1855. I. 158.
— De l'état auquel se trouve . . . l'azote. 1856. I. 158.
— De l'importance comparée des agents de la production végétale. 1860. I. 151.[1]—1861. I. 158.
— Note sur l'assimilation de l'azote de l'air. 1850. I. 158.
— Note sur un nouveau moyen pour doser l'azote. 1855. I. 158.
— Nouvelles recherches sur le rôle des principes inorganiques. 1858. I. 158.
— Quel est le rôle des nitrates dans l'économie des plantes? 1855. I. 158.
— À quel état l'azote . . . est-il absorbé. 1856. I. 158.
— Recherches expérimentales sur la végétation. 1852. I. 158.— 1853. I. 170.
— Remarques . . . concernant l'influence que le phosphate de chaux . . . exerce. 1857. I. 158.
Ville de Bruges. Plantations. 1899. III. 42.[1]
Villedieu, Influence de l'humidité sur le phylloxera. 1875. III. 568.
Villefranche, *marquis* de, (*député*, *Yonne*). Opinion sur l'article 24. du projet de loi des voies et moyens. 1819. IV. 326.
— Opinion sur le chapitre II. de la troisième partie du budget de 1824. 1823. IV. 275.
— Opinion sur le projet de loi concernant l'aliénation des bois. 1817. IV. 326.
Villejean, E. *See* REGNAULD, Jules & VILLEJEAN, E.
Villemin, Eugène. Herbier poétique. 1842. I. 94.
Villemotte, Gonzalve de. Du défrichement des forêts. 1845. IV. 275.
Villemus, A. Du café. 1875. III. 742.[1]
Villeneuve, L. P. COURET-. *See* COURET-VILLENEUVE, L. P.
Villepoix, R. MOYNIER DE. *See* MOYNIER DE VILLEPOIX, R.
Villeroy, Félix & Muller, Adam. Manuel de l'irrigateur. 186.? III. 150.[2]
Villers, Georges de. Sur les Ifs séculaires du cimetière de Castillon. 1879. II. 11.[1]

Villette. Nouveau manuel de botanique. 1838. I. 87.
Villevêque, Laisné de. Opinion sur le projet de loi concernant les échangistes. 1818. IV. 326.
Villevieille, Greffe d'Echinocactus et de Mamillaires. 1845. III. 618.[2]
Villez, E. von RANSONNET-. *See* RANSONNET-VILLEZ, E. von.
Villiers. Sur la curarine du Strychnos toxifera. 1885. III. 685.[2]
Villiers, A. Recherches sur le mélézitose. 1877. III. 466.[2]
— *See also* TANRET, Charles & VILLIERS, A.
— & **Fayolle**, M. Sur une réaction des aldéhydes. 1894. I. 177.
Villon, A. M. La industria de las traviesas de ferrocarril. 1895. IV. 557.[2]
Vilmorin. Question relative à l'une des variétés du Peuplier blanc. 1828. II. 96.[2]
— & **Michaux**. Rapport . . . . à l'occasion de rejetons de Pinus rigida. 1831. III. 308.[1]
Vilmorin, Henri Lévêque de. Sur la conservation du Melhania melanoxylon. 1890. II. 539.[2]
— Exposé . . . de l'École forestière des Barres. 1863. I. 58,[1] IV. 54.[2]
— Exposé de la composition de l'École des Pins silvestres. 1864. II. 46.[2]
— Flowers of the French Riviera. 1893. III. 463,[1] 634.[1]
— Sur les formes occidentales du Pinus Laricio. 1893. II. 43.[2]
— Note sur l'indifférence de quelques plantes. 1859. I. 232.[1]
— Sur l'origine du Lilas-Varin. 1873. II. 715.[1]
— La sélection. 1900. I. 248.[1]
— Selection, and its effects on cultivated plants. 1900. I. 248.[1]
— La villa Thuret. 1883. I. 59.
Vilmorin, Louis. De l'Ajonc sans épines. 1850. III. 489.[2]
— Note sur un projet . . . de créer une race d'Ajonc sans épines. 1851. III. 489.[2]
— Note sur une variété. 1850. III. 489.[2]
— Observations sur le Pin de Corte. 1846. III. 307.[2]
— Sur une variété non épineuse de l'Ajonc. 1850. III. 489.[2]
Vilmorin, Maurice Lévêque de. Arbres étrangers. 1890. IV. 127.[1]
— Arbres forestiers étrangers. 1900. IV. 126.[2]
— Arbres forestiers étrangers; recueil de notes. 1900. IV. 127.[1]
— Le bois de Pichepin. 1897. IV. 462.[2]
— Buddleia variabilis. 1898. II. 718.[1]
— The Calabrian Laricio. 1889. II. 43.[2]
— Cèdres de l'Atlas et Sapin du Babor. 1896. I. 483,[2] IV. 89.[1]
— Les Conifères du parc de Cheverny. 1892. I. 59, III. 291.
— The Corsican Pine at home. 1897. II. 43.[2]
— Ensayos de árboles exóticos en el monte de Eberswalde. 1900. IV. 545.[1]
— Essais d'arbres exotiques dans la forêt d'Eberswalde. 1900. IV. 126,[2] 545.[1]
— Le Frêne de Kabylie. 1895. IV. 536.[1]
— L'horticulture française à Chicago. 1894. III. 117.[1]
— Introduction d'arbres étrangers. 1888. III. 124.[1]
— Juglans Vilmoriniana. 1897. II. 114.[2]
— Le Mont Babor, Cèdres de l'Atlas. 1896. I. 483,[2] IV. 89.[1]
— Note sur le Pacanier. 1894. III. 354.[1]
— Notes sur quelques Ficus du jardin du Hamma. 1890. III. 369.[1]
— Le Pin Laricio de Calabre. 1889. III. 308.[1]
— Le Pin Laricio en Corse. 1897. II. 43.[2]
— Pinus palustris in France. 1897. III. 308.[1]
— Rare trees and shrubs in the Arnold Arboretum. 1894. I. 39.
Vilmorin, Pierre Louis François Levêque de. Revue des nouveautés horticoles. 1858. III. 87.
Vilmorin-Andrieux & Cie. Des Eucalyptus. 1878. III. 633.[2]
— Les fleurs de pleine terre. 1863. III. 87.
— Vilmorin's illustrirte Blumengärtnerei. 1863. III. 87.
Vimand. Nature and cure of dry rot. 1802. IV. 414.[1]
Vimont, Eugène. Almanach du poiré et du cidre. 1894. III. 444.[1]
Vimont, G. Album des syndicats champenois pour l'étude des principales maladies de la Vigne. 1881. III. 573.
Vincens, J. C. & **Baumes**. Topographie de la ville de Nismes. 1802. I. 406.
Vincent. Dégâts de l'hiver 1890–91. 1891. III. 49.[1]

Vincent. Nouvelles recherches sur la fibre du Phormium. 1848. III. 233.²

Vincent, Camille. Carbonisation des bois en vases clos. 1873. IV. 432.²

— Mode de production des méthylamines. 1873. III. 37.¹

— & **Delachanal.** Sur l'extraction de la sorbite. 1889. II. 311.²

— — Sur un hydrate de carbone contenu dans le gland du Chêne. 1887. IV. 515.¹

— — Note sur l'hydrogénation de la sorbine. 1890. II. 311.³

— — Sur la présence de la mannite . . . dans les fruits du Laurier-cerise. 1892. III. 438.¹

— — Sur la " quercine." 1888. IV. 515.¹

— — Sur la sorbite. 1889. II. 311.²

— — Sur la sorbite et sur sa présence . . . de la famille des Rosacées. 1889. II. 257.¹

— & **Meunier,** J. Sur un nouveau sucre accompagnant la sorbite. 1898. II. 311.²

Vincent, F. D'A. Forest administration of Ceylon. 1883. IV. 295.¹

— The forests of Ceylon. 1882. IV. 373.

— Mahogany in Ceylon. 1884. IV. 525.²

— Timber trees at the Cape. 1883. IV. 401.¹

Vincent, J. B. M. BORY DE SAINT-. See BORY DE SAINT-VINCENT, J. B. M.

Vincent, Louis. The Calabar bean. 1872. III. 484.¹

— Sur la fève d'épreuve du Calabar. 1872. III. 484.¹

— Theatrum naturae mirandum. 1706. I. 289.

Vincent, M. Tests of hardiness of fruit trees. 1886. III. 182.

Vincent, P. See DAVID, Ph., FOUCAUD, Julien & VINCENT, P.

Vincent de Beauvais. See VINCENTIUS BELLOVACENSIS.

Vincenti, Carl, Ritter von. Die Dattelpalme, ein Lebensbaum. 1879. III. 329.³

Vincentius Bellovacensis. Speculum naturale. 1264. I. 274.

Vincenzo, Maria. Il viaggio all' Indie Orientali. 1672. III. 277.

Vincey, Paul. L'ouragan du 26 juillet. 1896. III. 184.²

Vinchon, J. L'École forestière et l'Institut agronomique. 1888. IV. 34.²

Vinci, Lionardo da. Trattato della pittura. 1817. I. 33.

Vine diseases (brunissure, browning.). 1893. III. 580.

The **Vine** in Uruguay. 1900. III. 551.¹

The **Vine** manual; or, Instructions. 185.? III. 553.²

Vinen, E. Hart. Sur les noix de galles anglaises. 1856. IV. 574.²

Vines, Sidney Howard. On epinasty and hyponasty. 1889. I. 194.

— The influence of light upon the growth of leaves. 1882. I. 190,² *230.*

— Lectures on the physiology of plants. 1886. I. 148.

— Metamorphosis in plants. 1898. I. 101.²

— A students' text-book of botany. 1894. I. 92.

— The suction-force of transpiring branches. 1890. I. 108.

— See also BOWER, F. O. & VINES, S. H.

Vineto. See ESTIENNE, Charles. 1537. III. 554.¹

Vinetum. See ESTIENNE, Charles. 1537. III. 554.¹

The **vineyard.** See J., S. 1727. III. 553.²

Les **vingt** livres de Constantin Caesar. See CASSIANUS BASSUS. 1538. III. 98.

Vingtain, Léon. Note sur les semis de bois résineux. 1869. IV. 441.

Vino di Mirtillo. 1863. IV. 534.²

Vinson, Auguste. Sur les essais d'acclimatation des Arbres à quinquina à l'Île de la Réunion. 1874. III. 717.¹

— Mémoire sur les essais d'acclimatation des Arbres à quinquina à l'Île de la Réunion. 1875. III. 717.¹

— Notes [sur la " Flore de l'Île de la Réunion."] 1896. I. 432.

— See also MORIN, Édouard & VINSON, Auguste.

Vinson, Jean François Dominique Émile. Essai sur quelques plantes utiles de l'île Bourbon. 1855. III. 93.¹

Viola, C. Sulle condizioni geologiche dei monti della provincia Romana. 1897. IV. 70.

Violette. Mémoire sur la carbonisation du bois. 1848. IV. 394.

— Mémoire [1–2] sur les charbons de bois. 1851. IV. 431.²

— Propriété du charbon de bois pour favoriser la germination. 1853. IV. 431.²

Violette, A. Dunes et landes de Gascogne; gemmage du Pin maritime. 1900. IV. 468.² ·

Violette, Henri. Distillation des térébenthines et des résines. 1853. IV. 436.²

— Sur les résines. 1866. III. 227, 233.¹

Viollet-Le-Duc, E. Les glaciers du Mont-Blanc. 1877. IV. 48.²

Vion, Réné. L'Exposition forestière au concours régional d'Amiens. 1881. IV. 360.

Virág, József. Hibiscus Manihot. 1896. III. 587.²

Virchow, Ernst. Betrachtungen über einige zu Unterholzpflanzungen verwendbare Gehölze. 1888. III. 216.

— Dendrologisches aus Cleve. 1894. I. 49.

— Interessante Gehölze in Rastede. 1887. I. 48.

Virchow, Hans. Ueber Bau und Nervatur der Blattzähne. 1896. III. 260.¹

Virchow, Rudolf Ludwig Karl. Zwei Riesentannen in den Voralpen. 1888. II. 24.²

Viret, Georges. Législation et jurisprudence concernant les insectes. 1896. III. 191.

Virey, Julien Joseph. Arbre à beurre du Soudan. 1830. III. 667.¹

— Arbre fontaine des nègres. 1832. III. 341.²

— Arbres pluvieux. 1826. II. 339.²

— Atchar de l'Inde. 1823. III. 219.¹

— Autres emplois des Sumachs. 1831. III. 526.²

— Sur les avortements des parties des fleurs. 1838. I. 114.²

— Du baume aracouchini de la Guyane. 1825. III. 511.²

— Bois amer de l'Île de Bourbon. 1822. III. 687.¹

— Sur un bois antinéphrétique dit Espénille. 1844. III. 743.²

— Bois de Carapa et de Mapou. 1839. III. 512.¹

— Bois de Gayac faux. 1835. III. 707.²

— Sur le bois de Naghas. 1823. III. 610.²

— Botanique médicale. 1828. III. 56.

— Café du Soudan ou noix de gourou. 1827. III. 590.¹

— Sur le camphre de Bornéo. 1832. III. 611.¹

— Des caractères distinctifs de la graine de Croton tiglium. 1825. III. 517.¹

— Sur Carapa. 1821. III. 511.¹

— Carapa- und Mapou-Holz. 1839. III. 512.¹

— Sur les Châtaignes du Brésil. 1818. III. 631.¹

— Considérations sur la matière médicale de l'Indostan. 1828. III. 277.

— Considerations sur le froid et ses effets. 1816. I. 211.

— Du crajuru, ou carajuru et chica. 1844. III. 705.

— Sur la découverte de l'arbre du bdellium. 1833. II. 418.¹

— Description d'une plante célèbre. 1821. III. 754.²

— Description de l'écorce de Strychnos pseudoquina. 1830. III. 685.¹

— Des différentes sorte de thé. 1815. III. 222, *606*.

— Des diverses espèces de cacao. 1831. III. 594.

— Éclaircissements relatifs à l'arbre qui produit la résine copal. 1842. III. 233,² *489.²*

— D'une écorce amère . . . cascanoqui. 1820. III. 506.¹

— De l'écorce de Belabé. 1831. III. 282.¹

— Sur une écorce dite virginale. 1832. III. 481,² *488.²*

— Écorce fébrifuge . . . de Prunier de la Calabre. 1830. III. 400.²

— Écorce Jubaba. 1820. III. 417.¹

— De l'état actuel de nos connaissances sur . . . Quinquinas. 1812. II. 812.

— Études nouvelles sur la glaucité du feuillage. 1846. I. 185,² 236.²

— Examen des recherches . . . sur le lycion des anciens. 1843. II. 155,¹ *III. 543.²*

— Examen physiologique d'un phénomène de la végétation. 1824. I. 525.

— Falsches Guajachols. 1835. III. 707.²

— Flore nocturne. 1831. I. 220.²

— Du fruit de Mangoustan. 1822. III. 609.²

— Ueber die Goura- oder Gouru-Nuss, such Kola. 1832. III. 590.¹

— Gousses astringentes tinctoriales. 1825. III. 236.

— Gousses de Libidibi ou Dibidivi. 1835. III. 468.²

— Guarana. 1820. III. 632.¹ ·

— Sur l'histoire naturelle des beurres végétaux. 1835. III. 224.¹

— Histoire naturelle des médicamens. 1820. III. 52.

— Sur l'histoire naturelle du kino ou gambir. 1812. III. 748.¹

— Histoire naturelle médicale de l'encens. 1813. III. 523.¹

— Histoire naturelle médicale du suc . . . . Guarana. 1840. III. 539.²

— Hülsen, genannt Libidibi oder Dibidivi. 1835. III. 468.²

— Huile amygdaline du Prunier des Alpes. 1818. III. 439.¹

— Huile de Chalef ou Chalaf. 1843. III. 628.²

— De l'huile de touloucouna du Sénégal. 1834. III. 512.¹

Virey, Julien Joseph (*continued*).
— Huile et teinture de Tiglium. 1823. III. 517.[1]
— Sur une huile naturelle de Laurier de la Guyane. 1824. III. 403.[2]
— Importation de nouvelles espèces d'extraits. 1842. III. 236.
— Inégalité de la pousse des végétaux. 1832. I. 191.[1]
— Influence chimique . . . de quelques nourritures végétales. 1832. III. 219.[1]
— Insectes produisant de la manne. 1827. III. 612.[2]
— Sur les insectes qui produisent . . . cire d'arbre. 1840. III. 225.
— Ueber den Kampher von Borneo. 1832. III. 611.[1]
— Du kerfé, écorce du Sénégal. 1823. III. 280.[2]
— Du kino véritable. 1827. III. 485.[1]
— Du kino véritable de la Gambie. 1827. III. 485.[2]
— Lait potable d'une apocynée. 1832. III. 219.[1]
— Laits végétaux comestibles. 1838. III. 219.[2]
— Liste des noms des thés. 1824. III. 606.
— Manna aus Australien. 1832. IV. 533.[2]
— Manne de l'Australie. 1832. IV. 533.[2]
— Massoy. 1820. III. 407.[1]
— Ueber Mate oder Paraguay-Thee. 1832. III. 530.[2]
— Matière médicale d'Hippocrate. 1815. III. 238.[2]
— Sur un médicament precieux chez les anciens. 1819. III. 758.[1]
— Des médicaments aphrodisiaques. 1813. III. 244.
— Memoire sur l'histoire naturelle de la laque. 1821. III. 232.[2]
— Monesia or Buranhem of Brazil. 1844. III. 668.[1]
— Nannari; salseparejlle nouvelle. 1831. III. 693.[1]
— Native oil of Laurel used in Spanish Guyana. 1824. III. 403.[2]
— Naturgeschichte der vegetabilschen Butter. 1835. III. 224.[1]
— Naturwissenschaftliche Neuigkeiten. 1839. III. 544.[2]
— Sur la noix d'Arec. 1821. III. 320.[1]
— Note sur des médicamens peu connus. 1820. III. 244.
— Note sur l'Avoira, ou Palmier Aouara. 1819. III. 325.[1]
— Note sur l'origine de la gomme, dite de Bassora. 1819. III. 592.[1]
— Note sur la fève Tonka. 1829. III. 475.[2]
— Note sur la manne. 1828. III. 221.[1]
— Note sur le bois de Cailcédra. 1823. III. 512;[1]
— Note sur le Maté, ou Thé du Paraguay. 1832. III. 530.[2]
— Note sur le poison appelé Woorara. 1824. III. 689.[1]
— Note sur le Rita de l'Indostan. 1837. III. 540.[1]
— Note tendant à prouver qu'il n'y a point d'exception absolue aux propriétés médicinales des familles. 1821. III. 259.[2]
— Notes sur des objets nouveaux d'histoire naturelle médicale. 1839. III. 244.
— Notice de plusieurs plantes usitées dans la médecine. 1813. III. 218.[2]
— Notice sur l'arbre Carapa. 1821. III. 511.[2]
— Notice sur la noix de goura. 1832. III. 590.[1]
— Notice sur la racine dite cainca. 1829. III. 711,[2] 744.[1]
— Notice sur le tanguin de Madagascar. 1822. III. 691.[1]
— Notice sur un bois de teinture rouge d'Afrique. 1827. III. 167.[2]
— Notice sur un Café dit d'Éden. 1822. III. 738.
— Notice sur un medicament . . . souline. 1813. III. 690.[1]
— Notice sur un nouveau médicament. 1815. III. 467,[2] 516.[1]
— Nouveau bois de Santal citrin. 1826. III. 384.[2]
— Nouveau bois néphrétique. 1832. III. 706.[2]
— Nouveau Quinquina. 1828. III. 745.[2]
— Nouveaux éclaircissements sur . . . Monesia. 1844. III. 668.[1]
— Nouveaux éclaircissements sur . . . poison ipo. 1841. III. 366.[2]
— Nouvelle au bois nepherétique-noir du Brésil. 1822. III. 396.[2]
— Nouvelle écorce fébrifuge de l'Inde. 1818. III. 506.[1]
— Nouvelle espèce de Camphrier de Sumatra. 1821. III. 233,[1] 611.[1]
— Nouvelle espèce de Smilax antisyphilitique. 1824. III. 338.[2]
— Nouvelle plante anthelminthique. 1823. III. 424.[1]
— Nouvelle substance astringente . . .; algarovilla. 1826. III. 485.[1]
— Nouvelles considérations sur l'histoire . . . dû café. 1816. III. 741.[2]
— Observation sur des végétaux de la Perse. 1823. I. 477.[1]
— Observations sur des végétaux de la Perse. 1823. III. 279.[2]
— Observations sur l'Alcanna. 1824. III. 630.[1]
— Observations sur la production des corps gras. 1844. I. 182.[1]
— De l'organization des tissus végétaux dans les . . . galles. 1823. I. 214.[1]
— Sur l'origine de l'extrait tinctoria . . . de Buenos Ayres. 1842. III. 464,[2] 468,[2] 481.[2]
— Sur l'origine de la myrrhe. 1829. III. 511.[1]
— Origine du vrai Styrax d'Asie. 1832. III. 417.[2]
— Du paraguatan. 1833. III. 743,[2] 747.[1]
— Pharmacon hieron. 1832. I. 513.
— Plantes usitées contre les morsures des serpens. 1817. III. 244.
— Propriétés médicales de la Piscidia. 1832. III. 484.[1]
— Sur les Pseudo-quinas. 1830. III. 517.[1]
— Quelques considérations nouvelles sur l'acidité dans les plantes irritables. 1839. I. 197.[1]
— De quelques médicamens des sauvages américains. 1833. III. 268.[2]
— Sur quelques poisons végétaux peu connus. 1838. III. 685.[1]
— De la racine de Chiococca anguifuga. 1825. III. 711.[2]
— Racine de Jean Lopez. 1820. III. 506.[1]
— Rapport sur un mémoire relatif à la chenille nommée conque. 1825. III. 562.[2]
— Rapport . . . sur une dissertation botanique de M M. Nees d'Esenbeck. 1824. II. 224.[1]
— Recherches d'histoire naturelle . . . du Carnauba. 1834. II. 68.[1]
— Recherches d'histoire naturelle médicale sur les Poivriers. 1826. III. 342.[1]
— Recherches historiques et bibliques sur la marine. 1818. III. 221.[1]
— Recherches . . . sur la matière cireuse du Carnauba. 1834. III. 324.[1]
— Remarques sur la disposition géographique des végétaux alimentaires. 1817. III. 217.
— Remarques sur la flore' économique des Îles Marquises. 1843. III. 253.[2]
— Remarques sur le premier Quinaquina. 1829. III. 482,[1] 724.[1]
— Remarques sur les variétés des couleurs. 1838. I. 184.
— Remède des Hindous contre le cholera-morbus. 1831. III. 684.[2]
— De la résine de Mancenilier. 1829. III. 519.[1]
— Resine Kilcekwnemalo. 1820. III. 510.[1]
— Du sandaron, ou sandarous. 1819. III. 299.[2]
— Des semences de plantes legumineuses. 1822. II. 321.[2]
— Substances médicale . . . extraits de Takaoly. 1835. III. 632.[1]
— Sur le Tapioca, ou Tipiaca. 1817. III. 521.[1]
— Des thés les plus célèbres de la Chine. 1824. III. 606.
— Traité de pharmacie théorique et pratique. 1811. III. 257.[2]
— Ursprung der ächten asiatischen Storax. 1832. III. 417.[2]
— Usage de l'écorce de la racine de Grenadier. 1832. III. 630.[2]
— Des végétaux qui servent à enivrer les poissons. 1831. III. 260.[2]
— Vues nouvelles sur la cause physiologique des torsions volubiles. 1842. I. 196.[1]
— *See also* D'A . . . & VIREY, J. J.
Virgander, David Magnus. Frutetum suecicum. *See* LINNÉ, Carl von. 1758. I. 350.[1]
Virgilius, Marco Publius. The Bucoliks of Virgil. 1749. III. 99.
— Les Bucoliques de Virgile. 1749. III. 99.
— Georgicorum libri IV. 1741. III. 99.
Virginia — Agricultural and mechanical college — Agricultural experiment station. Annual report. Bulletin. III. 9.
Virginia — Agricultural experiment station. *See* VIRGINIA—AGRICULTURAL AND MECHANICAL COLLEGE . . . III. 9.
The Virginia Fringe-tree. 1882. III. 671.[2]
Die virginische Sumpfcypresse. 1889. III. 311.[1]
Viridarium adriaticum. 1686. III. 126.[2]
Virkninger af Foraarsfrosten paa Pæretræers Blomster. 1857. III. 182.
Virlet d'Aoust, Pierre Théodore. Sur le système de tannage rapide. 1870. III. 481.[2]
Viruly Verbrugge, W. A. Iets over het belang van den tuinbouw. 1881. III. 122.[2]
Visart, Amédée. De l'enlèvement des feuilles mortes dàns les bois. 1896. IV. 438.[1]

Visart de Bocarmé, A., *comte* & others. Enlèvement des bourgeons de Pin. 1898. IV. 482.²
—— Taillis simples. 1898. IV. 132.²
Visart de Bocarmé, Étienne. Une visite au domaine des Barres. 1895. IV. 539.²
Vischer, Edward. The forest trees of California. Sequoia gigantea. 1862. II. 50.²
Vischer, G. D. Ueber den Holzdiebstahl. 1820. IV. 313.
Vischio. 1888. IV. 519.²
Viscio, Giuseppe del. Coltivazione degli Agrumi. 1898. III. 497.²
Visiani, Roberto de. Sopra l' Acanto. 1857. V. xxv.¹
— Di alcune piante storiche del Giardino di Padova. 1856. I. 63.
— Delle benemerenze de' Veneti nella botanica. 1854. I. 81.¹
— Bericht über einen Regen einer vegetabilischen Nahrungs-Substanz. 1864. III. 221.¹
— Catalogo delle piante . . . delle provincie venete. 1857. I. 427.
— Considerazioni intorno al genere ed alla specie. 1847. I. 252.
— Drei neue Koniferen. 1857. II. 12.²
— Due nuove piante dell' Orto botanico di Padova. 1860. II. 782.²
— Flora dalmatica. 1842. I. 447.
— Florae dalmaticae supplementum. 1871. I. 428.
— Florae dalmaticae supplementum alterum adjectis plantis in Bosnia. 1876. I. 447.
— Sopra la Gastonia palmata. 1841. II. 653.¹
— Illustrazione botanica del Cusso vermifugo. 1852. II. 264.²
— Illustrazione delle piante . . . dell' Orto botanico di Padova. 1840. I. 63.
— Illustrazione di alcune piante della Grecia. 1842. II. 766.¹
— Di una nuova specie di manna caduta. 1864. III. 221.¹
— Della origine ed anzianità dell' Orto botanico di Padova. 1839. I. 63.
— L' Orto botanico di Padova. 1842. I. 63.
— Osservazioni sull' erbario di Linneo. 1870. I. 270.
— Di una pioggia di sostanza vegetabile alimentare. 1864. III. 221.¹
— Plantae dalmaticae nunc primum editae. 1830. 1826. I. 447.
— Plantae quaedam Aegypti. 1836. I. 487.
— Plantae quaedam . . . in Aegypto . . . detectae. 1836. I. 487.
— Plantarum serbicarum pemptas. 1860. II. 478.¹
— Recensio altera plantarum . . . quas Hortus patavinus eoht. 1858. I. 63.
— Relazione intorno alla malattia dell' Uva. 1854. III. 576.
— Revisio plantarum minus cognitarum quas Hortus patavinus colit. 1855. I. 522.¹
— stirpium dalmaticarum specimen. 1826. I. 447.
— Sulla vegetazione . . . dell' isola di Lacroma. 1863. I. 427.
— & **Saccardo,** P. A. Catalogo delle piante vascolari del Veneto. 1869. I. 428.
A visit to a vegetable giant. 1847. II. 149.²
A visit to the Big trees. 1866. II. 51.¹
Una visita 'á la Escuela de montes. 1887. IV. 540.³
Visites au Muséum d'histoire naturelle. 1900. I. 60.¹
Visitor, (*pseud.*). The Araucaria imbricata. 1880. III. 299.¹
Vislotzki, S. M. *See* Вислоцкий, С. М.
Visschere, P. de. L'Abelia floribunda Done. 1897. III. 748.¹
Visser, H. C. Over het werkzame bestanddeel van den bast van Streblus asper. 1896. III. 381.¹
Visser, R. Coffea stenophylla. 1898. III. 743.¹
— De cultuur van Ceara-rubber. 1900. III. 520.²
Vitale, A. Le cubage des Sapins. 1888. IV. 218.
— É legale l' accertamento mancando l' avviso. 1897. IV. 277.
— Sopra un nuovo metodo di cubatura degli Abeti. 1888. IV. 218.
— Un' osservazione sulla moltiplicazione agamica del Faggio. 1898. IV. 496.
Vitalis, L. De invoering . . . van het stelsel van kultures op Java. 1851. III. 128.
Le Viti americani. III. 23.³
La viticulture algérienne. *See* BERTRAND. 1889. III. 559.¹
Vitman, Fulgenzio. De medicatis herbarum facultatibus liber. 1770. III. 238.¹ .

— Saggio dell' istoria erbaria délle alpi di Pistoja. 1773. I. 424.
— Summa plantarum. 1789. I. 258.
Vito, Giuseppe. Della ramificazione nelle Solanacee. 1895. II. 775.¹
Vito Fiscicelli, Francesco de. Memoria sulla conservazione del legname di Quercia. 1819. IV. 513.
Vitray, BOUCHÉ DE. *See* BOUCHÉ DE VITRAY.
Vitturi, Rados Antonio Michieli, *conte*. Sopra la manna di Frassino. 1791. IV. 536.¹
— Memoria sull' introduzione degli Ulivi. 1792. III. 675.¹
Viulmen (= ? Vuillemin). *See* BIONЛЬMEHЪ.
Vivenot-Lamy. Emploi du bois cru dans les hauts-fourneaux. 1859. IV. 431.¹
Vivet. Note sur la culture des Erythrines. 1861. III. 475.²
— Note sur le kermès du Laurier-rose. 1869. III. 689.¹
Viviand-Morel, Victor. Cas de tératologie observés sur un Fuchsia. 1883. II. 643.²
— Exemple d'inflorescence anticipée. 1879. II. 280.¹
— Figue prolifère. 1890. II. 150.².
— Hybridations de Rosiers. 1888. III. 450.
— Multiplication des Bruyères. 1867. III. 650.¹
— Note sur l'Acer Pseudo-Platanus L. 1890. II. 479.²
— Note sur les Genista pilosa. 1896. II. 360.²
— Polymorphisme des feuilles du Lierre. 1891. II. 649.²
— Production et mérite des hybrides. 1893. I. 246.¹
— On Rosa polyantha. 1889. III. 456.¹
Viviani, Dominicus. Appendix ad Florae corsicae prodromum. 1824. I. 419.¹
— Elenchus plantarum hor. botanici J. Car. Dinegro. 1802. I. 61, V. VIII.²
— Florae corsicae specierum novarum . . . diagnosis. 1824. I. 419.¹
— Florae italicae fragmenta. 1804. I. 425.
— Florae italicae fragmenta; seu, Plantae rariores. 1808. I. 425.
— Florae libycae specimen. 1824. I. 484.
— Memoria sopra alcuni plagi in botanica. 1838. I. 268.
— Plantarum aegyptiarum decades. 1830. I. 487.
— Saggio sulla maniera d' impedire la confusione. 1800. I. 253.²
— Della struttura degli organi elementari nelle piante. 1831. I. 86.
— Voyage dans les Apennins de la cidevant Ligurie. 1807. I. 425.
Vivier. Le cubage des Sapins. 1881. IV. 218.
Vivier. Étude sur les formes de la tige du Sapin. 1870. IV. 446.¹
Vivier, A. De l'exploitabilité relative au maximum de rente. 1884. IV. 252.
Vivier, Édouard. L'administration des eaux et forêts . . . Gers. 1885. IV. 27.²
Vivier, F. & **Deiss,** E. Plantes à caoutchouc de Malaisie. 1899. III. 232.¹
Vlaanderen, C. L. & **Mulder,** G. J. Over de zuren uit koffy. 1859. III. 740.²
Vlaanderen, N. C. Waterzucht in de Koffiebessen. 1898. III. 737.
O **vlastnostech** a užitku Jeřábu. 1858. III. 460.¹
Vlissingen, P. FENTENER VAN. *See* FENTENER VAN VLISSINGEN, P.
Vlugtige blikken op den plantengroei van Suriname. 1855. III. 268.¹
Vochenberg, Johann, TOLLAT VON. *See* TOLLAT VON VOCHENBERG, Johann.
Vocke, A. Niedere Sträucher.. 1855. III. 121.²
— *See also* KOEHNE, Emil, VOCKE, A. & DRUDE, Oscar.
Voechting, Hermann. Der Bau . . . des Stammes der Melastomeen. 1875. II. 635.²
— Über die Bedeutung des Lichtes für . . . Cacteen. 1894. II. 588.²
— Beiträge zur Morphologie . . . der Rhipsalideen. 1873. II. 588.¹
— Die Bewegungen der Blüthen und Früchte. 1882. I. 197.²
— Über Blüthen-Anomalien. 1898. I. 115.²
— Du développement des organes dans le règne végétal. 1884. III. 37.¹
— Ueber den Einfluss der strahlenden Wärme auf die Blüthenentfaltung der Magnolia. 1898. II. 211.²
— Ueber den Einfluss niedriger Temperatur auf die Sprossrichtung. 1898. I. 194.
— Ueber den Fruchtstand von Raphia. 1876. II. 74.²
— Ueber die Lichtstellung der Laubblätter. 1888. I. 230.
— Ueber Organbildung im Pflanzenreich. 1878. I. 187.

Voechting, Hermann (*continued*).
— Ueber Spitze und Basis an den Pflanzenorganen. 1880. I. 195,² *III. 204.³*
— Ueber Transplantation am Pflanzenkörper. 1892. I. 208.³
— Ueber die Ursachen der Zygomorphie. 1885. I. 115.¹
— Über Zygomorphie und deren Ursachen. 1886. I. 100.¹
Voeikof, Aleksandr Ivanovitch. Der Einfluss der Wälder auf das Klima. 1885. IV. 54.
— On the influence of forests upon climate. 1885. IV. 54.
Voelcker, Augustus. On the composition . . . of Palm-nut kernel meal. 1865. III. 319.¹
Voelcker, B. Ueber Holzsamengewinnung. 1895. IV. 148.
Völcker, Karl. Untersuchungen über das Intervall zwischen der Blüthe und Fruchtreife von Aesculus. 1891. II. 482,² *840.¹*
Völker. Recherches sur l'huile de Ben. 1849. III. 409.¹
Völker, H. L. W. Forsttechnologie. 1803. IV. 381.
— Handbuch der Forsttechnologie. 1803. IV. 381.
— *See also* Фельькеръ, Г. Л. В.
Völter. Spät treibender Nussbaum. 1865. II. 114.¹
Vogel. Index plantarum Horti medici altorfini. 1790. I. 521.²
Vogel, (*jr.*). Notice sur le gutta-percha. 1848. III. 668.²
Vogel, August. Ueber die Absorption der Salze. 1841. I. 157.
— Sur l'absorption des sels. 1842. I. 161.
— Action of camphor on plant life. 1873. I. 211.
— Beiträge zur Kenntniss der sogenannten falschen China-rinden. 1876. III. 724.³
— Beitrag zur Kenntniss des Copal's. 1881. III. 233.²
— Beobachtungen über das Keimen. 1854. I. 203.
— Ueber den chemischen Vorgang des Keimens. 1854. I. 203.
— Einfluss des Stickstoffoxydgases. 1846. I. 211.
— Einige Versuche über das Keimen der Samen. 1870. I. 203.
— Expériences sur la germination. 1854. I. 203.
— Ueber den Gehalt der weinsauren Salze in . . . der Wein-rebe. 1848. II. 508.¹
— De l'influence du gaz de protoxyde d'azote. 1846. I. 211.
— Quaestio de hesperidum Malis. 1832. II. 402.¹
— Ueber Säurereaktion der Blüthen. 1879. I. 185.¹
— Ueber die Veränderung einiger Blumen- und Blüthen far-ben durch Ammoniakgas. 1870. I. 184.
— Ueber das Verhältniss der Camphergruppe zum Pflan-zenleben. 1873. I. 211.
— Ueber die Verschiedenheit der Aschen einzelner Pflanzen-theile. 1861. I. 153.
— & **Reischauer**, C. Über einen . . . Körper in den Frucht-schaalen der Juglans. 1856. II. 114.¹
— & **Wittwer**, W. C. Ueber den Einfluss der Vegetation auf die Atmosphäre. 1851. I. 170.
— — De l'influence de la végétation sur l'atmosphère. 1851. I. 170.
Vogel, C. J. de. De Koffie-cultuur op de onderneming Kan-dangan. 1895. III. 731.
Vogel, Christoph. Einige empfehlenswerte Sorbus-Arten. 1897. III. 459.¹
— Pirus Pollveria. 1897. III. 460.¹
Vogel, E. Central-afrikanische Datteln. 1854. III. 328.²
Vogel, E. F. Chronologischer Raupenkalender. 1837. IV. 91.³
Vogel, H. Flora von Thüringen. 1875. I. 387.
— Der Holzschwemmbetrieb. 1869. IV. 390.²
Vogel, H. A. von. Notice sur l'art de revivifier les fleurs fanées. 1819. I. 191.²
Vogel, J. & others. Forest management. 1875. IV. 244.
Vogel, J. R. Theodor. De Caesalpinieis Brasiliae. 1837. II. 318.²
— Dalbergiearum genera brasiliensia. 1837. .II. 318.²
— Generis Cassiae synopsis. 1837. II. 342.³
— De Hedysareis Brasiliae. 1858. II. 318.²
— Leguminosae. 1843. II. 318.¹
— Leguminosae adjectis quas cl. Ehrenberg in Hispaniola collegit. 1836. II. 318.¹
— Observationes de Bauhiniis americanis. 1839. II. 334.²
— De Swartzieis observationes. 1837. II. 318.¹
— Synopsis generis Cassiae. 1837. II. 342.²
— Synopsis generis Cassiae altera pars. 1837. II. 342.³·¹
— *See also* SCHLEIDEN, M. J. & VOGEL, Theodor.
Vogel, Sir Julius. New Zealand forests. 1874. IV. 380.²
Vogel, Louis. Das Pfropfen der Resinosen. 1868. III. 294.¹

Vogel, Rudolph Augustin. Historia materiae medicae. 1758. III. 238.¹
— De statu plantarum, quo noctu dormire dicuntur. 1759. I. 198.
— De verioribus balsami Meccani noctis. 1763. III. 510.²
Vogelgesang, H. Aphoristische Betrachtungen über den Aus-bau der Holzarten. 1887. IV. 69.
— Beiträge zur Naturgeschichte der essbaren Kastanie. 1877. IV. 492.³
— Gedanken über Forstorganisation. 1881. IV. 287.
— Ueber Holzverkauf und Holztaxen. 1876. IV. 388.¹
— Künstliche Maikäfer-Brutstätten. 1876. IV. 203.
— Noch ein Wort zur Engerlingsfrage. 1887. IV. 203.
Vogel, Felix. Flore fourragère. 1836. III. 223.¹
Vogelmann, Vollrath. Die Forstpolizei-Gesetzgebung. 1871. IV. 317.²
— Die Reutberge des Schwarzwaldes. 1871. IV. 118, *133.*
Vogelsberger, Albert. Ueber die systematische Bedeutung der anatomischen Charaktere der Hedysareen. 1893. II. 321.¹
Ueber **Vogelschutzgehölze**. 1885. III. 215.¹
Ueber **Vogelschutzgehölze** zur Anlegung von Nistplätzen. 1882. III. 215.¹
Voget. Ueber die Benutzung des Samens des gemeinen Spill-baums auf Brennöl. 1833. III. 532.¹
Voget, A. R. L. Anleitung zur Kenntnis der vorzüglichsten Giftpflanzen. 1829. III. 59.³
Vogl, August Emil. Über den Bau des Holzes von Ferreira. 1873. II. 358.¹
— Beiträge zur Kenntnis der Milchsaftorgane. 1866. I. 136.¹
— Beiträge zur Pflanzenanatomie. 1869. II. 813.¹
— Ueber die Chinabäume. 1867. II. 812. — 1868. III. 718.
— Die Chinarinden des Wiener Grosshandels. 1867. II. 813.¹
— Ueber Harzkörner in der Rinde von Portlandia. 1866. II. 827.²
— Kamala. 1865. II. 447.²
— Zur Kenntniss der chinesischen Gelbbeeren. 1871. II. 817.³¹
— Ueber den Milchsaft der Pflanzen. 1867. I. 181.²
— Die Milchsaftorgane der Cinchonen. 1869. II. 813.¹
— Zur näheren . . . Kenntniss des Bitterholzes. 1864. II. 415.¹
— The origin of the gum of Quebracho Colorado. 1881. II. 360.¹
— Ueber Pfeilgifte. 1870. III. 260.²
— Ueber Pflanzenwachs. 1870. III. 226.¹
— Phytohistologische Beiträge, I. 1865. II. 447.²
— Ueber Tamarisken-Gallen. 1875. III. 612.¹
— Ueber den Thee. 1870. III. 607.
— Untersuchungen über den Bau . . . der wichtigsten Farbe-hölzer. 1873. I. 125, *III. 256.*
— Ueber vegetabilische Fette und Fett liefernde Pflanzen. 1869. III. 224.²
— Über das Vorkommen von Gerb- und verwandten Stoffen in unterirdischen Pflanzentheilen. 1866. I. 183.
Vogler. Einführung des metrischen Masses. 1875. IV. 214.
— Introduction des mesures métriques. 1875. IV. 214.
— Sind in Folge der Konkurrenz . . . Aenderungen in der Ver-jüngung . . . unserer vorherschend Buchen enthaltenden Bestände nothwendig. 1884. IV. 498.
Vogler, H. Verzeichniss seiner auserlesenen Sammlung bo-tanischer Werke. 1818. I. 1, *III. 1.*
Vogler, K. W. 502.¹
Vogler, Johann Philipp. Versuche mit den Scharlachbeeren. 1780. IV. 502.¹
Vogler, K. W. M. De invloed van het water op de Koffie. 1900. III. 728.¹
— Is er al dan niet degeneratie? 1900. III. 733.²
— De keuze van Koffiezaad. 1900. III. 733.²
— Onderhoud van Koffietuinen. 1900. III. 728.¹
— Het schoonhouden der tuinen. 1899. III. 727.
— Het uitdunnen van vrucht. 1899. III. 727.
— Veredeling door vermenigvuldiging hybridisatie. 1899. III. 731.
Voglino, Pietro. I funghi più dannosi. 1891. III. 194.
— Di una nuova malattia dell' Azalea indica. 1899. III. 660.²
Vogt, Carl. Leçons sur les animaux utiles et nuisibles. 1875. IV. 90.¹
Vogt, Traugott Karl August. De Junipero Sabina. 1803. III. 304.¹
Vogtherr, Max. Ueber die Früchte der Randia dumetorum. 1894. III. 747.¹

Vohl, Hermann. Sur la chlorophylle. 1865. ˙I. 141.
— Darstellung des reinen schwefligsauren Kupferoxydul-Ammoniaks. 1865. I. 141.
Vohralík, F. Pěstování Angreštu a Rybízu v zahradách. 1883. III. 413.[2]
— O pěstování Oříšků Lískových. 1879. III. 357.[2]
— Pěstování Růží. 1884. III. 452.
— Růže ů onkovité. 1883. III. 450.
The voice of a tree from the Middlesex Fells. See WRIGHT, Elizur. 1883. V. xxx.[2]
Voigt, (*Amtsrath*). Mittheilung über Schälwaldanlagen. 1857. IV. 505.
Voigt, Albert. Ueber den Bau . . . des Samens . . . von Myristica. 1885. II. 221.[1]
— Die Botanischen Institute der freien und Hansestadt Hamburg. 1897. I. 49.
— Untersuchungen über Bau . . . von Samen mit ruminiertem Endosperm. 1888. II. 63,[1] *215,*[2] *220.*[3]
Voigt, Friedrich Ernst. De Junipero Sabina. 1826. III. 304.[1]
Voigt, Friedrich Siegmund. Almanach der Natur. 1832. V. VII.[2]
— Catalogus plantarum . . . in . Hortis ducalibus . . . jenensi et belvederensi. 1812. I. 45.
— Darstellung des natürlichen Pflanzensystems. 1806. I. 259.
— Dissertatio sistens conspectum tractatus de plantis hybridis. 1802. I. 245.
— Geschichte des Pflanzenreichs. 1847. I. 269.
— Handbuch der praktischen Botanik. 1850. I. 383.
— Handwörterbuch der botanischen Kunstsprache. 1803. I. 70.
— Lehrbuch der Botanik. 1808. I. 85.
— Plantarum rariorum in Horto belvederensi cultarum descriptiones. 1825. I. 46.
— System der Botanik. 1808. I. 85.
— Wörterbuch der botanischen Kunstsprache. 1803. I. 70.
Voigt, Johann Otto. Hortus suburbanus calcuttensis. 1845. I. 66.[2]
Voigt, R. Weniger bekannte Treibsträucher. 1900. III. 177.[1]
Voigtlander-Tetzner, Walter. Pflanzengeographische Beschreibung . . . des Brockengebietes. 1895. I. 389.
Voigts, J. von. Beherzigungen für diejenigen welche sich dem Forsthaushalte als Vorgesetzte zu widmen gedenken. 1782. IV. 213.
— Forst-Catechismus. 1775. IV. 95.
Voiry, Raymond Paul Eugène. Contribution á l'étude chimique des huiles essentielles de quelques Myrtacées. 1888. III. 633.[1]
— Sur l'essence d'Eucalyptus globulus. 1888. IV. 533.[2]
— Sur l'essence de Cajéput. 1888. III. 636.
— See also BOUCHARDAT, G. & VOIRY, R.
. & Bouchardat, G. Sur l'essence d'Aspic. 1888. III. 69.[2]
Voisin, (*abbé*). See JULIEN, Stanislas & VOISIN, (*abbé*).
Voisin, Auguste & Liouville, Henry. Sur quelques effets produits par l'emploi thérapeutique du curare. 1867. III. 683.[1]
Voith, Ignaz von. Ueber ein sonderbares Gebilde in der Ulme. 1837. II. 143.[1]
Volbehr, Berend F. K. J. Untersuchungen über die Quellung der Holzfaser. 1896. I. 149,[1] *IV. 412.*[2]
Volck, Phil. De iurisdictione forestali. 1635. IV. 313.
Volckamer, Johann Christoph. Continuation der Nürnbergischen Hesperidum. 1708. II. 400.[2]
— Hesperidum Norimbergensium sive de Malorum Citreorum . . . cultura et usu libri IV. 1708. II. 400.[2]
— Nürnbergische Hesperides. 1708. II. 400.[2]
Volckamer, Johann Georg. Opobalsami orientalis . . . examen. 1644. III. 510.[2]
Volckamer, Johann Georg, (*jr.*). Flora noribergensis. 1700. I. 289, *372.*
Volckmann, J. Ueber die Anwendung . . . des Pfropfens als Veredlungsmethode. 1878. III. 162.
Volger, Otto. Die Tanne als Ansiedler auf einer Weide. 1860. I. 234.[2]
Volkens, Georg. Ueber bemerkenswerte Bäume des Kilimandscharo. 1895. I. 493.
— Ueber die Bestäubung einiger Loranthaceen. 1899. VI. 159,[1] *174.*[1]
— Die cactusartigen Euphorbien Ostafrikas. 1897. II: 441.[2]
— Chenopodiaceae. 1893. II. 381.[1]
— Die Flora der aegyptisch-arabischen Wüste. 1887. I. 489.

— Zur Flora der aegyptisch-arabischen Wüste. Eine vorläufige Skizze. 1886. I. 489.
— Zur Frage der Aufforstung in Deutsch-Ost-Afrika. 1897. IV. 168.[2]
— Ueber Gambia-Mahagoni in Ostafrika. 1897. II. 421.[1]
— Gummi aus Deutsch-Ostafrika. 1897. III. 463.[2]
— Die Kalkdrüsen der Plumbagineen. 1884. II. 696.[1]
— Zur Kenntniss der Beziehungen zwischen Standort und anatomischem Bau. 1884. I. 218.
— Kulturerfolge des Versuchsgartens von Victoria. 1897. III. 131.[2]
— Kulturnachweisungen ostafrikanischer Stationen. 1897. III. 131.[2]
— Kulturnotizen aus der Kaiserl. Versuchsstation Kwai. 1897. III. 131.[2]
— Ueber Pflanzen mit lackirten Blättern. 1890. I. 135.
— Ueber Wasserausscheidung . . . an den Blättern. 1882. I. 169.[1]
— See also GÜRKE, Maximilian & VOLKENS, Georg; SCHWEINFURTH, Georg & VOLKENS, Georg.
Volkmann, Heinrich. Ueber die Bedeutung, Anlage und Bewirthschaftung der Bannwälder. 1878. IV. 177.[1]
Der **Volksgärtner**. III. 25.
De **Volksvlijt**. III. 15.
Vollmann, Franz. Katalog der Bibliothek der Kgl. botanischen Gesellschaft in Regensburg. 1895. I. 3.[1]
Vollmar, Georg. Der gegenwärtige Stand der Waldschutzfrage. 1880. IV. 177.[1]
— Waldverwüstung und Überschwemmung. 187.? IV. 50.
Vollmer. Einige Mittheilung über die forstlichen Verhältnisse in der Provinz Pommern. 1892. IV. 354.
Vollständige Anleitung zu einer systematischen Pomologie. See MANGER, H. L. 1780. III. 70.
Vollständige Anweisung schöne Rosen . . . zu erziehen. 1820. III. 451.[2] V. xxix.[1]
Vollständige nach dem Decimalmass berechnete Tabellen. See DUVE, G. C. 1801. IV. 221.
Vollziehungsverordnung über das Bundesgesetz betreffend . . . Oberaufsicht über die Forstpolizei. See RÉGLEMENT d'exécution . . . 1876. IV. 330.
Vollziehungs-Verordnung zum Bundesgesetz betreffend die eidgenössische Oberaufsicht über die Forstpolizei. 1879. IV. 306.
Volmar, P. Ueber den Anbau der Lärche. 1868. IV. 449.
— Zur Aufastungsfrage. 1873. IV. 171.
— Zur Buchenzucht. 1863. IV. 494.
— Fehler beim Buchenhochwaldbetriebe. 1869. IV. 495.
— Fichten-Stecklinge. 1898. II. 36.[1]
— Das Forstmeister- oder das Oberförster-System. 1876. IV. 287.
— Zur Forstwegebau-Frage. 1890. IV. 389.
— Ein Frass vom Rothschwanze. 1879. IV. 497.
— Ueber Holzvertrieb. 1899. IV. 388.[2]
— Die neuen Betriebsarten. 1880. IV. 198.
— Zur Pressler'schen Theorie. 1873. IV. 256.
— Die Ueberführung herabgekommener Eichen-Mittelwaldungen in gemischten Hochwald. 1870. IV. 128, *506.*
— Die Verjüngung in Löcher- und Koulissen-Hieben. 1890. IV. 508.
— Zur Verjüngung der Maikäferlarve. 1873. IV. 203.
— Ueber Vorhauungserträge. 1877. IV. 244.
Vulmerange, Marcel. Procédé graphique pour figurer les éléments constitutifs d'une forêt. 1890. IV. 245.
Volmerange, R. Mémoire sur les réformes à opérer dans le service forestier. 1896. IV. 293.[1]
Voln. Le caoutchouc. 1863. III. 229.
Volney, Constantin François, *comte de*. Tableau du climat et du sol des États-Unis. 1803. III. 262.[1]
Volodkevitch, S. N. See Володкевичъ, С. Н.
Volovitch, G. B. See Воловичъ, Г. Б.
Volta, Giovanni Serafino. Nuove ricerche . . . sopra il sessualismo di alcune piante. 1795. I. 199.
Volume sur pied de futaies de Hêtre de l'Ardenne. 1898. IV. 499.[1]
Volynski. See Волынскій.
Volz, (*Oberreallehrer*). Rebsorten . . . in Württemberg. 1852. III. 552.
Volz, K. W. Beiträge zur Geschichte der Zierpflanzen. 1851. I. 241.[2]
— Beiträge zur Kulturgeschichte. 1852. I. 241.[2]
Vonck, L. M. De Benzoëcultuur in de Residentie Palembang. 1891. III. 671.[1]
Vonhausen, Wilhelm. Die Beförderung der Keimung durch Chlor. 1858. I. 203.

Vonhausen, Wilhelm (*continued*).
— Ein Beitrag zur Behandlung der Forstgärten. 1880. IV. 150.
— Ein Beitrag zur Eichenschälwaldwirthschaft. 1877. IV. 506.
— Die Benutzung des Wassers in den Forstgärten. 1877. IV. 144.[1]
— Die Düngung der Forstgärten. 1872. IV. 144.[2]
— Einige Modificationen der Hügelpflanzung. 1876. IV. 153.[2]
— Das Einschlagen des Blitzes in die Bäume. 1861. IV. 193.[2]
— Der Eisbruch in der Winterhauch. 1864. IV. 190.
— Die Erziehung der Akazien- und Platanenpflanzen. 1876. IV. 520,[2] 523.[1]
— Ein interessanter Blitzschlag. 1879. IV. 510, 543.[1]
— Die natürliche Verjüngung der Holzbestände. 1871. IV. 139.[2]
— Die Raubwirthschaft in den Waldungen. 1867. IV. 71.
— Der schlagweise Hochwaldbetrieb. 1882. IV. 128.
— Das Stocksprengen. 1877. IV. 386.
— Untersuchung über den Rindenbrand. 1873. IV. 192.[1]
— Verdient die horst- und streifenweise oder die Einzelinsprengung den Vorzug? 1881. IV. 137.[2]
— Die Verjüngungsdauer der Weisstanne. 1870. IV. 444.[2]
— Die Volumveränderung des Holzes . . . als Ursache der Frostrisse. 1861. IV. 191.[1]
— Der Waldschneckenbohrer. 1876. IV. 152.
— Zurückweisung der Angriffe des Herrn Medicinalraths Mohr. 1863. IV. 190.
Vonhöne, Heinrich. Ueber das Hervorbrechen endogener Organe. 1880. I. 103.
Voordeelen van de aankweeking der carolinischen Wasbooms. 1827. III. 353.[1]
Voordeelen van de cultuur der Acacia. 1806. IV. 522.[2]
Voorhees, Eduard B. Manuring orchards. 1896. III. 152.
Voorneman, F. K. Iets over semoet graman. 1861. III. 735.
Voorst, Adolph van. Catalogus plantarum Horti academici Lugduni Batavi. 1633. I. 50.
Voort, J. A. van der. De gouvernements-Koffie-kultur op Java. 1872. III. 729.[2]
Voralberg — Ferdinandeum. *See* FERDINANDEUM . . . I. 27.
Vorarbeiten zu einer Flora Bayerns. 1896. II. 195.[2]
Vorarlberg — Forstverein. *See* FORSTVEREIN FÜR NORDTIROL. IV. 14.
Die Vorbereitung der Eleven für den Staatsforstdienst. 1878. IV. 36.[2]
Vorderman, A. G. Eurycoma longifolia. 1890. III. 508.[1]
— Over het gebruik der Djamblang zaden. 1888. III. 638.[1]
— Inlandsche namen van eenige Madoereesche planten. 1900. I. 76.[1]
— Jambulsamen gegen Diabetes. 1888. III. 638.[1]
— Javaansche geneesmiddelen I. 1894. III. 276.[1]
— Klapper en Malindjo-cultuur in Bantam. 1896. III. 312,[2] 323.[1]
— Kritische beschouwingen over Dr. C. L. van der Burg's "Materia medica." 1886. III. 274.[2]
— Mangga's kunstmatig onder bescherming van mieren. 1895. II. 457.[1]
— Pala Lelaki. 1894. III. 402.[1]
— De Pangium edule Reinw. 1900. III. 615.[1]
— Planten-animisme op Java. 1897. I. 512.
— Rasamala. 1894. III. 416.[2]
— De transmigratie en signatuurleer in de Javaansche geneeskunde. 1894. III. 259.[2]
— De zaadkernen van den Pitjoeng. 1891. III. 615.[1]
Die "Vorhauungen" im Buchen-Hochwalde. 1865. IV. 494.
Ueber das Vorkommen . . . der Cypresse. 1894. IV. 484.[2]
Das Vorkommen der Eibe. 1896. II. 11.[2]
Ueber das Vorkommen der Zirbelkiefer. 1867. II. 41.[1]
Vorkommen des Mannits. 1839. III. 407.[2]
Das Vorkommen und die Cultur der einheimischen Rhododendra. 1864. III. 656.
Vorländer, (*Oberförster*). Ueber das Ausästen der Bäume. 1841. IV. 170.
Vorlaender, J. J. Die Waldwirthschaft im Wiehengebirge. 1863. IV. 118.
Vorläufige Instruktion für die fürstlich Oranien-nassauischen Amts- oder Forstjäger. 1801. IV. 301.
Vorläufige Instruktion für die fürstlich Oranien-nassauischen Förster. 1801. IV. 301.
Vorläufige Instruktion für die fürstlich Oranien-nassauischen Oberförster. 1801. IV. 301.

Vorlege-Blaetter zum Gebrauch beim Unterricht im Situations-Zeichnen. n. d. IV. 263.
Voronof, Genadi. *See* Воронов, Генадій.
Vorreith. Ueber die Anzucht exotischer Holzpflanzen. 1850. IV. 127.[2]
Non vorremmo essere gli ultimi. 1899. III. 192.[1]
Vorschläge nach welchen der Transport der Bäume . . . *See* DU HAMEL DU MONCEAU, H. L. 1753. III. 154.[2]
Vorschläge zur Verbesserung der Kiefernholzsaat. *See* B. 1785. III. 309,[1] IV. 471.
Vorschlag einer nützlichen Zimmeranlage. 1752. IV. 115.
Vorschlag zur bessern Pflegung . . . der Wälder. 1842. IV. 277.
Vorschrift für die Vermessung, Schätzung und Betriebseinrichtung der Reichs-Forste. 1857. IV. 307.[1]
Vorschrift über die Beobachtung der Lärchenkrankheit. 1872. IV. 450.
Vorschrift zu der Aufstellung der Hauungs-Controle. 1840. IV. 300.[2]
Vorschrift zur Erziehung von Fichten- und Weisstannen-Pflanzen. 1877. IV. 146.[2]
Vorschriften für die Abschätzung und Einrichtung der Staatsforste in Württemberg. 1850. IV. 247.[2]
Vorschriften für die Ausführung der Forstvermessungs- und Abschätzungs-Arbeiten. 1899. IV. 302.
Vorschriften für die Bearbeitung der Wirthschaftspläne in den Domanialforsten. 1880. IV. 301.
Vorschriften für die Bearbeitung der Wirthschaftspläne in . . . Hannover. 1860. IV. 248.[1]
Vorschriften für die Forstvermessung und Forsteinrichtung. 1866. IV. 302.
Vorschriften für die grossh. badischen Bezirks-Forstbehörden zur Besorgung der Kaufs- und Tauschgeschäfte. 1846. IV. 289,[2] 299.
Vorschriften für die periodischen Revisionen des Waldstandes. 1849. IV. 247,[2] 300.[1]
Vorschriften für die Vermessung der Domanialforsten. 1860. IV. 301.
Vorschriften für die Vermessung und die Bearbeitung von Wirthschaftsplänen. 1866. IV. 302.
Vorschriften für die Verwaltung und Bewirthschaftung der Waldungen der Gemeinden. 1894. IV. 298.[2]
Vorschriften für Forstkartirung, Flächenberechnung. 1833. IV. 263.
Vorschriften über Ausbildung, Prüfung und Anstellung für die unteren Stellen des Forstdienstes. 1880. IV. 33.[1]
Vorschriften über Ausbildung, Prüfungen und Anstellung im Forstdienst. 1880. IV. 33.[1]
Vorschriften über die Anwendung des metrischen Maasses. 1872. IV. 299.
Vorschriften über die Ausbildung und Prüfung für den Forstverwaltungs- und Forstschutzdienst. 1880. IV. 33.[1]
Vorschriften über die Benutzung . . . der Dienstgehöfte der Staats-Forstverwaltung. 1893. IV. 302.
Vorschriften über die Legung der Forst-Geld-Rechnungen. 1893. IV. 302.
Vorschriften wegen Ausführung der Forst-Vermessungs- und Abschätzungs-Arbeiten. 1891. IV. 246.
Vorschriften zur Anwendung der Instruction für die Holzhauer in den Communalwaldungen. 1827. IV. 300.[2]
Vorschriften zur Vollziehung der Verfügung des K. [württembergischen] Finanzministeriums. 1850. IV. 303.[2]
Vorst, van der. Les plantations feuillues en Campine. 1898. IV. 119.[2]
Vorst, P. van der. Nog iets over het weghalen van strooisel. 1891. IV. 72.
Vorster, Karl, *Freyherrn* von. *See* Von den REBENSTICHERN. 1771. III. 562.[1]
Vorsterman van Oijen, A. A. Perzikboomen uit zaad. 1876. III. 441.[1]
Vorsterman van Oyen, G. A. De behandeling der fruitboomen. 1875. III. 140.[1]
"Vorsündfluthliche" Eiche. 1886. IV. 515.[2]
Vort Havebrug. Ed. by P. Hansen. 1911. III. 11.
Vort Havebrug. Ed. by J. Uldall. III. 11.
Ueber die vortheilhafteste Behandlungs-Methode bei Besamung . . . der Kiefern. *See* BJÖRN, Sören. 1807. IV. 471.
Vorträge aus dem Gebiete der Naturwissenschaften. I. 15.
Vortrag betreffend die Verminderung der Forsten. 1841. IV. 282.[2]
Vorzeitiges Zapfentragen. 1890. IV. 484.[1]
Die vorzüglichsten Giftpflanzen Deutschlands. 1801. III. 72.

Vos, André de. *See* DE Vos, Andre.
Vos, C. de. Het Acer of Eschdoorngeslacht. 1878. III. 533.²
— De bevruchting van Aucuba. 1883. III. 645.¹
— Boomen en heesters met witte takken. 1880. III. 208.¹
— Buxus. 1876. III. 522.²
— Het Fraxinus-geslacht. 1877. III. 672.¹
— Het geslacht Magnolia. 1876. III. 399.¹
— Hydrangea. 1876. III. 411.¹
— Iets over Cytisus Laburnum purpurascens. 1863. III. 480.²
— Iets over treurboomen. 1879. III. 204.¹
— Korte schets van de geschiedenis der plantkunde. 1888. I. 80.¹
— Mijn laatste woord over de zaaikwestie. 1877. I. 247.
— Padus Lauro-Cerasus. 1878. III. 437.²
— Populus canadensis. 1886. III. 345.²
— Populus canadensis aurea. 1876. III. 345.²
— Roest op de Pereboomen. 1881. III. 446.¹
— De Roos. 1879. II. 290,² III. 449.
— Het Sambucus geslacht. 1877. III. 751.²
— Woordenboek der voornaamste heesters. 1867. III. 75.²
Les Vosges. 1899. IV. 544.²
Vosges — Société d'émulation du département . . . *See* So-
    CIÉTÉ . . . I. 23.
Vosges — Société d'horticulture. *See* SOCIÉTÉ . . . III. 22.
Voskressensky, A. Sur la théobromine. 1841. III. 594.
Voss, (*Hofgärtner, Sanssouci*). Ueber Pflaumentreiberei. 1830. III. 432.²
Voss, Andreas. Deutzia scabra Thunbg. 1896. II. 239.¹
— Grundzüge der Gartenkultur. 1894. III. 36.¹
— Vilmorin's Blumengärtnerei. 1894. III. 75.² *See also* Voss, A. & SIEBERT, A. 1896. I. 271.¹
— Warum und inwieweit schadet das Zútiefpflanzen . . . den Gehölzen? 1886. III. 169.²
— Wurzelschnitt . . . bei Palmen. 1897. III. 318.²
Voss, C. Kurze Anleitung zur Veredlung . . . der Rosen. 1872. III. 452.
Voss, Leopold. Bibliotheca physico-medica. 1835. I. 2, *III. 1.*
Voss, Wilhelm. Merkwürdige Verwachsungen von Stämmen der Rothbuche. 1887. I. 209,¹ *IV. 497.*
Vossfeldt, (*Oberförster*). Angaben über ein neues Verfahren zur Erziehung von Eichenschälwald. 1867. IV. 506.
— Beitrag zur Erziehung von Eichenschälwaldungen. . 1867. IV. 506.
— Bericht über die Exkursion . . . in das königl. Forstrevier Scheidelwitz. 1865. IV. 353.
— Beschreibung und Anwendung des Rayolbohrers. 1853. IV. 152.
— Dimensionen und Ausnutzung einer . . . Weisstanne. 1853. IV. 447.¹
— Dimensionen und Sortiments-Massenergebniss einer . . . Fichte. 1854. IV. 460.¹
— Zur Erziehung der Eiche. 1855. IV. 505.
— Ueber die Erziehung von Kiefern- und Fichten-Mischbe-ständen. 1865. IV. 138.¹
— Holzmassen-Ergebniss eines . . . Weisstannen- und Fichten-Bestandes. 1855. IV. 236.
— Holzmassen-Ergebniss . . . eines 12jährigen Weisserlen-bestandes. 1858. IV. 489.²
— Neues Verfahren bei der Anlage von Nadelholz-Saat-kämpen. 1865. IV. 150.
— Ueber die sociale Frage . . . in der Forstwirthschaft. 1873. IV. 269.
— Ueber Waldschönheitspflege. 1855. IV. 136.²
Vossion, L. Notice sur la culture du ver à soie. 1893. III. 148.²
Votchal, E. *See* BOTЧALЬ, E.
Vothmann, J. G. Lærebog i' den oekonomiske Haugedyrk-ning. 1817. III. 100.³
Votum zur beabsichtigten Vereinigung der K. k. Forsta-kademie zu Mariabrunn mit der . . . landwirthschaftlichen Hochschule. 1871. IV. 36.²
Vouga, Albert. Le Poirier Bataillard. 1867. II. 280.²
Vouga, E. Flora alpina. 1874. I. 436.
Voulgre. Le Congo français. 1897. I. 491.
Voute, Rapporten over Koffie. 1873. III. 729.²
Voute, E. J. Araucaria excelsa R. Br. 1890. III. 298.²
— Een en ander over tuinbouw. 1899. III. 129.¹
— Rozen. 1890. III. 453.¹
Voute, Robert. Korte beschouwing . : . van den Theehandel. 1792. III. 606.
Voûte, W. Caoutchouc uit schorsen. 1900. III. 232. ²
— Caoutchouc-winning uit schorsen. 1900. III. 232.²

Voyage à l'Isle de France, à l'Isle de Bourbon. *See* SAINT-PIERRE, J. H. B. de. 1773. III. 279.²
Voyage à la Martinique. *See* CHANVALON, J. B. T. de. 1763. I. 334, *III. 266.*
Voyage au Mont-Pilat. *See* LATOURRETTE, M. A. L. C. de. 1770. I. 405.
Voyage autour du monde par la frégate du roi la Boudeuse. *See* BOUGAINVILLE, L. A. de. 1771. I. 301.
Voyage autour du monde . . . sur la corvette La Coquille . . . 1822–25. *See* LESSON, R. P. 1826. I. 347.
Voyage autour du monde sur la frégate la Vénus . . . Bota-nique. *See* DECAISNE, Joseph. 1846. I. 303.
Voyage dans l'empire de flore. *See* HANIN, L. 1800. I. 84.
Voyage dans le Finistère. *See* CAMBRY, Jacques. 1799. I. 406.
Voyage de l'Arabie Heureuse. *See* LA ROQUE, Jean de. 1716. III. 738.
Voyage de Siam des pères jesuites. .*See* TACHARD, Guy. 1687. III. 276.¹
A voyage to Arabia Fœlix. *See* LA ROQUE, Jean de.' 1716. III. 738.
A voyage to the East Indies. *See* WESDIN, J. P. 1796. III. 277.
Vrabata, Josef. *See* WRABATA, Josef.
Vrangel, W., *baron*. *See* ВРАНГЕЛЬ, В., *барона*.
Vray, G. Le forçage de l'Acacia . . . dealbata. 1898. III. 465.¹
— Les Palmiers sur la côte méditerranéenne. 1897. III. 318.²
Vrbata, Josef. *See* WRABATA, Josef.
Vreeden, W., BUURMAN VAN. *See* BUURMAN VAN VREE-DEN, W.
Vremenniya massoviya tablitzy. *See* Временныя массовыя таблицы.
Vries, Hugo de. A. Mayer's antwoord op mijne beschouwinge. 1875. I. 180.¹
— Über abnormale Entstehung secundärer Gewebe. 1891. I. 124.
— Adam's Gouden regen. 1894. II. 368.²
— De ademhaling der planten. 1878. I. 170.
— Over het algemeen voorkomen van circulatie. . . in de veef-selcellen. 1882. I. 165.
— Over den anatomischen bouw van wondhout. 1875. I. 207.³
— Über die Bedeutung der Kalkablagerungen. 1881. I. 176.
— Bestuivingen van bloemen door insekten. 1875. I. 239.²
— Over de beteekenis der organische zuren. 1875. I. 180.¹
— De bevruchting der Berken. 1896. II. 118.²
— Over de beweging van het water. 1892. I. 168.
— Beweging van ranken en slingerplanten. 1872. I. 196.²
— On biastrepsis in its relation to cultivation. 1899. I. 245.
— Boschbeplanting der duinen. 1890. IV. 160.²
— Sur les causes des mouvements auxotoniques. 1880. I. 194.
— Sur le dédoublement des phyllopodès. 1893. I. 145.¹
— Ueber den Einfluss des Druckes auf die Ausbildung des Herbstholzes. 1872. I. 127.²
— Ueber den Einfluss des Rindendruckes auf den anato-mischen Bau des Holzes. 1875. I. 127.¹
— Über einige Nebenprodukte des pflanzlichen Stoffwechsels. 1881. I. 176.
— Ueber einige Ursachen der Richtung bilateralsymmet-rischer Pflanzentheile. 1874. I. 194.
— Ueber erbungleiche Kreuzungen. 1900. I. 246.¹
— Over de erfelijkheid der fasciatiën. 1894. I. 144.²
— Over de erfelijkheid van synfisen. 1895. I. 144.¹
— Over das Erfrieren der Pflanzen. 1878. I. 212.
— Flora van Nederland. 1870. I. 391.¹
— Sur la fonction des matières résineuses. 1882. I. 181.¹
— Ueber halbe Galton-Curven. 1894. I. 244.³
— Sur l'hérédité de la fasciation. 1894. I. 144.²
— Sur l'hérédité des soudures. 1895. I. 144.¹
— Hybridising of monstrosities. 1900. I. 246.¹
— Iets over de beweging van het water. 1882. I. 167.
— De l'influence de la pression du liber. 1876. I. 527.
— Sur l'injection des vrilles. 1880. I. 196.²
— Over den invloed der bastdrukking op den bouw der jaar-ringen. 1873. I. 127.²
— De invloed der temperatuur op de levensvershijnselen. 1870. I. 232.¹
— De kola-noot. 1886. III. 590.²
— Längenwachsthum der Ober- und Unterseite sich krüm-mender Ranken. 1874. I. 196.²

Vries, Hugo de (*continued*).
— Het leven der bloem. 1877. V. x.²
— Levensduur der zaden. 1888. I. 527.
— Over den levensduur van eenige zaden. 1888. I. 527.
— Matériaux pour la connaissance de l'influence de la température. 1870. I. 232.¹
— Zur Mechanik der Bewegungen von Schlingpflanzen. 1874. I. 196.²
— Over eene methode om in plantensappen gebonden zuren te bepalen. 1882. I. 156.²
— Eine Methode zur Analyse der Turgorkraft. 1884. I. 150.¹
— Eine Methode, Zwangsdrehungen aufzusuchen. 1894. I. 144.¹
— Monographie der Zwangsdrehungen. 1892. I. 144.¹
— Een nieuw orgaan van het plantaardig protoplasma. 1882. I. 137.
— Ueber die Periodicität der partiellen Variationen. 1899. I. 245.
— Sur la periodicité des anomalies. 1899. I. 144.¹
— Over het periodisch optreden der anomalien. 1899. I. 144.¹
— Over de rol van melksap, gom en hars. 1879. I. 147.
— Over de schadelijkheid van gas voor planten. 1889. III. 185.¹
— Das Spaltungsgesetz der Bastarde. 1900. I. 246.¹
— Over de spanning tusschen celinhoud en celwand. 1876. I. 149.²
— Studien over zuigwortels. 1886. I. 165.
— Sur les unités des caractères spécifiques. 1900. I. 246.¹
— Over verdubbeling van phyllopodien. 1893. I. 145.¹
— De voeding der planten. 1876. I. 159.
— Vogellym. 1895. II. 179.²
— Ueber das Welken abgeschnittener Sprosse. 1874. I. 149.²
— Ueber Wundholz. 1876. I. 207.²
— Zaaien en planten. 1899. III. 36.¹
— *See also* OUDEMANS, C. A. J. A. & VRIES, Hugo de.
Vries, S. de. Curieuse aenmerckingen der bijsonderste Oosten West-Indische verwonderenswaerdige dingen. 1682. I. 285.¹
Vriese, Willem Hendrik de. Aanteekeningen betreffende getah-pertjaboomen. 1860. III. 229.
— Aanteekeningen omtrent . . . Encephalartos Altensteinii. 1846. II. 5.²
— Aanwyzing voor de teelt van de Kakao. 1860. III. 592.¹
— Adnotatio de flore Dryobalanopsidis. 1856. II. 560.¹
— Analecta Goodenoviearum. 1849. I. 498. — 1851. II. 846.²
— De Araliaceën van Java en Japan. 1856. II. 646.¹
— Araliacées de Java et du Japon. 1856. II. 646.¹
— L'Arbre du quinquina. 1858. III. 725.¹
— Bemerkungen über einige Palmen aus Surinam. 1855. II. 61.¹
— Bericht über Versuche mit Versendungen lebender Pflanzen. 1840. III. 155.
— Berigt aangaande een . . . Cycas circinalis. 1842. II. 4.²
— Berigten van proefnemigen angaande het overbrengen van levende planten. 1840. III. 155.
— Bijdrage tot de statistiek der kacao. 1859. III. 594.
— Bijdragen tot de kennis der flora van Sumatra. 1846. I. 467.
— Ueber den Campherbaum von Sumatra. 1851. II. 560.¹
— On the Camphor tree of Sumatra. 1853. III. 611.¹
— On the Camphor-tree of Sumatra. 1851. II. 560.¹'
— Over eene Casuarina op Sumatra. 1844. II. 92.¹
— Chloris medica. 1847. III. 58.
— De Deodara-Ceder en zijn nut. 1855. IV. 448.¹
— Descriptions et figures des plantes . . . du jardin . . . de Leide. 1847. I. 269.
— Sur deux nouveaux genres de Pandanées. 1854. II. 56.¹
— Doornia en Rykia. 1854. II. 56.²
— Over dusgenaamde Wardsche toestellen. 1855. III. 155.
— Eenige opmerkingen aangaande . . . Cycas circinalis. 1841. II. 4.²
— Over eenige verscheidenheden van Clematis florida azurea. 1855. III. 390.¹
— De Encephalarto Lehmanni. 1843. II. 6.¹
— Encephalartos Marumii. 1838. II. 5.²
— Enting (?) van eenen Glimboom. 1855. III. 164.²
— Ueber die erhöhte Temperatur der männlichen Blüthe der Cycadeen. 1851. II. 3.²
— Fred. Lud. Splitgerberi reliquiae botanicae surinamenses. 1848. I. 339.¹

— De getah-pertja-boomen van Nederlandsch Oost-Indië. 1856. III. 228.²
— Het gezag van Kaempfer . . . omtrent den botanischen oorsprong van den Steranijs. 1836. II. 209.¹
— Goodeniaceae. 1844. II. 846.²
— Goodenovieae. 1854. II. 846.²
— De handel in getah-pertja. 1856. III. 229.
— Herinnering aan de tentoonstelling. 1838. II. 5.²
— Hortus Spaarn-Bergensis. 1839. I. 51.¹
— Hoya variegata. 1852. II. 739.²
— L'Hoya variegata. 1853. III. 693.¹
— De invloed der kruidkunde op de belangen van den staat. 1857. III. 34.¹
— De invloed van den bliksem. 1855. IV. 193.²
— De Japansche Hiba-levensboom. 1850. II. 53.¹
— De Japansche Hiba-levensboom, Thuyopsis dolobrata Sieb. & Zucc. 1854. III. 312.¹
— Japansche Was-bloem van Motoske. 1855. II. 740.¹
— De Kamferboom van Sumatra. 1851. II. 560.¹
— De Kina-Boom overgebragt uit Amerika. 1855. III. 715.
— De Kina-boom uit Zuid-Amerika overgebragt. 1855. III. 717.²
— De Kina-inzamelaars in de bosschen van Peru. 1855. III. 717.²
— Kruidtuinen en herbarien. 1849. I. 38.¹
— Materiaux pour la connaissance de la flore de Sumatra. 1846. I. 467.¹
— Mededeelingen over het eiland Baroe. 1861. I. 465.
— De Medicijn-hof. 1852. III. 58.
— Die Meinungen von Kämpfer . . . über die Mutterpflanzen des Steranises. 1836. II. 209.¹
— Mémoire sur le Camphrier de Sumatra. 1856. II. 560.¹
— Minjak Tangkawang. 1861. II. 560.¹ III. 276.¹
— Nadere toelichting omtrent Zamia muricata. 1848. II. 7.¹
— Nieuwe onderzoekingen aangaande den Kampferboom. 1856. II. 560.¹
— Nieuwe planten van 1855. 1856. III. 77.
— Nieuwe waarnemingen over eene verhoogde temperatuur bij . . . Cycas circinalis. 1851. II. 4.¹
— De nieuwste nomenclatuur der Nederlandsch Oostindische Palmen. 1855. II. 62.¹
— Nog een woord over den stam van Cycas. 1845. II. 4.¹
— Note sur le Zamia muricata. 1846. II. 7.¹
— Notice sur une espèce peu connue d'Encephalartos. 1838. II. 5.²
— Novae species Cycadearum Africae. 1837. II. 5.²
— Observations sur la haute témperature des fleurs mâles des Cycadées. 1851. II. 3.²
— Observations upon the elevated temperature of the male inflorescence of the Cycadaceous plants. 1851. II. 3.²
— Oratio de progressu physiologiae plantarum. 1835. I. 146.
— De Palmen van Suriname. 1846. II. 61.¹
— Die Palmen von Surinam. 1846. II. 61.¹
— Over papier. 1853. III. 235.¹
— Le Pin pesse blanc Link. 1855. III. 305.²
— Plantae Indiae batavae orientalis. 1856. I. 465.
— Plantae novae et . . . Indiae Batavae orientalis. 1845. I. 465.
— Plantarum javanicarum . . . sylloge. 1844. I. 468.
— Plantenkunde voor apothekers en artsen. 1835. III. 57.
— Remarks on Doornia and Rykia. 1854. II. 56.²
— Remarques sur les arbres qui produisent le getah-pertja. 1860. III. 229.
— Responsio ad questionem . . . Quid hactenus . . . de forma . . . et functione radicum innotuerit. 1829. I. 160.
— De reusachtige boomen van Californië. 1855. II. 50.¹
— De Rijstpapier-plant. 1855. III. 644.¹
— De soorten van het geslacht Aeschynanthus. 1856. II. 792.²
— Splitgerbers botanische nalatenschap. 1845. I. 339.¹
— Over de Ster-anijs. 1834. II. 209.²
— Ueber den Stern-Anis. 1834. II. 209.²
— Stukken over de overbrengst van de West-Indische Cassave naar Java. 1855. III. 521.¹
— Ueber eine auf Sumatra . . . entdeckte Casuarina. 1844. II. 92.¹
— Synoecia (Ficus) Guillielmi I. 1861. II. 150.¹
— Teregtwyzing van C. L. Blume's Naamsverwarring van Pinus Merkusii. 1851. II. 42.²
— On the transplantation of the Peruvian Bark tree into Dutch East India. 1855. III. 715.
— Tuinbouw-Flora van Nederland. 1855. III. 77.

— De uitkomsten der Kina-kultuur in Nederlandsch Indië. 1857. III. 715.
— Vroege japansche Mume-Abrikoos. 1855. II. 275.[1]
— De Waringing van Java, Ficus Benjamina. 1855. II. 150.[1]
— De Witte Pijnboom. 1855. II. 37.[2]
— Een woord over den Sambinoer-boom. 1851. II. 8.[2]
— Zamia Galeotti. 1845. II. 4.[1]
— See also SIEBOLD, P. F. von & VRIESE, W. H. de.
— & Teysmann J. E. Bosscheria Minahassae. 1861. II. 152.[1]
Vriese, K. de. Kijkjes in de plantenwereld. 1891. I. 96.
Vrij, Johan Eliza de. Over de aanwezigheid van kinidine. 1866. III. 722.
— Action comparée des écorces . . . de Grenadier. 1891. III. 31.[1]
— Alkaloidbepaling in kinabasten. 1870. III. 722.
— Over de amorfe alkaloiden in den kinabast. 1896. III. 724.[1]
— Over het amorphe kiha-alcaloid. 1892. III. 724.[1]
— Over de amorphe kinine van Winckler. 1866. III. 721.
— On the amount of alkaloids in the Cinchona trees. 1864. III. 722.
— Over aqua en oleum Lauro-Cerasi. 1842. III. 438.[1]
— Over de benaming der Kina-alcaloiden. 1896. III. 724.[1]
— Over de bepaling der hoeveelheid alcaloiden in kinabasten. 1864. III. 722.
— Over de bepaling van het zoogenaamde kinovazuur. 1878. III. 723.
— Bereiding van tannas chinini. 1894. III. 724.[1]
— Bereiding van tannas chinini met constante samenstelling. 1891. III. 724.[1]
— Berigt omtrent een scheikundig onderzoek van Cinchona Pahudiana. 1863. III. 725.[2]
— Bijdrage tot de kennis der . . . china pseudo-regia. 1857. III. 722.
— Bijdrage tot de kennis der Cinchona Pahudiana. 1865. II. 814.[1]
— Bijdrage tot de kennis der kina-alcaloiden. 1857. III. 722. — 1860. III. 722.
— Bijdrage tot de kennis van het naucleine zuur. 1860. III. 746.[3]
— Over cerberine. 1884. III. 687.[2]
— Over chinoidinum. 1880. III. 723.
— Chromas kalicus als reagens. 1889. III. 723.
— On the Cinchona bark of British India. 1864. III. 714, 724.[2]
— Cinchona caloptera. 1872. III. 725.[2]
— Sur le Cinchona Hassk'arliana. 1874. II. 813.[2]
— On the cultivation of Quinine in Java. 1865. III. 713.[1]
— Sur la culture des arbres à Quinquina à Java. 1855. III. 713.[1]
— Sur les écorces de Quinquina de l'Inde anglaise. 1864. III. 714.
— Eenvoudige bepaling van het alcaloidgehalte van het extractum cinchonae liquidum. 1887. III. 723.
— Eenvoudige reactie op hydrokinine. 1897. III. 724.[1]
— Ueber die Einführung der Chinakultur in Ost-Indien. 1865. III. 715.
— Extraction de la quinamine. 1877. III. 726.[1]
— Extractum cinchonae liquidum. 1889. III. 723.
— A fast growing Cinchona. 1879. III. 726.[1]
— Gebruik van den kinine-herapathit. 1876. III. 721.
— Over het gebruik van kinovazuur. 1864. III. 721.
— Gevoeligheid der chromaatproef voor het onderzoek van kininezouten. 1898. III. 724.[1]
— Over de hoeveelheid Kina-alcaloiden. 1864. III. 722.
— Over den kinabast en zijne alcaloiden. 1875. III. 723.
— Over het in de kinabasten aanwezige kalk zout. 1896. III. 724.[1]
— Over kinabasten, geoogst in Jamaica. 1872. III. 722.
— Over de Kinabasten van Britsch Indië. 1864. III. 714.
— De Kinakultuur op Java. 1865. III. 713.[1]
— Kininebereiding in Java. 1885. III. 718.
— Kinologische studien. 1868. III. 724.[2]
— Kinologische studien tannas chinini. 1891. III. 724.[1]
— Over het kinovazuur. 1860. III. 721.
— Onderzoek van het melksap van Antiaris. 1885. III. 366.[2]
— Onderzoek van sulfas chinini. 1889. III. 723.
— Onderzoek van tannas chinini. 1893. III. 724.[1]
— Dans quel état les alcaloïdes des quinquinas des Indes existent-ils dans l'écorce? 1878. III. 723.
— Sur le quinetum. 1879. III. 726.[1]

— Rapport van het scheikundig onderzoek. 1863. III. 722.
— Resultaten van het scheikundig onderzoek. 1863. III. 722.
— Scheikundige onderzoekingen . . . tot de kennis . . . Kinaboomen. 1860. III. 722.
— Over het spontaan ontstaan der C. Calisaya. 1880. II. 813.[2]
— Sur le sucre de Palmier. 1865. III. 321.[1]
— Over de suiker van den Palmboom. 1865. III. 321.[1]
— Sur la teneur en alcaloïdes . . . de Cinchonas. 1869. III. 722.
— Veiling van Java-kina te Amsterdam. 1873. III. 718.
— Voortdurend gebruik van het Quinetum. 1894. III. 718.
— See also JUNGHUHN, Frans & VRIJ, J. E. de.
— & Ludwig, Ernst. Ueber das Antiar-Gift. 1868. III. 366.[2]
— — Chemische Untersuchung . . . der Antiaris. 1868. III. 366.[2]
Vrijberghe de Coningh, C. van. Praktyk en theorie. n. d. III, 104.
Vrijdag Zijnen, T. D. Aanteekeningen bij de Quinologie van Delondre. 1854. II. 812.
— China scrobiculata. 1850. III. 726.[1]
— Chinae verae et Pseudo-chinae. 1860. III. 338,[2] 724.[2]
— De gewassen uit de Nederlandsche kolonien. 1855. III. 28.[1]
— De in den handel voorkomende kinabasten. 1835. III. 724;[2] see also ZIJNEN, T. D. V. 1835. III. 721.
— Iets over vermeende Huanuco-kina. 1858. III. 725.[1]
— De kina-basten van het Rijks herbarium. 1860. III.724.[2]
— De Kinabasten van het Rijks herbarium . . . vergeleken met exemplaren. 1857. II. 812.
— De quinologische waarde. 1858. III. 721.
— Over de vermeende identiteit van den Lagosbast. 1857. III. 508.[1]
— Verwisseling der zaagbladige Wegedoorns-bexien. 1826. III. 543.[1]
Vrolik, Gerard. Catalogus plantarum medicinalium. 1805. III. 55.
— De Cycasstam met bollen vergeleken. 1846. II. 4.[1]
— Over eenige physiologische eigenschappen van het Viscum. 1857. II. 178.[2]
— Elenchus plantarum Horti medici amstelodamensis. 1807. I. 51.[1]
— Elenchus plantarum, quae in Horto amstelaedamensi coluntur. 1814. I. 51.[1]
— Over gelijkvormige oorzaak en verschijnselen bij het afvallen van bladen. 1851. I. 192.[1]
— Merkwaardige verschijnselen bij den groei eener Lonicera Periclymenum. 1857. II. 839.[1]
— Over merkwaardige verschijnselen . . . door eene oplossing van bijtend kwiksublimaat. 1842. I. 211.
— Naamlyst der geneesryke Plantgewaschsen. 1804. III. 55.
— Observationes de defoliatione. 1796. I. 191.[1]
— Oratio de eo, quod Amstelodamenses ad rem botanicam exornandam contulerunt. 1797. I. 80.[3]
— Over het verme igvuldigen van naalddragende boomen door wortelende uitspruitsels. 1858. II. 20.[1]
— Vervolg der waarnemingen over het afvallen van boomtakjes. 1852. I. 192.[1]
— Waarschuwing tegen de gemeene verwisseling der bladen van Dioema crenata. 1835. III. 495.[1]
— & others. Verslag over den paalworm. 1861. IV. 414.[1]
Vroom, James & others. A list of flowering plants and ferns found in Charlotte county. 1887. I. 310.
Vrtiška, Al. Ovocnická studie z Ruska. 1896. III. 135.
Vruchtboomen langs de wegen. 1900. III. 211.[1]
Vserossiski siezd liesokhozyayev. See Всероссійскій съѣздъ лѣсохозяевъ.
Vuillemin, Paul. Sur les affinités des Frankéniées. 1889. II. 561.[2]
— Antibiose et symbiose. 1900. I. 234.[1]
— Sur une bactériocécidie . . . du Pin d'Alep. 1888. IV. 464.[1]
— Le bois verdi. 1898. IV. 414.[1]
— Les broussins des Myrtacées. 1895. III. 633.[1]
— Cancer et tumeurs végétales. 1900. I. 206.[1]
— Sur les causes anatomiques de l'enracinement des tiges de Ronce. 1885. III. 306.[1]
— Les Chalazogames de M. Treub. 1892. II. 92.[1]
— Sur les fleurs doubles. 1893. I. 145.[2]
— Sur la genèse des tumeurs bactériennes du Pin d'Alep. 1889. IV. 464.[2]

Vuillemin, Paul (*continued*).
— Sur une maladie des Amygdalées. 1887. III. 431.[1]
— Sur une maladie des Cerisiers et des Pruniers. 1887. III. 431.[1]
— La maladie du Peuplier pyramidal. 1889. III. 346.[2]
— Sur une maladie du Prunellier. 1895. III. 443,[1] 534.[2]
— Sur une maladie parasitaire du Peuplier pyramidal. 1889. III. 346.[2]
— Modifications de l'éperon chez les Tropaeolum. 1893. II. 390.[1]
— Les mycorhizes. 1890. I. 234.[1]
— Polymorphisme normal dans les fleurs du Cornus sanguineus. 1894. II. 655.[2]
— Recherches sur les rouilles des Pins. 1894. IV. 462.[1]
— Recherches sur quelques glandes épidermiques. 1887. I. 113.[1]
— Sur les relations des bacilles du Pin d'Alep. 1888. IV. 464.[1]
— Sur des Roses à carpelles biovulés. 1893. II. 290.[1]
— La subordination des caractères de la feuille dans ... Anthyllis. 1892. II. 321.[1]
— Les tubercules radicaux des· Légumineuses. 1888. II. 321.[2]
— Sur des tumeurs ligneuses . . . chez les Eucalyptus. 1894. IV. 531.[1]
— *See also* BARTET, E. & VUILLEMIN, Paul; ? Вюилльменъ.
Vuillet. Culture de l'Indigotier. 1900. III. 479.[1]
— Quelques plantes intéressantes . . . du Niger. 1900. III. 93.[1]
Vuillier. Opinion et projet de décret sur l'administration. 1792? IV. 275.
— Réponse . . . aux objections que l'on a faites contre l'aliénation des forêts nationales. 1792? IV. 275.
Vuitzitzki, S. *See* Вуйцицкій, C.
Vukotinović, Ljudevit FARKAŠ-. Beitrag zur Kenntniss der croatischen Eichen. 1889. II. 130.[1]
— Formae Quercuum croaticarum. .1883. II. 130.[1]
— Neue Eichen Kroatiens. 1875. II. 129.[2]
— Neue Eichenformen. 1888. II. 135.[1]
— Neue Pflanzen und zweiter Nachtrag zur Flora Croatiens. 1875. I. 447.
— Novae formae Quercuum croaticarum. 1880. II. 130.[1]
— Novae Quercuum croaticarum formae. 1879. II. 130.[1]
— Novi oblici Hrvatskih hrastovah. 1880. II. 130.[1]
— Opis Ružah okoline zagrebačke. 1884. II. 288.[1]
— Rosae croaticae. 1884. II. 288.[1]
— Zur Rosenflora von Agram. 1887. II. 288.[1]
— *See also* SCHLOSSER, J. C. & VUKOTINOVIĆ, L. F.
Vukotinović, Ludwig von. *See* VUKOTINOVIĆ, Ljudevit FARKAŠ-
Vulgarisation de la sylviculture. 1897. IV. 540.[1]
Vulpius, Gustav. Écorce de Quinquina officinal. 1886. III. 723.
— Sur le glycoside du condurango. 1885. III. 693.[1]
Vultejus, von, (*Oberförster*). Ueber die Erziehung des besten Culturmaterials. 1879. IV. 150.
— Erziehungsresultate ausländischer Nadelhölzer. 1881. IV. 125.[2]
— Die Grasnutzung im Forstreviere Walkenried. 1881. IV. 135.[1]
— Die künstliche Verjüngung der Mittelwälder. 1881. IV. 131.[1]
— Der Lärchen-Krebspilz. 1882. IV. 451.
Vuurden, C. van. Rozen voor Indië. 1900. III. 451.[1] ·
Vuyck, L. Het geslacht Rubus. 1900. II. 302.[1]
— Nieuwe indigenen. 1900. I. 391.[1]
— De·plantengroei der duinen. 1898. I. 391.[1]
Vuyst, Paul de. La laine de bois comme litière. 1895. IV. 557.[1]
— Manuel pratique et raisonné des cultures spéciales. 1897. III. 113.
Vvedenski, A. N. *See* Введенскій, A. H.
Vvodnye doklady. *See* Вводныя доклады.
Vylezhinski. *See* Выложинскій.
Vypiska iz voinskago ustava. *See* Выписка изъ воинскаго устава.
Vysotzki, G. *See* Высоцкій. Г.
Vystavka predmetov. *See* Выставка предметовъ.

W. The Allamandas. 1886. III. 686.[1]
W. Ampelopsis Veitchi var. purpurea. 1893. III. 545.[1]
W. Zum Anbau der Fichte. 1897. IV. 454.
W. Aphelandra Margaritae. 1887. III. 708.[2]
W. Beaumontia grandiflora. 1890. III. 687.[1]

W. Camellias. 1890. III. 599.[1]
W. Caryota sobolifera. 1888. III. 321.[2]
W. The Climbing Hydrangea. 1879. III. 415.[2]
W. The Coco-de-Mer. 1890. III. 327.[1]
W. The Coral trees. 1891. III. 476.[1]
W. Die Cultur des Eucalyptus in Italien. 1881. IV. 532.[2]
W. Cycads in flower at Kew. 1885. III. 284.[1]
W. Daisy trees (Olearias). 1888. III. 756.[1]
W. Drawbacks to the Ailanthus. 1886. IV. 525.
W. Über Durchforstungen. 1894. IV. 175.[1]
W. Eenige opmerkingen naar aanleiding van Dr. Burck's verhandeling. 1897. III. 731.
W. Eichenwaldungen am badischen Oberrhein. 1859. IV. 505.
W. Frühjahrs- oder Herbstpflanzung im Gebirge? 1885. IV. 154.[2]
W. The great Wistaria of Salt Hill, near Slough. 1873. III. 490.[2]
W. Greenhouse Rhododendrons. 1898. III. 662.[1]
W. The Illiciums. 1889. III. 398.[1]
W. The Ivy and its uses. 1872. II. 642.[2]
W. Zur Kenntniss der forstwirthschaftlichen Verhältnisse Kroat.-Slavoniens. 1884. IV. 373.
W. Die Nachtheile der Cultur der Ailanthus. 1886. IV. 525.
W. The Neilgherry Rhododendron. 1889.· III. 657.[2]
W. Ueber das Nutzholzprozent in Buchenhochwaldungen. 1899. IV. 499.
W. Orange culture in Florida. 1889. III. 500.[1]
W. Ueber die Para-Nüsse. 1853. III. 631.[2]
W. Physianthus albens. 1887. III. 692.[1]
W. Русскія древесныя породы. 1868. III. 67.[2]
W. Rhododendron arboreum. 1890. III. 657.[2]
W. Die Rinde des Faulbaumes. 1883. IV. 528.[1]
W. Sabal Blackburniana at Kew. 1886. III. 331.[1]
W. Die Schwarzpappel als Nutzbaum im Walde. 1898. IV. 486.[2]
W. Something about nuts. 1872. III. 358.[1]
W. Spring-flowering Rhododendrons. 1890. III. 662.[1]
W. De stikstofvoeding van Koffie. 1897. III. 734.[1]
W. Thunbergia affinis. 1887. III. 710.[1]
W. The Umbrella China tree. 1896. III. 512.[2]
W. Die Waldbäume in Mähren. 1860. IV. 86.[2]
W. Weisse Heidelbeeren. 1890. II. 688.[2]
W. Welchen Gefahren ist die Kiefer . . . ausgesetzt? 1894. IV. 457, 478.
W. Wie ermittelt man den Wertzuwachs. 1894. IV. 252.
W. & others. Was hat der Forstmann bei Anlage eines Kiefersaatkampes zu beobachten? 1888. IV. 473.
W., van. Extraheeren van ruw alcaloid uit Kinabast in Indië. 1887. III. 718.
W., von. Die Pflanzung einjähriger Kiefern. 1850. IV. 472.
W., von. Die Verwüstung der Seestrandkiefer-Bestände in der Sologne. 1881. IV. 467.[1]
W., von. Welche Insekten beherbergen Eichel? 1893. IV. 208.[1]
W., A. The Hydrangeas. 1873. III. 412.[2]
W., A. Observations sur le développement des racines de l'Orme. 1895. IV. 518.[2]
W., A. Weissföhrensaat und Humus. 1864. IV. 480.
W., A. D. Fastigiate trees. 1891. ·III. 204.[1]
W., A. D. A Kentish hedgerow. 1892. III. 214.[2]
W., A. D. The Linden and its varieties. 1891. III. 585.[1]
W., A. D. Ornamental hedges. 1887. III. 214.[2]
W., A. D. Prince Albert's Fir. 1888. III. 312.[2]
W., A. D. The Siberian Salt tree. 1889. III. 478.[1]
W., A. D. Tree growth in 1892. 1892. III. 38.[2]
W., A. F. Gegen Rüsselkäferfrass. 1868. IV. 207.
W., A. F. Die Wahl des forstlichen Wirthschafts-Zinsfusses. 1875. IV. 256.·
W., A. P. Manure for Conifers. 1857. III. 291.
W., B. The Cantuas. 1885. III. 694.[2]
W., B. The Croweas. 1886. III. 503.[2]
W., B. The Podalyrias. 1885. III. 484.[2]
W., B. v. V. Ophouden van vruchtbaarheid van gronden, waarop jarenlang Koffie is geteeld. 1893. III. 727.
W., C. Elaeagnus reflexa. 1843. III. 629.[1]
W., E. The Mustard tree of Scripture. 1865. II. 473.[1]
W., E. H. Sea-side vegetation. 1875. III. 41.[2]
W., E. P. The Chestnut tree of Mount Etna. 1871. II. 124.[2]
W., E. V. De Doorn-Rolpalm. 1784. II. 70.[1]
W., F. Die Anwendung der Photographie im forstlichen Haushalte. 1897. IV. 37.[2]

W., F. Aufforstungen und Verbauungen im mittäglichen Frankreich. 1898. IV. 164.[1]
W., F. Dipladenias. -1873. III. 687.[2]
W., F. Der Holzimport nach Oberösterreich. 1886. IV. 406.[2]
W., F. Unsere Bewaldungsprocente. 1894. IV. 368.
W., F. Die Waldwirthschraft in Russisch-Polen. 1900. IV. 114.
W., F. Die Wildbachverbauung in Frankreich. 1896. IV. 186.[1]
W., F. X. Der Maulbeerbaum. 1847. III. 376.
W., G. Winter bedding with evergreen shrubs. 1879. III. 201.
W., G. E. Hemlock for tanneries. 1896. III. 312.[2]
W., G. E. The wood pulp supply. 1896. IV. 430.
W., G. J. Der herrschende Wind und der . . . Wälderwuchs. 1859. IV. 189.[1]
W., H. R. New varieties of Lilac. 1900. III. 681.[1]
W., H. T. Forest tree planting on the Great Plains. 1871. IV. 111.[2]
D.W., I. O. Weevils destructive to Cycads. 1887. III. 284.[1]
W., J. Abies magnifica. 1888. III. 296.[2]
W., J. Ardisia mamillata. 1887. III. 666.[1]
W., J. Une excursion forestière à Gooreynd. 1894. IV. 556.[1]
W., J. Large British Oaks. 1867. II. 138.[2]
W., J. Vinetum britannicum. See WORLIDGE, John: 1676. III. 141.
W., J. von. Beschädigung von Lärchenbeständen durch Nager. 1884. IV. 198.[1]
W., J. B. Planting on peat bog. 1885. III. 41.[1]
W., J. O. Rose insects. 1850. III. 453.[2]
W., J. R. The Lawson Cypress and its varieties. 1877. III. 301.[1]
W., J. R. Lawson's Cypresse. 1877. III. 301.[1]
W., J. S. Beech trees and underwood. 1878. IV. 495.
W., J. S. Clipped and natural hedges. 1881. III. 214.[1]
W., J. S. Gummifluss nicht ansteckend. 1884. I. 528.[1]
W., J. S. Gumming not contagious. 1884. I. 528.[1]
W., J. S. Trees and shrubs for exposed situations. 1876. III. 42.[1]
W., J. T. Decay of Oak woods in South Yorkshire. 1878. IV. 510.
W., L. Ueber die ästhetische Bedeutung des Waldes. 1887. IV. 55.[2]
W., L. von. Beweis dass die Verbindung der höhern Wissenschaften mit dem Forstwesen, ganz unentbehrlich seye. 1790. IV. 56.
W., M. Die Lohrindengewinnung in den bayerischen Staatswaldungen. 1892. IV. 513.
W., M. Le Pin Laricio de Corse en Flandre. 1895. IV. 466.[2]
W., N. Wood used by cabinet makers. 1896. IV. 427.[1]
W., S. Draped trees. 1874. I. 516.
W., S. Pitch-Pine. 1882. IV. 467.[1]
W., S. Transplanting evergreens. 1878. III. 169.[1]
W., S. E. On the Spanish Oaks. 1841. II. 129.[1]
W., S. S. Evergreen underwood. 1877. III. 215.[2]
W., T. F. Solanum Wendlandi. 1900. III. 702.[1]
W., V. . . . . G . . . . , Baron. Verhandeling over eenige weinig bekende buitenlandsche houtsoorten. 1819. IV. 126.[2]
W., W. The Aristolochias. 1888. III. 385.[2]
W., W. The Double Cocoa-nut at Kew. 1893. III. 327.[1]
W., W. Dracaena Godseffiana. 1897. III. 336.[2]
W., W. Echinopsis Decaisneana. 1894. II. 593.[2]
W., W. Fourcroeas. 1891. III. 341.[2]
W., W. Giant Cactus (Cereus giganteus). 1900. II. 590.[1]
W., W. Jacobinia magnifica. 1892. II. 800.[1]
W., W. Kentia Forsteriana. 1890. II. 69.[1]
W., W. Licuala Jeanenceyi. 1899. III. 326.[2]
W., W. Macaranga Porteana. 1894. II. 447.[1]
W., W. Ptychorhaphis augusta. 1892. III. 330.[2]
W., W. A survivor. 1890. III. 539.[2]
W., W. Washingtonia filifera. 1892. III. 332.[1]
W., W. See also WATSON, William.
W . . . . . , F. Ueber die Erträge der Fehmelwaldungen. 1859. IV. 446.[1]
Waadt. Staatliche Musteralp. 1898. IV. 136.[1]
Waage, Th. Ueber haubenlose Wurzeln der Hippocastanaceen. 1891. II. 480.[2]
— Ueber das Vorkommen . . . des Phloroglucins. 1890. I. 177.
— See also SIEDLER, Paul & WAAGE, Th.
Waal van Anckeveen, G. de. Bereiding van Liberia Koffie. 1887. III. 743.[1]

— Kort begrip van de leer der bemesting en toepassing . . . van Koffietuinen. 1896. III. 734.[1]
— Kort begrip van de leer der bemesting, gevolgd door de toepassing . . . van Koffietuinen. 1896. III. 152.
Waanders, BLOEMEN. See BLOEMEN WAANDERS.
De waarde der boschen. 1875. IV. 376.[2]
Waby, John F. Tropical gardening in British Guiana. 1893. III. 100.[1]
Wace, E. G. & Reynolds, W. H. Correspondence on the demarcations of the reserved forests in Hazara. 1874. IV. 295.[1]
Wach, Charles. Le Thé. 1860. III. 607.
Wachendorff, E. I. van. Horti ultraiectini index. 1747. I. 51.[1]
Wachi, G. La question des forêts en Algérie. 1885. IV. 279.[2]
Wachi, P. La question des forêts en Afrique. 1899. IV. 279.[2]
Der Wacholder. 1900. II. 31.[2]
Wachs, Rudolph. Vergleichende Untersuchung des Quercitrins. 1893. I. 177.
Wachsthum der Paulovnia imperialis. 1872. III. 703.[2]
Wachsthum der Platanen. 1872. II. 255.[1]
Wachsthum und Ertrag der Weymouthskiefer. 1890. IV. 470.[2]
Wachsthumsgang der Holzbestände. 1866. IV. 232.
Ueber die Wachsthumsleistung der Rotheiche. 1884. IV. 516.[1]
Ueber die Wachsthumsverhältnisse der Douglas-Tanne. 1884. II. 49.[1]
Wachtel, Georg. Beschreibung der . . . Domäne Neuhaus. 1894. IV. 372.
— Beschreibung der Exkursionstour . . . in den Forsten der Herrschaft Neuhaus. 1894. IV. 372.
— Popis . . . velkostatku Jindřichova Hradce. 1894. IV. 372.
— Popis vychâzky . . . do lesů velkostatku Jindřicho-Hradeckého. 1894. IV. 372.
Wachter, H. Wegweiser zur Erhöhung der Erträge kleinerer Privatwaldungen. 1874. IV. 244.
Wachtl, Fritz A. Beiträge zur Kenntniss der Gallen erzeugenden Insecten Europas. 1881. I. 216.[2]
— Beschreibung der Metamorphose . . . von Hedobia. 1877. IV. 210.[1]
— Cephaleia lariciphila n. sp. 1897. IV. 451.
— Die doppelzähnigen europäischen Borkenkäfer. 1884. IV. 92.
— Ein einfacher . . . Apparat zum Präpariren von Larven. 1878. IV. 92.
— Entomologisch-biologische Studien. 1879. IV. 210.[1]
— Die gesellige Fichten-Gespinstblattwespe. 1893. IV. 457.
— Die Krummzähnigen europäischen Borkenkäfer. 1895. IV. 93.
— O naroślach na Dębach . . . w zachodniej Galicyi. 1876. IV. 510.
— Ein neuer Megastigmus als Samenverwüster von Pseudotsuga. 1893. IV. 483.[2]
— Die Nonne. 1892. IV. 201.
— Serropalpus barbatus Schall. 1877. IV. 445.
— Die Weisstannen-Triebwickler. 1882. IV. 445.
— Zwei Feinde der Tanne. 1877. IV. 445.
— Zwei neue europäische Cynipiden. 1877. IV. 501.[1]
— & Kornauth, Karl. Beiträge zur Kenntniss der . . . Nonne. 1893. IV. 201.
Wackenroder, Heinrich. On Coca leaves. 1854. III. 492.[2]
Wacker, H. Uebersicht der Phanerogamenflora von Culm. 1861. I. 384.
Wacker, Johann. Die Beeinflussung des Wachsthums der Wurzeln. 1898. I. 188.
Waddel, L. A. See WARDEN, J. H. & WADDEL, L. A.
Waddy, E. A year with the wild flowers. 1873. I. 402.
Wade, Edward. A proposal for improving and adorning the island of Great Britain. 1755. IV. 120.
Wade, Walter. Catalogus systematicus plantarum . . . in comitatu dublinensi. 1794. I. 396.
— Plantae rariores in Hibernia inventae. 1804. I. 396.
— Salices. 1811. II. 98,[2] III. 347.
— Syllabus of a course of lectures on botany. 1802. I. 33.
Wäber, A. Die Wälder der Stadt Bern. 1870. IV. 367.
Waeber, Nikolai. Chemische Untersuchung der Samen der Butea. 1886. III. 468.[1]
Waeher, Robert. Lehrbuch für den Unterricht in der Botanik. 1885. V. x.[2]

Wächter, J. K. Über den Anbau fremder Gewächse. 1832. IV. 125.[2]
— Blicke in die Urgeschichte unserer Wälder. 1839. IV. 25.
— Über die Gewinnung der s. g. Rauhenborke. 1836. IV. 512.
— Ueber künstliche Baumfiguren. 1846. III. 202.[1]
— Nachricht von den Insecten-Verheerungen. 1831. IV. 206.
— Über die Reproduktionskraft der Gewächse. 1840. I. 199, IV. 65.[2]
— Säen und Pflanzen. 1833. IV. 25, 117.
— See also Bextreps.
Wächter, K. F. Om vore Skovtraeers successive Aftagelse i Højde. 1804. I. 350,[1] IV. 79.[1]
Wähner, Adolf. Kubirunge-Methoden der Rundhölzer. 1867. IV. 226.
Die **Wälder** Abchasiens. 1894. IV. 348.[1]
Die **Wälder** Afrikas. 1889. IV. 379.[2]
Die **Wälder** Amerikas. 1889. IV. 337.[1]
Die **Wälder** Australiens. 1889. IV. 380.[1]
Die **Wälder** Dalmatiens und seines Hinterlandes. 1895. IV. 374.[1]
Die **Wälder** des Syr-Darja-Gebietes. 1888. IV. 376.[1]
Wälder des westlichen Altai. 1870. I. 453,[1] IV. 87.[2]
Die **Wälder** im Amurgebiet und dem Seedistrikt. 1897. IV. 376.[1]
Die **Wälder** in Uri im Allgemeinen und Besonderen. n. d. IV. 364.
Die **Wälder** Norwegens. 1885. IV. 344.[1]
Die **Wälder** Transkaukasiens. 1883. IV. 348.[1]
Wälder und Holzindustrie in Australien. 1894. IV. 380.[2]
Der **Wälderverkauf** der katholischen Korporation zu St. Gallen im Jahre 1856. 1857. IV. 261.[2]
Wännman, Carolus Henr. Flora capensis. See LINNÉ, Carl von. 1759. I. 493.
Die **Wärme** im Juli 1845. 1846. IV. 192.[1]
Wäser, J. W. Der Berliner Kunstgärtner. 1794. III. 103.
Waey, H. W. van. De bereiding van de indigo. 1859. III. 479.[1]
— Bijdrage tot de kennis der kultuur . . . van Java. 1859. III. 128.
— De Kakao-kultuur. 1861. III. 592.[1]
— Ontginning van woeste boschgronden. 1858. III. 128.
— Producten van Java. 1860. III. 275.[2]
Wafelbakker, N. Iets over aqua Laurocerasi. 1842. III. 438.[1]
Waga, Anton. Ukazieiel polskich nazwisk na rodzaje królestwa roślinnego. 1848. I. 73.[1]
Waga, Jacob. Flora polonica phanerogama. 1847. I. 361.
— Flora polska jawnokwiatowych rodzajów. 1847. I. 361.
Die für den **Wagenbau** tauglichsten Holzarten. 1860. IV. 427.[1]
Wagener, Gustav. Anleitung zur Regelung des Forstbetriebs. 1875. IV. 241.
— Ueber die Aufstellung von Ertragstafeln. 1889. IV. 237.
— Die Begründung der nachhaltig einträglichsten Waldwirthschaft. 1900. IV. 259.[2]
— Ueber die Berechnung der Nutzungs- und Zuwachsbeträge. 1891. IV. 234.
— Die " Bestandswirthschaft." 1880. IV. 256.
— Ueber die Bestimmung der finanziellen Umtriebszeiten. 1871. IV. 251.[2]
— Controversen auf dem Gebiete der Walderstrags-Regelung. 1878. IV. 244. — 1879. IV. 236.
— Ueber den Einfluss der Verjüngungsart auf die Astbildung in Fichtenbeständen. 1890. IV. 454.
— Ergebnisse eines zwanzigjährigen Lichtwuchsbetriebs. 1892. IV. 130.
— Die Erziehung der Hochwald-Bestände. 1900. IV. 130.
— Expériences comparatives sur la production de l'Épicéa. 1885. IV. 233.
— Gedrängte Darstellung der . . . Waldbau-Regeln. 1875. IV. 107.[1]
— Ueber die Massnahmen der Eisenbahn-Verwaltungen zum Schutze der deutschen Waldwirthschaft. 1881. IV. 274.[1]
— Das " nationale System " des forstlichen Betriebs. 1880. IV. 270.
— Ueber die Pressler'sche Berechnungsart der Wirthschafts-Nutzeffecte. 1879. IV. 236.
— Ueber die principiellen Aufgaben der Waldwirthschaft. 1878. IV. 244
— Regeln der Wald-Werthberechnung. 1883. IV. 257.
— Streitfragen auf dem Gebiete des Waldbaues. 1885. IV. 18.

— Ueber die Untauglichkeit der Pressler'schen Berechnungsmethode. 1876. IV. 236.
— Vergleichende Darstellung der Beantragung und Verrechnung der Material- und Geld-Erträge . . . in den Staatswaldungen. 1880. IV. 261.[1]
— Vergleichende Untersuchungen über die Produktion der Fichte. 1885. IV. 233.
— Ueber die Wachsthumsleistung der Kiefer. 1879. IV. 481.
— Ueber Wachsthumsleistungen der Rothbuche. 1882. IV. 498.
— Ueber die Wachsthumsleistungen der verbleibenden Abtriebsstämme. 1888. IV. 234.
— Ueber die Wachsthumsleistungen der Fichte. 1878. IV. 58.
— Der Waldbau. 1884. IV. 107.[1]
— Die Waldrente. 1899. IV. 241.
— Ueber die wirthschaftliche Leistungsfähigkeit des Buchenhochwald-Betriebes. 1880. IV. 495.
— Die Zielpunkte und die bisherigen Zuwachs-Ergebnisse des Lichtwuchsbetriebes. 1887. IV. 130.
— Ueber Zuwachs-Berechnungs-Arten. 1889. IV. 234.
Wagener, Hermann. Essbare Früchte Venezuela's. 1849. III. 267.[1]
— Reise-Bemerkungen über Venezuela. 1850. I. 338.[1]
Wagener, Philippe Christian & Gruber, Friedrich. Flora von Hildesheim. 1798. I. 375.
Wagener, R. Die selbstständige Wieder-Entstehung einer Pflanzen-Varietät. 1874. II. 707.[2]
Wagenseil, J. C. De venatione et forestae jure. 1703. IV. 313.
Waghorne, Arthur Charles. A summary account of the wild berries . . . of Newfoundland. 1888. III. 262.[1]
Wagler, Paul. Die Eiche in alter und neuer Zeit. 1891. II. 132.[1]
Wagner. Les diverses variétés de tannin. 1867. III. 237.[2]
Wagner, (Besirksförster, Waldkirch). Bericht . . . über eine . . . forstliche Reise durch das Frankenland. 1862. IV. 356.[1]
— Forstliche Reisebilder aus dem Frankenland. 1862. IV. 356.[1]
Wagner, (Forstmeister). Kurze Mittheilung über Pyrus Aria. 1849. IV. 520.[2]
— **Blankenburg,** (Oberförster, Zedlitz) **& Rosenberg,** Baron von. Nachweis derer aus . . . Weisserlen-Beständen erhobenen Ertragsresultate. 1850. IV. 489.[2]
Wagner, (Oberförster). Die schädlichen Kiefern-Raupen. 1873. IV. 477.
Wagner, (Oberförster, Katholisch-Hammer). Ueber die Nachsucht der Buche. 1855. IV. 494.
— Notizen über Pinus rigida. 1852. IV. 468.[2]
— Ueber Raupenfrass in . . . Katholisch-Hammer. 1856. IV. 206.
— Ueber Schneebruch in . . . Katholisch-Hammer. 1856. IV. 190.
— Ueber das weitere Auftreten . . . der Forleule. 1852. IV. 475.
— **& Schulemann,** (Oberförster, Karlsberg). Generelle Beschreibung des k. Forstreviers Proskau. 1851. IV. 352.
Wagner, A. Die Heizungen und Moore Schleswig-Holsteins. 1875. IV. 354.
— Zur Kenntniss des Blattbaues der Alpenpflanzen. 1892. I. 220.[1]
— Die Nadelhölzer in der Provinz Schleswig-Holstein. 1871. IV. 118.
— Die Waldungen des ehemaligen Kurfürstenthums Hessen. 1886. IV. 354.
Wagner, Christian. Lehrbuch der praktischen Geometrie. 1799. IV. 57, 263.
— **& Hebig,** G. J. C. Botanisches Forsthandbuch. 1800. IV. 81.
Wagner, Christian Rudolph. Gyros Convolvulorum . . . evolvere tentabit. 1705. I. 196.[1]
Wagner, Daniel. Pharmaceutisch-medicinische Botanik. 1828. III. 56.
Wagner, F. Treets almindelige Teknologi. 1883. IV. 408.
Wagner, G. Beispiel aussergewöhnlicher . . . Werth-Vermehrung eines Fichtenstammes. 1859. IV. 458.
— Beiträge zur Kenntnis der Coleosporien . . . der Kiefern. 1896. IV. 462.[1]
— Beiträge zur Kenntniss der Pflanzenparasiten. 1896. III. 195.[1]
— Gloeosporium Myrtilli Allesch. 1896. III. 664.[1]
Wagner, Georg Friedrich. Discursus de balsamo. 1683. III. 510.[2]
— De natura et virtutibus plantarum. 1688. III. 238.[1]

Wagner, Hermann. Die Donauauen bei Wien. 1895. IV. 369.
— Illustrirte deutsche Flora. 1871. I. 386.
— Die Pflanzendecke der Erde. 1857. I. 299.
— Pflanzenkunde für Schulen. 1857. I. 90.
Wagner, J. A. Podręcznik dla dozorców lasów i gajowych skréslit. 1875. IV. 123.[2]
Wagner, J. P. Le mouvement syndical et les plantations fruitières sur les routes. 1898. III. 211.[1]
Wagner, János. A bazai vadon termő Juharfák. 1898. II. 476.[3]
— Ritka növények. Az Omorika Fenyő. 1900. III. 305.[2]
— Ritka növények. Pinus peuce. 1900. III. 308.[1]
Wagner, Johannes Gerhard. Arboreti sacri perfectioris specimen. 1732. II. 225.[2]
Wagner, Johannes Jakob. Historia naturalis Helvetiae curiosa. 1680. I. 432.[2]
Wagner, Karl. Zur Empfehlung der Rosa canina uralensis. 1890. III. 455.[1]
Wagner, Károly. See DIVALD, Adolf & WAGNER, Károly.
Wagner, Ludwig. Versuch über Holzbahnen. 1829. IV. 425.[3]
Wagner, Max. Das Zeidelwesen. 1895. IV. 439.
Wagner, Moriz. Ueber den Charakter ... der Vegetation in den Cordilleren. 1866. I. 330.
— Naturwissenschaftliche Reisen im tropischen Amerika. 1870. I. 330.
— Reise nach dem Ararat. 1848. I. 478.
— & Scherzer, Carl. Die Republik Costa Rica. 1856. I. 333.
—— Vegetations-Gemälde von Costa Rica. 1856. I. 333.
Wagner, P. Die Anwendung künstlicher Düngemittel. 1892. III. 151.
— A applicação de adubos artificiaes. 1892. III. 151.
Wagner, Rudolf. Zur Anisophyllie einiger Staphyleaceen. 1900. II. 473.[1]
— Sur la contenance en huile de quelques graines d'essences forestières. 1861. III. 224.[2]
— Ueber die Farbstoffe des Gelbholzes. 1851. III. 368.[1]
— Ueber die Farbstoffe des Gelbholzes (Morus tinctoria). 1850. III. 368.[2]
— Sur les matières colorantes du bois jaune. 1850. III. 368.[2]
— Eine neue Carludovica. 1899. II. 76.[1]
— Ueber den Oelgehalt einiger forstlicher Samen. 1860. I. 182,[1] III. 353,[1] 585,[1] IV. 462,[2] 500.[1]
— Quantity of oil furnished by the seeds of various forest-trees. 1861. III. 224.[2]
Wagner, Theodor. Statisticko-topografický a lesnický popis ... lesů svěřenského panství Nových Hradů. 1895. IV. 372.
— Statistisch-topographische Beschreibung der ... Fideicommiss-Herrschaft Gratzen. 1895. IV. 372.
Wahl. Zur Generation und Vertilgung von Hylesinus. 1897. IV. 204.
Wahl, Carl von. Vergleichende Untersuchungen über den anatomischen Bau der geflügelten früchte. 1896. I. 120.
Wahlberg, Peter Fredrik. Flora gothoburgensis. 1820. I. 352.
— Fröfäste uttrångande ur capseln med omogna frön. 1849. II. 609.[1]
— Iakttagelser på växter. 1851. I. 198.
— Notis om Pelargonium med geranielik blomma. 1863. II. 390.[1]
— Samtidiga (fenologiska) observationer. 1847. I. 223.[1]
— Växtfärgernas förändring i Lappmarken. 1845. I. 184.
— Växtformer i Luleå Lappmark. 1844. I. 354.
— & Winberg, Leopold. Anvisning till de svenska pharmaceutiska växternas igenkännande. See THUNBERG, C. P. 1826. III. 67.[1]
Wahlbom, Carl Adolph. De Oelandia. 1786. I. 352.
Wahlbom, Johannes Gustav. Sponsalia plantarum. See LINNÉ, Carl von. 1746. I. 198.
Wahlenberg, Göran (Georg). De camphora ejusue usu therapeutico. See FLODBERG, J. E. & HEDRÉN, E. 1834. III. 233.[1]
— Flora Carpatorum. 1814. I. 445.
— Flora lapponica. 1812. I. 352.
— Flora suecica. 1824. I. 353.
— Flora upsaliensis. 1820. I. 352.
— Gewächse im Morgenland gesammelt. 1828. I. 536.[1]
— Historisk Underrättelse om Upsala Universitetets Botaniska Trädgård. 1837. I. 40.
— Novitiae florae gotlandicae. See AFZELIUS, P. C. 1844. I. 354.

— Synopsis florae gothlandicae. 1837. I. 353.
— Tractatio anatomica. 1806. I. 98.
— Utkast till Gottlands flora. 1805. I. 352.
— Växter i Österländerne. 1826. I. 353.
— De vegetatione et climate in Helvetia. 1813. I. 433.
Wahlroos, A. Lyhykäinen metsänhoiton oppi. 1871. IV. 104.[1]
— Metsäoloista länsi-ja luoteis-Satakunnassa. 1891. IV. 348.[1]
Wahlström, J. E. Plantarum vascularium in regione Telgae borealis. 1847. I. 355.
Wahluch, Adolphe. A dictionary of materia medica. 1868. III. 243.
Wahrhaftige neue Zeitung wie ... wunderbarliche Gewächs auf den Eichbäumen sich erzeigt haben. 1582. IV. 509.
Wahrlich, W. Einige Details zur Kenntniss der Sclerotinia Rhododendri. 1892. III. 657.[1]
Waidmann, A. Der rechnende Forst- und Landwirth. 1872. IV. 59.[1]
Wailes, B. L. C. Report on the agriculture ... of Mississippi. 1854. III. 263.[3]
Wainio, Edward August. Anmärkningsvärda hybrider af slägtet Salix. 1882. II. 100.[2]
— Cotoneaster nigra från Suursaari. 1900. II. 260.[1]
— Cotoneaster vulgaris nigra ny för Finland flora. 1881. II. 259.[3]
— Florula Tavastiae orientalis. 1878. I. 363.
— Käsvistonsuhteista Pohjois-Suomen ja Venäjän-Karjalan rajaseudulilla. 1878. I. 364.
— Monströst päron. 1888. II. 280.[1]
— Notes sur la flore de la Laponie finlandaise. 1891. I. 531.[2]
— Salixhybrider från östra Finland. 1883. II. 101.[1]
Waisbecker, Anton. Beiträge zur Flora des Eisenburger Comitates. 1897. II. 305.[1]
Wait & **Judson**. The annual trade report of the business of the Muskegon valley. 1873. IV. 403.[2]
Waite, Merton Benway. The cause and prevention of Pear blight. 1896. III. 446.[1]
— The fertilization of Pear flowers. 1892. II. 280.[2]
— The pollination of Pear flowers. 1894. III. 445.[1]
— Pollination of pomaceous fruits. 1899. II. 257.[2]
— The pollination of Pear flowers. 1894. II. 280.[2]
Waite, Percival C. See TURNBULL, Robert & WAITE, P. C.
Waitz. Über die zweckmässigste Eintheilung der Rosen. 1842. II. 282.[1]
Waitz, Friedrich August Karl. Practische waarnemingen over eenige Javaansche geneesmiddelen. 1829. III. 275.[1]
— Praktische Beobachtungen über einige javanische Arzneimittel. 1829. III. 275.[2]
— Rosa Reichenbachiana. 1824. II. 298.[1]
Waitz, Karl Friedrich. Beschreibung der ... Heiden. 1805. II. 664,[1] III. 649.[2]
Wajgel, Leopold. Szkodniki naszych pól, ogrodów i lasów. 1875. III. 179.
Wakefield, Priscilla. Flore des jeunes personnes. 1796[?] I. 93.
— An introduction to botany. 1796. I. 93.
Wakker, J. H. De aanzwellingen aan de takken van Ribes. 1889. III. 414.[1]
— Aleuronkorrels zijn vacuolen. 1888. I. 137.
— Bau ... des Stengels von Abrus. 1889. II. 382.[1]
— Of bolgewassen gevaar opleveren voor overbrengen der Phylloxera. 1884. III. 573.
— Contributions à la pathologie végétale. 1889. III. 414.[1]
— De elaioplast. 1886. I. 137.
— La formation des cristaux d'oxalate de chaux. 1886. I. 139.
— Gnomonia erythrostoma. 1888. III. 435.[2]
— Over den invloed van parasietische fungi. 1892. III. 195.[1]
— Onderzoekingen over adventieve knoppen. 1885. I. 108.[2]
— Les renflements des branches ... de Ribes. 1889. III. 414.[1]
— Studien über die Inhaltskörper der Pflanzenzelle. 1888. I. 137.
— Untersuchungen über den Einfluss parasitischer Pilze. 1892. III. 195.[1]
— Een verbond tusschen boomen en mieren. 1888. I. 235.[1]
— De vorming van kristallen van oxalzure kali. 1886. I. 139.
Wal, H. H. Iets over het enten en oculeren. 1847. III. 160.
Walafridus Strabo. Hortulus. 849. I. 274.

Walbaum, Heinrich & **Bertram**, J. Beitrag zur Kenntnis der Fichtennadelöle. 1893. IV. 443.[2]
— & **Erdmann**, Hugo. Sur l'essence de néroli. 1899. III. 499.[1]
— & **Stephan**, Karl. Sur l'essence de Roses allemande. 1900. III. 454.[2]
Walberg, C. von. Neueste Beobachtungen zur Veredelung . . . der Forstwissenschaft. 1810. IV. 100.[2]
Walberg, T. W. von. Beschreibung der verschiedenen besonders nützlichen . . . Holzgattungen. 1787. IV. 86.[2]
Walberg, Theobald von. Etwas über den allgemeinen Holzmangel. 1805. IV. 283.[1]
— Ueber die Kultur . . . des inländischen und ausländischen Ahornbaumes. 1810. III. 534.[2]
Walcher, G. Ueber die Verwendung des "Holzstoffes." 1883. IV. 429.[1]
Walchner, Franz Hermann. Beiträge zur Naturgeschichte des Fichtenspinners. 1840. IV. 206.
— Der Botaniker. 1844. I. 88.
— Darstellung der wichtigsten . . . Verfälschungen der Arzneimittel. 1842. III. 258.
— Der practische Naturforscher. 1844. I. 88.
Walcott, Charles Doolittle. The United States forest reserves. 1898. IV. 179.[1]
Walcott, H. L. T. Is the amber-colored Choke-Cherry entitled to a distinct name? 1888. IV. 277.[2]
Walcott, John. Flora britannica indigena. 1778. I. 395.
Der **Wald** als Retter in der Futternoth. 1864. IV. 135.[2]
Der **Wald** auf dem Kyffhäuser-Gebirge. 1898. IV. 355.[1]
Wald-, Forst-, Jagt-, Wild-, Weyd-, Wercks- und Fischerey, Ordnung . . . Johann Philipsen . . . zu Mayntz, Ertzbischoffen. 1666. IV. 319.[2]
Wald- Forst- und Jägerey-Lexikon. See G., F. C. V. 1764. IV. 22.[1]
Wald-, Holz- und Forstordnung für die k. k. österreichische Vorlande. 1787. IV. 331.[1]
Der **Wald** in Griechenland. 1890. IV. 375.[2]
Der **Wald** in Gross- und Weiss-Russland. 1868. I. 358, IV. 80.
Der **Wald** und die Waldverminderung in Böhmen. 1861. IV. 278.[2]
Wald und Flur. IV. 11.
Ueber **Wald**- und Gartenraupen. 1806. IV. 206.
Wald und Holzindustrie in Oesterreich. 1893. IV. 407.[1]
Wald und Regen. 1889. IV. 51.
Wald- und Strafordnung für den Ziegelhäuser Forst. 1798. IV. 318.
Die **Wald**- und Weidabtheilung in . . . Todtnau. 1859. IV. 25.
Wald und Wild. Allgemeines Liederbuch. See WIEMANN, A. 1827. IV. 101.
Wald, Waldnutzung und Holzhandel in Mexiko. 1888. IV. 403.[2]
Wald-Arbeiter-Verhältnisse. 1860. IV. 311.[2]
Waldau. Welche Gründe sprechen für die Aufforstung von Ödland? 1899. IV. 159.
Ueber **Waldausreutungen.** 1853. IV. 43.
Waldbauliche Betrachtungen mit theilweiser Bezugnahme auf . . . die Waldungen der Gr. Hess. Rhein-Main-Ebene. 1869. IV. 118.
Waldbau-Schule [bei Aachen]. 1853. IV. 32.
Waldbauschulen. 1860. IV. 36.[1]
Waldbeerenertrag. 1865. IV. 439.
Die **Waldbestände** der Erde. 1885. IV. 636.[1]
Der **Waldbestand** Böhmens. 1886. IV. 371.
Der **Waldbestand** Europas. 1888. IV. 342.[2]
Der **Waldbestand** Grossbritanniens. 1892. IV. 357.[2]
Waldbestand in den Vereinigten Staaten. 1889. IV. 338.[1]
Der **Waldbestand** Preussens. 1894. IV. 354.
Waldbestand und Besitzverhältnisse der Forsten Preussens. 1894. IV. 354.
Waldbilder aus dem nordöstlichen Ausläufer des Fichtelgebirges. 1868. IV. 118.
Ueber **Waldbrände** und Waldbrandversicherungen. 1897. IV. 182.[2]
Waldbruehl, Wilhelm von. Die deutschen Pflanzennamen. See ZUCCALMAGLIO, A. W. von. 1841. I. 73.[2]
Waldburg, H. Der Kubikpreisrechner. 1879. IV. 402.[2]
Waldcultur und Steinkohlen in Ungarn. 1853. IV. 123.[2]
Walden, Werner. Der Wald und seine Bewohner im deutschen Liede. 1897. IV. 55.[2]
Walderträge aus dem Aargau. 1853. IV. 261.[2]
Waldertrag und Holzverbrauch. n. d. IV. 277.

Waldfeldbau. 1851. IV. 133.
Waldfeldbau in den Gemeindswaldungen der Stadt Zofingen. 1852. IV. 365.
Zur **Waldfeldbaufrage.** 1892. IV. 134.[1]
Der **Waldfeldbetrieb** im . . . Forstbezirk Ochsenhausen. 1884. IV. 134.[1]
Der **Waldfeld**-Betrieb im Kanton Aargau. 1856. IV. 133.
Die **Waldfläche** Böhmens. 1882. IV. 371.
Waldheim. Der Kiefernmarkkäfer. 1887. IV. 478.
Waldheim, Alexander, FISCHER VON. See FISCHER VON WALDHEIM, Alexander.
Waldhütte. IV. 15.
Die **Waldkrankheit** im Wallis. 1857. IV. 450.
Die **Waldkultur** durch Erdwälle. 1853. IV. 152.
Waldlieb, A. Ein verschwundener deutscher Waldbaum. 1892. IV. 440.[2]
Waldmann, V., (*pseud*.). Les Lapins et les Pins du Lord Weymouth. 1872. IV. 469.
Waldner, Henri. Beiträge zur Flore vogéso-rhénane. 1883. II. 284.[2]
— Botanicorum crux et scandalum. 1883. II. 302.[1]
— Ueber europaeische Rosentypen. 1885. II. 283.[2]
— Excursionsflora von Elsass-Lothringen. 1876. I. 387.
— Merkwürdige Rubus-Form. 1883. II. 309.[2]
— Les Rosiers de l'Alsace-Lorraine. 1882. II. 284.[2]
— Ueber das Schwanken der Vegetationsgrenze. 1881. I. 218.
Waldner, M. Über eigenthümliche Öffnungen in der Oberhaut der Blumenblätter von Franciscea. 1878. II. 769.[1]
Wald-Ordnung betreffend die Marggrevischen Unterthanen. 1535. IV. 318.
Wald-Ordnung dess Hochlöblichen Ercz-Stiffts Saltzburg. 1713. IV. 331.[1]
Waldordnungen für den heiligen Forst bei Hagenau. 1887. IV. 317.[1]
Ueber das **Waldpflanzen** . . . bei der Genossame Dorf-Binzen. 1865. IV. 366.
Der **Waldreichthum** Europas. 1890. IV. 342.[2]
Waldreichthum Russlands. 1884. IV. 346.
Waldron, C. B. Tree plantations or groves? 1896. IV. 112.
— & others. The flowering of the Virgilia. 1893. II. 346.[2]
Waldron, Lawrence Root. The development of the buds of the Wild Plum. 1900. II. 272.[1]
— See also BOLLEY, H. L. & WALDRON, L. R.
Zur **Waldsamen-Aufbewahrung.** 1859. IV. 147.[2]
Waldschmidt, F. Studien zur waldeckischen Flora. 1865. I. 385.
Waldschmidt, Johann Jakob. De potu Theae. 1685. III. 605.
Waldschmiedt, W. W. De sexu ejusdem plantae gemino. 1705. I. 198.
Waldschmiedt, Wilhelm Ulrich Huldreich. De usu et abusu potus Thee in genere. 1692. III. 605.
Der **Waldstand** Oesterreichs. 1888. IV. 368.
Waldstands-Übersicht . . . der Königl. Forstreviere Waldaschaff. 1858. IV. 351.[1]
Waldstands-Uebersicht . . . derjenigen Reviere . . . bei den Excursionen der süddeutschen Forstwirthe in Kaiserslautern betr. 1861. IV. 351.[1]
Waldstands-Übersicht . . . im königl. Forstamte Würzburg. 1862. IV. 248.[1]
Waldstein, Franz Adam, *Graf* von & **Kitaibel**, Paul. Descriptiones et icones plantarum rariorum Hungariae. 1802. I. 444.
Waldt-Ordnung dess durchleuchtigen, hochgebornen Fürsten . . . Marggrafen zu Brandenburg. 1613. IV. 319.[1]
Die **Waldungen** Frankreichs. 1886. IV. 361.
Die **Waldungen** im Grossherzogtum Baden. 1891. IV. 350.[2]
Die **Waldverhältnisse** in Tirol und Vorarlberg. 1891. IV. 369.
Waldverheerungen durch den Kiefernspanner in Bayern. 1895. IV. 479.
Waldverwüstung in Russland. 1890. IV. 282.[1]
Die **Waldverwüstungen** in Wälschtirol. 1885. IV. 283.[2]
Der **Waldwegebau** im Herzogthume Sachsen-Gotha. 1864. IV. 266.[2]
Der **Waldwegebaubetrieb** in Kurhessen. 1865. IV. 266.[2]
Zur **Waldwertberechnung** in den Staatsforsten Payerns. 1885. IV. 261.[1]
Waldwirthschaft in den Hochgebirgskantonen. 1858. IV. 123.[1]
Waldwirthschaft und Holzausfuhr. 1856. IV. 278.[1]
Die **Waldwolle.** 1853. IV. 482.[2]

Walford, T. Scientific tourist. 1818. I. 397.
Walichanoff, (*Stabs-Capitän*). Naturverhältnisse der kleinen Bucharei. 1883. I. 457.
Walker, *Rev. Dr. See* A SHORT account of the late donation of a botanic garden to the University of Cambridge. 1763. I. 52.
Walker, E. H. RAWSON-. Report on Tea raising in South Carolina. 1894. III. 600.[2]
Walker, Ernest. Some factors in the distribution of Gleditschia triacanthos. 1895. II. 362.[1]
Walker, Frank J. The Sequoia forests of the Sierra Nevada. 1890. II. 50.[1]
Walker, Inches CAMPBELL-. The forests of New.Zealand. 1876. IV. 380.[1]
— Les forêts de la Nouvelle-Zélande. 1876. IV. 380.[2]
— Report on English and Scotch forests. 1872. IV. 357.[2]
— Report on the transport of timber from the hill forests. 1873. IV. 389.
— Reports on forest management in Germany; Austria, and Great Britain. 1873. IV. 342.[1]
— The Sandal wood oil stills of South Canara. 1884. III. 384.[2]
— State forestry. 1877? IV. 280.[1]
— State forestry; its aim and object. 1876. IV. 269, 380.[2]
— On state forests . . . in Germany. 1875. IV. 349.[1]
— Utilization of the less valuable trees. 1894. IV. 382.[2]
— & others. Reports on forest management in Germany. 1873. IV. 244.
Walker, J. Die Baumzucht im Königreich Württemberg. 1815. III. 136.
Walker, J. R. Plant distribution. 1895. I. 301.
Walk , John. A catalogue of . . . trees in Scotland. 1812. V. xm.[1]
— An economical history of the Hebrides. 1808. IV. 358.[2]
— Essays on natural history. 1812. V. xx.[2]
— Experiments on the motion of the sap. 1788. I. 163.
— Salicetum. 1812. III. 347. —
— Versuche über die Bewegung des Saftes. 1788. I. 163.
Walker, John M. An experimental inquiry into . . . Cornus florida and sericea. 1803. III. 645.[2]
Walker, Joseph Burbeen. An address upon the forests of New Hampshire. 1872. IV. 338.[2]
— The forests of New Hampshire. 1883. IV. 339.
— Our New Hampshire forests. 1891. IV. 339.
Walker, Richard. The flora of Oxfordshire. 1833. I. 398.
Walker, Wilhelm. Die Erziehung der Obstbäume. 1844. III. 137.
— Nieuwe handleiding voor de oofthoom kweekerij. 1849. III. 139.
— Die Obstlehre der Griechen und Römer. 1845. III. 32.[1]
Walker, William. Forest trees of British landscape. 1877. I. 393,[2] 521.[1]
— The forests of British Guiana. 1874. IV. 342.[1]
— Suggestions for a new forest-law. 1882. IV. 315.[1]
Walker-Arnott, George Arnott. *See* ARNOTT, G. A. WALKER-.
Wall, Otto A. *See* OLDBERG, Oscar & WALL, O. A.
Wall, W. A. Westmanlands Flora. 1852. I. 355.
Wall-und Hügel-Pflanzungen. 1855. IV. 153.[2]
Wall Bake, H. W. A. van den. Djattihout. 1897. IV. 538.[1]
Walla, Ferdinand. Die Samen-Darren. 1874. IV. 148.
Wallace, Alexander. Ailanthiculture. 1865. III. 506.[2]
— A noted horticulturist at home. 1893. I. 39.
Wallace, Alfred Russel. Acclimatisation. 1878. III. 43.
— On the Bamboo and Durian of Borneo. 1856. III. 315,[1] 589.[2]
— Ueber Bambus und Durian auf Borneo. 1856. III. 315,[1] 589.[2]
— Guilielma speciosa Martius. 1853. III. 320.[2]
— Epping forest. 1878. IV. 358.[1]
— On Epping forest. 1878. IV. 358.[1]
— Insulinde. 1869. I. 466.
— Insulinde. 1869. I. 466.
— Island life. 1880. I. 218.
— The Malay Archipelago. 1869. I. 466.
— A narrative of travels on the Amazon. 1853. I. 342.
— De natuur der tropen en andere schetsen. 1878. I. 219.[2]
— Palm trees of the Amazon. 1853. II. 61.[1]
— A profitable Sugar-Palm. 1887. III. 320.[2]
— On some anomalies in zoological and botanical geography. 1864. I. 300.
— Tropical nature and other essays. 1878. I. 219.[2]
Wallace, Berkeley. A glimpse of a Californian Olive ranch. 1893. III. 676.[2]
Wallace, James. A description of the isles of Orkney. 1693. I. 394.

Wallace, Peter. The Areca Palm. 1873. II. 64.[2]
— The Cocoa-nut Palm. 1873. III. 324.[1]
— Cypress groves of the southern states. 1872. II. 51.[2]
— The Date Palm in Egypt. 1874. II. 72.[1]
— The gardens and Orange-grounds of St. Michael's. 1852. I I. 131.[2]
— The Indian Thorny or spreading Acacia. 1873. II. 323.[2]
— The large-flowered Magnolia at home. 1872. II. 212.[1]
— Pecan Nut tree. 1872. III. 354.[1]
— Seaside planting. 1873. III. 41.[2]
Wallenius, Johan Frederic. Om Finska allmogens nödbröd. *See* HELLENIUS, C. N. 1782. III. 219.[1]
Waller, A. D. Experiments on leaves of Iris. 1900. I. 231.[2]
— Four observations concerning the electrical effects of light. 1900. I. 231.[2]
Waller, J. L. De Liberia Koffie. 1887. III. 743.[1]
Wallerius, Johan Gotschalk. L'agriculture réduite à ses vrais principes. 1761. III. 35.
— De artificiosa foecundatione. 1752. I. 199.
— Chemische Grundsätze des Ackerbaues. 1761. III. 35.
— Élémens d'agriculture physique et chimique. 1761. III. 35.
— Elementa agriculturae physico-chemica. 1761. III. 35.
— De historiae naturalis usu medico. 1740. III. 238.[1]
— De principiis vegetationis. 1751. I. 31.
— Von der Ursachen, welche bei dem Wachsthum der Pflanzen bemerkt werden. 1751. I. 31.
— De vegetatione seminum vegetabilium. 1761. I. 527.
Walley. Remarks on . . . poisoning of a cow by leaves of Populus balsamifera. 1873. III. 345.[2]
Wallich, Nathaniel. An account of a new species of a Camellia. 1820. II. 550.[2]
— Account of the new genus Melanorrhoea. 1830. II. 457.[1]
— On Cassia lanceolata. 1836. II. 343.[1]
— Description of the tree which produces the Nipal Camphor wood. 1823. II. 224.[2]
— Description of two new genera . . . from Nepal. 1822. II. 763.[1]
— Descriptions of some rare and curious plants. 1835. I. 471.
— Descriptions of some rare Indian plants. 1820. I. 471.
— Descriptions of two new species of Sarcolobus. 1816. I. 471.
— Effects of the late gale at the Botanic garden. 1842. III. 184.[1]
— Emploi du Melanorrhaea usitata. 1830. III. 525.[1]
— List of Indian woods. 1831. IV. 17.
— Notes on Cassia lanceolata. 1836. II. 343.[1]
— Notes on the drugs called mishme teeta. 1837. III. 697.[2]
— Notice of the progress of botanical science in Bengal. 1819. I. 471.
— Notice regarding the American Sumach. 1845. III. 468.[2]
— Notice respecting Dr. Wallich's journey in Nepaul. 1822. I. 471.
— A numerical list of dried specimens of plants. 1828. I. 471, V. xxiii.[2]
— Observations on the Burmese . . . Varnish tree. 1840. II. 457.[1]
— Observations sur le nouveau genre Mélanorrhaea. 1830. II. 457.[1]
— Plantae asiaticae rariores. 1830. I. 471.
— Upon the preparation . . . of plants during a voyage from India. 1832. III. 155.
— Tentamen florae napalensis illustratae. 1824. I. 471.
Walliczek, Heinrich. Studien über die Membranschleime officieller Pflanzen. 1893. I. 181.[2]
— Studien über die Membranschleime vegetativer Organe. 1893. I. 135.
Wallin, Georg, jr. Γαμος φυτων; sive, Nuptiae arborum. 1729. I. 517.[1]
Wallinger, W. A. The treatment of Casuarina on sand-dunes. 1896. IV. 485.[1]
Wallis. A note . . . upon Mr. Lister's observation concerning the veins in plants. 1673. I. 133.
Wallis. Aufforstungen in der Rhône-Ebene. 1897. IV. 167.[1]
— Wildbachverbauung. 1896. IV. 187.[2]
Wallis, A. *See* MITTEN, W. & WALLIS, A.
Wallis, Gustav. Bereisung der Hochebene von Curitiba. 1859. I. 342.
— Die brasilianische Guiana. 1870. I. 339.[1]
— Einige Worte über die Leopoldinien. 1870. III. 326.[2]
— Gärtnerisch-botanische Streifzüge am Amazonenstrom. 1869. I. 343.

Wallis, Gustav (*continued*).
— La Guyane brésilienne. 1870. I. 339.[1]
— Die Kulturgewächse der deutschen Colonie Blumenau. 1856. III. 65.[1]
— Die Manglewaldung. 1870. I. 219.[2]
— Ueber den Manzinella-Baum. 1873. III. 519.[1]
— Les plateaux d'Euritiba. 1859. I. 342.
— Reisebericht über den Purusfluss. 1870. I. 343.
— Reise-Erinnerungen. 1876. I. 330.
— Schilderung des südbrasilianischen Urwaldes. 1856. I. 342.
— Ueber tropische Obstarten. 1861. III. 220.[1]
— Tropische Pflanzen als natürliche Wohnstätten der Ameisen. 1870. I. 235.[1]
— Ueber vegetabilisches Wachs. 1874. III. 226.[1]
— La végétation de la Guiane brésilienne. 1870. I. 339.[1]
— Voyages et découvertes dans l'Amérique du Sud. 1876. I. 330.
Wallis, J. Natural history of Northumberland. 1769. I.
Wallis, John. Dendrology. 1833. I. 163, *IV. 69.*[1]
— Fruiting of Trachelospermum jasminoïdes. 1877. III. 691.[2]
Wallis-Tayler, Alex. J. Tea machinery and tea factories. 1900. III. 600.[2]
Wallman, Johan Hacquinus. De systematibus vegetabilium. 1818. I. 251.
Wallmann, (*Forstcandidat*). Einiges über das Stammgrundflächen-Verhältniss . . . der Erle. 1852. IV. 489.[2]
— Notizen über die Schätzung von Lerchenbeständen. 1851. IV. 452.[1]
Wallmann, (*Oberförster*). Zur Waldwerthberechnung in Expropriationssachen. 1874. IV. 256.
Wallmann, (*Revierförster*). Ein Versuch der Buchenzucht. 1864. IV. 494.
Wallner, J. Lettre relativement à la greffe du Paeonia Moutan. 1830. III. 392.[2]
Wallner, J. K. Spis pierwszy roślin Zakładu ogrodowego w Antoninie. 1854. III. 68.[1]
Der **Wallnussbaum**, Juglans regia. 1877. III. 355.
Wallroth, Karl Friederich Wilhelm. Annus botanicus; sive, Supplementum tertium ad C. Sprengelii Floram halensem. 1815. I. 376.
— Beiträge zur Botanik. 1842. II. 107.[1]
— Geschichte des Obstes der Alten. 1812. III. 32.[1]
— Rosae plantarum generis historia. 1828. II. 282.[1]
— Schedulae criticae de plantis florae halensis. 1822. I. 377.
Wallström, Ol. Andr. Plantarum japonicarum novae species. *See* THUNBERG, C. P. 1824. I. 461.
The **Walnut** and its varieties. 1876. III. 354.[1]
A **Walnut** tree farm. 1896. IV. 488.[2]
Of the **Walnut**-tree, its etymology. 1733. III. 354.[1]
Walpers, E. Zur Erklärung der . . . Form der Schmetterlingsblüthe. 1839. II. 320.[1]
— On the irregular form of the flower of the Papilionaceae. 1839. II. 320.[1]
Walpers, Wilhelm Gerhard. Abyssinische Bandwurmmittel. 1853. III. 280.[2]
— Ueber Adansonia digitata. 1852. II. 529.[1]
— Animadversiones criticae in Leguminosas capenses. 1839. II. 319.[2]
— Bemerkungen über Schepti-Früchte. 1853. III. 388.[2]
— Beschreibung des Senecio mikanioides Otto. 1845. II. 865.[2]
— Beschreibung einer neuen blühenden Sophora. 1839. II. 384.[2]
— Beschreibung einer neuen Kennedya. 1846. II. 367.[1]
— Compositarum novarum decades. 1840. II. 848.[1]
— Ueber Feigen. 1851. II. 148.[2]
— Eine neue strauchartige Verbesina. 1851. II. 867.[2]
— Noch ein Paar Worte über Erythrina L. 1853. II. 356.[1]
— Notiz über Cortex Assa-Cou. 1851. II. 148.[2]
— Repertorium botanices systematicae. 1842. I. 268.
— Versuch einer morphologischen Deutung der Blüthe von der Gattung Coulteria. 1838. II. 338.[2]
— Zufällige Ursachen für die Verbreitung der Gewächse. 1853. I. 299.
— Zwei neue Pflanzen-Gattungen. 1851. II. 356.[2]
— *See also* DUCHASSAING, Placide & WALPERS, G. W.
— & **Mueller**, Karl. Annales botanices systematicae. 1848. I. 269.
Walpert, H. Alphabetisch-synonymisches Wörterbuch der deutschen Pflanzennamen. 1852. I. 73.[2]

— Ueber eine merkwürdige Bildung von Blüthen an einer Fuchsie. 1852. II. 643.[1]
— Synonyma der Phanerogamen . . . in Deutschland. 1855. I. 383.
Walpole, Horace. Essay on modern gardening. 1785. III. 123.[2]
Walser, *Dr.* Die grosse Linde in Leutkirch. 1861. II. 516.[2]
— Phytotopographische Skizze der Umgegend von München-roth. 1847. I. 382.
Walser, Emil. Der Baum in Winter. 1894. I. 294,[2] *III. 89.*[1] *IV. 84.*[1]
Walsh, Benjamin Dann. An instance . . of symphysis. 1836. I. 209.[1]
Walsh, George Ethelbert. Cultivation of the Pecan. 1889. III. 354.[1]
— Forest culture of to-day. 1897. IV. 112.
— The Guava in Florida. 1889. III. 637.[2]
Walsh, Joseph M. Coffee; its history. 1894. III. 740.[1]
— Tea; its history and mystery. 1892. III. 608.[1]
— Tea-blending as a fine art. 1896. III. 608.[1]
Walsh, Philip. On the disappearance of the New Zealand bush. 1897. I. 508.[1]
— On the future of the New Zealand bush. 1899. I. 506,[1] *IV. 89.*[2]
Walter. Om nogle af de Beskjærmelsesmidler . . . ved de Træsorters Overvintring i det Frie. 1836. III. 183.[1]
Walter. Cedrus Deodara var. viridis Hügelii. 1885. III. 300.[1]
Walter, C. & **Mueller**, Ferdinand, *Baron* von. Names of different woods . . . used by the Yarra natives. 1867. III. 282.[2]
Walter, Charles. Records of plants new to Victoria. 1900. I. 505.
Walter, E. Baum- und Coniferen-Schule von Wilhelm Weisse. 1899. III. 306.[1]
Walter, F. Verzeichniss der auf den Friedländischen Gütern cultivirten Gewächse. 1815. I. 45; *see also* WILLDENOW. 1815. III. 27.[2]
Walter, Fr. Einiges über Rosen. 1873. III. 452.
Walter, J. Die Krafft-Reuss'sche selbstregistrirende Kluppe. 1883. IV. 231.[2]
Walter, Johann Jacob. Allgemeines deutsches Gartenbuch. 1779. III. 103.
Walter, M. Bemerkungen über die Verheerungen des Fichten-Rüssel-Käfers. 1826. IV. 455.
Walter, Philippe. Composition de l'huile de Ben. 1846. III. 409.[1]
— Recherches sur l'huile de Ben. 1846. III. 409.[1]
Walter, Thomas. Flora caroliniana. 1788. I. 317.[2]
Walther, (*Oberförster*). Die Aussonderung der Holzsortimente. 1891. IV. 252.
— Die Behandlung der Pflanzgärten. 1893. IV. 151.[1]
— Beschädigung der Kiefer durch . . . Unterbau von Buchen. 1886. IV. 473.
— Blitzschläge im Walde. 1892. IV. 478.
— Ueber die Cubirung des Stammholzes. 1887. IV. 218. .
— Entgegnung auf die Abhandlung des Herrn M. von Sivers. 1895. IV. 474.
— Erfahrungen . . . über das Vorkommen und Wachstum der Eiche. 1894. IV. 508.
— Das forstliche Verhalten der Lärche. 1890. IV. 450.
— Hohe oder niedere Umtriebe. 1888. IV. 252.
— Die Holzverwerthung durch Submission. 1890. IV. 388.[2]
— Kiefern-Ueberhälter. 1806. IV. 474.
— Die Rindenmasse bei der Kiefer. 1888. IV. 481.
— Statische . . . Mittheilungen aus dem Eichen-Schälwalde. 1886. IV. 513.
— Untersuchungen über das Wachsthum der Kiefer. 1888. IV. 481.
Walther, Augustin Friedrich. Designatio plantarum quas hortus A. F. Waltheri complectitur. 1735. I. 43.
— Plantarum exoticarum indigenarumque index tripartitus. 1732. I. 43.
— Programma de plantarum structura. 1740. I. 97, 123.[2]
Walther, C. J. H. Etwas über Pflanzen-Emballage. 1862. III. 155.
— Gehölze mit schönem Herbstcolorit. 1867. III. 207.[1]
— Ueber die Kultur der einheimischen Alpenröschen. 1865. III. 654.[2]
— Neue Varietäten von Eichen. 1865. III. 362.[1]
— Ueber Pflanzenvermehrung durch Wurzelstecklinge. 1866. III. 158.[1]
— Rhus Toxicodendron, Giftsumach. 1864. III. 528.[1]

Walther, Friedrich Ludwig. Vom Anbau der vorzüglichsten . . . Holzarten. 1789. IV. 105.
— Beschreibung und Abbildung der in der Forstwirthschaft vorkommenden. . . . Geräthe. 1796. IV. 176.¹
— Einige Bemerkungen über die wissenschaftlichen Eintheilungen der Holzarten. 1805. I. 259.
— Flora von Giessen. 1802. I. 375.
— Grundlinien der teutschen Forstgeschichte. 1816.· IV. 25.
— Grundriss der Forstwissenschaft für Vorlesungen. 1789. IV. 95.
— Handbuch der Forsttechnologie. 1802. IV. 381.
— Handbuch der Forstwissenschaft. 1787. IV. 95.
— Holzarten. 1790. IV. 81.
— Kurgefasste ökonomische Naturgeschichte. 1787. IV. 56.
— Landwissenschaft. 1804. III. 136.
— Lehrbuch der Forstphysiographie. 1800. IV. 56.
— Lehrbuch der Forstwissenschaft. 1795. IV. 95.
— Theoretisch-praktisches Handbuch der Naturgeschichte der Holzarten. 1793. IV. 81.
— Die vorzüglichsten in- und ausländischen Holzarten. 1813. III. 72.
Walther, Israel. Von den Rebenstichern; drey Schriften. See Von den REBENSTICHERN. 1771. III. 562.
— Von den Rebenstichern; vier Preisschriften. See Von den REBENSTICHERN. 1767. III. 562.
Walther, Ludwig August. Pharmakognostisch-pharmakologische Tabellen. 1838. III. 258.
Walther, Ph. Untersuchung einer 70jährigen Weymouthskiefer. 1883. IV. 470.¹
Walther, Philipp. Die Ermittelung der Bestandsholzmassen. 1886. IV. 218.
Waltl, Joseph. Das Amylon und Inulin. 1829. I. 174.
— Handbuch der Naturgeschichte. 1837. I. 255.
Walton, Elijah. Flowers from the upper Alps. 1869. I. 435.
Walz, Georg Friedrich. Beiträge zur Cultur des Weinstocks. 1846. III. 582.
— Die Weintraube in verschiedenen Reifeperioden. 1847. III. 582.
Walz, Gustav. Ueber die Waldstreu. 1850. IV. 71.
Walz, Lajos. A Viscum album L. gazdanövényei Kolozsvár vidékén. 1885. II. 179.³
Walz, Rudolf. Zur Flora des Leithagebirges. 1890. I. 443.
Wand, Th. Berühmte Bäume. 1873. IV. 75.¹
Wanderings through the conservatories at Kew. See GOSSE, P. H. 1856. I. 54.
Wanderley, Germano. Die Constructionen in Holz. 1873. IV. 423.¹
— Handbuch der Bau-Constructionslehre. 1873. IV. 423.¹
Wang, Ferdinand. Die Anwendung der Photogrammetrie im forstlichen Haushalte. 1892 IV. 37.³
— Die Arbeiten der Wiederbewaldung in Britisch-Indien. 1891. IV. 168.¹
— Die Bedeutung des Waldes im Wildbachgebiete. 1888. IV. 184.³
— Die Ermittelung der Durchflussprofile. 1898. IV. 188.¹
— Die Ermittelung der Wasserabflussmengen. 1895. IV. 188.¹
— Die forstlichen Verhältnisse Mexicos. 1890. IV. 341.²
— Fortschritt und Erfolg auf dem Gebiete der Wildbachverbauung. 1890. IV. 188.¹
— Fortschritt und Erfolg auf dem Gebiete der Wildbachverbauung in Oesterreich. 1889. IV. 188.¹
— Die Gesetze der Bewegung des Schiebes. 1896. IV. 188.¹
— Die Gesetze der Bewegung des Wassers. 1895. IV. 188.⁴
— Die Inanspruchnahme forstlicher Bauten. 1899. IV. 188.¹
— Ueber den neuesten Stand der Wildbachverbauung in Oesterreich. 1894. IV. 188.¹
— Die photogrammetrischen Instrumente. 1893. IV. 265.
— Welche Erfahrungen liegen über Wildbach- und Lawinenverbauungen vor? 1890. IV. 184.³
— Die Wildbachverbauung. 1896. ·IV. 184.²
Wang, Nikolaus. Populäre Anleitung zur Cultur des Maulbeerbaumes. 1862. III. 377.
Wangenheim, von, (Forstmeister zu Klein-Tabars bei Gotha). Fortdauer des Holz-Wachsthums an abgehauenen Stöcken. 1835. I. 528.¹
Wangenheim, Friedrich Adam Julius von. Bemerkungen über die graue preussische Fichte. 1789. IV. 455.
— Bemerkungen über die nordische weisse Eller. 1789. II. 116.²

— Beschreibung der Poleyblättrigen Kalmia. 1788. II. 483,¹ 672.¹
— Beschreibung einiger Nordamericanischen Holz- und Buscharten. 1781. I. 304, IV. 75.³
— Beytrag zur teutschen holzgerechten Forstwissenschaft. 1787. I. 304, IV. 81.
— Der rothe Maulbeerbaum. 1826. II. 155.¹
Wanger, K. L. Der Lichtungshieb. 1888. IV. 174, 175.³
Wanklyn, J. A. Tea, coffee, and cocoa. 1874. I. 156.²
Wann ist die beste Zeit, Bäume zu pflanzen? 1849. III. 168.²
Wann ist ein Wald haubar? 1853. IV. 382.¹
Wanner, Steph. Excursionsflora für die deutsche Schweiz . . . Holzgewächse. 1885. I. 432.¹
Wantig, R. Haine und Gärten im griechischen Altertum. 1893. III. 32.⁵
Wappes, Lorenz. Die Bekämpfung der Kiefernschütte. 1900. IV. 480.
— Contribution à l'histoire naturelle du Weymouth. 1896. IV. 469.
— Ueber den Genauigkeitsgrad bei der Bestandsausscheidung. 1893. IV. 246.
— Zur Kenntniss und Würdigung der Weymouthskiefer. 1897. IV. 469.
— Zur Naturgeschichte der Weymouthskiefer. 1896. IV. 469.
— Plänter-Durchforstung im Jahre 1811. 1892. IV. 24,¹ 174.
— Vergleichende Untersuchungen über die Waldeinteilung. 1893. IV. 251.²
— Welche Ansprüche macht die Weisstanne? 1896. IV. 444.³
— Ueber die Weymouthskiefer. 1897. IV. 469.
Warburg, Otto. Acacia Perrotii Warb. 1897. II. 327.²
— Die afrikanischen Kautschukpflanzen. 1899. III. 688.³
— Ueber Bau . . . des Holzes von Caulotretus. 1883. II. 335.¹
— Die Bedeutung der Kolanuss-Kultur. 1897. III. 591.¹
— Über die Bedeutung der organischen Säuren. 1886. I. 176.
— Begoniaceae. 1894. II. 583.¹
— Begoniaceae africanae. 1897. II. 583.¹
— Beiträge zur Kenntnis der papuanischen Flora. .1891. I. 499.¹
— Bergpflanzen aus Kaiser Wilhelmsland. 1893. I. 499.¹
— Ein Besuch der Kina-Districte. 1887. V. xxxiii.²
— Bijdrage tot de kennis van den kanker der Kinaboomen. 1887. III. 717.²
— Bixaceae. 1895. II. 565.³
— Carpodinus und Clitandra. 1897. III. 687.²
— Castilloa-Kautschuk. 1898. III. 368.³
— Ceara-Kautschuk. 1899. III. 520.¹
— Zur Charakterisirung . . . der Myristicaceen. 1895. II. 220.¹
— Datiscaceae. 1894. II. 583.¹
— Die aus den deutschen Kolonien exportirten Produkte. 1896. III. 218.¹
— Ueber den Einfluss der Verholzung. 1893. I. 190.³
— Einige Bemerkungen über die Litoral-Pantropflanzen. 1898. I. 219.³
— Einige Bemerkungen zur südwestafrikanischen Gummifrage. 1898. III. 463.¹
— Ficus-Kautschuk. 1899. III. 360.¹
— Flacourtiaceae. 1894. II. 568.³
— Die Flora des asiatischen Monsungebietes. 1890. IV. 88.³·¹
— Eine neuer Gelbfärben benutzte Akazie. 1898. III. 465.¹
— Über die Haarbildung der Myristicaceen. 1895. II. 220.³
— Identifizierung der sog. Ochoconüsse. 1895. III. 221.¹
— Kautschuk in Deutsch-Ostafrika. 1899. III. 230.
— Die Kautschukpflanzen und ihre Kultur. 1900. III. 230.
— Kickxia africana. 1897. III. 688.¹
— Kautkultur. 1898. III. 590.¹
— Die Kulturpflanzen Usambaras. ·1894. III. 93.¹
— Mangabeira-Kautschuk. 1899. III.·688.¹
— Monographie der Myristicaceen. 1897. II. 220.¹
— Monsunia. 1900. I. 453,¹ 467.¹
— Moraceae africanae, II. Ficus. 1895. II. 149.¹
— Die Muskatnuss, ihre Geschichte. 1897. III. 402.¹
— Ueber eine neue Muskat-Fettnuss. 1895. II. 220.³
— Ein neuer Kaffeeschädling aus Afrika. 1895. III. 736.
— Über die nutzbaren Muskatnüsse. 1892. III. 402.¹
— Pandanaceae. 1900. II. 56.¹

Warburg, Otto (*continued*).
— Para-Kautschuk. 1898. III. 518.²
— Das Pflanzenkleid . . . Neu-Guineas. 1899. I. 499.²
— Plantae Hellwigianae. 1894. I. 499.¹
— Eine Reise nach den Bonin- und Volcano-Inseln. 1891. I. 463.¹
— Die Rohprodukte unserer Kolonieen. 1897. III. 218.¹·
— Sanbiaceae. 1896. II. 490.²
— Sansibar-Kopal. 1899. III. 489.²
— Die Steinnusspalme der Salomons-Inseln. 1898. III. 327.²
— The useful varieties of nutmegs. 1892. III. 402.¹
— Vegetationsschilderungen aus Südost-Asien. 1893. I. 466.
— Die Vegetationsverhältnisse von Neu-Guinea. 1892. I. 499.¹
— Ueber Verbreitung . . . der polynesischen Steinnuss-Palmen. 1896. II. 71.²
— Verschiedene Kautschukpflanzen. 1899. III. 230.
— Wer ist der Entdecker der Gewürz-Inseln? 1896. III. 275.¹
— Wilde Kaffeearten des Congostaates. 1900. II. 814.²
— Winteranaceae (Cancellaceae). 1895. II. 566.²
Warburton, G. E. Names and synonyms of British plants. 1889. I. 74.¹
Ward, E. W. New Zealand woods. 1857. IV. 402.¹
— Report on experiments . . . on New Zealand woods. 1875. IV. 410.
Ward, Edward. Gaultheria Shallon. 1886. III. 652.¹
Ward, Fannie B. A cochineal hacienda in Guatemala. 1885. III. 624.¹
Ward, Harry Marshall. Beech-wood. 1889. IV. 499.
— Coffee leaf disease. 1880. III. 735.
— Koffie-bladziekte. 1879. III. 735.
— The Oak. 1892. II. 132.¹
— Some recent publications . . . of the sources of nitrogen in plants. 1887. I. 234.¹
— Symbiosis. 1899. I. 234.¹
— Timber and some of its diseases. 1888. IV. 414.¹
— & **Dunlop**, John. On some points in the histology . . . of Rhamnus. 1887. II. 497.¹
Ward, J. K. Timber of Canada. 1896. IV. 403.¹
Ward, J. Slinger. Note on Manna collection in Sicily. 1894. III. 672.²
Ward, Julius H. White Mountain forests in peril. 1893. IV. 272.
Ward, Lester Frank. Decumaria barbara. 1882. II. 238.¹
— Diamond Willow. 1885. II. 106.²
— Guide to the flora of Washington. 1881. I. 319.
— List of plants added to the flora of Washington. 1885. V. xvii.²
— A new Fir of the Rocky Mountains. 1876. II. 22.²
— Oaks of the Potomac side. 1875. II. 128.²
— Origin of the Plane-trees. 1890. II. 254.²
— On the position of the gamopetalae. 1883. I. 252.
— Quercus Leana Nutt. 1880. II. 135.¹
— Timber-trees of the Dismal Swamp. 1877. I. 317,¹ IV. 77.³
Ward, Marshall. The diseases of Conifers. 1892. IV. 442.
Ward, N. M. Over het gebruik der Koffiebladen. 1854. III. 739.
Ward, Nathaniel Bagshaw. Account of the vegetation of the cliffs of Kilkee. 1864. I. 401.
— Aspects of nature. 1864. I. 401.
— Letter . . . to Sir W. J. Hooker, on the growth of plants. 1837. I. 187.
Ward, R. Notes on scale and other parasitical insects. 1890. III. 188.¹
Ward, R. Halsted. Plant organization. 1890. I. 101.¹
Ward, Stephen H. On the growth of plants in closely-glazed cases. 1854. III. 155.
Ward, Swinburne. On the Double Cocoa-nut of the Seychelles. 1865. II. 70.¹
— Preservation of the Coco de mer. 1867. II. 70.¹
Ward, William. Report on the use of the " Bouillie Bordelaise." 1895. III. 562.¹
Wardall, Thomas. Hedging with Thorn. 1868. III. 421.¹
— Raising groves and timber-belts in northern Iowa. 1868. III. 117.³
Warden, Charles James Hislop. Embelia Ribes. 1888. III. 666.¹
— Note on Erythroxylon . . . in India. 1888. III. 492.¹
— Note on the fruit of Erythroxylon. 1890. III. 493.²
— *See also* DYMOCK, William & WARDEN, C. J. H.
Warden, J. H. & **Waddel**, L. A. "Madar." 1886. III. 692.¹

Wardenburg, B. D. G. De Brem. 1857. III. 475.¹
— Verhandeling over de beste wijze, op welke . . . een bron van volksbestaan . . . kan geopend worden. 1829. IV. 159.
Warder, John Aston. Address on arboriculture. 1882. III. 117.¹
— Address on forestry. 1878. IV. 271.²
— American pomology; Apples. 1867. III. 425.²
— An essay on timber planting. 1880. V. xxx.¹
— Evergreens, their uses for shelter: 1858. III. 60.
— Forest trees adapted to . . . Illinois. 1881. IV. 112.
— Forestry and its needs. 1878. IV. 111.³
— Forestry for Indiana. 1881. IV. 112.
— Forestry meetings. 1882. IV. 271.²
— Forests of New Jersey. 1878. IV. 338.²
— The future orchards and forests of Nebraska. 1878. IV. 111.³
— Has the time come in Ohio for planting for timber? 1880. IV. 271.²
— Hedges and evergreens. 1858. III. 213.
— Larch-mere. 1882. IV. 449.
— Larch-wood. 1882. IV. 449.
— Notes from Arkansas. 1881. II. 123.²
— The Pear orchard. 1862. III. 445.²
— Philosophy of pruning. 1866. III. 170.
— Poplars, Aspens and Cotton-Woods. 1878. III. 344.¹
— The relations of forestry to agriculture. 1881. IV. 538.²
— Report on forests and forestry. 1875. IV. 336.¹
— Some trees for planting on the open prairies of northern Illinois. 1881. IV. 112.
— Thinning, trimming and pruning. 1880? IV. 171.
— Tree-planting for railroads. 1883. IV. 112.
— Tree planting in shelter-belts. 1882. IV. 154.²
— Tree-seeds. 1883. IV. 148.
— Trees. 1881. IV. 112.
— The trees of the Rocky Mountains. 1872. III. 60.
— The two Catalpas. 1879. II. 786.¹
— The western Catalpa. 1881. IV. 538.²
— The-western Catalpa tree. 1880. IV. 538.²
— What are forest trees? 1882. IV. 314.²
— The Wild-cherry tree. 1883. IV. 520.²
— The wine culture of the United States. 1857. III. 550.
— & others. The Catalpa. 1882. IV. 538.²
— **James**, D. L. & J. F. Woody plants of Ohio. 1882. *I. 312*, IV. 76.¹
Wardle, John. Trees and shrubs suitable for towns. 1884. III. 42.²
Wardle, Thomas. On the history and growing utilisations of tussur silk. 1891. III. 148.²
— Monograph on the wild silk industry of India. 1882. III. 148.³
— Monographs on the tusser and other wild silks of India: 1878. III. 148,³ 236.
— Report on Tasar silk and native dye-stuffs of India. 1880. III. 148.²
— Royal commission and government of India silk culture court. 1886. III. 148.¹
Wardleworth, Theo. H. Some pharmaceutical . . . plants of Jamaica. 1900. III. 64.²
Wardrop, J. Note on the connection between the chemical and morphological character of plants. 1856. I. 151.¹
Waring, Edward John. Bibliotheca therapeutica. 1878. III. 1.
— Notes on some of the principal indigenous tonics of India. 1858. III. 278.
— Pharmacopoeia of India. 1868. III. 257.¹
Waring, Richard H. A letter on some plants . . . of England. 1772. I. 395.
Waring, W. The fruit-grower's handbook. n. d. III. 132.¹
Waring, W. G. Prunus pennsylvanica as a stock. 1878. III. 439.¹
Warington, Robert. Additional observations on the green teas. 1852. III. 607.
— Observations on the green teas of commerce. 1845. III. 606.
— Observations on the teas of commerce. 1851. III. 607.
Wark, David. An account of the use of Furze. 1762. III. 489.²
Warming, Johannes Eugen Bülow. Den almindelige Botanik. 1880. I. 91.
— Bidrag til Cycadeernes Naturhistorie. 1879. II. 3.¹
— Ueber die Biologie der Ericineën Grönlands. 1886. II. 659.¹
— Om biologiska förhållanden hos Grönlands Ericineer. 1886. II. 659.¹

— Biologiske Optegnelser om grønlandske Planter. 1886. I. 220,[1] II. 659.[1]
— Die Blüthe der Compositen. 1876. II. 850.[1]
— Om Bygningen og den formodede Bestøvningsmaade af nogle grønlandske Blomster. 1886. I. 239.[2]
— Contributions à l'histoire naturelle des Cycadées. 1879. II. 3.[1]
— Sur les Cycadées. 1879. II. 3.[1]
— Den danske botaniske Literatur. 1880. I. 3.[1]
— Une excursion aux montagnes du Brésil. 1883. I. 343, V. xviii.[1]
— Exkursionen til Skagen. 1897. I. 358.
— Forgreningsforhold hos Fanerogamerne. 1872. I. 106.[2]
— Ueber Grönlands Vegetation. 1888. I. 309.[1]
— Om Grønlands Vegetation. 1888. I. 309.[1]
— Haandbog i den systematiske Botanik. 1879. I. 256.
— A handbook of systematic botany. 1879. I. 256.
— Handbuch der systematischen Botanik. 1879. I. 256.
— Kinatræerne. 1869. II. 812, III. 718.
— Lagoa Santa. 1892. I. 343.
— Lagoa Santa (Brésil). 1892. I. 343.
— Lehrbuch der ökologischen Pflanzengeographie. 1895. I. 219.[1]
— Ueber die Luftwurzeln von Avicennia. 1885. II. 753.[2]
— Om nogle arktiske växters biologi. 1886. I. 239.[2]
— Note sur la biologie ... des Vellosiacées. 1893. II. 90.[1]
— Notes biologiques sur des plantes de Groenland. 1886. I. 220.[1]
— De l'ovule. 1878. I. 122.
— Ein Paar nachträgliche Notizen über die Entwickelung der Cycadeen. 1878. II. 3.[2]
— Plantesamfund. 1895. I. 219.[1]
— Om Plantevæxten i det tropiske Amerika. 1892. I. 330.
— Recherches et remarques sur les Cycadées. 1877. II. 2.[2]
— Recherches sur la ramification des phanérogames. 1872. I. 106.[2]
— Rhizophora Mangle L. 1883. II. 614.[1]
— Om Rhizophora Mangle L. 1877. II. 614.[1]
— Skildringer af Naturen i det tropiske Brasilien. 1867. I. 343.
— Om Skudbygning, Overvintring og Foryngelse. 1884. I. 238.
— Symbolae ad floram Brasiliae centralis. 1868. I. 343.
— Tabellarisk Oversigt over Grønlands ... flora. 1887. I. 357.
— Tropische Fragmente. 1883. II. 614.[1]
— Om tropisk Agerbrug. 1894. III. 116.[1]
— En Udflugt til Brasiliens Bjærge. 1869. I. 343.
— Undersøgelser og Betragtninger over Cycadéerne. 1877. II. 2.[1]
— Untersuchungen über pollenbildende Phyllome. 1873. I. 116.[1]
— On the vegetation of tropical America. 1899. I. 331.
— Vochysiaceae et Trigoniaceae. 1875. II. 428,[1] 422.[2]
Warnecke, Hermann. Wie sind unsere Kiefernbestände zu durchforsten? 1888. IV. 473.
— Sur la wrightine. 1888. III. 692.[1]
Warneken, H. B. Die Kultur des Obstbaumes im Topfe. 1889. III. 139.
Warner, Richard. Plantae woodfordienses. 1771. I. 395.
Warnier, W. L. A. Bijdragen tot de kennis der Koffie. 1899. III. 741.[1]
Warnstedt, C. von. Das Wesen ... der lebendigen Feldbe-friedigungen. 1864. III. 214.[2]
Warnstedt, H. A. von. See REVENTLOW-FARVE, Ernst & WARNSTEDT, H. A. von.
Warnstorf, Karl. Betula pubescens × humilis. 1869. II. 119.[1]
— Blütenbiologische Beobachtungen. 1896. I. 240.[1]
— Blütenbiologische Beobachtungen bei Neuruppin. 1896. I. 240.[1]
— Weitere Beiträge zur Flora der Ukermark. 1891. II. 302.[1]
— Zwei Tage in Havelberg. 1880. II. 302.[1]
Waroe-vezel. 1870. III. 587.[2]
Warren. Sur le camphre de Formose. 1891. III. 404.[1]
— Formosa camphor. 1891. III. 404.[1]
Warren, Gouverneur Kemble. Preliminary report of explora-tions in Nebraska and Dakota. See HAYDEN, F. V. 1875. I. 324.
Warren, J. C. The great tree on Boston Common. 1855. II. 143.[2]
Warren, John Byrne Leicester, Lord de Tabley. On the Dume-torum group of Rubi in Britain. 1870. II. 303.[1]

— The flora of Cheshire. 1899. I. 404.[1]
— Flora of Hyde Park. 1871. I. 402, V. xxi.[1]
— Notes on a projected Cheshire flora. 1873. V. xxi.[1]
— Notes on ... Cheshire flora. 1873. I. 402.
— Some account of Cheshire Rubi. 1869. II. 303.[1]
— Suggestions on the " species " question as regards Rubus. 1870. II. 300.[1]
Warren, Pet. A genuine account of the manner of making best Russian pot-ashes. 1753. IV. 395.
Warren, Thomas Thomas Peter Bruce. On the cultivation of medicinal plants. 1865. III. 150.[1]
— On a new source of india rubber. 1874. III. 229.
— Report of examination of india rubber. 1884. III. 692.[2]
Warren, William H. Australian timbers. 1892. IV. 401,[2] 409.
— Some applications of the results of testing Australian tim-bers. 1890. IV. 415.[2]
— The strength ... of ironbark timber. 1887. IV. 531.[1]
— The strength ... of New South Wales timbers. 1887. IV. 410.
Warszewicz, Joseph von. Briefliche Mittheilung. 1852. I. 340.[2]
— Briefliche Mittheilung über die Reise des Herrn v. Warsze-wics in Central-Amerika. 1848. I. 329.
— Ueber einige Fuchsien-Bastarde ... durch kreuzende Befruchtung ... gezogen. 1842. III. 639.[2]
— Handelspflanzen ... für ostindische Colonisten wichtig. 1866. III. 128.
— Mittheilung über einen ... neuen hybriden Cactus. 1843. II. 591.[2]
— Nuttige gewassen ... voor de cultuur in Nederlandsch Oost-Indie. 1866. III. 128.
— See also CZERWIAKOWSKI, I. R. & WARSZEWICZ, Joseph.
Warszewitz, von, (Kunstgärtner, Insterburg). Mittheilung über das Verfahren den ... Cactus schneller zur Blüthe zu bringen. 1841. III. 618.[2]
Wartegg, Ernst von HESSE-. See HESSE-WARTEGG, Ernst von.
Wartenberg, Eberhard ERBACH-ERBACH UND WARTENBERG, Graf. See ERBACH-ERBACH UND WARTENBERG, Eberhard, Graf.
Wartenberg, Wilhelm. Beiträge zur Pharmakognosie von Psidium Araça. 1895. II. 632.[1]
Warth, H. Analysis of wood ashes. 1882. I. 155.
— Ash composition of some Indian woods. 1884. I. 155.
— On the impregnation of timber. 1877. IV. 420.
— Memorandum on the establishment of a factory for impreg-nating Pine sleepers. 1878. IV. 420.
— Memorandum on the preparation of kath. 1891. IV. 464.[1]
— The oils of turpentine from Pinus excelsa. 1889. IV. 463.[1]
— Report on the impregnation of timber. 1878. IV. 420.
— Report on the yield of catechin. 1890. III. 464.[1]
— Resin production in the Jaunsar forests. 1888. IV. 463.[1]
— Results of forest meteorology. 1871. IV. 59.[2]
Warthausen, Richard, Baron KÖNIG-. See KÖNIG-WARTHAU-SEN, Richard, Baron.
Wartmann, Bernhard. Beiträge zur St. Gallischen Volks-botanik. 1860. I. 75.[1]
— Bitterstisse mit schneeweissen Blüthen. 1876. II. 776.[1]
— Botanische Notizen. 1861. I. 143.
— Heidelbeere mit rein weissen Früchten. 1876. II. 686.[2]
— & Schlatter, Theodor. Kritische Uebersicht über die Ge-fässpflanzen der Kantone St. Gallen und Appenzell. 1879. I. 436.
Wartmann, E. Recherches sur la végétation. 1881. I. 203.
Wartmann, Jakob. Botanik für die weibliche Jugend. 1841. I. 94.
— St. gallische Flor. 1847. I. 434.
Warton, Simon. Schola botanica. 1689. I. 56.
Wartość pożywna żołędzi. 1860. IV. 514.[2]
Die Wartung und Pflege der vorzüglichsten deutschen Holz-arten. 1797. IV. 116.
Warum kommt die Fichte ... in Pommern nicht vor? 1892. IV. 454.
Warwick, William. See LANDERS, A. H. & WARWICK, William.
Was kann geschehen, um sogleich der Konsumtion mehr Holz darzubieten? 1840. IV. 281.[1]
Was soll die Forststatistik eines grössern Landes enthalten? 1851. IV. 336.[1]
Was soll eine Forstbotanik enthalten? 1859. IV. 75.[1]
Was soll eine forstliche Bodenkunde enthalten? 1857. IV. 68.
Washington — Agricultural experiment station. See WASH-INGTON — STATE AGRICULTURAL COLLEGE ... III. 9.

Washington — Biological society. *See* BIOLOGICAL . . . I. 5.

Washington — Fruits and flowers. *See* FRUITS . . . III. 3.

Washington — State agricultural college and school of science — **Experiment station.** Annual report. Bulletin. III. 9.

Washington, D. C. — National institute for the promotion of science. *See* NATIONAL . . . I. 6.

Washington academy of sciences. Proceedings. I. 7.[1]

The **Washington** Oak at Fishkill. 1888. II. 136.[1]

Washingtonia filifera. 1893. III. 332.[1]

Wasmann, Eric. Die Reblaus. 1895. III. 762.

Wasmer. Die Weisstanne in Mischung mit der Buche. 1861. IV. 444,[1] *494.*

— *See also* SCHERER & WASMER.

Wasowicz, Mieczyslaw Dunin. Dziworześnia sechelska. 1880. II. 71.[1]

— Wynik wycieczek botanicznych . . . w okolicach Mysłowic. 1886. I. 443.

Wassali, Friedrich. Ueber das Vorkommen der Traubenkrankheit. 1856. III. 577.

Der **Wassergehalt** des Bodens. 1885. IV. 51.

Der **Wassergehalt** von Bäumen. 1877. I. 149.[1]

Die **Wasserleitung** im Walde. 1868. IV. 73.[3]

Wassink, G. Enumeratio plantarum in Horto botanico nosocomiali bataviensi. 1851. I. 67.[3]

— Kinakultuur op Java. 1851. III. 715.

— Onderzoek van een vérfstof . . . in de Padangsche bovenlanden. 1864. III. 744.[1]

Watanabe, Hadjime. Die Anzucht von Zwangsformen. 1891. III. 176.[1]

Watbled-Defiennés. Importance de la multiplication par semis. 1853. III. 84.[1]

Watel, Maurice. La production . . . du Thé à Ceylan. 1899. III. 604.[1]

— Le thé de Ceylan. 1899. III. 608.[1]

Waterhouse, Benjamin. The botanist. 1811. I. 85.

Waterhouse, Sylvester. The influence of our northern forests on the Mississippi River. 1892. IV. 46.[1]

Waters, Campbell E. Witches' broom on the Locust. 1897. IV. 523.[3]

Waters, George Franklin. Character and cultivation of Eucalyptus globulus. 1874. IV. 529.[3]

Waterston, Robert Cassie. Story of the old Elm on Boston Common. 1876. II. 143.[3]

Waterton, Charles. Example in a Poplar tree. 1859. III. 180.[1]

— On self-renovation in timber-trees. 1859. I. 207,[3] III. 180.[1]

Watford natural history society. Transactions. I. 20.

Watier, H. Diagrammes comparatifs des divers éléments de production des essences feuillues. 1889. IV. 234.

— De la révolution du taillis dans les futaies sur taillis. 1896. IV. 131.

— Les taillis sous futaie des Vosges. 1896. IV. 131.

Watkins, B. M. *See* SOUTHALL, H. & WATKINS, B. M.

Watkins, C. R. W. Principles and rudiments of botany. 1858. I. 90.

Watkins, John. Notices of the natural history . . . of Louisiana. 1809. I. 318.

Watkins, William. A treatise on forest-trees. 1753. IV. 107,[3] 120.

Watney, Helen. The Elder. 1878. III. 752.[3]

Watrous, C. L. The effects of forests on climate. 1887. IV. 54.

Watson, (*Dr.*). On the resin of Ceradia furcata. 1846. III. 756.[1]

Watson, Benjamin M. American shrubs for ornamental planting. 1897. III. 203.

— American trees for ornamental planting. 1897. III. 203.

— Forcing hardy plants. 1893. III. 176.[3]

— The propagation of Cactuses. 1890. III. 619.

— Some American trees and shrubs. 1897. III. 61.[1]

Watson, Hewett Cottrell. Bemerkungen über die geographische Vertheilung und Verbreitung der Gewächse Grossbritanniens. 1832. I. 398.

— Calluna vulgaris in Cape Breton. 1865. II. 661.[3]

— Comparison between the upper . . . lines of trees and shrubs in Britain. 1835. I. 393.[3]

— Cybele britannica. 1847. I. 400.

— Erica Mackaii. 1835. II. 667.[3]

— The geographical distribution of British plants. 1832. I. 398.

— The London catalogue of British plants. 1844. I. 399, 533.

— The new botanist's guide. 1835. I. 398.

— Notes of a botanical tour in the western Azores. 1843. I. 497.

— Outlines of the geographical distribution of British plants. 1832. I. 398.

— Remarks on the geographical distribution of British plants. 1832. I. 398.

— Supplementary notes on the botany of the Azores. 1847. I. 497.

— Topographical botany. 1873. I. 402.

Watson, John. History of the parish of Halifax. *See* BOLTON, James. 1775. I. 395.

Watson, John Forbes W. A classified . . . catalogue of the Indian department. 1873. III. 278.

— Index to the native and scientific names of Indian . . . economic plants. 1866. III. 92.[3] — 1868. *I. 75.*[3]

— Plants of Kumaon. 1874. I. 474.

— Prize essay on the cultivation . . . of Tea in India. 1872. III. 603.

— Report on the preparation . . . of Rheea fibre. 1875. III. 382.[1]

— *See also* MONEY, E. & WATSON, J. F. W.

Watson, Peter William. Dendrologia britannica. 1825. I. 293, *III. 78,*[1] *IV. 84.*[3]

Watson, Sereno. Amelanchier alnifolia. 1888. II. 257.[3]

— Amelanchier oligocarpa. 1888. II. 258.[1]

— Berberis Fendleri. 1888. II. 203.[3]

— Berberis Fremonti. 1888. II. 203.[3]

— Bibliographical index to North American botany. 1878. I. 307.

— Botany [of California]. 1876. I. 324.

— Botany [of the fortieth parallel]. 1871. I. 323.

— Catálogo de las plantas del norte de México. 1882. I. 324, *332.*

— Upon a collection of plants made . . . about Guaymas, Mexico. 1889. I. 332.

— Contributions to American botany. 1879. I. 308. — II. 77.[1] — 1882. I. 324, *332.*[1] *IV. 84.*[3]

— Descriptions of new species . . . chiefly Californian. 1876. II. 61.[3] — 1888. I. 332, II. 313,[3] 801.[1] — 1889. I. 332, II. 801.[1]

— Descriptions of new species . . . chiefly Californian. 1876. I. 324.

— Descriptions of new species . . . from the Pacific states and Chihuahua. 1886. I. 325, *332.*

— Descriptions of new species of plants. 1879. II. 185.[3]

— Descriptions of some new species of North American plants. 1879. I. 308.

— Descriptions of some new species of plants. 1889. II. 801.[1]

— Descriptions of some plants of Guatemala. 1888. II. 801.[1]

— On the flora of Guadalupe Island. 1876. I. 332.

— The genus Ceanothus. 1875. II. 492.[3]

— On the genus Eriogynia. 1890. II. 265.[3]

— A history and revision of the Roses of North America. 1885. II. 283.[1]

— List of plants collected in Nevada, Arizona. 1874. I. 323.

— List of plants collected . . . in southwestern Chihuahua. 1886. I. 332.

— List of plants collected . . . in the state of Jalisco. 1887. I. 332.

— List of plants from southwestern Texas. 1882. I. 324, *332.*

— Neillia Torreyi. 1889. II. 270.[1]

— New plants of northern Arizona. 1873. I. 323.

— Notes upon plants collected in the department of Yzabal. 1886. I. 333.

— Notes upon some Palms of Guatemala. 1886. II. 61.[3]

— Palms of Southern California. 1876. II. 65.[1]

— Philadelphus Coulteri. 1888. II. 242.[1]

— Picea Breweriana. 1885. II. 37.[3]

— A point in nomenclature. 1887. II. 461.[3]

— The Poplar family. 1883. IV. 486.[1]

— The relation of the Mexican flora to that of the United States. 1891. I. 308.

— Revision of . . . North American species of the genus Lupinus. 1873. II. 370.[3]

— Revision of the extra-tropical North American species of . . . Potentilla. 1873. II. 270.[1]

— Revision of the genus Ceanothus. 1875. II. 492.[3]

— A revision of the North American Chenopodiaceae. 1874. II. 187.[1]

— Revision of the North American Liliaceae. 1879. II. 77.[1]

— Rosa Engelmanni. 1889. II. 293.[1]

— Rosa foliolosa. 1890. II. 293.[3]

— Rosa humilis var. triloba. 1889. II. 295.[1]

— Rosa minutifolia. 1888. II. 296.[1]
— Rosa nutkana. 1888. II. 296.[2]
— Schubertia grandiflora. 1890. II. 742.[2]
— Some new species of Mexican plants. 1888. I. 332.
— Some new species of plants of the United States. 1888. II. 313.[2]
— & others. Catalogue of plants collected in the years 1871–73. 1874. I. 307.
Watson, W. The forester's manual. 1837. IV. 108.[1]
Watson, Sir William, (1715–1787). An account of the Bishop of Lnodon's [sic] garden at Fulham. 1753. I. 52.
— An account of the Cinnamon-tree. 1753. III. 405.[2]
Watson, William, (of Kew). Abutilon vexillarium. 1890. III. 587.[1]
— Acacia déalbata. 1892. III. 464.[2]
— Acalypha Godseffiana. 1899. III. 514.[2]
— Acalypha Sanderiana. 1898. III. 514.[2]
— Aeschynanthus Hildebrandii. 1895. III. 708.[1]
— African Gardenias. 1890. III. 744.[1]
— Alberta magna. 1898. III. 711.[1]
— Allamanda grandiflora. 1891. III. 686.[1]
— Allamanda violacea. 1890. III. 686.[1]
— Azaleas. 1899. III. 656.
— Begonia Haageana. 1894. III..618.[1]
— Bismarckia nobilis. 1893. III. 320.[2]
— Boronias. 1889. III. 495.[2]
— Bougainvilleas. 1892. III. 388.[1] — 1894. III. 388.[1]
— Brugmansias. 1894. III. 700.[1]
— Cactus culture for amateurs. 1889. III. 619.
— Un Cactus médicinal. 1896. III. 622.[1]
— Cape Ivy. 1892. III. 756.[2]
— The Chinese Rose. 1891. III. 588.[1]
— Clematis Stanleyi. 1891. III. 391.[2]
— Clerodendron splendens. 1898. III..696.[2]
— Climbing Solanums. 1892. III. 701.[1]
— Coltivazione all' aria aperta di piante tropicali e sub-tropicali. 1889. III. 150.[1]
— Cool cultivation of tropical and sub-tropical plants. 1889. III. 150.[1]
— Crinodendron Hookeri. 1890. III. 584.[1]
— The cultivated species of Begonia. 1893. III. 618.[1]
— Dais cotinifolia. 1891. III. 626.[2]
— Dipladenia atropurpurea. 1893. III. 687.[2]
— Dipladenias. 1897. III. 687.[2]
— Drymophlœus olivæformis. 1891. III. 325.[1]
— Encephalartos Frederici Guilelmi. 1891. III. 285.[1]
— Eranthemum nervosum. 1897. III. 709.[1]
— Erica Chamissonis. 1899. III. 651.[2]
— Erica hyemalis. 1892. III. 651.[1]
— Eucalyptus calophylla. 1896. III. 634.[2]
— Eucalyptus globulus. 1900. III. 634.[2]
— Fuchsia triphylla. 1892. III. 640.[2]
— Fuchsias; species of. 1899. III. 640.[1]
— Fugosia hakeaefolia. 1900. III. 597.[1]
— Garden Palms. 1884. III. 318.[1]
— The genus Cycas. 1891. III. 284.[2]
— A giant African Aloe. 1890. II. 78.[1]
— Hibiscus Archeri. 1899. III. 587.[2]
— Hibiscus Cameroni. 1898. III. 587.[2]
— Hibiscus Manihot. 1898. III. 587.[2]
— Hoodia. 1897. III. 693.[1]
— Jubaea spectabilis. 1893. II. 09.[2]
— Kew notes. 1891. I. 55.
— The Lilac-flowered Daphne. 1892. III. 627.[1]
— Livistona Mariae. 1887. II. 70.[2]
— The Manettias. 1899. III. 746.[1]
— A medicinal Cactus. 1896. III. 622.[2]
— Metford's Lemon. 1900. III. 502.[1]
— A month at the Cape. 1887. I. 495.
— The Natal Laburnum. 1897. III. 469.[2]
— New Rhododendrons. 1899. III. 656.
— Night-flowering Cacti. 1892. III. 621.[1]
— Oxera pulchella. 1888. III. 697.[1]
— The Palm Veitchia Joannis. 1883. III. 331.[2]
— Les Palmiers cultivés. 1884. III. 318.[1]
— Pandanus odoratissimus. 1895. III. 313.[2]
— Paper-spined Opuntias. 1898. III. 625.[1]
— Passiflora amabilis. 1899. III. 615.[2]
— Passiflora racemosa. 1891. III. 616.[2]
— Passifloras — Passion-flowers. 1888. III. 616.[2]
— Pelargonium crithmifolium. 1899. II. 390.[2]
— Pereskia Bleo. 1896. II. 597.[2]
— Phyllocactuses. 1889. III. 625.[2]
— Plagianthus Lyalli. 1893. III. 587.[1]

— Plants flowering at Kew. 1888. I. 55.
— Plants of Kumaon. 1882. I. 474.
— Pleroma macranthum. 1893. III. 639.[1]
— Pleromas. 1897. III. 639.[1]
— Polycarpic Agaves. 1897. II. 89.[1]
— Protea cynaroides. 1895. III. 383.[2]
— Protea nana. 1889. III. 383.[2] — 1891. III. 383.[2]
— Ramie and China grass. 1896. III. 381.[2]
— Ravenea Hildebrandtii. 1891. III. 331.[1]
— Rhipsalis Houlleti. 1885. III. 626.[1]
— Rhododendron Ceres. 1892. III. 660.[2]
— Rhododendron keweïsæ. 1892. III. 660.[2]
— Rhododendron Kingianum. 1899. III. 657.[2]
— Rhododendron Maddeni var longiflora. 1894. III. 661.[1]
— Rhododendron Schlippenbachi. 1894. III. 662.[1]
— Rhododendrons. 1892. III. 655.
— Rhododendrons, new and other. 1896. III. 655.
— Richea pandanifolia. 1892. III. 665.[2]
— The sacred plant of the Druids. 1898. II. 180.[1]
— Senecio macroglossus. 1884. III. 756.[2]
— Shrubby Clerodendrons. 1892. III. 696.[1]
— Solandras. 1898. III. 701.[1]
— Solanum crispum. 1893. III. 701.[2]
— Solanum Wendlandi. 1893. III. 702.[1]
— Solanum Worsleyi. 1900. III. 702.[1]
— Some observations upon the sex of flowers. 1753. I. 199.
— Talaumas. 1895. III. 400.[2]
— Tecoma Mackenii. 1887. III. 707.[1]
— Tecoma Smithii. 1893. III. 707.[2]
— Tecomas and their culture. 1885. III. 705.
— Tenacity of life in a Yucca. 1890. II. 87.[1]
— Thunbergias. 1893. III. 710.[1]
— A yellow Ixora. 1897. III. 745.[1]
— Yunnan Rhododendrons. 1892. III. 662.[1]
— See also STEP, Edward & WATSON, William.
Watson, Winslow Cossoul. Forests, their influence, uses. 1865. IV. 43.
Watt, Koffie in Coorg an Wynaad. 1900. III. 732.[1]
Watt, George. Acacia catechu, catechu or cutch and kath. 1895. III. 464.[2]
— Brief statement . . . regarding tanning materials. 1896. III. 237.[2]
— Does India give promise of being . . . field for Rhea fibre production? 1894. III. 381.[2]
— Economic products of India. 1883. III. 278.
— Extract of cutch. 1896. III. 464.[2]
— First step in botany . . . of Bengal. 1876. I. 474.
— The forests of Manipur. 1888. IV. 378.
— Garjan or kanyin oil. 1893. III. 611.[1]
— The isolation of catechu and of kath. 1895. III. 464.[2]
— Ledger record of economic plants. 188.? III. 278.
— Memorandum on woods used for tea boxes. 1884. IV. 427.[1]
— Notes on the vegetation etc. of Chumba state. 1880. I. 474.
— Pamphlet on indigo. 1890. III. 479.[2]
— The pests and blights of the Tea plant. 1898. III. 604.[2]
— The present condition of the dyers. 1895. III. 746.[1]
— Review of the recent correspondence on the Letpet tea. 1896. III. 763.[2]
— & others. A dictionary of the economic products of India. 1885. III. 278.
Watt, Hugh Boyd. Scottish forests and woodlands in early historic times. 1900. IV. 27.[1]
Wattel, Casimir RAVERET-. See RAVERET-WATTEL, Casimir.
Wattel, H. Cacao boven-goud. 1900. III. 593.[2]
Wattenwyl, von. Waldbeschädigungen durch Eichhörnchen. 1883. IV. 198.[1]
Wattle bark. 1893. III. 463;[2] see also MÜLLER, Ferdinand, Baron von. 1892. III. 463.[2]
Wattle bark; report of the Board of inquiry. 1878. III. 463.[2]
Wattle cultivation. 1898. IV. 521.[1]
Wattles. 1880. III. 463.[2]
Wattles, and Wattle planting in California. 1890. III. 463.[1]
Watts, Francis. Citrate of lime and concentrated lemon. 1892. III. 499.[1]
— Tree planting in Antigua. 1900. IV. 342.[1]
Watts, Henry. A dictionary of chemistry. 1863. I. 151.[1]
— Watts' dictionary of chemistry. 1863. I. 151.[1]
Watts, Ralph Levi. Persimmons. 1899. III. 670.[1]
Watts, W. M. School flora for the use of elementary classes. 1878. I. 403.

Watzel, Cajetan. Ueber Pflanzenfrüchte. 1851. I. 119.
— Vegetationsbeobachtungen im Horizonte von Böhmisch-Leippa. 1854. I. 227.[1]
Wauchope, John Don. Extraordinary case of bleeding. 1873. I. 168.
Waugh, Frank Albert. Check list of hybrid Plums. 1900. III. 433.[1]
— Classification of Plums. 1897. III. 433.[1]
— The climbing Prairie-Rose. 1892. III. 457.[1]
— A contribution to the knowledge of physiological constants. 1898. I. 222,[1] II. 272.[1]
— The early botanical views of Prunus domestica. 1898. II. 274.[1]
— Geography of variation in . . . Prunus in America. 1899. II. 271.[1]
— Hybrid Plums. 1898. III. 433.[1]
— Maple sugar in Vermont. 1896. IV. 527.[2]
— The new view of the Hortulana Plum. 1897. III. 437.[1]
— Notes on sundry American Plums. 1898. II. 270.[1]
— The pollination of Plums. 1896. II. 272.[1]
— Some notes on timber-culture. 1895. IV. 112.
— Trees of minor importance for western planting. 1896. IV. 112.
— Utilizing Choke Cherry. 1896. III. 443.[1]
— The Wayland group of Plums. 1897. III. 437.[1]
— What is Prunus institita? 1899. II. 274.[2]
Wauters, Pierre Engelbert. Dissertatio botanico-medica de quibusdam plantis belgicis in locum exoticarum sufficiendis. 1785. III. 270.[2]
— Repertorium remediorum indigenorum. 1810. III. 270.[1]
Wauthier, Eugène. Commentarius in quaestionem . . . ut plantae . . . enumerentur, quae . . . pigmentum Indicum . . . largiuntur. 182. ? III. 479.[1]
— De pigmento indico. 1824. III. 479.[1]
Waverley Oaks. 1877. II. 132.[1]
The **Waverley** tree-guard and support. 1894. III. 199.
The **Waverly** [sic] Oaks. 1890. II. 132.[2]
Wavrechin, S. de. L'écorçage à la vapeur. 1866. IV. 434.
— L'écorçage à la vapeur devant l'Administration des-forêts. 1877. IV. 434.
Wawra von Fernsee, Heinrich, *Ritter*. Beitrag zur Flora der Hawai'schen Inseln. 1872. I. 509.[2]
— Botanische Ergebnisse der Reise . . . nach Brasilien. 1866. I. 343.
— Diagnoses plantarum novarum brasiliensium. 1879. I. 343.
— Ueber die Eucalyptus-Anpflanzung in Pola. 1875. IV. 529.[2]
— Itinera principum S. Coburgi. 1883. I. 303.
— Neue Pflanzenarten. 1881. I. 270.
— Neue Pflanzenarten gesammelt auf der transatlantischen Expedition. 1862. I. 270.
— Plantae Peckoltianae. 1864. I. 343.
— Ternstroemiaceae. 1886. II. 547.[2]
— Ueber Ternströmiaceen. 1887. III. 596.[2]
— & **Peyritsch**, Johann. Sertum benguelense. 1860. I. 491.
The **Wax** tree. 1893. III. 226.[1]
Wayne. Oil of Pignut Hickory. 1857. III. 353.[2]
Wayne, Edw. S. Researches upon Buchu. 1876. III. 495.[2]
Waynesse, L. de. Bericht wegens het aanleggen van Eiken-bosschen. 1794. IV. 504.
Wasgird, Michal. Sposób zachowania drzew owocowych od wymarznięcia. 1814. III. 183.
The **Weather** plant. 1890. II. 322.[2]
Webb. Cob Filberts. 1884. IV. 492.[1]
Webb, James. Cape Cod Cranberries. 1886. III. 663.[2]
Webb, O. Le Graptophyllum picturatum hort. Bull. 1896. III. 709.[1]
Webb, Philip Barker. Appendix to the Spicilegia gorgonea. 1850. I. 497.
— De Campylanthi fabrica. 1845. II. 779.[2]
— De Dicherantho. 1846. II. 194.[2]
— Fragmenta Florulae aethiopico-aegypticae. .1854. I. 488.
— Sur le genre Retama. 1845. II. 359.[1]
— Iter hispaniense. 1838. I. 420.
— De nova specie generis Sarothamni. 1848. II. 350.[2]
— Observations sur le groupe des Ulicinées. 1852. II. 387.[1]
— Observations sur le Tamarix gallica. 1841. II. 562.[2]
— Otia hispanica. 1839. I. 420.
— On the position to be assigned to the genus Cneorum. 1842. II. 366.[2]
— Spicilegia gorgonea. 1849. I. 497.
— Tamarix gallica of Linnaeus. 1841. II. 562.[2]

— *See also* **Parlatore**, Filippo & **Webb**, P. B.
— & **Berthelot**, Sabin. Géographie botanique. 1840. I. 497.
— — Phytographia canariensis. 1836. I. 497.
Webb, Robert Holden & **Coleman**, W. H. Flora hertfordiensis. 1849. I. 400.
— — Report on . . . Flora hertfordiensis. 1843. I. 399.
Webb, W. Notes on Nuytsia floribunda. 1894. II. 177.[1]
Webb, William Seward. Before the Forest commission . . . in the matter of the purchase of lands of W. S. Webb. 1895. IV. 314.[2]
Webber, Herbert John. Catalogue of the flora of Nebraska. 1890. I. 325.
— The development of the antherozoids of Zamia. 1897. II. 7.[1]
— Diseases and insects of Citrus. 1896. III. 498.[2]
— Fertilization of the soil as affecting the Orange. 1895. III. 500.[2]
— Improvement of plants by selection. 1899. I. 248.[1]
— Influence of environment in the origination of plant varieties. 1897. I. 245.
— Manures and Oranges. 1897. III. 500.[2]
— Methods of propagating the Orange. 1897. III. 497.[2]
— Notes on the fecundation of Zamia. 1897. II. 7,[1] 8.[1]
— Peculiar structures . . . in the pollen tube of Zamia. 1897. II. 6.[2]
— The reproduction of the Orange from seed. 1896. III. 500.[2]
— Sooty mold of the Orange. 1897. III. 501.[1]
— Studies on the dissemination . . . of Yucca. 1895. II. 87.[1]
— Treatment for sooty mold of the Orange. 1895. III. 501.[1]
— The two freezes of 1894–95 in Florida. 1896. III. 44.[1]
— Work of the United States department of agriculture on plant hybridisation. 1900. III. 51.
— *See also* **Bessey**, C. E. & **Webber**, H. J.; **Swingle**, W. T. & **Webber**, H. J.
— & **Bessey**, E. A. Progress of plant breeding in the United States. 1900. I. 248.[1]
Webber, Thomas Wingfield. The forests of England. 1872. IV. 358.[1]
— Reports . . . on some of the forests in England. 1871. IV. 357.[2]
Weber. Note sur un febrifuge annamite. 1862. III. 276.[2]
Weber, (*Professor, Munich*). Die Abnahme der Grösse von Buchenblättern. 1885. IV. 500.[2]
— Eine Theorie des Höhenwachsthums. 1890. I. 166, 187.
— Ueber die Vertheilung der Aschenbestandtheile. 1887. I. 155.
Weber, (*Regierungsforstassessor*). Die Bekämpfung der Kiefernschütte. 1899. IV. 480.
Weber, (*Regierungsrat*). Bericht der Direktion der Domänen und Forsten, betreffend das Auftreten des Borkenkäfers. 1871. IV. 204.
— Bericht über Erstellung meteorologischer Stationen. 1868. IV. 59.[2]
— Forststatistische Mittheilungen über den Amtsbezirk Bern. 1863. IV. 366.
— Forststatistische Mittheilungen über den Amtsbezirk Neuenstadt. 1863. IV. 366.
— Die Holztransporteinrichtungen im Schlierenthal. 1871. IV. 389.
— Quel est le meilleur moyen de donner à toutes les stations d'essais en Suisse une seule et même organisation? 1878. IV. 38.[2]
— Statistique forestière du district de Berne. 1863. IV. 366.
— Statistique forestière du district de Neuveville. 1863. IV. 366.
— Wie kann das schweiz. forstliche Versuchswesen . . . einheitlich organisirt werden? 1878. IV. 38.[2]
— & **Bertholet**, Charles. Statistique forestière. 1872. IV. 367.
Weber, Albert. Agaves et Cactées. 1896. II. 586.[1]
— Les Cactées de la Basse-Californie. 1895. II. 587.[2]
— Les Cactées des Îles Galapagos. 1899. . II. 587.[2]
— Cactées nouvelles du genre Rhipsalis. 1892. II. 586.[2]
— Les Echinocactus de la Basse Californie. 1898. II. 591.[2]
— Le Figuier de Barbarie. 1900. II. 596.[2]
— Notice sur la floraison de l'Epiphyllum Russellianum. 1900. II. 598.[1]
— Nouvelles Cactées. 1896. III. 620.[1]
— Les Pereskia et Opuntia Pereskioides du Mexique. 1898. II. 587.[2]

Weber, Anton. Clavis analytica ... Compositarum. 1843. II. 848.[1]

Weber, C. O. *See* BÄRSCH, G. & WEBER, C. O.

Weber, Carl. Die Bodenwirthschaft im Vogelsberg. 1894. IV. 351.[2]

Weber, E. Die volkswirtschaftliche Bedeutung des Waldes. 1895. IV. 45.

— *See also* WIEDEMANN, F. L. & WEBER, E.

Weber, F. C. Gründliche Einleitung zum Garten-Bau. 1725. III. 102.

Weber, Friedrich. Encephalartos villosus Lem. mit 4 Zapfen. 1885. II. 6.[1]

— Hortus kiliensis. 1822. I. 46.

Weber, Friedrich Benedict. Handbibliothek der deutschen forstwirthschaftlichen Literatur. 1803. IV. 1.

Weber, George Heinrich. Plantarum minus cognitarum decuria. 1784. I. 263.

— Primitiae Florae holsaticae. 1780. I. 374.

— Spicilegium florae goettingensis. 1778. I. 374.

Weber, J. Bericht der ständeräthlichen Commission ... betreffend eidgenössische Oberaufsicht über die Forstpolizei im Hochgebirge. 1875. IV. 330.

Weber, J. B. Dégats occasionnés par les froids pendant l'hiver 1870–71. 1870. III. 48.

— Greffe du Châtaignier sur le Chêne. 1867. III. 359.[1]

— Le Sureau à fleurs verdâtres. 1889. III. 752.[1]

Weber, Johann Karl. Die Alpenpflanzen Deutschlands. 1856. I. 532,[1] V. xxi.[2]

Weber, Johannes. Ueber das aetherische Oel ... von Cinnamomum. 1892. III. 406.[1]

Weber, John F. Culture and management of the Grape. 1860. III. 550.

— Grape-vine culture and wine-making. 1862. III. 550.

— The native Grapes of Pennsylvania. 1860. III. 546.

Weber, Josef. Lexeburjesch-latein-fransesch-deitschen Dixionèr fun de Planzen. 1890. I. 73.[3]

Weber, Josef Carl. Flora von Bayern in Abbildungen. 1851. I. 383.

Weber, K. *See* BEBEPЪ, K.

Weber, Karl Albert. Ein Beitrag zur Frage nach dem Endemismus der Föhre und Fichte. 1897. II. 15.[1]

— Ueber den Einfluss höherer Temperaturen auf die Fähigkeit des Holzes. 1885. I. 165.

— Über die Vegetation zweier Moore bei Sassenberg. 1897. I. 390.

Weber, Karl Otto. Beiträge zur Kenntniss der pflanzlichen Missbildungen. 1860. I. 143.

— Ueber das Regelmässigwerden unregelmässiger Blüthenkronen. 1850. I. 145.[1]

— Ueber Ursprung, Verbreitung und Geschichte der Pflanzenwelt. 1857. I. 299.

— Ueber das Verhältniss pflanzlicher Missbildungen. 1849. I. 143.

— *See also* BÄRSCH, G. & WEBER, C. O.

Weber, L. Handleiding voor eenige kultures op Java. 1863. III. 128.

Weber, Ludwig. Nonnulla ad camphoram spectantia. *See* SCHULZE, J. H. 1745. III. 404.[2]

Weber, Mary F. The practical influence of forestry. 1895. IV. 54.

Weber, Rudolf. Die Abnahme der Grösse von Buchenblättern. 1885. IV. 73.[1]

— Ansprüche des Buchen- und Eichenhochwaldes an den Boden. 1877. IV. 495, 506.

— Aschenanalysen von Buchen- und Eichen-Musterstämmen. 1877. II. 126,[2] 137.[2]

— Die Aufgaben der Forstwirtschaft. 1888. IV. 270.

— Ueber die Bedeutung der Holz verarbeitenden Industriezweige. 1883. IV. 426.[2]

— Beiträge zur agronomischen Statik des Waldbaues. 1876. IV. 60.[2]

— Ueber den Einfluss der Samenproduktion der Buche. 1892. II. 127.[1]

— Ergebnisse von Stammanalysen an Fichten. 1894. IV. 446,[2] 453.

— Kurze Uebersicht über das bisherige Forsteinrichtungsverfahren in den k. bayer. Staatsforsten. 1888. IV. 248.[3]

— Ueber den laufenden und durchschnittlichen Flächenzuwachs ... der Kiefer. 1900. IV. 482.[1]

— Lehrbuch der Forsteinrichtung. 1891. IV. 241.

— Messungen der Blattgrössen von Buchenblättern. 1885. II. 126,[2] V. 73.[1]

— Physiologische Untersuchungen über den Einfluss des Lichtes. 1876. IV. 67.[2]

— Recherches comparées sur les exigences du Sapin et de l'Épicéa. 1881. IV. 69.

— Uebersichtliche Zusammenstellung der ... aufgestellten Ertragstafeln. 188.? IV. 236.

— Untersuchungen über das Höhenwachstum der Fichte. 1895. IV. 458.

— Untersuchungen über den Grundstärken und Grundflächenzuwachs der Fichte. 1895. IV. 459.[1]

— Untersuchungen über die agronomische Statik des Waldbaues. 1877. IV. 69.

— Vergleichende Untersuchungen über die Ansprüche der Weisstanne und Fichte. 1881. IV. 69.

— Ueber den Volumen-Zuwachs von Fichtenklassenstämmen. 1896. IV. 459.[1]

— Der Wald im Haushalte der Natur. 1874. IV. 44.

— *See also* HARTIG, Robert & WEBER, Rudolf.

Weber von Ebenhof, Alfred, *Ritter*. Die Aufgaben der Gewässer-Regulirung. 1886. IV. 188.[1]

Weberbauer, August. Beiträge zur Anatomie der Kapselfrüchte. 1898. I. 120.

— Ueber Bildungsabweichungen in den Blüthenständen einer Eiche. 1899. II. 133.[2]

— Rhamnaceae. 1896. II. 491.[2]

Webern, Josef von. Immergrüne Traubeneiche. 1886. IV. 516.[1]

Webster. Extraordinary productiveness of the Orange-trees of St. Michael's. 1822. III. 499.[1]

Webster, Angus Duncan. Amelanchier canadensis. 1890. III. 419.[2]

— The Antarctic Beech. 1889. III. 360.[2]

— Berry-bearing plants. 1885. III. 208.[1] — 1889. III. 208.[1] 293.

— The best Conifers for ... the British Isles. 1889. III. 293.

— The Bhotan Pine. 1885.[7] III. 307.[1]

— The Black Jack Oak. 1890. III. 362.[2]

— The Californian Redwood. 1887. III. 310.[2]

— Carpets for trees. 1884. III. 205.[1]

— Cephalotaxus pedunculata fastigiata. 1886. III. 287.[1]

— Charcoal, its manufacture and use. 1885. IV. 395.

— The Chili Pine. 1887. III. 299.[1]

— The Cluster Pine. 1887. III. 308.[2]

— The Cluster Pine (Pinus Pinaster). 1882. III. 308.[1]

— The comparative value of exotic Coniferae. 1890. IV. 442.

— Conifers for chalky soils. 1888. III. 293.

— Conifers for economic planting. 1892. IV. 443.[1]

— The Cork tree. 1889. IV. 517.[1]

— The Corsican Pine. 1883. IV. 466.[1] — 1887. IV. 465.[2]

— On the culture and management of Picea Nordmanniana. 1881. IV. 444.[1]

— Cupressus macrocarpa lutea. 1896. III. 302.[2]

— Daphne Blagayana. 1897. III. 627.[1]

— The Douglas Fir. 1887. III. 309.[2]

— The Douglas Fir (Abies Douglasii Lindley). 1887. IV. 483.[2]

— The Douglas Fir at Penrhyn Castle. 1887. II. 49.[1]

— The Douglas Fir (Pseudotsuga Douglasii). 1884. IV. 483.[2]

— The Dropmore Douglas Fir. 1887. III. 309.[2]

— Dwarf Lebanon Cedar. 1896. III. 300.[2]

— The Eucalypti. 1891. III. 634.[2]

— Field and hedgerow trees. 1891. III. 215.[1]

— The forest flora of Carnarvonshire. 1885. V. xxi.[2]

— The formation ... of game coverts. 1885. III. 215.[1]

— The Giant Arbor-Vitae. 1887. III. 311.[3]

— The giant Arbor-Vitae (Thuia gigantea). 1886. III. 311.[2] — 1890. III. 312.[1]

— The glaucous African Cedar. 1889. III. 299.[2]

— The Great Silver Fir. 1885. III. 296.[1]

— Growth of Conifers after being felled. 1888. I. 210.[1]

— Hardy coniferous trees. 1896. III. 291.

— Hardy ornamental flowering trees. 1893. III. 78.[2]

— The Heart-leaved or Naples Alder. 1889. III. 356.[2]

— Hedgerow and field timber. 1887. III. 215.[1]

— Hedges, useful and ornamental. 1883. III. 214.[1]

— The Himalayan Fir. 1886. III. 306.[2]

— Holwood House and park. 1890. II. 127.[1]

— The Huon Pine. 1888. III. 287.[1]

— The Indian Bean. 1888. III. 706.[1]

— Insects injurious to forest trees. 1893. IV. 442.

— The Japan Cedar. 1886. III. 302.[1]

— Juniperus pachyphlaea. 1896. III. 304.[1]

— Juniperus rigida. 1896. III. 304.[1]

— King John's Oak. 1890. II. 139.[1]

Webster, Angus Duncan (*continued*).
— Knight's Cypress. 1890. III. 302.[1]
— Knole Park and its trees. 1890. II. 126.[1]
— The Lace-bark Pine. 1889. III. 307.[1]
— The large-coned Pine. 1887. III. 307.[1]
— Lawson's Cypress. 1887. III. 301.[1]
— Lord Aberdeen's Pine. 1887. III. 308.[2]
— The Mammoth tree. 1887. III. 310.[2]
— Manufacture of charcoal at Penrhyn Castle. 1881. IV. 395.
— Menzies' Spruce. 1886. III. 306.[1]
— The Monterey Cypress. 1886. III. 302.[2]
— The native trees . . . of Carnarvonshire. 1887. I. 394.
— On the new . . . Coniferae at Penrhyn Castle. 1887. III. 293.
— Notes about some fine Conifers. 1900. III. 123.[1] *293.*
— Notes from the Colonial-exhibition. 1886. IV. 20.[1]
— The Nut Pine. 1888. III. 308.[2]
— Oak bark. 1884. IV. 513.
— Old . . . trees on Holwood estate. 1890. I. 297.[1]
— The One-leaved Scotch Pine. 1893. II. 47.[1]
— Ornamental Barberries. 1887. III. 394.[1]
— Ornamental berry-bearing plants. 1888. III. 208.[1]
— Ornamental Oaks. 1888. III. 361.[1]
— Ornamental wall plants. 1884. III. 205.[1]
— Parasitical plants. 1882. IV. 211.[1]
— Paulownia imperialis. 1892. III. 703.[2]
— Peculiar growth of a Portugal Laurel. 1884. I. 528.[1]
— Pinus Balfouriana var. aristata. 1896. III. 306.[2]
— Pinus monticola. 1887. III. 307.[1]
— Pinus parviflora. 1887. III. 308.[1] — 1897. III. 308.[1]
— Pinus Pinaster prolifera. 1896. II. 44.[2]
— The plantations on the Penrhyn estate. 1890. IV. 358.[1]
— la   g chalky soil on the sea-coast. 1890. III. 41.[1]
4f⁰ ntin
— Plants for shady positions. 1882. III. 42.[1]
— The Plum-fruited Yew. 1880. III. 287.[2]
— Practical forestry. 1893. IV. 108.[3]
— Privets and their uses. 1887. III. 673.[2]
— Quality of British grown coniferous timbers. 1895. IV. 398.[1]
— Remarkable trees on Penrhyn estate. 1885. I. 297.[1]
— Renovating impoverished Conifers. 1886. III. 292.
— The Scarlet-berried Elder. 1889. III. 752.[1]
— Sequoia gigantea pendula. 1896. III. 310.[1]
— The Silver Fir. 1890. III. 297.[1]
— The Spanish Savin. 1889. III. 304.[1]
— The Spanish Silver Fir. 1886. III. 297.[1]
— The Syrian Juniper. 1896. III. 303.[2]
— Thinning plantations. 1894. IV. 175.[1]
— Thuya orientalis falcata. 1897. III. 311.[1]
— Town planting. 1892. III. 42.[2]
— Transplanting evergreens. 1882. III. 169.[1]
— Tree guards. 1886. III. 199.
— Trees and shrubs . . . for planting as shelter. 1890. III. 215.[1]
— Trees and shrubs for planting in towns. 1893. III. 42.[2]
— Trees and shrubs suitable for seaside planting. 1885. III. 41.[2]
— Trees best adapted for various soils. 1891. III. 41.[1]
— Trees for chalky soil. 1888. III. 41.[1]
— Trees for chalky soils. 1891. III. 41.[1]
— Trees for ironstone soils. 1891. III. 41.[1]
— Trees in Greenwich Park. 1899. III. 359.[2]
— Trees on the seacoast at Dover. 1890. III. 41.[2]
— Turkey Oak struck by lightning. 1890. IV. 194.
— The Umbrella Pine. 1888. III. 309.[2]
— Unsightly Araucarias. 1887. III. 299.[1]
— The upright Cephalotaxus. 1897. III. 287.[1]
— The Upright Indian Silver Fir. 1886. III. 297.[1]
— Useful fences. 1887. III. 214.[1]
— The utilisation of waste produce of forests. 1892. IV. 434.
— The value of Willow timber. 1897. IV. 487.[2]
— Weeping Elms. 1891. III. 364.[1]
— The Weeping Indian Juniper. 1889. III. 304.[1]
— The Weeping Larch. 1889. III. 304.[2]
— The Weeping Silver Fir. 1897. III. 297.[1]
— Weeping Willows. 1888. III. 351.[2]
— The Weymouth Pine. 1887. III. 309.[1]
— Willow growing. 1887. III. 349.
Webster, B. On the stem and branch pruning of Conifers. 1874. III. 295.[1]
Webster, J. Ring grafting. 1868. III. 161.

Webster, John. Old . . . trees on the estate of Gordon Castle. 1881. I. 297.[1]
Webster, John Blaikie. Athrotaxis. 1888. III. 299.[2]
— Berberis Darwini and japonica. 1883. III. 394.[1]
— The Black Mountain Fir. 1883. III. 296.[1]
— Cupressus (Retinospora) obtusa. 1893. III. 301.[2]
— Deer forest planting in the Highlands. 1890. IV. 136.[2]
— On the diseases of forest trees. 1871. IV. 195.[3]
— Extended introduction of hardy, useful and ornamental trees. 1894. I. 242.[1]
— Growing Larch in bogs. 1885. IV. 449.
— On the growth and management of Scotch Fir forests. 1874. IV. 472.
— On the growth of the roots of coniferous trees. 1871. II. 20.[3]
— Hedges. 1890. III. 214.[1]
— The Hornbeam. 1889. III. 357.[2]
— Influence of soil on Scotch Fir. 1885. IV. 473.
— The Rhododendron as a covert plant. 1888. III. 655.
— Subjects for underwood in game coverts. 1893. III. 215.[1]
Webster, Noah, (*jr.*). On the effects of evergreens on climate. 1799. IV. 52.
Die wechselnde und vorübergehende Benutzung des Forstgrundes zur Ackerkultur. 1840. IV. 133.
Weck, L. Beiträge zur Pflanzen-Pathologie. 1854. II. 103.[2]
Wecker, Louis de. Sur l'ophtalmie purulente. 1883. III. 462.[2]
— L'ophtalmie purulente factice. 1882. III. 462.[3]
Weddell, Hugh Algernon. Additions à la flore de l'Amérique du Sud. 1850. I. 329.
— Aperçu d'un voyage dans le nord de la Bolivie. 1852. I. 340.[2]
— Bemerkungen über das Material aus dem die sogenannten Guayaquil-Hüte bereitet werden. 1851. III. 332.[1]
— On Calisaya bark. 1850. III. 725.[1]
— Chinabarkens Naturhistorie. 1849. II. 812.
— Chloris andina. 1855. I. 329.
— On cinchona barks. 1850. III. 724.[2]
— On Cinchona calisaya. 1850. III. 724.[3]
— Coca. 1853. III. 492.[1]
— Considérations générales sur la famille des Urticées. 1856. II. 156.[1]
— Sur la culture des Quinquinas. 1867. III. 712.[1]
— Sur les cystolithes. 1855. I. 138.[3]
— De la distribution géographique des Urticées. 1856. II. 156.[1]
— Sur l'extraction du caoutchouc. 1854. III. 519.[1]
— On the extraction of caoutchouc. 1854. III. 519.[1]
— Histoire naturelle des Quinquinas. 1849. II. 812.
— On the leaves of the Coca of Peru. 1855. III. 492.[1]
— Sur la méthode . . . pour obtenir l'écorce du Quinquina. 1879. III. 718.
— Monographie de la famille des Urticées. 1856. II. 156.[1]
— The natural history of Cinchonas. 1849. II. 812.
— Naturgeschichte der Chinabäume. 1849. II. 812.
— Note sur la paille dont on fait les chapeaux dits de Guayaquil. 1851. III. 332.[2]
— Notes sur les Quinquinas. 1869. II. 812.
— Notes sur les Quinquinas. 1869. II. 812, V. xxvii.[3]
— Notice sur la Coca, sa culture. 1854. III. 492.[1]
— Notice sur quelques Rubiacées de l'Amérique tropicale. 1854. III. 721.
— Sur l'origine botanique du Quinquina rouge. 1855. III. 718.
— Plantes inédites des Andes. 1864. I. 330.
— Sur quelques écorces officinales. 1855. III. 722.
— Remarks on the generic name Cascarilla. 1871. II. 822.[1]
— Revue de la famille des Urticées. 1854. II. 156.[1]
— Revue du genre Cinchona. 1848. II. 812.
— Het stroo der hoeden van Guayaquil. 1851. III. 332.[2]
— Table of Cinchona barks. 1850. III. 721.
— Uebersicht der Cinchonen. 1849. II. 812. — 1869. V. xxvii.[2]
— Urticaceae. 1869. II. 156.[1]
— The vegetation of Brazil, Bolivia and Peru. 1851. I. 329.
— Voyage dans le nord de la Bolivie. 1853. I. 340.[2]
— *See also* Cosson, Ernest, Germain de Saint-Pierre, Ernest & Weddell, H. A.; Sweet, Robert & Weddell, H.
Wedderburn, J. W. *See* Jones, J. M., Wedderburn, J. W. & Hurdis, J. L.
Weddik, A. L. De Notenmuskaat-Kultuur op Java. 1839. III. 402.[1]
— Proeve over de teelt van den Kruidnagelboom. 1840. III. 635.[1]

Wedekind, Georg Wolfgang, *Freiherr* von. Anleitung zur Betriebsregulirung und Holzertragsschätzung der Forste. 1834. IV. 240.
— Anleitung zur Forstverwaltung. 1831. IV. 287.
— Das Auftreten des Harz-Rüsselkäfers. 1863. IV. 455.
— Bemerkungen über Gegenstände der Forstverfassung und Forstverwaltung. 1821. IV. 287.
— Die drei Stufen der forstlichen Beaufsichtigung der Privatwaldungen. 1859. IV. 285.[2]
— Einige Bemerkungen über den Besoldungsaufwand verschiedener Forstorganisationssysteme. 1821. IV. 288.[1]
— Encyklopädie der Forstwissenschaft. 1847. IV. 101.
— Die Fachwerksmethoden der Betriebsregulirung. 1843. IV. 250.[2]
— Forstwissenschaft. 1847. IV. 101.
— Instruction für die Betriebsregulirung und Holzertragsschätzung der Forste. 1839. IV. 240.
— Ueber die landwirthschaftliche Zwischennutzung. 1847. IV. 133.
— Ueber Liberalität und Popularität in Forstsachen. 1832. IV. 268.
— Ueber die Privatwaldungen. 1844. IV. 308.[1]
— Semis artificiels et plantations de Hêtre. 1845. IV. 494.
— Umriss der Forstwissenschaft. 1838. IV. 97.
— Versuch einer Forstverfassung im Geiste der Zeit. 1821. IV. 287.
— Welche Erfahrungen sind . . . bezüglich der Verbindung des landwirthschaftlichen mit dem forstwirthschaftlichen Betriebe . . . gemacht? 1855. IV. 133.
Wedel, Christian. De Terebinthina. *See* WEDEL, G. W. 1700. III. 525.[2]
Wedel, Georg Wolfgang. De Camphora. 1697. II. 224.[2]
— De cinnamomo. 1707. III. 405.[1]
— De corona Christi spinea. 1696. I. 512.
— Dissertatio . . . de Cubebis. 1705. III. 342.[1]
— De Hyperico. 1716. III. 609.[2]
— De lignis thyinis Apocalypseos in genere. 1707. I. 512.
— De Ligno Aloes. 1693. III. 626.[2]
— Propempticon inaugurale de anil. 1689. III. 479.[1]
— Propempticon inaugurale de mensis citreis. 1707. I. 511.
— Propempticon inaugurale de resina ægyptia Plauti. 1700. III. 227.
— De Sabina. 1707. III. 304.[1]
— De Sabina scripturae. 1707. II. 30.[1]
— De Sambuco. 1720. III. 752.[1]
— De Terebinthina. 1700. III. 525.[2]
— De Thea. 1707. III. 605.
— Usus novus catechu. 1671. III. 464.[1]
Wedel, Johann Adolph. De Camphora. *See* WEDEL, G. W. 1697. II. 224.[2]
Wedel, Johann Wolfgang. Tentamen botanicum flores plantarum in classes . . . dividendo . . . inserviens. 1747. I. 250.
Wedell, G. M. L. von. Beurtheilung der Preisschrift des Hrn. von Brocken von Vermehrung des Wachsthums. 1776. IV. 116.
— Beurtheilung der Schrift des . . . von Brocken . . . Von Vermehrung des Wachsthums der Bäume. 1775. IV. 169.[1]
Wedell, Wilhelm von. Ueber Sturmschäden in Gebirgsforsten. 1802. IV. 188.[2]
Wedge, Clarence. The Norway Maple. 1898. III. 535.[2]
Weeber, Heinrich Cesar. Die beweisführenden Untersuchungen der fossilen Brennstoffe. 1863. IV. 413.[1]
— Boden und Clima . . . im österreichischen Kaiserstaate. 1860. IV. 68.
— Leitfaden für den Unterricht . . . des Forstschutz- und technischen Hilfspersonales. 1856. IV. 99.[2]
— Die Riesen der Pflanzenwelt. 1859. IV. 65.[1]
— Die vorzüglichsten Waldbäume. 1859. IV. 86.[2]
Weed, Clarence Moores. The brown rot of stone fruits. 1890. III. 431.[1]
— Fungi and fungicides. 1894. III. 193.[2]
— Injurious insects and their transformations. 1899. III. 188.[1]
— The insect record for 1899. 1900. III. 188.[1]
— Insects and insecticides. 1891. III. 187.
— Spraying crops. 1892. III. 197.
— Ten New England blossoms. 1895. II. 104,[2] 663.[2]
— The White Pine louse. 1890. IV. 470.[1]
Weed, Howard Evarts. Spraying for profit. 1899. III. 198.[1]
Weed, James. Early history of Iowa horticulture. 1884. III. 118.[1]
Weeder, Alois. Der Bauernwald. 1900. IV. 309.[2]

Weekly florists' review. III. 9.
The **Weekly** miscellany for the improvement of husbandry. III. 18.
Weeping Ash tree ready for removal. 1893. III. 168.[1]
The **Weeping** Beech. 1872. III.-360.[2]
A **Weeping** Beech. 1888. II. 127.[1]
A **weeping** Elm at Kensington. 1897. III. 366.[1]
The **Weeping** Japanese Cherry. 1896. III. 439.[1]
The **Weeping** Larch 1887. III. 304.[2] — 1888. III. 304.[2]
Weeping, or drooping trees. 1854. III. 204.[1]
The **weeping** Sophora japonica. 1876. III. 488.[1]
The **Weeping** Spruce. 1897. III. 305.[2]
The **weeping**-tree mystery. 1890. I. 213.[2]
Weeping trees. 1872. III. 488.[1]
Weeping Wellingtonia. 1876. III. 310.[1]
Wefers Bettink, H. De bestanddeelen van het sap der Antiaris. 1889. III. 366.[2]
— Cijaanwaterstof uit de bladeren van Kigellaria. 1891. III. 614.[1]
— Sur la composition du suc de l'Antiaris toxicaria. 1889. III. 366.[2]
— Over den wortel van Ophioxylon serpentinum. 1888. II. 31.[2]
Wegelin, H. Die alten Zierpflanzen. 1898. III. 89.[1]
Wegelin, Theodor. Enumeratio stirpium florae helveticae. 1838. I. 434.
Wegelius, Herman. Rön och Anmärkningar om utländska waxter. *See* GADD, P. A. 1777. III. 120.[1]
Wegener, (*Oberförster, Zobten*). Beitrag zur Beantwortung der Frage: Ist die Beschattung . . . nützlich, werthlos oder schädlich? 1844. IV. 146.[2]
— Mittheilungen über den Zustand der k. Oberförsterei Zobten. 1850. IV. 352.
Wegener, H. Ein Beitrag zur Rostocker Anlagenflora. 1893. I. 49.
Wegener, L. Hebt den Obstbau! 1888. III. 139.
Wegener, Th. Beschreibung einiger neuen Cacteen. 1844. II. 585.[2]
Węgleński, Franciszek. O ustawie rolniczej dla mieszkańców dóbr Hrubieszowskich. 1847. IV. 296.[2]
Wegscheider, J. Ein Massenauftreten des Fichtenhohlnadelwicklers. 1891. IV. 457.
Wegscheider, R. Spektroskopische Notizen über die Farbstoffe grüner Blätter. 1884. I. 142.
Wegscheider, R. Ansichten über die . . . Bewirthschaftung der Mittelgebirgswaldungen zwischen dem Eger- und Bilathale. 1850. IV. 249.[2]
Wehmann, Achatz Friedrich. Hortus Caspar Bosianus. 1723. I. 43.
Wehmer, Carl. Das Calciumoxalat der oberirdischen Theile von Crataegus. 1889. II. 262.[2]
— Die Eichenblättrigkeit der Hainbuche. 1896. II. 121.[1]
— Ueber einige abnorme Lindeninflorescenzen. 1891. II. 516.[1]
— Einige weitere Beiträge zum Parasitismus der Nectria. 1895. III. 195.[1]
— Ueber Färbungen und Flecke der Rosenblätter. 1900. III. 453.[2]
— Über einen Fall intensiver Schädigung einer Allee durch . . . Leuchtgas. 1900. III. 185.[2]
— Zur Frage nach der Entleerung absterbender Organe. 1892. I. 192.[2]
— Die dem Laubfall voraufgehende . . . Blattentleerung. 1892. I. 192.[1]
— Monilia fructigena Pers. 1898. III. 195.[2]
— Die Oxalatabscheidung im Verlauf der Sprossentwickelung von Symphoricarpus. 1891. II. 842.[1]
— Zum Parasitismus von Nectria. 1894. III. 195.[1]
— Ueber das Verhalten der Formose. 1887. I. 177.
— Das Verhalten des oxalsauren Kalkes. 1889. I. 156.[1]
Wehrli, Ludwig. Ueber einen Fall von vollständiger Verweiblichung der männlichen Kätzchen von Corylus. 1892. II. 121.[2]
— Verweiblichung männlicher Kätzchen bei Corylus. 1893. II. 122.[2]
Wehrs, Carl von. Die nützlichen Amphibien, Insekten. 1872. III. 95.
Wehrs, G. F. von. Der Ahornzucker. 1813. IV. 526.[1]
Wehsarg, K. *See* SCHWARZ, C. & WEHSARG, K.
Weibel. Wem gehört der Stechtenknubelwald? 1885. IV. 331.[1]
Weichert, G. S. De virtute corticis peruviani antiphlogistica. *See* BÜCHNER, J. A. E. 1768. III. 720.
Die **weichhaarige** Eiche in Oesterreich. 1863. II. 135.[1]

Weichselcultur in Ungarn. 1878. III. 438.¹

Die Weichselholzkultur. 1801. III. 438.²

Das Weichselrohr, dessen Cultur. 1873. III. 438.¹

Ueber Weichselrohrzucht. 1881. ' III. 438.²

Weidel, H. Untersuchung des Sandelholzes. 1870. III. 384.¹

Weidemann & Kienitz, Max. Sind vollkommen reife von unreifen Kiefernzapfen zu unterscheiden. 1883. ' IV. 473.

Weidner, F. Die in Mecklenburg wildwachsenden Giftpflanzen. 1856. III. 73.

Weigel, Christian Ehrenfried von. Flora pomerano-rugica. 1769. I. 373.

— Fructus Javae esculenti. See HORNSTEDT, C. F. 1786. III. 275.²

— Index seminum et plantarum Horti gryphici. 1773. I. 44.

— Observationes botanicae. 1772. II. 840.¹

— Programma quo dissertationem . . . disserit. 1786. III. 404.²

Weigel, Georg. Über die Harzbalsame von Larix . . . und Abies. 1900. II. 21.²

— See also TSCHIRCH, Alexander & WEIGEL, Georg.

Weigel, Johann Adam Valentin. Schlesischer Pflanzenkalender. 1791. I. 374.

Weigel, Th. Ueber die ästhetische Schönheit der Bäume. 1881. I. 516.

Weigelt, C. Die japanische Mammut Kastanie. 1890. III. 358.²

— Syringa japonica. 1890. III. 681.¹

— See also REHDER, Alfred & WEIGELT, C.

Weight of bark from Cinchona trees. 1887. III. 725.²

Weigl, Anton. Zur Baumkubirung. 1870. IV. 217.

— Hackstreu-Ertragniss. 1870. IV. 437.²

— Ueber Holzvorrath. 1864. IV. 236.

Weigl, K. Die agrarischen Operationen und deren Bedeutung für die Forstwirthschaft. .1895. IV. 279.¹

Weigl, L. O rozmieszczeniu Kosodrzewiny i Rododendronów w okolicy Czarnohory. 1888. I. 438.

Weihe, Karl Ernst August. De nectariis. 1802. I. 118.¹

— Prunus floribunda, P. fruticans. 1826. II. 271.¹ '

— Rubus. 1825 II. 301.²

— Rubus Sprengelii. 1819. II. 310.¹

— & Nees von Esenbeck, C. G. Die deutschen Brombeersträuche. 1822. II. 301.¹

— — Rubi germanici descripti -et figuris illustrati. 1822. II. 301.²

Die Weihmuthskiefer. 1852. IV. 469.

Ein Weihnachtsbaum im Frühling. 1869. IV. 194.

Weijenbergh, H. (jr.). Over coleophoren en andere kleine motten. 1869. III. 190.

Weilbach, August. Aalholm. 1866. I. 40.

— See also ØRSTED, A. S. & WEILBACH.

Weiler, H. Die Weinrebe und ihre Kultur unter Glas. 1895. III. 553.¹

Weimar, Henry. See POWER, F. B. & WEIMAR, Henry.

Weimar, Wilhelm. Die Schwester der Königin-der Nacht. 1892. III. 621.²

Weimelka, Rudolf. Einiges über das Springen der Klötze. 1861. IV. 416.¹

Weinbau. III. 14.

Weinbau und Weinbereitung für Grünberg. 1845. III. 552.

Weinberg, J. See Вейнбергъ, Я.

Weinelt, J. E. Die Bisenzer Riesenlinden. 1896. IV. 528.¹

— Die Drahtriese. 1897. IV. 392.

— Die " grosse Tanne " bei Eisenstein. 1895. IV. 447.¹

— Wahl der Betriebsform. 1896. IV. 129.

Weiner, C. Unsere Obstsorten. 1899. III. 135.

Weinert. Die Gebirgs- und Waldverhältnisse der Krym. 1893. IV. 348.¹

Weinheimer, C. Die dienstlichen Rechte und Pflichten der Feldschützen. 1879. IV. 322.²

— Die dienstlichen Rechte und Pflichten der Gemeindediener in Württemberg. 1878. IV. 291.²

— Die dienstlichen Rechte und Pflichten der Holzhauer in Württemberg. 1879. IV. 291.²

— Die dienstlichen Rechte und Pflichten der Körperschaftsförster in Württemberg. 1878. IV. 291.²

— Die dienstlichen Rechte und Pflichten der Waldschützen in Württemberg. 1879. IV. 291.¹

— Das württembergische Forststraf- und Forstpolizeistrafgesetz. 1880. IV. 322.²

Weinkauf, Die Nutzholzerziehung der Kiefer mit Hilfe der Weymoutskiefer. 1896. IV. 469, 474.

— Ueber den Unterbau von Kiefern mit Buchen. 1896. IV. 138.²

Weinkauff, Humus oder Streuzersetzung? 1900. IV. 70.

— Warum und in welchem Masse brauchen wir im Pfälzer Wald . . . noch die Tanne. 1900. IV. 119.¹

Weinkauff, B, Die Lärche auf Pfälzer Buntsand. 1899. IV. 450.

Weinkauff, K. Mittelwald oder Hochwald in Gemeindeforsten. 1899. IV. 309.¹

Weinke, Franz Carl. Der Eucalyptus globulus. 1877. IV. 533.¹

Weinlaube. III. 25.

Weinlig, Albert. Die Pflanzenchemie. 1839. ' I. 151.²

Weinmann (Oberförster). See LANDOLT, Elias, HERTENSTEIN, (Forstmeister) & WEINMANN, (Oberförster).

Weinmann, J. A. Bestimmung einiger neuen Gewächse. 1820. II. 523.²

— Der botanische Garten der kaiserlichen Universität zu Dorpat. 1810. I. 41.

— Descriptiones aliquot plantarum ex Horto imperiali pawlowskiensi. 1824. I. 41.

— Descriptiones aliquot plantarum novarum . . . in Horto caesareo pawlowsciensi. 1821. I. 41.

— Elenchus plantarum Horti imperialis pawlowskiensis. 1824. I. 42.

— Enumeratio stirpium in agro petropolitano. 1837. I. 361.

— Nomina . . . nonnularum [sic] plantarum in gubernio permensi. 1850. II. 196.²

— Observationes botanicae ex Horto imperiali pawlowskiensi. 1825. I. 42.

— Observationes quaedam botanicae. 1837. II. 851.²

— Plantae novae . . . ex Horto . . . pawlowskiensi. 1825. I. 42.

— Plectranthus divaricatus.' 1824. II. 764.² '

Weinmann, Johann Georg. Dissertatio . . . fasciculum plantarum patriae urbi . . . vicinarum. See GMELIN, P. F. 1764. III. 72.

Weinmann, Johann Wilhelm. Duidelyke vertooning eeniger duizend . . . boomen, stammen, kruiden. 1735. I. 290.

— Eigentliche Darstellung . . . nebst einem in meisten Sprachen vollkommenem Register. 1735. I. 290.

— Multilinguis phytanthoza-iconographiae Weinmannianae index. 1735. I. 290.

— Phytanthoza iconographia. 1735. I. 290.

— Représentation de quelques milliers d'arbres, arbrisseaux, herbes. 1735. I. 290.

— Taalryk register der plaat- ofte figuur-beschryvingen der bloemdragende gewassen. 1735. I. 290.

— Thesaurus rei herbariae. 1787. I. 263.

Weinmeister, J. W. Die Blitzschläge der sächsischen Staatsforstreviere. 1898. IV. 195.¹

Weinrich, Georg Albert. Dissertatio inauguralis de Haematoxylo. 1780. III. 478.¹

Weinschenk, J. M. Ueber die Behandlung der mit Heide übersogenen jungen Kiefer-Schonungen. 1857. IV. 472.

— Bericht über die Anwendung der patentirten Schuster'schen Stock-Rodemaschine. 1859. IV. 386.

— Ueber Hügel-Pflanzung. 1861. IV. 153.²

— Ratzeburg, J. T. C. Vier Schriftstücke, den Frass des Rüsselkäfers betreffend. 1852. IV. 475.

Weinzierl, Theodor von. Beiträge zur Lehre von der Festigkeit . . . vegetablischer Gewebe. 1878. I. 149.¹

— Die Momente der Qualitätsbestimmung des forstlichen Saatgutes. 1889. III. 157.

— Die Production . . . der Nadelholzsamen. 1888. V. XXXII.²

— Ueber die Verbreitung des Phloroglucins. 1876. I. 176.

Weir, Harrison. Laburnum. 1899. III. 480.²

Weir, John. Mission of collector to Brazil. 1862. I. 342.

— On the Myroxylon Toluiferum. 1864. III. 482.²

Weis, Ludwig. Die Elemente der Botanik. 1869. I. 256.

Weise, Ernst. Die Resultate der im Winter 1877/78 augestellten Sägeversuche. 1879. IV. 393.

Weise, Johann Christoph Gottlob. Deutschlands Pflanzen-Blüthe-Kalender. 1831. I. 378.

— Encyclopädisches Garten-Wörterbuch. 1830. III. 31.

Weise, Wilhelm. Die Abstandszahl. 1880. IV. 244.

— Ueber das Absterben der alten Eichen. 1895. IV. 511.

— Ueber Aufstellung von Kiefern-Ertragstafeln. 1879. IV. 236, 481.

— Die Bestimmung von mittleren Probestämmen. 1880. IV. 218.

— Die Buchennutzholzfrage. 1881. IV. 499.

— Der deutsche Wald und die fremdem Holzarten. 1894. IV. 126.¹

— Die Durchforstungen im Lichte neuer Veröffentlichungen. 1894. IV. 175.¹

— Eine einfache Methode für die Aufstellung von Ertrags-
tafeln für die Kiefer. 1896. IV. 482.[1]
— Einiges über das Nutzungsprocent. 1882. IV. 244.
— Erfahrungen . . . aus dem Forstgartenbetriebe. 1892.
IV. 151.[1]
— Ergebniss der Holzsamen-Ernte. See ERGEBNISS. 1875.
IV. 438.[1]
— Ertragstafeln für die Kiefer. 1880. IV. 481.
— Festrede gehalten bei der 25jährigen Jubelfeier der Forst-
akademie Münden. 1893. IV. 33.[2]
— Ueber Formzahlen der Kiefer. 1881. IV. 481.
— Formzahlen und Ertragstafeln für die Kiefer. 1890. IV.
481.
— Zur Frage der Bestandsnormalität. 1885. IV. 245.
— Zur Frage der Wachsthumsleistungen nicht geschlossener
Bestände. 1885. IV. 233.
— Frostwirkungen im Jahre 1886. 1886. IV. 191.[3]
— Zur Kenntniss des Weisstannenkrebses. 1892. IV. 457.
— Die Kiefernertragstafeln von 1880. 1896. IV. 482.[1]
— Ueber die Kluppung. 1881. IV. 218.
— Die Kulmination des Durchschnittszuwachses. 1893. IV.
234.
— Laufend jährlicher und Durchschnittszuwachs. 1895. IV.
234.
— Leitfaden für den Waldbau. 1888. IV. 107.[1]
— Die Nachzucht der italienischen Pappel. 1885. III. 346.[1]
— Zur natürlichen Verjüngung der Kiefer. 1894. IV. 482.[1]
— Ein neuer Keimapparat für Holzsamen. 1876. III. 156.[3]
— Observations phénologiques. 1887. IV. 73.[1]
— Ueber phänologische Beobachtungen. 1887. IV. 73.[1]
— Die Plenterdurchforstung. 1893. IV. 174.
— Plenterdurchforstung oder Hochwald in Fichten? 1893.
IV. 454.
— Die Renten der Plenterung und des Hochwaldes. 1893.
IV. 258.
— Rhus vernicifera. 1885. III. 529.[1]
— Robinie und Weymouthskiefer. 1897. IV. 469, 523.[2]
— Die Rothbuche als Nutzholz. 1893. IV. 498.
— Das Schwinden der Breter. 1889. IV. 409.
— Studien über den Schluss der Bestände. 1889. IV. 234.
— Die Taxation der Privat-und Gemeinde-Forsten. 1883.
IV. 251.[1]
— Die Taxation des Mittelwaldes. 1878. IV. 241.
— Untersuchungen auf Kiefernkahlschlägen. 1885. IV.
218.
— Das Vorkommen gewisser fremdländischer Holzarten in
Deutschland. 1882. IV. 125.[2]
— Wann fliegt der Lärchensame? 1887. IV. 450.
— Ueber Weisstannen-Ertragstafeln. 1897. IV. 444.[1]
— In welchen Punkten bedürfen die Baur'schen Angaben
über Ertrag . . . der Revision? 1897. IV. 458.
— Wie weit kann der Femelschlagbetrieb in Deutschland
Platz greifen? 1894. IV. 131.
— Die Wirkung von Unterholz auf Eschenoberholz. 1885.
IV. 535.[1]
— Wolkenbildung, Regen und Wald. 1898. IV. 52.
— Die Zerlegung des Normalvorraths im Mittelwalde. 1880.
IV. 244.
— Zwei alte Höhenmesser in neuer Form. 1879. IV. 215.
Weismann, C. Skove og Skovbrug paa Fyn. 1900. IV.
343.[3]
— See also ROSTRUP, Emil & WEISMANN, C.
Weismüller, (Oberförster a. D.). Massregeln zur Hinterhal-
tung von Wasser . . . im Gebirge. 1899. IV. 185.[1]
Weiss, Adolf J. Beitrag zur Kenntniss der Spaltöffnungen.
1857. I. 131.[2]
— Die Bewegungserscheinungen sensitiver Pflanzen. 1862.
I. 197.[2]
— Über ein eigenthümliches Vorkommen von Kalkoxalat-
massen in . . . Acanthaceen. 1884. II. 796.[2]
— Ueber ein neues Vorkommen der Spaltöffnungen. 1857.
I. 131.[2]
— Die Pflanzenhaare. 1867. I. 112.[2]
— Untersuchungen über die Entwickelungsgeschichte des
Farbstoffes. 1865. I. 184.
— Untersuchungen über die Trichome von Corokia. 1891.
II. 656.[1]
— Untersuchungen über die Zahlen- und Grössenverhältnisse
der Spaltöffnungen. 1865. I. 131.[2]
— Weitere Untersuchungen über die Zahlen- und Grössen-
verhältnisse der Spaltöffnungen. 1891. I. 131.[2]
— & Wiesner, Julius. Vorläufige Notiz über die directe
Nachweisung des Eisens. 1860. I. 153.
Weiss, Alois. Der Borkenkäfer. 1882. IV. 204.

Weiss, C. Rhus Toxicodendrum. 1863. III. 528.[1]
Weiss, Emanuel. Beiträge zur Flora von Griechenland. 1869.
I. 449.
— Floristisches aus Istrien, Dalmatien. 1866. I. 447.
Weiss, F. Ueber die chemischen Bestandtheile der Cheken-
blätter. 1888. II. 631.[1]
— Examen chimique des feuilles de Cheken. 1888. II. 631.[1]
Weiss, Friedrich Wilhelm. Entwurf einer Forstbotanik.
1775. IV. 61.[3]
Weiss, Gustav Adolf. Allgemeine Botanik. 1878. I. 101.[1]
Weiss, Johann Christoph. De Malo Punica. 1712. III.
630;[1] see also BAIER, J. J. 1712. II. 611.[1]
Weiss, Johann Ev. Beiträge zur Kenntniss der Korkbildung.
1890. I. 131.[1]
— Die Blasenkrankheit der Birnenblätter. 1899. III. 447.[1]
— Die Blattbräune der roten Johannisbeere. 1899. III. 415.[1]
— Die Blattfallkrankheit der Johannisbeersträucher. 1900.
III. 415.[1]
— Borkensucht der Aprikosen. 1900. III. 435.[1]
— The caoutchouc-containing cells of Eucommia. 1892.
II. 254.[1]
— Clasterosporium Amygdalearum. 1899. III. 431.[1]
— Clasterosporium Amygdalearum auf Süss und Sauer-
kirschen. 1900. III. 432.[2]
— Der echte Mehltau des Apfelbaumes. 1899. III. 428.[2]
— Eine eigenartige Krankheit der Blätter des Apfelbaumes.
1899. III. 428.[2]
— Die Fliedermotte. 1899. III. 680.[2]
— Gefährliche Krankheiten des Birnbaumes. 1899. III.
447.[1]
— Gefässbündelverlauf bei Chavica Roxburghii. 1876. II.
94.[2]
— Die Heidelbeere. 1887. III. 664.[1]
— Die Kiefernschütte und ihre Bekämpfung. 1899. IV. 480.
— Ueber Korkbildung. 1885. I. 130.
— Das markständige Gefässbündelsystem. 1883. I. 134.[1]
— Die Moniliakrankheit an Apfelbäumen. 1900. III. 428.[2]
— Eine neue Spritze. 1900. III. 198.[2]
— Die Palme. 1887. III. 318.[1]
— Die Pflanzengeographie. 1888. I. 301.
— Die Schorfkrankheit des Kernobstes. 1900. III. 444.[2]
— Die schwarze Kirschblattwespe. 1900. III. 435.[2]
— Die Schwarzfleckigkeit der Rosen. 1900. III. 453.[2]
— Die Ursachen eines schlechten Erfolges bei Bespritzungen.
1900. III. 198.[2]
— Verpflanzung einer grossen Cryptomeria. 1900. III.
302.[1]
— Die Vertilgung der Feldmäuse. 1900. III. 186.[2]
— Verzeichniss der Pflanzen des deutschen Florengebietes.
1888. I. 389.
— Wachsthumsverhältnisse . . . der Piperaceen. 1876. II.
93.[2]
— Welche Spritzen sind die geeignetsten. 1899. III. 198.[2]
— Krause, M. & Bleibinhaus, J. Die Hasselmann'sche
Imprägniermethode. 1899. IV. 421.
Weiss, Leopold I. Beiträge zur Kenntniss der südbrasiliani-
schen Provinz Parana. 1886. III. 269.[3]
Weiss, Simon. Dissertatio physica de excrescentiis planta-
rum. 1694. I. 213.[3]
Weisse, Arthur. Beitrag zur Entwickelungsgeschichte der
Onagraceen-Blüthe. 1899. II. 643.[1]
— Zur Kenntniss der Anisophyllie von Acer. 1895. II.
479.[2]
— Ueber Lenticellen . . . bei Monocotylen. 1897. I. 132.[2]
— Eine monströse Frucht von Citrus Aurantium. 1900. II.
403.[1]
— Eine monströse Fuchsiablüte. 1893. II. 643.[2]
— Neue Beiträge zur . . . Blattstellungslehre. 1894. I. 103.
— Ueber Veränderung der Blattstellung. 1899. I. 103.
— Ueber die Wendung der Blattspirale . . . der Coniferen.
1891. II. 18.
Weisse, J. C. G. Anweisung zur Kultur einiger . . . Holzar-
ten. 1805. IV. 117.
Weisse, W. Igen szép Konifera. 1900. III. 306.[1]
Weisse, Wilhelm. Zur Massenanpflanzung empfehlenswerter
. . . Nadelhölzer. 1899. IV. 443.[1]
— Veredlung der Picea-Formen. 1891. III. 305.[1]
Weissenseeer Blumen-Zeitung. See BLUMEN-ZEITUNG. III.
11.
Weiss's height measurer. 1888. IV. 216.
Weisshand, F. W. Das Verpflanzen von Parkbäumen. 1894.
III. 169.[1]
Weissker, Ferdinand. Ueber Widerstandsfähigkeit ver-
schiedener Bäume. 1873. III. 45.

Weissker, R. Ueber die Grasnutzung im Walde. 1879. IV. 438.¹

Weissmann, Johann Friedrich. Balsamum verum quod vulgo opobalsamum dicitur. See SLEVOGT, J. H. 1705. III. 510.²

Ueber Weisstannenpflanzungen und Saaten. 1851. IV. 444.¹

Weisstannenstöcke mit Stockausschlägen. 1851. I. 209.²

Weisswasser — Böhmische Forstschule. See BÖHMISCHE ... IV. 14.

Weissweiler, Urban. Die Zucht des Maulbeerbaumes. 1875. III. 378.

Weitenweber, Wilhelm Rudolf. Der arabische Kaffee. 1835. III. 741.²

— Einige Bemerkungen über Bastardformen. 1854. II. 99.¹

— Die Tinctura Rhois Toxicodendri. 1836. III. 528.¹

Weitere Beiträge zu der Aufgabe des forstlichen Ausschusses. See COTTA, W. 1849. IV. 291.¹

Weitere Beiträge zur Rosenflora von Oberösterreich. See KELLER, J. B. von. 1893. II. 288.¹

Weitere Bemerkungen über mejicanische Pinus-Arten. See HARDINESS. 1844. III. 291.¹

Weitershausen, Freyherr von. Ueber den Anbau des Lerchenholzes. 1801. IV. 448.²

— See also DRAIS, F. H. G., Freyherr von, WEITERSHAUSEN, Freyherr von & GATTERER, C. W. J. ·

Weitershausen, Heinrich, Freiherr von. Die grossherzoglich hessische Oberförsterei Erbach. 1875. IV. 351.²

Weitgand, A. Der Versuchsgarten (Jardin d'essai du Hamma). 1898. I. 69.¹

Weitzner, Fr. Schulbotanik. 1853. I. 89.

Weizenbeck, Georg Anton. Anzeige der meisten um München wildwachsenden ... Pflanzen. 1786. I. 374.

— Botanische Unterhaltungen. 1784. I. 93.

Welch, E. S. Grafts. 1899. III. 426.²

Welche fremden Holzarten empfehlen sich für den Anbau als Waldgehölze? See BOOTH, John. 1878. IV. 125.¹

Welche Gegenstände sind behufs des Erlasses eines ... Forstpolizei- und Kulturgesetzes zu untersuchen? 1854.· IV. 307.²

Welche Holz- und Betriebsarten sind der Weidenutzung am nachtheiligsten. 1840. IV. 135.¹

Welche Spiräen-Arten ... behalten am längsten ihre Belaubung. 1885. III. 314.¹

Welchen Grad der Genauigkeit muss man bei der nachhaltigen Ertragsermittelung ... verlangen? IV. 235.²

In welcher Weise ist mit der Bildung von Förstervereinen vorzugehen. 1887. IV. 40.²

Welcher Werth ist auf eine bestimmte Gruppirung der Altersklassen zu legen? 1844. IV. 480.

Welcker, H. Notiz über das Ausspritzen des Saftes. 1860. I. 149.²

Welcker von Gontershausen, H. Die technischen Hölzer. 1854. IV. 396.¹ ·

Weid, Isaac. An essay on evergreen Oaks. 1829. III. 362.¹

Welden, Ludwig, Freiherr von. Monographie des Monte-Rosa. 1824. I. 433.

— Der Monte-Rosa. 1824. I. 433.

Well, Johann Jakob von. Kurz verfasste Gründe zur Pflanzenlehre. 1785. I. 83.

Wellcome, Henry S. A visit to the native Cinchona forests. 1880. II. 813.¹

Wellebil, Carl. Eine neue Culturmethode für Flugsandflächen. 1882. IV. 145.

— Die Verwerthung des Buchenholzes. 1874. IV. 499.

Wellenberg, (Oberförster-Candidat). See DALLWITZ, von & WELLENBERG.

The Wellhouse or zinc-tannin process ... for preserving wood. 1881. IV. 420.

Welling, Christoph Friedrich von. Allgemeine historischphysiologische Naturgeschichte der Gewächse. 1791. I. 93.

Wellingtonias. 1879. IV. 484.¹ ·

Wells, C. E. On the pinetum at Highnam Court. 1863. III. 292.

Wells, William V. Explorations and adventures in Honduras. 1857. III. 265.¹

Welsch, Christian Ludwig. Basis botanica. 1697. I. 97, 233.

Welser von Neunhof, P. C. Freiherr. Lehrbuch der ... Holzzucht von J. Friedel. 1811. IV. 106.

Welsh, Herbert. The teacher and the forest. 188.? IV. 29.

Welter, Henri. Essai sur l'histoire du Café. 1868. III. 739.

— Le Gui, Viscum album L. 1868. II. 179.¹ ·

Aus allen Weltheilen. I. 11.

Welwitsch, Friedrich. Apontamentos phyto-geographicos sobre a flora ... de Angola. 1858. I. 491.

— Extract from a letter ... on the botany of West Africa. 1861. II. 55.¹

— On the Loranthaceae of Angola. 1872. II. 174.¹

— Observations on the origin ... of the gum copal. 1867. III. 233.²

— Pungo Adongo und die schwarzen Felsen. 1868. I. 491.

— On a remarkable species of Cissus from ... Benguella. 1865. II. 503.¹

— Sertum angolense. 1869. I. 491.

— Synopse explicativa das amostras de madeiras ... de Angola. 1862. III. 281.¹

— Sur la végétation du plateau de Huilla. 1861. I. 491.

Wenck, Julius. Die Lehre von den Baumaterialien. 1863. IV. 423.¹

Wenckebach. See LEEMANS, J. F. & WENCKEBACH.

Wencker, Daniil. De potu café. See MAPPUS, Marcus. 1693. III. 741.¹

Wenda, K. Kola. 1890. III. 590.²

Wendeburg. Wie ist die Mischung mit Laubholz in den Nadelholzforsten der Heide zu fördern? 1869. IV. 138.¹

Wenderoth, Georg Wilhelm Franz. Analecten kritischer Bemerkungen. 1852. I. 269.

— Zur Birkenfrage. 1846. II. 117.²

— Blühender Cactus hexagonus. 1820. II. 590.¹

— Dissertatio ... Materiae pharmaceuticae hassiacae specimen. 1802. III. 72.

— Ueber Edwardsia microphylla und myriophylla. 1840. II. 85.¹

— Einige Bemerkungen über Azalea indica. 1837. II. 683.²

— Einige Bemerkungen über Betula pubescens Ehrh. 1846. II. 117.²

— Einige Bemerkungen über Cassia obovata. 1838. II. 343.¹

— Einige Bemerkungen über ... neue Pflanzenarten des Botanischen Gartens in Marburg. 1831. I. 47.

— Etwas über eine monströse Form der Amorpha. 1836. III. 467.¹

— Etwas über Laurus borbonia. 1834. II. 225.²

— Flora hassiaca. 1846. I. 382.

— Index plantarum Horti marburgensis. 1807. I. 45.

— Ueber Kultur-Palmen. 1853. II. 66.¹

— Lehrbuch der Botanik. 1821. I. 85.

— Nachträgliche Bemerkungen über Cassia cana. 1841. II. 343.¹

— Ueber eine neue Atragene. 1837. II. 200.¹

— Ueber eine neue Edwardsia. 1830. II. 384.¹

— Observationes botanicae. 1826. I. 267.

— Observationes botanicae. Ilex chrysocarpa. 1829. II. 463.²

— Observationes botanicae in Horto bot. marburgensi. 1831. II. 267.²

— Die Pflanzen botanischer Gärten ... Coniferae. 1851. II. 12.²

— Der Pflanzengarten der Universität Marburg. 1850. I. 47.

— Über die vegetabilischen Erzeugnisse Kurhessens. 1839. III. 121.¹

— Versuch einer Charakteristik der Vegetation von Kurhessen. 1839. I. 380.

Wendland, Heinrich Ludolph. Acacia pugioniformis, A. Browniana. 1819. II. 323.¹

— Alternation of function. 1869. II. 68.²

— Aster tomentosus, A. ferrugineus. 1819. II. 620,¹ 852.¹

— Bemerkungen über die in Blüthe stehende Dracaena Draco. 1836. III. 336.¹

— Beschreibung zweier neuer Pflanzen. 1850. II. 846.¹

— Bestimmung einiger neuen ... Mespilus. 1823. II. 260.²

— Commentatio de Acaciis aphylis. 1820. II. 323.¹

— Descriptiones plantarum novarum. 1825. I. 267.

— Ueber die im Garten zu Kew cultivirten ... Dryandra. 1819. II. 160.¹

— Kurze Beschreibung und Berichtigung einiger Pflanzen. 1833. I. 268.

— Nachrichten über Cereus extensus. 1836. III. 621.¹

— Supposed alternation of function in Palms. 1869. II. 68.¹

— See also BARTLING, F. G. & WENDLAND, H. L.

Wendland, Hermann. Aristolochia Goldieana. 1888. III. 386.²

— Beiträge zu den Borassineen. 1881. II. 61.[1]
— Beiträge zur Kenntniss der Palmen. 1878. II. 61.[1]
— Beiträge zur Palmenflora der Südseeinseln. 1862. II. 62.[1]
— Beiträge zur Palmenkultur. 1866. III. 317.
— Beitrag zur Palmenflora Amerika's. 1880. II. 66.[1]
— Bemerkungen über einige Palmengattungen Amerika's. 1860. II. 61.[2]
— Beschreibung dreier neuen Chamaedoreen. 1853. II. 66.[1]
— Beschreibung einer neuen Chamaedorea. 1852. II. 66.[1]
— Beschreibung einer neuen Palme . . . Maiorties. 1853. II. 71.[1]
— Beschreibung einiger neuer Pflanzen. 1863. II. 797.[1]
— Beschreibungen neuer Palmen. 1858. II. 60.[2]
— Ueber Brahea oder Pritchardia filifera Hort. 1879. II. 75,[2] III. 332.[1]
— Ueber Chamaedorea elatior. 1853. II. 66.[1]
— Chamaedorea Warscewiczii. 1862. II. 66.[2]
— Ueber Cyclanthus Poit. 1866. II. 76.[2]
— Descriptio duarum specierum . . . Carludovicae. 1854. II. 76.[1]
— Descriptio speciei novae . . . Ceratozamiae. 1854. II. 4.[1]
— De deux nouveaux genres de Palmiers. 1865. II. 72,[1] 75.[2]
— Einige neue Palmen Amerika's. 1856. II. 61.[1]
— Ueber einige Palmen Central-Amerika's. 1853. II. 61.[1]
— Einiges über Trauben-Krankheit. 1852. III. 575.[1]
— Enumeratio systematica Chamaedorearum. 1854. II. 66.[1]
— Die habituellen Merkmale der Palmen mit fächerförmigem Blatt. 1879. II. 61.[1]
— Index Palmarum, Cyclanthearum, Pandanearum, Cycadearum. 1854. II. 2,[1] 56,[1] 60.[2]
— Die Königlichen Gärten zu Herrenhausen bei Hannover. 1852. I. 47, III. 28.[1]
— Kritische Bemerkungen über einige . . . Iriarteen. 1863. II. 68.[1]
— Eine neue Palmengattung. 1858. II. 75.[1]
— Eine neue Palmen-Gattung aus Guatemala. 1853. II. 71.[1]
— Eine neue Pflanze der Gärten. 1859. II. 80.[1]
— Ueber die Palmengattung Synechanthus. 1859. II. 75.[1]
— Ueber Seaforthia elegans hort. 1858. II. 64.[1]
— Ueber die systematische Eintheilung der Palmen. 1856. II. 60.[2]
— Washingtonia robusta. 1888. II. 332.[1]
— Washingtonia robusta Herm. Wendl. 1883. II. 75.[1]
— See also MANN, GUSTAV & WENDLAND, Hermann.
— & Drude, Oscar. Palmae australasicae. 1875. II. 60.[2]
Wendland, Johann Christoph. Bemerkungen über einige Pflanzen. 1796. II. 731,[1] 855.[2]
— Botanische Bemerkungen über Glycine monoica. 1798. II. 550.[1]
— Botanische Beobachtungen. 1798. I. 264.
— Collectio plantarum. 1808. I. 265.
— Ericarum icones et descriptiones. 1798. II. 664.[1]
— Hortus herrenhusanus. 1798. I. 45.
— Observationes botanicae in Rosam centifoliam. 1809. II. 292.[1]
— Sammlung ausländischer und einheimischer Pflanzen. 1808. I. 265.
— Verzeichniss der Glas- und Treibhauspflanzen . . . auf dem Königl. Berggarten zu Herrenhausen. 1797. I. 44.
Wendler. Die Riesen-Eiche von Buschkau. 1900. II. 139.[2]
Wendt, Georg Friedrich Carl. Baumzucht Deutschlands. 1804. IV. 82.
— Deutschlands Baumzucht. 1804. III. 68.[2]
Weniger, H. L. See MEIGEN, J. W. & WENIGER, H. L.
Wenken en aanwijzingen betreffende Kinakultuur. 1882. II. 713.[1]
Wennberg, Ericus Samuel & Widmark, F. O. Stirpium in Guinea medicinalium species novae. See AFZELIUS, Adam. 1818. III. 93.[1]
Wennerström, Nils Gustaf. Om Pilplanteringar. See FRIES, Elias. 1836. III. 350.[1]
Wensjoe, Thure. Horti upsaliensis plantae. See THUNBERG, C. P. 1826. I. 40, II. 100.[1]
Went, Friedrich August Ferdinand Christian. Der Dimorphismus der Zweige von Castilloa. 1898. II. 147.[1]
— Étude sur la forme du sac embryonnaire des Rosacées. 1887. II. 256.[1]
— Ueber Haft- und Nährwurzeln. 1893. I. 104, 234.[2]
— De kultuurtuin te Tjikeumeh. 1891. III. 129.[1]
— De strijd tegen de ziekten der cultuurgewassen. 1899. III. 197.
— Over tropische vloedbosschen. 1892. I. 219.[2]

Wentz, Johann Georg. Praktische Bemerkungen über das Forstwesen. 1792. IV. 116, 230.[2]
Wentzel, V. Eigenthümlicher Blitzschlag in Buchen. 1882. IV. 194.
Wentzell, W. T. Sur le principe colorante des fleurs. 1890. I. 185.[1]
Wentzky, von, (Glambach). Bemerkungen über einen kleinen Akazienbestand. 1854. IV. 524.[1]
Wenzig, Theodor. Blüthenkalender der Pomaceen. 1881. II. 257.[1]
— Die Eichen Europas, Nordafrikas. 1886. II. 128.[1]
— Die Eichen Ost- und Südasiens. 1886. II. 131.[1]
— Die Eichenarten Amerika's. 1884. II. 128.[1]
— Die Eschen, Fraxinus. 1883. II. 707.[1]
— Die Familie Pomariae. 1874. II. 255.[1]
— Die Gattung Fraxinus Tourn. 1883. II. 707.[1]
— Die Gattung Spiraea L. 1888. II. 314.[1]
— Neue Beobachtungen in der Familie der Pomaceen. 1882. II. 256.[1]
— Die in Norddeutschland kultivirten Juglandeen. 1881. II. 111.[2]
— Nova ex Pomaceis. 1888. II. 256.[1]
— Die Pomaceen. 1883. II. 256.[1]
— Pomariae Lindley. 1874. II. 255.[2]
— Ueber die Wichtigkeit des Artbegriffes. 1882. I. 253.[2]
Wendlaff, Franciscus. De defoliatione plantarum. 1844. I. 191.[2]
Weppen, H. Acide cinnamique. 1874. III. 607.
Werbke, Norbert C. See POWER, F. B. & WERBKE, N. C.
Werck, Joseph. Die Kultur der Zwergobstbäume. 1881. III. 146.[1]
Werden auch Buchen vom Blitze getroffen? 1833. IV. 496, 543.[1]
Werden in der Jugend verpflanzte Fichten . . . kernfaul? 1853. IV. 453.
Werekha, Petr Nikolayevitch. An account of the forests of Russia. 1873. IV. 345.
— Notice sur les forêts et leurs produits. 1873. IV. 345.
— See also BEPEXA, П. Н.
Werkmeister, R. Über das Ringeln der Obstbäume. 1824. III. 174.[2]
— & Lenné. Auszug aus dem Gutachten über die . . . Heusinger'sche Anweisung. 1827. III. 136.
Werktuig van Howe om boomen te rooyen. 1866. IV. 386.
Werlitz, Gustav Adolph. Observationes de Olei Citri aetherei. 1828. III. 499.[1]
Werminski, F. Ueber die Natur der Aleuronkörner. 1888. I. 140.[2]
Werneburg, A. Ueber Absprünge der Laubholzbäume. 1875. II. 137.[2]
— Zur Durchforstungsfrage. 1886. IV. 174.
— Ueber den geregelten Plänterbetrieb. 1875. IV. 130.
— Noch etwas über das Ringeln der Spechte. 1876. I. 207,[2] IV. 199.[1]
— Schaden durch Engerlinge. 1872. IV. 202.
— Tortrix viridana. 1873. IV. 510.
— Zur Vogelschutzfrage. 1869. IV. 199.[1]
— Der Wanzenbaum. 1873. I. 207,[2] IV. 198.[2]
Werneck, F. I. von. Einleitung in das Studium der Natur- und Forstwissenschaft. 1808. IV. 96.
Werneck, Ludwig Friedrich Franz, Freyherr von. Anleitung zur Ahorn-Zucht. 1815. IV. 526.[1]
— Anleitung zur gemeinnützlichen Kenntniss der Holzpflanzen. 1791. IV. 61,[1] 81.
— Gemeinnützige Entdeckungen . . . im Gebiete der praktischen Forstwissenschaft. 1811. IV. 213.
— Physikalisch-chemische Abhandlungen über die spezifischen Gewichte der . . . Holzarten. 1808. IV. 407.[1]
— Versuch einer Pflanzen-Pathologie. 1807. I. 206,[1] IV. 195.[1]
— Vollständiger Forstcalender. 1777. IV. 95.
Wernek, (Oberforstmeister). Nachricht von einem tannenzerstörenden Schabkäfer. 1790. IV. 455.
Wernekinck, Franz. Icones plantarum . . . in Episcopatu monasteriensi. 1798. I. 375.
Werner, (Forstgehülfe). Waldbaulicher Wert der Hasel. 1890. IV. 492.[1]
Werner, Alexander. De herba Rubi Chamaemori. 1815. III. 458.[1]
Werner, Emil. Ueber "Ricinin." 1870. III. 522.[1]
Werner, Georg Heinrich. Mathematischer Unterricht in Verbesserung des Forstwesens. 1775. IV. 57.

Werner, Hermann. Beobachtungen über jährlich periodisch wiederkehrende Erscheinungen im . . . Pflanzenreich. *See* SCHÜBLER, Gustav. 1831. I. 224.[2]

Werner, Ludwig Reinhold von. De scriptoribus historiam plantarum borussicarum illustrantibus disserit. 1756. I. 80.[3]

Werner, William C. New phænogams for the Ohio flora. 1893. II. 106.[2]

— *See also* KELLERMAN, W. A. & WERNER, W. C.; LAZENBY, W. R. & WERNER, W. C.

Wernerian natural history society. Memoirs. I. 20.

Wernich, Waldemar. Der Wald- und Fruchtbaum. 1894. III. 99, *IV. 112.*

Wernicke. Sur la germination des graines. 1895. I. 204.

Wernicke, W. S. E. Axiomatische Forstbeschreibungen. 1847. IV. 242.

Wernigerode — **Naturwissenschaftlicher Verein des Harzes** . . . *See* NATURWISSENSCHAFTLICHER . . . I. 14.

Werbischek, Jakob. Genera plantarum. 1763. I. 257.

Wernz, Joh. Eine Auswahl von Kernobstsorten. 1881. III. 71.

Werth, (*Hofgärtner, Berlin*). Notizen über die Vermehrung . . . durch Stecklinge. 1838. III. 157.

Werth, Emil. Blütenbiologische Fragmente aus Ostafrika. 1900. I. 240.[1]

Werth der Krummholzkiefer. 1852. IV. 465.[1]

Die **Werthberechnung** der zur willkührlichen Benutzung zu veräussernden Mittelwälder. 1855. IV. 254.

Wertheim, C. J. M. *See* PLANTEN, H. O. W. & WERTHEIM, C. J. M.

Wertheim, Guillaume. *See* CHEVANDIER, Eugène & WERTHEIM, Guillaume.

Werthier, William. Notes on the Buckeye and Viburnum nudum. 1883. II. 481.[1]

Wertmueller, K. H. De catechu. 1779. III. 464.[1]

Wesche, Valentin Julius. Quaedam de chininio. 1828. III. 721.

Wesdin, J. P. Des Fra Paolino da San Bartolomeo Reise nach Ostindien. 1796. III. 277.

— Viaggio alle Indie Orientali. 1796. III. 277.

— A voyage to the East Indies. 1796. III. 277.

Weselsky, Philipp. Ueber eine neue Säure aus der Aloë. 1873. III. 333.[1]

Wesley naturalists' society. Journal. *See* JOURNAL of microscopy . . . I. 18.

Wesmael, Alfred. American Oaks in Belgium. 1890. III. 361.[1]

— American species of Ash. 1892. II. 707.[1]

— Les arbres calomniés. 1896. IV. 485.[1]

— Catalogue raisonné des arbres forestiers. 1864. I. 293, *III. 77, IV 84.*[3]

— Considérations sur les hybrides. 1866. I. 245.

— L'école d'arboriculture de Tournai. 1877. III. 154.[1]

— Énumeration des Conifères observés après l'hiver. 1881. III. 292.

— L'Érable Sycomore dans les parcs. 1900. IV. 536.[1]

— Étude sur quelques Bouleaux de la flore belge. 1863. II. 17.[2]

— Exposition internationale de sylviculture à Namur. 1869. III. 271.[1]

— De la fécondation au point de vue des croisements. 1863. I. 245.

— Flore forestière de Belgique. 1866. I. 391,[2] *IV. 84.*[2]

— Frène parasol. 1883. III. 672.[2]

— Le Hêtre. 1896. IV. 496.

— L'industrie forestière aux États-Unis d'Amérique. 1895. IV. 555.[2]

— Kort overzicht der in Belgie gekweekte Populieren. 1886. II. 96.[1]

— Monographie botanique . . . des Chênes de l'Amérique septentrionale. 1870. II. 128.[1]

— Monographie botanique . . . des Peupliers cultivés en Belgique. 1862. II. 96.[1]

— Monographie de toutes les espèces connues du genre Populus. 1869. II. 96.[1]

— Monographie des espèces du genre Fraxinus. 1892. II. '07.[1]

— Monographie des Groseilliers. 1864. II. 243.[1]

— Monographie des Peuphers. 1869. II. 96.[1]

— Monographie des Saules de la flore belge. 1865. II. 99.[1]

— Monographie des Saules hybrides de la flore belge. 1864. II. 102.[1]

— Naturalization of American Conifers. 1890. III. 293.

— Note sur le Tilleul à petites feuilles. 1872. II. 517.[1]

— Note sur quelques arbres de l'Himalaya. 1869. I. 470,[1] *IV. 88.*[2]

— Note sur une particularité de nervation . . . du genre Crataegus. 1865. II. 261.[1]

— Notice sur les Peupliers de l'Himalaya. 1868. II. 96.[1]

— Notice sur les Tilleuls forestiers de Belgique. 1880. II. 515.[1]

— Notice sur quelques espèces . . . d'Érables. 1859. II. 476.[1]

— Notice sur quelques espèces de Saules. 1860. II. 99,[1] *III.* 347.

— Observations critiques sur le polymorphisme de certains organes chez les Chênes. 1894. II. 130.[2]

— Observations critiques sur les Conifères des États-Unis. 1895. II. 14.[2]

— Observations sur quelques plantes . . . de la flore de Belgique. 1862. II. 102,[1] *262.*[2]

— Observations tératologiques. 1864. II. 507.[3]

— Oorsprong onzer fruitboomen. 1883. I. 247.

— Les Ormes forestiers et d'ornement. 1863. II. 142.[2]

— De parasolvormige Esch. 1883. III. 672.[2]

— Pépinières forestières. 1895. IV. 546.[1]

— Les ia an cultivés dans les jardins de Belgique. 1868. II. 254[2] t es

— Les Platanes . . . de Belgique. 1894. II. 254.[2]

— À propos du Thuya Lobbi. 1894. IV. 484.[2]

— Quelques considérations sur les phénomènes de la floraison. 1861. I. 220.[1]

— Quelques observations horticoles faites en 1873. 1874. III. 335.[1]

— Résumé de l'histoire des peupliers forestiers. 1893. IV. 485.[1] — 1894. IV. 486.[1]

— Revue critique des espèces du genre Acer. 1890. II. 476.[1]

— Le Saule à bois bleu. 1863. III. 351.[3]

— Le Saule à bois bleu (Salix daphnoides). 1875. III. 351.[3]

— Les Saules des bois, des marais . . . 1895. II. 99.[1]

— Tentoonstelling te Namen. 1869. III. 271,[1] *V. xxix.*[1]

— Transformation d'une vrille . . . chez le Vitis. 1864. II. 507.[3]

— Transformation des étamines en carpelles chez le Salix Caprea. 1862. II. 106.[1]

— Utilisation des terris charbonniers. 1894. IV. 546.[1]

— Une visite à l'arboretum . . . de Groenendael. 1895. IV. 539.[3]

— *See also* HEURCK, Henri van & WESMAEL, Alfred; THIELENS, Armand & WESMAEL, Alfred.

— & **Mélard,** A. Le Pitch-pine. 1894. IV. 462.[1]

Wessberge, (*Revierförster, Hannover*). Ueber Pflanzenverpacken. 1869. V. 151.[3]

— Ueber den zweialterigen Eichenschälwaldbetrieb. 1867. IV. 506.

Wessel, A. W. Flora Ostfrieslands. 1858. I. 384.

Wesselhöft, Johannes. Die Kultur der Rosen in Töpfen. 1887. III. 452. — 1897. III. 453.[1]

— Der Rosenfreund. 1866. III. 449.

— Ueber das Varüren der Rosen. 1876. III. 39, *449.*

— Die verschiedenen Anzuchtsmethoden der Rosen. 1881. III. 452.

Wessels, L. De geleidelijke oplossing van de gouvernements-Koffiecultuur. 1888. III. 730.

— De gouvernements Koffie cultuur in de Minahassa. 1891. III. 730.

— De gouvernementskoffiecultuur op Java. 1889. III. 730.

— De nieuwe toekomst der gouvernements Koffiecultuur. 1893. III. 730.

— De voorstellen van de Indische regeering omtrent de gouvernements Koffiecultuur op Java. 1892. III. 730.

Wessely. 'Bisherige Ergebnisse und Schicksale der Holztränkung nach Boucherie. 1861. IV. 418.

— Die Lärche. 1851. IV. 449.

Wessely, Franz. Einiges über die Vegetationsverhältnisse . . . der Stadt Kremsier. 1855. I. 441.

Wessely, Joseph. Die beweglichen Triftrechen. 1863. IV. 390.[1]

— Dienstunterricht für die Forst- und Jagdwachen beider Hälften des Kaiserthums Oesterreich. 1855. IV. 294.[2]

— Dienstunterricht für die öffentlichen Forst- und Jagdwachen des österreichischen Kaiserstaates. 1855. IV. 294.[1]

— Eichenkultur-Proben. 1856. IV. 503.

— Die Einrichtung des Forstdienstes in Oesterreich. 1861. IV. 294.[2]

— Der europäische Flugsand. 1873. IV. 145.

— Die Forste, die Staatsgüter. 1873. IV. 368.

— Forstliches Jahrbuch für Österreich-Ungarn. 1879. IV. 368.
— Das Futterlaub. 1877. III. 223.²
— Gedanken über unsere forstliche Unterrichtsfrage. 1880. IV. 36.¹
— Die grosse Forstausstellung der ungarischen Länder. 1873. III. 272.¹
— Ueber den [sic] hauptsächlichsten Holzhauerzeug. 1855. IV. 383.²
— Das Karstgebiet Militär-Kroatiens. 1876. IV. 167,¹ 373.
— Die Korkeiche mit Bezug auf Oesterreich. 1861. IV. 516.²
— Merkwürdige Fichtenastverbreitung. 1852. IV. 460.¹
— Niederösterreichs Weichselrohrzucht. 1881. III. 438.²
— Die österreichischen Alpenländer. 1853. IV. 368.
— Die österreichisch-steirische Hochgebirgs-Forstwirtschaft. 1851. IV. 139,¹ 141.
— Oesterreich's Lohstoffe. 1860. IV. 435.
— Oesterreichs Waldschätze. 1867. IV. 406,²
— Les richesses forestières de l'Autriche. 1867. IV. 406.²
— Statistik Niederösterreichs für Forst. 1868. IV. 369.
— Unterricht im öffentlichen Forst- und Jagdwachdienst des österreichischen Kaiserstaates. 1855. IV. 294.¹
— Der v. Manzonische Trift-Rechen. 1858. IV. 390.¹
— Die venetianischen Brettmühlen. 1860. IV. 393.
— Verrechnung der Urproduktion. 1870. IV. 262.
— Der Vorraths-Holzfang Alsacco. 1859. IV. 390.¹
— Das Ziehen und Schleppschlitteln des Brennholzes. 1857. IV. 389.
— See also LORENZ VON LIBURNAU, J. R., Ritter & WESSELY, Josef.
Wessén, Carl Johan. Plantae . . . in paroecia Ostrogothiae Kärna. 1838. I. 354.
West, Hans. Beyträge zur Beschreibung von St. Croix. 1793. I. 335.
— Bidrag til Beskrivelse over Ste Croix. 1793. I. 335.
West, John. Remarks on the management . . . of woods. 1842. IV. 120.
West, Tuffen. On the structure of the seed in Solanaceae. 1866. II. 768.¹
West African annatto. 1890. III. 613.¹
West African bass fibre. 1891. III. 330.²
West African Cinchona bark. 1894. III. 726.¹
West African indigo plants. 1888. III. 236.
West African Mahogani. 1894. IV. 401.¹
West African rubbers. 1889. III. 231.
West-American scientist. I. 7.¹
West coast and Puget Sound lumberman. See WEST coast lumberman. IV. 5.²
West coast lumberman. IV. 5.²
West Indian bulletin. III. 10.¹
West Indian Palms. 1887. II. 75.¹
West Indië. Bijdragen tot de bevordering van de kennis van de Nederlandsche West-Indische kolonien. III. 10.¹
West Riding consolidated naturalists' society. Journal. See The NATURALIST. Huddersfield. I. 19.
West Virginia — Medical society. See MEDICAL . . . I. 6.
West Virginia — Agricultural experiment station. Annual report. Bulletin. III. 9.
Westbeck, Zacharias. Om skogars och bränslo fulla besparning. 1760. IV. 282.¹
Westberg, Paul. Ueber den Hoftüpfel und dessen Geschichte. 1888. II. 17.¹
Westbrook, B. A. White Huckleberries. 1889. II. 672.¹
Westcott, Frederic. See KNOWLES, G. B. & WESTCOTT, Frederic.
Westen, Gustav von d. Ueber Augenstecklinge. 1863. III. 158.
Westenberg, B. Invoer van houtsoorten uit Ned. Oost en West Indië. 1892. IV. 407.¹
Westenberg, E. W. Viridarii Academiae Ducat. Gelriae et Comit. Zutphaniae. 1709. I. 49.
Westerhoff, Rembert. Accurata descriptio botanica . . . plantarum, in solo groningano. 1820. I. 394.
Westerholz. De iure forestali. 1674. IV. 313.
Westerhout, J. W. List of timber trees of the province of Malacca. 1845. IV. 400.²
Westerloo, comte de MÉRODE. See MÉRODE-WESTERLOO, comte de.
Westerlund, Carl Agardh. Blekinges Rubus-arter. 1854. II. 301.¹
— Spridda anteckningar till Skandinaviens flora. 1863. I. 356.
Westermaier, Max. Über Bau und Funktion des pflanzlichen Hautgewebesystems. 1884. I. 129.²
— Beiträge zur Kenntniss des mechanischen Gewebesystems. 1882. I. 134.²
— Bemerkungen zu der Abhandlung von Gregor Kraus: "Grundlinien." 1889. I. 183.
— A compendium of general botany. 1893. I. 92.
— Zur Embryologie der Phanerogamen. 1890. I. 122.
— Zur Kenntniss der osmotischen Leistungen des lebenden Parenchym's. 1883. I. 150.¹
— Kompendium der allgemeinen Botanik. 1893. I. 92.
— Ueber das markständige Bündelsystem der Begoniaceen. 1879. II. 583.²
— Neue Beiträge zur Kenntniss der physiologischen Bedeutung des Gerbstoffes. 1887. I. 183.
— Zur Physiologie und Morphologie der Angiospermen-Samenknospe. 1896. I. 122.
— Sur le rôle physiologique du tannin. 1887. I. 183.
— Ueber Spaltöffnungen und ihre Nebenapparate. 1899. I. 132.¹
— Untersuchung über den Bau . . . des pflanzlichen Hautgewebes. 1882. I. 129.²
— & Ambronn, Hermann. Beziehungen zwischen Lebensweise und Structur der Schling- und Kletterpflanzen. 1881. I. 236.¹
Westermeier, (Kgl. Oberförster). Wie steigern wir unsere und unserer Arbeiter Leistungen bei den Kulturen? 1889. IV. 310.¹
Westermeier, G. Leitfaden für das preussische Jäger- und Förster-Examen. 1878. IV. 98.¹
— Systematische forstliche Bestimmungstabellen der Waldbäume. 1886. IV. 84.¹
Western American Oaks. 1890. II. 129.¹
The western Arbor-vitae. 1891. II. 53.¹
Western Australia. See FRASER, Sir Malcolm. 1882. IV. 380.¹
Western Australia — Woods and forests department. Annual progress report. IV. 17.¹
Western Australian timber. 1896. IV. 401.¹
Western Australian timbers. 1900. IV. 402.¹
Western Australia's forests. See WESTERN Australian timber. 1896. IV. 401.²
The western Catalpa tree. 1890. IV. 538.²
A western forest. 1892. I. 504.
Western Grape grower, (pseud.). My vineyard at Lakeview. 1866. II. 550.
Western horticultural review. III. 9.
The western journal of the medical and physical sciences. I. 7.¹
The Western Larch. 1896. II. 33,² IV. 558.¹
Western medical and physical journal. I. 7.¹
Western New York horticultural society. Proceedings. III. 9.
Western Pine. 1900. II. 27.¹
Western pomologist. III. 9.
Western review. I. 7.²
Western review of science and industry. See KANSAS CITY review . . . I. 5.
The western Shad-bush. 1892. II. 257.²
Westerotien van Meeteren. Surinaamsche planten en cultuurgewassen. 1883. III. 64.²
Westerode, W. de WOLFF VAN. See WOLFF VAN WESTERODE, W. de.
Westersheim, Richard, Ritter, WETTSTEIN VON. See WETTSTEIN VON WESTERSHEIM, Richard, Ritter.
Der Westfälische Holzhändler. IV. 11.
Westfälischer Provincial-Verein für Wissenschaft und Kunst. Jahresbericht. I. 520.¹
Westgalizischer Forst-Verein. Jahres-Schrift. Vereinsschrift. IV. 15.
Westh, Th. Claudi. Hedeselskabets Virksomhed pas Øerne. 1899. IV. 156.²
Westland, A. B. Botanical rambles in China. 1886. I. 459.
— Plantes intéressantes de la Chine. 1894. III. 203.
— A rich field for the plant collector. 1894. III. 203.
— Vegetable sculpture in China. 1894. III. 202.²
Westland, George. Bouvardias as decorative plants. 1877. III. 711.¹
— Indoor berry-bearing plants. 1879. III. 695.²
— Winter-flowering Eupatoriums. 1877. III. 755.¹
Westmaas, E. A. de ROO VAN. See ROO VAN WESTMAAS, E. A. de.
Westmacott, Wilham. Θεολοβοτονολογια [sic]; sive, Historia vegetabilium sacra. 1694. I. 512.

Weston, Richard. Botanicus universalis et hortulanus. 1770. I. 262.
— A catalogue of stove plants. 1775. III. 81.
— The English flora. 1775. I. 262.
— Flora anglicana. 1775. I. 262.
— The gardener's and planter's calendar. 1773. III. 109.
— Tracts on practical agriculture. 1769. I. 3.[1]
— Tracts on practical agriculture and gardening. 1769. III. 109.
— The universal botanist and nurseryman. 1770. I. 262.
Westphalia — Forstverein für Westfalen und Niederrhein. *See* FORSTVEREIN . . . IV. 8.
Westphalia — Naturhistorischer Verein der preussischen Rheinlande . . . *See* NATURHISTORISCHER . . . I. 13.
Westring, Johan Peter. Afhandling om gula Kinan. 1800. III. 722.
— De Ledo palustri. *See* LINNÉ, Carl von. 1775. III. 653.[1]
— Ledum palustre. *See* LINNÉ, Carl von. 1785. III. 653.[1]
Westrum, A. S. van. De Bamboe als grondstof voor papier. 1881. III. 315.[3]
Westwood, John Obadiah. On caprification. 1837. II. 150.[3]
— The Laburnum leaf miner. 1881. III. 450.[3]
— Notice of a congregation of moths. 1836. IV. 523.[3]
— The Orange Coccus parasite. 1886. III. 501.[1]
Wetche, A. Ontarie-Poppelen. 1873. III. 345.[3]
Wetherell, Leander. Forest trees. Hampshire. 1855. IV. 111.[3]
— Planting shade and shelter trees. 1885. III. 215.[1]
Wetherill, H. Emerson. List of plants obtained on the Peary auxiliary expedition. 1895. I. 309.[1]
Wetterhan, J. David. Ueber die allgemeineren Gesichtspunkte der Pflanzengeographie. 1872. I. 300.
Wetterwald, Xaver. Blatt- und Sprossbildung bei Euphorbien und Cacteen. 1888. II. 435,[1] 588.[3]
Wettstein & Sohn. Begonia hybrida Wettsteini. 1885. III. 618.[1]
Wettstein von Westersheim, Richard, *Ritter*. Ueber das Androeceum von Philadelphus. 1893. II. 242.[1]
— Ueber das Auffinden der Pinus Cembra. 1887. II. 41.[1]
— Auffindung der Daphne Blagayana Frey. in Bosnien. 1888. II. 601.[1]
— Beitrag zur Flora Albaniens. 1892. I. 450.
— Beitrag zur Flora des Orientes. 1889. I. 479.
— Über bemerkenswerte neuere Ergebnisse der Pflanzengeographie. 1895. I. 301.
— Berichtigung zu . . . Was ist Pinus Wettsteinii. 1892. II. 49.[1]
— Der botanische Garten . . . der K, k. deutschen Universität in Prag. 1899. I. 522.[1]
— Die botanischen Anstalten Wiens. 1894. I. 66.[1]
— Daphne Blagayana Frey. in Bosnien. 1888. II. 601.[1]
— Über die einheimischen Betula-Arten. 1890. II. 117.[3]
— Flora von Oesterreich-Ungarn. 1889. I. 443.
— Der gegenwärtige Stand unserer Kenntnisse betreffend die Neubildung von Formen. 1900. I. 243.[1]
— Die Geschichte unserer Alpenflora. 1896. I. 438.
— Globulariaceae. 1895. II. 795.[3]
— Grundzüge der geographisch-morphologischen Methode der Pflanzensystematik. 1898. I. 253.[1]
— Myoporaceae. 1895. II. 805.[3]
— Neuere Anschauungen über die Entstehung der Arten. 1897. I. 243.[1]
— Nolanaceae. 1895. II. 767.[3]
— Notiz betreffend die Verbreitung der Lärchenkrankheit. 1888. IV. 451.
— Die Omorika-Fichte, Picea Omorica. 1891. II. 38.[1]
— Pflanzen und Ameisen. 1889. I. 235.[1]
— Die Pflanzenwelt der Polargegenden. 1900. I. 220.[1]
— Ueber Picea Omorica Panč. 1890. II. 38.[1]
— Pinus digenea. 1889. II. 41.[3]
— Ueber die Resultate . . . den Cytisus Alschingeri Vis. betreffenden Untersuchungen. 1890. II. 368.[3]
— Scrophulariaceae. 1895. II. 778.[3]
— Solanaceae. 1895. II. 767.[3]
— Ueber die Systematik der Solanaceae. 1892. II. 767.[3]
— Untersuchungen über die Section Laburnum. 1890. II. 68.[1]
— Über die Verwerthung anatomischer Merkmale zur Erkennung hybrider Pflanzen. 1888. II. 30,[3] 40.[3]
— Das Vorkommen der Picea Omorica. 1890. II. 38.[1]
— Vorläufige Mittheilung über Cytisus Laburnum. 1890. II. 369.[1]

— Die weibliche Blüte von Ginkgo. 1899. II. 8.[1]
— Die wichtigsten pflanzlichen Feinde. 1890. IV. 211.[1]
— & Wiesner, Juhus. Untersuchungen über die Wachsthumsgesetze. 1884. I. 187.
Wetzel. Ueber Düngung mit . . . Excrementen. 1877. IV. 144.[1]
Wetzstein, Albert. Willow notes. 1900. II. 108.[3]
Wex, Gustav, *Ritter* von. Treatise on the decrease of water in springs. 1873. IV. 50.
— Ueber die Wasserabnahme in den Quellen. 1873. IV. 50.
Weyd, Paul Marie. Pline. 1897. IV. 24.[3]
Weyda, H. Der chinesische Thee. 1844. III. 606.
Weyl. Die in der Umgegend Rastenburgs . . . vorkommenden seltnern Pflanzen. 1847. I. 382.
Weyland, Georg Carl. Kurze Abhandlung von Jagd- und Forstsachen. 1765. IV. 94.
Weyler y Lavina, Fernando. Catálogo de las plantas . . . (del imperio Marroqui). 1860. I. 484.
— Elementos de botánica. 1843. I. 88.
Weymayr, Thassilo. Die Gefässpflanzen der Umgebung von Gratz. 1867. I. 441.
Weymouth Pine fungus. 1892. IV. 470.[1]
Die **Weymouthskiefer.** 1895. IV. 470.[3]
Die **Weymouthskiefer** . . . in den zum Dominium Boskowitz (Mähren) gehörigen Waldungen. 1860. IV. 469.
Weymouthskiefern-Blasenrost. 1899. IV. 470.[1]
Die **Weymuthskiefer** . . . als Schutzholz. 1855. IV. 469.
Die **Weymuthskiefer** in Steiermark. 1865. IV. 469.
Weyn, de & Fabis. Huile d'olives. 1892. III. 679.[1]
Weyrich, Rudolf. Ein Beitrag zur Chemie des Thees. 1872. III. 607, 740.[3]
— *See also* WURTNER, LIEVENTHAL & WEYRICH, Rudolf.
Wgr. Beitrag zur Wirthschaft in Hochgebirgsforsten. 1874. IV. 149.[1]
— Die Holzgewächse und die Wohnlichkeit unseres Erdballes. 1874. IV. 44.
Whale, W. Egham wild flowers. 1875. I. 402.
Wharton, J. E. Report on forest tree planting. 1875. IV. 271.[3]
From what countries have the islands in the West Indies derived their plants? 1828. I. 335.
What is a Sycamore? 1889. II. 255.[1]
What is a tree? 1888. I. 106.[3]
What time shall we cut timber? 1858. IV. 384.[3]
Wheatley, G. Sago-cultuur in Britsch Noord-Borneo. 1895. III. 327.[3]
Wheeler. *See* KOCH, WHEELER & TOLLENS.
Wheeler, C. Further remarks on Coffee cultivation at Hazareebaugh. 1854. III. 732.[1]
Wheeler, Charles Fay. A sketch of the original distribution of White Pine. 1898. II. 46.[1]
— *See also* BEAL, W. J. & WHEELER, C. F.
— & Smith, E. F. Catalogue of the . . . plants of Michigan. 1881. I. 315.
Wheeler, George. Some plants observed . . . in his voyage to Greece. 1738. I. 451.
Wheeler, George M. Report upon the United States geographical surveys west of the one hundredth meridian. *See* ROTHROCK, J. T. 1878. I. 324.
Wheeler, J. H. Investigation du phylloxéra en Californie. 1882. III. 761.
Wheeler, James. The botanist's and gardener's new dictionary. 1763. III. 81.
Wheeler, James Love. Catalogus . . . plantarum . . . in horto Societatis pharmaceuticae. 1830. I. 54.
Wheeler, Timothy. Making maple-sugar. 1893. IV. 527.[3]
Wheeler, Wilham Archie. A contribution to the knowledge of the flora of southeastern Minnesota. 1900. I. 327.
Wheelock, William E. The genus Polygala in North America. 1890. II. 420.[3]
Whishaw, Francis. Further experiments with the Shan black vegetable dye. 1845. III. 236.
Whistling, Christian Gottfried. Oekonomische Pflanzenkunde. 1805. III. 51.
Whitby, Tobias. Tractatus de sanguine uvae. 1655. III. 582.
Whitaker, W. Notes on trees. 1894. I. 394, IV. 497, 511.
Whitcher, G. H. The growth and nutrition of plants. 1890. III. 151.
White. The productive resources of Cyprus. 1864. III. 272.[1]
White, Arnold H. Manuring of estates. 1875. III. 732.[1]
White, Charles Abiathar. Adaptability of the prairies for artificial forestry. 1884. IV. 155.[1]
— A curious method of propagating trees. 1897. III. 345.[3]
— Tuna and its distribution. 1897. II. 597.[3]

hite, Edmund. Report on botany: Timber and its diseases. 1888. IV. 414.¹

White, Edward. A descriptive account of the tree which produces the gutta percha. 1845. III. 223.²

White, F. S. Currants. 1898. III. 415.¹

— Gooseberries. 1898. III. 414.²

— Gooseberries and Currants. 1899. III. 414.¹

White, Francis Buchanan White. The Black wood of Rannoch. 1876. II. 46,² IV. 358.²

— The collecting and study of Willows. 1889. II. 99.¹

— The flora of Perthshire. 1898. I. 404.¹

— A list of British Willows. 1889. II. 102.¹

— Notes on some Willows. 1889. II. 102.¹

— A revision of the British Willows. 1891. II. 102.¹

— Salix fragilis, S. Russelliana, and S. viridis. 1888. II. 102.¹

— The Willows of the district of the North-East of Scotland. 1889. II. 102.¹

White, Francis J. Inaugural dissertation on the geography of plants. 1838. I. 299.

White, Gilbert. The natural history and antiquities of Selborne. 1789. I. 395, 533.

— The natural history of Selborne. 1789. I. 533.

— A naturalists calendar. 1795. I. 226.¹

White, H. C. Ash analyses of native woods. 1889. I. 156.¹

White, James. Large trees on the Annandale estate. 1879. IV. 85.¹

White, James C. On the action of Rhus venenata. 1873. III. 526.²

White, James Walter. A new British Rubus. 1899. II. 306.²

— Rubus discolor W. & N. var. leucocarpus. 1882. II. 307.¹

White, John. Journal of a voyage to New South Wales. See SMITH, Sir J. E. 1790. I. 500.

White, Joseph J. Cranberry culture. 1870. III. 663.²

White, R. B. Schaduwboomen voor Koffie. 1895. III. 484,² 734.²

— Shade tree for Coffee. 1895. III. 484.²

White, Taylor. A discourse on the Cinnamon. 1759. II. 224.¹

White, Theodore G. Mechanical elevation of the roots of trees. 1897. I. 188.

White, Wilham. Observations . . . on the Broad-leaved Willow bark. 1798. III. 351.²

White, William Hale. The culture and varieties of Roses. 1878. III. 449.

— Materia medica, pharmacy. 1892. III. 244.

The White Ash. 1894. II. 707.²

The White Oak. 1891. II. 132.²

The White Oak at Shandy Hill, Maryland. 1892. II. 132.²

The White Oak, Quercus alba. 1900. IV. 502.²

White-pine lumber in the United States. 1897. IV. 470.²

The White-Pine supply. 1882. IV. 470.²

White Pine timber supplies. See FERNOW, B. E. 1897. IV. 470.²

White Pines. 1892. II. 43.²

White tea of Persia. 1896. III. 608.¹

White Willow. 1895. III. 351.²

Whitehead, Charles. Fifty years of fruit-farming. 1889. III. 142.

— Fruit-farming in Kent. 1884. III. 142.

— Insecten nadeelig voor de vruchtenteelt. 1887. III. 190.

— Profitable fruit-farming, an essay. 1004. III. 142.

— Tree and timber-culture. 1888. III. 117.²

Whiting, C. E. Timber growing. 1874. IV. 111.²

Whiting, George. The products and resources of Tasmania. 1862. III. 283.¹

Whiting, Margaret Christine. See MILLER, Ellen & WHITING, M. C.

Whitley, Brames & Milne. Fulham nursery. 1817. I. 53.

Whitley, George, Jephson, George & Hunter, Alexander. Correspondence respecting the Box-wood of the Himalayas. 1861. IV. 400.¹

Whitman, Sidney. The German forest. 1895. IV. 349.²

Whitmarsh, Samuel. Eight years experience . . . in the culture of the Mulberry tree. 1839. III. 375.

Whitmore, O. S. The most desirable trees for street . . . planting in Chicago. 1898. III. 42.²

Whitney, Josiah Dwight. The Pine, the Sequoia. 1872. II. 51.¹

— See also FOSTER, J. W. & WHITNEY, J. D.

Whitney, Peter. An account of a singular Apple-tree. 1782. II. 266.²

Whitney, W. D. Botany [of the Lake Superior land district]. 1851. I. 314.

Whitten, John Charles. The emergence of Pronuba. 1894. II. 87.¹

— Forestry. 1892. IV. 112.

— Phenological notes at the Missouri botanical garden. 1894. I. 222.¹

Whittlewood forest. 1878. IV. 358.¹

Whitton, J. Sycamore buds and squirrels. 1890. III. 186.¹

The Whortleberry. 1868. III. 652.²

Whyte, Alexander. Report on the botanical aspects of British Central Africa. 1895. III. 131.²

Whyte, James. On the management of Oak coppice woods. 1858. IV. 505.

— Reclamation of neglected plantations. 1858. IV. 169.²

Whytes, G. Bignonia venusta at Syon. 1892. III. 705.

Wiazemsky, W. Verzeichniss der im elatomschen Kreise . . . gesammelten Pflanzen. 1870. I. 363.

Wibel, August Wilhelm Eberhard Christoph. Dissertatio . . . florae werthemensis sistens prodromum. 1797. I. 375.

— Primitiae florae werthemensis. 1799. I. 375.

Wichan, Jos. Pflanzet nur geschulte Bäume! 1882. III. 166.

Wichelhaus, H. Ueber die Lebensbedingungen der Pflanze. 1868. I. 217.

Wichers, J. Bemestingsrapport der onderneming Brangak. 1899. III. 734.¹

— Holz-Tabellen. 1841. IV. 223.

Wichers, P. J. Heide-ontginning; de Mosbes. 1889. III. 663.²

— Welke is de waarde van de Vaccinium macrocarpon. 1894. III. 664.¹

Wichmann, C. Ueber einige Coniferen unserer Gärten. 1887. III. 290.

Wichmann, Heinrich. Anatomie des Samen von Aleurites. 1880. II. 436.²

Die wichtigsten botanischen Kunstausdrücke. 1887. I. 71.

Die wichtigsten Obstschädiger. See HOLLRUNG, Max. 1898. III. 191.

Wichura, Max. Ein Ausflug nach Luleå-Lappmarken. 1859. I. 107,¹ 355.

— Die Bastardbefruchtung im Pflanzenreich. 1865. II. 9.¹

— Bemerkungen über das Blühen, Keimen und Fruchttragen der . . . Bäume. 1856. I. 147.

— Sur des hybrides de Saules. 1854. II. 100.¹

— Ueber künstlich erzeugte Weidenbastarde. 1853. II. 101.¹

— Observations on hybridization. 1866. I. 245.

— Der schiefe Verlauf der Holzfaser an den Bäumen Lapplands. 1859. I. 107.¹

— Ueber die in Schlesien vereinzelt vorkommenden nordischen Pflanzen. 1858. I. 384.

— Ueber schraubenförmig gewundene Baumstämme. 1851. I. 107.¹

— Ueber die Stellung der Samen bei den Akanthaceen. 1851. II. 796.²

— Ueber das Winden der Blätter. 1852. I. 190,¹ 289.

— Ueber die Zusammensetzung der weiblichen Blüthe . . . bei den Winden. 1848. II. 103.¹

Wicke, Wilhelm. Fernere Versuche über das Vorkommen des Amygdalins. 1852. III. 431.²

— Sur la présence de l'amygdaline. 1851. I. 175.

— Présence de la propylamine. 1854. III. 420.¹

— On the sources of amygdaline. 1851. I. 175.

— Ueber das Vorkommen des Amygdalins. 1851. I. 175.

— Ueber das Vorkommen von Propylamin. 1854. III. 423.¹

Wickede, A. J. O. Versuch einer Wald-Taxation. 1815. IV. 242.

Wickham, Henry Alexander. The introduction of the India-rubber tree into India. 1878. III. 518.²

— Rough notes of a journey . . . from Trinidad to Pará. 1872. III. 269.¹

Wickham, William. Memoranda respecting the culture of Fig trees. 1818. III. 369.¹

Wickham, William H. Canada Balsam. 1878. III. 295.²

Wickson, Edward J. The California fruits and how to grow them. 1889. III. 133.

— Irrigation in fruit growing. 1900. III. 151.

— Twig-budding and grafting the Olive. 1894. III. 676.²

Widdrington (formerly COOK), Samuel Edward. On the genera Pinus and Abies. See COOK, S. E. 1839. III. 289.

— On the Pinus and Abies. See COOK, S. E. 1839. III. 15.¹

— Sketches in Spain. See COOK, S. E. 1834. I. 420.

— On some species of European Pines. 1842. II. 39.¹

— Spain and the Spaniards. 1844. I. 420.

Widegren, Pehr David. Försök til en ny beskrifning af Östergöthland. 1817. I. 352.
Widenmann, A. von. Abnorme Blattformen an Syringa. 1894. II. 716.[1]
— Über den Einfluss von Insekten auf die Gestaltung der Blätter. 1894. I. 214.[1]
Widenmann, D. A. von. Die Bedeutung der Haarbekleidung an . . . der Silberlinde. 1893. II. 518.[1]
— Ueber geschlitzte (laciniate) Blattformen. 1893. I. 145.[1]
Widenmann, W. Darstellung des durch die würtembergischen Forstdienstinstruktonen vorgeschriebenen Forstabschätzungsverfahrens. 1828. IV. 247.[3]
— Geschichtliche Einleitung in die Forstwissenschaft. 1837. IV. 25.
— Literarische Berichte für Forstmänner. *See* LITERARISCHE . . . 1832. IV. I.
— Das System der Forstwissenschaft. 1824. IV. 56.
— Ueber den Zweck und Begriff der Forstwirthschaft. 1826. IV. 56.
Widerstandsfähigkeit unbewurzelter Gehölzstecklinge gegen Kälte. 1897. III. 182.
Widman, Oskar. O sztucznem trawieniu zapomocą soków roślinnych. 1882. III. 617.[1]
Widmann, Ergebniss eines Eichenschälwaldschlages. 1877. IV. 513.
Widmark, Fredericus Ol. Florula javanica. *See* THUNBERG, G. P. 1825. I. 468.
— *See also* WENNBERG, E. S. & WIDMARK, F. O.
Widmann, Friedrich. Catalogue des arbres . . . dans l'ancien jardin . . . d'Eystett. 1805. I. 78.[1]
— Catalogus systematicus . . . Horti eystettensis. 1805. I. 78.[1]
Wie erzieht man den meisten Brennstoff? 1854. IV. 431.[1]
Wie ist dem so sehr einreissenden Holzmangel vorzubeugen? *See* KEYSER, G. A. 1794. IV. 158.
Wie kann man dem überhandnehmenden Holzmangel · abhelfen? 1791. IV. 282[1] ¹ *see also* GERRATH; von. 1790. IV. 280.[1]
Wie viel Kubikzoll? Ausführlicher und genauer Holzberechner. n. d. IV. 219.
Wie vollsieht sich der Einbau alter Laubhölzer? 1897. IV. 138.[2]
Wie wird Waldstreu entbehrlich? 1856. IV. 437.[1]
Wiebecke. Taxus baccata L. in der Niederlausitz. 1885. II. 11.[1]
Wieber, Franz. Die Ausnutzung des Eichenhölzes. 1874. IV. 514.[1]
— Eichelaufbewahrung und Eichelsaaten. 1870. IV. 506.
Wied-Neuwied, Maximilian Alexander Philipp, Fürst von. Beitrag zur Flora Brasiliens. 1823. I. 341.
— Reise in das Innere Nord-America. 1839. I. 307.
— Reise nach Brasilien. 1820. I. 341.
— Travels in the interior of North America. 1839. I. 307.
— & Nees von Esenbeck, C. G. Zollernia, novum plantarum genus. 1827. II. 389.[1]
Wiedenmann, F. L. & Weber, E. Beschreibung der phanerogamischen Gewächse Est-, Liv- und Curlands. 1852. I. 361.
Wiedenmann, W. Das System der Forstwissenschaft. 1824. IV. 29.
Wiederausschlag der durch Sonnenbrand beschädigten jungen Buchen. 1849. IV. 496.
Wiedereintheilung des Kantons in vier Forstkreise. 1876. IV. 306.
Wiederhold. Zur Maikäfer-Frage. 1879. IV. 477.
— Ein Wort über die Eichen-Nachzucht. 1878. IV. 507.
Wiederhold, (*in Höxter*). Über die mit dem Namen Brand . . . belegte Krankheit der Obstbäume. 1826. III. 193.[2]
Wiederhold, E. HEDRICH VON: *See* HEDRICH VON WIEDERHOLD, E.
Wiedermann, Leopold. Rhodologische Notizen. 1886. II. 288.[1]
Wiefel, Carl. Abnormitäten an Pelargonium. 1887. II. 391.[2]
— Einige Formen von Prunus spinosa. 1885. II. 277.[3]
Wiegand, Karl McKay. Some varieties of Potamogeton and Spiraea. 1900. II. 315.[1]
— *See also* ROWLEE, W. W. & WIEGAND, K. M.
Wiegers, F. A. Collection d'arbres, arbrisseaux, plantes. 1809. I. 49.
Wiegmann, A. F. Über die Bastarderzeugung im Pflanzenreiche. 1828. I. 245.
— Ueber das Einsaugungs-Vermögen der Wurzeln, 1828. I. 160.
— Die Krankheiten . . . der Gewächse. 1839. III. 178.
— Om Planternes Sygdomme. 1839. III. 178.

— Over de ziekten . . . der gewassen. 1839. III. 178.
— *See also* BITMARΒ, A. Φ.
— & Polstorff, L. Over de anorganische bestanddeelen der planten. 1842. I. 152.[2]
— — Ueber die anorganischen Bestandtheile der Pflanzen. 1842. ·I. 152.[2]
— — Over ·de onbewerktuigde bestanddeelen der planten. 1842. I. 152.[2]
Wiehl, Julius. Zur Cubierung des Rundholzes. 1899. IV. 229.
— Welche Erfolge wurden mit der allgemein üblichen " schonenden " Durchforstung erzielt? 1898. IV. 176.[1]
Wiel, Johann Peter. Observationes de usu interno nucis vomicae. 1764. III. 682.[1]
Wieler, Arwed L. Analysen der Jungholzregion von Pinus sylvestris. 1886. II. 48,[1] 108.[2]
— Ueber Anlage und Ausbildung von Libriformfasern. 1889. I. 126.
— Über den Antheil des secundären Holzes der dicotyledonen Gewächse an der Saftleitung. 1888. I. 166.
— Beiträge zur Kenntniss der Jahresringbildung. 1887. I. 190.[1]
— Ueber die Beziehung der Reservestoffe zu der Ausbildung der Jahresringe. 1896. ·I. 128.[1]
— Ueber die Beziehung zwischen Wurzel- und Stammholz. 1891. I. 525.
— Ueber Beziehungen zwischen dem sekundären Dickenwachsthum und den Ernährungsverhältnissen. 1892. I. 527,[1] V. XII.[1]
— Das Bluten der Pflanzen. 1892. I. 169.[1]
— Dégâts invisibles causés aux Conifères par la fumée. 1897. IV. 178.[1]
— Einwirkung der sauren Gase auf die Vegetation. 1899. III. 185.[1]
— Erwiderung auf R. Hartig's Bemerkungen. 1889. I. 166.
— Die Function der Pneumathoden. 1898. I. 171.
— Ueber den Funktionswechsel der Markstrahlinitiale bei Holsgewächsen. 1886. I. 126.
— Holzbildung auf Kosten des Reserve-materials. 1897. I. 527, IV. 65.[1]
— Ist das Markstrahlcambium ein Folgemeristem? 1886. I. 125.
— Ueber die jährliche Periodicität im Dickenwachsthum. 1898. I. 527, IV. 65.[1]
— Ueber die Jahresperiode im Bluten der Pflanzen. 1893. I. 526.[1]
— Ueber den Ort der Saftleitung im Holze. 1889. I. 166.
— Ueber den Ort der Wasserleitung im Holzkörper. 1888. I. 166.
— Ueber die Periodizität in der Wurzelbildung. 1894. I. 191,[1] IV. 65.[1]
— Ueber unsichtbare Rauchschäden. 1897. IV. 193.[1]
— Ueber die Ursachen der Jahresringbildung der Pflanzen. 1889. I. 128.[1]
Wiemann, A. Wald und Wild. Allgemeines Liederbuch. 1827. IV. 101.
Wien. *See* VIENNA.
Wien — Internationaler pomologischer Kongress . . . 1873. *See* INTERNATIONALER . . . III. 25.
Wien — K. k. Ackerbauministerium. *See* K. K. ACKERBAU-MINISTERIUM. III. 25.
Wiener, (*Langen*). Aufastung von Kiefernstangenhölzern. 1898. IV. 474.
Wiener, Moreo. Eine Holzbahn. 1894. IV. 392.
— Ungarns Forstwirthschaft. 1896. IV. 374.[1]
— Ungarns Forstwirthschaft auf der Millenniumsausstellung in Budapest. 1896. IV. 21.[2]
— Ungarns Forstwirthschaft im abgelaufenen Jahrtausend. 1896. IV. 28.[2]
Wiener Alleebaumfrage. 1871. III. 209.
Wiener entomologische Monatsschrift. III. 25.
Wiener Handels-Akademie. Jahresbericht. 1891. III. 25.
Wiener illustrirte Garten-Zeitung. *See* WIENER Obst- und Garten-Zeitung.
Wiener Journal für das gesammte Pflanzenreich. III. 25.
Wiener landwirtschaftliche Zeitung. III. 25. *See also* ALLGEMEINE land- und forstwirthschaftliche Zeitung. IV. 13.[2]
Wiener Museum der Naturgeschichte. Annalen. I. 28.[1]
Wiener Obst- und Garten-Zeitung. III. 25.
Der **wienerische** Baum- und Obstgärtner; oder, Anleitung . . . zur Wartung der Obstbäume. 1798. III. 146.[1]
Der **Wienerwald.** 1870. IV. 369.
Wier, D. B. The curculio in the Cherry. 1878. III. 432.[1]
— Wier's Cut-leaved Maple. 1877. III. 536.[1]

Wier's Cut leaf Maple. 1898. III. 536.[1]

Wierzbike. Om Overvintringen . . . af den undseelige Mimosa. 1803. III. 481.[2]

Wiesbauer, Johann Baptist. Beiträge zur Flora von Presburg. 1871. I. 446.

— Ueber Eichenformen. 1875. II. 129.[3]

— Foristische Beiträge. 1879. II. 287.[2]

— Ist der Eibenbaum . . . giftig? 1894. III. 288.[3]

— Neue Rosen vom östlichen Erzgebirge. 1886. II. 288.[1]

— Die Rosenflora von Travnik. 1883. II. 287.[2]

— Verwachsung von Populus . . . und Abies. 1885. I. 209,[1] III. 40,[2] 346.[2]

— & Haselberger, Michael. Beiträge zur Rosenflora von Oberösterreich. 1891. II. 288.[1]

Wiese. Die neue Tanne im Peloponnes und das Verhalten unserer Fichte. 1860. II. 36.[2]

Wiese, Ernst. Allgemeine Forstwirthschaftslehre. 1874. IV. 98.[1]

— Ansichten über Bewirthschaftung der Privatforsten. 1869. IV. 308.[2] — 1874. IV. 101, 307,[2] 308.[2]

— Die Bedeutung der Durchforstungen. 1882. IV. 173.

— Beschädigungen junger Lärchenpflanzen. 1872. IV. 450.

— Die Durchforstungen. 1874. IV. 173.

— Der Faulbaum . . . auch Pulverholz genannt. 1869. IV. 528.[1]

— Flüchtige Bemerkungen eines durch die Forsten Ostpreussens flüchtig reisenden Forstmannes. 1860. IV. 353.

— Die Forst- und Jagdpolizei-Gesetze Preussens. 1870. IV. 320.

— Hylesinus piniperda L. 1877. IV. 477.

— Der Kieferndreher. 1872. IV. 476.

— Eine neue Krankheit der Kiefer. 1865. IV. 476.

— Die Pyramiden- (Spitz-; Italienische) Pappel. 1882. III. 346.[1]

— Die Schwarzerle. 1861. II. 116.[2]

— Der Sturm . . . 1872 an der Ostsee. 1875. IV. 139.[1]

— Das Verhalten der Kiefer auf ausgebautem Ackerboden. 1866. IV. 472.

— Welche Vortheile erwachsen den belasteten Forstfiskus aus Aufhebung des Holzrechts? 1871. IV. 333.

— Welche Vortheile kann die mit der Waldweide belastete k. Oberförsterei J. aus deren Ablösung erwarten? 1871. IV. 333.

Wiesecke. Le café purifié. 1847. III. 741.[2]

Wiesend, Otto. De Dulcamara. 1837. III. 701.[2]

Wiesenhavern, L. H. J. Abhandlung über das Theer- oder Pechbrennen. 1793. IV. 436.[1]

— Anleitung zu der neuen auf Physik und Mathematik gegründeten Forstschätzung. 1794. IV. 250,[2] 253.

Wiesner, H. Ueber das zu tiefe Pflanzen der Formobstbäume. 1883. III. 169.[2]

Wiesner, Julius. Der absteigende Wasserstrom. 1889. I. 166.

— Anatomie und Physiologie der Pflanzen. 1890. I. 92.

— Beiträge zur Kenntniss der indischen Faserpflanzen. 1870. III. 234.

— Bemerkungen über den factischen Lichtgenuss der Pflanzen. 1894. I. 230.

— Beobachtungen über den Einfluss der Erdschwere auf . . . Blätter. 1000. I. 168.

— Beobachtungen über die Anisophyllie einiger tropischer Gewächse. 1894. I. 111.

— Beobachtungen über die Wachsüberzüge der Epidermis. 1871. I. 129.[1]

— Beobachtungen über Stellungsverhältnisse der Nebenblätter. 1861. I. 111.

— Ueber die Bewegung des Imbibitionswassers im Holze. 1875. IV. 412.[1]

— Die Blattbögen und ihre Berechnung. 1861. I. 112.[1]

— Über das Eindringen der Winterknospen kriechender Brombeersprosse in den Boden. 1883. II. 306.[1]

— Ueber einige im laufenden Winter beobachtete Vegetationserscheinungen. 1873. I. 227.[2]

— Einleitung in die technische Mikroskopie. 1867. I. 36.[1]

— Elemente der wissenschaftlichen Botanik. 1881. I. 91.

— Die Entstehung des Chlorophylls. 1877. I. 141.

— Über die Entstehung des Harzes. 1865. I. 181.[1]

— Ueber die Epitrophie der Rinde. 1894. I. 190.[2]

— Zur Erklärung der wechselnden Geschwindigkeit des Vegetationsrhythmus. 1889. I. 200, 218.

— Experimenteller Nachweis paratonischer Trophieen. 1896. I. 190,[1] II. 36.[1]

— La faculté motrice des plantes. 1883. I. 194.

— Ueber ein Ferment, welches . . . die Umwandlung der Cellulose in Gummi . . . bewirkt. 1885. I. 181.[1]

— Die Flora der Umgebungen von Brünn. 1854. I. 440.

— Ueber den geometrischen Charakter . . . des . . . Laubblattes von Liriodendrum. 1859. II. 210.[1]

— Zur Geschichte des Laubblattes. 1857. I. 109.[2]

— Die Gesetze der Riefentheilung an den Pflanzenaxen. 1860. I. 105.

— Grundversuche über den Einfluss der Luftbewegung auf die Transpiration. 1888. I. 168.

— Über das Gummiferment. 1886. I. 181.[1]

— Die heliotropischen Erscheinungen. 1879. I. 195.[1]

— Ueber Heliotropismus. 1898. I. 195.[1]

— Influence de la lumière solaire diffuse. 1898. I. 230.

— Ueber die krystallinische Beschaffenheit der geformten Wachsüberzüge pflanzlicher Oberhäute. 1876. I. 129.[2]

— Die Lebensdauer der Gewächse. 1864. I. 193.[1]

— Die Lichtwuchs der Holzgewächse. 1897. IV. 67.[2]

— Die natürlichen Einrichtungen zum Schutze des Chlorphylls. 1876. I. 141, 230.

— Ueber eine neue Form der falschen Dichotomie. 1898. I. 107,[1] II. 438.[2]

— Note über das Verhalten des Phloroglucins. 1878. I. 155.

— Note über die angebliche Function der Wurzelspitze. 1884. I. 195.[2]

— Pflanzenphysiologische Mittheilungen aus Buitenzorg. 1894. I. 111, 233.[2]

— Photometrische Untersuchungen. 1893. I. 230.

— Recherches sur l'influence de la lumière. 1876. I. 167.

— Die Rohstoffe des Pflanzenreiches. 1873. III. 218.[2]

— Ueber die Ruheperiode . . . der Samen von Viscum. 1897. II. 180.[1]

— Der im Stamme absteigende Wasserstrom. 1889. IV. 63.[2]

— Studien über angebliche Baumbast-papiere. 1892. III. 235.[2]

— Studien über das Welken von Blüthen. 1897. I. 167.

— Studien über die Anisophyllie tropischer Gewächse. 1894. I. 111.

— Die technisch verwendeten Gummiarten. 1869. III. 227.

— Ueber Trophieen. 1895. I. 111.

— Die undulirende Nutation der Internodien. 1878. I. 187.

— Ueber das ungleichseitige Dickenwachsthum. 1892. I. 190.[2]

— Untersuchung einiger Treibhölzer. 1872. I. 242.[1]

— Untersuchung über die Lage der charakteristischen Riefen an den Axenorganen der Pflanzen. 1859. I. 105.

— Untersuchungen über den Bogenwerth der Blattbasen. 1861. I. 112.[1]

— Untersuchungen über den Einfluss der Lage auf die Gestalt der Pflanzenorgane. 1892. I. 524.[1]

— Untersuchungen über den Einfluss des Lichtes. 1876. I. 167.

— Untersuchungen über den Heliotropismus. 1880. I. 195.[1]

— Untersuchungen über den Lichtgenuss der Pflanzen. 1895. I. 230.

— Untersuchungen über die Bewegung des Imbibitionswassers. 1875. I. 165.

— Untersuchungen über die Beziehungen des Lichtes zum Chlorophyll. 1874. I. 141.

— Untersuchungen über die herbstliche Entlaubung. 1871. I. 191.[2]

— Untersuchungen über die mechanische Wirkung des Regens. 1897. I. 233.[1]

— Untersuchungen über die Organisation der vegetabilischen Zellhaut. 1886. I. 129.[2]

— Untersuchungen über die Wachsthumsbewegungen der Wurzeln. 1884. I. 526.[2]

— Untersuchungen über . . . Eucaliptgummi. 1871. III. 634.[1]

— Versuch einer Bestimmung . . . der heliotropischen Empfindlichkeit. 1893. I. 195.[1]

— Versuch einer Erklärung des Wachstums der Pflanzenzelle. 1890. I. 137.

— Versuche über den Ausgleich des Gasdruckes. 1879. I. 168.

— Ueber die Vertheilung der appendiculären Organe an den Axen von Hibiscus. 1857. I. 524.[2]

— Über den vorherrschend ombrophilen Charakter des Laubes der Tropengewächse. 1894. I. 233.[1]

— Vorläufige Mittheilung über die Elementargebilde der Pflanzenzelle. 1891. I. 137.

Wiesner, Julius (*continued*).
— Vorläufige Mittheilung über die ... Exotrophie.   1892.
I. 100.[1]
— Vorläufige Mittheilung über die Lage der Blattbasis.   1862.
I. 112.[1]
— Die Wechselbefruchtung.   1865.   I. 201.[1]
— Über die Zerstörung der Hölzer an der Atmosphäre.   1864.
I. 206.[2]
— Ueber den Zusammenhang ... Eigenschaften des Holzes
mit dessen anatomischem Baue.   1869.   IV. 543.[1]
— *See also* WEISS, A. J. & WIESNER, Julius; WETTSTEIN,
Richard von & WIESNER, Julius; Βίσνερος, Ἰούλιος.
— & **Molisch**, Hans.   Untersuchungen über die Gasbewegung
in der Pflanze.   1890.   I. 166.
— & **Pacher**, Johann.   Ueber die Transspiration entlaubter
Zweige.   1875.   I. 167.
Wiesner, Z.   Von den vertheilten Gemeindewäldern.   1897.
IV. 309.[2]
Wiest, Anton.   Untersuchungen über die pflanzengeogra-
phischen Verhältnisse Deutschlands.   *See* SCHÜBLER, Gustav.
1827.   I. 377.
Wietlisbach, J. W.   Aus dem Aargau.   Abschätzung einer ...
Waldfläche.   1862.   IV. 249.[2]
— Beschädigungen durch Curculio notatus.   1861.   IV. 476.
— Canton d'Argovie.   Taxation d'une parcelle de bois plantée
d'après le système.   1862.   IV. 249.[2]
— Dommages causés par le Curculio notatus.   1861.   IV.
476.
— Mittheilungen aus dem Aargau.   1866.   IV. 366.
— Notice forestière sur le canton d'Argovie.   1866.   IV. 366.
— Sur la production ... de l'écorce de Chêne.   1863.   IV.
512.
— Ueber die Production ... der Eichenrinde.   1863.   IV. 512.
— Rapport sur le thème: Quelles modifications peut-on con-
stater en Suisse dans l'importation des bois?   1863.   IV. 406.[1]
— Referat über die Frage: Welche Veränderungen lassen sich
... in der Einfuhr und Ausfuhr von Bauholz ... nachweisen?
1863.   IV. 406.[1]
— Ueber die Verbesserung der Wirthschaft in den Gemeinds-
waldungen.   1856.   IV. 242, 308.[1]
— Welche Beobachtungen sind über den Lichtungszuwachs
... gemacht worden?   1884.   IV. 175.[3]
— Welche Vortheile gewährt die natürliche Verjüngung.
1885.   IV. 140.
Wigand, Albert.   Beiträge zur Pflanzenteratologie.   1854.
I. 143. — 1887.   I. 144.[1]
— Der Botanische Garten zu Marburg.   1867.   I. 48.
— Botanische Untersuchungen.   1854.   I. 34.
— Über Deorganisation der Pflanzenzelle.   1863.   I. 181.[1]
— Desorganisation der Zellenwand.   1865.   I. 138.[1]
— Einige Beispiele anomaler Bildung des Holzkörpers.   1856.
I. 127.[1]
— Einige Sätze über die physiologische Bedeutung des Gerb-
stoffes.   1862.   I. 183.
— Über die feinste Structur der ... Zellenmembran.   1857.
I. 138.[1]
— Flora von Hessen und Nassau.   1891.   I. 389.
— Grundlegung der Pflanzen-Teratologie.   1850.   I. 143.
— Intercellularsubstanz und Cuticula.   1850.   I. 137.
— Über Intercellularsubstanz und Cuticula.   1854.   I. 137.
— Kritik und Geschichte der Lehre von der Metamorphose
der Pflanze.   1846.   I. 101.[2]
— Ueber Krystall-Plastiden.   1887.   I. 137.
— Mikroskopische Untersuchungen.   1872.   I. 91.
— Die rothe und blaue Färbung von Laub und Frucht.   1887.
I. 185.[1]
— Ueber den Sitz der China-Alkaloïde.   1862.   II. 813.[2]
— Versuche über das Richtungsgesetz der Pflanze beim
Keimen.   1854.   I. 203.
Wigand, F.   Ueber den Anbau der Lärche.   1841.   IV. 449.
Wigand, Johann.   Catalogus herbarum in Borussia nascen-
tium.   1590.   I. 372.
— Vera historia de succino borussico.   1590.   I. 372.
Wigand, Julius Wilhelm Albert.   Der Baum.   1854.   I. 82.[1]
— Flora von Kurhessen.   1859.   I. 384.
— Flora von Kurhessen und Nassau.   1859.   I. 384.
— Sur le Quassit.   1837.   III. 508.[2]
Wiggers, A.   Ueber den Quassit.   1837.   III. 508.[2]
Wiggers, F. H.   Primitiae florae holsaticae.   *See* WEBER,
G. H.   1780.   I. 374.
Wight, Robert.   Addenda to the foregoing [Wallich, N.
Notes].   1837.   II. 343.[1]
— Catalogue of Indian plants.   1833.   I. 471.
— Contributions to Indian botany.   1837.   II. 527.[1]

— Contributions to the botany of India.   1834.   I. 471.
— Description de deux genres nouveaux des Indes orientales.
1837.   II. 527.[1]
— Directions for preserving plants.   1837.   I. 35.
— Further observations regarding the homóothermal method.
1837.   III. 43.
— On the homóothermal method of acclimating extra-tropical
plants.   1837.   III. 43.
— Icones plantarum Indiae orientalis.   1840.   I. 472.
— Illustrations of Indian botany.   1840.   I. 472.
— Illustrations of Indian botany, principally of the southern
parts of the peninsula.   1831.   I. 471.
— Ueber Laurus Cassia Linné.   1839.   III. 405.[1]
— On the Laurus Cassia of Linnaeus.   1839.   II. 224,[1] III.
405.[1]
— Letter on Dr. Graham's discovery.   1837.   II. 555.[2]
— Notes on Indian botany.   1845.   I. 472, II. 842.[2]
— Notice of the Cassia Burmanni.   1837.   II. 344.[2]
— Observations on Mudar.   1835.   III. 692.[2]
— Observations on the flora of Courtallum.   1835.   I. 472.
— Remarks on Cambogia Gutta.   1839.   II. 555.[1] — 1840.
II. 225,[1] 554.[2]
— Remarks on the tree which yields the gamboge of com-
merce.   1836.   II. 552.[2]
— On the separation of the Pomegranate.   1840.   II. 610.[2]
— Spicilegium neilgherrense.   1846   I. 472.
— On the structure of the ovarium ... of Viburnum.   1845.
II. 842.[2]
— Suggestions for a new application of grafting.   1836.   III.
160.
— Synopsis of the genera of Indian Compositae.   1867.   II.
849.[2]
— On the tree which produces the gamboge.   1838.   III.
609.[2]
— & **Arnott**, G. A. WALKER.   Characters of some new ...
genera of plants.   1833.   I. 268.
— — Illustrations of Indian botany.   1835.   I. 472.
— — m florae peninsulae Indiae orientalis.   1834.
I. 47 Prodro us
— & **Gardner**, George.   Observations on the structure ...
of the genus Azima.   1845.   II. 472.[2]
Wighton, J.   Evil effects of trees in hedge-rows.   1874.   III.
214.[2]
— Mistleto roots.   1869.   III. 385.[1]
— On the Mistletoe.   1864.   III. 385.[1]
Wigman, H. J.   De bergwouden van Java.   1893.   IV. 376.[2]
— Bloemen als voedsel enz.   1897.   III. 219.[2]
— Bontbladerige planten.   1893.   III. 206.[2]
— Cacao.   1890.   III. 592.[2]
— Caryota urens Linn.   1900.   III. 321.[2]
— Cassia.   1894.   III. 470.[1]
— Causerie over Rozen.   1897.   III. 453.[1]
— Coniferen (Cupressus).   1892.   III. 302.[1]
— Eriobotrya japonica.   1889.   III. 424.[1]
— Eriobotrya japonica en Macadamia.   1889.   III. 383.[2]
— Eucalyptus.   1894.   III. 634.[1]
— Fraaie boomen.   1895.   III. 204.[1]
— Fraaie boomen Pterocarpus saxatilis.   1894.   III. 485.[2]
— De gele Pinang.   1890.   III. 320.[1]
— Hooge boomen in 's Lands plantentuin.   1890.   I. 298.
— Hybridisatie bij Koffie.   1900.   III. 733.[2]
— Iets over ... geoultiveerde Rozen.   1897.   III. 451.[1]
— Kiemkracht van zaad.   1897.   I. 204.
— Landbouw-causerie.   1890.   III. 727.
— Liberia-Koffie.   1887.   III. 742.[2] — 1890.   III. 742.[2]
— Manihot Glaziovii Muell. Arg.   1899.   III. 520.[2]
— Een merkwaardige boom.   1890.   III. 589.[1]
— Eene merkwaardige Klapperboom.   1890.   II. 67.[2]
— Nieuwe vruchtboomen: Cyphomandra.   1889.   III. 669,[2]
699.[2]
— Het nut van boomen.   1897.   IV. 45.
— Onze vruchtboomen.   1899.   III. 147.[1]
— Onze vruchten.   1900.   III. 275.[1]
— Ooftteelt in Ned. Indie.   1899.   III. 147.[1]
— Ooftteelt op Java.   1900.   III. 147.[1]
— Palmen.   1893.   III. 318.[1]
— Het planten van boomen ter herinnering.   1898.   III. 34.[1]
— Quelques mots sur la culture des Roses.   1876.   III. 452.
— Reuzen-Papaja.   1886.   II. 582.[2]
— De roode Pinang.   1890.   III. 324.[2]
— De Roos.   1892.   III. 453.[1]
— Rozen.   1894.   III. 451.[1]
— Tuinbouw-causerie.   1892.   III. 129.[1]
— Het uitzaaien van Palmzaden.   1898.   III. 318.[2]

— Vezelstof leverende planten. 1897. III. 235.[1].
— Vruchtboomen. 1894. III. 92.[1]
— Vruchtenteelt. 1898. III. 147.[1]
— Welke cultures komen na Koffie in aanmerking. 1899. III. 129.[1]
— See also ROMBURGH, Pieter van & WIGMAN, H. J.
Wigman, J. R. Verslag der verrichte werkzaamheden in den cultuurtuin te Paramaribo. 1900. III. 119.[1]
Wignier, L. D. Variété du Hêtre commun, Hêtre pleureur. 1846. II. 125.[2]
Wiig, O. E. OLSEN-. See OLSEN-WIIG, O, E,
Wimholdt, K. E. Forslag til Skovopelskning. 1802. IV. 156.[1]
Wiinholt, C. E. Bemærkninger samlede paa en Forstreise i Storbrittanien. 1806. IV. 357.[2]
Wijers, P. G. Onderzoek van het hout van Saprosma. 1854. II. 831.[1]
Eene **wijze** om week hout duurzaam te maken. 1859. IV. 418.
Wijze van beplanting der duinen. 1805. IV. 159.
Wikström, J. A. Provinsen Helsinglands fanerogama växter. 1868. I. 356.
Wikström, Johan Emanuel. Beskrifning af ett nytt slägte . . . Lonchostoma. 1818. II. 251.[2]
— Bidrag till kännedomen om sällsyntare växters geografiska utbredning inom Sverige. 1824. I. 353.
— Conspectus litteraturae botanicae in Suecia. 1831. I. 3.[1]
— De Daphne. 1817. II. 600.[2]
— Dissertatio botanica de Daphne. 1817. II. 600.[2]
— Enumeratio specierum generis Daphnes. 1818. II. 599.[2]—1820. II. 600.[2]
— Granskning af de till Thymelaearum växtordning hörande slägten. 1818. II. 599.[2]
— Mindre kända växter. 1822. I. 266.
— Några arter af växtslägtet Rosa. 1820. II. 282.[1]
— Öfversigt af ön Guadeloupe's flora. 1827. I. 335.
— Öfversigt af ön Sanct Barthelemi's flora. 1825. I. 335.
— Öfversigt af Stockholma-tractens naturbeskaffenhet. 1839. I. 354.
— Stockholms flora. 1840. I. 354.
Wilber, G. M. A white-fruited Blackberry. 1881. II. 310.[2]
Wilberding, J. H. A. De Aurantiis eorumque eximio usu medico. See HEISTER; Lorenz. 1741. III. 499.[1]
Wilbouchewitch, Jean. See VILBOUCHEWITCH.
Wilbrand. Der Blitz als Waldverderber. 1875. IV. 194.
Wilbrand, (Oberförster, Viernheim). Dreifacher Hochwald-betrieb. 1879. IV. 129.
Wilbrand, (Oberforstrath, Darmstadt). Forstästhetik in Wissenschaft und Wirthschaft. 1893. IV. 55.[2]
— Mittheilungen aus der Forst- und Cameralverwaltung des Grossherzogthums Hessen. 1886. IV. 351.[2]
— Statistische Mitteilungen aus der Forstverwaltung. 1882. IV. 351.[2]
Wilbrand, Johann Bernhard. Allgemeine Physiologie. 1838. I. 148.
— Handbuch der Botanik. 1819. I. 376.
— Die natürlichen Pflanzenfamilien. 1834. I. 260.
— Uebersicht der Vegetation Deutschlands. 1824. I. 377.
— & Ritgen, F. A. Gemälde der organischen Natur. 1821. I. 298.
Wührink, G. J. Wat is te verwachten uit het zaad der bestaande Appelsoorten. 1877. I. 248.[1] III. 426.[2] ·
Wilbuschewicz, Eugen. Histiologische und chemische Untersuchungen der gelben und rothen . . . Chinarinden. 1889. III. 725.[1]
— Histiologische und chemische Untersuchungen . . . gelber Chinarinden. 1889. III. 725.[1]
Wilbuszewitsch, V. Untersuchungen der Gerbsäuren der Cortex adstringens brasiliensis. 1886. III. 464,[1] 488.[2]
Wilcke, George Wilhelm Constantine von. Versuch einer Anleitung die wilden Bäume und Sträucher . . . erkennen . . . zu lernen. 1788. I. 370, IV. 81.
Wilcke, Samuel Gustav. Flora gryphica. 1765. I. 373.
— Hortus gryphicus. 1765. I. 44.
Wilckens, H. D. Eine Aeusserung über die Bildung des teutschen Forstmannes. 1801. IV. 31.
— Die Anfangsgründe der künstlichen Holzzucht. 1800. IV. 140.
— Die Anfangsgründe der natürlichen Holzzucht. 1801. IV. 105, 139.[1]
— Die forstmännische Lehre von dem Oertlichen. 1800. IV. 68.[1]
Wilckens, M. Der Hochschul-Unterricht für Land- und Forstwirthe. 1879. IV. 36.[2]

Wilcox, Reynold W. Strophanthus, a clinical study. 1897. III. 690.[1]
Wilczek, Ernst. L'influence du climat sur la végétation dans les Alpes. 1899. I. 438.
Wild. Die Ausscheidung von Wald und Weide. 1881. IV. 136.[1]
— Ueber Durchforstungen in Gebirgs- und Alpenwäldern. 1876. IV. 173.
— Eclaircies . . . dans les montagnes. 1876. IV. 173.
— Das Einschlagen der Pflanzen. 1889. IV. 153.[1]
— Weidenkultur und Korbflechterei. 1882. III. 348.
— Die Wirkungen der Fröste vom Winter 1879/80. 1881. IV. 191.[2]
Wild, A. E. · On the advantages and disadvantages of the natural and artificial systems of rearing forest trees. 1869. IV. 141.
— Report . . . on the forests . . . of Cyprus. 1879. IV. 375.[2]
Wild, Josef. Projekte über Aufforstung auf Haide und Oedgründen. 1884. IV. 158, 387.[1]
— Projekte über Aufforstung von Haiden. 1878. IV. 158, 389.
Wild, M. Die Alpenwälder, einst und jetzt. 1893. IV. 367.
— Aménagement provisoire. 1878. IV. 249.[2]
— Die Angriffe gegen das Forstgesetz. 188.? IV. 330.
— Anleitung für die Erstellung provisorischer Wirthschaftspläne im Kanton St. Gallen. 188.? IV. 249.[2]
— Beschädigungen der Lärchen durch Eichhörnchen. 1875. IV. 198.[1]
— Chilitanne oder Schmucktanne. 1883. III. 299.[1]
— Dommages causés aux Mélèzes par les écureuils. 1875. IV. 198.[1]
— Dommages causés par les écureuils. 1873. IV. 198.[1]
— Ein Gang durch die Thusner Wälder. 1887. IV. 367.
— Kleinere Mittheilungen. 1883. III. 190.
— Lehrsätze für den Unterricht im Zwergobstbau. 1882. III. 146.[1]
— Die Nutzniessung der Genossenschaftsgüter im Kanton St. Gallen. 1879. IV. 334.[2]
— Ein provisorischer Wirthschaftsplan. 1878. IV. 249.[2]
— Rentabilität einer Waldpflanzung in den Alpen. 1893. IV. 278.[2]
— Ueber Servitut-Ablösungen. 1885. IV. 334.[2]
— Der Tannenheher. 1883. IV. 464.[1]
— Die Verjüngung der Alpenwälder. 1893. IV. 140.
— Wald-Beschädigung durch Eichhörnchen. 1873. IV. 198.[1]
— Die Wirkungen der Fröste vom Winter 1879–80. 1880. III. 49.[1]—1881. III. 49.[2]
The **Wild** Black Cherry. 1885. III. 442.[2]
Wild with the wild flowers. See GOING, Maud. 1894. I. 96.
With the wild flowers. See FOLEY, F. A. 1850. I. 400.
Wild flowers of Dover. See FOLEY, F. A. 1850, I, 400.
Wild Rose, (pseud.). Budding. 1892. III. 164.[1]
— On some single Roses. 1889. III. 450.
Wild Roses. 1897. III. 451.[1]
Die **Wildbachverbauung** in Oesterreich. See L'endiguement des torrents. 1900. IV. 188.[1]
Die **Wildbachverbauung**. 1888. IV. 188.[1]
Die **Wildbachverbauung** in den Jahren 1883–1894. 1895. IV. 188.[1]
Die **Wildbachverbauung** in der Schweiz. See SALIS, Adolf von. 1890. IV. 187.[1]
Wilde, H. de. De Cupuliferen en de Mycorhiza. 1900. III. 167, IV. 74.[1]
— Les Cupulifères et le Mycorhiza. 1900. III. 167, IV. 74.[1]
— Le Gingko biloba. 1898. II. 8.[1]
Wilde, O. Die Pflanzen und Raupen Deutschlands. 1860. I. 384, III. 189, V. XIX.[2]
Wilde, R. de. Le Chêne d'Affligem. 1896. . II. 139,[1] IV. 516.[1]
Die **wilde** Dattelpalme. 1871. III. 328.[2]
De **wilde** zijde-soorten van Indië. 1882. III. 148.[2]
Wildeman, Émile de. See DE WILDEMAN, Émile.
Die **wilden** Rosen. 1899. III. 451.[1]
Wildenberg, C. Azalea mollis en Az. pontica. 1876. III. 655.
Wildenhayn. Abhandlung vom Pottaschsieden. 1771. IV. 395.
Wilder, Burt Green. Symmetry . . . in the leaves of Elms. 1868. II. 122,[2] 143.[1] ·
Wilder, Marshall Pinckney. Address on the semi-centennial anniversary. 1880. III. 32.[2]

Wilder, Marshall Pinckney (continued).
— Cultivation of the Azalea indica. 1875. III. 660.¹
— The horticulture of Boston and vicinity. 1881. III. 117.²
— Hybridization and production of new plants from seed. 1872. I. 247.
— The hybridization of the Camellia. 1847. III. 599.²
— Improvements in Japan Lilies. 1868. III. 671.²
— The most desirable varieties of fruit. 1886. III. 61.²
— The nomenclature of fruits. 1884. I. 518.²
— The production from seed of new varieties. 1855. III. 50.²
— The ripening and preservation of fruits. 1886. III. 173.²
— & others. Report on the causes of the injurious effects upon vegetation. 1873. III. 44.¹
Wildermet, von. See ФОНЪ ВИЛЬДЕРМЕТЪ.
Die Wildföhre. 1859. IV. 464.²
Wildhagen, Ferdinand. Waldbau und Wildzucht. 1875. IV. 136.²
Wildschaden im Kanton Aargau. 1858. IV. 196.²
Wildschälen. 1872. IV. 196.²
Wildsmith, W. Replanting large trees. 1881. III. 168.¹
— Upright Cypress. 1888. III. 303.¹
Wildvogel, Christian. De eo quod iustum est circa arbores. 1767. IV. 313.
— De jure florum. 1691. I. 288.
Wiley, Harvey Washington. Industrie sucrière aux États-Unis. 1893. IV. 527.²
— Maple sugar. 1885. IV. 527.¹
— The sugar industry of the United States. 1891. III. 220.²
— Sweet Cassawe. 1889. III. 521.¹
— See also EWEL & WILEY, H. W.
Wilhelm, (Professor). Viehvergiftung durch Eibenblätter. 1878. III. 288.²
Wilhelm, Gottlieb Tobias. Unterhaltungen aus der Naturgeschichte. 1810. I. 93.
Wilhelm, Gustav. Ein Keimversuch mit Zirbensamen. 1888. IV. 463.²
— Ungarisch-Altenburg und Hohenheim. 1868. IV. 32, 86.²
— Die Verwendung der Holzwolle als Streumaterial. 1888. IV. 429.
Wilhelm, Johann Georg. Dissertatio insuguralis, tradens Juniperum. 1718. III. 303.²
Wilhelm, Karl. Die Anatomie des Holzes der Douglastanne. 1886. IV. 484.¹
— Der Bau des Jahresringes. 1895. I. 525.¹
— Die Bedeutung unterirdischer Pilze. 1885. IV. 73.²
— Beiträge zur Kenntniss des Siebröhrenapparates. 1880. I. 133, II. 507.¹
— Die Beziehungen der Rindenspannung zur Bildung der Jahresringe. 1883. IV. 64.¹
— Ueber eine Eigenthümlichkeit der Spaltöffnungen bei Coniferen. 1883. II. 18.
— Der Fichtenblasenrost. 1883. IV. 456.
— Forstbotanische Streifzüge im Süden. 1895. IV. 87.¹
— Der " graue Riese." 1886· IV. 484.²
— Die Hängefichte. 1886. IV. 460.¹
— Die Hängefichte, Picea. 1887. II. 35.¹
— Das Harz der Nadelhölzer. 1894. IV. 62.²
— Eine immergrüne " Schwarzeiche." 1886. IV. 503.²
— Zur Kenntniss einiger beachtenswerther nordamerikanischer Holzarten. 1883. IV. 127.²
— Ein neuer Parasit der Weisstanne. 1884. IV. 445.
— Die Omorikafichte. 1892. IV. 460.²
— The sieve tubes of dicotyledonous plants. 1880. II. 507.¹
— Ueber Stellung und Bau der Nadeln der Tanne. 1889. IV. 447.¹
— Die Verdoppelung des Jahresringes. 1883. IV. 62.²
— Die Verdoppelung des Jahresringes (Vorläufige Mittheilung). 1883. I. 128.¹
— Über Wachsthum und Form der Bäume. 1897. I. 107.¹
— Waldpflanzungen an der norwegischen Küste. 1890. IV. 156.¹
— Zapfensucht bei Schwarzkiefer. 1886. IV. 466.²
— Zwei Parasiten der Birke. 1884· IV. 490.²
— See also HEMPEL, Gustav & WILHELM, Karl.
Wilhelmi, Carl. Eine Excursion in die Grampians. 1872. I. 502.
— Über eine Excursion . . . nach dem Murray. 1874. I. 502.
— Ueber nutzbare australische Bäume. 1872. IV. 401.²
— Die Pflanzen des australischen Continentes. 1874. III. 94.¹

Wilhem, Hieronymus de. De manna, χεχρυμμενφ, 1744. III. 221.¹
Wilhjelm, G. Om Udhugning i Egeskov. 1899. IV. 509.
Wilke, Christian Heinrich. Abhandlung über die fürstl. Jablonowskische Preisaufgabe. 1770. V. xxxi;¹ see also AUER, Andreas. 1767. IV. 263.
Wilke, Karl Adolph Oskar. Ueber die anatomischen Beziehungen des Gerbstoffs. 1883. I. 135, 183.
Wilken, G. A. De betrekking tusschen menschen, dieren en plantenleven. 1884. I. 518.
Wilken, N. P. Iets over den landbouw in de Minahassa. 1870. III. 128.
Wilkes, Benjamin. One hundred and twenty copper-plates of English moths. 1773. I. 395.
Wilkeson, Samuel. Wilkeson's notes on Puget Sound. 187.? IV. 397.
Wilkie, Thomas. On the advantages of forming belts of plantations. 1890. III. 215.²
— On the best method of seasoning timber. 1878. IV. 416.¹
— On the cause of ringshake in trees. 1879. IV. 414.¹
— On the comparative value of exotic Coniferae. 1890. III. 291.
— A gigantic Silver Fir. 1878. II. 24.¹
— On the management of plantations. 1878. IV. 120.
— Old . . . trees on the estate of Ardkinglas. 1881. I. 297.¹
— On the rearing . . . of hardwood plantations. 1881. IV. 137.²
— Replanting . . . in Scotland. 1889. IV. 359.¹
— Report upon the rearing of underwood. 1890. III. 215.¹
— On the system of Oak coppice management. 1881. IV. 507.
— On two new modes of fencing. 1878. III. 213.
— The varieties of trees . . . for planting as shelter. 1889. III. 215.²
Wilkins, A. J. Quelques explications au sujet . . . la généalogie présumée des variétés des Pêches du Ferghana. 1885. II. 276.¹
Wilkinson, Lady C. C. Weeds and wild flowers. 1858. I. 511.
Wilkinson, George. Experiments . . . on the cortex Salicis latifoliae. 1803. III. 351.²
Wilkinson, W. Percy. Preliminary survey of Eucalyptus-oils of Victoria. 1894. IV. 532.¹
Wilkinson, William. Memorials of the Minnesota forest fires. 1895. IV. 182.¹
Will, Alfred. Beiträge zur Kenntniss von Kern- und Wundholz. 1899. IV. 66.¹
Will, Hans. Untersuchungen über das Verhältniss von Trockensubstanz und Mineralstoffgehalt im Baumkörper. 1882. I. 155, II. 48.¹
Will, Heinrich. Einiges über Störung des Zuwachses . . . durch Insekten. 1865. IV. 207.
— See also RAMANN, Emil & WILL, Heinrich.
— & Fresenius, C. R. Untersuchungen über die unorganischen Bestandtheile der Vegetabilien. 1844. I. 152.²
Will, Hermann. See GORUP-BESANEZ, E. F. C. Freiherr von & WILL, Hermann.
Will, W. Sur la naringine. 1886. II. 403.¹
Will it pay to plant timber in America? 1885. IV. 260.¹
Willard, E. M. Forest products. 1896. IV. 398.¹
Willard, S. D. The future outlook for the fruit grower. 1900. III. 134.¹
— & Bailey, L. H. Notes upon Plums for western New York. 1897. III. 433.¹
Willard, W. O. Pruning the Grape vine. 1890. III. 549.¹
— Street or roadside trees. 1900. III. 208.²
Willbrand, W. Eine Lücke in der Ausbildung unserer Forstleute. 1893. IV. 137.¹
Willcocks, William Richard. Rosa devoniensis. 1859. III. 455.¹·
Willdenow. Verzeichnis der auf den Friedländischen Gütern kultivierten Gewächse. 1815. III. 27.²
Willdenow, Karl Ludwig. Anleitung zum Selbststudium der Botanik. 1804. I. 255.
— Ueber die Arten der Gattung Calyptranthes. 1796. II. 622.¹
— Berlinische Baumzucht. 1796. I. 293, III. 63.¹
— Beschreibung der Gattung Tamarix. 1816. II. 562,² 873.²
— Beyträge zur geographischen Geschichte des Pflanzenreichs. 1797. I. 298.
— Détermination de quelques nouvelles espèces de Figuier. 1801. II. 148.²
— Dialium guineense. 1796. II. 354.²
— Drei neue Pflanzen-Gattungen. 1801. I. 333.

— Duae plantae africanae descriptae. 1793. II. 514,²
'23.¹
— Einige neue Feigenarten. 1801. II. 148.³
— Einige seltene Gewächse beschrieben. 1801. I. 265.
— Enumeratio plantarum Horti regii botanici berolinensis.
1809. I. 45.
— Florae berolinensis prodromus. 1787. I. 374.
— Ueber die Gattung Fuchsia. 1792. II. 643.¹
— Ueber die Gattungen Brunia und Staavia. 1809. II. 251.¹
— Geraniologia in amicorum usum seorsim impressa. 1800.
II. 389.²
— Grundriss der Kräuterkunde. 1792. I. 83.
— Handleiding tot de kennis der planten. 1792. I. 84.
— Hortus berolinensis. 1816. I. 45.
— Ueber das Keimen der Pflanzen. 1796. I. 202.²
— Mémoire sur l'écorce d'Angustura. 1804. III. 503.²
— Nähere Bestimmung eines brasilianischen Gewächses,
Pilophora. 1815. II. 71.¹
— Eine neue Pflanzengattung Usteria. 1792. II. 720.²
— Observationes botanicae. 1788. I. 263.
— Observations on the genus Ficus. 1801. II. 148.²
— Phytographia. 1794. I. 264.
— The principles of botany. 1792. I. 84.
— De quelques nouveaux Palmiers de l'Amérique. 1801.
II. 61.¹
— Schradera et Rottlera. 1798. II. 439,² 452.¹
— Sur trois espèces . . . du genre Aristolochia. 1809. II.
181.¹
— Udkast till en Laerebog. 1792. I. 84.¹
— See also GUIMPEL, Friedrich, WILLDENOW, C. L. & HAYNE,
F. G.
— & Homeyer, A. H. Gekrönte Preisschriften über die . . .
pomologischen Preisfragen. 1801. III. 136.
Wi , Alwin. Zur Diagnostik des Coniferenholzes. 1887.
IIId7.¹
Wille, John Nordal Fischer. Kan og bör der gjöres noget ad
lovgivningens vei for at hindre skadeplanters udbredning i
vort land? 1892. III. 200.²
— Kritische Studien über die Anpassungen der Pflanzen an
Regen. 1887. I. 232.²
— Om podningsbastarder. 1896. I. 246.³
— Om Stammens . . . Bygning hos Avicennia. 1882. II. 753.²
— Sur la structure de la tige . . . de l'Avicennia. 1882. II.
'53.²
— Yderligere om regnopfangende planter. 1890. I. 232.²
— Om ympningsbastarder. 1896. I. 246.²
Willem, (pseud.). Behandeling . . . van den Koffieboom.
1900. III. 728.¹
Willemet, Hubert Felix SOYER-. See SOYER-WILLEMET, H. F.
Willemet, Pierre Remi, (sr.). Catalogus plantarum Horti bo-
tanici nanceynensis. 1802. I. 57.
— Nouveaux genres de plantes . . . dans les iles de France.
1805. I. 482.
— Observations sur les plantes dans les îles de France
1811. I. 482.
— Phytographie économique de la Lorraine. 1780. III.
85.
— Phytographie encyclopédique. 1805. I. 406.
— See also COSTE, J. F. & WILLEMET, Remi.
Willemet, Pierre Remi François de Paule. Herbarium
mauritianum. 1796. I. 481.²
— An virea plantarum ex characteribus botanicis sunt info-
rendae? 1782. III. 259.¹
Willer, A. K. See THORPE, T. E., ROBINSON, H. & WILLER,
A. K.
Willer, T. J. Het eiland Boeroe, zijne exploitatie. 1858.
I. 465.
— Overzigt van land en volk in Mandheling. 1846. III.
275.¹
Willermoz, C. F. Choix de plantes sarmenteuses. 1860. III.
204.²
— Observations sur le genre Poirier. 1849. III. 444.¹
— Observations sur les maladies des végétaux. 1854. III.
559.²
— Projet d'une classification de fruits. 1850. III. 84.²
Willett, R. S. Hedge culture in central Iowa. III. 111.
213.
William, Wilson P. Dwarf trees. 1891. III. 176.¹
William the Conqueror's Oak. 1876. II. 138.²
Williams, A. G. Forestry. 1890. IV. 112.
Williams, Benjamin Samuel. Areca purpurea. 1879. III.
320.¹
— Choice stove and greenhouse flowering plants. 1869. III.
82.

— Choice stove and greenhouse ornamental-leaved plants.
1870. III. 82.
— Einige neue in den Handel gegebene Pflanzen. 1879.
III. 83.¹
Williams, Charles. The vegetable world. 1833. I. 94.
Williams, D. Account of a three years' bearing Mango tree.
1845. III. 524.²
Williams, E. Pruning shrubs. 1880. III. 172.
Williams, H. C. Native Grapes of Arkansas or Texas. 1860.
III. 546.
— Native grapes of Texas. 1861. III. 546.
— Nut-trees in Virginia. 1857. III. 133.
Williams, J. The botanist's vade mecum. 1855. I. 35.¹
— Dissertatio . . . de succi circuitu. 1825. I. 163.
Williams, J. GREVILLE-. See GREVILLE-WILLIAMS, J. & MÜL-
LER, Hugo.
Williams, J. Lloyd. The sieve-tubes of Calycanthus. 1894.
II. 214.³
Williams, J. O. Mammoth trees of California. 1871. V.
XXV.²
Williams, John. Faunula Grustensis. 1830. I. 533.
Williams, L. O. Value of Currants and Gooseberries. 1897.
III. 414.¹
Williams, Newlin. Minor forest products. Maple sap. 1897.
IV. 527.²
Williams, R. Catalogue of the . . . plants of La Salle county.
1877. I. 314.
— The uses of the Bamboo. 1863. III. 315.¹
— Notices of Chinese agriculture. 1861. III. 273.¹
Williams, Samuel Wells. Chinese fruits, etc. 1851. III.
116.²
Williams, Stephen West. Report on the indigenous medical
botany of Massachusetts. 1849. III. 62.
Williams, Theodore. Japanese Plums. 1897. III. 443.²
Williams, Thomas. The Elder tree. 1873. III. 751.²
— Honeysuckles as bushes and pillar plants. 1872. III.
749.²
Williams, Thomas Albert. The Diamond Willow in S. Da-
kota. 1895. II. 106.²
— Native trees and shrubs of South Dakota. 1895. I. 320,
IV. 78.¹
Williams, W. S. Lemon growing and curing. 1897. III.
502.¹
Williamson, A. T. The commercial aspect of bark peeling.
1890. IV. 434.
— On the creation of leasehold timber farms. 1890. IV.
274.²
— The effect of the railway and canal traffic act. 1890. IV.
274.²
— The manufacture of home-grown timber. 1893. IV.
398.²
— Our timber supplies from abroad. 1893. IV. 398.²
— The utilisation of small-wood for turnery. 1893. IV.
428.¹
Willich, Christian Ludwig. Illustrationes quaedam botani-
cae. 1766. I. 262.
— Circa plantas quasdam singularia aliqua notata. 1770.
I. 262.
— De plantis quibusdam observationes. 1762. I. 261.
Willich, J. E. Bemerkungen . . . zur Verbesserung der Forst-
wirthschaft. 1793. IV. 123.²
Willich, Moritz Ulrich. Observationes botanicae. See WEIGEL,
C. E. 1772. II. 840.¹
Willig. Ueber Buchen-Starkholz. 1860. IV. 494.
Willigk, Erwin. Untersuchungen der Blätter von Ledum.
1852. III. 653.¹
Willis, Bailey. The Mount Rainier national park. 1899.
I. 327.
Willis, (Mrs.) Elizabeth L. H. The Palmetto and its uses.
1884. III. 331.¹
Willis, J. J. On the falling leaves. 1884. I. 155.
— On the growth . . . of Azalea indica. 1893. III. 660.¹
— Importance of phosphoric acid in soils. 1897. III. 41.²
— A naturalist's calendar. 1894. I. 226.¹
— Rearing of Citrus . . . from seed. 1893. III. 156.²
— Walnuts, Chestnuts and Almonds. 1897. I. 156.¹
— Wood-ashes. 1898. I. 156.¹
Willis, J. T. Citrus fruits. 1888. III. 497.²
Willis, John-Charles. Caoutchouc or indiarubber. 1899. III.
230.
— On gynodioecism. 1894. I. 239.¹
— A manual and dictionary of the flowering plants and ferns.
1897. I. 92.
— Panama rubber, Castilloa. 1899. III. 368.²

Willis, John Charles (*continued*).
— Rubber cultivation in Ceylon. 1898. III. 518.[2]
— Tea blights. 1899. III. 604.[2]
—& Burkill, I. H. Flowers and insects in Great Britain. 1895. I. 240.[1]
— — Observations on the flora of the Pollard Willows. 1894. I. 234.[2]
—& Green, E. E. The Cacao canker. 1897. III. 593.[2]
Willis, Joseph. Remarks on various specimens of fibre. 1857. III. 234.
Willis, Oliver R. Catalogue of plants … of New Jersey. 1874. I. 314.
— Erica and Calluna on Nantucket. 1886. II. 658.[1]
— A practical flora for schools and colleges. 1894. I. 256.
— Report of the flora of Westchester county. 1881. I. 315.
Willits, Edwin. Spraying fruits for insect pests. 1892. III. 198.[1]
Willkomm, Heinrich Moritz. Anleitung zum Studium der wissenschaftlichen Botanik. 1854. I. 89.
— Die Arten der Section Eusideritis. 1859. II. 766.[2]
— Ueber die atlantische Flora. 1884. I. 452.
— Bemerkungen über kritische Pflanzen der Mediterranflora. 1859. II. 766.[2]
— Bemerkungen über … Pflanzen des pyrenäischen Halbinsel. 1879. I. 422.
— Bemerkungen zu Pinus obliqua. 1886. II. 43.[1]
— Beobachtungen über die Bewegung der Vegetation. 1879. I. 224.[1]
— Die Bewegung des Safts im Pflanzenkörper. 1870. I. 164.
— Über die Bildungsweise der samentragenden Schuppe … der Abietineen. 1880. II. 19.
— Botanical notices from Spain. 1844. I. 420.
— Botanische Berichte aus Spanien. 1844. I. 420.
— Der botanische Garten der kaiserl. Universität Dorpat. 1873. I. 42.
— Die botanischen Gärten von Madrid. 1851. I. 522.[1]
— Der Buchenkrebs. 1867. IV. 496.
— Die "Ceder von Goa." 1890. II. 29.[2]
— Ueber Charakterpflanzen der Mittelmeerländer. 1895. I. 452.
— Sur le Chêne-liège de l'occident. 1866. II. 135.[2]
— Deutschlands Laubhölzer im Winter. 1859. I. 294,[2] *IV.* 83.
— Diagnoses plantarum … in insulis Balearicis. 1875. II. 86,[2] 497.[2]
— Die Dünen an den … preussischen Küsten. 1865. IV. 145.
— Entomologische Notizen. — Insectensachen, III. 1857. IV. 206.
— Enumeratio plantarum … in Hispania. 1852. I. 421.
— Especies nuevas ó críticas de la flora española. 1890. I. 422.
— Estatística da vegetação das steppes e da beiramar na península ibérica. 1895. I. 422.
— Forstliche Flora von Deutschland. 1875. I. 371, *IV.* 83.
— Führer in das Reich der Pflanzen Deutschlands. 1863. I. 385.
— Führer ins Reich der deutschen Pflanzen. 1863. I. 385.
— Ueber den gegenwärtigen Stand und Umfang der botanischen Wissenschaft. 1868. I. 79.[2]
— Grundzüge der Pflanzenverbreitung auf der iberischen Halbinsel. 1896. I. 423.
— Das Herbar. 1892. I. 36.[1]
— Ueber die Herkunft der "Ceder von Goa." 1890. II. 29.[2]
— Aus den Hochgebirgen von Granada. 1882. I. 422.
— Icones et descriptiones plantarum novarum … Europae austro-occidentalis. 1852. I. 421.
— Illustrationes florae Hispanicae. 1881. I. 422.
— Index plantarum … in insulis Balearibus. 1876. I. 423.
— Ueber Insectenschäden. 1874. IV. 205.[2]
— Die Insectenverheerungen in Ostpreussen. 1864. IV. 207.
— Zur Kenntniss der Pirus prunifolia. 1882. II. 266.[1]
— Die Korkeiche in Spanien. 1856. II. 140.[1]
— Die Lärchenkrankheit. 1867. IV. 450.
— Luontaisjärjestöllinen kasvikunnan kuvasto. 1893. I. 271.[1]
— Die mikroskopischen Feinde des Waldes. 1866. IV. 195.[2]

— Zur Morphologie der samentragenden Schuppe des Abietineenzapfens. 1880. II. 19.
— Ueber die Nadelhölzer. 1890. II. 13.[2]
— Zur Naturgeschichte der Zirbelkiefer. 1861. II. 41.[1]
— Ueber neue und kritische Pflanzen der spanisch-portugiesischen und balearischen Flora. 1890. I. 422.
— Ein neuer Nadelholzbaum Europa's. 1877. IV. 460.[2]
— Ein neuer Rostpilz der Fichte. 1870. IV. 455.
— Die Nonne, der Kiefernspinner. 1858. IV. 207.
— Observations sur quelques plantes … de la flore d'Espagne. 1880. II. 431.[2]
— Die Onorikasichte und verwandte Arten. 1885. II. 38.[1]
— Die Orangengewächse. 1877. III. 497.[1]
— Orangetraernes Historie. 1877. III. 497.[1]
— Ueber eine durch parasitische Pilze verursachte Krankheit der Kiefer. 1857. IV. 475.
— Der Park und die Baumschulen von Segrez. 1878. I. 59.
— Die Pflanzenwelt und die Gärten Portugals. 1884. III. 26.[1]
— Pugillus plantarum novarum peninsulae pyrenaicae. 1860. I. 421.
— Reiseerinnerungen aus Frankreich. 1878. I. 59. — 1879. I. 416.
— Die Riga'schen Stadtforsten. 1872. IV. 347.
— Saftbewegelsen hos Planterne. 1870. I. 164.
— Der Schlosspark zu Klösterle. 1890. I. 66.[1]
— Sertum florae hispanicae. 1851. I. 421.
— Spicilegium florae hispanicae. 1847. I. 420.
— Statistik der Strand- und Steppenvegetation der iberischen Halbinsel. 1895. I. 423.
— Die Strand- und Steppengebiete der iberischen Halbinsel. 1852. I. 420.
— Streifzüge durch die baltischen Provinzen. 1872. IV. 347.
— Ueber Südfrüchte. 1877. III. 119,[1] 220.[1]
— Tortrix ferrugana. Der rostgelbe Eichenwickler. 1863. IV. 509.
— Vegetations-Charakter der Normandie. 1879. I. 416.
— Vegetationsskizzen aus Spanien und Portugal. 1850. I. 421.
— Vegetationsverhältnisse der Umgegend von Tharand. 1866. I. 521.[2]
— Vegetationsverhältnisse von Traz os Montes. 1890. I. 422.
— Ueber die Veränderungen, welche die … Vegetation der iberischen Halbinsel … erlitten hat. 1853. I. 421.
— Verbreitung und Anbau der Dattelpalme. 1876. III. 328.[2]
— Verdient der Blaugummibaum als Forstculturgewächs in Europa angebaut zu werden? 1883. IV. 530.
— Versuch einer Monographie der europäischen Krummholzkiefern. 1861. II. 39,[2] 43.[1]
— Verwendung des Espenholzes in Livland. 1874. IV. 486.[2]
— Vorläufige Mittheilung über die Rothfäule der Fichte. 1865. IV. 455.
— Vorläufige Mittheilung über einen neuen Feind der Rothbuche. 1876. IV. 497.
— Waldbüchlein. 1889. I. 371.
— Wanderungen durch die nordöstlichen und centralen Provinzen Spaniens. 1852. I. 421.
— Wilde und verwilderte Obstgehölze. 1877. I. 242.[1]
—& Lange, Johan. Prodromus florae hispanicae. 1870. I. 421.
— — Supplementum; sive, Enumeratio et descriptio omnium plantarum … usque ad annum 1893 detectarum. 1870. I. 421.
Willmott, John, (*jr.*). An alphabetical enumeration of the plants contained in the Hortus kewensis. 1798. I. 522.[1]
Willoughby, Francis. An extract of a letter … containing some observations … made on some Sycamore-trees. 1670. I. 168.
— Extract of a letter … relating to some particulars … in M. Lyster's communications. 1671. I. 162.
— *See also* Tonge, Ezerel & Willoughby, Francis.
—& Wray. Experiments concerning the motion of the sap. 1669. I. 162.
The Willow. 1842. III. 350.[3]
Willow-farming. 1894. III. 349.
Wills, A. Wanderings. 1856. I. 435.
Wills, G. S. V. Dictionary of botanical terms. 1880. I. 71.
Wilshire, William Hughes. Contributions to structural botany. 1842. I. 98.
— The principles of botany. 1839. I. 88.
— Remarks on some points of vegetable structure. 1842. I. 133.

Willversch, Joseph. De praestante, sed cauto camphorae usu. 1789. III. 404.[2]

Wilmanns, C. A. Commentatio de anthelminthicis. 1826. III. 244.

Wilmer, Bradford. Observations on the poisonous vegetables. 1781. III. 80.

Wilmot, A. The book of South African industries. 1892. III. 281.[2]

Wilmot, John. Remarks on the present mode of budding. 1812. III. 159.[2]

Wilmot, Sainthill EARDLEY-. Growth of Sâl. 1885. IV. 529.[1]

— Notes on improvement fellings in Sâl forests. 1900. IV. 528.[2]

— Notes on Sâl forests. 1898. IV. 528.[2]

— Notes on the regeneration of Sâl. 1900. IV. 528.[2]

— Notes on the Sâl coppice forests of Oudh. 1900. IV. 528.[2]

— Notes on the Shisham and Khair. 1898. IV. 521.[1]

— On the treatment of Bamboo forests. 1890. IV. 485.[1]

Wilms, Theodor. Missbildung von Salix alba. 1877. II. 104.[2]

Wilsdorf, E. Procédés pour extraire les substances utiles ... de Kola. 1893. III. 590.[2]

Wilski, (*Forstmeister zu Görlitz*). Ein Beitrag zur Geschichte der Waldcalamitäten. 1874. IV. 195.[2]

Wilski, (*Oberförster*). See ROSCH, (*Oberförster*) & WILSKI, (*Oberförster*).

Wilson, Ernest Henry. Conifers. 1899. III. 293.

Wilson, Frances. Notes on Carya tomentosa. 1893. II. 112.[1]

Wilson, George. On the fruits of the Cucurbitaceae. 1859. III. 704.[2]

Wilson, George F. Andromeda japonica. 1900. III. 654.[1]

— Japanese Rose hedge. 1885. III. 456.[2]

Wilson, Henry W. Some considerations regarding ... mulching. 1885. III. 151.

— A winter visit to the Bahama Islands. 1891. III. 118.[2]

— A winter visit to the Bahamas. 1893. I. 337.

Wilson, Herbert M. Relation of forestation to water-supply. 1898. IV. 52.

Wilson, J. Aperçu statistique de l'agriculture, de la sylviculture et des pêcheries en Russie. 1876. IV. 345.

Wilson, James. A missionary voyage to the southern Pacific Ocean. 1799. III. 283.[2]

Wilson, James G. A twin-fruit of the Cocoa-nut. 1862. II. 67.[2]

Wilson, Jeremiah. Maple Sugar. 1845. III. 536.[1]

Wilson, John, (—1751). Synopsis of British plants. 1744. I. 394, V. xx.[2]

Wilson, John. Account of a visit to the falls on the Shiráwati River. 1838. II. 59.[2]

Wilson, John, (*Park keeper, Newcastle-upon-Tyne*). The influence of situation and soil on the growth. 1895. IV. 70.

— Suitable trees for various soils. 1884. III. 41.[1]

— Town and suburban planting. 1895. III. 42.[2]

— The uses and beauties of trees. 1889. I. 394.

Wilson, John H. The leaves and stipules of Larrea mexicana. 1893. II. 395.[2]

— The mucilage- and other glands of the Plumbagineae. 1889. II. 696.[2]

— Passiflora Margaret-Wilson. 1899. III. 615.[2]

— The structure of certain new hybrids. 1900. II. 244,[2] 577.[1]

Wilson, Kate Eastman. Double flowers of the Epigaea repens. 1890. II. 663.[2]

Wilson, Nathaniel. On the antidote Cacoon. 1863. III. 753.[2]

— Cinchona culture ... in Jamaica. 1864. III. 712.[2]

— On the Cinchona plantations ... at Bath, Jamaica. 1864. III. 713.[1]

— Die zu Geweben ec. verwendbaren Pflanzen Jamaica's. 1855. III. 267.[1]

— On the useful vegetable products ... of Jamaica. 1855. III. 267.[1]

— & Thwaites, C. H. K. Introduction of the Cinchona tree. 1862. III. 713.[2]

Wilson, Silas. Domestica Plums. 1899. III. 433.[1]

— New Iowa Plum culture. 1896. III. 433.[1]

— Propagating Cherry and Plum. 1900. III. 431.[1]

— Winter protection. 1889. III. 183.[2]

Wilson, Thomas. Enemies to the Tea plant. 1880. III. 604.[2]

Wilson, W. G. St. Helena. 1888. III. 282.[1]

Wilson, W. T. Forest vegetation and the air. 1890. IV. 54.

Wilson, William. Economy of the kitchen-garden. 1828. III. 133.

Wilson, William (of Warrington; 1799–1871). On the buds of Robinia Pseudacacia. 1843. II. 382.[2]

— On the glandular woody tissue of Coniferae. 1843. II. 16.[2]

— Myrica Gale with androgynous flowers. 1842. II. 111.[1]

— Observations on some British plants. 1834. I. 398.

— Researches in embryogeny. 1844. I. 121.

— On the structure ... of the pollen granules. 1843. I. 117.[1]

Wilson, William Powell. The Bald Cypress. 1889. II. 51.[2]

— On the cause of the excretion of water on the surface of nectaries. 1881. I. 118,[2] 169.[1]

— The development ... of the so-called Cypress- "knees." 1891. II. 52.[1]

— Note on Epigaea repens. 1877. II. 663.[2]

— Observations on Epigaea repens. 1892. II. 663.[2]

— The Palmetto of the southern states. 1890. II. 74.[2]

— The production of aerating organs on the roots. 1889. I. 171.

— Some observations on Epigaea repens. 1892. II. 663.[2]

— Tree-forms as determined by water supply. 1893. II. 52.[1]

— On the use of the Bambusa stem. 1890. III. 315.[1]

Wilsone, Charles. Destruction des Arbres de gutta percha. 1857. III. 668.[2]

— Destruction of the Gutta percha trees. 1857. III. 668.[2]

Wilts, (*pseud.*). The best firewood. 1886. IV. 431.[2]

Wiltshire archaeological and natural history magazine. I. 20.

Wimmenauer, Karl. Ueber altrömische Forstwirtschaft. 1895. IV. 28.[1]

— Die Bestandsformzahlen der Rothbuche. 1893. IV. 498.

— Ertragstafeln für Buchenhochwald. 1893. IV. 498.

— Ertrags-Untersuchungen im Buchenhochwald. 1880. IV. 498. — 1885. IV. 498. — 1889. IV. 498.

— Die finanzielle Seite der Kiefernwirthschaft. 1891. IV. 481.

— Die Formzahlen der Kiefer. 1889. IV. 481.

— Grundriss der Waldwegbaulehre. 1896. IV. 267.

— Grundriss der Waldwertrechnung. 1891. IV. 253.

— Die Hauptergebnisse zehnjähriger forstlich-phänologischer Beobachtungen. 1897. I. 225,[1] IV. 73.[1]

— Der jährliche Hiebsatz während der Verjüngungsdauer. 1893. IV. 252.

— Mittelstamm, Baum- und Bestands-Formzahl. 1890. IV. 218.

— Das mittlere Bestandsalter. 1890. IV. 218.

— Die Schaftmassen-Ermittelung. 1890. IV. 218.

— Wachsthum und Ertrag der Rothbuche. 1893. IV. 498.

— Wald- und Boden-Reinertrag. 1890. IV. 258.

— Weiserprozent und Bodenerwartungswert. 1890. IV. 258.

Wimmer, Christian Friedrich Heinrich. Einige Formen von Salix. 1850. II. 101.[2]

— Einige interessante Weiden-Formen. 1867. II. 101.[2]

— Über einige wichtige biologische ... Verhältnisse der Weiden. 1848. II. 103.[1]

— Flora von Schlesien. 1832. I. 378.

— Zur Flora von Schlesien. Bastardbildungen. 1848. II. 101.[2]

— Flora von Schlesien preussischen und österreichischen Antheils. 1841. I. 380.

— Über die Hybridität der Weiden. 1848. II. 100.[1]

— Zur Kenntniss der Salix-Arten. 1845. II. 101.[1]

— Zur Kenntniss der Salix-Arten. Anmerkung zu Fries's Monographie. 1846. II. 100.[2]

— List of the Silesian indigenous Willows. 1849. II. 101.[2]

— Neue Formen von Salix. 1851. II. 101.[2]

— Das Pflanzenreich. 1853. I. 256.

— Salices Europaeae. 1866. II. 100.[1]

— Ueber Salix silesiaca. 1857. II. 110.[1]

— Ueber die schlesischen Arten der Sippe Rubus. 1855. II. 301.[1]

— Seltnere und neuere Formen von Salix. 1852. II. 101.[2]

— Ein Ueberblick über die Geschichte der Kenntniss der Weiden. 1861. II. 99.[1]

— Uebersicht der ... Bastarde von Salix. 1850. II. 100.[1]

— Uebersicht der in Schlesien wildwachsenden Weiden-Arten. 1861. IV. 488.[1]

— Verzeichniss der in Schlesien wildwachsenden Weiden. 1849. II. 101.[1]

— Wildwachsende Bastardpflanzen. 1853. I. 271.[2]

— Zwei neue Arten aus der Flora der Schweiz. 1854. II. 107.[2]

Wimmer, Christian Friedrich Heinrich (*continued*).
— *See also* GÜNTHER, C. C., GRABOWSKI, Heinrich & WIMMER, Friedrich; BИММЕРЪ, Ф.
— & Grabowski, Heinrich. Flora Silesiae. 1827. I. 377.'
Wimmer, F. *See* BИММЕРЪ, Ф.
Wimmer, Martin. De calcisae radice. 1832. III. 744.'
Wimpfen, F. von. Oversigt over Penge-Udbyttet af Stats-skovene i Kongeriget Danmark. 1860. IV. 260.'
— Skov-Taxationen. 1836. IV. 253.
Winberg, Leopold. Florula javanica. *See* THUNBERG, C. P. 1825. I. 468.
Winch, Nathanael John. The botanist's guide through ... Northumberland. 1805. I. 396.
— Contributions to the flora of Cumberland. 1833. I. 398.
— An essay on the geographical distribution of plants through the counties of Northumberland. 1819. I. 397.
— Flora of Northumberland and Durham. 1831. I. 398, V. xx.³
— Remarks on the distribution of the indigenous plants of Northumberland and Durham. 1831. I. 398.
— Remarks on the flora of Cumberland. 1825. I. 397.
— Versuch über die geographische Verbreitung der Pflanzen in den englischen Grafschaften Northumberland. 1819. I. 397.
Winchell, Alexander. The fruit-bearing belt of Michigan. 1867. III. 133.
Winchell, N. H. List of trees and shrubs [of the Black Hills]. 1875. I. 320, IV. 77.³
Winckler, E. L. W. Blüthenkalender der deutschen und schweizer Flora. 1848. I. 224.³
Winckler, Emil. Geschichte der Botanik. 1854. I. 79.³
Winckler, Friedrich Ludwig. Chinova bitter. 1843. III. 725.'
— Sur la constitution chimique ... du Laurier-cerise. 1839. III. 438.'
— Die echten Chinarinden. 1834. III. 721.
— On Maracaibo bark. 1851. III. 722.
— Sur une nouvelle sorte de Kinkina. 1846. III. 725.²
Winckler, Hugo. Die Maydanpeker Waldungen. 1858. IV. 375.'
Winckler, Nicolaus. Chronica herbarum, florum, seminum. 1571. I. 281.
Windblad, Jacob Emil. Afhandling om de wäxter som i Bibelen omtalas. *See* THUNBERG, C. P. 1828. I. 513.
Winding, M. C. Stirpes agri femsionensis. *See* FRIES, E. M. 1825. I. 353.
Windmüller, Louis. A plea for trees and parks in cities. 1900. III. 202.'
Windsor, John. Flora cravoniensis. 1873. I. 402, 534.'
Windsor forest and great park. 1881. IV. 358.'
Windt, L. G. Der Berberitzenstrauch. 1806. III. 394.'
The wine crop of New South Wales. 1867. III. 559.²
Winfree, Philip. Culture of Indigo. 1846. III. 479.'
Wing, Rumsey, & others. El cundurango. 1872. III. 693.²
Wingate, D. Orange culture in South California. 1900. III. 500.²
Winge, P. Om Auktions- og Underhaandssalg af Skovpro-dukter. 1894. IV. 404.'
— Indført eller dansk Naaletræ. 1897. IV. 404.'
— Privatskovbrugets Forretningsorden. 1895. IV. 308.'
— Om Skovreguleringens rare Skat. 1889. IV. 245.
— Om Tilvirkning af Tagspaan og den petriske Imprægnering. 1872. IV. 428.²
Wingelmüller, Karl. Ein lästiger Bewohner unserer Nutz-bäume. 1890. III. 191, IV. 208.'
— Retinia resinella L. 1896. IV. 479.
— Der Rothschwanz. 1897. IV. 210.'
— Sphinx pinastri L., Kiefernschwärmer. 1896. IV. 479.
Wingfield, Charles & others. Report on various specimens of fibres from Bijnore. 1857. III. 234.
Winkel-Horn, F. Tabeller for Beregninger af Blokke. 1823. IV. 222.
Winkelbauer, Alois. Ueber das Aussasten der Waldbäume. 1887. IV. 172.'
Winkelblech, Karl. Bemerkungen zu Schleiden's offenem Sendschreiben. 1842. I. 157.
— Ueber Liebig's Theorie der Pflanzenernährung. 1842. I. 157.
Winkelmann, J. Kautschuk und Gutta-Percha. 1875. III. 231.
— Die Terpenthin- und Fichtenharz-Industrie. 1880. IV. 436.²
Winkler, Constantin. Zur Anatomie von Araucaria brasili-ensis. 1872. I. 139, II. 26.'

— Decas Compositarum novarum Turkestaniae. 1886. II. 54.'
— Literatur und Pflanzenverzeichniss der Flora baltica. 1877. I. 363.
Winkler, Eduard. Abbildungen der Arzneigewächse. 1834. III. 57.
— Abbildungen sämmtlicher Arzneigewächse Deutschlands. 1832. III. 73.
— Anfangsgründe der Botanik. 1836. I. 87.
— Ausführliche Beschreibung sämmtlicher Arzneigewächse. 1836. III. 57.
— Charactere der Gattungen und Arten sämmtlicher offici-nellen Pflanzen. 1846. III. 58.
— Getreue Abbildung aller in den Pharmacopöen Deutsch-lands aufgenommenen officinellen Gewächse. 1846. III. 58.
— Handbuch der Gewächskunde. 1834. III. 57.
— Handbuch der medicinisch-pharmaceutischen Botanik. 1846. III. 58.
— Pharmaceutische Waarenkunde. 1844. III. 258.
— Sämmtliche Giftgewächse Deutschlands. 1831. III. 73.
— Vollständiges Real-Lexicon der medizinisch-pharmaceu-tischen Naturgeschichte. 1840. III. 258.
Winkler, Fr. Ueber das Pflanzen grosser Bäume. 1888. III. 168.'
Winkler, Georg Johann, *Edler von Brückenbrand*, Anleitung zur Construction ... eines einfachen Taschen-Dendrometers. 1834. IV. 231.'
— Lehrbuch der angewandten Mathematik. 1821. IV. 58, 59.'
— Lehrbuch der Arithmetik und Algebra. 1813. IV. 57.
— Lehrbuch der Geometrie. 1814. IV. 58.
— Lehrbuch der Mechanik, Hydrostatik und Hydraulik. 1821. IV. 59.'
— Lehrbuch der Rechenkunst und Algebra. 1813. IV. 57.
— Logarithmische und logarith-trigonometrische Tafeln. 1834. IV. 58.
— Die praktische Geometrie. 1858. IV. 264.
— Waldwerth-Schätzung. 1835. IV. 253.
Winkler, Karl Gustav Adolf. Anomale Keimungen. 1895. I. 204, 125.'
— Beiträge zur Morphologie der Keimblätter. 1882. I. 123.'
— Ueber hypokotyle Sprosse ... über Verwachsung der Keimblätter. 1881. I. 123.'
— Die Keimblätter der deutschen Dicotylen. 1885. I. 123.'
— Ueber die Keimblätter der deutschen Dicotylen. 1874. I. 123.'
— Die Keimpflanze der Corylus Avellana. 1888. II. 121.³
— Die Keimpflanze des Sarothamnus. 1880. II. 351.²
— Die Keimpflanzen der Koch'schen Clematis-Arten. 1888. II. 196.'
— Polygala Chamaebuxus L. in Thüringen. 1882. II. 431.'
Winkler, Moritz. Reiseerinnerungen an Spanien. 1874. I. 421.
Winkler, Tiberius Cornelis. Boomen en bloemen in de bos-schen van Guiana. 1897. I. 339.²
— Een wandeling op het veen. 1860. I. 391.'
Winkler, Wilibald. Zur Anatomie der durch die Fichten-rindenlaus ... entstehenden Zapfengallen. 1878. IV. 456.'
— Sudetenflora. 1900. I. 390.
Winneberger, Das Vorkommen der Moos- oder Schwarz-föhre. 1858. II. 43.'
Winnecke, Charles. Plants collected in Central Australia. 1886. I. 503.
Winneken, Christian. Beschreibung des wahren Opobalsam-baumes. 1745. III. 510.²
Winning, C. H. O. M. von. De Kinahandel. 1892. III. 716.
Winslow, Andreas Pettersson. Göteborgstraktens Salix- och Rosaflora. 1877. II. 100,² 284.'
— Rosae scandinavicae. 1880. II. 284.'
— Satu talouden hoidolle tärkeätä Suomen kasvia. 1884. III. 68.²
Winslow, C. F. The Big tree. 1855. II. 50.'
Winslow, Jacob. Spicilegium anatomico-botanicum ... 1694. I. 30.
Winter. Zur Geschichte der französischen Forsteinrichtung im Reichslande. 1884. IV. 249.'
Winter, Alexander. Coffee cultivation in Berbice. 1882. III. 729.'
Winter, August. Vollständiges Gartenbuch. 1865. III. 104.
Winter, Ferdinand. Beiträge zur Flora des Saargebiets. 1877. II. 301.²
— Die Flora des Saargebietes. 1875. I. 387.
— Über eine neue Prunus-Art. 1886. II. 271.'

Winter, Georg. Die durch Pilze verursachten Krankheiten der Kulturgewächse. 1878. III. 194.
— See also SCHOCH, G. & WINTER, G.
Winter, J. Remarks on the cultivation of the Carob. 1882. III. 471.[2]
Winter, L. On the cultivation of the Olive. 1873. III.'675.[2]
Winter, Luigi. Cenno fisiologico sopra la Phoenix dactylifera. 1887. II. 73,[1] *III. 518,[1] 323.[3]*
— Structure as a guide to cultivators of Palms. 1887. II. 73,[1] *III. 518,[1] 323.[3]*
The winter aspect of trees. 1895. III. 360.[1]
Winter beauty in the home grounds. 1891. III. 208.[1]
Winter-berry-bearing plants. 1884. III. 208.[1]
A winter-flowering Clematis. 1874. III. 390.[1]
The winter-flowering Heaths. 1898. III. 651,[1] *651.[2]*
Winter-flowering Honeysuckle. 1879. III. 750.[2]
Winter-flowering plants. 1878. III. 401,[1] *673.[1]*
Winter-flowering shrubs. 1878. III. 352.[2]
Winter flowers. 1889. III. 207.[2]
Winter pruning. 1880. III. 170.
The Winter Sweet. 1896. III. 401.[1]
The Winter-sweet (Toxicophlaea spectabilis). 1877. III. 685.[3]
Winterfeld, von. Das sogenannte Aderlassen der Bäume. 1853. III. 174.[1]
Winterfeld, L. Baron von. Ueber das Vorkommen einiger Opuntia-Arten. 1845. II. 596.[1]
Die Winterfröste von 1880. 1880. IV. 191.[2]
Winterl, Joseph Jacob. Index horti botanici Universitatis hungaricae. 1788. I. 65.[2]
Winterschmidt, Johann Samuel. Bayrische Flora. 1819. I. 376.
— Naturgetreue Darstellung aller inn- und ausländischen Material-Samen. 1818. I. 120, *III. 220.[1]*
— Nürnbergische Flora. 1818. I. 376.
Wintershausen, Freiherr von. Gedanken über Behandlung der Waldungen. 1800. IV. 268.
Wintershoven, J. B. van. Handboek voor liefhebbers van vreemde plantzoenen. 1795. III. 75.[2]
— Handleiding tot de kennis van ... boomen, planten. 1829. III. 76.
Winterstein, E. Sur l'amyloïde végétal. 1893. I. 177.
— Sur les matières sucrées ... de la gomme chagual. 1898. II. 76.[2]
— Sur la substance mère de la gomme de bois. 1893. I. 181.[2]
— Sur les sucres provenant ... de Chagual. 1898. II. 76.[2]
Winterthur — Naturwissenschaftliche Gesellschaft. See NATURWISSENSCHAFTLICHE ... I. 26.[2]
Winther, M. Literaturae scientiae rerum naturalium in Dania, Norvegia & Holsatia ... enchiridion. 1829. I. 3.[1]
Winthrop, John. An extract of a letter ... concerning some natural curiosities. 1670. III. 262.[2]
Winton, T. C. Roses in California. 1885. III. 452.
Wionius, Georgius. Botanotrophium; seu, Hortus medicus Petri Ricarti. 1644. I. 56.
Wipacher, David. Flora lipsiensis bipartita. 1726. I. 373.
— Kurtzer doch gründlicher Bericht von denen jenigen Kräutern ... um Leipzig. 1726. I. 373.
Wirkung der Leucaena glauca auf Haustiere. 1900. III. 481.[1]
Wirkung des Blitzes auf die getroffenen Bäume. 1880. IV. 194.
Die Wirkung des Lichts und der Feuchtigkeit auf die Stecklinge. See The ACTION of light and moisture upon cuttings. 1844. III. 157.[2]
Die Wirkungen des Blitzschlages auf Bäume. 1875. IV. 194.
Wirnan, Johannes. Euphorbia ejusque historia naturalis. See LINNÉ, Carl von. 1752. II. 441.[2]
Wirschinger, F. L. Die Unfallverhütung in der Land- und Forstwirtschaft. 1894. IV. 311.[1]
Wirsing, Adam Ludwig. Eclogae botanicae. 1778. I. 262.
Wirt, George H. Stumpage prices. 1900. IV. 260.[1]
Wirtgen, Ferdinand. Beiträge zur Flora der Rheinprovinz. 1899. I. 390.
Wirtgen, Philipp. Anomalien in der Gattung Rubus. 1869. II. 305.[2]
— Beiträge zur Flora der nördlichen Pfalz. 1866. I. 386.
— Beiträge zur Flora des Regierungsbezirkes von Coblenz. 1839. I. 380.
— Beiträge zur rheinischen Flora. 1869. I. 386.
— Erster[-sechster] Nachtrag zum Prodromus der preuss. Rheinlande. 1844. I. 381.
— Flora der preussischen Rheinlande. 1870. I. 386.

— Flora der preussischen Rheinprovinz. 1857. I. 384.
— Flora des Regierungsbezirks Coblenz. 1841. I. 380.
— Die Gruppe der Hundsrosen. 1869. II. 284.[2]
— Ueber im Jahr 1847 beobachtete Missbildungen. 1848. II. 267.[1]
— Leitfaden für den Unterricht in der Botanik. 1839. I. 380.
— Ueber die pflanzengeographischen Verhältnisse der preussischen Rheinprovinz. 1837. I. 379.
— Prodromus der Flora der preussischen Rheinlande. 1842. I. 381.
— Rheinische Reiseflora. 1857. I. 384.
— Ueber Rubus tomentosus Borkh. 1869. II. 310.[2]
— Ueber die Vegetation der ... Eifel. 1865. I. 385.
— Zweiter Nachtrag zu meiner systematischen Uebersicht der .. Pflanzen des Rheinthales. 1837. II. 284.[1]
Wirth, C. Phänologische Beobachtung der Pflanzen. 1895. I. 221.
Wirth, Max. Ungarn und seine Bodenschätze. 1885. IV. 373.
Ueber die wirthschaftlichen und Ertrags-Verhältnisse der Reviere Frankenhofen. 1858. IV. 351.[1]
Wirthschaftseinrichtung und Ertragsberechnung der Erlenbrüche. 1847. IV. 489.[1]
Die Wirthschaftseinrichtung vom Revier Altdorf. 1865. IV. 248.[1]
Die Wirthschafts-Einrichtung vom Revier Schwann. 1880. IV. 248.[1]
Wirthschafts-Ergebnisse bezüglich der Forsten ... Sachsen-Altenburg. IV. 11.
Wirthschafts-Ergebnisse der landesfiscalischen Forst-Verwaltung [Anhalt]. 1883. IV. 350.[1]
Wirthschaftsregeln für den fränkischen Wald. 1851. IV. 247.[2]
Wirthschaftsregeln für die mit Tannen bestockten ... Waldungen. 1892. IV. 444.[2]
Wirtschaftsergebnisse der würtembergischen Staats-Forst- und Jagdverwaltung. 1899. IV. 261.[1]
Wirz, Joh. Flora des Cantons Glarus. I. Holzgewächse. 1893. I. 432.[2]
— Flora des Kantons Glarus. 1893. I. 437.
— Die Veränderungen in der Pflanzenwelt unseres Landes. 1898. I. 438.
Wirrén, Johannes Ernst Adhem. De balsamis. 1849. I. 180,[2] *III. 344.*
— Enumeratio plantarum officinalium Fenniam sponte inhabitantium. See ILMON, Imman. 1837. III. 68.[1]
— Geographica plantarum per partem provinciae easanensis distributio. 1839. I. 361.
— Scriptores rei herbariae fennicae. 1843. I. 80.[1]
Wisboom van Giessendam, D. W. P. De teelt van griendenteenhout. 1878. III. 348.
Wisconsin — Agricultural experiment station. See WISCONSIN UNIVERSITY OF ... III. 9.
Wisconsin — Naturhistorischer Verein. ·See NATURHISTORISCHER ... I. 6.
Wisconsin academy of sciences, arts and letters. Transactions. I. 7.[2]
Wisconsin Arbor day annual. 1892. IV. 42.[1]
Wisconsin geological and natural history survey. Bulletin. IV. 5.[2]
Wisconsin natural history society. Bulletin. See NATURHISTORISCHER VEREIN VON WISCONSIN. I. 6.
Wisconsin state agricultural society. Transactions. III. 9.
Wisconsin state board of agriculture. Biennial report. See WISCONSIN STATE AGRICULTURAL SOCIETY. III. 9.
Wisconsin state Cranberry growers' association. 1900. III. 664.[1]
Wisconsin state horticultural society. Annual report. Transactions. III. 9.
Wisconsin, University of — Agricultural experiment station. Annual report. Bulletin. III. 9.
Wise, John A. The new forest. 1863. I. 401, 511. — 1883. IV. 358.[1]
Viselius, J. A. B. Beknopte handleiding voor de Jute-cultuur. 1887. III. 128.
— Een kunstbewerking by de Koffiekultuur. 1875. III. 726.[2]
Wislicenus, Hans. Resistenz der Fichte gegen saure Rauchgase. 1898. IV. 460.[1]
Wislizenus, A. Memoir of a tour to northern Mexico. 1848. I. 331.
Wismer, J. J. Die Blutlaus. 1886. III.·428.[1]
Wisocky. Versuche über den Wasserverlust verschiedener Holzarten. 1855. IV. 411.[3]

Wisselingh, C. van. Over cuticularisatie en cutine. 1894. I. 129.²
— La gaine du cylindre central dans la racine. 1886. I. 104.
— Over de kurklamel en het suberine. 1892. I. 131.¹
— Sur la lamelle subéreuse. 1892. I. 131.¹
— Sur la paroi des cellules subéreuses. 1888. I. 138.² .
— Sur les revêtements des espaces intercellulaires. 1887. I. 138.²
Wissenbach, C. Group of Spruces at Wilhelmshöhe. 1883. II. 37.¹ .
— Picea nigra. 1892. III. 305.²
— A pyramidal Oak. 1883. II. 138.²
Wissenschaftliche Mittheilungen aus Bosnien und der Herzegovina. I. 28.¹
Wissenschaftlich-praktische Forschungen auf dem Gebiete der Landwirthschaft. *See* CENTRALBLATT für Agrikulturchemie. III. 11.
Wisser. Sur divers insectes nuisibles aux Caféiers. 1899. III. 737.¹
Wissmann. Das Blühen junger Buchen-Stockausschläge. 1858. II. 126.²
Wissmann, O. Ueber den Kiefernkrebs. 1869. IV. 476.
— Eine merkwürdige Abänderung des Eibenbaums. 1872. II. 10.¹
— Sonst und jetzt. 1876. IV. 26.
— Woher entsteht die Ringelkrankheit der Buche ? 1869. IV. 496.
Wisst, Aloys. Aliénation des forêts de l'état. 1866. IV. 275.
— Note sur l'annexion de l'administration des forêts. 187.? IV. 292.
— Réorganisation du service forestier. 1875. IV. 292.
Wistaria chinensis in Japan. 1898. III. 491.¹
The **Wistaria** in Japan. 1900. III. 490.²
Wistrand, A. T. Flora gothoburgensis. *See* WAHLBERG, P. F. 1820. I. 352.
Wit, C. DUDOK·DE. *See* DUDOK DE WIT, C.
Witch-Hazels (Corylopsis spicata). 1874. III. 416.²
Witchell, Charles A. & **Strugnell,** W. B. Fauna and flora of Gloucestershire. 1892. I. 534.²
—— The Lassington Pear tree. 1892. II. 280.²
—— Maud's Elm at Cheltenham. 1892. II. 144.²
With, J. T. Forsøg paa et tilstrækkeligt Middel at opfinde, hvorved Skovene i Norge kunne spares. 1761. IV. 273.¹
Witherell, L. R. The origin . . . of fruit in the prehistoric ages. 1888. III. 50.²
Withering, William. An arrangement of British plants. 1776. I. 395.
— A botanical arrangement of all the vegetables . . . in Great Britain. 1776. I. 395.
— A botanical arrangement of British plants. 1776. I. 395.
— Florae ulysipponensis specimen. 1822. I. 420.
— The miscellaneous tracts. . 1822. I. 420.
— A systematic arrangement of British plants. 1776. I. 395.
Withering, William, (jr.). Withering's British plants. 1830. I. 397.
— A systematic arrangement of British plants. 1830. I. 397, 533.
Withers, J. T. Celtis occidentalis. 1899. II. 142.¹
Withers, William. The Acacia tree. 1829. IV. 523.¹
— A letter to Sir Henry Steuart, bart. on the improvement in the quality of timber. 1829. IV. 120.
— A memoir . . . on the planting and rearing of forest-trees. 1827. IV. 120.
Withy, (pseud.). The Willow as a timber-tree. 1872. IV. 487.¹ — 1886. IV. 487.¹
Witkowsky, Ludwig. *See* HARNACK, Erich & WITKOWSKY, Ludwig.
Witman, Ernst. Entwurf einer-tabellarischen Darstellung der Terminologie der Phänogamisten. 1812. I. 70.
Witowski, Hippolit. Historya naturalna obejmująca. 1849. I. 89.
Witsch, Rudolf. Urbarmachung des Flugsandes. · 1809. IV. 167.¹
Witt, Johann Constantin. De legibus quibusdam ad processum vegetationis pertinentibus. 1802. I. 146.
Witt Hamer, H. M. de; Flora delfensis. 1868. I. 391.¹
Wittamer, Édouard. La rouille de l'écorce de Pin. 1894. IV. 559.²
Witte. *See* RAUHUT & WITTE.
Witte, (Oberförster). Eine astlose Weisstanne. 1895. II. 23.¹
Witte, (Oberförster Schöneberg). Schutz der Schonungen gegen Wild. 1869. IV. 146.²

Witte, Heinrich. Das Alter der Bäume. 1856. I. 193.¹
— Aralia (Fatsia) japonica. 1860. III. 642.¹
— Les Araliacées des jardins hollandais. 1861. II. 646.²
— Arauja albens G. Don. 1860. III. 692.¹
— Het blad. 1870. I. 110.
— Das Blatt. 1870. I.·110.
— De bloem. 1877. I. 237.
— Een bonte Larix. 1876. III. 304.²
— De boomreuzen van Noord-Amerika. 1878. I. 295.²
— Chamaebatia foliolosa Hartw. 1861. II. 259.¹
— Over den duur van het kiemvermogen der zaden. 1855. I. 527.
— Enting van den Kastanjeboom. 1881. III. 359.¹
— Enumeratio alphabetica . . . Palmarum. 1859. III. 317.
— Eriococcus gracilis Hasskl. 1861. III. 521.²
— Fatsia japonica. 1861. III. 642.¹
— Figuur boomen. 1878. III. 202.²
— Flora; afbeeldingen . . . van boomen, heesters. 1868. III. 77.
— Floraison automnale du Cydonia japonica. 1861. III. 420.¹
— Floraison d'une grande Pandanée. 1859. III. 313.²
— Floraison du Pandanus furcatus. 1861. III. 313.²
— Handleiding voor den bloementuin. 1866. III. 106.¹
— Hoe de planten reizen. 1874. I. 240.²
— Hoya macrophylla Bl. 1859. II. 740.¹
— Hybridisatie. 1881. III. 50.²
— De Liberia-Koffie. 1877. III. 742.¹
— Een monstreuse Kokosnoot. 1898. II. 67.²
— Les Myrtacées de la Nouvelle Hollande. 1860. II. 619.² — De ouderdom der boomen. 1856. I. 193.¹ — 1878. I. 193.²
— Het Palmhout. 1876. III. 523.¹
— Passiflora Impératrice Eugénie. 1868. III. 615.
— Een pelgrimage door België. 1875. III. 122.²
— Pisonia sylvestris. 1859. II. 192.¹
— De Plant. 1869. III. 37.²
— De plant en de mensch. 1877. III. 218.¹
— Plantkunde voor school en huis. 1873. I. 91.
— Raphidepis japonica Sieb. et Zucc. 1859. II. 281.²
— Schetsen uit het plantenrijk. 1870. I. 270, V. xiii.²
— Verslag omtrent de Internationale tuinbouwtentoonstelling te Hamburg. 1870. III. 121.²
— Weigelia amabilis Looymansii aurea. 1876. III. 748.²
— Wilde Rozen. 1888. III. 122.²
Witte, Louis. Ueber den Bau des Holzes einiger Lianen. 1886. I. 127.¹
Wittewaal, Jan. *See* WYTEWAAL, Jan.
Witthauer, J. G. Die Forsten der freien und Hansestadt Lübeck. 1857. IV. 353.
Wittich, Christoph. Pflanzen-Areal Studien. 1889. I. 372.
Wittlin, J. Ueber die Bildung der Kalkoxalat-Taschen. 1896. I. 139.
Wittmaack, Theodor. Pharmakopoea germanica. 1860. III. 249.
Wittmack, Max Karl Ludwig. Eine abnorme Fuchsie. 1887. III. 643.²
— Acalypha hispida Burm. 1899. II. 435.²
— Acer macrophyllum Pursh. 1881. III. 535.¹
— Der Akademische Forstgarten zu Münden. 1885. I. 48, IV. 18.²
— Allgemeiner Katalog des K. landwirthschaftlichen Museums. 1869. III. 28.¹
— Alnus glutinosa L. var. laciniata Ehrh. 1888. III. 356.²
— Alnus incana L. var. laciniata. 1887. II. 116.²
— Die australischen Lanzen-Grasbäume. 1876. II. 86.¹
— Die beiden alten Eiben . . . zu Berlin. 1899. II. 11.²
— Betula verrucosa Ehrh. var. laciniata. 1887. II. 120.²
— Die Blätter von Bauhinia racemosa. 1876. III. 467.²
— Bougainvillea glabra Choisy var. Sanderiana. 1899. II. 191.¹
— Bouvardia hybrida "Hogarth" fl. pl. 1887. II. 810.¹
— Bromeliaceae. 1888. II. 76.²
— Die Buche in Norwegen. 1889. II. 127.¹
— Callistemon lanceolatum Smith. 1890. III. 633.¹
— Choisya ternata. 1881. III. 496.¹
— Combretum coccineum Lam. 1887. II. 616.²
— Crataegus coccinea . . . als Wildfutter. 1898. III. 421.²
— Crossandra infundibuliformis. 1883. III. 709.¹
— Cycas Tonkinensis. 1886. II. 5.¹
— Dioon edule und Dioon edule var. lanuginosum. 1899. II. 5.²
— Dracaena arborea. 1897. III. 336.¹
— Dracaena Aubryana Brongn. 1894. III. 337.¹

— Ueber eine durchwachsene Birne. 1884. II. 280.[1]
— Echinocereus pectinatus var. robustus. 1890. II. 593.[1]
— Ueber einige Eigenthümlichkeiten der Rhizoboleen. 1884. II. 546.[1]
— Ueber essbare Eicheln. 1884. IV. 503.[2]
— Ueber die Familie der Marcgraviaceae. 1879. II. 546.[1]
— Die Fichte im Norden. 1887. II. 35.[1]
— Früchte von Akebia quinata. 1899. III. 393.[2]
— Führer durch die vegetabilische Abtheilung des Museums der Kgl. landwirthschaftlichen Hochschule. 1886. III. 28.
— Die Gärten Oberitaliens. 1883. I. 64.
— Ueber Gallen an Zweigen von Salix Caprea. 1879. III. 351.[2]
— Eine gehörnte Orange. 1884. II. 403.[1]
— Über das Grösserwerden der Blätter . . . im Norden. 1886. I. 218.
— Die grösste Eiche in Norwegen. 1888. II. 139.[1]
— Die grosse Weymouthskiefer, Pinus Strobus. 1877. II. 46.[1]
— Hamamelis japonica. 1886. III. 417.[1] — 1900. II. 253.[1]
— Hardenbergia Comptoniana. 1883. III. 480.[1]
— Ueber eine japanische Birne. 1884. II. 281.[1]
— Juniperus communis L. var. suecica. 1886. II. 31.[1]
— Eine keimende Kokosnuss. 1896. II. 67.[2]
— Die Keimung der Cocosnuss. 1896. II. 67.[2]
— Knospenmissbildungs : . . Syringa. 1882. III. 681.[2]
— Ueber den Kronenapfel. 1889. II. 267.[1]
— Licuala grandis Wendl. 1881. III. 326.[2]
— Eine liegende Birke. 1888. II. 118.[1]
— Luftwurzeln an Birken. 1887. I. 183.
— Macrozamia Moorei. 1885. III. 286.[1]
— Magnolia Watsoni. 1899. III. 400.[2]
— Marcgraviaceae. 1878. II. 546.[1]
— Ueber die Marcgraviaceen. 1879. II. 546.[1]
— Die Marcgraviaceen und ihre Honiggefässe. 1879. II. 546.[1]
— Ueber den Melonenbaum. 1878. II. 582.[2]
— Merkwürdig gewachsene Fichte in Norwegen. 1887. II. 36.[1]
— Der Milchsaft der Pflanzen. 1881. III. 218.[2]
— Monströser Apfel. 1888. II. 267.[1]
— The nectar-cups of the Marcgraviaceae. 1880. II. 546.[1]
— Neue griechische Gehölze. 1875. I. 448.[2]
— Neue und empfehlenswerte Pflanzen. 1887. III. 75.[2]
— Neuheiten aus der Baumschule von L. Späth. 1890. III. 437.[2]
— Die Nutzpflanzen aller Zonen. 1879. III. 29.[1]
— Die Nutzpflanzen der alten Peruaner. 1888. III. 32.[2] 64.[2] V. x.[1]
— Der Obst- und Gartenbau in den Vereinigten Staaten. 1894. III. 117.[1]
— The Papaw. 1878. II. 582.[2]
— Philadelphus mexicanus Schlechtd. 1883. II. 242.[2]
— Pieris japonica. 1883. III. 654.
— Pirus usguriensis Max. 1884. II. 281.
— Prunus Cerasus Rhexii fl. pl. 1886. II. 273.[1]
— Prunus Davidiana Franchet. 1895. II. 274.[1]
— Pueraria Thunbergiana. 1896. II. 380.[2] V. xxvi.[2]
— Die Reblaus. 1875. III. 568.
— Rhizoboleae. 1886. II. 546.[1]
— Rhododendron triflorum. 1883. II. 683.[2]
— Eine Rieseneiche in Norwegen. 1888. II. 139.[1]
— Riesige Blätter von Sambucus nigra. 1889. II. 841.[1]
— Russlands Pflanzenschätze in unsern Gärten. 1899. I. 242.[2]
— Die Schlangenfichte . . . in Norwegen. 1887. II. 35.[1]
— Schöne Birken in Norwegen. 1887. II. 118.[2]
— Schöne Koniferen in Lausanne. 1895. III. 299,[1] 310.[2]
— Smilax aspera L. 1897. III. 338.[1]
— Sparmannia africana. 1881. III. 585.[1]
— Stephanandra incisa. 1888. II. 316.[1]
— Syringa Emodi Wallich var. rosea. 1895. III. 681.[1]
— Thuja plicata Don. 1886. III. 311.[2]
— Tilia cordata var. pyramidalis. 1896. III. 586.[1]
— Ueberwallung eines Eisengitters. 1891. I. 210,[2] III. 672.[1]
— Ulmus montana With. in Norwegen. 1888. II. 145.[1]
— Vergrünte Blüte von Calycanthus. 1888. II. 214.[2]
— Der Vermont Ahorn-Zucker. 1896. IV. 527.[2]
— Verzeichniss brasilianischer Hölzer. 1873. IV. 398.[2]
— Vielköpfige Fichte. 1888. II. 37.[2]
— Washingtonia robusta. 1889. III. 332.[2]
— Wilhelmshöhe und seine Pflanzenschätze. 1885. I. 48.
— Xanthoceras sorbifolia Bunge. 1892. III. 540.[2]
— Xanthoceras sorbifolia Bunge (Sapindaceae). 1884. II. 490.[1]

— Ein Zapfen von Abies nobilis. 1885. III. 296.[2]
— Zapfen-Anhäufung an . . . Pinus Pinaster. 1884. II. 44.[2]
— Zapfenanhäufungen an einer gemeinen Kiefer. 1885. II. 47.[2]
— Zapfenhäufung an . . . Pinus halepensis. 1884. II. 42.[1]
— Zapfenkolonie an . . . Pinus Pinaster. 1887. II. 44.[2]
— Zwei werthvolle Granaten-Varietäten. 1881. III. 630.[2]
— See also BRANDT, R. & WITTMACK, Ludwig; GAERDT, Heinrich & WITTMACK, Ludwig; KOOPMANN, Karl & WITTMACK, Ludwig; KUNTZE, Otto & WITTMACK, Ludwig; LAUCHE, Wilhelm & WITTMACK, Ludwig; SPÄTH, Ludwig & WITTMACK, Ludwig.
— & Baillon, Henri. La flore et les essais de culture au Congo. 1887. III. 131.[1]
— & Brettschneider, F. Robinia neomexicana. 1892. III. 45.[1] 46.[1]
— & Müller, R. Abnormität von Colutea arborescens. 1888. II. 347.[1]
Wittman, F. J. Over de zwavelzure quinine. 1826. III. 721.
Wittrock, Veit Brecher. Om fanerogam- och thallogam-vegetationen i Skandinaviens Ilex-region. 1868. I. 356.
— Ueber die Geschlechtervertheilung bei Acer platanoides. 1886. II. 477.[1]
— De Horto botanico bergiano. 1891. I. 521.[2]
— Om könsfördelningen hos Acer platanoides. 1885. II. 477.[1]
— Om Linnaea borealis L. 1878. II. 835.[2]
— Notiser om Hedera Helix. 1886. II. 649.[2]
— En ny varietet af Tranbärsbusken. 1885. II. 687.[1]
— Oxycoccus palustris Pers. var. citriformis. 1885. II. 687.[1]
— De Picea excelsa (Lam.) Lk. f. acutissima Hort. 1891. II. 35.[1]
— De radice Quercus Roboris L. 1891. II. 137.[1]
— & Juel, H. O. Catalogus plantarum . . . in Horto botanico bergiano . . . cultarum. 1891. I. 40, 521.[2]
Wittstein, Georg Christian. Anleitung zur Analyse der Asche. 1862. I. 156.[2]
— Anleitung zur chemischen Analyse von Pflanzen. 1868. I. 156.[2]
— Chemische Versuche mit . . . Populus balsamifera. 1858. II. 97.[1]
— Etymologisch-botanisches Handwörterbuch. 1852. I. 76.[2]
— Handwörterbuch der Pharmakognosie. 1882. III. 259.[1]
— The organic constituents of plants. 1868. I. 156.[2]
— Pharmakognostisch-anatomische . . . Untersuchung der Coto-Rinde. 1875. III. 397.[2]
— Über das Vorkommen der Milchsäure. 1858. I. 180.[1]
— & Apoiger, F. Entdeckung der Borsäure. 1857. III. 666.[1]
— — Présence de l'acide borique. 1857. III. 666.[1]
Wittwer, (Oberförster, Karolath). Bemerkungen zur Schütte der Kiefer. 1859. IV. 476.
— Beobachtungen über den Absprung der Eichen. 1860. IV. 516.[1]
— Beschreibung der Einrichtung . . . der Nadelholz-Samendarre. 1859. IV. 147.[1]
— Erfahrungen, inwieweit sich die Kulturen bei dem Hochwasser . . . erhalten haben. 1855. IV. 185.[1]
— Erläuterungen zur Pflanzmethode mit dem eisernen Pflanzspaten. 1856. IV. 152.
— Mancherlei aus dem Gebiete des Waldbaues. 1856. IV. 152.
— Pflanzmethode mit dem eisernen Pflanzspaten. 1856. IV. 152.
Wittwer, Johann Philipp. Beyträge und Erläuterungen zu des Herrn . . . G. L. Hartig Lehrbuch für Förster. 1819. IV. 96.
Wittwer, Wilhelm Constantin. Geschichtliche Darstellung der verschiedenen Lehren über die Respiration der Pflanzen. 1850. I. 170.
— See also VOGEL, August, (jr.) & WITTWER, W. C.
Witzell, Karol. Catalogue des plantes d'ornement . . . Jardin botanique de Volhynie à Krzemeniec. 1821. I. 41.
— Spis roślin ozdobnych . . . w ogrodzie botanicznym Liceum . . . w Krzemieńcu. 1821. I. 41.
Witzleben, C. D. von. Untersuchungen über die Material- und Kapital-Versfasung. 1861. IV. 255.
Witzleben, Friedrich Ludwig von. Abhandlung über einige Ursachen des Holzmangels. 1800. IV. 280.[2]
— Ueber Baumschulen und Pflanzungen. 1794. IV. 149.[2]
— Beyträge zur Holzcultur. 1797. IV. 116.
— Die Direction des Forstwesens. 1791. IV. 287.

Witzleben, Friedrich Ludwig von (*continued*).
— Ueber die rechte Behandlung der Rothbuchen-Hoch- oder Saamen-Waldung. 1795. IV. 493.[2]
— Regulativ, wornach sich bey eintretenden Mastjahren ... zu achten ist. 1805. IV. 139.[1]
—... Vom Wiederanbau verödeter ... Waldungen. 1798. IV. 142.
Wizlsberger, C. Die Holzwolle als Ersatz für die Waldstreu. 1887. IV. 429.
Wo die Zürbel-Kiefer angebaut worden? 1835. IV. 463.[1]
Wo gehört die Fichte hin? 1867. IV. 453.
Wobst. Cultur der indischen Azaleen. 1870. III. 660.[1]
— Vermehrung der Pflanzen durch Wurzelstecklinge. 1868. III. 159.[1]
Wobst, Karl A. Beiträge zur Brombeerflora des Königreichs Sachsen. 1891. II. 302.[1]
— Veränderungen in der Flora von Dresden. 1880. I. 388.
Wochenblatt für Land- und Forstwirthschaft. IV. 11.
Wochenschrift für deutsche Förster. IV. 11.
Wochenschrift für Gärtnerei und Pflanzenkunde. *See* VEREIN ZUR BEFÖRDERUNG DES GARTENBAUES IN DEN KÖNIGLICH PREUSSISCHEN STAATEN. III. 14.
Wocke, E. Zwei immergrüne Zwergsträucher. 1900. III. 523,[1] 749.[2]
Woditschka, Anton. Aylanthus glandulosa vor dem Froste. 1864. IV. 525.
— Die Drahtriese. 1894. IV. 392.
— Die Drahtriese; eine neue und billige Bringungsart. 1897. IV. 392.
— Der Pinien-Processionsspinner. 1895. IV. 479.
— Die Zirbe .. und ihre Cultur. 1900. IV. 464.[1]
— Die Zirbe und ihre Cultur in Gröden. 1893. IV. 463.[2]
— Zürbelnusssaat und Erdbedeckung. 1864. IV. 463.[2]
Wodziski, Stanisław. 'O hodowaniu, użytku, mnożeniu i poznawaniu drzew, krzewow, roślin. 1818. III. 90.[2]
Woehl, Eugen. Aus den Forstrevieren des oberschlesischen Industriebezirkes. 1898. IV. 193,[1] 202.
Wöhler, Friedrich. Over eenige bestanddeelen der Canella alba. 1844. III. 613.[2]
— Sur l'huile essentielle du Pinus Abies. 1844. IV. 459.[2]
— Sur la présence de l'acide quinique dans l'aubier du Sapin. 1845. II. 23.[2]
— Sur quelques principes de la Cannelle blanche. 1844. III. 613.[2]
— & Haidinger, W. Über das Cocaïn. 1860. III. 492.[2]
— & Niemann, Albert. Sur l'alcaloïde du Coca. 1860. III. 492.[2]
Wölfer, Marius. Gemeinnütziges mathematisch-techuelogisches Taschenbuch. 1827. IV. 58.
— Gründliche und praktische Anweisung zur Berg- und Forstmesskunst. 1846. IV. 264.
— Gründliche und vollständige Anweisung zur practischen Forst- und Feldmesskunst. 1828. IV. 263.
— Der praktische Forst- und Feldmesser. 1846. IV. 264.
Woellner, Jo. Georg Magnus. De generibus plantarum ... potius augendis. *See* HEISTER, Lorenz. 1751. III. 54.
Woening, Franz. Die Pflanzen im alten Aegypten. 1886. I. 81.[1]
Woerlein, Georg. Bemerkungen über neue oder kritische Pflanzen der Münchener Flora. 1885. I. 388.[1]
— Nachträge zu Garckes Flora. 1883. II. 101.[2]
— Die Phanerogamen- und Gefäss-Kryptogamen-Flora der Münchener Thalebene. 1893. I. 389.
Wörmann & Godemann. Das praktische Feldmessen. 1894. III. 200.[1]
Wörnle, Paul. Anatomische Untersuchung der durch Gymnosporangium-Arten hervorgerufenen Missbildungen. 1894. IV. 212.
Wörterbuch der gebräuchlichsten Ausdrücke der Forst- und Waidmanns-Sprache. 1823. IV. 23.[1]
Wörz. Der Röderlandbetrieb im Allgäu. 1843. IV. 133.
Woher kommt es, dass die Wurzeln der Bäume leichter erfrieren? 1864. III. 182.
Wohler, G. Künstliche Befruchtung der Haselnüsse. 1895. III. 358.[1]
Wohlfarth & Lehr, W. Zweihundertundsiebzig Jahre altes Buchenbauholz. 1886. IV. 499.
Wohlfarth, Rud. Botanische Mittheilungen. 1888. II. 299.[2]
— Die Pflanzen des Deutschen Reichs. 1881. I. 388.
Wohlfromm, H. Verzeichniss ... der für ... Gumbinnen geeigneten Obstsorten. 1888. III. 72.
Wohlgemeinte Andeutungen zur Waldwirthschaft. *See* HERIGOYEN, Karl d'. 1854. IV. 118.

Der wohlgeübte und erfahrene Förster. *See* ZANTHIER, H. D. von & KROHNE. 1785. IV. 95.
Wohlleben, Johann Friedrich. Flora halensis. Supplementi fasciculus I. *See* LEYSER, F. W. von. 1761. I. 373.
— Supplementi ad Leysseri Floram halensem. 1796. I. 375.
Wohltmann, F. Bericht über seine Togo-Reise. 1900. III. 131.[1]
— Die B - und Klima-Ansprüche des Kolabaums. 1899. III. 590often
— Der Kakaobau am Kamerun-Gebirge. 1897. III. 593.[1]
— Zur Methode des Kaffeepflanzens in Deutsch-Ostafrika. 1898. III. 732.[2]
Wohmann, W. Die Lohrinden. 1865. IV. 435.
— Neubauer, C. & Lotichius, C. A. Die Schälung von Eichenrinden. 1873. IV. 512.
Wójcicki, Z. Przyczynek do kwestyi zapłodnienia u roślin nagonasiennych. 1897. I. 200.
Wojsbun, Edward. O służebnościach leśnych. 1869. IV. 333.[2]
Wokral, Theodor. Die "Bärenfichte." 1880. IV. 456.
Woldřich, Johann Nepomuk. Zur Morphologie der Apfelfrucht. 1868. II. 267.[1]
— Zwei morphologische Seltenheiten. 1864. II. 267.[1]
Wolf, Christian. *See* WOLFF, Christian.
Wolf, E. Den norske Last-Drager eller Bord-Reduction. 1785. IV. 220.
Wolf, Egbert L. Acer Trautvetteri Medw. 1891. II. 480.[2]
— Lonicera syringantha Maxim. 1892. II. 840.[1]
— Lonicera tangutica Max. 1891. II. 840.[1]
— Lonicera tatarica L. var. grandibracteata. 1891. III. 51.[2]
— Spiraea bullata Maxim. 1892. II. 314.[2]
— Spiraea opulifolia L. var. heterophylla. 1890. III. 430.
— Zwei Formen des gewöhnlichen Trauben-Hollunders. 1891. III. 752.[2]
— *See also* BOLLE, Ж. Д.
Wolf, F. O. Botanische Notizen aus dem Obern Rhonethal. 1887. I. 437.
— Notice sur quelques plantes ... rares pour le Valais. 1890. II. 105.[2]
Wolf, Georg Armin. De radice caincae. 1831. III. 744.[1]
Wolf, Helmhard, *Freiherr* von Hohberg. *See* HOHBERG, Wolfgang Helmhard, *Freiherr* von.
Wolf, John de. *See* DE WOLF, John.
Wolf, Nathanael Matthaeus von. Concordantia botanica. 1780. I. 77.
— Genera plantarum ... definita. 1776. I. 258.
Wolf, Rudolf. *See* SCHLÄFLI, Alexander & WOLF, Rudolf.
Wolf, Theodor. Ein Besuch der Galápagos-Inseln. 1879. I. 510.[2]
Wolfart, Peter. De china chinae. *See* VALENTINI, M. B. 1695. III. 719.
Wolfbauer. *See* HÖHNEL & WOLFBAUER.
Wolff, (*Braubach*). Waldwolle und Waldflachs. 1855. III. 233.[2]
Wolff, Christian, *Freiherr* von. Phaenomenon singulare de Malo pomifera. 1727. II. 266.[2]
— De Pomo ex trunco arboris enato. 1741. II. 266.[2]
Wolff, E. Praktische bemestingsleer. 1872. III. 151.
Wolff, Emil Theodor. Aschen-Analysen von land- und forstwirthschaftlichen Produkten. IT. 153.
— Aschen-Analysen von landwirthschaftlichen Produkten. 1871. I. 153.
— Die chemischen Forschungen auf dem Gebiete der Agrikultur. 1847. I. 151.[1]
— La chimica agraria. 18 ..? III. 36.[1]
— Ueber den Gerbstoffgehalt der Eichenrinde. 1861. IV. 514.[2]
— Die mittlere Zusammensetzung der Asche aller land- und forstwirthschaftlich wichtigen Stoffe. 1865. I. 153.
Wolff, H. Traitement des taillis de Hêtre. 1882. IV. 495.
Wolff, J. Bemærkninger over de Fordele, som Skibs ... erholde ved ... Opfindelse, til at forhindre Forraadnelse. 1832. IV. 416.[2]
Wolff, Jules. Présence de l'alcool méthylique dans les jus fermentés de divers fruits. 1900. I. 179.[2]
Wolff, Kaspar Friedrich. Theoria generationis. 1759. I. 199.
— Theorie von der Generation. 1759. I. 199.
Wolff, Reinhold. Beitrag zur Kenntnis der Schmarotzerpilze. 1877. IV. 461.[2]
Wolff, Robert von. Schutzwaldungen. 1891. IV. 321.
— & others. Ueber Verpflanzen der Coniferen. 1891. III. 2[9]5.[1]

Wolff, Salomon Beer. De ligno nephritico. *See* CARTHEUSER, J. F. 1749. III. 244.

Wolff van Westerrode, W. de. Bereidung van Javaansch papier. 1899. III. 367.[2]
— Djeroek-cultuur. 1899. III. 497.[2]
— Inlandsche plantennamen. 1893. I. 76.[1]

Wolfner, Wilhelm. Botanische Bemerkungen zur Flora Ungarns. 1857. II. 350.[1]
— Einige Worte über Thesium carnosum. 1858. II. 352.[1]
— Kritische Bemerkungen über mehrere ... Pflanzen der Flora Böhmens. 1856. II. 116.[2]
— Zwei neue Pflanzenarten aus Böhmen. 1854. II. 352.[1]

Wolfram, C. Chr. A. Cubiktafeln, welche ... den Inhalt runder Hölzer ... angeben. 1847. IV. 223.
— Hülfstafeln zur Berechnung der Holzpreise. 1847. IV. 402.[2]

Wolfram, R. Flora von Borna. 1878. I. 387.

Wolkenstein, F. L'arboriculture dans la Russie du nord. 1871. III. 292.

Wolkoff, A. de. *See* MAYER, August & WOLKOFF, A. de.

Wollaston, G. H. Paulownia imperialis. 1896. III. 703.[2]

Wolleb, Daniel. Observationes botanico-medicae. *See* LA CHENAL, Werner de. 1776. II. 262.[1]

Wollebius, Lucas. Dissertatio medica de methodo herbas lustrandi. 1711. I. 97.

Wollenhaupt. Eine alte Eibe in Mähren. 1893. IV. 440.[2]

Wollny, E. Importancia que para el cultivo de las plantas tienen las propiedades físicas del suelo. 1879. IV. 69.

Wollrath, Johan G. Horticultura academica. *See* LINNÉ, Carl von. 1754. III. 120.[1]

Wołoszczak, Eustach. Bemerkung zu der Abhandlung von A. Jenčič. 1900. II. 109.[1]
— Einige im Wechselgebiete neue Weiden. 1876. II. 102.[2]
— Ein für Galizien neuer Cytisus. 1886. II. 351.[2]
— Z granicy flory zachodnio i wschodniokarpackiej. 1896. I. 446.
— Kritische Bemerkungen über siebenbürgische Weiden. 1889. II. 103.[1]
— Materyały do flory Gór Łomnickich. 1892. I. 446.
— Przyczynek do flory Pokucia. 1887. I. 443.
— O roślinności Karpat. 1894. I. 446.
— O roślinności Karpat między Łomnicą a Oporem. 1892. I. 446.
— O rozróżnianiu Wierzb w stanie bezlistnym. 1886. II. 102.[2]
— Salices hybridae. 1898. II. 103.[1]
— Salices novae vel minus cognitae. 1891. II. 103.[1]
— Salix bifax und S. Mariana. 1888. II. 102.[2]
— Salix scrobigera. 1886. II. 110.[1]
— Sprawozdanie z wycieczek botanicznych w Karpaty Stryjskie. 1893. I. 446.
— O stosunku flory Pokucia do flory obszarów ościennych. 1889. I. 443.
— Uwagi nad " Roślinną szatą Gór Pokucko-Marmaroskich." 1890. I. 446.
— Zapiski botaniczne z Karpat Sądeckich. 1895. I. 446.

Wolski, Tomasz. O szkodach przez owady w lasach zrządzanych. 1830. IV. 209.[2]

Wolter, A. Führer in die Feldmess- und Nivellierkunst. 1883. III. 200.[1]

Woltersdorff, A. Broussonetia papyrifera L. und Cupressus funebris. 1854. II. 90,[1] 147.[1]
— Einige flüchtige Notizen über die Vegetation von Texas. 1849. I. 322.

Womačka, A. F. Abtriebsalter und Umtrieb. 1899. IV. 252.
— Das Capital im aussetzenden und jährlichen Betriebe. 1898. IV. 259.[1]
— Die Erhaltung der Wälder. 1876. IV. 177.[1]
— Der forstliche Wirthschaftszinsfuss. 1899. IV. 259.[1]
— Der Nutzeffect im aussetzenden und jährlichen Betriebe. 1899. IV. 259.[1]

Wondrák, Franz. Bemerkungen über den Wassertransport der Hölzer. 1899. IV. 390.[2]
— Zur Ehrenrettung der österreichischen Cameraltaxation. 1888. IV. 250.[1]
— Einige Bemerkungen über Formzahlen. 1895. IV. 259.[1]
— Zur Frage der Zirben-Kultur. 1880. IV. 463.[2]
— Zur Frage des galizischen Holzexportes. 1885. IV. 406.[2]

Wondrak, Ignaz. Verheerung junger Fichtenbestände. 1880. IV. 456.

Wonfox, W. J. & Pontifex, S. R. On the amount of tannine in some astringent substances. 1862. III. 237.[1]

Wood, Alphonso. The American botanist and florist. 1870. I. 307.

— A class-book of botany. 1845. I. 307, V. XVI.[2]
— Flora atlantica. 1879. I. 308.
— Leaves and flowers. 1877. V. X.[2]

Wood, Charles Henry. The progress of Cinchona cultivation ... in Bengal. 1878. III. 714.

Wood, Edward Septimus. Flowering of the large Bamboo at Dehra Dun. 1882. II. 59.[2]
— Note on strip fellings for Sál coppice. 1885. IV. 529.[1]
— Working plan of the Akona Sál forests. 1886. IV. 529.[1]
— *See also* BRANDIS, Sir Dietrich, STEWART, J. L. & WOOD, E.
— & Cotes, E. C. Beetle destructive to Sál coppice shoots. 1888. IV. 528.[2]

Wood, E. W. Dwarf Pear trees. 1874. III. 445.[2]
— Fruits best adapted for market purposes. 1881. III. 61.[2]

Wood, George Bacon & Bache, Franklin. The dispensatory of the United States. 1833. III. 246.

Wood, H. A season among the wild flowers. 1883. I.[*]534.[2]

Wood, Henry Trueman. Reports on the colonial sections of the exhibition. 1887. III. 28.[2]

Wood, Horatio C. Preliminary note on a new medicinal plant. 1877. III. 488.[2]
— *See also* MARSHALL, John & WOOD, H. C.

Wood, J. Eugenia Ugni. 1859. III. 638.[1]

Wood, J. O. Plum growing. 1900. III. 433.[2]

Wood, John Bland. Flora mancuniensis. 1840. I. 399.

Wood, John Medley. An analytical key to ... Natal indigenous plants. 1888. I. 495.
— Catalogue of plants in Natal botanic gardens, Durban. 1890. I. 69.[1]
— Furcraea gigautea var. 1898. III. 341.[2]
— A guide to the Natal botanical gardens. 1883. I. 69.[1]
— Guide to the trees and shrubs in the Natal botanic gardens, Durban. 1897. I. 69.[1]
— Natal. 1888. III. 281.[2]
— Preliminary catalogue of indigenous Natal plants. 1894. I. 495.
— & Evans, M. S. Natal plants. 1898. I. 495.
— — New Natal plants. 1897. I. 495.

Wood, Joseph. Notes of a botanical ramble in the north of Spain. 1858. I. 421.

Wood, Samuel. The tree planter and plant propagator. 1880. III. 153.
— The tree pruner. 1880. III. 172.

Wood, Thomas F. The North Carolina Crocus. 1882. II. 663.[2]
— Notes from North Carolina. 1882. II. 663.[2]
— & McCarthy, Gerald. Wilmington flora. 1886. I. 319.

Wood, W. Zoography. 1807. V. x.[2]

Wood, William. Nevv England's prospect. 1634. III. 262.[2]

Wood, William. Autumn and winter fruit-bearing trees. 1852. III. 207.[2]
— On the conditions of growth necessary to the production of bloom in Inga pulcherrima. 1848. III. 469.[2]
— Im Herbst und Winter fruchtragende [sic] Bäume. 1852. III. 207.[2]

Wood-Mason, James. *See* MASON, J. WOOD-.

Wood and iron. IV. 5.[2]

Wood and metal preservative. 1893. IV. 421.

Wood as a fuel for steam boilers. 1897. IV. 431.[2]

The wood business in Russia. 1884. IV. 383.[1]

Wood for cigar boxes. 1886. IV. 427.[1]

Wood for paving. 1893. IV. 533.[2]

Wood for railway sleepers. 1865. IV. 423.[2]

Wood for street paving. 1894. IV. 426.[1]

Wood for veneers. 1900. IV. 427.[1]

Wood for war-ships. 1885. IV. 425.[1]

Wood gas. 1889. IV. 433.[2]

The wood of the American turpentine tree. 1893. IV. 467.[1]

On wood oil. 1858. III. 610.[2]

Wood paper. 1885. IV. 430.

Wood paving from India. 1893. IV. 426.[1]

Wood-pulp. 1900. IV. 430.

Wood wool. *See* LAINE végétale ... 1853. IV. 482.[2]

The wood-worker. [Chicago]. *See* HOLZARBEITER. IV. 4.

Wood worker. [Indianapolis.] IV. 5.[2]

Wood-working machinery for estate purposes. 1880. IV. 393.

Wood-working trades journal. IV. 5.[2]

Woodall, Edward H. Fourcroya Beddinghausii. 1891. III. 341.[2]
— Tasmanian vegetation. 1878. I. 506.[1]
— Trees of the future. 1879. III. 123.[1]
— *See also* ROBERTS, Arkew & WOODALL, Edwards.

Woodcock. De Olijven en de Vijgencultuur op Sicilie. 1884. III. 126.[2]

Wooden and willow-ware trade review. IV. 5.[2]
Wooden cannons. 1897. IV. 425.[1]
Woodforde, James. A catalogue of the indigenous pheno-
gamic plants . . . of Edinburgh. 1824. I. 397.
Woodhouse, C. M. & C. Cinchona bark and quinine. 1899.
III. 719.
Wooding, John. Trees growing through a tombstone. 1885.
I. 187.
The woodland companion. See AIKIN, John. 1802. I. 393.[1]
Woodland gleanings. See TYAS, Robert. 1837. I. 393.[2]
Woodland rambles; conversations on timber trees. 1839. I.
393.[2]
Woodland sketches; portraits of trees. 1839. I. 393.[2]
Woodrow, G. Marshall. The cultivation of Oranges . . . in
India. 1891. III. 147,[1] 369,[1] 497.[2]
— The flora of western India. 1897. I. 475.[2]
— Gardening in India. 1889. III. 116.[1]
— List of drugs grown in the Botanical gardens, Gunesh
Khind, Poona. 1876. I. 67.[1]
— Note on Cassia grandis. 1891. III. 470.[1]
— Notes on a journey from Haveri to Kumta. 1894. I. 475.[2]
— Notes on a journey from Poona to Nagotna. 1895. I.
475.[2]
— Plants of a Bombay swamp. 1897. II. 562.[2]
— Seedling Orange trees. 1897. III. 500.[2]
Woodruff, E. Préparation de l'aloïne. 1890. III. 333.[2]
Woodruff, Samuel. The rattle-snake . . . disarmed by the
leaves of the White Ash. 1833. IV. 534.[2]
Woods, Albert Fred. Diseased Hydrangea leaves. 1899.
III. 411.[1]
— Notes on the cañon flora of Sioux county. 1893. I. 326.
— Observations on the Cottonwood. 1889. II. 97.[1]
— Principles of pruning. 1896. III. 171, 180.[2]
— See also BESSEY, C. E. & WOODS, A. F.; GALLOWAY, B. T.
& WOODS, A. F.
Woods, Charles D. & Merrill, L. H. Nuts as food. 1899.
III. 220.[2]
Woods, Joseph. Über die brittischen Gattungen von Rosa.
1818. II. 285.[1]
— On the genus Rubus. 1855. II. 300.[1]
— A synopsis of the British species of Rosa. 1818. II. 285.[1]
— The tourist's flora. 1850. I. 349.
Woods, Julian Edmund TENISON-. On Arauja albens Don.
1880. II. 736.[1]
— Botanical notes on Queensland. 1883. I. 503.
— The forest resources of Tasmania. 1879. I. 505, IV. 89.[2]
— On the relations of the Brisbane flora. 1880. I. 502.
— Tasmanian forests; their botany. 1879. I. 505, IV. 89,[1]
402.[1]
— On the vegetation of Malaysia. 1890. I. 466.
— See also BAILEY, F. M. & WOODS, J. E. TENISON-.
The woods! 1852. IV. 269.
Woods and forests. IV. 12.[1]
The woods and forests act. 1882. IV. 332.[2]
Woods and forests and timber price current. IV. 12.[2]
Woods and forests in the United Kingdom. 1900. IV. 261.[2]
Woods and manufactures of wood shown at the International
exhibition. 1863. IV. 19.[1]
Woods grown at Madras.—Cedrela Toona. 1856. IV. 525.
Amongst the woods of Morayshire. See AMONGST the woods of
Morayshire. 1881. IV. 359.[1]
The woods of New Zealand. 1885. IV. 402.[1]
Woods of the Philippine Islands. 1864. IV. 399.[1]
Woodville, William. Medical botany. 1790. III. 55.
Woodward, John. Some thoughts and experiments concern-
ing vegetation. 1700. I. 157.
Woodward's record of horticulture. III. 9.
Woodworth, D. A. First lessons in botany. 183.? I. 86.
Wooler, W. A. To grow the Mistleto. 1878. III. 385.[1]
— The Hawthorn, worked on the Pear. 1870. III. 422.[2]
Woolls, William. Botanical notes. 1887. II. 404.[2]
— Botanik der Eschen-Insel in Australien. 1862. I. 502.
— On the classification of Eucalypts. 1885. II. 623.[1] —
1892. II. 623.[2]
— A contribution to the flora of Australia. 1867. I. 502.
— The destruction of Eucalyptus. 1892. IV. 530.
— Double flowers. 1885. I. 145.[2]
— Eucalypts of the county of Cumberland. 1881. II. 623.[1]
— Sur les Eucalyptus. 1880. II. 623.[1]
— On the genus Dodonaea. 1891. II. 485.[2]
— A glance at the flora of Mount Wilson. 1888. I. 504.
— Lectures on the vegetable kingdom. 1879. I. 502.
— On the Myrtaceae of Australia. 1885. II. 619.[2]
— Note on Crowea exalata. 1887. II. 404.[2]

— Note on Eucalyptus leucoxylon. 1887. II. 625.[1]
— Notes on some specimens of plants collected at King
George's Sound. 1893. I. 504.
— Plants indigenous and naturalised . . . Sidney. 1880. I.
502.
— Plants indigenous in the neighborhood of Sydney. 1880.
I. 502.
— The plants of New South Wales. 1882. I. 503.
— Plants of N. S. Wales having medicinal properties. 1888.
III. 94.[1]
— Progress of botanical discovery in Australia. 1869. I. 82.[1]
— The Proteaceae of Australia. 1886. II. 158.[2]
— Remarks on the past . . . of the Australian flora. 1900.
I. 505.
— On the sanitary properties of Eucalyptus. 1886. IV. 531.[2]
— Sapindaceae of Australia. 1889. II. 483.[2]
— Species of Eucalypts first known in Europe. 1883. II. 623.[1]
— Species plantarum paramattensium. 1871. I. 502.
— Specimens of plants collected at King George's Sound.
1890. I. 504.
Woolrych, L. F. Uses of the Eucalypti. 1900. IV. 532.[1]
Woolson, G. A. The story of Trailing Arbutus. 1890. III.
643.[2]
Woolson, George C. Pachystima Canbyi in cultivation.
1891. III. 533.[1]
Woolverton, L. Fruits of Ontario. 1898. III. 62.
Wooster, David. Alpine plants. 1872. III. 83.[1]
Wooton, Elmer Ottis. New plants from New Mexico. 1898.
I. 327.
— A new southwestern Rose. 1898. II. 299.[1]
A word about timber. 1873. IV. 396.[1]
Worgitzky, Georg Eugen. Vergleichende Anatomie der
Ranken. 1887. I. 236.[1]
The world-old Yew. 1892. II. 11.[1]
World's industrial and Cotton centennial exposition. See
ALBRECHT, Joseph. 1885. I. 317.[1] — McLERAN, Benja-
min. 1885. IV. 19.[1]
Worlidge, John. A compleat system of husbandry. 1716.
III. 108.
— Systema agriculturae. 1669. III. 107.
— Systema horti-culturae. 1677. III. 107.
— Vinetum britannicum. 1676. III. 141.
Worm, Olaf. Museum Wormianum. 1655. I. 286.
A worm out river. 1894. IV. 46.[1]
Woronin, Michael. Ueber den Bau des Stammes von Caly-
canthus. 1860. II. 214.[1]
— Bemerkung zu dem Aufsatze von Herrn H. Möller über
Plasmodiophora Alni. 1885. IV. 488.[2]
— Zur Black-Rot-Frage in Russland. 1898. III. 582.
— Exobasidium Vaccinii. 1867. III. 663.[1]
— Kurze Notiz über Monilia fructigena. 1897. III. 431.[1]
— Observations sur certaines excroissances . . . de l'Aune.
1867. II. 115.[2]
— Ueber Peziza baccarum. 1885. III. 663.[1]
— Ueber die Pilzwurzel . . . von B. Frank. 1885. I. 233.[2]
— Über die bei der Schwarzerle . . . auftretenden Wurzel-
anschwellungen. 1866. III. 141.
— Die Sclerotienkrankheit der gemeinen Traubenkirsche.
1895. III. 439,[1] 459.[2]
— Über die Sclerotienkrankheit der Vaccinieen-Beeren. 1888.
III. 663.[1]
— & Nawaschin, S. Sclerotinia heteroica. 1896. III. 647.[1]
Worrall, Thomas D. On the destruction of the Big tree.
1883. I. 295.[1]
Worsdell, W. C. The anatomical structure of Bowenia.
1900. II. 3.[2]
— The anatomy of the stem of Macrozamia. 1896. II. 3.[2]
— The comparative anatomy of certain genera of the Cycada-
ceae. 1898. II. 3.[2]
— The comparative anatomy of certain species of Encepha-
lartos. 1900. II. 3.[2]
— Observations on the . . . female flowers of Coniferae.
1899. II. 20.[1]
— On the origin of "transfusion tissue." 1897. II. 18.
— The principles and practice of grafting. 1898. III. 163.[2]
— The principles and practice of pruning. 1898. III. 171.
— The structure of the female flower in Coniferae. 1900.
II. 20.[1]
— On transfusion-tissue. 1897. I. 111, II. 1.
— The vascular structure of the ovule of Cephalotaxus. 1900.
II. 8.[1]
— The vascular structure of the sporophylls of the Cyca-
daceae. 1898. II. 3.[2]
— See also BOODLE, L. A. & WORSDELL, W. C.

Worsley, C. F. Roadside arboriculture in Bengal. 1893. III. 211.[1]

Ein **Wort** über die Behandlung . . . der Wälder in Bünden. 1812. IV. 123.[1]

Worth, James. An account of the insect so destructive to the Peach tree. 1823. III. 441.[2]

Worth, R. Hansford. The relation of leaf and stem. 1899. I. 103.

Wortmann, Julius. Einige Bemerkungen zu der . . . gegen meine Theorie des Windens gerichteten Erwiderung. 1886. I. 196.[2]

— Ueber die Natur der rotirenden Nutation. 1886. I. 196.[2]

— Ueber die rotirenden Bewegungen der Ranken. 1887. I. 197.[1]

— Über das sogen. "Stippen" der Äpfel. 1892. III. 428.[1]

— Theorie des Windens. 1886. I. 196.[2]

Woschkius, Christoph. Discursus de balsamo. See WAGNER, G. F. 1683. III. 510.[2]

Wossidlo, Paulus. Quaedam additamenta ad Palmarum anatomiam. 1860. II. 62.[2]

— Über die Structur der Jubaea spectabilis. 1861. II. 69.[2]

— Ueber Wachsthum und Structur der Drachenbäume. 1868. I. 81.[2]

Wragg, John. Forestry. 1859. IV. 112.

— New ornamental plants and trees. 1894. III. 60.

— Propagation and uses of the Conifers. 1885. III. 294.[1]

— Seedling evergreens. 1888. III. 293.

Wragg, M. J. Not well known trees, shrubs and Conifers. 1886. III. 60.

— Ornamental trees and shrubs. 1885. III. 118.[1]

— Propagation of stone fruits. 1892. III. 430.[2] — 1898. III. 431.[1]

— Rocky mountain Conifers. 1900. III. 293.

Wragg, N. C. How I plant evergreens. 1896. III. 295.[1]

Wrangel, W., baron. See Врангель, В., барон.

Wray. An extract of another letter . . . containing some experiments about the bleeding of the Sycamore. 1670. I. 168.

— See also WILLOUGHBY, Francis & WRAY.

Wray, Leonard, (jr.). Gutta-producing trees. 1883. III. 229.

— On the Malayan fish poison. 1893. III. 475.[1]

— Notes on the cultivation . . . of Patchouli. 1890. III. 698.[1]

— On rubber and ramie cultivation in Perak. 1898. III. 518.[2]

Wrbata, Josef. Die Exkursion . . . in den Wiener Wald. 1874. IV. 371.

— Ueber Forstaervitute. 1869. IV. 335.

— Lesní kázáni. 187.? IV. 111.[1]

— Die Mineralkohle und die Forstwirthschaft in Böhmen. 1880. IV. 279.[1]

— Nachtrag zur Frage über . . . Rothfäule der Fichte. 1871. IV. 455.

— Pralea a les uudle pěstovaný. 1872. IV. 123.[2]

— Die Rothfäule der Fichte. 1870. IV. 455.

— Die Schnee- und Windbruch-Schäden . . . 1868. 1869. IV. 190.

Wrede, Ernst Christian Conrad. Verzeichniss meiner Rosen. 1814. III. 447.[2]

Wrede, J. H. P. Pomologisches Handbuch. 1803. III. 70.

Wredow, Johann Christian Ludwig. Gartenfreund. 1818. III. 103.

— Oekonomisch-technische Flora Meklenburgs. 1811. III. 72.

— Tabellarische Uebersicht derin Meklenburg wildwachsenden . . . Pflanzengeschlechter. 1807. I. 376.

Wretschko, Mathias. Beitrag zur Entwicklung der Inflorescens . . . der Asperifolien. 1866. II. 747.[2]

— Beitrag zur Entwickelungsgeschichte getheilter und gefiederter Blattformen. 1865. I. 110.

— Zur Entwicklungsgeschichte des Laubblattes. 1862. I. 110.

— Über Metamorphose der Pflanzen. 1867. I. 101.[2]

— Ueber Saftbewegung. 1868. I. 164.

— Vorschule der Botanik. 1865. I. 90.

Wright, A. H. On the manna of the Scriptures. 1847. III. 221.[1]

— Notices of Koordistan. 1847. III. 221.[1]

Wright, Albert Allen. Preliminary list of . . . plants of Lorain county, Ohio. 1889. I. 315.

Wright, Alder. See PIESSE, Charles & WRIGHT, Alder.

— & **Patterson**, G. Sur l'acide citrique des Mûres. 1878. III. 381.[1]

— & **Rennie**, E. H. Glycyphylline. 1881. III. 338.[2]

Wright, Charles Henry. Cocos Weddelliana. 1898. II. 68.[1]

Wright, Charles Romley Alder. On the essential oil of Nutmegs. 1873. III. 403.[1]

— On the essential oil of orange. 1873. III. 501.[2]

— Isomeric terpenes and their derivatives. 1873. III. 499.[1]

— & **Piesse**, C. H. The oxidation products of essential oil of orange-peel. 1871. III. 501.[2]

— On the oxidation products of the essential oil of orange peel. 1871. III. 501.[2]

Wright, Charles W. On Liquidambar styraciflua. 1857. III. 417.[2]

Wright, Edward Percival. Contributions towards . . . flora of the Seychelles. 1869. I. 482.

— Note sur la culture de Coco de mer. 1880. III. 327.[1]

— Notes on the Lodoicea sechellarum. 1868. II. 70.[2]

— Six months at the Seychelles. 1868. I. 482.

Wright, Elizur. The voice of a tree from the Middlesex Fells. 1883. V. xxxi.[2]

Wright, F. W. Oregonian forms of Umbellularia. 1895. II. 228.[2]

Wright, Floy L. The Sugar Maple. 1892. II. 480.[2]

Wright, John. The fruit grower's guide. 1892. III. 142.

— & **Hall**, James. A catalogue of plants . . . in the vicinity of Troy. 1836. I. 313.

— Notes on the Cypress swamps of Knox county. 1898. II. 51.[2]

Wright, Philip B. See BRISTOWE, L. W. & WRIGHT, P. B.

Wright, S. G. Leaf movement in Cercis canadensis. 1894. II. 345.[2]

— The minute structure . . . of the motile organ in the leaf of the Red Bud. 1894. II. 345.[2]

Wright, S. T. Fruit-culture for amateurs. 1897. III. 142.

Wright, Thomas. Vegetable fibres used in brush-making. 1898. III. 235.[1]

— On vegetable ivory. 1891. III. 330.[1]

Wright, William. Bible helps. 1896. I. 513.

— The illustrated Bible treasury. 1896. I. 513.

Wright, William, (1735–1819). An account of the medicinal plants growing in Jamaica. 1787. III. 64.[1]

— A botanical . . . account of the Quassia Simaruba. 1778. III. 509.[2]

— Description and use of the Cabbage-bark tree. 1778. II. 361.[1]

— Description of the Jesuits bark tree of Jamaica. 1778. II. 816.[1]

— Ueber die auf Jamaika wachsenden . . . gebräuchlichen Pflanzen. 1787. III. 64.[1]

Wrightson, Mathias. Fr. Analyse der Asche des Holzes . . . von Ulmus. 1845. II. 144.[1]

Wróblewski, W. O pochodzeniu stepów południowowschodniej Europy. 1895. I. 366.

Wroughton, R. C. A Japanese timber slide. 1893. IV. 390.[1]

Wskazówki krótkie do zakładania i utrzymywania szkołek owocowych. 1865. III. 138.

Wszechświat. I. 28.[2]

Wttewaal, Jan. Over het aankweeken van Doorns tot heggen. 1848. III. 213.

— De aanwending van zwavel tegen druivenziekte. 1857. III. 577.

— De arborum sylvestrium plantatione. 1839. IV. 119.[1]

— Het Beekberger woud. 1836. IV. 356.[1]

— Het behandelen van opgaande boomen. 1856. III. 121.[2]

— Over de behandeling van niet gesnoeide boomen. 1847. III. 121.[2]

— Iets belangrijks over het aankweeken van vruchtboomen. 1847. III. 139.

— Berken-spintkever. 1858. IV. 490.[3]

— Bladluizen. 1853. III. 189.

— Bosschen in de gemeente voorst. 1860. IV. 71.

— De dennenscheerder. 1849. IV. 475.

— Deugdzaamheid van het hout in verband met het jaargetijde, waarin de boom gekapt wordt. 1861. IV. 384.[2]

— De Douglas-Den. 1853. III. 309.[2]

— De Gaspeldoorn. 1851. III. 490.[1]

— Hoe kan eene vermindering van meikevers het best verkregen worden. 1861. IV. 202.

— De iepen-spintkever. 1858. III. 364.[1]

— Iets over het gebruik van het hout der Wilgen tot klompen. 1859. IV. 487.[3]

— Iets over het ontstaan . . . van den stengel. 1837. I. 105.

— Kort verslag van . . . de schadelijke insecten. 1861. III. 189.

Wttewaal, Jan (*continued*).
— Over het kweeken van plantsoen. 1856. IV. 119.[1]
— De Larix-mot. 1853. IV. 450.
— De Larix-schorsluis. 1855. IV. 450.
— Het leiden van een Perzikboom. 1857. III. 440.[2]
— De Moeras-eik. 1854. III. 362.[2]
— Over het nadeelige van het snoeijen. 1839. III. 169.[1]
— De nieuwe arkadische Spar. 1861. II. 24.[3]
— Nog iets over het vernielen der bosschen door de Bombyx dispar. 1848. IV. 549.[3]
— Over de noodzakelijkheid om de stompen . . . te rooijen. 1859. IV. 388.[3]
— Het ophouden der vernieling door de dennenrupsen in Nederland aangericht. 1847. IV. 549.[2]
— Opmerkingen bij het bepalen van de sterkte der onderscheidene houtsoorten. 1856. IV. 415.[2]
— Opmerkingen wegens Appelboomgaarden. 1841. III. 426.[1]
— De Paarden-kastanje als veevoeder. 1848. III. 538.[1]
— Plant de boomen ruim. 1849. III. 169.[1]
— Het planten van Dennen zonder kluit. 1852. IV. 472.
— Het rooijen van stompen in de jonge Dennenbosschen. 1859. IV. 386.
— Schadelijke insekten. 1860. III. 189.
— Le semis des Bouleaux. 1852. III. 357.[1]
— Snoei toch geen halfwassen opgaande boomen. 1860. III. 170.
— De snuitkever van het eikenblad. 1848. IV. 509.
— Sterke rupsenvraat aan eikenhakhout. 1848. IV. 509.
— De Surinaamsche houtsoorten. 1856. IV. 398.[1]
— Vernieling van insecten in dennenbosschen. 1851. IV. 442.
— Het verpoten van boomen in den nazomer. 1858. III. 168.[2]
— Het verpoten van groote boomen. 1861. III. 167.
— Verslag van den landbouw in Nederland. 1852. III. 122.[1]
— Volksboek over schadelijke en nuttige insecten. 1864. III. 189.
— Weerden-hakbosschen tot Hoephout. 1847. IV. 487.[1]
— Het wegnemen van de schors bij vruchtboomen. 1852. III. 175.[3]
— Wijze om . . . boomen te enten. 1851. III. 161.
Wucher, Peter. Ueber Waldverwüstung und Güterzertrümmerung. 1875. IV. 274.[1]
Wucherer, Johannes. Etwas über Rosenkultur. 1886. III. 452.
Ueber das **Wuchsverhalten** einiger exotischer Coniferen. 1889. IV. 127.[2]
Wüling, M. *See* ВЮЛЬФИНГЪ, M.
Wuensche, Johan Georg. Enumeratio plantarum circa Vitebergam. 1804. I. 375.
Wünsche, Otto. Die Alpenpflanzen. 1893. I. 437.
— Excursionsflora für das Königreich Sachsen. 1869. V. XIX.[2]
— Die Pflanzen des Königreichs Sachsen. 1869. V. XIX.[2]
— Die Pflanzen Deutschlands. 1871. I. 532.[1]
— Schulflora von Deutschland. 1871. I. 532.[1]
Wünscher, Friedrich. Ori at formere Rhododendron. 1838. III. 656.
— Die Vermehrung des Rhododendron arboreum. 1836. III. 657.[1]
Würdigung der Wälder. 1854. IV. 269.
Würnitzer, Franz Sales. Versuch über die Waldkultur. 1796. IV. 110.[3]
Würtemberg Schwarzwald. 1900. IV. 356.[1]
Würtembergische Lehranstalt für Land- und Forstwirtschaft in Hohenheim. *See* Die KÖNIGL. Württembergische . . . 1842. IV. 31.
Würtembergischer landwirthschafter Verein. *See* KÖNIGL. WÜRTEMBERGISCHER . . . III. 12.
Würtenberger, Alexander. Die einträgliche Beerenkultur. 1891. III. 147.[3]
Württemberg — **Forststatistische** Mittheilungen. *See* FORSTSTATISTISCHE . . . IV. 8.
Württemberg — **Verein für vaterländische Naturkunde**. *See* VEREIN . . . I. 15.
Württembergischer Forstverein. Bericht. Vorträge. IV. 11.
Württembergisches Wochenblatt für Landwirthschaft. *See* WOCHENBLATT für Land . . . IV. 11.
Wuertz, Georg Christoph. Conamen mappae generalis medicamentorum simplicium. 1778. IV. 450.
Würzburg — **Botanisches Institut**. *See* BOTANISCHES . . . I. 11.

Würzburg — **Physikalisch-medicinische Gesellschaft**. *See* PHYSIKALISCH-MEDICINISCHE . . . I. 14.
Würzburger naturwissenschaftliche Zeitschrift. *See* PHYSIKALISCH-MEDICINISCHE GESELLSCHAFT, WÜRZBURG. I. 14.
Wüst, Valentin. Farbenveränderung unserer Laubhölzer. 1900. IV. 492.[1]
Wüstemann, Einiges über das Veredeln der Bäume. 1854. III. 164.[2]
Wüstemann, Ernst Friedrich. Ueber die Kunstgärtnerei bei den alten Römern. 1846. III. 33.[2]
— Die Rose. 1859. II. 290.[2]
— Unterhaltungen aus der alten Welt für Garten- und Blumenfreunde. 1854. III. 32.[2]
Wuestenfeld, Ferdinand. Geschichte der arabischen Aerzte und Naturforscher. 1840. I. 81.[1]
Wüthrich, E. Ueber die Einwirkung von Metallsalzen. 1892. III. 197.
Wukasinović, Anton. Praktisch-populäre Regeln zur Maulbeerbaum- und Seidenzucht. 1808. III. 377.
Wu K'i-stin. Chi wu ming shi t'u k'ao. 1848. V. XXIII.[2]
Wulf, J. B. de. Traité abregé de la culture des arbres fruitiers. 1819. III. 140.[1]
Wulfen, Franz Xaver. Flora norica phanerogama. 1858. I. 441.
— Plantae rariores carinthiacae. 1778. I. 438.
— Plantarum rariorum descriptiones. 1805. I. 348.[3]
Wulff, J. Beobachtungen über das Verderben der Bucheckern. 1899. IV. 496.
— Die Buchenverjüngung in Schleswig-Holstein. 1893. IV. 496.
Wulff, Johann Christoph. Flora borussica. 1765. I. 373.
— Specimen inaugurale plantas xxiii in Borussia . . . comprehendens. 1744. I. 373.
Wulff, T. Studien über verstopfte Spaltöffnungen. 1898. I. 132.[1]
Wulfsberg, N. G. I. Holarrhena Africana. 1880. II. 726.[2]
Wullschlegel, J. Der japanes. Eichenseidenspinner. 1865. IV. 501.[2]
— Mittheilungen über einen Feind des Weinstockes. 1869. III. 563.
— Mittheilungen über Einführung . . . neuer Seidenspinner. 1863. III. 148.[1]
Wullstein, (*Forst- und Baurath, Töppendorf*). Ueber Bauholz-Berechtigungen und deren Ablösung. 1844. IV. 333.
— Zur Beantwortung der Frage: Wie ist eine Fläche, welche im Sommer zwar sehr trocken . . . anzubauen? 1852. IV. 141.
— Zur Beantwortung der Frage: Wie klein kann ein Forst-Grundstück sein? 1852. IV. 242.
— Einige Bemerkungen über das Verhalten der Weisserle. 1857. IV. 489.[2]
— Erfahrungen über . . . Ertrag aus eingeschlagenen jungen Nadelhölzern. 1863. IV. 260.[3]
— Ueber die Hinwirkung bei dem Holzanbau darauf, dass derselbe . . . Boden verbessernd sei. 1852. IV. 68.
— *See also* BRUNNEMANN & WULLSTEIN.
Wunderbar, R. J. Biblisch-talmudische Medicin. 1850. III. 238.[3]
Wunderlich, W. F. H. Insulinde, land en volk. 1895. I. 466.
Die **Wundertanne** im Peloponnes. 1860. II. 24.[3]
Die **wundervollen** Eichenforste der slavonischen Militärgrenze. 1869. IV. 373.
Wundram, C. L. Ueber Anlegung und Wartung lebendiger Hecken. 1803. III. 212.[3]
— Nachricht von dem . . . wildwachsenden Bohnenbaume. 1799. II. 368.[2]
— Ueber die successive Abnahme der Höhe und Stärke unserer Waldbäume. 1803. IV. 117.
Wunschmann, Friedrich. Deutschlands gefährliche Giftpflanzen. 1833. III. 73.
Wurfbain. Liberia-Koffie. 1895. III. 743.[1]
Wurm, W. Waldgeheimnisse. 1895. V. X.[2]
Wurmb, von. Ueber die Verkohlung des Holzes. 1830. IV. 394.
Wurmb, F. van. De krullende Moespalm. 1787. II. 4.[1]
— De orde der Palmboomen. 1781. II. 61.[2]
Wurstemberger. Einiges über den Holzfrevel. 1858. IV. 196.[2]
— Quelques mots sur les délits forestiers. 1858. IV. 196.[2]
Wurster. Procédé pour reconnaître le papier fabriqué avec du bois. 1890. IV. 430.
Wurthner, **Lieventhal** & **Weyrich**, Rudolf. Dosage de la théine. 1873. III. 607.

Wurtz, Charles Adolphe. La Papaina. 1882. III. 617.[2]
— Sur la papaine. 1880. III. 617.[2]
— & **Bouchut**, E. Sur le ferment-digestif du Carica. 1879. III. 617.[1]
Die **Wurzelbergstannen**. 1895. IV. 447.[1]
Wurzelbildung einer Libanotischen Ceder. 1886. I. 526,[2] II. 83.[1]
Der **Wurzelbrecher**. 1859. IV. 386.
✓**Wyatt**, W. & **Thornton**, C. G. Flora repandunensis. 1866. I. 402.
Wybrand, K. Eenige opmerkingen . . . voor den bijplant van Koffie. 1899. III. 731.
Wydler, Heinrich. Ueber accessorische Sprossen. 1852. I. 106.[1]
— Ueber dichotome Verzweigung der Blüthenaxen. 1843. I. 113.[1]
— Über einige Eigenthümlichkeiten der Gattung Passiflora. 1852. II. 577.[1]
— Ueber einige Fälle dichasialer . . . Verzweigung vegetativer Axen. 1876. II. 410.[1]
— Extrait d'une lettre sur la formation de l'embryon. 1838. I. 121.
— Fragment zur Kenntniss der Verstäubungsfolge der Antheren. 1851. I. 524.[1]
— Kleinere Beiträge zur Kenntniss einheimischer Gewächse. 1859. · I. 99.
— Die Knospenlage der Blätter. 1850. I. 109.[2]
— Zur Morphologie . . . der dichotomen Blüthenstände. 1878.. I. 113.[2]
— Morphologische Beiträge. 1845. I. 113.[1]
— Morphologische Mittheilungen. 1857. I. 99.
— Morphologische Notizen. Ilex Aquifolium. 1854. II. 463.[3]
— Morphologisches. 1857. II. 289.[1]
— Note sur la formation de l'embryon. 1838. I. 121.
— Plantarum quarundam descriptiones. 1830. II. 771.[2]
— Ueber die Stellung des Blüthenzweiges bei den Linden. 1846. II. 516.[1]
— Ueber die symmetrische Verzweigungsweise dichotomer Inflorescenzen. 1851. I. 113.[1]
— Verstäubungsfolge der Antheren von Lonicera. 1856. II. 833.[1]
Wydrzyński, Klemens. Przewodnik służby leśnej rządowej. 1853. IV. 289.[1]
— Urządzenie lasów w Królestwie Polskiem. 1862. IV. 345.
Wyeth, N. B. & **Nuttall**, Thomas. A catalogue of a collection of plants . . . Rocky Mountains. 1834. I. 321.
Die **Wylerlinde**. 1890. II. 517.[1]
Wylie, Jacob. Pharmacopœia castrensis ruthená. 1808. III. 247.[2]
— Pharmacopœia castrensis ruthenica. 1808. III. 247.[2]
— Russische Militärpharmakopöe. 1808. III. 247.[2]
Wyneken, B. Zwangs-Versicherungs-Genossenschaften der Rebcultur-Besitzer. 1878. III. 760.
Wyniki akcyi zalesienia wydm piaszczystych. 1899. IV. 168.[1]
Wynne, Arthur Beever. Note on submerged peat mosses. 1886. I. 393.[1]
Wynne, Gabriel. De cortice peruviano. 1779. III. 720.
Wynveldt, J. F. De Pepercultuur in de Lampongdistricten. 1887. III. 343.[1]
Wyoming—Agricultural experiment station. *See* WYOMING, UNIVERSITY OF . . . III. 9.
Wyoming, University of—**Agricultural** college department — Wyoming experiment station. Annual report. Bulletin. III. 9.
Wyplel, Martin. Beiträge zur näheren Kenntniss der Nutation. 1879. I. 194.
Wyssotzky, G. Einfluss des Waldes auf die Regenmenge. 1899. IV. 46.[2]
— L'humidité du sol et du sous-sol. 1900. IV. 46.[1]
Wyżycki, Józef Gerald. Zielnik ekonomiczno-techniczny. 1845. III. 52.

—**x**—. Die Acclimatisation fremder Holzarten. 1875. IV. 125.[1]
X. Over den aanleg van Koffie-tuinen. 1872. III. 726.[2]
X. Beitrag zur Höhen-Mess-Kunde. 1869. IV. 215.
X. Comisión de repoblación de la cuenca del Júcar. 1890. IV. 546.[2]
X. La comisión de repoblación de la cuenca del Segura. 1893. IV. 547.[1]
X. Commerce des bois. 1895. IV. 557.[1]

X. Compte rendu des excursions de 1897. 1897. IV. 544.[2]
X. La corteza de Mimosa. 1887. IV. 521.[1]
X. Les coupes blanches. 1897. IV. 545.[1]
X. El cuerpo de montes en la Exposición de Murcia. 1900. IV. 540.[1]
X. De la délimitation des forêts communales dans les Ardennes belges. 1895. IV. 551.[2]
X. La desamortizacion de los montes del estado. 1883. IV. 276.[2]
X. Das Diensteinkommen der grossherzoglich hessischen Forstbeamten. 1863. IV. 290.[2]
X. Les droits d'entrée sur les bois. 1894. IV. 552.[2]
X. Een en ander over Liberiakoffie. 1893. III. 742.[2]
X. Eenige wetenswaardigheden omtrent de theebereiding. 1900. III. 608.[2]
X. Ueber den am 1. Juni 1890 stattgehabten Spätfrostschaden. 1891. IV. 191.[2]
X. Estimation des bois incendiés. 1894. IV. 551.[1]
X. Greffe-racine. 1897. III. 164.[1]
X. Iets over de bemesting der Koffietuinen. 1897. III. 734.[1]
X. Importation des bois. 1894. IV. 552.[1]
X. Inyección de maderas con la creosota. 1878. IV. 420.
X. Koffiebladziekte. 1893. III. 736.[1]
X. Liga forestal del imperio alemán. 1899. IV. 541.[1]
X. Note sur les Bambous: 1850. III. 315.[1]
X. Nouveau procédé d'extraction du caoutchouc. 1900. III. 232.[2]
X. Nuevos trabajos agricolas y forestales en los Estados Unidos. 1887. IV. 551.[1]
X. Observations sur la greffe en fente. 1849. III. 160.
X. Pantógrafo de precision. 1885. IV. 265.
X. Le parc de la Zangerey. 1894. III. 28.[2]
X. Ueber das Pfropfen in den Spalt. 1849. III. 160.
X. Des plantations d'arbres à haute et basse tige. 1889. III. 200.[2]
X. Un problema forestal. 1884. IV. 257.
X. Producción de los montes de las Landas. 1885. IV. 361.[2]
X. Proyecto de ley sobre concesión á los pueblos de terrenos. 1887. IV. 551.[2]
X. Situation de la production des écorces de Chêne. 1898. IV. 515.[2]
X. Les Sureaux. 1899. III. 752.[2]
X. Les tarifs de transport des bois. 1894. IV. 552.[2] — 1895. IV. 552.[2]
X. De toekomst der Koffie en Suikercultuur. 1888. III. 128.
X. Unificación ó división de servicios. 1887. IV. 553.[1]
X. Utilisation particulière du Genêt d'Espagne. 1881. III. 477.[1]
X. Sobre la venta de los montes. 1892. IV. 552.[1]
X. Volume ou contenance? 1897. IV. 238, 550.[1]
X., M. Forêts particulières. 1893. IV. 261.[2]
X, Y, Z. L'embellissement des campagnes. 1896. IV. 137.[1]
X —. L'écorcement artificiel. 1878. IV. 434.
X ***. Maladies du Caféier en Cochinchine. 1898. III. 737.
Xanthopoulos, S. *See* Ξανθόπουλος, Σ.
Xérica, Ramón de. La teoria y la práctica de la resinación. 1869. IV. 436.[2]
Xuarez, Gaspare. *See* GILII, F. L. & XUAREZ, Gaspare.
Xylophilus, (*pseud.*). Landbouwbrieven. Houttuett. 1858. IV. 119.[1]

—**y**. The capabilities of the Weymouth Pine. 1881. IV. 470.[2]
—**y**. Forstliche Verhältnisse in Bulgarien. 1894. IV. 375.[1]
—**y**. Zum Forstwesen in Algier. 1892. IV. 262.
—**y**. Die Forstwirthschaft in Tirol. 1899. . IV. 370.
—**y**. Forstwirtschaftliches aus Rumänien. 1893. IV. 375.[1]
—**y**. Die Leistungsfähigkeit der Weymuthskiefer. 1881. IV. 470.[2]
—**y**. Zierstecklinge. 1885. III. 158.
—**y** —. Die Organisation des Forstbetriebes. 1886. IV. 368.
—**y** —. Die Schneesaat. 1884. IV. 149.[1]
—**y** —. Die Stammgrundstärkenmessung an Berglehnen. 1884. IV. 218.
—**y** —. Täuschungen bei der Massenertragsschätzung. 1883. IV. 218.
—**y** —. Ueber Verbauung von Schneelawinen. 1896. IV. 183.[2]
—**y** —. Die Versicherung . . . der forstwirthschaftlichen Arbeiter. 1887. IV. 311.[1]
Y. Aufforstungen . . . in Turkestan. 1894. IV. 168.[1]

Reorganización del servicio forestal. 1892. IV. 553.[2]
Uses of Larch wood. 1891. IV. 452.[1]
Y. Wie kann man den Waldfrevel gründlich abschaffen? 1799. IV. 313.
Y. (*Dr.*). Die Waldungen Korsika's. 1890. IV. 361.
Y., van. Koffie-cultuur in Serdang. 1900. III. 732.[1]
Y., A. Conifères nouveaux. 1845. III. 289.
Y., A. H. Zanthoxylum americanum. 1877. III. 506.[1]
Y., C. E. d'. A propos du bêchage dans les taillis. 1896. IV. 132.[2]
Y., D. J. The Ash and its uses. 1885. IV. 535.[2]
Y., D. J. English firewood. 1886. IV. 431.[2]
Y., D. J. The White Beam tree. 1888. III. 459.[2]
Y., D. Y. The care of unsawn timber. 1886. IV. 416.[2]
Y., E. A propos des plantations routières. 1900. III. 211.[1]
Y., V. O. Robiniers. Note relative aux chancres. 1899. IV. 524.[1]
Y., X. Spari contro le nubi da grandine. 1899. IV. 191.[1]
Yachnoff, L. *See* YASHNOF, L.
Yahito, Foukouba & others. Situation de la Vigne dans l'empire du Japon. 1886. III. 559.[1]
Yahyâ ibn Muhammad ibn Ahmad ibn al 'Awâmm. Le livre de l'agriculture. 1864. III. 99.
Yale forest school. 1900. IV. 30.[1]
Yanishevski, D. *See* ЯНИШЕВСКІЙ, Д.
Yanitzki, I. *See* ЯНИЦКІЙ, I.
Yarde, H. H. Pterocarpus santalinus. 1883. IV. 522.[1]
Yardley Oaks and other notable Oak-trees. 1874. II. 138.[2]
Yaroshevski, K. F. *See* ЯРОШЕВСКІЙ, K. Ѳ.
Yashnof, L. Description générale de la forêt de Krasnostanskaia. *See* YACHNOFF. 1900. IV. 347.
— Description générale de la forêt des apanages de Nelengsko-Kokovinskaia. *See* YACHNOFF. 1899. IV. 347.
— Die günstigste Temperatur für Keimproben. *See* JASCHNOFF. 1884. III. 156.[2]
— Die Wälder des russischen Nordens. *See* JASCHNOW. 1894. IV. 346.
— *See also* ЯШНОВЪ, Л.
Yatabe, Ryōkichi. Iconographia florae japonicae. 1891. I. 463.[1]
— A new Japanese Wikstroemia. 1891. II. 606.[2]
— New names of Japanese plants. 1892. I. 463.[1]
— New or little known plan of Japan. 1891. I. 463.[1]
— A new variety of Chrysanthemum sinense. 1891. II. 854.[2]
— Two new species of Japanese plants. 1890. II. 822.[2]
Yatchevski, A. A. *See* ЯЧЕВСКІЙ, A. A.
Yates, James. Opening of a Palm-spathe with an audible report. 1862. II. 3.[2]
Yates, Richard. Essay on the cultivation of Oak. 1802. III. 361.[2]
— Observations on the cultivation and growth of Oak timber. 1802. III. 361.[2]
Ydewalle, van OUTRYVE D'. *See* OUTRYVE D' YDEWALLE, van. Year-book of pharmacy. I. 20.
Y., a, s, Alexander. Douglas Fir on the Durris estate. 1900. IV. 483.[2]
Yeats, John. The natural history of commerce. 1870. III. 218.[1]
— The natural history of the raw materials of commerce. 1870. III. 218.[1]
Yekoussima. *See* TANAKA & YEKOUSSIMA.
Yelin. Ueber nütaliche Astungen. 1886. IV. 172.[1]
On **yellow** dye extracted from the Berberidaceae. 1865. III. 393.[2]
The **Yellow** Phœ. 1825. III. 758.[1]
The **Yellow** Wood, Cladrastis (Virgilia) tinctoria. 1874. III. 472.[2]
Yensh, F. *See* IEНШЪ, Ѳ.
Yeo, D. J. Trees for clay soils. 1886. III. 41.[1]
De la **yerba** maté de Paraguay. 1850. III. 485,[1] 530.[2]
The **Yew.** 1843. II. 10.[2]
Yew trees. 1896. II. 10.[2]
The **yield** of White Pine in the native forest. 1898. IV. 470.[2]
Yoeda, BRATA-. *See* BRATA-YOEDA.
Yokohama Nursery Co. How the Japanese grow the dwarfed trees. 1899. III. 176.[1]
— Maples of Japan. 1898. III. 534.[1]
Yokusai, JINUNIA. *See* JINUNIA YOKUSAI.
Yon, (*Frère*). Thé de Martinique. 1704. III. 222.
Yonge, Charlotte M. Keble's parishes. 1898. I. 535.
Yonne — Société des sciences historiques et naturelles. *See* SOCIÉTÉ . . . I. 23.

Yorke, Philip. On the spicula contained in the wood of the Welwitschia. 1864. II. 55.[2]
Yorkshire agricultural society. Transactions. III. 18.
The **Yorkshire** naturalists' recorder. *See* The NATURALIST. Huddersfield. I. 19.
Yorkshireman, (*pseud.*). Peeling standing timber. 1886. IV. 434.
Yoruba Indigo. 1888. III. 481.[2]
Yoshida, Hikorokurō. On aluminium in the ashes of flowering plants. 1887. I. 154.
— On the chemistry of Japanese lacquer. 1885. III. 529.[1]
— Lacquer. 1885. III. 529.[1]
— Sur la laque du Japon. 1884. III. 529.[1]
— Lindera sericea. 1891. III. 406.[2]
— *See also* KORSCHELT, O. & YOSHIDA, Hikorokuro.
Yoshii, T. *See* KELLNER, O.; YOSHII, T. & NAGAOKA, M.
Young, Arthur. The farmer's letters to the people of England. 1768. III. 123.[2]
— Travels . . . with a view of ascertaining the cultivation . . . of France. 1792. III. 271.[1]
— Voyage en Italie. 1796. III. 271.[1]
— Voyages in France. 1792. III. 271.[1]
Young, Charles, James & Peter. Hortus epsomensis. 1828. I. 54.
Young, H. W. *See* MILLER, E. S. & YOUNG, H. W.
Young, Herbert A. The flora of Oak Island. 1883. I. 315.
Young, J. T. Waarnemingen over het geneeskundig gebruik . . . van den Americaanschen Tulpenboom. 1793. III. 398.[2]
Young, James. Management of woods. 1848. IV. 120.
— Remarks on planting and the management of woods. 1846. IV. 120.
Young, Maud J. Familiar lessons in botany with flora of Texas. 1873. I. 323.
Young, Maurice. Aucuba sports. 1872. III. 645.[1]
Young's Cypress. 1887. III. 301.[1]
Ypey, A. Verhandeling over de opslurpende tepelen der plantgewassen. 1773. I. 160.
Ysabeau, A. L'Aubépine à fleur simple. 1854. III. 422.[1]
— Floraison du Paulownia. 1853. III. 703.[2]
— Flowering of the Paulovnia. 1853. III. 703.[2]
— Les forêts du globe. 1854. IV. 336.[1]
— Le Mûrier à papier. 1868. III. 368.[1]
— Le Robinier d'Utterhart. 1859. III. 486.[2]
— Traité des arbres fruitiers. 1851. III. 140.[1]
— De la Vigne et des arbres fruitiers. 1867. III. 144.
Ysabeau, V. F. A. Naturalisation de l'Araucaria en Angleterre. 1845. III. 298.[2]
Yu., S. *See* IO., C.
Die **Yucca** oder Stärkewurzel. 1856. III. 521.[1]
The **Yucca** Palm. 1892. II. 87.[2]
Yucca pendula en pleine terre. 1859. III. 340.[1]
Yuccas. 1883. III. 340.[2]
Yûhannâ ibn Masawaih. Opera de medicamentorum. 1623. V. xxviii.[2]
— Supplementum in secundum librum. 1623. V. xxviii.[2]
Yule, John. Notice of a collection of rare plants from India. 1820. III. 28.[2]
— Observations on the presumed analogy of certain organs of the embryo. 1823. I. 121.
— On the physical distribution of the Coniferae. 1819. II. 12,[1] 13,[2] IV. 452.[1]
Yūyō mokusai seiran. 1873. I. 37,[2] IV. 18.[1]
Yūyō Mokusai Shorau. n. d. IV. 399.[1]
Yūyō shokubutsu zusetsu. *See* TANAKA, Yoshio. 1888. III. 91.[2]
Yvart, Jean Augustin Victor. Coup d'œil sur le sol, le climat . . . de la France. 1807. III. 125.
— Object d'intérêt public. 1816. III. 394.[1]
Yzarn-Freissinet, d', *vicomte.* Coup d'œil sur les Landes de Gascogne. 1837. IV. 359.[2]

— **z.** Ueber Forsteinrichtung. 1894. IV. 246.
— **z.** Der Plänterwald in der Forstbetriebseinrichtung. 1898. IV. 131.
— **z —.** Die Anwendung der Plenterdurchforstung. 1898. IV. 175.[1]
— **z —.** Streifenweise Plenterungen. 1898. IV. 130.
z. Unser heutiges Durchführungssystem der Betriebseinrichtung. 1894. IV. 246.
Z. Bamboos. 1871. III. 315.[1]
Z. Begründung eines Eichen- und Buchenmischbestandes. 1898. IV. 131.[2]
Z. Eine bemerkeswerte Zuwachsleistung der Weymouthskiefer. 1899. IV. 471.

Z. Einige Gedanken über die "Methode du contrôle." 1897. IV. 238.

Z. Der kalifornische Ahorn. 1881. III. 535.[1]

Z. Ein kolossales Exemplar von Taxodium mucronatum. 1884. II. 52.[1]

Z. Sobre la legitimación de las roturaciones. 1897. IV. 552.[1]

Z. Los notarios en los deslindes de los montes públicos. 1898. IV. 555.[1]

Z. Privatbesitz und neues Forstgesetz. 1898. IV. 331.[1]

Z. Tessin. Lawinenverbauungen. 1897. IV. 188.[2]

Z. Les traitements des agents forestiers . . . en Allemagne. 1895. IV. 552.[2]

Z., A. Encephalartos. 1881. III. 255.[2]

Z., A. A. Das Imprägniren des Holzes. 1854. IV. 417.

Z, A—. *See* A — Z.

Z., G. *See* O., W. & Z., G.

Z., H. M. Voxtrœrne. 1857. III. 353.[1]

Z., H. M. Die Wachabäume. 1857. III. 353.[1]

Z., S. Sciółka leśna. 1860. IV. 71.

Z., V. Die älteste Akazie Deutschlands. 1891. II. 383.[1]

Zaailing-Appels. Wat is te verwachten uit het zaad der bestaande Appelsoorten. 1877. III. 426.[1]

Zaayer, H. G. de. Recherches sur l'andromedotoxine. 1889. III. 647.[1]

Zabel, Heinrich. Acer platanoides L. var. integrilobum. 1887. II. 479.[2]

— Die asiatischen Diervilla-Arten. 1886. II. 834.[2]

— Beiträge zur Kenntnis der Gattung Staphylea. 1888. II. 473.[1]

— Berberis Thunbergii de Cand. 1899. III. 395.[1]

— Bruckenthalia spiculiflora Reichenb. 1885. II. 661.[2]

— Celastrus bullata. 1886. II. 466.[2]

— Cercocarpus betulaefolius Nutt. 1886. II. 258.[1]

— Cytisus glabrescens Sartorelli. 1886. II. 350.[2]

— Cytisus praecox hort. 1899. III. 474.[2]

— Cytisus purgans Benth. et Hook. 1886. II. 351.[2]

— Dendrologische Beiträge. 1881. III. 46.[1]

— Ueber einige Formen von Quercus pubescens. 1886. II. 135.[1]

— Die erste nordwestamerikanische Bryanthus in deutscher Kultur. 1890. III. 653.[2]

— Evonymus obovata Nutt. 1888. II. 468.[2]

— Ueber den fibrösen Bau der Zellwand. 1861. I. 138.[1]

— Forsythia intermedia. 1885. II. 706.[2]

— Aus den Gärten der Forst-Akademie Münden. 1889. I. 48.

— Ein Gang durch die Gärten der Forstakademie Münden. 1895. I. 49, *IV. 18.[2]*

— Ueber die Gattung Abelia. 1893. II. 834.[1]

— Die Gattung der Zwergmispeln. 1897. II. 259.[2]

— Die Gattung Symphoricarpus. 1887. II. 841.[2]

— Ginkgo biloba. 1899. III. 287.[1]

— Hedysarum multijugum. 1894. III. 478.[2]

— Jamesia americana Torr. et Gray. 1889. II. 241.[2]

— Über den japanischen Schneeball. 1886. II. 842.[2]

— Lonicera gigantea Hort. gall. 1886. II. 837.[2]

— Lonicera splendida Boiss. 1890. II. 839.[2]

— Magnolia stellata Maxim. 1885. IIII. 400.[2]

— Ueber eine neue Catalpa. 1880. II. 787.[1]

— Neuere Mittheilungen über die sog. Mycorhiza. 1888. I. 529.

— Neues und Interessantes über Laubgehölze. 1899. II. 560,[1] 678.[1]

— Die nordamerikanischen Viburnum-Arten. 1889. II. 842.[2]

— Philadelphus microphyllus Gray. 1890. II. 242.[2]

— Ueber Pirus floribunda. 1876. III. 429.[1]

— Polygonum baldschuanicum Rgl. 1888. II. 186.[1]

— Ueber Prunus Jacquemonti Hook. fil. 1892. II. 274.[2]

— Quercus Garryana. 1898. III. 362.[1]

— Ribes succirubrum. 1896. II. 246.[2]

— Rosa multiflora Thunb. 1886. III. 456.[1]

— Spiraea bracteata Zbl. 1886. II. 314.[1]

— Spiraea- und Rubus-Bastarde. 1897. II. 308,[1] 315.[1]

— Stephanandra incisa. 1885. II. 316.[1]

— Die strauchigen Spiräen der deutschen Gärten. 1893. II. 250,[1] 314.[1]

— Synoptische Tabellen . . . häufigsten deutschen Pflanzen-Gattungen. 1872. I. 387.

— Systematisches Verzeichniss der in den Gärten der K. Preuss. Forstakademie zu Münden kultivirten Pflanzen. 1878. I. 48, *IV. 18.[2]*

— Uebersicht der Flora von Neu-Vorpommern. 1859. I. 384.

— Übersicht der kultivirten strauchigen Spiraeen. 1884. II. 314.[1]

— Unsere Vitis-Arten mit gefiederten Blättern. 1888. III. 544.[1]

— Vaccinium macrocarpum in Deutschland. 1884. II. 686.[1]

— Viburnum molle Mchx. 1891. III. 753.[2]

— Vitis tricuspidata. 1891. III. 545.[1]

— Weitere Beiträge zur Kenntnis der Gattung Staphylea. 1897. II. 473.[1]

— Wie verbreitet sich Linnaea borealis? 1876. II. 835.[2]

— Ueber wilde Rosen. 1876. III. 449.

— Zwei neue Staphylea Formen. 1898. II. 473.[1]

— Zwei schöne nordamerikanische Weiden. 1887. II. 107,[2] 108.[2]

Zabel, N. E. *See* Цабель, H. E.

Zabriskie, J. L. The fungus, Phyllactinia . . . on . . . Celastrus seadens. 1888. III. 532.[1]

— Hairs of the Peach in relation to hay fever. 1887. III. 442.[2]

— The lenticular markings of various Coniferae. 1885. II. 17.[1]

— Notes on the structure of the fruit-stone of the Date. 1892. II. 73.[1]

— Stamen of the Deerberry. 1886. II. 687.[1]

Zabucajo, a new esculent nut. 1849. III. 631.[2]

Zabystrzan, Johann. Allgemeine Beschreibung des . . . Reviers Swinoschitz-Lelekowitz. 1899. IV. 370.

Zach, *baron* von. Thé. 1825. III. 606.

Zacharias, E. Ueber die chemische Beschaffenheit von Cytoplasma. 1893. I. 137.

— Ueber Secret-Behälter mit verkorkten Membranen. 1879. I. 135.

Zache, Eduard. Über Anzahl und Grösse der Markstrahlen. 1886. I. 126.

Zacher, Gustav. Ueber Bewirthschaftung von Erlenbrüchern. 1895. IV. 488.[2]

— Zur volkswirthschaftlichen Bedeutung des Waldes. 1897. IV. 271.[1]

— Die Wälder Dalmatiens. 1889. IV. 283.[2]

Zahlbruckner, Alexander. Beitrag zur Flora von Neu-Caledonien. 1888. I. 509.[1]

— Eine bisher unbeschriebene Sapotacee. 1889. II. 698.[2]

— Ueber einige Lobeliaceen des Wiener Herbariums. 1891. II. 845.[1]

— Neue Breiträge zur Kenntniss der Lenticellen. 1885. I. 132.[2]

— Novitiae peruvianae. 1892. I. 340.[2]

— Plantae novae herbarii vindobonensis. 1897. I. 330.

— Plantae Pentherianae. 1900. I. 496.

— Revisio Lobeliacearum boliviensium. 1897. II. 845.[1]

— Trematocarpus. 1894. II. 845.[2]

Zahlbruckner, Johann. Beiträge zur Länderkunde Oesterreichs unter der Enns. 1831. I. 439.

— Darstellungen der pflanzengeographischen Verhältnisse des Erzherzogthums Oesterreichs. 1831. I. 439.

Zahn, Hermann. Altes und Neues aus der badischen Flora. 1895. II. 102.[1]

Zahn, Johann Heinrich. Dissertatio inauguralis de Rhododendro chrysantho. 1783. II. 678.[2]

Der Zahnbrecher, ein Werkzeug zum Stockroden. 1858. IV. 386.

Zahradnik, H. Zur Ansicht von Azalea indica. 1883. III. 660.[1]

Zahrt, Pflanzung ballenloser Kiefern. 1886. IV. 473.

Zahrtmann, K. M. Sandflugtskoven ved Rønne. 1893. IV. 146.[1]

Zajíček, Friedrich. Lehrbuch der praktischen Messkunst. 1882. IV. 265.

Zalenski, V. *See* Rothert, Wladislaw & Zalenski, W.,

Zalewski, Aleksander. O florze Lipnowskiej. 1890. I. 366.

— O Jemiole. 1891. II. 179.[2]

— Krótki przegląd roślin nowych dla Królestwa Polskiego. 1896. I. 367.

— Neue Pflanzenformen aus . . . Polen. 1897. II. 101.[1]

— Rozbiór prac dotyczących flory polskiej od roku 1880 do 1895 włącznie. 1896. I. 367.

— Zapiski roślinnicze z królestwa Polskiego. 1886. I. 443.

Zallinger, Johann Baptista. Abhandlung von dem Ursprung der Früchten. 1769. I. 118.[2]

— De incremento frugum. 1771. I. 118.[2]

— Die Krankheiten der Bäume. 1809. IV. 195.[1]

— De morbis plantarum. 1773. I. 206.[1]

— De ortu frugum ex mechanismo plantarum. 1769. I. 118.[2]

Zaluziansky à Zaluzian, Adam. Methodi herbariae libri tres. 1592. I. 30.

Zamboni, Giuseppe. Parnassi botanici fragmenta. 1721. I. 290.

Zambrano, Gaetano. La coltivazione del Melagrano. 1897. III. 630.³

De zamenstelling en vervalsching van de thee, koffie. 1883. III. 222.

Zaminer, Eduard. Geschichte des Waldwesens der ... Stadt Kronstadt-Brassó. 1891. IV. 28.¹

Zamora, J. L. La corteza de la Yaba. 1877. III. 467.¹

Zamorano, Francisco Torres. Manual de legislación de montes. 1896. IV. 555.¹

Zamyetchaniya o niekotorykh. See Замѣчанія о нѣко- торыхъ.

Zanardini, Giovanni. Prospetto della flora veneta. 1847. I. 427.

Zancla, Aurelio. Di alcune particolarità anatomiche degli aculei. 1897. I. 113.¹

Zander, Johannes. Primitiae Viridarii medici stettinensis. 1672. I. 43.

Zandovsky, J. Das Einrichtungsverfahren in den Forsten der Stadt Lemberg. 1895. IV. 246.

Zanger, A. I. Waldämtlich-geprieft-bestättigt- ... Beschrei- bung ... über die Kohlungsart. 1773. IV. 394.

Zannichelli, Gian Girolamo. Opuscula botanica. 1736. I. 424.

— De Rusco. 1727. III. 338.¹

— & G. J. Istoria delle piante ... ne' lidi intorno a Venezia. 1735. I. 424.

Zannichelli, Gian Jacopo. Lettera intorno alle facoltà dell' Ippocastano. 1733. III. 537.³

— Osservazioni intorno all abuso della coffea. 1755. III. 222.

Zanon, Antonio. Dell' agricoltura. 1763. III. 126.¹

Zanoni, Giacomo. Indice delle piante portate ... nell viag- gio di Castiglione. 1652. I. 424.

— Istoria botanica. 1675. I. 287, V. XVI.¹

— Rariorum stirpium historia. 1675. V. XVI.¹

Zantedeschi, Francesco. Cenni di alcuni studi sperimentali. 1848. I. 229.

— Della electricità degli stami e pistilli. 1853. I. 200.

— De l'influence qu'exercent sur la végétation des plantes ... les rayons solaires ... colorés. 1843. I. 229.

— Dell' influenza dei raggi solari ... colorati. 1843. I. 229.

— Des mouvements que présentent quelques végétaux ex- posés à l'action de la lumière lunaire. 1852. I. 195.¹

— Piante rare rinvenute ... alpi Bresciane. 1825. I. 426.

Zanthier, Hans Dietrich von. Abhandlungen über das ... Forstwesen. 1799. IV. 100.¹

— Kurzer systematischer Grundriss der practischen Forst- wissenschaft. 1764. IV. 94.²

— Sammlung vermischter Abhandlungen ... Forstwesen be- treffend. 1778. IV. 100.¹

— & Krohne. Der wohlgeübte und erfahrene Förster. 1785. IV. 95.

— & Lassberg. Forst-Calender; oder, Verzeichniss der Ver- richtungen. 1772. IV. 116.

О западном Tchinarye. See О западномъ Чинарѣ.

Zapałowicz, Hugo. Kilka slow o geografii roślin. 1891. I. 446.

— Przyczynek do roślinności Czarnej Hory, Czywczyna i Alp Rodnańskich. 1882. I. 443.

— Roślinną szatą Gór Pokucko-Marmaroskich. 1889. I. 446.

— Roślinność Babiej Góry. 1880. I. 443.

— Zapiski florystyczne z wschodnich Karpat. 1897. I. 447.

Zapasnik, K. See Запасникъ, К.

Zapf, L. B m k ng über die Kultur der Cacteen. 1843.

Zapiski Komiteta. See Записки Комитета.

Zappe, Ed. Die Zubereitung des Pflanzenwachses in Japan. 1873. III. 527.³

Zappella, M. Attuazione del regime silvano. 1898. IV. 277.

— Conservatore forestale. 1898. IV. 91.¹

— Diritti d' uso gravanti i boschi. 1897. IV. 329.

— Effetti del regime forestale. 1897. IV. 277.

— L' eterna questione forestale. 1898. IV. 329.

— Ferrovia economica. 1897. IV. 392.

— Impero del regime forestale. 1897. IV. 277.

— Innestiamo i nostri Olivi selvatici. 1896. III. 676.³

— E legale l' accertamento mancando l' avviso. 1897. IV. 277.

— Una legge santa. 1897. IV. 329.

— Organizzazione dell' amministrazione forestale italiana. 1898. IV. 293.²

— Reati e pene in materia forestale. 1898. IV. 329.

— Rimboschimento. 1897. IV. 166.¹

— La Talpa. 1898. IV. 90.²

Zarb, J. H. Rapport ... sur les spécimens botaniques. 1879. I. 489.

Zasiedaniya liesokhozyaistvennago siezda. See Засѣданія лѣсохозяйственнаго съѣзда.

Zatecki, Johann. Ueber die Kultur des Orangenbaumes. 1852. III. 499.²

Zaustinski, L. See Заусцинскій, Л.

Zavira, Constantin Johann. Onomatologia botanike tetra- glottos. 1787. I. 72.¹

Zawada, Karol. Das anatomische Verhalten der Palmen- blätter. 1890. II. 871.³

Zawadski, Alexander. Enumeratio plantarum Galiciae. 1835. I. 440.

— Flora der Stadt Lemberg. 1836. I. 440, 535.²

Zawodny, J. F. Betrachtungen über die Rostflecke der Aep- fel. 1897. III. 195.²

— Die Reblaus; ein Mahnwort an unsere Winzer. 189.? III. 574.

— Sklerotina. 1897. III. 195.²

Zawodny, Joseph. Begiessen und Pflanzen. 189.? III. 38.¹

— Zur Naturgeschichte des Ahorns. 1899. II. 476,³ IV. 526.²

— Verwachsung zweier Kiefern. 1889. IV. 66.²

— Der Weinbau in der Bukowina. 1898. III. 558.²

Zayas Enriquez, R. de. Les États-Unis mexicains. 1899. III. 265.¹

Zdárek, Robert. Aus dem Leben der Werre. 1881. IV. 207.

— Prunus Salzeri. 1893. II. 275.³

— Trockene Destillation des Holzes. 1900. IV. 433.¹

— Der Wald in der Hochlage. 1892. IV. 130.

Zdeněk, Josef Raušer. See Raušer Zdeněk, Josef.

Zdrowie. III. 10.¹

Zea, Francisco Antonio. Memoria sobre la quina. 1800. III. 720.

Zebe, (Oberförster, Volpersdorf). Beitrag zur Naturgeschichte der Birke. 1841. IV. 490.¹

— Curculio Lapathi Linn. 1843. IV. 488.²

— Die Ebresche. 1843. IV. 520.³

— Ueber den Getreidebau im Walde. 1842. IV. 133.

— Phalaena Tortrix. 1843. IV. 475.

— Ueber den Werth der Fichtenzapfen als Brennmaterial. 1844. IV. 489.²

Zed, (pseud.). The Fulham nursery. 1877. II. 134.¹

Die Zedern auf dem Libanon. 1886. II. 28.¹

Zedtwitz, C. M. Graf & Hoenig, Max. Die Zoll- und Verkehrs- frage in Bezug auf Land- und Forstwirthschaft. 1890. IV. 284.¹

Zeeb, Heinrich. Die Waldstreu-Frage. 1871. IV. 71.

Zeephout en zeepwortel. 1882. III. 265.²

Zeerleder. Notizen über den Schneedruckschaden ... Bern. 1897. IV. 191.¹

Zeeuwsch genootschap der wetenschappen. Nieuwe ver- handelingen. Verhandelingen. I. 16.

Zefkof, Otto. See Зефковъ, Отто.

Zehender, E. F. Anleitung zur Obstbaumzucht. 1857. III. 145.¹

— Die Mängel des Obstbaues. 1857. III. 145.²

Zehender, Friedrich. Auswahl einiger der besten ... Aepfel- sorten. 1865. III. 89,¹ 425.²

— Auswahl von Birnsorten. 1866. III. 89,¹ 445.²

Zehir-ed-din. See Baber Muhammad.

Zehnpfund, (Forstassessor). Die Aestungsleiter. 1892. IV. 172.¹

Zehnter, H. De dierlijke vijanden der Koffiecultuur. 1899. III. 737.

— De dierlijke vrienden der Koffiecultuur. 1900. III. 728.¹

Zehntner, L. De dierlijke vrienden der Koffiecultuur. 1899. III. 737.

Zeichnung der Stamm-Ruine einer riesenhaften Rüster. 1854. IV. 518.⁴

Zeichnung eines Eichen-Stammes auf dem Rittergut Lab- schütz. 1847. IV. 515.³

Zeichnung eines seltnen Rüster-Stammes. 1854. IV. 518.³

Zeidler, (Forstrath, Sagan). Beschreibung des herzoglich Saganer Hauptforstes. 1854. IV. 352.

Zeidler, C. W. De corticis peruviani usu. 1804. III. 720.

Zeidler, Josef. See Hofmann, Josef & Zeidler, Josef.

Zeil, M. A. *See* Цейль, M. A.

Zeile, Jakob Friedrich. Ueber die männlichen Blüthen der Coniferen. *See* MOHL, Hugo von. 1837. II. 18.

Zeiller, Paul. Rusticité du Chamaerops excelsa. 1889. III. 331.[2]

— Le Sapin de Douglas. 1890. IV. 483.[2]

Zeiner-Lassen, A. Formering af Roser. 1887. III. 452.

— Formering og Dyrkning af Azalea indica. 1883. III. 60.[1]

— Rosa rugosa Regeliana. 1896. III. 457.[1]

— Rosen, dens Historie. 1882. III. 450.

— Rosen i Nutid og Fremtid. 1890. III. 450.

— Saaning af Frø af Rosa canina. 1886. III. 452.

Zeise, W. C. Sur la fabrication des huiles essentielles. 1866. III. 224.[3]

Zeising, R. Die Beziehungen der Forstwissenschaft zu den Staats- und Wirthschaftswissenschaften. 1892. IV. 56.

— Die forstlichen Verhältnisse von Schottland. 1880. IV. 359.[1]

— Der Hacker'sche Verschulungsrechen. 1893. IV. 151.[1]

Zeiske, M. Flora des Ringgau's. 1898. I. 390.

— Ueber die Gliederung der Flora von Hessen. 1899. I. 390.

— Die Pflanzenformationen in Hessen. 1900. I. 390.

Zeithammer, L. M. Die Kleinholzindustrie des Böhmerwaldes. 1895. IV. 407.[1]

Zeithammer, Leopold. Einfluss des Waldes auf die Niederschlagsmenge. 1877. IV. 50.

Zeitner, S. F. Analysis chemica ... seminum Crotonis Tiglii. 1827. III. 517.[1*]

Zeitschrift der deutschen Forstbeamten. IV. 11. ·

Zeitschrift für Acclimatisation. III. 14.

Zeitschrift für bildende Gartenkunst. *See* JAHRBUCH für Gartenkunde. III. 12.

Zeitschrift für Chemie und Pharmacie. *See* KRITISCHE Zeitschrift. I. 13.

Zeitschrift für das Forst- und Jagdwesen in Baiern. IV. 11.

Zeitschrift für die Forstwissenschaft. IV. 5.[1]

Zeitschrift für die gesammte Staatswissenschaft. IV. 12.[1]

Zeitschrift für die gesammten Naturwissenschaften. I. 15.

Zeitschrift für Ethnologie. I. 15.

Zeitschrift für Förderung ... der Obstkunde. *See* MONATS-SCHRIFT für Pomologie. III. 13.

Zeitschrift für Forst- und Jagdwesen. Berlin. IV. 12.[1]

Zeitschrift für Gärtner, Botaniker. III. 14.

Zeitschrift für Gartenbau. *See* JAHRBUCH für Gartenkunde. III. 12.

Zeitschrift für Landschaftsgärtnerei. III. 14.

Zeitschrift für Nahrungsmittel-Untersuchung. III. 25.

Zeitschrift für Natur- und Heilkunde in Ungarn. I. 28.[2]

Zeitschrift für Naturwissenschaften. *See* ZEITSCHRIFT FÜR DIE GESAMMTEN NATURWISSENSCHAFTEN ... I. 15.

Zeitschrift für Obst- und Gartenbau. *See* SÄCHSISCHE Obstbau-Zeitung. III. 13.

Zeitschrift für Pflanzenkrankheiten. III. 14.

Zeitschrift für tropische Landwirtschaft. *See* Der TROPEN-PFLANZER. III. 14.

Zeitschrift für wissenschaftliche Botanik. I. 27.

Zeitschrift für wissenschaftliche Mikroskopie ... I. 15.

Zeitschrift für wissenschaftliche Zoologie. I. 15.

Zeitung für Holzhandel. *See* HANDELSBLATT für Walderzeugnisse. IV. 9.

Zellén, J. O. af. Handledning vid skogars indelning til ordnad hushållning. 1869. IV. 288.[2]

Zeller, E. A. Untersuchungen über die Einwirkung verschiedener Stoffe ... auf das Leben der Pflanzen. *See* SCHÜBLER, Gustav. 1826. I. 206.[1]

Zeller, Hanna. Feldblumen aus dem Heiligen Land. 1875. I. 480.

— Fleurs de la Palestine. 1875. I. 480.

— Wild flowers of the Holy Land. 1876. I. 480.

Zeller, Phil. Die Forst-, Jagd- und Fischerei-Polizei in den preussischen Staaten. 1830. IV. 301.

— Die Forst-, Jagd- und Fischerei-Polizei in den preussischen Staaten ... bearbeitet. 1830. IV. 320.

Zeller, W. Beobachtungen über das Gedeihen fremder Nadelhölzer. 1877. III. 292.

— Beobachtungen über die Wirkung der Frühfröste am 26. und 27. September. 1878. III. 46.[1]

— Die empfehlenswertesten Ziergehölze. 1886. III. 203.

— Das Reichsgesetz betreffend die Unfall- und Krankenversicherung. 1886. IV. 310.[2]

— Verpflanzung ... einer hundert (?) jährigen Dattelpalme. 1887. III. 328.[2]

Zeltner, A. de. Sur la noix de Cédron. 1867. III. 509.[1]

Zeman, Julius. Eine Ferial-Reise durch die Slavuta'er Waldungen. 1872. IV. 345.

— Kahlschlag oder natürliche Besamung. 1876. IV. 128.

— Der Kieferndreher. 1873. IV. 477.

Zemlitčka, Wilhelm. Das Vorkommen von Waldbeständen der gemeinen Kastanie. 1876. IV. 492.[2]

Zendrini, Bernardo. Trattato della China China. 1715. III. 338.[1]

Zenker, Jonathan Karl. Flora von Thüringen. 1836. I. 379.

— Historisch-topographisches Taschenbuch von Jena. 1836. I. 379.

— Merkantilische Waarenkunde. 1831. III. 218.[1]

— Naturgeschichte schädlicher Thiere. 1836. IV. 89.[2]

— Die Pflanzen und ihr wissenschaftliches Studium überhaupt. 1830. I. 86.

— Plantae indicae. 1835. I. 472.

Zenker, Josef von. Das Benagen der Kiefern durch Eichhörnchen. 1873. IV. 476.

— Zur Birkenzucht. 1884. IV. 490.[1]

— Der Bodenwerth des Nachhaltswaldes. 1882. IV. 257.

— Einfache Kubirungsmethode stehender Bäume. 1868. IV. 217.

— O finanční výslednosti dřevin. 1888. IV. 259.[2]

— O intensivnosti polního hospodářství. 1886. IV. 102.

— Zur Lösung der Frage des Lichtungsbetriebes. 1886. IV. 174.

— Lyda hypotrophica. 1892. IV. 457.

— Rundholz-Kubaturen als Walze. 1885. IV. 228.

— Samenruhe von Ulmus campestris. 1868. II. 144.[2]

— Die Schwarzföhrenharzung. 1868. IV. 466.[2]

— Die staatliche Forstaufsicht. 1883. IV. 286.[1]

— Der Stand der Forstwirthschaft ... im Königreiche Böhmen. 1890. IV. 372.

— Statististicko-topografický a lesnický popis lesů královského města Písku. 1889. IV. 372.

— Statistisch-topographische und forstliche Beschreibung der der königlichen Stadt Pisek gehörigen Wälder. 1889. IV. 372.

— Der Waldfeldbau. 1882. IV. 134.[1]

Zenkoffsky. Nonnulla ad processum vegetationis Coniferarum. 1846. II. 16.[1]

Zenneck, Ludwig Heinrich. Flora von Stuttgart. 1822. I. 377.

— Oekonomische Flora. 1822. III. 73.

— Über die Unterscheidbarkeit der entlaubten Bäume und Gesträuche. 1858. I. 294.[2]

Zentella, Arcadio. Catálogo de los productos ... de Tabasco. 1899. III. 265.[1]

Zeper, P. De Caesalpinia dasyrachys. 1882. III. 483.[1]

Zepnick. Beitrag zur Eriken-Cultur. 1835. III. 649.[2]

Zerapha, C. Stephano. Florae melitensis thesaurus. 1827. I. 451.

Zersi, Elia. Piante vascolare della provincia di Brescia. 1872. I. 428.

— Prospetto delle piante vascolari ... di Brescia. 1871. I. 428.

Zerweck. Erfahrungen über die Erziehung der Forchenpflanzen. 1887. IV. 473.

Zeserin. Ueber Durchforstungen. 1828. IV. 172.[1]

Zesselliers. Empoisonnement par l'écorce de Panama. 1804. III. 447.[1]

Zeti, Franc. Altro parere intorno alla natura ... della cioccolata. 1728. III. 594.[1]

Zetterlund, C. G. Branntwein aus Sägespänen. 1871. IV. 431.[1]

Zettermann, A. J. & Brander, A. E. Bidrag till sydvestra Finland's flora. 1867. I. 362.

Zetterstedt, Johann Emanuel. Om gamla träd. 1863. I. 296.[1]

— Om några hybrider af slägtet Salix. 1878. II. 100.[2]

— Plantes vasculaires des Pyrénées principales. 1857. I. 421.

— Pyreneernas vegetation. 1856. I. 421.

— Den tidiga våren 1878. 1878. I. 223.[1]

— Om växtgeographiens studium. 1863. I. 300.

— Om vegetationen i de högländtaste trakterna af Småland. 1867. I. 356.

— Vegetationen på Visingsö. 1878. I. 357.

— Vegetations-skizzer från Pyreneerna. 1859. I. 412.

Zetterstedt, Johann Wilhelm. Conspectus plantarum in horto botanico ... Universitatis lundensis. 1838. I. 40.

— De foecundatione plantarum. 1810. I. 199.

Zetterstedt, Johann Wilhelm (*continued*).
— De plantis cibariis romanorum. *See* RETZIUS, A. J. 1808. III. 88.[1]
— Resa genom Sveriges och Norriges Lappmarker. 1822. I. 353.
— Resa genom Umeå Lappmarker. 1833. I. 353.
Zetzel, F. Rön om brasilianska bönan Pecuris . . . nytta. 1759. III. 403.[2]
Zeumer, Hans. Untersuchungen über die Fichte. 1886. II. 36.[1]
Zeviani, Giovanni Verardo. Della moltiplicazione delle legne nel territorio veronese. 1772. IV. 122,[2] *393*.
Zeyher, & Rieger, J. C. Schwezingen und seine Gartenanlagen. 1826. III. 28.[1]
Zeyher, Carl. *See* ECKLON, C. F. & ZETHER, Carl.
Zeyher, Ch. L. Botanical notes on a journey into the interior of Southern Africa. 1846. I. 494.
Zeyher, Johann Michael. Verzeichniss der sämmtlichen Gewächse in dem Grossh. . . . Garten zu Schwezingen. 1818. I. 45.
— Verzeichniss sämmtlicher Bäume und Sträucher in den Grossh.-Badischen Gärten. 1806. I. 45.
— & **Roemer**, G. C. Beschreibung der Gartenanlagen zu Schwetzingen. 1809. I. 45.
Zeyher, N. J. Chemische Untersuchung der Rinde von Atherosperma. 1861. III. 403.[2]
Zeyss, Johann Heinrich Wilhelm. Versuch einer Geschichte der Pflanzenwanderung. 1855. I. 241.[1]
Zhebenko, F. *See* Жебенко, Ф.
Zhelyeznof, Nikolai Ivanovitch. *See* Géléznow, Nicolas.
Zhilinski, *general*. *See* Жилинскій, генералъ.
Zhudra, P. I. *See* Жудра, П. И.
Zhukof, A. I. *See* Жуковъ, А. И.
Zhukovski, N. *See* Жуковскій, Н.
Zhurnal spetzialnago po liesnoi. *See* Журналъ спеціальнаго по лѣсной.
Ziablovski. *See* Зябловскій.
Ziebarth, Karl. Das Forstrecht. 1887. IV. 317.[1]
Die Ziege als Waldverwüsterin. 1876. IV. 197.[1]
Ziegenhorn, Friedrich. Anleitung zur wohlfeilen Cultur der Waldgründe. 1846. IV. 141, 148.
Ziegenmeyer. Forstgeschichtliches vom braunschweigischen Solinge. 1881. IV. 26.
Ziegler. Die Gesetzgebung über die Privatwaldungen. 1859. IV. 317.[1]
Ziegler, Anton. Die Seidenzucht. 1842. III. 376.
Ziegler, E. Die Cultur und Gewinnung der Band- und Korbweide. 1861. III. 347.
Ziegler, H. von, **Klipphausen & Miessler**, Otto. Forst-Rechenhelfer. 1870. IV. 59.[1]
Ziegler, Julius. Beitrag zur Frage der thermischen Vegetations-Constanten. 1875. I. 221.
— Erläuternde Bemerkungen zur pflanzen-phänologischen Karte . . . von Frankfurt a. M. 1883. I. 225.
— Pflanzenphänologische Beobachtungen. 1891. I. 225.
— Pflanzenphänologische Karte . . . von Frankfurt a. M. 1883. I. 225.
— Ueber phänologische Beobachtungen. 1879. I. 225.
— Plaudereien aus dem Gemeindewalde der Eifel. 1898. IV. 119.[1]
— Ueber thermische Vegetations-Constanten. 1879. I. 221.
— Verwachsene Buchen. 1886. I. 209,[1] *IV. 497.*
Ziegler, Louis. Die officinellen Gewächse in tabellarischer Uebersicht. 1845. III. 57.
Ziegler, Wilhelm. Phänologische Beobachtungen. 1878. I. 225.
Ziegner-Gnüchtel, H. Der Forstdiebstahl. 1888. IV. 317.[1]
Ziegra, Christian Samuel. De morte plantarum. 1680. I. 146.
Ziel, B. Das Aufhören der Reblaus. 1894. III. 762.
Zielaskowski. Standortsuntersuchungen. 1898. IV. 70.
Zieliński, Ignacy. Ogrodnictwo praktyczne. 1817. III. 134.[2]
Zienkowski, Wincenty. Ogólny spis roślin . . . w ogrodzie Antonińskim. 1856. I. 42.
— Spis pierwszy roślin zakładu ogrodowego w Antoninie. 1852. I. 42.
Zier, L. Die Agricultur-Chemie. 1830. IV. 60.[2]
— Über Entwaldung und Holztheuerung. 1843. IV. 281.[1]
— Grundriss der Chemie, als Propädeutik der chemischen Technologie. 1843. IV. 60.[2]
Zierwein-Arten. 1882. III. 544.[1]
Zigra, Johann Hermann. Ausführliches Verzeichniss derjenigen Obstbäume und Sträucher . . . welche in Riga . . . gezogen. 1819. I. 41.
— Ausführliches Verzeichniss derjenigen Obstbäume und Sträucher, welche in Riga . . . gezogen. 1817. III. 68.[1]
— Ausführliches Verzeichniss derjenigen Pflanzen . . . welche in Riga . . . gezogen werden. 1817. I. 41.
— Ausführliches Verzeichniss über 2000 Species der seltenen exotischen Pflanzen. 1805. I. 41.
— Der Baum-Gärtner. 1803. III. 134.[2]
— Dendrologisch-öconomisch-technische Flora der im Russischen Kaiserreiche. 1839. III. 67.[2]
— Der nordische Baumgärtner. 1803. III. 134.[2]
— Ogrodnictwo zastosowane do klimatu północnego. 1825. III. 101.[1]
— Tabellarische Uebersicht der in den Wäldern der Ostsee-Provinzen befindlichen Baum-Arten. 1833. I. 358. *IV. 79.*[2]
— *See also* Цигра, Ив.
Ziino, Nunzio. Un caso importante di estimo forestale. 1898. IV. 259.[1]
Zijnen, Theodor Daniel VRIJDAG. *See* VRIJDAG ZIJNEN, T. D.
Zikmundowsky, (*Oberförster*). Die Eichenrinde der slavonischen Grenzforste. 1876. IV. 515.[1]
— Eukalyptuse in Dalmazien. 1880. IV. 532.[2]
— Wirkungen der Bora. 1883. IV. 189.[2]
Zillich, (*Oberförster*, *Preuss*). Massengehalt zweier Rüster-Stämme. 1857. IV. 518.[2]
Ziment, J. P. Darstellung, wie es zugehen muss, dass die Waldraupen . . . in unendlicher Menge erscheinen? 1834. IV. 206.
— Ideen über ein allgemeines Kulturgesetz wie es in forstlicher Hinsicht sein soll. 1831. IV. 313.
— Ueber den Verkauf von Staatswaldungen in Baiern. 1819. IV. 273.[2]
Zimmer. Beobachtungen . . . bei der Kultur der Kiefer und Fichte. 1856. IV. 123.[2]
— Conservation du bois. 1859. IV. 418.
— Cultur und Wachsthum der Lerche. 1849. IV. 449.
— Der Curculio pini. 1858. IV. 476.
Zimmer, (*Förster*). Insektensachen. 1833. IV. 475.
Zimmer, (*Oberförster*, *Glogau*). Aufforstung verarmter Ackerländereien. 1885. IV. 158.
— & *others*. Welche Erfahrungen liegen über den Nutzen der Einsprengung von Eichenheistern . . . vor? 1887. IV. 138.[1]
Zimmer, (*Professor*). Ueber das Versetzen der Holzpflanzen. 1847. III. 168.[2]
Zimmer, C. W. Lodoicea sechellarum. 1893. III. 327.[1]
Zimmer, Heinrich. Die Vermehrung der Coniferen. 1887. III. 294.[1]
Zimmer, Karl. Phänologische Beobachtungen über . . . Spartium scoparium. 1891. II. 352.[1]
Zimmerauer, Friedrich von. Les écoles agricoles et forestières en Autriche. 1900. IV. 36.[1]
Zimmerman, Charles D. Protection of trees from the sun. 1880. III. 184.[1]
Zimmerman, F. C. Forest culture in Prussia. 1881. IV. 354.
Zimmermann, Mittler & Grumbach. Kritik der Patriotischen Winke . . . Barons . . . von Seckendorf. 1801. IV. 100.[2]
Zimmermann, Albrecht. Over aaltjesziekte in de Thee. 1899. III. 604.[2]
— De aaltjesziekte . . . van de Koffie. 1899. III. 737.
— Beiträge zur Morphologie . . . der Pflanzenzelle. 1893. I. 137.
— De bestrijding der nematoden met zwavelkoolstof. 1900. III. 737.
— Bestrijding van den "Oeler tjäleng." 1900. III. 737.
— Botanical microtechnique. 1892. I. 37.[1]
— De botanische Mikrotechnik. 1892. I. 37.[1]
— Ueber die Chromatophoren in panachirten Blättern. 1890. I. 185.[1]
— Eenige Koffiezikten. 1899. III. 737.
— Over de enchytraeiden . . . in de Koffiewortels. 1899. III. 737.
— Enting van Liberiakoffie. 1900. III. 733.[2]
— Zur Godlewski'schen Theorie der Wasserbewegung in den Pflanzen. 1885. I. 165.
— Het groepsgewijze afsterven der Koffieheesters. 1897. III. 736.
— De kanker . . . van Coffea arabica. 1900. III. 737.
— Ueber den Krebs von Coffea arabica. 1900. III. 737.
— Zur Kritik der Böhm-Hartigschen Theorie der Wasserbewegung. 1885. I. 165.
— Lésing . . . over eenige Koffiezikten. 1899. III. 737.
— Über mechanische Einrichtungen zur Verbreitung der Samen. 1879. I. 240.[1]

—Molecular-physicalische Untersuchungen. 1883. I. 149.¹—1884. I. 125, 138.¹
— Die Morphologie ... des pflanzlichen Zellkernes. 1896. I. 137.
—De nematoden der Koffiewortels. 1898. III. 737.
—Die Nematodenkrankheit der Kaffeepflanzen. 1900. III. 737.
—Over een nieuwen Koffieboorder. 1899. III. 737.
—Plagen van Koffie- en bijcultures. 1900. III. 180.¹
—Ueber die radialen Stränge der Cystolithen von Ficus elastica. 1891. II. 151.²
—De Rostrella ziekte (kanker) in de Koffie. 1900. III. 737.
—Over eene schimmelepidemie der groene luizen. 1899. III. 737.
—Over de sluipwespen in de eieren der sprinkhanen. 1899. III. 737.—1900. III. 737.
—De stand der aaltjes- en andere Koffieziekten. 1899. III. 737.
—Tylenchus acutocaudatus Zn. in de Thee. 1900. III. 604.¹
—Ueber das Verhalten der optischen Elasticitätsaxen vegetabilischer Zellmembranen. 1884. I. 138.¹
—Voorloopig rapport over de aaltjes op Karanganjer. 1900. III. 737.
—Over ziekten en plagen in de Koffie. 1899. III. 737.
—Ueber den Zusammenhang zwischen der Richtung der Tüpfel und der optischen Elasticitätsaxen. 1884. I. 125.
—Ueber den Zusammenhang zwischen Quellungsfähigkeit und Doppelbrechung. 1883. I. 149.¹
Zimmermann, Ferdinand Joseph von. Grundzüge der Phytologie. 1831. I. 86.
Zimmermann, Hermann. Ueber Vaccinium Myrtillo — Vitis idaea. 1869. II. 685.²
Zimmermann, Johann Georg. Dubia ex Linnaei Fundamentis botanicis. 1751. I. 291.
Zimmermann, O. E. R. Die Palmen. 1873. II. 63.³
Zimmermann, W. F. A. De grondslagen der chemische plantenphysiologie. 1900. I. 152.¹
Die Zimmtgärten bei Colombo auf Ceylon. 1832. III. 405.²
Zin, K. See Цинъ, К.
Zinck, Christoph. Pomologia. 1766. III. 70.
Zinger, V. J. See Цингеръ, В. Я.
Zinke, Georg Gottfried. Aufruf ... zur Vertilgung der schädlichen Waldraupen. 1797. IV. 205.³
—Bemerkungen über die schädliche Waldraupe. 1797. IV. 205.¹
—Naturgeschichte der schädlichen Nadelholz-Insekten. 1798. IV. 91,¹ 441.
—Vertheidigung gegen die Angriffe ... in Jägers Waldraupen- und Borkenkäfergeschichte. 1798. IV. 206.
Zinn, Johann Gottfried. Catalogus plantarum Horti academici et agri gottingensis. 1757. I. 44.
—Observationes quaedam botanicae. 1753. I. 142.
Zippe, Franz Xaver Maximilian. Botanica dla niższych szkół realnych. 1857. I. 90.
Zippel, Hermann. Ausländische Handels- und-Nährpflanzen. 1885. III. 53.
—Dadelpalmen. 1900. III. 329.²
—Kaffeträet. 1896. III. 740.¹
—Kokospalmen. 1897. III. 324.¹
—Olietriet. 1900. III. 679.²
—Theebuskèn. 1897. III. 645.¹
—& Bollmann, Carl. Ausländische Culturpflanzen. 1876. I. 256.
——— Repräsentanten einheimischer Pflanzenfamilien. 1879. I. 256.
Zippelius. Uittreksel uit eenen Brief aan C. L. Blume. 1829. I. 465.
Zipperer, Paul. Untersuchungen über Kakao. 1887. III. 595.¹
Zipperlen, Otto. Bougainvillea glabra Sanderiana. 1896. III. 388.¹
Die Zirbelkiefer auf der Pfaueninsel. 1896. III. 307.¹
Eine Zirbelkiefer in Norwegen. 1886. II. 41.¹
Zircher. Theorie und Praxis in der Buchenwirtschaft. 1900. IV. 496.
Zirngiebl, H. Zwei Obstblattschaben. 1900. III. 192.²
Zitný, Thomas. Der Plattensäer. 1882. IV. 149.¹
Živa. III. 26.¹
Živa; časopis přírodnický. I. 28.²
Živný, M. Azalea mollis. 1899. III. 660.²
Ziz, J. B. See Koch, W. D. J. & Ziz, J. B.
Zlamal, Johann. Der Mittelwald. 1899. IV. 132.¹

Zobof, N. See Зобовъ, Н.
Zoe. I. 7.²
Zoega, Johann. Flora islandica. 1772. I. 351.
Zölffel, Georg. Ueber die Gerbstoffe der Algarobilla. 1891. III. 237.²
Zöller, Philipp Hugo. Chemische Untersuchung eines Himalaja-Thees. 1871. III. 607.
—Untersuchung eines Himalyathees. 1871. III. 607.
— & Grete, E. A. Sur l'amyloxanthate de potassium. 1875. III. 568.
—Note sur l'emploi du xanthate de potasse. 1875. III. 86³
Zöpfl, Gottfried. Die Eisenbahntariffrage unseres Holzverkehrs. 1896. IV. 284.³
Zoeppritz, Adolf. Waldungen und Holzgewinnung in Nordschweden. 1883. IV. 344.²
Zoest, J. van. Hoe het bederven van den grond ... door gas te voorkomen. 1881. III. 185.²
— Het wit in de Perzikboomen. 1859. III. 441.²
Zöd, Gottlieb. Behandlung und Anlegung der Bannwaldungen im Hochgebirg. 1844. IV. 181.¹
— Del governo dei boschi sacri. 1844. IV. 181.¹
— Handbuch der Forstwirthschaft. 1831. IV. 110.²
Zollickoffer, William. A materia medica of the United States. 1819. III. 262.¹
Zollikofer, Caspar Tobias. Versuch einer Alpenflora der Schweiz. 1828. I. 433.
Zollinger, C. vo. Praktisches Handbuch über ... Kultur des Maulbeerbaumes. 1843. V. xxviii.²
Zollinger, Heinrich. Ueber die Anonaceen des ostindischen Archipels. 1858. II. 215.¹
—Over het begrip en den omvang eener Flora Malesiana. 1857. I. 465.
—Bijdrage tot de natuurlijke geschiedenis van de houthommel. 1846. IV. 210.²
—Bijdragen tot de kennis van de gebergte systemen in het oostelijk Java. 1846. I. 468.
—Het eiland Lombok. 1847. I. 468.
—Gedachten over plantenphysiognomie ... van Java. 1846. I. 468.
— et over de natuurlijke geschiedenis van Madoera. 1858. I. 466.
—De Lampongsche districten. 1847. I. 467.
—Ueber ein neues Palmengeschlecht. 1856. II. 75.¹
—Observationes botanicae novae. 1857. I. 465.
—Observationes phytographicae. 1844. I. 465.
—Observationes phytographicae. Leguminosae. 1846. II. 319.²
—Die Pflanzenphysiognomie von Java. 1854. I. 469.¹
—Quelques observations sur l'histoire naturelle de l'île de Madoura. 1858. I. 465.
—Ueber die Rottlera-Arten ... zu Buitenzorg. 1856. II. 447.¹
—Over de soorten van Rottlera. 1856. II. 434.¹
—Systematisches Verzeichniss der im Indischen Archipel ... gesammelten ... Pflanzen. 1854. I. 462, 465.
— Togt naar den Salakh. 1843. I. 468.
—Een uitstapje naar het eiland Balie. 1845. I. 465.
—Vegetation around the volcanic craters of the island of Java. 1858. I. 469.¹
—Sur la végétation autour des cratères volcaniques de l'île de Java. 1858. I. 469.¹
—Verslag van eene reis naar Bima en Soembawa. 1850. I. 465.
Zondervan, H. Bangka en zijne bewoners. 1895. I. 466, III. 275.¹
Zoological and acclimatisation society of Victoria. Proceedings. See Acclimatisation society of Victoria. III. 27.¹
Zoologisch-botanische Gesellschaft in Wien. See Kaiserlich-königliche zoologisch ... I. 27.
Zoologisch-botanischer Verein in Wien. Verhandlungen. See Kaiserlich-königliche zoologisch-botanische Gesellschaft ... I. 27.
Zoologische Jahrbücher. III. 14.
Zoologische Station zu Neapel. Mittheilungen. I. 15, V. vii.²
Zorgenfrei. See Зоргенфрей.
Zorn, Bartholomaeus. Botanologia medica. 1714. III. 54.
Zorn Johannes. Abbildungen von Arzeneygewächsen. 1779. III. 55.
—Auswahl schöner und seltener Gewächse. 1795. I. 264.
—Dreyhundert auserlesene amerikanische Gewächse. 1785. I. 328.
— Icones plantarum medicinalium. 1779. III. 55.

Zornow, B. Die um Gumbinnen wildwachsenden Phanerogamen. 1870. I. 386.

Zotos, Zotos N. Ein Beitrag zur Kenntniss des Cerberins. 1892. III. 687.[2]

Zouteveen, Hermann F. HARTOGH HEYS VAN. See HARTOGH HEYS VAN ZOUTEVEEN, H. F.

Zprávy lesnické. See HÁJ. IV. 14.

Zr. Finanzielle Umtriebszeit und Fideikommisswald. 1872. IV. 251.[2]

Zschimmer. Ueber den Anbau der Korbweide. 1888. IV. 487.[2]

Zschimmer, (*Oberförster*). Holzstoff- und Holzcellulosefabrikation. 1890. IV. 430.

— Massenermittelung eines Fichten- und eines . . . Eichenbestandes. 1882. IV. 237.

— Mittheilungen über den Anbau von Korbweiden. 1887. IV. 487.[1]

— Mittheilungen über die Fabrikation von Cellulose. 1881. IV. 430.

— Eine neue Holzverwendung. 1875. IV. 430.

— Zuwachsuntersuchungen an einer aufgeasteten Kiefer. 1880. IV. 481.

Zschokke, Achilles. Ueber den Bau der Haut . . . unserer Kernobstfrüchte. 1897. I. 120.

— Ergebnisse der Beobachtungen an den im Kanton Bern . . . errichteten meteorologischen Stationen. 1891. IV. 60.[1]

Zschokke, Eugen. Verzeichniss der in der Umgegend von Aarau wild-wachsenden . . . Pflanzen. 1847. I. 434.

Zschokke, Heinrich. Der Gebirgs-Förster. 1806. IV. 99.[1]

— Der schweizerische Gebürgs-Förster. 1806. IV. 99.[1]

Zschokke, J. H. D. Die Alpenwälder. 1804. IV. 123.[1]

Zubrzycki, J. Flora Pienin. 1894. I. 446.

Zuccagni, Attilio. Centuria 1. Observationum botanicarum, quas in Horto regio florentino. 1806. · I. 61.

— Synopsis plantarum horti bot. Musei regii florentini. 1782. I. 61.

— **Desfontaines, R. L. & L'Héritier de Brutelle, C. L.** Cadiae arabicae descriptio. 1796. II. 338.[2]

Zuccalmaglio, A. W. von. Die deutschen Pflanzennamen. 1841. I. 73.[2]

Zuccarini, Joseph Gerhard. Beiträge zur Morphologie der Coniferen. 1843. II. 16.[1]

— Bemerkungen über einige wenig gekannte Pflanzengattungen. 1846. II. 5,[1] 225.[2]

— Beschreibung des Dasylirion graminifolium. 1841. II. 81.[1]

— Ueber die Bildung des Fruchtfleisches bei . . . Citrus. 1845. II. 401.[2]

— Charakteristik der deutschen Holzgewächse. 1829. I. 294,[2] *IV. 82.*

— Ueber Damnacanthus Gaertn. und Bahmannia. 1846. II. 816.[1]

— Über einige Pflanzen aus . . . Agave und Fourcroya. 1833. II. 88.[1]

— Über einige . . . Pflanzengattungen aus Japan. 1846. II. 816.[1]

— Einiges über Geschichte . . . von Viscum und Loranthus. 1833. II. 173.[1]

— Erläuterung der Gattung Lindera. 1846. II. 225.[2]

— Flora der Gegend um München. 1829. I. 378.

— Über die Flora japonica. 1841. I. 462.

— Knospen und Blätter der Cacteen. 1837. II. 587.[2]

— Über die Kohle . . . zur Fortpflanzung der Gewächse. 1841. III. 157.

— Leichtfasslicher Unterricht in der Pflanzenkunde. 1834. I. 87.

— Monographie der amerikanischen Oxalis-Arten. 1825. II. 392.[?]

— Über eine monströse Feige. 1842. II. 150.[1]

— On the morphology of the Coniferae. 1843. II. 16.[1]

— Naturgeschichte des Pflanzenreichs. 1843. I. 269.

— Ueber eine neue Gattung . . . der Bromeliaceae. 1838. II. 80.[2]

— Plantarum novarum . . . in Horto botanico herbarioque regio monacensi. 1832. I. 47.

— Ueber Rhododendron intermedium. 1837. · II. 681.[1]

— Ueber Vegetationsgruppen in Bayern. 1833. I. 378.

— Ueber Verbreitung und Benutzung der Cacteen. 1837. II. 585.[1]

— Ueber zwei merkwürdige Pflanzen-Missbildungen. 1844. II. 150,[1] *591.*[1]

— *See also* SIEBOLD, P. F. von & ZUCCARINI, J. G.

Zuccarini, K. Berichtigung . . . über die Mutterpflanze des Sternanises. 1836. II. 209.[2]

Lo zuccaro di Castagne. 1865. IV. 493.[2]

Zuccheri, P. G. Origine e progressiva coltivazione del bosco . . . del torrente Tagliamento. 1881. IV. 165.

Zucchini, Andrea. Sulla coltura e usi dell' Acacia. 1800. IV. 522.[2]

Zuchold, E. A. Additamenta ad G. A. Pritzelii Thesaurum literaturae botanicae. 1853. I. 2, V. VII.[1]

— Catalogus librorum botanicorum in Pritzelii thesauro omissorum. 1855. I. 2.

Zucht des Futterlaubgehölzes. 1877. III. 223.[1]

Zuckergehalt der Fichtennadeln. 1884. IV. 459.[2]

Die Zuckerpalme, Jubaea spectabilis. 1890. III. 326.[1]

Zueckert, Johann Friedrich. Die Naturgeschichte einiger Provinzen des Unterharzes. 1763. I. 373.

— Von den Speisen aus dem Pflanzenreich. 1778. III. 219.[1]

Zürcher, G. Aufforstung oder Verbauung? 1894. IV. 166.[2]

— Grosse Fichten bei Burgdorf. 1887. II. 37.[2]

Zürcherische botanische Gesellschaft. Jahresbericht. *See* SCHWEIZERISCHE BOTANISCHE GESELLSCHAFT. I. 26.[2]

Zürich. 1866. IV. 190. — 1874. II. 24.[1]

Zürich — **Botanisches Museum der Universität.** *See* BOTANISCHES . . . I. 26.[2]

Zürich — **Naturforschende Gesellschaft.** *See* NATURFORSCHENDE . . . I. 26.[2]

Zürn, E. S. Die Mistel. 1900. II. 180.[1]

Zufällige Gedanken von der Natur. *See* BROCKE, H. C. von. 1752. IV. 115.

Zuidergebergte bewoner, (*pseud.*). Middel tegen de aaltjesziekte in de Koffie. 1900. III. 737.

— Mishandeling van Koffieaanplant. 1900. III. 728.[1]

Zuidewyn, L. de ROY VAN. *See* ROY VAN ZUIDEWYN, L. de.

Zukal, Hugo. Zur Frage vom grünfaulen Holze. 1887. I. 207.[1]

Zulueta, José. La riqueza forestal. 1894. · IV. 552.[1]

Zumaglini, Antonio Mauritius. Flora pedemontana. 1849. I. 427.

— Della malattia attuale dell' Uva. 1851. III. 575.[2]

El Zumaque y la filoxera. 1893. III. 527,[1] *574.*

Zunk, Hermann Leopold. Die natürlichen Pflanzensysteme. 1840. I. 252.

Zurich. *See* ZÜRICH. 1874. II. 24.[1]

Zur Mühlen, A. von. Beitrag zur Frage über den Waldschutz. 1877. IV. 180.[1]

Zur Mühlen, Max von. Eine Syringa mit zweierlei Blüthen. 1889. II. 715.[1]

Zuruf an die Bewohner der Oberpfälzischen Herzogthümer wegen Vertilgung der . . . Waldraupen. 1798. IV. 205.[2]

Zurunić, T. P. Die bosnische Pflaume. 1895. III. 433.[1]

Zusätze und Bemerkungen zu der . . . Broschüre: "Über die bayerische Forstverwaltung." 1850. IV. 289.[2]

Zusätze zur Nachtrags-Instruktion vom 6. April 1846. 1854. IV. 302.

Zusammenstellung allgemeiner Verfügungen der königlich württembergischen Forstdirektion. 1864. IV. 322.[2]

Zusammenstellung der Besitzveränderung in der landesfiscalischen Forstverwaltung. *See* WIRTSCHAFTS-ERGEBNISSE . . . 1883. IV. 350.[1]

Zusammenstellung der Bestimmungen über Ausbildung und Prüfung für den preussischen Staatsforstverwaltungsdienst. 1882. IV. 33.[1]

Zusammenstellung der Ergebnisse der Holzfällungen in den Staatswaldungen [von Württemberg]. 1871. IV. 356.[1]

Zusammenstellung der forstlich-meteorologischen Beobachtungen im Kanton Bern. 1873. IV. 59.[2]

Zusammenstellung der im Königreiche Hannover geltenden Vorschriften über die Verwaltung der Forsten. 1860. IV. 301.

Zusammenstellung der in Würtemberg . . . in Forst- und Jagdsachen gegebenen Gesetze. *See* FORSTLICHE BLÄTTER für Würtemberg. IV. 8.

Zusammenstellung der Mittheilungen über die durch . . . Schneefall und Sturmwind . . . in . . . Böhmens verursachten Waldschäden. 1870. IV. 190.

Zusammenstellung der Probeaufgaben beim prakt. Staatsexamen für die Aspiranten des bayerischen Staatsforstverwaltungsdienstes. 1887. IV. 33.[1]

Zusammenstellung der . . . Wirthschafts-Ergebnisse in den Staatsforsten . . . Anhalt. IV. 12;[1] *see also* WIRTSCHAFTS-ERGEBNISSE. 1883. IV. 350.[1]

Zustand der Forst-Verwaltung im Jahr 10. der fr. Rep. 1802. IV. 292.

Ueber den Zustand der Kiefern-Waldungen. 1835. IV. 471.

Zuverlässige Nachricht von demjenigen Holtz-Cabinet. *See* CLODIUS, Christian. 1729. I. 37,[1] IV. 17.

Die Zuwachsberechnung im haubaren Holze. 1857. IV. 232.

Zuwachs-Ergebnisse aus dem Lichtwuchs-Betriebe der gräflich Castell'schen Waldungen. 1886. IV. 233.
Zuwachsverhältnisse in den Hochgebirgswaldungen. 1887. IV. 233.
Zuylichem, EYCK VAN. See EYCK VAN ZUYLICHEM.
Zvonař, E. Zalesňování půdy pro polní hospodářství nezpůsobilé. 1878. IV. 167.²
Zwaan, N. de. Salix acutifolia en S. uralensis. 1877. III. 348.
Zwanziger, G. A. Botanische Reise im Juli 1862. 1863. V. xxiii.¹
Zwanziger, Ignaz. Flora von Lungau. 1853. I. 440.
Zwanziger, J. G. Die vortheilhafteste Benutzung öder ... Gründe. 1836. IV. 167.¹
Zwart, H. C. Lichtgas en boomen. 1877. III. 185.²
Ein zweckmässiges Taxationsverfahren. 1859. IV. 243.
Ueber die zweckmässigste Art der Anpflanzung von Alleen. 1835. III. 209.
Ueber das zweckmässigste Verfahren bei Heisterpflanzungen. 1847. IV. 154.¹
De zweedsche apotheek. See PHARMACOPOEA suecica. 1775. III. 247.¹
Zweerus, C. Memorie over het njondollen. 1899. III. 731.
Zwei besondere Zainungsarten. 1863. IV. 387.²
Zwei buntblättrige Ahornarten. 1859. III. 533.²
Zwei Eichenriesen. 1886. II. 139.¹
Zwei empfehlenswerthe Palmen. 1880. III. 325.²
Zwei Euphorbiaceen, als Blattpflanzen. 1859. II. 444.¹
Zwei Heckensträucher, der Osagen- und Weissdorn. 1857. III. 213.
Zwei Pracht-Coniferen. 1890. III. 296,¹ 318.³
Zwei Predigten, in welchen zur Werthschätzung der Fruchtbäume ermuntert. 1799. IV. 280.¹
Zwei Riesenbuchen im Grossherzogthume Luxemburg. 1896. · IV. 500.³

Die zweite deutsche Nordpolarfahrt ... unter Führung des Kapitän Karl Koldewey. 1873. I. 303.
Zweites oder wiederholtes Blühen. 1890. I. 221.
Zwelfer, Johann. Animadversiones in pharmacopoeiam augustanam. 1652. III. 247.³
— Königliche Apotheek oder Dispensatorium. 1652. · III. 247.³
— Pharmacopoeia augustana reformata. 1652. III. 247.²
Zwenger, Constantin. Ueber das Aesculin. 1854. III. 627.²
— Ueber Brenncatechin und Ericinon. 1859. III. 480.¹
— Ueber die Gewinnung der Chinasäure. 1860. III. 664.¹
— Nonnulla de catechino. 1841. III. 464.¹
Ein Zwergwald im Canton Appenzell. 1885. IV. 72.
Ueber zwey neue Maschinen zum Ausroden der Stöcke. 1792. IV. 385.²
Zwickau — Verein für Naturkunde. See VEREIN ... I. 15.
Zwickauer Forst-, Geschäfts ... Kalender. IV. 12.¹
Zwicker, J. M. J. Depositorium ... aus den weiten Gebieten der Forst-, Jagd- und Naturkunde. 1805. IV. 100.³
— Der patriotische Forstmann. 1805. IV. 100.²
Zwierlein, K. A. Deutschlands Eichbaum. 1824. IV. 514.¹
— Vom grossen Einfluss der Waldungen. 1806. IV. 42.³
Zwinger, Johann Jakob. Dissertatio medica inauguralis de valetudine plantarum. 1708. III. 259.¹
Zwinger, Theodor. Dissertatio ... Amygdalarum fructus analysin exhibens. 1703. III. 434.²
— Lucubrationes academicae circa plantarum doctrinam. 1698. I. 288.
— Theatrum botanicum. 1696. I. 288.
Zwirner, Ludwig. Das Gefrieren und Erfrieren der Pflanzen. 1888. III. 182.
Zygophyllum arboreum of Jacquin. 1832. IV. 524.²
Zylker, A. J. Koffie-bladziekte. 1879. III. 735.
— De landbouw in de bergstreken. 1872. III. 128.

INDEX OF GREEK AUTHORS AND TITLES

Ἀγρονομικὰ, συνερανισθέντα ἐκ διαφόρων γαλλικῶν βιβλίων. 1833. III. 116.¹
Ἀριστοτέλης [Aristoteles.] See ARISTOTELES. 321. I. 271.²

Βάλβης, Ἀλέξανδρος. [Balbes, Alexandros.] Τὸ δένδρον Βαοβάβ. 1890. II. 529.¹
— Τὸ Θεόβρωμα. 1890. III. 595.¹
Βαχαβιόλος, Ἰ. [Bachabiolos, I.] Ἡ σημασία τῶν δασῶν παρὰ τοῖς Ἀρχαίοις. 1900. IV. 271.¹
— See also WIESNER, Julius.
Βίσνερος, Ἰούλιος. [Wiesner, Julius.] Στοιχεῖα ἐπιστημονικῆς φυτολογίας. See WIESNER, Julius. 1881. I. 91.
Βούρος, Ἰωάννης. [Bouros, Joannes.] See BOUROS, Julianus.
— Λάνδερερ, Ξαυέριος & Σαρτόριος, Ἰωσήφ. [Bouros, Johannes, Landerer, Xaver, & Sartorios, Josef.] Ἑλληνικὴ Φαρμακοποιΐα. 1837. III. 256.¹

Γεννάδιος, Παναγιώτης. [Gennadios, Panagiotes.] Περὶ Ἀϊλάνθου. 1885. III. 507.¹
— Περὶ ἀκαριδώσεως τῆς Ἀμπέλου. 1892. III. 564.¹
— Περὶ τῆς Ἀμυγδαλῆς. 1893. III. 434.¹
— Περὶ ἀνθοβολίας ἢ ῥυάδων Ἀμπέλου. 1888. III. 561.
— Περὶ τοῦ ἀνθρακος τῆς Ἀμπέλου. 1891. III. 580.
— Περὶ τῆς ἀποπληξίας τῆς Ἀμπέλου. 1889. III. 561.
— Περὶ τῆς Ἐλαίας. 1892. III. 678.¹
— Ἀσθένειαι τῶν Ἐσπεριδοειδῶν. 1885. III. 498.²
— Περὶ τινων ἀσθενειῶν ἀναπτυχθεισῶν εἰς τοὺς ἡμετέρους Ἀμπελῶνας. 1890. III. 561.
— Περὶ τινων ἀσθενειῶν τῆς Ἐλαίας. 1885. III. 677.³
— Περὶ Βοχμηρίας τῆς ἰσχυροτάτης. 1885. III. 382.¹
— Περὶ τῆς ἐν Γαλλίᾳ πορείας τῆς φυλλοξήρας. 1884. IV. 375.²
— Τὰ δάση μας. 1887. IV. 375.²
— Ἔκθεσις περὶ τῆς ἐν Καρύστῳ νόσου τῶν Ἐσπεριδοειδῶν. 1885. III. 498.²
— Ἔκθεσις περὶ τῆς ἐν Κύπρῳ γεωργίας. 1895. III. 127.³
— Ἐκσάρκωσις τῆς Ἀμπέλου. 1894. III. 561.
— Περὶ Ἐλαίας. 1892. III. 676.²
— Τὰ Ἐσπεριδοειδῆ. 1893. III. 497.³
— Περὶ Εὐκαλύπτων. 1890. IV. 530.
— Περὶ τῆς καλλιεργείας τῶν Εὐκαλύπτων. 1890. IV. 530.
— Ἡ Καμέλλεια. 1893. III. 599.¹
— Κατάλεγος τῶν παρασίτων τῆς Ἀμπέλου. 1885. III. 561.
— Περὶ τῆς κηκιδομυίας τῆς Ἀμπέλου. 1893. III. 564.¹

— Περὶ κομμιώσεως τῆς Ἀμπέλου. 1886. III. 561.
— Περὶ τῶν Μορεῶν. 1893. III. 378.
— Περὶ οἰκονομικωτέρας μεθόδου πρὸς καλλιέργειαν τῆς Ἀμπέλου. 1885. III. 559.¹
— Περὶ τοῦ Περονοσπόρου τῆς Ἀμπέλου. 1892. III. 580.
— Περὶ τῆς Πυραλίδος τῆς Ἀμπέλου. 1885. III. 563.
— Περὶ τῆς Πυραλίδος τῆς Δρυός. 1890. V. 501.¹
— Περὶ τοῦ Πυρηνοσπόρου τῆς Ἐλαίας. 1890. III. 678.¹
— Περὶ Ῥοιᾶς. 1893. III. 630.³
— Περὶ ῥυγχείου τοῦ πενθίμου. 1885. III. 563.
— Φιλλόξηρα ἢ φθοροποιός. 1879. III. 760.
— Περὶ φυλλοξήρας. 1888. III. 574.
— Περὶ φυλλοξήρας τῆς φθοροποιοῦ. 1880. III. 574.
— Ἡ χρυσομηλία τῆς Ἀμπέλου. 1887. III. 564.¹
— Περὶ Χυλοκεράτας. 1894. III. 471.³
— Περὶ Ψίλλου τοῦ Τουκκερίου. 1885. III. 579.
— See also GENNADIUS, Panagiotes.
Γερμανός, Νικόλαος. [Germanos, Nicolaos.] Διάγνωσις καὶ θεραπεία τῆς ἀσθενείας τῆς Ἀμπέλου, ἀνθρακος. 1890. III. 380.
— Περὶ τοῦ Περονοσπόρου τῆς Ἀμπέλου. 1890. III. 580.
Γεωπονικά. III. 26.¹
Γεωπονικά. De re rustica selectorum libri xx. See CASSIANUS BASSUS. 1538. III. 98.
Γεωπονικά, geoponicorum. See CASSIANUS BASSUS. 1538. III. 98.
Γιδόνης, Εὐγένιος. [Gidones, Eugenios.] Πρακτικὰ παραγγέλματα πρὸς καταπολέμησιν τοῦ περονοσπόρου. 1893. III. 581.

Δασικῆς νομοθεσίας. Τεῦχος Α΄. 1900. IV. 332.¹
Δημητριάδης, Ῥαϊνόλδος. [Demetriades, Rhainoldos.] Γεωργικά. 1891. III. 116.¹
Διοσκορίδης, Πεδάκιος Ἀναζάρβευς. [Dioscorides, Pedakios Anazarbeus.] Πεδακίου Διοσκορίδου Ἀναζαρβέως περὶ ὕλης ἰατρικῆς βιβλία. See DIOSCORIDES. 77. V. xiv.¹
— Πεδακίου Διοσκορίδου τοῦ Ἀναζαρβέως περὶ εὐπορίστων ἁπλῶν βιβλία. See DIOSCORIDES. 77. I. 272, V. xiv.¹
— Πεδακίου Διοσκορίδου τοῦ Ἀναζαρβέως περὶ εὐπορίστων ἁπλῶν βιβλία. See DIOSCORIDES. 77. I. 272.
— Πεδακίου Διοσκορίδου τοῦ Ἀναζαρβέως τὰ σωζόμενα ἅπαντα. See DIOSCORIDES. 77. I. 272.
— See also DIOSCORIDES, Pedakios Anazarbeus.

Έλληνική γεωργία. III. 26.¹

Ίβος, Γεώργιος. [Ibos, Georgios.] Ἡ ἀμπελουργία ἐν Ξηροχωρίῳ. 1900. III. 559.¹

Ιόνιος ἀνθολογία. Ionian anthology. See MAZZIARI, Domenico. 1834. I. 448.²

Κονδύλης, Παναγιώτης. [Kondyles, Panagiotes.] Γεωλογία καὶ βοτανική. 1892. I. 92.

Κόσμος. See Les MONDES. III. 20.

Κόφινα, Γ. Ν. [Kophina, G. N.] Μελέται περὶ δασῶν. 1895. IV. 124,¹ 375.³

Κρίνος, Σ. Δ. [Krinos, S. D.] Περὶ Στύρακος διατριβή. 1862. II. 705.¹

— Περὶ Στύρακος, διατριβὴ φαρμακογραφική. 1862. III. 671.²

Κυριακός, Γεώργιος. [Kyriakos, Georgios.] Ἡ Συκῆ ἐν Μεσσηνίᾳ. 1891. III. 369.³

Κών, Φερδινάνδος. [Cohn, Ferdinand.] Φυτολογίαι ὁμιλίαι. 1882. I. 96.

— See also COHN, Ferdinand.

Κωστῆς, Ν. [Kostes, N.] Ἐγχειρίδιον φαρμακολογίας. 1855. III. 258.

Λαβρᾶνος, Χριστόφορος. [Labranos, Christophoros.] Στοιχεῖα βοτανικῆς. 1853. I. 89.

Λάνδερερ, Ξαυέριος. [Landerer, Xaver.] Ἐγχειρίδιον τῆς βοτανικῆς. 1845. I. 88.

— See also ΒΟΥΡΟΣ, Ἰωάννης, ΛΑΝΔΕΡΕΡ, Ξαυέριος & ΣΑΡΤΟΡΙΟΣ Ἰωσήφ; LANDERER, Xaver.

Λισμάνης, Μιχαήλ. [Lismanes, Michael.] Δασονομικαὶ μελέται περὶ βελτιώσεως τῶν ἐν Ἑλλάδι δασῶν. 1897. IV. 375.²

Λοβέρδος, Ἰωάννης. [Loberdos, Joannes.] Ἡ ἡλικία τῶν φυτῶν. 1890. I. 193.²

— Περὶ ἱερῶν δένδρων. 1890. I. 517.¹

Λογοθέτης, Α. [Logothetes, A.] Περὶ τῆς καλλιεργείας τῆς Ῥοδῆς. 1888. III. 454.¹

— Περὶ οἰκονομικωτέρας μεθόδου πρὸς καλλιέργειαν τῆς Ἀμπέλου. 1885. III. 559.¹

Μανταφούνης, Ἀ. [Mantaphounes, A.] Περὶ δενδροστοιχιῶν. 1884. III. 209.

Μηλιαράκης, Σπυρίδων. [Meliarakes, Spyridon.] Ἐγχειρίδιον βοτανικῆς. 1899. I. 93.

— Ἐγχειρίδιον φυτολογίας. 1888. I. 92.

Μητσόπουλος, Κωνσταντῖνος. [Metsopoulos, Constantinos.] Περὶ ἐξανθρακώσεως ξύλων ἤτοι περὶ ἀνθρακοποιίας. 1886. IV. 395.

Τὰ νέα γεωπονικά. See ΓΕΩΠΟΝΙΚΑ. III. 26.¹

Ξανθόπουλος, Σ. [Xanthopoulos, S.] Περὶ τοῦ ἄνθρακος τῆς Ἀμπέλου. See ΞΑΝΘΟΠΟΥΛΟΣ (error for Ξανθόπουλος), Σ. 1900. III. 582,² V. xxix.¹

Ὀρφανίδης, Θεόδωρος. [Orphanides, Theodoros.] Περὶ Ἀβουτίλου τοῦ σημαιοφόρου. 1874. III. 586.¹

— Περὶ Ἀγμαλείου. 1873. III. 655.

— Περὶ ἀνατροφῆς τῶν νεαρῶν δένδρων ἐν φυτωρίοις. 1873. III. 154.¹

— Περὶ τοῦ ἐν Ἄνδρῳ ἀναφανέντος σκώληκος. 1873. III. 190.

— Περὶ Ἀρδισίας τῆς ἐπαλξωτῆς. 1873. III. 666.¹

— Ἀσθένειαι, ἐμπόρια, καὶ εἴδη τῶν Ἑσπεριδοειδῶν. 1872. III. 499.¹

— Περὶ Βεγωνίας τῆς τουϊδιανῆς. 1874. III. 705.

— Περὶ Γαρδενίας τῆς εὐανθοῦς. 1872. III. 744.²

— Περὶ δενδροφυτείαs. 1873. III. 166.

— Περὶ ἐγκεντρισμοῦ. 1873. III. 162.

— Περὶ ἐγκεντρισμοῦ ἢ ἐμβολιασμοῦ. 1873. III. 162.

— Εἴδη καὶ καλλιέργεια τῶν Ἰασμίνων. 1872. III. 672.²

— Εἰδήσεις περὶ τῶν ἀσθενούντων Ἑσπεριδοειδῶν. 1873. III. 498.¹

— Ἔκθεσις . . . ἀφορῶσα τὴν βοτανικὴν συλλογήν. 1874. I. 522.¹

— Περὶ τῶν ἐν Ἑλλάδι μαστιχοφόρων Σχίνων. 1872. III. 525.²

— Περὶ τῆς Ἑλληνικῆς ἀμπελουργίας. 1874. III. 558.¹

— Περὶ ἐνοφθαλμισμοῦ. 1874. III. 164.¹

— Περὶ τῆς ἐνσκηψάσης νόσου εἰς τὰ Ἑσπεριδοειδῆ. 1873. III. 498.¹

— Περὶ τοῦ ἐπιδημικῶς ἐνσκήψαντος σκώληκος εἰς τὰς Ἀμπέλους. 1872. III. 563.

— Περὶ Ἐρυθρίνης τῆς Ἀλεκτροδόφου. 1874. III. 476.¹

— Περὶ Εὐκαλύπτου τῆς σφαιροκάρπου. 1872. III. 634.²

— Περὶ τοῦ εὔόσμου Χειμωνάνθου. 1873. III. 401.¹

— Περὶ Ἐχίτου τοῦ ἥδυόσμου. 1874. III. 689.¹

— Περὶ ἡλιοντληξίας τῶν δένδρων ἤτοι αἰφνιδίου θανάτου φυτῶν. 1872. III. 184.¹

— Ἱστορία καὶ καλλιέργεια τῶν Ἑσπεριδοειδῶν. 1872. III. 497.¹

— Ἱστορία τῆς Ἀμπέλου καὶ καλλιέργεια αὐτῆς. 1875. II. 509.¹

— Καὶ πάλιν περὶ Εὐκαλύπτου. 1873. III. 633.²

— Καλλιέργεια Ἀκακίας ἢ Μιμόσης τῆς αἰθήμονος. 1872. III. 481.²

— Καλλιέργεια Βοιχμερίας τῆς χιονώδους. 1872. III. 382.¹

— Καλλιέργεια Σχίνου τοῦ κάπαλοῦ, κοινῶν Πιπεριά. 1872. III. 529.¹

— Καλλιέργεια τῆς Ἰαπωνικῆς Μεσπιλέας. 1872. III. 423.³

— Περὶ καλλιεργείας τῆς Πιστακίας. 1872. III. 526.¹

— Περὶ τῶν καλλιεργουμένων ἐν Ἑλλάδι Μορεῶν. 1872. III. 378.

— Περὶ Καλλιστημόνος ἢ Μετροσιδήρου τοῦ εὐειδοῦς. 1874. III. 633.¹

— Κλάσεις τῶν Μαγνολιοειδῶν, τάξις τῶν Μαγνολιομόρφων. 1875. III. 397.¹

— Περὶ μεγέθους καὶ ἡλικίας τῶν γηραιοτέρων δένδρων. 1874. I. 295.¹

— Μονογραφικὸς κατάλογος καὶ σύντομος περιγραφὴ τῶν γνωστοτέρων Ἑσπεριδοειδῶν. 1872. II. 401.¹

— Περὶ τοῦ διὰ μοσχευμάτων πολλαπλασιασμοῦ. 1873. III. 158.

— Περὶ τῆς ἐν Νάξῳ ἐνσκηψάσης νόσου τῶν Ἑσπεριδοειδῶν. 1872. III. 498.¹

— Νέαι περὶ τοῦ ἐντόμου τῶν Ἀμπελώνων μας παρατηρήσεις. 1872. III. 563.

— Νέον εἶδος ἢ διαφορὰ τοῦ φυτοῦ Βοιχμηρία. 1872. III. 381.¹

— Νεώτεραι περὶ φυλλοξήρας εἰδήσεις. 1874. III. 567.²

— Περὶ τῶν νεωτέρων καὶ ἀξιολογωτέρων φυτικῶν ἀνακαλύψεων. 1874. III. 91.¹

— Ὀδηγίαι πρὸς συλλογὴν τῆς . . . μαστίχης. 1872. III. 525.²

— Περὶ Οἰνετερίας τῆς συκῆς καὶ Οἰνετερίας τῆς θαμνώδους. 1874. III. 490.¹

— Περιγραφὴ καὶ καλλιέργεια τῆς Ἰαπωνικῆς Καμελλίας. 1872. III. 599.²

— Περιγραφὴ καὶ καλλιέργεια τῆς Ὑδραγγείας τῆς Ὀρτενσίας. 1872. III. 411.²

— Περὶ Πιττοσπόρου τοῦ σινικοῦ. 1873. III. 415.¹

— Πολλαπλασιασμὸς τῶν δένδρων διὰ παραφυάδων. 1872. III. 159.¹

— Περὶ Πολυγάλου τοῦ εὐειδοῦς. 1874. III. 514.¹

— Περὶ προφυλακτικῶν διὰ τὰ Ἑσπεριδοειδῆ δένδρα. 1873. III. 497.¹

— Περὶ Στεφανωτὸς τῆς πολυανθοῦς. 1873. III. 694.¹

— Στοιχεῖα βοτανικῆς. 1872. I. 96.

— Συμβουλὴ πρὸς τοὺς καλλιεργητὰς τῶν Λιμονεῶν. 1872. III. 502.¹

— Σύντομος εἰσαγωγή, καὶ ἰδίως περὶ φυτωρίων. 1872. III. 156.¹

— Περὶ Σφαιρανθέμου τοῦ Ἀλύγου. 1874. II. 795.²

— Περὶ Τεκώματος ἢ Βεγωνίας τῆς ἀκρορτπιανῆς. 1873. III. 707.²

— Περὶ Φιλύρου, ἰδίως δὲ περὶ τῶν ἐν Ἑλλάδι φυομένων. 1873. III. 585.¹

— Φυτῶν ἀσθένειαι. 1873. III. 179.

— Φυτῶν ἀσθένειαι ἐνδόμυχοι. 1874. III. 179.

— See also ORPHANIDES, Theodoros.

Παλαιολόγος, Γρηγόριος. [Palaiologos, Gregorios.] Περὶ ἀμπελουργίας καὶ οἰνοποιίας. 1836. III. 558.²

— Γεωργικὴ καὶ οἰκιακὴ οἰκονομία. 1833. III. 116.¹

Περίληψις ὀδηγίαι περὶ ἐκτελέσεως τοῦ ΒΧΜΒ' νόμου. 1899. IV. 332.¹

Πονηρόπουλος, Εὐστάθιος. [Poneropoulos, Eustathios.] Ἀμπελουργία καὶ οἰνοποιία. 1876. III. 558.²

— Ὀλίγαι λέξεις περὶ τῆς ἐν Ἑλλάδι γεωργίας. 1875. III. 127.¹

— Στοιχεῖα βοτανικῆς. 1880. I. 91.

Προμηθεύς. III. 26.¹

Πύρρος, Ἀριστείδης. [Pyrros, Aristeides.] Περὶ τῆς ἐν τῇ Ἀττικῇ ἐμφυτεύσεως τῆς Ἀμπέλου. 1887. III. 559.¹

Πύρρος, Διονύσιος. [Pyrros, Dionysios.] Βοτανικὴ πρακτική. 1838. III. 37.²

Ριονδέ, Ἀλέξις. [Riondet, Alexis.] Περὶ τῆς Ἐλαίας. 1882. III. 676.¹

— See also RIONDET, Alexis.

Σακελλάριος, Ἀθανάσιος. [Sakellarios, Athanasios.] Τὰ Κυπριακὰ ἤ γεωγραφία, ἱστορία. 1890. I. 452.

Σάμιος, Κωνσταντῖνος. [Samios, Constantinos.] Εἰκόνες ἐκ τῶν Ἑλληνικῶν δασῶν. 1900. IV. 375.²

Σαρακωμένος, Δ. [Sarakomenos, D.] Περὶ τῆς καλλιεργείας τῆς Ῥοδῆς. 1890. III. 453.¹

Σαρτόριος, Ἰωσήφ. [Sartorios, Joseph.] See ΒΟΥΡΟΣ, Ἰωάννης, ΛΑΝΔΕΡΕΡ, Ξαυέριος & ΣΑΡΤΟΡΙΟΣ, Ἰωσήφ.

Σταματιάδης, Σ. [Stamatiades, S.] Περὶ τῆς λιπάνσεως τῆς Ἀμπέλου. 1888. III. 549.¹

Στέφανος, Ἰ. [Stephanos, I.] Διπλώματα Πορτοκαλεῶν καὶ Λιμονεῶν. 1900. III. 498.¹

Σφέτσος, Γεώργιος. [Sphetsos, Georgios.] Ἀσθένειαι τῶν ὀπωροφόρων δένδρων. 1900. III. 180.¹
Σχέδιον νόμου περὶ δασῶν. Μέρος Α΄. 1899. IV. 332.¹

Ὑπουργεῖον ἐσωτερικῶν τμῆμα γεωργίας. Ἐκθέσεις. III. 26,¹
V. xxvii.¹

Φιλάρετος, Πέτρος. [Philaretos, Petros.] Περὶ τῆς δι ἀρότρου
καλλιεργείας τῆς Ἀμπέλου. 1886. III. 559.¹
— Περὶ ἐκφυλλίσματος . . . τῆς Ἀμπέλου. 1887. III. 549.¹
— Περὶ οἰκονομικωτέρας μεθόδου πρὸς καλλιέργειαν τῆς Ἀμπέλου.
1885. III. 559.¹
— Πῶς καὶ πότε πρέπει νὰ καθαρίζωνται τὰ δένδρα. 1895. III.
171.
Φιλοδασικὴ ἕνωσις. Λογοδοσία. IV. 15.
Φράας, Ν. Κ. [Phraas, N. K.] Στοιχεῖα τῆς βοτανικῆς. 1839.
I. 87.

Χασιώτης, Σπυρίδων. [Chasiotes, Spyridon.] Ὁ ἔλτης τῆς
Ἀμπέλου. 1900. III. 564.²
— Ἡ Ἀμυγδαλέα. 1900. III. 434.²
— Ἀσβέστωσις τῶν ὀπωροφόρων δένδρων καὶ τῶν Ἐλαιῶν. 1900.
III. 197.
— Βαμβακίασις τῆς Ἐλαίας. 1900. III. 678.¹
— Ἐγκεντρισμὸς καὶ ἐνοφθαλμισμὸς τῆς Ἀμυγδαλῆς. 1890. III.
434.¹
— Ἐγκεντρισμὸς καὶ ἐνοφθαλμισμὸς τῆς Βερικοκέας καὶ Κερασέας.
1890. III. 430.²
— Ὁ ἐγκεντρισμὸς καὶ ἐνοφθαλμισμὸς τῆς Ἐλαίας. 1890. III.
676.¹
— Ἐγκεντρισμὸς καὶ ἐνοφθαλμισμὸς τῆς Μωρέας καὶ Καρυᾶς. 1890.
III. 355, 378.
— Ἐγκεντρισμὸς τῆς Ἀμπέλου. 1900. III. 548.²
— Ἐγκεντρισμὸς τῆς Ἀμπέλου. 1890. III. 548.²
— Ἐμβολιασμὸς τῆς Δαμασκηνῆς Ἀπιδέας καὶ Μηλέας. 1890. III.
164.¹
— Ἐμβολιασμὸς τῆς Κυδωνέας, Καστανέας. 1890. III. 164.¹
— Περὶ ἐμβολιασμοῦ τῶν ὀπωροφόρων δένδρων. 1890. III. 164.¹ —
1900. III. 164.²
— Ἐνοφθαλμισμὸς καὶ ἐγκεντρισμὸς τῆς Πορτοκαλέας. 1890. III.
497.²
— Ἐνοφθαλμισμὸς καὶ ἐγκεντρισμὸς τῆς Συκῆς. 1890. III. 369.²
— Περὶ θεραπείας τῶν φθειριάσεων τῶν ἐσπεριδοειδῶν. 1900. III.
197.
— Καλλιέργεια Πιστακίας τῆς γνησίας. 1900. III. 526.¹

— Καλλιέργεια τοῦ Φίκου τοῦ ἐλαστικοῦ. 1900. III. 370.²
— Περὶ καλλιεργείας τῆς Λεπτοκαρυᾶς. 1900. III. 358.¹
— Κανία τῆς Ἐλαίας. 1900. III. 678.¹
— Μαγνολία ἡ μεγανθής. 1900. III. 400.¹
— Ἡ Μεσπιλέα τῆς Ἰαπωνίας. 1900. III. 424.¹
— Νέον γεωργικὸν ἡμερολόγιον. 1894. III. 116.¹
— Ὁ Περονόσπορος. 1900. III. 582.
— Περὶ πολλαπλασιασμοῦ τῶν Μορεῶν. 1900. II. 154,¹ III.
378.
— Ἡ σταφυλὶς τῆς Ἀμπέλου ἐν Ἠλείᾳ. 1900. III. 564.²
— Πῶς φυτεύονται τὰ δένδρα. 1900. III. 166.
— Τὸ Ῥόδον τῆς Ἰαπωνίας. 1900. III. 412.²
— Ὁ σκάθαρος — Ὀπιωρυγχίτης ὁ αὐλακωτός. 1900. III. 192.¹
— Σκώληκες εἰς Ἀμπέλους. 1900. III. 564.²
— Σκώληξ τῆς Ἐλαίας. 1900. III. 678.¹
— Ἡ Συκῆ. 1900. III. 369.²
— Ἡ Τριανταφυλλέα. 1900. III. 455.¹
— Φθειρίασις τῆς Συκῆς. 1900. III. 370.¹
— Ἡ φυματίωσις τῶν Ἐλαιῶν. 1900. III. 678.¹
— Περὶ φυτεύσεως Ἀμπέλων κατὰ τελειότερον σύστημα. 1900. III.
559.¹

Χλδραϊχ, Θεόδωρος. [Heldreich, Theodor.] Περὶ τῆς ἀναφυεί-
σης εἰς τὰς Ἀμπέλους καὶ σταφιδαμπέλους νόσου. 1878. III. 560.
— Ὀλίγα τινα περὶ φυλλοξήρας. 1879. III. 571.
— Περὶ συμβολικῆς καὶ λατρείας τῶν δένδρων καὶ δασῶν. 1875. I.
517.¹
— Χλωρὶς ψημιριχή. 1895. I. 514.²
— Ἡ Χλωρὶς τῆς Αἰγίνης. 1899. I. 451.
— Ἡ Χλωρὶς τῆς Θήρας. 1899. I. 451.
— Ἡ Χλωρὶς τοῦ Παρνασσοῦ. 1890. I. 450.
— See also HELDREICH, Theodor.
Χλωρός, Νικόλαος Α. [Chloros, Nicholas.] Περὶ ἀναδασώσεων.
1893. IV. 168.¹
— Οἱ ἄσπονδοι ἐχθροὶ τῶν ἐλληνικῶν δασῶν. 1886. IV. 210.¹
— Περὶ βαλανιδίων. 1887. IV. 502.¹
— Περὶ δ᾽ ἀεὶ ἡ σπουδαιότης αὐτῶν ὑπὸ ὑγιεινὴν ἔποψιν. 1891.
IV. 55.¹
— Ἐγκυκλοπαιδεία τῆς δασολογίας. 1891. IV. 23.¹
— Εἰδικὴ ἢ συστηματικὴ βοτανικὴ κατὰ Eichler. 1894. I. 256.
— Ἔμμισσον ἀξία τῶν δασῶν μας. 1890. IV. 48.³
— Ξυλολογία. 1887. I. 126.
— Ἡ Πεύκη καὶ τὰ ῥητινώδη προϊόντα. 1883. IV. 462.¹
Χριστίνης, Δημήτριος. [Christines, Demetrios.] Πραγματεία
περὶ μεταφυτεύσεως δένδρων καθ' ὅλας τὰς ὥρας τοῦ ἔτους. 1868.
III. 168.²

INDEX OF RUSSIAN AND SERVIAN AUTHORS
AND TITLES

А., С. [A., S.] Краткій очеркъ степного лѣсоразведенія въ Велико-Анадольскомъ лѣсничествѣ. 1894. IV. 157.

Абазадзе, А. [Abazadze, A.] Справочная карманная книжка для лѣсничихъ. 1889. IV. 298.[1]

Аггеенко, В. Н. [Aggeyenko, Vladimir Naumovitch.] Замѣтки о растительности Прибалханскихъ степей. 1886. I. 457.

— Обзоръ растительности Крыма. 1897. I. 370.

— О распространеніи растеній на Таврическомъ полуостровѣ. 1886. I. 369.

— О растительныхъ формаціяхъ Таврическаго полуострова. 1887. I. 369.

— Флора Крыма. 1890. I. 369.

Адамовић, Лујо. [Adamović, Lujo.] О вегетацији југоисточне Србије. 1892. I. 450.

— О шумама југоисточне Србије. 1899. I. 448,[2] IV. 87.[2]

— See also Адамовић, Lujo.

Акинфіевъ, И. Я. [Akinfiyef, I. Y.] О древесной растительности Екатеринославскаго уѣзда. 1895. I. 359, IV. 81.

— Краткій предварительный отчетъ о ботаническомъ изслѣдованіи Верхнеднѣпровскаго уѣзда. 1895. I. 366.

— Обзоръ древесной растительности Екатериносл. губ. 1894. I. 359, IV. 81.

— Обзоръ древесной растительности Екатеринославской губ. Лѣса Новомосковскаго уѣзда. 1895. I. 359, IV. 81.

— Растительность Екатеринослава. 1889. I. 365.

— О растительныхъ преимущественно лѣсныхъ зонахъ въ центральномъ Кавказѣ. 1897. I. 369.

— Флора центральнаго Кавказа. 1894. I. 369.

Акціонерное общество разработки лѣсныхъ произведеній и торговли ими. 1859. IV. 308.[1]

Акціонеръ (pseud.). Русскіе милліарды. 1867. IV. 260.[1]

Аладьинъ, П. [Aladin, P.] Пособіе лѣсовладѣльцамъ осматривать и оцѣнивать. 1875. IV. 256.

Александровичъ, Р. [Aleksandrovitch, G.] О семействѣ верескoвыхъ растеній. 1844. II. 658,[1] III. 647.[1]

Альбовъ, Н. М. [Albof, N. M.] Изъ Абхазіи (состояніе лѣсовъ). 1893. IV. 348.

— Лѣса Абхазіи. 1892. IV. 348.[1]

— Матеріалы къ флорѣ Колхиды. 1895. I. 370.

— Результаты ботаническихъ изслѣдованій Абхазіи. 1893. I. 370.

— See also Alboff, Nicolas.

Альмединген, А. [Almedingen, A.] Какую пользу можно извлечь изъ Сосни и Ели? 1895. IV. 443.[2]

— Ботаническій словарь; справочная книга. See Анненковъ, N. 1878. I. 73.[1]

— Лѣсоводство. 1851. IV. 103.[2]

Альтумъ, Бернардъ. [Altum, Bernard.] Мыши и значеніе ихъ въ лѣсномъ хозяйствѣ. 1880. IV. 198.[1]

— See also Altum, Bernard.

Анджейковичъ, А. [Andzheikovitch, A.] О лѣсахъ Франціи. 1882. IV. 361.

Андреевскій, Г. [Andreyevski, G.] Замѣчанія о лѣсоводствѣ. 1836. IV. 114.

Анненковъ, Н. [Annenkof, Nicolaus.] Ботаническій словарь или собраніе. See Annenkof, N. 1859. I. 73.[1]

— Ботаническій словарь; справочная книга. See Annenkof, N. 1878. I. 73.[1]

— Лѣсоводство. 1851. IV. 103.[2]

— Описаніе Кювескаго ботаническаго сада. 1851. I. 522.[1]

— See also Annenkof, N. I.

Анненковъ, С. [Annenkof, S.] О лѣсномъ богатствѣ Россіи. 1856. IV. 273.[1]

Антоновъ, А. А. [Antonof, A.A.] Матеріалы къ флорѣ Новгородской губерніи. 1888. I. 365.

Арнольдъ, (полковникъ). [Arnold, (Colonel).] Руководство къ лѣсоводству. 1854. IV. 104.[1]

Арнольдъ, Ѳ. К. [Arnold, Friedrich.] Вспомогательная книжка для лѣсничихъ и лѣсовладѣльцевъ. 1890. IV. 104.[2]

Исторія лѣсоводства въ Россіи, Франціи и Германіи. 1895. IV. 24.[1]

— Курсъ лѣсоводства для лѣсныхъ школъ. 1892 IV. 104.[2]

— Курсъ лѣсоводства для низшихъ лѣсныхъ школъ. 1889. IV. 104.[1]

— Лѣсная таксація. 1858. IV. 240.

— Лѣсной товаръ. 186.? IV. 426.[1]

— Лѣсоводство. 1860. IV. 104.[1]

— Оцѣнка дѣйствующихъ въ лѣсахъ капиталовъ. 1884. IV. 257.

— Простой и удобный способъ къ скорому и вѣрному опредѣленію количества лѣса. 1861. IV. 217.

— Русскій лѣсъ. 1890. IV. 346.

— Справочная книга для землевладѣльца и лѣсничаго. 1862. IV. 214.

— Хозяйство въ русскихъ лѣсахъ. 1880. IV. 104.[1]

— Шестидесятилѣтній юбилей. See Шестидесятилѣтній юбилей... 1898. IV. 2.

— See also Arnold, Friedrich von.

Арнольдъ, Ѳ. & Нидерреферъ, Э. [Arnold, F. & Nidergefer, E.] Вспомогательная книжка. See Арнольдъ, Ѳ. К. 1890. IV. 104.[2]

Арсеньевъ, С. [Arsenyef, S.] Алфавитный указатель статей, напечатанныхъ въ лѣсномъ журналѣ. 1851. IV. 1.

Архиповъ, С. Н. [Arkhipof, S. N.] Важное значеніе лѣса. 1899. IV. 45.

— Какъ слѣдуетъ хозяйничать въ лѣсу для полученія наибольшихъ выгодъ. 1900. IV. 114.

— Наставленіе къ искусственному разведенію лѣса. 1896. IV. 142.

— Опытъ практическаго примѣненія въ лѣсномъ дѣлѣ военно-глазомѣрной... съемки. 1895. IV. 214.

— Практическое наставленіе къ смолокуренію. 1899. IV. 437.[1]

— Разведеніе лѣса. 1900. IV. 114.

Ассмусъ, Э. [Assmuss, Eduard.] Сухая перегонка дерева. See Assmuss, E. 1867. IV. 432.[2]

— See also Assmuss, E. P.

Астауровъ, А. [Astaurof, A.] Объ опредѣленіи доходности лѣсовъ. 1856. IV. 236.

Астафьевъ, Р. Ѳ. [Astafef, R. F.] О поврежденіи лѣса короѣдами. 1893. IV. 204.

Ауэрсвальдъ, Э. See Россмесслеръ, Э. А. & Ауэрсвальдъ, Э.

Афанасьевъ, П. А. [Afanasef, P. A.] Курсъ механической технологіи дерева. 1879. IV. 408.

Ахенбахъ, Г. [Achenbach, H.] О лѣсосѣчныхъ общинахъ въ горахъ Зигерланда. 1878. IV. 134.[1]

Ахматовъ, М. & Касяненко, В. [Akhmatof, M. & Kasyanenko, V.] Пятомникъ и семянной складъ при Черкасскомъ лѣсничествѣ. 1897. IV. 347.

Ашикъ, В. А. [Ashik, V. A.] Сухая перегонка дерева. 1864. IV. 432.[2]

Б—а, Н. Ѳ. [B—a, N. F.] О лѣсныхъ продуктахъ, какъ о богатствѣ. 1860. IV. 273.[2]

Баварскія массовыя таблицы. 1869. IV. 230.

Базаровъ, А. и Монтеверде, Н. [Bazarof, A. & Monteverde, Nikolaj.] Душистыя растенія и эфирныя масла. 1894. III. 227.

Байковъ, Дм. [Baikof, Demetrius.] Ботаническая географія. 1844. I. 299.

— О строеніи растительной клѣтицы. 1843. I. 525.[1]

Баранецкій, О. В. [Baranetzki, O. V.] О причинахъ направленія вѣтвей деревьевъ и кустарниковъ. 1899. I. 524.[1]

Баранецкій, П. В. [Baranetzki, P. V.] Лѣсоохраненіе. 1880. IV. 177.[1]

Баркъ, Л. [Bark, L.] Лѣсоразведеніе на югѣ Россіи. 1880. IV. 157.

Барсуковъ, А. Ѳ. [Barsukof, A. F.] Очеркъ Флоры южной части Лохвицкаго уѣзда. 1898. I. 367.
Баталинъ, А. Ѳ. [Batalin, Alexander.] Матеріалы для Флоры Псковской губерніи. 1884. I. 364.
— See also BATALIN, Alexander.
Баумъ, О. М. [Baum, O. M.] Статистическій обзоръ лѣсоводства въ Пензенской губерніи. 1872. IV. 345.
Бауръ, Ф. [Baur, Franz.] Лѣсная таксація. See BAUR, Franz. 1861. IV. 214.
— See also BAUR, Franz.
Бедемаръ, Варгасъ де. See Варгасъ-де-Бедемаръ.
Бекаревичъ, Н. [Bekarevitch, N.] Матеріалъ къ флорѣ Костромской губерніи. 1883. I. 364.
Бекетовъ, А. Н. [Beketof, A.] Объ Архангельской флорѣ. 1884. I. 364.
— Вліяніе возраста, климата ... на поперечной возрастаніе Сосны ... Лиственницы. 1872. II. 20.[2]
— Ботаническіе очерки. 1858. I. 520.[2]
— Географія растеній. 1896. I. 301.
— Курсъ ботаники. 1862. I. 523.[2]
— Очеркъ Тифлисской флоры. 1853. I. 368.[2]
— See also BEKETOF, Andreas.
Бекманъ, I. Г. [Beckmann, J. G.] Лѣсной временникъ. See BECKMANN, J. G. 1764. IV. 116.
— See also BECKMANN, Johann Gottlieb.
Бержинскій, В. О. [Berzhinski, V. O.] Краткое обозрѣніе выгодъ лѣсоводства. 1841. IV. 268.
Берингеръ, Мартинъ. [Beringer, Martin.] О вліяніи хозяйственныхъ мѣръ на ходъ прироста. 1892. IV. 246.
Бернацкій, А. [Bernatzki, A.] Важнѣйшія задачи лѣсосохраненія въ Пермской губерніи. 1893. IV. 180.[1]
— О мѣрахъ въ лѣсосохраненіи. 1893. IV. 273.[2]
Бетсъ, В. Г. [Bates, H. W.] Натуралистъ на Амазонской рѣкѣ. 1863. I. 342.
— See also BATES, Henry Walter.
Бехагель-фонъ Адлерскронъ. [Bekhagel von Adlerskron.] Таблицы для опредѣленія кубическаго содержанія деревъ въ кругломъ видѣ. 1852. IV. 223.
Блюменталь, Ю. [Blumenthal, Ju.] Записка коммиссіи, учрежденной въ г. Казани для составленія таксъ на лѣсные матеріалы. 1867. IV. 284.[1]
Богословскій. [Bogoslovski.] Описаніе болѣзней сѣверной Сосны. 1872. IV. 476.
Богуслов, I. [Boguslof, I.] Статистическое обозрѣніе лѣсовъ. .. по Владимірской губерніи. 1849. IV. 345.
Боде, А. К. [Bode, Adolph Friedrich.] Карманная книга. See BODE, A. K. I. 6.
— Лѣсная технологія. 1846. IV. 381.
— Руководство къ разведенію лѣсовъ. 1853. IV. 104.[1]
— Ручная книга для хозяйственнаго обращенія съ лѣсами. See BODE, A. 1840. IV. 94.
— О свойствахъ русскихъ древесныхъ породъ и преимущественно дуба. 1851. IV. 398.[2]
— See also BODE, Adolph Friedrich.
Боковъ, В. Е. [Bokof, V. E.] Къ вопросу о колонизаціи Чердынскаго края. 1898. IV. 273.[2]
— Древообрабатывающая промышленность въ Пермской губ. 1899. IV. 404.[2]
— Куренная операція на Уральскихъ горныхъ заводахъ. 1898. IV. 395.
— Углеженіе въ лѣсахъ Пермской губерніи. 1897. IV. 395.
— Объ углеженіи на Уральскихъ горныхъ заводахъ. 1898. IV. 395.
— Химическая обработка дерева въ горно-заводскихъ дачахъ Пермской губерніи. 1898. IV. 433.[1]
Болегъ. [Boleg.] Современные пріемы переработки живицы и канифоли. 1898. III. 228.[1]
Боровскій, I. [Borovski, I.] Изслѣдованіе анатомическаго строенія ... древесины Pistacia mutica. 1886. II. 457.[2]
Бородинъ, И. П. [Borodin, I. P.] Анатомія растеній. 1887. I. 524.[1]
—: О диффузномъ отложеніи щавелево-кальція. 1892. I. 526.[2]
— О дыханіи почекъ, распускающихся на срѣзанныхъ вѣтвяхъ. 1893. I. 526.[2]
— Краткій очеркъ микологіи. 1897. III. 195.[1]
— Курсъ анатоміи растеній. 1887. I. 524.[1]
— Курсъ ботаники. 1882. I. 523.[2]
— Курсъ дендрологіи. 1891. IV. 81.

— Физіологическія изслѣдованія надъ дыханіемъ листоносныхъ побѣговъ. 1876. I. 526.[1]
— See also BORODIN, Johann.
О ботанической географіи (о флорѣ) южной Европы. 1837. I. 349.
Ботаническій садъ Имп. С.-Петербургскаго универси-тета. Ботаническія записки. See HORTUS UNIVERSITATIS IMPERIALIS PETROPOLITANAE. I. 9.
Боярышникъ. 1840. III. 421.[1]
Бранке, В. Ю. фонъ. [Branke, Vladimir von.] Древесная растительность южнаго берега Крыма. 1896. I. 368,[1] IV. 81.
— Изъ экскурсій по лѣсамъ Кавказскаго берега Чернаго моря. 1895. IV. 348.[1]
Бремзенъ, Н. [Bremzen, I.] Зелькова. 1873. III. 366.[1]
Бремъ, А. & Россмесслеръ, Е. [Brehm, A. E. & Rossmässler, E. A.] Лѣсныя животныя звѣри. See BREHM, A. E. & ROSSMÄSSLER, E. A. 1864. IV. 90.[1]
— — Охранители и истребители лѣса. 1890. IV. 90.[1]
— — See also BREHM, A. E. & ROSSMÄSSLER, E. A.
Буличъ, А. [Bulitch, A.] Ботаническія наблюденія во время экскурсіи по Волгѣ. 1892. I. 366.
Булычевъ, Н. П. [Bulytchef, N. P.] Очеркъ флоры и фауны Иркотскаго уѣзда. 1878. I. 454.[1]
Бульмерингъ, М. [Bulmerincq, M.] Указанія для опредѣленія цѣнности лѣсовъ Европейской Россіи. 1848. IV. 254.
— See also BULMERINCQ, M. E. von.
Бунге, А. [Bunge, Alexander von.] Астрагаловыя. See BUNGE, A. von. 1880. II. 376.[1]
— Описаніе новыхъ родовъ и видовъ китайскихъ и монгольскихъ растеній. See BUNGE, A. von. I. 460.[1]
— See also BUNGE, Alexander von.
Буницкій, К. [Bunitaki, K.] Руководство для древоразведенія въ Александровскомъ уѣздѣ. 1867. III. 101.[1]
Бургсдорфъ, Ф. [Burgsdorf, F.] Руководство къ надежному воспитанію и насажденію иностранныхъ и домашнихъ деревъ. 1801. IV. 103.[1]—See also BURGS-DORF, F. A. L. von. 1787. IV. 105.
— See also BURGSDORF, F. A. L. von.
Буркгардтъ, Г. [Burckhardt, Heinrich.] Посѣвъ и посадка лѣса. See BURCKHARDT, Heinrich. 1855. IV. 106.
— See also BURCKHARDT, Heinrich.
Бурый, Н. [Bury, N.] Лѣса Баваріи. 1893. IV. 351.[1]
— Лѣса Богеміи. 1894. IV. 372.
— Лѣса Франціи. 1893. IV. 361.
— Распространеніе лѣсахъ Баваріи. 1891. IV. 548.[2]
— Швейцарская центральная лѣсная опытная станція въ Цюрихѣ. 1892. IV. 38.[2]
Буттацъ, Ф. [Buttatz, F.] Начертаніе способа какъ заводить при недостаткѣ въ дровахъ лѣса. 1805. IV. 114.
— Примѣчанія о распространяющемся недостаткѣ въ лѣсѣ. 1805. IV. 280.[2]
Бушъ. [Busch.] Таблицы объема полѣнницъ и плотовъ. 1882. IV. 228.
Бушъ, Н. А. [Busch, N. A.] Ботанико-географическія изслѣдованія въ нагорной части Козмодемьянскаго уѣзда. 1891. I. 366.
— Краткій очеркъ растительности Вятской губерніи. 1891. I. 366.
— Матеріалъ къ флорѣ Вятской губерніи. 1889. I. 365.
Быковъ, Н. Л. [Bykof, N. L.] Лѣсныя культуры въ Каменно-Степномъ опытномъ лѣсничествѣ. 1900. IV. 347.
Бычихинъ, А. [Bytchikhin, A.] Значеніе защитныхъ насажденій для степной полосы. 1893. III. 215.[2]
Бѣлозерскій, О. М. [Byelozerski, O. M.] О разведеніи лѣса въ степной полосѣ. 1879. IV. 157.

В. Н. [V. N.] Посадка деревьевъ. 1882. IV. 153.[1]
Варгасъ-де-Бедемаръ, графъ. [Vargas de Bedemar, Graf.] Изслѣдованія запаса и прироста лѣсонасажденій въ С.-Петербургской губерніи. 1850. IV. 345.
— See also VARGAS DE BEDEMAR, E. A., Graf.
Васильевъ, Я. К. [Vasilyef, J. K.] Какими мѣрами могли-бы частные лѣсодѣльцы Кавказа поднять производительность своихъ лѣсовъ? 1890. IV. 383.[1]
— Значеніе рѣкъ Кубанской области въ лѣсномъ хозяйствѣ. 1895. IV. 383.[1]

Васнѣвскій, Ю. Н. [Vasnyevski, Yu. N.] Анатомическое строеніе... Parrotia persica. 1891. II. 254.¹

Введенскій, А. Н. [Vvedenski, A. N.] О размноженіи нѣкоторыхъ хвойныхъ... растеній черенками. 1882. III. 158.

Вводные доклады пятому всероссійскому съѣзду лѣсохозяевъ въ Москвѣ. 1882. IV. 40.¹

Веберъ, К. [Weber, K.] Практическое руководство по лѣсопильному производству. 1890. IV. 393.

— Руководство по смолокуренію. 1890. IV. 437.¹

— Сооруженіе сельско-хоз., лѣсныхъ заводскихъ и вообще промышленныхъ подъѣздныхъ путей. 1892. IV. 392.

Ведровъ, С. В. [Vedrof, S. V.] О лѣсоохраненіи по русскому праву. 1878. IV. 180.¹

— Труды всероссійскихъ съѣздовъ лѣсохозяевъ по вопросу о лѣсоохраненіи. 1877. IV. 180.¹

Вейнбергъ, Я. [Weinberg, J.] Лѣсъ, значеніе его въ природѣ и мѣры къ его сохраненію. 1884. IV. 44.

О Венгерскомъ Дубѣ. 1833. IV. 503.¹

Вереха, П. Н. [Verekha, P. N.] Лѣсоводство въ журналѣ "Сельское хозяйство и лѣсоводство." 1891. IV. 2.

— Опытъ лѣсоводственнаго терминологическаго словаря. 1898. IV. 23.¹

— Порядокъ отпуска лѣсныхъ матеріаловъ. 1875. IV. 297.¹

— Систематическій сборникъ дѣйствующихъ циркулярныхъ распоряженій. 1877. IV. 297.

— Систематическій указатель лѣсного журнала, издаваемаго С.-Петербургскимъ лѣснымъ обществомъ, за двадцать лѣтъ 1871-1890 годовъ. 1892. IV. 2.

— Систематическій указатель лѣсоводственныхъ статей Лѣсного журнала. 1899. IV. 2.

— Систематическій указатель отдѣльныхъ книгъ по лѣсоводству, изданныхъ на русскомъ языкѣ по 1887 году. 1888. IV. 2.

— Систематическій указатель предметовъ. 1888. IV. 289.¹

— & **Рудзскій, А.** [Verekha, P. & Rudzski, A.] Литература русскаго лѣсоводства. 1878. IV. 2.

Верманъ, Э. [Verman, E.] Лѣсная промышленность. 1847. IV. 426.¹

Вехтеръ. [Wächter.] О естественныхъ и искусственныхъ дѣятеляхъ, способствующихъ... возрожденію растеній. 1844. I. 527.²

— See also WÄCHTER, J. K.

Вигманъ, [А. Ф.] [Wiegmann, A. F.] О болѣзняхъ и нѣкоторыхъ уродливостяхъ растеній. 1836; III. 178.

— See also WIEGMANN, A. F.

Вильбушевичъ, Н. О. [Vilbushevitch, Jean.] Лѣсоразведеніе въ черноморской экономіи А. И. Фальцъ-Фейнъ. 1888, IV. 157.

— See also VILBUSHEVITCH, Jean.

Виммеръ, Ф. [Wimmer, Friedrich.] Растительное царство. See WIMMER, Friedrich. 1853. I. 256.

— See also WIMMER, С. F. H.

Вислоцкій, С. М. [Vislotzki, S. M.] Государственное значеніе лѣсовъ Тобольской губерніи. 1897. IV. 273.²

Воловичъ, Г. В. [Volovitch, G. B.] Ревизія пущъ и переходовъ звѣриныхъ въ бывшемъ великомъ княжествѣ Литовскомъ. 1867. IV. 345.

Володкевичъ, С. Н. [Volodkevitch, S. N.] Объяснительная записка по Вайдарскому лѣсному дѣлу. 1891. IV. 346.

— See also VILBUSHEVITCH, Jean.

Вольфъ, Э. Л. [Wolf, Egbert L.] Дендрологическій садъ С.-Петербургскаго Лѣсного Института. 1891. I. 521.² IV. 18.¹

— Деревья и кустарники въ зимнемъ состояніи. 1893. I. 294.² IV. 81.¹

— Листва деревьевъ и кустарниковъ. 1892. I. 294.¹ IV. 81.¹

— Матеріалы для изученія Ивъ, растущихъ дико въ Европейской Россіи. 1900. II. 101.¹

— Матеріалы для изученія русскихъ видовъ Жимолостей. 1899. II. 836.¹

— Новая пестролистная Таволга. 1891.· III. 430.¹

— See also WOLF, Egbert.

Волынскій. [Volynski.] Краткое основательное и опытное Россійскаго Государства лѣсоводство. 1820. IV. 103.²

Вороновъ, Генадій. [Voronof, Genadi.] Дешевый лѣсомѣръ. 1893. IV. 231.²

Вотчалъ, Е. [Vottchal, E.] Къ вопросу о распространеніи... солянина в растеніяхъ. 1887. I. 526.²

— Отложеніе крахмала въ древесныхъ породахъ. 1888. I. 526.²

Врангель, В., баронъ. [Wrangel, W., baron.] Исторія лѣсного законодательства Россійской Имперіи. 1841. IV. 315.¹

Временныя массовыя таблицы. 1886. IV. 228.

Всероссійскій съѣздъ лѣсохозяевъ. Труды. IV. 6.

Вуйчицкій, С. [Vuitzitzki, S.] Оплодотвореніе у Хвойныхъ. 1899. II. 21.²

Вылежинскій. [Vylezhinski.] Сухая перегородка дерева. n. d. IV. 432.¹

Выписка изъ воинскаго устава о пѣхотной службѣ для лѣсной стражи. 1855. IV. 296.²

Высоцкій, Г. [Vysotzki, G.] Растительность Великоанадольскаго участка. 1898. IV. 347.

Выставка предметовъ, относящихся къ лѣсо- и древоразведенію. 1885. IV. 19.²

Вѣщицкій, А. Ф. [Veshtchitzki, A. F.] О разведеніи лѣса на Ѳеодосійскихъ горахъ. 1881. IV. 157.

Вюильменъ. [Vuilmen =? Vuillemin.] Біологія растеній. 1897. I. 219.¹

Вюльфингъ, М. [Wülfing, M.] Руководство къ ботаникѣ. 1814. IV. 61.²

Г., П. В. [G., P. B.] Лѣса—спасеніе Новороссійскаго края. 1872. IV. 273.²

Габлицель. [Hablizl, K. L.] Физическое описаніе Таврической области. 1785. I. 368.¹

Газета Лѣсоводства и Охоты. IV. 6.

Гамрекеловъ, А. С. [Gamrekelof, A. S.] Самшитъ или Кавказская Пальма. 1891. IV. 525.

— See also Медвѣдевъ, Я. С. & Гамрекеловъ, А. С.

Ганггоферъ, А. [Ganghofer, August.] Лѣсное опытное дѣло. See GANGHOFER, August. 1881. IV. 37.¹

— See also GANGHOFER, August.

Гартвигъ, [Hartwig, G. L.] Тропическій міръ. See HARTWIG, G. L. 1860. I. 528.²

— See also HARTWIG, G. L.

Гартигъ, Робертъ. [Hartig, Robert.] Болѣзни деревьевъ. See HARTIG, Robert. 1882. IV. 195.²

— Изслѣдованіе хода роста, запаса Дубовыхъ. See HARTIG, Robert. 1865. IV. 232.

— See also HARTIG, Robert.

Гейеръ, Густавъ. [Heyer, Gustav.] Руководство къ оцѣнкѣ лѣсовъ. See HEYER, Gustav. 1865. IV. 253.

— Руководство къ статикѣ лѣсоводства. See HEYER, Gustav. 1871. IV. 255.

— See also HEYER, Gustav.

Гейеръ, Карлъ. [Heyer, Carl.] Лѣсовозращеніе. See HEYER, Carl. 1854. IV. 106.

— See also HEYER, Carl.

Гельмъ, П. [Helm, P.] Ботаническая поѣздка изъ Богословска въ Тагилъ. 1874. I. 363.

Генъке, К. Ф. Р. [Henke, Karol.] Объ устройствѣ лѣсовъ. See HENKE, Karol. 1846. IV. 240.

— See also HENKE, Karol.

Гензенъ, А. [Hensen, A.] Повторительный курсъ ботаники. 1898. I. 523.

Генько, Н. К. [Henko, N. K.] Разведеніе лѣса. 1896. IV. 157.

— Къ статистикѣ лѣсовъ Европейской Россіи. 1888. IV. 346.

— See also HENKO, N. K.

Гердеръ, Ф. Е. [Herder, Ferdinand von.] Наблюденія надъ періодичностью явленій въ развитіи растеній. 1877. I. 224.¹

— Сравнительная таблица начала развитія листьевъ, цвѣтовъ. 1875. I. 224.¹

— Сравнительная таблица средняго времени развитія на открытомъ воздухѣ листьевъ. 1872. I. 224.¹

— See also HERDER, F. G. von.

Гернетъ, К. [Gernet, Carl A. von] Виды аномальнаго строенія стеблей. 186.? I. 524.¹

— See also GERNET, Carl von.

Герценштейнъ, В. О. [Herzenstein, V. O.] Предохраненіе дерева. 1877. IV. 420.

— See also HERZENSTEIN, V. O.

Гибель, К. Г. [Giebel, C. G.] Птицы, полезныя. See GIEBEL, C. G. 1868. IV. 90.¹

— See also GIEBEL, C. G.

Гильдеманъ, А. [Gildeman, A.] Вліяніе электричества. 1850. I. 529.
— О лѣсныхъ, грушевыхъ и яблоновыхъ породахъ. 1841. III. 425,[2] 444.[2]
— Монографія Китайскаго Ясеня. 1843. III. 506.[2]
— Объ орѣшниковыхъ породахъ. 1840. III. 357.[2]
— О произрастающихъ въ Россіи тополевыхъ породахъ. 1840. III. 344.[1]
— О рябиновыхъ породахъ. 1840. III. 459.[1]
— О Чишковыхъ и Боярышниковыхъ породахъ. 1841. III. 421.[1]
Глинскій, Ф. А. [Glinski, F. A.] Бѣловѣжская пуща и зубры. 1899. IV. 347.
— See also GLINSKI, Fr.
Гоби, Хр. [Gobi, Christoph.] О вліяніи Валдайской возвышенности на географическое распространеніе растеній. 1876. I. 363.
Годовой отчетъ Училища Св. Анны. See HERDER, F. G. von. 1872. I. 217.
Голенкинъ, М. И. [Golenkin, Mikhail.] Матеріалы для флоры юго-восточной части Калужской губерніи. 1890. I. 365.
— See also GOLENKIN, Mikhail.
Головинъ, В. [Golovin, Vasil.] Разсужденіе о жизни растеній. 1825. I. 524.[1]
Гомилевскій, Василій. [Gomilevski, Vasili.] Австрійская черная Сосна. 1893. IV. 466.[2]
— Грецкій или Волошскій Орѣхъ. 1894. III. 355.
— Основаніе лѣсоразведенія въ степяхъ южной Россіи. Акація. 1880. IV. 523.[1]
— Предварительное естественное возобновленіе спѣлыхъ сосновыхъ лѣсовъ. 1891. IV. 474.
— Сельско-хозяйственная пользованіе въ лѣсахъ. 1897. IV. 134.[1]
— Типичный способъ облѣсенія оголенныхъ отъ лѣса пространствъ. 1895. IV. 157.
— Тутовое дерево или Шелковица. 1894. III. 378.
— Хозяйство въ дубовыхъ лѣсахъ, ради производства дубильнаго корья. 1900. IV. 509.
Горбунова, Е. [Gorbunof, Mrs. E.] Наши зеленые друзья-деревья. 1899. I. 82.[2]
Гордягинъ, А. [Gordyagin, Andrej.] Естественно-историческое описаніе Казанской губерніи. 1889. I. 365.
— Матеріалы для познанія почвы и растительности западной Сибири. 1900. I. 454.[2]
— Очеркъ растительности окрестностей г. Красноуфимска. 1888. I. 365.
— Растительность извѣстковыхъ скалъ на рѣкѣ Турѣ въ Пермской губерніи. 1895. I. 454.[2]
Горицкій, К. С. [Goritzki, K. S.] Матеріалы для флоры Харьковской губерніи. 1872. I. 363.
— Списокъ русскихъ и нѣмоторыхъ инородческихъ названій растеній. 1886. I. 522.[2]
Горожанкинъ, И. Н. [Gorozhankin, I. N.] О корпускулахъ . . . у голосѣмянныхъ растеній. 1880. II. 1.
— Матеріалы для флоры Московской губерніи. 1888. I. 365.
— See also GOROZHANKIN, I. N.
Горяниновъ, П. [Goryaninof, P.] Основанія ботаники. 1841. I. 522.
Гофманъ, С. О. [Hofman, S. O.] Календарь. See Календарь. IV. 6.
— Новый лѣсной календарь. See Календарь. IV. 6.
Гоше, Н. [Gaucher, Nicolas.] Теоретическое и практическое руководство къ облагороженію, воспитанію и размноженію. 1885. III. 153.
— See also GAUCHER, Nicolas.
Гребнеръ, В. фонъ. [Grebner, W. von.] Значеніе Осины въ русскомъ лѣсоводствѣ. 1859. IV. 486.[2]
— Копченіе древесной сажи. 1840. IV. 394.
— Руководство къ добыванію смолы и вара. 1859. IV. 436.[1]
Гребницкій, А. [Hrebnitzki, Adam.] Лѣсной отдѣлъ на всемірной выставкѣ въ Чикаго. 1893. IV. 19.[1]
Гребницкій, А. С. [Grebnitzki, A. S.] Крахмалъ, какъ запасной матеріалъ нашихъ деревьевъ. 1884. I. 526.[2]
— О періодичности накопленія и исчезанія крахмала въ вѣтвяхъ нашихъ деревьевъ. See GREBNITZKI, A. S. 1883. I. 526.[2]
Греве, В. [Greve, V.] See Шелгуновъ, Н. & Греве, В.
Гризебахъ, А. [Grisebach, August H. R.] Растительность земного шара. 1872. I. 300.
— See also GRISEBACH, A. H. R.

Гукеръ, I. [Hooker, J. D.] Начатки ботаники. See HOOKER, Sir J. D. 1876. I. 523.
— See also HOOKER, Sir J. D.
Гульбе, Л. А. [Gulbe, L. A.] О періодичной дѣятельности камбія въ корняхъ нашихъ деревъ. 1888. I. 525.
Гумбольтъ, Ф. Г. А. фонъ. [Humboldt, F. H. A. von.] О физіогноміи растеній. See HUMBOLDT, F. H. A. von. 1806. I. 217.
— See also HUMBOLDT, F. H. A. von.
Гурьяновъ, А. & **Маковецкій**, А. [Guryanof, A. & Makovetzki, A.] Практическое руководство лѣсоразведенія въ степяхъ южной Россіи. 1895. IV. 157.
Гюнтеръ, IA. [Günther, A.] Матеріалы къ флорѣ Обоянежскаго края. 1880. I. 364.

Д. [D.] О вліяніи электричества на ростъ дерева. 1857. I. 529.
Даніель-Бековъ. [Daniel-Bekof.] Опытъ статистическаго изслѣдованія казеннаго лѣсного хозяйства. 1900. IV. 25.
Дашковъ, Д. [Dashkof, D.] О мѣрахъ къ сохраненію лѣсовъ въ Рязанской губерніи. 1871. IV. 180.[1]
Двигубскій, Ив. [Dvigubski, Ivan A.] Легкій способъ распознавать дико-растущія на поляхъ московскихъ растеній. 1827. I. 360.
— Московская флора. 1828. I. 360.
Де-Бари, А. [Bary, H. A. de.] Сравнительная анатомія вегетативныхъ органовъ явнобрачныхъ и папоротниковыхъ растеній. See BARY, H. A. de. 1877. I. 524.[1]
— See also BARY, H. A. de.
Декандоль, А. [Candolle, Alphonse de.] Введеніе къ изученію ботаники . . . See CANDOLLE, Alphonse de. 1835. I. 87.
— See also CANDOLLE, Alphonse de.
Деларю, Е. [La Rue, Eugène de.] Выдѣленіе воды надземными органами растеній. 1868. I. 526.[1]
— Гистологическое изслѣдованіе сердцевиннаго влагалища нѣкоторыхъ Хвойныхъ. 1871. II. 16.[1]
— See also LA RUE, Eugène de.
Демонси, П. [Demontzey, Prosper.] Практическое руководство къ облѣсенію и задерненію горъ. See DEMONTZEY, Prosper. 1878. IV. 163.
— See also DEMONTZEY, Prosper.
Дзержановскій, В. [Dzerzhanovski, V.] Краткое описаніе казенныхъ лѣсовъ Кржепицкаго лѣсничества. 1878. IV. 345.
Дзѣвульскій, Л. [Dzievulski, L.] Опредѣленіе удѣльнаго вѣса древесныхъ волоконъ. 1886. IV. 411.[2]
Дивовъ, П. [Divof, P.] Краткое руководство къ сбереженію . . . въ Россійскомъ государствѣ. 1809. IV. 179.[2]
Диппель, [Dippel, Leopold.] Начальныя основанія ботаники. 1859. I. 523.
— See also DIPPEL, Leopold.
Длатовскій, А. [Dlatovski, A.] Курсъ лѣсовозобновленія и лѣсоразведенія. 1843. IV. 141.
Дмитріевъ, А. М. [Dmitriyef, A. M.] Предварительный отчетъ объ изслѣдованіяхъ флоры Ярославской губерніи. 1900. I. 368.[1]
Дмитріевъ, М. [Dmitrief, M.] Древесное сѣмо. 1897. III. 223.[2]
Добровлянскій, В. Я. [Dobrovlyanski, Vasili.] Задачи и урочныя данныя для составленія проэктовъ лѣсокультурныхъ работъ. 1890. IV. 114.
— Лѣсоустройство во Франціи. 1891. IV. 249.[1]
— О нѣкоторыхъ признакахъ древесныхъ сѣмянъ. See DOBROVLYANSKI, Vasili. 1892. I. 121.
— Практическая Дендрологія. See Тюбефъ, К. Сѣмена, плоды и всходы. 1891. I. 119, Вольфъ, Э. Л. Листва деревьевъ. 1893. I. 294,[1] and Вольфъ, Э. Л. Деревья и кустарники. 1893. IV. 81.[1]
— Изъ русскихъ лѣсовъ. 1888. IV. 346.
— Сравнительная анатомія листьевъ новыхъ. 1891. II. 103.[2]
— Урочныя нормы для лѣсокультурныхъ работъ. 1890. IV. 114.
— Частные случаи искусственнаго лѣсоразведенія. 1894. IV. 157.
Додель-Портъ, А. [Dodel-Port, A.] Очерки по анатоміи, физіологіи и исторіи развитія растеній. See DODEL-PORT, Arnold & Carolina. 1880. I. 523.[3]
— See also DODEL-PORT, Arnold.

Докладъ и проэктъ устава о лѣсахъ. 1809. IV. 315.[1]
Докладъ 3-й коммиссіи по вопросу о мѣрахъ борьбы противъ появившагося . . . шелкопряда-монашенки. 1895. IV. 202.
Докладъ Харьковскому Губ. Земскому Собранію особой коммиссіи по вопросу о сбереженіи лѣсовъ . . . въ Харьковской губерніи. 1876. IV. 180.[1]
Докучаевъ, В. В. [Dokutchayef, V. V.] Методы изслѣдованія вопроса: были-ли лѣса въ южной степной Россіи? 1889. I. 359, IV. 80.
— Предварительный отчетъ о дѣятельности особой экспедиціи . . . по испытанію и учету различныхъ способовъ и пріемовъ лѣсного. 1893. IV. 114.
—See also DOKUTCHAYEF, V.
Доллемъ, фанъ. See Фанъ Доллемъ.
Дю Брейль, А. [Du Breuil, Alphonse.] Курсъ древоводства. See DU BREUIL, A. 1846. III. 110.[1]
— See also DU BREUIL, Alphonse.
Дютуръ, П. [Dutour, P.] Руководство къ общей и лѣсной ботаникѣ. 1856. IV. 80.

О Ели. 1848. IV. 458.
Еттингенъ, А. Н. See OETTINGEN, Arthur von & MAYDELL, T. Лѣсные законны. 1898. IV. 316.

Жебенко, Ф. [Zhebenko, F.] Лѣсная дача имѣнія Порѣчье Смоленск губ. 1876. IV. 345.
Желѣзновъ, Н. [Zhelyeznof, N.] О происхожденіи зародыша. 1842. I. 527.
— See also GELEZNOW, Nicolas.
Жилинскій, (генералъ). [Zhilinski, (general).] Краткое обозрѣніе Полѣсья. 1892. IV. 346.
Жудра, П. Н. [Zhudra, P. I.] Монашенка (Ocneria monacha), ея образъ жизни. 1893. IV. 201.
Жуковскій, Н. [Zhukovski, N.] Права и обязанности лѣсной стражи. 1884. IV. 315.[2]
Жуковъ, А. Н. [Zhukof, A. I.] Лѣсоводство для русскихъ владѣльцевъ. 1849. IV. 114.
Журналъ спеціальнаго по лѣсной части комитета. 1885. IV. 114.

Заленскій, В. [Zalenski, V.] О кристаллоносныхъ клѣткахъ съ опробковѣлыми оболочками. 1897. I. 525.[1]
—See also ROTHERT, W. & ZALENSKI, W.
Замѣчанія о нѣкоторыхъ сѣверо-американскихъ лиственныхъ деревьяхъ. 1844. IV. 125.[1]
О западномъ Чинарѣ. 1850. III. 419.[1]
Запасникъ, К. [Zapasnik, K.] Разведеніелѣса въ степномъ краѣ. 1895. IV. 157.
Записки Комитета лѣсоводства. т. II-й. 1859. IV. 345.
Засѣданія лѣсохозяйственнаго съѣзда въ г. Уфѣ. 1873. IV. 40.[1]
Заусцинскій, Л. [Zaustsinski, or Zauscinski, L.] Нѣсколько замѣчаній о прозябеніи и . . . распространеніи обыкновенной Сосны въ Европѣ. 1844. II. 45.[1]
— Очеркъ двухсѣмянодольныхъ древесныхъ организмовъ вообще. 1857. IV. 61.[2]
Зефковъ, Отто. [Zefkof, Otto.] Таблицы для измѣренія дерева въ брусьяхъ и доскахъ. 1876. IV. 228.
Зобовъ, Н. [Zobof, N.] Лѣсная таксація и лѣсоустройство. 1873. IV. 244, 253.
— Начальныя основанія ботаники. 1864. I. 523,[1] IV. 80.
Зоргенфрей. [Sorgenfrei.] О Ясенахъ. 1837. III. 672.[1]
Зяблоцкій. [Ziablovski.] Начальныя основанія лѣсоводства. 1804. IV. 103.[1]

Иваницкій, Н. А. [Ivanitzki, N. A.] Списокъ растеній Вологодской губерніи. 1883. I. 364.
— See also IVANITZKY, N. A.
Ивановъ, А. [Ivanof, A.] Ботаническія и почвенныя изслѣдованія въ Юрьевскомъ и Суздальскомъ уѣздахъ. 1897. I. 367.
Ивановъ, М. [Ivanof, M.] Практическое смолокуреніе для крестьянъ. 1873. IV. 436.[1]
— Таблицы. 1874. IV. 227.
Объ Ивѣ. 1838. III. 347.
Извлеченіе изъ законовъ объ охраненіи и защитѣ лѣсовъ, принадлежащихъ частнымъ лицамъ. 1873. IV. 315.[1]

Извлеченіе изъ отчета по лѣсному управленію за 1866 годъ. 1868. IV. 289.[1]
Изслѣдованія о запасѣ и приростѣ лѣсовъ въ Тульской губерніи. 1858. IV. 345.
Императорскій С.-Петербургскій ботаническій садъ. Труды. See HORTUS PETROPOLITANUS. I. 9.
Императорскій Томскій Университетъ. Извѣстія. I. 519.[1]
Императорскій Юрьевскій университетъ. Труды ботаническаго сада. See UNIVERSITAS IMPERIALIS JURIEVENSIS. I. 10.
Императорское Вольно-экономическое общество. Лѣсной журналъ. IV. 6.
Императорское Россійское Общество Садоводства въ С.-Петербургѣ. Вѣстникъ. III. 10.
Инструкція для заготовленія. . . . дѣловыхъ лѣсовъ, употребляемыхъ на постройку артиллеріи. 1854. IV. 296.[2]
Инструкція для отграниченія лѣсныхъ надѣловъ. 1874. IV. 297.
Инструкція для отпуска лѣсныхъ матеріаловъ изъ дачъ вѣдомства. 1900. IV. 298.[1]
Инструкція для оцѣнки лѣсовъ. 1872. IV. 297.
Инструкція для оцѣнки лѣсосѣкъ, единичныхъ деревьевъ и насажденій. 1883. IV. 298.[1]
Инструкція для производства культуръ. 1844. IV. 296.[2]
Инструкція для производства работъ по изслѣдованію обширныхъ лѣсныхъ пространствъ. 1897. IV. 298.[1]
Инструкція для производства работъ по лѣснымъ надѣламъ государственныхъ крестьянъ. 1871. IV. 297.
Инструкція для производства работъ по лѣснымъ надѣламъ государственныхъ крестьянъ въ 13 губерніяхъ. 1869. IV. 297.
Инструкція для работъ по отграниченію лѣсныхъ надѣловъ. 1874. IV. 297.
Инструкція для ревизіи лѣсовъ, устроенныхъ по упрощеннымъ правиламъ. 1870. IV. 297.
Инструкція для устройства защитныхъ лѣсовъ. 1889. IV. 298.[1]
Инструкція для устройства и ревизіи лѣсовъ. 1855. IV. 298.[1]
Инструкція для устройства казенныхъ лѣсовъ. 1888. IV. 298.[1]
Инструкція для устройства казенныхъ лѣсовъ на Кавказѣ. 1896. IV. 298.[1]
Инструкція для устройства лѣсныхъ дачъ. 1900. IV. 298.[2]
Инструкція для устройства лѣсовъ крестьянскаго надѣла въ губерніяхъ великороссійскихъ. 1865. IV. 297.
Инструкція для устройства удѣльныхъ лѣсовъ. 1859. IV. 297.
Инструкція лѣснымъ ревизорамъ состоящимъ при управленіи Государственныхъ Имуществъ. 1875. IV. 297.
Инструкція о порядкѣ отпуска саженцевъ и древесныхъ сѣмянъ изъ казенныхъ лѣсничествъ. 1893. IV. 298.[1]
Инструкція о счетоводствѣ и отчетности лѣсныхъ офицеровъ. 1851. IV. 296.[1]
Инструкція объ управленіи лѣсною частью на горныхъ заводахъ хребта Уральскаго. 1833. IV. 296.[2]
Ипполитовъ, В. П. [Ippolitof, V. P.] Сухая перегонка дерева. 1884. IV. 433.[1]
Исаевъ, А. А. [Isayef, A. A.] Что принесъ 1888 годъ для сохраненія русскихъ лѣсовъ? 1889. IV. 180.[1]

Іенигъ, Ф. [Yensh, F. or Jensch?] Руководство къ разведенію лѣсовъ въ степяхъ. 1843. IV. 157.
Іоельсонъ. [Ioelson.] О возращеніи дубовыхъ низкоствольниковъ. 1889. III. 361.[2]

Кабештовъ, Н. М. [Kabeshtof, I. M.] Лѣсонасажденіе, питомники и школы въ имѣніяхъ графа М. М. Толстого. 1900. IV. 347.
Казицынъ, Н. [Kazitzyn.] Собраніе задачъ для кадетъ лѣсной роты Лѣсного и ежевого института. 1859. IV. 264.
Казначеевъ, К. А. [Kaznatcheyef, K.A.] Механическая технологія дерева. 1885. IV. 408.
Кайгородовъ, Д. [Kaigorodof, D.] Начальная ботаника. 1900. I. 523.[1]

Кайгородовъ, Дм. Н. [Kaigorodof, Dmitri N.] Бесѣды о русскомъ лѣсѣ. Краснолѣсье. 1880. I. 358, *IV. 80.*
— Бесѣды о русскомъ лѣсѣ. Чернолѣсье. 1881. I. 358, *IV. 80.*
— Къ вопросу о соотношеніи между шириною годичныхъ слоевъ и удѣльнымъ вѣсомъ еловой древесины. 1900. IV. 459.[2]
— Временныя и переносочныя дороги для сельскаго и лѣсного хозяйства. 1882. IV. 391.
— Дерево и его жизнь. 1897. I. 82.[2]
— Еловый короѣдъ. 1883. IV. 456.
— Краткій обзоръ растительнаго царства по климатическимъ поясамъ. 1884. I. 218.
— Лекціи лѣсного инженернаго искусства. 1892. IV. 266.[1]
— Лѣсной отдѣлъ на... выставкѣ въ Бременѣ. 1874. IV. 19.[2]
— Русскій толковый лѣсотоварный словарь. 1883. IV. 404.[1]
— Таблица для опредѣленія древесины важнѣйшихъ родовъ лѣсныхъ. 1891. I. 525,[1] *IV. 62.*[2]
Календарь и справочная книжка для лѣсохозяевъ. IV. 6.
Калинскій, В. [Kalinski, V.] О казенныхъ пихтовыхъ лѣсахъ Кѣлецко-Сандомірскаго кряжа. 1898. IV. 347.
Калифорнская Сосна. 1834. IV. 464.[2]
Калугинъ, Ив. [Kalugin, Ivan.] Опытъ примѣненія рѣзки изъ тонкихъ древесныхъ вѣтвей въ кормъ скоту. 1900. III. 224.[1]
Камснно-степное лѣсничество. 1900. IV. 38.[1]
Канадскія лѣсная древесныя породы. 1877. I. 531.
Каргинъ, Г. А. [Kargin, G. A.] Искусственное лѣсоразведеніе въ Воронежскомъ уѣздѣ. 1897. IV. 157.
Карельщиковъ, С. [Karelshtchikof, S.] О размѣщеніи и развитіи устицъ. 1867. I. 525.
— *See also* KARELTCHIKOFF, S.
Карманная дендрологія, важнѣйшихъ и употребительнѣйшихъ породъ для кораблестроенія. 1835. IV. 425.[1]
Карманная книга для русскаго лѣсничаго. IV. 6.
Карышевъ, Н. [Karyshef, N.] Атласъ подъѣзной статистики. 1885. IV. 336.[2]
Касяненко, В. [Kasyanenko, V.] *See* Ахматовъ, М. & Касяненко, В.
Кауфманъ, А. [Kaufmann, A.] О мѣрахъ къ охраненію лѣсовъ Россіи. 1873. IV. 180.[1]
— Разборъ извѣстныхъ до нынѣ способовъ сушенія и предохраненія дерева. 1870. IV. 419.
— *See also* KAUFMAN, A.
Кауфманъ, Н. [Kauffmann, Nicolaus.] Московская флора. 1866. I. 362.
— Отношеніе листа къ стеблю. 1862. I. 524.[1]
— *See also* KAUFFMANN, Nicolaus.
Кедръ. 1839. IV. 448.[1]
Кейзерлингъ, Л. А., *графъ.* [Keiserling, L. A., *Graf.*] Подготовка лѣсниковъ. 1895. IV. 114.
Кенигъ, Г. [König, Gottlob.] Лѣсная математика. *See* König, Gottlob. 1835. IV. 58.
— *See also* König, Gottlob.
Кеппенъ, П. [Köppen, P.] О мочальномъ промыслѣ. 1041. III. 900.[2] *See* КОЕРРЕN. 1942. III. 585.[2]
— *See also* КОЕРРЕN, Pet. von.
Кеппенъ, Федоръ. [Köppen, Friedrich Theodor.] Дикорастущія древесныя породы Европейской Россіи и Кавказа. 1880. *I. 358,* III. 190, *IV. 80.*
— Географическое распространеніе хвойныхъ древъ въ Европейской Россіи и на Кавказѣ. 1885. I. 359, *IV. 80.*
— Географическое распространеніе хвойныхъ древъ. 1885. II. 15.[1]
— *See also* КОЕРРЕN, Friedrich Theodor.
Кернъ, Э. Э. [Kern, Eduard.] Бесѣды о лѣсѣ. Облѣсеніе. 1897. IV.
— Наставленіе къ уходу за насажденіями. 1897. IV. 104.[2]
— Овраги, ихъ закрѣпленіе. 1892. IV. 185.[1]
— *See also* KERN, Eduard.
Кильштетъ, К. Е. [Kilshtet, K. E.] Къ вопросу о средствахъ для предохраненія дерева. 1900. IV. 421.
Кирпичниковъ, Д. [Kirpitchnikof, D.] Техническія работы по сухой перегонкѣ дерева. 1879. IV. 432.[1]
Киттары, М. [Kittary, M] Переработка хвои въ лѣсную шерсть. 1857. IV. 443.[2]

Кіевское общество Естествоиспытателей. Записки. I. 519.[2]
Классонъ. [Klasson.] Еще нѣсколько замѣчаній о образованіи напдавовъ на пняхъ Пихтовыхъ. 1844. I. 528.[1]
— Нѣкоторыя свѣдѣнія о произростаніи Лиственницы въ Россіи. 1844. IV. 449.
— О образованіи новыхъ слоевъ древесины или наплавовъ на пняхъ срубленныхъ Пихтовыхъ деревъ. 1843. I. 528.[1]
Клаусъ, К. [Claus, Carl.] Флоры мѣстныя приволжскихъ странъ. *See* CLAUS, Carl. 1851. I. 361.
— *See also* CLAUS, Carl.
Клеръ, О. [Clerc, O.] Замѣтка о хмѣльнолистной Костянкѣ. 1874. II. 307.[2]
— О нѣкоторыхъ Уральскихъ растеніяхъ. 1874. I. 363.
— Матеріалы о флорѣ Уральскаго края. 1874. I. 363.
— *See also* CLERC, G. O.
Клингенъ, Н. [Klingen, I.] Краткое описаніе удѣльнаго чаквинскаго подтропическаго хозяйства. 1900. III. 601.[1]
Кнорре, П. [Knorre, P.] Очеркъ Чернышевской лѣсной дачи. 1882. IV. 346.
Кожевниковъ, Д. и Цингеръ, В. [Kozhevnikof, D. & Zinger, V.] Очеркъ флоры Тульской губерніи. 1880. I. 364.
Коковцовъ, Д. [Kokovtzof, D.] Уставъ лѣсной. 1876. IV. 315.[1]
Колесовъ, А. [Kolesof, A.] Природа песковъ и ихъ облѣсеніе. 1900. IV. 158.
— Сосновая посадки на пескахъ. 1899. IV. 474.
— Сравнительная доходность лѣса и поля. 1895. IV. 259.[2]
Колмовскій, А. И. [Kolmovski, A. I.] Къ флорѣ Новгородской губерніи. 1896. I. 366. — 1899. I. 367.
Кольманъ, В. [Kohlmann, V.] Кубическія таблицы круглыхъ и обитыхъ дровъ измѣренныя по футовымъ мѣрамъ. *See* KOHLMANN, W. 1862. IV. 224.[2]
Колюпановъ, Н. [Kolyupanof, N.] Объ охраненіи владѣльческихъ лѣсовъ. 1861. IV. 179.[2]
Колядинъ, С. [Kolyadin, S.] Физіологія растеній. 1826. I. 525.[2]
Комаровъ, В. [Komarof, Vladimir.] Дополненіе къ списку растеній западныхъ уѣздовъ Новгородской губерніи. 1896. I. 366.
— Краткій очеркъ растительности горнаго Зеравшана. 1893. I. 457.
— Матеріалы по флорѣ Туркестанскаго нагорья. 1896. I. 457.
Конардовъ, С. [Konardof, S.] Общедоступная лѣсная таксація. 1892. IV. 253.
Конончукъ, П. И. [Konontchuk, P. I.] О мѣстной или односторонней твердослойности дерева. 1888. IV. 414,[1] 482.[1]
— *See also* KONONTCHUK, P. O.
Контоевскій. [Kontoyevski.] Практическія удобопонятно. 1882. IV. 432.[1]
— Спутникъ заводчика по части обработки продуктовъ дерева. 1871. IV. 426.[1]
Коншинъ, А. Ю. [Konshin, A. J.] Объ отвѣтственности за лѣсныя нарушенія. 1889. IV. 315.[1]
Коптевъ. [Koptef.] Бѣглый взглядъ на растительность Алтайскаго горнаго округа. 1857. I. 454.[1]
— О лѣсоботаническихъ признакахъ хвойныхъ породъ. 1856. II. 15.[2]
Корневичъ, К. [Korneven, K.] Ядовитыя растенія и отравленія ими причиняемыя. 1894. III. 59.[2]
Коржинскій, С. И. [Korzhinski, S. J.] Замѣтка объ Abies Semenowi. 1900. II. 25.[1]
— Очеркъ флоры окрестности г. Астрахани. 1882. I. 364.
— Предварительный отчетъ о ботанической экскурсіи въ дельту рѣки Волги. 1884. I. 364.
— Предварительный отчетъ о почвенныхъ и геоботаническихъ изслѣдованіяхъ. 1887. I. 365.
— Сѣверная граница черноземной области восточной полосы Европейской Россіи. 1888. I. 365.
— Флора востока Европейской Россіи. 1892. I. 366.
— *See also* KORZHINSKI, S. J.
Корфъ, баронъ. [Korf, baron.] Отчетъ... о дѣятельности по уничтоженію филлоксеры въ Крыму. 1882. III. 761.

Коршъ, Д. В. [Korsh, D. V.] Сборникъ законоположеній о сбереженіи и охраненіи лѣсовъ частныхъ и общественныхъ. 1888. IV. 315.[2]
— *See also* Korsch, D. V.
Космовскій, К. А. [Kosmowski, K. A.] Ботанико-географическій очеркъ западной части Пензенской губерніи. 1890. I. 365.
Костяевъ, А. В. [Kostyayef, A. V.] Краткое наставленіе къ укрѣпленію . . . летучихъ песковъ. 1900. IV. 146.[1]
Косяненко, В. *See* Ахматовъ & Косяненко, В.
Котта, Генрихъ. [Cotta, Heinrich.] Основанія лѣсоводства. *See* Cotta, Heinrich. 1832. IV. 97.
— Руководство ко введенію правильнаго въ лѣсахъ хозяйства и таксаціи лѣсовъ. 1820. IV. 239.
— *See also* Cotta, Heinrich.
Кравчинскій, Дм. [Kravtchinski, Dm.] Лѣсовозращеніе. 1883. IV. 104.[1]
— О хозяйствѣ въ лѣсахъ. 1888. IV. 104.[1]
— *See also* Kravtchinski, D.
О Красильномъ Дубѣ. 1836. IV. 518.[2]
Красновъ, А. Н. [Krasnof, A. N.] Географія растеній. 1899. I. 301.
— Замѣтки о растительности Алтая. *See* Krasnoff, A. 1886. I. 457.
— Кавказскія цѣпи горъ. 1895. I. 370.
— Матеріалы для флоры Полтавской губерніи. 1891. I. 366.
— Новые виды Сванетской флоры. 1892. I. 369.
— Опытъ исторія развитія флоры южной части восточнаго Тянь Шаня. 1888. I. 457.
— О современной флорѣ сѣверо-восточнаго Тянь Шаня. 1887. I. 457.
— Къ флорѣ бассейна р. Чаквы. 1895. I. 370.
— *See also* Krasnof, A. N.
Краткое наставленіе къ разведенію лѣсныхъ деревьевъ. 1872. IV. 104.[1]
Краткое описаніе важнѣйшихъ красильныхъ растеній. 1812. III. 236.
Краткое понятіе о составѣ древесины. 1856. IV. 432.[1]
Краткое содержаніе "Трудовъ" изданія 1900 года. 1900. IV. 38.[1]
Краузе, А. К. [Krause, A. K.] Критическая оцѣнка лѣсоустроительнаго метода царства польскаго. 1881. IV. 247.[1]
— Направленіе и организація лѣснаго опытнаго дѣла. 1880. IV. 37.[3]
— Народо-хозяйственное значеніе дѣятелей лѣснаго производства. 1891. IV. 270.
— Нѣмецко-русскій лѣсной словарь. *See* Krause, A. 1889. IV. 23.[1]
— Отзывъ по поводу книги Ѳ. К. Арнольда, "Исторія лѣсоводства." 1895. IV. 24.[1]
— Очеркъ лѣсной статистики. 188. ? IV. 336.[1]
— Экономическое значеніе лѣснаго капитала. 1893. IV. [2]59.[1]
— *See also* Krause, A.
Краузе, Г. Ф. [Krause, G. F.] О мѣрахъ отклоненія недостатка въ деревѣ . . . въ Германіи. 1839. IV. 180.[1]
— *See also* Krause, G. F.
Кразъ, Л. П. [Krahe, J. A.] Краткое руководство къ культурѣ корзиночной Ивы. *See* Krahe, J. A. 1882. III. 348.
— *See also* Krahe, J. A.
Крячагинъ, Н. [Kritchagin, N.] Учебникъ ботаники. 1896. I. 523.
Круберъ, В. [Kruber, V.] Оренбургская Башкирія въ лѣсохозяйственномъ. 1887. IV. 346.
Крутицкій, П. Я. [Krutitzki, P. Y.] Практическія занятія по гистологіи растеній. 1882. I. 524.[2]
Крыловъ, А. [Krylof, A.] Древоводство. 1871. II. 101.[1]
— Разведеніе торговыхъ растеній. 1870. III. 101.[1]
Крыловъ, П. Н. [Krylof, P. N.] Липа на предгорьяхъ Кузнецкаго Алатау. 1891. II. 515.[2]
— Матеріалъ къ флорѣ Пермской губ. 1878. I. 364. 1885. I. 364.
— Матеріалъ къ флорѣ Тобольской губерніи. 1893. I. [3]54.[3]
— О народныхъ лекарственныхъ растеніяхъ, употребляемыхъ въ Пермской губ. 1876. III. 68.[1]
— Нѣкоторыя свѣдѣнія о народныхъ лекарственныхъ средствахъ, . . . въ Казанской губерніи. 1882. III. 68.[1]

— Предварительный отчетъ о ботанической экскурсіи въ Пермскую губернію. 1876. I. 363.
— Тайга съ естественно-исторической точки зрѣнія. 1898. I. 454.[2]
— Къ флорѣ Вятской губерніи. 1885. I. 364.
Крюгеръ, В. [Krüger, V.] Лѣсоботаническое описаніе главнѣйшихъ сорныхъ (вредныхъ) въ лѣсахъ растеній. 1838. IV. 79.[1]
Кузминцевъ, П. [Kuzmintchef, P.] О лѣсахъ и кустарникахъ, растущихъ на Камчаткѣ. 1836. I. 454,[2] *IV.* 87.[1]
Кузнецовъ, Н. И. [Kuznetzof, N. I.] Вліяніе лѣса на образованіе источниковъ. 1895. IV. 51.
— Изслѣдованіе флоры Шенкурскаго и Холмогорскаго уѣздовъ. 1888. I. 365.
— Лѣса Европейской Россіи и значеніе ихъ въ хозяйствѣ страны. 1896. IV. 346.
— О русскомъ лѣсѣ. 1895. IV. 346.
— *See also* Kuznetzof, N. I.
Кулагинъ, Н. М. [Kulagin, Nicolai Mikhailovitch.] Вредное для лѣсовъ насѣкомое монашенка. 1894. IV. 201.
Кулишеръ, М. [Kulisher, M.] Лѣса Волынской губерніи подъ надзоромъ казны. 1888. IV. 346.
Куницкій, В. А. [Kunitzki, B. A.] Ботаническая и лѣсоводственная характеристика Осины. 1888. IV. 486.[2]
— О разновидностяхъ Осины. 1888. II. 98.[1]
Кунштиковъ, . [Kunshtchikof.] Переугливаніе въ стоячихъ кострахъ. 189. ? IV. 395.
Кунце, Максъ. [Kunze, Max.] Учебникъ древоизмѣренія. 1873. IV. 214.
— *See also* Kunze, Max Friedrich.
Курдюмовъ, В. [Kurdyumof, V.] Матеріалы для курса строительныхъ работъ. I. Дерево. 1894. IV. 423.[2]
Курисъ, Ив. [Kuris, Iv.] Докладъ Одесскому уѣздному земскому собранію о лѣсоразведеніи. 1876. IV. 157.
Кутузовъ, В. Н. [Kutuzof, V. N.] Нѣмецко-русско-французскій и французско-русско-нѣмецкій лѣсотехническій словарь. 1896. IV.23.[1]
— *See also* Kutuzof, V. N.
Клытмановъ, П. [Kytmanof, A. I.] Матеріалы для флоры Енисейскаго округа. 1894. I. 454.[2]
Кюри, [Cürie, P. F.] Руководство къ опредѣленію растеній. 1861. I. 362.
— *See also* Cürie, P. F.

Лабзинъ, Н. [Labzin, N.] Станки для обработки дерева. 1869. IV. 422.[1]
— Технологія дерева. 1878. IV. 408.
Леббокъ, [Lubbock, Sir Jehu.] Цвѣты, плоды и листья. *See* Lubbock, Sir John. 1886. I. 218.
— *See also* Lubbock, Sir John.
Левавасеръ, Т., сынъ. [Levavasseur, T. (jr.)] Практическое изслѣдованіе растеній и возобновленіе лѣсовъ. *See* Levavasseur, T. (jr.) 1878. IV. 163.
— *See also* Levavasseur, T. (jr.)
Левановскій, Н. [Levanovski, N.] Къ вопросу о вытѣсненіи однихъ растеній другими. 1871. I. 528.[1]
— Значеніе сѣмянъ. 1872. I. 529.[1]
Левитовъ, И. [Levitof, I.] Сибирскіе коршуны. 1894. IV. 279.[1]
Леонтьевъ, А. [Leontef, A.] Лѣсъ. Значеніе лѣса. 1885. IV. 104.[1]
Лепехинъ, Ив. [Lepechin, Iwan.] Дневныя записки путешествія по разнымъ провинціямъ Россійскаго государства. *See* Lepechin, Iwan. 1774. I. 359.
— Продолженіе дневныхъ записокъ. *See* Lepechin, Iwan. 1774. I. 359.
Лидовъ, А. П. [Lidof, A. P.] Смолы и эфирныя масла. 1886. III. 228.[1]
Линдеманъ, Э. [Lindemann, Eduard von.] Очеркъ флоры Херсонской губерніи. 1872. I. 363.
— Списокъ употребительнѣйшихъ растеній Херсонской флоры. 1872. III. 68.[1]
— *See also* Lindemann, Eduard von.
Линдлей, I. [Lindley, John.] Теорія садоводства. *See* Lindley, John. 1840. III. 35.
— *See also* Lindley, John.

Липскій, В. Н. [Lipski, Vladimir.] Замѣтка о флорѣ Крыма. 1894. I. 369.
— Изслѣдованіе о флорѣ Бессарабіи. 1889. I. 365.
— Отъ Каспія къ Понту. 1892. I. 369.
— Матеріалы для флоры средней Азіи. 1900. I. 457.
— Новыя данныя для флоры Бессарабіи. 1894. I. 366.
— Очеркъ растительности Предкавказья. 1894. I. 369.
— Флора кавказа. See LIPSKI, Vladimir. 1899. I. 370.
— See also LIPSKI, Vladimir.
Лисицынъ, П. А. [Lisitzyn, P. A.] Необходимыя мѣры къ облѣсенію степей. 1898. IV. 158.
Лисневскій, В. И. [Lisnevski, V. I.] Горные лѣса Ферганской области. 1885. IV. 376.[1]
— О разрушительныхъ силахъ горныхъ потоковъ. 1899. IV. 185.[1]
Лиственныя деревья въ хозяйственномъ отношеніи. 1850. IV. 396.[1]
Литвиновъ, Д. И. [Litvinof, D. J.] Ботаническія экскурсіи въ Сызранскомъ уѣздѣ. 1895. I. 366.
— Очеркъ растительныхъ формацій степной юго-восточной части Тамбовской губерніи. 1883. I. 364.
Липинъ, И. А. [Lishin, I. A.] Къ вопросу обводненія . . . Самарской губерніи. 1892. IV. 157.
Ломакинъ, А. А. [Lomakin, A. A.] Наблюденія надъ раздвѣтаніемъ растеній въ Кутаисѣ. 1897. I. 224.[2]
— Списокъ растеній, собранныхъ въ Талышѣ. 1895. I. 370.
Ломиковскій. [Lomikovski.] Разведеніе лѣса въ сельцѣ Трудолюбовѣ. 1837. IV. 157.
Лѣса Пріамурскаго края. 1883. IV. 376.[1]
Лѣсной вопросъ. 1876. IV. 273.[2]
Лѣсной календарь. IV. 6.
Лѣсной словарь. 1843. IV. 23.[1]
О лѣсной торговлѣ съ Англіею. 1840. IV. 404.[1]
Лѣсопромышленникъ. See Уставъ товарищества.
О лѣсоразведеніи и ирригаціи въ Одесскомъ уѣздѣ. 1875. IV. 157.
Лѣсохозяйственный статистическій атласъ. 1873. IV. 336.[1]
Любименко, В. Н. [Liubimenko. V. N.] Объ отложеніи кристаловъ щевелевокислаго кальція въ органахъ цвѣтка. 1900. I. 524.[2]
— О спящихъ почкахъ. 1900. I. 524.[1]
Любомудровъ. [Liubomudrof.] Лѣсоразведеніе. 1896. IV. 157.
Любшицъ, О. & **Триніусъ**, К. [Liboschitz, Joseph & Trinius, Karl.] Флора С. Петербургская и Московская. See LIBOSCHITZ, J. & TRINIUS, K. 1811. I. 360.
— See also LIBOSCHITZ, Joseph & TRINIUS, K.
Лясковскій, В. [Liaskovski, V.] Посадка деревьевъ въ средней полосѣ Россіи. 1898. III. 101.[1]
Ляслетъ: [Laslett, Thomas.] Лѣсъ и строевыя деревья. 1875. IV. 396.[1]
— See also LASLETT, Thomas.

М., В. [M., V.] Сѣверная лѣсная почва. 1896. IV. 70.
М-ча. [M-tcha.] Дивное дерево. 1870. III. 634.[2]
Маакъ, Р. К. [Maack, Richard.] Путешествіе на Амуръ въ 1855 г. 1859. I. 455.
Маевскій, П. Ф. [Mayevski, P. F.] Весенняя флора средней Россіи. Таблицы. 1886. I. 365.
— Ключъ къ опредѣленію древесныхъ растеній по листьѣ для . . . Россіи. 1890. I. 359, IV. 81.
— Таблицы для опредѣленія древесныхъ растеній въ ихъ зимнемъ состояніи для западной и средней Россіи. 1882. I. 294,[1] 359, IV. 80.[1]
— Таблицы для опредѣленія древесныхъ растеній по листымъ для западной и средней Россіи. 1882. I. 359, IV. 80.[1]
— Флора средней Россіи. 1892. I. 366.
Майеръ, А. [Mayer, A.] Ученіе о питаніи зеленыхъ растеній. 1898. I. 526.[1]
— See also MAYER, A.
Майеръ, Францъ. [Maier, Franz.] Первый приступъ къ приведенію въ порядокъ лѣсныхъ угодій, досель безъ правилъ, разсчетъ и порядка порубаемыхъ. 1841. IV. 169.[2]
— Полное собраніе сочиненій. 1850. IV. 157.
— Степное лѣсоводство. 1860. IV. 114.
Маковецкій, А. See Гурьяновъ, А. & Маковецкій, А.
Максимовичъ, Карлъ Ив. See MAXIMOWICZ, Carl Johann.

Максимовичъ, Михаилъ А[лександровичъ]. [Maximowicz, Michail.] Списокъ растеній Московской флоры. 1826. I. 360.
Малаховъ, М. В. [Malakhof, M. V.] Изслѣдованія въ Уральскомъ край. 1887. I. 365.
Мальгинъ, Н. [Malgin, N.] Объ акклиматированіи растеній въ Россіи. 1857. III. 120.[1]
— Нѣсколько замѣчаній о Лиственницѣ на Альпахъ. 1856. IV. 449.
Малюга, И. [Malyuga, I.] Причины порчи дерева въ сооруженіяхъ. 1885. IV. 413.[2]
Малютинъ, Ф. [Malyutin, F.] Руководство къ веденію дѣлъ, со стороны казны по нарушеніямъ Лѣсного Устава. 1874. IV. 315.[2]
Мамаевъ, С. [Mamayef, S.] See Черновъ, К. & Мамаевъ, С.
Маргграфъ, В. [Marggraf, V.] Нѣсколько данныхъ объ искусственномъ разведеніи лѣса. 1872. IV. 157.
Маргграфъ, О. [Marggraf, O.] Сампитъ или кавказская пальма въ Черноморскомъ округѣ. 1874. II. 453.[1]
Марковичъ, В. В. [Markovitch. V. V.] Забытый вязъ. 1900. II. 144.[2]
— Въ лѣсахъ Имеретіи. 1897, 1898. IV. 347.
Марковъ, Р. & **Рышковъ**, В. [Markof, R. & Ryshkof, V.] О лѣсахъ и водахъ Курской губерніи. 1894. IV. 346.
Мартыновъ, Иванъ. [Martynof, Johann.] Словарь родовыхъ именъ растеній. See MARTINOV, Joh. 1826. I. 77.
— Техно-ботаническій словарь, на латинскомъ и россійскомъ языкѣ. 1820. IV. 23.[1]
Мартьяновъ, Н. [Martyanof, N. M.] Матеріалы флоры Минусинскаго края. 1882. I. 454.[1]
Марченко, А. [Martchenko, A.] Къ вопросу объ искусственномъ разведеніи Тополей. 1898. IV. 485.[2]
Массальскій, В., князь. [Massalski, V., prince.] Лѣсоразведеніе безъ поливки въ Туркестанѣ. 1892. IV. 168.[1]
Матеріалы къ ближайшему познанію произведомыхъ Россійской имперіи. See BEITRÄGE zur Pflanzenkunde . . . I. 9.
Матеріальная отчетность лѣсного вѣдомства. 1869. IV. 289.[1]
Матернъ, А. [Matern, A.] Лѣсной альманахъ. 1880. IV. 346.
Медвѣдевъ, Я. С. [Medvyedef, J. S.] Деревья и кустарники Кавказа. 1882. I. 368,[1] IV. 80,[1] V. xxx.[1]
— Кавказскій подъалпійскій Клёнъ. 1882. II. 873.[1]
— Нѣсколько замѣчаній объ отличительныхъ признакахъ кавказской Пихты. 1882. II. 23.[1]
— Очерки Кавказскихъ лѣсовъ. 1882. I. 368,[1] IV. 80.[2]
— & **Гамрекеловъ**, А. [C.]. [Medvyedef, J. S. & Gamrekelof, A.] Статистическое описаніе лѣсовъ Боржомскаго имѣнія. 1889. IV. 346.
Мейеръ-Гирсау. [Meier-Girsau.] О назначеніи и свойствахъ бородавчатыхъ возвышеній или чеченчевъ на корѣ. 1843. I. 525.[1]
Меліоранскій, М. [Melioranski, M.] Ботаники весною. 1879. I. 523.[2]
— Наши деревья и кустарники. 1887. I. 359, III. 68,[1] IV. 80.
Мельниковъ, А. [Melnikof, A.] Указатель лѣсного журнала, издаваемаго С.-Петербургскимъ лѣснымъ обществомъ, за пять лѣтъ, 1891–1895 гг. 1896. IV. 2.
Мельниковъ, Н. П. [Melnikof, N. P.] Очерки производства бумаги изъ дерева въ Россіи. 1873. IV. 429.[1]
— Производство экстракта дубоваго дерева для кожевеннаго дѣла. 1895. IV. 157.[1]
Мерклинъ, Карлъ. [Mercklin, K. E. von.] Анатомія коры и древесины. See MERCKLIN, K. E. von. 1857. I. 124.
— О воспроизведеніи бересты на нашей Березѣ. 1864. I[1]. 118.[1]
— See also MERCKLIN, Karl Eugen von.
Мечъ, А. [Metch, A.] Матеріалы къ познанію флоры южнаго Урала. 1896. I. 367.
Миглинскій, А. [Miglinski, A.] Посадка дерева. 1899. IV. 153.[2]
— Руководство къ разведенію въ лѣсахъ нашихъ Сосны. 1896. IV. 474.
Миллеръ, К. [Müller, K.] Древесныя и кустарныя растенія. 1838. III. 67.[2]
Милютинъ, С. Н. [Milyutin, S. N.] Матеріалы по флорѣ известняковъ р. Оки. 1890. I. 365.

Министерства Государственныхъ имуществъ. Журналъ. IV. 6.
Мисѣвичъ, В. [Misyevitch, V.] Изслѣдованіе техническихъ свойствъ древесины Красной Осины. 1886. IV. 486.[2]
Мицуль, М. [Mitzul, M.] О произведеніяхъ лѣсоводства . . . на Парижской всемірной выставкѣ. 1869. IV. 20.[1]
Мнѣніе Государственнаго совѣта о предоставленіи компаніи капитана Крузенштерна привилегіи. 1864. IV. 273.[2]
Мокржецкій, С. А. [Mokrzhetzki, S. A.] Вредныя животныя и растенія. 1897. III. 179.
Молчановъ, А. П. [Moltchanof, A. P.] Краткій историческій очеркъ лѣсокультурныхъ мѣропріятій . . . по 1-му Одоевскому л-ву, Тульской губерніи. 1895. IV. 24.[2]
Монкевицъ, А. [Monkevitz, A.] Описаніе Нидербартаускоѣ казенной лѣсной дачи. 1876. IV. 347.
Монографія сибирскаго Кедра. 1843. IV. 463.[1]
Монтеверде, Н. [Monteverde, N.] See Базаровъ, А. и Монтеверде, Н.
Монтрезоръ, В. [Montresor, V.] Обозрѣніе растеній, входящихъ въ составъ флоры губерній Кіевскаго учебнаго округа. 1886. I. 365.
— Списокъ растеній, собранныхъ въ Кіевскомъ учебн. округѣ. 1888. I. 367.
Москальскій, П. [Moskalski, P.] Сборникъ рѣшеній . . . состоявшихся по дѣламъ о нарушеніи лѣсного устава. 1873. IV. 315.[2]
Мошковъ, П. С. [Moshkof, P. S.] Хозяйственная записка и посадка лѣса въ примѣненіи ихъ въ Юрсовской лѣсной дачѣ. 1900. IV. 347.
Мрозовскій, В. [Mrozovski, V.] Краткій очеркъ лѣсной промышленности. 1900. IV. 404.[2]
Муравьевъ. [Muravef.] Перечень и описаніе экспонатовъ лѣсного отдѣла . . . въ г- Кіевѣ. 1897. IV. 19.[2]
Мясоѣдовъ, А. И. [Miasoyedof, A. I.] Альбомъ наиболѣе вредныхъ древесныхъ паразитныхъ грибовъ. 1896. III. 195.[1]
— "Латы" для пересадки большихъ деревьевъ съ глыбами. 1894. III. 168.[1]

Навашинъ, С. [Navashin, S[ergej].] Болѣзнь березовыхъ сережекъ. 1893. IV. 490.[1]
— Объ обыкновенной Березѣ. See NAWASCHIN, S. 1894. II. 118.[1]
— Склеротинія Березы. 1893. IV. 491.[1]
— See also NAWASCHIN, Sergius.
Наказъ лѣсному объѣздчику при казенныхъ лѣсахъ. 1869. IV. 297.
Наказъ полѣсовщику и лѣсному сторожу. 1845. IV. 296.[1]
О нарастаніи слоевъ древесины и коры. 1838. I. 527.[1]
Нарушевичъ, К. [Narushevitch, K.] Инструкція и справочная книжка для лѣсныхъ сторожей. 1895. IV. 298.[1]
Насажденіе защитныхъ опушекъ. See Ю., С.
Наставленіе для составленія таксъ на лѣсные матеріалы изъ казенныхъ лѣсныхъ дачъ. 1883. IV. 298.[1]
Наставленіе завѣдующимъ лѣсоустроительными партіями, по употребленію получаемыхъ ими авансовъ и по представленію о нихъ отчетности. 1866. IV. 297.[1]
Наставленіе какъ легкимъ и выгоднымъ способомъ гнать деготь. 1836. IV. 491.[1]
Наставленіе какъ собирать и сохранять древесныя сѣмена. 1828. IV. 147.[1]
Наставленіе къ мочальному производству и къ . . . мелкаго подѣлочнаго лѣса. 1856. IV. 297.
Наставленіе къ производству лѣсныхъ посѣвовъ. 1856. IV. 297.
Наставленіе къ уходу за лѣсомъ. 1897. IV. 114.
Наставленіе лѣснымъ офицерамъ, командированнымъ для устройства лѣсовъ. 1858. IV. 297.
Наставленіе о разведеніи Желтинника. 1848. III. 524.[1]
Наставленіе о разведеніи лѣсныхъ древесныхъ породъ посредствомъ посѣва. 1831. IV. 148.
О неорганическихъ началахъ въ растеніяхъ. 1840. I. 526.[1]
Нердлингеръ, Г. [Nördlinger, Hermann.] Обзоръ свойствъ древесины отдѣльныхъ древесныхъ породъ. 1868. IV. 408.

— Техническія свойства древесины. See NÖRDLINGER, Hermann. 1860. IV. 408.
— See also NÖRDLINGER, Hermann.
Нероновъ, И. [Neronof, I.] Новая Пальмовая оранжерея Импер. С.-Петербургскаго ботаническаго сада. 1847. II. 871.[2]
Нестеровъ, Н. С. [Nesterof, N. S.] Сахарный Кленъ. 1895. IV. 527.[1]
— Фабрикація древесной стружки и ея примѣненіе. 1891. IV. 428.[2]
Нетыкса, М. А. [Netyksa, M. A.] Практическій курсъ токарнаго искусства по дереву. 1888. IV. 427.[2]
Нидергеферъ, Э. [Nidergefer, E.] See Арнольдъ, Ѳ. К. &Нидергеферъ, Э.
Николаевъ, Ѳ. Я. [Nikolayef, F. J.] Справочная книжка для лѣсопромышленниковъ. 1900. IV. 403.[2]
Николсъ, Т. [Nichols, Thomas.] Разсужденіе о произращеніи дубовыхъ деревъ. See NICHOLS, Thomas. 1791. IV. 504.
— See also NICHOLS, Thomas.
Новиковъ, С. [Novikof, S.] Дерево, его свойства и сохраненіе. 1889. IV. 114.
Новицкій, Тр. [Novitzki, Tr.] Айлантовое лѣсоводство. 1864. IV. 525.
Ново-Александрійскій институтъ сельскаго хозяйства и лѣсоводства. Записки. IV. 6.
Новороссійское общество естествоиспытателей. Записки. I. 519.[2]
Норманъ, А. [Norman, A.] Ставропольская флора. 1881. I. 364.
Нѣкоторыя замѣчанія о вліяніи температуры на жизнь . . . древесныхъ растеній. 1843. I. 525,[2] IV. 78.[1]
Нѣкоторыя замѣчанія по предмету физіологіи древесныхъ растеній. 1845. I. 525.[2]
Нѣкоторыя свѣдѣнія и замѣчанія о корабельныхъ лѣсахъ Вологодской губерніи. 1843. IV. 344.[2]
Нѣсколько замѣчаній объ Уральской Лиственницѣ. 1857. IV. 449.

Общее описаніе Неленгско-Коковинской удѣльной дачи 4-го Сюмскаго вѣдомства. 1895. IV. 346.
Общество для вывоза заграницу лѣсныхъ произведеній. 1869. IV. 39.[2]
Общество для поощренія лѣсного хозяйства. Лѣсной журналъ. IV. 6.
Общество естествоиспытателей при Императорскомъ Казанскомъ Университетѣ. Труды. I. 519.[2]
Общество испытателей природы при Императорскомъ Харьковскомъ Университетѣ. Труды. I. 519.[2]
Общій кратко-хозяйственный обзоръ Ольгинской Шермяткской дачи. 1867. IV. 345.
Объяснительная записка къ плану лѣсныхъ насажденій произведенныхъ въ Каменноватскомъ имѣніи. 1895. IV. 346.
Оверинъ, А. [Overin, A.] Перечень Пятигорской флоры. 1872. I. 363.
— & Ситовскій, Н. [Overin, A. & Sitovski, N.] Опытъ Русско-Кавказской флоры. 1858. I. 369.
Огіевскій, Василій. [Ogievski, Vasili.] Борьба съ вредными лѣсными насѣкомыми въ Баваріи. 1895. IV. 208.[1]
— Какая опасность угрожаетъ сосновымъ культурамъ отъ хруща? 1900. IV. 480.
— О сосновыхъ сѣменникахъ. 1898. IV. 474.
Оливеръ, Д. [Oliver, D.] Уроки элементарной ботаники. See OLIVER, Daniel. 1864. I. 523.
— See also OLIVER, Daniel.
Описаніе древесныхъ породъ сѣверной, средней и южной полосъ Россіи. 1841. IV. 80.
Описаніе дубоваго лѣса, употребляемаго въ судостроеніи. 1861. IV. 514.[1]
Описаніе и изображеніе дегтярной печи. 1835. IV. 436.[1]
Описаніе наиболѣе вредныхъ лѣсныхъ насѣкомыхъ въ средней полосѣ Россіи. 1893. IV. 205.[2]
Описаніе различныхъ способовъ переугливанія дерева и добыванія древеснаго угля. 1857. IV. 394.
Описаніе способовъ и размѣровъ укрѣпленія . . . пескомъ въ Россіи. 1876. IV. 157.
Описаніе шелкопряда-монаха. 1857. IV. 200.

Опытный практический лѣсоводецъ. 1834. IV. 114.
Ординація королевскихъ пущъ въ лѣсничествахъ бывшаго великаго Княжества литовскаго. 1871. IV. 297.
Орловъ, М. М. [Orloff, Michail M.] О лѣсахъ Россіи. 1900. IV. 347.
— Изъ лѣсовъ юго-западнаго края. 1898. IV. 347.
— Русское лѣсное хозяйство. 1895. IV. 25.
— Таксація срубленнаго лѣса. 1900. IV. 403.[1]
Основаніе лѣсного банка въ Вѣнѣ. 1869. IV. 309.[2]
Отоцкій, П. В. [Ototzki, P. V.] Къ вопросу о вліяніи лѣсовъ на грунтовыя воды. 1899. IV. 52.
— Гидрологическая экскурсія 1895 года въ степные лѣса. 1896. IV. 46.[1]
— Шиповъ лѣсъ. 1894. IV. 346.
Отчетъ общества для поощренія лѣсного хозяйства за 4 годъ его существованія. 1836. IV. 346.
Отчетъ по лѣсной части Закаспійской области. 1899. IV. 376.[1]
Отчетъ по лѣсному управленію. 1872 (1874). IV. 289,[1] 345, 539.[1]
Очеркъ дѣятельности П. А. Кочубея по лѣсоразведенію въ Полтавской губерніи. 1892. IV. 157.

Палимпсестовъ, И. У. [Palimpsestof, I. U.] Одинъ изъ отвѣтовъ на вопросъ: были-ли лѣса на югѣ Россіи? 1881. I. 358, *IV. 80.*
— Степи юга Россіи были-ли искони вѣковъ степями? 1890. IV. 157.
Павловичъ, Б. Э. [Pavlovitch, B. E.] Лѣсная съемка. 1872. IV. 264.
Павловичъ, П. Э. [Pavlovitch, P. E.] Краткій очеркъ Старогутской лѣсной дачи. 1897. IV. 347.
Палладинъ, В. [Palladin, W.] Анатомія растеній. 1895. I. 524.[1]
— Вліяніе кислорода на распаденія бѣлковыхъ веществъ въ растеніяхъ. 1889. I. 526.[2]
— Значеніе кислорода для растеній. 1886. I. 526.[1]
— *See also* PALLADIN, W.
Палласъ, С. [Pallas, P. S.] Описаніе растеній россійскаго государства съ ихъ изображеніями. *See* PALLAS, P. S. 1784. I. 360.
— Путешествіе по разнымъ провинціямъ Россійской Имперіи. *See* PALLAS, P. S. 1771. I. 359.
— *See also* PALLAS, P. S.
Памятная книжка для межевыхъ чиновъ, состоящихъ въ вѣдомствѣ лѣсного департамента. 1861. IV. 297.
Памятная книжка для чиновъ губернскаго лѣсного управленія. 1845. IV. 289.[1]
Панасевичъ, В. [Panasevitch, V.] Производство торговъ на продажу лѣсныхъ матеріаловъ изъ казенныхъ дачъ. 1881. IV. 298.[1]
Панцеръ, В. М. фонъ. [Panzer, V. M. von.] Наставленіе о введеніи правильнаго лѣсоводства. 1855. IV. 297.
Панчичъ, Josiф. [Pančić, Josef.] Живи песак у Србији и биље што на ньему расте. 1863. I. 449.
— Копаоник и ньегово подгорје. 1869. I. 449.
— Нешто о нашим шумама. 1880. IV. 124.[1]
— Нова грађа за флору кнежевине Бугарске. *See* PANČIĆ, Josef. 1886. I. 450.
— Флора кнежевине Србије. 1874. I. 449.
— Флора у околини Београдској по аналитичној системи. 1865. I. 449.
— Шумско дрвеће и шибље у Србији. 1871. I. 448,[1] *IV. 87.*[1]
— *See also* PANČIĆ, Josef.
Партанскій, Н. Н. [Partanski, N. P.] Лѣсъ, его вліяніе. 1895. IV. 45.
Патцигъ, О. Н. [Patzig, O. I.] О доходности лѣсовъ и лѣсныхъ посадокъ. 1900. IV. 260.[1]
Пачоскій, І. К. [Patchoski, I. K.] Описаніе новыхъ и мало извѣстныхъ растеній Херсонской губерніи. 1889. I. 365.
— Очеркъ флоры окрестностей Переяславля. 1894. I. 366.
— Флорографическія . . . изслѣдованія Калмыцкихъ степей. 1892. I. 366.
— Флоры Полѣсья. 1897. I. 367.
— Къ флорѣ Крыма. 1890. I. 369.
Пашкевичъ, В. [Pashkevitch, V.] Орѣхъ лѣсной и его культура. 1894. III. 358.[1]
— Очеркъ флоры цвѣтковыхъ растеній Минской губерніи. 1882. I. 364.

Перекрестовъ, К. [Perekrestof, K.] Сосновая плеяжденія и естественное возобновленіе ихъ. 1900. IV. 474.
Перелыгинъ, Н. [Perelygin, P.] О лѣсоботаническихъ системахъ. 1836. IV. 75.[1]
— Лѣсоохраненіе. 1835. IV. 177.[1]
— Начертаніе правилъ лѣсоводства. 1831. IV. 114.
— Теоретическая ботаника. 1818. I. 523.
Перечень вопросовъ возбужденныхъ Съѣздами лѣсничихъ 1897 года. 1898. IV. 40.[1]
Песоцкій, Н. А. [Pesotzki, N. A.] Древесная шерсть, ея употребленіе и производство. 1895. IV. 429.
Петровичъ, Sava. [Petrović, Sava.] Флора околине Нишка. 1882. I. 449.
— *See also* PETROVIĆ, Sava.
Петровскій, Ѳ. [Petrovski, F.] Смолокуреніе и выгонка дегтя. 1896. IV. 491.[3]
Петунниковъ, А. Н. [Petunnikof, Alexis.] Abies Semenowii Fedcz. 1900. II. 25.[1]
— Иллюстрированное руководство къ опредѣленію растеній . . . въ Московской губерніи. 1890. I. 365.
— Критическій обзоръ Московской флоры. 1900. I. 368.[1]
— Метаморфозъ клѣточной стѣнки. 1866. I. 525.[1]
— Сводъ ботаническихъ терминовъ. 1898. I. 522.[3]
— *See also* PETUNNIKOF, Alexis.
Піотровскій, В. [Piotrovski, V.] Изслѣдованіе техническихъ свойствъ . . . древесины и коры Arbutus Andrachne. 1886. II. 660.[2]
Пискаревъ, Н. [Piskaref, N.] Записки по межевому законовѣдѣнію. 1856. IV. 315.[1]
Планъ хозяйства на Плебанишскую лѣсную дачу. 1898. IV. 247.[1]
Плетеніе дерева и соломы. 1879. IV. 429.
Плющъ (Hedera). 1839. III. 642.[1]
Повало-Швыйковскій, Я. [Povalo-Shvikovski, J.] Объ истребленіи лѣсовъ въ общихъ дачахъ. 1833. IV. 282.[1]
Поганковъ, И. [Pogankof, I.] Руководство къ ботаникѣ. *See* Вюльфингъ, М. 1814. IV. 61.[2]
Поздняковъ, Н. [Pozdnyakof, N.] *See* Шафрановъ, Н. С. & Поздняковъ, Н.
Поземельно - торгово - промышленно - лѣсной банкъ. 1869. IV. 308.[1]
Полетаевъ, Н. [Poletayef, N.] Замѣтки о степномъ лѣсоразведеніи. 1879. IV. 157.
— Лѣсоразведеніе въ Херсонской губерніи. 1880. IV. 157.
Полетаевъ, О. [Poletayef, O.] *See* Шафрановъ, Н. С. & Полетаевъ, О.
Положеніе о Велико-Анадольскомъ учебномъ степномъ лѣсничествѣ. 1859. IV. 31.
Положеніе о денежномъ вознагражденіи лѣсной стражи за разведеніе Дуба. 1854. IV. 296.[1]
Положеніе о лѣсной стражѣ въ округахъ пахатныхъ солдатъ. 1847. IV. 296.[1]
Положеніе о лѣсномъ и межевомъ институтѣ. 1847. IV. 296.[1]
Положеніе о новомъ устройствѣ лѣсной части въ южныхъ поселеніяхъ. 1859. IV. 297.
Положеніе о сборѣ, порядкѣ требованія и разсылки сѣмянъ. 1854. IV. 296.[2]
Полонскій, Ф. [Polonski, F.] Статистическія свѣдѣнія о Рязанской губерніи въ лѣсномъ отношеніи. 1874. IV. 345.
— О съѣздахъ лѣсничихъ Вятской губерніи. 1877. IV. 40.[1]
— Объ устройствѣ въ губерніяхъ съѣздовъ лѣсничихъ. 1871. IV. 39.[3]
Поляковъ, И. С. [Polyakof, J. S.] Отчетъ объ изслѣдованіяхъ на островѣ Сахалинѣ. 1884. I. 456.
— Путешествіе на островъ Сахалинъ. 1883. I. 456.
Поповъ, Н. [Popof, N.] Лѣсная технологія. 1871. IV. 381.
Поповъ-Веденскій, В. Н. [Popof-Vedenski, V. N.] Деревья и кустарники въ зимнемъ состояніи. 1888. I. 294,[2] *IV. 80.*
Порядокъ управленія казенными лѣсами. 1860. IV. 289.[1]
Посадка деревъ. *See* В., Н. Посадка деревьевъ. 1882. IV. 153.[1]
Посниковъ, А. В. [Posnikof, A. V.] Русскія древесныя сѣмена. 1896. IV. 149.[1]

Постель, Э. [Postel, Emil.] Для ботаническихъ экскурсій. 1875. I. 363.
Потебня, А. [Potebnya, A.] Очеркъ флоры крымскихъ солончаковъ. 1894. I. 370.
Правила для измѣренія мантовыхъ, лиственничныхъ и дубовыхъ деревьевъ. 1836. IV. 222.
Правила для оцѣнки мелкихъ казенныхъ лѣсныхъ дачъ. 1876. IV. 256.
Правила для пріема и браковки въ адмиралтействахъ корабельныхъ лѣсовъ. n. d. IV. 296.[2]
Правила о заготовкѣ и пересылкѣ сѣмянъ, древесныхъ и кустарныхъ породъ. 1899. IV. 298.[1]
Правила о назначеніи денежныхъ выдачъ по вѣдомству Лѣсного Департамента. 1864. IV. 297.
Правила о пастьбѣ скота въ казенныхъ лѣсахъ въ Царствѣ Польскомъ. 1870. IV. 297.
Правила о порядкѣ пользованія лѣсами обремененными крестьянскими сервитутами въ губерніяхъ царства Польскаго. 1876. IV. 297.
Правила о порядкѣ присужденія медалей, обучающимся въ Лисинскомъ учебномъ. 1860. IV. 297.
Правила о пріемѣ казенныхъ . . . въ Лѣсной и межевой институтъ. 1847. IV. 30.[2]
Правила о продажѣ лѣсныхъ матеріаловъ изъ дачъ Вѣдомства государственныхъ имуществъ. 1860. IV. 297.
Правила объ отпускѣ лѣсныхъ матеріаловъ. 1869. IV. 297.
Правила объ устройствѣ пасѣкъ въ лѣсныхъ дачахъ казеннаго лѣсного управленія. 1871. IV. 297.
Правила объ учебной конференціи Лисинскаго учебнаго лѣсничества. 1859. IV. 31.
Правила объ учебной части лѣсныхъ кондукторовъ Лисинскаго учебнаго лѣсничества. 1859. IV. 31.
Правила объ учебныхъ занятіяхъ воспитанниковъ Лисинскаго егерскаго училища. 1859. IV. 31.
Правила преслѣдованія нарушеній лѣсного устава. 1876. IV. 315.[3]
Практическое простое краткое руководство къ разведенію строевыхъ . . . лѣсовъ. 1855. IV. 114.
Пресслеръ, М. Р. [Pressler, M. R.] Двадцать пять формулъ Пресслера. See Pressler, M. R. 1868. IV. 232.
— Измѣритель. See Pressler, M. R. 1852. IV. 230.
— See also Pressler, Max Robert.
Прессъ, А. [Press, A.] Искуственная сушка подѣлочнаго лѣса. 189 .? IV. 416.[2]
Пржевальскій, Н. М. [Przhevalski, N. M.] Изъ Зайсана черезъ Хами въ Тибетъ. See Przhevalski, N. M. 1884. I. 536.[1]
— Путешествіе въ Уссурійскомъ краѣ. 1870. I. 456.
— See also Przhevalski, N. M.
Программа для собиранія свѣдѣній о положеніи лѣсной торговли въ Россіи. 1880. IV. 404.[1]
Программа годовыхъ занятій для кондукторовъ и вольныхъ слушателей. 1860. IV. 31.
Программа лѣсного отдѣла Московской политехнической выставки 1872 г. 1871. IV. 19.[1]
Программа обмѣра деревъ. 1875. IV. 214.
Программа предметамъ, преподаваемымъ въ Лисинскомъ лѣсномъ училищѣ. 1875. IV. 31.
Программы для поступленія въ 1-й (младшій) классъ Лисинскаго лѣсного училища. 1875. IV. 31.
О прорастаніи сосудистыхъ растеній вообще. 1844. IV. 65.[2]
Протоколы засѣданій перваго съѣзда г. г. лѣсничихъ Екатеринославской губерніи. 1888. IV. 40.[1]
Проэктъ инструкціи для таксаціонныхъ работъ. 1842. IV. 296.[1]
Проэктъ лѣсоохранительной билетной системы. 1865. IV. 297.
Проэктъ новой таксаціонной инструкціи. 1863. IV. 297.
Проэктъ положенія объ устройствѣ Лѣсного и межевого института. 1839. IV. 30.[3]
Проэктъ правилъ о мѣрахъ содѣйствія Воронежскаго земства къ лѣсоразведенію. n. d. IV. 296.[2]
Пупоревъ, К. [Puporef, K.] Взглядъ на Вятскую флору. 1856. I. 362.
Пурингъ, Н. Н. [Puring, N.] Изслѣдованіе флоры Псковской губерніи. 1900. I. 368.[1]
— Краткій очеркъ частительности Водзентинскаго лѣсничества. 1899. I. 367.

— Новыя добавленія къ флорѣ Псковской губерніи. 1897. I. 367.
Путеводитель по Имп. Никитскому саду. 1878. I. 521.[2]
Пятницкій, А. Н. [Piatnitzki, A. P.] Улучшенный способъ углеженія на Уралѣ. 189 .? IV. 395.

Р., М. [R., M.] Краткое наставленіе къ разведенію лѣсовъ въ Оренбургской губ. 1892. IV. 114.
Р., Н. [R., N.] Какія мѣры должны быть приняты, чтобы остановить воровское истребленіе лѣсовъ? 1885. IV. 196.[2]
Раевскій, Николай. [Rayevski, Nicolaus.] Ботаника для реальныхъ училищъ. 1896. I. 523.[2]
— Приготовительный курсъ ботаники. 1866. I. 523.[2]
— Разведеніе ивняка для производства плетеныхъ издѣлій. 1882. III. 348.
О разведеніи строевыхъ лѣсовъ. 1805. IV. 114.
Рамштедтъ. [Ramstedt.] Таблица для показанія кубическаго содержанія круглыхъ деревъ. 1849. IV. 223.
Ратковъ, А. П. [Ratkof, A. P.] Корзиночное производство и плетеніе. 1898. III. 351.[1]
Рауэръ, От. [Rauner, St.] Дюны, ихъ укрѣпленіе и облѣсеніе. 1884. IV. 146.[1]
— Укрѣпленіе . . . летучихъ песковъ. 1888. IV. 146.[1]
Рачинскій, А. [Ratchinski, A.] Лѣсъ и климатъ. 1893. IV. 54.
Рачинскій, С. [Ratchinski, S.] О движеніяхъ высшихъ растеній. 1858. I. 527.
— See also Ratchinsky, S.
Рашевскій, П. И. [Rashefski, P. I.] Точный способъ опредѣленія времени рубки сочлененныхъ деревьевъ. 1897. IV. 385.[1]
Регель, Е. Л. [Regel, E[duard von.] Деревья и кустарники, выносящіе на воздухъ Петербургскій климатъ. 1870. III. 67.[2]
— Жимолость и ея разновидности. 1870. III. 840.[1]
— Каталогъ растеній находящихся въ саду Николая Тимоѳеевича Аксакова. 1860. I. 42.
— Лиственницы. See Regel, Eduard von. 1871. II. 32.[2]
— Обрѣзка деревъ. 1889. III. 171.
— Отчетъ по заграничной его командировкѣ въ Англію, Бельгію. 1871. III. 119.[1]
— Петербургская дендрологія. 1873. III. 67.[2]
— Путеводитель по Имп. С.-Петербургскому ботаническому саду. 1873. I. 521.[2]
— Русская дендрологія. 1870. I. 293, III. 7,[2] IV. 30.
— Русская помологія. See, Regel Eduard von. 1868. III. 68.[2]
— Списокъ деревьевъ и кустарниковъ произрастающихъ въ Петербургѣ и его окрестностяхъ. 1858. I. 358.
Рейнгардъ, Л. В. [Reinhard, Ludwig Vasilevitch.] Очеркъ флоры южной части Словянскаго уѣзда. 1891. I. 366.
Реутовичъ. [Reutovitch.] Практическое наставленіе къ добыванію смолистыхъ веществъ. 1864. IV. 436.[2]
Ризположинскій, Р. [Rizpoloshinski, R.] Цвѣтковыя растенія окрестностей с. Салмана. 1887. I. 365.
Рисунки къ лѣсному словарю. 1845. See Лѣсной словарь. 1845. IV. 23.[1]
Ришаръ, А. [Richard, Achille.] Основанія ботаники. 1819. I. 85. See Richard, Achille.
— See also Richard, Achille.
Роговичъ, А. [Hogovitch, A.] Обзоръ . . . растеній . . . флоры Кіевскаго учебнаго округа. 1869. I. 363.
Розенъ, Г. Г. [Rozen, G. G.] Очеркъ степного лѣсоразведенія. 1897. IV. 158.
Роллофъ, А. Х. [Rollof, A. X.] Разведеніе Маслины. 1898. III. 676.[2]
Романовскій, М. [Romanovski, M.] Курсъ русскаго лѣсного законодательства. 1881. IV. 315.[3]
Россійская фармакопея. 1866. III. 247.[2]
Россмесслеръ, Э. А. [Rossmässler, E. A.] Лѣсъ. See Rossmässler, E. A. 1863. I. 82,[1] IV. 55.[1]
— Опытъ анатомической характеристики древесныхъ тѣлъ. See Rossmässler, E. A. 1847. I. 525,[1] IV. 48.[2]
— See also Rossmässler, E. A.
— & Ауэрсвальдъ. [Rossmässler, E. A. & Auerswald, Bernard.] Ботаническія бесѣды. 1865. I. 362.
— See also Времъ, А. & Россмесслеръ, Э. А.
Ростовцевъ, П. В. [Rostovtzef, P. V.] Наши деревья и кустарники. . . . Сосна. 1894. IV. 461.[1]

Ростовцевъ, С. Н. [Rostovtchef, S. I.] Патологія растеній. 1899. III. 193.[1]

Ротертъ, В. [Rothert, Wladislaw.] Анатомія растительной клѣтки. 1895. I. 525.[1]
— О геліотропизмѣ. 1892. I. 527.
— О послѣдствіяхъ обезглавливанія. 1893. I. 528.[1]
— О строеніи оболочки растительныхъ сосудовъ. 1897. I. 525.[2]
— *See also* ROTHERT, Wladislaw.

Рохель, Л. [Rochel, L.] Сирень. 1866. III. 680.[1]

Рудзскій, А. [Rudzski, Alexander.] Краткій очеркъ исторіи лѣсоустройства. 1889. IV. 245.
— Краткій очеркъ лѣсной промышленности. 1882. IV. 426.[3]
— Лѣсная таксація. 1880. IV. 253.
— Лѣсныя бесѣды. 1881. IV. 114.
— Массовыя таблицы переложенныя на русскую мѣру. 1878. IV. 230.
— Настольная книжка по лѣсоводству. 1897. IV. 104.[3]
— Нѣсколько данныхъ для описанія деревьевъ и кустовъ Крыма. 1859. I. 368,[1] *IV. 80.*
— Нѣсколько матеріаловъ къ статистикѣ лѣсныхъ посѣвовъ. 1872. IV. 114.
— Руководство къ устройству русскихъ лѣсовъ. 1888. IV. 247.[1]
— Справочная книга для лѣсничихъ. 1869. IV. 22.[2]
— *See also* Вереха, П. & Рудзскій, А.

Рудольфъ, Л. [Rudolph, Ludwig.] Картины растительности земного шара. *See* RUDOLPH, Ludwig. 1853. I. 299.
— *See also* RUDOLPH, Ludwig.

Руководство для лѣсничихъ и любителей лѣсовъ. 1813. IV. 94.

Руководство къ собиранію ... древесныхъ сѣмянъ. 1856. IV. 147.[3]

Русское Лѣсное дѣло. IV. 6.

Руссовъ, І. Я. [Rousseau, Jean Jacques.] Руссовы письма о ботаникѣ. *See* ROUSSEAU, J. J. 1771. I. 93.
— *See also* ROUSSEAU, Jean Jacques.

Рышковъ, В. [Ryshkof, V.] *See* Марковъ, Р. & Рышковъ, В.

С., П. [S., P.] Лѣсъ, лѣсные промыслы и лѣсная торговля Вятской губерніи. 1882. IV. 404.[1]

Савицкій, П. [Savitzki, P.] Лѣсоразведеніе въ Бердянскомъ лѣсничествѣ. 1881. IV. 157.

Садоводства, Плодоводства и Огородничества Вѣстникъ. *See* Императорское Россійское Общество Садоводства. III. 10.

Саксъ, Ю. Д. [Sachs, Julius.] Руководство къ опытной физіологіи растеній. *See* SACHS, Julius. 1865. I. 525.[3]
— *See also* SACHS, Julius.

С.-Петербургская императорская академія наукъ.
Вѣдомости. Извѣстія. *See* ACADEMIA SCIENTIARUM IMPERIALIS PETROPOLITANA. I. 519.[2]

С.-Петербургскій Лѣсной Институтъ. Ежегодникъ. Извѣстія. IV. 6.

С.-Петербургское лѣсное общество. Лѣсной журналъ. IV. 6.

С.-Петербургское общество естествоиспытателей. Труды. I. 519.[3]

Саницкій, П. П. [Sanitzki, P. P.] Очеркъ флоры Калужской губерніи. 1883. I. 364.

Сахаровъ, В. [Sakharof, V.] Отчетъ о послѣднемъ засѣданіи IV. всероссійскаго съѣзда лѣсохозяевъ. 1879. IV. 40.[1]

Сборникъ вводныхъ докладовъ по вопросамъ, предложеннымъ къ обсужденію членовъ ... съѣзда лѣсохозяевъ. 1874. IV. 40.[1]

Сборникъ удѣльныхъ постановленій по лѣсной части 1868 года. 1892; IV. 298.[1]

Свида, А. [Svida, A.] Лѣсное дѣло Вятской губерніи до 1870 года и нѣкоторыя мѣры къ его улучшенію. 1870. IV. 345.

Свѣдѣнія о способѣ доктора Бушри для сбереженія деревьевъ. 1841. III. 196.

Селивановскій, И. [Selivanovski, I.] Изобрѣтатель берестяныхъ тростей. 1897. IV. 491.[1]

Сельское хозяйство и лѣсоводство. Журналъ Министерства Госуд. имуществъ. *See* Министерство Государственныхъ имуществъ. IV. 6.

Семеновъ [Semenof.] О вліяніи почвенной силы на растенія вообще. 1835. IV. 68.

— О внутреннемъ строеніи растеній вообще. 1836. I. 524.[2]
— О развитіи и возрастаніи древесныхъ растеній. 1835. I. 525.[3]
— О сокахъ древесныхъ растеній. 1835. I. 526.[1]

Семеновъ, П. [Semenof, P.] Придонская флора. 1851. I. 361.

Семеновъ, В. [Semenof, V.] Лѣсоохраненіе. 1843. IV. 179.[3]
— Таксація лѣсовъ. 1843. IV. 253.
— Уставъ лѣсной. 1899. IV. 316.

Сидка дегтя изъ осиновой коры. 1879. IV. 487.[1]

Сидоровъ, В. [Sidorof, V.] Вооруженіе растеній и защита ихъ отъ враговъ. 1887. I. 235.[2]
— Матеріалы для изученія Екатеринославской флоры. 1897. I. 367.

Сидоровъ, М. [Sidorof, M.] Лиственница. 1871. IV. 452.[1]
— *See also* SIDOROF, M.

Силантьевъ, А. А. [Silantef, Anatoli A.] Монашенка (Ocneria monacha). 1895. IV. 202.
— Цѣли и проэктъ всесторонняго изученія парка Лѣсного института. 1896. IV. 31.

Симиренко, Л. П. [Simirenko, Leon.] Крымское промышленное плодоводство. n. d. III. 68.[1]
— *See also* SIMIRENKO, Léon.

Систематическій каталогъ библіотеки Императорскаго С.-Петербургскаго ботаническаго сада. *See* CATALOGUS systematicus bibliothecae ... 1852. I. 2.

Систематическій сводъ и краткое содержаніе циркуляровъ. 1861. IV. 297.

Систематическій указатель предметовъ. 1892. IV. 289.[1]

Ситовскій, Н. [Sitovski, N.] *See* Оверинъ, А. & Ситовскій, Н.

Скалозубовъ, Н. Л. [Skalozubof, N. L.] О томъ, какіе продукты могутъ быть получены изъ дерева? 1898. IV. 437.[1]

Скробишевскій, В. Я. [Skrobishevski, V. J.] О наливаніи плодовъ. 1883. I. 528.[1]
— О происхожденіи нитчатаго аппарата у Viscum. 1883. II. 178.[1]
— *See also* SKROBISHEVSKI, V. J.

Слезкинъ, П. Р. [Slezkin, P. R.] Къ вопросу о вліяніи среды на развитіе корневой системы. *See* SLEZKIN, P. R. 1893. I. 196.[1]

Слѣпцова, М. [Slieptzof, Mrs. M.] Дерево и лѣсъ. *See* SLEPTZOF, Mrs. M. 1900. I. 82.[1]

Смирновъ, Н. [Smirnof, N.] Явнобрачныя растенія окрестностей с. Николаевскаго. 1885. I. 364.

Снѣгиревъ, С. Д. [Smirnof, S. D.] Надѣлы изъ луба и мочальный промыселъ. 1880. III. 585.[3]

Смѣта по Лѣсному департаменту Мин. госуд. имуществъ. 1882. IV. 345.

Собичевскій, В. Т. [Sobitchevski, Vasili T.] Задача лѣсоводства и средствъ для ея рѣшенія. 1871. IV. 269.
— Лѣсной отдѣлъ московской политехнической выставки. 1872. IV. 19.[1]
— Матеріалы для лѣсной географіи Россіи. 1886. I. 359, *IV. 80.*[1]
— Матеріалы для лѣсной статики. 1869. IV. 67.[1]
— *See also* SOBITCHEWSKI.
— & **Шафрановъ**, Н. С. Лѣсной календарь. *See* Лѣсной календарь. IV. 6.

Собелевскій, Г. [Sobolevski, Gregor.] Санктпетербургская флора. 1801. I. 360.
— *See also* SOBOLEWSKI, Gregor.

Соболевъ, А[лексей] Н. [Sobolef, A[lexei] N.] О возвышеніи Дуба. 1898. IV. 509.
— Летучіе пески и борьба съ ними. 1900. IV. 146.[1]
— Лѣсное хозяйство Пруссіи. 1899. IV. 355.[1]

Соколовъ, Н. Н. [Sokolof, N. N.] Жуки, повреждающіе дерево въ складахъ. 1900. IV. 210.[1]

Соображенія объ устройствѣ эмеритальной кассы для чиновъ корпуса лѣсничихъ. 1871. IV. 310.[1]

Сорокинъ, Н. В. [Sorokin, N. V.] Гниль нашихъ древесныхъ породъ. 1882. IV. 415.[1]
— Матеріалы для флоры Урала. 1876. I. 363.
— Матеріалы для среднеазіатскихъ растеній. 1888. I. 457.
— Способы опредѣленія сахаристыхъ веществъ въ растеніяхъ. 1889. I. 526.[1]
— *See also* SOROKINE, N. V.

Состояніе и нужды казеннаго лѣсного хозяйства въ
Сибири. 1899. IV. 294.[1]
Спасскій, В. [Spasski, V.] Носѣвъ деревьевъ и кустар-
никовъ. 1869. III: 156.[1]
Списокъ растеній гербарія русской флоры. See SCHEDAE.
1898. I. 367.
Списокъ растеній и сѣмянъ, собранныхъ въ юго-запад-
ныхъ областяхъ Кавказа г. Іеппемъ. 1842. I. 368.[1]
Способъ предохранить лѣсъ отъ гнили скораго возго-
ранія. 1849. IV. 417.
Спрыгинъ, И. [Sprygin, I.] Матеріалы къ флорѣ гу-
берній Пензенской и Саратовской. 1896. I. 367.
Срединскій, Н. К. [Sredinski, N. K.] Дикая Маслина
или Лохъ. 1887. III. 628.[1]
— Древесные питомники вдоль . . . желѣзныхъ дорогъ.
1878. III. 154.[1]
— Въ интересѣ степного лѣсоразведенія. 1882. IV. 157.
— Краткій историческій очеркъ лѣсоразведенія. 1887.
IV. 157.
— Краткое наставленіе для укрѣпленія летучихъ песковъ.
1887. IV. 146.[1]
— Краткое наставленіе при выкопкѣ, перевозкѣ и по-
садкѣ лиственныхъ древесныхъ. 1887. III. 166.
— Культура Вяза, Береста и Карагача. 1883. III. 364.[1]
— Лѣсоводство на всероссійской сельскохозяйственной
выставкѣ въ г. Харьковѣ въ 1887 году. 1890. IV.
19.[2]
— Матеріалы для флоры Новороссійскаго края и Бесса-
рабіи. 1872. I. 363.
— Очеркъ растительности Piонскаго бассейна. 1874. I.
363.
— Работы по устройству защитныхъ насажденій. 1881.
III. 215.[1]
— Phillyrea Medwedewi, Sred. 1875. II. 714.[1]
Статковскій, В. И. [Statkovski, V. I.] Защита дорогъ
отъ овражныхъ насыпей. 1895. IV. 157.
Стецеръ, Г. [Stötzer, H.] Руководство къ постройкѣ
лѣсныхъ дорогъ. See STÖTZER, H. 1877. IV. 266.[2]
— See also STÖTZER, H.
Стойковичъ, Алекса. [Stojković, Aleksa.] О мерама за
унапређенье шумарства у Србіи. 1880. IV. 41.[1]
Столѣтіе учрежденія лѣсного департамента. 1898. IV.
289.[1]
Страсбургеръ, Э. [Strasburger, Eduard.] Учебникъ
ботаники. See STRASBURGER, Eduard & others. 1894.
I. 523.[1]
— See also STRASBURGER, Eduard.
Страховъ, П. [Strakhov, P.] Русская ботаническая
литература. See STRAKHOV, P. 1859. I. 3.[2]
О строеніи ствола двусѣмянодольныхъ растеній. 1838.
I. 524.[1]
Сукачевъ, В. [Sukatchef, V.] Нѣсколько словъ о кур-
ской Daphne altaica Pall. 1900. II. 602.[1]
Сукковъ, Г. А. [Suckow, G. A.] Экономическая бота-
ника. See SUCKOW, G. A. 1777. III. 51.
— See also SUCKOW, G. A.
Сурожъ, О. И. [Surozh, O. I.] Лѣса и лѣсная промыш-
ленность Швеціи. 1896. IV. 344.[2]
— Масло, какъ запасное вещество нашихъ деревьевъ.
1893. I. 526.[2]
Сутчковъ, Вл. [Sutchkof, Vl.] Лѣсоохраненіе въ Харь-
ковской губерніи. 1893. IV. 180.[1]
Съѣздъ (VII.-VIII.) Русскихъ естествоиспыта-
телей и врачей . . . Протоколы. I. 519.[2]
Сюзевъ, А. [Siuzef, A.] Механическая обработка де-
рева. 1874. IV. 422.[1]
Сюзевъ, П. В. [Siuzef, P. V.] О нѣкоторыхъ новыхъ
растеніяхъ Московской флоры. 1900. II. 101.[1] · ·
— Очеркъ растительности Билимбаевскаго Завода. 1890.
I. 365.
— Растенія Билимбаевскаго Завода. 1893. I. 366.

Таблица площадей круговъ въ квадратныхъ сантиме-
трахъ при діаметрѣ въ сантиметрахъ. 1876. IV. 59.[1]
Таблица сортиментовъ древесины для лѣсныхъ дачъ
Виленской губерніи. 1897. IV. 229.
Таблицы для опредѣленія процента прироста. 1891.
IV. 234.
Таблицы объема цилиндровъ въ кубическихъ футахъ
при поперечникѣ. 1865. IV. 225.
Таблицы сортиментовъ древесины для казенныхъ лѣс-
ныхъ дачъ Тобольской губерніи. 1888. IV. 228.

Таблицы сортиментовъ древесины для казенныхъ лѣсныхъ дачъ Томской губерніи. 1893. IV. 228.
Таировъ, Василій. [Tairof, Vasili.] Библіографическій
указатель книгъ . . . по виноградарству и винодѣлію.
1891. III. 545.[2]
Такса на продажу лѣса изъ казенныхъ дачъ Карской
области. 1890. IV. 298.[1]
Такса на продажу лѣса изъ казенныхъ дачъ Эриванской
губерніи. 1888. IV. 298.[1]
Такса на продажу лѣсныхъ матеріаловъ изъ дачъ вѣдомства. 1899. IV. 298.[2]
Таксы на Кедровыя, Сосновыя . . . жерди и бревна изъ
дачъ Иркутской губерніи. 1900. IV. 298.[1]
Таксы на лѣсные матеріалы отпускаемые изъ казенныхъ
дачъ Акмолинской . . . областей. 1899. IV. 298.[2]
Таксы на лѣсные матеріалы отпускаемые изъ казенныхъ дачъ Тобольской губерніи. 1899. IV. 298.[2]
Таксы на продажу лѣса изъ казенныхъ дачъ Терской
области. 1895. IV. 298.[1]
Такса на продажу лѣсныхъ матеріаловъ изъ казенныхъ
· . . по Енисейской губерніи. 1900. IV. 298.[1]
Таліевъ, В. И. [Taliyef, Valeri Ivanovitch.] Къ вопросу
о реликтовой растительности ледниковаго періода.
1897. I. 367.
— Матеріалы для ботанико-географическаго описанія До-
нецкой возвышенности. 1900. I. 368.[1]
— Растительность Ильинской горы. 1897. I. 367.
— Растительность крайняго юго-восточнаго пункта Ека-
теринославской губерніи. 1896. I. 367.
— Растительность окрестностей г. Сергача. 1894. I.
366.
— Сѣверная граница черно зема, Сергачскій уѣздъ. 1895.
I. 366.
— Флора Крыма. 1900. I. 370.
— See also TALIEW, W. I.
Танфильевъ, Г. И. [Tanfilef, Gavril Ivanovitch.] Пре-
дѣлы лѣсовъ на югѣ Россіи. 1894. I. 359, IV. 81.[1]
— See also TANFILEF, G.
Таратчковъ, А. [Taratchkof, A.] Карачевскіе лѣса.
1859. IV. 345.
— See also TARATCHKOFF, Al.
Таргонскій, В. А. [Targonski, V. A.] Къ вопросу о
вліяніи лѣсовъ на явленіе града. 1879. IV. 46.[2]
Теплоуховъ, А. Е. [Teploukhof, A. E.] Записка объ
углеженіи. 1879. IV. 395.
— Историческій взглядъ на лѣсохозяйство въ пермскомъ
нераздѣльномъ имѣніи графовъ Строгановыхъ. 1881.
IV. 24.[2]
— Устройство лѣсовъ въ помѣщичьихъ имѣніяхъ. 1848.
IV. 368.[1]
Теплоуховъ, Ѳ. [Teplokhof, Theodor.] Лѣсной от-
дѣлъ на Московской политехнической выставкѣ. 1873.
IV. 19.[1]
— See also TEPLOUCHOF, Theodor.
Тисъ. 1840. III. 287.[1]
Титовъ, А. [Titof, A.] Лѣсное хозяйство въ Ростов-
скомъ уѣздѣ. 1881. IV. 346.
Тифлисскій ботаническій садъ. Труды. See TIFLISSKI.
I. 10.
Тихановъ, Левъ. [Tikhanof, Leo.] О разводкѣ дубо-
выхъ рощей. 1876. IV. 506.
Тихомировъ, В. А. [Tikhomirof, V. A.] О микрохими-
ческихъ свойствахъ . . . сѣмянъ Abrus praecatorius. 1883.
II. 322.[1]
— Къ морфологіи . . . цвѣтка Pilocarpus pinnatifolius.
1883. II. 409.[2]
— See also TIKHOMIROF, V. A.
Тихоновъ, В. [Tikhonof, V.] Очеркъ лѣсного хозяй-
ства Сѣверной Америки. 1898. IV. 337.[1]
Тищенко, В. [Tishtchenko, V.] Канифоль и скипи-
даръ. 1895. IV. 437.[1]
Токмаковъ, И. [Tokmakof, I.] Краткій обзоръ матеріа-
ловъ къ исторіи лѣсоводства. 1887. IV. 24.[2]
Толвинскій, А. А. [Tolvinski, A. A.] Устройство за-
щитныхъ отъ снѣжныхъ заносовъ насажденій. 1889.
III. 215.[2]
Тонковъ, Р. Н. [Tonkof, R. N.] Программа составленія
массовыхъ таблицъ. 1899. IV. 247.[2]
Торговля въ 1892 году. Выпускъ 3-й. Торговля лѣсомъ.
1893. IV. 404.[1]
Траутфеттеръ, Р. Е. [Trautvetter, E. R.] Объ извѣст-
ныхъ нынѣ видахъ Ивъ. 1836. II. 98.[1]

— — Имп. С.-Петербургскій ботаническій садъ. 1872. I. 21.¹
— Исторія изслѣдованія флоры губерній Кіевскаго Учебнаго Округа. See TRAUTVETTER, R. E. 1854. I. 3.²
— Краткій очеркъ исторіи . . . С.-Петербургскаго ботаническаго сада. See TRAUTVETTER, R. E. 1873. I. 42, 521.²
— О растительно-географическихъ округахъ Европейской Россіи. 1851. I. 361.
— See also TRAUTVETTER, E. R. von.
Триніусъ, К. See Либошицъ, О. & Триніусъ, К.
— See also TRINIUS, C. B.
Труды съѣзда . . . лѣсохозяевъ. 1887. IV. 40.¹
Труды экспедиціи, снаряженной Лѣснымъ департаментомъ, подъ руководствомъ профессора Докучаева. 1894. IV. 37.²
Тулиновъ, А. [Tulinof, A.] Труды IV. всероссійскаго съѣзда лѣсохозяевъ. 1879. IV. 40.¹
Тумскій, К. И. [Tumski, K. I.] Лѣсные промыслы. 1897. IV. 437.¹
Турскій, М. К. [Turski, M. K.] Бѣловѣжская пуща. 1893. IV. 346.
— Къ вопросамъ о неизбѣжности выборочной рубки. 1894. IV. 140.
— Изслѣдованія лѣсоводственнаго отдѣла экспедиціи . . . Бассейнъ Оки. 1898. IV. 347.
— Краткій предварительный отчетъ по лѣсоводственному отдѣлу экспедиціи изслѣдованія источниковъ главнѣйшихъ рѣкъ Европ. Россіи. 1896. IV. 347.
— О лѣсныхъ плугахъ. 1878. IV. 143.¹
— Лѣсоводственные орудія и инструменты. 1893. IV. 176.²
— Лѣсоводство. 1892. IV. 104.²
— Образованіе лѣса посадкою саженцевъ. 1893. IV. 53.¹
— Описаніе лѣсной дачи Петровской Сельскохозяйственной академіи. 1893. IV. 346.
— Изъ поѣздки въ нѣкоторыя лѣса средней и южной Россіи. 1884. IV. 346.
— Разведеніе Ели, Инъ. 1893. IV. 114.
— О разведеніи лѣсныхъ деревъ. 1884. IV. 114.
— Сборникъ статей по лѣсоразведенію. 1894. IV. 157.
— Сборъ древесныхъ сѣмянъ. 1893. IV. 148.
— Таблицы для таксаціи лѣса. 1872. IV. 243.
— Устройство древеснаго питомника. 1893. IV. 151.¹
— Устройство древеснаго питомника при народной школѣ. 1889. III. 120.¹
— Устройство Никольской лѣсной дачи. 1886. IV. 247.¹
— See also TURSKI, M. K.
— & Яшновъ, Л. Опредѣленіе . . . древесныхъ и кустарныхъ породъ по таблицамъ. 1885. I. 294,¹ IV. 80, V. XVI.¹
Туцевичъ, В. К. [Tutzevitch, V. K.] Пособіе к лѣсоустройству. 1877. IV. 244.
Тыдельскій, В. И. [Tydelski, V. I.] Казенный лѣсъ и частная купля подъ Тулою. 1096. IV. 270.¹
Тюбефъ, К. [Tubeuf, Karl.] Сѣмена, плоды и всходы важнѣйшихъ древесныхъ породъ. See TUBEUF, Karl, Freiherr von. 1891. I. 119.
— See also TUBEUF, Karl, Freiherr von.
Тюрмеръ, К. Ф. [Thürmer, K. F.] Пятьдесятъ лѣтъ лѣсохозяйственной практики. 1891. IV. 102.
— See also THÜRMER, C.

Удинцевъ, С. А. [Udintzef, S. A.] Предварительный очеркъ растительности Ирбитскаго уѣзда. 1889. I. 365.
Объ употребленіи дровъ вмѣсто угля въ доменныхъ печахъ. 1830. IV. 431.¹
Упрощенныя правила для устройства казенныхъ лѣсовъ. 1859. IV. 297.
Уральское общество любителей естествознанія. Записки. I. 519.²
Успенскій, П. П. [Uspenski, P. P.] О размноженіи Picea Parryana glauca прививкою. 1891. III. 306.¹
— See also USPENSKI, P. P.
Уставъ лѣсной. 1857. IV. 315.² — 1896. IV. 315.²
Уставъ лѣсной. See Семеновъ, В. 1899. IV. 316.
Уставъ Лѣсного общества въ С.-Петербургѣ. 1871. IV. 39.²
Уставъ Общества Балтійскихъ Лѣсоводовъ вспот. See STATUT des Vereins Baltischer Forstwirthe. 1890. IV. 40.¹
Уставъ товарищества технической разработки лѣсныхъ произведеній подъ фирмою "Лѣсопромышленникъ." 1871. IV. 39.²

Фадѣевъ, А. Ф. [Fadyeyef, A. F.] О карпологическихъ коллекціяхъ вообще. 1895. I. 521.¹
— Медоносныя растенія Урала. 1894. III. 270.²
Фаерманъ, Л. [Faermann, L.] О химической древесной массѣ и искусственномъ пергаментѣ. 1879. IV. 432.²
Фанъ Доллекъ. [Van Dollen.] Сборникъ древесныхъ породъ русскихъ и заграничныхъ. 1872. III. 67,² IV. 80.
Фармацевтическій журналъ. See PHARMACEUTISCHE Zeitschrift. I. 519.²
Федоровичъ, Ф. [Fedorovitch, F.] Новыя наблюденія надъ сибирскою Елью. 1876. II. 38.¹
Федотьевъ, П. [Fedotyef, P.] Добываніе поташа изъ золы. 1896. IV. 396.¹
Федченко, Б. А. See Федченко, О. А. & В. А; FEDTCHENKO, B. A.
Федченко, О. А. & В. А. [Fedtchenko, O. A. & B. A.] Матеріалы для флоры Уфимской губерніи. 1893. I. 366.
— — Ranunculaceae Русскаго Туркестана. 1899. II. 195.¹
— See also FEDTCHENKO, O. A. & B. A.
Фелькеръ, Г. Л. В. [Völker, H. L. W.] Лѣсная технологія. See VÖLKER, H. L. W. 1803. IV. 381.
— See also VÖLKER, H. L. W.
Филипповъ, И. [Filippof, I.] О лѣсоразведеніи въ Псковской губерніи. 1891. IV. 157.
— Посѣвъ Сосны и Ели. 1891. IV. 441.
Филипповъ, Н. [Filippof, N.] Объ опытахъ подсочки Сосны. 1899. IV. 437.¹
Фишеръ, Б. [Fischer, F. E. L.] Деревья и кустарники способные к разведенію въ окрестностяхъ Петербурга. 1852. III. 67.³
— Обозрѣніе древесныхъ и кустарныхъ растеній. 1839. III. 67.³
— О разныхъ видахъ душистой осокори, разводимой въ Россіи. See Fischer, F. E. L. 1841. II. 96.¹
— See also FISCHER, Friedrich Ernst Ludwig von.
Фишеръ-фонъ-Вальдгеймъ. [Fischer von Waldheim, Alexander.] Курсъ ботаники. . . . Органографія и морфологія сѣмянныхъ растеній. 1891. I. 523.
— See also FISCHER VON WALDHEIM, A. A.
Флавицкій, Ф. [Flavitski, Flavian.] Изслѣдованіе естественныхъ смолъ разныхъ Хвойныхъ. 1883. II. 20,¹ III. 227.
Фокель, (Форстмейстеръ.) [Fockel.] Описаніе естественнаго состоянія растущихъ въ сѣверныхъ россійскихъ странахъ лѣсовъ. 1766. I. 358, IV. 79,² 344.²
Фокъ, А. [Fock, A.] Лѣсная съемка за границей. 1890. IV. 265.
— Проходныя рубки. 1890. IV. 174.
Фонъ Вильдерметъ. [Wildermet, von.] Перечень наблюденій произведенныхъ въ 1837 году надъ питаніемъ и возрастаніемъ произбяемыхъ. 1839. I. 526.¹
Фонъ-Бранке, В. Ю. [Branke, von.] See Бранке, В. Ю. фонъ.

Хамбергъ. [Hamberg, H. E.] О вліяніи лѣсовъ на климатъ Швеціи. See HAMBERG, H. E. 1885. IV. 46.¹
— See also HAMBERG, Hugo Emanuel.
Холодковскій, Н. [Kholodkovski, N.] О ходахъ короѣдовъ. n. d. IV. 203.
Хорватъ, А. [Khorvat, A.] Къ ученію о корневой шейкѣ. 1893. I. 526.¹
Хрущовъ, Д. [Khrushtchof, J.] Бесѣда о лѣсѣ. Лѣсные пожары. 1895. IV. 182.²
— Бесѣда о лѣсѣ. Разведеніе лѣса на вспаханныхъ мѣстахъ. 1895. IV. 134.¹

Цабель, Н. Е. [Zabel, N. E.] Древесныя и кустарныя породы разводимыя въ Россіи. 1884. III. 68,¹ IV. 80.
— Курсъ общей ботаники. 1887. I. 523.¹
— Обзоръ физіологическихъ-отправленій органовъ. 1863. I. 525.³
— Растительная гистологія. 1864. I. 524.¹
О цвѣтоизмѣненіи листьевъ и хвои осенью. 1851. I. 526.³
Цейль, М. А. [Zeil, M. A.] Уставъ лѣсной. 1898. IV. 316.
Цигра, Ив. Г. [Zigra, J. H.] Древесная флора. See ZIGRA, J. H. 1842. I. 358, IV. 80.
— Подробное руководство к заведенію плодовыхъ деревъ для нашего сѣвернаго климата. See ZIGRA, J. H. 1803. IV. 134.¹
— See also ZIGRA, J. H.

Цингеръ, В. Я. [Zinger, V. Y.] Сборникъ свѣдѣній о флорѣ средней Россіи. 1885. I. 364.
— See also Кожевниковъ, Д. & Цингеръ, В.
Цинъ, К. [Zin, K.] О Каштановомъ деревѣ. 1850. III. 359.[1]
Цюндзевицкій, В. [Tziundzevitzki, V.] Практическія наставленія лѣсовлаѣльцамъ продающимъ лѣсъ. 1897. IV. 388.[2]
— Въ чемъ состоитъ правильное лѣсное хозяйство. 1898. IV. 246.

Чебышевъ, В. Л. [Tchebyshef, V. L.] Сохраненіе лѣсовъ о дробленіе селеній. 1894. IV. 270.
Черновъ, К. & **Мамаевъ**, С. [Tchernof, K. & Mamayef, S.] Простые корчевальные снаряды. 1889. IV. 387.[1]
Чернышевъ, Н. Е. [Tchernyshef, N. E.] Лѣсъ въ степи. 1894. IV. 346.
Чернышевъ, С. А. [Tchernyshef, S. A.] Деревья и ихъ польза. 1898. IV. 271.[1]
Черняевъ, В. М. [Tchernyayef, V. M.] О значеніи украинскихъ лѣсовъ. 1857. IV. 273.[1]
— Конспектъ растеній . . . въ окрестностяхъ Харькова и на Украйнѣ. 1859. I. 362.
— О лѣсахъ Украйны. 1858. IV. 345.
Чистяковъ, Д. [Tchistyakof, D.] Замѣтка по поводу южной границы сплошныхъ еловыхъ лѣсовъ . . . Московской губерніи. 1868. II. 34.[2]
— See also Тснιstιαкоff, I. D.

Шавровъ, Н. Н. [Shavrof, N. N.] О возможности введенія и развитія культуры нѣкоторыхъ цѣнныхъ растеній въ Закавказѣ. 1894. III. 120.[2]
— Пробковый Дубъ. 1887. IV. 517.[1]
— Шелковица, какъ плодовое дерево на Кавказѣ. 1894. III. 380.[1]
Шапиро, С. [Shapiro, S.] О развитіи въ Россіи смолокуренія на артельныхъ началахъ. 1872. IV. 436.[2]
— О сухой перегонкѣ дерева въ Швеціи и Норвегіи. 1872. IV. 432.[2]
Шатиловъ, И. Н. [Shatilof, I. N.] Лѣсоразведеніе въ с. Моховомъ. 1885. IV. 157.
— Руководство къ разведенію лѣсовъ на черноземѣ. 1897. IV. 114.
— Семидесятилѣтній опытъ искусственнаго лѣсоразведенія на черноземѣ. 1893. IV. 114.
Шафрановъ, Н. С. [Shafranof, N. S.] Лѣсовозращеніе. 1875. IV. 104.[1]
— Лѣсоохраненіе. 1872. IV. 177.[1]
— Изъ области государственнаго лѣсного хозяйства. 1870. IV. 289.[1]
— Отрывочныя замѣтки по лѣсоводству. 1888. IV. 102.
— Пренія и заключенія II-го всероссійскаго съѣзда лѣсохозяевъ. 1875. IV. 40.[1]
— See also Собичевскій, В. Т. & Шафрановъ, Н.
— & **Поздняковъ**, Н. [Shafranof, N. S.] & Pozdnyakof, N.] Лѣсной отдѣлъ на Парижской Всемірной выставкѣ 1867 года. 1868. IV. 20.[1]
— & **Полетаевъ**, О. [Shafranof, N. S. & Poletayef, O.] Объяснительная записка къ проектамъ таксъ на лѣса губерній Минской. 1868. IV. 345.
Шахтъ, Г. Дерево. See Schacht, Hermann. 1853. I. 82.[1]
Швапахъ, Адамъ. [Schwappach, Adam.] Руководство къ управленію лѣсами. See Schwappach, Adam. 1884. I. 55.
— See also Schwappach, Adam.
Швыйковскій, Новало-. See Повало-Швыйковскій.
Шевыревъ, Ив. [Shevyref, Ivan.] Вредныя лѣсныя насѣкомыя въ 1891 году. 1893. IV. 204.
— Вредныя лѣсныя насѣкомыя южной Россіи. Гусеницы листогрызы. 1892. IV. 205.[1]
— Вредныя лѣсныя насѣкомыя южной Россіи. Наблюденія 1891 года. 1892. IV. 205.[1]
— Дѣятельность короѣдовъ. 1888. IV. 204.
— Можно-ли дѣлать борьбу съ монашенкой обязательной для всѣхъ лѣсовлаѣльцевъ средней Россіи? 1894. IV. 201.
— Описаніе вредныхъ насѣкомыхъ степныхъ лѣсничествъ и способовъ борьбы съ ними. 1893. IV. 205.[2]
— Практическая ентомологія. Короды. 1887. IV. 549.[1]
— Шелкопрядъ монашенка. 1894. IV. 201.
Шелгуновъ, Н. В. [Shelgunof, N. V.] Исторія русскаго лѣсного законодательства. 1857. IV. 315.[2]

— Лѣсоводство. 1856. IV. 104.[1]
— Съемка и нивелляровка. 1857. IV. 264.
— & **Греве**, В. [Shelgunof, N. & Greve, V.] Лѣсная технологія. 1858. IV. 381.
Шелль, Ю. К. [Schell, Julius.] Матеріалы для ботаническоѣ географіи Уфимской и Оренбургской губ. 1881. I. 364.
— О Сиренгинѣ. 1872. II. 715.[2]
— Списокъ явнобрачныхъ растеній окрестностей Талицкаго Завода. 1878. I. 363.
— О хлорозности Pelargonium zonale. 1876. III. 181.[1]
Шендеровичъ, З. [Shenderovitch, Z.] Лѣсоторговыя исчисленія. 1898. IV. 229.
Шенрокъ, Э. И. [Schönrock, E. I.] Обзоръ устройства лѣсного управленія въ Германіи, Австріи и Франціи. 1889. IV. 288.[1]
— Романовско-Таволжанская казенная дача близъ г. Липецка. 1874. IV. 345.
Шеннинъ, Н. С. [Shenshin, N. S.] Древесные питомники общества Кіево-Воронежской желѣзной дороги. 1894. III. 154.[2]
Шестериковъ, П. С. [Shesterikof, P. S.] Нѣсколько дополненій къ флорѣ юго-западной части Одесскаго уѣзда. 1899. I. 368.[1]
— Матеріалы для флоры юго-западной части Одесскаго уѣзда. 1894. I. 366.
Шестидесятилѣтній юбилей Ѳ. К. Арнольда. 1898. IV. 2.
Шиловъ, Д. [Shilof, D.] Лѣсной уставъ изд. 1876 года. 1880. IV. 315.[1]
— Порядокъ преслѣдованія нарушеній лѣсного устава. 1879. IV. 315.[1]
— Проэктъ инструкціи о порядкѣ отпуска лѣса. 1893. IV. 298.[1]
— Сборникъ законоположеній о сбереженіи и охраненіи лѣсовъ частныхъ и общественныхъ. 1889. IV. 315.[1]
Шлейденъ, М. И. [Schleiden, M. J.] Дерево и лѣсъ. See Schleiden, M. J. 1870. IV. 44.
— Растеніе и его жизнь. See Schleiden, M. J. 1847. I. 524.[1]
— See also Schleiden, M. J.
Шмальгаузенъ, И. [Schmalhausen, Johannes.] Краткій учебникъ ботаники. 1887. I. 523.[1]
— О растительныхъ помѣсяхъ. 1874. I. 271.[1]
— Флора средней и южной Россіи, Крыма и сѣвернаго Кавказа. 1895. I. 366.
— Флора юго-западной Россіи. Руководство. 1886. I. 365.
— Шиповники окрестностей Кіева. 1891. II. 572.[1]
— See also Schmalhausen, Johannes.
Шмидтъ, Ф. Б. [Schmidt, Friedrich.] Труды сибирской экспедиціи Имп. Русскаго географическаго общества . . . Ботаническая часть. See Schmidt, Friedrich. 1868. I. 455.
— See also Schmidt, Friedrich.
Шнейдеръ, Э. [Schneider, E.] Карманная книга явнобрачныхъ растеній С.-Петербургской губерніи. 1858. I. 362.
Шредеръ, Р. И. [Schröder, R. I.] Живыя изгороди и лѣсныя опушки. 1869. III. 213.
— Наблюденія надъ растеніями, воспитываемыми въ питомникѣ Лѣсного Института въ С.-Петербургѣ. 1862. III. 67.[3]
— Списокъ древесныхъ породъ. 1890. I. 42.
— Указатель растеній дендрологическаго сада. 1899. I. 42.
— See also Schröder, R.
Штецеръ, Г. See Стецеръ, Г.
Штромбергъ, Ч. [Stromberg, T.] Лѣсные оазисы. 1894. IV. 157.
Шульгинъ, Н. [Shulgin, N.] Статистическое описаніе казенныхъ лѣсовъ Черниговской губерніи. 1858. IV. 345.
Шульцъ, [К. Г.] [Schultz-Schultzenstein, K. H.] Новыя наблюденія надъ сокосокращеніемъ въ растеніяхъ. 1840. I. 526.[1]
— See also Schultz-Schultzenstein, K. H.

Щегловъ, Н. [Shtcheglof, N.] Хозяйственная ботаника. 1828. III. 52.
Щекотовъ, I. Н. [Shtchekotof, I. P.] Лѣсопольная система хозяйства. 1884. IV. 134.[1]

—Проектъ наивыгоднѣйшей эксплоатаціи лѣсовъ сѣвера Россіи. 1884. IV. 383.[1]

Щепкинъ, С. [Shtchepkin, S.] О преобразованіи управленія казенными лѣсами въ Царствѣ польскомъ. 1881. IV. 289.[1]

Щуровскій, Г. Е. [Shtchurovski, G. E.] Были-ли лѣса въ южной степной Россіи въ историческое время? 1880. I. 358, *IV. 80.*

Эльсъ, В. [Els, V.] Опыты по физіологіи растеній. 1894. I. 525.

Энгель, А. [Engel, A.] Венгерская лѣсная промышленность. *See* ENGEL, A. 1882. IV. 406.[2]

— *See also* ENGEL, Alexander.

Энгельфельдъ, В. А. [Engelfeld, V. A.] О лѣсахъ Западной Сибири. 1888. IV. 376.[1]

Энгельманъ, Г. [Engelmann, G.] Наставленіе, какимъ образомъ съ выгодою пережигать сосновые пни и валежникъ. 1823. IV. 436.[1]

Ю., С. [Yu., S.] Насажденіе защитныхъ опушекъ. 1897. III. 215.[2]

Юдейхъ, Фридрихъ. [Judeich, Friedrich.] Лѣсоустройство. *See* JUDEICH, Friedrich. 1871. IV. 241.

— *See also* JUDEICH, Friedrich.

Яницкій, I. [Yanitzki, I.] Значеніе казенныхъ лѣсовъ для крестьянскаго населенія Привислянскаго края. 1899. IV. 273.[2]

Янишевскій, Д. [Yanishevski, D.] Матеріалы для флоры Бузулукскаго уѣзда. 1898. I. 367.

Ярощевскій, Е. Ѳ. [Yaroshevski, K. F.] Учебникъ ботаники. 1888. I. 523.

Ячевскій, А. А. [Yatchevski, A. A.] Паразитные грибы русскихъ лѣсныхъ породъ. 1897. IV. 212.

— Практическія указанія о сообщеніи матеріала для распознаванія грибныхъ болѣзней растеній. 1900. IV. 212.

Яшновъ, Л. [Yashnof, L.] Очерки заграничныхъ лѣсныхъ хозяйствъ. 1889. IV. 245.

— *See also* Турскій, М. & Яшновъ, Л; Ycknof, L.

Ѳедосѣевъ, С. К. [Fedosyeyef, S. K.] Флора окрестностей г. Николаева. 1898. I. 367.

— Къ флорѣ Полѣсья. 1897. I. 367.

SUBJECT INDEX TO VOLUMES I–V

Botanical names in *italics* are synonyms.

Abatia, II. 569.
Abauria, II. 367.
Abelia, II. 834; III. 748.
Abelia, II. 835.
Abelicea, II. 145.
Abena, II. 760.
Aberemoa, II. 217.
Aberia, III. 614.
Aberia, II. 570.
Abies, II. 21; III. 295; IV. 444, 558.
Abies, II. 32, 33, 49, 53; III. 304, 305, 309, 312; IV. 452, 483.
Abietineae, see Pinaceae.
Abroma, II. 532; III. 763.
Abrophyllum, II. 237.
Abrus, II. 322; III. 462.
Absorption of fluids and gases, I. 160.
Absorption of water by timber, IV. 411.
Abuta, II. 206.
Abutilon, II. 519; III. 586.
Abutilon, II. 526.
Abyssinia, phytography, *see* North East Africa, I. 486.
—— vernacular names, *see* Africa, I. 76.
Acacia, II. 322, 872; III. 462; IV. 520; V. xxvi.[1]
Acacia, II. 330, 338, 340, 354, 369, 371, 377; III. 466, 484.
Acaena, II. 257.
Acalypha, II. 435; III. 514.
Acalypha, II. 438, 452.
Acamptopappus, II. 850.
Acanthaceae, II. 795, 874; III. 708.
Acanthinophyllum, II. 155.
Acanthocladus, II. 430.
Acantholimon, II. 696.
Acantholippia, II. 758.
Acantholoma, II. 448.
Acanthopanax, II. 647; III. 641.
Acanthophoenix, II. 64; III. 319.
Acanthophyllum, II. 194.
Acanthorhiza, II. 64; III. 319.
Acanthosicyos, II. 844.
Acanthosyris, II. 168.
Acanthus, II. 796; III. 708.
Acclimatization and naturalization, III. 43.
Acer, II. 476, 873; III. 533; IV. 526; V. xxvi.[1]
Aceraceae, II. 476, 873; III. 533; IV. 526; V. xxvii.[1]
Aceratium, II. 510.
Achania, II. 525; III. 588.
Achillea, II. 850.
Achilleopsis, II. 537.
Achimenes, II. 792.
Achras, II. 697; III. 666.
Achras, II. 698, 699, 700; III. 667.
Achyranthes, II. 189.
Achyranthes, II. 190.
Achyronia, II. 379.
Achyrospermum, II. 762.
Acicalyptus, II. 620.
Acids, I. 180.
Aciella, II. 174.
Acioa, II. 257.
Acipetalum, II. 636, 641.
Acisanthera, II. 635.
Acksma, II. 250.
Acmadenia, II. 397.
Acmadenia, II. 408.
Acmena, II. 633.
Acmopyle, II. 8.
Acnistus, II. 768.

Acocanthera, II. 722; III. 685.
Acokanthera, II. 722; III. 685.
Acradenia, II. 397.
Acranthera, II. 808.
Acridocarpus, II. 424.
Acrocarpidium, II. 93.
Acrocarpus, II. 329; IV. 521.
Acrocephalus, II. 762.
Acrocoelium, II. 474.
Acrocomia, II. 64; III. 319.
Acrodiclidium, II. 223; III. 403.
Acrolobus, II. 171.
Acronychia, II. 397.
Acronychia, II. 408.
Acrophyllum, II. 250; III. 416.
Acrosepalum, II. 512.
Acrosanthus, II. 558.
Acrotriche, II. 688; III. 664.
Actephila, II. 435.
Actinidia, II. 540; III. 595.
Actinodaphne, II. 223.
Actinophora, II. 512.
Actinophyllum, II. 652.
Actinostemon, II. 435.
Actinostigma, II. 538.
Actinostrobus, II. 25.
Actinotinus, II. 842.
Acustelma, II. 737.
Adambea, II. 609.
Adamia, II. 239; III. 410.
Adansonia, II. 528; III. 589; IV. 528; V. xxvi.[1]
Adaptation to mechanical outside forces, I. 236.
Adaptations, protective, I. 235, 529.
Addisonia, II. 850.
Adelaster, III. 709.
Adelia, II. 436.
Adelia, III. 437, 445, 706.
Adelobotrys, III. 638.
Adelosa, II. 753.
Adenandra, II. 397; III. 495.
Adenanthera, II. 329; III. 466.
Adenanthos, II. 159.
Adenaria, II. 608.
Adenia, II. 576, 873.
Adeniloma, II. 268.
Adenium, II. 722.
Adenobasium, II. 511.
Adenocalymna, II. 784; III. 704.
Adenocarpus, II. 329; III. 466.
Adenochlaena, II. 436.
Adenodiscus, II. 512.
Adenodus, II. 510.
Adenogyne, II. 570.
Adenopeltis, II. 436.
Adenopetalum, II. 502.
Adenoplea, II. 716.
Adenoplusia, II. 716.
Adenopodia, II. 355.
Adenoropium, II. 445.
Adenosacme, II. 824.
Adenostemum, II. 221.
Adenostephanus, II. 160.
Adenostoma, II. 257; III. 419.
Adesmia, II. 329.
Adhatoda, II. 800; III. 709.
Adina, II. 808.
Adinandra, II. 547.
Administration of private, communal and corporation forests, IV. 307, 554.
Admiralty Islands, *see* Bismarck Archipelago, I. 499.
Adotia, II. 499.
Adolphia, II. 492.

Adriana, II. 436.
Adromischus, II. 235.
Aedemone, II. 330.
Aegialitis, II. 696.
Aegiceras, II. 692.
Aeginetia, II. 810.
Aegiphila, II. 753.
Aegiphila, II. 755.
Aegle, II. 398; III. 495.
Aegle, III. 496.
Aegopricon, II. 447.
Aegotoxicum, II. 436.
Aeolanthus, II. 763.
Aeonium, II. 237.
Aeration of the soil, III. 211.
Aerial roots, growth, I. 188, 526.
Aerva, II. 189.
Aerva, II. 189.
Aeschynanthus, II. 792; III. 708.
Aeschynomene, II. 330; III. 466.
Aeschynomene, II. 348, 375, 376, 377, 383.
Aesculus, II. 481; III. 536; IV. 527.
Aextoxicon, II. 436.
Affinity, relation of properties to, III. 259.
Affonsea, II. 330.
Afforestation, IV. 154, 546; V. xxx.[1]
Afghanistan, descriptive botany, III. 92.
—— economic products, III. 279.
—— forest descriptions, IV. 378.
—— phytography, I. 477.
Africa, afforestation, IV. 168, 547.
—— bibliography, I. 4.
—— botanic gardens, I. 68, 522.
—— cinchona cultivation, III. 717.
—— coffee cultivation, III. 732.
—— collections, III. 29.
—— cultivation of exotic trees, IV. 127.
—— cultivation of fruit trees, III. 147.
—— dendrography, IV. 89.
—— descriptive botany, III. 93.
—— East, afforestation, IV. 168; descriptive botany, III. 93; economic products, III. 281; forest description, IV. 379; forest products, IV. 401; miscellaneous publications on arboriculture, III. 131; phytography, I. 492, 536; V. xxiv.[1]
—— economic products, III. 279; V. xxviii.[1]
—— exhibitions, IV. 21.
—— financial results of forest management, IV. 262.
—— forest descriptions, IV. 379, 556.
—— forest devastation, IV. 283.
—— forest exploitation, IV. 383, 556.
—— forest fires, IV. 184; V. xxx.[1]
—— forest influences, IV. 49.
—— forest laws, IV. 332.
—— forest policy, IV. 279.
—— forest products, IV. 401.
—— forest regulations, IV. 307.
—— forest servitudes, IV. 335.
—— history, I. 81, 523; III. 33; IV. 28; V. x.[1]
—— injuries caused by insects, III. 192.
—— insects, IV. 210.
—— manuals of arboriculture, III. 116.
—— miscellaneous publications on arboriculture, III. 130.
—— miscellaneous publications on silviculture, IV. 124.
—— North, botanic gardens, I. 68, 522; *see also* Mediterranean States of Africa.

Africa, Northeast, economic products, III. 280; phytography, I. 486; V. xxiv.[1]
—— periodicals, I. 29; III. 26; IV. 16.
—— phytography, I. 482, 536; V. xxiv.[1]
—— reproductive interrelations, I. 240.
—— South, see South Africa.
—— state forest administration, IV. 295, 554.
—— street trees, III. 211.
—— taxes, tariffs, IV. 285.
—— tea cultivation, III. 604.
—— timber trade, IV. 407.
—— Tropical, dendrography, IV. 89.
—— vernacular names, I. 76.
—— viticulture, III. 559.
—— West, descriptive botany, III. 93; economic products, III. 280; forest description, IV. 379; forest products, IV. 401; miscellaneous publications on arboriculture, III. 131; phytography, I. 490.
Afromendoncia, II. 796.
Afzelia, II. 330, 872; III. 466.
Agalma, II. 652; III. 644.
Agalmyla, II. 793.
Aganosma, II. 722.
Aganosma, II. 730, 737.
Agapetes, II. 659; III. 647.
Agarista, II. 659.
Agarista, II. 673.
Agastachys, II. 159.
Agatea, II. 567.
Agathis, II. 25; III. 297; IV. 447; V. xxxii.[1]
Agathisanthemum, II. 825.
Agathophyllum, II. 227; III. 407.
Agathophylla, II. 398; III. 495.
Agathosma, II. 408.
Agathus, IV. 447.
Agati, II. 383; III. 487.
Agation, II. 567.
Agauria, II. 659; III. 647.
Agave, II. 88; III. 340.
Agave, II. 89.
Agdestis, II. 192.
Age, mixed woods in regard to, IV. 138.
Age of, forests, determination of, IV. 232, 235.
Age of trees, I. 193, 527; III. 181; IV. 55, 543.
Agelaea, II. 316.
Ageratum, II. 862, 866.
Agiabampoa, II. 850.
Aglaia, II. 419; 873.
Agnostus, III. 384; see also Stenocarpus, II. 167.
Agnus-Castus, II. 761; III. 697.
Agonandra, II. 169.
Agonis, II. 620; III. 633.
Agricolaea, II. 755.
Agriculture combined with raising of timber, IV. 134, 545.
—— combined with silviculture, IV. 132, 545.
Agrostistachys, II. 436.
Agyneia, II. 444, 449.
Aichryson, II. 237.
Ailanthus, II. 413; III. 506; IV. 524; V. xxvi.[2]
Ainsliaea, II. 850.
Aiouea, II. 223.
Aitonia, II. 419.
Aisoaceae, II. 193, 872; III. 388; V. xxvi.[1]
Akania, II. 484.
Akebia, II. 201; III. 393.
Akeesia, II. 484.
Alabama, see United States, Southeastern.
Alafia, II. 722.
Alangiaceae, II. 614; III. 632.
Alangium, II. 615; III. 632.
Alaska, economic products, III. 262.
—— phytography, I. 311, 531.

Alberta, II. 808; III. 711.
Albertinia, II. 850.
Albizzia, II. 330, 872; III. 466; IV. 521.
Albizzia, II. 322, 377.
Alchemilla, II. 257.
Alchornea, II. 436; III. 514.
Alchornea, II. 452.
Aldabra Islands, see Mascarene and Seychelle Islands, I. 481.
Alectryon, II. 484.
Aletris, II. 81.
Aleurites, II. 436; III. 514.
Aleurodendron, II. 536.
Aleutian Islands, economic products, III. 262.
—— phytography, I. 311.
Alexa, II. 331.
Alexandra, II. 331.
Algarobia, II. 379; III. 485.
Algeria, botanic gardens, see North Africa, I. 68, 522.
—— cultivation of exotic trees, IV. 127.
—— exhibitions, IV. 21.
—— financial results of forest management, IV. 262.
—— forest descriptions, IV. 379.
—— forest devastation, IV. 283.
—— forest fires, IV. 184; V. xxx.[2]
—— forest laws, IV. 332.
—— forest policy, IV. 279.
—— forest products, IV. 401.
—— forest servitudes, IV. 335.
—— miscellaneous publications on silviculture, IV. 124.
—— periodicals, IV. 16; see also Africa, I. 29.
—— phytography, see Mediterranean States of Africa, I. 483.
—— state forest administration, IV. 295.
—— taxes and tariffs, IV. 285.
—— vernacular names, see Africa, I. 76.
—— see also Mediterranean States of Africa.
Alhagi, II. 331; III. 466.
Alibertia, II. 808.
Alibrexia, II. 767.
Alicastrum, II. 146; III. 367.
Alicteres, II. 567.
Alimentary uses of wood products, IV. 433, 558.
Allaeanthus, II. 145.
Allaeophania, II. 809.
Allamanda, II. 723; III. 686.
Allanblackia, II. 553; III. 608.
Allasia, II. 761.
Allexis, II. 567.
Allocarpus, II. 854.
Allomorphia, II. 635.
Allophylus, II. 484.
Alloplectis, II. 793; III. 708.
Allospondias, II. 455.
Allotment, IV. 350.
Almeidea, II. 398; III. 495.
Alnus, II. 115; 871; III. 356; IV. 488.
Aloe, II. 77; III. 333; V. xxvi.[1]
Aloë, II. 79, 83.
Aloexylon, IV. 529.
Aloexylum, II. 600; III. 626.
Aloineae, see Liliaceae.
Alona, II. 767.
Alonsoa, II. 779.
Aloysia, II. 758.
Alphitonia, II. 492.
Alphonsea, II. 215.
Alpine regions, ecology, I. 219.
Alps, see Switzerland.
Alsace-Lorraine, forest descriptions, IV. 349.
—— forest laws, IV. 317.
—— forest regulations, IV. 298.
—— state forest administration, IV. 289.
—— see also German Empire.

Alseis, II. 809.
Alseodaphne, II. 223.
Alseuosmia, II. 834.
Alsinidendron, II. 194.
Alsodea, II. 568.
Alsodeia, II. 568.
Alsodeiopsis, II. 474.
Alsomitra, II. 844.
Alstonia, II. 723, 874; III. 686.
Alstonia, III. 670, 688.
Althoffia, II. 512.
Altingia, II. 252; III. 416; IV. 520.
Alvaradoa, II. 414.
Alvesia, II. 334.
Alvordia, II. 850.
Alysicarpus, II. 331.
Alyxia, II. 723; III. 686.
Alzatea, II. 465.
Amaioua, II. 809.
Amalocalyx, II. 724.
Amanoa, II. 436.
Amaraboya, II. 636; III. 638.
Amaralis, II. 809.
Amarantaceae, II. 189; III. 388.
Amaria, II. 334.
Amaroria, II. 414.
Amaryllidaceae, II. 88; III. 340.
Amasonia, II. 758; III. 695.
Ambelania, III. 686.
Amblyanthus, II. 692.
Amblyocalyx, II. 724.
Ambora, II. 222.
Amboraria, II. 825.
Ambrosia, II. 850.
Ameghinoa, II. 850.
Amelanchier, II. 257; III. 419.
America, see Central America, North America and South America.
Amherstia, II. 331; III. 466.
Amicia, II. 331; III. 466.
Amirola, II. 487.
Ammodendron, II. 331.
Ammothamnus, II. 331.
Ammyrsine, II. 673.
Amoora, II. 419.
Amorpha, II. 332; III. 467.
Ampalis, II. 145.
Ampelidaceae, see Vitaceae.
Ampelocissus, II. 501.
Ampelopsis, II. 501; III. 544.
Ampelopsis, II. 504; III. 544.
Ampelosicyos, III. 754.
Ampelovitis, II. 505; III. 545.
Amperea, II. 436.
Amphiblemma, II. 635.
Amphidonax, II. 59.
Amphilochia, II. 428.
Amphilophium, II. 785.
Amphipappus, II. 858.
Amphirrhox, II. 567.
Amphitecna, II. 785; III. 704.
Amphithalea, II. 332.
Amphodus, II. 366.
Amphorocalyx, II. 635.
Amygdalaceae, see Rosaceae.
Amygdalopsis, II. 270; III. 430.
Amygdalus, II. 270; III. 430.
Amyris, II. 398; III. 495.
Amyris, II. 403, 416, 417, 460; III. 510, 511.
Anabasis, II. 187.
Anabasis, II. 188; IV. 519.
Anacampseros, II. 194.
Anacardiaceae, II. 454; III. 523; IV. 525.
Anacardium, II. 455; III. 523.
Anacolosa, II. 170.
Anadenia, II. 160.
Anagallis, II. 605.
Anaglypha, II. 850.
Anagyris, II. 332; III. 467.
Anagyris, II. 377.
Analectis, II. 761.
Analysis (chemical), methods, I. 156, 526.

Anamirta, II. 206; III. 396.
Anamomis, II. 625, 631.
Anamorpha, II. 536.
Anaphrenium, II. 456.
Anarthrophyllum, II. 332; III. 467.
Anastraphia, II. 850.
Anatomy, IV. 62, 543; *see also* Morphology and anatomy, I. 97, 524; V. xl.[1]
—— of wood, *see* Structure of wood, I. 124, 524.
Anauxanopetalum, II. 461.
Anaxagorea, II. 215.
Anaxeton, II. 851.
Anchietea, II. 567.
Ancient literature, plants in, I. 514; V. xxv.[1]
Ancistrocarpus, II. 512.
Ancistrocladaceae, II. 584.
Ancistrocladus, II. 584.
Ancistrolobus, II. 554.
Ancylanthos, II. 809.
Ancylobothrys, II. 727.
Anda, II. 446.
Andersonia, II. 690.
Andira, II. 332; III. 467.
Andira, III. 476.
Andrachne, II. 436.
Andradaea, II. 190.
Andreusia, II. 806.
Andriapetalum, II. 165.
Androecium, I. 116, 524.
Androglossum, II. 491.
Andromeda, II. 659; III. 647.
Andromeda, II. 659, 662, 663, 670, 673, 674, 675, 687; III. 647, 649, 653, 664.
Androphylax, II. 207.
Andryala, II. 851.
Anemopaegma, II. 785; III. 704.
Anerincleistus, II. 635.
Aneuriscus, II. 558.
Angeja, II. 869.
Angelesia, II. 258.
Angiopetalum, II. 692.
Angiospermae, II. 56, 871; III. 313, 758; IV. 485; V. xxv,[2] xxviii,[2] xxxii.[2]
Angola, bibliography, *see* Africa, I. 4.
—— economic products, III. 281.
—— phytography, I. 491; V. xxiv.[1]
—— *see also* Africa.
Angophora, II. 620; III. 633.
Anguillaria, II. 692.
Anhalonium, II. 589, 591; III. 620, 622.
Anhalt, forest descriptions, IV. 350.
—— *see also* Germany.
Aniba, II. 223; III. 404.
Animals, injuries caused by, III. 186; IV. 196, 548.
—— interrelations with, I. 234.
Anisacanthus, II. 797.
Anisocentrum, II. 635.
Anisocycla, II. 206
Anisomallon, II. 474.
Anisomeles, III. 697.
Anisomeria, II. 192.
Anisomeris, II. 811.
Anisonema, II. 449.
Anisophyllea, II. 613.
Anisoptera, II. 559.
Anisoptera, II. 561.
Anisopus, II. 736.
Anisostemon, II. 317.
Anisotes, II. 797.
Annam, economic products, III. 276.
—— forest descriptions, IV. 377.
—— phytography, I. 469, 536.
—— *see also* Indochina.
Anneslea, II. 548.
Anneslia, II. 340; III. 469.
Annona, II. 215.
Annual rings, I. 127, 525.
Annularia, II. 734.
Anoda, II. 521.
Anoda, II. 527.

Anodendron, II. 724.
Anodopetalum, II. 250.
Anogeissus, II. 615.
Anoma, II. 234.
Anomalous structure of wood, I. 126, 525.
Anomospermum, II. 435.
Anona, II. 215; III. 401.
Anona, II. 216, 217, 218, 701.
Anonaceae, II. 215, 872; III. 401; IV. 520.
Anonychium, II. 379.
Anopterus, II. 237; III. 409.
Anotea, II. 525.
Anplectrum, II. 636.
Anplectrum, II. 635.
Anstrutheria, II. 614.
Antarctic Islands, phytography, I. 510.
—— *See also* Indian Ocean Islands, I. 481, 536; New Zealand, I. 506, 536; and Tierra del Fuego, I. 347.
Antihacantha, II. 441.
Anthacanthus, II. 797.
Anthemis, II. 854.
Antherotriche, II. 559.
Antherura, II. 809.
Antherylium, II. 609.
Antholobus, II. 168.
Anthobryum, II. 561.
Anthocephalus, II. 809; IV. 538.
Anthocercis, II. 788; III. 698.
Anthocleista, II. 716.
Anthocyan, *see* Autumnal coloration, I. 185, 526; Chlorophyll, I. 140.
Anthodiscus, II. 546.
Anthodon, II. 472.
Antholoma, II. 509.
Anthopterus, II. 659.
Anthospermum, II. 809.
Anthotroche, II. 768.
Anthyllis, II. 332; III. 467.
Anthyllis, II. 333, 355, 356.
Antiaris, II. 145; III. 366.
Antiaropsis, II. 146.
Antidesma, II. 437; III. 515.
Antidesma, II. 436, 444.
Antigonon, II. 184; III. 386.
Antilles, *see* West Indian Islands.
Antirrhinum, II. 779.
Antirrhoea, II. 809.
Antistrophe, II. 692.
Antstaris, II. 208.
Antsizoma, II. 206.
Antonia, II. 717.
Antrocaryon, II. 455.
Ants, *see* Myrmecophilism, I. 235.
Aotus, II. 332; III. 467.
Apalatoa, II. 349.
Apama, II. 181; III. 385.
Apatelia, II. 542.
Apeiba, II. 512; III. 584.
Apetrn, II. 513
Apetahia, II. 845.
Aphaerema, II. 569.
Aphananthe, II. 141.
Aphania, II. 484.
Aphanocalyx, II. 332.
Aphanomyrtus, II. 620.
Aphelandra, II. 797; III. 708.
Aphelexis, II. 858.
Aphloia, II. 572.
Apiaceae, see Umbelliferae.
Apicra, II. 79.
Apiocarpus, II. 473.
Apiocarya, II. 767.
Apiopappus, II. 851; III. 754.
Apocynaceae, II. 721, 874; III. 685; IV. 536.
Apocynum, III. 688.
Apodocephala, II. 851.
Apodostachys, II. 192.
Apodynomene, II. 386.
Apodytes, II. 474.

Apollonias, II. 223.
Apophyllum, II. 229.
Apoplanesia, II. 332.
Aporocactus, II. 589.
Aporosa, II. 437.
Appendages, I. 112.
Aprevalia, II. 332.
Aptandra, II. 170.
Aptandra, II. 171.
Apteron, II. 492.
Aptosimum, II. 779.
Apuleia, II. 333.
Apuleja, II. 853.
Aquifoliaceae, II. 462; III. 529; IV. 526.
Aquilaria, II. 600; III. 626; IV. 529.
Aquilicia, II. 503.
Arabia, coffee cultivation, III. 732.
—— economic products, III. 279.
—— history, *see* Asia, I. 81.
—— phytography, I. 480, 536; V. xxiv.[1]
—— vernacular names, *see* Western Asia, I. 76.
Arachis, I. 385.
Arachnothrix, II. 830; III. 747.
Aragoa, II. 779.
Aralia, II. 647; III. 641.
Aralia, II. 647, 648, 649, 650, 651, 652; III. 532, 641, 642, 643, 644.
Araliaceae, II. 646; III. 641; IV. 534.
Aralidium, II. 648.
Araucaria, II. 25; III. 297; IV. 447.
Araujia, II. 736; III. 692.
Arbor day, IV. 41, 541; V. xxix.[2]
Arboretums, I. 38, 521; III. 27; IV. 18, 539; V. viii,[1] xxvii.[2]
Arboricultural operations, various, III. 174.
Arboriculture, III. 96, 757; V. xxviii.[1]
—— laws, III. 200.
—— management and organization, III. 200.
—— manuals and general treatises of, III. 96, 757.
—— miscellaneous publications on, III. 116.
—— principles and fundamental sciences of, III. 35.
—— reports, III. 116.
—— statistics, III. 116.
—— *see also* Silviculture.
Arbutus, II. 659; III. 647; IV. 534.
Arbutus, II. 660, 661, 674, 684; III. 648.
Arceuthobium, II. 174.
Arceuthobium, II. 174.
Arceuthos, II. 30.
Archichlamydeae, II. 92, 871; V. xxvi.[1]
Archontophoenix, II. 64; III. 319; V. xxvi.[1]
Archytaea, II. 548.
Arctic zone, ecology, I. 219.
Arctocalyx, II. 794.
Arctostaphylos, II. 660; III. 648.
Arctotis, II. 851; III. 754.
Arctous, II. 661.
Arcynospermum, II. 521.
Ardisia, II. 692; III. 665.
Ardisia, II. 692, 693, 694, 695; III. 666.
Ardisiaceae, see Myrsinaceae.
Arduina, II. 724; III. 687.
Areca, II. 64; III. 320; V. xxvi.[1]
Areca, II. 68, 69, 71; III. 324, 325, 326; V. xxvi.[1]
Arechavaletaia, II. 569.
Arenga, II. 64; III. 320.
Argania, II. 697; III. 666.
Argentina, bibliography, *see* South America, I. 3, 519.
—— descriptive botany, III. 65.
—— economic products, III. 269.
—— forest descriptions, IV. 342.
—— forest products, IV. 398; V. xxxi.[2]
—— miscellaneous publications on arboriculture, III. 119.

Argentina, periodicals, *see* South America, I. 7, 519.
—— phytography, I. 344; V. xviii.[2]
Argithamnia, II. 437.
Argophyllum, II. 237.
Argylia, II. 785.
Argyranthemum, II. 854.
Argyreia, II. 744; III. 694.
Argyrolobium, II. 333.
Argyrothamnia, II. 437.
Aria, II. 311.
Aricuryroba, II. 67.
Ariocarpus, II. 589; III. 620.
Aristolochia, II. 181; III. 385.
Aristolochiaceae, II. 180, 872; III. 385.
Aristotelia, II. 509; III. 584.
Arizona, *see* United States, Western.
Arkansas, *see* United States, Western.
Armeniaca, II. 270; III. 430.
Armeniastrum, II. 771.
Aromadendron, II. 213.
Aronia, III. 419.
Aronia, II. 257, 311.
Arouna, II. 354.
Arrabidaea, II. 785; III. 705.
Arrest of growth, I. 191, 527.
Arrudea, II. 554.
Artabotrys, II. 216; III. 401.
Artanthe, II. 93; III. 342.
Artemisia, II. 851; III. 754.
Arthroclianthus, II. 333.
Arthrocnemum, II. 187.
Arthrophyllum, II. 648.
Arthrosolen, II. 603.
Arthrosprion, II. 322.
Arthrostemma, II. 636.
Arthrostemma, II. 640, 641.
Arthrostylidium, II. 59.
Arthrotaxis, II. 76.
Artificial selection, III. 50; *see* Evolution of cultivated plants, I. 243, 529.
Artocarpaceae, *see* Moraceae.
Artocarpus, II. 146; III. 367; IV. 519.
Aruba, II. 398.
Arundinaria, II. 58; III. 315.
Arundo, II. 59.
Arytera, II. 484.
Asaemia, II. 852.
Asagraea, II. 352.
Ascarina, II. 95.
Ascium, II. 546.
Asclepiadaceae, II. 735; III. 692.
Asclepias, II. 736; III. 692.
Asclepias, II. 736, 738, 740; III. 692, 693.
Ascyrum, II. 553.
Asemnantha, II. 809.
Asia, acclimatization, IH. 50.
—— afforestation, IV. 168.
—— arbor day, IV. 42.
—— bibliography, I. 4.
—— botanic gardens, I. 66, 522; V. ix.[1]
—— cinchona cultivation, III. 713.
—— collections, III. 29.
—— cultivation of fruit trees, III. 147.
—— dendrography, IV. 87, 544.
—— descriptive botany, III. 91.
—— diseases and injuries, III. 180.
—— diseases caused by fungi, III. 195.
—— economic products, III. 272.
—— erosion, IV. 188.
—— exhibitions, IV. 21, 540; V. xxix.[2]
—— financial results of forest management, IV. 262.
—— forest descriptions, IV. 375, 556; V. xxxi.[1]
—— forest devastation, IV. 283.
—— forest exploitation, IV. 383.
—— forest fires, IV. 184, 547.
—— forest influences, IV. 48.
—— forest laws, IV. 332.
—— forest management, IV. 250.
—— forest policy, IV. 279.
—— forest products, IV. 399, 557.

Asia, forest protection, IV. 181.
—— forest regulations, IV. 307.
—— forest schools, IV. 37, 541.
—— forest servitudes, IV. 335.
—— history, I. 81; III. 33; IV. 28; V. x.[1]
—— individual noteworthy trees, I. 298.
—— injuries caused by insects, III. 192.
—— insects, IV. 210, 550.
—— manuals of arboriculture, III. 116.
—— miscellaneous publications on arboriculture, III. 127.
—— miscellaneous publications on silviculture, IV. 124.
—— periodicals, I. 28; III. 26, 757; IV. 16, 539.
—— pharmacopoeias, III. 256.
—— phytography, I. 452, 536; V. xxiii.[1]
—— silviculture and pasturing, IV. 136.
—— state forest administration, IV. 294, 554.
—— street trees, III. 211.
—— taxes and tariffs, IV. 285.
—— tea cultivation, III. 601.
—— textbooks and manuals of forestry, IV. 100.
—— textbooks and manuals of silviculture, IV. 111.
—— timber trade, IV. 407.
—— vernacular names, I. 75; V. ix.[2]
—— viticulture, III. 559.
—— Western, dendrography, IV. 89; forest influences, IV. 49; phytography, *see* Asiatic Turkey and Arabia, I. 477, 536, *also* Persia, Afghanistan, Baluchistan and Pamir, I. 477; vernacular names, I. 76.
Asiatic Russia, afforestation, IV. 168.
—— descriptive botany, III. 91.
—— forest descriptions, IV. 376.
—— forest devastation, IV. 283.
—— forest influences, IV. 48.
Asiatic Turkey, afforestation, IV. 168.
—— descriptive botany, III. 93.
—— economic products, III. 279.
—— miscellaneous publications on arboriculture, III. 130.
—— phytography, I. 477, 535; V. xxiv.[1]
—— a a names, *see* Western Asia, I. 76ern cul r
—— *see also* Asia, Western.
Asimina, II. 216; III. 401.
Asiphonia, II. 181.
Aspalathus, II. 333.
Asparagus, II. 79. 1
Asperifoliaceae, *see* Borraginaceae.
Asperula, II. 809.
Aspicarpa, II. 424.
Aspidandra, II. 437.
Aspidopterys, II. 424.
Aspidopterys, II. 425.
Aspidosperma, II. 724; III. 686; IV. 536.
Aspidospermum, II. 724.
Aspidostigma, II. 411.
Assam, phytography, I. 475.
Associations, forestry, IV. 39, 541.
—— publications of, *see* Periodicals, IV. 3, 539.
—— reports of and notes on, *see* Measures promoting silviculture, IV. 39; *see also* Publications relating to officers and employees, IV. 310.
Assyria, history, *see* Asia, I. 81.
—— *see also* Persia.
Astelma, II. 859.
Astemon, II. 763.
Astephanocarpa, II. 852.
Astephanus, II. 736.
Aster, II. 852.
Aster, II. 855, 857, 858, 860, 861; III. 756.

Asteranthos, II. 611.
Asteriscium, II. 653.
Asterochiton, II. 539.
Asterolasia, II. 399.
Asteropeia, II. 548.
Asterotrichion, II. 526.
Astianthus, II. 785.
Astiria, II. 532; III. 590.
Astragalus, II. 333; III. 467.
Astranthus, II. 571.
Astrapaea, II. 533; III. 591.
Astrocaryum, II. 64; III. 320.
Astrocaryum, II. 72.
Astroloma, II. 690; III. 665.
Astronia, II. 636.
Astronidium, II. 636.
Astronium, II. 455.
Astrophyllum, II. 399.
Astrophytum, II. 591; III. 622.
Astropus, II. 539.
Astrostemma, II. 736.
Astrotricha, II. 648.
Astyria, III. 590.
Asystasia, II. 797; III. 709.
Atalantia, II. 399; III. 495.
Atalaya, II. 484.
Atamisquea, II. 229.
Atelandra, II. 490, 763.
Ateleia, II. 334.
Athanasia, II. 852.
Atherolepis, II. 736.
Atherosperma, III. 403.
Athrixia, II. 852.
Athroostachys, II. 59.
Athrotaxis, II. 26; III. 299.
Athrotaxis, II. 9.
Atlantic Islands, afforestation, IV. 169.
—— botanic gardens, *see* Canary Islands, I. 69.
—— economic products, III. 282.
—— (Madeira) phenology, I. 228.
—— phytography, *see* Azores, etc., I. 496, 536, *and* South Atlantic Islands, I. 498.
—— (Madeira) vernacular names, I. 76.
Atmospheric influences, I. 233; V. xii.[2]
Atmospheric relations, III. 42.
Atractogyne, II. 809.
Atractylis, II. 860.
Atragene, II. 195; III. 388.
Atraphaxis, II. 184; III. 387.
Atriplex, II. 187; III. 387.
Atropa, II. 768, 771, 772, 774.
Atrugia, II. 217.
Attalea, II. 64; III. 320.
Attalea, III. 327.
Atylosia, II. 341.
Aubertia, II. 406, 411.
Aubletia, II. 495, 512.
Aubrya, II. 393.
Aucoumea, II. 416.
Aucuba, II. 654; III. 644.
Aucubaephyllum, II. 819.
Audibertia, II. 765.
Audouinia, II. 251.
Augusta, II. 809.
Augusta, II. 866.
Aukland Islands, *see* New Zealand, I. 508.
Aulacocalyx, II. 809.
Aulacophyllum, III. 286.
Aulacostigma, II. 392.
Aulax, II. 159.
Aulomyrcia, II. 631.
Aulonemia, II. 59.
Aurantiaceae, *see* Rutaceae.
Australasia, acclimatization, III. 50.
—— afforestation, III. 169.
—— arbor day, IV. 42.
—— botanic gardens, I. 69, 522; V. ix.[1]
—— cinchona cultivation, III. 717.
—— coffee cultivation, III. 733.
—— cultivation of fruit trees, III. 147.
—— dendrography, IV. 89.
—— descriptive botany, III. 93.

Australasia, economic products, III. 282.
—— forest descriptions, IV. 380; V. xxxi.²
—— forest gardens, IV. 18.
—— forest laws, IV. 332.
—— forest policy, IV. 280; V. xxxi.¹
—— forest products, IV. 401; V. xxxi.²
—— forest protection, IV. 181; V. xxx.²
—— galls, see Australia, I. 216.
—— history, see Australia, I. 82.
—— individual noteworthy trees, I. 298.
—— injuries caused by insects, III. 192.
—— miscellaneous publications on arboriculture, III. 132; V. xxviii.¹
—— miscellaneous publications on silviculture, IV. 124; V. xxx.²
—— periodicals, I. 29, 520; III. 27; IV. 17.
—— phenology, I. 228.
—— phytography, I. 498, 535; V. xxiv.²
—— reproductive interrelations, I. 240.
—— textbooks and manuals of silviculture, IV. 111.
—— viticulture, III. 559.
Australia, collections, III. 29.
—— dendrography, IV. 89.
—— descriptive botany, III. 94.
—— diseases and injuries, III. 180.
—— economic products, III. 282.
—— exhibitions, IV. 21.
—— forest description, IV. 380.
—— forest devastation, IV. 283.
—— forest exploitation, IV. 383.
—— forest influences, IV. 49.
—— forest laws, IV. 332.
—— forest policy, IV. 280; V. xxxi.¹
—— forest products, IV. 401; V. xxxi.²
—— forest protection, IV. 181; V. xxx.²
—— galls, I. 216.
—— history, I. 82.
—— insects, IV. 210.
—— manuals of arboriculture, III. 116.
—— miscellaneous publications on arboriculture, III. 132; V. xxviii.¹
—— miscellaneous publications on silviculture, IV. 124; V. xxx.²
—— phytography, I. 499, 536; V. xxiv.²
—— ¡ta te forest administration, IV. 295.
—— tea cultivation, III. 604.
—— timber trade, IV. 407.
—— see also Australasia.
Austria, forest descriptions, IV. 368.
Austria-Hungary, acclimatization, III. 50.
—— administration of private forests, IV. 309.
—— afforestation, IV. 167, 547.
—— bibliography, I. 4, 519.
—— botanic gardens, I. 66, 522; V. ix.¹
—— collections, III. 29.
—— cultivation of exotic trees, IV. 127.
—— cultivation of fruit trees, III. 146.
—— dendrography, IV. 86.
—— descriptive botany, III. 89.
—— economic products, III. 272.
—— erosion, IV. 187.
—— exhibitions, IV. 21.
—— financial results of forest management, IV. 262.
541forest
—— forest descriptions, IV. 367.
—— forest devastation, IV. 283.
—— experiment stations, IV. 38, 541forest
—— forest fires, IV. 184.
—— forest gardens, IV. 18.
—— forest influences, IV. 48.
—— forest laws, IV. 331.
—— forest management, IV. 249; V. xxxi.¹
—— forest officers and employees, IV. 311.

Austria-Hungary, forest policy, IV. 278.
—— forest products, IV. 399.
—— forest regulations, IV. 307.
—— forest schools, IV. 36, 541.
—— forest servitudes, IV. 334.
—— galls, I. 216.
—— history, I. 81, 523; IV. 28.
—— individual noteworthy trees, I. 298.
—— insects, IV. 209, 550.
—— manuals of arboriculture, III. 115.
—— measures promoting sylvicultures, IV. 41.
—— miscellaneous publications on arboriculture, III. 127.
—— miscellaneous publications on silviculture, IV. 123.
—— periodicals, I. 27, 520; III. 24; IV. 13, 539; V. vii.²
—— pharmacopoeias, III. 256.
—— phenology, I. 227, 528; V. xii.²
—— phytography, I. 438; V. xxii.²
—— silviculture and pasturing, IV. 136.
—— state forest administration, IV. 294.
—— textbooks and manuals of forestry, IV. 99.
—— textbooks and manuals of silviculture, IV. 110.
—— timber trade, IV. 406.
—— vernacular names, I. 75.
—— viticulture, III. 558.
Austrian Littoral, forest descriptions, IV. 374.
—— phytography, I. 447; V. xxiii.¹
Autumnal coloration, I. 185, 526; III. 207; V. xii.²
Auxemma, II. 748.
Auxiliary and introductory publications, arboriculture, I. 757; V. xxvii.¹
—— dendrology; see Auxiliary publications, and Introductory publications.
—— forestry, IV. 1, 539; V. xxix.¹
Auxiliary publications, dendrology; I. 1, 519; V. vii.¹
Avalanches, IV. 188.
Avellanita, II. 437.
Avenue trees, see Street and shade trees, III. 208.
Averrhoa, II. 392; III. 491.
Averrhoidium, II. 484.
Avicennia, II. 753; III. 695.
Axanthes, II. 833.
Axanthopsis, II. 833.
Axinaea, II. 636.
Axinandra, II. 636.
Azyris, II. 188.
Ayenia, II. 532.
Azadirachta, III. 511.
Azalea, II. 673, 674, 675; III. 654.
Azaleodendron, II. 675; III. 654.
Azaola, II. 649.
Azara, II. 569; III. 614.
Azara, II. 572.
Azima, II. 472.
Azores, miscellaneous publications on arboriculture, III. 131.
—— phytography, I. 496.

Babbagia, II. 188.
Babingtonia, II. 620.
Baccaurea, H. 437.
Baccharis, II. 852; III. 754.
Baccharis, II. 863.
Backhousia, II. 620.
Baconia, II. 825.
Bactris, II. 65; III. 320.
Bacularia, II. 65.
Baden, forest descriptions, IV. 350.
—— forest laws, IV. 317.
—— forest regulations, IV. 298.
—— state forest administration, IV. 289.
—— see also German Empire.
Badiera, II. 430.

Badula, II. 693.
Badula, H. 694, 695.
Baeckea, H. 620.
Baeobotrys, II. 694.
Bahama Islands, see West Indian Islands.
Baikiaea, II. 334.
Baillonia, II. 753.
Baillonodendron, II. 560.
Baissea, II. 724.
Bakeria, II. 651; III. 644.
Balanites, II. 395.
Balanocarpus, II. 559.
Balanopsidaceae, II. 111.
Balanostreblus, H. 146.
Balansaephytum, II. 146.
Balaustion, II. 620.
Balbisia, II. 389.
Balbisia, II. 864.
Balboa, II. 386.
Balearic Islands, phytography, I. 423.
Balfouria, II. 734.
Balfourodendron, II. 399.
Balkan Peninsula, acclimatization, III. 50.
—— afforestation, IV. 168.
—— botanic gardens, I. 66, 522.
—— dendrography, IV. 87.
—— descriptive botany, III. 91.
—— economic products, III. 272.
—— forest influences, IV. 48.
—— forest schools, IV. 37.
—— history, III. 33.
—— insects, IV. 210.
—— manuals of arboriculture, III. 116.
—— miscellaneous publications on arboriculture, III. 127.
—— miscellaneous publications on silviculture, IV. 124.
—— periodicals, III. 26; IV. 15; V. xxvii.¹ xxix.¹ see also Greece, I. 28.¹
—— pharmacopoeias, III. 256.
—— phenology, I. 227.
—— phytography, I. 448, 536; V. xxiii.¹
—— timber trade, IV. 407.
—— vernacular names, I. 75.
—— see also Bulgaria, Greece, Montenegro, Rumania and Servia.
Ballota, II. 763.
Baloghia, II. 437.
Balsamea, II. 417.
Balsamocarpon, II. 338; III. 468; V. xxix.¹
Balsamodendron, II. 417, III. 510.
Baltic Provinces, forest descriptions, IV. 347.
—— see also Russia.
Baluchistan, phytography, I. 477.
Bambos, II. 59,
Bambusa, II. 59; III. 316.
Bambusa, II. 60; III. 315, 316.
Banara, II. 569.
Banisteria, II. 424; III. 513.,
Banisteria, II. 425, 427.
Banksia, II. 159; III. 382.
Banksia, II. 264.
Baphia, II. 334; III. 467.
Baptisia, II. 377.
Baranda, II. 611.
Barbacenia, II. 90; III. 341.
Barbados, see West Indian Islands.
Barbeuia, II. 192.
Barbeya, II. 141.
Barcena, II. 492.
Bark, as a forest product, IV. 434, 558.
—— increase, I. 189, 527; V. xii.¹
—— structure of, I. 130, 525; IV. 62, 543; V. xi.¹
—— various economic uses, IV. 436; see also Tanbarks, IV. 435.
—— wounds to, IV. 180.
Bark-beetles, see Scolytidae, IV. 203.
Bark cleaning, III. 175.
Bark stripping, IV. 434.

Barklya, II. 334.
Barleria, II. 797; III. 709.
Barleria, II. 819.
Barnadesia, II. 853; III. 754.
Barnadesia, II. 854.
Baronia, II. 455.
Barosma, II. 399; III. 495.
Barraldeia, II. 613.
Barringtonia, II. 611; III. 631.
Barringtoniaceae, see Lecythidaceae, II. 611; III. 631.
Barrotia, II. 56.
Barteria, II. 569.
Barthea, III. 638.
Barilingia, II. 380, 827.
Baryosma, II. 399.
Basanacantha, II. 809; III. 711.
Baseonema, II. 736.
Basiloxylon, II. 532.
Bassia, II. 187; III. 387.
Bassia, II. 697, 698, 699; III. 667; IV. 534.
Bassovia, II. 768.
Bastardia; II. 521.
Batesanthus, II. 736.
Bathysa, II. 809.
Batidaceae, II. 114.
Batschia, II. 206, 364.
Baudouinia, II. 334.
Bauera, II. 238; III. 409.
Bauerella, II. 399.
Bauhinia, II. 334; III. 467.
Baumannia, II. 816.
Baumgartenia, II. 235.
Bavaria, forest descriptions, IV. 350, 555.
—— forest laws, IV. 318.
—— forest regulations, IV. 299.
—— state forest administration, IV. 289.
—— *see also* German Empire.
Beatsonia, II. 561.
Beaucarnea, II. 84; III. 337.
Beaufortia, II. 620; III. 633.
Beauharnoisia, II. 558.
Beaumontia, II. 724; III. 687.
Beauprea, II. 159.
Beaulempsia, II. 230.
Beccariodendron, II. 217.
Becium, II. 764.
Beckea, II. 620.
Beddomea, II. 419.
Bedfordia, II. 853.
Bee plants, III. 224.
Beesha, II. 60.
Befaria, II. 661; III. 648.
Begonia, II. 583; III. 618.
Begoniaceae, II. 583; III. 618.
Behnia, II. 79.
Beilschmiedia, II. 223; IV. 520.
Bejaria, II. 661; III. 648.
Belangera, II. 250.
Belencita, II. 229.
Belgium, acclimatization, III. 46.
—— afforestation, IV. 160, 546.
—— botanic gardens, I. 49, 521; V. VIII.[2]
—— collections, III. 28.
—— cultivation of exotic trees, IV. 126, 545.
—— cultivation of fruit trees, III. 140.
—— dendrography, IV. 84.
—— descriptive botany, III. 77.
—— economic products, IV. 270.
—— exhibitions, IV. 19, 540; V. XXIX.[1]
—— financial results of forest management, IV. 261, 551.
—— forest descriptions, IV. 357; V. XXXI.[2]
—— forest devastation, IV. 282.
—— forest experiment stations, IV. 38.
—— forest fires, IV. 182, 547.
—— forest gardens, IV. 18, 539.
—— forest influences, IV. 542.

Belgium, forest laws, IV. 322, 554.
—— forest management, IV. 248, 550; V. XXXI.[1]
—— forest policy, IV. 274, 551.
—— forest protection, IV. 180.
—— forest regulations, IV. 303.
—— forest schools, IV. 33, 540.
—— forest servitudes, IV. 334, 555.
—— history, I. 80; III. 33; IV. 27.
—— individual noteworthy trees, I. 296.
—— insects, IV. 208, 549.
—— manuals of arboriculture, III. 106.
—— measures promoting sylviculture, IV. 40, 541.
—— miscellaneous publications on arboriculture, III. 122.
—— miscellaneous publications on silviculture, IV. 119, 544.
—— periodicals, I. 16; III. 15; IV. 12, 539; V. VII.[1]
—— pharmacopoeias, III. 250.
—— phenology, I. 226.
—— phytography, I. 391; V. XX.[1]
—— reproductive interrelations, *see* Europe, I. 239.
—— silviculture and pasturing, IV. 545.
—— state forest administration, IV. 291, 552.
—— taxes, tariffs, etc., IV. 284, 552.
—— textbooks and manuals of forestry, IV. 98.
—— textbooks and manuals of silviculture, IV. 107.
—— timber trade, IV. 404, 557.
—— vernacular names, I. 73; V. IX.[2]
—— viticulture, III. 553.
Bellendena, II. 159.
Belliolum, II. 209.
Bellonia, II. 793.
Bellota, II. 225.
Bellucia, II. 636.
Belonophora, II. 809.
Beloperone, II. 798; III. 709.
Beloperone, III. 709.
Belotia, II. 512.
Belvisia, II. 612.
Bembicia, II. 569.
Bembycodium, II. 852.
Bending and pressing of wood, IV. 422.
Bennettia, II. 569.
Bennettia, II. 444.
Benthamia, II. 654; III. 645.
Benthamiella, II. 768.
Bentia, II. 798.
Bentinckia, II. 65; III. 320.
Benzoin, II. 225, 704; III. 670.
Berberidaceae, II. 201; III. 393, 758.
Berberidopsis, II. 569; III. 614.
Berberis, II. 201; III. 393, 758.
Berberis, III. 395.
Berchemia, II. 492; III. 541.
Berchemia, II. 496.
Berckheya, II. 853, 855.
Berendtia, II. 779.
Berendtiella, II. 779.
Bergera, II. 408; III. 504.
Berghesia, II. 809.
Berginia, II. 798.
Bergsmia, II. 573.
Berkheya, II. 853.
Berlinia, II. 336.
Bermuda, *see* West Indian Islands.
Bernardia, II. 437.
Bernardia, II. 251.
Bernardinia, II. 316.
Bernieria, II. 223.
Bernoullia, II. 529.
Berrebera, II. 371.
Berria, II. 512.
Berrya, II. 512.
Bersama, II. 491.
Bertholletia, II. 611; III. 631; IV. 529.
Bertiera, II. 809.
Bertolonia, II. 806.

Bertya, II. 437.
Berzelia, II. 251.
Beschorneria, II. 89; III. 341.
Besenvalia, II. 869.
Besleria, II. 793.
Besleria, II. 794.
Bessera, II. 451.
Betula, II. 117; III. 357; IV. 490.
Betula, II. 115.
Betulaceae, II. 115, 871; III. 356; IV. 488; V. XXVI.[1]
Beureria, II. 748.
Beverages, III. 221.
Beyeria, II. 437.
Bhesa, II. 469.
Biancaea, II. 338.
Biasolettia, II. 228.
Bible plants, I. 512; V. XXV.[1]
Bibliography, I. 1, 519; III. 1; IV. 1, 539; V. VII.[1]
Bidaria, II. 738.
Bidens, II. 863.
Bigelowia, II. 853.
Bignonia, II. 785; III. 705.
Bignonia, II. 718, 731, 785, 786, 787, 788, 789, 790, 791, 792; III. 704, 705, 706, 707.
Bignoniaceae, II. 784; III. 704; IV. 538; V. XXVII.[2]
Bikkia, II. 809.
Bikkiopsis, II. 809.
Billardiera, II. 247; III. 415.
Billardiera, II. 249.
Billardieria, II. 815.
Billbergia, II. 76.
Billia, II. 483; III. 539.
Billotia, II. 621.
Binnendijkia, II. 536.
Biography, *see* History.
Biophytum, II. 392.
Biota, II. 52; III. 311.
Biporeia, II. 415.
Birds, IV. 90, 544.
—— injuries caused by, IV. 198.
Bischofia, II. 437.
Bismarck Archipelago, economic products, III. 282.
—— phytography, I. 499.
—— reproductive interrelations, *see* Australasia, I. 240.
Bismarckia, II. 65; III. 320.
Bivonea, II. 445.
Bivonia, II. 437.
Bixa, II. 565; III. 613.
Bixaceae, II. 565; III. 613.
Bixagrewia, II. 513.
Blaberopus, II. 723.
Blachia, II. 437.
Blackburnia, II. 411.
Blackwellia, II. 571.
Bladhia, II. 692.
Blaeria, II. 661.
Blakea, II. 636; III. 638.
Blastostrophe, II. 722.
Blastus, II. 636.
Blastus, II. 635.
Blatti, II. 610.
Blechum, II. 802.
Blechnum, II. 729.
Bleeding, I. 168, 526.
Ble hara, II. 798.
Blepharispermum, II. 853.
Blepharocarya, II. 455.
Blepharodon, II. 736.
Blighia, II. 484; III. 539.
Blinkworthia, II. 744.
Blondea, II. 511.
Blumea, III. 754.
Blyttia, II. 737.
Boat building, IV. 424; V. XXXII.[1]
Bobea, II. 809.
Bobea, II. 832.
Bobua, II. 703.
Bocagea, II. 217.

Bocconia, II. 229; III. 408.
Boehmeria, II. 156; III. 381.
Boehmeria, II. 156, 157; III. 382.
Boenninghausenia, II. 399.
Boerhaavia, II. 190.
Boerhaavia, II. 191.
Boerlageodendron, II. 648.
Bohadschia, II. 575.
Bohemia, forest descriptions, IV. 370.
—— *see also* Austria-Hungary.
Bolbostylis, II. 856.
Boldoa, II. 191.
Boldoa, II. 222.
Bolivaria, II. 712.
Bolivia, descriptive botany, III. 64.
—— economic products, III. 268.
—— miscellaneous publications on arboriculture, III. 119.
—— phytography, I. 340.
—— *see also* South America.
Bombacaceae, II. 528, 873; III. 589; IV. 528; V. xxvii.[1]
Bombax, II. 529; III. 589; IV. 528.
Bombax, II. 529, 566; III. 589.
Bombycospermum, II. 745.
Bonamia, II. 744.
Bonania, II. 437.
Bonannia, II. 484.
Bonellia, II. 691.
Bonnetia, II. 548.
Bonplandia, II. 746.
Bonplandia, II. 405; III. 503.
Bontia, II. 805; III. 710.
Bookkeeping, IV. 311.
Boraginaceae, see Borraginaceae.
Borassus, II. 65; III. 320; IV. 485.
Borassus, II. 66; III. 320.
Borbonia, II. 336.
Borbonia, II. 259, 379, 381.
Boretta, II. 662.
Borneo, economic products, III. 276.
—— phytography, I. 469; V. xxiii.[2]
—— *see also* Malay Archipelago.
Boronia, II. 399; III. 495.
Boronia, II. 413.
Borraginaceae, II. 747; III. 695.
Borrichia, II. 853.
Borya, II. 706.
Boschia, II. 529.
Boscia, II. 230.
Bosea, II. 189.
Bosnia, forest description, IV. 374.
—— phytography, I. 441; V. xxiii.[1]
—— *see also* Austria-Hungary.
Bosqueia, II. 146.
Bosscheria, II. 148.
Bossiaea, II. 336; III. 467.
Boswellia, II. 416; III. 509; IV. 525.
Botanic gardens, I. 38, 521; V. viii.[1]
Botanical names, *see* Etymology, I. 76; V. ix;[1] Nomenclators, I. 76; V. ix;[1] and Nomenclature, I. 253, 529.
—— terms, *see* Terminology, I. 69, 522.
Botany, descriptive, *see* Descriptive botany.
—— emblematic, I. 515; V. xxv.[2]
—— esthetic, I. 516, 536; V. xxv.[2]
—— general, I. 82; III. 37; IV. 61; V. x.[1]
—— silvicultural, IV. 61, 543.
Bothriospora, II. 810.
Botryceras, II. 456.
Botrydendrum, II. 650.
Botryodendron, II. 650; III. 643.
Botryoropis, II. 611.
Boucerosia, II. 736.
Bouchardatia, II. 400.

Bouardia, III. 744.
Bouzetia, II. 400.
Bowdichia, II. 337; III. 467.
Bowenia, II. 3; III. 284.
Bowkeria, II. 779.
Boxes, wood for the manufacture of, IV. 427.
Boymia, II. 406; III. 504.
Bracea, II. 724.
Brachistus, II. 768.
Brachyachenium, II. 855.
Brachychiton, II. 532; III. 590; V. xxvii.[1]
Brachyclados, II. 853.
Brachyglottis, II. 853; III. 755.
Brachyglottis, II. 861.
Brachylaena, II. 853.
Brachyloma, II. 688.
Brachylophon, II. 424.
Brachynema, II. 700.
Brachyotum, II. 636.
Brachypterum, II. 353.
Brachyris, II. 858.
Brachysema, II. 337; III. 468.
Brachystegia, II. 337; III. 468.
Brachystephanus, II. 798.
Brachytome, II. 829.
Brachytropis, II. 430.
Brackenridgea, II. 544.
Bracteolaria, II. 334.
Bracts, I. 111.
Bradburya, II. 345.
Braddleya, II. 567.
Bradlea, II. 444.
Bragantia, II. 181, 190; III. 385.
Brahea, II. 65; III. 321.
Brahea, II. 68; III. 332.
Branches, casting off, I. 192; V. xii.[1]
Branching, *see* Ramification, I. 106, 524.
Brandisia, II. 779.
Brandzeia, II. 337.
Brassaia, II. 652.
Brassaiopsis, II. 648; III. 641.
Brassica, II. 234.
Bravaisia, II. 798.
Brayera, III. 424.
Brayera, II. 264.
Brazil, botanic gardens, *see* South America, I. 39.
—— coffee cultivation, III. 728.
—— dendrography, IV. 78.
—— descriptive botany, III. 65.
—— economic products, III. 268.
—— exhibitions, IV. 19.
—— forest descriptions, IV. 342.
—— forest products, IV. 398.
—— miscellaneous publications on arboriculture, III. 119, 757.
—— periodicals, *see* South America, I. 7, 519.
—— phytography, I. 340, 531; V. xviii.[1]
—— vernacular names, *see* South America, I. 72.
—— *see also* South America.
Braxzeia, II. 512.
Bredemeyera, II. 430.
Bredia, II. 636.
Brehmia, II. 525, 719.
Bremontiera, II. 364.
Breonia, II. 810.
Breweria, II. 744.
Breweria, II. 744, 746.
Brexia, II. 238; III. 409.
Breynia, II. 438.
Brickellia, II. 853.
Bridelia, II. 438; III. 515.
Bridge building, IV. 424.

British India, botanic gardens, I. 66, 522.
—— cinchona cultivation, III. 713.
—— coffee cultivation, III. 732.
—— cultivation of fruit trees, III. 147.
—— dendrography, IV. 88.
—— descriptive botany, III. 92.
—— economic products, III. 276.
—— exhibitions, IV. 21; V. xxix.[1]
—— financial results of forest management, IV. 262.
—— forest description, IV. 377, 556;
V. xxxi.[2]
—— forest fires, IV. 184.
—— forest influences, IV. 48.
—— forest laws, IV. 332.
—— forest management, IV. 250.
—— forest policy, IV. 279.
—— forest products, IV. 400, 557.
—— forest protection, IV. 181.
—— forest regulations, IV. 307.
—— forest schools, IV. 37, 541.
—— forest servitudes, IV. 335.
—— history, *see* Asia, I. 81.
—— individual noteworthy trees, *see* Asia, I. 298; V. xvi.[1]
—— insects, IV. 210, 550.
—— manuals of arboriculture, III. 116.
—— miscellaneous publications on arboriculture, III. 129.
—— miscellaneous publications on silviculture, IV. 124.
—— periodicals, I. 28; III. 26; IV. 16.
—— pharmacopoeias, III. 257.
—— phytography, I. 470; V. xxiii.[2]
—— silviculture and pasturing, IV. 136.
—— state forest administration, IV. 294, 554.
—— taxes, tariffs, etc., IV. 285.
—— tea cultivation, III. 602, 763.
—— textbooks and manuals of forestry, IV. 100.
—— textbooks and manuals of silviculture, IV. 111.
—— timber trade, IV. 407.
—— vernacular names, I. 75.
British Islands, acclimatization, III. 46.
—— afforestation, IV. 161.
—— arbor day, IV. 42.
—— bibliography, I. 3.
—— botanic gardens, I. 51, 521; V. viii.[2]
—— collections, III. 28.
—— cultivation of exotic trees, IV. 126.
—— cultivation of fruit trees, III. 140.
—— dendrography, IV. 84.
—— descriptive botany, III. 78.
—— economic products, III. 271.
—— erosion, IV. 185.
—— exhibitions, IV. 19.
—— financial results of forest management, IV. 261.
—— forest descriptions, IV. 357, 556;
V. xxxi.[2]
—— forest experiment stations, IV. 38.
—— forest fires, IV. 183.
—— forest gardens, IV. 18.
—— forest influences, IV. 47.
—— forest laws, IV. 323.
—— forest management, IV. 248.
—— forest policy, IV. 274, 551.
—— forest products, IV. 398.
—— forest protection, IV. 180.
—— forest schools, IV. 34, 540.
—— galls, I. 215.
—— history, I. 80; III. 33; IV. 27.
—— individual noteworthy trees, I. 296;
V. xvi.[1]
—— insects, IV. 208.

British Islands, miscellaneous publications on silviculture, IV. 119, 544; V. xxx.[2]
—— periodicals, I. 17; III. 16, 757; IV. 12, 539.
—— pharmacopoeias, III. 250.
—— phenology, I. 226.
—— phytography, I. 393, 533; V. xx.[2]
—— reproductive interrelations, see Europe, I. 239, 529.
—— state forest administration, IV. 291.
—— taxes, tariffs, etc., IV. 284.
—— textbooks and manuals of forestry, IV. 98.
—— textbooks and manuals of silviculture, IV. 107, 544; V. xxx.[1]
—— timber trade, IV. 404, 557.
—— vernacular names, I. 73, 522.
—— viticulture, III. 553.
Brocchia, II. 453.
Brocchinia, II. 76.
Bromeliaceae, II. 76; III. 333.
Brongniartia, II. 337; III. 468.
Bronnia, II. 563.
Brookea, II. 779.
Brosimopsis, II. 146.
Brosimum, II. 146; III. 367.
Broussaisia, II. 238.
Broussonetia, II. 147; III. 367.
Broussonetia, II. 148, 153, 384; III. 368.
Browallia, II. 768; III. 698.
Brownea, II. 337; III. 468.
Brownetera, II. 9.
Brownlowia, II. 512.
Brucea, II. 414; III. 507.
Bruckenthalia, II. 661.
Bruea, II. 147.
Brueckea, II. 753.
Brugmansia, II. 771, 772; III. 699.
Bruguiera, II. 613; III. 632; IV. 529.
Bruguiera, II. 617.
Bruinsmania, II. 820.
Bruinsmia, II. 704.
Brunellia, II. 250.
Brunellia, II. 409.
Brunelliaceae, II. 250.
Brunfelsia, II. 769; III. 698.
Brunia, II. 251; III. 416.
Brunia, II. 251, 252.
Bruniaceae, II. 251; III. 416.
Brunnichia, II. 184; III. 387.
Brunsfelsia, II. 769.
Brunswick, forest descriptions, IV. 351.
—— forest laws, IV. 319.
—— forest regulations, IV. 300.
—— state forest administration, IV. 290.
—— see also German Empire.
Bruschia, II. 712.
Brya, II. 338.
Bryanthus, II. 661.
Bryanthus, III. 675; III. 653.
Bryophyllum, II. 235; III. 409.
Bryophyllum, II. 236.
Bubbia, II. 209.
Bubon, II. 653.
Bucco, II. 398.
Buceras, II. 615.
Buchanania, II. 455; III. 524.
Buchenavia, II. 615.
Buchenroedera, II. 338.
Buchholzia, II. 230.
Buchnera, II. 779.
Buchnera, II. 780.
Buchnerodendron, II. 569.
Buchozia, II. 831.
Bucida, II. 615.
Bucklandia, II. 252; III. 416.
Buckleya, II. 168.
Bud, morphology and anatomy, I. 107, 524.
—— variation, I. 244.
Budding, III. 164.

Buddleia, II. 717; III. 681.
Buddleia, II. 718, 719, 780.
Buechnera, II. 779.
Buena, II. 815, 819; III. 745.
Buergeria, II. 211.
Buettneria, II. 582.
Buettneria, II. 214.
Buettneriaceae, see Sterculiaceae.
Bugainvillaea, II. 191.
Buginvillaea, III. 388.
Buildings, IV. 266.
Bulbostylis, II. 853, 856.
Bulgaria, forest description, IV. 375.
—— see also Balkan Peninsula.
Bulnesia, II. 395.
Bumelia, II. 697; III. 667; IV. 534.
Bunchosia, II. 424.
Bunchosia, II. 427.
Buphthalmum, II. 853, 861.
Bupleurum, II. 653.
Bupleurum, II. 653.
Burasaia, II. 206.
Burchardia, II. 753.
Burchellia, II. 810; III. 711.
Burckhardia, II. 753.
Burkea, II. 338.
Burma, phytography, I. 475.
—— see also British India.
Burmeistera, II. 845.
Burneya, II. 809, 832.
Bursaria, II. 247; III. 415.
Bursera, II. 416; III. 510; IV. 525.
Bursera, II. 418; III. 511.
Burseraceae, II. 416, 873; III. 509; IV. 525.
Burainopetalum, II. 656.
Burtonia, II. 338; III. 468.
Burtonia, II. 380.
Busbeckea, II. 230, 714.
Bush fruits, see Small fruits, cultivation of, III. 147.
Butea, II. 338; III. 468.
Butneria, II. 214.
Butyrospermum, II. 697, 874; III. 667.
Buxaceae, II. 452; III. 522; IV. 525.
Buxus, II. 452; III. 522; IV. 525.
Byronia, II. 462.
Byrsanthus, II. 569.
Byrsocarpus, II. 316.
Byrsonima, II. 425.
Bystropogon, II. 763.
Bytteria, III. 508.
Byttneria, see Buettneria.

Cabinet makers' wood, IV. 426.
Cabralea, II. 419.
Cacalia, II. 853, 857, 864.
Cacosmanthus, II. 699.
Cacoucia, II. 615.
Cacoucia, II. 616.
Cactaceae, II. 584, 873; III. 618; IV. 529; V. xxvii.[1]
Cactus, II. 589, 591, 593, 594, 595, 597, 598; III. 620, 623, 624, 625, 626.
Cadaba, II. 230; III. 408.
Cadamba, II. 819.
Cadia, II. 338.
Caesalpinia, II. 338, 873; III. 468; IV. 521; V. xxix.[1]
Caesalpinia, II. 388; III. 483.
Caesalpiniaceae, see Leguminosae.
Cahota, II. 554.
Caillica, II. 354; III. 475.
Cajanus, II. 339, 873; III. 469.
Calamintha, II. 766.
Calampelis, II. 788.
Calamus, II. 65; III. 321.
Calamus, III. 319.
Calanchoe, II. 236; III. 409.
Calandrinia, II. 194.
Calanthea, II. 230.
Calantica, II. 569.
Calceolaria, II. 779; III. 702.
Calceolaria, II. 780.

Calcium oxalate, see Crystals, I. 138, 525.
Calea, II. 854.
Calea, II. 861.
Calectasia, II. 79; III. 334.
Calendars, see Periodicals, IV. 3; and Miscellaneous publications on silviculture, IV. 111.
Calendula, II. 854.
Calendula, II. 855, 867.
Calesiam, II. 456.
Caletia, II. 448.
Calicophyllum, II. 810.
California, see United States, Western.
Caligula, II. 659; III. 647.
Calliandra, II. 340; III. 469.
Calliandra, II. 377.
Callicarpa, II. 753; III. 695.
Callicarpa, II. 757.
Callicoma, II. 250; III. 416.
Calligonum, II. 184; III. 387.
Calliphysa, II. 184.
Callistachys, II. 375.
Callistemon, II. 621; III. 633.
Callistemon, II. 628.
Callitris, II. 27; III. 299; IV. 447.
Calluna, II. 661; III. 648.
Calocedrus, II. 33.
Calocephalus, II. 854.
Calochlamys, II. 757.
Calococcus, II. 449.
Calodendrum, II. 400; III. 496.
Calodracon, II. 79.
Calodryum, II. 422.
Calopetalon, II. 247.
Calophaca, II. 340; III. 469.
Calophanes, II. 799.
Calophylica, II. 495.
Calophyllum, II. 553; III. 608.
Calopogon, II. 558.
Calopyxis, II. 615.
Calosanthes, II. 789; III. 707.
Calothamnus, II. 621.
Calotropis, II. 736; III. 692.
Calpicarpum, II. 727.
Calpidia, II. 191.
Calpigyne, II. 438.
Calpurnia, II. 340; III. 469.
Calvaria, II. 697.
Calycanthaceae, II. 214; III. 401.
Calycanthus, II. 214; III. 401.
Calycanthus, II. 214; III. 401.
Calycogonium, II. 636.
Calycomis, II. 250.
Calycopeplus, II. 438.
Calycophyllum, II. 810.
Calycophyllum, II. 823.
Calycopteris, II. 616.
Calycosia, II. 827.
Calycothrix, II. 622.
Calycotome, II. 340.
Calycotomon, II. 340.
Calypso, II. 472.
Calypteriopetalum, II. 439.
Calyptranthes, II. 622.
Calyptranthes, II. 625, 633; III. 635.
Calyptraria, II. 636.
Calyptrion, II. 567.
Calyptrogyne, II. 65; III. 321.
Calyptronoma, III. 325.
Calyptrosm, II. 437.
Calyptrostigma, II. 834; III. 748.
Calyptrotheca, II. 230.
Calysaccion, II. 558; III. 610.
Calysphyrum, II. 834.
Calythrix, II. 622.
Calyx, see Perianth, I. 115.
Camara, II. 758.
Camarea, II. 425.
Camarotea, II. 798.
Cambessedesia, II. 636.
Cambium, I. 128, 525.
Cambogia, II. 554.
Camellia, II. 548, 550; III. 597; IV. 528.

Cameraria, II. 724.
Cameraria, II. 734.
Camoensia, II. 341, 873; III. 469.
Campanula, II. 845.
Campanulaceae, II. 845; III. 754.
Campbell Islands, see New Zealand, I. 506.
Campderia, II. 184.
Campelepis, II. 741.
Camphor, III. 233, 757.
Camphora, II. 224; III. 404; IV. 520.
Camphusia, II. 847.
Campnosperma, II. 455.
Campomanesia, II. 622.
Campsiandra, II. 341; III. 469.
Campsidium, II. 786; III. 705.
Campsis, II. 786; III. 705.
Camptocarpus, II. 736.
Camptopus, II. 810.
Camptosema, II. 341; III. 469.
Camptostemon, II. 529.
Camptostylus, II. 569.
Camptotheca, II. 614.
Campuloclinium, II. 856.
Campylanthera, II. 249.
Campylanthus, II. 779.
Campylogyne, II. 616.
Campylostemon, II. 471.
Campylotropis, II. 369.
Canada, botanic gardens, I. 38; V. VIII.[1]
—— cultivation of fruit trees, III. 132.
—— dendrography, IV. 76.
—— East, phytography, I. 309, 531; V. XVI.[2]
—— economic products, III. 261.
—— exhibitions, IV. 19.
—— forest descriptions, IV. 337, 555.
—— forest devastation, IV. 281.
—— forest exploitation, IV. 382.
—— forest fires, IV. 181.
—— forest laws, IV. 314.
—— forest policy, IV. 271.
—— forest products, IV. 397; V. XXXI.[2]
—— forest protection, IV. 177.
—— forest regulations, IV. 295.
—— forest schools, IV. 30.
—— history, see North America, I. 80.
—— measures promoting sylviculture, IV. 39.
—— miscellaneous publications on arboriculture, III. 116.
—— miscellaneous publications on silviculture, IV. 111; V. XXX.[1]
—— periodicals, I. 4; III. 2; IV. 3.
—— a e forest administration, IV. 288t t
—— taxes, tariffs, etc., IV. 284.
—— timber trade, IV. 403, 557.
—— West, phytography, I. 311.
Canala, II. 719.
Canalia, II. 603.
Cananga, II. 917; III. 401.
Canarium, II. 417; III. 510.
Canary Islands, botanic gardens, I. 69.
—— dendrography, IV. 89.
—— forest description, IV. 380.
—— miscellaneous publications on arboriculture, III. 131.
—— phytography, I. 496, 536; V. XXIV.[2]
—— see also Atlantic Islands.
Canavalia, II. 341; III. 469.
Candelabria, II. 438.
Candidea, II. 867.
Candollea, II. 541.
Canella, II. 566; III. 613.
Canella, II. 566.
Canellaceae, II. 566; III. 613.
Canopus, II. 168.
Canotis, II. 465.
Cansjera, II. 169.
Cantharospermum, II. 341.
Canthiopsis, II. 829.
Canthium, II. 826, 832.
Cantua, II. 746; III. 694.

Cantua, II. 778.
Cantuffa, II. 380.
Caopia, II. 558.
Caoutchouc, products and utilization, III. 230.
—— sources of, III. 228.
Cape Colony, see South Africa.
Cape Verde Islands, descriptive botany, III. 93.
—— phytography, I. 496.
Capellenia, II. 441, 543.
Capellia, II. 543.
Capirona, II. 810.
Capparidaceae, II. 229; III. 408.
Capparis, II. 230; III. 408.
Capraria, II. 780.
Capraria, II. 780, 806.
Caprifoliaceae, II. 833; III. 748; IV. 538; V. XXVII.[2]
Caprifolium, II. 835; III. 749.
Capsicum, II. 769; III. 699.
Caracasia, II. 546.
Caragana, II. 341; III. 469.
Caraipa, II. 553; III. 608.
Carallia, II. 613.
Caralluma, II. 736.
Carapa, II. 419; III. 511.
Carbonization, IV. 393.
Cardiacanthus, II. 798.
Cardiandra, II. 238.
Cardiocarpus, II. 416.
Cardiogyne, II. 147.
Cardiopetalum, II. 217.
Cardiophora, II. 416.
Cardiopteris, II. 474.
Cardiopteryx, II. 474.
Cardiospermum, II. 484.
Carduus, II. 854.
Cardwellia, II. 159.
Careya, II. 611; III. 631.
Cargillia, II. 701.
Carica, II. 582; III. 617.
Caricaceae, II. 582; III. 617.
Cariniana, II. 611.
Carionia, II. 636.
Carissa, II. 724; III. 687.
Carissa, II. 726, 816.
Carlea, II. 703.
Carlina, II. 854.
Carlowizia, II. 854.
Carlowrightia, II. 798.
Carludovica, II. 76; III. 332.
Carmichaelia, II. 342.
Carmona, II. 750.
Caroline Islands, phytography, I. 510.
Carolinea, II. 530; III. 589.
Carozylon, II. 188; III. 387.
Carpacoce, II. 810.
Carpenteria, II. 238; III. 409.
Carpidiopterix, II. 489.
Carpinus, II. 120; III. 357; IV. 491.
Carpodetus, II. 238
Carpodinus, II. 724; III. 687.
Carpodiptera, II. 512.
Carpodontos, II. 544.
Carpolobia, II. 430.
Carria, II. 548.
Carriage building, IV. 427.
Carrierea, II. 570.
Carroa, II. 352.
Carruthersia, II. 725.
Carumbium, II. 445; III. 519.
Carya, II. 112; III. 353; IV. 488.
Caryocar, II. 546; III. 596.
Caryocaraceae, II. 546; III. 596.
Caryodaphne, II. 225.
Caryodendron, II. 438.
Caryophyllaceae, II. 194.
Caryophyllus, II. 627; III. 635.
Caryopteris, II. 754; III. 695.
Caryospermum, II. 470.
Caryota, II. 65; III. 321.
Cascarilla, II. 822; III. 745.
Casearia, II. 570; III. 614.

Casimiroa, II. 400; III. 496.
Cassandra, II. 662; III. 649, 653.
Casselia, II. 754.
Cassia, II. 342; III. 470; V. XXVI.[2]
Cassidispermum, II. 697.
Cassine, II. 466.
Cassine, II. 467, 474, 476.
Cassinia, II. 854; III. 755.
Cassinopsis, II. 474.
Cassiope, II. 662; III. 649.
Cassipourea, II. 613.
Cassupa, II. 810.
Casuarium, III. 523.
Castanea, II. 123; III. 358; IV. 492.
Castanea, II. 125; III. 360.
Castaneaceae, see Fagaceae.
Castanola, II. 317.
Castanopsis, II. 125; III. 360.
Castanospermum, II. 345; III. 471.
Castela, II. 414.
Castelia, II. 414.
Castilleja, II. 780.
Castilloa, II. 147; III. 368.
Casting off of branches, I. 192; V. XII.[1]
Casuarina, II. 92, 871; III. 342; IV. 485.
Casuarinaceae, II. 92, 871; III. 342; IV. 485.
Catakidozamia, II. 6; III. 285.
Cataleuca, II. 862.
Catalpa, II. 786; III. 705; IV. 538.
Catalpium, II. 786.
Catamixis, II. 854.
Catappa, II. 617.
Catesbaea, II. 810; III. 711.
Catesbaea, II. 831.
Catha, II. 466; III. 531.
Catha, II. 466, 469.
Cathartocarpus, II. 342; III. 470.
Cathastrum, II. 471.
Cathedra, II. 170.
Cathormion, II. 377.
Catocoma, II. 430.
Catonia, II. 744.
Catophractes, II. 787.
Catostemma, II. 529.
Caucanthus, II. 425.
Caucasus, forest descriptions, IV. 348.
—— phytography, I. 368, 531.
—— see also Russia.
Caulotretus, II. 334.
Cavanillesia, II. 529.
Cavendishia, II. 662; III. 649.
Cavinium, II. 659.
Cayaponia, II. 844; III. 753.
Cayratia, II. 502.
Ceanothus, II. 492; III. 541.
Ceanothus, II. 494, 496; III. 543.
Cebipira, III. 467.
Cecropia, II. 147; III. 368.
Cedrela, II. 420; III. 512; IV. 525.
Cedrela, II. 422.
Cedrus, II. 27; III. 299; IV. 447, 558.
Ceiba, II. 529, 873; III. 589.
Celastraceae, II. 465; III. 531; IV. 526.
Celastrus, II. 466; III. 531.
Celastrus, II. 168, 248, 453, 466, 467, 469, 470.
Cell wall, I. 137, 525.
Cellulose, IV. 430, 558.
Celosia, II. 189.
Celosia, II. 190.
Celsia, II. 780.
Celtis, II. 141, 872; III. 363; IV. 518.
Celtis, II. 142, 500.
Centaurea, II. 854.
Centradenia, II. 636; III. 638.
Central America, acclimatization, III. 44.
—— afforestation, IV. 155, 546.
—— bibliography, I. 3, 519.
—— botanic gardens, I. 39.
—— cinchona cultivation, III. 712.
—— coffee cultivation, III. 728.

Central America, collections, III. 27.
—— dendrography, IV. 78.
—— descriptive botany, III. 63.
—— economic products, III. 264.
—— education, III. 32.
—— forest descriptions, IV. 341.
—— forest influences, IV. 46.
—— forest laws, IV. 315.
—— forest policy, IV. 272.
—— forest products, IV. 398; V. xxxi.[1]
—— forest protection, IV. 179.
—— history, I. 80.
—— injuries caused by insects, III. 188.
—— individual noteworthy trees, I. 295.
—— manuals of arboriculture, III. 99.
—— miscellaneous publications on arboriculture, III. 118.
—— miscellaneous publications on silviculture, IV. 113.
—— periodicals, I. 7; III. 9.
—— pharmacopoeias, III. 247.
—— phenology, I. 222.
—— phytography, I. 327, 531; V. xviii.[1]
—— state forest administration, IV. 288.
—— timber trade, IV. 403.
—— vernacular names, I. 72.
—— viticulture, III. 551.
Central American Republics, coffee cultivation, III. 728.
—— economic products, III. 265.
—— forest descriptions, IV. 341.
—— history, see Central America, I. 80.
—— miscellaneous publications of arboriculture, III. 118.
—— periodicals, see Central America, I. 7.
—— phytography, I. 333.
Central Asiatic Russia, miscellaneous publications on arboriculture, III. 127.
—— phytography, I. 456.
—— see also Asiatic Russia.
Centrandra, II. 446.
Centroclinium, II. 862.
Centrolobium, II. 345; III. 471; IV. 521.
Centronia, II. 636.
Centropogon, II. 845.
Centrosema, II. 345.
Centrosolenia, II. 794; III. 708.
Centrostemma, II. 739.
Cephaelis, II. 810.
Cephaelis, II. 827; III. 746.
Cephalanthus, II. 811; III. 711.
Cephalocereus, II. 591; III. 620; V. xxvi.[1]
Cephalocroton, II. 438.
Cephalocroton, II. 436.
Cephalotaxus, II. 8; III. 287.
Cephalotomandra, II. 191.
Ceradia, II. 862; II[?]. 756.
Ceraseidos, II. 270.
Cerasus, II. 270; III. 430; IV. 520.
Ceratephorus, II. 699.
Ceraticla, II. 453.
Ceratolobus, II. 65.
Ceratonia, II. 345; III. 471.
Ceratopetalum, II. 250; III. 416, by error also 415.
Ceratophorus, II. 699; III. 669.
Ceratopyxis, II. 811.
Ceratosepalum, II. 512.
Ceratosepalum, II. 576.
Ceratostema, II. 684.
Ceratozamia, II. 4; III. 284.
Cerbera, II. 725; III. 687.
Cerbera, II. 727, 729, 732, 733; III. 691.
Cercidiphyllaceae, II. 195; III. 388.
Cercidiphyllum, II. 195; III. 388.
Cercidium, II. 345.
Cercidium, II. 376.

Cercis, II. 345; III. 472.
Cercocarpus, II. 258.
Cercodia, II. 646.
Cercopetalum, II. 232.
Cereus, II. 589; III. 620.
Cereus, II. 591, 593, 597, 598; III. 620, 622, 625' 626.
Ceriops, II. 613; III. 632.
Ceropegia, II. 736; III. 692.
Ceroxylon, II. 66; III. 321.
Ceroxylon, II. 69.
Cervantesia, II. 168.
Cespedesia, II. 544; III. 596.
Cestrum, II. 770; III. 609.
Cestrum, II. 722, 774.
Ceylon, economic products, III. 279.
—— forest products, IV. 401.
—— phytography, I. 476; V. xxiii.[2]
—— see also British India.
Chadsia, II. 345.
Chaenestes, II. 772.
Chaenomeles, II. 258; III. 419.
Chaenopleura, II. 640.
Chaenostoma, II. 780; III. 702.
Chaetacanthus, II. 798.
Chaetachme, II. 142.
Chaetaea, II. 532.
Chaetocalyx, II. 345.
Chaetocarpus, II. 438.
Chaetogastra, II. 641; III. 639.
Chaetolepis, II. 636.
Chaetoptelea, II. 142.
Chaetostoma, II. 636'
Chaetosus, II. 725.
Chaetothylax, II. 798.
Chailletia, II. 422.
Chalepoa, II. 247.
Chalepophyllum, II. 811.
Chamaebatia, II. 259; III. 420.
Chamaebatiaria, see Sorbaria.
Chamaebuxus, II. 103.
Chamaecerasus, II. 835; III. 749.
Chamaecyparis, II. 28; III. 300; IV. 448.
Chamaedaphne, II. 662; III. 649.
Chamaedorea, II. 66; III. 321.
Chamaedorea, II. 71.
Chamaelaucium, II. 622.
Chamaemeles, II. 259.
Chamaemeles, II. 269.
Chamaeranthemum, III. 709.
Chamaerops, II. 66; III. 322; IV. 485.
Chamaerops, II. 64, 74, 75; III. 319, 331.
Chamelaucium, II. 622, 634.
Chamissoa, II. 189.
Champereia, II. 170.
Champion, IV. 431.'
—— manufacture of, IV. 393.
Charianthus, II. 636.
Charidion, II. 544.
Chariessa, II. 474.
Charlwoodia, II. 79; III. 334.
Charpentiera, II. 189.
Charpentiera, II. 825.
Chasalia, II. 811.
Chasmanthera, II. 206.
Chasselovpia, II. 703.
Chastenaea, II. 636.
Chatham Islands, see New Zealand, I. 506.
Chaulmoogra, II. 571; III. 614.
Chaunochiton, II. 170.
Chaunostoma, II. 763.
Chavarnesia, II. 734; III. 691.
Chavica, II. 93; III. 342.
Cheiranthera, II. 247; III. 415.
Cheiranthus, II. 234.
Cheiranthus, II. 234.
Cheirodendron, II. 648.
Cheirostemon, II. 532; III. 590.
Chelonecarya, II. 475.
Chelonespermum, II. 697.

Chemical extracts, IV. 432, 558.
Chemistry, III. 36; IV. 60.
—— physiological, I. 150, 525; IV. 63, 543.
Chenolea, II. 187.
Chenopodiaceae, II. 186; III. 387; IV. 519.
Chenopodium, II. 188.
Cherries, III. 431.
Chersodoma, II. 854.
Cheynia, II. 620'
Chibaca, II. 223.
Chichaea, II. 538.
Chickrassia, II. 420.
Chile, botanic gardens, see South America, I. 39.
—— descriptive botany, III. 65.
—— economic products, III. 269.
—— forest descriptions, IV. 342.
—— galls, see South America, I. 214.
—— individual noteworthy trees, see South America, I. 295.
—— miscellaneous publications on arboriculture, III. 119.
—— periodicals, see South America, I. 7.
—— phytography, I. 345; V. xviii.[1]
—— reproductive interrelations, see South America, I. 239.
—— vernacular names, see South America, I. 72, 522.
Chileranthemum, II. 798.
Chilianthus, II. 718.
Chiliophyllum, II. 854.
Chiliotrichum, II. 854.
Chilocalyx, II. 798.
Chilocarpus, II. 725.
Chilodia, II. 765.
Chilopsis, II. 787; III. 706.
Chimaphila, II. 658.
Chimonanthus, II. 214; III. 401.
China, afforestation, IV. 168.
—— bibliography, see Asia, I. 4.
—— botanic gardens, I. 66.
—— dendrography, IV. 87.
—— descriptive botany, III. 91.
—— economic products, III. 272.
—— forest devastation, IV. 283.
—— forest products, IV. 399, 557.
—— history, see Asia, I. 81; V. x.[1]
—— individual noteworthy trees, see Asia, I. 298.
—— manuals of arboriculture, III. 116.
—— miscellaneous publications on arboriculture, III. 127.
—— periodicals, I. 28; IV. 16.
—— pharmacopoeias, III. 256.
—— phytography, I. 457, 536; V. xxiii.[1]
—— tea cultivation, III. 601.
—— timber trade, IV. 407.
—— vernacular names, I. 75; V. ix.[2]
Chinchona, see Cinchona.
Chiococca, II. 811; III. 711.
Chiococca, III. 743.
Chiogenes, II. 662; III. 649.
Chionanthus, II. 705; III. 671.
Chionanthus, II. 706, 712.
Chione, II. 811.
Chionothrix, II. 189.
Chionotria, II. 407.
Chiranthodendron, II. 532; III. 590.
Chiratia, II. 610.
Chirita, II. 794.
Chirita, III. 356.
Chironia, II. 721; III. 685.
Chirostemon, see Cheirostemon.
Chisocheton, II. 420.
Chisocheton, II. 420.
Chitonia, II. 395.
Chlaenaceae, II. 511.
Chlanis, II. 572.
Chloanthes, II. 754.
Chloanthes, II. 760.
Chloranthaceae, II. 95; III. 343.

Chloranthus, II. 95.
Chlorocodon, II. 737.
Chloromyrtus, II. 625.
Chlorophora, II. 147; III. 368.
Chlorophyll, I. 140, 525.
Chlorosis, III. 180.
Chloroxylon, III. 496; IV. 524.
Chloroxylon, III. 509.
Choisya, II. 400; III. 496.
Chomelia, II. 811.
Chomelia, II. 832.
Chondodendron, II. 206; III. 396.
Chondrostylis, II. 438.
Chonemorpha, II. 725; III. 687.
Choretrum, II. 168; III. 384.
Choretrum, II. 168.
Chorilaena, II. 400.
Chorilaena, II. 409.
Choriophyllum, II. 438.
Choripetalum, II. 693.
Chorisema, see Chorizema, II. 345.
Chorisia, II. 530; III. 589.
Choristylis, II. 238.
Chorizanthe, II. 185.
Chorizema, II. 345; III. 472.
Chorisema, II. 366.
Chorosema, II. 345.
Chorosema, II. 472; *see also* Chorizema, II. 345.
Chotekia, II. 763.
Chresta, II. 856.
Christannia, II. 573.
Christiana, II. 512.
Christya, II. 731.
Chrozophora, II. 438; III. 515.
Chrysactinia, II. 854.
Chrysalidocarpus, III. 325.
Chrysanthemum, II. 854; III. 755.
Chrysobalanaceae, see Rosaceae.
Chrysobalanus, II. 259; III. 420.
Chrysocalyx, II. 348.
Chrysochlamys, II. 553.
Chrysocoma, II. 854.
Chrysocoma, II. 854, 867.
Chrysomallum, II. 761.
Chrysophyllum, II. 697; III. 667.
Chrysophyllum, II. 697, 698; III. 667.
Chrysopia, II. 558.
Chrysopsis, II. 854.
Chrysorrhoe, II. 634.
Chrysoscias, II. 381.
Chrysothamnus, II. 853.
Chrysoxylon, II. 378, 827.
Chukrasia, II. 420.
Chuncoa, II. 617.
Chuquiraga, II. 854.
Chuquiragua, II. 854.
Chusquea, II. 60; III. 316.
Chymococca, II. 600.
Chytranthus, II. 484.
Cicca, II. 414, 449; III. 521.
Cichoriaceae, see Compositae.
Ciconium, II. 389.
Cienfuegosia, II. 521; III. 587.
Cienkowskya, II. 748.
Cinchona, II. 811; III. 712; IV. 538; V. XXVII.[2]
Cinchona, II. 816, 820, 822, 830, 832; III. 743, 744, 745.
Cineraria, II. 855.
Cineraria, II. 852, 857, 864.
Cinnamodendron, II. 566.
Cinnamomum, II. 224; III. 404; IV. 520.
Cinnamosma, II. 566.
Cipadessa, II. 420.
Ciponima, II. 703.
Cissampelos, II. 206; III. 396.
Cissampelos, II. 206, 207.
Cissodendron, II. 650.
Cissus, II. 502, 873; III. 544.
Cissus, II. 501, 504; III. 544, 545.
Cistaceae, II. 563; III. 612.
Cistanthera, II. 513.

Cistellaria, II. 869.
Cistus, II. 563; III. 612.
Cistus, II. 565; III. 613.
Citharexylum, II. 754.
Citharexylum, II. 760, 806.
Citriobatus, II. 247.
Citrosma, II. 222.
Citrus, II. 400; III. 496, 758.
Citta, II. 373.
City planting, III. 42.
Cladostemon, II. 232.
Cladostigma, II. 744.
Cladothamnus, II. 662.
Cladrastis, II. 346; III. 472; IV. 521.
Clambus, II. 449.
Claoxylon, II. 438.
Clappertonia, II. 514.
Clarisia, II. 148.
Classification, I. 250, 529; V. XII.[2]
Clausena, II. 403; III. 503.
Clausena, II. 397.
Clausena, II. 408; III. 503.
Clavigera, II. 853.
Clavija, II. 691; III. 665.
Clear cutting, IV. 129, 545.
Clearing of the felling area, IV. 388.
Cleghornia, II. 725.
Cleidion, II. 438.
Cleisocratera, II. 827.
Cleistanthus, II. 438; III. 515.
Cleistocactus, II. 589.
Cléistochlamys, II. 217.
Clelia, II. 340.
Clematis, II. 576.
Clematis, II. 195, 872; III. 388; V. XXVI.[1]
Clematoclethra, II. 541.
Clementea, II. 341.
Cleome, II. 232.
Cleomodendron, II. 232.
Clermontia, II. 845.
Clerodendron, II. 755; III. 696.
Clethra, II. 657; III. 646.
Clethraceae, II. 657; III. 646.
Cleyera, II. 548; III. 596; IV. 528.
Cleyera, II. 547, 550.
Clianthus, II. 346; III. 472.
Clianthus, II. 385.
Clibadium, II. 855.
Clidemia, II. 637; III. 638.
Clidemia, II. 638, 640, 641.
Cliffortia, II. 259.
Cliftonia, II. 461; III. 529.
Clinacanthus, II. 693; III. 665.
Climatic and atmospheric relations, III. 42.
Climatic conditions, forest influence on, IV. 52, 542.
Climatic influences, injuries caused by, IV. 188, 548; V. XXX.[2]
Climatic relations, IV. 72, 543.
Climbing plants, ecology, I. 236, 529.
Climbing shrubs, III. 204.
Clinacanthus, II. 798.
Clitandra, III. 687.
Clitoria, II. 346; III. 473.
Clitoria, II. 345, 355, 358.
Cloezia, II. 622.
Clomenocoma, III. 755.
Clusia, II. 554; III. 608.
Clusia, II. 558.
Clusianthemum, II. 554.
Clutia, II. 438.
Cluytia, II. 438; III. 516.
Clypea, II. 208.
Clytostoma, II. 787; III. 706.
Cnemidostachys, II. 451.
Cneòrlaceae, II. 396.
Cneoridium, II. 404, 873.
Cneorum, II. 396.
Cnestis, II. 316.
Cnidoscolus, II. 439, 445.
Cobaea, II. 746; III. 694.
Coccoloba, II. 185; III. 387.

Coccoloba, II. 185.
Coccolobis, II. 185; III. 387.
Coccomelia, II. 437.
Coccothrinax, II. 67.
Cocculus, II. 207; III. 396.
Cocculus, II. 206, 207, 208; III. 397.
Cochin-China, botanic gardens, I. 66.
—— phytography, *see* French Indo-china, I. 469, 535.
—— *see also* Indochina.
Cochlospermaceae, II. 566; III. 613.
Cochlospermum, III. 613.
Cockburnia, II. 795.
Cockchafer, *see* Melolontha vulgaris, IV. 202.
Cocos, II. 67; III. 322, 758; IV. 485.
Cocos, II. 68; V. XXVI.[1]
Codarium, II. 354; III. 475.
Codazzia, II. 788.
Codiaeum, II. 438; III. 515.
Codiaeum, II. 437.
Codonandra, II. 340.
Codonanthus, II. 718.
Codonium, II. 171.
Codonocarpus, II. 192; III. 388.
Codoriocalyx, II. 354.
Coelebogyne, II. 436.
Coelocarpum, II. 757.
Coelocaryon, II. 220.
Coelocline, II. 402.
Coelococcus, II. 71; III. 327.
Coelodepas, II. 439.
Coelopyrum, II. 869.
Coelospermum, II. 814.
Coffea, II. 814; III. 726; V. XXIX.[2]
Coffea, II. 811, 815, 820, 825, 830, 832.
Cohnia, II. 79.
Coilotapalus, II. 147.
Coilotapalus, II. 148.
Cola, II. 533, 873; III. 590.
Coldenia, II. 748.
Colea, II. 787; III. 706.
Colebrookea, II. 763.
Colebrookia, II. 763.
Colecocma, II. 855.
Coleogyne, II. 259.
Coleonema, II. 404; III. 503.
Coleophora, II. 602.
Coleosanthus, II. 853.
Coleus, II. 763; III. 697.
Colicodendron, II. 230.
Colinil, II. 386.
Collaea, II. 358.
Culleuting, technique of, I. 35, 520, V. VIII.[1]
Collections, general, I. 35, 520; III. 27, 757; IV. 17, 539; V. VIII.[1] XXVII.[2] XXIX.[1]
Collections of wood, *see* Wood collections.
Colletia, II. 493; III. 541.
Colletia, II. 494; III. 541.
Colliguaja, II. 439.
Colmeiroa, II. 451.
Colombia, coffee cultivation, III. 729.
—— descriptive botany, III. 64.
—— economic products, III. 268.
—— history, *see* South America, I. 80.
—— phytography, I. 339; V. XVIII.[1]
Colona, II. 513.
Colophonia, II. 417; III. 510.
Color, ecology, I. 236.
—— physiology, I. 184, 526; V. XII.[1]
Colorado, *see* United States, Western.
Coloration, autumnal, I. 185, 526; III. 207.
Coloring of wood, IV. 422, 557.
Colpoon, II. 384.
Colquhounia, II. 763; III. 697.
Colubrina, II. 494; III. 541.
Columbia, II. 513.
Columella, II. 795.
Columelliaceae, II. 7
Columnar trees, III.

Columnea, II. 793; III. 708.
Columnea, II. 795.
Colutea, II. 347; III. 473.
Colutea, II. 385.
Colvillea, II. 347; III. 473.
Comarostaphylis, II. 660.
Comatoglossum, II. 489.
Combretaceae, II. 615; III. 632; IV. 529.
Combretopsis, II. 475.
Combretum, II. 616; III. 632.
Comesperma, II. 430; III. 513.
Comesperma, II. 430.
Commemorative tree planting, III. 34.
Commersonia, II. 533.
Commersonia, II. 537.
Commianthus, II. 830.
Commidendrum, II. 855.
Commiphora, II. 417, 873; III. 510.
Communal forests, administration, IV. 307, 554.
—— state supervision, IV. 285, 552.
Comocladia, II. 455; III. 524.
Comoro group, economic products, III. 281.
—— phytography, I. 496.
Comoroa, II. 411.
Compositae, II. 847; III. 754.
Composition of forests, IV. 137.
Comptonia, III. 352.
Conanthodium, II. 858.
Conchium, II. 162.
Conchocarpus, II. 405.
Condalia, II. 494.
Condalia, II. 496, 499.
Condamines, II. 815; III. 743.
Conductibility of timber, IV. 412.
Conduction of fluids and gases, I. 162, 526; V. xi.[1]
Condylocarpon, II. 725.
Congea, II. 757.
Congo State, economic products, III. 281; V. xxviii.[2]
—— forest description, IV. 379, 556.
—— forest policy, IV. 279.
—— miscellaneous publications on arboriculture, III. 131.
—— phytography, I. 491; V. xxiv.[1]
—— *see also* Africa.
Coniferae, *see* Pinaceae, *also* Ginkgoaceae, *and* Taxaceae.
Coniferous forests, IV. 138.
Conifers and hardwood, IV. 138.
Connaraceae, II. 316; III. 462; IV. 520.
Connaropsis, II. 392.
Connarus, II. 317; III. 462.
Connarus, II. 316, 317, 458.
Connecticut, *see* United States, Northeastern.
Conocarpus, II. 615.
Conocephalus, II. 148.
Conocephalus, II. 156.
Conohoria, II. 568.
Conomorpha, II. 693.
Conosiphon, II. 831.
Conospermum, II. 160.
Conostegia, II. 637.
Conostegia, II. 636.
Conradia, II. 794.
Conradina, II. 763.
Consolea, II. 595.
Constituents of plant body, I. 152, 525; IV. 63, 543.
Construction of roads and buildings, IV. 266.
—— timber for, IV. 422, 557; V. xxxii.[2]
Consuegria, II. 869.
Contents of felled timber, IV. 219, 550.
Conversion of timber, IV. 387, 392; V. xxxi.[1]
Convolvulaceae, II. 743, 874; III. 694; IV. 536.
Convolvulus, II. 744; III. 694.
Convolvulus, II. 744, 745, 746.

Conyza, II. 855.
Conyza, II. 864.
Cookia, II. 403; III. 503.
Cooperage, IV. 427.
Copaiba, II. 347; III. 473.
Copaifera, II. 347; III. 473.
Copal, III. 233.
Copernicia, II. 68; III. 324.
Coppice, IV. 132, 545.
Coppice with standards, IV. 130, 545.
Coprosma, II. 815; III. 743.
Coptosapelta, II. 815; III. 743.
Coquebertia, II. 389.
Corallobotrys, II. 662.
Corallospartium, II. 347.
Corchoropsis, II. 513.
Corchorus, II. 513; III. 584.
Corchorus, II. 265.
Cordia, II. 748; III. 695.
Cordia, II. 750.
Cordyla, II. 473.
Cordyline, II. 79; III. 334.
Cordyline, II. 81.
Cordyloblaste, II. 703.
Corema, II. 453; III. 523.
Coreopsis, II. 855.
Corethrostylis, II. 535.
Coriaria, II. 454; III. 523.
Coriariaceae, II. 454; III. 523.
Cork, IV. 455.
Cormonema, II. 494.
Cornacchinia, II. 755.
Cornaceae, II. 654; III. 644; IV. 534.
Cornidia, II. 240.
Cornulaca, II. 188.
Cornus, II. 654; III. 645; IV. 534.
Corokia, II. 757.
Corokia, II. 656; III. 646.
Corolla, *see* Perianth, I. 115.
Coronilla, II. 347; III. 473.
Corporation forests, administration, IV. 307, 554.
—— state supervision, IV. 285, 552.
Correa, II. 404; III. 503.
Corsica, phytography, I. 419, 535.
—— *see also* France.
Cortesia, II. 749.
Corylaceae, *see* Betulaceae.
Corylopsis, II. 252; III. 416.
Corylus, II. 121; III. 357; IV. 492.
Corynanthe, II. 815.
Corynanthelium, II. 860; III. 755.
Corynella, II. 348.
Corynitis, II. 348.
Corynocarpaceae, II. 462; III. 529.
Corynocarpus, II. 462; III. 529.
Corynostylis, II. 567; III. 613.
Corypha, II. 68; III. 324.
Corypha, II. 68, 74; III. 326.
Corythea, II. 439.
Cosbaea, II. 213.
Coscinium, II. 207; III. 396.
Cosmelia, II. 638; III. 664.
Cosmibuena, II. 815.
Cosmophyllum, II. 857.
Cossignia, II. 484.
Costa Rica, *see* Central American Republics.
Costaea, II. 462.
Cotinus, II. 455; III. 524; IV. 525.
Cotinus, II. 458.
Coteoneaster, II. 259; III. 420.
Cotoneaster, II. 278; III. 419, 421, 443.
Cotyledon, II. 235; III. 409.
Cotyledon, II. 235, 236.
Coublandia, II. 374.
Couepia, II. 260; III. 421.
Coula, II. 170; III. 384.
Coulterella, II. 855.
Coulteria, II. 338.
Couma, II. 725; III. 687.
Coumarouna, II. 355; III. 475.
Courantia, II. 235.
Couratari, II. 612.

Couratari, II. 611.
Courbonia, II. 232.
Couroupita, II. 612; III. 631.
Coursetia, II. 348.
Cousstpoa, II. 148; III. 368.
Coussaria, II. 815.
Coutarea, II. 815; III. 743.
Couthovia, II. 718.
Covellia, II. 148; III. 368.
Covillea, II. 395.
Cowania, II. 260.
Craepaloprumnon, II. 574.
Crambe, II. 234.
Crantzia, II. 452, 793.
Craspidospermum, II. 725.
Crassula, II. 236.
Crassula, II. 237; III. 409.
Crassulaceae, II. 234; III. 409.
Cratae-mespilus, II. 268.
Crataego-Mespilus, II. 260; III. 421.
Crataegus, II. 260; III. 421.
Crataegus, II. 257, 264, 269, 278; III. 429, 430, 443.
Crataeva, II. 232; III. 409.
Crataeva, III. 495.
Craterispermum, II. 815.
Cratoxylon, II. 554; III. 609.
Creaghiella, II. 637.
Creeping plants, III. 205.
Cremanium, II. 640.
Cremaspora, II. 815.
Cremastostemon, II. 599.
Crematomia, II. 748.
Cremophyllum, II. 440.
Cremostachys, II. 444.
Crenes, II. 608.
Crepidospermum, II. 418.
Crepidotropis, II. 355.
Crepinella, II. 648.
Crescentia, II. 787; III. 706.
Crescentia, II. 785, 787, 789; III. 704.
Crete, *see* Mediterranean Islands.
Crimea, forest descriptions, IV. 348.
—— phytography, I. 368.
—— *see also* Russia.
Crinodendron, II. 509; III. 584.
Crioceras, II. 725.
Cristaria, II. 516.
Critonia, II. 856.
Crossandra, II. 798; III. 709.
Crossonephelis, II. 484.
Crossopetalum, II. 470, 471.
Crossopteryx, II. 816; III. 743.
Crossosoma, II. 255.
Crossosomataceae, II. 255.
Crossostylis, II. 613.
Crotalaria, II. 348; III. 473.
Crotalaria, II. 333, 364, 369, 370, 388.
Croton, II. 489; III. 516.
Croton, II. 157, 438, 447; III. 515.
Crowea, II. 404; III. 503.
Crossophora, II. 438.
Cruciferae, II. 233.
Cruckshanksia, II. 389.
Crudia, II. 349.
Cryphaea, II. 95.
Cryptadenia, II. 600.
Cryptandra, II. 494.
Crypteronia, II. 610.
Crypteroniaceae, *see* Sonneratiaceae, II. 610.
Cryptocarpus, II. 191.
Cryptocarya, II. 225; III. 406.
Cryptocarya, II. 223.
Cryptolepis, II. 737.
Cryptomeria, II. 28; III. 301; IV. 448.
Cryptophragmium, II. 799.
Cryptosepalum, II. 349.
Cryptostegia, II. 737; III. 692.
Cryptostemon, II. 622.
Crystals, I. 138, 525; V. xi.[1]
Ctenodon, II. 330.
Ctenolophon, II. 392.
Cuba, *see* West Indian Islands.

Cubaea, II. 386.
Cubeba, II. 93; III. 342.
Cubilia, II. 484.
Cubing-tables, IV. 229.
Cucifera, II. 69.
Cucurbitaceae, II. 844; III. 753.
Cudrania, II. 148.
Cudrania, III. 368.
Cullenis, II. 530.
Cullumia, II. 855.
Cumingia, II. 530.
Cuminia, II. 763.
Cultivated plants, evolution, I. 246, 529.
—— introduction, *see* Introduction by man, I. 241.
Cultivation of exotic trees, IV. 124, 545.
Cunninghamia, II. 29; III. 302.
Cunonia, II. 250; III. 416.
Cunoniaceae, II. 250; III. 416.
Cunuris, II. 440; V. xxvi.²
Cupania, II. 485; III. 539.
Cupania, II. 422, 484, 485, 487, 488, 489.
Cupaniopsis, II. 485.
Cuphea, II. 608; III. 629.
Cupheanthus, II. 622.
Cupheanthus, II. 627.
Cuphocarpus, II. 651.
Cupia, II. 829.
Cupressus, II. 29; III. 302; IV. 448.
Cupressus, II. 28; III. 300, 310; IV. 448, 484.
Cupuliferae, *see* Fagaceae, *and also* Betulaceae.
Curatella, II. 541.
Curcas, II. 445; III. 519.
Cusparia, II. 405; III. 503.
Cuspidaria, II. 787.
Cussambium, II. 488.
Cussonia, II. 648.
Cussonia, II. 651; III. 644.
Cuttings, reparative processes, I. 208.
—— and layers, III. 157.
Cuviera, II. 816.
Cyanea, II. 845.
Cyanobotrys, II. 374.
Cyanocarpus, II. 160.
Cyanophyllum, II. 640; III. 638.
Cyanospermum, II. 381.
Cyanostegia, II. 757.
Cyanothamnus, II. 399.
Cyathocalyx, II. 217.
Cyathodes, II. 600.
Cyathodes, II. 691.
Cyathodiscus, II. 604.
Cyathogyne, II. 440.
Cybele, III. 394.
Cybianthus, II. 693.
Cybianthus, II. 690, 695.
Cybiostigma, II. 532.
Cybistax, II. 787.
Cycadaceae, II. 2, 871; III. 284.
Cycas, II. 4; III. 284.
Cyclandrophora, II. 269.
Cyclanthaceae, II. 76; III. 332.
Cyclanthera, II. 844.
Cyclanthus, II. 76; III. 332.
Cyclea, II. 207.
Cyclea, II. 206.
Cyclocarpus, II. 406.
Cyclocheilon, II. 757.
Cyclogyne, II. 385.
Cyclonema, II. 755.
Cyclopedias, *see* Miscellaneous publications, I. 30.
Cyelophyllum, II. 816.
Cyclopia, II. 349; III. 473.
Cyclostemon, II. 440.
Cycnopodium, II. 637.
Cydista, II. 787.
Cydonia, II. 263; III. 423.
Cydonia, II. 258; III. 419.
Cylicadenia, II. 729.

Cylicodaphne, II. 226; III. 406.
Cylista, II. 349.
Cylista, II. 381.
Cymbopetalum, II. 217.
Cymbosepalum, II. 349.
Cymelonema, II. 833.
Cyminosma, II. 397.
Cynanchum, II. 737.
Cynanchum, II. 737, 738, 740, 743; III. 693.
Cynoctonum, II. 737.
Cynoglossum, II. 749.
Cynometra, II. 349; III. 473.
Cyphokentia, II. 68.
Cyphomandra, II. 771; III. 699.
Cyprus, forest description, IV. 375.
—— viticulture, III. 558.
—— *see also* Mediterranean Islands.
Cypselocarpus, II. 188.
Cyrilla, II. 462; III. 529.
Cyrilla, II. 247.
Cyrillaceae, II. 461; III. 529.
Cyrtandra, II. 794; III. 708.
Cyrtandra, II. 794.
Cyrtandreae, *see* Gesneriaceae.
Cyrtandromoea, II. 794.
Cyrtanthera, II. 798, 800; III. 709.
Cyrtocarpa, II. 455.
Cyrtoceras, II. 739; III. 693.
Cyrtophyllum, II. 718.
Cyrtospermum, II. 455.
Cyrtostachys, III. 324.
Cystanthe, II. 690.
Cystidianthus, II. 742.
Cystoliths, *see* Crystals, I. 138, 525.
Cytisus, II. 349; III. 473; IV. 521.
Cytisus, II. 329, 333, 339, 359, 368, 376; III. 469, 480, 483; IV. 521.
Cytology, II. 139, 525; V. xi.¹

Daboecia, II. 662; III. 649.
Daboecia, III. 649.
Dacrydium, II. 8; III. 287.
Dacrydium, II. 9.
Dacryodes, II. 418; III. 511.
Dactylocladus, II. 637.
Dactylopetalum, II. 613.
Dactylostemon, II. 435.
Daedalacanthus, II. 799.
Daemia, II. 737.
Daemonorops, II. 65; III. 321.
Dahlia, II. 254.
Dais, II. 600; III. 626.
Dais, II. 604, 600.
Dalbergia, II. 352; III. 475; IV. 521.
Dalbergia, II. 370; III. 484.
Dalea, II. 352.
Dalechampia, II. 440; III. 517.
Dalhousia, II. 353.
Damages caused by trees, III. 34.
Dammara, II. 25; III. 297; IV. 447.
Dammaropsis, II. 148.
Damnacanthus, II. 816; III. 743.
Dampiera, II. 846.
Danaë, II. 80; III. 336.
Danaea, II. 864.
Danais, II. 816; III. 743.
Daniella, II. 353; III. 475.
Dapania, II. 392.
Daphne, II. 600; III. 626.
Daphne, II. 602, 603, 606; III. 628.
Daphnidium, II. 225.
Daphniphyllopsis, II. 614.
Daphniphyllum, II. 440; III. 517.
Daphnopsis, II. 602.
Darbya, II. 168.
Dartus, II. 771.
Darwinia, II. 622; III. 633.
Dasianthera, II. 573.
Dasycarpus, II. 511.
Dasycarpa, II. 455.
Dasycoleum, II. 420.
Dasylepis, II. 570.
Dasylirion, II. 80; III. 336.

Dasylirion, II. 84; III. 337.
Dasymalla, II. 760.
Dasynema, II. 511.
Datiscaceae, II. 583.
Datiscace*, II. 583.
Datura, II. 771; III. 699.
Datura, II. 771.
Daubentonia, II. 383; III. 487.
Davidia, II. 614.
Davidsonia, II. 250; III. 416.
Daviesia, II. 353; III. 475.
Daviesia, II. 388.
Davilla, II. 541.
Davya, II. 639.
Debility of trees, III. 181.
Debregeasia, II. 156.
Decachaeta, II. 855.
Decaisnea, II. 201.
Decaschistia, II. 521; III. 587.
Decaspermum, II. 622.
Decaspora, II. 691; III. 665.
Decatoca, II. 688.
Decatropis, II. 405.
Decortication, I. 192.
Decostea, II. 656.
Decumaria, II. 238; III. 410.
Dedea, II. 238.
Deer, forests, *see* Game keeping, IV. 13¹
Dearingia, II. 190; III. 388.
Defects and unsoundness of timber, IV. 413.
Defoliation, *see* Leaf-fall, I. 191.
Deforestation, effects of, IV. 42, 541; V. xxix.²
Degeneration, I. 248.
Deguelia, II. 353.
Dehaasia, II. 225.
Deherainia, II. 691; III. 665.
Deidamia, II. 576.
Deinanthe, II. 238.
Deinbollia, II. 485.
Delabechea, II. 532; III. 590.
Delairea, II. 864.
Delarbrea, II. 648; III. 641.
Delaria, II. 334.
Delavaya, II. 485.
Delaware, *see* United States, Southeastern.
Delima, II. 541, 543.
Delimopsis, II. 543.
Delissea, II. 845.
Delostoma, II. 788.
Delpydora, II. 698.
Dematophyllum, II. 695.
Dendrium, II. 673.
Dendrobangia, II. 474.
Dendrocalamus, II. 60; III. 316; IV. 455.
Dendrocharis, II. 726.
Dendrography, I. 292, 530; IV. 75, 544; V. xvi,¹ xxx.¹
—— *see also* Descriptive botany, *and* Phytography.
Dendrology, economic and horticultural, *see* subdivision Dendrological in the geographical arrangement *under* Descriptive botany, III. 60–92.
—— ornamental, *see* Ornamental uses and properties of trees and shrubs, III. 201.
Dendromecon, II. 229; III. 408.
Dendropanax, II. 649.
Dendrophthoë, II. 175.
Dendrophthora, II. 174.
Dendroseris, II. 855.
Dendrostylis, II. 572.
Denhamia, II. 467.
Denisonia, II. 757.
Denmark, administration of private forests, IV. 308.
—— afforestation, IV. 155.
—— forest descriptions, IV. 342.
—— forest devastation, IV. 281.
—— forest laws, IV. 315.

Denmark, forest officers and employees, IV. 310.
—— forest policy, IV. 272.
—— forest regulations, IV. 296.
—— measures promoting silviculture, IV. 39.
—— miscellaneous publications on silviculture, IV. 113.
—— periodicals, I. 8; V. VII.[1]
—— state forest administration, IV. 288.
—— taxes, tariffs, etc., IV. 284.
—— textbooks and manuals of forestry, IV. 94.
—— textbooks and manuals of silviculture, IV. 103.
—— see also Scandinavia.
Density and hardness of timber, IV. 411.
Density of plantations, see Distance in planting, III. 169.
Deplanchea, II. 788.
Deppea, II. 816.
Depth of planting, III. 169.
Dermatobotrys, II. 780; III. 702.
Dermatocalyx, II. 780.
Derris, II. 353; III. 475.
Description of plants, principles of, I. 254, 530.
Descriptive botany, economic, III. 51, 757.
—— medicinal, III. 53; V. XXVIII.[1]
—— miscellaneous, III. 59.
—— toxicological, III. 59.
—— see also Dendrography, and Phytography.
Desfontainea, II. 718; III. 682.
Desfontainesia, II. 706.
Desmanthodium, II. 855.
Desmanthus, II. 354; III. 475.
Desmanthus, II. 354, 374.
Desmochaeta, II. 190.
Desmodium, II. 354; III. 475.
Desmodium, II. 369; III. 481.
Desmogyne, II. 662.
Desmoncus, II. 68.
Desmostachys, II. 474.
Desmostemon, II. 448.
Destrugesia, II. 230.
Detandra, II. 208.
Detarium, II. 354; III. 475.
Determination of age, IV. 232, 235, 550.
Determination of increment, IV. 232, 550.
Determination of yield, IV. 232, 235, 550.
Deutzia, II. 238; III. 410.
Devastation, forest, IV. 280, 552.
Development, see Growth, I. 187, 526, and Histology, I. 123, 524.
Dewevrea, II. 354.
Diacicarpium, II. 615.
Dialium, II. 354; III. 475.
Dialyanthera, III. 402.
Dianthera, II. 799, 800.
Diapensiaceae, II. 691.
Diaspis, II. 425.
Diberara, II. 251.
Dibrachion, II. 445.
Dicalymma, II. 857.
Dicalyx, II. 703.
Dicarpidium, II. 533.
Dicentranthera, II. 797.
Dichaetanthera, II. 637.
Dichapetalaceae, II. 432.
Dichapetalum, II. 432.
Dicheranthus, II. 194.
Dichilanthe, II. 816.
Dichopsis, II. 699; III. 668.
Dichosema, II. 373; III. 482.
Dichostemma, II. 441.
Dichotomanthes, II. 263.
Dichroa, II. 239; III. 410.
Dichrostachys, II. 354; III. 475.
Diclidanthera, II. 704.

Diclidocarpus, II. 513.
Dicliptera, II. 799.
Dicliptera, II. 797.
Dicoelia, II. 441.
Dicoma, II. 855.
Dicophe, II. 252.
Dicoryphe, II. 252.
Dicotyledoneae, II. 92, 871; III. 342, 758; IV. 485, 529; V. XXVI,[1] XXVIII,[2] XXXII.[2]
Dicranolepis, II. 603, 874.
Dicranopetalum, II. 490.
Dicranostyles, II. 744.
Dicrastylis, II. 757.
Dicraurus, II. 190.
Dictionaries, I. 69, 522; III. 29; IV. 23; V. IX,[1] XXVII.[2]
Dictyanthus, II. 737; III. 692.
Dictyocarpus, II. 527.
Dictyocaryum, II. 68.
Dictyocaryum, II. 59.
Dictyoloma, II. 405.
Dictyosperma, II. 68; III. 324.
Dicypellium, II. 225; III. 406.
Didelotia, II. 354.
Didelta, II. 855.
Didesmandra, II. 541.
Didierea, II. 485.
Didymeles, II. 869.
Didymeria, II. 404.
Didymocarpus, II. 794.
Didymochiton, II. 420.
Didymopanax, II. 648.
Didymosperma, III. 325.
Didymosperma,[2] II. 68.
Didymotheca, II. 192.
Diemenia, II. 258.
Diervilla, II. 834; III. 748.
Dietrichia, II. 237.
Digitalis, II. 780.
Diglottis, II. 405.
Digomphia, II. 788.
Digyroloma, II. 799.
Dilivaria, II. 796; III. 708.
Dilkea, II. 576.
Dillenia, II. 541; III. 595.
Dillenia, II. 541.
Dilleniaceae, II. 540, 873; III. 595.
Dillwynia, II. 354; III. 475.
Dillwynia, II. 345, 358; III. 472.
Dilobeia, II. 160.
Dimorpha, II. 356.
Dimorphandra, II. 356.
Dimorphanthus, II. 647; III. 641.
Dimorphocalyx, II. 441.
Dimorphotheca, II. 855.
Dinemagonum, II. 425.
Dinemandra, II. 425.
Dinklagea, II. 317.
Dinochloa, II. 60.
Dinophora, II. 637.
Dioclea, II. 355.
Diodia, II. 816.
Diodontium, II. 858.
Diomedea, II. 857.
Dioncophyllum, II. 570.
Dioon, II. 5; III. 285.
Dioryktandra, II. 568.
Dioscorea, II. 90.
Dioscoreaceae, II. 90; III. 341.
Dioscoreophyllum, II. 207.
Diosma, II. 405; III. 504.
Diosma, II. 251, 397, 398, 399, 404, 408; III. 495.
Diospyros, II. 701; III. 669; IV. 534.
Diospyros, II. 702, 703.
Diostea, II. 753.
Diotolotus, II. 333.
Diotostemon, II. 235.
Dipelta, II. 835.
Dipetalum, II. 411.
Diphaca, II. 375.
Diphasia, II. 405.
Dipholis, II. 698.

Diphysa, II. 355.
Diplacus, II. 781; III. 703.
Dipladenia, II. 725; III. 687.
Dipladenia, II. 729; III. 689.
Diplandra, II. 643.
Diplanthera, II. 788, 800.
Diplarche, II. 663.
Diplectria, II. 636.
Diplesthes, II. 472.
Diplocalyx, II. 795.
Diploclisia, II. 207.
Diplocnema, II. 698.
Diplocrater, II. 170.
Diplodiscus, II. 513.
Diplodon, III. 630; see also Diplusodon, II. 609.
Diplodonta, II. 637.
Diploglottis, II. 485; III. 539.
Diplokeleba, II. 485.
Diploknema, II. 698.
Diplolaena, II. 405; III. 504.
Diplolepis, II. 737.
Diplolepis, II. 743.
Diplolobium, II. 385.
Diplolophium, II. 653.
Diplomorpha, II. 606.
Diplopappus, II. 852.
Diplopeltis, II. 485.
Diplophractum, II. 513.
Diplorhynchus, II. 725.
Diplospora, II. 832.
Diplostephium, II. 856.
Diplostylis, II. 751.
Diplothemium, II. 68; III. 325.
Diplusodon, II. 609.
Diplycosia, II. 663; III. 649.
Dipogon, II. 355.
Diporidium, II. 355.
Dipsacaceae, II. 844.
Dipteracanthus, II. 802; III. 710.
Dipterocalyx, II. 758.
Dipterocarpaceae, II. 559, 873; III. 610; IV. 528; V. XXVII.[1]
Dipterocarpus, II. 559; III. 610; IV. 428.
Dipteronia, II. 480.
Dipteropeltis, II. 744.
Dipterospermum, II. 791.
Dipteryx, II. 355; III. 475.
Dipyrena, II. 757.
Dirachma, II. 389.
Dirca, II. 603; III. 628.
Dirichletia, II. 816.
Disadvantages and damages caused by trees, III. 74.
Disanthus, II. 252; III. 416.
Discanthus, II. 76.
Discaria, II. 494; III. 541.
Dischidia, II. 737.
Dischisma, II. 780.
Disciphania, II. 207.
Discocalyx, II. 693.
Discospermum, II. 832.
Discostigma, II. 554.
Disease caused by phylloxera, III. 564, 758.
Diseases and injuries, IV. 195.
—— and their treatment, III. 178, 757.
—— caused by fungi, III. 193, 575; IV. 211, 550.
—— caused by insects, III. 562; IV. 199, 548; V. XXXI.[1]
—— caused by meteoric and similar influences, III. 181.
—— caused by phylloxera, III. 564, 758.
—— caused by plants, III. 193; IV. 210, 550.
—— manuals and general treatises, IV. 195.
—— prevention of, III. 196.
—— street trees, III. 212.
—— various publications, IV. 195.
—— see also Injuries.

Disemma, II. 576; III. 615.
Disepalum, II. 217.
Disisocactus, II. 597.
Disocactus, II. 597; III. 625.
Dispensatories, III. 245.
Dispersal of seeds, *see* Dissemination, I. 240.
Disposal of timber, IV. 388, 557.
Dissemination, I. 240; IV. 74.
Dissocarpus, II. 187.
Dissochaeta, II. 637.
Dissolaena, II. 731.
Dissotis, II. 637, 874.
Distance in planting, III. 169; IV. 154.
Distegocarpus, II. 120.
Distemma, II. 576; III. 615.
Distichostemon, II. 485.
Distictis, II. 788.
Distillation, IV. 432, 558.
Distomanthera, II. 239.
Distribution, geographical, I. 298, 531.
—— of seeds, *see* Dissemination, I. 240.
District of Columbia, *see* United States, Southeastern.
Distylium, II. 252; III. 417.
Ditassa, II. 737.
Ditaxis, II. 441.
Ditomostrophe, II. 534.
Ditta, II. 441.
Dittoceras, II. 737.
Diuroglossum, II. 534.
Dizygotheca, II. 648; III. 641.
Dobera, II. 473.
Dobinea, II. 456.
Docynia, II. 263.
Dodecas, II. 608.
Dodecastemon, II. 440.
Dodonaea, II. 485.
Dodonaea, II. 410, 485.
Dolia, II. 767.
Dolichandra, II. 788.
Dolichandra, II. 785; III. 707.
Dolichandrone, II. 788.
Dolichogyne, II. 861.
Dolicholobium, II. 816.
Dolichos, II. 355.
Dolichos, II. 341, 349, 355, 368.
Doliocarpus, II. 541, 873.
Doliocarpus, II. 569.
Dolophyllum, II. 53.
Dombeya, II. 533, 873; III. 591.
Dombeya, II. 536, 539.
Donaldsonia, II. 576.
Donatia, II. 239.
Dondia, II. 189.
Dondisia, II. 826, 833.
Donzellia, II. 441.
Doona, II. 560.
Doornia, II. 56.
Dorstenia, II. 148.
Doryalis, II. 570.
Doryanthes, II. 99.
Doryphora, II. 221; IV. 520.
Doryxylon, II. 452.
Double flowers, I. 145; V. xi.[1]
Dovyalis, II. 570; III. 614.
Doxantha, II. 788; III. 706.
Dracaena, II.·81; III. 336; IV. 485; V. xxvi.[1]
Dracaena, II. 79; III. 334, 339.
Dracaenopsis, II. 79.
Dracontomelon, II. 456.
Dracophyllum, II. 688; III. 664.
Drainage, III. 150; IV. 143.
Drapetes, II. 603.
Draytonia, II. 542.
Drebbelia, II. 171.
Dregea, II. 737.
Drejera, II. 800.
Drepanocarpus, II. 355.
Drepanocarpus, II. 370.
Driftwood, I. 242.
Drimys, II. 209; III. 397.
Drimyspermum, II. 604; III. 628.

Drought, injuries caused by, III. 183; IV. 192.
Drugs, III. 239, 757; V. xxviii.[1]
Drummondita, II. 409.
Drupaceae, *see* Rosaceae.
Dry fallen wood, IV. 438.
Dryandra, II. 160; III. 382.
Dryas, II. 263.
Drymis, II. 209.
Drymonia, II. 794.
Drymophloeus, II. 68; III. 325.
Dryobalanops, II. 560; III. 611; IV. 528; V. xxvii.[1]
Drypetes, II. 441.
Duabanga, II. 610.
Duboisia, II. 771; III. 700.
Duboscia, II. 513.
Dubouzetia, II. 510.
Duchartrea, II. 794.
Duchassaingia, II. 356.
Dufrenoya, II. 168.
Dugesia, II. 869.
Duguetia, II. 217; IV. 520.
Duhaldea, II. 859.
Duhamelia, II. 819.
Dulacia, II. 171; III. 384.
Dulongia, II. 242.
Dumeritia, III. 756.
Dunalia, II. 771.
Duparquetia, II. 355.
Duperreya, II. 746.
Dupinia, II. 550.
Durability of timber, IV. 413.
Durandea, II. 393.
Duranta, II. 757; III. 696.
Durio, II. 530; III. 589.
Durio, II. 530.
Dutch East Indies, *see* Malay Archipelago.
Duttonia, II. 807, 859.
Duvalia, II. 364.
Duvaliella, II. 560.
Duvaua, II. 460.
Duvernoia, II. 799.
Duvernoya, II. 799.
Dwarf plants, III. 205.
Dwarfing of plants, III. 175; *see also* Nanism, I. 236.
Dyckia, II. 76.
Dyera, II. 726; III. 688.
Dyerophyton, II. 696.
Dyes, III. 235.
Dyschoriste, II. 799.
Dysodia, III. 755.
Dysodidendron, II. 831.
Dysophylla, II. 763.
Dysoxylum, II. 420.
Dyssochroma, II. 771.

Eadesia, II. 768.
East Africa, *see* Africa, East.
—— reproductive interrelations, *see* Africa, I. 240.
East Indies, *see* British India.
—— Dutch, *see* Malay Archipelago.
Ebenaceae, II. 700; III. 669; IV. 534.
Ebenoxylum, II. 702.
Ebenus, II. 355.
Ebermaiera, II. 803.
Ecastaphyllum, II. 352.
Ecbolium, II. 799.
Ecclinusa, II. 698.
Eccremanthus, II. 488.
Eccremocarpus, II. 788; III. 706.
Ecdysanthera, II. 726.
Ecdysanthera, II. 724.
Echeveria, II. 235; III. 409.
Echidnopsis, II. 737.
Echinocactus, II. 591; III. 622.
Echinocactus, II. 593; III. 622.
Echinocarpus, II. 511; III. 584.
Echinocereus, II. 593; III. 622.
Echinocereus, II. 589.
Echinopanax, II. 648; III. 642.

Echinopsis, II. 593; III. 622.
Echinopsis, III. 622.
Echinopterys, II. 425.
Echinothamnus, II. 576.
Echinus, II. 447.
Echites, II. 726; III. 688.
Echites, II. 722, 725, 728, 729, 730, 731; III. 686, 689.
Echium, II. 749; III. 695.
Echium, II. 751.
Echyrospermum, II. 355.
Eckebergia, II. 420.
Ecology, I. 217, 528; III. 40; V. xii.[1]
—— of forest growth, IV. 67, 543.
Economic botany, *see* Descriptive botany, economic, III. 51, 757.
—— *see also* subdivision Economical in the geographical arrangement *under* Descriptive botany, III. 62–92.
Economic products and their uses, III. 217, 757; V. xxviii.[1]
—— placed according to countries, III. 261; V. xxviii.[1]
—— technology of, III. 218.
Economics, IV. 268.
Ectadium, II. 737.
Ectinocladus, II. 726.
Ecuador, descriptive botany, III. 64.
—— periodicals, *see* South America, I. 7.
—— phytography, I. 339; V. xviii.[1]
—— *see also* South America.
Edgeworthia, II. 603; III. 628.
Edgeworthia, II. 700.
Edmonstonia, II. 573.
Education, I. 78; III. 31; IV. 28, 540; V. xxix.[1]
Eduardia, II. 533.
Eduardsia, II. 384; III. 487.
Eduinia, II. 241.
Effect of various poisonous substances, III. 185.
Efulensia, II. 576.
Eganthus, II. 171.
Eggersia, II. 191.
Egypt, botanic gardens, *see* North Africa, I. 68.
—— dendrography, *see* Mediterranean States of Africa, IV. 89.
—— history, *see* Africa, I. 81, 523; V. x.[1]
—— miscellaneous publications on arboriculture, III. 130.
—— periodicals, *see* Africa, I. 29.
—— phytography, *see* Northeast Africa, I. 486.
Ehrenbergia, II. 809.
Ehretia, II. 750; III. 695.
Ehretia, II. 702, 748, 772.
Eichlerodendron, II. 570.
Eichwaldia, II. 562.
Eickebergia, II. 420.
Elaeagia, II. 816; III. 743.
Elaeagnaceae, II. 607; III. 628.
Elaeagnus, II. 607; III. 628.
Elaeis, II. 68; III. 325.
Elaeocarpaceae, II. 509; III. 584.
Elaeocarpus, II. 510; III. 584.
Elaeocarpus, II. 561.
Elaeococca, II. 436; III. 514.
Elaeodendron, II. 467; III. 532.
Elaeodendron, II. 407, 466, 567, 697; III. 666.
Elaeogene, II. 441.
Elais, II. 68.
Elaphrium, II. 418; III. 510.
Elasticity of timber, IV. 409.
Elateriospermum, II. 441.
Elatostema, II. 157.
Elatostema, II. 157.
Elcomarhiza, II. 737.
Electricity, conductibility of, IV. 412.
—— and Magnetism, I. 230, 529.
Eleutherococcus, II. 647.
Eliaea, II. 554.
Elichrysum, II. 858, 863.

Eliea, II. 554.
Elliottia, II. 663.
Ellipanthus, II. 317.
Ellipeia, II. 217.
Elsass-Lothringen, *see* Alsace-Lorraine.
Elsholtzia, II. 763.
Elutheria, II. 421.
Elvasia, II. 544.
Elytranthe, II. 174.
Elytropus, II. 726.
Embelia, II. 693; III. 666.
Embelia, II. 473, 694, 695.
Emblematic botany, I. 515, 536; V. xxv.²
Embothrium, II. 160; III. 382; V. xxvi.¹
Embothrium, II. 160, 162, 167.
Embryogonia, II. 616, 617.
Embryology, I. 121, 524.
Emeorhiza, II. 816.
Emerus, II. 347.
Eminia, II. 355.
Emmenanthus, II. 393.
Emmenopterys, II. 816.
Emmenosperma, II. 494.
Emmenospermum, II. 494.
Emmeorhiza, II. 816.
Emmotum, II. 474.
Emorya, II. 718.
Empetraceae, II. 453; III. 523.
Empetrum, II. 453; III. 523.
Empetrum, II. 453.
Emplectocladus, see Prunus, II. 270.
Empleurum, II. 405; III. 504.
Employees, IV. 310, 554.
Empogona, II. 816.
Enantia, II. 217.
Encelia, II. 856.
Encentrus, II. 469.
Encephalartos, II. 5; III. 285.
Encephalartos, II. 6.
Enchidium, II. 452.
Enchylaena, II. 188.
Enckea, II. 93.
Encliandra, II. 643.
Enclosures in trees, I. 210, 528; V. xii.¹
Encomiums, I. 79, 522; V. ix.²
Encopea, II. 817.
Encouraging the development of reproductive organs, III. 174.
Encouraging the maturation of wood, III. 174.
Encyclopedias, III. 30; IV. 22.
—— *see also* Miscellaneous publications, I. 30, 520.
Endespermum, II. 352.
Endiandra, II. 225.
Endlichera, II. 816.
Endodesmia, II. 554.
Endolasia, II. 823.
Endoleuca, II. 860.
Endospermum, II. 441.
Endosteira, II. 513.
Endrachium, II. 745.
Endusa, II. 171.
Energy, *see* Physics of plant body, I. 149.
Engelhardtia, II. 112.
Engineering, IV. 262, 551; V. xxx.²
England, forest descriptions, IV. 357; V. xxxi.²
—— *see also* British Islands.
Engravers' wood, IV. 427.
Enkianthus, II. 663; III. 649.
Enkleia, II. 603.
Enkyanthus, II. 663; III. 649.
Enkylista, II. 810.
Entada, II. 355; III. 475.
Entada, II. 376.
Entandrophragma, II. 421.
Entelea, II. 513.
Enterolobium, II. 356.
Enterospermum, II. 816.
Entrecasteauxia, II. 771.
Environment, *see* Ecology, I. 217, 528.

Epacridaceae, II. 687; III. 664.
Epacris, II. 688; III. 664.
Epacris, II. 690; III. 665.
Eperua, II. 356.
Ephedra, II. 53; III. 312.
Ephedranthus, II. 217.
Ephedranthus, II. 217.
Ephielis, II. 757.
Ephippiandra, II. 221.
Epicarpurus, II. 155.
Epicharis, II. 420.
Epicostorus, II. 269.
Epigaea, II. 663; III. 649.
Epigynium, II. 662, 684; III. 663.
Epiphyllum, II. 593; III. 623.
Epiphyllum, II. 597; III. 625, 626.
Epiphytism, I. 234; IV. 73, 543.
Episcia, II. 794; III. 708.
Epithinia, II. 831.
Eranthemum, II. 799; III. 709.
Eranthemum, II. 801, 802; III. 710.
Erblichia, II. 575.
Ercilla, II. 192; III. 388.
Ercilla, II. 193.
Eremanthus, II. 856.
Eremia, II. 663.
Eremodendron, II. 805.
Eremolepis, II. 174.
Eremomastax, II. 799.
Eremophila, II. 805; III. 710.
Eremopyxis, II. 633.
Eremosparton, II. 356.
Eremothamnus, II. 856.
Eriandrostachys, II. 486.
Eribroma, II. 538.
Erica, II. 663; III. 649; IV. 534.
Erica, II. 661, 662; III. 648; V. xxix.²
Ericaceae, II. 657; III. 646; IV. 534; V. xxvii.¹ xxix.²
Ericinella, II. 670.
Erigeron, II. 856.
Erigeron, II. 855, 868.
Erica, H. 356; III. 475.
Eriobotrya, II. 264; III. 423.
Eriocephalus, II. 856.
Eriococcus, III. 521.
Eriococcus, II. 449.
Eriocoma, II. 856; III. 755.
Eriodendron, II. 529; III. 589.
Eriodictyon, II. 747; III. 695.
Erioglossum, II. 486; III. 539.
Eriogonum, II. 185.
Eriogynia, II. 265.
Eriolobus, II. 264.
Erio, II. 763.
Eriosema, II. 356; III. 475.
Eriosema, II. 381.
Eriostemon, II. 405; III. 504.
Eriostemon, II. 409, 510.
Erisma, II. 428.
Erismanthus, II. 441.
Erithalis, II. 816; III. 743.
Erithalis, II. 832.
Ernodea, II. 816.
Erodendrum, II. 165.
Erodium, II. 389.
Erosion, protection from, IV. 184, 547.
Eroteum, II. 548.
Erycibe, II. 744.
Eryngium, II. 653.
Erythea, II. 68; III. 325.
Erythracanthus, II. 803.
Erythrina, II. 356; III. 475.
Erythrochilus, see Erythroehylus, II. 438.
Erythrochiton, II. 406; III. 504.
Erythrochiton, II. 550.
Erythrochlamys, II. 763.
Erythrochylus, II. 438.
Erythrococca, II. 441.
Erythropalum, II. 171.
Erythrophila, II. 486.
Erythrophleum, II. 353; III. 476; V. xxvi.²

Erythrophysa, II. 486.
Erythropyxis, II. 540.
Erythrospermum, II. 570.
Erythrostemon, II. 338.
Erythrostigma, II. 317.
Erythroxylaceae, II. 394; III. 492.
Erythroxylum, II. 394; III. 492.
Escallonia, II. 239; III. 410.
Eschweilera, II. 612.
Eschweilera, II. 648.
Esenbeckia, II. 406; III. 504.
Espadaea, II. 771.
Espeletia, II. 856.
Esterhazia, II. 780.
Esterhazya, II. 780.
Esthetic botany, I. 516, 536; V. xxv.²
Esthetic influences, III. 34; IV. 55, 542.
Esthetic principles, in arboriculture, III. 201.
—— in silviculture, IV. 136.
Etaballia, III. 358.
Ethic influences of forests, IV. 55, 542.
Ethnobotany, I. 511, 536; V. xxiv.³
Etymology of botanical names, I. 76; V. ix.²
—— of forest terms, IV. 23.
—— of vernacular names, I. 71, 522.
Euadenia, II. 232; III. 409.
Eucalyptus, II. 622, 874; III. 633; IV. 529.
Euchaetis, II. 406.
Euchilus, II. 380.
Euchresta, II. 358; III. 476.
Euclea, II. 702.
Eucommia, III. 418.
Eucommiaceae, II. 254; III. 418.
Eucryphia, II. 544; III. 596.
Eucryphiaceae, II. 544; III. 596.
Eudesmia, II. 622.
Eugeissona, II. 68; III. 325.
Eugenia, II. 625; III. 635.
Eugenia, II. 627, 631, 633, 634, 639; III. 635, 637, 638; V. xxvii.¹
Eukylista, II. 810.
Eulychnia, II. 589.
Euonymus, *see* Evonymus.
Euonymus, II. 467.
Euosma, II. 719.
Eupatorium, II. 856; III. 755.
Eupatorium, II. 853, 855.
Euphorbia, II. 441; III. 517.
Euphorbia, II. 448.
Euphorbiaceae, II. 433; III. 514; V. xxvi.²
Euphoria, II. 486.
Euphoria, II. 484, 487; III. 539.
Euphorianthus, II. 486.
Euplassa, II. 160.
Eupomatia, II. 217; III. 401.
Euptelea, II. 194.
Europe, acclimatization, III. 44.
—— administration of private forests, IV. 308, 554.
—— afforestation, IV. 155, 546; V. xxx.²
—— arbor day, IV. 42, 541.
—— bibliography, I. 3, 519.
—— botanic gardens, I. 40, 521; V. viii.¹
—— cinchona cultivation, III. 713.
—— coffee cultivation, III. 729.
—— collections, III. 27, 757.
—— cultivation of exotic trees, IV. 125, 545.
—— cultivation of fruit trees, III. 134; V. xxviii.¹
—— dendrography, IV. 78, 544; V. xxx.¹
—— descriptive botany, III. 66, 757; V. xxviii.¹
—— diseases and injuries, III. 178, 757.
—— diseases caused by fungi, III. 193.
—— economic products, III. 269.
—— education, III. 32.
—— erosion, IV. 184, 547.

Europe, exhibitions, IV. 19, 540; V. XXIX.[1]
—— financial results of forest management, IV. 260, 551.
—— forest descriptions, IV. 342, 555; V. XXXI.[2]
—— forest devastation, IV. 281, 552.
—— forest exploitation, IV. 383.
—— forest fires, IV. 182, 547.
—— forest gardens, IV. 18, 539.
—— forest influences, IV. 46, 541; V. XXX.[1]
—— forest laws, IV. 315, 554.
—— forest management, IV. 247, 550; V. XXXI.[3]
—— forest policy, IV. 272, 551.
—— forest products, IV. 398.
—— forest protection, IV. 179, 547; V. XXX.[2]
—— forest regulations, IV. 296, 554.
—— forest schools, IV. 30, 540.
—— forest servitudes, IV. 333, 555.
—— forest statistics, IV. 342, 555; V. XXXI.[1]
—— galls, I. 214.
—— history, I. 80, 523; III. 33, 757; IV. 24, 540; V. X.[1]
—— individual noteworthy trees, I. 296, 531; V. XVI.[1]
—— injuries caused by insects, III.[.] 188, 757; IV. 205, 544, 549; V. XXXI.[1]
—— insects, IV. 91.
—— inundation, IV. 184, 547.
—— land-slides, IV. 184, 547.
—— manuals of arboriculture, III. 100, 757.
—— measures promoting sylviculture, IV. 39, 541.
—— miscellaneous publications on arboriculture, III. 119.
—— miscellaneous publications on silviculture, IV. 113, 544; V. XXX.[2]
—— periodicals, I. 8, 519; III. 10, 757; IV. 5, 539; V. VII.[1] XXVII.[1] XXIX.[1]
—— pharmacopoeias, III. 247.
—— phenology, I. 222, 528; V. XII.[2]
—— phytography, I. 348, 531; V. XVIII.[2]
—— reproductive interrelations, I. 239, 529.
—— silviculture and pasturing, IV. 134, 545.
—— state forest administration, IV. 288, 552.
—— state supervision of forests, IV. 286.
—— street trees, III. 208.
—— taxes, tariffs, etc., IV. 284, 552.
—— tea cultivation, III. 601.
—— textbooks and manuals of forestry, IV. 94; V. XXX.[1]
—— textbooks and manuals of silviculture, IV. 103, 544; V. XXX.[1]
—— timber trade, IV. 403, 557.
—— vernacular names, I. 73, 522; V. IX.[1]
—— viticulture, III. 551.
Eurotia, II. 188.
Eurya, II. 548; III. 596.
Eurya, III. 597.
Eurybia, II. 861; III. 756.
Eurycoma, II. 414; III. 508.
Eurygania, II. 684.
Eurylobium, II. 757.
Euryops, II. 857; III. 755.
Euryspermum, II. 164.
Euscaphis, II. 473; III. 533.
Eusideroxylon, II. 225, 872.
Eustathes, II. 869.
Eustigma, II. 252.
Eustrephus, II. 83.
Eutacta, II. 25; III. 297.
Eutassa, III. 297.
Eutaxia, II. 358; III. 477.
Eutaxia, II. 354.

Euterpe, II. 68; III. 325.
Eutetras, II. 857.
Euthemis, II. 544.
Euxenia, II. 863.
Euxomodendron, II. 234.
Evaporation, see Transpiration, I. 166.
Evergreen foliage, III. 205.
—— hedges, III. 214.
Evergreens, planting of, III. 169.
—— pruning of, III. 173.
—— see also Pinaceae and Taxaceae.
Eversmannia, II. 358.
Evodia, II. 406; III. 504; IV. 524.
Evodia, II. 397, 406.
Evodianthus, II. 76.
Evolution, I. 243, 529; III. 50; IV. 74.
Evolvulus, II. 744.
Evonymus, II. 467; III. 532; IV. 526.
Exacum, II. 721.
Excentric growth, see Stem, I. 104, 524.
Excoecaria, II. 444; III. 518.
Excoecaria, II. 435, 437, 445.
Exhibitions, III. 27; IV. 19, 540; V. XXIX.[1]
Exocarpus, II. 168.
Exochorda, II. 264; III. 424.
Exogonium, II. 745.
Exolepta, I. 662.
Exospermum, II. 209.
Exostemma, II. 816; III. 743.
Exostyles, II. 358.
Exotic trees, cultivation of, IV. 124, 545.
Experimental stations, IV. 37, 541.
Experimental work, IV. 37, 541.
Exudation of water, I. 169, 526.
Eytrea, II. 473.
Eysenhardtia, II. 358; III. 477.
Eystathes, II. 869.

Fabiana, II. 771; III. 700.
Fabricia, II. 331, 620, 628.
Fadogia, II. 825.
Faeroe Islands, see Scandinavia, I. 350.
Fagaceae, II. 122, 872; III. 358, 758; IV. 492, 559; V. XXVI.[1]
Fagara, IV. 524.
Fagara, II. 406, 411.
Fagelia, II. 779.
Fagonia, II. 395; III. 493.
Fagraea, II. 718, 874; III. 682; IV. 536.
Fagus, II. 125, 872; III. 360; IV. 493; V. XXXI.[2]
Fagus, II. 127; III. 360.
Falconeria, II. 451.
Falkland Islands, phytography, I. 347.
Falling of branches, see Casting off of branches, I. 192.
Falling of leaves, see leaf fall, I. 191.
Fallugia, II. 264.
Faradaya, II. 757; III. 696.
Faramea, II. 817.
Fargesia, II. 60.
Farnesia, II. 322.
Faroe Islands, see Scandinavia, I. 350.
Farsetia, II. 234.
Fasciation, see Teratology of stem, I. 144.
Fatioa, II. 609.
Fatoua, II. 148.
Fats, I. 181, 526; III. 224; V. XI.[2]
Fatsia, II. 648; III. 642.
Fatsia, II. 648, 652; III. 644.
Faujasia, II. 857.
Faures, II. 160.
Fecundation, I. 200, 527; V. XII.[1]
Feijoa, II. 632; III. 637.
Felicia, II. 857; III. 755.
Felled timber, contents of, IV. 219, 550.
Felling, IV. 383, 556.
—— esthetic principles in, III. 202.
—— season of, IV. 384, 557.
Felling area, clearing of, IV. 388.
Fencing, IV. 146, 545.
Fendlera, II. 240; III. 411.

Fendlerella, II. 240.
Fenzlia, II. 627.
Ferdinanda, II. 857; III. 755.
Ferdinanda, II. 788.
Ferdinandusa, II. 817; III. 744.
Feretia, II. 817.
Fernandia, II. 788.
Fernelia, II. 817.
Feronia, II. 407; III. 504; IV. 524.
Ferreirea, II. 358.
Fertilization, III. 175.
—— see also Fecundation, I. 200, 527, and Reproductive interrelations, I. 236, 529.
Feuillea, II. 844; III. 753.
Fevillea, II. 844; III. 753.
Fibre balls, I. 242.
Fibres, III. 233; V. XXVIII.[1]
Ficalhoa, II. 670.
Ficoideae, see Aizoaceae, II. 193.
Ficus, II. 148, 872; III. 368; IV. 519.
Ficus, III. 368.
Fieldia, II. 794.
Fiji Islands, botanic gardens, see Pacific Islands, I. 69.
—— descriptive botany, III. 94.
—— economic products, III. 283.
—— phytography, I. 510; V. XXIV.[2]
Filicium, II. 485.
Fillaea, II. 358, 380.
Fimbristemma, II. 737.
Financial aspects of thinning, IV. 175.
Financial results of forest management, IV. 259, 551.
Finland, see Russia.
Finschia, II. 160.
Fires, IV. 181, 547.
Firewood, IV. 431.
—— see also Heating power of wood, IV. 412.
Firmiana, II. 534.
Fischera, II. 673.
Fischeria, II. 737; III. 692.
Fissicalyx, II. 358.
Fissility of timber, IV. 411.
Fitchia, II. 857.
Fitchia, II. 160.
Fitzroya, II. 30; III. 303.
Fixation of movable soil, IV. 145, 545.
Flacourtia, II. 570; III. 614.
Flacourtia, II. 574.
Flacourtiaceae, II. 568, 873; III. 614.
Fleischeria, II. 527.
Flemingia, II. 358, III. 477.
Flemingia, II. 804.
Fleurya, II. 157.
Flindersia, II. 407; III. 504.
Floras, see Dendrography, IV. 75; descriptive botany, III. 51; phytography, I. 250, 529.
Florida, see United States, Southeastern.
Flotovia, II. 854.
Flourensia, II. 857.
Flowering, season of, III. 207.
Flowers, double, I. 145.
—— ecology, see Color and Reproductive interrelations, I. 236, 529.
—— forcing and retarding of, III. 176.
—— morphology and anatomy, I. 114, 524.
—— ornamental, III. 207.
—— teratology, I. 145.
Flueckigeria, II. 193.
Flueggea, II. 444.
Fluggea, II. 444.
Fluids, absorption, I. 160.
—— conduction, I. 162, 526; V. XI.[2]
Flumes, transport of timber by, IV. 390.
Fockea, II. 738.
Fodder, II. 223; IV. 438, 558.
Foetidia, II. 612.
Foliage, III. 205.
Folk-lore, Plants in, see Plant lore, I. 517, 536.

Fontainea, III. 518.
Fontanesia, II. 706; III. 671.
Fontenellea, II. 281.
Food, III. 219.
—— *see also* Alimentary uses of wood products, IV. 433, 558.
Forchhammeria, II. 233.
Forcing and retarding of flowers and fruits, III. 176.
Fordia, II. 358.
Forest administration, IV. 287, 552.
—— state, IV. 288, 552.
Forest conditions, reports on, IV. 336, 555; V. xxxi.^{2}
Forest descriptions, IV. 336, 555; V. xxxi.^{2}
Forest devastation, IV. 280, 552.
Forest economics, *see* Forest policy, IV. 268, 551; V. xxxi.^{1} *and* Timber trade, IV. 402; *see also* Forest products, IV. 396.
Forest engineering, IV. 263, 551; V. xxxi.^{1}
Forest experiment stations, IV. 37, 541.
Forest exploitation, IV. 381, 556; V. xxxi.^{1}
Forest fires, IV. 181, 547; V. xxx.^{2}
Forest gardens, IV. 18, 539.
Forest growth, ecology of, IV. 67, 543.
Forest influence, esthetic, IV. 55, 542.
—— ethic, IV. 55, 542.
Forest influence, on climatic conditions, IV. 52, 542.
—— on moisture and water supply, IV. 49, 542.
—— sanitary, IV. 54, 542; V. xxx.^{1}
Forest influences, IV. 42, 541; V. xxix.^{2}
Forest laws, IV. 313, 554; V. xxxi.^{1}
Forest litter, IV. 70, 437, 543, 558.
Forest management, IV. 239, 550; V. xxxi.^{1}
—— financial results of, IV. 259, 551.
—— manuals of, IV. 239; V. xxxi.^{1}
Forest officers and employees, IV. 310, 554.
Forest policy, IV. 268, 551; V. xxxi.^{1}
Forest products, IV. 396, 557; V. xxxi.^{2}
Forest products other than wood, IV. 433, 558; V. xxxii.^{1}
Forest protection, IV. 177, 547; V. xxx.^{2}
Forest regulations, IV. 295, 554.
Forest reports, IV. 336, 555; V. xxxi.^{1}
Forest reservations, *see* Forest protection, IV. 177; *see also* Forest descriptions, IV. 336.
Forest schools, IV. 30, 540.
Forest seeds, IV. 438; V. xxxii.^{1}
—— gathering, keeping and preparing of, IV. 147, 546.
Forest servitudes, IV. 332, 555.
Forest statistics, IV. 336, 555; V. xxxi.^{1}
Forest technology, manuals of, IV. 381.
Forest utilization, IV. 381, 556; V. xxxi.^{1}
Forest valuation, IV. 239, 252, 550; V. xxxi.^{1}
—— manuals of, IV. 252.
Forestiera, II. 706.
Forestry, IV. 94, 544; V. xxx.^{1}
—— measures promoting, IV. 39, 541.
—— miscellaneous publications on, IV. 100, 544.
—— principles of, IV. 56, 542; V. xxx.^{1}
—— textbooks, and manuals, IV. 94; V. xxix.^{2}
Forestry associations, IV. 39, 541.
Forestry societies, IV. 39, 541.
Forests, composition of, IV. 137.
—— insurance of, IV. 284, 552.
—— state supervision of, IV. 285, 552.
—— tending of, IV. 169, 547.
—— volume of, IV. 216.
Formation of woods, IV. 140, 545.

Formosa, phytography, I. 463.
—— *see also* China.
Fornasinia, II. 371.
Forsoleaco, II. 445.
Forsteronia, II. 726; III. 688.
Forsythia, II. 706; III. 671.
Forsythiopsis, II. 799.
Fortunaea, II. 114.
Fothergilla, II. 252; III. 417.
Fouquieria, II. 563; III. 612.
Fouquieriaceae, II. 563; III. 612.
Fourcraea, II. 89.
Fourcroya, *see* Furcraea, II. 89.
Fourneaux Islands, *see* Tasmania.
Foveolaria, II. 704.
France, acclimatization, III. 47.
—— administration of private forests, IV. 309.
—— afforestation, IV. 161, 546; V. xxx.^{2}
—— arbor day, IV. 42, 541.
—— bibliography, I. 3.
—— botanic gardens, I. 56, 522; V. viii.^{2}
—— collections, III. 29.
—— cultivation of exotic trees, IV. 126, 545.
—— cultivation of fruit trees, III. 142; V. xxviii.^{1}
—— dendrography, IV. 85.
—— descriptive botany, III. 83; V. xxviii.^{1}
—— economic products, III. 271.
—— education, III. 32.
—— erosion, IV. 185, 547.
—— exhibitions, IV. 20, 540; V. xxix.^{1}
—— financial results of forest management, IV. 261, 551.
—— forest descriptions, IV. 359, 556; V. xxxi.^{1}
—— forest devastation, IV. 282.
—— forest experiment stations, IV. 38, 541.
—— forest fires, IV. 183; V. xxx.^{1}
—— forest gardens, IV. 18, 539.
—— forest influences, IV. 47, 542; V. xxx.^{1}
—— forest laws, IV. 323, 555.
—— forest management, IV. 248.
—— forest officers and employees, IV. 311, 554.
—— forest policy, IV. 275, 551.
—— forest products, IV. 398; V. xxxi.^{2}
—— forest protection, IV. 180, 547.
—— forest regulations, IV. 303.
—— forest schools, IV. 34, 540.
—— forest servitudes, IV. 334, 555.
—— galls, I. 215.
—— history, I. 81, 523; III. 33; IV. 27, 540.
—— individual noteworthy trees, I. 297.
—— insects, IV. 209, 549.
—— manuals of arboriculture, III. 110.
—— measures promoting silviculture, IV. 41, 541.
—— miscellaneous publications on arboriculture, III. 124.
—— miscellaneous publications on silviculture, IV. 104, 544.
—— periodicals, I. 20, 520; III. 18; IV. 12, 539; V. vii, xxvii.^{1}
—— pharmacopoeias. III. 255.
—— phenology, I. 226.
—— phytography, I. 404, 535; V. xxi.^{2}
—— silviculture and pasturing, IV. 135, 545.
—— state forest administration, IV. 291, 553.
—— taxes, tariffs, etc., IV. 285, 552.
—— textbooks and manuals of forestry, IV. 98; V. xxx.^{1}
—— textbooks and manuals of silviculture, IV. 108; V. xxx.^{1}
—— timber trade, IV. 405, 557.

France, vernacular names, I. 74, 522; V. ix.^{2}
—— viticulture, III. 554.
Franchetia, II. 253.
Franciscea, III. 769; III. 698.
Pranpula, II. 496.
Frankenia, II. 561.
Frankenia, II. 746.
Frankeniaceae, II. 561.
Franklandia, II. 160, 872.
Franklinia, II. 548.
Franseria, II. 857.
Frappieria, II. 864.
Fraxinus, II. 706; III. 672; IV. 534.
Fregirardia, II. 768.
Fremontia, II. 534; III. 591.
Fremontia, II. 188.
Fremontodendron, II. 534.
Fremya, II. 634; III. 638.
French Congo, forest administration, IV. 295.
—— *see also* Africa.
French Indochina, botanic gardens, *see* Cochin-China, I. 66.
—— coffee cultivation, III. 732.
—— phytography, I. 469, 536.
Frenela, II. 27.
Freycinetia, II. 56; III. 313.
Freycinetia, II. 56.
Freylinia, II. 780; III. 702.
Freziera, II. 548; III. 596.
Fridericia, II. 788.
Friedrichsthalia, II. 752.
Friendly Islands, phytography, I. 510.
Friesia, II. 509, 510; III. 584.
Froebelia, II. 688.
Propiera, II. 573.
Frost, IV. 66.
—— effects, I. 211.
—— injuries caused by, III. 181; IV. 191, 548; V. xxx.^{2}
—— protection from, III. 182.
Fruit trees, as street trees, III. 211.
—— cultivation of, III. 132; V. xxviii.^{1}
—— pruning of, III. 171.
—— and silviculture, IV. 134.
Fruits, III. 219.
—— forcing and retarding of, III. 176.
—— gathering of, III. 173.
—— metabolic processes, I. 178.
—— morphology and anatomy, I. 118.
—— ornamental, III. 207.
—— packing of, III. 173.
—— shipping of, III. 173.
—— storing of, III. 173.
—— teratology, I. 145, 525.
—— utilization of, III. 174.
Fuchsia, II. 643; III. 639.
Fuel, *see* Firewood, IV. 431; *see also* Heating power of wood, IV. 412.
Fugosia, II. 521; III. 587.
Fumana, II. 565.
Fumes, *see* Gases, injuries caused by, IV. 192.
Fumigating, III. 198.
Fundamental sciences of forestry, IV. 56; V. xxx.^{1}
—— of arboriculture, III. 35, 757; V. xxviii.^{1}
Fungi, diseases caused by, III. 193, 575; IV. 211, 550.
—— timber attacked by, IV. 414, 557.
Funifera, II. 603.
Furcraea, II. 89; III. 341.
Furcroya, II. 89.
Fusanus, II. 118.

Gabila, II. 208.
Gaertnera, II. 817; III. 744.
Gaertnera, II. 426.
Gagnebina, II. 358.
Gaiadendron, II. 174.
Gaillonia, II. 817.
Galactia, II. 358.

Galactia, II. 341.
Galactodendron, III. 367.
Galactodendrum, II. 146.
Galapagos Islands, phytography, I. 510.
Galbulimima, II. 209.
Galearia, II. 444.
Galedupa, II. 378.
Galega, II. 358, 386.
Galenia, II. 193.
Galiniera, II. 817.
Galipea, II. 407.
Galipea, II. 405; III. 503.
Galium, II. 817.
Gallesia, II. 192.
Galls, I. 213, 528.
Galphimia, II. 425; III. 513.
Galpinia, II. 609.
Gambelia, II. 779.
Gamblea, II. 649.
Game, injuries caused by, IV. 196.
—— covers, III. 215.
Game-keeping, with silviculture, IV. 136.
Gamolepis, II. 857.
Gamopoda, II. 208.
Ganophyllum, II. 486; III. 539.
Garapatica, II. 817.
Garberia, II. 857.
Garcia, II. 444.
Garcinia, II. 554; III. 609.
Gardenia, II. 817; III. 744.
Gardenia, II. 809, 814, 818, 823, 825, 829, 832; III. 747.
Gardens, III. 27, 757; V. xxvii.[2]
Gardneria, II. 718.
Gardoquia, II. 763.
Garnieria, II. 160.
Garretia, II. 421.
Garruga, see Garuga, II. 418.
Garrya, II. 110; III. 352.
Garryaceae, II. 110; III. 352.
Garuga, II. 418.
Garugandra, II. 361.
Garuleum, II. 858.
Gas, illuminating, IV. 443, 558.
Gases, absorption, I. 160.
—— conduction, I. 162, 526; V. xi.[2]
—— injuries caused by, III. 185; IV. 192, 548.
Gaslondia, II. 633.
Gasteria, II. 83.
Gastonia, II. 649.
Gastonia, II. 653.
Gastranthus, II. 803.
Gastrolobium, II. 358; III. 477.
Gastrolobium, II. 375; III. 486.
Gaudichaudia, II. 425.
Gaudichaudia, II. 426.
Gaultheria, II. 670; III. 652.
Gaultheria, II. 659, 662, 663; III. 649.
Gaura, II. 645.
Gautiera, II. 670.
Gaya, II. 521; III. 587.
Gaylussacia, II. 671; III. 652.
Geblera, II. 451.
Geeria, II. 648.
Geigera, II. 407.
Geijera, II. 407.
Geissanthus, II. 694.
Geissaspis, II. 359.
Geissois, II. 250; III. 416.
Geissoloma, II. 599.
Geissolomaceae, II. 599.
Geissomeria, II. 799; III. 709.
Geissospermum, II. 726; III. 688.
Gela, II. 397.
Geleznowia, II. 407.
Gelonium, II. 444.
Gelsemium, II. 718; III. 682.
Gemella, II. 584.
General botany, popular works, I. 93, 524.
—— textbooks, I. 82, 523.
Generation of heat, I. 186; V. xii.[1]

Genesiphylla, II. 449.
Genetyllis, II. 622; III. 633.
Geniostoma, II. 719.
Genipa, II. 818.
Genipa, II. 808.
Genista, II. 359; III. 477.
Genista, II. 332, 349; III. 467, 473.
Gentianaceae, II. 721; III. 685.
Geodesy, III. 200; IV. 263, 551; V. xxxi.[1]
Geoffraea, II. 361; III. 477.
Geoffraea, II. 332; III. 467.
Geoffroya, II. 361; III. 477.
Geographical distribution, I. 298, 531; V. xvi.[1]
Geology, III. 37; IV. 60, 542.
Geonoma, II. 68; III. 325.
Geonoma, II. 65; III. 321.
Geophila, II. 819.
Georgia, *see* United States, Southeastern.
Geotropism, I. 195, 527.
Geraniaceae, II. 389; III. 491.
Geranium, II. 389.
Geranium, II. 389, 392; III. 491.
Gerardia, II. 780; III. 702.
Gerascanthus, II. 748.
German Empire, acclimatization, III. 45.
—— administration of private forests, IV. 308.
—— afforestation, IV. 158, 546.
—— bibliography, I. 3.
—— botanic gardens, I. 42, 521; V. viii.[1]
—— collections, III. 27.
—— cultivation of exotic trees, IV. 125, 545.
—— cultivation of fruit trees, III. 135.
—— dendrography, IV. 81.
—— descriptive botany, III. 68; V. xxviii.[1]
—— economic products, III. 270.
—— education, IV. 32.
—— erosion, IV. 185.
—— exhibitions, IV. 19.
—— financial results of forest management, IV. 260.
—— forest descriptions, IV. 348, 555; V. xxxi.[2]
—— forest experiment stations, IV. 38, 541.
—— forest fires, IV. 182.
—— forest gardens, IV. 18, 539.
—— forest influences, IV. 46.
—— forest laws, IV. 316.
—— forest management, IV. 247, 550.
—— forest officers and employees, IV. 310.
—— forest policy, IV. 273.
—— forest products, IV. 398.
—— forest protection, IV. 180.
—— forest regulations, IV. 298.
—— forest schools, IV. 31.
—— forest servitudes, IV. 333.
—— galls, I. 215.
—— history, I. 80; III. 33, 757; IV. 25; V. x.[1]
—— individual noteworthy trees, I. 296, 531.
—— injuries caused by insects, IV. 205, 549; V. xxxi.[1]
—— manuals of arboriculture, III. 101.
—— measures promoting sylviculture, IV. 40, 541.
—— miscellaneous publications on arboriculture, III. 120.
—— miscellaneous publications on silviculture, IV. 115, 544.
—— periodicals, I. 10, 520; III. 11, 757; IV. 6; V. vii.[1]
—— pharmacopoeias, III. 247.
—— phenology, I. 224, 528; V. xii.[1]

German Empire, phytography, I. 370, 531; V. xix.[1]
—— reproductive interrelations, *see* Europe, I. 239.
—— silviculture and pasturing, IV. 135.
—— state forest administration, IV. 289, 552.
—— a supervision of forests, IV. 289t te
—— taxes, tariffs, etc., IV. 284.
—— textbooks and manuals of forestry, IV. 94; V. xxx.[1]
—— textbooks and manuals of silviculture, IV. 104, 544; V. xxx.[1]
—— timber trade, IV. 404.
—— vernacular names, I. 73; V. ix.[2]
—— viticulture, III. 551.
Germaria, II. 278.
Germination, I. 202, 528.
Gerontogea, II. 825.
Gerrardanthus, II. 844.
Gerrardina, II. 571.
Gesneria, II. 794; III. 708.
Gesneria, II. 794, 795.
Gesneriaceae, II. 792; III. 708.
Gesnouinia, II. 157.
Geunsia, II. 757.
Gevuina, II. 160; III. 383.
Ghiesbreghtia, II. 780.
Ghikaea, II. 780.
Gigalobium, II. 355.
Giganthemum, II. 341.
Gigantochloa, II. 60.
Gigliolia, II. 68.
Gilia, II. 747; III. 694.
Gilibertia, II. 649.
Gilibertia, II. 653.
Ginalloa, II. 174.
Ginkgo, II. 7; III. 286; IV. 440.
Ginkgoaceae, II. 7; III. 286; IV. 440.
Ginoria, II. 609.
Girdling, IV. 385.
Gironniera, II. 142.
Givotia, II. 444.
Glands, *see* Appendages, I. 112.
Glandulifolia, III. 397.
Glaphyria, II. 628.
Glaziophyton, II. 58.
Glaziova, III. 322.
Glechon, II. 763.
Gleditschia, II. 361; III. 477.
Gliricidia, II. 362.
Glischrocaryon, II. 646.
Globularia, II. 795; III. 708.
Globulariaceae, II. 795; III. 708.
Glochidion, II. 444.
Gloeospermum, II. 567.
Gloneria, II. 827.
Glossaries, I. 69, 522; III. 29; IV. 23; V. ix.[1] xxvii.[1]
Glossarrhen, II. 568.
Glossocalyx, II. 221.
Glossocarya, II. 757.
Glossogyne, II. 858.
Glossolepis, II. 486.
Glossopetalon, II. 469.
Glossostemon, II. 534.
Glossostephanus, II. 738.
Gloxinia, II. 794.
Gluta, II. 456; III. 524; IV. 526.
Glycideras, II. 858.
Glycine, II. 362; III. 477.
Glycine, II. 356, 366, 381, 387, 388; III. 486, 490.
Glyciphylla, II. 662.
Glycosmis, II. 407; III. 504.
Glycosmis, II. 408.
Glycycarpus, II. 457.
Glycyderas, II. 858.
Glyphaea, II. 513; III. 584.
Glyptopetalum, II. 469.
Glyptostrobus, II. 30.
Gmelina, II. 757; III. 696; IV. 536.
Gnaphalium, II. 858, 859.

Gnetaceae, II. 53; III. 312.
Gnetum, II. 54; III. 312.
Gnidia, II. 603, 874; III. 628.
Gochnatia, II. 858.
Godmania, II. 788.
Godoya, II. 544.
Goethea, II. 521; III. 587.
Goetzea, II. 771.
Goldfussia, II. 803; III. 710.
Gomortega, II. 221.
Gomortegaceae, II. 221.
Gomphandra, II. 475.
Gomphia, II. 545; III. 596.
Gomphocarpus, II. 738; III. 692.
Gomphocarpus, II. 743.
Gompholobium, II. 362; III. 478.
Gompholobium, II. 333, 866.
Gomphosia, II. 817; III. 744.
Gomphrena, II.,190.
Gomphrena, II. 190.
Gomutus, II. 64.
Gongronema, II. 738.
Gongylocarpus, II. 645.
Gongylolepis, II. 866.
Goniorrhachis, II. 362.
Goniothalamus, II. 217.
Gonocalyx, III. 663.
Gonocaryum, II. 474.
Gonocitrus, II. 407.
Gonocrypta, II. 737.
Gonocytisus, II. 359, 385.
Gonolobus, II. 738; III. 693.
Gonolobus, II. 737; III. 692, 693.
Gonoptera, II. 395.
Gonostylus, III. 584.
Gonus, II. 414.
Gonyanera, II. 819.
Gonystylaceae, II. 512; III. 584.
Gonystylus, II. 512; III. 584.
Gonzalagunia, II. 819; III. 744.
Gonzalea, II. 819; III. 744.
Goodallia, II. 604.
Goodenia, II. 846.
Goodeniaceae, II. 846; III. 754.
Goodia, II. 362; III. 478.
Goodia, I. 333.
Gorceixia, II. 858.
Gordonia, II. 548; III. 596.
Gordonia, II. 549, 703; III. 596.
Gorteria, II. 853, 855.
Gossania, II. 494.
Gossypium, II. 521; III. 587.
Gouania, II. 494; III. 541.
Gouania, II. 496.
Gouldia, II. 819.
Goupia, II. 469.
Gouriiea, II. 362.
Gowania, II. 494.
Grabowskia, II. 772.
Graderia, II. 780.
Graffenrieda, II. 637.
Graft hybrids,·I. 246.
Grafting, III. 159.
— natural, I. 209, 528; IV. 66.
— reparative processes, I. 208.
Grahamia, II. 194.
Gramineae, II. 57; III. 314; IV. 485.
Granateae, see Punicaceae.
Grand Duchy of Hesse, forest descriptions, IV. 351.
— forest laws, IV. 319.
— forest regulations, IV. 300.
— state forest administration, IV. 290.
— see also German Empire.
Grandidiera, II. 571.
Grangeria, II. 264.
Graphistemma, II. 738.
Graptophyllum, II. 799; III. 709.
Grass as forest product, IV. 438, 558.
Gravity of timber, IV. 411.
Grayia, II. 183.
Grazing animals, injuries caused by, III. 186; IV. 197, 548.

Great Britain, see British Islands.
Greece, forest descriptions, IV. 375.
— forest laws, IV. 332.
— history, IV. 28.
— periodicals, I. 28.
— state forest administration, IV. 294.
— viticulture, III. 558.
— see also Balkan Peninsula.
Greenea, II. 819.
Greenhouse plants, cultivation of, III. 150.
Greenland, dendrography, IV. 76.
— galls, see North America, I. 214.
— phytography, I. 308.
— reproductive interrelations, see North America, I. 239.
Greggia, II. 264.
Grenacheria, II. 694.
Grevea, II. 240.
Grevellina, II. 422.
Grevillea, II. 160, 872; III. 383.·
Grewia, II. 513, 873; III. 584.
Grewia, II. 512.
Grewiopsis, II. 514.
Greyia, II. 491; III. 540.
Grias, II. 612; III. 631.
Griffithia, II. 829.
Griffonia, II. 363.
Grindelia, II. 858.
Grischowia, II. 640.
Grisebachia, II. 663.
Grisebachiella, II. 726.
Griselinia, II. 656; III. 646.
Grisia, II. 809.
Grislea, II. 610; III. 630.
Grisollea, II. 474.
Ground, preparation of, III. 150; IV. 142, 545.
Groutia, II. 170.
Growth, I. 187, 526; III. 38; IV. 64, 543; V. XII.[1]
— arrest of, I. 191, 527; V. XII.[1]
— ecology of, IV. 67.
— of leaf, I. 190.
— of roots, I. 188, 526.
— of wood and bark, I. 189, 527; V. XII.[1]
Grubbia, II. 170.
Grubbiaceae, II. 170.
Grumilea, II. 819.
Grymania, II. 269.
Guachamaca, III. 690.
Guadua, II. 59.
Guaiacum, II. 395; III. 493; IV. 524.
Gnapira, II. 758.
Guares, II. 421; III. 512.
Guarea, II. 421.
Guatteria, II. 217.
Guatemala, see Central American Republics.
Guatteria, II. 218, 219, 872; III. 402.
Guazuma, II. 534; III. 591.
Guerkea, II. 724.
Guettarda, II. 819.
Guevina, II. 160; III. 383.
Guiacum, II. 396.
Guiana, botanic gardens, see South America, I. 39.
— coffee cultivation, III. 729.
— descriptive botany, III. 64.
— economic products, III. 267.
— exhibitions, IV. 19.
— forest descriptions, IV. 342.'
— forest products, IV. 398.
— miscellaneous publications on arboriculture, III. 118.
— phytography, III. 528, 531; V. XVIII.[1]
— see also South America.
Guibourtia, II. 347; III. 473.
Guichenotia, II. 540.
Guidonia, II. 570.
Guiina, II. 547.

Guilandina, II. 338.
Guildingia, II. 640.
Guilielma, II. 65; III. 320.
Guindilia, II. 490.
Guinea, see Africa, West.
Guioa, II. 486.
Gumillea, II. 250.
Gumira, II. 760.
Gummosis, I. 213, 528; III. 180.
Gums, III. 227, 757; IV. 436.
— and resins, I. 180; V. XI.[2]
Gunisanthus, II. 701.
Gunpowder, IV. 432.
Gussonia, II. 435, 451.
Gustavia, II. 612; III. 631.
Gutenbergia, II. 858.
Gutierrezia, II. 858.
Gutta percha, products and utilization, III. 230.
— sources of, III. 228.
— trees, cultivation of, III. 148.
Guttenbergia, II. 823.
Guttiferae, II. 552; 873; III. 608; IV. 528.
Gyminda, II. 469.
Gymnanthera, II. 738.
Gymnanthes, II. 445.
Gymnanthus, II. 194.·
Gymnartocarpus, II. 153.
Gymnema, II. 738; III. 693. ·
Gymnocarpus, II. 194.
Gymnocladus, II. 363; III. 478; IV. 521.
Gymnococca, II. 605.
Gymnolaema, II. 739.
Gymnolomia, II. 858.
Gymnopentzia, II. 858.
Gymnospermae, II. 1, 871; III. ·284, 758; IV. 440, 558; V. XXV,[1] XXVIII,[2] XXXII.[1]
Gymnosporia, II. 469.
Gynaecium, I. 117.
Gynandropsis, II. 233.
Gynocardia, II. 571; III. 614.
Gynoon, II. 444.
Gynopachis, II. 829.
Gynopogon, II. 723.·
Gynotroches, II. 613.
Gynoxis, II. 858.
Gynoxys, II. 858.
Gynozys, II. 864.
Gypsophila, II. 194.
Gyrandra, II. 440.
Gyrinops, II. 604.
Gyrinopsis, II. 604.
Gyrocarpus, II. 228.
Gyrostemon, II. 193.
Gyrostemon, II. 192.
Gyrotaenia, II. 157.

Habit, I. 106, 524.
— artistic aspect, see Esthetic botany, I. 516, 536.
— relation of properties to, III. 259.
— of trees and shrubs, III. 204.
Habrothamnus, II. 770, 772; III. 699.
Hackeria, II. 859.
Haemanthus, II. 803.
Haemadictyon, II. 731.
Haematostaphis, II. 456.
Haematoxylon, II. 363; IV. 521.
Haematoxylum, III. 478.
Haemocharis, II. 549.
Haemospermum, II. 719.
Haenianthus, II. 709.
Haenkea, II. 397.
Hagenia, II. 264; III. 424.
Hail, injuries caused by, III. 184; IV. 189, 548.
Hairs, see Appendages, I. 112.
Hakea, II. 162; III. 383.
Hakea, II. 167.
Halesia, II. 704; III. 670.
Halesia, III. 670.

Halgania, II. 750.
Halimium, II. 565; III. 613.
Halimodendron, II. 363; III. 478.
Halleria, II. 780.
Hallia, II. 363.
Halochloa, II. 60.
Halocnemum, II. 188.
Halodendron, II. 753.
Halopeplis, II. 188.
Haloragidaceae, II. 646.
Haloragis, II. 646.
Haloragis, II. 613.
Halorrhagis, II. 646.
Haloxylon, II. 188; III. 387; IV. 519.
  520.
Hamamelidaceae, II. 252; III. 416; IV.
  520.
Hamamelis, II. 253; III. 417.
Hamamelis, II. 253.
Hamelia, II. 819; III. 744.
Hamiltonia, II. 819; III. 744.
Hampea, II. 530.
Hancea, II. 447.
Hancornia, II. 726; III. 688.
Handbooks, see Manuals.
Hannoa, II. 414.
Hansemannia, II. 363.
Haplanthera, II. 803.
Haplopappus, II. 851, 852; III. 754.
Haplopetalon, II. 613.
Haplophyllum, II. 410.
Haplostichanthus, II. 217.
Hardenbergia, II. 366; III. 479.
Hardiness, III. 43.
Hardwood and conifers, IV. 138.
Hardwood forests, IV. 137.
Harfordia, II. 185.
Hariota, II. 594; III. 623.
Hariota, II. 598.
Harmandia, II. 171.
Harmogia, II. 620.
Harpsia, II. 534.
Harmsiopanax, II. 649; III. 642.
Haronga, II. 555.
Harpagophytum, II. 792.
Harpalyce, II. 363.
Harpephyllum, III. 424.
Harpullia, II. 486.
Harrachia, II. 798.
Harrisonia, II. 414.
Harrisonia, II. 740.
Hartighsea, II. 420.
Hartigia, II. 640.
Hartogia, II. 469.
Hartogia, II. 406.
Hasseltia, II. 569.
Hasskarlia, II. 445.
Hastingia, II. 758.
Haussmannia, II. 788.
Hanya, II. 645.
Hawaiian Islands, descriptive botany,
  III. 94.
—— forest descriptions, see Pacific
  Islands, IV. 380.
—— forest influence, see Pacific Islands,
  IV. 49.
—— forest laws, IV. 332.
—— phytography, I. 509.
—— see also Pacific Islands.
Haworthia, II. 83; III. 337.
Haxtonia, II. 861.
Hazardia, II. 858; III. 755.
Healing of wounds, see Reparative pro-
  cesses, I. 297, 528.
Heat, conductibility, IV. 412.
—— generation of, I. 186; V. xii.[1]
—— injuries caused by, III. 184; IV.
  192.
Heating power, timber, IV. 412.
Hebecladus, II. 772.
Hebeclinium, II. 856; III. 755.
Hebradendron, II. 554; III. 609.
Hecatoclesis, II. 858.
Hecastophyllum, II. 352.
Hecalea, II. 448.

Heckeldora, II. 421.
Heckeris, II. 93.
Hedaroma, II. 622; III. 633.
Hedeoma, II. 763.
Hedera, II. 649; III. 642; IV. 534.
Hedera, II. 504, 647, 648, 649, 650, 651,
  652; III. 641, 643.
Hederella, II. 637.
Hedgerows, III. 214.
Hedges, III. 212.
—— in tropical and subtropical coun-
  tries, III. 214.
Hedwigia, II. 418; III. 511.
Hedycaria, II. 222.
Hedycarpus, II. 486.
Hedyosmum, II. 95.
Hedyotis, II. 820, 825.
Hedysarum, II 363; III. 478.
Hedysarum, II. 331, 354, 369, 370, 388;
  III. 466.
Hedyscepe, II. 69.
Heeria, II. 456.
Heeria, II. 637.
Height of standing trees, IV. 215, 550.
—— of trees and shrubs, III. 204.
Heimia, II. 609; III. 629.
Heinsia, II. 819.
Heintzia, II. 793.
Heisteria, II. 171.
Helianthemum, II. 565.
Helianthemum, II. 565; III. 613.
Helianthostylis, II. 153.
Helichrysum, II. 858; III. 755.
Helichrysum, II. 859, 860, 863.
Helicia, II. 163.
Helicostylis, II. 153.
Helicteres, II. 534; III. 591.
Helictonema, II. 471.
Helietta, II. 407.
Heligme, II. 730.
Helinus, II. 495.
Heliocarpus, II. 514.
Heliophila, II. 234.
Heliotropism, I. 194, 527.
Heliotropium, II. 750; III. 695.
Helipterum, II. 859.
Helleria, II. 393.
Helmia, II. 90.
Helminthospermum, II. 142.
Helospora, II. 832.
Helwingia, II. 656.
Helygia, II. 730.
Hemecyclia, II. 445.
Hemiandra, II. 763; III. 697.
Hemiandrina, II. 316.
Hemichaena, II. 780.
Hemiclidia, II. 160.
Hemicyclia, II. 445.
Hemidesmus, III. 693.
Hemigenia, II. 763.
Hemigenia, II. 764.
Hemigymnia, II. 740.
Hemimeris, II. 779.
Hemiphractum, II. 561.
Hemiptelea, II. 142.
Hemistemma, II. 541.
Hemistephus, II. 541.
Hemistylis, II. 157.
Hemistylus, II. 157.
Hemizonia, II. 859; III. 755.
Hemprichia, II. 417.
Henfreya, II. 797; III. 709.
Henlea, II. 425, 831.
Henleophytum, II. 425.
Hennecartia, II. 222.
Henonia, II. 190.
Henricia, II. 859.
Henriettea, II. 637.
Henriettella, II. 637.
Henriquézia, II. 819.
Henrya, II. 804.
Henschelia, II. 228.
Henslowia, II. 168.
Henslowia, II. 610.

Heptaca, II. 540, 572.
Heptapleurum, II. 652.
Heptoneurum, II. 652.
Herbaceous grafting, III. 163.
Heredity, I. 248.
Heritiera, II. 535; III. 591.
Hermannia, II. 535; III. 591.
Hermbstaedtia, II. 190.
Hermesia, II. 436, 437.
Hermesias, II. 337.
Herminiera, II. 330; III. 466.
Hermandesia, II. 228.
Hernandia, II. 228, 872; III. 408.
Hernandiaceae, II. 228, 872; III. 408.
Herniaria, II. 194.
Herrania, II. 535; III. 591.
Herreria, II. 83.
Hertia, III. 755.
Herzegovina, forest description, IV. 374.
—— phytography, I. 447; V. xxiii.[1]
—— see also Austria-Hungary.
Hersogia, II. 406.
Hesperaloe, II. 83.
Hesperelaea, II. 709.
Hesperomannia, II. 859.
Hesperomeles, II. 264.
Hesse-Darmstadt, see Grand Duchy of
  Hesse.
Hesse-Nassau, see Prussia.
Heterapithmos, II. 869.
Heterocentron, II. 637; III. 638.
Heterochlamys, II. 446.
Heterocladus, II. 454.
Heterocroton, II. 439.
Heterodendrum, II. 486.
Heterolaena, II. 605.
Heterolepis, II. 859.
Heteromeles, II. 269.
Heteromorpha, II. 653.
Heteromeuron, II. 638.
Heteronoma, II. 636.
Heterophragma, II. 788.
Heterophyllaea, II. 819.
Heteropteris, II. 425; III. 513.
Heteropyxis, II. 874.
Heterosmilax, II. 83.
Heterospathe, III. 325.
Heterostemma, II. 739.
Heterostemon, II. 363.
Heterotrichum, II. 637.
Heudelotia, II. 417; III. 510.
Hevea, II. 445; III. 518.
Hewittia, II. 745.
Hexacentris, II. 804; III. 710.
Hexagonotheca, II. 512.
Hexalobus, II. 217.
Heyderia, III. 305; see also Libocedrus,
  II. 33.
Heynea, II. 423.
Heynichia, II. 422.
Hibbertia, II. 541; III. 595.
Hibiscus, II. 522; III. 587, 762.
Hibiscus, II. 525, 526.
Hicoria, II. 112; III. 353.
Hidalgoa, II. 859.
Hieronyma, II. 445.
Higginsia, II. 820.
High forest and clear cutting, IV. 129,
  545.
Hildebrandtia, II. 745.
Hillia, II. 820; III. 744.
Hillia, II. 718.
Hilsenbergia, II. 533.
Hindsia, II. 820; III. 744.
Hippia, II. 859.
Hippocastanaceae, II. 480; III. 536; IV.
  527.
Hippocratea, II. 471.
Hippocrateaceae, II. 471.
Hippodamia, II. 794.
Hippomane, II. 445; III. 519.
Hippophaë, II. 607; III. 629.
Hiptage, II. 426.
Hiraea, II. 426.

Hiraea, II. 425, 428.
Hirpicium, II. 859.
Hirtella, II. 264.
Hirtella, II. 265.
Hisingera, II. 574.
Histology, I. 123, 524; V. xi.[1]
History, I. 79, 523; III. 32, 757; IV. 23, 540; V. ix.[2]
—— of materia medica, III. 238.
Hitoa, II. 820.
Hitseria, II. 417.
Hocquartia, II. 181.
Hoepfneria, II. 322.
Hoffmannia, II. 820; III. 744.
Hoffmanseggia, II. 363.
Hofmeisteria, II. 859.
Hoheria, II. 524.
Hoitzia, II. 747.
Holacantha, II. 414.
Holalafia, II. 726.
Holarrhetia, II. 726; III. 688.
Holboellia, II. 201; III. 393.
Holigarna, II. 456; III. 524.
Holland, acclimatization, III. 46.
—— administration of private forests, IV. 309.
—— afforestation, IV. 159, 546.
—— bibliography, I. 3.
—— botanic gardens, I. 50, 521.
—— collections, III. 28, 757.
—— cultivation of exotic trees, IV. 126.
—— cultivation of fruit trees, III. 139.
—— dendrography, IV. 84.
—— descriptive botany, III. 75.
—— economic products, III. 270.
—— education, III. 32.
—— exhibitions, IV. 19, 540.
—— forest descriptions, IV. 356.
—— forest influences, IV. 47.
—— forest policy, IV. 274.
—— forest products, IV. 398.
—— forest protection, IV. 180.
—— forest schools, IV. 33.
—— history, I. 80; III. 33; IV. 27.
—— individual noteworthy trees, I. 296.
—— insects, IV. 208, 549.
—— manuals of arboriculture, III. 104.
—— measures promoting silviculture, IV. 40.
—— miscellaneous publications on arboriculture, III. 121.
—— miscellaneous publications on silviculture, IV. 119.
—— periodicals, I. 15, 520; III. 14, 757; IV. 12.
—— pharmacopoeias, III. 249.
—— phenology, I. 226.
—— phytography, I. 390, 532; V. xx.[1]
—— reproductive interrelations, *see* Europe, I. 239.
—— textbooks and manuals of silviculture, IV. 107.
—— timber trade, IV. 404.
—— vernacular names, I. 73; V. ix.[2]
—— viticulture, III. 553.
Hollandaea, II. 163.
Hollboellia, II. 201.
Hollrungia, II. 576.
Holmskioldia, II. 758.
Holochiloma, II. 760.
Holochilus, II. 702.
Holodiscus, II. 264; III. 424.
Hololachne, II. 562.
Holostemma, II. 738.
Homalanthus, II. 445; III. 519.
Homalium, II. 571, 873.
Homalocalyx, II. 627.
Homaloclados, II. 817.
Homalolepis, II. 415.
Hombronia, II. 56.
Homochaete, II. 859.
Homoianthus, II. 863.
Homonoia, II. 445.
Homonoya, II. 445.

Homostylium, II. 860.
Honckenya, II. 514; III. 585.
Honduras, *see* Central American Republics.
Honey-dew, I. 213.
Hongkong, botanic gardens, *see* China and Japan, I. 66.
—— history, *see* Asia, I. 81.
—— periodicals, *see* China and Japan, I. 28.
—— phytography, I. 460.
—— *see also* China.
Hoodia, II. 739; III. 693.
Hooibrenckia, III. 533.
Hoopesia, II. 345.
Hopea, II. 560; III. 611.
Hopea, II. 560, 703.
Hopkirkia, II. 864.
Hoplophyllum, II. 859.
Hormogyne, II. 700.
Hornemannia, II. 672.
Hornera, II. 869.
Hornschuchia, II. 218.
Hornschuchia, II. 554.
Horsfieldia, II. 220; III. 403.
Horsfieldia, II. 649; III. 642.
Horsfordia, II. 525.
Hortensia, II. 240; III. 411.
Hortia, II. 408.
Hortonia, II. 222.
Hosackia, II. 363.
Hoslundia, II. 763.
Hosta, II. 757.
Hostmannia, II. 544.
Hounea, II. 571.
House building, IV. 422.
Houstonia, II. 820; III. 744.
Houstonia, II. 810.
Hovea, II. 363; III. 478.
Hovenia, II. 495; III. 541.
Howardia, II. 827; III. 746.
Howea, II. 69; III. 325.
Hoya, II. 739; III. 693.
Hoya, II. 737, 742.
Hualania, II. 430.
Huberia, II. 637.
Hubertia, II. 864.
Hudsonia, II. 565; III. 613.
Hufelandia, II. 223.
Hugonia, II. 393.
Hulletia, II. 153.
Hulthemia, II. 281.
Humbertia, II. 745.
Humblotia, II. 445.
Humboldtia, II. 364.
Humea, II. 859.
Humidity, I. 232.
Humiria, II. 393; III. 492.
Humiriaceae, II. 393; III. 492.
Humirium, II. 393; III. 492.
Hungary, forest description, IV. 373.
—— phytography, I. 444, 536; V. xxiii.[1]
—— *see also* Austria-Hungary.
Huonia, II. 397.
Hura, II. 445; III. 519.
Huttia, II. 541.
Hyaenanche, II. 452; III. 522.
Hybanthera, II. 743.
Hybanthus, II. 567.
Hybridism, I. 245, 529.
Hybridization, improvement by, III. 50.
—— a a by, *see* Hybridism, I. 245, 529. ri tion
—— *see also* Reproductive interrelations, I. 236.
Hybrids, Graft, I. 246.
Hydathodes, *see* Stomata, I. 131, 525.
Hydnocarpus, II. 571; III. 614.
Hydnocarpus, II. 570.
Hydnophytum, II. 820; III. 744.
Hydrangea, II. 240; III. 411.
Hydristeele, II. 69.
Hydrocotyle, II. 653.

Hydrolea, II. 747.
Hydromestus, II. 797.
Hydrophyllaceae, II. 747; III. 695.
Hydrotropism, *see* Movements and Irritability, I. 193, 527.
Hyeronima, II. 445.
Hyeronyma, II. 445.
Hygrophila, II. 799.
Hymenaea, II. 364; III. 478.
Hymenaea, III. 489.
Hymenandra, II. 694.
Hymenanthera, II. 567; III. 614.
Hymenocalyx, II. 522.
Hymenocardia, II. 445.
Hymenoclea, II. 859.
Hymenocnemis, II. 820.
Hymenodictyon, II. 820; III. 744.
Hymenolobium, II. 378.
Hymenolophus, II. 727.
Hymenopyramis, II. 758.
Hymenosporum, II. 247; III. 416.
Hyophorbe, II. 69; III. 325.
Hyospathe, III. 325.
Hypelate, II. 486.
Hyperanthera, II. 234.
Hyperbaena, II. 207.
Hypericum, II. 555; III. 609.
Hypericum, II. 548, 553, 554, 703; III. 609.
Hypertrophism, I. 213, 528.
Hyperum, II. 392.
Hyphaene, II. 69; III. 325.
Hypobathrum, II. 820.
Hypocalymma, II. 627; III. 635.
Hypocalyptus, II. 364.
Hypocalyptus, II. 378.
Hypocyrta, II. 794.
Hypoëstes, II. 800.
Hypophyllanthus, II. 406, 534.
Hypopogon, II. 703.
Hypopterygium, *see* Julianiaceae, II. 114.
Hypothronia, II. 763.
Hypserpa, II. 207.
Hypserpa, II. 207.
Hysophila, II. 469.
Hyptianthera, III. 826.
Hyptis, II. 763.
Hyssopus, II. 763.
Hysterionica, II. 859.

Ibatia, II. 740.
Ibbetsonia, II. 349.
Iberian Peninsula, acclimatization, III. 49.
—— bibliography, I. 3.
—— botanic gardens, I. 60, 522.
—— cultivation of fruit trees, III. 145.
—— dendrography, IV. 85, 544.
—— descriptive botany, III. 88.
—— economic products, III. 271.
—— forest influences, IV. 47, 542.
—— forest management, IV. 249, 550.
—— galls, I. 216.
—— history, I. 81.
—— i a noteworthy trees, I. 292nd vidu l
—— manuals of arboriculture, III. 114.
—— miscellaneous publications on arboriculture, III. 126.
—— periodicals, I. 24; III. 23.
—— phenology, I. 226.
—— phytography, I. 419, 535; V. xxii.[1]
—— reproductive interrelations, *see* Europe, I. 239.
—— vernacular names, I. 74.
—— viticulture, III. 558.
—— *see also* Portugal and Spain.
Iboga, III. 733.
Icacina, II. 474.
Icacinaceae, II. 474; III. 533.
Iacorea, II. 692.
Iceland, *see* Scandinavia.
Ichnocarpus, II. 727; III. 688.
Ichthyomethia, II. 377; III. 484.

Icica, II. 418; III. 511.
Icosandra, II. 225.
Idaho, *see* United States, Western.
Idesia, II. 571; III. 614.
Idria, II. 563.
Ignatia, II. 719; III. 682.
Ilex, II. 462; III. 529.
Ilex, II. 469, 614.
Ilicineae, see Aquifoliaceae.
Illicium, II. 209; III. 397.
Illigera, II. 228.
Illinois, *see* United States, Northeastern.
Illipe, II. 698; III. 667; IV. 534.
Illuminating gas, IV. 433, 558.
Illustrating, I. 37, 521.
Imantina, II. 823.
Imbricaria, II. 699.
Improvement by hybridization, III. 50.
Incarvillea, II. 788.
Increase of wood and bark, I. 189, 527.
Increment, IV. 232, 550.
—— determination of, IV. 232, 550.
—— influence of thinning on, IV. 175.
India, *see* British India.
Indian Ocean Islands, afforestation, IV. 168.
—— botanic gardens, I. 68.
—— descriptive botany, III. 93.
—— economic products, III. 279.
—— forest description, IV. 378.
—— forest devastation, IV. 283.
—— forest influences, IV. 49.
—— forest laws, IV. 332.
—— periodicals, III. 26; *see also* Mauritius, I. 29.
—— phytography, I. 481, 536.
—— a forest administration, IV. 293st te
Indiana, *see* United States, Northeastern.
India-rubber, *see* Gutta percha, III. 228.
Indigofera, II. 364; III. 478.
Indigofera, II. 381.
Individual noteworthy trees, I. 295, 531; V. xvi.¹
Indochina, botanic gardens, *see* Cochinchina, I. 66.
—— dendrography, IV. 88.
—— descriptive botany, III. 92.
—— economic products, III. 276.
—— forest description, IV. 377.
—— forest products, IV. 400.
—— miscellaneous publications on arboriculture, III. 129.
—— periodicals, III. 26.
—— phytography, I. 469, 535.
Indovethia, II. 544.
Inflorescence, I. 113.
Influence, forest, IV. 42, 541.
—— of thinning on increment, IV. 175.
Infusions, III. 221.
Inga, II. 365
Inga, II. 330, 340, 377; III. 469, 483.
Injuries caused by animals, III. 186; IV. 196, 548.
—— caused by birds, IV. 198.
—— caused by climatic influences, IV. 188; V. xxx.¹
—— a by drought, III. 183; IV. 192½ used
—— caused by frost, III. 181; IV. 191, 548; V. xxx.¹
—— caused by game, IV. 196.
—— caused by gases, III. 185; IV. 192, 548.
—— caused by grazing animals, III. 186; IV. 197, 548.
—— caused by hail, III. 184; IV. 189, 548.
—— caused by heat, IV. 192.
—— caused by heat and insolation, IV. 184.
—— caused by insects, III. 186, 757; IV. 199, 548; V. xxxi.¹
—— caused by lightning, IV. 193, 548.

Injuries caused by man, IV. 196, 548.
—— caused by meteoric influences, IV. 188, 548; V. xxx.²
—— caused by plants, III. 193; IV. 550.
—— caused by rain, III. 184; IV. 189, 548.
—— caused by rime, III. 184; IV. 189, 548.
—— caused by rodents, III. 186; IV. 197, 548.
—— caused by smoke, III. 185; IV. 192, 548.
—— caused by snow, III. 184; IV. 189, 548.
—— caused by vascular plants, IV. 210.
—— caused by water, III. 185.
—— caused by wind, III. 184; IV. 188, 548.
—— of street trees, III. 212.
—— prevention of, III. 196.
—— *see also* Diseases and injuries, *and* Wounds and mutilations.
Inocarpus, II. 366; III. 479.
Inodaphnis, II. 366.
Inscriptions in trees, I. 210, 528; V. xii.¹
Insects, IV. 91, 544, 549.
—— diseases and injuries caused by, III. 186; IV. 199, 548.
—— timber attacked by, IV. 414, 557.
—— *see also* Interrelations with the animal kingdom, I. 234, Myrmecophilism, I. 235, *and* Reproductive interrelations, I. 236, 529.
Insolation, injuries, caused by, III. 184.
Institutions, botanical, *see* Botanic gardens, etc., I. 38, 521.
Instruments of measurement, IV. 231.
Insurance, of employees, IV. 310, 554.
—— of forests, IV. 284, 552.
Interrelations with animals, I. 234.
Interrelations of employees, IV. 310, 554.
Introduction by man, I. 241; V. xii.²
Introduction of trees and shrubs, *see* Acclimatization, III. 43.
Introductory publications, dendrology, I. 79, 522; V. ix;² *see also* Auxiliary and introductory publications.
Intsia, II. 366; IV. 521.
Intsia, II. 330.
Inula, II. 859.
Inundation, IV. 184, 547.
Iochroma, II. 772; III. 700.
Iodes, II. 475.
Iodina, II. 168.
Ioedes, II. 475.
Ionidium, II. 567.
Iowa, *see* United States, Western.
Iozylon, II. 153.
Iphiona, II. 859.
Ipomoea, II. 745; III. 694.
Ipomoea, II. 744
Ireland, forest descriptions, IV. 359, 556.
—— *see also* British Islands.
Iresine, II. 190; III. 388.
Iriartea, II. 69; III. 325.
Irina, II. 488.
Irmischia, II. 740.
Irrigation, III. 150; IV. 144.
—— of street trees, III. 211.
Irritability, I. 193, 197, 527.
Irvingia, II. 414; III. 508.
Iryanthera, II. 220.
Isertia, II. 820.
Isodendrion, II. 567.
Isoloma, II. 794.
Isomeris, II. 233; III. 409.
Isonandra, II. 698.
Isonandra, II. 698, 699; III. 668.
Isonema, II. 727.
Isopogon, II. 163; III. 383.
Isoptera, III. 560; III. 611.
Isora, II. 534.
Isotrema, II. 181.
Isotropis, II. 366; III. 479.

Isotypus, II. 862.
Italy, acclimatization, III. 49.
—— administration of private forests, IV. 309.
—— afforestation, IV. 165.
—— arbor day, IV. 42.
—— bibliography, I. 4.
—— botanic gardens, I. 60, 522; V. viii.²
—— collections, III. 29.
—— cultivation of exotic trees, IV. 127.
—— cultivation of fruit trees, III. 145.
—— dendrography, IV. 86.
—— descriptive botany, III. 88.
—— economic products, III. 271.
—— erosion, IV. 186.
—— exhibitions, IV. 20.
—— forest descriptions, IV. 363.
—— forest devastation, IV. 283.
—— forest fires, IV. 183.
—— forest gardens, IV. 18.
—— forest influences, IV. 47.
—— forest laws, IV. 327.
—— forest management, IV. 249.
—— forest officers and employees, IV. 311.
—— forest policy, IV. 276.
—— forest products, IV. 399.
—— forest protection, IV. 181; V. xxx.²
—— forest regulations, IV. 304.
—— forest schools, IV. 35, 541.
—— forest servitudes, IV. 334.
—— galls, I. 215.
—— history, I. 81; III. 33; IV. 28.
—— individual trees, I. 297.
—— insects, IV. 209.
—— manuals of arboriculture, III. 114.
—— measures promoting silviculture, IV. 41, 541.
—— miscellaneous publications on arboriculture, III. 126.
—— miscellaneous publications on silviculture, IV. 122.
—— pharmacopoeias, III.-256.
—— phenology, I. 226.
—— phytography, I. 423, 535; V. xxii.²
—— reproductive interrelations, *see* Europe, I. 239.
—— silviculture and pasturing, IV. 135.
—— state forest administration, IV. 293.
—— state supervision of forests, IV. 286.
—— taxes, tariffs, etc., IV. 285.
—— textbooks and manuals of forestry, IV. 99.
—— textbooks and manuals of silviculture, IV. 109.
—— timber trade, IV. 405.
—— vernacular names, I. 74.
—— viticulture, III. 557.
Itea, II. 241; III. 412.
Itea, II. 462.
Iva, II. 859.
Ixerba, II. 241.
Ixianthes, II. 780; III. 702.
Izionanthes, II. 393.
Ixonanthes, III. 393.
Ixodia, II. 859.
Ixora, II. 820; III. 745.
Ixorhea, II. 751.

Jacaranda, II. 788; III. 706.
Jacaratia, II. 582.
Jackia, II. 821.
Jackia, II. 432.
Jacksonia, II. 366.
Jacobinia, II. 800; III. 709.
Jacquemontia, II. 746.
Jacquinia, II. 691; III. 665.
Jacquinia, III. 665.

Jamaica, *see* West Indian Islands.
Jambolifera, II. 397, 625.
Jambosa, II. 627; III. 635.
Jambosa, II. 625.
Jamesia, II. 241; III. 413.
Janipha, II. 447; III. 520.
Jansonia, II. 366.
Janusia, II. 426.
Japan, afforestation, IV. 168.
—— arbor day, IV. 42.
—— bibliography, *see* Asia, I. 4.
—— botanic gardens, I. 66.
—— cultivation of fruit trees, III. 147.
—— dendrography, IV. 87.
—— descriptive botany, III. 91.
—— economic products, III. 273.
—— exhibitions, IV. 21, 540.
—— forest description, IV. 376.
—— forest products, IV. 399.
—— history, *see* Asia, I. 81.
—— individual noteworthy trees, *see* Asia, I. 298.
—— miscellaneous publications on arboriculture, III. 127.
—— periodicals, I. 28; III. 26; IV. 16, 539.
—— pharmacopoeias, III. 256.
—— phytography, I. 461; V. xxiii.²
—— tea cultivation, III. 601.
—— vernacular names, I. 75; V. ix.²
Jaracatia, II. 582.
Jasminum, II. 709; III. 672.
Jateorhiza, II. 207; III. 397.
Jatropha, II. 445; III. 519.
Jatropha, II. 447; III. 514, 520.
Jatrorrhiza, II. 207.
Jaundea, II. 317.
Java, botanic gardens, I. 67, 522; V. ix.¹
—— cinchona cultivation, III. 715.
—— dendrography, IV. 88.
—— economic products, III. 275.
—— forest devastation, IV. 283.
—— phytography, I. 457; V. xxiii.²
—— *see also* Malay Archipelago.
Jenkinsia, II. 475.
Jenkinsonia, II. 389.
Joanessia, *see* Joannesia.
Joannea, II. 854.
Joannesia, II. 446; *see also* Joanessia, III. 520.
Johanesia, II. 446.
Johannia, II. 854.
Joiners' wood, IV. 426.
Jollydora, II. 317.
Jonesia, II. 383; III. 487.
Jonidiopsis, II. 567.
Joosia, II. 821.
Josinia, II. 625; III. 635.
Jovellana, II. 780.
Jovellana, II. 782.
Juan Fernandez, economic products, III. 283.
—— *see also* Society Islands, etc.
Juania, II. 69; III. 326.
Juanulloa, II. 772; III. 700.
Juanulloa, II. 771.
Jubaes, II. 69; III. 326.
Jubelina, II. 426.
Jucunda, II. 640.
Juglandaceae, II. 111, 871; III. 353; IV. 488; V. xxvi.¹
Juglans, II. 112, 871; III. 354; IV. 488; V. xxvi.¹
Juglans, II. 112.
Juliania, *see* Julianiaceae, II. 114.
Juliania, II. 400.
Julianiaceae, II. 114.
Julocroton, II. 446.
Julostyles, II. 525.
Juncaceae, II. 77.
Jungia, II. 859.
Juniperus, II. 30, 871; III. 303; IV. 448, 558; V. xxviii.²
Jurgensenia, II. 661.

Jussiaea, II. 645.
Jussieua, II. 645.
Justicia, II. 800; III. 709.
Justicia, II. 797, 798, 799, 800, 801, 802, 803, 804; III. 709.

Kadsura, II. 210; III. 398.
Kadua, II. 821.
Kageneckia, II. 265.
Kakosmanthus, II. 699.
Kalanchoe, II. 236; III. 409.
Kaleniczenkia, II. 337.
Kaliphora, II. 656.
Kalmia, II. 672; III. 652.
Kalopanax, II. 647.
Kamptzia, II. 633.
Kanahia, II. 740.
Kandelia, II. 613.
Kansas, *see* United States, Western.
Karlea, II. 495.
Karwinskia, II. 495.
Kayea, II. 557.
Kellaua, II. 702.
Kelleria, II. 603.
Kelleria, III. 395.
Kelletia, II. 573.
Kendrickia, III. 638.
Kennedya, II. 366; III. 479.
Kennedya, II. 341.
Kentia, II. 69; III. 326; V. xxvi.¹
Kentia, II. 68, 69; III. 325, 326.
Kentiopsis, II. 69; III. 326.
Kentucky, *see* United States, South-eastern.
Keratophorus, II. 699.
Keraudrenia, II. 535.
Kerguelen Island, *see* Indian Ocean Islands.
Kermadec Islands, *see* New Zealand.
Kermadecia, II. 163.
Kerria, II. 265; III. 424.
Keteleeria, II. 32; III. 304.
Khaya, II. 421; III. 512.
Kibara, II. 222, 872.
Kibara, II. 222.
Kibessia, II. 637.
Kickxia, II. 727; III. 688.
Kielmeyera, II. 557.
Kiesera, II. 386.
Kigelia, II. 789; III. 707.
Kiggelaria, II. 572; III. 614.
King Island, *see* Tasmania.
Kingia, II. 83.
Kingsboroughia, II. 490.
Kippistia, II. 860.
Kirpanelia, II. 449.
Kirkia, II. 414.
Kissodendron, II. 650.
Klainedoxa, II. 414.
Kleinhovia, II. 535; IH. 591.
Kleinia, II. 864.
Knema, II. 220.
Knightia, II. 163.
Knoxia, II. 822.
Kochia, II. 188; III. 387.
Koeberlinia, II. 566.
Koeberliniaceae, II. 566.
Koellea, II. 765.
Koelreuteria, II. 487; III. 539.
Kohleria, II. 794.
Kokoona, II. 469; III. 533.
Kokoschkinia, II. 791.
Kolbia, II. 576.
Kolomikta, II. 540.
Koniga, II. 234.
Kookia, II. 403.
Koompassia, II. 367.
Koordersiodendron, II. 456.
Kopsia, II. 727; III. 688.
Kordelestris, II. 788.
Korea, phytography, I. 461.
Korthalsella, II. 174.
Korthalsia, II. 70.
Kosteletzkya, II. 525. ¿

Kotschya, II. 384.
Kowalewskia, II. 657.
Krameria, II. 367; III. 480.
Kraunhia, II. 388.
Kraussia, II. 832.
Krugia, II. 628.
Kuala, II. 406.
Kuestera, II. 798.
Kuhlia, II. 569, 718.
Kunthia, III. 321.
Kunzea, II. 628; III. 636.
Kunzia, II. 278.
Kurria, II. 820.
Kurrimia, II. 469.
Kydia, II. 525.
Kydia, II. 525.

Labatia, II. 698.
Labatia, II. 700.
Labiatae, II. 762; III. 697.
Labichea, II. 368.
Labisia, II. 694; III. 666.
Lablab, II. 368.
Lablabia, II. 368.
Laboratory technique, I. 36, 521; V. viii.¹
Labordia, II. 719.
Laboucheria, II. 358.
Labourdonnaisia, II. 698.
Laburnum, II. 368; III. 480; IV. 521.
Lac, III. 232.
Lacathea, II. 548.
Lacepedea, III. 473.
Lachanodes, II. 864.
Lachnaea, II. 604.
Lachnocapsa, II. 234.
Lachnocephalus, II. 759.
Lachnopetalum, II. 487.
Lachnopylis, II. 719.
Lachnosiphonium, II. 829.
Lachnostachys, II. 758.
Lachnostoma, II. 814.
Lachnostylis, II. 446.
Lacistema, II. 95.
Lacistemaceae, II. 95.
Lacmellia, II. 727.
Lactaria, II. 729.
Lactoridaceae, II. 215.
Lactoris, *see* Lactoridaceae, II. 215.
Ladenbergia, II. 822; III. 745.
Ladoicea, II. 70.
Laetia, II. 572; III. 614.
Lagascea, II. 859.
Lagenanthus, II. 721.
Lagerstroemia, II. 609; III. 629; IV. 529.
Lagerstroemia, II. 610.
Lagetta, II. 604; III. 628.
Lagetta, II. 602.
Laggera, II. 863.
Lagonychium, II. 379.
Laguna, II. 522, 525.
Lagunaea, II. 525.
Lagunaria, II. 525.
Laguncularia, II. 617.
Lalage, II. 336; III. 467.
Lamarchea, II. 628.
Lamarckia, II. 773.
Lambertia, II. 163.
Lamellisepaluin, II. 495.
Lamourouxia, II. 780; III. 703.
Lampaya, II. 758.
Lamprolobium, II. 369.
Lamprothamnus, II. 822.
Landolphia, II. 727; III. 688.
Landscape effect, IV. 136, 545.
Landscape gardening, *see* Ornamental uses and properties of trees and shrubs, III. 201.
Land-slides, IV. 184, 547.
Land surveying, *see* Geodesy, IV. 263.
Laneasagum, II. 440.
Lanessania, II. 153.
Langsdorfia, II. 411.
Lankesteria, II. 801.
Lannea, II. 456; III. 524.

Lanneoma, II. 456.
Lansium, II. 421; III. 512.
Lantana, II. 758; III. 696; IV. 536.
Lantana, II. 758.
Lanthorus, II. 175.
Lapageria, II. 84; III. 337.
Lapathum, II. 186.
Laplacea, II. 549.
Laportea, II. 157; III. 382.
Lardizabala, II. 201; III. 393.
Lardizabalaceae, II. 200; III. 393.
Larix, II. 82, 871; III. 304, 758; IV. 448, 558.
Larix, II. 49; III. 309.
Larochea, II. 236.
Larrea, II. 395; III. 494.
Larrea, II. 363.
Laseguea, II. 727.
Lasiadenia, II. 604.
Lasiandra, II. 641; III. 639.
Lasianthera, II. 475.
Lasianthus, II. 822.
Lasiobema, II. 334.
Lasiocarpus, II. 426.
Lasiococca, II. 446.
Lasiocorys, II. 764.
Lasiodiscus, II. 495.
Lasionema, II. 822.
Lasiopetalum, II. 535.
Lasiopetalum, II. 537, 539.
Lasiosiphon, II. 603.
Lasiostemum, II. 405.
Lasiostoma, II. 719, 820; III 682.
Lasiostyles, II. 438.
Lassonia, II. 210.
Latania, II. 70; III. 326.
Latania, II. 70; III. 326.
Latex, physiology, I. 181, 526.
Latex cells, morphology, I. 135,·525.
Latua, II. 772; III. 700.
Laugeria, II. 822.
Laugeria, II. 809.
Launaea, II. 860.
Lauraceae, II. 222, 872; III. 403; IV. 520.
Laurelia, II. 222.
Laurencellia, III. 755.
Laureria, II. 772.
Lauridia, II. 470.
Laurineae, see Lauraceae, II. 222.
Laurocerasus, II. 270; III. 430.
Laurophyllus, II. 456.
Laurus, II. 223; III. 406; IV. 520.
Laurus, II. 223, 224, 225, 226, 227, 228; III. 403, 404, 407.
Lavalleopsis, II. 171.
Lavandula, II. 764; III. 697.
Lavatera, II. 525; III. 588.
Lavoisiera, II. 638.
Lawrencella, II. 858.
Laws relating to arboriculture, III. 200.
Lawsonia, II. 609; III. 629.
Layers, III. 159.
Layia, II. 375.
Leandra, II. 638.
Leaf, fall, I. 191; V. xII.[1]
—— , see Photosynthesis, I. 172—function.
—— growth, I. 190.
—— morphology and anatomy, I. 109.
—— teratology, I. 144.
Leaves, autumnal coloration, I. 185, 526; III. 207; V. xII.[1]
—— propagation by, III. 159.
Lebeckia, II. 360.
Lebeckia, II. 364.
Lebetanthus, II. 689.
Lebidieropsis, III. 520.
Lebretonia, II. 526.
Lecananthus, II. 822.
Lecanosperma, II. 822.
Lechea, II. 565.
Lechenaultia, II. 847.
Lecocarpus, II. 860.

Lecontea, II. 825.
Lecostemon, II. 265.
Lecythidaceae, II. 611; III. 631; IV. 529.
Lecythis, II. 612; III. 631; IV. 529.
Lecythopsis, II. 612.
Ledenbergia, II. 193.
Ledocarpum, II. 389.
Ledonia, II. 563.
Ledothamnus, II. 672.
Ledum, II. 672; HI. 652.
Ledum, II. 673.
Leea, II. 503, 873; III. 544.
Legislation, see Forest laws, IV. 313.
Leguminosae, II. 318, 872; III. 462, 758; IV. 520; V. xxvi,[3] xxix,[1] xxxii.[2]
Leianthus, II. 721.
Leichhardtia, H. 740.
Leioclusia, II. 557.
Leiophyllum, II. 673; III. 653.
Leiothamnus, II. 721.
Leitneriaceae, II. 111; III. 353.
Lembotropis, II. 349.
Lemonia, II. 410; III. 505.
Lencymmaea, II. 869.
Lenidia, II. 543.
Lennea, II. 369; III. 481.
Lenticels, I. 132, 525.
Lentiscus, II. 457.
Leonhardia, II. 387.
Leonia, II. 567.
Leonia, II. 476.
Leonotis, II. 764; III. 698.
Leopoldinia, II. 70; III. 326.
Lepargyraea, II. 608.
Lepidadenia, II. 226; III. 406.
Lepidagathis, II. 801.
Lepidanthus, II. 436.
Lepidium, II. 234.
Lepidocarpa, II. 269.
Lepidocaryum, II. 70.
Lepidoceras, II. 175.
Lepidopetala, II. 453.
Lepidopetalum, II. 487.
Lepidophyllum, II. 860.
Lepidospartum, II. 860.
Lepidostachys, II. 437.
Lepidostemon, II. 781.
Lepidothamnus, see Dacrydium, II. 8.
Lepidoturus, II. 446.
Lepidosamia, II. 6.
Lepinia, II. 727.
Lepinionsis, II. 727.
Lepionorus, II. 170.
Lepipogon, II. 822.
Lepisanthes, II. 487.
Lepismium, II. 598.
Lepistemon, II. 746.
Leptactina, II. 822; III. 745.
Leptadenia, II 740
Leptaulus, II. 475.
Leptochlaena, II. 511.
Leptoclados, II. 719.
Leptoclinium, II. 857.
Leptodactylon, II. 747; III. 694.
Leptodermis, II. 822; III. 745.
Leptogonum, II. 185.
Leptolaena, II. 511.
Leptomeria, II. 168.
Leptonema, II. 444.
Leptonium, II. 170.
Leptonychia, II. 536.
Leptopetalum, II. 825.
Leptosema, II. 337.
Leptospermum, II. 628; III. 636.
Leptospermum, II. 620, 628.
Leptostachya, II. 800.
Lepurandra, III. 366.
Leschenaultia, II. 847; III. 754.
Lespedeza, II. 369; III. 481.
Lessertia, II. 369.
Lestibudesia, II. 189.
Lethedon, II. 226.

Lettsomia, II. 548.
Leucadendron, II. 164; III. 383.
Leucadendron, II. 164, 165.
Leucaena, II. 369; III. 481.
Leucas, II. 764.
Leucaster, II. 191.
Leuchtenbergia, II. 594; III. 623.
Leucocarpum, II. 467.
Leucocodon, II. 822.
Leucocroton, II. 446.
Leucomeris, II. 860.
Leucomphalos, II. 369.
Leuconotis, II. 727.
Leucophae, II. 766.
Leucopholis, II. 860.
Leucophyllum, II. 780.
Leucophyta, II. 854.
Leucopogon, II. 689; III. 665.
Leucosalpa, II. 780.
Leucosceptrum, II. 764.
Leucoria, II. 432.
Leucosidea, II. 265.
Leucœmia, II. 604.
Leucospermum, II. 164.
Leucosphaera, II. 190.
Leucosyke, II. 157.
Leucothamnus, II. 539; III. 595.
Leucothoë, II. 673; III. 653.
Leucothoë, II. 659, 675.
Leunisia, II. 860.
Lezarza, II. 531.
Leycesteria, II. 835; III. 749.
Leyssera, II. 860; III. 755.
Lhotskya, II. 629.
Liabum, II. 860.
Liatris, II. 857.
Libanothamnus, II. 856.
Liberia, see West Africa.
Libocedrus, II. 33; III. 305; IV. 452.
Libonia, II. 800; III. 709.
Licania, II. 265.
Licaria, III. 406.
Lichtensteinia, II. 175.
Licuala, II. 70; III. 326.
Licutautia, II. 640.
Light, ecology, I. 229.
Light requirement, IV. 67, 543.
—— mixed woods in regard to, IV. 138.
Lightning, injuries caused by, IV. 193, 548.
Lightfootia, II. 845.
Lightfootia, II. 572.
Lightia, II. 428.
Ligularia, II. 389.
Ligustrina, II. 714; III. 680.
Ligustrum, II. 711; III. 673.
Ligustrum, III. 697.
Lijndenia, II. 638.
Lilac, II. 714.
Liliaceae, II. 77; III. 333; IV. 485; V. xxvi.[1]
Limacia, II. 207.
Limacia, II. 207, 208.
Limonia, II. 408.
Limonia, II. 399, 407, 411; III. 495, 506.
Limoniastrum, II. 696.
Linaceae, II. 392; III. 492.
Lindackeria, II. 572.
Lindenia, II. 822; III. 745.
Linders, II. 225; III. 406.
Lindleya, II. 265; III. 425.
Linkia, II. 165.
Linnaea, II. 835; III. 749.
Linociera, II. 712.
Linodendron, II. 604.
Linospadix, II. 70; III. 326.
Linospadix, II. 65.
Linostoma, II. 604.
Linosyris, II. 853.
Linschotenia, II. 846.
Linum, II. 393; III. 492.
Linum, II. 393.
Liparia, II. 370.
Liparia, II. 379.

Liparis monacha, IV. 200, 548.
Lipochaete, II. 860.
Lippia, II. 758; III. 697.
Lippia, II. 753; III. 696.
Liquidambar, II. 253; III. 417; IV. 520.
Liquidambar, II. 252; III. 416; IV. 520.
Liquids, see Fluids.
Lirayea, II. 796.
Liriodendron, II. 210; III. 398; IV. 519.
Lirioema, II. 171; III. 384.
Lisianthus, II. 721; III. 685.
Lissanthe, II. 690.
Lissanthe, II. 688; III. 665.
Lissocarpa, II. 704.
Litchi, II. 487; III. 539.
Literature, plants in, I. 514, 535.
—— see also Bibliography.
Lithocarpus, II. 128.
Lithosanthes, II. 822.
Lithospermum, II. 751; III. 695.
Lithoxylon, II. 435.
Lithraea, II. 456.
Lithraea, II. 458.
Litosanthes, II. 822.
Litrea, II. 456.
Litsaea, II. 226.
Litsea, II. 226, 872; III. 406; IV. 520.
Livistona, II. 70; III. 326.
Livistona, II. 73, 74; III. 330.
Llagunoa, II. 487.
Llanosia, II. 550.
Llavea, II. 869.
Llerasia, II. 867.
Loasaceae, II. 583.
Lobadium, II. 458.
Lobbia, II. 183.
Lobelia, II. 845; III. 754.
Lobelia, II. 845, 846.
Lobostemon, II. 751.
Lobularia, II. 234.
Locellaria, II. 334.
Lochnera, II. 728.
Loddigesia, II. 370.
Lodoicea, II. 70; III. 327.
Lodoicea, II. 72.
Lbeselia, II. 747.
Loevigia, II. 640.
Loewia, II. 574.
Logania, II. 719.
Loganiaceae, II. 716, 874; III. 681; IV. 536.
Logging, see Felling, IV. 383, and Transportation, IV. 388.
Loiseleuria, II. 673.
Lomatia, II. 164; III. 383.
Lomatophyllum, II. 84.
Lonchocarpus, II. 370; III. 481.
Lonchostoma, II. 251.
Longetia, II. 446.
Longevity of trees, see Age, I. 193, 527.
Lonicera, II. 835; III. 749; V. xxvii.[2]
Lonicera, II. 810, 834, 835.
Lopezia, II. 645; III. 640.
Lopholaena, II. 860.
Lophopappus, II. 860.
Lophopetalum, II. 470.
Lophopetalum, II. 467.
Lophophora, III. 620.
Lophopyxis, II. 475.
Lophospermum, II. 780, 782; III. 703.
Lophostylis, II. 432.
Lophozonia, II. 127.
Lopimia, II. 526.
Lopping, IV. 172; see also Pollarding, III. 173.
Loranthaceae, II. 172, 872; III. 385; IV. 519; V. xxvi.[1]
Loranthus, II. 175, 872; III. 385.
Lord Howe Island, phytography, I. 508.
Lorenzanea, II. 490.
Loreya, II. 638.
Loricaria, II. 867.
Loropetalum, II. 253; III. 418.
Lotononis, II. 370.

Lotus, II. 370; III. 481.
Loudonia, II. 646.
Louisiana, see United States, Southeastern.
Lourea, II. 370.
Loureira, II. 445.
Louteridium, II. 801.
Low Archipelago, phytography, I. 510.
Lowea, II. 281.
Loxococcus, II. 71.
Loxodiscus, II. 487.
Loxopterygium, IV. 526.
Lozopterygium, II. 460; III. 529.
Loxostylis, II. 456.
Loyalty islands, phytography, I. 508.
Losania, II. 95.
Lucinaea, II. 822.
Luculia, II. 822; III. 745.
Lucuma, II. 698; III. 667.
Lucuma, II. 700.
Ludia, II. 572.
Ludolfia, II. 68.
Ludovia, II. 76; III. 332.
Ludovia, II. 76.
Luehea, II. 514.
Luehea, II. 760.
Luetkea, II. 265.
Lugonia, II. 740.
Luma, II. 631.
Lumber trade journals, see Periodicals, IV. 3.
Lumbering, forest exploitation, IV. 383, 556; V. xxxi.[2]
Lumnitzera, II. 617; IV. 529.
Lunania, II. 572.
Lunasia, II. 408; III. 504.
Lundia, II. 789; III. 707.
Lundia, II. 785.
Lupinus, II. 270; III. 481.
Luvunga, II. 408; III. 504.
Luxemburg, acclimatization, III. 46.
—— afforestation, IV. 160, 546.
—— cultivation of fruit trees, III. 140.
—— dendrography, IV. 84.
—— descriptive botany, III. 77.
—— forest descriptions, IV. 357.
—— forest laws, IV. 323.
—— individual noteworthy trees, I. 296.
—— periodicals, I. 15.
—— phytography, I. 391, 532.
—— vernacular names, I. 73.
—— see also Belgium.
Luxemburgia, II. 544.
Lychnophora, II. 860.
Lycioplesium, II. 768, 772; III. 700.
Lycium, II. 772; III. 700.
Lycium, II. 747, 768, 772, 774, 827, 831.
Lycoseris, II. 860.
Lygisma, II. 740.
Lygodisodea, II. 825.
Lyonia, II. 673; III. 653.
Lyonothamnus, II. 265.
Lyonsia, II. 728.
Lyperia, II. 780; III. 702.
Lysicarpus, II. 629.
Lysidice, II. 370.
Lysiloma, II. 370; III. 481; IV. 521.
Lysimachia, II. 695.
Lysimachiopsis, II. 695.
Lysinema, II. 690; III. 665.
Lysionotus, II. 792.
Lysiostyles, II. 746.
Lytanthus, II. 795.
Lythophilum, II. 869.
Lythraceae, II. 608; III. 629; IV. 529.
Lythrum, II. 609.

Maackia, II. 346; III. 472.
Maba, II. 700.
Mabea, II. 446.
Macadamia, II. 164; III. 383.
Macaglia, II. 724.
Macairea, II. 638.

Macaranga, II. 446; III. 520.
Macarisia, II. 613.
Macarthuria, II. 193.
Macfadyena, II. 789.
Macfadyena, II. 790.
Macfadyenia, II. 803.
Machaerium, II. 370.
Machaerium, II. 387; III. 489.
Machaonia, II. 822.
Machilus, II. 226; III. 407.
Machinery, wood for, IV. 427.
—— and tools used in silviculture, IV. 176.
Mackaya, II. 801; III. 709.
Mackaya, II. 171.
Macleania, II. 673; III. 653.
MacLeayia, II. 342.
Maclura, II. 153; III. 372; IV. 519.
Maclura, II. 147, 148.
Macnemaraea, II. 869.
Macowania, II. 860.
Macphersonia, II. 487.
Macquarie Islands, see New Zealand, I. 508.
Macraea, II. 392, 860.
Macranthosiphon, II. 789.
Macreightia, II. 702.
Macria, II. 748.
Macrocarpaea, II. 721.
Macroceratides, II. 373.
Macrocnemum, II. 822; III. 745.
Macrocnemum, II. 810, 823, 833; III. 743.
Macrocymbium, II. 356.
Macrodendron, II. 547.
Macrodiscus, II. 789.
Macrolobium, II. 371, 873.
Macrolobium, II. 330.
Macromiscus, II. 330.
Macropanax, II. 650.
Macropeplus, II. 222.
Macropiper, II. 93.
Macropodandra, II. 453.
Macrorhamnus, II. 491.
Macroscepis, II. 740.
Macrosiphon, II. 820.
Macrosphyra, II. 823.
Macrostegia, II. 605.
Macrostigma, II. 316.
Macrostylis, II. 408.
Macrozamia, II. 6; III. 285.
Macuna, II. 373.
Madagascar, afforestation, IV. 547.
—— dendrography, IV. 89.
—— descriptive botany, III. 93.
—— economic products, III. 281.
—— forest description, IV. 380, 556.
—— forest laws, IV. 332.
—— forest policy, IV. 280.
—— forest products, IV. 401.
—— miscellaneous publications on arboriculture, III. 131.
—— periodicals, I. 29.
—— phytography, I. 496; V. xxiv.[1]
—— reproductive interrelations, see Africa, I. 240.
—— state forest administration, IV. 295, 554.
Madarosperma, II. 740.
Maddenia, II. 265.
Madeira, forest description, IV. 380.
—— forest devastation, IV. 283.
—— miscellaneous publications on arboriculture, III. 131.
—— phenology, see Atlantic Islands, I. 228.
—— phytography, I. 496; V. xxiv.[2]
—— vernacular names, I. 76.
—— see also Atlantic Islands.
Madhuca, II. 698; III. 667.
Maerua, II. 233.
Macas, II. 694; III. 666.
Maesobotrys, II. 447.
Maesopsis, II. 495.

Mafureira, II. 422.
Magellan Territory, phytography, I. 347.
Magnetism, I. 230.
Magnolia, II. 211; III. 398; IV. 520.
Magnolia, II. 213; III. 400.
Magnoliaceae, II. 208; III. 397; IV. 519.
Magonia, II. 487.
Mahaleb, II. 270; III. 430.
Mahernia, II. 536; III. 591.
Mahonia, III. 395.
Mahonia, II. 201.
Mahures, II. 557.
Maieta, II. 638, 641.
Maihuenia, II. 594.
Maillardia, II. 154.
Maine, *see* United States, Northeastern.
Maingaya, II. 253.
Majidea, II. 486.
Makokoa, II. 604.
Malache, II. 526.
Malachodendron, II. 549.
Malachra, II. 525; III. 763.
Malacocarpus, II. 395, 591; III. 622.
Malacoxylum, II. 502.
Malaisia, II. 154.
Malanca, II. 823.
Malaspinaea, II. 692.
Malay Archipelago, afforestation, IV. 168.
—— botanic gardens, I. 67; V. ix.[1]
—— coffee cultivation, III. 729.
—— cultivation of fruit trees, III. 147.
—— dendrography, IV. 87.
—— descriptive botany, III. 91.
—— economic products, III. 274.
—— forest descriptions, IV. 376.
—— forest influences, IV. 48.
—— forest policy, IV. 279.
—— forest products, IV. 399.
—— forest regulations, IV. 307.
—— forest schools, IV. 37.
—— individual noteworthy trees, I. 298.
—— insects, IV. 210.
—— manuals of arboriculture, III. 116.
—— miscellaneous publications on arboriculture, III. 127.
—— miscellaneous publications on silviculture, IV. 124.
—— periodicals, I. 29; III. 26, 757.
—— phytography, I. 464, 536; V. xxiii.[2]
—— a forest administration, IV. 90 bis to
—— tea cultivation, III. 601.
—— timber trade, IV. 407.
—— vernacular names, I. 76.
Malay Peninsula, botanic gardens, I. 67.
—— cultivation of fruit trees, III. 147.
—— economic products, III. 274.
—— forest products, IV. 399.
—— miscellaneous publications on arboriculture, III. 129.
—— periodicals, I. 29; IV. 16.
—— phytography, I. 464.
—— tea cultivation, III. 601.
Malesherbia, II. 575.
Malesherbiaceae, II. 575.
Mallea, II. 420.
Mallophora, II. 759.
Mallotus, II. 447; III. 520.
Malortiea, II. 71; III. 331.
Malouetia, II. 728; III. 689.
Malpighia, II. 426; III. 513.
Malpighia, II. 424, 425, 426.
Malpighiaceae, II. 423; III. 513.
Malta, *see* Mediterranean Islands.
Malus, II. 266; III. 425; V. xxix.[1]
Malva, II. 525.
Malva, II. 525, 528; III. 589.
Malvaceae, II. 518; III. 586, 762.
Malvastrum, II. 525.
Malvaviscus, II. 525; III. 588.
Malvaviscus, II. 522.

Malveopsis, II. 525.
Mamillaria, II. 594; III. 623.
Mammals, IV. 90.
Mammea, II. 557; III. 610.
Mammea, II. 558.
Mammillaria, II. 594; III. 623.
Mammillaria, II. 589, 591; III. 620.
Man, injuries caused by, IV. 196, 548.
Managa, II. 869.
Manchuria, *see* Siberia, East.
Mandevilla, II. 728; III. 689.
Mandirola, II. 792.
Manettia, II. 823; III. 746.
Manettia, II. 823.
Mangifera, II. 456; III. 524.
Mangifera, III. 508.
Manglesia, II. 620, 872; III. 383.
Manglietia, II. 213.
Mangitilla, II. 695.
Manicaria, II. 71.
Manihot, II. 447; III. 520.
Manihtoa, II. 371.
Manna, III. 220.
Manna, ii. 331.
Mannia, II. 414.
Manniophyton, II. 447.
Manotes, II. 317.
Manuals, diseases and injuries, IV. 195.
—— forest management, IV. 239; V. xxxi.[1]
—— forest valuation, IV. 252.
—— forestry, IV. 94.
—— pharmacognosy and pharmacology, III. 257, 758.
—— silviculture, IV. 103; V. xxx.[1]
—— *see also* Textbooks.
Manuals and general treatises of arboriculture, III. 96, 757.
Manufacture of miscellaneous articles from wood, IV. 428, 557.
Manulea, II. 780.
Manulea, II. 780.
Manuring, III. 151; IV. 144, 545.
Maoutia, II. 157; III. 382.
Maoutia, II. 759.
Mapouria, II. 823.
Mappa, II. 520.
Mappia, II. 475.
Mappia, II. 446.
Mapping, *see* Geodesy, IV. 263.
Maprounea, II. 447.
Maquiera, II. 153.
Maralia, II. 651.
Maranthes, II. 269.
Marcellia, II. 745.
Marcetia, II. 638.
Marcgravia, II. 546.
Marcgravia, II. 546.
Marcgraviaceae, II. 546; III. 596.
Marenteria, II. 729.
Mareya, II. 447.
Margaritopsis, II. 822.
Margyricarpus, II. 268.
Marianthus, II. 247.
Marignia, II. 407, 418.
Marila, II. 557.
Maripa, II. 746.
Markea, II. 773.
Marlea, II. 615.
Marlierea, II. 629.
Marlothia, II. 495.
Marquartia, II. 56.
Marquesas Islands, phytography, I. 510.
Marrubium, II. 763; III. 697.
Marsana, II. 408.
Marsdenia, II. 740; III. 693.
Marshall Islands, descriptive botany, III. 94.
—— phytography, I. 510.
—— *see also* Pacific Islands.
Marsypopetalum, II. 218.
Martha, II. 827.
Martinezia, II. 71; III. 327.
Martiniera, II. 392.

Martiusia, II. 371.
Marumia, II. 638.
Marumia, II. 542.
Marupa, II. 414.
Maryland, *see* United States, Southeastern.
Mascagnia, II. 427.
Mascarene Islands, cinchona cultivation, III. 717.
—— miscellaneous publications on arboriculture, III. 130.
—— phytography, I. 481.
—— *see also* Indian Ocean Islands.
Mascarenhasia, II. 728; III. 689.
Massachusetts, *see* United States, Northeastern.
Massoia, III. 407.
Mastacanthus, II. 754.
Mastixia, II. 656.
Matayba, II. 487.
Matches, IV. 428.
Materia medica, III. 237, 757; V. xxviii.[1]
—— history of, III. 238.
Material for paper making, III. 235.
Mathematics, III. 36; IV. 57, 542.
Mathiola, II. 234.
Mathurina, II. 574.
Matisia, II. 530.
Matthiola, II. 234.
Mauneia, II. 572.
Maurandia, II. 780; III. 703.
Mauris, II. 457.
Mauritia, II. 71; III. 327.
Mauritius, forest description, IV. 378.
—— periodicals, I. 29.
—— tea cultivation, III. 604.
—— *see also* Indian Ocean Islands.
Maurocenia, II. 470.
Mavia, II. 358; III. 476.
Maximiliana, II. 71; III. 327.
Maximiliana, II. 566.
Maximowiczia, II. 213; III. 400.
Maxwellia, II. 530.
May-bug, *see* Melolontha vulgaris, IV. 202.
Mayepea, II. 712.
Mayna, II. 572.
Mayodendron, II. 789.
Maytenus, II. 470; III. 533.
Maseutoxeron, II. 404.
Measurement, instruments of, IV. 231.
—— *see also* Mensuration, IV. 213.
Measures promoting sylviculture and forestry, IV. 39, 541.
Mechanical forces, adaptations to, I. 236.
Mechanical tissues, I. 134.
Mecostylis, II. 446.
Medea, II. 439.
Medeola, II. 79.
Medinger, II. 371.
Medical botany, history of, III. 238.
—— *see also* Descriptive botany, medicinal, III. 53.
Medical properties, their relation to affinity and habit, III. 259; V. xxvii.[2]
Medical uses of wood products, IV. 433, 558.
Medicia, II. 718.
Medicinal plants, cultivation of, III. 149.
Medicinal products, III. 239, 757; V. xxviii.[1]
Mediocosma, II. 408.
Medieval literature, plants in, I. 514.
Medieval writers, I. 275, 530.
Medinilla, II. 638; III. 638.
Mediterranean Islands, afforestation, IV. 168.
—— botanic gardens, I. 66.
—— descriptive botany, III. 91.
—— economic products, III. 272.
—— forest descriptions, IV. 375, 556.

Mediterranean Islands, phytography, I. 451, 536.
Mediterranean region, phytography, I. 451; V. xxiii.[1]
—— and islands, miscellaneous publications on arboriculture, III. 127.
Mediterranean States of Africa, afforestation, IV. 168, 547.
—— botanic gardens, see North Africa, I.·68, 522.
—— dendrography, IV. 89.
—— descriptive botany, III. 93.
—— economic products, III. 279.
—— forest influences, IV. 49.
—— miscellaneous publications on arboriculture, III. 130.
—— periodicals, see Africa, I. 29.
—— phytography, I. 483; V. xxiv.[1]
—— vernacular names, see Africa, I. 76.
—— see also Algeria and Egypt.
Medusagyne, II. 557.
Medusanthera, II. 475.
Megaphyllaea, II. 421.
Megistostigma, II. 447.
Meladenia, II. 379.
Melaleuca, II. 629; III. 636; IV. 534.
Melaleuca, II. 620, 621, 628, 633.
Melananthus, II. 773.
Melanocarya, II. 467.
Melanochyla, II. 457.
Melanodendron, II. 860.
Melanophylla, II. 656.
Melanopsidium, II. 823.
Melanorrhoea, II. 457; III. 525.
Melanoselinum, II. 653; III. 644.
Melanthea, II. 438.
Melasanthus, II. 760.
Melastoma, II. 638; III. 638.
Melastoma, II. 635, 637, 640, 641.
Melastomataceae, II. 634, 874; III. 638.
Melhania, II. 536; III. 591.
Melhania, II. 539.
Melia, II. 421; III. 512; IV. 525.
Melia, III. 511.
Meliaceae, II. 418, 873; III. 511; IV. 525.
Melianthaceae, II. 491; III. 540.
Melianthus, II. 491; III. 541.
Melicocca, II. 487; III. 539.
Melicocus, II. 487.
Melicope, II. 408.
Melicytus, II. 567.
Melicytus, II. 467.
Melidora, II. 663; III. 649.
Melientha, II. 170.
Melio-Schinzia, II. 420.
Meliosma, II. 490.
Meliphlea, II. 528.
Mellera, II. 801.
Mellissia, II. 773.
Melloa, II. 789.
Melocactus, II. 595, 873; III. 623.
Melocactus, II. 591.
Melocanna, II. 60.
Melochia, II. 536; III. 591.
Melodinus, II. 728.
Melodorum, II. 218.
Melolobium, II. 371.
Melolontha vulgaris, IV. 202, 548.
Memecylon, II. 639; III. 638.
Memora, II. 789.
Menabea, II. 741.
Menarda, II. 449.
Mendoncia, II. 801.
Mendosia, II. 801.
Menispermaceae, II. 205; III. 396.
Menispermum, II. 207; III. 397.
Menispermum, II. 206, 207; III.. 396, 397.
Menodora, II. 712.
Mensuration, III. 200; IV. 213, 550.
Mentzelia, II. 583.
Menziesia, II. 674.
Menziesia, II. 662, 675; III. 649.
Mephitidia, II. 822.

Meratia, III. 401.
Meratia, II. 214.
Mercklinia, II. 162.
Meriania, II. 639.
Meriania, II. 641.
Merinthopodium, II. 773.
Meristematic tissues, I. 132.
Merkusia, II. 847.
Mertensia, II. 141.
Meryta, II. 650; III. 643.
Mesembryanthemum, II. 193; III. 688; V. xxvi.[1]
Mesogyne, II. 154.
Mespilus, II. 268; III. 429.
Mespilus, II. 260, 269, 278; III. 421, 443.
Messerschmidia, II. 750, 751.
Mesua, II. 557, 873; III. 610; IV. 528.
Metabolic processes and products, I. 174, 526; V. xi.[1]
Metachlamydeae, II. 657, 874; V. xxvii.[2]
Metagonia, II. 684.
Metalasia, II. 860.
Metamorphosis, I. 101.
Metaplexis, II. 741.
Metaplexis, II. 738.
Metastelma, II. 741.
Meteoric influences, diseases and injuries caused by, III. 181.
—— injuries, IV. 188, 548.
Meteorology, III. 36; IV. 59, 542.
Methorium, II. 534.
Methyscophyllum, II. 466.
Metrocynia, II. 349.
Metrodorea, II. 408; III. 504.
Metrosideros, II. 630, 874; III. 636.
Metrosideros, II. 620, 621, 625, 628; III. 633.
Metroxylon, II. 71; III. 227.
Metroxylon, III. 325, 330.
Metternichia, II. 774; III. 701.
Mexico, coffee cultivation, III. 728.
—— dendrography, IV. 78.
—— descriptive botany, III. 63.
—— economic products, III. 264.
—— forest descriptions, IV. 341.
—— forest laws, IV. 315.
—— forest policy, IV. 272.
—— forest protection, IV. 179.
—— miscellaneous publications on arboriculture, III. 118.
—— phytography, I. 331, 531; V. xviii.[1]
—— state forest administration, IV. 288.
—— timber trade, IV. 403.
—— see also Central America.
Meyenia, II. 801.
Meyenia, II. 770, 804; III. 710.
Meyna, II. 833.
Mezierea, II. 583.
Mezilaurus, II. 226.
Mezoneurum, II. 371; III. 481.
Mezzettia, II. 218.
Michelia, II. 213; III. 400.
Michigan, see United States, Northeastern.
Miconia, II. 640; III. 638.
Micrandra, II. 448; III. 521.
Micranthemum, II. 641.
Micranthemum, II. 448.
Micranthera, II. 558.
Micranthes, II. 763.
Micrantheum, II. 448.
Micrantheum, II. 448.
Microcachrys, II. 9; III. 287.
Microcalamus, II. 58.
Microchones, II. 728.
Micrococus, II. 69.
Microcorys, II. 764.
Microcos, II. 513.
Microcycas, II. 6.
Microdesmis, II. 448.
Microdon, II. 781.

Microëlus, II. 437.
Microglossa, II. 860.
Microkentia, II. 68.
Microlicia, II. 640.
Microlobium, II. 332.
Microloma, II. 741.
Micromeles, II. 311.
Micromelum, II. 408.
Micromeria, II. 766.
Micromyrtus, II. 631.
Micronychia, II. 457.
Microphoenix, II. 72; III. 328.
Micropora, II. 226.
Microptelea, II. 142.
Micropteryx, II. 356.
Microrhamnus, II. 495.
Microrhamnus, II. 496.
Microscopy, see Microtechnique.
Microsemma, II. 572.
Microstachys, II. 451.
Microsteira, II. 427.
Microtechnique, I. 36, 521; V. viii.[1]
Microtropis, II. 470.
Mida, II. 168.
Migration, I. 241; V. xii.[2]
—— and succession of forest growth, IV. 74, 543.
Mikania, II. 860; III. 755.
Mikania, II. 856, 864, 866.
Mildea, II. 487.
Miliusa, II. 218.
Millettia, II. 371.
Millingtonia, II. 789.
Millingtonia, II. 490.
Milnea, II. 419.
Mimetes, II. 164; III. 383.
Mimia, II. 371; III. 481.
Mimosa, II. 322, 330, 340, 354, 356, 358, 365, 369, 377, 379; III. 462, 484.
Mimosaceae, see Leguminosae.
Mimulopsis, II. 801.
Mimulus, II. 781; III. 703.
Mimusops, II. 699; III. 668; IV. 534.
Mineralogy, III. 37; IV. 60, 542.
Mining, timber used in, IV. 425.
Minkeletria, II. 373.
Minnesota, see United States, Western.
Minquartia, II. 171.
Minuria, II. 860.
Mionandra, II. 427.
Miquelia, II. 475.
Mirasolia, II. 867.
Mirbelia, II. 373; III. 482.
Mirbelia, II. 375.
Misanteca, II. 226.
Miscantheca, II. 226.
Miscellaneous publications including reports and statistics on arboriculture, III. 116, 757; V. xxviii.[1]
Miscellaneous publications on general forestry, IV. 100.
Miscellaneous publications on silviculture, IV. 111, 544; V. xxx.[1]
Miscellaneous publications, partly botanical, I. 30, 520; V. vii.[2]
Mischodon, II. 448.
Misodendron, II. 167.
Mississippi, see United States, Southeastern.
Missouri, see United States, Western.
Mitragyna, II. 823.
Mitraria, II. 795; III. 708.
Mitrasacme, II. 782.
Mitrastigma, II. 826.
Mitrephora, II. 218.
Mitriostigma, II. 829; III. 747.
Mitscherlichia, II. 191.
Mixed coniferous forests, IV. 138.
Mixed forests, treatment of, IV. 137.
Mixed hardwood forests, IV. 137.
Mixed woods, in regard to age, IV. 138.
—— in regard to light requirement, IV. 138.
Mocinna, II. 582.

Mocquerysia, II. 572.
Modecca, II. 576.
Modern literature, Plants in, I. 514.
Moghania, II. 358.
Mogiphanes, II. 190.
Mogorium, II. 709.
Mohlana, II. 193.
Mohrodendron, II. 704.
Moisture, forest influence on, IV. 49, 542.
—— *see also* Humidity. I. 232.
Moisture conditions, IV. 73.
Moldenhauera, II. 475.
Mollia, II. 514.
Mollinedia, II. 222.
Mollinedia, II. 221, 222.
Molloya, II. 160.
Mollugo, II. 193.
Molopanthera, II. 823.
Monachochlamys, II. 801.
Monadenium, II. 448.
Monanthochloë, II. 60.
Monanthotaxis, II. 218.
Monardella, II. 764.
Monetia, II. 472.
Mongolia, phytography, I. 460.
—— *see also* China.
Monimia, II. 222.
Monimiaceae, II. 221, 872; III. 403; IV. 520.
Monisia, II. 653.
Monnina, II. 430; III. 513.
Monocera, II. 510.
Monochaetum, II. 640; III. 639.
Monococcus, II. 193.
Monocotyledoneae, II. 56, 871; III. 313, 758; IV. 485; V. xxv.²
Monodora, II. 218; III. 401.
Monographidium, II. 259.
Monopanax, II. 650.
Monoporandra, II. 560.
Monoporus, II. 694.
Monopyrena, II. 759.
Monosis, II. 867.
Monospora, II. 574.
Monotes, II. 560.
Monotheca, II. 700.
Monoxora, II. 633.
Monsonia, II. 389.
Montagnaea, II. 856; III. 755.
Montagnea, see Montagnaea.
Montana, *see* United States, Western.
Montanoa, II. 856; III. 755.
Montenegro, forest description, IV. 374.
—— *see also* Balkan Peninsula.
Montinia, II. 241.
Montrouziera, II. 557.
Monttea, II. 781.
Moon, supposed influence, *see* Atmospheric influences, I. 233; *see also* Plant lore.
Moquilea, II. 265.
Moquinia, II. 860.
Mora, II. 355.
Moraceae, II. 145, 872; III. 366; IV. 519; V. xxviii.¹
Morelia, II. 823.
Morelosia, II. 748.
Morenia, II. 71.
Moricandia, II. 234.
Morierina, II. 823.
Morinda, II. 823; III. 746.
Morinda, II. 822.
Moringa, II. 234; III. 409.
Moringaceae, II. 234; III. 409.
Morisonia, II. 233.
Morocarpus, II. 156, 158.
Morocco, *see* Mediterranean States of Africa.
Morongia, II. 383.
Moronobea, II. 557; III. 610.
Moronobea, III. 610.
Morphology and anatomy, I. 97, 524; IV. 62, 543; V. xi.¹

Mortonia, II. 470.
Morus, II. 154; III. 372; IV. 519; V. xxviii.²
Morus, II. 147; III. 368.
Moschoxylum, II. 422; III. 513.
Mosquitoxylum, II. 457.
Mostuea, II. 719.
Motandra, II. 728.
Mound planting, IV. 153, 546.
Mouriria, II. 640.
Mourucoa, II. 746.
Moutabea, II. 430.
Movements, I. 193, 527.
——, nyctitropic, I. 197.
—— of tendrils, I. 196.
Moya, II. 469.
Mozinna, II. 445.
Msuata, II. 861.
Mucilaginous matter, *see* Gums and resins, I. 180.
Mucuna, II. 373; III. 482.
Muehlenbeckia, II. 185; III. 387.
Muellera, II. 374.
Mulching, III. 151.
Mulinum, II. 653.
Mullera, II. 374.
Munchausia, II. 609.
Mundia, II. 430.
Mundulea, II. 374.
Munronia, II. 421; III. 513.
Muntingia, II. 511.
Muraltia, II. 430; III. 513.
Murraya, II. 408; III. 504.
Murucuja, II. 576.
Musaceae, II. 90; III. 341; IV. 485.
Musanga, II. 155.
Museums, I. 38, 521; III. 27; IV. 18, 539; V. viii.¹
Musgravea, II. 164.
Musical instruments, wood for, IV. 428.
Mussaenda, II. 823; III. 746.
Mussaenda, II. 826, 829, 833; III. 744.
Mussaendopsis, II. 824.
Musschia, II. 845.
Mutilations, *see* Wounds and mutilations.
Mutisia, II. 861; III. 755.
Myagrum, II. 234.
Myaris, II. 403.
Mycetia, II. 824.
Myoorrhiza, *see* Symbiosis, I, 233, 529.
Myginda, II. 470.
Myginda, II. 469, 471.
Mylocaryum, II. 461.
Myodocarpus, II. 650.
Myonima, II. 824.
Myoporaceae, II. 805; III. 710.
Myoporum, II. 806; III. 710.
Myoschilos, II. 169.
Myosurandra, II. 251.
Myracrodruon, II. 455.
Myrceugenia, II. 631.
Myrcia, II. 631.
Myrcia, II. 622, 632, 639.
Myriantheia, II. 571.
Myrianthus, II. 155.
Myrica, II. 111; III. 352.
Myrica, II. 694, 706.
Myricaceae, II. 110; III. 352.
Myricaria, II. 562; III. 612.
Myriocarpa, II. 157; III. 382.
Myriophyllum, II. 741.
Myriotriche, II. 569.
Myripnois, II. 861.
Myristica, II. 220; III. 402, 758.
Myristica, III. 402.
Myristicaceae, II. 220; III. 402, 758.
Myrmecodia, II. 824; III. 746.
Myrmecodia, II. 824.
Myrmecophilism, I. 235.
Myrmedoma, II. 824.
Myrmephytum, II. 824.

Myrocarpus, II. 374.
Myrodia, II. 531.
Myrospermum, II. 873.
Myrospermum, II. 374; III. 482.
Myrothamnaceae, II. 251.
Myrothamnus, II. 251.
Myroxylon, II. 374; III. 482.
Myrrhidendron, II. 653.
Myrrhinium, II. 631; III. 637.
Myrsinaceae, II. 692; III. 665.
Myrsine, II. 694.
Myrsine, II. 693, 695, 700.
Myrstiphyllum, II. 827.
Myrtaceae, II. 618, 874; III. 633; IV. 529; V. xxvii.¹
Myrtella, II. 620.
Myr:illocactus, II. 589.
Myrtillus, II. 684; III. 663.
Mytophyllum, II. 569.
Myrtopsis, II. 408.
Myrtus, II. 631; III. 637.
*Myrtus,.*II. 625, 627, 631, 632, 633, 703; III. 635, 637.
Mytilicoccus, II. 408.
Myxopyrum, II. 712.
Myzodendraceae, II. 167.
Myzodendron, II. 167.

Naegelia, II. 494.
Nageia, II. 9; III. 287.
Nagelia, II. 257.
Nahusia, II. 643.
Nallogia, II. 170.
Names of plants, *see* Etymology, I. 76; V. ix.¹ Nomenclators, I. 69, 522; V. ix.¹ and Nomenclature, I. 253, 529; V. ix.¹
Nandina, II. 205; III. 396.
Nania, II. 620.
Nanism, I. 236.
Nannorrhops, II. 71; III. 327.
Nanopetalum, II. 438.
Nanophyton, II. 188.
Napaea, II. 526.
Napoleona, II. 612; III. 631.
Naravelia, II. 195.
Nardophyllum, II. 861.
Naregamia, III. 512.
Nassauvia, II. 861.
Nastus, II. 60.
Natalia, II. 491.
Nathusia, II. 714.
Natsiatum, II. 475.
Natural grafting, I. 209, 528.
—— and root fusion, IV. 66.
Natural regeneration, IV. 139, 545.
Natural selection, *see* Evolution, I. 243, 529.
Naturalization, III. 43.
Nauclea, II. 346.
Nauclea, II. 825; III. 746.
Nauclea, II. 808, 823, 831, 832; III. 748.
Naudinia, II. 408.
Nebraska, *see* United States, Western.
Nectandra, II. 227; III. 407.
Nectandra, II. 227; III. 403; IV. 520.
Nectaries, morphology and anatomy, I. 118.
—— ecology, *see* Reproductive interrelations, I. 236, 529.
Neca, II. 191.
Neesia, II. 530.
Neglected woods, restoration of, IV. 169.
Negria, II. 795.
Negundium, II. 476.
Negundo, II. 476.
Neillia, II. 268.
Neillia, II. 269.
Neilreichia, II. 864.
Neja, II. 859.
Nelitris, II. 622, 832.
Nematanthera, II. 93.
Nematanthus, II. 795.
Nematolepis, II. 408.

Nematophyllum, II. 386.
Nematostylis, II. 825.
Nemesia, II. 781.
Nemopanthes, II. 465.
Nemopanthus, II. 465.
Nemopanthus, II. 462.
Nenax, II. 825.
Nenga, II. 71.
Neobaronia, II. 376.
Neoboutonia, II. 448.
Neogoetzea, II. 448.
Neolindenia, II. 801.
Neolüderitsia, II. 395.
Neoscortechinia, II. 448.
Neosparton, II. 759.
Nepa, II. 387.
Nephelium, II. 487; III. 539.
Nephelium, II. 484, 486, 488.
Nephradenis, II. 741.
Nephroia, II. 207.
Nephropetalum, II. 537.
Nephrosperma, III. 327.
Neptunia, II. 374; III. 482.
Neraudia, II. 157.
Neriacanthus, II. 801.
Neriandra, II. 731; III. 691.
Nerium, II. 728; III. 689.
Nerium, II. 732, 734; III. 691.
Nesaea, II. 609.
Nesaea, II. 609.
Nesiota, II. 495.
Nesodaphne, IV. 520.
Nesogordonia, II. 869.
Nesopanax, II. 651; III. 644.
Nestlera, II. 861.
Netherlands, *see* Holland.
Nettoa, II. 514.
Neumannia, II. 572.
Neuracanthus, II. 801.
Neurocarpum, II. 346.
Neurolaena, II. 861.
Neuropeltis, II. 746.
Nevada, *see* United States, Western.
Neviusia, II. 268; III. 429.
New Caledonia, dendrography, IV. 89.
—— economic products, III. 283.
—— forest description, IV. 380.
—— miscellaneous publications on arboriculture, III. 132.
—— phytography, I. 508.
New Guinea, descriptive botany, III. 93.
—— economic products, III. 282.
—— phytography, I. 499, 535.
New Hampshire, *see* United States, Northeastern.
New Hebrides, miscellaneous publications on arboriculture, III. 132.
—— phytography, I. 508.
New Jersey, *see* United States, Northeastern.
New Mexico, *see* United States, Western.
New South Wales, *see* Australia.
New York, *see* United States, Northeastern.
New Zealand, afforestation, *see* Australasia, IV. 169.
—— arbor day, *see* Australasia, IV. 42.
—— botanic gardens, *see* Australasia, I. 69.
—— dendrography, IV. 89.
—— descriptive botany, III. 94.
—— economic products, III. 283.
—— forest description, IV. 380.
—— forest gardens, IV. 18.
—— forest policy, IV. 280.
—— forest products, IV. 402.
—— forest protection, IV. 181.
—— miscellaneous publications on arboriculture, III. 132.
—— miscellaneous publications on silviculture, IV. 124.

New Zealand, periodicals, *see* Australasia, I. 29, 520.
—— phytography, I. 506, 535.
—— reproductive interrelations, *see* Australasia, I. 240.
Newbouldia, III. 707.
Newcastlia, II. 759.
Newfoundland, economic products, III. 261.
—— forest policy, IV. 271.
—— phytography, I. 309; V. xvi.²
—— *see also* Canada.
Newtonia, II. 374.
Nicaragua, *see* Central American Republics.
Nicodemia, II. 719.
Nicotiana, II. 774; III. 701.
Nidorella, II. 861.
Niebuhria, II. 233.
Niederleinia, II. 561.
Nierembergia, II. 774; III. 701.
Nile Valley, *see* Africa, Northeast.
Nimmonia, II. 419.
Niota, II. 736.
Nipa, II. 71; III. 327.
Nisa, II. 571.
Nissolia, II. 374.
Nitraria, II. 395; III. 494.
Nivenia, II. 165.
Noaea, II. 188.
Nocca, II. 859.
Noisettia, II. 567.
Noisettia, II. 567.
Nolanaceae, II. 767.
Nolina, II. 84; III. 337.
Noltia, II. 701.
Nomenclators, I. 76; V. ix.²
Nomenclature, I. 253, 529; V. xii.²
Nopalea, II. 595; III. 623.
Norantea, III. 546; III. 596.
Norfolk Island, economic products, III. 283.
—— phytography, I. 508.
Normandia, II. 825.
Noronhia, II. 712.
Norrisia, II. 719.
North Africa, *see* Africa, North.
North America, acclimatization, III. 44.
—— administration of private forests, IV. 308.
—— afforestation, IV. 155.
—— arbor day, IV. 41, 541; V. xxix.²
—— bibliography, I. 3; V. vii.¹
—— botanic gardens, I. 38, 521; V. viii.¹
—— cinchona cultivation, III. 712.
—— collections, III. 27; V. xxvii.²
—— cultivation of exotic trees, IV. 124.
—— cultivation of fruit trees, III. 132.
—— dendrography, IV. 75, 544.
—— descriptive botany, III. 60.
—— diseases and injuries, III. 178.
—— diseases caused by fungi, III. 193.
—— economic products, III. 261; V. xxviii.²
—— education, III. 32.
—— erosion, IV. 184.
—— exhibitions, IV. 19.
—— financial results of forest management, IV. 259.
—— forest descriptions, IV. 336, 555.
—— forest devastation, IV. 281, 552.
—— forest exploitation, IV. 382.
—— forest fires, IV. 181.
—— forest influences, IV. 45.
—— forest laws, IV. 314.
—— forest management, IV. 247.
—— forest policy, IV. 271, 551; V. xxxi.¹
—— forest products, IV. 396; V. xxxi.²
—— forest protection, IV. 177.
—— forest regulations, IV. 295.
—— forest schools, IV. 30.
—— forest statistics, IV. 336, 555.

North America, galls, I. 214.
—— history, I. 80; III. 32; IV. 24; V. x.¹
—— individual noteworthy trees, I. 295; V. xvi.¹
—— injuries caused by insects, III. 186; IV. 205.
—— insects, IV. 91, 205.
—— manuals of arboriculture, III. 99.
—— measures promoting silviculture, IV. 39.
—— miscellaneous publications on arboriculture, III. 116.
—— miscellaneous publications on silviculture, IV. 111; V. xxx.¹
—— periodicals, I. 4, 519; III. 2, 757; IV. 3, 519; V. vii.¹
—— pharmacopoeias, III. 246.
—— phenology, I. 222, 528.
—— phytography, I. 304, 530; V. xvi.¹
—— reproductive interrelations, I. 239.
—— state forest administration, IV. 288.
—— street trees, III. 208.
—— taxes, tariffs, etc., IV. 284.
—— tea cultivation, III. 600.
—— textbooks and manuals of forestry, IV. 94.
—— textbooks and manuals of silviculture, IV. 103.
—— timber trade, IV. 402, 557.
—— vernacular names, I. 72.
—— viticulture, III. 549.
North Carolina, *see* United States, Southeastern.
North Dakota, *see* United States, Western.
Northea, II. 699.
Northeast Africa, *see* Africa, Northeast.
Northeastern United States, *see* United States, Northeastern.
Norway, afforestation, IV. 156.
—— forest descriptions, IV. 343.
—— forest devastation, IV. 282.
—— forest laws, IV. 315.
—— forest policy, IV. 273.
—— forest regulations, IV. 296.
—— miscellaneous publications on silviculture, IV. 113.
—— periodicals, I. 8.
—— state forest administration, IV. 288.
—— textbooks and manuals of silviculture, IV. 103.
—— *see also* Scandinavia.
Notelaea, II. 712.
Notelaea, II. 712.
Noteworthy trees, I. 295, 531; V. xvi.¹
Nothocestrum, II. 774.
Nothocnestis, II. 469.
Nothofagus, II. 127; III. 360; IV. 500.
Nothopanax, II. 650.
Nothopegia, II. 457.
Nothoprotium, II. 457.
Notobuxus, II. 453.
Notonia, II. 864.
Notopora, II. 674.
Notospartium, II. 374; III. 482.
Notothixos, II. 176.
Nouelia, II. 861.
Nouettea, II. 729.
Nucleus, *see* Cytology, I. 136, 525.
Nudilus, II. 706.
Nun-moth, *see* Liparis monacha, IV. 200.
Nunnesharia, II. 66.
Nursery management, III. 153; IV. 149; 546.
Nutation, *see* Movements and Irritability, I. 193, 527.
Nutrition, I. 150, 157, 525, 526; III. 37; IV. 64, 543; V. xi.¹
Nutritive adaptations, I. 228, 529; V. xii.²
Nuttallia, II. 268; III. 429.

Nuxia, II. 719.
Nuytsia, II. 177.
Nyctaginaceae, II. 190; III. 388.
Nyctanthes, II. 712; III. 674.
Nyctanthes, II. 709.
Nycterium, II. 774.
Nyctitropic movements, I. 197.
Nyctocalos, II. 789.
Nylandtia, II. 430.
Nyrophylla, II. 227.
Nyssa, II. 614; III. 632.
Nyssaceae, II. 614; III. 632.

Oakesia, II. 453.
Obbea, II. 809.
Obelanthera, II. 542.
Obetia, II. 157.
Obione, II. 187.
Obolaria, II. 835.
Ochanostachys, II. 171.
Ochetophila, II. 493, 494.
Ochna, II. 544; III. 596.
Ochnaceae, II. 544; III. 596.
Ochocoa, III. 403.
Ochocoa, II. 221.
Ochradenus, II. 234.
Ochranthe, II. 473.
Ochrocarpos, II. 558; III. 610.
Ochroma, II. 530.
Ochrosia, II. 729.
Ochroxylon, II. 411.
Ochthocharis, II. 640.
Ochthocosmus, II. 393.
Ocimum, II. 764.
Ocotea, II. 227; III. 407; IV. 520.
Ocotea, III. 403.
Octas, II. 869.
Octoclinis, II. 27.
Octoknemataceae, II. 172.
Octolepis, II. 604.
Octolobus, II. 537.
Octomeles, II. 583.
Octotropis, II. 825.
Ocymum, II. 764.
Ocyroe, II. 861.
Odina, II. 456, 461; III. 524.
Odonia, II. 358.
Odontadenia, II. 729; III. 689.
Odontandra, II. 421.
Odonteilema, II. 435.
Odontocarya, II. 208.
Odontonema, II. 801; III. 709.
Odontonemella, II. 802.
Odontospermum, II. 861.
Odostemon, II. 201.
Odyendea, II. 414.
Oecology, *see* Ecology, I. 217, 528.
Oedera, II. 861.
Oedera, II. 81, 859.
Oedmannia, II. 381.
Oenocarpus, II. 71.
Oenothera, II. 646; III. 640.
Oenothera, II. 645.
Oenotheraceae, II. 642; III. 639.
Office work, III. 200; IV. 311.
Officers, IV. 310, 554.
Oftia, II. 806.
Ohio, *see* United States, Northeastern.
Ohlendorffia, II. 779.
Oianthus, II. 741.
Oils and fats, I. 181, 526; III. 224; V. xi.[2]
Oklahoma, *see* United States, Western.
Olacaceae, II. 170; III. 384.
Olacineae, see Olacaceae.
Olax, II. 171.
Oldenburg, forest descriptions, IV. 352.
—— forest regulations, IV. 301.
—— *see also* German Empire.
Oldenlandia, II. 825.
Oldfieldia, II. 448.
Olea, II. 712; III. 674; IV. 536.
Olea, II. 712, 713; III. 679.
Oleaceae, II. 705; III. 671; IV. 534.
Olearia, II. 861; III. 756.

Oleobachia, II. 538; III. 591.
Oligosmilax, II. 83.
Oligostemon, II. 490.
Olinia, II. 599.
Oliniaceae, II. 599.
Olmedia, II. 155.
Olmedia, II. 153.
Olmediella, II. 572.
Olmediophaena, II. 155.
Olmediopsis, II. 155.
Olneya, II. 374; III. 482.
Olostyla, II. 814.
Omalanthus, II. 445; III. 519.
Omphacarpus, II. 513.
Omphacomeria, II. 169.
Omphalea, II. 448; III. 521.
Omphalobium, IV. 520.
Omphalobium, II. 317.
Omphalocarpum, II. 699; III. 668.
Omphalococca, II. 753.
Omphalogonus, II. 741.
Onagraceae, see Oenotheraceae.
Oncinema, II. 738.
Oncotheca, II. 869.
Ongokea, II. 171; III. 384.
Onobrychis, II. 374.
Ononis, II. 374; III. 482.
Ononis, II. 348, 370, 371.
Onoseris, II. 862.
Onosma, II. 751.
Ontogeny, I. 101.
Operculina, II. 746.
Ophiocaryon, II. 490.
Ophiocaulon, II. 576.
Ophioxylon, II. 731; III. 690.
Ophiria, II. 71.
Ophryosporus, II. 862.
Ophthalmoblapton, II. 448.
Opilia, II. 170.
Opiliaceae, II. 169.
Opulaster, II. 269.
Opuntia, II. 595, 874; III. 624; IV. 529.
Opuntia, II. 594, 595; III. 623.
Orania, II. 72.
Orania, II. 65.
Oraoma, II. 419.
Orbignia, II. 72.
Orbignya, II. 72.
Orchards, *see* Cultivation of fruit trees, III. 132.
Orchipeda, II. 734.
Orectospermum, II. 869.
Oregon, *see* United States, Western.
Oreobambos, II. 60.
Oreocallis, V. xxvi.[1]
Oreodaphne, II. 223, 227, 228; III. 408.
Oreodoxa, II. 72; III. 328.
Oreomunnea, II. 114.
Oreopanax, II. 650; III. 643.
Oreopanax, II. 649.
Oreosphacus, II. 764.
Oricia, II. 409.
Origin of cultivated plants, I. 246, 529.
Orites, II. 164.
Orixa, II. 409.
Orixa, II. 466.
Ormocarpum, II. 375.
Ormosia, II. 375.
Ornamental flowers, III. 207.
Ornamental fruits, III. 207.
Ornamental hedges, III. 214.
Ornamental properties of trees and shrubs, III. 202.
Ornamental uses of trees and shrubs, III. 201.
Ornus, II. 706; III. 672.

Orophea, II. 218.
Orospodias, II. 270.
Orothamnus, III. 383.
Orothamnus, II. 164.
Oroxylum, II. 789; III. 707.
Orphanidesia, II. 674.
Orphium, II. 721.
Orihaea, II. 684.
Orthosiphon, II. 764.
Orthostemon, II. 632; III. 637.
Orthothecium, II. 534.
Osbeckia, II. 640; III. 639.
Osbeckia, II. 637.
Osbornia, II. 632.
Osmanthus, II. 713; III. 679.
Osmaronia, II. 268; III. 429.
Osmelia, II. 572.
Osmhydrophora, II. 789.
Osmidrophora, II. 789.
Osmohydrophora, II. 789.
Osmosis, 150.
Osmoxylon, II. 651.
Ossaea, II. 641.
Ossaea, II. 637.
Osteocarpum, II. 188.
Osteocarpus, II. 767.
Osteomeles, II. 269; III. 430.
Osteomeles, II. 264.
Osteospermum, II. 862.
Osteospermum, II. 858.
Ostodes, II. 448.
Ostrearia, II. 253.
Ostrya, II. 122; III. 358; IV. 492.
Ostryocarpus, II. 375.
Ostryopsis, II. 122; III. 358.
Osyridocarpos, II. 169.
Osyridocarpus, II. 169.
Osyris, II. 169; III. 384.
Otanthera, II. 641.
Othera, II. 462, 466.
Othonna, II. 862; III. 756.
Othonna, II. 857; III. 755.
Ohrys, II. 232.
Otiophora, II. 825.
Otolepis, II. 487.
Otomeria, II. 825.
Otopappus, II. 868.
Otophora, II. 487.
Otostegia, II. 764.
Ototropis, II. 354.
Otonia, II. 93.
Oubanguia, II. 514.
Oudemansia, II. 534.
Oudneya, II. 234.
Ougeinia, IV. 522.
Ourates, II. 545; III. 596.
Ourouparia, II. 832.
Outea, II. 371.
Ovary, *see* Gynaecium, I. 117.
Ovieda, II. 755.
Owataria, II. 558.
Owenia, II. 421; III. 512.
Oxalate of lime, *see* Crystals, I. 138, 525.
Oxalidaceae, II. 392; III. 491.
Oxalis, II. 392; III. 492.
Oxandra, IV. 520.
Oxanthera, II. 400.
Oxera, II. 759; III. 697.
Oxleya, II. 407.
Oxyanthus, II. 825; III. 746.
Oxycarpus, II. 554.
Oxycladium, II. 373.
Oxycladus, II. 781.
Oxycoccus, see Oxycoccus.
Oxycoccus, II. 684; III. 663.
Oxydendrum, II. 674; III. 653.
Oxylobium, II. 375; III. 483.
Oxylobium, II. 358.
Oxymeris, II. 638.
Oxymitra, II. 218.
Oxymitus, II. 785.
Oxypetalum, II. 741.
Oxyramphis, II. 369.
Oxyspora, II. 641.

Oxystelma, II. 741.
Oxytenanthera, III. 316.
Oxytenia, II. 862.
Oxytropis, II. 376.
Oyedaea, II. 862.
Ozoroa, II. 456.
Ozothamnus, II. 854, 858; III. 755.

Pachira, II. 530; III. 589.
Pachistima, II. 470; III. 533.
Pachycentria, II. 641.
Pachydendron, II. 77.
Pachygone, II. 208.
Pachygone, II. 207.
Pachylobus, II. 418; III. 511.
Pachynema, II. 542.
Pachynocarpus, II. 560.
Pachyphytum, II. 235.
Pachypodium, II. 729.
Pachyrhizus, III. 483.
Pachyrhizus, II. 380.
Pachysandra, II. 453.
Pachyanthus, II. 830.
Pachystachys, II. 802.
Pachystela, II. 700.
Pachystigma, II. 825.
Pachystigma, II. 409.
Pachystima, II. 470.
Pachystroma, II. 448.
Pacific Islands, botanic gardens, I. 69.
—— coffee cultivation, III. 733.
—— descriptive botany, III. 94.
—— economic products, III. 283.
—— forest descriptions, IV. 380.
—— forest influences, IV. 49.
—— forest laws, IV. 332.
—— forest products, IV. 402.
—— miscellaneous publications on arboriculture, III. 132.
—— periodicals, III. 27.
—— phytography, I. 509; V. xxiv.²
—— reproductive interrelations, I. 240.
Pacific States, see United States, Western.
Packing of fruits, III. 173.
Packing plants, see Shipping, III. 154.
Padus, II. 270; III. 430.
Paederia, II. 825.
Paeonia, II. 200; III. 392.
Pagamea, II. 825.
Pagetia, II. 409.
Pahudia, II. 376.
Paivaeusa, II. 448.
Palafoxia, II. 862.
Palaquium, II. 699; III. 668.
Palenga, II. 450.
Palestine, phytography, I. 479; V. xxiv.¹
Palicourea, II. 825; III. 746.
Palicourea, II. 827.
Palicurea, II. 830.
Paliurus, II. 495; III. 542.
Paliurus, II. 500.
Palmae, II. 60, 871; III. 316, 758; IV. 485; V. xxv.³
Palmeria, II. 222.
Pamir, phytography, I. 477.
Pamphilia, II. 704.
Panama, see Central American Republics and Colombia.
Panax, II. 651; III. 643.
Panax, II. 647, 648, 650, 651; III. 641, 642.
Pancheria, II. 250.
Panciatica, II. 338.
Pancovia, II. 486; III. 539.
Panda, II. 869.
Pandaca, II. 732.
Pandanaceae, II. 56; III. 313.
Pandanus, II. 56; III. 313.
Pandora, II. 789; III. 707; V. xxvii.³
Pangium, II. 572; III. 615.
Panopsis, II. 165.
Papaveraceae, II. 229; III. 408.
Papaya, II. 582; III. 617.

Papeda, II. 400.
Paper making, material for, III. 235.
—— see also Wood pulp, IV. 429.
Paphia, II. 674.
Papilionaceae, see Leguminosae.
Pappea, II. 487; III. 539.
Pappostylum, II. 815.
Parabaena, II. 208.
Paracelsea, II. 721.
Paragenipa, II. 825.
Paragonia, II. 789.
Paraguay, descriptive botany, III. 65.
—— economic products, III. 269.
—— phytography, I. 344; V. xviii.³
Parameria, II. 729.
Paramignya, II. 409.
Paranephelium, II. 487.
Paranomus, II. 165.
Parapetalifera, II. 399.
Parartocarpus, II. 155.
Parashorea, II. 560.
Parasitism, I. 233, 529; IV. 73, 543; V. xii.³
Parasponia, II. 142.
Parastemon, II. 269.
Parathesis, II. 695.
Parathesis, II. 692.
Paratrophis, II. 155.
Paratropia, II. 651, 652; III. 644.
Paravallaris, II. 730.
Parechites, II. 734.
Parinarium, II. 269; III. 430.
Parishia, II. 457.
Paritium, II. 522; III. 587.
Parivoa, II. 356.
Parkia, II. 376; III. 483.
Parkinsonia, II. 376; III. 483.
Parmentiera, II. 789; III. 707.
Paropsia, II. 572; III. 615.
Parosela, II. 352.
Parquetina, II. 741.
Parrotia, II. 253; III. 418.
Parryella, II. 376.
Parsonsia, II. 730; III. 689.
Parthenocissus, II. 504; III. 544.
Parthenogenesis, I. 202.
Parthenopeïs, II. 867.
Parvatia, II. 201.
Paryphosphaera, II. 376.
Pasania, II. 128.
Paschanthus, II. 576.
Passerina, II. 604.
Passerina, II. 600, 603, 604, 606.
Passiflora, II. 576; III. 615.
Passiflora, II. 581; III. 616.
Passifloraceae, II. 575, 873; III. 615.
Passovia, II. 177.
Pasturing and silviculture, IV. 134, 545.
Patabea, II. 827.
Patagonia, phytography, I. 344; V. xviii.³
Patagonula, II. 751.
Patagua, II. 164.
Patascoya, II. 549.
Pathology, I. 206, 528; III. 40; IV. 65; V. xii.³
Patrisia, II. 573.
Pauletia, II. 334.
Paullinia, II. 487; III. 539.
Paullinia, II. 488; III. 540.
Paulownia, II. 781; III. 703; IV. 538.
Pauridiantha, II. 825.
Pavetta, II. 448.
Pavetta, II. 825; III. 746.
Pavetta, II. 817, 820, 829; III. 745.
Pavia, II. 481.
Pavonia, II. 526; III. 588.
Pavonia, II. 521, 522, 525; III. 587.
Paxia, II. 317.
Paxia, II. 317.
Paxiodendron, II. 222.
Payena, II. 699; III. 669.
Payera, II. 826.
Payeria, II. 422.

Paypayrola, II. 567.
Peat, IV. 438.
Peckia, II. 693.
Pedagogy, I. 78.
Pedaliaceae, II. 792; III. 708.
Peddiea, II. 604.
Pedilanthus, II. 448.
Peganum, II. 395.
Peganum, II. 395.
Pegia, II. 457.
Peireskia, II. 597.
Péixotoa, II. 427.
Pelargonium, II. 389; III. 491.
Pelea, II. 409.
Pelecyphora, II. 597; III. 625.
Pellacalyx, II. 614.
Pelliciera, II. 549.
Peltanthera, II. 719.
Peltogyne, III. 483.
Peltophorum, II. 376; III. 483.
Peltostigma, II. 409; III. 504.
Pemphis, II. 610.
Penaea, II. 599.
Penaea, II. 599.
Penaeaceae, II. 599.
Pendulous trees, III. 204.
Penianthus, II. 208.
Penicillanthemum, II. 393.
Pennantia, II. 475.
Pennsylvania, see United States, Northeastern.
Penstemon, II. 781.
Pentacaena, II. 194.
Pentace, II. 514.
Pentachondra, II. 690.
Pentaclethra, II. 376; III. 483.
Pentacme, II. 873.
Pentacoca, II. 393.
Pentacoelium, II. 806.
Pentadesma, II. 558; III. 610.
Pentadiplandra, II. 515.
Pentagonaster, II. 628.
Pentagonia, II. 826.
Pentaloba, II. 568.
Pentamorpha, II. 406.
Pentanopsis, II. 826.
Pentanura, II. 742.
Pentapanax, II. 651.
Pentapera, II. 663; III. 649.
Pentapetes, II. 536, 539.
Pentaphalangium, II. 558.
Pentaphylacaceae, II. 462.
Pentaphylax, II. 462.
Pentaptera, II. 617.
Pentapterygium, II. 674; III. 653.
Pentapyxis, II. 835.
Pentarhaphia, II. 794; III. 708.
Pentas, II. 826; III. 746.
Pentaspadon, II. 457.
Pentastemon, II. 781.
Pentatropis, II. 741.
Pentstemon, II. 781; III. 703.
Pentzia, II. 863.
Peperomia, II. 93.
Pepinia, II. 76.
Pera, II. 448.
Peraphyllum, II. 269.
Perdicium, II. 867.
Pereskia, II. 597; III. 625.
Perezia, II. 863; III. 756.
Perfumes, I. 182; III. 226.
Pergularia, II. 741.
Pergularia, II. 737.
Perianth, I. 115.
Pericambium, see Cambium, I. 128, 525.
Pericampylus, II. 208.
Periclistia, II. 567.
Pericycle, see Cambium, I. 128.
Peridiscus, II. 572.
Peridium, II. 448.
Periestes, II. 802.
Periploca, II. 764.
Periodicals and serials, I. 4, 519; III. 2, 757; IV. 3, 539; V. vii,¹ xxvii,¹ xxix.¹

Periodicity of growth, I. 101,'527; V. xii.[1]
Periomphale, II. 795.
Peripeplus, II. 826.
Periploca, II. 741; III. 694.
Periploca, II. 737; III. 693.
Periptera, II. 521.
Peristrophe, II. 802; III. 709.
Perithrix, II. 736.
Pernettya, II. 674; III. 653.
Perojoa, II. 689.
Peronema, II. 759.
Perrottetia, II. 470.
Persea, II. 227; III. 407; IV. 520.
Persea, II. 225, 226.
Persia, economic products, III. 279.
—— miscellaneous publications on arboriculture, III. 130.
—— phytography, I. 477; V. xxiv.[1]
Persica, II. 270; III. 430.
Persoonia, II. 165.
Persoonia, II. 419; III. 511.
Pertya, II. 863.
Peru, descriptive botany, III. 64.
—— economic products, III. 268.
—— history, see South America, I. 80.
—— miscellaneous publications on arboriculture, III. 118.
—— phytography, I. 340.
Perymenium, II. 863.
Peschiera, II. 732; III. 690.
Petalacte, II. 863.
Petalactella, II. 863.
Petalidium, II. 802.
Petalinia, II. 171.
Petalonyx, II. 583.
Petalopogon, II. 495.
Petalostemon, II. 352.
Petalostigma, II. 448.
Petalostylis, II. 376.
Petals, see Perianth, I. 115.
Petastoma, II. 790.
Petersia, II. 230.
Petesia, II. 820, 830.
Petiole, I. 112.
Petiveria, II. 193.
Petraea, II. 760.
Petraeovitex, II. 760.
Petrea, II. 760; III. 697.
Petrobium, II. 863.
Petrocarya, II. 269.
Petrophila, II. 165.
Petrophila, II. 163.
Petteria, II. 376; III. 483.
Petunga, II. 826.
Peucedanum, II. 653.
Peucephyllum, II. 863.
Peumus, II. 222; III. 403.
Phacellaria, II. 169.
Phaeanthus, II. 218.
Phaedranthus, II. 790; III. 707.
Phaeocoma, II. 863.
Phaeocephalus, II. 867.
Phaeoneuron, II. 641.
Phaeoptilon, II. 191.
Phaeoptilum, II. 191.
Phagnalon, II. 863.
Phaleria, II. 604; III. 628.
Phanerà, II. 334.
Pharmacognosy, III. 257; V. xxviii.[2]
—— manuals, III. 257, 758.
Pharmacology, III. 257; V. xxviii.[2]
—— manuals, III. 257.
Pharmacopoeias, III. 245, 758.
Pharmacosycea, II. 148.
Pharnaceum, II. 194.
Phaulothamnus, II. 193.
Phebalium, II. 409.
Phebalium, II. 399.
Phelline, II. 465.
Phellodendron, II. 409; III. 504; IV. 524.
Phenax, II. 157.
Phenology, I. 220, 528; V. xii.[2]
Phenomenology, see Phenology.

Pherosphaera, II. 9.
Phislanthus, II. 826.
Philadelphus, II. 241; III. 413.
Philadelphus, II. 628.
Philageria, II. 84.
Philagonia, II. 406.
Philesia, II. 84; III. 337.
Philetaeria, II. 563.
Philibertia, II. 742.
Philippia, II. 675.
Philippine Islands, coffee cultivation, III. 729.
—— dendrography, IV. 87, 544.
—— descriptive botany, III. 91.
—— economic products, III. 273.
—— exhibitions, IV. 21, 540.
—— forest descriptions, IV. 376, 556.
—— forest fires, IV. 547.
—— forest products, IV. 399.
—— miscellaneous publications on arboriculture, III. 127.
—— phytography, I. 463.
—— state forest administration, IV. 294, 554.
—— textbooks and manuals of forestry, IV. 100.
—— timber trade, IV. 407.
Philippodendrum, II. 526.
Phillipsia, II. 803.
Phillyrea, II. 714; III. 680.
Philomeda, II. 545.
Philosophy, I. 79, 522; V. ix.[2]
—— and principles of forestry, IV. 56, 542.
Philotheca, II. 409.
Phitopis, II. 826.
Phleocalymma, II. 474.
Phlebolithis, II. 700.
Phlebophyllum, II. 803.
Phlebotaenia, II. 430.
Phloga, II. 72.
Phlogacanthus, II. 802.
Phlomis, II. 764.
Phlomis, II. 764.
Phlox, II. 747.
Phlyarodoxa, II. 711.
Phoberos, II. 573.
Phocea, II. 470.
Phoebe, II. 227; IV. 520.
Phoebe, II. 224.
Phoenicophorium, II. 72; III. 328.
Phoenicospermum, II. 511.
Phoenix, II. 72; III. 328; IV. 485.
Pholidia, II. 807.
Pholidocarpus, II. 73.
Phoradendron, II. 177; III. 385.
Phornothamnus, II. 641.
Photinia, II. 269, 872; III. 430.
Phoxanthus, II. 491.
Phradus, II. 774.
Phryganocydia, II. 790.
Phthirusa, II. 177.
Phygelius, II. 782; III. 703.
Phylacium, II. 376.
Phylica, II. 495; III. 542.
Phylica, II. 251, 252.
Phylicanthus, II. 826.
Phyllagathis, II. 641; III. 639.
Phyllanthodendron, II. 449.
Phyllanthus, II. 449; III. 521.
Phyllanthus, II. 436, 444.
Phyllarthron, II. 790.
Phyllis, II. 826.
Phyllobotryum, II. 572.
Phyllocactus, II. 597; III. 625.
Phyllocalyx, II. 625.
Phyllochlamys, II. 155.
Phyllocladus, II. 9; III. 287.
Phyllocosmus, II. 393.
Phyllodoce, II. 675; III. 653.
Phylloma, II. 84.
Phyllonoma, II. 242.

Phyllostachys, II. 60; III. 316.
Phyllostylon, II. 142.
Phyllota, II. 376.
Phyliota, II. 380.
Phyllotaxy, I. 102.
Phylloxera, III. 564, 758.
Phylloxylon, II. 376.
Phylogeny, I. 249, 529.
Phymanthus, II. 389.
Physanthemum, II. 232.
Physena, II. 573.
Physetobasis, II. 726.
Physianthus, II. 736, 742; III. 692.
Physical and technical properties of timber, IV. 407.
Physics, III. 36; IV. 59.
—— of plant body, I. 149; V. xi.[2]
Physiological chemistry, I. 150, 525; V. xi.[2]
Physiology, I. 146, 525; III. 37; IV. 63, 543; V. xi.[1]
—— of chlorophyll, I. 140, 525.
—— of starch, I. 139, 525.
Physocalycium, II. 235.
Physocalymma, II. 610; III. 630.
Physocalymna, see Physocalymma.
Physocalyx, II. 782.
Physocarpus, II. 269; III. 430.
Physodium, II. 536.
Physolobium, II. 366.
Physopodium, II. 610.
Physopsis, II. 760.
Physostelma, II. 742.
Physostigma, II. 376; III. 683.
Phytelephas, II. 73; III. 330; IV. 485.
Phytocrene, II. 475.
Phytogeography, see Geographical distribution, I. 298, 531, also Dissemination, I. 240, and Migration, I. 240.
—— ecological, I. 217, 528; V. xii.[1]
Phytography, I. 250, 529; V. xii.[1]
—— see also Dendrography and Descriptive botany.
Phytolacca, II. 193; III. 388; IV. 519.
Phytolaccaceae, II. 192; III. 388; IV. 519.
Picea, II. 33, 871; III. 305; IV. 452, 558; V. xxxii.[1]
Picea, II. 21, 53; III. 295; IV. 444.
Pickeringia, II. 376; III. 484.
Pickeringia, II. 692.
Picraena, II. 415; III. 508.
Picralima, II. 730.
Picramnia, II. 414; III. 508.
Picrasma, II. 415; III. 508.
Picrella, II. 415.
Picrodendron, II. 415.
Picrolemma, II. 415; III. 508.
Picrolemna, see Picrolemma.
Pictetia, II. 376.
Pierardia, II. 437.
Pieris, II. 675; III. 653.
Pierotia, II. 393.
Pierrea, II. 560.
Pierrea, II. 571.
Pigafettia, III. 330.
Pilea, II. 157.
Pileanthus, II. 632.
Pileostegia, II. 242.
Pileostegia, II. 462.
Pileostigma, II. 334.
Piliocalyx, II. 632.
Pilocarpus, II. 409; III. 504.
Pilocereus, II. 598; III. 626; V. xxvii.[1]
Pilocereus, II. 591; III. 620.
Pilophora, II. 71.
Pimelandra, II. 692.
Pimelea, II. 605; III. 628.
Pimeleodendron, II. 450.
Pimelodendron, II. 450.
Pimenta, II. 632; III. 637.
Pimentelia, II. 826.
Pimia, II. 537.

Pinaceae, II. 12, 871; III. 289, 758; IV. 440, 558; V. xxv,[1] xxviii,[2] xxxii;[1] see also Conifers, IV. 138.
Pinanga, II. 73; III. 330.
Pincenectia, II. 84.
Pincenectitia, II. 84.
Pinckneya, II. 826.
Pinckneya, II. 827.
Findarea, II. 74.
Pineda, II. 573.
Pinus, II. 38, 871; III. 306, 758; IV. 460, 559; V. xxv,[3] xxxii.[3]
Pinus, II. 21, 27, 32, 33, 49, 53; III. 295, 305, 312; IV. 4u8, 452.
Pinzona, II. 541.
Pionandra, II. 771, 774; III. 699.
Piper, II. 93; III. 342, 758; V. xxvi.[1]
Piper, II. 93.
Piperaceae, II. 92; III. 342, 758; V. xxvi.[1]
Piperodendron, II. 460.
Piptadenia, II. 376; III. 484.
Piptanthus, II. 377; III. 484.
Piptocalyx, II. 222; III. 403.
Piptocelus, II. 869.
Piptocoma, II. 863.
Piptolaena, II. 734.
Piptosaccos, II. 869.
Piptostigma, II. 218.
Piptostylis, II. 403.
Pipturus, II. 157.
Piqueria, II. 863.
Pirounia, II. 193.
Piriqueta, II. 575.
Piscidia, II. 377; III. 484.
Piscidia, II. 383.
Pisonia, II. 191; III. 388.
Pistacia, II. 457; III. 525.
Pistacia, II. 418.
Pistil, see Gynaecium, I. 117.
Pitavia, II. 873.
Pitcairnia, II. 76.
Pith, I. 128.
Pithecoctenium, II. 790; III. 707.
Pithecoctenium, II. 785; III. 707.
Pithecolobium, II. 377; III. 484; IV. 522.
Pithecolobium, II. 365.
Pittiera, II. 844.
Pittoniotis, II. 809.
Pittosporaceae, II. 247; III. 415.
Pittosporum, II. 248; III. 416.
Pittosporum, II. 247; III. 416.
Pituranthus, II. 653.
Pityrodia, II. 760.
Placocarpa, II. 826.
Pladarozylon, II. 864.
Plagianthus, II. 526; III. 588.
Plagianthus, II. 521; III. 587.
Plagiopteron, II. 573.
Plagiospermum, II. 270.
Plagiostyles, II. 450.
Planaltoa, II. 863.
Planarium, II. 345.
Planchonella, II. 700.
Planchonia, II. 612.
Planera, II. 142.
Planera, II. 145; III. 366.
Planetary influences, Supposed, see Atmospheric influences, I. 233.
—— physics, I. 149.
Plant constituents and composition, I. 152, 525; V. xi.[2]
Plant lore, I. 517, 536; V. xxv.[2]
Plantaginaceae, II. 807.
Plantago, II. 807.
Planting, III. 165; IV. 151, 546.
—— depth of, III. 169.
—— distance in, III. 169; IV. 154, 546.
—— mound, IV. 153, 546.
—— season for, III. 168; IV. 154.
—— of evergreens, III. 169.
—— of street trees, III. 211.
Plants, diseases and injuries caused by, III. 193; IV. 210, 550.

Plants, propagation and raising of, III. 152.
—— shipping of, III. 154; IV. 151, 546.
Platanaceae, II. 254; III. 418; IV. 520.
Platanus, II. 254; III. 418; IV. 520.
Platen, II. 475.
Plathymenia, II. 378.
Flatonia, II. 558.
Platycarpidium, II. 653.
Platycarpum, II. 826.
Platycarya, II. 114; III. 356.
Platychilum, II. 363.
Platycrater, II. 243; III. 413.
Platydesma, II. 410.
Platygyna, II. 450.
Platykeleba, II. 742.
Platylobium, II. 378; III. 484.
Platylobium, II. 336.
Platylophus, II. 250.
Platymiscium, II. 378.
Platymitium, II. 873.
Platymitium, II. 473.
Platymena, II. 428.
Platysace, II. 653.
Platysepalum, II. 378.
Platystigma, II. 450.
Platytheca, II. 429; III. 513.
Platysamia, II. 5.
Plecospermum, II. 148.
Plectaneia, II. 730.
Flectocomia, II. 74.
Plectranthus, II. 764.
Plectrocarpa, II. 395.
Flectronia, II. 826.
Plegorhiza, II. 696; III. 666.
Pleiocarpa, II. 730.
Pleiochiton, II. 641.
Pleiogynium, II. 458.
Pleiosmilax, II. 85.
Pleiotaxis, II. 863.
Pleocarphus, II. 859.
Pleonotoma, II. 790.
Plerandra, II. 651; III. 644.
Pleroma, II. 636, 641; III. 639.
Plethiandra, II. 641.
Pleuradenia, II. 441.
Pleurandra, II. 541.
Pleurocalyptus, II. 632.
Pleurocoffea, II. 827.
Pleuropetalon, II. 474.
Pleuropetalum, II. 190.
Pleurophora, II. 610.
Pleurostylia, II. 471.
Plinia, II. 625.
Plocama, II. 827.
Plocosperma, II. 719.
Plocostemma, II. 739; III. 693.
Ploesslea, II. 416.
Pluchea, II. 863; III. 756.
Plukenetia, II. 450.
Plumbaginaceae, II. 695; III. 666.
Plumbago, II. 696; III. 666.
Plumeria, II. 730; III. 690.
Plumiera, II. 730.
Plums, III. 432.
Podachaenium, II. 857.
Podalyria, II. 378; III. 484.
Podanthus, II. 863.
Podiopetalum, II. 352.
Podocarpus, II. 9, 871; III. 287; IV. 440.
Podocarpus, II. 8, 9, 782.
Podococcus, II. 74.
Podocytisus, II. 368; III. 480.
Podolobium, II. 375; III. 483.
Podonephelium, II. 488.
Podoon, II. 456.
Podopetalum, II. 378.
Podophania, II. 863.
Podopterus, II. 186.
Podostelma, II. 742.
Poecilandra, II. 545.
Poecilochroma, II. 774.
Poecilodermis, II. 532; III. 590.

Poeciloneuron, II. 558.
Poeppigia, II. 378.
Poga, II. 614.
Poggea, II. 573.
Poggendorffia, II. 581.
Pogonanthera, II. 641.
Pogonanthus, II. 823.
Pogonia, II. 806.
Pogonophyllum, II. 448.
Pogonopus, II. 827; III. 746.
Pogonotrophe, II. 148.
Pogopetalum, II. 474.
Pogostemon, II. 765; III. 698.
Pohlana, II. 411.
Poikilospermum, II. 157.
Poinciana, II. 378; III. 484.
Poinciana, II. 338; III. 468; V. xxix.[1]
Poinsettia, II. 441; III. 517.
Poiretia, II. 378.
Poiretia, II. 690.
Poisonous substances, effect of, III. 185.
Poissonia, II. 378.
Poitaea, II. 378.
Poitea, II. 378.
Poivrea, II. 616.
Pokornya, II. 617.
Poland, see Austria-Hungary, Germany and Russia.
Polemoniaceae, II. 746; III. 694.
Polichhrysis, II. 573.
Pollarding, III. 173.
Pollen, morphology, I. 116, 524.
—— physiology, I. 201, 527.
Pollination, see Reproductive Interrelations, I. 236, 529.
Polyacanthus, II. 469.
Polyachyrus, II. 863.
Polyalthia, II. 218.
Polyalthia, II. 217.
Polyaster, II. 410.
Polycardia, II. 471.
Polycarpa, II. 571; III. 614.
Polyclados, II. 860.
Polycoelium, II. 806.
Polydragma, II. 450.
Polygala, II. 430; III. 514.
Polygala, II. 430; III. 513.
Polygalaceae, II. 429; III. 513.
Polygonaceae, II. 183; III. 386.
Polygonum, II. 186; III. 387.
Polygonum, II. 184, 185; III. 387.
Polylepis, II. 270.
Polymnia, II. 863; III. 756.
Polyosma, II. 243.
Polyphragmon, II. 832.
Polyporandra, II. 475.
Polyscias, II. 651; III. 644.
Polysphaeria, II. 599.
Polyspora, II. 548.
Polytropia, II. 381.
Polyzone, II. 622.
Pomaceae, see Rosaceae.
Pomaderris, II. 496; III. 542.
Pomaderris, II. 492, 494, 499.
Pomaria, II. 338, 363.
Pomatoderris, II. 496.
Pombea, II. 869.
Pometia, II. 488.
Pometia, II. 484.
Pomology, see subdivision Pomological in the geographical arrangement under Descriptive botany, III. 61–90.
Pongamia, II. 378; III. 484.
Pongamia, II. 353; III. 475.
Poortnannia, II. 778.
Pootia, II. 734.
Popowia, II. 218.
Popular Works, general botany, I. 93, 523; V. x.[2]
Populus, II. 96; III. 344; IV. 485.
Porana, II. 746; III. 694.
Poranthera, II. 450.
Poraqueiba, II. 475.
Porcelia, II. 218.

Porcelia, II. 216.
Porlieria, II. 396.
Porodittia, II. 782.
Porophyllum, II. 8o3.
Porphyrocoma, II. 802; III. 710.
Portaea, II. 772.
Portenschlagia, II. 407, 467.
Porteria, II. 844.
Portesia, II. 422.
Portlandia, II. 827; III. 746.
Portlandia, III. 743.
Portugal, afforestation, IV. 164, 546.
—— collections, III. 29.
—— cultivation of exotic trees, IV. 127.
—— forest descriptions, IV. 362.
—— forest devastation, IV. 283.
—— forest gardens, IV. 539.
—— forest schools, IV. 35.
—— miscellaneous publications on silviculture, IV. 122.
—— periodicals, IV. 539; V. XXIX.[1]
—— pharmacopoeias, III. 256.
—— a forest administration, IV. 293at te
—— textbooks and manuals of silviculture, IV. 109.
—— *see also* Iberian Peninsula.
Portulacaceae, II. 194.
Posoqueria, II. 827; III. 746.
Potalia, III. 682.
Potameia, II. 227.
Potaninia, II. 270.
Potash, IV. 395; V. XXXI.[3]
Potentilla, II. 270; III. 430.
Poterium, II. 270.
Pothomorphe, II. 93.
Pottingeria, II. 243.
Pottsia, II. 731.
Poulsenia, II. 155.
Poupartia, II. 458.
Fouroumа, III. 381.
Pourretia, II. 76, 529.
Pourthiaea, II. 269.
Pouteria, II. 700, 874.
Pouzolzia, II. 157.
Prainea, II. 155.
Prameria, III. 690.
Praravinia, II. 827.
Pre-Linnean botany, I. 271, 530; V. XIII.[1]
—— Latin names, *see* Dictionaries, I. 71, 522.
—— literature, keys to, I. 77.
Premna, II. 760; III. 697.
Prenanthes, II. 860, 866.
Preparation of the ground, III. 150; IV. 142, 545.
Preservation of timber, IV. 416, 557.
Pressing of wood, IV. 422.
Prestoea, II. 74.
Prestonia, II. 731; III. 690.
Prestoniopsis, II. 725.
Prevention of diseases and injuries, III. 196.
Prevostea, II. 746.
Prickles, *see* Appendages, I. 112.
Priestleya, II. 379.
Primulaceae, II. 695.
Principles and fundamental sciences of arboriculture, III. 35, 757; V. XXVIII.[1]
—— of forestry and fundamental sciences, IV. 56, 542.
Prinos, II. 462.
Prinsepia, II. 270.
Printzia, II. 864.
Prionium, II. 77.
Prionotes, II. 689.
Prioria, II. 379; III. 485.
Prismatocarpus, II. 846.
Prismatomeris, II. 827.
Pritchardia, II. 74; III. 330.
Pritchardia, II. 70; III. 326, 332.
Private forests, administration, IV. 307, 554.

Private forests, state supervision, IV. 285, 552.
Problastes, II. 617.
Prockia, II. 573; III. 615.
Prockia, II. 574.
Prockiopsis, II. 573.
Procris, II. 157.
Products, economic, III. 217, 757.
—— forest, IV. 396, 557; V. XXXI.[3]
—— various, III. 218.
Pronaya, II. 249; III. 416.
Pronaya, II. 247.
Propagation, III. 38, 152; IV. 146, 545.
—— vegetative, IV. 65, 149, 546; *see also* Cuttings, *and* Grafting.
—— *see also* Reproduction, I. 198, 527.
Proscephaleium, II. 827.
Prosopis, II. 379; III. 485, 758; IV. 522; V. XXVI.[3]
Prosorus, II. 449.
Prostanthera, II. 765; III. 698.
Prostea, II. 485, 488.
Protea, II. 165; III. 383.
Protea, II. 159, 163, 164, 165, 167.
Proteaceae, II. 158, 872; III. 382; V. XXVI.[1]
Protection from frost, III. 182.
—— of forests, *see* Forest protection, IV. 177.
Protective adaptations, I. 235, 529.
Protium, II. 418; III. 511.
Proustia, II. 864; III. 756.
Prumnopitys, II. 9; III. 287.
Pruning, II. 169; IV. 170, 547.
—— esthetic principles in, III. 202.
—— evergreens, III. 173.
—— fruit trees, III. 171.
—— plantlets, IV. 154.
—— shrubs, III. 172.
—— street trees, III. 211.
Prunopsis, II. 270.
Prunus, II. 270; III. 430; IV. 520; V. XXVI.[3]
Prunus, II. 540.
Prussia, forest descriptions, IV. 352, 555; V. XXXI.[3]
—— forest laws, IV. 319.
—— forest regulations, IV. 301.
—— state forest administration, IV. 290, 552.
—— *see also* Germany.
Psammisia, II. 675; III. 654.
Psathura, II. 827.
Pselium, II. 208.
Pseudais, II. 604.
Pseudaleia, II. 171.
Pseudaleioides, II. 171
Pseudanthus, II. 450.
Pseudehretia, II. 462.
Pseuderanthemum, II. 802, 874; III. 710.
Pseudima, II. 488.
Pseuditea, II. 248.
Pseudoacacia, II. 382.
Pseudobaeckea, II. 251.
Pseudocarpa, II. 421.
Pseudocalyx, II. 802.
Pseudocarapa, II. 421.
Pseudoeugenia, II. 625.
Pseudolarix, II. 49; III. 309.
Pseudolmedia, II. 155.
Pseudomorus, II. 155.
Pseudopanax, II. 651; III. 644.
Pseudophoenix, II. 74.
Pseudopteris, II. 488.
Pseudosmodingium, II. 458.
Pseudosorocea, II. 155.
Pseudospondias, II. 458.
Pseudotrophis, II. 155.
Pseudotsuga, II. 49; III. 309; IV. 483.
Pseudotsuga, II. 32.
Psiadia, II. 864.
Psidium, II. 632; III. 637.
Psilanthus, II. 827.
Psilobium, II. 827.
Psilosoler.a, II. 604.

Psilostachys, II. 438.
Psilotrichum, II. 190.
Psiloxylon, II. 573.
Psittacanthus, II. 177.
Psoralea, II. 379; III. 485.
Psoralea, II. 352.
Psorospermum, II. 558.
Psorospermum, II. 555.
Psychotria, II. 827; III. 746.
Psychotria, II. 811, 815, 819, 820, 825, 830; III. 747.
Psyllothamnus, II. 194.
Ptelea, II. 410; III. 505.
Pteleocarpa, II. 751.
Ptelidium, II. 471.
Pteridophyllum, II. 486.
Pterigium, II. 560.
Pterilema, II. 112.
Pterisanthes, II. 504; III. 545.
Pternandra, II. 641.
Pterocactus, II. 598.
Pterocalymma, II. 609.
Pterocarpus, II. 380; III. 485; IV. 522.
Pterocarpus, II. 349, 352.
Pterocarya, II. 114; III. 356.
Pterocelastrus, II. 471.
Pteroceltis, II. 142.
Pterocephalus, II. 844.
Pterochiton, II. 187.
Pterococcus, II. 184, 450.
Pterocoelion, II. 515.
Pterocymbium, II. 537.
Pterodiscus, II. 792; III. 708.
Pterodon, II. 485.
Pterolobium, II. 380.
Pteronema, II. 415.
Pteropetalum, II. 232.
Pterosiphon, II. 420.
Pterospermum, II. 537; III. 591.
Pterostegia, II. 185.
Pterostelma, II. 739.
Pterostemon, II. 243.
Pterostyrax, II. 744; III. 670.
Pterygocarpus, II. 737.
Pterygota, II. 537.
Pterygota, II. 532.
Ptilocalyx, II. 748.
Ptilochaeta, II. 427.
Ptilotus, II. 190.
Ptychopetalum, II. 171.
Ptychopyxis, II. 450.
Ptychorhaphis, III. 330.
Ptychosperma, II. 74; III. 330.
Ptychosperma, II. 68; III. 330, V. XXVI.[3]
Ptychostigma, II. 817.
Ptyssiglottis, II. 802.
Ptyxostoma, II. 251.
Publications relating to the cultivation of particular groups, III. 132; V. XXVIII.[1]
Pueraria, II. 380; III. 485; V. XXVI.[3]
Pukateria, II. 656.
Pulicaria, II. 864.
Pultenaea, II. 380; III. 486.
Pultenaea, II. 332, 345, 354, 373, 375; III. 467.
Puneeria, II. 778; III. 702.
Punica, II. 610; III. 630.
Punicaceae, II. 610; III. 630.
Pupalia, II. 190.
Purdiaea, II. 462.
Pure forests, treatment, IV. 137.
Purkinjia, II. 748.
Purpurella, II. 641.
Purshia, II. 278; III. 443.
Putoria, II. 829.
Putrangiva, III. 521.
Putranjiva, II. 450; III. 521.
Putzeysia, II. 483; III. 539.
Puya, II. 76.
Pycnanthemum, II. 765.
Pycnanthus, II. 221; III. 403.
Pycnarrhena, II. 208.
Pycnobotrya, II. 731.

Pycnocoma, II. 450; III. 521.
Pycnosandra, II. 440.
Pycnospora, II. 381.
Pycnostachys, II. 765.
Pygeum, II. 278.
Pyracantha, II. 278; III. 443.
Pyramis, II. 641.
Pyramidal trees, III. 204.
Pyramidocarpus, II. 573.
Pyrenacantha, II. 475.
Pyrenaria, II. 549.
Pyrenees, *see* Iberian Peninsula *and* France.
Pyrethrum, II. 854.
Pyrola, II. 657.
Pyrolaceae, II. 657.
Pyrospermum, II. 469.
Pyrostegia, II. 790; III. 707.
Pyrostria, II. 829.
Pyrrhanthus, II. 617.
Pyrrhocoma, II. 851.
Pyrrhosa, II. 403.
Pyrularia, II. 169.
Pyrus, II. 278; III. 444; V. xxix.[1]
Pyrus, II. 257, 258, 264, 266, 311; III. 419, 425, 459.
Pyxidanthera, II. 691.
Pyxidaria, II. 869.

Quadriala, II. 168.
Qualea, II. 428.
Qualea, II. 428.
Quapoya, II. 558.
Quararibea, II. 531.
Quartinia, II. 380.
Quassia, II. 415; III. 508.
Quassia, II. 415; III. 508, 509.
Quebrachia, II. 460.
Quercus, II. 128, 872; III. 361, 758; IV. 500, 559; V. xxvi.[1]
Quesnelia, II. 77.
Quiina, II. 547.
Quiinaceae, II. 547.
Quillaja, II. 281; III. 447.
Quinaria, II. 504.
Quinio, II. 207.
Quinsonia, II. 248.
Quintinia, II. 243.
Quisqualis, II. 617; III. 632.
Quivisia, II. 422.

Rabelaisia, II. 408; III. 504.
Racaria, II. 489.
Radamaea, II. 782.
Raddisia, II. 472.
Rademachia, II. 146.
Rademachera, II. 790.
Radermachia, II. 790.
Radermachia, II. 791.
Radlkofera, II. 488.
Radlkoferella, II. 698.
Radojitskya, II. 604.
Rafnia, II. 381.
Rafnia, II. 386.
Rail, transport of timber by, IV. 391.
Raillardia, II. 864.
Railway construction, timber used in, IV. 423, 557; V. xxxii.[1]
Railway sleepers, *see* Railway construction, IV. 423.
Rain, injuries caused by, III. 184; IV. 189, 548.
Rainfall, *see* Humidity, I. 232.
Raising of plants, III. 152.
Raleighia, II. 569.
Rameya, II. 208.
Ramification, I. 106, 524.
Ramisia, II. 192.
Ramona, II. 765.
Randia, II. 829; III. 747.
Randia, II. 817, 823.
Randonia, II. 234.
Ranunculaceae, II. 195, 872; III. 388; V. xxvi.[2]

Rapanea, II. 695.
Raphia, II. 74; III. 330.
Raphiacme, II. 742.
Raphides, *see* Crystals, I. 138, 525.
Raphiolepis, II. 281; III. 447.
Raphionacme, II. 742.
Raphiostylis, II. 475.
Raphistemma, II. 742.
Raphistemma, II. 737.
Raphithamnus, II. 760; III. 697.
Rapinia, II. 760.
Raputia, II. 410.
Raspalia, II. 251.
Rathea, II. 75, 581.
Ratonia, II. 485, 487.
Rania, II. 410.
Ravia, II. 405.
Rauwolfia, II. 731; III. 690.
Rauwolfia, II. 734, 754.
Ravenala, II. 91; III. 341; IV. 485.
Ravenea, II. 74; III. 330.
Ravenia, II. 410; III. 505.
Ravensara, II. 227; III. 407; IV. 520.
Razoumofskya, II. 174.
Rea, II. 855.
Reafforestation, *see* Afforestation. IV. 154.
Reaumuria, II. 562.
Redia, II. 438.
Reevesia, II. 537.
Reforestation, *see* Afforestation, IV. 154.
Refuse wood, IV. 433, 558.
—— utilization, IV. 431, 558.
Regelia, II. 633.
Regeneration, natural, IV. 139, 545.
Regnaldia, II. 438.
Regulations, *see* Forest regulations, IV. 295.
Reichardia, II. 780.
Reichenbachia, II. 192.
Reichenbachia, II. 191.
Reidia, II. 449.
Reifferscheidia, II. 541.
Reineckia, II. 75.
Reinhardtia, III. 331.
Reinhardtia, II. 71.
Reinwardtia, II. 393; III. 492.
Reinwardtia, II. 542.
Reissekia, II. 496.
Rejoua, II. 725, 732.
Relhania, II. 864.
Remijia, II. 830; III. 747.
Removal of stumps, IV. 385, 557.
Renardia, II. 574.
Renggeria, II. 558.
Renggeria, II. 554.
Rennellia, II. 823.
Reparative processes, I. 207, 528; V. xii.[1]
Reports on forest conditions, IV. 336; V. xxxi.[2]
Reproduction, I. 198, 527; III. 38; IV. ғ 65; V. xii.[1]
—— vegetative, I. 204, 528.
Reproductive interrelations, I. 236, 529.
—— organs, encouraging the development of, III. 174.
—— parts, morphology, I. 113, 524; V. xi.[1]
Reptonia, II. 700.
Resedaceae, II. 234.
Reserve material, storage and transfer, I. 179, 526; V. xi.[2]
Resin tapping, IV. 436.
Resins, I. 180; III. 227, 757; IV. 436; V. xi.[2]
Respiration, I. 169, 526.
Restoration of neglected woods, IV. 169.
Resuscitation of old trees, III. 181.
Retama, II. 359; III. 477.
Retanilla, II. 496.
Retarding of flowers and fruits, III. 176.
Retiniphyllum, II. 830.
Retinispora, II. 28; III. 300, 311.

Retinodendron, II. 561.
Retinodendropsis, II. 560.
Reunion, forest description, IV. 378.
—— *see also* Indian Ocean Islands.
Reversion of shoots and trees, I. 196, 527.
Revolving movements, I. 196.
Reynoldsia, II. 652.
Reynosia, II. 496.
Rhabdadenia, III. 690.
Rhabdia, II. 751.
Rhabdostigma, II. 830.
Rhabdothamnus, II. 795.
Rhacoma, II. 471.
Rhapanus, II. 491.
Rhagodia, II. 188; III. 387.
Rhagodia, II. 188.
Rhamnaceae, II. 491; III. 541; IV. 527.
Rhamnella, II. 496.
Rhamnus, II. 496; III. 542; IV. 527.
Rhamnus, II. 458, 492, 494, 495, 496, 499, 500, 872; III. 542.
Rhaphidanthe, II. 702.
Rhaphiolepis, II. 281; III. 447.
Rhaphiostylis, II. 475.
Rhaphispermum, II. 782.
Rhaphistemma, II. 742.
Rhaphithamnus, II. 760; III. 697.
Rhapidophyllum, II. 74.
Rhapis, II. 74; III. 331.
Rhaptonema, II. 208.
Rhaptopetalum, II. 540.
Rhazya, II. 731.
Rheedia, II. 558.
Rheirophyllum, II. 792.
Rhetinodendron, II. 864.
Rhexia, II. 641.
Rhexia, II. 636, 641.
Rhigiophyllum, II. 846.
Rhigozum, II. 790.
Rhinacanthus, II. 802; III. 710.
Rhinostegia, II. 169.
Rhipidodendron, II. 77.
Rhipidostigma, II. 702.
Rhipogonum, II. 84.
Rhipsalis, II. 598; III. 626.
Rhipsalis, II. 594.
Rhisobolese, *see* Caryocaraceae.
Rhizophora, II. 614; III. 632; IV. 529.
Rhizophora, II. 613, 692; III. 632.
Rhizophoraceae, II. 612; III. 631; IV. 529.
Rhodamnia, II. 633.
Rhode Island, *see* United States, North-eastern.
Rhodochiton, II. 782; III. 704.
Rhodoclada, II. 548.
Rhododendron, II. 675; III. 654.
Rhododendron, II. 684, 755; III. 662.
Rhodolaena, II. 511.
Rhodoleia, II. 254; III. 418.
Rhodomyrtus, III. 633; III. 637.
Rhodora, II. 675.
Rhodorhiza, II. 744.
Rhodostoma, II. 825; III. 746.
Rhodothamnus, II. 684; III. 662.
Rhodothamnus, II. 675.
Rhodotypos, II. 281; III. 447.
Rhodotypus, *see* Rhodotypos.
Rhoicissus, III. 545.
Rhombospora, II. 819.
Rhopala, II. 166; III. 383.
Rhopalandra, II. 207.
Rhopalocarpus, II. 215, 573.
Rhopalopilia, II. 170.
Rhopalostigma, II. 774.
Rhopalostylis, II. 69.
Rhus, II. 458; III. 526; IV. 526.
Rhus, II. 413, 415, 455, 456, 461; III. 524.
Rhynchanthera, II. 641.
Rhynchocalyx, II. 610.
Rhynchopetalum, II. 845.
Rhynchosia, II. 381; III. 486.

Rhynchosia, II. 354, 356, 386; III. 475.
Rhynchospermum, II. 864.
Rhynchospermum, II. 734; III. 691.
Rhynchostigma, II. 742.
Rhynchotechum, II. 795.
Rhynchotheca, II. 392.
Rhyssocarpus, II. 823.
Rhyticarpus, II. 654.
Rhytidandra, II. 615.
Rhytidophyllum, II. 795.
Rhytiglossa, II. 800; III. 709.
Ribeirea, II. 281.
Ribes, II. 243; III. 413.
Ricaurtea, II. 541.
Richaeia, II. 614.
Richea, II. 690; III. 665.
Richella, II. 218.
Richeria, II. 450.
Richetia, II. 559.
Ricinocarpus, II. 450.
Ricinodendron, II. 450; III. 521.
Ricinus, II. 450; III. 521.
Ricinus, II. 445.
Riedleia, II. 536, 539.
Rigiolepis, II. 684.
Rigiostachys, II. 415.
Rime, injuries caused by, III. 184; IV. 189, 548.
Ring-barking, III. 174.
Rinorea, II. 568.
Riocreuxia, II. 742.
Rissoa, II. 399.
Ritchiea, II. 233.
Rittera, II. 386.
Rivea, II. 746.
Rivina, II. 193.
Rivina, II. 193, 473.
Roads, IV. 266.
Robinia, II. 382; III. 486; IV. 522; V. XXXI.²
Robinia, II. 341, 363, 370, 374, 375, 383; III. 469, 481.
Robinsonella, II. 527.
Robinsonia, II. 864.
Roches, II. 237; III. 409.
Rochea, II. 236.
Rochefortia, II. 751.
Rochefortia, II. 750.
Rochonia, II. 864.
Rockery shrubs, III. 205.
Rodents, injuries caused by, III. 186; IV. 197, 548.
Rods, manufacture of, IV. 128.
Roella, II. 846; III. 754.
Roepera, II. 396.
Roettlera, II. 794.
Roezlia, II. 640.
Regiera, II. 830; III. 747.
Rohria, II. 853, 855.
Rolandra, II. 864.
Rollawils, II. 340.
Rollinia, II. 218.
Rondeletia, II. 830; III. 747.
Rondeletia, II. 819, 820, 831; III. 744.
Ronnowia, II. 448.
Root, morphology and anatomy, I. 103; V. XI.¹
Root cuttings, III. 158.
Root fusion, I. 209, 528; IV. 66.
Root grafting, III. 164.
Root growth, I. 188, 526.
Root pressure, I. 168, 526.
Root pruning, III. 173.
Ropalocarpus, II. 573.
Rosa, II. 281, 872; III. 447; IV. 520; V. XXIX.¹
Rosaceae, II. 255, 872; III. 419, 758; IV. 520; V. XXVI,² XXIX.¹
Rosalesia, II. 853.
Roscheria, II. 74.
Rosenbergia, II. 746.
Rosenia, II. 864.
Rosmarinus, II. 765; III. 698.
Rospidios, II. 701.

Rostellaria, II. 800; HI. 709.
Rostelleria, see Rostellaria.
Rotantha, II. 609.
Rotation, IV. 251, 551.
Rothmannia, II. 817, 829.
Rottlera, II. 446, 447, 452; III. 520.
Roucheria, II. 393.
Rough conversion of timber, IV. 387, 557.
Roulinia, II. 742.
Roumania, *see* Rumania, *also* Balkan Peninsula.
Roumea, II. 570, 574.
Roupala, II. 166; III. 383.
Roupala, II. 160, 163.
Roupellia, II. 731; III. 690.
Rourea, II. 317; III. 462.
Roussaeaceae, see Saxifragaceae.
Roussea, II. 246.
Roydsia, II. 233.
Royena, II. 703.
Ruagea, II. 421.
Rubia, II. 830.
Rubiaceae, II. 807; III. 710; IV. 538; V. XXVII,² XXIX.²
Rubus, II. 300; III. 457; V. XXVI.²
Rudgea, II. 830; III. 747.
Rudolphia, II. 383.
Ruehssia, II. 740.
Ruelingia, II. 194, 537.
Ruellia, II. 802; III. 710.
Ruellia, II. 797, 798, 799, 801, 803.
Ruizia, II. 537.
Ruizia, II. 222.
Rulingia, II. 537.
Rumania, erosion, IV. 188.
—— forest descriptions, IV. 375, 556.
—— forest laws, IV. 332.
—— forest policy, IV. 279.
—— measures promoting silviculture, IV. 41.
—— state forest administration, IV. 294.
—— *see also* Balkan Peninsula.
Rumea, II. 574.
Rumex, II. 186.
Rupala, II. 166.
Ruprechtia, II. 186.
Rusbya, II. 659.
Ruscus, II. 84; III. 338; IV. 485.
Ruscus, II. 85; III. 336.
Russelia, II. 782; III. 704.
Russia, acclimatization, III. 44.
—— administration of private forests, IV. 308.
—— afforestation, IV. 157.
—— Asiatic, *see* Asiatic Russia.
—— bibliography, I. 3.
—— botanic gardens, I. 41, 521; V. VIII.¹
—— cultivation of exotic trees, IV. 125.
—— cultivation of fruit trees, III. 134.
—— dendrography, IV. 79, 78, V. XXX.¹
—— descriptive botany, III. 67.
—— economic products, III. 270.
—— education, III. 32.
—— erosion, IV. 185.
—— exhibitions, IV. 19.
—— financial results of forest management, IV. 260.
—— forest descriptions, IV. 344, 555.
—— forest devastation, IV. 282.
—— forest experiment stations, IV. 37.
—— forest fires, IV. 182.
—— forest gardens, IV. 18.
—— forest influences, IV. 46.
—— forest laws, IV. 315.
—— forest management, IV. 247.
—— —— officers and employees, IV. 310for st
—— forest policy, IV. 273.
—— forest products, IV. 398.
—— forest protection, IV. 179.
—— forest regulations, IV. 296.
—— forest schools, IV. 30, 540.
—— forest servitudes, IV. 333.

Russia, galls, I. 215.
—— history, I. 80; III. 33; IV. 24.
—— individual trees, I. 296.
—— insects, IV. 205, 549.
—— manuals of arboriculture, III. 101.
—— measures promoting sylviculture, IV. 39.
—— miscellaneous publications on arboriculture, III. 120.
—— miscellaneous publications on silviculture, IV. 113.
—— al , I. 9, 519; III. 10; IV. 6, 538periodic s
—— pharmacopoeias, III. 247.
—— phenology, I. 223.
—— phytography, I. 358, 531; V. XIX.¹
—— silviculture and pasturing, IV. 135.
—— state forest administration, IV. 289.
—— a supervision of forests, IV. 286t te
—— taxes, tariffs, etc., IV. 284.
—— textbooks and manuals of forestry, IV. 94.
—— textbooks and manuals of silviculture, IV. 103.
—— timber trade, IV. 404, 557.
—— vernacular names, I. 73, 522.
—— viticulture, III. 551.
Rustia, II. 831.
Ruta, II. 410; III. 505.
Ruta, II. 399.
Rutaceae, II. 396, 873; III. 494, 758; IV. 524; V. XXIX.¹
Ruttya, II. 803.
Ruyschia, II. 547; III. 596.
Ryania, II. 573.
Rykia, II. 56.
Rylstonea, II. 633.
Ryparia, II. 573.
Ryparosa, II. 573.
Ryssopterys, II. 427.
Rytidophyllum, II. 795.
Rytidotus, II. 809.
Rytigynia, II. 833.

Sabal, II. 74; III. 331.
Sabal, III. 331.
Sabia, II. 491.
Sabiaceae, II. 490.
Sabicea, II. 831.
Sabina, II. 30.
Sabinea, II. 383.
Saccellium, II. 751.
Saccocalyx, II. 765.
Saccogloitis, II. 393.
Saccopetalum, II. 219.
Sacoglottis, II. 393.
Sageraea, II. 219.
Sageretia, II. 489.
Sagotia, II. 451; III. 522.
Sagraea, II. 637.
Saguerus, II. 64; III. 320, 330.
Sagus, II. 71, 74; III. 327, 330.
Sahagunia, II. 155.
Sakersia, II. 641.
Salacia, II. 472.
Salacia, II. 471.
Salaxis, II. 684.
Salazaria, II. 765.
Saldanhaea, II. 790.
Sale of timber, IV. 388, 557.
Salicaceae, II. 95, 871; III. 343; IV. 485; V. XXVI.¹
Salicornia, II. 188.
Salicornia, II. 188.
Salisburia, II. 7; III. 286.
Salix, II. 98, 871; III. 346; IV. 487; V. XXVI.¹
Salmea, II. 864; III. 756.
Salmeopsis, II. 864.
Salmia, II. 76; III. 332.
Salpichros, II. 774.

Salpigophora, II. 869.
Salpingantha, II. 803.
Salpinzantha, II. 803.
Salpixantha, II. 803.
Salsola, II. 188; III. 387.
Salsola, II. 188, 189.
Salsolaceae, see Chenopodiaceae.
Salvadora, II. 473; III. 533.
Salvadoraceae, II. 472; III. 533.
Salvia, II. 765; III. 698.
Salwedelia, II. 359.
Samadera, II. 415; III. 509.
Samara, II. 693.
Samaroceltis, II. 142.
Sambucus, II. 840; III. 751; IV. 538.
Samoa Islands, economic products, III. 283.
—— phytography, I. 510; V. xxiv.²
Samyda, II. 573.
Samyda, II. 570.
Samydaceae, see Flacourtiaceae.
Sanchezia, II. 803; III. 710.
Sand, as minor forest product, IV. 438.
Sandoricum, II. 421; IV. 525.
Sandwich Islands, see Hawaiian Islands, I. 509.
Sanfordia, II. 407.
Sanitary forest influences, III. 34; IV. 54, 542; V. xxx.¹
Santalaceae, II. 167, 872; III. 384; IV. 519.
Santalina, II. 831.
Santalum, II. 169; III. 384; IV. 519.
Santalum, II. 168.
Santiria, II. 418.
Santiriopsis, II. 418.
Santolina, II. 864.
Santolina, II. 850.
Sapindaceae, II. 483; III. 539.
Sapindus, II. 488; III. 540.
Sapindus, II. 421, 484, 485, 486.
Sapium, II. 451; III. 522.
Sapium, II. 437; III. 615.
Sapota, II. 700.
Sapota, II. 697, 699; III. 666, 668.
Sapotaceae, II. 696, 874; III. 666; IV. 534.
Sapranthus, II. 218.
Saprophytism, see Epiphytism, I. 234.
Saprosma, II. 831.
Saraca, II. 383; III. 487.
Sararanga, II. 57.
Sarcinanthus, II. 76.
Sarcobatus, II. 188; III. 387.
Sarcocaulon, II. 392.
Sarcocephalus, II. 831; III. 747.
Sarcococca, II. 453; III. 523.
Sarcocolla, II. 599.
Sarcoponum, II. 185.
Sarcolaena, II. 511.
Sarcolobus, II. 742; III. 694.
Sarcomphalus, II. 499.
Sarcomphalus, II. 496.
Sarcophyllum, II. 369.
Sarcophysa, II. 772.
Sarcopteryx, II. 485.
Sarcostemma, II. 742; III. 694.
Sarcostigma, II. 475; III. 533.
Sarcostyles, II. 240.
Sarcotheca, II. 393.
Sarcotheca, II. 460.
Sarcozygium, II. 396.
Sargentia, II. 410; III. 505.
Sariava, II. 703.
Saribus, II. 70.
Sarmienta, II. 795.
Sarotes, II. 534.
Sarothamnus, II. 349; III. 473.
Sarotheca, II. 800.
Sarothrostachys, II. 451.
Sassafras, II. 228; III. 407.
Sassafridium, II. 228.
Satanocrater, II. 803.
Satureia, II. 766.

Saurauia, II. 542; III. 596.
Sauropus, II. 451.
Sauvagesia, II. 545.
Savia, II. 451.
Saw mills, operation of, IV. 392.
Sawdust, IV. 431, 558.
Sawing of timber, IV. 392.
Saxegothaea, II. 10; III. 287.
Saxifragaceae, II. 237; III. 409.
Saxony, forest descriptions, IV. 352.
—— forest laws, IV. 321.
—— forest regulations, IV. 302.
—— state forest administration, IV. 291.
—— see also German Empire.
Scabiosa, II. 844.
Scaevola, II. 847; III. 754.
Scalesia, II. 864.
Scandinavia, acclimatization, III. 44.
—— bibliography, I. 3.
—— botanic gardens, I. 40, 521.
—— cultivation of exotic trees, IV. 125.
—— cultivation of fruit trees, III. 134.
—— dendrography, IV. 79.
—— descriptive botany, III. 66, 757.
—— economic products, III. 269.
—— financial results of forest management, IV. 260.
—— forest descriptions, IV. 342.
—— forest fires, IV. 182.
—— forest influences, IV. 46.
—— forest management, IV. 247; V. xxxi.¹
—— forest schools, IV. 30.
—— galls, I. 215.
—— history, I. 80; III. 33; IV. 24.
—— individual noteworthy trees, I. 296.
—— insects, IV. 205, 549.
—— manuals of arboriculture, III. 100.
—— miscellaneous publications on arboriculture, III. 119.
—— periodicals, III. 10; IV. 5, 539; V. xxvii;¹ see also Denmark, I. 8, Norway, I, 8, and Sweden, I. 8.
—— pharmacopoeias, III. 247.
—— phenology, I. 222.
—— phytography, I. 350, 531; V. xviii.¹
—— reproductive interrelations, see Europe, I. 239.
—— silviculture and pasturing, IV. 134.
—— timber trade, IV. 404, 557.
—— vernacular names, I. 73.
—— viticulture, III. 551.
—— see also Denmark, Norway and Sweden.
Scaphopetalum, II. 537.
Scepa, II. 437.
Schaefferia, II. 471.
Schanginia, II. 189.
Schaueria, II. 803.
Schaueria, II. 763.·
Schea, II. 874.·
Scheadendron, II. 616.
Scheelea, II. 64; III. 320.
Schefflera, II. 652; III. 644.
Schepperia, II. 230.
Schieckea, II. 466.
Schiedea, II. 194.
Schima, II. 591; III. 596.
Schima, II. 548.
Schimmelia, II. 398; III. 495.
Schindleria, II. 193.
Schinopsis, II. 460; III. 529.
Schinus, II. 460; III. 529.
Schinus, II. 456.
Schisandra, II. 213.
Schismatoclada, II. 831.
Schistocarpaea, II. 499.
Schistocarphs, II. 864.
Schistocodon, II. 742.
Schizandra, II. 213; III. 400.
Schizanthera, II. 640.

Schizocalyx, II. 473.
Schizocarpum, II. 845.
Schizochiton, II. 420.
Schizolaena, II. 511.
Schizolobium, III. 487.
Schizonotus, II. 311.
Schizophragma, II. 247; III. 415.
Schizopeis, II. 792.
Schizoscyphus, II. 383.
Schizosiphon, II. 383.
Schizostachyum, II. 60.
Schizostemma, II. 737, 741.
Schlechteria, II. 234.
Schlegelia, II. 790.
Schleinhera, II. 488; III. 540.
Schlumbergera, II. 597.
Schmaltzia, II. 458.
Schmardaea, II. 421.
Schmidelia, II. 484.
Schnella, II. 334.
Schoberia, II. 189.
Schoenleinia, II. 809.
Schoepfia, II. 171.
Schoepflopsis, II. 171.
Scholiera, II. 663.
Schollia, II. 739.
Schollia, II. 739.
Schotia, II. 383; III. 487.
Schottia, III. 487.
Schoutenia, II. 512.
Schradera, II. 831.
Schradera, II. 439, 810.
Schrankia, II. 383.
Schrebera, II. 714; III. 680.
Schrebera, II. 51, 740; III. 310.
Schubertia, II. 742; III. 694.
Schubertia, II. 51, 740; III. 310.
Schuermannia, II. 622.
Schufia, II. 643.
Schumacheria, II. 543.
Schuurmansia, II. 545.
Schwannia, II. 427.
Schweigeria, II. 568.
Schwenkfeldia, II. 831.
Schwenkia, II. 774.
Schwerinia, II. 639.
Sciadicarpus, II. 872.
Sciadodendron, II. 652.
Sciadopanax, II. 652.
Sciadophila, II. 496.
Sciadophyllum, II. 652; III. 644.
Sciadopitys, II. 49; III. 309; IV. 484.
Sciadotenia, II. 208.
Sciences, fundamental, of arboriculture, III. 35, 757.
—— of forestry, IV. 56; V. xxx.¹
Scion and stock, mutual influence, I. 246, 529; III. 39.
Sciophila, II. 157.·
Sciuris, II. 407.·
Sclerenchyma, see Mechanical tissues, I. 134.
Sclerocarpa, II. 461.
Sclerocarya, II. 461.|
Sclerochiton, II. 803.
Sclerolobium, II. 383.
Scleroolaena, II. 512.
Scleropyrum, II. 169.
Sclerostylis, II. 399.
Sclerotheca, II. 846.
Scleroxylon, II. 697.
Scolopia, II. 573; III. 615.
Scolosanthus, II. 831.
Scolytidae, IV. 203, 549.
Scoparia, III. 704.
Scorodocarpus, II. 172.
Scortechinia, II. 448.
Scotland, forest descriptions, IV. 358.
—— see also British Islands.
Scottellia, II. 570.
Scottia, II. 336.
Scrophularia, II. 782.
Scrophulariaceae, II. 778, 874; III. 702; IV. 538.

Scutellaria, II. 766; III. 698.
Scutia, II. 499.
Scutia, II. 492.
Scutinanthe, II. 418.
Scyphaea, II. 557.
Scyphiphora, II. 831.
Scyphocephalium, II. 221; III. 403.
Scyphochlamys, II. 831.
Scyphostegia, II. 222.
Scypbosyce, II. 155.
Scytanthus, II. 739, 804.
Scytopetalaceae, II. 540.
Sczegleewia, II. 537.
Seaforthia, II. 74; III. 319; V. xxvi.[1]
—— see also under Archontophoenix, II. 64.
Seaside planting, III. 41.
Season of felling, IV. 384, 557.
—— of flowering, III. 207.
—— of planting, III. 168; IV. 154.
Seasoning of timber, IV. 416.
Sebastiania, II. 451; III. 522.
Secamone, II. 742.
Secretory tissues, I. 134, 525; V. xi.[1]
Securidaca, II. 432; III. 514.
Securinega, II. 451; III. 522.
Securinega, II. 435.
Seddera, II. 746.
Sedgwickia, II. 252.
Sedum, II. 237.
Sedum, II. 235.
Seed catalogues, see Botanic gardens, I. 38.
Seed testing, IV. 147, 545.
Seedlings, I. 122; V. xi.[1]
Seeds, I. 120.
—— dissemination, I. 240.
—— forest, IV. 438; V. xxxi.[2]
—— gathering, keeping and preparing, IV. 147, 546.
—— selection of, IV. 147, 545.
—— shipping of, III. 154.
—— sowing of, III. 155; IV. 148.
—— testing of, III. 156.
—— vitality, I. 193, 527.
Seguiera, II. 193.
Seguieria, II. 193.
Selaginaceae, see Scrophulariaceae, II. 778.
Selago, II. 782.
Selago, II. 781.
Selection, artificial, III. 50; see also Evolution of cultivated plants, I. 246, 529.
—— natural, see Evolution.
—— system, coppice with standards, IV. 130, 545.
Selinum, III. 644.
Selkirkia, II. 751.
Semecarpus, II. 461; III. 529.
Semeiandra, II. 646.
Semele, II. 85; III. 338.
Sempervivum, II. 237.
Senapea, II. 869.
Senecio, II. 864; III. 756.
Senefeldera, II. 451.
Senegambia, see Africa, West.
Senna, II. 342; III. 470.
Senra, II. 527.
Sensitive plants, see Irritability, I. 193, 527.
Sepals, see Perianth.
Sequoia, II. 49; III. 309; IV. 484; V. xxv.[2]
Serenaea, II. 75.
Serenoa, II. 75; III. 331.
Serials, see Periodicals and serials.
Sericobonia, II. 800; III. 709.
Sericocoma, III. 190.
Sericodes, II. 396.
Sericographis, II. 800; III. 709.
Sericospora, II. 801.
Sericostoma, II. 751.
Seringia, II. 538.

Seringia, II. 535.
Serissa, II. 831; III. 748.
Serissa, II. 826.
Serjania, II. 488; III. 540.
Serjania, II. 490.
Serraea, II. 527.
Serronia, II. 93.
Serruria, II. 167.
Sersalisia, II. 700.
Servia, forest description, IV. 375.
—— measures promoting silviculture, IV. 41.
—— see also Balkan Peninsula.
Servitudes, forest, IV. 332, 555.
Sesamothamnus, II. 792.
Sesbania, II. 383; III. 487.
Sesses, II. 774.
Sesuvium, II. 194.
Sethia, II. 394.
Severinia, II. 399.
Seychelle Islands, phytography, I. 481, 536.
Shade trees, III. 208.
Sheadendron, II. 616.
Shedding of branches, see Casting off of branches, I. 192.
—— of leaves, see Leaf fall, I. 191.
Shelter plantations, III. 212, 215; IV. 154.
Shepherdia, II. 608; III. 629.
Sherbournia, II. 809.
Shingles, IV. 428.
Ship building, timber for, IV. 424; V. xxxii.[1]
Shipping of fruits, III. 173.
—— of plants, III. 154; IV. 151, 546.
—— of seeds, III. 154.
Shoes, wooden, see Wooden shoes, IV. 428.
Shoots, reproduction by, see Vegetative reproduction.
—— reversion, I. 196, 527.
Shorea, II. 560; III. 611; IV. 528.
Shorea, II. 559.
Shrubs, climbing, III. 204.
—— dwarf and creeping, see Dwarf and creeping plants, III. 205.
—— for rockery, III. 205.
—— for walls, III. 205.
—— pruning of, III. 172.
—— see also Trees and shrubs.
Shuteria, II. 384.
Siam, economic products, III. 276.
—— forest description, IV. 377.
—— phytography, I. 469.
—— see also Indochina.
Sibangea, II. 451.
Siberia, dendrography, IV. 87.
—— economic products, III. 272.
—— forest description, IV. 375.
—— forest policy, IV. 279.
—— phytography, I. 453; V. xxiii.[1]
—— state forest administration, IV. 294.
Siburatia, II. 694.
Sicily, phytography, I. 430, 535; V. xxii.[1]
—— see also Italy.
Sickingia, II. 831.
Sicklera, II. 768.
Sida, II. 527; III. 589.
Sida, II. 519, 521, 526; III. 586, 588.
Sidalcea, II. 528.
Sideranthus, II. 851.
Sideritis, II. 766.
Sideroxylon, II. 700, 874.
Sideroxylon, II. 462, 694, 697, 698, 700; III. 669.
Sigmatosiphon, II. 792.
Signatures, doctrine of, see Relation of properties to affinity, III. 259; V. xxviii.[1]
Silkworm trees, cultivation of, III. 148.
Silvia, II. 226.

Silvianthus, II. 841.
Silvics, see Ecology, IV. 67, Physiology, IV. 63, and Evolution, IV. 74; also Forest influences, IV. 42.
Silviculture, IV. 103, 544; V. xxx.[1]
—— measures promoting, IV. 39, 541.
—— miscellaneous publications on, IV. 111, 544; V. xxx.[1]
—— systems and methods of, IV. 127, 545.
—— textbooks and manuals of, IV. 103, 544; V. xxx.[1]
—— tools and machinery for, IV. 176, 547.
—— see also Arboriculture.
Silviculture and agriculture combined, IV. 132, 545.
Silviculture and fruit-trees, IV. 134.
Silviculture and pasturing, IV. 134, 545.
Silviculture with game-keeping, IV. 136.
Silviculture with regard to landscape effect, IV. 136, 545.
Simaba, II. 415; III. 509.
Simaruba, II. 415; III. 509.
Simaruba, II. 415.
Simarubaceae, II. 413; III. 506; IV. 524; V. xxvi.[2]
Simmondsia, II. 453; III. 523.
Sinapidendron, II. 234.
Sinapodendron, II. 234.
Sinclairia, II. 860.
Sindechites, II. 731.
Sindora, II. 384; III. 487.
Siolmatra, II. 844.
Sipanea, II. 831.
Siparuna, II. 222.
Siphocampylus, II. 846; III. 754.
Siphocampylus, II. 845.
Siphocodon, II. 846.
Siphocolea, II. 790.
Siphonandra, II. 811.
Siphonia, II. 445; III. 518.
Siphonodon, II. 471.
Siphonoglossa, II. 803.
Sipolisia, II. 866.
Sizygium, II. 633.
Skimmia, II. 411; III. 505.
Skytalanthus, II. 731.
Skytanthus, II. 731.
Slackia, II. 795.
Sladenia, II. 543.
Slides, transport of timber, IV. 390.
Sloanea, II. 511; III. 584.
Sloetia, II. 155, 879.
Small fruits, cultivation of, III. 147.
Smeathmannia, II. 572; III. 615.
Smilacaceae, see Liliaceae.
Smilax, II. 85; III. 338.
Smirnowia, II. 384.
Smithia, II. 384.
Smodingium, II. 461.
Smoke, injuries caused by, III. 185, IV. 192, 548.
Smythea, II. 499.
Snow, injuries caused by, III. 184; IV. 189, 548.
Soaresia, II. 148.
Societies, forestry, IV. 39, 541.
—— publications of, see Periodicals; see also Associations.
Society Islands, descriptive botany, III. 94.
—— economic products, III. 283.
—— phytography, I. 510.
Socotora, III. 741.
Socotra, see Africa, Northeast.
Soil, aeration of, III. 40.
—— as minor forest product, IV. 438.
—— fixation of, IV. 145, 545.
—— vegetative interrelations, I. 228.
Soil and its relation to tree growth, III. 40.
Soil relations, IV. 68, 543.

Solanaceae, II. 767, 874; III. 698.
Solandra, II. 7'·4; III. 701.
Solandra, II. 771.
Solanum, II. 774; III. 701.
Solanum, II. 771; III. 699.
Solenandra, II. 816.
Solenantha, II. 567.
Solenixora, II. 831.
Solenophora, II. 795.
Solenospermum, II. 469.
Solenostemma, III. 694.
Solenostigma, II. 141.
Solidago, II. 855, 860, 864.
Sollya, II. 249; III. 416.
Solmsia, II. 512.
Solomon Islands, see Bismarck Archipelago.
Somaliland, see Africa, Northeast.
Sonchus, II. 866.
Sonneratia, II. 610.
Sonneratiaceae, II. 610.
Sophora, II. 384; III. 487; IV. 524.
Sophora, II. 331, 349, 378, 388, 389.
Sorbaria, II. 311; III. 459.
Sorbus, II. 311; III. 459, 758; IV. 520; V. xxvi.[2]
Sorbus, III. 430.
Sorindeia, II. 461.
Sorocea, II. 155.
Sorting of timber, IV. 387.
Sotor, II. 789.
Soulamea, II. 416; III. 509.
Soulangia, II. 495.
Souroubea, II. 547; III. 596.
South Africa, afforestation, IV. 169.
—— bibliography, see Africa, I. 4.
—— botanic gardens, I. 69.
—— descriptive botany, III. 93.
—— economic products, III. 281.
—— exhibitions, IV. 21.
—— forest descriptions, IV. 379.
—— forest influences, IV. 49.
—— forest policy, IV. 280.
—— forest products, IV. 401.
—— miscellaneous publications on arboriculture, III. 131.
—— periodicals, IV. 16; see also Africa, I. 29.
—— phytography, I. 493; V. xxiv.[1]
—— reproductive interrelations, see Africa, I. 240.
South America, bibliography, I. 3.
—— botanic gardens, I. 39, 521; V. viii.[1]
—— cinchona cultivation, III. 713.
—— coffee cultivation, III. 728.
—— collections, III. 27.
—— cultivation of exotic trees, IV. 125.
—— dendrography, IV. 78.
—— descriptive botany, III. 63.
—— diseases and injuries, III. 178.
—— economic products, III. 264.
—— exhibitions, IV. 19.
—— forest descriptions, IV. 341.
—— forest exploitation, IV. 382.
—— forest laws, IV. 315.
—— forest products, IV. 398; V. xxxi.[2]
—— forest protection, IV. 179.
—— galls, I. 214.
—— history, I. 80; III. 32; V. x.[1]
—— individual noteworthy trees, I. 295.
—— injuries caused by insects, III. 188.
—— manuals of arboriculture, III. 99, {757.
—— miscellaneous publications on arboriculture, III. 118, 757.
—— miscellaneous publications on silviculture, IV. 113.
—— periodicals, I. 7, 519; III. 10, 757; IV. 5.
—— pharmacopoeias, III. 247.
—— phytography, I. 327, 531; V. xviii.[1]
—— reproductive interrelations, I. 239.

South America, tea cultivation, III. 601.
—— vernacular names, I. 72, 522.
—— viticulture, III. 551.
South Atlantic Islands, miscellaneous publications on arboriculture, III. 132.
—— phytography, I. 498.
South Carolina, see United States, Southeastern.
South Dakota, see United States, Western.
South Sea Islands, see Pacific Ocean Islands.
Southeastern United States, see United States, Southeastern.
Southwellia, II. 538.
Sowing, III. 155.
—— methods of, IV. 148.
—— and propagation, IV. 146, 545.
Soyauxia, II. 573.
Soymida, II. 421; III. 513.
Spadostyles, II. 380.
Spaendoncea, II. 338.
Spain, administration of private forests, IV. 554.
—— afforestation, IV. 164, 546.
—— arbor day, IV. 541.
—— erosion, IV. 186, 547.
—— exhibitions, IV. 20, 540.
—— forest descriptions, IV. 363, 556.
—— forest devastation, IV. 283.
—— forest fires, IV. 183.
—— forest laws, IV. 327, 555.
—— officers and employees, IV. 555.forest
—— forest policy, IV. 276, 551.
—— forest protection, IV. 181, 547.
—— forest regulations, IV. 304, 554.
—— forest schools, IV. 35, 541.
—— forest servitudes, IV. 334.
—— insects, IV. 209, 550.
—— measures promoting silviculture, IV. 41, 541.
—— miscellaneous publications on silviculture, IV. 122, 544.
—— periodicals, IV. 13, 539.
—— pharmacopoeias, III. 255.
—— silviculture and pasturing, IV. 135.
—— state forest administration, IV. 293, 553.
—— state supervision of forests, IV. 286.
—— taxes, tariffs, etc., IV. 552.
—— textbooks and manuals of forestry, IV. 99.
—— textbooks and manuals of silviculture, IV. 109.
—— timber trade, IV. 405, 557.
—— see also Iberian Peninsula.
Spanoghea, II. 484, 487.
Sparattanthelium, II. 229.
Sparattosperma, III. 707.
Sparmannia, II. 515; III. 585.
Spartianthus, II. 385.
Spartina, II. 60.
Spartium, II. 385; III. 488.
Spartium, II. 340, 349, 359; III. 473; IV. 521.
Spartocytisus, II. 349; III. 473.
Spartothamnus, II. 760.
Spathacanthus, II. 803.
Spathelia, II. 411.
Spathodea, II. 790; III. 707.
Spathodea, II. 788, 789, 790, 791.
Spatholobus, II. 385.
Speirostyla, II. 515.
Spermacoce, II. 831.
Spermadictyon, II. 819.
Spermolepis, II. 633; III. 637.
Sphacele, II. 766.
Sphacophyllum, II. 866.
Sphaeralcea, II. 528; III. 589.
Sphaerocarya, II. 169, 172.
Sphaerocoma, II. 194.
Sphaerodendron, II. 648.

Sphaerogyne, III. 639.
Sphaerolobium, II. 385; III. 488.
Sphaeroma, II. 528.
Sphaerophora, II. 823.
Sphaerophysa, II. 385.
Sphaerosepalum, II. 566.
Sphaerostema, II. 213; III. 400.
Sphaerothalamus, II. 219.
Sphalanthus, II. 617.
Sphedamnocarpus, II. 427.
Sphenodesma, II. 760.
Sphenogyne, II. 867.
Sphenostemon, II. 465.
Sphenotoma, II. 690.
Sphinctanthus, II. 831.
Sphragidia, II. 440.
Sphyranthera, II. 451.
Sphyrospermum, II. 684.
Spices, III. 221.
Spielmannia, III. 806.
Spigelia, II. 719.
Spilanthes, II. 866.
Spilanthes, II. 863.
Spines, ecology, I. 236.
—— morphology, I. 107.
Spinovitis, II. 505; III. 545.
Spiraea, II. 313; III. 460.
Spiraea, II. 264, 268, 269, 311, 316; III. 424, 430, 459.
Spiraeanthemum, II. 250.
Spiraeanthus, II. 316.
Spiraeopsis, II. 250.
Spiranthera, II. 411.
Spirolobium, II. 379.
Spiropetalum, II. 317.
Spirospermum, II. 208.
Spizia, II. 448.
Spondias, II. 461; III. 529.
Spondias, II. 416, 455, 456, 458.
Sponia, II. 141, 142.
Sportella, II. 278.
Spraying, III. 197.
Sprengelia, II. 690; III. 665.
Springalia, II. 690.
Spyridium, IV. 499; III. 543.
Squamellaria, II. 831.
Staavia, II. 252.
Stability of characters, see Heredity, I. 248.
Stachyanthus, II. 475.
Stachyarrhena, II. 832.
Stachyarpus, II. 9.
Stachycrater, II. 572.
Stachys, II. 767.
Stachys, II. 763, 766.
Stachystemon, II. 452.
Stachytarpheta, II. 760.
Stachyuraceae, II. 574; III. 615.
Stachyurus, II. 574; III. 615.
Stacking of timber, IV. 387.
Stadmannia, II. 489.
Stadmannia, II. 489; III. 539.
Stadtmannia, see Stadmannia.
Staehelina, II. 866.
Staehelina, II. 858.
Stagmaria, II. 456.
Stahlia, II. 385.
Staking trees, see Tree guards and supports, III. 198.
Stalagmites, see Stalagmitis.
Stalagmitis, II. 554; III. 609.
Stamens, see Androecium, I. 116, 524.
Standing trees, height of, IV. 215, 550.
—— volume of, IV. 216, 550.
Stangeria, II. 6; III. 286.
Stanleya, II. 234.
Stannia, II. 827.
Stapelia, II. 743.
Staphidium, II. 637.
Staphylea, II. 473; III. 533.
Staphylea, II. 473.
Staphyleaceae, II. 473; III. 533.
Staphylorhodos, II. 316.
Staphysora, II. 452.

Starch, I. 139, 525; III. 220.
State forest administration, IV. 288, 552.
State supervision of forests, IV. 285, 552.
Statice, II. 696; III. 666.
Statice, II. 696.
Statistics, forest, IV. 336; 555; V. xxxi.²
Staudtia, III. 403.
Stauntonia, II. 201; IH. 393.
Stauntonia, III. 393.
Stauracanthus, II. 387.
Stauranthus, II. 411.
Staurogyne, II. 803.
Stearodendron, II. 553; III. 608.
Steffensia, II. 93.
Steganthera, II. 222.
Stegnosperma, II. 193.
Stelechocarpus, II. 219.
Stellera, II. 606.
Stelmacrypton, II. 742.
Stelmatocrypton, II. 742.
Stem, morphology and anatomy, I. 104, 524.
—— teratology, I. 144, 525; V. xi.¹
—— torsion, I. 107.
Stemmadenia, II. 731.
Stemodia, II. 782; III. 704.
Stemonacanthus, II. 802.
Stemonoporus, II. 561.
Stemonurus, II. 475.
Stemotria, II. 782.
Stenanthera, II. 690; III. 665.
Stenocalyx, II. 427.
Stenocarpus, II. 167; III. 384.
Stenochilus, II. 805.
Stenocline, II. 866.
Stenodon, II. 641.
Stenolobium, II. 791.
Stenosiphonium, II. 803.
Stenostephanus, II. 803.
Stenostomum, II. 309.
Stenotropis, II. 356.
Stephanandra, II. 316; III. 462.
Stephania, II. 208; III. 397.
Stephania, II. 208.
Stephanodaphne, II. 606.
Stephanogastra, II. 636.
Stephanophysum, II. 802; III. 710.
Stephanotis, II. 742; III. 694.
Stephegyne, II. 823.
Sterculia, II. 538, 873; III. 591; V. xxvii.¹
Sterculia, II. 533; III. 590.
Sterculiaceae, II. 531, 873; III. 589, 763; V. xxvii.¹
Stereospermum, II. 791; III. 707.
Steriphoma, II. 233; III. 409.
Stevensia, II. 832.
Stevensonia, II. 72; III. 328.
Stevia, II. 866; III. 756.
Stewartia, II. 549.
—— see also Stuartia.
Sticks, walking and umbrella, see Rods, walking sticks, IV. 428.
Stiftia, II. 866; III. 756.
Stigmaphyllon, II. 427; III. 513.
Stigmatococca, II. 692.
Stigmatophyllum, II. 427.
Stilbaceae, see Verbenaceae.
Stilbanthus, II. 190.
Stilbe, II. 760.
Stillingia, II. 452.
Stillingia, II. 444; III. 522.
Stilpnophyllum, II. 832.
Stimulants, III. 221.
Stipules, morphology and anatomy, I. 111.
—— physiology, see Respiration, I. 169, 526.
Stironeurum, II. 700.
Stixis, II. 233.
Stizolobium, II. 373; III. 482.
Stocksia, II. 489.

Stoebe, II. 866.
Stoerkia, II. 81.
Stomata, morphology and anatomy, I. 131, 525.
Storage of reserve material, I. 179, 526; V. xi.²
Storckiella, II. 385.
Storing of fruits, III. 173.
Stormia, II. 217.
Storthocalyx, II. 489.
Strakaea, II. 181.
Stranvaesia, II. 316; III. 462.
Stranvaesia, II. 872.
Strasburgeria, II. 546.
Straussia, II. 832.
Strawadium, II. 611; III. 631.
Streblocarpus, II. 233.
Streblorrhiza, II. 385.
Streblosa, II. 827.
Streblus, II. 155; III. 381.
Street paving, IV. 425, 557.
Street trees, III. 208.
—— diseases and injuries of, III. 212.
—— planting of, III. 211.
—— pruning of, III. 211.
Strelitzia, II. 91.
Strength and elasticity of timber, IV. 409.
Streptodesmia, II. 329.
Streptosolen, II. 778; III. 702.
Streptostigma, II. 486.
Streptotrachelus, II. 731.
Strigilia, II. 704.
Strobilacanthus, II. 803.
Strobilanthes, II. 803; III. 710.
Strobilorachis, see Strobilorhachis.
Strobilorhachis, II. 797; III. 708.
Stroemia, II. 230.
Strombocarpa, II. 379; III. 485.
Strombosia, II. 172.
Strombosiopsis, II. 172.
Strongylodon, II. 385.
Strophanthus, II. 731; III. 690.
Structure of wood, I. 124, 524.
—— anomalous, I. 126, 525.
—— and bark, IV. 62, 543.
—— see also Stem, morphology and anatomy, I. 104, 524.
Strumpfia, III. 748.
Struthanthus, II. 177.
Struthiola, II. 606.
Strychnodaphne, II. 227.
Strychnos, II. 710; III. 682.
Strychnos, III. 688.
Stryphnodendron, II. 385; III. 488.
Strzeleckya, II. 407.
Stuartia, II. 549; III. 596.
Stübelia, II. 233.
Stumps, removal of, IV. 385, 557.
Sturtia, II. 521; III. 587.
Stylaithropus, II. 904.
Stylobasium, II. 316.
Styloceraceae, see Buxaceae.
Stylocoryna, II. 829.
Stylogyne, II. 695; III. 666.
Stylosanthes, II. 385.
Stypandra, II. 86.
Styphelia, II. 690; III. 665.
Styphelia, II. 688, 689.
Styphonia, II. 458.
Styracaceae, II. 704, 874; III. 670; V. xxvii.²
Styrax, II. 704, 874; III. 670; V. xxvii.²
Suaeda, II. 189; III. 387.
Suaeda, II. 188.
Succession of forest growth, IV. 74, 543.
Sudan, East, see Africa, Northeast.
Sudan, West, see Africa, West.
Sumatra, economic products, III. 275.
—— phytography, I. 467.
—— see also Malay Archipelago.
Sumbavia, II. 452.

Sundry forest products, IV. 438, 558.
Sun-scald, see Injuries caused by heat, III. 184.
Supports, III. 198.
Suregada, II. 444.
Suriana, II. 416.
Suringaria, II. 611.
Sutherlandia, II. 385; III. 488.
Suttonia, II. 695.
Suttonia, II. 695.
Swainsona, II. 385; III. 489.
Swainsonia, II. 385; III. 489.
Swammerdamia, II. 858; III. 755.
Swartzia, II. 386; III. 489.
Sweden, afforestation, IV. 156.
—— forest descriptions, IV. 344.
—— forest devastation, IV. 282.
—— forest laws, IV. 315.
—— forest policy, IV. 273.
—— forest protection, IV. 179.
—— miscellaneous publications on silviculture, IV. 113.
—— periodicals, I. 8, 519.
—— state forest administration, IV. 288.
—— textbooks and manuals of forestry, IV. 94.
—— textbooks and manuals of silviculture, IV. 103.
—— see also Scandinavia.
Sweetia, II. 386.
Swietenia, II. 422; III. 513; IV. 525.
Swietenia, II. 420, 421; III. 513.
Swintonia, II. 461.
Switzerland, acclimatization, III. 49.
—— administration of private forests, IV. 309.
—— afforestation, IV. 166.
—— arbor day, IV. 42.
—— bibliography, I. 4.
—— botanic gardens, I. 65.
—— cultivation of exotic trees, IV. 127.
—— cultivation of fruit trees, III. 145.
—— dendrography, IV. 86.
—— descriptive botany, III. 89.
—— economic products, III. 271.
—— erosion, IV. 187, 548.
—— exhibitions, IV. 20.
—— financial results of forest management, IV. 261.
—— forest descriptions, IV. 364.
—— forest devastation, IV. 283.
—— forest experiment stations, IV. 78.
—— forest fires, IV. 183.
—— forest influences, IV. 48.
—— forest laws, IV. 329, 555.
—— forest management, IV. 249.
—— forest officers and employees, IV. 311.
—— forest policy, IV. 277.
—— forest products, IV. 300.
—— forest protection, IV. 181.
—— forest regulations, IV. 305.
—— forest schools, IV. 36.
—— forest servitudes, IV. 334.
—— galls, I. 216.
—— history, I. 81; IV. 28.
—— individual noteworthy trees, I. 297.
—— insects, IV. 39.
—— manuals of arboriculture, III. 115.
—— measures promoting silviculture, IV. 41.
—— miscellaneous publications on arboriculture, III. 126.
—— miscellaneous publications on silviculture, IV. 123.
—— periodicals, I. 26, 520; III. 24; IV. 13.
—— pharmacopoeias, III. 256.
—— phenology, I. 227.
—— phytography, I. 432, 535; V. xxii.²
—— silviculture and pasturing, IV. 135.
—— state forest administration, IV. 294.

Switzerland, state supervision of forests, IV. 286.
—— textbooks and manuals of forestry, IV. 99.
—— textbooks and manuals of silviculture, IV. 110.
—— taxes, tariffs, etc., IV. 285.
—— timber trade, IV. 406.
—— vernacular names, I. 75.
—— viticulture, III. 558.
Syagrus, II. 67; III. 322.
Sycocarpus, II. 421.
Sycomorphe, II. 148.
Sycopsis, II. 254.
Sykesia, II. 817.
Symbiosis, I. 233, 529; IV. 73, 543.
Symbolanthus, II. 721.
Symmeria, II. 186.
Symphonia, II. 558; III. 610.
Symphorema, II. 761.
Symphoria, II. 841; III. 752.
Symphoricarpos, II. 841; III. 752.
Symphyllanthus, II. 432.
Symphyopappus, II. 866.
Symphyopetalon, II. 408.
Symphysia, II. 672.
Symphytonema, II. 743.
Sympieza, II. 684.
Symplocaceae, II. 703, 874; III. 670.
Symplocos, II. 703, 874; III. 670.
Symplocos, II. 558.
Synadenium, II. 452.
Synaedrys, II. 128.
Synanthereae, see Compositae.
Synaphea, II. 167.
Synaptea, II. 561.
Synaptolepis, II. 606.
Synarrhena, II. 699.
Syncarpia, II. 633; III. 637; IV. 534.
Synchodendron, II. 867.
Synclisia, II. 208.
Syncleisia, II. 208.
Syncolostemon, II. 767.
Syndesmis, II. 456.
Syndiclis, II. 228.
Synechanthus, II. 75.
Synisoon, II. 832.
Synoecia, II. 148.
Synoum, II. 422.
Synsepalum, II. 700; III. 669.
Syphocampylus, II. 846.
Syria, phytography, I. 479; V. xxiv.[1]
—— see also Asia, Western, and Asiatic Turkey.
Syrings, II. 714; III. 680.
Syringodea, II. 663.
Syrmatium, II. 363.
Systemon, II. 407.
Systems and methods of silviculture, IV. 127, 545.
Syzygium, II. 633; III. 637.

Tabebuia, II. 791; III. 707.
Tabernaemontana, II. 732; III. 690.
Tabernaemontana, II. 728, 731.
Tabernanthe, II. 733; III. 691.
Tacazzea, II. 743.
Tachiadenus, II. 721.
Tachigali, II. 386.
Tachigalia, II. 386.
Tacsonia, II. 581; III. 616.
Tacsonia, II. 576; III. 615.
Taeniochlaena, II. 317.
Tafalla, II. 867.
Talauma, II. 213; III. 400.
Talbotia, II. 90.
Talguenea, II. 499.
Talinella, II. 194.
Talinopsis, II. 194.
Talinum, II. 194.
Talinum, II. 194.
Talisia, II. 489.
Tamaricaceae, II. 561, 873; III. 612; IV. 529.

Tamarindus, II. 386; III. 489.
Tamariscineae, see Tamaricaceae.
Tamarix, II. 562, 873; III. 612; IV. 529.
Tamarix, II. 562.
Tamatavia, II. 811.
Tambourissa, II. 222.
Tamonea, II. 640.
Tamonopsis, II. 758.
Tan barks, IV. 435, 558.
Tanacetum, II. 854, 863.
Tanaecium, II. 791.
Tanaecium, II. 790.
Tanghinia, II. 733; III. 691.
Tanghinia, II. 725.
Tannin, I. 182; III. 237.
Taonabo, II. 550.
Tapeinosperma, II. 695.
Tapirira, II. 461.
Tapiscia, II. 473.
Tapura, II. 433.
Tar, manufacture of, IV. 436.
Taractogenos, II. 571.
Tarchonanthus, II. 867.
Tarenna, II. 832.
Tariffs, IV. 284, 552.
Tariri, II. 414.
Tarrietia, II. 539.
Tashiroea, II. 641.
Tasmania, botanic gardens, see Australasia, I. 69.
—— economic products, III. 283.
—— forest description, IV. 380.
—— forest products, IV. 402.
—— individual noteworthy trees, see Australasia, I. 298.
—— periodicals, see Australasia, I. 29.
—— phytography, I. 505.
—— see also Australasia.
Tasmannia, II. 209; III. 397.
Tassadia, II. 741.
Taubertia, II. 207.
Tauschia, II. 672.
Taverniera, II. 386.
Taxaceae, II. 8, 871; III. 287; IV. 440, 558.
Taxes, tariffs, etc., IV. 284, 552.
Taxodium, II. 51; III. 310; IV. 484; V. xxv.[2]
Taxodium, II. 49; III. 309.
Taxonomy, general, I. 254, 530; V. xiii.[1]
—— miscellaneous, I. 261, 530; V. xiii.[1]
—— textbooks, I. 254, 530; V. xiii.[1]
Taxotrophis, II. 155.
Taxus, II. 10, 871; III. 287; IV. 440, 558.
Technical terms, see Terminology.
Technique of collecting, I. 35, 520; V. viii.[1]
—— of illustrating, I. 37, 521.
—— of microscopy, see under Microtechnique, I. 36, 521; V. viii.[1]
Technology of economic products, III. 218.
—— of wood, IV. 407, 557.
Teclea, II. 411.
Tecoma, II. 791; III. 707; V. xxvii.[2]
Tecoma, II. 785, 786, 787, 789, 790, 791, 792; III. 705, 707.
Tecomaria, II. 792; III. 707.
Tecomella, II. 792.
Tectona, II. 761; III. 697; IV. 536; V. xxvii.[2]
Teedia, II. 782.
Tegumentary tissues, I. 129, 525; V. xi.[1]
Telanthera, II. 190.
Telectadium, II. 743.
Telfairia, III. 754.
Teline, II. 349.
Telopea, II. 167; III. 384.
Telotia, II. 208.
Temminckia, II. 847.
Temperate zone, ecology, I. 219.

Temperature, ecology, I. 231, 529.
—— see also Generation of heat, I. 186.
Templetonia, II. 386; III. 489.
Tending of forests, IV. 169, 547.
Tendrils, movements, I. 196.
Tennessee, see United States, Southeastern.
Tenorea, II. 411, 867.
Tension, I. 149; V. xi.[2]
Tephrosia, II. 386; III. 489.
Tephrosia, II. 374.
Tepualia, II. 633.
Teramnus, II. 387.
Teratology, I. 142, 525; III. 40; IV. 63; V. xi.[1]
Terebinthaceae, see Anacardiaceae.
Terechovskya, II. 869.
Terminalia, II. 617; III. 632; IV. 529.
Terminalia, II. 644.
Terminology, I. 69, 522; III. 29; V. ix,[1] xxvii.[2]
Ternstroemia, II. 550; III. 597; IV. 528.
Ternstroemia, II. 542.
Ternstroemiaceae, see Theaceae.
Terpnanthus, II. 411.
Ternopyllum, II. 554.
Tessarandra, II. 716.
Tessaria, II. 867.
Testing of seeds, III. 156.
—— of timber, IV. 415.
Tetracarpaea, II. 247.
Tetracentron, II. 214.
Tetracera, II. 543.
Tetrachyron, II. 854.
Tetracoccus, II. 452.
Tetracocyne, II. 573.
Tetracrypta, II. 613.
Tetractinostigma, II. 437.
Tetractomia, II. 408.
Tetradenia, II. 767.
Tetradenia, II. 226.
Tetradium, II. 406.
Tetradynia, II. 867.
Tetragastris, II. 418; III. 511.
Tetraglochin, II. 316.
Tetraglossa, II. 438.
Tetragonia, II. 194.
Tetragyne, II. 452.
Tetralopha, II. 832.
Tetrameles, II. 583.
Tetramerista, II. 550.
Tetramerium, II. 804.
Tetramerium, II. 817.
Tetranthera, II. 226, 228; III. 406; IV. 520.
Tetrapanax, II. 652; III. 644.
Tetrapathaea, II. 582.
Tetraplasandra, II. 653.
Tetrapleura, II. 521.
Tetrapteris, II. 427.
Tetrapteris, II. 426.
Tetrapterys, II. 426.
Tetrastemon, II. 631.
Tetrastigma, II. 504.
Tetrastylidium, II. 172.
Tetrastylis, II. 576.
Tetratheca, II. 429; III. 513.
Tetratheca, II. 429.
Tetrathylacium, II. 573.
Tetratome, II. 222.
Tetrazygia, II. 641.
Tetrazygia, II. 636, 640.
Tetreilema, II. 761.
Teucrium, II. 767.
Texas, see United States, Western.
Textbooks and manuals of forestry, IV. 94; V. xxx.[1]
—— and manuals of silviculture, IV. 103, 544; V. xxx.[1]
—— of general botany, I. 82, 523; V. x.[1]
—— of general taxonomy, I. 254, 530; V. xiii.[1]
—— of morphology and anatomy, I. 100, 524.

Textbooks, of physiological chemistry, I. 151; V. xi.[3]
—— of physiology, I. 148, 525.
—— see also Manuals.
Teysmannia, II. 75.
Thacombauia, II. 452.
Thamnea, II. 252.
Thamnia, II. 572.
Thamnocalamus, II. 58.
Thamnoseris, II. 867.
Thamnosma, II. 411.
Thea, II. 550; III. 597, 763; IV. 528; V. xxix.[2]
Theaceae, II. 547; III. 596, 763; IV. 528; V. xxix.[2]
Theaphyllum, II. 470.
Thecacoris, II. 452.
Thelira, II. 269.
Themistoclesia, II. 659.
Thenardia, II. 733.
Theobroma, II. 539; III. 592, 763.
Theobroma, III. 591.
Theodora, II. 383.
Theodorices, II. 869.
Theophrasta, II. 691; III. 665.
Theophrasta, II. 691; III. 665, 667.
Theophrastaceae, II. 691; III. 665.
Thermopsis, II. 387.
Thermopsis, II. 377; III. 484.
Thermotropism, see Movements and Irritability, I. 193.
Thesiaceae, see Santalaceae.
Thesium, II. 169.
Thespesia, II. 528.
Thespesocarpus, II. 701.
Thevetia, II. 733; III. 691.
Thibaudia, II. 684; III. 663.
Thibaudia, II. 659, 684; III. 647, 649, 654.
Thiersia, II. 832.
Thilachium, II. 233.
Thilos, II. 618.
Thinning, III. 173; IV. 172, 547.
—— esthetic principles in, III. 202.
—— financial aspects of, IV. 175.
—— influence on increment, IV. 175.
Thinouia, II. 489.
Thollonia, II. 474.
Thomandersia, II. 804.
Thomasia, II. 539; III. 595.
Thorelia, II. 870.
Thottea, II. 183.
Thouinia, II. 489; III. 540.
Thouinia, II. 448, 484, 490, 712, 745, 873.
Thouinidium, II. 490.
Thrinax, II. 75; III. 331.
Thryallis, II. 427.
Thryptomene, II. 633.
Thuja, II. 52; III. 311; IV. 484.
Thuja, II. 33, 53, 56?; IV. 299; IV. 447.
Thujopsis, II. 53; III. 312.
Thunbergia, II. 804; III. 710.
Thunbergia, II. 801.
Thuringian States, forest descriptions, IV. 355.
—— forest laws, IV. 322.
—— forest regulations, IV. 303.
—— a forest administration, IV. 291st te
—— see also German Empire.
Thuya, II. 27, 28, 52; III. 311; IV. 484.
Thuyopsis, II. 53; III. 312.
Thyana, II. 489.
Thylachium, II. 233.
Thymelaea, II. 606; III. 628.
Thymelaea, II. 604.
Thymelaeaceae, II. 599, 874; III. 626; IV. 529.
Thymelaeaceae, see Thymelaeaceae.
Thymelina, II. 603.
Thymus, II. 767.
Thyrsacanthus, II. 801, 802; III. 709.
Thyrsanthus, II. 388, 726.

Thyrsodium, II. 461.
Thyrsostachys, II. 60.
Tibet, phytography, I. 460, 536.
—— see also China.
Tibouchina, II. 641; III. 639.
Ticorea, II. 411.
Ticorea, II. 407.
Tierra del Fuego, phytography, I. 347.
Ties, railway, IV. 423; V. xxxii.[1]
Tiglium, II. 439; III. 516.
Tilesia, II. 868.
Tilia, II. 515; III. 585; IV. 528; V. xxvii.[1]
Tiliaceae, II. 512, 873; III. 584; IV. 528; V. xxvii.[1]
Tilicora, II. 208.
Tilsoides, II. 515.
Timbalia, II. 278.
Timber, attacked by fungi, IV. 414, 557.
—— attacked by insects, IV. 414, 557.
—— conversion of, IV. 392; V. xxxi.[2]
—— defects and unsoundness of, IV. 413, 414, 557.
—— density and hardness of, IV. 411.
—— disposal of, IV. 388, 557.
—— felled, contents of, IV. 219, 550.
—— physical and technical properties, IV. 407.
—— preservation of, IV. 416, 557.
—— rough conversion of, IV. 387, 557.
—— sale of, IV. 388, 557.
—— seasoning of, IV. 416.
—— sorting, IV. 387.
—— stacking, IV. 387.
—— suited for construction under ground or in water, IV. 426.
—— testing of, IV. 415.
—— transport of, IV. 388.
—— uses in construction, IV. 422, 557; V. xxxii.[1]
Timber-raising, combined with agriculture, IV. 134, 545.
Timber trade, IV. 402, 557.
Timeroyea, II. 192.
Timonius, II. 832.
Tina, II. 490.
Tinnaes, see Tinnea.
Tinnea, II. 767; III. 698.
Tinospora, II. 208; III. 397.
Tipuana, II. 387; III. 489.
Tirania, II. 233.
Tisonia, II. 574.
Tissues, anatomy, see Histology, I. 123, 524; V. xi.[1]
Tithonia, II. 867.
Tittmannia, II. 252.
Tobago, economic products, III. 267.
—— phytography, I. 338.
Tocoyena, II. 832.
Toddalia, II. 411; III. 506.
Toechima, II. 490.
Tolpis, II. 867.
Toluifera, II. 374; III. 482.
Tomex, II. 226.
Tomostylis, II. 613.
Tonkin, forest description, IV. 377.
—— phytography, I. 469, 536.
Tonsella, II. 472.
Tontelia, II. 472.
Tools, wood for, IV. 427.
—— and machinery used in silviculture, IV. 176, 547.
—— used in arboriculture, III. 177.
Top dressing, see Manuring, mulching, III. 151.
Topiary work, III. 202.
Toricellia, II. 656.
Torresea, II. 387.
Torreya, II. 12; III. 288.
Torsion of the stem, I. 107.
Touchiroa, II. 349.

Toulicia, II. 490.
Tounalea, II. 386.
Tournefortia, II. 751; III. 695.
Tournefortia, II. 750, 833.
Touroulia, II. 547.
Tourretia, II. 792.
Tovomita, II. 558.
Toxic effects, I. 210.
Toxicodendrum, II. 452; III. 522.
Toxicology, III. 260.
—— see also Descriptive botany, toxicological, III. 59.
Toxicophlaea, II. 722; III. 685.
Toxocarpus, II. 742.
Tozophoenix, II. 64.
Tozotropis, II. 348.
Toxylon, II. 153.
Trachelospermum, II. 734; III. 691.
Trachycarpus, II. 75; III. 331.
Trachylobium, II. 387; III. 489.
Trachymene, II. 654.
Tragia, II. 452.
Tragopyrum, II. 184.
Tramways, transport of timber, IV. 391.
Transcaucasia, forest descriptions, IV. 348.
—— phytography, I. 368, 531.
—— see also Russia.
Transfer of reserve material, I. 179, 526; V. xi.[2]
Transpiration, I. 166.
Transplanting large trees, III. 167.
Transport of timber, IV. 388.
Trattinickia, II. 418.
Traunia, II. 743.
Travels, I. 301, 531; V. xvi.[2]
—— notes of, see Forest descriptions, IV. 336.
Traversia, II. 864.
Treatises, general, see Miscellaneous publications.
Treatment of pure and mixed forests, IV. 137.
—— of wood, IV. 421.
Treculia, II. 155; III. 381.
Tree growth, soil and its relation to, III. 40.
Tree guards and supports, III. 198.
Tree lore, I. 517.
Tree planting, commemorative, III. 34.
Trees, disadvantages and damages caused by, III. 34.
—— large, transplanting of, III. 167.
—— mensuration of, see Mensuration, IV. 213.
—— utility and influences of, III. 34.
Trees and shrubs, flowering, see Ornamental flowers, III. 207.
—— fruiting, see Ornamental fruits, III. 207.
—— habit of, III. 204.
—— height of, III. 204.
—— ornamental properties of, III. 202.
—— ornamental uses of, III. 201.
—— pendulous, III. 204.
—— pyramidal and columnar, III. 204.
—— sanitary and esthetic influences, III. 34.
—— for temperate regions, III. 202.
—— for tropical and subtropical regions, III. 203.
—— see also Dendrography, IV. 75; also Forest products, IV. 396.
Trema, III. 142.
Tremandra, II. 429; III. 513.
Tremandraceae, II. 429; III. 513.
Tremanthera, II. 552.
Tremtanthera, II. 552.
Trematocarpus, II. 845.
Trematosperma, II. 475.
Trembleya, II. 642.
Tresanthera, II. 832.
Treutlera, II. 743.
Trevesia, II. 653; III. 644.

Trevoa, II. 499.
Trewia, II. 452.
Triadenia, II. 555.
Triainolepis, II. 832.
Trianaea, II. 778.
Trianosperma, II. 844, III. 753.
Trianthema, II. 194.
Trianthera, II. 782.
Triarthron, II. 177.
Triaspis, II. 428.
Tribeles, II. 247.
Tribrachya, II. 823.
Tribulus, II. 396.
Tricalysia, II. 832.
Tricera, II. 452.
Tricerma, II. 470.
Triceros, II. 461.
Trichadenia, II. 574.
Trichantha, II. 795.
Trichantha, II. 744.
Trichilia, II. 422, 873; III. 513.
Trichinium, II. 190.
Trichocaulon, II. 743.
Trichocladus, II. 254.
Trichodesma, II. 752.
Tricholobus, II. 317.
Trichomes, see Appendages, I. 112.
Trichosacme, II. 743; III. 694.
Trichosandra, II. 743.
Trichoscypha, II. 461.
Trichospermum, II. 513.
Trichosporum, II. 792.
Trichostema, II. 767.
Trichostigma, II. 193.
Triclisia, II. 208.
Tricomaria, II. 428.
Tricuspidaria, II. 509.
Tricycla, II. 191.
Tridesmis, II. 554.
Tridianisia, II. 476.
Tridimeris, II. 219.
Trigonia, II. 428.
Trigoniaceae, II. 428.
Trigoniastrum, II. 428.
Trigonochlamys, II. 418.
Trigonopleura, II. 452.
Trigonostemon, II. 452; III. 522.
Trigonotheca, II. 466.
Trigynaea, II. 219.
Trigyneia, II. 219.
Trilepisium, II. 870.
Trilix, II. 573.
Trimeranthus, II. 636.
Trimeris, II. 574.
Trimerisma, I. 250.
Trimming, see Pruning, III. 169.
Trinidad, botanic gardens, see South
  America, I. 39, 521.
—— economic products, III. 267.
—— phytography, I. 338.
Triolena, II. 642.
Triomma, II. 418.
Tripetaleia, II. 684.
Tripetalum, II. 558.
Triphasia, II. 411; III. 506.
Triphasia, II. 399; III. 496.
Tripinna, II. 761.
Triplandron, II. 554.
Triplaris, II. 186.
Triplochiton, II. 539.
Tripoli, see Mediterranean States.
Tripteris, II. 867.
Tripterygium, II. 471.
Triptolemaea, II. 352.
Trisciadia, II. 814.
Trisema, II. 541.
Tristan d' Acunha, see South Atlantic
  Islands.
Tristania, II. 633; III. 638.
Tristania, II. 629.
Tristaniopsis, II. 633.
Tristellateia, II. 428.
Tristemma, II. 642.
Tristira, II. 490.

Tristylium, II. 548.
Tritaenicum, II. 653.
Trithrinax, II. 75; III. 331.
Tritomodon, II. 663.
Triumfetta, II. 513.
Trivalvaria, II. 219.
Trixis, II. 867.
Trixis, II. 863.
Trochetia, II. 539; III. 595.
Trochocarpa, II. 691; III. 665.
Trochodendraceae, II. 194.
Trochodendron, II. 194.
Trochomeria, II. 845.
Trochostigma, II. 540.
Troostwykia, II. 317.
Trophis, II. 156.
Trophis, II. 154, 155; III. 381.
Tropical zone, ecology, I. 219, 528.
Tropidolepis, II. 854.
Tropidopetalum, II. 870.
Trujanoa, II. 452.
Trymalium, II. 499.
Trymalium, III. 543.
Trymatococcus, II. 156.
Tschudya, II. 638.
Tsuga, II. 53; III. 312; IV. 484; V.
  XXV.²
Tsuga, II. 49; III. 309.
Tsusiophyllum, II. 684.
Tuberaria, II. 613.
Tuckermannia, II. 453.
Tulicia, II. 490.
Tumboa, II. 55.
Tumion, II. 12; III. 288.
Tunis, forest description, IV. 379.
—— see also Mediterranean States.
Tupa, II. 845; III. 754.
Tupeia, II. 177.
Tupeia, II. 168.·.
Tupidanthus, II. 653.
Turgidity and tension, I. 149; V. XI.²
Turkestan, forest policy, IV. 279.
—— forest schools, IV. 37.
—— insects, IV. 210.
—— see also Russia, Central Asiatic.
Turkey, Asiatic, see Asiatic Turkey.
—— forest descriptions, IV. 375.
—— forest regulations, IV. 307.
—— see also Balkan Peninsula.
Turnera, II. 575; III. 615.
Turnera, II. 575.
Turneraceae, II. 574; III. 615.
Turners' wood, IV. 427.
Turpentine, manufacture of, IV. 436.
Turpinia, II. 473.
Turpinia, II. 473, 867.
Turraea, II. 422; III. 513.
Turraea, II. 421.
Turraeanthus, II. 423.
Tweedia, II. 741.
Twining plants, see Climbing plants, I.
  236, 529; III. 204.
Tylanthus, II. 495.
Tylecarpus, II. 476.
Tylophora, II. 743; III. 694.
Tylophora, II. 737.
Tylophoropsis, III. 743.
Tylosepalum, II. 452.
Tympananthe, II. 737.
Tynanthus, II. 792; III. 707.

Uapaca, II. 452.
Ucriana, II. 809.
Ugni, II. 634; III. 638; V. XXVII.¹
Uhdea, II. 856; III. 755.
Ulex, II. 387; III. 489.
Ulmaceae, II. 141, 872; III. 363; IV.
  518.
Ulmus, III. 366.
Umbelliferae, II. 653; III. 644.
Umbellularia, II. 228; III. 408.
Unanuea, III. 704.
Uncaria, II. 832; III. 748.

Uncaria, II. 823.
Underground construction, timber, IV.
  426.
Undergrowth, III. 215; IV. 132.
Ungeria, II. 539.
Ungnadia, II. 490; III. 540.
United States, administration of private
  forests, IV. 308.
—— arbor day, IV. 41, 541; V. XXIX.²
—— bibliography, see North America,
  I. 3.
—— botanic gardens, I. 38, 521; V.
  VIII.¹
—— cultivation of fruit trees, III. 132.
—— economic products, III. 262; V.
  XXVII.²
—— exhibitions, IV. 19.
—— forest descriptions, IV. 337, 555.
—— forest devastation, IV. 281, 552.
—— forest exploitation, IV. 382.
—— forest fires, IV. 182.
—— forest laws, IV. 314.
—— forest management, IV. 247.
—— forest policy, IV. 271, 551; V.
  XXXI.¹
—— forest products, IV. 397; V. XXXI.²
—— forest protection, IV. 178.
—— forest schools, IV. 30.
—— galls, see North America, I. 214.
—— history, see North America, I. 80.
—— individual noteworthy trees, see
  North America, I. 295; V. XVI.¹
—— measures promoting silviculture,
  IV. 39.
—— miscellaneous publications on arboriculture, III. 116.
—— miscellaneous publications on silviculture, IV. 111; V. XXX.¹
—— Northeastern, dendrography, IV.
  76, 544; economic products, III. 262;
  forest descriptions, IV. 338; miscellaneous publications on arboriculture,
  III. 116; phytography, I. 312, 531;
  V. XVII.¹
—— periodicals, I. 4, 519; III. 2, 757;
  IV. 3, 539; V. VII.¹
—— pharmacopoeias, III. 246.
—— phenology, see North America, I.
  222, 528.
—— phytography, I. 312, 317, 320, 531.
—— phytography, see also Alaska, I.
  311.
—— reproductive interrelations, see
  North America, I. 239.
—— Southeastern, dendrography, IV.
  77; economic products, III. 263;
  forest descriptions, IV. 339; miscellaneous publications on arboriculture,
  III. 117; phytography, I. 317, 531;
  V. XVII.¹
—— a forest administration, IV.
  288t te
—— taxes, tariffs, etc., IV. 284.
—— timber trade, IV. 403.
—— vernacular names, see North America, I. 72.
—— Western, dendrography, IV. 77,
  544; economic products, III. 264; V.
  XXVIII.²; forest descriptions, IV. 340,
  555; miscellaneous publications on ar-
  boriculture, III. 117; phytography, I.
  320, 531; V. XVII.²
Unona, II. 219.
Unona, II. 216, 217; III. 401.
Urania, II. 870; III. 341.
Uragoga, II. 810, 827.
Uraria, II. 388; III. 490.
Urceola, II. 734; III. 691.
Urechites, III. 691.
Urena, II. 528; III. 589.
Urera, II. 158; III. 382.
Urocarpus, II. 399.
Urophyllum, II. 833.
Urostigma, II. 148; III. 368.

Ursinia, II. 867.
Urtica, II. 148, 156, 157, 158; III. 381, 382.
Urticaceae, II. 156; III. 381.
Uruguay, descriptive botany, III. 65.
—— economic products, III. 269.
—— periodicals, *see* South America, I. 7.
—— phytography, I. 344; V. xviii.[2]
Urvillea, II. 490.
Urvillea, II. 488.
Uses of timber in construction, IV. 422, 557; V. xxxi.[1]
Uses of wood in manufacture, IV. 426, 557.
Usteria, II. 720.
Utah, *see* United States, Western.
Uterveria, II. 230.
Utility and influences of trees, III. 34.
Utilization of fruits, III. 174.
Utleria, II. 743.
Uvaria, II. 219, 872; III. 402.
Uvaria, II. 216, 218, 219.

Vacciniopsis, II. 684.
Vaccinium, II. 684; III. 663; IV. 534; V. xxvii.[2]
Vaccinium, II. 659, 663, 671, 672, 674; III. 652, 653.
Vahea, II. 727.
Vahlia, II. 533.
Valenzuelia, II. 490.
Valeriana, II. 844.
Valerianaceae, II. 844.
Vallaris, II. 734.
Vallea, II. 511.
Vallesia, II. 734.
Valuation, II. 200.
—— of forests, *see* Forest valuation.
Vangueria, II. 833.
Vanhouttea, II. 795.
Vanieria, II. 541.
Vantanea, II. 393.
Varenna, III. 477.
Vargasia, II. 546.
Variation, I. 243.
—— by hybridization, I. 245, 529.
Variegated foliage, III. 206.
Varilla, II. 867.
Varnish, III. 232.
Varronia, II. 748.
Varthemia, II. 867.
Vasconcellea, II. 582; III. 617.
Vasconcellia, II. 785.
Vasconellosia, II. 502.
Vasconella, III. 617.
Vascular plants, diseases and injuries caused by, IV. 210.
—— tissues, I. 133.
Vateria, II. 561; III. 611.
Vateria, II. 561.
Vateriopsis, II. 561.
Vatica, II. 561; III. 611.
Vatica, II. 560.
Vauquelinia, II. 316.
Vavaea, II. 423.
Vavanga, II. 833.
Veatchia, II. 461.
Vegetative interrelations, I. 228, 529; V. xii.[2]
Vegetative parts, morphology and anatomy, I. 103, 524; V. xi.[1]
Vegetative propagation, IV. 65, 149, 516; *see also* Cuttings, *and* Grafting.
Vegetative reproduction, I. 204, 528.
Veitchia, II. 75; III. 331.
Velasquezia, II. 186.
Vella, II. 234.
Vellosia, II. 90.
Vellozia, II. 90.
Velloziaceae, II. 90; III. 341.
Venegasia, II. 867.
Venezuela, coffee cultivation, III. 729.
—— descriptive botany, III. 64.
—— economic products, III. 267.

Venezuela, forest products, IV. 398.
—— miscellaneous publications on arboriculture, III. 118.
—— periodicals, *see* South America, I. 7.
—— phytography, I. 338.
—— vernacular names, *see* South America, I. 72.
Ventenatia, II. 572.
Ventilago, II. 499; III. 543.
Veprecella, II. 642.
Vepris, II. 411.
Vepris, II. 397, 411.
Verbena, II. 761.
Verbena, II. 753, 758, 760.
Verbenaceae, II. 752; III. 695; IV. 536; V. xxvii.[2]
Verbesina, II. 867.
Verbesina, II. 860.
Vereia, II. 236.
Vermont, *see* United States, Northeastern.
Vernacular names, I. 71, 522; V. ix.[1]
Vernicia, II. 436.
Vernonia, II. 867; III. 756.
Vernonia, II. 852.
Veronica, II. 782, 874; III. 704.
Verschaffeltia, II. 75; III. 332.
Verschaffeltia, II. 74.
Verticordia, II. 634; III. 638.
Vesalea, II. 834.
Vesicaria, II. 234.
Vestia, II. 778.
Vetrix, II. 98.
Vexillaria, II. 345.
Vialia, II. 536.
Viborgia, II. 388.
Viborquia, II. 358.
Viburnum, II. 842; III. 752.
Vicentia, II. 617.
Victoriperrea, II. 56.
Vieillardia, II. 192, 345.
Vigna, III. 490.
Viguiera, II. 868.
Villamilla, II. 193.
Villaresia, II. 476; III. 533.
Villaresia, II. 432, 474.
Villaresia, II. 476.
Villaria, II. 833.
Villebrunea, II. 158; III. 382.
Viminaria, II. 388; III. 490.
Vinca, III. 691.
Vinca, II. 728, 731, 738.
Vinsentia, II. 519.
Vincetoxicum, II. 737.
Vines, *see* Climbing plants, I. 236, 529, *and* Climbing shrubs, III. 204.
Vintenatia, II. 690.
Viola, II. 568.
Violaceae, II. 566; III. 613.
Virecta, II. 833.
Virgilia, II. 600.
Virgilia, II. 340, 346, 384; III. 472.
Virginia, *see* United States, Southeastern.
Virola, II. 221; III. 403.
Viscainoa, II. 396.
Viscum, II. 177, 872; III. 385; IV. 519.
Viscum, II. 174, 176, 177.
Visenia, II. 536; III. 591.
Visiania, II. 711.
Vismia, II. 558.
Visnea, II. 552; III. 608.
Vitacese, II. 501, 873; HI. 544, 758; V. xxvii.[1] xxix.[2]
Vitality, I. 192, 527; V. xii.[1]
Vitex, II. 761; III. 697.
Vitex, II. 760.
Viticastrum, II. 760.
Viticulture, III. 548.
Vitis, II. 505, 873; III. 545, 758; V. xxix.[2]
—— pathological, III. 559.
Vitis, II. 501, 502, 504; III. 544, 545.

Vitmannia, II. 415.
Vittadinia, II. 868.
Viviania, II. 392.
Viviania, II. 392, 819, 823.
Voacanga, II. 734.
Vochysia, II. 428.
Vochysia, II. 428.
Vochysiaceae, II. 428.
Vogelia, II. 696.
Vohemaria, II. 743.
Volkameria, II. 755.
Volkensia, II. 868.
Volkmannia, II. 755.
Volume, change of, in timber, IV. 411.
Volume of standing trees, IV. 216, 550.
Volume of whole forests, IV. 216.
Volume tables, IV. 229.
Vouacapoua, II. 332; III. 467.
Vouapa, II. 371.
Vyenomus, II. 467.

Wagatea, II. 388; III. 490.
Wahlbomia, II. 543.
Wahlenbergia, II. 846.
Wahlenbergia, II. 832.
Waldemaria, II. 675.
Walking sticks, IV. 428.
Wall shrubs, III. 205.
Wallenia, II. 695.
Wallenia, II. 692, 693.
Wallichia, II. 75; III. 332.
Wallichia, II. 833; III. 325.
Wallisia, II. 721; III. 685.
Walpersia, II. 495.
Walsura, II. 423.
Waltheria, II. 844.
Warionia, II. 868.
Warszewiczia, II. 833.
Washington, *see* United States, Western.
Washingtonia, II. 75; III. 332.
Washingtonia, II. 49.
Water, evaporation, *see* Transpiration, I. 166.
—— exudation, I. 169, 526.
—— injuries caused by, III. 185.
—— transport or timber by, IV. 390.
Water supply, forest influence on, IV. 49, 542.
Watering, III. 150.
Wax, III. 225; *see also* Oils and fats, I. 181, 526.
Webera, II. 832.
Wedelia, II. 868.
Weeping trees, *see* Pendulous trees, III. 204.
Weigela, II. 834; III. 748.
Weigeltia, II. 695.
Weihea, II. 614.
Weinmannia, II. 250.
Weinmannia, II. 250.
Welfia, II. 75; III. 332.
Wellingtonia, II. 49; III. 309; IV. 484.
Wallstedtia, II. 752.
Welwitschia, II. 55; III. 312.
Wendlandia, II. 833.
Wendlandia, II. 207.
Wendtia, II. 392.
Wensea, II. 765.
West Africa, *see* Africa, West.
West Indian Islands, coffee cultivation, III. 728.
—— dendrography, IV. 78.
—— descriptive botany, III. 63.
—— economic products, III. 265.
—— forest descriptions, IV. 341.
—— forest products, IV. 398.
—— miscellaneous publications on arboriculture, III. 118.
—— phytography, I. 334; V. xviii.[1]
—— *see also* Central America.
West Virginia, *see* United States, Southeastern.
Westia, II. 388.
Western Asia, *see* Asia, *and* Asiatic Turkey.

Western United States, *see* United States, Western.
Westringia, II. 767; III. 698.
Wetria, II. 452.
Wettinia, II. 75.
Whipplea, II. 247.
Whipplea, II. 240.
Whitfieldia, II. 805.
Whitia, II. 794.
Wiborgia, II. 388.
Wickerwork, IV. 429.
Widdringtonia, III. 312.
Widdringtonia, II. 27; III. 299; IV. 447.
Wigandia, II. 747; III. 695.
Wightia, II. 783.
Wikstroemia, II. 606; III. 628.
Wikstroemia, II. 856.
Wilbrandia, II. 752.
Wilkiea, II. 222.
Willardia, II. 388.
Willoughbeia, III. 691.
Willughbeia, II. 734; III. 691.
Wilsonia, II. 746, 870.
Wilsonia, II. 757.
Wimmeria, II. 471.
Wimmeria, II. 471.
Wind, injuries caused by, III. 184; IV. 188, 548.
—— *see also* Atmospheric influences, I. 233; Dissemination, I. 240; Migration, I. 241; Reproductive interrelations, I. 236, 529.
Windbreaks, *see* Shelter plantations.
Windmannia, II. 250.
Winter effects, III. 208.
Winter state of trees and shrubs, I. 294.
Wintera, II. 209; III. 397.
Winteraceae, *see* Magnoliaceae.
Winterana, II. 566.
Winteranaceae, *see* Canellaceae.
Winterania, III. 613.
Wisconsin, *see* United States, Northeastern.
Wissadula, II. 528.
Wistaria, II. 388; III. 490.
Wisteria, II. 388.
Withania, II. 778; III. 702.
Witheringia, II. 768.
Wittelsbachia, II. 566.
Wolkensteinia, II. 545.
Wollastonia, II. 868.
Wood, bending and pressing, IV. 422.
—— chemical composition, I. 154, 526; V. XI.[2]
—— coloring, IV. 422, 557.
—— defects and unsoundness, IV. 413, 557.
—— encouraging the maturation, III. 174.
—— increase, I. 189, 527; V. XII.[1]
—— pathology, I. 206.
—— refuse, *see* Refuse wood.
—— structure, I. 124, 524; IV. 62, 543.
—— technology, IV. 407, 557.
—— treatment, IV. 421, 557.
—— uses in manufacture, IV. 426, 557.

Wood wounds, *see* Wounds and mutilations.
Wood for machinery, IV. 427.
Wood for tools, IV. 427.
Wood-carving, wood for, IV. 427.
Wood collections, I. 37; IV. 17, 539; V. VIII.[1]
Wood famine, IV. 280, 552.
Wood fibres, IV. 429.
Wood products, medical uses of, IV. 433, 558.
Wood pulp, IV. 429, 557.
Wood structure, I. 124, 524; V. XI.[1]
—— *see also* Stem, morphology and anatomy, I. 104, 524.
Wood-wool, IV. 429, 558.
Wood-working machinery, IV. 421.
Wooden shoes, IV. 428.
Woodfordia, II. 610; III. 630.
Woods, formation of, IV. 140, 545.
Working of wood, IV. 421.
Wormia, II. 543.
Wounds and mutilations, I. 207, 528; V. XII.[1]
—— to bark and wood, III. 180.
Wrightia, II. 734; III. 691.
Wulffia, III. 868.
Wulfhorstia, II. 423.
Wunderlichia, II. 868.
Wurtemberg, forest descriptions, IV. 356.
—— forest laws, IV. 322.
—— forest regulations, IV. 303.
—— state forest administration, IV. 291.
—— *see also* German Empire.
Wurtzia, II. 449.
Wyoming, *see* United States, Western.

Xanthoceras, II. 490; III. 540.
Xanthocercis, II. 389.
Xanthochymus, II. 554; III. 609.
Xanthophyllum, II. 432; III. 514.
Xanthorhiza, II. 200; III. 393.
Xanthorrhoea, II. 86; III. 339.
Xanthosia, II. 654.
Xanthostemon, II. 634; III. 638.
Xanthoxylon, II. 411; III. 506.
Xenia, I. 201, 528.
Xenostoma, II. 766.
Xeranthemum, II. 858, 859, 863.
Xerochlamys, II. 511.
Xeropetalum, II. 533.
Xerophyta, II. 90; III. 341.
Xerosollya, II. 249.
Xerotia, II. 194.
Ximenia, II. 172; III. 384.
Ximenia, II. 172.
Xiphocarpus, II. 386.
Xolisma, II. 673.
Xylia, II. 389; III. 491; IV. 524.
Xylinabaria, II. 734.
Xylocarpus, II. 423; III. 513.
Xylococcus, II. 660.
Xylolaena, II. 512.
Xylomelum, II. 167.
Xylophylla, II. 449.

Xylopia, II. 219, 872; III. 402.
Xylosma, II. 574.
Xylosteum, II. 835; III. 749.
Xylotheca, II. 572.
Xylothermia, II. 376.
Xymalos, II. 222.
Xynophylla, II. 168.
Xysmalobium, II. 743.

Yangua, II. 787.
Year rings, *see* Annual rings, I. 127, 525.
Yield, determination of, IV. 232, 235, 550.
Yucca, II. 86; III. 339.
Yulania, II. 211.

Zaczatea, II. 742.
Zalacca, II. 75; III. 332.
Zalusania, II. 868.
Zaluzianskya, II. 783.
Zamia, II. 6; III. 286.
Zamia, II. 6; III. 285.
Zanha, II. 418.
Zanthorhiza, II. 200; III. 393.
Zanthoxylum, II. 411; III. 506, 758.
Zanthoxylum, II. 222, 316, 406; III. 504.
Zapania, II. 758.
Zappania, II. 758.
Zarcoa, II. 444.
Zataria, II. 787.
Zauschneria, II. 646; III. 641.
Zelkova, II. 145; III. 366; IV. 519.
Zenkeria, II. 333.
Zenkerella, II. 382.
Zenobia, II. 687; III. 664.
Zexmenia, II. 868.
Zichya, II. 366; III. 479.
Zieria, II. 413.
Zilla, II. 234.
Zinowiewia, II. 471.
Zizyphus, II. 500; III. 544.
Zizyphus, II. 494, 495; III. 542.
Zollernia, II. 389.
Zollikoferia, II. 860.
Zollingera, II. 490.
Zollingeria, II. 490.
Zollingeria, II. 864.
Zombiana, II. 807.
Zonanthus, II. 721.
Zoölogy, III. 94; IV. 89, 544.
Zornia, II. 389.
Zosima, II. 741.
Zschokkea, II. 734.
Zuccagnia, II. 389.
Zurloa, II. 419.
Zwaardekronia, II. 811.
Zygia, II. 330.
Zygodia, II. 734.
Zygogynum, II. 214.
Zygolepis, II. 487.
Zygoon, II. 833.
Zygophyllaceae, II. 394; III. 493; IV. 524.
Zygophyllum, III. 396.
Zygophyllum, IV. 524.
Zymum, II. 428.

Lightning Source UK Ltd.
Milton Keynes UK
UKHW031847290119
336364UK00006B/129/P